POST O
LONDON DI

W. KELLY & Co.
1846

Facsimile Text Edition of 1,950 copies
ISBN 0 9504069 9 6

Published by
Michael Winton 5 Lynn Road Castle Rising King's Lynn

UNDER THE IMMEDIATE AND SPECIAL PATRONAGE OF HER MAJESTY'S POSTMASTER-GENERAL.

THE JUNE EDITION OF THE

POST OFFICE LONDON DIRECTORY, 1846.

COMPRISING, AMONGST OTHER INFORMATION,

OFFICIAL DIRECTORY; COMMERCIAL DIRECTORY; COURT DIRECTORY: PARLIAMENTARY DIRECTORY; POSTAL DIRECTORY; BANKING DIRECTORY; &c. &c. &c.

THE FORTY-SEVENTH ANNUAL PUBLICATION.

LONDON:
PRINTED AND PUBLISHED FOR FREDERIC KELLY, PROPRIETOR
BY W. KELLY & CO.,
19 & 20, OLD BOSWELL COURT, TEMPLE BAR;
AND SOLD BY ALL BOOKSELLERS.

PREFACE.

It is confidently believed that the very high reputation this work has so long enjoyed will, in this, its *Forty-seventh* annual Edition, be fully maintained.

In the "Parliamentary Directory," commencing at page 1637, will be found the address during the *present Session* of every Peer and Member of Parliament, and the results of the recent Elections; and the "Official Directory," commencing at page 33, has been corrected to the *date of publication.*

The advantages possessed by the Proprietor are of no ordinary character; the most important being the means placed at his disposal through the favour of Her Majesty's Postmaster General: the General Post Letter-Carriers, under the sanction of his Lordship, collect, each on his own district, the information from which the Volume is compiled. To ensure accuracy in such a book, the collection of the information should be *simultaneous;* and how completely this is effected, is proved by the fact that an intelligent Letter Carrier performs *within twenty-four hours* all the duties *annually* required of him for the purposes of the "*Post Office London Directory.*"

The matter thus collected has, in the following pages, and under the supervision of competent Editors, been passed into every variety of combination likely to be of practical utility; and the arrangements adopted are such that all or either of the contents of this large volume may, *without difficulty*, be referred to.

That every part of the book should admit of easy reference is indispensable to the purposes for which it is intended; the "Post Office Directory" being the only work consulted in all cases of commercial letters to London imperfectly addressed. That the book is sufficient for this important part of the Post Office duty, and therefore that proper diligence and care have been devoted to its compilation, experience has amply proved.

The "Postal Directory," commencing at page 1673, has been enlarged and improved. The opinion entertained by the highest authorities of the Post Office, as to the value of this division of the book, is indicated by the fact that it has, during the current year, been officially supplied to all the Postmasters of the United Kingdom, as the best digest of Postal matters extant.

It is impossible to adduce better evidence of the value of the "Post Office London Directory" for official purposes; and superfluous to add more than that the volume is as indispensible to the Tradesman as to the Merchant and Banker of the Metropolis, it being the only book which has ever included a Street Directory of London, shewing at *one view* all the inhabitants of each street or place.

Of *such* a work the cost will not usually be a primary consideration. Still it may not be entirely irrelevant to direct attention to the fact, that the *Post Office Directory*, though containing more than double the amount of matter ever contained in any similar book (to say nothing of its superior accuracy), is published at a lower price than that at which any other complete annual Directory of London has ever been produced.

In the course of the collection of the information from which the following sheets have been compiled it has been necessary to make application to various Government Officers besides those of the Post Office. For the unfailing courtesy with which all such applications have been received, and the promptitude and politeness with which accurate information has been supplied, from those holding humble to those occupying the most important offices, the Proprietor respectfully returns his most grateful thanks.

Post Office Directory Offices,
19 & 20 Old Boswell Court.

*** The "Parliamentary Directory" is corrected to the latest moment, this will be perceived by referring to any of the late changes—for instance, the death of the late Earl of Yarborough, and the vacancy caused in the House of Commons for North Lincolnshire by the succession of the present Earl to the House of Peers; and the still more recent succession of the present Earl of Waldegrave.

The "Banking Directory" has been submitted to and corrected by every London and every Provincial Banker, and the Proprietor offers his best thanks for the uniform assistance he has received from them in compiling so important a portion of this work.

PREFACE

GENERAL INDEX TO LONDON.

See also Index to Postal Directory, page 725; also Index to Parliamentary, page 689.

CARSON'S

ORIGINAL ANTI-CORROSION PAINT,

Specially patronised by the British and other Governments, the Hon. East India Company, the principal Dock Companies, and most public bodies, is particularly recommended to the Nobility, Gentry, Agriculturists, West India Proprietors, and others, it having been proved, by the practical test of nearly 60 years, to surpass all other paints as an out-door preservative ; it is adapted for every description of iron, wood, brick, stone, compo, or stucco work, however exposed to sun or weather. It is also very economical, any labourer being able to lay it on, thereby avoiding the enormous charge generally made by painters.

Colours—Light Stone, Drab, or Portland ditto, Bath ditto, Yellow ditto, Light and Dark Oak, Light and Dark Lead, Light and Dark Chocolate, Bright and Dark Red and Black, 34s. per cwt.; Invisible Green, 50s. ; Bright and Deep Green, 60s. ; in casks of 28 lbs., 56 lbs., and 112 lbs. each.

OIL AND BRUSHES.

More detailed particulars will be sent free of Post.

The original Anti-corrosion Paint is only to be obtained of Walter Carson (successor to the inventors), 15, Token House Yard, back of the Bank of England, London, who will show nearly **THREE HUNDRED** Testimonials from the Nobility, Gentry, and Glergy, who have used the Anti-corrosion for many years.

NO AGENTS.—ALL ORDERS TO BE SENT DIRECT.

"And where the gardener, Robin, day by day,
Drew me to school, along the public way;
Delighted with my bauble coach, and wrapped
In scarlet mantle warm, and velvet capp'd."

Of high value in the Preservation & Restoration of Health.

CHILDREN'S CARRIAGES,

Of a very superior, elegant, and com. pact make, and so perfectly secure and easy, that children may be trusted with impunity to the most careless hands- In use from the palace to the cottage. Also self-moving Chairs, for house or garden. On Sale or Hire.

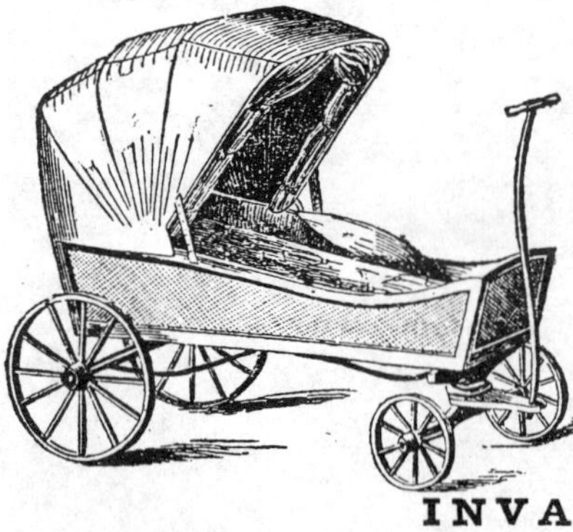

INVALID CARRIAGES.

To be disposed of, a number of out-door and in-door WHEEL CHAIRS, constructed especially for the comfort of invalids ; comprising the plainest as well as the most expensive builds, second-hand as well as new, from £3 to £35. Self-acting Wheel Chairs, by which any degree of exercise for the arms can be obtained, suitable for the drawing-room or garden. Long Bed or Spinal Carriages for the very debilitated. Any of the above can have hoods of Leather, Macintosh or Canvas, to let up and down. On Sale or Hire.

AT INGRAM'S MANUFACTORY, 29, CITY ROAD, FINSBURY SQUARE.

A Variety of Children's Carriages on Sale, from 10 shillings to 20 guineas.—Illustrated Catalogues may be had per Post.

CHEAP & DURABLE ROOFING.

BY HER MAJESTY'S ROYAL LETTERS PATENT.

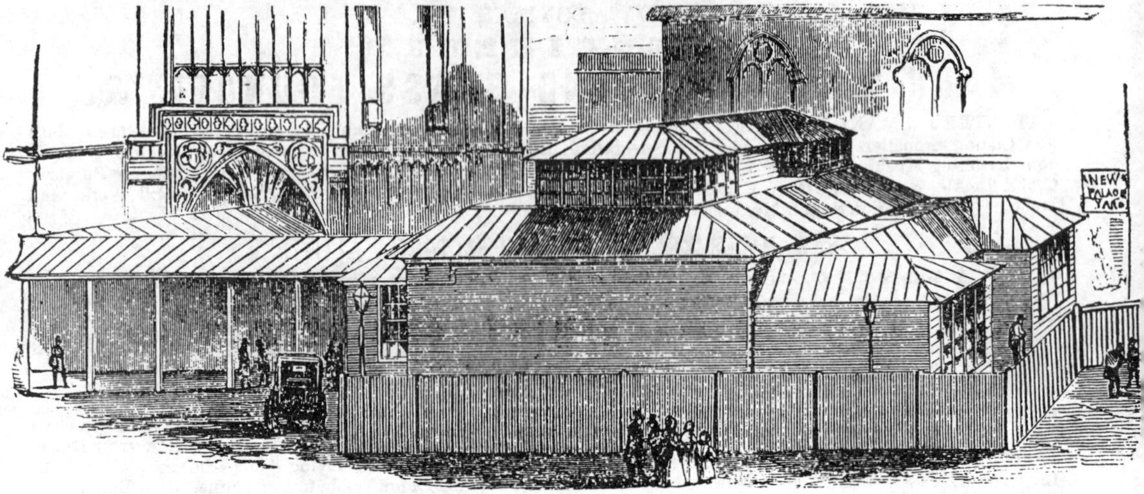

View of the New Vice Chancellor's Courts, and the Offices and Passages leading to Westminster Hall, which are roofed entirely with F. M'Neill and Co.'s Asphalted Felt, under the direction of Charles Barry, Esq., R.A., by order of Her Majesty's Commissioners of Woods and Forests. Dr. Reid's Offices and other Buildings at the New Houses of Parliament are also roofed with the same Felt.

F. M'NEILL AND CO.

(Of Lamb's Buildings, Bunhill Row, London), Manufacturers and only Patentees of the

PATENT ASPHALTED FELT FOR ROOFING

HOUSES, COTTAGES, VERANDAHS, SHEDS, AND EVERY DESCRIPTION OF BUILDINGS;

PATRONIZED BY

THE COMMISSIONERS OF WOODS AND FORESTS.
THE COMMISSIONERS OF CUSTOMS.
HER MAJESTY'S ESTATE, ISLE OF WIGHT.
ROYAL BOTANICAL GARDENS, REGENT'S PARK.
THE HONOURABLE THE EAST INDIA COMPANY.
THE HONOURABLE THE BOARD OF ORDNANCE.

And IT IS THIS FELT which has been exhibited at the great Agricultural shows of England, Scotland, and Ireland, *and obtained the* PRIZE, for being the Cheapest and Best description of Roofing, in lieu of Thatch, Slate, Tiles, &c. It is also used under slates, at the Royal Agricultural Society's House, Hanover Square; and for every description of Farm Buildings, on the estates of the Dukes of Northumberland, Sutherland, Norfolk, Bedford, and Rutland, the Marquis of Northampton, the late Earl Spencer, and most of the Nobility and Gentry.

For Garden Sheds and Frames, being a non-conductor, is a great protection for seeds, plants, and flowers, in cold and frosty weather.

For lining Granaries and Storehouses, and the outside and inside of walls of wooden buildings, and as a protection to ceilings under flooring from wet and damp, at the same time deadening sound.

It is also used under slates, tiles, &c., and adds greatly to the warmth of the building, especially of attics, while it secures the tightness of the roof, and contributes greatly to its durability. In Churches, and large open buildings, it is particularly desirable, preventing the falling of rain or hail upon the roof from being heard.

For Cattle and Sheep Sheds it is a portable and warm covering, and well adapted for the lambing season.

For covering Corn and Hay Ricks it is well adapted, and effects a great annual saving to the farmer; enabling him to feed his cattle, and manure his land, with the straw which is now used for thatching his Corn and Hay Ricks.

For Work Shops, Rope Walks, and every kind of Manufacturing Premises.

For Shipping to the Colonies it is in great request, as it resists the external heat of the sun, and does not crack with changes of temperature.

In point of economy, it has decided advantages. The expense of the Felt, as compared with slates, tiles, or thatch, is, in most cases—particularly when slates or tiles are brought from a distance—CONSIDERABLY LESS THAN ONE-HALF; and in the wood work there is a still greater saving, as the weight of the Felt is only 2¼lb. per square yard.

Price of the Roofing Felt is One Penny per Square Foot.

It is made to any length, by 32 inches wide. Parties sending their Orders to the Manufactory in Town, can have it cut off from the Machines in lengths best suited to their Roofs, so that they pay for no more than they actually require.

Samples, with full directions as to its uses, and manner of applying it, and Testimonials (some of them of seven years' experience) from Noblemen and Gentlemen, Members of the Royal Agricultural Society, also from Architects, Builders, &c., SENT FREE to any part of the Town or Country, and Orders by Post executed.

Messrs. F. McNeill and Co., also Manufacture a FELT FOR RAILWAYS, which for several years past they have solely supplied to the Great Western, London and Birmingham, Bristol and Exeter, and Bristol and Gloucester Lines.

The Public are respectfully cautioned against misrepresentation.

The only Works in Great Britain where the above description of Roofing is made, are F. M'NEILL & Co.'s Manufactories, LAMB'S BUILDINGS, BUNHILL ROW, **London**, where Roofs covered with the Felt are to be seen, and every information afforded.

COTTAM AND HALLEN,

Engineers, Iron Founders, Smiths, Agricultural Implement Makers, and General Ironmongers,

No. 2, WINSLEY STREET, OPPOSITE THE PANTHEON, OXFORD STREET, LONDON;

Estimates and Lists of Prices can be had on application at above.

Green-houses, and Hot-houses fixed, complete with Hot Water Apparatus, upon the most improved principles.

HATCHER'S BENNENDEN TILE MACHINE.

This is the most efficient Machine that has been invented for the purpose of making Drain Tiles. Any shape Tile can be made—it requires but few hands, viz., one man and three boys. With this amount of labour, the product of a day of 10 hours is as follows :—

1 inch diameter of Tile................	11,000	$1\frac{3}{4}$ inch diameter of Tile................	5,800
$1\frac{1}{4}$ ditto......ditto....................	8,000	$2\frac{1}{2}$ ditto......ditto	3,200

No charges made for patent dues or license ; the purchase of the machine includes free use of it.

Furnishing Ironmongery.

Iron Fire-Proof Book Cases, and Deed Boxes, which stood the test in the late Fire at Liverpool.
Kitchen Ranges.
Belgian Cooking Stoves.
Broiling Stoves.
Economical Cooking Ranges.
Hot Plates.
Hot Closets.
Register Stoves in great variety, for Drawing Rooms, Dining Rooms, &c.
Fenders and Fire-irons for ditto, to suit.
Arnott's Stoves.
Hot Air Stoves.
Tin and Copper Ware of every description, &c., &c.
Iron and Brass Bedsteads.

Horticulture.

Green-houses and Hot-houses upon the most improved principle, either all of Iron, or of Iron and Wood combined, at a very low rate of charge.
Hot Water Apparatuses for Heating Hot-houses, Public and Private Buildings, &c., with Cottam's patent, or Roger's Boilers.
Rendle's Tank system, carried out upon improved principles.
Materials for Hot Water work may be had by those who wish to fix their own apparatus.
Garden Engines and Syringes.
Superior Garden Tools of every description.
Garden Rollers.
Hand Glass Frames for Cucumbers, &c.
Fancy Wire-work for Gardens.
Flower Stages.
Garden Seats and Chairs.
Cast-Iron Flower Sticks, from 12 to 18 inches in the ground ; 4 feet, 4 feet 6 inches ; 5 feet, 6 feet, 7 feet.
Flower Bordering of various Patterns.
Annual Pins.
Garden Labels.
Metallic Wire.
Garden Vases in great variety.
Pedestals for ditto, &c.

Stable Furniture.

Mangers.
Racks.
Ramps.
Cills.
Guttering to prevent Horses slipping.
Rack and Biting Chains.
Stable Ramps.
Ditto Grates and Frames.
Bridle Hooks.
Saddle Brackets.
Capping for Wood Mangers.
Horse and Mare Pots, &c.

Agriculture.

Ploughs.
Harrows.
Cultivators.
Drills of all kinds.
Horse and Hoe Ploughs.
Thrashing Machines.
Chaff Cutters.
Pumps and Iron-work for liquid Manure Carts.
Weighing Machines of all kinds for Sheep, Cattle, Carts, &c.
Mills for various purposes.
Turnip Cutters.
Scotch Carts.
Dynamometers or Plough Gauges.
Field Rollers of all sizes.
Cast-iron Rickstands.

Iron Work for Builders.

Girders.
Columns.
Straps and Bolts.
Sash Weights.
Balconies.
Ornamental Staircase Railing.
Area Railing of all kinds.
Ditto Gratings.
Chimney Bars.
Rain Water Pipes.
Eaves Gutter and Angles.
Water and Gas pipe.
Cast-iron Pumps.
Suction Pipe for ditto, &c.

Sundries.

Wrought Iron, Sheep, Light Cattle, Strong Cattle, Ox, and Deer Hurdles at very low prices, C. & H. making them in large quantities.
Best Wire, for Strained Wire Fencing at 8s. 6d. per bundle of 150 yards each.
Uprights for ditto. 7d. each.
The Improved Continued, and every other kind of Fencing.
Sugar Mills.
Saw Mills.
Tread Mills.
Iron Water Wheels.
Hydraulic Presses, &c., &c., and every description of Wrought and Cast-Iron, and Brass work

Extensive Show Rooms at their Manufactory, 2, Winsley Street, Oxford Street, where a large Stock of Ironmongery, and every description of Implement used in Agriculture and Horticulture are to be seen.

Ornamental Iron and Wire Work for gardens and other purposes.

FAMILY MOURNING

AT THE LONDON GENERAL MOURNING WAREHOUSE,

247 & 249, REGENT STREET.

The Proprietors of this Establishment, in respectfully addressing themselves to the attention of the Nobility, the Gentry, and the Public, beg leave to renew their thanks for the extraordinary support they have received. Every article necessary for a complete Outfit of Mourning, for either the family or household, may be had here, and made up, if required, at the shortest notice; whilst the habitual attendance of competent persons connected with the establishment upon families of rank, and of every respectable denomination, enables the proprietors or their assistants to at once suggest or supply every thing necessary for the occasion, and suited to any grade or condition of the community. Skirts, &c., for Widowhood, and for Family Mourning, are always kept made up, and a note descriptive of the relation of the parties to the deceased, will insure at any time the proper supply of mourning being forwarded, both as to quality and distinction, according to the exigencies of the case; it being needful only to send dresses for patterns, when every requisite will be carefully prepared and chosen to render the appointments complete.

W. C. JAY & Co., PROPRIETORS.

SHERWIN, COPE, & CO.,

ENGINEERS AND MILLWRIGHTS,

5, CUMBERLAND STREET, SHOREDITCH, LONDON.

INVENTORS AND MANUFACTURERS OF THE

Imperial Printing Press.

S., C., & Co., Inventors of the IMPERIAL PRINTING PRESS, in acknowledging the liberal patronage awarded to their Press during a period of nearly twenty years, beg to inform the Trade that they have *greatly reduced the prices of their Presses*;—they have also *enlarged the Plattens*, and by the addition of *Double Springs*, increasing the strength of the staples, and other recent improvements, they have spared no expense to render their Imperial Presses easy and accurate in their working, and enduring in quality.

Merchants and Mission Societies will find these Presses peculiarly adapted for exportation.

S., C., & Co. are also Manufacturers of the Imperial Printing Machines, Arming Presses, Rolling Machines, Screw and Hydraulic Presses, Cutting Machines, Steam Engines, and every description of Machinery for Printing, Bookbinding, and general purposes.

Imperial Screw Press with Extra Power.

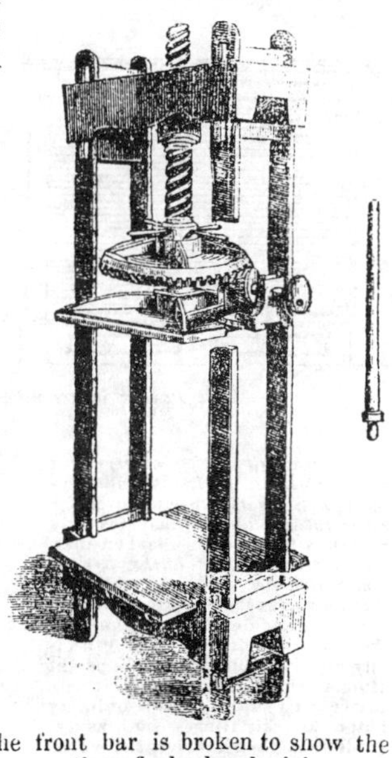

The front bar is broken to show the action of wheel and pinion.

Testimonials, and other information, may be obtained at the Manufactory.

PATENT PORTABLE AND FIXED WATER CLOSETS.

ROBERT WISS,

Invites an inspection of his New Method of Fixing WATER CLOSETS, by which contrivance the whole Apparatus is contained under the seat. They are sent out ready for fixing, and all expenses of Cisterns overhead and Carpenters' Work is saved. They can be placed in any room, and made to imitate any article of Furniture.

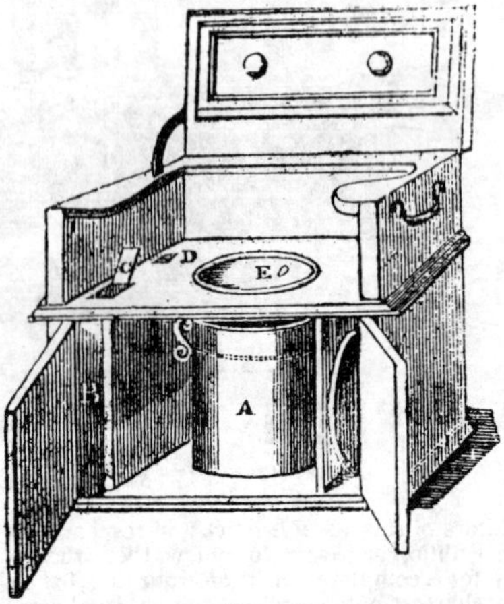

CAUTION.—**In consequence of unprincipled imitators having copied WISS'S various Patent Water Closets and advertised them as New and Improved, ROBERT WISS, the actual Inventor, very respectfully cautions th public against the same, and begs to acquaint them, that during the last Twelve Years all the real improvement have been effected by R. W. himself.**

TO BE SEEN AT THE MANUFACTORY,

No. 38, CHARING CROSS, NEAR THE ADMIRALTY.

IMPROVED PATENT CONVEX IRON REVOLVING SAFETY SHUTTERS.

IMPROVED PATENT IRON SLIDING SAFETY SHUTTERS.

PATENT REVOLVING PERFORATED BLINDS.

PATENT OUTSIDE SHUTTER, VENETIAN, CORRUGATED, AND CARRIAGE BLINDS.

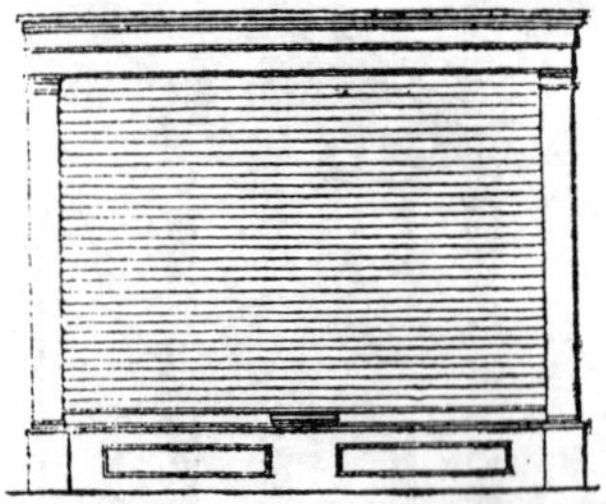

The attention of Architects, Builders, Blind Makers, and the Trade generally, is particularly requested to the IMPORTANT PATENTED IMPROVEMENTS in the above enumerated Articles, and inspection invited, at the Manufactory of the Patentees, R. HOWARD & Co., 115, Old Street, London; and at PATRICK CLARK & Co.'s, Engineers and Machinists, Tunnel Iron Works, 238, Wapping.

Engravings and Prospectusses may be had at either address, or will be forwarded on application.

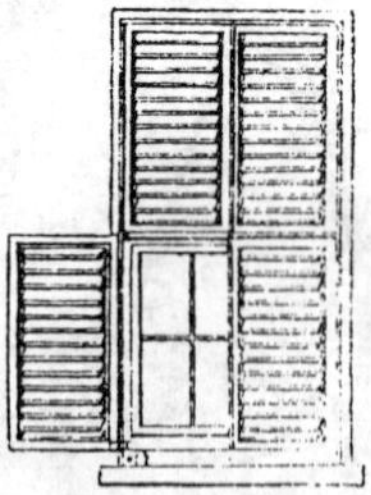

***This Patent is described in the Civil Engineer and Architects' Journal, for May,* 1845.—Page 160.**

The great importance of ***strength*** and ***stiffness*** in the Laths of Revolving Iron Shutters, when required for ***security,*** is so obvious that it is only necessary to point out the fact that, the *Patent Convex Laths are* 12 *times stronger than the ordinary flat Laths,* (as shown by the annexed engraving and description), to ensure their general adoption; and especially when combined with the patent Hinges, which will be found in use to be greatly superior to the ordinary butt or knuckle Hinges, both as regards strength and ***increase of working surface,*** as well as the addition of other material improvements.

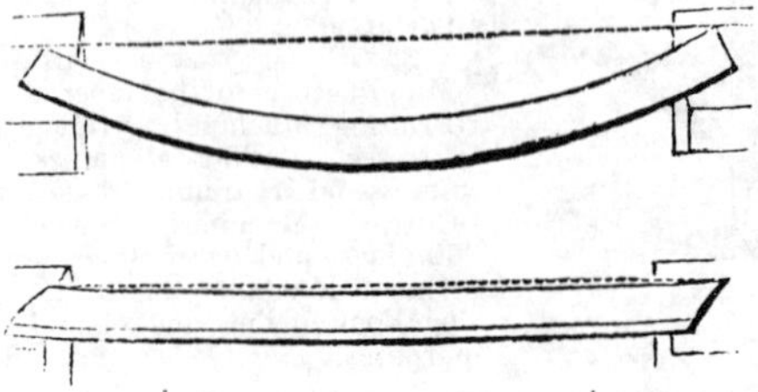

A flat Lath, and a Patent Convex Lath of corresponding length, (both cut from the same hoop; were supported on blocks, and a 28lb. weight suspended from the centre of each; the flat Lath gave a dip of $1\frac{1}{2}$ inch, while the Patent Convex Lath dipped $\frac{1}{8}$ inch only. Again, two Laths were tested to a given dip, the Patent Convex Lath, with a 56lb. weight gave exactly $\frac{1}{4}$ inch dip, and the flat Lath gave the same dip ($\frac{1}{4}$ inch) required but $4\frac{1}{2}$ lbs. **THUS THE PATENT CONVEX LATH IS TWELVE TIMES STRONGER THAN THE ORDINARY FLAT LATH.**

GLASS SHADES,

EITHER ROUND, OVAL, OR SQUARE, FOR THE PROTECTION OF CLOCKS, ALABASTER ORNAMENTS, MODELS, WAX FLOWERS, AND BIJOUTERIE OF EVERY KIND,

ARE SOLD AT GREATLY REDUCED PRICES AT

CLAUDET AND HOUGHTON'S

WHOLESALE AND RETAIL GLASS SHADE WAREHOUSE,

89, HIGH HOLBORN, LONDON.

COLOURED GLASS FOR WINDOWS.

CLAUDET AND HOUGHTON,

89, HIGH HOLBORN,

Beg to notify that they now supply Coloured Glass at prices so greatly reduced, as to make it available for many purposes from which it has hitherto been excluded on account of its expense. C. & H. have always on hand the largest variety of colours which can be obtained, of which they invite an inspection.

PAINTED AND ORNAMENTED GLASS

For Windows, executed in ancient or modern style, and at moderate prices, from the simplest to the most elaborate in design.

PATENT PLATE GLASS,

BRITISH PLATE GLASS, SHEET WINDOW GLASS, CROWN WINDOW GLASS, AND HORTICULTURAL (or Common Sheet) GLASS:

ALL AT THE LOWEST PRICES,

Wholesale and Retail, at

CLAUDET AND HOUGHTON'S

WINDOW GLASS WAREHOUSE,

89, HIGH HOLBORN, LONDON.

Lists of Prices forwarded free on application.

BY HER MAJESTY'S ROYAL LETTERS PATENT.

SUPERIOR FOOD FOR INFANTS, CHILDREN, AND INVALIDS.

ROBINSON'S PATENT GROATS and ROBINSON'S PATENT BARLEY, celebrated for making a delicate nutritious gruel and superior barley water in 10 minutes, are universally admitted by the faculty as the safest, purest and best food for the infant from its birth, and for mothers while nursing; also strongly recommended as a nourishing diet for all persons of weak digestion, and those under medical regimen.

The Patent Barley is likewise highly esteemed for making a delicious custard pudding, preferable to ground rice, tapioca, or arrowroot.

Sold by all respectable druggists, grocers, &c., in town and country, in packets of 6d., 1s., and in family canisters at 2s., 5s., and 10s. each.—ROBINSON and BELVILLE, sole manufacturers, purveyors to Her Majesty, 64, Red Lion Street, Holborn, London.

Under the Especial Patronage of

HER MAJESTY, THE QUEEN,

H. R. H. PRINCE ALBERT, THE SEVERAL SOVEREIGNS AND COURTS OF EUROPE.

THE ROYAL FAMILY, & NOBILITY OF GREAT BRITAIN.

AND UNIVERSALLY PREFERRED AND ESTEEMED.

ROWLAND'S MACASSAR OIL.

This ELEGANT, FRAGRANT and TRANSPARENT OIL, in its *preservative*, *restorative* and *beautifying* qualities for the Human Hair, is unequalled throughout the whole world.—Price 3*s.* 6*d.*, 7*s.*, Family Bottles (equal to four small) 10*s.* 6*d.*, and double that size 21*s.* per Bottle.

ROWLAND'S KALYDOR,

An ORIENTAL BOTANICAL PREPARATION of singular efficacy for rendering the SKIN SOFT, CLEAR and FAIR, for bestowing a healthy roseate hue on the COMPLEXION, and for eradicating all Cutaneous Eruptions and Discolorations. Price 4s. 6d., and 8s. 6d. per Bottle.

ROWLAND'S ODONTO, OR PEARL DENTIFRICE,

A FRAGRANT WHITE POWDER, *prepared from Oriental Herbs*, of inestimable virtue for *preserving and beautifying the TEETH, strengthening the GUMS, and for giving sweetness and perfume to the BREATH. Price 2s. 9d. per Box.*

IMPORTANT INFORMATION.

UNPRINCIPLED SHOPKEEPERS, for the sake of gaining a trifle more profit, vend the most SPURIOUS COMPOUNDS, under the same names; some under the implied sanction of Royalty; they copy the *labels, bills, advertisements and testimonials* (substituting *fictitious* names and addresses for the real) of the original preparations, and use either the word "GENUINE," or a FEIGNED name, in the place of "ROWLAND'S."—It is therefore highly necessary to see that the word "**ROWLAND'S**" is on the wrapper of each article.

☞ All others are **FRAUDULENT IMITATIONS.**

The genuine Preparations are Sold by the Proprietors,

A. Rowland & Son, 20, Hatton Garden, London.

And by Chemists and Perfumers.

POST OFFICE DIRECTORY PRINTING OFFICE.

THE CAPACITY OF THIS OFFICE FOR THE PRODUCTION OF BOOKS OF MAGNITUDE IS PROVED BY THE **CELERITY** WITH WHICH THIS THE

MOST MAGNIFICENT IN SIZE OF ANNUAL WORKS

HAS PASSED ITS STEAM PRESSES; FEW OTHER OFFICES COULD **UNASSISTED** UNDERTAKE IT AND ALTHOUGH THIS EDITION HAS BEEN COMPLETED

WITH SUCH RAPIDITY,

ITS PAGES EXHIBIT NO TRACES OF THIS EXTREME DESPATCH.

IT WILL BE SEEN THAT THE TYPOGRAPHY AND ARRANGEMENT ARE WORTHY OF A WORK

UNRIVALLED IN RESOURCES AS IN CIRCULATION.

W. KELLY & CO.,

STEAM MACHINE AND GENERAL PRINTERS,

Will undertake, *at the most reasonable charges*, all works, from those of a size equal to the present to the *smallest handbill*, at their Offices,

19 & 20, OLD BOSWELL COURT,

TEMPLE BAR.

ASYLUM FOREIGN AND DOMESTIC LIFE OFFICE,

70, CORNHILL, AND 5, WATERLOO PLACE, LONDON.

Established in 1824.

DIRECTORS.

Major-Gen. Sir James Law Lushington, G.C.B., Chairman
Charles William Hallett, Esq., Deputy-Chairman.
J. Harvey Astell, Esq.
Thomas Fenn, Esq.
George Palmer, Jun., Esq.
W. Edmund Ferrers, Esq.
E. Bedwell Kemble, Esq.
Foster Reynolds, Esq.
John Clarmont Whiteman, Esq.
G. Farren, Esq., Resident Director.

MEDICAL OFFICERS IN LONDON.

R. Ferguson, M.D., 9, Queen Street, Mayfair.
J. Forbes, M.D., F.R.S., 12, Old Burlington Street.
T. Callaway, Esq., Wellington Street, Borough, Southwark.

Persons suffering from Chronic Disease or irregularity of form, in pregnancy, or old age, are insured at proportionate rates, the ASYLUM being the Company which originally (in 1824) extended the benefits of life insurance to such cases.

RENEWABLE TERM INSURANCES FOR HEALTHY LIVES.

The advantages of a whole life Policy are secured by the smallest necessary outlay in the first instance,—the contract being continued year by year, whatever the future health of the assured (after the primary examination), at a stipulated slight increase of premium, little exceeding the price of an ordinary term insurance, up to the age of 70, when the rate remains stationary.

Extracts from RENEWABLE TERM rates for select lives.

Age.	1st year.	2nd year.	3rd year.	4th year.	5th year.	6th year.	7th year.
30	1 6 4	1 7 1	1 7 11	1 8 9	1 9 7	1 10 5	1 11 4
50	2 7 3	2 8 8	2 10 1	2 11 7	2 13 1	2 15 11	3 0 4

Extracts from the EVEN RATES for select lives.

Age.	20	30	40	50	60	70	80
Prem.	1 11 9	2 2 0	2 17 1	4 2 0	6 10 9	10 18 6	19 1 8

ALTERNATIVE.

Two thirds, only, of the even rates, whether for select or diseased lives, or for the risks of foreign climates, may be paid down, and the balance, with interest at 4 per cent. deducted from sum assured.

FOREIGN, AND MILITARY AND NAVAL INSURANCE.

Distinct classifications of places, according to salubrity of climate; a specific price for any particular place, or for a voyage or voyages.

Officers whose destinations are not known, covered to all parts of the world at a small but fixed extra rate of premium.

GEO. FARREN, Resident Director.

THE AUSTRALASIAN, COLONIAL AND GENERAL LIFE ASSURANCE AND ANNUITY COMPANY,

1, LEADENHALL STREET, (GRACECHURCH STREET END),

(*Removed from* 126, *Bishopsgate Street.*)

CAPITAL £200,000 IN 2,000 SHARES.

DIRECTORS.

Edward Barnard, Esq.
Robert Brooks, Esq.
Henry Buckle, Esq.
John H. Capper, Esq.
Gideon Colquhoun, Esq.
Charles E. Mangles, Esq.
Richard Onslow, Esq.
William Walker, Esq.

TRUSTEES—Edward Barnard, Esq.; J. H. Capper, Esq.; Edward Thompson, Esq.

AUDITORS—James Easton, Esq. and C. Richardson, Esq.

SOLICITORS—Messrs. Maples, Pearse, Stevens and Maples.

BANKERS—The Union Bank of London.

COLONIAL BANKERS—The Bank of Australasia (Incorporated by Royal Charter, 1835), 8, Austin Friars, London.

PHYSICIAN—Dr. Fraser, 62, Guildford Street, Russell Square.

ACTUARY AND SECRETARY—Edward Ryley.

To the purchasers of Annuities this Company, in addition to participation in profits, holds out the advantage of a much higher rate of Annuity than can be granted with safety by Companies which make their investments entirely in this Country.

The following are specimens of the rates of Annuity granted for every £100 sunk :—

Age.	Male Lives.	Female Lives.	Age.	Male Lives.	Female Lives.
	£ s. d.	£ s. d.		£ s. d.	£ s. d.
40	7 8 3	6 18 2	65	12 12 0	10 19 0
50	8 13 6	7 14 4	70	15 0 8	13 2 6
60	10 16 3	9 9 0	75	18 9 2	16 3 5

Prospectuses, with Tables, Forms of Proposal for the purchase of an Annuity or for making an Assurance, and every information, may be obtained by application at the Office of the Company.

POST OFFICE LONDON

OFFICIAL DIRECTORY

FOR 1846.

Lords of Her Majesty's Most Honourable

PRIVY COUNCIL.

HIS ROYAL HIGHNESS ALBERT, PRINCE OF SAXE COBURG AND GOTHA, K.G. CONSORT OF HER MAJESTY.

Aberdeen Earl of, K.T
Adair Sir Robert, G.C.B
Adam Sir Frederick, G.C.B
Albemarle Earl of
Amherst Earl
Anglesey Marquis of, K.G., G.C.B., K.P
Arbuthnot Charles
Ashburton Lord
Auckland Earl of, G C.B
Baring Francis Thornhill, M.P. *for Portsmouth*
Baring Hon. Wm. Bingham, M.P. *for Thetford*
Beauvale Lord, G.C.B
Becket Sir John, bart
Beresford Viscount, G.C.B
Besborough Earl of
Beverley Earl of
Bexley Lord
Bloomfield Lieut. Gen. Lord
Bosanquet Sir John Bernard
Boyle David
Brougham and Vaux Lord
Bruce Lord Ernest Augustus Chas. Brudenell, M.P. *for Marlboro'*
Brydges Sir Harford Jones, bart
Buccleuch and Queensbury Duke of, K.G
Buckingham and Chandos Duke of, K.G
Bulwer Henry Lytton, *Ambassador at Madrid*
Byng George Stephens, M.P. *for Chatham*
Cambridge Duke of, K.G. G.C.B. G.C.H
Campbell Lord
Canning Sir Stratford, G.C.B. *Ambassador to Turkey*
Canterbury Archbishop of
Carlisle Earl of, K.G
Carteret Lord
Castlereagh Viscount, M.P. *for Down county*
Chesterfield Earl of
Cholmondeley Marquis of, *Joint Hereditary Grand Chamberlain*
Clanricarde Marquis of, K.P
Clare Earl of, K.P
Clarendon Earl of, G.C.B
Clerk Sir George, M.P. *for Stamford*
Cockburn Sir George, G.C.B., M.P. *for Ripon*
Combermere Viscount, G.C.B., G.C.H
Conyngham Marquis of, K.P., G.C.H
Corry Hon. Hen. Thos. Lowry, M.P. *for Tyrone county*
Cottenham Lord
Cowley Lord, G.C.B
Croker John Wilson, LL.D., F.A.S
Cumberland Duke of, K.G., G.C.B., G.C.H., *King of Hanover*
Dalhousie Earl of
Damer Hon. Col. George Lionel Dawson, M.P. *for Portarlington,*
Dawson George Robert
De Grey Earl, K.G., K.P
De La Warr Earl, D.C.L
Denbigh Earl of, G.C.H
Denman Lord, *Chief Justice of the Queen's Bench*
Derby Earl, K.G
Devonshire Duke of, K.G
D'Eyncourt Charles Tennyson, M.P. *for Lambeth*
Donegal Marquis, G.C.H
Dunfermline Lord
East Sir Edward Hyde bart
Egerton Lord Francis, M.P. *for South Lancashire*
Ellenborough Earl of, G.C.B
Ellice Edward, M.P. *for Coventry*
Ellis Henry
Elphinstone Lord
Errol Earl of, K.T., K.C.H
Erskine Thomas
Exeter Marquis of, K.G
Falkland Viscount, G.C.H
Fitzroy Lord Charles, M.P. *for Bury St. Edmunds*
Foley Lord
Forester Lord
Fortescue Earl of
Foster Sir Augustus John, bart
Fremantle Sir Thomas Francis, bart. M.P. *for Buckingham*
Fremantle Sir William Henry, G.C.H
Frere John Hookham
Glenelg Lord
Gladstone Wm. Ewart, M.P. *for Newark*
Gordon Sir Robert, G.C.B. *Ambassador to Austria*
Gosford Earl of, G.C.B
Goulburn Henry, M.P. *for Cambridge University*
Graham Sir Jas. Rt. Geo. bart. M.P. *for Dorchester*
Grenville Thomas
Grey Earl
Grey Sir Charles Edward, G.C.H
Grey Sir George, bart. M.P. *for Devonport*
Grosvenor Lord Robert, M.P. *for Chester*
Haddington Earl of, *Elder Brother of the Trinity House*
Hamilton Duke of, K.G
Hardinge Sir Henry, G.C.B. *Governor General of India*
Harrowby Earl of, D.C.L., F.S.A
Hatherton Lord
Herbert Hon. Sidney, M.P. *for South Wiltshire*
Herries John Charles
Heytesbury Lord, G.C.B. *Governor of the Isle of Wight*
Hill Lord Arthur Marcus Cecil, M.P. *for Evesham*
Hobhouse Henry
Hobhouse Sir John Cam, M.P. *for Nottingham*
Hope Charles
Hope John, *Lord Justice Clerk of Scotland*
Howe Earl, G.C.H
Jenner-Fust Sir Herbert, knt. *Judge of the Prerogative Court of Canterbury*
Jermyn Earl, M.P. *for Bury St. Edmunds*
Jersey Earl of
Johnstone Sir Alexander, F.R.S
Kempt Sir James, G.C.H
Kinnaird Lord
Knatchbull Sir Edward, bart
Knight-Bruce, Sir James Lewis, knt. *a Vice Chancellor*
Labouchere Hen. M.P. *for Taunton*
Langdale Lord, *Master of the Rolls*
Lefevre Charles Shaw, M.P. *for North Hants, and Speaker of the House of Commons*
Lansdowne Marquis of, K G
Leinster Duke of
Lewis Thomas Frankland
Litchfield Earl of, D.C.L
Lincoln Earl of, M.P. *for South Notts*
Liverpool Earl of
London Bishop of
Londonderry Marquis of, G.C.B., G.C.H., B.E., S.P., *Lord Lieut. Durham*
Lonsdale Earl, F.R.S., F.S.A
Lushington Stephen, D.C.L., *Judge of the Admiralty*
Lushington Stephen Rumbold
Lyndhurst Lord, F.R.S
Macauley Thomas Babington, M P *for Edinburgh*
Mackenzie Holt
Mackenzie James Alex. Stewart
Maule Fox, M.P. *for Perth*
Melbourne Viscount. *Elder Brother of the Trinity House*
Melville Viscount, K.T. *Lord Privy Seal in Scotland*
Metcalfe Lord, *Governor General of Canada*
Minto Earl of, G.C.B
Monteagle Lord
Montrose Duke of, K.T
Morpeth Viscount
Murray Lieut. Gen. Sir Geo. knt
Newport Sir John, bart
Nicholl John, D.C.L., M.P. *for Cardiff*
Norfolk Duke of, *Earl Marshal of England*
Normanby Marquis of
Northumberland Duke of, K.G
Ouseley Sir Gore, G.C.H
Palmerston Viscount, G.C.B
Pakenham Richard, *Ambassador at Washington*
Parke Sir James, knt. *a Baron of the Exchequer*
Peel Sir Robert, bart., M.P. *for Tamworth*
Peel William Yates
Pemberton-Leigh Thomas, Q.C
Pierrepoint Hon. Henry Mauver,
Planta Joseph, G C.H
Plunket Lord
Pollock Sir Frederick, knt. *Chief Baron of the Exchequer*
Portland Duke of, K.G
Pottinger Sir Henry, G.C B
Richmond Duke of, K.G
Ripon Earl of
Roden Earl of, K.P
Rose Sir George Henry, G.C.H
Rosebery Earl of, K.T., D.C.L
Rosslyn Earl of
Russell Lord John, M.P. *for London*
Ryan Sir Edward, knt

St. Germans Earl of
Salisbury Marquis of, K.G., D.C.L
Shadwell Sir Lancelot, *Vice Chancellor of England*
Shaftesbury Earl of
Shiel Richard Lalor, M.P. *for Dungarvon*
Somerset Lord Granville Charles Henry, M.P. *for Monmouthshire*
Stanley Hon. Edward John
Smith Robert Vernon, M.P. *for Northampton*
Stanley Lord (of Bickerstaffe),
Strangford Viscount, G.C.B., G.C.H
Stuart de Rothesay Lord, G.C.B
Sugden Sir Edward Burtenshaw,
Talbot Earl, K.G., K.P
Tankerville Earl of
Taylor Sir Brook, G.C.H. *Chief Clerk in the Signet Office*
Thornton Sir Edward
Tindal Sir Nicolas Conyngham, *Chief Justice Common Pleas*
Uxbridge Earl of
Vaughan Sir Charles Rd. G.C.H
Warrender Sir George, bart
Wellington Duke of, K.G., G.C.B *Lord Lieut. Hampshire, &c. &c. &c*
Westmoreland Earl of, K.C.B. *Ambassador to Prussia*
Wharncliffe Lord
Wigram Sir James, knt. *a Vice Chancellor*
Willoughby de Eresby Lord
Wilton Earl of
Winchester Marquis of
Wynn Charles Watkin Williams, M.P. *for Montgomeryshire*
Wynn Sir Henry Watkin
York Archbishop of

PRIVY COUNCIL OFFICE, *Downing street.*

Hours 11 to 4.

OFFICERS OF THE PRIVY COUNCIL.

Clerks in Ordinary, Charles Cavendish Fulke Greville, esq. Hon. William Lennox Bathurst
Chief Clerk, John Barrett Lennard, esq
First Class, Henry Gaitskell, Charles Anthony Hamilton, esqrs
Second Class, Harry Chester, Edmund Stephen Harrison, esqrs
Third Class, Peter Francis De Barry, Charles George Villiers Bayly, Charles Edward Boothby, Thomas Kay, Lister Lester Kaye, esqrs
Appeal Clerk, Henry Reeve, esq
Clerk for Clergy Returns, Rev. W. Harness, M.A
Keepers of Council Chamber, John Baker, Charles Hodges, esqrs
Messengers, John Neal, John Dix
Office Keeper, James Evenden
Housekeeper, Mrs. Elizabeth Russell

ALPHABETICAL LIST OF

PERSONS HOLDING SITUATIONS UNDER THE CROWN,

IN THE

East India House, Bank of England,

THE VARIOUS LAW, CITY, AND ALL OTHER

PUBLIC OFFICES.

Abbot Rt. C. Duchy of Cornwall Of
Abbott Fras. Geo. Petty Bag Office
Abbott Hen. Bethune, Gen. Post Of
Abbott K.E. Conslr. Agent at Tehran
Abbott Ralph Dilnote, Custom Ho
Abdy Geo. Burlton, Custom Ho
Abercromby Hon. Ra. Amb. Srdinia
Aberdeen Earl, Privy Councillor
Abingdon Earl of, Ld. Lieut. of Berks
Aborn Geo. L. Millbank Prison
Acland Sir T.D. Excr. Bill Ln. Office
Adair Sir R. T. Privy Councillor
Adams Sir Chas. Elder Bro. Trinity H
Adam Sir Fredk. B. of Gen. Officers
Adam B. Samuel R. House of Lords
Adams Benj. General Post Office
Adams Ben. Gen. Register Office
Adams Chas. Thos. Custom House
Adams Edw. Richd. City Bridewell
Adams Fras. Woods' & Forests Offic
Adams Henry, Custom House
Adams Hy. Bentall, Woods & Forests
Adams John Berry, Gen. Post Office
Adams Mayow W. Woods & Forests
Adams Serjt. Middlesex Sessions
Adams Wm. Excise (Salisbury)
Adams William, Sewers' Office
Adams Wm. Woods' & Forests' Office
Adams Wm. Hawkins, Gen. Post Offi
Adams Wm. Chargé d'Aff. Peru
Adams Wm. Pitt, Consul at Lima
Adcock James, City Officer
Adderley Rd. Boyle, Exchr. Seal Offi
Adley John, Customs (Feversham)
Adlington T. E. Chancery Reg. Off
Adrian Emperor, Poor Law Office
Adrian William Thos. Treasury
Aitchison Jn. Paymaster-Gen's. Off
Aitken David, Admiralty, Somerset House
Akers James H. Seaman's Reg. Off
Albemarle Earl of, Privy Councllr
Albert H.R.H. Prince, K.G. Trinity House, & Ld. Wrdn. of Cornwall
Alchin Wm. T. Librarian, Guildhll
Alcock R. Consul at Foo-chow-foo
Alderson Sir Edwd. H. Brn. of Exchr
Alderson Thos. J Chancery Reg. Off
Aldrich Steph. Ct. of Bankruptcy
Aldridge Edwd. H. Queen's Bnch. Off
Aldridge John, Custom House
Aldridge Rd. General Post Office
Alexander H. Com. Lt. of London
Alexander Henry, East India Ho
Alexander Robert, Custom House
Alexander Rt. Dupre, Excheqr. Offi
Alexander Wm. Board of Ordnance
Alfred D. Col. & Emigration Board
Alfred Wm. Millbank Prison
Allen Anthony, House of Lords
Allan Wight Rt. Ecclstl. Com. Offi
Allen Arthur, Board of Ordnance
Allen Chas. P Westminster Sessions
Allen Chas. P. Middlesex Sessions
Allen Herbert, Custom House
Allen James, Excise Office
Allen John, Colonial Office
Allen John Fred. Board of Ordnance
Allen Joseph, Greenwich Hospital
Allen Joseph, War Office
Allen Robt. Board of Ordnance
Allen Thomas, Stamp & Tax Office
Allen Wm. Lndn. Dist. or T. Py. Post
Allen Wm. Hen. Court of Chancery
Allerton Richard, Custom House
Allfrey George, Lloyd's
Allin F. Queen's Remembrancer's O
Alsager Thos. M. Ct. of Bankruptcy
Alston Fras. Beilby, Foreign Office
Alston Willm. Vere, Audit Office
Althorpe Enoch, Quarter Master General's Office
Alton H. Consul at Terceira
Amedroz Hy. F. sen. Admty. Whitel
Amedroz Hy. F. jun. Admty. Whitel
Amedroz Hy. Fk. Admty. Somt. Ho
Amey Francis, Excise (Bristol)
Amherst Earl, Privy Councillor
Amphlett James, Custom House
Anderson Charles T. Py. Post
Anderson Chas. H. General Registr
Anderson Geo. Hay, Cstms. (Chestr)
Anderson Jas. Admlty. Smst House
Anderson Saml. Chncy. Affidvt. Offi
Anderson Thos. Russia Company
Anderson William, Excise Office
Anderson William, War Office
Anderson Wm. Geo. Paym. Gen's. Off
Anderson Wm. L. Admlty. Smst. Ho
Anderson Jas. Under Sheriff & Commission of Lieutncy. of Lndn
Andoe William, Audit Office
Andrew J. Customs (Maryport)
Andrewes Rev. G.T. Ho. of Commons
Andrews Grenville, Custom House
Andrews John, Gen. Post Office
Andrews Jn. Lambeth st. Police Ct
Andrews Thos. R. East India House
Andrews W.H. Hammrsmth. Pol. Ct
Angell Chas. Fd. Brd. of Ordnance
Angell Thos. Wm. Genl. Post Office
Angelo Hen. jun. Addiscombe
Anglesey Marq. of, K.G., G.C.B., K.P., Lord. Lt. of Angl. & Privy Councl r
Angus James, General Post Office
Angus John, General Register Office
Anketel Wm. Robert, Custom House
Annesley Jas. Consul at Barcelona
Annesley Jas. Consul, Amsterdam
Annesley Rev. F. British Museum
Ansell Chas. Queen Anne's Bnty. Of
Ansell Henry, Custom House
Anson Chas. Customs (Guernsey)
Anson G. Ed. Duchy of Cornwall Offi
Anson Col. Geo. Comm. in Chiefs Offi
Anson Sir Wm. Board of Gen. Officers
Ansted Dav. Thos. Addiscombe Sem
Anstruther Robert, Home Office
Appleton David, Admlty. Smst. Ho
Appleton Geo. East India House
Apps William, Tithe Commisson
Arber Hen. Bentick, Audit Office
Arbuthnot Chas. Privy Councilr
Arbuthnot George, Treasury
Arbuthnot Henry, Audit Office
Archer Geo. Samuel, Custom House
Archer Thomas, Treasury
Archer Wm. General Post Office
Archibald Lewis, M. London Director Post Office
Argent Jas. U. Customs (Colchester)
Arms John, Adjutant-Gen's. Office
Armstrong Chas. F. Gen. Post Offi
Armstrong Edward, Custom House
Armstrong Edwd. Gen. Post Office
Armstrong Ed. Paymaster Gen. Offi
Armstrong Geo. S. Gen. Post Office
Armstrong Jas. W. Seamans' Reg. O
Armstrong John A. Genl. Regist. Off
Arnaud Elias, Custom House
Arnaud Elias, Customs (Liverpool)
Arnaud J. M'Aulay, Custom House
Arnold Wm. R. South Sea House
Arnold Wm. R. Stamp & Tax Office
Arnot G. Customs (Berwick)
Arrowsmith Jsph. Insolvent Court
Ash George, Court of Chancery
Ash John, Board of Ordnance
Ash Wm. Woods & Forests' Offic
Ashford E. B. Gen. Register Office

Ashburton Lord, Privy Councillor, &Comr. for Promoting Fine Arts
AshfordE.B.Metropoltn.PoliceOffi
Ashley Lord, Commis. in Lunacy
Ashley George, City Officer
Aspain Henry, Home Office
Astell Wm.Govnr.RussiaCompany
AstonBenj.Rd.Ecclstl.Com.of Eng
Aston Benj.Richd. Qu. Anne'sBnty. Off. & Clk.TobaccoPipe Mak. Co
Aston Geo. Queen Anne's Bnty. Of
Aston JosephK.Queen Anne's Bnty
Aston Josias, Stamp & Tax Office
Atchison Geo. Court of Chancery
Atchley Wm. Henry, Treasury
AtkinsAnthony,Paymstr.Gen'sOffi
Atkins Fred.PaymasterGen'sOffice
Atkins Lionel, Land Revne. Recds
AtkinsSam.E.Clk.Clockmakers'Co
AtkinsonBeamont,Admlty.Smst.H
Atkinson John, Gen. Post Office
Atkinson Robt. Admlty. Smst. Ho
Atkinson Thos. Gen. Post Office
Atkinson Thos. G. Gen. Post Office
AtkinsonWm.Court of Bankruptcy
Atterbury Jas. LondonD.Post Offic
Attree Joseph, Board of Ordnance
Attree W. W. Tithe Commission
Attwater Wm. General Post Office
Attwell Joseph, Excise Office
Auckland Earl of, Privy Councilr
Auckland John, Custon House
Austin Alfred, Board of Ordnance
Austin Alfred, Poor Law Asst.Com
Austin Joshua, Excise Office
Austin Thomas, Poor Law Office
Avery Thomas, Customs (Truro)
Ayers James, Foreign Office
Ayrton W. S. Court of Bankruptcy

Bach Edmund, British Museum
Bache Henry, Board of Ordnance
Backhouse Geo. Canning, Forgn.O
BaconAugustusEdwd.K.WarOffice
Bacon Charles, Stamp & Tax Office
Bacon Rd. Taxing Masters' Office
Bacon Thomas, Court of Chancery
Badcock John, Excise (Sheffield)
Baggaley Wm. Walter, Gen.Post O
Bagster George, Audit Office
Bailey George, Stamp & Tax Office
Bailey Henry Chas. Gen. Post. Offi
Bailey James, Treasury
Bailey James Thos. Custom House
Baily Robert, House of Commons
Baines Cuthbert John,Gen.PostOff
Baines Henry, Court of Exchequer
Baines T. Custom House
Baird James, War Office
Baird Wm. M.D. British Museum
Baker Henry, Board of Ordnance
Baker James, Board of Ordnance
Baker James, Court of Chancery
Baker John, Privy Council Office
Baker John Strange, Gen.Post Offi
Baker Joseph, Treasury
Baker Rd. General Post Office
Baker Robert, Home Office
Baker T. Lndn. Dist.(or T. Py.) Pst
Baker William, jun. Sewers' Office
Baker Wm.jun.Dep.Cor.ofMiddlsx
Baker Wm.sen.Coroner for Middlx
BakerW.A.Lndn.Dist (orT.Py.)Pst
Balfour Charles, Home Office
Balgue George, Custom House
Balguy John, Com. of Bankruptcy
BallF.L.Sec.of Leg. Rio de la Plata
Ballantine Wm. Thames Police Ct
Ballard George, Excise Office
Ballard James, Bank of England
Baller John, Customs (Bideford)
Baly Dr. William, Millbank Prison
Bamford Thomas, Treasury
Bandinel James, Foreign Office
Banitt S. S. Stamp & Tax Office
Bankes Geo.Curstr.Baron of Exchr
Bankhead Charles, Amb. toMexico
Banks Benjamin, Poor Law Office
Banks Wm. Bank of England
Banning Charles, Gen. Post Office
Banton Wm. East India House
Barber Dean, Board of Trade
Barber George, Poor Law (Ireland)
Barber Gilbert, Stamp & TaxOffice
Barber James, Prerogative Court
Barber Jnthn. Excise Off. LondonN
Barber John,Com.ofCoalWhippers
Barber Wm. Court of Bankruptcy
Barber William, Custom House
Barchard Rt. Wm. CoalWhlprs.Co

Barfield Thomas, Excise (Wales)
Barfoot Oliver, Genl. Register Offi
Baring Francis T. Privy Councillor
Baring Thos.Excheqr.BillLoanOffi
Baring Hon. W. B. Privy Councillor, & Commissioner of Revenue Inquiry, & Tithe Commissioner & Chelsea Hospital
Barker Arthur Rd.Stamp&TaxOffi
Barker Wm.Bennett,Woods & For
Barker Wm. John, Woods&Forests
Barker Wm. W. Consul at Messina
Barlow Fra. Sec. of Presentations, Mast. in Lunacy &Visitor of Lun
Barlow G.B. Crown Off. Qn's.Bnch
Barlow Geo. Chinner,Gen.Post Off
Barlow James Pratt, Archdeacon of Surrey's Registry
Barlow Thos. Judgment Office, Queen's Bench
Barnard Benj. Com. Ltncy. Lndn
Barnard C.T.Sec.of Leg.atDresden
Barnard Chas. Wm. Gen. Post Off
BarnardWm.Williams,Gen.PostOf
Barne George, Custom House
Barnes George, Custom House
Barnes Hen.E. ClerktoMercers'Co
Barnes Henry Hickman, Solicitor to Exchequer Bill Loan Office
Barnes John, Crt. of Bankruptcy
Barnes Saml. Ct. of Queen's Bnch
Barnett Col. Consul, Alexandria
Barnett Ebnzr. East India House
Barnett Wm. National Debt Office
Barney Richard, Poor Law Office
BarnhamChs.Wyndham,Bd.Ordnc
Barr Henry, General Post Office
Barratt Chas. Exchequer Office
Barrie Col. Consulr. Asst. Madrid
Barron Eustace, Consul, San Blas
Barrow George, Colonial Office
BarrowJohn,Admiralty,Whitehall
Barrow Peter, Consul at Caen
Barrow Ths. C. Admiralty, Somerset House
BarryChas.Com.for Imp.Metropols
BarryRobert,Gen.Ship Owners'Soc
Barth Chas.Edmd.Gen. Post Office
Barth Wm. Gen. Post Office
Barth Wm. Thos. Gen. Post Offi
Bartlett Joshua, Excise Office
Bartlett John, General Post Office
Bartlett Rd. Consul, Teneriffe
Bartlett Wm. Admlty.SomersetHo
Bartley Robert, Bd. of Ordnance
Barton John, Vice Consul, Callao
Barton William Henry,Royal Mint
Basilico Andrew, Admlty.Smst.Ho
Bassano WalterW. ArmyMedcl.Bd
Bassett John, Excise (Chester)
Bassett Mrs. Cath. Millbank Prison
Bassit J. Loveless,GreenwichHosp
BastickJhn.Lndn.Dist.orT.Py.Post
Batchelour George, Treasury
Bate John, General Post Office
Bates George, General Post Office
Bates James, Home Office
Bates Joah Furey, Custom House
Bates Robert, Custom House
Batho Henry, Excise Office
Bathurst E. Consul, Copenhagen
Bathurst Hen. Thos. D. Audit Off
Battcock Charles, Gen. Post Off
Batten Wm. Henry, East India Ho
Batterbee Jas. House of Peers
Batty Espine, Irish Office
Bauldry Robert, General Post Offi
Bawden Tobias, Custom House
Bax Capt. Henry B.Trinity House
Baylee Henry Wm. Admlty.Whthl
Bayley John, Crt. of Queen's Bnch
Bayley Wm. General Register Off
Bayley Wm. B. Director East India Company
Bayliffe John, Custom House
Baylis A. J. Sup.Regr.(London ea)
Baylis R. Clerkenwell police ct
Bayly Chas. Geo. V. Council Off
Bayne Ralph, Board of Ordnance
Baynes Sir E. S.ConsulSt.Ptrsburg
Baynton Edward, Audit Office
Beachcroft Rt. Z. Genl. Post Office
Beal John, Home Office
Beale Bernard Geo. Gen.PostOffice
Beales Joseph, Custom House
Beard Edward, Stamp & TaxOffice
Beard John M. Stamp & Tax Office
Beatty John, Stamp & Tax Office
Beauchamp Jsph. Sidney, Treasury
Beauclerk Henry W. India Board

Beaufort Capt.Fras.Admlty.Whthl
Beaufort John, Gen. Post Office
Beaumont Charles, Custom House
Beaumont Edward, Custom House
Beaumont Jn.N.Cstms.(Montrose)
Beauvale Lord, G.C.B.,Privy Cncllr
Beck Robert, Custom House
Becket SirJohn,bt.PrivyCouncillor
Beckley Benj. Stamp & Tax Office
Beckwith John M. Royal Mint
Bedder Joseph, Woods & Forests
Beddoe Chas. M. Gen. Post Office
Beddome Samuel, City Officer
Bedford Chas.St.C.Cor.ofWestmnr
Bedford Lieut. Fred.Grenwh.Hsptl
Bedford Henry, Admlty.Whitehall
Beeby James, Admlty. Somset. Ho
Beeston John, Custom House
Beetham Fras. IrishDeeds Registry
Beevor Hen.Ths.BoardofOrdnance
Behneke W. L. Consul at Lubeck
Belcher Alex. B. Ct. of Bankruptcy
Bell Adolphus, Home Office
Bell Edw. Customs(Newport,Mon)
Bell John, Genl. Post Office
Bell John, Consul at Oran
Bell Richd. Customs (Yarmouth)
Bell Richard S. Genl. Post Office
Bell Robert, Admiralty, Whitehall
Bell Robert, Genl. Post Office
Bell Robert, Sewers' Office
Bell Robert, Custom House
BellSaml. Londn.Dist.orT.Py.Post
Bell Wm. Paymaster Genl.'s Office
Bell Wm.H. Admiralty, Whitehall
Bellairs Geo. Woods & Frsts. Offi
Bellamy Edmund, House of Com
Bellamy J. Poor Law Office
Bellamy Rd. Chelsea Hospital
Bellamy Wm. Customs (Penzance)
Bellamy Wm. House of Commons
Bellis Jonath. W. Bd. of Ordnance
Belton John, General Post Office
Beltz Samuel, Treasury
Benbow Thos. Messgr.toBd.Gn.Off
BengeFred.Wms.Admlty.Somst.H
Benham George, Custom House
Bennett Abm. Stamp & Tax Office
Bennett Charles, Gen. Post Office
BennettEdwd.Master inExchequer
Bennett Geo. Stamp & Tax Office
BennettJas.Customs(Bridlington)
Bennett John, Gen. Post Office
Bennett John J. British Museum
Bennett Saml. Board of Ordnance
Bennett Thomas, Excise Office
Bennett Thos. Edwd. Excise Office
BennettW.WolleyL.Remembr.Offi
Benson Rev. Sam. Hrsmgr.la.Gaol
Benthall John, PettyBagOff.Chncy
Bentinck Rev. W.H.E.SignetOffice
Bentley Henry Wm. Custom Ho
Bentley John, Bank of England
Bentley Matthew, Admiralty, Somerset House
Bentley Wm. Bank of England
Berdmore Chas. General Post Off
Berdmore W.DeLisle,Gen.Post Off
Bere Montague B. Commissioner of Bankruptcy
Berens Hy. Exchequer Bill Office
Berens Hy.CommonLtncy.London
Berens H. H. Hudson's Bay Comp
Berens Jsph. Exchr. Bill Loan Offi
Beresford Visct. Privy Councillor
BeresfordJn.G.Customs(Dundalk)
Bergne John Brodribb, Foreign Off
Bernard Charles, Custom house
Bernard Edward, Custom Kouse
Bernard sol.toExch.Bl.LoanOf
Bernard Philip, War Office
Berrey JohnA.Clk.Records&Writs
Berridge George, Irish Office
Berrill John, Custom House
Berry Denham, Admlty. Somst.Ho
Berry Rd. Judge Advct.Gnls.Office
Berthorn Peter Hen.Trinity House
BertolacciFrankRt.Bd.ofOrdnance
Bertram Chas. A. Gen. Post Office
Besborough Earl, Ecclesiastical Com. for England, & Privy Councillor
Bester Joseph, Insolvent Court
Beswick Anthony S. Board of Ord
Bettell Wm. Stamp & Tax Office
Beverley Earl of,Privy Councillor,
Beverley Richard, Custom House
Beverly Philip, Custom House
Bexley Lord, Privy Councillor
Beynon John, Custom House

Bezer George, Custom House
Bezer Henry, Custom House
Bezer Wm. Joseph, Custom Ho
Bicknell Hen. Clerk to Grocers' Co
Bicknell Hen. E.Chncy.Regstr.Off
Bicknell Thos. Supt. of Police (V)
Biddle Edward, War Office
Biddulph M. Lord Lieut. Denbigh
Bide John, Custom House
BidgoodR.Com.of P.Cncl.forTrade
Bidwell John, Foreign Office
Bidwell John,jun. Foreign Office
Biggar John, Admlty.Somst.House
Bignell Thomas, General Post Off
Biller Jho. Lndn. Dist.orT.Py.Post
Billinge William, Custom House
Bincks Jas.Lndn.Dis. orT.Py.Post
BinghamHon.R.Sec.ofleg.atTurin
Bingham Joseph, Stamp & Tax Off
Bingham Prgrne. Wrship. st.Pol.ct
Bingley Henry, Royal Mint
Binney John Thos. Colonial Office
Birch James N. House of Lords
Birch John Wm. House of Lords
Birch Peregrine, House of Lords
Birch Samuel, British Museum
BirchamF.T.Under-Sherf.of Lndn
Bird Robert, General Post Office
Bird Thomas, General Post Office
Birt John, Custom House
Bishop George, Home Office
Bishop John Drinkwater, Audit Of
Bishop Wm. Marlboro'st.PoliceCrt
Bissett Rd. Board of Ordnance
Black Alexander, Custom House
Black Joseph, Customs (Derry)
Black Patrick, Customs (Whitby)
Black Wm. Hen. Public Record Of
Blackburn John Edwd. Foreign Of
Blackburn William, Excise Office
Blackburne Wm. Ireland, India Bd
Blacker Latham,Csts.Sol.forIrelnd
Blackler Rt. Seamans' Register Of
Blackett Chas. Robt.CustomHouse
Blackwood Arthur, Colonial Office
Blackwood Thomas, CustomHouse
Blades Joseph, Stationery Office
Blagend Jas. Customs (Chichester)
Blaiklock John, Genl. Post Office
Blair W. E. Com. of P.C. forTrade
Blake George, Custom House
Blake Jas.Jos.Sup.Reg.St.Saviours
Blake John K. Exchequer
Blakesley Richd. Custom House
Blakston John, Custom House
BlamireWm. Tithe Commissioner, & Copyhold Commissioner
Bland George, Gen. Post Office
Bleaden John, City Officer
Blencowe Sam. Jas.Stamp&TaxOff
Bligh Hon. J. D.Ambsr.toHanover
Blink Geo.LondonDist.orT.Py.Pos
Bliss Wm. General Post Office
Bloomfield Hon. John A.D. Envoy Ex. & Min. Plen. to Russia
Bloomfield Lord, Privy Councillor
Blott Wm. General Post Office
Blount George, Audit Office
Blount Walter A. Herald's Col
Bluett Wm. Stamp & Tax Office
Blunt Chas. Consul at Salonica
Blunt Joseph, Solr. to Royal Mint
Blunt Sam. Jasper, Colonial Office
Blyth George, Audit Office
Board William, Custom House
Boatwright John, Gen. Post Office
Bock Henry, Bank of England
Bocquet Francis, Bank of England
Bocquet Robert, Bank of England
Boddy E.J.Writ Office,Qn's.Bench
Boddy Hen. D. Admlty. Somst. Ho
Boddy John, Treasury
Boddy John M. Admlty. Somst.Ho
Bokenham Wm. General Post Offi
Bolden G. Hammersmith Pol. Ct
Boler William, Royal Mint
Bolton Jsph. L. Presentation Offi
Bomeester Geo. Consul at Cagliair
Bonatti G. Consul at Scutari
Bond Benj McDermott,Custom Ho
Bond Benjamin, Custom House
Bond Edward A. British Museum
Bond John Jas. Public Record Offi
Bond R.DownerWebb,Poor Law O
Bond Wm. Marylebone Police Ct
Bond Wm. Westminster Police Ct
Bonham E. W. Consular Agent at Tabreez
Bonneau Cornelius,Bd.ofOrdnance
Bonner Col. John Geo.India House

Bonnet L. G. I. Genl. Register Offi
Bentein John Pitt, Gen. Post Offi
Booth James, House of Commons
Booth James, Stamp & Tax Office
Booth John, Custom House
Booth Robert, Stamp & Tax Office
Boothby Sir Wm. Custom House
BOothby Chas. E. Privy CouncilOff
Borradaile J. H. Stamp & Tax Offi
Borrow Cornelius Jago, War Office
Borrow John, War Office
BosanquetChas.Comn.Ltncy.Lndn
Bosanquet Chas.Exchr.Bill Ln.Offi
Bosanquet Sir J. B. Privy Counclr
Bosanquet S. R. South Sea House
Boston James, Custom House
Boswell J. Woods & Forests Office
Boswood Daniel, Gray's Inn
Boteler Wm. Fuller, Lincoln's Inn
BottChas.Joseph,Natnl.DebtOffice
Boucher John, Ct. of Exchequer
Bouchier John, Ct. of Exchequer
Bouchier John E.East India House
Bouchier Thomas, Gen. Post Office
Bouchier Thos. Stamp & Tax Office
Bouffler John, Paymaster Gen. Offi
BoulcottJoseph,Ordnance Offi.Tow
Boult Thomas, Court of Chancery
Boulton James, Stamp &Tax Office
BoultonJas.C.Report Off.Chancery
BourdillonEdw.Dewar,IndiaHouse
Bourdin MarkA.Stamp &TaxOffice
BourlieurJohn Stephen,Custom Ho
Bourne Edwd. General Post Office
Bourne Henry, General Post Office
BourneJas.Johnstone, Ordn.Board
Boustred J.A. G. Bow st. Police Ct
BouverieHon.P.P.Com.Ltcy.Lndn
Bowden Jas. Admlty. Somrst. Ho
BowditchStephenH.Gen.Registr.O
BowenFras.Metropltn.PoliceOffice
Bowen Hen.Lond. Dist. Post Office
BowenJas.Hill,Rg.of DesignsOffice
Bowen John, Exchequer Office
Bower E. Geo. Ordnance Board
Bowker John, Greenwich Hospital
Bowles Charles, Addiscombe Sem
Bowles John, Adjutant Genl's. Offi
Bowman Peter, Treasury
Bowness John, Custom House
BowringEdgarA.Com.of P.C.forTd
Bowyer Jas. Taxing Master's Offi
Bowyer John, Court of Chancery
Boxall Alfred, Custom House
Boyce Wm. Fras. Bd. of Ordnance
Boyd Charles, Custom House
BoydCharles,jun.Seaman'sReg.Offi
Boyd Edwin, Custom House
Boyd George, Treasury
BoydJames, Seaman's RegisterOffi
Boyd Maitland W. Gen. Post Offi
Boyden Thos. General Post Office
BoyerGeo. Phelps,Ordnance Board
Boyer James, Clerk to Coopers' Co
Boyes John, Custom House
Boyle David, Privy Councillor
Boyle John, Customs' (Glasgow)
Boys William, Excise Office
Brackenbury J. M. Consul, Cadiz
Bradford J. Custom House
Bradley Chas. L. Pentonvll. Prison
Bradley John, Rolls Court
Bradley Rt. Board of Ordnance
BradlyWm.Wyborn B.ofOrdnance
Brady Antonio, Admlty. Smst. Ho
Brady Wm. General Post Office
Bragg Henry A. Custom House
Bragg John, Royal Engineers' Offi
Braithwaite Thos. W.Ct.of Chncry
Braithwaite Wm. Custom Office
Brand Ferdinand, City Officer
Brand William, City Officer
Brande George William, Treasury
Brande William Thos. Royal Mint
Brander Alfd.L.Board of Ordnance
Brandon W.Lord Mayor's Ct.Office
Brant James, Consul at Erzeroom
Brant Rd. Wm. Consul at Smyrna
Branwell Thos. Bronte, War Office
Bray Reginald, Sol. British Musm
Braysher John, Custom House
Breeze John Scott, Bd.of Ordnance
Brent Wm. Brent, Palace Court
Breton Eliab, Metro. Police Office
BrewerSydneyJohn, CustomHouse
Brickhill James, Custom House
BrickwoodJohnS.Exr.BillLoanOffi
Bridges Rbt.Lndn.Dist.orT.Py.Pos
BridgesWm. Queen Anne's Bounty Office
Bridgwater J. Excise (Rochester)
Bridgwater Jn. Pugh, Stmp.& Tax
Bridseye J. Stamp & Tax Office
Briers Daniel, Ordnance Board
Briers Edwd. P. Board of Ordnance
BrietzckeE.I.Admlty.Somst.House
Briggs Edmund George, War Office
Briggs John Hen. Admlty.Whiteh
BriggsJohn Thos.Admlty.Smst.Ho
Bright Dr.John,Visitor of Lunatics
Bright John, Poor Law Office
Bright John, jun. Poor Law Office
BrittenDan.Commsn.Ltncy.Londn
Britten J.Meek,Comn.Ltncy. Lond
Britton James, Custom House
Broad Chas. Henry, Ordn. Board
Broad Chas. M. Ct.ofQueen'sBench
Broadhurst Wm. Ct. of Exchequer
Brock James, Custom House
BrockmanChas.Paymstr.Gen's.Off
Brockman J. D.Cnsl.atKonigsberg
BrockwellGeo.Edwd.Genl.PostOffi
Broderip Wm. J. Thames PoliceCt
BrodieChas.Geo.Alex.Bd.ofOrdnce
Brodie James, General Post Office
BrodieStuart,Admiralty,SomerstH
Brogden Jas. Comn.Ltncy.London
Bromley James, Greenwich Hospl
BromleyRdMadox,Admlty.Smst.H
Brooke&WarwickEarlLd.Lt.Wark
Brooks John Wm.Bank ofEngland
Brooks W. Sup. Reg. (Rotherhith)
Brooksbank Thomas C. Treasury
Brooksbank Thos.C.ChelseaHosptl
Brooksby Chas.House of Commons
Bros Thomas, Bank of England,&c
Broster James, Treasury
Broster Wm. Customs (Poole)
Brothers Fras. Excise (Dover)
Brougham&VauxLd.PrivyCouncIr
BroughamWm.Master inChancery
BroughtonRt.E.Worshipst.Plce.Ct
Brown Anthony,Chambln.ofLondn
Brown Archibald, Stamp & Tax
Brown Charles, Home Office
Brown DavidS.Seaman'sRegstr.Of
Brown Chas. Remembrancer's Offi
Brown Chas. James, Excise Office
Brown Major-GeneralGeorge,K.H. Deputy-Adjutant General
Brown Fredk.Josh.Gen.Post Office
Brown Henry Chas. Custom House
Brown James, Customs (Poole)
Brown James, General Post Office
Brown Jas. Masters' Off. Chancery
Brown Jas. Southwark Police Crt
Brown JamesSam.Genl.Post Office
Brown John, Audit Office
Brown John, Custom House
Brown John, Stamp & Tax Office
Brown John Marmaduke, Cust.Ho
Brown JohnS.Seaman'sRegstr.Offi
Brown Martin, Board of Ordnance
Brown Nevill, City Officer
Brown Robert, Ct. of Bankruptcy
Brown Rt. D. Admrly.Somrset.Ho
Brown Robert, British Museum
Brown Sam. C. Excise (Coventry)
Brown Sidney M. Genl. Post Office
Brown Spencer, Board of Ordnance
Brown Thomas, General PostOffice
Brown Thomas,Seaman'sRegistr.O
Brown Timothy Y.Consul at Genoa
BrownWalter,Lndn.Dist.orTPvPst
Brown Wm. General Post Office
Brown William, War Office
Brown Wm. A. Admlty. Smst. Ho
Brown Wm. Jas. Woods & Forests
Brown W.R.H.Ct ofCommonPleas
Browne Agst.F.D.Admlty.Smst Ho
Browne Charles, Custom House
Browne Edmund, Stamp &TaxOffi
Browne Edward J. Poor LawOffice
Browne George, East India House
Browne Geo. jun. East IndiaHouse
Browne Geo.H.Paymastr.Gen'sOffi
Browne Hen. M.Ecclesias.Com.Off
Browne John, Gen. Post Office
BrowneJohnH.Seaman'sRegstr.Of
Browne JohnMarmaduke,Customs
Browne Neville, Mansion House
BrowneNich.E.Cstms.(Beaumaris)
Browne Peter,Sec.of Leg.Cophagn
Browne Richd. AdmiraltyRegistry
Browne Thos. Customs(Alderney)
BrowneWm.Lawrence,Grnl.PostO
Browne William R. Custom House
Browning Thos. Clk.toDistillersCo
Brownlow Earl,LordLieut.Lincoln
Brownrigg John, Audit Office
Browse Hen. MetropolisRds.Office
Bruce Chas. Adjutant Gen's. Office
Bruce Ld. Ernest,Privy Councillor
Bruce Sir J.L.Knight,Vice-Chnclr. & Judge of the Court of Review
Bruce Jas. R. Ecclesias. Com. Off
Bruce Lewis B. Knight,Ct.ofChncy
Bruce Wm. Jsph. AdjutantGen's.O
Brumell John, Custom House
Brumfit C. Genl. Register Office
Brummell J. Custom House
Brummell William, Treasury
Brunker John, Gen. Post Office
Brush Samuel, LondonD.PostOffice
Brutten Rt.Supr.Regr.Bethnal grn
Bryan Frederick, Stationery Office
Bryan Jsph. Woods &ForestsOffice
Bryant Edward, Bank of England
Bryant George, Inner Temple
Brydges Sir H. J. Privy Councillor
Bryer John G.Worship st.PoliceCt
Buccleuch Jno. F. Ct. of Chancery
Buccleuch Duke of, Lord Lieut. of Roxburgh, Privy Councillor, & Com. of Health of Towns
Buchan Ralph, Treasury
Buchanan And. Sec. of Leg.Russia
BuchananJamesG.GreenwichHosp
Buckett Nich. M. Customs (Scilly)
Buckham John, Royal Mint
Buckingham Duke of, Privy Counc
Buck James, General Post Office
Buckland Wm. D.D. Dean of Westminster
Buckland Edward C. Treasury
Buckle Henry, Lloyd's
Buckle John, Excise (Barnstaple)
Buckle Robert,Excise(Cambridge)
BuckleWm.Hill,Cstms.(Ramsgate)
Buckley Mrs. Ann, Qtr.Mst.Gen.Of
Budd Geo.London Dist.Post Office
Bulkley Edwd.Stamp & Tax Office
Bulgin Thos.A.Ct.ofCommonPleas
Bull J. Journal Offi.House of Coms
Bull James, Customs (Scilly)
Buller James, Tithe Commissioner
Buller Thomas Wentworth, Tithe Commissioner & Copyhold Comr
Bullivant John, C. of Common Pls
Bullock Ed. Deputy Judge Advt. Gen. & Judge of Sheriff's Court
Bullock Frederick, Custom House
Bullock James Stephens, Customs
Bullock Watts E. Ct. of Bnkptcy
Bulpit Henry, General Post Office
Bumell George, Custom House
Bulwer Henry Lytton, Ambas. at Madrid & Privy Councillor
Bunce Jas. Masters' Office, Q. Ben
Buncombe Thos. BoardofOrdnance
Bunnett George, Custom House
BunnettWm.J.HAdmlty.Somst.Ho
Bunster Hen.Exchr.BillLoanOffice
Bunter Fredk. Stamp & Tax Office
Burbidge William, Excise Office
Burchell Jas.Sheriff's Office,Middx
BurchellWm.Sheriff'sOffice,Middx
Burckhardt Fras. H. Gen. Post Of
Burder Jno.Sol.toQn.Ann'sBnty.O
Burdon Thos. Kpr. Whitecross st
Burgess Hen.G. Board of Ordnance
Burgoyne Maj. Gen.Sir John Fox, Board of Ordnance
Burke Benj. Stamp & Tax Office
Burke J. Woods & Forests' Office
BurkeJsph.PoorL. Office (Ireland)
Burkitt Edwd. Clerk to Curriers' & to Tin Plate Workers' Companies
Burltom Henry, Custom House
BurmanJohn S.Exchr. of Pleas Off
Burman Rd. Exchr. of Pleas Off
Burmester John I. Admlty.Smst.H
Burn James, Custom House
Burnaby Robert, Custom Ho
BurnabyWm.Dyott,Bowst.PoliceC
Burnard Hugh Piper, Custom Ho
Burnet John, Custom House
Burnett Hen.P.D.PaymstGen.'sOff
Burnett Sir W. Admlty. Somst. Ho
Burningham Thos. Mstr. Off. Chy
Burra Jas. Clk. to Embroids'. Co
Burrell John P.WestminsterPolice Court
Burridge Edw.Hen. Southwk.P. Ct
Burridge Stph. Cstms. (Padstow)
Burrow Alfred A. Gen. Post Off
Burrow William, Poor Law Office
Burslem Hen.Paymaster Gen.'s Off
Burton John, General Post Off
Burton F. Greenwich Police Court
Burton Harry, Custom House
BurtonJsph.Lndn.Dist.orT.Py.Pst
Burton Saml.W.Admrlty.Somst.H
Burt Joseph, Public Record Office
Burwood Hen.Custms.(Southwold)
Bury James, Home Office
Bussell Thos.Arthur(CustomHous)
Busson William, Royal Mint
Bute Marqs.of,L.Lieut.Glamorgan
Butler George, Board of Ordnance
Butler George Hen. Custom House
Butler Hen.Admlty. Somst. House
Butler James, Consul at Tetuan
Butler John, Bank of England
Butler Miles, Excise (Lincoln)
Butler P. O'Bryan,Stamp&Tax Off
Butler Thomas, British Museum
Butterfield Chas. Trinity House
ButterworthHen Com.Ltncy.Lndn
Buzzard Geo.Sup.Regr.(St.James')
Byers AlfredC.Stamp & Tax Office
Byers Wm.Coppin,BoardofOrdnce
Byham George, Ordnance Board
Byham Henry, Board of Ordnance
Byham Richard, Board of Ordnce
Byham Wm. Rd. Board of Ordnce
Byng George S. Privy Councillor
Bynner Henry, Consul at Trieste
Byron Francis, Treasury
Byron William, East India House

Caddy James, General Post Office
Cahill Edward, Admlty. Smst. Ho
Cain John, Westmr.r. Police Crt
Caldewood Upton, Bd.of Ordnance
Caldwell George, Custom House
Caldwell William, Custom House
Cale Rd. Julian, Genl. Post Office
Cambridge Duke of,Privy Counclr
Cameron Eneas, Custom House
Cammille Henry, Custom House
Campbell Lord, Privy Councillor
Campbell Sir Hen.Fred.Palace Crt
Campbell SirRt.Coms.Ltncy.Lndn
Campbell SirR. Direc.EastIndiaCo
Campbell Alexr. Custom House
Campbell Archibald, Custom Ho
Campbell Christphr.Jas. Gen.Pt.O
Campbell Colin, Excise Office
Campbell Duncan, East India Ho
Campbell James, Genl. Post Office
Campbell John,Crt.of Bankruptcy
Campbell Dr. John, Greenwh. Hos
Campbell John R. Greenwich Hospital School
Campbell Lieut. Consul at Milan
Campbell Thos. East India House
CampbellThs.C.R.Seaman'sReg.Of
Campbell Ths. Theodore, Audit Off
Campbell Wm. Genl. Post Office
Cancellor J. H. Mastr. Cmn. Pleas
CandlerBenj.L.Cstms.(Southwold)
Cane Rd. Basil, Poor Law Office
Canney Thos. Admlty. Somrst. Ho
Canning Sir S. Ambssdr. to Turkey
Cannon JohnEdwd.Stamps&TaxOf
Cannon Rd. Adjutant Genl's. Off
Cannon Walter,Stamp & TaxOffice
Canterbury Archbishp.Privy Cnclr
Cape Rev.Jonath. AddiscombeSem
Capes Joseph, Royal Mint
Capper John Henry, Home Office
CapperSam. Js. Cmsn.Ltncy.Lndn
Capps Sampson, Custom House
Carbould Rd. Thos. Bank of Engld
Card Hen. Benson, Genl. Post Offi
Carlisle Earl of, Privy Councillor
Carlisle John, Customs (Dundalk)
Carlisle Nicholas, British Museum
Carmichael Chas. Ct. of Chancery
CarmichaelWm.Court ofChancery
Carpenter Wm.Hen.Brtsh.Museum
Carr Andrew Merton, Excise Office
Carrington Lord, Lord Lieutenant Buckinghamshire
Carrington Rev. Henry Court of Peculiars
Carrington Wm. Hen. Custom Ho
Carroll Sir Geo. Aldermn. of Lndn
Carroll Wm. General Post Office
Carruthers Peter, Exchequer Off
Carter Chas. Admlty. Somerst. Ho
Carter George, Exchequer Office
Carter John, City Officer
CarterJohn,Southwk.Ct.of Record
Carter Joseph, Cmsn. Ltncy. Lndn
Carter Stephen,Board of Ordnance
Carter Thomas, Adjutant Gen's.Off
Carter Thos. Emmerson, Customs

Carter William, Custom House
Carteret Lord, Privy Councillor
CartledgeThos.Secrety.of Lunatics
Cartwright Chas.Sharp,Custom Ho
Cartwright Edwd. Gen. Post Off
Cartwright Sir T.Ambsr.to Sweden
Carver Rev. Jas. Ord. Whtcrs. st
Casberd Robert M. Exchequer Bill Loan Office
CaseyLieut.D.O'Brien,Grnwh.Hptl
Cassell Fred. Customs (Douglas)
Cassell F. Customs (Hull)
Cash Wm. Com. of Coal Whippers
Cassidi Chas. Board of Ordnance
Casterton H.Customs(Lynn Regis)
Castleden M. J. Genl. Regstr. Of
Castleden S. Metrop. Carriage Of
Castlereagh Visct. Privy Councir
Castley Wm. General Post Office
Cater Thos. Duff, Bd. of Ordnance
Cates James, British Museum
Catterson Stepn. Bank of England
Cattley C. R. Consul at Kertch
Cattley Henry, Russia Company
Cattley John, Russia Company, & Eastland Company
Cattley Steph. W. Eastland Compy
Cattlin Samuel, Genl. Post Office
Caulier Henry, Custom House
Cavan Charles, Custom House
Cayley Henry, Eastland Company
Chadwick Edwin, Poor Law Office
Chalk Jas.G.Ecclesiastical Com.Of
Chalkey Thomas, Insolvent Court
Challis Henry W.Bank of England
Challis Thomas, Alderman
Chalmer Jas. A. Board of Ordnance
Chalmers Robert, House of Cmns
Chambers Thomas, Audit Office
Champ Chas. Admlty. Somrst. Ho
Champ Philip, Custom House
ChampneyDaniel,Bank of England
Chance George, Treasury
ChaneyJph.Lndn. Dist.or T.Py.Pst
Chant Jas. Col. Emigration Board
Chaplin Rev. Edward, Gray's inn
Chaplin Richard Piper,Admiralty, Somerset House
ChaplinWm.J.Aldmn&Shrf.of Lon
Chapman Abel, Hudson's BayCom
Chapman Capt. Aaron, Trinity Ho
Chapman Capt. Abel, Trinity Ho
ChapmanLieut.F.E.Rl.Enginrs.Off
Chapman Edwd. Hen. Bank of Eng
Chapman James, Custom House
Chapman John, Audit Office
Chapman Robert, Custom House
Chapman Thos. Chairman Lloyd's
ChapmanW.Greenwood,Colonl.Off
Chappell Samuel, Custom House
Chappell Thomas B. Sup.Registrar
Charlton T. jun. Ct. of Peculiars
Charnaud J. Consul at Smyrna
Chasseaud G.V.Consul Alexandria
Chatfield A.T.Customs(Stornaway)
Chatfield Fred. Cnsl. San Salvador
Chatterton Joseph, Custom House
Cheatham James, Custom House
Cheesewright Rd. City Officer
Cheetham Jsph. Brd. of Ordnance
Cheetham W. Board of Ordnance
Chenery Henry, Genrl. Post Office
Cheshire Wm. General Post Office
Chester Harry, Privy CouncilOffice
ChesterWilliamDouglas, CustomH
Chesterton Chas. Sewers' Office
Chesterton G. L. House of Correc
Chesterfield, Earl of, Privy Cnclr
Chetwynd Geo. Genl. Post Office
ChetwyndWm. J.General Post Offi
Chichester, Earl of, Ecclesiastical Commissioner (England)
Chichester Hon. F. A. H.Audit Offi
Child James, Treasurer
Ching Chas. Ct. of Queen's Bench
Ching Hen. Ct. of Queen's Bench
Chinner William Henry, War Offi
Chisholm Hen. W. Exchequer Offi
Chivers Wm. Stamp & Tax Office
Cholmondeley Marquis of, Privy Councillor
Choun Wm. Admiralty, Whitehall
Christie John, Admlty. Whitehall
Christmas C. G. Land Revenue Offi
Chubb John, Excise Office
Chubb John, Stamp & Tax Office
Church Frederick, Custom House
Church John T. Ct. of Bnkruptcy
Churchill Benj. Genl. Post Office
Churchill Edwd. Genl. Post Office
Churchill James, Excise Office
Churchill John B. Genl. Post Offi
ChurchillThos. General PostOffice
Clack Thos. Edw.Board of Ordance
Clague Rt. D. Customs (Bridport)
Clanricarde Marqs. Privy Counclr
Clapham George Erasmus, Custom House
Clapham James, Woods & Forests
Clapperton Jhn. Consul at Tarsons
Clarac J.S.Ldn. Dist. or T.Py. Post
Clarac Lewis S. Genl. Post Office
Clare Earl of, K.P. Privy Councllr
Clare Willis, Genl. Post Office
Clarendon Earl of, Privy Councir
Claridge Charles, Custom House
Clark Edwd. Admlty.Somst. House
Clark Francis, East India House
Clark George, Insolvent Drs.' Ct
Clark Henry, Treasury
Clark James, Excise Office
Clark Jas. Rd. Admlty. Somst. Ho
Clark John M.D. Army Medical Board
Clark John, City Officer
Clark John, Clerk of the Peace
Clark John, Consul at Bilboa
Clark John, Excise (Leeds)
Clark John, General Post Office
Clark John, National Debt Office
ClarkJohn,PaymasterGenl's. Office
Clark Stephen, Custom House
Clark Wm. Court of Queen's Bench
Clarke Charles, Consul at St. Jago
Clarke Geo. S. Army Medcl.Bd.Off
Clarke Giles, Clk. to Saddlers' Co
Clarke Hen. Jas. Customs(Maldon)
Clarke John Jas. Stamp & Tax Offi
Clarke Richd. Bankruptcy Court
Clarke Richard, Court of Chancery
Clarke Rd. Fredk.Bank of England
Clarke Thos. Board of Ordnance
Clarke Thomas Robt. Addiscombe
Clarkson Charles, Excise Office
Clay John Dodd, General Post Off
Clavell Cpt. Jhn. Greenwh.Hospitl
Cleaver Thos. Henry,StationeryOff
Cleere Edward, Custom House
Cleere Henry William, Treasury
Clegg William, Queen sq. PoliceCt
Clements Hon. Chas.S.PoorLawOff
Clements George, Custom House
Clements George, Excise (Surrey)
Clements Hn. Dawson,Gen.PostOff
Clements John, Custom House
ClementsThos. Marlboro'st.Pol.Ct
Clementson Jhn. Serj.ArmsHo.Cm
ClevelandDukeof,Ld.Lt.ofDurham
Clerk Alexander, Treasury
Clerk Jas.Com.of PrivyC.forTrade
Clerk Sir Geo. bart. Privy Council
Clerk Edward Thomas, CustomHo
Clerke Wm. Henry, Treasury
Clifford Sir Aug. Wm. House of Lords
Clift Jas. Clerk to Glass-sellers' Co
Clifton Thomas, Audit Office
Clifton Waller, Admlty. Whitehl
Clinton Gen. SirW.Hen.G.C.B.Brd. of Genl. Off. & Royal Hosp.Chel
Clive G. Hammersmith Police Ct
Clode Wm. Genl. Register Office
Clogg John, Custom House
Close John Douglas, India House
Close Jn. Frank,ConsulatCharente
Clutton John, Ecclesias. Comrs.Of
Clutton Robt. Ecclesias. Comrs. Of
Clyde Henry Grant, Custom Ho
Cobban James H. Customs (Alloa)
Cobbe Chas. Paymaster Gen's. Off
Cobham Francis J. City Officer
Cobham Geo. Grosvenor,CustomH
Cobham Geo. Strode, Custom Ho
Cochrane Geo. Elphick,Ea.Ind.Ho
Cochrane Col.Wm. Adjt. Gen's.Off
Cockburn SirGeorge,Privy Council
Cockburn Hen. D. Board of Ordn
Cockburn John, Custom House
Cockburn Wm. A. Brd.ofOrdnance
Cocke Charles A. General Reg. Off
Cockell Teesdale, Stamp & Tax Off
Cockerell Chs. Rt. Archt.toBk.Eng
Cockerell Jhn. Cmmsn. Ltny.Lond
Cockerell S.P.Cnsl.Qn.An.Bnty.Of
Cocking Hen. Valentine,Home Off
Cocking Valentine, War Office
Cocks Walter Carew, Audit Office
Cocks Wm. Henry, Gen. Post Offi
Cockshott John, Custom House
CoddingtonCapt.R.N.Board of Trad
Coggin Thomas, Sewers' Office
Coggins Chas. Duchy of Lncstr. Off
Coggins Charles, Stamp&TaxOffice
Coghlan Thos. Court of Chancery
Colborne Lord, Comsn. of FineArts
Cole Chas.Augsts.PublicRecordOff
Cole Henry, Public Record Office
Cole James Henry, Treasury
Cole Julius William,Trinity House
ColeWelcome,Lndn.Dis.orTy.Post
Cole Wm. Slave Compensatn. Offi
Coleman Chas. Ct. of Exchequer
ColemanEverardH.SeamansReg.O
Coleman Jos. Ct. of Exchequer
Coleman Joseph, Ct. of Com. Pleas
Coleman Leonard,Comdr. in Chf.O
Coleman Matthew L. War Office
Coleridge SirJno.T.Just.ofQn's.Bh
Coles Augustus L. Foreign Office
Coles Wm. L. PaymasterGeneral's Office
Collen Geo. Wm. Herald's College
Collett Charles, Gen. Post Office
CollettEdmund,Court ofQn's.Bnch
Collett Edwin, Gen. Post Office
Collett James, Home Office
Collett Thos.Wtng.Room,Ho.ofCo
Collett Wm. General Post Office
Collier Henry, Custom House
Collier John, Excise Office
Collier Jn. Dowsett, Stamp & Tax Office
Collier John Pycroft, Treasury
Collier Thos. N.Board of Ordnance
Collier Wm. P. Stamp&Tax Office
Collings Thos. Admrlty.Somrst.Ho
Collingwood Lewty, Gen. Post Off
Collingwood Wm.East IndiaHouse
Collins Francis, Gen. Post Office
Collins Jas.J.VoteOff.Ho.ofComms
Collins Rt. Vote Office House of Commons
Collins Rt.Jsph.VoteOff.Ho.ofCms
Collins Wm. Chas. Gen. PostOffice
Collinson James, Gen. Post Office
Collis Joseph, ChanceryRegisterOf
Collot Mrs. Agnes, Poor LawOffice
Collot Thomas, Poor Law Office
Collot Thos. PoorLawOff.(Ireland)
Colman John, General Post Office
Colquhoun Danl. Customs (Rye)
Colquhoun Rd.G.ConsulBucharest
ColtmanSirThos.Justce.Cmn.Pleas
Coltson John, Custom House
Colvile A. Hudson's Bay Company
Colville Edw.D.ChanceryRegis.Off
Colville Edw.D.jun.Chancy.Rgis.O
Combe Boyce, Clrknw.PoliceCourt
Combermere Visct. Privy Councir
Compton Anthony, Custom House
Compton Charles, Gen. Post Office
Compton Henry, Gen. Post Off
Compton John Aug. Gen. Post Offi
Conder John, Bank of England
Congreve Charles, Ho. of Lords
Connal Michael, Admlty.Somst.Ho
Connell Chas. H. BoardofOrdnance
ConnollyP.J.Lndn.Dist.orT.Py.Po
Conquest Jno. Clk. to Plaistrs'. Co
Conquest William, Sewers' Office
Const J. H. City Officer
Conway Rbt.H.PaymasterGen's.Of
Conyngham Marqs. of, PrivyConcl
Conyngham,see Lenox-Conynghm
Coode George, Poor Law Office
Cook Abraham, Customs (Ipswich)
Cook Lieut. Thomas, Addiscombe
Cook Robt. Ecclesias. Comrs. Off
Cook Thos. Burgess, Gen. Post Off
Cook Thos. London Dist. Post Offi
Cook Thos. B.Lndn.Dist.orT.PyPt
Cook William, House of Commons
Cook William, War Office
Cooke Mrs. Elizabeth, Home Office
Cooke Geo. W. Tithe Commission
Cooke James, Lambeth st.PoliceCt
Cooke James, Custom House
Cooke John,Admiralty, Somst. Ho
Cooke William, Custom House
Cookes John, General Post Office
Cookes William, Foreign Office
Coombes George, Excise Office
Coombs Robt. William, Audit Off
Cooper Alfred, Stamp & Tax Office
Cooper Alfred Wm.Gen.Post Office
Cooper Chas. P. Duchy LancasterO
Cooper Hay, Audit Office
Cooper Henry, Royal Marine Offi
Cooper Henry Augustus, Consul, Pernambuco, Brazil
Cooper James William, Treasury
Cooper John, Bank of England
Cooper John, Board of Ordnance
Cooper John, Excise Office
Cooper Rd.B.Col.&Emigration Bd
Cooper Samuel, Queen's Prison
Cooper Thos. Gen. Register Office
Cooper Wm. Geo. Pub. Record Off
CooteChas.John,C.of Cmmn.Pleas
Cope Augustus Lidbrook, Customs
Cope Jas. De Reimer, Custom Ho
Cope Thomas, Custom House
Cope Thomas, Secty. to Russia & Eastland Comps
Cope Walter, Consul at Guayaquil
Cope Wm. W. Keeper of Newgate
Copeland Wm.T.Alderman of Lond
Coppock Charles, Custom House
Corbett Charles Hen. Excise Office
Corbett Robert, India Board
Corbett Rt. F. Consul Maranham
Corbyn Comndr.Jsph.Grenwh.Hos
CorchialFrancesco,Consul,Otranto
Corder James, Sup. Regr. Strand
Corder Micah, Bank of England
Cornelius Rd.Lndn.Dist.orT.Py.Pt
Cornell Geo.Woods&Forests Office
Cornell S. Sup. Regr. Kensington
Corner A. B. Crown Office,Q.Bnch
Cornock Jas. Lnd. Dis. Post Office
Cornwall Gustavus C.Gen.Post Offi
Corrie William, Palace Court
CorryHen.Thos.L.PrivyCouncillor
Corsbie D. W. Stamp & Tax Office
Costerton Henry,Customs (Boston)
Cotman John, Custom House
Cottell John, East India House
Cottenham Lord, Privy Councillor
CottinghamJohn,Southwk.PoliceC
Cotton Benjamin, Trinity House
Cotton Hugh Powell, Treasury
Cotton John,Commsn.Ltncy.Lndn
Cotton John, Direc.EastIndiaCom
Cotton M. C. Customs (Greenock)
Cotton William, Audit Office
Cotton Wm. Commsn. Ltncy.Lndn
Cotton Wm.Govnr.Bank of Englnd
Cotton Wm. Metropls. Chs.Fnd.Of
CottonWm.H.PaymasterGeneral's Office
Cottrell Geo. Archd. Excise Office
Couch Thos. Wm. House of Lords
Court Charles, General Post Office
Court Chas.Thos.Genrl.Post Office
Court Francis, General Post Office
Court Henry,National Debt Office
Court Wm. General Post Office
Courtenay Edwd. House of Lords
Courtenay Josceline, India Board
Courtenay Francis F. Committee of Privy Council for Trade
Courtenay Thos. P. Revenue Inqry
Courthorp Wm. Heralds' College
Covey John, Custom House
Cowan Rbt. Sproule, Excise Office
Cowcher Edward, Custom House
Cowing Joseph, Custom House
Cowley Duncan John, Custom Ho
Cowley Lord, Privy Councillor
Cowling LawrenceD. Stamp & Tax Office
Cowper Fredk. General Post Office
Cowper Hon.Chas. Spencer, Secretary of Legation at Stockholm
Cowtan Mawer, British Museum
Cox Charles, Colonial Office
Cox Charles John, Custom House
Cox Edward, Army Med. Board O
Cox Frederick, General Post Office
Cox Henry, Admiralty, Whitehall
Cox Jas. R. S. Woods & ForestsOff
Cox John Edmund, Custom Ho
Cox Richard Wait, Custom House
Cox Robert, Custom House
Cox Wm. Saurin, Gen. Post Offi
Coxe Thomas, Custom House
Coxworthy Franklin, Bd. of Ordn
Cozens Matt. Queen's Bench Office
Crabb Edmund, Custom House
Crafer Charles Long, Treasury
Crafer Edwin Turner, Treasury
Crafer Frederick, Treasury
Crafer Thomas John, Treasury
Craib Wm. Woods & Forests' Offi
Crampton John, Cstms. (Newry)
Crampton J.F. Sec. ofLeg.America
Crandell Geo. Admlty. Somst. Ho
Crandell Wm. Admlty. Somst. Ho
Crandell Wm. Paymaster Gen Offi
Craufurd Clifford, EastIndiaHouse

Craven Augustus,S.ofLg.Stutgardt
Crawford John, Consl.at N.Orleans
Crawford J.T. Consul at Havanna
Crawford Wm.Inspector of Prisons
Creasy Elisha, Union Hall PoliceCt
Creed Hen.H.Electn.Of.Ho.ofCom
Creed Charles, Audit Office
Creswell Geo. Hen.Gen.Post Office
Cresswell SirCresswell,Just.Com.P
Crewe Fred.Richard, CustomHouse
Cribb Nevill Oliver, Custom House
CribbWm.London Dist.orT.Py.Pst
Criddle John, Stamp & Tax Office
Cridland Rd. Genl. Register Office
Crippen Henry, GeneralPostOffice
Crispin Alfred Thos. Treasury
Crispin Henry Musgrave,Treasury
Croft Sir Archer D.Mastr.ofQns.B
Croft Wm. Commsn. Ltncy. Lndne
Croft Wm.Paymaster Gen's. Office
Crofton Marcus L. Custom House
Croix Fierra la, Consul at Nice
Crokat Chas. Board of Ordnance
Crokat Chas. Stamp & Tax Office
Croke Chas. John, Gen. PostOffice
Croker John W. Privy Councillor
Croker Thos.C. Admlty. Whitehall
CromarHen.Lndn.Dist.orT.Py.Pst
Crome Joseph, Excise Office
Crompton Thos. Consul, Isla, Peru
Croner J. Customs (Tralee)
Croomes John, War Office
Crosbie Malcolm Douglas,Customs
Crosby Jas. Paymaster Gen. Office
Crosby John Admlty. Somerset Ho
Crosby Robert, Ct. of Chancery
Crotch James, Foreign Office
Crouch Walter, GeneralPostOffice
Crowe George W. Consul at Patras
Crowe John R. Consul,Christiana
Crowe Wm. Consul at Sfax, Tunis
Crowne C.Judgement Office QnsBh
Crowther Sam. Excise (Hereford)
CrumbleholmeJas.Custms. (Prstn)
Crutch John, Gen. Post Office
Cubitt Wm. Com.ofHealthofTown
Cuell William, Bank of England
Cuff Christr. Westr.Ct.of Requests
Cullum John, Board of Ordnance
CullumRt.Customs (NewportMon)
CulverwellSam.Hen.Stamp&TaxO
Cumberbatch A.C. Consul General at Constantinople
Cumberland Duke of, Privy Coun
CumberlandRchd.E.CustomHouse
CumberlandRichd.F.G.RoyalMint
Cumberland Sydney,Stamp&TaxO
Cumberland Thos. Jas.AuditOffice
Cumming Henry, Custom House
CummingLochlan, Custms(Invrns)
Cummins Chas.Remembrancer'sOf
Cummins Fred. Genl. Post Off
Cummins James, East India House
Cunningham Chas. Consul, Galatz
Cunningham Peter, Audit Office
Cunningham R.Cnsl.atConcepcion
CuretonRev.Wm. British Museum
Curgenven Peter, Custom House
Curling Daniel, Custom House
Currey Benjamin, House of Lords
Currey John, Ct. of Queen's Bench
Currie Francis Gore, Home Office
Currie Thomas, Board of Ordnance
Curry E. Thompson,Cons.atOstend
Curtis Fras. H. Court of Chancery
Curtis Horace Goad, Audit Off
CurtisJohn, Clk. toTilw.Chndrs.Co
Curtis Robert, City Officer
Curtis Thos. Lndn.Dist.orT.Py.Pst
CurzonHon.E.Cecil,Reg.ofDesigns
CurzonHon.Fras.J.Ct of Bnkrptcy
Curzon Hon.Hen.Geo. R.Audit Off
Cuthbert LewisM.Mrstrs.Of.Chncy
Cutten Chas. Court of Bankruptcy
Cutto Abraham, Genl. Post Office

Dabbs Thos. Tyrrell, Custom Ho
Dace James, General Post Office
Dadley Wm. Clerk toPewterers'Co
DalbiacSirJas. C.Bd.ofGen.Officers
Dalbiac Hen. E.Stmp. & TaxOffice
Dalbiac Wm. W.Stamp&TaxOffice
Dalhousie Earl, Privy Councillor
Daller George A. Chelsea Hospital
Daller Hen.Sam.Paymsr.Gen's.Off
Dalton John, Court of Chancery
Dalton Joseph, Stamp & TaxOffice
Daly Christopher, Custom House
Dalyell Com.Wm. C. C. Greenwich Hospital
Dalzell Robt. A. Consul at Mahon
Damaschino T. ViceCon. at Janina
Damer Col. D. Privy Councillor
Dampier Digby, Custom House
DampierJohnL.DuchyofCrnwll.Of
Dance Chas. Insolvent Debtors Ct
Daniel Stephen,Lond.D.PostOffice
Daniell Edmd.Rt.Com.ofBankptcy
Daniell Wm. Tonkin, Custom Ho
Dann R. Westminster Court
DanversFred.D.DuchyofLncser.Of
Danvers Fredk. Saml.EastIndiaHo
Darby Geo. Enclosure Comrs. Of
D'Arcy Edmd. Malone,Exchqr.Off
Dare Saml. Master Ct. of Exchqr
Darling SirRalph,Bd.ofGen.Officrs
Darvill James, Genl. Post Office
Date Joseph, Seaman's Register Of
Davern Captn. J. Chelsea Hospital
David Joshua, General Post Off
Davidson Alexr. Greenwich Hospital School
Davidson H. Com. Lty. of London
Davidson H. Customs (Wick)
Davidson T. Woods & Forests Off
Davie Cyrus, Customs (Gloucester)
Davie M. Customs (St. Ives)
Davies David, Genl. Post Office
Davies David Chas. Custom Ho
Davies Edwd. General Post Office
Davies Edward, Home Office
Davies Frederick, Custom House
Davies George, Genl. Post Office
Davies Griffith, Gen. Post Off
Davies Henry, Custom House
Davies John, Board of Ordnance
Davies John Speed, Custom Ho
Davies Robt. Pigot, Gen. Post Off
Daviniere Wm. Thos. Ea. IndiaHo
Davis Fras. H. Chancy. Regsr. Off
Davis George, Westmn. Police Ct
Davis Hart, Excise Office
Davis Henry, General Post Office
Davis James, Treasury
Davis John, Court of Exchequer
Davis John, Excise Office
Davis John, Queen's Bench Office
Davis John Fras. Plenipo. to China
Davis Rev.John,OrdinaryNewgate
Davis Oliver H. Admlty. Smst.Ho
Davis Philip,London Dist.PostOffi
Davis Rd. Vaughan, Excise Office
Davis Rt. Lambeth st. Police Ct
Davis Samuel, Customs (Whitby)
Davis Thomas, Custom House
Davis William, Custom House
Davison John, East India Comp
Daw Joseph, jun. Sewers Office
Daw Robert, Customs (Cardiff)
Dawkins Clinton Geo. Foreign Off
Daws Richard, Custom House
Dawson Frederic, Treasury
Dawson Rd. Crosbie, MillbankPrsn
Dawson Rt.Honble. GeorgeRobert, Commissioner of Customs
Dawson Rt. Sharrock, Home Off
Dawson Wm. Customs (Wells N)
Dax Edwd.Thos. Exchegr. of Pleas
Dax Richard, Court of Exchequer
Dax Thos. Master of Exchegr.of Pl
Day Mrs.Caroline F. State PaperOf
Day Edward, General Post Office
Day James, Custom House
Day Marcellus, Milibank Prison
Day Thomas Smith, Custom Ho
Dayas Thomas, Custom House
Daysh Geo.Wm. Admrlty. Smst.Ho
Deacon John, Admiralty Registry
Dealty Peregrine, Ct. of Qn's.Bnch
Dealtry Wm. Colonial Office
Dealtry Wm. D.D. Archd.of Surrey
Dean Isaac, General Post Office
Dean Rd. Betenson, Custom House
Dean Thomas, Excise (Hertford)
Dean William, House of Lords
Deane George, Greenwich Hospital
Deane John Wood, Bank of Engld
Deane Joseph, Custom House
Deans Peter, Stamp & Tax Office
De Barey PeterFrs.Pvy.Council Off
Debenham Fredk. Stamp & TaxOff
De Courcy Henry, Poor Law Office
Dedman William, Audit Office
Deedes Hen. Charles, India Board
Deedes William Hen. India Board
DeeringWm.Com.ofCoalWhippers
De Eresby Lord, Com. Fine Arts
De Fonblanque Thos. F. Audit Offi
Deforge Felix, General Post Off
Defrier Edward, Custom House
DeGreyEarl,K.G.,K.P.,PrivyCncllr
Deighton Rt.Commndr.inChf's.Off
De la Beche Sir Henry Thomas, kt. Comr. of Health of Towns
Delacourt Thomas, Custom House
Delaney BernardM.Stamp&TaxOff
Delap Wm. Customs (Coleraine)
De la Warr Earl, Privy Councillor
De Lisle&Dudley Lord,D.ofCnwl.O
Dell James, War Office
De Mole HenryWm.CustomHouse
De Montmorency Jas.Greenwh.Hos
Denbigh Earl of, Privy Councillor
Dene Richard, Stamp & Tax Office
Denman Lord,Chf.Justice,Qn's.Bn
Denman Hon. Thos.Ct.ofQun's.Bn
Dennis John, jun. Excise Office
Dennison Robert, Gray's Inn
DennisonW.T.HealthofTownsCom
Denton James, Custom House
Denton Robert Cross, Excise Off
De Pinn A. Court of Admiralty
Derby Earl of, K.G., Ld. Lt. Lancashire, & Privy Councillor
Dering Charles, Custom House
Dermer Edw, National Debt Office
DevallWm.Customs(Scarborough)
De Valmer Charles A. Audit Office
Devereux Edward, Custom House
Devereux Nich. Stamp&Tax Office
Devon Earl of, Patentee Subpœna Office & Ecclesiastical Commis
Devon Fred. Public Record Office
Devonshire Duke of, Ld. Lt. Derby
Dewar George, Custom House
Dewes Robert, Custom House
Dewey Robt. Customs (Shoreham)
Dewguard Edward, Custom House
Dewing Chas. Marlboro' st. Police Court
D'Eyncourt Chas.T.PrivyCouncllr
Dibley John Wm. Custom House
Dickens Frederick Wm. Treasury
Dickens Jas. Stamp & Tax Office
Dickenson Isaac W. Stamp&TaxOf
Dickenson William, Gen. Post Off
Dicker John, General Post Office
Dickins George, Custom House
Dickins George, Gen. Post Office
Dickinson John, Custom House
Dickinson John D. East India Ho
Dickinson John P.Stamp&Tax Offi
Dickinson Rd.Jrnl.Off.Ho. of Com
Dickinson Rt.Laycock,Custom Ho
DickinsonThomasP.Custom House
Dickinson Wm. Hen. Custom Hou
DicksonHenryE.Seaman's Reg.Offi
Dickson Wm. Custom House
Digby Earl, Lord Lieut. Dorset
Diggens James, Stationery Office
Dike George John, House of Lords
Dike Wm. Henry, House of Lords
Dillon Hon. Arthur, Home Office
Dillon Hon. Gerald, India Board
Dipnall Sidney Smith, Customs
Disbrowe SirE.C.Amba. to Holland
Disney Brab, Excise Office
Disney Henry Cathrow,Custom Ho
Disney Jas. Cathrow, Heralds' Col
D'Israeli Ralph Chan. Reg. Office
Dix John, Privy Council Office
Dixon James Wylde, Custom Ho
Dixon John,Com.of CoalWhippers
Dixon Martin, General Post Office
Dixon Matthew, General Post Off
Dixon Richard, Excise Office
Dixon Robert, Custom House
Dixon William, Custom House
Dixson A. O. Customs (Stockton)
Dobell Henry Wm. Custom House
Dobinson William, Genl. Post Offi
Dobson John, Custom House
Dobson Thomas, Excise Office
Dodd Edward Harvey, Excise Offi
Dodd Geo.Commsn.Ltncy. London
Dodge John, Audit Office
Dodgson George, Stamp & Tax Offi
Dodson Sir John, Master of Faculties & Advocate General
Dodsworth Thos. Colonial Office
Dodsworth Rev. W.Mtro.Ch. fnd.O
Doggett Edw. Bowers, India House
DoggettWm.DuchyofLncstr.Office
Dolman Arnold H. Custom House
Dombrain Sir Jas. kt. Customs
Domett Nathaniel, Lloyd's
Donald David, Geo. Genl. Post Offi
Donald Thomas, Bank of England
Donegall Marq. Privy Councillor
Donnan John, Custom House
Donne John Geo. Privy Seal Office
Dorant Wm. Vice Consul at Naples
Dorehill A. Stamp & Tax Office
Dorington J.E.Pb.Bus.Of. H.Coms
Dornford Josiah, Greenwich Hsptl
Doubleday Edwd. British Museum
DouglasAlexander,Seaman'sReg.O
DouglasSirC.E.GreenwichHospital
Douglas G.O. Genl. Register Office
Douglas James. Genl. Post Office
Douglas Job, Excise, (Stafford)
Douglas John Wm. Custom House
Douglas Wm.H.Admlty.Somst. Ho
Doull William, Sewers' Office
DouroMarquis,Com.in Chief Office
Doutty John, Admiralty, Somst.H
Dove Jas. Douglas, Audit Office
Dover Henry National Debt Office
Dowdeswell JohnE.Mastr.inChncy
Dowding Charles, Custom House
Dowley John, Sewers' Office
Dowley John Henry, Sewers' Office
Dowling Charles, Foreign Office
Dowling Thurlow, Bd. of Ordnance
Downes Thomas Rd. Audit Office
Downes W.Robeson, Stamp & Tax Office
Downs Thomas, Custom House
Dowsley Rd. J. Customs (Galway)
Dowson Robert, Chelsea Hospital
Dowton George Wm. Audit Office
Doyle M. Customs (Baltimore)
Doyle P. Wm. Sec. of Leg. Mexico
Doyle Richard, Lincoln's inn
Doyle Sir Fras. H.C. Bt. Excise Offi
Doyle Wm. Gen. Post Office
D'Oyley Gen.Hen.Bd.of Gen.Officers
Draffen Joseph Wright, Foreign Of
Drake Edward, General Post Office
Drake John, Commdr. in Chfs. Offi
Drake Richard, Audit Office
Drake Thos. Masters' Off. Chncy
DrakeThs.jun.Mastrs.Off.Chancery
Drake Wm. Seaman's Register Offi
Draper GeorgeWm. Stationery Off
Drew Beriah, Sewers' Office & Sup. Registrar, Bermondsey
Drew David, Clerk of Enrolments
Drew Dyer, Custom House
DrewGeo.SouthwarkCt.ofRequests
Drew Richard, Lloyd's
Drewry Hen. Runciman,WarOffice
Drinkwater Joseph, Excise Office
Driver Edw. Court of Exchequer
Druce Chas. Clk. Innholders' Co
Drummond Maurice, Treasury
Drummond Spencer, Treasury
Drury Arthur J. Foreign Office
Drury Robert, Excise Office
Dryden William, Excise Office
Drysdale Stoddart, East India Ho
Dubois E. Middx. Ct. of Requests
DuBourg Augsts.W.Houseof Lords
Duck John, General Post Office
Duckett John B. Chelsea Hospital
Duckworth Saml. Mstr. in Chncry
Dudgeon Danl. Customs(Wexford)
Duffy John, C.B.Bd.of Gen.Officers
Dugdale Geo. Greenwich Hospital
Duke Sir Jas. Alderman of London
Duke Robt. Clerkenwell Police Ct
Dunbar Lewis, Excise Office
Duncan George, Custom House
DundasHon. Rt.Admlty.Somerset House
Dunfermline Lord, Privy Councir
Dunlop Jas. National Debt Office
Dunn Francis, General Post Office
DunnRalph,Sol.to South SeaComp
Dunn Richd.Marsh, Custom House
Dunn Fredk. Wm. Custom House
Dunn Wm. Travis, Gen. Post Office
Dunne Fred. Wm. Custom House
Dunsmure James, East India Ho
Dunstall Wm.George,Gen Post Off
DuPasquier Geo. Brd. of Ordnance
Dupont Chs. Graham,General Post Office
Durant Edmund, Gen. Post Office
Durrant Wm. Board of Ordnance
Dutch Henry, Genl. Post Office
Dutton H. H. Consul at Cuxhaven
Dutton Wm. Coles, Custom House
Duval Philip S. Trinity House
DwarrisSirF.Mas.Office,Qns.Bench
Dwarris F. W. Queen's Bench Office
Dwight Henry Thos. Treasury
Dwight William Moss, Treasury
Dwyer Edm. Army Medcl. Brd.Offi
Dyer John J.Admiralty, Whitehall

Dyer Richard T. S. Audit Office
Dyke Francis, H. Queen's Proctor
Dyke George C. Custom House
DyneleyChas. Prerogatv. (Will)Off
Dynevor Lord, Ld. Lt. Carmarthen
Dyson Geo. Election Off. Ho. Com
Eade William, East India House
Earle Thomas, Excise Office
Earnshaw Alfred, Treasury
East Sir Ed.H.Judicial Com.of P.C
Easthope Jno.Admiralty, Somt.Ho
Eastlake Chas.L. Com. of Fine Arts
Eastmure Samuel V. Custom House
Easton Arthur, Home Office
Eastwick Lt.Edwd.B.Hayleyby.Col
Eastwood John, Audit Office
Eavres John, City Officer
Ebhart Mrs. Elizth. Chelsea Hosptl
Eckley J. Custom House
Eddrup Edward Chas. Audit Offi
Ede Joseph, Audit Office
Eden Arthur, Exchequer Office
Eden Ralph, Privy Seal Office
EdenWalter D.AdmiraltySomt.Ho
Eden Gen.Wm.Brd.of Gen. Officers
Edgar John, Custom House
Edgcumbe Hon.G.Sec.Lg.Hanover
Edkins Rt. Pitt, City Lndn. School
Edmeades Fredk. Custom House
Edmeades Geo. Paymast. Gen. Office
EdmundsLeond.CrownOff.Chncry. and Patent office
Edwardes Thos. Genl. Post Office
Edwards Lt. Chas. Chelsea Hospitl
Edwards Edwd. Genl. Register Offi
Edwards Edwd. Ct. of Bankruptcy
Edwards Ed.Lndn.Dist.orTPy.Post
Edwards Fred.Genl. Register Office
Edwards Fred.E Mstrs.Off.Chancery
Edwards Fredk. H. Custom House
Edwards John, Bank of England
EdwardsJohn, PublicRecord Office
Edwards Rd.Westmnr.PoliceCourt
Edwards Sam.P.Custms.(Sthmptn)
Edwards Wm. General Post Office
Edwards Wm.J.General Post Office
Edwin N. Southwark Police Court
EdyeJohn,Admlty.SomersetHouse
Egerton SirChas.B.Bd.of Gn.Offcers
EgertonLord Fras.PrivyCouncillor
EickeChas.Sam.W.Genl.PostOffice
Eld Howard, General Post Office
ElderWm.Thos.Board of Ordnance
Elderfield Thos. Stamp & Tax Off
Elderton Chas.Fred.Metpn.Pol.Offi
Eldred Chas. Excise (Macclesfield)
Eldred Charles, Excise Office
Eldred Edgar, Excise Office
Eldred Edward, Middle Temple
Eliot Chas. Turbeville, AuditOffice
Eliot Lionel Ducket, Audit Office
Ellard William, Poor Law Office
EllenboroughEarl of,G.C.B.,P.Cncr
ElierbyCapt.StephensonTrinityHo
Ellice Edw.Hudson'sBay Company
Ellice Edward, Privy Councillor
Ellice Russell,Comns. Ltncy.Lndn
Ellinkhuyson H.Consul atFlushing
Elliot Edward, Board of Ordnance
Elliot Hen. Board of Genl. Officers
Elliot Thos.F.Colnl.Emigratn. Brd
ElliottChas.Capt.R.N.Con.Gen.Tex
Elliott Chas. S. Board of Ordnance
Elliott EdwardJohn,CustomHouse
Elliott John Hay, Admlty.Smst.Ho
Ellis Chas.A.H.H.Middlesex Sessns
Ellis Charles Jas. Ordnance Office
Ellis Edward, General Post Office
Ellis Fredk. Chas. Public Recd. Off
Ellis Geo. Thames Police Court
Ellis Sir Henry, British Museum
Ellis Henry, Privy Councillor
Ellis John, Home Office
Ellis Robert, Custom House
Ellis Robert, Comn. Ltncy. London
EllisThos.F.Duchyof Lncstr. Office
Ellison Nath. Com. of Bankruptcy
Elmer J. Lunatic Office
Elmes James, City Officer
Elouis Charles, Royal Mint
ElphickJas.Lndn.Dist.orT.Py.Post
Elphick Jas. Hen. Genl. Post Office
Elphinstone Lord,PrivyCouncillor
ElringtonCapt.J.H.Tower of Lndn
Elsasser C. Consul at Pillau
Elssy John G. Bank of England
Elsey Joseph R. Bank of England
Elwin Jeken, Ordnance Board
Elwyn Robert, Excise (Durham)
Ely Daniel, General Post Office
Ely William, Palace Court
EmanThomas, ExciseOffice, (Hull)
Emerson Joseph, Custom House
Emery Henry, General Post Office
Emmens Thomas,Stamp&TaxOffice
Emmens Thomas, Treasury
Empson Wm. Hayleybury College
Enfield H.jun.Lunatic Offi.Chancy
EngelbachAlfH.Clnl.Emigratn.Bd
English Robert, Custom House
Enoch Cap.John,Qurtr. Mas.Gns.O
Erford John, Excise Office
Erle Hon. Sir William, knt. Court of Common Pleas
Erle William, Bank of England
Errol Earl of, Privy Councillor
Erskine Charles, Home Office
Erskine Thos. F. Admlty.Smst. Ho
Escreet Thomas, Bank of England
Essell George, Archdeacon of Rochester's Registry Office
Estcourt T.G.B.M.P.Exch. Bl.Ln.O
Estwick Richard, Customs (Cowes)
Etherington Wm. Stamp & TaxOff
Eustace Alfred, Gen. Post Office
Evans Capt. A. F. Chelsea Hospital
Evans Evan, Excise (Bath)
Evans George, Custom House
Evans James, Supt. of. Police(T.D)
Evans Joshua, Ct. of Bankruptcy
Evans Pierce, Cstms. (Aberistwth)
Evans Richard, Audit Office
Evans Rt. Eccltstl. Commsrs. Office
EvansRt.M. Seaman's Registr. Offi
Evans Rt.Speke. Admrlty.Whitehl
Evans Samuel, Sup. of Police (M)
Evans Wm. F. Admiralty, Whitehl
Evenden Jas. Privy Council Office
Everest George, Home Office
Everett Ellis, Stamp & Tax Office
Everett Wm. Stamp & Tax Office
Evett George, Stamp & Tax Office
Evison Lieut.J. C.R.N.Queen'sPris
Ewbank Samuel, Gen. Post Office
Ewen David, Customs (Ayr)
Ewings Joseph, Home Office
Exeter Marquis of, Lord Lieut. of Rutland & Northampton
Exley John, Customs (Aberdeen)
EyreWm.Jekin,PayMaster Gen.Of

Fabian Charles, Custom House
Fache Wm. Mich. Crt. of Exchqr
Fagan John, Comdr. in Chief's Offi
Faggetter Jas. Colonial Office
Fairbairns William, CustomHouse
FairmanJohn Nicholas,Custom Ho
Falcon Wm. General Post Office
Falkland Visct. Privy Councillor
Fall Richard, Custom House
Fane Rt. Geo.C.Crt.of Bankruptcy
Fanning Edm. General Post Office
Farebrother Chas.Aldrmn. of Lndn
Farmer Wm. General Post Office
Farncomb Thos. Alderm. of Lndn
Farquhar James, Archdeacon of Rochester's Registry Office
Farquharson Capt.Chas. TrinityHo
Farquharson John, Custom House
Farr Charles, Excise Office
Farr Wm. General Register Office
Farrall Marshall, Genl. Post Office
Farrence George John, Comm. of French & Danish Claims
Farren J. W.P.Cons.Philipine isle
Farrer Capt. Wm. E. Trinity Ho
Farrer Jas. Wm. Master in Chncry
Farrer Jonathan, Genl. Post Office
Fascutt Wm. National Debt Office
Fasson Ben. Paymstr. Genl's Office
Fasson John, Chelsea Hospital
Faulls George, Genl. Post Office
Fauquier Wm. Edwd. Treasury
Fawcett George, Poor Law Office
Fawkener Lyon, Bd. of Ordnance
Fawn George, Genl. Post Office
FearnsideT.R.Lnd.Revn.Record Of
Fearon Anthy.Fred.Stamp& TaxOf
Featherstone Jas.H.Bd.ofOrdnance
Featherstonhaugh George William Consul at Havre de Grace
Feild Thomas Merrick, War Office
Fell Jas. Marylebone Police Ct
Feltham Edwd. Gomer, Custom Ho
FenemoreEdwd.J.BankofEngland
Fenn Rt. Living, National Debt Off
Fenner Geo. Remembrancer's Offi
Fenner Thos. Remembrancer's Offi
Fennessy Robert, Foreign Office
Fenning George, Lloyd's
Fennings JamesPulham, Cusm. Ho
Fennings Philip, Customs
Fennings Wm. National Debt Offi
FenwickManners,Public RecordOff
Ferguson Chas. Genl. Post Office
Ferguson Daniel, Sup.of Police(S)
Ferguson James, Genl. Post Office
Fergusson Frs.Comndr. in Chf.'sOff
FergussonMrs.A.Comndr.inChf'sOf
Fernyhough Richd. Custom House
Ferriere Lewis, Consul at Tunis
Ferris Rd. J. Customs (Penzance)
Ferris Thos. Customs (Padstow)
FfinchJn. Drake,Grnwch.Police Ct
Ffinch Thomas Drake, Audit Office
Ffolkes Wm. John B. Excise Office
Field Abraham, Stationary Office
FieldChas.Fred.Admlty.Somst.Ho
Field Henry Wm. Royal Mint
Field Josiah, Bank of England
Fielding T. H. Addiscombe, E. I. C
Figg Mrs. Fanny, Greenwich Hsptl
Fillingham Rd. B.General Post Off
Fillippe Chas. Consul at San Lucar
FiltonFredk. F.Seam's.RegisterOffi
Finch Edwd. General Post Office
Finch John, Clerk to Long Bow String Makers', Fletchers', & Gardeners' Companies
Fincham James, Woods & For. Off
Findlay Henry, Board of Ordnance
FinlaisonAlex.Glen, Natl.Debt Offi
Finlaison Domett,Natl. Debt Office
Finlaison John, Natl. Debt Office
Finlay George Wm. Poor Law Off
FirminFrancisF.Seamn's.Regstr.Of
Firth George, Customs, (Kirkwall)
Firth James F. Clerk to Patten Makers Company
Fisher Charles, Genl. Post Office
Fisher Douglas, GeneralPost Office
Fisher Rev.Geo.Grenwh. Hos. Schl
Fisher Capt. John, City Officer
FisherJn.Wm. Srgeon.Metro.Polic
FisherSam.ClerktoMrchnt.Tailor's
Fisher William, City Officer
Fisher Wm.Court of Queen's Bnch
Fisher William, Gen. Post Office
FitchJ.H.Sup.Rg.St.Grge.'sSthwk
Fitch Thos. Metrop. Carriage Offi
Fitze Edward, Custom House
Fitze Wm. Beard, Custom House
FitzGerald Chas. Rbt. Home Office
FitzGerald Frederick, Treasury
Fitzgerald Geo. Stamp & Tax Offi
FitzgeraldJamesE.British Museum
Fitzhardinge Earl, Lord Lieut. of Gloucestershire
FitzmayerEdw.Chas.Custm. House
Fitzpatrick Michael John, Marlborough-street Police Court
Fitzpatrick Mrs. Worship st. P. Ct
Fitzroy Lord C. Privy Councillor
Fitz-Stephens John, Customs (Lymington)
Fladgate Thomas, Customs
Flamontz Robert, Excise Office
Fleet John, General Post Office
Fleming Henry, Tithe Commission
Fleming John, Custom House
Fletcher Charles Wm. India Board
Fletcher Charles, Bd. of Ordnance
Fletcher Francis, Poor Law Office
Fletcher G.C.Hammersmith Pol.ct
Fletcher Joseph, Ordnance Board
Fletcher Wm. Custom House
Flewker H. Excise (Liverpool)
Flint Andrew G. House of Lords
Flint James, Custom House
Flinter John W. Custom House
Flood Jas. Masters' Off. Qn's. Bnch
Florey Jethro, Tower of London
Fluck G. Poor Law Office
Fogg John, General Post Office
Foggo Wm. Customs (Perth)
Foley Lord, Privy Councillor
Follett Rt. Bayly, Taxing Master
Fonblanque J.S.M.Courtof Bankrp
Fonblanque Thomas de Grenier, Consul General at Belgrade
Foot William, Custom House
Foote Ambrose, Customs (Leith)
Foote George, Treasury
Forbes Hon. F.R.Ambsdr.to Saxny
Forbes George, Royal Mint
Ford Benjamin, Treasury
Ford Lieut. John,Chelsea Hospital
Foreman Thomas, Custom House
Forester Lord, Privy Councillor
Forester William, Audit Office
Forkath Geo. Stamp & Tax Office
Forrest Augustus, Genl.Post Office
Forrest Edmund, Genl. Post Office
Forrest Horton, General Post Offi
Forrest Lt. Gov. Emig. Agt. (Leith)
Forrest Robert, Home Office
Forrest Thomas, Lloyd's
Forrester John, Custom House
Forshall Rev. J. British Museum
Forster Chas. Millbank Prison
Forster Edw. jun. Eastland Compy
Forster Edw. sen. Eastland Compy
Forster Henry Fred. Foreign Office
Forsyth John, Custom House
ForsterW.Hen.Customs (Grimsby)
Fortescue Earl, Ld. Lieut. of Devon
Fortune John, Woods& Forests Offi
Fosdick Edward, Gen. Post Office
Fossett Benj. Admirlty. Somst. Ho
Fossett Wm. Admirlty. Somst. Ho
FossettW.King, Admlty.Somst.Ho
Foster Sir A. J. Privy Councillor
FosterHenry,Guildhall JusticeRm
Foster Morgan H.Paymaster General's Office
Fountain Wm. General Post Office
Fowler Charles Case, Custom Ho
Fowler Hen. Customs (Scarboro')
Fowler John, Custom House
FoxCol.C.R.Duchy of LancasterOff
Fox Florance, GeneralRegister Offi
Fox Jas.London Dist.or T.Py. Post
Fox Thomas, General Post Office
Fox Thomas Hall, Excise Office
Fox William, Commissary Court
FoysterJas. Customs (Beaumaris)
Franc George, Custom House
Francis Chas. W. Genl. Post Office
Francis Frederick, Custom House
Frankish Thos. Excise (Colchester)
FranklynThos. Marylebn.Police ct
Franklyn Richard,sen. Royal Mint
Franks Chas. Govnr. South Sea Ho
FranksW.Adams,East India House
Fraser Alex.Clinton,Custom House
Frederick Geo.S. Exchequer Office
Fredericks Thos. General Post Offi
Freeling John Clayton, Excise Offi
Freeman Richard, City Officer
Freeman Thos. Genl. Post Office
Freeth Col.Jas Qtr.Master.Gen.Offi
FreethJ.W.D'Urban,Com.inChfs.O
Fremantle Capt.Steph.R.N.IrishOff
Fremantle Sir Thos.F. Privy Cnclr
Fremantle Sir W. H.Privy Counclr
French Joseph, Genl. Post Office
Frere Chas. Election Off. Ho.Cmns
Frere John H. Privy Councillor
Freshfield F. Customs (Sligo)
Freshfield J. & C. Solictrs. to Bank
Freshfield Jas.Wm.Surrey Sessions
Fricker Fredk. Foreign Office
Friend George, East India House
Friend Lieut. C. Emig. Agt. (Cork)
Friend Richd. Admlty. Somst. Ho
Fry George, Rolls Court
Fry Danby Palmer, Poor Law Offi
Fry Jas.Thos.Chancery Regstr.Offi
Fryer Joseph, Marylebn. Police t
FulcherJohn Britling,Gen.PostOffi
Fuller John, Stamp & Tax Office
Funge Chas. Vice Chancellor's Ct
Funge Thos. Vice Chancellor's Ct
Furber John, Gen. Post Office
Fyfe Chas.Burges, Gen.Post Office

GageJohn, Signet Office
Gairdner Gordon, Colonial Office
Gairdner JohnS.Stamp&TaxOffice
Gaitskell Henry, Council Office
Galabin Thos. General Post Office
Galbraith W.G.Admlty. Somst. Ho
Gale Thos.Aug. ReportOff Chancry
Gale William, Custom House
GallandJohn, Cmndr.inChief's Offi
Gallin Rd. General Post Office
Gallop George, New Model Prison
Gallot Rd. Fuller, Genl. Post Offi
GallowayMaj.Gen.Archibald,Com. Ltncy. Lndn. &Ea. Ind. Director
Gallwey Capt. Thos. Consul, Naples
Galton Edward Earl, Custom Hse
Galton John, Custom House
GaltonJosephWest,Gen.PostOffice
GammanRt.Com.of CoalWhippers
Gapes Thos.Lnd. Dist.or T.Py.Post
Gandle John H. Custom House
Gandon Isaac, General Post Office
Gandy Edwd.Admiralty,Soms.Ho
GandyHen. Paymaster.Genl. Office

GandyJohn,Admiralty,SomersetH
Gardiner James,Stamp & TaxOffice
Gardiner John, General Post Office
GardinerJ.R.Duch. of Cornwl. Offi
GardnerFrancis Geary,CustomHse
Gardner H.P.Customs(Lancaster)
Gardner John, Gen. Post Office
Gardner Samuel, Consul at Jassy
Garerd William, Excise (Lynn)
Garman William C. Custom House
Garner Wm. General Post Office
GarnettFredk. B.Stamp&TaxOffice
Garnett Wm. Stamp & Tax Office
Garnett Rev. Rd. British Museum
GarrattJohn,Commsn.Ltncy.Lndn
Garrett Edwd. Greenwich Hosptl
Garrett R. C. Seaman's Reg. Office
Garrett Wm. B.Stamp & TaxOffice
GarrettRev.John, SurreyBridewell
Garrett Saml. Silver,Bd. of Ordnce
Garry Nicholas,Exchqr.Bil. Ln Offi
Gaskell James M. Lord Com. of Revenue inquiry & Tithe Comm
Gate Wm. Alex. Poor Law Office
Gates Richd. Customs (Shoreham)
Gates Thos. Customs (Brighton)
Gates William, Stamp & Tax Office
Gathen Phillip, Excise Office
GattieWm.Popham, Bank of Engld
Gatty George, Taxing Master
Gatty Rbt.Clk.to Needle makers Co
Gatty Robt. Court of Exchequer
Gaunt Wm. Board of Ordnance
Gauntlet Samuel, Genl.Post Office
Gay William, General Post Office
Geddings Samuel, Stamp &Tax Off
Geer Chas. Poor Law Office
Geesin John, QueenAnne's Bnty.O
Gell William, War Office
Gem Francis, Custom House
Genet Edward, Custom House
George David, Court of Exchequer
Gibb Wm.Admiralty, Somerset Ho
GibbesGeo.Commandr.inChief's Of
Gibbon Edward H. Herald's Coll
Gibbons Rt. ElectionOff.Hou. Com
GibbonsW.LondonDist.or T.Py.Ps
Gibbs Alf. John, Stamp & Tax Off
Gibbs David, Bridgemaster
Gibbs Michl. Alderman of London
GibbsSaml.Court of Common Pleas
Gibbs Thomas, General Post Office
GibsonAlf. Percy, Genl. Post Office
Gibson Chas. Fred.South SeaHouse
GibsonJamesCross, Custom House
GibsonJas.Edwd.PublicRecord Off
Gibson William, Custom House
GibsonWm.Benn, Genl.Post Office
Gidley Gustavus, Excise (Plymth)
Giffard Edwd. Admiralty, Whithll
Giffard Fras. Consul at Vera Cruz
Gilbert Edwd. Board of Ordnance
Gilbert Fras. H. Con. Cape Haytien
Gilbert John,Admiralty, Somst.Ho
Gilbert John, Audit Office
Gilbert Thos. W.Clk.to.Butcher'Co
Gilbert William, Excise Office
Gilchrist Joseph T.Bd.of Ordnance
Giles James B. Custom House
Gill John, Custom House
Gill Joseph, General Post Office
Gill Richard, General Post Office
Gill Wm. Chan. Lunacy Office
Gillespie Jas. Greenwich Hospital School
GillyWm. S. Admiralty, Whitehall
GingerWm.Journl.Off.H.of Comns
Ginger Wm. S. Stationary Office
Gipps John Methuen, Custom Ho
Girling John A.Adjutant Gen.'s Off
Gladstone Wm. Genl. Post Office
Gladstone Wm. Russia Company
Gladstone Rt. Hon. Wm. E. Com. forRevenue Inquiry, &TitheCom
Glass Jas. Wm. Consul at Tampico
Gleig Rev. Geo. Rt. Chelsea Hospl
Glen Wm. Cunningham,PoorL.Off
Glenelg Lord, Privy Councillor
Glennie John Irving, Archdeacon of Rochester's Registry, & Dean & ChapterofWestminster'sRgsty
Glibbery Jas. Worship st.Police ct
Gliddon John, Col. Emigration Bd
Gloag Thos. C.K.Admy. Somst. Ho
Glover Matt. Paymaster Gen. Offi
Glyn Geo Carr,Commiss.Lncy.Lnd
Glyn Sir Rd. P. South Sea House
Glynn Andrew, Genl. Post Office
Glynne Sir S. R. Ld. Lt. of Flintsh
Godby Chas.Geo.Stamp&TaxOffice
Godby John Palmer, Gen. Post Offi
Godby Wm. John, Gen. Post Offi
Goddard Archdeacon, Foreign Offi
Godfrey Jas. Brown, Gen. Post Offi
Godfrey Jeremiah, Gen. Post Office
Godfrey Pole, PaymasterGen.'sOffi
Godfrey Thos. Woods & ForestsOff
Godson Wm. Coker, Somerset Hou
Golden Thos. Metrop. Police Office
Golden Thos. Henry, Metropolitan Police Office
Goldham John, Custom House
Goldie Basil Heron,Bd.ofOrdnance
Goldie Wm.Admirlty.SomersetHo
Goldney Rev.John, K.Grnwh.Hosp
Goldsmith Malcolm, Admt. Smt.H
Gooch Henry, Audit Office
Gooch Joseph H. Duchy of Lancstr
Gooch Rd.StephenG.W.CustomHo
Gooch Sir Ts.Exchequer Bill Loan Office
Good Hen. Paymaster Gen.'s Office
Good John, General Post Office
Good Wm.Ecclesiastical Coms.Offi
Good William, Stamp & Tax Office
Goodall John Wm.Gen.Post Office
Goodbody George, House of Lords & Court of Chancery
Goodearl A. Taxing Masters' Office
Goodhall Wm. Excise Of.(Lond.E)
Gooding JamesYoung,Gen.Post.Of
Goodinge RomaineWm.CustomHo
Goodlif Fras. M.Admlty.Somst. Ho
Goodman Sam.R.Clk. to Ld.Mayor
Goodrich Rd.Mastrs.Office Qns.Bh
Goodrich Rd.Edmd.Queen's Bch.O
Goodrich Wm.Geo.Stamp&TaxOffi
Goodsir Thomas, General Post Off
Goodson Fras. Bow st. Police Ct
Goodson Wm. General Post Office
Goodwin Geo.Nunn, Genl. Post Off
Goodwin John, Consul at Palermo
Goodwin John, General Post Office
Goodwin John Thos. Excise Office
Goodwin Jph.F.Admlty. Somst.Ho
Goodwin Robert C. Custom House
Goodwin Wm. Privy Seal Office
Goodwin Wm. J.Ecclstl.Comm.Off
Goody J. Court of Common Pleas
Gordon Alexander, India Board
Gordon Sir Alex. Duff, Treasury
Gordon Geo. Huntly, Statinry. Offi
Gordon Geo. Rt. Sec. of Leg. Stckm
Gordon Robert, Comm. in Lunacy
GordonSirJs.A.Lt.Gov.Grnwh.Hpl
Gordon Gen. Sir. Jas. W. Quartermaster General's Office
Gordon John, Customs (Coleraine)
Gordon Sir Rt. G.C.B. Ambassador to Austria
Gordon Capt.Robt.R.N. Trinity Ho
Gore Chas. Alex. Woods & Forests
Gore Hon. Charles, Commissioner for improving the Metropolis
Gore John, Commsn. Ltncy.Londn
Gore Ralph, Stamp & Tax Office
Gorton James, General Post Office
Gorton Thomas, Customs (Dublin)
Gosford Earl of,G.C.B.,PrivyCncllr
Gosselin Gen. Bd. of Gen. Officers
Gossett Jackson, Custom House
Gosset Ralph A.Serj.ArmsHo.Com
Gosset SirWm.Serj.ArmsHo.Cmns
Gosset Wm.D.ElectionOff.Ho.Com
Gosling W.F.Prerogative(Will)Off
Goulburn Fredk. Custom House
Goulburn Hen. Privy Councillor
Goulburn Mr.Serj.Com.ofBnkptcy
Gould Nathaniel, Lloyd's
Gower Abel Lewes,BankofEngland
Gowland John, Excise Office
Gowland Wm. Edwd. Excise Office
Gowllard Richard, Custom House
Gozna Chas. Edwd. Custom House
Gozna Thomas W. Custom House
Grabham John, British Museum
Grace William, Consul at Mogador
Grace Wm. Lee, Stamp & Tax Offi
Gracewood Andrew, Foreign Office
Graff Jas. Admiralty,Somst. House
Graham Arthur, Gen. Post Office
Graham David, Custom House
Graham Fergus J. Consul,Bayonne
Graham G. Com.of HealthofTowns
Graham George Gen. Register Off
GrahamGeo.Jn.CourtofBankrptcy
GrahamGeo.Wm Genrl.PostOffice
Graham SirJ.R.G.PrivyCouncillor
Graham James, Excise Office
Graham John L. Custom House
Graham JohnS.Paymstr.Gen.'sOffi
Graham MissM. M.Admlty.Smst.H
Graham Thos. General Post Office
Graham William, Home Office
Grange Alex. Porter, General Post Office
Grant Sir Alex. C.bart.Audit Office
Grant James, Custom House
Grant James, Masters' Offi.Chancy
Grant Owen E. House of Lords
Grant Thos. G. Admiralty, Whithl
Grant Wm. Court of CommonPleas
Granville Earl, Privy Councillor
Grasswell Rd. N. East India House
Grattan T.C.Consul, Massachusetts
Graves Francis, Admiralty, Whthl
Graves Philip,Paymaster General's Office
Gray Andw. F. Customs (Glasgow)
Gray Benjamin, Stamp&TaxOffice
Gray Chas. Jrnl. Office, HouseCom
Gray Geo. Earle, Bank of England
Gray George Robt. British Musum
Gray Hen. J. Seaman's Regstr. Of
Gray James, Custom House
Gray John Edw. British Museum
Gray John jun. Clk.toFounders'Co
Gray Robert, General Register Offi
Gray Robert, Custom House
Gray Robert A. Lloyd's
Gray William, Consul at Virginia
Green Chas. Com.of CoalWhippers
Green Chas. Ernest, Custom Ho
Green Chas. Wm. House of Lords
Green Geo. Court of Bankruptcy
Green George, Custom House
Green George, Paymaster Genl. Off
Green Hen. Wm. Adjutant Gen. Of
Green Jas. Exchequer BillLoan Off
Green James, General Post Office
Green John, Consul at Athens
Green Michael, Court of Chancery
Green Peter, Custom House
Green Rt. Lndn.Dist. orT.Py.Post
Green T. Com. Lieutcy. of London
Green Ths. Moses, PublicRecordO
Green Wm. General Post Office
Green Wm. A. House of Lords
Greene Octavius, East India House
Grenfell Chas. P. Bank of England
Greenland T.H.Examrs.Offi.Chanc
Greenstreet Jas. Stamp & Tax Offi
Greenwood Chas.Carroll,AuditOffi
Greenwood John B. Clerkenwell Police Court
Gregory MarkH.Clk.toWaxChndlr
GregsonSamuel,Comn.Ltncy.Lond
Gregson Wm. London Gazette Offi
Greig William, Custom House
Grenville Thos. Privy Councillor
Greville Charles Cavendish Fulke Clerk in Ordinary of Council
Grey Earl, Privy Councillor
Grey Sir Chas. E. Privy Councillor
Grey Charles, Treasury
Grey Charles Samuel, Treasury
Grey Robert, Custom House
Grey Sir Geo. Privy Councillor & Ecclesiastical Commissioner
Grey Sir Hen. G. Bd. of Gen. Offi
Grey Rt. Jas. Moring, Trinity Ho
Grey William, Chelsea Hospital
GreyWm. Hen.Lndn.Dist.orTPy.P
Grieve David, Customs (Blakeney)
Griffin Henry, Genl. Post Office
Griffin Wm. John, War Office
Griffith Edwd. Master Comn. Pleas
Griffith John, Board of Ordnance
Griffith P. Sec. of Leg. in Greece
Griffith Thomas, Gray's inn
Griffith Wm. Board of Ordnance
Griffiths Chas. Consl.Buenos Ayres
Griffiths James G. Custom House
GriffithsPeterWm.Admlty.Smst.H
Grigg Robert, Consul at Mobile
Grimer Thos. General Post Office
Grimes John, City Officer
Grimes John, Customs (Liverpool)
GrimwoodW.Edgar, Sup.Police(E)
Grindrod James M. Custom House
Groom Jas. F.Court of Bankruptcy
Groom Rd. Solicitor toIndia Board
Gross William, Audit Office
Grosvenor Lord Robert,Priv.Coun
Grout George, Court of Admiralty
Grove Henry L. Customs (Exeter)
Grove John, Treasury
Grove Wm. PoliceMag.Greenwich
Grove Wm. Worship st. Police Ct
Groves Capt. J. R. MilbankPrison
Groves Thos. General Post Office
Groves William, Custom House
Gruaz Henry Thos. Board of Ordn
Grubb Joshua Johnson, WarOffice
Gruggen Chas. Price, Custom Ho
Gruggen Price, Custom House
Guarracino F. Consul at Batoom
Guazzaroni Joseph John, Treasury
Gude Richard, jun. City Officer
Gudge Jas. Jornl. Off. House Cmns
Gudgeon T. W. Stamp &TaxOffice
Gulson Edward, Poor Law Office
Gunn L. Lambeth st. PoliceCourt
GunnellChas.ElectionOff.HoCmns
Gunnell Geo. JournalOff.Ho.Cmns
GunnellSamuel,Jornl.Off.Ho.Cmn
GunnellSaml.B.BillOff.Ho.of Com
Gunnell Wm. S. Paymsr.Gen's Off
GunningThomas, Genl. PostOffice
Gunston Henry, Trinity House
Gurney Joseph, House of Lords
Gurney John Gregory, War Office
Gurney Wm. Brodie, Houses of Lords & Commons
Gurwood Col. John, C.B. Tower
Gutch Jas. Wm. Geo. Home Office
Guy James, Custom House
Gwatkin Fredk. Clerk to Mason'sC
Gwyn Robert, Board of Ordnance
Gwyther Geo. Customs(Ramsgate)

Habbijam James, Custom House
Hackman Henry, Custom House
HaddingtonEarl of,PrivyCouncillr
Haggar George, Custom House
Haggard Edmund, Stamp &TaxOff
Haggard Dr. Archdeacon of Surrey's Registry Office
Haggard Wm. D. Bank of England
Hahn GeorgeH.Comn.Ltncy.Lndn
Haigh Joseph, Board of Ordnance
Haines Geo.Hen.Stamp&TaxOffice
Haines Henry, Court of Chancery
Haines John, Treasury
Haines Mrs. Mary, Treasury
Haines Thomas, Custom House
Haines W. Custom House
HainesWm.Henry,House of Lords
Haines Wm. Thos. Genl.PostOffice
Hair John, Court of Chancery
Halcombe C. Stamp & Tax Office
Hale John Blagden, CustomHouse
Hale Samuel, Colonial Office
Hale Ven. Wm. H. Archd. of Lond
Halfhide Geo.Engvr.toStmp.&T.O
Haliburton Jas.C.Admlty.Smst.Ho
Haliday Michael, House of Lords
Halksworth Wm. Colonial Office
HalkettSir Colin,Bd.ofGenl.Officrs
Halkett John,Hudson'sBayCompy
Hall John, General Post Office
Hall Maj.L.A.RoyalEngineer'sOffi
Hall Lieut.Thos. Tower of London
Hall George, General Post Office
Hall John, Excise Office
Hall Jn. Hancock, Com. inLunacy
Hall Richard, General Post Office
HallRichard,PoorLawAsst.Commr
Hall Thos. J.ChiefMagistrt.Bow st
Hall Wm. Woods & Forests Office
Hallam Henry, Comr. of Fine Arts
Halligan Thomas, Treasury
Halse John, Stamp & Tax Office
Halton Walton Fox, Genl. PostOff
Hamber Thos.Court of Bankruptcy
Hamer Nathaniel, Rolls Court
Hamer James Henry, Audit Office
Hamer Nat. Court of Exchequer
Hamer Samuel, Genl. Post Office
Hamerton Capt. A. Consul,Muscat
Hamilton Duke of, Privy Councilr
HamiltonChas. Anthony,Cuncil.O
HamiltonSirG.B.Sec.of Leg.Berlin
Hamilton Geo. C.Customs(Milfrd)
Hamilton H. C. J. Ambasador to Brazil
Hamilton James, Gen. Post Office
Hamilton Jas. Greenwh. Hos. Schl
Hamilton JohnJas.Stamp&TaxOff
Hamilton Otho H. Audit Office
HamiltonRd.W.Admlty.Whitehall
Hamilton Thos. Court of Excheqr
Hamilton Wm. Consul at Boulogne
Hamilton Wm. Gen. Post Office
Hammack Jas. Thos. Gen. Rgstr.Of
Hammersley John, GeneralPost Of
Hammond Charles, CustomHouse
Hammond Edward, Foreign Office
Hammond George S.CustomHouse
Hampton Wm. Custom House

Hampton Wm. Custom House
Hanby George, Board of Ordnance
Hanby John, War Office
Hanby Joseph, War Office
Hanby William, Audit Office
Hancock Edwin Alex.Gen.Post Offi
Hancock John, Custom house
Hancock John Wm. Poor Law Off
Hankey George, Lloyds
HankeyJno.Alex.Comn.Ltncy.Lon
Hankey Thos. Comsn. Ltncy. Lond
Hankey Thos.A.Comsn.Ltncy.Lon
Hankins Henry, Stationery Office
Hankins Richard, Treasury
Hanley Jas. Worship st. Police cr
Hann George, Greenwich Hospital
Hansard James & Luke Jas. House of Commons
HansardWm.M.Judgmt.Of.Qn's.B
Hanson John, Lloyds
Hanson JohnO. Direct.Bank ofEng
Harden Chas. Court of Com. Pleas
Hardie Andrew, Seaman's Reg.Off
Hardie A. H. Customs (Maryport)
Harding DavidSaml.CustomHouse
Harding G. Sol. British Museum
Harding Thos.Perfect,ExciseOffice
Hardinge Sir Hy. Gov. Gen.ofIndia
HardistyFred.A.SubpœnaOf.Chncy
Hardman John, Excise Office
Hardwick Jn. Marlbro' st.Police Ct
HardwickeEarl,Ld.Lt.Cambridgsh
Hardy Alf. Lndn. Dist.orT.Py.Post
Hardy George, General Post Office
Hardy Jonthn. Cons.atConstantnpl
Hardy Rt. Admiralty Somst.House
Hardy Thos.D.PublicRecordOffice
Hardy Wm. Duchy of Lancstrs.Off
Hargood Hezkh.Stamp&Tax Office
Hargrave L. Consul atBalearicIsles
Hargraves Matthew, Excise Office
Harisson Alfred, Bd. of Ordnance
Harkness Rt. Stationery Office
Harkness Wm. Custom House
Harloe Charles, Custom House
HarmanChs.A.Luntc.Of.Ct.ofChcy
Harness Rev. W. Privy Council Of
Harnett William Chapman, Lloyds
Harper Thomas,Stamp&Tax Office
Harran Edward, Foreign Office
Harries Thos. Poor Law Office
Harris Daniel, Colonial Office
Harris Fras.C.Admlty.Somst. Hou
Harris Henry, Custom House
Harris Henry Geo.Bd. of Ordnance
Harris Jas. Greenwh.Hospt.School
Harris John G. Com. Insolvent Ct
Harris John W. Admlty.Somst.Ho
Harris Joseph, General Post Office
Harris Joseph, Stamp & Tax Office
Harris Robert, Custom House
Harris Rt. Clerk to Lord Mayor
Harris Thomas, GeneralPostOffice
Harriskine Wm. Insolvent Court
Harrison Ben. Exchequer Bill Off
Harrison Douglas, Custom House
Harrison Edm.Step.Py.CouncilOffi
Harrison Sir Geo.DuchyCornwl.Of
Harrison George, Stamp & Tax Of
Harrison George F. Gen. Post Off
Harrison Geo.H.R.Heralds'College
Harrison Henry A. Paymaster General's Office
Harrison James, Foreign Office
Harrison John, Excise Office
Harrison John, Gen. Post Office
Harrison Matthew, Treasury
Harrison Matt. South Sea House
Harrison Samuel,Bank of England
Harrison Thomas, Excise Office
Harrison Thomas Chas. Treasury
Harrison William, Gen. Post Off
Harrison Gibbs C. Admlty. Smst.H
Harrod Geo. Gateland, Excise Offi
Harrold Thomas, Treasury
Harrowby Earl of, Privy Councir. and EcclesiasticalCommissioner
Hart Sir H. Com. Greenwich Hsptl
Hart Capt. Home Office
Hart Joseph, War Office
Hart Napthali, Custom House
Hart Thos.Lndn.Dist.or T.Py.Post
Harting John, General Post Offi
Hartshorne John, ChelseaHospital
Hartwell George B. Custom House
Harvey Anthy. Bd. of Ordnance
Harvey Dan. W. City Commsnr.Po
Harvey Fredk. Custom House
Harvey Hen.Ellis,Stamp &Tax Off
Harvey J. Russia & Eastland Cos
Harvey John W. Geo. Gen. Pst.Off
Harvey Wm. Stamp & Tax Office
Harvey Wm. Tuck, Custom House
Haskoll James, Custom House
Hast Henry Chas. Custom House
Hast Rt. Grimes, Custom House
Hastings Thos. Customs (Glo'ster)
Hatherton Lord, Privy Councillor
Hathorn Geo.Exchqr.Bill Loan Off
Hatton Geo.PaymasterGen.'sOffice
Hatton Geo. Sydney, Sewers Offi
Haughton Richd. AddiscombeSem
Haviland Robert, Foreign Office
Hawdon Matthew, Custom House
Hawes Benjamin,Commissioner of Fine Arts
Hawes Wm. Bill Offi.House Comns
Hawker Chas.Fred.Bd.of Ordnance
Hawker Fran. Alfred, Audit Office
Hawker Joseph, Heralds' College
Hawkes John, Bank of England
Hawkes Roger, Gen. Post Office
Hawkins Chas.JohnM.Gen.PostOff
Hawkins Edwd. British Museum
Hawkins John Rd. Custom House
Hawkins JohnThos.Gen.PostOffice
Hawkins Wm. Excise (Reading)
Hawley Wm.Hy.Toovey,Poor L.O
Hay Charles, Stamp & Tax Office
HayEdwd.Holman,Admlty.Som.H
HayJ.H.Drummond,Con.atTngier
Hay Henry, Stamp & Tax Office
Hay Jn.Holman, Admrlty. Whiteh
Hay Jn.H.jun. Admiralty, Whiteh
HayCapt.Wm.Metropn.PoliceOffic
Hayes Sam. A.Admiralty,Somerset House
Hayles George, Stamp & Tax Offic
Hayman Capt. John,Trinity House
Haynes Chas. General Post Office
Haynes Edward, Stamp & Tax Offi
Haynes Fredk.jun.Ct. of Chancery
Haynes Henry J.Court of Chancery
Haynes John,Admiralty,Whitehall
Hayward John, Treasury
Hayward Jph.Ldn.Dist.orT.Py.Pst
Hazard Chas. Genl. Register Office
Hazell William, Custom House
Head SirEdmundW.PoorLawCom
Head John, Custom House
Head Thomas, Sewers' Office
Hearle Nathaniel, Audit Office
Hearle Thos. Customs (Falmouth)
Hearnden Isaac, Custom House
Hearsum Harry L.Board of Ordnce
Heath D. D.Middx Ct. of Requests
Heath George Fredk.Gen.Post Offi
Heath J.B.Dep.Gov. of BankofEng
Heath W.LondonDist.orT.Py.Post
Heather Thomas, Customs
HeavisideRev.J.W.L.Haylybry.Co
Hebden G.W.Admiraly. Somst. Ho
Hebert Lewis J. Quartermaster General's Office
Heckford Jas. Court of Exchequer
Heddell Fras. Customs (Lerwick)
Hemans Chas.Lloyd,CustomHouse
Hemington James, Custom House
Hemmans Lieut.Government Emigration Agent (Greenock)
Hemmens John, Gen. Post Office
Henderson Alex. Gen. Post Office
Henderson Geo.Clk.to Horners'Co
Henderson John B. Custom House
Heneage George Heneage Walker, Courts of C.P. & Exchequer
Henning George, Custom House
Henry Lieut.Gov.Emg.Agt.(Livpl)
Henry Thos. Lambeth st. Police ct
Hepburne Wm.Henry,Gen.PostOff
Herbert Frederick,Gen.Post Office
Herbert George, Custom House
Herbert George, Trinity House
Herbert Jacob, Trinity House
Herbert Rt. Hon. Sidney, M.P. Privy Councillor & War Office
Herbert William, Excise Office
Herdson John, Excise (Exeter)
Heron Wm.Woods&Forests' Office
Herries Chas.J.Commiss.of Excise
Herries Rt. Hon. John C. Com. for Improving the Metropolis
Herries Sir W. Lewis, Audit Office
Herschel Sir Jn.F.W.bart.Bri.Mus
Hersee Henry, Custom House
Hertslet James, Foreign Office
Hertslet Lewis, Foreign Office
Hertslet Lewis, Home Office
HertsletLewisCooke,Sewers' Office
Hertslet W. J. Consul at Memel
Hervey LordWm. Sec.of Leg.Paris
Hesketh Rt. Consul,Rio de Janeiro
Hester Henry, Insolvent Court
Hester J. Court of Queen's Bench
Hewitt John, Board of Ordnance
HewittThos.Young,Gen.PostOffice
Hewlitt JohnC.Palace Court Office
Heytesbury Lord, Privy Councillor
Heyward Charles, Custom House
HeywoodSir Ben.Exchr. Bll.Ln.Off
HibbardWm.H.General Post Office
Hick Ch. Wm. City Sword Bearer
Hickes Weston, Home Office
Hickman Poole, Chelsea Hospital
Hicks Robert, Stamp & Tax Office
HideGeo.Edwd.General Post Office
Higgins Jas. W. Metropo. Bldg.Off
HigginsWarner C.Woods&Forests
Higgins Wm. Fred. Colonial Office
Higginson Hen. Custms.(Wexford)
Higgs John, Westminster Court
Higgs T.Coroner for Dy. of Lancstr
Higgs William, Millbank Prison
Higham Jas. National Debt Office
Higham Sam. National Debt Office
Higley Chas. General Post Office
Hildyard Rt.C.Dh.of Lancas.Office
Hill Chas. Geo. Gen. Post Office
Hill C. T. Consul at Fiume
Hill David, East India House
Hill Fredk. Inspector of Prisons
Hill Hen. Slave Compens. Office
Hill James, Royal Mint
Hill Lord A. M. C. Privy Councllr
Hill Rev. Jas. Greenwich Hospital
Hill Richard, Excise (Sussex)
Hill Sam. Queen's Bench Office
Hill Thomas, Home Office
Hill William, Stamp & Tax Office
Hill Viscount, Ld. Lieut. Salop
Hillary Mrs. Eliz. Millbank Prison
Hillborne Edwd. Excise(Cornwall)
Hillman Robert, Custom House
Hillmer Wm. General Post Office
Hills James, Excise Office
Hilson James, Custom House
HindHy.J.Admiralty, SomersetHo
HindeWm.Thos.AdmirltySmst.Ho
Hindes Barth.N. Stamp & TaxOffi
HineRev.Geo.Hen.Totl.filds.Brdwl
Hingston C.L. Customs (Westport)
Hinton John, General Post Office
Hirsch Francis, Court of Chancery
Hitchens Robert, Gen. Post Office
Hoar James, Custom House
Hoar Joseph, Custom House
Hoare John,Lndn.Dis. or T.Py. Pst
Hoare JohnWm. Exchequer Office
HobartBenj. P.Admiralty,Somst.H
Hobart Frederick, India Board
HobartVereH.Com.ofP.C.forTrade
HobbsHenry, General Post Office
HobbsJohn Coleman,Gen. PostOffi
Hobbs Rd.M. Paymaster Gens.'Offi
Hobbs Samuel, City Officer
Hobbs Thomas, Excise Office
Hobbs William, City Officer
HobbsWm.Hen. Remembrncrs.Offi
Hobhouse SirJohnC. PrivyCouncIr
Hobhouse Rt. Hon. H. State Paper Office & Ecclesiastical Commis
HobhouseHen.HealthofTownsCom
Hoblyn Edward, Stamp & Tax Offi
Hobson Christopher, Gen. Post Offi
Hodd Edwd. Gen. Post Office
Hodder John, Customs (Cowes)
Hodder Lieu.Gov.Emigr.At.(Dbln)
Hodges Chas. Privy Council Office
Hodges Geo. H. Stationery Office
Hodges Geo.L. Consul at Hamburg
Hodgkin James, Poor Law Office
HodgkinWm.Pri.BillOf.Ho.Comm
Hodgkinson Thos. Bk. of England
Hodgson Amos,Board of Ordnance
Hodgson Chas.Geo. Sup.City Pol
HodgsonChristopher,QueenAnne's Bounty Office, & Office of the Dean & Chapter of St. Paul's
Hodgson Christph. Genl. Post Offi
HodgsonHen.John,Ct.Comn.Pleas
Hodgson Jeremiah, Ct. of Bankrup
HodgsonK.D. Commn. Ltncy. Lon
HoffmeisterC.W. Cs. (Portsmouth)
Hogg Jas. W.DirectorEastIndiaCo
Hogg Peter, Woods & Forests Offi
Hogwood Robert, House of Peers
Holden Hen. Geo. PublicRecordOf
Holden Henry Wm. Petty Bag Off
Holder Saml. Stationery Office
Holdway James, Somerset House
Hole John Boger, Foreign Office
Holford John, Qn. Anne's Bnty.Off
Holgate Wm. General Post Office
Holland Lord, Ambasdr.toTuscany
Holland HenryL. Bank of England
Hollings John, War Office
Hollingworth Edwd. Custom Ho
Holmes Alex. Board of Ordnance
Holmes George, Foreign Office
Holmes Geo.Vinter,Gen.PostOffice
Holmes John, British Museum
Holmes Ray, Patent Office
Holmes William, Custom House
Holmes Wm. A.Board of Ordnance
Holmes W. H. Customs, Maldon
Holroyd Edward,BankruptcyCourt
HoltFras.L.Exchqr.BillLoanOffice
Holworthy Chas.W.Gen.PostOffice
HolyoakFras.Qrtr.Mastr.Gens.Of
Honey John, General Post Office
Honeybourne Thos. D. Customs
HoodM. T. ViceCon.atMonteVideo
Hood William S. Custom House
Hook Wm. General Post Office
Hookey Fras.B.Comn. Ltncy.Lond
HookeyWm.Hen.Admlty.Somst.H
Hooper James, General Post Off
Hooper John K. AldermanofLondn
Hooper Mrs. M.Grnwh.Hsp.School
Hooper Rt. Little, Queen's Prison
Hooper Thomas, Custom House
Hooper Wm. Thos. East India Ho
Hope Chas. Privy Councillor
HopeHen.T.MetropolisImpr.Comr
Hope John, Privy Councillor
Hope Rt. Wallis, Bd. of Ordnance
Hoper Fredk. Stamp & Tax Off
Hopkins Hen. J.GeneralPostOffice
Hopkins Thos. Stamp & Tax Office
Hopper Christopher, Gen.Post Offi
Hopper Edw. Lythgoe, CustomHse
Hopper W. H. Poor LawCommissn
Hore James Smyth, Excise Office
Hornby Capt.CustomHouse&Coast Guard Comp. Fund
Horne SirWm.Master in Chancery
Horner Anthony, Ct. of Exchequer
Horner Leonard, Home Office
Hornidge Marma. EastIndiaHouse
Hornidge Wm. Court of Chancery
Horsfall John, Stamp & Tax Office
Horsfall John, jun., Custom House
HorsfieldDr.Thos. EastIndiaHouse
Hosken Richard Finlay, Customs
Hosken Wm. General Post Office
Hosking Robt. Pentonvl. Prison
Hosking William, Metropolitan Building Office
Hoss George, Excise Office
Hotchkin Francis, Excise Office
Hotson Robert Money, East India House
HoughThos.G.Masters'Off. Chancy
Houghton Arthur, Admiralty
Houghton Jn.H.N.Admlty. Whithl
Houndle Edwd. AdjutantGens. Offi
Hovenden John E. Tithe Comsnrs
Hovendon NicholasE.Gen.Post Off
How Thomas, Custom House
Howard Chas. Fredk.Stamp&TaxO
Howard Chas. TitheCommsnrs.Brd
Howard Charles Ed. CustomHouse
Howard Hy. F. Sec.ofLeg.at Hague
Howard Jas. General Post Office
Howard Thomas,BoardofOrdnance
Howard Thos. Court of Com. Pleas
Howard Thomas, Custom House
Howard Thomas Brown, Stamp & Tax Office
Howden Wm. B. Excise (Howden)
Howe Earl, G.C.H. Privy,Councillr
Howe Edward, Tower of London
HowellClarence Rd.PoorLawOffice
Howell Lewis Hen. Customs(Deal)
Howell Owen, General Post Office
Howell Th.J.Factorydep. Home Of
Howes Henry, AdjutantGenl.'s Off
Howes Mrs.Sarah,AdjutantGens.O
Howlett Sam. Burt,BrdofOrdnance
HowlettWm.Cullen,Gen.PostOffice
Howse George,Stamp & Tax Office
Howse Geo. F.AdjutantGens.Office
Howson William, Custom House
Hubbard Alf.Roots,Gen.PostOffice
Hubbard John, Russia Company
Hubbard John, jun. Custom House
Hubbard John G.Bank of England
Hubbard Jn.G.Comsn.Ltncy.Lndn
HuddlestoneGeo.R.Gen.PostOffice
Huddy Jos. Hoskin, Gen. Post Off

Hudson Capt.J.R.N.Queen'sPrison
Hudson Corris, Stamp &TaxOffice
HudsonJ.Sec.ofLeg.atRio-de-Janr
Hudson James, City Officer
Hudson John G. Bank of England
Hudson John, General Post Office
Hudson Jn. C. Stamp & Tax Office
Hudson John Peter, Home Office
Hughes Edwd.Grenwh.Hos.School
HughesEdwardBest,CustomHouse
HughesFred.Lndn.Dist.orT.PyPst
Hughes John, Court of Exchequer
Hughes John,Customs(Carnarvon)
Hughes Joseph, Poor Law Office
Hughes Philip, Treasury
Hughes Philip Alex. Audit Office
Hughes William,Bank of England
Hughes W. H.JudgeAdvct.Gens.Of
Hughes W.H.jun.Comsn.Ltny.Ln
Hughes W. T. ArmyMedicalBoard
Hulbert Jas. Michael, Excise Off
Hulburd Thomas, Gen. Post Office
Hull Thomas, Custom House
Hullah John, Greenwich Hos. Schl
Humber Rd. Board of Ordnance
Humbert Lewis, East India House
Hume Dr. John Rt. East India Ho. & Commissioner in Lunacy
Hume William, Stamp &TaxOffice
Humphery John, Alderman of London, & Com. for Improving the Metropolis
HumphreysGeorge,Gen.PostOffice
Humphries George, Treasury
HunnemanBladen,Stamp&TaxOffi
Hunt Charles, Custom House
Hunt Edward, Millbank Prison
HuntEd.H.Lunatc.of.Ct.of Chncry
Hunt J.H.S.L.GeneralRegisterOffi
Hunt John, Stamp & Tax Office
Hunt JosephOffwood,Gen.PostOffi
Hunt Marriott, Gen.RegisterOffice
HuntPercyS.Leigh,Pblc.Recrd.Off
Hunt Richard, Ct. of Exchequer
Hunt Thomas, Court of Chancery
HuntThos.C.Consul atSt.Michael's
Hunt Thos. Newman, Bank of Eng
Hunt WilliamBoyse,CustomHouse
Hunter Sir Claudius S. Alderman
Hunter Hen. Lannoy, India Board
HunterJohn Dixon,Gen.PostOffice
Hunter John, Tower of London
Hunter Rev.Jsph.PublicRecordOff
Hunter Wm. Alderman of London
Huntingdon Hen. Stamp & Tax Off
Huntley Richard, Custom House
Hurles John, City Officer
Hurlstone J. Worship st. Police ct
Hurrell Samuel, Excise Office
Hurry Edward, Lloyd's
Huskisson F. Greenwich Hospital
Huskisson Wm. Foreign Office
Hussey Hen. Chancery RegisterOffi
Hutchins Henry, Gen. Post Office
Hutchings Edwin, Poor Law Office
Hutchinson Fras. Sup. Registrar
Hutchinson Robert, Excise Office
Huth Chas. Fredk.Bank of Englnd
Hutt Thomas, Foreign Office
Huttner John C. Foreign Office
Hutton T. S. Consul at Prevesa
Huxley Jas. Clerk to Musicians' Co
Hyett David, Bank of England

Ibbott R. G. City Officer
Iggulden John, Prerogative Office
Illingworth Rev.E.A.Ho.ofCorrect
Ince Wm. Hen. Paymsr. Gen's. Off
Inchbald Rev.Robt.B.A.Addiscomb
Indis H. F. Com. of P. C. for Trade
Ingall Thomas, Bank of England
InglisSirRt.H.Metro.Chrch.Fnd.O. & Com. for Impr. the Metropolis
Inglis Henry, Custom House
Inglis Thomas, Custom House
Inglis Walter, Custom House
Inglis Wm. Price, Gen. Post Office
Ingpen Alfred Wm.InsolventCourt
Ingpen Edwd. Insolvent Drs. Court
Inman Wm. Woods &ForestsOffice
Innes Geo. M. Admiralty,Som. Ho
Innes JohnWm.Admirlty.Whitehl
Innes Wm.A.Admiralty,Whitehall
Instan Chas. Excise (Birmingham)
Ireland John, Ct. of Bankruptcy
Irons Ebenezer, Ct. of Bankruptcy
Irvine Thos. Greenwh. Hos. School
IrvineWalker,Ctms.(PortGlasgow)
Irving Chas. Mitchell, Audit Office
IrvingJno.Excheqr.BillLoanOffice
Irving Matthew, Custom House
Irving Thos.Com of P.Cncl.for Trd
Irving William, Custom House
Irwin James, Admiralty,Somst.Ho
Irwin Thomas, Audit Office
Ivimey J. Sup. Regr. (St. Pancras)

Jackaman R. F. Custom House
Jackson Chas. R.M.Ct ofChancery
Jackson Fred. Rowland,Gen.PostO
Jackson Geo. Admiralty,Somst.Ho
Jackson Henry Bates, Treasury
Jackson John, Admlty. Whitehall
Jackson Joseph, War Office
JacksonMaj.Basil,AddiscombeSem
Jackson Thos. Crown Of.Chancery
Jackson William, Foreign Office
Jackson William, Gen. Post Off
Jacob Rd. Thos. Gen. Post Office
Jacob Wm.James,Bank ofEngland
Jacob Wm. Stamp & Tax Office
Jadis Henry F.Com.ofP.C.forTrade
Jadis Vane, Colonial Office
Jago William, Custom House
James Chas. Henry, City Officer
James Edward,General Post Office
James James, Customs (Gweek)
James Jno.Secndy,Giltspurst.Cmp
James Joseph, Gen. Post Office
JamesR.Ctms.(Ramsey.St.IvesCnl)
James Thos. Admiralty, Whitehall
James Thos.Rt.General Post Office
James Thos. Stamp & Tax Office
James Wm.R.Sup.Regr.(Holborn)
Jameson Hen.Lndn.Dist.orT.P.Pst
Jameson Hugh, Excise Office
Jaques William, City Officer
Jardine David,Bow st.Police Court
Jarman Egbert, Gen. Post Office
Jarvis Thos. Hen. Poor Law Office
Jautard William, Audit Office
Jay Alfred T.Adjutant Gen.'sOffice
Jay John L. Greenwich Hospital
Jay Lieut. Chas. H. Admlty. Whthl
JayneThomas,Admiralty,Somst.H
Jacks Williams, Bk. of England
Jeffcott Thos. W. Court of Chncry
Jefferson John, Chancy.Affidvt.Off
Jefferson Matt. G.Admlty.Smst.Ho
Jefferson Thomas, Excise Office
Jeffreys Geo.Ct. of Common Pleas
Jeffreys W. J.Customs(Stornaway)
Jelf G. Archdeacon of Middx.Office
Jelly Wm. Coleman, Custom Ho
JellicoeAbrahamB.K.Stmp.&TaxO
Jemmett Wm. T. Comn. of Bkptcy
Jenkins Edwd. NationalDebtOffice
Jenkins SirRd.Comsn. Ltncy.Lndn
Jenkins Wm.Ed.Admlty.Somset.H
Jenkyns Edward, East IndiaHouse
Jenner Ed. Fras. Ct. of Peculiars
Jenner-Fust Sir H. knt. Arches Ct
Jennings Richd.Stamp&Tax Office
Jennings Wm. E. Custom House
Jennings William, State Paper Off
Jennings Wm. Earle, Ct. of Exchr
Jephson Robt.Holmes,PoorLawOff
Jepson Rev.G.Clrknwl. NewPrison
Jeremie Rev.Jas.A.HayleyburyCol
Jeremy Hy.GreenwichPoliceCourt
Jermyn Earl, Privy Councillor
Jerningham Hon. G.S.Sec. Lg.Mad
Jersey Earl of, Priuy Councillor
Jerwood Tas.M.A.Tithe Comrs. Bd
Jesse Edwd. Woods&Forests Office
Jesse John, South Sea House
JesseJohn H.Admiralty,Whitehall
Jessep Thos.F. Greenwich Hospital
Jiggins W. W. Court of Exchequer
Johnes John, Tithe Commissrs. Bd
Johnson Mrs. Ann, Colonial Office
Johnson Mrs.Ann,Exchr.BillLn.Of
Johnson Mrs. Ann,SouthSeaHouse
Johnson Arthur E. Gen. Post Off
Johnson Capt. CecilG. Foreign Offi
Johnson Charles, Gen. Post Office
Johnson Charles D. Stationery Off
Johnson Edwin, Consul at Oporto
Johnson Francis, Hayleybury Col
Johnson Geo. H. Admrlty.Somst.H
Johnson Godschall, Cnsl. Antwerp
Johnson James, Genl. Post Office
Johnson JamesJohn,CustomHouse
Johnson Rt.Hon John, Lord Mayor
Johnson John, Stamp & Tax Office
Johnson Joseph,BillOffi.Ho.ofCom
Johnson Patrick,Ct.of Bankruptcy
Johnson Richd. Stamp & Tax Off
Johnson William, Excise Office
Johnson Wm. General Post Office
Johnston James, Custom House
Johnston James, Supt.of Police(N)
Johnston Morrice,General Post Off
Johnston Thomas, Poor Law Office
Johnstone Sir A. Privy Councillor
Johnstone David G. Patent Office
Johnstone Frdk. Chs. Gen. Post Off
Johnstone James,Ct.ofBankruptcy
JohnstoneRev. W.H.AddscmbSem
Johnstone Wm.H.AddiscombeSem
Jolly David M. Customs (Dundee)
Jones Arthur,Pblc.Bus Of.Ho.Com
Jones Charles, Audit Office
Jones David, Poor Law Office
Jones Danl.Lloyd, Genl.Post Office
Jones Edward, Custom House
Jones Edwd.Marylebone Police Ct
Jones Edward Dewe, Signet Office
Jones Evan, Court of Admiralty
Jones Geo. Customs (Plymouth)
Jones Geo.Dundas,Genl.Post Office
Jones Harvey B.Clk.to Wlmen'sCo
Jones Henry, General Post Office
Jones Henry, General Post Office
Jones Henry Storer, India Board
Jones Hugh Bearer, Custom House
Jones John, Excise Office
Jones John, Board of Ordnance
Jones John,QuarterMastr.Gen's.Of
Jones JohnWinter,BritishMuseum
Jones Lewis, Treasury
Jones Marmaduke, Gen. Post Off
Jones Rev. Richard, Tithe Commissioner and Copyhold Com
Jones Rev. Richd. Hayleybury Col
Jones Ricd. L. Comn. Ltncy. Lndn
Jones S. L. Southwark, Ct. of Record, Clerk to Carmen's Co
Jones Thos. Admlty. Somst. Ho
Jones Thomas, Custom House
Jones Thos. Clerk to Bowyers' Co
Jones T. Customs (Wick)
Jones William, Bank of England
Jones Wm. Customs (Bridgewater)
Jones Wm. Masters' Off. Chancery
Jones Wm. Reduc.of Nat.Debt Offi
Jones William, Stamp & Tax Off
JonesWm.S.CrownOff Qun's.Bnch
Jopling Chas. Adjutant Gen's. Off
Jordan Henry, Stamp & Tax Office
Jorden John, Poor Law Office
Jouve L. E. Consul at Toulon
Jowett John T.PublicRecord Office
JoyWm.Com.ofPrvy.Cncl.forTrad
Joyce G. Com. of P. C. for Trade
Joyce G.jun.Com. of P.C.for Trade
Joyce John, Customs (Cork)
Jude Richd. General Post Office
Julians Thomas, Excise Office
Jull Thomas, Custms. (Feversham)
Jupp Rd. Sl. City Ct. of Requests
Jupp Sam. Clerk to Carpenters' Co

Kaines Fras.Lndn.Dist.orT.Py.Pst
Kains John, General Post Office
Kane George, Ordnance Board
Karstadt Edward, Genl. Post Offi
Karstadt Fredk.West.Gen.Post Off
Karstadt Geo. Hen. Gen. Post Off
Kay John Charles, Excise Office
Kay Jsph. Archt. to Grnwh. Hsptl
Kay Thomas, Privy Council Offic
Kaye Lister L. Privy Council Off
Kaye William, Foreign Office
Kebbell James, Clerk to Tilers' Co
Keddell John, Custom House
Keen Alfred, Board of Ordnance
Keene Jno, Horsemonger La. Gaol
Keene Wm.John,Genrl.Post Office
Keilor John,Southwk.Ct.ofRecord
Keith Thos.Hilton,Ea.IndiaHouse
Keith William, East India House
KelleyWmQueen'sRemembrncrsO
Kellner George, Genl. Post Office
Kelly Frederic, General PostOffice
Kelly Thomas,AldermanofLondon
Kelly Thos.Arnold,GeneralPostOff
Kelly Wm. Henry, Audit Office
Kelsey Hugh Stuart, Colonial Off
Kelsey JamesHenry,Custom House
Kelsey Jas. Sumner,Cstms.(Dovr.)
Kemp James, Excise Office
Kemp James, Stamp & Tax Office
Kemp W. R. Queen's Bench Office
Kempt Sir J. Privy Councillor
Kendall Wm. House of Commons
Kendall William S. Custom House
Kendle John, General Post Office
Kendrick Henricus, War Office
Kennedy Alex.L'Amillaiere,Cstms
Kennedy J. Consul, Galveston
Kenrick Wm.Admiralty,Somst.Ho
KensitHenry,Masters'Of.Chancery
Kensit Thos.G.Clrk.toSkinners'Co
Kent George, General Post Office
Kent Samuel Saville, Home Office
Kent Wm. George, City Officer
Kentish John Benj. City Officer
Kentish John Thos.PublicRecrd.Of
Keogh Thomas, Stamp&Tax Office
Ker James, Londn.Dist.orT.Py.Pst
Ker John, Customs (Bristol)
KerbyJsph.Londn.Dist.orT.Py.Pst
Kerr Niven, Consul at Cyprus
Kerrison SirEdw.Bd.ofGen.Officers
Kershaw George, Gen. Post Office
Kerton Walter,JudgmentOf.Qns.B
Key Henry, General Post Office
Key Sir John, Alderman ofLondon
Key John, Stamp & Tax Office
Key Jonathan,M.Comn.Ltncy.Lnd
Key William, General Post Office
Keys Richard, Customs(Wisbeach)
Kibble Jno. Court of Bankruptcy
Kiddle Wm. Commndr.inChfs'.Off
Kiddle Wm.F.jun.Com.inChfs'.Off
Kienitz Francis, Consul at Liebau
Kilgour Robt.S.Customs(Lerwick)
Kilpin James, House of Lords
Kilsby Thos.W.Clrknwell.Nw.Prsn
Kimpton Francis, War Office
Kimpton Wn. General Post Office
Kincaid Capt. J. City Bridewell
King Berkeley,QuarterMstr.Gen.O
King Edward, Custom House
King Edwd. Chas.Brd.ofOrdnance
King Henry, Board of Ordnance
King H. Stamp & Tax Office
King John, Custom House
King John Masters, Genl. Post Off
King Jonathan, Gen. Post Office
King Joseph, Admlty. Smrst. Hou
King Paul John, ChanceryReg.Off
King Rd. Paymaster Gen.'s Office
King Robert, South Sea House
KingThomasEdwd.OrdnanceOffice
King Thos. K. Regis.Irish DeedsOf
King Thos. Wm. Herald's College
King Ven. Walk. Archdn. of Roch
King Wm. Clk. to Blacksmith's Co
King Wm. Lndn.Dist.or T.Py.Post
King Wm. Irish DeedsRegistryOffi
Kingdom Jas. B.Admrlty.Smst.Ho
Kingscote Hen. Cmsn.Ltncy.Lndn
Kingsmill Rev.J.Pentonvll.Prison
Kingston Alfred,Public RecordOff
Kinkead Richd. Addiscombe Sem
Kinnaird Lord, PrivyCouncilOffice
Kinsey H. Customs (Newry)
Kirby Frederick Wm. War Office
Kirby Richard Chas. War Office
Kirk Conran A. AdjutantGenls.Off
Kirby John, General Post Office
Kirkman John,Clk.toCmbmkrs.Co
Kitchen Edwin, Treasury
Kitching Joseph Fras.Home Office
Kitson George, Court of Chancery
Kitson Wm. Buller, CustomHouse
Kitson Wm. Butler, Custom Ho
Kitson Wills, Court of Chancery
Knaggs William, Excise Office
Knapp H. Clk. to Haberdashers'Co
Knapton John, Excise (North'ton)
Knatchbull Sir E. bart. Pvy.Cnclr
Knevett Thomas, Custom House
Knewstub Robert, Custom House
Knight Bruce, Sir J. L. *see* Bruce
Knight John, Bank of England
Knight John C. British Museum
Knight Hen. G.Comsnr.ofFineArts and forImproving theMetropolis
Knight Valentine, Custom House
Knowlden F. F. Paymstr.Gen.s'Off
Knowlden Wm. Hen.Grnwh.Hsptl
Knox Charles, Custom House
Knox Hollis, Custom House
Know Rev.Hen.Barry,Office of the Peculiar of the Dnry.of Bocking
Knyvett Henry John, Home Office
Koch Chris. F. Consul,atFrankfort
König Charles, British Museum
KortrightC.E.K.ConsulCarthagena
KuczynskiVincentF.StatePaperOff
Kuper Hen.Geo.Consul atElsineur
Kyan John Howard, Audit Office
Kyring Mrs.S.L.Admlty.Somst.Ho

Labouchere Rt. Hon. Henry, Exchequer Bill Loan Office
Labouchere John, Exchqr.BillOffi

Lack Chas. Parry, Custom House
LackFredk.Com.ofPvy.C.forTrade
Lack Jno.Edw.CornReturns Office
Lack Rd.Wm.Com.ofP.C.forTrade
Lacon Henry Rosewell,Custom Ho
Lacon J. E. Customs (Grimsby)
La Coste Frederick, Custom House
La Croix Pierre, Consul at Nice
Lacroix Wm. Giles,Gen.PostOffice
Laidman Hy. Adjt.General's Office
Laing Sam. Comn.ofCoalWhippers
Lalor Florence, Custom House
Lalor John, Custom House
Lamb SirChas.Montolieu,PalaceCt
Lamb Hen. Wm. Insolvent Drs. Ct
Lambert Charles, Board of Trade
Lambert Henry, Custom House
Lambert Spencer, Custom House
Lambert William, Custom House
Lammin James, Masters'Of.Chncy
Lampert Wm. ReportOffice,Chncy
Lancaster Henry, Brd. of Ordnance
Lancaster Henry, jun.OrdnanceOff
Land Thos. Revenue InquiryOffice
Lander Chas. A.Cnsl.(Dardanelles)
Lane John, Clk. to Goldsmiths' Co
Lane William, Customs (Ipswich)
Lanfear Thomas, Custom House
Lang Chas. Ed. Admlty. Somst. Ho
Lang John, SeamensRegisterOffice
Langdale Lord, Master of Rolls
LangdonThos.Geo.Turner,G.PostO
Langford J. Exchqr. Bill Loan Off
Langford Richd. Stamp&TaxOffice
Langham Frs. Lndn.Dist.orT.Py.P
Langley John I. Greenwh. Hsptl
Langley Rd. General Post Office
Lansdowne Mq. of,K.G.Ld.Lt.Wilts
Lantit Robert, Customs (Kirkwall)
Laplume Geo. P. Admlty. Whitehl
Larkins Walter,Com.ofP.C. forTra
Lascelles Wm. Public Record Off
Lass Francis, Poor Law Office
Last Bernard John,Stamp&TaxOff
Last Wm. General Post Office
Latham Alfred, Bank of England
Latham Chas. Stamp & Tax Off
Latham Hen. ChanceryRegisterOff
Latham John Henry, Exchr. Off
Laughton John Jas. Custom House
Laurie John, Alderman and Sheriff of London
Laurie Sir Peter, Aldmn. of Lndn
Laurie Peter, Common Pleader, City, & Comsn. Ltncy. London
Laurie Robert, Heralds' College
Lavender Chas.Qn.Anne'sBnty.Off
Lavie John P. Custom House
Lavies John, Surgn.to Tothill flds. Bridewell, & Acting Ordnance Surgeon to Invalid Artillery
Law Benj. Keeper of Boro'Comptr
Law Hon. C.Ewan,Recrdr.of Lndn
Law John, Audit Office
Law William, Treasury
Law Wm.John, Comr. InsolventCt
Lawes Serj. Court of Bankruptcy
Lawford Edwd. Clerk to Drapers' Company, & Sol. toE. India Co. & Comm. Lieutncy. London
Lawless Thomas, Custom House
Lawrance J. V. Millbank Prison
LawrenceChas.Phillips,CustomHo
Lawrence Freeling J. Gen.Post Off
Lawrence Thomas, Genl. Post Offi
Lawrence Wm. Stationery Office
Laws William, India Board
Lawson Chas. John, Surrey Sessns
Lawson John, General Post Office
Lawson JohnPinhorn,PoorLawOff
Laxton Matt. Customs (Bristol)
Laycock Edmund, Gen. Post Off
Lea John Geo. General Post Office
Lea R. Custom House
Leach Edwyn Evans, Stamp & Tax
Leach Rd.Howell,Chncy.Rgstr.Off
Leach William, India Board
Leach Wm. Sup. Regr. (Stepney)
Leadley George, Thames Police Ct
Leake John M. Middle Temple
Leake John Martin, Treasury
Leake Stephen Ralph M. Treasury
Lean John, Board of Ordnance
Lean Lieut. Govnmnt. Emigrtn. Of
LearyJohnFred.T.S.A.Houseof Lds
Leaver John, Lon.Dist.orTpy.Post
Leaver Joseph, Enrolment Office
Le Blanc Geo. Middlesex Reg. Off
Le Blanc Lieut. Cl.Hen.Chls.Hsptl
Lechmere Charles, State Paper Off
Le Breton Philip Hem. Sup. Regr. (St. Martin's-in-the-Fields)
LeCointe John F.ReportOff.Chncy
Ledger George, Custom House
Le Dieu Thos. Fras. Ct. of Chncy
Lee Charles, Greenwich Hospital
Lee Charles, National Debt Office
Lee John, Stamp & Tax Office
Lee John Rt. S. Cstms (Woodbdge)
Lee Thomas, Customs (Drogheda)
Lee Timothy, Custom House
Leech James, Stamp & Tax Office
Leech John L. General Post Office
Leek James, Lon. Dist. orTpy.Post
Lees William, Board of Ordnance
LeesWm. James,BoardofOrdnance
LeFeuvreEdmundP,CustomHouse
LefevreChas.S.SpeakerofHo.Cmns
Lefevre Hen. Shaw, Russia Compy
Lefevre John Geo.S.Com.forTrade
LefroyChas.Edwd.HouseCommons
Lefroy James Austin, Custom Ho
Le Geyt Philip C. Grnwch. Hsptl
Legge Henry, Custom House
Legge Henry William, Custom Ho
Legoux Charles, Custom House
LegrandCharles,Stamp&TaxOffice
Leigh C. H. Lord Lieut.Monmouth
Leigh Edward, Customs (Llanelly)
Leigh Henry Francis, India Board
Leinster Duke of, Privy Councilr
Leitch Neil, Customs (Berwick)
LeithCornl.Forbes,Stamp&TaxOffi
Le Maire G.A. Queen'sBenchOffice
Leman Edwd. John, Crown Office
Lemay George Thomas, CustomHo
Lemon Sir Charles, bart. Com. for Improving the Metropolis
Lemon Robert, State Paper Office
LemonSamuelBuller,Custm.House
Lennard John B.Privy Council Offi
Lennox Lord Henry, Foreign Off
Lenon Thos.Bunbury, India Board
Lenox-Conyngham Geo.Forgn.Offi
Lepard Sam.Ck.toWireDrawer'sCo
Leslie Francis Seymour, HomeOffi
L'Estrange Edwd. Woods & Forests
Lethbridge J. A. Secretary to Greenwich Hospital
Lethbridge John C. Chels. Hospt
Lethbridge Samuel, HouseofLords
Lethbridge Wm. P. Greenwh.Hsptl
Lettis JohnWeeds, Gen. Pst. Office
Levermore Edwin Wm.ExciseOffic
Levermore Fred. Excise Office
Levett Hugh B. Bow st. Police Crt
Levett John Wm. Treasury
Levett William, Custom House
Lewes Alf. T.S. Admrlty.Somst.Ho
Lewes Edwd. M. Stamp&TaxOffice
Lewes John, General Post Office
Lewes John S. Col.Emigration Brd
Lewes Saml.S.AdmiraltySomst.Ho
Lewis Benj. Court of Chancery
Lewis Benj. jun. Court ofChancery
Lewis Charles, Stamp & Tax Office
Lewis Chas. T. Marshal'sOffice,Q.B
Lewis Frederick, Treasury
Lewis Geo Cornewall, PoorLawOffi
Lewis James, General Post Office
Lewis Jas. Slave Compensat. Offi
Lewis John, Excise Office
Lewis John, General Post Office
Lewis John, Excise (Canterbury)
Lewis Richd. Seaman'sRegisterOff
Lewis Thomas, Court of Chancery
Lewis Thos. A. Consistory Court
Lewis Thos. F. Privy Councillor
Lewis Wm. Garrett, General Post Office
Ley Edward, House of Commons
Ley Geo. T. Consul at Amoy
Ley Henry, House of Commons
Ley John Hen. House of Commons
LeyWm. ClerksOfficeHse.ofComns
Ley Wm. Journal Off. Hse.ofComns
LeyburnW.Admiralty,Smst.House
Lichfield Earl of, Privy Councillor
Liddell Hen. T. Consul Gottenberg
LiddellJohn, M.D.Greenwich Hsptl
Liffen John Fowler,Gen.PostOffice
Light Henry,Woods&ForestsOffice
Lightfoot Geo. Stamp & Tax Office
Lightfoot Isaac, Gen. Post Office
Lightfoot John, Eclstcl. Com.'s Off
Lightfoot Thos.Stamp & Tax Office
Lightfoot Thos. WestminsterCourt
Lilburn Geo. Admiralty,Somst. Ho
Lilley John H. Custom House
Lincoln John, Super. of Police (D)
Lincoln Earl of, Privy Councillor, Com. for Imp. the Metropolis and Health of Towns
Lindegren John, Consul PortoRico
Lindley Geo. Court of Exchequer
Lindsay D. A. Poor Law Commissioners Office
Lindsay Fred. Hen.Comndr.inChfs
Lines Chas. Lndn.Dist.orTpy.Post
Lings Thos. Admiralty, Whitehall
Linwood Jas. Lndn Dist.orTy. Post
Litchfield Charles, Treasury
Liston Wm. Stamp & Tax Office
Little William, Bank of England
Liveing Chas. National Debt Office
Liverpool Earl of,Privy Councillor
Livingstone Wm.ThamesPolice Ct
Llambias John, Consul at Bona
Llewelyn John, Audit Office
Lloyd Edwd. General Post Office
Lloyd Hen. Clements,PoorLaw Of
Lloyd J. Stamp & Tax Office
Lloyd Jas.A.Customs(Sunderland)
Lloyd John, General Post Office
Lloyd St. Vincent, Consl. at Ibraila
Lloyd Wm. General Post Office
Loch James, Exchqr. Bill LoanOffi
Loch John, Director East India Co
Locke Capt. John, Trinity House
Locker Frederick,Admiralty,Whtl
Locke John, Lord Mayor's Court
Lockett Jabez, Gen. Post Office
LockhartJohn G.Duchyof Lancastr
LockyerWm. Customs (Plymouth)
LoganRt. Masters'Office, Chancery
LoganWm.T.Sup.Reg.(Kengtn.gr)
LomasThos. Admiralty, Smst. Ho
Lomas Wm. Stamp & Tax Office
Lomax Major J. Stamp &Tax Office
Lomax Thos. East, Poor Law Offi
London Bishop of, Privy Councilr
Londonderry Marqof, Pvy.Councir & Lord Lieut. of Durham
Long Charles, Treasury
LongFred.B.Registrar of DesignsOf
Long George, Treasury
Long Geo. Marylebone Police Crt
Long Hen. Christphr. Bank of Eng
Long William, City Officer
Long Walter B. Stamp & Tax Off
Longden Thos.Hayter, Archdeacon of Surrey's Registry Office
Longley George,, Genl. Post Office
Longrigge Jsph.Excise(Cumbrlnd)
Lonsdale Earlof, P.C.,F.R.S.,F.S.A., Lord Lieut. of Cumberland & Westmoreland
Lord James, General Post Office
Lording Wm. Court of Chancery
Lorimer John, Customs (Kircaldy)
Loton Joseph, Home Office
Loudon P. Admiralty, Somest. Ho
Loundes N. Lndn. Dist.orTpy.Post
Lovatt George, Court of Chancery
Lovejoy Chas. Tench,Stamp &Tax
Lovelace Earl of, Ld.Lieut. Surrey
LovelandThos. M.Sup. Reg.(Chels)
Lovell Chas.H.Clerk toGlazier's Co
Lovell Francis, Ordnance Board
Lovell George, Ordnance Board
LovettJas.Crowdy, Gen.Post Office
Low David W. Custom House
Low Joseph, General Post Office
Lowe William, Custom House
LoweWillisHenry,EastIndiaHouse
LowryEdwd.Suprnd., of Police (B)
Lowther James, GeneralPost Office
LowtherThos.Master's Off.Chancery
Lowthian Jos. Admlty. Smrst. Ho
LoxdaleHenry,Admiralty, Whithll
LoydSam.Jones,Exchr.Bill LoanO
LubbockSir JohnWm.RussiaComp
Lucan Lord, Lord Lieut. of Sligo
Lucas David P.Customs (Cardigan)
LucasHenry Alfred,Custom House
Lucas John, Bankruptcy Court
Lucas John, Westminster PoliceCt
LucasMatthiasP.Aldermn.of Lndn
Luckhurst John, Genl. Post Office
Lucock John, Custom House
Lucy Fredk.Phelps,Gen.PostOffice
Ludlam Joseph Thos. India Board
Ludlow Mr.Serj.Com. of Bnkrptcy
Lugsdin Wm. General Post Office
Lukin CecilEdwd.Geo.India Board
Lumb Robt. C. M. Gen. Post Offi
Lumley Wm.Golden, Poor LawOff
Lund John, Tower of London
Lundie Robert, Stationery Office
Lundie Rt. Sam. Stationery Office
LuptonHarry, Admiralty,Somst.H
Lurton Thomas, Genl. Post Office
Luscombe John, Custom House
Lush JamesWilmot, Sewers' Office and Tower of London
Lush William, Treasury
Lushington Charles M.India Board
Lushington SirJ.L.Cms.Ltcy.Lndn
LushingtonRt.Hn.S.Ct.of Admrlty
Lushington Stephn. G. Custom Ho
Lushington Stephen R. Pvy. Cnclr
Luson John, Bank of England
Luttly B C.Clerk to Dyer's Compy
Luttrell Henry F. Audit Office
Lutwidge Robt.W.S.Com.in Luncy
Lyall Geo. Direct. of E. India Co
Lynch Andrew Hy. Mstr. in Chncy
LynchRd.Gov.Em'gtn.Agt.Limrck
Lyndhurst Lord, Privy Councillor
Lyne George P. Court of Chancery
Lyne Lewis Stephens, Excise Office
Lyons David, Audit Office
Lyons Sir Edmd. Ambsd.to Greece
LyttonBulwerRt.Hon.Ambs.Spain
Lyttelton Lord, Ld. Lt. Worcester
Maberly Col. General Post Office
Maberly Edward, Genl. Post Office
MaberlyFrederick,Genl. PostOffice
Maberly Stephen, Gen. Post Office
M'AdamSirJs.Metropls.RoadsOffic
M'Arter Daniel,Quarter MasterOffi
M'Auley Wm. Customs (Greenock)
M'Bean Alex. Consul at Leghorn
M'Caskey James, Customs(Dublin)
M'Culla John, Custom House
McCulloch John, Excise Office
M'Culloch JohnR.StationeryOffice
McCullum George, Excise Office
M'Cutcheon Jas. Bd. of Ordnance
McDermottW.H.Seaman'sReg.Offi
McDonaldLieut.Rd.Wm.HomeOffi
McFarlane Wm. Gen. Post Office
M'Gauran Chas Qn's.Rmbrncr.Offi
M'Gedy Francis, Lndn. Gazette Off
McGiloray J.Ctms.(Borrowstonnes)
McGregorDuncanCom.ofP.C.forTr
M'Grigor Sir Jas.Army Mdcl.Bd.of
McIntyre John Ewen, Custom Ho
M'Jannet James, Bd. of Ordnance
M'Kay William, Stationery Office
M'Kaye Mackenzie, Lon. Dist.Post
M'Kenzie Donald,Pymstr. Gen.'s O
M'Kenzie Finlay,Com.of P.C.forTr
M'KenzieKenneth,Cstms.(Carlisle)
M'KenzieRich.RoyalEngineersOffi
M'Kinlay J.Customs(Whitehaven)
M'KittrickThomas,Bd.ofOrdnance
M'Laughlin Edward, Excise Office
M'LeanSirJohn,Bd.of Gen.Officers
M'Lean Lachlan, Gen. Post Office
M'Leay Alex. R. Customs (Goole)
M'Mahon Edward, Foreign Office
M'MahonJohnCicero,Gen.PostOffi
M'MahonSirThs.Bd.ofGen.Officers
M'Neil Alexr. Customs (Stranraer)
M'Phail G.A.Sup. Regr.(Clerknwl)
M'Phee Ewen, Gen. Post Office
M'Pherson D. Customs (Inverness)
M'Pherson J. Custom House
M'QuoidSam.jun. Stamp& TaxOffi
M'Quoid Samuel, Stamp & Tax Off
M'TavishJohn, Consul atMaryland
M'Ternan Jas. Greenwich Hosptl
M'Whirter J. Consul at Puerto Cabello
MacaulayJ.B.M.P.Cmsn.of Fn.Arts
Macauley Thos. B. Privy Councir
Macdonald Geo. R. Poor Law Off
Macdonald Sir Jn. Adjutant Genl
Macdonald Robert, Custom House
MaceRd.G.Bow street PoliceCourt
Macgregor Fras. C. Consul Canton
Macgregor John, Comtt. for Trade
Macgregor John, Vi. Cons. Elsineur
Mackay James, Board of Ordnance
Mackay Robert, Custom House
Mackenzie Holt, Privy Councillor
Mackenzie Jas. A. S. PrivyCouncilr
Mackenzie John, Thames Police Ct
MackenzieRt. Shelton, Custom Ho
MackenzieThomas, Custom House
MackesonGeo.Admiralty,Smst.Ho
Mackintosh E.C. Consul at Mexico
MackmurdoG.W.Surgeon of Nwgt
Machlachlan Dan. Chelsea Hosptl
Maclaurin Arch.Admlty.Somst.Ho
Maclean Arch.D.Paymas. Gen's.Of
Maclean Chas. John Allan, Custom House

MacleanHenryJohn,CustomHouse
Maclean JohnH.Cstms.(Wisbeach)
MacleanSaml.B.Boardof Ordnance
Maclean William, Custom House
MacleanW.C.Custms.(Aldborough)
Macnaghten Eliot, East India Dir
Macquean John, Custom House
MacRae Kenneth, Treasury
Macvicar Neil, Custom House
Madan Capt. Fredk. Trinity House
Madden Sir Fred. British Museum
Maddison Fred. Admlty. Smst. Ho
Madox William, Ordnance Office
Maffey John, Custom House
MagenisA.C.Sec.of Emb.at Vienna
Maggs James, Custom House
MagnayGeorge,Comn.Ltncy.Lndn
MagnaySirWm.bt.Alderm.of Lond
Magrath Jas.Lawson,PoorLaw Offi
MaguireJas.Com.ofP.Cnl.forTrade
Maidlow Jas. General Post Office
Main Robert, Custom House
Maisey Geo. Superint. of Police(G)
MaitlandW.F.Commsn.Ltncy.Lnd
Maitland Gen.Fredc.Bd.ofGen.Offi
Maitland Joseph, East India House
Major Ebenezer, Chelsea Hospital
Makeham Jhn. M. Col. Emigra.Bd
Makeham J.P.Sup.Regr.(Westmr)
Makin Henry, Custom House
Malcolmson James, Bank of Eng
Males H. C.Enclosure Commiss.Of
Malet Sir Alexr.Amb.atStuttgardt
Maling Henry, Home Office
Malkin Robt. S. Stamp & Tax Offi
MallalieuF.M.Supern.tofPolice(R)
Mallet Charles, Audit Office
Mallet John Lewis, Audit Office
Mallet Louis, Audit Office
MallettThos. Clerkenwell PoliceCt
Maloney Wm. House of Lords
Mallons Hugh, House of Commons
Maltby Brough Geo. Trinity House
Maltby Edw. H. Marlboro' Plce.Ct
Maltby George, Custom House
Malyon Jas. Court of Com. Pleas
Malyon Jas. W. H. Common Pleas Office
Man John Hudson, Gen.PostOffice
Mandeville Thos. Gen. Post Office
Mann James Montague,CustomHo
Mann Thos. General RegisterOffice
Manners John, Excise (Lancaster)
Manning Chas.J.Cmsnr.Ltncy.Lnd
Manning Fred. J. MarshalseaCourt
Manning Jas. T. Custom House
Mansell Wm. Metro. Carriage Off
Mantle Joseph, General Post Office
Manwell Thomas, Excise Office
March Earl of,Comm.in Chief'sOff
March Alex. Geo.Hen. Custom Ho
MarchFredk.E.Board of Ordnance
MarchF.GeorgeHen.CustomHouse
March Henry Arth. Ordnance Brd
Mardon James How, Admiralty, Somerset House
Margetson James,Gen. Post Office
Mark Edward,Consul at St.Martha
Mark Wm. Adolphus, ExciseOffice
MarkWm.Penrose,Consl atMalaga
Markby Montague, Audit Office
Marks William, Excise (Norwich)
MarlboroughDukeof,Ld.Lt.ofOxfd
Marquard C. H. Sup. of Polce (K)
Marrable Geo. DuchyofCnwall.Offi
MarrableJohnFred.T.Gen.PostOffi
Marriott Geo.Jsph.T.Bd.of Ordnce
Marriott Robert, House of Comms
MarsdenRd.Andrew,BankEngland
Marsh Charles Edwd.Genl.PostOff
Marsh Thomas, Quarter Master General's Office
Marsh Thos. Wm. Genl. Post Off
Marshall Sir Chapman, Alderman
Marshall Charles, Poor LawOffice
Marshall Edward, War Office
Marshall Edward jun. War Office
Marshall John Long, Genl.PostOffi
MarshallMatthew,BankofEngland
Marshall Mathew, City Officer
Marshall Matthew, Nat. DebtOffice
MarshallNesbitW.Seaman'sReg.Of
Marshall Rd. Matt.Bd.of Ordnance
Marshall SamuelG.ConsulatCalais
Marshall William, Custom House
Marshall William, War Office
Marshall Wm. B. NationalDebt.Off
Marshall Wm. Ord, War Office
Marston Edward, Brd.of Ordnance
MartenGeo.Clk.toFellshp.Prtrs.Co
Martin Edw.Horatio,InnerTemple
Martin Edwd. Z. Custom House
Martin F. Customs (Arbroath)
Martin Francis, Heralds' College
Martin F. O. Tithe Comsnrs.Board
Martin Geo. CourtofCommonPleas
Martin George, City Officer
Martin James R. Health of Towns Commission
Martin John,Admiralty,Somst.Ho
Martin Leopold Chas.StationeryOf
Martin Nat. Clk. to Vintners' Com
MartinNath.Clk.toFruiterers'Com
Martin Richard, Genl. Post Off
MartinSaml.DuchyofLancastr.Offi
Martin Sir Thos.Byam,TrinityHou
Martindale C.M.Paymstr.Gn's.Offi
Martindale T. Gen. Register Office
Martineau H. Genl. RegisterOffice
Martineau Philip, Taxing Master
Martiny Emanl.Board of Ordnance
MarymanRobt.Woods&ForestsOffi
Mason James, Customs (Belfast)
Mason John Chas. EastIndiaHouse
Mason Joseph, Courtof Exchequer
MasonJosephHenry,CustomHouse
Mason Wm.Ambrose,PoorLawOffi
Masset Alfred, Custom House
Massey John, Insolvent Court
Masson William, Custom House
Masterman J. Comm. Ltncy. Lond
Masterman J.jun.Com.Ltncy.Lond
MastermanT.Admiralty,Whitehall
MastertonChas.Consl.Cochabamba
MatherGeo.QuarterMastGen's.Offi
Mathers Jas.Wm.NationalDebtOffi
MathesonRobt.Woods&ForestsOffi
Mathews James, Foreign Office
Mathison Gilbert Farquhar, Mint
MatsonJohn,Admiralty,Somst.Offi
MatthewJohn, Woods&Forests Offi
Matthew Thos. Patrick,War Office
Matthews Henry, Gen. Post Office
Matthews Robt. Gen. Post Office
MatthewsW.A.Cstms.(Cmbelltwn.)
Maude A. G. Clerkenwell Session
Maugham John. Custom House
Maule Geo. Solicitor to Treasury
Maule Fox, Privy Councillor
Maule Sir Wm.Hy.JusticeCom.Pls
Maxey Wm. General Post Office
Maxton James, Ordnance Office
May Edmund, Metpln.PoliceOffice
MayEdw.C.Organst.Grnwh.Hosptl
May John, jun. Chelsea Hosptl
May Jn. Superintdnt. of Police(A)
May Thos.Erskine,Ho.ofCommons
May Wm. Sup. Register(Islington)
Mayal E. W. Thos. Custom House
Mayall Thomas, Custom House
Maye William, Board of Ordnance
Mayer George, Colonial Office
Mayhew John, Excise (Northwich)
Mayhew William, Excise Office
Maynard Visct. Lord Lieut. Essex
MayneEdward,Paymastr.Gen's.Off
Mayne Hy. Bill Office, Ho. of Com
Mayne Rd.Metroptn. Police Office
Mayne Wm. Hy. East IndiaHouse
Mayo John, Custom House
MayowRt.Brown,Woods & Forests
Mazzoni Geo. Woods&Forests Offi
Meacher John,Court of Exchequer
Meade HenryWhite, CustomHouse
Meade MajorR.AdjutantGenl's.Offi
Meader Henry Wm. CustomHouse
Meader Walter, Custom House
Meader Wm. Hy. Roberts,CstmHo
Meagher Jeremiah,Consl.atLisbon
Mears John, Stamp & Tax Office
Mears Wm. General Post Office
Measor Chas. P. GeneralPostOffice
MeasorEdw.Jonathan,Gen.PostOff
Measor Walter, Custom House
Meek George, Comm. Ltncy. Lodn
Meek Jas Admiralty, SomersetHo
Meers Ezra, Insolvent Debtors' Ct
Meheux Henry, Genl. Post Office
Melbourne Visc. Privy Councillor
Melhuish Robert, Excise Office
Mellersh Henry,GeneralPostOffice
Mellersh Robert, Genl. PostOffice
Mellish Rd. Charles,ForeignOffice
Melvill Rev. Hen. HayleyburyColl
MelvillJas.Cosmo.,jun.IndiaHouse
MelvillJas.Cosmo.EastIndiaHouse
Melvill Philip, East India House
Melvill Visct. Ld. Pvy. Seal,Scotld
Melvill Alex.L. SouthSeaCompany
Melvill Rev.Hen.Tower ofLondon
Melville Hon. J. T. L. Russia Co
Melville Hon.W.Hy.L.EastIndiaH
Mence George, Poor Law Office
Merest Jas. Tithe Commissrs Bd
Merewether Mr.Serj.TownClk.Lnd
Merivale John H.Ct.ofBankruptcy
Merivale John Lewis, Chancery Registry Office
Merritt Stephen, Home Office
Merry Geo.J.T.Admrlty.Somst.Ho
Merry Henry, Stamp & Tax Office
MessengerJohnAlex.CustomHouse
Metcalf Chas. Thos.Page,IndiaHse
Metcalf EdwardB.AddiscombeSem
Metcalfe Fredk. Chancery Reg. Off
Metcalfe Lord, Privy Councillor
Methold H. Master Common Pleas
Meyer Henry Lewis, Home Office
Meymott Chas. SurreyCountyGaol
Meymott J.G.Southwk.Ct.ofReqsts
Middleton Alex.Admlty.Whitehall
Midford Robt. Board of Ordnance
Midlane Maurice,Admlty.Whitehl
Milbanke JohnR.Ambas.toBavaria
Mildred Daniel,Comn.Ltncy.Lndn
Mildred Fredk.Comn.Ltncy.Lndn
Mileham John, Gen. Post Office
Miles Charles, Custom House
Mill Geo. Grote, East India House
Mill Jn. Stuart, East India House
Millar Fredk.Geo.BoardofOrdnanc
Millard Jas.J.Clk.toCordwanrs.'Co
Miller Charles, Treasury
Miller C. S. Customs (Westport)
Miller Daniel Thos. Custom House
Miller Geo. Customs (Waterford)
Miller G. T. Consul at Woahoo
Miller James, Customs (Banff)
Miller James, Treasury
Miller John, Customs (Ayr)
Miller John, Customs (Perth)
Miller John, Court of Chancery
Miller John F. Bankruptcy Court
Miller JosephThos.Col.Emigra.Bd
Miller Wm. Royal Engineers' Off
Milliken A. General Post Office
Milliken Ernest, General Post Off
Milliken Fredk. Genl. Post Office
Milliken Wm. General Post Office
Millings Samuel, Custom House
Millman John, Admlty. Somst. Ho
Mills Chas. Directr. East India Co
Mills Fredk. Russell, Home Office
Mills Geo. Ireland, Deputy Coroner of Middlesex (Western Division)
Mills Henry, East India House
Mills Henry, Taxing Masters' Off
Mills Richard, Taxing Master
Millward Wm. Ct. of Com. Pleas
Milne Alex. Woods & ForestsOffice & Com. forImprovingMetropolis
Milne Frank,ChanceryRegister Off
Milner John, Board of Ordnance
Milsted Wm. Hen. Excise Office
Milton Henry, War Office
Milton John, General Post Office
Milton John, War Office
Minchin J. Consul at Fayal
Minet James Wacker, Treasury
Mingaye George Kervé, CustomHo
Minney John, War Office
Minto Earl of, Privy Councillor
Mirehouse John, CommonSerjeant
Mitchell Chas. Stationery Office
Mitchell Geo.Cm.ofPy.C.forTrade
Mitchell George, Custom House
Mitchell Geo. House of Peers
Mitchell Henry D. Genl. Post Off
Mitchell James, Millbank Prison
MitchellR.Commsn.Ltncy.London
Mitchell Thos. Gen. Post Office
MitchellThos.Lond.Dist.orTpy.Pst
Mitchell T. Alexr. Lloyd's
Mitchell Wm. Board of Ordnance
Mitchell Wm. Chas. Genl.Post Off
Mitchell Wm. Marylebn. Police Ct
Mitford John, Excise Office
Mitford John,Registry of Deeds Of
Mogan Peter F. Gen. Post Office
Mole Wm. Court of Common Pleas
Moloney Wm. E. Stamp & Tax Off
Molyneux Edwd.Consul at Georgia
Molyneux Hon. Francis, Secretary of Legation at Frankfort
Money Wm.CourtofQueen'sBench
Monro Rev. Robert,City Bridewell
Monro Cecil,ChanceryRegisterOffi
Montagu Basil, Ct. of Bankruptcy
Montagu H. Seymour,Stamp&Tax
Montagu Hon. Spencer D.IrishOffi
Monteagle Lord, Exchequer Office
MontefioreSirM.Comsn.Ltcy.Lndn
Montgomery Arch. Poor LawOffice
Montgomery Rt. Customs (Irvine)
Montgomery William, Post Office
Montresor Hen.Board of Ordnance
Montrose Duke of,PrivyCouncillor
Montucci Antonio Henry, Poor Law Office
Monty Jas. Court of Chancery
Monypenny W.T.Cstms.(Kirkaldy)
Moody Jhn. Customs(Dartmouth)
Moody Robert, House of Lords
Moon Arthur, Stamp & Tax Office
Moon FrancisG.Alderman&Sheriff of London
Moon Robert, Stamp & Tax Office
Moon Theophilus, Custom House
MooreAmbrose,Cmnsn.Ltncy.Lnd
Moore Arthur, Poor Law Office
Moore B. Admiralty, Somerset Ho
Moore Frederick Wm. Gen.PostOf
Moore George, Consul at Ancona
Moore Rev.G.Prerogative(Will)Of
Moore Geo. Rd. Genl. Post Office
Moore John, Foreign Office
Moore John, General Post Office
Moore John, India Board
Moore John, Court of Peculiars, & Deanery of Bocking Office
Moore John, Thames Police Court
Moore Niven, Consul at Aleppo
Moore Philip Chas.Ct. of Faculties, Archdeacon of London's Court, & Deanery of Bocking Office
MooreRev.Rt.Prerogative(Will)Of
Moore Thomas, Custom House
Moore William, War Office
Moore Wm.Cheteley,Ordnance Bd
More Alexr. Customs (Rochester)
Morfee Edward, Excise Office
Morgan Arthur,EcclesiasticalCommissioners' Office
Morgan Chas. General Post Office
Morgan DavidThos.RussiaCompny
Morgan Hen. Paymaster Genl's.Off
Morgan Hen. Vouholte,Custom Ho
Morgan John, Custom House
Morgan Jhn.Lndn.Dist.orT.Py.Pst
Morgan Peter F. Genl. Post Office
Morgan William, East India House
Morgan Wm. Paymaster Gen. Offi
Morier D.R.Min.Pln.toSwitzerland
Morier Greville, Foreign Office
Morpeth Visct. Privy Councillor
Morris Ann, National Debt Office
Morris Hy. Exchequer of Pleas Off
Morris Jas.Commsn.ofLtncy.Lndn
Morris John, Court of Exchequer
Morris Jsph.Bemrose,Bd.ofOrdnce
Morris Rd. Court of Exchequer
Morris Thos. Paymaster Genl's.Off
Morris Thos. Woods&ForestsOffice
Morris Thos. H. National Debt Offi
Morris Wm.Hen.Stmp.&TaxOffice
Morrish Thos. Court of Chancery
Morrison James Wm. Royal Mint
Morrison Robert, Stamp &Tax Offi
Morsley John, Roy. Engineers'Offi
Morten Lewis, Treasury
Mortimer A.J. Paymaster Gen. Off
Mortimer Rv.G.F.W.CityLnd.Schl
Mortimer Walter S.CourtofChncry
Mortlock Sir John C. Excise Office
Morton Francis, Comsnr. ofSewers
Morton Thos. C. Greenwich Hosptl
Moss Wm. Burrowes, Genl.PostOff
Moss Wm. Geo. General PostOffice
Mostyn E.L.Lord Lieut. Merioneth
Mostyn Llewellyn W. Custom Ho
Mostyn William, Audit Office
Mott Henry C. Poor Law Office
Mould Jas.Fredk.Genl. PostOffice
Mould R. T. Clerkenwell Police Ct
Moulden Jsph.E.Clk.toFarriers'Co
Moule James, Genl. Post Office
Moule Thos. General Post Office
Moulting Wm. Geo. Stamp&TaxOf
Moulton George, Gen. Post Office
Mounsey John,General Post Office
Mountague James, City Officer
Mounteney Rt.B. Pymstr.Gen's. Of
Mullens Wm.H.Brokr.to Nat.Dt.O
Mumbray John,Court of Chancery
Mundy Frederic C. Colonial Office
Mundy Genl. G.B.Bd.of Genl.Ofcrs
Mundy James, Custom House
Mungeam Rv.Wm.M. B.A.Qn's. Pr
Munro Gordon, Bd. of Ordnance
Munro Mrs.Ellen C.Bd.ofOrdnance

Murdoch Thos.Wm.C.Colonial Off
Murdock Wm. Gen. Post Office
Mure Wm. Consul at NewOrleans
Mure Samuel Robert, Custom Ho
Muriel John, Audit Office
Murray And. Taxing Masters' Offi
Murray Hon.C.A.sec.ofLeg.of Npls
Murray Chas. K. Ecclstl. Com. Off
Murray Sir Geo. Privy Councillor
Murray Henry, Consul at Tangier
Murray James, Foreign Office
Murray Js.A.Und.Sec.Mstr.ofRolls
Murray John, Comsn. Ltncy.Lndn
Murry Charles, Tower of London
Musgrove John, Aldermanof Lndn
Mushet Robert, Royal Mint
Muskett Charles, Custom House
Muspratt JohnP.Drct.ofE.IndiaCo
Mustoe George, Audit Office
Mutter James, Excise Office
Muxworthy Joseph, Stamp&TaxOf
Myall James, Surrey Bridewell
MylneJamesWm.Comm.inLunacy

Nailer R.Com.ofPvy.Cncl.forTrade
Nalder Joseph, Clerk to Fanmakers' Company, and to Playing Card Makers' Company
Nanson Isaac, General Post Office
Nanson Isaac H. Customs (Boston)
Napier Francis, Custom House
Napier Macvey, East India House
Nash Edward, Treasury
Nash Geo. John, GeneralPostOffice
Naylor Elisha, Land Revenue Rcds
Naylor Jas. Rd. Crown Off. Chncy
Neal George, General Post Office
Neal Jas. John, Gen. Post Office
Neal John, Privy Council Office
Neale E. St. John, Cnsl. Alxndrtta
Neale John, Court of Chancery
Neale John, Custom House
Neale Pendock Wm.Genl. PostOffi
Neame Wm. Capt. R.N. Customs
Neave John, Custom House
Neave Richard, Chelsea Hospital
Neave S. Commsn. Ltncy. Lond
Neave SirT.Commn.Ltncy.London
Neech George, Stationery Office
Needle Thos.MastersOffice,Chancy
Neiland Wm. Custom House
Neilson Wm. Custom House
Nelson Capt. Hen. Trinity House
Nelson Henry, Russia Company
Nelson Park,Clk.toScriveners'Com
Nelson Walter,PublicRecordOffce
Nelthorpe Wm.Stamp & TaxOffice
Nesbitt John,Clerkenwell PoliceCt
Nevinson Edw.Hen.Exchequer Offi
New Charles D. Custom House
Newbery Gen.Fras.Bd.of Gen.Offcr
Newbery Wm. Sup.Regr. St.Giles's & St. George's
Newcombe Fred.S. Pymstr.Gen.Off
Newcombe Samuel,Poor LawOffice
Newcomen B. Consul at Paraiba
Newell Edward,General Post Office
Newell Rt.Coal Whippers' Commis
Newland John, Middle Temple
NewmanFrancisC.TitheCommissio
Newman H. Consul at Nantes
Newman Henry, Custom House
Newman James A. City Officer
Newman Jas.Henry,Genl.PostOffic
Newman John, City Officer
Newman John, Custom House
Newman Rd.Kent,Genl.Post Office
Newman Wm. Genl. Post Office
Newport Sir John,Privy Councillor
Newton Charles, British Museum
Newton Charles, Genl. Post Office
Newton Joseph, Bank of England
Nicholl J. D.C.L. Ecclesiastcl.Comr
NichollRt.Hon.J.CourtofPeculiars
Nicholls James, Excise Office
NichollsSirJasper,Bd.ofGen.Offcrs
Nicholls John, Court of Chancery
Nicholls John, Custom House
Nicholls Nat. Surrey Bridewell
Nichols John B. & Son,VotesOffice
Nichols Ambrose, Bank of Engld
Nichols J.W.Hammersmith Pol.Ct
Nichols Wm. Excise Office
Nicholson Geo. T. Surrey Sessions
Nicholson John, Genl. Post Office
Nicholson Ralph G. Seamen's Registry Office
Nicholson Ward, Custom House
Nicholson W.Crown Offi.Qun'sBnh
Nicol James, Customs (Banff)

Nicolas W.Giffard,Com.in ChiefsOf
Nicolson James, Chelsea Hospital
NightingaleJoseph,Bd.ofOrdnance
Nind Samuel L.General Post Office
Nippen George,Gen.Register Office
Nisbet Alex.M D.GreenwichHospitl
Nixon John Pigott, Addiscombe
Nixon W.Woods&Forests(Edinbr')
Noble John Padmore,BankofEngld
Noble Richard Hatt, Home Office
Noble Thomas, Custom House
Noble Timothy, Custom House
Noel Louis H.Admiralty,Somst.Ho
Nokes Wm. Greenwich Police Ct
Noon Edward, Custom House
Norfolk Duke of, Heralds' College
Norman Alfred,General Post Office
Norman G.W.DirectorsofBk.ofEgd
Norman John, Excise Office
Norman Wm. Stamp & Tax Office
Normanby Marqs.of,Prvy Councir
Norris Henry, House of Lords
Norris Hen. Chas. Colonial Office
Norris P. Poor Law Comm. Off
Norris Wm.Henry,Gen. Post Office
Norris Wm. John,Privy Seal Office
North B.CommissaryofSurryOffice & Bishop of Winchester's Office
North William, Chelsea Hospital
Northcote StaffdH.Com.ofP.C.forT
Northumberland Duke of, K.G. Lord Lieut. Northumberland
Norton Fredk. Court of Chancery
Norton Hon.G.C.Lambethst.Pol.Ct
Noss William, Custom House
NosworthyHen.Admrlty.Somst.Ho
Nott Geo. Francis, Gen.Post Office
Noyes C.Com.ofPvy.Cncl.forTrade
Nunns William, Gen. Post Office
Nutting John, Excise (Grantham)
Nye JamesM.Admiralty,Whitehall

Oak William, Sewers' Office
Oakeley Jhn.Lndn.Dist.orT.Py.Pst
Oakes Thomas, Gen. Registry Off
Oakeshott Jsph.Lndn.Dist.Post Off
O'Brien Donatus, Board of Trade
O'Brien Hen.M.S.Bow st.Police Ct
O'Brien Patrick, Gen. Post Office
O'Brien Capt. Wm. Home Office
O'Connor Patrick, Custom House
Odell John, Home Office
Ogden Thomas,Stamp & TaxOffice
Ogden William,Stamp & TaxOffice
Ogilvie John, East India House
Ogilvie Richd. Annesley, Customs
O'Grady Geo.Alf.M.Gen.PostOffice
Oldham Jph. Comn .Ltncy. Lndn
Oldham Thomas, Bank of England
Oldroyd William, Custom House
O'Leary D.F.Chr.d'Aff.NewGranad
OliphantMajorJames,EastIndiaHo
Olive Jermh.Commsn.Ltncy.Lndn
Olive Jeremiah Exchqr.BillLn.Offi
OliverChas.J.H.Marlboro'st.Pol.Ct
OliverWm.Cooper,Genl.PostOffice
O'Neale George, Customs (Tralee)
O'Neil John, Quarter Master General's Office
Ongley Hy. Sarell, Consul at Crate
Onslow Arthur Robt.East India Ho
Onslow Constantine P.CustomHou
Onslow Richard, Surrey Sessions
Oom Adolphus K. Foreign Office
Orde Gen.Jas.BoardofGenl.Officers
Ormonde,Marqs.of,LordinWaiting
O'Reilly Chas.Wm.Admlty.Whthll
Orum Thomas. P. Excise (Suffolk)
Osborn Sir John, Audit Office
Osborne Charles, Audit Office
Osman John, Queen's Bench Office
OswaldW.D.Com.ofPy.Cncl.forTd
Ottey Fras.Ferrand, Exchqr.Office
Ottley Jeremiah, Excise Office
Otway CæsarGeo. Poor Law Office
Ouseley Major J. W. J. Haleybury
Ouseley Sir Gore, Privy Councillor
Ouseley William Gore, Envoy Extraordinary to Rio de la Plata
Overton Charles, Custom House
Owen Anewrin, Tithe Commrs.Brd
Owen Hugh, Poor Law Office
Owen John, Board of Ordnance
Owen Sir Jn.Lord Lieut.Pembroke
Owen Col.John,K.H.RoyalMarineO
Owen Foster,HighConstableWestr
Owen John, Audit Office
Owen Rd.Com. of Health of Towns
Owen Wm. Genl. Register Office
Owstan William, Excise Office

Oxenford Henry, Custom House
Oxenford William, Custom House
Oxtoby Thomas,Stamp&Tax Office

Packham Daniel, Custom House
Packham Henry, Genl. Post Office
Packham Wm. General Post Office
Paddon Morris, General PostOffice
Page Edward, Colonial Office
Page Edward, General Post Office
Page Fredk. Sago,Genl.Post Office
Page Hen.Joseph,Ct.ofBankruptcy
Page Samuel, Stationery Office
Page Wm. James,Genl.Post. Office
Paget Augustus, Foreign Office
Paget Sir Edw.Bd.of Genl. Officers
Paice Fred.Lndn.Dist.or T.Py.Post
Pain Thos.Queen'sRemembers.Offi
Paine Wm. Greenwich Hospital
Pakenham Right Hon. Henry Rd. Ambassador to U.S.A
PalgraveSirFras.PublicRecordOffi
Palgrave John, Custom House
Palin Vyse, Gen. Registry Office
Palk Robert, House of Lords
Palmer Hen. Thos.Genl.PostOffice
Palmer Thomas, PublicRecordOffi
Palmer Roundell,Bank of England
Palmerston Visct.PrivyCouncillor
Panizzi Antonio, British Museum
Panter John L MetropolisRoadsOf
Panton Chas.Queen'sRemembr'sOf
Pape Richard, Excise Office
Papps George, Court of Chancery
Papworth Wyatt A. Sewers' Office
Pargeter Frederick, Excise Office
Paris Archibd. Eastland Company
Paris Charles Snell, Russia Comp
Paris Thomas, Russia Company
Parish Samuel, Bank of England
Park Alex.A.MasterCommonPleas
Parke Sir Jas. Baron of Exchequer
Parker Benjamin, Excise Office
Parker Chas. Millbank Prison
Parker Edward, Custom House
Parker Fowler, Stamp & TaxOffice
Parker Frederick, Gen. Post Office
Parker George, Stamp&Tax Office
Parker John, Stamp & Tax Office
Parker J. Custom House
Parkhurst Rodic, Gen. Post Office
Parkin Geo. P. Admlty. Somst.Ho
Parkinson James, Lloyd's
Parkinson Sam.jun.Ct.of Chancery
Parkinson Samuel, Ct. ofChancery
ParnellHugh,Clk.Slk.Throwers'Co
Parnther Chas. Hen. Foreign Office
Parodi Francis, Gen. Post Office
Parr Wm. S. General Post Office
Parratt Edward, House of Lords
Parratt Edw. M. House of Lords
Parratt George Fredk. Treasury
Parry Rd.P.LondonDist.orTpy.Pst
Parry Capt. Sir Wm. Ed. Admlty. Whitehall,&Royal MarineOffice
Parsey John James, War Office
Parsey John Leuson, War Office
Parson Saml. K. Stationery Office
Parsons Joseph,Stamp &TaxOffice
ParsonsRt.Wm.Board of Ordnance
Parsons William, Custom House
Parsons William, Gen. Post Office
Partridge Henry, Genl. Post Office
Partridge Jno.Lndn.Dst.orTpy.Pst
Partridge Robert, Gen. Post Office
Paskin Chas.VoteOf.Ho.ofCommns
Paskin William, Bank of England
Pasley Maj. Gen. Com.ofP.C.forTr
PastellJas.Com.ofPrivyCl.forTrade
Pate Charles, Stamp & Tax Office
PatersonDavid,PaymasterGen.'sOf
Patten Jonathan, Colonial Office
Patten King, Stamp & Tax Office
Patten Richard, Customs (Goole)
Patterson Lewis Hen. ColonialOffi
PattesonSirJno.JusticeQun's.Bnch
Pattison Jas. Direc. Bank of Engld
Pattison Jn. Paymaster Gen.'s Offi
Pattison Wm. Paymstr. Gen.'s Offi
Paul George, Audit Office
Paull Henry, Excise Office
Pawley Geo. Quartrmstr.Gen.'sOffi
Payne James, General Post Office
Payne Jas. Lndn.Dist.orT. Py.Post
Payne John Rt. Brd. of Ordnance
Payne Joseph, Board of Ordnance
Payne Samuel H. Ordnance Board
Payne Thomas, Stamp & TaxOffice
Payne William, Coroner of London
Paynter T. Hammersmith PoliceCt

Payton William, Custom House
Peachey Jas. Clk. to Feltmakers'Co
Peacock Edwd G. EastIndiaHouse
Peacock Mark B. Solr. toPostOffice
Peacock Richard, General Post Offi
Peacock Rt. Wm. Genl. PostOffice
Peacock Ths.Love,Ea.India House
Peake George, Foreign Office
Peake Jas.A.Lndn.Dist.orT.Py.Pst
Pearce Edgar, Gen. Post Office
Pearce Nicholas, Sup. of Police(F)
Pearkes B. Consul at Bremen
Peall Henry, Custom House
Pearce Samuel, Custom House
Pearce Thomas, Board ofOrdnance
Pearsall James, City Officer
Pearse Christopher, Bk. ofEngland
Pearson Charles, City Solicitor
Pearson Henry Robert, Treasury
Pearson John, Royal Mint
Peck John Crook, Natnl. Debt Off
Peckham Thos. Stamp & Tax Offi
Peel Sir Robt. Privy Councillor
Peel George, Custom House
Peel Wm. Yates, Privy Councir
Peevor George, Chelsea Hospital
Pell Wm. Court of Chancery
Pellatt George, General Post Office
Pellatt Thos. General Post Office
Pelly Capt. Sir John H. TrinityHo
Pelly SirJno.Hen.Eastland Comp. & Director Bank of England
Pemberton Christopher Rt.Trsury. & Court of Exchequer
Pemberton Ed. Owen, Custom Ho
Pemberton Henry, Treasury
Pemberton-Leigh Thomas, Privy Councillor
Pemberthy J.P.Customs(Bridport)
Pengelly Edwd. Brd. of Ordnance
Penleaze Jno. S. Consul Barcelona
Pennell Chas.Hen.Admlty.Whithll
Pennell J. Croker, Foreign Office
Pennell Wm. Court of Bankruptcy
Pennethorne Jas.Woods & Forests Office
Pennington Albert,Genl.PostOffice
Pennington Dymoke Wells, G.P.O
Pennington Edwd. Colonial Office
Pennington Geo. James, Treasury
Pennington Hen. Genl. Post Office
Pennington Jas.M.Gen.Post Office
Pennington Thos.Consul atCorsica
Penny Rev. John, Millbank Prison
PennyWilliam,General Post Office
Penrhyn Edward, Surrey Sessions
Pepper Edwd. G. Greenwh. Hospl
Peppercorne Rt.Seaman's Reg. Off
Pepperell James, Colonial Office
Perceval Hen. Spencer, Treasury
Perceval Lt. Col. Serjeant at Arms
Percival Thomas, Gen. Post Office
Percy Hon. Wm. Hen.ExciseOffice
Perigal Edwd. Admlty. Somst. Ho
PerigalFredk.Admiralty,Somst.Ho
Perkin George, Gen. Post Office
Perkins Benjamin, Gen.PostOffice
Perkins Frederick, Custom House
Perkins Hutton, General Post Off
Perkins Thomas, Custom House
Perrier John, Admiralty, Whitehl
Perrier Sir Anth. Consul at Brest
Perrin William, Excise (Oxford)
Perring Frdk. General Post Office
Perring Robert. Genl. Post Office
Perrior Jas. Paymaster Gen.s' Off
Perrott George, India Board
Perry Hen. J. Court of Chancery
Perry John, Custom House
Perry John, Gray's Inn
Perry Jno. Geo. Inspctr. of Prisons
Perry J. P. Lambeth st. Police Crt
Perry William, Consul at Panama
Perry Wm. Exchequer of Pleas
Peter Geo.Fras.C. Bd. of Ordnance
Peter Wm.Consul at Pennsylvania
Peters John Hatch, Poor Law Off
Peters JohnMorgan,CustomHouse
PetersWm.Commn.Ltncy.London
Petersen F. H. Consul at Stettin
Petherick Wm. Custom House
Petrie Samuel, Treasury
Pettefer Geo. Stamp & Tax Office
Pew James, Board of Ordnance
Pewtress Thos.CoalWhippers'Com
Peyton Oliver, Gen. Post Office
PhilippsTrenhamW.Woods&Frsts. & Metropolis Improvement Com
Philips Alfred, Stamp & TaxOffice
Phillips Edmund, Brd. of Ordnance

Phillimore Chas. B. India Board
Phillimore Joseph, D.C.L. Dean of St.Paul'sRy.& Com. of French & Danish Claims
Phillimore Rb.Jph.D.C.L.Archdeacon of London&MiddlesexCourts
Phillimore W. Visitor of Lunatics
Phillimore William, South Sea Ho
Phillipps Sam. March, Home Office
Phillips Chas. Commr.ofBankptcy
Phillips Hen. Marylebn. Police Ct
Phillips John, Sewers' Office
PhillipsRbt.Lndn.Dist.orTpy.Post
Phillips Thos. Gen. Post Office
Phillips William, Custom House
Philpot Chas. Gen. Reg. Office
Philpot Fredk.Paymaster Gen.'sOf
PhilpotJohn,MastersO.Ct.ofChncy
Philpot JohnT.PaymasterGen.'sOf
Phipps John,Clerk to Weavers' Co
Phipps John, Woods & Forests Off
Pick Daniel, Custom House
Pickering Fras. Stationery Office
Pickering John, Ecclestcl. Com.Of
Pickering Wm. Greenwich Hsptl
Pickford Charles T. Custom House
Pickford Thomas, Consul at Paris
Pierrepoint Hon. H.M.Prvy.Cnclr
Piers B. Admiralty, Whitehall
Pierse W. F. Supt. of Police (H)
Pierson Henry C. India Board
Pigot Henry Becher, Custom Ho
Pigott Geo. G. W. Poor Law Office
Pigott Robt. Hen. G. F. Cstm. Ho
Pike Anthony,Admiralty,Soms.Ho
Pilcher John, Stamp & Tax Office
Pilcher Robert, Custom House
Pincombe William, Custom House
Pincott James, Stamp & Tax Office
Pinhorn John, Admlty. Somst. Ho
Pinney Joel, Stamp & Tax Office
Pirie Sir John, bart. Alderman
Pistrucci Benedetto, Royal Mint
Pitcairn Thomas, Admlty.Somst.H
Pitt Col.Geo.Denn,Adjnt.Gen.'sOf
Pittar Thomas John, Custom Ho
Pittman Richd. Ordnance Board
PixleyCapt.William,Trinity House
Plank George, Custom House
Plank Geo. jun. Custom House
Plant Wm. Jas. General PostOffice
Planta Joseph, Privy Councillor
Plasket Thomas Hen. HomeOffice
Plasket Thos. Hen. Signet Office
Plat Col. G. C. du. Cnsl. at Warsaw
Platt Hon. Sir T.J.knt.Ct. of Exch
Platt S. Queen's Bench Office
Plaw Henry Rt. Con. Gen. Dantzic
Playfair L. M.D.Hlth.ofTownsCom
Playle John, General Post Office
Pledger William, City Officer
Plowden Chas. Henry C. India Bd
Plowden W. H. C.DirectE.IndiaCo
Plowright Wm. Gen. Post Office
Plumer Thomas Hall, Examiners' & Petty Bag Office, Chancery
Plunkett Lord, Privy Councillor
Plunkett V. W. Custom House
Pocock Charles, Custom House
Poer Samuel Wm. Custom House
Pohlman John Geo. Audit Office
Poignand Chas. Board of Ordnance
Poignand John Rt. Home Office
Poingdestre Jas.Msngr.toHo.Cmns
Poland Sir W. H.Com.Ltncy.Lond
Polden James, Stationery Office
Pole Chas. Election Off. Ho. Cmns
Pole William, South Sea House
Pollard Edwd. Exchequer Office
Pollard John, Sewers' Office
Pollard Jas. Prince, Audit Office
Pollard Peter, Sewers' Office
Pollock Sir Fred. Chief BaronExch
Pollock Dav. Com. Insolvent Ct
Pollock Jno.Excise (MiddleWales)
Ponder S. sen. Clerk to Joiners' Co
Ponsonby Hon. Spencer,For.Office
Pontifex John, Sup.Regr.(London west) & Clk. to Armourers' Co
Poole Henry R. Custom House
Poole Moses, Patent Office
Poole W. D. Stamp & Tax Office
Porrett Robt. Board of Ordnance
Porter Edward, Consul at Bahia
Porter Ed. Rt. Middlesex Reg. Offi
Porter George, Stamp & TaxOffice
Porter Geo.Richardson,Com.forTr
Portland Duke of, K.G.PrivyCnclr
Portman Lord, Ld. Lieut.Somerset
Postlethwaite Joseph, House Cmns

Potbury Benjamin, Custom House
Potter Chas. London Dist. PostOffi
Potter Geo. Wm. Killett, Clk. to Coachmakers' Co. & Secondary of Poultry Compter
Potter John, Custom House
Potter John, General Post Office
Potter Robert, General Post Office
Pottinger Sir Hen. Pri. Cnclr
Potts Wm.Fred.GeneralPostOffice
Poulter John,S.Commiss.of Surrey
Poulton George, Excise Office
Powell Col.Wm.E.LordLt.Cardign
Powell Caleb Edward, Royal Mint
Powell Charles, Custom House
PowellChas Geo.Stamp&TaxOffice
Powell David, Bank of England
Powell Edwd. Joseph, Royal Mint
Powell Eyre Burton, Stamp &TaxO
PowellGeo. Wm. Duchy of Lancast
Powell Henry, General Post Office
Powell Henry, Stamp & Tax Office
Powell John T.Paymaster Gen.'sOf
Powell Richard, Colonial Office
Powell Thos.Lloyd,Gen.PostOffice
Powell Wm. Stamp & Tax Office
Power Michael F. Custom House
Powis Earl of, Ld.Lt. Montgomery
Powis Charles, Custom House
Powis Thos.PaymasterGen.'sOffice
Powley John, General Post Office
Powley William, Gen. Post Office
Powys L.JournalOff.House of Com
Prall Henry, General Post Office
Pratt Alfred, Custom House
Pratt Edward, Colonial Office
PrattJohn,DoorkeepertoHse.Coms
Pratt Wm. Edwd. Genl. PostOffice
PrattWm.Wheatley,CustomHouse
Prendergast Jas. Ct. of Chancery
Prendergast JohnD.ExchequerOffi
Prescott Fredk. Joseph,War Office
Pressly Chas. Stamp & Tax Office
Preston John, Customs (Yarmouth
PriceSirChas.Exchegr.BillLn.Offic
Price A. Tithe Commissioner
Price Chas. H. Court of Chancery
Price Jeremiah Pawson, ExciseOffi
Price John, Bank of England
Price Ralph, City Bridewell
Price William, Stamp & Tax Office
Prichard Dr. Comsnr. in Lunacy
Prideaux Francis Wm.IndiaHouse
Pringle Alexdr.Comof Revene.Inq
Pringle Geo. Ecclestcl.Com. Office
Prior Hervey M. BoardofOrdnance
Prirnett Charles M. Custom House
Pritchard George, Consul at Navigators' Island
Pritchard Robert, Custom House
Pritchard Saml. Paymas.Gen.'s Off
Pritchard Stephen, Lon. Dist. Post
Pritchard W. Hi. Bailiff, Southwk
Proby Chas. Admrlty. Somst. Ho
Probyn Capt. Geo. Trinity House
Probyn Wm. Cstms. (Chepstow)
Procter Bryan W. Com. in Lunacy
Protheroe Thos. Ct. of Exchequer
Prout T. Custom House
Prowse StephenR.GreenwichHsptl
Puckle Thos. Surrey Sessions
Pudar George, Home Office
PughCharles, Masters'Offi.Chancry
Pugh James, War Office
Pugh T.B. Clk.Framewk.Knitrs.Co
Pullman Thos. Woods& Forests Off
Pulman James, F.S.A. Heralds' Col
Pulman James, House of Lords
Pulman James H. House of Lords
Pulman Thomas, British Museum
Purbrick James, Board ofOrdnance
Purchas Thomas, Excise Office
Purdue John, Stamp & Tax Office
Purdue Thomas, Middle Temple
Purdy Frederick, Poor Law Office
Purser Major Wm. Custom House
Puttuck John, General Post Office
Pye Wm. London Dist. or T.Py.Pst
PymRt. John,Chancery RegisterOff
PymChas. TitheCommissionersBrd
Pyne Ben. TitheCommissionersBrd

Quaife Thomas, Stamp &TaxOffice
Quaife William,Stamp&Tax Office

Rablah George, General Post Office
Rackley Wm. General Post Office
Radford George, Customs (Deal)
Raggett George B. Customs (Deal)
Raggett Wm. P. Ordnance Board

Rahill Thos. Hen.Genrl.Post Office
Railton Wm. Ecclestcl. Com. Of
Raines John, War Office
Rainsford W. H. Con. Gen. Bogota
Ralph John, Customs (Milford)
Ralph Rev. Jas. New Model Prison
RamsayLieut.Gov.Emg.Agt(Lndy)
Ramsay Thos. Geo.Gen. Post Office
Ramsey John, General Post Office
Randal Charles, Gen. Post Office
Randall Rd. Ross,Admlty.Somst.H
Randall Wm. C.Adjt.Genrl.'sOffice
Randell Hen. Common Pleadr.City
Rapley Wm. Stationery Office
Rassam Christian, Con. at Moossul
Ratcliffe Chas. General Post Office
Raven Henry Baldwin, Treasury
Ravenhill John, Chelsea Hospital
RawDavidB.Lndn.Dist.orT.Py.Pst
Rawlings S. General Register Offi
Rawlinson Henry C.Conl.atBagdad
Rawlinson John,Marylbn.PoliceCt
Rawlinson Jn.Job,TitheCommisnr
Rawlinson Wm. Hen. Audit Office
RawnsleyJsph. H.Admlty. Smst. H
Ray Henry, Lndn. Dist. orT.Py.Pos
RayHenryB. MasterCommonPleas
Ray Samuel Henry, Custom House
Raymond William, Sewers' Office
Raymont Augustus, East India Ho
Rayner Thomas, Excise Office
Rea Edward Hugh,Genl.PostOffice
Rea William, Stamp & Tax Office
Read James, Greenwich Hospital
Read John, City Officer
ReadThos. Lndn. Dist.orTy.P.Post
Read Thos. Rd. Board of Ordnance
Read Wm. R. Custom House
Readdy Wm. Thos. Custom House
Reade Sir Thomas, Consul at Tunis
Reay Joseph, Customs (Belfast)
Reay Joseph, Customs (Limerick)
Reavens Francis, Court of Exchqr
Reddie James, Admirlty.Somst.Ho
Redgrave Samuel, Home Office
Reding Henry, Stamp & Tax Office
Redington Jno. P.Public Record O
Redman Fred. Ct. of Exchequer
Redpath Wm. Customs (Boston)
Redwick Chas. Customs (Arundel)
Reed Henry, General Post Office
Reed Samuel, General Post Office
ReedWm.John, GeneralPostOffice
Reeks John, Excise Office
Rees Capt. John, Trinity House
Rees Owen,M.D.PentonvillePrison
Rees John, Lloyd's
ReesWm.LondonDist.orT.Py.Post
Reeve Hen. Privy Council Office
Reeve Richd. Hen. Gen. PostOffice
Reeves Chas. Freeling, Gen.PostOf
Reeves Hen. Charles,CustomHouse
Reeves Richd. General Post Office
Reeves Wm. Thos. Custom House
Reid David B. M.D.Com. of Health of Towns
Reid Edwd. Report Of. Chancery
Reid Hugh G. Stationery Office
Reid George, Russia Company
ReidHen.Andrew,Paymastr.Gen.O
Reid SirJn.R.Direct.Bankof Engld
Reid John, Report Of. Chancery
Reid John, Stamp & Tax Office
Reid Jsph.Exchr. Bill Loan Office
Reid William, Paymstr. Gen.Office
Renard Samuel, Court ofChancery
Renaud Peter Thos. Duchy of Lanc
Rendall J. Consl. Cape Verd Isles
Renton Jas. Home,Admlty.Smst.H
Renwick George, Admlty.Somst.H
Retallick John, Custom House
Retherden Maj. T. Addiscombe
Revell Mrs. Ann M. Chelsea Hsptl
RevellChas.Tamplin,Chelsea Hsptl
Revely George Fras. Gen. Post Of
Reynal Geo. T. R. City Officer
Reynell C. General Register Office
ReynellSirThos.Bd.ofGenl.Officers
Reynolds Geo. Cstms. (Weymouth)
ReynoldsGeorge,TitheCommission
Reynolds Hen. R.Com.InsolventCt
Reynolds Hen. R. jun.Sol.Treasury
Reynolds Jas.U.Ct.ofQueen'sBench
Reynolds Mrs.S. TitheCommission
Reynolds William,ChelseaHospital
Reynolds Wm.Lndn.Dist.orT.Py.P
Rhodes Wm. Stationery Office
Rice Hon. Chas. Spring, ForeignOff
Rice George, General Post Office
Rice Henry, General Post Office

Rice Richard, Excise Office
Rice Hon.Stephen,E.S.CustomHou
Rich Frederick, Custom House
Rich Fras. Hen. Chany. Regstr.Off
Rich William Osborne, War Office
Richards Rev.Wm.Upton,Brit.Mus
Richards Hen. C. Insolv. Drs. Ct
Richards Rd.M.P. Master inChancy
Richards Rt.Admiralty,Somrst.Ho
Richards S. Exchegr. of Pleas Offi
Richards Thos. Gen. Post Office
Richards Wm.Chas.Bd.ofOrdnance
Richardson Alfred, Gen. PostOffice
Richardson George, Genl. Post Off
Richardson Geo. F. BritishMuseum
RichardsonJohn,Customs(Galway)
Richardson Thos. S. Custom House
Riche Marcus Wm. Genl. Post Off
Richmond Dk.of,K.G.Ld.Lt.Sussex
Richmond Henry, Custom House
Richter William, Bank of England
Rickards Geo.Cmmsn. Ltncy.Lndn
Ricketts Edward W. Treasury
Ricketts Fras. S. Exchequer Office
Ricketts Jas. Chelsea Hospital
Ricketts Wm. Hy. Custom House
Rickford Thomas, MillbankPrison
Rickman Wm.G.Paymstr.Gen's. O
Rickon Abraham, Custom House
Ridding William, Custom House
Riddle Edwd.Grenwh.Hosp.School
Riddle Gabriel, Excise Office
Riddle John, Grenwh.Hosp.School
Rideout Chas. General Post Office
Rideout N. S. C. Genl. Post Office
Rider James, Customs (Jersey)
Rider Thos. Excise (Northwich)
Ridgway Geo. S. Ct. of Chancery
Ridley Anthony, Lloyd's
Ridoutt Rd. General Post Office
Rigge John, Registry of Deeds Offi
Riley S. Hy. Admiralty, Somst. Ho
Ribiey James, Chelsea Hospital
Ripley Jeremy Jephson,CustomHo
Ripley Thos.Edmd.T.Bd.of Ordnce
Ripon Earl of, Privy Councillor
Ritchie J. S. Stamp & Tax Office
Ritherdon Robt. East India House
Rivers H. E. Greenwich Hospital
Rivers Lieut.Wm. Greenwh.Hosptl
Rivington Chas. Clk. toStatners'.Co
RobartsA.G.jun.Exchr.BillLn.Offic
Robarts A. W. Commsn.Ltcy.Lndn
RobberdsCs.C.Com.ofCoalWhipprs
Robins Lieut. Stephens P.HomeOff
Robbins Lieut. S. P. Foreign Offi
Roberson Alfred F. Custom House
Roberts Ardine John, War Office
Roberts Charles, Custom House
Roberts Chas.Public Record Office
Roberts Mrs. E. Greenwh. Hospitl
Roberts E.R. Customs(Barnstaple)
Roberts George, Gen. Post Office
Roberts John, Custom House
Roberts John, War Office
Roberts John, jun. War Office
Roberts Jonathan, Genl. PostOffice
Roberts Thomas, Bank of England
Roberts Thos. Stamp & Tax Office
Roberts Thos.Evan,Genl.Rgstr.Off
Roberts William, Excise Office
Roberts Wm. General Post Office
RobertsWilliam,Stamp&TaxOffice
Roberts Wm. Jackson, Custom Ho
Robertson Genl.A.Dirc.Est.IndiaC
Robertson Charles, Trinity House
Robertson David, Solicitor to Customs in Scotland
Robertson JamesC. Custom House
Robertson John,Admlty.Somst.Ho
Robertson John, Gen. Post Office
Robertson J.H.W. Seaman'sReg.O
Robertson Miss, Chelsea Hospital
RobertsonPeter, Admlty.Somst.Ho
Robertson Richard, CustomHouse
Robertson Richd. Gen. Post Office
Robertson Rd.Metrpls.RoadsOffice
Robertson Wm.Admlty.Somst.Ho
Robilliard JohnN. Customs(Wells)
Robilliard Nicholas, CustomHouse
Robins Henry, Custom House
Robinson Charles, Russia Compy
RobinsonCmndr.Chas.Grnwh.Hspl
Robinson C.F. CrownOff.Qns.Bnch
Robinson Edward, War Office
Robinson G.J.Woods&ForestsOffic
Robinson George Rd. Chairman of Committee of Lloyd's
Robinson Henry, East India House
RobinsonHen.J.Woods&ForestsOf

Robinson James, Gen. Post Office
Scarth Thomas, Board of Ordnance
Robinson John, Sup. of Police (P)
Robinson J. H. House of Lords
Robinson Sam. Thos. City Officer
Robinson Thomas, Gen. Post Office
Robinson Wm. Stationery Office
Robinson Wm. R. Dirct. Bk. of Engld
Robison John, Custom House
Robson Edward, Bank of England
Robson John, Westminster Court
Robson Thos. General Post Office
Robson Wm. F. Admlty. Somst. Ho
Rodd Henry, Customs (Bideford)
Rodd Hen. Lewis, Duchy of Cornwall
Roden Earl of, Privy Councillor
Rodford John, Gen. Post Office
Rodmell Thomas, Customs (Leith)
Rodney Fredk. Exchequer Office
Rodway Thomas, Excise Office
Roe John, Guildhall Justice Room
Roe John, Sewers' Office
Roe Wm. Stiles, Cstms. (Whitehvn)
Rogers Fras. N. J. Deputy Judge Advocate General
Rogers Frederick L. Audit Office
Rogers James, Gen. Post Office
Rogers John, Westminster Court
Rogers John Chas. Woods & Forests
Rogers P. Wm. Chancery Reg. Off
Rogers Sam. Commnr. of Fine Arts
Rogers Saunders, Custom House
Rolfe Sir Rt. Monsey, Baron Exchqr
Romilly Edward, Audit Office
Ronayne Uniack, Genl. Post Office
Roney Cusack P. Royal Marine Offi
Rooke T. B. Examiners Off. Chancery
Roper Samuel, Board of Ordnance
Rorauer James, Treasury
Roscozla Francis, Excise Office
Rose Sir Geo. Master in Chancery
Rose Sir Geo. H. Privy Councillor
Rose Col. Hugh, Consul at Syria
Rose George, Stamp & Tax Office
Rose John, Election Off. Ho. Cmmns
Rose John, Filacers Off. Qun's. Bnch
Rose Thomas Hayley, Woods & Frsts
Rose William, House of Lords
Rose Wm. Public Bus. Of. Ho. Cmns
Rose Wm. Farr, Stamp & Tax Office
Rose Wm. Paterson, Custom Ho
Rosbery Earl of, Privy Councillor
Ross Alexander, Custom House
Ross Charles, Stamp & Tax Office
Ross Chas. jun. Stamp & Tax Office
Ross David, Consul at Coquimbo
Ross Frederick, Custom House
Ross George F. Excise (Portsmouth)
Ross James, Customs (Llanelly)
Ross Sir Jno. Consul at Stockholm
Ross Wm. Lee, Custom House
Rosslyn Earl of, Privy Councillor
Rossy Nichls. Consular Agt. Enos
Rothery W. jun. Com. of Surrey's Of
Rothery W. sen. Com. of Surrey's Off
Rothney Alexr. East India House
Round Wm. Nash, Wood & Forests
Rouse George, Custom, House
Rouse Hen. Vi. Cnsl. at Valparaiso
Rouse John, Greenwich Hospital
Rouse Lieut. J. W. Grnwh. Hosptl
Routledge Chas. Report Off. Chncy
Routledge John C. Report Of. Chncy
Rowan Lieut. Col. Met. Police Offi
Rowbotham J. Sup. Regr. (Nwngtn)
Rowe John, General Post Office
Rowed James, Custom House
Rowell Wm. Spink, City Officer
Rowland Chas. Jrnl. Of. Ho. Cmns
Rowland Chas. City Officer
Rowland Edward, Audit Office
Rowland John, Stamp & Tax Offi
Rowlatt Rev. John Hen. Midl. Templ
Rowlatt Rev. Wm. Hen. Inr. Tmpl
Rowley Francis, Custom House
Rowsell Evan Ed. Admlty. Smst. Ho
Rowsell Jn. T. Sup. Reg. (Lndn. Cty)
Ruddick Wm. Paymastr. Gen's. Offi
Ruddle Francis, Audit Office
Rudge James, Stamp & Tax Office
Rudlin Wm. Henry, Audit Office
Rule Chas. P. Admlty. Smst. House
Rule Chas. Hen. Excheq. of Pleas
Rumsey Lacy, Treasury
Rundall Thomas, East India House
Ruscoe T. Great Seal Pat. Office
Rushton William, Custom House
Rushton William, General Post Offic
Rushworth Chas. P. Stamp & Tax Of
Rushworth Edwd. E. Stamp & Tax Of
Ruspini Bladen, Audit Office
Shephard Jn. Archdcn. of Middx. Off
Russell Lord John, Privy Council
Russell Edwin, Rolls Court
Russell Edwd. Stamp & Tax Office
Russell George, Stamp & Tax Office
Russell John Jas. Stamp & Tax Offi
Russell Mrs. E. Privy Council Offi
Russell Thos. Gen. Post Office
Russell Rev. W. Inspector of Prisons
Russell Wm. Court of Chancery
Russell Wm. Stamp & Tax Office
Russell Wm. Mozart, City Officer
Ruston William, City Officer
Rutherford G. Clk. to Gunmakrs'. Co
Rutherford John, Custom House
Rutland Duke of, K.G. Ld. Lieut. Liecester
Rutson Richd. Court of Chancery
Rutt Anthony, Sup. of Police (L)
Ryan Sir Edwd. knt. Privy Council
Ryan Thomas, Custom House
Ryan John, Excise (Manchester)
Ryan Rd. Consul at Para, Brazil
Ryder Charles, Stamp & Tax Office
Rye Wm. Brenchley, Brtsh. Museum
Ryland Archer, Cmn. Pleader, City
Ryle Charles, East India House

Sabine Henry, Custom House
Sadgrove Wm. H. Clk. Poultrs'. Co
Sadler Wm. Thos. Stamp & Tax Offi
Safe James William, Custom Houe
Saffery John, Board of Ordnances
St. German's Earl of, Privy Cncllr
St. John Frederick, Custom House
St. John Rt. Wm. Consul at Algiers
St. Leger Arthur, Paymaster Gen. Off
St. Quintin Geo. Fredk. Custom Ho
Salisbury Marqs. of, Privy Counclr. & Lord Lieut. of Middlesex
Salisbury Francis, Gen. Post Office
Salisbury W. Lndn. Dist. or Tpy. Post
Salmon Jas. Excise (Dorchester)
Salt John, Lndn. Dist. or Tpy. Post
Salter John, Custom House
Salter John, Stamp & Tax Office
Salter Sidney Jas. Stamp & Tax Offi
Saltwell Geo. Robert, Genl. Post Offi
Saltwell W. Lndn. Dist. or Typ. Post
Salusbury Thomas, Audit Office
Salvage Samuel, Gen. Register Off
Salvage S. Stamp & Tax Office
Sample John, Board of Ordnance
Sampson Marmaduke B. Bnk. of Eng
Sampson William, Russia Company
Sandaver Richard, Gray's inn
Sandell Joseph, Stationery Office
Sanders George Williams, Roll's Ct
Sanders Henry Wm. Signet Office
Sanders W. Basevi, Pblc. Record Offi
Sanderson Chas. Gilchrist, Customs
Sandham John Mullins, War Office
Sandison Donald, Consul at Brussa
Sandoz Fred. East India House
Sandwich Earl of, L. Lt. of Huntingdn
Sansom C. T. Mstrs'. Of. Queen's Ben
Sansom Jas. General Post Office
Sargent Frederick, Treasury
Sargent Thos. Stamp & Tax Office
Sargent William, Audit Office
Sargent William, Treasury
Satchwell Geo. Board of Ordnance
Saul Joseph, Admiralty, Somrst. Ho
Saul William, Stamp & Tax Office
Saunders Charles, Custom House
Saunders John, Custom House
Saunders John, East India House
Saunders John, Excise Office
Saunders J. E. Court of Exchequer
Saunders Nathaniel, City Officer
Saunders Robert J. Home Office
Saunders Sidney S. Consul, Janina
Saunders Thomas, City Comptroller
Saunderson Chas. East India House
Saurin Edward, Stamp & Tax Office
Savage Christopher W. Poor Law Offi
Savio Fras. Royal Engineers' Office
Savory John, Excise (Bath)
Sawell John Pownall, Custom Ho
Sawyer Edward, Treasury
Sawyer George, Ordnance Office
Sawyer Henry, Board of Ordnance
Sawyer Wm. Customs (Rochester)
Say Chas. S. Paymastr. Gen's. Office
Sayers Christopher, Genl. Post Off
Sayers Rd. General Post Office
Scales Robert, General Post Office
Scamp Wm. Admiralty, Somerset Ho
Scanlan Edmund, Custom House
Scarborough, Earl of, Ld. Lt. Notihm
Scarman Thomas, India Board
Smirke Edwd. Duchy of Cornwls. Ofi
Scarlett Hon. Peter Campbell, Sec. of Leg. to Florence
Scarth William, Board of Ordnance
Schelling Geo. F. Custom House
Schetky John Chrisn. Addiscombe
Schofield Wm. Excise (East Wales)
Scollick Jonthn. Jdg. Adv. Gen's. Offi
Scollick J. jun. Jdg. Advo. Gen's. Off
Scory John, Stamp & Tax Office
Scott Alex. Admiralty, Somerset Ho
Scott Arthur, East India House
Scott Benj. Clk. to Wheelwrights' Co
Scott Chas. Lond. Dist. or Typ. Post
Scott Charles, Treasury
Scott Fras J. National Debt Office
Scott Hen. Morton, Foreign Office
Scott Jas. Hen. Paymaster Genl. Offi
Scott John, Admlty. Somst. House
Scott Jn. F. National Debt Office
Scott Nwn. S. Sec. of Leg. Switzerland
Scott Robert, Customs (Alloa)
Scott Thos. B. G. Consul at Bordeaux
Scott Wm. Board of Trade
Scott William, Board of Ordnance
Scovell Chs. Andrew, Custom House
Scrimes Fredk. Wm. Custom House
Scroggs Hy. General Register Offi
Scudamore Frank Ives, Gen. Post Offi
Scudamore John, Genl. Post Office
Sculthorpe W. R. Lndn. Dist. or Ty. P
Seaford Lord, Ambas. to Portugal
Sealy G. T. Consul at Lima
Search John, Bank of England
Searle George, City officer
Secarry Thomas, Custom House
Sedgewick Alfred, Genl. Post Office
Sedgewick George, Genl. Post Office
Sedgwick Wm. Board of Ordnance
Seel Edmund Molyneux, Audit Offi
Seeley Robert, Comn. Ltncy. Londn
Selby John Donaldson, Tithe Comn
Selkirk Earl of, Hudson's Bay Co
Sellars Wm. National Debt Office
Semple John, Customs (Stranraer)
Senior Edw. Poor Law Ass. Com
Senior Nassau Wm. Mstr. in Chancry
Sent John, Excise Office
Seppings N. L. Admlty. Somst. House
Sercombe Isaac H. Stamp & Tax Offi
Seton James G. Court of Chancery
Seton Wilmot, Treasury
Sevenoaks John, Court of Chancery
Sewell John, City Officer
Sewell John, Clerk to Loriners' Com. & to Spectacle Makers' Company
Sewell John, Qurtr. Mastr. Gen's. Off
Sewell Thos. Haywood, Cusm. House
Sewell Wm. General Post Off
Seymour Lord, Comm. in Lunacy
Seymour Sir G. H. Ambsr. to Belgium
Shadforth Gn. Hen. Bd. of Gn. Officrs
Shadwell Chas. Sec. to Vice Chncllr
Shadwell Sir L. knt. Vice Chncllr
Shaftesbury, Earl of, Privy Councilr
Shank Hen. Direct. East India Comp
Shank William, City Officer
Shannon Wm. Paymstr. Gen's. Off
Sharp Sir C. Customs (Newcastle)
Sharp Henry, State Paper Office
Sharp Thomas, India Board
Sharpe Arth. Queen Anne's Bnty. Off
Sharpe Hen. Jas. Public Record Of
Sharpe Joseph, Court of Faculties
Sharpe Joseph, Stamp & Tax Offi
Shave Thomas, Custom House
Shaw Alexander W. Custom Ho
Shaw Isaac, Custom House
Shaw Joseph, Excise (Southampton)
Shaw Wm. Norcliffe, Genl. Post Off
Shearman Montague, Middx. Sessns
Shearman Thomas, Custom House
Shearman Wm. Stamp & Tax Office
Shee Wm. Archer, East India Ho
Sheebon Jn. Cstms (Burrowstonnes)
Shefford George, Ordnance Board
Sheil Justin, Envoy to Persia
Sheil Rd. Lalor, Privy Councillor
Sheild M. Paymaster Gen's. Offi
Sheldrick George, Custom House
Shelley Spencer, Treasury
Shells Frederick, House of Lords
Shelswell T. Lambeth st. Police Ct
Shelton John W. Chelsea Hospital
Shepard John, Home Office
Shepherd Hn. John, Q.C. Counsel to Admlty. & Clerk of Presentations, Court of Bankruptcy
Southern Hen. Sec. of Leg. at Lisbon
Shepheard Edward W. Audit Offi
Shepherd Jas. Exchequer Bill L. Off
Shepherd John, India House
Shepherd Rd. Alexander, Custm. Ho
Shepherd Thos. Customs (Derry)
Shepherds Saml. Gen Register Office
Sheppard Edmund, Gen. Post Office
Sheppard Edward, Custom House
Sheppard Hen. Gen. Post Office
Sheridan John, Admlty. Whitehall
Sheridan Wm. Stewart, Excise Off
Sherwin Hen. Greenwich Police Ct
Sherwood Henry, Custom Houso
Sherwood J. T. Consl. Portland, U.S
Sherwood Thomas, Ct. Com. Pleas
Sherwood T. E. Clerk to Farriers' Co
Shield M. Paymaster General's Of
Shields Jas. Lambeth st. Police Ct
Shillingford Alex. N. Gen. Post Of
Shillito Jas. Francis, Ea. India Ho
Shipway George, East India House
Shirreff Chas. I. Clk. to Turners' Co
Shoemack Hen. Chas. Rl. Engrs. Off
Sholl Charles, Customs (Gweek)
Shoveller John, Gen. Register Off
Shrimpton Hy. M. Paym. Gen's. Of
Shurvin H. Greenwich Police Ct
Shuter Thos. George, Gen. Post Or
Shuttleworth Lieut. Government Emigration agent (Sligo)
Sicklen Wm. Woods & Forests Off
Sidebotham Thomas Rt. Excise Of
Sidney T. Alderman of London
Silk Wm. Henry, Custom House
Silk Daniel, General Post Office
Silk George Chas. Metro. Ch. Fnd. Off
Sills George, Chelsea Hospital
Simes Wm. Paymaster Gen's. Office
Simmonds John, Gen. Post Office
Simmons Bartholomew, Excise Off
Simmons John, Stamp & Tax Office
Simmons Lieut. James Lintorn Arabin, Royal Engineers' Office
Simner Abel, Poor Law Office
Simpkinson John A. F. Lincoln's inn
Simpson Capt. Jn. Greenwh. Hosptl
Simpson Hen. Ct. of Queen's Bench
Simpson Hen. Insolvent Debtors' Ct
Simpson T. F. Stamp & Tax Office
Simpson Joseph, Custom House
Simpson Robert, Ct. of Queen's Bnch
Simpson Willoughby, Custm. Ho
Sims George, Gen. Post Office
Sims R. E. Custom House
Sims Robert H. Custom House
Simson Edgar, General Post Offi
Simson Thomas May, Gen. Post Offi
Sinfield Thos. Lndn. Dist. or Tpy. Pst
Sivewright Geo. Admlty. Whitehall
Sivrac Chs. A. G. Com. of P. C. for Trd
Skaif J. General Register Office
Skelton George, Foreign Office
Skelton John, Bank of England
Skene Charles C. Custom House
Skinner Wm. J. Custom House
Skirrow W. Commis. of Bankruptcy
Skoiles N. H. Stamp & Tax Office
Skottowe Augustine, Pmstr. Gl's. Of
Slade Joseph, Gen. Post Office
Slade Septimus, Paymstr. Gen's. Offi
Slade William, Gen. Post Office
Slade Wm. M. Taxing Masters' Offi
Sladen Henry, Customs (Cardiff)
Sladen Joseph, jun. Archdeacon of Rochester's Registry Office
Sladen Joseph, sen. Archdeacon of Rochester's Registry Office
Slaney Rt. A. Health of Towns Com
Slater Alfred, Gen. Post Office
Slater Thomas, Bank of England
Slatford John, Adjutant Gen's. Offi
Slaughter James, Exchegr. Bill Off
Slee Rt. Sup. Rgr. (St. Olave's, Swk)
Slee Wm. Lon. Dist. or Tpy. Post
Sleeman William, Custom House
Sloan John, Customs (Dumfries)
Slocombe Alfred, Custom House
Slocombe James, Custom House
Slyfield Henry, Custom House
Smallfield Alfred, Genl. Post Office
Smallwood William Gen. Post Office
Smart J. Commander in Chief's Off
Smart Thomas, Ordnance Office
Smart William, Custom House
Smeddle Wm. Board of Ordnance
Smedley Frs. High Bailiff, Westmstr
Smee Alfred, Bank of England
Smee Wm. Bank of England
Smerdon Thomas, Custom House

Smirke Sir Rt. knt. Commissioner for Improving the Metropolis
Smith Algernon, Westmr. Police Ct
Smith Andrew M.D. Army Mdcl. Bd O
Smith Charles, Board of Ordnance
Smith Chas. T. Chan. Lunacy Offi
Smith Chas. Culling, Custom House
Smith David S. Admiralty, Smst. Ho
Smith Edward, Ct. of Bankruptcy
Smith Edmd. B. Cstms. (Southmtn)
Smith Edwd. Jas. Genrl. Post Office
Smith Fras. R. G. Genl. Register Offi
Smith Rev. Fredc. Hayleybury Co
Smith George, Customs (Chester)
Smith George, City Officer
Smith George, Excise Office
Smith George, Stamp & Tax Office
Smith Geo. Rd. General Post Office
Smith Henley, Clerk to Barber's Co
Smith Hen. Admiralty, Somrst. Ho
Smith Henry, Audit Office
Smith Henry, Board of Ordnance
Smith Henry, General Post Office
Smith Hen. Woods & Forests' Office
Smith H. jun. General Post Office
Smith H. sen. General Post Office
Smith Hen. Attwell, Audit Office
Smith Henry John, Custom House
Smith Henry Stone, House of Lords
Smith J. Custom House
Smith James, Gen. Post Office
Smith James, Health of Towns Com
Smith Jas. London Dist. or Tpy. Pst
Smith Jas. Marlboro' st. Police Ct
Smith John, Custom House
Smith John, General Post Office
Smith John, Sup. Regr. (Whtcpl)
Smith John Abraham, Custom Ho
Smith J. D. General Register Office
Smith John Rt. Board of Ordnance
Smith Jsph. Sup. Regr. (St. Luke's)
Smith Martin T. Dir. East India Co
Smith Newman, South Sea House
Smith Peter, Colonial Office
Smith Richard, Stamp & Tax Offi
Smith Rt. Customs (Campbeltown)
Smith Rt. Lndn. Dist. or Tpy. Pst
Smith Rt. Edwd. East India House
Smith Robert Rd. Gen. Post Office
Smith Rt. Sexton, Genl. Post Offi
Smith Rt. Vernon, Privy Councillor & Commissioner in Lunacy
Smith Sarah, Admiralty, Whitehall
Smith Sidney John, East India Ho
Smith Thos. Chancery Lunacy Off
Smith Thos. Genl. Post Office
Smith Thomas, Excise Office
Smith Thos. B. Gen. Post Office
Smith Thos. Chas. Bank of England
Smith Thos. C. Cmmsn. Ltncy. Lndn
Smith William, Consul at Lisbon
Smith Wm. jun. Gen. Post Office
Smith Wm. Paymast. Gen.'s Office
Smith Wm. Sec to Hudson's Bay Co
Smith William D. Custom House
Smith Wm. Jas. Woods & Forests
Smith William John, Custom Ho
Smith Wm. Rt. Chan. Lunacy Off
Smith Wm. T. Public Record Office
Smither James, London District or Twopenny Post
Smithers John. Cstms. (Aberdeen)
Smithers Jsph. Union Hall Plce. Ct
Smythe Henry, Stamp & Tax Office
Snelgar Homer, Audit Office
Snell Wm. Henry, Genl. Post Off
Snosswell W. Ths. Admlty. Smst. Ho
Soady Brooking, Audit Office
Soady Brooking, jun. Audit Office
Soady John, Audit Office
Soady John Williams, Audit Office
Soady Capt. Joseph, Bd. of Ordnance
Soane Fredk. Stamp & Tax Office
Solly Edward, Addiscombe Sem
Solly Isaac, Commsn. Ltncy. Lndn
Solly Samuel, Eastland Company
Somers Earl, Lord Lieutenant of Herefordshire
Somerset Ld. G. Chas. H. Commr. of Revenue Enquiry & Tithe Commissioner
Somes Joseph, jun. Lloyd's
Soper John D. Custom House
Sorrell Sir T. H. Con. Gen. at Trieste
South Montagu, General Post Office
Southam John Downes, Gen. Post Of
Southee Osborn, Custom House
Southee Pearce, Custom House
Southey Dr. Henry H. Commisr. in Lunacy, & Visitor of Lunatics

Southwell Hen. Wm. Qu.'s Bnch. O
Sowray George, Genrl. Register Oc
Spalding John, General Post Offi
Sparke Joseph H. Cstms. (Dartmt
Sparrow James, Cstms. (Newcastl
Sparshott Capt. Saml. Custom Hou
Speer Edward, Treasury
Spence Chas. Admiralty Somst. Ho
Spence William, Stamp & Tax Of
Spencer Edward, Genrl. Post Office
Spencer Wm. Admiralty, Somst. Ho
Sperry George, Custom House
Spikin Chs. Southwark Police Ct
Spittal Joseph, Admiralty, Smst. Ho
Spittall Francis, Custom House
Spong Frederick, General Post Offi
Sporle Thos. Thames Police Court
Spratlin C. F. Examnrs. Offi. Chncy
Spratt Alfred, Genl. Post Office
Spurrell Geo. Admiralty, Smst. Ho
Spurrell John H. Admlty. Somst. Ho
Squirrell John R. Custom House
Stable David Henry, Clerk of Peace, Tower Liberty & Sewers' Office
Stacey George, Board of Ordnance
Stacey John Stephen, Gen. Post Off
Stacy George, Coal Whippers' Com
Stahlschmidt Hen. Geo. Gen. Post Of
Staines Rt. Customs (Chepstow)
Stanbrough W. Board of Ordnance
Stanbury Robert, Custom House
Standen Wm. Paymaster Gen.'s Offi
Stanley A. Poor Law Commrs. Off
Stanley Lord, Privy Councillor
Stanley Hon. E. J. Privy Councillor
Stanley Barker, Custom House
Stanley Rt. S. Excise (Liverpool)
Stannard Thos. Exchqr. of Pleas Offi
Stannus Major Gen. Sir Ephraim G. knt. Addiscombe Seminary
Stansmore John S. Customs (Truro)
Stanton William, Excise Office
Stanwell Wm. Customs (Gainsbro')
Stap Thos. Randal, Custom House
Stapleton Wm. Henry, Audit Office
Stapylton Chs. Rt. Martin, Paymstr. G. O
Stark Hugh, India Board
Stark Lieut. Gov. Emig. Agt. Belfast
Stark Samuel Mozley, Gen. Post Of
Starling Jhn. Saunders Custom Ho.
Staughton Stephen, Gen. Post Off
Staughton S. Lndn. Dist. or Tpy. Pst
Staveley Geo. Foreign Office
Staveley Thomas, Foreign Office
Steel James, Excise Office
Steel James, General Post Office
Steele James, Chelsea Hospital
Steele Rd. Lndn. Dist. or Tpy. Post
Steers Robert, City Officer
Steggall Baker, Poor Law Office
Stein Chas. Messngr. to House Comns
Stennett Joseph, Bank of England
Stephen Mr. Serj. Com. of Bkptcy
Stephen James, Colonial Office
Stephen Thos. B. Custom House
Stephens Jas. F. Admlty. Somst. Ho
Stephens John May, War Office
Stephenson A. Customs (Arbroath)
Stephenson Capt. Dan. Trinity Ho
Stephenson Edwd. S. Ct. of Exchqr
Stephenson Ernest A. Pymstr. Gn. O
Stephenson Frank. H. Stamp & Tx. Of
Stephenson Hen. F. Excise Office
Stephenson John, Treasury
Stephenson Robert, jun. Health of Towns Commission
Stephenson Thomas, Custom Ho
Stephenson Thos. Russia Company
Stephenson William, Treasury
Stephenson Wm. Henry, Treasury
Sterkey Charles, Audit Office
Stevans C. Adjutant General's Off
Stevens Francis, Excise Office
Stevens F. J. Consul, Trebizond
Stevens John, Bank of England
Stevens John, City Surveyor
Stevens Nathaniel, Custom House
Stevens R. Consul at Samsoon
Stevens Rd. Consul at Gallipoli
Stevens Thos. Stamp & Tax Office
Stevens Wm. Admiralty. Somst. Ho
Stevenson Geo. Gen. Post Office
Stevenson Rd. Comm. of Bankruptcy
Stevenson Stephen, Gen. Post Office
Steward Thomas, Audit Office
Stewart Alex. Lon. Dist or Tpy. Post
Stewart Arthur, Cstms. (Lancaster)
Stewart Duncan, Cstms. (Falmouth)
Stewart Hon. Edwd. Rd. Custom Ho
Stewart James, Bank of England

Stewart Jas. Copyhold Commission
Stewart J. Lunatic Office
Stewart John, Customs (Dundee)
Stewart Patrick, Board of Ordnance
Stewart Patrick, Custom House
Stewart Rd. Hardinge, War Office
Stewart Rd. Hardinge, jun. War Off
Stewart Villers, City Officer
Stewart Wm. Jn. Cstms. (Sunderlnd)
Still Robert, City Bridewell
Stillwell Edward, War Office
Stillwell Richd. Stamp & Tax Off
Stilwell Geo. Admlty. Somst. House
Stilwell Jas. Admlty. Somst. House
Stinchcombe John, Gen. Regstr. Of
Stock Nathaniel, Bank of England
Stocker John, Court of Exchequer
Stockwell Ts. Lndn. Dst. or Tpy. Pst
Stoddard Geo. Consul at Madeira
Stoddard Jno. L. Consl. Alexandria
Stokes John A. Masters' Off. Chncry
Stone Charles, Seamans Reg. Off
Stone Fred. Customs (New Ross)
Stone Henry, General Post Office
Stone Lieut. Wm. City Officer
Stone Thos. Sup. Reg. (St. Geo's. ea)
Stoneham Thomas, Master's Office, Queen's Bench
Stopford Sir Rt. Gov. Grnwh. Hospl
Stow Charles, Audit Office
Stow George, General Post Office
Stow Thomas B. Greenwich Hospital
Stow William Audit Office
Strachan Matthias, War Office
Stradbroke Earl Ld. Lieut. Suffolk
Straith Major H. Addiscombe
Strangford Visct. Privy Councillor
Strangways Hon. Wm. F. Ambs. Frankfort-sur-Maine
Stratford Wm. Court of Exchequer
Stratford Wm. H. Stamp & Tax Of
Stratford Lt. W. S. Adlty. Somst. Ho
Streatfield John, Home Office
Strickland William, Custom House
Strike Wm. Customs (Harwich)
Strike W. Customs (Rye)
Stringer Robert, Custom House
Strong Geo. Qr. Master Gen.'s Off
Strong Thos. B. Adjutant Gen.'s Offi
Stronge Chas. Walter, Treasury
Stroude J. Chancery Report Office
Strutt Hen. W. Admiralty, Somerset House
Stuart de Rothesay Ld. Privy Council
Stuart Adam S. Admlty. Somst. Ho
Stuart Geo. C. C. Seaman's Reg. Off
Stuart Isaac O. P. Seaman's Reg. Off
Stuart James, Home Office
Stubbs Thos. Edwd. Bankruptcy Ct
Sturgis Everard R. Insolvent Ct
Sturgis Samuel, Insolvent Court
Sturt Matthew, Custom House
Sturton Jacob, Paymaster Gen.'s Off
Suckling Jas. Bow st. Police Court
Suckling W. N. Report Offi. Chancy
Suft Rt. Fras. Com. of P. Cl. for Trade
Suft Robert Francis, Royal Mint
Sulivan Laurence, War Office
Sugden Sir E. B. Privy Councillor
Surrey Earl of, Privy Councillor
Surur M. Consul at Damietta
Suter Hen. Consul at Kaiseriah
Suter H. B. Consul at Missolonghi
Suter Wm. Paymaster Gen. Office
Sutherland Capt. Chelsea Hosptl
Sutherland John D. Gen. Post Office
Sutherland Wm. Stamp & Tax Offi
Sutton, see Manners Sutton
Sutton Edward, Poor Law Office
Sutton Hen. Customs (Newhaven)
Sutton Hn. J. H. T. M. Ct. of Faculties
Sutton Wm. Excise (Abergavenny)
Sutton Wm. Paymater Gen.'s Off
Swabey Hen. B. Admlty. Registry
Swatman Frd. Customs (Lyme)
Swatman William, Customs (Lynn)
Sweet George Hyde, Custom House
Sweet William, Stamp & Tax Off
Sweetman John C. Gen. Post Office
Swell Wm. Greenwich Hospital
Swift Abraham, Gen. Post Office
Swift Robert John, Excise Office
Swifte Edmund L. Tower of London
Sykes John, Excise (Rochester)
Sykes Col. W. H. Direc. E. India Ho
Symers Colin, Customs (Dundee)
Symonds A. Metropolit. Bldg. Off
Symonds Capt. Sir W. Admiralty, Somerset House
Symonds John, Seaman's Reg. Off

Symonds William, Custom House
Symons Chas. Stamp & Tax Office
Symons Edwd. Royal Engineers' Off
Symons Edw. Wm. Thames Police Ct
Symons John, Sup. Regr. (Poplar)
Symons William, Custom House
Syms Edw. G. Adjutant Gen's. Offi

Tahourdin H. Chancery Reg. Offi
Talbot Earl, Lord Lieut. Stafford
Talbot Clere, Colonial Office
Talbot Hon. G. C. Privy Seal Office
Talbot Hon. John C. Attorney-Gen. to H.R.H. the Prince of Wales
Talman Frans. H. Chelsea Hospital
Tancred Hen. Wm. Lincoln's Inn
Tandy Wm. Southwark Police Ct
Tanfield John, Excise (Coventry)
Tankerville Earl of, Privy Council
Tanner Thomas, Custom House
Tatam W. C. Consul, Venice
Tatem Edmund Chas. Custom Ho
Tatham Thos. Tithe Commissrs. Bd
Tattam John James, Custom House
Tattersall John, Custom House
Tattum John S. Custom House
Tayler James George, Audit Office
Taylor Alfred, Westmr. Police Ct
Taylor Bridges, Foreign Office & Signet Office
Taylor Sir Brook, Signet Office
Taylor Chas. Richd. Genl. Post Office
Taylor David, Custom House
Taylor George, Excise Office
Taylor Geo. Copyhold Commission
Taylor George, Sewers' Office
Taylor George Rd. Genl. Post Office
Taylor Henry, Colonial Office
Taylor Henry, Genl. Post Office
Taylor James, Custom House
Taylor James, Court of Arches, & Prerogative Will Office
Taylor James, Ct. of Common Pleas
Taylor John Fitzgerald, Custm. Ho
Taylor J. H. Court of Exchequer
Taylor Robert, Custom House
Taylor Wilbraham, Ho. of Comns
Taylor William, Bank of England
Taylor William, Home Office
Taylor Wm. National Debt Office
Taylor Wm. Stamp & Tax Office
Taylor Wm. Southwark Police Ct
Tebbs John Searles, War Office
Teesdale Chas. L. M. Gen. Post Office
Teesdale Jn. Solc. to Dchy. Lncst. Off
Teissier Baron de, South Sea House
Temple Courtenay, Genl. Post Office
Temple Frederick, City Officer
Temple Frederick Wm. City Officer
Temple Thomas, State Paper Office
Temple Hon. W. Ambassdr. to Sicily
Tennant Wm. Custms. (Dumfries)
Tennent Jas. E. Col. Sec. Ceylon
Terry Matthew, Paymastr. Gen's. Of
Terry G. H. Stamp & Tax Office
Tetley Mrs. Mary, Greenwich Hspitl
Thacker Abraham, Genl. Post Office
Thanet Earl, Lord Lieut. Kent
Thatcher John, Stamp & Tax Office
Thirlwall Thomas, Excise Office
Thom Jas. Pattison, East India Ho
Thom Robert, Consul at Ningpo
Thomas C. F. Excise (Gloucester)
Thomas Edwd. Court of Arches
Thomas Fras. S. Public Recd. Office
Thomas Fredk. Chas. Excise Office
Thomas Henry, Customs (Aldboro)
Thomas Hen. National Debt Office
Thomas John, Court of Common Pleas
Thomas Rd. Clerk to Glovers' Co
Thomas Seth, Board of Ordnance
Thomas Wm. Board of Ordnance
Thompson Edw. Clerk to Salters' Co
Thompson Edwd. L. Dist. Post Office
Thompson Edward, Gen. Post Office
Thompson Frederick, Audit Office
Thompson George, Gen. Post Office
Thompson Jas. Excise (Newcastle)
Thompson Isaac Edwd. Gen. Post O
Thompson John, Custom House
Thompson John, General Post Office
Thompson John, Tithe Commission
Thompson John Hen. Stmp. & Tax O
Thompson Lionel H. House of Lords
Thompson Rt. Admlty. Somset. Ho
Thompson Robert, Genl. Post Off
Thompson Thos. Woods & Forest Of
Thompson Wm. Bank & Alderman of London

Thompson Wm. Mastrs. Off.Chncy
Thompson William, Custom House
Thoms Wm. J. House of Lords
Thomson Alex. Customs(NewRoss)
Thomson Alex.Christie,Gen.PostOf
Thomson James, Genrl. Post Office
Thorburn Jas. Greenwich Hospital
Thornborrow John, Woods&Forsts
Thorndich John, Excise Office
Thorne Wm. General Post Office
Thornley Jsph.D.Customs (Fowey)
Thornton SirEdward,PrivyCouncil
Thornton ClaudGeo.EastlandCom
Thornton Edwd. East India House
Thornton GeorgeSmith,Russia Co
Thornton Henry, Custom House
Thornton Hen.Ct.ofQueen'sBench
Thornton Henry M. Eastland Co
Thornton John,Exchqr.BillLn.Offi
Thornton J. GeneralRegisterOffice
Thornton John, Russia Company
Thornton John, Stamp &TaxOffice
Thornton Stephen, Eastland Co
Thornton Stephen Edwd.Russia Co
Thornton Wm.Thos.EastIndiaHou
Thornton Wm. Thos. Excise Office
Thorpe George, Custom House
Thorpe John, Custom House
Thorpe Thos. Courtenay, Customs
ThorpeThomasDurrant,CustomHo
ThurgoodThos.Admlty.Somset.Ho
Thyer Geo. Genl. Post Office
Thyer Joseph, Gen. Post Office
Tibbet John, Stamp & Tax Office
TibsonChas.Admlty.Somset.House
Tichborne Thos.Stamp&Tax Office
TicknerEdw.Commsn.Ltncy. Lndn
Tierney G.Comsnr.Grenwh.Hosptl
Tijou John Thos.T.Genl.PostOffice
Tilbury John, Bank of England
Tilbrook JohnJ.Qrtr.Mstr.Gen'sOf
Tilley John, General Post Office
Tilley Joseph, General Post Office
Tillman William, Custom House
Tillyard Frederic, Gen. Post Office
Tilsley Hugh, Stamp & Tax Office
Tilt Jas. Worship st. Police Court
Timbrell Capt. Andrew,Trinity Ho
Timm Jsph.Solctr.toStmp&TaxOff
TimmingsJ.B.Csts.(Grangemouth)
Tindal Chas. J.MarshalCommonPl
Tindal Chas. J.SouthSeaCompany
Tindal Sir N. C. Chief Justice C.P
Tindal Wm. Deputy Chairman of
Committee of Mnagemnt.Lloyd's
Tite Thomas, General Post Office
Titberidge W.H.W.Gen.Registr.Of
Tizard Wm. Hen. Audit Office
Tod Daniel, General Post Office
Todd George, Consistory Court
Todd Jn. Sheriffs' Courts, London
Todd Thomas S.Customs(Swansea)
Tollemache Arthur L. Custom Ho
Tomkins John, Admrlty.Somst.Ho
TomlinsP.N.Clk. to Paintr.Stnr.Co
Tomlinson Wm. Genl. Post Office
Tompkins Charles, Audit Office
Tooke Thos.jun.EastlandCompny.
& Russia Company
Toon Henry, Stationery Office
Tootell Chas.J.Ct.ofCommonPleas
Topper Thos. Gen. Post Office
Topping Henry,Board of Ordnance
Topping John, General Post Offi
Topping Saml. Genl. Post. Office
Torre Bryan Stephen,ExciseOffice
Tothill Webb, Woods &Forests Offi
Tournier Rt.C.Lndn.Dist.orTpy.Pt
TownleyLieut.Col.C.ForeignOffice
Townley Charles, Trinity House
Townley John, Metropn.PoliceOffi
Townsend Charles, Custom House
Townsend C. Stamp & Tax Office
Townsend Jas. TitheCommsnrs.Bd
Townsend Wm. High Ct.of Admlty
Townsend Wm. Court of Arches
Townshend Robert, Irish Office
Towse John B. Clerk to Plumbers'
& Cooks' Companies
TowseW.B.ClerktoFishmongrs'.Co
Tracey D. J. PoorLawComs. Office
Tracey Lieut.A.F.Tothlfds.Bridwl
Tracey MatthewJno.GeneralPostO
Trahar Wm. Exchequer Office
Traill Jas. Southwark PoliceCourt
Traill John Heddle, CustomHouse
Travis Wm. R. Board of Ordnance
Treherne Henry, Audit Office
Treherne H. Custom House
Trelawney SirWm.Ld.Lt.Cornwall

TrenchSirFred.Wm.Bd.ofOrdnanc
Trenow James, Board of Ordnance
Trent Wm. Excise Office
Tresider Richard, Custom House
Trevelyan Chas. Edwd. Treasury
Trevenan Jas. Customs (Colchstr)
Trevor Chas. Stamp & Tax Office
Trevor Fred.Wm.Cstms(Montrose)
Treyvaud Henry, Genl. Post Off
Tribe Thomas, Stamp & Tax Office
Trickey John,Remembrancer'sOffi
Trimmer Charles, Home Office
Trimmer John Alfred, India Board
Trinder Wm. Exchr. of PleasOffice
Tristom Chas. P. Commissioner of
Privy Council for Trade
Tritton George, Custom House
Trotter Jas. Admiralty,Somst.Hou
Troughton Rd.Zouch,CustomHous
Troy John James, Customs (Cork)
TrumanJohnOsbertus,Stamp&Tax
Truman Samuel,Stamp&TaxOffice
Trundle George, Irish Office
Tryon Rev. George Robert John,
B.A. Addiscombe Seminary
Tuck George, General Post Office
Tucker Benj.DuchyofCornwallOffi
Tucker H. St.Geo.Dir.EastIndiaCo
Tucker James, City Officer
TuckerStephenC.Paymast.Gen's.O
TuffnellEdwd.Carleton,PoorLawO
Tugwood John, Genl. Post Office
TulinAlexander, Consul at Algiers
Tull Wm. General Post Office
Tullett John,Lndn.Dist or Ty. Post
TullochJames, South SeaCompany
Tupper Alfred Martin, Customs
Tupper Nantes, Audit Office
Turing Sir James, bart. Consul
at Rotterdam
Turnbull Alex.Consul at Marseilles
Turnbull John, Consul, Granville
Turner Adolphus, Foreign Office
Turner Adolphus, Con. Gen. Monte
Video
Turner Alfred, Custom House
Turner Chas. Admiralty Smst. Ho
Turner Chas Rt.Mstrs.' Of.Qun's.B
Turner Chas.W.Cnsl.at Carthagena
Turner Jas.Customs (Bridlington)
Turner James, Genl. Post Office
TurnerJno.Alderson,Stamp&TaxO
Turner Peter, Public Record Office
Turner Thos. M.D. Com. in Lunacy
TurnerWm.Ambsdr.toNwGranada
Turnour Chas. Chad. Custom Ho
Turquand Wm. Court of Banktcy
Turton Robert, War Office
Turton Thomas, Stamp&TaxOffice
Tuttle Samuel, Audit Office
Tuxford Peter, Custom House
Twisleton Edwd.Turner Boyd, Poor
Law Commissioners' Office
Twiss Frank, Bank of England
Twyford Saml. Bow st. PoliceCourt
Tyler John, Foreign Office
Tyrrell Edwd. City Remembrancer
Tyrrell Fredk. Bow street Police Ct
Tyrrell Michael, Custom House
TyrrellMrs.Susannah,BankofEngd
TyrrellTim.Clerk to Upholders'Co
Tyte Alfred J. Custom House
Underwood Ths. Cstms.(Preston)
Unwin Charles, India Board
Unwin John Wm. Sewers' Office
Unwin Joseph, Sewers' Office
Unwin Rd.Admiralty, Smst. House
Unwin Wm. Colonial Office
UptonRt.B.Ck. to Apothecaries'Co
Ure David James, Custom House
Ure Fras. M. Custom House
Ure James, Customs (Leith)
UsherThs.Consul atPort-au-Prince
Uwins Zechariah, Bank of England
Uxbridge, Earl of, Privy Councilr
Vale John, Board of Ordnance
Valpy A. J. Commnsn. Ltncy.Lndn
Valpy Rd. Com. of P. C. for Trade
Vandergucht Benj. Genl.PostOffice
Vanderkiste F.W.Cstms (Glasgow)
Vanderpant John,Bank of England
Vane Frederick, House of Lords
Vane George, Custom House
Vardon Thos. Library,Ho. of Cmns
VaughanSir Chas R.Privy Counclr
VaughanHenry,Court of Chancery
Vaughan John, Bank of England
Vaughan John Stephen, Na.DebtOf
Vaughan Richard B. Audit Office
Vaughan Samuel, Custom House

Vaughan Thos.W.Westmn. Session
Vaus Thomas, General Post Office
Vautin James, Bank of England
VauxWm.Sandys, British Museum
Veal J. Clk. of Records & Writs
Veal Wm. P.Paymaster Gen. Office
Veary Richard, Custom House
Vedova G. D. Consul at Scio
Venfield John, Foreign Office
Vere Hobart, Board of Trade
Vereker J. Customs (Limerick)
VernonGanvilleE.H.Wds.&For.Off
Vesey E. Paymaster Gen.'s Office
VickeraThos.E.Lon.Dis.or Tpy.Pst
Vigne Henry, South Sea Company
VilliersHon.C. P.Exn.'s Offi.Chanc
Vincent Francis, Woods & Forests
Vincent Hen.Wm. Rgstry.of Deeds
VincentHen. W.Qun.'sRemmbrncr
Vincent Wm. Board of Ordnance
Vine Charles, Audit Office
Vine Norris, Worship st. Police Ct
Viner John Tickell, South Sea Ho
Vines William, Clerk to Brewers'
& Leathersellers' Companies
Violet William, Custom House
Virgo John, Sewers' Office
Vivian Geo. Commissr.of Fine Arts
Vizard Wm. jun. Ct. of Bankrupcy
Vodoz Mrs. Chrlt.Com. for Trade
Vosper Lt. Wm. Greenwh. Hosptl
Voules G. A. Genl. Register Office
VoulesHerbert P.Pentonville Prisn
Voyce John, Excise Office
WaddTs.M.Surgeon,Boro'Compter
Waddell G. Cstms. (Grangemouth)
Waddell HenryWm.CustomHouse
WaddiloveWm.A.Admlty.Smst.Ho
Waddington G. Clrkenwl.Police Ct
Wade Col. F. T. Poor Law Office
Waghorn James, East India House
Waight James, Custom House
Wainewright John, Taxing Master
Wainwright Thos. E. Custom Hse
Waite Rev. T. Giltspur st. Compter
WakeChas.D.Consul at Charleston
Wake William, Stationery Office
Wakefield Hen. House of Correctn
WakelinJames, Stamp&Tax Office
WakelingGeorge,Seaman'sReg.Off
Wakley Thos. Coroner for Middx
WalcotThos.King, Admlty.Smst.H
Walcott Stephen,Coln.Emigratn.B
Walford John Allbut,Gen.Post Off
Walford Joseph G. Solr.to Customs
Walker Daniel, Home Office
WalkerEdmund, Mastr.of Exchegr
Walker Fred. Paymstr. Gen.'s Off
Waker Hen. A. Woods & ForestOf
Walker Hen.W.R.Admlty. Smst.H
Walker Isaac, Customs (Lyme)
Walker James, Ct. of Chancery
Walker Michael, Admlty. Whitehl
WalkerPat.Consul,MusquitoShore
Walker Richd. General Post Office
Walker Rd. P. Stamp & Tax Office
Walker Rt.Oneby, Chncy.Rgstr.Off
WalkerWm.Clk.to Basket Makrs.C
Walker William, Excise Office
Walker Wm. Queen's Bench Office
Walker William, War Office
Walkinshaw Jas. Comn.Ltncy.Lon
Wallace Fras. Customs (Irvine)
Wallace Jas. Customs (Waterford)
Wallace William, Excise Office
Waller Alfred, Treasury
Waller Arthr. Greenwich Hospital
WallerJohn,Woods&Forests Office
Waller John Frost, Woods & Frsts
WallerThos.W.Sec.of Leg.Brussels
Walliker Samuel, Genrl.PostOffice
Wallis Fred. John, Custom House
WalmisleyChas. Thos. PoorLawOff
Walmisley Henry, House of Lords
Walmisley J.A.Court of Exchequer
Walmisley Rt. Court of Exchequer
Walmisley Wm.Elyard,Hse.of Lds
Walne Alfred S. Consul at Cairo
Walpole Chas. Stamp & Tax Office
Walpole Francis, Home Office
Walpole John, Colnl.Emigratn.Bd
Walpole John Fred. Excise Office
Walpole Lt. Col. Consul(Santiago)
WalshSir Jn.B.bt.Ld.Lt.of Radnor
Walsh Fred. Thos. Custom House
Walsh James, Custom House
Walsh Jas. Tower Liberty Sessions
Walsh Thomas, Excise Office
Walsh Thomas George, CustomHo
Walsham Sir John Jas.Poor LawOf

Walshe Edw. Fred. Gen. PostOffice
Walter Edward, Custom House
Walter John, Stamp & Tax Office
Walters Wm. Stationery Office
Walton John, General Post Office
Walton Wm. Clerk to Girdlers' Co
Walton Wm. General Post Office
Walton Wm.Steward of Tower Lib
WaltonW.F.J.Ecclesias.Comrs.Off
Walton Wm.H.Master of the Exch
Wand Jas.Towr.Hamlets Ct.of Req
Warburton Arthur, Stamp&Tax Of
Warburton Hen.Exchqr.Bl.LoanO
Warburton Peter, Custom House
Ward Chas.ChanceryReport Office
Ward John, Consul at Dresden
Ward John, Consul at Saxony
Ward John Francis, War Office
Ward Rd.C.Masters' Off. Chancery
WardRt. Marshal's, &c.Q.B. Office
Ward Seth Chas. Clerk of Records
Ward Seth M. Court of Chancery
WardThs.P.Cm.of Py.Cncl.for Tra
Ward Thos. Lawrence, Foreign Of
Ward Wm. Commissn.Ltncy.Lndn
Ward Wm. Exhcq. Bill Loan Office
Ward William, Royal Mint
Ward Wm. Joseph, Genl. Post Off
WandenF.Commsn. Ltncy.London
Warden Fras. East India Co
WardleyWm. Excise (Shrewsbury)
Ware Thos. Sup.Rgr. (Shoreditch)
Waring F. Customs (Guernsey)
Waring F.Cons. at Norfolk(U.S.A)
Waring Jaspar, Consul at Alicante
Waring John Edwd. Foreign Office
Warman Chas. House of Commons
Warner George, War Office
Warre Alex. Admrlty. Smst. Hou
Warre Thos. Cmmsn. Ltncy. Lndn
WarrenA. Solcr.toBritish Museum
WarrenEdw. Chas.Admlty. SmstH
Warren James, Audit Office
Warren Jas. Insolvent Drs.' Court
Warren John, General Post Office
Warren John Willing, South SeaH
Warren Joseph, Custom House
WarrenderSirGeo.PrivyCouncillor
Warrington H.G. Consul at Tripoli
Warwick Earl, Ld. Lt. Warwicksh
Waterfield Thos. Nelson, IndiaBrd
WaterhouseGeorgeR.Brit.Museum
WaterhouseWm. Audit Office
Waterman Ths. Admlty. Smst. Ho
Waters Edward, Custms. (Carlisle)
WatersFrancis, Ct. of Exchequer
WatersJas.Custms.(DouglasI.Man)
Waters Thos.Jno.Queen's BenchOf
WatersWm. CourtofQueen'sBench
WatersWilliam,General PostOffice
WatkinsChs. Queen'sRememb'.Off
Watkins John C. Custom House
Watson Mrs. Ann, Foreign Office
Watson Abrah. General Post Office
Watson David, War Office
Watson D. H. Custom House
Watson Edward, Custom House
Watson Francis Paget, Custom Ho
Watson George, GeneralPostOffice
Watson James, Custom House
WatsonJs.Lawson, Stamp&TaxOff
Watson John, Bank of England
Watson Joseph, City Officer
Watson Rv.R. Bishop of Lndn's Ct
WatsonRobt. Digby, CustomHouse
Watson Thomas, Custom House
WatsonThos.M.GeneralPost Office
Watson Wm. Stamp & Tax Office
Watt Alexander, Genl. Post Office
WattRobt. Duchy of Cornwall's Off
Watts Alaric A. Stamp & Tax Off
Watts Arthur Leigh, Custom Hou
WattsEdward,Consul, Pernambuco
WattsEdwin B. Ct. of Bankruptcy
Watts Fras. London Gazette Office
Watts Henry, Col. of Advocates
Watts Thomas, British Museum
Waud Christopher, East India Ho
Waugh Thomas, Bd. of Ordnance
Weale Robt. Poor Law Assist.Coms
Weale Thos. Judge Advct. Gen.Off
Wear Geo. Ecclesiastical Com. Off
Wearne Thos.M. Customs (Exeter)
WeatherleyChas.Hen.Gen.PostOff
Weaver Henry, Genl. Post Office
Weaver Robert, Stamp & Tax Off
Weaver Wm. H. Pentonvll. Prison
WebbErnestF.Ecclesiasticl.Com.O
WebbJohn, Lndn.Dist.or T. Py.Pst
Webb Sml. Com.of P. C. for Trade

Webb Stephen Fredk. Custom Hou
Webb Thomas, General Post Offi
Webb William, Custom House
Webber Henry, Sewers Office
Weblin Jas. Woods& Forests Office
Webster Edwin, Irish Office
Webster Joseph, General Post Off
Webster Philip, General Post Off
Webster Philip, Westmr. Police Ct
Webster Lt. Richard, Home Off
WeddellWm.H. Admlty.Somst.Ho
Wedderburn Alexr. Gen. Post Off
Wedderburn Wm.Ths.Gen.PostOff
Wedgwood H. Metro. Public Carriage Office
Weedon Geo. S. General Post Off
Weguelin Thos. M. Bk.of England
Weguelin Thos. Matts. Russia Co
Weigall Thos. Admlty. Somst. Ho
Weir John, Stamp & Tax Office
Weir J. J. Custom House
Welbank Robt. Board of Ordnance
Welch Edward, Exchequer Office
Welch Francis, General Post Offce
Welch Robert, Customs (Stockton)
Welch Robert, Customs (Harwich)
Welchman Simeon, Excise Office
Welford Jonathan Cope, Cstm. Ho
Wellbank Capt. Robt. Trinity Ho
Weller Capt. Charles, Trinity Ho
Weller Wm. Court of Exchequer
WellerW.Winton,Admlty.SmstHo
Wellesley Hon. H. R. C. Secretary of Embassy at Constantinople
Wellesley Richard, Foreign Office
Wellington, Duke of, K.G. P.C. Lord Lieut. of Hampshire,Govr. of Tower, &c. &c. &c
Wells G.sen. Admiralty, Somst. Ho
Wells G. jun. Admiralty, Smst. Ho
Wells Jas. Marylebone Police Ct
Wells Samuel, Audit Office
Welsh Edwin, Bank of England
Welshman, Mrs. I.Adjt. Gen.'s Offi
Welsman Sam.Adjutant Gen.'s Off
Welstead Augustus, CustomHouse
WelsteadG.R. Paymaster Gen.'sOff
Welton Benjamin, City Bridewell
Wenlock Lord, Lord Lieutenant of York, (East Riding)
Werry Nathl. W.Consul at Beyrout
Wesselhoeft C. Consul at Hambro'
WestAlfred C.L. Seaman's Reg. Off
WestCharles Loft, Stamp &Tax Off
WestGeo.Rep.&Ent. Off.Ct.Chncry
WestHenry,Lndn.Dist.orTpy.Post
West John, General Post Office
West Martin J. Comm. of Bnkptcy
West Richard, Court of Exchequer
Westall Edward, Addiscombe Sem
Westall Richard, Custom House
WestcottW.Lndn.Dist. or T.Py.Pst
Western Chas. General Post Office
WestleyJohn,Lndn.Dst.orT.Py.Pst
WestleyJohn,Com.ofP.C.for Trade
Westley W. Piercy, Custom House
WestmacottChas.Wm.Gen.PostOff
Westmacott Geo. Stamp & Tax Off
WestminsterMarqs.of,Ld.Lt.Chesh
Westmoreland E.of.Ambass.Berlin
Weston Roper W. Customs (Weymouth)
Weston Wm Roper,Custom House
Weynton Capt.Alex. TrinityHouse
WhalleyHenry,PaymasterGen.'sOf
Wharncliffe Lord, West Riding of York
WheatleySir Hen. Duchy Cornwall
WheatleyJsph.W.General Post Offi
WheelerJohn Edw.Paymstr.Gen.O
Wheeler Mrs. Mary, War Office
Wheeler John T. Parish Clerks' Co
WheelerWm. Customs (Aberistwh)
Whicher Wm. Gen. Post Office
Whiffen T. Admiralty, Somst. Ho
Whiffen Hen.Wm. OrdnanceBoard
WhiffenJohn, Admiralty, Somst.H
Whitaker Robert, Custom House
Whitchurch Robert, Custom Ho
Whitcombe George, Gen. Post Off
White Adam, British Museum
White Augustus, Custom House
White Charles, Custom House
White Chas. V. Insolvent Court
WhiteEdward,Duchyof Cornwl.Off
White Edw.L.Commr.inChief's Off
White Edw. M.Woods &ForestsOff
White George, War Office
WhiteGeo.Edw.Slave Compens.Off
WhiteGeo.Walpole,Et.IndiaHouse
White G. W. Poor Law Office
White Henry, General Post Off
White Henry Agar, Trinity House
White John. Stamp & Tax Office
WhiteJ.W.Report Office,Chancery
White Rd. Court of Queen's Bench
White Rd. General Post Office
White Rd. Customs (Barnstaple)
White Robt. Customs (Drogheda)
White Wm. Fredk. House of Lords
White Wm. Henry, War Office
WhiteheadJohn,Consul, Archangel
WhiteheadWm.H.Ct.of Bankrptcy
Whiteman JohnC.East IndiaHouse
Whitestone Robert, Audit Office
Whitford Parry, National Debt Off
WhitfordThomas, Bank of England
WhithairJ.R.Gov.Giltspur'st.Cmpt
WhitingChas.John,Gen.PostOffice
Whiting George, Audit Office
WhitingGeo.Master's Off.Chancery
Whiting William,General Post Off
WhitmanJames,Woods&ForestsOf
Whitmore Chas.Horatio, CustomH
Whitmore Geo.SouthSeaCompany
Whitmore George, Lloyd's
Whitmore Jas.Campigne.Custm. H
WhitmoreJohn,Comndr.inChfs.Off
Whitmore Richard, Custom House
WhitmoreThos.Greenslade,Custms
Whitmore Wm.Courtof Bankrptcy
WhitmoreWm.W.Pub.Wks.Ln.Off
WhitnallWm.B.Paymstr.Gen.'sOff
Whittam Geo.Electn.Offi. Ho.Com
Whittard Charles, General Post Off
Whittington Wm. Stationery Off
WickhamHen.Lewis,Stmp.&Tx.O
Wickins Saml. Board of Ordnance
Wickins S. jun, Board of Ordnance
Wickins Thos. Englesby, Treasury
Wickwar JamesJ. StationeryOffice
Wightman SirWm.Just. of Qn'sBh
Wigram Rt. Hon.Sir Jas.Vice.Chan
Wigram L.T.Q.C. East IndiaHouse
WigramWm.DirectorEastIndiaCo
Wilbraham Col. the Hn.E.B.Col.Of
Wilbraham Roger Wm. Treasury
Wilcox George, Customs (Belfast)
WilcoxJohn,Paymstr.Gen's Office
Wilcox Wm. Cstms. (Bridgewater)
Wild John, Custom House
Wild John, Excise Office
Wild John, General Post Office
WildeEdw.A. Incpted.Law Society
WildmanThos.Coote, CustomHous
Wildsmith Jsp. Court of Chancery
Wilkin John, Ct.of Queen's Bench
Wilkins John, ViceConsulatOdessa
WilkinsonEdw.Close,Bk.of Englnd
Wilkinson George, Poor Law Office
WilkinsonHarryBrown,Gen.Pst.Of
Wilkinson John, Audit Office
Wilkinson John Jas.House of Coms
Wilkinson Rd. Consul at Syra
Wilkinson Rt. Board of Ordnance
WilkinsonT. Admrlty. Somt.House
Wilkinson Thos.S. Ct.of Admiralty
WilksEdw.D.Marlboro'st.PoliceCt
Wilks Joseph B. East India House
Willdey John, General Post Office
Willey Thomas, Custom House
WilliamesPriceBuckley, India Brd
Williams Arth. Jas.Gen.Post Office
Williams Capt. Inspectr. of Prisons
Williams Charles, Custom House
Williams Charles, Custom House
Williams Chas. Seaman's Reg. Off
Williams Chas. C. Genl.Post Office
Williams David, Genl. Post Office
Williams David,Ctms.(Carnarvon)
WilliamsComnd.Edw.Grnwh.Hspl
WilliamsF.Doorkpr. toHouseCmns
Williams H. Lord Lieut. Brecon
Williams John, Bank of England
WilliamsJohn,Genl. RegisterOffice
Williams John, Excise Office
Williams John,Lloyds' Custom Ho
WilliamsRev.J.HouseofCorrection
Williams Sir John, Justice Qns.Bn
Williams Joseph, General Post Off
WilliamsMontgomery W.Gn.Pst.O
Williams Rhys, General PostOffice
Williams RichardJ. Custom House
WilliamsRobt.Comn.Ltncy.Londn
Williams Thos. Greenwh. Hospital
Williams William, Trinity House
Williams Wm. J. Customs (Dover)
WilliamsW.J. Paymaster Gen.'sOff
Williamson D. Super. of Police (T)
WilliamsonEdwd.A.Smn's.Reg.Off
Williamson Jas. Excise Office
Williamson T. Excise (Halifax)
Willimott John Sennitt, Cstm. Ho
Willimott Wm. jun. Custom Ho
Willingale Rt. Cstms. (Gainsbro')
Willis Arthur, Lloyd's
WillisWm.Admiralty,Somerset Ho
WillisWm. Greenwh. Hosp.School
Willis Wm. Stamp & Tax Office
Willisford John, Chelsea Hospital
WillockSir H.Dir.of East India Co
Willoughby D'Eresby Lord, Ld.Lt. Carnarvon, & Com. of Fine Arts
WilmotChester E.Stamp&Tax Offi
Willshire Wm.Cons. at Adrianople
Wilson Alf. Commsn. Ltncy. Lndn
WilsonBelfordH.Consl.at Caraccas
Wilson Charles G. Custom House
Wilson C.L. Commsn. Ltncy. Lndn
Wilson Edw.Commsn.Ltncy.Lndn
Wilson Fletcher. Eastland Compy
Wilson Francis, Bk. of England
Wilson Sir Giffin, Master Chancery
Wilson George, General Post Offi
Wilson Hen.Lndn.Dist.or Tpy. Pst
Wilson Horace Hayman, Addiscombe Seminary & Hayleybury College
Wilson Hugh, Consul Arica,(Peru)
Wilson H.C.Sup.Reg.(Marylebone)
Wilson Major J. Royal Marine Off
Wilson John, Admiralty,Somst.Ho
Wilson John, Customs (Arundel)
Wilson Rd.Lndn.Dist.or Tpy.Post
Wilson Sir JohnM. Chelsea Hosptl
WilsonJosiah,Comn. Ltncy.Londn
Wilson Mrs. Mary, Royal Mint
Wilson M. Commsn. Ltncy.Londn
Wilson Rd. L. Comsn. Ltncy.Lndn
Wilson Saml. Alderman of London
Wilson Thos. Custms. (Chichester)
Wilson Thos. Hen. Gen. Post Office
Wilson Wm. Westminster Court
Wilton, Earl of, Privy Councillor
Wimbridge J.Army Medicl. Bd. Off
Winch Wm. Stamp & Tax Office
Winchester,Marqs.of, Pvy.Counclr
Windsor Chas. Gen. Post Office
Windsor Hen. Marston, Treasury
Wing Joseph, Stamp & Tax Office
Wingfield John, Trinity House
Wingfield Nicholas, Custom House
Wingfield Nicholas, Trinity House
Wingfield Wm. Master in Chncry
Wingrave Geo. Excise (Tring)
Wingrave JohnHanmer,Excise Of
Wingrave Joseph, Excise Office
Winkley William, Treasury
WinkworthE. Cstms.(Portsmouth)
Winn James, Bank of England
Winniett Joseph, Bd. of Ordnance
Winning Jas. Crown Off. Queen's Bench
Windser Chas. Stamp & Tax Offi
Windslow Edward, Master in Lunacy & Visitor of Lunatics
Winstanley William, Audit Office
WinterHy. Solc.toExchr.BillLn.Of
Wintour Thos.F.Stamp&TaxOffice
WireDavid Wm.Und. SheriffofLdn
Wise Thos.Brice C.Gen.Post Office
WittEdwd.Admiralty,SomersetHo
Wodehouse Herb.Ct.of Com.Pleas
Wodehouse Ld. Ld. Lieut. Norfolk
WodsworthWm.Dudley,Pr.Lw.Off
Wogdon J. Custom House
Wolley Hen. Admiralty, Whitehall
Wolley Thos. Admiralty, Whitehll
Wood Chas.A.Col.Land &Emig.Bd
Wood Chas. Wm. Gen. Post Offi
WoodEdward J.Seaman's Reg.Offi
Wood George Excise (Hull)
Wood GeorgeW.Ecclestcl.Com.Off
WoodHugh, Chancy. Register Offi
Wood John, Excise Office
Wood Genl. John S.Tower London
Wood Joseph, Board of Ordnance
Wood Matthew, Gen. Post Office
Wood Richard, Audit Office
WoodRichard,Consul at Damascus
WoodSamuelJas. Exchequer Office
WoodThomas, AldermanofLondon
Wood Thomas, City Police Office
Wood Thomas, Consul at Bengazi
WoodWm.John,Stamp&TaxOffice
WoodfallGeo. Commsn. Ltncy.Ldn
Woodfall HernonThos.Exchеqr.Off
WoodfordSirAlex.Bd.ofGen.Offcr
WoodgateFrancis, Bd. of Ordnanc
Woodgate Francis Jn.OrdnanceBd
Woodgate Septimus; Duchy Crnwl
Woodgear Henry, Custom House
Woodger Wm.Stamp & Tax Office
Woodham Wm.Stamp&Tax Office
WoodhouseJn.Lon.Dist.orTpy.Pst
Woodhouse John Lennox, Exchq. Bill Offi. for W. I. Island Relief
Woodifield Rt.Denby,Cstm. House
WoodlandRichard,Stamp&TaxOff
Woodrooffe Wm. Assocte.Cmn.Pls
WoodruffThos.Stamp & Tax Office
Woods AlbertWm.Heralds'College
Woods Chas. J. Coroner of Surrey
Woods Peter, Custom House
Woods Peter Longford,Custom Ho
Woodthorpe Edmund, City Officer
Woodward Hy.Wm.Stamp&TaxOf
Woodward Wm.Jas.Stamp&TaxOf
WooldridgeChas.Bshp.Wnchstr.Of
Woollett Hen.Chas.Reg.of Designs
Woolley Thos. S. Tithe Commissnr
Woolsey O'Brien, Admty.Smst.Ho
Woolsey O'B.jun. Admty.Smst.Ho
Woolsey Thos. F. Admty. Smst.Ho
Woolsey Wm. Admty. Smst. Ho
Worcester Marq.of,Com.inChf.'sO
Worley Danl. Adjutant Gen.'s Offi
Worsfold William, Treasury
Worth Geo. Admiralty, Whitehall
Worth William, Custom House
Worthington Thos. Cstms.(Dublin)
Wrankmore Chas. Glyde, Cstm.Ho
Wrather William, Sewers' Office
Wray John, Metropln.PoliceOffice
Wreford C. Customs (Fowey)
Wrenford Wm. Excise Office
Wright — Mastrs. Office, Chancery
Wright Chas. Clerkenwell Sessions
Wright Chas. Sewers' Office
Wright Chas. J. Audit Office
Wright Fredk. Court of Chancery
Wright GeorgeWm.Custom House
Wright Henry, Court of Chancery
Wright Jas. Middx. Ct.of Requests
Wright Jas. Figg, Greenwh. Hsptl
Wright John, Bankruptcy Court
Wright John, Custom House
Wright Joseph, Gen. Post Office
Wright M. Consul at Wiborg
Wright Robert, Trinity House
Wright Stepn. A. Bd. of Ordnance
Wright Steph.P.Hen.Ordnance Bd
Wright Thos. Excise (Worcester)
Wright Thos. Gen. Post Office
Wright Lt. T. D. Home Office
Wright Thos.John,Customs (Hull)
Wright V. C. Metropls. Roads Off
Wright Wm. Thos. Paymstr.Gen's
Wrigley Alfred, Addiscombe Sem
Wybrow Sydney Hampden, G.P.O
Wybrow William, Custom House
Wybrow William, Excise Office
WykeChs.L.Cnsl.atPort-au-Prince
Wyld Thos. J. Court of Exchequer
Wylde William, Foreign Office
Wyndowne OliverT.Genl.PostOffic
Wynn Chas. W. W. Privy Cncilor
Wynn Geo. Huxham, Gen. P. O
Wynn Sir N. W. Amb. to Denmark
Wynn Hen. W. Privy Councillor
Wynn Huskisson C.General PostO
Wynne Geo. Paymstr. Gen.'s Off
Wynne Owen, Customs (Sligo)
Wynyard G. B. C. Consul at Riga
Wyon Leonard, Royal Mint
Wyon William, R.A. Royal Mint
Wyse Thos.Commissnr.of FineArts
Ximenes Sir David, Bd. Gen.Offcrs
Yardley Chas. Metropltn.Police Of
Yeames James, Consul at Odessa
Yeames W. Consul at Taganrog
Yeld Wm. Walter, Gen. Post Office
Yeomans Rd. Excise (Stourbridge)
Yeowell William, Custom House
York Archbishop of, Privy Councilr
Young SirChas.G.Heralds' College
Young Sir Wm.bart. East India Co
YoungGeo.Fred.Com.ofCoalWhips
Young George F. Lloyds
Young James, Stamp & Tax Office
Young John,Clk.toShipwrights'Co
Young Thomas,General Post Office
Young Thomas, Treasury
Younghusband John, Custom Ho
Zetland Earl of,Ld.Lt.York(N.Rd)
Zwinger Js. Crown Off. Ct. Chancy

LORDS-LIEUTENANT OF ENGLAND AND WALES.

England.

Bedford, Earl de Gray, K.G., K.P., P.C
Berks, Earl of Abingdon
Bucks, Lord Carington
Cambridge, Earl of Hardwicke
Chester, Marquis of Westminster
Cornwall, Sir William Trewlawney
Cumberland, Earl of Lonsdale, P.C
Derby, Duke of Devonshire, K.G
Devon, Earl of Fortescue, P.C
Dorset, Earl Digby
Durham, Marquis of Londonderry, G.C.B., G.C.H., P.C
Essex, Viscount Maynard
Gloucester, Earl Fitzhardinge
Hereford, Earl Somers
Hertford,
Huntingdon, Earl of Sandwich
Kent, Earl Thanet
Lancashire, Earl of Derby, K.G., P.C
Leicester, Duke of Rutland, K.G
Lincoln, Earl Brownlow
Middlesex, Marq. of Salisbury, K.G., P.C
Monmouth, C. H. Leigh, esq
Norfolk, Lord Wodehouse [P.C
Northampton, Marquis of Exeter, K.G.,
Northumberland, Duke of Northumberland, P.C
Nottingham, Earl of Scarborough, K.G
Oxford, Duke of Marlborough
Rutland, Marquis of Exeter, K.G., P.C
Shropshire, Lord Hill
Somerset, Lord Portman
Southampton, Duke of Wellington, K.G
Stafford, Earl Talbot, K.G., P.C
Suffolk, Earl of Stradbroke
Surrey, Earl of Lovelace
Sussex, Duke of Richmond, K.G., P.C
Warwick, Earl Brooke and of Warwick
Westmoreland, Earl of Lonsdale, P.C
Wilts, Marquis of Lansdowne, K.G., P.C
Worcester, Lord Lyttleton
York, East Riding, Lord Wenlock
— *North Riding*, Earl of Zetland
— *West Riding*, Lord Wharncliffe, P.C

Wales.

Anglesey, Marquis of Anglesey, K.G., P.C
Brecon, H. Williams, esq
Cardigan, Col. Wm. Edwd. Powell, M.P., G.C.B
Carmarthen, Lord Dynevor [P.C
Carnarvon, Lord Willoughby d'Eresby,
Denbigh, Middleton Biddulph, esq
Flint, Sir Stephen Richard Glynne, bart
Glamorgan, Marquis of Bute
Merioneth, Edward Lloyd Mostyn, eqs
Montgomery, Earl of Powis
Pembroke, Sir John Owen, bart. M.P
Radnor, Sir John Benn Walsh, bart

GOVERNMENT AND OTHER PUBLIC OFFICES.

ALPHABETICALLY ARRANGED.

ADJUTANT GENERAL'S OFFICE.

Horse Guards. Hours, 11 to 5.

ADJUTANT GENERAL, Lieut. Gen. Sir John Macdonald, K.C.B
Deputy Adjutant General, Major Gen. George Brown, K.H
Assistant Adjutant General, Colonel William Cochrane
Deputy Assistant Adjutant General, Major Roche Meade
First Clerk, Richard Cannon, esq
Confidential Clerk, Edward Griffiths Syms, esq
Senior Clerks, Charles Jopling, Henry William Green, John Slatford, esqrs [Howes
Clerks, Edward Houndle, Daniel Worley, George Fuller
Junior Clerks, Thomas Carter, William Cannon Randall, Christopher Stevans, Henry Laidman, & Henry Howes
Messengers, Samuel Welshman, John Arms, Peter Ridley
Officekeeper, Mrs. Sarah Howes

Recruiting Department, 17 *Duke street, Westminster.* Hours, 11 to 5.

Inspecting Field Officer & Superintendent, Colonel George Dean Pitt, K.H
Chief Clerk, William Joseph Bruce, esq
Senior Clerk, Charles Bruce, esq
Juniors, Conran Alphonso Kirk, Alfred Thomas Jay, John Andrews Girling, Thomas Banks Strong, esqrs
Messenger, John Bowles
Housekeeper, Mrs. Isabella Welshman

ADMIRALTY.

Civil Department, *Somerset House.*

Hours, 10 to 4.

SURVEYOR OF THE NAVY, Captain Sir William Symonds, R.N., F.R.S
Chief Assistant & Draftsman, John Edye, esq
Clerk, first class, George Patey Parkin, esq
Clerk, second class, Charles Edward Lang, esq
Clerks, third class, Walter Dicken Eden, Samuel Augustus Hayes, Stuart Brodie, esqrs
1st Class Draughtsman, John Wilson, *2nd Class Draughtsman*, Thomas Waterman, *3rd Class Draughtsmen*, James Graff & William Thomas Hinde
Superintendent of Nautical Almanac, Lieut. William Samuel Stratford, F.R.S [Briggs, esq
ACCOUNTANT GENERAL OF THE NAVY, John Thomas
Deputy Accountant General of the Navy, O'Brien Bellingham Woolsey, esq
First class Clerk, John Martlet Boddy, esq

Ledger and Bill Branch.

Clerk, first class, James Beeby, esq
Clerks, second class, Joseph Hefford Rawnsley, Richard Madox Bromley, & Henry William Routledge Walker, esqrs
Clerks, third class, Richard Ross Randall, Henry Butler, Thomas Cairns Kerr Gloag, Richard Piper Chaplin, David Aitken, James Anderson, James Reddie, Joseph Nash, John Cooke, & George Hilditch Johnson, esqrs

Invoice and Claim Branch.

Clerk, first class, Richard Unwin, esq
Clerks, second class, John Biggar, John Tomkins, John Whiffin, & Antonio Brady, esqrs
Clerks, third class, Francis Coleman Harris, Joseph Fielder Goodwin, Matthew Bentley, John Gilbert, O'Brien Woolsey, jun. Edward Holman Hay, & William Kenrick, esqrs

Imprest Branch.

Clerk, first class, Thomas Collings, esq
Clerks, second class, Francis Mitchell Goodliff, Charles Blachford Rule, Thomas Jayne, John Scott, David Appleton, George Wells, sen. & Charles Turner, esqrs
Clerks, third class, John Hulme Spurrell, Thomas Wilkinson, George Spurrell, Peter William Griffiths, Joseph King, Charles Frederick Field, Louis Horace Noel, William Woolsey, William Henry Douglas, Michael Connal, Samuel H. Riley, George J. T. Merry, esqrs

Wages Branch.

Clerks, first class, Thos. King Walcot, Benjmn. Moore, esqrs
Clerks, second class, John Millman, George Jackson, Henry Smith, Thomas Jones, George Wright Hebden, Oliver Henry Davis, John Pinhorn, Henry Warren Strutt, George Stilwell, Charles Spence, (*actg.*) Robert Atkinson, (*actg.*) & James Bowden, (*actg.*) esqrs
Clerks, third class, James How Mardon, Charles Carter, George William Daysh, John Martin, Joseph Saul, Edward Cahill, Robert Thompson, William Henry Hookey, Gibbs Crawfurd Harrison, Malcolm Goldsmith, Henry Dawes Boddy, Peter Robertson, William Robertson, Thomas Floyer Erskine, William Galliers Galbraith, George Renwick, Alexander Scott, Thomas Pitcairn, Samuel Warren Burton, John Gandy, Arthur Houghton, Henry Nosworthy, Thomas Lomas, & William H. Weddell, esqrs

Naval Prize and Wills Branch.

Clerk, first class, Edward Gandy, esq
Clerks, second class, Thomas Culliford Barrow, Andrew Basilico, Robert Hardy, esqrs
Clerks, third class, James Irwin, Frederick Maddison, William Stevens, John Matson, William Spencer, Edward Witt, James C. Haliburton, Edward Cahill, jun. & William Goldie, esqrs
STOREKEEPER GENERAL OF THE NAVY, the Hon. Robert Dundas
Clerk, first class, James Richard Clark, esq
Clerks, second class, John Robertson, James Home Renton, Edward Clark, Thomas Whiffen & John Crosby, esqrs
Clerks, third class, Edmund Isham Brietzcke, Edward Charles Warren, James Bowen Kingdom, William Gibb, Joseph Spittal, John Easthope, George Wells, jun. Thomas Frederick Woolsey, Robert Dundas Brown & Robert Richards, esqrs

Contract Office.

Chief Clerk and Registrar of Public Securities, John James, esq
Clerk, second class, John Doutty, esq
Clerks, third class, Augustus Frederick Douglas Browne, Adam Steuart Stuart & Harry Lupton, esqrs

Victualling & Transport Services.

COMPTROLLER, James Meek, esq
Chief Clerk, William Leybourn, esq

Supply Branch.

Clerk, first class, Denham Berry, esq
Clerks, second class, James Stilwell & Charles Champ, esqrs
Clerks, third class, Peter Loudon, William Edward Jenkins & Samuel S. Lewes, esqrs

Pursery Account Branch.

Clerk, first class, Edward Perigal, esq
Clerks, second class, John Ivison Burmester, Thomas Canney & William Thomas Snosswell, esqrs
Clerks, third class, Charles Tibson, Frederick Perigal, Alexander Warre, William Lanphier Anderson, William Willis, Anthony Pike, George Maitland Innes, Matthew Gotham Jefferson, William Alfred Waddilove & Richard Friend, esqrs

Store Account Branch.

Clerk, first class, Evan Edward Rowsell, esq
Clerks, second class, Joseph Lowthian, Beamont Atkinson & William Winton Weller, esqrs
Clerks, third class, James Francis Stephens, Nicholas Lockyer Seppings, William Alexander Brown, Henry James Hind, Alfred Thomas Sayer Lewes & William Bartlett, esqs

Transport Branch.

Clerks, second class, David Scott Smith & Thomas Weigall, esqrs
Clerks, third class, Frederic Williams Benge & John Webber Harris, esqrs
The office formerly called Physician General of the Navy is now entitled

Director General of Naval Hospitals & Fleets.

Sir William Burnett, knt. M.D., K.C.H.
Clerk, first class, Benjamin Fossett, esq
Clerks, second class, Benjamin Paul Hobart, William Fossett & William Crandell, esqrs
Clerks, third class, Archibald Maclaurin, John Hay Elliott, William King Fossett, George Mackeson, George Crandell & William J. H. Bunnett, esqrs

Director of Architectural & Engineering Works.

Captain Henry Brandreth, R.E., F.R.S.
Draughtsmen, William Scamp & James Trotter
Head Messengers, George Lilburn & Isaac Brookman
Porter, Thomas Thurgood
Housekeepers, Miss Magdalen Malcolm Graham & Mrs. Sarah Lewin Skyring

Commissioners for the Property and Income Tax for the Naval Department.

John Thomas Briggs, esq.; Hon. Robert Dundas; James Meek, esq.; Sir William Burnett, knt. M.D., K.C.H.; Henry Frederick Amedroz, esq
Assessor for the Naval Department, O'Brien Bellingham Woolsey, esq
Clerk to the Commissioners for the Naval Department, Richard Madox Bromley, esq

ADMIRALTY.

Naval Department.—*Whitehall.*—Hours, 10 to 5.
Lords Commissioners,

Chief Secretaries,

Chief Clerk, Henry Frederick Amedroz, sen. esq
Clerks, first class, John William Innes, John Holman Hay, William John Mountain, Thomas Crofton Croker, John Jones Dyer, George Worth & John Barrow, esqrs
Clerks, second class, Charles Henry Pennell, Robert Speke, Evans, John Henry Briggs, John Heneage Jesse, Alexander Middleton, John Horatio Nelson Houghton, Henry Wolley, Waller Clifton, Thomas Wolley, Edward Giffard, Maurice Midlane & John Jackson, esqrs
Clerks, third class, Henry Frederick Amedroz, jun. William Frederick Evans, Henry William Baylee, Richard Wynne Hamilton, Thomas James, John Holman Hay, jun. Barrington Piers, Charles William O'Reilly, John Sheridan, William Alexander Innes, Robert Bell, Charles Proby, Thomas George Grant, Francis Graves, John Perrier, Frederick Locker, Robert Jones, & William Shakespere Gilly, esqrs
Translator of Foreign Papers, Henry Frederick Amedroz, jun. esq
Counsel, Henry John Shepherd, esq. Q.C.
Solicitor, William Frogat Robson, esq
Hydrographer, Capt. Francis Beaufort, R.N., F.R.S., &c
Assistant, Michael Walker
Comptroller of Packet Service, Sir William Edward Parry, knt. Capt. R.N., LL.D., F.R.S.
Officer in charge of Semaphore, Com. Charles Hawse Jay
Printer, Henry Loxdale
Head Messenger, George Philip Laplume
Assistant Messengers, John Christie, John Haynes, George Sivewright, William Choun & Thomas Lings
Porter, Henry Cox
Housekeeper, Mrs. Sarah Smith
Barge Master, Thomas Masterman

ARMY MEDICAL BOARD OFFICE.

13 *St. James's place.*—Hours, 10 to 4.

DIRECTOR-GENERAL, Sir James M'Grigor, bart., M.D. F.R.S., K.T.S.
Professional Assistants, Andrew Smith, M.D., Deputy-Inspector General of Hospitals; Dr. John Clark, Staff-surgeon, second class
Apothecary to the Forces, Francis Mathias Bassano, esq
First Clerk, George Somers Clarke, esq
Juniors, William Thomas Hughes, John Wimbridge, Walter Waterfield Bassano
Messengers, Edward Cox, Edmund Dwyer

AUDIT OFFICE FOR PUBLIC ACCOUNTS,

Somerset House.—Hours, 10 to 4.

COMMISSIONERS, Col. Sir William Lewis Herries, C.B., K.C.H. *Chairman*; Henry Fownes Luttrell, esq.; Sir John Osborn, bart.; Henry Arbuthnot, esq.; Edward Romily, esq.; Sir Alexander Cray Grant, bart
Secretary, John Lewis Mallet, esq
Chief Inspector, Frederic Leman Rogers, esq
Inspectors, John Gilbert, Thomas Theodore Campbell William Henry Rawlinson, John Soady, Otho H. Hamilton, William Winstanley, Samuel Wells, George Blyth, Charles Jones, Henry Gooch, esqrs
Senior Examiners, first class, John George Pohlman, Homer Snelgar, Joseph Ede, Frederick Thompson, Charles Jones, Lionel Ducket Eliot, Thomas Salusbury, Richard Wood, Edward Charles Eddrup, Richard Drake, John Law, David Lyons, Charles J. Wright, William Cotton
Senior Examiners, second class, Charles Stow, William Andoe, Charles Turbeville Eliot, Charles Tompkins, William Henry Tizard, George Bagster, John Drinkwater Bishop, William Hanby, Edward Wallwyn Shepheard, Charles Sterkey, Robert Whitestone, Charles Mitchell Irving, James Henry Hamer, William Waterhouse, Edward Rowland, William Henry Stapleton, John Muriel, Henry Attwell Smith, William Stow & Richard Evans
Junior Examiners, Nantes Tupper, John Owen, William Henry Kelly, John Brownrigg, John Williams Soady, Thomas Drake Ffinch Thomas Irwin, John Wilkinson, Thomas James Cumberland, John Llewellyn, Nathaniel Hearle, Henry Thomas Dundas Bathurst, James Douglas Dove, Charles Creed, Charles Vine, William Henry Rudlin, Peter Cunningham, Bladen Ruspini, Brooking Soady, jun., George William Dowton, Charles Carroll Greenwood, John Howard Kyan, James George Tayler, William Vere Alston, George Blount, Francis Alfred Hawker, Thomas Steward, Philip Alexander Hughes, Louis Mallet & Richard Thomas Swinnerton Dyer
Assistants, Thomas Clifton, Richard Barnwell Vaughan, William Sargent, Hon. Henry George Roper Curzon, Edmund Molyneux Seel, Charles A. de Valmer, William Mostyn, Charles Mallet, Thomas Francis de Fonblanque, Montague Markby, Walter Carew Cocks, Charles Osborne, Hay Cooper, Henry Bentick Arber, Robert Salkeld, William Coker Godson, Horace Goad Curtis, Hon. Fredk. Arthur Henry Chichester, Henry Treherne & Robert William Coombs
Supernumerary Examiner, William Jautard
Examiner of Naval Accounts, George Whiting
Principal and Minute Clerk and Private Secretary to the Chairman, Brooking Soady, esq
Officer for Reporting on Military Expenditure, Henry Smith
Ledger Keeper, George Paul; *Assistant*, Edward Bayntun
Clerk of Records, James Prince Pollard
Letter Clerk, John Chapman
Clerk of the Requisitions, Francis Ruddle
Clerk of the Enrolments, Thomas Richard Downes
Office Keeper, Samuel Tuttle
Messengers, Thomas Chambers, William Gross, John Dodge, John Eastwood, William Forester, James Warren, William Dedman, David Davies, Thomas Fisher, James Holdway

BANK OF ENGLAND.

Threadneedle Street, Incorporated 1694.—Hours 9 to 5.

JOHN BENJAMIN HEATH, ESQ. *Governor.*

WILLIAM R. ROBINSON, ESQ. *Deputy Governor.*

Edward Henry Chapman, esq	James Malcolmson, esq
William Cotton, esq	James Morris, esq
Charles Pascoe Grenfell, esq	George Warde Norman, esq
Abel Lewes Gower, esq	James Pattison, esq
John Oliver Hanson, esq	Christopher Pearse, esq
Kirkman Daniel Hodgson, esq	Sir John Henry Pelly, bart
Henry Lancelot Holland, esq	David Powell, esq
John Gellibrand Hubbard, esq	Sir John Rae Reid, bart
Thomas Newman Hunt, esq	Thomas Charles Smith, esq
Charles Frederick Huth, esq	William Thompson, esq. & Aldn
Alfred Latham, esq	Thos. Matthias Weguelin, esq
William Little, esq	Francis Wilson, esq

Secretary, John Knight, esq
Deputy Secretary, John Bentley, esq
Assistant, James Stewart, esq
Secretary to the Committee of Treasury, Marmaduke Blake Sampson, esq
Chief Clerk, Edwin Welsh
Chief Accountant, William Smee, esq. *Deputy,* George Earle Gray, esq
Assistant, John Padmore Noble, esq
Chief Clerks, William James Jacob, Henry Williams Challis
Accountants Discount Chief Clerks, John Watson, Micah Corder [Thomas Escreet
Accountants Drawing Office Chief Clerks, John Search,
Bank Stock Chief Clerks, John Cooper, William Bentley

STOCK OFFICES.

Reduced 3 *per Cents. &c. Transfer Office,* Edward Close Wilkinson and James Winn
3 *per Cents. Consols, &c. Transfer Office,* William Cuell and Williams Jecks
3¼ *per Cents, &c. Transfer Office,* Richard Frederick Clarke and Thomas Ingall
3 *per Cents. Consols, & Reduced Dividend Office,* Joseph Newton and John Stevens
New 3½ *per Cents. &c. Dividend Office,* William Jones and Richard Thomas Corbould
Register Office, John Edwards
Power of Attorney Office, John Skelton
Chancery, John Vaughan
Cheque Office, Henry Christopher Long
Storekeeper, Samuel Harrison
CHIEF CASHIER, Matthew Marshall, esq
First Assistant, Joseph Ravenscroft Elsey, esq
Second Assistant, Thomas Bros, esq
Cashiers, James Ballard, Thomas Clayton Turner, William Hughes, John Butler, Nathaniel Stock, William Taylor, James Vautin, John Vanderpant, William Popham Gattie, Francis Bocquet, William Paskin, Zachariah Uwins, John Williams, John Hawkes, Thomas Roberts, John Luson, Henry Bock, Thomas Donald, Frank Twiss, Robert Bocquet, John Tilbury, Joseph Stennett, John Conder, Daniel Champney, Ambrose Nichols, Josiah Field, Thomas Slater, William Richter, John Wood Deane
Bullion Office, William Debonaire Haggard [Fenemore
First In Teller, John Price. *First Out Teller,* Edward John
First Inspector, Stephen Catterson
Post Bill Office, Edward Robson
Drawing Office for Private Accounts, Edward Bryant
Drawing Office for Public Accounts, Thomas Hodgkinson
Discount Office, John Green Elsey
Bill Office, John William Brooks [William Banks
Branch Bank Office Chief, Richard Andrew Marsden,
Cash Book Office, David Hyett
General Cash Book Office, Samuel Parish
Solicitors, Messrs. James & Charles Freshfield [Palmer, esq
Standing Counsel, Sir Fitzroy Kelly, knt. and Roundell
Surgeon, Alfred Smee, esq
Architect, Charles Robert Cockerell, esq
Engineer, Thomas Oldham
Housekeeper, Mrs. Susannah Tyrrell
FOR BRANCH BANKS, *see* page 1971

BOARD OF CONTROL, *see* "*India Board.*"

BOARD OF GENERAL OFFICERS, *see* "*General Officers.*"

BOARD OF ORDNANCE, *see* "*Ordnance.*"

BOARD OF TRADE, *see* "*Committee of Privy Council for Trade.*"

BRITISH MUSEUM.

Great Russell street, Bloomsbury.

FORTY-EIGHT TRUSTEES :—23 by virtue of their offices ; 1 by the appointment of the Queen ; 9 representing the Sloane, Cotton, Harleian, Townley, Elgin, and Knight families, marked *S. C. H. T. E. K.* ; and 15 chosen by the former 33.

OFFICIAL TRUSTEES.

Archbishop of Canterbury, Lord Chancellor, Speaker of the House of Commons, Lord President of the Council, First Lord of the Treasury, Lord Privy Seal, First Lord of the Admiralty, Lord Steward, Lord Chamberlain, Three Secretaries of State, Bishop of London, Chancellor of the Exchequer, Lord Chief Justice of Queen's Bench, Master of the Rolls, Lord Chief Justice of Common Pleas, Attorney General, Solicitor General, the Presidents of the Royal Society, the College of Physicians, the Society of Antiquaries, and the Royal Academy.

TRUSTEE APPOINTED BY HER MAJESTY.

The Duke of Northumberland

FAMILY TRUSTEES.

S. Earl Cadogan, Lord Stanley
C. George Booth Tyndale, esq., the Rev. Francis Annesley
H. Lord Henry W. Bentinck, Earl Cawdor
T. Peregrine Edward Townley, esq
E. Earl of Elgin
K. John Knight, esq

ELECTED TRUSTEES.

Earl of Harrowby, Earl of Aberdeen, Duke of Rutland, Marquis of Lansdowne, Lord Ashburton, Right Hon. Thomas Grenville, Sir Robert Peel, bart., Duke of Hamilton, Earl of Derby, Sir Robert Harry Inglis, bart., Henry Hallam, esq., Earl of Carlisle, William Richard Hamilton, esq. Duke of Sutherland, Sir John Frederick William Herschel, bart

PRINCIPAL LIBRARIAN, Sir Henry Ellis, K.H.

SECRETARY'S DEPARTMENT.

Secretary, Rev. Josiah Forshall, M.A., F.R.S. *First Clerk,* Mr. Thomas Butler. *Second Clerk,* Mr. John C. Knight. 4 attendants

MANUSCRIPT DEPARTMENT.

Keeper, Sir Frederic Madden, K.H., F.R.S., F.S.A. *Assistant Keeper,* Rev. William Cureton. *Assistants,* Mr. John Holmes, Rev. William Upton Richards, Mr. Edward A. Bond. 4 attendants

DEPARTMENT OF PRINTED BOOKS.

Keeper, Antonio Panizzi, esq. *Second Keeper,* Nicholas Carlisle, esq. F.R.S. *Assistant Keeper,* Rev. Richard Garnett, M.A. *Assistants,* Messrs. John Winter Jones, Thomas Watts, Edmund Bach, William B. Rye. 17 attendants

DEPARTMENT OF NATURAL HISTORY.

Keeper of Mineralogy, Charles König, esq. K.H., F.R.S. *Assistants,* Messrs. George Frederick Richardson, George Robert Waterhouse. 4 attendants
Keeper of Zoology, John Edward Gray, esq. F.R.S. *Assistants,* Messrs. George Robert Gray, Adam White, William Baird, M.D., Edward Doubleday. 10 attendants
Keeper of Botany, Robert Brown, esq. F.R.S. *Assistant,* Mr. John Joseph Bennett. 2 attendants

DEPARTMENT OF ANTIQUITIES.

Keeper, Edward Hawkins, esq. F.R.S. *Assistant Keeper,* Samuel Birch, esq. F.A.S. *Assistants,* Messrs. Charles Newton, William Sandys Vaux, James Edwd. Fitzgerald. 8 attendants

DEPARTMENT OF PRINTS AND DRAWINGS.

Keeper, William Henry Carpenter, esq. 2 attendants

READING ROOM.

First Superintendent, Mr. James Cates. *Second Superintendent,* Mr. John Grabham. 3 attendants
Accountant and Collector of Books under Copyright Act, Mr. Mawer Cowtan
Clerk of Works, Mr. Thomas Pulman. *Solicitors,* Messrs. Bray, Warren and Harding
3 Housemaids, 2 Porters, 3 Messengers, and 1 Hall Porter

The public admitted to the Museum on Mondays, Wednesdays and Fridays	Jan. 8 to April 30 . . 10 to 4 May to Aug. 31 . . 10 to 7 Sep. 8 to Dec. 31 . . 10 to 4
The Reading Room (entrance east end of Montague place) open, to persons holding tickets of admission, every day	Jan. 8 to April 30 . . 9 to 4 May 8 to Aug. 31 . . 9 to 7 Sep. 8 to Dec. 31 . . 9 to 4

The public are also admitted to the Museum during the Easter, Whitsun and Christmas weeks every day except Saturday
The Museum (and Reading Room) closed on Sundays, Ash Wednesday, Good Friday, Christmas-day, and any Fast or Thanksgiving days, ordered by Authority; also between the 1st and 7th January, the 1st and 7th May, and the 1st and 7th September, inclusive

CARRIAGES OFFICE (METROPOLITAN PUBLIC).

6 *Adelphi terrace, Strand.*—Hours 10 to 4.

Registrar, Hensleigh Wedgwood, esq
Deputy Registrar, William Mansell, esq. R.N
First Clerk, Mr. Samuel Castleden
Second Clerk, Mr. Thomas Fitch
Office Keeper, Edward Wells

CHELSEA ROYAL HOSPITAL, see "*Royal Hospital, Chelsea.*"

COLONIAL OFFICE.

14 *Downing street.*

PRINCIPAL SECRETARY FOR THE COLONIES,

Under Secretaries, { George William Hope, esq; James Stephen, esq
Private Secretary to Lord Stanley, Col. the Hon. Edward Bootle Wilbraham
Chief Clerk, Peter Smith, esq
Senior Clerks, Henry Taylor, Gordon Gairdner, Samuel Jasper Blunt, Arthur Blackwood, George Barrow, esqrs
Clerks, William Greenwood Chapman, William Unwin, Frederic Clinton Mundy, Hugh Stuart Kelsey, Clere Talbot, Vane Jadis, Thomas William Clinton Murdoch, Charles Cox, William Dealtry, William Frederick Higgins, Edward Pennington, William Halksworth, John Allen, Henry Charles Norris, John Thomas Binney, esqrs
Librarian, George Mayer, esq
Assistant Librarian, Lewis Henry Patterson, esq
Office Keepers, Thomas Dodsworth, Samuel Hale
Porters, James Pepperell, Richard Powell
Housekeeper, Mrs. Ann Johnson

COLONIAL LAND AND EMIGRATION BOARD.

9 *Park st. Westminster.*

Commissioners, Thomas Frederick Elliot, esq. John George Shaw Lefevre, esq. & Charles Alexander Wood, esq
Secretary, Stephen Walcott, esq
Assistant Secretaries, John Walpole, John Gliddon, esqrs
Clerks, Messrs. Alfred Harold Englebach, James Chant, Joseph Thomas Miller, John Sayer Lewes, Drummond Alfred, Richard Bell Cooper, John Matthew Makeham

Government Emigration Agents.

Hours, 10 to 4.

London, Lieut. Lean, R.N., office, 70 Lower Thames st.

At the Outports:—

Liverpool, Lieut. Henry, R.N
Plymouth, Lieut. Hemmans, R.N
Glasgow & Greenock, Lieut. Forrest, R.N
Dublin, Lieut. Hodder, R.N
Cork, Lieut. Charles Friend, R.N
Belfast, Lieut. Stark, R.N
Limerick, Richard Lynch, esq. R.N
Londonderry, Lieut. Ramsay, R.N
Sligo, Lieut. Shuttleworth, R.N

COMMANDER IN CHIEF'S OFFICE, HORSE GUARDS.

Whitehall.

COMMANDER IN CHIEF,
Military Secretary,
Private Secretary,
Aides de Camp, Col. Hon. George Anson, H.P. unattd.; Lieut. Col. Marquis Douro, H.P. unattd.; Cornet the Earl of March, Royal Horse Guards, Blues; Cornet the Marquis of Worcester, 1st Life Guards
Assistants to the Military Secretary, Frederick Henry Lindsay, Francis Fergusson
Clerks, first class, Robert Deighton, William Kiddle, John Drake, George H. Gibbs, esqrs
Clerks, second class, John Fagan, John Galland, John Walter D'Urban Freeth, esqrs
Clerks, third class, Leonard Coleman, Edward Lawson White, John Smart, William Giffard Nicolas, & William Francis Kiddle, jun. esqrs
Office Keeper, John Whitmore
Housekeeper, Mrs. Ann Fergusson
Messengers, John Dolton, James Farquhar, John Manderson

COMMISSIONERS OF FRENCH AND DANISH CLAIMS,

5 *Whitehall place.* Hours, 10 to 4.

Commissioner, Joseph Phillimore, D.C.L
Secretary, George John Farrance, esq

COMMISSIONERS FOR IMPROVING THE METROPOLIS,

1 *Whitehall place.*

Commissioners, Earl of Lincoln; Lord Lyttleton; Lord Colborne; Rt. Hon. Charles Herries; John Humphery, esq. Ald. M.P.; Rt. Hon. the Lord Mayor of London; Sir Robert Harry Inglis, bart.; Sir Charles Lemon, bart.; Henry Thomas Hope, esq.; Henry Gally Knight, esq.; Alexander Milne, esq.; Hon. Charles Gore; Sir Robert Smirke, knt.; & Charles Barry, esq
Secretary, Trenham Walshman Phillips, esq

COMMISSIONERS FOR PROMOTING THE FINE ARTS,

Gwydyr House, Whitehall.

Commissioners, H. R. H. Prince Albert; Lord Lyndhurst, P.C.; Duke of Sutherland, K.G., P.C.; Marquis of Lansdowne, K.G., P.C.; Earl of Lincoln, M.P., P.C.; Earl Aberdeen, P.C.; Lord John Russell, M.P., P.C.; Lord Francis Egerton M.P., P.C.; Lord Palmerston, M.P., P.C.; Viscount Melbourne, P.C.; Lord Ashburton; Lord Colborne; Lord Willoughby De Eresby; Rt. Hon. Chas. Shaw Lefevre, M.P.; Rt. Hon. Sir Robert Peel, bart. M.P.; Rt. Hon. Sir James R. G. Graham, bart. M.P.; Sir Robert Harry Inglis, bart. M.P.; Henry Gally Knight, esq. M.P.; Benjamin Hawes, jun. esq. M.P.; Henry Hallam, esq. F.R.S.; Samuel Rogers, esq. F.R.S.; George Vivian, esq.; Thomas Wyse, esq.; Lord Mahon, M.P.; T. B. Macauley, esq. M.P
Secretary, Charles Locke Eastlake, esq. R.A.
Office Keeper, Thomas Laud

COMMISSIONERS FOR THE REGISTRATION & REGULATION OF COAL WHIPPERS, IN THE PORT OF LONDON.

(Under the Act 6 & 7 Vic. cap. 101.)

King James's Stairs, Wapping Wall. Hours 7 A.M., to 6 P.M.

Commissioners appointed by the Lords of the Committee of the Privy Council for Trade, Charles Green, esq. *Chairman;* Robert Wildman Barchard, esq.; Robert Gamman, esq.; Samuel Laing, esq
Commissioners appointed by the Common Council of the City of London, Thomas Pewtress, esq. *Vice-Chairman;* William Cash, esq.; John Dixon, esq.; George Stacy, esq
Commissioner in term of the Act, Geo. Frederick Young, esq
Registrar, Mr. John Barber
Clerk to the Commissioners & Accountant, Mr. Charles Cooper Robberds
Clerks, Mr. Robert Newell, Mr. William Deering

COMMISSIONERS OF REVENUE ENQUIRY.

Gwydyr House, Whitehall. Hours, 10 to 4.

Commissioners, the Rt. Hon. Lord Granville Charles Henry Somerset, M.P.; the Rt. Hon. William E. Gladstone, M.P.; Hon. William Bingham Baring, M.P.; James Milnes Gaskell, esq. M.P.; Alexr. Pringle, esq. M.P
Secretary, Thomas Peregrine Courtenay, esq

COMMISSIONERS OF SEWERS.

WESTMINSTER AND PART OF MIDDLESEX, *Court House,* 1 *Greek street, Soho square.* Hours, 9 to 4
Lewis Cooke Hertslet, *Clerk*
Assistant Clerks, Geo. S. Hatton, Thos. Coggin, John Pollard
Surveyor, J. Dowley, esq
Assistant Surveyor, Wm. Doull
Clerks of the Works, Robert Bell, John Phillips, Henry Webber, Francis Morton
Drawing Clerk, Wyatt Angelicus Papworth
Collectors, Wm. Oak, Chas. Chesterton, Wm. Raymond, Geo. Taylor, Wm. Wrather, Thos. Head
Office Keeper & Crier, Peter Pollard
Bailiff & Messenger, Wm. Conquest
CITY OF LONDON (having jurisdiction over the Sewage, Paving, Lighting, & Cleansing of the City), *Guildhall,* Joseph Daw, jun. *Principal Clerk*
HOLBORN AND FINSBURY, *Court House,* 7 *Hatton garden*
David Henry Stable, James Wilmot Lush, *Clerks;* John Roe, *Surveyor;* Joseph Unwin, *Summoner & Crier;* Charles Wright, John Henry Dowley, *Inspectors*
TOWER HAMLETS, *Court House,* 15 *Great Alie street,* John William Unwin, *Clerk*
SURREY AND KENT, *Office,* 185 *Bermondsey st. Borough,* Beriah Drew, *Clerk*
St. KATHERINE'S, near the Tower, *Office,* 34 *Essex st. Strand* John Virgo, *Clerk*
POPLAR AND BLACKWALL, 10 *Church row, Limehouse* William Baker, jun. *Clerk*
REGENT STREET COMMISSION, *Office of Woods, &c. Whitehall place,* William Adams, *Clerk*

COMMITTEE OF PRIVY COUNCIL FOR TRADE.

Office, Whitehall. Hours, 10 to 4.

PRESIDENT,

VICE-PRESIDENT,

Committee, Archbishop of Canterbury, Lord Chancellor, First Lord of the Admiralty, the Principal Secretaries of State, Chancellor of the Exchequer, Speaker of the House of Commons, Chancellor of the Duchy of Lancaster, Paymaster General, Master of the Mint, those Officers of State in Ireland who are Privy Councillors in England, Bishop of London

Legal Assistant, Stafford Henry Northcote, esq

Joint Secretaries, { John MacGregor, esq; John George Shaw Lefevre, esq }

Assistants, Frederick Lack, Vere Henry Hobart, esqrs

Registrar & Keeper of Papers, Charles Noyes, esq

Clerks, Robert Francis Suft, Samuel Webb, Richard William Lack, Robert Nailer, Walter Larkins, Vere Hobart, Francis F. Courtenay, esqrs

Private Secretary to the President the Earl of Dalhousie, Francis F. Courtenay, esq

Private Secretary to the Vice-President, James Clerk, esq

Statistical Department.

Chief, George Richardson Porter, esq

Assistants, William Drummond Oswald, Rd. Valpy, esqrs

Clerks, Thomas Irving, Charles Andrew George Sivrac, Thomas Poole Ward, Edgar Alfred Bowring, esqrs

Railway Department.

The President and Vice President of the Board of Trade

Senior Member, George Richardson Porter, esq

Inspector General of Railways, Major General Pasley

Secretary, Donatus O'Brien, esq

Assistant Inspector of Railways, Capt. Coddington, R.E

Registrar, Duncan McGregor, esq

Clerks, Finlay McKenzie, Charles Lambert, esqrs

Office Keeper, George Mitchell

Assistant Office Keeper, William Joy

Housekeeper, Mrs. Charlotte Vodoz

Messengers, James Maguire, D. Barber, William Scott & John Westley

Porter, Robert Bidgood

Office of Comptroller of Corn Returns,

6 *Charing cross.*

Comptroller of Corn Returns, George Joyce, esq

Deputy Comptroller, Henry Fenton Jadis, esq

Clerks, George Joyce, jun., John Edward Lack, William Edward Blair, esqrs

Messenger, Charles Scott

Office of Registrar of Designs,

35 *Lincoln's inn fields.*

Registrar, Frederic Beckford Long, esq

Assistant Registrar, Hon. Edward Cecil Curzon

Clerk, James Hill Bowen, esq

Second Clerk, Henry Charles Woollett, esq

Office Keeper, Charles Tristom

Messenger, James Pastell

COPYHOLD COMMISSION,

9 *Somerset place, Somerset House.*

COMMISSIONERS, William Blamire, esq. Thomas Wentworth Buller, esq. Rev. Richard Jones

Secretary, James Stewart, esq. barrister at law

Clerk, Mr. George Taylor

CUSTOMS ESTABLISHMENT.

Custom House, Lower Thames street. Hours, Indoor offices, 10 *to* 4. *Waterside offices, from* 1*st March to* 31*st October,* 8 *to* 4; *from* 1*st November to* 28*th February,* 9 *to* 4

COMMISSIONERS, Richard Betenson Dean, esq. *Chairman;* Hon. Edward Richard Stewart, *Deputy Chairman;* Henry Richmond, esq. Stephen George Lushington, esq. Culling Charles Smith, esq. Hon. Stephen Edmund Spring Rice, Rt. Hon. George Robert Dawson, Frederick Goulburn, esq. Thomas Pargitor Dickinson, esq

Secretary, Charles Andrew Scovell, esq

Assistant Secretary, William Maclean, esq

Clerk to the Western Ports, Charles Williams, esq

Clerk to the Northern Ports, Jeremy Jephson Ripley, esq.

Plantation Clerk, Charles John Allen Maclean, esq

Secretary's Office.

Chief Clerk, William Coles Dutton, esq

Coast Guard Clerk, James Watson, esq

Clerk of the Minutes, Henry Grant Clyde, esq

Clerks, Charles Claridge, Francis Geary Gardner, George Dickens, Edward Owen Pemberton, William Foot, Richard Robertson, William Butler Kitson, Thomas Courtenay Thorpe, James Campigne Whitmore, Charles Horatio Whitmore, Ward Nicholson, John Clogg, Harry Burton, Robert Stringer, Henry Makin, Thomas Coote Wildman, Frederick Davies, William Boyse Hunt, Robert Henry Graham Foster Pigott, Daniel Curling, John Blagden Hale, Thomas John Pittar, George Maltby, Stephen Frederick Webb, Joah Furey Bates, John Neale, Charles Edward Howard, Robert Bates, John Pownall Sawell, George Dewar, Arthur Lionel Tollemache, William Robert Anketel, Robert Shelton Mackenzie, George Caldwell, Edward Hollingworth, Henry William de Mole, Henry John Maclean, Frederick Richard Crewe and George Burlton Abdy, esqrs

Doorkeepers to the Board, James Guy, Robert Pilcher

Post Office Messenger, Thomas Halnes

Doorkeeper to Committee, John Aldridge

Housekeeper & Storekeeper of Forms & Books, Henry Charles Hast, & *Six Messengers*

Comptroller of Housekeeper's Accounts, William Buller Kitson

Surveyor for Buildings, Henry Adams, esq

Clerk of Works, Robert Dewes; *Clerk,* James Morris Grindrod

LAW OFFICERS.

Solicitor, Joseph Green Walford, esq

Assistant Solicitor, John Rutherfurd, esq

Chief Clerk, James Stephen Bullock; *Clerks,* William Cooke, Benjamin Potbury, Philip Beverly, Richard Beverley, Edward Lythgoe Hopper, Richard Edward Cumberland, John Laurence Graham

Messengers, Henry Sabine, William Webb

SURVEYORS GENERAL, William Roper Weston, Charles Dowding, Alexander Ross, Philip Fennings, Charles Boyd, esqrs

Clerks, Samuel Buller Lemon, James Wilde Dixon, Edward Jones, W. D. Chester, esqrs

RECEIVER GENERAL, Sir William Boothby, bart

Assistant, John Cotman, esq

First Clerk, George Franc, esq. *Paymaster,* Timothy Lee, esq

Clerks, Thomas Noble, Daniel Thomas Miller, Charles Sharp Cartwright, Timothy Noble, James Cooke, Edward Beaumont, George Bezer, Spencer Lambert, Henry Robert Poole, Hugh Piper Burnard, Thomas Edwin Wainwright, Robert Whitchurch

COMPTROLLER GENERAL, (Vacant)

Assistant, John Dickinson, esq

First Class Clerks, William Tilman, Robert Digby Watson, Elias Arnaud

Second Class Clerks, Henry Slyfield, Frederick Perkins, Alfred Martin Tupper, John King

Third Class Clerks, Samuel Robert Mure, William Henry Dickinson, Valentine William Plunkett, Robert Cowan Goodwin, John Boyes, George Grosvenor Cobham

Fourth Class Clerks, John Jenner Weir, Charles Cavan, Alfred Solcombe, Frederick Richard Crewe, Digby Dampier, Charles Beaumont, Robert Barnaby

Messenger, William Gale

Accountant of Petty Receipts, Auditor of Solicitors' Accounts, & Comptroller of Fines, John Speed Davies, esq

Principal Clerk, William Gale, esq

Clerks, John Beeston, Robert Grimes Hast, William Lee Ross, Charles Ernest Augustus Green

Messenger, William Watson

Inspector & Examiner of Plantation Accounts, John L. Woodhouse, esq

Clerks, William Symons, John King Wilmot, Charles Aubrey Wildman

Clerk of Postage, John Frederick Bernard, esq

Comptroller of Postage, Richard Robertson

Examiner of Stationery, Charles Williams, esq

Imports and Exports.

INSPECTOR GENERAL, William Irving, esq

Assistant Inspector, Robert Denby Woodifield, esq

Clerks, Henry Davies, Henry Thornton, John Alexande, Messenger, John Burt, John Burnet, John Cockburn, Alexander Clinton Fraser, David Charles Davies, Charles Browne, William Howson, Edward Bernard, James Johnson, Osborn Southee, Joseph Warren, Richard Whitmore, William Masson, Charles Parry Lack, George Strode, Cobham, James Mundy, Henry Burlton, Edmund Crabb, Edward Defriez, Grenville Andrews, John Jackson Gossett

Registrar General.

REGISTRAR GENERAL OF TRADING SHIPS OF GREAT BRITAIN AND IRELAND, John Covey, esq

Clerks, William Noss, George Barne, John James Tatham, Theophilus Moon

Long Room of the Port of London.

Collector, John Braysher, esq } BENCH OFFICERS
Comptroller, William Willimet, esq }
Clerk to Bench Officers, John Wright
Messengers, James Day, William Barber, John Salter

Ships' Entries Office.

Principal Clerk & Collector, Richard John Williams, esq
Clerks, James John Johnson, Edward Thomas Clark, Edward Sheppard Holles Knox

First Branch.

Principal Clerk & Receiver, James Walsh, esq
Clerks, John Thompson, John Brettell Henderson, William D. D. Smith, George Hyde Sweet, William Joseph Bezer, Robert Mackay, Peter Woods, Edward Walter, Price Gruggen
Principal Clerk & Assistant Comptroller, Dyer Drew, esq
Clerks, John Downs Soper, Christopher Daly, Samuel Vaughan, Samuel Henry Ray, Edward Genet, George Evans

Second Branch.

Principal Clerk & Receiver, William Dickon, esq
Clerks, John Forster, Thomas Hayward Sewell, John R. Lavie, Major Wm. Purser, Stephen Clerk, John Forrester, Thomas Durrant Thorpe
Principal Clerk & Comptroller, James Gray, esq
Clerks, Charles Henry Legoux, William Low, Edward Devereux, Chas. Price Gruggen, H. Treherne, Henry Woodgear, Alfred Massett, Charles Phillips Lawrence, Florence Lalor, Henry Cathrow Disney

Outward Department.

FIRST BRANCH.

Principal Clerk & Receiver, Richard Fall, esq
Clerks, William Billings & Thomas Howard

SECOND BRANCH.

Comptroller, Thomas G. Whitmore, esq
Clerks, John Sennitt Willmott, Charles Roberts, Henry Bezer, William Jackson Roberts, Thomas Inglis, Edwin Boyd

Coast Department.

Principal Clerk & Receiver, William Wybrow
Augustus Welstead, William Caldwell, James Haskoll, William Haines

Bond Office.

Principal Clerk, William Richard Browne, esq
Clerks, James Slocombe, Charles Grey Wilson, Frederick Rich, John Richard Hawkins, Frederick Howarth Edwards

THIRD BRANCH.

Collector, Robert Ellis, esq
Clerks, Peter Green, John Wild, Francis Paget Watson, William Sloper Hood, Michael Francis Power, Francis Gem, George Bumell, Robert Main
Comptroller, Thomas Cope, esq
Clerks William Willmott, jun. Thomas Lawliss, John Keddell, John Saunders Starling, Edward Z. Martin, Thomas Mayall

Landing Department.

Inspectors General of Waterside and Warehousing Departments, Thomas How, William Smith Kendall, esqrs
Landing Surveyors, Joseph Beales, Charles Knox, William Parsons, Matthew Sturt, Frederick Lacoste, George Blake, Robert Chapman, Charles Hammond, George Duncan, John Luscombe, Frederick St. John, Henry Charles Brown, William Rushton, John Blakston, John Cockshott
Searchers, Landing Waiters, &c., John Horsfall, William Beverley, Thomas Shave, Edward John Eliot, Thomas Tyrrell Dobbs, James Rowed, Tobias Bawden, Robert Knewstub, John Farquharson, Charles Pocock, George Green, John Hancock, Robert Cox, William Marshall, Thomas Smerdon, Joseph Henry Mason, Patrick Stewart, Thomas Mackenzie, Alexander L'Amilliere Kennedy, Samuel William Poer, Joseph Deane, William Gibson, William Holmes, John Beynon, Richard Annesley Ogilvie, William Beard Fitze, Edward Coweher, Charles Miles, John McAulay Arnand, George Forsyth, William Neilson, David Henry Watson, George Henry March, William Webb, Thomas Emmerson Carter, David William Low, Charles Glyde Wrankmore, George Herbert, John Palgrave, Samuel Valentine Eastmure, Henry Inglis, Samuel Brent, Walter Inglis, Thomas Lanfear, Charles John Cox, John Lucock, Æneas Cameron, Anthony Compton, Thomas Ryan, Thomas Dugdale Honeybourn, Henry Sherwood, Robert Alexander, Joseph Chatterton, Charles White, Thomas Arthur Bussell, Edmund Scanlan, George Benham, John McPherson, Edward King, George Henry Butler, John Fowler, Alexander Campbell, John Nicholas Fairman, Francis M. Ure, Edward Charles Fitzmayer, Llewellyn Mostyn, Frederick Francis, George Tritton, Edmund Charles Tatem, John Thorpe, Charles Harloe, Charles Coppock, Edward Best Hughes, Henry Lambert, Richard Finlay Hosken, John Horsfall, Augustus Lidbrook Cope, John Lalor, William Phillips, Michael Tyrrell, George Vane, Francis Napier, Robert Pritchard, John Auckland, Edward Fitze, Edward Armstrong, Henry Becher Pigot, John Neave, Charles Muskett, Richard Waite Cox, David James Ure, John Berrell, Joseph Hoar, Douglas Harrison, Charles Gilchrist Sanderson, John Henry Lilley, Francis Spittall, Edward Earl Galton, Charles Powis, Charles Tindal Pickford, Charles Hayward, Frederick John Wallis, John James Laughton, Alfred Pratt, Henry John Smith, John Clements, Peter Tuxford, John Heddle Traill, Arthur Leigh Watts, John William Douglas, Robert Kindersley Heath, Frederick Bullock, Sidney John Brewer, Robert Hillman, James Oldham, John Macqueen, James Clayton, John Methuen Gipps, Thomas Blackwood, William Henry Silk, Matthew Hawdon, William Payton, John Lloyd Williames, John Tattersall, John Fleming, James Britton, Edward Watson, James Cross Gibson, Henry William Waddell, Nicholas Wingfield, Henry Caulier, William Fairbairns, Henry William Bentley, Henry Rosewell Lacon, Charles Bernard, James Glynn Griffiths, Charles Hunt, John Smith, Samuel Millings, John Abraham Smith, William Worth, Alfred Turner, Edmund Philip Le Feuvre, Valentine Knight, Thomas B. Stephen, James Austin Lefroy, Charles Chad Turnour, Archibald Campbell, James De Reimer Cope
Inspectors of Guagers, Richard Zouch Troughton, John Robison, Thomas Shearman
Principal Guagers, Abraham Rickon, William Thomas Ready, John Booth, William Hampton, William Carter, William C. Garman, John W. Flinter
Guagers, George Clements, John Younghusband, George S. Hammond, Joseph Simpson, Daniel Pick, Robert Whitaker, Patrick O'Connor, Thomas Delacourt, James Burn, William Henry Carrington, John Bayliffe, Thomas Hull, Henry Cumming, David Graham, Charles Overton, John C. Watkins, Alfred Boxall, David Taylor, Henry Cammille, John Parker, Richard Smith, John Wogdon, James Eckley, Wm. Kinderley Read, Jonathan Bradford, George C. Dyke, Nathaniel Stevens, Sampson Capps, William Fletcher, Richard Blakesley
Clerks to Landing Surveyor, Henry Robins and Charles Townsend
Clerk to Inspector General, George Sheldrick
Extra Clerk to Landing Surveyor, Henry Charles Hast
Messenger to the Landing Surveyors, John Cole

Jerquer's Department.

Jerquer, James Forsayth, esq
Clerks, John Marmaduke Browne, Richard Tresidder, James Hilson, William Tonkin Daniell, Frederick William Dunne, Thomas Jones, Alexander Black, John Brummell, John Bowness, John William Dibley, Philip Champ, Naphtali Hart, Edward Gomer Feltham, Frederick Harvey

Warehousing Department.

Clerks for General Business:—First Class, Henry Newman, John Galton, William Gale, Isaac Hearndon, William Noss, John Mayo, William Henry Roberts Meader, Sidney Smith Dipnall, William Symonds, William Groves, William Ridding, Edward Dewguard, Richard Smith, Samuel Buller Lemon, John Marmaduke Brown
Second Class, George Barnes, Robert Harris, James Amplett, Rd. Tressider, James Hilson, Wm. Tomkin Daniell, Thomas Hooper, William Lambert, William Davis, Frederick William Dunn, Thomas Jones, Charles Thomas Adams, George Samuel Archer, Joseph Emerson, John Beeston, George Thomas Lemay, Henry Legge, George Frederick St. Quintin, Daniel Packham
Third Class, Henry Charles Reeves, William Pincombe, Thomas Prout, William Oldroyd, Thomas Moore, Edward Noon, James Brichill, George Rouse, William Levett, Robery Bell, James Thomas Bailey, Robert Grimes Hast, Henry Peall, Henry Robins, Henry Collier, Henry A. Bragg, Thomas Coxe, John Saunders, William Harkness, George Mitchell, William Paterson Rose, Benjamin Bond, Alexander Black, George Bunnett, John S. Tatum, John Edgar, Edward Chambers, John Nicholls, James Taylor, Charles Powell, James Flint

Fourth Class, Robert Taylor, James W. Dixon, Theophilus Moon, Charles Townsend, Joseph Cowing, Richard Huntley, William Lee Ross, Richard Veary, Henry Wm. Dobell, George Sheldrick, Malcolm D. Crosby, George Thorpe, William Sleeman, John Brumell, Jonathan Cope Welford, Thomas Foreman, James Fisher, Edward Jones, James Habbijam, James Brock, Henry Alfred Lucas, Thomas Smerdon, John Head, Henry William Legge, Robert Dixon, Charles Ernest Green, John Ranfield Squirrell, Frederick Ross, Walter Meader, Richard Allerton, Frederick Church, R. F. Jackaman

Fifth Class, William Neiland, Samuel Chappell. George F. Schelling, John Bowness, Pearce Southee, George Sperry, John William Dibley, Thomas Perkins, William Thomas Reeves, Philip Champ, Henry Cole, Henry Harris, James Maggs, Napthali Hart, Frederick W. Scrimes, John Gill, William Jennings, Parker Stanley, Robert Beck, Alfred Francis Roberson, Herbert Allen, John Stephen Bourlier, Henry White Meade, Henry W. Cole, George E. Clapham, Alfred J. Tyte, E. J. Feltham, William Thompson, Thomas Davis, Richard Westall, Edward Cleere, John Morgan, George Haggar, Arnold Henry Dolman, George B. Hartwell, James Grant

Sixth Class, William J. Skinner, Frederick Harvey, James C. Robertson, James Montague Mann, William John Smith, Thomas Heather, John H. Gandle, Henry Cumming, Henry Robins, T. Baines, William Hazell, William Douglas Chester, John Fitzgerald Taylor, Charles Robert Blackett, Matthew Irving, John Ewen M'Intyre, Richard Gowlland, Charles C. Skene, Charles Dering, Hugh Beaver Jones, Thomas Dayas, Charles D. New, Robert Stanbury, Augustus White, Neville Oliver Cribb, George William Wright, George Ledger, William Henry Ricketts, William Coleman, Jelley Romani, William Goodnige, Walter Measor, Robert Laycock Dickinson, Richard Marsh Dunn, William Petherick, George Peel, Richard Stephen George Weathcote Gooch, Thomas Stephenson, Thomas Secarry, John Edmund Cox

Check Office.

Clerk of Check, Henry Vonholte Morgan, esq.; 60 *Supertendents of lockers, warehouses, &c.* 1st. class, 15, 2nd class, 20, 3rd class, 25.—Total 60

120 *Lockers*: 1st class 30, 2nd class 40, 3rd, 50

180 *Weighers;* 1st class, 50, 2nd class, 60, 3rd class 70

50 *Messengers;* 18 *Gate-keepers*

Queen's Warehouse.

Warehouse Keeper, Frederick Thomas Walsh, esq

First Clerk, George Bunnett; *Second Clerk,*

Third Clerk, ; *Messenger,* John Brown

Assistant Warehouse Keeper, for seized vessels, Willoughby Simpson

Fines' Office.

Receiver of Fines & Forfeitures, Frederick Thomas Walsh, esq

Clerks, Malcolm Douglas Crosbie, Parker Stanley

Coast Guard Office.

Comptroller General, Phipps Hornby, esq. Capt. R.N., C.B.

Deputy Comptroller General, Samuel Sparshott, esq. Commander, R.N.

Principal Clerk, James William Safe, esq

Clerks, Thomas Randall Stap, Thomas Smith Day, Henry Hersee, James Pulham Fennings, Thomas Willey, R.N., (Charles Midwinter Primet, *Chief Clerk in Dublin*), Thomas Gorton, R.N., George Henning, Peter Warburton, James Henry Kelsey, John Coltson, William Tuck Harvey, Thomas George Walsh, John Morgan Peters, John Retallick, Constantine Phipps Onslow, William Greig, Thomas W. Gozna Marcus, L. Crofton, Robert English, George Hervé Mingaye, William Dixon, Duncan John Cowley, Charles Edward Gozna, Frederick Edmeades

Messengers, Alexander Horne, John Pitman

Coast Guard Compassionate Fund.

Supported by voluntary subscriptions and contributions, established 5th January, 1840, for the payment of gratuities to widows, orphans, and other relatives of subscribers deceased [General

Treasurer, Captain Phipps Hornby, R.N., C.B. Comptroller

Committee.

Captain Samuel Sparshott, R.N. Deputy Comptroller General

Sir James Dombrain, knt. Inspector General at Dublin

Captain William Neame, R.N. Assistant Inspector General at Dublin

James Pulham Fennings, esq

Secretary, James William Safe, esq

Navigation and Sloop Office.

Surveyor for the Act of Navigation, Nicholas Robilliard, esq

Assistant Surveyor, William Board

Clerks, Benjamin M'Dermott Bond, James Taylor, George Erasmus Clapham

Water Guard Department.

Inspector General, Henry Ansell, esq

Inspectors of the River, William Smart, David Samuel Harding, Peter Curgenven, esqrs

First Class Tide Surveyors, Messrs. Thomas Downs, Richard Fernyhough, William Jago, James Cheatham, John M'Culla, Samuel Pearce, John Dobson, Ralph Dilnote Abbott, James Boston

Second Class Tide Surveyors, James Blackman Giles, John Potter, John Newman, Thomas Knevett, Thomas Sedgwick Richardson, John Donnan, James Denton, Saunders Rogers, Robert Grey

ACTING TIDE SURVEYORS.

Thomas Fladgate, James Hemington, John Bide, John Roberts, William Yeowell, Robert Macdonald, Richard Daws, Charles Case Fowler

Registrar of Tide Waiters, Francis Rowley

Assistant, George Frederick Schilling

Registrar of Watermen & Inspectors' Clerk, James Brock

Inspectors' Messenger, James Waight

520 *Tide Waiters,* in three classes

62 *Watchmen,* ditto

82 *Watermen,* ditto

Alien Registration Office.

Registrar of Aliens for Port of London, Chas. Fabian, esq

Clerk, John Maffey

Collectors & Comptrollers of Customs, Outports—England.

	COLLECTORS.	COMPTROLLERS.
Aberistwith	Pierce Evans, esq	William Wheeler, esq
Aldborough	W. C. Maclean, esq	Henry Thomas, esq
Arundel	John Wilson, esq	Charles Redwick, esq
Barnstaple	Edw. Rds. Roberts, esq	Richard White, esq
Beaumaris	Nicholas E. Browne, esq	James Foyster, esq
Berwick	Neil Leitch, esq	George Arnott, esq
Bideford	Henry Rodd, esq	John Baller, esq
Blakeney	Robert Bacon, esq	David Grieve, esq
Boston	Isc. Holmes Nanson, esq	William Redpath, esq
Bridgewater	William Wilcox, esq	William Jones, esq
Bridlington	James Bennett, esq	James Turner, esq
Bridport	J. P. Penberthey, esq	Robert D. Clague, esq
Bristol	John Ker, esq	Matthew Laxton, esq
Cardiff	Robert Daw, esq	Henry Sladen, esq
Cardigan	Dd. Powell Lucas, esq	
Carlisle	Kenneth McKenzie, esq	Edward Waters, esq
Carnarvon	David Williams, esq	John Hughes, esq
Chepstow	Robert Staines, esq	William Probyn, esq
Chester	George Hay Anderson, esq	George Smith esq
Chichester	James Blagden, esq	Thomas Wilson, esq
Clay	(*see Blakeney*)	
Colchester	James Trevenon, esq	Jas Underwood Argent, esq
Cowes	John Hodder, esq	Richard Estwick, esq
Dartmouth	John Moody, esq	Jph. Hake Sparke, esq
Deal	Lewis Hy. Howell, esq	George B. Raggett, esq
Dover	William J. William, esq	Jas. Sumner Kelsey, esq
Exeter	Hy. Leslie Grove, esq	Thos. Mat. Wearne, esq
Falmouth	Duncan Stewart, esq	Thomas Hearle, esq
Feversham	John Adley, esq	Thomas Jull, esq
Fowey	J. Dickson Thornley, esq	C. Wreford, esq
Gainsborough	Robert Willingale, esq	William Stanwell, esq
Gloucester	Thomas Hastings, esq	Cyrus Davie, esq
Goole	Richard Patten, esq	Alex. Rose McLeay, esq
Grimsby	J. E. Lacon, esq	Willm. Henry Forster, esq
Gweek	Charles Sholl, esq	James James, esq
Harwich	Robert Welch, esq	William Strike, esq
Hull	Thos. John Wright, esq	Fredk. Cassell, esq
Ilfracombe	(*see Barnstaple*)	
Ipswich	William Lane, esq	Abraham Cook, esq
Lancaster	Henry Pugh Gardner, esq	Arthur Stewart, esq
Liverpool	Elias Arnaud, esq	John Grimes, esq
Llanelly	James Ross, esq	Edward Leigh, esq
Lyme	Frederick Swafman, esq	Isaac Walker, esq

Lymington has a Small Custom House, being a Branch of the Port of Southampton; the Chief Officer is John Fitz-Stephens.

Lynn Regis	Wm. Swatman, esq	Henry Casterton, esq
Maldon	Henry Jas. Clarke, esq	W. H. Holmes, esq
Maryport	John Andrew, esq	A. H. Hardie, esq
Milford	Geo. Cooke Hamilton, esq	John Ralph, esq
Newcastle	Sir Cuthbert Sharp	James Sparrow, esq
Newhaven	Joseph Baldwin, esq	Henry Sutton, esq
Newport, Mon.	Edward Bell, esq	Robert Cullum, esq
Padstow	Stephen Burridge, esq	Thomas Ferris, esq
Penzance	Rd. Jewell Ferris, esq	William Bellamy, esq
Plymouth	George Jones, esq	Wm. Lockyer, esq
Poole	William Broster, esq	James Brown, esq

Portsmouth	Charles Hoffmeister, esq..	Charles Winkworth, esq
Preston	Thomas Underwood, esq..	JamesCrumbleholme, esq
Ramsgate	William Hill Buckle, esq	George Gwyther, esq
Rochester	William Saywers, esq ..	Alexander More, esq
Rye	Daniel Colquhoun, esq..	William Strike, esq
St. Ives (Crnwl.)	M. Davie, esq..........	Robert James, esq
Saxmundham ..	(*see Aldborough*)	
Scarborough....	Henry Fowler, esq......	William Devall, esq
Scilly	Nicholas Martyn Buckett, esq..	James Bull, esq
Shoreham	Robert Dewey, esq	Richard Gates, esq
Southampton ...	Samuel P. Edwards, esq .	Edm. Burke Smith, esq
Southwold......	Henry Burwood, esq....	Benj.Saddler Candler,esq
Stockton........	Alex. Ogilvie Dixson, esq	Robert Welch, esq
Sunderland	James Abbott Lloyd, esq	William JohnStewart,esq
Swansea........	Wm. Barker, esq	Thos. Stephen Todd, esq
Truro..........	John Scaplen Stansmore, esq	Thomas Avery, esq
Wells, Norfolk..	William Dawson, esq ..	Jn. Nichs. Robilliard, esq
Weymouth	Roper Willis Weston, esq	George Reynolds, esq
Whitby	Patrick Black, esq......	Samuel Davis, esq
Whitehaven	William Stiles Roe, esq..	John McKinlay, esq
Wisbeach	John Hope Maclean, esq..	Richard Keys, esq
Yarmouth......	R. Bell, esq...........	John Preston, esq
Guernsey	*Principal Officer*, Charles Anson, esq..	Francis Waring, esq
Jersey..........	*Principal Officer*, George Radford, esq	James Rider, esq
Alderney	*Regr. of Certificates* Thomas Browne, esq	
Isle of Man .... *at Douglas*....	Fred. Cassell,esq........	James Waters, esq

Ports of Scotland.

Solicitor for Scotland, David Robertson, esq

	COLLECTORS.	COMPTROLLERS.
Aberdeen	John Smithers, esq ...	John Exley, esq
Alloa	James H. Cobban, esq ..	Robert Scott, esq
Arbroath	F. Martin esq	A Stephenson, esq
Ayr............	David Ewen, esq	John Miller, esq
Banff	James Nicol, esq........	James Miller, esq
Borrowstonnes..	John McGiloray, esq...	John Sheebon, esq
Cambelltown	Robert Smith, esq.....	W. A. Matthews, esq
Dumfries	William Tennant, esq ..	John Sloan, esq
Dundee	John Stewart, esq	Dd. Milligan Jolly, esq
Glasgow........	Fregift W. Vanderkiste, esq	And. Farq. Gray, esq
Grangemouth ..	John Burton Timmings..	George Waddell, esq
Greenock	Michael CullenCotton,esq	William M'Auley, esq
Inverness	Dunc. M'Pherson, esq ..	Lochlan Cumming, esq
Irvine..........	Robert Montgomery, esq	Francis Wallace, esq
Kircaldy	William Tankerville Moneypenny, esq..	John Lorimer, esq
Kirkwall	Robert Lantit, esq......	George Firth, esq
Leith	Thomas Rodmell, esq ..	Ambrose Foote, esq
Lerwick........	Robert S. Kilgour, esq..	Francis Heddell, esq
Montrose	Frederick William Trevor, esq	John Nelson Beaumont, esq
Perth	John Miller, esq	William Foggo, esq
Port Glasgow ..	John Boyle, esq.........	Walter Irvine, esq
Stornaway	W. J. Jeffreys, esq	A. T. Chatfield, esq
Stranraer	Alexr. M'Neil, esq......	John Semple, esq
Wick	H. Davidson, esq	T. Jones, esq

Ports of Ireland.

	COLLECTORS.	COMPTROLLERS.
Baltimore......	Andrew Nugent, esq....	M. Doyle, esq
Belfast	George Wilcox, esq	James Mason, esq
Coleraine	William Delap, esq	John Gordon, esq
Cork	John James Troy, esq..	John Joyce, esq
Drogheda	Robert White, esq......	Thomas Lee, esq
Dublin	Thos. Worthington, esq..	James M'Caskey, esq
Dundalk	John Carlisle, esq	John George Beresford
Galway	John Richardson, esq ...	Richard J. Dowsley, esq
Limerick	Joseph Reay, esq........	J. Vereker, esq
Londonderry ...	Thos. Shepherd, esq	Joseph Black, esq
New Ross	Frederick Stone, esq....	Alexander Thomson, esq
Newry	John Crampton, esq....	H. Kinsey, esq
Sligo	Owen Wynne, esq	Frederick Freshfield, esq
Tralee..........	J. Cronn, esq	George O'Neale
Waterford	James Wallace, esq	George Miller, esq
Westport	C. S. Miller, esq........	Cleyton Love Hingston, esq
Wexford	Henry Higginson, esq ..	Daniel Dudgeon, esq

Solicitor for Ireland, Latham Blacker, esq

Customs Benevolent Fund, & Office of the Bills of Entry for England & Wales, and the Ports on the Clyde.

Established by Act of Parliament for the Benefit of Widows, Children, and Relatives of deceased Officers and Clerks of the Customs in England and Wales.

DIRECTORS.

President, Joseph Green Walford, esq

Vice-Presidents, John Braysher, esq; Charles Andrew Scovell, esq

William Roper Weston, William Willimott, Richard Fall, Charles Dowding, William Maclean, & Charles Saunders, esqrs

Trustees, Richard Betenson Dean, esq. Stephen George Lushington, esq. Charles Culling Smith, esq. Charles Andrew Scovell, esq. Joseph Green Walford, esq

Auditors, Thomas Cope, James Gray, Charles Knox, esqrs

Actuary, Charles Ansell, esq. Atlas Insurance Office

Standing Counsel, Richard Ryder Dean, esq

Solicitor, John Innes Pocock, esq

Medical Referees, Dr. Hodgkin (London), Mr. Haetin (Liverpool)

Secretary of the Fund, & Manager of the Bill of Entry Office, George Plank, esq

Comptroller, William Strickland, esq

Accountant & Cashier, Henry Hackman

Clerks, Richard Alexander Shepherd, Wm. Wheatley Pratt, HenryWm. Meader, Wm. PiercyWestley, Geo. Plank,jun

Messenger, William Braithwaite

Distributors, John Maughan, Geo. Balgue, William Violet

DUCHY OF CORNWALL.

Office, Somerset House.

Hours of business, 10 to 4.

The Prince of Wales' Council.

His Royal Highness Prince Albert, K.G.

The Right Hon. Thomas Pemberton-Leigh

Lord De L'Isle & Dudley

Sir Henry Wheatley, G.C.H

The Earl of Lincoln

Lord Portman

George Edward Anson, esq

Secretary, James Robert Gardiner, esq

Officers of the Duchy of Cornwall.

Lord Warden of the Stannaries & Chief Steward of the Duchy in Cornwall & Devon, H.R.H. Prince Albert

Secretary to the Lord Warden & Keeper of the Records of the Duchy, James Robert Gardiner, esq

Chancellor and Keeper of the Great Seal, The Right Hon. Thomas Pemberton-Leigh

Surveyor General, Lord De L'Isle and Dudley

Auditor, Edward White, esq

Receiver General, Major Gen. Sir Henry Wheatley, G.C.H

Deputy Receiver, Benjamin Tucker, esq

Attorney General, The Hon. John Chetwynd Talbot, Q.C

Solicitor General, Edward Smirke, esq

Clerks, Benjamin Tucker, Robert Courtney Abbot, George Marrable & Septimus Woodgate, esq

Record Clerk, Frederick Devon, esq

Vice Warden of the Stannary Court, John Lucius Dampier, esq

Sheriff of Cornwall, Henry Lewis Rodd, esq

Constable of Launceston Castle, The Duke of Northumberland, K.G

Surveyor of Land & Minerals in Cornwall & Devon, Rd. Taylor, esq

Surveyor of Lands in Somerset, Dorset & Wilts, Robert Watt, esq

Mineral Agent, John Williams Colenso, esq

Ranger & Master Forester of the Forest of Dartmoor, H.R.H. Prince Albert

Deputy Foresters, Baldwin Fulford, James Wentworth Buller, Servington Savery, & Paul Owry Treby, esqrs

Stewards of Estates & Revenues in divers Counties, viz—

Berks, Dorset, Somerset, Wilts, & Surrey, James Robert Gardiner, esq

Deputy Steward of Cornwall & Devon, appointed by the Lord Warden, George Freeth, esq

DUCHY OF LANCASTER,

Office, Lancaster place, Strand.

Hours of business, from 10 till 4.

Chancellor,

Attorney General, Thomas Flower Ellis, esq

Receiver General, Col. Charles Richard Fox

Auditor, John Gibson Lockhart, esq

Clerk of the Council & Register, Fredk. Dawes Danvers, esq

Clerks, Joseph Henry Gooch, Peter Thomas Renaud, George William Powell, esqrs

Queen's Serjeant, Charles Purton Cooper, esq. Q.C

Queen's Counsel, Samuel Martin, esq. Q.C; Robert Charles Hildyard, esq. Q.C

Clerk in Court & Solicitor, John Teesdale, esq

Clerk of the Records, William Hardy, esq
Usher, Mr. William Doggett
Messenger, Charles Coggins

EAST INDIA COMPANY.

Six Directors are elected annually, in April, when six go out by rotation. Each Director serves four years.

DIRECTORS.

Chairman—Sir Henry Willock, K.L.S., Little Campden house, Kensington
Deputy Chairman—James Weir Hogg, esq. M.P. 40 Upper Grosvenor st

Years to serve.	Committees. Finance and Home.	Political and Military.	Revenue, Judicial, and Legislative.	OTHER DIRECTORS.
3	Chairman.			
3	DeputyChairmn.			
1	F H	....	......	Wm. Astell, esq. M.P. Everton
4	....	P M	......	Wm. Wigram, esq. 56 Upper Harley st
3	F H	....	......	Sir Robert Campbell, bart. 5 Argyll place
1	F H	....	......	JohnMasterman,esq.M.P.Nicholas la.Lombardst
4	F H	....	......	John Petty Muspratt, esq. 21 Russell square
2	....	....	RJL	Henry Alexander, esq.Clarendon pl.Hyde pk.gar
4	....	P M	......	Maj.-Gn.SirJ.LawLushington,G.C.B.26Dorsetsq
2	....	P M	......	Sir Wm. Young, bart. 7 Westbourne street
4	....	....	RJL	George Lyall, esq. M.P. 17 Park crescent
1	....	....	RJL	Russell Ellice, esq. 5 Portman square
1	F H	....	......	Sir Richard Jenkins, G.C.B. 7 Mansfield street
1	....	....	RJL	Wm. Butterworth Bayley, esq. Hookwood
2	F H	....	......	J.Shepherd,esq.Holly lodge,Walton-on-Thames
2	....	P M	......	Francis Warden, esq. 28 Bryanston square
4	....	....	RJL	Martin Tucker Smith, esq. 13 Upper Belgrave st
3	F H	....	......	Lt.-Col.Wm. Hen. Sykes, 47 Albion st. Hyde pk
1	....	P M	......	Maj.-Gn.ArchibaldGalloway,C.B.19Up.Harley st
3	....	P M	......	Maj.-Gen. Archibald Robertson, 53 Baker st
4	....	....	RJL	Elliot Macnaghten, esq. Monkhams, Woodford
2	....	....	RJL	Major James Oliphant, Wimbledon
3	F H	....	......	John Clarmont Whiteman, esq. 7 Bryanston sq
2	....	P M	......	Hon. Wm. Hen. Leslie Melville, 3 Arlington st

THE FOLLOWING GENTLEMEN ARE OUT BY ROTATION.

John Cotton, esq. 30 Upper Harley street
John Loch, esq. Morden park, Surrey
Charles Mills, esq. Camelford house, Oxford street
Wm. H. Chicheley Plowden, esq. 8 Devonshire place
Henry Shank, esq. 62 Gloucester place
Henry St. George Tucker, esq. 3 Upper Portland place

Secretary's Office.

Secretary, James Cosmo Melvill, esq
Assistant Secretary, John Docwra Dickinson, esq
Minuting and Correspondence Branch, Assistant, Edward Thornton, esq
Clerks, Henry Mills, William Henry Mayne, Marmaduke Hornidge, Thomas Campbell, James Cosmo Melvill, jun. Frederick Samuel Danvers, esqrs
Buying Department Clerk, John Davison, esq
Cashier, Joseph Barber Wilks, esq
Clerks in Charge of Ecclesiastical Registrations, &c. Francis Clark, Frederick Samuel Danvers
Clerk to College Department, William Thomas Hooper
Superintendent of Extra Clerks, Ebenezer Barnett, esq
Assistant, William Adams Franks

Accounts Branch.

Assistant, William Keith, esq
Clerks, William Collingwood, George Friend, John Ogilvie, Thomas Hilton Keith, William Thomas Daviniere, Henry Robinson, Edward Jenkyns, Robert Money Hotson, George Walpole White, Duncan Campbell, Arthur Rt. Onslow, James Waghorn, esqrs

Pay Branch.

Assistant, Joseph Barber Wilks, esq
Clerks, William Morgan, Sidney John Smith, James Dunsmure, John Estcourt Boucher, Clifford Craufurd, esqrs

Audit Branch.

Assistant, Charles Ryle, esq
Clerks, George Browne, Frederic Sandoz, William Banton, Willis Henry Lowe, Charles Saunderson, George Browne, jun. esqrs

Marine Branch.

Assistant, John Charles Mason, esq
Clerks, Robert Ritherdon, William Thomas Thornton, William Byron, esqrs

Examiners' Department.

Examiner of India Correspondence, Thomas Love Peacock, esq
Assistant Examiner, David Hill, esq. *Assistants*, John Stuart Mill, Francis William Prideaux, esqrs
Clerk, Correspondence Department, Octavius Greene, esq
Seniors, Joseph Maitland, Thomas Rundall, Thomas Robert Andrews, John Douglas Close, esqrs
Clerks, Stoddart Drysdale, Macvey Napier, Edmund Dewar Bourdillon, James Francis Shillito, William Archer Shee, Arthur Scott, William Henry Batten, George Grote Mill, Edward Gryffydh Peacock, esqrs
Superintendent of Extra Clerks, Richd. Nelme Grasswell, esq

Book Office.

Registrar, Christopher Waud, esq
Assistant, John Cottell, esq

Military Department.

Secretary, Phillip Melvill, esq. *Assistant*, Wm. Eade, esq
Clerks, George Appleton, Robert Edward Smith, Charles Thomas Page Metcalfe, James Pattison Thom, Thomas Robert Clarke, George Elphick Cochrane, John Davison, esqrs
Clerk for Passing Cadets & Assistant Surgeons, Thomas Robert Clarke, esq
Inspector of Military Stores, Lieut. Col. John George Bonner
Clerk, Lewis Humbert, esq. *Sub Inspector*, Alexander Rothney, esq

---

Clerk to Finance & Home Committee, John Docwra Dickinson, esq
Clerk of Political & Military Committee, William Eade, esq
Clerk to Judicial Revenue & Legislative Committee, David Hill, esq
Examining Physician, John Robert Hume, M.D
Oriental Librarian, Professor Horace Hayman Wilson
Keeper of the Museum, Thomas Horsfield, M.D., F.R.S
Counsel, Loftus Tottenham Wigram, Q.C
Solicitor, Edward Lawford, esq
Doorkeeper, John Saunders
Under Doorkeepers, Augustus Raymont, James Cummins, Edward Bowers Doggett, George Shipway

Military Seminary.

Addiscombe, Surrey.

Public Examiner & Inspector, Major Genl. C. W. Pasley, C.B., F.R.S., F.R.A.S., F.G.S. and Hon. M. Inst. C.E. from the Royal Engineers
Lieut. Governor, Major Genl. Sir Ephraim G. Stannus, knt. C.B. Bombay Army
Chaplain, Rev. William Henry Johnstone, B.A
Surgeon, Edward Westall
Staff Captain, Major Talbot Retherdon, late Bombay Artillery
Orderly Officers, Lieutenant Richard Kinkead, Madras Artillery, John Pigott Nixon, Bombay Infantry
Public Examiner, Oriental Department, Horace Hayman Wilson, M.A., F.R.S. Sanscrit Professor, Oxford

PROFESSORS AND MASTERS.

Mathematics & Classics, Rev. Jonathan Cape, A.M. Alfred Wrigley, B.A. Wm. Hen. Johnstone, B.A. Rev. Robert Inchbald, B.A. Rev. George Robert John Tryon, B.A
Fortification, Major Hector Straith, Lieut. Thomas Cook, R.N., F.R.S
Military Drawing, Edward Barnard Metcalf
Military Surveying, Major Basil Jackson
Landscape Drawing, Theodore Henry Fielding, John Christian Schetky
Oriental Languages, Richard Haughton, M.R.A.S., Charles Bowles
Geology & Mineralogy, David Thomas Ansted, M.A. *Lecturer*
Practical Mechanics, Lieut. Thomas Cook, R.N., F.R.S
Chemistry, Edward Solly, *Lecturer*
Sword Exercises, Henry Angelo, jun
Clerk for passing Cadets, &c. Thomas Robert Clarke, esq. office, E. I. house

Civil College.

Hayleybury, Herts.

Visitor, The Right Rev. the Lord Bishop of London
Principal, Rev. Henry Melvill, B.D
Dean, Rev. James Amiraux Jeremie, A.M
Registrar, Rev. Frederic Smith, A.M

EUROPEAN DEPARTMENT.

Professors :—*Classics*, Rev. James Amiraux Jeremie, A.M
Mathematics, Rev. James William Lucas Heaviside, A.M., Rev. Fred. Smith A.M
History & Political Economy, Rev. Richard Jones, A. M
Law, Wm. Empson, esq. A.M., F.R.S.L

ORIENTAL DEPARTMENT.

Visitor, Horace Hayman Wilson, esq. A.M., F.R.S
Professors:—*Hindee, Hindustani, & Mahratta*, Lieut. Edward Backhouse Eastwick
Arabic & Persian, Major James Walker Jasper Ouseley
Sanscrit & Teloogoo, Francis Johnson, esq

EASTLAND COMPANY.

South Sea House.

Governor, Stephen Thornton, esq
Deputy Governor, William Astell, esq. M.P
Treasurer, Hon. John Thornton Leslie Melville
Assistants, Samuel Solly, Edward Forster, John Thornton, Claude George Thornton, Thomas Tooke, George Warde Norman, Edward Forster, jun. Stephen Edward Thornton, Henry Cayley, Henry Milnes Thornton, George Smith Thornton, Fletcher Wilson, John Harvey, Thomas Matthias Weguelin, Archibald Paris, Thomas Tooke, jun. William R. Robinson, Charles Robinson, John Hubbard, jun. esqrs. Sir John Henry Pelly, bart. John Cattley, William Gladstone, Stephen Wildman Cattley, Thomas Anderson, esqrs
Secretary, Thomas Cope, esq. South sea house, & Cockelwood villa, Kilburn

ECCLESIASTICAL COMMISSIONERS FOR ENGLAND.

5 Whitehall place.

The Archbishops and Bishops of England and Wales; the Lord Chancellor; First Lord of the Treasury; President of the Council; Secretary of State for the Home Department, and Chancellor of the Exchequer; the two Lord Chief Justices of England; the Master of the Rolls, and Lord Chief Baron, and the Judges of the Prerogative and Admiralty Courts; the Deans of Canterbury, St. Paul's, and Westminster; the Earls of Devon, Bessborough, Chichester, and Harrowby; Lord Ashley; the Rt. Hon. Henry Hobhouse, Sir George Grey, bart., and John Nicholl, D.C.L
Treasurer & Secretary, Charles Knight Murray, esq
Assistant Secretary, James Jell Chalk, esq
Auditor & Actuary, Arthur Morgan, esq
Accountant, Benjamin R. Aston, esq
First Class Clerks, George Watson Wood, William Good & George Wear, esqrs
Second Class Clerks, Robert Cook, George Pringle, James Richard Bruce, & Robert Allan Wight, Esqrs.
Solicitors, Messrs. J. Meadows White & John Murray, 7 Whitehall place
Architect, William Railton, esq
Surveyors, Messrs. Robert Clutton, John Clutton, & John Pickering
Third Class Clerks, Messrs. Robert Evans, John Lightfoot, William Frederick James Walton, Ernest Frederick Webb, Henry Michael Browne, & William John Goodwin
Office Keeper & Messenger, John Bubb
Second Messenger, William Henry

EMIGRATION. *See 'Colonial Land & Emigration Board.'*

ENCLOSURE COMMISSIONERS FOR ENGLAND & WALES.

Office, 5 New street, Spring gardens.

Chief Commissioner, Rt. Hon. Earl of Lincoln, M.P.
Commissioners, George Darby, esq. M.P. William Blamire, esq
Secretary, Henry Charles Males, esq

ENGINEERS' OFFICE. *See 'Royal Engineers' Office.'*

ESTABLISHMENT OF QUEEN'S MESSENGERS. *See 'Home Office.'*

EXCHEQUER (RECEIPT OF).

Office, 3 Whitehall Yard.

Comptroller-General, Right Hon. Lord Monteagle
Assistant-Comptroller, Arthur Eden, esq
Chief Clerk, Francis Ferrand Ottey, esq
Accountant, George Septimus Frederick, esq
First Clerk, Edward Welch
Second Clerk, Charles Barratt
Third Clerk, John Karslake Blake
Fourth Clerk, Edward D'Oyley Bird Tucker
Fifth Clerk, John William Hoare

Office of Paymasters of Exchequer Bills,

2 Whitehall Yard.

Paymasters, { Edward Henry Nevinson, esq; John Henry Latham, esq }
Accountant, Samuel James Wood, esq
Senior Clerk, Edward Pollard, esq
Clerks, William Trahar, Edmund Malone D'Arcey, John Dalrymple Prendergast, Francis Stephen Ricketts, Frederick Rodney, esqrs
Office Keeper & Messenger, James Slaughter

Office for preparing & issuing Exchequer Bills.

Senior Clerk, Henry Williams Chisholm, esq
First Assistant Clerk, Hernon Thomas Woodfall, esq
Second Assistant Clerk, Robert Dupre Alexander, esq

Office of Weights & Measures,

2A, *Whitehall Yard.* Hours 10 to 4.

Superintendent, John Bowen, esq
Assistant, Peter Carruthers

EXCHEQUER BILL OFFICE FOR WEST INDIA ISLAND RELIEF.

Acts 2 & 3 Wm. IV. cap. 125, and 5 & 6 Wm. IV. cap. 51

South Sea House.

COMMISSIONERS.

Chairman, Henry Berens, esq
Benjamin Harrison, John Labouchere, George Hathorn, John Lennox Woodhouse, esqrs
Secretary, John Strettell Brickwood, esq
Assistant Secretary, Henry Bunster, esq
Accountant, James Green, esq
Clerk, Mr. George Carter

EXCISE OFFICE.

Old Broad Street.—Hours 9 to 3.

COMMISSIONERS.

Chairman, John Wood, esq
Deputy Chairman, Hart Davis, esq
Commissioners—Sir John Cheetham Mortlock, knt.; Hon. William Henry Percy; Thomas Harrison, esq.; Henry Frederick Stephenson, esq.; Charles John Herries, esq
Secretary, John Clayton Freeling, esq
Under Secretary, George Ballard, esq
Assistant Secretary, James Williamson, esq
Clerks—First Branch. Charles Henry Corbett, Robert Melhuish, William Roberts, Charles Clarkson, Joseph Wingrave, esqrs
Clerks—Second Branch. Robert Sproule Cowan, Samuel Hurrell, Hugh Jameson, Thomas Edward Bennett, Thomas Earle, Joseph Crome, William John Browne Ffolkes
Correspondent (vacant)
Assistants, Jeremiah Ottley, William Trent, William Stanton, James Hills, Edward M'Laughlin, James Kemp, James Allen
Clerks, John Thomas Goodwin, Henry Paull, William Stewart Sheridan, John Chubb
Correspondent for Ireland & Scotland, John Norman, esq
Assistants, William Anderson, Thomas Jefferson, James Mutter, William Walker, Robert John Swift, Brabazon Disney, John Hardman, William Boys, Bartholomew Simmons
Solicitor, Andrew Merton Carr, esq. barrister at law
Solicitor for Criminal Prosecutions, Sir Francis Hastings Charles Doyle, bart
Registrar, Gabriel Riddle. *Clerk*, George Poulton

Accountants.

Accountant General, George Archibald Cottrell, esq
Assistant, Lewis Stephens Lyne, esq
Principal Accountants, Joseph Atwell, John Cooper, John Hanmer Wingrave, & John Gowland
Accountants, Jeremiah Pawson Price, William Burbidge, James Smythe Hore, Thomas Walsh, John Collier, Bryan Stephen Tore, Thomas Robert Sidebotham, Frederick Levermore, & James Michael Hulbert
Receiver General, William Thomas Thornton, esq
Clerks, Robert Drury, George Smith
Receivers, John King, Thomas Hobbs
Comptroller & Auditor General, Richard Vaughan Davis, esq.—*Deputy*, John Williams, esq
Clerks, Thomas Perfect Harding, John Reeks, Charles Farr, George Gateland Harrod, Thomas Purchas, Thomas Hall Fox, Edward Morfee, George Coombes, Francis Hotchkin
Clerk of the Securities,
Assistant, William Edward Gowland
Clerks, Edwin William Levermore, Henry Batho, Charles James Brown, Francis Stevens
Clerks of the Diaries, William Nichols, James Churchill
Inspector-General of Permits, William Mayhew
Chief Permit Examiner, Lewis Dunbar
Inspector of Permit Printing Office, John Frederick Walpole
Doorkeepers, John Erford, William Wybrow, James Nicholls

Warehouse Keepers of Seized Goods, John Saunders, John Hall
Port Surveyor, Thomas Bennett
Surveyor of Exports, Joshua Bartlett
Assistants, John Davis, William Henry Milstead
Storekeeper, Wm. Johnson, esq. *First Clerk*, Geo. Taylor
Distributor of Stamps, William Johnson, esq. [Clark
Office Keeper, Simeon Welsman, *Head Messenger*, James
Messengers, Richard Rice, John Charles Kay, John Sent, Philip Gathen, Frederick Pargeter
Surveyor of Buildings, William Herbert, esq

Surveying General Examiners.

First Class, James Steel, Thomas Julians, John Voyce, Richard Dixon, Edgar Eldred, esqrs
Second Class, John Wild, Frederick Charles Thomas, Thomas Manwell, John McCulloch, Joshua Bartlett, Charles Eldred, Francis Roscozla, William Adolphus Mark, William Dryden, William Knaggs, Thomas Thirlwall, Robert Hutchinson, Thomas Dobson, esqrs
Third Class, Benjamin Parker, William Blackburn, William Owsten, esqrs
Fourth Class, Colin Campbell, Robert Flamantz, Thomas Smith, James Graham, William Wrenford, Thomas Rayner, John Harrison, George McCullum, John Jones, Joshua Austin, Richard Pape, William Gilbert, Joseph Drinkwater, Matthew Hargraves, John Thorndich, Robert Cross Denton, Edward Harvey Dodd, & Thomas Rodway, esqrs

List of Permit Offices.

LONDON NORTH COLLECTION.

London 1st District	38 Cannon st. City 11 Castle court, Budge row 19 Sermon lane, City
Ditto 2d ditto	12 London st. City 42 St. Mary axe
Ditto 3rd ditto	19 Bridgewater sq. Barbican
Islington District	6 Pullens row, Islington 17 Red Lion st. Clerkenwell
London West District	23 Bartholomew close
Holborn 1st District	99 Gt. Russell st. Tottnhm. ct. rd
Ditto 2nd ditto	110 Fetter lane
Ditto 3rd ditto	66 St. Martin's lane
Marylebone District	35 Seymour pl. Bryanstone sq

LONDON SOUTH COLLECTION.

Milbank District	26 Denbigh st. Pimlico
Lambeth 1st ditto	137 Temple place, Blackfriars rd
Ditto 2d ditto	67 Vauxhall walk
Southwark 1st District	10 Devonshire buildings, Dover road, Borough
Ditto 2d ditto	6 Weston st. Southwark
Westminster 1st District	66 St. Martin's lane
Ditto 2d ditto	8 Marylebone st. Piccadilly

LONDON EAST COLLECTION.

London East District	5 Gt. Prescot st. Goodman's flds
Ratcliffe ditto	96 Old Gravel lane, Ratcliffe
Stepney ditto	1 North st. Mile end
Spitalfields ditto	14 Princes st. Brick lane
Hoxton District	43 Hoxton square
Hackney District	14 Newmarket ter. Cam. heath rd

Collectors of Excise.

Barnstaple	James Johnston, esq
Bath	Evan Evans, esq
Bedford	William Allen, esq
Birmingham	Charles Instan, esq
Bristol	Francis Amey, esq
Cambridge	Robert Buckle, esq
Canterbury	John Lewis, esq
Chester	John Bassett, esq
Colchester	Thomas Frankish, esq
Cornwall, see Falmouth	
Coventry	Sam. Crook Brown, esq
Cumberland	Joseph Longrigge
Derby	Richard Robertson Judd, esq *residence, Nottingham*
Dorchester	James Salmon, esq *residence, Weymouth*
Dover	Francis Brothers, esq *residence, Canterbury*
Durham	Robert Elwin, esq *residence, Sunderland*
Exeter	John Herdson, esq
Falmouth	Edward Hillborne, esq
Gloucester	Thomas Weston, esq
Grantham	John Forbes, esq *residence, Stamford*
Halifax	Thomas Williamson, esq
Hereford	Samuel Crowther, esq
Hertford	Thomas Dean, esq
Hull	Thomas Eman, esq
Isle of Wight, see Southampton	
Lancaster	John Manners, esq
Leeds	John Clark, esq
Lewes	Richard Hill, esq
Lincoln	Miles Butler, esq
Liverpool	Robert Swan Stanley, esq
London (East)	William Goodall, esq
London (North)	Jonathan Barber, esq
London (South)	William Wallace, esq
Lynn	William Garerd esq
Manchester	Patrick Kelly, esq
Newcastle	James Thompson, esq
Northampton	John Knapton, esq
Northwich	John Mayhew, esq
Norwich	William Marks, esq
Oxford	William Perrin, esq
Plymouth	Gustavus Gidley, esq
Portsmouth	George Foster Ross, esq
Reading	Wm. Hawkins, esq
Rochester	James Bridgewater, esq
Salisbury	William Adams, esq
Sheffield	John Badcock, esq
Shrewsbury	William Wardley, esq
Southampton (Isle of Wight)	Joseph Shaw, esq
Stafford	Job Douglas, esq
Stourbridge	Richard Yeomans, esq
Suffolk	Thomas Pocock Orum, esq
Surrey	George Clements, esq
Sussex, see Lewes	
Wales (East)	Wm. Schofield, esq *residence, Cardiff*
Wales (Middle)	John Pollock, esq *residence, Welchpool*
Wales (North)	Joseph Wood, esq *residence, Carnarvon*
Wales (West)	George A. Evans, esq *residence, Carmarthen*
Worcester	Thomas Wright, esq
Yarmouth (Noflk.) see Norwch	
York	John Stephenson, esq

FACTORY DEPARTMENT, *see "Home Office."*

FIRST FRUITS OFFICE, *see "Queen Anne's Bounty Office.*

FOREIGN OFFICE,

16 *Downing st.*

PRINCIPAL SECRETARY FOR FOREIGN AFFAIRS
Under Secretaries
Chief Clerk, George Lenox-Conyngham, esq
Senior Clerks, John Bidwell, James Bandinel, Thomas Staveley, Thomas Lawrence Ward, Richard Charles Mellish, K.H., Edward Hammond, esqrs
Clerks, Edward M'Mahon, Adolphus Kent Oom, James Murray, Henry Frederick Forster, Clinton George Dawkins, Bridges Taylor, John Edward Blackburn, William Huskisson, Augustus Leopold Coles, George Canning Backhouse, William Wylde, Richard Wellesley, esqrs., Hon. Charles Spring Rice, Francis Beilby Alston, Augustus Paget, esqrs., Hon. Spencer Ponsonby, John Boger Hole, John Bidwell, jun. Greville Morier, Thomas George Staveley, and J. Croker Pennell, esqrs
Clerks attached to the Chief Clerk's Department, Henry Dundas Scott, John Brodribb Bergue, esqrs
Private Secretary to the Earl of Aberdeen, Clinton George Dawkins, esq
Precis Writer, Lord Henry Lennox
Clerks attached to the Slave Trade Department, Charles Henry Parnther, Henry Charles Scott, George Skelton, esqrs
Collector of State Papers, Ven. Archdeacon Goddard, D.D
Librarian & Keeper of the Papers, Lewis Hertslet, esq
Sub Librarian, James Hertslet, esq
Translator, John Christian Huttner, esq
Chamber Keepers, John Venfield, John Tyler
Housekeeper, Mrs. Ann Watson
Door Porter, Andrew Gracewood
Office Printer, James Harrison

FOREIGN PLANTATIONS, *see "Committee of Privy Council for Trade."*

FORESTS, *see "Woods, Forests, Land Revenue," &c.*

GENERAL OFFICERS, BOARD OF.
Office for Military Boards, 6 *Whitehall yard.*
Hours, 10 to 4.
For the Inspection and Regulation of the Clothing of the Army, &c. &c. &c.

GENERALS—Henry William Marquess of Anglesea, K.G., G.C.B., G.C.H., Hon. Sir Henry George Grey, G.C.B., G.C.H., Sir Edward Paget, G.C.B., Frederic Maitland, Sir William Henry Clinton, G.C.B., Sir William Anson, bart., K.C.B., William Eden, Gerard Goselin, Sir James Willoughby Gordon, G.C.B., G.C.H., F.R.S., Sir Ralph Darling, G.C.H

LIEUTENANT GENERALS — James Orde, Sir Charles Bulkeley Egerton, K.C.H., Godfrey Basil Mundy, Sir Colin Halkett, K.C.B., G.C.H., Rt. Hon. Sir Frederick Adam, K.C.B., Sir Thomas Reynell, bart. K.C.B., Sir Edward Kerrison, bart. K.C.B., G.C.H., Sir Jasper Nicholls, K.C.B., Francis Newbery, Sir James Charles Dalbiac, K.C.H., Sir John McLean, K.C.B., Sir Thomas McMahon, bart. K.C.B., Sir Alexander Woodford, K.C.B

MAJOR GENERALS—Henry Shadforth, Sir David Ximenes, K.C.H., Henry D'Oyley, John Duffy, C.B

ACTING COMMITTEE—*President*, Lieut. Gen. Sir James Charles Dalbiac, K.C.H

Major Generals, Henry Shadforth, Sir David Ximenes, K.C.H., Henry D,Oyley, John Duffy, C.B

Secretary to Military Boards, Henry Elliot, esq

Messenger, Thomas Benbow

GENERAL POST OFFICE, *see "Post Office"*

GENERAL REGISTER OFFICE,
Nos. 7 & 8 *Somerset Place, Somerset House.*

REGISTRAR GENERAL—George Graham, esq

Chief Clerk, Thomas Mann, esq

Solicitor, Joseph Parkes, esq

First Clerk of Accounts & Cashier, Charles Henry Anderson, esq

First Clerk of Correspondence, George Sowray, esq

First Clerk of Records, Edward Edwards, esq.; *Assistant ditto*, William Owen, esq

Examiner & Compiler of Abstracts, William Farr, esq

Senior Clerks, Benjamin Adams, Thomas Cooper, John Denne Smith, Charles Philpot, William Henry Walter Titheridge, Francis Raleigh Grant Smith, George Ormond Douglas, John Shoveller, esqrs

Junior Clerks, John Skaif, Marriot Hunt, John Williams, Richard Cridland, Carew Henry Reynell, James Thomas Hammack, Smith Rawlings, John Thornton, Robert Gray, James Henry Sylvan Leigh Hunt, George Adolphus Voules, Charles Brumfit, Michael John Castleden, Louis Gabriel Isidore Bonnet, William Clode, John Angus, Thos. Oakes, Thos. Evan Roberts, Frederick Edwards, Charles Anthony Cocke, Thomas Martindale, Charles Vyse Palin, Florence Fox, Stephen Bowditch, Fredk. Spong, Samuel Salvage, Charles Hazard, John Atkinson Armstrong, & Henry Scroggs, esqrs

Office Keeper & Head Messenger, Thomas Hill

Messengers, Oliver Barfoot, George Nippin, John Stinchcombe, William Bayley, Samuel Shepherd, and Thomas Oliver

Non-Parochial Register Office.
(A branch of the General Register Office.)
3 *Roll's yard, Chancery lane.* Hours, 10 to 4.

Superintendent Registrars & Registrars in London

BERMONDSEY.

SUPERINTENDENT REGISTRAR—Beriah Drew, esq. 185 Bermondsey st

REGISTRARS—*Leather Market*, William Cross, 16 Bermondsey New road; *St. Mary Magdalen*, Richard Hellier, 1 George terrace, Crimscott street, Bermondsey; William Charles Ewbank, deputy ditto, 5 George terrace, Crimscott st. Bermondsey; *St. James'*, James Paul, 20 Prospect row, Dockhead, Bermondsey

BETHNAL GREEN.

SUP. REGISTRAR—Robert Brutton, esq. 18 Bethnal green

REGISTRARS—*The Green*, Thomas Howard, 29 Green street, Bethnal green; *Church*, George Reynolds, 271 Bethnal green road; *Town*, Henry Gregory, 7 White street, Bethnal green road; *Hackney road*, James Murray, 8 Suffolk place, Cambridge heath gate, Hackney road

CHELSEA.

SUP. REGISTRAR — Thomas Myddelton Loveland, esq. Shawfield cottage, King's road, Chelsea

REGISTRARS—*Chelsea, South*, Thomas Long, 15 Manor street, Chelsea; *Chelsea, North West*, William Larner, 12 Robert street, Chelsea; *Chelsea, North East*, W. C. Smith, Exeter place, Exeter st. Sloane st

CLERKENWELL.

SUP. REGISTRAR—George A. M'Phail, esq. 17 Wilmington square, Clerkenwell

REGISTRARS—*Pentonville*, George Pyne, 43 Henry st. Pentonville; *Amwell*, William Foster, 2 Soley terrace, Lloyd square, Pentonville; *Goswell st.* Robert Charles Fair, 3 Lower Charles st. St. John st. road; *St. James's*, Abraham Western, 5 Clerkenwell close

HOLBORN.
Office, Little Gray's Inn Lane.

SUP. REGISTRAR—William Roberts James, esq. 23 Ely place, Holborn

DEPUTY REGISTRAR—Edward Wallywn James, esq. 23, Ely place, Holborn

REGISTRARS—*St. George the Martyr & St. Andrew's, Western*, Richard Bardons, 75 Red Lion st. Holborn; *St. Andrew's, Eastern*, Lazarus Holmes, 14 Dorrington st. Leather lane; *Saffron hill*, Thomas Truman, 23 Vine st. Hatton garden

ISLINGTON.

SUP. REGISTRAR—William May, esq. 8 Prospect cottages, Thornhill road

REGISTRARS—*West District*, John Watts, 2 Albion place, Thornhill road; *East District*, Wm. Henry Butterfield, 2 Berlinda cottages, Canonbury sq

KENSINGTON.
Office, 1 *Canning place, Kensington New Town.*

SUP. REGISTRAR—Samuel Cornell, esq. 1 Canning place, Kensington

DEP. SUP. REGISTRAR—George Chance, esq. Durham cottage, Thistle grove, Brompton

REGISTRARS—*Paddington, St. John's*, Robert Holloway, 2 Upper Southwick st.; *Paddington, St. Mary's*, James Pursey, 27 Pickering place; *Fulham*, Graham Hackman, Wimberley house, Fulham road; *Hammersmith, St. Paul's*, D. T. Roy, Brook green, Hammersmith; *Hammersmith, St. Peter's*, T. W. C. Perfect, Hammersmith terrace; *Kensington Town District*, Francis Gorham, 2 Terrace, Kensington; *Brompton District*, James Stone, 3 Elm place, Brompton

LAMBETH.

SUP. REGISTRAR—W. T. Logan, esq. Kennington green

REGISTRARS—*Waterloo road, 1st part*, Charles Mears, 124 Waterloo road; *Waterloo road, 2nd part*, Jas. Green, 96 York road; *Lambeth Church, 1st part*, John Harwood, Walsingham place, Westminster road; *Lambeth Church, 2nd part*, William Henry Wheatley, 33 Esher st. Upper Kennington lane; *Kennington, 1st part*, Wm. Easter, Upper Dorset place, Clapham road; *Kennington, 2nd part*, J. R. Unwin, 8 Alfred place, North Brixton; *Brixton*, John Plumber, Brixton place; *Norwood*, C. J. Child, Norwood

LONDON, CITY OF.

SUP. REGISTRAR—John Thomas Rowsell, esq. 35 Cannon st

REGISTRARS—*North East*, Thomas Abraham 49 Old Broad st.; *North West*, George Hooper, Sion College gardens, Aldermanbury; *South West*, William Arnott, 39 St. Andrew's hill, Doctors' commons; *South*, Alfred Nelson Wickes, 8 Clement's lane, Lombard st.; *South East*, Richard Cranch, 15 London st. Fenchurch st

REGISTRARS OF MARRIAGES—John Paul, 35 Cannon st. & John H. Paul, 35 Cannon st

LONDON, EAST.

SUP. REGISTRAR—Alexander John Baylis, esq. 1 Devonshire square, Bishopsgate

REGISTRARS—*St. Botolph*, Thomas Lifford Smartt, 25 Sun st. Bishopsgate; *Cripplegate*, Joseph Defriez, 10 Nicholl square, Cripplegate

LONDON, WEST.

SUP. REGISTRAR—John Pontifex, esq. 5 St. Andrew's court, Holborn

REGISTRARS—*South District*, Francis Hutchinson, 92 Farringdon st.; *North District*, William Fortescue, 9 Smithfield bars

MARYLEBONE, ST.

SUP. REGISTRAR—Henry Charles Wilson, esq. Court house, Marylebone lane

REGISTRARS—*All Soul's*, Charles Benson Breary, 73 Great Portland st. Marylebone; *Cavendish square*, William Clapp, 62 Welbeck st.; *Rectory*, Edward Joseph, 99 High st. Marylebone; *St. Mary's*, Henry Martin, 44 Upper York st. Porman square; *Christ Church*, Henry Obré, 12 Grove place, Lisson grove; *St. John's Wood*, George Henry Bachhoffner, 6 Wellington terrace, St. John's Wood

NEWINGTON.

SUP. REGISTRAR—John Rowbotham, esq. 55 Queen's row, Walworth

REGISTRARS—*St. Mary's*, Godfrey Young, 7 Church row, Newington; *St. Peter's, Walworth*, Wm. St. John Turner, 16 Keen's row, Walworth; *Trinity*, William Seagrave, 16 West terrace, St. George's road, Old Kent road

REGISTRARS OF MARRIAGES—John Fuller, 23 Crosby row, Walworth road, & William Seagrave, 16 West terrace, St. George's road

PANCRAS, ST.

SUP. REGISTRAR—Joseph Ivimey, esq. 1 Ampthill square, Hampstead road

REGISTRARS—*Tottenham court road*, John Wells, 23 Percy st. Bedford square; *Gray's inn lane*, John Worrell, 28 Hunter st. Brunswick square; *Somers Town*, William Henry Matthews, 44 Upper Seymour st. Euston square; *Camden Town*, Joseph Curtis, 1 St. James's terrace, Kentish town road; *Regent's Park*, Charles Henry Spong, 7 Mornington place, Hampstead road; *Kentish Town*, Edward Hacker, 1 Moreton villas, Kentish town road

POPLAR.

SUP. REGISTRAR—John Symons, esq. 1 Kerbey st. Poplar

DEPUTY SUP. REGISTRAR—Thomas Wardell, Poplar union workhouse

REGISTRARS—*Poplar*, Thomas William Gagen, 278 High st. Poplar; *Bow & Bromley*, James Dunstan, near the Church, Bromley, Middlesex

ROTHERHITHE.

SUP. REGISTRAR—Walter Brooks, esq. 61 Paradise st. Rotherhithe

REGISTRAR—*Rotherhithe*, George Pitt, 23 Paradise row, Rotherhithe

ST. GEORGE'S, HANOVER SQUARE.

SUP. REGISTRAR—Thomas B. Chappell, esq. Board room, between 104 & 105 Mount st. Berkeley st. Berkeley sq

DEPUTY SUP. REGISTRAR—Alfred Butt, Board room, Mount st

REGISTRARS—*Hanover square*, Edward Jay, 51 Park st. Grosvenor square; *Mayfair*, Charles Edmund Chowne, 48 Hertford st. Mayfair; *Belgrave*, Wm. Prue Jordan, 9 Lower Belgrave st. Eaton square

ST. GEORGE'S IN THE EAST.

SUP. REGISTRAR—Thomas Stone, esq. 6 Wellclose square

REGISTRARS—*St. Paul's*, Henry Baddeley, 27 Colet place, Commercial road; *St. Mary's*, Wm. Lockwood Howell, 40 Ratcliff highway; *St. John's*, John Verrall, Raine's school, Charles st. Old Gravel lane

ST. GEORGE'S, SOUTHWARK.

SUP. REGISTRAR—John Henry Fitch, esq. 17 Union st. Southwark

REGISTRARS—*Kent road*, Richard Bell, 12 White st. Southwark; *Borough road*, James Bedwell, 44 Belvedere pl. Southwark; *London road*, Arthur Redford, 96 London road, Southwark

ST. GILES' & ST. GEORGE'S.

SUP. REGISTRAR—William Newbery, esq. 6 King st. Bloomsbury square

REGISTRARS—*South District*, Geo. Lee, 50 Gt. Queen st. Lincoln's inn fields; *North District*, James Wood, 6 Gt. Russell st. Bedford square; *St. George*, John Yardley, 5 Thorney st. Bloomsbury

REGISTRAR OF MARRIAGES—William Musson Newbery, 23 Charlotte st. Bedford square

ST. JAMES'S.

SUP. REGISTRAR—George Buzzard, esq. 50 Poland st. Oxford st

REGISTRARS—*Berwick street*, Henry Robinson, 4 Cambridge st. Golden square; *Golden square*, George Lawford, 6 Saville passage, Saville row; *St. James's square*, James Roberts, 38 Duke st. St. James's

ST. LUKE'S.

SUP. REGISTRAR—Joseph Smith, esq. Registry office, 6 Finsbury terrace, City road

REGISTRARS—*Finsbury*, George Sinclair, 4 Finsbury terrace; *Whitecross street*, John Austin, 11 Rahere st. Goswell st.; *City road*, Henry Hamlin, 24 City terrace, City road

ST. MARTIN'S IN THE FIELDS.

SUP. REGISTRAR—Philip Henry Le Breton, esq. 44 Castle st. Leicester square

REGISTRARS—*Charing cross*, James Leonard, 18 Craven st. Strand; *Long acre*, Edward Cobbett, 115 Long acre

ST. OLAVE'S, SOUTHWARK.

SUP. REGISTRAR—Robert Slee, esq. 1 Parish street, St. John's, Southwark

REGISTRARS—*St. Olave & St. Thomas*, Wililam Stainer, 2 Broadway, St. Thomas, Southwark; *St. John, Horselydown*, John Benstead, 36 Charles street, Horselydown

ST. SAVIOUR'S, SOUTHWARK.

SUP. REGISTRAR—James Joseph Blake, esq. 79 Blackfriars road, Southwark

REGISTRARS—*St. Saviour*, Francis Parr, 22 Bridge street, Southwark; *Christchurch*, John White, 15 Great Charlotte street, Blackfriars road

REGISTRAR OF MARRIAGES—*St. Saviour*, Wm. Norris, 9 New street, Bridge street

SHOREDITCH, ST. LEONARD.

SUP. REGISTRAR—Thomas Ware, esq. 98 Kingsland road

DEPUTY—John Ware, esq. Trafalgar place, Hackney road

REGISTRARS—*Hoxton New town*, William Harper Skegg, 39 Brudenell place, New North road; *Hoxton Old town*, Charles Packer, Pitfield street, Hoxton; *Holywell & Moorfields*, Edward Earles, 4 Worship square; *St. Leonard's*, George Yarrow, Shoreditch churchyard; *Haggerstone, East*, John Johnson, 4 Brunswick street, Hackney road; *Haggerstone, West*, Nathaniel Bowring, 78 Pearson street, Kingsland road

REGISTRAR OF MARRIAGES—James Colson Edwards, 10 Rutland street, Kingsland road

STEPNEY.

SUP. REGISTRAR—William Leach, esq. 1 Colet place, Salmon lane, Stepney

REGISTRARS—*Limehouse*, Adolphus Barnett, 3 Vittoria place, Limehouse; *Ratcliff*, George Wells, 1 Brunswick terrace, Commercial road; *Shadwell & Wapping*, Daniel Ross, 56 Shadwell High street; *Mile end Old Town, Upper*, Thomas Baddeley, 38 Gloucester terrace, Commercial road; *Mile end Old Town, Lower*, Samuel Castleden; 14 Devonshire terrace, Globe road, Mile end Old Town

STRAND.

SUP. REGISTRAR—James Corder, esq. 6 Bow st. Covent garden

REGISTRARS—*St. Clement Danes*, William Fitch, 48 Carey street; *St. Mary's*, Samuel Lovett, 23 Clare street; *St. Anne's*, Henry Derviche Jones, 23 Soho square

REGISTRARS OF MARRIAGES—Wm. Boswood, 6 Bow st. Covent garden, & Samuel Lovett, 23 Clare st. Clare mrkt

WESTMINSTER.

Register Office, 10 *Dartmouth street.*

SUP. REGISTRAR—John P. Makeham, esq. 10 Dartmouth st

DEPUTY—George Pearse, jun. 5 Regent street

REGISTRARS—*St. John's*, George Pearse, sen. 46 Marsham street, Westminster; *St. Margaret's*, William Martin, 50 King st. Westminster

REGISTRAR OF MARRIAGES—Thomas Binge, 76 York st

WHITECHAPEL.

SUP. REGISTRAR—John Smith, esq. 23 Leman street, Goodman's fields

REGISTRARS OF BIRTHS AND DEATHS—*Spitalfields*, George Deboos, 24 Wood street, Spitalfields; *Artillery*, Thomas Mason, 7 High street, Norton folgate; *Mile end New Town*, Charles Hastings Rich, 70 Church street, Mile end New Town; *Whitechapel, North*, Henry Chapman, 8 Osborn street, Whitechapel; *Whitechapel Church*, William Hems, jun. 39 High street, Whitechapel; *Goodman's fields*, William Kerby, 40 Leman street, Whitechapel; *Aldgate*, John James Harris, 11 Upper East Smithfield

REGISTRARS OF MARRIAGES.—William Tayler, 15 Church street, Spitalfields; William Mosely, 17 Whitechapel road

GOVERNMENT EMIGRATION OFFICE, *see "Colonial Land & Emigration Board."*

GREENWICH HOSPITAL.

MILITARY DEPARTMENT.

Governor, Admiral Hon. Sir Robert Stopford, G.C.B., G.C.M.G

Lieut.-Governor, Rear-Admiral Sir James Alexander Gordon, K.C.B

Captains, John Clavell, John Simpson, John Bowker

Commanders, Charles Robinson, William Cunningham Cavendish Dalyell, Joseph Corbyn, Edward Garrett

Lieutenants, Frederick Bedford, William Rivers, John Wood Rouse, David O'Brian Casey, Bassit J. Loveless, Josiah Dornford

Masters, James Read, William Pickering

Chaplain, Rev. John Kellow Goldney

Medical Inspector of Hospital, John Liddell, M.D

Deputy Medical Inspector of Hospital, Alexander Nisbet, M.D

Assisting Surgeon, James McTernan

Assistant Surgeon, James Gregory Buchanan

Dispenser

Matrons, Mrs. Fanny Figg, Mrs. Elizabeth Roberts, Mrs. Mary Tetley

SCHOOLS.

Superintending Lieutenant, John Wood Rouse
Chaplain, Rev. George Fisher
Head Mathematical Master, Edward Riddle. *Assistant ditto*, John Riddle

Upper School.

Head Master, Rev. James Hill. *Assistants*, John Ramage Campbell, Alexander Davidson

Lower School.

Head Master, Thomas Irvine. *Assistants*, Edward Hughes, James Gillespie, William Willis, James Hamilton, James Harris
Singing Master, John Hullah
Matron, Mrs. Mary Hooper

CIVIL DEPARTMENT.

Resident Commissioners, George Tierney, esq. Sir Charles Eurwicke Douglas, C.M.G., M.P. Sir Henry Hart, K.C.H. Capt. R.N
Secretary, John Arscott Lethbridge, esq
Assistant Secretary, John Livingston Jay. *Clerk*, Thomas Broughton Stow
Steward, Thomas Freeman Jessep, esq. *Clerks*, George Hann, James Thorburn, James De Montmorency, H. E. Rivers & F. Huskisson
Cashier, William Paine, esq
Clerks, William Henry Knowlden, Stephen Robert Prowse, James Figg Wright
Brewer, Thomas Calvert Morton
Mates of the Victualling, James Bromley, George Dugdale
Clerk of the Cheque, Philip Carteret Le Geyt, esq. *Clerks*, John Inwood Langley, Thomas Williams, George Deane, Arthur Waller, William Popham Lethbridge, John Rouse
Architect, Joseph Kay, esq
Inspectors of Works, Charles Lee & William Swell
Clerk, Edward George Pepper

HEALTH OF TOWNS (COMMISSIONERS OF).

Gwydyr House, Whitehall. Hours, 10 to 5.

Commissioners, The Duke of Buccleuch; Earl of Lincoln; Robert Aglionby Slaney, esq.; George Graham, esq.; Sir Henry Thomas De la Beche, knt.; Dr. Lyon Playfair; Dr. David Boswell Reid; Richard Owen, esq.; William Thomas Dennison, esq.; James Ranald Martin, esq.; James Smith, of Deanston, esq.; Robert Stephenson, jun. esq.; William Cubitt, esq
Secretary, Henry Hobhouse, esq
Office keeper, Thomas Land

HERALD'S COLLEGE.

Office, Bennett's hill, Doctor's Commons. Hours, 10 to 4.

EARL MARSHAL, Duke of Norfolk, P.C

KINGS OF ARMS:—

Garter, Sir Charles George Young, knt. F.S.A.
Clarenceux, Joseph Hawker, esq. F.S.A.
Norroy, Francis Martin, esq. F.S.A.

SIX HERALDS:—

Somerset, James Cathrow Disney, esq
Chester, Walter Aston Blount, esq
Richmond, James Pulman, esq. F.S.A.
Windsor, Robert Laurie, esq
Lancaster, Albert William Woods, esq
York, Edward Howard Gibbon, esq

FOUR PURSUIVANTS:—

Bluemantle, Geo. Harrison Rogers Harrison, esq. F.S.A.
Rouge Dragon, Thomas William King, esq. F.S.A.
Rouge Croix, William Cauthorpe, esq
Portcullis, George William Collen, esq
Registrar, James Pulman, esq. F.S.A.
Secretary to His Grace the Earl Marshal, Edward Howard Gibbon, esq.

HOME OFFICE.

Whitehall. Hours 9 to 7.

PRINCIPAL SECRETARY FOR HOME AFFAIRS,

Under Secretaries .... Samuel March Phillipps, esq
Chief Clerk, Thomas Henry Plasket, esq
Senior Clerks, Richard Hatt Noble, Francis Walpole, Francis Gore Currie, Robert Sharrock Dawson, esqrs
Clerks, Henry John Knyvett, Charles Robert Fitz Gerald, Francis Seymour Leslie, John Streatfield, Robert Anstruther, Charles Erskine, Samuel Redgrave, esqrs. Hon. Arthur Dillon, Henry Maling, esq
Precis Writer & Librarian, Frederick Russell Mills, esq
Clerk for Criminal Business, John Henry Capper, esq
Assistant Clerk for Criminal Business, Geo. Everest, esq
Keeper of Criminal Register, Samuel Redgrave, esq
Clerk for Alien Business, Joseph Francis Kitching, esq
Chamber Keepers, William Taylor, Robert Forrest
Assistant, Francis Collett
Housekeeper, Mrs. Elizabeth Cooke
Office Porter, Stephen Merritt
Door Porter, Joseph Loton

Factory Department,

Office, 15 *Duke st. Westminster.*

INSPECTORS.	SUPERINTENDENTS.
Leonard Horner, esq	William Graham Longsight, Manchester; Joseph Ewings, Preston; Jno. Beal, Rochdale; Edw. Davies, Ashton under Lyne; esqrs
Thomas Jones Howell, esq. Residence, Painswick, Gloucestershire	Charles Trimmer, esq. Bollington, near Macclesfield; Weston Hickes, esq. Painswick, near Stroud; Samuel Savil Kent, esq. Sidmouth, Devon; Chas. Brown, esq. Myford, near Welchpool
Robert John Saunders, esq...	Robert Baker, Leeds; James Bates, Holmforth, Huddersfield; James Bury, Nottingham; esqrs.; & Capt. Hart, Halifax
James Stuart, esq........	John Peter Hudson, Belfast; Charles Balfour, Glasgow; Daniel Walker, Dundee; esqrs

Messenger, John Syrett

Inspectors of Prisons.

William Crawford, esq., Rev. Whitworth Russell, M.A. John George Perry, esq., Capt. Williams, Frederick Hill, esq

Establishment of Queen's Messengers

Attending the Secretaries of State.

SUPERINTENDENT AND COMPTROLLER OF ACCOUNTS, Lewis Hertslet, esq

Messengers for Foreign Service.

Joseph Wright Draffen, James Crotch, John Robert Poignand, Robert Haviland, John Edward Waring, Robert Fennessy, John Moore, George Holmes, Frederick Fricker, esqrs.; Lieut. Richard William McDonald, Lieut. Richard Webster, Lieut. Thomas Daniel Wright, Capt. Cecil Godschall Johnson, Lieut. Stephens P. Robbins, Lieut. Col. Charles Townley, Lieut. Spencer Percival Robbins, Jas. Wm. Geo. Gutch, Arthur Jas. Drury, esqrs

Messengers for Home Service.

(*Home Office.*)

Messrs. Thomas Hill, John Ellis, John Odell, George Pudar, Henry Lewis Meyer, Adolphus Frederick Bell

(*Foreign Office.*)

Messrs. Thomas Hutt, James Ayres, James Matthews, Wm. Jackson, Henry Aspain, Edward Harran, John Shepard, Henry Valentine Cocking

(*Colonial Office.*)

Messrs. Jonathan Patten, Edward Page, James Faggetter, Daniel Harris, George Bishop

INDIA BOARD.

Cannon Row, Westminster.

COMMISSIONERS.

President

The Lord President of the Council, The Lord Privy Seal, The First Lord of the Treasury, Principal Secretaries of State and the Chancellor of the Exchequer
Secretaries, Viscount Jocelyn, M.P., Viscount Mahon, M.P
Assistant Secretary, Hugh Stark, esq
Senior Clerks:—
Revenue, Hugh Stark, esq.; *Financial*, William Leach, esq.; *Military*, Arthur Easton, esq.; *Public*, Charles Henry Chicheley Plowden, esq.; *Secret and Political*, Thomas Nelson Waterfield; *Judicial*, John Alfred Trimmer, esqrs
Assistant Clerks, Charles William Fletcher, William Henry Deedes, Robert Corbett, Henry Lannoy Hunter, Pryce Buckley Williams, Thomas Bunbury Lenon, esqrs
Junior Clerks, Henry William Beauclerk, Cecil Edward George Lukin, Charles Unwin, Charles Bagot Phillimore, Henry Francis Leigh, Henry Charles Deedes, Joceline Courtenay, William Ireland Blackburne, esqrs.; Hon.

Gerald Dillon, Charles Manners Lushington, Henry Cornelius Pierson, Frederick Hobart, Henry Storer Jones, esqrs., and Hon. Frederick Arthur Henry Chichester
Solicitor, Richard Groom, esq
Private Secretary to the President, Alexander Gordon, esq
Private Secretary to Viscount Jocelyn, M.P. Charles Bagot Phillimore, esq
Private Secretary to Viscount Mahon, M.P. Charles Unwin, esq
Registrar & Keeper of the Papers, John Moore, esq
Assistant ditto, Thomas Sharp, esq
Office Keeper, Thomas Scarman
Housekeeper, Mrs. Renshaw
Messengers, Joseph Thomas Ludlam, William Laws
Porter, George Perrott

Inspector of Prisons and Factories.
See "*Home Office*."

INSPECTOR OF RAILWAYS.
See "*Committee of Privy Council for Trade*."

IRISH OFFICE.
18 *Great Queen Street, Westminster*. Hours 11 to 5.
CHIEF SECRETARY TO THE LORD LIEUTENANT OF IRELAND, Sir Thomas Fremantle, bart
Chief Clerk, George Trundle, esq
Assistant, Hon. Spencer Dudley Montagu
Private Secretary to Chief Secretary, Capt. Stephen Fremantle
Counsel, Espine Batty, esq
Messengers, Edwin Webster, James Tompkins, Robert Townshend, George Berridge

JUDGE ADVOCATE GENERAL'S OFFICE,
35 *Great George Street*. Hours 10 to 4.
JUDGE ADVOCATE GENERAL, Right Hon. John Nicholl, D.C.L., M.P
Deputy, Francis Newman James Rogers, esq, Q.C
Chief Clerk, Jonathan Scollick, esq
Clerks, William Henry Hughes, Jonathan Scollick, jun
Office Keeper, Richard Berry
Messenger, Thomas Weale

LAND REVENUE RECORDS AND INROLMENTS.
11 *Spring Gardens*. Hours 10 to 4.
For the Registration of Deeds relating to Crown property
KEEPER OF THE RECORDS, Tarver Richard Fearnside, esq
Assistant Keeper of Records, Elisha Naylor, esq
Messenger, Lionel Atkins

Auditor of Land Revenue. *Office*, 11 *Spring Gardens*, Charles George Christmas, esq

LAND REVENUES, *see* "*Woods, Forests*," *&c*

LONDON GAZETTE OFFICE,
Cannon Row, Westminster. Hours 10 to 5.
Gazette Writer, William Gregson, esq
Publisher, Francis Watts, esq
Chief Clerk, Francis M'Gedy, esq

METROPOLIS CHURCHES' FUND,
79 *Pall Mall*. Hours 10 to 4.
VICE PATRON, The Archbishop of Canterbury
PRESIDENT, The Bishop of London
TRUSTEES, Bishop of London; Right Hon. Thomas Erskine; Sir Robert Harry Inglis, bart. M.P.; William Cotton, esq
Secretary, Rev. William Dodsworth, M.A
Assistant Secretary, George Charles Silk

METROPOLIS IMPROVEMENT OFFICE,
7 *Whitehall Yard*. Hours 10 to 4.
Architect & Surveyor, James Pennethorne, esq

METROPOLIS ROADS NORTH OF THE THAMES.
Office 22 *Whitehall place*. Hours 10 to 4.
Secretary, John Leach Panter, esq
Accountant, Richard Robertson, esq
Assistant Accountant, Vincent Charles Wright, esq
Surveyor General, Sir James M'Adam, knt
Inspector, Henry Browse, esq

METROPOLITAN BUILDINGS OFFICE.
7 & 8 Vic. c. 84.
3 *Trafalgar Square*. Hours of public business, 10 to 4.
Board for superintending the execution of the Metropolitan Buildings Act, and deciding on differences arising thereon
Official Referees, James White Higgins, and William Hosking, esquires
Registrar, Arthur Symonds, esq. barrister at law

MINT, *see* "*Royal Mint*."

NATIONAL DEBT OFFICE, *see* "*Reduction of National Debt Office*."

ORDNANCE BOARD,
86 *Pall Mall*. Hours 10 to 6.
MASTER GENERAL, Right Hon. Gen. Sir Geo. Murray, G.C.B
SURVEYOR GENERAL OF THE ORDNANCE, Colonel Jonathan Peel, M.P.
CLERK OF THE ORDNANCE, Lord Arthur Lennox, M.P.
PRINCIPAL STOREKEEPER, Capt. Sir Thomas Hastings
Secretary to the Master General, Major Gen. Sir Fredk. William Trench, K.C.H., M.P.
Chief Clerk, Edward Elliot, esq
Clerks, John Ash, Henry Gilbert Burgess, esqrs
SECRETARY TO THE BOARD OF ORDNANCE, Richard Byham, esq
Chief Clerk, George Butler, esq
Senior Clerks, William Sedgwick, Joseph Wood, Charles Poignand, Richard Matthew Marshall, Geo. du Pasquier, George Satchwell, Ralph Bayne, William Chas. Richards, Robert Midford, George Hanby, William Madox, Jekin Elwin, Charles Fletcher, Henry George Harris, William Richard Byham, Joseph Cheetham, esqrs
Junior Clerks, Edward Marston, Robert Gwyn, Charles Cassidi, Henry Montresor, Alexander Holmes, James Holderness Featherstone, Henry Byham, Frederick Geo. Millar, William Cheetham, John Frederick Allen, Charles Henry Connell, Thomas M'Kittrick, George Francis Carew Peter, Richard Bissett, Thurlow Dowling, William P. Raggett, Charles Henry Broad, George Byham, Wm. Francis Boyce, Charles Crokat
INSPECTOR GENERAL OF FORTIFICATIONS, Major Gen. Sir John Fox Burgoyne, K.C.B.
Surveyor, John Owen, esq
Senior Clerks, Henry Lancaster, Henry Sawyer, esqrs
Junior Clerks, Robert Wm. Parsons, Franklin Coxworthy, James M'Cutcheon, Henry Findlay, George Sawyer, Henry Lancaster, jun. Charles James Ellis
Keepers of Maps, Plans, &c. &c., Samuel Burt Howlett, Joseph Nightingale, esqrs
Chief Messenger, Gordon Munro
Master General's Messenger, George Shefford
Housekeeper, Mrs. Ellen C. Munro
SOLICITOR TO THE ORDNANCE, Thomas Clarke, esq

AT THE TOWER:—

Surveyor General's Office.
Chief Clerk, William Lees, esq
Senior Clerks, Robert Wallis Hope, Thomas Waugh, Joseph Payne, Robert Bartley, William Alexander, William Maye, Joseph Haigh, John Robert Payne, John Jones, James Pew, Thomas Richard Read, Thomas Howard, Daniel Briers, Richard Pittman, William Durrant, esqrs
Junior Clerks, Thomas Scarth, Charles Frederick Angell, Henry King, Anthony Harvey, William Scott, Charles Wyndham Barnham, James Maxton, William James Lees, Samuel Bennett, John Saffery, Samuel Silver Garrett, William Wyborn Bradly, Robert Bradley, Joseph Winniett, Spencer Brown, Stephen Carter, Joseph Todd Gilchrist, Frank Robert Bertolacci, Henry Dingley Cockburn, George Phelps Boyer, Thomas Buncombe, John Lean Charles Frederick Hawker, Alfred Harrisson, Alfred Keen, Stephen Groom, James Johnstone Bourne, Henry Arthur March
Assistant Clerks, William Lyon, Walter Whitsed Veasey

Store Account Examiner's Office.
Senior Clerks, Frederick Edward March, Arthur Allen, James Trenow, Richard Humber, Stephen Amand Wright, Thomas Currie, Robert Welbank, esqrs
Junior Clerks, Joseph Attree, John Scott Breeze, John Milner, John Sample, William Scarth, William Richardson Travis, John Vale, Stephen Peltro Henry Wright Edmund Philips, Henry Thomas Beevor, Thomas Dun Cater, Jonathan William Bellis, Robert Allen, William Gaunt
Assistant Clerks, Walter Stanbrough, & Samuel H. Payne
Clerk of the Check, Joseph Boulcott
Engine Keeper, Thomas Smart
Housekeeper, Mrs. Dora March

Clerk of the Ordnance Office.
Chief Clerk, Seth Thomas, esq
Senior Clerks, William Thomas Elder, Upton Caldewood, Henry Thomas Gruaz, Henry Smith, William Mitchell, Charles Smith, Edward Patrick Briers, John Griffith, Francis Woodgate, William Griffith, John Cullum, Emanuel Martiny, esqrs

Junior Clerks, John Peace Mitchell, Martin Brown, William Smeddle, Edmund George Bower, James M'Jannet, William Thomas, Patrick Stewart, Robert Wilkinson, Charles George Alexander Brodie, James Mackay, William A. Cockburn, Alfred Langdon Brander, Harry Leonard Hearsum, Alfred Austin, William Coppin Byers, Henry William Whiffin, Thomas Edmund Tyndale Ripley, James A. Chalmer, George Joseph Tanner Marriott, Francis John Woodgate
Assistant Clerks, Wm. Alexander, James Purbrick

Principal Storekeeper's Office.

Chief Clerk, Robert Porrett, esq
Senior Clerks, George Stacey, Lyon Fawkener, Samuel Wickins, John Cooper, Samuel Roper, Amos Hodgson, Joseph Bemrose Morris, Edward Charles King, James Baker, esqrs
Junior Clerks, William Vincent, Basil Heron Goldie, Thomas Norman Collier, John Robert Smith, Edward Gilbert, Thomas Pearce, Thomas Edward Clack, Henry Baker, Hervey Montmorency Prior, Cornelius Bonneau, Edward Pengelley, Joseph Fletcher, John Hewitt, Henry Bache, William Chetely Moore, Thomas Edward King, Samuel Baker Maclean, William Alexander Holmes, John Davies, Charles Sandys Elliott, Samuel Wickins, jun. George Kane
Assistant Clerk, Anthony Sutton Beswick
Messengers, George Clark, Thomas Stallwood

Superintendent of Shipping's Office.
Woolwich.

Superintendent of Shipping, Joseph Soady, Capt. R.N
Clerk, Henry Topping

SMALL ARM DEPARTMENT:—

Inspector of Small Arms, George Lovell, esq
Assistant Inspector of Small Arms, Francis Lovell, esq

PARLIAMENTARY OFFICES.

Officers of House of Peers.

Clerk of the Parliaments, Right Hon. Sir George H. Rose, 7 Old Palace yard
Clerk Assistant, John William Birch, esq. [Palace yard
Additional Clerk Assistant, Benjamin Currey, esq, 6 Old
Reading Clerk & Clerk of the Private Committees, William Rose, esq
Counsel to the Chairman of Committees, Robert Palk, esq
Clerk of Journals, Edward Parratt, esq
Chief Clerk, Henry Stone Smith, esq
Clerk of Engrossments, William Elyard Walmisley, esq
Librarian, John Frederic Leary, esq. F.S.A
Clerk of Enrolments, George John Dike, esq
Other Clerks in the Office, Messrs. William Atkinson Green, Lionel Hill Thompson, Edward Courtenay, William Frederick White, Andrew Guisti Flint Peregrine Birch, George Mitchell; James Nicholas Birch, Edward Meredith Parratt, Michael Haliday, Bartholomew Samuel Rowley, Adam William Henry Dike, William Henry Haines, Frederick Vane, Charles Congreve, Owen E. Grant, J. H. Robinson, Augustus W. Du Bourg, Henry Walmisley, William Maloney, Charles William Green, William J. Thoms
Assistant Librarian, Mr. James Heard Pulman
Collecting Clerk, Mr. Thomas William Couch
Offces of Enrolments of Engrossment, James Kilpin
Doorkeeper to Library, Samuel Lethbridge
Keeper of Parliament Office, Mrs. Mary Truscott
Messengers, James Batterbee, Henry Norris
Gentleman Usher of the Black Rod, Sir Augustus William Clifford, bart
Yeoman Usher, James Pulman, esq. F.S.A.
Serjeant at Arms, Colonel Percival
Deputy, Mr. George Goodbody
Receiver of Fees, Mr. Frederick Shells
Short-hand Writer, William Brodie Gurney, esq
Assistant, Mr. Joseph Gurney
Principal Doorkeepers, Messrs. Thomas Stamp, Frederick Shells, John Oldrini, Abraham Grainger, Robert Hogwood, John Maggs, Robert Moody
Assistant Doorkeepers, Messrs. Hermon Muhlenkamp, William Moyes, John Royal, William Howard, Anthony Allan, William Dean
Messengers, William Lilly, James Whetton
Housekeeper, Mrs. Brandish
Deputy, Mrs. Bennett
Necessary Woman, Mrs. Oldrini
Fire Lighter, Mrs. Scheiner
Bishop's Doorkeeper, John Gurr

Clerks and Officers of the House of Commons.

Clerk of the House of Commons, John Henry Ley, esq. (4 Richmond terrace)
Clerk Assistant, William Ley, esq. (15 Queen st. Mayfair)
Second Clerk Assistant, Henry Ley, esq. (4 Richmond terr.)
Public Business Office and for the Collection of the Fees, 43 Parliament st
Clerk of Fees, John Edward Dorington, esq
Clerks, Mr. Arthur Jones, Mr. Edward Ley, Mr. William Rose, Mr. Robert Marriott
Accountant, Mr. John James Wilkinson

Committee Clerks and Election Office, House of Commons.

Committee Clerks, Robert Chalmers, George Whittam, George Dyson, Robert Gibbons
Clerks, Mr. John Rose, Mr. Charles Pole, Mr. Charles Gunnell, Mr. Charles Frere, Mr. Henry H. Creed, Mr. William Durell Gossett, Mr. Lyttleton Powys

Journal Office, and for the Votes and Proceedings of the House, 43 Parliament st

Clerk of the Journals, James Gudge, esq
Clerks, Mr. Charles Rowland, Mr. Joseph Postlethwate, Mr. Charles Gray, Mr. James Bull, Mr. Richard Dickinson, Mr. William Ley
First Clerk of Engrossing Office, Samuel Gunnell, esq
Clerks, Mr. George Gunnell, Mr. William Ginger

Private Bill Office, 2 Parliament st

First Clerk in Private Bill Office, Mr. William Hawes
Clerks, Mr. William Hodgkin, Mr. Henry Mayne, Mr. Joseph Johnson, Mr. Samuel Burgess Gunnell
Examiner of Election Recognizances, & Counsel to the Speaker, James Booth, esq
Clerk of Election Recognizances (vacant)
Librarian, Thomas Vardon, esq
Assistant, Thomas Erskine May, esq
Short-hand Writer, William Brodie Gurnev, esq
Serjeant at Arms, Sir William Gossett
Deputy, John Clementson, esq
Assistant, Ralph Allen Gossett, esq

Vote Office.

Deliverer of Votes and Printed Papers, Chas. Paskin, esq
Clerks, Mr. Robert Collins, Mr. Robert Joseph Collins, Mr. James Jeremiah Collins
Deputy Housekeeper, Mr. Wilbraham Taylor
Assistant, Mr. Edmund Bellamy
Door Keepers, Mr. John Pratt, Mr. Francis Williams
Messengers, Mr. Charles Stein, Mr. William Cook, Mr. Robert Baily, Mr. Hugh Mallons, Mr. Wm. Bellamy, Mr. James Poingdestre
Superintendent of Members' Waiting Room, Mr. Thomas Collett
Assistant, Charles Warman
Receiver of Post Letters, Wilbraham Taylor
Assistant, William Kendall
Chaplain to the House of Commons, Rev. Gerrard Thomas Andrews, M.A. 8 Sackville st
Secretary to the Speaker, Charles Edward Lefroy, esq. House of Commons, and Farnham, Surrey
Train Bearer, Mr. Robert Bailey
Printers of the Journals, &c., James & Luke Jas. Hansard
Printers of the Votes, John B. Nichols & Son

PAYMASTER GENERAL'S OFFICE,
Whitehall.

HER MAJESTY'S PAYMASTER GENERAL, Right Hon. William Bingham Baring, M.P.
Assistant Paymaster General & Accountant, William George Anderson, esq
Paymaster, Thomas Powis, esq
Principal Clerks, Philip Graves, Thomas Morris, Henry Burslem, Frederick Philpot, Jacob Sturton, James Perrior, Henry Austen Harrison, & Augustine Skottowe, esqrs
Senior Clerks, William Thomas Wright, Henry Good, Charles Montagu Martindale, Robert Martin Stapylton, Mathew Terry, William Ruddick, James Henry Scott, Henry Samuel Daller, Ernest Augustus Stephenson, Pole Godfrey, & Henry Whalley, esqrs
Bookkeeper, David Paterson, esq
Assistant Clerks, William Lawrence Coles, William Burgess Whitnall, William Bell, George Wynne, John Turner Powell, John Clark, Benjamin Fasson, George Richards Welstead, William Croft, Edward J. Armstrong, Edward Mayne, George Hatton, Stephen Cochrane Tucker, Henry Morgan, Robert Henry Conway, George Green, & William Jekin Eyre, esqrs
Junior Clerks, Henry Andrew Reid, John Townshend Philpot, Charles Stoddart Say, Robert Barclay Moun-

teney, George Edmeades, Arthur St. Leger, Thomas Hawkes, George Henry Browne, & Marmaduke Shield, esqrs

CLERKS IN THE PAY BRANCHES AT THE PORTS, &c.

CHATHAM—*Senior Clerks,* Charles Brockman & James Crosby, esqrs

Assistant Clerk, Frederick Simon Newcomb, esq

SHEERNESS—*Senior Clerk* (vacant)

Assistant Clerk (vacant)

PORTSMOUTH—*Senior Clerks,* Charles Cobbe & William Greetham Rickman, esqrs

Assistant Clerk, William Reid, esq

Junior Clerk, Septimus Slade, esq

PLYMOUTH—*Senior Clerks,* Walter Reid & Henry Gandy, esqrs

Assistant Clerk, William Jeffryes Williams, esq

Junior Clerks, William Standen & Edward Vessey, esqrs

HANOVER—*Paymasters,* Albert John Mortimer & Morgan Hugh Foster, esqrs

Clerks, J. H. Behr & Adolph Bähr, esqrs

Office Keeper & Head Messenger, Mr. Frederick Atkins

Messengers at Whitehall, Messrs. William Simes, Anthony Atkins, Edward Wheeler, William Sutton, Donald Mackenzie, John Wilcox & John Bouffler

MESSENGERS AT

Chatham, William P. Veal, William Crandell

Sheerness, William Morgan

Portsmouth, William Suter, William H. Cotton

Plymouth, William Sutton, Matthew Glover

GREENWICH OUT PENSION OFFICE, TOWER HILL.

Cashier, John Smith Graham, esq

Assistant Clerks, Frederick Walker, William Smith, John Aitchison, Frederick Francis Knowlden, William Pattison, Henry Peter Dickason Burnett, & Robert Harris Conway, esqrs

Junior Clerks, William Henry Ince, John Pattison, George Henry Browne, William Smythe Gunnell, Archibald Donald M'Lean, Richard Marsh Hobbs & Marmaduke Sheild, esqrs

Messengers at the Greenwich Out Pension Office, Messrs. Henry Mills Shrimpton, Samuel Pritchard & William Shannon

POOR LAW COMMISSIONERS' OFFICE.

1 & 2 Somerset place, London; and Custom House, Dublin. Hours, 10 to 4.

COMMISSIONERS, George Nicholls, George Cornewall Lewis, esqrs. Sir Edmund Walker Head, bart. Edward Turner Boyd Twisleton, esq

Secretary, Edwin Chadwick, esq. barrister at law

Assistant Secretaries, George Coode, William Golden Lumley, esqrs. barristers at law

ASSISTANT COMMISSIONERS, William Henry Toovey Hawley, Richard Hall, Robert Weale, Edward Carleton Tuffnell, esqrs.; Sir John James Walsham, bart.; Alfred Austin, esq.; & Colonel Thomas Francis Wade, C.B. Edward Turner Boyd Twisleton, esq. & George Grenville Wandisfort Pigott, esq

Clerks, First Class, Messrs. Thomas Johnston, Francis Fletcher, Francis Lass, Richard Basil Cane, Edward Sutton, Antonio Henry Montucci, James Hodgkin, Hugh Owen.

Clerks of the Second Class, Messrs. Thomas Austin, Frederick Purdy, George Mence, Emperor Adrian, Thomas Henry Jarvis, John Pinhorn Lawson, Christopher Wren Savage, William Cunningham Glen, Clarence Richard Howell, Danby Palmer Fry, Henry Clements Lloyd

Clerks of the Third Class, Messrs. William Burrow, John Jorden, Edwin Hutchings, Abel Simner, Charles Marshall, Thomas Harries, Joseph Hughes, Charles Geer, David Jones.

Clerks of the Fourth Class, Messrs. George Fluck, John Bellamy, William Ambrose Mason, Henry C. Mott

Lithographer, Samuel Newcombe

Office Keeper, Thomas Collot

Messengers, John Bright, Thomas East Lomax, Baker Steggall, John Hatch Peters, John Bright, jun

Housekeeper, Mrs. Collot

Officers serving in Ireland.

Address, "Poor Law Commission," Custom house, Dublin.

ASSISTANT COMMISSIONERS, Edward Gulson & Alfred Power, acting under delegation as a board; Hon. Charles Skeffington Clements, Edward Senior, William John Hancock, Cæsar George Otway, Joseph Burke, esqrs

Chief Clerk, Arthur Moore, esq

Clerks, First Class, Messrs. Charles Thomas Walmisley, Benjamin Banks, William Dudley Wodsworth, Richard Downer Webb Boud

Clerks, Second Class, Archibald Montgomery, George Barber, Thomas Collot

Clerks, Third Class, Alexander William Gate, Henry de Courcy, William Ellard, G. W. White, George William Finlay

Clerks, Fourth Class, James Lawson Magrath, Edward Joseph Browne, Robert Holmes Jephson, George R. Macdonald, A Stanley, D J Tracey, D A Lindsay, P Norris

Architect, George Wilkinson, esq. 4 North Frederick st. Dublin

Assistants to Architect, W. H. Hopper, Richard Barney, J. F. Ryan

Office Keeper, George Fawcett

Messengers, Thomas Gray, Patrick White, John M'Quade

POST OFFICE, (General.)

Hours 10 to 4.

POSTMASTER GENERAL FOR THE UNITED KINGDOM, The Right Hon. William Earl of Lonsdale, P.C., F.R.S. F.S.A.

SECRETARY, Lieut. Col. William Leader Maberly

ASSISTANT SECRETARY, Thomas Lawrence, esq

Private Secretary to Postmaster-General, Richard Robertson, esq.

Chief Clerk to the Secretary, James Campbell, esq

Seniors, William Milliken, Charles Johnson, John Ramsey, esqrs

Seniors, Second Class, John Palmer Godby, Maitland Wilson Boyd, Rodie Parkhurst, William Thomas Barth, Henry Benson Card, Edward Ellis, esqrs

Juniors, First Class, William James Page, Montagu South, Charles Lennox Moore Teesdale, Edward Hugh Rea, Francis Hast Burckhardt, Henry Pennington, Gustavus Charles Cornwall, Edward Page, Frederick Cowper

Juniors, Second Class, Freeling Jones Lawrence, George Hardy, James Caddy, John Spalding, Marshall Farrall, Alfred Spratt, John Strange Baker, William Dobinson, George Robert Saltwell, Thomas M. Watson, Horton Forrest, George F. Harrison, James M. Pennington, John Hall

Surveyors and Clerks to Surveyors.

Surveyors, Benjamin Churchill, Charles Rideout, George Neal, William Johnson, John Tilley, George Henry Creswell, William John Godby, John Kains, esqrs

Clerks to Surveyors, John Smith, George Pellatt, John Scudamore, Henry Bethune Abbott, Robert Richard Smith, James Henry Newman, Frederick Maberly, Stephen Maberly, John Robertson, John Beaufort, Charles Banning, William Gay, Charles Windsor, Christopher Hodgson, Augustus Forrest, Ernest Milliken

Surveyors, Scotland, John Warren, John Good, esqrs

Clerks to Surveyors, Scotland, William Septimus Parr, Charles Western, Christopher Hobson

Mail Coach Office.

Surveyor & Superintendent, George Stow, esq

First Clerk, William Thomas Wedderburn

Seniors, George Moulton, Edward Jonathan Measor

Juniors, Edmund Fanning, Alfred Norman, William Jackson, Alexander Henderson

Inspectors of Mail Coaches, Alexander Wedderburn, James Brown Godfrey, Charles Morgan, John Dicker, James Rogers, John Rodford, Thomas Webb, Charles Battcock

Railway Clerks, Lachlan Mc Lean, Frederick West Karstadt, John Benjamin Churchill, John Willdey, Thomas Smith, John West, George Perkin, Henry Emery, Thomas Robert James, William Walter Baggaley, Sidney Maberly Brown, Bernard George Beale, William Walter Yeld, Edward Armstrong, George Dickins, Alexander Norton Shillingford, John Fogg, William Slade, N. S. C. Rideout, Edward Maberly, Henry Griffin, Joseph Thyer, Robert Perring, Langdon Thomas, George Turner, Robert Christian Murray Lumb, David George Donald, Thomas Mawson

Solicitor's Office.

Solicitor, Mark Beauchamp Peacock, esq

First Clerk, Robert William Peacock

Second, Howard Eld

Third, Thomas Phillips

Receiver General's Office.

Receiver General, Thomas Young, esq

Chief Clerk, George Edward Hide, esq

Seniors, Abraham Cutto, John Blaiklock, Alexander Porter Grange

Juniors, Frederick Sago Page, Thomas Young Hewitt, Frank Ives Scudamore, William Travis Dunn, John Downes

Southam, James Thomson, Christopher Hopper, Alexander Christie Thomson, Frederick Charles Johnstone
Extra Clerks, A. Milliken, Frederick Cummins
Messenger, Abraham Fletcher

Accountant General's Office.

Accountant General, Charles Thomas Court, esq
Deputy, Charles Compton, esq
Chief Clerk, Edward Lloyd
Principal Clerks, William Garner, Henry George Stahlschmidt, William Collett
Seniors, Thomas Atkinson, John Potter, George Henry Karstadt, Harry Brown Wilkinson, John Frederick Thomas Marrable, Charles Court
Juniors, William Williams Barnard, Robert Zoffany Beachcroft, William Lawrence Browne, Charles Burges Fyfe, Marmaduke Jones, Charles Ratcliffe, Alfred Slater, James Frederick Mould, John Wild, Thomas Edwardes, George Richard Moore, Henry Sheppard, John Augustus Compton, Morrice Johnston, William Court, Walter Fox Halton, John L. Leech, Robert James Hampton, Edmund Forrest

Money Order Office.

President, William Barth, esq
Chief Clerk, Frederick Rowland Jackson, esq
First Class, Senior Clerks, Daniel Tod, George Chetwynd, Edward Frederick Walshe, Henry Thomas Palmer
Second Class, Senior Clerks, Charles Henry Weatherley, Henry Bulpit, Alfred Sedgewick, Montgomery Walter Williams, Frederick Phelps Lucy, Charles John Croke, George Francis Nott, Francis Court, William Farmer, Joseph West Galton, John Coleman Hobbs, John Weeds Lettis, William Doyle, Courtenay Temple, Charles Frederic Armstrong, William Price Inglis, Walter Crouch, Richard Julian Cale, Edward Spencer, James Douglas, John Hudson, Christopher James Campbell, Thomas Percival, George Bates, Charles Augustus Bertram
Juniors, James Hamilton, William Thomas Haines, Henry Prall, John Walton, John Lloyd, James Young Gooding, Samuel Walliker, George Fawn, Charles Samuel Whitbread Eické, Richard Hall, Alfred Richardson, Edmund Sheppard, Thomas Wright, David Williams, Oliver Thomlinson Wyndowe, George Thompson, Richard Jude, George Shepherd Weedon, Egbert Jarman, Thomas George Ramsay, Henry Partridge, John Hudson Man, Frederick Parker, Arthur James Williams, John Thomas Hawkins, Edwin Alexander Hancock, John Mileham, Thomas Richards, Charles Bennett, George Francis Revely, Lewty Collingwood, Richard Peacock, Charles Edmund Barth, Henry Jordan Hopkins, Charles Berdmore, Christopher Sayers, Thomas Gunning, Richard F. Gallot, Charles P. Measor, Matthew Dixon, Frederick Milliken, William Rushton, George Hall, Isaac Nanson, George N. Goodwin, John M. King, George Stevenson, Edward Bourne, John D. Hunter, Stephen Daniell
Probationary Class, Samuel L. Nind, John C. Sweetnam, Thomas Hulburd, Hutton Perkins, Henry D. Mitchell, Henry Davis, John Thompson, Thomas Churchill, Felix Deforge, James John Neal, Thomas Robinson, Henry Compton, Edwin Collett, Thomas Gibbs, Henry White, John Harting, Richard Sandon Bell, Frederick Josh. Brown, Thomas Brice Cleveland Wise, Thomas Goodsir, Alfred Ashton Burrow, Charles John Matthew Hawkins, Robert Thompson, George Alfred Muskett O'Grady, Alfred Percy Gibson, Frederick Perring, John Harrison, Samuel Mozley Stark, John Pitt Bontein, Charles William Westmacott, John Kirkby, Edgar Pearce, William Benn Gibson, John Bell, Frederick William Moore, John Atkinson, Charles Edward Marsh, George Frederick Heath, William Hook, Henry Charles Bailey, Dymoke Wells Pennington, George Thyer, John Britling Fulcher, Jonathan Farrer, Joseph Gill, Robert Pigot Davies, John Gardiner, William Norcliffe Shaw, George Richardson, Samuel Ewbank, William Falcon, Edward Thompson, Joshua David Griffith Davies, John Browne, Charles George Hill, Isaac Lightfoot, George Bland, John Bate, Joseph James, William Nunns, Alfred Eustace, William Henry Cocks, William Henry Norris, William Henry Snell, William Charles Mitchell, Robert Bell, John Spornberg Furber, John Lewes, Richard Henry Reeve, William Henry Hepburne, Arthur England Johnson, Charles Fisher, William Whicher, Thomas William Marsh, Charles Collett, Thomas Burrough Smith, Isaac Edward Thompson, William Tomlinson, William Burrowes Moss, Edgar Simson, William Giles Lacroix, Thomas Ormandy, Joseph Hoskin Huddy, William Joseph Edwards, Nicholas Eylmar Hovenden, John Stephen Stacey, William Campbell, Oliver Peyton

Inland and Foreign Office.

Superintending President, William Bokenham, esq
Presidents, Benjamin Vandergucht, Jas. Lowther, Francis Welch, William Holgate, esqrs
Assistant President, William Blott, esq
Vice Presidents, George Huxham Wynn, Henry Bourne, George William Graham, esqrs
Senior Clerks, Benjamin Vandergucht, James Brown, Wm. Holgate, James Lowther, Thomas Moule, Lewis Silvester Clarac, William Key, William George Moss, Charles Wilmot Holworthy, esqrs
Assistants, Joseph Low, Thomas Bird, William Packham, Francis Welch, William Joseph Ward, Henry Bourne, Richard White, Thomas May Simson, Richard Kent Newman, John Cookes, Samuel Hamer, George William Graham, Morris Paddon, John Cicero M'Mahon, Edward Hodd, Henry Meheux, Frederick Herbert, Robert Partridge, Thomas Henry Wilson, Charles William Wood, George Huxham Wynn, Albert Pennington, William Blott, William Hawkins Adams, George Vinter Holmes, Rhys Williams, William Cheshire, Charles William Barnard, Charles Johnson, William Gladstone, John Hinton, James Brodie, Charles John Whiting
Clerks, Edward James, Edward James Smith, Henry Matthews, William De Lisle Berdmore, Arthur Graham, Henry Mellersh, Thomas Boucher, George Kellner, Henry Hutchins, George Davies, Henry Jones, John Nicholson, Uniack Ronayne, Thomas Turner, Daniel Ely, Charles Millard Beddoe, George Tuck, John Gardner, Edward Davies, John Lawson, William King, William Tull, George Dundas Jones, George Chinner Barlow, William Hamilton, John Fowler Liffen, Thomas William Angell, John William Goodall, John Milton, George Sheffington Armstrong, Benjamin Adams, Henry Chenery, John Luckhurst Edward Drake, William Garrett Lewis, William Maxey
Junior Clerks, Alfred Smallfield, Matthew Wood, William Carroll, William Hillmer, Francis Salisbury, John Bury Adams, Alfred Roots Hubbard, William Kimpton, Sidney Hampden Wybrow, Andrew Glynn, Edward Karstadt, Thomas Lloyd Powell, John Douglas Sutherland, William James Plant, John Allbut Walford, Thomas Grimer, Charles Cornwallis Williams, James Crowdy Lovett, Geo. Rablah, Robert Sexton Smith, James Sansom, William Roberts, Jonathan King, Benjamin Perkins, William Frederick Potts, David Davies, John Hemmens, James Margetson, William Walton, Stephen Stevenson, Abraham Watson, William Henry Hibbard, Henry Kev, Edward Churchill, Douglas Fisher, George Edward Brockwell, Frederick George Perring, John Topping, Huskisson Curtis Wynn, Ewen Mc Phee, James Collinson, William Dickenson, William Montgomery, Thomas Greenhall Atkinson, William Castley, Edmund Durant, William Harrison, James Moule, John Burton, William Brown
Clerks to the Superintending President, James Brodie, Charles William Barnard, Henry Jones
Inspector of Official Correspondence, Lewis Silvester Clarac, Samuel Hamer, James Brodie, Charles William Barnard
Officers in charge of Indian Mails, James Payne, Thomas Fredericks, John Long Marshall [John Nash
Packet Mail Clerks, Joseph Wottenburg Wheatley, George
Officers at Paid Window, William Joseph Ward, Thomas Henry Wilson, Albert Pennington, Rhys Williams
Clerks of Letter Carriers' Accounts, William Lugsdin, George Sedgewick
Instructor of Junior Clerks, William Holgate
Two Senior Messengers, 49 Junior ditto, and 2 Watchmen

Inspector of Letter Carriers and Newspaper Office.

Inspector of Letter Carriers, Frederic Kelly
Assistant Inspectors, William Rackley, John Playle, Thomas Russell, Thomas Boyden, Thomas Burgess Cook, Abraham Swift, Willis Clare.
Sub-sorters, Charles Higley, Robert Hitchins, Richard Baker, James Johnson, William Whiting, Daniel Sills, John Fleet, Henry Dawson Clements, Henry Reed, William Last, James Darvill, Charles Graham Dupont, Philip Webster, Thomas Topper, William Archer, John Crutch, William Attwater, William Thorne, Thomas Tite, Edward Fosdick, Frederick Cox, George Kent, Joseph Mantle, John Puttick, William John Reed, Henry Powell, William Newman, William Cooper Oliver, Thomas Freeman, Joseph Offwood Hunt, Henry Rice, Richard Aldridge, John Andrews, George Rice, John Bennett, Richard Reeves, Richard Langley, William John Keene, John Boatwright, Robert Scales, James Dace, Robert

Bird, Jonathan Roberts, James Maidlow, Alfred William Cooper, William Green, Thomas Henry Rahill, John Goodwin, Thomas Fox, Robert Bauldry, Richard Gallin, Thomas Brown, James Angus, John Belton, Thomas Vaus, Thomas Mitchell, Joseph Wright, James Steel, Henry Stone, Abraham Thacker, William Goodson, Alexander Watt, William Bliss, Robert Potter, John Clark, James Howard, James Lord, James Ferguson, George Faulls, Jeremiah Godfrey, John Colman, Isaac Dean, Henry Hobbs, Joseph French, Richard Thomas Jacob, Richard Sayers, William George Dunstall, James Green, Henry Weaver, Henry Smith, Samuel Cuttlin, Richard Ridoutt, Joseph Harris, James Robinson, Richard Gill, William Smith, Thomas Harris, Thomas Groves, George Humphreys, Charles Randal, Jabez Lockett, Martin Dixon, George Roberts, Henry Huddlestone, John Hammersley, William Saunders, Thomas Bignell, George Sims, Henry Crippen, Francis Dunn, George Watson, Richard Walker, John Moore, John Bartlett, Charles Haynes, William Waters, William Penny, Joseph Webster, James Lewis, James Hooper, Joseph Williams, Thomas Mandeville, James Smith, Samuel Reed, John Lewis, Joseph Tilley, William McFarlane, Patrick O'Brien, Richard Martin, Henry Smith, Henry Treyvand, James Turner, William Plowright, John Tugwood, Marcus William Riche, George Richard Taylor, John Honey, William Sewell, Henry Barr, William Fountain, George Kershaw, William Parsons, Isaac Gandon, Francis Collins, James Buck, William Charles Collins, Francis Parodi, John Thomas Tabley Tijou, Henry Taylor, Thomas George Shuter, William Fisher, Henry Dutch, George Wilson, Thomas Robson, William Brady, Thomas Lurton George Langley.

Ship Letter Office.

Inspector, George Richard Huddlestone, esq
Chief Clerk, Henry Packham
Senior Clerks, William Hosken, Charles Ferguson
Juniors, Cuthbert John Baines, Roger Hawkes, Edward Finch, James Gorton

Dead and Returned Letter Office.

Inspector, Charles Newton, esq
First Clerk, Edmund Laycock
Seniors, Frederic Tillyard, Charles Whittard, Thomas Galabin, Edward Cartwright, Charles Richard Taylor
Juniors, John Kendle, William Saurin Cox, Robert Mellersh, George Richard Smith, Thomas Pellatt, William Lloyd, James Henry Elphick, William Edward Pratt, Daniel Lloyd Jones, Charles William Francis, Pendock William Neale, William J. Chetwynd, Owen Howell, William Murdock

London District late (Twopenny) Post Office.

Superintending President, Robert Smith esq
Chief Clerk, David Bolton Raw
Assistant Clerks, Joseph Kerby, Henry Wilson, John Blurton, Charles Potter, William Henry Grey
Surveyor, Thomas Read
Remittance Clerk, Frederick Paice

Sorting Office.

Presidents, Samuel Bell, James Smith
Vice Presidents, George Blink, Walter Robertson Sculthorpe, James Fox, John Hoare
Windowmen, Henry Cromar, John Oakeley
Clerks of Division, Frederick Hughes, Charles Anderson, Henry Ray, William Salisbury, John Morgan, William Westcott, Thomas Hart, James Linwood, Alfred Hardy, Walter Brown, John Biller, James Ker, William Pye, William Cribb
First Assistants, Joseph Oakshott, Joseph Burton, John Partridge, John Silvester Clarac, William Rees, Richard Steele, James Alfred Peake, John Bastick, Edward Edwards, John Leaver, Charles Scott, James Cornock
Second Assistants, James Atterbury, Thomas Mitchell, William Slee, Lewis Morris Archibald, Mackenzie M'Kaye, James Leek, John Salt, Alexander Stewart, Henry Bowen, Robert Matthews, Thomas Graham, Richard Burne Fillingham
Sorters, William Smallwood, Matthew John Tracey, Thomas Arnold Kelly, John Dodd Clay, John Powley, John Mounsey, Joseph Slade, William Powley, Samuel Topping, & Richard Wilson
Sub-sorters, William Reynolds, William Gibbons, Francis Kaines, Joseph Hayward, Thomas Curtis, Thomas Baker, Richard Powell Parry, Thomas Sinfield, Robert Charles Tournier, Thomas Stockwell, Thomas Burrell Cook, James Payne, Thomas E. Vickers, Samuel Brush, John Woodhouse, George Budd, William Cullen Howlett, George Harvey, John George Lea, Edward Newell, Charles Lines, William Allen, Robert Green, Nathaniel Loundes, Peter F. Mogan, James Bincks, Henry West, James Elphick, Robert Phillips, Robert Bridges & John Tullett
Inspector of Letter Carriers, William Saltwell
Assistant Inspectors, James Payne, Henry Jameson
Junior Inspectors, Thomas Gapes, James Smither, William Heath, Thomas Cook, Welcome Cole, William Edwards, John Rowe, & William Austin Baker
Stampers, Francis Langham, Richard Cornelius, John Webb, Joseph Chaney, Stephen Pritchard, Philip Davis, Edward, Thompson, John Simmonds, Samuel Gauntlet, William Mears, Edward Day, John Duck, William King, John Brunker, George Whitcombe & Patrick J. Connelly

PRIVY SEAL OFFICE.

28 *Abingdon street.* Hours, 10 to 3.

Lord Privy Seal, His Grace the Duke of Buccleuch, K.G.
Patent Clerks, John George Donne, Ralph Eden, esqrs
Clerk, William Goodwin, esq
Keeper of Records and Receiver of Fees, Ralph Eden, esq
Private Secretary to Lord Privy Seal, The Hon. G. C. Talbot
Messenger, William John Norris

PUBLIC RECORD OFFICE.

ESTABLISHED BY THE ACT 1 & 2 VICTORIA, C. 94.

Head Office, Rolls' House, Chancery lane
Branch Offices, Rolls' Chapel, Rolls' yard; Tower; Chapter House, Poets' Corner; and Carlton ride; office hours, 10 to 4
Keeper and Custos of the Records, the Master of the Rolls
Deputy Keeper, Sir Francis Palgrave, K.H.
Secretary, Francis Sheppard Thomas, esq
Assistant Keepers, First class, Thomas Palmer, esq. Rolls' Chapel; Thomas Duffus Hardy, esq. F.S.A. Tower; Henry Cole, esq.; Rev. Joseph Hunter, F.S.A.
Assistant Keepers, Second class, Henry George Holden, esq. Rolls' Chapel; Charles Roberts, esq. Tower; Frederick Devon, esq. Chapter House; William Henry Black, esq. Rolls' House
Clerks, Henry James Sharpe, Tower; John Thomas Jowett, Joseph Burtt, Chapter House; Walter Nelson, Carlton ride; William Lascelles, Rolls' Chapel; John Palmer Redington, Thomas Moses Green, Carlton ride; John Edwards, Rolls' House; John Thomas Kentish, Rolls' Chapel; Charles Augustus Cole, John James Bond, Carlton ride; William Basevi Sanders, Tower; Manners Fenwick, Percy Shelley Leigh Hunt, Carlton ride; William George Cooper, Rolls' Chapel; Peter Turner, James Edward Gibson, Carlton ride; Frederick Charles Ellis, Tower; Alfred Kingston, Tower

PUBLIC WORKS AND BUILDINGS, *see* "*Woods, Forests, & Land Revenues.*"

PUBLIC WORKS, LOAN OFFICE.

Acts 57 Geo. III. cap. 34 & 124—3 Geo. IV. cap. 86—1 & 2 William IV. cap. 24—4 & 5 William IV. cap. 72—1 Victoria, cap. 51—1 & 2 Victoria, cap. 88, & 3 Victoria, cap. 10—5 Victoria, Session 2, cap. 9

South Sea House, Threadneedle Street.

Hours, 10 to 4.

COMMISSIONERS.

Chairman—Benjamin Harrison, esq
Deputy Chairman—George Hathorn, esq

Charles Bosanquet, esq. Viscount Melbourne. Earl Fortescue. Sir Thomas Dyke Acland, bart. M.P. Sir Thomas S. Gooch, bart. Sir Charles Price, bart. Lord Hatherton, Thomas Grimstone Bucknall Estcourt, esq. M.P. William Wolryche Whitemore, esq. John Loch, esq. Henry Warburton, esq. M.P. Sir Benjamin Heywood, bart. Rt. Hon. Henry Labouchere, M.P. John Irving, esq. M.P. John Thornton, esq. Joseph Berens, esq. Samuel March Phillipps, esq. Andrew Colvile, esq. Jeremiah Olive, esq. Josh. Reid, esq. Nicholas Garry, esq. Sir John Henry Pelly, bart. John Horsley Palmer, esq. Abraham George Robarts, jun. esq. Thomas Baring, esq. M.P. George Warde Norman, esq. George Carr Glyn, esq. Samuel Jones Loyd, esq. William Ward, esq

Secretary, John Strettell Brickwood, esq
Assistant Secretary, Henry Bunster, esq
Accountant, James Green, esq
Clerk, Mr. George Carter
Solicitors, Messrs. Barnes, Winter & Bernard
Door-keeper, James Shepherd
Messenger, John Langford
Housekeeper, Mrs. Ann Johnson

QUARTER-MASTER GENERAL'S OFFICE.
Horse Guards. Hours 11 to 5.

QUARTER-MASTER GENERAL, Lieut. Gen. the Right Hon. Sir James Willoughby Gordon, bart. G.C.B., G.C.H., F.R.S.
Assistant Quarter-Master General, Col. James Freeth, K.H.
Deputy Assistant Quarter-master General, Capt. John Enoch
Clerks, first class, Thomas Marsh, esq. (*chief clerk*), George Mather, esq., John O'Neil, esq. (*confidential clerk*)
Clerk, second class, John Sewell, esq
Clerks, third class, John James Tillbrook, George Strong, esqrs
Principal Military Draughtsman, George Pawley, esq
Assistant Military Draughtsman, Mr. Lewis John Hebert
Lithographic Draughtsman, Mr. Berkeley King
Officekeeper, Enoch Althorpe
Housekeeper, Mrs. Ann Buckley
Messengers, John Jones, Daniel M'Arter, Francis Holyoak

QUEEN ANN'S BOUNTY.
and First Fruits' and Tenths' Office.
3 *Great Dean's Yard, Westminster.*

Hours : { Treasurer's department, 10 to 2 ; Secretary's and First Fruits' & Tenths' departments, 10 to 4

Secretary & Treasurer, Christopher Hodgson, esq
Secretary's department — Clerks, Mr. John Holford, Mr. Arthur Sharpe
Treasurer's department—Cashier, Mr. George Aston
Clerks, Mr. Benjamin Richard Aston, Mr. Joseph Keech Aston, Mr. Charles Lavender
First Fruits' department—Clerk, Mr. John Geesin
Tenths' department—Clerk, Mr. William Bridges
Auditor, Charles Ansell, esq
Counsel, Samuel Pepys Cockerell, esq. Lincoln's inn
Solicitor, John Burder, esq. 27 Parliament st

QUEEN'S MESSENGERS (*Establishment of*), *see "Home office."*

RECEIPT OF EXCHEQUER OFFICE, *see Exchequer (Receipt of)*

RECORD OFFICE. *see "Public Record office."*

RECRUITING DEPARTMENT, *see "Adjutant General's office."*

REDUCTION OF NATIONAL DEBT OFFICE,
19 *Old Jewry.* Hours 10 to 3

COMMISSIONERS, The Speaker of the House of Commons, The Chancellor of the Exchequer, The Master of the Rolls, The Lord Chief Baron of the Court of Exchequer, The Accountant General of the Court of Chancery, The Governor & Deputy Governor of the Bank of England
Secretary & Comptroller General, Samuel Higham, esq
Assistant, James Higham, esq
Chief Clerk, John Crook Peck, esq
Clerks. Messrs. John Francis Scott, William Taylor, John Clark, William Fennings, James Dunlop, Charles Lee, James William Mathers, Henry Thomas, Edward Conduitt Dermer, Robert Liveing Fenn, John Stephen Vaughan, Edward Jenkins, Parry Whitford, William Fascutt, Henry Dover, Francis John Scott, & Henry Court

Cheque Department.

Actuary & Check Accountant, John Finlaison, esq
First Clerk, Charles Liveing, esq
Clerks, Alexander Glen Finlaison, Domett Finlaison, Charles Joseph Bott, William Barnett, esqrs
Agents, Matthew Marshall, Thomas Bros, esqrs
Brokers, William Herbert Mullens & William Benjamin Marshall
Messenger, Thomas H. Morris
Porter, William Sellars
Assistant Porter, William Jones
Housekeeper, Mrs. Ann Morris

REGISTER OFFICE, *see "General Register Office."*

REGISTER OF DESIGNS OFFICE,
see "Committee of Privy Council for Trade."

REVENUE ENQUIRY (COMMISSIONERS OF),
see "Treasury."

ROYAL ENGINEERS' OFFICE (*London District*),
11 *James Street, Buckingham Gate.* Hours 10 to 4.

Commanding Royal Engineer, Major Lewis Alexander Hall
Junior Engineers, Lieut. Frederick Edward Chapman, & Lieut. James Lintorn Arabin Simmons
Clerks of Works, John Bragg, William Miller
Clerks, Henry Charles Shoemack, Francis Savio
Foremen of Works, John Morsley, Edward Symons
Office Keeper, Richard M'Kenzie

ROYAL HOSPITAL, CHELSEA.
Hours of business, 10 to 4

COMMISSIONERS, The President of the Council, The First Lord of the Treasury, The Secretaries of State, The Paymaster General, The Secretary at War, Sir William Lewis Herries, K.C.H. Chairman of the Board of Audit, The Governor, The Lieutenant Governor, The Adjutant General of the Forces, The Quartermaster General, and the Deputy Secretary at War
Governor, Hon. Sir Edward Paget, G.C.B.
Lieut. Governor, Gen. Sir William Henry Clinton, G.C.B.
Major, Lieut. Col. Henry Le Blanc
Adjutant, Col. Sir John Morillyon Wilson, C.B., K.H.
Treasurer, Right Hon. William Bingham Baring, M.P. (Paymaster General)
Secretary & Registrar, Richard Neave, esq
Assistant Secretary, John Fasson, esq
Clerks, First Class, Francis Henry Talman & Charles Tamplin Revell, esqrs
Clerks, Second Class, William Grey, Richard Bellamy, George Augustus Daller & George Sills, esqrs
Agent & Paymaster for the Out-Pensioners, Thomas Constantine Brooksbank, esq
Senior Clerks, John Willisford, James Ricketts, esqrs
Junior Clerk, Thomas Frome Hall
Captains of Invalids, John Davern, Augustus F. Evans, George Peevor, Charles Edwards, John Ford & John Willington Shelton
Chaplain, Rev. George Robert Gleig, M.A.
Physician & Surgeon, Daniel Maclachlan, M.D.
Deputy Surgeon, John Hartshorne, esq
Apothecary, William North, esq
Storekeeper, Captain Sutherland
Housekeeper, Mrs. Ann Mary Revell
Whitster, Mrs. Elizabeth Ebhart
Organist, Miss Robertson
Solicitor, John Christopher Lethbridge, esq
Master Cook, James Ripley
Under Cooks, John May, jun. James Steele
Turncock, William Reynolds
Sexton, John Ravenhill

ROYAL MARINE OFFICE,
22 *New street, Spring gardens.*

Deputy Adjutant Gen. Col. John Owen, K.H.
Assistant Adjutant Gen. Major John Wilson
Clerk, Henry Cooper, esq
Comptroller of Steam Machinery, Capt. Sir William Edward Parry, R.N.
Clerks, Waller Clifton, Cusack Patrick Roney, esqrs

ROYAL MINT,
Little Tower hill, hours 10 to 4.

Master & Worker, Rt. hon. Sir George Clerk, bart. M.P.
Deputy Master & Worker, James Wm. Morrison, esq
Clerk Assistant to Deputy Master, Charles Elouis, esq
Comptroller, Deputy Comptroller, & Queen's Clerk of the Copper Coinage, William Henry Barton, esq
Queen's Assay Master, Henry Bingley, esq
Probationer Assayer, Henry William Field, esq
Queen's Clerk & Clerk of the Papers, George Forbes, esq
Superintendent of Machinery & Clerk of the Irons, William Thomas Brande, esq. F.R.S.
Master's Assay Master, John Malebysse Beckwith, esq
Master's First Clerk, Melter, & Refiner, Gilbert Farquhar Mathison, esq
Master's Second Clerk & Probationer Melter, Robert Mushet, esq
Provost of the Company of Moneyers, Richard Franklyn, sen. esq
Weigher & Teller & Stamper of Money Weights, James Hill, esq
Surveyor of Meltings, John Buckham, esq
Surveyor of Money Presses, William Busson, esq
Chief Clerk in Mint Office of Receipt, Joseph Capes, esq
Accountant, William Boler, esq
Clerks in Mint Office, Richard F.G. Cumberland & Robert Francis Suft, esqrs
Chief Engraver, William Wyon, esq. R.A.
Second Engraver, Leonard Wyon, esq
Medallist, Benedetto Pistrucci, esq
Solicitor, Joseph Blunt, esq
Assistant Solicitors, Caleb Edward Powell, & Edward Joseph Powell, esqrs
Bullion Porter, Mr. John Pearson

Master's ditto, William Ward
Office Keeper, Mrs. Mary Wilson

RUSSIA COMPANY.

South Sea House.

Governor, William Astell, esq
Consuls, Thos. Tooke, Hon. J.T.L. Melville, & Henry Cattley, & Thomas Paris, esqrs
Court of Assistants, Thomas Tooke, John Thornton, esqrs. Hon. John Thornton Leslie Melville, Henry Cattley, Stephen Edward Thornton, William R. Robinson, Thomas Paris, George Smith Thornton, Thomas Tooke, jun., John Harvey, Charles Robinson, John Hubbard, John Cattley, Charles Snell Paris, David Thomas Morgan, Thomas Matthias Weguelin, William Sampson, esqrs. Sir John William Lubbock, bart. George Reid, Thomas Anderson, William Gladstone, Henry Nelson, Henry Shaw Lefevre, John Thornton, Henry Cayley, Thomas Stephenson, & Henry Launcelot Holland, esqrs
Secretary, Thomas Cope, esq. South Sea House

SECRETARIES OF STATE.

Principal Secretary for Colonial Affairs, see "Colonial offi."
.. .. .. *Foreign* .. .. *"Foreign office."*
.. .. .. *Home* .. .. *"Home office."*

SEAMEN'S GENERAL REGISTER AND RECORD OFFICE.

Offices at the Custom House, and No. 2 Hammet street, Minories.

Hours of attendance from 10 to 4.

Registrar General, John H. Browne, esq
Assistant Ditto, Charles Boyd, jun. esq
Overseer of Ticketing, James W. Armstrong, esq
Clerks, First Class, James Boyd, Henry J. Gray, esqrs
Clerks, Second Class, Robert Peppercorne, Chas. Williams, Everard H. Coleman, Andrew Hardie, David S. Brown, John S. Brown, John Symonds, Thomas Wild, esqrs
Clerks, Third Class, Francis F. Firmin, Isaac O. P. Stuart, Thomas Brown, James H. Akers, Joseph Date, John Lang, Nesbit W. Marshall, Thomas C. R. Campbell, Robert M. Evans, John H. W. Robertson, George C. C. Stuart, Ralph J. Nicholson, Edward A. Williamson, Robert C. Garrett, William H. M'Dermott, George Wakeling, Frederick F. Filton, Charles Stone, William Drake, Robert Blackler, Richard Lewis, Alfred C. L. West, Alexander Douglas, Henry E. Dickson, Edward J. Wood, esq
Messengers, Joseph Tween, William S. Barthorp
Porter, Henry Pridgeon
House Keeper, Mrs. Margaret Hubbard

SEWERS, COMMISSIONERS OF, *see Commissioners of Sewers.*

SIGNET OFFICE.

28 *Abingdon st.*—Hours 10 to 3.

KEEPERS OF THE SIGNET, the Chief Secretaries of State
Chief Clerks (appointed by Patent for life), Right Hon. Sir Brook Taylor, G.C.H. Rev. William Harry Edward Bentinck, John Gage, esq
Deputies, Thomas Henry Plasket, Bridges Taylor, esqrs
Keepers of the Records & Receivers of Fees, Edward Dewe Jones, Henry William Sanders, esqrs

SLAVE COMPENSATION OFFICE,

45 *Parliament street*—Hours 10 to 4.

Arbitrator, James Lewis, esq
Secretary, Henry Hill, esq
Clerks, Messrs. George Edward White & William Cole

SOUTH SEA COMPANY,

South Sea House, Threadneedle st.—Hours 9 to 3.

GOVERNOR, Charles Bosanquet, esq
SUB-GOVERNOR, Charles Franks, esq
DEPUTY-GOVERNOR, the Hon. Philip Pleydell Bouverie

DIRECTORS.

Henry Berens, esq. Baron de Teissier, Sir Richard Plumtre Glyn, bart. Matthew Harrison, esq. Robert King, esq. William Fuller Maitland, esq. Charles John Manning, esq. Alexander Leslie Melville, esq. Henry Iltid Nicholl, LL.D. William Phillimore, esq. William Pole, esq. Newman Smith, esq. John Thornton, esq. Charles John Tindal, esq. James Tulloch, esq. Henry Vigne, esq. John Willing Warren, esq. George Whitmore, esq
Cashier, John Tickell Viner, esq
Secretary, Charles Frederick Gibson, esq
Accountant, William Rowland Arnold, esq
Chief of the Transfer, Dividend, Will, & Letter of Attorney Offices, John Jesse, esq
Counsel, Samuel Richard Bosanquet, esq
Solicitor, Ralph Dunn, esq
Housekeeper, Mrs. Ann Johnson

STAMP, LAND & ASSESSED TAXES & PROPERTY TAX OFFICE,

Somerset House—Hours 10 to 4.

COMMISSIONERS.

Chairman, Henry Lewis Wickham, esq
Deputy-Chairman, John Thornton, esq
Charles Poulett Rushworth, esq. Henry Seymour Montagu, esq. Edward Saurin, Capt. R.N.
SECRETARY, Charles Pressly, esq
Assistant Secretary, Thomas Keogh, esq
Chief Clerk, Joel Pinney, esq
Clerks, Thomas Sargent, Charles Hay, Hezekiah Hargood, Archibald Brown, Charles Lewis, John James Russell, William Quaife, Charles Symons, William Price, John Edward Cannon, Henry Smythe, William Lomas, Bernard Murray Delany, John White, Alaric A. Watts, Henry Reding, Thomas Frederick Simpson
Extra Clerks, George Russell, William Spence
Supernumerary Clerks, Edward Everard Rushworth, William Farr Rose, Abraham Bradley King Jellicoe, Pierce O'Brian Butler, George Bailey, Charles Pate
SOLICITOR, Joseph Timm, esq
Assistant Solicitor, Hugh Tilsley, esq
First Clerk, John Reid, esq
Clerks, Isaac Henry Sercombe, Henry Ellis Harvey, William Ogden, Charles Rider, John Chubb, Thomas Tichborne, William Jacob, Thomas Elderfield
Supernumerary Clerks, Thomas Roberts, King Patten, Thomas James, Walter Cannon, S. Salvage, William Roberts
Messenger, Thomas Ogden
RECEIVER GENERAL, William Everett, esq
First Clerk, William Good, esq
Clerks, Henry Huntingdon, Benjamin Gray, James Young, William Norman, Bladen Hunneman, James Gardiner, William Rea, Richard Langford, D. W. Crosbie, John Criddle
Supernumerary Clerks, A. Dorehill, Fowler Parker, H. King
ACCOUNTANT AND COMPTROLLER GENERAL, Thomas Lightfoot, esq
Assistant, Arthur Richard Barker, esq
First Clerk, Peter Deans, esq
Clerks, William James Woodward, Edward Bulkley, John Salter, Edwyn Evans Leach, Thomas Stevens, William Willis, Edmund Haggard, Ralph Gore, Robert Hicks, Henry Merry, Alfred Coppin Byers, William Richard Arnold, John Thatcher
Supernumerary Clerks, J. Lloyd, J. Bridseye, S. S. Banitt
Registrar of Bankers' Returns, Peter Deans, esq
Clerks, James Rudge, George Smith
INSPECTOR GENERAL, William Garnett, esq
Chief Clerk, Henry Hay, esq
Clerks, William Winch, George Henry Haines, Edward Russell, William John Wood, William Henry Morris, Charles Loft West, George Hayles, Mark Anthony Bourdin, George Porter
Additional Clerks, Frederick B. Garnett, Alfred Cooper, Henry William Woodward, C. Townsend, N. H. Skoiles
Registrar of Land Tax, Henry Hay, esq
Sub-Registrar, William Winch
Inspector of Stamp Duties, Benjamin Beckley, James Wakelin, George Dodgson, William Deloin Poole
Engraver of Dies and Copperplates, George Halfhide
Registrar of Fire Insurances, George Westmacott, esq
Clerks, Josias Aston, John Osbertus Truman, George Lightfoot, Charles Winser, Joseph Sharpe, Charles Tench Lovejoy, John Beatty, William Lee Grace, Richard Jennings, Nicholas Devereux, William E. Moloney, C. Halcombe
Registrar of Warrants, William Watson
Assistant Registrars, William Nelthorpe, William Russell, James Boulton, James Leech
Warehouse Keeper & Consignment Clerk, Thomas Allen
Clerks, Thomas Hopkins, James Booth, George Evett, John Johnson, William Woodger, Abraham Bennett, John Lee
Tellers of Stamps, William Hume, John Pilcher, William Woodham, Edward Beard
Packers, John Horsfall, Thomas Peckham, Thomas Payne, William Saul, Henry Jordan, William Taylor
Porter, George Pettefer
Examiner of Spoiled Stamps, Charles Crokat, esq
Clerks, Richard Peacock Walker, Arthur Warburton, Samuel M'Quoid, jun. Charles Ross, jun

Registrar and Distributor of Conveyancers' and Attorneys Certificates, and of Bankers' and other Licenses, Teesdale Cockell, esq
Clerks, William Powell, Edmund Browne, William W. Dalbiac, Joseph Wing, John Key
Registrar of Newspapers & Pamphlets, Charles Ross, esq
Sub-Registrar of Pamphlets, John Halse
First Assistant Registrar, William Beever Garret
Second Assistant Registrar, Frederick Debenham
Extra Assistant Registrar, William Harvey
Assessor of Stage Coach duties, Richard Smith, esq
Clerks, John Henry Thompson, Charles George Powell, William Hill, James Lawson Watson, Bernard John Last, Thomas Brown Howard, Robert Smith Malkin
Comptroller of Stage Coach duties, James Greenstreet
Clerks, William Sutherland, William Shearman, James Kemp
Supervisor of Stampers, Joseph Harris; *Deputy*, John Hunt
Rollingpress Officer, William Jones
Office Keeper, Anthony Frederick Fearon. *Board Messenger*, William Henry Stratford. *Messengers*, Thomas Tribe, Thomas Boucher, William Sweet, Thomas Turton, Charles Coggins, David Williams, William Liston, James Pincott
Door Porter, Thomas Woodruff
Watchmen, David Burrows, Nathan Sowden, Daniel Morrough, Thomas Haviland
Inspectors of Taxes for London District, John Purdue, John Walter, esqrs.
Chief Clerk, Charles Bacon
Clerks, Ellis Everett, Joseph Dalton
Additional Clerks, William Chivers, Robert Morrison
45 *Distributors of Stamps for England & Wales*
14 *Receiving Inspectors of ditto*
4 *Superintending Surveyors*
136 *Resident Surveyors*
90 *Stampers*

Sea Policy Office.

Distributor of Sea Policy Stamps, Samuel M'Quoid, esq
Clerks to Distributor, Robert Moon, Arthur Moon, Fredk. Hoper
Messenger, William Thomas Sadler

Legacy Duty Department.

Comptroller, Charles Trevor, esq
Chief Clerk, John Corrie Hudson, esq
Clerks of the First Class
Examiner of Wills, Samuel Truman
Superintendents, George Rose, Eyre Burton Powell, Thos. Quaife, John Mears
Register Comptrollers, George Harrison, Edward Meredith Lewes, William Bettell, Thomas Oxtoby, William Etherington, Sidney James Salter, George Howse, Lawrence D. Cowling, Henry E. Dalbiac, George Fitzgerald, Thos. Harper, & John Simmons
Clerks of the Second Class
Superintendents, William George Moulting, Edward Hoblyn, Thomas Emmens, John James Clarke, Frank Hall Stephenson, Charles Walpole
General Registrars, John Parker, John Brown, John Weir, John James Hamilton, Samuel Henry Culverwell, Chas. Latham, William George Goodrich, John Pugh Bridgewater, Alfred Phillips, Frederick Bunter, Charles Godby, Henry Powell, John Alderson Turner, Chester Eardley Wilmot, John S. Gairdner, Charles Frederick Howard, Bartholomew Norder Hindes, J. S. Ritchie
Clerks of the Third Class, Charles Legrand, Corrie Hudson, J. H. Borradaile, John W. Dixon, William P. Collier, George Forteath, Richard Woodlands, William Bluett, G. H. Terry, Richard Dene, Edward Haynes, James Tibbet, Samuel Geddings
Will Sorters, George Bennett and John Scorey
Messengers, Joseph Parsons, Benjamin Burke and George Parker

Income & Property Tax Department.

SPECIAL COMMISSIONERS.
John Fuller, James Dickens, esqrs
Clerks, William Gates, Isaac Wykeham Dickinson, Walter Bathurst Long, Richard Stillwell, John Dowsett Collier, Thomas Wayth Gudgeon, Gilbert Barber, Cornelius Forbes Leith, Robert Weaver, Frederick Soane, Robert Booth, Alfred John Gibbs, Major James Lomax, John Michael Beard, William Robeson Downes, Thomas F. Wintour, John Rowland, Samuel James Blencowe, Joseph Bingham
Messengers, Joseph Pomeroy, Richard Johnson

STATE PAPER OFFICE.

12 *Duke Street, Westminster*. Hours 11 to 4.
KEEPER, Rt. Hon. Henry Hobhouse, F.R.S., F.S.A
Deputy Keeper of State Papers, Charles Lechmere, esq
Senior Clerk, Robert Lemon, esq. F.S.A
Junior Clerk, Mr. Thomas Temple
Extra Clerks, Messrs. Vincent F. Kuczynski, Wm. Jennings
Housekeeper, Mrs. Caroline Frances Day
Messenger, Henry Sharp

STATIONERY OFFICE,

James Street, Buckingham Gate, Hours 10 to 4
COMPTROLLER, John Ramsay, M'Culloch, esq
Storekeeper, George Huntley Gordon, esq
Clerks, First Class, Samuel Kent Parson, William Wake, William Rapley, William Stanley Ginger, esq:s
Second Class, Joseph Blades, William Wake, Thomas Henry Cleaver, Robert Lundie
Third Class, Robert Samuel Lundie, William Lawrence, Robert Harkness, William M'Kay, James Joseph Wickwar, Frederick Bryan
Fourth Class, William Robinson, Leopold Charles Martin, George Neech, George Hughes Hodges, Hugh Galbraith Reid, Samuel Page, Charles Mitchell, Charles D. Johnson, George William Draper
Examiner of Paper, James Diggens
Assistant ditto, Joseph Sandell
Second Assistant ditto, Francis Pickering
Warehousemen, William Rhodes, James Polden, William Whittington, Henry Toon, Henry Hankins
Messengers, Abraham Field, William Walters
Resident Porter, Samuel Holder

TENTHS' OFFICE, *see "Queen Anne's bounty Office."*

TITHE COMMISSIONERS' BOARD.

9 *Somerset Place*. Hours, 9 to 4
COMMISSIONERS, William Blamire, esq. Thomas Wentworth Buller, esq. Reverend Richard Jones
ASSISTANT COMMISSIONERS, Capt. Robt. Kearsley Dawson, Thomas Smith Woolley John Donaldson Selby, John Johnes, Charles Howard, Thomas Tatham, James Merest, James Townsend, Charles Pym, Anewrin Owen, John Job Rawlinson, esqrs
Assistant Commissioners for Special Purposes, George Wingrove Cooke, F. O. Martin, & W. W. Attree, esqrs. James Jerwood, M.A
Secretary, John Eykn Hovendon, esq
Assistant Secretary, Henry Pyne, esq
Chief Clerk, William Apps, esq
Clerks to Board, John Thompson, Francis Cornish Newman, Henry Fleming, James Buller, A. Price, esqrs
Office Keeper, George Reynolds
House Keeper, Mrs. Sarah Reynolds

TRADE & FOREIGN PLANTATIONS, *see "Committee of Privy Council for Trade."*

TOWER OF LONDON.

Hours, 10 to 4
CHIEF GOVERNOR & CONSTABLE, Field Marshal the Duke of Wellington, K.G. &c. &c. &c
Lieutenant of the Tower, General John Sulivan Wood
Deputy Lieutenant, Colonel John Gurwood, C.B
Fort Major, Capt. John Henry Elrington
Master Gunner, Edward Howe
Chaplain, Rev. Henry Melville, M.A
Gentleman Porter, Charles Murray, esq
Gentleman Gaoler, Jethro Florey, esq
Barrack Master, Lieut. Thos. Hall
Apothecary, John Hunter, esq
Yeoman Porter, John Lund
Steward & Coroner, William Walton, esq
Chief Bailiff, James Wilmot Lush, esq
Keeper of the Regalia, Edmund Lenthal Swifte, esq

TREASURY.

Whitehall. Hours, 10 to 4
LORDS COMMISSIONERS, Rt. Hon. Sir Robert Peel, bart. M.P.; Rt. Hon. Henry Goulburn, M.P.; James Milnes Gaskell, esq. M.P.; Henry Bingham Baring, esq. M.P.; William Forbes Mackenzie, esq. M.P. & William Cripps, esq. M.P.
JOINT SECRETARIES, Edward Cardwell, esq. M.P. & John Young, esq. M.P
Assistant Secretary, Charles Edward Trevelyan, esq
Auditor of Civil List, George James Pennington, esq
Principal Clerk for Colonial Business, George Wililam Brande, esq

Principal Clerk Assistant to the Secretaries, Stephen Ralph Martin Leake, esq
Chief Clerks, Thomas Constantine Brooksbank, William Edward Fauquier, George Boyd, Thomas Charles Harrison, Henry Robert Pearson, esqrs
Senior Clerks, Joseph Baker, Charles Long Crafer, Charles Litchfield, Matthew Harrison, Edward Speer, William Brummell, esqrs
Assistant Clerks, Christopher Robert Pemberton, Frederick Sargent, George Arbuthnot, Spencer Drummond, Thomas Peregrine Courtenay, Edward W. Ricketts, William Stephenson, esqrs. Sir Alexander Duff Gordon, bart., Spencer Shelley, Edwin Turner Crafer, Charles Samuel Grey, Alfred Waller, Charles Walter Stronge, esqrs
Junior Clerks, Wilmot Seton, Lewis Jones, Roger William Wilbraham, William Law, Frederick Fitzgerald, George Frederick Parratt, Frederick Dawson, James Henry Cole, Maurice Drummond, William Henry Clerke, Edward Coplestone Buckland, Alexander Clerk, esqrs
Private Secretaries to the First Lord Commissioner, William Henry Stephenson, George Arbuthnot, esqrs
Private Secretary to the Rt. Hon. Henry Goulburn, Christopher Robert Pemberton, esq
Private Secretary to John Young, esq. Edwin Turner Crafer, esq
Private Secretary to Edward Cardwell, esq. James Henry Cole, esq
Private Secretary to Charles Edward Trevelyan, esq. Charles Samuel Grey, esq
Clerk of Bills & Receiver of Fees, Lacy Rumsey esq
Assistant, William Moss Dwight, esq
Law Clerk, Richard Hankins, esq
Clerk of Stationery, James Davis, esq
Clerk of Parliamentary Accounts, Chas. Long Crafer, esq
Assistant, George Bachelour, esq
Clerks of Revenue Department, Henry Thos. Dwight, Thomas Englesby Wickins, esqrs
Clerks to Auditor of Civil List, Edward Sawyer, Henry Marston Windsor, esqrs
SUPERINTENDENT OF PAPER & REGISTER DEPARTMENT, *Chief*, Edward W. Ricketts, esq
Assistant, William Thomas Adrian, esq
Clerks, William Winkley, Kenneth Mac Rae, Hugh Powell Cotton, & William Henry Atchley, esqrs
Other Clerks, John Stephenson, John William Levett, Edward Nash, George Chance, esqrs
Keeper of the Papers, Mr. Thomas Emmens
Housekeeper, Mrs. Mary Haines
Chamber-keeper & Superintendent of the Messengers, Mr. John Haines
Messenger of the Registry, James Child
Messenger of the Chamber, Thomas Halligan
Doorkeeper, Lewis Morton
Secretaries' Messengers, John Boddy, William Worsfold, James Wacker Minet
Messengers for Deliveries, &c. Charles Scott, Peter Bowman, George Foote, John Grove, James Broster, Thomas Young, Charles Long, James Bailey, George Long, & Benjamin Ford
Chamber-keeper & Superintendent of Messengers to the First Lord, Mr. Thomas Appleton
Messengers, Robert Harvey, Jonas Colburn, John Fitness, James Samways
Messengers to the Chancellor of the Exchequer, John Winter, George Humphries

Commissariat Branch.

Principal Clerk, Thomas Archer, esq
Chief Clerk, Samuel Petrie, esq
Senior Clerks, first class, James William Cooper, Phillip Hughes, Thomas John Crafer, esqrs
Senior Clerks, second class, James Rorauer, Frederick Crafer, Frederick William Dickens, esqrs
Junior Clerks, Francis Byron, John Pycroft Collier, Ralph Buchan, Henry Clark, Henry Bates Jackson, esqrs

Civil Service Pay Office.

Paymaster, William Sargent, esq
Chief Clerk, Samuel Beltz, esq
Cashiers, Edwin Kitchen, Henry Pemberton, esqrs
Accountant, James Miller, esq
Clerks, first class, Henry William Cleere, Joseph Sidney Beauchamp, William Lush, esqrs
Clerks, second class, Charles Miller, Frederick Lewis, Joseph John Guazzaroni, esqrs
Junior Clerks, Alfred Earnshaw, Henry Spencer Perceval, John Martin Leake, esqrs

Solicitor's Office.

Gwydyr House.

Solicitor, George Maule, esq
Assistant Solicitor, Henry Revell Reynolds, jun. esq
First Clerk, Henry Baldwin Raven, esq
Clerks, Thomas Bamford, Henry Musgrave Crispin, Alfred Thomas Crispin, esqrs
Clerk for Criminal Business, John Hayward, esq
Messenger, Thomas Harrold

Commission for Enquiry into the Customs, Excise, & Stamps & Taxes.

Gwydyr House.

COMMISSIONERS, Lord Granville Somerset, Right Hon. William Ewart Gladstone, Hon. William Bingham Baring, James Milnes Gaskell, esq. Alexander Pringle, esq
Secretary, Thomas Peregrine Courtenay, esq
Office Keeper, Thomas Land

TRINITY HOUSE, CORPORATION OF THE.

Trinity Square, Tower Hill. Hours, 10 to 4.

MASTER, the Duke of Wellington, K.G. &c. &c. &c.

Deputy, Capt. Sir John Henry Pelly, bart.

ELDER BRETHREN.

Capt. Abel Chapman	Rt. Hon. Sir R. Peel, bart. M.P.
Capt. Aaron Chapman, M.P.	Rt. Hon. Viscount Melbourne
Lord Viscount Melville	Rt. Hon. the Earl of Minto
Capt. Andrew Timbrell	Capt. Frederick Madan
Capt. Daniel Stephenson	Admiral Sir Charles Adam
Capt. Robert Wellbank	Capt. Stephenson Ellerby
Capt. John Hayman	H.R.H. Prince Albert, K.G.
Capt. John Rees	Capt. George Brobyn
Capt. Henry Nelson	Capt. William Pixley
Capt. John Locke	Capt. Charles Farquharson
Capt. Alexander Weynton	Capt. Robt. Gordon, R.N.
Admiral Sir Thomas Byam Martin, G.C.B.	Capt. William E. Farrar
	Capt. Henry Bonham Bax
Capt. Charles Weller	Earl of Haddington
Right Hon. Sir James Robert George Graham, bart, M.P.	(one vacant)

Secretary, Jacob Herbert, esq
Chief Clerk, Brough George Maltby, esq
Clerks, Messrs. Charles Butterfield, Peter Henry Berthorn, Robert James Moring Grey, Charles Robertson, Robert Wright, Henry Agar White, George Herbert
Clerks in Ballast Offiee, Henry Gunston, John Wingfield
Collector of Duties (Port of London), Benjamin Cotton, esq
Clerks over Sea Department, William Williams, Philip S. Duval
Clerks, Coastways, Julius William Cole, Charles Townley

TWOPENNY POST OFFICE. *See "Post Office."*

WAR OFFICE.

Horse Guards. Hours, 10 to 4.

SECRETARY AT WAR, Rt. Hon. Sidney Herbert, M.P.
Deputy Secretary at War, Laurence Sulivan, esq
Chief Examiner of Army Accounts, Edward Marshall, esq
First Clerk, John Borrow, esq
Clerks:—First class, Henry Milton, Richard Charles Kirby, John Mullins Sandham, John Croomes, Francis Kimpton, George White, Wm. Anderson, Joseph Hanby, esqrs
Second class, Thomas Patrick Matthew, Richard Hardinge Stewart, John Leuson Parsey, Henricus Kendrick, Edwd. Biddle, Phillip Bernard, John Roberts, William Osborne Rich, Edward Robinson, Frederic Joseph Prescott, David Watson, John Minney, George Warner, Henry Runciman Drewry, John Searles Tebbs, William Henry Chinner, Thomas Jones, esqrs
Book-keeper, John Hollings, esq
Third class, Matthew Leonard Coleman, William Marshall, Augustus Edwin, Kenrick Bacon, Joseph Allen, William Brown, Frederick William Kirby, Edward Stillwell, William Ord Marshall, William Cook, John James Parsey, John Francis Ward, Edmund George Briggs, John Milton, James Baird, Cornelius Jago Borrow, John Hanby, Edwd. Marshall, junr., William Henry White, Thomas Bronte Branwell, John Roberts, junr., Richard Hardinge Stewart, junr. John Gregory Gurney, esqrs
Private Secretary to Secretary at War, Ardine John Roberts, esq
Ditto to Dep. Secretary at War, Rd. Hardinge Stewart, esq
Head Messenger, Matthias Strachan
Messengers, Joseph Hart, William Walker, John May Stephens, William Moore, William John Griffin, Joshua Johnson Grubb, Valentine Cocking, Joseph Jackson, John Raines, William Gell, Robert Turton, James Pugh, James Dell
Housekeeper, Mrs. Mary Wheeler

WEIGHTS & MEASURES OFFICE.

See Exchequer (Receipt of).

WOODS, FORESTS, LAND REVENUES, PUBLIC WORKS AND BUILDINGS.

1 & 2 *Whitehall place.* Hours, 10 to 4.

COMMISSIONERS, Rt. Hon. the Earl of Lincoln, M.P. Alexander Milne, esq. Hon. Charles Alexander Gore
Private Secretary to the Chief Commissioner, Granville Edward Harcourt Vernon, esq
Secretary to Chief Commissioner & Clerk to the Board, Trenham Walshman Philipps, esq
Chief Clerks, George Cornell, & John Burke, esqrs
Principal Clerks, John Waller, Thos. Hayley Rose, esqrs
Senior Clerks, Webb Tothill, William Adams, Robert Brown, William Ash, Henry Joshua Robinson, esqrs
Assistant Clerks, Henry Augustus Walker, Mayow Wynall Adams, Henry Bentall Adams, Edward L'Estrange, William Wyatt, esqrs
Junior Clerks, Messrs. Robert Maryman, Thomas Davidson, George Mazzoni, Edward Marshall White, William John Barker, William Nash Round, George Bellairs, John Frost Waller, John Thornborrow, Francis Vincent, Warner Charles Higgins, John Charles Rogers, Francis Adams, esqrs
Book-keeper, William Heron, esq
Itinerant Surveyor of Woods & Forests, Edward Jesse, esq
Surveyors of Houses, Thomas Chawner, James Pennethorne, esqrs
Assistant Surveyor of Houses, William James Smith, esq
Clerk to Commissioners for paving the Regent's Park, Regent st. &c. William Adams, esq

Department of Works & Buildings in England.

Surveyor, Wm. Inman, esq
Assistant, John Phipps, esq
Professional Clerks, William Bennett Barker, Joseph Bedder, esqrs
Clerk of the Furniture, James Robinson Sanders Cox, esq
Clerks of the Works, Messrs. Thomas Morris, Thomas Pullman, John Matthew, John Fortune, William Craib, George Johnson Robinson, Peter Hogg, James Whitman, William James Brown, & James Finchman
Turncocks, Henry Smith, Thomas Thompson
Office Keeper, John Boswell
Messengers, William Sicklen, Joseph Bryan, Thomas Godfrey, James Clapham, Henry Light, James Weblin, William Hall
Porter, John Brooks

IN EDINBURGH.

Clerk of the Works, William Nixon, esq
Office Clerk, Mr. Robert Matheson

FOREIGN MINISTERS IN ENGLAND AND BRITISH MINISTERS ABROAD;

And British Consuls abroad, and Consuls of Foreign States in the United Kingdom.

Foreign Ministers in England, and British Ministers Abroad.

Country	*Ministers from, at London.*	*British Ministers at*
AMERICA (United States of)	Envoy Ex. & Min. Plen. Louis M'Lane, esq. Harley st.; Sec. of Legation, Gansevoort Melville, esq....	Env.Ex. & Min. Plen. Rt. Hon. Hen.Richard Pakenham,esq.P.C. (*Washington*); Sec. of Leg.John Fiennes Crampton, esq
AUSTRIA	Env. Ex.& Min. Plen. Baron Neumann,Chandos Ho., 7 Chandos st. Cavendish sq.; Councillor to the Embassy,Baron Koller; Sec.to the Embassy, Baron Brenner; Attachés, Baron Kübeck,Count Anthony Esterhazy, Count Alfred Potochi	Amb. Ex. & Min. Plen. Rt. Hon. Sir Rt. Gordon, G.C.B. (*Vienna*); Sec. of Emb. Arthur Charles Magenis, esq
BAVARIA	Env. Ex. & Min. Plen. Baron de Cetto, 3 Hill st. Berkeley sq	En.Ex.&Min.Plen. John Ralph Milbanke, esq. (*Munich*); Sec. of Leg. Stephen Henry Sulivan, esq
BELGIUM	Env. Ex. & Min. Plen. M. Sylvain Van de Weyer, 50 Portland pl.; office, 9A, Weymouth st.; Sec. M. Charles Drouet; Attaché, M. Octave Delepierre	Env.Ex. & Min.Plen.Sir George HamiltonSeymour(*Brussels*);Sec of Leg.Thomas Wathen Waller,esq
BRAZIL	Env. Ex. & Min. Plen. Le Commandeur Marques Lisboa, 10 York place, Portman sq.; Sec. of Leg. Chevalier Augustus de Paiva; Attaché, Chevalier de Pereira; Joaquim Thomaz do Amaral, esq....	Env. Ex. & Min. Plen. H. C. J. Hamilton, esq. (*Rio de Janeiro*); Sec. of Leg. James Hudson, esq
CHINA	*No Ambassador*	Plenipo. John Francis Davis, esq
DENMARK	Env. Ex. & Min. Plen. Count Reventlow, 52 Wilton crescent, Belgrave sq.; Sec. of Leg. M. De Beilke	Env. Ex. & Min.Plen. Sir H.W. Wynn(*Copenhagen*); Sec.of Leg. Peter Browne, esq
EQUATOR(REPUBLIC OF THE)	*No Ambassador—"see Consuls"*	
FRANCE	Amb. Ex. & Min. Plen. Count St. Aulaire, Hertford house, 20 Manchester sq.; First Sec. Count de Jarnac; Second Sec. Count Louis de Noailles; Attachés. Comte de la Grange, Monsieur Cottee; Chancelier, M. George de Rabaudy	Amb. Ex.& Min. Plen.Rt.Hon. Lord Cowley, G.C.B. (*Paris*); Sec. of Emb. Lord Wm. Hervey
FRANKFORT (FREE CITY OF) ON THE MAINE	*No Ambassador—"see Consuls"*	Min. Plen.Hon.W.Fox Strangways; Sec. of Leg. Hon. Francis Molyneux
GREECE	*No Ambassador—see "Consuls"*	Min.Plen.Sir.Edm.Lyons,bart. G.C.B.Sec.of Leg.Phil.Griffith,esq
HANOVER	Env. Ex. & Min. Plen. Count Kielmansegge, 44 Grosvenor place; Sec. Charles Klingemann, esq. 4 Hobart place, Eaton square	En. Ex.& Min. Plen. Hon. John D. Bligh, Sec. of Leg. Hon. Geo. Edgcumbe
HANSEATIC REPUBLICS OF LUBEC, BREMEN, AND HAMBURGH	*No Ambassador—see "Consuls"*	Chargé d'Affaires,G.L.Hodges, esq. (*Hamburgh*)
IONIAN STATES	Agent, Sir A. Wood, Colonial Office	—
MEXICO	Env. Ex. & Min. Plen. Don Thomas Murphy, 7 Sussex place, Regent's park; First Sec. Don Joseph Murphy	Min. Plen. Charles Bankhead, esq.; Sec. of Leg. Percy William Doyle, esq
MONTE VIDEO	*No Ambassador see "Consuls"*	Chargé d'Affaires & Consul General, Adolphus Turner, esq
MUSCAT	Special Envoy,Saeed Alli Ben Nassur,95Gt.Prtlnd. st	*No envoy—see "Consuls"*
NEW GRENADA	Chargé d'Affaires, Don Manuel Maria Mosquera, 52 Baker st. Portman sq.; Sec. to the Legation, Don Rafael de Ayala, 39 Upper Baker st. Regent's pk	Chargé d'Affaires & Consul General, Daniel Florence O'Leary, esq. (*Carthagena*)

NETHERLANDS	Min. Ex. & Plen. M. Dedel, 25 Wilton crescent; Sec. of Legation, A. J. L. Stratenus, 90 Cadogan place, Sloane st	Env. Ex. & Min. Plen. Sir Ed. C. Disbrowe (*The Hague*); Sec. of Leg. Henry Francis Howard, esq
PERSIA	....	Env. Ex. & Min. Plen. Justin Shiel, esq
PERU	*No Ambassador—see "Consuls"*	Chargé d'Affaires & Con. Gen. William Pitt Adams, esq
PORTUGAL	Env. Ex. & Min. Plen. Baron da Torre de Moncorvo, 57 Upper Seymour st.; Sec. of Leg. Le Chevalier Marcal José Ribeiro; Attachés, Mons. La Pinto de Soveral, 92 Milton st. Dorset square, Mons. Antonio Travassos Valdez, 3 Delahay st. Westminster	Env. Ex. & Min. Plen. Lord Seaford (*Lisbon*); Sec. of Leg. Henry Southern, esq
PRUSSIA	Env. Ex. & Min. Plen. Chevalier Bünsen, 4 Carlton house terrace; Councillor of Legation, Baron Thile	En. Ex. & Min. Plen. Rt. Hon. the Earl of Westmoreland, K.C.B. (*Berlin*); Sec. of Leg. Sir G. B. Hamilton
RIO DE LA PLATA (UNITED PROVINCES OF)	Env. Ex. & Min. Plen. Don Manuel Moreno, 23 Upper Wimpole st	En. Ex. Wm. Gore Ouseley, esq.; Sec. of Leg. Francis Leeson Ball, esq
RUSSIA	Amb. Ex. & Plen. Baron Brunow, 30 Dover st. Piccadilly; First Sec. M. de Berg; Second Sec. M. de Koudriaffsky	Env. Ex. & Min. Plen. Hon. John Arthur D. Bloomfield; Sec. of Leg. Andrew Buchanan, esq
SARDINIA	Env. Ex. & Min. Plen. Count Nomis de Pollon, 11 Grosvenor st.; Sec. of Leg. Count Bevel	En. Ex. & Min. Plen. Hon. Ralph Abercromby (*Turin*); Sec. of Leg. Hon. Richard Bingham
SAXONY	Resident Minister, Baron de Gersdorf, 14 Chester square	En. Ex. & Min. Plen. Hon. F. R. Forbes (*Dresden*); Sec. of Leg. Charles T. Barnard, esq
SICILY	Env. Ex. & Min. Plen. Prince Castelcicala, 15 Princes st. Cavendish sq.; Secs. of Leg. Mons. G. Canofari, 2 Old Cavendish street	En. Ex. & Min. Plen. Hon. W. Temple (*Naples*); Sec. of Leg. Hon. Charles A. Murray
SPAIN	Env. Ex. & Min. Plen. Duke of Sotomayor; 1st Sec. of Legation, Le Chevalier de Tacon; 2nd Sec. of Legation, Don Victoriano de Pedrorena; Attachés, Don Pedro Perez de Castro, Count Crescent, 9 Cavendish square; Don Juan Antonio Lopez de Cevallos, Marques del Arco, 30 Weymouth st. Portland place	En. Ex. & Min. Plen. Rt. Hon. Henry Lytton Bulwer (*Madrid*); Sec. of Leg. Hon. George Sulyarde Jerningham
SWEDEN AND NORWAY	Env. Ex. & Min. Plen. Count Bjornstjerna; Chargé d'Affaires, Baron Rehausen, 14 Halkin st. west, Belgrave square	En. Ex. & Min. Plen. Sir T. Cartwright, G.C.H. (*Stockholm*); Sec. of Leg. G. J. R. Gordon, esq
SWITZERLAND	*No Ambassador—see "Consuls"*	Min. Plen. D. R. Morier, esq. (*Berne*); Sec. of Leg. Newton Saville Scott, esq
TURKEY	Amb. Ex. & Min. Plen. Sarim Effendi, 1 Bryanstone square; 1st Sec. of Emb. Edib Effendi; 2nd Sec. & Interpreter, I. Agop; 1st Attaché, Edward Zohrab, esq.; 2nd Attaché, Hassen Effendi	Amb. Ex. & Plen. Rt. Hon. Sir Stratford Canning, G.C.B. (*Constantinople*); Sec. of Embassy, Hon. Henry Rd. Chas. Wellesley
TUSCANY	*No Ambassador—see "Consuls"*	Min. Resident, Lord Holland (*Florence*); Sec. of Leg. Hon. Peter Campbell Scarlett
VENEZUELA	*No Ambassador at present—See "Consuls"*	Chargé d'Affaires & Con. Gen. Belford Hinton Wilson, esq
WURTEMBERG	....	En. Ex. & Min. Plen. Sir Alex. Malet, bart. (*Stuttgard*); Sec. of Leg. Augustus Craven, esq

BRITISH CONSULS AND VICE CONSULS ABROAD.

Marked thus † are Vice Consuls.

Adrianople, *Turkey*, William Willshire, esq
Aleppo, *Syria*, Nathaniel Wm. Werry, esq
Alexandretta, *Syria*, † E. St. John Neale
Alexandria, *Egypt*, Lieut. Col. Barnett, *Consul General*; John Laurence Stoddart, esq; † & *Chancelier*, G. Chasseaud, esq
Algiers, *Agent & Consul General*, Robt. W. St. John, esq; † Alexander Tulin, esq
Alicante, *Spain*,
Amoy, *China*, George Tradescant Ley, esq
Amsterdam, *Holland*, James Annesley, esq
Ancona, *Roman States*, George Moore, esq
Antwerp, *Belgium*, Godschall Johnson, esq
Archangel, *Russia*, John Whitehead, esq
Arica, *Peru*, Hugh Wilson, esq
Athens, *Greece*. *see Piræus.*
Austrian States, Sir Thomas S. Sorrell, K.H. *Consul Gen*
Bagdad, *Turkey*, Henry Creswick Rawlinson, esq
Bahia, *Brazil*, Edward Porter, esq
Balearic Isles. *see Mahon*
Baltimore, John M'Tavish, esq
Barcelona, *Spain*, J. S. Penleaze, esq
Batoom, *Turkey*, F. Guarracino, esq
Bayonne, *France*, Fergus James Graham, esq
Bengazi, *Tripoli*, Thomas Wood, esq
Belgrade, *Servia*, Th. de Grenier Fonblanque, esq. *Con. Gen*
Beyrout, *Syria*, Niven Moore, esq
Bilboa, *Spain*, John Clark, esq
Bogota, *New Granada*, Daniel Florence O'Leary, esq. *Con. Gen.* † W. H. Rainsford, esq
Bona, *Algiers*, John Llambias, esq
Bordeaux, *France*, Thomas Brand Graham Scott, esq
Boston, *United States*, Thomas Colley Grattan, esq
Boulogne, *France*, William Hamilton, esq
Bremen, *Hanseatic Republic*, † B Pearkes, esq
Brest, *France*, Sir Anthony Perrier
Brussa, *Turkey*, Donald Sandison, esq

Bucarest, *Wallachia*, Robert Gilmour Colquhoun, esq
Buenos Ayres, Charles Griffiths, esq
Cadiz, *Spain*, John Macpherson Brackenbury, esq
Caen, *France*, † Peter Barrow. esq
Cagliari, *Sardinia*, George Bomeester, esq
Cairo, *Egypt*, Alfred Septimus Walne, esq
Calais, *France*, Samuel G. Marshall, esq
Callao, *Peru*, † John Barton, esq
Canary Isles, *Spain. see Teneriffe.*
Canton, *China*, Francis Coleman Macgregor, esq
Cape Haytien, *Hayti*, † Francis Hastings Gilbert, esq
Cape Verd Isles, *Portugal*, John Rendall, esq
Caracas, *Venezuela*, Belford Hinton Wilson, esq. *Con. Gen*
Carolina (North & South), *United States*, Charles Dunkin Wake, esq. at Charleston
Carthagena, *New Granada*, } Chas. Edward Keith Kortright, esq
Carthagena, *Spain*, Charles Walsingham Turner, esq
Central America. *see St. Salvador*
Charleston, *United States. see Carolina*
Charente, *France*, John Frank Close, esq
Christiana, *Norway*, John Rice Crowe, esq. *Consul General*
Cochabamba, *Bolivia*, Charles Masterton, esq
Concepcion, *Chili*, Robert Cunningham, esq
Constantinople, *Turkey*, *Con. Gen.* Abraham Carlton Cumberbatch, esq. & *Chancelier* Jonathan Hardy, esq
Copenhagen, *Denmark*, E. Bathurst, esq
Coquimbo, *Chili*, David Ross, esq
Corsica, Thomas Pennington, esq
Coruna, *Spain*, James Baker, esq
Crate, Henry Sarell Ongley, esq
Cuxhaven, *Hanseatic Republic*, † H. H. Dutton, esq
Cyprus, Niven Kerr, esq
Damascus, *Syria*, Richard Wood, esq
Damietta, *Egypt*, † M Surur, esq
Dantzic, *Prussia*, Henry Robert Plaw, esq. *Con. Gen*
Dardanelles, *Turkey*, Charles A. Lander, esq
Dresden, *Saxony*, John Ward, esq. *Con. Gen*
Egypt. *see Alexandria*
Elsineur, *Denmark*, Henry George Kuper, esq. † John Macgregor, esq
Enos, *Turkey*, Nicholas Rossy, esq. *Consular Agent*
Erzeroom, *Turkey*, James Brant, esq
Fayal (*Azores*), *Portugal*, † J Minchin, esq
Fiume, *Austria*, † C T Hill, esq
Florida (East & West), *United States*, *Mobile*
Flushing, *Holland*, H. Ellinkhuysen, esq
Foo-chow-foo, *China*, Rutherford Alcock, esq
Frankfort, *free city of*, Christian F. Koch, esq
Gallipoli, *Two Sicilies*, †Richard Stevens, esq
Galatz, *Moldavia*, †Charles Cunningham, esq
Galveston, *Texas*, William Kennedy, esq
Genoa, *Sardinia*, Timothy Yeats Brown, esq
Georgia, *United States. see Savannah*
Gottenberg, *Sweden*, Henry Thomas Liddell, esq
Granville, *France*, John Turnbull, esq
Guayaquil, *Equator*, Walter Cope, esq.
Hamburg, *Hanseatic Republic*, George Lloyd Hodges, esq *Con. Gen.* †C. Wesselhoeft, esq
Havana (*Cuba*), *Spain*, Joseph Tucker Crawford, esq. *Con. Gen.*
Havre, *France*, George William Featherstonhaugh, esq
Ibralia, *Wallachia*, St. Vincent Lloyd, esq
Islay, *Peru*, †Thos. Crompton, esq
Janina, *Albania*, Sidney Smith Saunders, †T. Damaschino, esq
Jassy, *Wallachia*, Samuel Gardner, esq
Jerusalem, *Palestine*, James Finn, esq
Kaiseriah, *Turkey*, Henry Suter, esq
Kertch, *Russia*, C. R. Cattley, esq
Kiel (vacant)
Konigsberg, *Prussia*, †J. D. Brockmann, esq
Leghorn, *Tuscany*, Alexander M'Bean, esq
Liebau, *Russia*, Francis Kienitz, esq
Lima, *Peru*, William Pitt Adams, esq. *Consul General*
Lisbon, *Portugal*, Wm. Smith, esq. †Jeremiah Meagher, esq
Louisiana, *see New Orleans*,
Lubeck, *Hanseatic Republic*, †W L Behneke, esq
Madeira, *Portugal*, George Stoddart, esq
Madrid, *Spain*, Col. Barrie. *Consular Assistant*
Mahon, *Spain*, †Robert Adam Dalzell, esq
Maine, *United States. see Portland*
Malaga, *Spain*, William Penrose Mark, esq
Maranham, *Brazil*, Robert Falconer Corbett, esq
Marseilles, *France*, Alexander Turnbull, esq
Maryland, *United States. see Baltimore*
Massachusetts. *see Boston*
Matamoros, *Mexico*, Francis Lowe Giffard, esq
Memel, *Prussia*, †W. J. Hertslet, esq
Messina, *Two Sicilies*, Wm. Wilton Barker, esq
Mexico, Ewen C. Mackintosh, esq
Milan, *Austria*, †Lieut. Campbell, R.N.
Missolonghi, *Greece*, †H. B. Suter, esq
Mobile, *Florida*, Robert Grigg, esq
Mogador, *Morocco*, William Grace, esq
Monte Video, Adolphus Turner, esq. *Con. Gen.* †M. T. Hood, esq
Moossul, *Turkey*, Christian Rassam, esq
Mosquito Territory, Patrick Walker, esq. *Agent & Con. Gen*
Muscat, Capt. Atkins Hamerton
Nantes, *France*, Henry Newman, esq
Naples, *Two Sicilies*, Capt. Thomas Gallwey, R.N. †William Dorant, esq
Navigator's Island, George Pritchard, esq
New Hampshire, *United States. see Portland*
New Orleans, *United States*, William Mure, esq
New York, *United States*, Anthony Barclay, esq
Nice, *Sardinia*, Pierre la Croix, esq
Ningpo, *China*, Robert Thom, esq
Norfolk, *Virginia*, Francis Waring, esq
Norway. *see Christiana*
Odessa, *Russia*, James Yeames, esq. *Con. Gen.* †John Wilkins, esq
Oporto, *Portugal*, Edwin Johnson, esq
Oran, *Algiers*, John Bell, esq
Ostend, *Belgium*, E. Thompson Curry, esq
Otranto, *Two Sicilies*, Francesco Corchia, esq
Palermo, *Two Sicilies*, John Goodwin, esq
Panama, *New Granada*, William Perry, esq
Para, *Brazil*, Richard Ryan, esq
Paraiba, *Brazil*, Beverly Newcomen, esq
Paris, *France*, Thomas Pickford, esq
Patras, *Greece*, George W. Crowe, esq
Pennsylvania, *United States. see Philadelphia*
Pernambuco, *Brazil*, Henry Augustus Cowper, esq
Philadelphia, *United States*, William Peter, esq
Phillipine Isles, John William Percy Farren, esq
Pillau, *Prussia*, †C. Elsasser, esq
Piræus, *Greece*, John Green, esq
Port au Prince, *Hayti*, Thomas Usher, esq. †Charles Lennox Wyke, esq
Porto Rico, John Lindegren, esq
Portland, *United States*, Joseph Thomas Sherwood, esq
Prevesa, *Albania*, †T. S. Hutton, esq
Puerto Cabello, *Venezuela*, J. M'Whirter, esq
Riga, *Russia*, George Bunbury Clinton Wynyard, esq
Rio Janeiro, *Brazil*, Robert Hesketh, esq
Rotterdam, *Holland*, Sir James Turing, bart
St. Jago (*Cuba*), *Spain*, Charles Clarke
St. Martha, *New Granada*, Edward Mark, esq
St. Michael's (*Azores*), *Portugal*, Thomas Carew Hunt, esq
St. Petersburgh, *Russia*, Sir Edward Stuart Baynes
Salonica, *Turkey*, Charles Blunt, esq
Samsoon, *Turkey*, R. Stevens, esq
San Blas, *Mexico*, Eustace Barron, esq
San Lucar, *Spain*, †Charles Fillippe, esq
SanSalvador, *Central America*, Fred. Chatfield, esq. *Con. Gen*
Santiago, *Chili*, Lieut. Col. Walpole, *Con. Gen*
Savannah, *Georgia*, Edmund Molyneux, esq
Saxony, see *Dresden*
Scio, *Turkey*, G. D. Vedova, esq
Scutari, *Albania*, G. Bonatti, esq
Sfax, *Tunis*, †Wm. Crowe, esq
Shanghai, *China*, George Balfour, esq
Smyrna, *Turkey*, Rich. Wm. Brant, esq. †*and Chancelier* J. Charnaud
Stettin, *Prussia*, †F. H. Petersen, esq
Stockholm, *Sweden*, Sir John Ross, Capt. R.N
Syra, *Greece*, Richard Wilkinson, esq
Syria, Col. Hugh Rose, *Con. Gen*
Tabreez, *Persia*, Edward W. Bonham, *Con. Gen*
Tahiti, *Society Isles*, G. C. Miller, esq
Tampico, *Mexico*, James Wm. Glass, esq
Tangier, *Morocco*, John Drummond Hay, esq. *Agent & Con. Gen.* †Henry Murray, esq
Tarsons, *Syria*, †John Clapperton, esq
Tehran, *Persia*, K. E. Abbott, esq
Teneriffe, *Spain*, Richard Bartlett, esq
Terceira, (*Azores*), *Portugal*, H. Alton, esq
Tetuan, *Morocco*, James Butler, esq
Texas, Charles Elliott, Capt. R.N. *Con. Gen*
Toulon, *France*, L. E. Jouve, esq
Trebizond, *Turkey*, F. J. Stevens

Trieste, *Austria*, Sir T. H. Sorreil, K.H. *Con. Gen.* †Henry Bynner, esq
Tripoli, Hanmer G. Warrington, *Agent & Con. Gen*
Tunis, Sir Thos. Reade, *Agt.& Con.Gen.* †Lewis Ferriere, esq
Tuscany. See *Leghorn*
Valparaiso, *Chili*, Henry Rouse, esq
Venice, *Austria*, †W. C. Tatam, esq
Vera Cruz, *Mexico*, Francis Giffard, esq
Virginia, *United States*. See *Norfolk*
Warsaw, *Russia*, Col. Gustavus Charles du Plat
Wiborg, *Russia*, M. Wright, esq
Woahoo, *Sandwich Isles*, William Miller, esq. *Con. Gen*

CONSULS OF FOREIGN STATES IN THE UNITED KINGDOM.

America (United States of).

CONSUL-GENERAL AND AGENT FOR CLAIMS—Col. Aspinwall, 1 Bishopsgate churchyard

Barbadoes, Wm. R. Hayes; *Belfast*, Thomas W. Gilpin; *Bermuda*, Alexdr. J. Bergen; *Bristol*, Francis B.Ogden; *Cork*, John Murphy; *Cowes*, Jsph. Rodney Croskey; *Deal*, E. Iggulden; *Dover*, Henshaw Latham; *Dublin*, Thos. Wilson; *Dundee*, Stewart Steel; *Falmouth*, Robert W. Fox; *Galway*, Michael Kennedy; *Glasgow*, Jsph. Cowdin; *Hobart town* (*Van Dieman's Land*), E. Hathaway, jun.; *Hong Kong*, Frederick J. Bush; *Hull* (*Kingston-upon*), Joshua Garsed, jun.; *Kirkwall*, Robert Scarth; *Leeds*, Albert Davey; *Leith* (*Port of Edinburgh*), Robert Grieve; *Liverpool*, Robert Armstrong; *Llanelly*, Robert Dunkin; *Londonderry*, Robert L. Longhead; *Margate*, W. Cobb. jun.; *Nassau* (*New Providence*), John F. Bacon; *Picton* (*Nova Scotia*), John J. Peavey; *Plymouth*, Thomas Were Fox; *Port Louis* (*Isle of France*), Robert P. de Silver; *Ramsgate*, Edward Hodges; *St. John's* (*New Brunswick*), Israel D. Andrews; *Sydney* (*Nova Scotia*), Charles H. Delavan; *Tenby*, Robert Dunkin; *Turk's Island*, Abraham Morrell; *Yarmouth*, J. Preston (*agent*)

Argentine Republic.

VICE-CONSUL—John Luscombe, Plymouth

Austria.

CONSUL-GENERAL—L. N. de Rothschild, esq. 3 New court, St. Swithin's lane
CONSUL—*North Shields*, Joseph Burrell

Baden.

CONSUL—John Simpson, esq. 1 Riches court

Bavaria.

CONSUL-GENERAL—Adolphus Frederic Schaezler, esq. 11 Bury court, St. Mary axe

Belgium.

CONSUL—Hermenegild Castellain, eq. 3 Copthall court
VICE CONSUL—Charles Castellain, esq

Aberdeen, Alexander Thom; *Belfast*, S. K. Mulholland; *Cork*, H. Barry; *Cowes*, Henry Francis Ross; *Deal & Ramsgate*, E. Hodges; *Dartmouth*, George Hingston; *Dover*, M. Latham; *Dublin*, J. Fottrell; *Dundee*, Patrick Just; *Falmouth*, Alfred Fox; *Glasgow & Greenock, &c.* Francis Reid; *Guernsey*, F. D. Putron; *Jersey*, Charles Godfrey; *Hull*, John Foster; *Leith*, consul, J. Mitchell; vice consul, John Cadell; *Lerwick*, Chas. Duncan; *Liverpool*, consul, J. Johnstone; vice consul, Edwd. Meugens; *Manchester*, Geo. Kissel; *Margate*, W.Cobb, jun.; *Newcastle* (*Tyne*), John Reed; *Orkney Islands* (*Lerwick*), Chas. Duncan; *Padstow & Penzance*, Alex. Marrack; *Portsmouth*, Alex. Beattie; *Plymouth*, Samuel Treeby; *Ramsgate*, E. Hodges; *St. Ives* (*Cornwall*), Alex. Marrack; *Salcombe bay & Torbay*, Geo. Hingston; *Southampton*, T. Jerningham; *Yarmouth*, — Preston; *Canton* (*China*), Crawford Kerr; *Gibraltar*, Longlands Cowell; *Cape of Good Hope* (*Graham town*), Chas. Maynard; *Demerara*, E. Pottiez; *Sydney*, Wm. Hart Gaden; *New Zealand*, Charles de Witt

Bolivia (Republic of).

CONSUL-GENERAL—Antonio Acosta, esq. 47 Lime st. Fenchurch st

Brazil.

CONSUL-GENERAL—Chevalier Antonio da Silva, jun. Liverpool
CONSUL IN LONDON—Chevalier Antonio da Costa, 3 Howford buildings, Fenchurch st

Dover, Henry Morris; *Llanelly*, Robert Dunkin; *Plymouth*, Thos. Were Fox; *Swansea*, Robert Dunkin

Buenos Ayres. *See Rio de la Plata.*

Denmark.

CONSUL-GENERAL—Fletcher Wilson, esq. Consulate office, 6 Warnford court

Marked thus † are likewise Consuls General

Banff, Garden Grant; *Belfast*, P. L. Munster; *Boston*, R. W. Stainbank; *Bridlington*, Thomas Lamplough; *Bristol*, Thomas Porter Jose; *Cowes*, Thomas Harling; *Deal*, E. Iggulden; *Douglas*, W. F. Moore; *Dover*, Henry Morris; *Dublin*, Robert Dedrichson; *Exeter*, James Blackmore Wilcox; *Falmouth*, Alfred Fox; *Faversham*, W. W. Bentham; *Folkstone*, F. M. Faulkner; *Gloucester*, John W. Hentig, jun.; *Goole*, John Dails; *Grimsby*, J. Skelton; *Guernsey*, H. Dobree; *Hartlepool*, J. Geddes; *Harwich*, S. Billingsley; *Hull*, †W. C. Good; consul, Clements Good; *Jersey*, †J. de St. Croix; *Leith*, W. Marshall; *Liverpool*, F. Engel; *Llanelly*, Robt. Dunkin; *Londonderry*, James Ross; *Lynn Regis*, P. Randulph; *Margate*, W. Cobb, jun.; *Newcastle*, Edward Dodd; *Padstow*, Thomas Rd. Avery; *Penryn*, Alfred Fox; *Penzance*, Edward Pearce; *Plymouth*, Thos. Were Fox; *Portsmouth*, Alexander Beattie; *Ramsgate*, E. Hodges; *Rochester*, W. W. Bentham; *St. Ives* (*Cornwall*), Edw. Pearce; *Scarborough*, Francis Hill; *Scilly Isles*, Henry Edwards; *Seaham*, R. H. Webb; *Sheerness*, W. W. Bentham; *Southampton*, C. Baker; *Stockton*, Anthony Harris; *Sunderland*, John Charleton; *Swansea*, John Grove; *Tenby*, Robert Dunkin; *Truro*, Alfred Fox; *Waterford*, Alex. Rd. Pope; *Yarmouth*, J. Preston

France.

CONSUL-GENERAL—Durant St. André, esq. 44 Montagu square; Consulate office, 3 Copthall buildings, Throgmorton st
VICE-CONSUL—Frederick Gautier, esq. 22 Princes st. Cavendish sq. & 3 Copthall buildings
CONSULS—*Dover* (agt.), Henry Morris; *Brighton*, Peter Black (agt.); *Dublin*, M. de Vaubricourt; *Edinburgh*, M. de Serre; *Falmouth*, G. Fox (agt.); *Folkstone*, F. M. Faulkner (agt.); *Gibraltar*, M. Bero; *Harwich*, I. Billingsley (agt.); *Malta*, M. de Sontag; *Liverpool*, M. Laine; *Newcastle*, M. Dillon; *Plymouth* (agt.), John Luscombe; *Port Louis* (*Mauritius*), Jacques Just Barbet; *Portsmouth*, A. Vanden Berg (agt.); *Ramsgate*, E. I. Curling (agt.); *Rochester*, W. W. Bentham; *Rye*, John Vidler (agt.); *Southampton*, W. J. Lefeuvre (agt.)

Frankfort (free City of).

CONSUL—John George Behrends, esq. 12 Broad st. buildings; *Gibraltar*, Frederick Schott

Greece.

CONSUL—Pantia Ralli, esq. 5 Connaught place west; Consulate office, 25 Finsbury circus

Hanover.

CONSUL-GENERAL—Sir John Hall, K.C.H. St. Katherine's Dock house; Consulate office, 6 Circus, Minories
VICE-CONSUL—*Aberdeen*, William Leslie Thomson
CONSULS—*Bristol*, Joseph Frankel Alexander; *Cardiff*, William Morgan Davies; *Cork*, R. L. Jameson; *Cowes*, William Stuart Day; *Dartmouth*, Richard Langworth Hingston; *Dublin*, John Elliot; *Dundee*, Jas. Edwards; *Falmouth*, Alfred Fox; *Glasgow*, John Dunstan Sheppard; *Guernsey*, Henry Dobree; *Harwich*, J. Sansum; *Hull*, John Tall; *Jersey*, F. D. de St. Croix; *Leith*, Alexander Patterson; *Liverpool*, Richard Bryan Smith; *Lynn*, W. Garland; *Margate*, William Cobb; *Newcastle-upon-Tyne*, Edward Dodds; *Padstow*, T. R. Avery; *Penzance*, Richard Pearce; *Peterhead*, Roderick Gray; *Portsmouth*, Adrianus Van Den Bergh; *Plymouth*, John Luscombe; *Ramsgate, Deal & Dover*, E. Spencer Curling; *Rye*, Wm. Jenner; *Scilly*, Henry George Edwards; *Sheerness & Chatham*, William Walker Bentham; *Sunderland*, Richard Greenwell; *Southampton*, John Bennet; *Weymouth*, Joseph Horsford; *Yarmouth*, E. H. L. Preston

Hanseatic Republics, of Lubeck, Bremen and Hamburgh.

DIPLOMATIC AGENT & CONSUL GENERAL—James Colquhoun, esq. LL.D., K.S.M. 12 St. James's place; Consulate Office, 76 Cornhill

VICE-CONSULS: LUBECK.

Cowes, T. Harling, jun.; *Dartmouth*, R. L. Hingston; *Deal*, Edward Iggulden; *Dover*, H. Latham; *Falmouth*, Alfred Fox; *Gloucester*, William Fox; *Goole*, R. Claye jun.; *Guernsey & Jersey*, W. H. Gardner; *Hull*, W. V. Norman; *Newcastle-on-Tyne*, Edward Dodd; *Newport* (*Monmouth*), C. H. Stonehouse; *Plymouth*, Thos. Were Fox; *Poole*, Robert Slade; *Portsmouth*, A. Van Den

Bergh; *Ramsgate*, E. S. Curling; *Stockton*, G. Wilkinson; *Southampton*, John Bennett; *Weymouth*, J. Horsford; *Cape Town* (Consul), M. Thalwitzer; *Gibraltar* (Consul), James Thomson; *St. Helena*, Saul Solomon (consul), Nathaniel Soloman, (Vice-consul); *Sydney*, Pelham Dutton

VICE-CONSULS: BREMEN.

Cowes, T. Harling; *Dartmouth*, R. L. Hingston; *Deal*, Edward Iggulden; *Dover*, H. Latham; *Dundee*, Patrick Just; *Falmouth*, A. Fox; *Harwich*, S. Billingsley; *Hull*, W. V. Norman; *Leith*, A. Robinow; *Newcastle-on-Tyne*, Edward Dodd; *Newport (Monmouth)*, C. H. Stonehouse; *Plymouth*, Thos. Were Fox; *Portsmouth*, A. Van Den Bergh; *Ramsgate*, E. S. Curling; *Southampton*, John Bennett; *Weymouth*, J. Horsford; *Adelaide (Australia)*, Hermann C. Slakemann (Consul); *Gibraltar* (Consul), James Thomson; *Cape Town* (Consul), M. Thalwitzer; *St. Helena*, William Carrol (Consul)

VICE CONSULS: HAMBURGH.

Aberdeen, W. L. Thomson; *Cork*, Simon Ring; *Cowes*, W. S. Day; *Dartmouth*, R. L. Hingston; *Deal*, E. S. Curling; *Dover*, H. Latham; *Dublin* (Consul), Thomas Wisdom; *Dundee*, Patrick Just; *Falmouth*, Alfred Fox; *Gloucester*, William Fox; *Guernsey*, W. V. de Quesne; *Hartlepool*, J. Romyn; *Hull*, W. V. Norman; *Manchester*, H. Hasche; *Newcastle-on-Tyne*, Edward Dodd; *Newport (Monmouth)*, C. H. Stonehouse; *Plymouth*, Thos. Were Fox; *Poole*, Robert Slade; *Portsmouth*, A. Vanden Bergh; *Ramsgate*, E.S.Curling; *Rye*, John Vidler; *Southampton*, John Bennet; *Stockton*, George Wilkinson; *Swansea*, H. Barth, jun.; *Weymouth*, J. Horsford; *Bombay* (Consul), August Henry Husche; *Calcutta* (Consul), T.Herman August Wallenbach; *Cape Town* (Consul), M. Thalwitzer; *Gibraltar* (Consul), James Thompson; *Graham's Town (Cape of Good Hope)*, (Consul) Charles Maynard; *Nassau (New Providence)*, Frederick Peat; *Port Elizabeth (Cape of Good Hope)*, (Consul) Charles Maynard; *Port Louis (Mauritius)*, (Consul) Robert Stein; *Quebec* (Consul), Edward Ryan; *Sydney (New South Wales)* (Consul), Pelham Dutton; *Sierra Leone* (Consul), John Godfrey Nagel; *Sincapore* (Consul), Theodore A. Behn; *St. Helena* (Consul), Saul Soloman; (Vice-consul) Nath. Soloman

Hesse Darmstadt.

CONSUL-GENERAL—Bernhard Hebeler, esq., K.C.R.E., 15 York place, Baker st.; Consulate Office, 106 Fenchurch st

Mecklenburg Schwerin.

CONSUL-GENERAL—Christopher Kreeft; Consulate Office, 9 Billiter square, City

Cardiff, John Owen; *Cowes*, Thomas Harling, jun.; *Dartmouth*, R. L. Hingston; *Deal and Ramsgate*, Edward Iggulden; *Glasgow*, James Grieve; *Hull*, John Christiansen; *Jersey*, H. Ch. Godfray; *Leith*, Henry Denovan; *Malta*, John Ross; *Newcastle-on-Tyne*, C. F. Eskuche; *Newport (Monmouth)*, Stephen Campbell; *Plymouth*, Samuel Treeby; *Stockton & Hartlepool*, Pieter Romyn; *Malta*, John C. Ross

Mexico.

VICE-CONSUL—José Maria Saenz, 3 Winchester buildings

Cowes, Edward Day; *Falmouth*, Robert William Fox; *Glasgow*, William Malcolm; *Liverpool*, Ignacio Tato; *Plymouth*, Thomas Were Fox

Monte Video.

CONSUL-GENERAL—Frederick de Lisle, esq. 1 York place, Portman square

Liverpool, John Hall

Netherlands.

CONSUL-GENERAL—John Wm. May, esq. 123 Fenchurch st

Aberdeen, Arthur Thomson; *Belfast*, F. Gregg; *Bristol*, Robert Bruce, jun.; *Cardiff*, H. H. Parry; *Chatham*, W. W. Bentham; *Cork*, Richard L. Jameson; *Cowes*, W. S. Day; *Deal*, E. S. Curling, H. C. Tryon (Vice-consul); *Dover*, Henshaw Latham; *Dublin*, B. M. Tabuteau; *Dundee*, George Thoms; *Falmouth*, R. R. Broad; *Glasgow*, John Macpherson; *Harwich*, John Sansum; *Hull*, J. C. Cankrien, C. L. Ringrose (Vice-consul); *Leith*, Alexander Paterson; *Lerwick*, J. R. Spence; *Liverpool*, D. Willink, W. W. Willank (Vice-consul); *Londonderry*, Wm. Davenport; *Lynn*, P. Randulph; *Margate*, W. Cobb, jun.; *Milford*, G. Starbuck; *Newcastle*, W. J. M. Lange; *Newport (South Wales)*, C. Stonehouse; *Penzance*, Richard Pearce; *Plymouth*, John Luscombe; Vice-consul, William Luscombe; *Portsmouth*, Louis A. Van Den Berg; *Ramsgate*, E. S. Curling, W. Curling (Vice-consul); *Rye*, W. Jenner; *St. Ives (Cornwall)*, Richard Pearce; *Scilly Isles*, Henr. Edwards; *Sheerness*, W. W. Bentham; *Southampton*, Louis Arnold Van Den Berg; *Stockton*, George Wilkinson, P. Romyn (Vice-consul); *Sunderland*, Richard Greenwell; *Swansea*, Thomas Grove; *Weymouth*, Joseph Horsford; *Yarmouth*, Isaac Preston

New Granada.

CONSUL-GENERAL—Jose Maria Saenz, 3 Winchester buildings; *Falmouth*, Alfred Fox; *Jamaica*, Juan de Francisco Martin

Oldenburgh.

CONSUL-GENERAL—Henry Fredk. Tiarks, 48 Fenchurch st. *Cowes*, Thomas Harling, esq.; *Hull*, George Cammell; *Liverpool*, Francis Prange, esq.; *Leith*, Henry Lewis Platen Denovan; *Newcastle*, John George Dodd; *Newport*, C. H. Stonehouse; *Ramsgate*, Edward Hodges, esq

Peruvian Republic.

CONSUL—William Parish Robertson, 17 St. Helen's place; *Liverpool*, Henry Lucas; *Plymouth*, Thomas Were Fox

Portugal.

CONSUL-GENERAL—Le Commandeur Francisco Ignacio Van Zeller, 40 Dorset sq.; Consulate Office, 5 Jeffery square

VICE-CONSUL—Francisco Rebello, 16 Upper Woburn place. *Birmingham*, George Richmond Cullis; *Brixham & Torbay*, R. W. Wolston; *Cowes*, Thomas Harling; *Dartmouth*, Richard Langworthy Hingston; *Deal*, Edward Spencer Curling; *Dover*, Richard Bushell; *Dundee*, Archibald Crichton; *Exeter*, Frederick Dashwood Lake Hirtzel; *Falmouth*, George Croker Fox; *Folkstone*, Alfred Lewton Hodges; *Glasgow & the Ports of the Clyde*, John Mitchell, jun.; *Guernsey, Jersey & Alderney*, John Mansell; *Harwich*, Samuel Billingsley; *Hull*, John Hollingworth; *Kingsbridge & Salcombe*, Gabriel Beer Lidstone; *Leith & the Ports on the Frith of Forth*, William Muir; *Newcastle*, Edward Bilton; *Orkney & Shetland*, Arthur Anderson; *Penzance & Scilly Islands*, Richard Pearce; *Plymouth*, John Collier; *Poole*, James Aldridge; *Portsmouth*, Arnaldus Van den Bergh; *Ramsgate*, Edw. Hodges; *Southampton*, N. M. Priaulx; *Stockton on Tees*, Geo. Wilkinson; *Sunderland*, Hugh Panton; *Weymouth*, Joseph Horsford; *Yarmouth*, Isaac Preston

Prussia.

CONSUL-GENERAL—Bernhard Hebeler, esq. K.C.R.E. 15 York place, Baker st.; Consulate Office, 106 Fenchurch st

VICE-CONSULS—*Aberdeen*, Arthur Thomson; *Belfast*, Gustavus Heyn; *Berwick*, James Sinclair; *Birmingham*, G. R. Collis; *Brighton*, Jn. Brown; *Bristol*, H. Visger; *Cardiff & Chepstow*, C. H. Stonehouse; *Cork*, R. Deaves; *Cowes*, W. S. Day; *Dartmouth*, R. L. Hingston; *Deal*, E. Iggulden; *Dover*, H. Latham; *Drogheda*, Thos. Carty; *Dublin*, John Walsh; *Dundee*, Wm. Thornton; *Edinburgh* (Consul), J. G. Thomson; *Exeter*, J. Luscombe; *Falmouth*, G. C. Fox; *Faversham*, W. W. Bentham; *Glasgow*, Robert Sanderson; *Gloucester*, Wm. P. Price; *Guernsey*, John Le Marchant; *Halifax, Nova Scotia*, Stephen Binney; *Harwich*, Samuel Billingsley; *Hartlepool*, C. Martin; *Hull*, H. S. Bright; *Isle of Wight*, W. S. Day; *Jamaica*, Joseph Gordon; *Jersey*, Philip de St. Croix; *Leith*, J. G. Thomson (Consul); *Lerwick*, A. Sutherland; *Limerick*, F. Spaight; *Liverpool* (Consul), Otto Burchardt; *Llanelly*, Rt. Dunkin; *Londonderry*, Chas. Stewart; *Lynn*, Wm. Garland; *Malta*, Raphael Ferro; *Margate*, Wm. Cobb, jun.; *Montreal*, J. M. Tobin; *Montrose*, R. Millar; *Newcastle (Tyne)*, Wm. Bush; *Newfoundland*, B. Scott; *Newport (South Wales)*, C. H. Stonehouse; *Padstow*, Thos. Rd. Avery; *Penzance*, R. Pearce; *Perth*, J. Lowe; *Peterhead*, A. Robertson; *Plymouth*, John Luscombe; *Poole*, Edward Patzcker; *Portsmouth & Gosport*, L. A. Van der Bergh; *Prince Edward's Island*, J. M. Peters; *Quebec*, G. Pemberton; *Ramsgate*, E. S. Curling; *Rochester*, W. W. Bentham; *St. Vincent*, Robert Cumming; *Scilly Isles*, Henry Edwards; *Sheerness*, W. W. Bentham; *Shoreham*, John Brown; *Southampton*, Charles Baker; *Stockton*, C. Martin; *Sunderland*, George Booth; *Swansea*, Rt. Dunkin; *Tenby*, Robert Dunkin; *Waterford*, W. M. Ardagh; *Weymouth*, J. Horsford; *Wisbeach*, Wm. Garland; *Yarmouth*, Isaac Preston

Rio de la Plata, United Provinces of.

CONSUL-GENERAL—George Fred. Dickson, esq. 20 Hanover terrace, Regent's park; Consulate Office, 1 Winchester buildings

Dover, H. Latham; *Falmouth*, Alfred Fox; *Liverpool*, William Jackson; *Plymouth*, John Luscombe

Russia.

CONSUL-GENERAL—Geo. Krehmer, esq. Consulate Office, 15 Saville row; 2 Winchester buildings, City

VICE-CONSULS—*Aberdeen*, Arthur Thomson; *Belfast*, John Galbraith; *Bideford*, Thomas B. Chanter; *Birmingham* (Commercial Agent), George R. Collis; *Brighton*, Peter Cazalet; *Bristol*, Abraham Alexander; *Cork*, Edward Burke; *Deal*, Edward Spencer Curling; *Dover*, Henshaw Latham; *Dublin*, John Astle; *Dundee*, Thomas Neish; *Falmouth*, Alfred Fox; *Glasgow*, Nicholas Handyside; *Gloucester*, James Maurice Shipton; *Gosport*, Matthias March; *Guernsey*, Joseph Collings; *Harwich*, Samuel Billingsley; *Hull*, Thomas Firbank; *Isle of Wight*, Matthias March; *Kirkwall*, Robert Scarth; *Llanelly*, Robert Dunkin; *Leith*, David Thom; *Lerwick*, Wm. Bain; *Liverpool* (Consul), James Leigh, (Vice-consul) Nicholas Mahs; *Milford*, Thomas Roberts; *Newcastle-on-Tyne*, John Thos. Carr; *Newport (South Wales)*, Christopher A. Stonehouse; *Portsmouth*, Matthias March; *Plymouth*, John Luscombe; *Ramsgate & Deal*, Edward S. Curling; *Sheerness*, Wm. Walker Bentham; *Teignmouth*, Sir Warwick H. Tonkin, knt.; *Yarmouth*, John W Shelly

Sardinia.

CONSUL-GENERAL—John Benjamin Heath, esq. 31 Old Jewry, & 66 Russell square

VICE-CONSUL—Robert Amédée Heath, esq. 21 Upper Woburn place; Consulate Office, 31 Old Jewry

VICE-CONSULS—*Cork*, William Deane Seymour; *Ramsgate*, Capt. E. Hodges; *Liverpool*, Wm. Carter; *Dublin*, John J. Wisdom; *Deal*, Ed. Iggulden; *Dover*, Henshaw Latham; *Cowes*, Thos. Harling; *Sheerness*, Wm. Edgcombe

Saxe Weimar.

CONSUL-GENERAL—Samson Cahlmann, 1 Copthall chambers, Throgmorton st

Saxony.

CONSUL-GENERAL—James Colquhoun, esq. LL.D., K.S.M. 12 St. James's place: Consular Office, 76 Cornhill

Sicily.

CONSUL-GENERAL—Henry Swinburne Minasi, esq. 15 Cambridge st. Hyde park square

Bristol, Wm. Wolf Alexander; *Cowes*, Wm. Stuart Day; *Deal*, Edward Iggulden; *Dover*, Henshaw Latham; *Dublin*, Thomas Snowe; *Falmouth*, W. R. Broad; *Gibraltar*, Don Giacomo di Martino; *Gloucester*, Wm. Reynolds Lloyd; *Greenock*, Joseph Mantica; *Guernsey*, Henry Dobree; *Hull*, Joseph Lambert; *Liverpool*, H. W. Ross; *Malta*, D. Ippolito Garrow; *Newcastle-on-Tyne*, Edward Bilton; *Penzance*, Thomas Simon Bolitho; *Plymouth*, John Luscombe

Spain.

CONSUL-GENERAL—The Chevalier Don José Maria Barrero, 37 Old Broad st. City, & Albany villa, 237 Maida vale

CONSULS—*Gibraltar*, Don Antonio Estefani; *Jamaica* (residing at Kingston), Don Juan del Cantillo; *Malta*, Don Carlos Espana; *New Providence* (residing at Nassau), Don Juan Maura; *Sierra Leone*, Don Alphonso Guillemard y Aragon; *Singapore*, Don Antonio Maria Segovia

VICE-CONSULS—*Belfast*, Theodore Bozzi, esq.; *Birmingham*, Don Fernando Villanueva; *Bristol*, Don Antonio Lopez Vildosola, knt. I.C.; *Cape of Good Hope*, Harrison Watson; *Cork*, Bartholomew O'Verling; *Dartmouth*, Richard Lungworthy Kingston; *Deal*, Edward Iggulden; *Dover*, Henshaw Latham; *Dublin*, Don Gregorio Jaun de Ysasi; *Dundee*, Francis Molison; *Exeter*, John Clampit Sercombe; *Falmouth*, George C. Fox; *Gibraltar*, Don Pedro Andres Garcia; *Glasgow*, Robert Wardrop; *Gloucester*, Don Antonio Lopez Vildosola; *Greenock*, Robert Wardrop; *Halifax (Nova Scotia)*, James George Creighton; *Harwich*, Samuel Billingsley; *Hull*, Robert Keddey; *Leith*, James Gordon; *Liverpool*, Robert Mc William; *Lune (Jamaica)*, John Campbell; *Llanelly*, Robert Dunkin; *Malta*, Carlos Espana; *Manchester*, Don Demetrio Duarte; *Montego Bay (Jamaica)*, Samuel Anderson; *Newcastle-on-Tyne*, Edward Bilton; *Newfoundland*, Aaron Hogsett; *Newport, Monmouthshire*, William C. Webb; *Orkney*, Arthur Anderson; *Penzance*, Richard Pearce; *Plymouth*, John Luscombe; *Port Antonio (Jamaica)*, Alexander José Bruner; *Portsmouth*, John Walter Wilkinson; *Ramsgate*, Edward Hodges; *Rochester*, William Edgcombe; *Scilly*, Henry Edwards; *Sheerness*, William Edgcombe; *Shetland*, Arthur Anderson; *Sierra Leone*, Don Juan José Garcia; *Southampton*, Arthur Strafford; *St. Ives*, Alex. Marrack; *Swansea*, John William Leach; *Tenby*, Robert Dunkin; *Weymouth*, Edward Day; *Yarmouth*, Samuel Paget; *Youghall*, Thomas John; *Island of Guernsey*, Albert Carey; *Island of Jersey*, Charles Le Quesne; *Isle of Wight*, Thomas Harling, jun.

As there are no other Vice-Consuls appointed at the several ports and towns of the United Kingdom of Great Britain and Ireland than those above-named, all documents issued or authenticated by any other parties, assuming the Vice-Consular functions in those places, will neither be held valid, nor will they be recognised by the Consul-General.

Captains of Vessels arriving at any of the ports of the Spanish dominions, unless provided with a Bill of Health, granted by the proper authority at the port whence they sailed, and legalized by the Spanish Vice-Consul, should there be one, will be subject to a heavy fine, decreed by the Supreme Board of Health.

No deed or Instrument, or other Documentary evidence, is legal in Spain unless executed or passed before a Notary Public of these kingdoms, as a security for being executed according to the forms required by the laws of this country; and the signature of such Notary must be legalised by the Consul-General or Vice-Consul of the place where such Notary resides. The Consul-General, as well as the Vice-Consuls are also authorised to prepare Spanish powers of attorney, as well as some other Spanish documents, of a notarial character, affecting the interests of subjects of Her Catholic Majesty.

Every signature, whether of a public authority or private party, intended to produce legal effect in Spain, is required to be authenticated by a notary public of these kingdoms, whose signature and public qualifications must be legalised by the Consul-General or Vice-Consul, at the place where the document may be signed.

Sweden & Norway.

CONSUL-GENERAL—Charles Tottie, esq. 52 Montagu square

VICE-CONSUL—William Tottie, esq. 6 Melcombe place, Dorset square.

CONSULATE OFFICE, 2 Crosby square.

Aberdeen, Arthur Thompson; *Banff*, Garden Grant; *Belfast*, P. L. Munster; *Berwick*, John Batters; *Bideford*, James Chappell; *Birmingham*, George Collis; *Boston*, John Bontoft; *Bridport*, J. B. Good; *Brighton*, John Brown; *Bristol*, C. P. B. Howell; *Cardiff & Chepstow*, C. H. Stonehouse; *Chichester*, James Biffin; *Cork*, Rueben Deaves; *Cowes*, W. Stuart Day; *Dartmouth*, R. L. Hingston; *Deal*, E. Iggulden; *Douglas*, J. Stephens, jun.; *Dover*, Henry Morris; *Drogheda*, Thomas Carty; *Dublin*, Charles Hayes; *Dundee*, Wm. Carr Lamb; *Eastbourne*, R. B. Stone; *Exeter*, John Follett; *Falmouth*, R. B. Fox; *Faversham*, W. W. Bentham; *Fowey*, John Mills Carkeet; *Galway*, James Copeland; *Glasgow*, William Brooks; *Gloucester*, A. H. Jenkins; *Goole*, John Clay; *Grangemouth*, James Brooks; *Grimsby*, John Clay; *Guernsey*, Albert Carey; *Gweek*, Wm. Mayn; *Harwich*, John Sansum; *Hastings*, S. Bevill; *Hull*, John Clay; *Ilfracombe*, Nathaniel Vye; *Ipswich*, Wm. Lane; *Jersey*, Joseph Deslandes, jun.; *Kinsale*, John Spiller Newman; *Kirkwall*, Robert Scarth; *Leith*, Thomas Hutchinson; *Limerick*; William White; *Liverpool*, G. A. Lilly; *Llanelly*, Robert Dunkin; *Londonderry*, A. H. Stewart; *Lynn Regis*, P. Randulph; *Margate*, Wm. Cobb, jun.; *Milford*, W. W. Herries; *Montrose*, Robert Millar; *Newport (Monmouth)*, C. H. Stonehouse; *Newry*, George Guy; *Padstow*, John Tredwen; *Penzance*, Richard Pearce; *Peterhead*, Keith Forbes; *Plymouth*, N. Fogelstrom; *Poole*, E. Patzcker; *Portsmouth*, Louis Arnold Van Den Berg; *Ramsgate*, George Hammond; *Rochester*, W. W. Bentham; *Rye*, J. Vidler; *St. Ives*, D. Bamfield; *Scilly Islands*, W. T. Johns; *Seaham*, E. H. Webb; *Sheerness*, W. W. Bentham; *Sheffield*, C. W. Bingley; *Shoreham*, John Brown; *Sligo*, P. O'Connor; *Southampton*, C. Baker; *Stockton*, G. W. Todd; *Sunderland*, L. T. Wang; *Swansea*, Michael J. Michael; *Tenby*, Robert Dunkin; *Thurso*, Hugh Davidson; *Topsham*, John Follett; *Truro*, Edward Sharp; *Waterford*, Alex. Richard Pope; *Westport*, W. H. Parker; *Wexford*, Samuel Elly; *Weymouth*, George Arden; *Whitby*, T. Marwood; *Wick*, James Waters; *Wisbeach*; J. H. Maclean; *Woodbridge*, W. Keeble; *Yarmouth*, Isaac Preston.

Switzerland.

AGENT AND CONSUL-GENERAL—John Lewis Prevost, esq. 24A, Gresham st

VICE-CONSUL—George Prevost, esq. 24A, Gresham street

CONSUL AT LIVERPOOL—Emanuel Zwilchenbart, esq.

Turkey.

CONSUL-GENERAL—Edward Zohrab, esq. 1 Bryanstone square

Birmingham, G. R. Collis; *Deal & Dover*, E. S. Curlin; *Dublin*, John Wisdom; *Falmouth*, R. B. Fox; *Gibraltar*, John Langslands Cowell; *Glasgow*, J. Mitchell, jun.; *Liverpool*, M. L. Mozley; *Malta*, Antonio Farrugla, esq.; *Plymouth*, T. W. Fox, jun.; *Ramsgate*, E. F. Curling.

Tuscany.

CONSUL-GENERAL—James Christian Clement Bell, esq. 15 Angel court, Throgmorton street

VICE-CONSUL—Robert Grant, 15 Angel court, Throgmorton street

Falmouth, Alfred Fox; *Plymouth*, Thomas Were Fox

Venezuela.

CONSUL-GENERAL—James Mulligan, esq. 16 Tokenhouse yard

CONSUL—*Belfast*, John Fergusson; *Demerara*, Henry Haines; *Trinidad*, Felix Pouchet.

Wurtemberg.

CONSUL-GENERAL—Bernard Hebeler, esq. K.C.R.E. 15 York place, Baker st.; Consulate Office, 106 Fenchurch st

PASSPORT OFFICES.

Country.

AMERICA (UNITED STATES OF):—no passports are required

AUSTRIA:—the viza is to be obtained only at the Embassy, 7 Chandos street, Cavendish sq. between the hours of 12 and 2

BADEN:—on personal application at the Consul's office, 1 Riches court, between 10 & 3

BAVARIA:—to individuals personally known to the Minister, 3 Hill st. Berkeley sq.; or to the Consul, 11 Bury court, St. Mary axe

BELGIUM:—at the Legation, 9A, Weymouth street, Portland place, between 11 & 3, and are delivered the following day between 11 & 2 gratis; also at the Consul's office, 3 Copthall court, between 10 & 4, delivered forthwith on payment of a fee of five shillings

BRAZIL:—at the Legation, 10 York place, Portman sq. between 12 & 2, gratis

BUENOS AYRES:—*see Rio de la Plata*

CENTRAL AMERICA:—no passports required

DENMARK:—at the Embassy, 52 Wilton crescent, under special circumstances, from 10 to 12; also at the Consul's office, 6 Warnford court, between 10 & 4, on payment of a fee of ten shillings & sixpence

FRANCE:—at the French Passport office, 6 Poland street, Oxford street; from 11 to 5 for receiving applications for passports, which are granted on the following day between 1 & 3, on personal application, gratis; also at the Consul's office, 3 Copthall buildings, between 12 & 4, delivered forthwith on payment of a fee of ten shillings

FRANKFORT (FREE CITY OF) ON THE MAINE:—at the Consul's office, 12 Broad st. buildings, between 10 & 3, on payment of a fee of five shillings; natives of Frankfort obtain the passport gratis

GREECE:—at the Consul's office, 25 Finsbury circus, between 11 & 4, on payment of a fee of half a crown

HANOVER:—for natives of Hanover, or persons known to the embassy and going to Hanover, at the Embassy, 44 Grosvenor place, or at the Secretary's, 4 Hobart place, Eaton square, between the hours of 10 & 3, and at the Consul's office, 6 Circus, Minories, between 10 & 3, gratis

HANSEATIC REPUBLICS OF LÜBECK, BREMEN, AND HAMBURGH:—at the Consular office, 76 Cornhill, to applicants not being citizens of the Hanse Towns, on production of a previous passport or letter of recommendation, between 10 & 4, on payment of a fee of five shillings; documents required to be used in the Hanse Towns are legalised between 10 & 4, on payment of a fee of ten shillings and sixpence; passports requiring the "vizé," may be left at the Legation, 12 St. James's place, between 10 & 4, and may be called for between 12 & 6 on the following day]

HESSE:—*see Prussia*

LUCCA:—*see Sardinia*

MECKLENBERG SCHWERIN:—only at the Consul's office, 9 Billiter square, between 10 & 4, on payment of a fee of five shillings

MEXICO:—at the Legation, 7 Sussex place, Regent's park, between 12 & 4, and are delivered the following day at the same hours

NAPLES:—*see Sicily*

NEW GRANADA, AND FOR THE CONTINENT:—to citizens of the Republic at the Embassy, 52 Baker st. Portman square, between 10 & 12, and are delivered on the following day; foreigners must present two known persons as guarantee, at the Consul's office, 3 Winchester buildings, Great Winchester st., between 11 & 4; to citizens of the Republic only on payment of a fee of seven shillings

NETHERLANDS:—no passports granted at the Embassy, 25 Wilton crescent; the "vizé" to other passports may be obtained by leaving them until the next day. Passports are granted at the Consul's office, 123 Fenchurch street, between 10 and 4, on payment of a fee of five shillings

OLDENBURG:—at the Consul's office, 48 Fenchurch street, between 11 & 4, on payment of a fee of five shillings

PERU:—at the Consul's office, 17 St. Helen's place, Bishopsgate street, between 11 & 4, and are delivered the following day, on payment of a fee of eight shillings

PORTUGAL:—at the Embassy, 57 Upper Seymour street, Portman square, between 11 & 4, gratis, and may be called for on the following day; also at the Consul's office, 5 Jeffrey's square, Mary axe, from 10 to 4 o'clock

PRUSSIA:—at the Prussian passport office, 4 Carlton House terrace, from 11 to 2, to Prussian subjects only; also at the Consul's office, 106 Fenchurch street, between 10 & 6, to British subjects, and are delivered forthwith, on payment of a fee of seven shillings

RIO DE LA PLATA (UNITED PROVINCES OF):—at the Embassy, 23 Upper Wimpole street, between 10 & 5; gratis to Argentine subjects, or to foreign residents

RUSSIA:—at the Embassy, 30 Dover street, Piccadilly; at the Consul's office, 2 Winchester buildings, to strangers on presenting a letter of recommendation, of which forms may be had at the office, between 10 & 4; passports delivered the following day, on payment of a fee of six shillings and four pence

SARDINIA:—At the Consul's office only, 31 Old Jewry, to subjects only, between 11 & 3, and are delivered, gratis, on the following day

SAXONY:—at the Legation; passports, for which the "vizé" is required, if sent before 12 o'clock, may be had after 8 the same day; if left before 8 may be had before 12 the following day. New passports are granted to Saxon subjects, furnished with the means of legitimation, or by exception to British subjects producing either a letter of recommendation, signed by one known to the Saxon Minister, or an old Saxon passport; hours as above; in the absence of the Minister, at 12 St. James place

SICILIES, THE TWO:—at the Sicilian Legation, 15 Princes street, Cavendish square, between 10 & 12, on Mondays and Thursdays, and are delivered on the following day, between 2 & 3, gratis

SPAIN:—at the Spanish Legation, 9 Cavendish square; passports are granted to Spanish subjects, and "vizés" to Foreign Office passports, and to those granted by Foreign Diplomatic or Consular agents, between 1 & 4, gratis; and only to Spanish subjects engaged in the merchant navy at the Consul's office, 37 Old Broad street

SWEDEN AND NORWAY:—at the Legation, 11 Halkin street west, Belgrave square, between 9 & 1, and are delivered the following day, on payment of a fee of five shillings to the poor box

SWITZERLAND:—at the Consul's office, 21A, Cateaton street, to Swiss citizens only

TURKEY:—at the Embassy, 1 Bryanstone square, between 12 & 4, every day, except Sunday, gratis

TUSCANY:—at the Consul's office, only, 15 Angel court, Throgmorton street, between 10 & 4, on payment of a fee of ten shillings, or five shillings for a "vizé"

VENEZUELA:—no passports required

WURTEMBERG:—*see Prussia*

_ Passports can also be obtained at the Foreign Office, Downing street, by British subjects going abroad.

POST OFFICE LONDON
COMMERCIAL
AND
PROFESSIONAL DIRECTORY,
FOR 1846.

AARON Benj.Wolfe, watch manfr.17A,Bury st.St.MaryAxe
Aarons Benjamin, ironmonger, 125 Tottenham court road
Aarons Lewis, cigar manufacturer, see Alexander & Aarons
Aarons Solomon, pawnbroker, 6 Sloane st. Knightsbridge
Abbett Fredk.J.&Wm.Hen.silk mrcrs.& draps.301 Hi.Holbrn
Abbey Chas. boring tool & auger mkr. 58 Peartree ct. Clkwl
Abbey James, nurseryman, 123 Camden road villas
Abbey James, stock & sharebroker, 75 Old Broad st. City
Abbey John, cooper, Commercial rd. ea. opp. Limehouse ch
Abbey John, *White Hart* P.H. 30 Liquorpond street
Abbey Richard, *Lion* brewery, 21 East st. Walworth road
Abbey Robt. tin plate worker, 18 Queen st. Grosvenor sq
Abbiss James & Co. teadealers, 60 Gracechurch street
Abbitt Charles Robert, butcher, 58 James st. Oxford st
Abbot Wm. & Sons, proctors, 7 Dean's ct. Doctors' commons
Abbot Frances (Mrs.), sailmaker, 6 Lower East Smithfield
Abbot John, carpenter, 17 Clifton st. Finsbury
Abbot Robert, grocer, 18 Blue Anchor alley, Bunhill row
Abbot Robert Page, lodging house, 82 Wells st. Oxford st
Abbot Sam. sec.to Lon.coff.&ea.ho.keep.ass.8 Bathst.Nwgt.st
Abbot Wm.Thos.prof.of music,12 Wellington rd.St.John's wd
Abbott, Jenkins & Abbott, attorneys, 8 New inn, Strand
Abbott Thomas & Son, plumbers, 10 Silver st. Golden square
Abbott & Wheatly, solicitors, Rolls yard, Chancery lane
Abbott Wm.John&Jsph.lampmakrs.(C.Mount,agt.)60 Frith st
Abbott Wm.&Son, patent hair felt manufrs.11 Bermondsey st
Abbott Alfred, horse hair manufactr.4 Anchor st. Shoreditch
Abbott Anthony Duke,prof.of music,54 Spencer st.Goswell rd
Abbott Arthur, bricklayer, 16 New st. Golden square
Abbott Benjamin, cowkeeper, 6 Gun lane, Limehouse
Abbott Charles, bootmaker, 25 Jermyn st. St. James's
Abbott Charles, cheesemonger, 4 Lambeth Lower marsh
Abbott Charles, oilman, 81 Regent st. Lambeth
Abbott Charles, woollendraper, 357 Oxford st
Abbott Daniel, butcher, 18 Mount row, Liverpool road
Abbott Daniel, cabinetmaker,60&61 Brill row, Somers town
Abbott Edward, oilman, 115 St. Martin's lane, Charing cross
Abbott Edwin, pale ale brewer, Bow, & 98 Gracechurch st
Abbott Fras.Geo.attorney&patent agnt.Rolls yd.Chancery la
Abbott Fred. furnishing undertaker &casema.8 Crooked lane
Abbott George, chair manufacturer, 25 Warren st. Fitzroy sq
Abbott George, sculptor & modeller, 4 Percy st. Bedford sq
Abbott Henry, black borderer, 22 Woodbridge st. Clerknwl
Abbott Isaac, carpenter, 26 Earl st. east, Lisson grove
Abbott James, auctioneer, 2 Agar st. West Strand
Abbott James, bricklayer, &c. 23 Great Pulteney st
Abbott James Robert, wine & spirit merchant, 31 Coleman st
Abbott John, accountant, 3 Wilmot sq. Bethnal green road
Abbott John, attorney, 10 Charlotte st. Bedford square
Abbott John, grocer & teadealer, 29 College st. Chelsea
Abbott John, *Harrow* P.H. 77 Poplar High st
Abbott John, *John Bull* P.H. 30 Tyer st. Lambeth
Abbott John, upholsterer, 25 Leigh st. Burton crescent
Abbott John Darton, *White Lion* P.H.16 High st. St.Giles's
Abbott Sarah (Mrs.), ladies' school, 115 St. Martin's lane
Abbott Thomas, carpenter, 31 Earl st. east, Lisson grove

Abbott Vernon Montagu, solicitor, 59 Chancery lane
Abbott Vernon Montague, solicitor,11 Millman st. Bdfd. rw
Abbott Wm.cabinet ma.&uphols.36 Chalton st. Somers town
Abbott William, clock engraver,10 Northampton st. Clrkwl
Abbott William, conveyancer, 3 Windsor place, City road
Abbott William, linendraper, 193 Poplar High st
Abbott William, plumber, 19 Millbank st. Westminster
Abbott William, tailor, 6 Bury st. St. James's
Abbott William Cole, baker, 141 Bishopsgate without
Abecasis Solomon de A. merchant, 78 Leman st. Goodm. fi
A'Beckett, Son & Sympson, solicitors, 7 Golden square
A'Beckett Gilbert Abbot, barrister, 3 Inner Temple lane
Abel Samuel & Co. chemists,&c.116 Albany st.Regent's park
Abel Benj. bone dealer,24 Green st.Wellington st.Blackfriars
Abel Geo. bone boiler, 25 Green st.Wellington st.Blackfriars
Abel George, general dealer, 5 Gate st. Lincoln's inn fields
Abel George, glove maker, 153 St. John st. road
Abel Henry, piece broker, 40 Curtain road, Shoreditch
Abel James,smith & wheelwright,2 Patriot row,Cambridge rd
Abel John L.pro.of music,16 Kennington ter.Up.Kennington la
Abel Samuel, builder, Well st. Hackney
Abel Thomas,painter &glazier,12 Hatton wall,Hatton garden
Abel Thomas, rag & bottle dealer, 41 Aldermanbury
Abeling Wm.chronomet.&clock ma.36 Spencer st.Goswell rd
Abell Henry & Co. merchants & ins. brokers, 8 Old Jewry
Abell Thomas & Co. straw hat makers & bleachers, 5 James place, Hackney road
Abell Edward,custom house & shipping agent,41 Fish st.hill
Abell Edward, agent to the general steam navigation company, 41 Fish st. hill
Abell Henry,*Admiral Hawke* P.H.7 Jamaica rw.Bermond.rd
Abell William, upholsterer, 43 Fish st. hill, City
Abelton Robert, bread & biscuit baker, 3 Mark lane
Abercrombie Susan & Mary Ann, ladies' school, 69 Warren st
Abercrombie Wm. fruiterer, 55 Theobald's road, Red Lion sq
Abercrombie Wm.Hy.brass found.&gasfitter,19 John st.Ftz.sq
Aberdour Thomas, stationer, 27 Ernest st. Regent's park
Abet Brothers, greek merchants, 4 Coleman st. buildings
Abethell John,pawnbroker,13&14 Calthorpe pl.Gray's inn rd
Ablett & Wheeler, hosiers & shirt makers, 234 Regent st
Ablett Henry Wm. fruiterer, 10 Cornwall road, Lambeth
Ablett Isaac, solicitor, 6 Newcastle st. Strand
Ablett John,mariner,3 Totford pl.Neckinger rd. Bermondsey
Ablett John Lee, ready made linen wa. see Wheeler & Ablett
Ablett Joseph, carpenter, Allen's court, 387½ Oxford st
Ablett Joseph, farrier, 109 Park st. Kennington cross
Ablewhite Edward &Co.coach builders,15 Vere st.Cavendish square ; & Gothic hall, Union place, New road
Abney Park Cemetery Company (John Conquest, secretary), 53 Moorgate st
Abohbot Abraham,spice&drug mer. 7 Castle st. Houndsditch
Aborigines' Protection Society, (Sir T. F. Buxton, bart. president ; Thos.Hodgkin,M.D.hon.sec.),9 Brook st.Grov.sq
Abrahall Theophilus Bennett Hoskyns, a registrar of the bankruptcy court, Basinghall st
Abraham George Fred. & Son,solicitors, 6 Gt. Marlborough st

Abraham & Gardiner, ready made linen & outfitting warehouse, 53 Houndsditch, & 9 Little St. Mary Axe
Abraham Robt.&Son,architect&surv. 1Torrington st.Rusl.sq
AbrahamAugustus Brown,barrister, 3 Carey st.Lincoln's inn
Abraham Benj. builder, 11 Winter ter. Trinity sq. Borough
Abraham Benjn.Victor,watch&clock ma.5 Lisle st.Lester.sq
Abraham Godfrey, watch & clock manfr. 51 Gt. Prescot st
Abraham Henry, *Bell tavern*,6Addle hill, Doctors'commons
Abraham Henry Robt. architect, 1 Torrington st.Russell sq
Abraham James, butcher, 145 Lambeth walk
Abraham John, fruiterer, 12 Rufford's bldgs. Islington
Abraham John H. printer,&c. 1 Clement's lane, Lombard st
Abraham Richard, carver & gilder, 8 Bruton st. Bond st
Abraham Robt. architect & surveyor,32 York ter.Regts. pk
Abraham Thos. brushmaker, 39 Frederick pl. Hampstead rd
Abraham Thos. carpent. & undert. 8 Camden st. Islington gr
Abraham Thomas, surgeon, 49 Old Broad st. City
Abraham Thomas Rt. merchant, see Charnley & Abraham
Abraham Victor, military embroidr. 5 Lisle st. Leicester sq
Abraham William Henry, *Five Bells* P.H. 2 Bermondsey sq
Abrahams & Danziger,jewellers, 125 Houndsditch
Abrahams Sam.S.&Benj.watch mfs. 23 Lit. Alie st. Goodm.fi
Abrahams Abraham,fancy cabinet maker,68 Hatton garden
Abrahams Alexander, bootmaker, 30 Well st. Wellclose sq
Abrahams Alfred, gold guard & neck chain manufacturer, 12 & 24 Bevis marks
Abrahams A.(Mrs.),watch & gold guard chain manufacturer, 9 Great Prescot st. Goodman's fields
Abrahams Benj. clothes salesman, 9 Bermondsey new road
Abrahams Eliza.(Mrs.),watch maker & jewller.27Hanway st
Abrahams Henry, printer & publisher, 25 Houndsditch
Abrahams John, cabinet manufacturer, 21 Bevis marks
Abrahams John, jeweller & diamond mercht. 21 Bevis marks
Abrahams John, *City of Salisbury* P.H. 1 Fair st. Horslydn
Abrahams Lewis, furniture broker, 1 & 2 Gt. Charlotte st. & 72 Blackfriars road
Abrahams Lewis, *St.James tavern* P.H.33Duke st.Aldgate
Abrahams Lewis, silversmith, jeweller, cutler & cabinet maker, Lowther house, 438 Strand
Abrahams Michael, oil & italian warehouse, 51 Mansell st
Abrahams Samuel, solicitor, 4 Lincoln's inn fields
Abrahams Saml.Benj.solicitor, Chancery chmbs.1Quality ct
Abrahams Soesman, who. grocer & teadealer, 46 & 115 Middlesex st. & 14 Little Tower st. City
Abram Geo. Jas. & Wm.law stationers, Middle Temple lane
Abram JohnFred.surgeon&apoth. 1St.George's ter. Kensgtn
AbramsJohnClairmonte,westindia mer. 11Chatham pl.Bkfrs
Absell James, upholsterer,&c. 10 Cambridge pl.Hackney rd
Absell William, cooper, Blossom st. Norton folgate
Absolom Edward, who. grocer, see Stubbs & Absolom
Absolon William Henry & Co. tailors, 10 Sloane square
Absolon John, baker, 36 Napier st. Ashley crescent
Absolon William Henry, tailor, 37 Haymarket
Abud John, stationer, 12 Warwick court, Holborn
Abud Richard, goldsmith, &c. see Kitching & Abud
Abud William Thomas, refiner, 1 St. James's st.Clerkenwell
Aburn John, goldbeater, 1 Little George st. Bermondsey
Aburrow William, druggist, &c. see Taylor & Aburrow
Accident Relief Society (Rd. Croxton,sec.), 26 Birchin lane
Accountant General in Chancery's Office, Chancery lane
Acfield John & Son, plumbers, 5 Up. Glos'ter pl. Dorset sq
Acker John, commission agent, Three Nun ct. Aldermanbury
Ackerman Joseph, tailor & draper, 4 Hayes court, Soho
Ackermann & Co., to Her Majesty, His Royal Highness Prince Albert, & the Royal Family, publishers, book & printsellers, color & pencil manufacturers, plain & fancy stationery, wholesale & retail, 96 Strand
Ackermann Rudolph, eclipse sporting & military gallery, printseller, bookseller, fancy statinr.& manufr.of superfine watercolors to Her Majesty&theRoyal Family,191Regnt.st
Ackery John, glass cutter,4 Southampton st. Camberwell rd
Acklam John Philip, goldsmith & watchmaker, masonic jeweller & clothing & furniture manufacturer, 138 Strand
Ackland Wm. medical galvanist, 8 Claremont pl. Pentnvlle
Acknowledgments of Deeds by Married Women (office for filing the certificates of), Serjeants' inn, Chancery lane
Ackva John, baker, 7 Bear st. Leicester square
Acock Arthur, bootmaker, 26 Henrietta st. Covent garden
Acock Charles, bricklayer, 48 Waterloo st. Camberwell
Acock Edward, glove manufactr. see Harborow, Acock &Co
Acock Rd. hairdresser & perfumer, 22 Bishopsgate without
Acocks Arthur,auctnr.&house agt.26 Up. Albany st.Rgts.pk
Acocks Thomas, cheesemonger, &c. 4 Great Trinity lane
Acocks Thomas, who. cheesemonger, see Yeats & Acocks
Acocks Wm.plumber & paper hanger, 9 Store st.Bedford sq
Acome George, tailor, 16 Robert st. Grosvenor square
Acret George Sims, truss maker, & author of the popular treatise on hernia, 39 Houndsditch
Acret William Henry, surgeon, 47 Torrington square
Acton George & Sons, emery, putty powder,scouring paper, rouge & black lead manufacturers, 72 Shoe lane, Fleet st
Acton Geo. Wm. tallow chandler & oilman, 66 Farringdon st
Acton Samuel, fruiterer, 10 Conduit st. Paddington
Acton Thomas, livery stables, 27 UpperKing st. Bloomsbury
Acton Thomas, lodging house, 50 Jewin st. Cripplegate
Acton William, surgeon, 46 Queen Anne st. Cavendish sq
Acut Charles Joseph, cabinet maker, 15 Bath st. City road
Acutt Richd.&Henry, linendrapers, 23 Bridge road,Lambeth
Acutt John, linendraper, 15 Park place, Kennington cross
Acutt Robert, dealer in paintings, 11 Holywell st. Strand
Acworth Edward, linendraper,8 Cornbury pl. Old Kent road
Acworth Nath.Brindley,barrister,26 Old sq.Lin.inn &Albany
Adair Major Jas. sec to ScottishHospital,7 Crane ct.Fleet st
Adam Alexander & Son, merchants, 5 Martin's la. Cannon st
Adam Geo. & Co. glass & china manufs. 3 Bishopsgate within
Adam John&James,fruit broks.11 Pudding la. Low.Thames st
Adam Arthur,wax & tallow chandler,30 Foleyst.Portland pl
Adam David, wholesale bookseller, see Hayward & Adam
Adam George, fruiterer & orange merchant, 39 New Bond st
Adam George, merchant, 4 White Lion ct. Cornhill
Adam George, tobacconist, 38 Crown st. Finsbury
Adam Jas. cabinet & guncase mkr.16 Brownlow st. Long acre
Adam James, fruiterer, 26 New street, Dorset square
Adam Thomas Wilkie, baker, 7 St. James's street, Pall mall
Adam William, west india merchant, see Nelson & Adam
Adami Geo.&Chas.army&navy cap ma.11 Leicester st.Regt.st
Adams & Co. engineers & carriage builders,Fairfield works, Mile end road
Adams & Ede (late Webb), robe makers to her Majesty, 193 Fleet st. corner of Chancery lane
Adams FrancisB.&Sons,watch manfrs.21St.John's sq.Clrkwl
Adams & Hooper, coachmakers, &c. 28 Haymarket; workshops, 9½ Great Smith st. Westminster
Adams John & Co. fringe mfrs. 57 Wood st. City & Coventry
Adams & Pollock, manchester wareh. 2 Godfrey's ct. Milk st
Adams Ralph & Co. tile makers, Belle isle, Maiden lane, King's cross; and 1 St. Chad's row, Gray's inn road
Adams Samuel & David, lace agents, 22 Lawrence lane,City
Adams Alfred, french polisher, 11 St. George's ter. Boro' rd
Adams Alfred, surgeon-dentist, 62 Brook st. Hanover sq
Adams Ann (Miss), ladies' school, 6 Theberton st. Islington
Adams Arthur R. barrister, 1 Mitre court buildings, Temple
Adams Benjamin, bootmaker, 42 Narrow st. Limehouse
Adams Borlase Hill, barrister, 11 New square, Lincoln's inn, & 36 Lincoln's inn fields
Aams Butler, pattern drawer, 11 Union ct. Old Broad st
Adams Charles, butcher, 1 Brighton place, Hackney road
Adams Charles, locksmith & bellhanger, 19 Monmouth st
Adams Chas. Harrison, furniture ma. 7 Mansion ho.pl.Cambl
Adams Charlt.(Mrs.),milliner,2Hopkins bldgs.Islgtn.Highst
Adams Edmonds, accountant, 5 Barge yard, Bucklersbury
Adams Edward, fruiterer, 38½ Roebuck pl.Gt.Dover rd.Boro
Adams Edward, hair manufacturer, 23 Dean st. Fetter lane
Adams Edward, oyster salesman, see Wilson & Adams
Adams Edward Richards, Bridewell Hospital,NewBridge st
Adams Edwd.Richards, jun. barrister,2 Old sq. Lincoln's inn
Adams Eliza (Mrs.),butcher,23 Shaftesbury terrace,Pimlico
Adams Elizabeth (Mrs.), cooper, 29 Bury st. St. Mary axe
Adams Elizth.(Mrs.),dress & cor. ma.4 Compton st.Brnswk st
Adams Elizabeth (Mrs.), farrier, 4 Church la.Commercial rd
Adams Frederic, beer retailer, 9 Holly st. Dalston
Adams Fred. Ibbs. law stationer, 4 Symonds inn,Chancery la
Adams George, artist, 4 Burton st. Pimlico
Adams Geo. beerretailer,47 Portland st. Walworth common
Adams Geo. currier, &c. White's grounds, Bermondsey
Adams Geo. *Crown & Barleymow* P.H. 23 Gray's inn lane
Adams Geo. professor of music, 40 Upper John st.Fitzroy sq
Adams George, furniture broker, 1 Powell's place, City road
Adams Harriet(Mrs.),toy dealer,5 Mansion ho.pl.Cambwl.rd
Adams Henry, auctioneer & surveyor, 5 Dean st. Finsbury
Adams Henry, cheesemonger, 38 Queen's road, Bayswater
Adams Henry, solicitor, see Yarborough & Adams
Adams Hy. Austin, *Grapes* P.H. 8 Sun ct.Curzon st.May fair
Adams Hori, tailor, King st. New town, Deptford
Adams Hugh Westren, linendr. see Christian,Adams&Dewey
Adams Isaac, butcher, 8 Lower Porchester st. Edgware road
Adams James, grocer, 166 Long lane, Bermondsey
Adams James, *Peacock* P.H. 23 Great Trinity la. Bread st
Adams James, tailor, 16 Church st. Camberwell
Adams James, tailor, 2 Star alley, Fenchurch st
Adams James, tailor, 14 Lewisham st. Westminster
Adams James Fredk. professor of music, 40 Upper John st

Adams James H. solicitor, 5 Raymond buildings, Gray's inn
Adams James John, surgeon, 39 Finsbury square
Adams Jesse, pump maker, 4 Pump row, Old st. road
Adams John, appraiser & house agt. 76 High st. Camden twn
Adams John, builder, &c. Albion road, Stoke Newington
Adams John, civil engineer, 7 Lit. Abingdon st. Westminster
Adams Jn. chron. & watchspring ma. 28 Perceval st. Clknwll
Adams John, feather mer. 4 George st. Thrawl st. Spitalfields
Adams John, glover, 47 Munster st. Regent's park
Adams John, muffin, &c. baker, 30 Goodge st. Tottenham ct. rd
Adams John, picture liner, 12 Gt. Newport st. Long acre
Adams John, serjeant at law, 1 Serjeants' inn, Chancery la
Adams John, servants' institu. 117 Gt. Russell st. Bloomsby
Adams John, *Shakespeare's Head* P.H. 31 Wych st. Strand
Adams John, surgeon, 31 New Broad st. City
Adams John, whitesmith, 19 King st. Seven dials
Adams John, jun. barrister. 1 Serjeants' inn, Chancery lane
Adams John Francis, solicitor, see Millard & Adams
Adams John Hilditch, solicitor, see Cornthwaite & Adams
Adams Joseph, agent for Glasgow Steam Packet Co. 82 Lombard st
Adams Joseph, butcher, 46 Adams st. west, Portman square
Adams Joseph, mast & block mkr. 39 & 41 Narrow st. Limehouse
Adams Joseph, wharfinger, Leith & Glasg. wf. Low. Ea. Smithfi
Adams Joseph A. furnhg. ironmonger, 15 King st. Seven dials
Adams Magaret (Mrs.), straw hat ma. 30 Warren st. Fitzroy sq
Adams Mary (Mrs.), lodging ho. 17 Weymouth st. Portland pl
Adams Mary Ann (Miss), *Fountain* P.H. 14 Blackman st. Boro
Adams Moses, auctioneer, valuer, surveyor & land agent, 29 Hart st. Bloomsbury; & at Isleworth
Adams Nath. beer retailer, 19 Shepperton st. Islington
Adams Ralph, brick, tile & pot manfr. Maiden la. Battle brdg
Adams Rd. locksmith & bellhanger, 62 King st. Seven dials
Adams Rd. *Salutation tav.* 32½ Tavistock st. Covent grdn
Adams Robert, baker, 11 King st. Lower road, Islington
Adams Robert, drysalter, 130 Fenchurch st
Adams Robert, farrier, 10 Little Ormond yard, Queen sq
Adams Robert, pro. of chemistry, &c. 21 Pembroke sq. Knsgt
Adams Robert, *Union* P.H. 22 Queen st. Pimlico
Adams Samuel, tailor & clothier, 79 Brewer st. Somers town
Adams Sarah (Mrs.), chndlr. shop, 43 Wellington st. Goswl. rd
Adams Sarah (Mrs.), ginger beer ma. 15 Fieldgate st. Whitech
Adams Sarah (Mrs.), milliner, 90 East st. Manchester sq
Adams Selina (Mrs.), ladies' school, 5 Lower Islington ter
Adams Stephen, marine store dealer, 29 Bermondsey sq
Adams Thomas, beer retailer, 53 Wells st. Oxford st
Adams Thomas, butcher, 27 Lower York st. Lowr. Rotherhithe
Adams Thomas, chronometer maker, 36 Lombard st
Adams Thomas, cooper & grocer, 3 Green st. Kentish town
Adams Thomas, grocer, 43½ Penton st. Walworth
Adams Thomas, fruiterer, 20 Harrow road, Paddington
Adams Thomas, *Grapes* P.H. 14 Lime st. City
Adams Thomas, professor of music, 77 John st. Fitzroy sq
Adams Thomas, seedsman, see Minier, Adams & Nash
Adams Thomas, wireworker, 14 Norfolk st. Middlx. hospital
Adams Thomas Jas. auctioneer, 14 Stafford row, Pimlico
Adams Walter, cowkeeper, 6 Theberton st. Islington
Adams Wm. bookseller & publisher, see Hamilton, Adams & Co
Adams Wm. bootmaker, 219 Hoxton old town
Adams Wm. cabinet ma. 8 Cumberland st. Mddlx. hospital
Adams Wm. fruiterer, 29 Gt. Turner st. Commercial road
Adams Wm. ironmonger, 45 Fore st. Limehouse
Adams Wm. last maker, 141 Southwark bridge road
Adams Wm. stockbroker, see Guy & Adams
Adams Wm. straw bonnet wareho. 3 Goldington st. Somers tn
Adams Wm. tailor, 3 Little Queen st. High Holborn
Adams Wm. weavers' turner & skittle ma. 24 Booth st. Spitalfi
Adams Wm. wood turner, 1 Ray place, Ray st. Clerkenwell
Adams Wm. sen. fruiterer, Centre row, Covent grdn. mrket
Adams Wm. James, newspaper publisher, 59 Fleet st
Adams Wm. Salkeld, ironmonger, 57 Haymarket
Adams Wm. Samuel, solicitor, 16 George st. Mansion house
Adams Wm. Stephen, tobacconist, 44 Haymarket
Adamson Robert & Co. wine merchts. 14 John st. Berkeley sq
Adamson George, grocer, 12 Charles st. Westminster
Adamson Henry Thomas, fishmonger, 333 Oxford st
Adamson Horatio, linendraper, 59 Exmouth st. Clerkenwell
Adamson James, attorney, 29 Ely place, Holborn
Adamson James, baker, 13 Warwick lane, Newgate st
Adamson James, barrister, 24 Lincoln's inn fields
Adamson Jane (Mrs.), dairy, 3 Carpenter st. Berkeley square
Adamson John, cheesemonger, 122 Mount st. Berkeley sq
Adamson John, physician, 13 John street, Adelphi
Adamson John, merchant, 3 Bond court, Walbrook
Adamson Margaret (Mrs.), baker, 20 Lime street, City
Adamson Robert, cowkeeper, 11 Gee street, Somers town
Adamson Thomas, baker, 50 Munster street, Regent's park
Adamson Thomas, corn & coal mer. 20 Church st. Islington
Adamson Wm. furniture dlr. 2 Upper Dorset pl. Clapham rd
Adamson William, market gardener, Richmond rd. Dalston
Adamson William, millwright & steam saw mills, 5 John street, Whitechapel
Adamthwaite John Allen, notary, 6 St. Michael's al. Cornhill
Adcock Benjamin, coachsmith, 52 Parker street, Drury lane
Adcock Charles, newsvender, 14 Gt. James st. Lisson grove
Adcock Christ. surgeon, 28 Chalcroft ter. New cut, Lambeth
Adcock Daniel, cigar manufr. 4 Camomile st. Bishopsgate st
Adcock Edward, hatter, 4 Princes street, Cavendish square
Adcock Geo. Chas. cigar manfr. 1 Railway pl. Fenchurch st
Adcock Hen. Joseph, attorney, 3 Copthall bldgs. Throgm. st
Adcock Chas. boot & shoe maker, 19 Fair st. Horselydown
Adcock James Clark, cigar manufacturer, 7 Cullum street
Adcock John Lowe, builder, 9 Somerset st. Portman square
Adcock Mary (Mrs.), baker, 6 Cobourg pl. Lower rd. Rotherhth
Adcock Rt. Hill, wine & spirit mer. 8 Lit. Argyll st. Regent st
Adcock Sidney, working jeweller, 9 Tyler st. Regent st
Adcock Thomas, baker, 7 & 8 Blenheim ter. Bond st. Chelsea
Adcock Thomas, tailor & draper, 33 New st. Dorset square
Adcock Wm. ostrich feather ma. 3 Princes st. Cavendish sq
Addams & Cresswell, proctors & notaries, 8 Godliman st
Addams Jesse, D.C.L. advocate, 17 College, Doctors' comms
Addams Rd. jun. proctor & notary, 8 Godliman st. Doct. com
Addecott Wm. carpenter, 5 Little York place, Marylebone
Addenbrooke Joseph & Co. fancy statnrs. 101 Hatton garden
Adderley John, boot & shoe warehouse, 145 Borough High st
Adderley Joseph, stockbroker, 7 Bank chambers, Lothbury
Addinell John & Co. merchts. & who. drugg. 187 Bishopsg. wtht
Addington Luke & Saml. woollen dra. 105 & 106 St. Martin's la
Addington James, color & varnish manufactr. 84 London rd
Addinsell Samuel, tailor & draper, 15 Lamb's Conduit st
Addis & Guy, solicitors, 10 Great Queen st. Westminster
Addis Timothy & Son, wharfingers, Freeman's whf. Tooley st
Addis William & Son, bone & ivory brushmakers, 8 Radnor st. St. Luke's, & 1 Gastigny place, Bath st. City road
Addis Charles, jun. barrister, 21 Old square, Lincoln's inn
Addis Edwd. Richd. cheesemonger, 25 Flagon row, Deptford
Addis John, granary keeper, 63 Rotherhithe st
Addis Joseph, carvers' tool maker, 4 Church st. Deptford
Addis Sam. Jos. jun. carvers' tool ma. 6 Lr. Fore st. Lambeth
Addis Thomas, carver, 23 Norfolk st. Middlesex hospital
Addis William, ironmonger, 6 Leicester st. Leicester square
Addison & Harrison, attorneys, 11 Staple inn, Holborn
Addison & Hodson, music sellers & publishers by special appointment to the Queen & H.R.H. the Duchess of Kent, 210 Regent st. & 47 King st. Golden square
Addison Wm. & Co. provision agts. & dlrs. 168 Up. Thames st
Addison Chas. Greenstreet, barrister, 2 Inner Temple lane
Addison Ford, ale agent, Homerton brewery, Hackney
Addison George, stockbroker, 12 Copthall court, Bank
Addison Harriet (Mrs.), staymaker, 133 High st. Camden tn
Addison John, civil engineer, 6 Delahay st. Westminster
Addison John Christr. grocer, 55 Margaret st. Cavendish sq
Addison Joseph, barrister, 1 King's bench walk, Temple
Addison Nathaniel, fruiterer, 26 Flagon row, Deptford
Addison Philip, pub. of equity reports, 36 Chancery lane
Addison Ralph, merchant, 23 Laurence Pountney lane
Addison Robert, linendraper, Broadway, Stafford
Addison Robt. manufacturer & patentee of the Royal Albert transforming pianoforte, 210 Regent st
Addison Thomas, boot & shoe maker, 8 James st. Oxford st
Addison Thomas, physician, 24 New st. Spring gardens
Addison William, boot & shoe maker, 3 Hoxton High st
Addison Wm. provision agent & dealer, see Lash & Addison
Addison William, sail maker, Emmett st. Limehouse
Addy George William, baker, 3 Vaughan place, City road
Addy Joseph J. baker, 13 Queen st. Lower road, Islington
Ade & Jones, linendrapers, 415 Oxford st
Ade George, solicitor, 6 King's road, Bedford row
ADELPHI THEATRE, 411 Strand
Adency Thos. S. wood engravr. 42 Frederick pl. Hampstead rd
Adeney Wm. tailor & habit maker, 16 Sackville st. Piccadilly
Aders Julius, importer of wines, 29 St. Dunstan's hill
Ades John, butcher, 38 Trafalgar st. Walworth rd
Adey Charles Francis, solicitor, 5 Barnard's inn, Holborn
Adey Daniel, stationer, 10½ Cross st. Newington butts
Adey Daniel Francis, grocer, 44 Up. Berkeley st. Portman sq
Adey Goodson, solicitor, 5 Barnard's inn, Holborn
Adey James, tailor, 12 Charles pl. Hertford rd. Kingsland
Adey Thomas Joseph, wheelwright, 3 & 4 Thrawl st. Brick la
Adey William, chemist, 2 Claremont place, Old Kent road
Adie Patrick, optician, 1A, Conduit st. Regent st
Adjutant General's Office, Horse Guards; hours 11 to 5

Adkin Marg. & Sons, tobacco manfs. 185 & 186 St. George st
Adkin George, bootmaker, 18 Norland road, Notting hill
Adkin Robt. grocer & cheesemonger, 15 Norland rd. Nottg. hl
Adkins Hen. agent to John Smith & Son, gun ma. 4 Thavies inn
Adkins Jesse, coal & potato wa. 14 King st. Westminster
Adkins Mary Ann (Mrs.), potato dlr. 2 Middle row, Knightsb
Adkins Peter, *Vine* P.H. 25 Minories
Adkins Ths. Fletcher, *Royal Oak* P.H. 72 Margaret st. Hack. flds
Adkins William, hairdresser, 5 Leather lane, Holborn
Adlard Charles & James, printers, 22½ Bartholomew close
Adlard Alfred, engraver & printer, 7 & 8 Wardrobe pl. Doc. com
Adlard Frederick, hatter, 225 High Holborn
Adlard Frederick, tailor & draper, 224 High Holborn
Adlard Henry, engraver & printer, 42 Hatton garden
Adlard James Wm. slate merchant, see Roberts & Adlard
Adlard John, bookbinder, 35 Villiers street, Strand
Adlard William Gates, wholesale stationer, 1 Queenhithe
Adlington Robert, corndealer, Union row, Kingsland
Admans Richard, stationer, 3 Cumberland pl. Old Kent rd
Admiralty Civil Department, Somerset house; hours 10 to 4
Admiralty Naval Department, Whitehall; hours 10 to 5
Admiralty & Appeal Registry Office, 2 Paul's Bakehouse court, Doctors' commons; hours 10 to 4
Adnam Jos. & John C. who. spice dl. Old Swan la. Up. Thames st
Adnam Benjamin, coal merchant, 27 Cross st. Islington
Adnam John, wine & spirit mercht. see Kingsley & Adnam
Adnam Joseph, oil & colorman, 126 High Holborn
Adnam Richard Benjamin, baker, 14 Cross st. Islington
Adnett Basill, *White Lion* P.H. King street, Old Gravel la
Adnum George Pyner, coffee rooms, 32 Farringdon st
Adnum John, upholstr. & house agt. 12 New Church st. Lisson gr
Adolph William, merchant, 9 Bury square, St. Mary Axe
Adolphus John Leycester, barrister, 3 Harcourt bdgs. Temple
Adron Wm. & Chas. statuaries, 2 Quickset row, New rd. Fitz. sq
Adshead & Gilbert, com. agts. & warehsemn. 42 Noble st. City
Adshead & Taylor, glovers, hosiers, &c. 53 Strand
Adshead Samuel, tailor, 22 Gt. Turner st. Commercial rd. Ea
Adson George, locksmith, 14 Bedfordbury, Covent garden
Adult Orphan Institution (Rev. Thos. Bowdler, hon. sec.), 11 St. Andrews place, Regent's park
Advocate General of India Office, 9 New sq. Lincoln's inn
Advocates' College, Doctors' commons; hours 10 to 4
Ady Robert Hill, truss maker, 89 Fenchurch street, City
Affidavit Office in Chancery, 10 Symond's inn, Chancery la
Affidavit Office for Courts of Chancery, Q. B., C. P. & Exchequer & Bankruptcy Courts, *Ireland;* for proofs & registry of deeds in Ireland, 10 Southampton buildings, Chancery lane; hours of business 10 to 4
Aflalo Isaac, merchant, 49 Gt. Prescot st. Goodman's fields
African Civilization Society (Robert Stokes, sec.), 15 Parliament street, Westminster
Agar Alex. merchant, [successor to Robinson Bros.] custom ho. shipping agt. & lighterman, 12 Water la. Tower st
Agar Thomas, gasfitter, 13 Windmill st. Tottenham court rd
Agars John, timber broker, Jamaica coff. ho. St. Michael's alley
Agasse James Laurent, artist, 83 Newman st
Agate Edward, butcher, 4 St. Mark's road, Camberwell New rd
Age & Argus Weekly Newspaper Offi. 4 Brydges st. Covent gdn
Aged Pilgrims' Friend Society (John Box & James Bisset, secs.), 60 Paternoster row, & 13 Northampton sq. Camberwell
Agent Samuel, grocer, Clifton st. Wandsworth road
Ager & Fisher, haircutters & perfumers, 149 Leadenhall st
Ager Mary Ann & Son, coopers, 3 Whitecross st. Cripplegate
Ager Frederick, surgeon, 10 Oval, Hackney road
Ager Joseph, physician, 85 Great Portland st. Oxford st
Ager Stride John, upholsterer, 5 St. Mary's ter. Camden twn
Ager Thomas, baker, 45 Wellington st. Newington causeway
Ager Thos. who. boot & shoe wa. 36 Charles st. Hatton garden
Agg James, bookbinder, 5 Wine office court, Fleet st
Aggas William, bottle mercht. 8 Steel yd. wf. Up. Thames st
Agland Samuel John, cooper, 8A, Marylebone lane, Oxford st
Agland Wm. chair maker, 7 Clarence place, Hackney road
Aglio Augustine, artist, 2 Osnaburgh st. Regent's park
Aglionby Henry Aglionby, M.P. barrister, 5 Brick ct. Temple
Agness Wm. livery stables, Burwood mews, Titchbrn. st. Edg. rd
Agriculturist Cattle Insurance Co. (W. Fenton, sec.) 8 Chatham, place, Blackfriars; see page 2013
Agricultural Protection Society of Great Britain & Ireland (Henry Byron, sec.), 17 Old Bond st
Agriculturist Newspaper Office, 72 Fleet st
Aiani Baldezar, cage ma. & wire worker, 148 High st. Shadwell
Aickin Thos. stained glass works, 107 Vauxhall st. Lambeth
Aikin Charles Arthur, surgeon, 1 Albion st. Hyde park
Aikin Charles Rochmond, surgeon, 7 Bloomsbury square
Aikin George, surveyor, &c. see Peyton & Aikin
Aimé E. sec. to Dutch Rhenish Rlwy. Of. 62 King William st. City
Ainge Joseph, tailor, 17 South Molton st. Bond st
Ainger Hanh. & Lydia (Misses) dressma. 56 Banner st. St. Luke's
Ainger Nathl. & Son, warehousemen, 12 Basing la. City
Ainger Alfred, architect & surveyor, 7 John st. Bedford row
Ainger David, carpenter & packing case maker, 21 Beer lane
Ainger James, grocer, Little Chelsea
Ainger William, ironfounder, 75 Upper Ground st. Blackfrs
Ainsley Saml. Jas. landscape painter, 14 Euston pl. New rd
Ainslie Henry Walter, surgeon, 10 Euston square
Ainslie John A. veterinary surgeon, 1 Nassau st. Middlx. hosp
Ainslie William, *Star* P.H. 190 Wapping
Ainsworth Joseph, baker, 23 Upper Clifton st. Finsbury
Air Alexndr. C. surgeon, 43 Esher st. Up. Kennington lane
Air Robert, *St. Andrew* P.H. 93 Lower East Smithfield
Air Robert, *Turk's Head* P.H. 326 Wapping
Aird Benjamin Lambert, draper, 6 Mount st. Lambeth
Aird Wm. baker, teadealer, &c. 33 Little Newport st. Long acre
Aire & Calder Bottle Co. Castleford, nr. Pontefract, green glass bottle ma. Stott Walker, Horseshoe whf. 10 Up. Thames st
Aires John & Son, boot & shoe makers, 7 Bishopsgate within
Airey & Bellingham, cabinet ma. 1 Charles st. E. Hampstead rd
Airey George, stationer & bookseller, 7 Throgmorton st
Airey Henry, butcher, 4 Ocean row, High st. Stepney
Airey John, teadealer & grocer, 57 Shoreditch
Airey Joseph, surgeon, &c. 16 Poland st. & 80 Berwick st. Soho
Airey William, butcher, 4 Salmon lane, Limehouse
Aiskell, Child & Co. wine merchants, 2 Brabant ct. Philpot la
Aitchison Robert & Co. wine merchants, 8 Great Windmill st
Aitchison George, architect & district surveyor, 6 Muscovy court, Trinity sq. Tower hill; & High st. Woolwich
Aitchison Geo. cabinet maker, 5 Princes st. Fitzroy sq
Aitken & Mapleton, leather dress. 14 Russell st. Bermondsey
Aitken Charles James, bookbinder, 4 George st. Adelphi
Aitken John, bookbinder, 49 Great Wild st. Lincoln's inn fields
Aitkens John, solicitor, 6 Symond's inn, Chancery lane; & 30 Upper Belgrave place, Pimlico
Aitkin Allan, *Rein Deer* P.H. 160 Old Gravel lane, Wapping
Akam Joseph, bootmaker, 91 Bunhill row
Akam William, cooper, 10 Neptune st. Rotherhithe
Aked Joseph, bookbinder, 1 Palsgrave place, Strand
Akerman Hen. steam saw mills, 11 Bowling green st. Kengtn
Akerman John, coal & potato dea. 59 & 60 Park st. Camden twn
Akerman John Yonge, sec. to Greenwich Railway, London term
Akerman Robert, fancy umb. stick ma. 17 Richmond st. St. Luke's
Akerman Thomas, linendraper, see Nelson & Akerman
Akerman Wm. cook & confectioner, 32 St. Martin's court
Akerman Wm. *Greyhound* P.H. 30 Milton st. Cripplegate
Akers Henry, gold beater, 21 Rahere st. Goswell road
Akers Joseph, plumber & glazier, 16 Gt. St. Andrew st. 7 Dials
Akers Rd. livery stables, 22 & 29 Arlington st. Sadler's wells
Akers Rd. livery stables, 123½ St. John st. road
Akers Susannah (Mrs.), milliner, 34 Somerset st. Whitechapl
Akers Thomas, beer retailer, 12 Pancras st. Tottenham ct. rd
Akins Sybilla (Mrs.), tobacconist, 49 Lambeth High st
Akroyd Joseph, tailor, 42 Thanet st. Burton crescent
Alabaster Charles, straw & fancy hat maker, 58 Piccadilly
Alabaster George, carpenter, 1 Queen st. Finsbury
Alabaster James, *Market House* P.H. Finsbury market
Alabaster Wm. straw hat maker, 7 Chapel st. Holywell mount
Aland Thos. & John, water gilders, 18 Gt. Sutton st. Clerknwl
Albano Benedict, civil engineer, 24 Essex st. Strand
ALBANY, Albany courtyard, 46 Piccadilly, & 5 Burlington grdns
Albany Baths, John Adams, proprietor, York rd. Lambeth
Alberry Chas. appraiser & underta. 17 Sekforde st. Clerknwl
Albers James, merch. & insur. agnt. 18 Philpot la. & Lloyd's
Albert Eugene, hairdresser, &c. see Unwin & Albert
Albert George, grocer & cheesemongr. 93 Long alley, Finsbury
Albert George, tailor, 1 Orford row, Old Kent road
Albert Hen. fruiterer & greengrocer, 121 Long al. Finsbury
Albert Henry, grocer & cheesemonger, 122 Long alley, Finsby
Albert (*Meyer*), dentist, 45 Ludgate hill
Albert William, tailor, Stockwell place, Clapham road
Albin William, law wig maker, 6 Essex court, Temple
Albin Wm. stationer & tobacconist, 1 Devereux court, Strand
Albino Clement & Co. birdcage & frame ma. 14 Up. Union ct. Holb
Albino John, lookg. glass & barometer mkr. 47 St. John st. Smthfd
Albion Insurance Company (Edwin Charlton, sec.), 42 New Bridge st. Blackfriars; see page 2010
Albon Edwd. bricklay. & plasterer, 21 Albion pl. St. John's la
Albon William, tobacconist, see Goode & Albon
Albrecht Henry Jas. & Co. east india merchts. 14 Eastcheap
Albrecht Edmund, professor of languages, 26 Dean st. Soho
Albrecht John, colonial broker, 48 Fenchurch st
Albright Eliz. (Mrs.), stationer, 36 Bridge ho. pl. Newing. cau
Albutt Solomon, tailor, 36 Notting hill, High st
Alchin Wm. Turner, librarian, Guildhall, City

Alcock Anthony, glass & chinaman, 6 Charles st. Westmins
Alcock Daniel, lath render, York st. Walworth road
Alcock Edward, grocer, 361 Rotherhithe
Alcock George, wheelwright, 1 Goulstone st. Whitechapel
Alcock John, rag merchant, 12 Addle hill, Doctors' commons
Alcock Robert, beer retailer, 85 Earl st. East, Lisson grove
Alcock Samuel, china warehouse, 89 Hatton garden
Alcock Wm. printers' joiner, 24 White Lion st. Norton folgate
Aldam William, barrister, 3 Plowden buildings, Temple
Aldebert Isaac J. coachmaker, see Hallmarke, Aldebert & Co
Alden Sarah (Mrs.), lodging house, 5 Cecil st. Strand
Alder Frederick, *Queen's Elm* P.H. 1 Up. Church st. Chels
Alder James, boot & shoe ma. 15 Wilmot sq. Bethnal gr. rd
Alder John Williams, builder, 28 Duke st. Lincoln's inn fields
Alder Samuel, coffee rooms, 77 Judd street, Brunswick sq
Alder Wm. toydealer, 8 Queen's head row, Newington butts
Alderdice George, tailor, 19 Arlington st. Sadler's wells
Alderman Wm. Hen. *Lord Nelson* P.H. 114 Bishopsgt. without
Alders Chas. (Mrs.), seminary, 32 Chester pl. Kennington cross
Aldersey Joseph Stephens, attorney, 8 Gower st. Bedford sq
Aldersey Richard Baker, who. stationer, 11 Cloak lane, City
Alderson Geo. D. & Co. lead mercs. 2 Blenheim st. Oxford st
Alderson Geo. & Son, tailors & drapers, 13 Wellington st. Boro'
Alderson George, tobacconist, 2 Drinkwater pl. Waterloo rd
Alderson George, *Woolpack* P.H. 3 Hart st. Cripplegate
Alderson Henry, *Bell* P.H. 2 Newton st. High Holborn
Alderson Rd. *Marquis of Anglesey* P.H. 77 Devonsh. st. Lis. gr
Alderson Robert, grocer & teadealer, 9 Lamb st. Spitalfields
Alderson Thos. veterinary surgeon, 32 Warner st. New Kent rd
Alderton & Poulden, house & estate agts. 37 North Audley st
Alderton Chas. ivory turner, 3 Arthur st. Gray's inn road
Alderton Geo. turner & saw mills, 7 Chapel row, Exmouth st
Alderton Hen. bootmaker, 16 Mount pleasant, Gray's inn la
Alderton Wm. hairdresser, 11 Cross st. Golden sq
Alderton Wm. Sibson, steel pen & percussion cap manufactr. North st. Wolverhampton; London wareho. 127 Chancery la
Aldhous Henry, *Nine Elms tavern*, Nine Elms
Aldhous John, *Coach & Horses* P.H. 120 Holborn hill
Aldhouse Fredk. stationer, Church row, Newington butts
Aldington John, bottle mercht. 13 Oxford market, Oxford st
Aldington Wm. corndealer, 46 Goodge street, Fitzroy sq
Aldis Chas. Jas. Berridge, physician, 13 Old Burlington st
Aldis Sir Charles, knt. surgeon, 13 Old Burlington st
Aldis William, dining rooms, 101 Fore st. Cripplegate
Aldon William, merchant, 15 Great St. Helens
Aldous Jas. & Son, pawnbrks. & silversmiths, 67 Berwick st. Soho
Aldous Henry, grocer, 110 Gt. Russell st. Bloomsbury
Aldous Henry, plumber, painter, &c. 50 Exeter st. Lisson gr
Aldous James, tailor, 2 Grange road, Bermondsey
Aldous James, tool warehouse, 1 London st. Fitzroy sq
Aldous John, *Valentine & Orson* P.H. 43 Long la. Bermondsey
Aldous Phineas, plumber, 25 Gresse st. Tottenham court road
Aldous Richard, beer retailer, 3 Grange road, Bermondsey
Aldous Wm. tailor & draper, 7 Devonshire bldgs. Dover road
Aldred Samuel Botson & Co. woollendrapers, &c. 81 Holborn bridge, & 9 Aldgate High st
Aldred Augustin, tailor, 9 Leicester place, Leicester square
Aldred Daniel, linendraper, see Lainson & Aldred
Aldred Geo. gen. agt. & warehousemn. 5 Two Swan yd. Bishpsgt
Aldred Henry, bricklayer, 3 Kennington st. Walworth
Aldred William, builder, 70 Harper st. New Kent road
Aldred William, tailor, 30 Monkwell st. Cripplegate
Aldrich James, chaise spring maker, 4 James st. Old st
Aldrich John, coach smith, 54 Brick lane, St. Luke's
Aldrich Richd. piano forte ma. 33 Windmill st. Finsbury
Aldrich Samuel, confectioner, 117 Bethnal green road
Aldrid James, bricklayer, 18 Gt. Mays bldgs. St. Martin's la
Aldridge Richard & Sons, lightermen, Galley quay, Lower Thames st. & Trinity chambers, 5 Water lane
Aldridge Ann (Mrs.), pawnbroker, 10 Orange st. Bloomsbury
Aldridge Anna M. (Miss), grocer, 22 Chenies st. Bedford sq
Aldridge Charles William, furnishing ironmonger, 7 Falcon st. Aldersgate; & 28 Beech st. Barbican
Aldridge George, oilman, 8 Aylesbury st. Clerkenwell
Aldridge Geo. plumber & glazier, 29 Kingsgate st. Holborn
Aldridge Jas. goldsmith, &c. 11 Northumberland st. Strand
Aldridge John, barrister, Inner Temple hall staircase
Aldridge Joseph, attorney, 42 Gt. Russell st. Bloomsbury
Aldridge Napoleon, law stationer, 1 Clement's inn, Strand
Aldridge Robert, plumber, 4 Eagle st. Red lion square
Aldridge Samuel, beer retailer, Pleasant row, Old Kent rd
Aldridge Sarah (Mrs.), furn. ironmonger, &c. 78 Goswell rd
Aldridge Thomas, hardwareman, 16 Queen's bldgs. Knightsb
Aldridge Walter Wm. solicitor, 10 Gray's inn pl. Gray's inn
Aldridge Wm. butcher, 2 Marlborough road, Chelsea
Aldridge William, *Friar* P.H. 33 Friar st. Blackfriars rd
Aldridge Wm. furn. ironmonger, 7 Crosby row, Walworth rd
Aldridge's repository, 6 Upper St. Martin's lane
Aldwinckle & Fryer, linendrapers, 9 Clark's place, Islington
Aldwinkle Henry, bedstead maker, 18 Exmouth st. Spafields
Aldwinkle Henry, upholsterer, 20 Hedge row, Islington
Aldworth William Henry, butcher, 78 Red lion st. Holborn
Alecock James, grocer, 26 Queen street, Bryanstone square
Alefounder Joshia, furn. broker, 21 Barrett's court, Oxford st
Alegre Huard (Mad.), embroiderer, 37 Gt. Castle st. Regent st
Alehouse E. D. (Mrs.), *King's Head* P.H. 34 Margaret st. Cav. sq
Alepson Brothers & Co. merchants, 3 Copthall buildings
Alerme Philbert, dining rooms, 39 Gerrard street, Soho
Alex & Jones, surgeon dentists, 26 New Bridge street, Blackfriars; & 22 Ludgate hill
Alexander & Aarons, cigar manufacturers, 263 Strand
Alexander Alex. & Naphtali H. wholesale jewellers, 3 George street, Minories; & 16 Hatton garden
Alexander Ann & Geo. Wm. & Co. bill brokers, 40 Lombard st
Alexander & Carter, dyers, 21 Wilson street, Finsbury
Alexander Chas. & Edw. pawnbrs. 12 Newchurch st. wt. Edgw. rd
Alexander & Clare, carriers, Castle & Falcon, Aldersgate st
Alexander, Cullen & Co. east india agents & merchants, 28 Great Winchester street, Broad street
Alexander Henry & Isaac, biscuit bakers, 112½ & 226 High Holborn, & 407 Oxford street
Alexander (Lesley) & Co. merchants, 53 Old Broad st. City
Alexander Rt. & Co. india commissn. agts. Hall of Commerce
Alexander Rt. F. & Jas. cotton ma. (R. Mutrie agt.) 93 Watling st
Alexander Wm. & Co. wine, brandy & whisky mer. 35 Walbrk
Alexander And. *Hoop & Grapes* P.H. 14 Widegate st. Bshpgt
Alexander Ann (Mrs.), alamode beef house, 26 Tichborne st
Alexunder Chas. carpenter, &c. 54 Jewin street, Cripplegate
Alexander Chas. surgeon, 6 East ter. St. Geo.' rd. New Kent rd
Alexander Chas. Wm. confectioner, 14 King st. Covent gard
Alexander Chrisr. brewery, Royal hill, Queen's rd. Bayswatr
Alexander George, architect, see Stevens & Alexander
Alexander George, physician, 6 Sussex terrace, Hyde park
Alexander Henry, barrister, 5 Bolton row, Picc. dilly
Alexander Hen. grocer & cheesemonger, 3 Hemming's row
Alexander Henry, surgeon oculist, 6 Cork street, Bond st
Alexander Israel, auctioneer & horse dealer, 4 Chiswell st
Alexander Jacob, fruiterer, 78 Sun street, Bishopsgate
Alexander James, baker, 81 Hill street, Walworth road
Alexander James, boot & shoe mak. 21 York pl. Kentish town
Alexander James, butcher, 14 Hill street, Walworth road
Alexander Jas. east india agt. see Fletcher, Alexander & Co
Alexander James, merchant, 33 Great Winchester st
Alexander James, music warehouse, 101 Leadenhall st
Alexander James, surgeon, &c. 12 North Audley st
Alexander John, baker, 55 Chapel st. Pentonville
Alexander John, baker, 32 Cursitor st
Alexander John, upholsterer, 32 Newman st. Oxford st
Alexander Joseph, fruiterer, 4 St. George's market, Borough
Alexander Joshua, solicitor, 6 South st. Finsbury
Alexander Lewis, carcase butcher, 9 Bury st. St. Mary Axe
Alexander Mary (Mrs.), boarding house, 3 America square
Alexander Morris, who. watch & clockma. 3 George st. Mnris
Alexander Peter, tailor, 7 Robson's place, Kennington road
Alexander Richard, beer retailer, Coburg row, Westminster
Alexander Robert, boot & shoe maker, 5 Chelsea market
Alexander Samuel, general ironmonger, 124 Goswell st
Alexander Saml. lodging ho. 4 Carpenter's bldgs. London wall
Alexander Sarah (Mrs.), tobaccnst. 5 Jamaica ter. Cmlr. rd. ea
Alexander Wm. auctioneer, &c. 2 Harrison st. Gray's inn rd
Alexander Wm. chairmaker, 5 Goldsmith pl. Hackney road
Alexander Wm. *Chancellor's Head* P.H. 5 Carey st. Linc. inn
Alexander William, general commission merchant & agent, Lloyd's, Royal Exchange; & 7 Stepney green
Alexander Wm. *Southwark Arms* P.H. 151 Tooley st
Alexander Wm. watch & clock maker, 10 Parliament st
Alexander Wm. John, queen's counsel, 7 Figtree court, Temple
Alexandre Auguste, foreign bookseller, 37 Gt. Russell st. Bloomsbury, & 50 Burlington arcade
Alexandre Edme, artificial florist, 16 Hamilton pl. King's cr
Alexandre Geo. C. for. bookseller, 50 Burlington arcade
Aley James, *Crown* P.H. Glasshouse st. East Smithfield
Aley Robert, straw hat maker, 3 Brompton terrace
Aley Thomas, watchmaker, 18 Park side, Knightsbridge
Aley William, poulterer, 2 Queen's buildings, Knightsbridge
Alford Fitzherbert & Co. cloth factors, 10 Ironmonger lane
Alford Ann (Mrs.), coachmaker, 9 Cumberland pl. Newington butts; & 9 Cumberland row, Walworth road
Alford Chas. *Rose & Ball* P.H. 11 Bennett's hill, Doctors' com
Alford James, cooper & oil bagma. 12 Bennett's hill Doc. com
Alford John, *Sussex Arms* P.H. Sussex pl. Camden town
Alford John Thomas, outfitter & clothier, 138 Tooley st

Alford Robert (now Muller John Henry), engraver & copper-plate, letterpress & gold printer, 13 Bridge st. Southwark
Alford William, tailor & draper, 5 Deptford bridge
Alford William, jun. *Old Antigallican* P.H. 110 Tooley st
Alford Wm. Jenkins, *Colonel Wardle* P.H. 139 Tooley st
Alfred Club house (George Biggs, sec.), 23 Albemarle st
Alfred Home & For. Life Assurance Company (J.W. Hampton, sec.), Lothbury. For Directors, &c. see page 2011
Alfred Wm. Hen. fishing rod & tackle maker, 41 Coleman st
Alfrey William, merchant, 31 Aldermanbury
Algar John R. fish factor, 98 Lower Thames st
Algar Joseph, tailor, 15 Allington st. Pimlico
Alger George, shoemaker, 7 Barnet st. Hackney road
Alger Owen Tickell, solicitor, 37 Bedford row, Bloomsbury
Alger Rowland, grocer, 23 Cannon st. rd. St. George's East
Alger Samuel, porter merchant, 29 Redman's row, Mile end
Alien Office, at the Home Office, Whitehall; hours 11 to 4
Alison, Cumberlege & Co. valparaiso, &c. mrchts. 4 New Broad st
Alison Jas. M. & Co. merchants, 59 Friday st. Cheapside
Alison James Edward, tobacconist, 18 Little Britain
Alison Somerville Scott, physician, 2 Fitzroy st. Fitzroy sq
Alkins William, hairdresser, 50 Princes st. Edgware road
Allaire René, dyer & scourer, 75 Charlotte st. Fitzroy sq
Allam William, barge builder, 65 Wapping wall
Allamby Thos. & Geo. plumbers, 2 & 5 St. Martin's st. Leicstr. sq
Allan David & Co. merchants, &c. 46 Coleman st. & 4 Lothbury
Allan Fred. & Co. merchants & insu. brokrs. 41 Threadneedle st
Allan James & Co. straw & tuscan hat manufs. 158 Cheapside
Allan James & Geo. lithographic printers, 14 Birchin lane
Allan & Smith, wholesale linendrapers, &c. 9 Friday st
Allan & Smyth, wine merchants, 11 Mark lane
Allan Thomas & Son, solicitors to *Indemnity Mutual Marine Assurance Company*, 1 Frederick's pl. Old Jewry
Allan Alexander, dentist, 7 Maddox st. Bond st
Allan Alexander, painter, 189 St. George st
Allan Charles, tailor, 21 Stockbridge terrace, Pimlico
Allan David, baker, 69 Charlotte st. Fitzroy square
Allan David, cabinet mkr. & upholstr. 152 Sloane st. Chelsea
Allan David, chemist, &c. 100 Freeschool st. Horselydown
Allan George, paper stainer, 8 Pritchard's pl. Hackney fields
Allan Georgiana (Miss), milliner, 25 Sherrard st. Golden sq
Allan James Gordon, special pleader, 2 Hare court, Temple
Allan John, paper stainer, 12 & 13 Wade's pl. Hackney rd
Allan John, shipowner, 2 Leadenhall st
Allan John, M.D. surgeon, 23 Milner square, Islington
Allan John B. linendraper, see Hall & Allan
Allan Mary A. (Mrs.), chandlr's. shop, 14 Gt. Cumbrlnd. st. Hckny
Allan Thomas, calico printer, see Peel, Allan & Co
Allan Thomas Robinson, barrister, 1 Mitre ct. bldgs. Temple
Allan Wm. for. booksell. & com. agt. 18 Warwick sq. Newgate st
Allan Wm. upholstr. & feather dresser, 4 Mount st. Lambeth
Allanson & Machons, sheffield plate wa. 31 Castle st. Holborn
Allanson James, boot & shoe maker, 39 Mount st. Lambeth
Allanson Mary (Mrs.), coal dealer, 34 Great Wild st
Allard John, boot & shoe maker, Mare st. Hackney
Allard Samuel, house painter, 5 Edmund st. King's cross
Allardyce Samuel, baker, 14 Borough market
Allars John, tinman, 9 Back church lane, Whitechapel
Allason Thomas, architect, 1 Connaught sq. Edgware road
Allaway William, brick agent, 4 Catherine court, Tower hill
Allbon Henry, haberdasher, 7 Baker's row, Walworth rd
Allbright Joseph, smith, 4 John's place, Camberwell new rd
Allbury Edmund, *Red Cow* P.H. Grange, Bermondsey
Allcock Geo. Fredk. & Co. refiners, 1 Cox's ct. Lit. Britain
Allcock John, wheelwright, 57 Chester st. Kennington
Allcock Thos. Francis, builder, 11 Welbeck st. & 2 North st. Manchester square
Allcock Thos. Francis, slate & sawmills, 32 Commercl. rd. Lmbth
Allcorn George, trussmaker, 26 Stanhope st. Clare market
Allcroft Fred. Wm. book & printseller, 62 Quadrant, Regt. st
Allcroft William, music seller, 15 New Bond st
Allden Thos. furn. ironmonger, 42 Freeschool st. Horselydn
Allder W. *Buffalo's Head* P.H. 1 Allsop ter. New rd. Marylebo
Allder Wm. cement mfr. 80 Bankside & 22 Seward st. Goswell st
Alldin Henry, coal mer. Arch House wf. Lombard st. Chelsea
Alldis Emma M. (Mrs.) belt & stayma. 2 Chapl. pl. S. So. Audley st
Alldis James, working cutler, 57 Gray's inn lane
Alldis John, dining rooms, 2 London road, Southwark
Alldridge Alfred, tailor, 29 New road, Sloane st
Alldridge Rd. Wm. wine merchant, see Hills & Alldridge
Alldridge Thomas, wine cooper, 177 Sloane st. Chelsea
Alleged Lunatics' Friends' Society (Luke James Hansard, hon. sec.), 36 Coleman st. City
Allen & Anderson, merchants, 15 College st. Dowgate hill
Allen & Brown, haberdashers, 2 Marsh place, Old Kent road
Allen Charles P. & John W. solicitors, 17 Carlisle st. Soho sq
Allen & Davison, commission agents, 27 Lawrence lane
Allen, Hanburys & Barry, chemists, 2 Plough ct. Lombard st
Allen & Holmes, ribbon & galloon maks. 38 Noble st. Cheapside
Allen & Holmes, solicitors, 31 Bedford row, Bloomsbury
Allen, Hudson & Co. regimental tailors, 124 New Bond st
Allen & Isaac, cigar manufacturers, 106 Houndsditch
Allen Jane & Harriet (Misses), school, Mare st. Hackney
Allen John & Son, indigo & drug brokers, 4 Billiter square
Allen & Mortimer, solicitors, 17 Clifford's inn, Fleet st
Allen & Nicol, solicitors, 88 Queen st. Cheapside
Allen Richd. Jas. & Son, coal mers. 20 Leman st. Goodman's fi
Allen, Robinson & Co, agricultural chemists, 80 Fenchurch st
Allen & Solly, who. hosiers & yarn mfrs. 5 Dyer's ct. Aldmnby
Allen & Spilsbury, who. ironmongers, 5 Hatton garden
Allen Stafford & Geo. drug grinders, 7 Cowper st. City road
Allen Thomas & Co. tailors & habit makers, 9 Gt. Vine st
Allen Thos. & Joseph, tobacco & snuff mfrs. 24 Norton folgate
Allen Wm. H. & Co. booksellers, publishers, stationers, map & chart sellers, 7 Leadenhall st
Allen Abraham, builder, 47 Canterbury st. York rd. Lambeth
Allen Alfred Victor S. academy, 120 Bunhill row
Allen Ann (Mrs.), grocer, 61 Theobald's road, Red Lion square
Allen Benj. copper plate printer, 6 Bury st. Bloomsbury
Allen Benj. William, stationer, 30 Ebury st. Pimlico
Allen Charles, copper plate printer, 10 Fetter lane
Allen Charles, dining rooms, 236 Upper Thames street
Allen Chas. engrav. tool cutter, 7 Ferdinand ter. Hampstead rd
Allen Charles, organ builder, 11 Sutton st. Soho
Allen Chas. Pettitt, treasurer for Middx. 17 Carlisle st. Soho
Allen Daniel, ironmonger, 8 Little Barlow st. Marylebone
Allen Edmund, indigo & drug broker, 4 Billiter square
Allen Edward, butcher, 29 South Audley st
Allen Edwd. coffee rooms, 14 Cumberland st. ea. Regent's park
Allen Edwd. furniture broker, 3 Cross st. Newington butts
Allen Edwd. music, &c. seller, 17 Percy st. Tottenham ct. road
Allen Edwd. umbrella, parasol, walking stick, fishing tackle & riding whip mak. 198 Oxford st. & 14 Burlington arcade
Allen Elizh. (Mrs.), grindery dlr. 48 Wellington st. Newingt. cau
Allen Francis, baker, 11 Mortimer st. Cavendish square
Allen Franklin, butcher, 5 Cannon st. rd. St. George's east
Allen Fred. riding school, 70 Seymour pl. Bryanstone sq
Allen George, architect & district surveyor, 69 Tooley st. & 2 Monmouth pl. New cross
Allen Geo. beer retailer, 11 Macclesfield st. south, City road
Allen George, butcher, 20 Bowling st. Westminster
Allen George, butcher, 4 Gerrard st. Soho
Allen George, ironmonger, 193 Kingsland road
Allen Geo. scaleboard & congreve ma. 4 Little George st. Beth. gr
Allen Geo. stove grate & range ma. Church st. Deptford
Allen George, undertaker, 132 Fetter lane
Allen George, watchmaker, 14 Red Lion passage, Holborn
Allen George Henry, working jeweller, 13 King st. Soho
Allen Gideon, boot maker, 2 St. John's lane, Clerkenwell
Allen Hannah (Mrs.), *King's Arms* P.H. Blackwall stairs
Allen Henry, fruiterer, 117 Blackfriars road
Allen Henry, greengrocer & coal dealer, 7 Great Wild st.
Allen Henry George, barrister, 24 Old square, Lincoln's inn
Allen Henry Hughes, law stationer, 123 Chancery lane
Allen Henry R. professor of music, 37 Baker st. Clerkenwell
Allen Isaac, blacklead pencil ma. 35 Middlesex st. Aldgate
Allen James, booksel. & publisher, 20 Warwick la. Newgate st
Allen James, confectioner, 56 Crawford st. Bryanstone sq
Allen James, stationer & bookbinder, 209 Tooley st
Allen James, tripe dresser, 1 Bird st. Oxford st.
Allen James B. artist, 108 Camden rd. villas, Camden town
Allen James Edward, wine & spirit merchant, 87 Great Tower st
Allen James Gorden, barrister, 2 Hare court, Temple
Allen James M. architect, 37 London st. Fitzroy square
Allen Jane (Miss), grocer, 6 North row, Grosvenor square
Allen Job, greengrocer, 1 Shoemaker row, Blackfriars
Allen John, carpenter, 28 New st. Brompton
Allen John, coach maker, see Johnson & Allen
Allen John, confectioner, 21 St. Martin's le grand
Allen John, dining rooms, 26 Butcher row, Ratcliff
Allen John, *Essex coffee house & P.H.* 41 Aldgate High st
Allen John, furrier, 80 Curtain road, Shoreditch
Allen John, grocer, 16 & 17 Great Russell st. Covent garden
Allen John, oil & colorman, see James & Allen
Allen John, oil & colorman, 7 John's row, St. Luke's
Allen John, rocking horse, &c. ma. 3 Clarence pl. Hackney rd
Allen John, ruling penmaker, 35 St. Swithin's lane, City
Allen John, solicitor, see Emmet & Allen
Allen John, tobacconist, 6 King street, Portman square
Allen John, trunk & camp equipage maker, 22 Strand
Allen John King, milliner & laceman, 218A, Regent street
Allen John Michael, dressing case ma. 37 Wardour st. Soho

Allen John S. surgeon, Marylebone Infirmary, New road
Allen John Wm. lithographer, 1 Coleman st. buildings
Allen John Wm. vestry clerk, and clerk to the paving commissioners & commissioners of land & assessed taxes, St Ann's, Westminster, 17 Carlisle street, Soho
Allen Joseph, confectioner, 16 Tooley street
Allen Joseph, fruiterer, 13 Chester terrace, Eaton square
Allen Joseph, hairdresser, 2 Caledonian road, Pentonville
Allen Joshua Jullian, attorney, see Norris, Allen & Simpson
Allen Leonard, auctionr. 18 Spring st. & 13 Conduit st. Padtn
Allen Mary (Mrs.), school, 108 Camden rd. villas, Camdn. tn
Allen Mary (Mrs.), wine fining ma. 12 Mount st. Whitechpl
Allen Matthew, baker, 10 St. Agnes terrace, Tabernacle sq
Allen Matthew, bricklayer& plasterer, 21 Worship st. Finsbry
Allen Rebecca (Mrs.), bookseller, 65 Sun st. Bishopgate
Allen Richard, butcher, 3 Victoria pl. Queen's rd. Dalston
Allen Richard, *Dundee Arms* P. H. 252 Wapping
Allen Richard (nephew to the late Cobbett), cricket bat & stump manufacturer, 27 North street, Lisson grove
Allen Richard, slate merchant & slater, Stangate, Lambeth, & 7 Palace new road, Lambeth
Allen Robert, boot & shoe maker, 224 Poplar High street
Allen Robert, oil&colorman, 16 Up. Dorset st. Bryanstone sq
Allen Robert, serjeant at law, 4 Serjeants' inn, Fleet street
Allen Robert, tobacco & snuff manufacturer, 131 Shoreditch
Allen Robert, writer & sign painter, 20 Hart st. Grosvenor sq
Allen Samuel, cabinet maker, 5 Princes street, Barbican
Allen Samuel, coal merchant, 4 Coborn street, Bow road
Allen Samuel, engraver, 11 Cross street, Islington
Allen Samuel, grocer, &c. 3 Southampton st. Camberwell road
Allen Samuel Young, wood turner, 63 King street, Borough
Allen Thos. barrister, 7 King's bench walk, Temple
Allen Thos. beer retailer, 1 Southampton st. Camberwell
Allen Thos. boot & shoe maker, 78 Charlotte ter. New cut
Allen Thos. *Bridgehouse tavern*, foot of Vauxhall bridge
Allen Thos. builder & undertaker, 21 Camden ter. Camden twn
Allen Thos. chemical light manufactr. 21 Staple st. Borough
Allen Thos. *Cock & Magpie* P. H. 88 Drury lane
Allen Thomas, engr.&bookbndr. tool cut. 25 New st. Cloth fair
Allen Thos. grocer & teadealer, 85 Chiswell street, Finsbury
Allen Thos. *Grosvenor Arms* P. H. 11 Lr. Belgrave pl. Pmlco
Allen Thos. hairdresser, 1 Pleasant place, King's cross
Allen Thos. hairdresser, 82 Broadwall, Blackfriars
Allen Thos. hardwareman, 133½ Great Suffolk st. Borough
Allen Thos. locksmith, 2 Little College st. Up. Thames street
Allen Thos. smith & bellhanger, 17 Lit. Trinity la. Queenhithe
Allen Thos. statuary & mason, 93 Paul st. Finsbury
Allen Thos. stone mason, 37 Brudenell place, New north rd
Allen Thomas, surgeon, 24B, Grafton st. Fitzroy sq. & 4 Holmes terrace, Camden town
Allen Thos. woollen draper, 3 Marylebone st. Piccadilly
Allen Thos. Duke, butcher, 38 Lower Kennington lane
Allen Thos. Windsor, pawnbroker, 21 Clare st. Clare market
Allen Wm. baker, 120 Edgware road, Marylebone
Allen Wm. dairyman, 42 Silver street, Golden square
Allen Wm. bookbinds' knifema. 27 Gt. St. Andrew st. 7 Dials
Allen Wm. carver & gilder, 31 Ebury st. & 82 Upper Ebury st. Pimlico
Allen Wm. cheesemonger, 188 Sloane st. Knightsbridge
Allen Wm. chemist, 2 Morgan's pl. Liverpool rd. Islington
Allen Wm. currier, 76 Paradise st. Rotherhithe
Allen Wm. grocer, 224 Bethnal green road
Allen Wm. grocer & cheesemonger, 13 Camden st. Walworth
Allen Wm. linendraper, 76 Edgware road, Marylebone
Allen Wm. linendraper, 53 Hatton garden
Allen Wm. paperhanging maker, see Horne & Allen
Allen Wm. plumber, 4 Avery row, Lower Grosvenor st
Allen Wm. scale board manufacturer, stationer, &c. 5 & 6 Cumberland street, Curtain road
Allen Wm. silversmith, 29 Rahere st. Goswell road
Allen Wm. stationer & tobacconist, Camberwell green
Allen Wm. surgeon, 9 Albion place, Hyde park square
Allen Wm. wheelwright, York road, Lambeth
Allen Wm. wheelwright, 26 Short's gardens, Drury lane
Allen Wm. wheelwright, 17 Granby st. Waterloo road
Allen Wm. *White Hart* P. H. 146 Bethnal green road
Allen Wm. *Yorkshire Stingo tavern*, New rd. Marylebone
Allen Wm. Josiah, hosier & shirt maker, 10 Holborn bars
Allen Wm. Woodgate, grocer, &c. 3 Church st. Stoke Newingtn
Allenby Everett, silk mercer, see Lewis & Allenby
Allendoorf Steven, baker, 36 York road, Lambeth
Allerton Richard, surveyor & land agt. 36 Norfolk st. Strand
Alleston Thos. *Feathers* P. H. 36 Lambeth walk
Alley George, stationer & newsvender, 89 Chiswell st.
Alley Thomas, earthenware dlr. 17 Cambridge rd. Mile end
Alleyn Joseph, coach maker, One Swan yard, Bishopsgate st
ALLEYN'S ALMSHOUSES, 1 to 10 Bath st. City road
Allford Edward, bed warehouse, 5 Stafford row, Pimlico
Allfrey George, merchant, Lloyd's
Allfrey William, barrister, 36 Lincoln's inn fields
Allgood William, button maker, 19 King st. & 266 Borough
Allhusen Frederick & Co. merchants, 15 Philpot lane
Alliance British & Foreign Life & Fire Assurance Co. (Andrew Hamilton, sec.), Bartholomew lane, Bank. For Directors, &c. see page 2011
Alliance Gas Company, 39 Finsbury circus
Allibon Wm. wine & spirit merchant, 15 & 16 Wapping wall
Allin Charles, tripe dresser, 48 Lambeth walk
Allin John, *Duke of Wellington* P.H. Morning lane, Hackney
Allin John, *Golden Lion* P.H. 26 Cannon st. rd. St. George's ea
Alling Harriet (Mrs.), dressmaker, 10 Church lane, Whitechpl
Alling Jas. watchmaker, 10 Church lane, Whitechapel
Allingham Wm. & Son, rug & worstedma. Up. Russel st. Bermnd
Allingham George, printer & publisher, 22 Blackfriars road
Allingham Geo. printer, Old Trinity ho. Water la. Tower st
Allingham Geo. *York Arms* P. H. 54 East st. Manchester sq
Allingham Mary (Mrs.), hairdresser, 10 Fleur-de-lis ct. Fleet st
Allington Wm. *Admiral Vernon* P.H. 107 Long Alley, Finsby
Allinson Samuel, america merchant, 78 Basinghall st
Allison & Co. (late W. Jennings), hat manufrs. 72 Cheapside
Allison & Allison, pat. piano ma. 75 Dean st. & 49 Wardour st. Soho
Allison E. (Mrs.), straw bon. ma. 34 Tichborne st. Edgwr. rd
Allison John, stonemason, 4 St. Martin's pl. St. Martin's le gr
Allison Joseph, silk mercer, 238 & 240 Regent street
Allison Mary (Mrs.), coffee rooms, 3 & 4 Ivy la. Newgate st
Allison Stephen, umbrell.&parasol ma. 17 Well st. Wellclose sq
Allison Thomas, butcher, 148 New Gravel lane
Allison Thomas, undertaker, 8 Southampton st. Camberwell
Allison Wm. Brown, bootmkr. 18&19 Portpool la. Gray's inn la
Alliston Charles & George, solicitors, see Smith & Alliston's
Allistone Richard, haircutter & wig ma. 28 Silver st. Wood st
Allkins Joseph, tailor, 27 Weymouth st. Portland place
Allkins William, butcher, 116 Upper Whitecross st
Allman Thomas, bookseller & publisher, 42 Holborn hill
Allnatt John Benwell, stockbroker, 12 Copthall court, City
Allnatt Richard Hopkins, F.S.A. physician, 4 Parliament st
Allnutt Jas. Barnett & Co. floorcloth mfr. 9 Pantechnicon ar
Allnutt Geo. Stevens, barrister, Chancery chambs. 30 Chancy la
Allnutt Henry, brush maker, 89 Piccadilly
Allnutt Wm. *Punch Bowl* P.H. 3 Farm st. Berkeley sq
Allnutt Zachary, agent to Frith & Co. 4 Bolt court, Fleet st
Allnutts & Arbouin, wine & brandy merchants, 50 Mark lane
Allom Thomas, architect, 14 Hart st. Bloomsbury
Allonby Edward, fruiterer, 27 Borough road
Alloway Jos. J. timber mer. Chester whf. Edward st. Regent's pk
Allowance Office for Spoiled Stamps, Somerset House
Alloway Joseph Jas. timber mer. 55 Lr. Queen st. Rotherhithe
Allport Chas. coach builder, 10 Rosamon bldgs. Islington
Allport Franklin, ship & ins. broker, see Wimble & Allport
Allport James, painter and glazier, 16 Grafton st. Soho
Allport James, silver plater, 4 Thavies inn, Holborn
Allpress Joseph, laceman, &c. 4 Barnsbury place, Islington
Allpress L. (Mrs.), who. stationer, 10 Gt. Russell st. Bloomsb
Allpress Thomas, coachmaker, 1 Crown terrace, Mile end rd
Allpress William, carpenter, 11 John st. North, Marylebone
Allpriss Joseph, haberdasher, 4 Felix ter. Liverpool rd
Allsop Elisha & David, builders, carpenters & house agents, 1 Arlington place, Back road, St. George's East
Allsop Anna (Mrs.), milliner, 280 Regent st.
Allsop George, turner & brush maker, 1 & 2 Hungerford st
Allsop Henry, tobacconist, 159 Alfred place, Waterloo rd
Allsop John, who. turner & brush maker, 174 Union st. Boro
Allsop Thos. stock broker, see Barclay, Allsop & Mercier
Allsopp Saml. & Sons, east india ale brewrs. 102 Leadenhall st
Allsopp Samuel & Sons, burton ale stores, 61 King William st. City; agent, John Edwards
Allsopp Jas. earthenware dealer, 41 Chapel st. Pentonville
Allsup John (late Pellatt & Green), glass, china & staffordshire warehouse, 16 St. Paul's churchyard, corner of Paul's chain
Allt Thomas & Co. seed crushers, Church st. Deptford
Allt Thomas, merchant, Baltic coffee house
Allum Chs. Alex. *Marquis of Granby* P.H. 48 Vine st. Wstmr
Allum Edwyn, oil & ital. wa. 17 Middle Queen's bds. Knightsb
Allum John, button & trimming seller, 66 Leather lane
Allum John, cork manufacturer, 92 Vauxhall walk, Lambth
Allum Manoah, cabinetmaker, 22 President st. East, King sq
Allway Samuel P. coal merchant, 13 George st. Adelphi
Allwood Jacob, coffee rooms, 54 Old Bailey
Allworth James, hatter, 7 Frederick place, Old Kent road
Allwright George, dairy, 45 William st. Regent's park
Allwright George, grocer & oilman, 32 Brook st. Ratcliff
Allwright John, haberdasher, 37 Rochester row, Westmr

Allwright Robert, haberdasher, 43 Rochester row, Westmr
Allwright Thomas, cheesemonger, 45 Rathbone place
Allwright William, poulterer & porkman, 56 Rathbone place
Alman Fennell A. sec. to Helion Light co. 18 Chas. st. St. Jas
Almond George & Wm. army contractors, 1 Old Bond st
Almond John, boarding house, 7 Clifford st. New Bond st
Almond Mary Ann (Mrs.), fruiterer, Covent garden frt. markt
Almond William, fruiterer, Covent garden fruit market
Almond William, tobacconist, 6 Mora place, City road
Almonry Office (Joseph Hanby, sec.), Middle Scotland yard
Almosnino Solomon, merchant, 11 Bevis marks
Almshouses for Deserving Poor, White's al. 54½ Moorgate st
Aloof Judah, merchant, 17 Gt. Alie st. Goodman's fields
Alsager Henry, packer, 14 George st. Mansion house
Alsager Thomas Massa, official assignee, 12 Birchin lane
Alsford George, beer retailer, 3 Portland st. Walworth com
Alsford Jas. timber merch. 23 Mid. Grove st. Commerl. rd. ea
Alsing Hans Jacob, timber mercht. 3 Printers pl. Bermondsy
Alsop Robert, chemist & druggist, 15 Sloane sq. Chelsea
Alstons' & Hallam, work. goldsmiths, 30 & 31 Bishopsgate within
Alston, Bevan & Co. merchants, 33 Great St. Helen's
Alston David Thos. merchant, 15 Savage gardens, Tower hill
Alston Hen. Douglas, appraiser & house ag. 24 Wellclose sq
Alston James, barge builder, 395 Rotherhithe wall
Alston Thos. saddler, &c. St. Ann's pl. Commercial rd. Limeho
Alston Thomas, saddler, 7 High street, Bow
Alston Wm. linendraper, High row, Silver st. Kennington
Alt & Blogg, wholesale jewellers & pearl workers, 8 & 9 Chichester rents, Chancery lane
Alten Mining Assoc. (E. J. Cole, sec.), 52 Old Broad st. City
Althans Henry, corn factor, 1 George street, Tower hill
Alto Douro Railway Offices, 29 Threadneedle st
Alton & Walker, pawnbrokers, 7 London terrace, Hackney rd
Alvarey Joseph, straw hat maker, 19 Litchfield st. Soho
Alvarez Joseph, merchant, 34 Threadneedle st
Alvarez Ramon, imp. of cigars, 17 Opera arcade, Haymarket
Alven Francis G. ostrich feather merchant, 29 Nicholas lane
Alves Duncan Davidson, merchant, 8 Lime street square
Alvey Frederick, lithographer & stationer, 128 London rd
Alvey John, bricklayer & plasterer, 2 Upper Rathbone place
Alvey Thomas, stationer, 34 Cumberland row, King's cross
Alway Wm. Taylor, tinman & brazier, 7 Northampt. r. Holwy
Alwin William, blacking maker, New King st. Deptford
Amable & Co. milliners, dress makers, & importers of silk & fancy french goods, 17 George st. Hanover square
Amadio Francesco, jun. optician, 35 Moorgate st
Amadio Joseph, optician, 6 Shorter's ct. Throgmorton st
AMBASSADORS, *see* General Index
Ambler Benjamin, hay salesman, 62 West Smithfield
Ambler Edward, bookbinder, 27 Compton st. Clerkenwell
Ambler Henry, boot maker, 11 Hand court, Holborn
Ambler Joseph, grocer, 16 Tottenham st. Tottenham ct. road
Ambridge & Andrews, corn merchts. 123 St. John st. Smithfi
Ambridge Harry, fancy cabinet makr. 5 West pl. City road
Ambridge James, corn merchants, 143 St. John st. road
Ambridge Rd. Henry, straw hat ma. 8 Church row, Up. st. Isling
Ambrogi Matthew, plaster cast figure maker, 51 Drury lane
Ambrose Charles, plumber, 32 New road, St. George's East
Ambrose Geo. watch escapmnt. ma, 49 New Glo'ster st. Hoxton
Ambrose John, umbrella maker, 9 Rose st. Covent garden
Ambrose Madame, dressmaker, 5 Bryanstone st. Portman sq
Ambrose Mary (Miss), straw hat manuf. Broadway, Stratford
Ambrose Thos. *Hen. the Eighth* P.H. 46 Gt. St. Andrew st. 7 dia
Ambrose Thomas Henry, solicitor, 89 Chancery lane
Ambrose William, florist, King st. Battersea
Ambrose Wm. rag & bottle mercht. 18 Homer st. Marylebn
Ambrose William, umbrella maker, 5 St. Clement's la. Strand
Ambross David, *King's Arms* P.H. 10 Pritchards rd. Hack. rd
Amelang Leopold, sealing wax maker, see Dovell & Amelang
Amer Charles, butcher, 108 Union st. Borough
Amer William, butcher, 70 Earl st. East, Lisson grove
American Loyalist (Pay) Office, Treasury; hours 10 to 4
Amery John, bricklayer, Portland ho. Portland pl. Walw. com
Amery John, hardwareman, 6 Up. Dorset st. Bryanstone sq
Amery Philip, builder, 1B, Chapel st. Somers town
Amery Philip, undertak. & carpen. 30 Chalton st. Somers tn
Amery Robert, packing case maker, 46 Bishopsgate without
Amery William, bricklayer, 37 Friar st. Blackfriars road
Ames John & Son, saw mills for brush board, cartridge boxes, &c. & plane & general tool maks. 25 Tothill st. Westminster
Ames Thomas & Son, undertakers, 108 Church st. Shoreditch
Ames Charles, hatter, 25 George st. Blackfriars road
Ames Charles Andrew, butcher, 8 Church st. Mile end New tn
Ames Edwd. Saml. shopkeeper, 60 Seabright st. Bthnl. gr. rd
Ames James, cheesemonger, 4 Spring st. Marylebone
Ames Jas. *Kent & Essex* P.H. Kent & Essex yd. High st. Whitech
Ames John Samuel, oilman, 225 Bethnal green road
Ames Joseph, watch jeweller, 131 St. John st. road
Ames Levi, banker, see Prescott, Grote, Ames, & Cave
Ames Sam. furn. broker, 1 & 2 Rosamon bldgs. Islington green
Ames Thomas, auctioneer & appraiser, 11 John st. Oxford st
Ames Thomas, braid manufacturer, 23 Bethnal green road
Ames Thomas Jas. ginger beer maker, 17 Shadwell High st
Ames Walter, tailor, 5 Frederick street, Hampstead road
Amesbury Joseph, surgeon, 12 Devonshire st. Portland pl
Amey Joseph, fruiterer, 19A, Cleveland st. Fitzroy square
Amicable Life Assurance Office, 19 Serjeants' inn, and 50 Fleet street; for directors, &c. &c. see page 2019
Amies Wm. S. & Co. mfg. chemists, Sunwhf. Canl. rd. Kingsld. bas
Amis James, silk mercer, &c. 48 Bishopsgate within
Amiss John, fruiterer, 51 York terrace, Regent's park
Amiss Robert, livery stables, 15 Doughty mews, Guilford st
Amner Henry, bootmaker, 55 Mortimer st. Cavendish sq
Amor John, coffee rooms, 1 Arcade, Hungerford market
Amor John, wine & brandy merchant, 135 New Bond st
Amor Thomas, brass founder & pump ma. 7 Osborne st. Whtchpl
Amor Thomas, fishmonger, 36 Thayer st. Manchester sq
Amor William, pawnbroker, 45 Lambeth walk
Amory, Sewell & Moores, solicitors, 25 Throgmorton st
Amos & Bostock, dlrs. in sponge & india rubber, 6 Walbrook
Amos Charles, corn dealer, 4 Assembly pl. Kennington grn
Amos Charles Edwards, millwright, see Easton & Amos
Amos Jacob, carpenter, 17 Russell st. Bermondsey
Amos John, bakers' peelmaker, 40 Charles st. Hampstead
Amos William, baker, 9 Etham place, Dover road
Amos William, linendraper, 5 Thornton st. Horselydown
Amoss Chas. ham & beef dlr. 14 Walbrook rw. New nrth. rd. Hxtn
Amoss Thomas, *Bell* P. H. 59 Mount st. Berkeley square
Amphlet Thos. boot & shoe maker, 22 York row, Kenngtn. rd
Amphlett Richard Paul, barrister, 5 Old sq. Lincoln's inn
Amsden George John, surgeon, 1 Critchill pl. New North rd
Amy John Fred. cotton broker, 21 Cullum st
Amyot Wm. Henry, barrister, 3 Carey st. Lincoln's inn
Ancell & Bryant, who. druggists, 2 & 11 Savage gardens
Ancell & Fagg, surgeons, 73 New Church st. Lisson grove
Ancell Henry, surgeon, 3 Norfolk crescent, Oxford square
Anchor Life Assurance Company (Edward Baylis, actuary), 30 Sackville st. Piccadilly. For list of directors, &c. &c. see page 2012
Ancona & Bagster, architects & surveyors, 42 Lombard st
Andalusian Mining Ass. (J. T. Wright, sec.), 30 Gracech. st
Anderdon John Lavicount, mercht. see Manning & Anderdon
Anderdon Thos. Oliver, queen's counsel, 9 Old sq. Lincoln's inn
Anderson Brothers & Co. merchants, 9 New Broad st. City
Andersons' & Cateley, soap works, Gt. Suffolk st. Southwark
Anderson Geo. Glenny & Alx. D. corn & flour factrs. 48 Mark la
Anderson Jas. & Geo. fruiterers, 4 Alfred ter. Cambridge hth
Anderson John & Co. distillers, 25 Holborn hill
Anderson John & Sons, merchants, 65 Old Broad st. City
Anderson & Newson, merchants, 58 St. Swithin's la. City
Anderson & Smith, auctioneers & est. agts. 4 Eldon st. Finsbury
Anderson & Smith, merchants, 3 Lime st. square
Anderson Thos. & Son, law stationers, 31 Southampton bldgs
Anderson William & Co. west india brokers, 6 Mincing lane
Anderson William, senior & Co. general & commission merchants, and insurance agents, 10 Austin friars
Anderson Aaron Geo. baker, 10 Southampton st. Camberwell rd
Anderson Alexander, surgeon, 17 York place, Portman sq
Anderson Alexander, tailor, 45 James st. Oxford st
Anderson Andrew, baker, 7 Baker's row, Whitechapel road
Anderson Andrew, dining rooms, 26 Lower East Smithfield
Anderson Andrew, pianoforte maker, 83 Great Titchfield st
Anderson Ann (Mrs.), *Union* P.H. 52 Baker st. Lloyd sq
Anderson Anthony, *George* P.H. 173 Lambeth walk
Anderson Benj. *Turk's Head* P.H. 8 East st. Red Lion sq
Anderson Charles, muslin warehouse, see Smith & Anderson
Anderson Charles, chemist, 23 Lower Belgrave st. Eaton sq
Anderson Chas, who. tin. & tin toy ma. 5 Webber st. Blkfrs. rd
Anderson David, baker, 47 Greek st. Soho
Anderson David, carpenter, 12 Stanhope st. & 3 Houghton st. Clare market
Anderson Duncan, corn mercht. 11 Virginia terr. Gt. Dover rd
Anderson Edw. Chas. watchma. 7 Parsonage rw. Newingt. butts
Anderson Edw. W. breeches & trousers ma. 52 South Audley st
Anderson Eliz. (Mrs.), *Antelope* P.H. 11 Phipps st. Curtain rd
Anderson Eustace, solicitor, 15 Lincoln's inn fields
Anderson Francis, baker, 1 Hertford st. Mayfair
Anderson George, baker, 35 Tonbridge street, New road
Anderson Geo. teach. of drawing, 234 Maida vale, Edgw. rd
Anderson Henry, glass shade maker, 8 Gt. Smith st. Westmins
Anderson James, barrister, 11 New square, Lincoln's inn
Anderson James, ironmonger, 10 King street, Holborn

Anderson James, ironmonger & scale maker, 19 Wardour st
Anderson James, merchant, 11 Mark lane
Anderson James, smith & bellhanger, 28 Kingsgate st. Holbn
Anderson James, tailor & trim.selr. 75 High st. Camden town
Anderson James, tobacconist, 43 King street, Snowhill
Anderson Sir James E. physician, 11 New Burlington street
Anderson James G. linen factor, see Gilfillan & Anderson
Anderson John, baker, Denmark hill, Camberwell
Anderson John, carman, 6 Portugal pl. Cambridge road
Anderson John, *Carpenters' Arms* P.H. 7 Adamst. Brynstn. sq
Anderson John, cheesemngr. 17 Northampton row, Holloway
Anderson John, china gilder, 21 Glo'ster st. St. John st. rd
Anderson John, coffee roaster & dlr. 3 Worcester pl. Up. Thas. st
Anderson John, fruiterer, 10 Orange street, Red Lion sq
Anderson John, grease merchant, 16 St. John street road
Anderson John, grocer, 46 Chapel street, Pentonville
Anderson John, *Royal Oak* P.H. 40 Turvile st. Shoreditch
Anderson John, surgeon, 18 Maida hill, Edgware road
Anderson John Hay, seedsman, see Hay, Anderson & Sangster
Anderson John Henry, solicitor, 80 Cornhill
Anderson Jonas, grocer, 8 Clark st. Commercial road east
Anderson Joseph, horse dealer, 108 Piccadilly
Anderson Joseph, merchant, 15 College st. Dowgate hill
Anderson Leonard, boot & shoe mkr. 16 Oakley st. Lambeth
Anderson Luke, tailor, 63 Oakley street, Lambeth
Anderson Mary (Mrs.), baker, 1 Northampton pl. Old Kent rd
Anderson Mary (Mrs.), *King's Arms tav.* 1 Kensington High st
Anderson Mary Ann (Mrs.), dyer, &c. 2 Howland st. Fitzroy sq
Anderson Peter, dealer in foreign securities, 4 Austin friars
Anderson Robt. baker, 9 Coleman st.
Anderson Robt. carpenter, 8 King st. Commercial rd. east
Anderson Robert, warehouseman, 1 Bread st. City
Anderson Robt. watch motion ma. 25 Westmoreland pl. City rd
Anderson Robt. wharfinger, see Brander & Anderson
Anderson Rt. Wm. tallow chand. 62 Marylebone la. Oxford st.
Anderson Samuel R. ship chandler, 92 Tooley street
Anderson Thos. baker, 2 High st. Marylebone
Anderson Thos. bottle mer. & lint ma. 7 Dorset st. Portman sq
Anderson Thos. coal merchant, 7 King's road, Pimlico
Anderson Thos. ship joiner & packing ca. ma. 33½ Haydon st
Anderson Thos. silk dresser & hot presr. 22 James st. Old st
Anderson Thos. Paterson, solicitor, see Beavan & Anderson
Anderson Wm. cabinet ma. 27 Circus st. New rd. Marylebone
Anderson Wm. druggist, 178 Tooley street
Anderson Wm. *Eldon Arms* P.H. Queen sq. Eldon st. Finsbury
Anderson Wm. ham dealer, 2 Winckworth buildings, City rd
Anderson Wm. livery stables, 77 Park street, & 43 Green street, & Wood's mews, Grosvenor square
Anderson Wm. stationer & tobacconist, 372 Rotherhithe
Anderson Wm. surgeon, 18 Brompton row
Anderson Wm. surgeon, 12 Chadwell st. St. John st. rd
Anderson Wm. tailor, see Whitehead & Anderson
Anderson Wm. tobacconist, 15 Broomfields, Deptford
Anderson Wm. vellum binder, 4 St. Benet's pl. Gracechurch st
Anderson Wm. watch manfr. 38 Little Sutton st. Clerkenwell
Anderson Wm. Fredk. cheesemgr. 32 Featherstone st. City rd
Anderson's soluble starch warehouse (John Forsyth, agent), 8 Great Bush lane, Cannon street
Anderton George Thomas, butcher, 98 Bermondsey st
Anderton Isaac, tea dealer, 60 Whitechapel rd. & 26 Old st
Anderton James, solicitor (resident manager of the West of England Assurance Co.), 20 New Bridge st. Blackfriars
Anderton William, tallowchandler, 27 Old st. St. Luke's
Andrade Abraham & Davd. jun. meat salsm. 2 New Newgate mk
Andrade Benjamin, butcher, 1 New Newgate market
Andrade David, meat salesman, 7 New Newgate market
Andrade Saul, meat salesman, 145 Kingsland road
Andrade Soln. H. ostrich feather man. & furr. 63 Leadenhall s
André Jas. P. & Sons, westind. merchs. 12 Camomile st. Bishopsgt
André Peter, hatter, 127 New Bond street
Andrew John & Co. cotton yarn manufs. & dyers, 7 Goldsmith st
Andrew & Wagner, engravers on wood, booksellers & stationers, 10 Crawley st. Oakley sq. Somers town
Andrew Alexander, russia broker, see Rayner & Andrew
Andrew Charlotte (Mrs.), plumber, 36 Dowgate hill
Andrew Frederick William, plain & ornamental painter, 23 Northumberland street, Marylebone
Andrew Frederick Wm. jun. stationer, 22 Coleshill st. Pimlico
Andrew George, plumber, 26 Widegate street, Bishopsgate
Andrew James, drysalter, 8 Billiter st
Andrew John James, solicitor, see Atkins & Andrew
Andrew John, bookseller & stationer, 10 Crawley st. Oakley sq
Andrew Joseph, *Portland Arms* P.H. 25 High st. Portland twn
Andrew Joseph Geo. oil & italian wareho. 8 New st. Dorset sq
Andrew Mary (Mrs.), market gardener, South Lambeth
Andrew Matthew, coffee rooms, 5 Cross st. Newington butts
Andrew Thomas, furn. broker, 36 South st. Manchester sq
Andrew Wm. Isaac, jun. beer retailer, South Lambeth
Andrewes Henry, tinplate worker, see Barber & Andrewes
Andrewes Henry, cheesemonger, 132 Hoxton Old town
Andrewes John, tailor, 131 Hoxton Old town
Andrewes Thos. wire wkr. & cagema. 17 Old Compton st. Soho
Andrews Charlotte, Sophia, Elizabeth, & Ellen (Misses), artificial florists, 16 Newman st
Andrews & Cooper, silk manufacturers, 21 Milk st. City
Andrews George & Co. tailors, 9 Cork st. Bond street
Andrews George & Co. tea dealers, 316 Oxford street
Andrews George William & Co. wine merchts. 62 Moorgate st
Andrews Hugh, Sons & Gee, calico prnts. & merchts. 55 Friday st
Andrews John H. & Co. ribbon & silk agts. 26 & 27 Addle st. City
Andrews Rd. & Co. blacking makers, 4 Panton st. Haymkt
Andrews William & Co. helmet makers, 9 Pall mall
Andrews Abraham, cooper, 14 Southampton st. Camberwl. rd
Andrews Alexander, printer, 27 Old Glo'ster st. Hoxton
Andrews (Mrs.), Amelia, wardrobe dlr. 17 Lamb's Conduit pas
Andrews Andrew, corn merchant, see Ambridge & Andrews
Andrews Ann (Mrs.), milliner, 18 Foley place, Portland place
Andrews Ann (Mrs.), undertaker, 8 Phœnix st. Crown st. Soho
Andrews Biggs, queen's counsel, 4 King's bench walk, Temple
Andrews Caroline A. (Miss), umbrel. ma. 10 Store st. Bedford sq
Andrews Catherine (Mrs.), coal dealer, 96 Gt. Peter st. Westm
Andrews Charles, baker, 16 Bath st. Hackney road
Andrews Charles, bird dealer, 50 Brick lane, Spitalfields
Andrews Charles, builder, 61 St. George's road, Borough
Andrews Charles, dining rooms, 59 Chiswell st
Andrews Charles, oilman & drysalter, 67 Chiswell st
Andrews Eliza (Mrs.), bookseller & librarian, 167 New Bond st
Andrews Eliza (Mrs.), hatter, &c. 3 Newman's row, Lincs. inn fi
Andrews Elizabeth (Mrs.), shoemakr. 19 Holywell la. Shordtch
Andrews Elizbth. (Miss), stationer, 14 Gloster ter. Kensington
Andrews George, engineer, 18 Spencer st. Goswell road
Andrews Harriet (Miss), ladies' school, 3 Millman pl. Bedfd. rw
Andrews Henry, bedstead ma. 17 Cross st. Blackfriars road
Andrews Henry, bottle dealer, 74 Long lane, Smithfield
Andrews Henry, fishmonger, 14 Freeschool st. Horselydown
Andrews Henry, invalids' chair mak. 18 Foley pl. Portland pl
Andrews Hen. paperhanger, 3 Angel pl. New rd. Pentonville
Andrews Henry John, hairdresser, 36 Water la. Blackfriars
Andrews Isaiah, furniture dealer, 108 Wardour st. Soho
Andrews James, beer retailer, 3 Crispin st. Spitalfields
Andrews James, beer retailer, Grange road, Bermondsey
Andrews James, carpenter, 24 Princess st. Portman market
Andrews James, silversmith & polisher, 10 Bull & Mouth st
Andrews James, *White Bear* P.H. Ratcliff cross
Andrews John, artist, 4 George st. New Kent road
Andrews John, cheesemonger, 24 Shaftesbury ter. Pimlico
Andrews John, fruiterer, 47 Upper North pl. Gray's inn road
Andrews John, grocer, 2 Waterloo st. Camberwell
Andrews John, leathercutter, 35 Weston st. Somers town
Andrews John, tobacconist, 18 Hedge row, High st. Islington
Andrews John Goldwyer, surgeon, 4 St. Helen's pl. Bishopsg
Andrews John Richard, brazier, 71 Tottenham court road
Andrews Jonathan, tailor, 15 Adam st. Adelphi
Andrews Joseph, surgeon, 1 Up. Belmont pl. Wandsworth rd
Andrews Joseph, teadealer, 3 High st. Kensington
Andrews Mary (Mrs.), *George IV.* P.H. 10 New st. Smithfld
Andrews Mary (Mrs.), grocer, 36 Brunswick st. Blackwall
Andrews Peter, catholic printer & publisher, 92 Bartholomew cl
Andrews Reginald, linendra. 16 Calthorpe pl. Gray's inn rd
Andrews Richard, muslin manufacturer, 54½ Friday st
Andrews Richard, surgeon, 96 Crawford st. Portman square
Andrews Robert, fruiterer, 99 Park st. Grosvenor square
Andrews Sarah (Mrs.), wardrobe dealer, 51 Paddington st
Andrews Thos. grocer, 24 Upper John st. Liverpool rd
Andrews Thos. japanner, &c. 8 Castle st. east, Oxford market
Andrews Thos. oilman, 51 Penton st. Pentonville
Andrews Wm. butcher, 44 White st. Borough
Andrews Wm. chimney sweeper, 1 Angel court, St. James's
Andrews Wm. city coffee rooms, 29 Farringdon st.
Andrews Wm. fruiterer, 2 Stepney High st
Andrews Wm. merchant, 14 New City chambers, Bishopsgate
Andrews Wm. physician, 2 Suffolk place, Haymarket
Andrews Wm. saddler, 2 Compton st. Clerkenwell
Andrews Wm. Dan. carpenter, Bolingbroke gardens, Battersea
Angas, Bevan & Co. merchants, 2 Jeffreys sq. St. Mary axe
Angel Richard, bootmaker, 77 Great Tower st. City
Angel William, poulterer, 35 Compton st. Brunswick square
Angell John & Son, silversmiths, 51 Compton st. Clerkenwell
Angell Joseph & Son, mnftg. silversmiths, 25 Panton st. Haymkt
Angell Alfred, solicitor, 23 Lincoln's inn fields
Angell Evan, carpenter & joiner, 6 Charterhouse lane
Angell George, warehouseman, 45 Friday st

Angell John, hair dresser, Nelson place, Old Kent road
Angell John Scott, leather factor, see Ward & Angell
Angell Samuel, architect & surveyor, 18 Gower st. Bedford square, & 5 Hatton garden
Angell Wm. tobacconist, 94 New Gravel la. Shadwell
Angelo Henry Charles, school of arms, 32 St. James's st
Angier Frères&Co.(cognac),Thos. Henshaw, agt. 3 Philpot la
Angier Samuel H. agent for shipping,&c. 75 Cornhill
Angliss John, tallow chandlers' mould frame, beer engine, & pewter pot manufacturer,merchants supplied, 6Allerton st. East road, City road
Angliss Thomas, butcher, Ferry road West, Poplar
Anglo Mexican Mining Association, 5 Broad st. buildings
*Anglo Mexican Mint Co.*G.B.Lonsdale,sec.5 Broad st. bdgs
Angold James Bernard, tobacconist, 72 Lambeth walk
Angold John, timber merchant,25 Tottenham st. Tottenham court road ; 49½ High st. St. Giles's ; & 5 Crown place, Soho
Angold Samuel, tobacconist, 85 Chalton st. Somers town
Angrave John, leather seller, 42 Up. Salisbury pl. Lock'sflds
Angus Wm. & Co. coach builders, Lancelot pl. Trevor sq
Angus Alexander, surgeon & accoucheur, 66 Frith st. Soho
Angus Andrew Wm. cheesemonger, 29 East st.Walworth rd
Angus Henry,wheelwright,7 GreenDragon yd.HighHolborn
Anichini Pompey, sen. metal broker, 21 Fenchurch st
Anley Wm. bootmaker, 15 Henrietta st. Manchester sq
Annan Isaac, baker, 17 Gordon st. Islington
Annan Wm. lithograph. & letter press printer, 46 Watling st
Annand John, proctor, 20 Gt. Carter lane, Doctors' commons
Annand Margaret(Mrs.),confectioner,101Bridge rd.Lambeth
Annand Wm. insurance agt. 3 Winchester bdgs. & Lloyd's
Annandale William, surgeon, 73 Piccadilly
Annesley George, solicitor, 64 Lincoln's inn fields
Annesley Sir James, physician, H 6, Albany
Anness Wm. marine storedealer,17Cambridge pl.Edgware rd
Annett James,professor of languages, 2Chester ter. Eaton sq
AnnettThos.Alfred, wor.goldsmith,23Wellington st.Goswl.rd
Anning Henry, shell dealer, 1 Cannon st. Ratcliff
Anning Robert, curiosity dealer, 60 Cannon st. Ratcliff
Anningson John, surgeon, 152 Whitechapel road
Annis John, pawnbroker, &c. 121 Minories
Annis Thomas, tailor, 24 Sackville st. Piccadilly
Annis William, bookbinder, 102 Park st. Kennington cross
Annis William, plumber, 13 Little Titchfield st. Portland pl
Anns Joseph, *Lord Nelson* P.H. Trafalgar st. Walworth rd
Annuity (Government) Office, 19 Old Jewry ; hours 10 to 3
Ansdell Samuel, bookbinder, 11 Adam st. West
Ansdell Hen. W. & Co. *City of Carlisle* P.H. 99 Shoreditch, [High st
Ansell Abraham&Co. importers of foreign goods, 56½ Wood st
Ansell & Edmondson,wine mers.18Lit.Knightridr.st.Drs.cms
Ansell & Hawke, medical glass & general fixture dealers, 8 Great Queen st. Lincoln's inn fields
Ansell Hyam & Co. merchts. 3 Howford bdgs. Fenchurch st
AnsellAbm.*Pr.ofBrunswick*P.H.Brunswickter.Barnsby.pk
Ansell Amos, beer retailer, 33 Rawstorne st. Goswell rd
Ansell Ann (Mrs.), glass & china dlr.61Upp.Ebury st.Pimlico
Ansell Ann (Mrs.), *WhiteHart*P.H.17 Windmillst.Tott.ct.rd
Ansell Charles, actuary, *Atlas Assurance Co.* 92 Cheapside
Ansell Charles, *Horse & Groom* P.H. 30 King st. 7 dials
Ansell Edward, commission agent, 15 Noble st. Cheapside
Ansell Edward, fruit salesman, 50 New church st. Lisson gr
Ansell George, clock spring maker, 25 Banner st. St. Luke's
Ansell George Wm.stationer,31 Bridport pl. NewNorth road
Ansell Hyam, commercial agt. 14 Gt.Prescot st.Gdmns. flds
Ansell James, city carman, 50 Minories
Ansell James, leather seller, 77 Long lane, West Smithfield
Ansell James Knottesford,bookseller,7 Russell pl.OldKent rd
Ansell John, boot & shoe warehouse, 66 Barbican
Ansell Joseph, optician, 27 Bury st. St. Mary Axe
Ansell Thomas, baker, High st. Bow, Middlesex
Ansell Thomas, bootmaker, 22 John st. West, Edgware road
Ansell Thomas, camden nursery,Gloucester pl.Camden town
Ansell Thomas, surgeon, Harley place, Mile end road
Ansell William, bootmaker, 23 Canterbury pl. Old Kent rd
Ansell William, brushmaker, 10 Great Ryder st. St. James's
Ansley Thos. sofa & couch ma. 9 Queen st.Short st. New cut
Anslie William, *Star* P.H. 190 Wapping High st
Anslow Ann (Mrs.), biscuit baker, 175 Union st. Borough
Anslow Thos. mahogany merchant, 17 Marlboro' st.Blkfrs rd
Anspach William, baker, 50 Brunswick st. Hackney road
Ansted John & Thos. fruit brokers, see Clark, Ansted & Co
AnstedChas.mercht.&ins.brok.8St.Benet'spl.Gracechurch st
Ansted James, merchant, 8 St. Benet's pl. Gracechurch st
Anstee Edward, butcher, 14 Oxford market
Anstee Thomas, boot & shoe maker, 26 Charterhouse lane
Anstey,LeGassick &Guthrie,tailors,18 George st.Hanover sq
Anstey Isaac, fur & horse hair cap ma. 4 Bridge rd.Lambeth
Anstey John, tea dealer, 144 High st. Hoxton Old town
AnsteySaml.meltingpot manfr.10 Devonshire st.NewNrth.rd
Anstey Thomas Chisholme, barrister, 54 Chancery lane
Anstiss Wm. bricklayer, &c. 9 Up. Cleveland st. Fitzroy sq
Answorth Robert, law stationer, 1 Clifford's inn, Fleet st
Answorth William, warehouseman, 1 Clifford's inn
Anthony Benjamin B & Co. french artists in dyeing, steaming & glazing, 53 Basing place, Waterloo road
Anthony John Galieb & Co. merchts. & ship agts. 71 Cornhill
Anthony Elizabeth (Mrs.), tailor & mercer, 78 Chancery la
Anthony Henry, pork butcher, 28 Goswell road (west side)
Anthony James Mark, silk manfr. 14 Wood st. Spitalfields
Anthony John Hollis, solicitor, 31 Nicholas lane
AnthonyRobt.poultry salesman,10Shiptav.pas.Leadenhl.mkt
Anthony Samuel Hollis, merchant, 29 Austinfriars
Anthony Wm. restorer of paintings, 19 Lisle st. Leicester sq
Anti Coal Monopoly Co. (J. A. Chowne), 31 Charing cross
Anti Corn Law LeagueHead Office(Geo.Wilson,chairman Abraham W. Paulton, secretary), 67 Fleet street
Anti Dry Rot Company (Kyan's patent), (T. Thompson sec.) 2 Lime st. sq. & 4 Macclesfield st. south, City road
Anti Monopoly Coal Co.(Jas. Ghagan,sec.),29Charing cross
Anti State Church Assoc. 12 Warwick sq. Newgate street
Antill Ann (Mrs.), orange merchant, 7 Borough market
Anton George, baker, 111A, Jermyn street, St. James's
Anton James, parliamenty. & scotch law agt. see Law&Anton
Antrobus Edmund, teaman to her Majesty, and to her Majesty Queen Adelaide, 446 West Strand
Antrobus John, academy, 10 Jermyn street, St. James's
Antrobus William, writing master, 5 Duke street, Adelphi
Antwerp Steam Co.(Lightly&Simon,agts.),123 Fenchurch st
Anwyl & Co. whol. trimming warehouse, 22 Lawrence lane
Anwyl Owen, oilman & grocer, 20 LowerBelgrave st.Pimlico
Anyon Thomas, silk dyer to her Majesty, 44 Greek st. Soho
Apel Henry, teacher of german, 5 College street, Chelsea
Aplin Benjamin, attorney, 5 Furnival's inn, Holborn
Aplin John D.french china dlr. 439 Strand& 2 Lowther arcade
Aplin Robert, french china dlr. 23 Lowther arcade, Strand
Apothecaries' Hall, R. B. Upton, clerk, Water lane, Blkfrs
Appach FrederickWm. insur.broker & agt.18 Tokenhouse yd
Appel George, baker, 122 Praed street, Paddington
Appelbee Samuel, baker, 271 Bermondsey street
Appelbee Wm. sen. baker, 13 Gt. Chapel street, Westminster
Appleby Chas. grocer & cheesemgr. 1 Conduit st. Paddington
Appleby Charles Robt. tailor, 17 St. John st. Clerkenwell
Appleby Jas. cheesemonger, 16 Freeschool st. Horselydown
Appleby James, dining rooms, New Cross road, Deptford
Appleby James, heraldic engravr.3Lowr.King st.Old Kent rd
Appleby John, working cutler, 48 Banner st. St. Luke's
Appleby Samuel, solicitor, 6 Harpur st. Red Lion square
Appleby Thos. cheesemonger, 5 Princess st. Edgware rd
Appleby Thomas Wm. tobacconist, 13 Bethnal green road
Appleford Fredk. account. & agt. see Jeffreys & Appleford
Appleford John Edward, city carman, 3 Gt. Tower street, & 12 Palentine place, Commercial road east
Appleford William, tailor & draper, 145 Holborn bars
Applegarth George, ladies' boot & shoe ma. 50 Marchmont st
Applegarth Jane (Mrs.), shoemaker, 3 George ct. Piccadilly
Applegate Thomas, haberdasher, &c. 30 Notting hill High st
Applegate William, tailor & trimming seller, 146 Tooley st
Applegath Thomas, lace cleaner, 27 Foley pl. Gt. Portland st
Appleton Anth. & Co. who. tea dlrs.10 Catherine ct. Tower hl
Appleton Chas. & Co. sydney merchants, 11 St. Benet's pl
Appleton Daniel & Co. book exporters, 16 Little Britain
Appleton Hen.&Son, lace ma.& worsted spinnrs. 29 Long acre
Appleton Francis,grocer, &c.2 Cable street,Wellclose square; & 75 Hackney road
Appleton George, auctioneer, &c. see Newton & Appleton
Appleton Hannah (Miss), milliner, 14 Philipps st.Kingsld. rd
Appleton Henry, baker,grocer & cornchandler,Battersea flds
Appleton Henry, surgeon, see Huxtable & Appleton
Appleton James, coppersmith & brazier,100 Old st. St. Luke's
Appleton James, grocer, 174 Drury lane
Appleton James Metcalfe, surgeon, 45 Curzon street
Appleton John, auctioneer, estate & house agent, land surveyor & valuer, 31 Nicholas lane, City; and at Leytonstone, & Harlow, Essex
Appleton John, patent and other line, rope, twine & door mat manufacturer, 1 Ernest st. White Horse lane, Mile end rd
Appleton John, country ale agent, Hungerford wf. Strand
Appleton John, solicitor, 3 Fenchurch buildings
Appleton Mary (Mrs.), baker, 5 Weston st. Somers town
Appleton Thomas, coppersmith & worm mak.69 Houndsditch
Appleton Thos. Ben.surgeon,10Newington ter.Horsemngr. la
Appleton Wm. hairdresser, 28 Thomas street, Oxford street
Appleton Wm. ironmonger, 81 Drury lane

Appleyard Charles, solicitor, 1 New square, Lincoln's inn
Appleyard Henry, *Magpie & Stump* P.H. 118 Newgate st
Appleyard Henry, news agent&bookseller,1 Duke st.Adelphi
Applin George, cheesemonger, 52Up. Berkeley st. Portman sq
Appold George, skin dyer, 23 Wilson street, Finsbury square
Apprenticeship Society, 7 Blomfield st. Finsbury
Apps Wm.&Co.coal merchts.Western whf.George st.Adelphi
Apps Charles,umbrellamaker,15Mansell st.Goodman's fields
Apps Danl. grocer & cheesemonger, 4Woburn ct.Bloomsbury
Apps James, picture dealer, 21 Pembroke pl. Vauxhall rd
Apps Robert, coffee rooms, 2 Calthorpe pl. Gray's inn road
Apps Thomas, coachmaker, 92 Blackfriars road
Apps William, tailor, 243½ Strand
Apsey Joseph, baker, 9 Waterloo road
Apsey Joseph, engineer, 10 Catherine st. Cornwall road
Apted George, baker, 15 Baker's row, Whitechapel road
Apted Susan (Mrs.),cheesmongr.41&42 Broad st.Bloomsbury
Apted Wm. bootmaker, 4 Norland road, Notting hill
Apted William, fishmonger, 28 Brewer st. Golden square
Arabin William, undertaker, 16 Kenton st. Brunswick sq
Arber Thomas, builder, 91½ Newman st. Oxford st
Arber Thomas, surveyor, &c. 29A, Brook st. Grosvenor sq
Arbery Sarah (Mrs.), bootmaker, 4 Windmill st. Finsbury
Arbouin & Butcher (late Samuel Arbouin), wine & spirit brokers, 21 Mark lane, Fenchurch st
Arbouin James, wine & brandy merc. see Allnutts & Arbouin
Arbuthnot, Latham & Co. merchts. 5½ Gt. St. Helen's passage
Arbuthnot & M'Combice, paper makers, 30 Walbrook
Arch John, carpenter, 2 Cornwall road, Lambeth
Archæological Institute of Gt. Britain & Ireland, (Albert Way, esq. hon. sec.) 12 Haymarket
Archard Matthew, carman, 1 Gould square, Crutched friars
Archbell & Hewland, sailmakers, ship chandlers, rope ma. & imp. of coir cordage, 105 Wapping, opposite Gun dock
Archbishop Tenison's Schools, 42 Castle st. Leicester sq.; Chapel pl. 172 Regent st. 4 & 18 High st. Lambeth
Archbold John Fredk. barrister, 4 King's bench walk,Temple
Archbutt John, grocer & ita. wa. 24 Motcomb st. Belgrave sq
Archbutt John, grocer, 26 Victoria road, Pimlico
Archbutt John, pawnbroker, &c. 20 Bridge road, Lambeth
Archbutt Robert, builder, Manor st. Chelsea
Archbutt Robert, pawnbroker, 109 & 110 Blackfriars road
Archbutt Samuel, solicitor, 9 Sloane square, Chelsea
Archbutt Samuel, jun. solicitor, 9 Sloane square, Chelsea
Archdeacon of London's Court, 10 Gt. Knightrider st
Archdeacon of Middlesex Office, 3 Godliman st
Archdeacon of Rochester's Registry, 19 Bennett's hill
Archdeacon of Surrey's Registry, 3 Paul's chain
Archdeacon Elizh.(Mrs.),fur.brkr. 2Constable rw.Mile end rd
Archer & Cressall, brass founders, finishers & gasfitters, 10 Horse shoe alley, Wilson st. Finsbury
Archer Francis & Co. blacking manufacturers, Old Ford
Archer George & Co. coach curriers, 21 Gerrard st. Soho
Archer Henry & Co.plumbers, 15 Bulstrode st.Manchester sq
Archer James & Son, tailors, 35 Charlotte st. Whitechapel
Archer Jane (Mrs.) & Sons, tobacconists, 1Broadway,Westm
Archer John & Peter, silk mfrs. 16 Steward st. Spitalfields
Archer, Perry&Archer,silk dressers & waterers,23Worship st
Archer & Taverner,paper stainers, 141 & 142Old st. St.Luke's
Archer Archibald, artist, 31 Liverpool st. King's cross
Archer EdwardWm.*MoneyersArms*P.H.28Provost st.City rd
Archer Edwin, chemist, 1 Upper King street, Holborn
Archer Elisha, stationer, 25 Frederick pl. Hampstead rd
Archer Elizh. (Mrs.), ship biscuit baker, 73 Lower Thames st
Archer Frederick, surgeon, 3 Chapel st. Grosvenor place
Archer Frederick S. artist, 18 Tavistock st. Covent garden
Archer George, attorney, 17 Harpur st. Red lion sq
Archer Henry, potato dealer, 31 George st. Blackfriars road
Archer Henry Goodwyn, barrister, 8 King's bench walk
Archer Henry Thomas, solicitor, 33 Gracechurch st. City
Archer Isaac, tailor, 27 Tichborne st. Haymarket
Archer James, baker, 71 King st. Deptford
Archer James, bootmaker, 1 Brook's row, Bagnigge wells rd
Archer James, carpenter, &c. 9 Cullum st. Fenchurch st
Archer Jessie (Miss), milliner, see Puddiphat, Archer & Hunt
Archer John, artist, 46 Clarendon st. Somers town
Archer John, baker & flour factor, 3 High Holborn
Archer John, linendraper, 71 Bunhill row
Archer John, *Pewter Platter* P.H. 10 Cock hill, Ratcliff
Archer John, regr. & cabinetmaker, 22 Banner st. St. Luke's
Archer John, window glass, oil & color mer. 115 Fore st. City
Archer John S. tallow melter, &c. see Cuthberts' & Archer
Archer John Tracey, ironmonger, 80 Cable st. Wellclose sq
Archer Joshua, engr. & prin. 2 Southampton terr. Pentonvil
Archer Robert, cutler, 3 Cumberland st. west, Regent's pk
Archer Robert, who. tea & coffee dealer, 93 Gt. Tower st
Archer Samuel Wm. clock & watch mak. Mare st. Hackney
Archer Sarah (Mrs.), *Ship* P.H. 32½ Gray's inn lane
Archer Sarah (Mrs.), *Old Three Colts* P.H. Old Ford
ArcherSophia(Mrs.),strawbonnetma.18Abbey st.Bthnl.gn.rd
Archer Thomas, tailor, 7 Tysoe st. Clerkenwell
Archer Thomas Henry, plumber, 65 Park st. Grosvenor sq
Archer William, bookseller, 88 Berwick st. Soho
Archer William, bricklayer, King st. Commercial rd. east
Archer William, carrier, see Deacon & Archer
Archer William, clockmaker, 20 Banner st. St. Luke's
Archer William, coffee rooms, 4 Surry place, Walworth rd
Archer William, flour factor, 177 Upper Thames st
Archer William, surgeon, 1 Montagu st. Portman square
Archer William, undertaker, 7 & 11 Church st. Rotherhithe
Archer William, wine & spirit merchant, 12 Mincing la. City
Archer Wm. Clare, grocer, 1 Dalgleish pl. Limehouse fields
Archer Wm. Hen. saw & tool maker, 11 Goodge st. Fitzroy sq
Arches Registry Office, 20 Gt. Knightrider st. hours 10 to 4
Archibald James, baker, 1 New Norfolk st. Lower rd. Islngtn
Archibald Thomas D. special pleader, 12 Paper bldgs.Temple
Archibell Charles, tailor, 10 Hosier lane, West Smithfield
Arden Joseph, barrister, 17 Cavendish square
Arding Jas.&Son,printers'joiners&bldrs.62Dorset st.Salisb.sq
Arding James, builder, 2 Water st. Blackfriars
Arding Thomas, boot & shoe maker, 56 Lambeth walk
Ardley Abraham,carpen.builder & undertak.11Gt.St.Helen's
Ardley Wm. coffee rooms, 12 Bluecross st. Leicester sq
Arene Auguste, hairdresser, 40 Manchester st. Manchester sq
Aresti Joseph, lithographer, 56 Greek st. Soho
Argent Ann (Mrs.), livery stables, 3½ Claremont pl. Pentonv
Argent Chas. Frdk.japanner, 19Lower Northampton st.Clkwl
Argent Edward, coach builder, 3 Claremont pl. Pentonville
Argent Henry, furniture japanner, 84 Long alley, Finsbury
Argent James, *Cock & Bottle* P.H. 83 Strand
Argent James, naturalist, 32 Bishopsgate without
Argent Joseph, fruiterer, 17 Bethnal green
Argent William, builder, 7 Seabright place, Hackney road
Argent William, plumber & glazier, 35 Church lane, Limehouse; & 27 Three Colt st. Limehouse
Argenti, Sechiari & Co. merchants, 43 Finsbury circus, & 3 Albion place, London wall
Argles Frank Atkinson, solicitor, see Walker, Grant & Co
Argus Life Assurance Co. Ed. Bates,res.dir.39 Thrgmtn. st
Ariel James, *Rent Day* P.H. 4 Cambridge st. Edgware rd
Ariell John, watch movement ma. 11 Perceval st.Clerkenwell
Ariell Sam. bookkeeper & account. 15 Maiden la. Covt. gdn
Arigna Iron Co.(N.S.Price,res. dir.) 9Liverpool st. Bishpsgt
Aris John, cattle salesman, 41 West Smithfield
Ariss Thomas, greengrocer, &c. 23 South st. Manchester sq
Arkell William, merchant, 11 Mark lane
Arkwright & Co. cotton spinners, 5 Dyer's court, Aldermnby
Arle Chas. fancy cabinet maker, 16 Whitmore rd, Hoxton
Armagh, Coleraine, & Portrush Railway Co. (Thomas Wm. Younghusband, secretary), 28 Threadneedle street
Armand Clement, printer, 46 Rathbone place, Oxford st
Armani Antoine N.&Co. merchants, 1 Scots yard, Gt. Bush la
Armer Fras. tea dealer & grocer, 43 Clarence st. Rotherhite
Armes Ann (Miss), confectioner, Mile end rd. op. Trinity gr
Armfield Geo. artist, 15 Princes st. Stamford st. Blkfrs rd
Armfield Joseph, butcher, 6, Brook st. Grosvenor square
Armfield Saml. lathe & tool ma. 10 Gt. St.Andrew st. 7 dials
Armfield Wm. ivory turner, 34 New Church st. Lisson grove
Arminger Rt. silk,cotton& woollen dyer,8 Mill st.Hanoversq
Armistead Alfred, notary, 28 Clement's lane, Lombard st
ArmisteadMary(Miss),baby lin.dlr.10 Crawfordst.Portmn.sq
Armitage Bros.woollen manufs.(J.Taylor,ag.),49Moorgate st
Armitage Benj. brush maker & cooper, Church st. Hackney
Armitage Edward, artist, 14 George st. Adelphi
Armitage Elizh. (Mrs.),tobacnst.2Brydges st. Coventgarden
Armitage Frederick, tailor, 60 Brook st. Lambeth
Armitage Joseph, paper hanger, 7 Orchard pl. Kingsland rd
Armitage Robert, baker, 290 Strand
Armitage Thos.bootmaker,31Shoemakers' row, Doctors' com
Armitage Wm. George,auctioneer,&c.14 Broadway,Deptford
Armitage Wm. Jos. plumber, Church st. Stoke Newington
Armitstead Henry, plater, 3 Hill st. Finsbury
Armour Philip, tailor, 12 Little Chapel st. Soho
Armourers' & Braziers' Alms Houses (John Pontifex,sec.), Britannia place, 184 & 185 Bishopsgate without
Armourers' & Braziers' Hall(J.Pontifex clk.),81Coleman st
Armsby Robert, carpenter, &c. 3 Little St. Thomas Apostle
Armson Francis, survey. & build. 22 Orchard st. Portman sq
Armstead Charles, oilman, 22 Foxley rd. CamberwellNew rd
Armstrong Chas.&Co. west india mers. 4 Finch lane,Cornhill
Armstrong Nicholas H. & Co. upholsterers' warehousemen, 11 Brewer street, Golden square

Armstrong & Jones, solicitors, 38 Red Lion square
Armstrong & Smith, builders, 15 Gillingham street, Pimlico; 85 Baker street, Portman square; & Savoy st. Strand
Armstrong Abraham, accountant, auctioneer, &c. 20 Lawrance lane, Cheapside; & Castle court, Cheapside
Armstrong Charles, hop merchant, see Jones & Armstrong
Armstrong Chas. oil wareh. 1 Heathpl.Commercial rd. East
Armstrong Charlt. (Mrs), who. potter, 8 Cock hill, Ratcliff
Armstrong Christopher, surgeon, 7 Tyndale pl. Islington
Armstrong Christ. surgeon, see Jeaffreson, Armstrong & Co
Armstrong Edmund, grocer, 6 Claremont place, Old Kent rd
Armstrong Elizh. (Mrs). oil & color wa. 67Chandosst.Cov.gar
Armstrong Elizabeth (Mrs.), tailor, &c. 12 St George street
Armstrong Francis, farrier, 13 Little Chapel st. Westminster
Armstrong George, oil & colorman, 62 Leather lane, Holborn; 23 High street, Islington; 47 Fore street, Cripplegate; & 1 Ann's terrace, Liverpool road
Armstrong George Hillas, surgeon, 10 York st. St. James's
Armstrong George Walford, solicitor, 33 Old Jewry
Armstrong Hen. grocer & biscuitbaker, 27 & 28 Wappingwall
Armstrong Hen. Stephen, oilman, 10 Munster st. Regent's pk
Armstrong Herman Harbusch, copper & brass worker, see Hopwood & Armstrong
Armstrong Isaac, saddle & harness makers' ironmonger, coach founder & plater, 35 & 36 King street, Snow hill
Armstrong John, beer retailer, 87 Devonshirest. Lisson grove
Armstrong John, coffee rooms, 63 Stanhope st. Clare market
Armstrong Joseph, cabinet maker, 21 Sherrard st. Golden sq
Armstrong Richard Baynes, attorney, 8 Staple inn, Holborn
Armstrong Robert, oilman, 15 Gray's inn lane
Armstrong Robt.plasterer&modeller, 24 Herculesbldgs. Lamb
Armstrong Rt. Baynes, queen's counsel, 2 Cloisters, Temple
Armstrong Samuel, cowkeeper, 23 Windmill st. Tott. ct. rd
Armstrong Thomas, bookbinder, 23 Villiers st. Strand
Armstrong Thomas, coal merchant, see Capper & Armstrong
Armstrong Wm.boot&shoemkr.10Catherine st. Comml. rd.Ea
Armstrong Wm. plumber, &c. 29 South st. Manchester sq
Armstrong Wm. tailor, &c. 4 Wigmore st. Cavendish sq
Armstrong Wm. James, upholsterer, 1 Church st. Cambrwl
Armstrong Wm. Jas. upholsterer, 4 Southampton st.Cambrwl
Armstrong Wm. Jones, barrister, 4 Elm court, Temple
Army Medical Board Office (Thos. Tanner, secretary), 13 St. James's place, St. James's; hours 10 to 4
Army Medical Officers' Benevolent Society (Thos. Tanner, sec.), 13 St. James's place, St. James's; hours 10 to 4
Army Medical Officers' Friendly Society (Thos. Tanner, sec.), 13 St. James's place, St. James's
Army & Navy Club House (T. Walcot, sec.), 20 St.James's sq
Arnall James, tobacconist, 5 Lower road, Islington
Arnall Joseph, butcher, 5 Stepney rents, Hackney road
Arnall Robert, livery stables, Elm tree road, St. John's wood
Arnatt James, grocer, 107 Praed st. Edgware road
Arnaud John, court plumasier, 27 Gt. Portland st. Oxford st
Arnell Dennis, jeweller, 39 Skinner st. Clerkenwell
Arnell John, corn & coal mer. 9 Stanhope st. Hampstead rd
Arnell John, sen. clock maker, 12 St. James's st. Clerkenwell
Arnell John, jun. watchmaker, 16 Chapel st. New road
Arnett Charles, tobacconist, 355 Oxford street
Arnett Frances (Mrs.), milliner. 2 High st. Newington Butts
Arnett Henry, tobacconist, 324 Oxford st. & 10 High Holborn
Arnett John, custom house agent, 8 St. Dunstan's hill
Arnett Richard George, silver engraver, see Rose & Arnett
Arnett Thomas B. gold cutter, &c.17 Sekforde st. Clerknwll
Arney George, undertaker, see Turner & Arney
Arney Geo. Alfred, barrister, Temple chmbs. 126 Chancery la
Arney Hector William, solicitor, 34 George st. Hanover sq
Arnison William, carpenter, 52 Marsham st. Westminster
Arnold & Frodsham, chronometer, watch & clockmakers, 84 Strand
Arnold George & Thomas, pawnbrokers, 188 Shoreditch
Arnold Hen.&Rt.fruit & potato salesmn.Mill la.&Sptfids.mkt
Arnold Pickard & John, wholes. druggists, 135 Aldersgate st
Arnold & Roxberry, perfumers, &c. 20 Kensington High st
Arnold Thos. &Co.booksellers &publishers, 53 Paternoster rw
Arnold Augustus Walter, attorney, 31 Golden square
Arnold Chas. tobacconist, 2 Melville ter. Caledonian road
Arnold Charles, who. tea dealer, 1 Cullum st. Fenchurch st
Arnold Ebenezer, printer, 37 Tabernacle walk, Finsbury
Arnold Elizabeth (Mrs), coal dlr. 15 Coleman st. buildings
Arnold Elizabeth (Mrs.), dress maker, 4 Buryst. Bloomsbury
Arnold Frederick, manufctrng. perfumer, 9 Budge row, City
Arnold Frederick, stationer, 9 Budge row, Cannon st. City
Arnold Frederick, tea dealer, 42 Ruffords bldgs. Islington
Arnold George, cabinet ma.&ho.agt.1 Michael's pl.Brompton
Arnold George, fruiterer, 38 Henry st. east, Avenue road
Arnold George, glover, 72 Berners street, Oxford st
Arnold George, grocer & teadealer, 49 Cross st. Islington
Arnold George, hat manufacturer, 57 Cheapside, & 1 Bow la
Arnold George, smith, 5 Trafalgar street, Walworth rd
Arnold George, tailor, &c. 49 Cross street, Islington
Arnold Harriet (Mrs.), artist, 2 Up. Gloucester st. Dorset sq
Arnold Hen. booksell. & statr. 45 Marchmont st. Brunswk.sq
Arnold James, cheesemonger, 344 Rotherhithe
Arnold Jas.surgicl.inst.mkr.&truss mfr.&inst.ma.to the royal veterinary coll. & dlr. in druggists' sundrs. 35 West Smithfi
Arnold James, tailor, 24 London st. Fitzroy square
Arnold Jane (Mrs.), leatherseller, 141 Gt. Suffolk st. Boro'
Arnold John, fishmonger, 7 Cannon st. road Commer. road
Arnold John, house painter, see Chittenden & Arnold
Arnold John, house painter, 25 London st. Fitzroy square
Arnold John, linen draper, 350 Oxford street
Arnold John, *Old King's Hd.* P.H. 1 Palace row, New road
Arnold John, plane, saw & tool maker, 2 High st. St. Giles'
Arnold Joseph, fancy toy wareho. 38 King William st. City
Arnold Joseph, ship & custom house agent, Morgan's lane, Tooley street; & 43 Charles st. Horselydown
Arnold Joseph Hayman, ship&ins.agt.3Clement's la.Lombd.st
Arnold Joseph W. ham&beef shop, 34 Hi.Holborn & 77 Long ac
Arnold Mary (Mrs.), ham & beef dealer, 19 Gracechurch st. & 66 Watling street
Arnold Mary A. (Mrs.), mus.inst.ma.15 Margaret st.Hackney
Arnold Matilda (Mrs.), furn. brok. 3 Sun tavern fi. St. Geo.ea
Arnold Sarah (Mrs.), baker, 135 Kent st. Borough
Arnold Thomas, baker, 8 St. Geo. st. Albany rd. Old Kent rd
Arnold Thomas, *Grapes* P.H. 41 Bread street, Cheapside
Arnold Thomas, straw hat warehouse, 69A, Lisson grove Nrth. & 97 Devonshire st. Lisson grove
Arnold Thomas James, barrister, 12 Serjeants' inn, Fleet st
Arnold Wm. butcher, 305 Rotherhithe street
Arnold Wm. dyer & scourer, 18 Greenhills rents, Smithfield
Arnold Wm. house & commission agt. 82 Regent st. Lambeth
Arnold Wm. rag &bottle dealer, 18 Lit.Guilford st.Brunswk.sq
Arnold Wm. rag & bottle dealer, 4 Darby pl. Jermyn st
Arnold Wm. shoe warehouse, 145 Church st. Shoreditch
Arnold Wm. Hen. linendraper, 2 Wharf rise, Kingsland road
Arnold Wm. John, wine broker, Coml.coffee ho. Mincing lane
Arnold Wm. John Delancey, coal mer. Norway wf. Millbank st
Arnott Henry, brushmaker, 11 Brewer st. north, Goswell rd
Arnott James Moncrieff, surgeon, 2 New Burlington street
Arnott Neil, physician, 38 Bedford square
Arnott Wm. bookbinder, 39 St. Andrew's hill, Doctors' com
Arnould Joseph, barrister, 10 Farrar's buildings, Temple
Arnull & Allender, stock brokers, 6 Bank chambs. Lothbury
Arnum William, academy, 18 Upper Belgrave place, Pimlico
Arpin John, haircutter & perfumer, 16 Crown ct. Pall mall
Arpthorp & Clark, grocers, 17 Clarendon sq. Somers town
Arpthorp Frances& Sarah, staymakers, 37 Bishopsgate within
Arpthorp William, surgeon, 3 Princes st. Leicester square
Arrah Henry, cheesemonger, 81 St. John st. Clerkenwell
Arrend Matthew, boot&shoe mkr. 50 Henry st.east, Avenue rd
Arrend Nicholas, boot maker, 1A, Up. Glo'ster st.Dorset sq
Arrington Wm. beer retailer, 5 Fields place, Lock's fields
Arrow John Hen. upholder, appraiser, &c. 5 Cowley st. Westm
Arrowsmith Hen.& Arthur, house decorators, 80 New Bond st
Arrowsmith Chas. jun. solicitor, 40 Devonshire st. Queen sq
Arrowsmith Jas. wine cooper & bottle mer. 2&3 Finsbury mkt
Arrowsmith John, hydrographer to the Queen, 10 Soho sq
Arrowsmith Thos. *Golden Anchor* P.H. 17 Coppice rw. Clknwl
Arrowsmith Thomas, tailor, 79 Berwick st. Soho
Arrowsmith Wm. brace & belt maker, 173 Aldersgate st
Arroyave Anselmo de, mercht. 16 George st. Mansion house
Art Union (monthly publication), 186 Strand
Art Union of London (George Godwin, esq. F.R.S. Lewis Pocock, esq. F.S.A. hon. secretaries, & Thomas S. Watson, assistant sec.), 4 Trafalgar square, Charing cross
Artaria Henry, dealer in works of art, 18 Golden square
Arscott Richard, teadealer, 56 Kingsland road
Artaud Wm. & Steph. upholsterers, 79 Wimpole st.Cavend.sq
Arter Charles, timber mercht. Queen's gardens, Brompton
Arter Omer, grocer, Church st. Deptford
Arthaud Henry, dairyman, 5 Mead's court, Old Bond st
Arthur's Club house (Jas. Milner, sec.), 69 St. James's st
Arthur & Belsham, boot & shoe warehouse, 128 Edgware rd
Arthur Ann (Mrs.), fringe & trimming maker, 4 Little Portland st. & 34 Maddox st. Regent st
Arthur Henry, manchester agent, 6 Bread st. City
Arthur Hy. Massey, pro. of music, 41 Charles st. Commercl.rd.E
Arthur James, corn &coal merc.2 Manifold pl.Kennington la
Arthur John, *Sir John Falstaff* P.H. 140 Kent st. Borough
Arthur John, surgeon, 164 Shadwell High st
Arthur Joseph, surgeon, High st. Deptford
Arthur Robt. who. leather&shoe wareh. 17 Wilson st. Finsbury

Arthur Thomas, paperhanger, decorator, &c. to the Queen, 3 Sackville st. Piccadilly
Arthur William, baker, 27 Peter st. Soho
Artillery & Armoury house, Artillery place, Finsbury
Artindale John, baker, 25 Cannon st. road, St. George's East
Artis Charles Dillon, poulterer, 16 Motcomb st. Belgrave sq
Artis Zachariah, zinc, tin & iron plate ma.269 PoplarHigh st
Artists' Gen. Ben. Fund Ins.(Wm. Roper, sec.)32Sackville st
ArtlettChas.carpet planner&upholst.23 Greville st.Hat.gard
Artlett David, baker, 31 Lower Sloane st
Artlett Henry, upholsterer, 28 Kenton st. Brunswick sq
Artlett Job, eating house, 12 High road, Knightsbridge
ArtúsJosé&Co.cigar importers, 3Duncannon st.Trafalgar sq. & 4 Opera colonnade, Pall mall
Arum James, fruiterer, 10 Arabella row, Pimlico
Arundale John, grocer, 40 Church rd. Commercial rd. East
Arundel Gerard, tobacconist, 60 Paradise row, Chelsea
Arundel James, upholsterer, 255½ Whitechapel road
Arundel John, silk manufr. see Henderson, Arundel & Co
Arundel Matthew, tailor, 68 Coleshill st. Eaton square
Arundell Hen.&Renfric, wine mers. 60 Mount st. Berkeley sq
Arundell John & Son, carpenters & undert. 14 St. George st
Arundell Charles Francis, solicitor, 3 Cork st. Bond st
Arundell Hy. timber mer. &lath render, 6Webber st.Blkfr.rd
ArundellWm.carpenter, 13 Wellington pl. Back rd.St.Geo.ea
Asals William, cabinet maker, 230 Whitechapel road
AsamTeaCompany(Richard Allen Cue, manager), 11Crooked lane, King William st. London bridge
AsberreyWm. fringe & trimming ma.2Abbey st. Bethnl.gr.rd
Asbridge Wm.Orton, *Coach&Horses* P.H.9 Grafton ct.Mrylb
Asby William, wholesale teadealer, 47 Watling street
Ascott Henry, dining rooms, 29 Seymour pl. Bryanstone sq
Ascott John, dining rooms, 38 Upper Marylebone st
Ascott Thomas, wheelwright, Lower road, Rotherhithe
Ascroft Thomas H. haircutter, 35 Paradise row, Chelsea
Asdell Thomas, furniture broker, 5Dorset pl. Pall mall east
AshClaudius&Sons, mineral teeth ma.8 & 9Broad st.Golden sq
Ash John & Sons, schoolmasters, 8 Cumming st. Pentonville
Ash Lawrence Williams & Co. corn & coal merchants, 53 & 54 White Lion st. Pentonville, & 4 Henry st. Pentonville
Ash & Lewin, woollendrapers & mercers, 110 Regent st
Ash Abraham, staymaker, 29 St. Martin's ct. Leicester sq
Ash Elizabeth (Mrs.), corset maker, 29 St. Martin's court, Leicester square, & 25A, Crawford st. Portman square
Ash Frederick, heraldic engraver, 23 Frith st. Soho
Ash George, dentist, 15 Great Marlborough street
Ash Henry, staymaker, 52 Mount st. Lambeth
Ash James Bryern, carpenter, 8 Belmont row, Vauxhall
Ash Lewis, engineer & millwright, 39 Oakley st. Lambeth
Ash Neville, merchant & insurance broker, see Ross & Ash
Ash Richard Holland, barrister, 6 Gray's inn square
Ash Robert, beer retailer, High st. Battersea
Ash Robt. engravr. printer & stationr. 5 Wellington st. Boro'
AshSarah(Mrs.), coal mercht.22 Smith st.King's rd. Chelsea
AshWalter, engineer & machinist, 4Lit.Mitchell st. St.Luke's
Ash William, boot & shoe maker, 24 Jewin st. Cripplegate
Ash Wm. Leigh, beer retailer, 31 Bear lane, Blackfriars rd
Ashbee Richd. & Wm. lamp makers, 18 Broad ct. Long acre
Ashbey James, window blind maker, 12 High row, Knightsbr
Ashbey John, windowblind maker7 Prince's pl. Coml. rd. East
Ashbey Thomas, blind ma.1High st.Portlnd tn.&Knightsbdge
Ashbey Wm. window blind ma. 9 Alfred pl. Newington caus
Ashbolt William, ale merchant, 22 Sloane square
Ashbridge John Simpson, pawnbroker, 101 Broad st. Ratcliff
Ashbridge John Simpson, pawnbroker, 2 Park pl.Mile end rd
Ashburner John, physician, 55 Wimpole st. Cavendish sq
Ashburner Robert, lodging house, 6 Castle st. Falcon sq
Ashbury Christophr. Hen. law statnr. 8 Hemlock ct.Careyst
Ashby & Co. engravers, printers, & bankers' agents, 79 King William st. City
Ashby Skidmore & John, groat&pearl barley makers, Horseshoe wharf, 10 Upper Thames street
Ashby Wm. & Co. roman cement and plaster of paris manfs. (J. Winkfield, agent), 41 Upper Thames street
Ashby Edwd. oil, italian, &brit.winewa.1&2 Old Broad st.City
Ashby Elizabeth (Mrs.), dairy, 5 Fonthill place, Clapham rd
Ashby Henry, builder, see Bridger & Ashby
Ashby Henry, grocer, 42 Lambeth walk
Ashby Ishmael Wm. baker, 2 Brunswick. ter. Barnsbury rd
Ashby Ishmael William, baker, 50 Goswell street
Ashby James Bennett, baker, Well street, Hackney
Ashby Jane (Mrs.), baker, 134 St. Alban's place, Edgware rd
Ashby John, carver & gilder, 14 Old Compton st. Soho
Ashby John, upholsterer, 17 West st. Seven dials
Ashby Joseph, fruit merchant, 9 Botolph lane, City
Ashby Mark, boot & shoe maker, 13 Sale st. Paddington
Ashby Richard, carpenter & builder, 24Bishopsgate without
Ashby Robert, cattle salesman, 60 West Smithfield
Ashby Wm. sen. baker, 19 Glo'ster st. St. John st. road
Ashby Wm.carpenter & undertaker, 36 Lower Kennington la
Ashcombe Wm.&Thos. Phillips, surgeons, 89 Gracechurch st
Ashcombe George, butcher, 8 High st. Notting hill
Ashcraft Wm. bootmaker, 9 Brydges st. Covent garden
Ashcroft Joseph, painter, 99 Hill st. Walworth road
Ashcroft Wm. sen. cooper, Butcher row, Ratcliff
Ashdown & Collinson, saddlers, 46 Gt. Marylebone st
Ashdown Charles, watchmaker, Stratford broadway
Ashdown Edward, fruit salesman, Covent garden fruit mrkt
Ashdown George, baker, 30 Cable st. Wellclose square
Ashdown George, tailor, 9 Basing lane, Bread st. Cheapside
Ashdown Henry, turner, &loom ma.23 Anchor st.Shoreditch
Ashdown Robert, coffee rooms, 16½ Castle st. Leicester sq
Asher Adolphus, foreign bookseller, 158 Fleet st. & Berlin
Asher Isaac Benj. clothes salesman, 2 Hanover pl. Minories
Ashfield & Clode, solicitors, 7 Staple inn, Holborn
Ashfield William, bricklayer, 3 Bayne's row, Coldbath fields
Ashfield William, bricklayer, 73 Red Lion st. Clerkenwell
Ashfield Wm. T. engraver & printer, 6 Church st. Lambeth
Ashford Charles, teadealer & grocer, 38 Bow lane, Cheapside
Ashford James, butcher, 12 Norland road, Notting hill
Ashford James, coffee rooms, 67 Shoe lane
Ashford John, builder & undertaker, High st. Deptford
Ashford Richard Henry, pawnbroker, 41 Bethnal green rd
Ashford Thos. Fras. merchant, 5 Salvador Ho. Bishopsgate
Ashford Wm. chinadealer&undertkr.22 Eastst.Manchestersq
Ashley Elizabeth Mrs. & Co. teadealers & grocers, 15 Strand
Ashley & Watts, solrs. Lord Mayor's court off. 7 Old Jewry
Ashley Wm. & David, carpenters, &c. 9 Duke st.Bishopsgate
Ashley hon. John Anthony, barrister, 3 Newsq. Lincoln's inn
Ashley Charles Henry, wine mercht. 3 Suffolk la. Cannon st
Ashley Edward, escapement maker, see Manser & Ashley
Ashley Edward fur. ironmonger, 21 Frederick st.Gray's innrd
Ashley Edward, watchmaker, 17 Chapel st. Pentonville
Ashley George, teadealer & grocer, 72 Piccadilly
Ashley Hannah (Mrs.), milliner, High st. Kingsland
Ashley Henry, solicitor, 9 Shoreditch & Hackney
Ashley Isaac, tailor, 17 Leigh st. Burton crescent
Ashley James, accountant & general agent, 14 Craven street, Strand; & 3 Gloucester place, New road
Ashley James, pewterer, 131 Minories
Ashley James, stationer, 13 Chandos st. Covent garden
Ashley John, jun. bricklayer, 11 Clayton pl. Kennington rd
Ashley Robt. potato dealer, 21 & 22 Strutton ground, Westm
Ashley Robt. Hen. *Ashley's hotel*, 30&31 Maiden la. Cov. gdn
Ashley Thomas, teadealer, 43 Great hall, Hungerford markt
Ashley Thos. Jas. T. pewterer, & *Jolly Coopers* P.H. 1 & 2 Short's buildings, Clerkenwell close
Ashley Wm. Thos. whfingr. Stonestairs wf. Broad st. Ratcliff
Ashlin John & Sons, cornfactors, 50 Mark lane
Ashlin William, plumber & glazier, 37 Clerkenwell close
Ashman James & Son, pawnbrs. & silversmiths, 65Long acre
Ashman Caleb, locksmith & bellhang. 91 Fetter la. Holborn
Ashman Charles, tailor, 69 Chancery lane
Ashman George, bookbinder, 3 Cherrytree court, Aldersgate
Ashmead Charles & Co. hatters, 7 Mount st. Berkeley sq
Ashmead Charles, hatter, 22 Davies st. Berkeley square
Ashmead Geo. Benj. brush ma. ivory turner, military & navy cockade maker & naturalist, 10 Duke st. Grosvenor sq
Ashmole John, merchant, Old Trinity house, Water lane
Ashmore Thomas & Sons, merchants, 15 Crosby hall chmbrs
Ashmore Elizb.(Mrs.), *WhiteBear* P.H. Lambeth st.Goodm.fl
Ashmore James, barrister, 3(north) King'sBench wk.Temple
Ashmore Wm. beer retailer, 15 Bartholomew sq. St. Luke's
Ashpited Arthur, architect, 5 Crown court, Old Broad st
Ashplant Thomas, coffee rooms, 36 Weston st. Somers town
Ashpole John, grocer, 68 Ossulston st. Somers town
Ashton & Evans, cheesemongers, 5 Park st. Borough
Ashton Geo. & Son, cattle salesmen, 60 West Smithfield
Ashton Herbert & Co. who. button wa. 76 Aldermanbury
Ashton Josh.&Sons.hat makers & inventors of the light elastic waterproof hat, 54 & 55 Cornwall rd. Waterloo bridge
Ashton Margt.&Charlte. straw bonnet manfs.42Cannon st.rd
Ashton Alfred, staymaker, 6½ Hanway st. Oxford st
Ashton Ann (Mrs.), tobacconist, 41 Mount st. Berkeley sq
Ashton Arthur, fur. undertaker, 83 Union st. Lambeth walk
Ashton Edmund, shoemaker, 47½ Hackney road
Ashton Francis, teadealer, 36 City road, Finsbury square
Ashton George, tobacconist, 2 Clarence pl. Camberwell road
Ashton Henry, architect, 50 Brook st. Grosvenor square
Ashton Henry, sculptor, 92 Piccadilly
Ashton Hy. Geo. paperhanging ma. 7 River st.Myddelton sq
Ashton Isabella(Mrs.), gunma.Swallow'sgrdn.Goodman'sflds

Ashton Job, corn&salt mer.2 Bridge pl.& 34Wharf rd.City rd
Ashton LouisaMaria(Mrs.),hotel keeper,seeBryant&Ashton
Ashton Mary (Mrs.), boarding house, 22 Cloak la.Cheapside
Ashton Richard, merchant, 3 White Lion court, Cornhill
Ashton Robt. John, attorney, 2 Pelham crescent, Brompton
Ashton Samuel, beer retailer, Ord st. Millwall
Ashton Sam.blacking ma.39 MiddleGrove st.Comml.rd.East
Ashton Sophia (Mrs.), boarding house, 1 Little Distaff lane
Ashton Sophia (Miss), dressma. 35 Gt.Alie st. Goodmn's flds
Ashton Thomas, corndealer, 13 Harrow road
Ashton Thomas, shipbroker&auctionr.9 George yd.Lombd.st
Ashton Thomas, statuary, &c. 29 Marylebone st. Piccadilly
Ashton Thomas, *White Bear* P. H. 15 Bride lane, Fleet st
Ashton Wm. undertaker, 63 Collier st. Pentonville
Ashton William, wireworker, 245 Oxford st
Ashurst & Son, solicitors, 48 Moorgate st. Lothbury
Ashurst William Henry, solicitor, 137 Cheapside
Ashurst Wm. Henry, jun. solicitor, 137 Cheapside
Ashwell & Paul, silkdyers, 11 Old Paradise row, Islington gr
Ashwell Mary (Mrs.), cowkeeper, 27 Hertford st. Fitzroy sq
Ashwell Samuel, physician, 16 Grafton st. Bond st
AshwellThomas,*RedHart*P.H.20&*Black Dog*P.H.83Shoela
Ashwin Richard Chas.chemist, 5 Up. Penton st. Pentonville
Ashwood Fredk. painter & decor. 11 Sherborne st. Blandfd sq
Ashworth Frederick Harold, barrister, 1 Paper buildings
Ashworth Emily (Mrs.), greengroc. 13 Glo'ster st.St.Jn st.rd
Ashworth Robt. grocer, 1 Hargrave pl. Bermondsey New rd
Ashworth Thos. cabinet ma. 1Gt.Turner st.Commerl.rd.East
Askew Edward, bootmaker, 6 Great St. Helen's
Askew Edward, butcher, 1 Cumberland row, King's cross
Askew John, linendraper, & carpet wareh. 110 Blackman st
Askey John, fruit salesman, Borough market
Aslet Andrew, fishmonger, 289 Oxford st
Aslett John, baker, 74 Newington causeway
Aslett Wm. cowkeeper, 19 Shouldham st. Bryanstone sq
Aslin Mary (Mrs.), morocco case mak. 35 Clerkenwell close
Aspden Andrew, coffee rooms, 4 London wall, City
Aspenlon Francis & Son, hat dyers, 89 Union st. Borough
Asperne Wm. Dent (manager of eastern branch of London & Westminster bank), 87 High st. Whitechapel
Asphalte of Seyssel Company (Claridge's patent), (J.Farrell, secretary), Stangate, Lambeth
Aspin William, carman, 7 Morgan's lane, Tooley st
Aspinall John Bridger, barrister, 11 Paper buildings, Temple
Aspinall Paul, stone merchant, Crown wharf, New North road bridge, Hoxton
Aspinwall James, upholsterer & cabinet maker, & manufr. of Dr. Arnott's hydrostatic beds, 70 Grosvenor st. Bond st
Aspland Algernon Sydney, sp. pleader, 4 Lamb bdg. Temple
Aspland William, bricklayer, 1 Porter's place, Holloway
Asplin William, hairdresser & perfumer, 13 New Bond st
Asprey Charles, stationer, see Kennedy & Asprey
Asprey Frederic, solicitor, 6 Furnival's inn, Holborn
Assam Comp. (Walter Prideaux, sec.) 57 Old Broad st. City
Assay Office, Goldsmiths' hall, Gutter lane, Cheapside
Assenden Thos. furniture broker, 8 St. Ann's pl. Limehouse
Assender James, cheesemonger, 30 New road, St.George'sEa
Assender Joseph James, fellmonger, 62 Bermondsey st
AsserJohn,corn&flour ag.6 Hart st. Crutched frs.&Corn exch
Asser Louis, china & glass warehouse, & agent for Yates's patent porcelain projecting letters, &c. 147 Regent st
Asser Louisa (Miss), baby linen wa. 56 & 57 Burlington arcade
Asser Nathaniel, tailor, 41 Aldenham st. Somer's town
Asser Solomon, plumasier & florist, 8 & 9 Burlington arcade
Assinder Richard, *Red Lion* P.H. 5 Cross lane, Long acre
Assistant Drapers' Soc. (Henry Mayhew, sec.), 355 Strand
Associate Fund (or Gospel Ministers' Fund) Society (Rev. Charles Gilbert, sec.), 4 Blomfield st. Finsbury
Associate Institution for the Protection of Women, 8½ St. Swithin's lane, King William st
Associated Catholic Charities' Orphan Asylum (Antonio Wm. Julien Harrison, sec.), 4 Lamb's bldgs. Bunhill row
Associate's Office (C.P.), 1 Staple inn; hours 10 to 5
Association for the Aid & Protection of Dressmakers & Milliners (R. D. Grainger, hon. sec.), 13 Clifford st. Bond st
Association for the Improvement of Street Paving (Chas. Sibley, sec.), 20 Vere st. Cavendish square
Aste Henry, corn & coal merchant, 169 Tottenham court rd
Astell Richard, dairyman, 8 Shepherd st. Mayfair
Astell Samuel, stenciller & painter, 61 Wilsted st. Somers town
Astle Mary & Sons, bookbinders, 2 Cloak lane, City
Astley Evan, tailor, 40 Windmill st. Tottenham court road
Astley Peter, manchester warehouse, 26 Wood st. Cheapside
Astley Peter, jun. tailor, 19 Castle st. Falcon square
Astley William, hatter, 115 Union st. Borough
Astly Peter, tailor & draper, 19 Castle st. Falcon square

Aston & Wallis, solicitors, 2 New Broad st. City
Aston & Scott, stockbrokers, 32 Throgmorton st
Aston Charles, cork manf. 23 Milton st. City
Aston Joseph, fancy trimming manfr. 6 Galway st. St.Luke's
Aston William, watchmaker, 12 Queen st. Tower hill
Astor & Co. (now Wolf & Figg), pianoforte & musical instrument makers, 20 St. Martin's le Grand
Astrope John, coffee rooms, 10 Rathbone place, Oxford st
Asturian Mining Co. (J. Charretie, esq.sec.), 9 Austin friars
Asylum Foreign & Domestic Life Office (G.Farren, resident director), 70 Cornhill, & 5 Waterloo place, Pall Mall; see page 2014
Asylum for Female Orphans (Miss Sarah Cockburn, matron), Mead place, Westminster road
Atcheler John, horse slaughterer, 6 Sharp's alley, Cowcross st
Atchinson Elizabeth (Mrs.), dairy, 9 George la. Botolph la
Atchison Robert, baker, 12 Brewer's green, Westminster
Athenæum Club House (Edwd.Magrath, sec.), 107 Pall mall
Athenæum Newspaper Office, 14 Wellington st. North, Strand
Atherfold Henry, chandler's shop, 10 Chapel st. St.Geo.'s East
Atherfold William, *Nag's Head* P.H. Mare st. Hackney
Atherly & Stillwell, gold&silver wire drawers, manufacturers of gold, silver & tinsel threads, bullions, spangles, embroidering threads, pearls, &c. 3 Bridgewater sq. Barbican
Atherly John, gold lace manufacturer, see Odell & Atherly
Atherton William, barrister, 2 Brick court, Temple
Athill John, nightman, 32 Belvedere road, Lambeth
Atkin John, *Castle* P.H. High st. Battersea
Atkin John, fan paper stainer, 46 Barbican, & 2 Garlick hill
Atkin John Horton, barrister, 13 Cursitor st. Chancery lane
Atkin Samuel, butcher, Borough market
Atkin Thomas, bootmaker, 2 Opera arcade, Haymarket
Atkin Thomas, butcher, 3 Borough market
Atkin Thomas, cattle salesman, 60 West Smithfield
AtkinWm. Pickworth, corn & coal dealer, 10Union pl. Islington
Atkins & Andrew, solicitors, 5 White Hart ct. Lombard st. & 1 Church st. Deptford
Atkins Geo. & Son, watchmakers, 6 Cowper's ct. Cornhill
Atkins Geo. & Wm. brushm. & turners, 1 Mount st. Berkeley sq
Atkins James & Son, lime burners, Wharf, Nine elms, Vauxhall
Atkins John & Son, merchants, 2 Walbrook buildings
Atkins & Sercombe, tailors, 20 St. James's st. Piccadilly
Atkins Arthur, plumber, 44 Princess st. Lisson grove
Atkins Ebenezer Thos. tobacconist, 79 Church st. Shoreditch
Atkins Edward, beer retailer, 87 Crown ct. Tudor st. Blackfrs
Atkins Edward Thomas, grocer, 79 Poplar High st
Atkins Francis Thos. chemist & druggist, 4 High st. Deptford
Atkins Frederic, solicitor, see Smith & Atkins
Atkins Henry, carpenter, 61 Harrow road, Paddington
Atkins James, butcher, Hertford road, Kingsland
Atkins James, fruiterer, 20 Cotton st. Poplar
Atkins James, oilman, 39 Princess st. Portman market
Atkins John, oilman, 98 Brick lane, Spitalfields
Atkins John, tobacconist, 31 Baldwin st. City road
Atkins John Payne, secret springr. 21 Peartree st. Goswell st
Atkins Joseph, appraiser, 28 London terrace, Hackney road
Atkins Jsph. Pinder, *Old Hob* P.H. 81 Brunswick st. Blackwall
Atkins Rachael (Mrs.), cheesemonger, 46 Broad st. Ratcliff
Atkins Richard, gasfitter, 8 Royal Hospital row, Chelsea
Atkins Richard, upholsterer, &c. 6 Argyll place, Regent st
Atkins Robt. *Fishing Smack* P.H. Coal harbour, Blackwall
Atkins Robert, grocer, 50 Baldwin st. City road
Atkins Susannah Mary (Mrs.), dressmaker, 17 Up. Baker st
Atkins Thos. lighterman, 20 John st. Commercial rd. Lambeth
AtkinsThos. timber mer. Northmptn. wf. 48 Edward st. Rgts. pk
Atkins Wm. hairdresser, 50 Princess street, Edgware road
Atkins Wm. surgeon, High street, Deptford
Atkins Wm. umbrella maker, Southampton st. Camberwell
Atkins Wm. jun. watchmaker, 71 Poplar High st
Atkins Wm. sen. clock & watchmaker, 3 Hoxton Old town
Atkins Wm. Hen. straw hat manuf. 13 Church st. Spitalfields
Atkinson Ann & Elizh. (Misses), academy, 20 Manchester bldgs
Atkinson & Biggar, manfg. chem. & drug grinds. 66 Aldersgate st
Atkinson & Coates, linendrapers, 35 Bridge road, Lambeth
Atkinson, Foster & Byers, silk & lace wareh. 42 NewBond st
Atkinson Fras. & Wm. stock & sharebrok. 61½ Threadneedle st
Atkinson James & Co. russia merchants, 108 Fenchurch st
Atkinson James & Edward, whol. perfumers, 24 Old Bond st
Atkinson James S. & Co. stuff, moreen, &c. manfrs. 65 Friday st
Atkinson John & Son, cuppers, 15 Abchurch lane, City
Atkinson Jonas & Co. russian merchants, Baltic coff. house
Atkinson & Musgrave, law and gen. stationers, 94 Chancery la
Atkinson & Pilgrim, solicitors, Church court, Lothbury
Atkinson Robt. & Co. woolstaplers, Up. Russell st. Bermondsey
Atkinson & Seelie, wine & brandy mercs. 34 St. Mary at hill
Atkinson Wm. & Anthony, merchants, 2 New Broad st. court

Atkinson Alexander, railway coffee rooms, 14 Tooley st
Atkinson Alfred Charles, tailor, &c. see Pinn & Atkinson
Atkinson Benjamin, surgeon, 12 King William st. City
Atkinson Fredk. fishmonger, 25 Victoria road, Pimlico
Atkinson Frederick Cox, coal merc. see Weddell & Atkinson
Atkinson George, barrister, 1 Inner Temple lane
Atkinson George, plumber & painter, 29 Prince's rd. Lambeth
Atkinson Henry, iron & steel wks. see Johnson, Atkinson & Co
Atkinson Henry, linendraper, 1 Eagle st. City road
Atkinson Henry John, manuftr. see Rowlandson & Atkinson
Atkinson Henry Tindal, barrister, 1 Pump court, Temple
Atkinson James, billbroker, 39 Clement's lane, Lombard st
Atkinson James, upholsterer, 8 York place, Westminster rd
Atkinson John, beer retailer, 6 Belmont row, Vauxhall
Atkinson John, boot & shoe maker, 10 Stepney High st
Atkinson John, grocer, 10 Felix terrace, Liverpool road
Atkinson John, hop & seedfactor, 69 Borough High st
Atkinson John, law stationer, 6 Quality ct. Chancery lane
Atkinson John, merchant & genl. agent, 31 Lawrence lane
Atkinson John Chas. surgeon, 16 Romney ter. Westminster
Atkinson Linton, oil & color warehouse, 75 Blackman st
Atkinson Martha (Miss), milliner, 7 Queen st. Tower hill
Atkinson Martin, cabinet maker, &c. 70 to 75 Bridge road, Lambeth; & Addington st. York road
Atkinson Mary (Mrs.), outfitting warehouse, 151 Kingsland rd
Atkinson Matthew, bricklayer, 37 Tottenham st. Fitzroy sq
Atkinson Richard, oil & colorman, 43 Red Lion st. Holborn
Atkinson Richard, who. confectioner, 10 Laurence Pountney la
Atkinson Richard Hollier, attorney, 27 Carey st. Lincoln's inn
Atkinson Robert, brass finisher, 7 Falcon pl. Ray st. Clknwl
Atkinson Samuel, ship & custom house agent, 34 Mark lane
Atkinson Samuel, turner, 12 Manchester st. Gray's inn road
Atkinson Solomon, barrister, 12 Warwick court, Holborn
Atkinson Thomas, grocer, 7 Norfolk pl. Lower road, Islington
Atkinson Thomas, wine cooper, 22 Greycoat st. Westminster
Atkinson Thomas Robert, law stationer, 63 Carey street
Atkinson Wm. cowkeeper, 17 Little Warner st. Clerkenwell
Atkinson Wm. dyer, &c. Lamb's passage, 37 Chiswell st
Atkinson Wm. haberdasher, 141 St. George street
Atkinson Wm. irish provision agent, 9 Arthur st. West
Atkinson Wm. provision brok. 2 Langbourn chmbrs. Fench. st
Atkinson Wm. surgical instr. manfr. 33 Market st. Boro' rd
Atkinson Wm. tailor, 71 Westbourne st. Pimlico
Atkiss Saml. lathe & tool maker, 19 Gt. St. Andrew st. 7dials
Atlas Life & Fire Assurance Company, 92 Cheapside. For Directors, &c. see page 2014
Atlas Newspaper Office, 6 Southampton street, Strand
Atlee Sophia (Mrs.), grocer, 17 Harrison st. Gray's inn road
Atlee Stephen, dining rooms, 36 Bow lane, Cheapside
Atloff John George, french boot & shoe maker, 20 Vere st
Atmore Harriet (Mrs.), boarding ho. 15 King st. Cheapside
Atmospheric Railway Office, (Samuda Brothers, proprietors,) Orchard place, Blackwall
Attenborough Geo. & Richard, pawnbrokers, 204 Fleet st
Attenborough George, pawnbroker, 31 Compton st. & 24 Kenton st. Brunswick square
Attenborough Richard, goldsmith, 68 Oxford street
Attenborough Richard, pawnbroker, 8 Bridgehouse pl. Boro'
Attenborough Richard, pawnbroker, 110 Shoreditch High st. & 31 Crown st. Finsbury
Attenborough Rt. pawnbroker, 93&94 Charlotte st. Fitzroy sq
Attenbrow Wm. Joseph, grocer, &c. 189 Oxford street
Atterbury John, watch motion maker, 2 Pool terr. City road
Attfield Benj. wax chandler & oilman, 50 Lisson grove north
Attfield Edward, dairyman, 1 King st. Camden town
Attfield Henry, butcher, Meadow place, South Lambeth
Attfield Henry, butcher, 2 Holland place, Clapham road
Attfield Richard, upholsterer, see Tratt & Attfield
Attfield Robert, law & general stationer, 15 Cursitor st
Atto John, surgeon, 67 Seymour place, Bryanstone square
Attorney General's Office, 2 King's bench walk, Temple
Attorneys' Certificate Office, Stamp office, Somerset House
Attorneys & Solicitors Registrar's Office (the Incorporated Law Society, *registrar*, Robert Maugham, secretary), Incorporated Law Society, Chancery lane; hours 10 to 4
Attree Elizbth. (Miss), baby linen ware. see Dominey & Attree
Attree Thos. Aug. solicitor, see Wimburn, Collett & Co
Attree William Wakeford, barrister, 1 Figtree ct. Temple
Attride Henry, stockbroker, 20 Throgmorton street
Attridge Jonas, tea agent, 5 Exmouth street, Spafields
Attryde John, stationer, 2 Adam st. West, Bryanstone sq
Attwater Wm. dyer & scourer, 25 Devonshire st. Queen sq
Attwater Wm. professor of music, 56 Great Portland st
Attwaters Charles, solicitor, see King & Attwaters
Attwaters Wm. surgeon, 3 Beaufort ter. West. King's rd. Chlse
Attwell Robert & Son, butchers, 17 Brown's lane, Spitalfields
Attwell Adolphus, butcher, 124 Union st. Borough
Attwell Alonzo Geo. butcher, 5 Devonshr. pl. Comml. rd. East
Attwell Augustus V. butcher, 28 Nassau pl. Commercl. rd. East
Attwell James, butcher, 2 Hayfield place, Mile end road
Attwell John, bookbinder, 2 Coldbath square, Clerkenwell
Attwell Orlando, butcher, 192 Kingsland road
Attwell Margt. (Miss), stationer & toy wa. High st. Kingsland
Attwell Rome Theodore, butcher, 69 Holywell la. Shoreditch
Attwood & Smith, window glass manufactr. 25 New Bridge st
Attwood Edward Marcus, barrister, 3 Old sq. Lincoln's inn
Attwood Eleanor (Mrs.), *Blue Anchor* P.H. 67½ Whitechpl. rd
Attwood Geo. de B. sec. to Bnk. of B.N. Ameri. 7 St. Helen's pl
Attwood Maria (Mrs.), bookseller, 39 Gt. Castle st. Regent st
Attwood Richard, baker, 7 Broomfields, Deptford
Attwood Thomas George, hairdresser, 25 Gt. Marlborough st
Atty George, barrister, 3 Garden court, Temple
Atwell John, hairdresser, 2 George court, Piccadilly
Atwell Robert, cowkeeper, 1 Little Sussex place, Hyde park
Atwood George W. com. merchant, 14 America sq. Minories
Atwood John, *Swan* P. H. 120 Piccadilly
Atwood Thomas, accountant, 30 Edward st. Blackfriars road
Atwood William, market gardener, Old Brompton
Auber Henry Peter, solicitor, 21 Lincoln's inn fields
Aubert & Klaftenberger, watch & clock makers & jewellers, 157 Regent street
Aubert & Thompson, ship & insurance brokers, 59 Fenchurch st
Aubert John Lewis, paper stainer, see Holmes & Aubert
Aubertin Brothers, merchants, 6 Great Winchester st
Aubery Sarah (Mrs.), coffee rooms, 18 John st. Minories
Aubin George Douglas, solicitor, see Holt & Aubin
Aubrey Adolphus A. baker, 20 Lower Smith st. Northampton sq
Aubrey Charles, coal merchant, 10 Vaughan ter. City road
Aubrey Wm. printer, 45 Freeschool st. Horselydown
Aucott John, hairdresser, 7 Little Bath st. Clerkenwell
Auction Mart, 3 Bartholomew lane, Bank
Auden Chas. oil & italian warehouse, 11 Cleveland st. Fitzr. sq
Audinet George, pork butcher, 6 Crown st. Soho
Audit Office for Civil List, Somerset house; hours 10 to 4
Audit Office for Public Accts. Somerset house; hours 10 to 4
Auditor's Office for Land Revenue, 11 Spring gardens; do
Augarde Chas. tobacconist, 9 Church row, Aldgate High st
Augarde Francis Joseph, hatter, 51 Oxford street
Augarde Henry, hairdresser, 1 Shorter's ct. Throgmorton st
Aughtie Thos. Wm. lodging house, 2 Giltspur st. Smithfield
Augmentation Office, Carlton ride; hours 10 to 4
Auguste Victoire, ladies' french shoe maker, 244 Regent st
Augustine Marie (Miss), milliner, 5 Pelham ter. Brompton
Aukland Joseph, grocer, 63 Whitecross st. Cripplegate
Aulaguier François, hairdresser, 4 Old Cavendish street
Ault Sophia (Miss), school, 66 Gt. Tower street
Aumonier David, jeweller, 6A, Dorset st. Manchester sq
Aumonier David, stock & sharebroker, 16 Cornhill
Aunger William, tailor, 8 New inn passage
Aungier William, tailor, 24 Redcross square
Ausender Thomas, jeweller, &c. 12 Short's bldgs. Clerkenwell
Aust David, brush manufac. 28 Somerset pl. Hoxton new town
Aust George, house agent, 12 Orchard st. Portman square
Aust Jane (Mrs.), boarding house, 68 Guilford st. Russell sq
Austen & Hobson, solicitors, 4 Raymond buildings, Gray's inn
Austen & Iorns, linendrps. 187 & 188 Oxford st. & 1 Thayer st
Austen Charlotte (Miss), prof. of music, 9 Gt. Castle st. Regt. st
Austen Francis Cobb, proctor, 17 Great Knightrider st
Austen Fred. Lewes, solicitor, see Hale, Boys & Austen
Austen George, barrister, 4 Inner Temple lane
Austen Henry, hop & seed factor, see Latter, Austen & Sons
Austen Henry Edgar, barrister, 7 New sq. Lincoln's inn
Austen James, dairyman, 8 Canterbury pl. Old Kent road
Austen Wm. carpenter, 27 Canterbury pl. Old Kent road
Austin & Chappell, stockbrokers, 4 Bank chambs. Lothbury
Austin Jas. & Jsph. jobmasters, Whitehorse yd. Kngtsbdge
Austin & Owen, bankrupts' register office, 10½ King's arms yd
Austin & Rammell, civil engineers & architects, 10 Walbrook
Austin Thos. & Wm. furniture cleaners & dyers, 11 Golden sq
Austin Abraham, baker, Holmes' terrace, Kentish town
Austin Charles, queen's counsel, 2 Plowden buildings, Tmpl
Austin Chas. saddler & harness maker, 52 Parliament st
Austin Chas. engrav. & copper plate printer, 25A, Hatton gardn
Austin Chas. Val. water gilder, 11 Glo'ster st. St. John st. Clkl
Austin Daniel Edwin, solicitor, 5 Sise lane, Bucklersbury
Austin Edward, surgeon, 3 Walker pl. Lower rd. Rotherhithe
Austin Edward Charles, surveyor, 5 Singleton st. Hoxton
Austin Elizab. (Mrs.), lodging ho. 36 Gt. James st. Bedford row
Austin Elizabeth (Mrs.), fringe ma. 22 Amelia st. Walwrth. rd
Austin Francis, tobacconist, 15 High st. Kensington
Austin George, baker, 42 Gt. Wild st. Lincoln's inn fields
Austin George, fringe maker, 46 Devonshire st. Queen sq

Austin George, stationer, 3 Orange row, Kennington road
Austin George, *WilliamFourth*P.H. Albion ter. Wandsworth
Austin Geo. Edward, cheesemonger, 4 Road side, Mile end rd
Austin Harriet (Mrs.), baker, Well street, Hackney
Austin Henry, carpenter, 92 Gt. Peter st. Westminster
Austin Henry, chemist & drysalter, 161 Bermondsey street
Austin Henry, civil engineer, 10 Walbrook, City
Austin Henry, smith, 84 Lambeth walk
Austin Henry, who. & retail tea & coffee dlr. 18 Philpot la
Austin Henry D. builder, 4½ Bathurst st. Sussex sq. Hyde pk
Austin H. Debrona, bricklayer, &c. 28 Winchester row, New rd
Austin James, sash & blind line maker, 31 St. John's square, Clerkenwell; & 9 Princes st. Finsbury
Austin James, ship & house smith, 21 Mill lane, Tooley st
Austin James, silk dyer, 19 Cumberland st. Shoreditch
Austin Job, organ & piano forte tuner, 35 Haydon st. Minories
Austin John, academy, 11 Rahere st. Goswell road
Austin John, auctioneer, 22 Southwark bridge rd. Borough
Austin John, boot & shoe maker, 9 St. Mary axe
Austin John, cabinet maker, 45 East st. Manchester square
Austin John, chaser, 21 Clerkenwell green
Austin John, fringe mkr. 9 Litt. Portland st. Gt. Portland st
Austin John, furn. broker, 2 Marlborough st. Blackfrs. rd
Austin John, goldsmith & watchmaker, 136 Oxford st
Austin John, registrar, 11 Rahere st. Goswell road
Austin John, rope maker, 37 Roebuck place, Gt. Dover rd
Austin John, straw plait dealer, 43 King st. Long acre
Austin John, surveyor, 7 Derby st. King's cross
Austin John, trunk maker, 372 Oxford st
Austin John, *White Hart* P.H. 64 Fetter lane
Austin John, jun. fringe manuf. 20 Wilmot st. Brunswick sq
Austin Joseph, bootmaker, 5 White lion street, Pentonville
Austin Morgan Fuller, surgeon, 15 Red lion st. Clerkenwell
Austin Peter, cheesemonger, 31 St. John st. Clerkenwell
Austin Peter William, pork butcher, 247 Poplar High st
Austin Ralph John, merchant, 31 St. Thomas' st. East, Boro'
Austin Richard, academy, 3 Old Compton st. Soho
Austin Robert, cork manfr. 2 Clarence gdns. Regent's park
Austin Sarah (Mrs.), hardware dlr. 2 Gt. Bath st. Clerkenwell
Austin Sarah (Mrs.), italian wareh. 8 New Bridge st. Vauxhl
Austin Thomas, baker, 169 Bermondsey street
Austin Thomas, baker, 4 Great George st. Bermondsey
Austin Thomas, carpenter, Bray's court, Lower rd. Islington
Austin Thos. cheesemonger, 4 Haberdashers' walk, Hoxton
Austin Thomas, tailor, Well street, Hackney
Austin Thos. Phipps, *Peele's coffee house*, 177 & 178 Fleet st
Austin Wm. boot & shoemaker, Camberwell grove
Austin Wm. builder, 5 Singleton street, Hoxton
Austin Wm. butcher, 12 Broadwall, Blackfriars
Austin Wm. ironfounder, 47 Ewer street, Borough
Austin Wm. orange merchant, Borough market
Austin Wm. pill box maker, 5 Furnival's inn place, Holborn
Austin Wm. rope & twine manufacturer, 431 Oxford st
Austin Wm. solicitor, 25 St. Swithin's lane
Austin Wm. *White Bear* P.H. 28 Lit. Newport st. Long acre
Austin Wm. Henry, attorney, 31 St. Martin's st. Leicester sq
Austin William R. wine merchant, see Robinson & Austin
Austing Henry John, bookbinder, 6 Tudor st. Blackfriars
Australian Agricultural Co. (George Engstrom, sec.), 12 King's arms yard, Coleman st
Australian Mining Co. 1 Adelaide place, London bridge
Australian Trust Co. 48 Moorgate street, Bank
Australasian, Colonial & General Life Assur. & Annuity Co. (Ed. Ryley, sec.), 126 Bishopsgate within, see page 2015
Austwick & Webb, wine merchants, 1 Walbrook
Authors' Institute (John Wilkes, director), 28 Surrey st
Avann John, *Mansion House* P.H. Prospect pl. Lr. rd. Deptford
Aveling John, timber mer. 6 Irongate wf. Paddington basin
Aveline Pindock Wm. surgeon, Camberwell green
Avenell Wm. packing case & block mkr. 78 Bethnal green rd
Avern George, cork cutter, 75 Oakley st. Lambeth
Avern Thos. coach plater & founder, 9 West st. Soho
Avern Thos. wine merchant, 15 Newcastle st. Farringdon st
Avern Wm. tailor, 12 John street, Adelphi
Avery & Dangar, blindmakers, 11 Gt. Portland st. Oxford st
Avery John & William, wholesale & retail haberdashers, 14 Church lane, Whitechapel
Avery & Mitchener, printers, 116 Gt. Russell st. Bloomsbury
Avery Henry, secretary to Commercial Gaslight & Coke Co. Ben Jonson's fields, Stepney
Avery James, *Old Gibraltar* P.H. Gibraltar row, Lr. rd. Dptfd
Avery James, jun. *World* P.H. Nelson pl. Old Kent road
Avery John, fruiterer, 11 Diddington pl. Caledonian road
Avery John, *Rose & Crown* P.H. 64 Parsons st. St. George st
Avery John, sugar & fruit broker, 25 Mincing lane
Avery John, surgeon, 17 Saville row, Piccadilly
Avery Joseph, cigar depôt, 5 Great Piazza, Covent garden
Avery Jsph. silvrsmth. & jewllr. 38 Manchester st. Manchtr. sq
Avery Mary Anne (Mrs.), stay & corset maker, 88 Oxford st
Avery Thomas, grocer, Stratford, Essex
Avery Wm. baker, 1 Melville place, Caledonian road
Avery William, bricklayer, 60 New Compton st. Soho
Aves John, turner, 15 White st. Bethnal green
Aves Thos. *Marlbro' Head* P.H. Pelham st. Spitalfields
Avila Sarah (Mrs.), pawnbroker, 16 Constable rw. Mile End rd
Avill Wm. pianoforte maker, 29 Cumberland st. Hackney rd
Aviolet Wm. G. undertaker, 36 Windsor terrace, City road
Avis James, fruiterer, 30 Stangate, Lambeth
Avis John, tailor, 2 John st. Titchfield ter. Regent's park
Avis Reeve, hair dresser, 6 High street, Portland town
Avis William, carpenter, 27 High street, St. Giles's
Avory Charles, basket maker, 5 Little Suffolk st. Borough
Avrill Wm. *Duke on Horseback* P.H. 9 Holland st. Blackfrs. rd
Awberry Eliz. & Cath. stationers, 48 Rupert st. Haymarket
Axford Elizabeth (Mrs.), milliner, 4 Maddox st. Bond st
Axford Frederick Pain, solicitor, 16 Cornhill
Axford James, dairyman, 21 Crown court, Pall mall
Axmann Paul, wine merchant, 4 Mark lane
Axon John William, bookbinder, 16 Bartholomew close
Axtell Sam. & John, curriers, 14 Russell street, Bermondsey
Axtell Ann (Mrs.), chandler's shop, 10 Chicksand st. Whtchpl
Axtell Thomas, toothpowder box maker, 54 Bunhill row
Axtell Wm. jun. leather dresser, 11 Russell st. Bermondsey
Axtill Thomas, dairy, 60 Swinton street, Gray's inn road
Ayann John, *Plough* P.H. 152 Hoxton old town
Ayers & Saunders, linendrapers, 171 Tottenham court road
Ayers Charles R. architect, 8 John st. Berkeley square
Ayers James, plumber, 11 Stanhope terrace, Hyde park
Ayers John, greengrocer, 87 Dean street, Soho
Ayers John, linendraper & laceman, 56 Whitechapel road
Ayerst Francis, solicitor, 2 Charlotte row, Mansion house, & 1 Jamaica place, Limehouse
Ayerst John, city carman, 64½ Low. Thames st. & 13 Kent st. Boro'
Ayles Stephen, cork cutter, 250 High street, Wapping
Aylesbury & Thame Junction Railway, 2 Furnival's inn
Aylett Isaac, builder, 31 Wilsted street, Somers town
Aylett William, grocer, 3 Church street, Rotherhithe
Aylett William, grocer, 8 Horseferry road, Westminster
Aylieff & Whitelaw, tailors. 5 Princes st. Hanover sq
Ayliffe Paul, coach smith, 16 Church st. Blackfriars road
Ayliffe Rich. *Perseverance* P.H. 1 Lupus st. Belgrave road
Ayling Thos. & Jas. bootmakers, 25 Collier st. Pentonville
Ayling James, wood carver, 3 Dean street, Soho
Ayling James, *King's Arms* P.H. 23 Poland st. Oxford st
Ayling James, sen. furnishing ironmonger, 32 Parliament st
Ayling Mary (Mrs.), fruiterer, 20 Exeter st. Sloane st
Ayling Thomas, carpenter, 45 Princess st. Lisson grove
Ayling William, grocer & tea dealer, 35 Gilbert st. Oxford st
Aylott & Jones, booksellers & publishers, 8 Paternoster row
Aylward Ann (Miss), ladies' school, 14 Camomile street, City
Aylward John, carcase butcher, 70 Aldgate High street
Aylward John, linendraper, 14 Monmouth pl. Old Kent rd
Aylwin, Bevan, Cole & Harris, oil & mediterranean produce brokers & warehouse keepers, 90 Lower Thames st
Aylwin George, sen. oil & drug broker, 96 Lower Thames st
Aylwin George Allen, merchant, 17 Finsbury square
Aylwin Gulielmus, grocer, 33 Weymouth st. New Kent rd
Aylwin William, lodging house, 28 Carey st. Lincoln's inn
Aynsworth Benjamin, patten maker, 273 Bermondsey st
Ayre George, tobacconist, 56 Exmouth st. Spafields
Ayre William, surgeon, Mare street, Hackney
Ayre William, tailor, 60 Poland street, Oxford street
Ayres Benjamin Wm. merchant, 9 Union court, Old Broad st
Ayres Edward James, artist in hair, 124 Gt. Portland st
Ayres George, *Crown* P.H. Orchard place, Blackwall
Ayres John Cobb, hatter & tobacconist, 204 Tooley street
Ayres Philip, pocket book ma. & fancy stationer, 18 Sise lane
Ayres Thos. chess & cribbage board ma. 28 Gt. Bath st. Clknwl
Ayres Thomas, cowkeeper, 46 Cartwright st. Rosemary lane
Ayres Thomas, fly propr. 8 Colchester ter. Old Brompton
Ayres Wm. carpenter & builder, 78 & 79 Redcross st. Boro'
Ayres Wm. newsvender, 18 University st. Tottenham ct. rd
Ayrton Wm. Scrope, reg. of ct. of review, Quality ct. Chancy. la
Ayshford William, *Fishmongers' Arms* P.H. 8 West st. Soho
Ayton Charles, organ builder, 16 Summer st. Hatton garden
Ayton Robert, undertaker, 9 Devonshire street, Globe road
Ayton Thomas, organ builder, 21 Gt. Bath st. Clerkenwell
Azemberg Francis, china manfrs'. agent, 89 Hatton garden
Azuelos Judah, feather mer. & com. agt. 4 Bury st. St. Mary axe

BAAB John Martin, mfr. of clocks, watches & jewelry to H.R.H. the Grand Duke of Hesse Darmstadt, 19 Gerrard st. Soho

Baalham Robert, carpenter & builder, Edward pl. Balls pond
Babb Benj. fishmonger, 16 Little Charlotte st. Goodge st
Babb Wm. straw hat maker & milliner, 296 High Holborn
Babbage William, surgeon, &c. 1 Bengal pl. New Kent rd
Babbington Jas. grocer, 16 Northumberland st. Marylebone
Babbs Robert, butcher, 206 Sloane st. Knightsbridge
Baber & Squire, bakers, 78 Jermyn st. St. James's
Baber Benjamin, boot & shoe maker, 6 Moorgate st. Bank
Baber Caroline (Miss), milliner, 6 Montague pl. Kentish tn
Baber John, floorcloth manufacturer, see Smith & Baber
Baber William, furn. broker, 1A, Lr. York place, Kentish town
Babin Aug. child's carr. & invalid chair mak. 3 New st. Old st
Babington Benjamin, barrister, 23 Old sq. Lincoln's inn
Babington Benjamin Guy, physician, 31 George st. Hanover sq
Bacchus George & Sons, plain & cut glass manufacturers, & union glass works, Birmingham, & 8 Tokenhouse yard
Bacchus Wm. *Rising Sun* P.H. 26 High road, Knightsbrdg
Bach Adolphus, foreign jurisconsult & agent for judicial transactions abroad, Sussex chambs. 10 Duke st. St. James'
Bache Rd. & Co. *Langbourn coffee ho.* 1 Ball alley, Lombard st
Bachhoffner Atkinson, oil & ital. wa. 9 Everett st. Brunswick sq
Bachhoffner George, currier, 69 & 70 Monmouth st. 7 dials
Bachhoffner Geo. upholsterer & cabinet maker, 6 Pied Bull yard, Bury street, Bloomsbury
Bachhoffner George H. reg. of births, &c. 6 Wellington ter. Mrylb
Bachhóffner Louisa (Mrs.), italian warehouse, 37 Museum st
Back George, *George & Vulture* P.H. 39 St. George st
Back George Walter, teadealer, 137 Whitechapel road
Back John, carpenter, 10 Boswell court, Queen square
Back John, commission agent, 14 Milk st. Cheapside
Back Thomas, cheesemonger, 5 Swan lane, Rotherhithe
Back William, physician, 13 St. Thomas's st. Borough
Back Wm. Hen. drawing master to Christ's hosptl. Newgate st
Backer George, stationer, 14 Union st. Clarendon square
Backer Henry, treacle maker, 1 Heneage st. Whitechapel
Backett Wm. manufacturing chemist, 25A, Stoney st. Borough
Backhouse Mary (Mrs.), pat. maltster, Cox's sq. Spitalfields
Backhouse Robt. copper pl. printer, 2 Red lion st. Clerkenwell
Backhouse Thos. stockbroker, 4 Angel ct. Throgmorton st
Backler Henry, tailor, 13 Bateman's buildings, Soho square
Backler Leonard, cheesemonger, 7 Pitfield st. Hoxton
Backley George, eatinghouse, 331 Strand
Backous William, tailor, 14 St. John st. road
Backway John, *Horns & Chequers* P.H. Limehouse stairs
Bacon John & Francis, tanners, Royal oak yard, 173 Bermondsey st. & Church st. Horselydown
Bacon & Wayman, wire weavers, paper & bank note mould manufacturers & sieve makers, 15 Barbican
Bacon Ann Hodge (Mrs.), engraver, 99 Chancery lane
Bacon Benjamin, bobbin silk dlr. 1 Anchor st. Spitalfields
Bacon Benjamin, dairyman, 110 Cromer st. Brunswick sq
Bacon Ebenezer, machine ruler, engine turner, medallion & ornamental scroll engraver, 3 Angel ct. Skinner st
Bacon Edward, firebrick & tilema. 8 Church ter. Cornwall rd
Bacon Francis, merchant, 147 Leadenhall st
Bacon Fras. Wills, cabinet ma. 33 Appleby st. Kingsland rd
Bacon Frederick, *Hotel Français*, 40 Charterhouse sq
Bacon Frederick, lodging house keeper, 40 Charterhouse sq
Bacon Geo. *Cape of Good Hope* P.H. 3 Gt. Titchfield st. Oxfd. st
Bacon George, writing master, 7 Paradise row, Chelsea
Bacon Henry, barrister, 2 Stone buildings, Lincoln's inn
Bacon Henry, tanner, Upper Russell st. Bermondsey
Bacon James, barrister, 10 New square, Lincoln's inn
Bacon James, boot & shoe maker, 30 Maze, Tooley st
Bacon James, fruiterer, 19 Mount st. Walworth road
Bacon James, staffordshire wa. Staffordshire pl. Old Kent rd
Bacon John, *George* P.H. 6 Billingsgate
Bacon John, horse dealer, Staffordshire pl. Old Kent road
Bacon John, sculptor, 17 Newman st. Oxford st
Bacon John, watch case maker, 5 Charles st. City road
Bacon John Edward, tanner, 1 Terrace, Old Kent road
Bacon John Francis, merchant, 26 Austinfriars
Bacon John Turner, chemist, &c. 21 Moorgate st. City
Bacon Joseph, *Ship & Shovel* P.H. Steel yard, Maze pond
Bacon Joshua B. engraver, see Perkins, Bacon & Petch
Bacon Nehemiah, currier, 15 Church st. Islington
Bacon Oliver R. jun. (Mad.), corset maker, 25 North Audley st
Bacon Rt. beer retailer, 1 Pleasant row, East st. Walworth
Bacon Samuel, *New George* P.H. 18 Drury court, Drury la
Bacon Samuel, surgeon, 41 Frederick pl. Hampstead road
Bacon Samuel Sampson, grocer, 38 White street, Borough
Bacon Stephen, corn & coal mer. 3 Northampton pl. O. Kent rd
Bacon Thomas Mich. *Freemasons' tav.* 62 Gt. Queen st. Lin. in. fl
Bacon Wm. silk mercer, see Sewell, Evans, Hubbard & Bacon
Bacon Wm. fishmonger, 4 Billingsgate
Bacon Wm. straw hat maker, 200 Tottenham court road

Bacon Wm. transparent painter, 40 Gt. Russell st. Bloomsby
Bacot John, surgeon, 4 Portugal st. Grosvenor square
Badcock Henry, cheesemonger, 1 Churchway, Somerstown
Badcock Harriet (Mrs.), confectioner, 6 Eagle terrace, City rd
Badcock Jas. toothbrush maker, 7 Newton st. New North rd
Badcock John, dining rooms, 80 Blackman st. Borough
Badcock John, grocer, 11 Blenheim st. Bond st. Chelsea
Badcock Thos. carpr. & undertkr. 21 Brunswick st. Cromer st
Badcock Wm. straw hat manufr. 65 Albany rd. Camberwell
Baddams Wm. Hen. tobacconist, 75 Lambeth Lr. Marsh
Baddeley John, Thos. & Hen. attorneys, 12 Leman st. Goodm. fl
Baddeley Charles, boot & shoe maker, 119 Oxford st
Baddeley George, bootmaker, 2 Upper King st. Holborn
Baddeley Henry, solicitor & rgstr. 27 Colet pl. Coml. rd. Ea
Baddeley Mary (Mrs.), library, Mason's pl. Little Chelsea
Baddeley John, boot & shoe maker, 48 Oxford st
Baddeley John, die sinker & letter cut. 20 Allen st. Goswl. st
Baddeley Richard Mumford, barrister, 5 Chancery lane
Baddeley Richard Rock, stamper & press piercer, 66 Rahere st
Baddeley Thos. solr. & registr. 38 Gloster ter. New rd. Whichpl
Baddeley William, boot & shoe maker, 130 Strand
Baddeley William, consulting engineer & patent agent, 26 Lombard st. City, & 29 Alfred st. Islington
Badder Mary (Miss), *Golden Fleece* P.H. 7 St. John st. rd
Badeley Edward, barrister, 3 Paper buildings, Temple
Baden Consulate, 1 Riches court, Lime st
Baden William, plumber, &c. 38 Star st. Edgware rd. & 3 Conduit st. Hyde park
Badger Thos. & Son, soot mrchts. 9 Gt. Bell Alley, Coleman st
Badger James, chaser, 15 Phœnix st. Crown st. Soho
Badger John, surgeon, 12 Melcolmbe place, Dorset square
Badger Mary Ann (Miss), board. house, 41 Craven st. Strand
Badger Thos. S. tin worker, 13½ Newmarket ter. Hackney road
Badger Wildsmith, surgeon, 4 Gutter lane, Cheapside
Badham & Gaunt, linendrapers, 19 Crosby row, Walworth
Badham, Houghton & Mayhew, attorneys, 4 Verulam bldgs
Badham Robert, grocer, 35 Park st. Grosvenor square
Badly John & Paul, cattle salesmen, 59 West Smithfield
Badollet John Moses, watchmaker, &c. 50 Greek st. Soho
Badrick Henrietta T. (Mrs.), dairy, 21 Old Boswell ct. Strand
Baetens Jph. & Son, bronze & ormolu ma. 18 Oxendon st. Haymkt
Baffin's Bay Co. furriers & skin importers, 242 Regent st
Bagg David, silk, satin, &c. dresser, 13 Brown's la. Spitalfields
Bagg Elijah, trunk & blind ma. 12 Frederick pl. Hampstead rd
Bagg Thomas, wood engraver, 63 Gower st. Bedford square
Bagg William, artist, 63 Gower st. Bedford square
Baggallay Richard, barrister, 11 New square, Lincoln's inn
Baggallay Richard, who. habdashr. see Spence, Baggallay & Son
Baggallay Thos. W. who. hosier, see Burbidge & Baggallay
Baggott William Herbert, beer retailer, 74 Boro' High st
Baglehole William, shipping agent, 24 Billiter st
Bagley James, grocer, 5 Motcomb street, Belgrave square
Bagley James, carpenter, 7 Aldermanbury postern
Bagley John, grocer, 15 Pitfield st. Hoxton
Bagley Mary (Miss), milliner, 20 White st. Bethnal green
Bagley Theophilus, baker, 75 Friar st. Blackfriars road
Bagley William, barrister, 5 Figtree court, Temple
Baglin Thomas, tailor, 39 Castle st. ea. Oxford st
Bagnall Wm. Henry, watchmaker, 195 Bishopsgate without
Bagot Henry Vincent, commerci l coffee rooms, 21 Cullum st
Bagshaw David Bunaur, watchmaker, 22 King st. Clerkenwll
Bagshaw George, printer, 11 Cross st. Hatton garden
Bagshaw Isaac Smith, zinc manufact. Broadway, Deptford
Bagshaw John, mercht. *Univers. Ass. Soc.* 1 King William st
Bagshaw Richard, newsvender, 31 Brydges st. Covent garden
Bagshaw William, accountant, see Broom & Bagshaw
Bagshawe Hen. Ridgard, barrister, 2 New sq. Lincoln's inn
Bagster Saml. & Sons, bookselrs. & publshrs. 15 Paternoster row
Bagster Henry, architect & surveyor, see Ancona & Bagster
Bagster Henry M. merchant, 81 Mark lane
Bagster Joseph, solicitor, 3 Sise lane, Bucklersbury
Bagster Wm. surgeon, 17 Compton st. East, Brunswick sq
Bagster William, tailor, 3 Southampton st. Strand
Bagwell John, carpenter, 25 Riley st. Chelsea
Bahia Steam Navigation Co. (Charles Saunderson, sec.), Lombard st. chambers, 33 Clements lane
Bahr George Frederick & Co. ship agents, 43 Mark lane
Bahr James, pork butcher, 27 Bagnigge wells road
Baigent Isaac, dining rooms, 9 Upper East Smithfield
Baigent James, cheesemonger, 80 Seymour pl. Bryanstone sq
Baigent James, dairyman, 29 Graham st. West, Pimlico
Baigent Thomas, undertaker, 45 Castle st. East, Oxford st
Baijer Otto B. west india mer. 14 New City chambs. Bishopsg
Bail Henry, florist, Centre row, Covent garden market
Baildon Richard, corn dealer, 16 Seymour st. Euston sq
Bailey Brothers, manufacturing chemists, 24 London wall

Bailey Danl. & Edwd. engineers, iron founders, ironmongers, manufacturers of bedsteads, hurdles, gates, fencing, &c. &c. smiths' work in general, pump makers, & hothouse builders, 271 & 272 High Holborn
Bailey & Fox, silk & velvet manufrs. 5 Russia row, Milk st
Bailey Jacob & Son, auct. & appraisers, 42 Wood st. Cheapsi
Bailey, James & Co. silk mercers, 77 St. Paul's churchyard
Bailey James Church & Co. merchants, 109 Fenchurch st
Bailey James Church & Co. wine merchants, 109 Fenchurch st
Bailey & Giddins, bakers, 79 Vauxhall walk, Lambeth
Bailey & Keatley, carpenters, 44 Up. George st. Bryanstn. sq
Bailey, Pegg & Co. iron merchants & iron founders, 81 Bankside, Southwark; Gun wharf, 64 Wapping wall; & Brierley Hill, Staffordshire
Bailey Richd. & Thos. town carmen & carriers, & contractors for cart horses, 70 Cannon st. City; & 14 Castle st. City rd
Bailey, Shaw & Smith, solicitors, 5 Berners st. Oxford st
Bailey, Shorter & Co. (of Oporto), 109 Fenchurch st
Bailey & Son, auction. & appraisers, 42 Wood st. Cheapside
Bailey Benjamin, shoemaker, 27 Old st. road
Bailey Charles, basketmaker, Piazza, Covent garden
Bailey Charles, builder, 47 London st. Fitzroy square
Bailey Charles, cheesemonger, &c. 45 High st. Kensington
Bailey Charles, coachmaker, 49 London wall
Bailey Charles, conveyancer, 5 Stratford place, Oxford st
Bailey Chas. furniture broker, 23 East pl. Walcot pl. Lambeth
Bailey Daniel, butcher, 41 Charles st. Hatton garden
Bailey David Alf. chandler's shop, 7 Cross la. Newton st. Holbn
Bailey Elizh. (Mrs.), beer retailer, 6 North st. Lisson grove
Bailey Edward, tobacconist & stat. 1 York pl. Westmnstr. rd
Bailey Francis, boot & shoe maker, 9 Aldersgate st
Bailey Frederick, solicitor, 1 Cloisters, Temple
Bailey George, architect & surveyor, 13 Lincoln's inn fields
Bailey George, beer retailer, 72 Park st. Camden town
Bailey George, button & trimming seller, 204 Boro' High st
Bailey George, fruiterer, 25 Saville st. Fitzroy square
Bailey George, horse hair & hair seating manufacturer, 27 Coppice row, & 1 Vineyard walk, Clerkenwell
Bailey George, *Unicorn* P.H. 79 Jermyn st. St. James's
Bailey George, tailor, 18 New st. Brompton
Bailey Geo. Norton, cloak ma. 6 Dufour's pl. Broad st. Goldn sq
Bailey Harriet (Mrs.) dressmaker, 32 Water lane, Blackfrs
Bailey Henry, butcher, 20 Tottenham court road
Bailey Henry, bookseller & stationer, 158 New Bond st
Bailey Henry, glass & china warehouse, 4 Bond st. Chelsea
Bailey Henry, *Goat* P.H. 3 Stafford st. Bond st
Bailey Henry, law stationer, 58 Carey st. Lincoln's inn
Bailey Henry, painter & glazier, 5 Stafford st. Bond st
Bailey Henry, *Pitt's Head* P.H. Grange road, Bermondsey
Bailey Henry, watch jeweller, 10 Tysoe st. Exmouth st
Bailey Henry, wholesale stationer, see Dobbs, Bailey & Co
Bailey Henry Edwin, solicitor, 6 King's road, Bedford row
Bailey Henry Saml. beer retailer, 32 Skinner st. Somers tn
Bailey James, builder & house agt. 5 Portman pl. Edgwr. rd
Bailey James, caneworker, 6 Great Mitchell st. St. Luke's
Bailey James, livery stable keeper, 57 London wall
Bailey James, mast, oar & block maker, 114 Shad Thames
Bailey James, tailor & piece broker, 11½ West st. Golden sq
Bailey John, beer retailer, 18½ Coburg st. Clerkenwell
Bailey John, *Blue Coat Boy* P.H. 5 Norton folgate
Bailey John, bookbinder, 8 Fisher st. Red Lion square
Bailey John, builder, 109 Vauxhall street, Lambeth
Bailey John, butcher, 12 East st. Walworth road
Bailey John, coffee rooms, 42 New Compton st. Soho
Bailey John, dyer & scourer, 6 Purbeck place, Lambeth
Bailey John, hairdresser, 18 Harrow road, Paddington
Bailey John, oil & colorman, 74 Friar st. Blackfriars road
Bailey John, plumber, 25 King st. Deptford
Bailey John, solicitor, 8 Barnard's inn, Holborn
Bailey John, window glass cutter, 338 Rotherhithe st
Bailey John Fredk. upholsterer, 32 Grove pl. Lisson grove
Bailey John Thos. undertak. 10 Carthusian st. Charterho. sq
Bailey Joseph, bootmaker, 6 Deptford bridge
Bailey Joseph, fruiterer, 66 Cornwall road, Lambeth
Bailey Joseph, fruiterer, 60 York st. Westminster
Bailey Joseph, *Sun tavern*, 31 Ludgate hill
Bailey Joseph, tobacconist, 83 Church lane, Whitechapel
Bailey Joseph, well sinker, Dunsany pl. Wandsworth road
Bailey Mary Ann (Miss), milliner, 2 Chapel st. Grosvenor pl
Bailey Matthew, bootmaker, 8 Wellington st. Kingsland rd
Bailey Nathaniel, tailor, 13 Cannon row, Westminster
Bailey Richard, hay salesman, see Mead & Bailey
Bailey Stephen, salesman, 30 Gray st. Blackfriars road
Bailey Thos. egg merchant, 242 Borough High st
Bailey Thos. *Fountain's Abbey* P.H. 94 Praed st. Paddington
Bailey Thos. grocer, &c. 53 Britannia st. Gray's inn road
Bailey Thos. hatter, 6 Brunswick st. Stamford st. Blackfrs
Bailey Thos. leather dresser, &c. 10 Skinner st. Snow hill
Bailey Thos. *Rose & Crown* P.H. 6 Booth st. Spitalfields
Bailey Thos. surgeon, 29 Three colt st. Limehouse
Bailey Thos. surgeon, 36 York st. City road
Bailey Thos. tailor, 29 Addle st. Wood st
Bailey Thos. tailor, 53 Exmouth st. Clerkenwell
Bailey Thos. tailor, High st. Notting hill
Bailey Thos. tailor, Kensington gravel pits
Bailey William, auctioneer, 27 Chiswell st. Finsbury
Bailey William, baker, 8 Little Earl st. Seven dials
Bailey Wm. biscuit baker & confectr. 7 James st. Oxford st
Bailey William, bookseller, 51 Oakley st. Lambeth
Bailey William, brass worker, 33 King st. Covent garden
Bailey William, cabinet maker, 43 Waterloo st. Camberwell
Bailey William, coal dealer, 34 Boston st. Dorset square
Bailey William, dining rooms, 26 Munster st. Regent's park
Bailey William, gasfitter, 20 Hart st. Covent garden
Bailey Wm. grocer & cheesemngr. 1 Newland ter. Kensington
Bailey Wm. looking glass, &c. mfr. 30 New Gloster st. Hoxton
Bailey Wm. parchment & vellum ma. 19 Lt. George st. Bermy
Bailey Wm. potato salesman, 22 & 35 Red Lion st. Spitalfds
Bailey Wm. window blind maker, 53 Grosvenor pl. Pimlico
Bailey Wm. H. surgical bandage & truss ma. 418 Oxford st
Bailey Wm. Thomas, hatter, 46 Fleet st
Bailey Wm. Thurston, builder, 2 Lit. Charlotte st. Blkfrs. rd
Bailey Wm. Willis, mineral engineer, 5 Jeffrey's square
Baillie, Kerr & Co. merchants, 3 White Lion court, Cornhill
Baillie Edward, glass stainer, 7 Henry street, Cumberland market; & 12 Cumberland market
Baillie Geo. agt. for crown colonies, 5 Cannon row, Wesminr
Baillie George, surgeon, 78 Poplar High st
Baillie John, coachmaker, 2 South place, Pimlico
Baillière Hippolyte, foreign bookseller, 219 Regent st
Baily Brothers, bookslrs. statnrs. & prntslrs. Freemans bldgs
Baily & Hammond, stock & share brokers, 13 Angel ct. Bank
Baily & Jackson, upholsterers, cabinet manufacturers & furniture printers, 92 New Bond st. & 3 Woodstock st
Baily John & Son, poulterers & dealers in live birds, 29 Davies st. Berkeley square
Baily & Roberts, engravers & printers, 13 Villiers st. Strand
Baily Thomas & Co. brewers, Wyndham road, Camberwell
Baily Wm. & Son, furnishg. ironmongers, 71 Gracechurch st
Baily Benjamin, solicitor, 37 Threadneedle st
Baily Charles, architect & surveyor, 72 Gracechurch st
Baily Edward Hodges, sculptor, 10 Percy st. Tottenham ct. rd
Baily Elliot Edward, dairy, 32 Brown st. Bryanstone square
Baily John, barrister, 8 New square, Lincoln's inn
Baily John, *Masons' Hall tav.* 4 Mason's al. 14 Basinghall st
Baily Thos. furn. broker, 29 Little Alie st. Goodman's fields
Baily William, teadealer, see Sweet & Baily
Bain Elizabeth & Son, news agents, 2 Duke st. Westminster
Bain Alexander, barrister, 1 Stone buildings, Lincoln's inn
Bain Edwin Sandys, barrister, 1 Tanfield court, Temple
Bain Geo. parliamentary agent, see Cameron & Bain
Bain Henry, barrister, 1 Cloisters, Temple
Bain James, bookseller, 1 Haymarket
Bain James, grocer, 4 St. George's pl. Back rd. St. George's ea
Bain Marcus, plasterer, &c. 3 Hampstead st. Fitzroy square
Bain Robert, carpenter, 11 King st. Clerkenwell
Bain Ross, bricklayer, 17 Clipstone st. Fitzroy square
Bain Wm. *White Bear* P.H. 66 King William st. City
Bain Wm. Pellew, srgn. 7 Brunswick ter. Brunswick st. Bkwl
Bainbridge & Mews, timber mer. Trin. wf. L. Trin. st. Rotherh
Bainbridge Charles, imitator of marble & wood to the trade, staircase & other papers painted by hand, 17 Chapel place, Crown st. Soho (late with Cubitt)
Bainbridge Henry, *Crown* P.H. 59 Wapping wall
Bainbridge Jas. *Prince Albert* P.H. 1 Sherborne st. Blnfrd. sq
Bainbridge John Nathan, M.D. surgeon, 86 St. Martin's lane
Bainbridge Joseph, chemist & druggist, 60 Leather lane
Bainbridge Wm. boot & shoe maker, 18 Duke st. Smithfield
Bainbridge Wm. ladies' shoemaker, 4 Southampton ct. Queensq
Bainbridge Wm. grocr. 27 Rotherhithe st. & Larkhall la. Clphm
Baines Benj. stockbroker, 2 Copthall court, Throgmorton s t
Baines Benj. tailor, 11 Church lane, Islington
Baines Edw. *Bacchus & Tun* P.H. 32 Perceval st. Clerkwell
Baines Elizabeth (Miss), dressmaker, 65 Coleman st. City
Baines Frederick, plumber & glazr. 18 Frederick pl. Hmpstd. rd
Baines Matthew Talbot, queen's counsel, 2 Tanfield ct. Temple
Baines Richard, tuscan & straw hat mnfr. 33 Greek st. Soho
Baines Robert Henry, solicitor, 13 Gray's inn square
Baines Thomas, *Caledonian* coffee rooms, 7 Museum st
Baines Thomas, saddler & harness ma. 44 Duke st. Mnchstr. sq
Baines Wm. Ferdinand, wine & spirit mercht. 14 Philpot lane
Bainfield Robert, grocer, 13 James st. Oxford st

Baird Elizabeth (Mrs.), matron, Orphan working school, Canal bridge, City road
Baird Jas. musician & music copyist, 9 Leigh st. Red Lion sq
Baird John, wholesale perfumer, 32 Eagle st. Red Lion sq
Bairnson Thomas, lodging ho. 5 Little Broad st.St.Geo's. ea
Baisler Francis, stationer & bookseller, 124 Oxford st
Baiss Brothers&Co. who. druggists, 125&126 Low. Thames st
Bajot Pierre, coffee rooms, 3 High st. St. Giles's
Baker's old established patent mangle & agricultural repository, & mangle maker by appointment to the Queen, 309 Oxford st. near Bond st.; proprietor, Thomas Wilkinson, nephew of the late Mr. Baker
Baker Dan. Sebbon & Son, auctioneers, 107 Upper st. Islgtn
Baker & Daniels, ship & insurance agents, 140 Fenchurch st
Baker & Davies, distillers, 13 Castle st. Finsbury
Baker & Dowden, linendrapers, 17 Upper Eaton st. Pimlico
Baker & Eastwood, warehousemen, 32 Cheapside
Baker Ezekiel & Son, gun manufactrs. 24 Whitechapel road
Baker George & Co. linen drapers, &c. 3 & 4 Ludgate hill
Baker George Leeke & Charles, solicitors to the Equitable Gas Light company, 52 Lincoln's inn fields
Baker Geo. & Son, builders, Palace New road, Lambeth
Baker George & Son, ironmongers, 1 Park terrace, Camden town; & 139 Tottenham court road
Baker Geo. & Son, stock & share brokers, 29 Threadneedle st
Baker Henry & Co. shetland hosiery wareh. 111 New Bond st
Baker Henry & Son, auctioneers & estate agents, Kilburn
Baker & Jackson, alum wareho. Griffin's wharf, 79 Tooley st
Baker Jane & Martha, milliners, 48 Shoe lane, Holborn
Baker John & Co. silk manufacturers, bandanna & corah printers, 28, 29 & 30, Lawrence lane, & 10 Trump st
Baker John & Son, furn. undertakers, 7 Cross st. Islington
Baker Joseph & Son, auctns. & apprs. 18 Windmill st. Finsby
Baker Juliana & Eliza, milliners, 41 Duke st. Manchester sq
Baker & Martin, commission agents, 75 Aldermanbury
Baker & Leach, cheesemongers, 280 Oxford st
Baker & Parson, solicitors, 4 Pancras lane, City
Baker Richard & Co. mangle, press & engine makers & machinists; agents for the sale of agricultural implements manufactured by Wedlake & Thompson, union foundry, Hornchurch, Essex; 65 & 66 Fore st. Cripplegate
Baker Samuel & Co. west india merchants, 106 Fenchurch st
Baker Samuel C. & Charles N. by special appointment to the Queen & H.R.H. Prince Albert, dealers in ornamental poultry, live wild fowl, gold, silver, white, pied & common tamebred pheasants; pheasants & poults, foxes & cubs for stocking, &c. &c. 3 Halfmoon passage, Gracechurch st. & at the Pheasantry, Beaufort st. King's road, Chelsea
Baker Thomas & Son, irish linen factors, 17 King st. Cheapsd
BakerWm.&Jno.builders& lookg.glss.frame ma.56Hatton gdn
Baker Wm. jun. & Robert B. solicitors, 3 Crosby sq. Bishopsgate; & 4 Albion terrace, Limehouse
Baker street Bazaar, 58 Baker st. Portman square
Bakers' Hall (Henley Smith, clerk), 16 Harp la. Tower st
Baker Ann Maria (Mrs.), working cutler, 186 Tooley st
Baker Benjn. beer retailer, 2 Williams pl. Walworth road
Baker Benjamin, confectioner, 144 Shoreditch High st
Baker Benjamin, dining rooms, 9 Church lane, Commercl. rd
Baker Benjamin, leather breeches maker, 215 Piccadilly
Baker Chas. cabinet maker, 10 Upper Ebury st. Pimlico
Baker Charles, meat salesman, see Harris & Baker
Baker Charles, solicitor, 3 Wells st. Gray's inn road
Baker Charles, upholsterer, 107 Upper st. Islington
Baker Chas. upholsterer & house agent, 18Brook st.Grsvnr. sq
Baker Charles, jun. butcher, 4 Torrington pl. Torrington sq
Baker Charles John, milliner, 5 Charlotte st. Fitzroy sq
Baker Chas.Lancaster,chemist& druggist,2Up.EastSmithfld
Baker Charlotte (Miss), matron, St. Bartholomew's hospital
Baker Dan. *Porto Bello* P.H. 5Turvile st.Church st.Shoredh
Baker Edmund, dyer & calenderer, 212 Whitechapel road, & 72 Blackman st. Borough
Baker Edmund, dyer & scourer, 15 Commercial pl. City rd
Baker Edmund, jun. dyer, 47 Exmouth st. Clerkenwell
Baker Edward, chronometer maker, 11 Angel ter. Pentonville
Baker Edward, potato dealer, Deptford bridge
Baker Edward, surgeon, 50 Walcot place east, Lambeth
Baker Edward, who. druggist, see Gale, Baker, Warde & Co
Baker Edwin, tailor, 9 Featherstone buildings, Holborn
Baker Elizabeth (Mrs.), coal mer. 15 Copenhagen pl. Limeho
Baker Elizth. (Miss), seminary, 10 Lower Kennington grn
Baker Elizabth. (Mrs.) lodging house, 24 Upp. Wimpole st
Baker Emanuel, cabinetma. 28 Exmouth st. Commer. rd. East
Baker Emanuel, surgeon, see Coyne & Baker
Baker Fras. straw hat maker, 36Chester pl. Kennington cross
Baker Francis, tobacconist, 36 Farringdon st
Baker Frank, shirt maker & glover, 1 & 2 Burlington arcade
Baker Frederick, plumber, 23 Up. Charlton st. Fitzroy st
Baker Frederick, tobacconist & snuff maker, 207 Fleet st
Baker Fredk. Matthew, surgeon, 11 North pl. Kingsland rd
Baker George, agt. to *Phœnix Fire Off.*28Lr.Kennington la
Baker George, cheesemonger, 17 King David la. Shadwell
Baker George, fruiterer, 16 Nottingham st. Marylebone
Baker George, grocer & italian wa. 3 Bruton st. Berkeley sq
Baker George, grocer, tea & italian wa. 37 Ludgate hill
Baker George, ironmonger, 6 Harrow road, Paddington
Baker George, ropemaker, 21 Bermondsey wall
Baker Henry, architect, 11 Upper Gower st. Bedford sq
Baker Henry, bootmaker, 12 Carlton st. Regent st
Baker Henry, manchester agent, 3 Lawrence la. Cheapside
Baker Henry, merchant, 79 Mark lane
Baker Henry, saddler, Church st. Battersea
Baker Henry Charles, builder, Peckham foot path, OldKt.rd
Baker Henry Sherston, barrister, 4 Old sq. Lincoln's inn
Baker Honor (Mrs.), *Auction Mart tavern*, Throgmorton st
Baker James, basket maker, 4 Hope st. Whitechapel
Baker James, *Britannia* coffee rooms, 117 Waterloo rd
Baker James, butcher, 57 Back Church lane, Whitechapel
Baker James, earthenware dlr.7Norfolkpl.Camberwell nw.rd
Baker James, *Prince of Orange* P.H. Mill st. Dockhead
Baker James, surgeon, 1Dorchester pl.NewNorth rd.Hoxton
Baker James, tailor to the Queen, 9 George st. Hanover sq
Baker James, tobacconist, 8 Edgware road
Baker James Rt. stock broker, 2 Bank chambers, Lothbury
Baker Jane (Mrs.), straw hat ma.32 Stanhope st. Clare mar
Baker John, bootmaker, 6 Wine office court, Fleet st
Baker John, butcher, Hen&Chicken lane, Walworth common
Baker John, butcher, 4 Nursery place, Old Kent road
Baker John, coachbody maker, 42 Carlisle st. Lambeth
Baker John, confectioner, 4 Jewin crescent, Cripplegate
Baker John, cowkeeper, 14 Hill road, St. John's wood
Baker John, *Four Swans tap* P. H. 84 Bishopsgate within
Baker John, grocer, 57 Tottenham court road
Baker John, grocer, 6 Surry place, Wandsworth road
Baker John, haberdasher, 19 Cotton st. Poplar
Baker John, ham & beef dealer, 3 Albemarle st. Piccadilly
Baker John, livery stables, 1 Brompton grove
Baker John, livery stables, 12 Up. Queen's bldgs. Brompton
Baker John, millstone ma. Brook's wf. Pickleherng. Tooley st
Baker John, surgeon, 48 Gray's inn lane
Baker John, surgeon, 1 Green st. Bethnal green
Baker John, undertaker, 4 Church lane, Islington
Baker John, watch cap mak. 14 Gt. Sutton st. Clerkenwell
Baker John George, harness ma.11Wellington st.Blackfrs.rd
Baker John James, *Unicorn* P.H. 35 Shoreditch High st
Baker John Law, merchant, Hall of Commerce, Threadndl.st
Baker JohnW.carpenter,&c.12Harleyfordst.Kennington com
Baker Joseph, fishmonger, 3 Whiterose court, Coleman st
Baker Joseph, fruiterer, 2 Keen's row, Walworth road
Baker Joseph, *George* P.H. 8 East Harding st. Gough sq
Baker Joseph, locksmith, 36 Gt. Wild st. Lincoln's inn fields
Baker Joseph, pawnbroker, 48 Stanhope st. Clare market
Baker Joseph, tobacconist, 110 Cheapside
Baker Joseph, *Tower* dining rooms, 60 Minories
Baker Joseph Alfred, bootmaker, 22 Charing cross
Baker Joshua, hay salesman, 12 & 32 Cumberland market
Baker Mark, box wood preparer, 4 Nevill's ct. Fetter lane
Baker Mark, carpenter, 32 Stanhope st. Clare market
Baker Mary (Miss), artist, 9 George st. Hanover square
Baker Mary Ann (Mrs.), dressmaker, 57 South Audley st
Baker MaryAnn(Mrs.),tobacconist,61Regent stHorseferry rd
Baker Moses, builder, Southampton st. Camberwell road
Baker Nathaniel, baker, 28 Green st. Bethnal green
Baker Peter, chandler's shop, 8 Gt. Carlisle st. Portman mkt
Baker Richard, tailor & draper, 40 Cheapside
Baker Richard, trunk maker, 41 Edgware road, Marylebone
Baker Richard, worsted manufacturer, 14 Fort st. Spitalfields
Baker Richard Grey, corn dealer, 12 Sidney st. Mile end
Baker Robert, baker, 26 Church st. Lambeth
Baker Robert, historic & ornamental engraver, 66 Goswell rd
Baker Saint Thomas, wireworker, hot water apparatus, green houses, &c. Manor house, King's road, Chelsea
Baker Samuel, brass & iron turner, 8 James st. Goswell rd
Baker Samuel, merchant, 106 Fenchurch st
Baker Sam. F.civil enginr.well borer,&c.3Oxford pl.Wsmr.rd
Baker Saml. Fras. *Oxford Arms* P.H. 3 Oxford pl.Westmr.rd
Baker Samuel Thomas, wine merchant, 8 Gt. Marlborough st
Baker Sarah (Miss), crt. millinr. & dress mak. 113 Piccadilly
Baker Sarah (Miss), seminary, 15 Barnes pl. Mile end road
Baker Sarah (Miss), staymaker, 23 Lisson grove north, Newrd
Baker Stephen, beer retailer, 26 Cumberland market
Baker Stephen, bootmaker, 24 Tokenhouse yard
Baker Thos. beer retailer, 109 Albany road, Camberwell

Baker Thos. cabinet maker, 1 Christopher st. Hatton garden
Baker Thos. corndealer, 7 Pleasant row, Cambridge rd
Baker Thos. fruiterer, 35 Providence row, Cloudesley sq
Baker Thos. linendraper, 31 Tavistock st. Covent garden
Baker Thos. livery stables, 6 Waterloo ter. Commercial rd. ea
Baker Thos. naturalist, Edward place, Balls pond
Baker Thos. solicitor, see Keddell, Baker & Grant
Baker Thos. upholsterer, 13 High st. Camberwell road
Baker Thos. Hen. conveyancer & parlmenty. agt. 29 Spring gdns
Baker Thos. James, *Cross Keys* P.H. 34 Marylebone la
Baker Thos. K. cutler & hardwareman, 73 Farringdon st
Baker Thos. K. gun & pistol maker, 1 Stonecutter st.
Baker Thos. Waghorn, watch maker & jeweller, 62 St. Martin's lane, Charing cross
Baker Wm. academy, Francis place, Holloway
Baker Wm. artist, 2 Harrington street, Hampstead road
Baker Wm. artist in fire works, 31 Cambridge rd. Mile end
Baker Wm. awl blade maker, 14 Allen st. Goswell st
Baker Wm. baker, 215 Bethnal green road
Baker Wm. baker, 3 Cottage pl. Green st. Kentish town
Baker Wm. baker, 26 Prior place, East street, Walworth
Baker Wm. basket ma. 7 Marylebone la. & 27 Gt. Titchfield st
Baker Wm. basket maker, 5 Osborne place, Spitalfields
Baker Wm. beer retailer, 3 Prior pl. East st. Walworth
Baker Wm. boot maker, 7 Charles st. Middlesex Hospital
Baker Wm. boot & shoe maker, Church st. Stoke Newington
Baker Wm. corn dealer, 9 Parnham pl. Salmon la. Limehouse
Baker Wm. coroner for Middlesex, 3 Crosby sq. Bishopsgate & 10 Church row, Limehouse
Baker Wm. hairdresser, 24 New st. Dorset square
Baker Wm. hatter & outfitter, 25 Clement's lane, Lombard st
Baker Wm. laceman, 3 Church st. Camberwell
Baker Wm. manufacturing chemist, see May & Baker
Baker Wm. musical instrument mk. 1 New Peter st. Westmr
Baker Wm. *Nag's Head* P.H. 10 James st. Covent garden
Baker Wm. *Osborne Arms* P.H. 9 Heneage st. Whitechapel
Baker Wm. picture dlr. & carver, &c. 95 Charlotte st. Fitzroy sq
Baker Wm. surgeon, 11 Wardrobe place, Doctors' commons
Baker Wm. tobacconist, 7 Gray's inn passage, Red Lion sq
Baker Wm. tobacconist, 6 Princes pl. Commercial rd. east
Baker Wm. undertaker, 22 Harrison st. Gray's inn road
Baker Wm. vestry clerk & solr. 1 Hatton ct. Threadneedle st
Baker Wm. watch finisher, 28 Glo'ster st. St. John st. rd
Baker Wm. watchmaker & jeweller, 35 Long acre
Baker Wm. Hen. tinplate worker, 27 Windmill st. Finsbury
Baker Wm. John, artist, 27 Dean st. Commercial rd. east
Baker Wm. Joseph, chemist, 14 Cornwall cres. Camden new tn
Baker Wm. Lloyd, sailmaker, 21 Bermondsey wall
Baker Wm. Mosely, *Green Dragon* P.H. 1&2 Botolph alley
Baker Wm. Pares, surgeon, 35 High st. Bow
Bakewell Henry, hatter, 151 Church st. Shoreditch
Bakewell James, butcher, 362 Rotherhithe
Bakewell John, publisher, 80 Newgate st
Bakewell Wm. artist in hair, 7 Berkley st. Clerkenwell
Balaam Frederick, corn dealer, 2 Whittlebury st. Euston sq
Balch Charlotte (Mrs.), dressmaker, 39 Great Windmill st
Balch Jane B. R. (Miss), ladies' school, 40 Gt. Alie st. Goodman'sfi
Balch John, butcher, 1 Ship tavern pass. Leadenhall market
Balchin Ann M. (Mrs.), milliner, 8 Watt's terrace, Old Kent rd
Balchin Francis, cattle salesman, 17 West Smithfield
Balchin James, currier, 8 Cumberland pl. Newington butts
Balchin James, coffee rooms, 34 Warwick st. Golden sq
Balchin William, tailor, 15 Kenton st. Brunswick sq
Balchin William, tailor, 77 Chalton st. Somers town
Balcombe & Evans, stock & share agts. 10 Tokenhouse yard
Balcombe Jas. *Blenheim Arms* P.H. 2 Blenheim st. Oxford st
Balcombe James, hairdresser, 2 Blenheim st. Oxford st
Balcombe Steph. *Norland Arms* P.H. 1 Addison rd. nth. Nott. hl
Balcon James, watch & clock maker, 56 Grove st. Camden tn
Baldacci Francesco, figure mak. 15 Up. Wellington st. Cov. gar
Balderson Abraham Thos. surgeon, 11 Poland st. Oxford st
Balderson Kent, pork butcher, 76 Long lane, Smithfield
Balding Ann (Mrs.), *Ship* P.H. Vauxhall bridge road
Balding Charles, oil & colorman, 43 Gt. James st. Lisson gr
Balding Edward, tailor, 12 Pont st. Sloane st
Balding Thomas, baker, 87 High st. Marylebone
Balding Thomas, teadealer & grocer, 22 New st. Dorset sq
Balding Thomas, jun. cheesemonger, 13 New st. Dorset sq
Balding Wm. *Bell inn* P.H. 31 Long lane, Smithfield
Baldock Lucretia (Mrs.), *Nightingale* P.H. 33 Alpha road
Baldock Robert, bookseller, 85 High Holborn
Baldock Wm. poultry dlr. 4 Bull & Mouth st. St. Martin's le grnd
Baldrey Jno. *Cherry Tree* P.H. 85 Up. Whitecross st. St. Luke's
Baldry Abraham, butcher, 5 Bolingbroke row, Walworth rd
Baldry William Carr, man's mercer, 166 New Bond st
Baldwin & Elliott, saddlers' ironm. 4 Martin's la. Cannon st
Baldwin Francis & Son, hame & chain ma. 43 Ray st. Clerknwl
Baldwin Hen. & John, *Tom's coffeehouse*, Cowper's ct. Cornhill
Baldwin Hen. & John, woollen drapers & tailors, 31 Cornhill
Baldwin & Waters, who. tea & coffee dealrs. 2 Bishopsgate ch. yd
Baldwin Benjamin, miniature painter, 27 Rathbone pl
Baldwin Charles, hame manufacturer, 42 Ray st. Clerkenwell
Baldwin Charles, printer, Union st. Bridge st. Blackfriars
Baldwin Charles, surveyor, 7 Coppice row, Clerkenwell
Baldwin Charles Barry, barrister, 6 Parliament st
Baldwin Eliza (Mrs.), milliner, 1 York pl. Upper st. Islington
Baldwin Frederick, cooper, 59 Bath st. City road
Baldwin George, coffee rooms, 3 Middle row, Knightsbridge
Baldwin Henry, carman, 93 Hoxton old town
Baldwin Henry, woollendraper & tailor, 101 Cheapside
Baldwin Hen. G. stone mason, 32 Squirries st. Bethnal gr. rd
Baldwin James, jun. paperstainer, 62 St. John st. Clerkenwell
Baldwin James, sen. paperstainer, 22 Whitechapel High st. & 13 Etham place, Kent st. Borough
Baldwin John, chandler's shop, 42 Bethnal green road
Baldwin John, statuary, &c. 1 Ward's row, Bethnal green rd
Baldwin Joseph, baker, 13 Leigh st. Red Lion square
Baldwin Joseph, marine store dlr. 57 Church st. Shoreditch
Baldwin Joseph, rope & rag mercht. 6 Fox's lane, Shadwell
Baldwin Richard, bricklayer, Camberwell green
Baldwin Robert, barrister, 2 Brick court, Temple
Baldwin Robert, bookseller & publisher, 47 Paternoster row
Baldwin Samuel, undertaker, 48 Amwell st. Pentonville
Baldwin Susan (Miss), stayma. & baby linen wa. 204 Sloane st
Baldwin Thomas, perfumer, 33 Great Tower st
Baldwin Thomas, watchmaker, 71 Old st. St. Luke's
Baldwin Wm. bracemaker, 20 Little Newport st. Long acre
Baldwin Wm. *Stewart Arms* P.H. 11 Norland rd. Notting hill
Baldwin William, tailor & draper, 2 Jewin st. Cripplegate
Bale (Mrs. Ann), furniture broker, 12 Vine st. Hatton wall
Bale Anthony, Norfolk house academy, Stepney green
Bale James, watch jeweller, 63 Gee st. Goswell st
Bale Rd. grocer & cheesemonger, 87 Union st. Lambeth walk
Bale Richard, *King on Horseback* P.H. 118 Borough High st
Bale Thomas, printer, 6 Brook st. New road
Bale William Stamp, dining rooms, 153 Blackfriars road
Bales Isaac, coal dealer, 30 Fleet lane, Farringdon st
Bales James, merchant, 4 Alderman's walk, New Broad st
Bales Mary (Mrs.), dining rooms, 9 Little Carter lane
Baley Thomas, livery stable keeper, 119 Aldersgate st
Balfour Brothers, silk merchants, 7½ Great Winchester st
Balfour Buchanan, ship & ins. broker, see Brooks & Balfour
Balfour Charles, merchant, 57½ Old Broad st. City
Ball Edward & Son, oil & italian warehouse, 81 New Bond st
Ball & Co. manufacturers & importers of ostrich, fancy & funeral feathers, artificial flowers, crape, silk & gimp trimmings, rouching, caps' springs, & general fancy warehousemen, 7 & 8 Foster lane, Cheapside
Ball Geo. & Co. manufacturers of mourning collars, widows caps, child bed linen, millinery, willow squares, bonnet shapes, whalebone, cane, dolls' heads, &c. &c. &c. 7 & 8 Foster lane, Cheapside
Ball Henry & Son, tailors, 307 High Holborn
Ball Isaac & Son, furnishing ironmongers, 61 Coleman st
Ball James & Son, boot & shoemakrs. 26 High st. Kensington
Ball & Macaire, watch case ma. 26 Myddleton st. Spa fields
Ball & Norcott, carpent. & undert. Gt. Green st. Kentish tn
Ball William Y. & Co. who. glove manufacturers, 32 Wood st
Ball Abraham N. bootmaker, 9 High st. Newington
Ball Charles, hatter, 2 Sloane st. Knightsbridge
Ball Charles Jas. coal merchant, Feltoe's whf. Belvedere rd
Ball Eliza Jane (Miss), *Albion hotel*, 25 Cockspur st
Ball George, coffee rooms, 3 Cecil court, St. Martin's lane
Ball George, grocer, 1 Dorset st. Clapham road
Ball George, stationer, Deptford High st
Ball George, wine merchant, see Taylor & Ball
Ball Geo. Fredk. gold & silver worker, 9 Glos'ter st. Queen sq
Ball Henry, *Cock* P.H. 129 Great Portland st
Ball Henry, barrister, Hall staircase, Inner Temple
Ball Henry, tinman & braziers' tool ma. 8 Seward st. Gswell. st
Ball Herbert, tailor & draper, 5 St. George's ter. Borough rd
Ball James, bookbinder, 20 Little Carter la. Doc. commons
Ball James, builder, 20 New Quebec st. Portman square
Ball James, chair maker, 3 Ewer st. Union st. Borough
Ball James, manufacturer of gold, silver, & silk braid, aiguillettes, watchguards, &c. 4 Great New st. Shoe la
Ball James, oilman to his late Royal Highness the Duke of Sussex, 12 Duke street, Grosvenor square
Ball John, accountant, see Quilter & Ball
Ball John, attorney, 18 Bedford row, Bloomsbury, & 58 Hercules buildings, Lambeth
Ball John, furnitr. broker, 7 Broker's row, Red Cross st. Boro'

Ball John, plumber, Union road, Clapham road
Ball John, Holloway dairy, 3 Northampton row, Holloway
Ball John, merchant, office of the London Zink Rolling Mill, 28 Martin's la. Cannon st; Rolling Mill, Wenlock basin
Ball John, tailor, 20 St. George's place, Knightsbridge
Ball John, tobacconist, 251 High Holborn
Ball Joseph, *Queen's Arms tavern*, 70 Newgate st
Ball Mary (Mrs.), *White Bear & Union hotel*, 221 Piccadilly
Ball Richd. grainer, &c. 16 Devonshire st. Queen sq. Bloomsb
Ball Rd. mason, 2 Sussexter. & 13 Up. Queen's bdgs. O. Brompton
Ball Richard, upholsterer, 15 Northumberland st. Strand
Ball Samuel, smith & machinist, 5 Globe road, Mile end rd
Ball Thomas, builder, 2 the Mall, & 37 Peel st. Kensington
Ball Thos. fishmonger, 10 & 11 Lr. Area, Hungerford mrkt
Ball Thos. Mugliston, chemist, 77 St. George's rd. Southwk
Ball Wm. alton ale house, 12 Smithfield bars
Ball Wm. bookseller, 5 Aldine chambrs. 13 Paternoster row
Ball Wm. butcher, 21 Little Randolph st. Camden town
Ball Wm. dairyman, 5 Earl st. west, Edgware road
Ball Wm. patent locksmith, see Bramah, Prestage & Ball
Ball Wm. plumber & painter, 56 George st. Blackfriars rd
Ball Wm. tailor, &c. 13 St. John st. Clerkenwell
Ball Wm. wine merchant, 19 Bloomsbury st. St. Giles's
Ball Wm. Hen. coachmaster, Park place, Kennington cross
Ballance Thomas & Son, silk manufrs. 15 Gutter lane, City
Ballance Thomas, firewood dealer, Deptford Lower road
Ballantine Arthur, stock & share broker, 25 Tokenhouse yd
Ballantine James, newsvender, 45 Great Guildford st. Boro'
Ballantine John Palin, plumber, 6 Jamaica ter. Coml. rd. ea
Ballantine Mary A. (Mrs.), *Golden Anchor* P.H. 182 Wapping
Ballantine Robert, commercial agt. 28 Noble st. Cheapside
Ballantine Wm. barrister, 5 Inner Temple lane
Ballantine Wm. magistrate at Thames Police Ct. 89 Cadogan pl
Ballantyne John, hosier & glover, 18 Bedford st. Bedford row
Ballantyne Wm. watchmaker, 12 White Lion st. Goodman's flds
Ballard Jas. & Thos. paper hanging ma. 45 Duke st. Manchst. sq
Ballard Thos. & Co. ornamental & gen. printers, 19 Basing la
Ballard Thos. & Co. surgns. & chemists, 81 Connaught ter. Edgw. r
Ballard Charles, paperstainer, 23 Red Lion st. Holborn
Ballard Chas. Edward, paperstainer, 47 High st. St. Giles's
Ballard Edward, surgeon, 2 King Edward ter. Liverpool rd
Ballard Edwin, tailor, see Daulby & Ballard
Ballard George, confectioner, 66 Sun st. Bishopsgate
Ballard Henry, *Red Lion* P.H. 48 Parliament st. Westmnstr
Ballard James, coal dealer, 44 Brick lane, St. Luke's
Ballard Joseph, veter. surgeon, Bell yd. Brown st. Brystne. sq
Ballard Mary (Mrs.), ironmonger, 3 Folly, Dockhead
Ballard Rd. fruiterer, &c. 58 Up. North pl. Gray's inn road
Ballard Samuel, fruiterer, 34 Weymouth st. New Kent road
Ballard Wm. bath proprietor, 3 Chapel place, Cavendish sq
Ballard Wm. engraver & printer, 14 Cannon st. St. Geo. east
Ballard Wm. undertaker, 7 Britannia row, Hoxton
Ballard Thomas, gardener, Asylum road, Old Kent road
Ballast Offices, Trinity House & Narrow st. Ratcliff
Balle William, linen draper, High st. Stoke Newington
Ballentine William, baker, 12 Crosier st. Lambeth
Balleny John (late George R. Elkington), gold, silver gilt & black ornamental manufacturer, 74 Hatton garden, & at 44 St. Paul's square, Birmingham
Baller Henry, surgeon, 26 Jewry st. Aldgate
Balli (Xenophon) & Co. merchants, 26 Broad st. buildings
Ballin George, coal merchant, 65 Bankside
Ballinger Henry, jun. confectioner, 350 Oxford st
Ballinger Thomas, artist, 44 Cornhill
Ballinger Thomas, confectioner, 148 High Holborn
Ballisat Sophia (Miss), milliner, 126 Upper st. Islington
Ballisat Wm. boot & shoemaker, 118 Upper st. Islington
Balls James & Son, music sellers & publishers, 408 Oxford st
Balls Adolphus, writing master, 12 Blandford pl. Dorset sq
Balls Charles, coffee rooms, 4 Cumberland row, Walworth rd
Balls Henry, boot & shoema. 3 Marlborough pl. Kenngtn. cross
Balls James, alamode & boiled beef dining rooms, 20 & 21 King Edward st. Newgate st. (late Butcherhall lane)
Balls James, *Granby tavern*, 28 South Audley st
Balls James, lodging house, 2 St. James's sq. south side
Balls John, builder, Balls cottage, Grange rd. Bermondsey
Balls John, upholsterer, 170 Oxford st.; 12 & 13 Bird st. & 36 Rathbone place
Balls Richard, tailor, 45 Regent st. Lambeth
Balls Mary Ann (Mrs.), *Ship* P.H. Lower Shadwell
Balls Thos. brushmaker & turner, 11 James st. Haymarket
Balls Thos. iron, tin plate & metal merchant & agent, 69 Old Broad st. City
Balltis Wm. Ellward, cabinet ma. 9 Lit. Windmill st. Gldn. sq
Bally John Hadley, commission mercht. 47 Moorgate st
Balme Paul, tobacco pipe manufactr. Canal wharf, Mile end
Balmer John, chemist, 91 St. John st. road
Balmer Thomas, millwright, &c. 8 Abbey st. Bermondsey
Balmer Wm. tailor, 1A, Winchester pl. Southwark bridge rd
Balsdon & Crookes, tailors, 6 Grosvenor st. New Bond st
Balsdon E. P. (Miss), wax & tallow chandler, 256 Oxford st
Balston & Co. paper manufs. 3 Crown court, Old Broad st
Baltic Coffeehouse (John Monger), 58 Threadneedle st
Baltazzi (Demetrius) & Co. merchants, 75 Old Broad st
Baly Ann (Mrs.), haberdasher, &c. 18 Seymour st. Euston sq
Baly Joseph, merchant, North & South American coffeehouse
Baly Price P. civil engineer, 14 Buckingham st. Strand
Baly William, physician, 28 Spring gardens
Bamber John Daniel, locksmith, 27 Wood st. Westminster
Bambrick Henry, bookseller & stationer, 26 St. James's st
Bambridge William, *Grapes* P.H. 60 Bunhill row, & 60 Featherstone st. City road
Bambridge Wm. sailmaker, 12 Bird st. Green bank, Wapping
Bambury Thos. Saml. brush maker, 35 Union st. Clarendon sq
Bamfield Charles, saddler, 20 Savage gardens, Tower hill
Bamford Charles Francis, attorney, 7 King's Bench walk
Bamford James, coach builder, 50 Tottenham court road
Bamford James, silk manufacturer, 6 Milk st. Cheapside
Bamford John, plumber, 4 Crombie's row, Commerl. rd. east
Bamford Robert, coach builder, 62½ Berwick st. Soho
Bamford William, baker, 26 Mount st. Lambeth
Bamford William, bricklayer, 16 White Lion st. Pentonville
Bampton James, coal dealer, 17 Brackley st. Barbican
Bampton Mary Ann (Mrs.), la. school, 18 North st. Lisson grv
Bampton Robert, tailor, 74 Salisbury st. Lisson grove
Banbury Edward, barrister, 4 Harcourt buildings, Temple
Banbury Frederick T. ribbon manufacr. see Peters & Banbury
Banbury Maria (Miss), milliner, see Rowley & Banbury
Banbury Thomas, beer retailer, 6 New Manor st. King's rd. Chls
Banbury William, fancy brush ma. 6 Barclay st. Somers tn
Bance Richd. grocer & cheesemonger, 8 Exeter st. Sloane st
Banchini Gasper, coal & coke dealer, 68 Shoe lane, Holborn
Banchini Geo. *Bull in the Pound* P.H. 42 Broadwall, Blkfs
Bancks Robert Olddiss, solicitor, 11 Cecil st. Strand
Bancroft's Hospitl. Rev. Rd. I. F. Thomas, res. min. Mile end rd
Banderet Henry, wine merchant, see Halse & Banderet
Bandrowski Albert, cornchandler, 12 Lit. Pulteney st
Bandy Samuel, baker, 5 Chapel place, Brompton
Banes & Fiskin, sewed muslin warehouse, 89 Watling st
Banes Benjamin, leather seller, see Sorrel & Banes
Banes William Thomas, baker, 18 Chandos st. Covent garden
Banfield Chas. *Green Dragon* P.H. 40 Maddox st. Regent st
Banfield Emma (Mrs.), grocer, 6 St. Andrews hill, Doc. com
Banfield James, coal & potato dealer, 82 Long lane, Smithfield
Banfield Lewis, shoemaker, 24 Bethnal green road
Banfield Thomas, tailor, 2 Belgrave st. south, Pimlico
Banfield Walter, tailor, 6 Dorset st. Portman square
Banfill Samuel, cabinet maker, 20 Edward st. Langham pl
Bangham Benjamin, shoemaker, 11 Salmon lane, Limehouse
Bangham Mary Ann (Mrs.) pewter toy ma. 4 Castle st. Saffronhl
Bangham Wm. furn. undertaker, 7 Stockbridge ter. Pimlico
Bangor John, tailor & drap. 9 Old Chapel row, Kentish town
Bangs Chas. & Co. painters, 15 Church st. King's rd. Chelsea
Bangs Henry, baker, 3 Goldington st. Somers town
Bangs Joshua, baker, 28 Chapel st. Somers town
Banham John, bookseller, 3 Devonshire place, Stepney
Banister Henry Joshua, professr. of music, 50 Burton crescent
Banister Isabella (Mrs.), tobacconist, 17 Sherrard st. Gldn. sq
Banister John, butcher & purveyor to her Majesty, 17 Threadneedle street
Bank of Australasia (Wm. Milliken, sec.), 8 Austinfriars; for directors, &c. see page 2007
Bank of British North America (George De Bosco Attwood, secretary), 7 St. Helen's place; for directors, &c. see page 2006
Bank of Ceylon (Hugh Mackay, sec.), 72 Old Broad st. City; for directors, &c. see page 2006
Bank of England, Threadneedle street. For directors, branches, &c. see OFFICIAL & BANKING Directories

Hours of business:—

Accountant's Department	9 to 5	Branch Bank Office	9 to 3
Cashier's Department	9—5	Chancery Offices	9—3
Bullion Office	9—3	Drawing Off. for Pub. Accs.	9—5
Bank Note Pay Office	9—5	Drawing Off. for Private do.	9—5
Post Bill Office	9—5	Discount Office	9—3
Dividend Warrant Office	9—3	Bill Office	9—5

Bankart Fred. solicitor, 34 Clement's lane, Lombard st
Bankers' Clearing House, Post Office court, Lombard st
Bankes James L. & Chas. ribbon manfrs. 8 Wood st. Cheapside
Bankes George, M.P. cursitor baron of the Exchequer, 5 Old Palace yard, Westminster
Bankruptcy, Court of, 82 Basinghall st. hours 10 to 4

Bankrupt Office, 2 Quality court, Chancery lane; hours of business during term & sittings, 10 to 4; in vacation, 11 to 3
Bankrupt & Insolvent Gazette, King's arms bldgs. Cornhill
Bankrupts' Registry Off. (Austin & Owen's) 10½ King's arms yd
Bankrupts' & Insolvent Registry Office (Perry's), King's arms building, Cornhill
Banks & Mann, teadealers, &c. 9 Bridge st. Westminster
Banks, Peacock, Wilsen & Banks, wholesale linen merchants 10 & 11 Friday st. Cheapside
Banks Anth. lodging house, 10, 11 & 13 Manchester bldgs
Banks Frederick, butcher, New cross
Banks Henry, fruiterer, 3 Thornton st. Horselydown
Banks Henry, tripe dresser, 109 Church st. Shoreditch
Banks James, house agent, 2 Grey terrace, Great Dover rd
Banks John Byng, lace manufr. 22 Lawrence lane, Cheapside
Banks John H. engr. & cop. plate printer, 7 Gt. Newport st
Banks Joseph, advertising agent, 11½ Wellington st. north
Banks Joseph, *Crown* P.H. 4 Cranbourne pass. Cranbourne st
Banks Joseph, estate agent, surveyor & valuer, 18 Fish st. hill
Banks Joseph, jun. accountant & arbitrator, 18 Fish st. hill
Banks Percival Weldon, barrister, 8 Gray's inn place
Banks Peter, hairdresser, 5 Cross ct. Carnaby st. Golden sq
Banks Richard, hatter, Nelson place, Old Kent road
Banks Richard, wholesale jeweller, see Green & Banks
Banks Rt. tallow chandler, 18 & 19 Stebonheath ter. Limeho
Banks Thomas L. tallow chandler, 229 Shoreditch High st
Banks William, butcher, Deptford High st
Banks Wm. horse dealer, 11 Gray's inn terrace
Banks Wm. livery stables, see Osborn, Son & Banks
Banks Wm. *Old Crown* P.H. 7 Crown st. Soho
Banks Wm. *Red Lion* P.H. 6 Dockhead, Bermondsey
Banks Wm. silk & commission agent, see Jameson & Banks
Banks Wm. tailors' trimming seller, 90 Holborn hill
Banks Wm. *Windmill* P.H. 18 Nicholas lane, Lombard st
Banks Wm. Henry, corn dealer, 62 Brick lane, Spitalfields
Banks Wm. Henry, tailor, 50 King st. terrace, New North rd
Bann Mary (Mrs.), bootmaker, 27 New Bond st
Banner Cicely F. (Miss), straw bonnet manfr. 78 St John st. rd
Banner Henry, plumber & glazier, 35½ Whitecross st
Banner John, music seller, 6 Hopkins bldgs. Upper st. Islington
Banner Mary Ann (Mrs.) statnr. 4 Manchester bldgs. Hollowy
Banner Samuel, surgeon, 26 Berkeley square
Banner Samuel, surgeon, see Higham & Banner
Banning Thos. & John, wine mers. 1 Hammond's ct. Mincing la
Banning Henry John, hatter, 4 Three Oak la. Horselydown
Banning John, sugar broker, 21 Great Tower st. City
Bannister Charles George, attorney, 13 John st. Bedford row
Bannister Cyrus, cane worker, 29 Hyde st. Bloomsbury
Bannister Mary A. (Mrs) cheesemnger. 13 Charles st. Hmpstd. rd
Bannister James, coachmaker, see Smith & Bannister
Bannister James, watchmaker, 32 Princes st. Leicester sq
Bannister John Edwd. engrav. 38 Southampton st. Pentnvl
Bannister John Henry, surgeon & chemist, 436 Oxford st
Bannister Joseph, butcher, 20 Newport ct. Newport market
Bannister Joseph, french polisher, 39 University st. Tott. ct. rd
Bannister Joshua, coal merchant, 35 Road side, Mile end road
Bannister Joshua, shpg. ironmgr. 40 New Gravel la. Ea. Lon. dk
Bannister Robert Dixon, shipsmith, 40 New Gravel lane
Bannister Thomas, barrister, 4 Middle Temple lane
Bannister Thomas, fruiterer, 8 Buckingham pl. Marlbro. rd
Bannister Thos. porkman, 23 Sidney pl. Commercial rd. east
Bannister Timothy, grocer, 22 New Church court, Strand
Bannister Wm. carver & gilder, 8 Pollen st. Hanover square
Bannister Wm. shoemaker, 52 Margaret st. Hackney fields
Bans James, wadding ma. 29 Lower Smith st. Northampton sq
Bansback David, baker, 21 Squirries st. Bethnal green road
Banson Thomas Hall, architect, &c. 9 Blomfield st. Finsbury
Banter Edward, *Cape of Good Hope* P.H. Devonshire mws. east
Banter Isaac, furn. broker, 49 Greenfield st. Coml. rd. east
Banter William, cabinet manufacturer, 5 Bethnal green rd
Banting James, architect, 5 Stanley pl. Paddington green
Banting John, carpenter, 3 Bedford st. Bedford row
Banting Wm. upholder & cabinet maker, 27 St. James's st
Bantock Hugh, butcher, Stratford broadway
Bantock John, carpenter, Stratford broadway
Banwell Charles, tailor, see Fraser, Banwell & Co
Banyard John, plumber, 5 Villa street, Walworth common
Banyard Wm. russia agt. 5 Adams ct. Old Broad st. & Baltic
Banyon Augustus, goldsmith & jeweller, 16 Frith st. Soho
Banyon John, clerk to Watermen's Co. 18 St. Mary at hill
Banyon Thomas H. stationer & engraver, 8 Greek st. Soho
Baptist Joseph, currier, 17 Goldsmith's row, Hackney rd
Baptist Guar. & Christ. Intell. (Frs. Newton, pblr.), 2 Crane ct
Baptist Missionary Soc. (Josph. Angus, sec.), 33 Moorgate st
Baptiste Violette, french boot maker, 15 Little Newport st
Barandon Chas. who. stationer & printer, 4 N. London st. City
Barbe Charles, artists' colorman, 60 Quadrant, Regent st
Barber & Andrewes, tin plate workers & wood meat screen makers, 65 John st. Fitzroy square
Barber Brothers, commission merchts. 7 Basinghall st
Barber Brothers, stock & share brokers, 7 Cowper's court
Barber & Calvert, tailors & clothiers, 123 Pall mall
Barber & Groom, who. tin plateworkers, Union ct. Holborn hill
Barber, Howse & Davis, woollenwarehmen. 19 St. Paul's ch. yd
Barber James & Co. cloth workers & packers, 4 Coleman st
Barber James & Co. ship & insurance brokers, & east india army agents, 17 St. Mary Axe
Barber, Nephew & Co. ea. india & col. brokers, 36 Fenchurch st
Barber & Smith, goldsmiths & jewellers, 36 Cornhill
Barber Widow & Son, hatters, 13 Royal Exchange
Barber William & Sons, grocers, 141 & 142 Lambeth Lower marsh, & 32 Gray's inn lane
Barbers' Hall (Henley Smith, clerk), 33 Monkwell st
Barber Abram, goldsmith & watchmaker, 56 Cheapside
Barber Benjamin, carpenter, &c. 36 Park st. Up. st. Islington
Barber Chas. ship & ins. broker, Chamberlains wf. Tooley st
Barber Chas. teadealer, 14 Rufford's blgs. High st. Islington
Barber Charles Chapman, barrister, 11 New sq. Lincoln's inn
Barber Charlt. (Miss), lace wa. 44 Up. North pl. Gray's inn rd
Barber Christphr. Wm. dentist, 12 Beaumont st. Portland pl
Barber Edward Field, *King's Head* P.H. 50 Gt. Tower st
Barber Frederick, billbroker, 7 Cowper's court, Cornhill
Barber George, clothes salesman, 10 Gt. Chapel st. Westmnr
Barber George, hatter, 41 George st. New Kent road
Barber George, linendraper, 8 Deptford High st
Barber Henry, dyer, 27 Henry st. Pentonville
Barber Henry, hosier & outfitter, 46 St. George st
Barber Henry, tailor, 25 Crawford street, Portman sq
Barber Henry, tailor & draper, 166 Goswell st
Barber Henry Joseph, solicitor, 2 Clement's la. Lombard st
Barber Isaac, potato salesman, South row, Covent garden
Barber Jas. cheesemonger, 2 Providence pl. York rd. Lmbth
Barber John, barrister, 10 Gray's inn place, Gray's inn
Barber John, confectioner, Broadway, Stratford
Barber John, corndealer, 47 Old st. St. Luke's
Barber John, dealer in birds, 27 Sclater st. Bethnal green
Barber John, livery stables, Church st. Hackney
Barber John, melter & bone merchant, 10 Baldwin's place, Gray's inn lane, & 37 Upper Fore st. Lambeth
Barber John, solicitor, 11 Furnival's inn, Holborn
Barber John, straw plait dealer, 9 Market st. Oxford mkt
Barber Joseph, chemist, 7 Orange st. Red Lion square
Barber Joseph, colonial broker, 9 Fenchurch st
Barber Joseph, die sinker & spoon ma. 53 Gt. Sutton st. Clkwl
Barber Joseph, wharfinger, Brewer's, Chester's & Galley quays, Lower Thames street
Barber Joseph, wharfinger, Chamberlain's wf. Tooley st
Barber Leonard, tobacconist, 5 Penton st. Pentonville
Barber Otho, butcher, see Hyem & Barber
Barber Peter, dyer, 3 Church st. Clapham rd
Barber Richard, bootmaker, 10 Gt. Woodstock st. Marylebone
Barber Richard Edward, grocer, 87 Chalton st. Somers town
Barber Samuel, haberdasher, 1 Exeter st. Strand
Barber Samuel, solicitor, 9 Warwick st. Charing cross
Barber Susannah (Mrs.), *Birdcage* P.H. 81 Wood st. Cheapsi
Barber Thomas, bootmaker, 30 Cross st. Hatton garden
Barber Thomas, dairyman, 3 Southampton bldgs. Chanceryla
Barber Thomas, grocer, 104 Aldersgate st. & 37 Cowcross st
Barber Thos. Archer, chemist, 2 Scott's pl. Lower rd. Islington
Barber Thos. Beetonson, custom ho. agent & agent for Mant's ale, Galley quay, Lower Thames st. & 10 Beer lane
Barber Thos. B. packer & calenderer, 33 Camomile st
Barber Thos. Hunt, commission merchant, 7 Basinghall st
Barber William, cabinet maker, 2 Leonard sq. Finsbury
Barber William, hairdresser, 16 Gt. Garden st. Whitechapel
Barber William, painter, 9 Green st. Theobalds road
Barber William, plated agent, 29 Bartlett's bldgs. Holborn
Barber William, upholsterer, 58 Charlotte st. Fitzroy sq
Barber Zachariah James, grocer, 17 Upper Marylebone st
Barbour & Co. coal merchts. Middle wf. Gt. Scotland yard
Barbut Geo. shoe mak. 3 Commercial pl. York rd. Lambeth
Barcham Ann (Mrs.), tobacconist, 6 Charles st. Commrcl. rd
Barchard Edward & Co. merchants & agents, 3 Philpot lane
Barchard Robt. Wildman, coal mercht. 6 Lr. Fore st. Lambth
Barchou Arsene, pattern drawer, reader, & card cutter for jacquard machines, 16 Church st. Spitalfields
Barclay Alex. & Co. wax bleachers, oil merchants & sealing wax makers, 2 Piccadilly; & Teddington
Barclay, Allsop & Mercier, stock & share brokers, 1 Royal Exchange buildings
Barclay, Bevan, Tritton & Co. bankers, 54 Lombard st
Barclay Brothers & Co. merchants, 12 Austin friars

Barclay & Friend, irish & foreign provision & general merchants, 102 Leadenhall st
Barclay & Friend, export agents for Allsopp & Sons' india ale in bulk & in bottle, 102 Leadenhall st
Barclay, Perkins & Co. brewers, Park st. Boro', & Stoney la
Barclay Robt. & Co. whitelead & color manufacturers, 102 Leadenhall st. & Little George st. Bermondsey
Barclay & Son, wax bleachers & oil merchts. 170 Regent st
Barclay & Sons, patent medicine wareho. 95 Farringdon st
Barclay David, leather dressr. 40 Crucifix la. Bermondsey
Barclay George, hatter & fur manufacturer, 42 St. James's st. Piccadilly; & 104 Quadrant, Regent st
Barclay George, engraver & printer, 22 Gerrard st. Soho
Barclay George, printer, 28 Castle st. Leicester square
Barclay Henry, surgeon dentist, see Heath & Barclay
Barclay James, fur manufctr. coat mak. & hatter, 212 Strand
Barclay Jas. watchma. 10 Jamaica ter. Commercial rd. Limeh
Barclay Jas. Lindsey, pat. medicine vend. 9 King's rd. Gray's in
Barclay John, mercht. & insur. broker, Lloyd's, & 7 Jeffrey's sq
Barclay Ralph, paperhanger, 46 Marchmont st. Burton crest
Bardell Jas. sen. horsedealer, 20 Gresse st. Tottenham ct. rd
Bardell James, jun. stables, 2 Stephen's mews, Gresse st
Barden Thos. tobacconist, &c. 2 Market st. Shepherd's markt
Bardgett Wm. cornfactor, Corn exch. & 53 Old Broad st. City
Bardin Elizabeth (Miss), globe mak. 16 Salisbury sq. Fleet st
Bardolph James, fish factor, 105 Lower Thames st
Bardons Ann (Mrs.), straw hat mak. 27 Bedford st. Bedford row
Bardons John, surveyor, 27 Bedford st. Bedford row
Bardons Richard, carpenter, 75 Red Lion st. High Holborn
Bardsley Elizab. (Mrs.), grocer, &c. 103 Tottenham court rd
Bardwell Wm. architect & surveyor, 11 Park st. Westminster
Bare James, sen. chandler's shop, 16 Caroline st. Commcl. rd. ea
Bare Jn. *Coal Meters' Arms* P.H. 31½ Heath st. Commcl. rd. ea
Bare John, *Red Lion* P.H. 17 Bevis marks
Bare Robert Hall, fishmonger, 2 Gray's inn passage, Red Lion square; & 13 & 14 Lower area, Hungerford market
Barefoot Wm. tallow chand. & oilman, 110 Upper st. Islingtn
Bareham Jas. cheesemonger, 61 Mortimer st. Cavendish sq
Barelli John & Co. merchants, 11 Castle st. Holborn
Barenger Wm. & Sons, plumbers & glaziers, 2 Green st. Kentsh. tn
Barfield George, carpenter, 4 Rodney st. North, Pentonville
Barfield William, dairy, 10 Corporation row, Clerkenwell
Barfoot Philip & Son, corn & coal dlrs. 70 Lit. Cadogan place
Barfoot Edward Way, surgeon, 18 William st. Regent's park
Barford James & Co. straw hat, plait & bonnet manufactur. 22 Wood st. City, & 5 Wilderness row, St. Luke's
Barford Charles, bookbinder, 27 Poland st. Oxford st
Barford Richard, timber merchant, 18 Wharf road, City road
Barge John, grocer, 52 Pratt st. Camden town
Bargman John, plumber, 4 Fort pl. Grange rd. Bermondsey
Barham Frederick, surgeon, 10 Osnaburgh st. Regent's park
Barham Henry, solicitor, 11 Austinfriars, Old Broad st
Barham Jas. *Shipwrights' Arms* P.H. 283 Bermondsey st
Barham Robert, greengrocer, 14 Windsor st. Islington
Baring Brothers & Co. merchants, 8 Bishopsgate within
Baring Hannah (Miss), ladies' wardrobe wa. 5 Exeter st. Lis. gr
Bark Joseph, boot & shoemaker, 174 Poplar High st
Bark Thos. veterny. surgeon, 7 Two Swan yard, Bishopsgate
Bark William, professor of music, 137 Fenchurch st
Barker & Bowker, solicitors, 1 Gray's inn square
Barker Chas. & Co. coachmakers, 66 Chandos st. Covent gdn
Barker & Co. goldsmiths, 142 Leadenhall st
Barker Edward & Co. tailors, 7 St. Michael's al. Cornhill
Barker Elizth. & Sophia (Misses), dress maks. 40 Mount st
Barker George & Robert, pawnbrokers, 91 Houndsditch, & 17 Aldgate High st
Barker & Howard, cornchandlers & livery stables, 55 Dorset place, Pall mall east
Barker Jas. T. & Co. merchants, St. Saviour's dock, Southwk
Barker John & Co. wine merchants, 9 Mincing lane
Barker & Morgan, surgeons, 5 Albion place, Hyde park sq
Barker Robert & Son, linendrapers, Church st. Hackney
Barker, Rose, & Norton, solicitors, 50 Mark lane, and 3 Park street, Westminster
Barker Sarah & Ann (Misses), school, 3 Sion vil. Hortulan pl
Barker & White, countrynewspaper & gen. adverti. off. 33 Fleet st
Barker Wm. & Chas. shoe thread & twine wa. 59 Watling st
Barker Wm. & Son, wine & brandy mers. 49 Bishopsgate without
Barker Aldred, dairyman, 49 Charles st. Westminster
Barker Ann (Mrs.), wine merchant, 26 Wilton place, Belgrave square, & 10 Lowndes terrace, Knightsbridge
Barker Benj. linendraper, 5 Beaufort terr. King's rd. Chelsea
Barker Chas. correspondent & advertisement agt. 12 Birchin la
Barker Charles, rush hassock & basket maker, 6 Providence st. City road
Barker Charles, *Three Spies* P.H. 11 Gt. Windmill st. Haymk
Barker Chas. Theodore, linendrap. 3 Grenada pl. O. Kent rd
Barker Christiana (Mrs.), *Jolly Butchers* P.H. Hi. st. Stok. New
Barker Edgar, surgeon, 40 Edgware road, Marylebone
Barker Edward, *Crown & Six Cans* P.H. 33 High Holborn
Barker Edward James, barrister, 59 Lincoln's inn fields
Barker Eliz. (Mrs.), haberdasher, 129 Edgware rd. Marylbo
Barker Francis, fruiterer, 18 Villa st. Walworth common
Barker Frederick, linendraper, see Barker Robert & Son
Barker George, confectioner, 10 Davies st. Berkeley square
Barker George, wine merchant, 340 Oxford st
Barker Henry, butcher, 6 Lower st. Islington
Barker Henry, tailor & draper, 45 Basinghall st
Barker Henry, tobacconist, 6 Middle row, Knightsbridge
Barker Jabez, watch jeweller, 42 Wynyatt st. Goswell road
Barker James, beer retailer, Maiden lane, King's cross
Barker James, bookseller, 19 Throgmorton st
Barker James, clockmaker, 38 Colet place, Commercial road east; & 28 Little Sutton st. Clerkenwell
Barker James, grocer, 26 Cable st. Wellclose square
Barker James, pastrycook, 38 Colet place, Commercial rd
Barker James, publisher & printseller, 7 Ely place, Holborn
Barker Jane (Mrs.), stables, 4 Mason's yd. Duke st. St. James'
Barker Jane (Mrs.), milliner, 42 Hedge row, High st. Islington
Barker Job, straw hat warehouse, 99 Edgware road
Barker Job, straw hat manufacturer, 292 High Holborn
Barker John, beer retailer, King st. New town, Deptford
Barker John, cheesemonger, 22 Exmouth st. Clerkenwell
Barker John, rag & rope merchant, see Codner & Barker
Barker John, tailor, 12 George st. Hanover square
Barker John, teapot handle maker, 22 Little Britain
Barker Jonas, plumber, 35 Spring st. Paddington
Barker John, surgeon, 22 Richmond pl. East st. Walworth
Barker Joseph, merchant, 5 Crown ct. Philpot lane
Barker Joseph, stock broker, 7 Tokenhouse yard, City
Barker Joseph, surgeon dentist, 191 Fleet st
Barker Joseph George, appraiser, 54 Broadwall, Blackfriars
Barker Margaret (Mrs.), fruiterer, 50 Crutchedfriars
Barker Nathaniel, plumber, &c. 2 Triangle, Kenningtoncross
Barker Oliver, veterinary forge, 9½ High st. St. Giles's
Barker Raymond H. barrister, 4 Garden court, Temple
Barker Richard, gunmaker, 77 Leman st. Goodman's fields
Barker Robert, pawnbrkr. & silversmth. 21 Gt. Portland st
Barker Robert, plumber & glazier, 154 Houndsditch
Barker Robert, tallowchandler, 210 Bermondsey st
Barker Samuel, bootmaker, 9 Yardley st. Clerkenwell
Barker Samuel, cowkeeper, 57½ Chiswell street, Finsbury
Barker Samuel, solicitor, 15 Gray's inn square
Barker Thomas, auctioneer & estate agt. 142 Blackfriarsroad
Barker Thomas, builder, Deptford High st
Barker Thomas, shipbroker, 75 Cornhill
Barker Thomas Alfred, physician, 15 Grafton st. Bond st
Barker Walter, solicitor, 87 Gt. Portland st. Oxford st
Barker Wm. boarding school, Lower st. Islington
Barker Wm. cabinet maker, 14 Elm st. Gray's inn lane
Barker Wm. who. cabinet maker, 5 Middlesex ter. Hackney rd
Barker Wm. coal merchant, New wharf, Whitefriars
Barker Wm. coffee rooms, 103 Blackfriars road
Barker Wm. ladies' shoemak. 18 Old Cavendish st. Oxford st
Barker Wm. *Maidenhead* P.H. 1 Albion pl. King's cross
Barker Wm. newsman, 187 Brick lane, Spitalfields
Barker Wm. shoemaker, 69 Strutton ground, Westminster
Barker Wm. smith & wheelwright, Morning lane, Hackney
Barker Wm. tobaccopipe maker, 28 Worship st. Nortonfolgt
Barker Wm. Joseph, scotch broker, 7 Tokenhouse yard
Barkley Geo. M. coach lace & worsted wareho. 68 High Holborn
Barkley Thomas, chemist, 15 Little Tower st
Barkley, William, butcher, 2 Aylesbury st. Clerkenwell
Barkly Henry, merchant, 6 Fenchurch buildings
Barkly Henry, west india merchant, 3 Fenchurch bldgs. City
Barkworth Thos. window blind ma. 5 High st. Newingtonbutts
Barland Adam, artist, 11 Southampton st. Fitzroy square
Barlee Edwd. Hobart, solicitor, 13 New North st. Red Lion sq
Barley Edmund Johnson, druggist, High st. Kingsland
Barley Robert, carpenter, 15 Brook st. St. Pancras
Barlin Jacob, Nathaniel & David, tobacco, snuff & cigar manufrs 48 & 49 St. John st. Smithfield, & 156 Upper Whitecross st
Barling Benjamin, jeweller & engra. 142 High st Camden tn
Barling Fredk. statr. & hardwa. man. 16½ Emmett st. Limeho
Barling George V. fruit salesman, Farringdon market
Barling Jacob, pianoforte maker, 34 Hart st. Bloomsbury
Barling Wm. bricklayer, 42 Wellington pl. Blackfriars road
Barlow & Anderson, soapmakers, Gt. Suffolk st. Borough
Barlow & Co. ironfounders, engineers & contractors for gas apparatus, 32 Bucklersbury & Wenlock iron wf. 19 Whf. rd. City rd
Barlow Fred. & Geo. wine merchants, 4 Little Bridge st. Blkfr g
Barlow & Gill, hopfactors, Calvert's bldgs. 241 Boro' High st

Barlow & Le Capelain, patent office, 5 Chancery lane
Barlow & Longden, proctors,3 Paul's chain, Doctors' comms
Barlow Chas.china & glass wa. 11 Fieldgate st. Whitechapel
Barlow Edmund, solicitor, see Robinson & Barlow
Barlow Eli, engraver, 42 Old Compton st. Soho
Barlow Elizab. Ann(Mrs.),linendr.8 St. George ter. Boro' rd
Barlow Francis, com. in lunacy,45 Lincoln's inn fields
Barlow Frederick, surveyor, 5 Foundling ter. Gray's inn rd
Barlow Frederick, wine merchant,see Clarke & Barlow
Barlow Frederick Pratt, solicitor,see Tustin & Barlow
Barlow George, newsvender & stationer, 32 Jewin st
Barlow George, press piercer, 7 Northampton bldgs. Clkwl
Barlow George, tailor, 82 Great Suffolk st. Borough
Barlow Geo. H.grocer & italian wareho.5A,Curzon st.May fr
Barlow George Hilaro, physician, 7 Union st. Borough
Barlow Henry Rd. *Telegraph* P.H. 34 Broomfield pl.Deptfd
Barlow James, ironmonger & manufacturer of the celebrated antique pattern self heating & improved shower baths, improved british plate, &c. 14 King William st. City
Barlow Jasper, coal merchant, 18 New st. Horseferry road
Barlow John, lisbon merchant, 62 Moorgate st. Bank
Barlow John, tailor, 23 Alfred st. Bedford square
Barlow Jonathan, coach plater, 6 Queen st. Grosvenor sq
Barlow Louisa (Mrs.), *Admiral Rodney* P.H. New King st. Deptford
Barlow P. B. barrister, 1 Plowden buildings, Temple
Barlow Saml. coal mercht. St.Ann's whf.Earl st. Blackfriars
Barlow Sydney, commssn. agt. 71 Gt. Russell st. Bloomsbry
Barlow Thomas, coffee rooms, 31 Queen st. Bryanstone sq
Barlow Wm. builder, Flora cottages, Queen's rd. Dalston
Barlow William, lace manufacturer, see Mason,Barlow&Butt
Barlow William, tinman & brazier, 96 London wall
Barlow Sir Wm. Owen, bart. barrister, 5 Figtree ct. Temple
Barmore James, jun. butcher, 9 Charles st. St. George's East
Barnaby James, fruiterer, 6 St. George's terrace, Boro' rd
Barnaby Thomas, oil & colorman, 23 Borough market, & 107 High st. Woolwich
Barnaby William, teadealer, 17 Warwick st. Pimlico
Barnard & Clark, auctioneers, appraisers & undertakers, 15 Blandford st. Portman square
Barnard, Corbould & Son, coal mers. 9 Bankside, Southwark
Barnard, Dimsdale, Barnard&Dimsdale,bankers, 50Cornhill
Barnard Edwd. & Sons,silversmiths,Angel st. St. Mrtn's le gr
Barnard F. E. & T. mastmaks.Acorn yd. Trinity st. Rotherhi
Barnard John & Co. timber merchts. Belvedere rd. Lambeth
Barnard John & Son, flatting mills,12 Nicholl sq. Aldersgate
Barnard's Inn, 22 Holborn hill
Barnard Charles, baker, 100 Wood st. Cheapside
Barnard Charles, boot&shoe mak. 2Surrey pl. ea.OldKent rd
Barnard Daniel, chandler's shop, 53 St. George st
BarnardEdwd.agt. gen.for crown colonies,5Cannon row,Wstr
Barnard Eliza (Mrs.), dress maker, 33 North Audley st
Barnard Franz, watch ma. 3 Magdalen row, Gt. Prescot st
Barnard Frederick, tailor, 32 Kenton st. Brunswick sq
Barnard George, artist, 85 Great Portland st
Barnard George, surgeon dentist, 33 Albany st
Barnard Hannah (Mrs.), shoemaker, Church st. Hackney
Barnard Hen. umbrella ma.15White Lion st. Norton Folgate
Barnard Jabez, oil & colorman, 339 Oxford st
Barnard James, house decorator, &c. 48 Up. Marylebone st
Barnard James,*London* coffee rms.1 Charles st. Midsx.Hosp
Barnard James Michael, undertaker, 24 Old Bailey
Barnard Jas.Townley, *White Swan hotel*,7 High st. Deptfrd
Barnard John,cabinet ma.&bath prop. 3 Belton st. Long acre
Barnard John, *Golden Fleece* P.H. 11 Bermondsey wall
Barnard John,leather cutr. &c. 39A,Phœnix st. Somers town
Barnard John Fuller, wine mercht. see Mansell & Barnard
Barnard Mark, solicitor, 28 Southampton st. Strand
Barnard Morris, umbrella maker, 34 Camomile st. City
Barnard Robert, oil & italian warehouse, 31 Carnaby st
Barnard Samuel, coal merchant, 113 Shad Thames
Barnard Samuel, tailor & draper, 38 Holborn hill
Barnard Semmy John, boot & leather imp. 30 Lime st
Barnard Sophia (Mrs.), baby linen waho.Church st. Hackney
Barnard Thos. auctioneer, &c. see Clark & Barnard
Barnard Thomas, wine merchant, 26 New Broad st. City
Barnard Thos.*Northumbrld.Arms*P.H.9Gt. Russell st.Cov.g
Barnard Thos.Vince, mgr. Deptford Gas wks.Creek st. Dptfd
Barnard Walter, fruit salesman, Borough market
Barnard Wm. cowkeeper, 31½ Charles st. Charles sq. Hoxton
Barnard Wm. engraver & printer,28 Lion st. New Kent road
Barnard Wm.Geo. potato & coal dealer,8Red Lion st. Borough
Barnard Wm. Tyndall, special pleader,9Old sq. Lincoln's inn
Barnby Jane (Mrs.), dining rooms, 48 Old Bailey
Barnby Robt. mathl. ins.case ma.17Baker's row,Coppice row
Barnes & Cock, wine merchants, 62 Lincoln's inn fields
Barnes Frederic & Co. ironmongers & manufacturers, 109 Fenchurch st.; 182 Livery st. Birmingham; & 13 Howard st. Sheffield
Barnes& Haines,wine merchts.11Mincing lane,& 149 Sloane st
Barnes & Hood, iron & brass founders, Deptford green
Barnes Philip & Sons, railway traffic & reference takers, 95 Gracechurch st
Barnes Richard & Co. merchants, Globe court, Fish st. hill
Barnes, Simpson&Co.merchts.& ins. broks. 22 Tokenhouse yd
Barnes Thomas & George, brace makers, 26 Goswell st
Barnes, Winter & Bernard, solicitors, 2 Gt. Winchester st
Barnes Alfred, stockbroker, 12 Copthall ct. Throgmorton st
Barnes Alfred B. surgeon, Gloster house, King's rd. Chelsea
Barnes Beatrice Ann (Mrs.), plasterer, see Clarke & Barnes
Barnes Catherine (Mrs.), builder, 46 East st. Manchester sq
Barnes Charles, butcher, 40 Leonard st. Finsbury
Barnes Charles, hatter, 66 Newington causeway
Barnes Christopher H. surgeon, Bellevue ho. Notting hill
Barnes Edward, fruiterer, 1 Goldington st. Somer's town
Barnes Edwin, baker, 12 White Hart st. Lwr. Kennington la
Barnes Elizh. (Mrs.), bonnet shape dlr. 87 Redcross st. Boro
BarnesElizh.(Mrs.),bonnet shape ma. 87Redcross st.Borough
Barnes Elizh. (Mrs.), linendraper, 22 Park ter. Regent pk. rd
Barnes Frances, (Mrs.) school, 134 Salisbury sq. Fleet st
Barnes Francis, schoolmaster, 20 Union st. Deptford
Barnes George, haberdasher, 3 Vere st. Clare market
Barnes Hector, painter & glazier, 39 Botolph lane
Barnes Henry, corn factor, Jack's coffee house, Mark lane
Barnes Henry, drysalter,129 Up. Thames st. & 110 Long acre; & oxalic acid manfr. Belle isle, Maiden lane, King's cross
BarnesHen.Eugene,clk.tomercers co.Mercers'hall,Irnmngr la
Barnes James, goldbeater, 15 Waterloo st. St. Luke's
Barnes James, grocer, 2 Union st. Borough road
Barnes James, hairdresser, 3 Rockingham pl. New Kent rd
Barnes James, tailor, 14 St. John st. Clerkenwell
Barnes James, *Two Sawyers* P.H. Redgate ct. 78 Minories
Barnes Jesse, wheelwright, Knightsbridge green
Barnes John, carpenter & builder, 21 Queen's row, Pentonville; & 15 Lower Queen's row, New road, Pentonville
Barnes John, filter manufacturer, 281 Poplar High st
Barnes John, general dealer, 19 Exeter st. Lisson grove
Barnes John, hairdresser & perfumer, 17 Tyler st. Regent st
Barnes John, M.D. surgeon, 32Tavistock place, Tavistock sq
Barnes John, teacher of music, 12 Swan st. Minories
Barnes Joseph, hatter, 20 Norton folgate, & 100 Minories
Barnes Joseph G. livery stables, Phœnix yd. 126 Oxford st
Barnes Keith, solicitor, see Lyon, Barnes & Ellis
Barnes Louisa (Mrs.), milliner, 70 New Bond st
Barnes Louisa (Miss), roasting jack ma. 5 Falcon pl. Clrknwl
Barnes Maurice, *Two Brewers* P.H. Giffin st. Deptford
BarnesPhœbe(Mrs.),straw hat ma.5St.George's st.OldKnt.rd
Barnes Richard, alderney dairy, 4 Kensington gravel pits
Barnes Rt. floor cloth ma. 11 City rd. & 28 Windmill st. Finsb
Barnes Robert, oil & tallow chand. 156 Brick la. Spitalfields
Barnes Robert, physician, 43 Notting hill High st
Barnes Robt. Cuthbertson, baker, 7Calcutta pl. East india rd
Barnes Samuel, brushmaker, 3 Shouldham st. Edgware road
Barnes Samuel, linendraper, 9 Pleasant row, Holloway rd
Barnes Simon, fruiterer, 13 Wilmot st. Russell square
Barnes Thomas, coffee roaster, 13 Umberston st. Comcl. rd
Barnes Thomas, corn dealer, 59 Lambeth walk
Barnes Thos. grocer & cheemgr. 15½ Prospect pl. O. Bromptn
Barnes Thomas John, land agnt. & auctionr. 33 Fenchurch st
Barnes Wm.agt. to A.&C. S. Mills, cheesefactors, 21Tooley
Barnes Wm. architect, 3 Church court, Old Jewry
Barnes Wm. grocer, 114 Edgware road, Paddington
Barnes Wm. hatter, &c. 70 New Bond street
Barnes Wm. potato dealer, 119 Church st. Shoreditch
Barnes Wm. printer, 44 Bridgehouse pl. Newington causew
Barnes Wm. *Rose & Ram* P.H. 83 Redcross st. Boro'
Barnes Wm. seal engraver, 107 Paul st. Finsbury
Barnes Wm. George, merchant, see Copland, Barnes & Co
Barnes Wm. Henry, builder, Hemingford road,Barnsbury rd
Barnes Wm. Hy. J. carpenter, 23 Brunswick parade, Pntnvl
BarnesWm.Josiah, bricklyr.&chinadl.7Garden rw.Cmbwl.rd
Barnes Wm. T. ship, &c. bro. & coal fac. 31 St. Mary at hill
Barnesley Hy.Charles,surveyor, 107 Gravel la.Houndsditch
Barnett Barnard & Son, watchma.2Mount st.Whitechapl.rd
Barnett&George(Misses),seminary,5Lr.Southwickst.Hydepk
Barnett & Good, teachers of cutting, &c. 10 London wall
Barnett, Hoares & Co. bankers, 62 Lombard st
Barnett John Edwd. & Sons,wholes. gunmakers,134 Minories
Barnett & Kimpton, ship & insur. brokers, 1 Leadenhall st
Barnett Louisa & Co. milliners, 74 Quadrant, Regent st
Barnett Abraham, clothier, 34 Holywell st. Strand
Barnett Adolphus, surgeon, 3 Vittoria pl. Comcl. rd. east

Barnett Alfred, umbrella maker, 47 Great Prescot st]
Barnett Asher, baker, 34 Middlesex st. Aldgate
Barnett Benjamin, wardrobe dlr. 35 Kenton st. Brunswick sq
Barnett Bennett, picture restorer, 21 Tichborne st. Haymkt
Barnett Bridges, beer retailer, 26 New King st. Deptford
Barnett Charles, stationer, printer & account book manufacturer, 2 Bucklersbury, Cheapside
Barnett David, baker, 5 Commercial road, Pimlico
Barnett David, tailor & shipping agt. 203 Shadwell High st
Barnett Elizh. (Mrs.), vertical jack maker, 43 Union st. Boro'
Barnett Emanuel, slopseller, 79 Cable st. Wellclose sq
Barnett Francis L. pawnbroker, &c. 5 Roebuck ter. Dover rd
Barnett George, tailor, 10 London wall
Barnett George Fred. boat builder, Creek rd. Deptford
Barnett George Thomas, tailor & outfitter, 129 Holborn hill
Barnett Harris, boot & shoe manufacturer, wholesale & for exportation, 13 Catherine Wheel alley, Bishopsgate
Barnett Hen. copper pl. printer, 6 Glo'ster st. St. John st. rd
Barnett Henry, egg merchant, New road, South Lambeth
Barnett Hyam, forgn. & hebrew bookslr. 2 St. James' pl. Aldgate
Barnett James, brass founder, see Pontifex & Barnett
Barnett James, carpenter, 13 York st. Covent garden
Barnett James, carrier, George yard, Aldermanbury
Barnett James, cowkeeper, 29 Riley st. King's road, Chelsea
Barnett John, academy, 6 Stafford st. Lisson grove
Barnett John, architect & survr. 3 Verulam bldgs. Gray's inn
Barnett John, clothes dealer, 44 Marylebone lane, Oxford st
Barnett John, engraver, 18 Castle st. Holborn
Barnett John, physician, 34 Chesham pl. Belgrave square
Barnett Joseph, slopseller, 46 Shadwell High st.
Barnett Joseph, butcher, 94 Berwick st. Soho
Barnett Joseph, tobacconist, 58 Strutton ground, Westminr
Barnett Josiah, watch case ma. 15 Lr. Charles st. Nthmp. sq
Barnett Lewis, pencil maker, 71 Leman st. Goodman's fields
Barnett Mary (Mrs.), milliner & dress ma. 27 Old Burlington st
Barnett Mary Anne (Mrs.), *D. of York* P.H. 8 Sheph. st. Oxfd. st
Barnett Michael, furniture broker, 2 Crown st. Walworth rd
Barnett Montague, watch & timepiece ma. 16 Swan st. Mino
Barnett Morris, *Cock* P.H. 51 Leadenhall st
Barnett Moses, carpenter, 6 Chapel mews, Belgrave square
Barnett Moses, fruiterer, 56 Church st. Minories
Barnett Nathan, fancy cap manufr. 35 Mitre st. Aldgate
Barnett Richd. custom house agent, 3 Love lane, Eastcheap
Barnett Robert, professor of music, 71 Dean st. Soho
Barnett Robert, stockbroker, see Tucker, Barnett & Co
Barnett Robert Augustus, chemist, 5 Three Colt st
Barnett Saml. pawnbroker, 10 St. George's circus, Obelisk
Barnett Samuel, potato warehouse, High st. Kingsland
Barnett Thomas, baker, 52 Lower George st. Chelsea
Barnett Thomas, furniture broker, 6 Vine st. Hatton wall
Barnett Thomas, *York Minster* P.H. 55 Bunhill row
Barnett Thomas William, surgeon, 26 Fore st. Limehouse
Barnett William, bootmaker, 18 Broadway, Tooley st
Barnett William, cheesemonger, 100 Lambeth Lwr. marsh
Barnett William, hairdresser, 95 Bartholomew close
Barnett William, master mariner, 16 Bedford square east
Barnewall Robert & Sons, merchts. 8½ Copthall ct. Throgm. st
Barney James D. & Co. gen. factors of iron goods, 14 Lit. Tower st
Barney Bond, clothes salesman, 29 Broad st. Bloomsbury
Barney Stephen, barrister, 2 New Temple bldgs. Mitre ct
Barney William, fruiterer, 127 Great Guildford st. Borough
Barnjum Thomas, wine merchant, 1 Chapel pl. Cavendish sq
Barns Ann Hannah (Mrs.), honiton lace mnfr. 304 Regent st
Barns Elizh. Lucy (Miss), milliner, 60 St. Paul's churchyard
Barns Francis, wholesale staymaker, 46 Baldwin st. City road
Barns Stephen, carpenter, 50 Bridport pl. New North road
Barns William, solicitor, see Evans & Barns
Barns William, tobacconist, 3 Vauxhall bridge foot
Barnsby Robert, barge builder, Creek road, Deptford
Barnsby Robert, grocer, 8 Bird st. Oxford st
Barnshaw Thomas, beer retailer, 12 Brunswick st. Blackwall
Barnstorff John Ludar, tailor, 38 Great Titchfield st
Barnwell & Rayner, cabinet maks. 1 Golden Lion ct. Aldersgt. st
Barnwell Frederick Lowry, attorney, 1 Lincoln's inn fields
Barnwell Charles Lowry, merchant, 15 Gt. St. Helen's
Barnwell Henry Lowry, miller, see Kingsford & Barnwell
Barnwell Joseph, coal merchant, 65 Great Titchfield street, Oxford st.; & Middle wharf, Great Scotland yard
Barnwell William, turner, 10 Bridgewater gardens, Barbican
Barnwell Wm. surgeon, 7 Queen Charlotte row, New rd. Maryl
Baron Charles, painter, &c. 2 Manchester ter. Liverpool road
Baron Charles, plumber, painter, &c. 26 Park st. Islington
Baron François, bookseller, 8 Rochester ter. Stoke Newingtn
Baron John, fishmonger, 3 Lumber court, Seven dials
Baron Thomas, printer, 18A, Symons st. Chelsea
Baron William, *Opera tavern*, 22 Haymarket
Baron William, shell fishmonger, 23 Haymarket
Barough & Fall, grocers, 1 New Cavendish st. Portland pl
Barough Francis, grocer & teadealer, 92 Hatton garden
Barough Francis, jun. teadealer, 65 Lamb's conduit st
Barr Alfred, carver & gilder, 21 Fleet st
Barr Chas. engra. brass & zinc plate mfr. 43 Chandos st. Str
Barr George, wholesale chair & couch maker to the trade, 30 Curtain road, Shoreditch
Barr Henry, bricklayer & plasterer, 28 Up. Marylebone st
Barr James, dairy, Dempsey st. Stepney
Barr James, engine turner, see Knight & Barr
Barr James, plumber & glazier, 2 New Turnstile, Holborn
Barr John, chair & sofa manfr. 70 Curtain rd. Shoreditch
Barr John, pawnbrkr. & silversmith, 11 Osborne st. Whtchpl
Barr John, wharfinger, 17 Copenhagen place, Limehouse
Barr John Cabourn, hatter, 21 Blackman st. & 10 Old Bailey
Barr John C. hat manufacturer, 80 Newgate st
Barr Joseph, carpenter, 9 Nassau st. Middlesex hospital
Barr Joseph, *Windsor Castle* P.H. 27 Long acre
Barr Martin, bricklayer, 75 Cowcross st. Smithfield
Barr Mary Ann (Mrs.), staymaker, 14 Tottenham court road
Barr Thomas, coal dealer, 17 Copenhagen place, Limehouse
Barr Wm. bricklayer, &c. 11 Nassau st. Middlesex hospital
Barr Wm. chair & sofa maker, 116 Curtain rd. Shoreditch
Barr Wm. sen. chair maker, 29 Rose & Crown court, Finsbury
Barrable John, actuary, 3 Park place ter. Paddington green
Barrack Office, 83 Pall Mall; hours 10 to 4
Barrack Elizth. (Mrs.), *Trafalgar hotel*, 34 & 35 Spring grdns
Barrack James, *Union hotel*, 4 Cockspur st. Charing cross
Barraclough Henry, farrier, 14 Upper Ogle st. Fitzroy sq
Barraclough Solomon, tobacns. &c. 46 Ludgate hl. & 70 Chpside
Barraclough Stephen, woolstapler, 85 Bermondsey
Barrada Hage Ally, merchant, 1 Mitre square, Aldgate
Barralet Jsph. cabinet lead liner, 8 Holywell row, Shordch
Barrall Henry, milliner, &c. 16 Gt. Chapel st. Westminster
Barras John Ryder & Co. tobacco ma. 16 Broad st. Bloomsbury
Barras George, tobacconist, 416 Oxford st
Barras Lucy (Mrs.), coml. boarding ho. 29 Arundel st. Strand
Barras Thomas, plumber & glazier, 5 Milton st. Dorset sq
Barrat Benjamin, gasfitter, 2 Brunswick pl. Brompton
Barrat James, carpenter & bldr. 34 Lit. Windmill st. Gldn. sq
Barrat John, pianoforte maker, 27 High st. Camden town
Barrat John, saddler & harness ma. 143 High st. Camden twn
Barrat Thomas, dyer, 10 Upper George st. Bryanstone sq
Barratt Benjamin, bricklayer, 4 William st. Blackfriars rd
Barratt John Chas. carver, gilder & picture dealer, 368 Strand
Barratt Joseph, carpenter, 39 Windmill st. Tottenham ct. rd
Barratt Maria (Mrs.), milliner, 4 Glo'ster pl. King's rd. Chel
Barratt Phineas, milliner, see Klugh & Barratt
Barratt Wm. bookbinder, 21 Portugal st. Lincoln's inn fields
Barraud & Lund, chron. watch & clockmakers, 41 Cornhill
Barraud & Welch, coal mers. & wharfingers, New wf. Whitefrs
Barraud Edward F. chemist, 5 Union row, Camberwell road
Barraud Henry, artist, 79 Park st. Grosvenor sq
Barraud William, artist, 79 Park st. Grosvenor sq
Barray Alexander, tailor, 27 Billiter st. Fenchurch st
Barrell Francis James, pill box maker, 26 Little Wild st
Barrell Robert, oilman, 3 Constable row, Mile end road
Barrell Salmon, linendraper, 1 Holloway pl. Holloway rd
Barrenger James, working jeweller, 59 Carlisle st. Lambeth
Barrero Don Jose Maria, span. consulgen. 37 Old Broad st. City
Barrett & Clay, wine & spirit merchants, 70 Mark lane
Barrett & Co. wax chandlers & lamp wareho. 10 Halkin st. West
Barrett & Condell, solicitors, 7 Copthall ct. Throgmorton st
Barrett & Corney, refiners, wire drawers, & gold & silver thread & lace manufacturers, 70 Little Britain
Barrett Rd. & Son, iron & brassfndrs. King's head ct. Beech st
Barrett Thomas & Co. insurance brokers, 70 Mark lane
Barrett Thomas & Daniel, teadealers, 24 Church st. Shoreditch; & 24 Three colt st. Limehouse
Barrett & Eyston's, attorneys, 5 Gray's inn square
Barrett Thomas & John, coach builders, 71 Up. Berkeley st
Barrett Andrew, brush & mat manufac. 118 Piccadilly
Barrett Ann (Mrs.), milliner, 22 Clipstone st. Fitzroy square
Barrett Ann (Mrs.), plumber, 157 Church st. Shoreditch
Barrett Ashley, miller, Narrow st. Ratcliff
Barrett Barkley Geo. wkg. jeweller, 12 Lit. Compton st. Soho
Barrett Benjamin, gasfitter, 6 Lt. Pulteney st. Golden square
Barrett Daniel, ho. agt. & undertaker, 27 Castle st. Southwark
Barrett David, painter, 10 Gt. Quebec st. Montagu square
Barrett Edwd. news agt. bookslr. & stationer, 136 Minories
Barrett Eleanor (Mrs.), grocer & teadealer, 95 Fetter la. Holbn
Barrett George, coal merchant, Gt. Scotland yard
Barrett George, hardwareman, 38 Charles st. Hatton garden
Barrett George, house agent, 57 Hill st. Walworth road
Barrett George, ironfounder, smith, &c. see Wood & Barrett

Barrett George, poulterer, 15 Red Lion passage, RedLion sq
Barrett George Goodin, barrister, 2 Tanfield court, Temple
Barrett Henry, baker, 175 Bethnal green road
Barrett Hen. Wm. watchmaker, 11 Judd st. Brunswick sq
Barrett Jacob, academy, 57 King square, Goswell road
Barrett James, baker, 6 Artichoke row, Mile end road
Barrett James, carpenter & undertak. 101 Hoxton old town
Barrett JamesFred.baker,13Clement's inn pas.Clare market
Barrett Jennison, cheesemonger, 147 Brick lane, Spitalfields
Barrett John, basket maker, 10 Gt.Crown ct. Lit. Pulteney st
Barrett John, bootmaker, 42 Bedford st. Strand
Barrett John, brushmaker & turner, 299 Oxford st
Barrett John, coal & potato dealer, 8 Hoxton old town
Barrett John, grocer, 9 Back Church lane, Whitechapel
Barrett John, oilman, 17 John st. Limehouse fields
Barrett John, tinplate worker, 20 Green st. Leicester sq
Barrett John, tinplate worker, 15 Wood st. Spafields
Barrett JohnWoodward, *Plough* P.H.Plough rd.Rotherhithe
Barrett Jonas, grocer, 21 Granby st. Hampstead road
Barrett Joseph, metal warehouse, 60 Shoe lane
Barrett Joseph, paper hanging wa. 75 Church st. Shoreditch
Barrett Richard, printer, &c. 13 Mark lane, City
Barrett Richard, surgeon & bath proprietor, 23 NewBond st
Barrett Robert Humphrey, *Crown* P.H. 75 Basinghall st
Barrett Samuel, barrister, 26 Old square, Lincoln's inn
Barrett Samuel, surgeon, 176 Sloane st. Chelsea
Barrett Samuel Broadbent, who. hosier,21Addle st.Wood st
Barrett Samuel B. C. surgeon, 25 Sloane st. Chelsea
Barrett Thomas, bricklayer, 2 New road, St. George's East
Barrett Thomas, cowkeeper, 15 Prospect pl. Old Brompton
Barrett Thomas, tripe dresser, 235 Tottenham court road
Barrett William, conveyancer, 2 Bell yard, Doctors' commons ; & 8 Rosamon house, Islington green
Barrett Wm. firewood cutter, 1½ Charles st.east.Hampstd. rd
Barrett William, *Green Man* P.H. & livery stable keeper, 37 Featherstone st. City rd
Barrett William, grocer & tobacconist, 69 Ossulston st
Barrett William, *Royal Oak* P.H. 10 Granby st.Waterloo rd
Barrett William, watchmaker, 86 Fetter lane, Holborn
Barreyman Ann(Mrs.), baby linen wa. see Todd&Barreyman
Barrick & Rose, anchor, chain & ship smiths, 180 Wapping
Barrick John, bootmaker, 3 Wilsted st. Somers town
Barrie Robert, carpenter, 9 Hart st. Covent garden
Barrie Robert, livery stables, 9 Hart st. Covent garden
Barrier James, shoemaker, 4 Surrey st. Strand
Barringer John, cowkeeper, 10 Snow's fields, Bermondsey
Barringer Thos. Stevens, surgeon, 96 St. John st. Clerkenwl
Barringer Wm. cheesemonger,15Henrietta st.Covent garden
Barringer Wm. Timson, coal mer. Union wf. Millbank st
Barritt & Co. wholesale bible & prayer book warehouse & embossers of book covers, 173 Fleet st
Barritt George, *Queen's Head* P.H. 16 Queen st. Golden sq
Barritt James,looking glass frame mkr.5Fashion st. Spitlflds
Barritt Saml.cabinetma.&furn.war.8Mansion ho.pl.Cambrwl
Barritt Simon, lighterman & baker, 38 Rotherhithe
Barron John L. & Co. merchants, 1 Leadenhall st
Barron & Son, ironmongers to her Majesty, smiths & locksmiths, 436 West Strand
Barron & Harvey, wholesale druggists, 6 Giltspur st
Barron & Smith,armyagents,4UpperCharles st.Westminster
Barron Ann (Mrs.), milliner, 86 Albany st. Regent's park
Barron Arthur, barrister, 89 Chancery lane
Barron Benjamin, tailor, 3 King st. Portman square
Barron Charles, wine & brandy merchant, 19 Pall mall
Barron Edward, solicitor, 29 Bloomsbury square
Barron Edwd. Enfield, surgeon, 16 St. Thomas st. ea. Sthwk
Barron Henry, paper stainer, painter &decorator, 68 Strand
Barron Mary (Mrs.), baker, 49 Kennington st. Walworth
Barron William, builder, Salisbury wharf, Strand
Barron William, galloon manufacturer, 56 Aldermanbury
Barrow, Golding & Barrow, wine & spirit merchants, 52 Coleman st. & cellars, 2 King's arms yard
Barrow & Nicolson, surgeons, 48 Davies st. Berkeley sq
Barrow Henry, math. instrumentma. see Robinson & Barrow
BarrowEdwd.Bradford,brass fndr.59Whitehor.st.Coml.rd.ea
Barrow Geo. door plate maker & engraver, 3Grafton st.Soho
Barrow John, bottle mer. & winecooper, 30 Mill la. Tooley st
Barrow John, carpenter, 4 Salisbury court, Fleet st
BarrowJohn,chandler's shop, 22 Dorchester st. New North rd
Barrow John, spirit merchant, 28 Mincing la. Fenchurch st
BarrowRichard, grocer & coal dlr.23 St. Clement's la. Strand
Barrow Robert P. wine, &c. merchant, see Corney & Barrow
Barrow Thomas, bootmaker, 37 Hatfield st. Stamford st
Barrow Thos. oil & color & varnish ma. 91 Lower Thames st
Barrowdale Charles, sheep salesman, 41 West Smithfield
Barrowforth John, merchant, 5 Martin's lane, Cannon st
Barrowforth John, wine mercht, &c. 5 Martin's la. Cannon st
Barrows James, seedsman, &c. Caledonian road, Pentonville
Barrows Jonathan, dyer, 60 Drummond st. Euston sq
Barrs Francis, beer retailer, 7 Homer st. Marylebone
Barry (Dykes) & Co. importers of chicory, chocolate & cocoa manfrs. 29 & 30 Ropemaker st. & 6 Type st. Finsbury
Barry (Dykes), teadealer, &c. 27 Skinner st. & 84 Snow hill
Barry & Co. stock & share brokers, 7 Birchin lane, Cornhill
Barry & Hayward, wholesale stationers, 18 & 19 Queenhithe
Barry John & Jas. bedding manufs. & upholst. 293½ Oxford st
Barry Jsph. & Geo. syringe ma. 74 White Lion st. Pentonville
Barry Wm. & Son, stationers, engravers, & account book ma. 122 Bishopsgate within, & Egyptian hall, 170 Piccadilly
Barry Arthur, corndealer, 44 High st. Notting hill
BarryCharles,R.A.architect,32Great George st.Westminster
BarryCharles,ship&insurancebroker,3 Brabant ct. Philpot la
Barry Francis, baker, 66 Strutton ground, Westminster
Barry Frederick, homœopathic surg. 9 Artillery pl. Finsbury
Barry Frederick, spice merchant, see Jarvis & Barry
Barry Garret, school, 9 Gough square, Fleet st
Barry Jarret, upholsterer, 7 Gilbert st. Oxford st
Barry John, job, post & fly master, 44 High st. & 1 Rosedale cottages, Notting hill
Barry John Thomas, chemist, see Allen, Hanburys & Barry
Barry Joseph, tailor, 7 Brown st. Bryanstone square
Barry Robert, ship owner, 20 New city chambers, Bishopsgate
BarrySusannah(Mrs.), grocer, 56 Baldwin's gdns. Leather la
Barry Thos. Wm. bricklayer & builder, 64 Paul st. Finsbury
Barry William, *King's Arms* P.H. 23 Great Titchfield st
Barry William Henry, plumber, painter, &c.94½Kingsland rd
Barsham, Lonsdale & Co. patent emery & glass cloth, black lead, emery & anti-corrosion paint manufacturers, 41 Threadneedle st. & Stratford, Essex
Barsham John B. surgeon & apothecary, 73 Theobald's road
Barsotellia Francis, figure maker, 22 George st. Portland pl
Barstow James P. barrister, 7 Figtree court, Temple
Barter Joseph, cabinetmaker, 40 Fleet lane, Old Bailey
Barter W. embosser & herald chaser, 19 Poland st. Oxford st
Barter Wm. commercial coffee rooms, 44 Crown st. Finsby
Barth Charles, carpenter, 13 St. James's place, Hampstead rd
Barth Wm. W. upholsterer, &c. 18A, Newman st. Oxford st
Barth Wm. Wright, bookseller, 4 Brydges st. Covent gardn
Barthés Antonin & Co. wine merchants, & french & spanish cork manufactory, 1 Savage gardens
Barthés & Lowell, foreign booksellers, late Bossange & Co. 14 Great Marlborough st
Barthold William, merchant, 2 Nun court, 74 Coleman st
Bartholomew Joseph & Son, rug ma. 9to11 Hackney rd. cres
Bartholomew&Walker,silk manfrs.11Steward st.Spitalfields
Bartholomew Wm.&Geo.carpet mnfrs.14Finsbury pavement
Bartholomew Wm.Hen.&Son,blckingma.42Parkst.Dorset sq
Bartholomew David, carpenter, 10 Felix pl. Liverpool road, & Charles st. Gibson sq
Bartholomew Edward, baker, 15 Silver st. Golden sq
Bartholomew Francis, hosier & glover, 143 Fleet st
Bartholomew John, bookedge gilder, 14St.John's sq.Clrknwl
Bartholomew John, cabinet maker, 3 Brownlow mews, Gray's inn road, & 219 Tottenham court road
Bartholomew John, fishing rod & tackle maker, 4 Crooked la
Bartholomew John, hosier, 10 Bishopsgate without
Bartholomew John, ivory turner, &c. 4 Crooked la. Cannon st
Bartholomew Joseph, hearthrug manufr. 64 Hoxton Old twn
Bartholomew Josiah, watch manuf. 25 Red Lion st.Clerknwl
Bartholomew Robert Henry, attorney, 5 New inn, Strand
Bartholomew Thos. rug manf. see Bartholomew Jos. & Son
Bartholomew Valentine, artist, 23 Charlotte st. Portland pl
Bartholomew Valentine(Mrs.),artist,23Charlotte st.Portld pl
Bartholomew William, solicitor, 3 Gray's inn place
Bartington Samuel, carver & gilder, 95 Wardour st. Soho
Bartington Silas, undertaker, 99 Bermondsey st
Bartle & Jarvis, tailors & drapers, 266 Strand
Bartleet Thos.&Sons,button ma. & manchest.& woollen warehousmn.18&19Noble st.Cheapside,&126Gt.Charles st.Birm
Bartleet Wm. & Sons, manufacturers of needles & fish-hooks (successors to Durnford Francis & Co. of Gracechurch st.), 73 Aldermanbury, & Redditch, Worcester
Bartleman George, surgeon, 74 Westbourne st. Pimlico
Bartlet James, physician, 10 Bentinck st. Cavendish sq
Bartlett & Beddome, attorneys, 27 Nicholas la. Lombard st
Bartlett Robt. & Co. teadls.&grocers,19 Foley st. Portland pl
Bartlett Abraham Dee, naturalist, 10 Lt. Russell st. Cov. gar
Bartlett Alfred Gregory, chronometer ma. 70 Rahere st
Bartlett Amery,dyer&scourer,20 Somers. pl. East, New rd
Bartlett Charles A. bookseller, &c. 32 Paternoster row
Bartlett Charles Scott, bookbinder, 8 Athol pl. Pentonville
Bartlett Edw. Barton, dentist, 11 Connaught ter. Edgw. rd

Bartlett Elizh. (Mrs.), grocer, 27 President st. Goswell road
Bartlett George, architecl. modeller, 33 Duncan ter. City rd
Bartlett George, cabinet maker, 229 Whitechapel road
Bartlett George, dentist, 15 Caroline street, Bedford square
Bartlett George, potato salesman, 4 Up. area, Hungerford mkt
Bartlett George, tinplate worker, 20 Earl st. East, Lisson gr
Bartlett Geo. Elliott, *New Inn* P.H. 1 Henry st.ea. Avenue rd
Bartlett Gyles, cabinet maker, 32 Drummond st. Euston sq
Bartlett Hannah (Mrs.), fruiterer, 33 Marylebone la. Oxford st
Bartlett Henry, carpentr. & undrtkr. 5 South st. Manchr. sq
Bartlett Hen. Geo. grocer, &c. 35 Lower Sloane st. Chelsea
Bartlett Isaiah, coachsmith, 4 Oxford place, Waterloo road
Bartlett James, builder, 7 Rolls buildings, Fetter lane
Bartlett James, coach builder, 15 Lower Kennington green
Bartlett James, fish salesman, Billingsgate market
Bartlett Jas. oil & colorman, 15 Southampton st. Cambrwl
Bartlett John, *Barnsbury Castle* P.H. Barnsbury park
Bartlett John, carpenter, 16 George st. Portland place
Bartlett John, coach lamp maker, 11 Leg alley, Long acre
Bartlett John, cheesemonger, 76 Great Tower st. City
Bartlett John, hairdresser, 83 Drury lane
Bartlett John, manuf. of pat. box beam scales, weighing machines, malt, sugar & coffeemills, &c. 182 Bishopsgate without
Bartlett Jsph. confectioner, 20 New Church st. W. Edgwre.rd
Bartlett Michael, surgeon, 24 Hatton garden
Bartlett Ridley, jun. baker, 51 Bath st. City road
Bartlett Ridley, sen. baker & corndealer, Kingsland green
Bartlett Robert, muslin, &c. printer, see Gates, Coats & Co
Bartlett Robert, straw bonnet ma. 10 Tottenham ct. New rd
Bartlett Samuel, gasfitter, 7 Brooke's market, Leather lane
Bartlett Thomas, fruiterer, 1 Swallow st. Regent st
Bartlett Thomas, printer, 169 Tooley st. Boro'
Bartlett Thomas, surgeon, 39 Chancery lane
Bartlett Thomas John M. solicitor, 9 Pall Mall East
Bartlett Wm. *Bay Malton* P.H. 48 Clipstone st. Fitzroy sq
Bartlett Wm. bread & biscuit baker, 117 Houndsditch, & 7 Little St. Mary axe
Bartlett Wm. chemist, 1 Bretten ter. King's rd. West, Chelsea
Bartlett Wm. dentist & cupper, 15 Park pl. South, Chelsea
Bartlett Wm. engraver, 23 Castle st. Leicester square
Bartlett Wm. japanner & gilder, 18 Blenheim st. Oxford st
Bartlett Wm. surgeon, 19 Notting hill terrace
Bartlett Wm. wholesale confectioner, 91 Goswell st
Bartley George Wm. & Co. teadealers, 41 Cannon st. City
Bartley & Southwood, attorneys, 30 Somerset st. Portman sq
Bartley Alexander, bootmaker, 251 Oxford st
Bartley James, venetian blind maker, 67 Long acre
Bartley Wm. stables, 11 & 12 Somers mews, Up. Southwick st
Bartley William Alexander, horse dealer, 232 Oxford st
Bartman George, watch wheel ma. 19½ Compton st. Clkwll
Barton Sam. & Jnthn. wine &c. mers. 79 Old Broad st. City
Barton William & Jeffery, wax & tallowchandlers & melters, 26 Bishopsgate within, & 36 St. Mary axe
Barton William & Son, tailors, 51 Cheyne walk, Chelsea
Barton Carrol Richard, solicitor, 4 Wolsingham pl. Lambeth
Barton Charles, butcher, 4 Portland row, Camberwell road
Barton Charlotte (Mrs.), baker, 6 Pleasant place, Holloway
Barton Edward, merchant, 27 Hatton garden
Barton Edward, seed mercht. 36 Gainsford st. Horselydown
Barton Edward, silversmith & cutler, 27 Hatton garden
Barton Elizth. (Miss), engrav. & print. 21 Grevillest. Hat. grd
Barton Francis, ironmonger, 3 Canal bridge, Old Kent road
Barton George, barrister, 3 Plowden buildings, Temple
Barton George, carpenter, 11 Brill place, Somers town
Barton George, confectioner, 164 High st. Camden town
Barton George, who & retail hat maker, 87 Houndsditch
Barton George Gray, india agt. see Crawford, Colvin & Co
Barton George Henry, solicitor, 6 Bloomfield ter. Pimlico
Barton Henry, butcher, 39 Bath st. Tabernacle square
Barton James, corn chandler, 28 St. Chad's row, Gray's inn rd
Barton James, fruiterer, High st. Kingsland
Barton Jane (Miss), milliner & stay ma. 12 Vere st. Cavendish sq
Barton John, auctioneer, 7 Cheltenham place, Westm. road
Barton John, cooper & wine & spirit mer. 24 Gt. Trinity lane
Barton John, doll maker, 2 Constitution row, Gray's inn rd
Barton John Everett, tailor, 14 Gt. Quebec st. Montagu sq
Barton John Geo. oil & color wareho. 10 Church la. Comcl. rd
Barton Joseph, bed sacking, door mat, &c. manfr. 48 Goodge st
Barton Joseph, florist, Borough market
Barton Joseph, stationer & news agent, 48 Goodge st
Barton Joseph, stock & share broker, 15 Angel ct. Throgmtn. st
Barton Marian (Mrs.), trunk, box & cypress paper manufr. & scaleboard maker, 119 Curtain road, Shoreditch
Barton Mary (Mrs.), enginr. & mechanist, 29 Providence row
Barton Mary Ann (Miss), dressmaker, 59 King st. Westminster
Barton Michael, bed sacking makr. 26 Weston st. Somers town
Barton Robert, oil & colorman, see Gurney & Barton
Barton Robt. Dodge, chemist & druggist, 95 St. John's wood ter
Barton Saml. tailor, hosier & outfitting wareho. 3 Strand
Barton Saml. *Royal George* P.H. Tanner's hill, New tn. Dptfrd
Barton Thomas, *Black Horse* P.H. 15 Ropemakersflds. Limeh
Barton Thomas, solicitor, 17 Buckingham st. Adelphi
Barton Wm. fruit salesman, Borough market, & 2 Park st
Barton Wm. leather seller & who. grindery dlr. 23 Redcross st. Cripplegate
Barton Wm. stockbroker, 10 Throgmorton st. & Stock Exchge
Barton Wm. umbrella maker & newsvender, Wandsworth rd
Barton Wm. upholsterer, 19 Winchester pl. Southwk. bdg. rd
Barton Wm. Hardy, tailor, 94 St. John's Wood terrace
Barton Wm. Thos. jeweller, 9 Queen's Head row, Newingtonbtts
Bartram Samuel, bricklayer, North place, Kingsland rd
Bartram Samuel, upholsterer, 257 Whitechapel road
Bartram William, grocer, 1 Arthur st. Trevor square
Bartram Wm. livery stables, 10 Raven row, Whitechapel rd
Bartram Wm. pawnbroker, 26 & 27 Princes st. Leicester sq
Bartrop Joseph, corn & coal mer. 5 Youl's pl. Old Kent rd
Bartrop Robert, corn & flour merchant, 176 High Holborn
Bartrop Robt. grocer & cheesemonger, 1 Portland st. Walw. com
Bartrum, Harvey & Co. woolln. draps. 73, 74 & 75 Holborn hill
Bartrum & Pretyman, merchants, wholesale ironmongers & copper nail manufacturers, Red Lion whf. Up. Thames st
Bartrum Thomas & Son, solicitors, 19 & 20 Austin friars
Bartrum Edwin, cattle salesman, 17 West Smithfield
Bartrum Thos. R. west india mer. Red Lion whf. Up. Thames st
Bartrup Wm. *Ship & Lion* P.H. 41 Ropemkrs. flds. ThreeColt st
Barttelot Wm. A. hairdresser, 20 Notting hill terrace
Barugh John, oil & colorman, 31 High Holborn
Barugh John, wine & spirit mer. see Sunley, Barugh & Co
Barwell Ann (Mrs.), *Marlbro'* P.H. 3 Blenheim st. Oxford st
Barwell Charles, butcher, 149 Bethnal green road
Barwell Edward, potato salesman, 30 Munster st. Regnt's. pk
Barwell Henry, market gardener, Bridge road, Battersea
Barwell Henry, market gardener, Park road, Battersea
Barwell Walter, lodging house, 3 Trinity pl. Charing cross
Barwick Edward, lithographer, 30 Rood lane
Barwick Geo. D. chandler's shop, 27 Brighton st. Cromer st
Barwick Henry Daniel, plumber, &c. 1 George st. Shoreditch
Barwick James, rag mer. 1 & 2 Denmark st. Ratcliffe highwy
Barwick James Fredk. wheelwright, 63 Old st. St. Luke's
Barwick Jane (Mrs.), coach plater & beader, 22 Laystall st
Barwick John, chandler's shop, 20 Oval, Hackney road
Barwick Richard, rag mercht. 4 Cambridge rd. Mile end rd
Barwick Thomas, coachmaster, Beresford st. Walworth
Barwick Thomas, livery stables, Williams pl. Walworth rd
Barwick Thos. window blind ma. 8 King John's ct. Holywell la
Barwick Wm. ironmonger, 5 Prospect pl. Lower rd. Deptford
Barwis William H. B. arbitrator, accountant & navy agent, 1 New Boswell court, Carey st. Lincoln's inn
Barwise Geo. plumber & glazier, 3 Wallington pl. Wandsw. rd
Barwise Jackson, sec. to Lough Corrib, &c. co. 18 Austin frs
Barwise John, watch & chronometer maker, 29 St. Martin's la
Basan George, merchant, 2 Church court, Clement's la. City
Basby Thos. carman & coal mer. 1 Marlbro' mews, Blenheim st
Bascomb William, tailor & habit maker, 19 Mortimer st
Baseden James, carman, 2 Well court, Queen st. Cheapside & King's Arms yard, Lower Whitecross st
Baseley Danl. cheesmngr, 18 Bolingbroke rw. Walworth rd
Baseley Edward, grocer, 9 Park ter. King's rd. West, Chelsea
Baseley Hen. Edwd. stationer & bookslr. 9 Old Broad st. City
Baseley James, who. cheesemonger, see Parry & Baseley
Basevi George, jun. architect, 17 Saville row, Piccadilly
Basevi Nathaniel, barrister, 19 Old square, Lincoln's inn
Basham George, solicitor, 7 Staple inn, Holborn
Basham John, timber mer. & sawyer, John st. Holywell mount
Basham John, vegetable salesman, North row, Covent garden
Basham Thos. retail brewer, 9 St. Mark's rd. Cambwll. nw. rd
Basham Wm. Richard, physician, 17 Chester st. Grosvenor pl
Bashford James, fruiterer, Clapham rise
Basire Jas. engraver & lithographer, 4 Red Lion square
Basker John, beer retailer, 5A, Middle row, Knightsbridge
Baskerville John, *Black Bull* P.H. Little Chelsea
Baskerville Thomas, cabinet manfr. 6 Worship sq. Finsbury
Baskett Elizh. (Mrs.), cornchandl. 95 St. George's rd. Southwk
Basley Wm. Hen. professr. of music, &c. 2 Tyndale pl. Islingtn
Basly Henry, tailor, 2 Goodwin's court, St. Martin's lane
Basman Henry, trimming seller, 37 Old Compton st. Soho
Basnett Edward, solicitor, 28 Carey st. Lincoln's inn
Bass & Cursons, engra. & printers, 3 Dove ct. St. Martin's le gr
Bass & Co's. pale east india ale stores, 3 Sherborne lane, City, (A. G. Favenc, agent)
Bass, Ratcliff & Gretton, burton & india ale stores, 49 Great Tower st. & 3 Wharf, city basin (William Stevens, agent)

Bass, Ratcliff & Gretton, pale india ale store, 67 Lower Thames st (Edward Phillips, agent)
Bass, Ratcliff & Gretton, pale ale store, 3 St.James's st. (H. & G. Berry & Co. agents)
Bass Elizh. (Mrs.), ladies' school, 37 Leman st. Goodman's fl
Bass Henry, pork butcher, High st. Deptford
Bass James, pharmaceutical chemist, 78 Hatton garden
Bass John, grocer, 7 Shepherd st. Mayfair
Bass John H. cork manufactr. 6 Featherstone st. City road
Bass William, barrister, 12 Serjeants' inn, Fleet st
Bass William, surveyor & builder, 66 Goswell st
Bassam Thomas, tailor, 107 Park st. Camden town
Bassano Walter, who.tea & coffee dlr. 73 Queen st. Cheapside
Bassell Elizh. (Mrs.), hairdresser, 114 Shadwell High st
Basset John S. baize, flannel, carpet & manchr.wa. 34 Wood st
Basset William, potato salesman, 60 Rosemary lane
Bassett Geo. & Son, surveyors, 1 Southampton st. Fitzroy sq
Bassett Edward, butcher, 16½ Gt. Crown ct. Soho
Bassett George, carpenter, 5 Church st. Clapham rd
Bassett Henry, architect, 1 Southampton st. Fitzroy sq
Bassett James, butcher, 201 Shoreditch High st
Bassett James, pawnbroker, 32 Gt. Queen st. Lincoln's inn fl
Bassett John, engineer & prin.press ma. see Coniston & Bassett
Bassett John, tailor, 59 Union st. Borough High st
Bassett John, tobacconist, 19 Union st. Borough
Bassett John, wax & tallow chandler, 115 Cromer st. New rd
Bassett Joseph, boot & shoemaker, 24 Cirencester place
Bassett William, beer retailer, 65 Seymour st. Euston sq
Bassett William, builder, 27 Store st. Bedford sq
Bassett Wm. plumber & glazier, 14 Barnsbury row, Islingtn
Bassham William, carpenter, 30 Tysoe st. Spafields
Bassil William, wheelwright, 12 St. John st. Clerkenwell
Bassingham Wm. gas fitting ma. 3 Whitecross st. Cripplegt
Bassington James, ironfounder, 8 Beech st. Barbican
Bassington Thos. G. engraver, &c. 46 Spencer st. Goswell rd
Bastable Hen. veterin. forge, 1 Chapel pl. Gt. Suffolk st. Boro
Bastable Robert, farrier, 6 New road, St. George's East
Bastard Alex. fishmonger, 9 Commercial pl. Kentish town
Basten Edward, baker, 73 Gt. Carlisle st. Portman market
Basten James, baker, 56 Vauxhall st. Lambeth
Basten John, baker, 23 Brown st. Bryanstone sq
Basten Joseph, baker, 7 Union st. Walcot pl. Lambeth walk
Bastenne, Asphalte or *Bitumen Co.* (Chas. Fred. Tilstone, sec.), 31 Poultry, & Mill wall, Poplar
Baster George, *Mulberry Tree* P.H. Bromley, Middlesex
Baster James, carpenter, 30 Primrose st. Bishopsgate st
Baster John, maker of farinaceous food, 7 Orange st. Blomsby
Bastick & Driver, scale, weight & weighing machine makrs; weights to foreign standards; 2 Holywell row, Worship st
Bastick Wm. operative chemist, 2 Brook st. Bond st
Bastin Wm. bedstead & chair ma. 8 Gibraltarwk. Bethn. gr. rd
Bastings Wm. bootmaker, 3 Felix bldgs. Liverpool road
Baston Ann (Miss), milliner, 42 Tavistock st. Covent Garden
Baston Wm. upholsterer, 28 Garden row, London rd. Boro'
Bastow William, grocer, 41 Museum st. Bloomsbury
Batard Thomas B. merchant, see Sampson, Batard & Co
Batch Celia & James, timber dlrs. 8 Broomfields, Deptford
Batchelar Daniel, printer, 14 Hackney road crescent
Batchelor Edward, shoe warehouse, 3 Oxford market
Batchelor George, chemist, &c. 24 High st. Newington butts
Batchelor Henry, gen. outfitter & com. agt. 24 Pudding la
Batchelor Henry, hardwareman, 14 & 15 Brook hill Clknwl
Batchelor Henry, linendraper, see Cooper & Batchelor
Batchelor James, bootmaker, 6 Upper John st. Golden sq
Batchelor James, fringe & trimming maker, 179 Oxford st
Batchelor John, eating house, 7 George court, Piccadilly
Batchelor Joseph, bookbinder, 112 Fetter lane
Batchelor Mary (Mrs.), pork butcher, 4 Kent st. Borough
Batchelor Thomas, butcher, Elliotts pl. Lower st. Islington
Batchelor Thomas, butcher, 118 Lambeth walk
Batchelor Thos. P. cabinet mak. & upholder, 111 Crawford st
Batchelor Wm. undertaker, 5 Great Quebec st. Montagu sq
Batchelour Wm. surgeon, 21 Finsbury place North
Batcock Rd. engineer, lathe & tool ma. 4 Gibson st. Lambeth
Bate George, tailor, 11 James st. Covent Garden
Bate Henry, oilman, 2 Cross st. Hoxton New Town
Bate John, bread & biscuit baker, 9 Maddox st. Regent st
Bate Joseph, confectioner, 48 Whitechapel High st
Bate Robert Brettell, optician to the Queen, chart agent to the Admiralty, hydrometer & mathematical instrument maker to her Majesty's Honourable Boards of Excise & Customs, 21 Poultry & 33 Royal Exchange
Bate Wm. baker, 5 Clare st. Clare mkt. & 126 Tottenham ct. rd
Bateman Benjamin & Co. brass founders, engineers, lamp manufacturers & gas fitters, 13 Budge row
Bateman & Bennett, solicitors, 2 New square, Lincoln's inn
Bateman John & Co. who. boot manfrs. 18 Sun st. Bishopsgt
Bateman Abraham, coach wheelwr. 14 Green st. Theobald's rd
Bateman Edward, fruiterer, 1 Park st. Upper st. Islington
Bateman Francis, cheesemonger, 96 Great Titchfield st
Bateman George, glass cutter & stainer, 90 Hatton garden
Bateman George, greengrocer, 149 Poplar High st
Bateman Geo. Mitchell, law stationer, 17 Took's ct. Chancy. la
Bateman Henry, surgeon, 6 Islington green
Bateman Henry, timber merchant, 35 Sun st. Bishopsgate
Bateman Henry, wheelwright, &c. King John's ct. Holywell la
Bateman Horace (Mrs.), anatml. mdlr. 12 Albert ter. Kngtsbr
Bateman Jacob, shoemaker, 27 Newland st. Kensington
Bateman John, cabinet maker, 8 John st. north, Marylebone
Bateman John, cheesemonger, 77 Leather lane
Bateman John, clock case ma. 98 St. John's st. Wst. Smithfield
Bateman John, surgeon & chemist, 46 Long Acre
Bateman John Alfred, surgeon, 174 Shadwell High st
Bateman Jonas, fruiterer, 101 Upper st. Islington
Bateman Joshua Wigley, solicitor, 2 Elm court, Temple
Bateman Mary Ann (Mrs.), law stat. & booksel. 16 Bucklersb
Bateman Richard Ellis, M.D. surgeon, 54 Crawford st
Bateman Sam. carman, King John's ct. Holywell la Shoredit
Bateman Sam. scavenger, Dowgate whf. Canal rd. Kingsld. rd
Bateman Sam. jun. scavenger, King John's ct. Holywell la
Bateman Thomas, attorney, 2 Elm court, Temple
Bateman Thomas, baker, 28 Minories
Bateman Thomas, bookbinder, 36A, Tottenham st
Bateman William, cheesemonger, 14 Tyler st. Regent st
Bateman William, fish salesman, Billingsgate
Bateman William, merchant, Baltic coffee house
Bateman William, printer, 95 Leadenhall st
Bates Chas. & Son, wheelwrights, 35 & 36 Borough road
Bates & Guillemard, stockbrokers, Founders' hall ct. Lothbury
Bates, Puttock & Holiday, auctioneers, house agents & valuers, &c. 5 Welbeck st. Cavendish square
Bates Alfred, *Crown & Apple Tree* P.H. 37 Berwick st. Soho
Bates Ann (Mrs.), tobacconist, 1 Up. Grenville st. Somers tn
Bates Charles, bootmaker, 6 Finsbury place south
Bates David, glass cutter, 24 Chalcroft terrace, New cut
Bates Eliza (Mrs.), corset ma. 1 Hopkins bldgs. Islington
Bates Hen. who. tuscan straw manuf. 6 Silver st. Wood st
Bates Jacob, grocer, 3 Brunswick terrace, Barnsbury road
Bates James, bootmaker, 73 Parsons st. St. George st
Bates John, coach builder, 26 Worship st. Finsbury
Bates John, furn. broker, 35 Chalcroft ter. New cut, Lambth
Bates John, lamp cotton manufactr. 8 Wilkes st. Spitalfields
Bates John, watch pinion mak. 40 Great Sutton st. Clerkenw
Bates John B. *Rose & Crown* P.H. 60 Dorset st. Salisbury sq
Bates John Christopher, cheesemonger, 3 Kent st. Borough
Bates John Jas. druggist, 17 Devonshire bldgs. Gt. Dover rd
Bates Josiah, commer. & custom ho. & gen. agt. see Hill & Bates
Bates Joseph, dairyman, 5 Christopher ct. St. Martin's le gd
Bates Richard, carver & gilder, 51 New Compton st. Soho
Bates Samuel, coal & potato dealer, 145 Houndsditch
Bates Samuel, dairyman, 150 Houndsditch
Bates Samuel, printer, 48 Howland st. Fitzroy sq
Bates Theodore Chas. pianoforte & organ & seraphine maker, 6 Ludgate hill, & Dorset st. Salisbury sq
Bates Thomas, barrister, 4 Old square, Lincoln's inn
Bates Thomas, ham & beef dealer, 130 Whitechapel road
Bates Thos. watch movement ma. 56 Wellington st. Goswell st
Bates Wm. coach spring mak. 3 Gt. Garden st. Whitechapel
Bates Wm. lace warehouse, 76 Whitechapel High st
Bates Wm. surgeon, 20 George st. Blackfriars road
Bates Wm. Davis, corn & coal merchant, 129 Whitechapel rd
Bates Wm. E. carver, gilder, & pict. dlr. 2 Back st. Horselydown
Bateson Henry, surgeon, 2 Haddon place, Waterloo road
Batey Joseph & Co. tailors & breeches makers to her Majesty's household & H.R.H. Prince Albert, 38 Pall Mall
Batey John, tailor, 40 Princes st. Portman market
Batger & Co. confectioners, 16 Bishopsgate without
Batger John Samuel, haberdasher, 44 Curtain rd. Shoreditch
Bath Ann (Mrs.), *Regent Arms* P.H. 1 Regent st. Horseferry rd
Bath Edw. John, corn chandler, 4 New rd. St. George's East
Bath James, carpenter, 75 Vauxhall walk, Lambeth
Bath Jane (Miss), lodging house, 19 Thavies inn, Holborn
Bath John, *Spanish Patriot* P.H. 34 Lambeth Lower marsh
Bath John, carpenter, 62 Walcot place east, Lambeth
Bath John, fruit & vegetable salesman, Borough market
Bath John, manufacturer of work boxes, tea chests, backgammon tables, chessmen, bagatelle boards, travelling cases, & leather portmanteaus of every description, 97 Cheapside, & 14 Poultry
Bath John, beer retailer, 144 High st. Camden town
Bath Michael, cork cutter, 67 High Holborn
Bath Wm. artist, 15 John st. Waterloo road

Bath Stephen, coal merchant, 211 Wapping High st. & 10 Calvert st. Old Gravel lane
Bathe & Breach, *London tavern*, 123 Bishopsgate within
Bathe & Kindon, floor cloth & cover ma. Swan st. O. Kent rd
Bathe John, *Green Dragon* P.H. 56 & 57 Fleet st
Bathe Joseph Geo. metal fan light ma. 125 Crawford st. Portman square, & 14 Salisbury mews, Gloucester place
Bathe William, *Plough tavern*, Blackwall stairs
Bather George, scale maker, 62 Haymarket
Batho & Bingley, banknote engr. printers, &c. 56 Lombard st
Batho Thomas, coal dealer, 5 Milford lane, Strand
Batho William, stockbroker, 6 Bank chambers, Lothbury
Batho Wm. Morse, solicitor; vestry clerk of St. Botolph, Aldgate; St. Ethelburga, Bishopsgate; ward clerk of Portsoken, & clerk to Paviors' Comp. 2 America sq. Minories
Bathurst & Bowdler, proctors, 12 & 13 Great Knightrider st
Bathurst Geo. booksel. & stationer, 1 Bathurst st. Hyde park
Bathurst George, custom house agent, 76 Lower Thames st
Bathurst Wm. Blakeway, sec. London Hospital, Whtchpl. rd
Batkin Chas. & Co. warehousemen, 9 Foster lane, Cheapside
Batkin John, ship ironmonger, &c. 29 King st. Tower hill
Batley Benjamin & Wm. oil & black lead mercs. 22 Barbican
Batley Wm. & Henry, polygon & spiral twist turners, importers & dealers in foreign woods, 6 Portland st. Soho
Batley Charles, horse dealer, 94 Whitechapel High st
Batley Henry, solicitor, 12 Gray's inn square
Batley James, shopkeeper, 192 Bethnal green road
Batley Richard, livery stables, Eaton row, Eaton square
Batley Robert, fishmonger, 28 Long alley, Finsbury
Batley Walter, plumber, 11½ Upper Porchester st. Edgware rd
Batsford Bradley Thomas, bookseller, 30 High Holborn
Batsford John James, comb & brush manufacturer, 1 St. Martin's court, Leicester square
Batsford Thos. cowkeeper, 7 Bleeding Hart yd. Hatton gdn
Batson George, grocer, 24 Gloucester ter. Vauxhall bdg. rd
Batstone John, baker, 59 Strutton ground, Westminster
Batstone Thomas, smith, &c. James st. Marlboro' rd. Chelsea
Batstone William, baker, 8 New Manor st. Chelsea
Batt & Rutley, seedsmen, 412 Strand
Batt Thos. & Co. cabinet ma. uphols. &c. 49 Gracechurch st. & 1 Barge yard, Bucklersbury
Batt Benjamin, watch & case gilder, 9 Gee st. Goswell st
Batt Charles, brush & turnery wareho. 11 New st. Dorset sq
Batt Dinah (Mrs.), china dealer, 30 Carnaby st. Golden sq
Batt George, merchant, 412 Strand
Batt James, engineer, 5 Salmon lane, Limehouse
Batt John, silk merchant, 39 Old Broad st. City
Batt John Wm. coach carver, 17 Herbert bldgs. Waterloo rd
Batt Richard, tailor & breeches ma. 9 Edwards st. Portman sq
Batt Thomas, dining rooms, 19 Bucklersbury
Batt Thomas, *Horse & Cart* P.H. 43 Tooley st
Battam & Craske, painters & paperhangers & house decorators, 54 Oxford st. & 45 Cheapside
Battam Thomas & Son, enamellers & gilders on china & glass, 2 Johnson's court, Fleet st
Battams Wm. & Sons, cattle salesmen, 41 West Smithfield
Battcock Thos. & Fred. corn & coal mer. Chelsea whf. Cheyne wlk
Battcock George, grocer, &c. 14 Marylebone st. Regent st
Batten Edwd. & Son, timber brokers, 11 Union ct. Old Broad st
Batten & Edwards, ship & insurance brokers, & commercial agents, 66 Lower Thames st
Batten & Son, cheesemongers, Ship tav. pas. Leadenh. mkt
Batten Edmund, barrister, 5 New sq. Lincoln's inn
Batteen James, grocer & teadealer, see Hart & Batten
Batten John, carpenter, 8 Bolingbroke row, Walworth road
Batten John, hairdresser, 24 Upper Ebury st. Pimlico
Batten John, shipbroker, 18 Arbour sq. Commercial rd. east
Batterbee Joseph, auctionr. & appr. 17 Winchester pl. Pntnvl
Batterbee Robt. tailor, hosier & glover, 87 Bishopsgate within
Batterbee Thomas, boot & shoe ma. 23 Rathbone pl. Oxford st
Battersby John, ladies' shoemaker, 39 Tottenham court rd
Battersby John, shoemaker, 133 Oxford st
Battersby John, *Leather Market tav.* New Weston st. Brmndsy
Battersby Wm. Thos. stationer, &c. 13 Percival st. Clrknwell
Battershill Saml. bricklayer, 8 Amelia st. Walworth road
Batterson Ann & Susan, hosiers & glovers, 165 Regent st
Battes John & Son, upholsterers, 7 Hardwick pl. Commcl. rd. ea
Battes John, upholsterer, 3 Jamaica ter. Commrcl. rd. Limeh
Battey James, fruiterer, 6 Norway place, Hackney road
Battie John, grindery wareh. 4 Gt. Crown ct. Lit. Pulteney st
Batting Wm. watch case springer, 17 Camomile st. Bishopsg
Battison Thomas, *Mercer's Arms* P.H. 44 Totton st. Stepney
Battle John, grocer, 83 Golden lane, St. Luke's
Battley Jph. & Co. lampblack mnfrs. 3 Courtney ter. Kingslnd
Battley Joseph, grocer, Stratford, Essex
Battley Rd. chemist & druggist, 32 Whitecross st. Cripplegate
Battram William, butcher, 3 White hart st. Newgate market
Battson Benjamin, baker, 2 Peacock st. Newington butts
Batty & Co. oil, italian & export pickle warehouse, 15 & 16 Finsbury pavement, & Providence row, Finsbury square
Batty, Melville & Co. wholesale stationers, 174 Aldersgate st
Batty Abraham, market gardener, Blue Anchor rd. Bermondsy
Batty Charles, oil & colorman, 272 Oxford st
Batty Joshua, currier, 10 Swan yard, & 69 Shoreditch
Batty Thomas, dairyman, 1 Earl's ct. Little Newport st
Batty William, solicitor, 26 Charles st. St. James's square
Battye Thomas, surgeon, 5 Woburn place
Battye William, ironmonger, 7 Courtney terrace, Kingsland
Battyll Rd. Collier, flannel agent, 83 Wood st. Cheapside
Baucher Elizabeth (Miss), tobacconist, 128 Tottenham ct. rd
Baucher Jas. Robt. cornchandler, 19 Hackney rd. cr. & 204 Brick lane, Spitalfields
Baud Benj. architect, Linc.'s inn fields chamb. Portsmouth st
Bauer Abraham & Co. bankers, 9 Arthur st. west, King William st. City, & at Manchester & Hamburgh
Bauer William, laceman, 85 Oxford st
Bauerman Hillery J. & Co. rag. mer. Beal's whf. Tooley st
Baugh Joseph, tailor & salesman, 26 Crescent st. Euston sq
Baugh William, hat manufacturer, see Stainburn & Baugh
Baughan Mary A. (Mrs.), wheelwright, 5 Lt. Cockpit yd. Bdf. rw
Baughan John Henry, army & navy agent, 9 Charing cross
Baughan Thomas, baker, 5 Belmont row, Vauxhall
Baughen Brothers, shag manufacturers, 9 Aldermanbury
Baughen John, house painter, 25 New st. Dorset square
Baughen Samuel, grocer, 25 New st. Dorset square
Baughen Samuel, tailor, 10 Stafford st. Lisson grove
Baugniet Charles, artist, 21 Beaumont st. Portland place
Bauly William, artist, 22 Crawford st. Portman square
Baum Peter Friedrich, Hamburgh mer. & agt. 10 Lombard st
Baumann Alfred, fancy cap manufacturer, 22 London wall
Baumer Charles, merchant, 33 Great St. Helen's, Bishopsgate
Baumgart Charles, watchmaker, 31 Gerrard st. Soho
Baumgarten Chas. B. accountant, 8 Barnes pl. Mile end road
Baumgartner Edw. J. barrister, 3 Plowden bldgs. Temple
Baven Wm. chairmaker, 5 Broker's row, Red cross st. Boro'
Baverstock & Gorton, *King & Queen* P.H. 30 Norton folgate
Baverstock & Parnell, brewers, 11 Westmoreland place, Walworth common
Baverstock James, dyer & embosser, 18 Dean st. Soho]
Bavin Benjamin, sealing wax & wafer maker, 52 King st. Boro'
Bavin William, lighterman, 14 Jewry st. Aldgate
Bawden John, boot & shoe maker, 17 Munster st. Regents pk
Bawden Margaret (Miss), milliner, see Wiltshire & Bawden
Bawden William, boot & shoe wareho. 8 Tyler st. Golden sq
Bawden William, mine agent, 2 Bank chambers, Lothbury
Bawdon William S. linendraper, 145 St. John st. Smithfield
Bawler Francis, fruiterer, 19 Harp alley, Farringdon st
Bawn John, block & mast maker, 17 Emmett st. Poplar
Bawn John, *Chequers* P.H. 16 Duke st. St. James's
Bawtree Thomas, fruit salesman, 61 Farringdon market
Bax Daniel, tailor & woollendraper, 46 & 48 Regent st. & umbrella manufacturer, 38 Regent circus
Bax Dorothy (Mrs.), *Hertford Arms* P.H. 14 Lit. Grosvenor st
Bax Edward, macintosh warehouse, 1 Charing cross; & umbrella & india rubber golosh ma. 7 Strand
Bax Thomas, corndealer & seedsman, 143 & 144 Bishopsgate without, & 309 Wapping
Baxendale, Tatham, Upton & Johnson, solicitors, 7 Great Winchester st. & 24 Lincoln's inn fields
Baxter, Boult & Co. soapmakers, 88 Carlisle st. Lambeth
Baxter Robt. Michael & Chas. attorneys, 48 Lincoln's inn fi
Baxter Alexr. baker, 27 Freeschool st. & 6 Folly, Dockhead
Baxter Charles, portrait painter, 33 Gt. St. Helens
Baxter David, baker, 7 Moor lane, Cripplegate
Baxter Ebenezer J. potato dlr. 10 Bolingbrook row, Walw. rd
Baxter Edmond, grocer, 134 Union st. Borough High st
Baxter Edward, grocer, 61 Cromer st. Brunswick square
Baxter George, chemist & druggist, 198 High Holborn
Baxter George, *Crown & Anchor tavern*, 189 Strand
Baxter George, currier, 4 Church st. Borough
Baxter George, dairyman, 3 Gray st. Manchester sq
Baxter George, patentee of oil color printing, engraver on wood & bronze printer, 11 Northampton square
Baxter Hector, bookbinder, 49 Little Bartholomew close
Baxter Henry, bricklayer, 40 Park st. Dorset square
Baxter Henry, who. pickle manfr. see Gordon, Baxter & Co
Baxter Henry Foster, surgeon, 5 George st. Hanover sq
Baxter Henry John, barrister, 5 Essex court, Temple
Baxter James, boot & shoe maker, 31 King st. Soho
Baxter James, button & trimming sel. 67 St. George st
Baxter James, *Crown* P.H. 50 Kent st. Borough
Baxter James, grocer, &c. 32 Sherborne st. Blandford sq

Baxter James, linen warehouse, 8 Bow lane, Cheapside
Baxter James, *Welsh Harp* P.H. 52 Carnaby st. Golden sq
Baxter Jane (Mrs.), baker, 8 Lucas pl. Commercial rd. east
Baxter Jefferson, tailor, 7 Nag's head court, Gracechurch st
Baxter John, breeches maker, 11 Finsbury st. Finsbury sq
Baxter John, fruiterer, 9 Newland terrace, Kensington
Baxter John, *Grapes* P.H. 129 High Holborn
Baxter John, japanner, 13 Clerkenwell green
Baxter Richard, barrister, 3 Garden court, Temple
Baxter Robert, baker, 44 Penton st. Pentonville
Baxter Robert, british & foreign stock & share broker, 8 Old Broad st. City
Baxter Robert, trunkmaker, 96 White Lion st. Pentonville
Baxter Stafford Stratton, solicitor, 41 Chancery lane
Baxter Thomas, who. & retail ironmonger, 148 Minories
Baxter William, bookseller, &c. 68 Paradise row, Chelsea
Baxter William, surgeon, 2 Middlesex place, New road
Baxter William, tobacconist, 150 Drury lane
Baxter William Edward, haberdasher, 21 Eyre st. hill
BaxterWm.Thos. *Marquis of Granby* P.H. 67 Union st. Boro'
Bayes Henry, trunkmaker, 20 Park side, Knightsbridge
Bayes James, starch maker, see Giles & Bayes
Bayes Jane (Mrs.), toy dealer, 142 Tooley st
Bayes Joseph, fruiterer, 1 Paulton st. Church st. Chelsea
Bayes William, surgeon, 29 Lloyd square
Bayfield & Malfatti, imprs. of foreign goods, 16 Watling st
Bayfield Sam. & Son, surgeons, 3 & 16 St. Thomas' st. Boro
Bayfield George, baker, 31 Tabernacle walk, Finsbury
Bayfield Henry M. *Bee Hive* P.H. 55 Brill row, Somers town
Bayfield William, pawnbroker, 73 Charlotte terr. New cut
Bayford John & James H. proctors & notaries, 12 & 13 Great Knightrider st. Doctors' commons
Bayford Augustus Fred. D.C.L. advocate, 3 Bell yd. Doc.com
Bayford Henry, potato salesman, Clare market
Bayler Thomas, bootmaker, 7 Little Windmill st. Golden sq
Bayles Frances (Miss), stay manf. 2 Woodbridge st.Clerknwll
Bayles Mary (Mrs.), grocer, Earls court, Old Brompton
Bayles William John, tailor, 44 Newington causeway
Bayless Sarah (Miss), academy, 38 Coppice row, Clknwll
Bayley & Blew, perfumers to the Royal Family, 17 Cockspur st. Charing cross
Bayley Elizh. E. & M. (Misses), fancy repos.Church st.Hckny
Bayley, Janson & Richardson, solicitors, 4 Basinghall st
Bayley Joseph & Richd. packers, &c. 34 Friday st. Cheapside
Bayley & Ridley, ship brokers, 3 George yd. Lombard st
Bayley Alfred, stockbroker, 39 Lothbury
Bayley Charles, smith & tinman, 24 King st. Clerkenwell
Bayley Charles John, barrister, 3 Essex court, Temple
Bayley Christopher, cheesemonger, 9 Gwynn's pl. Hackny. rd
Bayley Edmund, chemist, 12 Aldgate, High st
Bayley Edward Morshead, pork butcher, 65 Hackney road
Bayley Edward, tinplate worker, 1 Clarence pl. Deptford
Bayley Emilius, special pleader, 2 Essex court, Temple
Bayley Francis, barrister, 21 Old square, Lincoln's inn
Bayley George, chemist & druggist, 5 Crown pl. Old Kent rd
BayleyHenryGeorge, hairdresser, 1 Hampton st.Walworth rd
Bayley James, carman, 29½ Gt. Sutton st. Clerkenwell
Bayley John, bookseller, &c. 11 Kensington ter. Gravel pits
Bayley John, boot & shoe maker, 37 Low.Queen st. Rotherhithe
Bayley Robert, solicitor, Clarence chambers, 12 Haymarket
Bayley Saml. carpenter, 3 Theobald's road, Red Lion sq
Bayley Saml. piece brok. & list dlr. 8 Bedfordbury, Cov. gar
Bayley Sir John, bart. barrister, 2 Essex court, Temple
Bayley Thomas, plumber, Broadway, Deptford
Bayley Thomas, solicitor, 58 Lincoln's inn fields
Bayley Thomas, stockbroker, see Field, Son & Bayley
Bayley Thomas, jun. china dealer, 82 Hatton garden
Bayley Wm. cheesemonger, Church st. Hackney
Bayley Wm. gold & silver beater, 14 & 15 Gee st. Goswell st
Bayley Wm. grocer, 167 Shoreditch
Bayley Wm. ornamental painter, 7 Cottage place, City road
Bayley Wm. tailor, 21 George st. Adelphi
Bayley Wm. Chas. optician & spectacle ma. 76 St.John st. rd
Bayley Wm. Kennedy, barrister, 5 New sq. Lincoln's inn
Bayley Wm. Mitchell, butcher, 4 St.Martin's ct.Ludgate hill
Baylie Elie & Co. iron & tinplate merchants, ironplate workers & chain manufacturers, 39 & 40 Rosoman st. Clerkenwell
Baylie John, accountant, 5 Cook's court, Carey st
Baylie Lionel, coffee rooms, 20 King st. Tower hill
Bayliff Mary & Amelia, straw bonnet ma. 2 Pitfield st.Hoxton
Bayliff Richard & Co. hat makers, 9 Vine place, Old st. road
Baylis & Drewe, solicitors, 84 Basinghall st
Baylis Henry Francis & Co. printers' ink, japan & varnish makers, & color manufacturers, 21 Old Montague st
Baylis Alexander John, vestry clerk, 22 Redcross st. Cripplegate
Baylis Richard & John, orange merchants, 16 Botolph lane
Baylis Charles, oilman, 149 Whitechapel road
Baylis Edwd. actuary of *Anchor Life Ass. Co.* 30 Sackville st
Baylis Edward, orange merchant, 23 Pudding la. Eastcheap
Baylis Edward, pawnbroker, 8 Adams row, Hampstead rd
Baylis George, butcher, 23 Strutton ground, Westminster
Baylis George, grocer, 100 Uxbridge st. Newington causeway
Baylis George, scale ma. 8 Winchester pl. Southwark brdg.rd
Baylis George, tailor, 19 Little Queen st. Westminster
Baylis Henry, cowkeeper, 29 Church st. Mile end new town
Baylis James, coal merchant, 52 Beaumont st. Portland pl
Baylis John, crape manufacturer, 14 Owen's row, Goswell rd
Baylis John, grocer, 25 Exeter st. Lisson grove
Baylis John, fruiterer, 39 North Audley st
Baylis Joseph, baker, 8 Adam st. west, Bryanstone square
Baylis Joseph, baker, 73 Lisson grove north, Marylebone
Baylis Joseph, wholesale grocer, see Hicks, Baylis & Hicks
Baylis Joseph Rt. silversmith & pawnbrok. 41 Aldersgate st
Baylis Mary (Miss), straw hatmaker, 5 Sloane st. Chelsea
Baylis Mary (Mrs.), grocer, &c. 53 High st. Portland town
Baylis Mary (Mrs.), staymaker, 4 Youl's pl. Old Kent road
Baylis Samuel, coal merchant, 11 Exeter st. Lisson grove
Baylis Thos. *Griffin* P.H. 5 Liquorpond st. Gray's inn lane
Baylis Thos. Hen. special pleader, 11 King's bench wlk. Temple
Baylis William, baker, 11 North street, Edgware road, & 12 Exeter st. Lisson grove
Baylis William, furniture bro. 11 Brook st. New rd. St. Pancras
Baylis William, jeweller, 9 Upper Rupert st. Soho
Baylis William, linendraper, Bridge road, Battersea
Bayliss Moses, tailor, 14 Queen's buildings, Knightsbridge
Bayliss Thomas, grocer, 8 Coppice row, Clerkenwell
Bayliss Thomas, ironmonger, brazier & tinman, 273 Strand
Bayly Thos. Tanner & Co. ship insurance & general commission agents, 1 London st. Mark lane
Bayly Bethune, barrister, 4 Mitre court chambers, Fleet st
Bayly Charles, chemist & druggist, 30 Lamb st. Spital sq
Bayly Daniel Rodgers, *Commercial* coffee ho. 85 Cannon st
Bayly George, brushmaker, 146 Fenchurch st
Bayly Geo. sailmaker & shipchandler, Fountain strs. Bemnds
Bayly Jas. Dudgeon, stationer, &c. 10 George yd. Lmbrd. st
Bayly Robert, barrister, 3 Harcourt buildings, Temple
Bayly Thomas, baker, 66 New Church st. Lisson grove
Bayly Thomas, sen. bootmaker, 279 Bermondsey st
Bayly William, carver & gilder, 15 Marshall st. Golden sq
Bayman Henry, hand screw makr. 35 Old Gravel la. Wapping
Bayne & Ellery, merchants, 52 Mark lane
Bayne William, oilman, 13 Vauxhall bridge road
Baynes John & Son, dyers & scourers, 100 Blackman st. Boro
Baynes Frederick, ironmonger, 6 Marchmont st. Brnwk. sq
Baynes Henry, wholesale stationer & account book maker, printer & bookseller, 9 Clement's lane, Lombard st
Baynes Henry Saml. bookseller, 40 St. John's sq. Clerkenwll
Baynes James, hairdresser, 29 Bear lane, Blackfriars road
Baynes John, dyer, &c. 6 Brooke st. Holborn, & Clapham com
Baynes Richard, bookseller, 28 Paternoster row
Baynes Thomas Mann, artist, 41 Burton st. Burton crescent
Bayntin Walter James, surgeon, 28 Lower Eaton st. Pimlico
Baynton Jas. umbrel. & hat shag silk manf. 17 Wood st. Sptlfds
Bayond Antoine, fruiterer, 75 High st. Marylebone
Bays Francis & Alfred, cheesemongers, 57 Blackfriars road
Bays Ann Roberts (Miss), ladies' school, 13 Great Alie st
Bays Richard, baker, 5 Priory place, Camberwell road
Bayst William, pork butcher, 138 Church st. Shoreditch
Bazalgette Evelyn, barrister, 8 Old sq. Lincoln's inn
Bazalgette Jsph. Wm. civil engineer, 24 Gt. George st. Westm
Bazin John, fishing tackle mkr. 8 Duncan pl. London fields
Bazzoni Anthony, wax & composition doll maker & maker of the speaking dolls, 128 High Holborn
Beacall William, dentist, 15 Newman st. Oxford st
Beach Thomas & Joshua, coopers, 4 Little New st. Shoe lane
Beach William & Sons, white & oil leather manufacturers, Wright's buildings, Grange road, Bermondsey
Beach Edward, wax & tallowchandler, 37 Lime st
Beach George, ironmonger, 176 Poplar High st
Beach Mary Ann (Mrs.), oil & itali. wareho. 13 North Audleyst
Beach Thomas, cork cutter, 35 William st. Whitechapel
Beacham John, saddler, 2 Dover place, Old Kent road
Beacham Lewis, saddler, 253 Whitechapel road
Beacham Thomas, silk mercer, &c. 28 Bagnigge wells road
Beachcroft Charles, surveyor, 48 High st. Notting hill
Beachcroft Richard, solicitor, see Maltby & Beachcroft
Beachcroft Robt. wine merchant, 1 Dunster ct. Mincing la
Beachcroft Samuel, architect & surveyor, 75 Old Broad st. City, & 83 Cadogan place, Sloane st
Beachim Thomas, butcher, 5 Gilbert's passage, Clare market
Beackon Frederick, baker, Stratford, Essex

Beacon George, baker, Deptford green
Beadel & Foulkes, aucts. survr. & estate agts. 25 Gresham st
Beadell George, dairyman, 8 St. James' place, Hampstead rd
Beadell Wm. baker, 17 Jubilee pl. north, Commerl. rd. east
Beadell William, cook & confectioner, 8 Vere st. Cavendish sq
Beadell William, marine store dealer, 6 Leather lane
Beadle James, cheesemonger, 5 Ironmonger row, Old st
Beadman Thomas, porkman, 164 Lambeth walk
Beadnell William, stationer, 114 Bethnal green road
Beadon Abraham, bookbinder, 41 Gloucester st. Queen sq
Beadon Wm. Fredk. barrister, 1 King's Bench walk, Temple
Beagle James, featherbed & upholstery warehouse, 68 & 90 Bridge road, Lambeth
Beal's wf. Chas. & Geo. Griffin & Co. Mill la. Tooley st
Beal Abraham, shoemaker, 9 Keen's row, Walworth road
Beal Edmund, furn. broker, 5 Gt. James st. Lisson grove north
Beal Frederick, tobacconist, High st. Deptford
Beal James, cooper, 78 Cowcross st. West Smithfield
Beal John, saddler, 2 Gresse st. Rathbone place
Beal Rd. *Royal Standard* P.H. 1 Up. Dorset st. Bryanstone sq
Beal Samuel, *Coach & Horses* P.H. 20 Eyre st. hill, Hat. gar
Beal Sarah (Mrs.), straw hat ma. 3 Mansion house pl. Cambwl
Beal Thomas, corn factor, Corn exchange tavern, Mark lane
Beal William, hat maker, 8 Cumberland place, New road, & 8 Commercial place, City road
Beal Wm. Ebenr. furrier, &c. 12 Bolingbroke rw. Walworth rd
Bealby John, builder, carp. & under. 10 Lit. Queen st. Holborn
Bealby Robert, printer, 33 Arlington st. Clerkenwell
Beale Frederick & Co. patent euphonicon pianoforte manufacturers, 201 Regent st. & 55 King st. Golden sq
Beale Hen. & Co. frenchdyers & scourers, 35 Blackman st. Boro
Beale John & Co. chemists, 108 Long acre
Beale & Kine, hop mers. 8 Wellington chambers, Londonbridge
Beale Wm. John & Henry, oil brokers & agts. 4 Jeffrey's sq
Beale Alfred, cabinet carver, 9 Fuller st. Bethnal green
Beale Ann (Mrs.), hat manf. 15 Bennett st. Stamford st. Blkfrs
Beale Edward, baker, 1 South place, Tibberton sq. Islington
Beale Elizabeth Ann (Mrs.), midwife, 13 Chapel pl. Cav. sq
Beale George, painter, &c. 9 Norfolk st. Middlesex hospital
Beale James, hosier, glover & shirtmaker, 131 New Bond st
Beale James, shoema. 34 Bridgehouse pl. Newington causew
Beale James, wholesale tea & coffee dealer, 91 Great Tower st
Beale James Hen. cabinet mkr. 13 Westmoreland pl. City rd
Beale John, baker, 6 West st. Hackney
Beale John, cooper, 10 Smith's buildings, City road
Beale John, grocer & oilman, 24 Osnaburgh st. Regent's pk
Beale John Franks, butcher, 173 Union st. Borough
Beale Joseph, hatter, 56 Brunswick st. Stamford st
Beale Lionel, surgeon, 108 Long acre
Beale Miles, surgeon & apothecary, 41 Bishopsgate within
Beale Thomas, surgeon, 30 Bedford sq. Commercial rd. east
Beale Thomas James, printer, 19 Webb st. Bermondsey st
Beale Thos. Fredk. music seller, see Cramer, Beale & Chappell
Beale Thos. G. (sec. *Queen Adelaide inst.*) 13 Chapel pl. Cav. sq
Beale William, brass finisher, 110 Cornwall rd. Lambeth
Beale Wm. furn. broker, 1 King st. Lower rd. Islington
Beale William, who. coffee dealer, 14 Little Tower st
Beales Edmond, barrister, 4 Stone buildings, Lincoln's inn
Beales John Edward, solicitor, 7 John st. Adelphi
Beales Samuel, chemist, &c. 196 Bishopsgate without
Beales William, tobacconist, 27 Union st. Clarendon sq
Beales William, *Windmill* P.H. 35 New Park st. Borough
Beall & Webster, pawnbrokers & general salesmen, 20 Gt. Charlotte st. Blackfriars road
Beaman George, surgeon, 32 King st. Covent garden
Beament Henry, glass & china dlr. 1 Napier st. New North rd
Beamish John, academy, 14 Wellington st. Goswell road
Beamish John, fur skin dresser, 16 White st. Borough
Beamish John, fruiterer, 133 Bethnal green road
Beamish Sarah (Mrs.), library, 30 Grenville st. Somers town
Bean Edward & Sons, surgeons, 14 Clarence pl. Camberwl. rd
Bean James & Co. military & nav. tailors, 62 Brook st. Bond st
Bean, Son & Gaselee, surgeons, Denmark hill
Bean Edward, basket maker, 12 Borough market
Bean Elizth. (Mrs.), wholes. confectioner, 36 Rawstorne st
Bean Francis, butcher, 3 Dean st. Holborn
Bean Fred. hosier, 13 Northumberland pl. Commercial rd. east
Bean Geo. livery stables, Cumberland mews nrth. Adam st. west
Bean John, butcher, 6 Shepherd st. Hertford st. Mayfair
Bean John, pork butcher, 8 Courthrope ter. Bermndsy new rd
Bean John, pork butcher, 62 Freeschool st. Horselydown
Bean John, wharfinger & coal mer. Bowle's wf. Cockhl. Ratcliff
Bean John, *Fountain* P.H. 141 Lambeth walk
Bean Peter, grocer, 5 Southampton ct. Queen sq. Bloomsbury
Bean Sophia (Miss), milliner, 37 Edgware road
Bean Thomas, baker, 25 Clifton st. Finsbury
Bean William, florist, Dean's row, Walworth road
Bean William, silk dealer, 2 Wilkes st. Spitalfields
Beane Robert, corn & flour merchant & factor, 5 Kensington High st.; & Jacks coffee house, Mark lane
Beanlands Benjamin, solicitor, 14 Cook's ct. Lincoln's inn
Bear Daniel, *Admiral Tyrrel* P.H. Bermondsey wall
Bear John, straw hat maker, 37 Freeschool st. Horselydown
Bear William, bricklayer, 7 Wimbourne st. New north rd
Beard Richard & Co. agents for the sale of Dauptain's ultramarine, 85 King William st. City
Beard Richd. & Co. coal merchs. Purfleet whf. Earl st. Blkfrs
Beard Abraham, seal engraver, 32 St. John's sq. Clerkenwell
Beard Charles, cloth worker & presser, 25 Castle st. City rd
Beard David, baker, 16 Love lane, Eastcheap
Beard Edward, lodging house, 74 Connaught ter. Edgware rd
Beard Francis Carr, surgeon, 215 Oxford st
Beard George, confectioner, 6 Sydney alley
Beard Geo. decorative needlework repository, 287 Regent st
Beard George, pin & needle manufr. see Kirby, Beard & Co
Beard George Gifford, *White Swan* P.H. 108 Fetter lane
Beard James C. printer & schoolstatnr. 25 Crown rw. Walworth
Beard John, carpenter, Church st. Deptford
Beard John, engine turner, 12 Red Lion st. Clerkenwell
Beard Joseph, baker, 267 Borough High st
Beard Neville, currier & leather factor, morocco & roan dresser, 6 Beech st. Barbican
Beard Richard, photographic portrait rooms, Royal Polytechnic Institution, 309 Regent st.; 34 Parliament st.; 85 King William st. City; manufactory 18½ Wharf rd. City rd
Beard Thomas, coach maker, 7 Mount pleasant, Gray's inn la
Beard William, butcher, 16 Peerless place, City road
Beard Wm. fancy cabinet maker, 5 Cook's ct. Lincoln's inn
Beard Wm. fancy cabinet maker, 32 Gloucester st. Queen sq
Beard Wm. oil, tar, turp. & seed broker, &c. 75 Old Broad st
Beard William Durnsford, custom house, general shipping & passengers' agent, Hall of Commerce
Beard Wm. John, plumber & painter, 35 Southwark bridge r
Beardmore John, baker, 60 Lambeth walk
Beardmore John Thos. confectioner, 152 Princes rd. Lambth
Beardmore Letitia (Miss), dressma. see Burton & Beardmore
Beardmore William, hatter, see Williams & Beardmore
Beardon George, cab builder, 26 Tavistock mews, Tavistk. sq
Beards Thomas, gasfitter, 3 Hayward's pl. St. John st. Clerknw
Beardshaw Thomas, grocer, 32 St. Albans st. Lambeth
Beardwell Joseph, baker, 8 Woburn buildings, Tavistock sq
Beare John, patentee of pumps & fire engines, 16 Holborn hl
Beare Philip, tobacconist, 77 Bethnal green road
Bearman Thomas, baker, 1 Essex place, Mare st. Hackney
Bearne Philip, grocer, 14 Little Compton st. Soho
Bearns Mary Ann (Mrs.), shoema. 28 Robert st. King's rd. Chels
Beart John, solicitor, 4 Bouverie st. Fleet st
Beasley Edmund, linendraper, 5 Gt. Chapel st. Westminster
Beasley Fred. *Olive Branch* P.H. 58 Crawford st. Portman sq
Beasley John, boot & shoe maker, 8 Salmon lane, Limehouse
Beasley John, plumber, 2 Beauvoir place, Kingsland
Beasley Peter, chandler's shop, 105 Hoxton Old town
Beasley William, *Black Horse* P.H. 6 Rathbone place
Beasley William Cole, special pleader, 5 Brick ct. Temple
Beaten George, *Prince Regent* P.H. 16 Devonshire terrace, Globe road, Mile end road
Beater Mary (Mrs.), milliner, 9 Wellington ter. Clapham rd
Beathen & Tallent, pianoforte maks. 13 & 14 Borough road
Beaton & Dawes, tailors, 129 Upper st. Islington
Beaton Andrew, silversmith, &c. 110 Whitechapel High st
Beaton John, chemist, 174 Shoreditch High st
Beaton George, baker, 9 Lion st. New Kent road
Beatson John, shipbreaker & timber mercht. 81 Rotherhithe
Beatson Wm. architect & surveyor, 3 Bartholomew la. City
Beattie Alexander & Co. merchants, 39 Nicholas lane
Beattie Andrew, silk, cotton & woollen dyer, 70 & 71 Oakley st. Lambeth; Emanuel place, Camberwell road, & 11 Charles st. Westbourne terrace, Hyde park
Beattie Henry, pawnbroker, see Notley & Beattie
Beattie Jas. gunmak. 52 Up. Marylebone st. & 223 Regent st
Beattie John, tea dealer, 15 Tyler st. Regent st
Beattie Wm. artist & sculptor, 74 Great Portland st
Beau Thomas, china & glass dealer, 47 Great Titchfield st
Beauchamp John, british plate manufactr. 94 High Holborn
Beaufoy & Co. vinegar & wine makers, & manufacturers of acetic acids & chlorides of soda & lime, & millers, South Lambeth, & Wandsworth road, North side
Beauman Francis, artist, 14 Augustus sq. Park village east
Beaumont & Thompson, solicitors, 19 Lincoln's inn fields, & Cutlers' hall, 6 Cloak lane
Beaumont James, solicitor, Cutlers' hall, 6 cloak lane, & 19 Lincoln's inn fields

Beaumont Philosophical Institution, John Owen, librarian, 32 to 37 Beaumont square, Mile end
Beaumont Abr. chem. see Corbyn, Beaumont, Stacey & Messer
Beaumont Alfred, architect, 5 Beak st. Regent st
Beaumont Hannah (Mrs.), coffee rooms, 53 Long acre
Beaumont Henry, pork butcher, 38 High st. Poplar
Beaumont Henry, solicitor, Warwick chmbs. Beak st. Regnt. st
Beaumont Henry, wine merchant, 4 Pancras la. Bucklersbury
Beaumont John, coachmaker, 10 Commercial pl. City road
Beaumont John Henry, bootma. 15 Mortimer st. Cavendish sq
Beaumont John Wm. greengrocer, 2 Glo'ster pl. Walworth rd
Beaumont Joseph, *Red Lion* P.H. 9 Lit. Guilford st. Brunswk. sq
Beaumont Joseph, tailor & clothier, &c. 11 Finch la. Cornhill
Beaumont Robert, fruiterer, 20 Brewer st. Somers town
Beaumont Thomas, boot & shoe maker, 28 Gray's inn lane
Beaumont Thomas, butcher, 187 Poplar High st
Beaumont Thomas, furng. ironmng. 16 Union st. Hoxton New tn
Beaumont Thomas, plumber, 1 Sutton st. Commer. rd. East
Beaumont Wm. tin plate worker, 6 Aylesbury st. Clerkenwell
Beavan & Anderson, solicitors, 2 Adelphi terrace, Strand
Beavan & Stuart, woollen manufacturers, 17 Gresham st
Beavan Charles, barrister, 1 New square, Lincoln's inn
Beavan Edward, barrister, 4 Middle Temple lane
Beavan John, hairdresser & wigmaker, 48 Lamb's Conduit st
Beavan Thomas Drew, goldsmith, 31 Marylebone st. Piccadly
Beavan Wm. toy dealer & stationer, 11 Bridge st. Southwark
Beaven James, *White Horse* P.H. 10 Cripplegate buildings
Beaver Alexander, mast maker, Mill wall, Poplar
Beaver Charlte. (Miss), stationer, 13 Pleasant rw. Hlwy. rd
Beaver Dennis, boot & shoe ma. 108 Chalton st. Somers town
Beaver Richard, livery stables, 7 Whitehorse yd. Coleman st
Beaver William, butcher, 100 Fore st. Cripplegate
Beavers Thomas, dentist, 29 Gt. Windmill st. Haymarket
Beavis Edwin, cheesemonger, 67 St. Mary Axe
Beavis John, bookseller, &c. 1 Portland pl. Lower rd. Islngtn
Beavis Wm. cheesemonger, 9 Cornwall road, Stamford st
Beavis Wm. law stationer, 2 Bride court, New Bridge st
Beazley Edward, tailor, 9 Narrow st. Limehouse
Beazley John, cheesemonger, see Hughes & Beazley
Beazley John, drysalter, 3 Spicer st. Spitalfields
Beazley Raymond, tailors' trimming seller, 1 Thomas street, Grosvenor sq. & 20A, Cleveland st. Fitzroy sq
Beazley Samuel, architect, 29 Soho square
Beazley Thomas, carpent & undert. 43 Cornwall rd. Lambeth
Bebb & Rose, attorneys & agents, 12 Argyll st. Regent st
Bebbington Henry Atkinson, stationer, 426 Strand
Bebell Charles, tobacconist, 8½ Union st. Borough
Beck, Henderson & Co. seedsmen, Middle wharf, Adelphi
Beck (Henry Edward & Herbert Browne), surgeons, &c. 82 Bridge road, Lambeth
Beck Michael & Co. glass & china dlrs. 63 Sun st. Bishopsgate
Beck Robert & Co. hair cutters & wig makers, 79 Cheapside
Beck Ann Rebecca (Miss), haberdasher, 184 Whitechapel rd
Beck Chas. Turner, law stationer, 15 Castle st. Holborn
Beck Edward, scotch ale agent, 7 Hungerford wharf, Strand
Beck Edward Hall, corndealer, 1 Hoxton Old town
Beck Fred. fruiterer, 2 Walbrook pl. Hoxton New town
Beck James, plasterer, 52 Tabernacle walk, Finsbury
Beck James Fenn, grocer, &c. 23 Bolingbroke row, Walworth
Beck John, tailor, 4 King st. Holborn
Beck John, wine merchant, see Lister, Beck & Beck
Beck Richard, watchmaker, see Brugger, Beck & Co
Beck Richard Low, wine merchant, see Lister, Beck & Beck
Beck Robert, shoemaker, Denmark hill, Camberwell
Beck Simon Adams, solicitor, 118 Fenchurch st
Beck Sydney, tinman & brazier, 1 New King st. Deptford
Beck Thomas, brushmaker, 4 Tavistock row, Covent garden
Beck Thos. Geo. tailor & mercer, 4 Tavistock row, Covent garden
Beck Thos. S. surgeon, 53 Upper Marylebone st.
Beck Wm. Richard, goldsmith, see Grayhurst, Harvey & Co
Beckenham James, importer of cigars, 64 York rd. Lambeth
Beckenham Richd. carpenter, 2 Southampton mws. Eustn sq
Becker Francis Paul & Co. writg. engrs. 12 Paternoster row
Becker Charles, furrier, 28 Cannon st. road, St. George's ea
Becker Fras. Paul, writ. engr. 27 Southampton pl. Euston sq
Becker Samuel, importer of dantzic spruce, 59 Gt. Prescot st
Becket & Young, grocers, 3 High st. Islington, & 3 Wells row
Becket John, scotch agent, 27 Farringdon st
Beckett Ann (Mrs.), & Son, general printers, 45 Marylebone la
Beckett Charles, printer, 135 Kingsland road
Beckett Edward, solicitor, 16 Warwick st. Golden square
Beckett Geo. bootmaker, 41 Fenchurch st. & 37 Gracechurch st
Beckett George, fruitererer, Mare st. Hackney
Beckett James, corn chandler. Mare st. Hackney
Beckett James, *White Raven* P.H. 38 Raven st. Whitechpl. rd
Beckett John, corndealer, &c. 49 Barbican
Beckett John, rope & twine mfr. 1 Hen. & Chicken la. Wlwth. com
Beckett John, tobacconist, 1 Blackman st. Borough
Beckett Joshua William, printer & engraver, 9 Cannon st. rd
Beckett Samuel, wholesale oilman, see Grayling & Beckett
Beckett Wm. John, *Turk's Head* P.H. 2 Butcher row, Ratcliff
Beckford George Hen. law & genl. stationer, 122 Chancery la
Beckford William, tailor, 70 Hercules buildings, Lambeth
Beckford William, west india merchant, 11 Lime st
Beckingham Charles Henry, tobacconist, 415 Strand
Beckingham Henry, baker, 44 Wells st. Oxford st
Beckingham Honey B. grocer, 54 Rawstorne st. Goswell road
Beckitt Henry Hugh, attorney, see Loveland & Beckitt
Beckitt John Ducker, glass wareho. see Brameld & Beckitt
Beckles Samuel Husbands, barrister, 3 Elm court, Temple
Beckley Aaron, fishmonger & poult. 11 Conduit st. Padgtn
Beckley Richard, lodging house, 37 Green st. Grosvenor sq
Beckwith Ambrose, *Fox & Hounds* P.H. 37 Hare st. Bethnalgn
Beckwith Charles, woollen factor, see Friend & Beckwith
Beckwith Joseph, *Clarendon* coffee rooms, 77 Shoe lane
Beckwith Joseph, engraver, 3 Wilderness row, Clerkenwell
Beckwith Samuel, turner, 10 Princes st. Fitzroy square
Beckwith Thomas, coffee rooms, 31 Hatton wall, Hatton gdn
Beckwith Wm. *Shoulder of Mutton* P.H. 77 Brunswk. st. Blkwl
Beckwith William, smith, Stratford, Essex
Beckwith William Andrews, gun manufacturer to the Honorable East India Company & her Majesty's Board of Ordnance; fire arms of every description, wholesale, retail, & for exportation, 58 Skinner st. Snow hill
Bedale John, merchant, 76 Coleman st
Beddome Richard Boswell, solicitor, see Bartlett & Beddome
Beddome William, warehouseman, see Favell, Beddome & Co
Beddow Benjn. linendraper, 61 Strutton ground, Westmr
Beddow Josiah, accountant, 26 Beauvoir ter. Kingsland
Beddeson Henry, grocer, 27 Carnaby st. Golden sq
Beddells Caleb & Co. manufacturer of elastic india rubber fabrics, 6 Dyer's court, Aldermanbury
Bedford, Geddes & Co. cut-glass manufacturers (Edward Barton, agent), 27 Hatton garden
Bedford Joshua Thos. & Sons, undertakers, 35 Farringdon st
Bedford & Middleton, proctors, 2 Godliman st. Doctors' com
Bedford Office, Montague st. Russell sq. hours 10 to 3, monday, wednesday & friday
Bedford United Mines, G. W. Harrison, sec. 51 Old Broad st. Cty
Bedford Chas. St. Clare, solicitor, see Vincent & Bedford
Bedford Elizabeth (Miss), milliner, 5 Wells row, Islington
Bedford Francis, architect, 28 Granville square
Bedford Francis, bookbinder, see Clarke & Bedford
Bedford Frs. draughtsman & lithgphr. 17 Wells st. Gray's i. rd
Bedford Francis, grocer, 51 Coppice row, Clerkenwell
Bedford Francis, imitative enamlr. 7 Woodbridge st. Clrknwl
Bedford George, solicitor, 31 Norfolk st. Strand
Bedford Harriet (Miss), grocer, 19 Shoe lane, Fleet st
Bedford Henry, solicitor, 4 Gray's inn square
Bedford James, straw hat manufacturer, 52 Bunhill row
Bedford James, upholstr. & cabinet ma. 5 Notting hill, High st
Bedford John, wire weaver, 91 & 92 Long lane, Bermondsey
Bedford Robert, saddler, see Laurie, Bedford & Rand
Bedford Samuel, undertaker, 26 Villiers st. Strand
Bedford Thomas, cowkeeper, 3 Litt. Coram st. Brunswick sq
Bedford Thomas, statuary & mason, 256 Oxford st
Bedford Wm. ale & stout house, 3 Railway pl. Fenchurch st
Bedford William, grocer, 17 James st. Oxford st
Bedford William, poultry salesman, 61 Newgate market
Bedford Wm. hatters' trimg. ma. 20 Brunswick st. Hackney rd
Bedford William, insurance broker, Lloyd's
Bedgood Daniel, bootmaker, 1 Cross st. Hoxton new town
Bedggood Thos. coachmakr. & wheelwright, 3 Wharf rd. City rd
Bednall William, carpenter, 3 Blandford pl. Dorset square
Bedsor Thomas, butcher, 43 Fetter lane
Bedsor Wm. poulterer, High st. Kensington
Bedward & Matthews, woollendrapers, &c. 3 Vigo st
Bedwell, Yates & Co. wholesale grocers & teadealers, 103 St. John st. West Smithfield
Bedwell Henry Augustus, tobacconist, Camberwell green
Bidwell Lumley Benj. stockbroker, 5 Angel ct. & Stock exch
Bedwell Richard, butcher, 54 Gt. Guildford st. Borough
Bedwell Richard George, butcher, 31 Gt. Guildford st. Boro'
Bedwell Thos. hydrometer & saccharometer ma. 3 Lit. Alie st
Bee Benjamin, timber dealer, 114 Gt. Titchfield st. Oxford st
Bee Peter, meat salesman, 14 New Newgate market
Beebe James, silver spoon maker, 67 Red Lion st. Clerkenw
Beebe William, hide & skin salesman, Bermondsey skin mkt
Beeby Francis, gold cutter, 39 Sekforde st. Clerkenwell
Beeby Henry, *Princes st. ale house* P.H. 53 Princes st. Soho
Beech Lydia (Miss), dressmaker, 44 Gower pl. Euston sq
Beech Thomas, haberdasher, 188 Drury lane

Beech William, hatter, 7 Miles lane, Upper Thames st
Beech William, wood turner, 3 Portland st. Soho
Beech Wm. Philip, shipbreaker,Lavender whf. 140 Rotherh
Beecham Geo. Fredk. marine store dlr. 163 Brick la. Spitalfi
Beecham Wm. greengrocer, 10 Russell st.LowerRotherhithe
Beecher Henry, painter & glazier, 1 Wood st. Westminster
Beechey Mary & Son,silk & crape trim.ma.52 Aldermanbury
Beechey Wm. Nelson, solicitor, & clerk to the Haberdashers' Company, Haberdashers' hall, 8 Gresham st
Beeck Thomas, physician, Princes place, Kennington road
Beecroft John, ironmonger, 4 Leicester pl. Cambwl. new rd
Beedle Ann (Mrs.), chinadealer,202 Sloane st. Knightsbridge
Beedle Charles, painter, 27 Albion place, Walworth road
Beedle John, painter & plumber, 4 Charles st. Trevor square
BeedleRobert, linendraper, 4 Crown st. Finsbury
Beedle Thomas, baker, 70 Shoreditch
Beeker John, tailor, see Mette, Beeker & Mette
Beekes William, tobacconist, 107 Blackfriars road
Beels Geo. bird dealer, 45 Gt. Andrew st. Seven dials
Beeman Isaac, hop & seed factor, George inn yard, 70 Boro'
Beer Henry, tobacco manuf. 40 New road, St. George's east
Beer John, carpenter, 36 Union st. Middlesex hospital
Beer Robert, fruiterer, 64 Goswell road
Beer William, locksmith, 18 Warren st. Fitzroy square
Beer Wm. tobacconist, 15 Swan lane, Upper Thames st
Beerbohm Julius E.& Co. com. mers. & agents, 26 Austin frs
Beere John, kid leather dyer, 10 Turner square, Hoxton
Beese Henry, *King's Head* P.H. 51 Orchard st. Westminster
Beesley Sophia & Charlotte, milliners, 5 Charles st. Soho sq
Beesley Wm. painter & glazier, 10 Barclay st. Somers town
Beeson Jas. carthorse dlr.&contractor, 92 Long la.Smithfield
Beeson Thomas, tailor, 12 David st. York pl. Marylebone
Beeson William, hairdresser, 89 Berwick st. Soho
Beeson William, stationer, 3 Constable row, Mile end road
Beeston Alfred, sec. to Grand Union Railway, 78 Cornhill
BeestonFredk.Robt.architect,&c.15Northumberlandst.Strnd
Beeston Joseph, painter, &c. 1 Tyndale pl. Upper st. Islington
Beeston Sarah (Miss), dressmaker, see Patterson & Beeston
Beeswank John Wm. grocer, 8 Paradise st. Rotherhithe
Beetham & Foulger, solicitors, 2 Tanfield court, Temple
Beetham Albert Wm. barrister, 3 Serjeants' inn, Fleet st
Beetham Francis, solicitor, extraordinary commiss. for ex. of witnesses in the Court of Chancery & Exchequer, Ireland, & registry of deeds, &c. 2 Tanfield court, Temple
Beetholme George, solicitor, 52 Brompton row
Beetholme John Law, attorney, 1 New Inn, Wych st. Strand
Beetlestone George, printer, 1 Paul's head ct. Fenchurch st.; & 68 Freeschool st. Horselydown
Beeton Henry, baker, 1 Essex place, Mile end road
Beeton Robt. Fras. *King's Head* P.H. Broadway, Stratford
Beeton Samuel Powell, *Dolphin* P.H. 39 Milk st. Cheapside
Beetson Wm. brass & cock founder, 17 Brick la. St. Luke's
Beetson Jane (Mrs.), lodging ho. 13 Fludyer st.Westminster
Beevers Wm. stonemason, 63 Borough road
Beevor Charles, surgeon, 49 Berners st. Oxford st
Beevor & Buckley, solicitors, 2 Gray's inn square
Begbie & Young, cornfactors, 27 Mark lane
Begbie Charles, solicitor, 27 East st. Red Lion square, & 2 Love lane, Eastcheap
Begbie George Coryndon, accountant, 10 Coleman st
Begbie John, *Grosvenor hotel*, 19 Park st. Grosvenor sq
Begbie Matthew Baillie, barrister, 77 Chancery lane
Begbie Wm. beer retailer, 24 St. Chad's row,Gray's inn road
Begg Thomas & Co. west india mercs. 8 St. Michael's alley
BeggThomas,fancyboxma.5Queen'sHead passage,Newgatest
Beggi Fran. Oratio, physician, 2 Marylebone st. Golden sq
BeharrellAbrahamWm.who.tea&coffee agt.13Fenchrch.bdgs
Behenna Richd. hand screw mkr. 75Westmoreland pl. City rd
Behnes William, sculptor, 13 Osnaburgh st. Regent's park
Behrends John George, consul for the free city of Frankfort, 12 Broad st. buildings
Behrends John George, merchant, 12 Broad st. buildings
Behrens Joseph, jeweller & picture dlr. 236 High Holborn
Beichteller Robert, net maker, 104 Bermondsey st
Beighton Francis Glossop,wax chandler, 8 Gt. Marylebone st
Beioley Rd. Wm. Fletcher, solicitor, see Vallance & Beioley
Beisley Sidney, solicitor, see Gem, Pooley, & Beisley
Beisiegel Jacob, baker, 98 York st. Westminster
Bekenn Wm. Fred. translator & accountant, 30 Lit. Bell alley
Beland Francis, jeweller, 5 Baron st. Pentonville
Belasco Abraham, *Gun & Star* P.H. 51 Middlesex st. Aldgate
Belchar Richard, baker, 3 & 4 Poplar High st
Belchar William, baker, 51 Brunswick st. Blackwall
Belchem Cornelius, grocer, 4 Lit. Russell st. Covent garden
Belcher & Gould, milliners, 28 Henrietta st. Covent garden
Belcher & Swift, shoe agts. 127 St. John st. West Smithfield
Belcher Alex. B. offi. assignee, 9 King's arms yd. Moorgate st
Belcher George, tailor & trimming seller, 29 Bow lane
Belcher Hannah (Mrs.), hatter, 1 Stangate st. Lambeth
Belcher James, baker, 8 Gray's place, Fulham road
Belcher Jane (Mrs.), leather dresr. 67 Snow's fields, Bermond
Belcher John, architect, 3 Montague terr. Trinity sq. Boro'
Belcher John, architect & surv. 5 Adelaide pl. London bridge
Belcher Jsph. dining rooms, 15 Peel pl. Kensingtn.gravel pts
Belcher Joseph, linendraper, 55 Edgware road, Marylebone
Belcher Samuel, hatter, 4 London road, Southwark
Belcher Samuel, linendraper, 276 High Holborn
Belcher Thomas, butcher, 20 Newport ct. Newport market
Belcher William, grocer, 2 Holles st. Cavendish square
Belcher William, locksmith, 19 Duke st. Chelsea
Beldam Joseph, barrister, 3 Plowden buildings, Temple
Belford John, tailor, 5 Gt. Chapel st. Westminster
Belgic Embassy Office, 9A, Weymouth st
Belgrave Henry, teadealer, see Tipper & Belgrave
Belinaye Henry, physician, 41 King st. Golden square
Belk Edwin, *King's Arms* P.H. 18 Moor st. Soho
Bell, Broderick & Bell, solicitors, 9 Bow church yd. Cheapside
Bell Daniel, Son & Co. american stockbroks. 23Birchin la.City
Bell, Dodgson & Co. silk merchants, 50 Old Broad st. City
Bell E. M. & M. A. (Misses), corset makers, 63 Margaret st
Bell Geo. & Walter, engrav.& enamelers, 21 Portland st.Soho
Bell & Grant, merchants, 15 Angel court, Throgmorton st
Bell & Hughes, commn. wine merchants, 38 Fenchurch st
Bell, Hunter & Co. genl. com. & paper agts. 16St.Dunstan's hill
Bell John & Co. chemists & druggists, 338 Oxford st
Bell John Thos. & Co. who. quill & pen manf. 4 Dowgate hill
Bell John & Co. coal mer. Collier quay, Narrow st. Ratcliff
Bell Joseph & Son, warehousemen, 50 Bow lane, City
Bell (Mrs.&Miss), teachers of music, 3 Barnes pl. Mile end rd
Bell & Pyman, receivers of fee farm rents, 6Gough sq. Fleet st
Bell Robt. & Son, boot&shoe ma. 4Paddington st. Marylebone
Bell & Son, fish factors, 15 Lower Thames st
Bell & Son, newsvenders, 16 Finch lane, Cornhill
Bell, Rannie & Co. wine merchants, 49 Pall mall, & at Leith
Bell, Steward & Lloyd, solicitors, 59 Lincoln's inn fields
Bell's Life in London weekly newspaper office, 170 Strand
Bell's New Weekly Messenger newspaper office, 299 Strand
Bell's Weekly Messenger newspaper office, 2 New Bridge st
Bell Alex. corn & seed factor, Winchester wharf, Clink st. Bankside, & 3 New London st. Crutched friars
Bell Alex. engineer & machinist, 1 Chapel pl. Long la. Berm
Bell Alfred, printer, 17 Kirby st. Hatton garden
Bell Alexander, merchant, 2 Brabant court, Philpot lane
Bell Alexander, professor of elocution & for the removal of stammering & other impediments of speech, 58 Upper Norton st. Portland place
Bell Alex. Carlisle, fruiterer, 7 Great. Russell st. Bloomsby
Bell Alfred Hen. *Old Crown* P.H. 110 Brick la. Bethnal green
Bell Allan, baker, 86 Hoxton Old town
Bell Amelia (Mrs.), coffee rooms, 48 Bridge house pl. Boro'
Bell Chas. engraver, &c. 4 Dufours pl. Broad st. Golden sq
Bell Chas. grocer, 17 Sidney place, Commercial road east
Bell Chas. saddler, &c. 34 Wigmore st. Cavendish square
Bell Chas. solicitor, 36 Bedford row, Bloomsbury
Bell Chas. wharfinger & carman, 11 South st. Paddington basin
Bell Chas. Lambert, accountant, 12 Copthall court, City
Bell David, stove grate maker, 3 Eldon st. Finsbury
Bell Edward, fancy repository, 9 Burlington pl. Old Kent rd
Bell Edward, fishmonger, 4 New st. Covent garden
Bell Edward, grocer & tea dealer, 28 Lambeth walk
Bell Edward, grocer, 7 North st. Lisson grove
Bell Elizh. (Mrs.), pianoforte ma. 4 Lit. Russell st. Drury la
Bell Elizh. M. (Mrs.), gold burnisher, 26 Lr. Smith st. Nthptn.sq
Bell Elizh. Sarah (Miss), ladies' schl. 32 George st. Euston sq
Bell Fras. (Mrs.), milliner & straw warehouse, 34 Wigmore st
Bell Fras. rag & bottle dealer, 24 Lit. Welbeck st. Cavendish sq
Bell Frederick, carver & gilder, 25 Sekforde st. Clerkenwell
Bell George, butcher, 6 Old North st. Red Lion square
Bell George, picture frame maker, 6 Middle row, Old st.
Bell George, salmon salesman, &c. 125 Lower Thames st. & Salutation court, 100 Lower Thames st
Bell George, tobacconist, 2 Ward's pl. Hoxton Old town
Bell George, university bookseller & publisher, 186 Fleet st
Bell Henry, auctioneer & estate agent, 10 Oxford st
Bell Henry, currier, 15 Peter st. Saffron hill
Bell Henry, grocer, Knotts ter. Tanners hill, New tn. Deptford
Bell James Christian Clement, consul general for Tuscany, 15 Angel court, Throgmorton st
Bell James, baker, Church st. Deptford
Bell James, *Bell* P.H. 21 Pall mall
Bell James, fish factor, 120 Lower Thames st
Bell James, fishmonger, 34 Fish st. hill

Bell James, special pleader, 1 Churchyard court, Temple
Bell James Thos. watchmaker, see Dwerrihouse & Bell
Bell John, bricklayer, 12 Foley st. Portland place
Bell John, carpet manufacturer, see Watson, Wood & Bell
Bell John, corn & coal merchant, 160 Upper Whitecross street
Bell John, currier & leather cutter, 54 Union st. Borough
Bell John, fish factor, 116 Lower Thames street
Bell John, musical clockmaker, 8 Elm st. Gray's inn lane
Bell John, potato salesman, 26 James st. Covent garden
Bell John, potato salesman, South row, Covent garden market
Bell John, sculptor, 1 Madeley villas, Kensington New tn
Bell John, sculptor, 1 Marlbro' ter. Kensington New town
Bell John, solicitor, 28 Craven street, Strand
Bell John, solicitor, 24 Austin friars
Bell John, statuary, 25 Buckingham place, Fitzroy square
Bell John, tailor, 31 Deptford High street
Bell John, tailor & draper, 37 Ludgate street
Bell John Lewis, grocer, 20 Bedford pl. Commercial rd. east
Bell John P. quill & pen maker, 4 Dowgate hill
Bell John P. ship & insurance broker, 4 Dowgate hill
Bell John Thos. pianoforte maker, 17 Old st. St. Luke's
Bell John Thos. picture frame ma. 5 Hatfield st. Goswell st
Bell John Thos. wareho. keep. & agt. Fresh wf. Lo. Thames st
Bell John William, insurance broker, Lloyd's
Bell Jonathan, bootmaker, 3 Great James st. Lisson grove
Bell Joseph, confectioner, 11 High Holborn
Bell Lewis, *Ben Jonson* P.H. Stepney Old road
Bell Louise (Mrs.), bookbinder, see Egleton & Bell
Bell Luke, *Cow & Calf* P.H. 36 Eastcheap
Bell Margaret (Mrs.), milliner, 73 Wimpole st. Cavendish sq
Bell Maria (Miss), ladies' school, 27 Hornton st. Kensington
Bell Peter, east india agent & merchant, see Scott, Bell & Co
Bell Richard, embosser & lucifer match manufacturer, 16 Basing lane, Bread street, & Wandsworth, Surrey
Bell Richard, grocer, 32 Cumberland market, Regent's park
Bell Richard, manufactur. see M'Dougal, Sambourne & Bell
Bell Richard, oil & colorman, 133 Great Suffolk st. Borough
Bell Richard, undertaker & sexton, 12 White st. Borough
Bell Robert, lead, color & glass merchant, & manufacturer of lead pipe, 162 Sloane street
Bell Robert, porkman, 80 Charlotte st. Fitzroy sq
Bell Robert, surveyor, 41 Howland st. Fitzroy sq
Bell Robert, warehouseman, see Harrison & Bell
Bell Robert Chas. *Opera coffeehouse*, 8 Exeter st. Strand
Bell Samuel, tailor, 1 Francis place, Holloway
Bell Sydney Smith, barrister, 21 Old square, Lincoln's inn
Bell Thomas, baker, 42 Nelson st. Long lane, Borough
Bell Thomas, *Blue Anchor* P.H. 3 Coleman st. City
Bell Thomas, bookbinder, 21 Laurence Pountney lane, City
Bell Thomas, butcher, 17 Upper Dorset st. Bryanstone sq
Bell Thomas, *King's Head* P.H. 47 Gravel lane, Southwark
Bell Thomas, surgeon, 47 King William st. City
Bell Thomas, surgeon dentist, 17 New Broad st. City
Bell Thomas William, stockbroker, see Ewart & Bell
Bell Walter, hairdresser, 170 Aldersgate st
Bell Wm. baker, 69 Great Tower st
Bell Wm. confectioner, High st. Deptford
Bell Wm. engraver & enameller, 44 Dean st. Soho
Bell Wm. hosier & haberdasher, 25 King st. Portman sq
Bell Wm. looking glass & cabinet maker, upholder, undertaker & appraiser, 26 Great Winchester st
Bell Wm. official assignee, 3 Coleman st. buildings
Bell Wm. painter & glazier, 22 Francis st. Tottenham ct. rd
Bell Wm. physician, 37 Albemarle st
Bell Wm. physician, 13 Holles st. Cavendish square
Bell Wm. piece broker & woollen draper, 14 Duke st. Aldgate, & 1 Aldgate High st
Bell Wm. pork butcher, 263 Oxford st
Bell Wm. *Red Lion* P.H. 2 Hanway st. Oxford st
Bell Wm. solicitor, 30 Cloudesley st. Islington
Bell Wm. surgeon & chemist, 13 Crosby row, Walworth rd
Bell Wm. surveyor & land agent, see Dickson & Bell
Bell Wm. tailor & clothier, 7 Church st. Borough
Bell Wm. woollen draper, 1 Aldgate High st
Bell Wm. Joseph, carver & gilder, 25 King st. Clerkenwell
Bell Wm. Errington, coal factor, 16 St. Dunstan's hill
Bellamy & Smith, wine merchts. 42 Parliament st. Westmnr
Bellamy Alexander, wine merchant, see Legh & Bellamy
Bellamy Charles, barrister, 6 New square, Lincoln's inn, & 4 Lamb building, Temple
Bellamy Esther (Mrs.), furniture broker, 12 Old st. St. Luke's
Bellamy George, bootmaker, 5 Lit. Carter la. Doctors' com
Bellamy Henry, grocer, 90 Green st. Bethnal green
Bellamy John, bootmaker, 25 Arlington st. Sadlers' wells
Bellamy John, butcher, 7 Lumber court, Seven dials
Bellamy Lewis Robert, solicitor, 4 South square, Gray's inn
Bellamy Richard, plumber, 25 Adam st. East, Portman sq
Bellamy Samuel, bricklayer, 24 Clarence pl. Camberwell rd
Bellamy Samuel L. druggist, 5 Bridgehouse pl. Newingtn. cau
Bellamy Thomas, architect, 8 Charlotte st. Bedford sq
Bellamy William, dining rooms, 1 Essex st. Strand
Bellamy Wm. H. sec. to pat. concentrated tea Co. 2 Moorgate st
Bellars John, lodging house, 19 Manchester buildings
Bellars William, manchester agent, 22½ Milk st
Bellasis Edward, serjeant-at-law, 9 New square, Lincoln's inn, & 17 Bedford square
Bellatti Louis, plumber & painter, 3 Carter st. Walworth rd
Bellchamber Stephen, undertaker, 8 Union st. Lambeth wk
Bellchambers & Wilders, importers & dealers in foreign wines & spirits & hop merchts. 101 St. John st. Smithfield
Bellchambers Jonathan, bookseller, 10 King Wm. st. Strand
Bellefontaine Augustus, watchmaker, 59 Brewer st. Somerstn
Bellenie William, stonemason, 7 Fisher st. Red Lion sq
Bellenger Thomas, poulterer, 47 Lisle st. Leicester sq
Belles George, cutler, 4 Queen st. Chelsea
Bellett John, poulterer, 6 Church st. Camberwell
Belletti Augustine, mahogany mer. 6 Railway pl. Fenchch. st
Belletti Joseph, mahogany mer. 6 Railway pl. Fenchurch st
Bellew James, tombstone engr. 24 Mansion ho. st. Kennington
Bellew John, artifl. flower ma. 44 Gibson st. Waterloo rd
Bellgrove George, grocer, 7 Portsdown ter. Kilburn gate
Bellingham Brothers, chemists, 390 Strand
Bellingham G. & Co. coal mrs. Gt. Cambridge st. Hackny. flds
Bellingham Jane A. (Miss) ladies' schl. 32 King sq. Goswell rd
Bellingham John, spirit mer. 76 Gt. Cambdge. st. Hackney rd
Bellingham Thomas, tailor, 25 Southampton row, Russell sq
Bellingham William, carpenter, see Airy & Bellingham
Bellingham Wm. *Flying Horse* P.H. 22 Blackman st. Boro'
Bellis James, butcher, 4 Limehouse old road
Bellis John, proctor, 20 Gt. Carter lane, Doctors' commons
Bellman Vincent, plasterer & scagliola manufacturer, 14 Buckingham street, Fitzroy sq
Bellot Lewis Fredk. merchnt. 10 Barge yd. chambs. Bucklsby
Bellringer Henry, butcher, 317 Strand
Bellringer Sarah (Mrs.), shoe ma. 1 Surrey pl. Cambl. newrd
Bellringer William, beer retailer, 6 Heartley pl. Old Kent rd
Bellville John B. teadealer, see Robinson & Bellville
Belmer Emanuel, engineer, 5 King st. Golden square
Belsey John, watch & clock maker, 126 Gt. Suffolk st. Boro'
Belsham James, bootmaker, 22 Gt. Windmill st. Haymarket
Belsham John Andrew, boot & shoema. 20 Little Pulteney st
Belshaw George, *Britannia* P.H. 33 James st. Covent garden
Belshaw George, *Gordon hotel*, 3 Piazzas, Covent garden
Belshaw Thomas, plumber, &c. 2 London st. Fenchurch st
Belt William Charles, barrister, 7 Chancery lane
Belton Edward, linendrap. & haberdash. 57 Lisson grove North
Belton Elizabeth (Mrs), fruiterer, 19 Bryanstone st
Belton John, *Coopers' Arms* P.H. Poplar High st
Belton John Charles, chemist & druggist, 27 Gt. Tower st
Belton Peter, auctioneer & appraiser, 15 Leather la. Holborn
Belton Samuel Thomas, fruiterer, 9 King st. Portman sq
Belton Samuel Wm. stationer, 23 King st. Portman sq
Belton Wm. *White Swan* P.H. 19 Road side, Mile end road
Belward Richard, plumber & glazier, 70 Provost st. City rd
Beman Lucy & Son, tallow chandlers, 13 Down st. Piccadilly
Bemand Richd. linendraper, &c. 19 Albion terr. Wandsworth
Bemand Wm. linendraper, &c. see Kidd, Gemmill & Bemand
Bembridge John Wm. carpenter & joiner, 9 Barclay st
Beminster Samuel, *Lion & Lamb* P.H. 35 Aske st. Hoxton
Bemman Wm. Robert, goldbeater, 3 Gravel lane, Borough
Benassit Emile, merchant, 66 Mark lane
Benazus Mahomed, merchnt. 28 Camomile st. Bishopsgate
Benbow Jas. eagle iron foundry, Bear garden, 27 Bankside
Benbow John, attorney, 26 Mecklenburgh square
Benbow John Henry, solicitor, 1 Stone bldgs. Lincoln's inn
Benbow Richard, printer, 93 Cornwall road, Stamford st
Benbrook Ann (Miss), toy dealer, 5 York bldgs. Millpond st
Bench John Holt, baker, 24 St. John st. rd. Clerkenwell
Benda Gabriel, fancy goods & toy imp. 11 Camomile st
Bendall Elizh. (Mrs.), umbrella wa. 18 St. Martin's ct. Lestr. sq
Bendall James Longman, tailor, 28 Edmund pl. Aldersgt. st
Bendall Robt. Smith, linendraper, 3 Watts terr. Old Kent rd
Bendel Nathaniel, coffee rooms, 114 London wall
Bendell Elizh. (Mrs.), fishmonger, 18 Gt. Coram st. Brnswk. sq
Bender Ann (Mrs.), milliner, 14 High st. Marylebone
Bender Ehrenreich, tailor, 13 Gt. Prescot st. Goodman's flds
Bending William, bootmaker, 2 King st. Holborn
Bendixen Sigfried, portrait painter, 5 Percy st. Bedford sq
Bendy Richard, oilman, 41 Chapel st. Somers town
Benecke Brothers, wool merchants, 17 Moorgate st
Benesh & Banbury, lace manufacturers, 15 Addle st. City
Benetfink & Jones, furnishing ironmongers, 81 Cheapside

Benett George, wine merchant, 93 Charlotte st. Fitzroy sq
Benett William Morgan, solicitor, see Cotton & Benett
Benevolent Society of Blues (Christ's hospital), Queen's Arms tavern, Newgate st. (T. R. Sidebotham, sec. 9 Manchester ter. Liverpool road)
Benevolent Society of St. Patrick (Edward Hastings, sec.), Upper Stamford st. Blackfriars
Benfield Enos, tailor, 35 George st. Hanover square
Benfield George, bootmaker, 143 Leadenhall st
Benfield William, *Torrington Arms* P.H. Mill wall, Poplar
Benford Joseph, jun. skein silk dyer, 34 Whiskin st. Clerkenw
Bengal Indigo Co. Black swan yd. 72 Bermondsey st
Bengal Military Orphan Society (Major William Turner agent), 69 Cornhill
Bengough Geo. Robt. trunk, &c. maker, 4 Tichborne st. Haymkt
Benham Dan. sec. to City of London Gas Co. Dorset st. Salisby. sq
Benham Ebenezer, wholesale furrier, see Lütge & Benham
Benham Ebenezer, jun. solicitor, 12 South sq. Gray's inn
Benham Frederick, baker, 88 Bridge road, Lambeth
Benham James, carpenter, 6 Warwick st. Charing cross
Benham George, bookseller, 10 Water st. Blackfriars
Benham John Lee, ironmonger, bath maker, stove grate & kitchen range manufacturer, & hot water engineer, 19 Wigmore st. Cavendish sq
Benham John Thos. baker, 46 New Church st. Lisson grove
Benham Thomas, greengrocer, 23 Raven st. Whitechapel rd
Benham Wm. furn. ironmonger & bath manufr. 56 Blackfriars rd
Benham Wm. Ash, grocer, 52 Lamb's Conduit st. Foundling
Beningfield Jas. Hen. conveyancer, see Hockley & Beningfield
Beniacour Gaicoma, turkish bazaar, 13 Piccadilly
Beniowski Major, the discoverer of phrenotypics & publisher, 8 Bow st. Covent garden
Benjamin Abrm. & Jph. cigar imp. 14 Lit. Charlotte st. Blkfrs. rd
Benjamin Wm. jun. & Co. amer. merchts. 28 Noble st
Benjamin Angel, general salesman, 87 Long alley, Finsbury
Benjamin Benjamin, genl. factor & job wa. 126 Minories, & 8 New square, Minories
Benjamin David, pen & pencil ma. who. stationer, 25 Lit. Alie st
Benjamin Dinah (Mrs.), merchant, 1 Lime st. square
Benjamin Emanuel, clothes salesman, 103 Up. Whitecross st
Benjamin Ephraim, clothes salesman, 66 High st. St. Giles's
Benjamin Henry, tailor, 102 Fleet st
Benjamin Jacob, child bed linen wareh. 73 Leadenhall st
Benjamin Joseph, cigar manfr. 98 Middlesex st. Whitechapel
Benjamin Joseph, fishmonger, 12 Duke st. Aldgate
Benjamin Lewis, *Howard's* coffeeho. 3 St. James' pl. Aldgate
Benjamin Louis, jeweller, 37 Princes st. Leicester square
Benjamin Mark, fruiterer, 43 Marylebone lane
Benjamin Michael, merchant, 102 Fleet st
Benjamin Michael, watch manfr. 19 Bevis marks, St. Mary axe
Benjamin Moses, fishmonger, 17 Duke st. Aldgate
Benjamin Nathan, tailor, 78 Bridge road, Lambeth
Benjamin Philip, glass lustre maker, 105 Hatton garden
Benjamin Simon, *Black Lion* P.H. 8 Vinegar yard, Drury la
Benjamin Solomon, clothes salesman, 163 Up. Whitecross st
Benkert Andrew, gasfitter, &c. 29 Eldon st. Finsbury
Benn Joseph, iron & brass foundry, see Brook & Benn
Bennell Joseph, carrier, *White Horse* inn, Cripplegate bldgs
Bennet Edward, architect & surveyor, 19 Henrietta st. Cov. gar
Bennet Henry, physician, 9 Cambridge square, Hyde park
Bennet Henry, potato salesman, 68 Leather lane, Holborn
Bennet James, livery stables, see Spice & Bennet
Bennet John F. wax & tallow chandl. 21 Princes st. Cavdh. sq
Bennet Mary (Mrs.), general smith, 11 Seward st. Goswell st
Bennet Thomas, city carman, Blue Anchor rd. Rotherhithe
Bennet Wm. Heath, barrister, 36 Chancery lane
Bennett, Bolding & Pope, solicitors, 9 Scot's yd. Bush la. City
Bennett Dan. & Son, south sea ship owners, 294 Rotherhithe
Bennett Fras. & Co. furn. ironmongers, 14 & 15 Lr. st. Islngtn
Bennett & Field, hat & cap manufacturers, 11½ Gt. Dover st
Bennett John & Co. tailors, &c. 5 Charles st. St. James's
Bennett John & Co. tailors, 32 Maddox st. Regent st
Bennett John & Henry, working jewellers, &c. 175½ Oxford st
Bennett Joseph & Wm. builders, Rochester rw. Westminster
Bennett & Lloyd, bricklayers, 47 & 48 Weymouth ter. Hckn. rd
Bennett & Paul, solicitors, 1 Sise lane, Bucklersbury
Bennett & Sadler, chemists, 85 Goswell road
Bennett Solomon & Son, pickled tripe warehouse, 130 Bishopsgate without; boiling house, 16 Acorn st. Bishopsgate
Bennett Thos. & Son, wine & brandy mers. 81 Low. Thames st
Bennett Wm. & Co. wholesale teadealers, 47 Cannon st
Bennett William & Son, carvers & gilders, 1 Milton place, Islington green, & 8 Princes st. Bedford row
Bennett Wm. & Son, woollendrapers, 170 & 171 Boro' High st
Bennett Abraham, fruiterer, 17 Princes st. Fitzroy square
Bennett Ann (Mrs.), baker, 5 Kennington cross
Bennett Ann (Mrs.), lodging house, 9 Surrey st. Strand
Bennett Arthur, carpenter, Well st. Hackney
Bennett Barnard D. cheesemonger, 20 James st. Covent grdn
Bennett Benjamin, tailor, 28 Hertford st. Fitzroy square
Bennett Benjamin, whitesmith, 49 High st. Kensington
Bennett Caroline (Mrs.), brassfounder, 22 Pennyfields, Poplar
Bennett Charles, boot & shoe mkr. 3 Tavistock row, Cov. grd
Bennett Charles, coal merchant, Broken wharf, Wapping, & 2 Copthall chambers, Throgmorton st
Bennett Charles, corn merchant, College whf. Belvedere rd
Bennett Charles, earthenware dealer, 7 Port pl. Walworth com
Bennett Charles, grocer & teadealer, 124 Lower Thames st
Bennett Charles, hairdresser, 59 Gt. James st. Lisson grove
Bennett Charles, stock & share bkr. 1 Copthall chmbrs. City
Bennett Charles, jun. stockbrkr. 12 Copthall ct. Throgmo. st
Bennett Clara (Miss), hosier, glover, &c. 16 Piccadilly
Bennett Cordelia (Miss), hosier & glover, 40 Fenchurch st
Bennett Daniel, chemist, 355 Rotherhithe st
Bennett Edmund, corn merchant, Church st. Hackney
Bennett Edward, master of the Exchequer, 7 Stone bldgs. Lincoln's inn
Bennett Edward, carpenter & case maker, 7 Bull & Mouth st
Bennett Edward, grocer, 96 York st. Westminster
Bennett Edward, plumber & gasfitter, 67 Friar st. Blackfrs. rd
Bennett Edwin, surgeon, King's pl. Commercial rd. Whitcha
Bennett Elizabeth (Mrs.), tripe dresser, 127 Bethnal grn. rd
Bennett Elisha, butcher, Bridge road, Battersea
Bennett Elizabeth (Mrs.), lodging house, 6 Craven st. Strand
Bennett Frederick Danl. surgeon, 3 Commercial pl. Old Kt. rd
Bennett Fredk. Wm. locksmith & bellhanger, 4 Fore st. Crippleg
Bennett Frederick Debell, surgeon, see Gowar & Bennett
Bennett George, baker, 149 Kingsland road
Bennett George, *Lillie Arms* P.H. New Richmond road, Flhm
Bennett George, pork butcher, 151 Hoxton Old town
Bennett George, solicitor, 19 Castle st. Falcon square
Bennett George, *Star & Garter* P.H. 44 Pall mall
Bennett George, *White Lion* P.H. 29 Leather lane, Holborn
Bennett George Frederick, seal engraver, 88 Regent st
Bennett George Thomas, timber merchant, 58 Tottenham court road, & 127 St. John street, Clerkenwell
Bennett Henrietta (Mrs.), 3 *Compasses* P.H. 23A, Orchard st
Bennett Henry, baker, 2 Somerset terrace, Kensington
Bennett Henry, boot & shoe maker, 10 Harrow rd. Paddingtn
Bennett Henry, glass cutter, 5 Drury court, Drury lane
Bennett Henry, linendraper, 59 Upper North pl. Gray's inn rd
Bennett Henry, *Sovereign* P.H. 1 Taunton pl. Regent's park
Bennett Henry John, pilot, 310 Wapping High st
Bennett Henry Lee, merchant, 28 Botolph lane
Bennett James, builder, see Willcock & Bennett
Bennett James, carver & gilder, 28 Billiter st
Bennett James coachmaker, Wandsworth road
Bennett James, dentist & cupper, 40 Fenchurch st
Bennett James, dining rooms, 120 Whitechapel road
Bennett James, enginr. coppersmth. & foundr. 107 Kingsland rd
Bennett James, gas fitter, 255 Tottenham court road
Bennett James, herbalist, Centre row, Covent garden
Bennett James, linendraper, Battersea square
Bennett James, *Lord Keith* P.H. 21 York st. Portman sq
Bennett James, naturalist, 40 Fenchurch st
Bennett James, plumber, &c. 42 Up. Berkeley st. Portman sq
Bennett James, sen. plumber, 45 Seymour pl. Bryanstone sq
Bennett James, surgeon & dentist, Deptford bridge
Bennett James, tobacconist, 83 Edgware road
Bennett James Danl. ropemaker, 293 Rotherhithe st
Bennett James Douglas, ropemaker, Silver st. Rotherhithe
Bennett James Risdon, physician, 24 Finsbury place north
Bennett Jane (Mrs.), china wareho. 37 Queen st. Bryanstone sq
Bennett John, builder, 12 Belgrave st. south, Pimlico
Bennett John, bricklayer, 41 Marshall st. Golden square
Bennett John, cabinet ma. & undertaker, 174 St. John st. rd
Bennett John, camel hair pencil ma. 28 Hart st. Bloomsbury
Bennett John, corn dealer, 26 Long lane, Smithfield
Bennett John, druggist, 85 Broad st. Ratcliff
Bennett John, shipping & general agent, 28 Botolph lane
Bennett John, solicitor, 44 Bloomsbury square
Bennett John, tailor, 2 Trinity st. Borough
Bennett John, tinplate worker, 56 High st. Lambeth
Bennett John Edmd. watch & clockma. 45 Seymour pl. Brynstn. sq
Bennett John Edward, accountant, 36 Throgmorton st
Bennett John Edwards, hay salesmn. see Edwards & Bennett
Bennett John Fletcher, hat manufr. 135 Union st. Borough
Bennett John Heffert, fruiterer, 18 Warner st. New Kent rd
Bennett John Morris, surgeon, 46 Up. Baker st. Regent's pk
Bennett John Thomas, goldsmith & jeweller, 3 Cross st. Finsby
Bennett John Thos. solicitor, 12 Queen square, Bloomsbury
Bennett John Wm. solicitor, 12 Warwick court, Gray's inn

Bennett Joice(Mrs.),hat lining cut. 3 Lit. Charlotte st. Blkfrs
Bennett Joseph, confectioner, 14 Norton folgate
Bennett Joseph, dining rooms, 85 Bunhill row
Bennett Joseph, hatter, see Lincoln, Bennett & Son
Bennett Joseph, hairdresser, 6 Marylebone lane, Oxford st
Bennett Joseph, mathl. cabinet ma.2 Bartlett's pas.Fetter la
Bennett Joseph, wholesale milliner, 45 Wood st
Bennett MaryAnn(Mrs.),chinashop,13Charles st.Portmansq
Bennett Matilda(Miss),grocer, 23 Duke st. Lincln.'s inn flds
Bennett Nehemiah, wheelwright, Church st. Waterloo road
Bennett Nicholas, solicitor, 2 Bartlett's buildings, Holborn
Bennett Obadiah, tailor & breeches maker, 16 Gresham st
Bennett Rebecca(Mrs.),carver & gilder, 6 St. John st. Clknwl
Bennett Reb.(Mrs.),pastrycook & corn dlr.60&61Hackney rd
Bennett Richd. brushmak.9 Chancery pl.CamberwellNew rd
Bennett Robert, coal dealer, 20 Fleet lane, Farringdon st
Bennett Robt. tinman, &c. 22 Shoemaker row, Ludgate hill
Bennett Rowland Nevitt, solicitor, see Bateman & Bennett
Bennett St. John, barrister, 2 Cloisters, Temple
Bennett Samuel, lace manfr.36 Hedge row, High st.Islington
Bennett Samuel, farmer, Stoke Newington green
Bennett Samuel, furniture bro. 6 Brown st. Bryanstone sq
Bennett Saml. Chas. tailor, 10 Richmond st. Leicester sq
Bennett Saml. Geo. sackcloth & tarpaulin ma. 250 Tooley st
Bennett Sarah (Mrs.), bootmaker, 28 Grafton st. Soho
Bennett Sarah(Mrs.), *WellesleyArms* P.H. 27 Robertst.Chels
Bennett Sarah Ann, grocer, 1 Augustus row, Spa road
Bennett Solomon, butcher, 3 St. George's market, Borough
Bennett Stephen, tailor, 8 Charles st. Manchester sq
Bennett Susannah(Mrs.), furn. ironmonger, 171 Aldersgate st
Bennett Thomas, beer retailer, 53 Vauxhall walk
Bennett Thos. butcher, 103 Mary st. New rd. Regent's park
Bennett Thos. gold & silver beatr. 11 Woodbridge st.Clerknwl
Bennett Thos. hairdresser, Southampton st. Camberwell
Bennett Thos. oilman, &c. 20 King's road East, Chelsea
Bennett Thos. *Plough* P.H. 26 Museum st. Bloomsbury
Bennett Thos. porkman, 10 Dorset crescent, New north road
Bennett Thos. solicitor, 12 Queen square, Bloomsbury
Bennett Thos. special pleader, Devereux chambers, Temple
Bennett Thos. tailor, 14 White horse yard, Drury lane
Bennett Thos. teadealer, 37 Little Pulteney st
Bennett Thos. timber merch. 12 King Edward st. Lambeth
Bennett Thos. tobacconist, 25½ Bollingbrook row, Wlwth. rd
Bennett Thos. umbrella manufactr. Church st. Hackney
Bennett Wm. beer retailer, 24 Gibson st. Waterloo road
Bennett Wm. bookseller & publisher, 53 Paternoster row
Bennett Wm. bricklayer, 17 Great Chapel st. Oxford st
Bennett Wm. coal merchant, Canal bridge, Old Kent road
Bennett Wm. confectioner, 115 Shoreditch
Bennett Wm. florist & seedsman, 139 High st. Camden town
Bennett Wm. fruiterer, 8 John st. Oxford st
Bennett Wm. furniture broker, 12 New King st. Deptford
Bennett William, grocer, 27 Frederick st. Hampstead rd
Bennett Wm. jeweller, 38 Castle st. Leicester square
Bennett Wm. livery stables, 7 Parham pl.King'srd.Chelsea
Bennett William, oil & colorman, 3 Churchway, Chalton st
Bennett Wm. shaving brush maker, 80 Britannia st. City rd
Bennett Wm. shoe thread manufr. 10 Worcester st. Boro'
Bennett Wm. teadealer, &c. 12 Jamaica st. Comml. rd. East
Bennett Wm. who. boot warehou. 6 Swan st.Trinity sq. Boro'
Bennett Wm. Gipps, *Triumph* P.H. 36 Skinner st.Somerstn
Bennett Wm. Peter, tailor, 4 Paul's chain, Doctors' commons
Bennett Wm. Waring, grocer, 6 Chapel place, Liverpool rd
Benning Wm. & Co. law booksellers, 43 Fleet st
Benning James, cheesemonger, 82 Gt. Portland st. Oxford st
Bennicke Jas. John, coach mast. see Bennicke & Jardine
Bennington John & Son, ironmongers, braziers & lamp ma. to her Majesty & the Royal Family, 97 Jermyn st. St. James's
Bennington Samuel, plumber, 7 Camberwell grove
Bennison & Lennard, discount & exchange brokers, 75 Old Broad st. City, & Baltic coffee house
Bennett Aaron, bootmaker, 2 New st. Covent garden
Bennoch & Twentyman, silk agents, 78 Wood st. Cheapside
Benns George, *Fox & Bull* P.H. Park side, Knightsbridge
Benoimont Henry Horatio, tobacconist, 34 Goodge st
Benoimont James, tobacconist, 15 Mount st. Lambeth
Bensen Gerd Jacob, *GoldenLion* P.H. 9 Leman st. Gms.flds
Benskin Joseph, *Rose* P.H. 59 Snows fields, Bermondsey
Bensley James, linendraper, 6 Three Colt st. Limehouse
Benson Harriott, Jane & Emma, la. schl. 12 Barnsbury villas
Benson, Logan & Co. merchants, & patent metallic cement manufacturers, 4 New Broad st. City, & Lime wharf; Bridge wharf, King's road, Camden New town
Benson Thomas & Son, ship owners & sailmaks. 60 Low. Shadwl
Benson William & Thomas, carvers, gilders & looking glass manufacturers, 2 Greenfield st. Commercial road
Benson Chas.(sec. to Clarence Railway), 80 Old Broad st.City
Benson Florance John, barrister, 2 Paper buildings, Temple
Benson Jabez, carver & gilder, 39 Warwick st. Golden sq
Benson John Levett, surgeon, 41 Upper Seymour st. Euston sq
Benson Joseph, solicitor, 6 Gray's inn square
Benson Joseph S.pl. glass grinder, 28 Chicksand st.Whitchpl
Benson Richard, fruit salesman, Borough market
Benson Robert, newsvender, 9 Parliament st
Benson Thomas, horse hair manufr. 93 Church st. Mile end
Benson Thomas, linendraper, 40 Upper st. Islington
Benson Thomas, merchant, Lloyd's
Benson Thomas, jun. shipwright, Ratcliffcross dock, Ratcliff
Benson Thomas, stationer, &c. 21 King's road, Bedford row, & 109 Gray's inn lane
Benson Thomas Starling, merchant, 26 Gainsford st
Benson William, coal dealer, 60 St. John st. Clerkenwell
Benson William, solicitor, 4 Carey st. Lincoln's inn
Benson Wm. tobacconist, 133 Oxford st
Benson Wm. watch spring ma. 16 Wilderness row, Clerknwl
Benson Wm. Henry, cigar manufr. 1 Castle st. Houndsditch
Benstead John & Co. plumbers, 2 New Church st. Lisson grove
Benstead Charles, blindmaker, Prospect row, 1 Neckinger rd
Benstead Chas. undertaker, 1 Prospect row, Bermondsey rd
Benstead John, plumber, &c. see Star & Benstead
Benstead Rosetta (Mrs.), grocer, 16 Tower st. Westmstr. rd
Bensted Danl. smith & farrier, 5 Eagle ct. Dean st. Holborn
Bensted George, grocer, 1 Westmoreland pl. Walworth cmn
Bensted John, day school, 36 Charles st. Horselydown
Bensted John, grocer, King st. New town, Deptford
Bensusan M.L.&Co. merchants, 6 Magdalen row, Gt.Prescotst
Bensusan Abraham Levi, merch. 1 ThreeKing ct. Lombard st
Bensusan Joshua, merchant, 60 Gt. Prescot st. Goodman's fi
Bensusan Thomas, merchant, 27 Austin friars
Bent's Literary Advertiser Newspaper, 13 Paternoster rw
Bent Edward Rowley, bookseller, 20 Cursitor st
Bent James, coal merchant, 1 Inwood pl. Kentish town
Bent Jas. who. & retail shoe warehouse, 3 Beech st. Barbican
Bent Joseph, genl. agent, 6 Somersetpl. New rd.Commerl.rd.ea
Bent Wm. coal mercht. Cannonwhf. Cannon row, Westminster
Bentall Henry, coal mer. Beaufort wf. Beaufort bldgs, Strand
Bentall John, *Britannia* P.H. Wandsworth road
Bentall William, cabinet ma. Southampton st. Camberwllrd
Benthall Francis, solicitor, see Freeman, Bothamley & Benthall
Bentham Alfred, fruiterer, 43 Great Marylebone st
Bentham Jabez, cheesemonger, 14 Theobalds road
Bentham Wm. emery & glasspaper ma. 48 Marsham st.Westmr
Bentley & Chant, opticians, 12 Nicholl square
Bentley Robert & Co. warehousemen, 136 Cheapside
Bentley (Saml.&John), Wilson & Fley, printers, 64&65 Shoe la
Bentley Arthur, printer, 19½ Pitfield st. Hoxton
Bentley Chas. linendraper, 7 Cumberland row, Islingtn. grn
Bentley Chas. pewterer, 12 Woodstock st. Oxford st
Bentley Edward, physician, 35 Trinity square, Southwark
Bentley Francis, corn & coal dealer, 170 Bethnal green road
Bentley George, stationer, 10 Collier st. Pentonville
Bentley Harriet (Mrs.), tobacconist, 11 Lit. Russellst. Druryla
Bentley James, *Ship* P.H. Horseferry road, Westminster
Bentley John, artist, 114 Sloane st. Knightsbridge
Bentley John, chimney sweeper, 24 Brick st. Park lane
Bentley John, linendraper, 80 St. John st. road, & 4 Union pl. Lisson Grove north
Bentley John, picture & curiositydeal. 16 Bedford st.Cov.gar
Bentley John, who. & retl. cheesemonger, 5 Smithfield bars
Bentley John William, *Falcon* P.H. 1 Bethnal green
Bentley Joseph, ivory carver & turner, 16 Princes st. Soho
Bentley Michael, attorney, 1 Brick court, Temple
Bentley Nathaniel, who. & export ironmonger, 4 Fen ct. City
Bentley Richard, bookseller & publisher, 8 New Burlington st
Bentley Richard, timber merchant, 51 Old st. St. Luke's
Bentley Thomas, smith, King st. Lower rd. Islington
Bentley Wm. furniture broker, 4 Chapel st. New road
Bentley Wm. pastrycook, 1 Athol place, New rd. Pentonville
Bentley William, trunk maker, 10 South st. Manchester sq
Bentley Wm. George, raised letter maker, 234 High Holborn
Bentley Wm. George, wholesale perfumer, 220 High Holborn
Benton Benjamin, silk manufacturer, 24 Addle st
Benton Cornelius, tailor, 13 Little Marylebone st
Benton Edward, pawnbroker, 23 Tottenham court road
Benton George, fruiterer, 6 Little St. Mary Axe
Benton Geo. pawnbroker & silversmith, 244 High Holborn
Benton John, lodging house keeper, 6 Arundel st. Haymkt
Benton Luke, fruiterer, Spitalfields market
Benton Wm. *John O'Groat* P.H. 24 Gray st. Blackfriars rd
Benwell Benjamin, baker, 14 Gower st. north, Euston square
Benwell James, *King's Head* P.H. 11 Baker's row, Whitech
Benwell Joshua Proctor, merchant, see Holland & Benwell

Benzoni Charles, dairyman, 17 Duke st. St. James's square
Beolchi Charles, LL.D. prof. of italian,&c. 48 Upper Albany st
Berdoe Joseph, tailor, 70 Goswell road
Berdoe Walter, tailor, 69 Cornhill
Berens, Blumberg & Co. importers of & dealers in french, german & british fancy goods, 33 St. Paul's churchyard, & 60 Rue de Bondy, Paris
Berens Richard Beauvoir, barrister, 2 New sq. Lincoln's inn
Beresford Fras. M. wharfinger, Pickleherring Upper wharf, Tooley st
Benwell William, coal & potato dealer, 31 Drury lane
Benzie William, baker, 10 Acton pl. Bagnigge wells road
Beresford George, writer on glass, 17 Vine st. Hatton wall
Beresford Henry, sup. of police, 12 Richmond bldgs. Soho
Beresford William, special pleader, 5 Essex court, Temple
Bergareche & Co. merchants, 33 Great Winchester st
Berger Francis & Co. colonial brokers, 23 Mincing lane
Berger John & Samuel, color manfrs. Water lane, Homerton
Berger Lewis & Sons,color maks.7Well ct.Queenst.Cheapside
Berger Samuel & Co. pat. rice starch man. Bromley, Middsx
Berger Elizb. (Mrs.), tallowchandler, 117High st.Marylebone
Berger Geo. bookseller & publisher, 19 Holywell st. Strand
Berger Lewis, oil & roman vitriol ma. 1Citywf.Up.Thames st
Berger Michael, clockmaker, 6 Leman st. Goodman's fields
Berginstein Shoreham, watchmaker, 113 Gt. Titchfield st
Berkeley Charles, solicitor, 52 Lincoln's inn fields
Berkeley Chas. Clement, barrister, 5 New sq. Lincoln's inn
Berkeley Comyns Rowland, solicitor, 35 Lincoln's inn fields
Berkeley Geo. Brackenbury, who. tea & coffee dlr. 1½ Sise la
Berkeley Maurice Henry, solicitor, 27 Lincoln's inn fields
Berkeley Thomas, solicitor, see Weall & Berkeley
Berkley & Dunnell, color ma. Star&Garter yd. Ratcliff hiway
Berkley Jas.Thos. stockbroker, 18 Threadneedle st.&Stock ex
Berks & Hants Railway, 449 West Strand
Berks Jonathan, greengrocer, 10 Camden st. Walworth road
Berkshire John, who. & retail coal dlr. 45 Geo. st. Blkfrs. rd
Berlandina David, merchant, 36 Duncan ter. City road
Berliner Benjamin, baker, 45 Duke st. Aldgate
Berles, Römcke & Co. merchants, 40 Commercial sale rooms
Bermes Adam, baker, 169 Drury lane
BerminghamGeo.surgeon &c.5Moretonvilla,Kentish town rd
Bermingham John, boot & shoe maker, 75 Long acre
Bermingham Walter, bootmaker, 33 Sun st. Bishopsgate, & 3 Star alley, Fenchurch st
Bernal Abraham, earthenware dealer, 12 Whitechapel road
Bernard Ann (Mrs.), milliner, 11 Lit. Russell st. Drury la
Bernard Harrt.(Miss), pro. of phalacromiasy,14John st.Adel
Bernard John, fishg.tack.ma. & turner,4Church pl.Piccadilly
Bernard John Fredk. solicitor, see Barnes, Winter & Bernard
Bernard Sophie Madame, stay & corset ma. 48 Frith st. Soho
Bernard Sigrist, tin pl. worker, 42 Monkwell st. Falcon sq
Bernard William, baker, 22 John's row, St. Luke's
Bernasconi & Riddell, architectural modellers, & plain & ornamental plasterers, 27A, Francis st. Tottenham court rd
Bernasconi Fredk. trunk mkr. 26 Gt. Quebec st. Montagu sq
BernaysAdolphus,professor of German,4Powis pl. Blmsby.sq
Berncastel Albert & Co. furriers, 7 Great Dover st. Borough
Berney Wm. timber dealer & sawyer, 9½ Totton st. Stepney
Bernhard Francis, baker, 30 Edward st. Stepney
Berni & Melliard, hat makers, 56 Gt. Guildford st. Borough
Bernie George, shipwright, 40 Wapping High st
Bernoulli E. merchant, 4 Austin friars
Bernstein Aaron, furrier & skin dlr. 4 & 5 Cutler st. Hndsdch
Berquez Francis, watch maker, 27 Henrietta st. Cavendish sq
BerrallWm.&Son,boot & shoemfs.60Marylebone la.Oxford st
Berrell Peter, surgeon, &c. 53 Mount st. Lambeth
Berrey George James, barrister, 61 Chancery lane
BerridgeJsph.(sec. of*Freemasons' Ass. Office*),11Waterloo pl
Berridge Joseph, translator, 22 St. Swithin's lane
Berridge Richard, bootmaker, 66 Chapel st. Pentonville
Berrier Fontaine Camille, physician, 3 Foley place
Berriman John, grocer, 23 King st. St. Luke's
Berriman Robert, hosier, 17 Church st. Camberwell
Berriman Thomas, carpenter, 10 Vine st. Waterloo road
Berriman Thomas, haberdasher, 226 Shadwell High st
Berringer John, turner, 29 Gun st. Bishopsgate
Berrollas Jsph. Anthony, watch ma. 15 Spencer st.Goswell rd
BerrowRd. french polisher, 7 James pl. Larkhall la. Clapham
Berry Henry & Co. sole inventors, patentees & manufacturers of the patent portable inkstands, & instantaneous lights, with indian rubber stoppers, importers of french wax taper matches, &c. 21 Long acre (late of 134 Drury lane, & 21 Bedford st. Covent garden), see Webster
Berry Henry&George,jun.agents for Bass&Co.india pale ale, & ale & stout merchants, 3 St. James's st
Berry John & Chas. cabinet makers, 40 East st. Red Lion sq
Berry Wm. & George, plate case makers, 48 Old Bailey
Berry Augustine, academy, 19 Gt. Smith st. Westminster
Berry Chas. flour factor, 14 Leman st. Goodman's fields
Berry Chas. plane & toolmaker, 6 Long la. West Smithfield
Berry Charles, *Stevens' hotel*, 18 New Bond street
Berry Christ. baker, 12 Camden st. East st. Walworth
Berry Cornelius, accountant, 132 Fenchurch st
Berry Edward Unwin, surgeon, 7 James st. Covent garden
Berry Frederick, watchmaker, 2 Arcade, Hungerford market
Berry George, baker, Bridge road, Battersea
Berry George, carver & gilder, Church st. Hackney
Berry George, grocer, 3 St. James's st. Pall mall
Berry George, plane & toolmaker, 5 George's pl. Old st. rd
Berry George Smith, engraver, 27 Church st. Soho
Berry Graham, linendraper, 56 Paradise row, Chelsea
Berry Henry, cheesemonger, 7 Bedford st. Mile end road
Berry Henry, solicitor, 12 Grove place, Lisson grove
Berry James, grocer, &c. 5 Shepperton pl. New North road
Berry James, solicitor, see Gray & Berry
Berry James Wm. M. barrister, 1 Paper buildings, Temple
Berry John, baker, 4½ Scott's place, Lower road, Islington
Berry John, butcher, 4 Broomfields, Deptford
Berry John, butcher, 9 Clift st. New North road
Berry John, butcher, 11 Shadwell High st
Berry John, cooper, 10 Goswell road, east side
Berry John, linendraper, 64 New Church st. Lisson grove
Berry John, plumber & glazier, 33 Anchor st. Spitalfields
Berry John, tailor, 42 Clarendon square, Somers town
Berry Joseph, potato dealer, 177 Lambeth walk
Berry Kemp, flour factor, 43 Commercial sale rooms, & at Jack's coffeehouse, Mark lane
Berry Richard, *European* coffeehouse, 2 Mansion house st
Berry Robt. glass & chinaman, 28 Featherstone st. City rd
Berry Samuel, cooper & stave mer.ThreeOakla.Horselydown
Berry Thomas, brushmaker, 1 London terrace, Hackney rd
Berry Thomas, engraver, see Draper, Berry & Hearse
Berry Thomas, toy wareho. 20 Royal Hospital row, Chelsea
Berry Wm. bootmaker, 233 Bermondsey st
Berry Wm. flour factor, 2 Clark st. Stepney
Berry Wm. meat salesman, Leadenhall market
Berry Wm. painter & glazier, 4 High st. Stepney
Berry Wm. poulterer, 32 King st. Portman square
Berry Wm. tailor, 19 William st. Regent's park
Berry Wm. *York& Albany tavern*, Glo'ster gate, Regent's pk
Berry Zephaniah Deacon, ironmonger, 3 King's rd. Pimlico
Berryman & Ditchner, brokers, 19 Henrietta st. Mnchstr.sq
Berthold G. F. A. tortoiseshell & horn comb maker, 35 Nottingham place, Whitechapel
Bertin James Chas. chairmaker, 39 Holywell la. Shoreditch
Bertin Samuel George, chairmaker, 42 Hoxton square
Bertini Auguste, prof. of the piano, 71 Gt. Portland st
Bertolini John Dominique, *Newton hotel & French restaurateur*, 34 St. Martin's street, Leicester square
Berton Numa, tailor, 18 Princes st. Hanover square
Bertram Elizh.(Mrs.), upholder, 8 Devonshire bds. Gt. Dover rd
Bertram Henry, wine mercht. 18 & 25 Elizabeth st. Eaton sq
Bertram Mons. prof. of dancing, 8 Gloucester rd. O. Brompton
Bertram MoritzB.soapma.&perfmr.1Crescent,Cambridgehth
Bertram William, upholsterer, 100 Dean st. Soho
Bertrand Louis, dancing mast. 3 Ebenezer ter. Kenngtn. com
Bertrand Marian (Mrs.), fancy repository, 34 Gt. Portland st
Bertrand Susanna (Mrs.), tobacnist. 23Arlington st.Sdlrs.wls
Berwick Alex.&Co.ale brewers, Old Swan whf.Up.Thames st
Berwick Steam Shipping Co. (Alexander Thomson, agent), Downe's wharf, Lower East Smithfield
Berwick Ann (Mrs.), embroiderer, 7 Union st. Berkeley sq
Besant Charles, bookbinder, 2 Marshall st. Golden square
Besant Geo. solicitor, 1 Bond ct. Walbrook
Besant Mary Ann(Mrs.), linendrpr.7 Oddy's row, Islington gn
Besant Thomas, *Boar & Castle hotel*, 6 Oxford st
Besch Frederick, tailor, 11 Hanover st. Hanover sq
Bescoby Francis, oilman, 15 & 16 Stanhope st. Clare market
Bescoby Henry, tallowchandler, 71 Milton st. Cripplegate
Besemeres John & Sons, clothiers, ready made linen warehousemen, outfitters, & contractors for complete equipments of every kind & value, 61, 62, 63, 64 Houndsditch
Besemeres John & Wm. wholesale shirt makers, 119½ Wood st
Besemeres Wm. surgeon, 13 Marlborough pl. Old Kent road
Besford Sarah (Miss), embroideress & artist in german needle work to the Queen by special appointment, 9&19 Hanway st
Besley Daniel, tailor, 19 Queen st. Soho
Besley Fredk. wharfinger, &c. see Nicholson, Besley & Co
Besley Mary (Mrs.), *Sir John Barleycorn* P.H. 15½ Drury la
Besley Robert, typefounder, see Thorowgood & Besley
Besley Thomas, grocer, 47 Weymouth st. New Kent rd
BesleyWm.grocer&cheesemonger,36New rd.St.George's east

Besly Saml. Peter L. surgeon,13Camden st.north,Camden tn
Bessan Auguste, for. flowers imp. & com. agt. 4 Wood st.City
Bessant Uriah, corndealer, 50 Mansfield st. Kingsland road
Bessell John, glaziers' patent diamonds & vice manufacturer, &c. 151 St. John st. road
Bessemer Hen. bronze & gold paint manufacturer, Baxter house, Old St. Pancras road
Besset Jacques, gen. merchant, 3 Sherborne lane
Best Benjamin, coal merchant, 7 St. John st. Clerkenwell,& 6 Warlters buildings, Holloway
Best Charles, printer, 5 St. James's walk, Clerkenwell
Best Chas. Fred. sen. upholder & ho. ag. 60Berners st.Oxfd.s
Best Charles F. jun. upholsterer, 54 Henry st. east,Avenue rdt
Best Charlotte (Miss), milliner, 39 Maiden la. Covent garden
Best Elizh. (Mrs.), lodging ho. 3 North crescent, Bedford sq
Best George, coffee rooms, 2 Belton st. Long acre
Best George, fruiterer, 7 Royal Hospital row, Chelsea
Best Hiram William, boot, &c. maker, 36 York st. City road
Best James, tailor, 42 Rosoman st. Clerkenwell
Best John, coffee rooms, 205 Shoreditch High st
Best Read, cigar case ma. 27 Bennett st. Blackfriars
Best Thos. stationer&acct.book ma.26Redcross st.Cripplegate
Best William, carpenter, 21 Whittlebury st. Euston sq
Best William, dairy, 22 Henrietta st. Cavendish square
Best William, *George* P.H. 19 Queen Anne st. Cavendish sq
Best Wm. imp.of minrl.waters,22B,Henrietta st.Cavendish sq
Best William, jeweller, 16B, Wimpole st. Cavendish square
Best William, paperhanger, 12 Adam st. Portman sq
Best William, solicitor, 35 Lincoln's inn fields
Best William, tailor, 54 Upper North place, Gray's inn road
Best Wm. Francis, furniture broker, 35 St. John st. road
Best William Richd. leather cutter, 93 Blackfriars road
Best William Mawdesley, barrister, 89 Chancery lane
Best Wm. Robert, straw hat ma.15&16 Newington causeway
Beste George, merchant, 14 Mark lane
Bestow Wm. haberdasher, 4 Vernon pl. Bagnigge wells rd
Beswick Charles, tailor, 6 Moorgate st. Bank
Beswick Jas. coach wheelwrt. 59 Gt. Titchfield st. Oxford st
Beswick James, plumber, 2 Wellington st. Blackfriars rd
Beswick John, *White Hart* P.H.Gt.Turner st.Commer. rd
Beswick John Jas. undertaker, 3 Gt. Wild st. Drury lane
Beswick P.(Mrs.),*Grn. Dragon*P.H.Spring garden pl.Stepny
Beswick Thos. leech imp. 6Whitfield st. Leonard st.Finsbury
Beswick William, *Prince Albert* P.H. Orchard pl. Blackwall
Betham John,custom house & com.ag.Cox quay,Lr.Thames st
Bethel Charles, morocco case ma. 26 Gt. Chart st. Hoxton
Bethel Richard, fruiterer, Centre row, Covent garden
Bethell John, pitch, turpentine & tar works, Bow common & Battersea fields
Bethell John, furnishing undertaker, 30 Farringdon st
Bethell John, solicitor, 78 King William st. City
Bethell Richd. queen's counsel, 3 Stone bldgs. Lincoln's inn
Bethlehem Lunatic Hospital (Nathaniel Nicholls, steward), corner of Lambeth &St.George's roads,Obelisk,Southwark
Bethnal House Lunatic Asylum(John Warburton,proprietor, James Phillips, surgeon), Cambridge road, Mile end
Betson George, surgeon, 111 Wapping High st
Betteley Jacob, glass&china dealer,90Tottenham court road, & 128 High st. Camden town
Bettell Joshua, carpenter, 18 Hastings st. Burton crescent
Betteridge Ezekiel, ivory & wood turner, 1 Craven st. City rd
Betteridge Wm. grocer, 32 Guildford place, Spafields
Bettles John & Co. anatomical bootma. 45 Greek st. Soho
Bettridge John, papier maché ma. see Jennens & Bettridge
Betts Henry & Son, cuppers, 70 Wimpole st
Betts John Thos.jun.&Co. french brandy disty.7 Smithfi. bars
Betts & Sons, sweepsmelters & refiners, 131 Long acre
Betts Ann M. (Mrs.),lighterman,4 Church row, Horselydown
Betts Arthur, musical instrument maker, 27 Royal Exchange
Betts Benjamin, chaser, 11 Wilderness row, Clerkenwell
Betts Hannah(Mrs.),dining rooms, 13 Norland rd. Nottg.hill
Betts James, *Prince Regent* P. H. High st. Deptford
Betts John, bookseller & publisher, 115 Strand
Betts John, butcher, 29 St. George's pl. Knightsbridge
Betts John, general agent, 5 Goldsmith st. Cheapside
Betts John, map publisher,bookseller & stationer, 115 Strand
Betts John, tailor, 38 Coleshill st. Eaton square
Betts John Fletcher, teadealer, 262 Oxford st
Betts Sally (Mrs.),*King's Arms* P.H. 51 Sloane sq. Chelsea
Betts Thomas, ivory turner, 18 Ironmonger st. St. Luke's
Betts Thos. *Marquis Lansdown* P.H.Thomas st.Hackney rd
Betts Thomas, tinplate worker, 82 Leather lane, Holborn
Betts Thomas John, patent capsule manufacturer& importer of Selters water, 1 Wharf road, City road
Betts William, fruiterer, 44½ St. George st
Bettsworth Thos.corn & coal mer.Kg's Arms wf. Davis pl.Chel
Bettyes John, coachmaker,28 Manchester st.& 53 & 54 Dorset st. Manchester square
Beuler Jacob, engraver, 4 Bury place, Bloomsbury
Beurle Mark Ludwig, *Royal Midshipman* P.H. 25 to 27 Skinner st. Clerkenwell
Bevan, Iron & Bevan, importers of farina,irish & foreign provisions, & preservers of patent fresh provisions, 2 Birchin lane, Cornhill, & Dublin
Bevan Charles Dacres, barrister, 3 Paper buildings, Temple
Bevan Chas. Stanley,book bind.5Chapel pl.south,S.Audley st
Bevan Clara(Miss),tchr. of music, 52 Devonshire st.Queen sq
Bevan Edward, wharfinger, &c. see Holl & Bevan
Bevan George, egg salesman, 224½ Hoxton Old town
Bevan Henry Augustus, merchant, see Alston, Bevan & Co
Bevan John, agt. for Watkins Dublin stout, 2 Birchin lane
Bevan John C. De la Rue,oil broker,see Aylwin,Bevan & Cole
Bevan Nathaniel, glass mounter & patent screw ink manufacturer, 3 Glo'ster st. Commercial road east
Bevan Thomas, beer retailer, 14 Burdett st. Walworth com
Bevan Thomas, physician, 20 Finsbury circus
Bevan Richard, currier, see Jones & Bevan
Bevan Wm. decorator, house painter & gilder, 1 Welbeck st
Bevan William, solicitor, 6 Old Jewry
Bevans Geo.&Hen.*D.of Albemarle* P.H.6 Stafford st.Bond st
Beven Thomas, jun. baker, 93 Bethnal green road
Beven William, egg merchant, 27 Bateman's row,Shoreditch
Beverton Benjamin, tinman, George st. Camberwell
Beverton Geo. Fredk. tin toyma. 1 St.George's st. O. Knt. rd
Beverton James,tinplate work. 36 Devonshire st. Kenningtn
Beverton Sam. gasfitter & locksmith, 23 Lambeth walk
Beverton Wm. tin plate worker, 3 Pleasant row, Old Kent rd
Beville Francis, upholsterer, 48 Wells st. Oxford st
Bevington Henry & Son, organ builders, 48 Greek st. Soho
Bevingtons' & Sons, manufrs. of morrocco, spanish, roan & skiver leather, dressers of kid & lambskins, cape, sheep, oil & gloving leather & wool staplers, Neckinger mills, Bermondsey, & Worcester
Bevington Alexander, insurance broker, 33 Clement's lane
Bevington Alfred, glue maker, Neckinger road, Bermondsey
Bevington (Miss), berlin warehouse, Stratford, Essex
Bevington Timothy, furrier, leather seller, & lapland wool rug manufacturer, 67 King William st. City
Bevington Timothy, seal, nutria & mock sable skin dresser & dyer, 1 Weavers la. Tooleyst.; wareho. 67King Wm.st.City
Bevington Timothy, lapland wool rug & cavalry skin manf. 106 Bermondsey st.; wareho. 67 King William st. City
Bevins Daniel Wm. brass & cockfndr. 37 Georgest. Blkfrs. rd
Bevir Edward James, barrister, 20 Old sq. Lincoln's inn
Bevis Alexander, tobacconist, 9 Church st. Chelsea
Bevis Catherine (Mrs.), coach ma. & smith, Tennis ct. King st. Borough
Bevis Daniel, silk broker, 69 Basinghall st
Bevis Harriet (Mrs.),strawhatmak. 22 Mount st. Berkeley sq
Bevis James, general salesman, 105½ High st. Camden town
Bevis James N. coach painter, 62 Seymour pl. Bryanstone sq
Bevis Thomas, coffee rooms, 4 Jamaica ter. Coml. rd. Limeho
Bew & Bishop,drapers &mercers,20 Frederick pl. Hampstd.rd
Bewick John, milliner, 7 Bermondsey New road
Bewlay Thomas, tobacconist & snuff manufacturer to the royal family, wholesale & retail, 49 Strand
Bewley & Evans, chemists & manufrs. of mineral waters, 55 Berners st. & Sackville st. Dublin
Bewsher Thomas, bootmaker, 11 Museum st. Bloomsbury
Beyer Martin, bootmaker, 65 Burlington arcade, Piccadilly
Beyer Wm. confectioner, 122 Chalton st. Somers town
Beyerman Andw.coffeerooms&transr.oflanguages,167 Wapg
Beynon, Jones & Beynon, herald chasers, 78 Margaret st
Beynon & Stocken, tobacco manufacturers, 10 Gracechurch st
Beynon James, *Crown* P.H. 23 Aberdeen pl. Maida hill
Beynon John, straw bonnet wareh. 15 Newington causeway
Beynon Lucy (Miss), straw hat mnftr.14 High st. Camberwll
Beynon William, manufacturer of hooks & eyes, needles, stay holes, thimbles, buttons, silk purses, buckles, clasps, snaps, &c. 7A, Falcon sq. & Newhall works, Birmingham
Bezant Wm.&Alfred, pawnbrokers,96Chalton st.Somers twn
BezzellHenryThomas & John, builders, 10 High st. Deptford
Bibb Reuben, spur maker, 6 Tower st. Seven dials
Bibbing John, bricklayer, 1 White st. Bethnal green road
Bibby Richard, bricklayer, 7 Priest alley, Great Tower st
Bibby Samuel, surgeon, 9 North Audley st
Bibby Thomas, *Rodney's Head* P.H. 296 Rotherhithe st
Bichner Otto Fred. barrister, 30 Southampton buildings
Bick George, locksmith, 28 Britannia st. City road
Bickell John, baker, 7 Northampton row, Holloway
Bicker John, cooper, 14 Hardington st. Portman market
Bickerdike Rev. John, academy, Green st. Kentish town

Bickers & Bush, booksellers, 1 Leicester sq. & 9 Leicester st
Bickers Wm.&Son, grocers&oilmen,4 Charles st.Berkeley sq
Bickers John, plumber, painter & glazier, 129 Long acre
Bickers Wm. coal merchant, 79 Sloane st. Knightsbridge
Bickerton Jas.&Son,hat mnfrs. 51 & 52 Castle st. Southwark
Bickerton James, jun. hat mnfr.36&37Stamford st.Blkfrs. rd
Bickerton John, parliamentary agent, 18 Gt. George st
Bickerton Richard Palin, surgeon, 92 St. John's wood ter
Bickerton William, grocer, 4 Mount place, Walworth road
Bickford Huldah & Lucina (Misses), lace dealers, 59 Lamb's Conduit st
Bickford John & E. fruiterers, 10 Goldsmith rw. Hackney rd
Bickford Fras. John, statnr. & library, 5 Queen's rd. Dalston
Bickford Jonathan, beer retailer, Bow lane, Bromley
Bickham Thomas, surgeon, Ferry road west, Poplar
Bickley George, solicitor, 5 Barge yard, Bucklersbury
Bickley James, chandler's shop, 15 Earl st. ea. Lisson grove
Bickley Samuel, insurance broker, Lloyd's
Bickmore Elizth.(Miss),livery stables,50½Blackman st.Boro'
Bicknell & Davidson, solicitors, 38 Bloomsbury square
Bicknell & Jennings, trimming sellers, 52 Wardour st. Soho
Bicknell Thomas & Co. grocers, 64 & 65 Conduit st. Regent st
Bicknell Christopher & Samuel, solicitors, 48 Manchester st
Bicknell Elhanan, sperm oil mercht. see Langton & Bicknell
Bicknell Henry, lodging house, 4 Green st. Grosvenor sq
Bicknell Hen.solicitor,& clerk to the co. Grocers'hall,Poultry
Bicknell James, perfumer, 8 Henry street ea. Avenue road
Bicknell Samuel, tailor, &c. 29 High st. Marylebone
Bicknell Wm. Valentine, hosier, &c. 3 Blackman st. Borough
Biddecome John, cheesemonger, 13 Princes st. Westminster
Biddell Wm. & Co. brass founders, &c. 4 West Smithfield
Biddell Alfred, coal mercht. Child's Belvedere whf. Lambeth
Biddell Frederic, hatter, 7 Brook hill, Clerkenwell
Biddell Thos. Wm. button & milty. ornamt. mak. 55 Drury la
Biddell William, butchers' clothier, 4 West Smithfield
Biddell William, engraver, 3 Allen st. Goswell st
Bidden James & Son, stockbrokers, 22 Finch la
Bidder Geo. Parker, civil engineer, see Stephenson & Bidder
Biddle Elizh. ladies' school, 19 Hemus terrace, Chelsea
Biddle George, cowkeeper, 46 Bath st. City road
Biddle George, leather seller, 22 New st. Brompton
Biddle George, tailor, Stratford, Essex
Biddle Jacob, cheesemonger, 12 Hereford pl. Coml. rd. east
Biddle John, tobacconist, &c. 119 York rd. Lambeth
Biddle Paul, oil & italian wareho. 79 Judd st. Brunswick sq
Biddle Richard, baker, 1 Compton st. east, Brunswick sq
Biddle Richard, truss maker, 90 Leadenhall st
Biddle William, fishmonger, &c. 127 Holborn hill
Biddlecombe Harriet (Mrs.), *Horse & Groom* P.H. 23 Gresse st
Biddlecombe James, coachmaker, 22 St. James' place, Hampstead road, & 40 Whittlebury st. Euston square
Biddles James, dairyman, 1 Robert st. Hoxton
Biddles James, tobacconist, 8 Chetenham pl. Westmr. road
Biddulphs, bankers, see Cocks & Biddulph
Biddulph Wm. & Co. tailors & drapers, 120 High st. Shadwell
Biddulph John, coffee rooms, 116 Drummond st. Euston sq
Biddulph William, baker, 101 Cromer st. Brunswick sq
Biden John, seal & copperplate engraver, 37 Cheapside
Bidet Charles, manuftg. goldsmith, 19 King st. Clerkenwell
Bidgood, Jones & Wilson, woollen warehsmn. 6 Vigo st. Reg. st
Bidgood Henry, button & trimming seller, 7 Vigo st. Regent st
Bidlake James Hodgson, watchmaker, 10 North pl. Kingsld. rd
Bidlake Wm. Seth, watch & clock ma. &c. 43 Threadneedle st
Bidmead David & Co. linendrapers, 7 Crombies rw. Coml. rd
Bidmead Moses Chas. & Co. hos.&glovers, 51&52 Holborn hill
Bidmead Wm. Horatio, printer, 7 Bream's bldgs. Chancery la
Bieber Nicholas Elert, merchant, 9 New Broad st. City
Biehl Thomas, stockbroker, 75 Old Broad st. City
Bielefeld Chas. F. papier maché orna. mfr. & pat. of the quaquaversal toilet glass stand, 15 Wellington st. Nth. Strnd
Bielefeld Chas. Henry, tobacconist, 188 Brick la. Spitalfilds
Bielefield Samuel Augustus, coal mercht. Milford la. Strand
Bielfeld Henry, artist, 31 Rathbone place, Oxford st
Bienemé Angelo, sculptor, imp. of marble work, 22 Newman st. & 20½ Clipstone st. Fitzroy sq. & Cirencester wharf, 8 Augustus st. Regent's park
Biers & Stringer, furnish. undertakers, 13 Broad st. Golden sq
Biers Hugh, surveyor, 12 Dorset place, Dorset square
Biertumpfel & Clark, improved candle mould & frame makers, 68 Albany st. Regent's park, & 38 Lt. Albany st. north
Biffen Charles, tailor, Southampton st. Camberwell
Biffen John, tailor, 62 Davies st. Berkeley square
Biffen William, tailor, 27 Villiers st. Strand
Bigelsford John, brazier, 7 Gt. Crown ct. Lit. Pulteney st
Bigg James & Son, booksellers, 53 Parliament st. Westminster
Bigg William & Son, dentists, 3 Langham place, Portland pl
Bigg Edward Smith, solicitor, 38 Southampton buildings
Bigg Frances (Miss), lodging ho. 37 St. Andrew's hill, Blkfrs
Bigg Fred. sec. to *Ipswich, &c. rail.* 12 Old Jewry chamb
Bigg Harriet (Mrs.), milliner, 50 Bishopsgate without
Bigg Henry, surgical instrument maker & anatomical machinist, 9 St. Thomas's st. Southwark, & 29 Leicester sq
Bigg Hugh, engraver & printer, 37 St. Andrew's hill
Bigg James, fruiterer, North row, Covent garden market
Bigg John, fruiterer&orange mer. North row, Cov.gard.mrkt
Bigg Richard, baker, 44 Gray's inn lane
Bigg Thomas, chemist, 15 Crawford st. Portman square
Bigg William Robert, barrister, 23 Old square, Lincoln's inn
Biggar Douglas, manufactg. chemist, see Atkinson & Biggar
Bigge Arthur, barrister, 1 Mitre court buildings, Temple
Biggenden John, attorney, 5 Walbrook
Biggerstaff Wm.&John, wine mers.&bankers, 8 WestSmithfld
Biggerstaff Robt. oil & colorman, 43 Strutton ground, Westm
Biggs & Annis, tailors, 24 Sackville st. Piccadilly
Biggs Joshua&Son, pocketbk.ma. 1 Francis ct. Berkly st. Clkwl
Biggs Charles, ship & insur. broker, 122 Bishopsgate within
Biggs Edward, cattle salesman, 41 Smithfield
Biggs Edward, cowkeeper, 31 Edgware road
Biggs Edward, hatter, 4 Jamaica row, Bermondsey
Biggs Elizth. (Mrs.), baker, 27 Devonshire st. Lisson grove
Biggs Elizabeth (Mrs.), ironmonger, 37 Baldwin st. City road
Biggs George, baker, 2 Maida hill east
Biggs George, bookseller & publisher, 421 Strand
Biggs George, coal mercht. 11 Coal Exchange, Lower Thames st
Biggs George, shoemaker, 21 Little Chapel st. Westminster
Biggs Henry, carpenter & builder, 18 Brewer st. Golden sq
Biggs Henry, hairdresser, 4 Creed lane, Ludgate st
Biggs Henry, tobacconist, 1 Crescent place, Brompton
Biggs Jeremiah, job & postmaster, & livery stables, South place, Finsbury
Biggs John, carpenter, 52 King st. Soho
Biggs John, undertaker & coffin maker, 41 Houndsditch
Biggs John, upholster. & underta. 3 Holloway pl. Holloway
Biggs Joseph, baker, 50 Pennyfields, Poplar
Biggs Kirkman, italian warehouse, 237 Oxford st
Biggs Martha (Mrs.), wholesale stationer, 108 Fore st. Cripplg
Biggs Michael, cattle salesman, 17 West Smithfield
Biggs Rachael (Mrs.), *Anchor & Hope* P.H. 8 Shadwell Dock st
Biggs Thomas, desk & dressing case ma. 57 Rathbone place
Biggs Thomas, livery stables, 23 Brick st. Park lane
Biggs Wm. carver, gilder & picture restorer, 31 Conduit st
Biggs William, cutler, Stratford broadway
Biggs Wm. imp. of french wines & cognac brandy, 39 Cornhill
Biggs Wm. tea dealer, 4 Kennington cross
Biggs Wm. upholsterer & berlin wool wareho. 28 Edgware rd
Bigmore Job, windsor chair manufr. 1 White st. Bethnal gr
Bigmore John, furnit. brok. 16 Baldwin's gardens, Leather la
Bigmore Stephen, plumber & painter, 22 Museum st. Blmsby
Bignall Charles, funeral coachmaster, 58 Tothill st. Westminster
Bignall John, grocer, &c. 31 Chapel st. Pentonville
Bignel Robert, bootmaker, 2 Panton st. Haymarket
Bignell Elizbth. (Mrs.), strawhat ma. 1 Robart'ster. Com. rd. ea
Bignell Henry, builder, 23 Wardour st. Soho
Bignell William, builder, 6 Norfolk pl. Marlboro' rd. Chelsea
Bigney George, hatter, 55 Bath st. City road
Bignold Geo. poulterer, 11 Ship tav. pas. Leadenhall market
Bignold Saml. sec. Norwich Ins. Co. 6 Crescent, New Bridge st
Bigsby Thomas, french polisher, 8 Eagle st. Red Lion sq
Bigwood John, blacksmith, 24 Fieldgate st. Whitechapel
Bilbe Thos. & Co. ship joiners, Nelson dock, Rotherhithe st
Bilboe William, hat box maker, 5 Friar st. Blackfriars rd
Bilbrough Geo. carpenter, 24 Up. Salisbury pl. Lock's fields
Biles Peter, smith & farrier, 5 Dorset st. Clapham road
Biles William, clothier, 104 Regent st. Horseferry road
Biles Wm. *Railway tav.* P.H. 9 Wellington pl. We. In. dk. rd
Bilke Henry, stockbroker, 7 King's Arms bldgs. Change alley
Bill Francis, grocer & oilman, 27 South Audley st
Bill John Walker, *King's Head* P.H. 56 Middlesex st. Somrs. tn
Billes Joseph, bone boiler, Upper Fore st. Lambeth
Billing Archibald, physician, 6 Grosvenor gate, Park lane
Billing Edward, printer & engraver, 186 Bermondsey st
Billing Geo. lodging house, 4 Bell's buildings, Salisbury sq
Billing John, butcher, 4 Earl st. east, Lisson grove
Billing John, plumber & glazier, 90 Lambeth walk
Billing John Turner, solicitor, 33 King st. Cheapside
Billing Samuel, baker, 2 Freeschool st. Horselydown, & 4 Portland st. Walworth common
Billing Sydney, barrister, 2 Churchyard court, Temple
Billing Thomas, baker, 62 Lucas st. Commercial road
Billing Thos. printing ink agt. Blue Anchor rd. Bermondsey
Billing Thos. William, engraver, 11 Aske terrace, Hoxton
Billing William, tailor, 60 Southampton st. Camberwell

Billingham Joseph & Son, curriers & wholesale boot & shoe manufacturers, 126 St. John st. Smithfield
Billinghurst William, ship owner, 10 Austinfriars
Billings Charles, lodging house, 21 Finsbury square
Billings Robt. Wm. architect, 44 Lr. Belgrave pl. Pimlico
Billings Thomas, cattle salesman, 60 West Smithfield
Billings William Henry, cattle salesman, 60West Smithfield
Billingsley Wm. lighterman, 9 Pell st. Ratcliff highway
Billington John, fishing rod, &c. ma.93Chalton st.Somers tn
Billiter Henry & Son, curriers, 9 Robert st. Grosvenor sq
Billiter John, leather factor,4 New leather mkt. Bermondsey
Billiter Richd. corn & flour dlr. 17 Holland pl. Clapham rd
Billiter Richard Henry, oil merchant, see Harris & Billiter
Billiter William, tailor, 4 Great Marlborough st
Bills Samuel, *Fox & Goose* P.H.40 Shakspear's wlk.Shadwell
Billson Charles, who. coffee dealer, see Turner & Billson
Billson Thomas, cabinet maker, 7 Gt.Titchfield st.Oxford st
Billson William, butcher, 81 St. George st
BillsonWm. cabinet maker& undertaker, 4 Meard's st. Soho
Bilney Robert, carpenter, 14 Bentinck st. Berwick st. Soho
Bilsborough Sophia(Mrs.),beer ret.12South wf. rd. Padngtn
Biltar William, boot & shoe maker, 32 Thomas st. Oxford st
Biltcliff Joseph, engineer, millwright, &c. 25 Wilderness row
Bilton Edward, shoe warehouse, Kensington gravel pits
Bilton Edwin, bootmaker, 203 Tottenham court road
Bilton George, chemist, &c. 19 Three Colt st. Limehouse
Bilton George(Mrs.),straw bonnet ma.84Mount st.Berkly.sq
Bilton Henry, tobacconist, &c. 211 Blackfriars road
Bilton James, boot & shoe maker, 100 High st. Notting hill
Bilton James Read, bootmaker, 45 Beech st. Barbican
Bilton John, conveyancer, 1 King's road, Bedford row
Bilton John, musical instrum. ma. 93 Bridge rd. Lambeth
Bilton Samuel Francis, barrister, 5 New sq. Lincoln's inn
Bilton Thos. solicitor, 3 Kennington pl. Up.Kennington lane
Bilton Wm. wheelwright & tiresmith,9Plough yd.Shoreditch
Binckes Ann(Mrs.), cheesemonger, 1 Little Bath st.Clerknwl
Binckes Henry Ashbey, artist, 163 Fenchurch st
Binckes Litchfield, pianoforte mak.10Fredk's.pl.OldKent rd
Binckes Thomas, tea & coffee dealer, 163 Fenchurch st
Binden Henry, cheesemonger, 204 Shadwell High st
Binder Hannah (Miss), grocer, 29 Tottenham court road
Binder Joseph,carpenter& ho.agent, 75 Park st.Grosvenor sq
Binfield Henry, hosier & haberdasher, 18 Old Fish st
Bindley William, watchmaker, 24 Rahere st. Goswell road
Binge Edward, *British Oak* P.H. 9 Baltic st. Golden lane
Binge Louisa (Miss), fancy repository, 9 Lowther arcade
Binge Thomas, chemist & druggist, 76York st. Westminster
BingemanJacob,baker,164Unionst.Borough,&21Whitchpl.rd
Bingemann Jacob, baker, 35 Minories
Bingham Chas. Edwd. newsman, stationer, &c. 62 Mount st
Bingham Francis, surgeon & accoucheur, 1 Back Church la
BinghamFras.watch movemt.ma.81 Murray st.NewNorth rd
Bingham George, tailor, 29 Conduit st. Regent st
Bingham George, veterinary surgeon,32Bell st. Edgware rd
BinghamHenry,auctioneer&ho.agt.19Ryder's ct.Leicester sq
Bingham Henry, *Horse & Groom* P.H.3 Chapel place mews, Chapel st. Belgrave square
Bingham John, fruiterer, 4 Portman st. Portman square
Bingham Joseph, carman, 7 & 8 Chapel st. Cripplegate
Bingham Peregrine, magistrate at Worship st. police court
Bingham Thos.galloon & double manuf.21Milk st.Cheapside
Bingham Thomas, marble mason, &c. 13 Vauxhall bridge rd
Bingle Edward, undertaker, 27 St. John's sq. Clerkenwell
Bingle Fredk. bootmaker, 51 George st. Blackfriars road
Bingley & Batho, engravers, &c. see Batho & Bingley
Bingley Benjamin, *King's Arms* P.H. 123 Shoreditch
Bingley Charles Bentley, tailor, 22 Gt. Marlborough st
Bingley James, furn. ironmonger, 3 Pleasant row,Pentonvill
Bingley Jas.& Pettigrew,tailors,&c.27 Duke st.Grosvenor sq
Bingley Mark,statnr. account bk. mk. & printer,60 Cannon st
Bingley Wm. Richard, barrister, 52 Lincoln's inn fields
Binmore Henry, *St. Ann's* coffee rooms, 437 Oxford st
Binmore John, coffee & chop house,3 Brook st. Grosvenor sq
Binmore John, coffee rooms, 12 Carnaby st. Golden square
Binnie & Foay, french stay wareho. 41 Judd st. Brunswick sq
Binnie & Richardson, tailors, 31 Old Bond st
Binnie John, baker, 11 Thornton st. Dockhead,& 29 Thomas st. Horselydown
Binning Thos. *White Lion* P.H. 6 St. Alban's pl. Haymarket
Binnington Josiah, carpent.& builder, 29 Primrose st. Bishpsg
Binnington Stephen, chemist, 35 Haymarket
BinnsJohn&Joshua, bldg.materl. dlrs.5Munsterst.Regnt's.pk
Binns William & Co. agents for patents & the registration of designs, civil engineers & mechan.draftsmen,27 Carey st
Binns John, haberdasher, &c. 4 Newland place, Kensington
Binns John, hatter, 13 King st. Lower road, Islington
Binns Nimrod, cabinet maker, 2 Ocean row, Stepney
Binns Wm. & Samuel, cabinet makers, 243 High Holborn
Binns Thomas, plumber, 39 Harrison st. Gray's inn road
Binyon Alfred, musical instr. ma. 40 Tavistock st. Covnt gdn
Binyon Alfred, patent St. James's chest expander depot, 40 Tavistock st. Covent garden
Binyon Alfred, wholesale sheffield plate & cutlery warehouse, 40 Tavistock st. Covent garden
Binyon Edward, sheffield agent, 4 Bride lane, Fleet st
Birbeck James, fruiterer, 14 Collier st. Pentonville
Birch & Bramah, solicitors, 6 Great Winchester st
Birch Eliza & Maria, grocers, 84 St. John st. Clerkenwell
BirchJohnB.&Eugenius,civil enginrs.3 Cannonrow,Westmtr
Birch Samuel & Co. cooks & confectioners, 15 Cornhill
Birch Abel, undertaker, 5 Middle row, Knightsbridge
Birch Baynes, carriage lamp maker, 66 Fetter lane, Holborn
Birch Chamberlain, hosier, 5 Vere st. Cavendish square
Birch Charles, irish repository, 16 & 17 Vere st. Cavendish sq
Birch Charltt. (Miss), prof. of music, 2 Tavistock st. Bdfd.sq
Birch Emanuel, coffee rooms, 7 Frances ter. Hampstead rd
Birch James, grocer, 6 Brecknock place, Camden new town
Birch Henry William, solicitor, see Rooper, Birch & Ingram
Birch John, artist, 47 Brewer st. Golden square
Birch John, carman, 3 Wharf, Macclesfield st.South, City rd
Birch Joseph, butcher, 4 Clement's inn pass. Clare market
Birch Joseph, tailor, 7 Leicester place, Leicester square
Birch Richard, solicitor, 14 Clifford's inn, Fleet st
Birch Thomas, solicitor, 2 Tavistock st. Bedford square
Birch Thomas Henry, barrister, 5 Inner Temple lane
Birch Thomas Jacob, barrister, 5 Inner Temple lane
Birch Tryce Wm. accountant, 37 Garden row, London road
Birch Wm. carpenter, 22 High st. Notting hill
Birch Wm. pipe maker, 4 Weymouth st. New Kent road
Birch Wm. stationer, &c. High st. Kensington
Birch William, surveyor, 24 Great Russell st. Bloomsbury, & 33 Little Russell st. Bloomsbury
Birch William, undertaker, 2 Grove place, Brompton
Birch Wm. watch manufacturer, 173 Fenchurch st
Birch Wm. Richardson, linguist, Scarsdale ter. Kensington
Birchall James, watchmaker, 8 Wellington st. Goswell st
Birchall Robert, stationer & account book maker, 8 Poultry
Bircham & Dalrymple, solicitors, 15 Bedford row
Bircham William, solicitor, 38 Connaught ter. Edgware rd
Birchmore William, tobacconist, 4 & 5 New Kent road
Bird & Dudley, yeast dlrs. 8 Charlotte mews,Tottenham ct.rd
Bird Elizth. &Martha(Misses), school, 25 Bethnal gr. ea. side
Bird George & William, bricklayers, builders & brickmakers, 7½ Thayer st. Manchester sq. & Hammersmith
Bird & Jervis, surgeons, 16 Orchard st. Portman square
Bird Stephen & Hen. builders & brick ma. 24 Kensgtn. Hi. st
Bird William & Co. iron & tinned plate merchants, 5 Martin's lane, Cannon st
Bird Adam, carpetwa. & linendraper, 79 Whitechapel High st
Bird Benj. cabinet ma. & undertaker, 9 New inn st.Curtain rd
Bird Charles, barrister, 4 Stone buildings, Lincoln's inn
Bird Charles, egg merchant, 16 Ivy lane, Newgate st
Bird Charles, linendraper, 90 Lambeth Lower marsh
Bird Christian Elizh. (Mrs.), dressma. 10 Gate st.Linc. inn fi
Bird David, painter & glazier, 23½ Swan st. Minories
Bird Edward, painter & decorator,20Charlotte st. Portland pl
Bird Elizabeth (Mrs.), printer, 67 New Compton st. Soho
Bird Frances (Mrs.), wardrobe dlr. 28Lt. Guilford st. Bruns.sq
Bird George, builder, 38 Edgware road
Bird George, china warehouse, 33 Providence row, Islington
Bird George, painter & decorator, 49 Portman pl. Edgware rd
Bird George, paperhanger, 7 Spur st. Leicester square
Bird George, surgeon, 7 Union place, New road
Bird Gervase, tailor, see Erratt & Bird
Bird Geo. Jas. timber mer.Waterl. br. wf. Comcl.rd. Lambth
Bird Golding, physician, 19 Myddelton square
Bird Henry, china wareh. 28Park pl.Mile end rd.nr. *Red Cow*
Bird Henry, fruiterer, 47 North st. Sloane st
Bird Henry, jeweller & silversmith, 109 Cheapside
Bird Henry, stationer, 5 Ave Maria lane
Bird Henry, surgeon, Milan cott. Caroline pl. Hampstead rd
Bird Henry, teadealer, Camberwell grove
Bird Henry H. civil engineer, 5 Robert st. Adelphi
Bird Henry Peale, solicitor, 58 Lincoln's inn fields
Bird Hugh, scumboiler & saw mills, Green bank, Wapping
Bird Isaac, architect&surveyor,72Seymour pl. Bryanstone sq
Bird Isaac, coffee rooms, 65 St. George st
Bird James, horsehair manufacturer, 15 West st. Smithfield
Bird James, solicitor, 5 New inn, Strand, & Hammersmith
Bird James, timber mer.12&13Club rw.Church st.Bethnal gr
Bird John, bookbinder, 52 Hatton garden
Bird John, carpenter & blind mak. 17 Union st. Whitechpl. rd

Bird John, coach laceman, 19 King st. Soho
Bird John, ladies' boot & shoe maker, 86 Oxford st
Bird John, *Stag's Head* P.H.13 Nw.Cavndsh. st. Portland pl
Bird John, stationer & bookseller, 8 Spring st. Paddington
Bird John, surgeon, 2 Regent place west, Regent square
Bird John, tailor, Mare st. Hackney
Bird John Lorence, barrister, 21 Old square, Lincoln's inn
Bird John Proctor, solicitor (at Mr. Hume's), 10 Great James st. Bedford row
Bird John Sanders, grocer,&c. 6 Church st. Stoke Newington
Bird John W. baker, 12 Judd st.&17 Brunswick st. Cromer st
Bird John William, surgeon, 102 St. George st
Bird Joseph, builder, 21 Seymour place, Bryanstone square
Bird Joseph, cabinet ma. & undertak. 24 New North st. Finsb
Bird Joseph, *Harrow* P.H. Stratford
Bird Joshua, greengrocer, 39 Lower Kennington lane
Bird Richard, baker, 70 London road, Southwark
Bird Richard, coal dealer, 13 Arthur st. Knightsbridge
Bird Richard, *Granby Arms* P.H. Granby st. Hampstd. rd
Bird Samuel, bottle dealer, 34 North row, Grosvenor sq
Bird Samuel, *Jolly Gardeners* P.H. Princes road, Lambeth
Bird Samuel, pork butcher, 71 Bethnal green road
Bird Samuel Joseph, bed.screw mak. 3 Lit. Compton st. Soho
Bird Sarah (Mrs.), *Three Colts tavern*, 45 London wall
Bird Thomas, cabinet maker, Ship yard, 36 Wardour st. Soho
Bird Thomas, cabinet maker, 7 Richmond buildings, Soho sq
Bird Thomas, corndealer, 7 Artichoke row, Mile end road
Bird Thomas, linendraper, 21 Langley pl. Comrcl. road east
Bird Thomas, fruiterer, 16 Gray's inn lane
Bird Wm. baker, 7 Weston st. Borough
Bird Wm. chair & couch maker, Eden place, Ivy la. Hoxton
Bird Wm. chemist, &c. see Pyman & Bird
Bird Wm. bootmaker, 11 West st. Golden square
Bird Wm. potato dealer, 133 Church st. Shoreditch
Bird Wm. metal, wire, tubing, steel, &c. wa. 37 Basinghall st
Bird Wm. Fredk. Wratislaw, solicitor, 5 Verulam buildings
Bird Wm. Henry, carpenter, 8 Holland st. Brixton road
Bird Wm. John, bookseller, see Hamilton & Bird
Birdsey Thomas & Wm. grocers, 47 Ernest st. Regent's park
Birdsey John, butcher, 20 Munster st. Regent's park
Birdsey Wm. grocer & teadealer, 41 Goodge st Tottnhm. ct. rd
Birdseye Ann (Mrs.), bootmaker, 125 Waterloo road
Birdseye Ann (Mrs.), grocer, 4 Cobourg place, Bayswater
Birdseye John Clark, ale & stout mer. see Derrick & Birdseye
Birdseye Michael, trimming seller, 17 Houndsditch
Birdseye Thomas, hair dresser, 5 Hornsey row, Islington
Birkbeck Wm. Lloyd, barrister, 6 Stone bldgs. Lincoln's inn
Birkett Danl. & John & Co. corn factors, 3 Lime st. square
Birkett John & Son, solicitors, 3 Cloak lane, City
Birkett Daniel, jun. mercht. Bell ct. Mincing la. & Bordeaux
Birkett Dan. jun. wine mer. Bell ct. Mincing la. & Bordeaux
Birkett Edmund Lloyd, physician, 3 Cloak lane, Cheapside
Birkett Henry John, stationer, 4 Salmon lane, Limehouse
Birkett James, ironfounder, 6 Three Colt lane, Bethnal gr
Birkett John, surgeon, 2 Broad st. buildings, City
Birkett Rd. stationer & account bookma. 27 Norton folgate
Birkin Ebenezer, cheesemonger, 20 Penton row, Walworth rd
Birkin Ebenezer Thos. poulterer, 22 Beckford row, Wlwth. rd
Birkit James, baker, 12 Little Newport st. Long acre
Birkitt Geo. *Green Dragon* P.H.4 Shadwell dck. st. Lw. Shdwl
Birley Henry, engineer, see Miller, Ravenhill & Co
Birley John, plumber, 26 Brompton row
Birley Samuel, *Lamb & Flag* P.H. 2 Crutched friars
Birmingham Plate Glass Co's. warehouse, 141 Fleet st
Birmingham Railway, see London & Birmingham Railway
Birmingham Railway clearing house, 111 Drummond st
Birmingham & Oxford Railway, 449 West Strand
Birmingham & Manchester Direct Railway Company (Abraham Augustus Flint, secretary), 1 Moorgate
Birnie William, baker, 6 Oxford st. Mile end
Birrel John, baker, 24 Stamford st. Blackfriars
Birrell Cath. (Miss), ladies' school, 53 Rosoman st. Clerknwl
Birt & Burt, solicitors, 1 Southampton st. Fitzroy square
Birt Charles, linendraper, see Ludgate & Birt
Birt Daniel, linendraper, 190 Borough High st
Birt Francis, carpenter, 76 Milton st. Dorset square
Birt Hugh, *Red Cow* P.H. Princes st. Lambeth
Birt James, linen & woollen draper, 168 Hoxton Old town
Birt Mary (Mrs.), printer, 39 Gt. St. Andrew st. Seven dials
Birt William, dairyman, 9 New Quebec st. Portman square
Birt William, linendraper, 143 Up. Whitecross st. St. Luke's
Birt William Radcliff, academy, 2 Cambridge rd. Mile end
Birtles Richard, fruiterer, 24 Leather lane, Holborn
Birtles Richard, printer, 24 Leather lane
Birtley Iron Company (Charles Perkins, manager), 67 Mark lane, & Scott's wharf, Bankside, Southwark
Birts Mary A. (Miss), boarding ho. 13 Warwick ct. Gray's inn
Bischoff & Coxe, solicitors, 19 Coleman st. City
Bischoff Jas. & Sons, mers. & ins. brokers, 28 Threadneedle st
Bischoffsheim Louis Raphael, mer. 2 Copthall chamb. Bank
Bisgood Thomas, solicitor, 36 Carey st. Lincoln's inn
Bish George, engineer, Stratford, Essex
Bishop Geo.& Chas. herald paints. to the Queen, 3 Bennett's hl
Bishop & Horsfall, steel pen ma. 19 John st. Tysoe st. Spafields
Bishop Joseph & Sons, merchants, 13 Crutched friars, & Colonial chambers, 4 John st. Minories
Bishop & Pell, distillers, british wine makers & brandy merchants, 18 Ropemakers' st. Finsbury
Bishop of London's Registry Office, 3 Godliman st. 10 to 5
Bishop of Rochester's Registry, 19 Bennett's hill, Doctors' commons; hours of business ½ past 9 to 5
Bishop of Winchester's Registry Office for Surrey, 12 Great Knightrider st.; hours 10 to 5
Bishop Ann (Mrs.), bonnet maker, 11 Abbey st. Bermondsey
Bishop Benj. brushmaker, 208 High Holborn
Bishop Benj. grocer & cheesemgr. 1 Aylesbury pl. Old Kent rd
Bishop Charles, fruiterer, 15 Gainsford st. Horselydown
Bishop Charles Wm. herald painter, 28 Pelham rd. Bromptn
Bishop Edwin, tobaccopipe ma. 3 Gloucester st. Hackney flds
Bishop Elizh. (Mrs.), dairy, 44 Queen st. & 24 Molyneux st. Bryanstone square
Bishop Elizh. (Mrs.), milliner, 6 Everett st. Brunswick sq
Bishop Fredk. cutler & dressing case ma. 3 Royal Exchange
Bishop Fredk. *Hawley Arms* P.H. Francis ter. Hampstd. rd
Bishop Fredk. Augustus, wine & spirit mer. Church st. Hckny
Bishop George, builder, 13 Thanet st. Burton crescent
Bishop Geo. *Northumberland Arms* P.H.2 Charles st. Westm
Bishop Geo. ship ins. & gen. com. agent, 31 Gt. St. Helen's
Bishop Geo. whipmaker, 8 St. Margaret's ct. Boro' High st
Bishop Hannan (Mrs.), tobacco pipe m. 106 Old st. St. Luke's
Bishop Henry, carver, 47 Baldwin st. City road
Bishop Henry Edward, hosier, 6 Grosvenor row, Pimlico
Bishop James, coach wheelwright, 18 Little Russell st. & 12 Gilbert st. Bloomsbury
Bishop James, boot & shoe maker, 27 York st. Walworth rd
Bishop Jas. haircutter & wig maker, 5 Little Vine st. Piccadilly
Bishop James, lace warehouseman, 213A, Piccadilly
Bishop James, machine ruler, 35 St. Swithin's lane
Bishop James, newsvender, 1 Lillypot lane, Noble st
Bishop James, painter, plumber, &c. 32 Gower pl. Euston sq
Bishop Jas. Chapman, organ bldr. Lisson grove South, New rd
Bishop Jas. Griffin, ironmonger & smith, 102 Fetter lane
Bishop Job, ladies' wardrobe dlr. 11 Chalton st. Somers town
Bishop Job, *Orange Tree* P.H. 4 Orange st. Red Lion sq
Bishop John, baker, 28 Crown st. Finsbury
Bishop John, baker, 21 Poplar row, New Kent road
Bishop John, basket maker & turner, 21 Chiswell st
Bishop John, foreign commis. agt. see Morgan & Bishop
Bishop John, jeweller, 3 Kenton st. Brunswick sq
Bishop John, jeweller, 3 Poland st. Oxford st
Bishop John, shipwright, 24 Rotherhithe wall
Bishop John, solicitor, 14 Lincoln's inn fields
Bishop John, surgeon, 38 Bernard st. Russell sq
Bishop John, tailor & draper, 46 Glo'ster st. Queen sq
Bishop John, umbrella & parasol manufacturer to her Majesty, 12 Ludgate hill
Bishop John Crompton, wine merchant, 23 Savage gardens
Bishop John Dommett, surgn. 5 Rochester ter. Stoke Newngtn
Bishop John Skynner E. warehousemn. see Morgan & Bishop
Bishop Joseph, oilman, &c. 51 Brewer st. Golden sq
Bishop Joseph, *Swan* P.H. 3 George st. Foley pl
Bishop Joseph, tailor & clothier, 45 Goswell st
Bishop Joseph, agent to Reid & Co. New wharf, Whitefriars
Bishop Mary (Mrs.), copp. plate print. 2 New Church st. Berm
Bishop Mary (Mrs.), milliner, 4 Cannon st. St. George's East
Bishop Matilda (Mrs), grocer, 1 North st. East st. Walworth
Bishop Matthew Thos. commission agt. 30 Queen st. Cheapside
Bishop Nathaniel, baker, 111 Bishopsgate without
Bishop Robert, dairyman, 18 Crown court, Pall mall
Bishop Robert, manchstr. & button wareho. 34 St. Martin's le gr
Bishop Robert, *Sieve* P.H. 3 Church st. Minories
Bishop Robert, tailor, 49 Rufford's bldgs. High st. Islington
Bishop Robert, wine merchant, 3 Church st. Minories
Bishop Samuel, dining rooms, 3 Greenland place, Cromer st
Bishop Sam. Robt. builder, Kingsland basin, Kingsland rd
Bishop Stephen, linendraper, 11 Red Lion square, Holborn
Bishop Thomas, baker, 23 North Wharf road, Paddington
Bishop Thomas, bricklayer, 43 Edward st. Regent's park
Bishop Thomas, cheesemonger, 2 Torrington pl. Torrington sq
Bishop Thomas, coal dealer, 20 Circus st. New road
Bishop Thomas, general salesman, 2 Gravel lane, Borough
Bishop Thomas, grocer, 62 Great Suffolk st. Borough

Bishop Thomas, plumber, 62 Gt.Carlisle st. Portman market
Bishop Wm. coffee rooms, 20 Norfolk st. Middlesex hospital
Bishop Wm. goldsmith & gunmaker's agent, 170 New Bond st
Bishop Wm. grocer, 1 New Portland pl. Wandsworth rd
Bishop Wm. news agent, 9 Aldermanbury postern
Bishop Wm. plumber & painter, 1 & 2 William st. Shoreditch
Bishop Wm. tailor & gen. clothier, 16 Judd st. Brunswick sq
Bishop Wm. trunk maker & upholsterer, 155 Leadenhall st. & 11 Nag's Head court, Gracechurch st
Bishop Wm. umbrella maker, 24½ Marchmont st. Brswk. sq
Bishop Wm. wholesale stationer & printer, 66 Cheapside
Bishop Wm. Henry, baker, 165 Kingsland road
Bishop Wm. Renauded, grocer, 27 Hart st. Bloomsbury
Bisley Frances (Mrs.), carpenter, &c. 7 Jamaica rw. Bermndsy
Bisley Henry, *Ship Argo* P.H. 214 Rotherhithe
Bisney Esther (Mrs.), butcher, 1 Church place, Piccadilly
Biss John Geo. furnishing undertak. 6 Gilbert st. Clare market
Bissell Ann (Mrs.), baker, 29 Cowper st. City road
Bissell James, boiler & tank manfr. 106 Up. East Smithfield
Bisset Andrew, barrister, 6 Stone buildings, Lincoln's inn
Bissett James, baker, 16 William st. Caledonian road
Bissex William, plasterer, 38 Albany road, Camberwell
Bissmire George, silversmith, 36 Pear Tree court, Clerknwll
Bithray Stephen, optician, 29 Royal Exchange
Bitmead Wm. window blind mak. 67 Freeschool st. Bermonds
Bitter John Herman, dining rooms, 2 Warwick pl. Bedford rw
Bitting Elizabeth (Mrs.), baker to her Majesty & the Queen Dowager, 11 Bury st. St. James's
Bittleston Adam, barrister, 4 Brick court, Temple
Bittner William, watchmaker, 30 Dean st. Soho
Bixley James, coach joiner, see Esau & Bixley
Blaber Eliza (Miss), milliner, 20 Dorset st. Portman square
Blachford Caleb, baker, 49 Philipps st. Kingsland road
Blachford John, solicitor, 36 Moorgate st. Bank
Black & Bidmead, umbrella & parasol makers, 11 Wellclose sq
Black Hen. & Co. coach bldrs. 1 Berners st. & 2 Perry's pl. Oxfd. st
Black (Neil), & Co. linen merchants, 11 Bread st. Cheapside
Black Alexander, for. bookseller, 8 Wellington st. North
Black Alexander, wine & spirit merchant, 32 Fenchurch st
Black Alfred, butcher, 21 Back st. Horselydown
Black Archibald, merchant, 34 Lime st. City
Black Benjamin, carriage lamp maker, 49 South Molton st
Black Charles, general agent, 5 Adam st. Adelphi
Black Chas. Chris. irish linen factor, see Crocker, Black & Co
Black Charles Wm. gen. commission agent, 24 St. Swithin's la
Black Edward, *Albemarle Arms* P.H. 71 South Audley st
Black James, baker, 57 John st. Holland st. Blackfriars rd
Black James, bread & biscuit baker, 24 Lamb's Conduit st
Black Jas. Shuter, irish linen factor, 3 Lawrence la. Cheapside
Black John, baker, 3 Nursery place, Old Kent road
Black John, carpenter, 2 Windsor court, Strand
Black John, carver, 33 Ernest st. Regent's park
Black John, fruit salesman, Covent garden fruit market
Black John, hairdresser, 5 Wilsted st. Somers town
Black John, tailor, 2 Greville st. Hatton garden
Black John, wine merchant, 11 Great Tower st. City
Black Joseph, gardener, Wellington nursery, Balls Pond rd
Black Patrick, physician, 13 Bedford sq
Black Robert, baker, 34 Queen st. Short st. New cut, Lambth
Black Robert, baker, 29 Long alley, Finsbury
Black Thomas, baker, 18 Hunter st. Great Dover road
Black William, brush, &c. manufacturer, see Taylor & Black
Black William, solicitor, 148 Southwark bridge road
Blackall John, ship & insur. broker, 12 Langbourn chambers
Blackall John George, surgeon, 14 Henry st. ea. Avenue rd
Blackall Thomas, clothworker, packer, &c. 59 London wall
Blackall Thomas, physician, 13 Queen st. Mayfair
Blackborn Thomas, pawnbroker, 4 Skinner st. Somers town
Blackborn Wm. pawnbroker, 62 Myddelton st. Spafields
Blackboro Henry, draper, 67 Brewer st. Somers town
Blackbourn Cuthbert, carpenter & builder, 123 Goswell st
Blackbourn Robert, fishmonger, 1 Charlotte st. Whitechapel
Blackburn George H. & Co. wine merchts. 58 Old Broad st
Blackburn & Pardon, printers, 6 Hatton garden
Blackburn Charles, painter, 7 Grosvenor st. West, Eaton sq
Blackburn Chas. Pettit, furn. undertak. 101 Gt. Portland st
Blackburn Colin, barrister, 5 King's bench walk, Temple
Blackburn Edwd. L. architect & surveyor, 16½ Clement's inn
Blackburn Edwin, wine, &c. mer. 10 Savage gardens, Tower hill
Blackburn Edwn. Jas. jun. fun. carriage mastr. 101 Gt. Portl. st
Blackburn Elizabeth (Mrs.), builder, 4 Salmon la. Limehouse
Blackburn George, fruiterer, 10 Eliza place, Sadler's wells
Blackburn Henry, proctor, 9 Gt. Knightrider st. Doctors' com
Blackburn Isaac, engineer, general machinist & manufacturer of improved steel mills, beams, scales, weights & measures, 128 Minories, & City engine works, Northumberland alley, Fenchurch st
Blackburn James Watson, hosier & outfitter, 47 Cheapside
Blackburn John, *Eight Bells* P.H. 5 Lit. Denmark st. Soho
Blackburn John, oil & italian wa. 19 Bedford st. Covt. grdn
Blackburn John, stationer, 11 Park ter. Regent's park road
Blackburn Joseph, russia mat. wa. 4 Wormwood st. Bishopsg
Blackburn Richard, prof. of music, 5 St. Ann's pl. Coml. rd. ea
Blackburn Thos. *Brewers' Arms* P.H. 29 Millbank st. Westm
Blackburn Thomas, butcher, 250 Poplar High st
Blackburn Thomas, corn dealer, Rose alley, Bankside
Blackburn Thomas, iron plate worker, 1 Peartree ct. Clerkwl
Blackburn Wm. barrister, 10 Old square, Lincoln's inn
Blackburn Wm. carpenter, 8 Avery row, Low. Grosvenor st
Blackburn Wm. stationer, 32 St. George's pl. Knightsbridge
Blackburn Wm. tailor, 65 Millbank st. Westminster
Blackburn Wm. tobacconist, 15 Victoria road, Pimlico
Blackburne George, merch. 60 Mark la. & 20 Lr. rd. Islingtn
Blacker & Earith, shawl manufr. & warehou. 12 Gresham st
Blacker Edward, builder, 2½ Upper Yardley st. Clerkenwell
Blacker Harriet (Miss), wardrobe dlr. see Looker & Blacker
Blacker Mary (Mrs.), bricklayer, 12 Mansell st. Goodman's fi
Blacker Rowland Hill, warehouseman, 16 Gresham st. City
Blacker William, fishing tackle maker, 54 Dean st. Soho
Blacket & Tomkins, woollen dps. & tailors, 85 Boro' High st
Blacket Jas. butchers' clothier & slopsllr. 31 West Smithfield
Blacket George, painter & glazier, 31 Henry st. Hampstd. rd
Blacket Wm. Steven, tailor & draper, 1 Skinner st. Snow hill
Blacketer Thomas, picture frame ma. 20 Wych st. Drury la
Blackett John Wilson, coal mer. Phœnix whf. Clink st. Boro'
Blackett John Wilson, insurance broker, 39 Threadneedle st
Blackett Thomas, wine fining maker, 24 Crutched friars
Blacketter Elizh. (Mrs.), tallowchandler, 72 Silver st. Stepney
Blackford Harry, coach lace maker, see Cooper & Blackford
Blackford Henry, plumber & glazier, Morning la. Hackney
Blackford John, wire blind maker, 17 Charterhouse st
Blackford Thomas, horse hair & hair seating manufacturer, 20 Little Wild st. Lincoln's inn fields
Blackham Charles James, bootmaker, 26 Aldgate
Blackie John & Son, bookslrs. & publishers, 11 Warwick sq
Blackie Alex. pianoforte mak. 81 Margaret st. Cavendish sq
Blackie Alex. B. stock & share bro. 35 Abchurch lane, City
Blackie George, escapement ma. 12 Woodbridge st. Clerknwl
Blackler William, cider merchant, Hay's wharf, Tooley st
Blackley Matthew, stationer & bookselr. 27 North Audley st
Black Lion wf. Jas. Smith, between 31 & 95 Lr. East Smithfield
Blacklock John, boot & shoe maker, 42 Bernard st. Russell sq
Blacklock John, stationer, 118 Whitechapel High st
Blacklock Thomas, shoemaker, 35 Brown st. Bryanstone sq
Blacklock Wm. printer, see Bradshaw & Blacklock
Blacklock William James, artist, 40 London st. Fitzroy sq
Blackman Josiah & Mrs. Wm. music sellers & instrument makers, 5 Bridge st. Southwark
Blackman Chas. Wm. grocer, 76 Charlotte st. Portland pl
Blackman Edwd. L. shirt ma. & outfitter, 14 Gracechurch st
Blackman George, cooper, 1 & 7 Gower's walk, Church lane, Whitechapel, & Rupert st. Goodman's fields, & Phœnix place, Ratcliff cross
Blackman Geo. juvenile color maker, 53 St. John st. road
Blackman Geo. tailor, 3 Bath bldgs. Baldwin st. City road
Blackman James, tallowmelter, 180 Blackfriars road
Blackman John, bacon drier, Tennis ct. King st. Borough
Blackman John, grocer, 3 Limehouse Old road
Blackman John, hatter, 10 & 16 Baker's row, Mile end New tn
Blackman Mary (Miss), school, 34 New North st. Red Lion sq
Blackman Thomas, bedstead mak. 1 Bucks row, Whitechapl
Blackman Wm. coach plat & founder, 3 Hanover st. Long acre
Blackman Wm. *Delaware Arms* P.H. 220 Oxford street
Blackman Wm. solicitor, see Wilton & Blackman
Blackman Wm. Chas. grocr. & oilman, 11 Bedfordbury, Cov. gar
Blackmore Brothers, axminster carpet manfrs. 12 Friday st. Cheapsde [late 7 King's Arms bldgs. Wood st.], & Wilton, Wilts
Blackmore Chas. P. & Walter, bolting cloth ma. Wandsworth
Blackmore Christopher & Co. tailors, &c. 10 Cork st. Bond st
Blackmore & Co. solicitors, 2 New inn, Strand
Blackmore Benjamin, grocer, 69 Brunswick st. Blackwall
Blackmore Henry, hosier & outfitter, 33½ Strand
Blackmore Isabel (Miss), artist, 16 Up. Montagu st. Mntgu. sq
Blackmore James Thos. surgeon, see Collyer & Blackmore
Blackmore John, tailor, 17 Park pl. Kennington cross
Blackmore Martin, leatherseller, 56 Bread st
Blackmore Mary (Miss), milliner, 11 Davies st. Berkeley sq
Blackmore Philip, saddler, &c. 8 Little James st. Bedford rw
Blackmore Robert, solicitor, 3 St. Martin's pl. Charing cross
Blackmore Wm. Hen. cotton merchant & manufacturer of cotton waste for wiping engines, & sack & bag manufacturer, & dealer in bags & mats, 11 Cres. Minories

Blackmore Wm. Hen. oyster ware. 5 Hart st. Crutchedfriars
Blackmore Wm. Hen. painter & glazier, 11 Dean st. Soho
Blackmur George, umbrella furn. manf. 98 York st. Coml.rd
Blackmur Samuel Richd. cabinet mak. 46 Bethnal green rd
Blackmur Wm. Henry, grocer, &c. 95 & 97 Bethnal green rd
Blackshaw Wm. carp. & build. 62 Pritchard's rd. Hackney flds
Blackstone John, leather cutter, 34 Saville st. Fitzroy sq
Blackstone Jph. corn lighterman, 7 Thomas st. Horselydown
Blackstone Joseph, surgeon, 31 Bayham ter. Camden town
Blackwall Railway Co. see "London & Blackwall"
Blackwell & Farnell, printers' ink ma. 14 King st. Clerkenwl
Blackwell Samuel & Robert, saddlers & harness manufrs. &c. 259 Oxford street
Blackwell & Stembridge, tailors, 34 Leicester square
Blackwell & Williams, general com. agents & manufacturers of congreves, &c. Old Montague street, Whitechapel
Blackwell Charles, butcher, 8 Churchway, Somers town
Blackwell Charles, tailors' shears ma. 5 Noel st. Soho
Blackwell Elizh. (Mrs.), bootma. 19 NewQuebec st. Portman sq
Blackwell Francis, stationer, &c. 9 North pl. Gray's inn lane
Blackwell Henry, french polisher, 100 John st. Fitzroy sq
Blackwell James, engine turner, see Liston & Blackwell
Blackwell John, ironmonger, 9 Charles st. Middlesex hospital
Blackwell Thomas, oilman, see Crosse & Blackwell
Blackwell Thomas Seal, surgeon, 7 Crawley st. Oakley sq
Blackwell William, *Roebuck* P.H. 256 High Holborn
Blackwell William, surgeons' instrument & table knife ma. & manufacturing cutler, 3 Bedford ct. Covent garden
Blackwood William & Sons, publishers, 37 Paternoster row
Blade John, grocer & cheesemonger, 53 ThreeColt st. Limeho
Blades & East, engravers & printers, 11 Abchurch la. City
Blades James, truss maker, 11 Leathersellers buildings
Blaenavon Iron & Coal Company (J. Booth. sec.), 4 Pancras la
Blagden Richard, surgeon, 26 Albemale st. Piccadilly
Blagden Thomas, coal & corn merchant, 14 Goswell road
Blagg James Peter, coffee rooms, 198 Tooley st
Blagg Thomas, cheesemonger, 15 Sidney pl. Commercial rd
Blagrove Wm. & Chas. professors of music, 88 Norton st
Blagrove Henry, professor of music, 71 Mortimer st
Blaikley Alexander, artist, 6 Percy st. Bedford square
Blain John Samuel, tinplate worker, 102 Bethnal green road
Blain Wm. bedstead maker, 10 Little Earl st. Seven dials
Blain Wm. boot & shoe maker, 30 Aldermanbury
Blaine Henry & Robert S. merch. 5 Barge yd. Bucklersbury
Blair George, saddler, &c. see Renton & Blair
Blair James, cabinet maker & upholsterer, 33 King st. Holborn
Blair John, baker, 1 Frederick place, Mile end road
Blair Robert, surgeon, 90 Great Russell st. Bloomsbury
Blake Geo. & Bros. inlay & cabinet ma. 8 Stephen st. Tot. ct. rd
Blake & Boyle, solicitors, 17 Clement's inn, Strand
Blake Bros. buhl furniture manf. 8 Stephen st. Rathbone pl
Blake Chas. & Co. pianoforte manf. 16½ Lawrence la. Cheaps
Blake & Cherrill, proctors, 6 Gt. Knightrider st. Doc. com
Blake John A. & Co. gunmakers & sword cutlers, 253 Wapping
Blake, Sandford & Blake, chemists & mineral water manufacturers to her Majesty, 47 Piccadilly
Blake & Sellwood, job masters, 24 King st. Kensington
Blake & Tamplin, solicitors, 6 King's road, Bedford row
Blake Thomas & Co. tea warehouse, 4 Fenchurch buildings
Blake Barnabas, physician, Camberwell grove
Blake Benjamin, furniture broker, 8 Mint st. Borough
Blake Benj. Wm. insura. broker, 13 City rd. & Hall of Com
Blake Charles, *Hop Pole* P.H. 28 Edgware road
Blake Charles, solicitor, see Bridger & Blake
Blake Charles, solicitor, see Wood & Blake
Blake Charles, tailor, 16½ Lawrence lane, Cheapside
Blake Dodshon, jun. foreign agent, 23 St. Swithin's lane
Blake Edmund, grocer & cheesemonger, 192 Poplar High st
Blake Geo. *King of Prussia* P.H. 23 Cartwright st. Rosemryla
Blake George, solicitor, Carlton chambers, 8 Regent st
Blake George, wire worker, 88 John st. Fitzroy square
Blake Geo. Henry, cabinet ma. & inlay. 53 Mount st. Berkly. sq
Blake George John, wine merchant, 21 Great Tower st
Blake Henry, carman, 48 White Lion st. Pentonville
Blake Henry, shoeing smith, 2 Ormond yd. Yorkst. St. James's
Blake James, boot & shoemaker, 58 Pennyfields, Poplar
Blake James, hosier & glover, 13 Lowndes st. Belgrave sq
Blake James, surgeon, 16 Pall mall
Blake James, tobacconist, 21 Aldgate High st
Blake James, tobacconist, 7 Exeter pl. Gt. Dover st
Blake James Joseph, solicitor, 79 Blackfriars road
Blake John, baker, 2 Granby st. Waterloo road
Blake John, coffee broker, see Williams & Blake
Blake John, *Golden Lion* P.H. 4 Warwick pl. Bedford row
Blake John G. solicitor, see White, Blake, Tylee & Fawkener
Blake John Judd, law stationer, 1 Great Knightrider st

Blake Jonathan, cheesemonger, 1 High st. Hoxton Old town
Blake Joseph, *Prince of Wales* P.H. 22 East road, Cityroad
Blake Joseph Wm. *Globe & Dolphin* P.H. 25 Liquorpond st
Blake Nathan, linendraper, 75 Edgware road, Marylebone
Blake Richard, butcher, 20 St. Martin's st. Leicester sq
Blake Robert, boot & shoemaker, 13 Robert st. Bedfordrow
Blake Robert, straw hat wa. 107 St. John st. West Smithfield
Blake Robert, surgeon, 13 White st. Borough
Blake Samuel, dining rooms, 30 Princess st. Portmn. market
Blake Samuel, *Horse & Groom* P.H. 50 Great Portland st
Blake Thomas, D.C.L. advocate, 1 College, Doctors' commons
Blake Thomas, coffee & dining rooms, 4 Postern rw. Tower hl
Blake Thomas, smith & farrier, 2 Globe road, Mile End road
Blake Wm. accountant & coml. agt. Chancy. chambs. Qualityct
Blake William, cheesemonger, 114 Chalton st. Somers town
Blake Wm. *East India Arms* P.H. 225 Poplar High st
Blake Wm. hair dresser, 5 Upper York st. Bryanstone sq
Blake Wm. music publisher, 12 Vigo st. Regent st
Blake Wm. plumber & glazier, Morning lane, Hackney
Blake Wm. tailor, 50 Church st. Minories
Blakebrough Stphn. ironmonger, 32 Camden st. Walworth
Blakeley & Thomas, feather dressers, merchants & mattress & palliasse makers, 133 Bishopsgate without, & 26 Acorn st
Blakelock & Fiddey, solicitors, 3 Paper buildings, Temple
Blakeman George, steel wrkr. & polisher, 25 Gt. Crownct. Soho
Blakeman Hugh Stevenson, grocer, Bromley, Middlesex
Blakemore Robert, teadealer, 14 Orange st. Red Lion sq
Blakemore William, dentist, 21 Grosvenor st. Grosvenor sq
Blakeney John, solicitor, see Dufaur & Blakeney
Blaker Elfred, picture cleaner & repairer, 126 Long acre
Blaker Mary (Mrs.), *George* P.H. Stratford broadway
Blakesley Benjamin, trunk & pack. case ma. 47 Friday st
Blakeway John, wine merchant, see Durand & Blakeway
Blaksley Hen. Jas. ship & ins. broker, 2 New City chambers
Blamire Frederick, boot & shoe maker, 19 Bow High st
Blamire Robert, cheesemonger, 12 Chapel st. East, May fair
Blamire Wm. artificial florist, 22 Gt. Russell st. Covent gardn
Blanch Thos. & David, coach smiths, Ham yd. Gt. Windmill st
Blanch John, gun maker, 29 Gracechurch st
Blanch John, leather seller, 2 Green st. Bethnal green
Blanchard Wm. & Sons, prntrs. 20½ Warwick la. & 62 Millbank st
Blanchard Ann (Miss), milliner & straw hat ma. 118 Oxford st
Blanchard David, butcher, 6 Courthope ter. Bermnsy. New rd
Blanchard Edwin, leech dealer, 4 Crawford passage, Clknwl
Blanchard Harriet (Mrs.), milliner, 22 Victoria rd. Pimlico
Blanchard Henry, eel pie house, 101 Union st. Boro' High st
Blanchard Mark Henry, plasterer, 13 Melina pl. Westmr. rd
Blanchard Thomas, surgeon, 17 Upper Ebury st. Pimlico
Blanchard Wm. pastrycook, 33 Liquorpond st. Gray's inn la
Blanchett Edwd. *Waterman's Arms* P.H. Bevedere rd. Lmbth
Blanchett Thomas, hat maker, 106 Hare st. Bethnal green
Bland Joseph & Co. tailors & habit ma. 4 Argyll st. Regent st
Bland Cornelius, surgeon, 5 Mount Etna, Mile end road
Bland Elizabeth (Mrs.), butcher, 43 Charlotte ter. New cut
Bland George, barrister, Devereux chambers, Strand
Bland George, dining rooms, 35 Adam st. west, Bryanston sq
Bland George, *Garraway's Coffee House*, see Funge & Bland
Bland George, watch maker, Church st. Hackney
Bland Henry, yeast merchant & brewer, 47 York st. City rd
Bland John, butcher, 115 St. John st. road
Bland John, chemist, see Griffiths & Bland
Bland Joseph Napoleon, coach, &c. maker, 56 South Audley st
Bland Mielje (Miss), ladies' schl. 12 Virginia pl. Gt. Dover rd
Bland Robert, gasfitter, &c. 24 Cromer st. Brunswick square
Bland Stephen, cutler, 8 Percy pas. Charlotte st. Fitzroy sq
Bland Thomas, butcher, 14 Rufford's bldgs. High st. Islington
Bland William, tailor, 11 Earl st. Finsbury
Bland Wm. H. annatto manufacturer, see Fullwood & Bland
Bland Wm. James, teainsp. Commrcl. coffeehouse Minc. la City
Bland Wm. Richd. tobacconist, 106 Up. Whitecrosst. St. Luke's
Blandford John F. & Co. chemists, 97 Charlotte st. Fitzroysq
Blandford Lucy (Mrs.), clothes dlr. 15 Crucifix la. Bermndsy
Blandford Silas, surgeon, R.N. 9 Chester square, Pimlico
Blandford Thomas, bootma. 3 Hereford ter. King's rd. Chelsea
Blandford Thos. russia broker, Baltic coffee house
Blane Samuel, bookbinder, 15 Cross st. Hatton garden
Blane Wm. beer retailer, 59 Southampton st. Camberwell
Blanford George, watchmaker, 28 Phœnix st. Somers town
Blanford Wm. who. looking glass, picture frame, moulding maker, carver, gilder & oval turner, 29 Bouverie st. Fleet st
Blank Emilius, merchant & agent for swiss & german good 18 King st. Cheapside
Blankley William, poulterer, 33 Museum st. Bloomsbury
Blanshard John, chandler's shop, 15 Charlotte st. Pimlico
Blanshard Robert, surgeon, 21 Poplar High st.
Blashfield John, artist, 7 Upper Stamford st. Blackfriars

Blashfield John M. office of works, 3 Kensington gardens
Blatch Hen. sec. to court of examiners, Apothecaries' hall
Blatchford Charles, baker, 1 Whiskin st. Clerkenwell
Blatchford John, tailor, 8 Carlisle st. Soho square
Blatchley Edward, cook & confectioner, 362 Oxford st
Blatchly John, tobacconist, 1 West st. Golden sq
Blatherwick Richard, hosier, 131 Bishopsgate without
Blatspiel Frederick Ernest, furrier, 9 Warwick ct. Holborn
Blatt John, french bootmaker, 127 Jermyn st. St. James's
Blatz Andrew, baker, 22 Well st. Wellclose square
Blaxland George, solicitor, see Jones & Blaxland
Blaxland Samuel, wine & spirit mercht. 12 Devonshire sq
Blaxland Wm. surgeon, 16 Clarence place, Camberwell
Blay Edwd. Hen. *Duke of York* P.H. 18 Northwf.rd. Pddngtn
Blay Wm. oil & colorman, 5 Albert ter. Queen st. Chelsea
Blaylock George, milliner, 14 Fore st. Cripplegate
Bleakley Robert, coffee rooms, 82 Sun st. Bishopsgate
Blease Alfred Whitter, wine & spirit broker, 21 Mark lane
Blease Robert, confectioner, 3 Torrington pl. Torrington sq
Bleeze Thos. coffee & eating house, 27 Plumbers st. City rd
Blenco John, tailor, 23 Brompton row
Blencowe Rt. barrister, 1 New Boswell ct. Carey st
Blencowe William, baker, 5 Broadley terrace, Blandford sq
Blenkarn Thomas, bookseller & publisher, 19 Chancery lane
Blenkarne David, solicitor, 11 Clement's lane, City
Blenkarne Henry, surgeon, 39 Dowgate hill
Blenkhorn John Alex. tailors'trim. sel. 237 Shoreditch High st
Blenkins Chs. coal mer. Haggerstone wf. Brnswck. st. Hckny. rd
Blenkinsop Henry, hosier & haberdasher, 53 Gracechurch st
Blenkinsop Jas. boarding ho. 5 Christopher st. Finsbury sq
Blenkiron Wm. stock & collar manufacturer & general agent, 123 Wood st. Cheapside
Blessed Barnabas Chas. shoe ma. 6 Southampton st. Cmbwl
Bletchley John, bath & bristol carrier, see Budd & Bletchley
Blew William, perfumer, see Bayley & Blew
Blewett Ann (Mrs.), shoemaker, 4 Charles st. Commercial rd
Blewitt Henry, livery stables, Trinity st. Borough
Blick Richard Granger, special pleader, 2 Brick ct. Templ
Blick William, tailor, 1 Harcourt st. New road
Bligh S.&J.S. ironm.& tool wa. 72 Church la. Whitechapel
Bligh George, ropemaker, 8 Cherry Garden st. Rotherhithe
Blight Gilbert, jun. stationer, 67 Gracechurch st
Blight Samuel, professor of music, 24 Hastings st. Burt. cres
Blincoe William, auctioneer, see Cotterell & Blincoe
Blind Man's Friend (John Simpson, treasurer), 29 Saville row
Blindell John, coppersmith, 3 New road, Whitechapel road
Blindell W. *Mallard Arms* P.H. 31 Mid. Grove st. Comcl. rd. ea
Blinkhorn Benjamin, *Red Lion* P.H. 1 Breezer's hill, Ratcliff
Blinko William, cattle salesman, 37 West Smithfield
Blisett Charles, tobacconist, 14 Creed lane, Ludgate hill
Bliss David, gasfitter & brass mfr. 3 Carlisle st. Lambeth
Bliss Edwin, brushmaker, stationer, & gen. wareho. 8 Barbican
Bliss Fredk. *Butchers' Arms* P.H. 4 South st. Spital market
Bliss Henry, attorney, 11 Bentinck st. Manchester st
Bliss Henry, barrister, 11 King's Bench walk, Temple
Bliss Henry John, undertaker, 123 Church st. Shoreditch
Bliss Isaac, fruiterer, 28 Rotherhithe st
Bliss Richard, creditors' agent, 71 Cornhill
Bliss Rt. (Mrs.), ladies' school, 3 & 4 Addison road south
Bliss William, boarding house, 19 Adam st. Adelphi
Bliss William, bootmaker, 1 Perceval st. Clerkenwell
Bliss William, brace tool ma. 4 Charles st. Brandon st. Wlwth
Bliss William, grocer, 98 Shoe lane, Fleet st
Blissatt Edward, tailor, 28 Dean st. Soho
Blissett Ann (Mrs.), hatter & fancy cap maker, 13 Middle row, Holborn, & 1 & 2 Holborn bars
Blissett Isaac, gun & pistol maker, 69 Leadenhall st
Blissett John, gun & pistol maker, 321 High Holborn
Blizard Geo. *Devonshire Arms* P.H. 21 Duke st. Portland pl
Block & Grey, wine merchants, 10 Old Broad st. City, & Park lane, corner of Mount st
Block Samuel & Sons, worsted & fringe makers, 52 & 53 Newgate st. & 3 Paternoster row
Blockey Geo.& Josph. H. wine mer. 21 Duke st. & 80 Jermyn st
Blockey John, wine & spirit mer. 104 Ebury st. Eaton sq. Pimlico
Blockley William, dairyman, 1 Lower Duke st. Stamford st
Blockley William, stationer, 8 Seymour pl. Camden town
Blofeld John H.& Co. mappublishrs. 12 Millman st. Bedford row
Blofeld Thomas & Co. ink manufacturers, 5 Greville st
Blofeld Thos. G.& Co. cutlers & razor ma. 6 Middle row, Holbn
Blofeld George, pastrycook, 27 Parker's row, Bermondsey rd
Blofeld Richard, solicitor, 12 Millman st. Bedford row
Blofeld William, tinman & brazier, 145 Tooley st
Blofield George, baker, 144 Tooley st
Blofield James, butcher, 136 Up. Whitecross st. St. Luke's
Blogg & Martin, commission agents & auctioneers in diamonds & jewels, 23 Bucklersbury
Blogg Wm.& Co. Union brewery, 11 Cobham row, Clerkenwell
Blogg Frederick, brewer, 1 West st. Skinner st. Somers town
Blogg John, merchant, 6 Laurence Pountney pl. Cannon st
Blogg Wm. Gottey, paper stainer, Dalston sq. Storer st. Cml. rd
Blomfield Wm.& Sam. table & cork knifema. 7 Newton st. Holbn
Blomfield John, plumber, 4 Union ter. Commercial rd. East
Blomfield John, carman, *Rose Inn*, 25 Farringdon st
Blomfield Stephen, butcher, 8 Hoxton old town
Blondell Thos. *Duke of Wellington* P.H. 232 Shoreditch Hi. st
Blood Abraham, newsvender, 16 East st. Manchester square
Bloom John, tailor, 6 Carpenter street, Berkeley square
Bloom John, tailor, &c. 15 Shepherd's market, Mayfair
Bloomer John, grocer, &c. 1 Up. Gloucester pl. Dorset sq
Bloomfield Ann (Mrs.), *King's Head* P.H. 6 Swinton st
Bloomfield Hy. *Harmood Arms* P.H. 29 Harmood st. Hmstd. rd
Bloomfield Horatio, surgeon, 3 David pl. Bow lane, Poplar
Bloomfield John, lodging house, 54 Rupert st. Haymarket
Bloomfield Noah Read, surgeon, 125 Wapping
Bloomfield Robert, bricklayer, Harlow house, Mile end road
Bloomfield Wm. ship owner, 13 Virginia terr. Gt. Dover rd
Bloomfield Zachariah, furniture bro. 7 York pl. Westmr. rd
Bloomsbury Dispensary, 62 Gt. Russell st. Bloomsbury
Bloomsbury Savings' Bank (G. Knox, manager), 30 Montague st. Russell square
Bloor Robert, derby china manufacturer, 34 Old Bond st
Bloor Wesley, timber merchant, 86 Paul st. Finsbury
Blore Chas. Hen. carpenter, &c. 9 Kinnerton st. Belgrave sq
Blore Edward, architect, 7 Welbeck st. Cavendish square
Blore Hen. beer retailer, Caledonian ter. Caledonian road
Blore John, architect, 8 Michael's place, Brompton
Blore John, butcher, 5 Westbourne st. Pimlico
Blore Rt. mgr. of Lond. Convce. Co. 13 St. Alban's pl. Edgwr. rd
Blossom Thomas, *Globe* P.H. Globe court, 23 Fish st. hill
Blott Benjamin, butcher, 185 Shoreditch
Blott James, baker, 239 High Holborn
Blott William, baker, 26 Islington High st
Blount Arnold, east india warehouse, 71 New Bond st
Blount Charles, solicitor, see Parkes, Cary, Blount & Co
Blount Thomas, fruiterer, 19 Vine st. Hatton wall
Blount Thomas, *Hotel de Versailles*, 2 Leicester pl. Le'ster sq
Blount William, chemist, 47 Cheyne walk, Chelsea
Blount William, leather cutter, 14 High st. Marylebone
Blow George Fordham, currier & machine strap, hose pipe, & bucket maker, 21 Great Dover st. Borough
Blow James, fruiterer, 28 Fieldgate st. Whitechapel
Blowen Saml. Thos. fishfact. 132 Long la. Bmsy.& Billingste
Blower, Vizard & Parson, attorneys, 61 Lincoln's inn fields
Blower Edward, butcher, 5 Providence st. City rd
Blower John, carver & gilder, 40 George st. Portman sq
Blower Samuel, fruiterer, 11 Powell st. west. King square
Blower Thomas, butcher, 5 Stevens place, New North road
Blower William, butcher, 18 Felix terrace, Liverpool road
Blowfield Henry Matthew, *Rose & Crown* P.H. 21 Crucifix la
Blowfield Sophia (Mrs.), straw hat ma. 17 Finsbury pl. North
Bloxam & Ellison, solicitors, 1 Lincoln's inn fields
Bloxam & Sanderson, milliners, 6 Triangle, Kenngtn. cross
Bloxam Alfred B. wine merch. 14 Southampton st. Strand
Bloxam Chas. livery stables, 8 Philpot ter. Edgware rd
Bloxam Edward, solicitor, see Hawkins, Bloxam & Co
Bloxam George B. proctor & notary, 23 Lit. Knightrider st
Bloxam Geo. F. wine mercht. 33 Broad st. bldgs. New Broad st
Bloxam James Mackenzie, barrister, 41 Chancery lane
Bloxam Matthew, paperhngr.& paintr. 99 Gt. Russell st. Blmsb
Bloxam Richard, solicitor, see Hawkins, Bloxam, Stocker & Co
Bloxam William, surgeon, 28 Duke st. Grosvenor square
Bloxham Thomas, tailor, 154 St. George st
Bloxsome George Frederick, surgeon, 59 Ebury st. Pimlico
Bloyd Joseph, lead mer. Topping's whf. & 11 Duke st. Tooley st
Bluck Edwin & Co. ironmongr. 22 Theobald's rd. Red Lion sq
Blue Coat School, Little Chapel st. Westminster
Blue Sinclair, surgeon, 186 High st. Poplar
Bluel Victor, cabinet maker, 7 Borough road
Bluett Benj. G. shipjoiner & mast ma. Coal harbour, Blackwll
Bluett John, surgeon, 4 Bentinck pl. High st. Portland twn
Bluett John, surgeon, 5 St. Ann's villas, Acacia rd. St. John's wd
Bluett Wm. grocer, 39 Old Gravel lane, Wapping
Blumberg, Berens & Co. for. goods im. see Berens, Blumberg & Co
Blumenthal Adol. & Co. wine & sp. mer. 16 John st. Crtchd. friars
Blumfield Benjamin, house agt. & valuer, 11 Upper North pl
Blumfield George, bookbinder, 22 Well st. Cripplegate
Blumfield William, cooper, 1 West st. Walworth road
Blundell, Spence & Co. paint, color & varnish manfrs. & patent. of the palm wax candles & machinery oil, 69 Up. Thames st
Blundell Benson, barrister, 10 Serle st. Lincoln's inn

Blundell Bezer, solicitor, 1 & 3 Mitre court chambers, Fleet st
Blundell Edward Straw, physician, 18 Lower Seymour st
Blundell Elizabeth (Miss), ladies' school, 139 Wapping
Blundell Geo. dairyman, 53 Henry st. east, Avenue road
Blundell Henry, fishmonger, 2 Billingsgate
Blundell Henry, clock maker, 7 Red Lion st. Clerkenwell
Blundell Henry, coffee rooms, 2 Brownlow mews, Gray's inn la
Blundell James, physician, 1 Great George st. Westminster
Blundell Joseph, cheesemonger, 13 Dean st. Holborn
Blundell Joseph, ham dealer, 60 Seymour st. Euston square
Blundell Josh. Birkbeck (sec. to Thames Tunnel Co.) Rotherhith
Blundell Mary (Mrs.), straw hat ma. 20 Cross st. Newgtn. bts
Blundell Thomas, fruiterer, 9 East road, City road
Blundell Thos. Chas. rope & matting ma. 123 St. John st. Clrkwl
Blundell Thomas Leigh, physician, 39 Lombard st
Blundell William, fishfactor, 18 Love lane, Eastcheap, & 131 Long lane, Bermondsey
Blunden George, haberdasher, Mortimer rd. Kingsland
Blundell William, dentist, see Fisher & Blundell
Blunden William, livery stables, 84 Bridge road, Lambeth
Blunden Wm. Henry, tailor & hatter, Camberwell green
Blunderfield Benjamin, carpenter, 10 Parker's row, Dockhead
Blunsum James, tailor, 8 Leathersellers bldgs. London wall
Blunt Arthur, cheesemonger, 135 Lambeth walk
Blunt Charles, typefounder, 15 Little Mitchell st. St. Luke's
Blunt Edmund, haberdasher, 6 Globe road, Mile end
Blunt Edward, pocketbook manf. 23 Weston st. Pentonville
Blunt George Saml. tailor, 10 Shepperton pl. New North rd
Blunt James Tillyer, stockbroker, 7 Warnford court, City
Blunt John, fancy cabinet maker, 10 Coppice row, Clerknwl
Blunt John, merchant, Lloyd's
Blunt John Elijah, barrister, 4 New square, Lincoln's inn
Blunt Joseph, solicitor to the Mint, 5 Raymond bldgs. Gray's in
Blunt Joseph, jun. solicitor, see Roy, Blunt, Johnstone & Co
Blunt Robert, druggist, 4 Prospect pl. Cheyne walk, Chelsea
Blunt Samuel, newsvender, see Tatchell & Blunt
Blunt William, grocer, &c. 2 Church row, Pancras road
Blunt Wm. hardwareman, 12 Hemmings' row, St. Martin's la
Blyth & Co. carpet warehouse, 52 Little Britain, sole agents to Gregory, Thomsons & Co. Kilmarnock
Blyth Henry David & James, merchants, 9 Austin friars
Blyth Charles & Co. manufacturers of knit hose, frocks, caps, cravats, &c. at Hawes & Askrigg, Yorkshire, & general warehousemen, 2 Trump st. King st
Blyth, Hamilton & Blyth, bed feather, horse hair & rug manufacturers, 52 Little Britain, near the Gen. Post Office; manufactory, steam mills, Elizabeth st. Hackney road
Blyth John & Alfred, engineers, millwrights, boiler makers & ironfounders, Fore st. Limehouse
Blyth John, architect & surveyor, 113 Aldersgate st
Blyth Joseph Daniel, oil & color man, 62 Leather lane
Blyth Robert, saddler & harness maker, 4 Park lane
Blyth Thomas, boot & shoe maker, 2 Crombie's row, Commercial road East, & 31 Lambeth walk
Blythe John & Co. brassfounders, 7 Grove, Gt. Guildford st
Blythe Samuel, sawmaker, Glebe place, King's road, Chelsea
Blythe Thos. tanner, 21 Richardson st. Long la. Bermondsey
Blythe William, bootmaker, 33 Cheyne walk, Chelsea
Boaden Ann (Miss), card board box ma. 1 Lovell's ct. Ptnstr. rw
Boag Hannah (Mrs.), babylinen wareh. 101 Mount st. Berkely sq
Boag John M. G. *Alton ale rooms*, 126 Fleet st
Boag William, music seller, 11 Great Turnstile, Holborn
Boak Joseph, linendraper, 2 Glo'ster ter. Commercial road
Boakes William, chandler's shop, 12 Barnard st. Hackney rd
Boam Barnett, dealer in watches & plate, 8 Great Alie st
Board of Control for the Affairs of India, Cannon row
Board of General Officers, 6 Whitehall yd. hours 10 to 4
Board of Green Cloth, St. James's palace, hours 11 to 4
Board of Trade & Plantations, Whitehall, hours 10 to 5
Board Amos, carpenter, 5 Charles st. East, Hampstead road
Board Charles, corn & coal mer. 7 Sparrow corner, Minories
Board Gregory, whiting ma. Lovegrove st. Canal, Old Kent rd
Board Jeremy, cowkeeper, 24 Middle Grove st. Coml. rd. East
Board Joseph, bricklayer, Lovegrove st. Old Kent road
Board Rt. carpent. & undrtk. 2 Westmoreland st. Marylebone
Boardman John Charles, carpenter, Downham rd. Kingsland
Boards John, pawnbroker, 1 Commercial road East, Whitchpl
Boarer John, butcher, 7 Surrey place, Wandsworth road
Boase John, carpenter & builder, 47 Whitechapel High st
Boast Chas. Bird & Co. pat. inorganic manure mfrs. Old Ford
Boast David, surgeon, 100 Blackfriars road
Boast John, surgeon, 61 Trinity square, Borough
Boatwright, Brown & Co. sealing wax, wafer & patent wafer manufacturers, 17 St. Saviour's churchyard, Boro'
Bobart Henry, tobacconist, 134 Goswell st. West side
Bobbitt Edwin Elijah, auctioneer, 27 Judd st. New road
Boccius Light Office (Gottlieb Boccius, patentee), 6 John st. Adelphi
Bockett Daniel Smith, solicitor, 60 Lincoln's inn fields
Bockhorn Johanna (Mrs.), violn strngma. see Seiler & Bockhorn
Bocking Charles, basket maker, 1 King st. Covent garden
Bocking Isaac, *Red Deer* P.H. 18 Patriot row, Cambridge rd
Boddington & Bourne, appraisers 58 Museum st. Bloomsbury
Boddington & Co. west india mers. 9 St. Helen's pl. Bishpsgt
Boddington Carter, silk & worsted ware. 84 St. Martin's lane
Boddington Henry John, artist, 5 Acton st. Gray's inn road
Boddington William, house agent, see Pinner & Boddington
Boddington William, potato factor, 1 Old road, Stepney
Boddy & Morton, ladies' school, 10 Calthorpe st
Boddy George, beer retailer, 17 Robinhood lane, Poplar
Boddy John, lodging house keeper, 6 Manchester buildings
Boddy Thomas, meat salesman, see Woodham & Boddy
Boddy William Barnard, surgeon, 3 Saville row, Walworth rd
Bodecker Wm. Geo. Chas. corn merchant, New Corn Exch
Boden Henry & Co. fringe & trimming manufrs. 75 Wood st Cheapside
Boden John Acton & Co. needle ma. 20 Lawrence la. Cheapsd
Boden George, barrister, 11 Paper buildings, Temple
Boden Henry, vet. surgeon, 1 Up. Russell st. Bermondsey st
Boden John, coach ironmonger, &c. 21 Paget pl. Waterloo rd
Boden Thos. H. smith & farrier, 1 Up. Russell st. Bermondsey st
Boden William, sugar refiner, see Friend & Boden
Bodfield James & Joseph, tammy, moreen, damask & stuff manufacturers, 15 Milk st. Cheapside
Bodger Dennis, builder, 19 Cross st Hatton garden
Bodger Dennis, carpenter & builder, 2 Leather la. Holborn
Bodger Edward, carpenter & undertaker, 75 Fetter lane
Bodger Thomas, jun. carpenter & joiner, 9 Hatton garden
Bodkin Thos. surgeon, &c. 3 St. James's pl. Bermondsey rd
Bodkin William Henry, barrister, 4 Paper bldgs. Temple
Bodley & Etty, gold & silver lacemen, 31 Lombard st
Bodman Henry & Co, tailors, 17 Beaufort bldgs. & 95 Strand
Bodman Benjamin, solicitor, 24 Queen st. Cheapside
Body John Edmond & Co. merchants, 32 Mark lane
Body Martin, buildg. matrl. dlr. Lwr. Salisbury pl. Lock's fi
Boffey William, tailor, 5 Myddelton place, Sadler's wells
Bogarts Peter, upholsterer, 43 Duke st. Grosvenor sq
Boggas John, block maker, East India road, Poplar
Boggess William, bootmaker, 22 Three Colt st. Limehouse
Boggett & Reynolds, buttonmks. 50 St. Martin's la. Charing cr
Boggi Peter, wax & plastr. figure ma. 11 Margaret st. Clknwl
Boggis Edwd. chandler's shop, 26 Mansfield st. Kingsland rd
Boggis Henry, gasfitter, 132 Middlesex st. Aldgate
Boggis Henry, smith & bellhanger, 6 St. Mary at hill
Boggon John, *Three Suns* P.H. 88 New crane, Shadwell
Bogue David, bookseller & publisher, 86 Fleet st
Bogue John, Albion ho. boys' academy, King st. Battersea
Bohling Ludwig, grocer & cheesemongr. 7 Duncan pl. London flds
Bohm Daniel, herald painter, 31 Church row, Pancras road
Bohn Frederic, eng. & for. bookseller, 19 Henrietta st. Cov. gar
Bohn George, baker, 1 Barnes pl. Mile end rd. nr. the turnpike
Bohn Henry Geo. english & foreign library of the fine arts, natural history & belles lettres 4, 5 & 6 York st. Covent grdn
Bohn James, english & foreign bookseller, 12 King William st. West Strand
Bohn John, bookseller, 12 King William st. Strand
Bohn John Christian, baker, 128 Drury lane
Bohté Augustus, tailor, 9 Sackville st. Piccadilly
Boidin Henry, linendraper & haberd. 44 High st. Kensington
Boileau Frederique, die sinker, 7 Regent place, City road
Boinville Ernest de, french advocate, 82 Dean st. Soho
Boiteux Louis Antoine, draftsman & embroiderer, 5 King st. Golden square
Bolaffey Samuel, house agent & appraiser, 25 Everett st
Boland Jane (Mrs.), tobacconist, 92 Shadwell High st
Bolanos Mining Co. (John Head, sec.), 2 Duke st. Adelphi
Bolch John, tailor, 19 Union st. Middlesex Hospital
Bolden Gilbert, solicitor, 22 Paternoster row
Boldin John, plumber, 21 Whitcomb st. Pall mall East
Bolding Thomas & Son, engine, pump & soda water engine manufacturers, 19 South Molton st. Bond st
Bolding Henry Jas. stock & share broker, 27 Tokenhouse yd
Bolding John Parker, solcr. see Bennett, Bolding & Pope
Bolding Wm. trimming wa. 4 Bray's bldgs. Lower rd. Islington
Boldock John, tobacconist, 6 Folly dock head, Bermondsey
Boles Mary (Mrs.), fruiterer, 5 Thornton st. Horselydown
Bolitho Thos. & Wm. merchants & tin smelts. 28 Fenchurch st
Bolland Wm. Proctor, barrister, 10 Farrar's bldgs. Temple
Bollen Fredk. lace mercht. & warehomn. 13 St. Paul's church yd
Bollen Wm. carpntr. & undrtk. 74 Tyer st. Princes rd. Lambeth
Bollington Joseph, tea dealer, 51 A, Park st. Camden town
Bolnois John, cabinet manufacturer, 93 John st. Fitzroy sq.

Bolt François, baker, 1 Crown st. Walworth road
Bolt Sarah (Mrs.), china wareh. 25½ Union st. Bishopsgate
Bolton Henry & George, tailors, 63 Pall mall
Bolton, Merriman & Dunning, solicitors, 25 Austinfriars
Bolton Chas. forge & house bellows maker, 138 Houndsditch
Bolton Edward Jones, butcher, 45 Chapel st. Pentonville
Bolton Edward Jones, butcher, 28 Islington High st
Bolton George, coachmaker, 119 Albany st. Regent's park
Bolton George, coffeerooms, 140 Tottenham court road
Bolton George Buckley, surgeon, 9 Pall mall
Bolton George John, upholsterer, &c. 85 High st. Marylebone
Bolton Henry, grocer & teadlr. 20 Lloyd's row, St. John st. rd
Bolton Jas. lace, ribbon & embroid. wareho. 146 Oxford st
Bolton Jas. tobacconist, 26 St. George's pl. Hyde park corner, & 7 Middle Queen's buildings, Brompton
Bolton James W. grocer, 169 Shadwell High st
Bolton Jane (Miss), milliner, 163 Tottenham court road
Bolton John, corn & coal mer. 112 & 113 Albany st. & Westbourne mews, Bayswater
Bolton John, dining rooms, 45 Exmouth st. Clerkenwell
Bolton John, glove maker, 17 Church st. Lambeth
Bolton John, pattern & clog maker, 32 New st. Cloth fair
Bolton John Henry, solicitor, see Price & Bolton
Bolton John T. dust contractor, 1 Brunswick st. Blckfrs. rd
Bolton Joseph, chemist, 8 Stafford street, Old Bond street
Bolton Joseph Edwd. pork butcher, 2 Pleasant pl. Holloway rd
Bolton Richard, grocer, 13 Lower Shadwell
Bolton Robert, fruiterer, 5 Barnsbury place, Islington
Bolton Robert. staymaker, &c. 11 Stanhope st. Clare market
Bolton Robert, surgeon, 11 Belmont place, Wandsworth rd
Bolton Thomas, oilman, 21 Charles st. Clarendon square
Bolton Thos. John, omnibus pro. 32 Dudley grove, Harrow rd
Bolton Thos. John, coach & omnibus pro. Commercil. rd. Lmbth
Bolton Thomas Whalley, solicitor, 4 Elm court, Temple
Bolton Wm. cabinet maker, 93 Albany st. Regent's park
Bolton William, commission brewer, King st. Kensington
Bolton Wm. Hen. house painter, 6 St. James's pl. Bermondsey rd
Bolton Wm. Henry, *Plough* P.H. 305 Oxford st
Bolton Wm. Treacher, chemist, 12 Well's row, Islington
Bolwell Wm. Johnson, lodging house, 25 Charlotte st. Fitzy. sq
Bonallack Jacob, wheelwright, 11 Church la. Commrl. rd. east
Bonallack Rebecca (Mrs.), coal dlr. 180 Montague st. Whtchp
Bonce Wm. grocer & cheesemonger, 25 King st. Soho
Bond Edward & William, gun makers & archery wareh. 45 Cornhill, & at Hooper's square, Goodman's fields
Bond George & Henry, chasers, 67 Wynyatt st. Goswell road
Bond Sarah Elizth. & Mary A. (Misses) seminary, 62 Goswell rd
Bond & Morgan, shawl manufacturers & furriers, 25 Oxford st
Bond Thos. & Nephews, mast & block ma. 80 & 27 Fore st. Limeho
Bond Thomas & Son, fishing rod & tackle maks. 62 Cannon st
Bond Ann (Mrs.), printer & engraver, 32 Castle st. ea. Oxford ma
Bond Charles, dining rooms, 8 Long lane, Bermondsey st
Bond Charles, mourning warehouse, 27 Oxford st
Bond Elizabeth (Mrs.), dressmaker & milliner, 27 Oxford st
Bond George, dairyman, 33 George st. Portland place
Bond Geo. *Jacob's Well* P.H. 25 New inn, Broadway, Shoredith
Bond Geo. painter & glass stain. 14 Commercial road, Lambeth
Bond George, wine merchant, 4 Arthur st. West, London brdg
Bond Henry, chemist & cuppr. 11 Cross st. Hoxton new town
Bond Henry, ladder maker, 65 Kingsland road
Bond Henry, *Running Horse* P.H. 58 Davies st. Berkeley sq
Bond Isaac, grocer & cheesemongr. 30 Gt. George st. Bermondsy
Bond Jas. Bryant, silk mercer, 25 Lamb's Conduit st. Foundg
Bond John, butcher, 65 Davies st. Berkeley square
Bond John, cabinet maker, 6 Grange road, Bermondsey
Bond John, carpenter, 15 Woodbridge st. Clerkenwell
Bond John, chemist & marking ink ma. 28 Long la. Smithfield
Bond John, grocer, 22 Brick lane, St. Luke's
Bond John, pianoforte maker, 19 Frederick pl. Hampstead rd
Bond John, plumber, &c. 2 Little Randolph st. Camden town
Bond John Jas. cabinet ma. & undertak. 24 & 25 St. George st
Bond John Player, stockbro. 13 Copthall ct. Throgmorton st
Bond Richard, appraiser, 54 Seymour st. Euston square
Bond Richard, beer retailer, 14 East st. Walworth road
Bond Richard, bootmaker, 5 Church passage, Basinghall st
Bond Robert, hosier, 7 Palace row, New road
Bond Samuel, grocer & cheesemongr. 27 Marketrow, Oxfrd. mkt
Bond Thomas, cooper, 7 Gravel lane, Southwark
Bond Thomas, barrister, 7 Figtree court, Temple
Bond Thomas Robert, butcher, 99 Lambeth Lower Marsh
Bond Timothy, cabinet carver, 1 Whitmore place, Hoxton
Bond William, bootmaker, 37 Lisle st. Leicester square
Bond William, *Bull inn*, 122 Holborn hill
Bond William, gun maker & sword cutler, 59 Lombard st
Bond William, hairdresser, 24 Blandford st. Manchester sq
Bond William, police magistrate, Queen sq. police court
Bond William, tea dealer, 8 Norfolk st. Middlesex hospital
Bond William Henry, law bookseller, 8 Bell yd. Temple bar
Bond Wm. Henry, wine, ale & stout mer. 15 Bow la. Cheapsi
Bond Wm. Jas. plane, saw & tool ma. 23 King David la. Shadwell
Bone William & Son, bookbinders, 76 Fleet st. & 28 Shoemaker row, Blackfriars
Bone Andrew J. com. mer. Hall of Commerce, Threadneedle st
Bone Andrew James, coal merchant, Hermitage bridge whf. & Jerusalem coffee house
Bone Barnabas, carpenter, 41 Guildford pl. Lr. Kengton. la
Bone Charles, *Robin Hood* P.H. 9 & 10 Millbank st.
Bone George, tea dealer & grocer, 44 Minories, & 117 Whitechapel road
Bone Henry P. artist, 12 Percy st. Tottenham court road
Bone James, *Horse Shoe* P.H. 15 Little George st. Westmr
Bone James Andrew, coal merchant, Hermitage bridge whf. Wapping, & Jerusalem coffee house
Bone John, linendraper, 13 & 14 Great Dover st. Boro'
Bone John, stockbroker, Stock excha. & 5 Bank chambers
Bone Robert, confectioner, 9 Road side, Mile end road
Bone Samuel Vallis, barrister, 2 Stone bdgs. Lincoln's inn
Bone Wm. grocer & teadealer, 251 Poplar High st
Bone Wm. jun. artist, 12 Percy st. Tottenham court road
Bone Wm. Thos. *Royal George* P.H. 24 Lower George st. Chelsa
Boner Thomas, butcher, 26 Pennyfields, Poplar
Bonfield Wm. & Son, coal & corn merchants & granary keepers, Whiting's wharf, 40 Broad st. Ratcliff
Bonfield Wm. dining rooms, 188 Kingsland road
Bonham Charles, coal dealer, 54 Exeter st. Lisson grove
Bonham George, pawnbroker, &c. 105 Whitechapel High st
Bonham Hen. who. boot & shoe maker, 15 Gerrard st. Soho
Bonham Maria (Mrs.), chandler's shop, 52 Snowfield, Brmnds
Bonham Thomas, engineer & pump ma. 408½ Oxford st
Bonham Thomas Richard, baker, Church st. Hackney
Bonhote John, merchant, 12 Union court, Old Broad st
Boniface John, butcher, 4 South place, Camberwell New rd
Boniger Paul, furniture broker, 2 Castle st. Long acre
Boniwell Robert, coffee rooms, 6 Lit. Vine st. Piccadilly
Bonnell James P. theolgl. bookseller, 22 Holywell st. Strand
Bonnella Wm. cabinet ma. & timber mer. 57 Worship st. Finsbury, & 32 Pollard's row, Bethnal green
Bonner Hen. Wm. professor of music, 16 Bridge st. Pimlico
Bonner James, tailor, 15 Lower Sloane st. Chelsea
Bonner John, baker, 107 Aldersgate st
Bonner John, butcher, 47 Charlotte st. Whitechapel
Bonner John, *Harlequin* P. H. 69 Drury lane
Bonner John George, solicitor, see Temple & Bonner
Bonner Letitia, general dlr. 11 Clark's pl. Bagnigge Wls. rd
Bonner Richard Henry, surgeon, see Challice & Bonner
Bonner Thomas, cowkeeper, 18, Golden lane, Barbican
Bonner William, colonial broker, see Dummelow & Bonner
Bonnett James, looking glass fra. ma. 4 Middle row, Holborn
Bonnett James, livery stable keeper, 6 Farm st. Berkeley sq
Bonnett John Charles, surgeon, 29 Queen Anne st. Cavdish. sq
Bonney Edward, 3 *Horse Shoes* P.H. 7 Milford lane, Strand
Bonney Fras. Augustus, surgeon, 3 Halkin ter. Belgrave sq
Bonney James, wax & tallow chandler, 14 Adam st. West
Bonney John, carpenter, 51 Pear Tree court, Clerkenwell
Bonney William, fishmonger, 35 Bath st. City road
Bonney Wm. Woolfe, wine merc. 2 William st. Knightsbridge
Bonnick John, coachmaker, 14 Chapel place, Brompton
Bonnin James, jun. builder, 9 Onslow terrace, Fulham road
Bonnin James, sen. builder, 8 Sussex terrace, Old Brompton
Bonnin John, grocer, 43 Kensington High st
Bonning Elizth. (Miss), ladies' school, 8 Marlborough square
Bonning Saml. cheesemonger, 10 Gray's pl. Fulham road
Bonnor Thos. general agent, 14 Angel ct. Throgmorton st
Bonny Henry, baker, 9 Henry's place, Old Kent road
Bonny Mary (Mrs.), grocer, &c. 40 Trafalgar st. Walworth
Bonom Anne (Miss), baby linen wa. 11 Popham ter. Tibbrtn. sq
Bonsall Chas. *Glo'ster Arms*, P.H. 5 Up. Park pl. Regent's pk
Bonsall John, *White Swan* P.H. Vauxhall bridge road
Bonsall John, whipmaker, 168 Tottenham court road
Bonser Thomas, meat salesman, 20 Newgate st. & 7 & 8 Rose st. Newgate market
Bonser Wm. birmingham & sheffield agt. 89 Long la. Wt. Smithf
Bonsor Joseph & Co. who. stationers, 132 Salisbury sq. Fleet st
Bonsor Henry, fishmonger, 4 Little Bell alley, Coleman st
Bonsor Joseph, fishmonger, 4 Cross st. Hoxton New town
Bonsor Joseph, printer, 134 Fenchurch st
Bonsor Martha (Mrs.), grocer, Church st. Hackney
Bonsor Samuel, wax & tallow chandler, 433 Oxford st
Bonter John, fishmonger, Church st. Hackney
Bonus John, ship & insurance broker, see Carter & Bonus
Bonython John, appraiser, 88 Salisbury st. Lisson gr
Booby Noel Henry, chemist & druggist, 72 Crawford st

Boobbyer David&J.H.who.ironmong.14 Stanhope st.Druryla
Boodle's Club House(JohnGeo.Fuller,sec.) 28 St. James's st
Boodle & Co. conveyancers, 9 Davies st. Berkely sq
Boodle Edward, barrister, 23 Old sq. Lincoln's inn
Boodle John, jun.solicitor&clerk to the trustees of Grosvenor place district, 43 Lower Belgrave place
Book Society for Promoting Religious Knowledge (James Palmer, sec.), 19 Paternoster row
Bookbinders' Provident Institution (J. England, sec.), Balls Pond road
Booker & Sons, coach builders, 13 & 14 Mount st. Grosvenor sq. & Edmonton
Booker Thomas, Sons & Co. merchants, 59 Mark lane, City
Booker Fanny (Miss), millinr.&dressma.43Comptonst.Clkwl
Booker Geo. fishmonger, 21 Upper King st. Bloomsbury
Booker Henry, furn. broker, 61 Earl st. ea. Lisson gr.North
Booker John, butcher, 5 Sun st. Bishopsgate
Booker Wm. linendraper, 3 Middlesex ter. Hackney rd
Booker Wm. rope & twine maker, 44 Kent st. Borough
Booker Wm. upholsterer, 14 Lower Seymour st. Portman sq
Booksellers' Prov. Inst. (S. Ives, hon. sec.), 60 Patnstr.row
Bool Jas. statuary&mason, 84 Arthur st. King's rd. Chelsea
Boolds Jas. Almond, carver, 1 Warren mews, Warren st
Bools Edward, hairdresser, 4 Robson's pl. Kennington road
Boome Henry, tailor, 20 Wilderness row, Clerkenwell
Boon George, grocer, 60 Castle st. Southwark
Boon Henry, marine store dealer, 13 Coppice row, Clerknwl
Boon Jas. tobacconist, 1 Monyers st.&4 Cross st. Hoxton
Boon William, been retailer, 5 Surrey place, Walworth rd
Boone Thos. & Wm. booksellers & publishers, 29 Nw. Bond st
Boone Wm. butcher, Larkhall lane, Clapham
Boone Wm. furniture broker & undertkr. 110 Gray's inn lane
Boor John Thos. coffee rooms, 122 Lower Thames st
Boord Joseph, distiller, see Swain, Boord & Co
Boore Chas. bricklayer, 112 Waterloo road
Boore Chas. coppersmith, 34 Lit. Charlotte st. Blackfrs. rd
Boore Geo. lapidary, 16 Little Compton st. Soho
Boore Wm. dyer & scourer, 23 Maiden lane, Covent garden
Boore Wm. prepar. school, 6 St. James's ter. Camden town
Boorer Ann (Mrs.), wheelwright, 10 Glo'ster row, Wlwth.rd
Boorer Henry, linendraper, Deptford bridge
Boorman Jas. *Castle*, P.H. Youl's place, Old Kent rd
Boorman John, *Golden Hind* P.H. 16 Little Moorfields
Boorman Thomas Hughes, merchant, Baltic coffee house
Boorman Wm. grocer, 70 Upper Berkeley st. Portman sq
Boosey Thos. & Co. musicsellers, 28 Holles st. Cavendish sq
Boosey Abraham, cabinet maker, 53 Bermondsey st
Boosey Geo. Bockett, engraver & printer, 10 Rood la. Fench.st
Boote John, chemist, 24 Exmouth st. Spa fields
Booth & Co. distillers, 55 Cowcross st. West Smithfield
Booth & Fox, feather purifiers, 80 Hatton garden, & Cork
Booth Robert & Son, brokers & auctioneers to the Lords of the Admiralty, & valuers to the Court of Bankruptcy, 7 Ironmonger lane, Cheapside
Booth Benj. writer & sign pntr. 68 Monmouth st. Seven dials
Booth Charles B. solicitor, see Taylor & Booth
Booth Edwin, surgeon, 3 Great Queen st. Westminster
Booth George, brazier, 14 Ship alley, Wellclose square
Booth George, portmanteau ma. 7 Queen's sq. Barthlmw. cl
Booth George, solicitor, 4 Newman st. Oxford st
Booth Geo. Fredk. watchma. 38 Nicholas st. Hoxton new town
Booth Henry, corndlr. & seedsman, 1 Union rd. Rotherhithe
Booth Henry, stone merchant, see Brown, Rusby & Booth
Booth James, baker, Anderson's buildings, City road
Booth James, beer retailer, 11 Baker's row, Walworth road
Booth James, butcher, 13 Market st. Mayfair
Booth Jas. potato mer. 41 Baalzephon st. & Davis' wf. Boro'
Booth John, plumber, &c. 2 Palace row, New road
Booth John, stationer, 11 Frederick's place, Old Kent road
Booth John, stone mer. Willingtonwf. Augustus st. Regt.'s pk
Booth Joseph, *Duke's Head* P.H. Priest's alley, Gt. Tower st
Booth Joseph, oil & colorman, 16 Brandon st. Walworth
Booth Lionel, bookseller & stationer, Duke st. Portland pl
Booth Philander Rd. cheesemonger, 34 Freeschool st. Horsldn
Booth Richd. carpenter & undertak. 6 Huntley st. Bedford sq
Booth Richd. mechanical tool ma. & wa. 233 Blackfriars rd
Booth Robert, builder, 5 Gibson st. Waterloo road
Booth Stephen, chair manufactr. 102 Lambeth lower marsh
Booth Wm. artist, 53 Charlotte st. Fitzroy square
Booth Wm. *Ship* P.H. 19 New st. Horselydown
Booth Wm. tobacconist, 32 Edward st. Regent's park
Booth Wm. tobacconist, 28 Munster st. Regent's park
Booth Wm. Joseph, archit. & surv. 34 Red Lion sq. Holborn
Boothby Benjamin, barrister, 3 Serjeants' inn, Fleet st
Boothby Frederick, pianoforte maker, see Clark & Boothby
Boothby Margaret (Mrs.), ironm. 13 Cleveland st. Fitzroy sq
Boothby William, plumber, &c. 25 Lisle st. Leicester square
Bootheey Ann (Mrs.), earthenwa.wa. 5 High st. Stoke Newngtn
Boother John, beer retailer & grocer, Mill row, Kingsland
Bootland George, cabinet maker, 29 Hampstead road
Boott Francis, physician, 24 Gower st. Bedford square
Booty James, oil merchant, see Stringer & Booty
Booty John Gillam, solicitor, see Cameron & Booty
Boram Arthur Wm. linendraper, 3 Bowyer pl. Camberwell
Boram John, leather gun case maker, 30 Berwick st. Soho
Boraman Wm. greengrocer, 4 Prospect pl. Old Brompton
Borchardt Adolph Salomon, chiropodist, & razor strop ma. 7 New Weston st. Bermondsey
Borckhardt Chas. fruiterer, 12 Lit. Charlotte st. Goodge st
Bord Richard, wax & tallow chandler, 38 Watling st
Bord Richard, wine merchant, 6 Aldermary churchyard
Bordeaux, Toulouse & Cette Railway Company (C. T. Beke, sec.), 31 Lombard st
Bordier Julius, merchant, 3 Austinfriars
Boreham Edward, butcher, 30 South st. Manchester sq
Boreham Hen. builder, plumber, &c. 26 Wilmot st. Brunswick sq
Boreham John, bootmaker, 13 Stepney causeway
Boreham Wm. Hugh, tailor, 1 Albert pl. Hoxton Old town
Borehenger John, baker, 38 Brick lane, Spitalfields
Boreman Fred. Felix, gold laceman, 69 Sloane st.&432 Strand
Boreman John, butcher, 1 Barnsbury st. Liverpool road
Borer Chas. grocer&cheesemngr. 5 & 6 Elliott's row, Islington
Borer George, teadealer, 1 Great Chapel st. Westminster
Borer John, grocer, 37 Exmouth st. Clerkenwell
Borer Richard, grocer, 111 Upper Whitecross st. St. Luke's
Borer William, brush mnfr. see Matthew Brothers & Borer
Borley George Thos. cornchndlr. 1 Adam's terr. Hamst.road
Borley Hanh. Maria (Miss), school, 4 Bedford sq. Comml.rd
Borley John, grocer, 27 Cromer st. Brunswick square
Borley John, jeweller, 17 Princes st. Leicester square
Borley John Henry, jeweller, 75 London wall
Borley Wm. *Prince of Wales* P.H. 22 Gt. Barlow st. Maryleb
Borman James, hosier & glover, 60 Bishopsgate without
Borman Thomas, bookbinder, see Wood & Borman
Born Ambrose, merchant tailor, 13 Hanover st. Hanover sq
Born Richard, baker. 13 Rupert st. Haymarket
Borough Compter (Benjn. Law, govr.), Mill lane, Tooley st
Borough of Marylebone Joint Stock Loan & Discount Company, 127 Gt. Portland st. Oxford st
Borough of Marylebone Reform & Registration Association (Wm. Allen, secretary), 62 Warren st. Fitzroy sq
Boroughs James, baker, 16 Chichester place, Gray's inn rd
Borradaile John W. & Abraham, merchants, 34 Fenchurch st
Borradaile Wm. Sons & Ravenhill, merchts. 34 Fenchurch st
Borradaile Wm. solicitor, 20 King's Arms yard, Coleman st
Borras Robert, warehouseman, see Sugden & Borras
Borrell Geo. H. oil & color wa. 3 Haberdashers' pl. east, Hoxton
Borrell Maximilian John, wholesale watch manufacturer, 19 Wilderness row, Clerkenwell
Borrett Charles Wm. barrister, 8 New square, Lincoln's inn
Borrett Francis T. madeira mercht. see Krüger & Borrett
Borrett George, tailor, 10 Staining lane, City
Borrett James, share broker, 5 Bank chambers, Lothbury
Borrett Thomas, pork butcher, 153 Brick lane, Spitalfields
Borrett Thomas, solicitor, see White & Borrett
Borrie Peter, engineer, 3 Crescent, Minories
Borroff John, cheesemonger, 136 Church st. Shoreditch
Borrow William, tailor, 43 Amelia st. Walworth road
Borthwick George, hat manufacturer, 14 Thornton st. Dockhd
Borthwick John, baker, 30 Bell yard, Temple bar
Borthwick Michael Andrew, civil engineer, 1 Furnival's inn
Borton Edward, barrister, 1 New square, Lincoln's inn
Borton Henry, baker, 11 Long lane, West Smithfield
Borton Richard Edward, plumber, 103 Bethnal green road
Borwick George, wholesale agent for Hudson's washing & bleaching powder, 18 Aldermanbury
Bos John, professor of languages, 3 Acton pl. Kingsland rd
Bosankoe Joseph, beer retailer, 44 Jubilee st. Commercl. rd
Bosanquet, Franks & Whatman, bankers, 73 Lombard st
Bosanquet & Naghten, merchants, 32 Fenchurch st
Bosanquet Wm. Henry Francis, barrister, 1 Inner Temple la
Bosbery Thomas, linendraper, see Smith & Bosbery
Bose Henry, tailor, 146½ Leadenhall st
Bose Hermann C. *Exchange* dining rooms, 2 Change al. Cornh
Bosher Charles, grocer, &c. 10 Chichester rents, Chancery la
Bosher Esther (Mrs.), carrier, 5 South end, Knsgtn. New tn
Bosher Henry, fishmonger, 38 Theobald's rd. Red Lion sq
Bosher Leonard, cork manufacturer, 75 High Holborn
Bosher Thomas, toy warehouse, 167 Kingsland road
Bosomworth John, potato salesman, 16 Counter st. Borough
Bospidnick Wm. dairyman, 3 Tharney st. Bloomsbury
Boss Samuel & Co. tailors & habit makers, 57 Frith st. Soho

Boss Fredk. gold chain maker, 32 Sekforde st. Clerkenwell
Boss Isaac Abraham, merchant & manufacturer of glaziers' patent diamond, importer of foreign provisions & wines, coal merchant, & sole importer of the improved patent german metallic ribbed umbrella frames, 6 Bury st. St. Mary Axe
Boss Thomas, beer retailer, 45 Gt.Queen st.Lincoln's inn flds
Boss Thomas, patent gun manufacturer, 73 St. James's st
Bossey Charles, greengrocer, 2½ Hackney road
Bosswell George, stonemason, 6 Vauxhall walk
Bossy Alfd.Horsley, surgeon,3&4Brunswk pl.StkeNwngn rd
Bossy Frederick William, surgeon, East road house, City rd
Bostel Daniel Thos. carp. & builder, 17 Well st. Cripplegate
Bostell Daniel, coffee rooms, 24 Great Winchester st. City
Bostock George Western, tailor, 52 George st. Blackfriars rd
Bostock Henry Jas. who. sponge dealer, see Amos&Bostock
Bostock James, stenciller, 5 Hackney road
Bostock Jas. *BlackwallRailway hotel*, 7 London st.Fench.st
Bostock John, physician, 22 Up. Bedford place, Russell sq
Bostock Robert, coal merchant, 12 Wharf, City road basin
Bostock Thomas, copper plate printer, 6 Broad st.Golden sq
Boston David, coffee rooms, 95 Goswell st
Boston Edwin, tobacconist, 86 Goswell st
Boston Francis, hairdresser, 47 Long Acre
Boston Henry, tailor, 6 Church passage, Basinghall st
Boston James, sen. furniture broker, 10 Porter st. Soho
Boston John, beer retailer, 1 Alfred ter. Cambridge heath
Boston John, jun. brick mould maker, 79 Hackney road
Boston Joseph, *George* P.H. 58 Monmouth st. 7 dials
Boston Thomas Lamprell, tobacconist, 94 Kingsland road
Boston Wm.locksmith&bellhanger,Triangle,Mare st.Hackny
Boswall George, tripe seller, 60 Brick lane, Spitalfields
Boswall John, wine cooper, 6 Little Bush lane, Cannon st
Boswell Thomas & Samuel, plumbers, 1 New st. Kennington
Boswell Eusebius, plumber, 30 George st. Euston square
Boswell George, wheelwright, Grey Eagle st. Spitalfields
Boswell John, coal mer. Union whf.Wilton rd. Pimlico basin
Boswell John, proctor, 10 Godliman st. Doctors' commons
Boswell Sam. jun.paperhanger,18 Mansion ho.st.Kennington
Boswood John, accountant, 17 Great Winchester st. City
Boswood Thomas, chemist, 40 Lower George st. Chelsea
Boswood William, registrar of marriages, Strand Union district, 6 Bow st. Covent garden
Bosworth George, painter & glazier, 9 Ball alley, Lombard st
Bosworth George Cooper, hosier, 6 & 7 Addle st. Wood st
Bosworth James, china warehouse, 48 Poplar High st
Bosworth John, butcher, 6 Cambridge pl. Edgware road
Bosworth John, herald painter, 69 Seymour st. Euston sq
Bosworth Richard, wine merchant, 289 Regent st
Botanical Society, Geo. E. Denne, sec. 20 Bedford st. Covent garden
Boteler William, jun. barrister, 21 Old sq. Lincoln's inn
Boteler Wm. Fuller, queen's counsel, 21 Old sq.Lincoln's inn
Botevyle Thomas, tailor, 13 Duke st. Smithfield
Botham Frederick, hatter, 170 Kingsland road
Botham James, grocer, &c. 15 Goldsmith's row, Hackney rd
BothamleyThos.H.solictr.seeFreeman, Bothamley&Benthall
Botibol Isaac, feather cleaner, 24 Rathbone pl. Oxford st
Botibol Moss, plumasier & florist, 3 King st. Holborn
Botly Christphr. Geo. silver chaser, 57 Rahere st.Goswell rd
*Botolph wf.*Wilkinson&Stennett,betw.9& 13 Low. Thames st
Botschan Margaret (Mrs.), cutler, 44 Worship st. Finsbury
Bott Charles, dairyman, 57 Mount st, Berkeley sq
Bott Clement, engraver & printer, 1 Well st. Cripplegate
Bott Philip, cheesemonger, 13 Southampton st. Camberwell
Bott Thomas, upholder, &c. 28 Margaret st. Cavendish sq
Bott Wm. Robt. builder, 3 Somerset st. Portman square
Botten Charles, engineer, gas meter manufactr. brass & cock founder,&c.23 Farring.st.&10 Crawford passage, Clerknwl
Botten James, coffee rooms, 10 Exeter st. Sloane st
Botterill Brothers, upholders, 37 Northumberland pl.Com.rd
Botterill Geo. coffee rooms, 113 Shoe la. & 129 Chancery la
Botting Henry, dairyman, 34 George st. Portman sq
Botting Wm. carpenter & builder, 26 East st. Manchester sq
Botting Wm. trimming seller, 15 St.George's pl.Cambwl.rd
Bottjer Gerd, cheesemonger, 260 Poplar High st
Bottom Joseph, butcher, 39 Chapel st. Pentonville
Bottomley Albert David & Co. outfitters & ship agents, 81 Gracechurch st
Bottomley Henry, embosser, 2 Bell yd.Gt.Carter la.Doct.Com
Bottomley Rachel (Miss), furrier, 9 Essex pl. Mare st.Hackny
Bottomley Sampson Hugh, grocer, 26 Warner st.NewKent rd
Bottomley Thomas, confectioner, 60 Strutton ground, Westm
Bottomley Thos. Gabriel, seal engra.60 Strutton grnd.Westm
Bottomley Wm. merchant & ship owner, 13 Broad st. bldgs
Botton Henry, butcher, 76 George st. Portman sq
Botton James, tailor, 59 Berwick st. Soho
Bottone Emilio, wine merchant, 1 Old Cavendish st
Bottrell Thomas, boot & shoe maker, 273 Poplar High st
Bottrell Thomas, hosier & glover, 17 Barnsbury pl. Islington
Bottriell Thomas, baker, 1 White st. Bethnal green
Bottrill Wm. butcher, 41 New Rochester row, Westminster
Botwright & Kemp, chemists, 2 Trinity row, Upper st. Islingt
Botwright John, baker, 86 London road, Southwark
Bouard Alfred Francois, french advocate, 5 Chancery lane
Bouch John & Co. cigar boxmaker, 26 Old Glos'ter st.Hoxton
Bouch Joseph & Co. who. linendrap. 7 Russia row & 2 Milk st
Bouch Benjamin, *Bakers' Arms* P.H.48Crescent st.Euston sq
Bouch John, warehouseman, see Luck, Bouch & Coath
Bouchard Thomas, beer retailer, 39 Chicksand st. Whitech
Bouche Edward, furniture brok. 9 Watts bldgs. Kingsld. rd
Boucher William & John, butchers, 201 Kingsland road
Boucher Wm. Richard & Co. potters & glassmen to her Majesty & the Hon. East India Company, 128 Leadenhall st
Boucher Anthony, solicitor, 6 Gray's inn square
Boucher Benj. John, cheesemonger, 26 George st. Portm. sq
Boucher James, tobacconist, 61 Myddelton st. Clerkenwell
Boucher James, *King's Arms* P. H. 27 Aldersgate st
Boudard Hypolite, importer of french kid, 56 Bread st
Bouffler James, tailor, 6 Cloth fair, West Smithfield
Boughey Catherine (Mrs.), hosier, 12 Union ct. Old Broad st
Boughey William F. F. barrister, 3 Brick ct. Temple
Boughton & Grinsted, stockbrokers, 11 Throgmorton st
Boughton George, tailor, 63 King st. Soho
Boughton Thos. grocer & cheesemonger, Bridge rd. Battersea
Boulcott John & Co. oil merchts. Paul's whf. 23 Up.Thames st
Boulcott John & Son, ship biscuit bakers, 80 Wapping wall
Boulcott Joseph & Co. timber merchants, Narrow st. Ratcliff
Bould Jonathan, *Champion* P. H. Bond st. Vauxhall
Boulden John Tonge, grocer, 23 Earl st. East, Lisson grove
Boulding Edward, musical ins. ma. 7 New st. Kennington rd
Boulding James, bookseller &c. 140 Upper st. Islington
Boullancourt Augustus, surgeon dentist, 19 Frith st. Soho
Boully Peter, chemist & drugst. 6 Grove ter.Qn's.rd.Bayswa
Boulnois John, upholsterer, 14 Charlotte st. Rathbone place
Boulnois William, bazaar, 58 Baker st. & 5 King st.Portm.sq
Boult Amelia (Miss), dressmaker, 13 Bedford st. Covent gar
Boult Henry, soapmaker, see Baxter, Boult & Co
Boult Henry, merchant, &c. Red Lion wharf, Up. Thames st
Boult John Stphn. coffee rooms, 30 Russell court, Drury la
Boult Joseph, architect, 38 Gower place, Euston square
Boult Joseph, wheelwright, Hornton st. Kensington
Boult Louisa A.(Miss), prof. of music, 13 Bedford st. Covent gar
Boulter Edward & Co. cotton mnfr. 11 Queen st. Cheapside
Boulter Edmund, gen.commer. agt.5 Northampton sq.Clkwl
Boulter John, turner, 190 Kent street, Borough
Boulter Joseph, tobacconist, 68 Brunswick st. Blackwall
Boulter Robert, tailor, 62 Bridge road, Lambeth
Boulter Samuel, *Bell* P.H. 5 Leicester st. Leicester sq
Boulter Samuel, cooper, Baldwin st. Old st. St. Luke's
Boulter Sam. watchma.12UpperGlos'ter pl.King'srd.Chelsea
Boulter Samuel John, surgeon, 11 King's road east, Chelsea
Boulter Thomas, fruiterer, 53 Albany st. Regent's park
Boulter Thomas Beavois, baker, 230 Bethnal green road
Boulter William, *Waterloo Arms* P.H. George st.Camberwell
Boulting George, locksmith, &c. 32 Warren st. Fitzroy sq
Boulting John, jun.ironmonger, 16&17 Union st. Middlesex hos
Boulting William, house painter, &c. 60 George st. Euston sq
Boulton, Watt & Co. engineers, 18 London street, Fenchurch street, & Soho, Birmingham
Boulton Benjamin, haberdasher, 2 Dorset st. Clapham road
Boulton Elizabeth (Mrs.), butcher, 3 Princes rd. Lambeth
Boulton Francis, *Coach & Horses* P.H. 4 Flood st.Westminst
Boulton Fredk. Horatio, solicitor, see Pool & Boulton
Boulton Geo. pin & needle maker, by special appointment to H.M. Qu. Victoria & the Qu. Dowager, 12 Gt. Dover st. Boro',& 58 Kent st. Boro
Boulton John, patten ma. 54 Vauxhall walk, & 32 Cloth fair
Boulton Robt. laceman & hosier, 21 Lamb st. Spitalfields
Boulton Samuel, wh. milliner, 2 Whiskin st. Clerkenwell
Boulton Thos.boot & shoe maker, 2 St.Dunstan's all. Tower st
Boulton Thomas, needle maker, 13 Cook's ct. Lincoln's inn
Boulton Wm. potato salesman, South rw. Covent gardn. mkt
Boulton William, builder, 15 Compton street, Clerkenwell
Boulton William, tailor, 15 Marchmont st. Brunswick sq
Boulton William James, attorney, 21A, Northampton square
Bound Henry, tailor, 5 St. James place, Hampstead road
Boundy James, *Apollo* coffee rooms, 26 Mercer st. Long acre
Boundy Joseph, bricklayer, 12 Ivy lane, Hoxton
Bounsall John Tyesh, hosier, &c. 24 Burlington arcade
Boura Emily & Fanny (Misses), milliners, 26 Maddox st
Boura Aimé, dyer & scourer, 31 Rathbone place

Bourdieu James & Sons, merchants, 45 Lime st
Bourdillon James & Son, solicitors, 2 Austin friars passage, & 30 Great Winchester st
Bourdillon Charles, barrister, 9 Old square, Lincoln's inn
Bourdillon Thos. barrister, 3 Stone buildings, Lincoln's inn
Bourdin Dominick F. teacher of dancing, 36 Bryanstone st
Bourdin Madame, teacher of dancing, 36 Bryanstone st
Bourdon Frederick, silk dyer, 50 Worship st. Finsbury sq
Bourdon Jacques Louis & Co. woolcombers (french system), 196 Bermondsey st
Bourgeard Louis, boot maker, 46 Castle st. Leicester sq
Bourgoin Helene (Mrs.), artificial florist, 34 Manchester st
Bowin Edward Cook & Sons, tailors, 66 Lamb's Conduit st
Bourn Joseph, boot & shoe maker, 207 Bermondsey st
Bourn Joseph, ship & insurance agent, 49 Lime st
Bourn Wm. jun. lighterman, 12 Garford st. Limehouse hole
Bourne Edward Cook&Son,furriers&hat.19Lamb'sConduit st
Bourne & Gye, agency office, 16 Bouverie st. Fleet st
Bourne & Son, tailors, 66 Lamb's Conduit st. & 2 Princes st. Hanover square
Bourne Alfred, butcher, 31 Watling st. City
Bourne Alfred, carpenter, 30 President st. East
Bourne Alfred, merchant, 30&31, Clement's lane, Lombard st
Bourne George, grocer, 23 Wellington place, Stepney
Bourne Herbert, imp. & french ware. see Collin & Bourne
Bourne James, artist, 7 Somerset st. Portman square
Bourne James, bootmaker, 46 Roebuck place, Gt. Dover st
Bourne John, boot & shoe maker, 47 Leadenhall st
Bourne John, tailor & lodging ho. 10 & 11 Crutchedfriars
Bourne John, teadealer, 4 Friendly place, Old Kent road
Bourne John Cook, artist, 14 Buckingham st. Strand
Bourne Joseph, derbyshire stone bottle & jar warehouse, 126 London wall, & 4 Wharf, south side, Paddington basin
Bourne Maria (Mrs.), lodging house,37Somersetst. Prtmn.sq
Bourne Sarah (Mrs.), beer retlr. 115 Eastfield st. Limeho. fds
Bourne Thos. cheesemonger, 31 Lit. Newport st. Long acre
Bourne Thos. china dealer, 64 Tower st. Westminster rd
Bourne Thomas, fruiterer, 2 Aylesbury pl. Old Kent road
Bourne William, appraiser, 58 Museum st. Bloomsbury
Bourne William, cabinet manufr. 23 Aldgate
Bourne Wm. sec. to North.& Eastern Railway Co. Shoreditch
Bourne William, grocer, 109 Blackman st
Bourner Jas. & Co. van office, *Lewes Arms*, Grey terrace, Gt. Dover st. & Moore's, *New inn*, Old Change
Bourquin Francis Henry, watch manf. 65 Coleman st
Boursot Adolphe, wine mer. & agent, 9 Hart st. Crutched frs
Bourton Joseph, saddler & harness maker,64Borough High st
Bousfield Geo. & Co. woollen warehomen. 60 Gracechurch st
Bousfield John R. & Co. who. clothes wareh. 26 Houndsditch
Bousfield John R. & Thos. & Wm. who. slopsellers, see Favell & Bousfield's
Bousfield Saml. & Co. linen warehsmn.15 King st. Cheapside
Bousfield Chas. P. silk manufactr. see Lea, Bousfield & Co
Bousfield Fredk. stationer & accountant, 29 Thayer st
Bousfield Robt. woollen draper, see Regless, Sherret & Co
Bousfield Sarah (Mrs.), lodging house, 31 Surrey st. Strand
Bousfield Stephen, grocer, 135 Edgware road, Marylebone
Bousfield Thomas, slopseller, see Favell & Bousfield
Bousfield William, slopseller, see Favell & Bousfield
Bousfield Wm. stout & pale ale agent, 30 St. Mary at hill
Bousfield Wm. wine & spirit merchant, 30 St. Mary at hill
Bousfield William Cheek, solicitor, 7 Coleman st. city
Boutcher, Mortimore&Co. leather fac.6 Leather mkt. Bermond
Boutcher Emanuel, merchant, see Ricketts, Boutcher & Co
Boutcher William, tobacconist, 27 Water lane, Blackfriars
Boutcher Wm. wine merchant, see Ricketts, Boutcher & Co
Boutell Sarah (Mrs.), carpenter & joiner, 8 George ct. Picdily
Boutillier David, linendraper, 4 Northumberld. pl. Com. rd. e
Boutle John, shoe manufacturer, 21 King street, Tower hill
Boutroy Henry, tailor, 3 Argyll street, Regent street
Bouts & Ellis, hide, &c. factors, 1 Leadenhall st. Hide mrkt
Bouts Thomas & Son, wine & spirit merchants, 25 Barbican
Bouts John, *WeymouthArms* P.H.33Weymouthter.Hcknyrd
Bouts William, importer of cigars, 25 Barbican
Boutwell Thomas, carpenter, 35 Chapel street, New road
Bouverie, Norman & Murdoch, bankers, 11 Haymarket
Bovet Frederic & Alphouse, merchants,24 East India chambers; & 7 Duncan terrace, City road
Bovey Chas. engine turner, 5 Corporation row, St. John st
Bovey Edward, oil & colorman, 1 Steven's pl. New North rd
Bovey John, *King's Arms* P.H. 7 Old Compton street, Soho
Bovey John, tailor, 24 Little Bell alley, Coleman st. City
Bovey Mary Ann (Mrs.), lace cleaner, 21B, Frith st. Soho
Bovill Benj.&Sons, corn&coalmer. Milford la. Strand&Corn Ex
Bovill Benjamin, corn & seed factor, 75 Mark lane
Bovill George Hinton, engineer, see Swayne & Bovill
Bovill William, barrister, 11 Paper buildings, Temple
Bovingdon James, teadealer, 2 Crown place, Old Kent road
Bovingdon Susanna (Miss), milliner, &c.60Lamb'sConduit st
Bovingdon William, pork butcher, 24 Gray's inn lane
Bow Charles, cabinet maker, 21 Crawford st. Portman sq. & 24 Harcourt st. New road, Marylebone
Bow Robt. carpenter & builder, 52 Crawford st. Portman sq
Bowcher Fred. James, engraver, 56 Newman st. Oxford st
Bowcher John, bricklayer, 30 Great Bush lane, Cannon st. & 8 Somerset street, Aldgate
Bowcher John, currier & leather peak ma. 28 Greek st. Soho
Bowden Edw. & Ambrose, chemists, 13 Charles st. St. James'
Bowden John Saunders & Son, attorneys, 66 Aldermanbury
Bowden Charles, dyer, 27 Ebury street, Pimlico
Bowden Charles, hairdresser, Mare street, Hackney
Bowden Eliza (Miss), tobacconist, 49½ Cheyne walk, Chelsea
Bowden George, cabinetmaker, 4WhiteLion st. Norton folgate
Bowden George, house, &c. painter 14 Bland terr. Gt. Dover rd
Bowden George, *Wenlock Arms* P.H. Wenlock rd. City rd
Bowden Henry Martin, general merchant, 43 Lime st
Bowden Hugh Charles, general & commission merchant, 18 New East India chambers, Leadenhall street
Bowden HughCharles, agent for McKibbins' boiler sheathing, roofing & rail felts, 18 Ea. India chambers, Leadenhall st
Bowden John, *Belvedere* brewery, Vine street, Lambeth
Bowden John Thomas, tailor, 4 Hand court, Holborn; & 16 North place, Kingsland road
Bowden Joseph, cabinetmaker, 4 James pl. Hoxton fields
Bowden Mary (Mrs.), hairdresser, 63 King st. Westminster
Bowden Susannah (Mrs.), hat manufr.13Charles st. Blkfrs.rd
Bowden William, *Chalk Farm* P.H. Hampstead road
Bowden William, tailor, 23 Kingsgate street, Holborn
Bowdery & Kerby, booksellers & stationers, 190 Oxford st
Bowdery Geo. soapmaker, 32 Green st. Wellington st. Blkfrs
Bowdery William, tailor, 78 Lisson grove, North
Bowdigde Hen. stables, 4 South mews, Manchester sq
Bowditch Henry, corndealer, 13 Old Dorset pl. Clapham rd
Bowditch Henry, miller & corn dlr. 1 Dorset st. Clapham rd
Bowditch Hugh, corndealer, &c. 64 Blackfriars road
Bowditch James, solicitor, 70 Chancery lane
Bowditch Thomas, corn factor, High street, Deptford
Bowditch William, coal dealer, 9 Russell pl. Old Kent road
Bowdler Amos, bootmaker, 12A, Allington st. Pimlico
Bowdler Charles, proctor, see Bathurst & Bowdler
Bowdler Nathaniel, *Nag's Head* P.H. 70 Cotton st. Poplar
Bowdler Nathaniel, plumber, 11 Bulstrode mews, Marylbn. la
Bowdon Jas. trunk&portmanteau ma. 259 Borough High st
Bowdon William, *King's Head* P.H. 17 Leather la. Holborn
Bowe Elizabeth (Mrs.), commerc. boarding ho. 29 Falcon sq
Bowe John Joseph, furrier, 29 Falcon sq. Aldersgate street
Bowe Thos. linendraper & hosier, 70 Gt. Queen st. Linc. inn fl
Bowen Charles & Co. wine & spirit merchants, 22 Harp lane
Bowen & Godwin, paper stainers, 1 Macclesfield st. Soho
Bowen John & Son, poulterers, &c. 66 George st. Portman sq
Bowen & Sanford, wholes. & retail stationers, 315 Oxford st
Bowen Ann (Mrs.), haberdasher, 4 Cow cross st. Smithfield
Bowen Arthur, potato salesm. 17½ Mill lane & 53 Tooley st
Bowen Augustus Fred. bootmaker, 1 Earl's ct. Leicester sq
Bowen Cornelius, coffee rooms, 47 Baalzephon street
Bowen David, tailor, 78 John street, Fitzroy square
Bowen Edward, stationer, 70 Great Suffolk street, Borough
Bowen Henry, hatter, 131 High street, Camden town
Bowen James, glove manufacturer, 23 Queen's row, Pimlico
Bowen Jas. oilman&tallowchandler, 8 Panton st. Haymarket
Bowen Jas. wine & beer merchant, 30 Swallow st. Piccadilly
Bowen John, greengrocer, 3 Charles street, Westminster
Bowen John, tailor, 19 Hastings st. Burton crescent
Bowen John, watch ma.&goldsmith, 2 Tichborne st. Haymrkt
Bowen John, jun. poulterer, 50 Wigmore st. Cavendish sq
Bowen John Robert, carman, 4 Heneage st. Whitechapel
Bowen Mary A. (Mrs.), brass&bellfndr. 62 Redlion st. Clerkenwl
Bowen William, *Adam & Eve* P.H. 82 York st. Westminstr
Bowen William, linendraper, 238 High st. Poplar
Bower Benjamin & Son, orangemerch. 106 Lower Thames st
Bower Emma & Maria (Misses), art. florists, 67 Hatton gdn
Bower James & Son, bakers, 5 Tothill street, Westminster
Bower Joshua & Co. orange merchants, 8 Botolph lane
Bower Joshua & Co. crown glass&gluemanufacturers, wholesale & retail & for exportation, 15 Old Bailey; manufactory at Leeds
Bower (Thos. Holme) & Son, solicitors, 46 Chancery lane
Bower Alethea (Miss), teadealer, 40 Carnaby st. Golden sq
Bower Alfred, surgeon, 102 Curtain road, Shoreditch
Bower Charles, grocer, 39 Salisbury st. Lisson grove
Bower Charles, upholsterer, &c. Belmont row, Wandsworth rd
Bower Charles, solicitor, 52 Welbeck st. Cavendish sq

Bower Francis, working jeweller, 9A, Mill st. Hanover sq. & 10 Maddox st. Bond st
Bower George, solicitor, see Willis, Bower & Willis
Bower John dining rooms, 158 Church street, Shoreditch
Bower John, engine, lathe & tool mak. 13 King st. Clerkenwl
Bower Mark Noble, surgeon, 95 Hatton garden
Bower Sidney, wine & spirit merchant, 13 Sise lane
Bower Thos. architect & surveyor, 10 James pl. Hoxton fld
Bower William, baker, 5 Sloane square, Chelsea
Bower William, chemist, 96 Tottenham court road
Bower William, dining rooms, 92 Golden lane, Barbican
Bower Wm. linendraper, 2 Gray's place, Fulham road
Bower William, staymaker, 30 Beech st. Barbican
Bowerbank Edward & Sons, distillers, 77½ Sun st. Bishopsg
Bowerman Benjamin, butcher, 7 St. James pl. Bermondsey
Bowerman Chas. butcher, Grangepl. Grange rd. Bermondsy
Bowerman Thomas, tobacconist, 60 Upper Ebury st. Pimlico, & 15 Arabella row, Pimlico
Bowers Nathaniel & Son, comb makers, 43 Cannon st
Bowers Chas. Hyatt, linendraper, 18 Cannon st. road
Bowers Charles Read, sack hire wareho. mast, oar & block maker, Flockton's whf. Potter's fields, & 9 Horselydown la
Bowers George, house painter, 12 Orange st. Red Lion sq
Bowers John, butcher, 54 Golden lane, Barbican
Bowers John, linendraper, &c. see North & Bowers
Bowers John, *Percy Arms* P.H. 1 Great Percy st. Clerkenwl
Bowers Joseph, ladder maker, 32 Hayfield pl. Mile end road
Bowers Thomas, *Horse & Groom* P.H. 3 Turnmill st. Clerknwl
Bowers Thomas, painter, 87 Paul street, Finsbury
Bowers Wm. butcher, 12 Thornton st. Freeschool st. Dock hd
Bowers Wm. fruiterer, 15 Old Fish st
Bowers Wm. potato dealer, 3 Devonshire pl. Commrcl. rd. East
Bowers Wm. wheelwright, 13 Thornton st. Dock head
Bowes, Son & Johnston, insurance, oil, and russia brokers, 73 Old Broad street, City
Bowes Charles, carpenter & surveyor, Battersea rise
Bowes Philip, accountant & arbitrator, 11 Powell st. East, King square, & 4 Whiterose court, Coleman st.
Bowie John, *Golden Shears* P.H. 84 Wood st. Cheapside
Bowie Robert, surgeon, 12 Billiter square & 44 Burr st. East Smithfield
Bowie Robert, jun. surgeon, 135 Whitechapel High st
Bowker David, coffee rooms, 68 Aldersgate st
Bowker James, bootmaker, 119 Fetter lane, Fleet st
Bowker James, solicitor, see Barker & Bowker
Bowker Thomas, beer retailer, Battersea
Bowker William, attorney, 1 Gray's inn square
Bowkett Thos. Edwd. surgeon, 6 & 7 India row, East India rd
Bowland Samuel, tobacconist, 95 Wardour st. Soho
Bowler James, hat manufactr. Bridge st. Southwark
Bowler Charles, baker, 184 Fleet street
Bowler Elizabeth (Mrs.), straw hat ma. 25 Grafton st. Soho
Bowler Jas. last maker, 22 Upper Cleveland st. Fitzroy sq
Bowler Martha (Mrs.), *Star & Garter* P.H. Church st. Batrsea
Bowler Robert Ewen, artist, 17 Judd place West, New road
Bowler Wm. *Antigallican* P.H. 5 Darkhouse la. Billingsgate
Bowles & Gardiner, wholesale stationers, 49 Newgate st
Bowles Ann (Mrs.), coffee rooms, 3 Hart st. Grosvenor sq
Bowles Barnard, greengrocer, 4A, St. Mary at hill
Bowles Frances (Mrs.), milliner, 10 Blandford st. Portman sq
Bowles George, basket & chair mfr. 5 Upper Rupert st. Soho
Bowles George, carman, 179 Drury lane
Bowles George, chandler's shop, Wandsworth road
Bowles James, printer, 1 Taymouth ter. Philpot st. Com. rd. Ea
Bowles James, stationer, &c. 188 High Holborn
Bowles John, butcher, 48 Broad st. Bloomsbury
Bowles John, *Coach & Horses* P.H. 29 Greek st. Soho
Bowles John, *Coach & Horses* P.H. 56 Minories
Bowles John, wheelwright, 118 Tyer st. Lambeth
Bowles John, saddle & harness ma. 5 Wilson st. Drury lane
Bowles John Christopher, general agent, 77 Cannon st. City
Bowles John Henry, barrister, 2 Middle Temple lane
Bowles Stephen, shell fishmonger, 15 New st. Covent garden
Bowles Wm. auctioneer & ho. agt. 58 Gt. Coram st. Brunswick sq
Bowles Wm. silk & cotton dyer, 33 Gt. Bush la. Cannon st
Bowles William, surveyor, 23 Haverstock hill
Bowley James & Co. ship joiners, Emmett st. Poplar
Bowley Thomas & Co. tea brokers, 25 Eastcheap
Bowley Charles John, tobacconist, 3 Deptford High st
Bowley Joseph, tallow chandler & soap maker, 67 Tothill st. Westminster & 52 Paradise row, Chelsea
Bowley Robert Kanzow, bootmaker, see Taylor & Bowley
Bowley Wm. carpenter, 69 Tothill st. Westminster
Bowley Wm. oilman & tallow chandler, 110 Tottenham ct. rd
Bowling Iron Company, **(Joseph Freeman, agent,) 8 St. Swithin's lane, City**
Bowling Jacob Saml. wire worker, 146 High st. Camden twn
Bowling, Walker & Co. druggists & italian wa. 18 Kent st. Boro'
Bowman Frederick & Son, sugar refiners, 27 Great Alie st
Bowman & May, scotch and manchester warehousemen, 3 Wood st. & 34 Milk st. Cheapside
Bowman Charles, sugar refiner, Church lane, Commercl. rd
Bowman David, grocery, oil & italian warehouse, 3 Tottenham court road, & 118 Wardour st. Oxford st
Bowman Frederick, dealer in Bramah's patent locks & pens, manufacturer of desks, dressing cases, &c. 9 Old Bond st
Bowman George, auctioneer, appraiser, house & estate agent, 7 High st. Deptford
Bowman Henry, undertaker, 3 Brownlow st. Drury lane
Bowman John, grocer, 14 Middle Queen's blds. Knightsbridge
Bowman Joseph, merchant, 2 Walbrook buildings
Bowman Joseph, mercht. see Monkhouse, Winter & Bowman
Bowman Joseph, warehouseman, see May & Bowman
Bowman Kemp, furniture broker, see Redshaw & Bowman
Bowman Robert, carver & gilder, 136 Fleet st
Bowman Robert, chaser, 18 Great James st. Hoxton
Bowman Robert, wine & brandy mer. 3 Clement's la. Lombard st
Bowman Robert Moore, wine merchant, Auction mart
Bowman Sarah (Mrs.), baker, 45 Southampton blds. Chancy. la
Bowman Thomas, tailor, 9 Beauchamp st. Holborn
Bowman William, F.R.S. surgeon, 14 Golden square
Bowne John, coal mercht. Union wf. Grosvnr. basin, Pimlico
Bowness Geo. & Son, fishing tack. ma. 12 & 14 Bell yd. Temple bar
Bowness Geo. jun. fishing tack. ma. 33 Bell yard, Temple bar
Bowness William, artist, 14 Fitzroy st. Fitzroy square
Bowra Henry Goodeve, surgeon, 12A, Charterhouse square
Bowring Brothers, hosiers & outfitters, 11 Fenchurch st
Bowring & Pfleger, brokers, 123 Fenchurch st
Bowring George, archery manufactr. 127 Drummond st
Bowring Henry, colonial broker, Commercial coffee house
Bowring Henry, *Commercial coffee house*, Mincing lane
Bowring John, hosier, glover & outfitter, 38 Lombard st
Bowring Nathl. house est. agt. & regstr. 78 Pearson st. Kgsld. rd
Bowring Samuel, colonial broker, 82 Great Tower st
Bowron Geo. bookbinder & seller & stationer, 213 Oxford st
Bowron John, cheesemonger, 62 Earl st. East, Lisson grove
Bowron John, cheesemonger, 88 Salisbury st. Lisson grove
Bowron Wm. cheesemonger, 43 Grosvenor row, Pimlico
Bowry Chas. oil & italian wareho. 11 Southampton st. Fitz. sq
Bowry Edmund, oilman, 33 Ashley crescent, City road; & 54 Fetter lane, Holborn
Bowry John, engr. & printer, 8 King's ter. Bagnigge wells rd
Bowry Thos, coffee rooms, 18 Royal Hospital row, Chelsea
Bowser Ann & Harriet, ladies' school, 3 Muscovy ct. Tower hl
Bowser & Corbett, trimming sellers, 19 Dears pl. Somers tn
Bowser John, mahogany merchant, see Browning, Bowser & Co
Bowser Wm. engineer, 50 Parson's st. St. George st
Bowstead Joseph, barrister, 5 Essex court, Temple
Bow street Police court, Covent garden, hours 10 to 5
Bowtell John & Joseph, boot & shoe makers, 131 Piccadilly, & 42 Crawford street, Portman square
Bowtell Thos. & Wm. boot ma. 19 Strand, & 152 Tottm. ct. rd
Bowtell John R. linendraper, 4 Notting hill High street
Bowtell Thos. boot & shoe ma. 58 Cheapside, & 49 Skinner st
Bowyer & Vaughan, packers, North mews, North bds. Finsbury
Bowyer Ann (Miss), stay maker, 11 Blackman st. Borough
Bowyer Edmund, wine & spirit mercht. Hungerford wharf
Bowyer George, barrister, 21 Old square, Lincoln's inn
Bowyer Jane (Mrs.), *Crown* P.H. 4 Grey Eagle st. Spitalfields
Bowyer John, french polisher, 24 Lr. Northampton st. Clknwl
Bowyer John, *New Grapes* P.H. 82 Fenchurch street
Bowyer Thomas, bricklayer, &c. 30 Weston st. Somers town
Bowyer Thomas, coal mercht. 13 Ratcliff row, John st. City rd
Box Alexander, coach wheelwright, 43 Market st. Boro' road
Box Alfred Marten, grocer & cheeseman, Bridge rd. Battersea
Box James, academy, 25 Princes st. Spitalfields
Box John, carver & gilder, 2 Gt. Smith street, Westminster
Box John (hon. sec. to the *Aged Pilgrims' Friend Society*), 13 Northampton square, office, 60 Paternoster row
Box Joseph, academy, 14 King's road, Gray's inn
Box Robert Dixon, ladies' boot & shoe maker, 187 Regent st
Box Sam. *Ben Jonson's Head* P.H. 2 Westmrlnd. bdgs. Aldrsgt
Box Thomas, fruiterer, 17 Hackney road crescent
Box William, grocer, 91 Albany st. Regent's park
Box William B. watch & chronometer manufr. 21 Upper Charles street, Northampton square
Boxall Catherine Ann (Miss), baker, 3 King st. Golden sq
Boxall Richard, booking office, 90 Gracechurch street
Boxall Rd. corndlr. & coach propr. 4 Clarence pl. Clapham rd
Boxall Stephen, bootmaker, 16 Upper East Smithfield
Boxell John, hair cutter & perfumer, 39 Norton folgate
Boxell John, *Middleton Arms* P.H. 38 Norton folgate

Boxer James, solicitor, 61 Moorgate street
Boxer Thomas, haberdasher, 33 Surrey place, Old Kent road
Boxley William, grocer, 16 Queen street, Pimlico
Boxsius Philip, furrier, 62 Chiswell street, Finsbury
Boxwell Richard, *Mischief* P.H. 414 Oxford street
Boyall Elizabeth (Mrs.), tobacconist, 10 Poultry
Boyce & Husk, meat salesmen, 3 Newgate market
Boyce Eleanor (Mrs.), cheesemonger, 79 Fenchurch street
Boyce George John, pawnbroker, 59 Lisson grove North
Boyce Geo. John, pawnbroker, 51 Theobald's rd. Red Lion sq
Boyce James, butcher, 7 King street, Cloth fair
Boyce James, tailor, 22 Clifton street North, Finsbury
Boyce John, carpenter, 9 Essex st. & 14 Hemlock ct. Carey st
Boyce John, commercial coffee ho. &c. 71 Pennyfields, Poplar
Boyce Joseph, undertaker & auctioneer, 185 Kingsland road
Boyce Mary (Miss), coffee rooms, 25 Cullum st. Fenchurch st
Boyce Richard, fruiterer, 58 Drury lane
Boyce Robert, tobacconist, 137 Waterloo road, Lambeth
Boyce Saml. Clinch, accountant & arbitrator, 4 Dowgate hill, & 79 Fenchurch st
Boyce Stephen, dairyman, 43 Park st. Camden town
Boyce Thomas, oil & colorman, 54 York road, Lambeth
Boyce Thomas, pork butcher, 18 Marylebone la. Oxford st.; & 24 Harrow road, Paddington
Boyce Wm. beer retailer, 99 Princes road, Lambeth
Boyce Wm. bootmaker, 44 Grosvenor mews, Grosvenor st
Boyce Zimri, bricklayer, 1 Glo'ster row, Lock's fields, Wlwth
Boyd Benjamin & Mark, stock brokers & resident directors of the North British Insurance Co. 4 New Bank blds. Lothbury
Boyd & Coleman, cheesemongers, 5 Pitfield street, Hoxton
Boyd & Forrett, scotch shawl ware. 24½ Friday st. Cheapside
Boyd & Harmer, silk manufacturers, 20 Spital square
Boyd James & Son, furnishing ironmongers & smiths, bath, stove, kitchen range & smoke jack makers, bell hangers, patentees of the himalaya funnel for smokey chimneys, also of the hermetic chimney valve for preventing downward currents in chimneys, when without a fire, 78 Welbeck street, Cavendish square
Boyd John & Co. hop & seed mers. 1 Wellingtn chambs. Londnbdg
Boyd John & Co. imps. of guano, 1 Wellingtn. chambs. Londonbdg
Boyd John & Christopher, warehousemen, 5, 6 & 7 Friday st
Boyds' & Thomas, merchants, 2 Moorgate street, City
Boyd Alexander (late Summers), furnishing ironmonger, stove & bath maker & bellhanger, 105 New Bond street
Boyd Archibald, upholsterer, cabinet maker & undertaker 5 Upper Marylebone street, Portland place
Boyd Edwd. resident dir. United Kingdom As. Of. 8 Waterloo pl
Boyd E. Lennox, assist. res. dir. United Assur. Of. 8 Waterloo pl
Boyd George, fruiterer, 3 Duke street, Grosvenor square
Boyd George, lace agent, 15 Staining lane, Wood street
Boyd James, sugar refiner, see Hall & Boyd
Boyd James, jun. commission agent & broker, 59 Mark lane
Boyd John Edmond, baker, 11 Grosvenor street West
Boyd Mary (Mrs.), baker, 41 Castle street East, Oxford st
Boyd Robert, baker, 17 Abingdon street, Westminster
Boyd Robert, printer, 2 York place, Upper st. Islington
Boyd Robert, res. physician, Marylebone infirmary, New rd
Boyd William, cheesemonger, 79 Bunhill row
Boyde Thomas, writer & grainer, 7 Oxford street, Stepney
Boyde William, bootmaker, 13 Gt. White lion st. Seven dials
Boydell Samuel & Charles, solicitors, 41 Queen sq. Bloomsby
Boyden John, *Duke of Wellington* P.H. 41 Lucas st. Commrcl. rd
Boyden William, dairyman, 23 Low. Smith st. Northampton sq
Boyens Henry, engineer, 45 Back Church lane, Comml. rd
Boyer James, clerk to Coopers' Company, 71 Basinghall st. & 93 Newgate st
Boyer James, grocer & teadealer, 93 Newgate street
Boyer James, painter & glazier, 119 Fetter lane
Boyer James, painter, 62 Upper Ground st. Blackfriars
Boyer Joseph Marie, mercht. 3 St. Michael's alley, Cornhill
Boyer Nicholas, leather gilder, 21 Gloucester st. Queen sq
Boyes George M. auctioneer, accountant, estate agent, &c. 35 Abchurch lane
Boyes James Wm. foreign cigar mer. 14 Angel court, Bank
Boyes Jane (Mrs.), lodging house, 6 Cecil st. Strand
Boyland James Wallis, cupper & dentist, 34 Sloane st
Boyle, Bryden & Co. surveyors & house & land agents, 290 Regent st. & 10 Albion place, Hyde park square
Boyle Jas. W. & Co. hearth rug ma. 7½ Cleveland st. Fitz. sq
Boyle William & Co. house decorators, 41 Ludgate hill
Boyle Alexander, law stationer, 10 Gray's inn pl. Gray's inn
Boyle Cornelius, who. stationer, see Williams, Coopers' & Co
Boyle Edward, silkmercer & linendraper, 43 Farringdon st. & 79 Holborn bridge
Boyle Frederick, solicitor, see Hoppe & Boyle
Boyle James, barrister, 4 Essex court, Temple
Boyle James, law stationer, 50 Carey st. Lincoln's inn fields
Boyle James, *Victoria* P.H. 30 Ernest st. Regent's park
Boyle Patrick A. surgeon, 31 Cardington st. Hampstead rd
Boyle Patterson, umbrella maker, 333A, Oxford st
Boyle Robert, school, 9 Steyman's row, Holloway road
Boyle Salome (Mrs.), linendraper, 36 St. John st. Clerkenwell
Boyle Wallace, mineral album works, 28 George's row, Cityrd
Boyle William, jeweller & watch maker, 28 Cheapside, & 5 Castle st. Falcon square
Boyle Wm. watchmaker & undertaker, 11 Arundel st. Strand
Boyle Wm. Ansell, solicitor, see Blake & Boyle
Boyle Wm. Robt. Augustus, barrister, 5 New sq. Lincoln's inn
Boyls Rebecca (Mrs.), library, 19 James st. Oxford st
Boyls Wm stationer & news agent, 4 Bowling st. Marylebone
Boyman Boyman, sec. *Brighton, Lewes & Hastings Railway*, 11 King William st. City
Boyn John, wine & spirit mercht. 2 Catherine st. Tower hill
Boyn John, jun. wine mer. & com. agt. 2 Crooked la. chambers
Boyne Charles, tobacconist, 3 Amelia pl. Walworth road
Boyne Robert, tobacco & snuff manfr. 1 St. George st
Boyne Robert, tobacco manufacturer, 115 St. George st
Boynton Robert, greengrocer, 1 Pelham rd. Brompton
Boys James & Co. wholesale teadealers, 12 Gt. St. Helen's
Boys Daniel, solicitor, see Hale, Boys & Austen
Boys George, lodging house, 29 Bread street, Cheapside
Boys Henry, teacher of music, 15 Dorset st. Portman square
Boys James, tailor, 18 Great Smith street, Westminster; & 11 Stockbridge terrace, Pimlico
Boys John, tailor, 82 Cornwall road, Lambeth
Boys Mary S. (Mrs.), straw bonnet ma. 18 Gt. Smith st. Westm
Boys Nicholas, law statnr. 22 Henrietta st. Cavendish sq
Boys Thos. builder & bricklayer, 29 Up. Clifton st. Finsbury
Boys Thomas, butcher, Bath terrace, Camberwell New road
Boys Thomas, print publisher, 11 Golden square
Boyse George, painter & glazier, 30 Paradise row, Rotherhithe
Boyse Robert, bricklayer, Stringer's row, Lwr. rd. Rotherhithe
Boyson & Hoyer, merchants, 1 Crown ct. Threadneedle st
Boyson Augus. ship & insu. broker, 11 Gould sq. Crutched frs
Boyton Chas. silver spoon ma. 26 Wellington st. Goswell st
Boyton William, tailor, 56 Park street, New st. Dorset sq
Bozier Joseph, chair & sofa maker & upholsterer, 74 Willow walk, Curtain road, Shoreditch
Bozon Frederick, solicitor, 27 Bucklersbury
Brabant Wm. Hughes, solicr. see Capron, Brabant & Capron
Brabham Eliz. (Mrs.), chemist & druggist, 141 Poplar High st.
Brabrook John, tobacconist, 55 Parliament street
Braby Jas. & John, wheelwrights, &c. 22 Duke st. Stamford st
Braby Edward, veterinary surgeon, 20 Park st. Boro
Brace Edward, dairy, 40 Rawstorne street, Goswell road
Brace Eliza (Miss), baby linen wareh. 11 Crown st. Finsbury
Brace George, solicitor, 24 Surrey street, Strand
Brace James George, baker, 39 Shouldham st. Edgware rd
Brace Joseph, tanner, Richardson st. Long lane, Bermondsey
Brace Thomas, solicitor, 25 Surrey st. Strand
Brace Wm. brewer, Goodman's yard, Minories
Brace Wm. cooper, 6 Little Marylebone st. Cavendish sq
Bracebridge Jas. & Edwd. Chas. watchma. 8 Red Lion st. Clkwl
Bracey William, solicitor & notary, 63 Old Broad st. City
Bracher Edward B. meat salesman, 29 Newgate market
Bracher Frederick, breeches ma. & tailor, 23 Old Jewry
Bracher George, breeches maker, 2 Copthall buildings
Bracher William, painter & decorator, 15 Gt. Ormond st
Bracher William, turner, 6 Red Lion court, Spitalfields
Brack John, painter, 21 York st. Commercial road East
Brackenbury Samuel, bootmaker, 10 Long la. Bermondsey
Bradbear William, cabinetmaker, 123 Curtain road, Shoreditch
Bradbee Geo. Whiffin, fringe & trimmg. ma. 115 Newgate st
Bradbee Rebecca (Mrs.), fancy trimming wareh. 54 Wood st
Bradbeer John, builder, 16½ Up. Southwick st. Edgware rd
Bradberry & Co. spectacle maks. 28 Holles st. Cavendish sq
Bradbery Sarah (Mrs.), bookseller, 2 Michael's pl. Brompton
Bradbrook Edwin, cowkeeper, 3 High Timber st. Up. Thames st
Bradbrook Geo. plumbr. paintr. & glazr. 108 Park st. Camdn. tn
Bradbrook Jas. *Cherry Tree* P.H. 1 Bowling green la. Clerkwl
Bradbrook Susanh. (Miss), tobacconist, 7 Compton st. Clerkwl
Bradbrook William John, baker, 43 Bethnal green road
Bradbury & Evans, printers, 1 to 6 Lombard st. Whitefriars, & 90 Fleet street
Bradbury, Greatorex & Beall, warehousemen, 79 Basinghall st
Bradbury Thos. S. & Co. mustard ma. & drug gr. 2 Moor la. Criplg
Bradbury Thomas & Son, silverplaters, 30 Bouverie st
Bradbury Ambrose, pawnbrok. & clo. salesm. 40 London rd
Bradbury Geo. *Masons' Arms* P.H. Richmnd. pl. Ea. st. Wlwth
Bradbury Geo. who. ironmonger, see Dodgson & Bradbury
Bradbury Henry, dentist, 8 Laurie terrace, Westminster road
Bradbury John, soda water maker, 19 Worship st. Finsbury

Bradbury William, tailor, 2 Mortimer st. Cavendish sq
Bradbury Wm. water cress salesman, Long market, Cov.gar
Braddick James, cheesemonger, 24 Grosvenor row, Pimlico
Braddick William, dairyman, 422 Oxford st
Braddock Mary (Mrs.), grocer, 38 Lower Islington terrace
Braddon Henry, attorney, 15 Cook's court, Carey st
Braden Alex.& Co. grocer&groat mfs.84 St.John st. Smithfd
Braden Alexr. Samuel, teadealer, 13 High st. Pentonville
Braden Herman, sugar refiner, 11 Denmark st. St. Geo.East
Braden Robt. fishmonger, 22 Upper York st. Bryanstone sq
Bradfeild Jsph. Crathorne,gasfitter,9Warwick st. Regent st
Bradfield James, blindmaker, 5 Clarence place, Regent's pk
Bradfield John, teadealer & brewer, 48 London wall
Bradfield Rebecca(Miss),millnr.21LittleWindmill st.Hymkt
Bradfield William Henry, optician, 31 Royal st. Lambeth
Bradford & Harrison, bedding wareho.1 Gt. Dover st. Boro'
Bradford Robt. & Co. merchts. & ins. broks. 27 Austinfriars
Bradford Alfred, *WhiteHorse*P.H.38Assembly row,Mile end
Bradford Charles, cheesemonger, 70 Boston pl. Dorset sq
Bradford David, cooper, Nelson place, Old Kent road
Bradford Edward, tailor, 8 Huntley street, Bedford square
Bradford Eliza (Mrs.), lodging house, 34 Arundel st. Strand
Bradford George, cptician, 99 Minories
Bradford John, undertaker, 34 Golden la. Barbican
Bradford John, haberdasher, 9 Stepney Old road
Bradford John, paper hanger & decorator, 4 Bride la. Fleet st
Bradford John, teadealer, 56 Gt. Titchfield st. Oxford st
Bradford Samuel Jas. fishmonger, 1 Lower Kennington green
Bradford Thomas, tailor, 15 Stepney High street
Bradford Wm. bonnet maker, 125 St. George street
Bradford Wm. George, tailor, 38 Bucklersbury
Bradfute Wm. insurance broker, Lloyd's
Bradick William, bedstead maker, 10 West st. Seven dials
Brading Hen. *RoyalAlbertSaloon*,17Shepherdess wk.City rd
Bradley, Barnard & Co. accountants, arbitrators & agents, 6 Bow church yard, City; & Albion chamb. Small st. Bristol
Bradley James & Andrew, china & glass dealers, 47 Pall mall
Bradley Joseph & Son, bricklayers, 125 Upper st. Islington
Bradley Wm.&Co. globe iron foundry, 2 Gt.Guildford st.Boro'
Bradley Ann (Mrs.), shoemaker, 109 Shoreditch
Bradley Benjamin, commission agent, 63 Hatton garden
Bradley Charles, gasfitter, lamp manufacturer, lock smith & bellhanger, 59 Chapel st. Pentonville
Bradley Charles, gasfitter, 38 Old street road
Bradley Edmund Bick, maltster, Fairfield, Wandsworth; & Church street, Battersea
Bradley Edward, baker, 3 King street, Aldgate
Bradley Edward, wine merchant, see May & Bradley
Bradley Edward Gould, solicitor, 11 Berners st. Oxford st
Bradley Elizabeth (Mrs.), baker, 2 Brunswick st. Blackwall
Bradley Francis, bricklayer, see Bradley Joseph & Son
Bradley George, china & glass dealer, Church st. Hackney
Bradley George, lighterman, 10 Limehouse causeway
Bradley George, working jeweller, 5Sugar loaf ct. Leadnhll.st
Bradley Giles, furn. undertaker, see Cressall & Bradley
Bradley Grace (Miss), dress&costume maker to her Majesty's theatre, 52 Rathbone place, Oxford street
Bradley Henry, confectioner, 20 Poplar High street
Bradley Henry, solicitor, see Raven & Bradley
Bradley Henry, tailor, 30 Newman street, Oxford street
Bradley Hugh, *Artichoke* P.H. 121 Lambeth Lower marsh
Bradley Jane (Mrs.), chandler's shop, 11 Park ter. Chelsea
Bradley John, chemist, 10 Pont street, Belgrave square
Bradley John, foreign bird dealer, 5 King's pl. Comcl.rd. East
Bradley John, grocer, 31 Brook street, Ratcliff
Bradley John, house, &c. agency office, 95 Goswell road
Bradley John, printer, 78 Great Titchfield st. Oxford st
Bradley John, straw plt. leather slr.&dlr.2Church st.Spitalfi
Bradley John, jun. professor of music, 5 Gower pl. Euston sq
Bradley John, sen.prof. of music, 12Buckingham pl. Fitzroy sq
Bradley John, *UnionArms* P.H. 12 Union court, Holborn hill
Bradley Joseph, grocer, 35 Millbank st. Westminster
Bradley Maria E. (Miss), milliner, 11 Grove st. Camden town
Bradley Philip, lighterman, 58 Limehouse causeway
Bradley Samuel, malt & hop factor, 82 Mark lane
Bradley Stephen, fruiterer, 5 Blenheim st. Bond st
Bradley Thomas, *Rose & Crown* P.H. 18 Clare ct. Drury la
Bradley Thomas Edward, baker, Bromley, Middlesex
Bradley Wm. artist, 54 Charlotte st. Fitzroy square
Bradley Wm. lighterman, 59 Limehouse causeway
Bradley Wm. machine ruler, 4 Mitre st. Aldgate
Bradley Wm. straw plait wa.8&9 Parsnage. rw. Newingtn. btts
Bradley Wm. wheel & fuzee cutter, 63 Old st. road
Bradly Brothers, for. wine & spirit imprts. 2 Gt. St. Helen's
Bradly Henry, tailor, 4 Colvill ter. King's road, Chelsea
Bradly Rd. B. jeweller, cutler, &c. 96 Bishopsgate without

Bradnam James, butcher, 31 Aylesbury st. Clerkenwell
Bradney Saml.&Son, ironmongers, 16 & 17 New rd. St.Geo.Ea
Bradock John, broker & agent, 12 Mark lane
Bradsell Benj. fruiterer, 4 & 5 Cumberland st. Mddsx. hospital
Bradsell Benj. fruiterer, 4 Wellington ter. Kensingtn. gravl. pits
Bradsell William, potato dealer, 6 New st. Dorset square
Bradshaw & Blacklock, lithographic & letter press printers, 59 Fleet st. & 3 Pleydell st. Whitefriars
Bradshaw, Rhodes & Co. calico printers, 20 Basing la. City
Bradshaw, Son&Co. military tailors, 27Warwick st. Golden sq
Bradshaw's General Railway Publication Office, 59 Fleet st
Bradshaw Charles, hosier & glover, 11 Eastcheap
Bradshaw Edward, cowkeeper, Ferry road West, Poplar
Bradshaw George, fishmonger, 7 Duke st. Smithfield
Bradshaw Geo. hosier, glov.&shirtmak. 103 Bishopsgt. within, & 25 Hedge row, High street, Islington
Bradshaw Henry, *GlengallArms* P.H. Ferry rd. West, Poplar
Bradshaw James, high constable for the Holborn division, 2 Hawley terrace, Hampstead road
Bradshaw James, tailor, 1Trinity sq.&1Postern row, Towr. hill
Bradshaw James, woollen draper, see Fergusson & Bradshaw
Bradshaw Louisa (Mrs.), butcher, 19 Buckinghm. pl. Fitzroy sq
Bradshaw Mary (Miss), milliner, 6 Conduit st. Hanover sq
Bradshaw Sam. landscape engr. 11Harrington st. N. Hmpstd. r
Bradshaw Susan Matilda (Mrs.), clear starcher, lace veil cleaner, gold & silver muslin blondes, chalies, cashmeres, print & chantilly laces, &c. 9 Packenham st. Calthorp st
Bradshaw Thomas, boot ma. 20 Elizabeth pl. Balls pond rd
Bradshaw Thomas K. dairyman, 6 Poppin's court, Fleet st
Bradshaw William, cattle salesman, 37 West Smithfield
Bradshaw Wm. conveyancer, Auction mart, Bartholomew la
Bradswell Benj. sen. fruiterer, 4 & 5 Cumberland st. Mddx. ho
Bradswell Benj. jun. fruiterer, 4 Wellington ter. Knsngtn
Bradwell Edmund, theatrical decorator, 21 Chester pl. Kennington cross
Brady Charles & John, surgeons, &c. 194 Blackfriars road
Brady Jas. & Geo. Wm. solicitors, 1 Staple inn, Holborn
Brady Charles, merchant, 3 Clement's lane, Lombard street
Brady Emma (Miss), seminary, 22 & 23 Portland pl. Islington
Brady Margaret (Mrs.), *Three Compasses* P.H. Glasshouse st
Braess William, cabinet maker, 4 Crawford st. Portman sq
Brafield Edward, cabinet maker, 21 Spring st. Marylebone
Bragg Henry, bottle mer. Mann's wharf, Montague cl. Boro'
Bragg Isabella (Mrs.), baker, 17 Ratcliff rw. John's rw. St. Luke's
Bragg James, stone merchant & builder, 153 & 239 Wapping
Bragg John, fishmonger, Spitalfields market
Bragg John, stockbroker, 6 Throgmorton st
Bragg John, surveyor, 6 Hollywell street, Millbank
Bragg Richd. beer retailer, 7 Hyde pl. Bridport pl. Hoxton
Bragg Robert, *Britannia* P.H. 1 Britannia row, Islington
Bragg Thomas, seal engraver, 54 Rathbone place
Bragg Wm. chair manufactr. 7 Nichols row, Bethnal green
Bragg Wm. oilman & engraver, 7Acton pl. Bagnigge wells rd
Bragg Wm. Allan, baths, 23Queen's row, New rd. Pentonville
Bragger Charles, smith, 82 Rotherhithe st
Bragger Wm. Henry, *NorthPole* P.H. 55Church rd. Com. rd. E
Braggiotti Dominick & Co. merchants, 32 Lombard st
Braggs Marian (Miss), dancing aca. 6Greyhound pl. UpGrng. r
Braggs Robt. rifle & gun maker, 151 Strand, & 43High Holborn
Braham George & Co. pen manfrs. 6 Freeman st. Spitalfields
Braham James, boot & shoe maker, 25 Pitfield st. Hoxton
Braham John, rag & bottle dealer, 4Lit. Guildford st. Brnsk. sq
Braham Joseph, watchmaker, 54 Jubilee st. Commerl rd. Ea
Braham Lewis Henry, solicitor, 101 Chancery lane
Braham Louis, watch & clock maker, 30 King st. Portman sq
Braikenridge William, solicitor, see Hicks & Braikenridge
Brailey Wm. &Son, brushm.&turners, 21Skinner st. Bishopsgt
Brailey John, carpenter, 3 Church st. Blackfriars road
Braidwood James, superintendent of the London Fire Engine Establishment, 68 Watling st
Brain & Payne, foreign booksellers & publishers & commission agents, 12 Paternoster row, & at Leipsic
Brain Abraham, stonemason, 2Gt. Union st. Newington csway
Brain Ephraim, copperplate printer, 48 Salisbury square
Brain Ephraim, woollen warehsmn. 9 Lit. Bell al. Coleman st
Brain Frederick, ivory cutter, ivory & box comb maker, & four-holed bone button manufacturer, & manufacturer of & dealer in artificial manures, steam mills, Thomas st. Stamford st. Blackfriars road
Brain Richard, *Goat* P.H. 1 Kensington High st
Brain Richard, jun. currier, 8 High st. Deptford
Brain Thomas, leather seller, 85 Shadwell High st
Brain Wm. furniture brok. 32 Southampton st. Camberwell
Brain William, wire worker & bird cage maker & umbrella & fishing rod maker, 158 High Holborn; & at 4 Park side, Knightsbridge

Braine JamesWilliams, surgeon, 5 Cleveland row, St. James's
Braine William, bootmaker, 4 Norwich court, Fetter lane
Braithwaite & Jones, jewellers, 3 Cockspur st. Charing cross
Braithwaite Frederick, civil engineer, 1 Bath place, New road
Braithwaite John, civil engineer, 4 Trafalgar square
Braithwaite John, engineer, 39 Bedford square
Braithwaite Isaac, stock broker, see Foster & Braithwaite
Braithwaite Joseph, china & glass wa. 5 Lamb's Conduit pass
Braithwaite Joseph Bevan, barrister, 3 New sq. Lincoln's inn
Braithwaite Moses, compos.ornam.ma. 2 Paradise st. Finsbury
Braithwaite Robert, baker, 8 Bedford pl. Lr. rd. Rotherhith
Braithwaite Thomas, barrister, 2 Mitre court bldgs. Temple
Braithwaite William, solicitor, 15 Serjeants' inn, Fleet st
Brake David, saddler, &c. 41 Rufford's bldgs. Islington High st
Brake Henry, carpenter, 2 Odell pl. Little Chelsea
Brake James, grocer, 5 Berkley st. Clerkenwell
Brake James, *Red Lion* P.H. 48 Red Lion st. Clerkenwell
Brakenbury Robert, butcher, 358 Rotherhithe street
Braker Thomas, tailor, 25 Holles st. Stanhope st. Clare mkt
Bramah, Prestage & Ball, manufacturers of Bramah's patent locks, pens & water closets, iron & brass founders, &c. 124 Piccadilly
Bramah & Robinson (now Charles Robinson), engineer, millwright, founder, &c. Pimlico road
Bramah Edward Henry, solicitor, see Birch & Bramah
Brambini Donatto & Jsph. framema. 18 Summers st. Hattn. grdn
Bramble Edward, watchmaker, 10 Wells st. Oxford st.
Brameld & Beckitt, china manuftrs. top of the Haymarket
Bramrs & Smart, coal merchts. 3 Davies st. Berkeley square
Bramley Thomas Charlesworth, solicitor, see Shoubridge & Bramley
Brampton & White, tobacconist, 27 Greek st. Soho
Brampton Samuel, butcher, High st. Stoke Newington
Brampton Thos. *White Bear* P.H. 19 Kent st. Boro'
Brampton Wm. corn mercht. 9 Royal hl. Queen's rd. Bayswtr
Bramston Edmund, patent leather manfr. & military wareho. 37 Parker st. Drury lane; & Maiden lane, King's cross
Bramwell George, solicitor, 6 Furnival's inn, Holborn
Bramwell George Wm. barrister, 2 Paper buildings, Temple
Branburgh Geo. *D. of Clarence* P.H. 1 Rotherfld. st. nth. Islngtn
Branch Benjamin, carpenter, &c. 41 Great Alie st. Goodm. fl
Branch James, wheelwright, 22 Waterloo road
Branch John, baker, 16 Paradise street, Marylebone
Branch John, shoemaker, 1 White st. Bethnal green
Branch Wm. bricklayer, &c. 4 Thanet st. Burton crescent
Brand George & Son, upholsterers & cabinet manufacturers, 14 Berners street, Oxford street
Brand H. W. & Co. alimentary preserve ma. 11 Lt. Stanhope st
Brand James & Co. merchants, 49 Lime street
Brand James & Son, brushmakers, 43 Blackman st. Borough
Brand Catherine (Miss), milliner, 29 Duke st. Manchester sq
Brand Edmd. Cameron, tobcnst. 2 Newmrkt ter. Cmbrdg hth
Brand Ferdinand, solicitor, comptroller of Bridge house estates, Guildhall
Brand George, hatter, 11 Little St. Andrew st. Seven dials
Brand Henry, currier, 7 Upper East Smithfield, &163 Union st. Borough
Brand James, builder, Bromley High street, Middlesex
Brand James, merchant, 9 New Broad st. City
Brand James, merchant, see Harvey, Brand & Co
Brand Richard, butcher, 11 Harrow road
Brand Thomas, clerk sitter of the Poultry & Giltspur compters, Sheriffs' court office, Whitecross st. Cripplegate
Brand William, *Brown Bear* P.H. 89 Leman st. Goodman's flds
Brand Wm. marine store dealer, 33 Chapel st. Somers town
Brand Wm. oil & colorman, 9 Ivy lane, Newgate street
Brand Wm. *Stag's Head* P.H. Canal road, Kingsland road
Brandard Edward, engraver, 27 Hemingford ter. Islington
Brandau Frederit Wm. prof. of singing, 22 Gt. Portland st
Brandeis Ephraim, imp. foreign goods, 5 St. Dunstan's hill
Brander & Anderson, wharfingers, lightermen & granary keepers, Butler's wharf, 13 Shad Thames, Horselydown
Brander Edw. fishing tackle mk. 27 Wormwood st. Bishopsg
Brander John, silk dyer, Mile end road
Brandon Abraham, whol. shoe warehouse, 49 Houndsditch
Brandon Alfred, china wareh. 4 Beaufort terr. King's rd. Chels
Brandon David, merch. *Hall of Commerce*, Threadneedle st
Brandon Elizabeth (Mrs.), milliner, 60 Mortimer st. Cav. sq
Brandon Gilbert, south american mer. 3 Copthall chambers
Brandon John, hairdresser, 10 Up. Lisson st. Lisson grove
Brandon John, working jeweller, 32 Rose st. Covent garden
Brandon Lucinda (Miss), prof. of music, 1 Burton crescent
Brandon Raphael, architect, 11 Beaufort buildings, Strand
Brandon Robert, surgeon, 1 Wyndham pl. Bryanstone sq
Brandon Samuel, market gardenr. 33 Paradise row, Rotherhi
Brandon Samuel, tobacconist, 163 Strand
Brandon Thomas, lace & millinery warehouse, 139 Oxford st
Brandon Thomas, milliner, 226 Regent st
Brandon Thomas, preserver of birds, 5 John st. Old Kent rd
Brandon Thomas Henry, architect, see Wyatt & Brandon
Brandon William, silk manufacturer, 23 Spital square
Brandram Brothers & Co. merchants, saltpetre & vitriol & white lead manufs. 17 Sise lane, Bucklersbury, & Lower road, Rotherhithe, & 38 Shad Thames
Brandt Charles, professor of languages, 41 Frith st. Soho
Brandt Fras. Fredc. special pleader, 2 Figtree ct. Temple
Brandts Emanuel Hen. Son & Co. merchts. 33½ Gt. St. Helen's
Brandum Charles, oilman, 99 Whitechapel road
Brannam Thomas, tailor, 8 Leigh street, Red Lion square
Brannan Chas. prof. of music, 32 Up. North pl. Gray's inn rd
Brannan Henry, carver & gilder, 13 Duke st. Grosvenor sq
Brannan John, herald painter, 1 King's head yd. Lit. Wild st
Brannan Matthew, fruiterer, 47 Clipstone st. Fitzroy sq
Brannan Patrick, fruiterer, 21 Rufford's buildings, Islington
Brannd Henry, carpenter, 6 Devonshire st. Queen sq
Branscomb Walter, solicitor, 1 Wine office court, Fleet st
Branscomb Wm. grocer & beer retlr. 20 Harmood st. Hmpd. rd
Branscombe John & Co. teadealers, 88 Pall mall
Bransford George, umbrella maker, 4 Cock lane, Smithfield
Bransgrove Alex. carriage lamp ma. 24 Mercer st. Long acre
Bransgrove Charles, farrier, 14 Whf. Paddingtn. basin, Nth. sd
Bransgrove Charles, grocer, 51 Dudley grove, Harrow road
Bransgrove James, painter, 3½ North st. Sloane st
Bransgrove James, tailor, 4 Little James st. Bedford row
Bransom William, slopseller, 37 Wapping High st
Branson Thos. & Son, cattle salesmen, 37 West Smithfield
Branson William, baker, 19 Norton Folgate
Branston George, law stationr. see Hill, Branston & Wootton
Branston Robert Edw. wood engraver, 36 St. Andrew's hill
Brant John Charles, oil & italian warehouseman & british wine manufacturer, 298 Oxford st. & 92 Aldersgate st
Brant John, tailor, 55 Baldwin st. City road
Brant Robert, coachmaker, 2 Hatton yd. Hatton wall
Brant William, bedstead maker, 60 Baldwin's gardens
Branton Henry, soda water maker, 31 Sydney st. Mile end
Brasher Sarah (Mrs.), furniture dealer, 29 Broad st. Golden sq
Brashier Benjamin, hairdresser, 1 Up. Ashby st. Nthmptn. sq
Brashier James, baker, 82 Milton st. Cripplegate
Brasier & Reichell, fishmongers, 20 King st. Westminster
Brasier Samuel, merchant, 8 Broad st. buildings
Brass & Stanes, insurance agents, 5 America square
Brass William & Son, builders, 5 Silver st. Wood st. & 5 Islington green
Brass George, tailor, 43 Marshall st. Golden square
Brass Mary (Mrs.), dining rooms, 64 Fore st. City
Brassington John, bookseller, &c. 27 Kensington High st
Brasted Henry, teadealer & grocer, 18 Up. Marylebone st
Bratt George, *New Cross inn*, New cross
Bratt H. (Mrs.), *Blue Last & Sugar Loaf* P.H. 50 Water l. Bkfr
Bratt Saml. & Son, ship smith, 9½ Gainsford st. Horselydown
Bratt Joseph, *Rose & Crown* P.H. 21 Dartmouth st. Westm
Braun & Krotowski, fancy cap manufact. 111 London wall
Braun Louis, fancy cap manufacturer, 65 Wood st. Cheapsi
Braund John, lodging house, 26 Mount st. Grosvenor sq
Braund John George, tobacconist, 35½ Pitfield pl. Hoxton
Braund Joseph, bootmaker, 27 King street, Soho square
Brawn George, brushmaker, 4 Hayes place, Kingsland road
Brawne Houston, barrister, 2 Churchyard court, Temple
Bray, Warren & Harding, attorneys, 57 Gt. Russell st. Bloomsby
Bray Ambrose, hairdresser, 2 Haberdashers pl. East, Hoxton
Bray Ann (Mrs.), *White Swan* P.H. 104 Long alley, Finsbury
Bray Charles, furnishing ironmonger, stove grate & range manufacturer, 14 Cranbourn st. Leicester square
Bray Edwd. bootmaker, 12 Upp. Park pl. Regent's park rd
Bray Frederic, tailor, 16 Barbican
Bray George, sen. butcher, 5 Bartholomew terrace, City rd
Bray Henry M. teacher of music, 29 Grove pl. Lisson grove
Bray James, builder, 53, Percival street
Bray John, composition seal maker, Park road, Battersea
Bray John, grocer & cheesemonger, 15 Newton st. Holborn
Bray John, oil & colorman, 176 Drury lane
Bray John, shoemaker, 16 Tonbridge st. New road
Bray John Wm. *Six Bells* P.H. 14 Adams pl. King's rd. Chelsea
Bray Richard, cheesemonger, 3 Princess pl. Westminster rd
Bray Robert, grocer & coal dlr. 1 Clandon st. Walworth com
Bray Sarah (Mrs.), milliner, 100 Lambeth walk
Bray William, blacksmith, 45 Compton st. Clerkenwell
Bray Wm. turner & fire screen maker, 24 Saville st. Fitzroy sq
Bray Wm. F. sec. to Craig Ddu Slate Co. 9 Lincoln's inn flds
Bray Wm. F. jun. auctioneer & appraiser, 259 High Holborn
Bray Wm. Thomas, watchmaker, 29 London road, Southwark, & 6 Surrey pl. Newington butts

Bray William F. sen. surveyor, valuer & land agent; mortgage & annuity office; registry for the sale of estates, houses, life interests, and reversions, 123 Chancery lane
Brayne Henry, coal mer.&wharfinger, NineElms whf.Vauxh
Brayne John, brown stone potter & filter maker, Nine Elms
Bray's Institution for founding Libraries (Rev. Arthur Trollope. sec.), 52 Hatton garden
Brayshaw Christopher, tailor, 322 Regent st
Brayshay William, stuff agent, 5 Carey lane, Cheapside
Brazier Chas. chandler's shop, 20 Duke st. Lisson gr. Nth
Brazier Charles Thomas, artist, 106 Blackfriars road
Brazier Emma (Mrs.), milliner, 11Southampton row,New rd
Brazier John, plumber & house decor. 106 Blackfriars road
Brazier Richard, *Blue Posts* P.H. 18 King st. Golden sq
Brazier Thomas, grocer, 7 St. Ann's court, Soho
Brazilian Company, 6 Broad st. buildings, City
Brazilier George, tailor, 58 South Molton st. Bond st
Breach James Gaby, *London tavern*, see Bathe & Breach
Breadcutt John, butcher, 22 Newgate market
Breaden George, fruiterer, 8 Camberwell grove
Breading Thomas, tailor & draper, 3 Gt. Hermitage st
Breaithwaite Chas. bootmaker, 17 Wade's pl. Hackney road
Breakspear John, linendraper, 81 St. John st. road
Brealey Richard, surgeon, 141 Kingsland road
Brealey Richard, tailor, 34 Hosier lane, West Smithfield
Brearey Charles Benson, surgeon, 73 Gt. Portland st
Brearey Thomas, flannel & drugget agent, 50 Aldermanbury
Breckles Saml. cabinet mak. & upholsterer, 265 Boro' High st
Brecknell, Turner & Sons, wax & tallow chandls. 31 Haymkt
Brecknell Henry Byerley, linendraper, 184 Oxford st
Brecks John, tailor, &c. 22 Stephen st. Tottenham ct. road
Brecon & Merthyr Tidvil Railway, 3 Park st. Westminst
Bredall John, surgeon, 1 Bilby place, Up. Kennington lane
Brede George Wm. fishmonger, 12 Webb st. Bermondsey st
Bredee Charles, cook, 5 Bride lane, Fleet st
Bredel Charles Andrew, merchant, 5 Great Winchester st
Breedon Frederick, cowkeeper, 80½ Friar st. Blackfriars rd
Breedon Jarvis, beer retailer, 1 Paradise row, Chelsea
Breedon Thomas, wheelwright, 9 Type st. Finsbury
Breem Edward, coffee rooms, 4 Gt. Windmill st. Haymarket
Brees John, birm. & sheffield wareh. 15½ West st. Smithfield
Breese James, clock manufactr. &c. 5 North pl. Gray's inn rd
Breeze & James, linendrapers, 19 Kensington High st
Breeze Robert baker, 43 Walnut tree walk, Lambeth
Breidenbach Francis Henry, hairdresser, perfumer & distiller of eau de cologne to her Majesty, H.R.H. Prince Albert & Duchesses of Kent & Cambridge, & the Royal family, 87 & 88 Park st. Grosvenor square
Breillat Joseph potter & glass seller, 27 Blackman st. Boro'
Brellisford Jane (Mrs.), coffee rooms, 37 Gresham st
Brelsford John, beer retailer, 24 Canterbury pl. Old Kent rd
Bremer M. F. merchant, 19 London st. Fenchurch st
Bremer John, *Bell* P.H. 106 Middlesex st. Aldgate High st
Bremer Martin Fredk. ship agt.& ins.bro.seeSack,Bremer&Co
Bremner & Till, tobacco brokers, 118 Fenchurch st
Bremner Alexander, baker, 51 Warren st. Fitzroy square
Bremner Alexander, merchant, 11 Billiter square
BremnerHugh,agt. to *City of Glasgow Ass. Co.*120Pall mall
Bremner John, baker, 203 Piccadilly
Bremner Wm. carver & gilder, 1 Spur st. Leicester square
Bremridge Edwin Rd. auctioneer, see Lovell & Bremridge
Bremridge James, barrister, 1 Pump court, Temple
Bren Thomas, bootmaker, 18 Union st. East, Spitalfields
Brenan Robert & Son, shipbrokers, 5 Gt. Tower st
Brenan James, oil works, 15 Old Montague st. Whitechapel
Brenan John, coffee rooms, 4 Charles st. Grosvenor sq
Brenchley Edmund, grocer, 41 Freeschool st. Horselydown
Brenchley James Bishop, ship & gen. agt. 150 Fenchurch st
Brendel & Roberts, *Artichoke tavern*, Blackwall stairs
Brendell John, furniture broker, 21 Earl st. West, Edgw. rd
Brendling John, wind instru. ma. 13 Elder st. Norton folgate
Brengeri Jean Baptiste, merchant, 27 Mincing lane
Brennan James, merchant, 5 Barge yard, Bucklersbury
Brennan John, lamp & gasfitter, 10 Gt. Sutton st. Clkenwll
Brennan Thomas, grocer & cheesemongr. 2 Brook st. Lambeth
Brennand Pearson, veterinary instru. ma. 217 High Holborn
Brennand Robt. woollen warehouseman, 15 Addle st. Wood st
Brennen John, boot maker, 24 Royal st. Carlisle st. Lambeth
Brent Samuel & Daniel, ship smiths, Plough rd. Rotherhithe
Brent Charlotte (Miss), preparatory school, 24 Albany st
Brent George Smith, surgeon, 28 Berwick st. Pimlico
Brent Grace(Mrs.), *Red Lion & Key* P.H.25 Mill la.Tooley st
Brent Hugh, lodging ho. 51&37 Manchester st. Manchester sq
Brent Thomas, chemist, 37 Red Lion st. Holborn
Brent William Brent, barrister, 37 Gower st. Bedford square
Brentano Herman, merchant, 7 Bury court, St. Mary Axe
Brentnall Teresa (Mrs.), oil wa. 2 South pl. Tibberton sq
Brereton Wm. Pellott, tailor, 10 Lit. Stanhope st. May fair
Bressey John, pawnbroker, Stratford
Bressey Robt. Nath. coachmaker, High st. Stoke Newington
Bretland George, upholsterer, 2 Crawley st. Euston square
Breton John, baker, 1 Anglesea place, Commercial rd. east
Brett Brothers & Co. woollen warehousemen, 74 Wood st
Brett Henry & Co. proprietors of the improved British cognac and the liqueur ginger brandy, 139 & 140 Holborn bars
Brett Sarah & Son. vellum binders, 5Nag's head ct. Gracech. st
Brett Bayly, artist, 26 Nicholas lane, City
Brett Benjamin, baker, 139 Lambeth Lower marsh
Brett Benjamin, boot & shoe maker, 138 Poplar High st
Brett Benjamin, boot & shoe maker, 101 St. George st
Brett Christopher Russell, lamp glass wa. 19 Farringdon st. & 1 Wheatsheaf yard, Farringdon st
Brett Frederick, hairdresser, 2 Little St. Thomas Apostle
Brett Frederick Harrington, physician, 24 Brompton sq
Brett George, seal engraver, 21 Tysoe st. Clerkenwell
Brett George Wm. tailor & draper, 2 Wells row, Islington
Brett Henry, *Brett's hotel*, 139 Holborn bars
Brett James, butcher, 1 Little Chester st. Grosvenor place
Brett James, *Fountain* P.H. 12 New st. Dockhead
Brett John, butcher, 2 Clare court, Drury lane
Brett John, cabinet maker, 53 Bunhill row, St. Luke's
Brett John, hairdresser, 4 Osborne st. Whitechapel
Brett Kitty (Mrs.), baker, 17 New North st. Red Lion sq
Brett Robert, baker, 8 Litchfield street, Soho
Brett Robert *Grapes*, P.H. 27 Silver st. Golden square
Brett Robert, plumber, 17 St. George's road, Southwark
Brett Robert, surgeon, see Reynolds & Brett
Brett Robert, surgeon, Stoke Newington green
Brett Thomas, cabinet manufacturer, 16 Lamb st. Spital sq
Brett Thomas, greengrocer, 20 Rosoman st. Clerkenwell
Brett Thomas, florist, 48 Great Hall, Hungerford market
Brett Uriah, ham dealer, 22 Penton row, Walworth road
Brett Wilford Geo. barrister, 22 Portugal st. Linc. inn fields
Brett Wm. butcher, Kingsland High street
Brett Wm. cabinet maker, 27 Guildford place, Spafields
Brett Wm. *King's Arms tap*, 23 Old Castle st. Whitechapel
Brett Wm. livery stables, 18 Swan st. Trinity sq. Borough
Brett Wm. surgeon, 6 Warwick st. Golden square
Brettell Geo. shoemaker, 2 South st. King's rd. Chelsea
Brettell Janns John, solicitor, see Sawyer & Brettell
Brettell Joseph C. sec. to *Royal Naval Ass.* 13 Waterloo pl
Brettell Thomas, printer, 25 Rupert st. Haymarket
BretttinghamRd F. *Ld. Somers Arms* P.H.68Union st.Clrnd.sq
Brettle Geo. & Co. wholesale hosiers, haberdashers, flannel factors & glovers, 119 Wood street
Brettle Thomas, locksmith & bellhanger, 8 Counter st. Boro'
Bretton & Tunwell, upholsterers, 21 Charlotte st. Fitzroy sq
Brevetor Thomas, builder, West st. Hackney
Brewer Fras. & Son, corndealers, 35 Notting hill High st
Brewer & Hallworth, builders, 5 Chequer yd. Dowgate hill
Brewer & Long, brewers, 25 Gibson st. Waterloo road
Brewer Alfred, paper mould ma. 19 Surrey pl. Old Kent rd
Brewer Charles, dining rooms, 8 Boston st. Dorset sq
Brewer Chas. omnibus prop. 43 Addison rd. Nth. Notting hill
Brewer Geo. fruiterer, 8 Grange ter. Grange rd. Bermondsey
Brewer Henry, mast & block maker, 80 Bermondsey wall
Brewer Henry, poulterer, 1 Exeter st. Sloane st
Brewer Henry, *Queen's Head* P.H. 19 Fashion st. Dockhead
Brewer Henry N. *Surrey Arms* P.H. Surrey sq. Old Kent rd
Brewer James, bootmaker, 3 Lime st. passage, Lime st
Brewer James, painter, 14 Upper Fountain place, City road
Brewer James, tin & japan ware manfr. 5 Red Lion st. Clkwl
Brewer John, bldng. matrl. dlr. 4 Caledonia pl. Caledonia rd
Brewer John, brushmaker & warehouseman, 264 Boro'High st
Brewer John, carpenter & builder, see Hallworth & Brewer
Brewer John, packer, see Wheelton, Brewer & Buckland
Brewer John Hibberd, special pleader, 4 Pump court, Temple
Brewer Joseph, fruiterer, 55 Rosoman st. Clerkenwell
BrewerNath.grocer&cheesemonger,20Harper st.NewKent rd
Brewer Rhoda (Mrs.), *Spread Eagle* P. H. Stangate st. Lmbth
Brewer Richard, beer retailer, 11 Lit. Hermitage st. Wapng
Brewer Richard Lawrence, tailor & glover, 162 Fenchurch st
Brewer Samuel, academy, 42 Princes st. Upper Stamford st
Brewer Saml. brazier, 4 Thatched house rw. Lwr. rd. Islingtn
Brewer Samuel Wells, ham dealer, 29 Bishopsgate without
Brewer Thomas, cowkeeper, 3 Church st. Horselydown
Brewer Thomas, tinplate worker, 44 Whitecross st. Cripplgt
Brewer Thomas Gibson, solicitor, 13 Gray's inn square
Brewer William, physician, 21 George st. Hanover sq
Brewer William, trunkmaker, 120 Oxford street
Brewer Wm. Henry, draftsman, &c. 6 Red lion ct. Fleet st
Brewers' Alms Houses, Oxford st. Whitechapel road

Brewers' Hall (Wm. Vines, clerk), 18 Addle st. Wood st
Brewers', Chester's & Galley Quays, Joseph Barber, wharfinger, between Custom house & Tower
Brewington Sier, boot & shoe maker, 7 Vauxhall row
Brewood Thomas, wadding maker, Neate st. Coburg rd. Old Kent road
Brewster Chas. coachbuilder, 9 Margaret st. Cavendish sq
Brewster & West, printers, 6 Hand court, Upper Thames st
Brewster James, cattle salesman, 8 West Smithfield
Brewster James, *Fortune of War* P.H. 92 East st. Manchester sq
Brewster John, *Yorkshire Grey* P.H. 54 Eagle st. Red Lion sq
Brewster Sam. potato salesman, 38 Stoney st. Boro' market
Brewster Walker, manufacturer of ornamental hair to the royal family, 48 New Bond street
Brian Benjamin, plasterer, 1 Bouverie st. Paddington
Briant Adam, coal dealer, 12 Back hill, Hatton garden
Briant Henry, *Chequers* P.H. 11 Abingdon st. Westminster
Briant James, auctioneer, 12 Kennington row
Briant James, carpenter, Mare st. Hackney
Briant John, hatter, 5 Whitecross street, Borough
Briant Nathaniel, civil engineer, 11 Adam st. Adelphi
Briant Richard Wippell, carman, 41 Princes square, Ratcliff highway; & London dock entrance
Briant Rt. Fred. wheelwright, 33 Princes sq. Ratcliff highway
Briant William, *Horns tavern*, Kennington common
Briarly Thos. Edwd. barrister, 8 King's bench walk, Temple
Brice Dan. organ bldr. & masqr. wa. 8 Brownlow st. Drury la
Brice Elijah, coal dealer, 80 Long alley, Finsbury
Brice John, *Horse & Groom* P.H. 48 Whitehorse st. Stepney
Brice Joseph, currier, 10 Tyer's gateway, Bermondsey st
Brice Samuel, tailor, 50 St. John st. Clerkenwell
Brice Thomas, *Exmouth Arms* P.H. 1 Exmouth st. Euston sq
Brice Wm. painter & paper hanger, 111 Upper st. Islington
Bricheno Charlt. (Mrs.), baker, 52 Featherstone st. City rd
Brickdale James, haberdasher, 18 Church rd. Commerl. rd. Ea
Brickdale Matthew S. barrister, 4 Stone bldgs. Lincoln's inn
Brickhill Wm. printer, 4 Cumberland pl. Newington butts
Brickley Henry, linendraper, 2 Sol's row, Hampstead road
Brickman Robert, trunkmaker, 22 Lime st. City
Brickman Rt. Jas. undertaker, 24 Princes sq. Ratcliff highway
Brickman William, tailor, 8 Cecil st. Strand
Brickwood Edwd. Clanfield, proctor & notary, 6 Dean's court
Bridegroome Mary (Mrs.), baker, 53 Hoxton square
Briden John, corn dealer, 30 Paddington st. Marylebone
Brideson Arthur, cheesemonger, 6 Clare st. Clare market
Brideson Arthur, cheesemonger, 44 Gt. Hall, Hungerford mkt
Bridewell Hospital, 14 New Bridge st. Blackfriars
Bridge Alfred Charles, barrister, 5 Pump court, Temple
Bridge Ann (Mrs.), tailor, 5 Haberdasher's place West, Hoxton
Bridge George & Co. cork manufctrs. 29 High st. St. Giles's
Bridge George, tobacconist, 2 Exeter st. Sloane st. Chelseaa
Bridge Henry, solicitor, see Cookney & Bridge
Bridge James Southby, essence of spruce mercht. 21 Bread st
Bridge Mary (Miss), milliner, 24 Sloane terrace, Chelsea
Bridge Robert, *Oxford Arms* P.H. 1 Seymour pl. Camden tn
Bridge Thos. Andrew, chemist, 270 Regent circus, Oxford st
Bridge Walter, academy, 47 Roebuck pl. Gt. Dover st
Bridge Wm. fruiterer, 15 James pl. Marlboro' road, Chelsea
Bridge Wm. fruiterer, 35 New Manor st. Chelsea
Bridge Wm. tailor, 5 Gloucester ter. Vauxhall bridge road
Bridge-house Comptroller's Office, Guildhall, hours 10 to 5
Bridgeman Benjamin, *White Hart* P.H. 11 Clifton st. Finsby
Bridgeman Mary (Mrs.), dairy, 2 Borough road
Bridgemaster's Office, Guildhall; hrs. 10 to 2, saturdays only
Bridgen & Cronk, milliners, &c. 28 Conduit st. New Bond st
Bridger & Ashby, builders, 7 Aldgate
Bridger & Blake, solicitors, Carpenters' hall, 68 London wall
Bridger Chas. *Blue Anchor & Eight Bells* P.H. 115 Bermndsy st
Bridger Benjamin, hosier, 31 Little Newport st. Long acre
Bridger Daniel, carpenter, &c. 5 Princes rd. Kenningtn. cross
Bridger Elizth. (Mrs.), builder, 31 Chapel st. Grosvenor sq
Bridger George, pork butcher, 53 Chapel st. Somers town
Bridger James, cowkeeper, 7 Goulstone st. Whitechapel
Bridger John, coffee rooms, 72 Commercial road, Lambeth
Bridger Mary (Mrs.), cheesemnger. 12 Hastings st. Burton cres
Bridger Richard, cork cutter, 10 Homer st. Marylebone
Bridger William, coal merchant, see Olley & Bridger
Bridger Wm. Melton, barrister, 1 Old square, Lincoln's inn
Bridges & Mason, solicitors, 23 Red Lion square, Holborn
Bridges Arthur, porkman & cheesemonger, 138 Lambeth walk
Bridges Caroline (Miss), organist, 3 Titchborne st. Edgw. rd
Bridges Charlotte (Miss), school, Camberwell grove
Bridges Edward, grocer & teadealer, 32 Cheyne wk. Chelsea
Bridges Frederick, locksmith, 18 Pitt st. Old Kent road
Bridges George, oil & colorman, 24 Newcastle st. Strand
Bridges George Talbot, solicitor, 7 Lincoln's inn fields
Bridges Henry, brushmaker, turner & matlayer to the Queen, & wainscot furniture manufacturer, 406 Oxford st
Bridges Sir Hen. gunpowder manufacturer, 35 St. Swithin's la
Bridges Henry, painter & plumber, 56 Dudley grove, Harrow rd
Bridges Henry, painter & plumber, &c. 5 Lit. Sussex pl. Hyde pk
Bridges Hen. Joseph, *P. of Wales* P.H. Princes rd. Notting hl
Bridges James, artist, 18 Charles st. Berners st
Bridges John, artist, 18 Charles st. Berners st
Bridges James, grocer, 30 Great Bath st. Clerkenwell
Bridges John, shawl & parasol fringer & silk weaver, 14 Brown's lane, Spitalfields
Bridges John Wm. wine & spirit merchant, 5A, Warnford ct
Bridges Richard, corndealer, 6 Silver st. Clerkenwell
Bridges Thomas, builder, 18 Old Quebec st. Portman square
Bridges Thomas, shoemaker, 23 Cole harbour st. Hackney rd
Bridges Thomas, solicitor, see Lacy & Bridges
Bridges Thomas B. straw hat maker, 55 Church st. Shoreditch
Bridges William, hat block turner, 8 Gravel lane, Southwark
Bridgett Joseph & Co. silkmen, 63 Aldermanbury
Bridgett Thomas, silk manufacturer, 63 Aldermanbury
Bridgewater James, printer, 31 South Molton st. Bond st
Bridgins John, baker, 14 George st. Blackfriars road
Bridgins John, general salesman, 8 Clarence pl. Hackney rd
Bridgland Robt. Stileman, brewer, Pilgrim st. Up. Kugtn. la
Bridgman Fred, confectioner to her Majesty, 10 Wigmore st. Cavendish square
Bridgman James, marine store dlr. 31 Eagle st. Red Lion sq
Bridgman Jesse, gen. agent, 5 Hercules pas. & 56 Threadndle st
Bridgman Thomas, corn & coal mercht. Mare st. Hackney
Bridgwater & Minehead, junc. rail. off. 3 Bishopsgate ch. yd
Bridle Edward, timber merch. 3 Canning pl. Old st. St. Luke's
Bridle Hannah (Mrs.) wheelwrght. 1 New inn yd. Tottnhm. ct. rd
Bridle William, news agent, 47 Chapel st. Somers town
Briearley Mary (Mrs.), *Old Star* P.H. 11 Calvert st. Wapping
Briebach & Mogge, sugar refiners, 11 Denmark st. Ratcliff hi
Briebach Herman, baker, 42 Cannon st. rd. St. George's East
Briellat James, china warehouse, 7 King st. Holborn
Brien & Harding, surgeons, 13 Spencer st. Goswell road
Brien Hen. greengrocer, 3 Middle st. Cloth fair, Smithfield
Brier John, horn, bone & engine oil merchant, 11 Castle st. Saffron hill
Briers Thomas, chemist, 18 Blenheim terrace, Kingsland
Brigden Joseph, cowkeeper, 38 Cable st. Wellclose sq
Brigden William, dairyman, 37 Phœnix st. Somers town
Brigg Thomas, umbrella & stick maker, 23 St. James's st
Briggs George & Chas. coachmaks. 45 Wigmore st. Cavndsh. sq
Briggs George & Son, fishmongers, 54 Wigmore st. Cavndsh. sq
Briggs Hen. Rt. & Co. seedcrushers, 5 Primrose st. Bishopsgt
Briggs & Lees, furnishing undertakers, 71 Kingsland road, opposite Shoreditch church
Briggs Thomas & Son, solicitors, 55 Lincoln's inn fields
Briggs Ann (Mrs.), dyer, 1 Brunswick pl. Stoke Newingtn. rd
Briggs Constantine, upholsterer, 20 Bridgehouse pl. Borough
Briggs Edmund, *Crown* P.H. 89 Park st. Grosvenor sq
Briggs Edward, warm & cold baths, 75 Harley st. Cavendish sq
Briggs Edwin, chemist & drug. 48 Wigmore st. Cavendish sq
Briggs George, bootmaker, 1 Queen st. Lower road, Islington
Briggs Henry, baker, 9 Bolingbroke row, Walworth road
Briggs Henry, *Bell & Mackerel* P.H. Essex pl. Mile end road
Briggs Henry, dyer, 2 East st. Walworth road
Briggs Henry, *Kg. of Prussia* P.H. 27 High st. Kensington
Briggs Hy. *Old Rum Puncheon* P.H. Rose & Crown ct. Eldon st
Briggs James, dyer & scourer, 9½ London ter. Hackney road
Briggs James, surgeon, 30 Edgware road, Marylebone
Briggs John, butcher, 57 Great Tower st. City
Briggs John, cowkeeper, 65 Pritchard's road, Hackney road
Briggs John, dyer, 2 Seward cottages, Seward st. Goswell st
Briggs John, undertaker, 62 Kingsland road
Briggs John Edmund, *Grapes* P.H. 206 Upper Thames st
Briggs John H. toy maker, 33 Greenhill's rents, Smithfield
Briggs Joseph, general agent, 4 Crown court, Cheapside
Briggs Joseph, silk dyer, 52 Brewer st. Golden square
Briggs Luke, coal merchant, 116 London road, Southwark
Briggs Robert, tailor, 57 Poland st. Oxford st
Briggs Rt. John, drugg. & grocer, 1 Clarendon st. Somrs. tn
Briggs Samuel, coachmaker, 6 Constable row, Mile end rd
Briggs Samuel, dyer, 6 Calcutta pl. East India road, Poplar
Briggs Samuel, hatmaker, 98 Gracechurch st
Briggs Sarah (Mrs.), straw bonnet ma. 15 James st. Haymkt
Briggs Thomas, dressing case manufacturer, 27 Piccadilly
Briggs Thomas, furn. broker, 2, 3, 6 & 7 Castle st. Long acre
Briggs Thomas Carter, barrister, 6 Old sq. Lincoln's inn
Briggs Wm. tallowchandler & oilman, 6 Brewer st. Golden sq
Briggs William, turner, 14 Princes st. Little Queen st
Brigham John, *Skinners' Arms* P. H. 25 Coburg st. Clrknwl
Brigham Joseph, livery stable keeper, 79 London wall

BrighamSarah(Mrs.), *Wheatsheaf* P.H.219 WappingHigh st
Bright, Martin & Birtles, saddlers' ironmong. 30 Bow st
Bright Thomas & Wm. brushmakers, 6 Brompton road
Bright Brailsford, who. druggist, see Hearon, Bright & Co
Bright Charles, baker, 20 York row, Kennington road
Bright Edward, barrister, 11 King's Bench walk, Temple
Bright Frederick, coffee rooms, 15 Borough market
Bright George Wm. builder, &c. 16 Queen st. Grosvenor sq
Bright Henry, artist, 11 Park place villas, Paddington
Bright Henry, barrister, 2 Paper buildings, Temple
Bright James, baker, 8 Upper Albany st. Regent's park
Bright James, bootmaker, 44 Church street, Shoreditch
Bright James, physician, 12 Cambridge square, Hyde park
Bright John, butcher, 34 Bath st. City road
Bright John, farina & custard mfr. 5 Holland st. Clapham rd
Bright John, physician, 19 Manchester square
Bright John Edward, barrister, 5 Old square, Lincoln's inn
Bright John Knighton, boot & shoe ma.83 Mount st.Berkly.sq
Bright Samuel, cowkeeper, 99½ Bunhill row, Chiswell st
Bright Richard, watchmaker, see Upjohn & Bright
Bright Rd. (late Argand), lamp & oil wa.37 Bruton st.Bond st
Bright Richard, physician, 11 Saville row, Piccadilly
Bright Thos. brush ma. cooper & turner, 2 Albion pl. Hyde pk
Bright Thomas, umbrella ma. 37 Gt. St. Andrew st. 7 Dials
Bright Thos. Goldsmith, tailor & draper, 18 Gt. Dover st. Boro
Bright William, milliner, &c. 12 Ludgate st. Ludgate hill
Bright Wm. tailor & woollendraper, 51 Whitechapel road
Bright Wm. Oliver, solicitor, 13 Furnival's inn, Holborn
Brightman John & Co. e. i. merchants & agents, 30 Cornhill
Brighton & Cheltenham Direct Railway, 1 Moorgate
Brighton & Chichester Railway Co. (Frederick Otley, secretary), 4 Dean st. Tooley st
Brighton, Croydon & Dover Joint Station Committee (Geo. Harrison, sec.), 1 Joiner st. Tooley st
Brighton & Hove Gen. Gas Co. (Geo. Garraway, sec.), 29 St. Swithin's lane
Brighton Incorporated Gas Light & Coke Co. (Samuel Thomas, secretary), 27 Austinfriars
Brighton Railway, see "London & Brighton"
Brighton Edward, carpenter & builder, White Bear yard, Back hill, Hatton garden
Brighton James, butcher, 67 Park st. Camden town
BrightonJas. *SeymourArms* P.H.42Up.Seymour st. Eustonsq
Brighton John, plumber, &c. 212 Tooley st
Brignall James, butcher, 3 New st. St. Thomas's st. Borough
Brignell Charles, nurseryman, Well st. Hackney
Brillard Ann & Catherine, dressmakers, milliners & straw bonnet makers, 2 Little Chapel st. Soho
Brimblecombe William, dairyman, 26 Laurence st. Chelsea
Brimelow James, dairyman & coal dealer, 34 Gray's inn lane
Brind Edward & Co. coal mer. St. Ann's whf. Earl st. Blkfrs
Brind Chas. wine, &c. merch. 14 Devonshire st. Bishopsgate
Brind Chas. Bourn, grocer & who. stationer, 28 Old change
Brindle Joseph G. plate & plated ag. 17 Cross st. Hatton grdn
Brindley Catherine (Mrs.), coal mer. Bermondsey wall
Brindley John, saddler, 2 Princess st. Lisson grove
Brindley John, tailor, 5 Penton place, Pentonville
Brindley John, tobacconist, 9 High st. Marylebone
BrindleyRupert, slate mer. Mill stairs whf. Mill st. Dockhead
Brindley Thomas, pocket book manufr. 21 Castle st. City road
Brine Chas. & Augustus, marble & stone merchts.statuaries & masons, 17 & 18 South row, New rd. & Northern wf. Horsfall basin, Maiden lane, Battle bridge
Brine William Halett, baker, 122 Golden lane
Brinjes John Fred. engineer, Backchurch lane, Whitechapel
Brinkman Henry, watchma. 56 Cannon st. Ratcliff highway
Brinkman Philip, watchmaker, 12 Union st. Bishopsgate
Brinley John Short, ship broker, 14 Little Tower st
Brinsden Jn. *Bridport Arms* P. H. 34 Bridpt. pl. New N. rd
Brinsden Joseph, baker, 14 Brighton st. Cromer st
Brinsden Wm. C. furniture wa. 6 Victoria road, Pimlico
BrinsleyCharles, fancytea box ma.25Mitre st.New cut, Lmbth
Brinsley John, silk manufr. see Critchley, Brinsley & Co
Brinsmead Hen. pianoforte ma. 3 Up. Grafton st. Fitzroy sq
Brinsmead John, pianoforte ma. 15 Charlotte st. Fitzroy sq
Brinsmead Susan(Mrs.), staymaker, 15Charlotte st. Fitzroysq
Briscoe Thomas & Son, corn dealers, 8 Green st. Bethnal gn
Briscoe Benj. printer, 8 Three Herring ct. Red Cross st
BriscoeCharles, Hyde park dairy, 9 Park side, Knightsbridge
Briscoe Joseph, engraver & printer, 28 Banner st. St. Luke's
Briscomb Geo. tailor & draper, 52 Grosvenor row, Pimlico
Brisen Samuel, china dealer, 7 Somerset pl. New rd. Whtchpl
Brisley Pierce Sweeting, solicitor, 4 Pancras la. Cheapside
Brissenden Ann(Mrs.), lodging house, 34 New st. Horseferry rd
Brissenden James, tailor, 4 Regent place, Horseferry road
Brister Wm. baker, 17 Somerset pl. New rd. Commercial rd

Bristol Bottle Company (Powell Brothers & Co.), 22 Steel yard, 86 Upper Thames street
Bristol & English Channel Connection Railway, 3 Park street, Westminster
Bristol, Poole Harbour & Lymington Junction Railway Company, (Wm. Edwards, sec.) 55 King William st. City
Bristoll Thos. engrvr. & printer, 19 Buckingham st. Strand
Bristow, Edmonds & Co. wholesale druggists, 27 Gt. Bush la
Bristow & Tarrant, solicitors, 2 Bond court, Walbrook
Bristow Abraham, linendraper, see Dix & Bristow
Bristow Angelie (Mrs.), dairy, 14 Exeter st. Lisson grove
Bristow Frederick, dining rooms, 28 Compton st. Burton cr
Bristow Geo. carpent. & builder, Lit. George st. Bermondsey
Bristow George, potato dealer, 19 Clare st. Clare market
Bristow Hen. E. berlin wool imp. see Lindsay, Bristow & Co
Bristow James, dairyman, 9 Wardour st. Soho
Bristow John, cheesemonger, 1 Carnaby st. Golden sq
Bristow John, fire engine maker, 1 Holloway st. Whitechapel
Bristow John, hosier, 1 Samson's pl. Grange rd. Bermondsey
Bristow John, cheesemonger, 20 Silver st. Golden square
Bristow John Hen. cheesemonger, 38 Kingsgate st. Holborn
Bristow Joseph, boatbuilder, Horseferry stairs, Rotherhithe
Bristow Jsph. *Cheshire Cheese* P.H.20 Phillips bdgs. Smrs.tn
Bristow Michael, meat salesman, Leadenhall market
Bristow Robert James, oil & dry cooper, Dockhead, Bermond
Bristow Thomas, dairyman, 42 Gt. Castle st. Regent st
Bristow William, butcher, 2 White st. Borough
Bristowe John Syer, surgeon, 2 Nth. Addington pl. Camberwell
Bristowe Simon, barrister, 3 Essex court, Temple
Britannia Life AssuranceCo. (Peter Morrison, res. director), 1 Princes st. Bank; for list of directors, &c. see page 2016
Britannia & Conservative weekly newspaper, 26 Bride la
Britcher Wm. pastrycook, 6 Tothill st. Westminster
Britchwell William, baker, 127 St. John st. road
British American Land Co. (Jas. J. Cummings), 4 Barge yard, Bucklersbury
Brit. AnnuityCo. (J. Mendham, mangr.), 36 NewBroad st. City
Brit. Anti-State Church Association (Rev. F. A. Cox, D.D. J. M. Hare & E. Miall, secs.) 12 Warwick sq. Newgate st.
British Archæological Association (Thos. Crofton Croker, esq. Admiralty, & Chas. Roach Smith, esq. 5 Liverpool st. City, hon. secs.), 4 York st. Covent garden
British Artists' Society (Edward Hassell, secretary), 6½ Suffolk st. Pall mall East
British Association for the Advancement of Science (John Taylor, esq. F.R.S. general treasurer), 2 Duke st. Adelphi
British Buildg. Invest. Co. (J.R. Macarthur, man.) 3 Ivy la
British Coffeehouse & Tavern, 27 Cockspur st.
British Colonial Bank & Loan Co. (J. R. Hollway, accountant), 50 Moorgate street
British Colour Company, 27 Poultry
British Commercial Life Assurance Co. (Eben. Fernie, mg. director), 35 Cornhill
British Fluid Company (C. Wheeler, sec.), 28 Leadenhall street
British Coal Company, 27 Poultry
British & Foreign Anti-Slavery So. (John Scoble, sec.), 27 New Broad st. City
British & Foreign Bible Society (Rev. Andrew Brandram & Rev. George Browne, secretaries), 10 Earl st. Blackfrs
British & Foreign Institute (James S. Buckingham, resident director), 13 George street, Hanover square
British & Foreign School Society (Henry Dunn, secretary) central establishment & normal school for the training of teachers, Borough road. For list of schools, see "Schools" in TRADES' DIRECTORY
British & Foreign Seaman & Soldier's Friend Society (Joseph Wm. Tomkins, secretary), 17 Wellclose square
Brit. & For. Temperance Intelligencer, 20 Paternoster row
British & Foreign Temperance Society (Rev. Owen Clarke secretary), Aldine chambers, 13 Paternoster row
British & Foreign Unitarian Association (Thomas Richard Horwood, sec.), 31 St. Swithin's lane
British Gas Light Company, office, 11 George yard, Lombard street (John Woodrooffe, sec.); office of works (Geddie Pearse, superintendent), 105 Broad st. Ratcliff
British Gas Works (George Woodrow, secretary), Old Ford
British Hong Kong Tea Company, 13 King William st City, & 12 & 13 Nicholas lane
British Illuminated Glass Co. 77 Cornhill
British Institution (George Nicol, secretary), 52 Pall mall
British & Irish & City of Dublin SteamPacket Co.'s Office (Jas. Hartley & Co.) 137 Leadenhall st.; & 33 Regent circus & Dublin Steam wharf, Low. East Smithfield
British Lying in Hospital (Yewd & Truwhitt, secretaries Mrs. Harriet Simson, matron), 34 Brownlow st. Drury la

British Museum, Great Russell street, Bloomsbury; the public are admitted on Monday, Wednesday, & Friday, from January 8 to April 30, between 10 & 4; May 8 to August 31, 10 & 7; September 8 to December 31, 10 & 4. The *reading room* of the Museum (entrance, east end of Montague place) is open every day; except on Sundays, on Ash Wednesday, Good Friday, Christmas Day, and on any fast or thanksgiving days ordered by authority; except also between the 1st & 7th of January, the 1st & 7th of May, & the 1st & 7th of September inclusive
British Mutual Life Assurance Society (Chas. Jas. Thicke, resident sec.), 17 New Bridge st. Blackfriars; for directors, &c. see page 2013
British Orphan Asylum (Rev. John Davis & Rev. Chas. Kemble, hon. secs. Jas. Leach, sec.), Clapham rise; office, 11 Abchurch lane, City; attendance, Wednesdays, 11 till 4
British Paper Warehouse, 46 Cornhill
British Plate Glass Company (Edward Wilson, secretary), 1 Albion place, Blackfriars road, & 2 Upper Ground st
British Penitent Female Refuge (Rev. John Glanville, sec.), Heath herne, Cambridge heath
British Reformation Society (Geo. Finch, esq. hon. sec.), 8 Exeter hall, 372 Strand
British Rock & Patent Salt Company (James B. Lobb, secretary), 6 Great Winchester st
British Shipping Co. (Thos. Geo. Edgley, sec.), 10 Cullum st
British Society for the Propagation of the Gospel among the Jews (George Yonge, sec.), 1 Crescent pl. New Bridge st
British Star Blacking Co. New North road, Hoxton
Britnell Benjamin, baker, 34 Silver st. Golden sq
Britnell Cranley, pork butcher, 33 Silver st. Golden sq
Brittain & Holland, brass cock mnfs. 8 St. James's bldgs. Clkwll
Brittain & Houston, woollen manufacturers, 2 Basinghall st
Brittain Thos. & Jas. undertakers, 17 Southampton pl. Euston sq
Brittain George, carpenter, 2 Streatham, st. Bloomsbury
Brittain John, undertaker, 14 Great Peter st. Westminster
Brittain Joseph, baker, 84 Westbourne st. Pimlico
Brittain Richd. working jeweller, 15 Gt. Maze pd. Tooley st
Brittain Stephen, horse hair manfr. 59 Church st. Shoreditch
Brittain William, bookseller, 11 Paternoster row
Brittain Wm. gen. salesman, 147 Up. Whitecross st. St. Luke's
Brittain Wm. wardrobe dealer, 68 Oakley st. Lambeth
Britten John & Son, clothworkers & packers, 21 Basinghall st
Britten John, city measurer of woollen cloth, 21 Basinghall st
Britten John Meek, solicitor, see Fox & Britten
Britten Joseph, butcher, 2 Sloane st. Knightsbridge
Britten Joseph Procter, teadealer & grocer, 110 Fleet st
Britten Thomas, wine merchant, 5 Suffolk lane, Cannon st
Britten William, bookseller, 7 Russell court, Drury lane
Britten Wm. birmingham agent, 9 Lawrence lane, Cheapside
Britten William S. surgeon, 28 Henry st. East, Avenue rd
Brittian Bartholomew, bedstead maker, 149 Waterlood road
Brittle Ann (Mrs.), brassfounder, 20 King st. Borough
Brittle Joshua, gasfitter & turner, 6 City gardens, City rd
Brittlebank Wm. hairdresser, 3 Bozier's ct. Tottenham ct. rd
Britton John, butcher, 2 Eagle place, Jermyn st
Britton Richard, silversmith, 46 Gt. Sutton st. Clerkenwell
Brixey Elizabeth (Mrs.), florist, Borough market
Brize John Baker, stockbroker, 13 Angel ct. Throgmorton st
Broackes William, physician, 1 Cork st. Bond st
Broad Geo. & Sons, woolstaplers, 2 Market st. Bermondsey
Broad Abel, hairdresser, 22 High road, Knightsbridge
Broad Cath. (Mrs.), & Son, coach ironmgrs. &c. 149 Drury la
Broad Charles, cheesemonger, 154 Hoxton Old town
Broad Charles, surgeon, 51 Goswell road
Broad George, farrier, 4 Crawford mews, Bryanstone sq
Broad George, surgeon, &c. 8 Old Compton st. Soho
Broad John, chemist, 27 Coles terrace, Barnsbury road
Broad John, hairdresser, 61 Upper Ground st. Blackfriars
Broad Joseph, wax chandler, 19 High st. Bow, Middlesex
Broad Peter, oilman & grocer, 12 Tavistock st. Covent grd
Broad Peter, auctioneer & valuer, 12 Tavistock st. Covent garden & Tavistock villa, Shepherds' bush
Broad Samuel, brass turner, 204 Upper Thames st
Broad Steph. varnish ma. & colormn. 31 Broad st. Bloomsbry
Broad William, cheesemonger, 207 Shadwell High st
Broadbent & Whitcomb, milliners, 19 Sackville st
Broadbent John, warehouseman, 27 Budge row, City
Broadbent Wm. factor, &c. see Leach, Broadbent, Leach & Co
Broadbridge Ben. architect & surv. 172 Albany st. Regent's park
Broadbridge Charles, architect & survey. 87 Gt. Portland st
Broadbridge Chas. plumber, 10 Church st. Stoke Newington
Broadbridge Chas. tobacconist, 13 Church st. Stke. Nwngtn
Broadbridge George, coal merchant, 29 Up. Eaton st. Pimlico; & Milford lane, Strand
Broadbridge Isaac, grocer & cheesemonger, 2 High st. Bow
Broadbridge Thomas, plumber, &c. 2 Church st. Stoke Newgtn
Broadfoot, Brand, Thomson & Co. warehousemen, 21 Friday st. & 13 Gt. Distaff lane
Broadhead Alfred, barrister, 4 Gray's inn square
Broadhead Edwin, carpenter, 7 St. James's market, Haymkt
Broadhead Elizabeth (Mrs.), grocer, 43 Newington causeway
Broadhurst James Christr. *Crown* P.H. Bridge st. Lambeth
Broadhurst John, china dealer, 21 Dorset cres. New North rd
Broadhurst Mary (Mrs.), beer retailer, 6 Poplar High st
Broadhurst Thomas, shoemaker, Church st. Hackney
Broadhurst Wm. sugar broker, 13 & 16 Commercial sale rms
Broadribb Sarah (Mrs.), ladies' school, 115 Kingsland road
Broadwater Rob. ship, &c. agent, see Hopcraft & Broadwater
Broadwater Thomas, surgeon, 216 High st. Poplar
Broadway Cornelius, carpenter, &c. 31 Redcross st. Boro'
Broadwood, Mundell & Huggins, brewers, 50 Broad st. Goldn. sq
Broadwood & Sons, pianoforte makers, 32 & 33 Gt. Pulteney street, 9 Golden square & 69 Horseferry rd. Westminster
Broady Sarah (Miss), & Co. dealers in ornamental china, glass, perfumery, &c. 9 Halkin street West, Belgrave square
Brock Charles, butcher, 44 Upper Lisson st. Lisson grove
Brock Jane & Richd. coffee rooms, 106 Bishopsgate without
Brock John & Son, tailors, 10 Sackville st. Piccadilly
Brock Isaac, coffee rooms, 53 Piccadilly
Brock James, china dlr. 1 Lit. Cherry grdn. st. Rotherhithe
Brock Jane N. (Miss), straw hat ma. 20 Bromley st. Coml. rd. E
Brock John, haberdasher, 38 York st. City road
Brock John, watchma. & jeweller, 2 Darlington pl. Vauxhall
Brock John, watch & clock maker, 69 George st. Portman sq
Brock Thomas, upholsterer, see Druce & Brock
Brock Wm. artist in fireworks, 3 Baker's rw. Whitechapl. rd
Brock Wm. *Duke of Cumberland* P.H. 8 Kensington High st
Brockbank, Atkins & Son, chronometer, clock & watch makers, 6 Cowper's court, Cornhill
Brockbank John & Son, pianoforte ma. 3 Crawley st. Oakly. sq
Brockbank Robt. A perfumer, see Rigge, Brockbank & Rigge
Brockbank Wm. watch & clock maker, 75 Mount st. Brkly sq
Brockedon William, artist, 29 Devonshire st. Queen square
Brockelbank & Rolt, timber merchants, 72 Cornhill, & Acorn wharf, Lower Trinity st. Rotherhithe
Brockelbank Jas. lighterman & gen. agt. 30 Horselydown la
Brockelbank Lemuel, melter & candle ma. 127 Aldersgate st
Brockelbank Robert Hinde, oilman, 328 Strand
Brockelbank Thomas, turner, 5 Portland place, Boro' road
Brockell Thos. & Son, hosiers, glovers, &c. 133 New Bond st
Brockhan John, fur skin dyer, 180 Long lane, Bermondsey
Brocking Robert, grocer, Battersea square
Brockington Robert, tailor, 19 Red Lion st. Spitalfields
Brocklehurst John & Thomas & Sons, velvet, silk, ribbon & hat plush manufrs. 32 & 33 Milk st. Cheapside
Brocklesby & Wessels, commission merchants, 4 Muscovy ct
Brocklesby Charles, tailor, 89 Newman st. Oxford st
Brockley Wm. linendraper, 2 Brunswick pl. Old Kent road
Brockliss Wm. Henry, tailor, 4 Villa st. Walworth common
Brocksopp, How & Co. wholesale tea dlrs. 233 & 234 Boro' High st
Brocksopp Thomas, hosier & glover, 6 Old Bond st
Brocksopp Thomas, whol. hosier, 12 Wood st. Cheapside
Brockway Alex. asst. sec. to the *Peace Soc.* 19 New Broad st. Cty
Brockway William, grocer, 66 King st. Borough
Brockwell & Reed, teadealers, 10 Gt. Russell st. Covnt. grdn
Brockwell Ellen (Mrs.) milliner, 11 Princes st. Cavendish sq
Brockwell Henry, gasfitter, 39 Compton st. Clerkenwell
Brockwell James, tobacconist, 35 Vauxhall walk, Lambeth
Brockwell John, brass clock case ma. 50 Rahere st. St. Luke's
Brockwell John, bricklayer, 4 White Hart st. Kennington
Brockwell Josiah, merchant, 36 Old Broad st. City
Brockwell Nathaniel, bricklayer, 54 Regent st. Lambeth
Brockwell William, bricklayer, 121 Vauxhall walk
Broder Wm. building material dealr. 1 Granville pl. Clerknwl
Broderick Jas. & Son, vet. surgeons, 12 Regent st. City road
Broderick Benjamin, undertaker, 82 Chapel st. Pentonville
Broderip Fras. & Wm. solicitors, see Powell, Broderips' & Co
Broderip Wm. John. F.R.S. Magistrate at the Thames Police Court, 2 Raymond buildings, Gray's inn
Brodey Wm. *British Queen* P.H. 114 New Gravel lane
Brodie & Allen, manufacturing chemists, Bow common
Brodie Reuben J. & Co. surgeons, 27 Montague st. Bloomsbry
Brodie Sir Benj. C. bart. surgeon, 14 Saville row, Piccadilly
Brodie Harriet (Mrs.), baker, 2 Lower York pl. Kentish town
Brodie Henry Hugh, stationer, 12 Steyman's rw. Holloway road
Brodie James, *Fountain* P.H. 4 Foster lane, Cheapside
Brodie John, house & ship joiner, 34½ Wapping High st
Brodie John Clater, artists' colorman, & wholesale artists', painters', & grainers' brush manfctr. 79 Long acre
Brodie John George, straw bonnet manufr. 115 Waterloo rd
Brodie Martha (Mrs.), wkg. cutler, 30 Lit. Pulteney st. Gldn. sq

BrodieMary(Mrs.),babylinen wareho.25Holles st.Cavndsh.sq
Brodie Matilda (Mrs.), dressmaker, 26 Porter st. Soho
Brodie Peter Bellinger, barrister, 49 Lincoln's Inn fields, & Portsmouth street
Brodie William, baker, 112 Aldersgate st
Brodie Wm. house&ship joiner,17 Gt.Hermitage st.Wapping
Brodie Wm. John, plumber, 11½ Bennett's hill, Doctors' com
Brodigan Francis, barrister, 4 Garden court, Temple
Brodribb Edwd. tea broker, see Lloyd, Matheson&Brodribb
Brodribb Francis Bower, soapmaker, see Smith & Brodribb
Brodribb Henry, solicitor, 6 Child's place, Temple bar
Brodribb William Perrin, surgeon, 12 Bloomsbury square
Brodrick John, *Golden Lion* P.H. 25 King st. St. James's
Brodrick William, solicitor, see Bell, Brodrick & Bell
Brogden Henry,clothwork.&presser,8New inn yd.Shoreditch
Brogden Jas. composition doll ma. 5 Cross st. Hatton garden
Brogden John, who. jeweller, see Watherston & Brogden
Brokenshir Mary (Miss), milliner, 7 Rufford's row, Islington
Brokenshire Wm. furniture broker, 19 Little Marylebone st
Brokhes William, plumber, &c. 14 Up. Kennington la. Vauxh
Bromage Charles, dyer, & scourer, 6 Cleveland st.Mile end rd
Bromage Thos.acct.book mrf.&c.3 Southampton ct. Queen sq
Bromehead Jonath. Crawford, sol. see Reyroux & Bromehead
Bromehead Joseph Crawford, barrister, 3 Old sq. Linc. inn
Bromfield George, brush manufacturer, &c. 31 Gt. Dover st
Bromfield Samuel, Albany dining rooms, 190 Piccadilly
Bromley & Crush, pawnbrokers, 55 Museum st. Bloomsbury
Bromley David Matthew, *Sir John Falstaff* P.H. Lower Watergate, Deptford green
Bromley Edward, straw hat manufactr. see Gray & Bromley
Bromley Emma (Miss), ladies' school, 1 Grove ter. Brompton
Bromley Hen. window blind maker, 5 Athol pl. Pentonville
Bromley Hen. Thos. *Brecknock Arms tav.* Camden rd.villas
Bromley James, window glass merchant, 315 Oxford st
Bromley James, pawnbroker, 11 Broadway, Ludgate hill
Bromley James, pawnbroker, see Crush & Bromley
BromleyJane(Miss),straw hat ma.5Marchmont st.Brunsw.sq
Bromley Jeremiah, stove grate maker, 144 Whitechapel rd.
Bromley Jeremiah, wind. glass mer. 14 King's pl.Comcl.rd.Ea
Bromley John, stationer, &c. see Carter & Bromley
Bromley Joseph Warner, attorney, 1 South sq. Gray's inn
Bromley Maria (Mrs.), general dealer, 4 New Turnstile
Bromley Matthew,*Freemason'sArms*P.H.29King st.Deptfrd
Bromley Peter, news agent, 3 Great Ormond st
Bromley Robert Holme, bootma. 6 Copthall bldgs.Copthallct
Bromley Samuel, cheesemonger, 116 & 154 Lambeth walk
Bromley Thomas, surgeon, 2 Stangate st. Lambeth
Bromley Thomas, wine cooper,23Gt.Barlow st.Marylebone
Bromley Thos.How,*Paul Pindar*P.H.169Bishopgt.without
Bromley William, jun. solicitor, 12 Gray's inn square
Bromwich James, cattle salesman, 41 West Smithfield
Bromwich Owen, baker, 37 Crawford st. Portman sq
Bronckhorst Henry Adolphus, solicitor, 36 Basinghall st
Broodbank Joseph, coffee rooms, 205 Bermondsey st
Brook & Benn, iron & brass foundry, 15 Folly, Dockhead
Brook Joseph,Sons&Co.woolmer.18King'sarmsyd.Coleman st
Brook Richard & Son, goldsmiths, 1 Poultry
Brook & Smith, ship & insurance brokers & general agents, 2 Catherine court, Trinity square, Tower hill
Brook William Wicking & Richard, melters & tallow-chandlers, Southwark bridge rd. & 105 Blackman st. Boro'
Brook Abrm. John, boot & shoe ma.6 Albion pl. Holloway rd
Brook Benj. corndealer, 64 Seymour place, Bryanstone sq
Brook Charles, fruiterer, 4 New Church st. Lisson grove
Brook Charles, pork butcher, 9 Church st. Chelsea
Brook James, butcher, 8 Walker's court, Golden square
Brook Jas. Bird, solicitor, 12 Took's ct. chambs. Chancery la
Brook John, boot & shoe maker, 8 Hayes court, Soho
Brook Joseph, undertaker, Byde's place, Shoreditch
Brook Thos. pawnbroker, 130 Up. Whitecross st. St. Luke's
Brook Thomas George, miniature painter, 48 Crawford st
Brook Wm. harness mak.1Manor pl. Grange rd.Bermondsey
Brook Wm. Harvey, cheesemonger, 9 Peerless place, City rd
Brookbank Jabez Wm. printer, 1 Charles st. Mile end nw. tn
Brookbank Minns,fur.brokr.23Colville ct.John st. Fitzry. sq
Brookbank Thos. furniture brokr. 2&30 Batty st.Commerl.rd
Brookbank Wm. sen. tailor, 19 George st. Adelphi
Brookbank Wm. jun. tailor, 11 Up. York st. Bryanstone sq
Brooke Charles, F.R.C.S.E. surgeon, Keppel st. Russell sq
Brooke Edward Hornby, lamp & oilwa.53 Lamb's Conduit st
Brooke Elizabeth (Mrs.),ironmonger&fancytinmould maker, cutter & docker maker to pastrycooks, 117 High Holborn
Brooke Geo.coach ma.Queen's head yd.Gt.Queen st.Lin.in.fi
Brooke Geo. confectioner, 8 Smart's bldgs. Hoxton old town
Brooke George, poultry&game salesman,Leadenhall market
Brooke Hen. Dyson,game&poultry salesman,Leadenhall mkt
Brooke Hen. Jas. sec. to *Lon. Life Ass.*81 King Wm.st.Cit
Brooke Horace John, solicitor, 19 Thavies inn, Holborn
Brooke James, conveyancer & col. law agt. 16 Furnival's inn
Brooke John, greengrocer, 36 Jubilee pl. Commercial road
Brooke Leonard, haberdasher, 34 Chapel st. Somers town
Brooke Thomas, furniture broker, Park place, Old Kent rd
Brooke William, wholesale hardwareman, jeweller, cutler, ironmonger, & china dealer, 9 Tothill st. Westminster, and Brooke house, King's road, Chelsea
Brooke Zachary, attorney, 17 Featherstone bldgs. Holborn
Brooke Henry, grocer, Southampton st. Camberwell
Brooker & Harrison, copper & steel plate printers, 29 & 30 Castle st. East, Oxford st
Brooker John & Son,carvers&gilds.5Southmptn.rw.Russll.sq
Brooker George, grainer, 27 Berwick st. Pimlico
Brooker James, corndealer, 22 Lit. Coram st. Russell sq.
Brooker James, irish merchant, Hall of Commerce, & 3 Bridge row, Pimlico
Brooker John, cattle salesman, 17 West Smithfield
Brooker John, oil & colorman, Little Chelsea, North side
Brooker Robert, grocer, 53 Praed st. Paddington
Brooker Wm. corndealer, 8 Willow walk, Tabernacle sq
Brooker Wm. tobacconist, 30 City terrace, City road
Brookery Peter, fishmonger, 16 Lumber court, Seven Dials
Brookes' Club House (Isaac Halse & Henry Banderet, proprietors & wine merchants), 60 St. James's st. Pall Mall
Brookes Anna Maria (Mrs.), academy, 3 Golden square
Brookes Benjamin, *Shakspeare's Head* P.H. 60 Drury lane
Brookes Benjamin, surgeon, 37 Bedford st. Covent garden
Brookes George, gen. merchant & com. agent, 9 Lime st
Brookes James, locksmith, 71 Devonshire st. Kennington
Brookes John, furnishing ironmonger & bath manufacturer, 36 Old Compton st. Soho
Brookes Joseph, watch spring mak. 5 Berkely ct.Clerkenwell
Brookes Marian (Miss), academy, see Smith & Brookes
Brookes Richard, coffee rooms, 2 Osborne st. Whitechapel
Brookes Robert, loom broker, 25 Sclater st. Bethnal green
Brookes Robert, surgeon, 57 Mount st. Lambeth
Brookes Robert, jun. surgeon, 132 Waterloo road
Brookes Wm. baker, Vassall road, Camberwell New road
Brookes Wm. boot maker, 19A, Lission grove North, New rd
Brookes Wm. M'Intosh, architect & surv. 6 Adam st. Adelphi
Brookfield Ann (Mrs.), rope&twine dl. 17 New inn yd. Shored
Brookfield Chas. Austin, solicitor, see Parkes, Carey, Blount & Co
Brookfield Robert, grocer, &c. 161 Sloane st. Chelsea
Brooking Benjamin, surgeon, &c. 7 Bow st. Covent garden
Brooking Samuel Rowe, builder, 84 High st. Portland town
Brooking Thomas H. merchant, see Robinson & Brooking
Brookman & Langdon, black lead pencil manufacturers, 28 Great Russell st. Bloomsbury
Brooking Wm. furniture broker, 9 King st. Tower hill
Brookman Mary&E.millinrs.& staymkrs.63 Newngtn.causwy
Brookman Benj.*Half-moon* P.H. Half-moon pas.Leaden.ma
Brookman Benjamin, pork butcher, 16 Gt. Pearl st. Spitalfi
Brookman Chas. hairdresser, 14 Conduit st. Paddington, & 23 New Quebec st
Brookman William, auctioneer, 5 Ebenezer ter. Coml. rd Ea
Brookman John, tobacconist, 23 New King st. Deptford
Brookman Robert, currier, Church st. Hackney
Brooks & Balfour, ship & insurance brokers & commission merchants, 157 Fenchurch st.& Lloyd's & Jerusalem cof. ho
Brooks Benjamin & Son, *Crown* P.H. 100 Curtain rd. Shordh
Brooks Brothers, wholesale & retail stationers, booksellers, publishers & news agents, 87 New Bond st
Brooks & Claxton, drugbrokers, 2 Turnwheel la. Cannon st
Brooks Geo.& Co.turkey carpet wa.2 Turnwheel la.Cannon st
Brooks & Green,land agts.&surveyrs.&auctnrs.28Old Bond st
Brooks James & James W. attorneys, 29 John st. Bedford row
Brooks & Nephew, silk manufacturers, 26 Spital square
Brooks (Cox) & Sons, pianoforte hammer rail makers, 31½ Cumberland market, Regent's park
Brooks & Watson, wood dealers, Flagon row, Deptford
Brook's Wharf, John Graham, between 48 & 57 Upper Thames street
Brooks Alfred, wine merchant, see Justerini & Brooks
Brooks Amelia (Mrs.), orange merchant, 11 Borough market
BrooksAnn (Mrs.),*Fortune of War*P.H.King's rd.Camden tn
Brooks Benjamin, *King's Arms* P.H.27 Exmouth st.Clrknwl
Brooks Charles, carman, 14 Trinity square, Borough
Brooks Charles, chemist & druggist, Priory, Wandsworth rd
Brooks Chas, contractor & carman, Vine yard, Lant st
Brooks Charles, dining rooms, 11 Bishopsgate within
Brooks Charles, stockbroker, 3 Bartholomew lane, Bank
Brooks Charles John, *Angel* P.H. 8 Paradise st. Marylebone
Brooks Charles John, beer retailer, 42 Fetter lane

Brooks David, baker, 2 Shepperton place, New North road
Brooks Dorothy (Mrs.), grocer, 7 Marlborough rd. Chelsea
Brooks Edward, dairyman, 14 Bayham st. Camden town
Brooks Edward, wax & tallow chandler, 77 Strand
Brooks Elizabeth (Mrs.), dining rooms, 10 South st. Chelsea
Brooks Francis, pianoforte ma. 1 Granby st. Hampstead rd
Brooks Francis Henry, banker, see Dixon, Brooks & Dixon
Brooks George, butcher, 12 Flagon row, Deptford
Brooks George, fruiterer&coal dealer,40 Gilbert st. Oxford st
Brooks George, ironmonger, 18 Charles st. Grosvenor sq
Brooks George, *King's Arms* P.H. New King st. Deptford
Brooks George, who.lace wareho. 1 St.Paul's pl. Walwth com
Brooks Grove, shoemaker, 9 Page st. Westminster
Brooks Harriet (Mrs.) milnr.& dressma. 24 Denmark st.Soho
Brooks Henry, bootmaker, 11 Mile end road
Brooks Henry, carver, gilder, picture dealer & restorer, 113 Wardour st. Soho
Brooks Henry, newsvender, 33 Poland st. Oxford st
Brooks Henry, newsvender, 12 Warwick square
Brooks Hen. tobacconist, 4 Cadogan row, King's rd. Chelsea
Brooks Henry William,cheesemonger, 49, & pork butcher at 52 Bath st. City road
Brooks Jacob, dyer, 10 Upper Dorset place, Clapham road
Brooks James, baker, 103 Rosemary lane, Minories
Brooks James, hairdresser, 8 Porter st. Soho
Brooks John, butcher, 219½ Poplar High st
Brooks John, carpenter, 23 Gt.Warner st. Clerkenwell
Brooks John, carpenter & broker, 6 Salmon lane, Limehouse
Brooks John, chandler's shop, 23 Pool st. New North rd
Brooks John, fruiterer, 16 Clare court, Drury lane
Brooks John, grocer, 19 East st. Manchester square
Brooks John, grocer, 23 Pool st. New North road
Brooks John, *Lord Camden* P.H. 16 Camden st. Walworth
Brooks John, oil & colorman, 23 Norton folgate
Brooks John, solicitor, 2 Great James st. Bedford row
Brooks John, stanhope press man. 14 Wild ct. Lincoln's inn fi
Brooks John, timber merchant, Commercial road, Lambeth
Brooks John Griffiths, tailor, 36 Wilson st. Finsbury
Brooks John Hampton,snuff dlr. 23 & 24 Lit.Chapel st.Westr
Brooks John Henry, account book maker, 72 Farringdon st
Brooks Joseph, grocer, 3 Salisbury st. Lisson grove
Brooks Joseph, upholsterer, 92 Long lane, Smithfield
Brooks Mary (Mrs.), baker, 19 Old Gravel lane, Wapping
Brooks Michael,wood dealer, 3 Broomfields, Deptford
Brooks Michael Francklin, *Lamb* coffee rooms, 32 Lime st
Brooks Nathaniel, silk manufacturer, 25 Spital square
Brooks Nathnl. *Town of Ramsgate* P.H. 288 Wapping High st
Brooks Reuben, carver & gilder, 35 Thayer st
Brooks Richard,cheesemonger,&c. 13 Upper Berkeley st. West
Brooks Robt. butcher, 26 Leigh st. Burton crescent
Brooks Robt. loom broker, 25 Sclater st. Bethnal green
Brooks Robt. shipowner & mercht. St. Peter's chamb. Cornhill
Brooks Robt. tobacconist, 26 Parker's row, Dockhead
Brooks Robt. John, bookseller & stationer, 7 Torrington pl
Brooks Sam. law stationer, 4A, Took's court, Chancery lane
Brooks Sam. watchmaker, 52 Great Sutton st. Clerkenwell
Brooks Sarah (Mrs.), fruiterer, 49 Marchmont st. Burton crs
Brooks Sarah (Mrs.) tobacconist, 300 Strand
Brooks Thomas, baker, 37 Hoxton old town & 84 Rosemary la
Brooks Thomas, bookseller & publr. 8 Baker st. Portman sq
Brooks Thomas, bootmaker, 15 Mount st. Berkeley sq
Brooks Thomas, cheesemonger, 160 Shoreditch
Brooks Thomas, dining rooms, 2 Whiterose court, Coleman st
Brooks Thomas, grocer, 1 Houghton st. Clare market
Brooks Thomas, grocer, 19 Titchborne st. Edgware rd
Brooks Thomas, hide & skin broker, see Culverwell & Brooks
Brooks Thomas, lace &fancy rouche manufacturer, 13 Frederick place, Goswell road
Brooks Thomas, linendraper, 106 Borough, & 2 King st
Brooks Vincent, wholesale stationer, 421 Oxford st.
Brooks Walter, pitch&tar mer. Caroline whf. 63 Rotherhithe
Brooks William, architect, 13 Percey st. Tottenham court rd
Brooks Wm. builder, 10 Glasshouse st. East Smithfield
Brooks Wm. butcher, 10 Bolingbroke row, Walworth road
Brooks Wm. carver, gilder & printseller, 14 Great Queen st. Lincoln's inn fields
Brooks Wm. cheesemonger, 7 Cleveland st. Mile end road
Brooks Wm. *Hope* P.H. 28 Stephen st. Lisson grove North
Brooks Wm. pawnbroker, 2 Sydney place, King's rd. Chelsea
Brooks Wm. tailor, 25 King st. Westminster
Brooks Wm. tobacconist, 167 Hoxton old town
Brooks William, *Victory* P.H. 16 Newnham st. Edgware rd
Brooks William, window glass merchant, cutter & stainer, diamond setter, &c. 110 Strand
Brooks Wm. Geo. tailor, 16 Prior pl. East st. Walworth rd
Brooks William Tuck, oilman, 16 Carburton st. Fitzroy sq
Brooksbank Abm. & Sons, leather fact. 7 Bermondsey mrkt
Brooksbank & Farn, solicitors, 14 Gray's inn square
Brooksbank James, barrister, 1 Essex court, Temple
Brooksbank John, brush & mat maker, 307 High Holborn
Brooksbank Theodore, barrister, Devereux chambers, Strand
Brooksby Chas. feather & fur manuf. 4 Woburn bdgs. Tavst.sq
Broom & Bagshaw, accountants, 35 Coleman st. City
Broom Hen. Chas. who.teadealer, 11 Laurence Pountney hill
Broom Herbert, barrister, 5 Essex court, Temple
Broom Joseph, oil & colorman, 1 Rochester row, Vincent sq
Broom Sarah (Mrs.), buildg. material dlr. 156 Southw.bdg.rd
Broom Wm. tea agent, 7 Fen court, Fenchurch st
Brooman Edwd. sugar broker, Commercl.coff.ho. Mincing la
Brooman Rd. Arch. sec. G.P.O. & Reg. Canal R. Co. 11 Serjeant's Inn, Fleet st.
Broome Edward, grocer, 2 Brunswick parade, Pentonville
Broome Francis, meat salesmn.&provsn.agnt. 10 Newgate st
Broome George Alex. plumber & glazr. Morning la. Hackney
Broome John, butcher, 6 Barnsbury place, Islington
Broome John, *Rising Sun* P.H. 3 Air st. Piccadilly
Broome Jsph. carpenter, 10 Parsonage row, Newington butts
Broome Thomas, vapour baths, 1 Bridgewater sq. Barbican
Broomfield Robert, bootmaker, 37 Myddelton st. Clerkenwell
Broomhall Thos. indigo broker, 2 Swan lane, Up. Thames st
Broomhead Geo. grocer & cheesem. 4 Thomas st. Oxford st
Broomhead Luke, work. cutler, 8 Union st. East, Spitalfields
Broomhead Thompson, carpenter, 2 Low.Chester terr. Pimlico
Bros Joseph tobacconist, 11 Barking churchyd. Trinity sq
Bros Thomas, barrister, 10 King's Bench walk, Temple
Brosnan Andrew, tailor, 2 Wilson st. Drury lane
Brothers Charles, boot maker, 16 Chapel st. Somers town
Brothers James, shoemaker, 38 Chapel st, Somers rown
Brotherston Isaac, baker, 117 Long alley, Finsbury
Brotherston James, saddler, &c. 5 Commercial pl. City road
Brotherton Alfred, who. clothier, 105 Bishopsgate without
Brotherton Charles, hairdresser, 28 Up. Lisson st. Lisson gr
Brotherton Charles, tailor & draper, 67 Goswell st
Brotherton James, special pleader, 11 Crown office row
Brotherton James, tailor, &c. 20 Charterhouse st. City
Brotherton John, horsehr. mer. see Harms, Son & Brotherton
Brotherton Wm. oil mer. for steam machinery, 19½ Minories
Brothwell Benjamin, grocer, 23 Hill st. Walworth road
Brough John & Fred. tailors, 22 Southampton row, Russell sq
Brough Edward, bougie & catheter mak. 25 Bartholomew close
Brough John, beer retailer, 18 Hackney road crescent
Brough John, wood carver, 46 Barbican
Brough Thomas, *Ram tavern*, 78 West Smithfield
Brough William Thomas, baker, 81 Whitechapel road
Broughall Fras. *Coach & Horses* P.H. 118 Mount st. Berkeley sq
Broughall Richard, butcher, 30 High st. Portland town
Broughton John Vickery & Son, woolln. draprs. 382 Oxford st
Broughton Benj. liv. stables, 1A, Blenheim terr. St. John's wd
Broughton & Noakes, who.&expt. hardwmn. 135 Fenchurch st
Broughton Letitia (Miss), ladies' school, 2 Alie pl. Goodms.fi
Broughton Charles W. tailor, 16 Southampton st. Strand
Broughton Charl. (Mrs.), straw hat ma. 1 Aldrmnbry pstrn
Broughton Francis, solicitor, see Watson, Broughton & Son
Broughton Francis, jun. soltr. see Watson, Broughton & Son
Broughton Wm. black lead dlr. 3 Aldermanbury postern
Broughton Wm. smith & stove ma. 2 Aldermanbury postern
Broughton Rt. Edwards, magistrate, Worship st. police ct
Browell Wm. Faulkner, barrister, 35 Southampton buildings
Browett Wm. & Henry, fringe&ribbonma. 1 Lit. Lovela. Wood st
Browett Wm. & John, carpenters, 45 Featherstone st. City road
Browett Thomas, ironmonger, Church st. Stoke Newington
Brown Archibald & Co. silk gauze ma. 18 Friday st. Cheapside
Brown Arthur & Co. brewers, Earl's court, Old Brompton
Brown & Coaffee, dyers, 4 Bray's bldgs. Lower rd. Islington
Brown & Conway, wholes. grocers, White horse yd. Friday st
Brown & Cray, cap makers, 11 Long lane, Bermondsey
Brown & Davies, surgeons, 39 Connaught terr. Edgware road
Brown & Dickinson, imp. of for. wine, 25 Laurence Pountney la
Brown & Ellis, cooks & confectioners, 28 Ludgate st
Brown & Forster, man's mercers, 5 Vigo st. Regent st
Brown George & Co. tailors, 119 Jermyn street
Brown George & Co. tailors, 11 Princes st. Hanover sq
Brown George Thomas & Son, corn merchants & sack merchants & imperial measure makers, 32 Mark lane
Brown & Gilson, fishmongers, 3, 4 & 5 Hungerford market
Brown & Goodge, dressmakers, 17 Tabernacle row
Brown Isabella & Son, cheesemongers, 25 Cannon st. City
Brown Jane & Son, linendrapers, 9 White horse la. Stepney gn
Brown, Janson & Co. bankers, 32 Abchurch lane
Brown John & Co. discount bank, 50 Threadneedle st
Brown John & Co. wine merchants, 50 Threadneedle st
Brown John & Henry, nurserymen, Albion rd. Stoke Newingtn

Brown Jno. & Sons, linen & table linen mnfs. & bleachers (Baker & Son, agts.) 17 King st. Cheapside & Waringstown, Ireland
Brown & Jordeson, coal merchants, Purfleet wharf, Earl st. Blackfriars, & 2 St. Mary at hill
Brown & King, wholesale stationers, 239 Upper Thames st.
Brown, Lenox & Co. iron cable office, 8 Billiter square; manufactory at Mill wall
Brown & Mann, jewellers, 11 Tavistock row, Covent garden
Brown Mary & Co. newsagents, 19 Warwick square
Brown, Mason & Richardson, hay salesmen, 23 Old Bailey
Brown, Newth & Co. military, naval & general outfitters & agents for India & the colonies, 116 Jermyn st
Brown & Parnell, stationers, &c. 17 Old Broad st. City
Brown & Perry, builders, 1 Blenheim cott. Bond st. Chelsea
Brown & Redpath (C.J.), patentees & manufacturers of ships' fire hearths to H.M. Royal Navy, to the hon. East India Co. ironfounders, smiths, braziers, & export ironmongers, 5 Dean's buildings, near the West India docks, Commerl. rd
Brown Robert & Benj. & Co. linen agents, 9 to 11 Watling st
Brown Robert & Benjamin & Co. merchants, 157 Cheapside
Brown Robert & Co. muslin manufrs. 106 Wood st. Cheapside
Brown & Rodda, gun makers, 36 Piccadilly
Brown & Rogers, staymakers, 75 Houndsditch
Brown, Rusby & Booth, stone merchants, 42 Bankside & Kingsland road bridge
Brown Saml. & Co. patent metallic cask ma. 12 Gravel la. Boro
Brown & Sedgwick, silk printers, Stratford
Brown & Standfast, newsagents, 4 Lit. George st. Westmnstr
Brown, Sharps & Co. muslin manufacturers, 16 Bread st. & 18 Watling st. also at their manufactory at Paisley
Brown Susannah & Sons, carpenters, 10 & 11 Saville pl. Mile end
Brown Thos. & Co. pawnbroks. 55 Up. North pl. Gray's inn rd
Brown Thomas & Henry, cabinet makers, 16 Arnold pl. Walw. rd
Brown Thomas Leonard & Son, leather pipe & bucket makers, 1 Whitecross st. Cripplegate, & 37 Worship st. Shoreditch
Brown Thomas & Son, fringe & trimming mfrs. 38 Noble st. City
Brown Thomas & Sons, medical glass manufacturers, & bottle & phial merchants, 46 Farringdon st
Brown, Waddell & Co. carpet manufrs. 4 Star court, Bread st
Brown Wm. & Son, linendrapers, 20 Finsbury pavement
Brown William & Son, scotch manufacturers, 29 Bread st
Brown William & Son, tanners, 26 Long lane, Bermondsey, & 2 Bermondsey leather market
Brown Wm. Smith & Son, sailma. & ship ch. 53 Broad st. Ratcliff
Brown Wm. & Thos. law stationers, 16 Serle's pl. Lincoln's inn
Brown & Williams (Mesd.), milliners, 23 Sloane st. Chelsea
Brown & Wood, coal mers. Cannon wf. Cannon rw. Parliament st
Brown & Young, lightermen, wharfingers & granary keepers, 19 Thomas st. Horselydown, 333 Rotherhithe st. & Shad Thames
Brown Abraham, bootmaker, 63 Regent st. Westminster
Brown Abr. *Sunderland Arms* P.H. 25 Sackville st. Piccadilly
Brown Agnes (Mrs.), printer, High st. Deptford
Brown Alexander, butcher, 18 Boston st. Dorset square
Brown Alexander, embroiderer by appointment to the Queen, the Queen Dowager & the Duchess of Kent, 24 Portman st. Portman sq. manfty. 2 South Wm. st. Perth
Brown Alex. *Pr. Regent* P.H. 1 Wellington pl. Sidmouth st
Brown Andrew, baker, 11A, Duke st. Manchester square
Brown Ann (Mrs.), grocer, Lower road, Rotherhithe
Brown Ann (Mrs.), milliner, 2 Emanuel pl. Camberwell road
Brown Ann (Mrs.), tailor, 53 Banner st. St Luke's
Brown Anselm, manfg. stationer, 68 Red Lion st. Clerkenwell
Brown Anth. stringed music. inst. ma. 40 Up. Rosoman st. Clkwl
Brown Benjamin, carpenter, 34 Aske st. Hoxton
Brown Benjamin, clothworker & packer, 31 Aldermanbury
Brown Benjamin, hardwareman, 17 High st. Islington
Brown Benjamin, marine store dealer, 73 Praed st. Padngtn
Brown Charles, baker, Upper North st. Whitechapel road
Brown Charles, beer retailer, 7 Greenhill's rents, Smithfield
Brown Charles, china & glass warehouse, 35 Oxford st
Brown Charles, confectioner, 95 Limehouse Causeway
Brown Charles, dairyman, 147 Regent st. Lambeth
Brown Charles, fruiterer, 22 Shaftesbury terrace, Pimlico
Brown Charles, hat maker, 3 East st. Walworth road
Brown Chas. mast, block, oar, &c. mkr. Vine yd. 110 Tooley st
Brown Charles, muffin baker, 14 Clare court, Drury lane
Brown Charles, painter, 2 Eliza place, Sadler's wells
Brown Charles, plumber, &c. 5 Somerset street, Aldgate
Brown Charles, solicitor, 12 Buckingham st. Strand
Brown Charles, solicitor, 22 Duke st. Westminster
Brown Charles, statuary & mason, 62 Harrow rd. Paddington
Brown Charles, wire worker, 19 Up. York st. Bryanstone sq
Brown Charles B. physician, 38 Hill st. Berkely sq
Brown Charles Henry, brushmaker, 92 Upper st. Islington
Brown Charles James, solicitor, 10 New inn, Wych st. Strand
Brown Charles Rose, stationer, &c. 193 Bishopsgate without
Brown Christopher, brushmaker, 71 Old st. road
Brown Daniel, butcher, 68 Harrow road
Brown Daniel, bookseller & news agt. 51 Holywell st. Strand
Brown Daniel, carman, 8 Southampton street, Strand
Brown Daniel, pawnbroker, 4 & 5 Ryder's court, Leicester sq
Brown David, baker, 19 Queen's row, Cambridge road
Brown David, dining rooms, 1 Little Chapel st. Soho
Brown David, wine merchant, 5 Adam's court, Old Broad st
Brown David, scotch warehouseman, 29 Bread st. Cheapside
Brown David, stationer, 8 Orford pl. Marlboro' rd. Chelsea
Brown David, wholesale grocer, 86 Great Tower st. City
Brown Ebenezer, *Blue Anchor* P.H. 25 St. Mary at Hill
Brown Edmund, carpenter, &c. 99 High st. Marylebone
Brown Edmd. Jsph. stationer, 3 Saville row, Walworth rd
Brown Edward, baker, 142 Hoxton old town
Brown Edwd. blacking & polish mak. 25 Broad st. Golden sq
Brown Edwd. carpt. & build. 25 Hardington st. Portman mkt
Brown Edward, east india broker, see Ripley, Brown & Co
Brown Edward, cabinet maker, George st. Camberwell
Brown Edward, lathrend. & coaldlr. 32 New Montague st. Sptlds
Brown Edward, tailor, 6 Crown row, Walworth road
Brown Edward John, butcher, 21 James st. Oxford st
Brown Edward Robert, book & map selr. 10 Cullum st. City
Brown Edwin, chemist & druggist, 27 & 28 Lower st. Islgtn
Brown Eleanor (Mrs.), grocer, 10 New Manor st. Chelsea
Brown Eliza (Mrs.), dng. rooms, Old Barrack yd St. George's pl
Brown Eliza (Miss), dressmakr. 19 Bevenden st. East rd. City rd
Brown Elizabeth (Mrs.) *City of Quebec* P.H. 70 Wapping wall
Brown Eliz. (Mrs.), *Coopers' Arms* P.H. 76 Golden la. St. Luks
Brown Eliz. (Mrs.), diningrooms, Old Barrack yd. Knghtsbdg
Brown Elizabeth (Mrs.), dairy, opposite Park ter. Camden tn
Brown Elizh. (Mrs.), grocer, 10 Lit. Woodstock st. Marylebone
Brown Eliz. (Mrs.), straw hat ma. 13 Ernest st. Regent's park
Brown Ellen (Mrs.), egg importer, 21 Clink st. Bankside
Brown Emily (Mrs.), ladies' school, 1 Lower Islington ter
Brown Euphemia (Mrs.), bootmaker, 134 Union st. Borough
Brown Euphemia (Mrs.), picture dlr. 19 Tavistock st. Cov. gar
Brown Ferdinand, *Ship Afloat* P.H. 16 Beer la. Tower st
Brown Frances (Miss), prof. of music, 5 Up. Baker st. New rd
Brown Francis, beer retailer, 9 Queen's st. Lr. rd. Islington
Brown Francis, bootmaker, 29 Bishopsgate without
Brown Francis, fruiterer, 50 Drury lane
Brown Francis, furrier & hatter, 137 Upper st. Islington
Brown Fredk. architect, 32 Francis st. Tottenham court rd
Brown Frederick, beer retailer, 232 Hoxton old town
Brown Frederick, butcher, 12 New st. Dorset square
Brown Frederick, pianoforte maker, 47 Warwick st. Pimlico
Brown George, baker, 4 Little Coram st. Brunswick sq
Brown George, baker, 63 Upp. Ebury st. Pimlico
Brown George, breeches mak. 25 St. Martin's ct. St. Martin's la
Brown George, builder & bricklayer, 18 Lisson grove North
Brown George, cooper, 13 Kensington gravel pits
Brown George, cooper & turner, 154 Edgware rd. Marylebn
Brown George, cowkeeper, 9 Bulstrode mews, Marylebone la
Brown George, dairy, 3 Milton st. Cripplegate
Brown George, dressing & jewel case ma. 248 Tottenham ct. rd
Brown George, dyer & scourer, 2 Whitehall pl. Kentish town
Brown George, fruiterer, 14 Gt. Chapel st. Westminster
Brown George, glass & china wareho. 11 College st. Chelsea
Brown George, hairdresser, 17 Ludgate hill
Brown George, job master, 8 Keppel mews North, Keppel st
Brown George, plasterer, 15 Skinner st. Clerkenwell
Brown George, plumber, painter, &c. 2 Brompton pl. Brmptn
Brown George, shoemaker, 68 Brewer st. Somers town
Brown George, solicitor, 19 Southampton st. Holborn, & 24 Portman place, Edgware road
Brown George, tailor, 19 John st. Minories
Brown George, *Three Tuns* P.H. High st. Bow
Brown George, timber dealer, Broomfield pl. Deptford
Brown George, tobacconist, 5 Blackfriars road
Brown George, tobacconist, 10 Rochester row, Westminster
Brown George, tobacconist, 11 Gt. Crown ct. Lit. Pultny. st
Brown George, watch & clock maker, 9 Praed st. Paddington
Brown George, wine merchant, 80 Grosvenor st
Brown George Aug. candle ma. see Pateshall, Brown & Jones
Brown George Henry, grocer, 49 Rawstorne st. Goswell st
Brown George Henry, grocer 32 St. John st. Clerkenwell
Brown George J. C. confectioner, 28 High st. St. Giles's
Brown Harriet (Mrs.), *Tally Ho* P.H. 6 Willow ter. Kentish tn
Brown Harvey C. builder, &c. 1 Hawley pl. Kentish town
Brown Henry, artist, 67 Pearson st. Kingsland road
Brown Henry, auctioneer & appraiser, 22 Throgmorton st. & 16 Harleyford place, Kennington common
Brown Henry, baker, 182 Hickman's Folly, Dockhead
Brown Henry, beer retailer, 11 Gt. Trinity lane, Bread st

Brown Henry, bootmaker, 30 Shoreditch
Brown Henry, cheesemonger, 113 Upper st. Islington
Brown Henry, comb manufacturer, 187 Whitechapel road
Brown Henry, conveyancer, 50 Lincoln's inn fields
Brown Henry, engraver & printer, 14 Nicholl sq. Aldersgate
Brown Hen. *Half Moon & Punch Bowl* P.H. Buckle st. Whtcpl
Brown Henry, poulterer & porkman, 13 London ter. Hackney rd
Brown Henry, shell fish warehouse, 30 Aldersgate st
Brown Henry, shoemaker, High st. Kingsland
Brown Henry H. solicitor, 13 Gloucester gr. West, Brompton
Brown Henry, surgeon, 1 Charles st. Lowndes sq. Knhtsbrdge
Brown Henry, surgeon, 8 Ferdinand terrace, Hampstead rd
Brown Henry, tinplate worker, 18 Lower road, Islington
Brown Henry Edwards, solicitor, see Clark, Davidson & Co
Brown Henry Hill, solicitor, 50 Lincoln's inn fields
Brown Henry Wm. grocer, 7 Portland st. Walworth common
Brown Hugh, bread & biscuit baker, 78 Cornwall rd. Lambeth
Brown Hugh Joseph, baker, 1 Harper st. New Kent road
Brown Isaac, surgeon, 27 Oxford square, Hyde park
Brown Isabella (Mrs.), shipping grocer, 144 Wapping
Brown Jacob, grocer, &c. 26 King st. Portman square
Brown James, *Adam & Eve* P.H. 144 Church st. Shoreditch
Brown James, bootmaker, 19 Cumberland mkt. Regent's pk
Brown James, bricklayer, 102 Praed st. Paddington
Brown James, builder, 12 Cottage row, Bermondsey
Brown James, builder & decorator, 17 Up. George st. Ptmn sq
Brown James, butcher, 26 Union st. East, Spitalfields
Brown James, cabinetmaker, 72 Vauxhall walk, Lambeth
Brown James, cheesemonger, 23 William st. Lisson grove
Brown James, chemist, 22 Hereford pl. Commercial rd. East
Brown James, clk. vulcan iron wa. St. Ann's wf. Earl st. Blkfrs
Brown James, dining rooms, 51 Carey st. Lincoln's inn
Brown James, dining rooms, 25 Gt. James st. Lisson grove
Brown James, gasfitter, &c. 54 Newman st. Oxford st
Brown James, *Globe* P.H. 198 Rotherhithe st
Brown James, *Grey Eagle* P.H. 21 Grey Eagle st. Spitalfields
Brown James, grocer, 9 South Island place, Clapham road
Brown James, hairdresser, 99 Upper Thames st
Brown James, meat salesman, see Lawrance & Brown
Brown James, *Private Hotel*, 21 to 24 Dover st. Piccadilly
Brown James, shoemaker, 11 Haberdashers' walk, Hoxton
Brown James, straw bonnet bleacher, 24 Porter st. Soho
Brown James, violin & bow maker, 73 Wheeler st. Spitalfields
Brown James, watch & clock mak. 56 George st. Portman sq
Brown James Buckley, builder, 1 Cottage row, Bermondsey
Brown James Burrell, bootma. 9 Prior pl. East st. Walworth
Brown Jas. Crompton, law stationer, see Taylor & Brown
Brown James Miller, silkman, sewing silks & military sash-manufacturer; trams, &c. in shades, 27 Basinghall st
Brown Jane (Mrs.), boarding house, 19 Addle st. Wood st
Brown Jane (Mrs.), fruiterer, 18 South st. Manchester sq
Brown Jane (Miss), hairdresser, 75 Compton st. Clerkenwell
Brown Jane (Mrs.) [late Keating & Brown], catholic book-seller, 10 Duke st. Manchester square
Brown Jane (Mrs.), milliner, 28 Harcourt st. Kew road
Brown Jane (Miss), ladies' school, Stockwell comn. Clapham rd
Brown Jemima (Miss), shoe wa. 2 Victoria pl. Coml. rd. Limh
Brown Jeremiah, hairdresser, 16 Great Marylebone st
Brown John, alehouse, Hertford street, Fitzroy square
Brown John, auctioneer, &c. 7 Essex place, Mile end road
Brown John, baker, 8 Colvill terrace, King's road, Chelsea
Brown John, baker, 132 High st. Camden town
Brown John, baker, 13 Windsor place, Southwark bridge rd
Brown John, basketmaker, 20 & 33 Redlion st. Spitalfields
Brown John, blacking & ink manufr. 3 East road, City road
Brown John, bookseller, 1 Charlotte st. Fitzroy square
Brown John, bootmaker, 61 Charlotte st. Fitzroy sq
Brown John, boot & shoe maker, 20 Weston st. Somers town
Brown John, boot & shoe maker, 18 Queen st. Pimlico
Brown John, brushmaker, 298 Albany road, Camberwell
Brown John, builder, 1 Short st. Horselydown
Brown John, carpenter, see Perry & Brown
Brown John, carpenter & undertk. 15 George row, Bermdsy
Brown John, cheesemonger, 45 & 47 Fetter lane
Brown John, cheesemonger, 6 Staverton row, Walworth rd
Brown John, dairy, 22 Mercer st. Long Acre
Brown John, dairy 68 Pratt st. Camden town
Brown John, dyer, 13 Sidney st. Goswell road
Brown John, fancy paper ma. 145 Up. Whitecross st. St. Luke's
Brown John, farrier, 23 Whitefriar's st. Fleet st
Brown John, furnishing undertaker, 32 Edgware road
Brown John, furniture dealer, 6 Dean's row, Walworth road
Brown John, *Green Man* P.H. Surrey pl. Old Kent road
Brown John, grocer, &c. 4 John st. West, Edgware road
Brown John, grocer, 53 Paddington street, Marylebone
Brown James, *Hare & Hounds* P.H. Stoke Newington road
Brown John, ironmercht. Dowgate iron whf. Upper Thames st
Brown John, ivory turner, 23 Kingsland rd
Brown John, *Kettle Drum* P.H. 153 St. George st
Brown John, ladies' shoemaker, 60 Mansell st. Goodmn. fids.
Brown John, lapidary 2 Newcastle st. Clerkenwell
Brown John, linendraper, 95 High st. Camden town
Brown John, manufacturing goldsmith, see Eady & Brown
Brown John, milliner, 77½ Fore street, Cripplegate
Brown John, *Old George* P.H. 7 Lombard st. Lant. st. Boro'
Brown John, plate glass manufacturer to Her Majesty, 56 Great Queen st. Lincoln's inn fields
Brown John, plumber, painter, &c. 5 Lowndes pl. Holloway
Brown John, plumber, 3 Northampton st. Islington
Brown John, shoemaker, 73 Margaret st. Hackney fields
Brown John, *Regent's Arms* P.H. 50 York ter. Regent's pk
Brown John, silk mercer & linendraper, 137 Oxford st
Brown John, stock & sharebroker, see Price & Brown
Brown John, surgeon, 11 Suffolk place, Islington
Brown John, surveyor & builder, 34 Castle st. East, Oxford st
Brown John, tailor, 27 Frederick st. Regent park
Brown John, undertaker, 40 St. Andrew's road, Borough
Brown John, *White Hart* P.H. 30 Brook street, Ratcliff
Brown John, Geo. coachbldr & harn. ma. 4 Hope ter. Notting hl
Brown John Goldfinch, coal merchant, see Irving & Brown
Brown John Hall, saddler, 220 Blackfriars road
Brown John Martin, carpt. & builder, 106 Paul st. Finsbury
Brown John Richard, master mariner, 63 Judd st. New road
Brown Joseph, baker, 67 Farringdon st
Brown Joseph, baker, 82 Salisbury st. Lisson grove
Brown Joseph, carman, London dock entrance, Upper East Smithfield, & 19 Samuel st. St. George's East
Brown Joseph, chandler's shop, 75 Harrow road
Brown Joseph, chemist & druggist, 1 Lombard terr. Chelsea
Brown Joseph, coach lace manufr. 5 Belton st. Long acre
Brown Joseph, coach plat. & founder, 8 Charles st. Long acre
Brown Joseph, Hope coffee rooms, 27 King st. Snowhill
Brown Joseph, compos. ornamen. ma. 25 Newman st. Oxford st
Brown Joseph, gold laceman, &c. see Lambert, Brown, & Co
Brown Joseph, tobacconist, 3 Saville road, Walworth road
Brown Joseph, upholsterer, cabinet maker, & patent sea cot manufacturer, 37 Minories
Brown Joseph, special pleader, 2 Essex court, Temple
Brown Joseph, watch jeweller, 8 Buxton st. Goswell road
Brown Joseph, wax chandler, 75 Quadrant, Regent st
Brown Joseph Hullett, surgeon, 37 Euston square & 27 Melton st. Euston square
Brown Launcelot, tailor, 56 Gt. Marylebone st
Brown Lawrence S. wine mer. see M'Kenzie, Brown & Co
Brown Madis, beer retailer, 25 High road, Knightsbridge
Brown Mark, cowkeeper, 3 Cross st. King st. Golden square
Brown Mark, wharfinger, Potter's Fields, Tooley st
Brown Mary (Mrs.), dairy 66 Cromer st. Brunswick sq
Brown Mary (Mrs.), ladies' school, 4 Albion rd. Holloway
Brown Mary (Mrs.), oil & color warehouse, 28 Great Carter lane, & 5 Little Knightrider st. Doctors' Commons
Brown Mary (Mrs.), flatting mills, 4½ Clerkenwell close
Brown Mary (Mrs.), hairdresser, 17 Lambeth walk
Brown Mary (Mrs.), milliner, 16 Gt. Marylebone st
Brown Mary (Mrs.), *Star & Garter* P.H. 13 Green st. Leicester square
Brown Mary Ann (Mrs.), *Duke's Head* P.H. 16 Vine st. Hattn. wl
Brown Mary Ann (Mrs.), oil wareho. 199 Bethnal green road
Brown Mary Ann (Mrs.), umbrella ma. 30 Charlotte st. Whitech
Brown Mary Ann (Mrs.), *White Horse* P.H. 18 Cloak lane, City
Brown Matthew, ham & beef shop, 2 Colvill ter. Chelsea
Brown Michael, coal dealer, 77 Salisbury st. Lisson grove
Brown Philip, auctioneer, surveyor, & estate agent & address office, 2 Jermyn st. & 8 St. Paul's terrace, Islington
Brown Philip, pianoforte manuf. 53 Bartholomew close
Brown Rachael (Mrs.), baker, 23 King st. Snow hill
Brown Richard, baker, 7 Chapel st. New road
Brown Richard, boot & shoe ma. 47 Rufford's bldgs. Islngtn
Brown Richard, carriage lamp maker, 5 Princess pl. Southwrk
Brown Richard, cheesemonger, 20 Park terr. Regent's park rd
Brown Richard, gossamer hat maker, 69 Union st. Borough
Brown Richard, lapidary, 16 St. John's square, Clerkenwell
Brown Richard, oil & colorman, 40 Regent st. Horseferry rd
Brown Rich. organ builder, &c. 13 Triangle, Kennington cr
Brown Richard, surveyor & auctioneer, 6 Billiter st
Brown Rich. Thornton, oil & seed brok. 60 Old Broad st. City
Brown Robt. appraiser, &c. 2 Palentine pl. Comml. rd. East
Brown Robert, baker, 57 Lower Marsh, Lambeth
Brown Robert, basket maker, 3 Gravel lane, Southwark
Brown Robert, bootmaker, 8 Foster street, Bishopsgate
Brown Robert, coffee rooms, 31 Camden st. Islington
Brown Robert, cowkeeper, 29 Spring st. Paddington

Brown Robert, *Dr. Johnson's tavern*, 1 &2 Bolt ct. Fleet st
Brown Robt engineer & machinist, 26 Gibson st. Waterloo rd
Brown Robert, grocer, 2 Holland st. Brixton road
Brown Robert, mason, Bell court, 179½ Drury lane
Brown Robert, newsvender, 16 Little Coram st. Brnsk. sq
Brown Robert, sculptor, 58 Great Russell st, Bloomsbury
Brown Robert, shipowner, 62 Lowr e Shadwell
Brown Robert, Who. straw hat wareh. 94 Bartholomew cl.
Brown Robert Jacob, undertaker, &c. 3 Church st. Waterloo rd
Brown Robert Mansel, ship bro. & agt. see Stovell & Brown
Brown Roger, watch & clock maker, 25 Shepherd st. Mayfair
Brown Samuel, baker, 5 Denmark place, Camberwell
Brown Samuel, coal & potato dlr. 43 Saville st. Portland pl
Brown Samuel, fruiterer, 66 Devonshire st. Lisson grove
Brown Samuel, grocer & cheesemonger, 71 Park st. Camden town
Brown Samuel, hatter, 85 Broadwall, Blackfriars
Brown Samuel, ladder maker, 5 Cottage place, City road
Brown Samuel, map & print mounter, 33A, Red Lion sq.
Brown Samuel, *Steam Packet* P.H. 1 Park pl. Limeho. causwy
Brown Samuel, tailor, 27 Finsbury pavement
Brown Samuel James, stationer, 7 Blackmoor st. Claremarket
Brown Sarah (Mrs.), beer retailer, Blackwall stairs
Brown Sarah (Mrs.) carver & gilder, 43 Chapel st. Edgware rd
Brown Sarah (Mrs.), grocer, 19 Ebury square, Pimlico
Brown Sarah (Mrs.) *King William the Fourth*, 53 Margaret st. Wilmington square
Brown Susannah (Miss) stationer, 11A, Stanehope ter. Baysw
Brown Sarah (Mrs.) milliner & dressma. 14 Duke st. Manchr. sq
Brown Susan (Mrs.) tailor, 117 St. John st. Smithfield
Brown Thomas, baker, 8 Richmond pl. East st. Walworth
Brown Thomas, baker, 16 Bedford st. Commercial road
Brown Thos. bookslr. see Longman, Brown, Green, & Longmans
Brown Thos. bootmaker, 3 & 4 Connaught tr. Edgw. rd
Brown Thomas, builder, 1 Camberwell New road
Brown Thomas, butcher 5 Melbourne pl. Old Kent road
Brown (Mrs.), plumber, 9 Union pl. Lower rd. Islington
Brown Thos. cheesemonger, 1 Grafton st. & 1 West st. Soho
Brown Thomas, cheesemonger, 61 Leather lane, Holborn
Brown Thomas, cheesemonger, 40 Tottenham court road
Brown Thomas, coach maker, 127 Praed st. Paddington
Brown Thomas, coach maker, see Silk & Brown
Brown Thomas, fruiterer, 10 New Gravel lane
Brown Thomas, coal dealer, 12 White st. Drury lane
Brown Thomas, colorman to artists, 163 High Holborn
Brown Thomas, easy & elizabethan chair maker & inventor of the ottoman chair bed for exportation, 49 Curtain rd. Shoreditch
Brown Thos. glass & staffordshire wareh. 47 St. Martin's la
Brown Thos. grocer, 1 Lit. George st. York st. Westminster
Brown Thos. goldsmith & jeweller, 6 Guildford pl. Spafields
Brown Thomas, house agent, 9 Fountain place, City road
Brown Thomas, newsvender, 1 Avery row, Grosvenor st
Brown Thomas, nurseryman, Bedford nursery, Haverstk. hill
Brown Thomas, nurseryman, Powis place, Hampstead road, & Munster square, Regent's park
Brown Thomas, painter, &c. 38 Markham st. King's rd. Chelsea
Brown Thomas, paper stainer, 27 Dean st. Soho
Brown Thomas, physician, 6 Queen Anne st. Cavendish sq
Brown Thomas, plumber, &c. 15 Red Lion st. Whitechapel
Brown Thomas, soap manufacturer, 90 Old street road, & 4 New Inn st. Shoreditch
Brown Thomas, solicitor, 33 Hart st. Bloomsbury
Brown Thomas, staffordshire wareh. see Tidmarsh & Brown
Brown Thomas, statuary & mason, Camberwell green
Brown Thomas, surgeon, 10 Fenchurch buildings
Brown Thomas, surgeon, 2 Lit. St. Mary axe & 31 St. Mary axe
Brown Thomas, tailor, 33 Charles st. Westminster
Brown Thomas, tailor, 3 Lisle st. Leicester square
Brown Thomas, tailor, 17 Tower royal, Watling st
Brown Thomas, undertaker, 67 Buttesland st. Hoxton
Brown Thomas, who. straw hat mnfr. see Munt & Brown
Brown Thomas Boden, artist, 42 Howland st. Fitzroy sq
Brown Thomas Cowper, solicitor, see Brundrett, Randall & Co
Brown Thomas E. dairy, 1 Cumberland ter. Camden town
Brown Thomas Norton, pawnbroker, 39 & 40 Fetter lane
Brown Thomas W. *Red Lion* P.H. Batty st. Coml. rd. East
Brown Thos. Wm. Russell, *Flask tavern*, 9 Ebury sq. Pimlico
Brown Timothy, cork manufac. 7 Thornton st. Horselydown
Brown Wm. accountant, 17 Bull & Mouth st. St. Martin's le gr
Brown Wm. artist, 43 Chapel st. Edgware road
Brown Wm. baker, 19 Montpelier st. Brompton
Brown Wm. baker, 35 Surrey row, Blackfriars road
Brown Wm. baker, 36 Waterloo road, Lambeth
Brown Wm, barrister, 10 Gray's inn pl. & 12 Spencer ter. Islgn
Brown Wm. bedstead maker, 15 Gt. Warner st. Clerkenwell
Brown Wm. bookseller 130 & 131 Old st. St. Luke's
Brown Wm. bookseller, 104 High Holborn
Brown Wm. bookseller, printer, &c. see Royston & Brown
Brown Wm. butcher & poulterer, 6 Comrcl. pl. Old Kent
Brown Wm. carcase butcher, 48 Aldgate, High st
Brown Wm. carpenter & builder, 34 Chapel pl. Liverpool rd
Brown Wm. carpenter & undert. 13 Skinner st. Clerkenwell
Brown Wm. cheesemonger, 27 Bermondsey New road
Brown Wm. cheesemonger, Church st. Hackney
Brown Wm. chinaman, 12 Gower place, Euston square
Brown Wm. coachsmith, 10 Earl st. London road
Brown Wm. coal dealer, 6 Cobourg st. Euston square
Brown Wm. coal dealer, 13 Little Coram st. Brunswick sq.
Brown Wm coal mer. 32 New Manor st. King's rd. Chelsea
Brown Wm. cowkeeper, 32 Great Marylebone st
Brown Wm. draper, 4 York place, Portland town
Brown Wm. engineer, 32 John st. Holland st. Blackfriars rd
Brown Wm. english & foreign bookseller, 35 High Holborn
Brown Wm. fishmonger, see Gilson & Brown
Brown Wm. *Fountain tavern*, P.H. 41 Amwell st. Pentonville
Brown Wm. grainer & writer, 25 Rutland st. Hampstead rd
Brown Wm. grocer & cheesemonger, 64 High st. Lambeth
Brown Wm. haberdasher & hosier, 20 Gt. Russell st. Cov. ga
Brown Wm. hairdresser, 28 Sidney st. Goswell road
Brown Wm. *Jolly Sailor*, P.H. 7 Back road, St. George's Ea
Brown Wm. marine store dealer, 22 East road, City road
Brown Wm. marine store dlr. 2 & 3 New Montague st. Spitalf
Brown Wm. modeller & plasterer, 10 Chenise st. Bedford sq
Brown Wm. *New Wine Shades*, 15 Clement's lane, City
Brown Wm. *Norfolk Arms* P.H. 10 Burwood pl. Connaught ter
Brown Wm. oil & colorman, 25 King st. Seven dials
Brown Wm. painter & scagliola ma. 64 Gt. Marylebone st
Brown Wm. plumber & glazier, 58 Chapel st. Pentonville
Brown Wm. plumber, 4 Harcourt st. New road
Brown Wm. potato dealer, 11 Hayes court, Soho
Brown Wm. poulterer, 17 Winter ter. Trinity sq. Borough
Brown Wm. poultry salesman, 62 Newgate market
Brown Wm. sealing wax & waf. ma. see Boatwright, Brown & Co
Brown Wm. shoemaker, 3 Goldsmith place, Hackney road
Brown Wm. surgeon, 81 Piccadilly
Brown Wm. surgeon, &c. 8 Upper East Smithfield
Brown Wm. tailor, 34 Wyndham st. Bryanstone sq
Brown Wm. tailor, see Ollivier & Brown
Brown Wm. *Turk's Head* P.H. 1 Turk st. & 1 Virginia row, Bethnal green
Brown Wm. watchmaker, 14 Myddelton st. Clerkenwell
Brown Wm. chemist & druggist, 154 Sloane st. Chelsea
Brown Wm. window gl. & lead mer. 6 Parsonage rw. Newingtn
Brown Wm. Fras. cheesemngr. 3 Roberts pl. Commercial rd. Ea
Brown Wm. Hen. baker, Tanners hill, New town, Deptford
Brown Wm. Hen. beer retailer, 12 Bowling green la. Clknwll
Brown Wm. Henry, physician, 13 Bedford st. Bedford sq
Brown Wm. Pearson, cutler, 2 Beckford row, Walworth rd
Brown Wm. S. shipowner, 3 Brunswick ter. Commer. rd. East
Brown Wm. Thomas, cheesemonger, 29 Watling st
Browne, Cartwright & Browne, surgeon dentists, 22 Fleet st
Browne Geo. Elliott & Co. wool wareho. keepers, 80 Coleman st
Browne James Kendle & Nephew, corn factors, 80 Mark la
Browne Joseph & Co. scagliola works, 33 University st
Browne Thomas & Co. wholesale ironmongers, 44 Eastcheap
Browne Wm. & Jonas, merchnts. Grenada, & 123 Fenchurch st
Browne Wm. & Son, linendrapers, 10 Clark's pl. Islington
Browne & Wingrove, refiners, 30 Wood st. Cheapside
Browne Alexander, tallow chandler, 69 Wells st. Oxford st
Browne Asaph Ira, solicitor, 27 St. Mary at hill
Browne Charles, *Old Queen's Head* P.H. 1 Lower st. Islington
Browne Charles, solicitor, 8 Walbrook, City
Browne Chas. Fred. surgeon, 2 Brunswick ter. Walworth rd
Browne Daniel George, who. confectioner, 36 Chiswell st
Browne Edmund, tailor, see Story & Browne
Browne Edmd. Head, stock & share broker, 12 Angel ct. Bank
Browne Edward, east in. & col. broker, see Carey & Browne
Browne Edwd. cabinet, chair, feather bed manuf. & upholsterer, 3 & 4 Curtain road, Shoreditch
Browne Edward Hen. architect, 13 Beaufort bldgs. Strand
Browne Elizabeth (Mrs.), *White Hart* P.H. 21 Gravel la. Boro
Browne Francis Wm. newsvender, 5 Stepney Old road
Browne Frederick, wig maker & perfumer, & sole proprietor of the magic magnet or talismanic razor sharpener, 47 Fenchurch st
Browne Frederick, solicitor, see Day, Hughes & Browne
Browne George, fruiterer, 34 Somerset place, Hoxton
Browne George, surgeon, 37 Euston sq. & 27 Melton st
Browne George, whalebone cutter, 10 Foster st. Bishopsgate
Browne Geo. jun. alum & paper ag. Chamberlain's wf. Tooley st
Browne Geo. Dean, engraver & printer, 39 Crown st. Finsbury
Browne George Lathom, barrister, 57 Chancery lane

Browne Henry, paperhanger, 4 Bolingbroke row, Walwth.rd
Browne Henry Nibbs, sugar refiner, Albert st. Shadwell, & 13 John st. Minories
Browne James, builder, 24 College st. & 23 Old Fish st
Browne James, physician, 32 Cadogan st. Chelsea
Browne John, baker, 31 Munster st. Regent's park
Browne John, saddler & harness maker, 5 King's cross
Browne John, selector of Broadwood's pianofortes, 27 Soho sq
Browne John, shipowner, Freeman's wharf house, 96 Tooley st
Browne John, solicitor, see Coode & Browne
Browne John, *Turk's Head* P.H. 1 Melbourne pl. Old Kent rd
Browne John, Markham, solicitor, 2 Hinde st. Manchester sq
Browne John Ownsworth, surveyor, 8 Furnival's inn, Holborn
Browne Mackley, & Son, parliamntry. agts. 21 Parliament st
Browne Maria (Mrs.), grocer, 14 West st. Walworth rd
Browne Mary (Mrs.), window glass wa. 17 High row, Knightsb
Browne Neville (sec. *to Bude Light Co.*) 22 King Wm. st. Strand
Browne Philip, merchant, 37 Lombard st
Browne Rich. (Admiralty registry), 2 Paul's Bakehouse ct
Browne Richard, hairdresser, 166 Poplar High st
Browne Rd. shawl fringer & embroid. 1 Dudley ct. Silver st
Browne Richd. Lovell, barrister, 13 South sq. Gray's inn
Browne Robert, corndealer, Church st. Hackney
Browne Robert Fred. surgeon 13 William st. Knightsbridge
Browne Robert Palmer, architect, 30 Clement's la. Lombard st
Browne Rowland Jay, special pleader, 3 Hare court, Temple
Browne Sarah (Mrs.) stay maker, 3 Manners st. York rd.
Browne Simeon, linendraper, 199 High Holborn
Browne Thomas, butcher, 29 Munster st. Regent's park
Browne Thomas, fruiterer, 2 Aylesbury place, Old Kent rd.
Browne Thomas, ea. india agt. Hall of Com. Threadneedle st
Browne Thos. grammar school. 14 Henrietta st. Brunswick sq
Browne Thomas, merchant, 44 Eastcheap
Browne Thomas, wholesale & retail haberdasher, hardwareman, &c. 29 & 30 Union st. Bishopsgate
Browne Tobias, surgeon, see Forbes, Browne & Young
Browne Wm. alamode beef shop, 53 High st. St. Giles's
Browne Wm. (sec. *to the Travellers' Club*), 106 Pall Mall
Browne Wm. barrister, 5 New square, Lincoln's inn
Browne, Wm. *Two Eagles* P. H. 6 South st. West sq. Lambeth
Browne Wm. Geo. commis. agt. Hall of Commerce, Thdndle. st
Browne W. M. (actuary to *Westminster & Gen. Life Ass.*) 27 King st. Covent garden
Brownell Joseph, coal mercht. Phœnix wh. Clink st. Bankside
Browning, Bowser & Co. mahogany merchants, 36 Lit. Windmill st. Golden square and 102 Milton st. Dorset square
Browning Chas. & Hen. merchants, see Twiss & Brownings
Browning J. & T. *Marq. of Granby* P.H. 33A, Gt. Marylebne. st
Browning Jas. & Wm. H. & Co. oil mer. 113 St. John st. Smithfi.
Browning Thomas Richard & Wm. & Co. timber merchants, Waterloo Bridge Wharf, Commercial road, Lambeth
Browning Thomas & Son, distillers, 6 Smithfield bars
Browning Charles, surgeon, 99 Dorset place, Dorset square
Browning Charles James, tailor, 53 Britannia st. City road
Browning George, artist, 36 Lit. Windmill st. Golden sq.
Browning Henry, baker, 20 Spring st. Paddington
Browning Henry, grocer, 21 Crown st. Soho
Browning Hen. Harris, tailor & draper, 17, Finch la. Cornhill
Browning Jas. corndealer, 190 Up. Whitecross st. St. Luke's
Browning James, haberdasher, 84 Bermondsey st
Browning James, straw hat maker, 13 Shoemaker row, Blkfrs
Browning John, butcher, 27 Wimbourn st. New North rd
Browning John, *Coach & Horses* P. H. 133 Aldersgate st
Browning Samuel, grocer & cheesemonger, 47 King st. Soho
Browning Thos. boot & shoe maker, 5 Heartley pl. Old Kent rd
Browinng Thomas, solicitor, 1 Hatton ct. Threadneedle st
Browning Thos. John, *D. of Bridgewater* P.H. 29 Macclesfield st
Browning Wm. mathemat. inst. ma. see Spencer, Browning & Co
Browning William, saddler, 31 Broomfield place, Deptford
Browning William Weedon, tailor, 25 Eagle st. City road
Brownjohn Ann (Mrs.), coal dlr. 15 Hosier la. West Smithfi
Brownjohn John, butcher, 41 Whitechapel, High st
Brownjohn Thomas, locksmith, 19 Hosier la. West Smithfield
Browniess Antho. Colling, surgeon, 4 Albion pl. Barnsby pk
Brownley John, solicitor, 8 New Boswell ct. Carey st. Linc. inn
Brownley Mary (Mrs.), butcher, 211 Rotherhithe st
Brownlie James, cabinetmaker, 1 Richmond st. Leicester sq
Brownlow Robert, tobacconist, 2 Eagle terrace, City road
Brownly Richard, butcher, 5 Albion pl. Lower rd. Rotherhithe
Brownrigg Margaret (Mrs.), butcher, 41 South Audley st
Brownrigg James, *Sugar Loaf* P.H. 40 Gt. Queen st. Linc. inn. fi
Brownrigg Samuel, boot & shoemaker, 90 Mount st. Berkly sq
Brownrigg Wm. tailor 16 Mary st. New road, Regent's pk
Brownsell John, tripe dresser, 22 Little Earl st. Seven dials
Brownsmith Thomas G. worsted &c. ma. 9 Lisle st. Leicester sq
Brucciani Dominico, plaster fig. ma. 5 Lit. Russell st. Cov. gar

Bruce, Buxton & Co. billbrokers, 34 Abchurch lane, City
Bruce & Gibson, *Dark House* PH. 8 Three Tuns passg. Nwgt. mkt
Bruce G. S. & Co. merchants, 16 Gould sq. Crutched friars
Bruce, Hamilton & Co. (Teneriffe), merchants, 16 Gould sq
Bruce & Wyld, booksels. publish. & prints. 84 Farringdon st
Bruce Alex. ale & dining rooms, 24 Brunswick parade
Bruce Alexander, surgeon, 26 Montagu st. Portman sq
Bruce & Moore, med. & gen. fixture dealers, 24 St. Mary Axe
Bruce Andrew, mason, 1 Allan st. Cross st. Islington
Bruce Ann (Mrs), goldsmith, 63 Jermyn st. St. James's
Bruce Anthony, cheesemonger & purveyor to her Majesty, 19 Clarges st. Piccadilly
Bruce Geo. Henry, leather stainer, 1 New Glo'ster st. Hoxton
Bruce Jas. broker & appraiser, 19 & 20 Peters lane, St. John st
Bruce James, surgeon, 95 Old st. St. Luke's
Bruce John, baker, 74 Fore st. City
Bruce John, pianoforte maker, 11 Frederick st. Regent's pk
Bruce Joseph, leather cutter, 42 Gt. Titchfield st. Oxford st
Bruce Methven, baker, 1 Lamb st. Spital square
Bruce Robert, undertaker, 62 Whitecross st. Cripplegate
Bruce Samuel baker, 2 Collingwood place, Mile end road
Bruce William, baker, 7 Albany st. Regent's park
Bruce William, barrister, 4 Essex court, Temple
Bruce William, bootmaker, 50 Mortimer st. Cavendish sq.
Bruce Wm. builder & furn. undertaker, 44 Barbican, City
Bruce William, *King's Arms* P.H. 19 Castle st. Long acre
Bruce William, optical turner, 16 King's Head ct. Shoe lane
Bruce Wm. Hen. law & gen. stationer, 1 Trump st. Cheapside
Bruck Louis H. merchant, 10½ Tokenhouse yard
Brue Ann (Mrs.), boarding house, 36 Burton crescent
Bruff Peter Schuyler, surveyor, 35 Bloomsbury st
Bruford Chas. upholsterer & cabinet maker, 47 Wellclose sq
Bruford Wm. upholsterer & cabinet maker, 37 Wellclose sq
Brufton Mary Ann (Mrs.), lodging house, 26 Surrey st. Strand
Brugger, Beck, & Co. watch, &c. makers, 39 Blackman st. Boro'
Brugger Joseph & Bernhard, clock makers, 32 Hampstead rd
Brugger & Straub, german & french clock & watchmakers, & dealers in organs, musical boxes & weather glasses, 79 High Holborn
Bruin George, *Windmill* booking off. 115 St. John st. Smithfld
Bruin Thos. dep. gauger for the city of London, 84 Lr. Thames st
Bruin Thos. *Golden Lion inn*, 112 St. John st. West Smithfield
Bruin Thos. *White Hart* waggon offi. 121 St. John st. Smithfld
Brumbley, Joseph, furniture broker, 143 Drury lane
Brumbley Joseph, wine cooper, 144 Drury lane
Brumby John, bookseller, 24 Haymarket, & 1 Panton st
Brumby Thomas, glass & lustre manufacturer, 19 St. James's st
Brumell Charles, civil engineer, 2 Parliament street
Brummitt George, bootma. 4 Type st. Chiswell st. Finsbury
Brumwell John, *Grosvenor Basin* P.H. 14 Wilton ter. Pimlico
Brundrett, Randall, Simmons & Brown, solicitors, agents to Regstr. Supreme court, Madras, 10 King's Bench wk. Temple
Brunel Francis & Co. merchants, 147 Strand
Brunel Sir Mark Isambard, civil enginr. 1 Pk. prospect, St. Jams
Brunes John C. & Son, tailors & habitma. 13 Grove st. Camdn tn
Brunies Borchert, whalebone work. 6 Percy circus, Lloyd sq
Brunker Thomas, cotton merchant & Lancashire rush manufacturer, 7 Queen st. Worship st. Finsbury, & wadding manuf. upon an improved principle, 10 Angel alley, Bishpsgt. st
Brunning John & Son, builders, 6 Up. Grenville st. Somers twn
Brunsden James, *Grave Maurice* P.H. Bow lane, Bromley
Brunsden Thomas, tailor, 6 Waterloo st. Camberwell
Brunskill Charles & William, silk & ribbon manufrs. 9 Pater noster row, & mills, Battersea
Brunskill Henry, surgeon, 20 Pembroke pl. Vauxhall brdg. rd
Brunswick Charles & Co. furriers, 52 Wigmore st
Brunswick Steam Wharf (J. F. Kennell, secretary; A. Wightman, superintendent; T. Dyer, manager), Blackwall
Brunt Josiah & Co. silk manfrs. 12 Milk st. & Leek, Stafford
Brunt Ellen (Mrs.), pearl stringer, 14 Greville st. Hatton gdn
Brunt George, tar distiller, see Miles & Brunt
Brunt John, stationer, 221 Rotherhithe st
Brunt John Eldershaw, goldsmith, 14 Greville st. Hat. gdn
Brunt Matthew, *Red Cow* P.H. 9 Park place, Mile End rd
Brunton T. & W. ship tank makers, see Fuller & Smith
Brunton & Whiting, solicitors, 11 New inn, Strand
Brunton Archibald Jas. stockbrok. South Gallery Auc. mart
Brunton Catherine (Mrs.), chemist, 7 Waterloo pl. Com. rd. E
Brunton Edward, cabinet maker, 66 Old st. St. Luke's
Brunton James, baker, 44 Cheyne walk, Chelsea
Brunton James, *Queen's Head* P.H. 1 St. John's lane, & 1 Peter's lane, Smithfield
Brush Thomas, fishmonger, Warlter's bldgs. Old Kent road
Brush Wm. grocer & cheesemonger, 1 Strewan pl. King's rd. Chel
Brushfield Joseph Blackden, oilman, 198 Kingsland road
Brushfield Sarah (Mrs.), oil wareh. 5 Whitehorse st. Stepney

Brushfield Thomas, oil & color warh. 28 Union st. Bishopsgate
Brust John, baker, 19 Bethnal green
Brust John, baker, 106 York road, Lambeth
Bruton Wm. hearth rug ma. 5 Anderson's bldgs. City road
Brutton Robert, solicitor & super. registrar, 18 Bethnal green
Bruwenin Fred. Geo. balance wheel ma. 52 Gt. Sutt. st. Gosl. st
Bruxner Henry, merchant, 3 Crown ct. Old Broad street
Bryan & Donkin, engineers, Blue Anchor road, Grange rd
Bryan, Price & Co. tanners, coach & harness curriers, japanners & army contractors, 8 & 9 Dacre st. Westminster, & Willow walk, Bermondsey
Bryan & Ward, butchers, 5 Staverton row, Walworth road
Bryan Ann (Miss), baby linen wa. 12 Gt. College st. Camden tn
Bryan Cecilia (Mrs.), furn. brok. 2 Obelisk bldgs. Waterloo rd
Bryan Edward, *Hope* P.H. 13 Jewry st. Aldgate
Bryan George, livery stables, Clarence pl. Clapham road
Bryan George, oilman, 11 Great Chapel st. Westminster
Bryan Henry, hairdresser, 87 Drury lane
Bryan James Pridmore, coal mer. Somerset wf. Beauft. bgs. Stnd
Bryan John, bricklayer, &c. 6 Kinnerton st. Belgrave sq
Bryan Joseph, baker, 34 Gilbert st. Grosvenor sq
Bryan Sarah (Mrs.), pork butcher, 8 Berwick st. Soho
Bryan Thomas, baker, 14 Munster st. Regent's park
Bryan Thomas, brewer & spirit mer. 54 George st. Portman sq
Bryan Thomas, brewer, 54 George st. Portman square
Bryan Thomas, marine store dlr. 20 Union st. Clarendon sq
Bryan William L. *Bee Hive* P.H. Leadenhall market
Bryant & Ashton, *Berners hotel*, 6 & 7 Berners st. Oxford st
Bryant, Burnells & Co. sugar refiners, 20 Mining lane, & Plymouth
Bryant & Davies, export wine, beer & spirit merchants, & general merchants, 30 Nicholas lane, Lombard st
Bryant & May, patent blacking & grease ma. 133 Tooley st
Bryant & White, surgeons, 50 Edgware road, Marylebone
Bryant Adam Uriah, tinplate worker, 47 Beech st. Barbican
Bryant Charles, stationer, 3 Grove pl. Green st. Kentish tn
Bryant Christr. furrier, 13 Winchester st. Pentonville
Bryant Edward, surgeon, 29 Wellington rd. St. John's wood
Bryant Edward, *White Horse* P.H. 62 Orchard st. Westmr
Bryant Edward Newton, stockbroker, 16 Throgmorton st
Bryant Edwin, merchant, 1 Leadenhall st
Bryant Elijah, carpenter, 60 White Horse st. Stepney
Bryant Fred. Wm. *H. of Venison* P.H. 1 Bell yd. Temple br
Bryant Isaac, *Prince of Wales* P.H. 17 Beauvoir ter. Kgsld. rd
Bryant James, bootmaker, 38 City road
Bryant James, surgeon, 173 Kingsland road
Bryant John, baker, Great William st. Caledonian road
Bryant John, boot & shoe ma. 18A, Cleveland st. Fitzroy sq
Bryant John, butcher, 32 Queen st. Pimlico
Bryant John, chemist & druggist, 32 Up. Belgrave pl. Pimlico
Bryant John, grocer, 3 Queen's place, Holloway road
Bryant John, saddler, 1 Chapel place, Belgrave square
Bryant John, tailor, 8 Addle hill, Doctors' commons
Bryant John Berry, surgeon, 1 Bridge road, Lambeth
Bryant John C. inspr. Chelsea watr. wks. 27 Ebury st. Pimlico
Bryant Robert, boot & shoe maker, 123 Tottenham court road
Bryant Robert, coal dealer, 37 Ernest st. Regent's park
Bryant Thomas, dyer & scourer, 20 Wardour st. Soho
Bryant Thomas, grocer, 56 Hunter st. Old Kent road
Bryant Wm. livery stables, 108 Oxford st
Bryant Wm miscellaneous repository, 88 Aldgate High st
Bryant Wm. Lamboll, dealer in paintings, 30 St. James's st
Bryceson Henry, organ builder, 5 Tottenham ct. New road
Bryden Andrew, look. glass silverer, 12 George st. Minories
Bryden James, sec. to Newry Ennisk'n. &c. rlwy. 63 Moorgate st
Bryden Jas. surveyor & ho. & land agt. see Boyle, Bryden & Co
Bryden Wm. parliamentary agt. 4 New palace yd. Westmstr
Brydges Benjamin Kay, surgeon, 28 Coppice row, Clerkenwell
Brydon John, berlin wool repository, 58 Geo. st. Portman sq
Brydon Thomas, embroiderer, &c. 5 Maddox st. Bond st
Bryer John, watchmaker, 20 Northampton sq. Clerkenwell
Bryer Thomas, haberdasher, see Stone & Bryer
Bryer William Thomas, *Gun* P.H. 103 Wapping
Bryne James Hen. haberdasher, 110 Golden lane, St. Luke's
Bryning William, hairdresser, 15½ College st. Chelsea
Bryon Hen. *Fox & French Horn* P.H. 29 Clerkenwell green
Bryon Thos. *New Bell* P.H. 16 York st. York rd. Lambeth
Bryson Geo. accountant, auctionr. & aprsr. 11 Basing la. City
Bryson Jas. *Two Brewers* P.H. 13 Buckingh. row, Brewers gr
Bryson Jas. *Pindar of Wakefield* P.H. St. Chad's row, Gray's inn road
Bubb George, tailor, 28 James st. Buckingham gate
Bubb James, plasterer & modelr. 20 Clarendon st. Somers tn
Bubbers John R. cheesemonger, 72 Provost st. City road
Buchan, Welch & Pine, calico printers (H. I. Collett, agent), 39 Friday st
Buchan Thomas, pianoforte ma. 11 Mount pl. Whitechapel rd
Buchanan & Grainger, solicitors, 8 Basinghall st
Buchanan Andrew, surgeon, 61 Broad st. Ratcliff
Buchanan Charles, merchant, 2 Birchin lane
Buchanan Geo. butcher, 48 London road, Southwark
Buchanan George Adam, surgeon, 50 Myddelton st. Spafields
Buchanan Jane (Mrs.), milliner, 18 Frederick st. Hmpstd. rd
Buchanan John, upholsterer & cabinet ma. 47 Moorgate st
Buchanan Mary Ann (Mrs.), gold & silver caster, 4 Racquet ct
Buchanan Robertson, solicitor, 1 Walbrook buildings
Buchanan Wm. bookbinder, 19 Denmark st. Soho
Buchanan Wm. merchant & e.i. agent, 15 Old Jewry chambers
Buchanan Wm. Jas. nurseryman, Bowyer pl. Camberwell rd
Buchler, Thöl & Co. general merchants, 28 Mark lane
Buck Charles & Son, florists, 33 Portland terrace, Regent's park, & Keppel st. Marlborough road, Chelsea
Buck & Hickman, saw & tool mak. 8 & 9 Church la. Whitechapel
Buck & Co. merchants & commission agents, 52 Eastcheap
Buck & Straker, printers, 4 Cullum st. Fenchurch st
Buck Edward, pork butcher, 58 New Church st. Lisson grove
Buck Frederick, boot mak. 17 Gt. White Lion st. Seven dials
Buck George, bricklayer, 1 New st. Kennington
Buck Geo. saw, file, plane & tool maker, 245 Tottenham ct. rd
Buck John Oswald, solicitor, 38 Bow st. Covent garden
Buck John Smith, wholesale grocer, see Simkin & Buck
Buck Joseph, *Roe Buck* P.H. 11 Tooley st. Borough
Buck Joseph, saw, file & mechanical tool maker, wholesale, retail & for exportation, 124 Newgate street, City, & 91 Waterloo road, opposite the Victoria theatre, Lambeth
Buck Joseph, undertaker, Church street, Hackney
Buck Richard, ship & insurance broker, 52 Eastcheap
Buck Robert, builder, Morning lane, Hackney
Buck Robert, carpenter, Church street, Hackney
Buck Robert, merchant & ship insurance broker, 60 Mark la
Buck Sarah (Mrs.), livery stables, 8 Clay street, Marylebone
Buck Stephen, shoemaker, 4 Brunswick st. Cromer street
Buck Thomas, chemist, &c. 3 Kingsland green
Buck Thomas, physician, 6 Princes place, Kennington road
Buck Thomas Alpheus, surgeon, 14 Park pl. Kennington cr
Buck Thomas Stubbs, woollen draper, 2 Great Dover street
Buck Thos. Wills, stationer & coal mer. 33 Mount st. Lambeth
Buck Wm. bricklayer & coal dlr. 26 Bethnal green road
Buck Wm. hair dresser & wig maker, 48 Threadneedle st
Buck Wm. printer, 35 Glo'ster ter. New rd. Commercial rd
Buck Wm. solicitor, 35 Great James st. Bedford row
Buckee Edwd. coppersm. & braz. 14 Bleeding hart yd. Hat. gar
Buckee Elizh. (Mrs.), cornchandler, 21 Coppice row, Clerkenw
Buckenham John Clarke, hosier, 14 Baker st. Portman sq
Buckerfield Thos. H. solicitor, 36 Southampton bldgs, Chan. la
Buckett Chas. smith, 1 Vine yard, 110 Tooley street
Buckett John, cattle salesman, 70 West Smithfield
Buckett William, butcher, 22 Cloth fair, West Smithfield
Buckey Abraham, *Bull's Head* P.H. Well st. Mile end Newtn
Buckingham Alex. organ builder, 65 White Lion st. Islington
Buckingham Elizh. M. (Mrs.), straw hat ma. 2 Queen st. City
Buckingham George, carver & gilder, 48 Park st. Dorset sq
Buckingham Henry, chair ma. 4 Brokers' row, Red cross st
Buckingham John, flax dresser & spinner, ropemaker, curled hair & hair cloth maker, 33 Broad st. St. Giles's
Buckingham John, rope, colored twine, cocoa fibre, &c. other mattings, bed sacking & horse hair manufacturer, 9 High Holborn, opposite Middle row
Buckingham Richard, haberdasher, 122 Shoreditch
Buckingham Richard, hairdresser, 13 Old street, St. Luke's
Buckingham Rd. Holloway, linendraper, 124 Shoreditch
Buckingham Rt. linendraper, Southampton st. Camberwell road, & 6 Walworth place, Walworth road
Buckland Wm. & Son, wine mers. &c. 38 Newington causeway
Buckland Edward, cigar imp. 15 St. Benet's pl. Gracechurch st
Buckland Frederick, merchant, 26 St. Swithin's lane
Buckland Fredk. Lye, pastry cook, 4 Great Russell st. Cov. grdn
Buckland Geo. tallow chandler, 21 Richmond pl. East st. Wlwth
Buckland Geo. Alex. packer, see Wheelton, Brewer & Buckland
Buckland Henry, blind maker, 4 Circus st. New road
Buckland Henry, cabinet ma. 7A, Charles st. Manchester sq
Buckland Henry Y. *Royal Standard* P.H. Tannershill, Deptfd
Buckland James, ivory & hard wood turner, 105 Aldersgate st
Buckland James, tailor, 110 Waterloo road, Lambeth
Buckland Jane (Miss), milliner, 41 Chapel st. New road
Buckland Jerh. Geo. *Hen & Chickens* P.H. Hen & Chick. lane, Walworth road
Buckland John, boot & shoe ma. 1 Nottingham st. Marylebone
Buckland John, milliner & laceman, 6 Crosby row, Walwth rd
Buckland John Pelham, surgeon, 84 Watling st
Buckland Louis, insurance agent, see Davies & Buckland
Buckland Louis, insurance broker, 33 Threadneedle st. City

Buckland Richd. flatting mills, 11 Hop gardens, St. Martin's la
Buckland Sarah (Miss), milliner, 63 Grosvenor st. Bond st
Buckland Thomas, ship & insurance broker, Lloyd's
Buckland Thomas, chemist & druggist, 84 Watling st
Buckle Daniel, engraver & printer, 4 Up. Baker st. Lloyd sq
Buckle Daniel, furniture broker, 10 Vine st. Hatton wall
Buckle James, bricklayer & plasterer, 12 Goswell st
Buckle John, barrister, 1 Essex court, Temple
Buckler Jno. C. & Ch. architects, 15 Rockingham rw. N. Knt. rd
Buckler Henry, stenographer, Thornhill road, Islington
Buckler Henry Peach, woolbroker, 79 Basinghall st
Buckler John, F.S.A. artist, 15 Rockingham row, New Kent rd
Buckler William, artist, 47 Canterbury st. York road
Buckles & Co. merchants, 33 Mark lane
Buckley Charles, grocer, Cheshire st. Waterloo town
Buckley George, basket maker, 15 East st. Walworth road
Buckley George, painter, 2 Broadley ter. Blandford square
Buckley Elizh. (Mrs.), wardrobe dlr. 33 Croydon st. Bryan. sq
Buckley Henry, floor cloth manufctr. 39 Bridge rd. Lambth
Buckley Jas. coach plater, 55 & 56 Gt. Wild st. Linc's inn fields
Buckley James, plumber, &c. 2 Onslow place, Fulham road
Buckley John, plumber & glazier, 65 Bath st. City road, & 6 Charlton st. Fitzroy square
Buckley John Edmund, artist, 1 Newman st. Oxford st
Buckley John Arthur, solicitor, see Beevor & Buckley
Buckley Joseph, *Czar's Head* P.H. 48 Great Tower st
Buckley Richard James, baker, 92 Green st. Bethnal green
Buckley Titus Henry, cooper, 6 Dorset st. Clapham road,
Buckley William, coffee rooms, 21 Old Boswell court, Strand
Buckley William, beer retailer, 79 Green st. Bethnal green
Buckman Edward, oilman, 46 New cut, Lambeth
Buckmaster Wm. & Co. tailors & army clothiers, 3 New Burlington st
Buckmaster Eliza Ann (Miss), academy, 20 Bedford st. Cov. gar
Buckmaster John, *Swan tavern*, Lr. area, Hungerford markt
Bucknall Henry & Sons, corkmers. & manfrs. 22 Crutched friars
Bucknall & Sons, cork merchs. & manufrs. 31 Crutched friars
Bucknell Daniel, rubbish carter, North whf. rd. Paddington
Buckney Esther M. & Co. timber mercs. 66 Bankside, Southwark
Bucknole John, tobacconist & stationer, 10 Edward st. Soho
Buckoke Benjamin, butcher, 25 Henry st. East, Avenue rd
Buckoke Benj. jun. butcher, 16 New Church st. West, Edgwar. rd
Buckoke Charles, tailor, &c. 19 North row, Grosvenor sq
Buckoke Henry, butcher, 2 Salisbury st. Lisson grove
Buckoke Jabez, pork butcher, 75 Devonshire st. Lisson grove
Buckquet Charles, cooper, 5 Homer st. Marylebone
Buckridge John, to'az shawl mfr. 27 Patriot sq. Cambridge hth
Bucksey John, tobacconist, 31 Gt. James st. Lisson grove
Buckthorp Thomas & Co. tea & coffee agents, 2 Mincing la
Buckthorp Charles, gold beater, 3 Tabernacle sq. Finsbury
Buckton George, proctor & notary, 2 Gt. Knightrider st
Buckwell George, organ builder, 30 Hackney road
Buckwell Wm. timber, deal & mahogany merchant, Borough rd. & at Commercial wharf, Old Kent road
Budd & Bletchley, bath & bristol car. Angel inn, 54 Farringdon st
Budd & Hayes, solicitors, 33 Bedford row, Bloomsbury
Budd Jas. & Edwd. L. tinplate wa. Paul's whf. 25 Up. Thames st
Budd David C. merchant, see Carruthers & Budd
Budd Eliza (Mrs.), tobacconist, 31 Seymour st. Euston sq
Budd George, wine merchant, 158 Shoreditch
Budd George, physician, 20 Dover st. Piccadilly
Budd George William, bookseller, see Calkin & Budd
Budd Henry, breeches maker, 46 Lombard st
Budd Henry, bricklayer, 44 Wardour st. Soho
Budd Henry, coachmaker, Harriet mews, Lowndes square
Budd Henry, surgeon dentist, 5 Holles st. Cavendish square
Budd James, copper agent, Paul's whrf. 25 Upper Thames st
Budd John, *Three Sugar Loaves* P.H. 99 Union st. Borough
Budd John E. tallow chandler, 34 Brown st. Bryanstone sq
Budd Joshua Thos. grocer, oilman, &c. 82 Mount st. Berkeley sq
Budd Louisa (Mrs.), academy, 23 Gt. George st. Bermondsey
Buddell & Phipps, ladies' shoemak. Cadogan house, Sloane st
Budden George, tailor, 50 Gibson st. Waterloo rd
Budden Wm. leather & paper case mfr. 12 Waterloo pl. Clknwl
Budding William, baker, 2 Park terrace, King's rd. Chelsea
Budding William, butcher, 4 Wells st. Mile end New town
Buddle & Tildesley, saw & planing mills, & chimney piece manufacturers, 3 & 5 Irongate wharf, Paddington
Buddrich Geo. W. potter & glass seller, 104 Bishopsgt. without
Bude Light Off. (Neville Browne, sec.), 22 King Wm. st. Strand
Budge Benjamin, butcher, 87 Lambeth lower marsh
Budge Benjamin, hide & skin salesmn. Bermondsey skin markt
Budge Benjamin, jobmaster, Surrey square, Old Kent road
Budge John, butcher, 113 Lambeth lower marsh
Budge Nathan, butcher, 171 Lambeth walk
Budmoe Elizh. (Mrs.), *Waterman's Arms* P.H. 11 Barnham st
Buego Alexander, hairdresser, 4 Westmorlnd. blds. Aldgst. st
Buer John, butcher, 7 Norfolk st. Middlesex hospital
Buer William, pawnbroker, 51 & 52 York sq. Regent's park
Buffen George, haberdasher, 158 Lambeth walk
Buffini Henry, *Gerrard Arms* P.H. 41 Gerrard st. Islington
Buffrey David, brass finisher, 44 Wilsted st. Somers town
Bufton Ann (Miss), milliner, see Greyell & Bufton
Bugbee Jph. *Gr. Coat Boy* P.H. & carman, 34 Artillery rw. Wstr
Bugg George, builder, 2 Pilgrim st. Ludgate hill
Bugg John, tea dealer, 190 Hoxton Old town
Bugg William, *Two Brewers* P.H. Stratford
Bugiotti Louis, plaster cast figure maker, 4 Leather lane
Buglar Wm. mast & block maker, 79 Wapping wall
Buhl Frederick, boot & shoe maker, 58 Burlington arcade
Bühler Conrad J. *City of Norwich* P.H. 61 Wentworth st
Buhrer Abraham, impr. of for. glass, &c. 46 Skinner st. Snow hl
Buick George, baker, 2 Helmet row, Old st. St. Luke's
Builder Newspaper Office, 2 York st. Covent garden
Builder Thos. tailor, 1 Grange pl. Grange road, Bermondsey
Buisson John F. & Co. merchts. 8 Langbourn chmbs. Fench. st
Buist George, oil & colorman, 81 Waterloo road
Buist Geo. saddler, 7 Finsbury place South
Buist John, painter & paper hanger, 48 Hercules blds. Lmbth
Buist Robert, dentist, 105 York road, Lambeth
Buist Wm. plumber, &c. 20 White Hart pl. Lower Kennington la
Bukett George, tobacconist, 272 Bethnal green road
Bulbick James, beer retailer, Mill wall, Poplar
Bulbrook Charles, cabinet maker, 17 Lant street, Borough
Bulck Robert, bookbinder, 7 Litchfield st. Soho
Bulford Charlotte (Mrs.), plumber, 17 Lombard st. Cheyne wk
Bulford George, bricklayer, 33 Turner square, Hoxton
Bulford John, house agent, 5 James place, Hoxton fields
Bulford Sarah (Mrs.), milliner, 2 Charles pl. Charles sq. Hoxton
Bulford Thomas, bricklayer, 27 Wellington st. Kingsland rd
Bulgin Henry, bookseller & stationer, 221 Regent st
Bulgin James, optical turner, 8 Harrison st. Gray's inn rd
Bulgin William, undertaker, 8 Crown court, Temple bar
Bull Henry & Co. wood & millboard box makers, 138 London wall
Bull Martha & Sarah, milliners, 38 Pembroke sq. Kensington
Bull & Nash, dlrs. in bonded stores, wines, spirits, bottled ale & stout, & irish & foreign provision, 91 Minories
Bull & Smith, bookbinders, 33 Whitefriars st
Bull William & Co. cloth merchants, 6 & 7 Addle st. Wood st
Bull & Underwood, solicitors, 25 Ely place
Bull & Wilson, woollen warehousemen, 52 St. Martin's lane, & 224 Shoreditch High st
Bull wharf (John Wm. Goss), between 62 & 68 Upper Thames st
Bull Benjamin, boot & shoe maker, 8 Dean st. Westminster
Bull Benjamin, butcher, 153 Bethnal green road
Bull Benjamin, bricklayer & plasterer, 24 Warwick lane
Bull Chas. pocketbook lockmaker, 5 New ct. Farringdon st
Bull Daniel, butcher, 9 Gt. Chapel st. Westminster
Bull Daniel G. cheesemonger, 63 Aldersgate st
Bull Edward, public library, 19 Holles st. Cavendish sq
Bull Edward, currier & leatherseller, 89 Shoreditch High st
Bull George, fruiterer, 8 Cloth fair, Smithfield
Bull George, leatherseller, 10 Paradise st. Marylebone
Bull George, undertaker, 6 Hackney road
Bull Henry, merchant, 88 Great Tower st
Bull Henry, paper stainer, 7 Skinner st. Bishopsgate
Bull Henry, tailor, 7 John st. Minories
Bull Isaac, builder, 28 Herbert st. New North road
Bull James, beer retailer, 129 Brunswick st. Hackney road
Bull James, oil & colorman, 109 Upper Whitecross st
Bull John, cheesemonger, 8 Albion pl. Hyde park square
Bull John, lodging house, 15 Ely place, Holborn
Bull John, *Railway tavern*, New cross
Bull John, stockbroker at Mr. Bone's, 5 Bank chambers
Bull John, tailor & habit maker, 2 Argyll pl. Regent st
Bull John Edwd. chandler's shop, 5 Wellingtn. st. Kingsland rd
Bull John Thos. grocer, 5 Portman place, Edgware road
Bull Joseph, cattle salesman, 60 West Smithfield
Bull Joseph, staymaker, 35 Pitfield st. Hoxton
Bull Joseph, wax & tallow chandler, 113 Chancery lane
Bull Lawrence, butcher, 24 Baker's row, Whitechapel rd
Bull Martha (Mrs.), strawhat ma. 17 Bartholomew ter. St. Luke's
Bull Matthew, baker, George st. Camberwell
Bull Obadiah, bricklayer, 20 White Lion st. Spitalfields
Bull Reuben, furnishing ironmonger, 18 & 19 Adam st. West
Bull Richard, baker, 5 Holles st. Clare market
Bull Richard, grocer & cheesmg. 21 Lit. Bell alley, Coleman st
Bull Rd. Hen. lookg. glss. frame mfr. 34 Wilke's st. Spitalfields
Bull Sarah (Mrs.), packing case ma. 3 Artillery st. Bishopsgate
Bull Simeon Thomas, architect, &c. 16 Holles st. Cavendish sq
Bull Thomas, cabinet ma. 77 Shaftesbury st. New North rd
Bull Thomas, keybugle & trumpet ma. 34 Windmill st. Finsbury

Bull Thomas, linendraper, see Kent & Bull
Bull Thomas, physician, 27 Finsbury place North
Bull Thomas, tailor, 84 Dean st. Soho
Bull Thos. H. small workr. in gold & sil. 13 President st. East
Bull Thomas Love, corn & coal merchant, see Kruse & Bull
Bull Wm. bookseller, 8 Stationers' hall ct. Ludgate st
Bull William, boot & shoe maker, 3 Church st. Camberwell
Bull William, butcher, 6 Albion place, Hyde park square
Bull William, *Cat & Mutton* P.H. 1 Duncan pl. London fields
Bull William, dairyman, 4 Queen st. Soho
Bull Wm. Henry, dairy, 35 Windsor st. Lower st. Islington
Bull Wm. John, beer retailer, 8 Mayfield place, Kensington
Bullar Henry, special pleader, 11 King's Bench walk, Temple
Bullar John, barrister, 11 King's Bench walk, Temple
Bullard Benjamin, grocer, 37 Swan place, Old Kent road
Bullard Thos. Saml. parish clerk, 9 Grocers' hall ct. Poultry
Bullard Wm. bricklayer, &c. 91 Mount st. Berkeley sq
Bullas George, carcase butcher, 58 Aldgate High st
Bullbrooke Thos. chairmaker, 13 Garden row, London road
Bullen & Parker, surgeons & chemists, 10 Duke st. Boro'
Bullen Edward, special pleader, 3 Pump court, Temple
Bullen George, cattle salesman, 15 West Smithfield
Bullen Henry St. John, surgeon, 24 Judd st. Brunswick sq
Bullen John, auctioneer, 12 Wormwood st. Old Broad st
Bullen John, dairyman, 4 Brook st. Gloucester rd. Hyde pk
Bullen John, potato salesman, South row, Covent garden mkt
Bullen Joseph B. waggon *Vine* office, 70 Bishopsgt. st. within
Bullen Wm. grocer & cheesemonger, 16 Salmon la. Limehouse
Buller Richard & Co. merchants, 2 Brabant ct. Philpot la
Buller Vivian A. & Plumer A. wine mers. 2 Brabant ct. Philpot la
Buller Charles, jun. barrister, 5 Hare court, Temple
Buller Henry, dining rooms, 88 Park st. Camden town
Buller John Edward, solicitor, see Smart & Buller
Buller Martha (Mrs.), coffee rooms, 205 Tottenham court rd
Buller William Charles, barrister, 6 Old square, Lincoln's inn
Bulley Nicholas, plumber, &c. 33 Titchborne st. Edgware rd
Bullick Thos. Richardson, linen &c. wa. 60 Basinghall st
Bullin & Burt, surgeons, 26 Farringdon st
Bulling Ann (Mrs.), ladies' wardrobe dlr. 12 Brewer st. Pimlico
Bullions James, grocer, &c. 1 James pl. Lark hall la. Clapham
Bullivant Francis, teadealer, &c. see Philpott & Bullivant
Bullivant Henry, stationer, 40 Amwell st. Pentonville
Bullivant Isaac, hatmaker, 231 Shadwell High st
Bullivant Thos. beer retailer, 6 Colchester ter. Old Brompton
Bullman Ann (Mrs.), fruiterer, 13 Fair st. Horselydown
Bullman Jas. King, grocer & cheesem. 21 Lower rd. Islington
Bullmore & Patrick, gold lace manufacturers & embroiderers, 17 Bedford st. Covent garden
Bullmore William, gold & silver thread manufacturer & wire drawer, 28 Clerkenwell close
Bullock Edw. & Rd. H. auctioneers & landagts. 211 High Holbrn
Bullock & Luscombe, solicitors, 35 Lincoln's inn fields
Bullock Benjamin, ham & beef dealer, 83 Gray's inn lane
Bullock Charles, linendraper, 21 Bolingbroke rw. Walwth. rd
Bullock Edward, barrister, 10 Farrar's buildings, Temple
Bullock Harriet (Mrs.), tobacconist, 10 Limekiln hill, Limeho
Bullock John, livery stables, Denmark hill, Camberwell
Bullock John, tea dealer, 19 Duke st. Grosvenor square
Bullock John F. wholesale gilt jeweller & manufacturer of gold, silver & tinsel lace, 14 Bartlett's buildings, Holborn
Bullock Joseph B. attorney, 15 Laurence Pountney hill
Bullock Lloyd, operative chemist, 22 Conduit st. Bond st
Bullock Robert tailor, 3 Chichester pl. Gray's inn road
Bullock Thomas, baker, Stratford
Bullock Thomas, clothes dealer, 31 Cutler st. Houndsditch
Bullock William, bookseller, 3 Clerkenwell green
Bullock William, dairy, 41 Henry st. Hampstead road
Bullock William, velvet & silk manfctr. 11 Paternoster row
Bullpitt John & Sons, cork merchants & manufrs. 62 Minories
Bullwinckell Geo. Fred. *Archers* P.H. 11 Osborne st. Whitchpl
Bulwinckle Jos. bookbinder & gilder, 5 Cullum st. Fenchurch st
Bullwinkle Esther (Miss), cheesemonger, 35 St. George st
Bullworthy Mary Ann (Mrs.), pawnbrkr. 12 Aylesbury st. Clkwl
Bully John, bootmaker, 14 Little St. Thomas Apostle
Bulman Robert, carpenter, &c. 3 Little Vine st. Piccadilly
Bulmer & Stride, parliamentary agents, 44 Parliament st
Bulmer John Rubens, agent, 30 & 31 Wharf road, City road
Bulpit Edward, potato dealer, 37 Eagle st. Red Lion square
Bulstrode Christopher, cabinet maker, 50 Paddington st
Bulstrode Jas. oil & colorman, 1 Rufford's row, Islington
Bulstrode John, corn & coal merchant & van proprietor, 8 Cumberland place, Old Kent road
Bult James, Son & Co. (late Goodbehere & Bult), bankers, money changers, & dealers in bullion, 85 & 86 Cheapside
Bult Benjamin E. bookseller, 25 New Quebec st. Portman sq
Bult James Samuel, upholsterer, 9 Up. Albany st. Regent's pk
Bult John, tailor, 9 St. Ann's lane, St. Martin's le grand
Bult Mary (Mrs.), chandler's shop, 6 Corbet ct. Spitalfields
Bultitude Elijah, butcher, 1 Symons st. Chelsea
Bumpus Evan E. *Britannia* P.H. 51 Britannia st. Bagnigge wells road
Bumpus Thomas, bookseller & stationer, 6 Holborn bars
Bumpus Thos. jun. new & old bookseller, 1 Birchin lane
Bumpstead Elizth. (Mrs.), *Lamb* P.H. 12 Lamb pl. Kingslnd. rd
Bumstead George, bookseller, 180 High Holborn
Bumstead Henry, fruiterer, 7 Wells st. Jermyn st
Bumstead David & Co. Droitwich salt mer. 86 Lr. Thames st. 35 Bridge wf. City road basin, & 338 Wapping High st
Bumstead John Daniel & Samuel, merchants & agents, 86 Lower Thames st. & 338 High st. Wapping
Bumstead Daniel, beer retailer, 22 Cross st. Islington
Bunbury Edward Herbert, barrister, 15 Lincoln's inn fields
Bunce Frederick, bootmaker, 2 Gt. Pultney st. Golden sq
Bunce Harriott (Mrs.), glass mounter, 2 John st. Wlmngtn. sq
Bunce Joseph, baker, 1 Church st. Lambeth
Bunce Thomas, grocer, 203 Bermondsey st
Bunce Wm. bookseller & stationer, 8 Charles st. Westminster
Bunce Wm. music printer, 20 King's head court, Holborn
Buncombe Chas. Hope, surgeon, 27 Assembly row, Mile end
Buncombe Richd. boot & shoe maker, see Ferris & Buncombe
Bundey Abraham, builder, 4 Broadley terrace, Blandford sq
Bundey Geo. carpenter & undert. 38 North st. Manchester sq
Bundey Henry, builder, Weymouth terrace, Hackney road
Bundey Thomas, grocer, 203 Bermondsey st
Bundey Wm. carpenter, 77 Boston place, Dorset square
Bundock George, *White Swan* P.H. 20 Whitechapel High st
Bundock Jas. *North Country Pink* P.H. Risbie's rope walk, Limehouse
Bundy Daniel, academy, Little Chelsea
Bundy John, trunk maker, 7 Cheapside & 33 Hatton garden & 49 High Holborn
Bungay William, tailor, 5 Marsham st. Westminster
Bungey Henry, fruiterer, 4 Brecknock pl. Camden new twn
Bungey Stephen, whitesmith, 16 St. Martin's st. Leicester sq
Bunie Michael, tallow chandler, 68 Lisson grove north
Bunker Joel, cowkeeper, 17 Devonshire st. New North road
Bunker Joseph, builder, 28 Francis st. Newington butts
Bunker Samuel, fruiterer, 28 Churchway, Somers town
Bunker William, wheelwright, Stepney green
Bunn Edw. Thos. & Son, iron mer. & agts. 9 St. Michael's alley
Bunn Edw. Thos. mercht. & ins. brok. 9 St. Michael's alley
Bunn Henry, cabinet maker, 12 Spicer st. Spitalfields
Bunn John, linendraper, 16 St. Alban's place, Edgware road
Bunn Thomas, haberdasher, hosier & laceman, 8 Cheapside
Bunnell Peter, fancy wareh. & hosier, 24 St. Martin's-le-grand
Bunnett & Corpe, engineers, patentees of revolving iron safety shutters, ornamental metallic sash bars, concentric steam engines, &c. 26 Lombard st. & Newcross rd. Deptford
Bunnett Alfred, blind ma. 19 Bridge house pl. Newgtn. cau
Bunnett Wm. J. blind mak. 5 Mount st. Westminstr. bridge rd
Bunney Benj. silk warehouseman, 43 Noble st. Cheapside
Bunney Geo. (Mrs.), surgical belt mak. 27 Lr. Eaton st. Pimlico
Bunney George Hockley, florist, Conservatory, Covent garden & Maryland point, Stratford, Essex
Bunney Henry John, stationer & acct. book ma. 9 Pancras la
Bunning Chris. & Son, cop. pl. engravs. 28 Bedford st. Cov. gardn
Bunning Jas. Bunston, architect, &c. 34 Guilford st. Russ. sq
Bunny Brice Fred. barrister, 1 New sq. Lincoln's inn
Bunny George, butcher, 6 Queen's row, Pimlico
Bunter Richard W. cattle salesman, 17 West Smithfield
Bunting Ann (Mrs.), stationer, &c. 9 Manor pl. north, Chelsea
Bunting Christiana M. (Miss), milliner, 1 Bridge pl. Southw
Bunting George, tailor, 5 Adam st. West, Bryanstone sq
Bunting John, organ & pianoforte ma. 22 Swan st. Minories
Bunting John, shell fishmonger, 12 Plumber's row, City rd
Bunting Robert, lapidary, 35 Sekforde st. Clerkenwell
Bunting William, linendraper, &c. 13 King st. Covent gardn
Bunton John, who. umbrel. mfr. 15 Gresham st & 212 High Holbn
Bunyan John, *Three Tuns* P.H. 40½ Northampton st. Clkwll
Bunyard Charles & Co. grocers, 131 Aldersgate st
Bunyard & Metcalf, seedsmen, 9 City road, Old st
Bunyard Alfred, fruit salesman, Borough market
Bunyer William, *Old Bell hotel & tap.* 123 Holborn hill
Bunyon Ann (Mrs.), basket ma. 14 Parkside, Knightsbridge
Burbery & Merridew, manfrs. & imp. of ribbons, 26 Wood st
Burbey Richard, solicitor, see Dimmock & Burbey
Burbidge & Baggellay, who. hosiers, 25 Bridge st. Southwk
Burbidge & Healey, ironmongers, smiths & manufacturers of hot water apparatus for horticultural purposes, & of improved cooking apparatus, 130 Fleet st
Burbidge John & Son, desk & dressing case makers & undertakers, 8 Tysoe st. Clerkenwell

Burbidge Edward, solicitor, 88 Hatton garden
Burbidge Edwin, dairyman, 54 Lit. Clarendon st. Somers tn
Burbidge Geo. land & estate agt. see Hubbard & Burbidge
Burbidge George, tobacconist, 8 Aldenham st. Somers town
Burbidge James Thomas, *Pitt's Head* P.H. 53 Old Bailey
Burbidge Jonas, academy, 19 Penton st. Pentonville
Burbidge Thomas Bulcock, who.hatma. 25 Bridge st Southwk
Burbidge William, rectifier, 74 Aldersgate st
Burbridge John & Robt. grocers, 1 Jerusalem pas. St. John's sq
Burbridge Thomas, hairdresser, 71 Newgate st
Burch John & Son, habit makers, 75 Newman st. Oxford st
Burch & Lucas, tailors & drapers, 52 King William st. City
Burch Amelia (Mrs.), fruiterer, 45 Broad st. Ratcliff
Burch Clear, lead pencil manftr. 32 Platt ter. Pancras road
Burch Edw. Jas. gen. outfitting war. 35 Gt. Russell st. Blmsb
Burch John, coffee rooms, 7 Star corner, Bermondsey
Burch Wm. bootmaker, 26 Paradise row, Chelsea
Burch Wm. last & boot tree ma. 2 & 3 Back hill, Hatton gardn
Burch Wm. plumber, 33 Adam st. West, Bryanstone sq
Burch Wm. Walter, engraver & printer, 48 Lombard st
Burchall Charles, confectioner, Wandsworth rd. North side
Burcham Edmund, corndealer, 2 Albion pl. East, King's crs
Burcham Robt. Partridge, chemist, 14 Albany st. Regent's pk
Burcham Thomas Borrow, barrister, 12 Paper bldngs. Tmple
Burchardt Jacob, furrier & cap ma. 12 Cutler st. Houndsditch
Burchatt Elizabeth (Mrs.), academy, Old Brompton
Burchell, Kilgour & Parson, solicitors, 24 Red Lion sq. Holborn, & 47 Parliament st
Burchell Geo. Wm. grocer, Wyndham road, Camberwell
Burchell James, solicitor, 24 Red Lion square
Burchell Peter L. surgeon, &c. 1 Kingsland road
Burcher Frances (Mrs.), greengrocer, 10 North st Lisson grove
Burchett James Robt. & Son, proctors, 9 Gt. Knightrider st
Burchett George, bricklayer, 47 Waterloo st. Camberwell
Burchett Henry, boot & shoe manufacturer, 71 Oxford st
Burchett Wm. boot manuftr. 29 Cheapside, & 31 Holborn hill
Burchfield Thos. & Son, agricul. implmnt. ma. 83 West Smithfld
Burchfield Samuel, ropemaker, Pennyfields, Poplar
Burchfield Thos. & Son, scale, weight & weighing machine manufacturer, 1 & 83 West Smithfield
Burchfield Wm. butchers' cutler, 20 New Newgate market, & 11 West Smithfield
Burchmoore Thos. *Marquis of Hastings* P.H. 42 Ossulston st
Burchmore Wm. linendraper, 10½ Exmouth st. Clerkenwell
Burchnall William, meat salesman, 3 Newgate market
Burd John & Son, calico printers (T. Collins, agent), 6 Clement's court, Milk st
Burden Chas. Jones, *Coopers' Arms* P.H. 6 Strutton grnd. Westr
Burden Edward, chemist, 38 Duke st. Grosvenor square
Burden James John, beer retailer, 223 Bethnal green road
Burden John, builder, 28 East st. Red Lion sq
Burden Johnson Thos. grocer, 13 Parker's row, Bermonds. rd
Burden John Wm. appraiser, 107 York st. Comrcl. rd. Whitchpl
Burden Thomas, beer retailer, 12 Strutton ground
Burden Thomas, chemist, 6 Store st. Bedford square
Burden Wm. *Battle of the Nile* P.H. 57 Albion st. Rotherhithe
Burden Wm. smith & farrier, High row, Silver st. Kensington
Burden Wm. Thomas, butcher, 5 Coborn road, Mile end rd
Burder Henry Hardcastle, solicitor, 21 Abchurch lane
Burder John, solicitor & notary, 27 Parliament st. Westminstr
Burder John, jun. solicitor, 34 Bloomsbury square
Burdett Charles, linendrapr. 10 Chichester pl. Wandsworth rd
Burdett Frederick James, silkman, 54 Bethnal green road
Burdett Jas. Francis, *Dolphin* P.H. 38 Church st. Shoreditch
Burdett John, carpet & floor cloth dealer, 76 Bishopsgate within
Burdett Rd. plumber & glazier, 61 Seymour pl. Bryanstone sq
Burdett Wm. linendraper, 3 York terrace, Commercial rd. ea
Burdett Wm. Francis, dancing master, 7 Chalton st. Somrs tn
Burdge Frederick, currier, see Labdon & Burdge
Burdge William Labdum, ham & beef dealer, 258 High Holborn, & 30 Tottenham court road
Burdin Joseph, lodginghouse, 22 Beaumont st. Marylebone
Burditt Mary & Lucy (Misses), milliners, 4 Margaret st. Cav. sq
Burdock Catherine (Mrs.), clear starcher, 7 Queen st. Oxford st
Burdock William, grocer, 39 Boston place, Dorset square
Burdon & Gray, wine merchants & merchants, 1 New London st. Crutched friars
Burdon Cotsford, barrister, 23 Old square, Lincoln's inn
Burdon Henry, dairyman, 67 King st. Golden square
Burdon John, grocer, 6 Little Guildford st. Brunswick sq
Burdon Robert, goldsmith, 107 Chalton st. Somers town
Burdon Thomas, governor of debtors' prison, Whitecross st
Burdon Thomas, shoemaker, 11 Gt. Hermitage st. Wapping
Bureaud Riofrey, physician, 68 Wimpole st. Cavendish sq
Burfield Benjn. engin. & pat. axle ma. 20 Boro' rd. Southwark
Burfield Chas. granite agt. Wellington chmbrs. London br
Burfield Henry, chemist & druggist, 180 Strand
Burfoot Joseph, bootmaker, 9 Gt. Woodstock st. Marylebone
Burford David & Ephraim & Co. calico printers, 87 Wood st
Burford George & Thomas, linendrapers, Stratford broadway
Burford Alfred, *Royal Champion* P.H. Portland st. Walw. com
Burford Benjamin, tobacconist, 57 Greek st. Soho sq
Burford Ephraim, calico printer, Stratford
Burford Henry Thos. B. surgeon, 82 Hamilton ter. St. John's wd
Burford John Court, solicitor, 77 Cornhill, & 10 King's Bench walk, Temple
Burford Robert, panorama, 16 Leicester square
Burford Thos. fancy trimming ma. 32 Thomas st. Brick lane
Burford Thomas, oil & colorman, 71 Dury lane
Burford Thos. Wm. livery stables, 8½ Blackman st. Boro'
Burford Wm. baker, 3 Long lane, West Smithfield
Burford Wm. dealer in horses, 35 London road, Southwark
Burford Wm. house decorator, 69 Coleman st. City
Burgar John Wesley, watch manufr. 57 Banner st. St. Luke's
Burge Edmund, boot & shoe maker, 24 Queen st. Bryanstone sq
Burge Edward, cheesemonger, 51 Ernest st. Regent's park
Burge Elizh. (Miss), grocer, 17 Copenhagen st. Pentonville
Burge George, picture dealer, 19 Frith st. Soho sq
Burge George Wm. trimming manf. see Rooke, Son & Burge
Burge Henry, chandler's shop, 44 Waterloo st. Camberwell
Burge James, toy dealer, 135 Minories
Burge Joseph, tailor, 26 Charles st. Horselydown
Burge Rich. cabinet mak. 19 Lamb's Conduit pas. Red Lion sq
Burge Wm. queen's counsel, 1 Paper buildings, Temple
Burge Wm. bootmaker, 123 Gt. Saffron hill, Hatton garden
Burgeff & Co. sparkling hock merchants, 7 Hart st. Mark la
Burges Alfred, civil engineer, see Walker & Burges
Burges Francis, tailor, 18 Salisbury st. Strand
Burges George, bagatelle board ma. 4 Galway st. St. Luke's
Burges John, coal factor, see Clark & Burges
Burges John, tobacco pipe maker, 42 New Peter st. Westmr
Burgess Hen. & Co. agents for bankers, 29 St. Swithin's la. City
Burgess John & Son, old italian warehouse, 107 Strand
Burgess Alex. Innes, pawnbroker, 10 Clarence pl. Cmbrwl. rd
Burgess Charles, baker, 16 Charles st. Westminster road
Burgess Chas. *Globe* P.H. 22 Upp. Marylebone st. Portl. pl
Burgess Edmund William, builder, 51½ Wardour st. Soho
Burgess Edward, clock case mak. 8 Perceval st. Clerkenwell
Burgess Edwin, baker, 83 Hackney road
Burgess Edwin, cowkeeper, 47 & 49 Cornwall road, Lambeth
Burgess Herbert Sawyer P. coach mak. 1 Sloane sq. Chelsea
Burgess James, fruiterer, Church st. Hackney
Burgess James, leather seller, 2 Albion place, Holloway rd
Burgess James, shoemaker, 1½ Providence row, Finsbury
Burgess John, carpenter, 10 Upper Ranelagh st. Pimlico
Burgess John, general dealer, 53 Gt. James st. Lisson grove
Burgess John, pawnbroker, High st. Kingsland
Burgess John, *Railway tavern*, 5 Harmood pl. Camden twn
Burgess John, tailor, 38 Harleyford pl. Kennington common
Burgess John Hugh, barrister, 7 New square, Lincoln's inn
Burgess Joseph, pawnbroker, 35 Chichester place, Gray's inn road, & 124 Long acre
Burgess Joseph, tailor, 18 Crosby row, Walworth
Burgess Mary (Mrs.), broker, 12 Devonshire st. Lisson grove
Burgess Mary Anne (Mrs.), grocer, 19 Cleveland st. Fitzroy sq
Burgess Robert, cheesemonger, 23 East road, City road
Burgess Robert, hairdresser, 15 & 16 Opera arcade, Haymkt
Burgess Robert, livery stables, Kensington High st
Burgess Robert, smith, 2 Meard's court, Soho
Burgess Samuel Walter, librarian, 5 Harvey bldgs. Strand
Burgess Thos. medical bookseller, 28 Coventry st. Haymrkt
Burgess Thomas, oil & colorman, 135 Tooley st
Burgess Thomas, solicitor, 35 Essex st. Strand
Burgess Thomas, tailor & breeches maker, 275 Regent st
Burgess Warfe, lodging ho. 22 Portsea place, Connaught sq
Burgess Wm. baker, New cross
Burgess Wm. baker, 5 Temple place, Old Kent road
Burgess Wm. furniture broker, 60 Bethnal green road
Burgess Wm. lithographer, 25 Hart st. Bloomsbury
Burgess Wm. patent yeast maker, 2 Denmark st. St. George st
Burgess Wm. Henry, dealer in colonial produce, 5 Harp lane
Burgh James, carver & gilder, 19 Edward st. Hampstead rd
Burgh Robert, fringe & lace ma. 41 & 42 Lit. Bartholomew close
Burghart Frederick, tailor, 17 Clifford st. Bond st
Burghes James Mount & Co. merchants, 4 Billiter square
Burgin John, *Black Bull* P.H. 46 Freeschool st. Horselydn
Burgis James, plumber, glazier, &c. 4 Ferdinand terrace, Hampstead road, & Green st. Leicester square
Burgiss Martha (Mrs.), *Ship & Star* P.H. 4 Sparrow cor. Minors
Burgoine Charles, grocer & cheesemonger, 23 Queen st. Pmlco
Burgon John T. wholesale hardwareman & gun flint manufacturer, 35 Bucklersbury, City

Burgon Thomas Chs. e. i. & col. brokers, 11 Gt. St. Helen's
Burgoynes', Thrupp & Clark, solicitors, 160 Oxford st
Burgoyne John Charles, attorney, 160 Oxford st
Burini Nicolo, tobacconist, 66 Lisson grove North
Burk Mary (Mrs.), cheesemonger, 13 Grace's all. Wellclo. sq
Burke Eliz. & A. (Misses) school, 6 Bath ter. Cambrwll. New rd
Burke, Pritt, Venables & Co. parliamentary agents, 44 Parliament st
Burke Edmund, builder, 42 Queen st. Bryanstone square
Burke Edmund, iron merchant & agent, Hall of Commerce
Burke Henry, fishmonger, 2 Howard's place, Hackney road
Burke Henry, plumber, &c. 22 Stafford st. Lisson grove
Burke John Bernard, barrister, 2 Churchyard ct. Temple
Burke John Webb, beer retailer, Caledonian road
Burke Joseph (Mrs.), milliner, 2 Crawford st. Portman sq
Burke Joseph, straw & tuscan warehouse, 2 Crawford st. Portman square, & 62 High st. Camden town
Burke Michael, *Wheatsheaf* P. H. 46 Holywell st. Strand
Burke Patrick, surgeon, 13 Upper Montagu st. Montagu sq
Burke Peter, barrister, 2 Churchyard court, Temple
Burke Thomas, tailor, 25 Grafton st. Fitzroy square
Burke Thos. Haswell, embosser, 12 Bull Head ct. Newgate st
Burke Thomas Haviland, barrister, 27 Glo'ster pl. New road
Burket Charles, oilman, &c. 42 Queen's road, Bayswater
Burket Thomas, book lock & clasp ma. 18 Redcross st. Crplgt
Burkett John, secret springer, 44 Galway st. St. Luke's
Burkitt Edward, clerk & solicitor to the Curriers' Co. & Tinplate Workers' Co. Curriers' hall, betwn. 6 & 7 London wall
Burkitt Miles, stockbroker, 3 Shorter's court, Throgmorton st
Burkitt Miles, tinplate worker, 16 Wellington st. Borough
Burl George, beer retailer, 15 Harrow road, Paddington
Burland Benjn. willow square, &c. ma. 14 Pump row, Old st. rd
Burland Thomas, fish salesman, 9 Cross la. St. Mary at hill
Burleigh, Snelgar & Burleigh, wine mers. 7 Devonsh. sq. Bspg
Burleigh Richard Boyden, *New inn tavern*, 52 Old Bailey
Burleigh Rd. Clarke, surgeon, 19 Camden ter. Camden Newtn
Burleigh Wm. rag & bottle warehouse, 43 Up. Rathbone place
Burleton John Robert, *Blue Posts* P. H. 1 John st. Oxford st
Burletson Geo. haberdasher, 4 Saville pl. Mile end road
Burletson Geo. Charlton, linendra. 2 Hayfield pl. Mile end rd
Burletson Robert, linendraper, 11 Saville row, Mile end rd
Burletson Wm. linendraper, 11 Manor pl. nth. Kg's. rd. Chelsea
Burley David, potato dealer, 15 James st. Oxford st
Burley John, druggist, 314 Rotherhithe st
Burley John, solicitor, 8 New square, Lincoln's inn
Burley Joseph, working cutler, 18 Salisbury st. Lisson grove
Burley Richd. furniture bro. 8 Lit. Pulteney st. Golden sq
Burley Richard, jeweller, 29 St. John's square, Clerkenwell
Burley Samuel, coal dealer, 15 Up. Dorset st. Bryanstone sq
Burling James, timber & coal merchant, Stratford
Burlingham Charles, tailor, 10 Jermyn st. St. James's
Burlingson John Henry, bootmaker, 5 Vernon pl. Bloomsby
Burls & Gladstones, warehousemen, 1 Lit. Love la. Wood st
Burls Chas. (sec. to Gaslight & Coke Co.), 19 New Bridge st
Burls Chas. jun. (sec. to London Cemetery Co.), 15 New Bridge st. Blackfriars, & 281 Regent st
Burls Edward, baker, 18 Langley pl. Commercial rd. east
Burls Edward, pawnbroker, 1 & 2 King's row, Walworth rd
Burls John, warehouseman, 10 Wood st. Cheapside
Burls Thomas, baker, 3 Nutford place, Bryanstone square
Burlton George, beer retailer, 24 Lambeth walk
Burlton Richard, plumber, 21 Portland st. Walworth comn
Burlton Thomas, silversmith, 15 Beckford row, Walworth
Burluraux Andrew Joseph, french, dutch, & english basket manufacturer, 28 Tavistock st. Covent Garden
Burman Edward, whip thong ma. 37 Clarendon sq. Somers tn
Burman Eliza (Miss), milliner, 37 Clarendon sq. Somers twn
Burman James Meffett, grocer, 17 Berwick st. Soho
Burman John sen. ivory turner, 14 Cumberland st. Curtain rd
Burman Wm. composition letter ma. 12 St. John'sla. Smithfld
Burman Wm. surgeon, 12 Jewry st. Aldgate
Burman Wm. Edward, hatter, 120 Whitechapel High st
Burmeister Ferdinand D. ship broker, 16 John st. Minories
Burmester Brothers, merchts. 10 St. Helen's pl. Bishopsgate
Burmester John, barrister, 23 Old sq. Lincoln's inn
Burmester John George Henry, merchant, 110 Leadenhall st
Burmingham Benj. shoemaker, 16 Cumberland st. Curtain rd
Burmingham Wm. cheesemgr. 142 Edgware rd. Marylebone
Burn Daniel & Sons, sailmakers, 67 Lower Shadwell
Burn Adam, solicitor & scotch agt. 14 Gt. Carter la. Drs'.com
Burn Andrew, tailor to her Majesty, 27 Sackville st. Piccadly
Burn Elizabeth (Mrs.), fruiterer, Covent garden market
Burn Jacob Henry, coal merchant, 8 Gt. Newport street; & at Bridewell wharf, William st. Blackfriars
Burn James, bookbinder, 37 Kirby st. & 35 Hatton garden
Burn James, bookseller & stationer, 11 Up. Kennington green
Burn Jas. *Queen's Head* P.H. Queen's head ct. Gt. Windmill street, & 6½ Great Crown court, Little Pulteney st
Burn James, solicitor, 11 Tokenhouse yard
Burn James, tailor, 71 St. James's st
Burn John, tailor, see Harrison & Burn
Burn John Ilderton, solicitor, 6 South square, Gray's inn
Burn J. Southerden, solicitor, see Grimaldi, Stables & Burn
Burn Joseph, *Black Swan* P.H. Schoolhouse lane, Ratcliff
Burn Mardall W. coal merchant & agent, 76 & 77 Freeschool st
Burn Ralph, boot & shoemaker, 40 Piccadilly
Burn Sam. rectifier & brandy distil. 78 Freeschoolst. Horselyd
Burn Thomas Boyle, stationer, 5 Whitefriars street
Burn William, auctioneer, 87 Harrow road, Paddington
Burn William, auctioneer, 35 New church st. Lisson grove
Burn Wm. carman, 7 King's hd. yd. Duke st. Lincoln's inn fie
Burnaby John Dick, barrister, 2 Pump court, Temple
Burnaby Sherrard B. D.C.L. advocate, 12 College, Doct.com
Burnal George D. cabinet ma. 12 St. George'spl. St. Geo's. east
Burnand George & Co. stock & share brokers, 12 Cornhill
Burnand Francis, stock broker, 24 Change alley, Cornhill
Burnand Henry, underwriter, Winchester house & Lloyd's
Burnand Lewis, underwriter, Winchester house & Lloyd's
Burnand Theophs. underwri. to Marine Ins. Co. 27 Cornhill
Burnard George, tin plate worker, 225 Hoxton old town
Burnard John, tailor, 26 New North st. Red Lion square
Burnard John, *Weaver's Arms* P.H. Backchurch la. Whitech
Burnard Mary (Miss), milliner, 14 Edmund pl. Aldersgate st
Burnard Wm. tinplate worker, 7 Webber st. Blackfriars rd
Burnboom Wm. sugar refiner, 12 Finch st. Mile end new town
Burnby Joseph, china & glass dealer, 4 Deptford High st
Burncastle Andrew, furrier, 4 Blackman st. Borough
Burne Walter, corndealer, 57 Hoxton old town
Burne Wm. chandler's shop, 41 Salisbury st. Lisson grove
Burnell Thos. & Co. mers. 1 Gt. Winchester st. Old Broad st
Burnell Arabella (Miss), hosier, 12 Guildford pl. Spitalfields
Burnell Blomfield, solicitor, 58 Fenchurch st
Burnell Daniel, baker, 135 Houndsditch
Burnell Edward Henry, land surveyor, 122 Chancery lane
Burnell Henry, carpenter & builder, 25 Fetter lane
Burnell John, lantern leaf & horn plate ma. 131 Whitechapel
Burnell Thomas, glass & china dealer, 39 Moorgate st. & 1A, Coleman st. City
Burnell William, baker, 167 Old Gravel lane, Wapping
Burnell William, beer retailer, Maiden lane, King's cross
Burness James, commcl. agt. see Herring, Burness & Co
Burness James, merchant, 64 Cornhill
Burnet Richard & Co. linendrapers, 2 Piazza, Covent garden
Burnet Geo. R. oil & Italian war. 2 Beckford row, Walworth
Burnet Joseph, tailor, 4 New st. Brompton
Burnet William, baker, 59 Cromer st. Brunswick square
Burnett Fred. Jph. & Henry, ship & insu. agents, 30 St. Maryathill
Burnett Sir Robt. & Co. vinegar makers & distills. Vauxhall
Burnett's patent for the preservation of timber, canvas, cordage, cotton, woollen, &c. from dryrot, mildew, moth and premature decay (Charles Jackson, secretary), 53 King William st. London bridge.—Hydraulic apparatus & tanks for the expeditious preparation of the above materials, Millwall, Poplar, nearly opposite Greenwich
Burnett Duncan Pringle, navy agent, see Copland & Burnett
Burnett Henry, wholesale oilman, 19 Bedford square east
Burnett James, livery stables, 4 Hart st. Covent garden
Burnett Joseph, confectioner, 14 Blackfriars road
Burnett Richard, beer retailer, Montague close, Southwark
Burnett Robert French, barrister, 10 New sq. Lincoln's inn
Burnett Thomas, merchant, see Houghton, Burnett & Co
Burnett William, baker, 43 Minories
Burnett William, tailor, 211 Bethnal green road
Burnett Wm. Hope Whidby, solicitor, 4 Henrietta st. Cav. sq
Burnham Francis, *Albion* P.H. 35 Albion st. Hyde park
Burnham George, rug manfr. Neate st. Cobourg rd. Old Kent rd
Burnham James, carpenter, &c. 4 Beauchamp st. Leather la
Burnham James, silk mercer, 35 Edgware road
Burnham Josiah, cheesemonger, 8 Mortimer st. Cavendish sq
Burnie & Buckland, gen. com. & custom ho. agts. 157 Fenchrh. st
Burnie Wm. & Co. merchants, 22 New City chbs. Bishpsg. wi
Burnie Joseph, barrister, 54 Chancery lane
Burnie William, surgeon, 9 Claremont sq. Pentonville
Burnie Wm. jun. commission & custom house agent & ship broker, 22 New City chambers, Bishopsgate within
Burniston Mrs. Elizth. lodging house, 108 Mount street
Burnley Samuel, dyer, 23 Freeschool st. Horselydown
Burnman John, *Bagnigge Wells Tavern*, Bagnigge wells rd
Burns Jas. bookseller & stationer, 17 Portman st. Portman sq
Burns James, solicitor, 1 Willow walk, Kentish town
Burns Philip, brewer, 21 Regent st. Horseferry rd
Burns Thomas, bricklayer, &c. 37 Wilson st. Finsbury

Burnside Wm. who. stationer, see Hodgkinson, Son & Co
Burr Hen. clothes salesman, 5 Church st. Cheyne wlk. Chelsea
Burr Henry, shoemaker, 1 Brompton place, Brompton road
Burr John, bookseller, 47 Water lane, Blackfriars
Burr Robert, manufacturing upholsterer & decorator in all its branches, & sole maker of Hall's patent bedding, 18 Bentinck st. Manchester sq
Burr Thomas, goldbeater, 33 Cannon st. rd. St. George's east
Burr Thos. L. act. to Haggerston Savings Bank, 77 Hackney rd
Burr Thomas William, solicitor, 8 Devonshire st. City
Burr William, shoe & stay mercer, see Waite & Burr
Burra James, solicitor, 18 Bread st. Cheapside
Burrage Charles, meat salesman, 52 Newgate market
Burrage Henry, carpenter, 2 Bath buildings, City road
Burrell & Paterson, solicitors, 1 White hart ct. Lombard st
Burrell (Salmon), Son & Foley, linendraps. 13 Vere st. Cav. sq
Burrell Charles, cattle salesman, 17 West Smithfield
Burrell Charles, cheesemonger, Deptford bridge
Burrell Henry, beer retailer, 4 Edward st. Barnsbury road
Burrell Henry, *Bull & Mouth Tap* P.H. Bull & Mouth st. City
Burrell Henry, undertaker, 22 Bull & Mouth st
Burrell James Fitchet, merchant, 2 Gt. St. Helen's & Baltic
Burrell John Palfrey, magistrate, Queen sq. police court
Burrell John, architect, 27 Spring gardens
Burrell Joseph, barrister, 7 New square, Lincoln's inn
Burrell Joseph F. patent medicine prepa. 9 Gt. Titchfield st
Burrell Thomas, cattle salesman, 17 West Smithfield
Burrell Thomas, veterinary surgeon, 13½ Gt. Windmill st. Haymarket, & 2 Bathurst mews, Sussex sq. Hyde park
Burrell Walter W. barrister, 5 Richmond terrace, Whitehall
Burrell William, butcher, 140 Long lane, Bermondsey
Burren Jas. *Blakeney's Head* P.H. 34 Lit. Bartholomew close
Burrett James, tallow chandler, 39 James st. Oxford st
Burridge & Sparrow, linendrapers, 109 London rd. Southwrk
Burridge Wm. & Geo. coal merchts. whf. 13 Millbank st. Westmr
Burridge George, tailor, Deptford High st
Burridge Henry, ho. painter, &c. 15 Grenville st. Brunswick sq
Burridge Henry, tailor & undertaker, 21 St. Andrew's rd. Boro
Burridge Jas. Bryant, surgeon, 4 Paragon pl. Lock's fields
Burridge Joseph, house decorator, 7 Chenies st. Bedford sq
Burrill Ann (Mrs.), bottle wareho. 31 Leigh st. Burton cres
Burrill John, teadealer, 3 Warwick st. Belgrave road
Burrin & Nalder, wine & spirit mer. 5 Martin's la. Cannon st
Burrin Thomas, grocer, 99 Norton st. Fitzroy square
Burrough John, cheesemonger, 60 North st. Edgeware road
Burrough John, tailor, 24 Old Cavendish st. Oxford st
Burroughes & Watts, billiard table & cloth ma. 19 Soho sq
Burroughs & Carter, auctioneers & est. agts. 106 London wl
Burroughs Jeremiah, merchant, 18 Addle st. Wood st
Burroughs Robert, carpenter, Engine house, Bermondsey st
Burroughs Samuel, tobacconist, 95 East st. Manchester sq
Burroughs Zaccheus, tailor, 30 Budge row, City
Burrow H. N. lunatic asylum, Grove house, Stoke Newngtn. gr
Burrow James, marine store dlr. Church st. Deptford
Burrow John Thomas, clothier 15 Adams row, Hampstead rd
Burrow Thomas C. barrister, 3 Paper buildings, Temple
Burrowes John, jun. coal merchant, 9 Bankside
Burrowes Joseph, baker 21 Skinner st. Somers town
Burrowes Thos. corn & seed mer. see Hopkinsons' & Burrowes
Burrowes Thomas, lodging house, 7 Howard st. Strand
Burrows & Parker, coal mercts. 14 Phœnix wf. Cityroad basin
Burrows Jno. Wm. & Sons. who. confectioners, 130 Houndsditch
Burrows & Thoms, operative chemists, 289 Strand
Burrows Arthur, barrister, 89 Chancery lane
Burrows Charles, french polsh. 7 South Island, pl. Clphm. rd
Burrows Charles, plumber, &c. 52 Dorset st. Portman square
Burrows Charles, solicitor, see Healing & Burrows
Burrows Daniel, *King's Arms* P.H. 37 Arundel st. Strand
Burrows Edward, watch ma. 36 King's road East, Chelsea
Burrows George, grocer, Bow
Burrows George, lapidary, 8 St. John's lane, West Smithfield
Burrows George, physician, 45 Queen Anne st. Cavendish sq
Burrows George, working silversmith, see Pearce & Burrows
Burrows Geo. Mann, physician, 46 Upper Gower st. Bedford sq
Burrows Isaac, soda water manufacturer, see Paul & Burrows
Burrows James, coal mercht. Chester wf. 30 Low. Belgrave pl
Burrows James, lodging house, 14 Fludyer st. Westminster
Burrows James, *Rose & Crown* P.H. 56 Lower Thames st
Burrows Marg. (Mrs.), infant school, 179 Shadwell High st
Burrows Robert, tailor, 145 Praed st. Paddington
Burrows Robert R. teadealer, &c. 23 Skinner st. Somers tn
Burrows Sarah (Mrs.), *Old Margate Tow* P.H. George row, Bermondsey
Burrows Thomas, greencocer, 1 St. Martin's ct. Ludgate hill
Burrows Thos. fan & skylight mak. 3 Hampden st. Somers tn
Burrows Thos. Benj. beer retailer, 48 Brick la. Spitalfields
Burrows Walter, surgn. dentist, 12 Somerset pl. Nw. rd. Wtchpl
Burrows Walter, surgeon, 5 Low. Charles st. Northampton sq
Burrows Wm. carpenter, &c. 7 Stanhope st. Hampstead rd
Burrows Wm. corn dealer, 31 Charlotte st. Bagnigge wells rd
Burrows William, manufacturer of metal conservatory, greenhouse, fan & sky lights, 37 St. John's lane, Smithfield
Burrows Wm. plumber, &c. 3 Leicester st. Leicester sq
Burrows Wm. surgeon, 1 Park st. Islington
Burrup & Blight, stationers, 12 East front, Royal exchange
Burrup Richard, brush maker, 32 Castle st. east, Oxford st
Burry George, *Castle tav.* 12 Gresham st. & 26 King st. City
Burry John, butcher, 24 Newport market
Burry Sarah (Mrs.), *Angel* P.H. 8 Rotherhithe walk
Bursby Hen. *Bull's Head* P.H. 16 Aylesbury st. Clerkenwell
Bursell George, bootmaker, 21 Camomile st
Bursey Henry, surgeon, 11 Chandos st. Covent garden
Bursill Francis, house painter, 10 Cleveland st. Fitzroy sq
Bursill John, house decorator, 92 Stanhope st. Hampstead rd
Bursill William, milk & butterman, 4 Great Marylebone st
Burslem Willoughby M. physician, 36 Chester place West
Burstall Abraham & Son, builders, 38 St. Martin's la. Charing cr
Burstall Henry A. printr. & publishr. 2 Tavistock st. Cov. gar
Burston Moses, statuary, &c. 40 Southampton st. Pentonvl
Burt & Potts, smiths & ironmongers, 65 York st. Westmnstr
Burt Ann (Mrs.), ham & beef shop, 71 Fore st. Cripplegate
Burt Arabella (Mrs.), straw hat manufactur. 44 Holborn hill
Burt Elizabeth (Miss), ladies' school, 18 Gt. Prescot st
Burt George, surgeon, 7 Crescent place, New Bridge st. Blkfrs
Burt Henry, solicitor, see Birt & Burt
Burt Henry M. bill broker, &c. see Womersley & Burt
Burt James, *City of London* P.H. 104 Berwick st. Soho
Burt James, fruiterer, 12 Chelsea market, Chelsea
Burt James, portmanteau maker, 24 Buckingham st. Strand
Burt James, fishmonger, 44 Hedge row, Islington High st
Burt John, baker, 37 Flint st. East st. Walworth road
Burt John, smith & wheelwright, 32 Church st. Chelsea
Burt John G. K. M.D. surgeon, 13 Church row, Newingtn. buts
Burt Mary Ann (Mrs.), *Carpenter's Arms* P.H. 58 Marsham st
Burt Nathan, wine merchant, see Dennys & Burt
Burt Richard, grocer & cheesemonger, 42 Poplar High st
Burt Rosa (Miss), milliner, 3 Broad court, Long acre
Burt Stephen John, surgeon, see Bullin & Burt
Burt Thomas, wheelwright, 200 Bethnal green road
Burt William, bricklayer & builder, 5 Gt. Vine st. Regent st
Burtenshaw Hen. stationer & newsvender, 31 Leicester sq
Burtenshaw Thomas, bricklayer, Camden place, Peckham
Burtenshaw Thos. oven builder, 26 Southwark bridge road
Burtenshaw William, teadealer, 15 East road, City rd
Burton & Beardmore, dress ma. 89 Charlotte st. Fitzroy sq
Burton & Dent, plumbers & lead mers. 21 Newcastle st. Strand
Burton & Hammond, tinmen, 21 Philip lane, London wall
Burton Jas. & Sons, engineers, 5 John's pl. Holland st. Blkfrs
Burton & Moore, wine merchants & manufacturers of capillaire, cordials, &c. 62 St. Thomas's place, Great Dover st
Burton Thomas & Sons, builders, 151 & 152 Aldersgate st
Burton Anne (Mrs.), poulterer, 4 Gloucester pl. Islington grn
Burton Arthur, coal merchant, Ranelagh wharf & Draw dock, Commercial road, Pimlico
Burton Arthur, greengrocer, 2 Gt. Carlisle st. Portman mkt
Burton Benj. brazier & coppersmith, 15 Weston st. Somrs. tn
Burton David, cooper, Talbot inn yard, 17 Boro' High st
Burton Decimus, architect & surveyor, 6 Spring gardens
Burton Edward, butcher, 22 Robert ter. King's rd. Chelsea
Burton Edward, lodging house, 7 St. Alban's pl. St. James's
Burton Edward Downing, *King's Head* P.H. 265 Strand
Burton Edwd. Fredk. solctr. see Chilton, Burton & Johnson
Burton Elizabeth (Mrs.), baby linen wareh. 18 St. Martin's ct
Burton Elizabeth (Mrs.), tobacconist, 55 Fleet street
Burton Ephraim H. bootma. 16 Red Lion pas. Red Lion sq
Burton George, linendraper, 42 Wellington st. Goswell road
Burton George, linendraper & silk mercer, 37 Piccadilly
Burton George, watch ma. 1 Northampton st. Clerkenwell
Burton Henry, dining rooms, 38 Cannon st. City
Burton Henry, who. perfumer & hair mer. 18 Greek st. Soho
Burton Henry, physician, 41 Jermyn st
Burton Hen. *Princess Charlotte* P.H. 385 Albany rd. Cmbwl
Burton James, attorney, 3 Powis pl. Gt. Ormond st. Queen sq
Burton James, cabinetmaker, 18 Charles st. Manchester sq
Burton James, optician, 25 Pleasant row, Pentonville
Burton James, tailor, 21 Foley st. Portland place
Burton James, wireworker & blindmaker, 54 Hackney road
Burton Jane (Mrs.), milliner, 51 York st. Westminster
Burton John, carman, 8 Agar st. West Strand
Burton John, cooper, Stratford Broadway
Burton John, furniture broker, 7 St. George's pl. Walwth. rd
Burton John, ship & insur. agt. & mer. 122 Bishopsgate within

Burton John, upholst. & furn. deal. 55 Skinner st. Snow hill
Burton John, who. milliner & lacemanf. 8 Gresham st. City
Burton John Barlow, tobacco. & medallist, 12 Aldersgate st
Burton John Robt. spirit color maker, see Moore & Burton
Burton Jsph, *Catherine Wheel* P.H. Catherine Wheel alley
Burton Joseph, currier & leather seller, 30A, Gt. Sutton st
Burton Martha (Miss), stationer, Stratford Broadway
Burton Mary A. (Mrs.), bookslr. & statnr. 19 St. Martin's le gr
Burton Mary Ann (Miss), straw hat mak. Church st. Hackney
Burton Matilda M. (Miss), academy, 18 Whitehead's gr. Chel
Burton Parnell, *Horns tavern* P.H. 3 Gutter la. Cheapside
Burton Richard Francis, surgeon, 12 Wade's pl. Hackney rd
Burton Robert, pianoforte maker, 54 Goswell road
Burton Samuel, steam flour mills, Broad st. Lambeth
Burton Thomas, blind maker, 8 Essex place, Mile end road
Burton Thomas, cheesemonger, 37 Paddington st. Marylebone
Burton Thomas, fancy cabinet maker, 5 Galway st. St. Luke's
Burton Thomas, grocer, 12 Garden row, London road
Burton Thomas, livery stables, York mews South, Padngtn. st
Burton Thomas, plasterer & slater, 13 Wilsted st. Somers town
Burton Thomas, plumber & glazier, 51 York st. Westminster
Burton Thomas, who. teadealer, 61 King William st. City
Burton Thomas James, chemist & druggist, 22 Wellclose sq
Burton Thomas Stackhouse, solicitor, see Hodgson & Burton
Burton-upon-Trent, Stafford, Shrewsbury & Newtown Railway Company, George Webb, sec. 1 Moorgate
Burton William, cheesemonger, 28 Bow lane, Cheapside
Burton William, dairyman, 9 Stanhope st. Clare market
Burton William, hairdresser, 6 Avery row, Grosvenor st
Burton William, laceman, 96 Upper st. Islington
Burton William, plumber, &c. 7 Wilsted st. Somers town
Burton Wm. Bradshaw, onion & fruit salsmn. Fruit mkt. Cov. gdn
Burton Wm. Ford, gunpowder manufactr. 25 Broad st. bldgs
Burton Wm. Henry, chophouse, 38 Cannon st. City
Burton Wm. Samuel, ironmonger, see Rippon & Burton
Burton William Warwick, solicitor, 12 Serle st. Lincoln's inn
Burtt Charles, jun. limewharf, Canal wf. Albany rd. Cambwl
Burtt Eleanor (Mrs.), *York Arms* P.H. 87 High Holborn
Burtt John, boarding house, 12 Liverpool st. Bishopsgate
Burtt John, marine store dealer, 24 Weston st. Somers town
Burtt John, tinman, 17 Poplar High st
Burtt Thos. book lock & clasp ma. 45 Northampton st. Clrkwl
Burtwell Charles, plumber, 3 Youl's place, Old Kent road
Burtwell Charles, plumber, &c. 2 Brighton pl. Hackney rd
Burwash David, notary, 26 Birchin lane, Cornhill
Burwash Wm. Hen. undertaker, 78 St. James's wlk. Clerkenwl
Bury Edward, barrister, 1 New square, Lincoln's inn
Bury Francis, law agent, 77 Aldermanbury
Bury John, engraver, 5 Christopher ct. St. Martin's le grand
Bury John, hairdresser & perfumer, 205 Sloane st
Bury John, law stationer, 12 Castle st. Holborn
Bury John William, attorney, 20 Devonshire st. Portland pl
Bury Thomas, news agent, Southampton st. Camberwell
Bury Wm. sec. to *Hope Life Assurance Co.* New Bridge st
Busain James, military cap & belt maker, 8 Gerrard st. Soho
Busbridge Jas. corn & coal dealr. 1 Charles st. Commercl. rd
Busby Sarah (Mrs.), & Co. childbed linen wa. 174 Oxford st
Busby Charles, butcher, 57 Freeschool st. Horselydown
Busby George, tripeman, 64 Freeschool st. Horselydown
Busby Michael Horton, window blind, garden seat & flower stand maker, & ornamental wire work manufactory, 7 & 8 Anderson's buildings, City road
Busch Edward & Co. general merchants, 18 Mark lane
Busch John A. G. music master, 13 Queen Charlotte row, Nw. rd
Busfield Joseph, chairmaker, 139 Union st. Borough
Bush & Co. manufacturing chemists, Bow common
Bush & Mullens, solicitors to the Association of London Bankers, 7 St. Mildred's court, Poultry
Bush William & Co. tobacconists, 290 High Holborn
Bush George, *York Minster* P.H. 50 Wardour st. Soho
Bush James, butcher, 108 Star st. Edgware road
Bush John, coffee rooms, 7 Darkhouse lane, Billingsgate
Bush John, pianoforte string ma. 12 Grafton st. ea. Tot. ct. rd
Bush Joseph, sawmaker, 1 Somerset st. Aldgate
Bush Robert, bookseller & bookbinder, Church st. Hackney
Bush Robert John, bookseller, see Bickers & Bush
Bush Thomas, hop & seed merch. Londn. brdg. foot, Southwark
Bush Thomas, bookbinder & stationer, 15 Jewry st. Aldgate
Bushby James, greengrocer, 9 Thornton st. Horselydown
Bushby Joseph, merchant, St. Peter's chambers, Cornhill
Bushby Joseph, insurance broker, see Litt & Bushby
Buschek Charles, merchant, 133 Fenchurch st
Bushell George, tailor, 20 Temple st. Whitefriars
Bushell John, chemist, &c. 12 Hall place, Kennington lane
Bushell Robert, hatter, 114 Shoreditch
Bushell Thomas, beer retailer, 31 Brunswick st. Hackney rd
Bushell Thomas, *Coach & Horses* P.H. 324 Strand
Bushell Thomas, surgeon, 117 Crawford st. Portman sq
Busher Edward, coach & harness maker, 212 Piccadilly
Busher Henry, confectioner & soda water manufacturer, 6 & 7 Postern row, Tower hill
Bushnell Joseph, tailor, 48 Gibson st. Waterloo road
Bushnell Rich. livery stables, Mason's yd. Duke st. St. James's
Busk Hans, jun. barrister, 1 Figtree court, Temple
Busk Henry William, barrister, 16 Old square, Lincoln's inn, & 7 Powis place, Gt. Ormond st
Buskin George, tallow chandler, 179 St. George st
Buss & Leedham, who. cheesemgrs. 17 Gt. Trinity la. Bread st
Buss Charles, surgeon, 60 Broad st. Bloomsbury
Buss Robert, sen. baker, 107 High st. Camden town
Buss Robt. Henry, corn dealer, 76 Park st. Camden town
Buss Robert William, artist, 68 Warren st. Fitzroy square
Buss Wm. surgeon, 3 Melville terrace, Caledonian road
Buss William Church, engraver, 16 Great Newport st
Bussell John, cheesemonger, 40 Salisbury st. Lisson grove
Bussell Peter, appraiser, 100 York st. Commercial rd. east
Bussey Fredk. brass fndr. & finishr. 18 Gt. Mitchell st. St. Luke's
Bussey James, ironmonger & gasfitter, 16 Bear st. Le'ster sq
Bustead Richard, barrister, 26 Upper Marylebone st
Buswell Charles, cattle salesman, 60 West Smithfield
Buswell John, baker, 4 Hastings st. Burton crescent
Buszard William, haberdasher, 177 Hoxton Old town
Butchers' Hall (Thos. Webb Gilbert, clerk), 5½ Eastcheap
Butcher Ann (Mrs.), clothes dlr. 2 Devonshire st. Lisn. gr
Butcher Benjamin, fish salesman, 9 Mount row, New Kent rd
Butcher Charles, bedstead maker, 9 Sidney st. Mile end rd
Butcher Chas. bookseller, binder & stationer, 27 Cannon st. road, & 19 Warwick lane, Newgate st
Butcher Esther (Miss), hosier, Stockwell pl. Clapham rd
Butcher Francis, *Blue Pig* P.H. 30 St. Mary axe
Butcher Frederick, butcher, 36 Lamb's Conduit st
Butcher Henry, cheesemonger, 46 Lamb's Conduit st
Butcher Henry, tailor & gaiter maker, 8 Catherine st. Strand
Butcher James, weighing machine agt. 9 Earl st. Blackfrs
Butcher James, currier, 55 Turnmill st. Clerkenwell
Butcher James, linendraper, 81 Long lane, Smithfield
Butcher Michael, carpenter, &c. 183 Long lane, Bermondsey
Butcher Samuel, corndealer, 51 Rufford's bldgs. High st. Islgtn
Butcher Samuel, *Noah's Ark* P.H. 179 Rotherhithe st
Butcher Samuel, tinman & brazier, 54 Windsor st. Islington
Butcher Thomas, butcher, 10 Orchard st. Portman square
Butcher Thomas, commission broker, Camberwell grove
Butcher Thomas, lapidary, 78 Myddelton st. Clerkenwell
Butcher Thomas, pianoforte maker, 41 Great Titchfield st
Butcher Thomas, tin plate wkr. 22 Cambridge rd. Mile end rd
Butcher Thomas, wine & spirit broker, 21 Mark lane
Butcher Webster G. tailor & draper, 28 Bedford st. Covent gdn
Butcher Wm. baker, 25 Brydges st. Covent garden
Butcher Wm. carpet warehouseman (agent to Lea & Co. Kidderminster), 49 Gt. Marlborough st
Butcher Wm. coffee rooms, 3 Linden place, Bayswater
Butcher Wm. *Coopers' Arms* P.H. 22 Wellington pl. Stepney
Butcher Wm. grindery dealer, 9 Star corner, Bermondsey st
Butcher Wm. librarian, 44 Leader st. Chelsea
Butcher Wm. seal engraver, 6 Lwr. Smith st. Northampton sq
Butes George, ivory turner, 16 Clerkenwell green
Butheroyd Jonathan, grocer, 1 Fairfield place, Stepney
Butfoy Abia, *White Horse* P.H. 45 Spicer st. Spitalfields
Butiman Christopher, oil & colorman, 7 Dean st. Westminster
Butland Henry, tobacconist, 3 St. John st. Clerkenwell
Butler Elizabeth & Sons, wine merchants, 14 Water la. Tower st
Butler & James (W. B.) & Co. wine merchants, 6 Broad st. bldgs
Butler James & Son, copper, brass & iron wire weavers, workers & drawers & sieve manufacturers, 4 Elm st. Gray's inn lane
Butler John & Richard, ironmongers, 151 & 152 Edgware rd
Butler John & Wm. builders, 40 Botolph la. Eastcheap
Butler & Muckley, seedsmen & herblsts. South row, Cov. gdn
Butler & Phillips, law writers, 103 Chancery lane
Butler Rd. & Rt. & Co. merchts. & insur. broks. 6 Austin friars
Butler Richard & Robert & Co. wine merchants, 6 Austin friars
Butler Charles, baker, 64 Marylebone lane, Oxford st
Butler Charles, beer retailer, 77 Brandon st. Lock's fields
Butler Charles, cap maker, 1 Star corner, Bermondsey
Butler Charles, *Eagle* coffee rooms, 9 Pitt's pl. Old Kent rd
Butler Chas. furn. broker, 2 Wellington pl. Back rd. St. Geo. ea
Butler Charles, ordnance agent, Parade, Tower
Butler Charles, tobacco, &c. manuf. see Lambert & Butler
Butler Charles, undertaker, 20 Crucifix lane, Bermondsey
Butler Chas. Edwd. furnishing undertaker, 31 Farringdon st
Butler Daniel, baker, 3 Sol's row, Hampstead road
Butler Daniel, bootmaker, 13 Adam st. west, Bryanstone sq

Butler Daniel, furnishing undertaker, 17 Farringdon st
Butler Edward, baker, 3 York st. Middlesex hospital
Butler Edward, tailor, see Laffin, Butler & Laffin
Butler Edward, tailor, 9 Chapel place, Cavendish square
Butler Edward, tailor, 7 Chapel place, Liverpool road
Butler Edward Robert, solicitor, 7 Furnival's inn, Holborn
Butler Edwin, chemist, 76 Earl st. east, Lisson grove
Butler Elijah, coal dlr. & beer retlr. 9 Nottingham st. Maryleb
Butler Eliza (Mrs.), stationer, &c. 2 Westmoreland st. Maryleb
Butler Elizh. (Mrs.), *Gloucester coffee house*, 248 Oxford st
Butler Frederick, fruiterer, 12 Nelson pl. Old Kent road
Butler George, butcher, 19 St. John st. Clerkenwell
Butler George, grocer, 114 Drury lane
Butler George, haberdasher, 5 Broadway, Westminster
Butler Harriet (Mrs.), baker, 16 Wade's place, Hackney rd
Butler Henry, cowkeeper, 86 Waterloo road
Butler Henry, engraver & printer, 26 Abchurch lane, City
Butler Henry, furn. undertaker, 5 High st. St. Giles's
Butler Henry, wine & spirit mercht. see Greenwood & Butler
Butler James, architect & surveyor, 118 New Bond st
Butler James, fruit salesman, see Ramsdale & Butler
Butler James, fruit salesman, 4 Church st. Boro' market
Butler James, ginger beer mnf. & carman, 56 Tottnhm. ct. rd
Butler James, italian warehouse, see Hedges & Butler
Butler James, merchant, 6 Austinfriars
Butler James, smith & ironmonger, 40 Exeter st. Strand
Butler James, solicitor, 4 Young st. Kensington sq
Butler James, straw bonnet ma. 7 Thornton st. Dockhead
Butler James, surgeon, 34 Seething lane, Tower st
Butler James, wheelwright & tiresmith, 13 Deptford bridge
Butler James, who. & retail cheesemongr. 23 Shadwell High st
Butler Jane (Mrs.), brushmaker, see Ladley & Butler
Butler Jane (Mrs.), berlin repostry. 19 Crawford st. Portmn sq
Butler John, boot & shoe maker, 8 Princes st. Westminster
Butler John, boot & shoe maker, 100 Tottenham court rd
Butler John, *Golden Lion* P.H. 51 Dean st. Soho
Butler John, haberdasher, hosier & glover, 42 Wellclose sq
Butler John, horse hair manufr. 16 Princes st. Mile end New tn
Butler John, plumber & oilman, 111 Park st. Camden town
Butler John, jun. solicitor, 134 Tooley st. Borough
Butler Joseph, fishmonger, 11 Portman market
Butler Joseph, straw hat maker, 5 Blackman st. Borough
Butler Joshua, biscuit baker, 2 Goodge st. Tottenham ct. rd
Butler Mary Ann (Miss), milliner, 45 Ludgate hill
Butler Matthew, egg merchant, 114 Rosemary la. Minories
Butler Robert, furniture broker, 74 Old st. St. Luke's
Butler Richard, music seller & publisher, 6 Hand ct. Holborn
Butler Robert Kay, who. & ret. ironmonger, 174 High Holborn
Butler Sarah (Miss), milliner, 118 New Bond st
Butler Sarah (Mrs.), confectioner, 3 Hereford pl. Com. rd. east
Butler Thomas, brush manufacturer, 73 Houndsditch
Butler Thomas, chandler's shop, 3 Charles st. Long acre
Butler Thomas, chemist & druggist, 4 Cheapside
Butler Thomas, importer of sponge, & sole agent for emery stone in London, 93 Upper Thames st
Butler Thomas, linen draper, 58, 59, 74 & 75 Shoreditch High st
Butler Thomas, smith, 17 Broad st. Lambeth
Butler Thomas, wine merchant, 42 Trinity sq. Tower hill
Butler Thomas Holmes, glass cutter, see Elliott & Butler
Butler Timothy, sculptor, 1 Middlesex pl. New road
Butler William, brass manufactur. 4 Chenies st. Bedford sq
Butler William, cheesemonger, 8 Acton pl. Bagnig. wells rd
Butler William, eating house, 18 Robert st. Grosvenor sq
Butler William, hardwareman, 113 Rosemary lane, Minories
Butler William, *Old King's Arms* P.H. 104 Holborn hill
Butler William, plumber, &c. 11 Little St. Thomas apostle
Butler Wm. saddlers' tool ma. & ironmger, 1 Bell ct. Drury la
Butling Richard, cheesemonger. 25 Seething la. Tower st
Butt Jas. Lawrence & Co. tailrs. 1 Farringdon st. & 48 Ludgate hill
Butt Anne (Miss), stationer, 29 Rodney st. Pentonville
Butt Charles, umbrella manufr. 1 William st. Shoreditch
Butt Edward, lace & muslin ware, 7 Newcastle pl. Edgware rd
Butt George, coal merchant, 41 Upper Berkeley st. west
Butt George, fruiterer, 21 Henry st. Pentonville
Butt George Medd, queen's counsel, 3 Tanfield ct. Temple
Butt Henry, earthenware dlr. 10 Adam's pl. King's rd. Chelsea
Butt Henry, linendraper, 21 Mortimer st. Cavendish square
Butt Isaiah, lace manufacturer, see Mason, Barlow, & Butt
Butt James, butcher, 73 Welbeck st. Cavendish square
Butt John, bootmaker, 21 Sidmouth st. Gray's inn road
Butt John, fruiterer, 20 Millbank st. Westminster
Butt John, fruiterer, 3 Newland place, Kensington
Butt John, lime burner, Hackney whf. Wharf rd. Hackney
Butt John, pianoforte maker, 28 Goldsmith pl. Hackney rd
Butt John, tailor, 9 St. Ann's la. General Post Office
Butt John, auctioneer, 1 Bailey's pl. Marlboro' rd. Chelsea
Butt Joseph, bootmaker, 9 Little Turnstile, Holborn
Butt Mary (Mrs.), grocer, &c. 22 Henry st. Pentonville
Butt Mary (Mrs.), tobaccon. 1 Church st. Cheyne walk, Chelsea
Butt Richard, tailor, 47 Wellington place, Sepney
Butt Richard, trimming seller, 10 Tyler st. Golden square
Butt Robert, bugle warehouse, 2A, Welbeck st
Butt Robert, linendraper, 17 Bolingbroke row, Walworth rd
Butt Robert James, attorney, 97 Gt. Russell st. Bloomsbury
Butt Samuel, tailor, 9 Thornton st. Dockhead
Butt William, cheesemonger, 363 Rotherhithe st
Butter Francis, baker, 45 Ray st. Clerkenwell
Butterell Thomas, grocer, 150 Shoreditch High st
Butterfield Brothers, stuff manufacturers, 27 Wood st. & Bradford, Yorkshire
Butterfield & Co. oil & tallow merchants, 12 Bucklersbury
Butterfield Robert Steven & James, coal merchants, Norfolk wharf, 13 Water st. Strand
Butterfield John, *Grapes* P.H. 16 Farringdon st
Butterfield & Venour, attorneys, 5 Gray's inn square
Butterfield Wm. architect, 4 Adam st. Adelphi
Butterfield Wm. bird stuffer, 38 Seymour pl. Bryanstone sq
Butterfield Wm. Hen. registrar, 2 Belinda cot. Canonbury sq
Butterick Charles, grocer, Warlter's buildings, Old Kent rd
Butterick Wm. china & glassman, 33 & 34 Grove pl. Lisson gr
Butterley Iron Co. (Christph. Kreeft, agent), 9 Billiter sq
Butters Chas. oilman, plumber, &c. 14 Gwynn's pl. Hackney rd
Butters Henry, author & publisher, 40 St. John st. road
Butterworth John & Wm. leather & shoe warehouse, 9 Great Dover st. & 4 Swan st. Great Dover road
Butterworth & Radcliffe, grocers & teadealers, 34 St. John st rd
Butterworth (Sidney Aquilla) & Co. stuff mfrs. 2 Blue boar ct
Butterworth Wm. & Sons, flannel & baize manufrs. 83 Wood st
Butterworth Henry, law bookseller & publisher, 7 Fleet st
Butterworth Thomas, tailor, 7 York st. west, Commercial rd
Butterworth Wm. Hen. special pleader, Hall staircase, Temple
Buttery Charles, restorer of pictures, 46 Greek st. Soho
Buttfield Joseph G. & Son, grocers, 350 Rotherhithe st
Butti Alexander, carver & gilder, 96 Leather lane, Holborn
Buttle Henry, fruiterer, 168 Union st. Borough High st
Buttler Chas. liv. stabs. & van pro. 6 & 20 Little Portland st
Buttler Henry, baker, 3 King st. Snowhill
Button Charles, operative chemist, 146 Holborn bars
Button Henry, *Pewter Platter* P.H. 86 Gracechurch st
Button John, pawnbroker, 20 John st. West, Edgware rd
Button Lago, carpenter, 15 Brown st. Bryanstone square
Button Nathaniel, confectioner, 37 Poultry & 77 Holborn bridg
Button Samuel, marine store dealer, 1 Fell st. Wood st
Button Sophia E. (Miss), pastrycook & confectr. 187 Fleet st
Button Thomas, confectioner, 16 Middle row, Holborn
Button Wm. plumber & glazier, 42 Goodge st. Tottenham ct. rd
Button William, sailmaker, 12 Narrow st. Ratcliff cross
Buttress John Josiah & Son, silk manfs. 36 Steward st. Spitalfi
Butts Wm. & Son, hosiers & glovers, 52 Cornhill & 62 Leadnhl. st
Butts Thomas, currier, 7 Union st. Spitalfields
Butwell Joseph, coal dealer, 29½ Bell st. Edgware road
Buxton, Bruce & Co. bill brokers, see Bruce, Buxton & Co
Buxton & Rogers, comp. ornament ma. 13 Well st. Oxford st
Buxton & Slack, wool brokers, 76 Basinghall st
Buxton Wm. & Son, pa. sash line ma. 3 Eden pl. Ivy la. Hoxton
Buxton Elizabeth (Mrs.), lodging house, 3 King st. St. James's
Buxton Geo. coach maker, 4 Northampton pl. Old Kent rd
Buxton John, plumber, &c. 10 Little Grosvenor st
Buxton John, seedsman & florist, Dunsany pl. Wandswth. rd
Buxton John, M.D. surgeon, 5 Brownlow st. High Holborn
Buxton Thos. silk & cotton manufr. 57 Wood st. Cheapside
Buxton Wm. grocer, 9 Brown st. Bryanstone square
Buxton Wm. Henry, tailor, 3 Botolph alley, Thames st
Buzzacott Alexander, farrier, Broomfield place, Deptford
Buzzard Charles, painter, 11 Jewry st. Aldgate
Buzzard George, vestry clerk of St. James's, 50 Poland st
Buzzard Henry, *Globe* P.H. 5 Grosvenor pl. Borough road
Byam George, sec. to Paris & Lyons railway. 19 King's arms yd
Byam Wm. Jonathan, surgeon, 34 Welbeck st. Cavendish sq
Byard George, hat box maker, 26 White horse yard, Drury la
Byard Horatio, picture dealer, 20 Wardour st. Soho
Byars James, baker, 3 Southampton place, Nine elms
Byas Edward, lunatic asylum, Fairfield rd. Bow & Old Ford
Byas William, pawnbroker, 147 St George st
Byass Robert Blake, wine & spirit & export portermerchant, 1 Langbourn chambers, & Limehouse hole
Byatt Benjn. cheesemonger, 20 East st. Walworth road
Byatt William, cheesemonger, 18 King's row Pimlico
Bycroft John, silk mercer, 54 Leicester square
Byden George, confectioner, 67 Shadwell High st
Bye Charles, butcher, 2 Northampton row, Holloway
Bye George, upholsterer, 25 Queen's row, Pimlico

Bye James, shoe maker, 1 Pritchard's pl. Hackney fields
Bye John, printers' pressma. & joiner, 5 Tichborne ct. Holbrn
Bye Richard, appraiser, 2 Church la. Islington
Bye Thomas, wharfinger & timber mer. Nine elms, Vauxhall
Bye Thos. Wm. *Wheatsheaf* P.H. 25 Rathbone pl. Oxford st
Byers George, hatter & capmaker, 1 Pall mall
Byers George, *Volunteer* P.H. 28 Upper Baker st. New road
Byers Thos. *Sun* P.H. 7 Upper Lisson st. Lisson grove
Byfeld Ellen & Jane, ladies' school, 78 Stanhope st. Regent's pk
Byfield Elizabeth (Mrs.), staymaker, 9½ Gt. Smith st. Westm
Byfield Louis, undertaker, 14 Felix place, Liverpool road, & 30 Upper Park st. Islington
Byfield Mary (Miss), engraver on wood, 30 Up Park st. Islg
Byfield Robt. stationer, bookseller & news ag. 21 Charing cr
Byfield Thomas, fruiterer, 93 Crawford st. Portman sq
Byfield Thomas, grocer, 2 New King st. Deptford
Byford George, baker, 58 Church st. Shoreditch
Byford John, confectioner, 6 Steyman's row, Holloway rd
Byford Samuel, fruiterer, 122 Bermondsey st.
Byford Thomas, teadealer, 21 Bow High st.
Byford Wm. stuffer of birds & beasts, 23 St. Mary at hill
Bygate John, corndealer, 9 Roadside, Mile end road
Bygrave & Marshall, vet. surgeons, 17&18 Up. Bryanstone st
Bygrave Geo. fishmonger, 1 Chelsea market, Lower Sloane st
Bygrave Thos. surveyor & valuer, 14 Clement's inn, Strand
Bygrave Wm. tailor, 4 Lower Porchester st. Edgware road
Byles & Hart, surgeons, 15 Union st. east, Spitalfields
Byles Jas. Hodge, chemist & druggist, 86 Hackney road
Byles John Barnard, serjeant at law, 6 King's Bench walk
Bylow Jane Alice (Mrs.), chemist, 122 Poplar High st
Bynner Evan, grocer, 35 Little Newport st. Long acre
Byrd Jane (Mrs.), butcher 61 Kent st. Borough
Byres Wm. who. confectioner, 64 Broad st. Bloomsbury
Byrn, Trist & Byrns', merchants, 18 Philpot lane
Byrn Henry, ham & tongue dealer, 69 Barbican
Byrn Oscar, dancing master, 6 Burton crescent
Byrne Alexander, cooper, 25 Philip lane, London wall
Byrne Anna Maria (Mrs.), lodging house, 1 Manchester st
Byrne Edmund, solicitor, see Lowe, Sweeting & Byrne
Byrne Chas. appraiser, &c. 19 Duke st. Lisson grove
Byrne Dudley (sec. to Gt. Munster Railway), 63 Moorgate st
Byrne Edward, surgeon, &c. 47 Old Gravel lane, Wapping
Byrne Henry, poulterer, 14 Rufford's row, Upper st. Islington
Byrne John, dairyman, 11 Woburn buildings, Tavistock sq
Byrne John, surg. bandge. ma. 27½ Beckfrd. rw. Walwth. rd
Byrne John, tailor, 11 New Church st. West, Edgware road
Byrne Margaret (Miss), dressmaker, 2 Mid. New st. Fetter la
Byrne Timothy, carpenter & builder, 32 Theobald's road
Byrne Wm. *Grapes* P.H. 79 Fore st. City
Byrne Wm. August. surgeon, 94 St. Martin's la. Charing crs
Byrne Wm. Pitt, barrister, 16 Montagu st. Portman sq
Byrnes Ellen (Mrs.), ladies' school, East India rd. Poplar
Byron John Ballard & Co. timber merchants, Canterbury wharf, Belvedere road
Byron John, tailor, 15 High road, Knightsbridge
Byson Wm. Henry, oilman, 8 Canal place, Old Kent road
Bytham Richard, *Old George* P.H. the Stowage, Deptford
Bywater Matthew, saddler & harness maker, 99 Piccadilly
Bywaters Sageman, bricklayer, &c. 48 Carnaby st. Golden sq
Bywaters Samuel, bricklayer, 6 Adam's pl. Boro' High st
Byworth George, bookseller, 16 Duke st. West Smithfield
Byworth Mary (Mrs.), watch & clockma. 12 Bridge st. Lambeth

CAARTEN John Marius Bicker, barrister, 5 Figtree ct
Cabban John, cooper, 2 Lavender place, Rotherhithe
Cabbell Benj. Bond, barrister, 1 Brick court, Temple
Cabbell Thomas, barrister, 1 Essex court, Temple
Cabburn Jas. grocer, 1 High st. Portland town
Cabburn John Fras. B. anti-doloric oil mfr. 1 King's cross
Cabburn Jas. B. *White Hart* P.H. New rd. & Gray's inn rd
Cable Elizabeth (Mrs.), livery stables, 245 High Holborn
Cable Hen. cooper, turner, hoop & meas. ma. 47 Gt. Tower st
Cable John Richd. grocer, 7 Crosby row, King st. Borough
Cable Wm. painter & glazier, 8 Magdalen st. Bermondsey
Cadbury Mark & Son, cheesemongers, 24 New Bond st
Cadbury Jas. cheesemonger, 58 Wardour st. Soho
Cadbury Thomas, cheesemonger, 20 Victoria road, Pimlico
Cadby Chas. patent pianoforte mfr. 20 Alfred st. Bedford sq
Caddel Thos. & Edw. desk & dress. case ma. 113 Leadenhall st
Caddell Archibald, *Coach & Horses* P.H. 37 Hill st. Berkly. sq
Caddell David, solicitor, 13 Bell's buildings, Salisbury sq
Caddell Jas. *Running Footman* P.H. 5 Charles st. Berkly. sq
Cade Geo. *Castle* P.H. 16 Greenhill rents, Smithfield
Cadell John, dining rooms, Youls place, Old Kent road
Cadell Robert, publisher, 4 Lovell's ct. Paternoster row
Caden Margaret (Mrs.), coffeerooms, 39 Wilderness row, Clknw
Cadge Jason, grocer, 24 Gt. Windmill st. Haymarket
Cadman Wm. cutler, 221 High st. Shadwell, & 3 U. Ea. Smithfld
Cadman Jas. grocer, &c. 17 Park st. Camden town
Cadman John, umbrella manufacturer, 202 Strand
Cadogan reading rooms, Botanic gdns. Sloane st. Chelsea
Cadogan Wm. surveyor, 4 Pickett pl. & 2 Essex st. Strand
Cafe Henry Smith, Son & Reid, auctionrs. 48 Gt. Marlboro' st
Cafe Hamilton Henry, auctioneer, 48 Gt. Marlborough st
Cafe Henry Smith, auctioneer, 48 Gt. Marlborough st
Cafe Thos. jun. artist, 80 Newman st
Cafe Thos. Smith, artist, 80 Newman st. Oxford st
Cafe Wm. Smith, ho. agt. & valuer, 12 Commercial rd. Lambth
Caffary Patrick John, merchant, see Shaw & Caffary
Caffrey John, tailor, 3 Gillingham st. Pimlico
Caffyn Wm. stationer, 31 Oxford st. Mile end
Cahan Edward, tailor & draper, 371 Strand
Cahill & Hewett, surgeons, 12 Michael's place, Brompton
Cahill Cornelius, tailor, 11 Richmond st. Leicester sq
Cahill Thomas, physician, 3 William st. Albert gate
Cahill Wm. cheesemonger, 41 Hatfield st. Stamford st. Blackfrs
Cahlmann Bros. I. & S. merchts. 1 Copthall chamb. Throgmn. st
Cahlmann Samson, consul for Saxe Weimar, 1 Copthall chambers, Throgmorton st
Cahn David & Co. letter press, copper plate, and cromo-lithographic printers, 7 Great Queen st. Lincoln's inn flds
Cahn Salomon, mercht. 5 Langbourn chambs, Fenchurch st
Cailes James, *Hercules' Pillar* P.H. 18 Great Queen st
Caillard Camille Timothée, french teacher, 76 Up. Berkeley st
Cain Caleb, tailor, 13 York place, Westminster road
Cain John, hairdresser, 24 Spring st. Portman sq
Cain Joseph, fishmonger, 2 Star corner, Bermondsey
Cain Millen, carpntr. & undertkr. 42 Charles st. Commercial rd
Caines Charles, wholesale glover, 99 Wood st. Cheapside
Caines Geo. C. bookseller (by appointment to H.R.H. Prince Albert) & stationer, &c. 5 Halkin st. west, Belgrave sq
Caines G. C. (Mrs.), select educational agncy. 5 Halkin st. west
Cains John, grocer, 115 Shad Thames, Horselydown
Cairns Hugh M'Calmont, barrister, 5 New sq. Lincoln's inn
Cakebread Diana (Mrs.), plumber, &c. 1 Smith's bldgs. City rd
Cakebread George, fruiterer, 50 Kingsland road
Calais, Dunkirk & West Flanders Junction Railway Company (William Jesse, sec.), 11 King William st. City
Calcott Stephen, coal dealer, 2 Gt. White Lion st. Seven dials
Calcraft John, straw hat maker, 96 Bunhill row
Calcutt Charles, butcher, 2 Pleasant place, King's cross
Calcutt John, butcher, 4 Mid. Queen's bldgs. Knightsbridge
Calcutt Thomas, butcher, 2 Little Queen st. Westminster
Calcutt Thomas, jun. butcher, 30 George st. Portman sq
Caldecott, Powell & Wilcocks, warehousemen, 2 Mitre court & 20 Cheapside
Caldecott Wm. upholsterer, 53 & 54 Gt. Russell st. Bloomsbury
Calder Amelia (Mrs.), seminary, 11 Northamptn. pl. Cntrbry. sq
Calder Francis Wm. bookseller & stationer, 199 Oxford st
Calder Henry C. beer retailer, 10 Talbot ct. Gracechurch st
Calder William, hatter, 129 Lambeth Lower marsh
Calder William, tailor, 20 Sale st. Paddington
Calderara Serafino, barometer maker, &c. 78 Leather lane
Caldicott Robert & Richard, ribbon manufactrs. 24 Wood st
Caldwall Thomas, agent to *Guardian Fire & Life Office*, 68 Paradise row, Chelsea
Caldwell Adam & Co. silk dyers, 15 Adam st. east, Portman sq
Caldwell Bros. & Co. mers. & warehosmn. 34 Paternoster row
Caldwell John & Co. silk dyers, 83 Dean st. Soho
Caldwell David (parliamentary agent & secretary to the *Forth & Clyde Navigation & Crinan Canal Comps.*), 29 Golden sq
Caldwell Hen. S. physician, 3 North Addington pl. Cambrwl
Caldwell John, biscuit baker to her Majesty, 427 Strand
Caldwell John, picture restorer, 28 Marylebone st. Piccadilly
Caldwell Joseph, hide & skin salesman, Bermondsey skin mkt
Caldwell Wm. Chesworth, tailor, 8 Cannon st. road
Cale & Gibson, law writers, 5 Cook's court, Carey st
Cale Rich. fancy toilet & smelling bottle ma. 63 Hatton. grdn
Cale Thomas, tailor, 4 Castle st. east, Oxford st
Caledonian Asylm. (Jn. Burnie, sec.), Caledonian rd. Copnhg. fl
Caledonian Life Insu. Co. (J. Inglis, manager), 27 Moorgate st
Caledonian Steam Towing Co. 11 Milk yard, Shadwell
Caley Sophia (Miss), seminary, 6 Park pl. Kennington cross
Calf Sarah (Mrs.), bookseller, 116 Edgware rd. Marylebone
Calf John, *Round Table* P.H. 23 St. Martin's court
Calisé Ferdinand, italian confectioner, 13 Duke st. Grosvn. sq
Calisher Nathan J. jeweller & diamond mer. 88 Aldgate Hi. st
Calkin & Budd, booksellers to her Majesty, & dealers in ancient & modern classical music, 118 Pall mall
Call (Sir W. P. bart.), Marten & Co. bankers, 25 Old Bond st
Callaghan Frs. lace, &c. makr. 38 Windmill st. Tottenham ct. rd
Callaghan John, straw hat manufr. 6 Lillypot lane, Noble st

Callaghan Timothy, broker, 86 Salisbury st Lisson grove
Callaghan Wm. practl. optician, 45 Gt. Russell st. Bloomsby
Callander Alex. B. corn & foreign flour factor, 15 Mincing la
Callao & Lima Railway Co. (Wm. Bevan, solicitor), 6 Old Jewry
Callard Daniel, baker, 4 Upper Porchester st
Callard Henry, carpenter, 3 Commercial pl. Commerl. rd. East
Callard John, carver & gilder, 9 Crown st. Walworth road
Callard Susanna (Miss), stationer, &c. 2 Norris st. Haymkt
Callaway Henry, surgeon, 6 Bishopsgate st. without
Callaway John, fruiterer, 2 New Kent road
Callaway Thos. surgeon, 7 Wellington st. London br. Borough
Callaway Thos. watch dial painter, 52 Clerkenwell close
Callcott William, butcher, 1 New st. Kennington road
Callcutt Richard, leather cutter, 2 Clarence pl. Hackney rd
Callen Chas. Coombes, carver & gild. 5 Wellington pl. Goswl. rd
Callen Isabella (Mrs.), lodging house, 6 Church st. Soho
Calley John, *Red Lion* P.H. 29 Hart st. Covent garden
Callinder George, tailor, 5 King's row, Pimlico
Callingham Jas. & Son, bricklayers, 96 Vauxhall walk, Lambth
Callingham John, tailor, 4 Bedford st. Bedford square
Callingham Richard, baker, 26 Lit. Queen st. High Holborn
Callingham William, baker, 8 Museum st. Bloomsbury
Callop Sarah (Mrs.), grocer, 20 Charles st. Hampstead rd
Callow Thomas & Son, whipmakers to their R.H. the Duke of Cambridge & Prince George, 8 Park lane, Piccadilly
Callow Elizabeth (Mrs.), brass founder, Bow common
Callow Geo. cabinet ma. & undertk. 8 Abbey st. Bethnal gr. rd
Callow James, boys' school, 5 Old Quebec st. Portman sq
Callow John, builder & undertakr. 41 Paradise row, Chelsea
Callow John, *Butchers' Arms* P.H. 48 Pear Tree ct. Clerknwll
Callow Joseph, solicitor, 3 Walbrook buildings
Callow Thomas, *Crown & Anchor* P.H. 43 Paul st. Finsbury
Callow Thomas, crucible pot manufacturer, &c. Bow common
Callow William, artist, 20 Charlotte st. Portland place
Callow Wm. *Fox & Hounds* P.H. 32 Paradise row, Chelsea
Calloway Wm. John, tailor & outfitr. 2 & 3 Bridge rd. Lambeth
Calls John, tailor, Hope cottages, Wandsworth road
Calow John, house painter & decorator, 62 Kent st. Borough
Calow John Alfred, tailor, 5 Upper North pl. Gray's inn rd
Calow Robert, dyer, 5 Mount row, New Kent road
Calrow Joseph & Son, wine & spirit merchts. 36 St. Mary at hill
Calton Robt. rocking horse mnfr. 14 Lower Kennington green
Calver John, butcher, 6 Brook st. Ratcliff
Calver John, jun. stonemason, 10 Green st. Bethnal green
Calver Jas. *City of Hereford* P.H. 1 Union st. Middlesex hospital
Calver William, general salesman, 13 Gt. Suffolk st. Boro'
Calvert Felix & Co. brewers, 89 Upper Thames st
Calvert Christopher Alderson, barrister, 4 Serle st. Carey st
Calvert Chas. A. (sec. to Colonial bank), 13 Bishopsgate within
Calvert Frederic, barrister, 8 New square, Lincoln's inn
Calvert George, stove maker, 2 West place, Islington
Calvert Geo. stove range maker, 2 Camden st. Islington green
Calvert James, stove maker, 8 West place, Islington green
Calvert John, bookbinder, 3 Hitt's pl. Ray st. Clerkenwell
Calvert John Wm. physician, 11 Blandford pl. Dorset square
Calvert Robert, tailor, &c. 10 Oxford st. Stepney
Calvert Samuel, linendraper, 8 Crawford st. Portman sq
Calvert Wm. baker, 5 Hopkin's buildings, Upper st. Islington
Calway Bartholomew, linendraper & hosier, 119 Tooley st
Cam Wm. woollen warehouseman, 33 King st. Cheapside
Cambell John, *Bedford family hotel*, 41 & 42 Southampton rw
Cambers Thomas, gold chaser, 12 Hooper st. Clerkenwell
Cambourne Geo. preserver of birds, 9 Blenheim st. Bond st
Cambourne John, bird dealer, 19 Dartmouth st. Westminster
Cambourne Mary (Mrs.), artifi. florist, 9 Blenheim st. Bond st
Cambray Philip, fruit salesman, Covent garden fruit market
Cambray William, *Golden Cross* P.H. 3 Cross la. Long acre
Cambrian & Grand Junction Railway Company (Josephus Ferris, secretary), 12 Nicholas lane, King William st
Cambridge & Lincoln Railway Company (Cusack Patrick Roney, secretary), 30 Great Winchester st. City
Cambridge & Oxford Railway Company, 28 Poultry
Cambridge Ann (Mrs.), staymaker, 2 Holland st. Kensington
Camden Richd. coal & potato dealer, 124 Bermondsey st
Camden Society (Wm. John Thoms, sec.), 25 Parliament st
Camden Town Savings' Bank, Camden st
Camden & Kentish Town Almshouses, Little Randolph st
Camden Thomas, boneboiler, 13 Thomas st. Whitechapel rd
Camerer, Faller & Co. wooden clock ma. 2 Broad st. Blmsby
Cameron & Booty, attorneys, 1 Raymond buildings, Gray's inn
Cameron Alexander, baker, 166 Tooley st
Cameron Mrs. Mary, coal dealer. 7 Cross st. Golden square
Cameron Dugald Edward, solicitor, see Julius & Cameron
Cameron Ewen Henry, barrister, 37 Chancery lane
Cameron George, oil & colorman, 11 Market st. May fair
Cameron John, armyclothier, cap, &c. ma. 3 Gt. Ryder st. St. Jas'
Cameron John, for. timber. mer. 30 Red Lion yd. Gt. Warner st
Cameron Norman, fruiterer, 64 Great hall, Hungerford mkt
Cameron Richd. brace maker, 12 Dorrington st. Coldbath fl
Cameron Sarah (Mrs.), bootmaker, 15A, North Audley st
Cameron William, grocer, 65 Tyer st. Lambeth
Camfield Lydia (Mrs.), lodging house, 13 Water st. Blkfrs
Camfield Wm. coal dealer, 28A, Marylebone la. Oxford st
Camm James, hosier, 166 Church st. Shoreditch
Cammann John Thomas, bread & biscuit baker, 36 Cloth fair
Cammegh Sarah (Mrs.), furn. broker, 217 Whitechapel road
Cammerer Matthew, clock ma. 3 Back Church la. Whitech
Camp Elizabeth (Mrs.), dairy, 36 Lower Islington terrace
Camp George, cowkeeper, 20 Cobourg st. Euston square
Camp George, shawl merchant, 408 Oxford st
Camp John, bookbinder, 65 Margaret st. Wilmington sq
Camp John, carman, 6 Blenheim mews, Blenheim st. Oxford st
Camp Eliza (Mrs.), confectioner, 47 South Audley st
Camp Thomas, cowkeeper, 15 Drummond st. Euston square
Camp William, *Three Doves* P.H. 23 & 24 Berwick st. Soho
Camp Wm. wood, ivory, & metal turner, 81 Tottenham ct. rd
Campart John T. hosier & glover, 16 & 17 Burlington arcade
Campbell Alex. & Jas. & Co. merchts. 10 George yd. Lombard st
Campbell Archibald & Co. brewers (Edinburgh), Steel yard, Upper Thames st
Campbell (Dawson) & Co. wine merchants, 12 Little Tower st
Campbell, Harrison & Lloyd, silk mnfrs. 19 Friday st. City
Campbell James & Co. merchants, 56 Moorgate st. Bank
Campbell James F. & Co. shipbrokers, 4 Birchin lane
Campbell & Page, bootmakers, 12 Pall mall East
Campbell & Witty, solicitors, 21 Essex st. Strand
Campbell Alexander, baker, 4 Temple st. Whitefriars
Campbell Alexander, oil & colorman, 7 High st. Kingsland
Campbell Andrew, confectioner, 16 Church st. Shoreditch
Campbell Andrew, silversmith & jeweller, 43 Tottenham ct. rd
Campbell Andrew, scotch stores, 16 Rood lane, Fenchrch. st
Campbell Archibald, chemist, 4 Essex pl. Mare st. Hackney
Campbell Archibald, officer of the fishery, 26 Bedford sq. ea
Campbell Charles, coffee rooms, 3 Mount st. Lambeth
Campbell Charles, rag merchant, 133 Kingsland road
Campbell Dugald F. (un. sec. to Col. Bank), 13 Bishopsgate st
Campbell Edward Geo. coal dealer, 11 High st. Lambeth
Campbell Frances (Miss), ladies' school, 32 Camden rd. villa
Campbell Geo. Chas. woollen draper, see Wilson & Campbell
Campbell Hannah M. (Miss), boarding house, 19A, Golden sq
Campbell Henry Elmes, solicitor, 3 New inn, Strand
Campbell Hugh, fishmonger, 23 New rd. St. George's East
Campbell James, barrister, 2 New square, Lincoln's inn
Campbell James, *Berkeley Arms* P.H. 6 John st. Berkeley sq
Campbell James, dairyman, 8 College terrace, Chelsea
Campbell James, wine merchant, see Cockburn & Campbell
Campbell James, *Yorkshire Grey* P.H. 14 Cheynewlk. Chelsea
Campbell John, baker, Church st. Deptford
Campbell John, grocer, 12 Lambeth hill, Doctors' commons
Campbell John, *Paviors' Arms* P.H. Johnson st. Millbank
Campbell John Shaw, physician, 16 Weymouth st
Campbell M'Gregor, pawnbroker, 168 & 169 Shadwell
Campbell Peter, importer of foreign wines, 82 Mark lane
Campbell Robert, clothes salesman, 74 Davies st. Berkeley sq
Campbell Thomas, sculptor, 16 Great Marlborough st
Campbell Thomas Theodore, surgeon, 2 Burton crescent
Campbell Wm. coach trimmer, 32 Northumberland st. New rd
Campbell William, merchant, 2 Great St. Helen's
Campbell William, tailor & draper, 96 Fenchurch st
Campbell William George, barrister, 9 Inner Temple lane
Camper John, *White Hart* P.H. 4 Aylesbury st. Clerkenwell
Campin Henry, shawl manufac. see Towler, Campin & Co
Campion John & Son, who. shoe warehouse, 19 St. Mary Axe
Campion Sarah A. & Eliz. B. dress ma. 21 Up. North pl. Gr. in. rd
Campion Alfred, beer retailer, 46 Cornwall road Lambeth
Campion Celia (Mrs.), cooper, 7 Munster st. Regent's park
Campion Edward, gasfitter, 1 Church st. Clapham road
Campion Emma (Miss), school, 7 Albion ter. Canonbury sq
Campion George, cowkeeper, 38 Clipstone st. Fitzroy sq
Campion Richard, provision merchant & agent, 30 Tooley st
Campion Robert, grocer, Church st. Hackney
Campion Ruth (Mrs.), coffee rooms, 3 Leathersellers' bldgs
Campion Thos. oilman, 5 Leathersellers' blds. London wall
Campion Thos. rag & bottle dlr. 1 Cumberland st. west, Rgnt's pk
Campion Wm. tobacconist, 28 Park place, Kennington cross
Campkin Henry, bookslr. & law statnr. 14 Lit. New st. Shoe la
Campleman John, tailor, 9 Poland st. Oxford st
Camplin & Ingoldby, surgeons, &c. 11 Finsbury square
Camplin John, surgeon, 33 Compton terrace, Islington
Campling Thomas, coach builder, Up. Grange rd. Old Kent rd
Camps Joseph, chemical agt. 3 Worcester pl. Up. Thames st

Camps William, physician, 50 Green st. Grosvenor sq
Camroux F. F. (secretary to *Nat. Loan Fund LifeAss.*),26 Cornhill
Camroux Ferdinand Richard, merchant, 26 Birchin lane
Canada Company(JohnPerry,sec.),13St. Helen'spl. Bishops
Canapo Telesfro, looking glass frame ma. 22 Lit. Saffron hill
Cancellor Charles, stockbroker, 1 Cushion ct. Old Broad st
Cancellor Ellis, starchmaker, see Coward & Cancellor
Candelin Arnold, tinman, 14 Amelia st. Walworth road
Candland Chas. chaise saddle & harness ma. 96 Brownlow st
Candler Charlt. (Miss), school, 17 Brunswick pa. Barnsby rd
Candler Fredk. Alex. hosier & outfitter, 367 Oxford st
Candler Sam. ho.agt.&appraiser,4Angelter. New rd. Islingtn
Candler Sarah (Mrs.),tobacconist,37Shaftsburyst.NewNo.rd
Candler Thomas W. wine & beer merchant, 8 Billiter st
Candler Thos. Wagstaffe warehouse keeper, 8 Billiter st
Candin James, *Crown* P.H. 40 Narrow st. Limehouse
Candlin Thos. Jsph. *Bull's Head* P.H. 75 West Smithfield
Candy Charles & Co. foreign merchants, 4 & 5 Watling st
Candy James, butcher, 110 Murray st. New North road
Cane Richard&Co. watch manf. 46 Gt.Sutton st. Clerkenwell
Cane Ann (Mrs.), oil & italian warehouse, 92 Oxford st
Cane George, cheesemonger, 22 Jubilee place, Chelsea
Cane Geo. saddler,43Kingslandrd. &85 WheelerstSpitalfieds
Cane Henry, tailor, 12 Swan st. Great Dover road, Borough
Cane James, oilman, 4 Broadway, Ludgate hill
Cane John, linendraper, see Hoare & Cane
Cane John, shoemaker, 47 Water lane, Blackfriars
Cane Mary (Mrs.), *Three Compasses* P.H. 58 Up. Ebury st
Cane Mary Ann (Miss), cheesemngr.4& 5 Crown ct. Pall mall
Cane Robert, grocer, 24 Riley st. Chelsea
Cane Samuel, baker, 19 Marine street, Bermondsey
Cane Thos. tinplate worker, 3 Mansion house st. Kennington
Canet Theophilus, tailor, 63 South Molton st
Caney John, tinplate wrkr. 35 Clark's orchard, Rotherhithe
Canham Alfred, oil & colorman, 123 St. George st
Canham Harriet (Mrs.), oil & colorman, 230 Rotherhithe
Canham John, accountant, 5 King Edward st. Lambeth road
Canham Joseph, linen draper, 30 Lit. Earl st. Seven dials
Canham Samuel, furn. undertaker, 7 Oxford st. Mile end
Canham Thos. Edwd. corn & seed dlr.30 Hayfield pl. Mile end
Canham William, coffee rooms, 68 Fore st Cripplegate
Cankrien Hugh Ker, barrister, 23 Old square, Lincoln's inn
Cann Henry, bone boiler, 40 Upper Fore st. Lambeth
Cann John, *Robin Hood* P. H. Robin hood court, Shoe lane
Cann Jsph. bricklayer& slater, 24 Huntley st.Tottenhamct.rd
Cann Thomas, *King's Arms* P.H. 44 Blackman st. Borough
Cannadine Richard, plane & tool ma. 21 Gt. Smith st. Westmr
Cannall Mary(Mrs.),*GeorgeIV*.P.H.94Green st.Bethnal grn
Cannam John grocer, &c. 3 Foubert's place, Regent st
Canneaux Louis M. & Son, of Rheims, wine merchants, 8 Gould square, & 14 John st. Crutched friars
Canneaux Claude, wine cooper, 2 Catherine ct. Tower hill
Cannel Francis, coachsmith, 28 Charlotte st. Old st. road
Cannell John, tea dealer & grocer, 14 Great Newport st
Cannell Thomas, *Seven Stars* P. H. 3 Fleet st. Bethnal grn
Cannell Wm. dairyman, 67 Gt. Carlisle st. Portman market
Canner Robert, carpenter, 26 Northumberland st. New road
Canning Elizabeth (Mrs.), dairy, 3 Exeter st. Sloane st
Canning John, coach ironmonger & plater, 50 Long acre
Canning Margt. (Miss),babylinenwa.1Barnsburypl.Islington
Canning Wm. wholes.shoe wareh.3 Corbet ct.Gracechurch st
CannonWm. & Maria Ann (Miss),schl.16Aldenham st.Som.tn
Cannon Charles & Co. dyers to her Majesty, 6 Davies st. Berkeley square
Cannon Caroline (Miss), milliner, 69 Kingsland road
Cannon Charles, dyer & scourer, 23 Newcastle st. Strand
Cannon Charles, fish salesman, 21 Love lane, & 11 Philpot lane, Eastcheap
Cannon Daniel, tobacco manufacturer, 98 Rosemary lane
Cannon Elizh. (Mrs.), firework artist, 3Asylumbdgs.West.rd
Cannon Elizabeth (Mrs.), *WhiteHorse*P.H.51Rayst.Clrkwl
Cannon Geo. foreign booksel. 2 Gt.May's bldgs.St.Martin's la
Cannon James, baker, 31 Elizabeth st. Eaton square
Cannon John, brush ma. 15 Bedford pl. Commercial rd. east
Cannon John, tailor, 7 Wingrove place, Clerkenwell
Cannon Michael, *BrownBear* P.H.38 Millbank st.Wstmnstr
Cannon Samuel, bootmaker, 85 Church st. Shoreditch
Cannon Samuel, vet.surgeon, South Bruton mews, Bruton st
Cannon Stephen, stock & sharebrok. 26 Tokenhouse yard
Cannon Thomas, gen. sale shop, 41 Church st. Shoreditch
Cannon Thomas, *BlackHorse*P.H.10Bedfordbury,Covnt.gdn
Cannon Wm.ship&ins.brok.&cust.ho.agt.62Lower Thames st
Canns James, veterinary forge, 62 Snows fields, Bermondsey
Cansdale Thos. butcher, 5 Skinner's pl. Leadenhall market
Cansdell Thos. *Hoop& HorseShoe*P.H.10 Queen st.Tower hill
Canstatt Nathan, surgeon, 8 Bevis marks
Cant Geo.Wm.last, boot tree,patten & clog ma.69 HighHolbn
Cant James, baker, 13 New st. Brompton
Cant Samuel Henry, last maker,39 Phœnix st.Somers town
Cant Thos. Fred. last maker, 32 Phœnix st. Somers town
Cant William, hosier, 16 Elizabeth st. Eaton square
Canter Jsph.cloth&fancy cap ma. 17 Goulstone st.Whitechap
Canterford Wm. shell comb ma. 3 Prospect pl. Islington
Canti Chas. Antonio, glassblower,28 White st. Long la.Boro'
Cantis Henry, surgeon, 8 Maddox st. Regent st
Canton Alfred, surgeon dentist, 18 Old Bond st
Canton Edwin, surgeon, 104 St. Martin's lane, Charing cross
Canton George Augustus, dentist, 40 St. Martin's lane
Canton Henry, dentist, 2 Great Suffolk st. Borough
Canton James, *Lord Nelson* P.H. Robinhood lane, Poplar
Canton James John, oilman, 19 Eldon st. Finsbury circus
Canton John N. writing master,12 White Lion st.Spitalfields
Canton Maria (Mrs.), dentist, 3 Osborne st. Whitechapel
Canton Wm. Laurence,surg.dent. 18 Hanover st. Hanover sq
Canton Wm. L. surgeon dentist, 32 Penny fields, Poplar
Cantor Benj.& M. theatrical dr. wa.21 Goulstone sq.Whtchpl
Cantor Frances (Miss), lead pencil ma. 4 Bury st. Aldgate
CantorJosephJacob,quill,pen,sponge,&c.dealr.6Houndsditch
Cantor James,*D.ofCumberland's Hd.* P.H.11 New road,St. George's east
Cantrell Joseph, boot & shoemaker, Camberwell green
Cantrell Joseph Thomas, barrister, 21 Old sq. Lincoln's inn
Canute Thomas, stuff manufacturer, 5 Addle st
Canute Thomas, stuff warehouseman, 6 & 7 Addle st
Cantwell Robert, architect & surveyor, 20 Gt. Marlboro' st. 25 Wimpole st. Cavendish sq. & 10 Church st. Camberwell
Cape of Good Hope Trade Society, 5 Fen court, Fenchurch st. (James Sutherland, secretary)
Cape George Augustus, tailor, &c. 11 Old Bond st
Cape John, merchant, 12 Coleman st
Cape Lawson, physician, 64 Brook st. Hanover square
Cape Mary Ann (Miss), lodging house, 7 Panton square
Cape William, accountant, 13 Portsea place, Connaught sq
Capel, Cuerton & Lawford, stockbrokers, 7 Popeshead alley
Capel & Cundy, coal merc. Wilton wharf,Wilton rd. Pimlico
Capel Henry & Co. wine merchants, 17 Lit. Tower st
Capel Henry & Co. coopers, 17Lit.Tower st. &14 Seething la
Capel(Jas.),Norbury,Trotter&Co. stockbroks.9Throgmrtn.st
Capel Thomas Spencer & Co. coal merchants, Bridewell wharf, Bridewell precinct, William st. Blackfriars
Capel Arthur, tea broker, see Carlisle, Capel & Co
Capel J—— D——, engineer, see Seaward & Capel
Capell Edward, baker, 45 Margaret st. Wilmington sq
Capener Daniel, undertaker, 41 North st. Sloane st
Capener John, carpenter, &c. 24 Kinnerton st. Belgrave sq
Capener John, grocer, Ring cross, Holloway
Capern Hermon, hairdresser, 163 Hoxton Old town
Caperoe Elizth. (Mrs.), marine store dlr. 183 Kingsland rd
CapesJoseph & Co.booksellers & stationers,6Paternoster row
Capes & Stuart, solicitors, 1 Field court, Gray's inn
Capes Edward, saddler, 259 Whitechapel road
Capes Frederick, proctor, 11 Gt. Carter la. Doctors' comms
Capes George Augustus Harrison, surgeon, 22 Philpot lane
CapesJohnS. accountant, Australian chbs.33 Gracechurch st
Capey Sarah (Mrs.), haberdasher, 62 Aldersgate st
Capill John Jas. blind ma. 18 Charlotte st. Pentonville
Caplin Jean F. I. orthopœodist, 58 Berner's st. Oxford st
Caplin John, chaser, 34 King st. Clerkenwell
Caplin Madame R. G. milliner & corset ma. 58 Berners st
Capon Edward, grocer, 4 Little Vine st. Regent st
Capon Joseph, wire drawer & worker, 65 Farringdon st
Capon Samuel, see Winchester & Capon
Capon Stephen, bricklayer, &c. 28 Church row, Pancras rd
Capon Thomas, *Three Hats* P.H. 19 Islington High st
Capon Thomas, *Victoria* P.H. Lower road, Rotherhithe
Capon Thomas, jun. grocer, Gibraltar rw. Lr. road, Deptford
Caporn Jas. architect & surveyor, 10 Dyer's bldgs. Holborn
Capp Mark, baker, 2 Barnet st. Hackney road
Capp William, baker, 29 King st. East st. Walworth
Cappel Michael, tobacco & snuff manufacturer, 256 High st. Borough; manufactory, 21 Assembly row, Mile end road
Capper & Armstrong, coal merchants, 17 Salisbury st. Strand
Capper Geo. & Nephews, merchants, 1 Adelaide pl. London br
Capper & Gray, chocolate & cocoa manuf. 396 Strand
Capper & Gray, teadealers, 397 Strand
Capper John & Son, linendrapers to the Queen, 69 Gracechurch st. & 26 Regent st
Capper, Morley & Capper, warehomn.19Breadst.&17Watlingst
Capper & Waters, makers of the corazza & other shirts by measure, 8 Carlton chambers, Regent st. Waterloo place
Capper Charles, stockbroker, Lloyd's

Capper Henry, stock & share broker, 21 Tokenhouse yard
Capper Wm. Best, milliner & laceman, 62 Upper Stamford st
Cappi Wm. barometer frame ma. 11 Baker's row, Clerkenwl
Capps Dennis, carver & gilder, 46 Foley st. Portland place
Capps James, builder, 1 Grove ter. Queen's rd. Bayswater
Capps Joseph Fredk. grocer, 7 Grove ter. Queen's rd. Bayswtr
Capps Thomas, woollen & manchester warehouseman & general outfitter, 21 Leadenhall st
Cappur Ralph Thomas, surgeon, 8 Brook st. Grosvenor sq
Capron, Brabant & Capron, solicitors, 7 Saville place, New Burlington st
Capron John A. & Co. who. leathersellers, 23 Bishopgt. witho
Capron Abraham, carpenter, 11 Elizabeth st. south, Pimlico
Capron Geo. *Dolphin* P.H. 6 Union st. Walcot pl. Lambth. wlk
Capron Jas. *George IV.* P.H. 10 Guildford st. east, Spafields
Capron John, grocer, 7 Pembroke mews, Chapel st. Grosvnr. pl
Capstick Jane (Mrs.), milnr. 20 Camden cottages, Camd. new tn
Capt Jules, watchmaker, see Nicole & Capt
Captain Cook's Almshouses, Mile end road
Capua Lewis Pisman, fruit & nut mer. 3 St. James's pl. Aldgat
Capua Mordecai, fruit merchant, 3 St. James's place, Aldgate
Capue Mordecai, livery stables, Mitre st. Aldgate
Caraffa Henry, academy, 10 Pagoda ter. Bermondsey new rd
Carbery Christopher, turner, 44 Paul st. Finsbury
Carbery Patrick, tailor, see Place & Carbery
Carbonell & Co. wine merchants, 182 Regent st
Carbonell Antonio de Ramony, merchant, 34 Threadneedle st
Card & Dowling, pork butchers, 2 Halfmoon pas. Leadenb. mkt
Card, Dice & Stamp Office, Somerset house, hours 10 to 4
Card James, straw hat ma. 6 Lit. Titchfield st. Portland pl
Card Joseph (late Walker), watch & clock maker, & dealer in watch materials, 4 Somerset st. Aldgate
Card Martha (Mrs.), toy dealer, 6 Swan st. Minories
Card Thomas, tailor, 27 Pembroke place, Vauxhall bdg. rd
Card William, flute manufacturer, 29 St. James's st
Cardale, Cardale & Iliffe, solicitors, 2 Bedford row, Bloomsby
Carden & Hack, carpenters, 34 Penny fields, Poplar
Carden & Whitehead, stockbrokers, 61½ Threadneedle st
Carden George Frederick, barrister, 11 Carey st
Carden Michael, grocer, 34 Penny fields, Poplar
Carden Wm. Robinson, cheese & provision ag. 253 Tooley st
Carder John, builder, Bow
Cardinal Wm. importer of turkey carpets, 62 Princes st. Leicester sq. Levant warehouse, St. Helen's pl. Bishopsgt
Cardno James, baker, 3 North place, Ball's pond road
Cardwell James, butcher, Wandsworth road
Cardwell Wm. *George IV.* P.H. 27 Queen's row, Pimlico
Care James, grocer & teadealer, 13 Clare st. Clare market
Carel James, beer retailer, 38 Harrow road, Paddington
Careless Edmund, oil & colorman, 205 Tooley st
Careless Edmund, soda water, &c. manfr. 14 Threadneedle st
Careless Jas. soup, chop & dining rooms, 7 Finch la. Cornhill
Careless James, jun. wine rooms, 7 Finch lane, Cornhill
Careless Wm. oil & italian wah. 25 Wormwood st. Bishopsgt
Cares John, baker, 69 Upper Berkeley st. Portman sq
Caress James, grocer & cheesemonger, 18 Dean st. Holborn
Carette Emanuel, hat manufacturer, 7 Lombard st. Borough
Carew George, solicitor, 9 Lincoln's inn fields
Carew Sarah (Mrs.), grindery dlr. & beershop, 106 Bethnal gr. rd
Carey & Browne, east india & colonial brokers, 36 Mincing la
Carey James, coffee rooms, 29 Shaftsbury ter. Pimlico
Carey Thomas, baker, 3 Keppel st. Chelsea
Carey William, artificial florist, 95 Berwick st. Soho
Carey William, bricklayer, 4 Berners mews, Berners st
Carey William, surgeon, 8 Halfmoon st. Piccadilly
Carey Wm. Henry, ship & insurance broker, 21 Mark lane
Carfrae James A. publisher, 49 Essex st. Strand
Carle Chas. carver & gilder, 8 Cumberland pl. Newington butts
Carle Thos. machinist, lathe & tool ma. 60 Princes rd. Lambeth
Carles Hycinthe, peruke maker, 1 Conduit st. Regent st
Carless Eugene B. surgeon, 39 Warwick st. Belgrave road
Carless Henry, chaser, 16 Guildford st. East, Spa fields
Carless Robert, accountant, 15 Wine office court, Fleet st
Carless William John, butcher, 5 Duke st. Chelsea
Carleton Elizth. (Mrs.), milliner, 3 Bowling st. Westminster
Carley George, who. watchmaker, see Stoddart & Carley
Carlier John, commission agent, 1 Ampton pl. Gray's inn rd
Carlile John & Co. silk & stuff agents, 2 Mitre ct. Milk st
Carliles', Pittman & Co. who. haberdashers, 11, 12 & 13 Bow la
Carlin Brothers, tobacconists, 85 Gracechurch st
Carlin Mary (Miss), milliner, 20 Seymour pl. Bryanstone sq
Carlin William Henry, importer of cigars, 25 Ludgate st
Carlisle, Capel & Co. tea brokers, 1 Dunster ct. Mincing la
Carlisle Robert, hairdresser, 16 Lowther arcade, Strand
Carlisle Thomas, chandler's shop, 98 Green st. Bethnal grn
Carlisle Wm. cutler, Henry Adkins, agent, 4 Thavies inn
Carlisle Thomas, tailor, 1 Hampstead st. Fitzroy square
Carlon & Haynes, solicitors, 6 Palace chmbrs. St. James's st
Carlos Edward John, solicitor, 6 York pl. Walworth rd. & at Lord Mayor's court office, 7 Old Jewry
Carloss Elizh. (Mrs.), watch gilder, 26 Gt. Sutton st. Clrknw
Carloss George, watch & water gilder, 11 Hooper st. Clrknwl
Carlow Samuel Stewart Townsend, architect, 21 Old Jewry, City, & 12 Clapham road place
Carlton Charles, *Duke of Wellington* P.H. 15 Spring grdns
Carlton Club House (James Jephson, sec.), 94 Pall mall
Carlton Thomas, *Coach & Horses* P.H. 11 Avery rw. Grosv. st
Carly, Son & Wingrove, backma. Layton's bldgs. 143 Boro'
Carly Cornelius, upholstr. 6 & 7 Bolingbroke rw. Walworth rd
Carly Edmund, upholsterer, Portland row, Walworth com
Carmalt John, laceman & hosier, 16 Colvill ter. King's rd
Carman Edw. *King's Arms* P.H. 37 Freeschool st. Horselydn
Carman Henry, greengrocer, Flagan row, Deptford
Carman John, camp equipage & trunk ma. 2 Bruton st. Bond st
Carman Thos. jun. who. ironmonger & manufr. 120 Newgate st
Carman Wm. dairy, 6 Wallington pl. Wandsworth road
Carme Eloi, jewel casema. 8 Gt. May's bldgs. St. Martin's la
Carn Brea Mines' Off. (John Mc Donnell, sec.), 35 Broad st. blds
Carnaby George, furniture dealer, 21 Bermondsey square
Carnall Thomas, corkcutter, 9 Postern row, Tower hill
Carne Charles, chemist, 13 Caledonia ter. Caledonian rd
Carne Henry, sen. barge builder, Battersea fields
Carne Henry, jun. barge & lug builder, 21½ Stangate, Lmbth
Carne John, chemist, 55 Brompton row, Brompton
Carnell Thomas, *Coopers' Arms* P.H. 28 Hampden st. Somers tn
Carnelly John, *Hoop & Toy* P.H. Old Brompton
Caroline William, egg merchant, 54 King st. Borough
Carpenter Jas. & Thos. bookbinders, 4 Wardrobe ter. Doc. com
Carpenter & Westley, opticians, Microcosm, 24 Regent st
Carpenter Wm. & Son, clothwrkrs. Bowling all. 20 Whitecrss. st
Carpenter Smith's Wharf, Richard Willson & Co. Mill lane, between 53 & 56 Tooley st
Carpenters' Hall, (Jupp & Basil, clerks), 68 London wall
Carpenter Ambrose, tobacconist, 42 Margaret st. Wilmingt. sq
Carpenter Charles, cooper, 26½ Radnor st. St. Luke's
Carpenter Charles, hairdresser, 5 Church st. St. Geor.'s, Boro'
Carpenter Charles Edwd. carman, 6½ Foster st. Bishopsgate
Carpenter David, watch maker, 13 Nelson terrace, City rd
Carpenter Eliza (Mrs.), baker, 30 Exmouth st. Euston sq
Carpenter Elizh. (Mrs.), corn dea. 70 Harper st. New Kent rd
Carpenter George, hairdresser, 1 Little Queen st. Holborn
Carpenter Henry, miller, steam flour mill, Shad Thames
Carpenter Henry, news vender, 28 Seething lane, Tower st
Carpenter James, bookseller & publisher, 14 Old Bond st
Carpenter James, grocer, 54 Russell st. Lower Rotherhithe
Carpenter James, grocer, 9 Aylesbury st. Clerkenwell
Carpenter James, plumber, &c. 16 Cross st. Newington butts
Carpenter John, baker, 66 Clarendon st. Somers town
Carpenter John, baker, 102 Drummond st
Carpenter John, baker, 23 Drummond st. Euston square
Carpenter John, butcher, 26 Three Colt st. Limehouse
Carpenter John, *Coach & Horses* P.H. 11 King st. Westmr
Carpenter John, cooper, 9 Clerkenwell gr. & 18 Aylesbury st
Carpenter John, tailor, 26 Lower Belgrave st. Pimlico
Carpenter John Blake, grocer & cheesemgr. 30 Up. Seymour st
Carpenter Joseph, auctioneer, see Woollams & Carpenter
Carpenter Joseph, chandler's shop, 82 Cromer st. Brunswk. sq
Carpenter Joseph, oilman, 30 Pepper st. Union st. Borough
Carpenter Nicholas, publisher, 60 Spencer st. Goswell rd
Carpenter Percy, artist, 10 Nottingham place, Marylebone
Carpenter Prudence (Mrs.), *Anchor tap* P.H. 28 Horslydn. la
Carpenter Richard, omnibus builder, 7 Paddington green
Carpenter Richard, pawnbroker, 1 Chas. st. St. George's east
Carpenter Richard C. architect, 99 Guildford st. Russell sq
Carpenter Robert, chemist, 55 Backchurch la. Whitechapel
Carpenter Robert, wax & tallow chandler, 35 Duke st. Smithfl
Carpenter Saml. beer retailer, 110 Park st. Kengtn. cross
Carpenter Thomas, meat salesman, 88 St. John st. Smithfield
Carpenter Thomas, printer, 16 Gilbert st. Oxford st
Carpenter Wm. jun. artist, 10 Nottingham pl. Marylebone
Carpenter Wm. (Mrs.), artist, 10 Nottingham pl. Marylebone
Carpenter Wm. cooper, 82 St. George's road, Borough
Carpenter Wm. hairdresser, 3 Adelaide place, Grange road
Carpenter Wm. hairdresser, 103 Bermondsey st
Carpenter Wm. hairdresser, 7 Duke st. Chelsea
Carpenter Wm. miller, steam mills, Greenwich, & 68 Low. Shadwell; 59 New Corn Exch. Mark la. & Bromley, Middx
Carpenter Wm. solicitor, 11 Union court, Old Broad st
Carpenter Wm. watchmaker, 4 Perceval st. Clerkenwell
Carpenter Wm. Guest, surgeon, 1 West st. Finsbury
Carpentier Francis, goldsmith, 21 Perceval st. Clerkenwell
Carpmael Thos. who. coffee & spice dlr. 5 Vine st. Minories

Carpmael William, patent agent, see Poole & Carpmael
Carpue Joseph, physician, 45 Charlotte st. Fitzroy square
Carpue Joseph F. bookbinder, 11 Old Compton st. Soho
Carpue Nehemiah, surgeon, 16 Globe road, Mile end
Carr & Goodall, button & trimming sell. 4 Glassho. st. Reg.st
Carr & Jacob, wine merchants, 10 Laurence Pountney hill
Carr David & Wm. woollendrapers, 15 Warwick st. Golden sq
Carr James R. & Son, tailors, 11 Liverpool st. Bishopsgate
Carr Lamb & Co. coal factors & ship, &c. agts. 36 St. Mary at hill
Carr & Robertson, button & manch. warehomen. 130 Wood st
Carr Thomas & Co. silk manufacturers, 14 Addle st
Carr Wm. & Co cheesemongers, 22 Brewer st. Somers town
Carr Andrew, coach painter, 15 Northumberland st. New rd
Carr Andrew M. solicitor, Excise Office, Old Broad st
Carr Anthony, solicitor, see Miller & Carr
Carr Benjamin, horse hair manufr. 108 Bunhill row, St. Luke's
Carr Benjamin, poulterer, Bull's head pas. Gracechurch st
Carr Benjamin, teadealer, 4 Charlton pl. Gt. Dover rd. Boro'
Carr Charles, grindery dealer, 19 Fleet lane, Farringdon st
Carr Charles, *Pine Apple* P.H. 80 Hercules bldgs. Lambeth
Carr Charles, tailor, 46 Edgware road, Marylebone
Carr Charles, who. & retail confectnr. 223 Blackfriars rd
Carr Eliza (Miss), milliner, see Saunders & Carr
Carr Fenwick, oil & italian wareho. 57 Glos'ter st. Queen sq
Carr George, meat salesman, 2 White hart st. Newgate mkt
Carr George, oil & colorman, 99 Goswell st
Carr George Bownes, merchant, 10 Laurence Pountney hill
Carr Henry, cheesemonger, 29 Foley st
Carr Henry, ironfounder, 89 Great Peter st. Westminster
Carr Henry, wheelwright, 46 Hedge row, Islington High st
Carr Isaac, russia merchant, see Catleys' & Carr
Carr James, cowkeeper & dairyman, 39 Park st. Dorset sq
Carr James Joshua, shipbroker, see Ritherdon & Carr
Carr Jas. Wm. bread & biscuit baker, 37 Up. Parkpl. Dorset sq
Carr John, butcher, 8 Farringdon market
Carr John, haberdasher, 79 Church lane, Whitechapel
Carr John, plumber & glazier, 1 Belgrave mews ea. Belgrave sq
Carr John, wheelwright, 13 Robert st. Hampstead road
Carr John Smith, blackg. mkr. 57 Hatton gdn. & 10 Hatton wall
Carr John Wilson, meat salesman, 15 New Newgate market
Carr Lewis, silk dyer, 43 Spicer st. Spitalfields
Carr Matthew, tailor, see Maitland & Carr
Carr Ralph, cheesemonger, 33 Brook st. Ratcliff
Carr Robert, *Black Prince* P.H. 2 Black Prince rw. Wlwth.rd
Carr Samuel, beer retailer, 173 Southwark bridge road
Carr Theophilus, boarding ho. 4 Scott's yard, Cannon st
Carr Thomas, firebrick maker, 64 Lower Shadwell
Carr Thomas, woollen warehouseman, 1 Basinghall st
Carr Wm. bookbinder, 30 Holywell lane, Shoreditch
Carr Wm. cheesemonger, 25 Beckford row, Walworth road
Carr William, cheesemonger, 57 Kingsland road
Carr Wm. feather manufacturer, 20 King st. Covent garden
Carr Wm. hairdresser, 26 Thomas st. Oxford st
Carr Wm. merchant, see Carr, Lamb & Co
Carr Wm. merchant, 65 Old Broad st. City, & Baltic
Carr Wm. plumber & painter, 24 Montagu st. Portman sq
Carr Wm. tailor, 3 Avery farm row, Pimlico
Carr Wm. Thomas, barrister, 89 Chancery lane
Carrall James & Co. advertising agents, 289 Strand
Carrand Joseph, silk importer, see Thomel & Carrand
Carrell Robt. Hen. chinawareho. 12 King st. Covent garden
Carreras Frederick, grocer, 20 Wilsted st. Somers town
Carreras Joseph, linguist, &c. 20 Wilsted st. Somers town
Carrew John Wm. nautical instrument ma. 13 Wapping wall
Carrick John & Co. iron & brass founds. 55 St. George st
Carrick Ann (Mrs.), plumber & painter, 99 Fore st. Limehouse
Carrick James, chemist, 30 Duke st. Manchester square
Carrick Maria (Mrs.), baker, 4 Water lane, Blackfriars
Carrick Thomas, artist, 43 Upper Seymour st. Portman sq
Carriere Aglaée (Madame), dressmaker, 10 John st. Berkeley sq
Carriere Joseph, hairdresser & perfumer, 10 John st. Berkeley sq
Carrighan Terentius, solicitor, 23 Red Lion square, Holborn
Carrington Saml. & Thos. iron founders, 50 Upper Thames st
Carrington Abraham, baker, 1 North place, Kingsland road
Carrington Benjamin, surgeon, 5 Winchester pl. Pentonville
Carrington Fred. Augustus, barrister, 28 Lincoln's inn fields
Carrington Geo. horsedealer & livery stables, 255 Oxford st
Carrington Geo. Wm. civil engineer, 14 Duke st. Westmnr
Carrington John, grocer, 95 Vauxhall st. Lambeth
Carrington John, surgeon, 60 Leman st. Goodman's fields
Carrington Richard, malt distiller, see Smith & Carrington
Carrington Thomas, baker, 5 Goldsmith's row, Hackney rd
Carrington William, grocer, 2 Charles st. Long acre
Carritt Fk. attorney, 10 Basinghall st. & 11 Chapel st. Pentvil
Carritt Wm. for. & colnl. produce dealer, 6 Botolph lane
Carroll Alex. chemical stopperer, 5 Green Dragon yd. Snow hl
Carroll Ann Susan (Mrs.), coffeerooms, 9 Tavistock rw. Cov. gar
Carroll Anthony, furniture broker, 7 & 8 East st. Finsbury
Carroll James, bootmaker, 4 South st. King's road, Chelsea
Carroll James, coffee rooms, 24 Sun st
Carroll John, tailor & draper, 37 Worship st. Finsbury
Carroll Jthan. watch escapement mak. 35 Skinner st. Clkwl
Carroll Luke, oil & colorman, 14 King st. Tower hill
Carroll Philip, provision agent, 5 Wellington chbrs. Tooley st
Carroll Samuel, east india & colonial broker, 37 Mincing lane
Carroll Thomas, baker, 32 Ossulston st. Somers town
Carroll Thomas, grocer, 2 Back road, St. George's east
Carroll Wm. grocer & cheesemonger, 36 Worship st. Finsbury
Carron Company's Iron Warehouse (Henry Stainton, agent), 15 Upper Thames st
Carron Wharf, Henry White, 87 Lower East Smithfield
Carrow John Monson, barrister, Hall staircase, Temple
Carrs Robert, *Prince Regent* P.H. 8 St. George st
Carruthers & Budd, merchants & insur. broks. 9 Copthall ct
Carruthers Chas. *Friend at Hd.* P.H. 32 Colonnade, Russl.sq
Carruthers Charles, surgeon, 43 York road, Lambeth
Carruthers George Edwd. surgeon, 14 Redman's row, Mile end
Carruthers Jas. *King's Arms* P.H. Sun tav. fields, St. Geo. east
Carruthers Jas. plumber, 30 Charles st. Charles sq. Hoxton
Carruthers Richard, provision merchant, 1 Philpot lane
Carruthers Thomas, tailor, 43 Glo'ster st. Queen square
Carruthers Wm. *Harp* P.H. 26 New Church st. Lisson grove
Carslake George, grocer, 24 Regent st. Westminster
Carson Samuel, salting instrmt. depôt, 1 Bishopsgate within
Carson Walter, sole manuf. of anti-corrosion paint to the Hon. Board of Ordnance, & the Hon. E.I.Co. 15 Tokenhouse yd
Carss Jane (Mrs.), teadealer, 87 Broad st. Ratcliff
Carstairs John F. wine mer. 8 Claremont row, Barnsbury rd
Carstairs Joseph, inventor & teacher of the genuine systems of penmanship & arithmetic, & the useful branches of mathematics, 81 Lombard st. City
Carswell Mary (Mrs.), baker, 13 Halfmoon st. Piccadilly
Carter & Bird, linendrapers, 28 St. George's pl. Knightsbdg
Carter & Bonus, ship & insurance brokers, 11 Leadenhall st
Carter & Bromley, stationers, account book & copying machine manufacturers, 23 Royal Exchange, north side
Carter & Co. wharfingers, &c. West Kent Whf. Montague close
Carter Edward & Co. *White Hart* P.H. 35 Hoxton Old town
Carter & Gregory, solicits. Lord Mayor's ct. off. 7 Old Jewry
Carter Henry & Co. designers & engravers on wood, 114 Upper Stamford st
Carter John & Sons, uphols. & auctioneers, 53 Poplar High st
Carter & M'Hugh, cloth finishers, &c. &c. 13 Basinghall st
Carter & Strofton, importers of foreign wines & spirits, 65 South Molton st. Grosvenor square
Carter Thos. & Brothers, manchstr. mer. 58 Aldermanbury
Carter Thomas & Son, bacon driers, 6 John's pl. Blackfrs. rd
Carter Thomas & Son, house & ship joiners, Emmett st
Carter, Vavasseur & Rix, silk manuftrs. 9 Trump st. Cheapside
Carter William & Frank, boot & shoe makers, 55 Boro' High st
Carter Albinus, ship & insurance broker, commercial & custom house agent & public notary, 70 Lower Thames st
Carter Alfd. carver & gilder, 17 Judd st. Brunswick sq
Carter Alfred, porkman, 15 New road, St. George's east
Carter Alfred, stay, &c. manufacturer, 6 Blackfriars road; 13 Sloane sq. Chelsea, & 5 Stockwell st. Greenwich
Carter Anne (Mrs.), staymaker, 13 Sherrard st. Golden sq
Carter Arthur, grocer, 18 George st, New Kent road
Carter Benjamin, tailor, 21 East st. Manchester sq
Carter Catherine (Mrs.), *Jack's coffee ho.* Corn Exch. Mark la
Carter Chas. brassfounder & gasfit. 41 Exeter st. Lisson grove
Carter Charles, hairdesser, Church st. Hackney
Carter Charles, tea dealer, 293 Oxford st
Carter Cornelius Jas. plasterer, 6 Maze pond, Tooley st
Carter Daniel, plumber & glazier, 44 Fleet lane
Carter Edward, builder, 31 Murray st. Hoxton
Carter Edw. *Southampton Arms* P.H. 168 High st. Camden tn
Carter Edwd. sen. carver & gilder, 60 Exmouth st. Spafields
Carter Edwd. jun. ornamntl. carver, 26 Garnault pl. Spafields
Carter Eliza (Mrs.), milliner, 2 Francis place, Holloway
Carter Elizabeth (Mrs.), toy wareho. 29 Bishopsgate within
Carter Ellen (Mrs.), corn dlr. 34 Robert ter. King's rd. Chelsea
Carter Frances (Mrs.), *King's Head inn*, King's Head inn yard, 54 Borough High st
Carter Francis, bootmaker, 10 Wingrove place, Clerkenwell
Carter George, *Albion* P.H. Maiden lane, King's cross
Carter Geo. carpen. King's arms yd. Marylebone st. Piccadilly
Carter Geo. diamond setter, 3 Lower Smith st. Northampton sq
Carter George, dyer, 18 Earl st. Horseferry road
Carter George, market gardener, Battersea
Carter Hen. dentist, 9 Thanet place, Strand
Carter Henry, ironmonger, 24 King David's lane, Shadwell

Carter Hen. *Sprd.Eagle* P.H.47½Guildford pl.Lr.Kengtn.la
Carter Hen. trimming seller, 91 Lambeth Lower marsh
Carter Isaac, pianoforte maker, 7 Orchard st. Portman sq
Carter Isaac,steel plate manufr. 24 Aldenham st.Somers twn
Carter Isaac Mills, *Noah's Ark* P.H.216 Blackfriars rd
Carter James, beer retailer, 33 King's road east, Chelsea
Carter James, *Crown & Thistle* P.H. 42 Haymarket
Carter James, dyer, see Alexander & Carter
Carter James, *Grapes* P.H. 1 Union st. New Bond st
Carter James, grocer & cheesemonger, 2 North st. Lisson gr
Carter James, seedsman & florist, 238 High Holborn
Carter James Hewitt, artist, 41 Gt. Russell st. Bloomsbury
Carter James Mortimer, butcher, 127 Minories
Carter James Tunnadine, carver & gilder,65Berwick st.Soho
Carter Jane (Mrs.), tobacconist, 10 James st. Haymarket
Carter Jeremiah, woollen manuf.&merchant,65Basinghall st
Carter Jesse & Son, bricklayers, 7 Clayton st. Kennington
Carter Job,*Queen'sHead*P.H.73Gt.Queen st.Lincoln's i.flds
Carter John, alton ale rooms, 304 Oxford st
Carter John,archery warehouse, 36 Store st. Bedford sq
Carter John, artist, 3 Friedenstein ter. Hampstead rd
Carter John, auctioneer, see Burroughs & Carter
Carter John, baker, 28 Great Tower st. City
Carter John, chronometer maker to the Royal Navy, 61 Cornhill, & 207 Tooley st
Carter John, ivory comb ma. 5&6Fleur de lis st.Norton folg
Carter John, grocer, 11 Lombard st. Chelsea
Carter John, market gardener, Battersea
Carter John, outfitter, 59 Gracechurch st
Carter John, plumber, 6 Richmond st. East. st. Walworth
Carter John, pork butcher, 16 Friar st. Blackfriars road
Carter John, solicitor, Lord Mayor's ct. office, 7 Old Jewry
Carter John, surgeon, &c. 23 Dorset st. Portman square
Carter John, tripe dresser, 25 Homer st. Marylebone, & 34½ Munster st. Regent's park
Carter John, watch maker, 16 Hackney road crescent
Carter John,who.flour&corn dealr.22Clayton pl.Kenningtnrd
Carter John Adams, merchant, 147 Leadenhall st
Carter Joseph, bricklayer, High st. Deptford
Carter Joseph, bricklayer, &c. 1 Wellington st. Goswell st
Carter Joseph, cheesemonger, 139 Brick lane, Spitalfields
Carter Joseph, cheesemonger, &c. 18 Shepherd's ct. Mayfair
Carter Joseph, dairy, Hemingford ter. west, Islington
Carter Joseph, tripe dresser, 37 Grosvenor row, Pimlico
Carter Joseph Richd. *Castle* P.H. Providence pl.Kentish tn
Carter Mark, builder, 14 Rose st. Long acre
Carter Mary Terry (Mrs.), tobacconist, 1Darlington pl. Vxhl
Carter Nicholas, vellum binder, 28 London wall
Carter Patrick W. woollendraper, 14 Basinghall st
Carter Richard, wholesale cheesemonger, 3 Newgate st. & 2 Gerrard st. Soho
Carter Richard, confectioner, 110 Crawford st. Portman sq
Carter Robt. grocer & cheesemonger,50Gt.James st.Lissn. gr
Carter Robert, plumber, 17 Bethnal green road
Carter Robert, salesman & who. furniture war. 16 Minories
Carter Samuel, coal merchant, 50 OldGloucester st. Hoxton
Carter Samuel, livery stables, 1 Bray's pl. Low.rd. Islingtn
Carter Samuel, surgeon, &c. 9 Tabernacle sq. Finsbury
Carter Samuel, wax & tallow chandler, manufacturer of adamantean wax & composition candles, 65 Blackmn. st. Boro'
Carter Sarah (Mrs.), baker, 13 Gwynn's pl. Hackney road
Carter Susan(Mrs.),*Shepherd&Shphrds.*P.H.8Worcester st
Carter Thomas, composition letter maker, 7 Hatton wall
Carter Thomas, hopfactor, 241 Borough High st
Carter Thomas, market gardener, Falcon lane, Battersea
Carter Thomas, shipwright, Millwall dock, Poplar
Carter Thomas, stock broker, 21 Tokenhouse yard
Carter Thomas, tripe dresser, 33 St. James's market, & 1 Middle row, Knightsbridge
Carter Thomas Dicks, bricklayer, 1 Up. Charles st. Westmr
Carter Walter, *Olive Branch* P.H.37Earl st.West,Edgw.rd
Carter Wm. artist, 238 High Holborn
Carter Wm. baker, 101 St. John st. Clerkenwell
Carter Wm. *Bee Hive* P.H. Flagon row, Deptford
Carter Wm. berlin repository, 8 Crown st. Finsbury
Carter Wm. carpenter & cabinet maker, 17 Temple st. Whtfrs
Carter Wm. cheesemonger, 1 Union pl. Walworth road
Carter Wm. comb maker, 24 Primrose st. Bishopsgate
Carter Wm. *Green Gate* P.H. 15 Bethnal green road
Carter Wm.plumber,12Lit.Yorkpl.Gt.York mws.Portman sq
Carter Wm. stationer, 10 Judd st. Brunswick square
Carter Wm.who.coffee&spice mer.10 Cross la.St.Mary at hill
Carter Wm. wholesale staymaker, 2 Grocers'hall ct.Poultry; manufactory, Gt. Charlotte st. Landport, Portsmouth
Carter Wm. trimming manufacturer, 8 Crown st. Finsbury
Carter Wm. watch case maker, 7 President st. east, King sq
Carter Wm. Geo.attorney,Temple chambs.Falcon ct.Fleet st
Carter Wm. Grover, surgeon, 21 Aberdeen pl. Maida hill
Carter Wm. Henry, baker, Battersea square
Carter Wilson, coal agent, see Rhode & Carter
Carthew Jas. Hen. *ClockHouse*P.H.1Queen's blds.Knightsb
Carthew Thomas, plumber & glazier, see Knight & Carthew
Carthy Charles, bootmaker, 97 Park st. Kennington cross
Cartier Charles, merchant, see Stiffel & Cartier
Cartland James, corn & coal dlr. 6 Mount row, Liverpool rd
Cartledge Henry, leather gilder, 33 Hatton wall
Cartledge Joseph, stay ma. 2 Union pl. Lower rd. Islington
Cartmel Thomas, hatmaker, 59 King William st. City
Cartwright & Browne, dentists, see Browne, Cartwright&Co
Cartwright & Pritchard,law stationers&lithograph. printers, 1 Warwick place, Bedford row, & 57 Chancery lane
Cartwright Francis, dairy, 59 Park st. Dorset square
Cartwright Francis, tailor, 62 Grosvenor st. Grosvenor sq
Cartwright Henry, tobacconist, 1 St. James's st. Pentonville
Cartwright John, china enameller,4Gunpowder alley,Shoela
Cartwright John Edward, coffee rooms, 60 Red Cross st.City
Cartwright Joseph, black reviver maker, 41 Threadneedle st
Cartwright Richard, surgeon, 35 Bloomsbury square
Cartwright Samuel, surgeon dentist, 32 Old Burlington st
Cartwright Samuel, jun. surgeon dentist, 9 Sackville st
Carty, Son & Wingrove,back & vat maks.143 Boro' High st
Carughi Paul, barometer, thermometer, looking glass & picture frame maker, 38 Brook st. Holborn
Carvalho Raphael N. & Co. merchts. 8½ Cross st. Finsbury
Carvalho David Nunes, cheap book warehouse, & repository for second hand novels, travels, &c. 147 Fleet st
Carver JamesFrederick,ironmonger,1Gray'splace,Fulhamrd
Carver Ann (Mrs.), ladies' school, 1 Maida hill, Edgware rd
Carver Samuel Ebenezer, tobacconist, 27 Marylebone lane
Carver Thomas, boot & shoe ma. 25 Richard st. Comcl.rd. ea
Carver Thomas, butcher, 2 Commercial road east,Whitechpl
Carver Wm. gold engraver, 28 Wellington st. Goswell st
Carver Wm. Thos. tobacconist, 28 Norfolk st. Middlsx. hsptl
Carveth Thos. *Duke of Wellington* P.H. 20 Cross st.Hoxtn
Carwardine Richard, shoemaker, 41 Cumberland market
CarwardineThos.carpenter,builder,&c.9William st. Manch.sq
Carwell Geo. liv.stables, 12 Pied Bull yd. Bury st. Bloomsby
Carwood William, engineer, 9½ Back Church la. Whitechapl
Carey Brothers & Co. shippng.&com.agents, 5 Arthur st.ea
Cary George & John, map & globe sellers, 86 St. James's st
Cary Edward, carpenter, 10 Marlborough square, Chelsea
Cary Edward Augustus, surgeon, 25 New rd. St. George's ea
Cary Francis Stephen, artist, 6 Bloomsbury st. St. Giles's
Cary John, bootmaker, 1 Cross ct. Russell ct. Drury lane
Cary John, carpenter, 19 Molyneux st. Bryanstone sq
Cary Joseph, solicitor, 52 Moorgate st. City
Cary Thomas, tallow chandler & oilman, Church st. Hackney
Cary William, optician, 181 Strand
Caryl Alexander, saddler, &c. 63 St. John st. Smithfield
Casbard Elizabeth (Mrs.), butcher, 76 Shoe lane, Fleet st
Case Charles, tobacconist & snuff mak.34 Bishopsgate within
Case Charles Jas. watch &clock maker,34Bishopsgate within
Case Frederick, hatter, 80 Lambeth walk
Case Henry, whalebone & cane preparer, 44 Basinghall st
Case John March, navy agent, see Loudonsack & Case
Case Matthew,cabinet maker, 12 Bateman's buildings,Soho
Case Richard,house agent&appraiser,40Duke st. Bishopsgate
Case William, wine merchant, 56 Brook st. Grosvenor sq
Case Wm. Hen. italian & british wine wareh. 2 High holborn
Casella & Tagliabue, opticians & philosophical & mathematical instrument makers, drawing instrument, hydrometer & saccharometer, barometer, thermometer & telescope manufacturers, 23 Hatton garden
Casella Charles, coral merchant, 3 Brabant ct. Philpot lane
Casey & Phillips, silk manufacturers, 13 Spital square
Casey Charles, shoemaker, 66 Brick lane, St. Luke's
Casey Enoch, watch case joint finisher, 25 King st. Clknwll
Casey Henry Seymour, surgeon, 17 Gt. Coram st. Bruns. sq
Casey John, silk manfr. 6 White Lion st. Norton folgate
Casey John Archibald, artist, 17 Gt. Coram st. Brunswk. sq
Casey Maurice, dairyman, 32 New st. Dorset square
Casey Michael, tin plate worker, 32 Cloth fair, Smithfield
Casey Richard, fruiterer & greengrocer, 3 Cannon st. City
Casey Stephen, bricklayer, 27 Upper George st. Bryanstn. sq
Casey William John, teadealer, 25 Bear lane, Blackfriars
Cash & Ledgard, woollen & stuff warehousemen, St. Albans hall, 39 Wood st. & 2 Little Love lane
Cash Charles, ironmonger & zinc & iron plate works, & iron & brass founder, 74 Whitechapel road, 1 St. Mary st. Whitechapel road, & 1 Heneage st. Brick lane, Spitalfields
Cash George, hairdresser, 33 Brown's lane Spitalfields
Cash Henry, iron founder, 1 Heneage st. Whitechapel

Cash James, stay manufacturer, 19 Shoreditch
Cash John, tailor & costumer, 38 Tavistock st. Covt. garden
Cash Wm. bookslr. genl. agt. & undertkr. 120 Gt. Russell st
Cashmore Moses Joseph, jeweller & watch mak. 11 Bevis marks
Caslake William, butcher, 11 Brick lane, Spitalfields
Caslake Wm. coach builder, 28 Canterbury pl. Old Kent rd
Casley John, attorney, 31 Guilford st. Russell square
Caslon Henry, letter founder, 22 & 23 Chiswell st
Cason Wm. sou' wester & oil'd suit ma. 45 Shadwell High st
Caspar Nathan, watchmaker, 13 Bury st. St. Mary axe
Casper Judah, bead, plate, &c. mer. 17 Bury st. St. Mary axe
Casperd Henry, carpenter, 2 Paradise st. Lambeth
Cass (Sir John's) School, 12 Church row, Aldgate High st
Cass John, cheesemonger, 268 Bermondsey st
Cass Samuel, herald painter, 101 High st. Marylebone
Cassaigne Chas. & John & Co. wine mers. 12A, Salisbury st. Str
Cassavetti Demetrio G. & Co. merchts. 11 Broad st. buildings
Cassell Edwin Edward & Co. coal tar refiners, pitch, naptha & varnish manufacturers, turpentine distillers, patentees of the champhine & naptha lamp for streets & indoor lights, patentees of bitumen or asphalte for flooring arches of railroads & other purposes, Millwall, Poplar; 19 Minories; & Hall of Commerce, Threadneedle st
Cassell James Robert (executors of), pawnbroker, 155 Brick lane, Spitalfields
Cassell John Wm. pawnbroker, 118 & 119 High st. Camden tn
Cassell Mary A. (Mrs.), milliner, 17 White st. Bethnal green
Cassell Maurice, stockbroker, 15 Throgmorton st.
Casseltine Thomas, carpenter, 19 Albion gr. Thornhill road
Cassidy Richd. picture dealer, 10 Richmond st. Leicester sq
Cassin Henry, secretary to the Coventry & Leicester Railway, & Warwick & Cheltenham Railway, 36 Church ct. Old Jewry, & 79 Connaught terrace
Casson Elizabeth (Mrs.), grocer, 73 Pearson st. Kingsland rd
Casson John, grocer, 58 Bath st. City road
Casson Wm. grocer & cheesemngr. 10 Mansionhouse st. Kengtn
Casswell John, butcher, 23 Queen st. Bryanstone sq
Casswell John, medical glass maker, Forrest's wharf, Earl st
Castang Philip, dealer in foxes, &c. 11 Cottage pl. City rd
Castell James, hatter, 30 Devonshire st. Globe road
Castell John, boarding house, 26 Hunter st. & 1 Judd st
Castell John, dairyman, 20 Ironmonger lane, Cheapside
Castell John, who. confectioner, 44 & 45 Princes st. Leicester sq
Castell Susannah (Mrs.), milliner, 30 Devonshire st. Globe rd
Castell Wm. tobacconist, 15 Pearl cres. Bagnigge Wells rd
Castellain (Hermenegild), Sons & Co. merchants 3 Copthall ct
Castelli Giustiniani & Co. merchts. 10 Bury ct. St. Mary Axe
Castenada Miguel, spanish commissioner, 163 Albany st
Castendieck & Schlutow, ship brokers, 37 Mincing lane
Casterson Robert, coach builder, 69 Old st. St. Luke's
Casterton & Dixon, attorneys, 1 Angel court, Throgmorton st. & Radnor cottage, King's road, Chelsea
Castile Nath. carver & gilder, 6 Chapel st. Tottenham ct. rd
Castle John & Co. imp. of wines & spirits, 56 Aldersgate st
Castle, Jones & Wortley, warehousemen, 7 Love la. Wood st
Castle Eden Coal Of. W. S. Lindsay, agent, 35 Abchurch la
Castle & Turner, surgeons, 38 Bermondsey square
Castle Chas. chair & cabinet ma. 7 Castle st. east, Oxford st
Castle Charles, engraver & printer, 82 Fetter lane
Castle Charles, *Old Coventry Arms* P.H. Bromley, Middx
Castle George, beer retailer, 151 Blackfriars road
Castle George, bootmaker, 28½ Poultry
Castle George, timber merchant, 3 Beaufort pl. Chelsea
Castle Hen. ship breaker & timber mer. Baltic whf. Millbank
Castle Hen. surveyor & civil engineer, 6 John st. Adelphi
Castle Henry James, surveyor, 30 Queen sq. Bloomsbury
Castle James, baker, 157 Bethnal green road
Castle James, baker, 24 Globe road, Mile end
Castle James, blind maker, South Island pl. Clapham rd
Castle James, newsvender, see Woodward & Castle
Castle James, *White Bear* P.H. 2 Upper Thames st
Castle John, *Barnard's inn coffee house*, 20 Holborn
Castle John, *City of Salisbury* P.H. 44 Upper Salisbury pl. Lock's fields, Walworth
Castle Joseph, tobacconist, 62A, Paddington st
Castle Mary Ann (Mrs.), fishmong. 3 Halfmoon pas. Lednh. mkt
Castle Samuel, hosier & glover, 108 Oxford st
Castle Wm. grocer, &c. 1 Gt. College st. North, Camden town
Castle Wm. furniture broker, 4 Wilsted st. Somers town
Castleden Saml. registrar, 14 Devonshire ter. Globe road
Castleman Lawrence, cowkeeper, 42½ Clipstone st. Fitzroy sq
Castley Geo. grocer & cheesemonger, 133 Vauxhall walk
Caston Thos. ironmonger, 6 & 7 Bridgehouse pl. Newington cau
Caston Wm. coach plater & founder, 25 Gun st. Bishopsgate
Caston Wm. jun. smith, 3 Lower Trinity st. Rotherhithe
Caston Wm. sen. ship smith, 237 Rotherhithe st
Castro John, chandler's shop, 13 Powell st. east, King sq
Castro Peter, watch & case gilder, 55 Rahere st. Goswell rd
Castrique Louis & Co. merchants, 3 Philpot lane
Caswall Alfred, barrister, 3 Paper buildings, Temple
Caswall Charles, surgeon, 29 Park st. Islington
Caswell John & Co. teadealers, 217 Shoreditch High st
Caswell Job, newsvender, 5 Oxford place, Waterloo road
Caswell Samuel, baker, 4 York ter. Commercial rd. east
Caswell Wm. & Son, builders, 45 Paradise row, Chelsea
Catchpole & Williams, jewellers & silversmiths, 120 Regt. st
Catchpole Henry, wholesale slopseller, 77 Minories
Catchpole William, hairdresser, 9 Broadway, Ludgate hill
Catchpole Zachariah Rd. cheesemgr. 42 Up. Lisson st. Lisson gr
Caten James, bootmaker, 63 Richardson st. Long la. Boro'
Cater Mary Ann & Wm. Chas. hatters, cap, helmet & accoutrement makers & sword cutlers, 56 Pall mall
Cater Saml. & Co. drapers & silk mercers, 1 Finsbury pl. North
Cater Chas. coal & potato merchant, 8 Cross st. Islington
Cater Henry, boiler maker, 2 Winchester place, Southwark bridge road, & Grove, Great Guildford street, Borough
Cater Joseph, beer retailer, 60 Up. North pl. Gray's inn rd
Cater Robert, whitesmith, 158 Old Gravel lane, Wapping
Cater William, bookbinders' pressmaker, 95 Old st. road
Cater William Chas. upholsterer, 38 Newman st. Oxford st
Cates Dougal Rd. *George* P.H. 6 St. James's ter. Waterloo rd
Cates George, solicitor, 9 America square, Minories
Cates Joseph, livery stables, 61 New rd. Sloane st. Chelsea
Cates William, appraiser, 61 Star st. Paddington
Cates William, confectioner, 6 Park st. Borough
Catesby Fred. japanner, 14 Brown st. Bryanstone sq
Catherall Geo. fruiterer, 59 Praed st. Paddington
Catherall Harry, beer shop, 2 Orchard pl. Kingsland rd
Catherick Henry, cabinet maker, 74 Charlotte st. Fitzroy sq
Catherick Wm. cabinet maker, 14 Percy st. Tottenham ct. rd
Catherwood Alfred, physician, 21 Charles sq. Hoxton
Catherwood Geo. stockbroker, 3 Warnford ct. Throgmrtn. st
Catherwood Hen. who. teadealer, &c. 138 Borough High st
Catherwood William, watchmaker, 24 Nelson st. City road
Cathie Adam, baker, 13 Minerva terrace, Barnsbury park
Cathie Charles, *Coopers' Arms* P.H. 21 Union st. Borough
Cathie John, *Cock & Bottle* P.H. 7 China walk, Lambeth
Cathie John W. *Samson's Castle* P.H. 8 Samson's pl. Berm
Catholic Asylum for Female Orphans (John A. Kelly, master, James O'Leary, sec.), Tudor place, Tottenham court road, & Heath house, Hampstead
Catholic Institute of Gt. Britain (J. Smith, sec.), 14 Soho sq
Cathrow William, surgeon, 42 Weymouth st. Portland place
Catleugh Wm. florist, &c. Hans st. Hans place, Chelsea
Catley Joseph, bookseller, &c. 61 Chester st. Kennington la
Catley Thomas, salt merchant, 12 Cross st. Golden square
Catley Thos. *Mercers' Arms* P.H. 31 Jubilee place north, Commercial road east
Catley Zaccheus, cane worker, 1 & 2 Red lion row, Walwth. rd
Catlin Ann (Mrs.), baker, 48 Skinner st. Snow hill
Catlin Daniel, fruiterer, 74 Tothill st. Westminster
Catlin John Hallam, glover & hosier, 9 Huggin la. Wood st
Catlin William, baker, 2 White lion st. Pentonville
Catlin Wm. bookbinders' tool cutter, &c. 63 Chandos st. Cov. gar
Catlin William, hairdresser, 45 Russell st. Rotherhithe
Catline William Iliffe, printer, 3 Terrace, Old Kent road
Catling Frederick James, merchant, see Body & Co
Catling Geo. building material dlr. 82 Church st. Shoreditch
Catmore John Lake, bookbinder, 78 Britannia st. City road
Catmur Benjamin, optician, 28 Chamber st. Goodman's fields
Catmur Henry, bookbinder & dining rooms, 164 Bthnl. grn. rd
Catnur Alexander, fruiterer, 39 Shadwell High st
Cato Thomas & Son, wire workers, 89 Holborn hill
Caton Francis, working jeweller, 12 Cloak lane, Cheapside
Caton George, silkman, 21 Wilkes st. Spitalfields
Caton George, silk manufacturer, 21 Wilkes st. Spitalfields
Caton William, silkman, 25 Wilkes st. Spitalfields
Caton Wm. *White Hart* P.H. 96 Pennington st. St. George st
Cator Peter, barrister, 5 Old square, Lincoln's inn
Cattarns & Fry, solicitors, & secs. to the London, Westminster, & Vauxhall Steam Packet Co. & to the Old Woolwich Steam Packet Co. & to the Kew Junction Steam Boat Co. 62 Mark lane
Cattell John, goldbeater, 14 West st. Seven dials
Cattell John, teadealer, 11 Bolingbroke row, Walworth road
Cattell Peter, coachmaker, 32 Upper Park pl. Regent's pk
Cattell Richard, bootmaker, 5 Queen's row, Pimlico
Cattell Robert George, jeweller, 10 White Conduit st
Cattell Samuel, joiner, 13 Newland st. Eaton square
Cattell Thomas, *Cross Keys* P.H. Lawrence st. Cheyne wlk
Cattell Wm. pawnbroker, 21 Borough road
Catten Charles, coal dealer, 141 Hoxton Old town

Catterall Joseph, barrister, 4 Essex court, Temple
Cattermole James, surgeon, 50 Albany road, Camberwell, & 10 St. Peter's place, Walworth common
Catterns Henage Parker, undertaker, 27 Hart st. Bloomsby
Cattle Enoch, portable desk ma. 9 Gloucester st. St. John st. rd
Cattle Henry, tailor, 30 Southampton st. Covent garden
Cattley Henry Thompson, white lead, color & varnish manufacturer, 19 Cousin lane, Upper Thames st
Cattley & Stephenson, russia merchants, 10 St. Helen's pl
Cattleys & Carr, russia merchants, 9 Moorgate st. & Baltic
Cattley Stephen Wildman, merchant 68 Upper Thames st
Cattlin Fredk. Fisher, auctioneer, &c. 39 Ely pl. Holborn hill
Cattlin James, watchmaker, 58 Great Marylebone st
Cattlin Thomas Magnus, solicitor, 39 Ely place, Holborn
Cattlin Wm. crape dealer, 7 Devonshire st. New North road
Cattlin Wm. dentist, 6 Francis place, Holloway
Catton Charles, *Black Horse* P.H. 39 Leman st. Goodman
Catton John, patten & clog maker, 15 Vine st. Hatton wallfi
Catton John Alfred, plumber, &c. 4 Elizabeth st. Hans pl
Caudle Edward, surgeon, 18 Gt. Guildford st. Borough
Caudle George, scale maker, 19 Wych st. Strand
Caudwell Ann (Mrs.), *City Arms* P.H. Anderson's bdgs. City rd
Caufield Michael & Co. woollen warehousemen, 8 Basinghall st
Caulfield & Hunter, who. confectioners, 1 Old st. St. Luke's
Caulfield Michael, ship provision mer. 86 Tower hill
Caulfield Wm. bookseller, 6 Gray's inn passage
Caulfield Wm. Beare (secretary to Shipowners' Towing Company), 102 Leadenhall st. & 5 Fox lane, Shadwell
Caulton Charles, baker, Southampton st. Camberwell
Caulton John, baker, 71 Hare st. Bethnal green
Caunt Benjamin, *Coach & Horses* P.H. 90 St. Martin's lane
Caunt John, boot & shoe ma. 27 Beckford row, Walworth rd
Causeley Frederick John, oil & colorman, 18 Bath st. City rd
Causley George, *Crown* P.H. 46 Stanhope st. Clare market
Causse Augustus, perfumer & hairdresser, 267 Regent st
Causton Henry Kent & Co. publishers, 14 Birchin la. Cornhill
Causton Henry Kent, printer, 14 Birchin lane, Cornhill
Causton Jas. bootmak. 12 Buckingham pl. Marlbro' rd. Chelsea
Causton Joseph, printer & stationer, see Jones & Causton
Cautherley Geo. engraver, &c. 17 Warren st. Fitzroy square
Cavalier Cornelius, meat salesman, 3 Newgate market
Cavalier George, cowkeeper, 1 Langdale st. Cannon st. rd
Cavalier Peter, hairdresser, 47 Davies st. Berkeley square
Cavan Bros. & Co. east & west india mer. 29 Finsbury circus
Cave Amos, toy warehouse, 23 Paddington st. Marylebone
Cave Benjamin, turner & toyman, 1 Edwards st. Portman sq
Cave Daniel, banker, see Prescott, Grote, Ames & Cave
Cave David Allen, *King of Prussia* P.H. 30 Leather lane
Cave George, grocer, 12 Elder st. Norton folgate
Cave James, general engraver, 18 East road, City road
Cave Joseph, caneworker, 2 New st. Old st. St. Luke's
Cave Mary (Miss), milliner, see Maggi & Cave
Cave Robert, fishing tackle, &c. maker, 2 Oakley st. Lambeth
Cave Thomas, cut glass manufacturer, 149 Aldersgate st
Cave Thomas, commercial boarding ho. 149 Aldersgate st
Cave William, carver & gilder, 11 New inn yard, Shoreditch
Cave William, chair & couch ma. 2 Lit. Mitchell st. St. Luke's
Cave Wm. Geo. cut glass & shade ma. 23 Fenchuh. st. & 30 Rood la
Cavel Mary (Mrs.), chair ma. 26 Bridgehouse pl. Newngt. cau
Cavell George Frederick, *Noah's Ark* P.H. Narrow st. Rtclff
Cavell John, grocer & cheesemongr. 29 Nelson st. Bermondsey
Cavell John, law stationer, 7 Gray's inn place, Gray's inn
Cawkwell & Dalby, coal mers. Gun & shot wharf, 79 Tooley st
Cawley John, fruiterer, 16 Great Titchfield st
Cawley Thomas, hat trimming ma. 28 Lit. Guildford st. Boro'
Cawood Joseph, grocer, 13 Church st. Blackfriars road
Cawood Wm. yeast mercht. 32 Underwood st. Mile end new tn
Cawse Clara (Miss), artist, 8 Frith st. Soho square
Cawse George, *White Lion* P.H. 23 Curzon st. Mayfair
Cawston Mary Anne (Mrs.), trunk ma. 27 Burlington arcade
Cawston Saml. Wm. stockbroker, 3 Shorter's ct. Throgmortn. st
Cawthorn Maria H. (Mrs.), bookseller & library, 24 Cockspur st
Cawthorn William, wine merchant, 45 Great Tower st
Cawthorne Charles, who. coffee dealer, 16 St. Swithin's lane
Cawthron James, oil & colorman, 6 St. George's st. Albany rd
Cawthron Thomas, melter & candle maker, 136 Tooley st
Caybourn Robt. grocer, &c. 53 & 54 Brunswick st. Blackwall
Cayley Henry & Co. russia merchants, 28 Gt. Winchester st
Cayley Wm. & Sons, upholstrs. & undrtkrs. 122 Upper st. Islgtn
Cayley Alexander, baker, 1 Hyde pl. Bridport pl. Hoxton
Cayley John, who. & retail veterinary chemist & druggist, horse & cattle medicine chests, 18 Smithfield bars
Cayzer George, smith in general, 27 Gt. Guildford st. Boro'
Cazaly Thos. engraver, printer & statnr. 48 Tottenham ct. rd
Cazaly William, linendraper, 48 Red Lion st. Holborn
Cazaux Dominique, mineral water wa. 8 Jermyn st. St. James'
Cazenove John, sec. *Family Endowment Ass.* 12 Chatham pl
Cazenove Philip, stockbroker, see Laurence, Cazenove & Co
Cazotte Charles, cheesemonger, 23 Davies st. Berkeley sq. ; & confectioner, 10A, Mount st. Grosvenor square
Ceal Owen, snuff & cigar ma. 12 & 13 St. Benet's pl. Gracech. st
Cecil & Gaskin, builders, 14A, South st. Grosvenor sq
Cecil Charles, *Star* coffee rooms, 33 Golden lane, Barbican
Cecil William, *Lamb* P.H. 36 Wilmot st. Bethnal green
Ceely Charles Christopher, builder, 64 Poplar High st
Ceely John Thomas [from Mr. George Robins], auctioneer & yacht agent, &c. free register offices, 56 Cotton st. Poplar
Ceely Wm. Geo. sail ma. & ship chndlr. 78 Brunswick st. Blkwl
Ceeney Henry, veterinary surgeon, 17 Macclesfield st. City rd
Celerier Martl. & Co. (of cognac), brandy merch. 70 Mark la
Cemetery & General Funeral Co. united with Shillibeer's patent funeral carriages, 1 Commercial pl. City road, & 136 Union st. Southwark
Central Kent Railway Co. 4 Mansion house place, City
Central London Ophthalmic Institution, Henry Haynes Wolton, surgeon, 7 Everett st. Brunswick square
Central Providt. Buildg. Association, 13, Agar st. Strand
Central Servants' Home & Registry Office (Mrs. Mary Ann Crocker, superintedent), 5 Millman st. Bedford row
Centreton Doig D. who. cork mftr. 1 Eagle st. City road
Cereghetti Abondio, chandler's shop, 133 Cornwall rd. Lambeth
Cerrito Joseph, merchant, 8 Water lane, Tower st
Cesarini Adelaido Constance, coffee & dining rms. 20 Oxendn. st
Cetta & Crosta, lookg. glass & pictr. fr. mrs. 34 St. John's lane
Cetta John, looking glass manufr. 14 & 15 Brooke st. Holborn
Cetti John & Co. merchants, 25 Red Lion st. Holborn
Ceurvorst Joseph, merchant, 20 Gt. St. Helen's
Chabot Alfred, artist, 7 Thavies inn, Holborn
Chabot Chas. zincographic & lithographic draughtsman, & copper plate maker, engraver & printer, 9A, Skinner st
Chabot Edwin, surgeon, 1 Emanuel place, Camberwell road
Chabot Elizabeth (Mrs.), carman, 6 Bath st. Tabernacle sq
Chabot Philip, grain dyer, 61 Fashion street, Spitalfields
Chadborn James, grocer, 88 Drummond st. Euston sq
Chadwell Elizh. (Mrs.), lodging house, 16 Gt. Pulteney st
Chadwell John Spencer, oil & colorman, 122 Gt. Suffolk st. Boro'
Chadwick James & Brother, manufacturers of small wares, sewing cotton, &c. 4 Dyer's court, Aldermanbury
Chadwick Edwin, sec. to poor law com. 1 Somerset place
Chadwick Henry S. barrister, 1 Bury st. St. James'
Chadwick Jas. pavior & granite mer. Grosvr. wf. Millbank rw
Chadwick Jos. jeweller & watchma. 18 Gt Bath st. Clerknwll
Chadwick Richd. auctioneer, 35A, St. Martin's la. Charing cr
Chadwick Thomas, woolstapler, 61 Bermondsey st
Chadwick William, solicitor, 58 Lincoln's inn fields
Chadwin George Jonathan, builder & fire ins. ag. Battersea
Chafer Susan (Miss), milliner, 132 New Bond st
Chaffer Richard, ivory turner & importer of meerschaum pipes & boxes, 46 Lisle st. Leicester square
Chaffers Alexander, solicitor, see Kell & Chaffers
Chaffers William, jun. pawnbroker, 42 Watling st
Chaffey John & Son, wollen & man. waremn. 79 Queen st. Chpsid
Chaffin Henry Holland, furn. broker, 68A, Lambeth High st
Chaille John H. linendraper, 10 Melbourne pl. Old Kent road
Chaldecott Watts Thos. surgeon, 11 Alfred pl. Nwngtn. cswy
Chalener Sarah (Mrs.), milliner, 16 Charles st. Paddington
Chalenor Samuel, shell fishmonger, 43 Bell yard, Templebar
Chalfont Wm. dining rooms, 23 Salisbury st. Lisson grove
Chalfont William, stationer, see Jones & Chalfont
Chalie & Richards, wine merchants, 8 Wellington st. Strand
Chalk George, grocer, 17 Adam's row, Hampstead road
Chalk George, grocer, 2 Brompton road
Chalk Henry, pork butcher, 78 Tothill st. Westminster
Chalk James, timber mer. 10 & 48 Cannon st. rd. St. George's E
Chalk John, undertaker, 146 Long lane, Bermondsey
Chalk John Gustavus, solicitor, 45 Bedford row
Chalk Wm. Oliver, surgeon, 3 Nottingham terrace, New rd
Chalkley Ann & Margaret, butchers, 33 Brick la. St. Luke's
Challacombe & Mayou, silk mrs. 1 & 2 Lowndes' ter. Knighsb
Challen Caleb & Son, tailors & drapers, 240 High Holborn
Challen & Hollis, pianoforte makers, 41 Great Titchfield st
Challen Richard Jones, manchester agent, 43 Bread st. City
Challenor Francis C. genl. hardware dealer, 19 Ray st. Clknwl
Challenor John, grocer, 45 White st. Borough
Challice & Bonner, surgeons, 2 Crucifix lane, Bermondsey
Challice John, surgeon, 2 Grange road, Bermondsey
Challineor Thomas, muslin & lace wareh. 24 Wigmore st
Challis, Harris & Lee, meat salesmen, Leadenhall market
Challis James & Son, tailors, 3 Christopher st. Hatton wall
Challis & Phillips (late Allison, Knight & Co.), merchant tailors, outfitters, &c. 16 Cornhill
Challis Anthony, butcher, 15 Fieldgate st. Whitechapel

Challis Edward, boat builder, 1 East lane, Bermondsey wall
Challis John, *King's Arms* P.H. 6 Lit. James st. Bedford row
Challis Mary (Mrs.), fruiterer, 171 Sloane st. Knightsbridge
Challis Robert, butcher, 5 Southampton st. Camberwell
Challis Thomas, *Jane Shore* P.H. 103 Shoreditch
Challis Thomas, skin broker, 32 Wilson st. Finsbury; & hide & skin salesman, Leadenhall & Bermondsey leather mkts
Challiss Robert, tobacconist, 74 Drury lane
Chalmer & Simpson, stock & share broks. 23 Tokenhouse yd
Chalmers, Guthrie & Co. mers. & bankers, 9 Idol. la. Tower st
Chalmers David, grocer, &c. 49 Princess st. Edgware road
Chalmers John, stockbroker, 14 O. Broad st. City, & Stock Ex
Chalmers Wm. Robt. coal mer. 16A, Walcot pl. west, Lambeth
Chalon John James & Alfred Edward, artists, 10 Wimpole st
Chalon Henry Barnard, artist, 7 Queen st. Brompton road
Chaloner Edward, toy dealer, 5 Brewer st. Somers town
Chamberlain & Co. worcester royal porcelain, glass & earthenware wareho. 155 New Bond st. (late 1 Coventry st. Haymkt)
Chamberlain & Strachan, blackwell hall facts. 84 Basinghall st
Chamberlain's Wharf, Jsph. Barber, between 11 & 12 Tooley st
Chamberlain Archibald, cooper, 18 Charles st. Comml. road
Chamberlain Benjamin, carman, 36 Belvedere rd. Lambeth
Chamberlain Chas. undertaker, 59 Rahere st. Goswell rd
Chamberlain Charlt. (Mrs.), fishmngr. 3 Up. Duncan pl. City rd
Chamberlain Edward Hughes, barrister, 4 Elm ct. Temple
Chamberlain Elizth. (Mrs.), baker, 20 Wheeler st. Spitlflds
Chamberlain Geo. window glass & lead wareh. 90 Crawford st
Chamberlain James Bradley, optician, 203 High Holborn
Chamberlain Jas. Hardy, attor. 42 Grafton st. east, Tott. ct. rd
Chamberlain John, shoemaker, 74 Earl st. ea. Lisson gr. nth
Chamberlain Joseph, fruiterer & carman, 34 Belvedere road
Chamberlain Joseph, *Goat* P.H. Arabella row, Pimlico
Chamberlain Jsph. who. shoe wareh. 36 Milk st. & 2 Wood st
Chamberlain Rt. *White Horse* P.H. 71 White Horse st. Stpny
Chamberlain Thomas, coffee rooms, 1 White Rose ct. Colemn. st
Chamberlain Wm. brush manufactr. 71 Newington causeway
Chamberlain Wm. saddler, 7 West place, Islington green
Chamberlain Wm. wood letter cutter, 142 Gt. Suffolk st. Boro
Chamberland Thomas, hairdresser, 81 Snow hill
Chamberlayne & Meaden, solicitors, 31 Gt. James st. Bedford rw
Chamberlayne Hen. house decorator, 25 Gt. Chapel st. Oxfrd. st
Chamberlayne Jas. fruiterer, 8 Gt. Hall, Hungerford mrkt
Chamberlin Chas. furn. broker, 6 Brokers' row, Redcross st
Chamberlin Edward, grocer, 1 Rigman's rents, Limehouse
Chamberlin John, *Feathers* P.H. 16 Old Castle st. Bethnal grn
Chamberlin John, smith & farrier, 7 Harrow rd. Paddington
Chamberlin John, wheelwright, Neal's yd. Queen st. 7 Dials
Chamberlin William, butcher, 15 George st. Mansion house
Chamberlin William, teacher of music, 13 Gresse st
Chambers & Ellwood, wine & spirit mers. 18 Kings st. Chpsd
Chambers & Franklin, who. button & trimng. wa. 8 Gresham st
Chambers Geo. & Co. needle & fish hook mfr. 14A, Gresham st. & Astwood bank, near Redditch, Worcestershire
Chambers & Limby, chocolate manufacturers & tea & coffee dealers, 4 Tower Royal, Watling st
Chambers & Mathew, surgeons, 3 Trafalgar pl. ea. Hackney rd
Chambers Rd. & David, who. ironmongers, 41 Bishopsgt. witht
Chambers Alex. block & mast ma. see Ward & Chambers
Chambers Alexander, tailor, 104 St. George st
Chambers Benjamin, clothier, &c. 13 London rd. Southwark
Chambers Charles, coffee rooms, 2 King st. Westminster
Chambers Chas. silver & gold engrav. 11 St. James wk. Clrkwl
Chambers Chas. *Perseverance* P.H. 11 Stephen st. Lisson gr
Chambers Elijah, auctioneer & surveyor, 7 Great Tower st
Chambers Fanny (Miss), milliner, 130 Regent st
Chambers Francis, east & west india agent, & wine & spirit merchant, 22 St. Dunstan's hill, Great Tower st
Chambers Francis, tobacconist, 56 New Church st. Lisson gr
Chambers Geo. pat. stove & range ma. 205 Upper Thames st
Chambers Geo. ship & insur. broker, see Watson & Chambers
Chambers Geo. sen. butcher, 102 Shoreditch
Chambers Geo. Hy. merchant, see Watson & Chambers
Chambers Henry, surgeon, 34 Surrey place, Old Kent road
Chambers James, oil warehouse, 93 Union st. Borough
Chambers Jane (Mrs.), ship chandler, 240 Rotherhithe
Chambers John, coach painter, 26A, John st. Fitzroy square
Chambers John, dairyman, 3 Coborn road, Mile end road
Chambers John, dyer & fruiterer, 73 Seymour st. Euston sq
Chambers John, saddler & harness maker, 70 Long acre
Chambers John, surgeon, see Mathew & Chambers
Chambers John, tailor, 25 Sidmouth st. Regent square
Chambers John David, barrister, 6 Old square, Lincoln's inn
Chambers John Pink, pawnbro. 37 Regent st. Horseferry rd
Chambers Matthew, baker, King st. Turk st. Bethnal green
Chambers Montagu, queen's counsel, 3 Child's pl. Temple bar
Chambers Richard, academy, 24 Castle st. Leicester sq
Chambers Richard, beer shop, Newland st. Kensington
Chambers Robert. barrister, 13 Gray's inn square
Chambers Robert Byron, solicitor, 14 Basinghall st
Chambers Robert W. millwright, 24 Princes st. Lambeth
Chambers Solomon, corn & coal mer. 4 Lower Eaton st. Pimlico
Chambers Thos. barrister, Devereux chambers, Strand
Chambers Thos. cheesemonger, 47 Dorset st. Portman sq
Chambers Thos. cheesemonger, 11 High st. Marylebone
Chambers Thos. *Crown & Shears* P.H. 10 Sparrow cornr. Minors
Chambers Thos. engraver, 12 Leathersellers blds. London wall
Chambers Thos. grocer, &c. see Goddard & Chambers
Chambers Thos. grocer, 26 Silver st. Wood st
Chambers Thos. oilman, 31 Gravel lane, Southwark
Chambers Thos. K. physician, 42 Curzon st. May fair
Chambers Wm. *Barleymow* P.H. 60 Bath st. City road
Chambers Wm. fishmonger, 169 Poplar High st
Chambers Wm. oilman, &c. 6 Seabright pl. East, Hackney rd
Chambers Wm. tailor, 18 Grafton st. East, Tottenham ct. road
Chambers Wm. tailor, 8 Maddox st. Bond st
Chambers Wm. undertaker, 2 Blackman st. Borough
Chambers Wm. Fred. physician, 46 Brook st. Grosvenor sq
Chambers Wm. Mellish, barrister, 2 Paper buildings, Temple
Chamen Richd. T. wine merchant, 7 Charlotte st. Fitzroy sq
Champ George, potato dealer, 4 Clare court, Drury lane
Champ Robert, plumber & house decorator, 1 Burton cresnt
Champain John, engraver, 74 Lower Sloane st. Chelsea
Champion, Fishwick & Co. lead merchants & white lead manufacturers, 9 Laurence Pountney hill; Paul's wharf, Upper Thames st.; & Islington fields
Champion (Percival) & Co. merchants, 21 Throgmorton st
Champion Ann (Mrs.), straw bonnet ma. 5 Fisher st. Red Lion sq
Champion Charles, solicitor, 32 Ely place, Holborn
Champion Constant. gen. mercht. see Vermeir & Champion
Champion Elias, dairy, 7 Stafford st. & 15 Dover st. Piccadilly
Champion Henry, grocer, 2 Turk's row, Chelsea
Champion Henry, saddler, 8 Upper Spring st. Portman sq
Champion Henry S. ship & insur. broker, 10 Cullum st
Champion John, *John Kemble* P.H. 60 Long acre
Champion Percival & Co. merchants, 21 Throgmrtn st. & Lloyd's
Champion Robert, corn chandler, 68 Low. George st. Chelsea
Champion Sampson, gasfitter, 2 Union st. Middlesex hospital
Champken Matthew, beer retlr. 15 Sheppertn. pl. New North rd
Champken Wm. plumber, &c. 1 Commercial pl. Kingsland rd
Champness John. S. coal mer. Waterloo wf. 8 Fountain ct. Strand
Chance, Brothers & Co. manufacturers of plate, sheet & crown window glass, french shades & alkalis, 2 Coleman st. bldgs. Moorgate st. & at their glass works, near Birmingham
Chance William, Son & Co. american merchants, 2 Coleman st. buildings, & at 152 Great Charles st. Birmingham
Chance Edward, export ironmonger, hardwareman & general commission merchant, 2 Coleman st. buildings
Chance Edward John, surgeon, 49½A, Lincoln's inn fields
Chance George, *White Hart* P.H. 69 Long la. West Smithfl
Chance Henry, barrister, 38 Lincoln's inn fields
Chance James Hen. carver & gilder, 28 London st. Fitzroy sq
Chance Jane (Mrs.), *Albion* P.H. 4 Thornhill road, Islington
Chance Robert Lucas, window glass manufacturer, 2 Coleman st. buildings, Moorgate st. & at Birmingham
Chancellor of the Exchequers Office, 11 Downing st.; 10 to 7
Chancellor George, coach proprietor, 1 Cheyne rw. Chelsea
Chancellor John, funeral carriage master, 8 Lit. Warner st
Chancellor John, coach proprietor, Bridge rd. Battersea
Chancellor John, livery stables, White Lion st. Chelsea
Chancellor Thomas, jobmaster, Terrace, Kensington
Chancery, Lord Chancellor's Sec.'s Offi. Quality ct. 10 to 4 Perry Henry James, esq. sec
Chancery Subpœna Office, Rolls yard, Chancery lane
Chandler John & Son, boot & shoe makers, 9 Porter st. Soho
Chandler John Worster & Leonard, meat salesmen, 133 St. John st. Smithfield, & Newgate market
Chandler Richard & Sons, nurserymen, Wandsworth road
Chandler Allen, barrister, 3 Harcourt buildings
Chandler Arthur, solicitor, 39 Coleman st
Chandler Arthur, solicitor, 27 Southampton bldgs. Chancery la
Chandler Fredk. *Cheshire cheese* P.H. 10 Dean st. Holborn
Chandler Bentham, surgeon, 46 Weymouth st. Portland pl
Chandler Dennis, merchant & commission agent, 68 Mark la
Chandler Elizabeth (Mrs.), tobacconist, 197 Tooley st
Chandler Geo. pianoforte mak. 27 Tavistock pl. Tavistk. sq
Chandler James, boot & shoe ma. 1 Southampton st. Camberwell
Chandler James, *Grapes* P. H. 63 West Smithfield
Chandler John, baker, 3 Bridge st. Southwark
Chandler John, whip throng ma. 62 Turnmill st. Clerkenwel
Chandler John Wm. grocer & cheesem. 29 Notting hill, High st
Chandler Joseph, butcher, 6 Little Essex st. Strand
Chandler Lewin, butcher, 5 Crombie's row, Coml. road east

Chandler Lewis H.auctr.ho.&gen.agt.27Gt.Russell st. Blmby
Chandler Louisa (Mrs.), milliner, 20 Bevenden st. Hoxton
Chandler Mary (Mrs.), brush, carpet-broom, & sieve manufacturer, 195 High Holborn
Chandler Mary A.(Mrs.),tobacconist, 50 Brewer st.Golden sq
Chandler Matthew, cowkeeper, 5 Eaton lane north, Pimlico
Chandler Thomas, boat builder, Holywell st. Westminster
Chandler Thomas, chandler's shop, 2 Fair st. Horsleydown
Chandler Thos. *PelhamArms* P.H.18 George st. Grosvenor sq
Chandler Thomas, *Ship* P.H. Millbank row, Westminster
Chandler Thomas, steam flour mills, 18 Broad st. Lambeth
Chandler Thomas, surgeon, 58 Paradise st. Rotherhithe
Chandler Wm. cheesemonger, 118 Cromer st. Brunswick ter
Chandler William, dyer, 3 Cherrygarden st. Rotherhithe
Chandler Wm.Gibbs,stationer&library,3 Camberwell High st
Chandless Thomas, barrister, 13 Old square, Lincoln's inn
Chandless Thomas, linen draper,30 High st. Newington butts
Chandon Philip, wine merchant, see Moet V. & Chandon
Chaney Chas. W. *Queen's Head* P.H.25Paradise st. Rothrhith
Chanlieu Chas.prof.of pianoforte,9 St.George's pl.Cambwl.rd
Channell Wm.Fry,serjnt. at law, 2 Serjeants' inn,Chancery la
Channing Henry, *Wheatsheaf* P. H. 13 Vere st. Clare mkt
Channon John, cabinetmaker, 12 Poland st. Oxford st
Channon John, coal merchant, Beaufort wharf, Strand
Channon Thomas, haberdasher, 5 Brompton pl. Brompton
Channon William, baker, 17 Stoke Newington green
Chant George, surgeon, 17 Cross st. Wenlock road
Chant John, spectacle maker, see Bentley & Chant
Chant Samuel, stockbroker, 8 Throgmorton st. & Stock exch
Chantaume Pierre, french boot maker, 298 Regent st
Chanter John & Co. patentees & proprietors of the smoke consuming furnace & moveable fire bars,4A, Wine office ct. Fleet st
Chantler Edward Henry, lighterman, 31 Bankside
Chantrey Jeremiah, beer retailer, 9 Bride st. Liverpool road
Chantrey Thomas, wheelwright, 35 Bowling st. Clerkenwell
Chantry Chas. sec. of Vaccine Ins. 18 Providence row,Finsby
Chantry Edwd.tinplate wrkr.39 Brandonst.Lock's fi. Walwth
Chantry George, *Horse Shoe* P.H. 267 Tottenham ct. road
Chantry Samuel, cheesemonger, 36 Leather lane, Holborn
Chany Henry, engineer, brass & cock founder, manufacturer of pumps, water closets, beer machines, &c. & plumbers' brass work in general, 34 Clifton st. Finsbury square
Chaplain John, plumber, &c. 5 Brunswick place, Brompton
Chaplain Thos. wrkg.jeweller, 4 Spring pl. Bagnigge wls. rd
Chaplain John & Wm. news agents, 52 Fleet la. Farringdonst
Chaplin Thos. & Son, printers, &c.16 Webb st. Bermondseyst
Chaplin Valentine & Co. wine merchants, 25 Bucklersbury
Chaplin William & Co. booking office, 34 & 36 Regent circus
Chaplin (Wm. Jas.) & Horne (Benj. Worthy), wharfingers & railway carriers, Hambro' wharf, Upper Thames st
Chaplin Charlotte (Mrs.), *Clarendon hotel*, 169 New Bond st. & 19 & 20 Albemarle st. Piccadilly
Chaplin Edward Amos, attorney, 3 Gray's Inn square
Chaplin George, tailor,38 Maddox st. Regent st
Chaplin John, picture dealer & importer, 88 New Bond st
Chaplin John, *Spread Eagle inn*, 84 Gracechurch st
Chaplin John, upholsterer, 11 Hemmings row, St. Martin'sla
Chaplin Joseph, fishmonger, 64 Paddington st. Marylebone
Chaplin Rt. Jas. mourning & wedding ring ma. 17 Redcross sq
Chaplin Thomas, printer, 2 Red Lion court, Fleet st
Chaplin Valentine, merchant & agent, 26 & 27 Bucklersbury
Chaplin Wm.coach offi. *Spread Eagle inn*,84 Gracechurch st. & *Angel*, St. Clement's
Chaplin Wm. *Tiger* P.H. 24 Wells st. Oxford st
Chaplin Wm. *White Horse inn*, 90 Fetter lane
Chaplin Wm.sen.coach propr. *Swan with 2 Necks*, Gresham st
Chaplin Wm. jun. *Swan with Two Necks tavern*, 10Lad la
Chaplyn Henry Cleere, attorney, 53 Lincoln's inn fields
Chapman Brothers, distillers, Old Ford
Chapman Brothers, sugar refiners & coloring ma. Old Ford
Chapman& Day,coalmerchts.2NewLondon st.Crutched friars
Chapman & Elcoate, printers & publishers, office,63 Farringdon st. printing offices, 2 Peterborough court & 5 Shoe lane, Fleet st
Chapman Grorge & Charles, wine merchts. 9 St. James's st
Chapman & Hall, booksellers & publishers, 186 Strand
Chapman Harriet&Elzh.fringema.6St.Agnester.Tabernac.sq
Chapman Henry & Co. asphalte manfrs. Canal, St. George's st. Albany road, Old Kent road
Chapman James&Co.stock brokers,6Bank chmbrs.Lothbury
Chapman John & Co. ship owners, ship & insurance brokers, &c. 2 Leadenhall st
Chapman John & George, corn dealers, 33 Bath st. City rd
Chapman John & Son, goldsmiths, 14 Frith st. Soho
Chapman Misses, milliners, 16 Little Charlotte st.Goodge st
Chapman & Lambert,timber merchants, 31 Lower Belgrave place, & 2 wharf, Grosvenor canal
Chapman & Moore, hatters, 30 Old Bond st
Chapman & Page, leather merchants, 20 Gt. St. Helen's
Chapman Rt. & Co. rectifiers & sugar refiners,53 Drury lane
Chapman Thomas & William, merchants, 36 Old Broad st
Chapman&Warren,wine mer.2Nw.London st.Crutched friars
Chapman, Webb&Chapman,landag.&survey.3Arundel st.Std
Chapman Adden, brewer, Pearl crescent, Bagnigge wells rd
Chapman Arthur, linendraper, 34 Seymour st. Euston sq
Chapman Benedict Lawrence,barrister,3 Stone bds.Linc.inn
Chapman Benj. secret springer, 25 Wellington st.Goswell rd
Chapman Chas. Thos. dining rooms, 104 Bishopsgate within
Chapman Christr. coffee rooms, 177 Church st. Shoreditch
Chapman Cowdell, special pleader, 2 Cloisters, Temple
Chapman Daniel, furn. ironmonger, see Glenton & Chapman
Chapman Edward, plumber, 4 Brownlow st. Drury lane
Chapman Edward, *WhiteHart* P.H.College st.Belvedere rd
Chapman Edward Henry, merchant, 134 Leadenhall st
Chapman Eliza (Mrs.),beer retailer,50Up.Lisson st.Lisson g
Chapman Elizh.(Miss),dressmak.3Windmill st.Tottenh.ct.rd
Chapman Esther (Mrs.), tobacconist, 20 John st. Minories
Chapman George, cheesemonger, 12 Silver st. Wood st
Chapman George, coal & potato warehouse, 18 Drury lane
Chapman George,cowkeeper & dairyman,4High st.Islington
Chapman George, fruiterer, 25 Great Titchfield st. Oxford st
Chapman George, hatters' bow string & gut wheel band maker, 11 Noel st. Bermondsey New road
Chapman George, fruiterer, Spitalfields market
Chapman George, pawnbroker, 30 London st. Fitzroy sq
Chapman Geo. Benj. tobacconist, 25Wellington st.Goswell st
Chapman Henry, engineer, 11 Beaufort buildings
Chapman Henry, undertaker, 11 Osborne st. Whitechapel
Chapman Horatio, grocer, 35 St. George's pl. Knightsbridge
Chapman Isaac, cheesemonger, 27 Margaret pl.Hackney flds
Chapman Isaac, printer, 103 Star st. Edgware road
Chapman James, chemist & druggist, 23 Clifton st. Finsbury
Chapman James, cooper, &c. 36 Mansell st. Goodman's flds
Chapman James, flour factor, 11 Gt. Dover st. Borough
Chapman James, law stationer, 35 Cursitor st
Chapman James, looking glass frame maker, 26 Hoxton sq
Chapman Jas. china & glass wa. 10 Lamb's Conduit passage
Chapman James, vet. surgeon, 26 Riding ho. la. Langham pl
Chapman James Norris, coal mer. 1 Lit. Queen st. Holborn
Chapman James Saml. painter & glaz. 15 Low. Fore st. Lamb
Chapman Jane (Mrs.), stationer, 41 Gt. Dover st. Borough
Chapman Jeremiah Brown, cooper, 15 Harp lane, Lower Thames st. & 79 Bermondsey st
Chapman Jesse, picture frame, &c. ma. 2 Pitt st. Fitzroy sq
Chapman John, bookseller & publisher, 121 Newgate st
Chapman John, boot & shoe maker, 123 Waterloo road
Chapman John, bougie maker, 81 York place, Waterloo rd
Chapman John, cabinet maker, 5 Pritchard's pl.Hackneyflds
Chapman John, chairmaker, Hollen yard, Hollen st. Soho & 3 Dufour's place, Broad st. Golden square
Chapman John, chemist, 7 High st. Pentonville
Chapman John, *CityofCanton* P.H. 1 North st. East India rd
Chapman John, civil engineer, 6A, Lisson gr. North, New rd
Chapman John, colonial broker, 8 Commercial sale rooms
Chapman John, corndealer, 96 Shoe lane
Chapman John, fishmonger, 6 Vine place, Old st. road
Chapman John, grocer, 114 Brook st. Lambeth
Chapman John, leather cutter, 4 Saville st. Fitzroy square
Chapman John, oilman, 35 Brick lane, Spitalfields
Chapman John, porkman, 32 Fore st. Cripplegate
Chapman John, *Prince Albert* P.H. High st. Notting hill
Chapman John, robemaker, 115 Chancery lane
Chapman John, shoemaker, 26 Edward st. City road
Chapman John, surgeon, 25 Edward st. Langham place
Chapman John, undertaker,60John st.Holland st.Blackfrirs
Chapman John, jun. plumber, 63 Theobald's rd. Red Lion sq
Chapman John, sen. plumber, 15 Lamb's conduit st
Chapman Jonathan, merchant, see Thomas & Chapman
Chapman Joseph, shoemaker, 3 London st. Fitzroy sq
Chapman Joseph Henry, boot & shoe manufr. 196 Tooley st
Chapman Mark Hughes, baker, 10 Minories
Chapman Mary (Mrs.), beer retailer, 2 Goldsmiths row Hackney road
Chapman MaryAnn(Mrs.).grocer,4Ladbroke grv.Notting hll
Chapman Middleton, cabinetma. 51 Gt. Sutton st. Clerknwl
Chapman Miles Francis, builder,128Drummond st.Euston sq
Chapman Richard, *Union* P.H. 25 Marylebone st. Piccadilly
Chapman Robert, fruiterer, 43 South st. South Audley st
Chapman Rt. *Freemasons' Arms* P.H. Salmon la. Limehouse
Chapman Robert, *King's Arms* P.H. 264 Oxford st
Chapman Samuel, pawnbroker, 5Whitby place,Lock's fields

Chapman Thomas, carpenter & builder, 5 Stangate, Lambeth
Chapman Thomas, farrier, 1 Arthur st. King's rd. Chelsea
Chapman Thomas, fruiterer, 4&5 Gt. hall, Hungerford market
Chapman Thomas, lodging house, 9 Howard st. Strand
Chapman Thomas, manufacturer of fracture & invalid beds, chairs, spinal carriages, desks, dressing cases, 8 Denmark st. late of 9 New Bond st
Chapman Thomas, ladies' school, 64 Gt. Prescot st. Goodman's fi
Chapman Thomas, printer & stationer, High st. Battersea
Chapman Thomas, jun. dairy, 20 Chenies st. Bedford sq
Chapman Thomas, sen. dairy, 179 Tottenham court road
Chapman Thomas M. teadealer & grocer, 13 Gray's inn lane
Chapman Thomas Wood, flax & tow spinner, 6 Nelson sq
Chapman Thory, stockbroker, Stock exchange
Chapman Wm. boot & shoe wareho. 62 Mount st. Lambeth
Chapman Wm. chairmaker, 21 Old Boswell court, Strand
Chapman Wm. beer retailer, 1 Macclesfield st. North, City rd
Chapman Wm. cheesemonger, 64 Edgware rd, Marylebone
Chapman Wm. dentist, 82 Albert st. Mornington crescent
Chapman Wm. fruiterer, 71 Friar st. Blackfriars road
Chapman Wm. fruiterer, 1 & 2 New street, Cloth fair
Chapman Wm. grape grower, South Lambeth (South side)
Chapman Wm. nurseryman, South Lambeth (South side)
Chapman Wm. plumber, 19 Charterhouse st. Charterhouse sq
Chapman Wm. professor of languages, 1 Albion pl. Upper Kennington lane
Chapman Wm. *Ship* P.H. 67 Sun st. Bishopsgate
Chapman Wm. surveyor of taxes, 3 Church pl. Covent gdn
Chapman William, tobacconist, New cross, Deptford
Chapman Wm. wheelwright, 38 New st. mews, Dorset sq
Chapman Wm. jun. wine & spirit mer. 4 Pancras la. Bucklrsbry
Chapman Wm. Alex. pawnbroker, 74 Turnmill st. Clerkenwl
Chapman Wm. Chas. *Dyers' Arms* P.H. 55 Long alley, Finsbry
Chapman Wm. Cobb, grocer, 42 South st. Manchester sq
Chapman Wm. Cotton, corn merchant, 2 New London st
Chapman Wm. Edward, oilman, &c. 57 Lambeth walk
Chapman Wm. Henry, ship biscuit baker & potato salesman, 6 & 7 Mill lane, Tooley st
Chapman Wm. Henry, teadealer, 67 London rd. Southwark
Chapmans Lewis, flatting mills, 6 Ball court, Giltspur st
Chappel George, baker, 25 Windsor st. Lower st. Islington
Chappel Wm. carpenter, 61 Warren st. Fitzroy square
Chappell John & Co. stationers & newspaper agts. 84 Lombard st
Chappell Benjamin, smith, White's row, Whitechapel
Chappell Emily (Mrs.), music & musical instrumental seller to her Majesty, 50 New Bond st
Chappell Frederick C. stockbroker, 15 Angel court, Bank
Chappell Fredk. Patey, solicitor, 1 Quality ct. Chancery la
Chappell George, baker, 3 William st. Lisson grove
Chappell Geo. cooper & color. malt ma. 2 Silver st, Clerknw
Chappell Geo. *Swan & Horse Shoe*, P.H. 85 Gray's inn la
Chappell John, baker, 60 Flagon row, Deptford
Chappell John, brush manuf. & warehousema. 122 Long acre
Chappell John, cabinet maker, High st. Deptford
Chappell John, porkman, 56 Skinner st. Snowhill
Chappell John, stationer, 84 Lombard st. City
Chappell John, poulterer, 32 Great Hall, Hungerford market
Chappell John, stationer & bookseller, 146 Minories
Chappell John C. printer & stationer, 44½ St. George st
Chappell John Cramer, surgeon, 27 Jermyn st. St. James's
Chappell John Wm. solicitor, 10 Wyndham pl. Bryanstone st
Chappell Mary (Mrs.), pork butcher, 76 Fore st. Cripplegate
Chappell Mary (Mrs.), straw bonnet ma. 17 Gt. Smith st. Westm
Chappell Robert, stockbroker, see Austin & Chappell
Chappell Samuel, butcher, 82 Wood st. City
Chappell Sarah (Mrs.), plumber, 28 Walbrook
Chappell Thos. Bainard, registrar, Mount st. Berkeley sq
Chappell Thomas, bedstead mak. 17 Gt. Smith st. Westmin
Chappell William, butcher, 6 Farringdon market
Chappell William, tailor, 27 Tottenham pl. Tottenham ct. rd
Chappellsmith John, statnr. & bookslr. 13 Dean st. Westm
Chappelow & Petch, bridle cutters, wholes. harness makers, saddlers, ironmongers & leather sellers, 138 Long acre
Chappenden John Wm. tobacconist, 2 City rd. Finsbury sq
Chapple Rich. & Co. scagliolists, &c. 55 Milbank st. Westm
Chapple Charles, carpenter, 4 Foley st. Portland place
Chapple Edward, grocer & oilman, 1 Ranelagh ter. Pimlico
Chapple Henry, locksmith, 51 Leader st. Chelsea
Chapple John, confectioner, 19 Cross st. Newington butts
Chapple John, dyer, 9 Gibson st. Waterloo road
Chapple John, solicitor, 35 King st. Cheapside
Chapple John, trunkmaker, 31 Piccadilly
Chapple Richard, plasterer, 55 Millbank st. Westminster
Chapple Thomas, linendraper, 5 Borough road
Chapple William, tailor, 9 East st. Red Lion square
Chapple William, trunkmaker, 14 High Holborn
Chapple William, jun. trunkmaker, 17 King William st. City
Chapple Wm. Gould, *Castle* P.H. see Hayward & Chapple
Chappuis François, engine turner, 3 Corporation rw. Clrknwl
Chapter House, 68 St. Paul's churchyard
Chapter House Record Office, Poet's corner, Old Palace yd
Chapuy Louis, perfumer, 28 Litchfield st. Soho
Chard Wm. & Edward, navy agents, 3 Clifford's inn, Fleet st
Chard Charles Thomas, *White Hart* P.H. 18 Abchurch la
Chard James, china warehouse, 9 Up. Seymour st. Euston sq
Chard Thomas, smith, &c. 2 Great Sutton st. Clerkenwell
Chardin William Alfred, printer, Mare st. Hackney
Charie George, working jeweller, 84 Long lane, Bermondsey
Charing Cross Hospital (John Robertson, hon. sec.), Agar st. West Strand
Charitable Fund & Dispensary, 9 Fore st. Cripplegate
Charity Commission, 13 Great George st. Westminster
Charker Edward & Hen. butchers, 26 Marylebone st. Piccad
Charles & Fox, merchants, 161 Upper Thames st
Charles Edmund, veterinary surgeon, 26 Clarges st. Piccad
Charles Francis, oilman, 55 Great Ormond st. Queen square
Charles James, merchant & agent, 1 White Lion ct. Birchin la
Charles Joseph, tailor, 171 Fleet st
Charles Mary (Mrs.), straw hat ma. 5 Carthusian st. Ch'trho. sq
Charles Richd. clothes salesman, 1 Middle row, Knightsbrdg
Charles Robert, soap maker, see Paton & Charles
Charles Robert, tailor, 35 Lower Ranelagh st. Pimlico
Charles Thomas, fishmonger, 9 Arabella row, Pimlico
Charles Thos. Wm. law stationer, 5A, Took's ct. Chancery la
Charles Wm. bootmaker, 1 Southampton st. Euston square
Charles Wm. bricklayer, 2 Lower Trinity st. Rotherhithe
Charles Wm. David, grocer, 19 Elizabeth pl. Balls pond rd
Charlesworth John A. teabroker, 3 Nag's head ct. Gracech. st
Charlesworth Wm. tobacconist, 108 Union st. Borough
Charleton & Watson, coalfactors & ship & insurance brokers, 28 St. Mary at hill
Charlick Wm. hairdresser, 1 Duke st. Lincoln's inn fields
Charlton & Easton, grocers & teamen, 48 Charing cross
Charlton Chas. Hen. solicitor, see Lacy, Howard & Charlton
Charlton Edwin, sec. to *Albion Insurance Co.* New Bridge st
Charlton Geo. baker, 23 Marylebone st. Piccadilly
Charlton Geo. grocer, 9 Courthope ter. Bermondsey new rd
Charlton Geo. painting brush manufr. 175 Bermondsey st
Charlton Geo. teadealer, 9 Great Coram st. Brunswick sq
Charlton Geo. whiting & hearth st. ma. 92 Union st. Lambeth wk
Charlton Henry, corn & coal dealer, 146 Praed st. Paddington
Charlton Henry, paperhanger, 56 Regent st. Horseferry rd
Charlton Isabella (Miss), milliner, 16 Princes st. Cavend. sq
Charlton James, watch & clock maker, 14 Lisson grove north
Charlton Jas. whalebone cutter, 16 Cecil ct. St. Martin's la
Charlton John, coffee & chop ho. 15 Tichborne st. Haymarket
Charlton Richard, haberdasher, 3 Bowling st. Marylebone, & 40 Great Marylebone st
Charlton Charlotte (Mrs.), rope maker, 2 Brook st. Ratcliff
Charlton Wm. cheesemonger, 21 Aylesbury st. Clerknwl. gr
Charlwood Geo. seedsman, &c. 14 Tavistock row, Covent gdn
Charlwood William, cloth factor, 38 Coleman st
Charman Wm. manufacturing jeweller, 63 Berwick st. Soho
Charnley & Abraham, wine & spirit mers. 21 Harp la. Tower st
Charnley Thos. *Catherine Wheel* P.H. 11 Church st. Kensingtn
Charnock Rich. Stphn. & John, solicitors, 44 Paternoster row
Charnock Richard, barrister, 5 King's Bench walk, Temple
Charnock Wm. painter, &c. 20 Albion ter. Wandsworth road
Charrett William, baker, 46 Church rd. Commercial rd. east
Charrington, Head & Co. brewers, Mile end road
Charrington John & Co. coal merchants, 173 Fenchurch st. & 58 Lower Shadwell
Charrington Harry, coal merchant, 18 Upper Thames st
Charrington James, currier, 5 Winter sq. Long la. Bermondsy
Charrott Richard, dairyman, 9 Crescent place, Burton cresct
Chart John, tailor, 30 Dean st. Soho
Charter House, Charterhouse square
Chartered Gas Light Co. (Charles Burls, secretary), 19 New Bridge st. Blackfriars; Horseferry road, Westminster; Curtain road, Shoreditch; & Brick lane, St. Luke's; wharf, 7 Macclesfield st. south, City road
Charters, Holland & Newson, coachmakers, 30 New Bond st
Charters James, carpenter, &c. 3 Ann's place, Hackney rd
Charters Thos. Armstrong, pilot, 52 White Horse st. Stepny
Chartier & Hartley, trimming makers, 21 Pump row, Oldst. rd
Chartres Francis emery paper ma. 10 Noble st. Goswell st
Chartres James, bootmaker, Southampton st. Camberwell rd
Chase Chas. plumber & glazier, 53 Upper John st. Fitzroy sq
Chase John, plumber, 62 Charlotte st. Fitzroy square
Chase Sarah (Miss), milliner, 16 Hinde st. Manchester sq
Chase Thomas, chemist, 14 Holborn
Chasen Samuel, *Bromley Arms* P.H. 27 Cleveland st

Chasen Samuel, *Duke of Newcastle* P.H.34 Lt. Earl st. 7 Dials
Chassereau Henry, stationer, 97 High st. Camden town
Chassereau Thomas Purton, mer. 6 North buildings, Finsby
Chasteanneuf C.A. greengrocer, 16 Adam st. west, Prtmn. sq
Chater & Hayward, glass, lead, oil & color merchants, 21 St. Dunstan's hill, Tower st
Chater Charles, bootmaker, 6 Osborne st. Whitechapel
Chater Charlt. (Miss), boys' school, 26 Abbey pl. St. John's wd
Chater George, who. stationer, see Grosvenor, Chater & Co
Chater Rich. pap. stainr. &decoratr. 45 Tottenham court road
Chater Samuel, cheesemonger, 9 Brewer st. Somers town
Chater Thomas, grocer, 20 Richmond pl. East st. Walworth
Chater William, watchmaker, 163 Goswell st
Chaters John, shipowner, 40 King st. Redmond's row, Stepny
Chatfield, Wingate & Hart, solicitors, 16 Austinfriars
Chatfield James, dyer & scourer, 16 Old Compton st. Soho
Chatfield John, grocer, 10 Aldgate High st
Chatfield Thos. italian & brush wa. 3 Richmond rd. Dalston
Chatfields (Miss), ladies' academy, 4 Church row, Limehouse
Chatland Thos. coach harness pltr. 36 Brownlow st. Drury la
Chatley Joseph, boat builder, Eastern wharf, Adelphi
Chatley William, boat builder, Eastern wharf, Adelphi
Chatterley Wm. Weldon, dancg mstr. 5 Old Dorset pl. Clphmrd
Chatterton Fredk. professor of the harp, 52 Gt. Portland st
Chatterton Geo. R. silversmith, 2 Peter's ct. St. Martin's lane
Chatterton John Baslir, professor of harp, 32 Manchester st
Chatterton Susan (Mrs.), coal merchant, 6 Dorrington st
Chatterton Wm. coal & potato dlr. 1 Lit. Geo. st. Hampstd. rd
Chatting Edward, hatter & cap maker, 5½ Newgate st
Chatting Francis, wax chandler, 8 Ireland row, Mile end rd
Chatto John, surgeon, 23 Great Coram st. Russell sq
Chatwin Fred. potato salesman, 6 Up. area, Hungerford mkt
Chatwood John, chemist&druggist, 95 Old Gravel la. Wapping
Chauffourier Augustin, imp. of fr. provisions, 105 Quadrant
Chauncy Nath. S. west india mercht. 39 Wilson st. Finsbury
Chauntler & Westwood, solicitors, 8 Gray's inn sq
Chauntler John, laceman, 51 St. Paul's churchyard
Chavannes Mary (Mrs.), milliner, 16 George st. Portman sq
Chave & May, curriers & leather slrs. 34 Brick la. St. Luke's
Chave Elizab. (Mrs.), green grocer, &c. 29 Sidney st. Gosw. rd
Chavell Rd. Billett, lodging ho. 12 New North st. Red Lion sq
Chawner & Co. silver knife, fork, &c. makers, 16 Hosier lane, Smithfield
Cheal Henry, baker, High st. Battersea
Cheal Robt. carrier, original New inn, 20 Old Change Cheapsde
Cheale Wm. tailor, 24 Providence row, Finsbury
Cheap John, ship broker, 6 Rood lane, Fenchurch st
Cheape & Leslie, merchants, 19 Abchurch lane, City
Cheaston Edw. *Rose of Normandy* P.H. 32 High st. Marelb
Cheater Sarah (Mrs.), chairmaker, 6 Rose st. Soho
Cheatle Edward, butcher, 18 Gordon st. City road
Checkley Joseph, butcher, 27 Goswell rd
Checkley Wm. corn dealer, 7 Upper Wellington st. Strand
Chedgzoy Thos. potato dlr. South rw. Covent garden market
Cheek John, umbrella, whip & fishing rod maker & archery wa. who. retail & for exportation, 132 Oxford st. & 52 Strand
Cheek William, hairdresser, 87 East st. Manchester sq
Cheel Alexander, carpenter, 29 Little Marylebone st
Cheel Thos. bricklayer, 30 Lit. Marylebone st. Cavendish sq
Cheel Thos. jun. bricklayer, 14 Lit. Marylebone st. Cavend. sq
Cheeper, Watson & Jackson, silk & ribbon wareh. 36 Wood st
Cheere Charles, barrister, 11 King's bench walk, Temple
Cheere Robert, attorney, 11 King's bench walk, Temple
Cheese Sam. & Hen. *Flora* tea grds. & P.H. Uxbridg. rd. Bayswr
Cheese James, wholesale druggist, see Hancock & Cheese
Cheeseman Ann & Fred. farriers, 30 Wellington pl. Blkfrs. rd
Cheeseman Elizbth. (Mrs.), fruiterer, 14 Cannon row, Westmnr
Cheeseman Richard, china dealer, 2 Canal bridge, Old Kent rd
Cheeseman Richd. hairdresser, 26 Low. Queen st. Rotherhithe
Cheeseman Rd. Ellis, house agt. 25 Gt. Dover st. Borough
Cheeseright Thomas, academy, 8 Church st. Kensington
Cheesewright Chas. Wm. goldbtr. 54 Ossulston st. Somers twn
Cheesewright Sam. B. coal & timber mer. Baltic wf. Kingsld. rd
Cheesewright Wm. house painter, 97 Mary st. Hampstead rd
Cheesley David, dairyman, 11 Cumberland row, Islington
Cheesman Christian (Mrs.), stay manufacturer, 38 Holywell st. Strand, & 1 Harriet st. Sloane st
Cheesman Geo. carver & gilder, 20½ Lit. Newport st. Long acre
Cheesman George, tanner, leather dresser & dyer, 12 Great Newport st. & Neckinger road, Bermondsey
Cheesman Harriet (Miss), baker, 21 George row, Bermondsey
Cheesman Henry, mariner, 72 Great George st. Bermondsey
Cheesman John, plasterer, 62 Devonshire st. Lisson grove
Cheesman Thomas, tobacconist, 40 Bath st. City road
Cheesman Wm. cowkeeper, 13½ Henry st. Hampstead road
Cheeswright Fredk. G. coal merchant, 16 Up. Kennington gn
Cheeswright Henry, law stationer, 223 Piccadilly
Cheeswright Henry Cornfoot, notary, 62 Lower Thames st
Cheetham Charles, hatter, 49 Grosvenor row, Pimlico
Cheetham John, fruiterer, 8 Little Vine st. Piccadilly
Cheetham Mary (Mrs.), wdrobe. dlr. 9 Up. Copnhagn. st. Pntvl
Cheeves Mary (Mrs.), grocer, 4 Cobourgh pl. Rotherhithe
Cheinlander Henry baker, 76 Turnmill st. Clerkenwell
Cheffin Chas. *Running Horse* P.H. 18 Lit. Queen st. Holborn
Cheffins Chas. Fredk. surveyor, draughtsman & lithographer, 6 Castle st. Holborn, & 9 Southampton bdgs. Chancery la
Chelmsford & Bury (provisional committee) *Railway Company* (David Bartie, sec.), 61 Moorgate st
Chelsea, Brompton & Belgrave Dispens. 41 Sloane sq. Chelsea
Chelsea & Brompton Omnib. As. Off. 5 Bretten ter. King's rd
Chelsea Savings' Bank (T. L. Jeffree, sec.), Pulham ter. Kgs. rd
Chelsea Water works' Office (James Gascoigne Lynde, sec.), 16 Great Queen st. Westminster; *Works*, Thames bank
Cheltenham & Oxford Railway Company, 449 West Strand
Chemical Gazette newspaper, 7 Red Lion court, Fleet st
Chenery Charles, wholesale coffee dealer, 9 Mincing lane
Chenery George, *Old Pied Bull* P.H. 90 Upper st. Islington
Chenery Henry, grocer, 81 Great Guildford st. Borough
Chenery John, plumber & painter, 19 Bryan st. Pentonville
Chenery Joseph, hosier, glover, &c. 85 Newgate st
Chenery Martin, lodging house, 84 Park st. Grosvenor sq
Chenery Robert, coal merchant, 43 Bryanstone st
Cheney Chas. & Co. silk & velvet manfctrs. 36 Basinghall st
Cheney John, bricklayer & builder, 69 Acton st. Gray's inn rd
Cheney John, dairyman, 93 Mount st. Berkeley square
Chenning George, grocer, 47 Adam st. West, Portman sq
Chenoweth Edward, ironmonger, 5 Newland pl. Kensington
Chenoweth Samuel, shoemak. 120 Gt. Russell st. Bloomsbury
Chenu Fredk. tobacconist, 22A, Drummond st. Euston sq
Chenu Henry, hatter & jeweller, 32 Blackfriars road
Chepmell Edward Charles, M.D. 16 Hanover sq
Chepperfield Wm. A. butcher, 16 Moreton ter. Kentish twn
Chequer William, saddler, 248 Blackfriars road
Cherer George, short hand writer, 10 Lincoln's inn fields
Cherrey John, supt. grand junc. canal whf. 14 Paddington bas
Cherrill Sidney & Co. mnfg. jewellers, 6 Newcastle pl. Clrknwl
Cherrill Alfred Nelson, proctor, see Blake & Cherrill
Cherrill Ann (Miss), library, 8 Trinity st. Borough
Cherry Chas. who. patten tie & french clog ma. 126 Golden la
Cherry George, grocer, 16 Wells st. Oxford st
Cherry John, fruiterer, Long market, Covent garden market
Cherry Joseph, fishmonger, 42 Henry st. Hampstead rd
Cherry Morris, news agent, 14 Flagon row, Deptford
Cherry Peter, bottle dealer, 7 Lit. Cadogan pl. Sloane st
Cherry Peter, *British hotel*, 82 & 83 Jermyn st. St. James's
Cherry William, tailor, 35 Upper Seymour st. Portman sq
Cheshir Joseph, hat manufacturer, 39 Gravel la. Southwark
Cheshire Elizh. (Mrs.), who. earthnwa. dlr. 3 Wf. York rd. Cy. rd
Cheshire Jane (Mrs.), goldbeater, 112 Gt. Titchfield st. Oxford st
Cheshire John, butcher, 26 Brick lane, St. Luke's
Cheshire Joseph, plumber & glazier, Camberwell green
Cheshire Richard Francis, academy, 3 Cambridge st. Gldn. sq
Cheshire Samuel, druggist, 144 Whitechapel High st
Cheshire Wm. Jas. paper tea tray ma. to the Queen & royal family, 17 & 18 King st. Covent garden
Cheshunt College Rooms, 7 Blomfield st. Finsbury, 10 to 4
Chesley Joseph, beer retailer, 8 Ship yard, Temple bar
Chesnay, Eugene & Co. imps. of french hat trim. 2 Bouverie st
Chesney Richard, engraver, 25 Castle st. East, Oxford st
Chessall Matthew Rd. attorney, 51 Up. Baker st. Regent's pk
Chessher Thomas, coal dealer, 41 Long alley, Finsbury
Chessman Chris. S. commis. agent, 21 Addle st. Wood st
Chessney Jsph. Benj. printer, &c. 211 Bermondsey st
Chessor William, cooper, 1 Totton st. Commercial rd. east
Chessum Wm. carpenter & builder, 89 Leonard st. Finsbury
Chester Henry & Son, attorneys, 3 Parsonage row, Newingt
Chester, Toulmin & Chester, attorneys, 11 Staple inn, Holborn
Chester & Holyhead Rail. Co. (Geo. King, sec.), 61 Moorgate st
Chester Charles, attorney, 144 Blackfriars road
Chester Charles, livery stables, George yard, 80 Leather lane
Chester Fredk. Arthur, butcher, 17 Sussex pl. Old Kent road
Chester John, conveyancer, 5 Bond court, Walbrook
Chester Richard, cornchandler, 1 Up. Park pl. Regent's pk
Chester Robert, oil warehouse, 1 Bloomsbury market
Chester Robert, printer&newsagent, 10 Lit. Queen st. Westmr
Chester Thomas, baker, 12 Wellington st. Blackfriars road
Chester Thos. dealer in birds, 170 Brick la. Spitalfields
Chesterman Benj. carpen. & build. 4 Stanhope st. Clare mrkt
Chesterman Chas. pianoforte ma. 114 Crawford st. Portman sq
Chesterman Frederick, timber mer. 34 North st. Manchstr. sq
Chesterman Geo. furn. broker, 11 Glo'ster. ter. New rd. Whtchpl
Chesterman Jane (Mrs.), academy, 4 Southmptn. ter. Pentonvil

Chesterman Jesse, brass manufactr.&gas fitter,5 Eyre st. hill
Chesterman Wm. springer & liner,37 Meredith st.Clerkenwell
Chesterton Arthur, house agent & coal merchant, 2 Terrace, High st. Kensington, & Arundel wharf, Strand
Chesterton Chas. sen. estate agt. 2 Ter. High st. Kensington
Chesterton Elizh.(Mrs.), baker, 141 Long lane, Bermondsey
Cheston Chester, solicitor, 1 Winchester blds. Gt. Winch. st
Cheswright, Sheffield & Co. timber merchts. 120 Bunhill row
Chettle Geo. Rodney, hairdres. 14 Clayton pl. Caledonian rd
Chettle William, watchmaker, 35 Commercial rd. Lambeth
Cheveley James,attorney,2Up.Wharton st.Bagnigge wells rd
Chevalier Benj. fishing tackle ma. 12 Bell yd. Temple bar
Chevalier William, artist, 24 Tonbridge place, New road
Chevers Forbes M. & Norman, surgeons, 26 Up. Stamford st
Cheverton Emma(Mrs.),ladies'school,1 Cardigan pl. Nw.nth.rd
Cheverton Thomas, grocer, 107 Tottenham court road
Chevis Robert, hairdresser, 20 Felix terrace, Liverpool road
Chew Bradley, eating house, 64 Brewer st. Somers town
Chew John, baker, 22 Carnaby st. Golden square
Chew Robert, lighterman, 47 Broad st. Wapping
Chew Thomas, livery stable keeper, 20 & 22 Little Moorfields
Chew Thomas, teadealer, 25 Crawford st. Portman square
Chew William, baker, 7 Diddington pl. Caledonian road
Cheyne & Perry, beer retailer, 4 King st. Borough
Cheyne Robert Romley, surgeon, 43 Berners st. Oxford st
Cheyney Lucy(Miss),teach.of drawg.10 Hanover pl. Regt.pk.rd
Chibnall Wm. baker & corn chandler, 12 Tothill st. Westm
Chichester John Hopton R. barrister, 3 Stone blds. Linc's inn
Chichester Robert Bruce, barrister, 8 New sq. Lincoln's inn
Chick Charles, coal dealer, 118 Praed st. Paddington, & 5 Wharf, south side, Paddington basin
Chick James, lath render, Gravel lane, Southwark
Chick John, carpenter & undertaker, 5 Harper st. New Kent rd
Chick Joseph, dining rooms, 9 Moor st. Soho
Chick Samuel, oil & tallow chandlr. 7 Church row Aldgate High st
Chick Thomas, cabinetmaker, 7 & 8 Mount rw. Liverpool rd
Chick Wm. dining rooms, 72 Gt. Carlisle st. Portman markt
Chick William, butcher, 28 St. Mary Axe
Chickall Geo. shawl warehouse, 86 Quadrant, Regent st.
Chiddenton John, butcher, 211 Up. Whitecross st. St. Luke's
Chidell & Jones, wine merchants, 1 Hay's lane, Tooley st
Chidell George, grammar school, 186 Edgware road
Chidgey Cornelius, bricklayer, 24 Wilson st. Finsbury sq
Chidley John James, wholesale bookseller, 123 Aldersgate st
Chidley Richard, cheesemonger, 118 Whitechapel road
Chidley Richd. plumber & glazier,4 Sol's row, Hampstead rd
Chieslie Rt. J. writing master, 8 Seymour pl. Bryanstone sq
Chifferiel Fredk. law stationer, 2 Took's ct. Chancery lane
Chilcoot Michael, tailor, 63 Mount st. Berkeley square
Chilcot Jas. Wm.&Co.who. stayma.5 Falcon st. City & Portsea
Chilcot Joseph, livery stables, 1 Weymouth st. New Kent rd
Chilcote Geo. Henry, solicitor, 14 George st. Mansion house
Chilcote Paul, surgeon, 12 Golden square
Chilcott Isaac H. tailor & outfitter, 159 Fenchurch st
Chilcott Phœbe (Mrs.), milliner, 10 Upper st. Islington
Child & Co. bankers, 1 Fleet st. Temple bar
Child (Coles) & Co. coal merchs. coke burners & wharfingers, Belvedere wharf, next Hungerford bridge, Belvedere road, Lambeth, & Greenwich wharf, East Greenwich, Kent
Child Jsph & Co. agents for Guinness's stout, 43 Leicester sq
Child Charles, builder, 2 Halsey terrace, Cadogan st
Child Charles John, ironmonger, 68 George st. Portman sq
Child Daniel, pianoforte manufr. 10 Chester pl. Old Kent rd
Child Daniel, pianoforte maker, 33 High st. Notting hill
Child Edmund, builder, 7 Warwick st. Belgrave road
Child Edwd. jun. builder, 8 Halsey terrace, Cadogan st
Child Edward Edmund, pawnbroker, 217 Shadwell High st
Child Elizabeth (Mrs.), lodging house, 13 Cecil st. Strand
Child Francis, solicitor, 24 Cannon st. City
Child George, ship bro. & custom house agent, 2 Dunster ct
Child George, seed merchant, 119 Lower Thames st
Child Geo. Chaplin, physician, 27 Mortimer st. Cavendish sq
Child Helen (Mrs.), *Horse & Groom* P.H. 31 Bedfordbury
Child Henry, optician & painter on glass, 66 Vauxhall walk
Child Henry, solicitor, see Wire & Child
Child James, baker, 25 Three Colt st. Limehouse
Child James, grocer & italian wareho. 54 Amwell st. Pentonv
Child Jas. insp. of weights & meas. 9 Up. Gloucester st. Clknwl
Child James, veterinary surgeon, Church st. Hackney
Child John, plasterer, 34 North st. Edgware road
Child John, tailor, 120 Church st. Shoreditch
Child Joseph, oil & colorman, 8 Green st. Bethnal green
Child Joseph, plasterer & bricklyr. 34 Shoemaker row, Blkfrs
Child Matthew, fruiterer, 2 King st. Rotherhithe wall
Child Richard, tailor, 7 Princes road, Lambeth
Child Richd. umbrella, &c. mak. 8 Whitmore row, Hoxton
Child Robert, *Sovereign* P.H. 34 Munster st
Child Robert John, solicitor, see Fennell, Child & Kelly
Child Rt. Williams, who. jewllr. 13 Mount pleasnt. Gray's i. rd
Child Samuel Preston, merchant, Baltic coffee house; orchil & cudbear & extract of indigo ma. Chester pl. Bethnal green
Child Susannah (Mrs.), butcher, 37 South st. Manchester sq
Child Tobias, tanner, spanish & morocco leather manufacturer, &c. John st. Parker's row, Dockhead, Bermondsey
Child Wm. *Bee Hive* P.H. Holly st. south, Dalston
Child Wm. confectioner, 7 Aldenham st. Somers town
Child Wm. grocer, &c. 39 Gravel lane, Southwark
Child Wm. gun & pistol maker, 280 Strand
Child Wm. *Queen's Arms* P.H. Kilburn
Child Wm. Henry, wholesale fancy & general brush manufacturer, 22 Providence row, Finsbury
Childe James, artist, 39 Bedford st. Covent garden
Childerstone Fred. cheesemonger, 16 King st. Westminster
Childs George, artist, 12 Amwell st. Pentonville
Childs George, butcher, Southampton st. Camberwell rd
Childs George Borlace, surgeon, 34 Fore st. Cripplegate
Childs Richard, tailor, 18 Queen Anne st. Cavendish sq
Childs Samuel, wax bleacher, 11 Green st. Leicester square, & Earl's court, Old Brompton
Childs William, furnishing ironmonger, 40 North Audley st
Chiles Lewis, fishmonger, 222 Poplar High st
Chillingworth Chas. composition letter ma. 55 Gt. Dover st
Chillingworth William, importer of foreign wines to her Majesty by appointment, 43 Great Tower st. Tower hill
Chilmaid Henry, glass & china dealer, Camberwell green
Chilton, Burton & Johnson, solicitors, 7 Chancery lane
Chilton Frederick, baker, 15 Queen st. Ratcliff
Chilton George, queen's counsel, 9 Crown Office row, Temple
Chilton James, butcher, 86 Crawford st
Chilton John, warehouseman, 6 New court, Bow lane
Chilton Robert Henry, grocer, 9 Southampton st. Camberwl
Chilton Thomas Mills, butcher, 13 Portman mkt. Marylebn
Chilton William, plumber, &c. 4 Kinnerton st. Belgrave sq
Chilver Lewis, wheelwright, 16 Wharf, North side, Paddington basin, & Maiden lane, King's cross
Chilver Thomas F. surgeon, 14 New Burlington st
China Tea Company, Henry Blake, 106 Newgate st
Chinery Matthias, german paste mak. 28 Church st. Lambeth
Chinese Collection, 18 St. George's place, Hyde park corner
Chinn Joseph, carpenter, 7 Gate st. Lincoln's inn fields
Chinn Samuel, portrait painter, 140 Aldersgate st
Chinner Charles, butcher, Church st. Stoke Newington
Chinnery John F. wine merchant & customhouse agent, Customhouse chambers, 67½ Lower Thames st
Chinnock Frederick, auctioneer & estate agent, 28 Regent st
Chipchase Joseph, boot & shoe maker, 227 Shadwell High st
Chipp John, *Queen's Head* P.H. 20 Park side, Knightsbridge
Chipp Mary (Miss), fancy reposty. 109 Albany st. Regent's pk
Chipp Thomas Paul, prof. of music, 109 Albany st. Regent's pk
Chippen Jasper, bread & biscuit baker, Clapham rise
Chippendale Augustus, solicitor, 10 John st. Adelphi
Chippendale John, navy agent, 10 John st. Adelphi
Chippendale John, F.R.C.S. surgeon, 69 Great Queen st
Chipperfield John, oil & colorman, 10 Silver st. Clerkenwell
Chipperfield Robert, tailor, 11 Bloomsbury st. Bloomsbury
Chipperton Fras. W. cheesemonger, 8 Portsdown ter. Kilburn
Chippindale William & Charles, coopers, 130 Bunhill row
Chiquedance Jean, gold chain ma. 8 Ashby st. Northampton sq
Chiriaco & Co. merchants, 28 Broad st. buildings
Chirney Chas. & Thos. linendrapers, 12 Albion place, & 1 Caledonian place, Caledonian road
Chirney Charles, shawl warehouse, 40½ Friday st. Cheapside
Chirney Charles, shawl manufr. see Forbes, Chirney & Co
Chirnside Henry, painter & glazier, 75 Berwick st. Soho
Chisholm Alex. Bain, surgeon, 32 Devonshire st. Portland pl
Chisholm Andrew, *Old White Horse* P.H. 64 London wall
Chisholm Duncan, baker, 109 Bermondsey st. Tooley st
Chisholm John, baker, 3 Aylesbury pl. Old Kent road
Chisholm John, teadealer, 30 St. George st
Chisholme, Hall & Gibson, solicitors, 64 Lincoln's inn fields
Chisholme Henry, dyer, 32 Upper Ebury st. Pimlico
Chisholme John, attorney, 3 Cook's court, Carey st. & 29 Edward st. Hampstead road
Chislett Alfred (late Gilkerson), optician & mathematl. instrumt maker to H.M. Stationery Office, 27 Greenfield st. Coml. rd
Chislett Geo. *City* chop & coffee rooms. 22 St. Martin's le grnd
Chislett William Game, *Swan* P.H. 25 Fish st. hill
Chisman Isabella (Miss), milliner, 16 Chapel st. Ea. May fair
Chisman John, booksel. & stationer, 42 Albany st. Regent's pk
Chisnell James Edward, fruiterer, 2 Upp. Church st. Chelsea
Chissholme Hannah (Mrs.), milliner, 35 & 36 Maddox st

Chissholme James, pianoforte maker, 15 Great Pulteney st
Chiswell Geo. H. plumber&beer ret. 7Gt. George st. Bermondsy
Chittenden & Arnold, ho. painters, 109 Jermyn st. St. James's
Chittenden Brothers, undertakers, 42 & 43 Greek st. Soho
Chittenden Andrew, linendraper, 13 Charles st. Middlx. hos
Chittenden Charles, upholsterer, 193 Piccadilly
Chittenden George, baker, 28 St. George st
Chittenden Henry, corn, seed & flour factr. 3 New London st
Chittenden James, lath render, 149 Southwark bridge rd
Chittenden John, cheesemngr. 3 William's pl. Walworth rd
Chittenden John, corn dealer, 2 Windsor pl. Old Kent rd
Chittenden John Franks, surgeon, 71 Whitechapel High st
Chittick Thos. locksmith, 11 South st. King's rd. Chelsea
Chittle George, hairdresser, 34 Eyre st. hill
Chittleburgh John, curiosity dealer, 126 Gt. Portland st
Chittock Fredk. cheesemonger, 58 High st. Portland town
Chittock George, corn & coal mer. 20 North pl. Kingsland rd
Chitty Caleb, watch & clock ma. 19 York row, Kennington rd
Chitty Charles, stockbroker, Stock exchange
Chitty Edward, miller, Jack's coffee house, Mark lane
Chitty James, baker, 48 Francis st. Newington butts
Chitty Richard, working jeweller, 3 Charles st. Soho sq
Chitty Thomas, specl. pleader, 1 King's Bench walk, Temple
Chitty Tompson, special pleader, 6 Pump court, Temple
Chitty Wm. beer retailer, 7 Crombies row, Commerl. rd. East
Chitty Wm. coal & potato dealer, 18 Brownlow st. Drury la
Chiverhall George, greengrocer, 5 King st. Westminster
Chivers Charles, breeches maker, 2 Conduit st
Chivers Ebenezer, tailor, &c. 6 Creed lane
Chivers Saml. Fredk. paperhang. &c. 135Church st. Shoreditch
Chivers Thomas, tailor, 35 Warner st. Dover road
Chivers William, umbrella maker, Church st. Hackney
Choat Ebenezer, wool & horse&hair card maker to the honourable board of ordnance, 5 Star corner, Bermondsey
ChoatMaryAnn(Mrs.), trunk ma. 61 Lamb'sConduitst. Fndlng
Choice Emily (Mrs.), cupper, 2 Little Ormond st. Queen sq
Choice John, lodging house, 19 Lr. Belgrave pl. Pimlico
Cholerton James, grocer, 37 Palace st. Buckingham gate
Cholmeley Robert, barrister, 6 Old square, Lincoln's inn
Cholmeley Stephen, solicitor, see Frere, Foster, Goodford&Co
Cholmondeley Joseph, surgeon, 3 Nottingham pl. New rd
Choppin Wm. ironmonger, 11 Bell yard, Gracechurch st
Chopping Thos. fancy repos. 57 Westbourne gro. Bayswater
Chorley James, beer retailer, Nottingdale, Notting hill
Chorley Mary Ann (Mrs.), milliner, &c. 6Glo'ster pl. Islington
Chorley William, grocer, 28 Whitechapel High st
Chowles Geo. upholstr.&cabinet ma. 18 High st. Marylebone
Chown Henry, builder, 1 Gt. Quebec st. Montagu square
Chowne (Claude) & Co. importers, 265 Regent st
Chowne Chas. Edmd. surgeon & regr. 48 Hertford st. Mayfair
Chowne William D. physician, 14A, Princes st. Cavendish sq
Chretien Joseph, trunkmaker&carpenter, 4Russia ct. Milk st
Chrichton Francis, dairyman, 11 East st. Manchester sq
Chrimes Thomas, solicitor, 2 Frederick place, Gray's inn la
Chrisbian Michael, ironmongr. 2 Vittoria pl. Cambridge rd
Chrisp & Co. wine & spirit brokers, 26 Gt. Tower st
Christ's Hospital, Newgate st. City
Christchurch Savings Bank (H.P.Hinde, sec.), Albany st. Regent's park
Christey Alex. milliner, 1 Bedford pl. Lower rd. Rotherhithe
ChristeyAlexander, lighterman, Galley quay, Lower Thames street, & 4 Muscovy court, Tower hill
Christey Wm. lighterman & custom house agnt. Galley quay
Christian, Adams & Dewey, linendrapers, household, ready made & childbed linen & general outfitting warehouse, 12 Holles st. Cavendish square
Christian & Rathbone, outfitters, 11 Wigmore st
Christian Instruction Society, 60 Paternoster row
Christian Spectator newspaper, 56 Paternoster row
Christian& Philanthropic Institution House (Edward Turst Carver, secretary), 20 Red Lion square
Christian Tract So. (J. E. Clennell, sec.), 121 Newgate st
Christian Eleanor(Mrs.), artist, 32 Friedenstein ter. Regt. pk
Christian Cooke, oilman, 16 Lambeth High st
Christian Christopr. Baker, printer, 1 Whitefriars st
Christian Ewan, architect & surveyor, 44 Bloomsbury sq
Christian Henry, dealer in colonial produce, 9 Mincing lane
ChristianJohnA. land survey. 16St. MaryAbbotts ter. Kensingt-
Christian Cooke, baker, Camberwell green
Christian Michael, ironmonger, 3 Vittoria pl. Cambrdg. rd
Christian Richard, merchant, Railway pl. Fenchurch st
Christian Thomas, baker, 4 Fisher st. Red Lion square
Christie & Manson auctioneers, 8 King st. St. James's
Christie James Edward & Wm. bakers, 10 Queen's buildgs. Knightsbridge, & millers, steam mills, King's road, Chelsea
Christie Rt. & Co. linen factors & warehousemen, 12 Friday st
Christie Wm. & John Chr. gasfitters, 6 Somerset st. Aldgate
ChristieWm.&Robert &Co. merchants, 5 Fenchurch buildings
Christie Alfred, merchant, 34 Broad st. buildings
Christie Alex. *RoyalGeorge* P.H. 25 Drummond st. Euston sq
Christie Archibald, drug & drysalt broker, 17 Fenchurch st
Christie Archibald Jas. *Christie's hotel*, 57&58 St. James's st
Christie Charles, timber merchant, 19 &51 Broad st. Lambeth
Christie Charles Wm. barrister, 5 Old square, Lincoln's inn
Christie Chas. jun. engineer&machinist, 19 Broad st. Lambeth
Christie Edm. carpet & upholstery wareho. 54Old Compton st
Christie Elizh. (Mrs.), mar. store dlr. 50Wilsted st. Somers twn
Christie George, tailor, see M'Kellar & Christie
Christie Harriet (Mrs.), milliner, 68 Regent quadrant
Christie Jas. carpenter & joiner, 32 Maiden la. Covent garden
Christie John, timber merchant, 73 Lambeth Lower marsh
Christie Jonathan Hen. barrister, 6 Stone bldgs. Linc. inn
Christie Mary (Miss), ladies' school, 2 Sand's bldgs. Islingtn
Christie Thomas, who.&retail teadealer, 9 Whitechapel High st. 12 Norton folgate, & 1 Hereford place, Commercial rd
Christie Wm. bookbinder, 7 Wardour st. Soho
Christie Wm. chronomtr. watch&clockmak. 18Cannon st. City
Christie Wm. toydealer, 9 Strong's place, Brompton
Christie Wm. Dougal, barrister, 5King's Bench walk, Temple
Christie Wm. jun. fancy bread & biscuit baker, 51 Bow lane
ChristmasChas. G. (sec. to *Rev. Interest So.*), 17 King's Arms yd
Christmas George, bootmaker, 12 Mount st. Lambeth
Christmas James, eating house, 10 Brick lane, Spitalfields
Christmas James, general salesman, 93 Old st. road
Christmas James, grocer & oilman, 34 South Audley st
Christmas James, *Gun* P.H. 55 St. John st. Clerkenwell
Christmas John, statuary & mason, Stoke Newington rd
Christmas John Wm. attorney, 6 Raymond bldgs. Gray's inn
ChristmasLouisa(Mrs.), basket ma. 13 Hayfield pl. Mile end rd
Christmas John Wm. plumber, &c. 15 Holland st. Blkfrs. rd
Christmas Samuel, hatter & furrier, 62&63 Burlington arcade
Christmas Thos. pewterer, 3 Green st. Wellington st. Blackfrs
Christmas Thomas, turner, 1 Holywell row, Shoreditch
Christmas William, grocer, 2 Cornwall ter. Camden town
Christmas William, tailor, 8 Provost st. City road
Christoffers John, *Windmill* P.H. 49 Leather lane
Christopher William Thomas & Co. wine merchants, 16 Woburn place, & 55 Great Woburn st
Christopher Arthur Anstey, shipper & importer of french & german wines, 7 Hart st. Mark la. & 54 Crutched friars
Christopher Danl. hairdresr. & perfumer, Mare st. Hackney
Christopher Henry, architect, see Garland & Christopher
Christopher John Charles, district surveyor, see Garland & Christopher
Christopher John C. surgeon, 26 Gloucester pl. Portman sq
Christopher John Danby, solicitor, 26A, Argyll st. Regent st
Christophers John Crouch, surgeon, 8 Upper Montagu st
Christophers Joseph S. merchant, & cape of good hope emigration agent, 2 East India chambers, Leadenhall st
Christopherson Wm. who.&shippingironmongr. 55KingWm. st
Christy Frederick Collier & Co. engineers, boiler makers, iron & brass founders, Thames ironworks, 70 Rotherhithe
Christy John Fell & Co. flint glass ma. Palace Newrd. Lamb
Christy John Thos. jun. & Henry & Co. hatters, 35 Gracechurch st. manufactory 113 & 170 Bermondsey st
Christy Frances (Miss), ladies' school, 27 Warner
Christy James, grocer, 14 Northumberland st. Marylebone
Chrystal William, jeweller, 37 Granville square
Chubb Charles & Son, inventors & patentees of the patent fireproof strong rooms, safes & boxes, and of the new patent lock & combination latch, 57 St. Paul's churchyard, London, & 28 Lord st. Liverpool
Chubb Charles Francis, solicitor, 4 Raymond buildings
Chubb Henry, haircutter, & wig. ma. 7St. Peter'sall. Cornhill
Chubb John, enameller, 34 Coppice row, Clerkenwell
Chubb John, tailor & draper, 1 Queen st. Cheapside
Chubb Thomas, bookbindr. 5 Dean st. Fetter lane
Chubb Thos. A. (acct. to So. Ea. rail. co.), 4 Joiner st. Tooley st
Chuck King & Co. glass & lead merchants, 10 Norton folgate, & 9 Kingsland road
Chuck Danl. cabinet & chair carver, 222 Hoxton Old town
Chuck John, cabinet ma. & fur. broker, 90 Shoe la. Fleet st
Chuck John, painter, 23 Liverpool st. King's cross
Chumbley John, prof. of music, 4 Park pl. ter. Paddingtn. gn
Chumley George, tailor, 10 James st. Oxford st
Chunk Nail Company (George Chidley, agent), 31 Ely place
Church Chronicle newspaper, 5 Paternoster row
Church Commission & Comm. of Charities, 13Gt. George st
Church of England Life & Fire Assurance Institution (Wm. Emmens sec.), 5 Lothbury, see page 2015
Church of England Quarterly Review Office, 342 Strand
Ch. of Eng. Sunday Sch. Inst. 118 Dorset st. Salisbury sq

Church Extension Fund, 18 Serjeants' Inn, Fleet st
Church Missionary College, 12 Barnsbury place, Islington
Church Missionary Society (Rev. Henry Venn, B.D. Rev. Rd. Davies, M.A. & D. Coates, esq. secs.), 14 Salisbury sq
Church Pastoral Aid Society (Rev. Charles Clayton, M.A. sec.), Temple chambers, Falcon court, Fleet st
Church & State Gazette newspaper, 342 Strand
Church Daniel Wm. plumb. & painter, 40 Broad st. Lambeth
Church Edmund Boyle, solicitor, see Stenning & Church
Church Edmund Boyle, solicitor, 33 Essex st. Strand
Church Edward, attorney, 37 Spital square
Church Edward, carpenter, 26 Vere st. Duke st. Clare mrkt
Church George, brewer, Thames bank, Ranelagh road
Church Hannah (Mrs.), *Stag* P.H. 1 Castle lane, Westminster
Church Henry, carpenter, 14 Vauxhall ter. Vauxhall walk
Church Henry, grocer, 67 Banner row, St. Luke's
Church Henry, cheesemonger, Kingsland green
Church Henry Tyrrell, lithographer, 58 Watling st
Church John, watchma. & jeweller, 14 Bridge rd. Lambeth
Church John Thomas, solicitor, vestry clerk of the parish of St. George the Martyr, Queen square; & clerk of enrolments in Bankruptcy, 9 Bedford row
Church John Wm. beer retailer, 2 Penton st. Walworth rd
Church Joseph Saml. Cambridge heath brewery, Hackney rd
Church Mary (Mrs.), frankfort black ma. Maiden la. King's cr
Church Samuel, stationer, 62 Oakley st. Mount st. Lambeth
Church Swan (Mrs.), straw hat ma. 29 Penton st. Walworth rd
Church William, chandler's shop, 170 Upper Thames st
Church William, furniture broker, 121 Waterloo road
Church William, fruiterer & greengrocer, 107 Lambeth walk
Church William, general dealer, 169 Upper Thames st
Church William, *King's Arms inn*, 122 Leadenhall st
Church William Fredk. hairdresser, 2 Bread st. hill
Churcher Jas. & Son, hatters, 13 Beckford row, Walworth rd
Churcher Charles, hatter, 3 London terrace, Hackney road
Churcher Corn. tallow chandler, 43 Middlesex st. Aldgate
Churcher Maria (Miss), straw hat ma. 69 King st. Golden sq
Churcher Thos. who. perfum. & hair ma. 22 King st. Golden sq
Churcher Wm. earthenware dealer, 1 Dear's pl. Somers town
Churcher William, glass cutter, see Nutkins & Churcher
Churches & Chapels, Incorporated Society for Promoting the Enlargement, Building & Reparing of (Rev. Thomas Bowdler, secretary), 4 St. Martin's place, Trafalgar square
Churchill & Sim, wood brokers, 39 Old Broad st. City
Churchill (Smyth) & Co. wine merchants, 44 Southampton row
Churchill Charles, fruiterer, 93 Up. Seymour st. Euston sq
Churchill Chas. Stephen, chemist, 44 Strutton ground, Westmr
Churchill Henry, barrister, 2 Harcourt buildings, Temple
Churchill Henry, coachma. 12 Claremont mews, Claremont sq
Churchill Henry, surgeon, 16 Portland pl. north, Clapham rd
Churchill Hy. Blencowe, barrister, 2 Raymond bds. Gray's inn
Churchill James, doll maker, 6 Church st. Blackfriars road
Churchill Jas. fancy cabinet maker, 29 Charlotte st. Shoreditch
Churchill John, fishmonger, 44 Chapel st. Somers town
Churchill John, medical bookseller, 46 Princes st. Leicester sq
Churchill Robert Turner, wood broker, 3 Sun ct. Cornhill
Churchill Samuel, accountant, 38 Castle st. Holborn
Churchill Wm. carpenter, 12 John's row, Brick la. St. Luke's
Churchill Wm. timber merchant, Commercial rd. Lambeth
Churchlow Wm. hairdresser, 17 Old Bailey
Churchman Newspaper Office, 5 Paternoster row
Churchman George, bootmaker, 17 Marshall st. Golden sq
Churchman George, linendraper, 156½ Poplar High st
Churchman John, gold & silver drawer, 69 Red Lion st. Clkwl
Churchward John, cider mercht. Chamberlns. whf. Tooley st
Churchward Richard, builder, 11 St. Thomas st. East, Boro'
Churchman Richard, fruiterer, 18 Poplar High st
Churchyard Benj. coffee rooms, 26 Somerset st. Aldgate
Churchyard Isaac, cattle salesman, 60 West Smithfield
Churchyard Isaac, chemist, 24 Park ter. Regent's park rd
Churley James, butcher, 12 Eaton lane North, Pimlico
Churton Wm. & Son, hosiers, shirt & stock ma. 91 Oxford st
Churton Edward, bookseller & stationer, 26 Holles st. Cav. sq
Chuter Rt. export ironmonger & insu. broker, 3 Copthall bldgs
Chutter Jonathan, carpent. 35 Duke st. Commercl. rd. Lambeth
Ciceri Peter & Anthony & Co. wholesale wire workers & fancy birdcage manufacturers, 7 Eyre street hill, Hatton garden
Ciceri Joseph, grocer, 22 Eyre street hill, Hatton garden
Cicognani Mariano, tailor, &c. 19 Sherrard st. Golden sq
Circuit Isaac, hay & straw salesman, 19 West Smithfield
Circular to Bankers' Newspaper Offi. 29 St. Swithin's la. City
City Chamberlain's Office, Guildhall; hours 10 to 3
City Chronicle Newspaper Off. 14 Finch la. & 17 Royal Exch
City Club Ho. (John Towgood Kemble, sec.), 19 O. Broad st. City
City Corn Office (Wm. Rushton, collector), 10 Catherine ct. Tower hill; hours 10 to 6
City Comptroller's Office, Guildhall; hours 10 to 5
City Dispensary (John T. Rowsell, sec.), 76 Queen st. Chpsde
City Dues Office (Wm. M. Russell, collector, 10 to 4), 8 Coal ex
City of Dublin & Belfast & British & Irish Steam Packet Company (Jas. Hartley & Co. managers), 33 Regent st. Piccadilly, & Dublin Steam wharf, Lower East Smithfield
City of Glasgow Life Assurance Company, 120 Pall mall; for directors, &c. see page 2017
City Gauger's Office, 84 Lower Thames st.; hours 9 to 4
City Library (Wm. Herbert, librarian), Guildhall, City
City of London Conservative Association, 117 Bshpsgt st. withn
City of London Court of Requests, Guildhall bdgs.; Court days, Wednesday & Saturday, at 11; hours on other days 10 to 1
City of London Gas Co. (D. Benham, sec.), Dorset st. Slsbry. sq
City of London General Pension Society (Henry F. Richardson, sec.), 36 Coleman st
City of London Literary & Scientific Institution (George Stacey, secretary), 165 Aldersgate st
City of London Lying in Hospital (Jas. Clift, sec.), City road; committee meet every Wednesday at ½ past 10
City of London Parliamentary Registration Committee, League Registration Offices (Sidney Smith, sec. 15 & 18 East Temple chambers), 2 Whitefriars st. Fleet st
City of London School (Thos. Brewer, sec.), Milk st. Cheapside
City of London & Tower Hamlets Cemetery Company (Jas. Edward Shearman, sec. Joseph Hill, superint.), office, Cemetery, South grove, Mile end
City of London Truss Society (Wm. Eglinton, sec.), 76 Queen st. Cheapside
City of London Union Office, 35 Cannon st. City; house, Clarehall place, Stepney green
City of London Union & Register Office, & Registration of Births, Deaths & Marriages, 35 Cannon st.; hours 10 to 4
City Police Office (Daniel Whittle Harvey, esq. commissioner; Thomas Wood, sec), 26 Old Jewry; hours 9 to 5
City Remembrancer's Office, Guildhall yard; hours 9 to 8
City Solicitor's Office, Guildhall yard (Charles Pearson, city solicitor); hours 9 to 7
City Steam Boat Co. (Chas. Hancock, sec.) 17 Earl st. Blkfrs
Civil Engineer & Architects' Journal, 10 Fludyer st
Clabben William, potato dealer, 205 Bethnal green road
Clabon (John & John Moxon), solicitors, 76 Mark lane
Clack Henry, upholsterer, 49 George st. Portman square
Clack Hen. T. mgr. of Union Bank of London, 14 Argyll pl. Regt. st
Clack Robert, butcher, 7 Neptune st. Rotherhithe
Clack Susannah (Miss), childbed linen wareh. 102 Oxford st
Clagett Thomas William, america merchant, 8 Billiter sq
Clamp George, pawnbroker, 124 Aldersgate st
Clampit Gilbert, turner & bed plr. ma. 16 New inn yd. Shdtch
Clamtree Jsph. F. H. tobac. pipe manfr. 13 Hereford st Lissn. grv
Clapcott Charles, painter, 12 George st. Euston square
Clapham Benjamin, tanner, Willow walk, Bermondsey
Clapham Charles W. working jeweller, 104 High Holborn
Clapham Emma (Miss), milliner, 99 New Bond st
Clapham George, shawl manufacturer, 24 Friday st. Cheaps
Clapham Hen. Chas. surgeon, 29 Francis st. Tottenham. ct. rd
Clapham James George, cheesemonger, 65 Leather lane
Clapham Thomas J. oil & colorman, 6 Green st. Bethnal gn
Clapham William, shellfishmonger, 83 Snow hill
Clapham Wm. Henry, solicitor, 29 Gt. Portland st. Oxford st
Clapp John & Thos. vetnry. surgeons, 89 Red cross st. Boro'
Clapp Chas. musician, 40 Windmill st. Tottenham court road
Clapp Elizabeth (Miss), milliner, 7 John st. Oxford st
Clapp Jane (Mrs.), confectioner, 1 New Kent road
Clapp John, grocer, 6 South place, Camberwell new road
Clapp Robert, commission merch. & gen. agt. 80 Old Broad st
Clapp Samuel, coach smith, 35 North st. Sloane st
Clapp Saml. writing engraver, 1 Plumer's ct. High Holborn
Clapp Thomas, veterinary surgeon, 17 Park st. Boro' markt
Clapp William, surgeon, 62 Welbeck st. Cavendish square
Clapperton Alexander, baker, 5 Chenies st. Bedford square
Clapperton Francis, bookseller & publisher, 159 Fleet st
Clapperton Jas. *Kenilworth Castle* P.H. King st. New Nrth rd
Clapperton Robert, lodging house, 1 North cres. Bedford sq
Clapperton Simon, tailor, 3 Great Marlborough st
Clapperton William, herald painter, 54 Upper Stamford st
Clapshaw Aquila, cricket bat ma. 2 Nelson pl. New st. City rd
Clapshaw Charles, cricket bat ma. 3 West pl. Islington grn
Clapshaw James, grocer, Larkhall rise, Clapham
Clapton & Maythorn, straw hat manufrs. High st. Bow
Clarage Henry, hairdresser, &c. 31 Cannon st. City
Clarance John & Co. wholesale coffee dealers, 19 Cullum st
Clarance & Willes, imp. of guano & agricul. agt. 21 Cullum st
Clarance Thomas, tea & coffee broker, 14 Billiter st
Clare Geo. & Co. ho. decorators, 128 Mount st. Berkeley sq
Clare & Gimber, cheesemongers, 132 Tooley st

Clare Hy. & Sam. bed & mattress maks, 8 Clerkenwell close
Clare Ambrose, solicitor, 5 Sise lane, Bucklersbury
Clare Benj. secret springer, 29 Meredith st. Clerkenwell
Clare Elizh. (Miss), dressmaker, 15 Wilmot st. Russell sq
Clare Francis Knight, cabinet ma. 33 Rosoman st. Clrknwll
Clare Henry, solicitor, 8 Up. Chadwell st. Myddelton sq
Clare Henry F. surgeon, 1 Ladbroke terrace, Notting hill
Clare Henry James, watch maker, 15 Meredith st. Clerknwll
Clare James, cheesemonger, 1 Ann's place, Hoxton
Clare James, cheesemonger, 1 Whitmore road, Hoxton
Clare Michael, butcher, 161 Drury lane
Clare Michael, coal dealer, 22 Gt. Wild st. Lincoln's inn fields
Clare Patrick, coal dealer 141 & 144 Fetter lane, Fleet st
Clare Peter, stove grate maker, 12 Holland st. Blackfriars rd
Clare Samuel, carrier, see Alexander & Clare
Clare Samuel, cattle salesman 17 West Smithfield
Clare Thomas, artist, 6 Mabledon place, Burton crescent
Clare William, hairdresser, 69 Hoxton Old town
Clarenboll John, baker, 3 St. James st. Pentonville
Clarence Chambers, 12 Haymarket
Clarence Railroad Office (Chas. Benson, sec.), 80 Old Broad st. City
Clarence Edward Harper, pilot, 46 White Horse st. Stepney
Clarence James, fruiterer, 27 Elizabeth st. Eaton square
Clarence Thomas, fruiterer, 2 Church place, Piccadilly
Claret George, engraver, printer & publisher of masonic works & masonic instructor, 28 Up. Clifton st. Finsbury
Claridge, Day & Co. wine merchants, 21 Pudding lane
Claridge's Patent Asphalte of Seyssel Company (I. Farrell, sec.), Stangate, Lambeth
Claridge George, goldbeater, 18 Warwick lane, Newgate st
Claridge George, linendraper, 12 London ter. Hackney rd
Claridge George, tobacconist, 8 Southampton st. Cambrwell
Claridge John, butcher, Bromley, Middlesex
Claridge Mary (Mrs.), straw hat ma. 73 High st. Marylebone
Claridge Thomas, tailor, 51 High st. Marylebone
Claridge William, butcher & grocer, Bromley, Middlesex
Claringbold Wm. baker, 5 Chatsworth blds. Low. rd. Deptford
Claringbold Wm. baker, 7 New King st. Deptford
Claringbould Hen. Wm. *Barley Mow* P.H. 17 Norfolk st. Cambridge road
Clark Andrew & Son, plumbers & lead merchants & cast sheet lead manufacturers & agents for Delbruck's autogenous lead soldering process, manfrs. of chemical apparatus by patent, Bear garden, Bankside
Clark, Ansted & Co. fruit brokers, 39 Mincing lane
Clark & Barnard, auctioneers, 15 Blandford st. Portman sq
Clark & Boothby, pianoforte ma. 112 Gt. Portland st. Oxford st
Clark & Burges, coal factors, 6 Coal exchange
Clark, Charles & Augustus G. B. merchants & agents to Wm Clark & Co. of Bordeaux, 35 Seething lane
Clark & Collins, gold lacemen, embroiderers, military accoutrement & gold thread manfrs. 5 Glasshouse st. Regent st
Clark & Cooper, attorneys, Sessions house, Old bailey
Clark, Coulthard & Co. bottle mer. Dowgate whf. Up. Thames st
Clark, Davidson & Brown, solicitors, 36 Essex st. Strand
Clark George & Milbourne, merchants, 29 Pudding lane
Clark George & Co. ham & beef venders, 29 Hackney road
Clark Henry & Co. who. brush manufacturers, 26 Watling st
Clark John & Co. merchants, 5 Crescent, Minories
Clark John, jun. & Co. cotton spinners & thread manufacturers, Mile end, Glasgow, & 56 Aldermanbury
Clark John & Thomas, woollen manufactrs. 2 Basinghall st
Clark Matthew & Son, wine & spirit brokers, 72 Gt. Tower st
Clark Patrick & Co. engineers, lathe, tool & patent blowing machine manufacturers, Tunnel iron works, 238 Wapping
Clark Richard & Co. wax bleachers & oil refiners, lamp & chandelier manufacturers, &c. 447 West Strand
Clark Robert & Son, cork cutters, 99 Blackman st. Borough
Clark & Rogers, dentists, 5 Sackville st. Piccadilly
Clark Thomas & Chas. merchants, see Denny, Clark & Co
Clark Thomas & Co. who. jewellers, 51 Hatton garden
Clark Thomas & Son, mast makers, 34 Rotherhithe st
Clark William & Co. *Eagle* brewery & P.H. 52 Wellclose sq
Clark Wm. & Co. cheesemongers, 100 St. George st
Clark Wm. & Co. mnfrs. & imptrs. of ribbons, 33 Wood st. City
Clark Wm. & Son, timber merchts. 1 Southwark bridge road
Clark Abraham, wireworker, 4 Sun tavern fields, St. Geo. Ea
Clark Adam, printer, engraver, &c. 132 Jermyn st. St. James's
Clark Alexander, plumber, 111 Poplar High st
Clark Andrew, dentist, 57 Brook st. Grosvenor square
Clark Andrew, grocer & cheesemong. 70 Friar st. Blackfrs. rd
Clark Andrew, writer & grainer, 39 Rathbone place
Clark Ann (Mrs.), *Rose & Crown* P.H. 19 Commer. rd. Lambeth
Clark Anthony, umbrella, &c. maker, 15 King's rd. Bedford rw
Clark Benj. butcher, 17 Berkley st. Clerkenwell
Clark Benj. printing ink & gen. agt. 16 Kirby st. Hatton garden
Clark Charles, architect, 23A, Clapham road pl. Clapham
Clark Charles, barrister, 2 Middle Temple lane
Clark Charles, haberdasher, 46 Brick lane, St. Luke's
Clark Charles, hairdresser, 5 Edwards place, Hackney road
Clark Charles, grocer, 26 Gt. Barlow street, Marylebone
Clark Chas. merchant, 15 St. Benet's pl. Gracechurch st
Clark Charles, merchant, &c. see Denny, Clark & Co
Clark Chas. printer & wafer ma. 6 Tudor st. Blackfriars
Clark Charles, stationer, 4 Union row, Camberwell road
Clark Charles, timber merchant, 28 Princes st. Stamford st
Clark Chas. Thos. candlemould ma. see Biertumpfel & Clark
Clark Chas. Vane, stock & share agt. 2 Hatton ct. Threadndle. st
Clark Colin, *Star* coffee rooms, 19 Finch lane, Cornhill
Clark Daniel, coffee rooms, 1 Mount row, Davies st
Clark Daniel, paper hanger, 5 Brett's buildings, Cambwll. rd
Clark Edward, haircutter, 3 Queen's head pas. Paternoster rw
Clark Edward, builder, Church st. Stoke Newington
Clark Edward, oilman, 11 Whitmore row, Hoxton
Clark Edward, sculptor, 13 Wigmore st. Cavendish sq
Clark Edward, stockbroker, see Sparkes & Clark
Clark Edward, tailor, 11 Berkley st. Clerkenwell
Clark Edward, upholsterer, 10 Wyndham st. Bryanstone sq
Clark Edward Rawson, wine merch. 2 Clifford st. Bond st
Clark Elizabeth (Mrs.), haberdasher, 136½ Hoxton Old town
Clark Francis, confectioner, 118 Long alley, Finsbury
Clark Frederic, barrister, 3 Church yard court, Temple
Clark Frederick Le Gros, surgeon, 30 Finsbury square
Clark Geo. builder, 110½ Broadwall, Blackfriars
Clark Geo. butcher, 16 King David lane, Shadwell
Clark Geo. carpenter & builder, 14 Hatfield st. Stamford st
Clark Geo. chair & couch ma. 13 Goldsmith's row, Hackney rd
Clark Geo. coach builder, 38 Belvedere pl. Southwark brdg. rd
Clark Geo. coffee rooms, 4 Crown st. Finsbury
Clark Geo. linendraper, 149 Upper Whitecross st. St. Luke's
Clark Geo. picture dealer, 80 Wardour st. Soho
Clark Geo. rag & phial dealer, 47 Brick lane, St. Luke's
Clark George, *Shard Arms* P.H. Bridge pl. Old Kent rd
Clark Geo. solicitor, 28 Finsbury place North
Clark George, tailor, 6 Portland place, Borough road
Clark Geo. who. watch manfr. 7 Radcliffe ter. Goswell road
Clark Geo. Aram, pianoforte tuner, 48 Warwick st. Pimlico
Clark George Wood, *Crown & Anchor* P.H. 1 Rodney buildings, New Kent road
Clark Henry, button, trimming & manch. wa. 60 Aldermanbury
Clark Henry, colonial dealer, 13 Mincing lane
Clark Henry, fishmngr. & fruitr. 32 Aylesbury st. Clerkenwel
Clark Henry, grocer, 29 Great Wild st. Drury lane
Clark Henry, ironmonger, 159 Shoreditch, & 4 Kingsland rd
Clark Henry, lithographer & lithographic printer, 9 Pancras la
Clark Henry livery stables, 50½ Manchester st. Manchester sq
Clark Henry, oil, turpentn. & color mer. 21 Redcross st. Crplgt
Clark Henry Bingley, solicitor, see Burgoynes', Thrupp & Co
Clark Henry Bucknell, coffee rooms, 15 Wellington st. Boro'
Clark Henry Richard, ironmonger, 54 Upper North place
Clark Henry Richard, scale pan maker, 38 Cowcross st
Clark Isaac, butcher, 92 White Lion st. Pentonville
Clark James, baker, 46 Lower Queen st. Rotherhithe
Clark James, *Blackamore's Head* P.H. Dorset pl. Pall mall
Clark James, coal dealer, 100 Fetter lane, Holborn
Clark James, dairyman, 65 Nelson square, Blackfriars road
Clark James, grocer, &c. 41 Milbank st. Westminster
Clark James, *Horse & Dorsers* P.H. 13 Bread st. hill
Clark James, livery stables, George yard, 91 Long acre
Clark James, meat salesman, Leadenhall market
Clark Sir James, bart. physician, 22B, Brook st. Grosvenor sq
Clark James, plumber, 243 Poplar High st
Clark James, rag merchant, 33 Fleet lane, Farringdon st
Clark James, sofa maker, 18 City terrace, City road
Clark James, surgeon, 3 York place, Kingsland road
Clark James, tailor, 62 Berwick st. Soho
Clark James, tailor, 6 Devonshire st. Lisson grove
Clark James, teadealer, 8 Clare st. Clare market
Clark James, teadealer, 4 Crown row, Walworth road
Clark James, wholesale grocer & provision merchant, & shipping & insurance agent, 24 & 25 Billiter st
Clark James Anthony, baker, 424 Strand
Clark James Thomas, tinman & brazier, 1 Limekiln hill
Clark Janet (Mrs.), baker, 19 Jewin st. Cripplegate
Clark Jeremiah, stationer & account bk. ma. 13 Moorgate st
Clark Job, carpenter, 10 Seward st. Goswell st.
Clark John, baker, 5 Finch lane, Cornhill
Clark John, blacksmith, 1 Little Grove st. Lisson grove
Clark John, clerk of the peace for the City of London & Boro' of Southwark, & clerk of the Central Criminal Court, Sessions house, Old bailey

Clark John, clothes & stay manufacturer, Falcon hall, 17 & 18 Silver st. Wood st. & 20 Noble st. Falcon sq
Clark John, coal merchant, 1 Paragon, New Kent road
Clark John, coffee rooms, 43 Dean st. Soho
Clark John, furniture broker, Myrtle cot. Cross st. Islington
Clark John, glass & china dealer, 32 Newington causeway
Clark John, grocer, 8 Ordnance terrace, St. John's wood
Clark John, grocer, 175 Shoreditch High st
Clark John, italian warehouse, 60 Beaumont st. Portland pl
Clark John, jewellery case maker, 3 George st. Adelphi
Clark John, oilman, 90 Red cross st. Borough
Clark John, omnibus proprietor, 5 Eccleston place, Pimlico
Clark John, physician, 12 Beaumont st. Marylebone
Clark John, pork butcher, 10 Regent st. Horseferry road
Clark John, printer, 16 Maryland pl. Gt. Bland st. Dover rd
Clark John, pumpmaker, 10 Temple st. Whitefriars
Clark John, ship & insurance agent, see Denham, Clark & Co
Clark John, ship insu. & custom ho. agent, see Leach & Clark
Clark John, shipowner, 15 Fish st. hill
Clark John, straw hat maker, 15 George st. Blackfriars rd
Clark John, surgical inst. & truss maker, 38 Gt. Windmill st
Clark John, tailor, 153 Tottenham court road
Clark John, tanner, see Hackblocks', Clark & Meek
Clark John, *Three Colts* P.H. Cambridge road, Mile end
Clark John Benj. wine mer. 9 Guildford pl. Kennington la
Clark John Henry, plumber & painter, 3 Eagle st. City road
Clark John Horne, auctioneer & appr. 23 Holles st. Caven. sq
Clark John Joshua, baker, 5 Thornton st. Dockhead
Clark John Wm. bricklayer, 18 Peter st. Bishopsgate
Clark Joseph, *Bedford Arms* P.H. 79 Wapping wall
Clark Joseph, cigar maker, 5 Drury lane
Clark Joseph, clothier, 1 Aldgate
Clark Joseph, colonial broker, 13 Mincing lane
Clark Joseph, cooper, 44 Charles st. St. George's East
Clark Joseph, currier & leatherseller, see Marley & Clark
Clark Joseph, fishing tackle maker, 11 St. John's la. Smithfi
Clark Joseph, library, 6 Gravel lane, Southwark
Clark Joseph, oil & colorman, 23 Wapping wall
Clark Joseph, ship & insur. agt. 21 Cullum st. Fenchurch st
Clark Joseph, tailor, 12 Devonshire st. Queen square
Clark Joseph, teadlr. & grocer, 3 Gt. Chapel st. Westminster
Clark Joseph, timber merchant, 16 Waterloo road
Clark Joseph, turner, 16 Cumberland pl. Newington butts
Clark Joseph Henry, court headdresser, peruke maker & hair cutter, 1 Vigo st. Regent st
Clark Joseph William, pawnbroker, 55 Long acre
Clark Lavinia (Miss), dressmaker, 54 Dorset st. Portman sq
Clark Maria (Miss), millnr. & dress ma. 6 South st. Grosvnr. sq
Clark Maria (Mrs.), tobacconist, 2 Charlotte st. Portland pl
Clark Margaret (Miss), baker, 20 Clarence st. Rotherhithe
Clark Mary A (Mrs.), beershop, Stringer's rw. Lr. rd. Rotherhth
Clark Martha (Mrs.), newsvender, 17 Gt. Moore pl. Lambeth
Clark My. A. (Mrs.), licensed lighterman, Galley quay, Lr. Thames st. & 9 Crutched friars
Clark Mary A. (Mrs.), *Queen's Head* P.H. 51 Amelia st Wlwth. rd
Clark Matilda (Miss), milliner, 47 Skinner st. Snow hill
Clark Matthew John, grocer, 23 Prior pl. East st. Walworth
Clark Michael Robt. dairyman, 98 East st. Manchester sq
Clark Moses, baker, 104 Long acre
Clark Nicolas, tinman & brazier, 119 Praed st. Edgware rd
Clark Pamela (Mrs.), poulterer, 74 High st. Marylebone
Clark Peter, farrier, Cole st. Gt. Dover st
Clark Richard, carpenter, 41 Vauxhall bridge road
Clark Richard, cheesemonger, 2 Spectacle all. Whitechapel
Clark Richard, fruiterer, 125 Church st. Shoreditch
Clark Richd. jun. muffin baker, 55 Marylebone la. Oxford st
Clark Robert, academy, 12 Devonshire st. Queen sq
Clark Robert, coach maker, 1 Henrietta st. Manchester sq
Clark Robert, cowkeeper & dairyman, 7 Spring st. Paddington
Clark Robert, fringe maker, 2 Cranbourne st. Leicester sq
Clark Robert, hairdresser, 10 Finsbury market
Clark Robert, *Marq. of Granby* P.H. 7 Kemp's rw. Pimlico
Clark Robert, *Old Mansion ho.* P.H. 23 York row, Kennigtn. rd
Clark Robert, tailor & woollendraper, 62 Blackfriars road
Clark Robert J. tailor, 10 Upper Cleveland st. Fitzroy sq
Clark Robert, tobacconist, 191 Long lane, Bermondsey
Clark Sally (Mrs.), bootma, 50 Upper North pl. Gray's inn rd
Clark Samuel, carpenter, &c. 2 Little Vine st. Piccadilly
Clark Samuel, fruiterer, 10 High st. Kensington
Clark Samuel, hairdresser, 18 Lit. Chapel st. Westminster
Clark Samuel, *Ram's Head* P.H. Borough market
Clark Samuel, smith & bellhanger, 1 Edward pl. Ball's pond
Clark Samuel, tailor, &c. 2 Fore st. Limehouse
Clark Samuel, tailor, 3 Southampton st. Fitzroy square
Clark Samuel Bartholomew, upholsterer, 14B, Dean st. Soho
Clark Stephen, butcher, 16 Salmon lane, Limehouse
Clark Stephen, straw bont. presr. 61 Stanhope st. Clare mkt
Clark Susannah (Mrs.), locksmith, 28 Sherrard st. Golden sq
Clark Thomas, artesian well engineer, 2 Finsbury circus
Clark Thomas, barometer maker, 20 Kirby st. Hatton garden
Clark Thos. boot & shoe maker, 30 Old Change
Clark Thos. bricklayer, 24 Wells mews, Wells st. Oxford st
Clark Thos. *Bricklayers' Arms* P.H. 31 North st. Manchstr. sq
Clark Thos. butcher, 18 Nassau pl. Commercial rd. East
Clark Thos. carver & gilder & picture dealer, 20 Portman place, Edgware road, & 90 Strand
Clark Thos. chandler's shop, Mill row, Kingsland
Clark Thos. cheesemonger, 5 Salisbury st. Lisson grove
Clark Thos. chemist, 18 Barossa ter. Cambridge road
Clark Thos. clothwrkrs.' porter, Customho. quay, Lr. Thams. st
Clark Thos. fruiterer, 33 Rahere st. Goswell road
Clark Thos. furniture broker, 17 Gt. Moore pl. Lambeth
Clark Thos. grindery dealer, 2 Well st. Mile end new town
Clark Thos. ironmonger, 3 Bridge ho. pl. Newington causeway
Clark Thos. locksmith, 15 Rose & Crown court, Finsbury
Clark Thos. merchant, &c. see Denny, Clark & Co
Clark Thos. painter & glazier, 53 Northampton st. Clerkenwell
Clark Thos. projecting letter agt. see Hughes & Clark
Clark Thos. smith & farrier, 4 Cross st. Islington
Clark Thos. solicitor, 3 Dean's court, Doctors' commons
Clark Thos. tailor, Bow, Middlesex
Clark Thos. turner, 119 Old st. St. Luke's
Clark Thomas, wheelwright, 7 Sumner st. Bridge st. Southwark
Clark Thos. Joseph, *Green Lattice* P.H. 5 Billingsgate
Clark Thos. S. painter & glazier, Edward place, Ball's pond
Clark Wm. *Artichoke* P.H. 13 White Hart st. Drury lane
Clark Wm. baker, 55 Bell st. Edgware road
Clark Wm. baker, Hollywood, Lit. Chelsea (North side)
Clark Wm. baker, 17 Pelham road, Brompton
Clark Wm. baker, 33 Praed st. Paddington
Clark Wm. baker, 110 Wapping
Clark Wm. beer retailer, 65 Castle st. East, Oxford st
Clark Wm. beer retailer, 11 Cobham row, Clerkenwell
Clark Wm. bookbinder & embosser, see Westleys' & Clark
Clark Wm. bookseller, 170½ Bishopsgate without
Clark Wm. bootmaker, 133 Shadwell High st
Clark Wm. boot & shoe maker, 25 Union st. Clarendon square
Clark Wm. bricklayer, 29 King st. New North road
Clark Wm. bricklayer, 17 Queen st. Lower road, Islington
Clark Wm. *Buffalo* P.H. Brett's buildings, Finsbury
Clark Wm. builder & slate merchant, 37 Commercial road, Lambeth, & Cambridge heath road, Mile end
Clark Wm. cheesemonger, 20 Museum st. Bloomsbury
Clark Wm. corndealer & baker, Stratford
Clark Wm. dining rooms, 114 Edgware road
Clark Wm. lamp contractor, 4 Catherine st. Pimlico
Clark Wm. lead & color merchant, 27 Crosby hall chambers
Clark Wm. linendraper, 67 Castle st. Southwark
Clark Wm. marine store dealer, 16 Union st. Kingsland road
Clark Wm. *Nunny Castle* P.H. 37 Sun st. Bishopsgate
Clark Wm. nursery seedsmn. & florist, 25 Bishopsgat. within
Clark Wm. oil & color manfr. & hop mer. 74 St. John st. Smithfld
Clark Wm. picture dealer, 81 Dean st. Soho
Clark Wm. scale maker, 29 Great Sutton st. Clerkenwell
Clark Wm. skein silk dyer, see House & Clark
Clark Wm. straw hat maker, 21 Gt. Guildford st. Borough
Clark Wm. tailor, 25 Gt. Pulteney st. Golden sq
Clark Wm. tyne bottle warehouse, see Coulthard & Clark
Clark Wm. watchmaker, 5 Hope cottages, Wandsworth rd
Clark Wm. sen, teadealer, 116 Lambeth Lower marsh
Clark Wm. Cosmo, teacher of languages, 4 Brompton place
Clark Wm. Henry, bookseller & stationer, 6 Charing cross
Clark Wm. Lewis, baker & corn dealer, 62 Cotton st. Poplar
Clark Wm. Mark, machine printer, 10 Red Lion court, Fleet st
Clark Wm. Mark, bookseller & publisher, 17 Warwick lane
Clark Wm. Thomas, tea urn manufacturer, see Gibbs & Clark
Clarke & Addison, ready made linen wareho. 50 Houndsditch
Clarke & Barlow, wine merchts. 4 Lit. Bridge st. Blackfriars
Clarke & Barnes, plasterers, 15 Finch lane, Cornhill
Clarke & Bedford, bookbinders, 61 Frith st. Soho
Clarke & Dewey, foreign & british lace wareho. 2 Ludgate st
Clarke & Eaton, flour wharf, Maidstone wf. Queenhithe
Clarke Fredk. & Co. paper stainrs. 42 Poultry, & 348 Oxford st
Clarke, Fynmore, Fladgate & Clarke, solrs. to Hungerford Market Co. & to London & Westmr. Steam boat Co. & to the Royal Agricultural Society of England, 43 Craven st. Strand
Clarke & Gosling, solicitors, 24 Austinfriars
Clarke & Hedges, cabinet maks. 4 Spann's bldgs. St. Pancras
Clarke Henry Green & Co. publishers, 66 Old Bailey
Clarke Hyde & Co. merchants, 9 St. Michael's alley, Cornhill
Clarke James & Co. warehousemen, 3 Bow lane, Cheapside

ClarkeJane&Son, fishmongers, 11Orange row, Kennington rd
Clarke, Medcalf & Gray, solicitors, 20 Lincoln's Inn fields
Clarke & Musson, haberdashers, 29Hedge rw. High st. Islingtn
Clarke & Page, provn. brok. & agts. 8 Jeffrey's sq. St. Mary axe
Clarke Rd. E. & Son, paperstainers, 3 Chenies st. Bedford sq
Clarke Robert & Son, furriers, 6 Finsbury square
Clarke & Rowe, who. teadealers, 7 Arthur st. west, London br
Clarke Thomas J. & Edwd. S. solicitors, Bishopsgate churchyd
Clarke & Walden, floor cloth manufrs. 2 Neate st. OldKent rd
Clarke & Weemys, bookbinds. 13 Charles st. Hatton garden
Clarke Wm. & Son, watch manfrs. 21 Thavies inn, Holborn
Clarke Wm. & Sons, watch manufacturers, 8 Goswell road
Clarke Anthony Wm. surgeon, 72 Queen st. Cheapside
Clarke Arthur, lodging house, 4 Leigh st. Red Lion sq
Clarke Benjamin, bricklayer, 2 Robinson's row, Kingsland
Clarke Benjamin, jun. surgeon, Mare st. Hackney
Clarke Benjamin, sen. chemist & druggist, Mare st. Hackney
Clarke Charles, baker, Manor place, Holloway
Clarke Charles, brewer, 37 Little Sutton st. Clerkenwell
Clarke Chas. *Chester Arms* P.H. 115 Albany st. Regent's pk
Clarke Charles, grocer, 67 Walnut Tree walk, Lambeth
Clarke Charles, linendraper, 10 Great Dover st
Clarke Charles, livery stables, see Turner & Clarke
Clarke Charles Edward, surgeon, 10 Lower Grosvenor place
Clarke Charles Henry, basket maker, rod & rush dealer, 23 New st. & 14 Rose alley, Bishopgate
Clarke Christopher, linendraper, 13 Goswell road
Clarke Danl. math. inst. case ma. 27 Glo'ster st. John st. rd
Clarke David, *Coach & Horses* P.H. Lit. Ormond yd. Queen sq
Clarke David R. merchant, 35 Old Broad st
Clarke Edward, barrister, 2 Pump court, Temple
Clarke Edward, coal merchant, 2 Artillery ter. Westminster
Clarke Edward, coppersmith, brazier, &c. 23 Old st. St. Lukes
Clarke Edward, livery stables, Ebury mews, Chester square
Clarke Edward, *Pheasant* P. H. 35 Stangate, Lambeth
Clarke Edward, shoemaker, 12 Barrett's ct. Oxford st
Clarke Edward, solicitor, 5 Featherston buildings, Holborn
Clarke Edward, solicitor, see Richards, Clarke & Clarke
Clarke Edward M. optician, machinist & engineer, 428 Strand & Rodney iron works, Bolingbrooke gardens, Battersea
Clarke Edwd. W. boot & shoema. 12 Southampton rw. Russell sq
Clarke Elizabeth (Mrs.), linendraper, 9 London road, Sthwk
Clarke Francis, baker, 4 Kennington pl. Up. Kennington lane
Clarke Francis, coachmaker, see Tilbury, Son & Clarke
Clarke Francis, surgeon, 9 Marylebone lane, Oxford st
Clarke Francis, tailor, 7 Praed st. Paddington
Clarke Frederick, dentist, 61 Grosvenor st. New Bond st
Clarke Frederick, dining rooms, 30 Chancery lane
Clarke Frederick, paper stainer & decorator, 348 Oxford st
Clarke Frederick C. solicitor, see Richards, Clarke & Clarke
Clarke George, carpenter, 3 Felix st. Hackney road
Clarke George, carver, 17 Wells mews, Wells st. Oxford st
Clarke George, *King's Head* P.H. 48 Gerrard st. Soho
Clarke George, poulterer & game dealer, 50 Albany st
Clarke Geo. *Somers Arms* P.H. 69 Wilsted st. Somers town
Clarke George Adolphus, hosier, glover, &c 98 Strand
Clarke Geo. J. *Grd. Surrey Canal* P.H. Peckhamft. pth. O.K. rd
Clarke Geo. Miller, tallow chndlr. 55 Albany st. Regent's pk
Clarke Geo. Rich. teadealer & grocer, 176 Whitechapel rd
Clarke Geo. Rochfort, specl. pldr. 1 Mitre ct. bldgs. Temple
Clarke Giles, solicitor, Saddlers' hall, 143 Cheapside
Clarke Harriet L. (Miss), ladies' school, 25 Clarendon sq. Pntnv
Clarke Henry, brewer, 1 Honduras st. St. Luke's
Clarke Henry, cabinet mkr. 1 Church row, Bethnal gr. rd
Clarke Henry, linendraper, 52 New Bond st
Clarke Henry, lodging house, 33 Surrey st. Strand
Clarke Henry, seedsman, 39 King st. Covent garden
Clarke Henry, solicitor, 13 George st. Mansion house
Clarke Henry, tailor, 96 Praed st. Paddington
Clarke Hen. B. attorney, Chichester chambs. 22 Chancery la
Clarke Herbert, imp. french kid & glove ma. 4½ Bread st. Chpsi
Clarke Hyde, civil engineer, 9 St. Michaels alley, City
Clarke Isaac, architect, &c. 3 Charlotte row, Mansion house
Clarke Jacob Augustus, surgeon, 11 Warwick st. Belgrave rd
Clarke James, carpenter & build. 1 Rawstorne st. Brompton
Clarke James, carver, gilder & looking gl. maker, 163 Drury la
Clarke James, chandler's shop, 111 Green st. Bethnal green
Clarke James, coffee rooms, 13 Park pl. Kennington cross
Clarke James, confectioner, 20 London road, Southwark
ClarkeJames, duplex roller ma. &c. 34 Bartholomew ter. Kg. sq
Clarke James, oilman, 7 Folly, Dockhead, Bermondsey
Clarke James, stock broker, 3 Bartholomew lane
Clarke James, straw bonnet maker, 25 Buckingham st. Strand
Clarke James Blucher, cattle salesman, 17 West Smithfield
Clarke James Fernandez, surgeon, 23 Gerrard st. Soho
Clarke James Langton, barrister, 35 Southampton buildings
Clarke James Z. carriage clock, &c. ma. 4 Charles st. City rd
Clarke Jane (Miss), lace, fan & india shawl wa. 154 Regent st
Clarke Jeremiah, *Barleymow* P.H. 12 Romney ter. Westmr
Clarke Job, chandler's shop, Church st. Stoke Newington
Clarke Job Guy, jeweller & silversmith, 15 King Wm. st. City
Clarke John, bread & biscuit maker, Kilburn
Clarke John, butcher, 8 Upper area, Hungerford market
Clarke John, carpet manufacturer, worsted & yarn spinner & dyer, 13 Ropemakers' st.; 4 White st. Finsbury; manufactory, Market Harborough & Burton mills
Clarke John, currier, 36 Hereford st. Lisson grove
Clarke John, enameller, 8 Orchard st. St. Luke's
Clarke John, fruiterer, 29 Bermondsey New road
Clarke John, grocer, 24 New road, St. George's east
Clarke John, grocer, 15 Turnmill st. Clerkenwell
Clarke John, grocer, 180 Union st. Borough High st
Clarke John, *Horse Shoe inn* P.H. 7 Goswell st
Clarke John, library, 2 Harleyford st. Kennington common
Clarke John, painter & glazier, 6 Gt. Castle st. Regent st
Clarke John, printer, 55 Old Bailey
Clarke John, professor of music, 59 Bayham st. Pancras rd
Clarke John, boys' school, 6 Ladbroke place, Notting hill
Clarke John, spice merchant, 1 Little Distaff lane
Clarke John Chorley, *Falcon* P.H. 8 Falcon sq. Aldersgate
Clarke John Jeffkins, stockbroker, see Linton & Clarke
Clarke John Say, surgeon, 16 Brunswick pl. Barnsbury rd
Clarke John Thomas, watchmaker, 17 Eagle st. City road
Clarke Jonathan, ship bisc. baker, 5 Phœnix pl. Ratcliff crs
Clarke Joseph, architect, 1 Lincoln's inn fields
Clarke Joseph, butcher, 64 Strutton ground
Clarke Joseph, *Golden Horse* P.H. 108 Aldersgate st
Clarke Joseph, tailor, 109 Shoe lane, Fleet st
Clarke Joseph, turner, 21 Duck lane, Wardour st. Soho
Clarke Joseph Charles, accountant, 11 Goswell road
Clarke Joseph Samuel, surgeon, 50 Sloane st. Knightsbridge
Clarke Joshua, fruiterer, 25 Marylebone lane, Oxford st
Clarke Justinian B. *D. of Clarence* P.H. 1 Clarence pl. Camb. rd
Clarke Lavinia (Miss), dressmaker, 31 George st. Portman sq
Clarke Leonard, fruit salesman, Covent garden fruit market
Clarke Maria (Mrs.), ging. beer ma. 42 Fredk. st. Hmpsted. rd
Clarke Martin, dyer & scourer, 42 Tottenham st. Totnm. ct. rd
Clarke Mary (Mrs.), straw bonnet wa. 63 Castle st. Le'ster sq
Clarke Mary (Miss), straw hat ma. 56 Redcross st. Cripplgte
Clarke Nathaniel, ham & beef shop, 9 Up. Penton st. Pntvle
Clarke Nathaniel Richard, S.L. barrister, 5 Brick ct. Temple
Clarke Richard, coachmaker, 149 Southwark bridge road
Clarke Robert, china warehouse, 33 Edgware road
Clarke Robert, farrier, Great Scotland yard
Clarke Robert, surgeon dentist, 7 Jermyn st. St. James's
Clarke Rt. Bloomfield, plumber, 13 Gower st. North, New rd
Clarke Samuel, bookseller & publisher, 13 Pall mall east
Clarke Samuel, hairdresser, 2 Southampton st. Camberwell
Clarke Sarah (Mrs.), hotpresser, 206 Upper Whitecross st
Clarke Stephen, meat salesman, 49 Aldgate High st
Clarke Theophilus, honiton lace mfr. 18A, Margaret sq. Cav. sq
Clarke Susk. (Mrs.), *Adelaide* P.H. 2 Wellingtn. pl. Lrvpl. rd
Clarke Thos. joiner, 1 Regent place, Horseferry road
Clarke Thos. grocer, 84 Devonshire st. Lisson grove
Clarke Thos. jeweller, 2 Crown st. Finsbury
Clarke Thos. paperstainer & decorator, 60 High Holborn
Clarke Thomas, surgeon, 16 Charles st. Westbourne terrace
Clarke Thos. Sydenham, barrister, 6 New sq. Lincoln's inn
Clarke Wm. bookseller & newsman, 21 Finch lane, Cornhill
Clarke Wm. bricklayer & slater, 8 White Hart st. Kennington
Clarke Wm. cattle salesman, 60 West Smithfield
Clarke Wm. coal agnt. Claycross & Snibston whf. Caledonian rd
Clarke Wm. coal merchant, Milford wharf, Milford la. Strand
Clarke Wm. *Cock* P.H. Lower Kennington green
Clarke Wm. dairy, 2 Edward st. Kennington cross
Clarke Wm. dining rooms, 143 Fetter lane, Fleet st
Clarke Wm. *Duke of Glo'ster* P.H. 8 Glo'ster t. New rd. Coml. rd
Clarke Wm. dyer & scourer, 92 John st. Fitzroy sq
Clarke Wm. foreign & english bookslr. & newsmn. 21 Finch la
Clarke Wm. fruit salesman, Covent garden fruit market
Clarke Wm. glass & lead merchant, 50 High st. St. Giles's
Clarke Wm. law stationer, 5 Hemlock court, Carey st
Clarke Wm. manager of Claycross & Snibston coal wharf, Caledonian road, Pentonville
Clarke Wm. merchant, 33 Bloomsbury square
Clarke Wm. oil & colorman, 216 Upper Whitecross st
Clarke Wm. solicitor, 54 Chancery lane
Clarke Wm. stock & share broker, 7 Bank chmbrs. Lothbury
Clarke Wm. tailor, 3 Patriot row, Cambridge road
Clarke Wm. tailor, 37 Seymour place, Bryanstone square
Clarke Wm. woollendraper, see Evans & Clarke
Clarke Wm. Henry, beer shop, 152 Blackfriars road

Clarke Wm. Hislop, barrister, 4 New square, Lincoln's inn
Clarke Wm. Tredway, solicitor, 30 Gt. James st. Bedford row
Clarkson & Sharpe, grocers & italian warehouse, 171 Strand
Clarkson & Son, proctors & notaries, 25 Gt. Carter la. Doc. com
Clarkson Thomas & Co. furniture printers & manufacturers to the Queen, 17 Coventry st. Haymarket
Clarkson Wm. & Co. tea dealers, 11 Black Prince rw. Walwh. rd
Clarkson Catherine (Mrs.) grocer, 1 Marshall st. Golden sq
Clarkson Charles, tallowchandler, 9 Avery rw. Grosvenor st
Clarkson Christr. tailor, 28 Circus st. New rd. Marylebone
Clarkson Francis, lodging ho. 37 Halfmoon st. Piccadilly
Clarkson Geo. fruiterer, 48 Penton st. Pentonville
Clarkson Mary (Mrs.), turnery wareh. 4 Postern rw. Towerhill
Clarkson Samuel, tailor, &c. 42 Robert st. Hoxton
Clarkson Thos. jun. gold beater, 5 Middle New st. Fetter la
Clarkson Thos. Chas. tanner, see Hacker & Clarkson
Clarkson Wm. barrister, 1 Paper buildings, Temple
Clarkson Wm. Geering, proctor, 7 Bell yd. Doctors' commons
Clary Mary A. (Mrs.), *Prince of Wales* P.H. 7 North st. Pntvlle
Clary Wm. skein cotton dyer, 13 New inn yard, Shoreditch
Claudet & Houghton, glass shade, window glass & painted glass warehouse, 89 High Holborn
Claughton Henry, appraiser, 41 Church st. Rotherhithe
Claus William, cabinet maker, 5 Exeter st. Strand
Claussen Wm. Hen. engraver & printer, 60 Long la. Bermondy
Clashofska Davis, trimming manf. 16 Fort st. Spitalfields
Clavey Henry, carpenter, Denmark hill, Camberwell
Clavey Wm. Robt. surg. &c. 12 Lit. Queen st. Linc. inn flds
Claxton & Prothero, inst. ma. 27 Harrington st. nth. Hampstd. rd
Claxton Robert & Richard, cotton mfrs. George sq. Hoxton
Claxton Abraham, cabinet maker, 118 Britannia st. City rd
Claxton Elizabeth (Mrs.), boot & shoe maker, 38 Hampstead rd
Claxton John, coal merchant, see Wells & Claxton
Claxton John, *Red Lion* P.H. 19 Robert st. Oxford st
Claxton John, drug broker, see Brooks & Claxton
Claxton Marshall, artist, 6 Southampton st. Fitzroy sq
Claxton Richard, tailor, 10 Nelson terrace, City road
Claxton Wm. skein silk dyer, 5 Deal st. Mile end New town
Clay & Gillman, merchants & insu. agents, 28 Bucklersbury
Clay & Newman, droitwitch salt manuf. 86 Lower Thames st; Bridge wharf, 35 City road basin, & Dundee wf. 338 Wapping
Clay Richd. & Co. mer. 1 Winchester bldgs. Gt. Winchester st
Clay, Smith & Co. printers, 7 East Harding st. Gough sq
Clay Wm. & Son, woollen & manchr. warehmn. 140 Cheapside
Clay George, fancy hair worker, 88 Chapel st. Pentonville, & 16 St. John's sq. Clerkenwell
Clay George, woollendraper, see Woollett, Rowe & Clay
Clay George, jun. *Cock* P.H. 76 Snow hill
Clay Henry, manufacturer of paper tea trays to the Queen & the royal family, 17 & 18 King st. Covent garden
Clay Richard, printer, 7 & 8 Bread st. hill, City
Clay Robert R. surgeon, Springfield place, Wandsworth rd
Clay Samuel, tailor & hatter, High st. Stoke Newington
Clay Thomas, dining rooms, 148 Brick lane, Spitalfields
Clay Thomas, staymaker, 29 Edward st. Blackfriars rd
Clay Wm. butcher, 26 Newport court, Newport market
Clay Wm. painter & glazier, 32 Exeter st. Sloane st
Clay Wm. paper stainer, 10½ Devonshire ter. Globe rd. Mile e
Clay Wm. Charles Spencer, wine mercht. see Barrett & Clay
Clayard Robert, livery stables, 25 Lisle st. Leicester square
Clayden Henry, *Grapes* P.H. 40 Houndsditch
Clayden Thos. jun. bricklayer, Victoria pl. Coml. rd. Limeho
Claydon Charles Broadbelt, barrister, 2 Hare court, Temple
Clayfield Wm. tin plate worker, 7 Short's gardens, Drury la
Clayson John, *Talbot hotel*, 17 Montpelier st. Brompton
Clayton & Cookson, solicitors, 6 New sq. Lincoln's inn
Clayton James & O. surgeons, 3 Percy st. Tottenham ct. rd
Clayton Jsph. & Richd. *Princess of Wales* P.H. 46 London rd
Clayton & Square, attorneys, 3 Hare court, Temple
Clayton William & Co. who. perfumers, fine soap mkrs. & importers of foreign essences, eau de cologne, &c. 72 Watling st
Clayton Charles, fine soap manufacturer, wholesale & export & importer of perfumery, 72 Little Britain
Clayton Chas. saw & tool maker 22 Snow'sfields, Bermondsey
Clayton Edward, *Coach & Horses* P.H. 118 Edgware road
Clayton Edward, tailor, 191 Wellington ter. Waterloo road
Clayton George Hen. baker, 11 Copenhagen st. Pentonville
Clayton Henry, oil & colorman, 21 Upper Park place, Regent's park road
Clayton Henry, painter, 1 Milton st. Dorset square
Clayton Henry, patentee of the pipe, tile & brick machines, 21 Upper Park place, Dorset square
Clayton James, *Sutton Arms* P.H. Edwards ter. Caledonian rd
Clayton John, commsn. agt. & warehsmn. 1 Crownct. Cheapside
Clayton John, cooper, 11 Whitehart pl. Kennington lane
Clayton John, butcher, 47 Great Marylebone st
Clayton John, dining rooms, 113 Long alley, Finsbury
Clayton John, *Feathers* P.H. Deptford bridge
Clayton John, sec. of *Equitable Rev.* 10 Lancaster pl. Strand
Clayton John, solicitor, 10 Lancaster pl. Waterloo bridge
Clayton John, jun. architect, 38 Elizabeth st. Eaton square
Clayton Joseph, newspaper agent, 320 Strand
Clayton Joseph, printer, see Palmer & Clayton
Clayton Joseph, watchmaker, 64 Westmoreland pl. City rd
Clayton Mary A. (Mrs.), straw ma. 13 Alderson's blds. City rd
Clayton Robert, sen. manufacturer of blacking, inks & chemical lustre fluid & harness polish, congreves, fusees, &c. &c. 4½ Lower Northampton st. Clerkenwell
Clayton Robert, cheesemonger, 16 Langley pl. Comml. rd. ea
Clayton Thomas, leghorn hat press. 13 Fleur de lis st. Spitalfi
Clayton Thomas, coffee & chophouse, 236 Shoreditch
Clayton Wm. carver & gilder, 4 High st. Newington butts
Clayton Wm. coffee rooms, 2 Orange st. Bloomsbury
Clayton Wm. grocer, &c. 39 Lower Queen st. Rotherhithe
Clayton Wm. hairdresser, 2 St. George's ter. Borough road
Clayton Wm. linendr. & straw bonnet fctr. 27 Whitechapel rd
Clayton Wm. lodging house keeper, 18 Sherrard st. Golden sq
Clayton Wm. tallowchandler, 39 Langley pl. Commercial rd
Clayton Wm. wholesale perfumer, 72 Watling st. Cheapside
Clayworth Joseph, poulterer, 1 Ship tav. pas. Leadenh. mrkt
Clayworth Robert, poulterer, 168 Whitechapel road
Cleare Chas. lace & baby linen wareho. 48 Blackman st. Boro'
Cleare Samuel, boot & shoe maker, 16 Gwynn's pl. Hackney rd
Cleare William, boot & shoemaker, 3 Cannon st. St. Geo. eas
Clearson Charles, oil & italian wareho. 82 Leadenhall st
Cleary John, grocer, 55 New Church st. Lisson grove
Cleasby Anthony, barrister, 3 north, King's bench walk, Tmpl
Cleasby Edward, wine & spirit merchant, 61 Edgware road
Cleaton Edward, welch flannel manfr. 37 Gresham st. City, & at Llanidloes, Montgomeryshire
Cleaton Jane (Miss), lace & muslin wa. 161 Tottenham ct. rd
Cleave John, publisher & bookseller, 1 Shoe lane, Fleet st
Cleave Wm. timber & coal mer. 9½ Gt. Smith st. Westminster
Cleaveland & Holmes, *Craven's Head* P.H. 98 Drury lane
Cleaver Fred. S. who. perfum. & soap ma. 18 Red Lion sq
Cleaver Richard, carman, 17 Barnham st. Tooley st
Cleaver Samuel, barometer maker, 30 Theobald's road
Cleaver Saml. roman cement manfr. 3 Belgrave ter. Pimlico
Cleaver Wm. coffee rooms, 75 Seymour st. Euston sq
Cleaver Wm. Budd, woollen fac. & warehmn. 17 Lawrence lane
Cleaver Wm. Jones, bookseller & publ. 80 Baker st. Portmn. sq
Clee Wm. furniture broker, 24 Cleveland st. Fitzroy sq
Cleets William, gold & silver beater, 42 Drury lane
Cleeve George, grocer, 107 Junction terrace, Edgware road
Cleeves James, silk trimming mnf. 52 Sclater st. Bethnal grn
Cleeves John, teadealer, 11 John's row, St. Luke's
Cleeves John, trmng. mnfr. 20 Weymouth terr. Hackney rd
Clegg James & Co. merchants, 76 Coleman st
Clegg Edmund, merchant, 76 Coleman st. City
Clegg George, butcher, 12 Windmill st. Tottenham ct. rd
Clegg John, ostrich feather manufacturer, 20 Noel st. Soho
Clegg Joseph, *Harp tavern*, 19 Jermyn st. St. James's
Clegg Samuel, civil engineer, 16 Sidmouth st. Gray's inn rd
Clegg William, bootmaker, 3 Edward st. Blackfriars road
Clegg Wm. grocer & cheesemonger, 14 Salmon la. Limehouse
Cleghorn & Dunbar, hemp & flax merchants, 8 Billiter st
Cleghorn Thos. & Co. matting material dealers, 8 Billiter st
Cleggett George M. *Rose & Crown* P.H. 9 Ship tavern psge
Cleghorn Elizth. (Mrs.), leather cutter, Stratford broadway
Cleghorn Hen. enameller & dial plate ma. 42 King st. Clkw
Cleghorn John, engraver, 4 Charlton place, Islington green
Cleghorn Robert, crucible, charcoal blacking, coal dust & ink manufacturer, Weaver's lane, Tooley st
Cleghorn William, saddler, 5 Type st. Finsbury
Cleland Allan, surgeon, 118 Cock hill, Ratcliff
Cleland James, *Star & Garter* P.H. 33 St. Martin's lane
Clemence Edward, shoe warehouse, 21 Wilmot st. Russell sq
Clemence John, carpenter & builder, 6 Villiers st. Strand
Clemence John, newsvender, 29 City terrace, City road
Clemence Mark, lodging house, 36 Craven st. Strand
Clemence William, carpenter, 31 Villiers st. Strand
Clemens Francis, tailor, 6 Wych st. Strand
Clement's inn, 259 Strand
Clement Geo. tan dlr. & carman, 12 Russell st. Bermondsey st
Clement Henrietta (Mrs.), school, 3 Brunswick pl. Islington
Clement Henry Geo. eating house keeper, 29 Paddington st
Clement Henry George, ham & beef shop, 41 Aldersgate st
Clement John Turner, actuary, *Licensed Victuallers' & General Fire & Life Assurance Co.* 444 West Strand
Clement Wm. pork butcher, 11 Wade's place, Hackneyrd
Clements John & Wm. carpenters, 1 Barnet st. Hackney rd
Clements Edward, ham & tongue dealer, 165 Blackfriars rd

Clements Francis, bootma. 43 Baldwin's gardens, Leather la
Clements Francis W. boot&shoe ma. 17A, Aylesbury st. Clknwl
Clements George, coal mercht. 12 Took's ct. Chancery lane
Clements Hannah (Miss), milliner, 33 Up. King st. Bloomsby
Clements James, zinc workr. & brazr. 42 East st. Walworthrd
Clements John, hairdresser, Battersea square
ClementsJohn, who. bookseller, 21&22LitPulteneyst. Gldn. sq
Clements John Stphn. fruiterer, 16 Hertford rd. Kingsland
Clements John Thomas, butcher, Deptford broadway
Clements Joseph, jeweller & silversmith, 214 Oxford st
Clements Robert, corndealer, 111 Church st. Shoreditch
Clements Robert G. oilman, 93 Church st. Shoreditch
Clements Sobieski (Mrs), potato saleswoman, 45 Lambeth Lower marsh
Clements Thos. grocer&chsmngr. 32Lit. Guilfordst. Brnswk sq
ClementsThomasPackard, linendrap. 32 Judd st. Brunswk. sq
Clements Wm carpenter, see Clements John & William
Clements Wm. stationer, printer, &gum ticket manufacturer, 102 Wood street, Cheapside, & 1 Jewin crescent
Clementson John, cattle salesman, 41 West Smithfield
Clementson Joseph, silver caster, 53 Jewin st. Cripplegate
Clementson Richard, blackwell hall factor, 12 Coleman st
Clementson Wm. newsman & stationer, 122 Lambeth walk
Clemmans Geo. Thos. appraiser&house agent, 36 Hackneyrd
Clemmans James John, auctioneer, surveyor, appraiser, upholsterer & undertaker, 17, 18 & 21 Holywell row, Worship st. Finsbury
Clemmens James, butcher, 17 Green st. Bethnal green
Clemments George, tailor, 10 Little Sutton st. Clerkenwell
Clemmitt John, general carrying & shipping agent, Clemmitt's inn, GreenArbour court, Old Bailey; waggon, coach & errand cart office, corner of Skinner st. & Old Bailey
Clemow Francis, *Anderton's hotel & coffee ho.* 164 Fleet st
Clemow Robert, hosier & outfitter, 80 King William st. City
Clench James, bone&manure dlr. 8 Page's walk, Bermondsey
Clench Thomas, *Old Cock* P.H. 1 Market st. St. James's
Clendinning John, physician, 16 Wimpole st. Cavendish sq
Clendinning Robert, grocer, 12 Chester terrace, Eaton sq
Clendon Chitty, surgeon dentist, 15 Conduit st. Regent st
Clennell John Edward, boy's school, Mare st. Hackney
Cleobury Thomas Mortimer, solicitor, 30 Sackville st
Clephan James, architect, 18 Warwick st. Charing cross
Clerc Peter, watch case & dial maker, see Gilling & Clerc
Clerc Samuel, *Dunston Arms* P.H. 10 East road, City rd
Clergy MutualAssuranceSo.(Wm.Webb, sec.) 41 Parliamtst
Clergy Orphan School, St John's wood road
Clergy Orphan Society (Hen. Stretton, col.), 77, Gt. Queenst
Clerical Club & Ecclesiastical Registry Office (Richard Hayes, sec. & manager), 13 Henrietta st. Covent garden
Clerical, Medical & General Life Assurance Society (Geo. Hen. Pinckard, act.), 78 Gt. Russell st. Bloomsbury, see page 2018
Clerical Registry(JohnWilkes, director), 28 Surrey st. Strand
Clerk of Assize & Associate Office, Judges' chambers, Rolls garden, Serjeants' inn; hours 11 to 2 & 6 to 8
Clerk of the Peace Middlesex, Sessions house, Clerkenwell; hours 10 to 3 & 5 to 8
Clerk of the Peace (City) Office, Sessions house, Old bailey; hours 10 to 5
Clerk of the Peace for Surrey, 1 Nth. st. Lambeth; hrs. 10to4
Clerk of the Peace for Tower Liberty, 36 Wellclose square; hours 10 to 3; during sessions 11 to 3
Clerk of the Peace for Westminster (Deputy), 17 Carlisle st. Soho; hours 9 to 6.
Clerks of the House of Commons Office, 43 Parliament st
Clerks of Works Society (Chas. Jas. Minet, sec.), 19½ Exeter hall, Strand
Clerk John & Co. lithographers, 202 High Holborn
Clerk John, barrister, 9 King's Bench walk, Temple
Clerk Susan (Mrs.), straw hat m. 56 Redcross st. Cripplegte
ClerkeGeo. Jas. who. watchma. 3 Cherrytree ct. Aldersgate st
Clerkenwell Police Court, Bagnigge wells road; hours 10 to 5
Cleveland & Homes, slaughtermen, 52Marshall st. Golden sq
Cleveland Henry, seal engraver, 42 St John's sq. Clerkenwell
Cleveland Richard, tripe dresser, 14 Silver st. Golden sq
Cleveland Robert, seal engraver, 7 Berkeley st. Clerkenwell
Cleveland Samuel, oil & colorman, 1 Queen st. Chelsea
Cleveland Wm. merchant, see Houghtons, Cleveland & Co
Clever Chas. stationer&newsagt. 18 Commercial rd. Lambeth
Cleversley Wm. floor cloth mf. Cumberland pl. Old Kent rd
Cleverly John, haberdasher, 10 Russell pl. Old Kent rd
Clewett Emma (Miss), berlin wool repository, 5 Adelaide st. West Strand, & 12 Lowther Arcade
Clewett Felix, *Golden Cross tap* P.H. Duncannon st. Cha. cr
Clewley Daniel, dairyman, 3 Buckingham st. Strand
Clibbens Thomas, *Stuart Arms* P.H. 27 Critchill pl. Hoxton
Clies Geo. flour dressing machine m. 2½ Buross st. Coml. rd
Cliff & Husler, stone &coal merchants(John Trickett, agent), nr. the Ferry, Isle of Dogs, Millwall
Cliff Chas. copper plate printer, 7 Guildford st. East, Spaflds
Cliff Jane (Miss), butcher, 4 Sparrow corner, Minories
Clifford Augustin & John, masons, 24 York pl. Fulham rd
Clifford's inn, 186 Fleet st
Clifford Chas. plumber & glazier, 12 Baldwin st. St. Luke's
Clifford Chas. Hen. *Camden Head* P.H. 48 High st. Camden tn
Clifford Chas. Hy. *Crooked Billet* P.H. 20 King David la. Shadl
Clifford Edward, teadealer, 82 Grosvenor st. Grosvenor sq
Clifford Geo. *Sash & Cocoa Tree* P.H. 4 Whitecross pl. Finsby
Clifford James, butcher, 29 Great Marylebone st
Clifford James, fruiterer & greengrocer, 11 Lambeth walk
Clifford John, merchant, 58 Lombard st
Clifford John Mizelbrook, plumber, 6 Glo'ster pl. Walw. com
Clifford John Mizelbrook, plumber, 2 Portland tr. Walw. com
Clifford Thomas, poulterer, 15 John st. Oxford st
Clifford Thos. J. *Marq. of Granby* P.H. 33A, Gt. Marylebone st
Clifford Wm. barrister, 36 Lincoln's inn fields
Clifford Wm. gold chain maker, 7 Perceval st. Clerkenwell
Clifford Wm. grocer & teadealer, 112 Gt. Suffolk st. Borough
Clifford Wm. house agent, 151 Blackfriars road
Clifford Wm. sen. law stationer & news agt. 5 Inner Temple la
Clift Charles, optician, 3 New inn yard, Shoreditch
Clift George, laceman & milliner, 128 Oxford st
Clift James, solicitor, 30 Bloomsbury square
Clift Samuel, dairyman, 17 Air st. Piccadilly
Clifton Eugene & Co. importers of wines, 10 Tokenhouse yard
Clifton & Evans, pasteboard makers, 23Red Lion st. Clerknwl
Clifton Nathl. & Nathl. Hen. surgeons, 38 Cross st. Islington
Clifton Wm. & Son, poultry salesmen, 66 & 67 Newgate mkt
Clifton Edward Norton, architect & survyr. 9 Tokenhouse yd
Clifton George James, wine & spirit merchant, 47 Lime st
Clifton Geo. Wm. wine & brandy mer. 37 Jewry st. Aldgate
Clifton Isaac, oilman, 9 Upper North pl. Gray's inn road
Clifton Thos. glass factor, carver, &c. 8 Laurence Pountney la
Clilverd William, fruiterer, 41 Duke st. St. James's
Climpson George, dairyman, 14 Edward st. Dorset sq
Climpson Wm. carpenter & undertak. 9 Queen st. Bryanst. sq
Clinch John, merchant, 31 Abchurch lane
Clinch Joseph, pilot, 4 Globe st. Wapping
Clinch Thos. Wm. job master, 1 Keppel mews North, Russell sq
Clinch William, hairdresser, 37 Mitre st. Aldgate
Clinkscales Thomas, baker, 35 Haberdashers' st. Hoxton
Clint Alfred, landscape painter, 42 Robert st. Hampstead rd
Clint George, portrait painter, 4 Keppell st. Russell square
Clint Thomas, fruiterer, 14 Gordon st. City road
Clinton John, professor of music, 14 Greek st. Soho
Clipperton & Impey, solicitors, 17 Bedford row
ClippingdaleJosiah, superintend. St. Katharine's. dck steam wf
Clipson Charles, builder, 32 King st. Westminster
Clipson Wm. *Globe* P.H. 26 Great Dover st. Borough
Clisby Henry, baker, 14 Bishopsgate within
Clisby John, cheesemonger, 1 Cornwall ter. Camden town
Clisby Mary Elizh. (Mrs.), butcher, 32Liverpool st. Bishopsg
Clissold Joseph, stock & share broker, 1 Copthall chambers
Clitherow James, linendraper, &c. 63 Goswell st
Clitherow John, firework ma. 13 Weaver st. Bethnal green
Clitherow Wm. silk, &c. dyer & scourer, 24 Queen st. Chelsea
Clive George, magistrate, Hammersmith police court
Clixby Thomas, tailor, 6 West st. Golden square
Cloake Felicia H. (Mrs.), shop fixtr. dlr. 3 Liverpool st. City
Cloake George, shop fixture broker, 15&16 Eldon st. Finsbury
Cloake Thomas, tailor, 75 Kingsland road
Cloake Thomas, watchmaker, 5 Saville row, Walworth rd
Clode & Son, wine & spirit merchants, 78 Mark lane
Clode Charles Mathew, solicitor, see Ashfield & Clode
Close John, solicitor, 8 St. Mildred's court, Poultry
Close Samuel, coal dealer, 22 Mitre st. Blackfriars road
Close Wm. coal merchant, 5 Manchester bldngs. Westminst
Closs Saml. & Son, auctioneers, &c. 33 Clement's lane
Closs Samuel, saddler, &c see Skinner & Closs
Closs Samuel, saddler, 15 Spring st. Paddington
Clossmann F. F. & Co. french wine merchants, 16 Mincing la
Clothier & Tarrant, silversmiths, 8 Vigo st. Regent st
Clothier Wm. & Wm. pawnbrokers, 48 Borough road
Clothier Sam. & Wm. statuary&masons, 6Quickset rw. New rd
Clothier John, coal dealer, 9 Cromer st. Brunswick sq
Clothier Joseph, clothier, 51 Flagon row, Deptford
Clothier Robert, aurist, 13 Great James st. Bedford row
Clothworkers' Almshouses (Robert B. Towse, secretary), 26 Monkwell st. City, & Frog lane, Tibberton square
Clothworkers' Hall (Rob. B. Towse, clerk), 41 Mincing la
Cloudes Mary (Mrs.), dressmaker, 1 Botolph la. Thames st

Clough Edward, cooper, &c. 21 King David lane, Shadwell
Clough John, tin plate worker, 2 High st. Bow
Clough Robert, shirt & stock maker, 130 Oxford st
Cloghly Wm. irish stout & whisky importer, 26 Mincing la
Clout & Crowter, bakers, 1 Providence pl. Walworth commn
Clout Richard, butcher, 1 Clayton place, Kennington road
Clout Thomas. cotton broker, 20 Commercial sale rooms
Clouter Samuel, currier, 10 Kent st. Borough
Clover John, baker, Bromley, Middlesex
Clover Joseph, artist, 85 Newman st. Oxford st
Cloves' (Daniel & Peter) coal & corn merchants & wharfingers, St. Ann's wharf, Earl st. Blackfriars & Storehouse wharf, Cock hill, Ratcliff
Clow Joseph, haberdasher & silk mercer, 7 Ludgate st
Clowes, Wedlake & Clowes, solicitors, 10 King's bench walk
Clowes William & Sons, printers, Duke st. Stamford st. Blackfriars, & 14 Charing cross
Clowes Ellis, solicitor, 44 Lincoln's inn fields
Clowes Richard, tailor, 61 Drummond st. Euston sq
Clowes Thomas, wine merchant, see Lavell & Clowes
Clowser Mary Ann (Mrs.), calico glazer, 124 Bunhill row
Clowsley Henry, turner, 56 Oakley st. Mount st. Lambeth
Clowsley John, carpenter, 49 Leonard st. Finsbury
Clubb Wm. & Son, engravers & printers, 7 Charterhouse st
Clubb (Miss), ladies' school, 41 Park st. Islington
Clubb Henry Wm. grocer, 7 Buckingham pl. Marlbro'rd. Chelsea
Clubb James, *White Hart* P.H. 199 Bishopsgate st. without
Clubb Wm. Ebenezer, engraver & printer, 7 Charterhouse st
Clubb Wm. tobacconist, Sun tavern fields, St. Geo. East
Clube Louisa & Eliza, haberdashrs. 30 Kensington High st
Cluer Wm. tobaccopipe maker, 11 Narrow st. Limehouse
Clues Elizabeth (Mrs.), staymaker, 85 Shoreditch High st
Cluff William, silk manufacturer, 24 Spital square
Clunes William, pawnbroker, 29 Brydges st. Covent garden
Clunie John, bread & biscuit baker, 71 Watling st
Clunie Thomas James, baker, 10 Portman st. Portman sq
Clunn Philip Ellenton, grocer, 69 Gray's inn lane
Clunn Robert, gun maker, 2 Lit. Portland st. Gt. Portland st
Clunn Thomas, *Richardson's hotel*, Piazza, Covent garden
Cluse & Bose, general ironmongers, 35 City road
Cluse Sarah (Mrs.), baker, 11 Chiswell st. Finsbury
Clutterbuck Henry, physician, 1 Crescent, New Bridge st
Clutterbuck James, gasfitter, 26 Coppice row, Clerkenwell
Clutterbuck John, *Plough* P.H. 210 Bermondsey st
Clutterbuck Joseph, brickmaker, Kensington gravel pits
Clutton & Cooper, solicitors, 48 Borough High st
Clutton Henry, architect & surveyor, 8 Whitehall place
Clutton Owen, cornfactor, 3 Webb st. Bermondsey st
Clutton Robert, surveyor, 8 Whitehall place
Clutton Wm. goldsmith & jeweller, 21 Denmark st. Soho
Clyma John, tailor, 4A, West st. Seven Dials
Clymer & Dixon, original patentees & manufacturers of the improved columbian printing press, &c. 10 Finsbury st. Finsbury square
Clymer Geo. Augustus, builder, St. James pl. Old Kent rd
Coach & Harness Makers' Hall (G. W K. Potter, clerk), Noble st
Coad James, bootmaker, 13 Fisher st. Red Lion sq
Coaffee George Benjamin, dyer, see Brown & Coaffee
Coakley John, tailor, 63 Mark lane
Coal Exchange, 96 Lower Thames st.; hours 12 to ½ p. 2
Coal Meters' Office, 5 Coal Exchange; hours 9 to 7, & 9 to 4
Coales Danl. & Son, smiths & ironmongers, 75 Gray's inn la
Coates, Blizard & Co. coach & harness mkrs. 7 Park la. Piccadilly; factory, Pembroke mews, Chapel st. Grosvenor place
Coates & Co. american merc. 13 & 14 Bread st. Cheapside
Coates Henry & Co. tailors, 21 Down st. Piccadilly
Coates & Howes, wine & brandy mercht. 8 Baker st. Portman sq
Coates Ingle & Wood, manchester wa. 5 Wood st. Cheapside
Coates Charles James, stock & sharebrok. 4 Tokenhouse yd
Coates William & Co. wine importers & sole consignees of Watkins' Dublin stout, 25 Whitechapel High st
Coates Wm. & Son, brewers, 10 Cumberland pl. King's rd. Chelsea
Coates Edward, hatter, 64 High Holborn
Coates Edward, omnibus proprietor, Stratford
Coates Frederick, lodging house keeper, 33 Craven st. Strand
Coates Fred. architect & surveyor, 5 Lyon ter. Edgware rd
Coates George, surgeon, 43 Hart st. Bloomsbury
Coates Giles, clock maker, 15 Up. Belgrave pl. Pimlico
Coates James, beer retailer, Southampton st. Camberwell
Coates John, cheesemonger, 115 Up. Whitecross st. St. Luke's
Coates John, fruiterer, 157 Old Gravel lane, Wapping
Coates John, leather dresser, Jamaica level, Bermondsey
Coates John, linen, &c. draper, see Milsum & Coates
Coates Richard, merchant, 147 Leadenhall st
Coates Robert, shoemaker, 4 Foxley rd. Camberwell New rd
Coates Thomas, carman, 10 Wilton road, Pimlico
Coates Thomas, linendraper, see Atkinson & Coates
Coates Thomas, solicitor, 42 Bedford square, Bloomsbury
Coates William, plumber, Southampton st. Camberwell road
Coath Thomas, warehouseman, see Luck, Bouch & Coath
Coats Jsph. calico printer, see Gates, Coats, Bartlett & Co
Coats Martha (Mrs.), straw hat ma. 49 Up. North pl. Gray's inn rd
Coats Thomas, builder, 108 Sloane st. Chelsea
Cobb Charles Francis, solicitor, see Simpson & Cobb
Cobb Frederic, physician, 5 St. Helen's place, Bishopsgate
Cobb George, plumber, 3 Pelham st. Brick la. Spitalfields
Cobb George, glass, china, &c. warh. 114 High st. Marylebone
Cobb Henry, land agent & surveyor, 18 Lincoln's inn fields
Cobb James, brush maker, 23 Sidney st. Somers town
Cobb John, beer retailer, 6 Commercial ter. Com. rd. east
Cobb John, solicitor, 15 Northumberland st. Strand
Cobb John, tailor, 44 Dorset st. Portman square
Cobb John, watch jeweller, 5 Cobham row, Clerkenwell
Cobb Joseph, butcher, 22 King's road east, Chelsea
Cobb Richard, stock & sharebroker, 2 Copthall buildings
Cobb Robert, plumber & painter, see Green & Cobb
Cobb Robt. surg. dentst. & chemist, 10 Frederick's pl. Hampst. rd
Cobb Robt. C. (Mrs.), ladies' school, 45 George st. Euston sq
Cobb William, corkcutter, 78 Houndsditch
Cobb William, oilman, see Lodge & Cobb
Cobb Wm. Simms, *White Hart* P.H. 51 Leman st. Goodman's fi
Cobbe Charles, surgeon, 45 Bedford place, Kensington
Cobbe Thomas, barrister, 22 Portugal st. Lincoln's inn fields
Cobbett Jas. & Co. floorcloth & carpet mfs. 1 Deptford bridge
Cobbett Rd. & Son, glaziers, 25 Northumberland st. Strand
Cobbett Wm. & Henry, woollendrapers, 29 Sackville st
Cobbett Arthur, italian warehouse, 18 Pall mall
Cobbett Caroline (Miss), dressmaker, 4 Prince's st. Bdfd. row
Cobbett Daniel A. surveyor, 5 Railway pl. Fenchurch st
Cobbett Edward, carver & gilder, 115 Long acre
Cobbett Edward John, compos. ornam. ma. 16 Gt. Windmill st
Cobbett Edwin, who. teadealer, 111 High st. Marylebone
Cobbett James Paul, barrister, 17 Chancery lane, Fleet st
Cobbett John Morgan, barrister, 4 Fig tree court, Temple
Cobbett Thos. academy, 1 Queen's Head row, Lower st. Islingtn
Cobbin John Ingram, stockbroker, 7 Throgmorton st
Cobbin William, tailor, &c. 2 Woburn bldgs. Tavistock square
Cobbold Alfred, solicitor, see Wilkinson & Cobbold
Cobby Charles William, solicitor, 22 Paternoster row
Cobden Richard & Co. calico printers, 56 Bow lane
Cobden George, scotch agent, 40 Gresham st
Cobell Ann (Mrs.), grocer, 11 Russell st. Lower Rotherhithe
Cobham Wm. & Hen. statuaries, &c. Portland pl. Peckham rd
Cobham Edward Fage, oilman, 48 Bow lane, Cheapside, & 277 Kent st. Borough
Cobham Hannah (Mrs.), undertaker, 9 Augustus rw. Spa rd
Cobham Samuel, *St. Paul's* coffee house, 95 Newgate st
Cobham Samuel W. italian warehouse, 18 Lawrence la. City
Cobley Thomas, jun. coachmaker, 14 Whitechapel High st
Cobley William, goldbeater, 3 St. John's ct. King st. Snowhill
Cobon James, tailor, 36 East st. Walworth road
Cochran Ann (Miss), baker, 52 Burr st. East Smithfield
Cochran John, engraver, &c. 41 Harleyford pl. Kennington
Cochran Thomas, rag & bottle dlr. 2 Portugal pl. Cambridge rd
Cochran William, jeweller & silversmith, 266 Regent st. & 64 King's road, Brighton
Cochrane Charles, corn merchant, 26 Lamb st. Spital sq
Cochrane Geo. barrister, law chambers, 77 Chancery lane
Cochrane James, baker, 11 Francis st. Tottenham court road
Cochrane James, bookseller, 43 Stamford st. Blackfriars rd
Cochrane William, ship biscuit baker, 63 Wapping
Cock Astley & Chas. wine merchants (I. H. Vale & Co. Bordeaux), 3 Dunster court, Mincing lane
Cock John & Son, carpenters, 2 South row, Golden square
Cock, Spavin & Co. wholesale teadealers, 6 Old Jewry
Cock Anna (Mrs.), beer retailer, Battersea
Cock Brooker, jun. wind. glass cut. 7 Nassau pl. Comml. rd. east
Cock Brooker, sen. plumber & glazier, 35 York road, Lambeth
Cock Edward, surgeon, 12 St. Thomas st. Borough
Cock Edwin, writer & grainer, 26 Park pl. Kennington cross
Cock George, butcher, 70 Church st. Mile end new town
Cock George, meat salesman, 3 New Newgate market
Cock George, spring & roasting jack ma. 21 Union ct. Holbn. hl
Cock Gilbert, chandler's shop, Back road, Kingsland
Cock Henry, brass screw maker, 3 Clipstone st. Fitzroy sq
Cock Henry, plumber, 2 Middle row. Knightsbridge
Cock James, carpentr. & undert. 44 Marsham st. Westminster
Cock John, fruiterer, 63 King st. Borough
Cock John Diggory, stationer & acc. book mak. 7 High Holborn
Cock Richard Seymour, wine merchant, see Barnes & Cock
Cock Thomas, fruiterer, 271 Poplar High st

Cock William, engine turner, 21 Myddelton st. Spafields
Cock Wm. jun. short hand writer, 12 Took's ct. Chancery la
Cockburn Archbold & Co. wine merchants, 161 New Bond st
Cockburn Brothers & Co. merchants, 60 Mark lane
Cockburn George & Son, stationers & booksellers, 9 Aldgate
Cockburn J. & Campbell, wine merchants, 151 Piccadilly
Cockburn & Co. bankers, 4 Whitehall
Cockburn J. & Co. e.i. merchants & agt. 11 New Broad st. City
Cockburn Alex. J. E. queen's counsel, 3 Harcourt bldgs. Temple
Cockburn Eleanor (Mrs.), *White Hart* P.H. 32 Shadwell Hi. st
Cockburn Henry Milner, tobacconist, 63 Tottenham ct. rd
Cockburn James Robt. toy dlr. 44 Cannon st. Ratcliff highway
Cockburn John, silk dyer, 34 New st. Dorset square
Cockburn Robert, *Falcon* P.H. 28 Old Fish st
Cocke Alexr. irish & for. prov. broker, Commer. coff. ho. Mincg. la
Cocke Archibald, surgeon, 7 Ulster place, Regent's park
Cocke Arthur, surgeon, 32 Howland st. Fitzroy square
Cockell Edgar, surgeon, 6 Queen's ter. Queen's road, Dalston
Cocker Alfred Richard, attorney, 11 Nassau st. Soho
Cocker Douglas, modeller & sculptor, 88 Quadrant, Regent st
Cocker Edwin, manufacturer of chandeliers & every description of gas apparatus for lighting mansions, public buildings, manufactories, &c. &c. 22 Ely place, Holborn hill
Cocker Edwin (Mrs.), comml. boardg. ho. 22 Ely pl. Holborn
Cocker Elizabeth (Mrs.), boarding ho. 22 Ely pl. Holborn hll
Cocker George, wholesale warehouse for Derbyshire spar ornaments, 8 Chenies st. Bedford square
Cocker James, boarding house, 14 Charter house square
Cocker Robert, *William IV.* P.H. 1 Up. Boston st. Blandford sq
Cockerell & Co. merchants & east india agents, 8 Austinfriars
Cockerell Geo. Wm. & Son, auctioneers & agents, 47 Blackman st
Cockerell James & Son, billiard table makers, 32 Gt. Charlotte st. Blackfriars road
Cockerell Son, & Hoard, auctioneers, 26 Conduit st. Bond st. & 47 Blackman st
Cockerell & Stockwell, bootmakers, 65 Fleet st
Cockerell Geo. Joseph, coal mercht. see Gundell & Cockerell
Cockerell James, auct. & apprais. 32 Gt. Charlotte st. Blkfrs
Cockerell John Christr. coffee rooms, 16 King st. Westminr
Cockerell Samuel Pepys, barrister, 7 Old sq. Lincoln's inn
Cockerell William, grocer, 86 Gray's inn lane
Cockerell William, hairdresser, 5 Duke st. Smithfield
Cockerill Daniel, butcher, 12 Broadway, Ludgate hill
Cockerill Edward, cheesemonger, 2 Greenland pl. Cromer st
Cockerill Joseph, bricklayer, 40 Little Bartholomew close
Cockerill Wm. beer retailer, 38 Henry st. Hampstead rd
Cockerton Joseph & Son, merchants, 2 Austinfriars
Cockerton George Asser, grocer, 11 Lower Brompton grove
Cockerton John, *King's Head* P.H. 12 Pudding la. Eastchp
Cockerton Jsph. *Royal Hosp.* P.H. 22 & 23 Ryl. Hosptl. rw. Chlsa
Cocket George, sheep & calf salesman, 41 West Smithfield
Cockett Fred. *Crown tav.* 12 Vinegar yd. Brydges st. Cov. gar
Cockett Wm. *Acorn* P.H. 65 Great Cambridge st. Hackney rd
Cockhead Richard, *Red Lion & Still* P.H. 172 Drury lane
Cockin & Seamer, silk manufacturers, 5 Milk st. Cheapside
Cockin Wm. *White Hart* P.H. 10 Greenfield st. Whitechapel
Cocking Henry, tailor, 42 Sekforde st. Clerkenwell
Cocking James, tailor, 65 Southampton st. Pentonville
Cocking Joseph, fruiterer, 42 Lamb's Conduit st
Cocking Thomas, chemist, &c. 19 Gt. Portland st. Oxford st
Cockings Edward & Thomas, tin plate workers, 145 Long acre
Cockle James, oilman, 1 Chatwrth. bldgs. Lower rd. Deptford
Cockle James, oilman, High st. Deptford
Cockle Jas. special pleader, Grecian chmbs. 19 Devereux ct. Str
Cockle James, surgeon, 18 New Ormond st. Queen sq
Cockle John, physician, 107 Guildford st. Russell square
Cockle Richard, *Depository of the British & Foreign Bible Society*, 10 Earl st. Blackfriars
Cockle Stephen, timber merchant, Church st. Deptford
Cockman Walter & Henry, oil & colormen, 44 Whitechapel rd
Cockman & Windmill, saddlers, &c. 74 George st. Portman sq
Cockman James, dairyman, 44 Princess st. Edgware road
Cockman Newell, zinc worker, 2 West st. Walworth rd
Cockman Walter, oilman, 122 Tottenham court road
Cockman Walter, oil & colorman, 32 Aldersgate st
Cockram Elizh. (Mrs.), jobmaster, 100 High Holborn
Cockram John, builder, 25 Adam st. west, Bryanstone sq
Cockrell Fred. linendraper, Church st. Stoke Newington
Cockrell James, leather cutter, 53 Snows fields, Bermondsey
Cockrell John, grocer, 3 Samson's pl. Grange road, Bermondsey
Cockrill Joseph, meat salesman, 23 Newgate market
Cocks, Biddulph & Co. bankers, 43 Charing cross
Cocks John & Son, plumbers, 2 Frederick place, Mile end road, & 9 Ireland row, Mile end road
Cocks Robert & Co. by special appointment, imp. & publishers of foreign music to her Majesty, 6 New Burlington st
Cocks Alfred, oilman, 3 Broadway, Westminster
Cocks James, pork butcher, 35 High st. Kensington
Cocks John, painter, see Sargood & Cocks
Cocks John, *Shakspeare's Head* P.H. 46 Perceval st. Clrknw
Cocks Samuel, *White Swan* P.H. 7 Long acre
Cocksedge James, pawnbroker, 30 Church st. Shoreditch
Cockshott Mary (Mrs.), lodging ho. 32 Oxenden st. Haymarket
Cockshott Stephen, pilot, 5 Brunswick terrace, Blackwall
Cocksworth David, teadealer, 10 Broadway, Ludgate hill
Codd Messrs. army agents, 15 Fludyer st. Westminster
Codd William, tailor, 26 Dean st. Soho
Codling Mary (Miss), tobacconist, 28 High st. Notting hill
Codner Richard & Son, cider merchants, 31 Mill la. Tooley st
Cody Patrick, carpenter, 41 Ruffords buildings, Islington
Coe Charles Edwd. portfolio & music case ma. 84 Fetter lane
Coe Charles Skinner, ladies' boot & shoe maker, 97 Oxford st
Coe Daniel, baker, 1 Caroline st. Camden town
Coe George, coachmaker, York place, Westminster road
Coe James & Son, architects & surveyors, 29 Bridport place, Hoxton, & 1 Carpenter's buildings, London wall, & Victoria avenue, Gravesend
Coe James, solicitor, see Coe & Marshall
Coe John, shopkeeper, 33 Salisbury st. Lisson grove
Coe Richd. B. civil engineer & surveyor, 9 Adam st. Adelphi
Coe Thomas, boot & shoemaker, 14 Lucas st. Rotherhithe
Coe Thomas Henry, printer, 27 Old change
Coe William, looking glass maker, 5 New inn st. Shoreditch
Coe William, tailor, 30 St. Martin's st. Leicester square
Coell Robert, undertaker, 3 Limehouse causeway
Coen Charles, grocer, Grove lane, Deptford
Coeuret Jean Pierre Francis, confectioner, 53A, Drury lane
Coffee Henry, modeller, 6A, Oxford market
Coffey A. E. & Sons, civil engineers, Bromley, Middlesex
Coffey John, grocer, 25 Richmond pl. East st. Walworth rd
Coffey John, painter & glazier, 7 Gilbert st. Clare market
Coffey Thomas, tailor, 1 Warwick square, Newgate st
Cogan Robert, glass, lead, oil & color mercht. & glass shade & lamp glass warehouse, 5 Princes st. & 48 Leicester sq
Cogan William, gasfitter, 16 Munster st. Regent's park
Cogar Wm. Abram. bootmaker, 23 New st. Covent garden
Cogdon Edward, tailor, 14 Old st. St. Luke's
Cogdon William, brewer, 3 Gloucester ter. New rd. Whitechapl
Cogger James, tinman, 6 Queen's ter. Marlboro' rd. Chelsea
Cogger John, fruit salesman, 64 Farringdon market
Cogger Thomas, engineer & print. pr. ma. 3 Essex st. Bouverie st
Coggins John, fruiterer, 21 Upper Marylebone st
Coggins Joseph, public library, &c. Hornton st. Kensington
Coghill Donald, baker, 5 Maiden lane, Covent garden
Cogswell Benjamin, gun & pistol warehouse, 224 Strand
Coham John Joachim, surgeon, 27 Dorset st. Portman sq
Cohen Aaron & Co. rag, bottle & metal dlrs. 5 York ter. Kent st. rd. & 1 Roebuck ter. & 1 Charlton place, Gt. Dover rd
Cohen Henry Hymen & Co. merchants, 48 Lime st
Cohen Judah & Sons, west india merchants, 58 Mansell st
Cohen Moses & Co. china & for. lace dealer, 14 Hanway st
Cohen Aaron, tool & iron dealer, 64 Cowcross st
Cohen Abraham, carpet dealer, 88 Long alley, Finsbury
Cohen Abraham, marine store dealer, 2 Cross st. Islington
Cohen Abraham M. paperstainer, 100 Fenchurch st
Cohen Asher Jn. lead pencil ma. 23 Mid. Grove st. Com. rd. east
Cohen Barnet, cap peak ma. 18 Goulston sq. Whitechapel
Cohen Barnet Solomon, black lead, black lead pencil, sealing wax & wafer manufacturer, 9 Magdalen row, Gt. Prescot st
Cohen Daniel W. physician, 5 Highbury place
Cohen Dan, tobacconist, 25 Aldgate
Cohen David Abrahams, pencil maker, 40 Minories
Cohen Edward, shipping & forwarding agt. 14 Clement's inn
Cohen Elias, grocer, 113 Houndsditch
Cohen Emanuel, rag & phial dlr. 41 Cowcross st. Smithfield
Cohen Henry, general dealer, 9 Bell lane, Spitalfields
Cohen Herman Jacob, merchant, 12 Gt. Prescot st. Goodman's fl
Cohen Hyam, metal merchant, 5 Windsor st. Bishopsgate
Cohen Hyman Benjamin, tailor, &c. 70 Leadenhall st
Cohen Hymen (Mrs.), merchant, 38 Mansell st. Goodman's flds
Cohen Isaac, clothier, 41 Gt. James st. Lisson grove
Cohen Isaac, stockbroker, 59 Threadneedle st
Cohen Jacob, confectioner, 86 St. John st. Clerkenwell
Cohen John, professor of music, 26 Soho square
Cohen Joseph, tobacconist, 136 Houndsditch
Cohen Leam, furniture broker, 16 Lower marsh, Lambeth
Cohen Lewis, merchant, 65 Gt. Prescot st. Goodman's fields
Cohen Louis, stockbroker, 59 Threadneedle st
Cohen Maria (Mrs.), tool dealer, 40 Cowcross st. Smithfield
Cohen Michael, clothes dealer, 4 Sandy's row, Spitalfields
Cohen Moses, curiosity dealer, 12 Charles st. Soho square
Cohen Moses, clothes dealer, 42 Duke st. Aldgate

Cohen Moses, rag merchant, 1 Roebuck ter. Gt. Dover road
Cohen Nathan, clothes dealer, 104 Gt. Saffron hill
Cohen Philip, bottle merchant, 68 & 69 Lant st. Borough
Cohen Philip, phial & bottle mercht. 32 Lr. Kennington la
Cohen Phion, marine store dlr. 7 Artillery pass. Bishopsgate
Cohen Rachel (Miss), tobacconist, 31 Well st. Wellclose sq
CohenSamuel, furn.broker,9 Landers bdgs.Sandy's rw.Bpsgt
Cohen Samuel, tool dealer, 81 Cowcross st. Smithfield
Cohen Sim, china & glass wareho. 46 Leman st. Goodman's fi
Cohen Solomon, merchant,11 Leatherselrs'. bldgs. Lond.wall
Cohen Solomon Hyman, slopseller, 168 & 182 Tooley st
Cohn Marcus David & Son, calcutta merchts. 3 Barge yd
Cohu Andrew, jun. east india merchant, 33 St. Mary Axe
CoilettThomasA.accountant,18 Hemus ter. King'srd.Chelsea
CokerWm.&Son,riggers,shipchandlers,&c Narrow st.Ratcliff
Coker Betsey (Mrs.), fan manufacturer, 8 Racquet ct. Fleet st
Coker Wm. boot & shoe maker, 19 Rathbone place, Oxford st
Colas Ferdinand, paper box manufacturer, 55 Fleet st
Colam James, ham & tongue dealer, 5 Charterhouse st
Colbatch Wm. silk manufr. 48 Aldermanbury
Colbourn Thos. *MortimerArms* P.H. 11 Mortimer rd. Kingsld
Colbourne Benj. beershop, Peckham footpath, Old Kent rd
Colbourne James, butcher, 16 Cumberland row, King's cross
Colbourne Raleigh, grocer, 95 Gt. Peter st. Westminster
Colbran James, *Spread Eagle tavern*, 1 Pratt st. Lambeth
Colbron John, staymaker, 53 Rathbone place, Oxford st
Colbron Wm. tailor, 4 Mill st. Hanover square
Colburn Henry, booksell. & publisher, 13 Gt. Marlborough st
Colby George Wm. corn merchant, 70 St. George st
Colby John, hairdresser, Warlters' buildings, Old Kent road
Colby Joseph, bootmaker, 63 Freeschool st. Horselydown
Colby Joseph John, wood turner, 16 Fleet la. Farringdon st
Colchester & Nephew.russia brok.58Threadneedle st.&Baltic
Colchester Wm. Markham, chemist & druggist, 28 Old st. rd
Coldham James, *Crown* P.H. 30 George st. Blackfriars rd
Coldicoatt Wm. coal dlr. 11 & 12 Blue Anchor al. Bunhill row
Coldred Walter, grocer, 29 Phœnix st. Somers town
Coldrey George, merchant, & buying, shipping & insurance agent, 7½ Lawrence lane, & at Lloyd's
Coldrey George Gage, merchant & ship. agt. Lloyd's coffee ho
Coldrey Thomas, laceman, 119 Upper st. Islington
Coldrick Joseph, tailor, 34 University st. Tottenham ct. rd
Coldstream Guards' Hospital (surgeon-major, Wm. Hunter), 2 Vincent square, Westminster
Coldwell John, baker, 6 Aldenham terrace, Pancras road
Coldwell Robert, portable writing, dressing, & jewel case manufacturer,&c. 15 Great May's buildings, St. Martin's la
Coldwell William, baker, 88 Chalton st. Somer's town
Cole Geo. & John, masons & bldrs. 18 Cursitor st. Chancery la
Cole & Hussey, bootmakers, 23 Greek st. Soho
Cole Jonathan & Sons, builders, 27 Liverpool st. Bishopsgate
Cole, Nichols & Co. merchants, 34 Dowgate hill
Cole Samuel & Son, tailors, 60 Well st. Oxford st
Cole Wm. & Son, bricklay.&bldrs. 29 Gt. Barlow st. Marylebo
Cole Alfred, grocer, 22 Bridport place, New North road
Cole Alfred James, jun. importer of foreign toys, 25 Basing lane, Bread st. Cheapside
Cole Augustus, lace & embroi. wa. 17 Holles st. Cavendish sq
Cole Beaumont, coach currier, 4 Princes st. Bedford row
Cole Charles, artist, 71 Poplar High st
Cole Chas. corn dealer, 26 Upper Salisbury pl. Locks flds
Cole Chas. engraver & printer, 28 Myddelton st
Cole Charles Nicholas, solicitor, 13 Doughty st. Foundling
Cole Daniel, linendraper, 22 Blandford st. Portman sq
Cole David, carpenter, 108 Waterloo road, Lambeth
Cole Ebenezer, news agent, 16 St. Saviour's churchyd. Boro'
Cole Edward, cooper, 4 Harrow st. Lant st. Borough
Cole Edward, grocer, 16 New Church court, Strand
Cole Edward Joseph, sec. to *Alten Mining Association, & Great Wheal Martha Consolidated Mines Co.* 52 Old Broad st. City
Cole Elizabeth (Miss), school, see Cook & Cole
Cole Elizabeth (Mrs.), milliner, 33 Warwick st. Golden sq
Cole Elizabeth (Miss), toy dealer, 53 St. John st. Smithfield
Cole Elizabeth Rushon (Mrs.), engr. & printer, 140 Goswell st
Cole George, plumber & glazier, 112 Brook st. Lambeth
Cole George Fras. glasscutter, 15 Wild ct. Lincoln's inn flds
Cole George Mason, needle factor, &c. 12 Fell st. Cripplegt
Cole Henry Thomas, barrister, 2 Elm court, Temple
Cole Henry Warwick, barrister, 40 Chancery lane
Cole Hen. Wm. oil&mediter.prod.brok.see Aylwin, Bevan&Co
Cole Hester (Mrs.), fruiterer, Long market, Covt. garden mkt
Cole Jacob, hatter, 23 Bridge st. Westminster
Cole James, blind maker, 1A, Hannibal road, Stepney green
Cole James, cooper, 13 Fleet lane, Farringdon st
Cole James, hosier, 427 Oxford st
Cole James, surgeon, 25 Harley st
Cole James, *White Hart* P.H. 135 Poplar High st
Cole James, work. jeweller, 5 Charlotte st. Fitzroy square
Cole James F. chronometer ma. 9 Motcomb st. Belgrave sq
Cole Jas.Fras. pump ma.& well sink. NewWeston st. Bermsy
Cole Jane (Mrs.), mar.store dlr. 3 Gt. Carlisle st. Portm. mkt
Cole John, baker, 11 Upper East Smithfield
Cole John, boot & shoe maker, 85 Brunswick st. Blackwall
Cole John, boot & shoe maker, 15 Robinhood lane, Poplar
Cole John, *Brown Bear* P.H. 32 Devonshire st. Queen sq
Cole John, butcher, 21 Liquorpond st. Gray's inn lane
Cole John, fruiterer & greengrocer, 74 Gray's inn lane
Cole John, furniture broker, 83 Long alley, Finsbury
Cole John, grocer, 80 Park st. Kennington cross
Cole John, hairdresser, 21 Brown st. Bryanstone square
Cole John, painter & glazier, 32 Park st. Dorset square
Cole John, solicitor, 4 Adelphi terrace
Cole John, wholesale druggist, 101 High Holborn
Cole Jonathan, tailor, 1 Tredegar square, Mile end road
Cole Joseph, house agent, 2 Somers pl. west. Somers town
Cole Joseph, jun. auctioneer, &c. 15 Seymour st. Euston sq
Cole Matthew, painter & glazier, 43 Bedfordbury, Covt. gdn
Cole Michael, writer & grainer, 24 King st. Golden sq
Cole Richard, bootmaker, 210 Strand
Cole Richard, linendraper, 6 Essex pl. Mare st. Hackney
Cole Robert, pawnbroker, 28 East st. Walworth road
Cole Robert, solicitor, 14 Tokenhouse yard, & 57 Upper Norton st. Portland place
Cole Samuel, coach builder, 41 St. George st
Cole Samuel, crape dresser & dyer, 27 Wellington st. Gswl. rd
Cole Samuel, plumber, &c. 27 Museum st. Bloomsbury
Cole Sarah (Mrs.), window blind maker, 206 Whitechapel rd
Cole Simon, cabinet ma. 18 Dorchester st. New north road
Cole Thomas, boot tree maker, 92 Bethnal green road
Cole Thomas, carpenter, 9 Chapel pl. Liverpool road
Cole Thomas, carpet & rug manufacturer, 18 Newgate st
Cole Thomas, english & foreign second hand bookseller, 38 Princes st. Leicester square
Cole Thomas, coachmaker, see Wiseman & Cole
Cole Thomas, corndealer, 14 Lambeth Lower marsh
Cole Thomas, designer & maker of ornamental & portable clocks, 2 Upper Vernon st. Pentonville
Cole Thomas, grocer & cheesem. 5 Brown st. Bryanstone sq
Cole Thomas, hatter, 92 Gracechurch st
Cole Thos. mathematl. inst. ma. 21 Hannibal rd. Stepney grn
Cole Thomas, pawnbroker, 126 & 127 Waterloo road
Cole Thomas, teadealer, 33 Villiers st. Strand
Cole Thos. Hen. provision broker & agt. 2 Brabant ct. Philpot la
Cole Welcome, green grocer, 2 Melville pl. Caledonian rd
Cole Wm. auctioneer, appraiser, &c. 25 Old st. St. Luke's
Cole Wm. baker, 12 Manor place, Walworth road
Cole Wm. boot & shoe maker, 2 Ball alley, Lombard st
Cole Wm. bootmaker, 3 Union st. Deptford
Cole Wm. carpenter & builder, Jamaica level, Rotherhithe
Cole Wm. carver & gilder, 16 Pierrepoint row, Islington green
Cole Wm. grocer & cheesemgr. 1 Cadogan terrace, Sloane st
Cole Wm. paper hanger, 23 Frederick place, Hampstead rd
Cole Wm. tailor, 74 Old st. road
Cole Wm. tailor, 18 Regent st. Horseferry road
Cole Wm. tobacconist, 6 Seymour row, Little Chelsea
Cole Wm. Hen. baker, 3 Hope terrace, Notting hill
Cole Wm. Robert, barrister, 1 Elm court, Temple
Colebank James, tailor, 30 Elizabeth st. Eaton square
Colebatch Edward, builder, 52 Church st. Minories
Colebatch Geo. surveyor & builder, 52 Church st. Minories
Colebatch Jsph. wareho. keepr. & custom ho. & shipping agt. 60 Low. Thames st. & Trinity chambrs. 5 Water la. Tower st
Colebeck Thomas, bootmaker, 20 New Union st. Lit. Moorfi
Colebourn Henry, surgeon, 28 Harleyford pl. Kennington
Colebrook George, baker, New st. Deptford
Colebrook Henry, baker, 19 Wenlock road, City road
Colebrook Robert M. oyster salesman, 38 St. Mary at hill
Coleby Sam. cop. pl. & letter pr. print. 24 Tysoe st. Spafields
Coleby William, corn dealer, Stratford, Essex
Colee George, coach proprietor, 122 Holborn hill
ColegateEdward, tallowchandler, 32 Seymour pl. Brynstn. sq
Coleman Benj. & Co. soda wa. mfr. 32 Baalzephon st. Bmdsy
Coleman Brothers, hatters, 60 & 61 Chiswell st. Finsbury
Coleman Bros. wine & spirit mer. 2 Crown ct. Old Broad st
Coleman, Flockhart & Oakley, wine merchts. 8 Fenchurch st
Coleman, Flockhart & Oakley, merchts. & agts. 8 Fenchurch st
Coleman Hen. S. & Bros. wine mers. 2 Crown ct. Old Broad st
Coleman Jacob & Co. tailors & drapers, 74 Union st. Borough
Coleman James & Jonathan, builders, 7 Church st. Borough market, & 8 New Weston st. Bermondsey
Coleman Richard & William, trunkmakers, 13 Dowgate hill

Coleman Anne (Mrs.), undertaker, 13 Snow's flds. Bermondsey
Coleman Benjamin, clothes salesman, 19 Rosemary lane
Coleman Benj. potato salesman, South row, Covent gardn. mkt
Coleman Charles, baker, Providence place, Kentish town
Coleman Charles, merchant, 17 St. Mary Axe
Coleman David, bricklayer, 11 Hayfield pl. Mile end road
Coleman Dennis, engraver, 16½ Clarendon sq. Somers town
Coleman Edward, baker, 2 Colchester st. Whitechapel High st
Coleman Edward, linendraper, 99 High st. Camden town
Coleman Edward, stationer & printer, 36 Poplar High st
Coleman Edward, upholsterer, 77 London wall
Coleman Francis, hatmaker, 267 Borough High street
Coleman Fras. Brewer, linendraper, see Gawtrey & Coleman
Coleman Hen. Pearson, oyster salesman, 19 St. Mary at hill
Coleman George, fishmonger, 17 Mint st. Borough
Coleman George Fowler, saddler, 24 White Horse st. Stepney
Coleman Jacob, tailor, 36 Broad street, Bloomsbury
Coleman James, *Bear & Wheatsheaf tav.* 72 Lwr. Thames st
Coleman James, *Boston Arms* P.H. 20 Boston st. Dorset sq
Coleman James, cabinet bench ma. 10 Tottenham st. Tot. ct. rd
Coleman James, cattle salesman, see Ebsworth & Coleman
Coleman James, watchmaker, 6 Westmoreland st. Marylebone
Coleman James Edward, accountant, 21 Coleman street
Coleman John, news agent, 13 Cambridge st. Golden sq
Coleman John, wholesale druggist, see Howard & Coleman
Coleman Joseph, baker, 15 Mount row, Liverpool road
Coleman Mary (Mrs.), bookseller, 3 East street, Old Kent rd
Coleman Richd. bricklayer, &c. 19 Philip lane, London wall
Coleman Robert, fruiterer, 3 Pont st. Belgrave square
Coleman Robert, merchant & insurance brkr. 33 Clement's la
Coleman Robert, shopkeeper, 40 Old Castle st. Bethnal grn
Coleman Samuel S. who. milliner, 3 New Farringdon st
Coleman Thomas, cheesemonger, 63 Castle st. Leicester sq
Coleman William, baker, 16 Hamilton row, Bagnigge wells rd
Coleman William, bricklayer, 7 Church st. Clapham rd
Coleman Wm. butcher, 8 Lit. Chester st. Grosvenor place
Coleman Wm. cutler & dressing case maker, 4 Haymarket
Coleman Wm. stockma. & tailor, 5 Hemming's rw. St. Martin's la
Coleman William, tailor, 93 Broad street, Ratcliff
Colemans Mathew W. surgeon, 265 Whitechapel road
Coles & English, soapmakers, Belvedere road, Lambeth
Coles Mary & Rebecca, grocers, &c. 25 Robert st. Chelsea
Coles William & Son, tailors, 22 Paul street, Finsbury, & 29 Finsbury place north
Coles' Upper Wharf, 21 Shad Thames, Horselydown
Coles Barbara (Mrs.), cheesemonger, 47 Wigmore st. Caven. sq
Coles Benjamin, baker, 16 Vauxhall bridge road
Coles Charles, *Black Horse* P.H. 29 Poplar High st
Coles Charles, dining rooms, 1 Bedford st. Covent garden
Coles Charles, jun. east & west india broker, 86 Gt. Tower st
Coles Frances (Mrs.), school, 8 Brooksby st. Liverpool rd
Coles Geo. baker, 8 Phœnix street, Somers town
Coles Geo. carpenter & joiner, 24 Hoxton square
Coles Geo. grocer & cheesemgr. 43 Gt. Wild st. Lincoln's inn fl
Coles Geo. merchant & east india agent, see Dallas & Coles
Coles Harrison, butcher, 2 Portman street, Portman square
Coles Henry, indigo, drysalt. & col. broker, 46 Fenchurch st
Coles Hen. Josiah, laceman, hosier, & draper, 109 St. John st. rd
Coles Isaac, linendraper, 2 & 3 Pleasant row, King's cross
Coles James, fruiterer, 18 Arlington street, Sadler's wells
Coles James, newsvender & stationer, 39 Kingsgate street
Coles James, warehouseman, see Leaf, Coles, Smith & Co
Coles John, bricklayer, &c. 3 St. Andrew's hill, Doc. commons
Coles John, carman, 7 New London street, Crutchedfriars
Coles John, chemist, Chancery pl. Camberwell New road
Coles John, corndealer, 3 Brewer street, Somers town
Coles John, trussmaker, 27 James street, Covent garden
Coles Joseph, tobacconist, 233 Strand
Coles Lewis, tailor, 29 Little Windmill street, Golden sq
Coles Lewis R. umbrella ma. 42 Bridgehouse pl. Newngtn. cswy
Coles Mary (Mrs.), china wa. 69 Charlotte ter. New cut. Lmbth
Coles Richard, butcher, 50 Dorset street, Portman square
Coles Samuel, confectioner, 35 & 36 Hampstead road
Coles Sarah (Mrs.), bricklayer, 30 Gt. Carter la. Doctors' com
Coles Thos. baker, 3 Spring street, Paddington
Coles Thos. biscuit baker, 21 South st. Manchester sq
Coles Thos. cabinet maker, 2 Garnault place, Spafields
Coles Thos. dairyman, 2 Duke street, Bloomsbury
Coles Timothy Horsman, east india mer. see Grey & Coles
Coles Wm. baker, 17 Upper Charlton st. Fitzroy square
Coles Wm. coachmaker, 47 Whittlebury street, Euston sq
Coles Wm. coaldealer, 11 Brewer street, Somers town
Coles Wm. colonial broker, 7 Mincing lane
Coles Wm. cooper, 33 Addington place, Camberwell road
Coles Wm. stockbroker, 1 Warnford court, Throgmorton st
Coles Wm. tailor, &c. 6 Gloucester terrace, Hoxton
Coles Wm. sole inventor & patentee of the spiral spring trusses, & the medicated bands for curing rheumatism, do. of the true antifriction principle applied to railway carriages, locomotives, & other machinery, 3 Charing cross
Coles Wm. Frederick, cooper, 26 Crosby row, Walworth
Coley Chas. pawnbroker, 8 Norfolk pl. Lower rd. Islington
Coley Ellen (Mrs.), school, 5 Rotherfield st. north, Islington
Coley William, tailor, 31 Phœnix street, Somers town
Colgate George, silversmith & jeweller, 125 Boro' High st
Colhoun James, merchant, St. Peter's chambers, Cornhill
Colin Orlando, foreign agent, 84 Newman street, Oxford st
Colk George, chemist & druggist, 29 Fleet st
Collacott George, tailor, 21 Park place, Kennington cross
Collambell Charles, surgeon, 7 Canterbury place, Lambeth
Collar George, bootmaker, 9 Adam st. East, Portman sq
Collar George, locksmith & bellhanger, 33 Wych st. Strand
Collard & Collard, pianoforte manufacturers, 26 Cheapside, 195 Tottenham court road, & 6 High st. Camden town, & 12 Francis st. Tottenham court road
Collard George, plumber, 58 George st. Euston square
Collard James, fruiterer, 14 Charles st. Manchester square
Collard John, bootmaker, 22 Richmond pl. East st. Walworth
Collard John, cornfactor, Jack's coffee house, Mark lane
Collard Joseph, bootmaker, 19 Southampton st. Euston sq
Collard Robert, cheesemonger, 6 Charles st. Hatton garden
Collard Robert, wheelwright, 90 Lit. Cadogan pl. Sloane st
Collard Thomas, tobacconist, 9 Upper st. Islington green
Collard William, grocer, 5 Paradise row, Chelsea
College of Advocates, Doctors' commons, hours 10 to 4
College of Heralds, Bennett's hill, Doc. com. hours 10 to 4
College of Physicians (Royal) (Frs. Hawkins, reg.), 13 Pall mall East
College of Chemistry (J. Gardner, M.D. sec.), 16 Hanover sq
College of Surgeons (Royal), 40 Lincoln's inn fields
College for Civil Engineers Office, near the Bridge, Putney
Collegiate & Scholastic Institution (John Wilkes, proprietor), 28 Surrey st. Strand
Collen John & Thos. grocers, &c. 6 Broadway, Westminster
Collen Henry, artist, 29 Somerset st. Portman square
Collen John, wheelwright, 19 Lit. Turner st. Commercl. rd. East
Collender John, tailor, 9 Barbican
Collender Wm. paperhanger, &c. 54 Salmon lane, Limehouse
Collens Robert, hop & seed factor, 17 Maze pond, Boro'
Collens Wm. grocer & teadealer, 12 Bathurst st. Sussex sq
Colles Eliza (Miss), ladies' school, 21 Beauvoir ter. Kingsld
Collett Charles, fruiterer, 10 Aston place, Holloway
Collett Chas. M. solr. see Wimburn, Collett, Laurie & Attree
Collett Hannah (Mrs.), lace cleaner, 18 Manor pl. Walwth. rd
Collett Hen. John, fancy repository, 5 Seymour pl. Camdn. tn
Collett Hen. John & Co. manch. agts. & warehomn. 39 Friday st
Collett James, baker, 24 Beckford row, Walworth road
Collett John Richard, carpenter, 3 Ellis st. Sloane st
Collett Leonard, wheelwright, 9 Orange row, Kennington rd
Collett Mary Jane (Miss), milliner, 4 Waterloo pl. Pall mall
Collett Walter, cheesemonger, 4 Windsor pl. Old Kent rd
Collett William, bootmaker, 24 Betty st. Commercial road
Collette Charles H. solicitor, see Prichard & Collette
Colley George, livery stables, 6 North Portman mews
Colley Henry, fruiterer, 11 & 12 Ivy lane, Newgate st
Colley John & Son, hairdress. & perfum. 28 Bishopsga. within
Colley Richd. Bower, who. umbrella ma. see Evans & Colley
Colley Samuel, job master, 8 Marlborough road, Chelsea
Colley Thos. grocer & teadealer, 1 Princes st. Westminster
Colley Thomas, saddler & harness maker, 18 Cockspur st
Colley Wm. Edwd. *Tilt Boat* P.H. 4 Dark house la. Billingsgt
Colley Wm. John, millwright, 8 St. George's row, Pimlico
Colliard Jean Antoine, wine merchant, 15 Soho sq
Collick, Worsley & Co. who. druggists & chemists, 139 Up. Thames st. & 14 Laurence Pountney lane
Collick Richard, *Vine tap* P.H. 69 Bishopsgate within
Collicutt Edward, dairyman, 113 Chalton st. Somers town
Collie George, baker, 12 Motcomb st. Belgrave sq
Collie John, baker, 1 Bermondsey square
Collier Edmund & Sons, merchants, 15 New Broad st. City
Collier George & Son, bookbinders, 72 Hattongdn. & 4½ Cross st
Collier, Hedges & Steel, solicitors, & Steel, vestry clerk of St. Clement Danes & Liberty of the Rolls, 9 Carey st
Collier & Lownds, oil & italian wa. 11 Union ter. Nottinghill
Collier Samuel & Son, grocers, 1 Sussex ter. Old Brompton
Collier & Snee, navy agents, 3 Brick court, Temple
Collier Ship Office (John Anderson, mgr.), 5 Shadwell dock st.
Collier Benjamin, watchcase ma. 73 Rahere st. Goswell road
Collier Caleb, jeweller, 209 Sloane st. Knightsbridge
Collier Charles, physician, 20 Fitzroy square
Collier Elizabeth Mary (Mrs.), oil wareh. 31 Up. Marylebone s
Collier Francis, stables, Mason's yard, Duke st. St. James

Collier George, grocer, 2 Upper Kennington lane
Collier George Fred. physician, 32 Spring gardens, Charing cr
Collier James, coffee roaster, 10 Worship square, Finsbury
Collier James, coffee rooms, 190 Poplar High st
Collier Jesse, hat manufacturer, 67 Gt. Suffolk st. Borough
Collier Job, linen draper, 10 John's pl. Camberwell new rd
Collier John, cattle salesman, 8 West Smithfield
Collier John, haberdasher, 21 White Hart pl. Lwr. Kengtn.la
Collier Joseph Perkins, grocer, &c. 1 Albionter. Wandsworth rd
Collier Louisa (Miss), stationer, 1 Woburn bldgs. Tavistock sq
Collier Mary (Mrs.), cheesemonger, 13 Crawley st. Somers tn
Collier Noah, grocer & oilman, High st. Stoke Newington
Collier Thomas, plumber & glazier, Mare st. Hackney
Collier Thos. watch pendant ma. 6 President st. West, King sq
Collier Vincent J. auctioneer, brewery & estate agent, surveyor & valuer, 3 Moorgate st. City
Collier Wm. builder, &c. 23 Upper Bryanstone st. Portman sq. & 4 New Quebec st. Portman square
Collier William, carman, 39½ Rupert st. Haymarket
Collier William, tailor, 13 King st. Tower hill
Colliers Henry, tailor, 1 Oxford market
Collimore William, ham & beef dealer, 80 Whitechapel rd
Collin & Bourne, imp. & french wareh. 12 Skinner st. Snowhill
Collin & Errington, furriers, 6 Arabella row, Pimlico
Collin Henry & Co. furriers, 11 York row, Kennington road
Collin Geo. lodging house, 1 Belgrave st. south, Pimlico
Collin George, tailor, 21 Tavistock st. Covent garden
Collin Henry, fur manufacturer, 6 Albert st. Pimlico
Colling Cuthbert, currier, 87 & 88 Bartholomew close, City
Colling Joseph, shipowner, 44 & 45 Parsons st. St. George's st
Colling Robt. W. *Champion* P.H. 6 Salisbury st. Lissongrove
Colling Wm. beer retailer, 10 Portland ter. Walworth com
Collingbourn Mary (Mrs.), cowkeeper, 8 Church st. Cambwl
Collinge Charles & Co. patent axletree, sugar mill, & spherical hinge manufacturers, 64 Bridge road, Lambeth
Collingham Thomas, grocer, 46 Vauxhall walk, Lambeth
Collingridge & Davis, vinegar makrs. 227 Albany rd. Cambrwl
Collingridge Charles, solicitor, see Potter & Collingridge
Collingridge Elizh. (Mrs.), watchgilder, 27 Wilderness row
Collingridge Thomas, watchmaker, 136 Aldersgate st
Collingridge Thomas, *Yorkshire* coffee ho. 136 Aldersgate st
Collings Elizabeth & Sons, wine coopers & manufacturers of wine finings & spirit coloring, 30 Seething lane, Tower st
Collings Charles Wilkins, philosophical instrument maker, 12 Little Portland st
Collings Fred. Jas. optician, 15 Barnsbury row, Cloudsly sq
Collings Henry, bookseller, &c. 49 York road, Lambeth
Collings Henry, newsvender, 37 King st. Long acre
Collings John, chair & sofa maker, 12 George st. Portland pl
Collings, John, coffee rooms, 57 Aldermanbury
Collings John, sen. tailor, 20 Powell st. east, King sq
Collings John, jun. tailor, 14 Great Ormond st. Bloomsbury
Collings Louisa (Mrs.), plate powder ma. 3 City gdns. City rd
Collings Mary (Mrs.) fruiterer, Borough market
Collings Richard, tailor, 6 Lit. Ormond st. Queen sq. Bloomsby
Collings Robert, *Three Tuns* P.H. 83 Chancery lane
Collings Thos. cheesemonger, 1 Beckford row, Walworth rd
Collings Thomas, fruiterer, 3 Portman market, east side
Collings Wm. mast & block mkr. 6 Arch, Maze, Tooley st
Collings Wm. Henry, *Sugar Loaf* P.H. 8 King st. Drury la
Collington Samuel, oilman, 4 Gt. White Lion st. Seven dials
Collingwood Jas. & Edmund, butchers, 17 Lamb's Conduit st
Collingwood Hen. butcher, 9 Cumberland ter. Camden New tn
Collingwood John C. academy, 22 Brudenell pl. Nw. Nth.rd
Collingwood Mary (Mrs.), baker, 30 Langley pl. Cmmrcl.rd.ea
Collingwood Robert, jun. butcher, 4 Pratt st. Camden town
Collingwood William, meat salesman, 10 Newgate market
Collingsworth Samuel, tailor, 26 Shoemaker row, Blackfrs
Collins Brothers, clover, hay, &c. dlrs. 13 North wf. road, Paddington basin
Collins Chas. & Wm. Fred. linendrprs. 21, 22 & 23 Lr. Sloane st
Collins Edw. & Wm. paperhanging mnfr. see Duppa & Collins
Collins & Furber, refiners of gold, &c. 17 Jewin st. Cripplegate
Collins James & Son, butchers, 37 Marchmont st. Brunswick sq
Collins & Papprill, statnrs. 13 Bolingbroke row, Walworth rd
Collins & Rigley, solicitors, 5 Crescent pl. Bridge st. Black frs
Collins & Scarrot, engravers, 11 Gt. Winchester st. City
Collins Susannah & E. (Misses), dressma. 35 Wilson st. Finsby
Collins & Walker, who. grocers, 1 Turnwheel lane, Cannon st
Collins & Waters, linendrapers, 2 Lowndes terr. Knghtsbrdg
Collins William & Son, cattle salesmen, 60 West Smithfield
Collins Abel, *Roebuck* P.H. 50 Gt. Dover st. Borough
Collins Ann (Mrs.), boot & shoe maker, 56 Coleman st
Collins Ann (Mrs.), hatter, 21 High st. St. Giles's
Collins Benjamin, tinplate worker, 154 Shoreditch High st
Collins Charles, artificial florist, 109 Wood st. Cheapside
Collins Charles, *Brown Bear* P.H. 117 Up. East Smithfield
Collins Charles, butcher, 34 Upper Seymour st. Portman sq
Collins Charles, dining rooms, 54 Paradise row, Chelsea
Collins Charles, oilman, 9 Russell pl. Old Kent road
Collins Charles, painter & glazier, 6 Upper East Smithfield
Collins Charles, pat. metallic polshg. paste ma. 9 Bridgewatr sq
Collins Charles, *Seven Stars* P.H. 189 Brick la. Spitalfields
Collins Charles John. bookbndr. 16 Nassau st. Middlesex hsptl
Collins Charles Wm. phlsphcl. instrumt. mak. 12 Lt. Portland st
Collins Charles Wm. gold laceman, &c. see Clark & Collins
Collins Daniel, trunk & packing case maker, 310 Oxford st
Collins Edward, butcher, 17 Liquorpond st. Gray's inn lane
Collins Edwin, market gardener, Melbourne pl. Old Kent rd
Collins Eliz. (Mrs.), oil & italian wa. 9 Dorset st. Portman sq
Collins Eliz. (Mrs.), potato dealer, 2 Kingsgate st. Holborn
Collins Emma (Mrs.), awl blade ma. 47 Seward st. Goswell st
Collins Frances (Mrs.), sackingma. 9 & 17 Helmet rw. St. Luke's
Collins Francis, agent, &c. see Rheinlander & Collins
Collins Francis, goldsmith, 19 Green ter. New river head
Collins George, tailor, 8 Brown st. Bryanstone square
Collins George John, law stationer, 35 King st. Westminster, & 28 Cursitor st. Chancery lane
Collins Geo. Wm. barrister, 1 New square, Lincoln's inn
Collins Geo. Wm. harness deprtmnt. Bazaar, 5 Kingst. Portm.sq
Collins Goulding, bookbinder, 18 Holywell st. Millbank
Collins Henry, auctioneer & house agent, 3 Brook st. Bond st
Collins Henry, general salesman, 163 Shoreditch
Collins Henry, tailor, 56 Castle st. east, Oxford st
Collins Irvine, tailor, 14 Miles lane, Upper Thames st
Collins Isaac, coal merchant & charcoal burner, 6 Stafford place, Vauxhall bridge road
Collins James, *Giraffe* P.H. Penton place, Walworth
Collins James, gun & pistol repository, 115 Regent st
Collins James, hat manufactr. 31 Little Guildford st. Boro'
Collins James, silversmith & jeweller, 115 Regent st
Collins Jane (Mrs.), boot blocker, 7 Little Earl st. Seven dials
Collins Job Wm. chemist, 135 High st. & 33 Park st. Camden tn
Collins John, bootmaker, 39 Wardour st. Soho
Collins John, bootmaker, 42 Whitcomb st. Pall Mall east
Collins John, butcher, 6 Glo'ster ter. Vauxhall bridge road
Collins John, carpenter, 20 Lambeth High st
Collins John, cattle salesman, 60 West Smithfield
Collins John, cheesemonger, 13 Warwick st. Pimlico
Collins John, chemist & druggist, 51 Piccadilly
Collins John, fruiterer & coal dealer, 5 London wall
Collins John, paintr. & glaz. 12 Cannon st. rd. St. George's east
Collins John, printer, 44 King st. Soho
Collins John, silk hat maker, 19 Crown st. Soho
Collins John, tailor & breeches maker, see Hunt & Collins
Collins John, who. haberdashr. & fringe ma. 23 Fore st. Cripplgt
Collins John, wheelwright, Middle yd. Gt. Queen st. Linc. inn fi
Collins John, wholesale toy ma. 13 Hatfield st. & 20 Blkfrs. rd
Collins John Geo. teadealer & grocer, 62 Snow hill
Collins John Richard, chemist, 120 Crawford st
Collins John Wm. plumber, 6 Wyndham road, Camberwell
Collins Jonathan, butcher, 293 High Holborn
Collins Joseph, butcher, 17 Red Lion st. High Holborn
Collins Joseph, butcher, 19 Watling st
Collins Joseph, hairdresser, 17 Robert st. Grosvenor sq
Collins Joseph, statuary & mason, 16 NewChurch st. Lisn. gr
Collins Joseph, tailor, 3 Albion bldngs. Bartholomew close
Collins Julia (Miss), bookseller, 29 Orchard st. Portman sq
Collins Julius, surgeon, 89 Mary st. Regent's park
Collins Luke, hatter, 1 Brill row, Somers town
Collins Maria (Mrs.), hat mfr. 6 Back Church la. Whitechpl
Collins Maria (Mrs.), tobacconist, 154 Princes rd. Lambeth
Collins Martha (Mrs.), haberdasher, 6 Whitmore pl. Hoxton
Collins Robert, bedstead & cabinet maker, 1 Brook st. New rd
Collins Robert, beer retailer, 1 Canterbury pl. Old Kent rd
Collins Robert, coal dealer, 9 Hop gardens, St. Martin's la
Collins Robert, greengrocer, 19 Bedfordbury, Cov. grdn
Collins Robert, teadealer, 31 New road, St. George's East
Collins Robert Nelson, who. druggist, see Elliott & Collins
Collins Samuel, butcher, 21 New st. Covent garden, & 9 Crown court, Pall mall
Collins Samuel, ironmonger, 11 Rathbone pl. & 17 Wardour st
Collins Saml. Yeoman, bookslr. & pub. 17½ Holywell st. Strand
Collins Sarah (Mrs.), *Evelyn Arms* P.H. Grove st. Deptford
Collins Simeon, picture imptr. & cleaner, 118 Piccadilly
Collins Susannah (Mrs.), milliner, 11 Stucley ter. Camden tn
Collins Thomas (agent to Burd & Sons), calico printers, Manchester, 6 Clement's court, Milk st
Collins Thomas, builder, 11 Newland terrace, Kensington
Collins Thomas, butcher, 194 Piccadilly
Collins Thos. coffee rooms, 12 Ropemakers fields, Limeho
Collins Thomas, fruiterer, 4 Orange row, Kennington rd

Collins Thomas, ornmntl. paintr. 2 Villa pl. Walworth comn
Collins Thomas James, grocer, 4 Leman st. Goodman's fields
Collins Wm. artist, 1 Devonport st. Hyde park
Collins Wm. baker, 2 John's pl. Old Kent road
Collins Wm. baker, 64 Snow hill
Collins Wm. baker, 77 Whitechapel High st
Collins Wm. carver, 16 Paradise st. Finsbury
Collins Wm. dairyman, 28 Lisle st. Leicester square
Collins Wm. dealer in horses, 25 Mount st. Lambeth
Collins Wm. fancy cabinet maker, 3 Glo'ster st. St. John st. rd
Collins Wm. glass enameller to the Queen, & cut glass manufacturer to the royal family, 227 Strand
Collins Wm. greengrocer, 6 Upper James st. Golden square
Collins Wm. grocer, 35 Little Queen st. Holborn
Collins Wm. haberdasher, 37 Freeschool st. Horselydown
Collins Wm. horsedealer, North st. Lambeth
Collins Wm. painter, 11 Church st. Cheyne walk, Chelsea
Collins Wm. skinner & furrier, 2 Earl st. Finsbury
Collins Wm. *Star* coffee rooms, 8 Oxford market, Oxford st
Collins Wm. Anthony, barrister, 3 Old square, Lincoln's inn
Collins William Henry, artist, 14 Poultry
Collins Wm. Louis, white hart brewery, Wood st. Westminstr
Collinson Alfred, surgeon, 1 Monmouth place, Old Kent road
Collinson Edward, lampmaker & gasfitter, 95 Blackman st
Collinson Edward, upholsterer, 4 Allsop pl. Regent's park
Collinson George C. upholsterer, see Hurley & Collinson
Collinson Henry, chemist, 9 Aske st. Hoxton
Collinson John, carpenter, South Molton lane, Brook st
Collinson Joseph, *Bazaar tav.* P.H. 10 King st. Portman sq
Collinson Joseph, wholesale stationer, 3 Great Trinity lane
Collinson Joseph, saddler, see Ashdown & Collinson
Collinson Thos. tinplate worker & oilman, 35 Lombard st
Collinson Thos. Wm. Y. grocer, 8 Nottingham st. Marylebone
Collinson Wm. Fras. brassfounder, see Cope & Collinson
Collis Matthew & Wm. printers, 52 Bow lane, Cheapside
Collis Charles, hairdresser, 3 Shoe lane, Fleet st
Collis Edward, solicitor, 6 New Ormond st. Lamb's cond. st
Collis James, accountant, 10 Berkeley st. Clerkenwell
Collis James, architect, 2 Shaftesbury cres. Vauxhall bdg. rd
Collis James, paper hanger, 21 Platt terrace, Pancras rd
Collis Jas. Daniel, hairdresser, &c. 3 Mill st. Hanover sq
Collis Joseph, glass dealer, 23 Great Saffron hill
Collis Maria (Mrs.), straw hat ma. 21 William st. Regent's pk
Collis Thomas, *Black Dog* P.H. 34 Vauxhall walk, Lambeth
Collis Thomas, coffee rooms, 4 Princes st. Leicester sq
Collison Chas. & Co. patten tie french clog & clog material & patent leather manufrs. Star corner, Bermondsey, & 92 Blackman st. Borough
Collison Francis & Co. merchants, 32 Fenchurch st
Collison George, carpenter, 4 King st. Soho
Collison George (Rev.) school, Well st. Hackney
Collison John Webb, *Horse & Sacks* P.H. 26 Harrow rd. Paddng
Collison Maria (Miss & Co.), french clog & ladies' shoe warehouse, 92 Blackman st. Borough
Collison Wm. *British Lion* P.H. 14 & 15 Bartholomew terrace
Collison Wm. fruiterer, &c. 72 York st. Westminster
Colliss John, *World's End* P.H. 59 Newington causeway
Colliss Moses A. glass manufy. 100 Gt. Saffron hill, Hat. gar
Collisson William, solicitor, deputy clerk of assize for the Midland circuit, 28 Great James st. Bedford row
Colliver John, smith in general, 18 Compton st. Clerkenwell
Colliver Joseph, coffee & chop house, 54 Holywell st. Strand
Collman & Davis, decorators & upholsterers, 49 Curzon st
Collmann & Stolterfoht, merchants, 34 Broad st. buildings
Colls Charles & Co. discount agts. 38 Nicholas la. Lombardst
Colls Benjamin, plumber & glazier, 3 Union row, Camberwell
Colls Christmas Wm. *Rainbow tavern*, 15 Fleet st
Colls Letteus, silk warehouseman, 18 Charles st. St. James's
Colls Richard, artist, 18 Charles st. St. James's
Colls Thomas, chandler's shop, 11 King's Head ct. Shoe lane
Colls William, *Rainbow tavern*, 15 Fleet st.
Collyear & Lokier, butchers, 48 Cheyne walk, Chelsea
Collyer & Blackmore, surgeons, 24 Old st. road
Collyer Elizh. & Ann, booksels. 5 Prospectpl. Cheynewk. Chlsa
Collyer Chas. *Coopers' Arms* P.H. 19 Budge row, Cannon st.; & *Plough & Harrow* P.H. 1 Orange row, Kennington rd
Collyer Cornelius, window blind maker, 47 Salisbury square
Collyer George, boot & shoemaker, Denmark hill, Cambrwl
Collyer George Samuel, army agent, 9 Park pl. St James st
Collyer Henry, plumber & painter, 26 Broad st. Lambeth
Collyer James Wenden, *Rainbow* P.H. 24 Newgate st.
Collyer James Wendon, cattle salesman, 15 West Smithfield
Collyer John, barrister, 10 Serle st. Lincoln's inn
Collyer John, oil & colorman, 26 Princes st. Westminster
Collyer Joseph, plumber, 63 Gt. Carlisle st. Portman mrkt
Collyer Samuel, solicitor, 42 Southampton bldgs. Chanceryla
Collyer William, bricklayer, 45 East st. Kennington road
Collyhole Eleanora, (Mrs.), dressma. 14 Young st. Kensington
Colman Jeremiah & Jas. mers. & mustard manfs. 1 Dowgate hill
Colman Alexander, butcher, 5 Upper Church st. Chelsea
Colman Chas. Rt. ship agt. & whrfigr. Iron gate wharf tower
Colman Edward, tobacconist, 1 East India road, Poplar
Colman George Augustus, solicitor, 2 New inn, Strand
Colman John, laceman, 172 Regent st.
Colman Samuel P. hotpresser, see Shepherd & Colman
Colman Thomas, tobacconist, 25 Skinner st. Somers town
Colman Wm. Gooding, architect & survyr. 2 New inn, Strand, Colman's Wharf, St. Katherine's Tower
Colnaghi Paul & Dominic & Co. printsellers to her Majesty, 14 Pall mall east.
Colnet William, *Cock tavern*, 201 Fleet st.
Colomba & Hare, barometer & thermometer maker, 37 Charles st. Hatton garden, & 89 Chancery lane
Colombian Mining Ass. (L. R. Jones, sec.), 13 Austin friars
Colombine David Elwin, attorney, 8 Carlton chbs. Regent st
Colombo John, doll maker, 26 Litt. Russell st. Bloomsbury
Colonial Bank (Chas. A. Calvert, sec.), 13 Bishopsgatewithin
Colonial Bishopricks' Fund (Honble. Mr. Justice Coleridge, Archdeacon Hale & Rt. Honble. Wm. E. Gladstone, treasurers; Rev. E. Hawkins, B.D. hon. sec.), 79 Pall mall
Colonial Church Society (Capt. Cotton, sec.), 5 Exeter hall
Colonial Department Office, 13 & 14 Downing st
Colonial Gazette Office, 320 Strand
Colonial Land & Emigration Board & South Australian Commission, 9 Park st. Westminster, 11 to 5
Colonial Missionary Socy. (Rev. A. Wells, sec.) 4 Blomfieldst
Colosseum, Regent's park
Colquhoun Jas. hanseatic consul, 12 St. James's pl. St. James's
Colquhoun Patrick, LL.D. barrister, 12 St. James's place
Colson Jesson, harpist, 26 Store st. Bedford square
Colson John Thomas, auctioneer, 4 Water st. Blackfriars
Colson Wm. Drake, hat manufactr. 1 Frederick place, & straw hat manfr. 9 Upper st. Islington & 303 High Holborn
Colston Wm. & Co. woollen drapers, 23 Bridge rd. Lambeth
Colston Clara (Miss), brushwareh. 11 Peel pl. Kensng. gravl. pt
Colston Danl. Edwd. upholsterer, 97 High st. Notting hill
Colston Danl. E. upholster. 10 Peel pl. Kensington Gravel pits
Colston Samuel, grocer, 22 Vauxhall bridge road
Colthard Thomas, bookbinder, 19 Grove st. Camden town
Colthard Thos. Wm. engraver, 26 Red Lion st. High Holborn
Colthrup George, grocer, 1 Gloucester pl. Walworth common
Coltman Susan (Mrs.), milliner & dressmaker, 31 Pall mall
Colton James, tailor, 16 Dean st. Fetter lane
Colton Wm. hairdresser, 13 Whitcomb st. Pall mall East
Coltson John, coal marchant, 65 Bankside
Colven Richd. builder, 5½ Park st. Borough market
Colven Richd. *Prodigal's Return* P.H. Bridge rd. Battersea
Colven Thomas, builder, 5 Counter st. Borough
Colverd Henry, *Cherry Tree* P.H. Bromley, Middlesex
Colverd Saml. *Ship & Mermaid* P.H. 19 Snow's flds. Brmndsy
Colvile Andrew, west india merchant, 9 Fenchurch buildings
Colvile James William, barrister, 9 New sq. Lincoln's inn
Colvill Henry, engraver, &c. 32 Southampton st. Covnt. grdn
Colville John & Co. merchants, 6 Crosby sq. Bishopsgt. within
Colvin James, & Alexander & Bazett David, india agents; see Crawford, Colvin & Co
Colwell Chas. hat box ma. 2 Surrey row, Blackfriars road
Colwell Henry, boot & shoe maker, 71 Lambeth walk
Colwell Henry, truss maker, 2 Horse Shoe ct. Ludgate hill
Colwill Charles, carpenter, 16 Beaufort buildings, Strand, & 32 Brydges st. Covent garden
Colwill Robert, tin plate worker, 14 Church rd. Coml. rd. Ea
Colyer Joseph & Co. coopers, back & vat makers, & bottle beer dealers, 42 Leman st. Goodman's fields
Colyer Benjamin, jeweller, 28 Polygon, Clarendon square
Colyer Edward, engraver, printer & lithog. 17 Fenchurch st
Coman Robins Chas. *Sun & Sword* P.H. 66 Cable st. Wellclosesq
Combe Boyce, magistrate, Clerkenwell police court
Combe, Delafield & Co. porter brewers, Castle st. Long acre
Combe Henry, surgeon, 2 Caroline st. Bedford square
Combe Jas. civil engineer, Lombard st. chambs. 33 Clement's la
Combe John, attorney, 9 Staple inn, Holborn
Comber George, carpenter, 2 Denmark st. Ratcliff highway
Comber Richard, silk broker, 28 Great Winchester st
Combs John & Son, bottle merchants, 11 Gt. Bush la. Cannon st
Combs John, grocer & cheesemonger, Well st. Hackney
Combs Wm. A. flint glass warehouse, 11 Gt. Bush la. Cannon st
Comer Thomas, jun. merchant, see Staunton, Comer & Co
Comerford & Girdler, public notaries, 7 Tokenhse. yd. Lothby
Comerford Charles, solicitor, 72 Old Broad st. City
Comerford Michael, furniture broker, 58 Baldwin's grdns
Comfort & Falconer, furn. undertaks. 3 Bartlett's pass. Holborn

Comfort James & Joseph, woollen warehousemen, 123 Wood st
Comfort William & Son, butchers, 77 Farringdon st
Comfort Charles, tailor, &c. 73 Coleman st. Bank
Comfort Edward, bootmaker, 153 Goswell st
Comfort Edward, trimming seller, 43 Silver st. Golden sq
Comfort George, butcher, 92 Fetter lane, Holborn
Comfort Hen. caneworker, 20 Stephen st. Tottenham ct. rd
Comfort James, butcher, 150 Goswell st
Comfort John, butcher, Mare st. Hackney
Comfort John, upholsterer, 8 Wells row, Upper st. Islington
Comfort Robert, hair manufacturer, & tambor & skin parting worker, 5 Goodman's court, St. Martin's lane
Comfort Thomas, butcher, 3 Gloucester place, Islington
Comin Mary (Mrs.), boot war. 2 Church st. St. George's, Boro'
Comley Henry John, bootmaker, 7 Wells st. Oxford st
Comley John, boot & shoe maker, 92 Berwick st. Soho
Comley John, ivory & bone tooth, nail & hair brush manufacturer, 3 North st. Little Moorfields
Comley John, surgeon, 46 Gt. Alie st. Goodman's fields
Comley John, tobacconist, 87 Crown ct. Water st. Blackfriars
Comley John, tobacconist, 15 White Hart pl. Lr. Kengtn. la
Comley Thomas, coffee rooms, 125 Wardour st. Soho
Comley Wm. dentist & cupper, 7 Osborne st. Whitechapel
Comley William, boot & shoe maker, 5 Tyler st. Golden sq
Comley William, shoemaker, 24 George st. Portland place
Commander-in-Chief's Office, Horse Guards; hours 10 to 5
Commercial Bank of London (Alfred R. Cutbill, manager), 6 Lothbury; *Western Branch*, 6 Henrietta st. Covent gdn. see page 2003
Commercial Daily List Office, 42 Mincing lane
Commercial Dock Company's Office (H. K. Smithers, jun. sec.), 106 Fenchurch st
Commercial Gas Light & Coke Company (Henry Avery, sec.), Ben Jonson's fields, Stepney
Commercial & General Life Assurance Association (Frederic Lawrence, sec.), 112 & 113 Cheapside. For direct. see page 2017
Commercial Road Office, 3 Crosby square, Bishopsgate; hours 10 to 5
Commercial Sale Rooms, between 29 & 36 Mincing lane—*Accountant's Office*, 37 Sale Rooms; hours 10 to 3
Commercial Sale Rooms Coffeehouse, Mincing lane
Commercial Travellers' Society Office (Thomas Peach, sec.), 38 Ludgate hill
Commercial Wharf & Old Swan Pier, Leman & Bryan, between 98 & 101 Upper Thames st
Commin Mary Ann (Mrs.), dressma. 20 Everett st. Brunswick sq
Commins John, *White Lion* P.H. 13 Lit. James st. Bedford row
Commissary of London's Registry Office for Wills & Administrations, 16 Great Knightrider st.; hours 9 to 4
Commissary of Surrey's Off. 12 Gt. Knightrider st.; hrs. 10 to 5
Commissioners for Affidavits in Chancery, Q. B., C. P. & Ex. & Bankruptcy Courts, Ireland, & for Proof & Registry of Deeds in Ireland, 10 Southamp. bdgs.; hrs. 10 to 4
Commissioners for Building New Churches, 13 Great George street; 10 to 5
Commissioners of Clerkenwell Paving, 23 Upr. Rosoman st
Commissioners for Improving the Metropolis (Trenham Walsham Philips, secretary), 1 Whitehall place
Commissioners of Land & Assessed Taxes (St. Martin's), 19 Buckingham st. Strand; hours of business, Wednes. Thurs. & Fri. 12 to 2
Commissioners in Lunacy, 45 Lincoln's inn fields; 10 to 4
Commissioners for Paving St. John's District (Wm. Bartholomew, sec.), 56 St. John's square
Commissioners of Police, 4 Whitehall place; hours 10 to 4
Commission for Promoting the Fine Arts (Chas. Locke Eastlake, sec.), Gwydir house, Whitehall
Commissioners for the Registration, &c. of Coal Whippers, King James's stairs, 71 Wapping wall
Commiss. of Revenue Enquiry (Thomas Peregrine Courtenay, sec.), Gwydir house, Whitehall; hours 10 to 4
Commissioners of Sewers; see "Sewers"
Commissioners of Slave Compensation, 45 Parliament st.; hours 11 to 4
Commissioners of the Southampton Estate Paving Acts (John Walker Wilkins, survr.), 10 Edward st. Hampstead road; hours 10 to 4
Commissioners of Taxes for Holborn & Finsbury (James Buchell, clerk), 24 Red Lion sq.; hours 10 to 5
Commissioners of Whitechapel Paving, Kent & Essex yard, 114 Whitechapel High st
Committee of Spanish American Bondholders (Alfred Godfrey sec.), Stock Exchange.
Committee of Portuguese Bondholders, Old Swan wharf
Committee of Spanish Bondholders, Old Swan wharf
Common Pleas (Court of), Westminster Hall & Guildhall
Common Pleas, Serjeants' inn, Chancery la. hours of business (except in Rule department):—term, 11 to 5; vacation, 11 to 3; 10th August to 24th October, 11 to 2. In Rule department—term, 11 to 3 & 6 to 8; vacation, 11 to 3; & Aug. 10 to Oct. 24, 11 to 2
Compere Thos. paper mnfs'. agent, 16 Cleveland st. Mile e. rd
Compigne Henry, solicitor, 24 Bucklersbury
Complin Edward Thomas, surgeon, 24 Charterhouse sq
Compson Edward, fishmonger, 116 Vauxhall walk, Lambeth
Comptess Louis, watchcase maker, 10 East st. Red Lion sq
Compton & Foster, tin foil beaters, &c. 31 Dunning's alley
Compton & Fowler, chemists, &c. 14 Brewer st. Golden sq
Compton & Ritchie, printers, 23 Middle st. Cloth fair
Compton Edward, tailor, 1 Nicholas passage, Nicholas lane
Compton George, *Queen's Head* P.H. 44 Broad st. Lambeth
Compton Henry, pewterer & tin foil beater, 37 Fenchurch st. & 9 Booth st. Spitalfields
Compton Hen. Jas. *Cadogan hotel*, 75 Sloane st. Chelsea
Compton James, *City of London* P.H. 30 Dalby ter. City rd
Compton John, butterman, 7 Great Marylebone st
Compton Lemuel, beer retailer, 105 Drummond st. Eusto sq
Compton Nevin, architect, 51 Moorgate st
Compton Ralph, solicitor, see Crosby & Compton
Compton Thos. auctioneer, estate agent, &c. 51 Moorgate st
Compton Wm. Hen. letter pr. & copper pl. printer & engra. & agt. for Lon. Edinb. & Dublin Life As. Co. 55 Paddington st. Marylebone
Comptroller of Corn Returns Office (Geo. Joyce, receiver), Board of Trade, 52 Parliament st.; hours 10 to 4
Comptroller Gen. for Receipt of Exchequer, 3 Whitehall yd
Comrie Alexander, surveyor, 2 Bridge st. Westminster
Comyn Fitzwilliam, solicitor, see Vandercom, Cree, Law & Co
Comyn Richard, solicitor, 27 Lincoln's inn fields
Comyns Thomas R. carpet & commsn. agt. 5 New Farringdon st
Comyns Henry, optician, 5 Hereford ter. King's rd. Chelsea
Conant John Edward, barrister, 19 Upper Wimpole st
Conaway John, cheesemonger, 3 Gray's inn lane
Concanen Alfred, bookseller, stationer & advertising agent, 17 Southampton buildings, Chancery lane
Concanen George, solicitor, see Hodgson, Concanen & Noyes
Concanon James, bootmaker, 5 Opera arcade, Haymarket
Condell Charles, solicitor, see Barrett & Condell
Conder Edw. who. coffee dealr. 2 Salters' hall ct. Cannon st
Condon David, tailor, 84 Edgware rd. Marylebone
Condon John, oil & colorman, 1 Villa st. Walworth common
Condron Charles, crape & silk mfr. see Warland, Condron & Co
Conen Elizth. (Mrs.), watchcase ma. 14 Rahere st. Goswell rd
Conen Geo. desk & dressg. case mak. 41 Spencer st. Goswell rd
Coney Ann (Mrs.), poulterer, see Lyons & Coney
Coney Charles, french staymaker, 86 Oxford st
Coney James, statuary & mason, 24 Wharf, Paddington basin, North side
Coney William, stationr. & tobacconist, 60 Wardour st. Soho
Coneyheare John, *King's Arms* P.H. 48 Orchard st. Westminstr
Congerton Thomas, organ bldr. &c. 36 Salisbury st. Lisson gr
Congregational Committee on Gen. Education (Charles Hindley, esq. M.P. chairman, Rev. A. Reed, D.D. sec.), 4 Coleman st. buildings
Congregational Library (Ed. Churchyard, librarian), 4 Blomfield st. Finsbury
Congregational School Society (Rev. George Rose, secretary), 4 Blomfield st. Finsbury
Congregational Union Society (Rev. Algernon Wells, secretary), 4 Blomfield st. Finsbury
Congreve & De Lisle, druggists, 1 New Bridge st. Vauxhall
Congreve Rocket & Ordnance Stores Manufactory, 14 London st. Fenchurch st. & West Ham, Essex
Congreve John, painter, 19 Hardington st. Portman market
Congreve Wm. printer, 26 Duke st. Lincoln's inn fields
Coningsby John, cheesemonger, 78 Hackney road
Coningsby Wm. cheesemonger, 7 Broughton pl. Hackney rd
Coniston & Bassett, engineers & print. pr. ma. 57 Bunhill row
Conne Nicholas, engraver on glass, 33 Princes st. Leicester square, & 71 Great Portland st
Connell Cath. (Mrs.), dressmaker, 4 Low. John st. Golden sq
Connell Daniel, china wareho. 18 Union st. Bishopsgate
Connell Elizh. (Mrs.), milliner, Camberwell green
Connell John, parliament agent, see Richardson & Connell
Connell Mary Eliza (Miss), milliner, 147 New Bond st
Connell Philip, perfumer & berlin repos. Camberwell green
Connell Timothy, tailor, 14 King st. Soho
Connell Wm. chronometer ma. 22 Myddelton st. Spafields
Connell William, hat manufacturer, 154 Tooley st
Connell William, tailor, 4 Lower John st. Golden square
Connelly James, tobacconist, 5 Surrey pl. Newington butts
Conner Esther (Mrs.), *Elder Tree* P.H. 12 Elder st. Norton fol

Conner George, oil & colorman, 235 Shoreditch High st
Conner Henry, pianoforte maker, 9 George st. Euston sq
Connerton John Meredith, mast & oar ma. 2 Gt. Cherry grdn. st
Connett John, butcher, 11 Hastings st. Burton crescent
Connew Reginald, bricklayer, &c. 12 Brown's la. Spitalfields
Conneybeer John, coffee rooms, 161 High st. Camden town
Conningsby Thomas, cheesemonger, 249 Bethnal green road
Connolly James, tailor, 4 Belgrave mews East, Belgrave sq
Connolly Wm. Edw. *Angel* P.H. 37 Thayer st. Manchester sq
Connollys Sarah & Son, italian wa. 12 Blandford st. Maryleb
Connor Andrew, tailor, see Maney & Connor
Connor Barnard, tailor, 19 Castle st. East, Oxford market
Connor Chas. auctioneer & furniture brok. Mare st. Hackney
Connor John, chemist & druggist, 171 Waterloo road
Connor Joseph, tobacconist, Gibraltar row, Deptford lwr. rd
Connor Richard, cabinet maker, Mare st. Hackney
Connor William, M.D. surgeon, Devonshire house, Battersea
ConnortonJno. agt. to W. of Egld. fire ins. Alfred pl. Waterloo rd
Conolly Hugh, teadealer, 1 Old North st. Red Lion square
Conolly Wm. general dealer, Treport pl. Wandsworth road
Conquest Benj. Oliver, *Garrick tav.* 25 Leman st. Goodmn's. fi
Conquest Ebenezer, builder, &c. 4 Albion pl. Holloway road
Conquest George, seal engraver, 108 Shoe lane, Fleet st
Conquest George, tin plate worker, 27 Old Change
Conquest John, solicitor, 53 Moorgate st. Bank
Conquest John T. F.L.S. physician, 13B, Finsbury square
Conquest Wm. S. russia broker, 13 Finsbury sq. & Baltic
Conrath Henry, baker, 6 Lower Seymour st. Portman square
Cons Frederick, pianoforte, &c. key ma. 81 John st. Fitzroy sq
Conscience Peter & Co. clock & watch makers, 17 Basing la
Conservative Club (E. C. Hampton, sec.), 74 St. James's st
Consolidated Tretoil Mining Co. 8 George yard, Lombard st
Const John Heyborne & Co. house & estate agents, 6 Copthall buildings, & ivory turner, 31 Red Lion st. Clerkenwell
Const Chas. upholsterer & furn. wa. 207 Tottenham ct. rd
Const John Heyborne, jun. ivory & hard wood turner & maker of conjuring tricks & puzzling toys, 15 Lit. Queen st. Holborn
Constable & Finden, wholesale druggist, 254 Boro' High st
Constable Charl. (Mrs.), midwife, 18 Henrietta st. Manch. sq
Constable Eliza (Mrs.), baker, 32 Clark st. Stepney
Constable Henry, baker, 29 Assembly row, Mile end road
Constable Henry, grocer, 1 Broad st. Bloomsbury
Constable James, boot & shoe maker, 1 Hare pl. Fleet st
Constable John, cheesemonger, 24 Shoemaker row, Blackfrs
Constable John, west india merchant, 39 Lime st
Constable Joshua, hairdresser, 30 Strutton ground, Westminsr
Constable Thomas, ironmonger, see Green & Constable
Constable Thomas, tallowchandler, Church st. Hackney
Constable William, builder, 1 Regent st. Blackwall
Constable William, grocer, 7 Temple place, Old Kent road
Constable William, linendraper, 202 Tottenham court road
Constance & Fisher, dress ma. & milnrs. 79 Lisson grove Nth
Constance Wm. druggist, 5 Hanover pl. Regent's park rd
Constantine Thomas Wm. surveyor, 8 New Ormond st
CONSULS:—*See General Index*
Conti Graziano, wine merchant, 127 Regent st
Conves Thomas, baker, 364 Rotherhithe
Conway & Howe, wholesale teadealers, 2 Star court, Bread st
Conway, Phelps & Hayward, who. grocers, 4 Maiden la. Cheaps
Conway Charles, carver & gilder, Rose yard, Rose st. Soho
Conway Cornelius, coal & coke dlr. 21 Gravel la. Southwark
Conway Daniel, tailor, 40 Church road, Commercial rd. Ea
Conway Edwin, butcher, 73 Hackney road
Conway Henry, writer on glass, &c. 15 Old Compton st. Soho
Conway John Coggan, who. grocer, see Brown & Conway
Conway Philip, florist, Earl's court, Old Brompton
Conway Wm. furniture brkr. 2 Catherine st. Commerl. rd. Ea
Conwell William, carpenter, 41 King st. Clerkenwell
Conyers Ellen Miss, milliner, &c. 7 King st. Portman sq
ConyersThos. G. sec. of *Crown Life Assur. Co.* 33 New Bridge st
Conyers Wm. carpenter, 4 Wellington st. Blackfriars road
Coode, Browne & Kingdon, solicitors, 13 Bedford row
Cook & Cole (Misses) preptry. school, 27 & 28 Queen's rw. Walwth
Cook James & Mary (Mrs.), builders, 6 & 7 Penton row, & 5 Manor place, Walworth
Cook John & Edward, hard & soft soap makers, melters & dealers in tallow, 11 Goodman's yard, Minories
Cook John Richard & Co. printers, 76 Fleet st
Cook John & Son, melters & tallow merchts. Goodman's yard
Cook & Humphreys, solicitors, 28 St. Swithin's lane, City
Cook & Maple, carpet warehо. 22 & 23 Middle Queen's blds. Knightsbridge, & 145 & 147 Tottenham court road
Cook, Rowley & Co. coachbuilders & harness makers, 9½ King st. Golden square, & 37 Liquorpond st. Hatton garden
Cook & Piper, composition ornament mnfr. 90 Dean st. Soho
Cook Samuel & Son, cattle salesmen, 41 West Smithfield
Cook & Sanders, attorneys, 1 New inn, Wych st. Strand
Cook, Sons & Co. warehousemen, 21, 22, 23, 24, 25 & 26 St. Paul's church yard
Cook & Williams, tailors, 10 Princes st. Hanover sq
Cook Aaron Speechley, hairdresser, 3 Noel st. Wardour st
Cook Absolom, carver & gilder, 54 Upper Marylebone st
Cook Albert, boot & shoe maker, 56 Hoxton Old town
Cook Arthur, cheesemonger, 4 North st. Edgware road
Cook Bartholomew, tailor, 57 Drummond st. Euston sq
Cook Caleb, locksmith, 7 Marlborough road, Chelsea
Cook Charles, baker, 50 Duke st. Manchester sq
Cook Charles, boot & shoe maker, 20 Gt. Bath st. Clerkenwll
Cook Charles, butcher, 39 Red Lion st. Holborn
Cook Charles, furnishing ironmonger, 153 Houndsditch
Cook Charles, *George & Dragon* P.H. 6 Hoxton market
Cook Chas. hairdresser, 28 White Hart pl. Lr. Kenningtn. la
Cook Charles, news agent, 16 New North st. Red Lion sq
Cook Charles, painter & decorator, 41 North Audley st
Cook Charles, jun. butcher, 50 Sloane square
Cook Charles Bates, lathe & tool dealer, 124 Old st. St. Luke's
Cook David, glass grinder, 13 Great Chapel st. Oxford st
Cook Edward, *King's Arms* P.H. 20 Wilkes st. Spitalfields
Cook Elijah, grocer, 11 Little Newport st. Leicester sq
Cook Emma (Miss), dressmaker. 24 Lit. Charlotte st. Blkfrs. rd
Cook Francis, bootmaker, 1 Bengal place, New Kent road
Cook Frederick, cheesemonger, 126 High st. Camden town, & 1 Plumber's row, City road
Cook Frederick, fruiterer, 3 Freeman's pl. Mile end road
Cook George, *Blue Anchor* P.H. 17 Mile end road
Cook Geo. engraver & printer, 17 Gt. Windmill st. Haymarket, & 72 New Compton st. Soho
Cook George, grocer, 38 Greek st. Soho
Cook Geo. grocer, 36 Red Lion st. Clerkenwell green
Cook Geo. livery stables, 4 Connaught terrace, Edgeware rd
Cook Geo. *Marquis Cornwallis* P.H. 61 Collier st. Pentnv
Cook George, *Tower* P.H. 19 Artillery st. Bishopsgate
Cook Geo. spring ma. & tire smith, 7 Gt. Chapel st. Westminster
Cook Geo. Simon, solicitor, see Le Blanc & Cook
Cook Geo. Thomas, hosier, 21 Sun st. Bishopsgate
Cook George W. F. solicitor, 46 York st. Portman sq
Cook Henry, cab proprietor, 1 Brook mews, Gloucester rd
Cook Henry, coal mercht. Western wf. George st. Adelphi
Cook Henry, *Mogul* P.H. 167 Drury lane
Cook Henry, whiskey, brandy, & coal mercht. 22 Budge row
Cook Henry James, linendraper, 27 Hedge row, Islington
Cook Henry Joseph, bookbinder, New yard, Gt. Queen st. Hbrn
Cook Isaac, cabinet mak. & upholst. 24 Lit. Charlot. st. Blkfrs. rd
Cook James, baker, 9 Boundary st. Shoreditch
Cook James, bricklayer, 27 Singleton st. Hoxton new town
Cook James, cheesemonger, 171 Shoreditch High st
Cook James, furnishing undertaker, 31 Lambeth Lwr. marsh
Cook James, furniture broker, 34 Exeter st. Lisson grove
Cook James, general broker, see Trueman & Cook
Cook James, marine store dealer, 150 Brick lane, Spitalfields
Cook James, oil & colorman, 65 St. James's ter. Waterloo rd
Cook James, painter, &c. 40 Bow lane, Cheapside
Cook James, *Royal Oak* P.H. 19 Barnet st. Hackney road
Cook James, saddler, 18 Upper Berkeley st. west
Cook James, tailor, 2 Upper Charles st. Parliament st
Cook James, tobacconist, 268 Poplar High st
Cook James, watch cap maker, 5 Robert st. Hoxton
Cook James Richd. tailor, 54 Great Queen st. Lincoln's inn fi
Cook James S. baker, 15 Charles st. St. James's square
Cook James Smith, brass rule cutter, 1 Neville's ct. Fetter la
Cook Jane (Miss), ladies' school, 3 Union road, Rotherhithe
Cook Job, hatter, 68 Millbank st. Westminster
Cook John, baker, 48 Edgware rd. & 1 Queen st. Bryanstone sq
Cook John, *Beckford's Head* P.H. 161 Kent st. Borough
Cook John, bootmaker, High st. Deptford
Cook John, butcher, 49 Great Peter st. Westminster
Cook John, chimney sweeper, 17 Gt. Windmill st. Haymarket
Cook John, coach wheelwright, 20 Upper Bryanstone st
Cook John, coaldealer, 35 Red Lion st. Spitalfields
Cook John, confectioner, 5 Charlotte st. Whitechapel
Cook John, corn & seed merchant, 91 Whitechapel High st
Cook John, fur dyer, White's grounds, Bermondsey st
Cook John, gun & pistol manufactr. 6 Well st. Wellclose sq
Cook John, look. gl. & pict. framema. 10 Gt. Mitchell st. St. Luke
Cook John, *Running Horse* P.H. 82 Harrow rd. Paddington
Cook John Wm. stock & share broker, 36 Throgmorton st
Cook Joseph, export boot & shoe depôt, 3 Greville st. Hatton garden
Cook Joseph, fancy brushmaker, 3 Bethnal green road
Cook Joseph, hairdresser, High st. Notting hill
Cook Joseph, perfumer, Kensington gravel pits

Cook Joshua, artist, 109 Mount st. Berkeley square
Cook Livett, statr. & newsvender, 1 Maiden la.Covent gardn
Cook Loveday S. (Mrs.), staymaker, 1 Leicester st. Regent st
Cook Lucy (Miss), milliner, 78 Shoreditch High st
Cook Martha (Mrs.), *Birch Tree* P.H. 49 Gt. James st. Hoxton
Cook Mary (Mrs.), skein silk dyer, see Greive & Cook
Cook Richard, baker, 10 Norland road, Notting hill
Cook Richard, cheesemonger, 6 Constitution row, Gray's inn rd
Cook Richard, roller maker, 44 Bartholomew close
Cook Richard Philip, baker, 286 Oxford st
Cook Robert, butcher, 10 Commercial place, Coml. road east
Cook Robert, butcher, 31 Sloane square, Chelsea
Cook Robert, sheep salesman, 41 West Smithfield
Cook Robert, solicitor, 18 Warwick st. Golden square
Cook Robert, tailor, 17 Poland st. Oxford st
Cook Robert, tailor, 65 Red Lion st. Holborn
Cook Samuel, cheesemonger, 168 Lambeth walk
Cook Samuel, egg merchant, 31 Grange walk, Bermondsey sq
Cook Sarah (Mrs.), glassgrinder & silverer, 24 Up. St. Martin's la
Cook Sarah (Mrs.), grocer, New King st. Deptford
Cook Sarah (Mrs.), stationer, 19 Queen's road, Bayswater
Cook Sarah (Mrs.), stayma. 8 Northampton pl. Canonbury sq
Cook Silas Kemball, academy, 29 Paradise row, Rotherhithe
Cook Thomas, blind maker, 1 Steyman's row, Holloway road
Cook Thomas, boot & shoe maker, 19 Lombard st. Chelsea
Cook Thomas, bricklayer, 1 Little James st. Hoxton
Cook Thomas, bricklayer, &c. Monte video pl. Kentish town
Cook Thomas, butcher, 61 Exmouth st. Clerkenwell
Cook Thomas, cabinet maker, 86 Old st. St. Luke's
Cook Thomas, carver & gilder, 19 Hatton garden
Cook Thomas, fishmonger, 29 Shaftesbury terrace, Wilton rd
Cook Thomas, fruiterer, 47 Westbourne street, Pimlico
Cook Thomas, harness ma. 10A, Earl st. east, Lisson gro. north
Cook Thomas, *Horse & Groom* P.H. 24 Mount st. Lambeth
Cook Thomas, lighterman, 8 Maiden lane, Covent garden
Cook Thomas, livery stables, 43 Lamb's Conduit st
Cook Thomas, *Sun* P.H. 2 Gate st. Lincoln's inn fields
Cook Thomas, tailor & draper, 6 New Farringdon st
Cook Thomas, tobacco pipe maker, 5 Jacob's st. Dockhead
Cook Thomas Aynsley, seal & silver engraver, 16 Cornhill
Cook Thos. Galliard, yeast dlr. 4 York st. Charlotte st. Whitecpl
Cook Thomas Masters, basket ma. 43 St. John st. Smithfield
Cook Wm. baker, 12 Guilford st. Russell square
Cook Wm. beer retailer, 5 Ivy terrace, Hoxton
Cook Wm. bootmaker, 5 Church st. Soho
Cook Wm. boot & shoe maker, 12 King st. Soho
Cook Wm. bootmaker, 2 Clarence pl. Broadway, Deptford
Cook Wm. bootmaker, 11 Clement's inn pass. Clare market
Cook Wm. bootmaker, 6 Holles st. Stanhope st. Clare market
Cook Wm. butcher, 3 Newington causeway
Cook Wm. cheesemonger, 5 Constable row, Mile end road
Cook Wm. cheesemonger, 156 Whitechapel road
Cook Wm. coffee rooms, 2 Wilsted st. Somers town
Cook Wm. fruiterer, 49 Leader st. Chelsea
Cook Wm. glass grinder, 58 Wych st. Strand
Cook Wm. haberdasher, 4 Broad st. Golden square
Cook Wm. harness maker, 66 Friar st. Blackfriars road
Cook Wm. hot water apparatus ma. 2 Redcross sq. Cripplegte
Cook Wm. house and ship smith, 5 arch, Maze, Tooley st
Cook Wm. marine store dealer, 11 Salisbury st. Lisson grove
Cook Wm. printer, 73 Paul st. Finsbury
Cook Wm. stationer & bookseller, 44 Chalton st. Somers twn
Cook Wm. straw bonnet maker, 23 King st. Seven dials
Cook Wm. tobacco pipe maker, 4 Marygold st. Bermondsey
Cook Wm. trunk & portmanteau maker, 72 Chancery lane
Cook Wm. wine cooper, 4 Parish st. Tooley st
Cook Wm. jun. boot and shoe maker, 12 King st. Soho
Cook Wm. Christopher, coffee rooms, 267 Strand
Cook Wm. Hopson, coach builder, see Robinson & Cook
Cook Wm. Newton, brushmaker, see Newton & Cook
Cooke E. S. & M. A. birmingham & metal warehouse, 2 Brownlow st. Drury lane
Cooke John & Sons, sealing wax & wafer manfrs. 5 Cannon st
Cooke Thos. V. & Co. corn distillers, Thames bank, Pimlico
Cooke Wm. & Co. indian condiment & curry powder wareho. 24 Princes st. Cavendish sq.; removed from 99 Hatton gdn
Cooke Wm. & Son, surgeons, 39 Trinity sq. Tower hill
Cooke Wm. & John, hatters, 43 St. Mary Axe
Cooke Algern. Sidney, *Two Brewers* P.H. Stoney la. Tooley st
Cooke Ambrose M. trimming, &c. warehouse, 75 Cheapside
Cooke Augustus, surgeon, Denmark hill, Camberwell
Cooke Ann (Mrs.), poulterer, 21 Princes st. Leicester sq
Cooke Arthur, poulterer, 13 Great Hall, Hungerford market
Cooke Benjamin, cooper, see Wilson & Cooke
Cooke Charles, attorney, 7 Swinton st. Gray's inn road
Cooke Charles, clerical agent, see Spencer & Cooke
Cooke Charles, ship, commercial, custom house & treasury agent, 9 St. Dunstan's hill
Cooke Charles, seal wafer manufr. 14 Royley st. Old st
Cooke Charles Gomond, chemist, see Godfrey & Cooke
Cooke Charlt. (Mrs.), ironpl. work. 26 Herefrd. pl. Commercl. rd
Cooke Corbett, corn dealer, 12 Theobald's road
Cooke Dennis Francis, chemist, 18 Whitechapel High st
Cooke Edward, barrister, 2 Plowden buildings, Temple
Cooke Edward, barrister, 8 Southampton bldgs. Chancery la
Cooke Edward John, newsvendr. 2 Charles st. Hatton garden
Cooke Frederick, tailor, 20 South Molton st. Bond st.
Cooke George, plumber, glazier, painter, paperhanger, &c. 10 Bride's passage, Fleet st
Cooke George Francis, solicitor, 30 King st. Cheapside
Cooke George Frederick, solicitor, 4 Elm court, Temple
Cooke George Wingrove, barrister, 9 Inner Temple lane
Cooke Hannah (Mrs.), dress maker, 35 Park st. Grosvenor sq
Cooke Henry, stock & share agent, see Jones, Cooke & Green
Cooke Henry, tobacconist, 9½ Mortimer st. Cavendish sq
Cooke James, fruiterer, 13 Brewer st. Pimlico
Cooke James Hubert, poulterer, 78 Holborn bridge
Cooke John, boot & shoe maker, 8 Surrey pl. Wandsworth rd
Cooke John, chemist & druggist, 58 Hoxton Old town
Cooke John, hosier, 340 High Holborn
Cooke John, shop fixture broker, 23 Hatton wall, Hatton gdn
Cooke John, shorthand writer, 1 Warwick pl. Bedford row
Cooke John Annis, poultry salesman, 65 Newgate market
Cooke John Athanasius, barrister, 7 Old sq. Lincoln's inn
Cooke John Charles, physician, 4 Caroline st. Bedford sq
Cooke John Henry, barrister, 26 Old square, Lincoln's inn
Cooke Joseph, upholsterer, &c. 34 York bldgs. New road
Cooke Joseph Frederick, butcher, 158 High st. Camden town
Cooke Layton, estate agent, 7 John st. Adelphi
Cooke Mary (Mrs.), china dealer, 1 Marah pl. Old Kent rd
Cooke Masia Joscelin, solcitr. & pat. agnt. 20 Halfmoon st
Cooke Nathaniel, printer, see Ingram & Cooke
Cooke Robert, plumber, glazier, paperhanger & painter, 119 Salisbury sq. Fleet st. from St. Bride's passage
Cooke Robt. tobacco pipe ma. 8 York st. Church st. Bethnal gr
Cooke Robt. Humphrey, surgeon, Church st. Stoke Newingtn
Cooke Samuel, carpet, rug & blanket manufacturer, & yarn & worsted spinner, 12 Friday st. Cheapside, & Mill bridge, Leeds, late of 7 King's Arms bldgs. Wood st
Cooke Sarah (Mrs.), fancy cap mak. 3 Church la. Islington
Cooke Sarah (Mrs.), lodging ho. 20 Westbourne gro. Bayswtr
Cooke Sarah (Mrs.), toywareho. 16 High st. Newingtonbutts
Cooke Selby Ann (Mrs.), cloth cap ma. 32 Cross st. Islington
Cooke Thomas, tailor & habit maker, 3 King st. Holborn
Cooke Thomas, undertaker, 17 Cannon st. St. Georgs's east
Cooke Thomas, warehouseman, 10 Basinghall st
Cooke Thomas, *White Horse* P.H. Liverpool road
Cooke Wm. greengrocer, 14 Harrow road
Cooke Wm. haberdasher, 43 Marchmont st. Brunswick sq
Cooke William, hatter, 40 Lamb's Conduit st
Cooke Wm. E. pat. of electric telegraph, 1 Copthall bldgs
Cooke Wm. Geo. tobacco pipemaker, 4 Marygold st. Bermondsy
Cooke Wm. Henry, barrister, 4 Elm court, Temple
Cooke Wm. Henry, surgeon, 88 York road, Lambeth
Cookes & Long, ship & insurance brokers, 60 Mark lane
Cookes Alfred, varnish manufacturer, see Innell & Cookes
Cookes George, colonial broker, 2 Great Tower st
Cookes James, export stationer, patent ledger & account book, & patent inkstand manufacturer, 51 Fenchurch st
Cookman Elizb. (Mrs.), cutler & toy wareh. 50 Poplar High st
Cookman Samuel, greengrocer, 17 Queen st. Pimlico
Cookney & Bridge, solicitors, 5 Lamb's Conduit pl. Foundling
Cooks' Kitchen Mining Company (George William Harrison, sec.), 51 Old Broad st. City
Cooksey Daniel, furn. undertaker, 52 Amwell st. Pentonville
Cooksey Samuel, coach ironmonger, wholesale & for exportation, 5 King's Head court, St. Martin's le grand
Cooksey Thomas, hatter, 35 & 36 Mitre st. Blackfriars road
Cocksley John, slater, 3 Chapel st. Pentonville
Cookson, Cuthbert & Co. bottle manufacturers & merchants (Wm. Kidd, agent), Red Bull wharf, Upper Thames st
Cookson Isaac & Co. see R. W. Swinburne & Co
Cookson Hen. tailors' trimming wa. 10 Gt. Jas. st. Lissongr. north
Cookson John, fruiterer, 133 Praed st. Paddington
Cookson Wm. Strickland, solicitor, see Clayton & Cookson
Cookworthy Fredk. C. accountant, 24 Castle st. Falcon sq
Coole Wm. fruiterer, 54 Mount st. Berkeley square
Cooley Hen. grocer, 11 Anthony st. & 28 New rd. St. George's ea
Cooling Arthur, manufacturing perfumer, clarifier of marrow, lard & suet, 134 London wall
Cooling Richd. tailor & habit mkr. 7 Jermyn st. St. James's
Cooling Wm. tailor, 6 Maddox st. Bond st

Coombe Benjamin & Co. wire weavers, general wire workers & sieve manufacturers, 30 Mark lane
Coombe & Jones, solicitors, 2 Church ct. Clement la. City
Coombe Chas. pianoforte ma.26Leonard st. Tabernacle walk
Coomber John, purveyor of milk to her Majesty, & Queen Adelaide, 56 Margaret st. Cavendish square
Coomber Henry, tobacconist, 1 Park st. Boro' market
Coomber Jane (Miss), ladies' school, 4 Paradise row, Chelsea
Coomber John, booking office, White Hart inn yard, Boro'
Coomber John, coach & cart wheelwright, Wilton rd. Pimlico
Coomber Wm. dining rooms, 112 New Gravel lane
Coomber Wm. *Old Rising Sun* P.H. 79 High st. Marylebon
Coombes Edward, *York Minster* P.H. 8 North Audley st
Coombes Henry, plumber, painter, &c. 8 Poplar High st
Coombes Hen. H. manchstr. wareho. see Graham, Coombes & Murray
Coombes James, carver & gilder, 49 Holywell st. Strand
Coombes John, fruiterer, 15 Gwynn's place, Hackney road
Coombes John, plumber & painter, 163 Poplar High st
Coombes John, tailor, 60 Wilson st. Finsbury square
Coombes Nathaniel, china & glass wareh. 67 Lambeth walk
Coombes Robert, hairdresser, 33 Houndsditch
Coombes Thos. carpenter & furn. broker, 38 Penny flds. Poplr
Coombes Wm. Newman, plumbr. painter, &c. 35 Poplar High st
Coombs & Co. patent inkstand makers, 26 Denmark st. Soho
Coombs Wm. Hen. & Jas. carpntrs. 10 Bennett's hill, Doc. com
Coombs George, eating house, 22 New King's st. Deptford
Coombs Geo. *Green Man* P.H. Green St. Church st. Blkfrs. rd
Coombs George Cains, cheesemonger, 50 Cowcross st
Coombs Hen. Edw. fancy pill box ma. 9 Twister's all. Bunhl. rw
Coombs James, cheesemonger, 13 Regent pl. Horseferry rd
Coombs John, purfleet lime, sand & cement wharf, Earl st. Blackfriars, & Regent's canal, Hampstead road
Coombs Lydia (Miss), boarding house, 11 Salisbury square
Coombs Nathaniel George, coal mer. 20 Craven st. Strand
Coombs Philip, boot & shoe maker, 1 Beaufort pl. Chelsea
Coombs Theophilus, farrier, 27 Rose st. Covent garden
Coombs Thomas, baker, 179 Wellington ter. Waterloo road
Coombs Thos. Merriman, linen & silk wa. 13 & 14 Ludgate st
Coombs Wm. Hen. oil & colorman, 18 Old Paradise row, Islngtn
Coomes Francis, beer retailer, 114 Regent st. Lambeth
Coomes Michael, bookseller & stationer, 141 Regent st
Coomes Step. coal mer. 14 St. Thomas's st. east, Southwark
Cooney Edw. chandler's shop, 31 Pearson st. Kingsland rd
Coope Octavius Edwd. sugar refiner, 2 Mansell st. Goodman's fields, & 42 Bett's st. Ratcliff highway
Coope Octavius Edward, brewer, see Ind, Coope & Co
Cooper Ann (Mrs. & Miss), school, 11 President st. east
Cooper & Batchelor, linendrapers, 113 New Bond st
Cooper & Blackford, coach lace makers, 140 Long acre
Cooper Charles & Henry, bakers, 12 Drury lane
Cooper (Collingwood) & Co. silk manfrs. 6 Gutter la. City
Cooper Dan. & Co. merchts. 3 Copthall chamb. Throgmorton st
Cooper & Davis, builders, 19 Castle st. Southwark, & 7 Emerson st. New Park st. Southwark
Cooper Elizh. & S. & J. (Misses), ladies' school, 11 Bolt ct. Fleet st
Cooper Emanuel & Co. hat ma. 49 & 50 Castle st. Southwark
Cooper Geo. & Edwd. upholsterers, cabinet ma. looking glass manufrs. carvers, gilders & house decrtrs. 36 Piccadilly
Cooper & Green, varnish & color ma. 11 Tothill st. Westminst
Cooper James & Co. pianoforte makers, 48 Southampton row, Russell square
Cooper James & Nephew, house painters, 67 Gt. Tower st
Cooper James Binion & Son, ironfounders, 121 Drury lane
Cooper John & Co. silk warehousemen, 2 Gresham st. City
Cooper Joseph & Co. wholesale hatters & hatters' furriers, 12 Laurence Pountney lane, Cannon st
Cooper & Madgwicks', japanners, & wholesale furnishing ironmongers & tin plate dlrs. 27 St. John's la. Clerkenwll
Cooper Philip & Sons, silk mercers to her Majesty, 2 Waterloo place, Pall mall
Cooper & Phillips, quill merchants, pen cutters & manufactrs. of Walkden's inks, register ink, ink powder, vellum & parchment, 5, 6 & 7 Shoe lane, Fleet st
Cooper Thos. & Co. tea dealers & spice merchts. 5 Monument yd
Cooper & Wardell, shoemakers, 36 Dartmouth st. Westminr
Cooper Wm. & Co. cheesemongers, 65 Stones' end, Borough
Cooper Wm. & Thos. preservers of fresh provisions, bottled fruits, &c. & export oilmen, 7 St. John st. Clerkenwell, & 134 Leadenhall st
Coopers' Almshouses, Schoolhouse lane, Ratcliff
Coopers' Hall (James Boyer, clerk), 71 Basinghall st
Cooper Abraham, sen. R.A. artist, 19 New Millman st
Cooper Alexander, baker, 12 Northumberland st. Strand
Cooper Alexander D. jun. artist, 19 New Millman st. Foundling
Cooper Alfred, tailor, 2 Hanover place, Old Kent road
Cooper Alfred, who. stationer, see Poulter & Cooper
Cooper Anthony, butcher, 117 Bishopsgate without
Cooper Augustus, surgeon, 1 Wellington ter. Clapham rise
Cooper Aug. Hen. sec. to who. drapers, &c. soc. Ironmonger la
Cooper Bransby B. surgeon, 2 New st. Spring gardens
Cooper Caroline (Miss), dress ma. 8 Blenheim ter. Kingsland
Cooper Caroline M. (Miss), milliner, 37 Dorset st. Portman sq
Cooper Chas. chaise saddler, 17 Finsbury st
Cooper Chas. coffee rooms, 37 Charles st. Hatton garden
Cooper Chas. *Feathers* P.H. 11 Dean st. Westminster
Cooper Chas. undertaker, &c. 118 Gt. Russell st. Bloomsbury
Cooper Chas. wine mer. 33 Nag's Head ct. Gracechurch st
Cooper Chas. Purton, queen's counsel, 7 New Boswell ct
Cooper Daniel, grocer & oilman, 2 Lit. Bath st. Clerkenwell
Cooper Deborah (Miss), seminary, 6 Markham pl. Chelsea
Cooper Edward Priestley, barrister, 7 Old sq. Lincoln's inn
Cooper Elias, butcher, 19 Broadley ter. Blandford sq
Cooper Elizh. (Mrs.), coffee rooms, 13 Pollen st. Hanover sq
Cooper Elizabeth (Miss), milliner, 24 Maddox st. Regent st
Cooper Francis, wine merchant, Lloyd's
Cooper Frederick Chas. artist, 37 Dorset st. Portman sq
Cooper George, auctioneer, 6 Markham place, King's road, & 6 Elm terrace, Little Chelsea
Cooper George, bookseller, 5 St. Thomas pl. Gt. Dover st
Cooper George, linendraper, 1 Dockhead, Bermondsey
Cooper George, lighterman, 12 Globe st. Wapping
Cooper George, professor of music, 25 Ely place, Holborn
Cooper George, surgeon, 168 Fleet st
Cooper George, undertaker, 4 Jerusalem ct. St. John st. Clrknl
Cooper Geo. Armytage, tobacconist, 13 Dorrington st
Cooper Geo. Binion, iron & brass found. 5 Polygon. Clarend. sq
Cooper Geo. Edwd. stockbroker, 4 Shorter's ct. Thrgmrtn. st
Cooper George Lewis, surgeon, 35 Keppel st. Russell sq
Cooper George Pate, tailor to the Queen & Prince Albert, 6 Suffolk st. Pall mall east
Cooper Henry, artist, 9 Paddington green
Cooper Henry, bootmaker, 23 Little Russell st. Bloomsbury
Cooper Hen. mfr. of type for markg. linen, 17 Nelson st. Cock la
Cooper Henry, surgeon, 20 Moor st. Soho
Cooper Henry, tailor & habitmaker, 81 Park st. Grosvenor sq
Cooper Henry, warehouseman, 98 Wood st. City
Cooper Henry Robt. cabinetma. 8 & 9 Gt. Pulteney st. Golden sq
Cooper Henry Sarel, *Adam & Eve* P.H. 11 Terrace, Kensington
Cooper Henry Spencer, barrister, 3 Paper buildings, Temple
Cooper Hugh Welch, builder, 42 Wakefield st. Brunswick sq
Cooper Hugh, artificial florist, 53 Cromer st. Brunswick sq
Cooper Hugh William, builder, 95 Harrison st. Gray's inn rd
Cooper Isaac Augustus, confectioner, 209 Tottenham ct. rd
Cooper Jacob, tobacconist, 12 Lower st. Islington
Cooper James, coffee rooms, 209 Brick lane, Spitalfields
Cooper James, dining rooms, 19 Golden lane, Barbican
Cooper James, grocer, 35 & 36 Rochester row, Westminster
Cooper James, grocer & teadealer, 173 Brick la. Spitalfields
Cooper James, hairdresser, 33 Little Bell alley, Coleman st
Cooper James, manufg. jeweller, 37 Perceval st. Clerkenwell
Cooper James, oilman, 19 Exmouth st. Clerkenwell
Cooper James, paper stainer, 31 Duke st. Bishopsgate
Cooper James, plumber, &c. 34 & 35 Maiden la. Covent gardn
Cooper James, *Rose & Crown* P.H. 47 Broad st. St. Giles's
Cooper James, tailor, 35 Ernest st. Regent's park
Cooper James, tailor, 23 New Bond st
Cooper James, upholsterer, 11 George st. Euston square
Cooper James Charles, carriage draftsman, 109 Long acre
Cooper Jane (Mrs.), dining rooms, Church st. Hackney
Cooper Jeremiah, plumber, &c. 6 Hastings st. Burton cresct
Cooper John, animal preserver, &c. 29 Radnor st. St. Luke's
Cooper John, baker, 8 Mount place, Walworth road
Cooper John, *Bell Inn* P.H. 134 Shoreditch High st
Cooper John, builder, 33 Newland st. Eaton square, Pimlico
Cooper John, builder, 15 Warren st. mews, Fitzroy square
Cooper John, cattle salesman, 8 West Smithfield
Cooper John, chemist & druggist, 23 High st. Bow, Middlesex
Cooper John, confectioner, 27 Brompton row, Brompton
Cooper John, dining rooms, 82 Charlotte terrace, New cut
Cooper John, goldbeater, 101 Aldersgate st
Cooper John, greengrocer, 8 East st. Walworth road
Cooper John, grocer, 3 Temple st. Whitefriars
Cooper John, hay salesman, 62 Smithfield, & Hendon, Middx
Cooper John, *Mechanics' Inst. tav.* 29 Circus st. New road
Cooper John, *Mount hotel*, 78 & 79 Grosvenor st
Cooper John, *Pied Bull* P.H. 22 High st. Pentonville
Cooper John, plumber, 6 Hanover st. Hanover square
Cooper John, *Royal Oak* P.H. High st. Deptford
Cooper John, silversmith & plater, see Watson & Cooper
Cooper John, tobacconist, 24 New Church st. Lisson grove
Cooper John, wine merchant, 44 Southampton row, Russell sq

Cooper John, warehouse keeper for wool, &c. Chequer yard, Dowgate hill, & Ducksfoot lane
Cooper John Brooker, grocer, 6 Windmill st. Finsbury
Cooper John Edw. barrister, 10 Crown Office row, Temple
Cooper John Eggar, solicitor, Sessions house, Old Bailey
Cooper John Thomas, analytical & consulting chemist, 82 Blackfriars road
Cooper Joseph, artificial florist, 20 Tavistock st. Cov.garden
Cooper Joseph, *British Queen* P.H.1Sussex st.Tottnhm.ct.rd
Cooper Joseph, builder, 111 Stanhope st. Hampstead rd
Cooper Joseph, carman, 22 Old Gravel lane, Wapping
Cooper Joseph, dry salter, 29 White Hart pl. Lr. Kengtn. la
Cooper Joseph, gold chaser, 12 Hooper st.Gt.Sutton st.Clkwl
Cooper Joseph, newspaper agent & printer, 23 Poppin's ct. Fleet st. 8 York ter. Salmon lane, Limehouse
Cooper Joseph tailor, 12½ Bolingbroke row, Walworth rd
Cooper Jos. Hen. coal mer.wharfinger&whiting ma.Crooked Billet wf. 16 Millbank st. & Millbank wf. 18 Millbank st
Cooper Joseph Thos.organist, &c.6 Cross la.St Mary at hill
Cooper Margaret (Mrs.), straw bonnet ma. 40 Tottenham st
Cooper Mary (Mrs.),greengrocer,5 Aldenham ter.Pancras rd
Cooper Matthew, plasterer, Cobourg road, Old Kent road
Cooper Michael, grocer, 35 Uxbridge st. Nwngton. causeway
Cooper Michael, solicitor, see Clutton & Cooper
Cooper Michael, spectacle maker, 10 Long lane, Smithfield
Cooper Montague Ormsby, solicitor, &clerical&school agent, 8 Great James st. Bedford row
Cooper Richard, butcher, 54 Great Portland st. Oxford st
Cooper Rich. slate mer. Bangor wf. Belvedere rd. Lambeth
Cooper Richard Berkeley, oilman, 7 Charlotte st. Portand pl
Cooper Richard George Hen. stenciller,3West place, City rd
Cooper Robert, butcher, 3 Portland pl. Commercial rd. East
Cooper Robert, ship ins.&customho.agt.12 Harp la.Tower st
Cooper Robert, *Three Tuns* P.H.13 Houghton st. Clare mkt
Cooper Robert Webb, beer retailer, 30 Bell st. Edgware rd
Cooper Samuel, baker, Mare st. Hackney
Cooper Samuel, machinist, 15 Temple st. Hackney road
Cooper Samuel, porkman, 13 Eagle st. City rd
Cooper Samuel, surgeon, 7 Woburn place, Russell sq
Cooper Sarah (Mrs.), oil&color wa. 18 Turnmill st. Clerknwl
Cooper Sarah (Miss), milliner, 1 Glo'ster pl. Cmbrwl.New rd
Cooper Stafford Moore, solicitor, 9 Old Cavendish st
Cooper Taylor, pianoforte manufacturer, 43 Edgware road
Cooper Thomas, academy, 8 Greville st. Hatton garden
Cooper Thomas, baker, 37 Bermondsey st
Cooper Thomas, baker, 173 Tottenham court road
Cooper Thomas, baker, Wandsworth road
Cooper Thomas, builder, 9 Goldington st. Somers town
Cooper Thomas, carpenter, 39A, Arlington st. Camden town
Cooper Thomas, carpenter, Whitecross st. Borough
Cooper Thomas, chandler's shop, 41 Princess st.Edgware rd
Cooper Thomas, cheesemonger, 86 Paul st. Finsbury
Cooper Thomas, *Fleece & Sun* P.H. 16 Threadneedle st
Cooper Thomas, grindery dealer, 13 Long alley, Finsbury
Cooper Thomas, grocer, 36 Homer st. Marylebone
Cooper Thomas, mattress maker, 17 London road
Cooper Thomas, miniature painter, 184 Fleet st
Cooper Thomas, jun. nightman, 11½ Salisbury st. Lisson gr
Cooper Thomas, painter & paperhngr.26 Chas. st.Middlx. hos
Cooper Thomas, plumber, 8 St. Peter's pl. Walworth commn
Cooper Thomas, pork butcher, 2 Featherstone st. City road
Cooper Thomas, rubbish carter, 13 Wf. nth. si. Pddngtn. basin
Cooper Thomas, solicitor, 24 Lincoln's inn fields
Cooper Thomas, tailor, 3 Portland place, Borough road
Cooper Thomas, umbrella & stick manufr. 22 New Bond st
Cooper Thomas, upholsterer, 17 London road, Southwark
Cooper Thos. who. station. see Williams, Coopers,Boyle & Co
Cooper Thomas Crowder, herald painter,1Red Lion yd. Clerkn
Cooper Thos. Fredk. chronometer & watch ma. 6 Calthorpe st
Cooper Thos. Hen. surgeon,47 Camden st.south,Camden town
Cooper Thomas S. artist, 16 Wellington ter. St. John's wood
Cooper Wm. brewer, 50 Lower Shadwell
Cooper Wm. chair & sofa manufr. 42 London road,Southwark
Cooper Wm. cheesemonger, 6 Kenton st. Brunswick sq
Cooper Wm. coal& potato dlr.35Gt.St.Andrew st. Seven dials
Cooper Wm. contractor, 2 Vincent square, Westminster
Cooper Wm. *Excise* coffee house, 56 Old Broad st. City
Cooper Wm. flannel, blanket & stuff wareho. 69 Aldermanbry
Cooper Wm. hairdresser, 7 Broadway, Westminster
Cooper Wm. *Lion* coffee rooms, 45 Blackman st. Borough
Cooper Wm. lodging house, 42 Gt. Windmill st. Haymarket
Cooper Wm. meat salesman, Newport New market, Soho
Cooper Wm. paperstainer, 37 Old st. St. Luke's
Cooper Wm. pianoforte maker, 122 St. John st. road
Cooper Wm. pianoforte key maker, 24 William st.Hamps. rd
Cooper Wm. printer, 41 Clarendon square
Cooper Wm. sand merchant, 34 Millbank st. Westminster
Cooper Wm. shoemaker,30Cumberland row,Islington High st
Cooper Wm. silk manufacturer, see Andrews & Cooper
Cooper Wm. silversmith, 39 Kirby st. Hatton garden
Cooper Wm. stationer & newspaper agent, 52 Sloane st
Cooper Wm. straw hat & bonnet maker, 204 Poplar High st
Cooper Wm. Bush, solicitor, 5 Heathcote st.Mecklenbgh.sq
Cooper Wm. Fredk. solicitor,5 Grove end road, St. John's wd
Cooper Wm. Hen. archit. & survyr.1 Verulam bdgs.Gray's inn
Cooper Wm.Hen.chandler'sshop,8Gibraltarwk.Bethnl.gn.rd
Cooper Wm. Henry, tailor, 9 York st. Kingsland road
Cooper Wm. James, bootmaker, 45 Seward st. Goswell st
Cooper Wm. Joseph, butcher, 24 Newport ct. Newport mkt
Cooper Wm. Joseph, tailor, 21 Sackville st. Piccadilly
Cooper Wm. Wellington, barrister, 60 Chancery lane
Cooper Wm. Whatelerley, grocer, 120 Gt. Suffolk st
Cooper Wm. White, surgeon, 2 Tenterden st. Hanover sq
Coot Mark, dyer & scourer, 13 Fitzroy place, Kentish town
Coote John Eyre & Son, solicitors, 20 Austinfriars
Coote Benjamin, upholstr. & house agt. 104 Tottenham ct.rd
Coote Edward, grocer, Mid. 41 Grove st. Commercial rd. ea
Coote Henry Charles, proctor, 2 Gt. Knightrider st.Drs.com
Coote Holmes, surgeon, 24 Argyll st. Regent st.
Coote John, *Carpenters' Arms* P.H. 27½ Up. Southwick st
Coote Richard, barrister, 6 Gray's inn square
Coote Richard Holmes, barrister,1Stone bldgs.Lincoln's inn
Cooze Whitley Wm. house painter & decorator, 20 Frith st
Cope & Collinson, cabinet brassfounders, 53 Berwick st.Soho
Cope & Eales, architects & surv. 21 Cork st. Burlington ga
Cope, Hamerton & Co. ribbon manufs. 9 Wood st. Cheapside
Cope Benjamin, leather cutter, 100 White Lion st. Pentonvl
Cope Benjamin, stockbroker, 3 Bartholomew lane, Bank, & 22 New Church st. Bermondsey
Cope Charles, attorney, 58 Euston square, New road
Cope Chas. James, ship ins.& custom ho agt. 20 Fenchurch st
Cope Edward, accountant, 4 Pelham ter.Pelham rd.Bromptn
Cope Edward Henry, tobacconist, 163 Tottenham court rd
Cope Henry, cattle salesman, 17 West Smithfield
Cope Henry, jun. attorney & parliamentary agt. & solicitor, & sec. to Anti-bridge Toll Asso. 14 Agnes pl. Waterloo rd
Cope Henry, sen. solicitor, 14 Agnes place, Waterloo road
Cope Jacob George, painter & glazier, 133 Upper Thames st
Cope James, dairyman, 63 Castle st. Southwark
Cope James, engineer, see Hopkinson & Cope
Cope James, music engraver & printer, 32 Frith st. Soho
Cope John, coal & potato dealer, 75 Warren st. Fitzroy sq
Cope John, ginger beer maker, 33 Snow's fields, Bermondsey
Cope Samuel, chasers' tool maker, 7 Wood st. nth. Goswell rd
Cope Thomas, engraver, printer & stationer, 49 Cheapside
Cope Thomas, printer, 20 Buckingham st. Strand
Cope Thomas, trimming seller, &c. 10 Kenton st. Brnswk.sq
Cope Thomas S. barrister, 5 Mitre ct. chambers, Fleet st
Cope Wm. barrister, 3 Pump court, Temple
Cope Wm. dining rooms, 63 Cornwall road, Lambeth
Cope Wm. grocer & cheesemonger, 5 Lawson st. New Kent rd
Cope Wm. hat dyer, 16 Little Guildford st. Borough
Cope Wm. last maker, 52 Gray's inn lane, Holborn
Cope Wm. vellum binder, 85 St. Martin's lane, Charing cross
Cope Wm. Lidbrook, coal & wine mer.41 Keppel st. Russell sq
Cope Wm. Titley, wine cooper, 24 Kingsland row, Dalston
Copeland & Garrett (late Spode), porcelain, earthenware & glass manufacturers to the Royal Family, Portugal st. & 37 Lincoln's inn fl.; manufact. Stoke upon Trent, Staffordsh
Copeland Alfred, butcher, 24 Blackman st. Borough
Copeland George, chair & sofa ma. 21 Club row, Bethnal grn
Copeland George, tailor, 128½ High st. Camden town
Copeland Mrs. Jane, china dealer, 12 Grove ter. Bayswater
Copeland John, tailor, 16 Frederick st. Regent's park
Copeland Josiah, tailor, 101A, Gt. Titchfield st. Oxford mrkt
Copeland Thomas, surgeon, 17 Cavendish sq
Copeland William, carpenter, 30 Hertford st. Fitzroy square
Copelin James, ham dealer, 8 Sidney pl. Commercial rd. east
Copelin Wm. ham dealer, 10 Black Prince row, Walworth rd
Copelin Wm. ham & tongue dealer, 46 Newington causeway
Copestake Sampson, lace mfr. see Groucock, Copestake & Co
Copiapo Mining Co. (Fred. Grellet, sec.), 22 Austinfriars
CopiniGaetano, plate glass man.&carver, &c.37 Nortonfolgate
Copland, Barnes & Co. shipping grocers&oilmn. 46 Botolph la
Copland & Burnett, navy agents, 22 Surrey st. Strand
Copland James, F.R.S. physician, 5 Old Burlington st
Copley George, eatinghouse, 45 Seymour st. Euston square
Copley James, cutler, 4 Drury lane
Copling John, merchant, 14A, Gresham st
Copp James, ham & beef shop, 8 Lamb st. Spital square
Coppard Charles, beer retailer, 59 Charlotte st. Whitechapel
Coppard John Henry, beer retailer, 19 West pl. City rd

Coppen & Frank, linendraps.&haber.4&5Clark's pl.Islington
Coppen Thomas, cattle salesman, 17 West Smithfield
Copper Miners in England (Governor & Company offl), 57½ Old Broad st. City, & Castle Baynard wharf, 12 Up. Thames st. (William Inglis, secretary)
Coppin John, eating house, 1A, Amelia st. Walworth road
Coppin John, linendraper & silk mercer, 52 Goswell road
Coppin Joseph, fruiterer, 3 Bermondsey New road
Coppin William, baker, 9 Munster sq. Regent's park
Copping Elizabeth (Mrs.), grocer, 26 Sidney st. Somers town
Copping Frances (Mrs.), haberdasher, 36 Kingsland road
Coppins John, smith, 5 Rose st. St. Luke's
Coppley George Hobson, oil&colrmn.25York row,Kengtn.rd
Coppock James, attorney, 3 Cleveland row, St. James's
Copsey Samuel, fishmonger, 27 Kent st. Borough
Copus Charles, upholsterer & furniture broker, 3 Henrietta st. Manchester sq. & 16 Goodge st. Fitzroy square
Copyhold Commision, Somerset house, Strand; hours 9 to 6
Coram Daniel, coal dealer, 39 Cumberland mkt. Regent's pk
Corazza Jerome, academy, 20 Pelham road, Brompton
Corbaux Fanny (Miss), artist, 59 Up. Norton st. Fitzroy sq
Corben Chas. coach ma.30&31 Gt.Queen st.Lincoln's inn flds
Corbet Robert, butcher, 32 Bartholomew ter. St. Luke's
Corbett & Fountaine, clothiers & tailors, 46 Albemarle st
Corbett Benjamin, accountant, 5 Panyer alley
Corbett George, wine & spirit merchant, 8 Old Jewry
Corbett Jonathan, smith & farrier, 23 Princes st. Lambeth
Corbett Robert, trimming seller, see Bowser & Corbett
Corbett Thos. bookseller & stationer, circulating library, 218 Tottenham court road
Corbett Thos. Wm. picture restorer, 75 John st. Fitzroy sq
Corbett Uvedale, barrister, 22 Old square, Lincoln's inn
Corbishley Robt. silk warehouseman, 25 Wood st.Cheapside
Corbould Aster, coal merchant, see Barnard, Corbould & Son
Corbould Edward, artist, 21 Rutland gate, Hyde park
Corbould Eleanor (Mrs.), lodging house, 36 Southampton blgs
Corby Henry, glass & china dealer, Church st. Hackney
Corby Mary Ann (Miss), stationer, 176 Poplar High st
Corby Susan (Mrs.), tobacconist, 61 Brick lane, Spitalfields
Corby Thomas, *Craven tavern* P.H. 3 Craven ct. Strand
Corbyn, Beaumont, Stacey & Messer, wholesale & retail chemists & druggists, 300 High Holborn
Corbyn Clara (Mrs.), seminary, 42 Albany rd. Camberwell
Corcoran (Bryan) & Co. wire weavers & workers, manufc. of paper machine wires, felts, &c. woven malt kiln plates, screens, sieves, shovels, trucks, smut & flour cylinders, & brushes for all sorts of machinery, mill straps & driving bands of every description, importers & builders of french mill stones, agts. for Blackmore's bolting cloths, 36 Mark la
Cordaroy Frederick, hat maker, 50 Old st. road
Cordaroy George, hat manuf. 9 Cumberland row, New road
Cordell Thomas, cheesemonger, 3 Chalton st. Somers town
Cordell Thomas, *Northumbld. Arms* P.H.44Fashion st. Spfi
Corden Samuel, cheesemonger, 2 Comml. pl. Kingsland road
Corden Samuel, commission agent, 95 Wood st
Corder Charles, linendraper 3½ New Cavendish st. Portland pl
Corder Elizth. Mary (Mrs.), academy, Hollywood, Lit. Chelsea
Corder James, clerk to the Strand Union, & superintendent registrar of births, deaths & marriages, Strand Union offices, 6 Bow st. Strand; hours 10 to 4
Corder Jas. *Duke of York* P.H.1York ter.Salmon la.Limehou
Corder John, house agent, 28 Commercial road, Lambeth
Corder Robert & Son. maltsters, Deptford bridge
Corder William, linendraper, 32 High st. Kensington
Corderoy John & Edwd.provisionagts.32 Tooley st. &Hays la
Corderoy Wm.&Geo.surveyors&agents,98Highst.Marylebone
Cordeux Samuel, *Bedford Arms* P.H. Pont st. Cadogan pl
Cording Edmund, tailor, 200 Hoxton Old town
Cording George, jeweller, 232 Strand
Cording Gregory, fruiterer, 140 Waterloo road, Lambeth
Cording John Charles, hosier & glover, 231 Strand
Cording John Masheder, pawnbroker, 163 St. George st
CordingThomas,pawnbroker& silversmith,38Aldgate High st
Cordingly Wm. hop & seed factor, 5 Counter st. Borough High st. & Queen's Head inn yard, 84 Borough
Cordis John, locksmith, 11 Artichoke row, Mile end road
CordreyJas.&Fras.&Chas.fellmongers,34Longla. Bermondsey
Cordrey Evan, fellmonger, Wilds rents, Long la. Bermondsey
Cordrey Francis, fellmonger, Russell pl. Russell st. Brmndsy
Cordrey John, fellmgr. & leather dresser, 37 Long la. Brmdsy
Cordwainers' Hall (Jas.Josiah Millard,clk.),17Gt.Distaff la
Cordwell Sarah (Mrs.), pawnbroker, 31 Exmouth st. Spaflds
Cordwent Wm. cheesemonger, 8 Dean st. Westminster
Core Robert Lee, lighterman, 14 Paradise row, Rotherhithe
Corfe William, cattle salesman, 17 West Smithfield
Corfield Charles, farrier, 34 Marylebone lane, Oxford st
Corfield Charles Leopold, shorthandwriter, 88 Chancery lane
Corfield Edward, land agent, 31 Francis st. Tottenham ct. rd
Corfield George Keates, attorney, 20 Harley st. Cavendish sq
Corfield Jane (Mrs.), coaldealer, 26A, Upper Marylebone st
Corfield John, plumber & painter, 36 Fetter lane, Holborn
Corfield Joseph, book edge gilder, 44 Kirby st. Hatton gardn
Corfield William, cheesemonger, 21 King's rd. east, Chelsea
Corfield William, solicitor, 2 Robert st. Adelphi
Cork & Bandon & Irish Railway Company's Office, (Wm. Billing, sec.), 11 Adam st. Adelphi
Cork & Hall, coach builders, 137½ New Bond st
Cork & Killarney Rail. (Alex.Johnston, sec.), 63 Moorgatest
Cork & Waterford Railway Co. (George Henry Layard, sec.), 8 Delahay st. Westminster
Cork Daniel, meat salesman, Leadenhall market
Cork George, cattle salesman, 59 West Smithfield
Cork George, riding school, &c. 1 Tyndale pl. Up.st.Islington
Cork Harriet (Mrs.), city carman, Swan st. Dover rd. Boro'
Cork Henley, fruiterer, 13 Peerless pl. City road
Cork Robert, fruiterer, 1 Kenton st. Brunswick sq
Cork Thomas, grocer, 2 Temple st. Whitefriars
Cork Thomas, market gardener, Jamaica level, Bermondsey
Cork Wm. bricklayer, 17 Harp lane
Cork Wm. hosier & glover, 4 Trinity rw. Upper st. Islington
Corke Thomas, sheep salesman, 41 West Smithfield
Corker Daniel, watchma. 18 Langley pl. Commercl. rd. east
Corker Nathaniel, watchmaker, 48 South Molton st
Corker Richard, dairyman, 25 Frederick st. Regent's park
Corles Thos. Bingham, solicitor, 12 Featherstone buildings
Corless Thomas, beer retailer, 11 Narrow st. Ratcliff
Corley John, barrister, 4 Verulam buildings, Gray's inn
Cormack Thomas, solicitor, 1 Arundel terrace, Islington
Cormack Wm. rope & twine ma.12Gt. Guildford st. Borough
Cormack Wm. John, seedsman, New Cross
Cormie & Taylor, hairdressers, &c. 3 Finch lane, Cornhill
Corn Exchange (New& Old), Mark la.hoursof business 10to3
Corn Exchange Secretary's Office (Thomas Levick, sec.), 3 Fowkes's buildings, Great Tower st. hours 10 to 4
Corn Meter's Office, 61 Great Tower st. City, & 14 Broad st. Horselydown, & *Cock & Lion* P.H. Lower east Smithfield, & 51 Upper Thames st. hours of business, Nov. to Jan., 7 to 6; Feb. & Mar., 6 to 6; April to Aug., 5 to 7; Sept. to Oct., 6 to 6
Corn Reporter Office (The Universal), 42 Mincing lane
Corn Returns Office, see Comptroller of Corn Returns
Corn Edward, bootmaker, 10 Constitution row, Gray's inn rd
Corn James, bootmaker, 29 Henrietta st. Covent garden
Cornaby Henry, tailor, 61 King st. Borough
Cornelius Charles, cheesemonger, 20 Sussex pl. Old Kent rd
Cornelius James Connor, surgeon & chemist, 101 Goswell st
Cornelius William, carpenter, 31 Brewer st. Somers town
Cornell, Lyell & Webster, ribbon mfrs. 15 St. Paul's ch. yd
Cornell George, conveyancer, 66 Up. Norton st. Fitzroy sq
Cornell James, wine & spirit broker, see Long & Cornell
Cornell Robert, linendraper, &c. see Kirkpatrick & Cornell
Cornell Samuel, supt. registrar, &c.1 Canning pl.Kensington
Cornell Thos. carver & gilder, 72 Margaret st. Cavendish sq
Cornell Wm. boot & shoe maker, 5 Pratt st. Camden town
Cornell Wm. boot & shoe mak.9 Frederick pl. Hampstead rd
Corner Geo. Rd. & Charles C. solicitors, 1 Dean st. Tooley st
Corner George, stationer, 34 Clipstone st. Fitzroy sq
CornerJas.survey.&val. 4 Apollo bldgs. N. East st. Walworth
Corner John, chemist, 4 Edwards terrace, Kensington
Corner John, ladies' & children's shoe manufacturer, wholesale & export, 52 Paul st. Finsbury
Corner Richd. butcher, 25 Goodge st. Tottenham court road
Corner Richd. market coffee rooms, 46 Farringdon market
Corner Richard James, barrister, 2 Tanfield court, Temple
Corner Wm. Elgie, shipping butcher, 9 Lower Shadwell
Corney & Barrow, wine & brandy mer. 65 Old Broad st. City
Corney Charles, beer retailer, 12 York st. Hans place
Corney Charles, wheelwright, 12 York st. Hans pl. Sloane st
Corney Charles, wheelwright, 4 Middle row, Knightsbridge
Corney Charles Samuel, baths, Addington sq. Camberwell
Corney Eliza (Mrs.), grocer, 3 Freeschool st. Horselydown
Corney Isaac, surveyor of ships, 10 Arbour ter. Coml. rd. ea
Corney James, refiner, wiredrawer, &c. see Barrett & Corney
Corney Sarah, (Mrs.), clothier, 4 Surrey pl. Newington butts
Corney Thomas, *Blue Anchor* P.H. Bromley, Middlesex
Corney Thomas, drysalter, custom ho. agt.70Low.Thames st
Corney William, cheesemonger, 55 Whitechapel road
Cornfoot & Elmslie, west india merchants, 6 Copthall court
Cornick Joseph, beer retailer, Lower Calthorpe st
Cornish Charles, bread & biscuit baker, 85 Fenchurch st
Cornish Charles, fishmonger, New cross road, Deptford
Cornish Henry, broker & appraiser, 33 Bell st. Edgware rd

Cornish Henry, haircutter, 81 Baker st. Portman square
Cornish Henry, painter & glazier, 54 Chalton st. Somers town
Cornish James, bookseller & publisher, 1 Middle row, Holbn
Cornish John, builder, 2 Newcastle street, Strand
Cornish John, greengrocer, 79 Tottenham court road
Cornish John, cocoa & rush matting, hassock & door mat manufacturer, 33 Bedford street, Covent garden
Cornish John Robert, barrister, 11 Paper buildings, Temple
Cornish William, new & old bookseller, 7 Hanway st. Oxford st.; & 37 New st. Birmingham
Cornman Philip, livery stables, 10 Whitechapel High st
Corns Samuel, news agent, 64 William st. Regent's park
Cornthwaite & Adams, solicitors, 14 Old Jewry chambers
Cornwall Augustus Rd. dentist, 13 Egremont pl. New rd
Cornwall Henry Cobb, attorney, 3 Barnard's inn, Holborn
Cornwall James, chimney sweeper, Camberwell green
CornwellMary&Ann&Maria, prep.school, 24 Amwell st. Pentnv
Cornwell Rt. & Co. stock broks. Copthall cha. Copthall bldgs
Cornwell David, marine store dealer, 25 Bethnal green rd
Cornwell Edmund, fruiterer, High st. Stoke Newington
Cornwell H. Miss, milliner, 3 Wellington ter. Clapham rise
Cornwell John, baker, 91 Upper Whitecross st. St. Luke's
Cornwell Thomas, baker, 55 Kingsland road
Coronel Abraham, cigar manufacturer, 27 Gt. Prescot st
Coroner's of Middlesex Office, 35 Bedford square
Corpe Abraham, saddler, 15 Primrose st. Bishopsgate st
Corpe Alfred, tailor, see Rausch & Corpe
Corpe Edmund, ladies' shoe ma. 126 Mount st. Berkeley sq
Corpe Edwin, furniture warehouse, 13 Eldon st. Finsbury
Corpe George, solicitor, 3 Lincoln's inn fields
Corpe John Westbrook, engineer, &c. see Bunnett & Corpe
Corpe Samuel, saddler & harness maker, 142 Houndsditch
Corporation of the Amicable Society for a Perpetual Assurance of Lives (T. Galloway, registrar), 19 Serjeants' inn, & 50 Fleet street; see page
Corporation of the London Assur. see "London Assurance"
Corporation of the Sons of the Clergy (Oliver Hargreave, registrar), 2 Bloomsbury place
Corpus Chas. & Geo. furn. broks. 27 & 28 Barrett's ct. Oxfd. st
Corr Joseph, boot & shoe maker, 24 Sherrard st. Golden sq
Corrie & Co. colonial brokers, 29 Mincing lane
Corrie George, lock smith, 25 Gt. College st. Westminster
Corrie James, watch & clock ma. 33 Kirby st. Hatton garden
Corrie John, carpenter & stationer, Camberwell grove
Corrie Martin, tobacconist, 13 Mount row, Liverpool road
Corrie Thomas S. dancing master, 36 Bedford st. Covent gdn
Corrie William, barrister, 1 Pump court, Temple
Corrock Rebecca (Mrs.), robe maker, 29 King st. Cheapside
Corrock Rebecca (Miss), robe maker, 21 Lit. Knightrider st
Corrotti Jas. alabaster wa. 12 Black horse yd. Rathbone pl
Corsan John, lighterman, 16 Gt. Hermitage st. Wapping
Corsan Thomas, watchmaker, 119 Wapping
Corsbie George, silversmith, watchma. &c. 21 Bath pl. New rd
Corsby Charles, musical instr. maker, 9 Princes st. Leicester sq
Corsby George, jun. musical instrument mak. 28 Coventry st
Corsby Susan (Mrs.), silver string ma. 37 O. Compton st. Soho
Corse Henry, bootmaker, 26 New Union st. Lit. Moorfields
Corser Robert & Co. grocers & tea dealers, 152 Leadenhall st
Corsham Geo. gas fitter & lamp ma. 26 Lower Eaton st
Corson (Mrs.), grocer, 6 Belgrave place, Wandsworth road
Corss & Roberts, tailors, &c. 63 Shoreditch High street
Corsten Henry, florist & fruiterer, 19A, Davies st. Berkeley sq
Corston Chas. *Star & Garter* P.H. 6 Newland pl. Kensington
Cort Hen. Hannam, surgeon, 34A, York st. Portman sq
Cortazzi, Garland & Co. merchts. 2 Ingram ct. Fenchurch st
Cortazzi Frederic, merchant, Baltic coffee house
Corti Peter, barometer manufacturer, 30 Eyre street hill
Cortissos Hen. B. indigo & cochineal broker, 4 Lit. Tower st
Corvan Anthony, baker, 16 Adam's row, Hampstead road
Cory William & Son, coal merchants & coke burners, New Barge house wharf, Commercial road, Lambeth
Cory & Williamson, cheesemongers, 177 Bishopsgate without
Cory Edward A. M.D. surgeon, 7 Clarke's ter. Cannon st. rd
Cory Henry, barrister, 1 New square, Lincoln's inn
Cory Dr. Horace, chemical color works, 13 Narrow street, Limehouse, & 83 Upper Thames street
Cory John, *Woolpack* P.H. 14 Brick lane, St. Luke's
Cory Richard, coal merchant, see Green & Cory
Cory Wm. straw hat maker, 28 Gt. Charlotte st. Blackfrs. rd
Cory Wm. Hanrott, surgeon, 8 Air street, Regent street
Cosens Fred. wine merchant, 3 New London st. Mark lane
Cosens George Henry, drug broker, 8 Lime street, City
Cosgreave Peter, surgeon, 34 Norfolk street, Strand
Cosgrove John, ropemaker, 9&11 Raven row, Whitechapel rd
Cosham Joseph, baker, 16 New road, St. George's east
Cosi Lawrence, art. flower ma. 34 Greenhill's rents, Smithfield
Cosier Mary (Mrs.), lodging house, 20 Surrey st. Strand
Cosier William, hop merchant, 2 Three Crown sq. Borough
Cosins James, furniture broker, 16 Castle st. Long acre
Cosins William, furniture broker, 16 Gt. Earl st. Seven dials
Cosmorama Panoramic Exhibition, 207 & 209 Regent st
Cosnight Rich. coal dealer, 12 Mason st. Westminster bdg. rd
Cosomini Louisa (Miss), art. florist, 60 Stanhope st. Claremrkt
Cossar James, tobacconist, 31 Guildford place, Spafields
Cossart Wm. madeira mer. see Gordon (Webster), Cossart & Co
Cossens Lydia (Mrs.), milliner, 15 Lit. Queen st. Holborn
Cossens Thomas, bootmaker, 24 Back hill, Hatton garden
Cosser Walter & Son, timber mers. Acre wf. Belvedere rd. Lmbth
Cosser Andrew, carpenter & builder, 2 Charles place, York road, Lambeth, & 84 Bridge road, Lambeth
Cossey Robert, cowkeeper, 9 Queen st. Tower hill
Cossington John, lighterman, Stratford
Cosson Henry, *Blue Last* P.H. 113 Curtain rd. Shoreditch
Cosson Wm. fruiterer, 29 Adam st. west, Bryanstone square
Cossum Mary A. (Mrs.), linendraper, 3 Guildford pl. Spafields
Costa Manuel, italian warehouse, 131 Jermyn st. St. James's
Costeker William & Son, woollendrapers, 63 Cornhill
Costeker John, cloth merchant, 5 Paragon, New Kent road
Costell Henry, boot & shoe maker, 53 Gray's inn lane
Costello William Birmingham, M.D. surgeon, 10 Golden sq
Coster Jas. & Co. warehsmen. Fountain ct. & 4 Aldermanbury
Coster John, dairyman, 11½ Smith square, Westminster
Coster Joseph, furniture broker, 7 Bow lane, Bromley
Coster Wm. gold & silver piercer, 40 Lit. Sutton st. Clerknwll
Costiff James, baker, 2 Saville place, Lambeth
Costigan John, china warehouse, 27 Lower Sloane st
Coston Matthew, stockbroker, 5 Bank chambers, Lothbury
Cotchett Thos. grocer & butterman, 7 Trinity row, Islington
Cotes Charles, solicitor, 61 Russell square, Bloomsbury
Cotes Nathl. Hardcastle, bookseller & library, 139 Cheapside
Cotesworth, Powell & Pryor, mer. between 16&17 St. Helen's pl
Cotgreave Robt. blacking mak. 27 George st. Grosvenor sq
Cothay William, merchant, 37 Mincing lane
Cother Dunbar John, barrister, 4 Harcourt bldgs. Temple
Cother William, barrister, 4 Garden court, Temple
Cotman Henry, commercial ale house, 251 Tooley st
Cotman John Sell, artist, 8 Henrietta st. Brunswick sq
Coton Charles, dairyman, 7 New Manor st. King's rd. Chelsea
Coton John, cowkeeper, 19 New st. Brompton
Coton Wm. dairyman & porkman, 160 Sloane st. Chelsea
Cotsford Edward Jas. auctioneer, 7 Denmark ter. Pentnvlle
Cotsworth Thos. jun. builder, 5 Crescent, Southwark bridge rd
Cott James, carpenter & builder, 4 Whitehorse pl. Mile end rd
Cottage Wm. *D. of Northumberland* P.H. 64 Worship st. Shrdth
Cottam & Hallen, engineers, iron founders, agricultural implement makers, ironmongers, manufacturers of bedsteads, hurdles, gates, fencing, &c. &c. smiths' work in general, pump makers, wire workers & hot house builders, 2 Winsley st. & Cornwall road, Lambeth; (entrance, 76 Oxford st.)
Cottam James, colonial broker, 14 Commercial sale rooms
Cottam, Mortan & Co. west india merchants, 11 Lime st
Cottam Hen. pawnbroker, 25&26 Freeschool st. Horselydown
Cotter Thomas, furniture broker, 11 Vere st. Clare market
Cotterell & Blincoe, auctioneers, 37 Hart st. Bloomsbury
Cotterell & Rich, tallowchandlers, 32 High st. Kensington
Cotterell James, beer retailer, 16 Great Sutton st. Clknwell
Cotterell Thomas, pawnbroker, 163 Oxford st. & 99 Shoe lane
Cotterell Thomas, pawnbroker, see Vaughan & Cotterell
Cotterell Wm. John, plumber, 77 Manchester st. Gray's inn rd
Cotterill James Ward, oil & colorman, 282 Poplar High st
Cotterill William Henry, solicitor, 32 Throgmorton st
Cottingham John, magistrate, Union hall police court
Cottingham Joseph Orlibar, plumber, glazier, painter, & paperhanger, 12 Peter's hill, St. Paul's
Cottingham Lewis N. architect, 43 Basing pl. Waterloo rd
Cottle Robert, stockbroker, see Harrison & Cottle
Cottle Wm. sieve manufactu. 20 East st. Lamb's Conduit st
Cotton & Benett, solicitors, 2 Raymond bldgs. Gray's inn
Cotton James W. & Co. commissn. agts. 3 New ct. Moorgate st
Cotton & Hildyard, writers & grainers, 8 Titchborne st
Cotton, Fry & Co. metal & insurance brokers, 1 Riches ct
Cotton & Johnson, file, tool & metal wa. 21&22 Grafton st. Soho
Cotton William Henry & Samuel, solicitors, 7 Lothbury
Cotton's Wharf, John Hen. & Geo. Scovell, 20 & 21 Tooley st
Cotton Andrew, brass founder, 38 Union st. Borough rd
Cotton Benjamin, baker, 32 Henry st. east, Avenue rd
Cotton Chas. *Mason's Arms* P.H. 58 Devonshire st. Portland pl
Cotton Charles Rogers, cooper, & wood hoop merchant, Salisbury lane, near East lane stairs, Bermondsey
Cotton David, cabinet & bedstead maker, 49 King st. Borough
Cotton Francis, pawnbroker, 90 Shoreditch & 28 Hackney rd
Cotton George W. auctnr. & gen. agt. 24 Bishopsgt. st. wthn

Cotton Henry, basket & brush maker, cooper & turnery warehouse, 73 Tottenham court road
Cotton Henry Chas. architect & surveyor, 3 Islington green
Cotton Herminia Henrica (Mrs.), oilwa. 7 Gt. Bath st. Clerkenwl
Cotton James, furniture broker, 2 Duke st. Lisson grove
Cotton James, market pie house. 21 Long lane, Smithfield
Cotton James, who. hatter, 21 & 22 Princes st. Mile end New tn
Cotton John, chandler's shop, 16 Church rd. Comrcl. rd. East
Cotton John, oil & colorman, 3 College terrace, Chelsea
Cotton John, tailor, Robin Hood lane, Poplar
Cotton John, tailor, 20 Worship st. Finsbury
Cotton John W. currier, 24 Upper Lisson st. Lisson grove
Cotton Joseph, hatter, 62 Redcross st. Cripplegate
Cotton Joseph Lash, oilman, 1 Bridgehouse pl. Borough
Cotton Michael George, russia merch. 28 Gt. Winchester st
Cotton Robert, dining rooms, 10 Mill st. Hanover square
Cotton Robt. T. architect & surv. 2 North bldgs. Finsbury circ
Cotton Sarah (Mrs.), chandler's shop, 1 Hill st. Walworth rd
Cotton Thomas, watch spring mak. 11 Red Lion st. Clknwl
Cotton Wm. cornchandler, 13 King st. Westminster
Cotton Wm. merchant, 3 Crosby square, Bishopsgate st
Cotton Wm. plumber, &c. 63 East st. Manchester sq
Cotton Wm. who. cheesemonger, 4 Langley pl. Coml. rd. East
Cotton Wm. Augustus, tin & iron plate worker, 145 Minories
Cottrall Robert, last maker, 17 Cloth fair, Smithfield
Cottrell Chas. & Son, auctioneers, 89 London rd. Southwark
Cottrell Benjamin, manufacturer of braids, cords, & laces, Abbey st. Bethnal green road
Cottrell Charles, turner, 4 Portsmouth pl. Lr. Kennington la
Cottrell Edward, baker, 1 Salmon lane, Limehouse
Cottrell Elizabeth (Mrs.), grocer, 8 Robert st. Grosvenor sq
Cottrell George Henry, leather dresser & seller, 30 Barbican
Cottrell Henry, last, boot tree, & clog maker, 125 Holborn hill
Cottrell James, coal & potato dealer, 92 Star st. Edgware rd
Cottrell John, brassfounder, 29 Banner st. St. Luke's
Cottrell John, locksmith & bellhanger, 31 King st. Snowhill
Cottrell Levi, *Britannia* P.H. 83 High st. Camden town
Cottrell Thos. *Mother Red Cap* P.H. Greenland pl. Camden tn
Cottrill John, toymaker, 24 Plumber st. City road
Couch Charles, bookseller, 5 Mora place, City road
Couch Charles, coffee rooms, 66 Bunhill row
Couch George, lapidary & jeweller, 46 Clerkenwell green
Couch Richard, barrister, 7 Mitre court chambers, Temple
Couch Robert, grocer & cheesemonger, 9 Regent st. Hrsefry. rd
Couch William, coffee rooms, 25 Blackmoor st. Drury lane
Couchman Edward, engraver & printer, 10 Throgmorton st
Couchman Edward, undertaker, 11 Throgmorton st
Couchman Stephen, cheesemonger, 93 Upper Whitecross st
Couchman Thomas, *Windsor Castle* P.H. 1 Windsor terrace, Vauxhall bridge road
Couchman William, haberdasher, 80 Tothill st. Westminster
Coulborn Joseph, boot & shoe maker, 37 Ludgate st
Coulden Joseph, working cutler, 6 Red lion court, Spitalfields
Coulden Wm. tailor, 22 Coal harbour st. Hackney road
Coulderoy Alfd. beer shop, Tanners hl. Deptford new town
Couldery Thomas, tailor, 23 White st. Borough
Couldrey Joseph, math. inst. ma. 26 St. Thomas's st. east, Boro'
Couldrey Samuel, gold beater, 10 Eccleston st. east, Pimlico
Couldridge Chas. carpntr. & undertak. 15 Middle row, Holborn
Coule Chas. prof. of the accordion, 21 Gt. Mays bdgs. St. Mtns. l
Couling Hen. measuring tape mfr. 6 Hayward's pl. St. John st
Couling Maria (Mrs.), pianoforte mak. 9 Castle st. Long acre
Coulman Maria (Miss), milliner, 17 Southampton st. Euston sq
Coulsell Jas. Saml. plumber & glazier, 21 Green st. Bethnal gr
Coulsell Wm. jun. mathem. instrument ma. 9 Castle st. Boro'
Coulshaw Wm. tailor, 8 Cripplegate buildings
Coulson & Jackson, ladies' school, 32 Colet pl. Comr. rd. ea
Coulson (Jukes) & Co. export ironmongers, engineers & millwrights, 11 & 12 Clement's lane, Lombard st. & 7 St. Mary's row, Birmingham
Coulson Jas. bricklayr. & plastr. 4 Portman pl. Globe rd. Mile e
Coulson James, whiskey merchant, see Hill & Coulson
Coulson John, cheesemonger, 161 Shadwell High st
Coulson John, mason & lettr. cut. 15 Northumberld st. Marylebon
Coulson John, plumber, 15 King st. Lower rd. Islington
Coulson Philip, bricklayer, 42 Cromer st. Brunswick sq
Coulson Robert, *Coulson's hotel*, 45 Brook st. Grosvenor sq
Coulson Sam. sen. goldsmith & jewel. 7 Duke st. Grosvenor sq
Coulson Sam. jun. working jeweller, 17 Broad st. Golden sq
Coulson Thomas, boot & shoema. 38 Sekforde st. Clerkenwell
Coulson Walter, barrister, 7 New sq. Lincoln's inn
Coulson Watson, wine agent & com. merchant, 5 Mark lane
Coulson Wm. surgeon, 2 Frederick's place, Old Jewery
Coulston Peter, *City Arms* P.H. 22 King st. Aldgate
Coultas Charles, *Wheatsheaf* P. H. 12 Lower Grosvenor place, & 1 Upper Eaton st. Pimlico

Coulthard & Clark, tyne bottle warehouse, 34 Gt. Tower st
Coulthard, Manico & Co. paper, general merchants, alum & chemical agents, Brook's wharf, Upper Thames st
Coulthard Edward, attorney, 4 Gray's inn square
Coulthard Joseph, chain cable & anchor warehouse, 278 Wapping; office, 34 Great Tower st
Coulthard Joseph, merchant, 34 Gt. Tower st. City
Coulthred James, surgeon, 139 Southwark bridge road
Coulthurst Henry Utrick & Nicholas, solicitors, 13 New inn
Coulthurst Thurston, butcher, 35 Up. Park pl. Regent's pk
Coulton Charles, auctioneer & appraiser, 52 Union st. Boro'
Coumbe John, butcher, 24 Upper North pl. Gray's inn road
Coumbe Richard, butcher, 124 Crawford st. Portman sq
Counsell Wm. shorthand writer, 15 Cursitor st
Count Sarah (Mrs.), oil warehouse, 36 Cowcross st. Smithfi
Counter Richard, tobacconist, 42 South st. Manchester sq
County Chronicle newspaper Office, 5 Warwick square
County Court of Requests, 14 to 16 Kingsgate st. Holborn
County Fire Office (John A. Beaumont), 50 Regent st
County Herald newspaper Office, 5 Warwick sq. Newgate st
Countze George, coach & harness ma. see Pearse & Countze
Coup Sarah (Miss), milliner, 8 Little Queen st. Westminster
Coupar George, baker, 1 Little Compton st. Soho
Coupar John, baker, 50 Stanhope st. Clare market
Couper William, baker, 13 Elizabeth st. South Pimlico
Coupland & Gilbert, who. stay ma. 1 George yard, Bow la. City
Coupland Charles, solicitor, 30 Bucklersbury
Coupland Mary (Miss), wireworker, &c. 370 Oxford st
Coupland Michael, engineer, &c. Pond yd. New Park st. Boro'
Courage & Donaldsons', brewers, Shad Thames
Courrier de l' Europe newspaper Office, 1 Finch lane, Cornhill, & 10 Wellington st. Strand
Course & Gudgen, oil & colormen, 44 St. John st. Clerkenwll
Course of Exchange newspaper Office, 13 Copthall court
Court & Guy, ironmongers, 201 Oxford st.
Court Gazette newspaper Office, 12 Catherine st. Strand
Court Journal newspaper Office, 19 Catherine st. Strand
Court & Ladies' Magazine Office, 11 Carey st. Lincoln's inn
Court of Review Registrar's Office (Wm. Scrope Ayrton, regr.), Quality court, Chancery lane; hours during term & sittings, 10 to 4; in vacation, 11 to 3
Court George, carver & gilder, 11 Adam st. east, Portman sq
Court Henry, printer, 26 Brooke st. Holborn
Court John, cooper, 37 Chalcroft ter. New cut, Lambeth
Court John, plumassier & artificial florist, 13 Gt. Castle st
Court Wm. tailor, 17 Great Pulteney st. Golden square
Court Wm. Grimes, chemist & druggist, 282 Regent st
Courtauld (Samuel), Taylors' & Courtauld, crape, silk & velvet manufacturers, 1 & 2 Carey lane, Cheapside
Courtauld Wm. jeweller, 26 Brick lane, Spitalfields
Courteen Richard, solicitor, 17 Paradise row, Rotherhithe
Courtenay James & Wm. James, merchants, 11 Abchurch la
Courtenay Francis Burdett, surgeon, 289A, Regent st
Courtenay John, surgeon, 5 Finsbury terrace, City road
Courtenay Philip Warner, barrister, 10 Crown office row
Courthope (J. B. & John) & Bayly, stationers, paperhangers, &c. 33 Rotherhithe, & 10 George yard, Lombard st
Courthope Frederick Wm. wine merchant, 49 Mark lane
Courthope Henry Waide, coal merchant, 393 Rotherhithe
Courthope James, coal mer. 21 Paradise st. Rotherhithe
Courtier Chas. bible & prayer book wa. 3 Bouverie st. Fleet st
Courtnall Samuel, wheelwright, 1 North st. Pentonville
Courtnay Thomas, cheesemonger, 104 Drury lane
Courtney Emma (Miss), seminary, 54 Thurloe sq. Brompton
Courtney Greenwood Hen. locksmith, &c. 2 Lit. Grosvenor st
Courtney James, merchant, 21 Water lane, Great Tower st
Courtney James, tailor, 10 Gillingham st. Vauxhall brdg. rd
Courtney John, cheesemonger, 10 Bathurst st. Sussex sq. Hy. pk
Courtney Thomas, china & earthenware wareho. 34 Old Bond st
Courtney Thomas, wine cooper, 10 Gt. Thomas Apostle
Courtney Thomas, livery stables, 5 Gt. St. Thomas Apostle
COURTS OF REQUEST.—*See* LAW DIRECTORY
Cousens James & Sons, who. teadealers, 14 Sherborne la. City
Cousens & Whiteside, watchma. 20 Davies st. Berkeley sq
Cousens Rd. Thos. wool wareho. keeper, see Gooch & Cousens
Cousens Richd. Wm. watchma. 7 Providence pl. Comerl. rd. Ea
Cousin Louis, artificial florist, 8 Mabledon pl. Burton cresct
Cousins Wm. & James, carpenters, 45 Duke st. St. James's
Cousins Benj. printer, 18 Duke st. Lincoln's inn fields
Cousins Charles, corn & coal mer. 3 Shepherd pl. Up. Brook st
Cousins George, bootmaker, 18 Broadway, Deptford
Cousins George Mitchell, *Black Horse* P.H. 46 Haymarket
Cousins Henry, artist, 15 Osnaburgh st. Regent's park
Cousins Samuel, A.R.A. artist, 15 Osnaburgh st. Regent's pk
Cousins Thos. mkt. gardener, Cambridge row, Cambridgeheath
Cousins Wm. carpenter & joiner, 34 Devonshire st Queen sq

Couszens C. *Lord Wellington* P.H. 4 Baalzephon st. Bmdsy
Couta Gabriel, brass filagree worker, 12 Blenheim st. Oxfrd. st
Coutts & Co. bankers, 59 Strand
Coutts Elizabeth & Ann, bakers, & corn chandlers, 16 Notting hill, High st. & 6 Kensington High st.
Coutts Isabella (Mrs.), *White Hart* P.H. 21&22 Milbk row
Couty David upholsterer, 16 Alfred pl. Newington causeway
Couzens Charles, artist, 38 Upper Berkeley st
Couzens Joseph, boot & shoe ma. Southampton st. Cambwll. rd
Cove Luke Hinde, coal mercht. 11 Montpelier st. Brompton
Covell James, butcher, 26 Broadway, Deptford
Coveney Benjamin, wholesale export & fancy stationer, bristol board and account book manufacturer, 31 Bread st
Covent Garden theatre, Bow st. Covent garden
Coventon Joseph, clock case mak. 60 Red Lion st. Clerknwll
Coventon Philip, butcher, 22 Wells row, Upper st. Islington
Coventon Wm. instrument case maker, 19 Robert st. Bedfd. rw
Coventon Wm. Garlick, solicitor, 12 Highbury park, Islgtn
Coventry Elizabeth & Thomas, dyers & scourers, 39 Barbican
Coventry & Hollier, music publishers & and pianoforte manufacturers, 71 Dean st. Soho
Coventry, Nuneaton, Birmingham & Leicester Railway, (Henry Cassin, sec.) 3 Church court, Old Jewry
Coventry Sarah & Edw. silk manufact. 120 Union st. Boro'
Coventry & Sheppard, corn factors, 8 Whitehart court, Lombard st. & Corn exchange
Coventry Chas. grainer & writer, 130 Curtain road
Coventry Charlotte (Mrs.), dyer, 37 Road side, Mile end rd
Coventry Edward P. silk manufacturer, 120 Union st. Boro'
Coventry George, fruiterer, 1 Edward st. Stepney
Coventry John, engraver & printer, 80 King William st. City
Coventry John, printer & stationer, Church st. Hackney
Coventry Mary Elizb. (Mrs.), umbrella mak. 174 Oxford st
Coventry Millis, corn & flour factor, see Coventry & Sheppard
Coventry Millis, wharfinger, 20 Shad Thames (George strs)
Coventry Richard, goldsmith, 34 Perceval st. Clerkenwell
Coventry Thomas, barrister, 5 Old square, Lincoln's inn
Coventry William, plumber, &c. 32 Chapel st. Curtain road
Cover Ann (Miss), butcher, 15 South st. Grosvenor sq
Cover James, butcher, 12 James st. Covent garden
Cover John, *George & Dragon* P.H. 18 New North st
Cover John, packing case maker, 12 Charles st. Hatton gardn
Coverdale & Lee, solicitors, 4 Bedford row
Coverley James, carpenter, 1 King's head ct. Shoreditch
Coverlid Henry, hairdresser, 12 Royal Hospital rw. Chelsea
Coverlid John, hairdresser, 78 Salisbury st. Lisson grove
Covey William Henry, surgeon, 42 Charing cross
Covington Jas. & Co. whfingers & lighterm. 8 Whf. Cityrd. basin
Covington Charles, hatter, 10 Old Bailey
Covington James, lighterman & wharfinger, 1 Warkworth terrace, Commercial road east, & 8 Wharf, City road basin
Cow Peter & Kate, lace & baby linen wa. 42 Bishopsgate wthn
Cowan Alexander & Sons, paper makers, 45 Upper Thames st
Cowan John & Co. manufacturers of wax & sperm candles, sealing wax, &c. & dealers in sperm oil, 8 Mansion house st
Cowan Alexander, marine store dealer, 96 Aldersgate st.
Cowan David, chandelier lamp maker, gasfitter & oilman, 9 Hungerford st. Strand
Cowan Edward, tailor, 6 Gt. St. Thomas Apostle, Cheap side
Cowan Lewis, bone mer. & soap ma. 139 New Gravel la. Shadwl
Cowan Lewis, juvenile publisher, 19 Aylesbury st. Clerkenwell
Cowan Malcolm, scotch advocate & parliamentary counsel, New Temple bldgs. Mitre court, Fleet st. & 4 Devonport st. Hyde park
Cowan Solomon, general dealer, 15 Goswell st
Coward & Cancellor, starchmakers, 15 Princes st. Lambeth
Coward Chas. lead & oil mercht. 10 & 11 Lit. Knightrider st
Coward Chas. painter, 10 Lit. Knightrider st. Doctors' comns
Coward George, surgeon, 6 Woburn bldgs. Tavistock sq
Coward Geo. Fred. east india mercht. 27 Budge row, Cannon st
Coward Geo. Wm. chemist, 10 Norfolk st. Middlesex hospital
Coward Geo. Wm. Hen. surgeon, Herbert st. New North road
Coward James, academy, 91 Sloane st
Coward James, meat salesman, 3 Rose st. Newgate market
Coward John Wm. Smith, surgn. 11 Minerva ter. Barnsbury pk
Coward Richard A. who. drug. & merc. 10 Laurence Pountney la
Coward Thomas Christopher, surgeon, 5 Stepney High st
Coward Wm. dairy, 7 Powell st. east, King's sq. Goswell rd
Coward Wm. surgeon, 11 DeBeauvoir sq. Kingsland
Cowburn William, solicitor, 10 Lincoln's inn fields
Cowd Samuel, chinadealer, 97 Gt. Suffolk st. Borough
Cowden Thos. beer retailer, 9 Bird st. Oxford st
Cowderoy Edward, cheesemonger, 19 Gt. Suffolk st. Boro'
Cowderoy James, butcher, 1 Newcastle place, Edgware rd
Cowderoy Jas. cowkeeper, 3 Upper Berkeley st. Portman sq
Cowderoy John, baker, 8 Hardwick pl. Commercial rd. east
Cowderoy John, grocer, 73 York st. Westminster
Cowderoy John, teadealer & grocer, 19 Blackfriars road
Cowderoy John, grocer & teadealer, 29 Grafton st. Soho
Cowderoy Thomas, grocer, 40, Clapham road place
Cowderoy Wm. jeweller, High st. Kensington
Cowdry Esther (Mrs.), who. brushma. & wareho. 270 & 271 Strand
Cowell John & Son, malt factrs. New Corn Exchange, Mark la
Cowell Joseph & Son, tailors, 93 Great Russell st. Bloomsbury
Cowell & Thomas, carpenters, Ryder yard, St. James's
Cowell Frederick, wine merchant, 67 Borough High st
Cowell James, butcher, 17 Chandos st. Covent garden
Cowell John, stationer, 8 Monmouth pl. Old Kent road
Cowell Joseph, printer & bookseller, 22 Queen's row, Pimlico
Cowell Lucy (Mrs.), dyer, &c. 22 Queen's row, Pimlico
Cowell Richard, grocer, 57 Newington causeway
Cowell Thomas, jun. butcher, 3 Brook st. Glo'ster road
Cowell Thomas, sen. butcher, 31 St. George's pl. Knightsbridge
Cowell Wm. beer retailer, Lr. Salisbury pl. Locksfields
Cowell William, rope & twine ma. 40 Green st. Bethnal gr
Cowen Alfred, omnibus prop. Little Grove st. Lisson grove
Cowen Henry, hairdresser, 24 Bedfordbury, Covent garden
Cowen Jas. grocer & oilman, 15 Old Quebec st. Portman sq
Cowens Jas. cheesemonger, 15 Old Quebec st. Portman sq
Cowie Jas. & Son, foreign newspaper office, & foreign & english advertising agents. 2 St. Ann's la. Genl. Post office
Cowie, Jolland & Co. booksellers & stationers, 31 Poultry
Cowie David, shoemaker, 16 Colville ct. John st. Fitzroy sq
Cowie Elizth. (Mrs.), prep. school, 3 Marlbro' rd. St. John'swd
Cowie George, printer & publisher, 110 Shoe lane, Fleet st
Cowie John, sheffield plate establishment, 11 Holles st. Cav. sq
Cowing Elizabeth (Mrs.), lodging ho. 33 Bury st. St. James's
Cowing James, silk manufacturer, 18 Spital square
Cowing James, jun. silk manufacturer, 10 Fort st. Spital sq
Cowing John, beer retailer, 17 Brandon st. Locksflds. Walw
Cowland George, grocer, Neate st. Coburg rd. Old Kent rd
Cowland John B. herald painter, 38 Lisle st. Leicester sq
Cowland Joseph, *Yorkshire Grey* P.H. Stratford
Cowlard Henry, solicitor, 14 Lincoln's inn fields
Cowlard William, turner, 1 Dorrington st. Leather lane
Cowle Mary (Mrs.), poulterer, 90 Aldersgate st
Cowles Alfred, engraver, 111 St. Martin's lane
Cowles Chas. cabinet maker, 2 Hollen st. Wardour st. Soho
Cowles Isaac, coal dealer, 23 College hill, Up. Thames st
Cowles Michael, poulterer, 5 Belmont row, Vauxhall
Cowley Charles, baker, 26 Catherine st. Pimlico
Cowley Dan. *Sugar Loaf* P.H. 41 Gt. Hermitage st. Wapping
Cowley Eliz. (Mrs.), brushmak. 2 Cheltenham pl. Westmr. rd
Cowley George, baker, 10 Dean st. Westminster
Cowley Henry, grocer, &c. 14 Cherry garden st. Bermondsey
Cowley James Thomas, hatter, 48 Long lane, Smithfield
Cowley John, *King's Head* P.H. 40 Bridge road, Lambeth
Cowley John Christian, barrister, 1 Park cres. Portland pl
Cowley Thomas, baker, 13 Romney terrace, Westminster
Cowley William, bird & shell dealer, 31 King st. Tower hill
Cowley William, poulterer, 10 New Chapel pl. Kentish Town
Cowling John, barrister, 2 Mitre court buildings, Temple
Cowling Joseph, ropemaker, &c. 20 Gt. Suffolk st. Borough
Cowling Thomas, tailor, 29 Hart st. Bloomsbury
Cowlrick Wm. working jeweller, 25 Charles st. Middlx. hosp
Cownden Charles, boat builder, see Wentzell & Cownden
Cownden Charles, sen. boat builder, 48 Lr. Forest. Lambeth
Cowne Samuel, pawnbroker, 1 Huntworth ter. Portman mrkt
Cowne Samuel, surgeon, 25 Beaufoy terrace, Edgware road
Cowney Chas. *Dr. Butler's Head* tav. 5 White Rose ct. Coln. st
Cownley George, dairy, 12 Grocers' hall court, Poultry
Cowper John & Frederick & Co. warehousemen, 43 St. Paul's churchyard, & 51 Old change
Cowper James, linendraper, &c. 1 St. George's circus, Obelisk
Cowper Robert, carpenter, 23 Wakefield st. Regent square
Cowper Thomas, mercer, 144 Borough High st
Cowper Thos. tripe dresser, 24 Strutton ground, Westminster
Cowper William, grocer, 28 New st. Dorset square
Cowtan Henry, carpenter, 3 Richmond bldgs. Dean st. Soho
Cowthard Charles, baker, High st. Deptford
Cowthorpe Henry, lighterman, 2 Salisbury st. Bermondsey
Cowvan Barnard & Sam. canton strop ma. 164 Fenchurch st
Cox Benjamin & Co. wholes. cheesemongers, 50 Newgate st
Cox, Bros. & Co. leadmer. (Isaac Fisher, ag.), 8 Tooley st. Boro
Cox Charles & Son, royal marine agents, 44 Hatton garden
Cox & Co. (Rd. Hen. Cox; Chas. Hammersley; Henry Richd. Cox; & Fred Wm. Cox), army agents, 2 Craig's ct. Charing cr
Cox, Heisch & Co. merchants, 16 America square, Minories
Cox, Horner & Hogg, who. hosiers, 3 Clement's court, Wood st
Cox John A. D. & Henry M. printers 74&75 Gt. Queen st. Lin. in. fi
Cox & Jones, law stationers, 18 High Holborn
Cox Rd. S. & Co. fancy handf. & ribbon ma. 7 St. Paul's church yd

Cox & Stone, solicitors, 33 Poultry
Cox Wm. & Hen. Poore, stock & share brok. 16 Throgmorton st
Cox & Williams, solicitors, 62 Lincoln's inn fields
Cox Adam, hardwareman, 83, Houndsditch
Cox Alfred, fishmonger, Little Chelsea
Cox Algernon, barrister, 22 Portugal st. Lincoln's inn fields
Cox Amelia (Miss), grocer, 1 Upper Kennington lane
Cox Anthony, furniture broker, High st. Bow
Cox Benj. butcher, 9 Glasshouse st. 7 Swallow pl. Regent st
Cox Benjamin, hosier & glover, 94 Bishopsgate without
Cox Bridget (Mrs.), milliner, 39 Adam st. west, Bryanstone sq
Cox Catherine (Mrs.), grocer, 6 Water lane, Blackfriars
Cox Catherine (Miss), straw hat ma. 2 Mary pl. Bow la. Poplar
Cox Charles, butcher, 201 Bethnal green road
Cox Chas. *Ecclesiastical Gaz. Office*, 9 Southampton st. Strand
Cox Charles, gasfitter, 6 Little Queen st. Westminster
Cox Charles, plumber, 6 Little Mitchell st. St. Luke's
Cox Charles James, physician, 3 Beaumont st. Portland pl
Cox Daniel, butcher, Denmark hill, Camberwell
Cox Daniel, shoemaker, 25 Mansionhouse st. Kennington
Cox Ebenezer, bookbndrs.' toolcut. 6 Up. Southampton st. Pntvl
Cox Edward, law stationer, see Laidman & Cox
Cox Edward, *Lion & Goat* P.H. 5 Grosvenor st
Cox Edward, tobacconist, 31 Bell st. Edgware road
Cox Edward, tool & plane ma. 15 Gt. Queen st. Lincoln's inn fi
Cox Edward, translator of latin records, 119 Chancery lane
Cox Edward H. auctioneer & surveyor, 106 New Bond st
Cox Edward Wm. barrister, 3 Crown Office row, Temple
Cox Eleanor F. (Mrs.) med. bookseller, 13½ St. Thomas' st. Boro
Cox Eliza (Mrs.), chemist & druggist, 4 John's row, St. Luke's
Cox Elizabeth (Mrs.), dressmak. 16 Park ter. Regent's park
Cox Elizbth. (Mrs.), *Old Chelsea Water Wks.* P.H. Up. Belg. ter
Cox Francis, bookbinder, 15 St. Swithin's lane
Cox Frederick, optician, 100 Newgate st
Cox Frederic, wireworker, 98 Gt. Peter st. Westminster
Cox Fredk. George, proctor & notary, see Jennings & Cox
Cox George, baker, Church st. Hackney
Cox George, bread & biscuit baker, 61 Goswell road
Cox George, optician, jeweller & practical chemist, & proprietor of Cox's pure carbon blacking, 128 Holborn hill
Cox George, painter & glazier, 9 Seymour st. Euston sq
Cox George, solicitor, 14 Sise lane, Bucklersbury
Cox Geo. sup. of soc. for pro. christ. knowldg. 76 & 77 Gt. Queen st
Cox George, tailor, 13 Lit. Guildford st. Brunswick sq
Cox George, tennis court keeper, 16 James st. Haymarket
Cox George Jas. lithographer, 13 Little Guildford st. Russell square, & Royal Polytechnic Institution, 309 Regent st
Cox Hannah (Mrs.), tobacco pipe ma. 8 Queen's ct. 247 Hi. Hlbn
Cox Henry, cheesemonger, 4 Barnsbury st. Liverpool road
Cox Henry, coffee rooms, 32 Bell st. Edgware road
Cox Henry, corn chandler, 101 London road, Borough
Cox Henry, hatter, 11 Glasshouse st. Regent st
Cox Henry, soap boiler, 4 Eyre st. hill, & White Bear yard, Back hill, Hatton garden
Cox Henry, watchmaker, 2 Church lane, Islington
Cox Henry Edward, staymaker, 10 & 11 Castle st. Leicester square, & 37 Westminster bridge road
Cox Herman, merchant, 18 Mark lane
Cox Isaiah, cheesemonger, 1 Tothill st. Westminster
Cox Jacob, coal dealer, 11 Osborne st. Whitechapel
Cox James, furn. broker & appraiser, 11 Strutton gr. Westmr
Cox James, carman, 23 Little Carter la. Doctors' commons
Cox James, coke agent & gas inspector, 70 John st. Fitzroy sq
Cox James, *Cross Keys* P.H. 6 Belton st. Long Acre
Cox James, farrier, see Semington & Cox
Cox James, optical & mathemat. instrument mak. 5 Barbican
Cox James, printing press mnfr. & engineer, Wenlock road
Cox James, smith, 150 Hoxton Old town
Cox James, tailor, 17 King st. Soho
Cox James, wheelwright, 81 Upper East Smithfield
Cox James, jun. cook & confectioner, Camberwell green
Cox James Mitchell, artist, 12 Hanway st. Oxford st
Cox John, beer retailer, 24 Brick lane, St. Luke's
Cox John, brewer, White's grounds, Bermondsey st
Cox John, carp. & builder, 2 & 3 Grafton st. east, Tottnhm ct. rd
Cox John, coal merchant, 30 Bloomsbury st. Bloomsbury
Cox John, coffee rooms, 14 Fashion st. Dockhead
Cox John, *King's Head* P.H. 21 Lower st. Islington
Cox John, news agent & stationer, 78 Drury lane
Cox John, whiting & size maker, Russell st. Bermondsey
Cox John Alexander, greengrocer, 3 Pump yard, Ratcliff
Cox Joseph, brace & belt maker & undertaker, 75 London wal
Cox Joseph, butcher, 51 Bethnal green road
Cox Joseph, *Coopers' Arms* P.H. 9 Cowcross st
Cox Joseph, fringe maker & importer of berlin wools & patterns, 16 Park terrace, Regent's park road
Cox Joseph, wholesale & retail haberdasher, button & tailors' trimming seller, 59 High st. Bloomsbury
Cox Leonard Philip, wine merchant, 75 Old Broad st
Cox Mary (Mrs.), dairy, 5 New Compton st. Soho
Cox Matthias, working cutler, 8 Windsor pl. Southwk. brdg. rd
Cox Nathaniel, watchmaker, 140 Goswell st
Cox Ralph, shoe warehouse, 303 Oxford st
Cox Richard Benjamin, hosier & haberdasher, 41 Holborn hill
Cox Robert, builder, 6 Buckingham pl. Marlbro' rd. Chelsea
Cox Robert, coachmaker, 2 Bowyer pl. Camberwell road
Cox Samuel, plumber, 10 Cobham row, Clerkenwell
Cox Sarah (Mrs.), hatmaker, 78 Borough High st
Cox Stephen, jun. dealer in horses, 6 Stamford st. Blackfrs. rd
Cox Thomas, carman, 18 Bishop's court, Old Bailey
Cox Thomas, corn dealer, 26 Lambeth walk
Cox Thomas, grocer, 2 & 3 Peel pl. Kensington gravel pits
Cox Thomas, livery stables & fruiterer, 9 Lower Porchester st
Cox Thomas, nailfactor, 17 Lowr. Charles st. Northampton sq
Cox Thomas, shoemaker, 65 Green st. Bethnal green
Cox Thomas, solicitor, 7 Bennett st. Stamford st. Blackfrs. rd
Cox Thomas, clerical tailor & robe maker, 29 Southampton street, Strand
Cox Thomas, tailor, 62 Gt. Titchfield st. Oxford st
Cox Thomas, tobacconist, 39 Gibson st. Waterloo rd
Cox Thomas, wine cooper & bottle mer. 9 Singleton st. Hoxton
Cox Thomas Harford, *Plough* P.H. 11 Plough yd. Shoreditch
Cox Travers, physician, 2 Stanhope pl. Connaught square
Cox William, baker, 19 Ernest st. Regent's park
Cox William, carman, Wheatsheaf yard, Farringdon st
Cox William, carrier, 49 Chapel place, Brompton
Cox William, carpenter, 12 Smith square, Westminster
Cox William, carpenter, 7 Wood st. Cheapside
Cox William, carpenter & undertaker, 36 Clerkenwell close
Cox William, coal & potato wa. 27 George st. Grosvenor sq
Cox William, corn dealer, 51 Ossulston st. Somers town
Cox William, *Cox's hotel*, 55 Jermyn st. St. James's
Cox William, grocer, 13 Cornwall road, Stamford st
Cox William, shoemaker, see Knapp & Cox
Cox William, solicitor, 16 Pinner's hall, Gt. Winchester st
Cox William, watch jewlr. 15 Lr. Smith st. Northampton sq
Cox William, wine cooper, 18 Crown st. Soho
Cox Wm. Hen. barge builder, College wf. Belvedere rd. Lmbth
Cox William Henry, bootmaker, 6 Bear st. Leicester sq
Cox William Henry, ham dealer, 134 Bishopsgate without
Cox William Henry, poultry salesman, Leadenhall market
Cox William Henry, steam printer & printing ink maker, 5 Great Queen st. & 29 Parker st. Lincoln's inn fields
Cox William H. tanner, see Drake & Cox
Coxall Daniel, grocer & fruiterer, 12 & 13 St. Ann's place, Limehouse.
Coxe & Glover, sheriff's officers (Surrey), 57 George st. Blkfrs. rd
Coxe Philip Smith, attorney, see Bischoff & Coxe
Coxell Daniel Henry, leather seller, 85 Fore st. Limehouse
Coxeter James, surgical instrument maker to University College Hospital, 23 Grafton st. east, Tottenham court rd
Coxford John Wm. academy, 55 Gt. Prescot st. Goodman's fl
Coxford Philip, deal merchant, 3 Mary's pl. Kingsland road
Coxhead Andrew, portmanteau ma. 3 York pl. Westmr. rd
Coxhead Benj. Seager, ship & anchorsmith, Millwall, Poplar
Coxhead Frederick, *Bell tavern* 3 Lower Thames st
Coxhead Fred. coach builder, Villa st. Walworth common
Coxhead Hezekiah, boot & shoe ma. 22 Glo'ster row, Grange rd
Coxhead John, merchant, see Fordati, Coxhead & Co
Coxhead Phillip, *Duke of York* P.H. 93 York st. Commercial road east
Coxhead Robert Thomas, tailor, 3 Queen st. Golden square
Coxill Joseph, cooper, 43 Upper Seymour st. Euston square
Coxon John, gen. commission agent & warehmn. 43 Basinghall st
Coxon Robt. Jas. bookbinder & statnr. 1 Grenville st. Brnswk. sq
Coxwell Hen. surgeon dentist, 10 Claremont row, Islington
Coy Jeffery, warehsmn. 1 Flying Horse ct. Maiden la. Wood st
Coy John Underwood, woollen factor, 8 Wood st. Cheapside
Coyfe Thomas, confectioner, 2 Deptford bridge
Coyne & Baker, surgeons, 13 Bulstrode st. Manchester sq
Coysh Wm. *N. Guildford Barge* P.H. 9 Belvedere rd. Lamb
Cozens, Matthews & Thorpe, watchma. 10 Artillery pl. west
Cozens Chas. saddler, 29 Liverpool st. Bishopsgate
Cozens Edward, grocer, 104 Drummond st. Euston square
Cozens John, grocer, 31 Dorset st. Portman square
Cozens John, hairdresser, 51 Redcross st. Cripplegate
Cozens Leonard Abbot, coal merchant, Middle wharf, Great Scotland yard, & 50 Grove place, Brompton
Cozens Thomas, stonemason, 17 Lisson grove North
Crabb Edmund, miller, 52 Lower Shadwell
Crabb George, barrister, 16 Southampton bldgs. Chancery la
Crabb Jas. carpenter, corn ledger, 28 Parker's row, Dockhead

Crabb John, shoemaker, 44 Upper Marylebone st
Crabb Josph. *Sir Walter Scott* P.H. Pritchard's pl. Hcknyfi
Crabb Josiah, baker, 13 Clarence place, Hackney road
Crabb Wm. baker, 99 Albany st. Regent's park
Crabb Wm. Brooksby, shoemaker, 185 Sloane st. Knightsbr
Crabb Wm. Brooksby, jun. bootma. 22 Motcomb st. Belgrave sq
Crabb Wm. Kendrick, hairdresser, 230 Hoxton Old town
Crabtree Charles, baker, 2 Wigmore st. Cavendish sq
Crabtree Francis, fancy biscuit baker, &c. 8 Strand
Crabtree John, carman, 7 Burford ter. East India rd. Poplar
Crabtree Joseph, baker, 31 Little Alie st. Goodman's fields
Crabtree Mark, dyer & scourer, 16 King st, Seven dials
Crace Fred. & Son, house decorators, 14 Wigmore st. Caven. sq
Crack William, barge builder, 55 Lower Fore st. Lambeth
Cracklen John, butcher, 43 Charles st. Westminster
Crackles Thos. M. dining rooms, 6 Union pl. Lisson grove
Cracklow & Farrer, wine & spirit merchants, 23 Old Fish st
Cracknell & Simeon, baker, Broadway, Deptford
Cracknell Thomas, painter, plumber, &c. 9 Maida hill east
Cracknell William, grocer, 29 Stangate, Lambeth
Craddock & Co. booksellers & publishers, 48 Paternoster row
Craddock Charles, surgeon, 6 Chapel place, Cavendish sq
Craddock Chas. Rich. solicitor, see Wiglesworth, Ridsdale & Co
Craddock Geo. china &c. wa. 4 New Portland pl. Wandswth rd
Craddock Geo. surgical elastic bandage mak. 35 Leicester sq
Craddock John, hairdresser, Stratford broadway
Craddock John, printer, 8 Holywell st. Strand
Craddock John, wine cooper, 39 Vere st. Clare market, & 8 Symond's inn, Chancery lane
Craddock Joseph, perfumer, 7 Mount st. Lambeth
Cradduck Thomas, coffee rooms, 299 Kent st. Borough
Cradick Abraham, beer retailer, 14 Norfolk pl. East st. Walw
Cradock Charles, tobacconist, 11 Cock hill, Ratcliff
Cradock Edward, coffee rooms, 29 King st. Covent garden
Cradock Henry, shoemaker, 20 Strutton ground, Westmins
Cradock Thomas, oilman, Church st. Hackney
Crafford John, coffee rooms, 183 Shadwell High st
Crafford Thomas, *Hope* coffee rooms, 77 Fetter lane
Craft Harriet & Sarah, straw hat mak. 51 Dorset st. Prtmn. sq
Craft John, cheesemonger, 20 Philpot lane
Craft John, *John Bull Brewery*, Essex st. Whitechapel, office, 20 Philpot lane
Craft Rebecca (Mrs.), *Two Brewers* P.H. 83 Brick la. Spitalfi
Craft William, fishmonger, 41 Store st. Bedford sq
Crafter Edward, auctioneer, &c. 9 Arthur st. West, City
Crafter George, solicitor, 168 Blackfriars road
Crafter Moses, *Old King's Head* P.H. 1 Penton row, Walw
Crafter Richd. chemist & druggist, 171 Hoxton Old town
Crafter Wm. auctioneer & appraiser, 4 Stamford st. Blackfrs. rd
Crafts George Fred. engraver, 19 Artillery la. Bishopsgate
Crafts John, solicitor, 1 Scot's yard, Bush lane
Crafts Mary Ann (Mrs.), tailor, 30 Freeschool st. Horselydn
Cragg & Jeyes, solicitors, 22 Bedford row
Cragg George, butcher, 1 Harper st. New Kent rd
Cragg James, butcher, 117 Mount st. Berkeley square
Cragg John, who. watch manufacturer, 8 Northampton sq
Cragg Richard Riley, *Royal Oak* P.H. 221 Whitechapel rd
Cragg William, butcher, 71 New Church st. Lisson grove
Craggs George Frederic, fancy stationer, 6 Budge row, City
Craggs Wm. *Cottage of Content* P.H. Park pl. Walworth
Craig Andrew, lodging house, 7 Agar st. Strand
Craig Ddu Slate Company (Wm. F. Bray, sec.), 9 Lincoln's inn fields
Craig David, bootmaker, 70 Pennyfields, Poplar
Craig James, painter & glazier, 2 Coborn rd. Mile end rd
Craig Richard Davis, barrister, 3 Stone bldgs. Lincoln's inn
Craig Thomas, potato merchant, 72 London rd. Southwark
Craige John, livery stables, 28 King st. Portman sq
Craighead & Webb, watch & clock makers, 1 Royal Exchng
Craigie John Livingstone, surgeon dentist, 42 Finsbury sq
Craigmyle John, chronometer & watchma. 90 Park st. Grosv. sq
Crake Hy. T. B. carver & gilder, 181 Wellington ter. Watrloo. rd
Crake John, architect, Carlton chambers, 4 Regent st
Crake Vandeleur B. barrister, 6 King's Bench walk, Temple
Crakell Frederick, tailor, 10 Bolt court, Fleet st
Craker John, carpenter, 4 Shepherd place, Upper Brook st
Craker William, wheelwright, 38 North row, Grosvenor sq
Crambrook William, silversmith & jeweller, 379 Strand
Cramer, Beale & Chappell, music sellers & publishers, & musical instrument warehouse, 201 Regent st. & 67 Conduit st. & 55 King st. Golden square
Cramfield Joseph, butcher, 1 Linden place, Bayswater
Cramond John, ship insurance broker, 46 Lime st. City
Cramp Daniel, tailor, 23 Edward st. Blackfriars rd
Cramp Fredk. Wm. tailor, 20 Gibraltar wk. Bethnal green rd
Cramp George, coal dealer, 22 High st. St. Giles's
Cramp John, butcher, 3 Trinity st. Borough
Cramp John, butcher & salesman, 52 & 53 Whitechapel High st
Cramp Joseph, butcher, 13 Upper Park pl. Dorset sq
Cramp Joseph, fruiterer, 26 Sidmouth st. Gray's inn rd
Cramp Robert, shop thread, twine & rope warehouseman, 5 Smith's buildings, Somerset st. Whitechapel
Cramp Thomas, butcher, 19 Chapel st. New rd
Crampern John Burgh & Co. coal mer. Nottghm. wf. City bsn
Crampern & Winter, saw mills, 21 New North st. Finsbury
Crampern John Callis, corn dealer, 92 Jermyn st. St. James's
Crampin Saml. plumber, glaz. & paint. 3 Up. Bryanstone st
Crampten William, dentist, 53 St. Martin's lane
Cranch Joseph, grocer, 1 Chancery pl. Camberwell New rd
Cranch Richard, solicitor & registrar, 15 London st. City
Cranch Thos. butcher, 4 Portland pl. south, Clapham road
Crane, Son & Graham, manufacturing chemists, Stratford, White's row, Whitechapel, & Jamaica coffeehouse, St. Michael's alley, Cornhill
Crane Louisa & Jemima (Misses), milliners, 26 Duke st. Grosv. sq
Crane Thomas & Frederick, grocers, 2 Richmond rd. Dalston
Crane Alfred Thos. wine mer. 48 Southampton row, Russll. sq
Crane Daniel, bricklayer, 26 Rawstorne st. Goswell road
Crane Frederick, hosier, see Sandland & Crane
Crane George William, printer, 56 Flagon row, Deptford
Crane James, agent to the Anthracite Coal Company, 11 Crooked lane, King William st. City
Crane James, *Blue Anchor* P.H. 48 Rosemary lane
Crane James, maltster, Stamford bridge, Little Chelsea
Crane Jonas, *John Bull* P.H. 3 Brewer st. north, Goswell rd
Crane Joseph, linendraper, Commercial road east
Crane Sarah (Miss), pianoforte teacher, 2 Amwell terrace
Crane William, cornfactor & hopman, Strand st. Sandwich, Kent, & Jack's coffee house, Mark lane
Crane Wm. Camp, merchant, 12 Copthall court
Craney James Robinson, grocer, 202½ Shadwell High st
Craney John Eddison, grocer, 52 Fore st. Cripplegate
Cranfield Isaac & Sons, leash mfrs. 3 Hare st. Bethnal grn
Cranfield Ann (Mrs.), strw. hat ma. 2 Kinnerton st. Belgrave sq
Cranfield Charles, cooper, 5 George row, Bermondsey
Cranfield Richard, grocer, 103 Gt. Suffolk st. Borough
Cranfield Thomas, wood turner, 35 Brownlow st. Drury lane
Cranmer Thomas, *Three Tuns* P.H. 53 Red cross st. Cripplegt
Crannis & Kemp, patentees of wood paving, 47 Castle st. Boro'
Cranob William, grocer, 149 Hoxton Old town
Cranston John & Son, shoemakers, 16 Chapel st. Curtain rd
Cranston William, dyer & scourer, 244 Shoreditch
Cranstoun George, merchant, 37 Old Broad st. City
Cranwell George, bootmaker, 151 Long lane, Bermondsey
Cranwell Robt. plumber & glazier, 15 Edwards st. Portman sq
Cranwell Thomas, plumber, 153 Edgware road, Marylebone
Cranwell Thomas, tailor, 11 Star corner, Bermondsey
Crapnell George, grocer, 12 Circus st. New road
Crapp Eliza Sarah (Miss), milliner, 38 Lit. Queen st. Holbn
Crapp Elizh. (Mrs.), tobacconist, 38 Lit. Queen st. Holborn
Crask Wm. Bradford, 3 *Compasses* P.H. Raven rw. Whitec. rd
Craske John, painter & decorator, see Battam & Craske
Craswell Rich. *King of Prussia* P.H. 29 Somerset pl Hoxton
Crassweller Hen. ironmonger, 36 Welbeck st. Cavendish sq
Cratchley Joseph, ironmong. 6 Crombie's rw. Commercl. rd. East
Crate George Edward, hairdresser, 12 Park st. Borough
Crate Joseph, saddler, 11 Halkin st. West, Belgrave sq
Crate William, grocer & cheesemonger, 116 Waterloo road
Crause Edward, grocer, 25 Union row, New Kent road
Craven John & Co. whol. teadlrs. 18 Laurence Pountney hill
Craven & Lucas, sugar refiners, 7 to 9 Red Lion st. & Duncan st. Whitechapel
Craven Ann (Mrs.), tobacconist, 17 Grenville st. Somers town
Craven John, marble engraver, 10 Gillingham st. Pimlico
Craven Frederick, furniture broker, 20 Union st. Borough
Craven John, wholesale grocer, 3 Idol lane, Great Tower st
Craven William, grocer, 6 George st. Camberwell
Crawcour Abram, furniture dealer, 6 Lambeth Lower marsh, & 25 & 26 Chalcroft terrace, New cut, Lambeth ,11 Gt. Charlotte street, Blackfriars road
Crawcour David, dentist & cupper, 14 Windsor pl. City rd
Crawcour Isaac, tobacconist, corner Bermndsy. & Old Kent roads
Crawcour Isaac, tobacconist, 22 Crown lane, Walworth road
Crawcour Samuel, dentist, 33 Beckford row, Walworth road
Crawford, Walwyn & Co. wine merchants, 4 Savoy st. Strand, & 74 King's road, Brighton
Crawford, Colvin & Co. east india agts. 71 Old Broad st. City
Crawford Jas. & Alex. bookbinders, 18 Peerless row. City rd
Crawford Joseph T. tea & col. broker, 12 Mincing lane
Crawford & Lindsays, of Banbridge, Ireland, linen manfrs. & bleachers (J. S. Black, mngr.), 3 Lawrence la. Cheapside
Crawford Richard & Co. cheesemongers, 81 Gracechurch st

Crawford Robert & Co. wine merchants, 4 Savoy st. Strand
Crawford Christoph. *Waterman's Arms* P.H.22 Wappingwall
Crawford Geo. Morland, barrister, 3 Old sq. Lincoln's inn
Crawford Henry, turner, 50 Market st. Borough road
Crawford James, cutler, 20 Princes st. Drury lane
Crawford James, tailor, 25 Manchester st. Manchester sq
Crawford John, coal mercht. 63 St. George's rd. Southwark
Crawford John, painter & glazier, 71 Redcross st. Borough
Crawford John Nevin, umbrella & parasol ma. 28 Cheapside
Crawford Mervyn, physician, 62 Upper Berkeley st
Crawford Robt. veterinary surgeon, 2 Wood st. Westminster
Crawford William, bookbinder, 16 Peerless row, City road
Crawley George & Co. wine & spirit imptrs. 16 Mincing lane
Crawley Alfred James, pawnbroker, 100 Shadwell High st
Crawley Antony Gibbs, solicitor, 12 Southampton bldgs
Crawley Chas. *York hotel*, 10 Albemarle st. Piccadilly
Crawley Chas. Fred. bookseller, 19 Devonshire st. Queen sq
Crawley Chas. Jas. bricklayer, 21 Bridgeho. pl. Newing.cau
Crawley Cornelius, bootmaker, 237 Shadwell High st
Crawley Edmund, who. tea & coffee dlr. 11 Cullum st. City
Crawley Ellen (Mrs.), dressmaker, 432 Strand
Crawley Fredk. *Duke of Cambridge* P.H. Felix st. Hackny.rd
Crawley Geo. A. solicitor, see Pemberton, Crawley & Gardiner
Crawley George S. corn & coal mercht. 1 Harley pl. Bow rd
Crawley James, fruiterer, 3 Royal Hospital row, Chelsea
Crawley John, *Red Lion* P.H. 17 Silver st. Golden square
Crawley Patrick, shoemaker, 27 Broad st. Bloomsbury
Crawley Peter, *Queen's Hd. & Fr. Horn* P.H. 14 Dukest. Smthfi
Crawley Richard Walter, pawnbroker, 40 Bow High st
Crawley Samuel, bricklayer, &c. 34 Surrey pl. Old Kent rd
Crawley Thomas, fruiterer, 11½ Ropemakers' st. Finsbury
Crawley Wm. optician & spectacle ma. 21 Oxendon st. Haymk
Crawley William, *John Bull* P.H. Roman road, Old Ford
Crawshaw Sarah (Mrs.), oil & color wareh. 41 Shadwell High st
Crawshay Geo. pat. chain cable ma. see Hawks & Crawshay
Crawshay Wm. iron merchant, George yard wharf, 36 Upper Thames st
Crawter Thos. & Hen. land agts. 7 Southamptn. bldgs. & Cobham
Craxford John, lath render, Belvedere road, Lambeth
Cray Thomas, cabinet maker, 44 Henry st. Hampstead road
Cray Thomas, cap maker, see Brown & Cray
Creak Frederick, baker, 131 Lambeth Lower marsh
Creak George, baker, 154 New Gravel lane
Creak Thos. King, builder, 20 New Church st. Bermondsey
Creak William, pawnbroker, 14 George row, Bermondsey
Creaker Henry, baker, 49 High st. Camden town
Crealock Wm. Belton, solicitor, see Karslake & Crealock
Cream Charles, grocer, 12 Church st. Kensington
Creamer Wm. haircutter & perfumer, 156 Aldersgate st
Crease James & Son, colormen, varnish makers, & anti-corrosin paint manfs. 29 & 30 Cowcross st. West Smithfield
Creaser Thomas Wm. barrister, 4 Lamb buildings, Temple
Creason William, wholesale saddler, 83 Long acre
Creasor William, saddler, 85 Long acre
Creassey James, *Tam O'Shanter* P.H. 14 Grafton st. Soho
Creasy Edward Shepherd, barrister, 2 Mitre court chambrs
Creasy Robert, boot & shoema. Southampton st. Cambrwl.rd
Creaton Alfred & Frederick, grainers, 1 Lit. Moorfields
Creaton Thos. Albon, writer & decor. painter, 5 Bow la. City
Creaton Wm. Geo. porkman, 3 Bolingbroke rw. Walworth rd
Creber Richard, pianoforte mak. 11A, Berners st. Oxford st
Cree Thos. & Son, solicitors, 3 Verulam buildings, Gray's inn
Cree David, solicitor, see Vandercom, Comyn & Co
Creed Ebenezer, wholesale & retail fishing rod & tackle maker, 33 Wilderness row, Clerkenwell
Creed Giles, print & bookseller, 160 High Holborn
Creed James, lighterman, 61 Great Hermitage st. Wapping
Creed Richard, secretary to the London & Birmingham Railway Company, office at the Station, Euston square
Creed William, boarding house, 4 Circus, Minories
Creed William, glass & china dlr. 77 High st. Camden town
Creed William, tailor, 47 Chester st. Kennington cross
Creed Wm. tobacconist & woollen dr. 3 Hungerford st. Strand
Creedy James, baker, 41 Rawstorne st. Goswell road
Creek Henry, fruiterer, 6 Gray's inn lane
Creevy Ann (Mrs.), carman & wheelwright, 56 Drury lane
Creevy Mary (Miss), dairy, 250 Tottenham court road
Creffield John, grocer, 10 Lion st. New Kent road
Creke Wm. enamel letter works, 7 Pleasant pl. King's cross
Crellin James & Co. tailors, 4 St. James's st. Pall mall
Crellin Horatio Nelson, surgeon, 21 Surrey pl. W. Old Kent rd
Crellin Phillip, outfitter, 198 St. George's st
Crellin William, surgeon, 19 Wellington rd. St. John's wood
Crellin Wm. tailor & trousers ma. 3 George yard, Lombard st
Cremer John Thos. & Co, merch. & commis. agts. 52 St. Mary Axe
Cremer Wm. & Co. wine & spirit merchants, 16 Mincing lane
Cremer Geo. boot & brush ma. 9 Northampton pl. Old Kent rd
Cremer Henry, wine & general merchant, 40 Lime st
Cremer Peter, furnishing undertaker, 41 Hackney road
Cremer William, general merchant, 16 Mincing lane
Cremer Wm. Henry, brushmaker, 10 Bridge st. Westminster
Crenan Wm. Henry, boot & shoe ma. 29 Gower pl. Euston sq
Crespin Charles Henry, wine mercht. 114 Upper st. Islington
Cressall & Bradley, furn. undertakers, 5 Whitechapel road
Cressall Peter, undertaker, &c. 45 Clark st. Stepney
Cressall Thos. Geo. brass finisher, &c. see Archer & Cressall
Cressey Charles Waite, grocer, 12 Gt. Suffolk st. Boro'
Cressey Richard, genl. salesman, 48 Chalton st. Somers tn
Cresswell & Addams, proctors, see Addams & Cresswell
Cresswell & Forrester, glove manufrs. 1 Orange st. Bloomsbury
Cresswell Abraham, dining rooms, 8 Whitechapel road
Cresswell Henry Richd. herring mer. 117 Lower Thames st
Cresswell James, statnr. 5 Rufford's bldgs, High st. Islington
Cresswell John, bookslr. & newsv. 121 Crawford st. Portmn.sq
Cresswell Mary (Mrs.), *Old Vineyard* P.H. 1 Vineyd. walk, Clk
Cresswell Rt. Nathl. barrister, 8 Godliman st. Doctors' com
Cressy Frederick, turner, 5 Short's gardens, Drury lane
Cressy George, turner, 173 Drury lane
Cressy Sarah (Mrs.), bedstead mak. 6 Gt. Earl st. Seven dials
Cressy Thomas, umbrella maker, 158 Upper Whitecross st
Creswick Wm. paper maker & stationer, 5 John st. Oxford st
Cretté Louis, de Paris, manfr. & importer of preparations for artificial flower makers, 75 Judd st. Brunswick sq
Creuseton John, hairdresser 9 Portman st. Portman sq
Crew Francis, bookseller & stationer, 27 Lamb's Conduit st
Crew George, *Ship* P.H. 6 & 7 Bacon st. Bethnal green
Crew Henry, oil & colorman, 38 Brook st. St. George st
Crew John, engraver, 155 Aldersgate st
Crew Thomas Francis, attorney, 38 Essex st. Strand
Crew William, butcher, 1 Phœnix place, Ratcliff cross
Crew William, hairdresser & perfumer, 177 Tooley st
Crew William, shipping butcher, Butcher row, Ratcliff
Crews Ann (Miss), dressmaker, 89 Park st. Camden town
Crews John, hairdresser, 18 Shoe lane, Fleet st
Crews Philip, bootmaker, 24 Little Queen st. High Holborn
Crews Thomas, shape manufact. 19 Chalton st. Somers town
Cribb Brothers, lucifer matchma. 14 New Millman st. Foundling
Cribb Daniel, coal dealer, 10 Brewer st. Golden sq
Cribb George, surgn. dentist, 65 Gt. Russell st. Bloomsbury
Cribb Henry, *Ship* P.H. 23 Saville st. Fitzroy square
Cribb Mark, fruiterer, West side, Covent garden market
Cribb Robert, baker, 2 Bedford court, Covent garden
Cribb Robert, *Goat in Boots* P.H. Little Chelsea
Cribb Wm. carver, gilder & plate gl. wa. 34 King st. Covent gar
Cribb Wm. E. clock & watchma. 17 Southampton rw. Russell sq
Cribb Wm. sec. to St. Paul's savgs. bk. 15 Gt. Russell st. Cov.gn
Crichton & Barwick, plumbers, 15 Featherstone st. City rd
Crichton & Son, auctioneers, upholsterers & undertakers, 1 Marlborough pl. Walwth. rd. & 2 High st. Newington butts
Crichton Benj. Thos. shipowner & cooper, 6 Griffin st. Shadwell
Crichton David, biscuit baker, 50 Strand
Crichton James, merchant, Baltic, 58 Threadneedle st
Crichton John, math. inst. ma. & optician, 112 Leadenhall st
Crichton Patrick Chas. west india merch. 21 Finsbury circus
Crick Ann (Mrs.), butcher, 105½ St. John st. Clerkenwell
Crick Ann (Mrs.), fruit saleswoman, Covent garden fruit mkt
Crick Henry, butcher, 8 Great Bath st. Clerkenwell
Crick Hen. Thos. miscellaneous repos. 8 Deptford high st
Crick Susanna (Mrs.), bookseller, Broadway, Stratford
Crick Thomas, silk mercer, see Griffiths & Crick
Crick Thomas, silk mercer, 17 Cecil st. Strand
Crick William, fishmonger, Church st. Hackney
Crickett James & Son, linendrapers, 21 Cable st. Wellclosesq
Crickett John, linendraper, 36 Brick lane, Spitalfields
Crickitt & Son, proctors, 1 Godliman st. Doctors' commons
Crickmay Samuel, tripeman, 30 Brick lane, St. Luke's
Crickmay Wm. lodging house, 17 Pelham crescent
Crickmer Richd. Jex & Fred. engineers, Page'swk. Bermondsey
Crickmer Chas. wine & brandy mer. 24 Little Knightrider st
Crickmer Robt. millwright & engineer, Spa rd. Bermondsey
Criddle Harry (Mrs.), artist, 3 Upper Belgrave place
Cridland Charles, raised letter maker, 21 Porter st. Soho
Cridland Henry, cheesemonger, 4 Folly, Dockhead
Cridland John, butcher, 22 Devonshire st. Lisson grove
Crighton Henry, warehouseman, see Gunnis & Crighton
Crighton James, baker, 5 Leman st. Goodman's fields
Crighton Robert, butcher, 27 Whitechapel High st
Criminal Law Commission, 52 Lincoln's inn fields
Crimp & Ward, scotch, burton & east india pale ale & stout merchants, Hall of Commerce vaults, & 7 Old Broad st
Crinan Canal Co. (David Caldwell, sec.), 29 Golden square
Crine John Henry, picture frame ma. 25 Cannon st. road

Crippa Joseph, prof. of music, 5 Up. Belgrave ter. Belgrave sq
Crippen & Manton, whol. tea & coffee dealers, 8 Eastcheap
Crippen Charles, stock & share broker, 3 Bartholomew lane
Cripplegate Savingsbk.(John&C.Ellis, mgs.), 31 Whitecross st
Cripps John & Co. sword cutlers & belt makers, 23 Cursitor st
Cripps, Son & Starkey, who. stationers, &c. 31 Newgate st
Cripps Charles, artist, Brewers' hall, Addle st. Wood st
Cripps Charles, *King's Arms* P.H. Chester st. Kennington la
Cripps Edward, smith, &c. 19 Wharf, Paddingtonbasin, nor. side
Cripps Eliza (Mrs.), straw hat wa. 14 Peel pl. Knsgtn. gvl. pts
Cripps Henry, coal dealer, 1 New North st. Red Lion sq
Cripps Henry Wm. barrister, 13 Serle st. Lincoln's inn
Cripps John, hairdresser, 18 Brill row, Somers town
Cripps John, livery stables, 34 New Bond st
Cripps John, size maker, 8 Swan mead, Bermondsey
Cripps Sarah (Miss), corset maker, 14 Charles st. Soho sq
Cripps Thomas, baker, 25 St. Martin's le Grand
Cripps William, barrister, 2 Essex court, Temple
Cripps William, livery stable keeper, Dover yd. Berkeley st
Cripps Hen. Wm. equi. draftsman & conveyancer, 13 Serle st
Crips Robert, dealer in plait, 19 Wells st. Oxford st
Crisfield John, *Fitzroy Arms* P.H. Cardington st. Hampstd. rd
Crisp Thos. & Co. shipwrights, Mill st. Dockhead, Bermndsy
Crisp Charles, lodging house, 15 Villiers st. Strand
Crisp Edmd. *Wires Head* P.H. 17 Moreton ter. Kentish tn
Crisp Edward, surgeon, 31 Beckford row, Walworth road
Crisp Fortunatus, publisher, 7 Wellington st. North, Strand
Crisp James, bookbinder & printslr. 44 Newman st. Oxford st
Crisp James, tailor, 2 Church st. Shoreditch
Crisp Jas. upholst. & decorator, 43 King's rd. east. Chelsea
Crisp Jemima (Mrs.), grocer, 19 Queen st. York st. Wlwth. rd
Crisp Nathaniel, *White Hart* P.H. 10 Gt. White Lion st. 7 dials
Crisp Thomas, oilman, 22 Bow st. Covent garden
Crisp Wm. chronometer & clock ma. 20 Green ter. Clerknwl
Crisp William, goldsmith & jeweller, 64 Red Lion st. Clrkwl
Crisp William James, grocer, 1 Sidney pl. Commercial pl. East
Crispin William, tailor, 14 Bedford court, Covent garden
Cristall Joseph & Sons, shipbreakers, 294 Rotherhithe st
Criswick & Lepard, composition decorators, glass & picture frame manufacturers, 6 New Compton st. Soho
Critchett George, surgeon, 9 New Broad st. City
Critchfield James, tobacco pipe maker & clay merchant, 28 Maze, Tooley st. & 30 Snow's fields, Bermondsey
Critchfield Wm. Thos. *Old Queen's Head* P.H. 23 Gt. Maze pond
Critchley, Brinsley & Co. silk manufacturers, 121 Cheapside
Critic Newspaper Office, 29 Essex st. Strand
Crittle James, *White Hart tavern*, 197 Shoreditch High st
Croad Saml. glazier & water bed ma. 2 Providence row, Finsby
Croake James, china dealer, 116 Cromer st. Brunswick sq
Croaker Wm. building material dlr. 1 Napier st. Gt. Dover rd
Crocker, Black & Crocker, irish linen factors, 14 Gresham st
Crocker Jonathan & Albert, calico printers & warehousemen, 85 & 86 Watling st. & 51 Friday st. Cheapside
Crocker Edward, surveyor, 2 Belgrave road, Pimlico
Crocker Henry, solicitor, 7 Castle st. Holborn
Crocker Isaac, cheesemonger, 11 Beckford row, Walworth rd
Crocker James, *George inn & hotel*, 22 Aldermanbury
Crocker John, butcher, 9 Gray's place, Fulham road
Crocker John, carman, 25 Upper Marylebone st
Crocker Thomas, butcher, 6 Burlington pl. Old Kent road
Crocker William, bootmaker, 1 Bedford st. Strand
Crocker Wm. Hen. chronometer ma. 70 Leman st. Goodman's fi
Crockett John, pawnbroker, 93 High Holborn
Crockett Richard, solicitor, 60 Trinity square, Borough
Crockford George, artist, 11 Compton st. East, Regent sq
Crockford Henry, fishmonger, 65 Whitechapel High st
Crockford John, publisher, 29 Essex st. Strand
Crockford Joseph, grocer, 5 Queen's buildgs. Knightsbridge
Crockford Thos. butcher, 1 Spectacle al. Whitechapel Hi. st
Crockford Sarah Frances (Mrs.), wine mer. 10 St. James's st
Croff Sarah (Mrs.), school, 69 Poplar High st
Croft & Innocent, tea dealers, 40 Bedford st. Strand, & 31 High st. Kensington
Croft Abraham, tailor, 4 Wyndham st. New road
Croft Hen. Jas. & Co. shell fishmongers, 13 Hand court, Holborn
Croft Chas. Ilderton, surgeon, 23 Laurence Pountney lane
Croft Daniel, *Fox & Grapes* P.H. 49 Brewer st. Golden sq
Croft Sir Archer Denman, bart. master of Court of Queen's Bench, Queen's Bench office, Temple
Croft Edward, bricklayer, &c. 18 Castle st. Southwark
Croft Edward, hearth rug manuf. 3 West place, City road
Croft Geo. blacklead pencil maker, 4 Hanover st. Long acre
Croft George Thirmbeck, teadealer, 35 Whitechapel road
Croft George William Henry (secretary to General Cemetry Company), 95 Great Russell st, Bloomsbury
Croft John, oil & colorman, 18 York place, Kent st. road
Croft John, solicitor, 1 Walbrook buildings, City
Croft Richard, laceman, 18 Ludgate hill
Croft Samuel, grocer, 14 Henry st. Hampstead road
Croft Thomas, livery stables, Northumberland alley, Fenchurch st. & 9 Whitechapel road
Croft Thomas, plumber, 13 Green bank, Wapping
Croft William, *Bull's Head* P.H. 43 Gt. Windmill st. Haymkt
Croft William, draper, see Luck & Croft
Croft William, engraver, 27 Winchester st. Pentonville
Croft William, grocer, 92 Vauxhall st. Lambeth
Croft William, surgeon, 8 Surrey place, Kennington
Crofton & Rippon, tobacco manftrs, 61 Bartholomew close
Crofton Anthony, barrister, 7 New square, Lincoln's inn
Crofton Fred. Edwd. C. L. stockbroker, 1 Bank chamb. Lothby
Crofton Philip, cabinet mfr. & furng. undertaker, 113 Cromer st
Crofts Alfred & Sam. haberdashers, 37 East st. Walworth rd
Crofts James & Co. merchants, 4 King st. Cheapside
Crofts David, *Duke of Sussex* P.H. New st. Deptford
Crofts George, fruiterer, 26 Beaumont st. St. Marylebone
Crofts Jas. John, watchma. 19 St. George's pl. Camberwll. rd
Crofts John, solicitor, 1 Walbrook buildings
Crofts Josiah, baker & confectioner, 188 Piccadilly
Crofts Robert, *Waterford Arms* P.H. 50 Haymarket
Crofts William, *George's hotel*, 213 Strand
Crofts William, barrister, 10 Serle st. Lincoln's inn
Crofts Willoughby Rd. tailor, 16 Upper Ashby st. Nrthmptn. sq
Croger Thos. musical instrument mkr. 5 Epping pl. Mile end
Croggon Thomas John, commission agent, 2 Ingram court
Croggon Thos. John, patent asphalte roofing, sheathing & boiler felt manufacturer, 2 Ingram court
Croggon Thomas John, patent manure factor, 2 Ingram ct
Croggon Thomas John, roman cement factor, 2 Ingram ct. & 77 Wapping wall, & Railway wharf, Greenwich
Crohn Henry, merchant, 8 White Hart court, Lombard st. & 12 King st. Finsbury
Crokat Charles, merchant, see Wilkie & Crokat
Croker Thomas, *Star & Garter* P.H. 62 Poland st. Oxford st
Crokes John, saw maker, 30 Hosier lane, West Smithfield
Crole & Stevens, sworn for. exch. brkrs. 65 Old Broad st. City
Croll Alex. A. & Co. pat. dry gas meter mnfcty. Suffolk st. Clkwl
Crolls David, tailor, 79 John st. Fitzroy square
Crombie Lewis, secretary to London, Salisbury & Yeovil Railway, 63 Moorgate st
Cromer James, turner, 51 Wellington st. Blackfriars road
Crompton John & Thomas B. paper makers, 14 Earl st. Blackfriars, & Farnworth mills, Lancashire
Crompton Charles, barrister, 1 Paper buildings, Temple
Crompton Charles, merchant, 29 Great Ormond st
Crompton Chas. plumber, &c. 4 Royal hill, Queen's rd. Bayswtr
Crompton Thomas, stockbroker, 39 Lothbury
Cromwell Rd. carpenter & architect, 99 Guilford st. Russell sq
Cronchey Joseph, grocer, 1 Leader st. Chelsea
Cronchey William, grocer & cheesemonger, Little Chelsea
Croney Ann (Mrs.), baker, 60 Cotton st. Poplar
Cronin Daniel, auctioneer & appraiser, 12 East st. Red Lion sq
Cronin Denis, physician, 113 Strand
Cronin James Bartholomew, mfng. jewelr. see Wheeler & Cronin
Cronin Laurence, grocer, teadealer, &c. 60 Wapping High st
Cronin Philip, mat & rug maker, 3 Queen's ct. King st. Cov. grdn
Cronk Rebecca (Miss), milliner, see Bridgen & Cronk
Crook George & Son, linendrapers & silkmen, 48 Pall mall
Crook Chas. liverystable keeper, Angel inn yd. St. Clement's
Crook Chas. Hen. tin plate worker, 100 Regent st. Westmr
Crook Henry, builder, 24 Crosier st. Stangate, Lambeth
Crook Henry, tailor, 22 East road, City road
Crook Jacob, ironmonger, 3 Beauvoir place, Kingsland
Crook Jacob, tin plate worker, 72 Gt. Peter st. Westminster
Crook James, watch jeweller, 18 Ratcliff row, City road
Crook James Martin, surgeon, 17 Brook st. Grosvenor sq
Crook John, linendraper, 38 Cannon st. rd. St. George's east
Crook John Chas. cotton yarn manufactr. 7 Goldsmith st. City
Crook Joseph, watch jeweller, 47 Wynyatt st. Goswell rd
Crook Maria B. (Miss), tallowchand. 4 Salmon pl. Grange rd
Crook Mary Ann (Mrs.), hat manufactr. 67 Brick la. Spitalfi
Crook Thomas, sen. builder, Morning lane, Hackney
Crook Wm. carpenter & chandler's toolma. 9 Lit. Queen st. West
Crook William, jun. furnishing ironmonger & patent kitchen range maker, 55 George st. Portman sq
Crook Wm. sen. furn. ironmonger, smith & bell hanger, inventor & manufacturer of the open fire kitchen range, with oven & boiler, 5 Carnaby st. Golden sq
Crook William, plumber, 55 Seymour st. Euston sq
Crookes, Gibbons & Gibbons, who. teadlrs. St. Andrew's hill
Crookes Joseph & Son, tailors, 143 Regent st
Crookes George, tailor, 33 Maddox st. Regent st
Crookes John Farrar, surgeon, 5 Suffolk pl. Pall mall east

Crookes Joseph, tailor & habit maker, 143 Regent st
Crookes Wm. manufacturing cutler, 71 Brook st. Ratcliff
Crookes Wm. undertaker, 151 Shadwell High st
Crooks Chas. tailor, 16 Stamford st. Blackfriars
Crooks George, baker, 18 Kenton st. Brunswick square
Crooks George, grocer, 71 Leather lane, Holborn
Crooks Henry, surgeon, 47 George st. Portman square
Crooks Jas. *Euston Arms* P.H. 33 Melton st. Euston sq
Crooks Robert, tailor, 18 Throgmorton st
Croom Joseph, *Sussex hotel*, 17 & 18 Bouverie st. Fleet st
Croome Charles James, artist, 126 Albany st. Regent's park
Croome John Daniel, artist, 20 Albany st. Regent's park
Croot Abraham, brewer, York st. York road, Lambeth
Cropley Edward, *Black Horse* P.H. 1 Queen st. Tower hill
Cropley John, lapidary in general, 44 Gt. Sutton st
Cropley John Walter, hay salesman, 62 West Smithfield
Cropp John, grocer, 7 Barnsbury place, Islington
Cropp John (Mrs.), ladies' school, Hill house, Wandsworth rd
Cropp Thos. sen. *Blue Coat Boy* P.H. Brewer's green, Westmr
Cropp Thos. jun. *Plough* P.H. 18 Rochester row, Westmnstr
Gropper Mary (Miss), chandler's shop, 5 New rd. Whitechl
Cropper Wm. bricklayer, 61 Snow's fields, Bermondsey
Crosan George, *Star* P.H. 21 Duke st. St. George's east
Crosbie Robert, plumber, 4 Newland terrace, Kensington
Crosby & Compton, solicitors, 3 Church court, Old Jewry
Crosby Henry, saw maker, 19 Upper Ogle st. Fitzroy sq
Crosby John, carpenter, 71 Davies st. Berkeley sq. & 27 South Molton st
Crosby Mary (Miss), milliner, 15 Queen st. Brompton road
Crosby Robert, cutler, 5 Ball alley, Lombard st
Crosby Walter, surveyor of the Temple; office, 4 Plowden buildings, Temple, hours 11 to 4
Crosby Wm. paperhanger, 89 Grand Junction ter. Edgware rd
Crosby Wm. paperhanging manuftr. see Hennell & Crosby
Crosby Wm. pork butcher, 202 Bermondsey st
Crosby Hall Chambers, 24 Bishopsgate within
Crosby Hall Literary & Scientific Institution (Thos. Bax, treasr.; John Reid, sec.), 32 Bishopsgate within
Croser William, carpenter, 28 Duke st. Bishopsgate
Crosier David, oil & colorman, 16 & 17 Churchway, Somers tn
Crosier George, law stationer, see Druce & Crosier
Crosier James, oil & colorman, 18 William st. Caledonian rd
Crosier Jonathan Jas. oil & colorman, 15 Brewer st. Somers tn
Crosland John & Co. stationers, engrav. &c. 1 & 2 Fenchurch st
Crosley Henry, engineer, Emerson st. Southwark brdg. rd
Crosley James, oilman, 108 Great Suffolk st. Borough
Crosley Saml. gas meter & apparatus ma. Cottage la. City rd
Croson Geo. *Lord Hill* P.H. 22 North whf. rd. Paddington
Cross Algernon, grocer, 191 Lambeth walk
Cross Benjn. Beddoe, solicitor, 38 Southampton buildings
Cross Charles, *Hoop & Adze* P.H. 37 St. John st. Clerkenwl
Cross Charles, silk manuftr. & agent, 19 Gutter lane
Cross Charles, tobacconist, 37 Windmill st. Finsbury
Cross Christopher, plumber, painter, &c. 1 Kingsland green
Cross Diana (Mrs.), grocer & cheesemngr. 14 Gray st. Manch. sq
Cross Edward, cooper, &c. 15 Wallington pl. Wandsworth rd
Cross Edward, painter, 1 Canterbury pl. & Mill st. Lambeth
Cross Edward, royal zoological gardens, Walworth, Surrey
Cross Edward, wholesale grocer & teadealer, 57 Mansell st. Goodman's fields, & Goodman's yard
Cross Elizabeth (Miss), milliner, see Manning & Cross
Cross Geo. bed & mattress maker, 3 Primrose st. Bishopsgate
Cross George, bookbinder, 10 Rathbone place, Oxford st
Cross George, general agent, 12 Copthall ct. Throgmorton st
Cross George, map mounter & colorer, 98 Dean st. Soho
Cross George John, printer, 118 Gray's inn lane
Cross Geo. Wm. Coleman, linendraper, 175 Boro' High st
Cross Hannah (Mrs.), engraver & printer, 92 Leadenhall st
Cross Hannah (Miss), milliner, 6 Kingsland row, Dalston
Cross Henry, beer retailer, 46 Cowper street, City road
Cross Henry, *Black Cap* P.H. 91 High st. Camden town
Cross Hen. furniture bro. 17 Husband st. Broad st. Golden sq
Cross Henry, lodging house, 47 South street, Grosvenor sq
Cross Hen. Geo. *Angel & Crown* P.H. 19 Ship alley, Wellclose sq
Cross Henry Wright, solicitor, 5 New inn
Cross Isabella (Miss), milliner, 2 Devonsh. bldgs. Dover rd
Cross James, baker, 21 Windmill st. Tottenham ct. road
Cross James, dyer & scourer, 13 New Church st. West, Edgw. rd
Cross James, furniture dlr. 2 Cumberland row, Walwth. rd
Cross James, hairdresser, 49 Minories
Cross James, linendraper & grocer, Battersea
Cross James, solicitor, see Pownall & Cross
Cross James, tallowchandler & oilman, 27 Newgate st
Cross John, barrister, 5 Hare court, Temple, & 13 Victoria sq
Cross John, cabinet ma. & uphol st. 47 Commercial rd. Lmbth
Cross John, *Caledonian Arms* P.H. 20 Princess st. Lisson gr
Cross John, carpenter & underta. 6 Tichborne ct. Holborn
Cross John, grocer, 41 Charles st. Westminster
Cross John, grocer, 18 Chester st. Kennington cross
Cross John, house decorator, painter, &c. 22 Gt. Portland st
Cross John, meat salesman, Leadenhall market
Cross John, printer, 9 Poppin's court, Fleet st
Cross John, working jeweller, 3 Edwards st. Portman sq
Cross John B. watchmaker, 41 Charterhouse square
Cross Joseph, engraver, printer & mapseller, 18 Lower Holborn
Cross Joseph Aubrey, turner, 1 Charles st. St. George's East
Cross Philip, dairy, 49 Collier st. Pentonville
Cross Robert, physician, 21 Leicester square
Cross Samuel, bootmaker, 1 Dover pl. West, Kent st. Boro'
Cross Sarah (Mrs.), *Van Tromp* P.H. 53 Church st. Shoreditch
Cross Thos. bookbinder, 6 King's Head court, Holborn hill
Cross Thos. marine store dealer, 94 London rd. Southwark
Cross Thos. George, butcher, 10 Boziers ct. Tottenhm. ct. rd
Cross Thos. Jsph. boot & shoema. 22 Crosby row, Walworth rd
Cross Wm. fishmonger, 351 Rotherhithe st
Cross Wm. registrar of births, 16 Bermondsey New road
Cross Wm. tailor, Church st. Hackney
Cross Wm. tailor, 50 Kingsland road, east side
Cross Wm. Henry, solicitor, 28 Surrey st. Strand
Cross Wm. Sharp, spl. pleader, 7 King's Benchwalk, Temple
Crosse & Blackwell, oilmen by appointment to the Queen, 21 Soho square, & 11 King st. Soho
Crosse & Sismey, solicitors, 11 Serjeant's inn, Fleet st
Crosse Thos. & Son, solicitors, 3 Hatton ct. Threadneedle st
Crosse Edward Willson, proctor, 4 Bell yd. Doctors' com
Crosse Robt. Fredk. solicitor, 1 New Temple bldgs. Mitre ct
Crosse Susannah (Mrs.), chamois vest & sock ma. 80 Wood st. City
Crossfield Abraham, solicitor, 91 Whitechapel road
Crossfield George, cutler, 13 Orange st. Red Lion sq
Crossfield John J. bent & stained glass wks. 6 Bury st. Bloomsb
Crossingham Wm. teadealer & grocer, 39 Watling st. City
Crossland David, brushma. & turner, 10 Stafford st. Bond st
Crossland Jas. jeweller, 3 Bray's bldgs. Lower rd. Islington
Crossland John Mekle, artist, 21 Shaftesbury ter. Pimlico
Crossland Samuel, coffee rooms, 8 Bride la. Fleet st
Crossland Thomas, chemist, 6 Exmouth st. Clerkenwell
Crossley John & Co. chemists, 41 Bishopsgate st. within
Crossley George, tailors' trimming seller & haberdasher, 22 Newcastle st. Strand
Crossley Henry, currier, Church st. Deptford
Crossley James, fruiterer, Centre row, Covent gar. market
Crossley James, tailor, &c. 43 Little Britain
Crossley John, cheesemonger, 70 Holborn hill
Crossley John, hairdresser, 12 Bentinck st. Manchester sq
Crossley John, soapmaker, 8 Old Montague st. Whitechapel
Crossley John, wax & tallow chandlr. 78 High st. Marylebone
Crossley Michael, hairdresser, 9 Thayer st. Manchester sq
Crossley Richard, cheesemonger, 147 Holborn bars
Crossley Thos. zinc worker & ironmonger, Kingsland green
Crossley Thos. sewing silk, ribbon, &c. warehmn. 38 Noble st
Crosthwaite John Thos. mercht. Hall of Commerce, City
Crosswell Stephen Hawes, importer of lisbon wines, 1 Bishopsgate st. within
Crossweller David & Alfred, undertakers, builders, & blindma. 7 Clayton pl. Kennington rd. & 17 Low. Kennington green
Croswell Henry, jeweller, 63 St. Paul's churchyard
Crosthwaite John & Co. wine merchants, 8 Fenchurch st
Croton Wm. & Hen. cheesemngrs. 4 Lit. Sussex pl. Hyde pk. gns
Croton Sophia (Miss), cheesemonger, 17 John st. Oxford st
Croton Wm. jun. cheesemonger, 2 Blenheim ter. St. John's wd
Croton Wm. sen. cheesemngr. & poulterer, 5 Store st. Bedford sq
Crotty Elizabeth (Mrs.), tailor, James place, Hoxton fields
Crouch Stephen & Ambrose Rich. fish salesmen, 7 Billingsgate
Crouch's small parcels conveyance to & from London, & all parts of Scotland & Ireland, 5 Tudor st. Bridge st. Blackfrs
Crouch Ann (Mrs.), *Bricklayers' Arms* P.H. 22 Kingsgate st
Crouch Christr. attorney, 37 Southampton bldgs. Chancery la
Crouch Daniel Newton, barrister, 15 Chancery lane
Crouch Edward, *White Bear* P.H. Long Walk, Bermondsey
Crouch Fredk. haberdasher, 33 Gt. Wild st. Linc. inn fields
Crouch George, bookseller & binder, 1 Crown court, & 5 Tudor st. Blackfriars
Crouch George, ornamental carver, 77 Newman st. Oxford st
Crouch Henry Wm. manufacturing turner, 35 Gt. Sutton st
Crouch James, tailor & habit maker, 2 Bird st. Oxford st
Crouch James, warm & cold baths, 16 Laurence Pountney hill
Crouch John, oil & colorman, 35 James st. Buckingham gate
Crouch John C. pawnbrok. 33 Grafton st. East, Tottenham ct. rd
Crouch John H. surveyor, 2 Johnson st. Holywell st. Westmr
Crouch Jsph. brass turner & finisher, 13 Wellngtn. st. Kingslnd
Crouch Joseph, oil & colorman, 57 Chapel st. Somers town
Crouch Michael, grocer & tea dealer, 45 High st. Marylebn

Crouch Richd. linen draper, &c. 116 Whtchpl. High st
Crouch Samuel, hairdresser, 17 Clark's pl. High st. Islington
Crouch Saml. locksmith, &c. 5 Little Randolph st. Camden tn
Crouch Stephen, pocketbook ma. 8 New Union st. Lit. Moorfld
Crouch Thomas, fruit salesman, Fruit market, Covent garden
Crouch William, ironmonger, &c., see Hart & Crouch
Crouchy George, buil. matrl. dlr. 45 Coppice row, Ray st
Croucher John, bricklayer, 10 Bowl yard, St. Giles's
Croucher John Honour, accnt. & gen. agent, 11 Nag's head ct
Croucher John Thomas, chemist, &c, 223 Shadwell High st
Croucher Joseph, parliamentary, &c. agent, 31 New Broad st. City, 6 James st. Buckingham gate & 3 Trafalgar sq. Charing cross
Croucher Thomas, trunkmaker, 116 Fleet st.
Croucher Wm. painter & glazier, 23 Queen st. Cheapside
Croucher George, fringe maker, 12 New ct. Farringdon st
Croudace & Meeson, coal factors & ship & insurance brokers, 3 Cross lane, St. Mary at hill & Coal Exchange
Croughton & Harding, tobacconists, 100 Upper st. & 5 Barnsbury place, Islington
Croughton Thomas, tobacconist, 76 Kingsland road
Crout Thomas, gasfitter, 1 Ivy terrace, Hoxton
Croutel Walter, *Crown & Can* P.H. 110 St. John st. Clerkenwell
Crow Daniel, *Three Elms* P.H. 32 Gt. St. Anne st. Westminster
Crow George Francis, butcher, 54 York st. Westminster
Crow John, appraiser & broker, 3 & 4 Dean st. Westminster
Crow John, carver & gilder, 2 Crown terrace, Mile end road
Crow John, plasterer, 10 Boot st. Hoxton market
Crow Joseph, dining rooms, 53 Coleman st
Crow Robert, *Admiral Codrington* P.H. Green st. Chelsea
Crow Sutton Edward, linendraper, 38 Judd st. Brunswick sq
Crow William, bootmaker, 22½ Duke st. Lincoln's inn fields
Crow Wm. carpenter & undertaker, 51 Tothill st. Westminster
Crow Wm. grocer & oilman, 35 Sidmouth st. Gray's inn rd
Crow Wm. Richard, timber mer. 5 Benjamin st. Clerkenwell
Crowburst William, lath render, 56 Eagle st. Red Lion sq
Crowden James, tailor & draper, 33 Lombard st
Crowden Richard, bootmaker, 6 Foubert's place, Regent st
Crowden Wm. bootmaker, 3 Cross ct. Carnaby st. Golden sq
Crowder & Maynard, solicitors, 57 Coleman st
Crowder George, baker, Church st. Camberwell
Crowder George, whalebone cutter, cane preparer, & wood busk manufacturer, 13 Sun st. Bishopsgate
Crowder Richd. academy (Stamford ho.), Church st. Cambwell
Crowder Richd. Budden, Q.C. barrister, 1 Brick ct. Temple
Crowder Samuel, cane dealer, manufacturer of walking sticks, umbrella ribs, & every description of brushboards, 13 Sun street, Bishopsgate; & at Bishopsgate saw mills, George & Catherine Wheel yard, 80 Bishopsgate
Crowder Theophilus, importer of meerschaum pipes & every description of tobacconists' fancy goods, 11 & 12 Cripplgt. blds
Crowe Alexander, merchant, 35 Old Broad st. City
Crowe John, carpenter & builder, 12 Mount row, Berkeley square, & 10 Church st. Paddington
Crowe Mary (Mrs.), spur ma. 1 Whitcomb ct. Prince st. Lster. sq
Crowe Robt. tailor & draper, 12 Portugal st. Lincoln's inn flds
Crowe Spicer, ironmonger, see Marriott & Crowe
Crowe Thos. F. & Wm. clothiers, 95 Edgware rd. Marylebone
Crowe Thomas Worsfold, surveyor, 23 Nelson st. City road
Crowfoot John & Son, plumbers & glaziers, Well st. Hackney
Crowfoot Abel, grocer, 1 Charles st. Manchester square
Crowfoot John, jun. plumber & glazier, see Crowfoot John & Son
Crowgey Robert, accountant & linguist, 46 Threadneedle st
Crowhurst George, *Adam & Eve* P.H. Duke st. Chelsea
Crowhurst Samuel, builder, 4 Monmouth pl. Old Kent road
Crowley Abm. & Chs. S. & Hy. alton ale brews. U. Fore st. Lmbth
Crowley & M'Kinnell (Xerez de la Frontera) winemer. 18 Mark la
Crowley, Hicklin & Co. carriers by railway & canal, *Salisbury Arms*, King st. Smithfield, 30 & 31 wharfs, City road basin, Camden town, railway station, *Green Man & Still*, 122 Oxford st. & 40 Regent's circus, Piccadilly
Crowley James & Co. who. button wa. 9 Noble st. Cheapside
Crowley Charles, cork cutter, 167 Goswell st
Crowley Charles Alex. fruiterer, 48 Dean st. Oxford st
Crowley David, skinner, 18 Magdalen st. Bermondsey st
Crowley Nicholas Jph. R.H.A. artist, 13 Up. Fitzroy st. Fitzy. sq
Crown Life Assurance Company (Thomas G. Conyers, sec.), 33 New Bridge st. Blackfriars, see page
Crown Office in Chancery, Rolls yard, Chancery lane; hours, during session of parliament, 10 to 3; at other times 10 to 2
Crown Office (Queen's Bench), 2 King's Bench walk, Temple; hours of business, term, 11 to 5; vacation, 11 to 3
Crown Thos. pin ma. tin pl. mer. & wire drawer, 187 Union st
Crowne Mary & Fanny, dress mkrs, 71 Margaret st. Cvdsh. sq
Crowson John, corndealer, 81 High st. Camden town
Crowson John, hairdresser & perfumer, 21 Middle rw. Holbn
Crowter Susannah (Mrs.), baker, see Clout & Crowter
Crowther Ann (Mrs.), fruiterer, 38 Bartholomew close
Crowter Benj. ginger beer maker, 28 Stangate, Lambeth
Crowther Elizab. (Mrs.), stationer, 26½ Wilson st. Finsbury
Crowther Ely', chandler's shop, 1 North st. Whitechapel rd
Crowther Ely Walker, woollen manfr. & com. agt. 115 Fore st
Crowther Geo. Buckley, surgeon, 36 Lambeth Lower marsh
Crowther Jas. plumber & glazier, 33 Lit. Bartholomew close
Crowther John, grocer, 46 Carnaby st. Golden square
Crowther Robt. woollen draper, 4 Weston st. Bermondsey
Crowther Robt. Warmington, solicitor, 1 Trinity pl. Charingcr
Crowther Thomas, saddler, 26 Providence row, Finsbury
Crowther Thomas, stone mason, 30 East st. Walworth rd
Crowthers Mark, pewterer, 12 Gt. Carlisle st. Lisson grove
Croxen John, cornchandler, 4 William st. Regent's park
Croxford Jacob, grocer, 4 Bowling green lane, Clerkenwell
Croxon Anna (Mrs.), furn. broker, 2 Conduit court, Long acre
Croxon George, furnitr. broker, 1 Conduit court, Long acre
Croyden Charles, chemist, &c. 37 Wigmore st. Cavendish sq
Croyden John, coach lace, &c. mak. 12 Coal yard, Drury la
Croydon Railway Company (Robert Serrel Young, sec.), secretary's office, London bridge terminus; *Transfer Office*, 3 Joiner st. Tooley st
Croydon John, *Myddelton Arms* P.H. 24 Portland pl. Islngn
Croysdill Henry, accountant, 33 Old Jewry
Croxford John, timber dealer, Commercial rd. Lambeth
Crozier Henry, printer, 37 Silver st. Golden square
Crozier Robert, bookseller, 29 Bow st. Covent garden
Crozier William, bootmaker, 40 East st. Walworth road
Cruchley George Fred. mapseller, engraver, &c. 81 Fleet st
Crucknell Geo. woollen warehsman. see Rhodes & Crucknell
Crudgington Joseph, corn dealer, 78 Green st. Bethnal green
Cruickshank Fredk. artist, 56 Devonshire st. Portland pl
Cruickshank George, artist, 23 Amwell st. Pentonville
Cruickshank James, baker, 4 Johnson st. O. Gravel la. St. Geo. ea
Cruikshank, Melville & Co. merchants, 13 Austinfriars
Cruikshank Alex. hairdress. & perfumer, 3 Norris st. Haymarkt
Cruikshank Robert, artist, 66 Gray's inn lane
Crump Benjamin, plumber, &c. 1 Esher st. Up. Keningtn. la
Crump Charity (Mrs.), stay maker, Camberwell green
Crump Chas. combmaker, 47 Hatfield st. Stamford st. Blkfrs
Crump Chas. *Temperance hall*, Milton st. Cripplegate
Crump David, *Asylum Boy* beer shop, 1 Franklin rw. Chlsa
Crump Hannah (Mrs.), omnibus proprietor, Stratford, Essex
Crump James, *Coach & Horses* P.H. Stratford Broadway
Crump James Henry, cheesemonger, 59 Hackney road
Crump John, beer retailer, 3 Lower Islington terrace
Crump Joseph, furniture broker & dealer, 9 Great Smith st
Crump Peter, butcher, 6 Dean st. Westminster
Crump Susan (Mrs.), fruiterer, Southampton st. Camberwell
Crump Thomas, beer retailer, 9 Smart's bldgs. Hoxton Old tn
Crump Thomas, bootmaker, 5 William st. Regent's park
Crump Thomas, butcher, 3 Newport ct. Newport market
Crump Thomas, tailor, 23 Prospect place, Cambridge heath
Crump Wm. carpenter, Liverpool road
Crump Wm. cheesemonger, 49 Goswell road
Crump Wm. china dealer, 83 Paradise st. Rotherhithe
Crundall Wm. indigo merchant, see Hammond & Crundall
Cruse Archelaus, news agent, 73 Little Britain
Cruse Edward, professor of music, 66 Ebury st. Pimlico
Cruse Henry, stationer, 5 Compton st. Clerkenwell
Cruse Wm. bookseller, 22 Grove place, Brompton
Cruse Wm. greengrocer & coal mer. 3 Saville pl. Mile end rd
Crush & Bromley, pawnbrokers, 35 Hyde st. Bloomsbury
Cruso Fras. *Crn. & Sceptre* P.H. 27 Gt. Titchfield st. Foley st
Crussell John, carpenter, &c. 19 Nicholas lane, City
Crust John, cattle salesman, 8 West Smithfield
Crutch Geo. M.D. surgeon, 16 Bedford pl. Lower rd. Rothrhth
Crutch John, furn. ironmonger, 34 St. Martin's la. Charing cr
Crutch John Hampden, tea dealer, 8 St. John st. road
Crutcher Thomas, shipsmith & tinman, 167 Rotherhithe
Crutchley Richd. beer retailer, 1 Besom pl. Old Gravel lane
Crutchley Robert, M.D. surgeon, 59 Drury lane
Crutchley Wm. builder & surveyor, Oval rd. Gloucester gate
Crutchley Wm. builder & surveyor, Stafford pl. Glo'ster cres
Cruttenden John, *Ship* P.H. Great Garden st
Cruttwell Charles Jas. barrister, 9 New sq. Lincoln's inn
Cruttenden Thomas, dining rooms, 120 Wapping High st
Cruwys John, *Turk's Head* P.H. 35 King st. Holborn
Cruwys John, tailor, 11 Crown ct. Russell st. Covent garden, & 21 Church st. Soho
Crux Richard, *Argyll Arms* P.H. 18 Argyll st. Regent st
Cryer Thomas, livery stables, 2 Montague mews, Russell sq
Cubison Elizabeth (Mrs.), milliner, see James & Cubison
Cubit Wm. painter, 73 Oakley st. Lambeth

Cubitt Wm. & Co. builders, 20 Abchurch lane; Calthorpe place, Gray's inn rd.; & 3 Park lane, Piccadilly
Cubitt George, combmaker, 181 Tottenham court rd
Cubitt Honor (Mrs.), *Bunch of Grapes* P.H. Bermondsey wall
Cubitt James, jeweller, 11 Grafton st. east, Tottenham ct. rd
Cubitt John, auctioneer, 2 Up. Porchester st. Hyde park
Cubitt Joseph, civil engineer, 12 Manchester bldgs. Westmnr
Cubitt Joseph, stockbroker, 2 Founders' hall ct. Lothbury
Cubitt Lewis, architect, 77 Great Russell st. Bloomsbury
Cubitt Martin, builder, 200 High Holborn
Cubitt Robt. Harvey, chemist & druggist, 26 John's rw. St. Luke's
Cubitt Thomas, *Black Lion* P.H. Thorney st. Museum st
Cubitt Thomas, builder, 93 Eaton pl. & Thames bank, Pimlico
Cubitt Thomas, plait importer, see Gregory, Cubitt & Co
Cubitt Thos. Riches, upholsterer, &c. 6 Sherrard st. Golden sq
Cubitt Timothy, perfumer, 76 Oakley st. Lambeth
Cubitt Wm. civil engineer, 6 Gt. George st. Westminster
Cudby Mary A. & Carln. (Misses), dress ma. 31 Red Lion st. Holbn
Cucksey James, coal & potato dlr. 35 Leather lane, Holborn
Cuell Wm. Henry, mining agent, see Watson & Cuell
Cuendet Samuel, watch casemaker, 9 Wilmington square
Cuerton Charles Louis, importer of wines, 12 Mark lane
Cuerton Henry, stockbroker, see Capel, Cuerton & Lawford
Cuff Edwd. Geo. & Co. wine merchts. 41 Crutched friars
Cuff Joshua H. & Son, veterinary druggists, 10 West Smithfield
Cuff Christopher, solicitor, 12 Halfmoon st. Piccadilly
Cuff George, brazier & tinman, 20 White Hart st. Lr. Kengton. la
Cuff Isaac, fruiterer, 34 Norfolk st. Middlesex hospital
Cuff Robt. saddler, 50 Curzon st. Mayfair; & 11 Pall mall east
Cuffley Edward, butcher, 90 Vauxhall walk, Lambeth
Cufflin James, potato salesman, 3 Pleasant pl. King's cross
Cufflin Robt. Stephen, jeweller, 6 Oddy's row, Islington gr
Cugny William, *Yorkshire Grey* P.H. 20 Foley place
Cuisset Fras. seal engraver, 14 Greville st. Hatton garden
Cuisset John, jeweller & silversmith, 40 Blackfriars road
Culf Wm. who. & retail brush manufacturer, 4 East rd. City rd
Culham James, surgeon, 103 Drummond st. Euston square
Cull William, painter, glazier & plumber, 279 Strand
Cullam John, oilman, 20 Charlotte st. Fitzroy square
Cullen, Broom & Co. shawl manufacturers & warehousemen, 74 & 75 Aldermanbury
Cullen & Higgin, leech importers, 7 Budge row, Cannon st
Cullen Edward, butcher, 9 Bury st. St. James's
Cullen Elizth. (Mrs.), milliner, 17 Frederick pl. Old Kent rd
Cullen Hannah (Mrs.), grocer, 1 Moreton ter. Kentish tn. rd
Cullen William, chemist, &c. 37 Beckford row, Walworth rd
Cullerne & Sheppard, jewel case ma. 10 Greville st. Hatton gdn
Cullerne Chas. Pulteney, surgeon, 6 Air st. Piccadilly
Culley Henry, coffee rooms, 85 Long lane, Smithfield
Culliford Chas. J. lithographer, 22 Southampton st. Strand
Culliford Edward. lithogra. draftsman, 11 Howard st. Strand
Culliford Emma (Miss), coffee rooms, 7 King st. Snow hill
Culliford John, coffee rooms, 5 Dove court, Old Jewry
Culliford Thos. John, insur. broker, see Dewar & Culliford
Cullimore Danl. upholsterer, 63 Up. North pl. Gray's inn rd
Cullimore Enos, dairyman, 7 Greville st. Hatton garden
Cullimore James, road surveyor, 1 Holywell st. Millbank
Culling Daniel, grocer, &c. 8 Cain place, Kentish town
Culling Joseph, grocer, 48 Howland st. Fitzroy square
Cullingford Robert, *Crown* P.H. 84 Edgware road
Cullingham Charles, grocer & teadealer, 128 Houndsditch
Cullington Daniel & Son, solicitors, 2 Craven st. Strand
Cullum Austin, *Tiger Cat* P.H. New row, Deptford
Cullum Geo. furnishing ironmonger, 26 St. John st
Cullum Henry, tobacconist, 30 Fish st. hill
Culmer Henry, grocer & teadealer, 18 Lit. Earl st. Long acre
Culpeper Wm. Moe, surgeon, Marylebone Infirmary, New rd
Culver Geo. grocer & cheesemonger, 22 Webber st. Blkfrs. rd
Culver Thomas, fruiterer, Little Chelsea, North side
Culver Thomas, grocer, 1 Grundy st. East India road
Culverhouse Daniel, baker, 94 Bunhill row, Chiswell st
Culverhouse Wm. soda water manuf. 10 Osborne pl. Whitchpl
Culverwell & Brooks. hide & skin brokers, 21 Bow lane
Culverwell Wm. & Son, dealers in druggists' sundries, 24 William st. Charlotte st. Blackfriars road
Culverwell George, ladies' shoe ma. 6 Mercer st. Long acre
Culverwell James, baker, 30 Lambeth walk
Culverwell Richard, tailor & draper, 53 Gt. Marylebone st
Culverwell Robert, cupper, 4 Rathbone place, Oxford st
Culverwell Robert James, physician, 21 & 23 Arundel st. Strand
Culverwell Rt. J. warm, cold, &c. baths, 5 New Broad st. City
Culverwell Thos. fruiterer, 12 Little Chester st. Grosvenor pl
Culverwell William, potato salesmn. 20 Oxford st. Mile end
Culverwell Wm. surgeon, 5 Commercl. pl. York rd. Lambeth
Cumber Tho. & Son, bootmakers, 15 St. Alban's pl. Edgware rd
Cumberland John, publisher, 2 Cumberlnd. ter. Camdn. Newtn
Cumberlege Chas. N. architect & surveyor, 5 John st. Adelphi
Cumby Thomas, gasfitter, 28 East st. Manchester sq
Cuming Samuel, builder, 3 Cirencester place, Fitzroy square, & Haunch of Venison yard, Brook st. Bond st
Cuming William, coach builder, 12 Rathbone pl. Oxford st. & 19 Little Albany st. Regent's park
Cuming Wm. glass dealer, 80 John st. Fitzroy square, & 10 Charlotte mews, Tottenham court road
Cumming & Debenham, milliners, 15 Princes st. Hanover sq
Cumming Fredk. & Co. custom house & general agents, & sole agents for Swan's writing copybooks, 15 Fish st. hill
Cumming Wm. & Co. carpet ma. 98 Hatton grd. & 68 London wll
Cumming Alexander, blacksmith, 12 Swan st. Minories
Cumming Ann (Mrs.), butcher, 35 Salisbury st. Bermondsey
Cumming Edward, corkcutter, 75 Lower Thames st
Cumming Geo. saw ma. 108 Whitehorse st. Com. rd. Stepny
Cumming Jas. Cameron, physician, 27 Lowndes st. Belg. sq
Cumming John, watchmaker, 202 Oxford st
Cumming John Durant, carpet manuf. see Harris & Cumming
Cumming Richard, solicitor, 27 King st. Cheapside
Cumming Robert, bootmaker, 46 Red Lion st. Spitalfields
Cumming William, furrier, 62 Britannia st. City road
Cumming William, upholsterer & carpet wa. see Luck, Kent & Co
Cumming Wm. S. surgeon, 2 Vittoria pl. Commercial rd. East
Cummings Geo. Gordon, tea & col. & guano brokr. 14 Mincing la
Cummings John, carver & gilder, 13 Queen's rd. Bayswater
Cummings John, jun. bricklayer, 4 Johnson st. Somers town
Cummings John, gasfitter, 17 North st. Sloane st
Cummins Amelia & H. (Misses), ladies' school, 45 Stamford st
Cummins Alexander, tailor, 6 Douglas st. Vincent sq
Cummins Charles, crown agent, 22 Duke st. Westminster
Cummins Charles, chronometer & watchmak. 148 Leadenhall st
Cummins James, baker, 1 Upper Baker st. Regent's park
Cummins James, japanner, 36 Marshall st. London road
Cummins James John, merchant, 34 Abchurch lane
Cummins Judith (Mrs.), cheesemonger, 192 Up. Thames st
Cummins Richd. Swete, ship & insurance agt. 34 Abchurch la
Cummins William, baker, 78 Drummond st. Euston square
Cumner John, linendraper, 153 Borough High st
Cumper James, bootmaker, 5 North st. East st. Walworth
Cundale & Morgan, italian wareh. 42 Amwell st. Pentonville
Cundale John, coal mercht. Bridewell wf. William st. Blkfrs
Cundale Richard, lead mercht. 51 Marylebone la. Oxford st
Cundall Joseph, bookseller, 12 Old Bond st
Cundall Thomas, morocco leather dresser, 73 Bermondsey st
Cundell & Cockerell, coal mers. Purfleet wf. Earl st. Blkfrs
Cundell George Smith, general merchant, 17 Finsbury circus
Cundy Charles F. solicitor, Carlton chambers, 8 Regent st
Cundy Henry Capel, coal merchant, see Capel & Cundy
Cundy Samuel, stone merchant, mason & statuary, Belgrave wharf, Lower Belgrave place, Pimlico
Cundy Thomas, architect, 13 Chester square, Pimlico
Cuninghame John, agent to Lafitte, Blount & Co. bankers, 4 Castle court, Birchin lane, City
Cunliffes, Brooks & Co. bankers, 24 Lombard st
Cunliffe. Garratt & Co. merchants, 106 Fenchurch st
Cunliffe Roger, banker, 24 Bucklersbury
Cunningham & Forbes, wine mers. 4 Arthur st. West, London br
Cunningham Chas. A. surgeon, 31 Sidmouth pl. Gray's inn rd
Cunningham Hugh, bookseller, pub. & stationer, 193 Strand
Cunningham John, tailor, 51 Greek st. Soho
Cunningham Peter, tobacco pipe ma. 2 Henry st. Portland tn
Cunningham Robert, architect, &c. 30 Howland st. Fitzroy sq
Cunningham Rt. merch. & agent, Old Swan wf. Up Thames st
Cunningham Saml. saw mills, 31 Minerva st. Hackney road
Cunningham Susan (Mrs.), dress ma. 12 Cleveland st. Fitz. sq
Cunnington John, hosier & haberdshr. 9 Market st. Shpds. mkt
Cupit Hen. Phillips, oil & colorman, 31 Lisle st. Newpt. mkt
Cupitt John, oil & italian warehouse, 21 Pitfield st. Hoxton
Curates, Society for promoting the employment of additional, in populous places (Rev. John M. Rodwell sec.), 4 St. Martin's place, Charing cross
Curd John, cheesemonger, 92 High st. Camden town
Curd Richard, academy, 35 Cromer st. Brunswick square
Cureton Edward, who. ironmonger, 49 Bread st. Cheapside
Cureton Henry, medallist & coin dealer, 81 Aldersgate st
Cureton Joseph Richard, fishing tackle ma. 48 Snow's fields
Curie Paul Francis, physician, 30 Brook street, Grosvenor square, & 34 St. Martin's le Grand
Curle Charles, builder, 9 Ranelagh place, Pimlico
Curlewis Henry Chas. tailor, &c. 12 Hanover st. Hanover sq
Curling Chas. & Co. wharfingers, Davis' wharf, Tooley st
Curling George & Co. who. druggists, 4 Finch lane, Cornhill
Curling, Pixley & Co. rope makers, Ferry road West, Poplar, & 10 George yard, Lombard st
Curling & Procters, furniture printers, 18 Cheapside

Curling William & Jas. fish factors, 13 Lower Thames st
Curling, Young & Co. merchants, 5 George yard, Lombard st
Curling, Young & Co. shipbuilders, 5 George yard, Lombard st. & Emmett st. Poplar
Curling Frederick A. solicitor, 3 Crown ct. Old Broad st. City
Curling Jesse, woolstapler & fellmonger, 167 Bermondsey st
Curling John, baker, 4 Snow's fields, Bermondsey
Curling John, carpntr. & win.blind ma. Union rd. Clapham rise
Curling John, *Sugar Loaf* P.H. 24 Queen st. Cheapside
Curling Lydia Amelia (Mrs.), lace cleaner & clear starcher to the Queen, 20 Woodstock st. Oxford st
Curling Richard, lace cleaner, 11 Stafford row, Pimlico
Curling Robert, solicitor, see Fyson & Curling
Curling Thomas Blizard, surgeon, 37 New Broad st. City
Curll Robert & Co. coach wheelwrights, 12 Sutton st. Soho
Curnick John, carpenter, Battersea fields
Curnick Joseph, carpenter, 17 Chichester pl. Wandsworth rd
Curnock Thomas & Sons, wharfingers, road contractors, lime, cement, &c. merchants, 19 North Wharf road, Paddington
Curnock Thos. & Son, Hawley wharf, 13 Hawley ter. Camden tn
Curnock Alfred, wharfinger, see Curnock Thomas & Sons
Curnock John, wharfinger, see Curnock Thomas & Sons
Currall & Son, wine merchants, 35 Bishopsgate within
Curran James, *Seabright Arms* P.H. 2 Hill st. Hackney rd
Curran John Philpot, barrister, 36 Southampton buildings
Curran Thomas, academy, 8 Manor place, Walworth road
Currey Robert & Co. tobacco & snuff manufacturers, 8 Shoemaker row, Blackfriars & 106 Fleet st
Currey, Wilmer & Currey, solicitors, 6 Old Palace yd. Westmr
Currey Frederick, barrister, 3 New square, Lincoln's inn
Currey Hen. David, builder, 16 Clifton pl. Camberwell New rd
Currey James, tailor, 7 Upper York st. Bryanstone sq
Currey Thomas, beer retailer, 117 Cock hill, Ratcliff
Currey William, carman, 66 St. John st. Smithfield
Currie John & Co. distillers, Bromley, Middlesex
Currie & Seignette, merchts. & french agents, 26 Mincing la
Currie, Woodgate & Williams, attorneys, 32 Linc. innfields
Curries & Co. bankers, 29 Cornhill
Currie Archibald, grocer, 40 Munster st. Regent's park
Currie James, M.D. surgeon, 39 Clifton st. Finsbury
Currie James, saddler, &c. 2 Princes st. Cavendish sq
Currie James Charles, linendraper, High st. Deptford
Currie John, tailor, 166B, Oxford st
Currie Niel, baker, 84 Broadwall, Blackfriars
Currie William, tobacconist, 34 Theobald's road, Holborn
Curriers' Hall (Ed. Burkitt, clk.), Currs'. hall ct. 6 Lond. wall
Currington Samuel & Thomas, Rotherham Foundry Co. 50 Upper Thames st
Curry George, coffee rooms, 48 Seymour st. Euston sq
Curry George, potato dealer, 17 Brooke st. Holborn
Curry John, wine merchant, 39 Burton st. Burton crescent
Curry Joseph H. bookseller & stationer, 203 Sloane st
Curry Thomas, coppermining office, 3 Bond court, Walbrook
Curryer Geo. engraver & engineturner, 18 Perceval st. Clknwl
Curryer Thos. watch & clock glass ma. 134 Up. Whitecross st
Curryer Wm. seal engraver, &c. 4 Charles st. Hatton garden
Curryer Wm. stationer, 2 Cobourg place, Bayswater
Cursham George, physician, 5 Saville row, Piccadilly
Cursitors' (& Petty Bag) Office, Rolls yd. Chancery la.; 10 to 6
Curson Thomas, carpenter, 54 Belvedere pl. Southwark bdg. rd
Curson Thomas, carpenter, 24 Chapel st. Curtain road
Cursons Mary (Mrs.), engraver & printer, see Bass & Cursons
Curteis Fras. Tress. hop factor, see Nash, Selmes & Curteis
Curteis John, who. grocer, see Ryde, Curteis & Whitworth
Curteis Wm. C. D.C.L. advocate, 14 College, Doctors' comm
Curties Thomas, boot & shoe maker, 23 Chenies st. Bedford sq
Curties Thomas Stephen, cheesemonger, 97 York st. Wstmr
Curtin James & Co. tobacconists, 27 Fish st. hill
Curtis's & Harvey, gunpowder manufacturers, 74 Lombard st. & Hounslow Heath mills, Middlesex
Curtis James & Son, hatters' bowstring ma. 29 Green st. Bkfs
Curtis Joseph & Son, curriers, 20 Finsbury st. Finsbury sq
Curtis Robt. & Edwd. builders, 59 Fenchurch st. & Stratford
Curtis Charles, coach tire smith, 52 & 53 Ray st. Clerkenwell
Curtis Charles, cowkeeper, &c. 4 Royal Oak pl. Eaton sq
Curtis Charles, distiller, 6 Assembly row, Mile end road
Curtis Charles, lodging house, 13 Norfolk st. Strand
Curtis Charles, *London & St. Katharine's Docks hotel*, Upper East Smithfield
Curtis David, shaft bender, see Reed & Curtis
Curtis Edward, blind maker, 92 Edgware road, Marylebone
Curtis Edward, boot & shoe maker, 2 Queen's road, Dalston
Curtis Edward, *George* P.H. Foster's bldgs. 123 Up. White st
Curtis Edward, tailor, 23 Crown st. Westminster
Curtis Edwin, marine store dlr. 6 Denmark pl. Camberwell
Curtis Elizabeth (Mrs.), grocer, 22 Hosier la. West Smithfield
Curtis George, bonnet shape maker, 117 Lambeth walk
Curtis George, butcher, 9 Jewry st. Aldgate
Curtis George, haberdasher, 1 Salisbury st. Bermondsey
Curtis George, market gardener, Blue Anchor rd. Brmndsy
Curtis George, oil & colorman, 4 Church st. Camberwell
Curtis Henry, tailor & habit ma. 11 George ct. Piccadilly
Curtis Henry S. merchant, 17 Gt. St. Helen's, Bishopsgate st
Curtis Herman, wine, spirit & beer merchant, 53 St. Mary axe
Curtis James, butcher, 9 Upper East Smithfield
Curtis James, carver & gilder, 2 Old Compton st. Soho
Curtis James, grocer, 58 Albany st. Regent's park
Curtis James, linendraper, 42 Union st. Bishopsgate
Curtis James, wholesale druggist, 11 Old Fish st. City
Curtis James, fringe maker, 90 Drury lane
Curtis James Brydges, wine merchant, 5 Arthur st. west
Curtis James Charles, commission merch. 17 Gt. St. Helen's
Curtis Jas. Hen. *Royal Oak* P.H. 24 Gt. Earl st. Seven dials
Curtis James John, dentist, 13 Blandford st. Manchester sq
Curtis James John, music wire drawer, 11 Cobourg pl. O. Kent rd
Curtis John, baker, 9 Union st. Clarendon square
Curtis John, bootmaker, 11 North st. Manchester square
Curtis John, coach smith, 86½ Oxford st
Curtis John, coal merchant, Thornhill wharf, Caledonian rd
Curtis John, commission merchant & agent, 7 Jeffrey's sq
Curtis John, rag & bottle dealer, 42 Homer st. Marylebone
Curtis John, solicitor, 80 Basinghall st
Curtis John, *Swan* P.H. Thornhill bridge, Caledonian road
Curtis John, tailor, 3 Providence place, York road, Lambeth
Curtis John Harrison, aurist, 2 Soho square
Curtis John Wright, surgeon, 8 Finsbury pavement
Curtis Joseph, coal dealer, 6 Wharf, Macclesfield st. south
Curtis Joseph, surgeon, &c. 1 St. James's ter. Camden town
Curtis Lawrence S. beer retailer, 36 Union st. Bishopsgate
Curtis Philip, cabinet maker, 1 Rose & Crown ct. Moorflds
Curtis Rebecca (Mrs.), grocer, &c. 28 Princes road, Lambeth
Curtis Richard, corn & coal dealer, 2 James place, Holloway
Curtis Robert, *Coach & Horses* P.H. 73 Long la. Bermondsey
Curtis Robt. *Railway* coffee rooms, 1 St. James pl. Hampstd. rd
Curtis Samuel, bookbinder, 28 Milton st. Cripplegate
Curtis Stephen Stuart, hide & leather factor, 19 Coleman st. & Hide market, Leadenhall market
Curtis Stevenson, grocer, 55 Strutton ground, Westminster
Curtis Thomas, butcher, 52 Milbank st. Westminster
Curtis Thomas Vendem, surgeon, 16 Lr. Lisson st. New road
Curtis William, dairy, 118 Upper Seymour st. Euston sq
Curtis William, grocer, 32 George st. Blackfriars road
Curtis William, hay & straw salesman, 19 Giltspur st
Curtis William, turner, 40 Charlotte st. Old st. road
Curtis Wm. Benjamin, wiredrawer & pin maker, 37 Cannon st
Curtis William Hyne, carpenter, 10 Denbigh st. Pimlico
Curtis William Lamb, meat & butter salesmn. 25 Newgate st
Curtiss John Alfred, attorney, 32 Beaumont st. Portland pl
Curtoys John & Son, grocers, 65 St. John st. Clerkenwell
Curwer John, cheesemonger, 2 Bridge st. Vauxhall
Curwood John, barrister, 17 Clifford's inn, Fleet st
Curwood Jonathan, fruiterer, 12 Grocers' hall ct. Poultry
Curzon hon. Edward Cecil, barrister, 7 New sq. Lincoln's inn
Curzon hon. Francis James, barrister, 3 Brick ct. Temple
Curzons William, grocer, 93 Park st. Gosvenor square
Cusack Caleb, coach wheelwright, 20 Ann's pl. Whitmore rd
Cusel Herman & Co. merch. & for. agt. 3 Pinners' ct. O. Broad st
Cusens Thomas Hen. *Albion* P.H. 48 Long la. Bermondsey
Cushee Edward, shoe warehouse, 1 Lower st. Islington
Cushen William, fruiterer, 12 New Quebec st. Portman sq
Cushing Robert, carpenter, 67 Long alley, Finsbury
Cushion James Daniel, optician, 2 New Compton st. Soho
Cuss John, chimney sweeper, 4 Up. York st. Bryanstone sq
Cussans John, upholsterer, 36 Maiden lane, Covent garden
Cussons Geo. plumber, 1 Baden pl. Crosby row, Walworth rd
Custerson Robert, wheelwright, 69 Old st
Custom House, Lower Thames st.—hours *In-door offices*, 10 to 4; *Waterside offices*, Mar. to Oct. hours 8 to 4; Nov. to Feb. hours 9 to 4
Custom House & Wool Quay, William John Hall & Co. between Custom House & Tower
Cusworth John, statuary & mason, High st. Stoke Newngtn
Cutbert Margaret (Mrs.), grocer, 17 Grove lane, Deptford
Cutbell Richard Sam. grocer, 17 Charles st. Commercl. rd. ea
Cutbill Alfred R. mngr. of Commercial Bk. of London, Lothbury
Cutbill Thomas Samuel, sec. to United Peninsular Railway office, 1 Royal Exchange buildings
Cutbill Wm. A. chair & sofa ma. 10 Holywell row, Shordtch
Cutbush Henry, pork butcher, 2 Exmouth st. Clerkenwell
Cutbush Luke Flood, painter, 35 Fieldgate st. Whitechapel
Cutbush Thomas, painter, &c. 9 Woburn bldgs. Tavistock sq
Cutchey Walter, hosier & outfitter, 178 Borough High st

Cutforth Ashlin, sheep salesman, 41 West Smithfield
Cuthbert (Thomas & John) & Archer, tallow melters & wax & tallow chandlers, 42 & 43 Paternoster row
Cuthbert & Southey, printers & stationers, 155 Fenchurch st
Cuthbert Thos.&John, wax chandlers, 18 Gt.George st. Westm
Cuthbert & Wotherspoons, wholesale fur manufacturers, 60 Cheapside, & 54 & 55 Bow lane
Cuthbert Chas. math. instrument mak. 9 Clerkenwell green
Cuthbert Dorothy (Mrs.), lodging ho. 4 Lr.James st. Gldn sq
Cuthbert George, oilman & tallow chandler, 87 Fore st. City
Cuthbert George F. hosier & glover, 60 St. Martin's le grand
Cuthbert Henry, cheesemonger, 111 Wardour st. Soho
Cuthbert Henry, carpent. & underta. 2 Elder st. Norton folgt
Cuthbert Jas. coffee & ale rooms, 14 Gt. Distaff la. Friday st
Cuthbert John, cooper, &c. 24 High row, Knightsbridge
Cuthbert Mary Ann (Mrs.), haberdasher, 199 St. George st
Cuthbert Moses, cowkeeper, 73 Earl st. east, Lisson grove
Cuthbert Sarah (Mrs.), solder mfr. 18 Backchurch la. Whitech
Cuthbert Wm. bottle merchant, see Cookson Cuthbert & Co
Cuthbert Wm. Hastings, who. oil & color mer. 44 Bankside
Cuthbertson Geo. & Son, boot & shoe maks, 123 Aldersgate st
Cuthbertson & Harms, coal merchts. Maiden la. King's cross
Cuthbertson Charles, baker & corn dealer, 22 Sloane terrace
Cuthbertson James, bookseller & stationer, 4 Brompton rd
Cuthbertson John, linendraper, 1 Portland pl. Borough rd
Cuthbertson John, tailor, see Stucké, Cuthbertson & Stucké
Cuthbertson Thos. cheesemonger, 4 Lombard ter. Chelsea
Cutbush Joseph, *Star* P.H. 79 Blackman st. Borough
Cuthell John, builder, 13A, Avery row, Bond st
Cuthill James, florist & seedsman, Denmark hill, Camberwell
Cutler & Barker, corn, seed & meal men, 97 Farringdon st
Cutler & Co. (of Bordeaux), wine merchants, 3 Mansion house place, City, & 12 Hungerford st. Strand
Cutler Edward & Son, tailors, 8 Hanover st. Hanover square
Cutler John & Son, ironfounders, 16 Gt. Queen st. Linc. inn flds
Cutler & Reed, tailors, 25 St. James's st. & High st. Clapham
Cutler Ambrose, plumber, Larkhall lane, Clapham
Cutler Benjamin, steam boiler manufr. 143 New Gravel lane
Cutler Charles, solicitor, 8 Bell yard, Doctors' commons
Cutler Edward, grocer, 59 Wych st. Strand
Cutler Edward, surgeon, 15 New Burlington st. Piccadilly
Cutler Frederick, solicitor & colnl. law agt. 16 Furnival's inn
Cutler Helen (Miss), milliner, 73 Charlotte st. Fitzroy sq
Cutler James, bricklayer, 16 Frederick pl. Newington butts
Cutler John, *Carpenters' Arms* P.H. 34 Cambridge rd. Mile end
Cutler Joseph, hook & eye manfr. 15 Noble st. Cheapside
Cutler Thomas, livery stables, see Maddocks & Cutler
Cutler William, plumber, &c. 2 Radcliffe ter. Goswell road
Cutlers' Alms Houses, Balls pond road, Islington
Cutlers' Hall (James Beaumont, clerk), 6 Cloak lane, City
Cutmore Chas. Rd. & Co. piano ma. 17 Brecknock pl. Cmdn. N. tn
Cutmore Chas. dining rooms, 4 Royal Hospital row, Chelsea
Cutmore Fred. bricklayer, 39 York st. York road, Lambeth
Cutmore Geo. *Two Brewers* P.H. 26 Aylesbury st. Clerknwl
Cutmore James, grocer, 20 Queen st. Soho
Cutmore Richard, bricklyr. & plastr. 2 Gibson st. Waterloo rd
Cutmore Richard, *Fox & Peacock* P.H. 12 Gray's inn lane
Cutmore William, baker & corn merchant, 6 Grafton st. Soho
Cutress Geo. *Old Justice* P.H. 4 Windsor pl. Southwark br. rd
Cutress Wm. builder, 17 Winchester pl. Southwark br. rd
Cuttell George, lapidary, 52 New Compton st. Soho
Cutten E. & F. surveyors & auctioneers, 21 Coleman st. City
Cutter Charles, hatter, 172 Tottenham court road
Cutter Henry, linendraper, 34 Mount st. Lambeth
Cutter Robert, fancy bread & biscuit baker, 114 Strand
Cuttill Richard James, silk broker, 1 Crown ct. Old Broad st
Cutting John, french polisher, 42 London st. Fitzroy sq
Cutting John, furnishing ironmonger, 271 Oxford st. & toy, cutlery & british plate warehouse, 268 Oxford st
Cutler Wm. livery stables, Bell yd. 59 Mount st. Berkeley sq
Cutto Abraham, solicitor, 28 Back st. Horselydown
Cutton William, butcher, 110 Vauxhall st. Lambeth
Cuttriss George, *Piazza coffee house*, Covent garden
Cuttriss Henry, oil & colorman, 3 Green st. Bethnal green
Cutts George, greengrocer, 128 Praed st. Paddington
Cutts Jesse, turner, 140 Poplar High st
Cuxon Benjamin, butcher, 31 Tottenham court road
Cuxon Joseph, goldbeater, 228 Tottenham court road
Cwmorthin Slate Company (Thomas Arthur Corlett, sec.), New Adelphi chambers, 12 John st. Adelphi
Cymmrodorion, or Royal Cambrian Institution (John Parry, sec.), 63 Gt. Queen st. Lincoln's inn fields

DABBS Richard, grocer, 128 Brick lane, Spitalfields
Dace Wm. metal, wire, &c. wa. 13 Jerusalem psge. Clerkwnl
Dacie Wm. Scudamore, solicitor, 12 Throgmorton st
Da Costa Aaron & Isaac G. merchants, 11 Great St. Helen's
Da Costa Antonio, brazilian vice consul, 3 Howford bldgs
Dacre George, solicitor, Stratford, Essex
Dadd Robert, chemist, 54 Whitechapel High st
Dadd Stephen, french gilder & ormolu mnfr. 32 Gerrard st
Dade Wm. Coveney, manchester agt. 2 Blue boar ct. Friday st
Dadley William, solicitor, 6 Union st. Borough
Dadson Jesse, baker, 4 Oxford place, Hackney road
Dadswell David, teadealer, 58 London road, Southwark
Dadswell George, shoema. 1 Wyndham rd. Cmbrwll. New rd
Dadswell Jas. boot & sh. ma. 1 Devonshire pl. Walworth com
Dafforn John & Son, bookbinders' press & ruling machine manufacturers, 22 Great Mitchell st. St. Luke's
Dafft John, woollen draper, see Dudden & Dafft
Daft Henry, tailor, 5 Greenland place, Cromer st
Daft Robert, tailor, 13 Old Cavendish st. Oxford st
Dagg Martha (Mrs.), milliner, 32 Upper Marylebone st
Dagg Rebecca (Mrs.), school, 7 Lyon terrace, Maida hill
Dagg Thomas, newsvender, 25 Sussex st. Tottenham ct. rd
Dagg Wm. hairdresser, 32 Up. Marylebone st. Portland pl
Daggett Henry, dyer & scourer, 7 College terrace, Chelsea
Daggs George, butcher, 7 Richmond st. East st. Walworth
Dagley Elizabeth (Mrs.), oil wareho. 63 Allerton st. Hoxton
Dagley James, oilman, 7 Ebenezer pl. Lower Kennington la
Dagley James, solicitor, 45 Connaught square
Dagley Wm. greengrocer, 14 Gt. Trinity la. Bread st
Dagnall Charles, rope maker, Little Chelsea
Dagworthy Matthew, fishmonger, 11 Terrace, Kensington
Dailey & Inskipp, leather dress. & dyers, 137 Long la. Berms
Dailey Wm. Jas. printer, 1 & 2 Coleman pl. Lambeth marsh
Dain Major, brush & whisk broom maker, 70 Goswell st
Dain Major, brushmaker, 3 York terrace, Kent st. road
Daines John Benj. & Co. glass & lead merchants, & wholesale paper hanging warehouse, 6 Farringdon st
Daines Wm. *King's Head & Lamb* P.H. 50 Up. Thames st
Daintry Thos. carpenter, 19 Up. Dorset st. Bryanstone sq
Dainty William, pianoforte ma. 29 Newman st. Oxford st
Dakers Wm. barge builder, 21 New st. Bermondsey New town
Dakin William & Co. tea merchants, 1 St. Paul's churchyard
Dakin Harriet (Mrs.), boarding house, 41 Finsbury square
Dakin James, tailor, 6 Barking churchyard, Gt. Tower st
Dakin Jonathan, coachsmith, 1 Lit. Exeter st. Sloane st
Dakin Joseph, cheesemonger, 377 Oxford st
Dakin Jsph. chemist & export druggist, 248 Poplar High st
Dakin Thomas, wholesale chemist & druggist, 73 King William st. City, & 23 Abchurch lane, Lombard st
Dalby Chas. Edwd. fruiterer, 138 Brick lane, Spitalfields
Dalby Edward, dalby's carminative wareho. 230 Oxford st
Dalby Edward H. baker, 1 Pleasant row, Canal, Old Kt. rd
Dalby John, coal merchant, see Cawkwell & Dalby
Dalby Sam. boot & shoe mart, 151 Fleet st. & 126 Newgate st
Dalby Sarah Ann (Miss), milliner, 5 Curtain rd. Shoreditch
Dalby Thomas, wool dlr. & fellmong. Grange wk. Grange rd
Dalby William, potato dealer, 159 Church st. Shoreditch
Dalby William Thomas, surgeon, Blackman st. Borough
Dalcho John Wm. gold lace weaver, Peter's ct. St. Martin's la
Daldy Thomas, *Coach & Horses* P.H. 6 Charles st. Drury la
Daldy Thomas Mee, surgeon, 33 New Broad st. City
Daldy William, coffee rooms, 36 Tothill st. Westminster
Dale Daniel Robt. & Co. british & for. wine wa. 27 Coventry st
Dale George Thomas & George Cornelius, surgeons, 14 Commercial place & 19 King's place, Commercial road east
Dale Thos. & Fred. *Glo'ster hotel*, 76 & 77 Piccadilly & 1 Berkley st
Dale Thos. & Fredk. job masters & livery stables, 75 Piccadilly
Dale Daniel, miller, Lower road, Rotherhithe
Dale Daniel, tailor, 5 James place, Larkhall lane, Clapham
Dale Edw. *Marq. Cornwallis* P.H. 1 Marchmont st. Brunsw. sq
Dale Edward, surgeon, 23 Holborn hill
Dale Geo. cheesemonger, 1 Folly, Dockhead, Bermondsey
Dale Geo. undertaker, 4 Broad st. Golden square
Dale Geo. veterinary surgeon, 4 Emanuel pl. Camberwell rd
Dale Geo. Ellison, sailmaker, 273 Wapping
Dale James, grocer & teadealer, 82 Leader st. Chelsea
Dale John, boot & shoe maker, 3 Grove lane, Camberwell
Dale James, carman, 33 Fish st. hill, City, & Sumner st. Sthwrk
Dale John, carman, 3 Stoney lane, Tooley st
Dale John, insurance broker, see Ryan & Dale
Dale John, tobacconist & register office, 8 Marylebone lane
Dale John, tobacconist, 13 Plumber st. City road
Dale John, who. ironmonger, &c. 18 & 19 Chiswell st
Dale Jos. L. solr. 8 Furnival's inn & 8 Stanhope st. Hamps. rd
Dale Richard, brazier & coppersmith, 195 Upper Thames st
Dale Robt. hatters' trimming seller, 20 Earl st. Finsbury
Dale Robert, *Ordnance Arms* P.H. 1 York road, Lambeth
Dale Sarah (Mrs.), plated goods ma. 7 Bishop's ct. Chancy. la
Dale Thomas, bridle cutter, 10 Rupert st. Haymarket

Dale Thomas, grocer, 18 Pratt st. Camden town
Dale Thomas, plumber, &c. 8 Portland pl. south, Clphm.rd
Dale William, boot & shoe maker, 109 London wall
Dale William, tailor, 38 Praed st. Paddington
Dale William, tobacconist, 29 High st. Portland town
D'Alembert & Morgan, hatters, 19 Regent st
Dalgleish & Tayler, coal merchts. Gt. Scotland yard wharf
Dalgleish Wm. timber mercht. Irongate wharf, Paddington
Dalgliesh John, fruitbroker & genl. agent, 25 Mincing lane
Dalglish, Falconer & Co. calico printers (Daniel Johnson, agent), 16 Watling st
Dalibar William, tinplate worker, 37 New Manor st. Chelsea
Dallas & Coles, merchts. & ea. india agents, 29 Austinfriars
Dallas Rbt. cabinet mkr. & undertkr. 38 Red Lion st. Clknw
Dallas Wm. china & glass dealer, 33 High st. Kensington
Dallaway John, wkr. in minerals, 49 Union st. Clarendon sq
Dallen Rachel (Mrs.), *Lord Hill* P.H. 17 New Manor st. Chelsea
Dallman Samuel, builder, 1 Queen's Head lane, Islington
Dallor John, wine merchant, 9 Scot's yd. Bush la. Cannon st
Dallow Samuel, oil & colorman, 141 St. John st. road, & 3 Kingsland green
Dally George, newsvender, 21 Queen st. Seven dials
Dally Robert, *Ship-a-ground* P.H. 44 Broad st. Ratcliff
D'Almaine Thos. & Co. music sells. pianoforte mks. 20 Soho sq
D'Almaine William, embroiderer, 38 Gerrard st. Soho
D'Alphouse Jean, coffee rooms, 28 Panton st. & 7 Oxendon st
Dalman Robert, cutler, &c. 25 Marchmont st. Brunswick sq
Dalmas J— & M—, childbed linen warehouse, 79 Wood st
Dalphin John, oil & colorman, 49 Whitecross st. Cripplegate
Dalrymple Alexander, west india merchant, 11 Lime st
Dalrymple John, surgeon, 56 Grosvenor st. Grosvenor sq
Dalston Jonathan Norman, solicitor, see Manning & Dalston
Dalrymple Rt. Farre, solicitor, see Bircham & Dalrymple
Dalton John & Co. silk dressers, &c. 24 White st. Little Moorfields, & South pl. Finsbury
Dalton & Madeley, oil leather dressers, Godalming; warehouse, 2 Budge row, City
Dalton & Stokes, stockbrokers, see Stokes & Dalton
Dalton Wm. & John, coal merchts. Union whf. 24 Millbank st
Dalton Christr. slater, 9 Macclesfield st. north, City road
Dalton Edwin, artist, 5 Fitzroy st. Fitzroy square
Dalton Francis, grocer, &c. High st. Stoke Newington
Dalton Fred. combmaker, 31 St. Martin's ct. St. Martin's la
Dalton Henry, chemist, 1 St. Martin's pl. Trafalgar sq
Dalton Henry, straw hat maker, 8 Aldgate High st
Dalton Herbert, ea. in. & dye wood broker, 12 Lit. Tower st
Dalton John, oilman, Stratford broadway
Dalton John, satin dresser, embosser & waterer, Finsbury house, 4 South pl. Finsbury
Dalton Joseph, surgeon, 21 Bernard st. Russell square
Dalton Peter Joseph, surveyor, see Doyley & Dalton
Dalton Richard, confectioner, 154 Blackfriars road
Dalton Richard, hosier, 9 Inner Temple lane
Dalton Robert, gasfitter, 33 Royal st. Lambeth
Dalton Thomas, portable desk & writing case maker, 85 Quadrant, Regent st. & 6 Gt. Ormond st. Queen sq
Dalton Thomas, tobacconist, 95 Bermondsey st
Dalton William, beer retailer, 162 Alfred pl. Waterloo rd
Dalton Wm. plumber, &c. 11 Clark st. Commercial road east
Dalton Wm. Hen. bookseller & publisher, 28 Cockspur st
Dalton Winnall Thos. mast & block ma. Narrow st. Ratcliff
Dalvalley Thomas, ironmonger, 27 Brown st. Bryanstone sq
Dalwood Henry, beer retailer, 53 Whitcomb st. Haymarket
Daly Chas. bookseller & publisher, 17 Greville st. Hatn. gdn
Daly Fanny (Miss), haberdasher, 2 Welbeck st. Cavendish sq
Daly James, boot & shoe maker, 14 High st. St. Giles's
Daly John, glass & chinaman, 7 York st. Borough
Daly William, tobacconist, 38 Lower Sloane st
Daly William Henry, custom ho. ship & in. agt. 23 Harp la
Dalzell Robert M. accountant, 51 Lincoln's inn fields
Dalziel Jane (Mrs.), berlin repository, 59 Lamb's Conduit st
Damant John, grocer, 3 Little Hermitage st. Wapping
Damant John, wheelwright, 19 Old st. road
Damer William Jas. cabinet maker, 1 Church la. Islington
Dames & Bowman, sugar refiners, 2 Osborne st. Whitechapel
Dampier Christr. Edwd. solicitor, 48 Lincoln's inn fields
Dampier John Lucius, vice warden of stannaries, 24 Montague place, Russell square
Danby Charles, furniture & fancy fringe & trimming manufacturer, 43 New Bond st
Danby Joseph, engraver, 35 Wigmore st. Cavendish st
Danby Samuel, translator of latin records, 96 Chancery lane
Danby Stephen, carpenter, 27 Crosby row, King st. Boro'
Danby Steph. Wm. jun. carpenter, &c. 10 Crosby row, Boro'
Danby Thomas, grocer, 11 Whitechapel High st
Dancaster William, chemist, High st. Kingsland
Dance John, *Ship* P.H. 61 Minories
Dance William, artist, 1 Leadenhall st
Dance William, firewood dealer, Lower road, Rotherhithe
Dancer Elizabeth (Miss), milliner, 22 Conduit st
Dancer Thos. Jn. cabinet maker, 6 Winckworth bldgs. City rd
Dancocks Samuel, dairy, 6 Upper Church st. Chelsea
Dando, Sons & Co. hat manufacturers, 42 & 43 Cheapside
Dando Geo. coal dealer, 41 North st. Manchester sq
Dando James, jun. tailor, &c. 1 Church row, Fenchurch st
Dando James, sen. tailor & draper, 69 Old st. road
Dando John, tailor, 93 Farringdon st
Dando Joseph H. B. professor of music, 32 Bishopsgate within
Dando Rd. James, tallow chand. 13 Up. Rathbone pl. Oxford st
Dandridge Arthur, engraver, 1 High st. Deptford
Dane Jas. Saml. accountant & general agent, 14 Walbrook
Dane Nathaniel, collar maker, 8 Mercer st. Long acre
Dane Richard, collar maker, 30 Earl st. Finsbury
Dane William, *David & Harp* P.H. 114 Fore st. Limehouse
Danes Michael, cheesemonger, Montevideo pl. Kentish town
Danford John & Son, haberdsh. & hosiers, 81 Aldgate High st
Danford Jas. picture frame maker, 18 Thrawl st. Spitalfields
Danford John, fringe manufacturer, 22 Aldgate
Danford Mary Jane (Mrs.), bricklayer, Barnet st. Hackney rd
Dangar James, blind maker, see Avery & Dangar
Danger Hannah (Mrs.), gold & sil. cas. 2 Spann's blds. St. Panc
Dangerfield John & Abraham, solicitors, 68 Chancery lane
Dangerfield David, cheesemonger, 6 Foxley rd. Cambrwl. N. rd
Dangerfield Jonathan, cheesemonger, 247 Bermondsey st
Dangerfield Julius, carpenter, 10 Red Lion ct. Spitalfields
Daniel Thomas & Co. merchants, 4 Mincing lane
Daniel Ann (Mrs.), lodging house, 7 Warwick st. Regent st
Daniel Benjamin, fishmonger, 117 High st. Camden town
Daniel Charlotte (Mrs.), school, 1 York terrace, Kingsland
Daniel Edward, tailor, 80 Great Guildford st. Borough
Daniel Fredk. (Mrs.), baby linen wa. 8 Jubilee st. Mile end rd
Daniel George, accountant, 18 Canonbury sq. Islington
Daniel Geo. west india merchant, 20 Sun st. Bishopsgate
Daniel Hannah (Mrs.), plumber, 55 Flagon row, Deptford
Daniel Henry, stonemason, 27 Worcester st. Union st. Boro'
Daniel James, sec. to *London & Westminster Mutual Life Assurance*, 448 West Strand
Daniel John, currier, 45 Turvile st. Church st. Bethnal green
Daniel John, horse hair manuf. 51 Cloth fair, West Smithfield
Daniel Richd. bookseller & newsvender, 2 King st. Cov. garden
Daniel Robt. *Duke of Clarence* P.H. 1 Hope ter. Notting hill
Daniel Samuel, baker, 45 Trafalgar st. Walworth road
Daniel Samuel, beer retailer, 77 Curtain rd. Shoreditch
Daniel Thomas, fruiterer, 35 Chapel st. Pentonville
Daniel Thomas Henry, sugar & fruit broker, 83 Gt. Tower st
Daniel Wm. *Custom House tavern*, 77 Lower Thames st
Daniel Wm. grocer, 49 Parsons st. St. George st
Daniel Wm. perfumer, 37 Burlington arcade, Piccadilly
Daniel Wm. Thomas Shave, barrister, 41 Chancery lane
Danieli Chas. Geo. jeweller & silversmith, 315 Oxford st
Danieli James, jeweller, silversmith & clock ma. 304 Oxford st
Daniell Alfred B. & Richard P. chinamen by special appointment to her Majesty, 18 Wigmore st. & 129 New Bond st
Daniell Alex. Deanes & Geo. pawnbrokers, 5 Bowling st. Marylb
Daniell Alex. D. & Geo. trunkmakers, 34 Edwards st. Portman sq
Daniell, Dickinson & Co. east india agents, 5 St. Mildred's ct
Daniell Edward, bookseller, 53 Mortimer st. Cavendish sq
Daniell James, coal merchant, Western wharf, Geo. st. Adelphi
Daniell James N. merchant, 25 Bucklersbury
Daniell Jonathan, plumber & glazier, 20 Judd st. Brunswick sq
Daniell Neville, surgeon dentist, 15 Charlotte st. Fitzroy sq
Daniell Samuel, pocket book maker, 8 Cornhill
Daniels & Payne, iron & tin plate merchts, 29 Upper Thames st
Daniels Richd. & Thos. cheesemongers, 218 Shadwell High st
Daniels & Thompson, tailors, 90 Jermyn st. St. James's
Daniels Wm. & Arthur, woollen manufacts. 3 Aldermanbury
Daniels Abraham, who. perfumer, 1 Budge row, Cannon st
Daniels Ebenezer, tailor, 30 Jewin crescent
Daniels George, butcher, 24 Shadwell High st
Daniels George, tinman, 22 Easton st. Spafields
Daniels Godfrey, furn. dlr. 3 Cumberland row, Walworth rd
Daniels Henry, bread & bis. baker, 20 James st. Cannon st. rd
Daniels Jas. grocer & cheesemngr. 12 Murray st. New North rd
Daniels Jas. grocer, Downham road, Kingsland
Daniels Jas. painter & glazier, 62 Ossulston st. Somers town
Daniels Jeremiah, carpenter, 14 Whitfield st. Finsbury
Daniels John, stationer, 5 William st. Manchester sq
Daniels John, tailor, 169 Long lane, Bermondsey
Daniels Joseph, fruiterer, 4 East st. Spitalfields
Daniels Nathaniel, sworn broker in metals, 50 Threadneedle st
Daniels Philip, *Pantheon* dining rooms, 317 Oxford st
Daniels Saml. G. silkwinder, 2 Paradise row, Bethnal grn. rd

Daniels Wm. ship & insurance agent, see Baker & Daniels
Dann Johnson & Co. tea dealers & grocers, 84 New Bond st
Dann George, boot & shoe maker, 14 Charles st. Soho sq
Dann Richard, straw bonnet maker, 19 Queen st. Tower hill
Dann Stephen, grocer, 17 Colvill terrace, King's rd. Chelsea
Dann Thomas, tailor, 38 Gt. Queen st. Lincoln's inn fields
Dann William, fruit salesman, Borough market
Dannatt James, shoemaker, 319 Albany road, Camberwell
Dannell Edmond Geo. grocer, 1 Wyatt's pl. Buttler's ter. Dockhd
Dannell Rt. Benj. chandlers' shop, 4 St. James's pl. Bermdsy. rd
Dannells Mary (Mrs.), *King's Arms* P.H. 22 Bennett st. Blkfrs. r
Danofsky Frederick, tailor, 15 King st. St. James's
Danson Henry, chemist, 96 Oxford st
Danson John, currier & leather seller, 7 Carnaby st. Goldensq
Danziger Abraham, jeweller, see Abrahams & Danziger
Dantziger Jacob Wolf, dealer in ancient coins & medals in gold, silver & bronze, & natural curiosities, 29 Wardour st. Soho
Danvers C. & Co. who. ironmongs. & wine mers. 33 Wormwood st
Darben Joseph, shoemaker, 115 Bethnal green road
Darby Elizth. & Ann (Misses), dressma. 1 Old Compton st. Soho
Darby & Garland, woollen & fancy warehousemen, 35 Wood st
Darby Walter & Co. who. grocers, 13 Cannon st
Darby Edwd. plumber & glazier, 11 Chapel st. Grosvenor pl
Darby George, barrister, 1 Figtree court, Temple
Darby George Edwards, baker, 19 Penton row, Walworth rd
Darby Henry William, pyrotechnist, 98 Regent st. Lambeth
Darby John, smith, 18 East st. Walworth road
Darby Mary (Miss), milliner, 33 Thayer st. Manchester sq
Darby Rowland, tailor, 13A, Red Lion square, Holborn
Darby Wm. Absalom, surveyor, 3 Charles st. Westbourne ter
Darbyshire George, cabinetmaker, 8 Pancras lane
Darbyshire Mary Ann (Mrs.), *Cock* P.H. 7 New st. Broad st. Golden sq
Darcey Alexander, barrister, 4 Pump court, Temple
Darcey Patrick Byrne, sole consignee of Randal Plunkett's patent malt, & dealer in isinglass, 48 Mark lane
Darcy Thomas, teadealer, Bow lane, Bromley
Darcy William, turner, 10 George st. Portland place
D'Arcy William, tailor, 5 Buckingham st. Strand
D'Arcy Wm. Arthur, civil engineer, 23 Denbigh st. Pimlico
Dare & Holland, boot & shoe makers, 133 Shoreditch High st. 101 St. John st. road, 5 King's road east, Sloane sq. & wholesale, 11 Queen st. Cheapside
Dare & Slark, furnishing ironmongers, 16 Cockspur st
Dare Rd. Wallis & Co. boot & shoe wareho. 22 Finsbury pavmnt
Dare Hester (Mrs.), stationer & news agent, 55 Watling st
Dare Robert, butcher, High st. Stoke Newington
Dare Sarah (Mrs.), timber merchant, 1 Bermondsey New rd
Dare William, grocer, 8 Queen's buildings, Knightsbridge
Dargavel Alexander, confectioner, 77 Union st. Borough
Dark Argington Wm. tailor, 37 Chester pl. Kennington cross
Dark Fredk. *Pitt's Head* P.H. 7 Lit. Stanhope st. Mayfair
Dark James, fruiterer, 27 Robert st. Grosvenor square
Dark James Hen. Lord's cricket ground, St. John's wood rd
Dark Matilda (Mrs.), bat ma. Lord's cricket gd. St. John's wd
Darke John, cabinetma. & undertaker, 34 & 46 London wall
Darke John, wharfinger & dust contractor, 5 & 6 Wharfs, Paddington basin, & Cowley whf. Cmbdge. st. Old St. Pancrs
Darke John Rolle, baker, 144 Praed st. Paddington
Darke Sam. Wallwyn, solicitor, 56 Stamford st. Blckfrs. rd
Darke William, builder, 3 Clarehall place, Stepney green
Darke William, hairdresser, 24 Bridge st. Westminster
Darke William Argenton, tailor, 27 Wilmot sq. Russell sq
Darker Wm. H. jun. optical lapidary, 9 Paradise st. Lambeth
Darker Wm. Hill, sen. operative chemist, 9 Paradise st Lambth
Darkin John, teadealer, 11 New st. Bishopsgate
Darkin Martha (Miss), school, 33 St. James's pl. Old Kent rd
Darley Edwd. dyer & scourer, 10 Maiden la. Covent garden
Darley Elizabeth (Mrs.), smith, 11 & 12 Stoney la. Tooley st
Darley Timothy, ship chandler, 4 & 5 Russell st. Low. Rother
Darling John & Son, printers, 31 Leadenhall st
Darling Chas. cabin furniture wa. 55 Robin Hood la. Poplar
Darling Daniel, undertaker, Triangle, Hackney
Darling George, physician, 6 Russell square
Darling Jas. theologl. bkslr. 21, 22 & 23 Lit. Queen st. Holbn
Darling Thos. furniture broker, 6 Star corner, Bermondsey
Darling Thos. Rd. tobacconist & stationr. 144 Rosemary la
Darling Wm. pork butcher, 22 Gt. Hall, Hungerford market
Darlow John, engraver, 40 Gee st. Goswell st
Darlow John, linendraper, 61 St. John's st. Clerkenwell
Darnell George, academy, 26 Theberton st. Islington
Darnell John, coal dlr. 4 Halfmoon crescent, Pentonville
Darnell John, fancy cabinet ma. 37 Gt. Chart st. East rd. City rd
Darnell Wm. farrier, 5 Cheshire st. Bethnal green
Darnell Wm. granary kpr. Brooks whf. Pickle hrng. Tooley st
Darnell Wm. plumber, 189 Upper Thames st
Darnton William, pianoforte maker, 43 Cross st. Islington
Darrington Samuel, meat salesman, 47 Newgate market
Dart & Son, coach, saddle & livery lace manfrs. 143 Long acre
Dart John, furniture broker, &c. 12 Warren st. Fitzroy sq
Dart Joseph Henry, barrister, 20 Southampton buildings
Dart Richd. cabinet mak. 29 & 30 Park pl. Kennington cross
Dart Richard, merchant & shipowner, 3 Walbrook buildings
Darter George B. S. pianoforte mfr. 57 Baker st. Portman sq
Dartford Gunpowder manufrs. Office, 34 Throgmorton st
Darthez Brothers, merchants, 15 Austinfriars
Dartiguenave Victor, artist, 199 Piccadilly
Dartnall Jacob, butcher, 9 Long lane, Bermondsey
Dartnall William, butcher, 5 Kingsland road
Dartnell Edward Taylor, irish law agent, 6 Barge yard chambers, Bucklersbury, & 48 Lower Sackville st. Dublin
Dartnell John, livery stables, 9 Field place, St. John st. rd
Darton & Co. booksellers & publishers, 58 Holborn hill
Darton Ann (Mrs.), toy & fan. repos. 33 Bishopsgate st. within
Davall John, umbrella maker, 48 Bermondsey st
Darvell John, bootmaker, 1 Albion st. Rotherhithe
Darvies John Brutus, wine cooper, 32 Walbrook, City
Darvill Francis, saddler, 11 Notting hill, High st
Darvill James, fruiterer, 60 Ossulston st. Somers town
Darvill John Thomas, surgeon, 7 Dean's row, Walworth rd
Darvill William, chairmaker, 32 Tower st. Westminster rd
Darwin Henry, tailor, 11 Calthorpe place, Gray's inn road
Darwin James, baker, 55 Bridport place, New North road
Darwin Jonathan, grocer, 134 St. George st
Dasent Bury, surgeon, 11 Pall mall
Dasent John Bury, barrister, 2 Serjeants' inn, Fleet st
Dash Martha (Mrs.), hat & cap maker, 118 Tottenham ct. rd
Dash Sarah (Mrs.), fruiterer, 33 Wigmore st. Cavendish sq
Dashwood Wm. Halsey, solicitor, 3 Clifford's inn
Dashwood A. Wm. shoemkr. 23 White Hart pl. L. Kennington la
Dashwood James, paperhanger, 4 Francis st. Newngtn. butts
Dashwood Joseph, print colorer, &c. 1 Holywell st. Strand
Da Silva & Co. patent medicine wareho. 1 Bride la. Fleet st
Da Silva Henrique Joze & Co. merchants, 5 Warnford ct
Dastis German, merchant, 109 Fenchurch st
Datchens Henry, fruiterer, 8 Camomile st. Bishopsgate
Datchens John, fruiterer, &c. 2 Cullum st. Fenchurch st
Date Joseph, grocer, 4 Sarah place, Old st. road
Daubeny John, LL.D. advocate, 11 College, Doctors' commons
Daubuz Lewis Charles & William, tin smelters & merchants, 9 New Broad st. City
Daukes & Rodick, agents for stout & ale, 3 Exeter st. Strand
Daulby & Ballard, tailors, 23 Tavistock place, Tavistock sq
Daun Edward, distiller & wine mer. see Sewell, Daun & Co
Dauncey Thos. blackwell hall factor, 25 Milk st. Cheapside
Dauptain Jean, manfr. of ultramarine, 17 Wharf rd. City rd
Davall John, umbrella maker, 48 Bermondsey st
Davenes Amédée, poulterer & egg mer. 22 Turnmill st. Clknwl
Davenport Jas. & Chas. lamp & oil wa. 4 & 5 Bedford st. Cov. gar
Davenport John & Co. manufacturers of earthenware, china & glass, 82 Fleet st.; 28 Wharf rd. City road; Longport, Staffordshire; & Canning place, Liverpool
Davenport Burrage, merchant, 2 Dunster court, Mincing la
Davenport Charles, auctioneer, estate & house agent, 5 Mark lane, City
Davenport Chas. optician & cigar dealer, 33 Tabernacle row
Davenport Ellen (Miss), dressmaker, 9 Church st. Spitalflds
Davenport James, pewterer, 15 Gt. Smith st. Westminster
Davenport James, who. potato dealer, Spitalfields market
Davenport John, jun. bootmaker, 28 Wood st. Cheapside
Davenport John, hosiery commis. agt. 28 Addle st. Wood st
Davenport John T. chemist, 33 Gt. Russell st. Bloomsbury
Davenport Sam. historical engraver, 38 Myddelton st. Spaflds
Davenport Wm. solicitor, 21 Ely place
Daves Hannah (Mrs.), *Duke's Head* P.H. 10 Low. Kenningtn. la
Daves Wm. *Queen Adelaide* P.H. 12 Gwynn's pl. Hackney rd
Davey James & Co. tailors, 113 Edgware road, Paddington
Davey (Peter) & Pegg (Wm.), coal & coke mers. Old Barge ho. wharf, Up. Ground st. & Coal exch. 96 Lr. Thames st
Davey Alfred Edwd. trunk mkr. 59 Cannon st. St. George's ea
Davey Ambling, builder, 22 Queen's row, Pentonville
Davey Charles Gabriel, *Swan inn*, Broadway, Stratford
Davey Evan, carpenter, &c. 9 Copenhagen st. Pentonville
Davey George, glass & chinaman, 192 Tottenham ct. road
Davey Henry, baker, Hertford road, Kingsland road
Davey Henry, boot & shoe maker, 61 Park st. Camden tn
Davey Henry, carpenter, 129 Southwark bridge road
Davey Jacob Mills, surveyor, 5 Up. Charles st. Westmr
Davey James, house painter & stenciller, 5 Crown st. Soho
Davey John, furniture brok. 7 Union st. Middlesex hospital
Davey Joseph, baker, 149 St. John st. Smithfield

Davey Joseph, ginger beer manufact. 10 Cloth fair, Smithfi
Davey Nicholas, fruiterer, 2 Upper Kennington lane
Davey Robert, cabinet maker, 1 Eagle pl. Eagle st. City rd
Davey Robt. pork butcher, 8 James pl. Larkhall la. Clapham
Davey Robt. smith & farrier, 11 Brownlow mws. Gray's inn la
Davey Robt. surgeon, 19 Gt. Ormond st. Queen sq. Bloomsby
Davey Robt. Thos. Geo. grocer, 21 Marylebone la. Oxfd. st
Davey Samuel, cooper, 11 Pitman's buildings, St. Luke's
Davey Susan (Mrs.), cooper, 91 John st. Fitzroy square
Davey Thomas, baker, 31 Great James st. Hoxton
Davey Thomas, coffee rooms, 32 Church st. Lambeth
Davey Thomas, *Royal Standard* P.H. 56 Rotherhithe
Davey Thomas, silk machine maker, 19 Quakerst. Spitalfids
Davey William, builder, 8 Market st. Newport market
Davey William, coach & cart wheelwright, South Lambeth
Davey William, farrier, 65 Marylebone lane, Oxford st
Davey William, milliner, &c. High st. Stoke Newington
Davey William, india rubber & sponge manufr. 15 Walbrook
David Bouvot, merchant, manufacturer & wholesale dealer in precious & false stones & all articles generally used by jewellers; also cristles & other continental productions, 7 Finsbury pl. South & 22 Rue de Bondy, Paris
David Francis, painter & grainer, 55 Berwick st. Soho
David John, surgeon, 24 Brewer st. Golden square
David Robert, imitator of woods, &c. 21 City road
Davidge George, stockbroker, 13 Finch lane, Cornhill, & Stock Exchange
Davidge James, painter, 60 Gt. Titchfield st. Oxford st
Davidge James, tailor, &c. 40 Friday st. Cheapside
Davidge Thomas, cheesemonger, 48 Minories
Davidge William, beer retailer, 12 Crescent st. Euston sq
Davids David, cowkeeper, 11 Hart st. Covent garden
Davids Moss, fishmonger & poulterer, 30 Paternoster row
Davids Wm. Hy. bed sacking mfr. 24 Brandon st. Walworth
Davids William Henry, surgeon, 49 Brompton row
Davids William Thomas, artist, 5 Coventry st
Davidson Abraham & Son, chiropodist, 54 Fenchurch st
Davidson Alex. & Co. dantsic spruce imp. 28 Trafalgar sq. Step
Davidsons' & Co. west india merchants, 6 Lime st. square
Davidson Danl. M. & Co. metal agts. Cousin la. Up. Thames st
Davidson & Peter, merchants, 2 Scots yard, Bush lane
Davidson Adam, watch & clock maker, 44 Goswell st
Davidson Alexander, baker, 22 Devonshire st
Davidson Alexander, flour factor, see Hall & Davidson
Davidson Andrew, appraiser, 25 Harcourt st. New road
Davidson Charles, barrister, 6 Stone buildings, Lincoln's inn
Davidson Duncan, tailor, 24 Norfolk st. Middlesex hospital
Davidson Geo. letterpress printer, 16 Serle's place, Linc. inn
Davidson Geo. Henry, printer & publsh. 25 Water st. Blkfrs
Davidson Isaac, jeweller, 40 Mansell st. Goodman's fields
Davidson James, baker, 15 Belvedere road, Lambeth
Davidson James, solicitor, see Clark & Davidson
Davidson John, lamp manufac. & gasfitter, 40 Wych st
Davidson Madgwick Spicer, solicitor, see Bicknell & Davidson
Davidson Mary Ann (Mrs.), wardrobe dlr. 25 Russell ct. Druryla
Davidson Meyer, stockbroker, Stock exchange
Davidson Nathaniel, surgeon, 40 North st. Manchester sq
Davidson Septimus, solicitor, see Hardwick & Davidson
Davidson Thos. physician, Shaftesbury ho. Bayswater hill
Davidson Thos. P. solicitor, 4 Theberton st. West, Islington
Davidson William, haberdasher, 24 Little Gray's inn lane
Davidson William, hairdresser, 14 Cullum st. Fenchurch st
Davidson William, ship & commercl. agt. 8 Water la. Tower st
Davidson William, wine & spirit mercht. 8 Water la. Tower st
Davie John, hairdresser, 2 Betts st. Ratcliff highway
Davie Joseph, watch & clock maker, 201 High Holborn
Davie Peter, boot & shoe maker, 17 Moorgate st. Bank
Davies Brothers & Co. law stationers, 26 Change alley
Davies & Buckland, insurance agents, Lloyd's
Davies Daniel & Co. linendrapers, 155 Blackfriars road
Davies Daniel & Son, attorneys, 21 Warwick st. Golden sq
Davies Daniel & Thomas, linendrapers, 82 & 83 Waterloo rd
Davies David & Co. seedsmen, 8 Great Dover st. Borough
Davies George & Co. chemists, 2 Constable row, Mile end rd
Davies Geo. Fredk. & Co. woollen drapers, 189 Boro' High st
Davies, Hodgson & Co. who. teadealers, 9 & 10 Philpot la
Davies Jas. & Son, export boot & shoe war. 9 Gracechurch st
Davies Jas. & Son, work. jewllers, 8 Bloomsbury st. Blmsbury
Davies James & Thomas, attorneys, 25 Coleman st
Davies Jeremiah & Co. army clothiers & tailors, 49 Poland st
Davies Mary & D. (Misses), ladies' sch. 10 Dorset ter. Claphm. rd
Davies & Price, tailors, 4 Cork st. Bond st
Davies Robert & Co. bankers & merchants, 187 Shoreditch
Davies Robt. & F. plumbers, 106 Mount st. Berkeley square
Davies Thomas & Son, tailors, 19 Hanover st. Hanover sq
Davies Albert, *Dyers' Arms* P. H. 7 Webb st. Bermondsey
Davies Ann (Mrs.), furn. brok. 25 Lit. Pulteney st. Golden sq
Davies Ashmore, impt. for. fancy goods, 18 Lamb's Conduit st
Davies Benjamin, solicitor, 4 Devonshire sq. Bishopsgate
Davies Benj. Rees, engraver & printer, 16 George st. Eustonsq
Davies Charles, baker, 19 George st. Portman square
Davies Charles, butcher, 3 George's terrace, Kentish town
Davies Charles, tobacco & cigar mnfr. Cole st. Gt. Dover rd
Davies Charles James, *Star* P. H. 40 Wilkes st. Spitalflds
Davies Charlotte (Mrs.), rag & bottle dealer, 6 Sheffield st. & coffee rooms, 8 Sheffield st. Lincoln's inn fields
Davies Cornelius James, fancy cab. mak. 6 Rempstone pl. Hxtn
Davies David, boot & shoe ma. 1 Assembly row, Mile end rd
Davies David, cabinet maker, 120 Up. Seymour st. Euston sq
Davies David, childbed linen wareho. 15 Union st. Borough
Davies David, coachmaker, 15 Wigmore st. Cavendish sq. & 19 Osnaburgh st. Regent's park
Davies David, coal merchant & dealer, 142 Rosemary lane
Davies David, dairyman, 4 Conduit court, Long acre
Davies David, dairyman, 15 Whitcomb st. Pall mall
Davies David, grocer, 43 Marsham st. Westminster
Davies David, grocer, 43 Portland st. Walworth common
Davies David, silk warehouseman, see Lycett & Davies
Davies David, smith & engineer, 55 Collingwd. st. Blkfrs. rd
Davies David, solicitor, 4 Henrietta st. Covent garden
Davies David, surgeon, 17 Lower Belgrave st
Davies David, tea & coffee dealer, 12 Crown st. Finsbury
Davies Ebenezer, law stationer, 4 Bream's bldgs. Chancery la
Davies Edward, carp. & undert. 3 Jerusalem ct. St. John st
Davies Edward, oil & colorman, 67 Harrow road
Davies Edward, who. & retail tea dealer, 9 & 10 Philpot la
Davies Edward Clement, chemist, 48 Ernest st. Regent's pk
Davies Edw. Geo. lint ma. 2 Pagoda ter. Bermondsey New rd
Davies Edward Henry, boarding ho. 21 Castle st. Falcon sq
Davies Edward Henry, tailor, 19 St. Martin's le Grand
Davies Edwin C. blanket & horse clothing warh. 9 Goswell st
Davies Elizh. Hannah (Mrs.), milliner, 18 Lamb's Conduit st
Davies Esther (Mrs.), rag & bottle dealer, 2 Cross st. Golden sq
Davies Evan, dairyman, 4½ Church st. Blackfriars road
Davies Evan, tailor, &c. 33 Thomas st. Horselydown
Davies Frances Elizh. (Mrs.), law statr. 2 Serle's pl. Linc. inn
Davies Fred. umbrella & firescreen ma. 1 Gt. Warner st. Clknwl
Davies Fredk. confectioner, 5 Trinity rw. & 10 Islngtn. High st
Davies Frederick, surgeon, 19 Upper Gower st
Davies Gavin, hairdresser, 3 Castle st. Leicester square
Davies George, bookbinder, 1 Trig lane, Upper Thames st
Davies George, *Brown Bear* P.H. 7 Bridge st. Southwark
Davies George, grocer, 15 Windmill st. Finsbury
Davies George, hairdresser, 50 Marshall st. Golden square
Davies George, packer, 21 Duke st. Bishopsgate
Davies George, surgeon, 2 Constable row, Mile end road
Davies George, upholsterer, 50 Long alley, Finsbury
Davies George, writer & grainer, 1 Green st. Paddington
Davies Geo. Hugh, wine, beer, &c. merch. see Bryant & Davies
Davies Henry, carman, Warlters buildings, Old Kent road
Davies Henry, confectioner, 26 Gt. Charlotte st. Blkfrs. rd
Davies Henry, engine turner, 4 Baynes row, Coldbath fields
Davies Henry, hosier & tailor, 19 Oxford st
Davies Henry, physician, 18 Saville row, Piccadilly
Davies Henry, *Royal Victoria* P.H. 134 Waterloo road
Davies Henry, saddler, 11 Chapel pl. Vere st
Davies Henry Edward, chemist, 43 Wood st. Cheapside
Davies Hy. Philip, coal mer. Palace wf. Church st. Lambeth, & Middle wharf, Great Scotland yard
Davies Henry Tudor, barrister, Inner Temple hall staircase
Davies Herbert, surgeon, 27 New Broad st. City
Davies Horatio David, cabt. & bilrd. table ma. 17 Artillery la
Davies Hugh, carman, 19 Dowgate hill
Davies James, butcher, 36 Chapel st. Grosvenor square
Davies James, grocer, 2 Manor row, Queen st. Chelsea
Davies James, grocer, 1 Manchester st. Gray's inn road
Davies James, linendraper, 50 Oxford st
Davies James Harvey, tobacconist, 164 Kingsland road
Davies James Henshall, coal agent, 11 Poultry
Davies Jas. Wm. auctioneer, 4 Marlboro' pl. Kennington cross
Davies Jane (Mrs.), dairywoman, 19 Sherborne lane, City
Davies Jeffery, painter, &c. 98 Nicholas st. Hoxton New town
Davies Jenken, dairyman, 15 Long lane, Bermondsey
Davies John, archit. & surveyor, 4 Devonshire sq. Bishopsgt
Davies John, blacking maker, 10 Dorrington st. Leather la
Davies John bootmaker, 47 Gt. Queen st. Lincoln's inn fields
Davies John, butcher, 4 Peel pl. Kensington gravel pits
Davies John, cheesemonger, 19 Borough road
Davies John, dairyman, 26 Compton st. Brunswick square
Davies John, dairyman, 60 York st. City road
Davies John, dairyman, 21 Cloth fair, West Smithfield
Davies John, news agent, 70 George st. Portman square

Davies John, pork butcher, 124 Poplar High st
Davies John, *Rising Sun* P.H. Great Scotland yard
Davies John, surgeon, 3 Stepney High st
Davies John, tobacconist, 1 Vinegar yd. Brydges st.Cov. gdn
Davies John, wheelwright, 7 Thornton st. Dockhead
Davies John, *Welsh Harp* P.H. 23 Aylesbury st. Clerkenwell
Davies John Barnes, old bookseller, 15 Gt. Turnstile, Holborn
Davies John Francis, boot & shoe maker, 5 Shadwell High st
Davies John Prior, distiller & brandy mer. see Baker & Davies
Davies Jonathan, *Queen's Arms* P.H.31 Queen st.Cheapside
Davies Joseph, chemist & druggist, 27 Aldgate
Davies Joseph, *Holland Arms* P.H. Holland pl. Kensingtn
Davies Joseph, wholesale perfumer, see Lloyd & Davies
Davies Lewis, tailor & draper, 23 Dover place, New Kent rd
Davies Maria (Miss), pearl stringer, 3 Mill st. Hanover sq
Davies Margt.(Mrs.), tobacconist, 19 Cumberland rw. King's cr
Davies Mark Harrison, tailor, 56 South Molton st. Bond st
Davies Mary (Mrs.), haberdasher, 71 Up. Whitecross st. St. Lu
Davies Matthew Peter, tallow chandler, 63 St. Martin's lane
Davies Michael, cap maker, 57 Brick lane, Spitalfields
Davies Morgan, cowkeeper, Cumberland pl. Old Kent rd
Davies Philip, grocer & tea dealr. 1 Three Oak la. Horselydown
Davies Rebecca (Mrs.), grocer & cheesemgr. 18 Whittleburyst
Davies Richard, biscuit baker, 133 Lambeth, Lower marsh
Davies Richard, carman, 8 Lit. Knightrider st. Doctors' com
Davies Richard, engraver & jeweller, 211 Strand
Davies Richard Edward, surgeon, 140 Minories
Davies Richard, tailor, 34 Conduit st. Regent st
Davies Richard John, plumber, 49 Rupert st. Haymarket
Davies Richard Thomas, trunk, &c. maker, 225 Piccadilly
Davies Robert, brushmaker, 76 Regent st. Lambeth
Davies Robert, importer of dutch rushes, & chair manufacturer, 1 Market st. Finsbury
Davies Robert, solicitor, see Hill & Davies
Davies Robert, stationer & tobacconist, 4 Lit. Marylebone st
Davies Robert, surgeon, 126 Holborn hill
Davies Samuel, academy, 16 Brill place, Somers town
Davies Samuel, perfumer, Larkhall lane, Clapham
Davies Sophia (Mrs.), straw hat maker, 27 Charterhouse la
Davies Stephen, coal merchant, Somerset wharf, 58 & 59 Bankside, Southwark, & Times wharf, Wilton road, Pimlico
Davies Stephen, *Horse Shoe* P.H. 26 Clerkenwell close
Davies Stephen, tailor, 11 New Union st. Lit. Moorfields
Davies Thomas, bedsacking & hearthrug mf. 27 Mint st. Boro'
Davies Thomas, confectioner, 89 Poplar High st
Davies Thomas, cooper, 19 Bear st. Leicester square
Davies Thomas, cowkeeper, 28 Hastings st. Burton crescent
Davies Thomas, cowkeeper, 53 Old st. St. Luke's
Davies Thomas, cowkeeper, Violet hill, St. John's wood
Davies Thomas, grocer, 50 Rosoman st. Clerkenwell
Davies Thomas, jeweller & watchmk. 5 Middle row, Holborn
Davies Thomas, letterpress printer, 82 West Smithfield
Davies Thomas, surgeon, see Brown & Davies
Davies Thomas, tailor, 85 St. George's road, Southwark
Davies Thomas, toy warehouse, 43 Lr. George st. Chelsea
Davies Thomas White, chemist, 14 Old Dorset pl. Clapham rd
Davies Thomas Zaccheus, *Black Lion* P.H. 22 Bayswatr. ter
Davies William, artist, 15 Earl st. east, Lisson grove north
Davies William, baker, 25 Lower st. Islington
Davies Wm. carpenter & builder, 9 Providence row, Finsbury
Davies Wm. chandlers' shop, 11 Coburg st. Clerkenwell
Davies Wm. cheesemonger, 22 Gt. Charlotte st. Blackfrs. rd
Davies Wm. chemist, Well st. Hackney
Davies Wm. clock case & cabinet ma. 5 Percival st. Clerkenwl
Davies Wm. coal merchant, 30 Walbrook
Davies Wm. cowkeeper, 34 Bermondsey square
Davies Wm. dairyman, 4 Chapel st. Bedford row
Davies Wm. dining rooms, 68 Tottenham court road
Davies Wm. *King's Arms* P.H. Pitt's place, Old Kent road
Davies Wm. patent mangle maker & machinist, 351 Oxford st. & 66 Wells st. Oxford st
Davies Wm. plumber & painter 18 Clift st. New North road
Davies Wm. plumber, &c. 42 Upper North pl. Gray's inn road
Davies Wm. statnr. & cardmk. 110 St. John st. West Smithfield
Davies Wm. surgeon, &c. Dove row, Hackney fields
Davies Wm. surgeon, Well st. Hackney
Davies Wm. tailor, 38 Great Dover st. Borough
Davies Wm. Brisset, solicitor, 21 Red Lion square
Davies Wm. J. emery & black lead ma. New Weston st. Southw
Davies Wm. Thos. tailor, 52 Poland st. Oxford st
Davies Winifred (Mrs.), dairy, 3 Tavistock ct. Covent garden
Davis Aaron Dav. & Co. watchma. 43 Mansell st. Goodman's flds
Davis Alfred & Co. importers of toys, beads & other foreign fancy merchandise, birmingham & sheffield warehousemen, & general factors, 59 & 60 Houndsditch
Davis Charles & Co. ship brokers & mers. 133 Fenchurch st
Davis & Delaforce, wine, liqueur, &c. merchs. 87 Wimpole st
Davis Edward & Co. wholesale bootmakers, 114 Leadenhall st. & 43 Mansell st. Goodman's fields
Davis Edward Byrne & Co. lime merchants & wharfingers, east side, Grosvenor basin, Phœnix wharf, Whitefriars, & 19 Wharf, north side, Paddington basin
Davis Edward John & Co. repellent cloth, marquee, flag, rick cloth, twine & wheel grease manuf. 64 West Smithfield
Davis Esther & Julia (Misses), milliners, 7 Savage gardens
Davis Geo. & Horatio & Co. tobacco brokers, 107 Fenchurch st
Davis Geo. & Son, woolstaplers, Church st. Horselydown
Davis, Hesketh & Co. export oilmen, 126 & 127 Leadenhall st
Davis & Hopkins, lamp makers, 18 Ray st. Clerkenwell
Davis Jacob & Co. wholes. furriers, 5 Bull head ct. Newgate st
Davis James & Henry, surgeons, 66 Stanhope st. Hampstead road, & 23 Hampstead road
Davis John & Co. waterproof cloth mills, West Smithfield
Davis John Wilson & Son, who. grocers, Broadway, Deptford
Davis Joseph & Co. booksellers, 104 Sloane st. Knightsbridge
Davis & Levy, cigar manufacturers, 7 Mitre st. Aldgate
Davis & Lipman, cigar manufacturers, 4 Duke st. Smithfield
Davis Mark & Son, cigar manufacturers, 61 Borough road
Davis Matthew & Co. coach & army lace makers, 90 Long acre
Davis (Phineas) & Whittaker, sheriffs' officers, 3 Red Lion sq
Davis Sophia & Mary, grocers, 62 Leader st. Chelsea
Davis & Vigers, land surveyors, auctioneers, &c. 3 Frederick's place, Old Jewry
Davis Wm. & Co. musical instrument makers, 31 Coventry st
Davis's Almshouses, Queen's Head lane, Islington
Davis's wharf, Chas. Curling & Co. wharfingers, Tooley st
Davis Abraham, birmingham warehouse, 285 Oxford st
Davis Abraham, china & glass dealer, 281 Oxford st. & 113 Tottenham court road
Davis Alexander, printer & stationer, 16 John st. Minories
Davis Alexander, sponge mercht. brush manfr. & repository for horse clothing, harness, &c. 33 Strand & 20 Regent st
Davis Alexr. vinegar maker, see Collingridge & Davis
Davis Alexander, wine broker, 7 Savage gardens, Tower hil
Davis Aley, tobacconist, 84 Quadrant, Regent st
Davis Alfred, coffee rooms, 3 Dockhead, Bermondsey
Davis Allen, auctioneer & surveyor, 36 Old Jewry
Davis Ann, ready made linen wareho. see Hallett & Davis
Davis Ann (Mrs.), carpenter, 25 Church st. Chelsea
Davis Benjamin, bootmaker, 26 Hayfield pl. Mile end road
Davis Benj. bricklayer, 25 Church st. Cheyne walk, Chelsea
Davis Catherine (Mrs.), orange merch. 14 Russell ct. Drury la
Davis Charles, butcher, 61 Mount st. Lambeth
Davis Chas. confectr. & soda water ma. 161 Alfred pl. Wtrlo. rd. & 2 Grosvenor pl. Borough rd
Davis Charles, furniture dlr. 2 Cumberland pl. Newington butts
Davis Chas. leech imp. & pill box ma. 72 Frederick pl. Newngtn
Davis Charles, tin plate worker, 94 Broad st. Ratcliff cross
Davis Chas. Wm. conveyancer, 24 Charles square, Hoxton
Davis Chas. Wm. chronometer ma. 1 Foxton ter. Thornhill rd
Davis Chris. Hen. chemist, &c. 9 Acton pl. Bagnigge wells rd
Davis Coleman, music sellr. 8 Dover pl. west, Kent st. rd. Boro'
Davis Cyrus, *Plough* P.H. 19½ Giltspur st. Smithfield
Davis Daniel, bacon drier, 33 Allen st. Goswell st
Davis Daniel, coal dealer, 8 York st. Westminster
Davis Daniel, glass & china wareho. 45 Blackfriars road, & 62 Newington causeway
Davis Daniel, tobacconist, 297 Oxford st
Davis David, clothes dlr. & jeweller, 46 Marylebone lane
Davis David, clothes salesman, 23 Jermyn st. St. James's
Davis David, teadealer & grocer, 12 Crown st. Finsbury
Davis David John, wine merchant, 2 Parliament st
Davis David M. ship agent & merchant, 9 Trinity sq. Tower
Davis Edmund, fishing rod & tackle manfr. 15 New st. Cov. grdn
Davis Edward, beer retailer, 23 Russell st. Rotherhithe
Davis Edward, brown pottery, 3 Salisbury st. Bermondsey
Davis Edward, cattle salesman, 60 West Smithfield
Davis Edward, coachmaker, 1 Grove pl. Lisson grove
Davis Edward, dairyman, 4 Hosier lane, Smithfield
Davis Edward, grocer, 18 Portsmouth pl. Lr. Kennington la
Davis Edward, lime mer. Grosvenor whf. Wilton rd. Pimlico
Davis Edward, milliner, 2 Stevens pl. New north road
Davis Edward, sculptor, 17 Russell place, Fitzroy square
Davis Edward, surgeon, 17 Upper Belgrave place, Pimlico
Davis Edward, tailor, 28 St. John's wood terrace, Portland town
Davis Edward, tailor, 1A, New Church st. Lisson grove
Davis Elias, slopseller, see Moses, Son & Davis
Davis Evan James, baker, 11 Frith st. Soho
Davis Fanny (Miss), work. jeweller, 34 Southamptn. st. Strand
Davis Francis, zinc worker, 3 Albion pl. east, New road
Davis Francis Henry, boot ma. 39 Amwell st. Pentonville

Davis Fras. Viney, tailor, 2 Evaline pl. Commercial rd. east
Davis Fredk. Sidney, booksllr,&c. 25 High st. Newingtn.bts
Davis George, butcher, 13 Brick lane, St. Luke's
Davis George, cabinet maker, 40 Skinner st. Bishopsgate
Davis George, dancing master, 7 Grove place, Lisson grove
Davis George, *Fountain* P.H. 88 Shoreditch
Davis George, grocer, 47 Carlisle st. Lambeth
Davis George, saddler & harness maker, 100 Borough High st
Davis George, who.& export shoe ware. see Gamble & Davis
Davis George, *York* coffee rooms, 70 Gray's inn lane
Davis George Edw.printer, 2 Albion bldgs. Bartholomew close
Davis Hannah (Mrs.), carpenter, 3 Paulton st. Chelsea
Davis Hannah (Mrs.),shoemaker, 9 New Bridge st. Vauxhall
Davis Henry, furniture broker, 5 York pl. Westminster rd
Davis Henry, glass mounter, &c. 11 Gt. Sutton st. Clrknwl
Davis Henry, leather seller, 7 Whitby pl. Lock's fields
Davis Henry, plumber & glazier, 166 Sloane st. Knightsbridge
Davis Henry, shoemaker, 23 Little Queen st. Westminster
Davis Henry, wh.sodawa.mfr.&sack&bag ma.35St.Mary Axe
Davis Henry Joseph, day school, 146 Blackfriars rd
Davis Howell, tailor, &c. 4 Church row, Aldgate High st
Davis Isaac, furniture broker, 19 York pl. Westminster rd
Davis Isaac, music printer, 25 Berwick st. Soho
Davis Isaac, solicitor, 24 St. James's square
Davis Jacob David, furrier, 14 Saint Mary Axe
Davis James, boot & shoe maker, 16 College st. Chelsea
Davis James, boot & shoe maker, 17 Gibson st. Waterloo rd
Davis James, clock ca.mak. 11 Pear Tree court, Clerkenwell
Davis James, engine turner, 55 Wynyatt st. Goswell st
Davis James, dairyman, 8 South wharf rd. Paddington
Davis James, meat salesman, 17 New Newgate market
Davis James, poulterer, Poultry market, Leadenhall
Davis James Barnaby, dentist, 6 Quickset row, New road
Davis James Edward, barrister, 1 Elm court, Temple
Davis Jane (Mrs.),ivory turner&umbrella mak. 36 Goswell st
Davis John, baker, 40 Union row, New Kent road
Davis John, *Black Lion* P.H. Church st. Chelsea
Davis John, carpenter, 4 King's Head row, Old Brompton
Davis John, *Canning's Head* P.H. 26 Sidney st. Mile end
Davis John, cheesemonger, 104 Grt. Portland st. Portland pl
Davis John, coal mercht. Old Ferry wharf, Duke st. Chelsea
Davis John, manufacturing cutler, 69 Leadenhall st
Davis John, dyer, 91 High st. Marylebone
Davis John, fruiterer, 42 Cornwall road, Lambeth
Davis John, fruit salesman, Covent garden fruit market
Davis John, fruit salesman, Spitalfields market
Davis John, grocer, 5 Lower Porchester st. Edgware road
Davis John, grocer, 28c, Marylebone lane, Oxford st
Davis John, haberdasher, 7 Arcade, Hungerford market
Davis John, iron & wire fence mfr.3Sidney pl.King's rd.Chlsea
Davis John, ivory turner, 7 Charles st. Goswell road
Davis John, machinist & patent plough maker, 422 Oxford st
Davis John, news agent, 50 Broad st. Bloomsbury
Davis John, oilman, corner of Grove road, Mile end road
Davis John, oil & colorman, 10 St. Ann's place, Limehouse
Davis John, plumber, 11 Bartholomew terrace, City road
Davis John, pork butcher, 69 Broad st. Ratcliff
Davis John, pork butcher, 97 Shoe lane, Fleet street
Davis John, poulterer, 21 Leigh st. Burton crescent
Davis John, seal, dye&roller engraver, 19Perceval st.Clrknw
Davis John, sugar refiner, 64 Leman st. Goodman's fields
Davis John, tailor, 44 Cleveland st. Fitzroy square
Davis John, upholsterer, 138 Tottenham court road & 1 Tottenham court, New road
Davis John, wheelwright, 4 New st. Freeschool st. Dockhead
Davis John, sen. oilman, 122 Church st. Shoreditch
Davis John Grainge, *Crown & Still* P.H. 15Clare st.Clare mkt
Davis John Hall, physician, 17 Russell place, Fitzroy sq
Davis John Jas. *Three Crowns* P.H. High st.Stoke Newington
Davis John K. riding academy, 18 Motcomb st. Belgrave sq
Davis Joseph, chandler's shop, 11 Spicer st. Spitalfields
Davis Joseph, china & glass dealer, 43½ Hedge row, Islingtn
Davis Joseph, furrier, & china & glass dealer, 128 Goswell st
Davis Joseph, gun lock maker, 9 Chamber st. Goodman's fi
Davis Joseph, milkman, 10 Gt. Trinity lane, Bread st
Davis Joseph, pianoforte, organ & self playing pianoforte maker, 20 Southampton st. Strand
Davis Joseph, stockbroker, 75 Old Broad st. City
Davis Joseph, sugar broker & cooper, 23 Water la. Tower st
Davis Joseph, surgeon dentist, 123 Pall mall
Davis Jsph. Gordon, builder, 1 Hugh st. Eccleston sq.Pimlico
Davis Lawrence, merchant, 43 Mansell st. Goodman's fields
Davis Lazarus, tailor, 2 Gt. York mews, Portman square
Davis Lewis, grocer, 10 South st. King's road, Chelsea
Davis Margt.(Miss), mourng. mllnr. 6 Gt. Russell st. Blmsbry
Davis Maria A.(Mrs.), grocer&coal dlr.14Gt.Alie st.Goodm.fls
Davis Mary (Mrs.), cooper, 43½ Chapel st. Pentonville
Davis Mary (Miss), linendraper, 82 Upper Whitecross st
Davis Mary (Mrs.), vellum binder, 33 Dorset st. Spitalfields
Davis Mary Ann (Miss), haberdash. & milliner, 118 Minories
Davis Moses, linendraper, 23 Gt. Prescot st. Goodman's flds
Davis Moss, merchant, 35 Surrey st. Strand
Davis Nathaniel, carman, 2 Collin's court, Tooley st
Davis Phineas, wine merchant, 3 Red Lion square
Davis Peter, coffee rooms, 11 London rd. Southwark
Davis Priscilla (Mrs.), brush & sponge warehouse, & lodging house keeper, 49 Strand
Davis Reuben Thomas, law bksllr. 57 Carey st. Lincoln's inn
Davis Richd. agt. to Sunday School Union, 60 Paternoster row
Davis Richard, builder, see Cooper & Davis
Davis Richard, butcher, Holland st. Brixton road
Davis Richard, grocer, 3 Green st. Bethnal green
Davis Richard, livery stables, 23 Carey st. Lincoln's inn
Davis Richard, stationer, 46 Ernest st. Regent's park
Davis Richard, tailor, see Kolbe & Davis
Davis Richard, tailor & draper, 11 Amwell st. Pentonville
Davis Richard Francis, merchant, 37 Fenchurch st
Davis Richard Powell, iron merchant, firm Guest & Co
Davis Richd. S. surgeon, 12 Mecklenburgh sq. & 13 Chancy.la
Davis Robert, boot & shoe maker, 55 Lambeth High st
Davis Robert, painter, glazier, &c. 33 Store st. Bedford sq
Davis Robert, M.D. surgeon, 1 Worship sq. Finsbury
Davis Robert, tobacconist, 56 Penton st. Pentonville
Davis Robert, jun. umbrella manuf. 22 Bridge rd. Lambeth
Davis Robert Edwd. tobacconist, 124 Cornwall rd. Lambeth
Davis Robert Kirkup, auctioneer & surveyor; broker & valuer by appointment to the Court of Bankruptcy, 68 Mark lane
Davis Samson, surgeon, 19 Sydney sq. Commercial rd
Davis Samuel, cheesemonger, 47 Brewer st. Golden sq
Davis Samuel, cooper & back ma. 39 Southwark bridge rd
Davis Samuel, whitesmith, 3 Back hill, Hatton garden
Davis Samuel Forbes, operative chemist, 215 Oxford st
Davis Sarah (Mrs.), *Jamaica coffee house*, St. Michael's alley
Davis Susannah (Mrs.), pipe ma. 10 Southamptn.bldgs.Eustn.sq
Davis Thomas, academy, 1 Palace st. Pimlico
Davis Thomas, boot & shoe maker, 11 Bouverie st. Edgw. rd
Davis Thomas, bootmaker, 12 Lit. Carter la. Doctors' coms
Davis Thomas, tailor & breeches maker to the royal hunt, 12 Regent st. Waterloo place
Davis Thomas, butcher, 1 Bermondsey New rd
Davis Thomas, cane warehouse, 16 Princes st. Bedford row
Davis Thomas, carriage lamp ma. 7 Hart st. Duke st. Grosv. sq
Davis Thomas, cowkeeper, 13 John st. Fitzroy sq
Davis Thos. dairy, 31 Lower George st. Chelsea
Davis Thomas, cowkeeper&dairyman, 51 Church st. Minories
Davis Thomas, die, seal engraver, &c. 16 Broad st. Golden sq
Davis Thomas, insurance brok. 15 Angel ct. Throgmorton st
Davis Thomas, picture dealer, 5 Arabella row, Pimlico
Davis Thomas, porkman, 155 Bishopsgate without
Davis Thomas, surgeon, 69 Brook st. Hanover square
Davis Thomas, umbrella furniture ma. 5 Glo'ster pl. Old Kent rd
Davis Thomas, wine & spirit merc. 2 Cross la. St. Mary at hill
Davis Thos. wood let. & cabinet ma. 25 Liverpool st. City
Davis Thomas Edward, coal merchant, 159 Whitechapel rd. & 12 Cleveland st. Mile end rd. & New Crane wf. Wappg. wl
Davis Thomas Stevens, chimney sweep, 20 Theobald's rd
Davis Valentine, archtct.&surveyr. 4 King Edward st. Islngtn
Davis Waller Hamilton, solicitor, 1 New Boswell court
Davis Wm. bootmaker, 6 Lamb's Conduit st. Foundling
Davis Wm. brush ma. 13 Colvill ter. King's rd. Chelsea
Davis Wm. cabinet maker &undertaker, 22 King st. St. Luke's
Davis Wm. china mender, 18 Bedford court, Covent garden
Davis Wm. copperplate printer, 11 Red Lion court, Fleet st
Davis Wm. eating house, 10 Jerusalem pass. Clerkenwell
Davis Wm. engraver, 9 St. James's walk, Clerkenwell
Davis Wm. grocer, 29 Smith st. King's road, Chelsea
Davis Wm. grocer & cheesemonger, 4 Church pas. Chancery la
Davis Wm. hairdresser, 3 Bermondsey New road
Davis Wm. ivory turn. 3 Bentinck pl. High st. Portlandtown
Davis Wm. plumber & glazier, 9 Warwick st. Golden sq
Davis Wm. potato dealer, 40 Red Lion st. Spitalfields
Davis Wm. potato & pea salesman, Spitalfields market
Davis Wm. tailor, 21 Weymouth st. Portland place
Davis William, tobacconist, 175 Kingsland road
Davis Wm. *Victoria* P.H. 1 Mornington road, Regent's park
Davis Wm. writer & grainer, 32 Ernest st. Regent's park
Davis Wm. Hy. woollen warehman. see Barber, Howse & Davis
Davis Wm. Isaac, grocer, 4 Brandon row, Newington causeway
Davis Wm. Michael, *Blue Posts* P.H. 22 Berwick st. Soh
Davis Wm. Page, undertaker, 13 Throgmorton st
Davison, Newman & Co. grocers, &c. 44 Fenchurch st

Davison Robt. & Co. ship biscuit bakers, 45 Lower Shadwell
Davison, Thos. Robinson & Son, average staters, &c. 13 Birchin la
Davison Frederick, organ builder, see Gray & Davison
Davison George, upholsterer, 42 Foley st. Portland place
Davison Henry, cabinet maker, 18A, Harrow rd. Paddington
Davison Hen. special pleader, 10 King's Bench walk, Temple
Davison Henry, toy manufactr. 24 St. John's lane, Smithfld
Davison Horatio Wm. solicitor, 8 Virginia ter. Gt. Dover rd. & 77 Basinghall st. City
Davison John, bookbinder, 11 Jewin crescent, Cripplegate
Davison John, *Britannia tav.* 4 Caroline pl. City road
Davison John, coffee roaster, 3 White Lion court, Sevendials
Davison John, corn dealer & bone agent, 43 Old street road
Davison John, *New Merlin's Cave* P.H. 45 Up. Rosoman st
Davison John, surveyor of taxes, 3 Charlton pl. Gt. Dover rd
Davison Martha (Miss), milliner, 13 Bath st. City road
Davison Nicholas Francis, physician, 30 Russell square
Davison Robert, surveyor, Truman's brewery, Spitalfields
Davison Robert W. B. west india mer. 4 Jeffrey sq. St. Mary Axe
Davison Thomas, news agent, 6 Nowell's bdgs. Liverpool rd
Davison Thos. Hen. coal mercht. 19 High row, Knightsbridge
Davison William, solicitor, 48 Bread st. Cheapside
Davison William, surgeon, 12 York st. Covent garden
Daviss William, *Blakeney's Head* P.H. 217 Poplar High st
Daviss William, silk manufacturer, see Washington & Daviss
Davonport Alexander, surgeon, 1 Well ct. Queen st. City
Davoren Oliver, hairdresser, 39 Wych st. Strand
Davy Helen & Ann (Misses), milliners, 8 Gilbert st. Grsvr. sq
Davy John & Sons, printers, 15 Queen st. Seven dials
Davy, Mackmurdo & Co. druggists, 100 Up. Thames st. & manufacturing chemists, 25 Gt. George st. Bermondsey
Davy Charles, artists' colorman, &c. 83 Newman st. Oxford st
Davy Christopher, archt. & surv. 11 Furnival's inn, Holborn
Davy David, wheelwright, 1 Cobourg st. Euston square
Davy Edwd. confectioner, 19 Upper Seymour st. Euston sq
Davy Henrietta (Miss), milliner, 16 Upper King st. Blmsbry
Davy James, linendraper, 212 Poplar High st
Davy Jas. Gardiner, coal mer. White Lion wf. 18 Up. Thames st
Davy John, *Weavers' Arms* P.H. Stoke Newington green
Davy John, writer & frame ma. 94 St. George's rd. Boro'
Davy John Edward, grocer & cheesemonger, 46 Rochester row, Westminster, & 33 Berwick st. Soho
Davy John Henry, wheelwright, Parker st. Drury lane
Davy Mary (Mrs.), tobacconist, 6 Crawford st. Portman sq
Davy Robert, coffee rooms, 80 Snowhill
Davy Robert, jun. perfumer & hairdresser, 222 Strand
Davy Sarah (Mrs.), tobacconist, 55 Park st. Camden town
Davy Susan (Mrs.), fruiterer, 1 Wellington st. North, Strand
Davy Wm. printer & stationer, 8 Gilbert st. Grosvenor sq
Davy's patent elastic india rubber saddles & collars depôt (Agmon Canavan, agent), 107 Jermyn st. St. James's
Daw Chas. Nicholas, butcher, 46 High st. Portland town
Daw Edmund, map mounter & colorer, 114 Fetter lane
Daw George, confectioner, 3 Wimpole st. Cavendish sq
Daw Henry, bootmaker, 42 Cleveland st. Fitzroy sq
Daw Henry, butcher, 76 Crawford st
Daw Jas. John, statnr. & printer & vellum binder, 36 Friday st
Daw John, machine ruler, 26 Great Bush lane, Cannon st
Daw Joseph, pork butcher, 38 High st. Notting hill
Dawbin Joseph, watchmaker, 74 Paradise st. Rotherhithe
Dawe & Odling (Misses), milliners, 6 Theberton st. Islington
Dawe Elizabeth (Mrs.), stationer, 4 Gray's pl. Fulham rd
Dawe Frederick, *Ship* P.H. 61 Chandos st. Covent garden
Dawe George, *Bull's Head* P.H. 23 Walbrook
Dawe George, printer, 9 Southampton place, New road
Dawe George, printer, 9 Southampton mews, Euston square
Dawe Helen (Mrs.), haberdasher, 34 Bath st. City road
Dawe Wm. cabinet maker, 6 Theberton st. High st. Islington
Dawes Brothers, iron & steel merchants, 33 Abchurch lane
Dawes & Edwards, linendrapers, 13 Southampton row
Dawes Thos. & Sons, solicitors, 9 Angel ct. Throgmorton st
Dawes Bartholomew, cabinetmaker, &c. 20 Carlisle st. Soho
Dawes Charles, teadealer, &c. 19 Maddox st. Regent st
Dawes Elizh. (Miss), milliner, 9 Carthusian st. Charterho. sq
Dawes Fred. Wm. undertaker, 1 Lit. Windmill st. Golden sq
Dawes George, meat salesman, 19 Newgate st
Dawes Henry, tailor, see Beaton & Dawes
Dawes Henry, tailor, 1 Church st. Stoke Newington
Dawes Jesse, japanner, 12 Laystall st. Liquorpond st
Dawes Jesse, seraphine ma. 9 New Church st. Lisson grove
Dawes Jonathan, blindmaker, 3 Francis place, Holloway
Dawes Jonathan, blindmaker, 4 Porter's pl. Holloway
Dawes Richd. cheesemonger, 1 Wharf rise, Kingsland road
Dawes Rd. surgeon & chemist, 5 Blenheim ter. St. John's wd
Dawes Susannah (Mrs.), baker, 251 Blackfriars road
Dawes William, attorney, 15 Serjeants' inn, Fleet st
Dawes William, ivory turner, 12 Cannon st. St. George's east
Dawes Wm. Matthias, watchmaker, 131 Upper st. Islington
Dawkes David, oilman, tallow chandler, &c. 68 Shoreditch
Dawkes John, grocer, 9 John's row, Brick lane, St. Luke's
Dawkins Charles John, engraver & printer, 49 Bunhill row
Dawkins Geo. lighterman, 19 John st. Commercial rd Lamb
Dawkins Hannah (Mrs.), dairy & purveyor of asses' milk to the Royal Family, 6 Quickset row, New road, Fitzroy sq
Dawkins William, watch case springer, 11 St. John st. road
Dawn Wm. oriental designer, 9 Godliman st. St. Paul's
Daws Harry, veter. surgeon, 31½ Gresse st. Tottenham ct. rd
Daws Robt. pat. chair mnf. 19 Upper Dorset st. Bryanstn. sq
Dawson Joseph & Sons, shoe & leather wareho. 24 Old Jewry
Dawson Wm. & Sons, general newsvenders & advertising agents, stationers & printers, 74 Cannon st. City
Dawson & Williams, woollendrapers, 13 Newgate st
Dawson Andrew, barge bildr. Vauxhall bridge foot, Lambth
Dawson Anna Maria (Mrs.), stay & corset ma. 199 Regent st
Dawson Charles, law stationer, 2 Cursitor st. Chancery la
Dawson Charles, shoefactor, George inn yard, 70 Borough
Dawson Charles, fruit salesman, North row, Covent garden
Dawson Charles, law stationer, 2 Cursitor st. Chancery la
Dawson Charles, teach. of music, 1 Hopkins bldgs. Islington
Dawson Daniel, *Yorkshire Grey* P.H. 190 Piccadilly
Dawson Edward, china & glass wa. 1 Brook hill, Clerknwll
Dawson Francis Dennis Massey, barrister, 6 Pump ct. Temple
Dawson Frederick, barrister, 2 Pump court, Temple
Dawson Frederick, carriage lamp maker, 33 Long acre
Dawson Frederick, surgeon, 3 Union pl. Lower rd. Islington
Dawson George, livery stables, 57 Up. Crown st. Westminster
Dawson George, 3 *Compasses* P.H. Harrow alley, Houndsditch
Dawson George, *Two Brewers* P.H. 10 Millpondbdge. Brmnsy
Dawson George, wine merchant, 8 St. Swithin's lane
Dawson Harriot (Miss), imp. of isinglass, 126 Church st
Dawson Henry, barrister, 10 Farrar's buildings, Temple
Dawson Henry, hose & clog maker, 54 Broad st. Bloomsbury
Dawson Henry, spice merchant & dry salter, 51 Watling st
Dawson Henry, toy dealer, Camberwell green
Dawson James, biscuit baker, irish provision merchant, 9 Billiter square, & 324 Wapping, & Jamaica coffee house
Dawson James, railway carrier, see Scholefield, Dawson & Co
Dawson James, bookseller, 38 White Lion st. Pentonville
Dawson James, carpenter, 25 Gray st. Blackfriars road
Dawson James, sand wharf, Kingsland rd. West side
Dawson James, silk manufacturer, 26 Fort st. Spitalfields
Dawson Jas. who. tallow melter & candle ma. 37 St. Mary Axe
Dawson John, auctioneer, 21 Old Jewry
Dawson John, barrister, 5 Mitre court chambers, Temple
Dawson John, cabinetmaker, 8, 14 & 15 Wittam's buildings, Old st. road
Dawson John, cheesemonger, 5 Church st. Camberwell
Dawson John, coach joiner, 6 Castle st. Long acre
Dawson John, grocer, 27 & 28 North st. Poplar
Dawson John, hair dresser, Camberwell green
Dawson John, lighterman, Mill wall, Poplar
Dawson John, printer, 86 Theobald's road
Dawson John, *Rose* P.H. 51 Bridge road, Lambeth
Dawson John, shipowner & west india mercht. 9 Billiter sq
Dawson John, teadealer, 89 Church st. Shoreditch
Dawson John Wm. James, attorney, 7 Bloomsbury st. St. Giles's
Dawson Jonathan, academy, 36 Hunter st. Brunswick sq
Dawson Joseph, boarding school, High st. Bow
Dawson Nathaniel, woollen factor, 3 Basinghall st
Dawson Richard, *Red Lion* P.H. 51 Shoe lane Fleet st
Dawson Rd. M.D. consulting surgeon, 15 Finsbury circus
Dawson Richard, surgeon, see Mason & Dawson
Dawson Robert, carpenter, 109 Great Titchfield st.
Dawson Sarah (Mrs.), strawhat ma. 11 Chapel st. Holywell mt
Dawson Thomas, bookbinder, 27 New North st. Red Lion sq
Dawson Thos. carriage lamp ma. 32 Gt. St. Andrew st. 7 Dials
Dawson Thomas, chemist & drug. 7 Bride ter. Liverpool rd
Dawson Thomas, grocer, 5 Brompton place, Hackney road
Dawson Thomas, oil & italn. war. 1 Up. Barnsbury st. Islingtn
Dawson Thomas, teadealer & grocer, 41 High st. Marylebone
Dawson Vesey Thomas, barrister, 11 New sq. Lincoln's inn
Dawson Wm. fruiterer, 5 Rodney buildings, New Kent rd
Dawson Wm. ham & beef shop, 24 Pitfield st. Hoxton
Dawson Wm. laceman, 4 Staverton row, Walworth road
Dawson Wm. ladies' shoemaker, 6 Burlington arcade
Dawson Wm. *Old Jerusalem* P.H. 1 St. John's sq. Clerkenwell
Dawson Wm. *Rising Sun* P.H. 12 Charles st. Grosvenor sq
Dawson Wm. surgeon, 51 Lamb's conduit st
Dawson Wm. Isaac, cigar merchant, 12 Lime st
Dax Thomas, master of Ex. of Pleas, 8 Old sq. Lincoln's inn
Day & Haghe, lithographers to the Queen & to the Queen Dowager, 17 Gate st. Lincoln's inn fields

Day, Hughes & Browne, solicitors, 19 Margaret st. Cavendish sq
Day Jno. Christian, Alf. & Josh. surgeons, 6½ Palace row, New rd
Day John, Son & Watson, importer of wines & spirits, 2 & 3 Water lane, Tower st
Day & Martin, blacking manufacturers, 97 High Holborn
Day & Payne, millers, Malin's whf. Lwr. Fore st. Lambeth
Day Benj. & Co. oil & italian warehouse, 95 Gracechurch st
Day Richard & Martha (Miss), linendra. 171 Bethnal gr. rd
Day Wm. & Co. dealers in diamonds & gems, 1 Bulstrode st
Day Alfred, auctionr. & appraiser, 17 Smith's bldgs. City rd
Day Ann (Mrs.), crape dresser & printer, 17 Goswell st
Day Arch. bootmaker, 4 Green Dragon court, St. Saviour's
Day Charles, confectioner, 52½ Church st. Shoreditch
Day Charles, customhouse & shipg. agent, 60 Lowr. Thames st. & Trinity chambers, 5 Water lane, Tower st
Day Charles, poulterer, 18 Blackmoor st. Drury lane
Day Charles, surgeon, 5 Pleasant row, Holloway road
Day Charlotte (Mrs.), court millr. & dressma. 320 Regent st
Day David John, bricklayer, 66 New Compton st. Soho
Day Ebenezer, jun. estate agt. & surveyor, 29 Edgware rd
Day Ebenezer, sen. plumber & glazier, 29 Edgware road
Day Edward, coal merchant, John st. Cambridge heath
Day Edward, linendraper & coal mer. 20 Mare st. Hackney
Day Edward, linendraper, 2 Robart's ter. Commercl. rd. east
Day Edward, working goldsmith, 3 Lovell's ct. Paternoster rw
Day Edwin, tailor, 1 College st. Chelsea
Day Elizh. (Mrs.), clog & patten ma. 9 Union st. Kingsl. rd
Day Francis John, grocer, 114 Curtain road, Shoreditch
Day George, fruiterer, &c. 40 Margaret st. Wilmington sq
Day George, laceman, 11 Middle row, High Holborn
Day George, physician, 3 Lower Southwark st
Day George, *White Bear* P.H. 24 King st. St. Luke's
Day George Thomas, engineer, &c. patent ventilating works, Commercial road, Pimlico
Day Harvey, beer retailer, 25 Belvedere road, Lambeth
Day Henrietta (Miss), fancy reposty. 11 Crosby rw. Wlwth. rd
Day Henry Callis, surgeon, 5 Cornbury place, Old Kent rd
Day Isaac, carman, Camperdown house, Snow's flds. Brmndsey
Day Isaac, carman, 19 Eastcheap
Day James, bricklayer, 13 Lt. Chesterfield st. Marylebone
Day James, commission agent, 51 Aldersgate st
Day James, dairyman, 1½ Hampden st. Somers town
Day James, dyer & scourer, 10 St. James' pl. Bermondsey rd
Day James, engineer, 12 Whitfield st. Leonard st. Finsbury
Day James, fruit salesman, Spitalfields market
Day James, grocer & cheesmngr. 17 Gt. Mitchell st. St. Luke's
Day James, tailor & draper, 15 Lt. Alie st. Goodman's fields
Day Jane (Mrs.), copperplate printer, see Shaw & Day
Day John, boot & shoe maker, 17 Commercial road, Lambeth
Day John, butcher, 13 Newport court, Newport market
Day John, calenderer & packer, see Johnson & Day
Day John, coal mercht. Horseshoe whf. 10 Upper Thames st
Day John, coffee rooms, 33 Union st. Bishopsgate
Day John, haberdasher, 14 Stepney High st
Day John, hairdresser, 51 Gt. Portland st. Oxford st
Day John, jewellers' cabinet trayma. 46 St. John st. road
Day John, leather seller, 6 West place, Islington green
Day John, potato salesman, 28 & 29 Crispin st. Spitalfields, & Beal's wharf, Mill lane, 53 Tooley st. Borough
Day John, tailor, 10 Princes st. Rotherhithe
Day John Nash, attorney, 17 Bridge st. Southwark
Day Joseph, modeller & chaser, 53 Dean st. Soho
Day Lewis, surgeon, 9 Salisbury square, Fleet st
Day Mary Ann (Miss), librarian & news agent, 17 Goswell st
Day Matilda (Miss), school, 1 Norfolk pl. East st. Wlwth. rd
Day Peter, cotton broker & agent, 7 Commercial sale rooms
Day Philip, cornchandler, 27 Long lane, Bermondsey
Day Richard, jun. artist, 42 Commercial road, Lambeth
Day Richard, butcher, 28 Old Gravel lane, Wapping
Day Richard, grocer & cheesemnr. 38 Shouldham st. Edgwr. rd
Day Richard, modeller, 10 New Church st. Lisson grove
Day Robert, mechanicl. chimney sweep, 21 Newton st. Holborn
Day Robert, tailor, 37 Up. Rathbone pl. Tottenham ct. rd
Day Sarah (Mrs.), grocer, 25 Bride st. Liverpool road
Day Stephen, chandler's shop, 98 Old Gravel la. Wapping
Day Thomas, carpenter & undert. 31 Halfmoon st. Bishopsgate
Day Thomas, cheesemonger, 11 John st. Cambridge heath
Day Thomas, coal merchant, Rutland pl. whf. Up. Thames st. & 36 Frederick st. Gray's inn road
Day Thomas, fruiterer, 6 Fore st. Cripplegate
Day Thomas, grocer, 369 Rotherhithe st
Day Thomas, plumber, 44 Weymouth terrace, Hackney rd
Day Thomas Clark, woollenwarehomn. see Willott, Scott & Day
Day Thomas Fisher, artist, 26 Francis st. Newington butts
Day William, attorney, 1 Queen st. May fair
Day William, baker, Kensington gravel pits
Day William, baker, 22 Princes st. Westminster
Day William, barrister, 55 Lincoln's inn fields
Day Wm. bookbinders' tool cutter & engrav. 90½ Holborn hill
Day William, charcoal dealer, 29 Crown st. Soho
Day W. cook & confectioner, 20 Southampton row, Russell sq
Day William, leatherseller, 98 Gt. Titchfield st. Oxford st
Day William, *Sun & Falcon* P.H. 7 Down st. Piccadilly
Day William, tailor, 17 Liverpool st. Bishopsgate
Day William, tobacconist, 304 Oxford st.
Day William, trunk & camp equipage maker, 353 & 378 Strand
Day Wm. work. jeweller, 3 Regent pl. Horseferry rd. Westmr
Day Wm. Charles, cheesemonger, 42 Henry st. east, Avenue rd
Daybell George, tailor, 15 Devonshire st. Queen square
Dayes Charles, boot & shoe ma. 17 Lit. St. Andrew st. 7 dials
Daykin William, cheesemonger, Clare market
Dayman Chas. Orchard, barrister, 10 South sq. Gray's inn
Daymont Robt. James, tobacconist, 49 Bermondsey st
Days George Lewis, tailor, 18 Bowling green la. Clerkenwl
Dayson Thomas, compositionornament, looking glass, picture frame manf. carver & gilder, 18 Phœnix st. Soho
Deacock Thos. pianoforte mak. 4 Buckingham pl. Fitzroy sq
Deacon & Archer, carriers, White horse inn, Cripplegate
Deacon Dan. & Son, carriers, White horse inn, Cripplegate buildings, & 136 London wall
Deacon James & Sons, linen & cotton factors, sail cloth & bagging agents, 30 Gresham st. Blackwell hall, & Market st. Manchester
Deacon, Mack & Co. carriers, Whitehorse inn, Cripplegt. bdgs
Deacon Amos, carpenter, 6 Talbot court, Eastcheap
Deacon Chas. auctioneer & estate agt. 2 Berners st. Oxford st
Deacon George, timber merchant, Bond st. Vauxhall
Deacon Henry, accountant, 70 Basing place, Waterloo road
Deacon Henry, H. proctor, Doctors' commons
Deacon Jas. *Geo. & Dragon* P.H. 13 Buckingham pl. Fitzroy sq
Deacon James, lamp ma. & furn. ironmonger, 4 Moorgate st
Deacon James, pewterer, 87 St. John st. Clerkenwell
Deacon Jas. *Rose & Crown* P.H. 7 Ann's ter. Cambridge heath
Deacon John, builder, 20 Lambeth square
Deacon John, butcher, 8 Church st. Camberwell
Deacon John, marshal of Admiralty Ct. 2 Paul's Bakehou. ct
Deacon John Charles, watchmaker, 18 Gt. Guildford st. Boro'
Deacon Jsph. watch jeweller, 43 Sekforde st. Clerkenwell
Deacon Richard, bottle merchant, Gt. Scotland yard
Deacon Samuel, coffeehouse keeper, & london & country advertisement agent, 3 Walbrook
Deacon Thomas, fishmonger, 4 Lower st. Islington
Deacon Thomas, shell fishmonger, 49 Hedge row, Islington
Deacon William, baker, 4 Parker's row, Dockhead
Deacon William, bricklayer, 6 Lit. St. James's st. St. James's
Deadman George, wheelwright, 6 Lit. Vine st. Waterloo rd
Deadman James, *Admiral Carter* P.H. 3 Bartholomew close
Deaf & Dumb Asylum (Thomas James Watson, governor), Gloucester place, Old Kent road
Deakin Charles, cheesemonger, 5 Northampton row, Holwy
Deakin Henry, *Baptist Head* P.H. 50 Bermondsey st
Deakin Henry, *Lord Arran's Arms* P.H. 122 New Bond st
Deakin John, tallowchandler, 12 Little St. Andrew's st. 7 dials
Deakin William, *Sun* P.H. 12 Clare st. Clare market
Deakins James & Co. cocoa & chocolate manfrs. Steam mills, Flower & Dean st. Brick lane, Whitechapel
Deakins James, wine merchant, 76 Goswell road
Deal Pier Co. (Henry Jackson, sol.), 15 St. Helen's place
Deal James, *Mail Coach* P.H. 1 Camomile st. Bishopsgate
Deal Mark, *Swan* P.H. Upsdell's row, Kingsland road
De Allex Thomas, physician, 7 Nottingham terrace, New rd
Dean & Hatton, meat, poultry & butter salesman, 21 Newgate st
Dean John & Son, cheesemongers, 32 Gt. Tower st. City
Dean John & Sons, pianoforte makers, 19 Wilmot st. Russell sq
Dean & Law, engravers, printers, & wholesale lithographers, 26 Nicholas lane, City
Dean, Leeks & Dixon, solicitors, 13 St. Swithin's lane
Dean & Page, merchants, 3 Cross lane, St. Mary at hill
Dean & Winkley, jewellers & watchmakers, 169 Boro' High st
Dean Thomas & Charles, surgeons, 435 Oxford st
Dean Thomas & Co. lithographers, stationers & publishers, 35, 36 & 40 Threadneedle st
Dean William & Son, attorneys, 16 Essex st. Strand
Dean & Chapter of St. Paul's Registry, 5 Deans' court, Doctors' commons; hours ½ p. 9 to 5
Dean & Chapter of Westminster Registry, 19 Bennet's hill; hours of business ½ past 9 to 5
Dean Alfred, china & glass dlr. 12 Southampton st. Cmbrwl
Dean Andrew, *White Lion* P.H. 44 Liverpool st. Bishopsgate
Dean Arthur, civil engineer, 2 Broad Sanctuary, Westminstr
Dean Charles Rich. *Duchess of York* P.H. Battersea fields
Dean Charles Richard, *Prince's Head* P.H. Battersea

Dean Edwd. tailors' measure ma.30Frederick pl.Nwngtn.bts
Dean Edwin, porkman, 37 Gravel lane, Borough
Dean Edwin, *Two Ships* P.H.27 Old Compton st. Soho
Dean Elizabeth (Mrs.), baker, Grove st. Deptford
Dean Elizabeth (Mrs.), coffee rooms, 28 Hampstead road
Dean Emily (Mrs.),governess agent,10 Red Lion sq.Holborn
Dean Geo. grocer, 1Rothefield st. north, Lower rd. Islington
Dean Geo. Henry, stationer, 8 Cornbury pl. Old Kent road
Dean Henry, baker, 2Compton st. Brunswick square
Dean Henry, cheesemonger, 91 Fore st. Cripplegate
Dean Henry, hatter, 2 Mill st. Hanover square
Dean Henry, teadealer, 9 Haberdashers' walk, Hoxton
Dean James, corndealer, 5 Compton st. Burton crescent
Dean James, grocer, 68 Cornwall road, Stamford st
Dean Jeremiah, *Prince of Wales* P.H. 6 Exeter st. Knightsb
Dean John, baker, 61 Friar st. Blackfriars road
Dean John, carman, 19 Wilmot st. Russell square
Dean John, dairyman, 57Wynyatt st. Goswell st
Dean John, foreign money exchanger, see Selim, Dean & Co
Dean John, milliner, 22 Sidney place, Commercial rd. east
Dean John, plasterer, 12 Carlisle st. Lambeth
Dean John, surgeon, 32 Lucas st. Commercial road
Dean John Colpitt, barrister, 36 Chancery lane
Dean John Robt. grocer & teadlr. 52 Chapel st. Somers town
Dean John Wm. lighterman, 32 Trinity sq. Tower hill
Dean Joseph, corn & flour factor, 13 Worship st. Finsbury
Dean Joseph, tailor, 1 Leicester sq. & 48 Frith st. Soho
Dean Mary Ann (Mrs.), dining rooms, 57 Farringdon st
Dean Richard, builder, &c. 66 Basing place, Waterloo road
Dean Richard John, *George* P.H.22Mount row, Liverpool rd
Dean Richard Ryder, barrister, 2 New square, Lincoln's inn
Dean Samuel, broker & appraiser, 24Seymour pl.Bryanst.sq
Dean Samuel, russia merchant, 23 Abchurch lane
Dean Thos. *Coach & Horses* P.H. High st. Stoke Newington
Dean Thomas, *Goat* P.H. 25 Chenies st. Bedford square
Dean William, attorney, 109 Guilford st. Russell square
Dean William, baker, 46 Lower Trinity st. Rotherhithe
Dean William, corndealer, 11 Freeschool st. Horselydown
Dean William, grocer, Little Chelsea
Dean William, stationer, 11 York st. Westminster
Dean William, wireworker, 15 High st. St. Giles's
Dean Wm. Cockell, grocer,7 Wellington ter.Knsgtn.gra.pits
Dean Wm. Henry, auctioneer & survey. Stratford broadway
Dean William Henry, grocer, 91 Fleet st
Deane, Dray & Deane, stove, range & fireproof box & iron fence & hurdle makers, 86 Chiswell st. & 119 Bunhill row
Deane George & John, who. & ret. hardwaremen, ironmongers, cutlers, jewellers & lamp manufacturers, & agents for Windle's steel pens, at the opening to the Monument, 46 King William st. London bridge
Deane Geo. & John, ironmon. 3 Arthur st. West, London br
Deane George & John, London bridge gun manufactory, 30 King William st. City
Deane Geo. & John, saddlers, &c. 2 Arthur st. East, London br
Deane&Medland,druggists' sundries ma.1 Sidney st.Mile end
Deane Ann (Mrs.), court lace clnr. 2 Upp.James st.Golden sq
Deane Charles, artist, 8 Blandford pl. Dorset square
Deane Charles, lead office, 9 Martin's lane, Cannon st
Deane Charles, solicitor, 61 Lincoln's inn fields
Deane Dennis Wood, artist, 4 York place, City road
Deane Edward, grocer, 4 & 5 Shoreditch
Deane Esau, cheesemonger, 8 Lambeth walk
Deane Frances (Mrs.), grocer, 3 East india road, Poplar
Deane Fredk. soda water mfr.2Lit.Portland st.Gt.Portland st
Deane James, pilot, 5 Gt. Hermitage st. Wapping
Deane Jas.P.D.C.E.advocate,3Col.Drs.com.&6Porchester ter
Deane Joseph, grocer, 11 Eden pl. Old Kent road
Deane Stephen, silk mercer, &c. 65 Bishopsgate within
Deane Thomas, dairyman, 50 Green st. Grosvenor sq
Deane William Wood, architect, 4 York pl. City road
Deanery of Bocking Office, 10 Gt. Knightrider st. Drs.com
Deans, Dunlop & Hope, parlim. & scotch agts. 19 Fludyer st
Deans Thos. parliamentary agt. 23 Fludyer st. Westminster
Dear Edward & Son, bricklayers, 4 Charles st. Hatton grdn
Dear Ann (Mrs.), *Red Lion* P.H. 5 Fleet la. Farringdon st
Dear Arthur, sec. school of design, 37 Crispin st. Spitalfields
Dear Edmund, jeweller, 5 Woodbridge st. Clerkenwell
Dear Edwd. grocer & teadealer, 52 Red Lion st. High Holborn
Dear George, tan dealer, 25 Elizabeth pl. Bermondsey road
Dear James, potato mer. 3 Manor pl.south, King's rd. Chelsea
Dear John, baker, 19 Ropemakers' fields, Three Colt st
Dear Joseph, baker, 23 Three Colt st. Limehouse
Dear Margaret(Mrs.), lodging ho.keeper, 25Arundel st.Strnd
Dear Richard Edward, ink, sealing wax & wafer manufacturer, 20 & 21 Bishopsgate without
Dear Sarah (Mrs.), butcher, 23 Fetter lane, Fleet st
Dear Thomas, baker, 23 Bow st. Covent garden
Dear William, fly proprietor, 18 Bathurst mews, Sussex sq
Dear William, upholder, see Rogers & Dear
Dear Wm. upholsterer & undertaker, 103 John st. Fitzroy sq
Dearberg George, tailor, 13 Theberton st. Islington
Dearden James, trimming seller, 60 Myddelton st. Clerknwl
Dearden William, tobacco pipe ma. 51 Bell st. Edgware rd
Dearen Francis Thos. comp. ornament ma. 54 Greek st. Soho
Dearie Chas. east india mer. 13 Old Jewry chmbrs. Old Jewry
Dearing John, furn. undertaker, 35 Anchor st. Shoreditch
Dearing Thomas B. stationer & watch maker, 109 Goswell st
Dearle William, sculptor & mason, 15 Portland rd. Regt's. pk
Dearlove Edwin, timber bro. 5 Barge yd. chambers, Bcklsbr
Dearman John, tobacconist, 5 Belvedere road, Lambeth
Dearon Thos. Francis, comp. ornament ma. 54 Greek st. Soho
Dears James, furniture broker, 20 David st. Marylebone
Dearsley Henry, fishfactor, 96 Lower Thames st
Dearsly Henry Richard, barrister, 3 Plowden bldgs. Temple
Deason James, architect, 31 Keppel st. Russell sq
Dearth Hen. *Montague Arms* P.H. Montague mews, Russl.sq
Dearth James, looking glass & picture frame ma. 23 Up. St. Martin's lane, & 33 Tavistock st. Covent garden
Dearth Joseph, greengrocer, 23 Lower Ranelagh st. Pimlico
Deason Wm. *RoyalStandard* coff.ho.78Church la.Whitechpl
Death Arthur, baker, 72 Great Cambridge st. Hackney rd
Death Blucher, engraver & printer, 32 St. Martin's le grand
Death Francis, baker, 3½ Nile st. Hoxton
Death Francis, butcher, Bow common
Death Jeremiah, baker, 12 James's place, Hoxton
Death Mich. pastrycook, 4 Westmoreland bldgs. Aldersgate
Death Rt. workg. silversmith, 27 Wellington st. Goswell st
Death Samuel, beer retailer, 4 Albert place, City road
Death Thomas Edwd. haberdasher, 1 Bishopsgate without
Death William, builder, 64 Kennington st. Walworth
Death William, *Crown* P.H. 9 Sheffield st. Lincoln's inn fi
Deavill Eliza (Mrs.), *King's Arms* P.H. 29 Whitechapel rd
Debarfald Myers, cap manufactr. see Emanuel & Debarfald
Debaufer Catherine (Mrs.) & Son, brass founders, gas fitters in general, & lamp manufacturers, 10&11Creed la. Ludgate st
Debeger Charles, furniture broker, 12 St. Ann's court, Soho
Debegér Chas. Andrew, furniture broker, &c. 34 Wardour st
Debenham & Lanham, silk mercers, &c.26Edward's st.Prtm.sq
Debenham, Pooley & Smith, haberdashers, 44 Wigmore st
Debenham & Storr, auctioneers, 26 King st. Covent garden
Debenham George, carpenter & underta.25King st.Camdn. tn
Debenham George, solicitor, see Thompson & Debenham
Debenham Robert, linendraper, 2 Queen's road, Dalston
Debenham Samuel, *Golden Hart* P.H. 23 Lamb st.Spitalflds
Debenham Thomas, pawnbroker, 1 Queen's row, Pimlico
Debenham William, grocer, 39 King st. Camden town
De Bergue Charles, merchant, 9 Arthur st. west, City
De Bernardy Constantine William, foreign & general agent, 21 Cork st. Burlington gardens
De Beyer Alexander & Co. tailors, &c. 5 Burlington gardens
Debnam George, straw hat ma. 25 Broadley ter. Blandford sq
Debnam Henry, cowkeeper, 44 Hercules buildings, Lambeth
Debnam Jno. wine mercht. & cooper, 3& 6 Talbot ct. Gracech.st
Debnam Joseph, jun. straw bonnet ma, 29Rosoman st.Clknwl
Debnam Joseph, sen. straw bonnet manftr. 71 Theobald's rd
Debnam Mark, tuscan & straw hat ma.22 Old Comptn st.Soho
Debnam William, straw hat maker, 48 Hackney road
Debney Gerrard, plumber, 4 Red Lion st. Whitechapel
De Boo William, watchmaker, 46 Princess st. Lisson grove
Deboos Edward, skein silk dyer, 7 Elder st. Norton folgate
Deboos George, registrar, 24 Wood st. Spitalfields
De Buck Wynand John, merchant, 18 Broad st. buildings
De Caligny Edw. merchant, 4 George st.Trinity sq.Towerhill
De Casteras Sinibaldi (Madame), milliner, 10 Portman sq.
Decastro & Peach, teadealers & grocers, 65 & 66 Piccadilly
Decastro, Watson&Palmer, chemists, 25St.Geo.'s pl.Kngtsbr
De Charms William Mead, merchant, 106 Fenchurch st
De Costa Andrade & Co. importers & manufrs. of ostrich feathers, artificial flowers, &c. 9 Gresham st
Decosta Amelia (Miss), embroiderer, 3 Broad ct. Long acre
De Courcey Wm. appraiser, 106 Wardour st
De Custer John, tailor, 53 Newman st. Oxford st
Deddman Jsph. cheesemr. & poultr. 7 Harper st. New Kent rd
Dedman Ann (Mrs.), confectioner, 96 Waterloo road
De Douay John & Co. milliners, 22 Burlington arcade
Dee & Fargues, who. work. jewellers, 8 Sherrard st. Golden sq
Dee James, carpenter, 23 Shaftesbury terrace, Pimlico
Dee Richard, *Angel & Crown* P.H. 36 Warwick st. Regt. st
Deed James, leatherseller, 24 Stanhope st. Clare market
Deed John Simpkin, currier, leather dress. wool rug, bookbdrs.' cloth, canvas, mill bd. ma. &c. 9&10Lit.Newport.st. Lng. acre
Deedes John, barrister, 1 Essex court, Temple

Deedy John, house agent, 40 Great Dover st. Borough
Deeker Thomas, upholsterer, 49 Berwick st. Oxford st
Deeks Charles, cheesemonger, 5 Brompton road
Deeks George, auctioneer, 8 Porchester place, Edgware rd
Deeks Geo. auctioneer, 93 Grand Junction ter. Edgware rd
Deeks Wm. hairdresser, &c. 49 Hertford st. Mayfair
Deeks Wm.oil&clrmn.&builder,3Regent pl.Globe rd.Mile end
Deeks Wm. jun. news agent & statnr.49 Hertford st. Mayfair
Deeley Geo. & Co. engineers, &c. Buckley st. Whitechapel
Deeley Isabella (Mrs.), milliner, 9 Princes st. Fitzroy sq
Deeley Wm.plane mkr.12 Mortimer market,Tottenham ct.rd
Deen James & Co. tailors, 23 Saville row, Piccadilly
Deer Edward, butcher, 41 Banner st. St. Luke's
Deer Joseph, wheelwright, 20 Upper Bryanstone st
Deer Reuben, butcher, 27 Chapel st. Somers town
Deering Henry, fruiterer, 17 Seabright pl. west, Hackney rd
Deering John, poultry salesman, Leadenhall market
Deering Napoleon, law stationer, see Riches & Deering
Deering Susan (Mrs.), staymaker, 64 Bunhill row
DeeringJamesWilliam,butcher,1Hallpl.LowerKennington la
De Ferre J. J. E. silk merchant, 6 Great Winchester st
Deffee Daniel, fishmonger, 6 Lower Thames st
Deffee John, *Ship* P.H. 24 Wheeler st. Spitalfields
Deffee Michael, house agent, &c. 254 Bethnal green road
Deffell John Henry & Co. merchants, 3 Billiter ct.Billiter sq
Deffell John & Son, merchants, 3 Billiter court, Billiter sq
Deffell Henry, colonial broker, 14 Mincing lane
De Fontaine Louis,clock & watchma.18 Wilsted st.Somers tn
De Fontaine Moreau, patent office, 1 Skinner's place, Sise la
Defraies Stephen, coal dlr. 3 Bedfordbury, Covent garden
Defries Nathan, patent dry gas meter manf.67St.Martin's la
Defries Jonas, sole inventor of the solar paragon & vesta oxydator lamp cotton & glass manufacturer; also plain & cut flint glass of every description, 147 Houndsditch
Defriez Joseph, funl.featherman, 10 Nicholl sq.Aldersgate st
Defriez Josh. Geo. surgeon, 20 Belgrave ter.Queen's rd.Dlstn
Degerdon Ludwig, baker, 5 Little Earl st. Seven dials
De Gex John Peter, barrister, 5 New square, Lincoln's inn
De Grave, Short & Fanner (late M. De Grave & Son), scale ma. to her Majesty's exchequer, Royalmint, Gen. Post office & the Assay office, Goldsmiths' hall, 59St. Martin's legrand
De Gruchy Matthew, milliner, 20 Red cross sq. Cripplegate
De Hague & Holmes, stockbrokers, 1 Angel ct.Throgmrtn.st
De Horne Abraham, stockbroker, 2 Royal ex.bds.&Stock ex
Deighton Mary Ann(Miss),milliner,&c.10Bridge st.Lambeth
Deighton William, staymk. 9½ Orange row, Kennington rd
Deighton Wm. tailor & draper, 23 St. James's st. Pall mall
Deighton William, woollen warehouse, 46 Aldermanbury
Deighton Wm. James, surgeon, 33 George st. Blackfriars rd
Deinhard & Jordan, of Coblentz(agency), 13 Little Tower st
De Jersey Henry, solicitor, see Fisher & De Jersey
De Karcheski Xiavier, parisian stationer, 70 Mortimer st
De Keyser Constant, *Royal hotel*, 26 New Bridge st. Blkfrs
De Knock Edward, bookbinder, 37 Spring st. Paddington
De la Chaumette L. J. stock bro. 12 Angel ct. Throgmorton st
Delacour John F. french bonnet shape mfr. 31 Greek st Soho
De la Court Mary Ann (Mrs.), established 1835, dealer in fancy needlework, knitting & netting, with every article for the work table, & maker of fancy trimmings, 8 Clark's place, High st. Islington
De la Crouée & Co. merchants, 70 Lower Thames st
De la Fontaine Jn. coach plat. see Higgins & De la Fontaine
Delaforce & Davis, for. wine & spirit imp. 7 Westmoreland st
DelaforceEdwd.Jas.*Neptune*P.H. 8 Neptune st.Rotherhithe
Delaforce James, grocer, 31 Newland st. Kensington
Delafosse Frs. J. teabro. see Ewart, Maccaughey & Delafosse
Delafosse John Robert, teadealer, see Palmer, Delafosse &Co
Delagarde Gustavus, fancy goods imp. 17 Lowther arcade
DelahayJamesThomas, *RunningHorse* P.H. 128 Piccadilly
DelahuntThomas, haircutter, 13 Bedford pl. Comrl. rd. East
De Laistre Wm. Henry, tailor, 32 Goodge st.Tottenham ct.rd
De la Mare Brothers, silk manufs. 14 Duke st. Bishopsgate
De Lamare John, cooper, 13 Fair st. Horselydown
Delamotte Freeman G. wood engraver, 127 Chancery lane
De la Motte Jemima(Madame),milliner,45 Skinner st.Snwhll
Delane Wm. Fredk. Aug. barrister, 4 Chatham pl. Blackfrs
De Laney Hughes Paul, printer, 17 White st. Borough
Delaney John, wine & spirit merchant, 70 Mark lane
De Lannoy & Nash, manchesterwa.14Friday st.&90Watling st
Delano William, tailor, &c. 23 South Audley st
Delany Edward, physician, 98 Chalton st. Somers town
Delany Joseph, pawnbroker, Broadway, Church st.Rotherhi
Delany Michel, tailor, 26 Princes st. Drury lane
Delaporte Charles, hatter, 175 Church st. Shoreditch
Delaporte Michel P. foreign book & printseller, 116 Regent st
De la RueThos.&Co.cardma.&who.stationers,110Bunhillrow

De la Salle Jas.Thos.chronmtr.watch&clock ma.18Cannon st
Delatouchi Wm. chemist & druggist, 147 Oxford st
Delay James, furrier & fur skin dealer, 226 Kent st. Borough
De Lay John (Mrs.), milliner, 12 Chichester pl. Gray's inn rd
Delbos Ainé Louis, wine merchant (E. S. Polkinghorne & Co. agents), 12 Clement's lane, Lombard st
Delcour Henry, auctioneer & appraiser, 5 Frith st. Soho
Delcroix J. & Co. wholes. & retail perfumers, 158 NewBond st
Delcroix & Son, wholesale & retail perfumers, 66 Conduit st
Delegoute Fredk. lodging house, 13 Panton square, Haymkt
Delf John, hosier & laceman, 166 Drury lane
Delf Thomas, bookseller, 16 Little Britain
Delferier William, teacher of dancing, 40 Sloane square
Deligny Wm. manftg. jeweller, 10 Glos'ter st. St. John st. rd
Delille Charles Jean, professor of french, 32 Ely pl. Holborn
De Lisle, Janvrin & DeLisle, merchts. & bankers, 16 Devons. sq
Dell Jas.&Co.ink & blacking ma.27 A, Adam st.ea.Portman sq
Dell John, grocer, &c. 20 Berkley st. Clerkenwell
Dell Joseph, tobacconist, 150 Leadenhall st
Dell Samuel, bootmaker, 2 Church st. Stoke Newington
Dell Thomas, *Black Bull* P.H. High st. Stoke Newington
Dell William, shoemaker, 1 Prospect place, Old Brompton
Dell Wm. *Thatched House tavern*, Lower road Islington
Dellamore James, dyer, 2 William st. Whitechapel
Dellarocca Michael, plumber & painter, 53 Lambeth walk
DellaroccaWm.plumber&painter,29Geo.st.Princesrd.Lmbth
Della Torré Joseph & Co. merchants, 70 Lamb'sConduit st. & looking glass manufactrs. carvers & gilders, 9 Lamb's Conduit st
Deller Simeon, egg merchant, 133 Houndsditch
Dellewen James, *Royal Oak* P.H. 14 Abbey st. Bethnal gr.rd
Delley Joseph, coffee rooms, 3 Duke st. Lincoln's inn fields
Delley Thomas, coffee rooms, 56 Watling st
Dellow Ann (Mrs.), basket maker, 6 Star st. Shadwell
DellowRichard, basket maker, 13Garlickhill&Milkyd.Shadw
Delmar & Wynne, solicitors, 46 Lincoln's inn fields
Delmar Baldock, attorney, 10 New inn, Wych st. Strand
Delmar Charles, woollen draper, 9 Leicester st. Leicester sq
Del Mar Emanuel, pro. of languages, 18Savage gard.Tow.hill
Delmonte Eliza (Mrs.), tobacconist, 8 King st. Tower hill
Deloitte William Welch, accountant, 11 Basinghall st
Delolme Henry, watch & chronometer maker, 48 Rathbone pl
D'Elor Ann (Mrs.), military cap ma. 30Warwick st.Regent st
Delotz Geo. G. grainer, 35 Hastings st. Burton crescent
Delow George, coffee rooms, 3 Camomile st. Bishopsgate
Delowery Cornelius, beer shop, 87 Gt. Suffolk st. Borough
Delve George, confectioner, Mare st. Hackney
Delveau James, harpmaker, 210 Regent st
Delves Samuel, goldsmith & jeweller, 6 John st. Oxford st
Delves Thomas, baker, 26 New road, St. George's east
De Mattos & De Leon, merchants, 5 Copthall court
DeMattosWm.N.coal mercht.Child's Belvidere wf. Lambeth
De Medina H. Augustus, solicitor, 10 Argyle sq. King's cross
Demeur John, merchant, 9 Water lane, Tower st
De Morgan George, barrister, 30 Lincoln's inn fields
DempseyJohn, sen. paper stainer, 27Hunter st.Brunswick sq
Dempsey Geo. Drysdale, surveyor, 101Gt.Russell st.Blmsby
DempseyJohn, jun. paper stainer, 27 Hunter st.Brunswick sq
Dempsey Joseph, *Fountain* P.H. Stracey st. Stepney
Dempsey Joseph, smith & manufacturer of sugar refiners' iron moulds, 5 Abel's buildings, Goodman's fields
DempseyWm.Joseph, tailor, 2 Devonshire pl.Comml. rd.east
Dempster Henry, pawnbroker, 222 Blackfriars road, & 100 Union st. Borough
Denbigh John, hearth rug manufr. 15 Duncan ter. City rd
Denby Thomas, solicitor, see Oliverson, Denby & Lavie
Dence Robt. & Co. who. tea dlrs. 3 Brabant ct. Philpott la
Dence John, *Hermit* P.H. 34 Bedford sq.east, Commercialrd
DenchCharlesJohn, upholsterer, 65Seymour pl.Bryanstone sq
Dench Daniel, coffee rooms, 79 Gray's inn lane
Dench Henry, upholsterer, 58 Seymour pl. Bryanstone sq
Dench William, butcher, Church st. Deptford
Dench Wm. iron broker & dealer, 13 Church la.Whitechapel
Dench Wm. tailor, 27 New Millman st. Foundling
Dencher Anne (Miss), fancy repository, 26 South Audley st
Dendy & Morphett, solicitors, 3 Bream's bldgs. Chancery la
Dendy Walter Cooper, surgeon, 10 Tillotson pl.Waterloo rd
Denegri Francis, picture frame maker, 37 Gt. Saffron hill
Dènereaz Noel, commission merchant, 70 Lower Thames st
DeneulainDominique, *Hotel de Provence*, 17&18Leicester sq
Dengate Emma (Mrs.), grocer, &c. 27 Ferry rd.west, Poplar
Dengate William, druggist, 154 Waterloo road
Denham, Clark & Smith, ship & ins. agents, 35 Pudding la
Denham Edward Benjamin, smith, furnishing & general ironmonger, 16 & 17 Bull & Mouth st. & Blue Coat bldgs
Denham Elijah, tobacconist, 7 Park st. Borough market

Denham Emma (Miss), printer & stationer, 189 Regent st
Denham James, grocer, 24 Flagon row, Deptford
Denham John Chas. sec. to *Globe Ins. Co.* Pall mall & Cornh
Denham Mary (Mrs.), tailor, 100 Bermondsey st
Denham Robert, beer retailer, 78 Chapel st. Pentonville
Denington George, cabinet maker, 5 Sarah pl. Old st. rd
Denington Wm. coffee rooms, 10 Mortimer st. Cavendish sq
Denison, Heywood, Kennards & Co. bankers, 4 Lombard st
Denison Edmund Beckett, barrister, 10 New sq. Lincoln's inn
Denison Jane (Miss), haberdasher, 9 Margaret ter. Pdngton. gr
Denison Stephen Chas. barrister, 4 Harcourt bldgs. Temple
Denithorne Wm. wheelwright, 16 Macclesfield st. north
Denman Geo. L. surveyor & estate agt. 4 Curzon st. Mayfair
Denman Hannah (Mrs.), milliner, 27 Marchmont st. Brunsw. sq
Denman James, baker, 7 North st. Finsbury market
Denman James, harness ma. 27 South wharf. rd. Paddington
Denman John, fruiterer, 210 Blackfriars road
Denman John, fruiterer, 27 Marchmont st. Burton crescent
Denman John, grocer, 106 High st. Camden town
Denman John, shoemaker, 39 Banner st. St. Luke's
Denman Margt. (Mrs.), coffee ho. & beer retailr. 73 leather la
Denman hon. Richard, barrister, 3 Paper buildings, Temple
Denman Samuel, baker, 6 King st. Clothfair, W. Smithfield
Denman Thos. butcher, 39 Shaftesbury st. New North rd
Denman Thos. *Coopers' Arms* P.H. 3 Crown st. Finsbury
Denman Thomas, sculptor, 83 Quadrant, Regent st. & 7 Buckingham st. Fitzroy square
Dennant Elizabeth (Mrs.), milliner, 351 Oxford st
Dennant William, baker, 8 Albion road, Stoke Newington
Denne & Jellicoe, proctors, 2 Gt. Knightrider st. Drs. Coms
Denne Henry, baker, 5 Ebenezer pl. Commercl. rd. Limehou
Dennes & Wood, shirt & stock manfrs. 69 Wood st. Cheapside
Dennett Edward, law stationer, 9 Hemlock court, Carey st
Dennett James, printer, 121 Fleet st. & 48 Cumming st
Dennett Rt. Dean, coffee rooms, 8 Up. North pl. Gray's inn rd
Dennett Wm. builder, &c. 4 Wenlock road, City road
Dennett Wm. Alex. law stationer, 8 Serle's pl. Linc. inn
Denney Geo. clock case & cabt. mk. 4 Wellington st. Goswell st
Denney Samuel, brushmaker, 27 Holles st. Clare market
Denney Wm. Thos. fishmonger, 7 Newland ter. Kensington
Denning Henry, grocer & cheesemonger, 56 Marylebone la
Denning Isaac, goldsmith, 1 Tichborne st. Haymarket
Dennis Brothers & Co. tin & tinplate agents, 2 Whitehart court, Lombard st
Dennis & Price, builders & brick ma. Caledonian rd. Pentvile
Dennis Susan & Elizb. (Misses), fancy repository, 7 Lowther ar
Dennis Wm. & Co. florists, near World's end, King's rd. west
Dennis Charles, grindery dealer, 10 George ct. 32 Piccadilly
Dennis Chas. size & neatsfoot oil manfr. White's gr. Bermsy
Dennis Charles, woolstapler, White's grounds, Bermondsey, & 13 Grange road, Bermondsey
Dennis Edward, grocer, 16 College st. Chelsea
Dennis George, solicitor, 5 Great Vine st. Regent st
Dennis George, cowkeeper, 3½ Cleveland st. Fitzroy square
Dennis George, dairyman, 73 Devonshire st. Lisson grove
Dennis Henry, toy & stationery wa. 102 Albany st. Regent's pk
Dennis John, copper pl. printer, 11 Low. Smith st. Clerknwel
Dennis John, glasscutter, 19 Mount pleasant, Gray's inn lane
Dennis John, grindery warehouse, 17 Vere st. Clare market
Dennis John, *Rose & Crown* P.H. Turk's row, Chelsea
Dennis John, sheep & calf salesman, 59 West Smithfield
Dennis John Charles, astronomical, philosophical & optical instrument maker; inventor & only maker of the lunar sextant, calotype cameras, &c. 118 Bishopsgate st. within
Dennis John S. cattle salesman, 8 West Smithfield
Dennis Richard, cheesemonger, 141 Shoreditch
Dennis Richard, coffee rooms, 91 High Holborn
Dennis Thomas, bricklayer, 18 Paul st. Finsbury
Dennis Thomas, carpenter, 11 Brewer st. Pimlico
Dennis Wm. grindery wa. 17 Little Pulteney st. Wardour st
Dennis William, grocer & wine mer. Church st. Hackney
Dennish Wm. cooper & turner, 3 Fieldgate st. Whitechapel rd
Dennison Andrew, *Unicorn* P.H. 37 Henrietta st. Covent gdn
Dennison Ann (Mrs.), hairdresser, 42 Banner st. St. Luke's
Dennison Robert, butcher, 9 Chapel st. Somers town
Dennison Robt. sub-steward, steward's office, 9 Gray's inn sq
Denniss John & Son, linendrapers & hosiers, 68 Tooley st
Denny, Clark & Co. merchts. & east india agts. 21 Austinfriars
Denny Charles, corndealer, 26 Lower Marsh, Lambeth
Denny Charles, cornchandler, 100 Gt. Peter st. Westminster
Denny James, furnish. undertaker, 188 Brick la. Spitalfields
Denny John, alamode house, 124 Whitechapel High st
Denny John, surgeon, &c. 1 London rd. Southwark
Denny Thomas, corndealer, 16 Up. Ground st. Blackfriars
Denny Thomas A. merchant, 15 Fish st. hill
Denny Wm. french corset maker, 1 Broomfield pl. Deptford
Denny Warner, tobacconist, 2 Old st. road
Dennys & Burt, wine merchants, 14 Savage gdns. Tower hill
Denoon Alexander & Co. merchants, 6 Adam's ct. Old Broad st
Denston George, baker, 6 Tabernacle sq. Finsbury
Denston Michael, carpenter & builder, 1 East st. Old Kent rd
Denston Michael, carpenter, Bedford rw. East st. Walworth rd
Dent John & Wm. & Co. who. glovers, 97 Wood st. Cheapside
Dent Richd. & Son, house & land sur. 38 High st. Camden town
Dent Thos. & Son, watch glass ma. 50 Northampton st. Clknwl
Dent Edward J. chronometer, watch & clock maker to the Queen, & H. I. M. the Emperor of Russia, 82 Strand, 33 Cockspur st. Charing cross, & 34 Royal Exchange
Dent Geo. grocer & teadealer, 55 Blackman st. Borough
Dent John, *Printers' Arms* P.H. 23 New Church st. Strand
Dent John, silkmercer, 30, 31 & 32 Crawford st. Portman sq
Dent John, upholsterer & cabinet maker, 99 Crawford st
Dent John, upholsterer, 17 Spring st. Portman square
Dent Joseph, beer retailer, 21 Britannia st. City road
Dent Marmaduke, cheesemonger, 2 Marlboro' pl. Kenningt. crs
Dent Mary (Mrs.), butcher, 6 Blackmoor st. Clare market
Dent Peter, cheesemonger, 57 London road, Southwark
Dent Thomas, brassfounder & gasfitter, 27 Curtain road
Dent Thomas, merchant, see Palmer, Mackillop, Dent & Co
Dent Wm. butcher, 35 Poland st. Oxford st
Dent Wm. chandlers' shop, 4 Crosier st. Lambeth
Dent Wm. dyer, 26 Everett st. Brunswick square
Dent Wm. grocer, 18 Buckingham st. Fitzroy square
Dent Wm. grocer, &c. 80 Tooley st
Dent Wm. merchant, 11, King's Arms yard, Moorgate st
Dent Wm. plumber & lead merchant, see Burton & Dent
Dent Wm. tobacconist, 30 Spencer st. Goswell road
Dent Wm. wine & brandy mer. see Urwick, Son & Dent
Denton & Jutsum, oilm. & pat. grease ma. Bromley New town
Denton & Serjeant, lightermen & stone merchants, Quebec wharf, Rotherhithe
Denton Benj. waggon off. White Swan yd. 20 Whitechape High st
Denton Edward Yates, *Old Dundee Arms* P.H. 51 Wapping
Denton Henry, solicitor, see Kinderley, Denton & Kinderley
Denton Hughes Ridgway, barrister, 3 Garden ct. Temple
Denton James, bottle merchant, 9 Allhallows la. Up. Thamesst
Denton James, shipwright, &c. 183 Tooley st
Denton John, barrister, 3 Garden court, Temple
Denton John, *Rising Sun* P.H. 130 Princes road, Lambeth
Denton John Bailey, land & ho. surv. & agt. 9 Gray's inn sq
Denton Robert, coffee roaster, 10 Moor lane, Cripplegate
Denton Robert, fruiterer, 66, St. Mary Axe
Denton Robert, paperstainer, 89 Leadenhall st
Denton Samuel, attorney, 15 Gray's inn square
Denton Wm. oilman, 6 Brunswick place, Old Kent road
Denyer Barnard, gunmaker, 11 Seymour pl. Camden town
Denyer John, dyer, 16 White Hart pl. Lower Kennington la
Denyer Joseph M. *Crown & Anchor* P.H. 1 Finsbury pavemnt
Denyer Thomas, woollen dra. 34 King William st. London br
De Pass Danl. & Son, who. & export boot ma. curriers' leather factors & imp. of foreign leather, 20 Finsbury pl. north
Depecke John, teadealer, 104 Fenchurch st
De Pinna Abrão, notary & conveyancer, foreign & English & official translator to her Majesty's high court of admiralty of England, & judicial committee of her most honourable privy council for appeals from the vice admiralty & prize courts abroad, 3 Bartholomew lane, Royal Exchange
Depinna David, boot & shoe maker, 142 Shoreditch High st
Depledge Rachael (Mrs.), *Coach & Horses* P.H. 34 Grsvnr. mws
Depmore Albert, butcher, 11 Back Church la. St. George's ea
Depôt Wharf, J. Hen. & Geo. Scovell, betw. 32 & 42 Tooley st
De Porquet Fenwick, printer & publisher, & english & foreign school agent, 11 Tavistock st. Covent garden
De Prati Joachim, physician, 4 Mortimer st. Cavendish sq. & 23 Cloudesley sq
Depree Charles Templer, solicitor, 8 Lawrence lane, City
Deptford Benevolent Institution for Educating Youths (Absolom Davies, master), Deptford green
Deptford Grn. Coal & Coke Co. (Ths. G. Edgley, man.), Dptfd. gn
Deptford Gas Wks. (Ths. Vince Barnard, mgr.), Creek st. Dptfd
Deptford, Rotherhithe & Bermondsey Gas Company (Jas. Fortune, sec.), 19 Bishopsgate st. within
Derbishire John, surgeon, 3 Grafton st. Fitzroy square
Derby & Raven, solicitors, 2 Harcout buildings, Temple
Derby James, plumber, 65 Whitehorse st. Stepney
Derby Joseph, tobacconist, 120 Poplar High st
Derby William, artist, 12 Osnaburgh st. Regent's park
Derbyshire, Staffordshire & Worcestershire Junction Railway Co. (R. Shelton Mackenzie, D.C.L. sec.), 1 Moorgate
Dereier Chas. Jas umbrella ma. 41 Fleet la. Farringdon st
Derick James Rd. bottle dealer, 16A, Shepherd's ct. May fair

Derick John Macduff, architect, 12 Buckingham st. Strand
Derisley William, hosier, &c. 68 Bishopsgate within
Dermody Leonard, coffee rooms, 1 Tyler's ct. Golden sq
Dermott Christopher, surgeon, 29 Shaftesbury crescent, Vauxhall bridge road
Dermott George D. surgeon, 16 Bloomsbury st. St. Giles's
Dernen Fredk. & Co. french good imprtrs. 47 Bow la. Chpsde
Deroussiere George, dyer, 13 Duke st. Chelsea
Derrett Ann (Mrs.), painter, 46 Molyneux st. John st. west
Derrick & Birdseye, ale, stout&cider mers. 21 Swallow st. Pic
Derry Chas. mathemat. inst. ma. 7 Leigh st. Burton crescent
Derry Rd. *Duke of Wellington* P.H. 1 Elizabeth pl. Ball's pond
Derwent Bank, Hobart Town, 2 Alderman's walk
Derwent Mines Company, 9 Austinfriars, Old Broad st
Desanges Fras. G.M. skein silk dyer, 32 Chicksand st. Brick la
Desanges Louis William, artist, 34 Soho square
De Sausmarez James, barrister, Figtree court, Temple
Desbois Daniel, watch & clock maker, 9 Gray's inn passage
Desborough & Young, solicitors, 6 Sise lane, Bucklersbury
Desborough Henry, sec. to *Atlas Assur. Co.* 92 Cheapside
Deschamps Nicholas, bootmaker, 29 Burlington arcade
Descou Carina (Miss), milliner, &c. 11 Bruton st. Bond st
Desforges Jas. baker, 11 Jamaica st. Commercial rd. Stepney
Desnoy Edward, blind maker, 3 James st. Oxford st
Desormeaux William, butcher, 8 Park place, Mile end road
Desormeux James, porkman, 10 Bedford pl. Coml. road East
De Souza Madame, milliner, 4 Grafton street, Fitzroy sq
Dessoulavy & Williams, imps. of forgn. waters, 4 Albemarle st
Destitute Sailors' Asylum (William Partridge, superintendent), Well st. Wellclose sq
Dessurne Louis M. wine mer. 14 Cooper's row, Crutched frs
Dessurne Mark Bernard A. artist, 14 Cooper's row, Tower hill
De Sussex Stanislas Francis Meldon, mnf. chemist, 6 Rood la. Fenchurch st.; & works, Glengall whf. Millwall, Poplar
Desvignes Elisé Hubert, diamond merchant, 2 Golden sq
Desvignes Hubert, picture restorer, 34 Foley st. Portland pl
Dethridge Geo. brassfound. & gasfit. 4 Strutton grnd. Westmr
Detkins Eugene, bookselr. & statnr. 20 Brook st. Grsvnr. sq
Detmold & Richmond, merchants, 46 Lime st. City
Dettmer Wm. pianoforte maker, 60 Warren st. Fitzroy sq
Deurlacher Henry, jun. picture dealer, 131 Regent st
Devas (Wm. & Thos.) Minchener & Routledge, calico printers & warehousemen, 24 Lawrence lane, Cheapside
Devaux Charles & Co. merchants, 62 King William st. City
De Vear Thomas & Son, curriers, 44 Lisle st. Leicester sq
Deven Henry, fur skin dyer, 12 Anchor yard, St. Luke's
Devenish Rd. Hy. coff. refining powd. ma. 1 Union bdgs. Leathr. la
Devenport Charles, basket ma. 44 Red Lion st. Spitalfields
Dever Robt. cook, confectioner & venison dealer, 60 Cornhill
De Vere Paul & Co. vegetable & spice essence manufacturers, George Raphael, proprietor, Richmond road, Dalston, & 22 Abchurch lane, City
Deverell Elizabeth & Mary Ann (Misses), milliners 216 Oxford st
Deverell Wm. & Thos. linendrs. 197 Oxford st. & 1 Orchard st
Deverell Jane (Mrs.), straw plait dealer, 165 Union st. Boro'
Deverell John, linendraper, 143 Oxford st
Deverell John, solicitor, 5 Gray's inn square
Deverell Robert, manchester agent, 1 Star court, Bread st
Deverell Waller Ruding, sec. of School of Design, Somrst. ho
Devereux Lee, plumber & glazier, 99 St. John st. Smithfield
Devereux Stephen W. baker, 113 Union st. Borough
Devereux Thomas, baker, 97 Shoreditch
Devereux Thomas, french polisher, 10 Eldon st. Finsbury
Devernegoul Chas. New River Co. turncock, 2 Tichborne ct
Devey Mrs. Ellen & Miss, ladies' school, 3 Beaufort pl. Chels
Devey William & Son, brass founders, lead merchants, pump, closet & cock manufacturers, 8 & 9 Shoe lane, Fleet st
Devey Fredk. Nicholas, attorney, 34 Ely place, Holborn
Devey Wm. wine & spirit mer. 1 Savage gardens, Tower hill
Deville James, lamp manufacturer, bronzist, gasfitter, oil gas apparatus, & lighthouse lanthern & reflector maker, & dealer in lamp oils, 367 Strand
Devilliers Ann M. (Mrs.), school, 65 Westmoreland pl. City rd
De Vils Louis, tchr. of french, &c. 12 Brnswk. par. Barnsby. rd
Devin Adolphus, jeweller, 3 Frith st. Soho
Devine Dennis, shoemaker, 7 Essex pl. Mare st. Hackney
Devine Ellen (Mrs.), farrier, 12 Thornhaugh mews, Sussex st
de Vitery Joseph, merchant, 33 Gt. Winchester st. O. Brd. st
Devitt & Moore, ship & insurance bro. & gen. agts. 9 Billiter st
Devitt Joseph, confectioner, 130 Blackfriars road
Devitt Mary (Mrs.), marine store dlr. 79 Broadwall, Blkfrs
De Vos Auguste, merchant, see Walther & De Vos
Devnall John, dairyman, 4 Derby st. Mayfair
Devoll William, fruiterer, 1 Great Distaff lane, Friday st
Devon Chas. translator of records, 36 Queen sq. Bloomsbury
Devonald Erasmus L. surgeon 71 Gt. Titchfield st. Oxford st
Devonshire, the Great Consolidated Copper Mining Co 16 & 17 Barge yard chambers, Bucklersbury
Devonshire Catherine (Mrs.), grocer, 10 Water st. Blackfriars
Devoy George A. stockbroker, 39 Lothbury
Devy Eliza (Madame), milliner & court dressmaker, 73 Grosvenor st
Devy Mouchi, importer of foreign silks, &c. 73 Grosvenor st
Dew William Stephen & James Bernard, outfitters, hosiers, glovers, flannel drapers & cotton manufrs. 146 Cheapside
Dew John Hen. auctioneer, 20 King William st. West Strand
Dew Sarah (Mrs.), straw bonnet ma. 7 Gower pl. Euston sq
Dew Wm. coal merchant, 11 New Manor pl. King's rd. Chels
Dew Wm. undertaker, 20 Charterhouse lane, St. John st
Dewar & Culliford, insur. broks. 16 New City chambs. & Lloyd's
Dewar David, Son & Co. manufrs. of table linen, covers, &c. Dunfermline; warehouse, 6 King's Arms bldgs. Wood st
Dewar Alexander, fruiterer, 21 High st. Marylebone
Dewar Alexander, scots timber mercht. see Nicholl & Dewar
Dewar Hunter, gold cutter, 9 Coburg st. Clerkenwell
Dewar John, stationer & bookseller, 8 Roadside, Mile end rd
Dewdney George, perfumer, 172 Fenchurch st
Dewdney Saml. *Old Cheshire Cheese* P.H. 23 Addle st. Wood st
Dewell Wm. A. watch gilder & springer, 13 Cowper st. City rd
Dewer Ebenezer & Robert, smiths & ironfounders, 16 Old st. St. Luke's, & 2 Bevis marks
Dewey Edward, for. & brit. lace wareh. see Clarke & Dewey
Dewey George, lace manufacturer, see Smith & Dewey
Dewey John, linendraper, see Christian, Adams & Dewey
Dewey John, tailor, 52A, Mortimer st. Cavendish square
Dewick Mary & Son, printers & stationers, 46 Barbican
Dewick Edward, stationer, see Herring, Dewick & Hardy
De Wilde F. Augustus, ironmonger, brass founder & window blind manufacturer, 72 & 73 Wells st. Oxford st
Dewin Joseph, watchcase mak. 17 Red Lion st. Clerkenwell
Dewing John, undertaker, 3 New row, Deptford
Dewing Thomas, bootmaker, 14 Back st. Horselydown
Dewint Peter, artist, 40 Upper Gower st. Bedford square
De Winton Walter, engineering surveyor, 15 Abingdon st
Dewis Edw. fringe trmng. &c. ma. 146 Church st. Shoreditch
Dewsbury & Bushnell, livery stables, 2 Brick st. Park lane
Dewsbury Christopher, livery stables, 2 Duke st. St. James'
Dewsbury George, tailor, 36 Tabernacle walk, Finsbury
Dewsbury Margaret (Mrs.), grocer, 15 Crown ct. Pall mall
Dewsnap Frances (Mrs.), cutler, 315 Oxford st
Dewsnap Wm. table blade & cork knife manufacturer, metal & edge tool grinder & polisher, 8 Castle st. Saffron hill
Dewson John, dairyman, 20 Little Alie st. Goodman's fields
Dewy Susannah (Mrs.), milliner, 28 Church st. Camberwell
Dexter Chas. Wm. glover & gaiter ma. 15 Duke st. Smithfield
Dexter Elizh. (Mrs.), cowkeeper, 15 Kinnerton st. Belgrave sq
Dexter Francis, sack, tilt, & ropemanfr. 20 Roadside, Mileend rd
Dexter George, painter, 49 Oakley st. Mount st. Lambeth
Dexter James, chemist & druggist, 2 Queen's row, Pimlico
Dexter John, butcher, 11 Hatton wall, Hatton garden
Dexter John Creed, pawnbroker, &c. 125 Whitechapel road
Dexter Thos. pawnbroker, &c. 1 & 2 Union st. East, Spitalfields
Dexter Wm. *Black Horse* P.H. George yd. Whitechpl. High st
Dexton Michael, bootma. 2 Cumberlaad st. west, Regt.'s pk
Dey Ann (Mrs.), grocer, 5 Vine st. Romney st. Westminster
Dey Robert, baker, 35 Broad st. Bloomsbury
D'Eyncourt Louis Chas. Tennyson, barrister, 11 Paper bldgs.
Dezoete Samuel & Son, stockbrokers, 80 Old Broad st. City
Dhobah Company (R. Gardner, secretary), 46 Lime st
Diamond Hugh Welch, F.S.A. surgeon, 22 Frith st. Soho
Diamond Wm. Batchelor, surgeon, 17 Weston st. Somers tn
Diaper William, iron chest, door & bookcase maker, 29 Worship st. Norton folgate
Dias David, merchant, 54 Gt. Prescot st. Goodman's fields
Dias John, butcher, 11 Duke st. Aldgate
Dias Nathaniel, earthenware dealer, 173 Bethnal green rd
Dibb Wm. patten & cricket bat maker & dealer in all kinds of patten materials, 83 Friar st. Blackfriars road
Dibben & Henville, woollen drapers, 83 St. John st. road
Dibben George, grocer, see Hill & Dibben
Dibben George, tobacconist, 6 Park side, Knightsbridge
Dibbin Fras. Wm. engineer & surveyor 22 Chster. pl. Kenningtn. la
Dibbin Henry Edward, innholder, agent & wine merchant, Gerard's hall, 3 Basing lane
Dibdin Thomas Colman, artist, 23 Charlotte st. Fitzroy sq
Dibon James, oil & italian warehouse, 125 Drury lane
Dibsdall Charles, cheesemonger, &c. 20 Lit. Marylebone st
Dice Stamp Office, Somerset house; hours, 10 to 4
Dicey Geo. Augustus & Son, printers, 1 Dyer's bldgs. Holborn
Dick, Möller & May, ship & ins. agts. 3 Muscovy ct. Towr. hl
Dick Walter & Peter & Co. shawl warehmn. 13 Gt. Distaff la
Dick Adam, baker, 43 Tufton st. Westminster

Dick Charles George, barrister, 2 Cloisters, Temple
Dick Henry, jeweller, 43 Kenton st. Brunswick sq. & 3 Survey place, Camberwell New road
Dick John, pianoforte manufactr, 64 Newman st. Oxford st
Dick John, printer, see Luntley & Dick
Dick John, wig maker, 11 King st. Cheapside
Dick Joseph, boot & shoe maker, 3 Skinner st. Snowhill
Dick Matthew, *Blue Post tavern*, 59 Haymarket
Dick Robert, baker, 23 Southampton st. Pentonville
DickensChas. & Hen. brass founders, 7 Middle st. Cloth fair
Dickens John Thomas, grocer, 89 Kingsland road
Dickens Richard, carpenter, 50 New st. Vauxhall st. Lambeth
Dickens Thomas, agt. to the sun fire & life offi. 100 Chalton st. Somers town
Dickens Wm. stationer, 20 Cumberland row, Walworth rd
Dickens Wm. upholsterer, &c. 23 Norton st. Fitzroy sq
Dickenson, Lowes & Robert, artists, 114 New Bond st
Dickenson Ed. *Crown & Anchor* P.H. 72 Parson's st. St.Geo.st
Dickenson Geo. Grosvenor brewery, 14 George st. Grosvenor sq
Dickenson John, *Earl of Romney* P.H. Deptford green
Dickenson William, butcher, 5 Dover pl. Old Kent road
Dickenson Wm Thomas, tailor, 33 Mansion house st. Kennigtn
Dicker & Clark, envelope makers, embossers & fancy stationers, 2 Crane court, Fleet st
Dicker Martha (Mrs.) & Son, pawnbrokers, 1 & 2 Commercial terrace, Limehouse
Dicker John, butcher, 147 Kingsland road
Dicker Walter, cattle salesman, 59 West Smithfield
Dicker William, pawnbroker, 82 & 83 Lambeth Lower marsh
Dickerson John, farrier, &c. 25 Wilson st. Finsbury
Dickes Wm. designer & engraver, 48 Salisbury sq. Fleet st
Dickeson John, hat manufact. 4 Webber st. Blackfriars rd
Dicketts Caroline (Mrs.), dairywoman, 2 Gt. Ryder st. St. James
Dicketts Thomas, tailor, 2 Great Ryder st. St. James's
Dickie Chas. house agent, 5 Palatine pl. Stoke Newngtn. rd
Dickin Geo. & Co. wine & west india merchts. 29 Queen st. City
Dickins Frederick Owen & Co. coal merchants & ship owners, Jamaica wharf, 13 Upper Ground st. Blackfriars bridge
Dickins, Smith & Stevens, linendrapers, 232 Regent st
Dickins Giles, *White Hart* P.H. 199 Tottenham court road
Dickins John, *Britannia* P.H. 28 Nelson st. Long la. Bermndsy
Dickins Richard, chemist & druggist, 80 Holborn hill
Dickins Thos. bricklayer, 11 Northumberland st. Marylebone
Dickins Wm. lodginghouse keeper, 2 Norfolk st. Strand
Dickins Wm. Richard, paperhanger, 36 Leonard st. Finsbury
Dickinson George & Co. oil & italian wa. 88 Long la. Smithfield
Dickinson John & Co. wholesale stationers, 65 Old Bailey
Dickinson John & Geo. builders, 1 Waterloo pl. Commrcl. rd. ea
Dickinson Benj. wine importer, see Brown & Dickinson
Dickinson Edw. John, lithographer, 1 Crown ct. Old Broad st
Dickinson Geo. *London Stone* P.H. 82 Cannon st. City
Dickinson Geo. vet. surgeon, 5 Portman mews So. Portman sq
Dickinson Geo. Murray, surgeon, 183 Tottenham court road
Dickinson James, barrister, 24 Old square, Lincoln's inn
Dickinson John, tailor, 18 Munster square, Regent's park
Dickinson John Robt. solicitor, 33 Sidmouth st. Gray's inn rd
Dickinson Joseph, print & bookseller, 114 New Bond st
Dickinson Robert, tailor, 55 Poland st. Oxford st
Dickinson Wm. boot & shoe maker, 83 Bethnal green road
Dickinson Wm. chemist, 16 Cambridge st. Edgware road
Dickinson Wm. furnishing ironmonger, 8 Beak st. Regent st
Dickinson Wm. job master, 7 Curzon st. May fair
Dickinson Wm. surgeon, 37 Sloane st. Knightsbridge
Dickison Benjamin, spanish merch. see Vergara & Dickison
Dickman David, surgeon, 14 Porchester pl. Edgware road
Dickman John, pork butcher, 43 Ernest st. Regent's park
DicksJosephWhatley, chandlers' shop, 19 Tarling st. St. Geo's.e
Dicks Thomas, bootmaker, 5 King st. Covent garden
Dicks Thomas, hairdresser, 49 Brick lane, St. Luke's
Dicksee Robert John, portrait painter, 53 Old Compton st
Dicksee Thomas Francis, artist, 23 Howland st. Fitzroy sq
Dickson & Bell, surveyors & land agents, 30 Bucklersbury
Dickson, Brothers & Co. merchants, 62 Moorgate st
Dickson George Fred. & Co. merchants, 1 Winchester bldgs
Dickson & Overbury, attorneys, 4 Frederick's pl. Old Jewry
Dickson Peter & Co. merchants, 9 Liverpool st. Bishopsgate
Dickson Robert & Co. farriers, 8 Bulstrode mews, Marylebn
Dickson Adam, scotch bread & biscuit baker, 167 Strand
Dickson Commander (secretary to *Royal Naval Benevolent Society*), 18 Adam st. Adelphi
Dickson Edward, barrister, 24 Old square, Lincoln's inn
Dickson Geo. *Worcester Arms* P.H. 42 George st. Portmn. sq
Dickson George Fred. consul general for Buenos Ayres, 1 Winchester buildings, Great Winchester st
Dickson John, builder, Earl st. Horseferry road
Dickson Robert, physician, 5 Curzon st. Mayfair
Dickson Robt. veterin. surgeon, 26 Brook mews, Berkeley sq
Dickson Samuel, physician, 28 Bolton st. Piccadilly
Dickson Thomas, carver & gilder, 13 London st. Fitzroy sq
Dickson Wm. merchant, see Henderson, Dickson & Co
Dickson Wm. Hy. furniture dealer, 4 Crown st. Walworth rd
Didot F. & Co. french publishers, 8 Amen corner, Paternost. row
Didsbury Gilbert, bootmaker, 34 Poultry
Diether Jane (Miss), prof. of music, 28 Everett st. Brnswk. sq
Dietman Henry, baker, 21 Bath place, New road
Dietrichsen & Hannay, chemists & pat. medicine dl. 63 Oxford st
Dietrichsen's patent double action garden machine, fire engine, & ship's pump manufactory, 63 Oxford st
Dietrichsen Lionel, e. & w. india mer. 2 Wells st. Oxford st
D'Iffanger Thos. academy, 50 Portman pl. Edgware road
Digance Daniel & Co. hatters, 18 East side Royal Exchange
Digby Arthur, solicitor, 29 Coleman st. City
Digby Benj. Joseph, original bun. ho. 40 Grosvenor rw. Pmlco
Digby Edward, surgeon & chemist, 205 Fleet st
Digby Henry, hairdresser, 2 Charlotte row, Walworth road
Digby James, grocer, High st. Battersea
Digby John Marriott, grocer, 20 Cable st. Wellclose sq
Diggins Ann (Mrs.), toy warehouse, 37 Gibson st. Waterloo rd
Diggles George, attorney, 4 Great College st. Westminster
Diggs Edwin, carver, &c. 190 Wellington ter. Waterloo rd
Dighton Isaac, artist, 40 Torrington square
Dighton Thomas, artist & modeller, 2 Lower Grosvenor place
Dighton William, goldsmith, see Latham & Dighton
Dighton William Edward, artist, 40 Torrington square
Dignam James, warehouseman, see Westron & Dignam
Dignam Thomas, brace & belt maker, 25 New st. Covent gdn
Dignam Thomas, solicitor, see Richardson & Dignam
Dignum Charles, tailor & army clothier, 1 Cecil st. Strand
Dijon & Mulhouse Railway, 7 Tokenhouse yard
Dike George, *William IV.* P.H. Commercial rd. Pimlico
Dike James, stone & marble merchant, 44 Holywell st. Millbk
Dike William, boot & shoemaker, 2 Commercial rd. Pimlico
Dike Wm. Henry, leatherseller, 51 Lower George st. Chelsea
Dill Christian, baker to the Queen, 366 Oxford st
Dillamore & Rowley, corkcutters, 27 Castle st. Leicester sq
Diller David & John, desk & dress case ma. 5 Chandos st. Cov. grn
Diller Fredk. writing desk ma. 8 Lit. Russell st. Bloomsby
Diller George, *King's Head* P.H. 1 Stockbridge ter. Pimlico
Diller Thomas, silversmith, 1 Richmond buildings, Soho
Dilley Joseph, straw hat ma. 26 High st. Newington butts
Dilley Daniel, tailor, 1 Sermon la. Little Knightrider st
Dillimore Charles, livery stables, Crescent mews, Minories
Dillman Fred. coffee rooms, 2 Earl's court, Leicester square
Dillon George & Charles, printers, 77 Hatton garden
Dillon Chas. White, artists' colorman, see Rowney, Dillon & Co
Dillon John, warehouseman, see Morrison, Dillon & Co
Dillon Rebecca (Mrs.), coal dealer, 13 Upper Cleveland st
Dillon Sarah (Mrs.), bootmaker, 80 Drury lane
Dilnutt Wm. boot & shoemaker, 5 Bartlett's passage, Holborn
Dimbleby & Haddon, cattle salesman, 60 West Smithfield
Dimes Fredk. artists' colorman, 91 Gt. Russell st. Bloomsbury
Dimes Thomas, attorney, 26 Bread st. Cheapside
Dimes William, solicitor, 46 Lincoln's inn fields
Dimmack, Thompson & Firmstone, iron & tin plate merchants, St. Peter's chambers, Cornhill
Dimmett Robt. carpenter, &c. 10 Barking church yd. Trinity sq
Dimmock & Burbey, solicitors, 4 Skinner's place, Sise lane
Dimmock John, grocer, Albion terrace, Canonbury square
Dimmock John, porkbutcher, 7 Wyndham road, Camberwell
Dimock, Smith & Co. linendrapers, 123 High Holborn
Dimond Charles, jun. cheesemonger, 41 Carnaby st. Golden sq
Dimond Charles, sen. cheesemonger, 2 Chenies st. Bedford sq
Dimond Charles John, solicitor, see Simpson & Dimond
Dimond James, hairdresser, 1 Burlington gardens
Dimond Mary (Mrs.), baker, 21 Fetter lane, Fleet st
Dimond Samuel, fishmonger, 10 Seymour place, Camden twn
Dimsdale John, banker, see Barnard, Dimsdale & Co
Dimsdale Jsph. Cockfield, banker, see Barnard, Dimsdale & Co
Dimsdale Josiah, glass enameller, &c. 3 West place, City rd
Dinde Antoine, bootmaker, 156 Regent st
Dines George, *Coopers' Arms* P.H. 46 Lower Thames st
Dingle George, hairdresser & perfumer, 97 Tooley st
Dingle John, bootmaker, 18 Nassau st. Middlesex hospital
Dingle John King, surgeon, 31 Upper Eaton st. Pimlico
Dingley Thos. haberdasher, 2 Strutton ground, Westminster
Dingwall, Portal & Co. wine merchants, 2 Idol la. Tower st
Dingwall John, attorney, 8 Tokenhouse yard
Dinham Edmund, oilman & tallow chand. 226 Tottenham ct. rd
Dinham John, *Duke's Head* P.H. 56 Museum st. Bloomsbury
Dinmore Thomas William, stationer, &c. 3 City road, Old st
Dinmore Wm. stationer & accnt. book mak. 78 O. Broad st. City
Dinn Burgess, grocer, 2 Brunswick st. Cromes st

Dinn Thomas, corn chandler, 153 Brick lane, Spitalfields
Dinneford Charles, chemist, 172 New Bond st
Dinnis James, bookseller & publisher, 62 Paternoster row
DinscombeRobt. *Reindeer* P.H. 34 Richard st. Coml. rd. east
Dinsdale Geo. & Son, saddlers&harn.maks.17Finsby.pavmnt
Dinsdale Andrew, yarn merch. 5 Frederick's pl. Old Jewry
Dinsdale Henry, medical agent, 4 Middle row, Holborn
Dinsdale John, fire wood dealer, Lower road, Rotherhithe
Dinsdale William, tobacconist, 45 Old st. St. Luke's
Diorama, 18 Park square, Regent's park
Diplock Caleb, *Albion tavern*, 8 Duke st. Grosvenor sq
DiplockJohn,tea dlr. 10 Crosby row, & 2 Union pl.Walworth
Dippie Adam, cigar manuftr. 4 Lit. College st. Westminster
Dipple Edwin, publisher & printsel. 42 Holywell st. Strand
Dipple Richard, tobbacconist, 138 Brick lane, Spitalfields
Dipple Thos. John, prof. of music, 33 Theberton st. Islington
Diprose John, bookseller & binder, 312 Strand
Dipstale Charles, carpenter, 55 Baalzephon st. Bermondsey
DipstaleSarah(Mrs.),toolwa. 55 Baalzephon st. Bermondsey
Dircks & Co. furnace architects & engineers, office for the pat.argand furnaces of C. Wye Williams, 7 Nicholas lane
Dircks Henry, general agent for patent inventions, 7 Nicholas lane, City
Direct West End & Croydon Railway Co. (John Lucas Cotton, sec.), 34 Gracechurch st. City
*Direct London& Dublin Rail.Co.*4 Charlotte rw.Mansion ho
Direct London & Manchester Rail.(Edwd. L.Ogle,sec.), 64 Moorgate st
Direct Northern Railway to York, 64 Moorgate st
Direct Sheffield & Macclesfield Railway (George Fredk. Hire, sec.), Swan with two necks, Gresham st
Direct Tours & Honfleur Rail. Co. 4 Mansion ho. pl. City
Discombe John, turner, 4 Skinner st. Bishopsgate
Discombe Wm. bootmaker, 3 Lit.Torrington st.Torrington sq
Dismore Danl. *King's Arms* P.H. 11 Smart's buildgs. Hlbrn
Dismore Thos. & Son, mftg. jewellers, 11 Clerkenwell green
Dison Hen. lace manufacturer to her Majesty, 237 Regent st
Dispensary for Diseases of the Lungs, 92 Newman st
Dispensary for Ringworm &Skin Dis. 2 Princes st.Lestr.sq
Dissenters' & General Life & Fire Assurance Co.(Dr.Thos. Price, sec.), 62 King William st. City ; see page 2020
Dissenters' (or Dr. Williams's) Library (Richard Cogan, librarian), 49 Red Cross st. Cripplegate
District VisitingSoc.(John Wood,sec.),19 Exeter ha.Strand
Dit Wm. surgeon, 17 Beresford ter. Kennington st.Walworth
Ditcham John, chandler's shop, 17 Sidney st. Goswell road
Ditchburn & Mare, iron ship builders, Orchard pl.Blackwall
Ditchburn Thomas, solicitor, 17 Old Broad st. City
Ditchburn Wm. tobacco pipe maker, 15 Edward st. Stepney
Ditchfield James, physician, 4 Gordon st. Gordon square
Ditchman John, house agent,&c. 1 Thurlow pl. Hackney rd
Ditchner Wm. furniture broker, see Berryman & Ditchner
Ditton Benjamin, grocer, South Lambeth new road
Diver Thomas, hairdresser, &c. 6 Penton st. Pentonville
Divers John, sugar broker, 1 Cullum st. & Commercl. cof. ho
Dives Thos. miller, Bolingbroke house, Mill wharf, Battersea
Divett, Alexander, academy, 10 Whitehead's grove, Chelsea
Divine James, dairyman, 27 Bowling st. Westminster
Dix & Bristow, linendrapers, 2 High st. Pentonville
Dix Benjamin, builder, 125 Long lane, Bermondsey
Dix David Edmund, lodging ho. 19 Up. Belgrave pl. Pimlico
Dix George, bootmaker, 79 Turnmill st. Clerkenwell
Dix George, corndealer, 27 Redcross st. Borough
Dix Harry, warehouseman & shipping agent, 3 Basinghall st
Dix James, engraver & printer, 6 Dorrington st. Leather la
Dix James Chas. engraver on gold, silver, stone, ivory, &c. & printer in general, 1 St. Ann's la. St. Martin's le grand
Dix John, baker, 39 Union st. Whitechapel road
Dix John, sen. indigo blue maker, 3 Aylesbury st.Clerkenwl
Dix John, jun. undertaker, 3 Aylesbury st. Clerkenwell
Dix John Aveling, manchester com. agt.49 Bow la.Cheapside
Dix Richard, solicitor, 10 Symond's inn, Chancery lane
Dix Wm. shipping butcher, 13 Ebenezer place, Limehouse
Dixey John, grocer & cheesemonger, 16 Brick st. Park lane
Dixey Charles Waslett, optician, mathematical & philosophical instrument maker to her Majesty & the Royal Family, 3 New Bond st.
Dixey William, optician, 241 Oxford st
DixieGeo.& Mark, *OneTun* P.H.127Gt.Saffronhill,Hattonwl
Dixie Thomas, blacksmith, 2½ Boundary st. Shoreditch
Dixie William, glasscutter, 18 Coppice row, Clerkenwell
Dixon Basil & Thos. cattle salesmen, 8 West Smithfield
Dixon, Brooks & Dixon, bankers, 25 Chancery lane
Dixon & Elmer, meat salesmen, 9 New Newgate market
Dixon Henry Jecks & Co. earpet manufrs. 71 Aldermanbury
Dixon Isabella & James, tailors & drapers, 7 Houndsditch
Dixon Joseph & Son, wholesale jewellers, 37 Hatton garden
Dixon Richard & Co. clothiers & outfitters, 12 Fenchurch st
Dixon & Ross, steel&cop.pl.prints.4 St. James' pl.Hampst.rd
Dixon & Whitings, hatters' furriers, Southwark bridge rd
Dixon Abraham, gold&silver beater, 1 Friar st.Blackfriars rd
Dixon Arthur, chemist, 3 Stockwell terrace, Clapham road
Dixon Benj. timber mer.Commer.wf.Commercial rd.Limeho
Dixon Charles, boot & shoe maker, 8 Bevenden st. Hoxton
Dixon Charles, dining rooms, 156 Upper Thames st
Dixon Chas. upholsterer, billiard & bagatelle table maker, 86 Crown court, Water st. Blackfriars
Dixon Charles, whitesmith, 6 Ring cross, Holloway
Dixon Edward, engraver, 31 Sekforde st. Clerkenwell
Dixon Edward, surgeon, 66 Wardour st. Soho
Dixon Edward, writer & grainer, 9 Up. Fountain pl. City rd
Dixon Eliz.(Mrs.),straw hat ma.10 Brydges st.Covent garden
Dixon Francis, lodging house, 13 Richmond buildings, Soho
Dixon Frederick, currier, 33 Long lane, Bermondsey
Dixon Frederick Seekamp, solicitor, see Casterton & Dixon
Dixon George, butcher, 12 Bedford st. Mile end
Dixon George Clarke,grocer,6 Foxley rd.Camberwl.New rd
Dixon Henry, manifold writer & tracing paper ma.194Strand
Dixon Henry, tobacconist, 113 High st. Camden town
Dixon Hezekiah, ivory turner, fishing tackle & archery manufacturer, 10 Ball alley, Lombard st
Dixon James, butcher, 2 King David la. Shadwell High st
Dixon James, coal factor, see Harris & Dixon
Dixon James, herald chaser, 93 Wardour st. Soho
Dixon James, surgeon, 37 Broad st. buildings
Dixon James, tailor, 5 Arundel st. Strand
Dixon James Henry, solicitor, see Dean, Leeks & Dixon
Dixon Jeremiah, butcher, 104 High st. Camden town
Dixon John, bird dealer, 10 Adam & Eve court, Oxford st
Dixon John, butcher, Charlotte st. Portland place
Dixon John, cabinet ma. & undertaker, 3 Gray's inn terrace
Dixon John, papier maché & gen. japan agt.18 Brownlowst
Dixon John, *Star & Garter* P.H. 21 King st. Westminster
Dixon John (Mrs.), grocer, &c. 6 Tower st. Westminster rd
Dixon John, stationer, 31 King st. Camden town
Dixon John, tailor, 84 Great Titchfield st. Oxford st
Dixon John Bond, solicitor, see Frankham & Dixon
Dixon Joseph, bootmaker, 10 Norfolk pl. East st. Walworth rd
Dixon Joseph, grocer, 8 Little Pearl st. Spitalfields
Dixon Martha (Mrs.), milliner, 14 Church row, Pancras rd
Dixon Mary (Mrs.), confectioner, 56 King William st. City
Dixon Matthew, man. of plated wares, 35 Castle st. Holbn
Dixon Pearson John, undertaker, 52 Bethnal green road
Dixon Richard, linendraper, 58 Blackfriars road
Dixon Richd. repositoryforhorses,carriages,&c.56 Barbican, & job master, 40 Lemon tree yard, Haymarket
Dixon Robert (sec. to *Poplar saving's bank*),Highst.Poplar
Dixon Rt.Stainton,coal mer.Providencewf.Collegest.Lambh
Dixon Samuel, carver& gilder, 12 Gt. Portland st. Oxford st
Dixon Sam.pat.columbianpress maker,&c.seeClymer&Dixon
Dixon Thomas, florist, Centre row, Covent garden market
Dixon Thomas, *Friend at Hand* P.H.3 Platt ter.Pancras rd
Dixon Thomas, house agt.&undertak.113 High st.Camden tn
Dixon Thomas, tobacconist, 2 Melina buildgs.Westminster rd
Dixon Thomas Henry, solicitor, 5 New Boswell ct. Carey st
Dixon William, *Anchor* P.H. 11 Temple st. Whitefriars
Dixon William, *Coach & Horses* P.H. High st. Bow
Dixon Wm. chronometer & watchma. 45 King sq. Goswell rd
Dixon William, provision agent, 12 Dowgate hill
Dixon William, surgical instru.maker.2Tonbridge st.Newrd
Dixson & Co. wholesale shoe warehouse, 147 Cheapside
Doane Charles, artist, 14 Berners st. Oxford st
Doane Richard, barrister, 2 New inn bldgs.Wych st. Strand
Dobbin Rebecca (Mrs.), baker, 26 Flagon row, Deptford
DobbinsAnn (Mrs.&Son),ironmongers,1Markhamst.Chelsea
Dobbins Benjamin, butcher, 22 St. John st. road
Dobbins William, butcher, 6 Drury lane
Dobbs, Bailey & Co. wholesale plain&ornamental stationers & pencil makers, 134 Fleet st. & 13 Soho square
Dobbs Hy. oil of, & romanvitriol ma.Citywhf.1Up.Thames st
Dobbs Samuel, who.& retail glover, 4 Princes st.Westminster
Dobbs Thomas, greengrocer, 77 Mary st. Hampstead rd
Dobby John, cutler, 16 Wych st. Strand
Dobby Thomas Wm. cutler, 54 Myddelton st. Clerkenwell
Dobell Benjamin, tailor & draper, 25 Gracechurch st
Dobell Henry, plumber & painter, 42 Robert st. Chelsea
Dobell Walter, grocer&cheesemgr.28Russell st.Bermondsey
Dober Jas. *Prince Regent* P.H. 55Kennington st.Walworth
Dobie Alexander, solicitor, &c. 2 Lancaster place, Strand
Dobie David, surgeon, &c. 43 Exmouth st. Spafields
Dobie John, solicitor, see Dunn & Dobie
Dobinson George, carpenter, &c. 103 East st. Manchester sq

Dobinson James George, attorney, 10 Gray's inn square
Dobinson Joseph, w. india mer. see Timperon & Dobinson
Dobinson Michael, upholsterer, 70 Berners st
Dobinson Mary (Mrs.), milliner & dressmaker, 70 Berners st
Dobinson Thomas, butcher, 27 Cleveland st. Fitzroy sq
Dobinson William, linendraper, 185 Shadwell High st
Doble Edward, baker, 72 White Lion st. Pentonville
Doble Henry, *Star* P.H. 19 Star st. Shadwell
Doble Henry, surgeon, 84 Parson's st. St. George st
Dobree Samuel & Sons, merchants, 6 Tokenhouse yard
Dobree George, pawnbroker, 68 & 69 Charlotte st. Fitzroy sq
Dobree George, solicitor, see Harrison & Dobree
Dobree Robert John, pawnbroker, 12 Gilbert st. Grosvnr. sq
Dobson John & Sons, chemists & druggists, 30 Coleman st
Dobson Eliz. (Mrs.), boarding ho. 22 Ironmonger la. City
Dobson Henry, livery stables, 3 Wharf, Macclesfield st. south
Dobson Henry, solicitor, 7 New Millman st. Foundling
Dobson Henry H. silversmith, &c. see Wilkinson & Dobson
Dobson James, laceman, 127 High st. Borough
Dobson James, pin manufacturer, 15 Noble st. Cheapside
Dobson John, carpenter & builder, 1 Old Gravel la. Wapping
Dobson John, fancy bread, &c. manuf. 31 Noble st. Cheapside
Dobson John, lace cleaner, 11 Charlotte st. Portland place
Dobson John, optician, 54 Newington causeway
Dobson Joseph, grocer, 69 Leather lane, Holborn
Dobson John Richd. hop & seed merch. 2 St. Thomas's st. Boro'
Dobson Thomas, importer of, & dealer in diamonds, pearls & other precious stones, bullion, &c. & general merchant, 147 Leadenhall st
Dobson Thomas, corn & flour factor, 3 Billiter square
Dobson Wm. architect & surveyor, 10 Jubilee st. Mile end rd
Dobson Wm. hardwareman & stationer, & writing, copying, shaving & dressing case manufacturer, 162 Strand
Dock Master's Office, St. Katharine's, Tower
Docker Charles, grocer & cheesemonger, 2 Gt. Chapel st. & 41 Strutton ground, Westminster
Dockerill, Duchesne & Dockerill, teadlrs. 97 Fenchurch st
Docking John Bristow, grocer, 66 Brewer st. Somers town
Docking Rt. E. *Coach & Horses* P.H. 1 Blue Anchr. al. Bunhl. rw
Dockray Rt. B. engineer, 13 St. Prancras vale, Hampstead rd
Dockree Jn. brassturn. & gasburn. ma. 16 Galway st. St. Luke's
Dockrell Wm. fishmonger, High st. Stoke Newington
Dockrell Wm. timber merchant, High st. Stoke Newington
Dockrey Jesse, tailor & draper, 47 Duke st. Aldgate
Dockwray Rt. B. res. engineer, Terminus, Euston grove
Docwra Stephen, beer retailer, 3 Southampton st. Cambrwl
Dod Alfred, printer, 6 Princes st. Leicester square
Dod & Wray, solicitors & foreign law & patent agents, 16 Great Marlborough st
Dod & Wray, solicitors & foreign law & patent agents 3 Little Argyll st. Regent st
Dodd & Humpage, surgeons, 1 Bryanstone st. Portman sq
Dodd, Rowsell, Grueber & Dodd, solicitors, 5 Billiter st
Dodd Charles, chemist & druggist, 43 Lamb's Conduit st
Dodd Daniel George, engraver, 40 Jewin st. Cripplegate
Dodd David, surgeon, 9 Wilderness row, Clerkenwell
Dodd Edward, clog & patten maker, 5 Whitmore pl. Hoxton
Dodd Edw. violin bow & string ma. 112 Vauxhall wk. Lamb
Dodd Elizabeth (Mrs.), *Ship* P.H. Sun Tavern fields, St. George's east
Dodd Elijah, surgeon & apothecary, 91 Bridge road, Lambeth, & at Staines, Middlesex
Dodd Grantham Robert, solicitor, 26 New Broad st. City
Dodd Henry, scavenger, carter & road contractor, City wharf, Eagle wharf road, New North road, Hoxton
Dodd Isaac, egg mer. 2 Union rw. Page's wk. Grange rd. Brmsy
Dodd James, builder, 25 East st. Red Lion square
Dodd James, tailor & trousers maker, 31 St. James's st
Dodd James B. surgeon, Fonthill place, Clapham road
Dodd John, grocer, &c. 68 Farringdon st
Dodd John, surgeon, 12 Portman st. Portman square
Dodd Joseph, butcher, 56 Back Church lane, Whitechapel
Dodd Mary (Miss), milliner, 18 Compton st. Brunswick sq
Dodd Moses, auctioneer & surveyor, 16 New Broad st. City
Dodd Philip George, jeweller, watchmaker & miniature painter, 25 Leadenhall st. & 79 Cornhill
Dodd Richard, beer retailer, 14 Lit. Chester st. Grsvnr. pl
Dodd Wm. farrier, 3 Craven yard, Drury lane
Dodd Wm. ropemaker, 1 Page's walk, Grange rd. Bermondsey
Dodd Wm. staymaker, 170 Church st. Shoreditch
Doddemeade Charles, tailor, 20 Newington causeway
Doddington Samuel N. hosier, &c. Albion ter. Canonbury sq
Dodds & Stowe, meat salesmen, 49 Newgate market
Dodds Walter Geo. beer merch. 3 Howford bdgs. Fench. st
Dodge Esau, boot & shoe maker, 104 Blackfriars road
Dodge James, lamp & gas fit. ma. 6 Cumberland rw. Walwth. rd
Dodge Joseph, fishmonger, 12 Cumberland row, King's cross
Dodging William, tailor, 6 Bell yard, Temple bar
Dodgson & Bradbury, who. ironmongers, 80 Bishopsga. witho
Dodgson George, artist, 21 Mornington pl. Hampstead road
Dodgson Hassard Hume, spec. pleader, 7 King's Bench walk
Dodgson Robert, silk merchant, see Bell, Dodgson & Co
Dodley Henry, butcher, 10 Limehouse causeway
Dodman James, glover, &c. 39 Freeschool st. Horselydown
Dodman Joseph, boot & shoe maker, 9 Symons st. Chelsea
Dodman Joseph, rod merchant & waggon office, Red Lion yard, 110 Aldersgate st
Dodman William, tobacco manufr. 73 Banner st. St. Luke's
Dods James, bookbinder, 16 Greville st. Hatton garden
Dods James Maitland, attorney, 102 St. Martin's la. Charing cross, & 115 Leadenhall st
Dods Samuel, butcher, 23 Church st. Blackfriars road
Dodsley Wm. Rogers, builder & material dlr. 12 Old st. rd
Dodson Daniel, bookseller, dealer in novels, &c. 137 Fleet st
Dodson David, poulterer, 260 Borough High st
Dodson George Peter, solicitor, 20 Southampton buildings
Dodson Henry, bread & biscuit baker & patentee of the unfermented bread, biscuits, &c. 98 Blackman st. Borough
Dodson James, ship, commercial, custom house & treasury agent, & to the east india company, 9 St. Dunstan's hill
Dodson Sir John, knt. D.C.L. advocate general & master of the faculties, 14 College, Doctors' commons
Dodson John, *Duke of York* P.H. 28 Stockbridge ter. Pimlico
Dodson John, *Geo. & Dragon* P.H. 1 Stepney rents, Hackney rd
Dodson John, straw bonnet ma. 28 Camden st. Islington grn
Dodson Joseph, potato salesman, 19 Mill lane, Tooley st. & bone manure manufacturer, 22½ Gt. George st. Bermondsey
Dodson Joseph, russia broker, 5 Commercial sale rooms
Dodson Robert, wheelwright, Edmunds pl. Battersea
Dodson Thomas, needle maker & cutler, 5 Bath st. Newgate st
Dodsworth William, chinaman, 11 Spring st. Marylebone
Dodwell Benjamin & Edw. grocers, 9 Church st. Kensington
Dodwell Thos. Wedon, wax & waferma. 12 Orchard st. St. Luke's
Dodworth Benjamin, cutler, Mare st. Hackney
Doe Joseph Bolton, ironfounder & patentee of the metallic soap frame, 8 Finch st. & Hope st. Montague st. Whitechp
Doering Frederick, merchant, 2 Crosby square
Doery Chas. fishmonger, 12 Lower area, Hungerford market
Doggett & Harryman, hop & seed factors, 230 Borough
Doggett & Tayler, bootmaker, 35 Davies st. Berkeley sq
Doggett Edward, grocer, 9 Plumber row, City road
Doggett Hen. counting ho. &c. stool mak. 15 Somerset st. Aldgt
Doggett John, ironmonger, 36 Shoreditch
Doggett Martin, oil & colorman, 14 Brompton Low. Grove
Doggett Martin, oilman, 46 Up. Marylebone st. Portland pl
Doggett Thos. upholder & appraiser, 25 High st. Marylebone
Doggett William, tailor, 15 South Molton st
Doggrell Henry, upholsterer & undert. 3 London rd. Southwrk
Doherty, Scrivens & Co. skinners, &c. Holland st. Blackfrs
Doherty James, brace ma. 18 Gt. Saffron hill, Hatton garden
Doig John, baker, 68 Fetter lane, Holborn
Doig William, baker, 50 Lower Queen st. Rotherhithe
Dolamore Ben. *Cheshire Cheese* P.H. 16 Wine offi. ct. Fleet st
Dolamore Henry, teadealer, 32 Bridge road, Lambeth
Dolans', Sunderland & Co. army clothiers, 97 St. Martin's la
Dolbey Sarah (Mrs.), baker, High st. Stoke Newington
Dolby Charlotte (Mrs.), *York* chophouse, 96 Wardour st
Dolby Joseph, linendraper, King's road West, Chelsea
Dole John, leather striper, 25 Fair st. Horselydown
Dole Lewis, carpenter, 10 Up. Marylebone st. Portland pl
Dolling Wm. Bruce, booksel. & statnr. 47 North st. Edgware rd
Dollman Chas. John, child bed linen wareho. 32 New Bond st
Dollman Edward, merchant, 32 Gt. St. Helen's
Dollman Edward Francis, bootmaker, 33 New Bond st
Dollman Francis Thos. architect, 27 Mornington pl. Hmpstd. rd
Dollond George, optician, 59 St. Paul's churchyard
Dolman Charles, bookseller & publisher, 61 New Bond st
Dolman Edward, surgeon & apothecary, Stratford, Essex
Dolman Frederick, jun. carver & gilder, 3 Brompton road
Dolman Frederick Wm. solicitor, 27 Carey st. Lincoln's inn
Dolman James, attorney, 14 Clifford's inn, Fleet st
Dolman Robert, coal dealer, 1 Berwick st. Soho
Dolphin Thos. law stationer, 24 Cursitor st. Chancery lane
Dolwin Richd. lighterman, 4 Market st. Westminster
Domett & Co. ship biscuit bakers, see Young, Domett & Co
Domett, England & Son, shipbroks. 7 George yd. Lombard st
Dominey & Attree, childbed linen wareh. 24 Hatton garden
Dommett Emanuel, surgeon, Rosamon bldgs. Islington green
Domone John, fruiterer, 31 Rose st. King st. Covent garden
Don James, tailor, 9 Lower James st. Golden sq
Donagan Mary (Mrs.), hairdresser, 58 Edgware rd. Maryleb
Donahoo Thomas, surgeon, 27 White Horse st. Com. rd. Stepney

Donald Peter, *Black Bull* P.H. 151 New Gravel lane
Donald Thos. Fran. grocer, &c. 49 Cumberland st. Hacky. rd
Donald Wm. cheesemonger, 8 Seymour st. Euston sq
Donald Wm. gas meter manufr. & the original manufr. of patent imperial raised dish covers, 35 Britannia st. City rd
Donalds Wm. & Jas. ornamental engrvrs. 29 Artillery pl. wst
Donaldson & Dixon, merchants, 35 Mark lane
Donaldson, Lambert & Co. merchants, 8 Broad st. buildings
Donaldson Thos. & Rt. brewers, see Courage & Donaldsons'
Donaldson Adam, schoolmaster, 48 Earl st. east, Lisson grove
Donaldson Charles, hatter, &c. 33 Warwick st. Golden sq
Donaldson Charles, wine merchant, 123 Fenchurch st.
Donaldson Daniel, tailor, 62 Frith st. Soho
Donaldson Elizh. (Miss), dressmaker, 54 Margaret st. Cav. sq
Donaldson George, watch & clock maker, &c. 121 Pall mall
Donaldson George H. merchant, 8 Broad st. buildings
Donaldson Harriet (Mrs.), hat & umbrella ma. 132A, Oxford st
Donaldson Hugh, surgeon, 23 Foxley rd. Camberwell new rd
Donaldson John, coachmaker, 294 Regent st. & 49 & 50 Margaret st. Cavendish square
Donaldson John, greengrocer, 44 Rochester row, Westmintr
Donaldson John Henry, dentist & cupper, 73 York st. Kngsld. rd
Donaldson Saml. ho. & land agt. & valuer, 40 Curzon st. Mayfair
Donaldson Stuart, merchant, 8 Broad st. buildings
Donaldson Thomas, baker, 78 Church st. Mile end New town
Donaldson Thos. baker, 8 Lit. Sussex pl. Hyde park gardens
Donaldson Thos. confectioner & corn dealer, 10 Kingsland rd
Donaldson Thos. Leverton, architect, 71 Russell sq.; & district surveyor, 3 Pelham terrace, Brompton
Donaldson Wm. baker, 1 Cross st. Islington
Donaldson Wm. dyer, 31 High st. Portland town
Donaldson Wm. tailor, 8 Northumberland st. Marylebone
Donaldson Wm. Leverton, solicitor, 18 Southampton st. Bloomsbury square
Doncaster John, blind maker, 18 Young st. Kensington
Donelly Felix Arthur, surgeon, 2 St. James's pl. Old Kent rd
Doneton John, jun. earthenware mer. & ma. 28 High st. Lambh
Dones James, plumber & zinc worker, 4 Baron st. Pentonville
Donges John, baker, 26 City gardens, City road
Dongworth Samuel, tinman, 68 Church st. Shoreditch
Donhue John, tobacconist, 3 Park st. Dorset square
Donia James, baths, 23 Sherrard st. Golden square
Donkin Bryan & Co. millwrights, Blue Anchor rd. Bermndsy
Donnahoe George, fruit salesman, Covent garden fruit mrkt
Donne Wm. & Sons, heraldic engravs. & prints. 6 Warwick st. Charing cross, & 51 Cheapside, & 2 Cranmer place, Waterloo road
Donne Charles, *Welsh Trooper* P. H. 37 Bankside
Donne Edward, barrister, 50 Upper Harley st
Donne Francis Thomas, solicitor, 1 Princes st. Spitalfields
Donne George, looking glass maker, 9 Eldon st. Finsbury
Donne Griffith, straw bonnet ma. 2 Denton st. Somers town
Donne John, wine merchant, 1 New court, Throgmorton st
Donne Samuel Edward, solicitor, 28 New Broad st. City
Donne William, butcher, 77 Paul st. Finsbury
Donne William, *George* P. H. 12 Bankside, Borough
Donner John, watch & clock ma. 6 Lr. George st. Chelsea
Donney David, glasscutter, 4 Gt. James st. Lisson grove
Donnison John, notary, 71 Cornhill
Donnison John, stationer & printer, 21 Liverpool st. Bishopsg
Donnison Wm. & Co. engravers, 8 Thornton st. Dockhead
Donoghue Daniel, fruiterer, 109 Gray's inn lane
Donoghue Michael, coffee rooms, 122 Up. Seymour st. Eustonsq
Donoughe John, coal merchant, 5 Vere st. Clare market
Donovan John & Co. warehouse for the sale of irish linen in any quantity, 40 Hart st. Bloomsbury sq
Donovan Joseph & Wm. fishmngs. & poulterers, 292 Oxford st
Donovan Cornelius Jas. fruiterer, 1 Howard's pl. Hackney rd
Donovan Fredk. beer retailer, 58 Cowcross st. Smithfield
Donovan James, potato salesman, 18 Sidney pl. Com. rd. East
Donovan James, *Windmill*, P. H. Robert st. Limehouse
Donovan Joseph, sen. fishmonger, 72 Tottenham ct. road
Donovan Richd. utrecht velvet imptr. 32 Broad st. Golden sq
Donovan Thomas, cooper, 10 Crown st. Soho
Donthorn John Wm. architect & surveyor, 18 Hanover st. Han. sq
Doody Peter, tailor, 16 Mercer st. Long acre
Doogood Henry J. short hand writer, 48 Carey st. Chancery la
Dooley John, *Bell* P. H. 61 Old Bailey
Doors William, ironplate worker, 14 Holland st. Blkfrs. rd
Doran Geo. glass & china dlr. 126 Edgware rd. Marylebone
Doran John, bricklayer, 12 Northampton st. Clerkenwell
Dordoy & Goodwin, chemists, 38 Blackman st. Borough
Dore Hezekiah, butcher, 28 Brown st. Bryanstone square
Dore John, plumber & zinc worker, 17 Exmouth st. Spafields
Dore John, tobacco & snuff manufacturer, 6 Eastcheap
Dore Joseph, pianoforte maker, 10 Polygon, Clarendon sq
Dore Richard, fruiterer, 11 Stockwell ter. Clapham road
Dore Wm. carrier, Elephant inn, 112 Fore st. Cripplegate
Dore William, *Grapes* P.H. 11 Duke st. Manchester square
Dore William Henry, butcher, 18 James st. Covent garden
Doren Mary (Mrs.), skinner & furrier, 19 Lant st. Borough
Dorey Fras. & Co. pat. horse shoe ma. 9 Middle rw. Knightsbdge
Dorey Josiah, family mourning warehouse, 42 Oxford st
Dorking, Brighton & Arundel Atmos. Rail. (Rt. Furner, sec.), Adelaide ho. London bdg. Parlmntry offi. 2 Bridge st. Westmr
Doria Adair Andrew, barrister, 4 Old square, Lincoln's inn
D'Orleans Pierre, egg merchant, 9 & 10 Grafton st. Soho
Dorley William, gas fitter, 9 Exmouth st. Clerkenwell
Dorling Henry, cheesemonger, 278 Bermondsey st
Dorling Henry, shoemaker, 42 Holywell lane, Shoreditch
Dorman Edward D. shell fish wa. 2 Railway pl. Fenchurch st
Dorman Frederick, painter, 122 Grove st. Camden town
Dorman Henry, *Antelope* P.H. 1 Eaton terrace, Eaton sq
Dorman Stephen, tailor, 4 Terrace, Davies st. Berkeley sq
Dormar Nicholas, *Betty's chophouse* tavern, 315 Strand
Dormer James, furn. undertaker, 29 Church st. Shoreditch
Dormer Joshua, undertaker, 279 Bethnal green road
Dorn Philip, baker, 9 Charles st. Westbourne terrace
Dornford Thos. Wm. wine & spirt mer. 1 Suffolk la. Cannon st
Dorrell Chas. Thos. ship smith, Salisbury la. Bermdsy. wall
Dorrell Edmund, artist, 43 Warren st. Fitzroy square
Dorrell John, boot & shoe maker, 44 Waterloo st. Camberwll
Dorrell John, marine store dlr. 24 Redcross st. Borough
Dorrell John, *Market* coffee house, 9 West Smithfield
Dorrell Joseph Henry, tailor, 37 Old st. road
Dorrell William, tailor, 70 Freeschool st. Horselydown
Dorrington, Hayward, Ellicombe & Curry, parliamentary agents, 16 Parliament st. Westminster
Dorrington George, wood engraver, 143 Blackfriars road
Dorrington Jane (Mrs.), *Union* P.H. 30 Union st. Kingsld. rd
Dorrington John, *Britannia* P.H. Church st. Hackney
Dorrington John, hairdresser, 158 Brick lane, Spitalfields
Dorset John & Son, tallow chandlers, &c. 52 King st. Westmin
Dorsett Elizab. (Mrs.), carwoman, 16 Tower Royal, Watling st
Dorville Lewis, beer retailer, 93 Salisbury st. Lisson grove
Dorward Andrew, baker, 84 Shadwell High st
Dorward John, chemist, 45 Kingsland road
Dosscher George Henry, sugar refr. 14 Finch st. Whitechapel
Dossetor & Peart, hosiers & glovers, 12 & 13 Poultry
Dossetor Daniel, butcher, 5 Gt. Russell st. Covent garden
Dossetter John, furng. ironmonger, &c. 29 Theobald's road
Dosson George, cheesemonger, 66 Marsham st. Westminster
Dosson John, cheesemon. 17 Gloucester ter. Vauxhall br. rd
Dottridge Sam. carpntr. & undertkr. 138½ Hoxton Old town
Doubble Thomas, linendraper & haberdasher, 38 Leatherlane
Doubbell Geo. Hy. oil & colorman, 81 Park st. Kenngton cross
Doubell Wm. linendraper, 2 Pullham ter. King's rd. Chelsea
Double Charles, law stationer, 34 Cursitor st. Chancery la
Double William, *Bull's Head* P.H. St. Katharine's
Doubleday Edward, surgeon, 249 Blackfriars road
Doubleday Edwd. Playal, grocer, 1 New Buckingham pl. Gt. Dover road
Doubleday John, dlr. in casts of coin, 5 Lit. Russell st. Blmby
Doublet Thomas & Hen. spectacle makers, 74 Paul st. Finsb
Doubosq Charles, zinc worker, 6 King's row, Knightsbridge
Doubtfire Thos. Hen. wire worker, 17 Upper East Smithfield
Douce John, prof. of music, 9 New North st. Red Lion sq
Doudney Brothers, tailors, 97 Fleet st. & at 17 Old Bond st
Doudney Edward P. & Son, tailors, 49 Lombard st
Doudney David Alfred, printer, 1 Long la. West Smithfield
Dougal George, auctioneer, 10 Melina pl. Westminster rd
Dougal Richard Cates, *George* P.H. 6 St. James terrace, Waterloo road
Dougan James, solicitor, New Cham. Foregate, Clmnt's. inn
Doughty Benjamin & Co. button makers, 103 St. Martin's la
Doughty Edw. D. surgn. & chemt. 4 William st. Knightsbr
Doughty Elizabeth (Mrs.), cutler, 431 West Strand
Doughty Henry, plumber, 4 St. Thomas's pl. Old Kent rd
Doughty Jas. printer & stationer, 22 Kensington, High st
Doughty James, stationer, 22 Young st. Kensington
Doughty John Joseph, baker, 11 Whitechapel road
Doughty Mary (Miss), boarding house, 10 Arundel st. Strand
Doughty Richard, shoemaker, 101 Star st. Edgware road
Doughty Sarah (Mrs.), beer ret. & brewer, 81 East st. Manchester square
Doughty Thomas, surgeon, 37 Fore st. Cripplegate
Doughty Thos. Neale, solicitor, 15 Queen's bldgs. Brompton
Doughty William, baker, 86 Blackman st. Borough
Douglas & Brown, surgeon, &c. 3 Trevor ter. Knightsbridge
Douglas Charles & Son, corn & seedfactors, 4 Gould square, Crutched friars, & Baltic wharf, 262 Wapping High st
Douglas & Hamer, wax & composition doll ma. 58 Shoe lane

Douglas & Mills, ship & insurance brokers, 23 Billiter st
Douglas Chas. M. commisn. mercht. 5 Goldsmith st. Waod st
Douglas Duncan, baker, 58 Charlotte st. Whitechapel
Douglas Frances (Mrs.), goldsmith, 13 St. James's st. Clrkw
Douglas Hargaretta (Mrs.), tobacconist, 171 Drury lane
Douglas James, baker, 14 John st. Holland st. Blackfriars
Douglas John, tailor, 10 Little York place, Glo'ster place
Douglas John, umbrella maker, 21 Belton st. Long acre
Douglas JohnMore, res.direc.ofgeneralwoodcutCo.Belvdre.rd
Douglas Joseph, barrister, 4 Garden court, Temple
Douglas Matthew, fruiterer, 9 Southampton st. Camden town
Douglas Richard, carriage lamp maker, 34 Wych st. Strand
Douglas Samuel, machine ruler, 6 Little Knightrider st.
DouglasSam. *Marqs. Westminster* P.H.1Warwick st. Pimlico
Douglas Sarah (Mrs.), boarding house, 17 Ely pl. Holborn
Douglas Sholto James, barrister, 10 Farrar's bldgs. Temple
Douglas Wm. cabinet maker, 4 Little Cadogan place, Sloane square, & 14 Lowndes st. Belgrave square
Douglas William, staymaker, 63 Gt. Portland st. Oxford st
Douglass Robert & Co. crape manufacturers, 3 Carey la. City
Douglass James Alex. solicitor, 11 Queen sq. Bloomsbury
Douglass Matthew, stockbroker, Stock exchange, Bank
Douglass Robt. lamp, china, glass, & oil wa. 184 Piccadilly
Douglass Sam. tin plate worker, 80Vauxhall walk, Lambeth
Douglass Ths. stationer & news ag. 2 Gt. Distaff la. Friday st
Doulton & Watts, potters, chemical apparatus, & filter makers, 28 High st. Lambeth
Doulton John jun. earthenware mer. 28, High st. Lambeth
Dourminney, James, fruiterer, 2, Britannia st. City road
Douse, Wm. Sam. bricklayer, 27Cumberland st. Middlx. hospl
Douthwaite & Griffiths, saddlers, &c. 31 Little Moorfields
Douthwaite Robert, bootmaker, 21 Tothill st. Westminster
Douthwaite William, currier, &c. 16 Star corner, Bermndsy
Dovaston Edward, builder, 9 Stucley terrace, Camden town
Dove Alexander James, tallow melter, see Marshall & Dove
Dove Ann (Mrs.), lodging house, 12 Fludyer st. Westminster
Dove Edwin, hairdresser, 3 Clifford street, Bond st
Dove Henry, grocer, &c. 4 Britannia pl. Wandsworth road
Dove Henry, linendraper, 102 Newgate st
Dove Hen. *Three Jolly Butchers* P.H.7 Warwick la. Newg. st
Dove Jamas, chandlers' shop, 5 North place, Dalston
Dove John, baker, 2, Elizabeth st. Hackney road
Dove Joseph, attorney, 9 New Millman st
Dove Michael, grocer, 15 Old Chapel row, Kentish town
Dove Samuel, plumber & glazier, 5Goldsmith pl. Hackney rd
Dove William, plumber & glazier, 54½ Gt. Guildford st. Boro'
Dove William Richard, butcher, 2 Bloomsbury market
Dovell & Amelang, sealing wax ma. 54 Red Lion st. Clerknwl
Dovell Wm. carpent. & undertak. 1 Buckingham st. Strand
Dovenor John Wilkinson, grocer, 77, Lower marsh, Lambeth
Dover, Deal, Ramsgate, & Margate Steam Packet Office, 65 King William st. City
Dover Henry John, solicitor, 12 South square, Gray's inn
Dover James, glass cutter, 40 Cornwall road, Lambeth
Dover John William, wine merchant, 124 Fenchurch st
Dover Wm. blindmaker, 70 Wells street, Oxford st
DoverWm.ho.agent & appraiser, 73Gt. Cambridge st. Hack.rd
Dovey & Stapleton (Misses), str. bon.ma. 5St. George's circus
DoveyChas. trnry. wa.&wireworker, 6 Seymour pl. Camden tn
Dovey John, fruiterer, 63 Lisson grove North
Dovey John Sam. toymaker, 48 Freeschool st. Horselydown
Dovey Sherlock, wireworker, 25 Crown st. Soho
Dovey Thomas, plumber, &c. 13 Rose & Crown ct. Finsbury
Dow James, gardener, 37 Lisson grove North
Dow James, watchcase manuf. 54 Perceval st. Clerkenwell
Dow Peter, bookbinder & gilder, 5 Staining lane, Wood st
Dow Thomas Wm. bootmaker, 16 York st. Covent garden
DowWm. Alexr. special pleader, 9King's bench walk, Temple
Dowbiggin Thos. & Co. cabinetma. & upholstrs. 23 Mount st
Dowdall James, glass cutter, 11 Neville's court, Fetter lane
Dowdall Jas. Edwd. chemical stopper mfr. 18 New st. sq
Dowde Anna Bell (Miss), milliner, 21 Queen sq. Westmnstr
Dowdell James, bootmaker, 287 Kent st. Borough
Dowdell Wm. grocer & teadlr. 23 Fieldgate st. Whitechapel
Dowden George, teadealer, 57 Edgware road, Marylebone
Dowden Joseph, linendraper, see Baker & Dowden
Dowdeswell Benj. carriage lamp maker, 14 Old Cavendish st
Dowdeswell George Morley, barrister, 5 Crown office row, & 1 Figtree court, Temple
Dowding Benj.&Co.who. cheesemrs. 5 Warwick la. Newgt. st
Dowding Wm.Jno.&Sml. paper ma.12NewWeston st. Brmdsy
Dowding Benjamin, meat salesman, see Titmuss & Dowding
Dowding John, bookseller, 82 Newgate st
Dowding John Paul, oilman, 14 New road, St. George's east
Dowding Richd. cooper, wine & beer mercht. 58Wapping wall
Dowding Walter Scott, bookseller, 18Cannon st. St. Geo. east
Dowell James, smite & farrier, Wandsworth road
Dowell Joseph, *Bay Tree tavern*, 33 & 35 St. Swithin's lane
Dowell William, shipping butcher, 25 Wapping wall
Dower John, mapengrav. & printer, 6 Cumming pl. Pentonvil
Dowers Thos. Wm. T. law stationer, 16 Took's ct. Chancery la
Dowgate Wharf, Anthony Nichol & Son, between 83 & 84 Upper Thames st
Dowie James & Co. pat. boot & shoe wareho. 455 West Strand
Dowie James, merchant, see Gould, Dowie & Moore
Dowker Thos. Stockton, picture cleaner, 29East la. Dockhead
Dowle John, dairyman, 38 Poland st. Oxford st
Dowle Richard, dairyman, 25 Gt. Titchfield st. Oxford st
Dowlen John Walter, grocer, 7 Seymour st. Euston square
Dowler Frederick, calenderer, &c. 6 Foster st. Bishopsgate
Dowler John, tobaccon. 7 Perseverance ter. Church st. Bthnl.gr
Dowler Joseph, hairdresser, 6 Piazza, Covent garden
Dowler Joseph, *Rainbow* P.H. 51 Queen st. Ratcliff
Dowler Matthew, blind, &c. manufr. 99 Fetter lane, Holborn
Dowley George, beer retailer, George st. Camberwell
Dowley Jas. Hy. shoemaker, 3 Southwark bridge road
Dowley John, surveyor, 35 Howland st. Fitzroy square
DowleyThos. *Crown* P.H.10Butlersbldgs. Up. EastSmithfield
Dowling Alfred Septimus, serj. at law, Tanfield chambers
DowlingBridget(Mrs.), *Phœnix* P.H. Phœnixpl. Ratcliffcross
Dowling Edmund, grocer & teadealer, 30 King st. Tower hill, & 10 King's road east, Chelsea
Dowling Henry, *Red Lion* P.H. 68 Blackman st
Dowling James, artist, 38 Foley place, Great Portland st
Dowling John, grocer, 186 Shadwell High st
Dowling Maria (Mrs.), stereotype found. 13 & 14 St. John's la
Dowling Richard Brinsley, barrister, 2 Brick court, Temple
Dowling Saml. bath ale agent, 23 Hungerford wharf
Dowling Sarah E. (Miss), dressma. 29 Princes sq. St. Geo. ea
Dowling Thos. engraver & printer, 24 Panton st. Haymarket
Dowling Thos. stone mason, 23 Compton st. Clerkenwell
DownWm.&Co. ironmongers&smiths, 1 Cobourgpl. Bayswater
Down Daniel John, tailor, 76 Albany st. Regent's park
Down Henry Sidney, hatter, 306 Holborn, 50 Bread st. 60 Long acre, & 359 Strand
Down Israel, plumber & glazier, 14 Featherstone bldgs. Hlbrn
Down Jeremiah, tailor & draper, 179 Strand
Down John, chemist, 1 Queen's row, Bayswater
Downe Daniel, sailcloth factor, 75 Queen st. Cheapside
Downe John, coal mer. Union whf. Wilton road, Pimlico
Downer C.J. sec. to Economic Life Assnce. Soc. 6&7N. Bridge st
Downer John, bookseller, 3 Surrey place, Wandsworth road
Downer Sam. iron platework. 11Greenhil's rnts. Smithfi. bars
Downer William, attorney & solicitor, law & gen. agent for the Canadas & United States, 16 George st. Mansion ho
Downes Chas. & Son, army & gen. agts. 14 Warwick st. Char.cr
Downes, Gamlen & Scott, attorneys, 7 Furnival's inn, Holborn
Downes & Scott, wholesale teadealers, 135 Up. Thames st
Downes Emma (Miss), toydealer, 46 Hedge row, Islington
Downes Edward, carver & gilder, 18 Chenies st. Bedford sq
DownesGeo. *Haberdashers' Arms* P.H.1Hbrdshrs.pl.e.Hxtn
Downes Henry, Commander R.N. hon. director United Service Museum, Middle Scotland yard, Whitehall place
Downes James, chemist, 39 Rathbone place
Downes John, carpenter, 10 Hooper st. Clerkenwell
Downes John, writer & grainer, 5 Bank chbrs. Lothbury, & 61 Church st. Shoreditch
Downes Joseph, coach broker, 8A, Lit. James st. Bedford rw
Downes Mary (Mrs.), china ware. 28Theobald's rd. Red Lion sq
Downes Robert, silversmith, 28 Cowper st. City rd
Downes Robert, watch & clock maker, 96 Upper st. Islngtn
Downes Thomas, cabinetmaker, 246 Whitechapel road
Downes Thos. Wm. jeweller, 40 Hedge row, High st. Islngtn
Downes Wm. stove & grate mak. 13 Bland ter. Gt. Dover rd
Downey Alice & Son, lightermen, 21 Commercial rd. Lmbth
Downey John & Son, lightermen, 11 Millbank row, Holywell st. Westminster, & Battersea fields
Downey Richard & Son, licensed lightermen, barge & boat builders & pile drivers, 11 Millbank row, & Nine Elms
Downey Francis, sen. plumber, 1 Duke st. St. James's
Downey William, engraver, 58 King st. Camden town
Downey William, *Plough* P.H. 41 Brook mews, Berkeley sq
Downham Geo. corndealer, 20 Camden st. East st. Walworth
Downham Geo. livery stables, 24 Chester st. Kenningn. cross
Downie James, baker, 44 Liquorpond st
Downie John, cabinaster, 12 Johnson st. Holywell st. Westr
Downie John, stationer & librarian, 64 King st. Soho
Downing George & John Henry, floorcloth manufacturers, 6 & 7 Lowndes' ter. Knightsbridge, & King's rd. Chelsea
Downing William & Co. furn. undertakers, 78 Hoxton Old tn
Downing Charles, surgeon, &c. 57 Gt. Coram st
Downing Edward, brushmaker, 19 Brown st. Bryanstone sq

Downing Edward, surgeon, 23 Broomfield place, Deptford
Downing Francis, solicitor, 13 King's road, Bedford row
Downing George, jeweller, 16 New st. Covent garden
Downing George, undertaker, 53 Walnut tree walk, Lambth
Downing Henry Bourne, general merchant, 11 Mark lane
Downing James W. carpet warehmn. see Muckalt&Downing
Downing John, stationer, 2 Queen's road, Bayswater
Downing Joseph, *Marquis of Granby* P.H. St. Katherine's
Downing Michael, stereotype founder, 62½ Snow hill
Downing Reb. (Mrs.), *Bridge hotel tap*, Montagueclose, Boro'
Downing Samuel, *Red Lion* P.H. 23 Rosoman st. Clknwell
Downing Thomas, coal mercht. 4 Kensington High st
Downing William, bargebuilder, 8 Abdy st. Horselydown, & 2 Bermondsey wall
Downing Wm. sailmaker, 24 Gainsford st. Horselydown; 2 Bermondsey wall; & Pickle Herring stairs, Tooley st
Downman Hugh H. tinplate merchant, 9 Laurence Pountney lane, & Hall of Commerce, Threadneedle st
Downs Henry & Edwin, maltsters, lightermen & corn merchants, 76 New Corn exchange, & Richmond, Surrey
Downs Daniel, beer retailer, 56 Chapel st. Pentonville
Downs Edwin, brewer, see Gaskell & Downs
Downs JohnHen.maltstr.&cornmr.76NewCorn exch.&Gray's
Downs Nathaniel, tailor, 17 Brewer st. Golden square
Downs Rd. baker, 205 Blackfrs. rd. & 111 Gt. Suffolk st. Boro'
Downs Robert, baker, 50 Great Guildford st. Borough
Downs Thomas, cheesemonger, 7 L. Porchester st. Edgware rd
Downs Wm. lighterman & corndealer, Battersea square
Downs Wm. undertaker, 52 Great Guildford st. Borough
Downton Jonathan, brass founder, patent pump, fire engine & water closet maker, Conant place, Commercial road, Limehouse; residence, 7 Jamaica place
Downton Matthew, bootmaker, 4 Limekiln hill, Limehouse
Dowse Henry & George & Co. merchts. 17 Broad st. buildings
Dowse George, merchant, N. & S. American coffeehouse
Dowse James, machine ruler, 106 Gt. Guildford st. Borough
Dowse James, potato dealer, 82 London road, Southwark
Dowse Thomas, artist, 39 Charlotte st. Fitzroy square
Dowse William, barrister, 1 Millman place, Bedford row
Dowse Wm. Heatrell, barrister, Law chambers, 77 Chancery la
Dowsee Sarah (Miss), straw hat maker, 28 Crawford st
Dowsett Henry, coffee rooms, 31 Friday st
DowsettJas.Finch,plumbr.&glazr.8Smith st.King's rd.Chlsea
Dowsett John, buildg. material dlr. 7 New rd. St. George's Ea
Dowsett John, wheelwright, Whitecross st. Borough
Dowsett Jonathan, builder, 3 Plough yard, Shoreditch
Dowsett Richard, coffee rooms, 33 Belvedere rd. Lambeth
Dowsett Wm. Bailey, gold & silver engra. 23 Wilderness row
Dowsing, F. Paul, J. G. & Co. lithographers, 7 Warwick ct. Hlbn
Dowson Christopher & Son, shipbuilders, Limehouse bdg. dock, Narrow st. & 23 Narrow st. Limehouse
Dowson Joseph & Co. mahogany, timber & stave merchants, Prince's whf. (late Lett's whf.) Commercial rd. Lambeth
Dowson Christopher, jun. ship builder, Limehouse
Dowson Christopher, sen. ship builder, 14 Church rw. Limeho
Dowson Henry, bookbinder, 28 Park st. Dorset square
Dowson Joseph, coal merchant, 76 Judd st. Brunswick sq
Dowson Joseph, copperfounder, 12 Church row, Limehouse
Dowson Josph. copper mer. & brass fou. see Young, Dowson & Co
Dowson Joseph Emerson, iron & brass founder, merchant & smith, stove grate manfr. gas fitter & general ironmonger, 67 Welbeck st. Cavendish sq & 5 Seymour pl. Brynstn. sq
Doxat & Co. merchants, 13 Bishopsgate without
Doy John, carpenter, 20 Charterhouse st
Doyle Andrew, *White Bear* P.H. 53 Kingsland road
Doyle Edwards, solicitor, see Nicholls & Doyle
Doyle Henry, oil & colorman, 4 Parkside, Knightsbridge
Doyle James, cabinet maker, 32 Tabernacle row, City road
Doyle Jamas, grocer, 25 Commercial road, Lambeth
Doyle John, *Marquis of Granby* P.H. 51&52 Chandos st. Str
Doyle John, scale & weighing machine mkr. 26 King st. Boro'
Doyle Michael, steward's office, 15 Old sq. Lincoln's inn
Doyle Peter, sen. sail maker & canvass merchant, 27 & 28 Shadwell High st. & 74 Wapping wall
Doyle Peter, jun. shipchandler, 27 & 28 Shadwell High st. & 74 Wapping wall
Doyle Sir Francis Hastings, bart. barrister, 17 Serjeants' inn
Doyle Thomas, fishmonger, 17 Lit. Windmill st. Golden sq
Doyle Wm. fancy cabinet ma. 31 Betts st. Ratcliff highway
Doyley & Dalton, architects & surveyors, 6 John st. Adelphi
Doyley John, surveyor, 36 Upper Barnsbury st. Islington
Doyley's warehouse (A. Walker & Co.), 346 Strand
Drabble Samuel, working cutler, 1 High st. Marylebone
Drabble William, chemist, 25 Bedford row, Bloomsbury
Drach Rebecca Wolf (Mrs.), merchnt. 10 Castle st. Houndsditch
Dracott Charles, cattle salesman, 17 West Smithfield
Draddy John, grocer, 95 Rosemary lane, Minories
Draeger George, tailor, 36 Leicester square
Drage Charles, chemist, 2 Brick hill la. Up. Thames st. City
Drage Charles, eau de cologne importer, 6 Tower Royal
Drage John, fruiterer, 24 Cleveland st. Fitzroy square
Drago Sophia (Miss), milliner, 9 Patriot row, Cambridge rd
Drain John, gardener & florist, Bridport place, Hoxton
Drake & Cox, tanners, Russell st. Bermondsey
Drake Ann (Mrs.), umbrella manuf. 3 St. John's la. Smithfi
Drake Caroline (Mrs.), *Ship* P.H. 12 Arcade, Hungerford mar
Drake Edwd. house agent, 11 Heathcote st. Mecklenbrgh. sq
Drake Edward, *St. Andrew* P.H. 24 George st. Portman sq
Drake Francis, solicitor, 34 Bouverie st. Fleet st
Drake Geo. silversm. &c. 1 Commerce row, Up. st. Islington
Drake Henry, potato dlr. 2 Jamaica ter. Coml. rd. Limehouse
Drake Hugh James, beer retailer, 22 Old st. road
Drake James, featherbed manufactory, 13 Oxford st
Drake James, ironmonger, 3 Caledonia ter. Caledonian road
Drake John, colonial broker, 9 Mincing lane
Drake John, grocer, 169 Kingsland road
Drake John Collard, patentee & manufacturer of improved lining for damp walls of houses, including the "butting" or invisible join for carpets, velvets, &c. or any suitable material, & patent mounted paper scales for surveyors, engineers, &c. 19 Elm tree road, St. John's wood
Drake Joseph, feather merch. 40 Brick lane, Spitalfields
Drake Joseph, feather, wool & horsehair manufacturer, 56 Wentworth st. & 40 Brick lane, Spitalfields; manufactory, George st. Spitalfields
Drake Joseph, lath render, 16 Quickset rw. New rd. Fitzroy sq
Drake Marmaduke, oil & colorman, 39 Gt. Peter st. Westmr
Drake Marmaduke, oilman & candle ma. 213 Blackfriars rd
Drake Philip, notary public, 42 Leicester square
Drake Robert, furrier to her Majesty & the Royal Family, hatter & army capmaker, 25 Piccadilly
Drake Samuel, boot & shoe mak. 30 Sidney st. Goswell road
Drake Theod. bone button ma. Vale royal, Maidn. la. King's cr
Drake Thos. surgeon, 8 Nassau pl. Commercial road east
Drake Wm. beer retailer, 171 Brick lane, Spitalfields
Drake William, fruiterer, 2 Old Fish st
Drake Wm. Bishop, clothes sales. 130 High st. Camden twn
Drake Wm. Rd. solicitor, see Walton, Forbes & Drake
Drakeford Charles, butcher, 3 New Grove, Mile end road
Drakeford Charles, potato dealer, 43 Leather lane, Holborn
Drakeford David, silk broker, 34 Great Winchester st
Dramatic Authors' Society, 1 Trinity place, Charing cross
Drane Jn. & Co. ivory & tortshl. & hardwood dlrs. 122 Minories
Drane & Sherwin, comb manufacturers, 122 Minories
Drane John, cabinet maker & furniture dealer, 25 Chichester place, Gray's inn road
Drane Wm. schoolmaster, see Fleming & Drane
Dransfield Joseph & Son, fancy stuff manufacturers, 21 Gutter lane; factory, Rookey mill, Huddersfield
Dransfield Ann (Mrs.), confectioner, 6 Pitts's pl. Old Kent rd
Drant Mary (Mrs.), tobacconist, 63 Chandos st. Cov. gardn
Drant Wm. grocer, 5 Stockbridge terrace, Pimlico
Draper, Berry & Hearse, engravers, 26 Change alley, Cornhill
Draper, Child & Co. Star brewery, 11 Oxford st
Draper Wm. & Thos. leatherdressers, &c. 107 High Holborn
Drapers' Almshouses, Cooper's row, Crutchedfriars; & Hill st. Blackfriars road; & 160 Whitechapel road
Drapers' Hall (Edward Lawford, clerk), 27 Throgmorton st
Draper Abrm. herbalist, 2 Halfmoon pas. Leadenhall market
Draper Chas. bookselr. & statnr. 68 St. John st. WestSmthfld
Draper Chas. *Sun* P.H. 140 Bishopsgate without
Draper Chas. tobacconist, 46 Gt. Queen st. Lincoln's inn fields
Draper George, locksmith, 3 Elm st. Gray's inn lane
DraperGeo.russia mer.4Gt.Winchester st.City,&Baltic cof.ho
Draper Hastings Dare, attorney, 45 Vincent sq. Westminster
Draper James Hilton, straw bonnet ma. 3 Evaline pl. Com. rd. E
Draper John, *Globe tavern*, 91 Hatton garden
Draper John, who. ret. & expt. stationer, &c. 50 Lombard st
DraperJohnWm. fruit salesman, &c. Centre row, Covent gar
DraperJoseph,smith&bellhang. 88 Gt.Titchfield st.Oxford st
Draper Moses, tailor, 7 Taunton pl. Brunswick st. Dover rd
Draper Richd. currier & shoe manf. 7 Church la. Whitechapel
Draper Robert, watch jeweller, 22 Ossulston st. Somers town
Draper Sarah (Mrs.), butcher, 14 Porter st. Soho
DrawaterGeo. baker & confectioner, 4 Albion pl. King's cross
Drawmer Thomas, linendraper, 19 Sussex place, Old Kent rd
Dray Frederick, grocer, &c. 13 Colonnade, Brunswick sq
Dray Thos. tus. & straw bon. manfr. 84 Chiswell st. Finsbury sq
Dray William, stove & range manufr. see Deane, Dray & Deane
Draycott Frederick, carver & gilder, 27 Duke st. Bloomsbury
DrayseyJohn, copperplate printer, 14 Primrose st. Bishopsgt
Drayson George, goldsmith, 16 Brewer st. Golden square

Drayton Thos. dressing case ma. 32 Up. Rosoman st. Clerkw
Drayton Wm.W. stayma.4Commerce row,Upper st.Islington
Dredge & Ross, smiths' & coopers' tool mak. 24 Gt. Alie st
Dredge John, printer & stationer, 67 Whitechapel High st
Dredge Joseph, bootmaker, 25 St. Swithin's lane
Dresden Edward Zodiac, merchant, 1 Lime st. square
Dresden R—— Z ——, merchant, 1 Lime st. square
Dresser Clement, wool merchant, 19 Basinghall st
Dresser Joseph, cheese & ham factor, Hay's wharf,Tooley st
Dresser Richard, accountant, 8 Eastcheap
Dressler Gustavus, merchant, 6 Idol la. Gt. Tower st
Drew,Heyward&Barron, who. druggists,2Gt.Bush lane,City
Drew Walter& Henry P. L. surgeons,79Gower st.Bedford sq
Drew&Wodderspoon,stationers,16&17Portugal st.Lin.in.flds
Drew Beriah, sup. reg. of births, &c. 185 Bermondsey st
Drew Chas. *Crown* P.H. 182 Church st. Shoreditch
Drew Danl.cabinet ma.& upholst. 36 Compton st.Clerkenwell
Drew David, carpenter, 34 Gt. Titchfield st. Oxford st
Drew Edw. stationer & toy wa.2 New Chapel pl.Kentish twn
Drew Elizh.(Mrs.), milliner, &c.27 Up. Albany st. Regent's pk
Drew Frances (Mrs.),boot & shoe wa.37A,Lamb'sConduit st
Drew Francis,boot&shoe manufacturer,11 Newington causeway, & 5 Brighton place, Brixton
Drew George, solicitor, 185 Bermondsey st
Drew Henry, horse dealer, 80 Blackman st. Borough
Drew Henry, surgeon, 33 Torrington square
Drew Henry, who. ironmonger, &c. see Rownson & Drew
Drew James, haberdasher, &c. 19 Bridge st. Westminster
Drew James Paul, artist, 8 Howland st. Fitzroy square
Drew Jeffery, currier, 13 Purim pl. Cambridge rd. Mile end
Drew John, law stationer, 8 Took's court, Chancery lane
Drew John, lighterman, 146 Upper Thames st
Drew John, plumber, 17 Newcastle st. Strand; & oil & colorman, 96 Drury lane
Drew John, ready made linen wareho. 70 Burlington arcade
Drew John, wine merchant, 19 Liquorpond st
Drew John Brown, carpenter, 11 Wittam's bldgs. Old st. rd
Drew Mary (Mrs.), lodging house, 14 Villiers st. Strand
Drew Robert, cheesemonger, 65 Clarendon st. Somers town
Drew Robert,*Crown tavern*, 7 Stationers' hall court
Drew Thomas, fruiterer, 71 Gt. Guildford st. Borough
Drew Thomas, grocer, 23 Bermondsey New road
Drew Thomas, grocer, &c. 55 Grundy st. East Ind.rd. Poplar
Drew Thomas, tobacconist, 3 Elwell pl. Grange rd. Brmdsy
Drew William, baker, 87 Charlotte st. Fitzroy sq
Drew William, builder, 27 Up. Albany st. Regent's park
Drew William, poulterer & fishmonger, 19 Finsbury pavmt
Drew Wm.Jno.builder, 1 Rosedale vil.Ladbroke gr.Notng.hl
Drewe Amelius Hen. W. solicitor, see Baylis & Drewe
Drewe Aurelius J. wharfinger, Steel yard, 86 Up. Thames st
Drewe Robt. John, oil& colorman, 118 Gt. Titchfield st
Drewell Saml. artist in fireworks, 6 Hatfield pl. Westmr. rd
Drewell Samuel, cowkeeper, Beaumont mews, Marylebone
Drewett & Fowler, bankers, 4 Princes st. Bank
Drewett & Mercer, carpenters, 59 King st. Borough
Drewett Ambrose, carpenter, 4 Red Lion st. Borough
Drewett Ann (Mrs.), sexton, 5 Church st. St.Saviour's, Boro'
Drewett James, booking office, *Spur inn* yd.97 Boro'High st
Drewett Thos.sack&bag dlr. 60 Snow's fields, Bermondsey
Drewett William, registrar, 4 Denmark pl. Well st. Hackney
Drewry Charles Stewart, barrister, 5 New sq. Lincoln's inn
Drewry Edward, *Ship& Sun* P.H.33 Crosby rw.Walworth rd
Drewry Edward, surgeon, 8 Park terrace, Highbury
Drewry James,*Gentleman & Porter* P.H. 33 Kingsland rd
Dreyer & Genetat, tailors, 26 Sackville st. Piccadilly
Dridge John, engraver, Wandsworth road, north side
Driffield Henry, whip maker, 21 Mercer st. Long acre
Dring & Fage, hydrometer, saccharometer & gauging instrument makers, 19 & 20 Tooley st. Southwark
Dring Samuel, grocer & cheesemgr. 21 Long alley, Finsbury
Drinkwater Jsph.*Coach& Horses* P.H.35 Notting hill High st
Drinkwater Wm. Leece, barrister, 3 Paper bldgs. Temple
Driscall John, tailor, 23 Back hill, Hatton garden
Driscoll Margaret & Samuel, bootmakers, 14New st. Cloth fr
Driscoll Bartholomew, shoemaker, 26 Rosemary lane
Driver Edward & George Neale, surveyors & land agents, 8 Richmond terrace, Whitehall
Driver Edward, baker, 52 Union st. Somers town
Driver George, oil & colorman, 74 Snow hill
Driver Henry, lace dealer, 116 Crawford st. Portman sq
Driver Henry A. coal merchant, Milford wharf, Strand
Driver Henry Austen, who. stationer, 28 King st. Cheapside
Driver Jas. pat. medicn. vend. 37 Lit. Charlot. st. Blkfrs. rd
Driver John Samuel, scale maker, see Bastick & Driver
Driver Robert, fishmonger, 206 Shadwell High st
Driver S.(Mrs.), *Experienced Fowler* P.H.Nightngl.la. Lmho
Driver Thos. *George& Dragon* P.H.17 Paradise row, Chelsea
Driver Thomas, grocer, High st. Stoke Newington
Droitwich Salt Company, 86 Lower Thames st. 35 Bridge wharf, City road basin, & 338 High st. Wapping
Drolenvaux & Stahlschmidt, ship&cust. ho.agts.14Mark lane
Dromgole John, window glass dealer, 20 Barbican
Dromgole Peter, coach, &c. spring maker, Stratford
Dron John, silk dyer, 25 Oakley st. Lambeth
Drouet Richard, butcher, 7 Kennington row
Drouet William, *Coach& Horses* P.H. 72 Broad st. Lambeth
Drouhet, Gardner & Co. merchants, 4 Finsbury circus
Drover George, marine store dlr. 10 George's row, City road
Droy Thomas, *Rose* P.H. 58 Hatton garden
Droy Thomas, timber merchant, see Knight & Droy
Druce Alex.copper mer.seeSims,Willyams,Nevill,Druce&Co
Druce & Brock, upholsterers, &c. 200 Regent st
Druce & Crosler, law stationers, 9 Quality ct. Chancery lane
Druce Charles & Sons, attorneys, 10 Billiter square
Druce Charles &Co. furn. depart. Bazaar,4King st.Portm.sq
Druce Thos. & Wm. timber&coal mers. Paradise row, Chelsea
Druce James, marine store dlr. 9 Eaton lane north, Pimlico
Druce John, butcher, 82 Farringdon st
Druce Joseph, butcher, 13 Skinner st. Somers town
Druce Mary Ann (Mrs.), butcher, 6 Pitfield st. Hoxton
Druce Thomas, butcher, 29 Weymouth st. Portland place
Druce Thomas, coal merchant, 42 Commercial rd. Lambeth
Druce William, *Feathers* P.H.75Commercial road, Lambeth
Druce Wm. *Feathers* P.H. 205 Wellington ter. Waterloo rd
Druce Wm. wharfinger & slate merchant, Druce's No. 2 wharf, Paradise row, Chelsea
Druce Wm. hanstown brewery, 31 Lower George st. Chelsea
Druckker Simeon Sam. for. goods imp. 3 Phill's bld. Houndsd
Drucquer John, importer of cigars, 334 Strand
Druggan Henry, boot & shoe maker, 60 Goswell road
Druggan James, bootmaker, 9 Goswell road
Druggan James, boot & shoe mak. 9 St. John st.Clerkenwell
Druitt Chas.zinc & metal worker, 49 Wellington pl.Stepney
Druitt Henry, tailor, 39 Albany road, Camberwell
Druitt Robert, surgeon, 39A, Curzon st. Mayfair
Druitt Thos. currier, 4 Ebenezer pl. Com. rd. Limehouse
Druitt Thomas, mason, 7 Ireland row, Mile end road
Druke Sarah (Mrs.), manufact. of fine colors, 5 Cloak lane
Drummond Archibald, tea dealer, 98 Whitechapel High st
Drummond Ellen (Miss), artist, 78 Wimpole st.Cavendish sq
Drummond Fenwick, porkman & poulterer, see Hughes & Drummond
Drummond Henry, Andrew Mortimer, Charles, Andrew Robert, George & Harvey, bankers, 49 Charing cross
Drummond James, baker, 78 Milton st, Dorset square
Drummond John, cork cutter, 147 Shadwell High st
Drummond John, tailor, 125 Bermondsey st
Drummond John T. *Crooked Billet* P.H. Hermitage stairs, Wpg
Drummond Myra (Miss), artist, 78 Wimpole st. Cavendish sq
Drummond Rob. pork butcher&game dlr. Bridge st. Vauxhall
Drummond Thos. smith, 38 Gravel lane, Southwark
Drummond William, cattle salesman, 15 West Smithfield
Drury Francis & Son, music. bellfndr. 60 Red Lion st. Clkwl
Drury Edw.Geo.clock case ma.15 Up.Charles st.Northam.sq
Drury Geo. goldsmith & cutler, & sword cutler, 32 Strand
Drury Henry D. wine mer. see Rutherford, Drury & Co
Drury Henry, straw hat maker, 45 Hackney road
Drury Lane Theatre, Brydges st. Covent garden
Drury Michael, surgeon, High st. Deptford
Dry Charlotte (Mrs.), china dealer, 6 Youl's pl. Old Kent rd
Dry Jemima(Mrs.), wheelwright, 5Horse&Groom yd. Westmr
Dry Thomas, solicitor, 21 Lincoln's inn fields
Dry Wm. *Bull's Head* P.H.&livery stables, 101 Tottenham ct. rd
Dry William Henry, surgeon, 40 Up. Salisbury pl. Locksflds
Drybrough Andrew, wine merchant, 6 Basing lane, Bread st
Dryden Charles Beville, solicitor, 21 Lincoln's inn fields
Dryden George, watchmakr, 30 Lit. Guilford st Brunswk. sq
Dryden Robert, who. grocer & com. agent, 30 Coleman st
Dryden Wm.millwright,&c.10Kinaston st. Oakley st. Lambeth
Dryhurst George, plumber, &c. 16 Gt. Quebec st. New rd
Dryland Wm.russia broker, 56Threadneedle st.&5Hercules pas
Drysdale Henry, auctioneer, 4 Lamb's Conduit st. Foundling
Drysdale James, beer retailer, 5 Boyton place, Walworth
Drysdale James, bookseller, 165 Goswell st
Drysdale James, carpenter, 34 Chapel st. New road
Drysdale John, Caledonian Stm. Towing Co. 11 Milk yd. Shdwl
Drysdale John, wine merchant, 59 Mark lane
Drysdale Mary (Mrs.), milliner, 4 Lamb's conduit st
Drysdale Thomas, general agent, 56 Aldermanbury
Dubbins Edward, *Somerset hotel*, & refrshmt. rms. 162 Strand
Dubery Richd. ginger beer mer. 13 Hastings st. Burton cres
Dubois Charles Edgar William & Co. bootma. 66 Old Bailey

Dublin & Galway Railway Co. (Jas. Brydon, sec.), 19 Moorgate st
Dubois Edward & Co.engineers, &c.75&76 Broad st.Lambeth
Dubois Charles, bootmaker, see Edgar & Dubois
Du Bois Edward, barrister, 3 Middle Temple lane
Du Bois Edward,clk.to comr.in lunacy,12Abingdon st.Wstm
Dubois Daniel, dentist, 65 Princes st. Leicester square
Dubois Hill E. F. barrister, Mitre court, Fleet st
Dubois John, plumber & glazier, 33 Upper Ebury st.Pimlico
Dubosc Jean Baptiste, wine mercht. see Gonzalez & Dubosc
Dubourg John, *Dubourg's hotel*, 60 & 61 Haymarket
Dubourg John, saloon of arts, 8 Gt.Windmill st. Haymarket
Dubourg John, tobacconist, 63 Haymarket
Du Bouisson, Henckell & Co. merchants, see Henckell & Co
Du Buisson James, merchant, 18 Laurence Pountney lane
Ducas Thomas, grocer & cheesemonger, Orchard pl. Blackwl
Duce John, gunlock ma.1Lambeth st.Whtchpl.&Wednesbury
Duchemin Hen. french polisher, 4 Birdcage walk, Hackney rd
Duchesne Clarke, surgeon, 22 White Lion st.Norton folgate
Duchesne Robert, teadlr.see Dockerill, Duchesne & Dockerill
Duchy of Cornwall Office, Somerset house; hours 10 to 4
Duchy of Lancaster Office, Lancast.pl.Strand; hours 10 to 4
Duck Geo. smith in general, 19 Freeschool st. Horselydown
Duck Wm. bricklayer, 2 Great Portland st. Oxford st
Duck Wm. sweep, 14 Princes st. Bedford row, & 2 Silver st. Bloomsbury
Duckitt Wm. & Mark, cowkeepers, 29 Gt.George st.Bermdsy
Duckrell & Dickins, straw hat ma. 6 Courtenay ter.Kngslnd
Duckrell Wm. coachmaker, 3 Virginia pl. Gt. Dover rd
Duckworth & Kennedy, meat salesmen, 30, 31 & 40Nwgt.mkt
Duckworth Wm. Thos. & Hen. cattle salesm.41 West Smthfld
Ducrow John, tobacconist, 15 & 26Lit.Windmill st.Golden sq
DuCroz John C. glass, china, lamp & lustre ma.112 Regent st
Dudbridge John, grocer, 1 Hunter st. Gt. Dover rd
Dudden & Dafft, woollendrapers, 123 Whitechapel High st
Dudden Wm. P. & Edmund, woollendrapers, 16 Coventryst
Dudderidge Hen. Wm. locksmith, 21 Anchor st. Shoreditch
DudderidgeHen.W. oil & colorm.3 Goldsmith's row, Hack.rd
Dudderidge Wm. furnitr. broker, 5 Rose & Crown ct.Eldon st
Duddy Charles, butcher, 164 Hoxton Old town
Duddy George, butcher, 3 Drummond st. Euston square
Dudfeild & Wicks, glove leather stainers, 1Castle st.Saff. hill
Dudeney Henry, beer retailer, 6½ East st. Walworth road
Dudgeon Robt. Ellis, physician, 82 Glo'ster pl. Portman sq
Dudgeon William, tailor, 5 Gray's inn passage, Red Lion sq
Dudin Henry, cornfactor, lighterman, wharfinger & granary keeper, Jerusalem wharf, Shad Thames, Horselydown; Springhall's wharf, Bermondsey wall; & East lane, Bermondsey wall; & Shad Thames
Dudley Chas. & Geo. whitesmiths, 18 John's row, St. Luke's
Dudley (Misses), ladies' school, 36 Duke st. Grosvenor sq
Dudley & Rutty, linendra. 3 Gerrard st.&1&2Nassau st. Soho
Dudley Benjamin, *Macclesfield Arms* P.H. City road
Dudley Francis F. bricklayer, 152 Old Gravel la. Wapping
Dudley James, *Crown* P.H. 154½ Upper Whitecross st
Dudley John, chairmaker, 38½ Charles st. City road
Dudley John, watch enameller, 15 Peerless row, City road
Dudley John, watch jeweller, 8 Radcliffe ter. Goswell road
Dudley Sophia (Mrs.), linendraper, 19 Spring st. Paddingtn
Dudley William, wholesale jeweller, 13 Thavies inn, Holbrn
Dudman David, *Wheatsheaf* P.H. 51 Red Lion st. Holborn
Dudman Joseph, boot & shoe maker, 20 King st.Coventgdn
Dudman Richard (agent to Robert Micklejohn & Son, ale merchants), Three cranes wharf, Upper Thames st
Dudman Richd. commrcl. traveller, 2 Dean st. sth. Tooley st
Dudman Thomas, coal mer. Horseferry branch rd. Ratcliff
Duer James, carpenter, 23 Paddington st. Marylebone
Duer Samuel, baker, 146 New Bond st
Duesbury Henry, architect, 1 Upper Gore, Kensington
Dufaur & Blakeney, solicitors, 3 Bedford row
Dufaur Frederick, navy agent, 13 Clement's inn, Strand, & 4 Grove cottage, Holloway
Dufaur Frederick, solicitor, 23 Queen Anne st. Cavendish sq
DufavilleWm. gelatine ma. Broughton ho.WhiteConduitflds
Duff-Gordon & Co. merchants, 24 Crutched friars
Duff & Hodgson, music sellers & publishers, 65 Oxford st. & pianoforte makers, 3 Berners st
Duff Jas. Gordon & Co. merch. & madeira ags.138Leadnhl st
Duff Alexander M. dentist, 2A, Welbeck st. Cavendish sq
Duff Chas. music string ma.9Harrington st. nth.Hampstdrd
Duff Jas. watch & clock maker, 24 Castle st. Houndsditch
Duff John, tailor, 4 Yeates court, Carey st
Duff Peter, linendraper, 8 Brewer st. Golden square
Duff Peter John, haberdasher, 2 Orange st. Red Lion sq
Duff Wm. à-la-mode beef house, 69 Castle st. Leicester sq
Duff Wm. notary, 5 Nicholas lane, Lombard st
Duff Wm. Hen. surgeon, 4 Mecklenburgh ter. Gray's inn rd
Duffell Henry, smith & engineer, 190 Shadwell High st
Duffell James, ironmonger, 1 Wandsworth road
Duffell James Henry, stock broker, 2 Adams ct.OldBroad st
Duffett Henry, ladies' shoemaker, 61 King st. Seven dials
Duffie Archibald, straw hat ma.27Norfolk st.Middlesex hosp
Duffield & Co. merchants, 2 Skinner's place, Sise lane
Duffield & Merriott, coach builders, 114 Aldersgate st
Duffield Sluices Offi.(Geo.Newman, sec.), Bermondsey wall
Duffield Ann (Mrs.), baker, 13 Duke st. Portland place
Duffield George, baker, 6 Portland pl. Commercial rd. east
Duffield John, bookseller & stationer, 62 Hackney road
Duffield JohnElder, harness manufac. 1Long lane, Smithfield
Duffield Joseph, turner & carver, 28 Brandon st. Walworth
Duffield Wm. tailor, 10 Canterbury place, Old Kent road
Duffill Elizth. (Miss), school, 9 Prospect pl. Wandsworth rd
Duffill George H. barrister, 7 King's Bench walk, Temple
Duffin Edward W. surgeon, 14 Langham pl. Portland place
Duffin Richard, tailor, 33 High st. Lambeth
Duffy John & Son, calico & muslin printers, 8 Friday st.Chpsd
Duffy Bernard, physician, 6 Upper Seymour st. Portman sq
Duffy James, grocer, 17 Ship yard, Temple bar
Duffy Patrick, *Fountain & Still*P.H. 2 Golden la. Barbican
Dufort Louis, confectioner, 11 Smithfield bars
Dufour Wm.stationer & music seller, 17A, Gt.George st.Wstr
Dugan James John, hairdresser, 37 Warren st. Fitzroy sq
Dugard Chas. & Edw. saddlers & harness ma.10Finsbry. pav
Dugard Geo.&Thos.workg.jewellers, 34RedLionst.Clerkenwl
Dugard Geo. & Thos. merchants, 34 Red Lion st. Clerkenwell
Dugard Charles, livery stables, Richmond road, Dalston
Dugard Wm. Thos. type founder, 18 Fulwood's rents
Dugdale John & Brothers, furniture & calico printers (H. James, agent), 6 Dyer's court, Aldermanbury
Dugdale Henry, blockmaker, 16 Gainsford st. Horselydown
Dugdale John, printer, 23 Russell court, Drury lane
Duggan Thomas, & Co. pipe clay & bath brick merchants, Chamberlain's wharf, 11 & 12 Tooley street
Duggan Henry, lighterman, 28 New Church st. Bermondsey
DugganJohnColeman, lighterman, 10Coleman's cre.Brmndsy
Duggan Mary (Miss), milliner, 1 Brook st. Grosvenor sq
Duggan Wm.congreve match manufr. 16 North st.Whtcpl.rd
Duggin James Frederick & Co. silk dyers, &c. 37 Duke st. Manchester square, & 12 King st. Holborn
Dugmore William, barrister, 4 New sq. Lincoln's inn
Dugood James, hairdresser, 7 Bath st. City road
Duguid Robert, teadealer, 138 St. George st
Duguid William, upholsterer, 1 Barton st. Westminster
Duhan Charles, cheesemonger, 33 Upper Eaton st. Pimlico
Duhy James, bootmaker, 20 Dartmouth st. Westminster
Dujardin John, artist, 5 Westbourne place, Sloane square
Duke & Bennett, worstd.& utrechtvelvet mfs. 46A, Newgt.st
Duke & Hill, coal factors & insurance brokers, 23 Botolph la
Duke & Jeffrey, general wire workers, sieve, birdcage, & fire iron manufacturers, 2 Allen's court, 387 Oxford st
Duke Thomas & Son, umbrella makers, 26 Crown st. Soho
Duke of Cornwall's Harbour & Launceston & Victoria Railway Co. (George Dyson, sec.), 10 Austin friars
Duke George, bricklayer, 63 Harrow road, Paddington
Duke Henry, linendraper, 16 King's pl. Commercial rd. east
Duke James, grainer, 2Chapel pl. north, South Audley st
Duke James, van proprietor, 39 Curtain road
Duke Mannin George, law & gen. stationer, 99 Chancery la
Duke Rd. mercht. & sailcloth factor, 31 Low. EastSmithfield
Duke Thos. Oliver, surgeon, 17 Harleyford pl. Kengtn. com
Duke William, *Fleece* P.H. Upper Russell st. Bermondsey
Duke William, tailor, 29 Jewry st. Aldgate
Dukes Chas. portrait painter, 33 Gt. St. Helen's, Bishopsgate
Dukes Esquire, surgeon, 5 Acton place, Kingsland road
Dukes George, watchmaker, 8 St. John st. Clerkenwell
Dukes Joshua, school, 7 Kingsland place, Kingsland road
Dulau Messrs. & Co. foreign booksellers, 37 Soho square
Dullea Owen, *IndiaArms*P.H. 62Gainsford st.Horselydown
Dulson Harriet (Mrs.), beer retailer, 12 High st. Deptford
Dumain Geo. cheesem. & grocer, 44&45NewChurch st.Liss.gr
Dumain James, cheesemonger, 32 Ashley crescent, City rd
Dumas & Wylie, merchants & insurance brokers, 33 Great Winchester st. & Lloyd's
Dumas Claudius, silk & cot. mer. 25 Anchor st. Bethnal green
Dumbarton Glass Co.(Wm. C. Smith, agnt.), 43 Trinity sq
Dumbrell Charles, butcher, 41 Theobald's road
Dumbrill Richard, fruiterer, 77 Fore st. City
Dumergue Francis, barrister, 13 Old square, Lincoln's inn
Dummelow & Bonner, colonial brokers, 48 Fenchurch st
Dummelow John Robert, wheelwright, Parker's row, Brmsy
Dummer MaryAnn(Mrs.), teadlr. & grocer, 16SouthAudleyst
Dummler Albert, merchant, 11 Mark lane

Dumville John, butcher, 1 Brunswick st. Cromer st
Dun Wm. chair maker, 8 China walk, Lambeth
Dunage Harminia (Mrs.), lace cleaner, 15 Grafton st. Fitzy. sq
Dunball Louisa (Mrs.), stay maker, 27 New rd. Sloane st
Dunball Robert, beer retailer, 8 Horse shoe alley, Finsbury
Dunbar & Cleghorn, hemp, flax & mat. mers. 11 Ireland row, Mile end road, & 8 Billiter st. Leadenhall st
Dunbar (Duncan) & Sons, wine merchants & ship owners, 95 Fore st. Limehouse
Dunbar David, sculptor, 15 Elizabeth st. south, Pimlico
Dunbar James, glasgow & manch. agent, 3 Lit. Friday st
Dunbar John, jun. iron foundry, 187 Tottenham court road
Dunbibin James Priest, dep. registrar, 51 Gt. Suffolk st. Boro
Duncalfe Wm. muffin baker, 19 Platt terrace, Somers town
Duncan & Garmston, hop & seed merchts. 9½ Counter st. Boro'
Duncan James & Co. calico printers, &c. 81 Watling st
Duncan Andrew, accountant, 10 Tokenhouse yard
Duncan Andrew, solicitor, 11 Featherstone bldgs. Holborn
Duncan David, baker, 17 Whittlebury st. Euston square
Duncan David, florist, Lower Queen st. Rotherhithe
Duncan Edward, artist, 2 Mornington place
Duncan Edward, surgeon & apothecary, 3 Leadenhall st
Duncan Geo. G. brushma. &c. 3 Albert pl. Hoxton Old town
Duncan James, scotch provision agent, 353 Wapping
Duncan John, solicitor & patent agent, 72 Lombard st. & solicitor to Eastern Counties Railway, 41 Shoreditch
Duncan John Busher, barrister, 2 Tanfield ct. Temple
Duncan John Francis, stationer, see Dunn & Duncan
Duncan Joseph, hatter, 8 Park side, Knightsbridge
Duncan Joseph, pub. of *Railway World* newspaper, 2 Crane ct
Duncan Peter King, leather factor, 17 Halfmoon st. Bishopsgt
Duncan Richard, wine merchant, 43 Lime st
Duncan Robert, baker, 1 Felix terrace, Liverpool road
Duncan Thomas, clothier, 112 Whitechapel road
Duncan Wm. baker, 124 Jermyn st. St. James's
Duncanson John, joiner, 14 Salisbury st. Strand
Dunch Thomas Wm. surveyor, 15 Stepney causeway
Duncomb John & Co. booksellers, &c. 10 Middle row, Holborn
Duncombe Benjamin, dentist, 2 Union st. Bishopsgate witht
Duncombe Daniel, coffee rooms, 48 Drury lane
Duncombe Frederick, attorney, 18 Devereux court, Strand
Duncombe Hy. Brandeth, chemist, 31 Robinson's rw. Kingsl. rd
Duncombe Henry Haynes, attorney, 6 Lyon's inn, Strand
Duncombe James, solicitor, 4 Gray's inn place
Duncombe Richard, builder, 8 Tavistock st. Covent garden
Duncombe Wm. law stationer, 14 New sq. Lincoln's inn
Duncombe Wm. law stationer, 30 King st. Holborn
Duncum John, rope & fancy mat maker, Bow
Duncumb Sarah (Mrs.), grocer, 12 Elizabeth st. sth. Pimlico
Dundas David, queen's counsel, 13 King's bench walk, Tmpl
Dundee, Perth & London Steam Company, Mrs. Elizabeth Hore, wharfinger, 272 Wapping
Dundee Wm. merchant & agent, see Elrington & Dundee
Dunford Jas. & Hen. saddlers, &c. 31 Paddington st
Dunford Charles Wm. stationer, 42 High st. Notting hill
Dunford Henry, die sinker, 6 Wellington st. Goswell road
Dunford James, picture dealer, 16 Gt. Newport st. Long acre
Dunford Richard, butcher, 22 Wilmot st. Russell square
Dunford Thomas, tobacconist, 7 Chelsea market
Dunford William, fruiterer, 22 Grosvenor row, Pimlico
Dungar George, *Leopard* P.H. 13 Seward st. Goswell st
Dungate Charles, coal & potato dlr. 11 Robert st. Grsvnr. sq
Dungate Rebecca (Mrs.), undertaker, 9 Broadway, Westmr
Dunger Rt. carpenter & underta. 6 Skinner st. Somers town
Dunham Danl. dairy, 30 Gough st. & 8 Henry st. Gray's inn la
Dunham John, french boot & shoe warehouse, 373 Oxford st
Dunhill Fredk. sacking manuf. 13 Dorset st. Clapham rd
Dunhill Thos. carriage & harness ma. Uxbridge rd. Bayswtr
Dunington Hen. pat. cloth & lisle glove ma. 61 Aldermanbury
Dunk Wm. & Albert, hop & seed factors, 9 Counter st. Boro'
Dunk David, baker, 16 Sidney pl. Commercial road east
Dunkin Henry, corn merchant, lighterman & wharfinger, Davis's Lower wharf, Shad Thames
Dunkin Joseph, plated manufr. 6 Rolls buildings, Fetter la
Dunkley Ths. & Son, frn. undertaks. 66 & 75 Tower st. West. rd
Dunkley Hen. stonemason, 14 Dorset crescent, New North rd
Dunkley James, springer & liner, 124 St. John st. Clerknwll
Dunkley Thomas, jeweller, 82 Bunhill row
Dunkley Thomas, plumber & glazier, 8 Plumber st. City rd
Dunkley Thomas Hen. bootmaker, 24 Queen's row, Pimlico
Dunkley Wm. Henry, turner in general, 43 Wardour st. Soho
Dunkly Henry, boot & shoe warehouse, 16 Aldgate st. High st
Dunlap Agnes (Mrs.), percus. cap ma. 44 East st. Manchtr. sq
Dunlap James, physician, 42 Baker st. Portman square
Dunlap Thos. prcus. cap & tube ma. 23 Gt. Queen st. Lin. in flds
Dunlop James & Co. merchants, 147 Leadenhall st
Dunlop Archibald, land & gen. agent, 52 Lower Belgrave pl
Dunlop Archibald, jun. sole wholesale agent for Maugham's patented carrara water, 78 Upper Thames st
Dunlop Donald Mackenzie, barrister, 10 Chancery lane
Dunlop John, engraver, &c. 3 Flying horse ct. Gresham st
Dunlop John James, general agent, 26 New City chambers
Dunlop Wm. parliam. & scotch agent, see Deans, Dunlop & Hope
Dunmoody John, coachsmith, 8 Compton mews, Brunswick sq
Dunmore George, butcher, 29, Strutton ground, Westminster
Dunn Brothers (Wm. W. & John M.), woolbroks. 17 Gresham st
Dunn & Dobie, attorneys, 2 Raymond buildings, Gray's inn
Dunn & Duncan, law & general stationers, 9 Fleet st
Dunn & Tilley hat dyers, 79½ Union st. Borough
Dunn Wm. & Son, comb maks. & hornpress. 6 Osborne pl. Brickla
Dunn, Wordsworth & Dunn, solicitors, 32 Threadneedle st
Dunn Alfred, bookbinder, 14 Chandos st. Covent garden
Dunn Alexander, ship agent, stone merchant & custom house agent, 8 Trinity square, Tower hill
Dunn Ann (Mrs.), beershop, 20 Windsor st. Lower st. Islington
Dunn Benjamin, oil & colorman, 4 White horse lane, Stepney
Dunn Charles, lace & millinery warehouse, 129 Oxford st
Dunn Charles George, tinman, 15 Queen st. Tower hill
Dunn Daniel, manufacturer of soluble chocolate, essence of coffee, &c. 9 King's row, New road, Pentonville
Dunn Daniel, ship & anchor smith, the Stowage, Deptford
Dunn Francis, tailor & draper, 22 Forston st. City road
Dunn Frederick, builder, 21 Southampton st. Camberwell
Dunn Frederick, machine ruler, 46 Barbican
Dunn Frederick Alex. chemist, 235 Oxford st
Dunn George, baker, 25 Robinson's row, High st. Kingsland
Dunn George, goldbeater, 1 Jewin court, Jewin st
Dunn George, pianoforte maker, 36 London st. Fitzroy sq
Dunn Hannibal, auctioneer & appraiser, 29 Poultry
Dunn Henry, chemist & druggist, 130 Shoreditch
Dunn Henry Lawrence, wax chndlr. & oilmn. 110 Aldersgate st
Dunn Jas. dlr. in rope, China hall gate, Lower rd. Rotherhi
Dunn Jas. patent rope manfr. 5 Vittoria pl. Mile end road
Dunn James John, baker, 55 Leonard st. Finsbury
Dunn John, bricklayer, &c. Dunsany place, Wandsworth rd
Dunn John, chairmaker, 109 Waterloo road, Lambeth
Dunn John, *Duke of York* P.H. 3 Fair st. Horselydown
Dunn John, muffin & crumpet baker, 58 Mount st. Berkeley st
Dunn John, oil & italian warehouse, 59 Cannon st
Dunn John, plumber, 31 Brewer st. Golden square
Dunn John, tailor, 6 Langley place, Commercial road east
Dunn John, warm & cold baths, 11 Bath st. Newgate st
Dunn John, wine & spirit merchant, 52 Great Tower st. City
Dunn John Miller, wool broker, 10 King st. Finsbury
Dunn Joseph, shoemaker, 43 Gibson st. Waterloo road
Dunn Joseph, tailor, 13 Newington causeway
Dunn Joseph G. boot & oyster wa. Nicholas pass. Lombard st
Dunn Mary (Mrs.), clothes dealer, 52 Myddelton st. Clerkenwel
Dunn Mary Ann (Mrs.), seminary, 7 Lamb's conduit passage
Dunn Mercy (Mrs.), hatter, 82 Chiswell st
Dunn Owen John, timber mer. 5 Philpot st. Commrl. rd. east
Dunn Richard, carver & gilder, 2 Norfolk st. Middlx. hosp
Dunn Richard, tailor, 8 Golden square
Dunn Robert, surgeon, 15 Norfolk st. Strand
Dunn Stephen, baker, 15 Ann's terrace, Cambridge heath
Dunn Thomas, ropemaker, 2 Stepney square
Dunn Thomas Robert, butcher, 177 Union st. Borough
Dunn Wm. baker, 15 King's road east, Chelsea
Dunn Wm. *Goldsmiths' Arms* P.H. 42 Bedfordbury, Covt. gar
Dunn Wm. *Man in the Moon* P.H. 13 Lit. Vine st. Regent st
Dunn Wm. plasterer, 22 South wharf road, Paddington
Dunn Wm. *Royal Exchange* P.H. 7 Adams mews, Grosv. sq
Dunn Wm. C. *Barleymow* P.H. 20 Cannon st. St. George st
Dunnage Wm. & Isaac, painters, &c. 11 Webb st. Bermondsey
Dunnage Thos. white lead agent, 3 Laurence Pountney pl
Dunne Margaret (Miss), milliner, 8 Brook st. Bond st
Dunnell John, *King's Head* P.H. 55½ Edgware road
Dunnell John, sen. *Bee Hive* P.H. 126 Crawford st. Portman sq
Dunnell Robert Geo. color manfr. see Berkley & Dunnell
Dunnell Thomas, cheesemonger, 1 Bread st. hill, City
Dunnett David, *Black Bull* P.H. 4 Brook st. Ratcliff
Dunnett John, cowkeeper, 13 Upper Eaton st. Pimlico
Dunnett William, importer of dutch toys, 3 Cheapside
Dunning Chas. *Three Mariners* P.H. 94 Fore st. Cripplegte
Dunning George, tobacconist, Wandsworth road
Dunning Gustavus, sheriff's officer, 130 Chancery lane
Dunning Henry, carpenter, 13 Woodstock st. Oxford st
Dunning Hen. Stephen, turner, 7 Queen st. Pitfield st. Hoxton
Dunning John R. grocer, 97 Grand Junction ter. Edgware rd
Dunning Mary (Miss), tobacconist, 3 Northampt. rw. Hollowy
Dunning Simon, solicitor, see Bolton, Merriman & Dunning
Dunsby & Mole, hairdressers & perfumers, 37 Nicholas lane

Dunsdon Thomas, boot & shoe maker, 138 Goswell st
Dunsford Harris, physician, 44 Up. Seymour st. Portman sq
Dunsford John, veterinary surgeon, 32 North row, Grosvr.sq
DunsmoreWm.carpen.& builder, 9 Bath pl. New rd. Fitzroysq
Dunsmore William, confectioner, 20 Middle row, Holborn
Dunstan George, cooper, 46 Exmouth st. Clerkenwell
Dunstan James, vestry clerk & registrar, Bromley, Middx
Dunster Richd. *Crown & Cushion* P.H. 17 Princes st. Barbican
Dunster William Hilliard, solicitor, see Jones & Dunster
Dunt John & Son, boot & shoewareho. 1 Cockspurst. Charing cr
Dunt John E. chandelier & lampma. see Hancock, Rixon & Dunt
Dunthorn Edward, linendraper, High st. Stoke Newington
Dunthorn Elizh. (Mrs.), lodging house, 14 Manchester bldgs
Dunthorn Josh. cornmer. 1 Com. rd. Lmbth. & 4 Broadw. Blckfrs
Dunthorne William, grocer, 19 Up. Cleveland st. Fitzroy sq
Du Pasquier Francis, surgeon, 62 Pall mall
Du Pasquier John M'Mahon, solr. Carltonchamb. 8 Regent st. & 62 Pall mall
Dupere AbrahamWm. poulterer. 21 Crown row, Walworth rd
Duplan Chas. & Edwd. grocers, 13 Munsterst. Regent'spark
Duplan Gilbert, grocer, 11 Regent's place, Horseferry road
Duplantier Ann (Madame), artificial florist, 9 Mount st
Duplex Henry, solicitor, 61 Lincoln's inn fields
Duplex Geo. cabinet & chairmaker, 23 Ropemaker's st. Finsb
Duplex George, surgeon, 28 Guilford st. Russell sq
Duplex George, surgeon, see Harris, Duplex & Harris
Duplock John, plumber, painter & glazier, 6 Noble st. Cheapside
Dupouy François & Co. wine mers. 4 Cross la. St. Dunstan's hill
Duppa & Collins', paperhanging manufrs. 314 Oxford st
Dupree John, wire worker, 26 High st. St. Giles's
Dupree John, wireworker & blindma. 21 Somerset st. Aldgate
Duprey Henry, cotton, rush & wadding mnfr. 60 Aldersgate st
Duprey Thos. Benjn. linendraper, 2 Nelson pl. Old Kent rd
Dupuis Jules, ladies' shoemaker, see Jacobs & Dupuis
Durand & Blakeway, wine merchts. 20 Bedford st. Cov. gar
Durand & M'Kenzie, american merchants, 37 Milk st
Durant & Co. brokers for silk, insurance, &c. 11 Copthall ct
Durant John, corn dealer, 289 Kent st. Borough
DurantMatilda (Mrs.), straw hatwareho. 50 High st. Notng.hl
Durbin Harriet (Mrs.), cheesemonger, 96 St. George st
Durbridge Robt. cheesemngr. 33 Felix ter. Liverpool road
Durham Alexander, *White Lion* P.H. 68 Shadwell High st
Durham Charles, teadealer, 2 King's pl. Commercial road
Durham Chas. Jacob, *Joiners' Arms* P.H. Camberwell green
Durham Cornelius, miniature painter, 191 Regent st
Durham Geo. Wm. Knight, pawnbr. 22 New King st. Deptford
Durham Henry, grocer, 47 Spencer st. Goswell road
Durham Joseph, artist, 6 North crescent, Bedford square
Durham Jsph. Banks, cutler, needle & razor ma. 261 Regent st
Durham Richd. cheesemonger, 14 NewQuebec st. Portman sq
Durham Robert, grocer, 15 Chester place, Old Kent road
Durie & Miller, warehousemen, 20 Watling st
Durieu Lewis Adolphus, oilman & tallow chndlr. 23 Drury la
Durlacher Louis, chiropodist, 15 Old Burlington st
Durley John cabinet ma. & upholsterer, 84 Wells st. Oxford st
Durlin Jane (Mrs.), ladies' shoemaker, 65 Burlington arcade
Durling William, livery stables, 31 Hermes st. Pentonville
Durnford John, gold & silver beater, 70 Compton st. Clerkenwell
Durnin Alexander, chemist, 7 Strutton ground, Westminster
Durrant, Stuart & Maxwell, solicitors, 6 Gray's inn square
Durrant George & Thos. coppersmiths, 121 Up. Whitecross st
Durrant James, *Bull's Head* P.H. 71 York st. Westminster
Durrant Jemima (Mrs.), grocer, Church st. Battersea
Durrant John, *Marlborough Head* P.H. 23 Fox's la. Shadwl
Durrant JohnRowland, stockbroker, 26 Change alley, Cornhill
Durrant Rd. watch & clock ma. 64 Gt. Russell st. Bloomsbury
Durrant Thos. *Hand in Hand* P.H. 23 Wynyatt st. Goswell st
Durrant Wm. plumber & painter, 5 Lower Trinity st. Rothrh
Durrell Samuel Joseph, print seller, 88 Wardour st. Soho
Durston Mary & Ellen (Misses), milliners, 233 Tottenham ct. rd
Durston Abraham, baker, 233 Tottenham court road
Durston Chas. Rt. win. blind ma. 9 Artichoke row, Mile end rd
Durston Robert, window blind maker, Mare st. Hackney
D'Usayer Henry, professor of languages, 122 Regent st
Dutch Almshouses, 23 Crown st. Finsbury
Dutch Rhenish Rail. Office (E. Aimé, sec.), 62 King William st. City
Dutch & Snelling, fishmongers, 5 Ivy la. Newgate st
Duterrau John Francis, watchmkr. see Perigal & Deterrau
Duthie Sarah (Mrs.), market gardener, Bromley, Middlesex
Duthie William, jeweller, 19 Gerrard st. Soho
Duthoit David, auctioneer & valuer, 41 Moorgate st
Duthoit Jonathan, silk manfr. 26 Steward st. Spitalfields
Dutt John, carpenter, 9 Hornsey row, Upper st. Islington
Dutton Thomas D. & Son, boot & shoe makers, 4 St. Martin's ct. & 53 Blackman st. & 29 Chapel st. Edgware road
Dutton Ann (Miss), dressmaker, 67 Poplar High street
Dutton Anne (Mrs.), milliner, 35 Bruton st. Bond st
Dutton Douglas, chemist & surgeon, 73 Connaught ter
Dutton Edwd. cabinet ma. &c. 94 Grand Junction ter. Edgw.rd
Dutton George Hill, brewer, 11 Dutton st. Cromer st
Dutton Henry, teadealer, 84 Upper Whitecross st
Dutton Joseph, oil & color warehouse, 8 Bath st. City road
Dutton Rd. for. & col. wool brok. 4 Sambrook ct. Basinghall st
Dutton Robert Wm. watch & clock maker, 148 Fleet st
Dutton Samuel, imptr. & dealer in tobacco & cigars, 84 Drury la
Dutton Thos. jun. boot & shoema. 3 Stavertonrow, Walworth rd
Dutton Thos. Goldsworthy, locksmith, &c. 78 Leadenhall st
Dutton Thomas Goldsworthy, marine & architectural lithographic artist, 2 Bale's cottages, Wandsworth rd
Dutton Thos. Rt. boot & shoe ma. 19 Beckford rw. Walworth rd
Dutton William Huddard, bootmaker, 6 St. Martin's court, & 5 Lowndes ter. Knightsbridge, & 172 North st. Brighton
Duval Chas. cheesemonger, 9 Crosby row, Walworth road
Duval Chas. water gilder, 3 Grosvenor st. Grosvenor sq
Duval Lewis, water gilder, 87 Charlotte st. Fitzroy square
Duval Wm. last, patten & clog ma. 17 Milton st. Cripplegate
Duvall Benjamin, who. cheesemonger, Broadway, Deptford
Duvall John, artist & engraver, 3 Northumberland st. Strand
Duvall Wm. bacon drier & corn mer. 61 Holland st. Blkfrs. rd
Dwarris Sir Fortunatus, knt. master of Queen's Bench, Queen's Bench office, Temple
Dwelley Sarah (Mrs.), wheelwright, Bow
Dwelly Jas. hardwa. & umbrella ma. 10 Gt. Turnstile, Holbrn
Dwelly John, wheelwright, 11 Well st. Wellclose square
Dwelly Wm. furnishing ironmonger, 197 Tottenham court rd
Dwerrihouse & Bell, watch & clock mkrs. 131 Mountst. Berkly.sq
Dwyer James, cigar depôt, 25 Gt. Portland st. Oxford st
Dwyer Michael, *Bell* P.H. 27 Felton st. Hoxton
Dyball John, wood dealer, 15 New road, Deptford
Dyce William, artist, 1A, Adelphi terrace
Dye Robert, livery stables, 21 White Lion st. Norton folgate
Dyer Elizabeth & Jane, hosiers, 24 East road, City road
Dyer & Emmett, merchs. & hempen cloth ma. 78 Lr. Thames st
Dyer John & Henry, shell fishmongers, 66 Haymarket
Dyer Thomas & Co. druggists, 37 Upper Marylebone st
Dyers' Almshouses, opposite Anderson's bldgs. City road
Dyers' Hall (Chas. B. Luttly, clerk), 3 College st. Dowgt.hill
Dyer Caroline (Mrs.), dining rooms, 102 York st. Westminster
Dyer Charles, architect, 36 Guilford st. Russell square
Dyer Charles K. merchant, 4 New Broad st. City
Dyer Daniel, ship owner, 52 Gainsford st. Horselydown
Dyer Edward, hardware dealer, 3 Union st. Boro'
DyerEd. *True British Sailor* P.H. 47 Nw. Church st. Lisson gr
Dyer Elizabeth (Mrs.), grocer, 238 Rotherhithe st
Dyer George, bookseller & publisher, 24 Paternoster row
Dyer George, ironmonger, 5 Gray's inn lane
Dyer Henry, coffee rooms, 12 Bury st. Bloomsbury
Dyer James, chair maker, 86 Britannia st. City road
Dyer Jas. col. broker, see Woodbridge, Dyer & Woodbridge
DyerJames, cheesemonger, 7 Orford pl. Marlboro' rd. Chelsea
Dyer James, job master, riding academy & livery stables, 42 Worship st.; 2 Finsbury place south; & Halkin st. west
Dyer James, solicitor, 27 Ely place, Holborn
DyerJames, tobacst. 7 Southampton ct. Southton row, Blmby
Dyer John, bed, mattress & cabinet maker, 62 Borough rd
Dyer John, bedstead maker, 56 New Gloucester st. Hoxton
Dyer John, builder & bricklayer, 2 Gower st. north, New road
Dyer John, painter & glazier, 65 East st. Manchester sq
Dyer John, wine merchant, 16 Cullum st. City
Dyer John Chas. Wm. surgeon, 11 St. Geo. ter. Liverpool rd
Dyer John Joseph, watch case & pendant maker, rolling & flatting mills, 11 Gloucester st. St. John st. road
DyerJohnParry, *Crn. & Anchor* P.H. 8 Up. Storer st. Com. rd. e
Dyer Joseph, cane rib maker, 27 & 28 Wilkes st. Spitalfields
Dyer Joseph Woodfield, cheesemonger, 61 & 62 Boro' High st
Dyer Robert, *Norfolk hotel*, 30 Surrey st. Strand
Dyer Saml. carpenter, 17 Portsmouth pl. Low. Kennington la
Dyer Sophia (Mrs.), grocer, 21 Lit. Alie st. Goodman's fields
Dyer Thomas, bookseller, 24 Princes st. Leicester square
Dyer Thomas, carpenter, 10 Gt. Chapel st. Oxford st
Dyer Thomas, grocer, &c. Bromley, Middlesex
Dyer Thomas, surgeon, 37 Upper Marylebone st
Dyer Wm. baker, 3 Nelson place, Old Kent road
Dyer Wm. customhouse & ship agt. 16 John st. Crutched friars
Dyer Wm. ship & custom house agt. 16 John st. Minories
Dyer Wm. grocer, 2 Perseverance ter. Church st. Bethn.gr.rd
Dyer Wm. greengrocer, 3 Narrow st. Limehouse
Dyer William, haberdasher, 161 Tooley st
Dyer William, plumber, Bromley, Middlesex
Dyer Wm. Andrew, merchant, 5 Catherine ct. Tower hill
Dyer Wm. Geo. T. surgeon, 23 Sackville st. Piccadilly

Dyet Frederick, grocer, 193 Upper Thames st
Dyke & Stokes, proctors & notaries, 2 Gt. Knightrider st
Dyke Decimus T. proctor, 2Gt.Knightrider st.Doctors'cmns
Dyke Frs.Hart, queen's proctor,&c.see Jenner,Dyke&Jenner
Dyke Gilbert, coffee rooms, 4 Edward st. Wardour st. Soho
Dyke Joseph, *Vine* P.H. Mile end gate, Mile end rd
Dyke Samuel, painter, 4 Trafalgar st. Walworth road
Dyke Thomas, draughtsman, 5 Spring st. Marylebone
Dyke Wm. tailor, 21 Grafton st. east, Tottenham ct. rd
Dyker Fras. sec. to Gaspé fishery & coal mine Co. 2 New Broad st
Dykes Geo. Pugh, carpenter & joiner, 73 Judd st. Brunsw. sq
Dykes Lamplugh Brougham, barrister, 1 Elm court, Temple
Dykes Mary (Mrs.), milliner, 73 Judd st. Brunswick square
Dykes William Henry, brassfounder, 12 Denmark st. Soho
Dymant John Felix, tailor, 23 Sherborne st. Blandford sq
DymesDanl.*CalthorpeArms*P.H.37Up.Nth.pl.Gray's inn rd
DymesJohn,*NewChesterfieldArms*P.H.Shepherd st. May fr
Dymock Francis, dyer & calenderer, &c. 46 Brick lane, St. Luke's, & 9 Norman's buildings, Brick lane
Dymott Mary (Mrs.), baker, 42 Millbank st. Westminster
Dyne Wm.Wilkins & Edwards, solicitors, 61 Lincoln's inn flds
Dyne Wm. corndlr.&seedsman,7Rochester ter.Stk.Newingtn
Dyneley Charles, proctor, see Willett & Dyneley
Dyson & Flavell, solicitors, 21 Bedford row, Bloomsbury
Dyson, Hall, Parkes & Coates, parliamentary agents, 25 Parliament st
Dyson Thomas & Co. silk shawl wa. 32 Noble st. Cheapside
Dyson Arthur, printer & publisher, 231 Shoreditch High st
Dyson Harman, horse dealer, 41 Cross st. Finsbury
Dyson Henry (late Messrs. Catherwood),brass manufacturer & gasfitter, sash fronts, stall board & door plates in brass & zinc, desk rods, &c. Bowling grn. walk, Pitfield st.Hoxtn
Dyson James, grocer, 30 Great Tower st
Dyson James Armstrong Francis, solicitor, 36 Carey st
Dyson John, carpenter, &c. 49 Swinton st. Gray's inn road
Dyson John, grocer & cheesemg. 64&65 High st. Portland twn
Dyson Richard, livery stables, 6 Park lane, Piccadilly
Dyson Robert, hairdresser, 44 Bridport pl. New north rd
Dyson William, hairdresser, 16 King st. Holborn
Dyson William, solicitor, 19 Chancery lane
Dyster, Nalder&Roper, hide, skin & tal. brok. 6 Leadenhall st
Dyte Hannah & Son, quill merchants, pen manufacturers, who. & gen. stationers, travelling desk & dressing case makers, 106 Strand
Dyte Maurice, chemist & surgeon, 44 Houndsditch
Dyte Henry, solicitor, 2 Hare court, Temple

EABY Francis,*YorkshireGrey* P.H.49 Whitechapel High st
Eade George, chemist & druggist, 39 Goswell st
Eade George, wine merchant, 14 Walbrook, City
Eade Wm. Aislabie, barrister, 10 Old square, Lincoln's inn
Eades & Goward, carpenters, Phœnix yd. Oxford st
Eades Danl. saw mills, measure maker & timber mer. Pump court, 66 Union st. & 38 Bear lane, Gravel lane, Borough
Eades Edmund, baker, 52, Wilton st. Westminster
Eades Henry, livery stables, 10 Brompton road, Brompton
Eades James, writer & grainer, 56 Paul st. Finsbury
Eades John, timber yard, 38 Bear lane, Blackfriars road
Eades Richard, baker, 31 Marshal st. Golden square
EadieAlex.Hart,bookedge gilder,&c.11Craven bdgs.Drury la
Eadon William, greengrocer, 8 Horseferry rd. Westminster
Eadson Christopher, butcher, 2 Market st. Newport market
Eady & Brown, mftg. goldsmiths, 26 Red Lion st.Clerkenwell
Eady Chas. & Son, plate polishers, 5 Little Dean st. Soho
Eady Ephraim Childe, academy,1 Lit. James st. Bedford row
Eagar Robert, merchant, see Home, Eagar & Co
Eagland Edwin Henry, surgical mechanician,20Coventry st
Eagle James & Co. linen factors, 26 Bread st. Cheapside
Eagle Life Assurance Company (Hen. P. Smith, actuary), 3 Crescent, New Bridge st. Blackfriars; for list of directors, &c. see page 2013
Eagle Steam Packet Co. (James S. Newborn, sec.), 6 Hungerford st
Eagle Francis King, barrister, 4 New square, Lincoln's inn
Eagle James, warehouseman, see Bell & Eagle
Eagle Richard, boot & shoema. 21 Peter's hill, Doctors' com
Eagle Robert, *Cricketers* P.H. 61 Grove st. Camden town
Eagle Robert, *Rose* P.H. 21 Saville place, Lambeth
Eagle William, barrister, 3 Plowden buildings, Temple
Eagle William, carpenter, 39 Milton street, Dorset square
Eagles Edward, boot & shoe ma. 3 Cambridge rd. Mile end rd
Eagles Edward, pocket book, &c. ma.106 Wood st.Cheapside
EaglesHenry, brass&cockfounder,9Buckingham rw.Westmr
Eagles James, organ builder, 4 Hackney road crescent
Eagles Thos.chandler's shop,6 Goldsmith's row, Hackney rd
EagletonEdward & Co.who.teadlrs.& grocers,83 Newgate st
Eagleton & Glover, tailors, woollendrapers & trimming sellers, 42 Borough High street
Eales Christphr. architect & surveyor, see Cope & Eales
Eales Chris. architect & surveyor, 4 Chapel pl. Cavendish sq
Eales John, undertaker, 23 Ernest street, Regent's park
Eales Wickham John, muffin baker, 2 West st. Seven dials
Eales William, surgeon, 23 Parliament street
Eames Alfred, *China Hall* P.H. Lower road, Rotherhithe
Eames John, undertaker, 3 Church place, Covent garden
Eames Wm. carver & gilder, 90 Great Portland st
Eamonson Jas. auctioneer & upholsterer, 252A, Oxford st
Eardensohn John, who. shoemaker, 10 Wellclose square
Eardley Andrew, *King's Arms* P.H. 9 Rolls buildgs. Fetter la
Earee Ann (Mrs.), coffee rooms, 185 Whitechapel road
Earee James, coffee rooms, 15 Hackney road crescent
EarethDaniel,*BridportArms* P.H.84Harrisonst.Gray'sinnr
Earith Charles & Son, dyers, 82 Goswell st
Earith Chas.shawl ma.& warehouseman,see Blacker&Earith
Earl Ann (Mrs.),painter & glazier,1Lit. George st.Westmstr
Earl Daniel, woollen warehouseman, 27 Basinghall st
Earl Henry, school slate maker, 17 William st. Lant st. Boro'
Earl James, cattle salesman, 41 West Smithfield
Earl James, tailor, &c. 117 Goswell st
Earl Richard, baker, 5 Dover place West, Kent st. Boro'
Earl Samuel, tailor, 70 Lambeth walk
Earl Thomas, fruiterer, 151 Goswell st
Earle Mary & Son, wine coopers, bottle mers. & wine fining mkrs. their old established house,3 Gt. St. Thomas Apostle
Earle Charles, wine cooper & bottle mer. 22 Queenhithe
Earle George, public library, &c. 67 Castle st. east, Oxford st
Earle Henry Edward,wine merchant, 81Grosvenor st.Bond st
Earle James, french polisher,45 Hastings st. Burton crescent
Earle Sarah (Miss), milliner & dress maker, 23 Up. Baker st
Earle Thomas, sculptor, 72 Upper Ebury st. Pimlico
Earle William, Alton ale agent, Nine elms, Vauxhall
Earle Wm. funeral carriage master, 7 Castle st. Long acre
Earle Wm. *Sun* P.H. 57 Newman st. Oxford st
Earles Edward, registrar of births,&c. 4 Worship square
Earles Eliza (Miss), haberdasher, 115 Shoreditch
Earles Jas. livery stables, Red Lion yd. 9 Lit. Guilford st
Earley John, builder, 53 Park st. Camden town
Earlidge & Headworth, arrow root dlrs.60 St.John's sq.Clkw
Early & Smith, wholesl. slopsellers, 11, 12 & 13 Houndsditch
Early Townsend & Co. (late Townsend, Hardwick & Ford), haberdashers, silk mercers & drapers,324&325High Holbn
Early Edward, bricklayer, 6 John st. Old Kent road
Early James, tailor, 2 Halstead pl.South Lambeth, New rd
Early Thos. plumber, 1 Halstead pl. South Lambeth,New rd
Earnshaw Hen. bridle cutter & harness ma. 18 Poland st
Earnshaw Thos.chronometer ma.2 Brewer st.Nth.Goswell rd
Earnshaw Thomas, sen. chronometer, watch & clock maker, 119 High Holborn
Earnshaw Wm. bootmaker, 10 Market st. Oxford st
Earnshaw Wm. Arthur,commcl.agt.13Harp la.Lr.Thames st
Earp James,*Dolphin* P.H. Dolphin court, 11½ Ludgate hill
Earp Mary Ann (Mrs.), milliner,&c. 22 Newland st. Pimlico
Earp Thomas, surveyor of pavements,23Marsham st.Westmr
Earratt John, saddler, officers' belt & sabretash manufacturer, 7 Leicester st. Leicester square
Earthrowl William, baker, 55 King st. Borough
EarthrowlWm.carpenter&undertaker,13Elizabeth.ter.Islgtn
Earwaker Hen.coach builder, 14Kendal's mews,Blandford st
Earwicker Joseph, straw bonnet mfr. 14Romney ter.Westmr
Earwood Elizth (Mrs.),eating ho.2 Francis pl. New North rd
Easey James, cheesemonger, 4 Scott's pl. Lower rd. Islingtn
Easley Humphrey, butcher, 165 Church st. Shoreditch
Easley Joseph, butcher, 2 Hatton wall, Hatton garden
Easley Thomas, butcher, 25½ Lamb st. Spital square
Eason Henry & James, curriers & tanners, 24 Berners st. Oxford st. & Grange, Bermondsey
Eason James, cheesemonger, 13 Parnham st. Limeho. fields
Eason Jane (Mrs.), lodging house, 24 Upper Ebury st
Eason John, bricklayer, &c. 1 Clarke st. Stepney
Eason John, laceman & importer of french flowers, millinery, &c. 11 & 14 Lowther arcade
Eason William, *Welsh Harp* P.H. 1 Essex st. Bouverie st
Easson James U. surgeon, 1A, Bedford place, Russell sq
East, Landon &Holland,man's mercers,34Sackville st.Piccad
East Country Dock Off. (Alexr. Shirreff, sec.), 50 Lombard st. & Rotherhithe
East IndiaArmyAgency (Grindley & Co.), 16 Cornhill, hrs. 9 to 5; & 8 St. Martin's place, Charing cross, hrs. 9 to 8
East India Chambers, 23 Leadenhall st
East India & China Association Committee (John Stikeman, secretary), 2 Cowper's court, Cornhill
East India Co.'s Almshouses, bet. 225 & 230 Poplar High st

East India Company (J.C.Melvill, sec.), 11 to 21 Leadenhall st. ; for particulars, see "OFFICIAL DIRECTORY"
East India Company's Recruiting Department, 28 Soho square ; hours, 8 A.M. to 9 P.M
East India Military Store Warehouse, 108 Leadenhall st
East India Tea Co. (Richd. Hughes, sec.), 9 Gt. St. Helen's
East Indian Rail. Co. (D. L. Noad, sec.), 8 Broad st. bldgs
East Lincolnshire Railway Office, (Thos. Reynolds, sec.), 7 Lothbury, & 3 Park st. Westminster
East London Cemetery (David Francis, sec.), Alfred ter. Step
East London Coal Company (Jos. Goddard, man.), Regent's canal dock, Limehouse
East London General Pension Society (George Kirby, secretary), 17 Tyssen st. Bethnal green
East London Lying-in Institution (Mark O'Shaunessy, secretary), 2 Ireland row, Mile end road
East London Pension Society (George Henderson, sec.), 5 Mitre st. Aldgate
East London Poor Law Union, 1 Devonshire sq. Bshpsgt. st
East London Registry Office for Families & Servants (Mrs. Elizth. Gordelier), 8 Assembly row, Mile end
East London Water Works' Office (Joseph Cecil, sec.), 16 St. Helen's place, Bishopsgate ; Works (Thos. Wicksteed, engineer), Old Ford
East Surrey Free Trade Registration & Qualification So. Sy. League Reg. Off. 19 & 20 Ea. Temple chbs. Whitefriars st
East Tamar Consolidated Mines (George William Harrison, sec.), 51 Old Broad st
East & West of England Junc. Rail. from Northmptn. to Cheltenham, broad gauge (R. Watkins, jun. esq. sec.), 35 Charing cross
East & West India Dock Co. (Geo. Collin, sec.), 8 Billiter sq. ; *East India Docks*, East India road, Poplar ; *West India Docks*, Isle of Dogs ; *Warehouses*, 70 to 78 Fenchurch st. & Billiter st
East & West London Coal Company, 458 West Strand
East Benjamin, cabinet maker, 11 Turner square, Hoxton
East Charles, hairdresser, 4A, Davies ter. Berkeley sq
East Geo. boot & shoe ma. 44 Richard st. Commercial rd. east
East Giles, boot & shoe ma. 4 Albert pl. Marlboro' rd. Chlsea
East James, boot & shoe maker, 181 Shadwell High st
East James, butcher, 5 Royal Hospital row, Chelsea
East James, poultry salesman, 59 Newgate market
East Jeffery, scavenger, Wright's bldgs. Spa rd. Bermndsey
East Jesse, cooper & hoop mfr. 1 & 2 Waterloo ter. Comm. rd. ea
East John, carver & gilder, 25 York buildings, New rd
East John, fishmonger, 53 Chandos st. Covent garden
East Joseph, engraver & printer, see Blades & East
East Joshua, job master, Rugby yd. 40 Lamb's Conduit st
East Robert, oilman, 65 Crawford st
East Samuel, bricklayer, 1 York st. Kingsland road
East Sarah (Mrs.), milliner, 38 Goodge st. Tottenham ct. rd
East Sarah Ann (Miss), dyer, 8 Wellington ter. Clapham rd
East Thomas, morocco leather dresser, 214 Bermondsey st
East Thomas, oil & colorman, 9 London terrace, Hackney rd
East Wm. carpenter & undertaker, 5 Green bank, Wapping
East Wm. Edmund, stationer, printer, &c. see Skipper & East
East Wm. Fred. architect & survey. 7 Winchester pl. New rd
East Wm. Thomas, hosier, 19 Providence row, Finsbury
Eastabrook Wm. grocer & cheesemngr. 115 Shadwell High st
Eastaugh Edw. who. boot & shoe ma. 189 Brick la. Spitlflds
Eastbury Robert, cheesemonger, 19 Park st. Camden town
Easter Wm. fur. undertaker, 11 Up. Dorset pl. Clapham rd
Easterbrook Wm. staymaker, 39 Duke st. Bishopsgate
Easterling Thos. brush, &c. ma. 62 Up. North pl. Gray's inn rd
Eastern Counties Railway Office (Archibald Bulkeley, secretary), 40 High st. Shoreditch
Eastern Dispensary (John Comley, surgeon), 46 Gt. Alie st
Eastern Literary & Scientific Institution (James Murray, hon. sec.), 88 Hackney road
Eastern Literary & Scientific Institution (William Houlder, sec.), Commercial road east
Eastey James, grocer, 100 Hill st. Walworth road
Eastgate Charles, coachsmith, 31 Long acre
Eastgate Michael, *Ship* P.H. Grove pass. Church st. Hackny
Eastgate Thomas, *Gate* P.H. 13 Harp lane, Tower st
Eastham William, plumber, Kingsland High st
Easthope John & Son, stockbrokers, 38 Throgmorton st
Eastick Robert Thos. saddler, 3 Garden row, Camberwell rd
Eastlake Charles Lock, R.A. artist, 7 Fitzroy square
Eastland Company (Thos. Cope, sec.), 25 Birchin lane
Eastman & Yeo, stationers, copperplate, lithographic & letterpress printers & account book manufrs. 100 Cheapside
Eastman James, carpenter & builder, High st. Battersea
Eastman Jas. leather dressr. & stripr. 165 Long la. Bermndsy
Eastman Sam. butcher, 5 Vittoria pla. Cambridge rd. Mile end
Eastman Sam. dairyman, Bridge road, Battersea
Eastman Wm. Thos. silk dyer, see M'Gill & Eastman
Eastman Wm. Thos. hatter, 3 Beckford row, Walworth rd
Easto Robert, who. tea & coffee dealer, 33 St. Mary at hill
Easton & Amos, millwrights, engineers, makers of Easton's improved hydraulic rams & lead pipe manufactrs. Grove, Great Guildford st. & Waterworks chambers, Orange st. Leicester square
Easton Elizh. (Mrs.), china & glass wa. 235 Bermondsey st
Easton Frederick Wm. surgeon, 2 Cleveland st. Mile end rd
Easton Henry, grocer & teaman, see Charlton & Easton
Easton James, solicitor, 6 New square, Lincoln's inn
Easton James, baker, 147 High Holborn
Easton James, civil engineer, 80 Blackfriars road, & Grove, Great Guildford st. Borough
Easton James, furniture brok. 8 Southampton st. Cambrwll
Easton James, hay & straw salesmn. Red Li. yd. 111 Edgware rd
Easton John, baker, Green st. near the Grove, Kentish town
Easton John, plumber, 1 Sun st. East st. Walworth road
Easton Thomas, barrister, 1 Hare court, Temple
Easton Thos. corn dealer, 31 White Hart pl. Kennington la
Easton Thomas, corn & coal mer. 1 Grange rd. Bermondsey
Easton Thomas, corn lighterman & agent, 11 Horselydown la
Easton Thomas, plasterers' hair manfr. 2 Spa rd. Bermondsey
Easton Thomas, veterinary surgeon, Stratford, Essex
Eastty Nathaniel, custom house agent & ship & insurance broker, 132 Upper Thames st
Eastty Nathaniel, wine merchant & dealer in London double stout, pale india ale, London stock ales, & cyder, 132 Upper Thames st
Eastway Elias, furn. ironmonger, 12 Old Dorset pl. Clapham rd
Eastwell Thos. beer retailer, 47 Brandon st. Walworth
Eastwood Chas. linendraper, 45 Newington causeway
Eastwood Sarah (Miss), shawl border ma. 33 Fore st. Crippleg
Eastwood Wm. butcher, 71 Strutton ground, Westminster
Eastwood Wm. copper & steelplate manuf. 4 Harp al. Shoe la
Eastwood Wm. auctioneer & accnt. 33 Fore st. Cripplegate
Easum Elizh. (Mrs.), fishmonger, 4 Constable rw. Mile end rd
Easum Robt. Hayes, ropemaker, Commercial rd. east, Stepney
Easum William, genl. salesman, 5 Robert's pl. Comml. rd. east
Easy Wm. cheesemonger, 4 Kingsland road, Dalston
Eates Thomas, toymaker, 22 Upper Rosoman st. Clerkenwell
Eaton Anne (Mrs.), wine mer. 21 Southampton st. Bloomsbury
Eaton John Matthews & James, tailors, 9 Lower st. Islington
Eaton John M. & James, tailors, 7 Islington green
Eaton Elizth. & Ellen (Misses), milliners, Camberwell green
Eaton Chas. pork butcher, 21 New Montague st. Brick la. Sptfs
Eaton Daniel, tailor, 55 George st. east, Euston square
Eaton Geo. fishing rod, hook & tackle mak. 6 & 7 Crooked la
Eaton Hy. solr. 35 Ebury st. Pimlico, & 10 New inn, Strand
Eaton Henry W. silk broker, 33 Old Broad st. City
Eaton James, plumber & glazier, 22 Lamb st. Spitalfields
Eaton James, stay haberdasher, &c. 60 Berwick st. Soho
Eaton John, butcher, 6 Silver st. Golden square
Eaton John, straw bonnet maker, 8 Church st. Shoreditch
Eaton John, tailor, 9 Duke st. Adelphi
Eaton Lucy (Miss), school, 11 Bury st. St. James's
Eaton Richard, butcher, 33 Featherstone st. City road
Eaton Susanna (Mrs.), *Elephant* P.H. 119 Fenchurch st
Eaton William, butcher, 16 Great Moore place, Lambeth
Eaton William, silversmith, 16 Jewin crescent, Cripplegate
Eaton William, tin manufacturer, 32 Banner st. St. Luke's
Eatwell Chas. *Albemarle's Head* P.H. 12 St. John's sq. Clkwl
Eavestaff Wm. pianoforte maker, 66 Gt. Russell st. Bloomsbury, & 17 Sloane st
Eayres Nathaniel, tailor, 23 New Church st. Lisson grove
Eayrs William, baker, 9 Green st. Paddington
Ebbels James, butcher, 54 London st
Ebbern Wm. & Co. canal carriers, White Horse, Cripplegate, 136 London wall, & 7 Wharf, south side, Paddington basin
Ebbetts Daniel, wine merchant, 16 Mincing lane
Ebbles James, butcher, 54 London st. Fitzroy square
Ebborn Francis, baker, 122 Grove st. Camden town
Ebbs & Smith, stationers & printers, 5 Postern row, Tower hill
Ebbs John, builder, &c. 29 Aberdeen place, Maida hill
Ebbs Thos. Barlow, laceman, 11 Up. Charles st. Nthmptn. sq
Ebbs Wm. Hawkins, merchant, &c. see Greenwood, Ebbs & Co
Ebers E—, S. & Co. booksellers & librarians, 27 Old Bond st
Ebert Henry, porkman, 22 Broad st. Bloomsbury
Eborall John, bricklayer, &c. 22 Smith st. King's rd. Chelsea
Eborall John, bricklayer, 12 Paradise row, Chelsea
Ebsworth & Coleman, cattle salesmen, 17 West Smithfield
Eburne Joseph, metal agent, 17 Thavies inn, Holborn hill
Eccles Ann (Mrs.), chandler's shop, 44 Bell st. Edgware rd
Eccles Ann (Mrs.), printer, engraver, &c. 101 Fenchurch st
Eccles Benjamin, general dealer, 52 Gt. James st. Lisson gr

Eccles Mary A.(Mrs.),fruiter.1 Pierepont rw.Islingtn.High st
Eccles William, grocer, &c. 9 Princess st. Edgware road
Eccles William, surgeon, 59 Old Broad st. City
Ecclesiastical Commissioners for England & Wales, 5 Whitehall place; hours of business 10 to 4
Ecclesiastical Gazette Office, 9 Southampton st. Strand
Ecclestone Alf. *Turkish Slave* P.H. 141 Brick la. Spitalfields
Echecopar & Co. wine merchants (Cadiz), Danl. Birkett, jun. agent, 1 Bell court, Mincing lane
Echevarri Juan, grocer, 3 Flower's buildings, Holloway
Echlin William Leahy, surgeon, 56 Dean st. Soho
Eck Thomas, carrot salesman, Borough market
Eckett Joseph, teadealer, 4 Ossulston st. Somers town
Eckford Hen. Geo. picture dlr. Peter's pl. 10 Hemming's row
Eckford John, carver & gilder, 59 Greek st. Soho
Eckroyd, Wm. leatherdresser, 1 Tyer's gateway, Bermondsey st
Eckstein & Addison, ironmongers & smiths, 294 Strand
Eckstein Geo. F. pat. range ma. furnish. ironmngr. & fitter up of hot water apparts. for warming bdgs. 13 Hi. Holborn
Eckstein John, furnishing & general ironmonger, smith, brazier & bellhanger, 3 High st. Notting hill
Economic Funeral Co. (Jas. Syer, mgr.) 29A, N. Bridge st
Economic Funeral Co. (Hy. Gregson, sup.), 29 N. Bridge st
Economic Life Assurance Office (C. J. Downer, sec.), 6 & 7 New Bridge st. Blackfriars; for directors, &c. see p. 2021
Economy Society, 147 Strand
Economist weekly newspaper, 6 Wellington st. Strand
Ecroyd Wm. leatherdres. Tyer's gateway, 211 Bermondsey st
Edbrook Sarah (Mrs.), dressmkr. & milliner, 5 New st. Brmptn
Edbury Joseph, organ builder, 67 Seymour st. Euston square
Eddels James C. tailor, &c. 7 Piccadilly
Eddels James Creed, hosier, 2 Coventry st. & 34 Piccadilly
Eddels Mary (Mrs.), hosier & glover, 64 Cheapside
Eddels Nathaniel, furniture warehouse, 153 Whitechapel rd
Edden Edwin, wholesale druggist, 154 Upper Thames st
Edden Richard, tailor & draper, 1 Ely place, Holborn
Eddington Wm. plasterer, 32 Shaftsbury st. New North rd
Eddis Arthur Shelly, barrister, 28 Southampton buildings
Eddis Eden Upton, artist, 78 Newman st. Oxford st
Eddis Henry William, merchant, 26 Broad st. buildings
Eddison Wm. Edward. wine & liqueur merchant, 2 Walbrook
Eddy Charles W. chemist. 30 Crown st. Finsbury square
Ede Francis & Son, merchants, 34 Gt. Winchester st. Broad st
Ede John Robert, surgeon, 1 Mathon place, Pentonville
Ede Joseph, manchester warehouseman, 120 Cheapside
Ede Joseph, robemaker, see Adams & Ede
Ede Sarah (Mrs.), coal dlr. 14 Buckingham pl. Fitzroy sq
Ede William, baker, 12 Chichester pl. Wandsworth road
Ede William, harnessmaker, 100 St. George's rd. Borough, & 3 East st. Walworth road
Edelsten & Williams, pin & needle mak. 5 Crown ct. Cheapside
Eden Thomas Edward & Son, surgeon dentists, 6 Langham place, & 45 Threadneedle st
Eden Michael, upholsterer, Conant place, Limehouse
Eden John, *Old Rose* P.H. Russell st. Bermondsey st
Eden Thomas, solicitor, 3 Salisbury st. Strand
Eden Wm. hairdresser, 10 Hastings st. Burton crescent
Edenborough Thos. & Co. wine merchants, 3 Pancras la. City
Edenborough William & Alfred, surgeons, 74 Coleman st
Edenborough Alfred, surgeon, 187 Bishopsgate st. without
Edenborough Jolland Jennings, surgeon, 41 Friday st
Edenborough Sam. Bolton, wool bro. see Marsh & Edenborough
Edensor Mary (Mrs.), lodging ho. 9 Up. Belgrave pl. Pimlico
Edey James, shipping butcher, Limehouse hole
Edgar Edwd. pianoforte music seller, 63 Lamb's Conduit st
Edgar James, tobacconist, 13 Wells st. Oxford st
Edgar John, gasfitter, 71 Marylebone lane
Edgar Thomas, merchant, 71 Cornhill
Edgar William, musician, 4 Bishop's walk, Lambeth
Edgar William, silk mercer, &c. see Swan & Edgar
Edgar William, tailor, 19 Argyll st. Regent st
Edgcomb Joseph & Co. fringe & fancy trimming ma. 24 Watling st
Edgcomb Wm. & Co. who. stationers, 8 Budge row, City
Edgcomb Charlotte (Mrs.), fringe mnfr. 54 Mount st. Lmbth
Edgcomb Joseph, fringemaker, 17 Newington causeway
Edgcombe James, bootmaker, 31 Old Compton st. Soho
Edgcombe Sarah (Miss), fancy wa. 7 Triangle, Kennington cr
Edgcumbe George, basket maker & turner, 99 Poplar High st
Edge George, painter, 48 William st. Regent's park
Edge Thomas, gold & gilt jewellery mnfr. 82 Hatton garden
Edge Thomas, manufacturer of gas & oil lamps, lustres, & every description of gas apparatus for lighting towns, mansions, public buildings, manufactories, &c. patentee & sole maker of gas meters with patent indexes & other important improvements; manufactory, 59 Great Peter st. Westminster, & city office, 6 Poultry
Edgecomb & Kimpton, who. general stationers, 8 Budge row
Edgecombe Wm. hairdresser, 4 Middle row, Knightsbridge
Edgeler William, bookbinder, 6 Apollo court, Fleet st
Edgeley Thomas, tailor, 44 Burlington arcade
Edgell Alexander, solicitor, 4 Verulam bldgs. Gray's inn
Edgell Harry, barrister, 21 Cadogan place, Knightsbridge
Edgell Henry Parsons, accountant, 13 Bouverie st. Fleet st
Edgeller Thomas, upholsterer, 32 Newland st. Eaton square
Edgerley Henry, *Golden Anchor* P.H. 105 Leadenhall st
Edghill Hen. pigeon & rabbit dlr. 1 Anderson's bldgs. City rd
Edghill Jeremiah, horsehair manufacturer, 40 Old st. St. Luke's
Edghill William G. tailor & draper, 401 Oxford st
Edgington Thomas & Co. marquee, tent, flag, rick cloth, tarpauling, tilt, sack & rope manufacturers; also marquees, tents, tarpaulings, &c. lent on hire; 17 Smithfield bars, & 2 Orford row, Old Kent rd
Edgington Benjamin, rick cloth, tent, marquee, flag & improved tarpauling manufacturer, 2 Duke st. Borough, (opposite the Greenwich railway), & 208 Piccadilly
Edginton Edwd. T. grocer, 10 Up. Glo'ster pl. King's rd. Chelsea
Edginton John, tobacconist, 135 Cornwall rd. Lambeth
Edgley Jas. F. coalfactor, Customh. chambrs. 70 Lr. Thames st
Edgley John, baker, 42 Radnor st. St. Luke's
Edie Euphemia (Mrs.), baker, 11 Market st. Fitzroy market
Edinburgh Life Assurance Company (C. Staniforth, resident director), 11 King William st. City. For list of Directors, &c. &c. see page 2022
Edinburgh & London Steam Packet Co. 35 Leadenhall st
Edington & Freeman, coal mercs. Blackfriars whf. 22 Earl st
Edington James Chas. working silversmith, 23 Leicester sq
Edington John James, jeweller, 10 Portland st. Soho
Edington Johnston, *Artichoke* P.H. 14 Church st. Camberwell
Edington William, jeweller & silversmith, 219 Oxford st
Edis & Low, sheep salesmen, 59 West Smithfield
Edis Joseph, butcher, see Garratt & Edis
Edis Robt. carpenter & builder, 5 Providence row, Finsbury
Edisburg John, bookseller, 1 Blenheim terrace, St. John's wd
Edison John Sibbald, barrister, 3 Plowden bldgs. Temple
Edkins Henry & Co. grocers, 18 Coventry st. Haymarket
Edkins Sam. S. silversmh. & globema. 16 Salisbury sq. Fleet st
Edlin Edward, dentist, 9 Queen's row, New rd. Pentonville
Edlin George, tobacconist & snuffmaker, 6 Aldgate
Edlin John, florist, 2 Queen's row, New rd. Pentonville
Edlin Saml. saddler & harness maker, 2 Green st. Grosvenor sq
Edlin Thomas, turner & toy manufacturer, 37 New Bond st
Edlin William, butcher, 118 Shadwell High st
Edlin Wm. Matthew, florist, 33 Queen's rd. Bayswater
Edlmann Joseph, merchant, 9 Liverpool st
Edmand James, straw hat ma. 7 Chester pl. Old Kent rd
Edmanson William, grocer & tea dlr. 42 High st. St. Giles's
Edmead Wm. baker, 49 Gower place, Euston square
Edmeades Wm. pianoforte ma. see Levesque, Edmeades & Co
Edmed Richard, hop, seed & corn factor, 20 King st. Boro'
Edmeston Jas. archt. & surveyor, Salvador house, Bishopsgt
Edmiston Charles & Son, tailors & trousers ma. 69 Strand
Edmiston Abraham, gun case maker, 12 Macclesfield st. Soho
Edmiston Chas. Jas. tailor & outfitter, 91 & 93 Gracechurch st
Edmond Alex. sec. to *Nth. of Scotl. Life Ass. Co.* 1 Moorgate st
Edmond Francis, ship chandler, 140 Wapping
Edmond John, solicitor, 60 Margaret st. Cavendish sq
Edmondes Henry, deputy clerk of the peace for Middlesex, Sessions house, Clerkenwell green
Edmonds Hy. & Geo. & Co. druggs. & perfumers, 27 Gt. Bush la
Edmonds John & Co. wholes. button, trimming & manchester warehousemen, 4 & 5 Gresham st. Wood st. City
Edmonds Sarah & Hen. law stationers, 7 Hemlock ct. Carey st
Edmonds Anthony, bandana & corah printer & silk manufr. 33 Lawrence lane, Cheapside
Edmonds Charles, bookseller & stationer, 154 Strand
Edmonds Charles, oil & colorman, 8 Whitefriars st
Edmonds Chas. share & stockbroker, 9 Change all. Cornhill
Edmonds Chas. J. *Feathers* P.H. 42 Brown st. Bryanstone sq
Edmonds Chris. Wm. C. arch. & surv. 2 Bridge st. Southwark
Edmonds Edwd. baker & corndlr. 146 Poplar High st
Edmonds Ezekiel, corndlr. 6 Cumberland pl. Newington butts
Edmonds Fras. (Mrs.), *Grapes* P.H. 18 St. Thomas's st. Boro'
Edmonds George, butcher, 37 Stanhope st. Clare market
Edmonds George, poultry salesman, Leadenhall market
Edmonds George, saddler & harn. manuf. 101 Leadenhall st
Edmonds Henry, beer retailer, 71 Marylebone lane
Edmonds Henry, dairy, 12 Charles st. Westbourne terrace
Edmonds Henry, solicitor, 62 Trinity square, Boro'
Edmonds Jacob, bookbinder, &c. see Remnant & Edmonds
Edmonds James, baker, 108 Brick lane, Spitalfields
Edmonds James, bootmaker, 7 Bruton st. Bond st
Edmonds James, bootmaker, 15 Salmon lane, Limehouse

Edmonds James, butcher, 4 Sussex st. Tottenham ct. road
Edmonds James, cheesemonger, 6 Brewer st. Somers town
Edmonds James, fruiterer, 41 North st. Lisson grove
Edmonds James, grocer, 4 New st. Kennington road
Edmonds James, grocer, 15 Limehouse causeway
Edmonds James Matthew, baker, 11 Kingsland row, Dalston
Edmonds John, cowkeeper, 23 Edgware road
Edmonds John, dairyman, 1 Upper Crown st. Westminster
Edmonds John, poulterer, 7 Halfmoon pas. Leadenhall mrkt
Edmonds John, *Steam Ship* P.H. Naval row, Blackwall
Edmonds John, workbox&dress.case ma. 3 Meredith st.Clkwl
Edmonds John, wine mercht. 19 Charles st. Hatton garden
Edmonds John Thomas, dentist, 27 George st. Hanover sq
EdmondsJn.Wm.*RoyalSovereign*P.H.15Park st.Limehouse
Edmonds Joseph, baker, 11 Hoxton Old town
Edmonds Maria (Mrs.), plumber, Meadow pl. South Lmbeth
Edmonds Mary(Mrs.),Guilford dairy,83Guilford st. Rusl. sq
Edmonds Sarah(Mrs.),dining rooms,6 Dover pl.W.Kentst.rd
Edmonds Simeon,fruiterer,8Up.Southwick st.Nth.Cmbge.ter
Edmonds Thos. news ag. & bank reading room, 2 Lit. Bell al
Edmonds Thomas, chemist, 24 Cross st. Blackfriars
Edmonds Thomas, dairyman,16Marchmontst. Brunswick sq
Edmonds Thos. ivory & hard wood turner, teapot handlemkr. & dealr. in ivory & hard woods, 1 Monkwell st. Cripplegate
Edmonds Thos. R. actuary, *Legal & Gen Life Ass. So.* 10 Fleet st
Edmonds Wm. carpenter, 8 Edward st. Kennington cross
Edmonds Wm. *Royal Standard* P.H. 10 White st. Borough
Edmonds Wm. umbrella & fishing rod ma. 15 East rd. City rd
Edmondson, Keniston & Co. woollen warehsmn.20Ludgate hl
Edmondson George, tailor, 4 Wapping wall
Edmunds Alfred Sayres, solicitor, see Rolfe & Edmunds
Edmunds Edward, carpenter, 18 Brown st. Bryanstone sq
Edmunds Edward, teadealer, 29 Gt. Russell st. Bloomsbury
Edmunds Geo. B. chemist, 2 Norfolk pl. Marlboro' rd. Chlsa
Edmunds John, silk manufacturer, 5 Fort st. Spitalfields
Edmunds John, stationer & rag merchant, 5 Lit. St. Thomas Apostle, & 18 Bread st. hill
Edmunds John Thomas, builder, 3 Gun st. Spital sq
Edmunds Samuel, cheesemonger, 209 Upper Whitecross st
Edmunds Thomas, grocer, 49 Seymour pl. Bryanstone sq
Edmunds Thomas, oil & colorman, 2 Holly st. Dalston
Edmunds Wm. wax & tallow chandler, 233 Hoxton Old tn
Edmunds Wm. painter & glazier, 2 Wilson st. Finsbury
Edney Ann (Mrs.), stationer & booksel. 2 St. Johnst.Clerkwl
Edney E. (Mrs.), *Garrick's Head* P.H. 1 Montague place, Lower road, Deptford
Edney John M. prof.ofsinging,7&8Pleasant row, Pentonville
Edney Wm. hairdresser, 93 Dean st. Soho
Edney Wm. upholsterer,&c. 9 Chapel st. Tottenham court rd
Edridge Freeman, tallow & oilman, 20 Red Lion st. Holborn
Edridge Sarah (Mrs.), rag & bottle wa. 8 Bloomsbury markt
Edridge Thomas, tallow chandler & oilman, 1 Oxford st
Edridge Thos. Rd. ship & ins. broker, see Marshall & Edridge
Edridge Wm. coppersmith, brazier & brassfounder, 43 Princes st. Rotherhithe, & 354 Rotherhithe wall
Edsall Richard, surgeon, 195 Bermondsey st
Edser James, bricklayer, 1 Buckingham row, Westminster
Education Board, Privy Council Office, Downing st
Edward Peter, tailor, 72 Cheapside
Edward's Almshouses, 1 Church st. Blackfriars road
Edwards & Bennett, hay salesmen, 39 West Smithfield, & Belvedere road, Lambeth
Edwards Brothers, groat manufacturers, & corn & flour merchants, 99 Blackfriars road
Edwards Chas.&Son, music string ma.20Sharp's all.Cow cross
Edwards Charles & Son, tailors, 5 Rupert st. Soho
Edwards Charlotte & Son,furriers,6Gt.Pulteneyst.Golden sq
Edwards D. & H. & Co. sole patentees of the preserved potato, 1A, Bishopsgate st. within
Edwards Edwd. & Son, who. teadealers,14 Abchurch la.City
Edwards & Fisher, ship & insurance bro. 5 Trinity sq.Twr.hl
Edwards Hen.Lees&Chas.&Co.wooln.manfs.9Gracechurch st
Edwards & Hopkins, ink, dye & chemical manf. 22 Harrowrd
Edwards & Hughes, booksel. & publishers, 12 Ave Maria la. & Stationers' Hall court
Edwards Joel & Sons, tailors, &c. 9 Hanover st. Hanover sq
Edwards John & Co. coal merchts. Salisbury wharf, Strand
Edwards John & Co. wholesale teadealers, 17 St. Mary Axe
EdwardsMy.&Elzh.(Misses) linendra.3Prospectpl.Kngsld.rd
Edwards (Misses), court milliners, 3 Old Cavendish st
Edwards & Nevins, painters, 30 Stangate st. Lambeth
Edwards & Peake, solicitors, 11 New Palace yard, Westmr
Edwards & Poucher, alamode beef house, 242 Strand
Edwards & Scott, naval & military tailors & habit makers, 52 Conduit st. Regent st
Edwards Thomas & Co.coal mer.Durham whf.Mlfrd.la.Strnd
Edwards & Mason, solicitors, 8 Moorgate st. City, & 8 Delahay st. Westminster
Edwards & Whiteway, attorneys, 51 Lincoln's inn fields
Edwards William & Son, tailors, 48 Basinghall st
Edwards Wm. & Co. linendrps. 28 & 29 Middle row,Holborn
Edwards Alexander, tin plate worker, 194 Bethnal green rd
Edwards Ann (Miss), tobacconist, 11 Union row, Lit. Chelsea
Edwards Ann (Mrs.), lodging house, 13 Oxendon st
Edwards Ann (Mrs.), milliner, 52 Mortimer st.Cavendish sq
Edwards Anthony Turner, builder & bricklayer, 12 Idol la
Edwards Benjamin, watch & clockmaker, 17 Shoreditch
Edwards Benjamin, milliner,141Up.Whitecross st.St.Luke's
Edwards Charles, cheesemngr. 44 Marchmont st.Brunswk.sq
Edwards Charles, chemist, 63 Gt. Russell st. Bloomsbury
Edwards Charles, haberdasher, 17 Piccadilly
Edwards Charles, linendraper, &c. see Dawes & Edwards
Edwards Charles (Mrs.), milliner, 13 Regent st
Edwards Charles, ship & insur.broker,see Batten & Edwards
Edwards Charles, *Swan tap* P.H. Bridge ct. Westminster
Edwards Charles, veterinary surgeon, 41 Little Moorfields, & 14 Ropemakers' st. Finsbury
Edwards Charles John, leather pipe & mill band maker & oilman, 3 St. John st. road
Edwards Chas. Rd. grocer & cheesemonger, 3 Brunswick st. Blackwall
Edwards Chrisr. grocer, 2 Charles pl.Hertford rd.Kingsland
Edwards Daniel, surgeon, 13 Queen st. Cheapside
Edwards Daniel, tailor, 6 Bloomsbury st. Bloomsbury
Edwards David, butcher, 101 Wapping
Edwards David, cowkeeper, &c. 57 East st. Manchester sq
Edwards David, dyer, 154 Hoxton Old town
Edwards David, furniture broker,8Wentworth pl.Mile end rd
Edwards David, glass & china dlr. 38 Somerset pl. Hoxton
Edwards David, *Queen's Head* P.H. 154 Whitechapel road
Edwards David, surgeon, 22 King st. Covent garden
Edwards David Owen, surgeon, 15 Cheyne walk, Chelsea
Edwards Edward, boot & shoemaker, 164 Oxford st
Edwards Edward, bricklayer, 50 Mansell st. Goodman's flds
Edwards Edward, fancy repository, 21 East rd. City road
Edwards Edward, linen draper, Kensington gravel pits
Edwards Edward, linen draper, 99 High st. Notting hill
Edwards Edward, official assignee, 7 Fredk.'s pl. Old Jewry
Edwards Edward, silversmith, 52 Red Lion st. Clerkenwell
Edwards Edwin, proctor, 1 Bennett's hill, Doctors' commns
Edwards Elizabeth (Miss), milliner, 241 Regent st
Edwards Elizabeth (Mrs.), *Bull* P.H. 190 Kingsland road
Edwards Eliz. (Mrs.), fruiterer, 22 Liverpool st. Bishopsgate
Edwards Evan. gen. furn. irnmngr.&hardwa.&c. 61 Barbican
EdwardsFran.(Miss),dressma.9Haberdashrs'.pl.west,Hoxton
Edwards Francis, architect & surveyor, 17 Hart st. Bloomsb
Edwards Francis, tailor & draper, 122 Newgate st
Edwards Fred. barrister, 4 Brick court, Temple
Edwards Fred. booksel. & printer, 56 Leman st. Goodman'sfi
Edwards Fred. pawnbroker, 162 Hoxton Old town
Edwards Fred.stove ma.&bellha.20 Polandst.&86½Oxford st
Edwards Fred. T. wine,ale & bot.stout mer. 3 Bond ct. Walbk
Edwards George, baker, 144 Edgware road, Marylebone
Edwards Geo. brushmaker, 197 Brick lane, Spitalfields
Edwards Geo. butcher, 5 Victoria place, Hoxton Old town
Edwards Geo. carpenter, 6 Vauxhall st. Princes rd. Lambeth
Edwards Geo. civil engineer, 13 George st. Adelphi
Edwards Geo. clothworker,13&14Peter's hill,Doctors'comns
Edwards Geo. engraver&printer, 9Albert pl.Shepherdess wk
Edwards Geo. milkman, 12 Beech st. Barbican
Edwards Geo. pork butcher, 5 Tabernacle square
Edwards Geo. *Ship* P.H. 11 Little Tower st
Edwards Geo. surveyor, 3 Montague place, Islington
Edwards Geo. Benj. linendraper, 19 Thornton st.Horselydwn
Edwards Geo. Frederick, baker, 20 Lit. Warner st. Clerkwl
Edwards Geo. Wm. wine broker, see Howes & Edwards
Edwards Harrison, carpenter, 27 King st. Clerkenwell
Edwards Henry, carp.&undertak.42 East. st. Manchester sq
Edwards Hen. chandler & oilman,10Cambridge st.Golden sq
Edwards Hen. insurance brok.&c. 75 Old Broad st.&Lloyd's
Edwards Hen. oil & seed brok.&c.75O.Broad st.&Baltic cof.ho
Edwards Hen. plumbr. & glazr.4 Prospect pl. Kingsland rd
Edwards Henry, solicitor, see Jacques & Edwards
Edwards Henry, surgeon, 67 Edgware road, Marylebone
Edwards Hen. surg.inst.case ma.31Bartlett's bldgs.Holborn
Edwards Henry, tobacconist, 42 Cannon st. City
Edwards Henry, tobacconist, 25½ Marchmont st. Brunsw.sq
Edwards Henry Barge, grocer, 150 Edgware rd. Marylebo
Edwards Henry Jas. *George* P.H. 24 St. John st.Clerknwell
Edwards Hen. P.block&mastma.40&40½Russell st.Rothrhith
Edwards James, *Black Bull* P.H.Old Montague st.Whitech
Edwards James, bookseller, 76 Bunhill row, St. Luke's

Edwards Jas. boot & shoe ma. 1 Up. Church st. Chelsea
Edwards James, cheesemonger, 18 Brown's la. Spitalfields
Edwards James, chronometer maker, see Hunter & Edwards
Edwards James, coachspringma. Denmrk.ct. Denmrk.st. Soho
Edwards James, dealer in second hand plate, 36 Jewin st
Edwards James, foreign bird dealer, 23½ Addle hill, Doc.com
Edwards James, fruiterer, 37 Cornwall road, Lambeth
Edwards James, fruiterer, 57 Hackney road
Edwards James, livery stables, Kinnerton st. Belgrave sq
Edwards James, oilman, Bow
Edwards James, oilman, 1 Walbrook st. New North rd
Edwards James, plumber, 18 Redman's row, Mile end road
Edwards James, shoemaker, 4 Prospect pl. Kingsland rd
Edwards James, *Somerset Arms* P.H.1 Seymour rw. Lit. Chel
Edwards James, staymaker, 25 King st. Holborn
Edwards James, surgeon, 2 Sion vil. Hortulan pl. Kgs.rd. Chls
Edwards James, tailor, 86 York st. Westminster
Edwards James Allon, merchant, see Maack & Edwards
Edwards James Hurd, hosier & shirt maker, 80 Oxford st
Edwards Jane (Mrs.), cheesemonger, 121 High st. Camden tn
Edwards Jane (Mrs.), lodging ho. 4 & 5 Charlotte st. Pimlico
Edwards Jeremiah, butcher, 24 Everett st. Brunswick sq
Edwards John, agent for Allsopp & Son's burton ale, 61 King William st. City
Edwards John, baker, 31 Gt. Quebec st. New road
Edwards John, baker, 59 North st. Edgware road
Edwards John, baker, 98 Paul st. Finsbury
Edwards John, baker, 57 Princes st. Lambeth
Edwards John, baker, 16 Whitehorse ter. Stepney
Edwards John, beer retailer, 32 Brill row, Somers town
Edwards John, bootmaker, 4 Up. North pl. Gray's inn rd
Edwards John, bootmaker, 63 Bath st. City road
Edwards John, bootmaker, 3 Crucifix lane, Bermondsey
Edwards John, builder, 8 Belgrave road, Pimlico
Edwards John, coal dealer, 272 Bermondsey st
Edwards John, carpenter, 138 Golden lane, St. Luke's
Edwards John, coffee rooms, 129 St. Alban's pl. Edgware rd
Edwards John, furniture printer, see Miles & Edwards
Edwards John, grocer, 39 Holborn hill
Edwards John, ham & tongue dealer, 87 Leadenhall st
Edwards John, lath render & furnit. bro. 15½ Lower st. Islgtn
Edwards John, nail ironm. & gen. coml. agt. 3 Nag's head ct
Edwards John, newsvender, 21 Harrow road, Paddington
Edwards John, tailor, 18 Upper Ground st. Blackfriars
Edwards John, tobacconist, 27 Charlotte st. Fitzroy sq
Edwards John, wheelwright, Prospect pl. Canal, Old Kent rd
Edwards John Brewen, solicitor, 61 Nelson square
Edwards John Jas. ornamental painter, 69 Gt. Titchfield st
Edwards John Scarlett, tea agent, 34 Fenchurch st
Edwards John Wm. cheesemonger, 11 Marchmont st. Bur.cres
Edwards Joseph, beer retailer, 17 Saville st. Fitzroy sq
Edwards Joseph, chemist & druggist, 12 New Cavendish st
Edwards Joseph, hairdresser, 9 Triangle, Kennington cross
Edwards Joseph, sculptor, 40 Robert st. Hampstead road
Edwards Joseph James, furn. broker, 11 Crucifix la. Bermdsy
Edwards Joshua, bootmaker, 107 Paul st. Finsbury
Edwards Lewis, bootmak. & tobaccon. 26 Park pl. Kenningt. cr
Edwards Lydia (Mrs.), tobacconist, 10 Carlton st. Regent st
Edwards Mary Ann (Mrs.), carter, 12 Barons pl. Waterloo rd
Edwards Mary Ann (Miss), dressma. 56 Gainsford st. Horsld
Edwards Nath. *Cock & Castle* P.H. 55 Elizabeth st. Hackney
Edwards Peter, timber merchant, 56 Lambeth Lower marsh
Edwards Philemon, ironmong. & stove ma. 16 Lower st. Islgtn
Edwards Reuben, carpent. & joiner, 49 Liverpool st. Bishpsg
Edwards Richard, haberdasher, 114 Shoreditch High st
Edwards Richard, *Merlin's Cave* P.H. 64 South Audley st
Edwards Richard, pat. emery cloth ma. 12 Fairfield pl. Bow
Edwards Richard, pianoforte ma. 1 Seymour st. Euston sq
Edwards Richd. printer & stationer, 42 Basing pl. Waterloo rd
Edwards Richd *Running Horse* P.H. 15 Chapel st. ea. Mayfair
Edwards Robert, bootmaker, 47 Chapel st. Pentonville
Edwards Robert, engraver & library, 26 Lisle st. Leicester sq
Edwards Robert, surgeon, 90 Oxford terrace, Edgware road
Edwards Rt. Morley, pat. medicine vendr. 22 Radnor st. St. Luke
Edwards Robert Levitt, baker, 201 Shadwell High st
Edwards Samuel, *Vulcan* beershop, Salmon la. Limehs. flds
Edwards Sam. *Sportsman* P.H. 8 Frederick st. Portland twn
Edwards Tenison, barrister, Law chmbrs. 77 Chancery lane
Edwards Thos. army clothier, 4 Charing cross
Edwards Thos. army contractor, 104 Up. Stamford st. Blkfrs
Edwards Thos. bootmaker, 4 Blenheim st. New Bond st
Edwards Thos. *Bull's Head* P.H. 6 Jewin crescent
Edwards Thos. coffee house, 35 Fetter lane
Edwards Thos. coal merchnt. White Lion wf. 18 Up. Thames st
Edwards Thos. dining rooms, Nutkin's corner, Bmdsy. wall
Edwards Thos. fruiterer & muffin bkr. 21 Cobourg st. Eustn. sq
Edwards Thos. dressing case maker to Her Majesty & the Royal Family, 21 King st. Holborn
Edwards Thos. grocer, &c. 20 Little Queen st. Westminster
Edwards Thos. lighterman, Galley quay, Lower Thames st
Edwards Thos. lighterman & coal merclt. 11 Beer la. Tower st
Edwards Thos. lodging ho. 19 Arundel st. & 23 Norfolk st. Strand
Edwards Thos. mahogany broker, 1 Pinner's hall, Old Broad st
Edwards Thos. mahogany frame ma. 51 Marshall st. Golden sq
Edwards Thos. silk mercer, 9 Soho square, Oxford st
Edwards Thos. solicitor, 4 Clement's inn
Edwards Thos. stockbroker, 76 Old Broad st. City
Edwards Thos. surgeon, 21 Union st. Clarendon square
Edwards Thos. tailor, 10 St. George's pl. Camberwell rd
Edwards Thos. Kersey, solicitor, 1 Raymond buildings
Edwards Thomas Richard, tailor, 1½ Queen's Head lane
Edwards Thos. Salmon, *Black Horse* P.H. 19 Tottenham ct. rd
Edwards Wm. accountant & valuer, 35 King st. City
Edwards Wm. beer retailer, Earl's court, Old Brompton
Edwards Wm. boot & shoe maker, 12 Princes st. Lambeth
Edwards Wm. cabinet maker, 40 High st. Camden town
Edwards Wm. carpenter, 36 Windmill st. Tottenham ct. rd
Edwards Wm. chemist, 30 Addington place, Camberwell rd
Edwards Wm. chemist, 29 King William st. City
Edwards Wm. coal mer. Bridge wf. Canal rd. Kingsland rd
Edwards Wm. coal merchant, 30 Whitmore road, Hoxton
Edwards Wm. cornchandler, 48 Charlotte ter. New cut, Lamb
Edwards Wm. druggist, 13 Goodge st. Tottenham court rd
Edwards Wm. fruiterer, 27A, Charlotte st. Fitzroy sq
Edwards Wm. furniture broker, 6 College ter. Chelsea
Edwards Wm. *George* P.H. 1 Portland st. Wardour st
Edwards Wm. grocer, 28 Edmund st. King's cross
Edwards Wm. grocer, 16 New King st. Deptford
Edwards Wm. grocer, 72 New Church st. Lisson grove
Edwards Wm. grocer, 18 North place, Kingsland road
Edwards Wm. haberdasher, &c. 20 High st. Marylebone
Edwards Wm. hatter, 6 Totford pl. Neckinger rd. Bermondsey
Edwards Wm. livery stables, 15 Wilmot st. Russell sq
Edwards Wm. merchant, 10 Liverpool st. Bishopsgate
Edwards Wm. *Old Fox* P.H. Southampton court, Queen sq
Edwards Wm. parisian repository, 183 Fleet st
Edwards Wm. pat. medicine war. 67 St. Paul's churchyard
Edwards Wm. pocket book lock mak. 73½ Queen st. Cheapside
Edwards Wm. *Red Lion* P.H. 72 King st. Deptford
Edwards Wm. silversmith, 19 Sekforde st. Clerkenwell
Edwards Wm. size & whiting ma. 9 Collier's rents, White st. Boro
Edwards Wm. tobacconist, 25 Kent st. Borough
Edwards Wm. warehouseman, 9 Aldermanbury
Edwards Wm. watchmaker, 4 Theberton st. Islington
Edwards Wm. wine merchant & broker, 17 Gt. Tower st
Edwards Wm. Aug. shoema. 6 Barrossa ter. Cambridge heath
Edwards Wm. Hen. beer retailer, 18 Leigh st. Burton cresc
Edwards Wm. Hen. pianoforte maker, 17 Bridge rd. Lambeth
Edwards Wm. Holmes, barrister, 1 Middle Temple lane
Edwards Wm. L. build. & und. 1 Charles pl. Westbn. ter. Padgtn
Edwards Wm. Staples, chemist, &c. 14 Etham pl. Kent st. rd
Edwin Isaac Edwin, scrivener, 4 Cook's court, Lincoln's inn
Edy John, elastic truss, &c. maker, 63 Dean st. Soho
Edy Thomas, saddler, 16 Stafford row, Pimlico
Edye John, bootmaker, 30 Redcross st. Borough
Edye Jsph. agt. to imprl. fire & life insu. 7 Church st. Lambeth
Edye Thomas, attorney, 14 Clement's inn, Strand
Edye Walter Oke, special pleader, 13 King's Bench walk
Eede Charles, butcher, 1 Newland place, Kensington
Eede Henry, teadealer, &c. 26 Marchmont st. Brunswick sq
Eedes John, accountant & bookseller, 14 Lit. Knightrider st
Eedes Robert, trunk & packing case maker, 49 Moorgate st
Eedle Edward, bookseller, 82 Chancery lane
Eedy Bennett, bookbinder, 17 New st. square, Fetter lane
Eekhoud Alexander, merchant, N. & S. American coffee ho
Eeles David, bricklayer, 17 George st. Grosvenor square
Eeles Thomas Robert, bookbinder, 22 Cursitor st
Egan Edward, merchant, see Kingston's, Lambert & Egan
Egan Elizth. (Mrs.), wig parting ma. 41 Kirby st. Hatton gard
Egan James, tailor, 6 Sussex st. Tottenham court road
Egan John, furn. ironmonger, 16 High row, Knightsbridge
Egan John, tailor, 21 Chenies st. Bedford square
Egan Pierce, bookseller, 2A, Grove ter. Bayswater
Egan William, solicitor, 58 Lincoln's inn fields
Egerton Mary & Sons, plumbers, 1 Temple st. Whitefriars
Egerton Henry, barrister, 6 Old square, Lincoln's inn
Egerton Jeremiah, daguerreotype agent, 8 Red Lion court Fleet st. & 1 Temple st. Whitefriars
Egg Charles & Henry, gun, rifle & pistol manufacturers, 1 Piccadilly (successors to the late Joseph Manton & Son)
Egg & Co. patent truss makers, 1 Piccadilly
Egg Augustus, artist, 30 Gerrard st. Soho

Egg Charles John, linendraper, Whitmore pl. Hoxton Old tn
Egg Durs, gunmaker, 4 Pall mall
Eggett William, beer retailer, 81 Broad st. Lambeth
Eggleton Charles, *Crown tav.* Clifford's inn passage, Fleet st
Eglese Joseph, jeweller, 30 Cornhill
Egleton & Bell, bookbind. & gold burnish. 17 Queen st. Clknwll
Egleton Charles & Thomas, bookbinders, 90½ Holborn hill
Egleton Charles, bookbinder, 5 East Harding st. Gough sq
Egleton Wm. Hen. engraver, 23 Edwards ter. Caledonian rd
Egley Thomas, bookseller, stationer & juvenile library, 69 New Bond st
Egley William, artist, 75 Connaught terrace, Hyde park
Eglinton Robt. & Co. eastindia agts. 13 Old Jewry cham. O. Jewry
Egyptian Agency Offices & India Rooms, 34 Cornhill; 10 to 5
Ehrenhoff & In de Betou, medical practitioners in therapeutic manipulation, 3 Upper Gower st. Bedford sq
Ehrensperger (Conrad) & Co. merchants & ultramarine agents, 4 Laurence Pountney place, Cannon st
Ehrhart Joseph, confectioner, &c. 437 Strand
Eicke John, conveyancer, 65 Gower st
Eiffe James S. chronometer maker, 48 Lombard st. City, & 1 South crescent, Bedford square
Einsle Edwd. surgical inst. ma. & cutler, 46 St. Martin's lane
Eisdell John Byles, brewer, Burdett st. Walworth common
Eisenberg John, surgeon chiropodist, 14 Cockspur st
Eitel Abraham, coppersmith & mould ma. 5 Villiers st. Strand
Eivers John, civil engineer, 12 Buckingham st. Strand
Eives James, ironmonger, 29 Gt. Titchfield st. Oxford st
Ekstedt Thos. James, pianofortema. 37 Bridge house pl. Boro'
Elam Alfred, truss maker, 403 Oxford st
Elam Benj. & Sons, woollen drapers, 33 Sackville st
Elam Benjamin, chemist, 196 Oxford st
Elam Thomas, ropemaker, 68 Marylebone lane, Oxford st
Eland & Son, sheep salesmen, 41 West Smithfield
Eland John, morocco leather manuf. Gun al. 85 Bermndsy. st
Eland Thomas Bult, butcher, Old Chapel row, Kentish town
Elborough Thomas & Co. wax & tallowchand. 51 South Audley st
Elburn Henry James, sen. coffee rooms, 181 Fleet st
Elcoate Luke, printer, see Chapman & Elcoate
Elcock Jacob, butcher, 20 Upper Ebury st. Pimlico
Elcock James, teadealer, &c. 15 Paddington st. Marylebone
Elcocks Thomas, builder, 9 Bridgewater gardens, Barbican
Elcom Richard, beer retailer, near the bridge, New North rd
Elcum Hugh William, solicitor, 187 Blackfriars road
Elden Chas. James, confectioner, 40 Red Lion st. Holborn
Elden William, musician, 18 New road, St. George's east
Elder & Jurdison, *Caledonian hotel*, 3 Robert st. Adelphi, & *Osborn's Adelphi hotel*, 1 to 4 John st. Adelphi
Elder, Smith & Co. booksellers & stationers, 65 Cornhill
Elder David, *George* P.H. 104 Houndsditch
Elder Henry Weston, bristle mercht. 7 Commercial pl. City rd
Elder Peter, coach builder, 17 Nassau pl. Commercial rd. ea
Eldered John, smith & farrier, 5 Swan st. Gt. Dover rd
Eldershaw Wm. stationer & newsman, 15 Adam st. west
Elderton Charles, butcher, 2 Well st. Wellclose square
Elderton Chas. Merrick, barrister, 9 New sq. Lincoln's inn
Elderton Edward Merrick, solicitor, 3 Lothbury
Elderton Harriet (Mrs.), ladies' school, 46 Wilmington sq
Elderton Thomas Rt. ironmonger, 2 Up. Gloucester pl. & 4 Boston st. Dorset square
Eldon Richard, *Red Lion* P.H. 8 Nag's Head ct. Gracech st
Eldred John H. survey. & build. 11 Bleeding Hart yd. Hatn. gn
Eldred Joseph, farrier, 25 Colchester st. Whitechapel
Eldred William, baker, 1 Artillery terrace, Westminster
Eldrid Thomas, saddlers' ironmonger, 21 Fore st. Cripplegate
Eldridge & Rapson, vet. surgeons, 33 Colonnade, Russell sq
Eldridge & Youngman, timber merchants, Grange road
Eldridge Harriet & Eliza, stay ma. 16 Leigh st. Burton cres
Eldridge Edward, baker, 15 Exeter st. Sloane st
Eldridge Francis, watch motion maker, 9 Rose st. St. Luke's
Eldridge Henry, carpenter, &c. 29 Cumberland st. Hackney rd
Eldridge James Wraight, dining rooms, 9 King st. Boro'
Eldridge Jesse, smith & farrier, 2 St. George's st. Albany rd
Eldridge John, oil & colorman, 10 Cromer st. Brunswick sq
Eldridge Louisa (Miss), dressmaker, 7 Judd st. Brunswick sq
Eldridge Thos. builder & house agt. 6 Judd st. Brunswick sq
Eldridge Thos. coachmaker, 27 Up. North pl. Gray's inn road
Eldridge Thomas, cooper, 64 Kent st. Borough
Eldridge Wm. coach builder, 79½ Charlotte st. Portland pl
Eldridge Wm. conveyancer, 36 Carey st. Lincoln's inn
Eldridge Wm. tailor, 27 Hyde st. Bloomsbury
Eldridge Wm. watch motion maker, 54 Rahere st. Goswell rd
Electric Telegraph Works (Philip Woodrow, superintendt.), 22 Church row, Limehouse
Element Wm. carpet warehouse & upholsterer, 108 Strand
Elems Robert, *Fox* P.H. 33 Kingsland crescent, Kingsland rd
Elen Charles, butcher, 23 Queen st. Edgware road
Eley Henry, chemist, 19 Providence place, Kentish town
Eley Joseph, carrier, 6 Commercial place, Kentish town
Eley Robert, coal & wood dealer, 5 York st. Hans pl. Sloane st
Eley William Thomas, wire cartridge, percussion cap & wadding manufacturer, 40 Old Bond st
Elford John H. & son, tailors, 3 Gt. Pulteney st. Golden sq
Elford & Hancock, smiths & farriers, 5 Lit. Exetr. st. Sloane st
Elford John Edward, grocer, 12 King street, Seven dials
Elford William, wax & tallow chandler, 65 Charing cross
Elgar Edwin, butcher, 4 Wellington terrace, Liverpool rd
Elgee John, *Swan* P.H. 1 Cornbury place, Old Kent road
Elger & Kelk, builders, 13 South st. South Audley st
Elger Charles, fruiterer, 99 White Lion st. Pentonville
Elger William, tobacconist, 2 Thornton st. Horselydown
Elgie Charles Wm. solicitor, 7 Warwick court, Holborn
Elgie George Thomas, solicitor, 2 Bucklersbury
Elgie Thos. plumber & painter, 52 Foley st. Portland place
Elgood John Garrard, house agent & auctioneer, 98 Wimpole st
Elias Benj. statr. & tobacconist, 23 Up. Seymour st. Euston sq
Elias Hyman, merchant, 33 Clement's lane, Lombard st. City
Elin John B. & Co. merchants, 80 King William st. & 9 Nicholas lane, City
Eling William, dealer in shells, 5 High st. Deptford
Eliot Geo. H. surveyor, &c. 17 Charlotte st. Portland pl
Elisha Caleb, watch & clock maker, 15 New Bond st
Elisha Chas. Rees, tallow chandler, 14 Cable st. Wellclose sq
Elisha George, bricklayer, 12 Paradise st. Finsbury
Elisha Henry, grocer, 10 King st. Cloth fair, Smithfield
Elisha James, wire blind maker, 192 Bishopsgate without
Elkan Isaac, merchant, 10 Bucklersbury
Elkin Benjamin & Sons, merchants, 4 Great Winchester st
Elkin Charles Mitton, grocer, 32 Chiswell st
Elkin Wm. ironfounder, 3 Kinaston st. Oakley st. Lambeth
Elkington & Co. patentees, electro platers & gilders & manufacturers & retailers of electro-plated & gilt articles of every description, 22 Regent st. & 45 Moorgate st. City
Elkington & Haworth, druggists, 132 St. Alban's place, Edgware road, & 6 Maida hill east
Elkington Alfred, woolstapler, 162 Bermondsey st
Elkington Edward, chemist, 10 Mount row, Liverpool road
Elkington Henry, woolstapler, 3 Russell st. & 1 Little Fendall st. Bermondsey
Elkington Jacob, chemist & druggist, 21 Broadway, Deptford
Elkington John, *White Hart* P.H. 296 Strand
Elkington Joseph, grocer, 11 Vauxhall bridge road
Elkington Mary (Mrs.), cowkeeper, 5 Keppel st. Marlbro' rd
Elkins Alfred, surgeon, 30 Foley place, Portland place
Elkins Chas. Jno. paperhanger, High st. Kensington
Elkins Edward, solicitor, 59 Newman st. Oxford st
Elkins Eliza (Mrs.), juvenile clothier, Kensington High st
Elkins George, plumber & painter, 6 Rawstorne st. Brompton
Elkins Harry, sculptor, 29 Crescent st. Euston square
Elkins James, *Nelson's Head* P.H. 1 Gt. York mews, Baker st
Elkins Valentine, bookseller, 1 Southampton pl. Euston sq
Elkins William Henry, bookseller & stationer, 47 Lombard st
Elkins William Morris, solicitor, 23 Fenchurch st
Elks Thomas, shirt maker, &c. see Ragsdale & Elks
Ell Charles, confectioner, 25 Kingsland road
Ell George, ladder & barrow maker, 3 Tottenham court New road, & 5 Drinkwater place, Waterloo road
Ell James, baker, 16 Copenhagen street, Pentonville
Ell Thos. ladderma. 1 Windsor ter. City rd. & 3 Singleton st. Hxtn
Ellaby Wm. Francis, solicitor, 2 Bedford row, Holborn
Ellamy Thomas, carpenter, 47 Edmund st. King's cross
Ellard Wm. plumber, 20 Windmill st. Tottenham court rd. & 1 Camden road, Camden New town
Elldred John, linen factor, see Phillips & Elldred
Ellen Thomas, coal merchant, 73 Gt. Russell st. Bloomsbury
Ellenden Geo. marine store dealer, 32 Up. Lisson st. Lisson gr
Ellenor Thos. boot & shoe ma. Hospital row, Chelsea
Ellerby Elizb. & Wm. who. sheffield wareho. 8 Ave Maria la
Ellerby John, hop mer. 3 Brunswick ter. Trinity sq. Borough
Ellerby Thomas, artist, 34 Gerrard st. Soho
Ellerd James, painter & glazier, 63 Coppice row, Clerkenwell
Ellerd Wm. carpenter, 15 Berner st. Commercial road east
Ellerman Charles F. & Co. merchants, 23 Philpot lane
Ellerthorp Jonathan, conveyancer, 37 Colet pl. Comm. rd. ea
Ellery Edmund B. merchant, see Bayne & Ellery
Ellery Edmund Boger, solicitor, 12 Gray's inn square
Elles James, baker, 6 Foster lane, Cheapside
Ellesmere & Chester canal co.'s rail. commit. of. 107 Jermyn st
Ellett Chas. Henry, baker, 12 Charles st. Mile end New town
Ellett Samuel, desk & pocketbook maker, 8 Jewin st
Elley Dan. stock & share broker, 1 Hatton garden & 8 Bartholomew lane, City

Elley John, fur. ironmonger, 1 corner Hatton garden & Holborn
Elley Thos. Benson, shoe & leather mfr. 4 New Farringdon st
Ellice, Kinnear & Co. merchants, 145 Leadenhall st
Ellicombe George Bradley, parlmnty. agt. see Dorrington & Co
Ellicott & Cook, watch & clock makers, 26 Lombard st
Ellicott James, tailor, 24 Dean st. Soho square
Elliman Cyrus, bootmaker, 3 Red Lion court, Fleet st
Ellington Hen. floor cloth ma. see Ridley, Son & Ellington
Elliot & Collins, wholesale druggists, 1 Oxford ct. Cannon st
Elliot Francis & Joseph, tailors, 116 Britannia st. City road
Elliot John Lettsom & Co. brewers, Stag brewery, Pimlico
Elliot Charles, upholsterer, 6 Clifton st. Finsbury
Elliot George, cheesemonger, 128 Jermyn st. St. James's
Elliot Geo. plumber, painter & glazier, 10 Chandos st. Covnt. gdn
Elliot John, cattle salesman, 37 West Smithfield
Elliot John, chicoree importer, 42 Milton st. Fore st
Elliot Margaret Ann (Miss), tabinet establshmnt. 43 Pall mall
Elliot Mary (Mrs.), printer & publisher, 14 Holywell st. Strand
Elliot Rebecca (Miss), portrait painter, 10 Chandos st. Cov. gn
Elliot Robert, coffee rooms, 63 Wych st. Strand
Elliot Robert, surgeon, Denmark hill, Camberwell
Elliot Walter, grindery & leather seller, 13 Bedfordbury
Elliot Wm. Timbrell, solicitor, 44 Great Russell st
Elliotson John, physician, 37 Conduit st. Bond st
Elliott & Butler, glasscutters, 5 Mount Pleasant, Gray's inn la
Elliott C. A. & J. A. surgeons, Cowper house, Retreat, Old Brompton
Elliott James & Thomas, bakers, 26 High st. Bow
Elliott & Symons, Cowper ho. lunatic asylum, Old Brompton
Elliott Stephen & Joseph, coachma. 85 Bridge rd. Lambeth
Elliott Wm. Venn & Son, carpntrs, 6 Hartshorn all. Leadnhl. st
Elliott Ann (Mrs.), tinplate worker, 3 Spring st. Portman sq
Elliott Chas. beer retailer, 29 Peacock st. Newington butts
Elliott Chas. butcher, 112 Park st. Kennington cross
Elliott Chas. carpenter, 5 Judd st. Brunswick square
Elliott Charlotte (Miss), pat. stay & belt ma. 34 Newman st
Elliott Daniel, baker, 25 Britannia row, Lower st. Islington
Elliott Daniel, cheesemonger, 268 Oxford st. & 24 Skinner st. Somers town
Elliott Edwd. commission agt. 4 Railway pl. Fenchurch st
Elliott Edwin, confectioner, 12 Broadway, Deptford
Elliott Emma (Miss), seminary, 8 Pelham ter. Brompton
Elliott Geo. bread & biscuit baker, 1 Wilmington st. Spafids
Elliott Geo. manufacturing jeweller, 5 Skinner st. Clerkenwll
Elliott Geo. oil & colorman, 9 Corporation row, Clerkenwell
Elliott Geo. oil & colorman, 12 Clement's in. pas. Clare mrkt
Elliott Geo. Percy, barrister, 2 Plowden bldgs. Temple
Elliott Henry, lapidary, 16 St. John st. road
Elliott Henry, linendraper, 40 Hackney road
Elliott Jabez, furrier, 14 Richmond pl. East st. Walworth
Elliott James, baker, 41 Primrose st. Bishopsgate
Elliott James, baker, 133 Whitechapel road
Elliott James, *Crown* P.H. 80 Chiswell st
Elliott James, grocer, 70 Princes st. Lambeth
Elliott James, potato dealer, 19 Counter st. Borough
Elliott James, *Sun* P.H. 145 Union st. Borough
Elliott James, upholsterer, 14 New Church st. west, Edge. rd
Elliott James, *White Horse* P.H. 62 Church st. Chelsea
Elliott James Branch, fishmonger, 29½ Hackney road
Elliott James Warner, silk dyer, 101 Jermyn st
Elliott Job, ironmonger & smith, 9 Beer lane, Tower st
Elliott John, cattle salesman, 59 West Smithfield
Elliott John, fruiterer, 1 Shepherd's market, Mayfair
Elliott John, furniture broker, 5 Chapel st. New road
Elliott John, machinist & phlspcl. instrmt. ma. 14 Stacey st. Soho
Elliott John, market gardener, Cadogan ter. Chelsea
Elliott John, merchant, Lloyd's coffee ho. Royal Exchange
Elliott John, general salesman, 35 Kingsland road
Elliott John, printer, 81 Princes road, Lambeth
Elliott John, saddlers' ironmonger, see Baldwin & Elliott
Elliott John, surgeon. &c. 2 Finsbury pavement
Elliott John, *White Hart* P.H. Earl's court, Old Brompton
Elliott John Dymoke, chemist, &c. 10 Giltspur st
Elliott Joseph, coal dealer, 36 Stanhope st. Clare market
Elliott Joseph, scalemaker, 5 Hosier lane, West Smithfield
Elliott Philip, artists' color wa. 50 Whittlebury st. Euston sq
Elliott Rd. *Tallow Chandlers' Arms* P.H. 30 King st. Gldn. sq
Elliott Richard, builder, 5 Devonshire ter. Camden new tn
Elliott Robert, cheesemonger, 233 Shadwell High st
Elliott Robert, coffee rooms, 21 Queen st. Soho
Elliott Robert, cork manfr. 17 Swan st. Minories
Elliott Robert, *Rodney's Head* P.H. 138 Whitechapel road
Elliott Samuel, pork butcher, 39 Tabernacle walk, Finsbury
Elliott Selina (Miss), milliner, Church st. Hackney
Elliott Thomas, linendraper, 158 Kingsland road
Elliott Thomas, linendraper, 7 Crown row, Mile end road
Elliott Thomas, mattress & bedstead ma. 52 Long alley, Fnsby
Elliott Thomas, merchant, 55 Old Broad st
Elliott William, baker, 8 Lower road, Islington
Elliott Wm. baker, 5 Trafalgar place, Walworth common
Elliott Wm. button manfacr. 10 Goldsmith st. Cheapside, & at Birmingham; patentee of the brocaded silk buttons
Elliott Wm. coal dealer, 19 New Compton st. Soho
Elliott Wm. confectioner & jeweller, 36 Broad st. Lambeth
Elliott Wm. dyer, 6 Wellington place, Goswell road
Elliott Wm. fruiterer, 1 Manor place, Walworth road
Elliott Wm. linendraper, 2 New Church st. west, Edgw. rd
Elliott Wm. mathematical, optical, philosophical & drawing instrument maker, 268 High Holborn
Elliott Wm. tailor, 12 Denmark terrace, Pimlico
Elliott Wm. Edwd. mathemticl. ins. ma. 139 Shadwell High st
Elliott Wm. Timbrell, solicitor, 44 Gt. Russell st. Blmsby
Ellis Barbara & W. (Misses), milliners, 42 Duke st. Grsvnr. sq
Ellis Edward & Co. stockbrokers, 53 Threadneedle st
Ellis, Everington & Co. warehousemen, 3 St. Paul's churchyard, & 17 Ludgate st
Ellis John Joseph & Geo. hop & seed merets. 81 Boro' High st
Ellis Richd. & Nathl. linendrapers, 6 Praed st. Paddington
Ellis Richard & Son, auctioneers, estate agents, & land surveyors, 36 Fenchurch st
Ellis Richard & Son, merchants, 33 Clement's lane, City
Ellis & Smith (Misses), academy, 25 Addington pl. Cmbwl. rd
Ellis & Spaull, tailors, 25 New Ormond st. Queen square
Ellis & Wales, auctioneers & surveyors, 150 Minories
Ellis Alexander, wholesale clothes warehouse, 74 Minories
Ellis Anthony, builder & undertaker, Mare st. Hackney
Ellis Arthur, solicitor, see Wetten & Ellis
Ellis Arthur, sec. to Royal Naval Female School Society, 32 Sackville st. Piccadilly
Ellis Benjamin, glaziers' diamond manufactr. 35 Goswell rd
Ellis Benj. upholder & undertaker, 67 Up. Ebury st. Pimlico
Ellis Charles, barrister, 2 Stone buildings, Lincoln's inn
Ellis Charles, cabinet maker, &c. 21, Bedford st. Covent gdn
Ellis Charles, carpenter, 27 King st. Golden square
Ellis Charles, engineer, 11 Chester st. Kennington cross
Ellis Charles, *Carved Red Lion* P.H. 1 Lower st. Islington
Ellis Chas. ship & custom ho. agent, 20 Harp la. Lr. Thames st
Ellis Chas. wholesale teadealer, 20 Harp la. Lowr. Thames st
Ellis Chas. Jas. muslin warehouseman, see Woolrich & Ellis
Ellis Chas. Jas. ship & com. bro. Hall of Com. Threadneedle st
Ellis Charlotte A. (Miss), teacher of music, 21 Up. Eaton st
Ellis Cydwelyn, surgeon, 31 Howland st. Fitzroy square
Ellis David, goldsmith & jeweller, 2 John st. Oxford st
Ellis Edmund, corn & coal mercht. 169 St. John st. road
Ellis Edward, architect, 131 Fenchurch st
Ellis Eleanor (Mrs.), blacksmith, 1½ Low. Duke st. Stamford st
Ellis Ellis, underwriter, 51 Old Broad st. City, & Lloyd's
Ellis Ellis, wine merchant, 1 Botolph lane, Thames st
Ellis Frederick, barrister, 6 Pump court, Temple
Ellis George, baker, 16 Stockwell terrace, Clapham road
Ellis George, butcher, 12 Munster st. Regent's park
Ellis George, corn meter, 15 Powell st. East, King's square
Ellis George, furniture broker, 6 Sun tavern fields
Ellis George, *Goat* P.H. 103 Golden lane, Barbican
Ellis George, oil & color warehouse, 14 Union st. Borough
Ellis George, potato dlr. 1 King's Arms pl. Commercl. rd. Ea
Ellis George Henry, solicitor, see Lyon, Barnes & Ellis
Ellis Gervase, grocer, Tanner's hill, Deptford new town
Ellis Henry, baker, 7 Ebury square, Pimlico
Ellis Henry, boot & shoe mkr. 20 Litt. Newport st. Le'stersq
Ellis Henry, human hair mercht. 11 Cambridge st. Golden sq
Ellis Henry, miller, black horse mill, Lower rd. Deptford
Ellis Henry, music sel. & statnr. 8 Wolsingham pl. Lambeth
Ellis Henry, solicitor, 40 Bernard st. Russell square
Ellis Henry Saml. *White Hart* P.H. 8 Park st. Borough
Ellis Henry William, barrister, 4 Elm court, Temple
Ellis Horatio Thos. Wm. silversmith, 11 King st. Cov. gar
Ellis James, chemical & general glass lamp mfr. 69 Fleet st
Ellis James, brassfounder, 144 Houndsditch
Ellis James, surgeon, 10 Henry's place, Old Kent road
Ellis James, tobacconist, 191½ Oxford st
Ellis John, bootmaker, 77 Albany street, Regent's park
Ellis John, bootmaker, 16 Marylebone st. Golden square
Ellis John, cheese & butterman, 11 Wardour st. Soho
Ellis John, cook & confectioner, see Brown & Ellis
Ellis John, drug & drysaltery broker, 1 Botolph lane
Ellis John, *Eagle* brewery, 12 Salmon lane, Limehouse
Ellis John, ham & beef dealer, 14 Castle st. Leicester sq
Ellis John, linen draper, 5 Brighton place, Hackney road
Ellis John, painter & glazier, 7 Tavistock row, Covent gard
Ellis John, tailor, 9 Brudenell place, New North road
Ellis John Robert, brushmaker, 43 Banner st. St. Luke's

Ellis John Robert, brush manufr. 153 Shoreditch High st
Ellis John Solomon, clothes warehouse, 2 Minories
Ellis John Thomas, *Constitution* P.H. 26 White st. Boro'
Ellis Joseph, beer retailer, 9 Blackfriars road
Ellis Joseph, jeweller, 66 London road, Southwark
Ellis Joseph, nightman & carman, Church st. Nwngtn. butts
Ellis Joseph, plumber, &c. 59 Brunswick st. Stamford st
Ellis Joseph, tailor, 40 Tufton st. Horseferry rd. Westminster
Ellis Lewis, wholesale job warehouseman, 74 Minories
Ellis Mary Isab. (Mrs.), butcher, 34 Hatton wall, Hatton gn
Ellis Michael, watchmaker, 18 Bevis marks
Ellis Peter, merchant, Lloyd's & Jamaica coffeehouse
Ellis Richard, baker, 40 Mount st. Berkeley square
Ellis Richard, carpenter, 2 & 3 Richmond st. Leicester sq
Ellis Richard, grocer & teadealer, 31 Chapel st. Somers town
Ellis Richard, provision broker, 33 Clements la. City
Ellis Robert, carpenter, 40 St. Andrew's hill, Blackfriars
Ellis Robert, cowkeeper, 8 Well st. Wellclose square
Ellis Robert, tobacconist, 15 Gloucester row, Grange rd
Ellis Robert, solicitor, 2 Cowper's court, Cornhill
Ellis Robert, surgeon, 59 Brompton crescent, Brompton
Ellis Samuel, baker, see Fisher & Ellis
Ellis Sam. drug, drysaltery & ivory broker, 131 Fenchurch st
Ellis Samuel, fruit salesman, Square market, Covent garden
Ellis Samuel, tailor, 32 Gracechurch st
Ellis Samuel, wholesale furrier, 48 Skinner st. Snowhill
Ellis Samuel Helbert, stock broker, 17 Throgmorton st
Ellis Sarah (Mrs.), corn dealer, 24 Salisbury st. Lisson grove
Ellis Sarah (Mrs.), dressmaker, 53 North st. Edgware rd
Ellis Sarah (Mrs.), grocer, 1 Northumbrlnd. ter. Bagnigewlls. rd
Ellis Thomas, bootmaker, 20 Wilson st. Finsbury sq
Ellis Thomas, coachmaker, 60 Whitechapel High st
Ellis Thomas, *Ellis's family hotel*, 59 St. James's st
Ellis Thomas, hide & leatherseller, see Bouts & Ellis
Ellis Thomas, wine cooper & fining maker, 10 Gt. St. Helen's
Ellis Thomas Flower, barrister, 3 Elm court, Temple
Ellis Thomas Henry, engraver, 2 Jewin st. Cripplegate
Ellis Walter, cowkeeper, 20 New st. Brompton
Ellis Wm. baker, 20 Felton st. Hoxton
Ellis Wm. boot & shoe ma. 1 Flower's buildings, Holloway
Ellis Wm. box & packing case maker, 6 Botolph alley
Ellis Wm. butcher, 16 Great Suffolk st. Borough
Ellis Wm. butcher, 20 Newport court, Newport market
Ellis Wm. butcher, 23 Crown row, Walworth road
Ellis Wm. furnishing undertaker, Lower road, Deptford
Ellis Wm. manufacturer of fancy goods in ivory, & sole inventor, patentee & manufacturer of glass cylinder anatomical syringes, 3 Thanet place, Temple bar
Ellis Wm. tailor, 22 Northumberland st. New road
Ellis Wm. tobacconist, 17 East road, City road
Ellis Wm. Jas. engraver & printer, 2 Great Dover st. Borough
Ellis Wm. Robert, barrister, 24 Chancery lane
Ellisdon William, draper, 113 Kingsland road
Ellison Thos. & John, bagatelle table makers, 13 Meredith st
Ellison Cuthbert, barrister, 4 Hare court
Ellison Elizabeth (Miss), milliner, 73 High st. Poplar
Ellison George Thomas, solicitor, see Bloxham & Ellison
Ellison John, tinplate worker, 27 Milton st. Cripplegate
Ellison Joseph, teadealer & grocer, 15 Shoemaker rw. Blackfrs
Ellison Nathaniel, barrister, 35 Up. Bedford pl. Russell sq
Ellison Samuel Kitching, surgeon, 22 Poplar High st
Ellison Thos. barrister & equity draftsman, 4 New Boswell ct
Ellison Thomas, bookbinder, 17 Ave Maria lane
Ellison William, musician, 45 Warwick st. Pimlico
Ellmers Hen. fur & skin dresser, 8 Shepherd st. Spitalfields
Ells Dagnall, *Five Bells* P.H. 105 Chancery lane
Ellson George, china & glass wa. 114 York road, Lambeth
Ellstow Thos. timber merch. 105 Snow's fields, Bermondsey
Ellsworth Wm. livery stables, 75 Grosvenor mews, Grosvnr. st
Ellwood John & Sons, hat mfrs. 24 Gt. Charlotte st. Blackfrs. rd
Ellwood George, wholesale furrier, 164 Aldersgate st
Ellworthy Richard, dairyman, 7 Fendall st. Bermondsey
Elmenhorst Theodore H. merchant, 20 Mark lane
Elmer Barnabas, meat salesman, see Dixon & Elmer
Elmes Harvey Lonsdale, architect, 11 Gordon st. Gordon sq
Elmes Henry John, bricklayer & builder, 19 Cloak lane
Elmes James, architect, civil engineer, &c. 19 & 20 Austin frs
Elmes Jane (Mrs.), wigmaker & perfumer, 62 High Holborn
Elmes John, toyman, 13 Gray's place, Fulham road
Elmes William, chandler's shop, 42 Three Colt st. Limehouse
Elmore & Clement, carpenters, 36 Duke st. St. James's
Elmore John & Co. coal merchants, 65 Bankside, Southwark
Elmore & Phillips, horse dlr. Albert ga. yd. Hi. rw. Kngtbdg
Elmore Alfred Walter, artist, 19 Charles st. Berners st
Elmore John Richard, M.D. surgeon, 9 New Cavendish st
Elms Daniel Fenwick, appraiser, &c. 16 Grafton st. Soho
Elms George, carpenter, see Poulton & Elms
Elms Wm. fruiterer, &c. 4 Bell yard, Temple bar
Elms Wm. *Kensington Arms* P.H. 29 Newland st. Kensington
Elmsley Wm. barrister, 8 Old square, Lincoln's inn
Elmslie & Preston, solicitors, 47 & 48 Moorgate st
Elmslie & Simpson [late Foster & Co.], tinfoil & pewter manufacturers & importers of quicksilver, 9 Union buildings, Leather lane, & 36A, Leather lane, Holborn
Elmslie (Jas.) & Stooks (Thos.), merchants, 2 Abchurch lane
Elmslie Edmd. Wallace, architect, 50 Berners st
Elnor Ann (Miss), rope & twine ma. 20 Star corner, Bermonds
Elphee Caleb, ham & beef shop, 9 Portland pl. Edgware rd
Elphee John, ham & beef dealer, 23 Middle row, Holborn
Elphick Edward, plumber, &c. 33 Cleveland st. Fitzroy sq
Elphick Henry, *Intrepid Fox* P.H. 75 Wardour st. Soho
Elphick John, plumber, &c. 28 Castle st. east, Oxford st
Elphinston John, bread & biscuit baker, 227 Regent st
Elphinstone George, baker, 21 Throgmorton st
Elphinstone Howard, D.C.L. advocate, 7 College, Doctors' com
Elphinstone James, tailor, 40 Rupert st. Haymarket
Elrington & Dundee, merchts. & agents, 1 Argyll pl. Regent st
Elsam Richard, furn. ironmonger, 10 Hungerford st. Strand
Elsback Jacob, leather cut. 1 Ann's place, Whitechapel
Elsden John, bricklayer, 18 Great Bush lane, Cannon st
Elsden John, grocer, 4 New row, Deptford
Elsden Wm. Buddry, linendraper, 4 Brunswick pl. Old Kent rd
Else John Ogle, surgeon, 78 Albany road, Camberwell
Else Wm. S. goldsmith & jeweller, 35 & 36 Burlington arcade
Elsegood Henry, surgeon, &c. 91 Park st. Grosvenor sq
Elsegood Henry Charles, surgeon, 14 Upper Brook st
Elsey Ann (Mrs.), lodging ho. 8 Queen st. Soho
Elsmore John, baker, 11 Broadway, Westminster
Elsom Frederic, chemist, 6 Salmon lane, Limehouse
Elson George, chemist, Bridge road, Battersea
Elson Richd. oil boiler & colorman, 11 William st. Whitechapel
Elster & Co. merchants, 41 Threadneedle st
Elster Daggi James, merchant, Baltic coffee house
Elston Wm. & Son, builders, 12 Wormwood st. & 9 Old Bailey
Elston Henry, *Globe tavern* P.H. 57 South Molton st
Elston James, blacksmith, Kensington High st
Elston John, file cutter, 7 Pear Tree court, Clerkenwell
Elston Richard, chinaman, 67 New Church st. west, Lisson gr
Elston Rd. engine turn. & gold dice finsh. 24 Myddleton st
Elston Sam. chandlr. shop, 19 Belgrave ter. Qn.'srd. Dalston
Elston Wm. plumber, painter, &c. 8 Wormwood st. Bishopsgate
Elsworth Wm. stock & sharebroker, 2 Bank chambrs. Lothby
Elt Chas. Hen. bookseller & statnr. 18 Hedge row, Islington
Elt Thomas R. *White Swan* P.H. 138 Salisbury ct. Fleet st
Elteen Ann (Mrs.), grocer & cheesemonger, 54 High st. Kensgton
Elton Cath. (Mrs.), who. ironmnger, 122 Whitechapel High st
Elton Edmund Lucas, fruiterer, 325 Oxford st
Elton Edward, dyer & scourer, 53 Sloane st. Knightsbridge, & 5 Holland place, Kensington, & 10 Edgware rd
Elton James, butcher, 16 James st. Oxford st
Elton William, clothfactor, 33 Basinghall st
Elton Susanh. (Mrs.), *King's Head* P.H. 1 Gt. Mitchell st. St. Lk
Elven Robert, coffee house keeper, 62 Tooley st
Elverson Geo. dog dealer & veter. surgeon, 19 Red Cross sq
Elverston Chas. draper, hosier, haberdasher, &c. 188 Tooley st
Elves Nehemiah, cheesemonger, 113 Brick lane, Spitalfields
Elves Thomas, butcher, 103 Drury lane
Elvidge George, baker, 14 Goldsmith place, Hackney rd
Elvin Eliza (Mrs.), grocer, 28 Maze, Tooley st
Elvin John, builder, 24 Garden row, London rd. Borough
Elvin Sophia (Mrs.), bookseller, 13 Tabernacle sq. Finsbury
Elvy John R. sugar broker, Commercial coffee ho. Mincingla
Elwall George, merchant, Lloyd's
Elwell Thomas, ironmonger, 24 Hedge row, Islington
Elwin Jeken, surgeon, 20 Broad st. buildings
Elwin Marsham, barrister, Chapel stairs, Lincoln's inn
Elwood Ann (Mrs.), bottle dealer, 46 North st. Sloane st
Elworthy Alfred, cowkeeper, 68 Tothill st. Westminster
Elworthy James, boot & shoema. 10 St. Martin's pl. Trafalgar sq
Elworthy Mercy (Mrs.), stockma. 4 Hemming's rw. St. Martin's la
Ely Charles John, engraver & printer, 252 Tottenham court rd
Ely Charles Joseph, *Grapes* P.H. 70 Milton st. Fore st
Ely George, grocer, 32 St. George's row, Pimlico
Ely Geo. Fred. engraver & copper pl. print. 5 Carlisle st. Soho
Ely James, gold & silversmith & jeweller, 8 Soho square
Ely Jacques, army & navy commission agent &c. 256 Strand
Ely John, *Eagle tavern* P.H. 14 Wentworth pl. Mile end rd
Ely Joseph, wine merchant, 8 Cadogan st
Ely Lydia (Mrs.), milliner, 8 Soho square
Ely Richard, bricklayer, &c. 432 Oxford st
Ely Thomas, woollen factor, see Nash & Ely
Emans Edward, grocer, 1 Church st. Chelsea

Emans Peter, *Edinburgh Castle tavern*, 322 Strand
Emanuel Brothers, wholesale jewellers, 5 Hanover square
Emanuel & Debarfald, cap manufacturers, 149 Houndsditch
Emanuel Abraham, bottle warehouse, 26 Gt. Titchfield st
Emanuel Abraham, watch maker, 31 Somerset st. Aldgate
Emanuel David, watch manufacturer, 36 Minories
Emanuel Emanuel, curiosity import. see Town & Emanuel
Emanuel Emanuel, diamond merchant, 39 Lamb's Conduitst
Emanuel Joel, merchant, 25 Bury st. St. Mary Axe
Emanuel Lewis, curiosity dlr. 20 Parliament st. Westminster
Emanuel Moses, glass dealer, 16 Gt. Prescot st. Goodman'sfi
Emary Frederick James, salt merchant, see Harris & Emary
Emberick James, cheesemonger, 194 Kingsland road
EmberleyJosephWm. mathetml.casema.1Broadst.Londondks
Emberson Thomas, working jeweller, 31 Fore st. City
Embery Henry, bookbinder, 19 New st. Cloth fair, Smithfld
Embleton Luke, smith & engineer, 40 New Park st. Boro'
Embleton Robert, shipowner, 3 George yard, Lombard st
Emblin John W. & Co. coal mer. Thornhill bridge, Caledn. rd
Emblin John, tripe dresser, 67 Leather lane, Holborn
Embling Thomas, surgeon, 31 Brompton row
Embry John, coal dealer, 7 Crown st. Soho
Embury Francis, cheesemonger, 51 Goswell st
Emerick John, clock casemaker, 8 Coburg st. Clerkenwell
Emerson Thomas & Co. auctioneers, surveyors, valuers & undertakers, 91 Newgate st
Emerson Thos. & Co. carpet wareho. &c. 305 High Holborn
Emerson Wm. & Co. furniture wareho. 11 Palace rw. St. Pancra
Emerson James, surgeon, 3 Blenheim ter. Bond st. Chelsea
Emerson Mary (Mrs.), herbalist, 28 St. Ann's court, Soho
Emerson Robert, cattle salesman, 37 West Smithfield
Emerson Robert, chemist, 5 Frederick's place, Old Kent rd
Emerson Thos. upholsterer & cabinet maker, 91 Newgate st
Emerson William, silk manufacturer, 28 Spital square
Emerton John, hairdresser, 3 Melbourne place, Old Kent rd
Emerton John, meat salesman, 27 New Newgate st
Emerton John Wm. boot & shoe ma. 117 Gt. Suffolk st. Boro'
Emerton John William, butcher, 33 & 34 Newgate market
Emerton William, dairyman, 2 Alexander place, Brompton
Emery Geo. & Co. linen drapers, 31&32Sidneypl. Coml. rd. ea
Emery & Winch, railway carriers, Geo. yd. Aldermanbury
Emery Aaron, *Hope* P.H. 15 Gravel lane, Southwark
Emery Alfred, boot & shoe maker. 23 Hedge row, Islington
EmeryAnn(Mrs.), lodginghouse, 3Carthusianst. Charterho. sq
Emery Chas. milliner & lace dlr. 11 Upper st. Islington
EmeryEdwin, lkg. glass ma. carver, &c. 37 Hunterst. Brnswk. sq
Emery Frederic Arthur, chemist, &c. 46 Notting hill, High st
Emery George, carpenter, &c. 21 Swallow st. Piccadilly
Emery George, draper, 31 Sidney pl. Commercial road east
Emery George, french polisher, 12 High st. Lambeth
Emery Isaac, chandler's shop, 61 Castle st. East, Oxford st
Emery Jubal, boot & shoe maker, 15 Westbourne st. Pimlico
Emery John, grocer, 13 Elizabeth st. Hans place, Sloane st
Emery Jsph. bread & bisct. ba. 16 Royal Hospital rw. Chelsea
EmeryLouisa (Miss), china dlr. 3Vernon pl. BagniggeWls. rd
Emery Richard, cooper, 6 Brunswick st. Blackwall
EmerySusannah (Miss), milliner, 23&25Hanway st. Oxford st
Emery William, beer retailer, 8 Aldgate
Emery Wm. coal & potato mercht. 16 Chandos st. Cov. garden
Emery William, tailor, 29 Little Bell alley, Coleman st
Emes John, tarpaulin manufr. Limehouse cut, Limehouse
EmesJohn, trunk&plate case mak. 108 Gt. Russell st. Bloomsb
Emes Thomas, ironmonger, 13 Marylebone lane, Oxford st
Emett William, baths, 1 Purim pl. Cambridge rd. Mile end
Emigration (Government) Office, 70 Lower Thames street (Lieut. Lean, R.N. manager); hours of business, 10 to 4
Emington John, coffee rooms, 71 Old st. St. Luke's
Emley Rich. drug. & drysalt brok. 27 Martin's la. Cannon st
Emly Henry, barrister, 3 New square, Lincoln's inn
Emmens James, stationer, 8 Grosvenor st. West
Emmens John, corn merchant, 33 Elizabeth st. Eaton sq
Emmens Samuel, ironmonger, 15 King st. Tower hill
Emmens Thomas, invalid chair ma. 23 Paget pl. Waterloo rd
Emmens William, secretary to *Church of England Assurance Institution*, 5 Lothbury
Emmerson John, *George* P.H. 74 Brunswick st. Blackwall
Emmerson Rd. nightman & beer seller, Britton st. Chelsea
Emmerson Richard, patent wrought iron tube manufacturer & cast iron merchant, 63 Brunswick st. Blackfriars
Emmerson Wm. *Albion* coffee rooms, 3 Little Moorfields
Emmerton Fras. builder & bricklayer, 57 Bartholomew close, & 40 King st. Snowhill
Emmerton George, baker, 25 Norland road, Notting hill
Emmerton Henry, bricklayer, 57 Bartholomew close, & 40 King st. Snow hill
Emmerton James, tailor, 1 Sudeley st. Islington
Emmerton Richard, beer retailer, 6 Tyssen place, Dalston
EmmertonRichard, straw hat mfr. 76 Waterloo ter. Wtrlo. rd
Emmett & Allen, attorneys, 14 Bloomsbury square
Emmett & Chadwick, architects, 9 John st. Adelphi
Emmett&Dyer, merchs.&hemp cloth ma. seeDyer & Emmett
EmmettElizh.(Mrs.), cutler&gen.hardwarem.27Holborn hill
Emmett Elizth. (Mrs.), tobacconist, Newcross rd. Deptford
Emmett William, wine cooler maker, 5 Broad st. Golden sq
Emmitt Geo. jun. grocer, 12Black Prince row, Walworth rd
Emmitt George, grocer, High st. Deptford
EmmottChris. fishsauce maker, 21Grange walk, Bermondsey
Emmott John, livery stables & job master, Barlow's mews, Bruton st. & 39½ Old Bond st
Emmott Walter Browning, fruiterer, 8 Trump st. Cheapside
Emms John, carpenter, 3 Black Lion yard, Whitechapel rd
Emms Robert, wheelwright, 14½ Macclesfield st. south, City rd
EmneyThos. lodging house, 17 St. Alban's place, St. James's
Emons Thomas, cooper, 7 Green st. Bethnal green
Emperor John, undertkr. St. John's Church yd. St. John's wd
Empriere William, tobacconist, 157 Goswell st
Empson George, fruiterer, 23 Chapel st. New road
Empson Henry, solicitor, 27 Bucklersbury
Emsden John, coffee rooms, 11 Bedford court, Covent garden
EmsleySaml. stay&shoewa. Norfolk st. Cambridge rd. Whchpl
EmsleyWm. cop. pl. printer, publr. & bookbdr. 41 Cloth fair
Emslie John, engraver, 6 Upper North place, Gray's inn road
EmsonCharles, cowkeeper, &c. 11 OldMontagu st. Whitechapel
EmsonJas. agt. for french & german goods, 2 St. Ann's la. City
EndE.&Co.(Mrs.), wireweavers&blindma. 91&92Longla. Brms
Endean John, teadealer, 9 Queen's buildings, Brompton
Endean Wm. brassfounder, 48 White st. Borough
Endean Wm. grocer & teadealer, 2 Hatfield pl. Westmnr. rd
Enderby Charles Henry & George, merchts. 13Gt. St. Helen's
Endersbee Wm. mathl. ins. maker & ship chnd. 28 Wapping
Endicott John, rule&baromtr. ma. 23 Lit. Saffron hl. Hattn. wa
EneferSam. carpent. build. &undertaker, 39Dorsetst. Prtmn. sq
Enever John, baker, 3 King st. Snowhill
Engall John & Son, boot & shoe ma. 4 Green st. Kentish town
EngehamThos. C. coach&harn. ma. 9Mansionho. pl. Cmbrwl. rd
Engel & Samuels, who. umbrella & parasol manufacturers, 26 & 27 Little Alie st. Goodman's fields
Engel Jones, umbrella maker, see Samuels & Engel
Engel Joseph, sculptor, 25 Castle st. Leicester sq
Engelhardt Frederick, merchant, 1 Fen court, Fenchurch st
Engelhart John, porkman, 23 St. Martin's le grand
Engineers' Office (London district), 11 James st. Buckingham gate; hours of business, 10 to 4
Engisch Christian Charles, baker, High st. Stoke Newington
England George & Co. engineers & patent screw jack manufacturers, Hatcham inn works, Old Kent road
England Wm. & Co. woollen manufacturers, 2 Basinghall st
England Alfred, teadealer, 22 New st. square
England George, painter & glazier, 218 Hoxton Old town
England George, woollen manufacturer, 2 Basinghall st
England James, bootmaker, 13 Paradise row, Rotherhithe
England John, plumber, see Stannard & England
England John, plumber & glazier, 2 Garter ct. Barbican
England Louis, builder, 3Shepperton st. NewNorth rd. Islngtn
England Mary Ann (Mrs.), dining rooms, 17 Whitechapel
England Sophia (Mrs.), straw bon. ma. 2Essex pl. Mare st. Hky
England Thomas, merchant, 7 George yard, Lombard st
England Thomas, shipbroker, see Domett, England & Son
Engleback Thomas, glass bender, 10 Thrawl st. Spitalfields
Engleburtt James, hatter, 54 Radnor st. St. Luke's
Engleburtt Wm. silk winder, 4 Elizabeth st. Hackney road
Englefield Charles, grocer, 30 North row, Grosvenor sq
Englefield Richd. confectioner, 11 Lower Eaton st. Pimlico
Engleheart Nathaniel B. & Son, proctors, 19Gt. Knightrider st
Engleheart Wm. Hayley, solicitor, 3 Great Knightrider st
Engley Thos. Fredk. linendraper, 4Grosvenor pl. Com. rd. east
English Churchman newspaper, 111 Fleet st
English Copper Company (Wm. Inglis, sec.), 57½ Old Broad st. City, & Castle Baynard, 12 Upper Thames st.
English Monthly Tract So. (Jhn. Stabb, sec.), 20 Red Lion sq
English Opera House, Wellington st. north, & Strand
English & Scottish Law Life Assur. & Loan Assoc. (James Butler Williams, actuary), 12 Waterloo pl. see page 2023
English & Casson, surgeons, 22 Gracechurch st
English Edward, soapmaker, see Coles & English
English George, paper borderer, 27 Castle st. Southwark
English Henry, mine agt. & sharebroker, 5 Shorter's court
English Henry Scale, attorney, 33 Old Jewry
English James, hop & seed merchant, 87 High st. Borough
English John, fur. broker & appraiser, 7 Gt. Earl st. 7 Dials
English John, mounter & inlayer of drawings, 19 Soho sq
English Joseph, dyer, 36 Gilbert st. Oxford st

English Joseph, pastrycook, 75 Bethnal green rd
English Robert, tailor, 8 Chapel st. Pentonville
English William, leather cutter, 20 Hatton wall
English William, millwright, &c. see Hunter & English
English William, surgeon, Denmark hill, Camberwell
English William, tailor, Hertford road, Kingsland
Engstrom, Luck & Co. merchs. 7 Gt. St. Helen's
Enoch Geo. architect & surveyor, 21 Edwards st. Portman sq
Enouy John C. pat. medicine wa. 6 Polygon, Clarendon sq
Enright Francis J. C. engineers', architects', surveyors,' & railway stationer for tracing & copying drawings & plans, & for copying writings, 9 John st. Adelphi
Enscoe David, wholesale ironmonger, 40 Dowgate hill
Ensoll Fredk. bookseller & stat. 45 Paddington st. Maryleb
Ensoll Richd. linendraper, 72 Drury la. & 66 Broad st. Blmsby
Ensom Joseph, *Swan* P.H. Swan yard, Shoreditch
Ensor Jonathan, painter, &c. 56 Charles st. Westminster
Ensor John Pople, *Duke of Glo'ster* P.H. Union rw. N. Kent rd
Ensor & Pittendreigh, solicitors, 14 South sq. Gray's inn
Enthoven (L. J.) & Co. merchts. 8 Moorgate st. City
Enthoven Hen. John, merchant, 8 Moorgate st. City
Entwisle John, merchant, 6 Great Winchester st
Entwistle Robert, *Hope* P.H. 1 Pollard's row, Bethnal green rd
Entwistle Wm. wood turner, 11 Wheeler st. Spitalfields
Episcopal Floating Church Society (Captain George Elliott, R.N. secretary), 32 Sackville st
Epps Jas. homœopathic chemist, 112 Gt. Russell st. Bloomsbry
Epps George N. surgeon, 79 South Audley st. Grosvenor sq
Epps John, physician, 89 Great Russell st. Bloomsbury
Epps Thomas, carved chair maker, 85 Vauxhall st. Lambeth
Eppy Charles William, surveyor, 21 Lincoln's inn fields
Epthorp Jas. lighterman, 5 Wellington pl. W. India dk. rd
Equitable Assurance Office (A. Morgan, F.R.S. actuary), New Bridge st. Blackfriars
Equitable Coal Co. (A. Osborn, sec.), 24 Bishopsgt. within
Equitable Funeral Company, 84 Hatton garden
Equitable Gas Light Company (George Johnson Gregory, secretary), 21 John st. Adelphi, & Thames bank place
Equitable Reversionary Interest Society (J. Clayton, sec.), 10 Lancaster place, Waterloo bridge, Strand
Equity & Law Life Assurance Society (James Joseph Sylvester, actuary & secretary), 26 Lincoln's inn fields; for list of directors, &c. see page 2024
Equivalent Company (Thos. G. Smith, sec.), 7 Dowgate hill
Era & Echo Steam Packet Office (Thomas Hancock, proprietor), 8 Cornwall road, Lambeth
Era weekly newspaper, 5 Catherine st. Strand
Erard Sebastian & Pierre, harp & pianoforte makers, by special appointment to her Majesty & Royal Family, 18 Gt. Marlborough st. & 3 Little Portland st
Erat Jacob & Jas. patent harp mnfrs. 23 Berners st. Oxford st
Erck George, habit maker & tailor, 35 Davies st. Berkeley sq
Erechtheum Club (William Holl, sec.), 8 York st. St. James'
Erewash Valley Extension, &c. Railway, 44 Finsbury circus
Erichsen Eric, merchant, 110 Fenchurch st
Erichsen John Edward, surgeon, 48 Welbeck st. Cavendish sq
Erlam (Mrs. & Misses), ladies' school, 16 Elm tree rd. St. Jn's wd
Erle Peter, barrister, 2 New square, Lincoln's inn
Erle William, queen's counsel, 20 Bedford square
Ernes William, veterinary surgeon, 23 John st. Dockhead
Ernest Henry, auctioneer, accountant, estate agent, surveyor & valuer, & patent & designs registration agent, 99 Cheapside
Ernsting John, tailor, 22 Salisbury st. Strand
Ernstring Fredk. A. linendraper, 10 New st. Brompton
Ernteman George, tailor, 6 Spring st. Portman square
Ernteman Peter, tailor, 17 Duke st. Lisson grove
Errand Cart Booking Office (T. Watkins, pro.), 18 Old bailey
Errand Cart Booking Offi. (Mrs. H. Phillips, pro.), 25 Oldbaily
Erratt & Bird, tailors, 3 Jones' st. Berkeley square
Erratt Stephen, breeches ma. & tailor, 3 Thayer st
Erratt Stephen, tailor, 11 Beak st. Regent st
Errington Charles, furrier, see Collin & Errington
Errington Edward, baker, 40 Marylebone lane, Oxford st
Errington George, farrier, 19 Collingwood st. Backfriars rd
Errington James, artificial florist, 30 Burlington arcade
Errington Frederick, watchmaker, Clarence pl. Clapham rd
Errington James, hosier, &c. 226 Piccadilly
Errington John, grocer, 45 Belvedere pl. Southwark bdg. rd
Errington John Edwd. civil engineer, 11 Adam st. Adelphi
Errington Matthew, cheesemonger, 88 High st. Marylebone
Erskine Henry Trail, barrister, 3 Stone bdgs. Lincoln's inn
Ersser Thos. Dan. lapidary & jeweller, 24 Broad st. Goldn. sq
Ersser Wm. furn. japanner & ho. paint. 33 Broad st. Golden sq
Erswell Henry, coachmaker, 3 Finsbury pavement
Erswell Henry, upholsterer, 24 Blenheim st. Bond st. Chelsea
Erwin Chas. carpenter & builder, 6 Albion st. Rotherhithe
Erwood Alfred, billiard table mak. 2 Charles st. Hatton grdn
Erwood Jas. billiard table maker, 3 Brownlow st. Bedfordrow
Erwood Thos. Snelson, plumber & glazier, Church st. Hackny
Erwood William, florist, 50 Gt. Hall, Hungerford market
Erwood William, paper stainer, 3 Hoxton Old town
Erxleben James, lithographer, 25 Leigh st. Burton crescent
Esam, manch. warehousemn. see Hadland, Shillingford & Esam
Esau & Bixley, coach joinrs. & blind mas. 17 Worship st. Finsby
Esberger Henry, tobacconist, 47 Carnaby st. Golden sq
Esch John Paul, merchant, 2 St. Mary at hill
Escombe & Sidebotham, shipping agents, 74 Gt. Tower st
Escombe Robert, wine merchant, see Robinson & Escombe
Escombe Wm. coal merchant, Savoy wharf, Savoy st. Strand
Escott William, beer retailer, Ferry road west, Poplar
Escreet Henry, architect, 77 Old Broad st. City
Esdaile Sir Jas. & Co. bankers, 9 St. Michael's alley, Cornhill
Esdaile James, metropolitan tepid & cold swimming, warm, vapour & shower baths, 23 Ashley crescent, City road
Esdailes & Margrave, veneer & deal sawyers, ships' block makers by machinery, bent timber & coach varnish manufacturers, & scale board cutters, City saw mills, Wenlock basin, Regent's canal, City road; & 7 Wellington place, West India Dock road, Limehouse
Edailes & Margrave, sole licensees for the metropolis, of Rankin's patent wood paving, City saw mills, Wenlock basin, Regent's Canal, City road
Esden James, *Rising Sun* P.H. 41 Fair st. Horselydown
Esden James Henry, slater, Bangor whf. 4 Union pl. Pimlico
Eshelby George, currier, 6 Princes st. Lit. Queen st. Holborn
Eslick Stephen, tailor, 35 Queen st. Brompton road
Esling Henry, ironmonger, 10 High st. Portland town
Espin John, conveyancer, 3 Elm court, Temple, & 3 New Boswell court, Carey st
'Espinasse James, barrister, 13 South square, Gray's inn
Espiner John, gasfitter, 11 Tyler st. Golden square
Esquilant Fred. stationer & account book mak. 346 Oxford st
Essam Joseph, *Bricklayers' Arms* P.H. 15 Fentonst. Com. rd. ea
Essery Matthew, tailor, 14 Abbey st. Bermondsey
Essex Wm. & Sons, coach curriers, 28 Stanhope st. Clare mkt
Essex Alfred, stationer & dressing case ma. 22 Crawford st
Essex Jas. bricklayer, 23 Britannia row, Lower st. Islingtn
Essex Jas. carriage rug maker, 1 Charterhouse lane
Essex James, tobacconist, 47 Park st. Camden town
Essex Richd. Hamilton, artist, 13 York bldgs. Newrd. Mryleb
Essex Wm. enamel painter in ordinary to her Majesty, & to H.R.H. Prince Albert, 32 Compton st. Brunswick sq
Essex William, tobacconist, 13 Water lane, Blackfriars
Essington Thomas, grocer, &c. 56 Robinhood lane, Poplar
Estall Wm. silk manufr. & haberdasher, 12 Bethnal green rd
Etches Wm. J. & Edw. derby cheesefactors, 253 Tooley st
Etches Wm. lodging house, 4 Bedford st. Bedford row
Esterbrooke Wm. water gilder, 31 Brownlow st. Long acre
Etheredge Fredk. Wm. agricultl. engi. 15 Park st. Westmr
Etheredge John Thos. haberdasher, 48 Cromer st. Brunswksq
Etheredge Thomas, hosier & glover, 167 Aldersgate st
Etheredge Thos. goldsmith & jeweller, 48 Rupertst. Haymkt
Etheridge Joseph, drysalter, 9 Great St. Helen's
Etheridge Wm. grocer & tea dlr. 5 Brooke's market, Holborn
Etherington Edward, smith, Temple place, Old Kent road
Etherington Jas. *King's Arms* P.H. 52 Tothill st. Westmr
Etherington Joseph, carpenter & bldr. 4 Morgan's la. Tooleys
Etherington Wm. boot tree maker, 83 Cow cross st. Smith t
Etherton Henry, smith, 1 Staple st. Long la. Bermondseyfi
Etherton Wm. carpenter & undertaker, 99 Church st. Chelsea
Ethnological Society (Rd. King, M.D. sec.), 27A, Sackville s
Eton Thomas, secret springer, 49 Wellington st. Goswell st
Etteridge Sarah (Mrs.), butcher, Mare st. Hackney
Etteridge Sarah (Mrs.), carrier, *White Horse inn*, Cripplegate
Ettling Leopold, mathemat. inst. mak. 151 St. George st
Etty Walter, gold & silver laceman, see Bodley & Etty
Etty William, R.A. artist, 14 Buckingham st. Strand
Etwell Thomas, fruiterer, 192 Bermondsey st
Etzerodt Christian, diamond mercht. 15 Old Compton st. Soho
Etzler John Adolphus & Co. merchants, 266 Strand
Euen Peter, straw hat maker, 13 East st. Manchester sq
Eungblut Peter, grocer, &c. 36 Henry st. Hampstead rd
European Gas Company, 39 Finsbury circus
European Life Assurance & Annuity Company (David Foggo, secretary), 10 Chatham place, Blackfriars; for directors, &c. see page 2023
Eustace George, cheesemonger, 21 Wormwood st. Bishopsgt
Eustace Patrick, shoemaker, 3 Market st. May fair
Eustace Sarah (Mrs.), baker, 175 St. John st. road
Eustice & Watts, ironfounders, 75 Market st. Edgware road
Evan Daniels, cheesemonger, 58 Red Cross st. Borough
Evance William, beer retailer, 224 Albany rd. Camberwell

Evans Anne & Son, book & print sllrs. 1 Gt. Queen st. Linc. inn fi
Evans & Barns, solicitors, 6 South square, Gray's inn
Evans Brothers, mercs. & drysltrs. 3 Cranes wf. 69 Up. Thames st
Evans Charles & Co. linendrapers, shawl & cloak warehouse, 119 Oxford st
Evans Charles & Henry, boot & shoe ma. 73 Lambeth walk
Evans & Clarke, woollendrapers, 65 Bishopsgate without
Evans & Colley, wholesale umbrella & parasol manufacturers, 4 Cripplegate buildings
Evans David & Co. silk manfctrs. & printers, 121 Cheapside
Evans Edward & Co. milliners, 13 Aldgate
Evans & Gould, pencil manftrs. 10 Up. Rosoman st. Clerknwll
Evans & Grant, tailors & habit makers, 8 Cork st. Bond st
Evans John & Sons, engineers, machinists & patent axletree makers, 104 Wardour street, Soho
Evans John & Co. surgical instrument maks. 10 Old Change
Evans John & Son, tailors, 12 Mortimer st. Cavendish sq
Evans Joseph & Francis, hatters & hosiers, 35 St. James's st
Evans Joseph & Sons, importers of foreign, & manufacturers of english toys & fancy articles, 114 & 116 Newgate st
Evans & Lascelles, coopers & stave mers. 88 & 89 Guildfrd. st
Evans & Lascelles, yeast agts. 88 Gt. Guildford st
Evans, Lescher & Evans, who. druggists, 60 Bartholomew close
Evans Matthew & Henry, stationers, King's rd. west, Chelsea
Evans Maurice Evan & Co. carpet & bedding warehouse, 12 Holborn bars, & 1 & 4 Castle st
Evans & Neville, colonial brokers, 131 Fenchurch st
Evans Richard & Co. coffee merchts. 62 Queen st. Cheapside
Evans Richard & Son, bricklayers, 7 West st. Walworth
Evans Robt. H. Thos. & Chas. booksellers, 106 New Bond st
Evans & Sherwin, iron founders, 21 Norton folgate, & Short st. Shoreditch
Evans Thomas & Co. tailors, 127 Mount st. Berkeley sq
Evans Thomas & Son, potato salesmen, 18 & 21 Tooley st
Evans & Webb, seal engravers & printers, 64 New Bond st
Evans William & John, tailors, 1 Duke st. Grosvenor sq
Evans Wm. & Thos. print & musicslrs. 12 & 13 Patriot rw. Cmbg. rd
Evans Ann (Mrs.), coffee rooms, 28 Falcon sq. Aldersgate st
Evans Ann (Mrs.), greengrocer, 4 Caledonian road
Evans Augustus Charles, mnfg. chemist, 11 Church la. Com. rd
Evans Benjamin, mast & block ma. Coal harbour, Blackwall
Evans Benjamin, prof. of music, 2 Barnsbury st. Felix pl. Livpl. rd
Evans Benjamin, surgeon, 11 Trinity st. Borough
Evans Benjamin, upholsterer, 48 Myddelton st. Clerkenwell
Evans Charles, coal & potato dlr. 18 Adam's row, Hampstead rd
Evans Charles, potato dealer, Spitalfields market
Evans Charles, coffee rooms, 36 Bishopsgate st. without
Evans Charles, hatter, 28 St. Thomas st. east
Evans Charles, publisher, 351 Strand
Evans Charles, silk mercer, see Saunders & Evans
Evans Charles, solicitor, see Shearman & Evans
Evans Charles, warehomn. &c. see Eyles, Evans, Hands & Co
Evans Charles, watch & clock ma. 50 Chiswell st
Evans Danl. bricklayer & plasterer, 44 Up. York st. Brynstn. sq
Evans Daniel, cowkeeper, 2 Dorset st. Clapham road
Evans Daniel, wax & tallow chandler, 217 Blackfriars road
Evans David, carpenter & undertaker, 10 Penton st. Walwth
Evans David, chimney & flue surveyor, engineer & patentee of the improved house ventilator, 61 Coleshill st. Eaton sq
Evans David, cowkeeper, 34 Banner st. St. Luke's
Evans David, cowkeeper, 13 Marsham st. Westminster
Evans David, dairyman, 42 Sloane square
Evans David, linendraper, Ring cross, Holloway road
Evans David, oil & italian warehouse, 407 Strand
Evans David, upholsterer, 13 Guildford place, Spafields
Evans Edward, argyll nursery, Paddington green
Evans Edward, carpenter, 11 Norfolk pl. Lower rd. Islington
Evans Edward, oil & colorman, 111 Curtain road, Shoreditch
Evans Edward, surgeon, &c. 2 Stone's end, Borough
Evans Edward (Mrs.), widows' milliner, 92 Fenchurch st
Evans Edward, engraver on wood, 91 Bartholomew close
Evans Edward John, sec. to Free Trade Club, 27 Regent st
Evans Edward Kendall, shoemaker, 33 Chapel st. New rd
Evans Edwin, artist, 11 Caroline st. Bedford square
Evans Edwin (Mrs.), prof. of dancing, 11 Caroline st. Bedfd sq
Evans Elizabeth (Mrs.), dairy, 10 Ropemakers' st. Finsbury
Evans Emma (Mrs.), grocer, Maiden lane, Battle bridge
Evans Enoch, baker, 95 Hoxton Old town
Evans Esther (Miss), milliner, &c. see M'Rae & Evans
Evans Evan, dairyman, 186 Hoxton Old town
Evans Evan, tailor, 61 Castle st. Southwark
Evans Evan, tailor, 16 Clipstone st. Fitzroy square
Evans Fanny (Mrs.), milliner, 15 Lower Brompton grove
Evans Fra. haberdshr. & statnr. 4 Prospect cot. Thornhill rd
Evans Frances (Miss), *Bee Hive* P.H. 20 King st. Comrcl. rd. Ea
Evans Frederick, cabinet maker, 8 Bedford st. Bedford row
Evans Fredk. Hodgson, barrister, 4 Stone bdgs. Lincoln's inn
Evans Fred. John, sup. of chartered gas works, 18 Brick la
Evans Frederick Mullett, printer, see Bradbury & Evans
Evans Frederic, Wm. dining rooms, 90 Church st. Shoreditch
Evans George, accountant & arbitrator, 11 City road
Evans George, *Black Swan* P.H. 26 Brown's lane, Spitalflds
Evans George, carver & gilder, 17 St. Chad's row, King's cross
Evans George, coal mer. 69 Parsons st. St. George st
Evans George, linendraper, 149 & 150 Tottenham court rd
Evans George, naval & military tailor, 3 Fleet st
Evans George, teadealer, 5 Queen st. Pimlico
Evans George John, furn. brok. 2 Earl st. east, Lisson grove nth
Evans Griffith, black lead pencil ma. 8 Up. Rosoman st. Clk
Evans Griffith F. D. physician, 21A, Hill st. Berkeley sq
Evans Henry, *Black Prince* P.H. 151 Princes rd. Lambeth
Evans Henry, colonial merchant, 21 Fenchurch st
Evans Thos. confectioner, 3 Upper Kennington lane
Evans Henry, hairdresser & perfumer, 7 Gutter la. Cheapsd
Evans Henry, *Highlander* P.H. 89 Dean st. Soho sq
Evans Henry Jas. coppersmith, 76 Leman st. Goodman's flds
Evans Henry Kay, curiosity dealer, 282 High Holborn
Evans Henry Thomas, cheesemonger, see Ashton & Evans
Evans Hugh, solicitor, 5 Lincoln's inn New square
Evans Humphrey, working jeweller, 86 Bartholomew close
Evans Jacob, teadealer, 7 Great George st. Bermondsey
Evans James, butcher, 23 Store st. Bedford square
Evans James, furniture broker, 4 Crescent st. Euston sq
Evans James, gold & silver refiner, 12 Up. King st. Blmsbry
Evans James, marine store dlr. 8 Cross st. Newington butts
Evans James, pastrycook & baker, 20 Lr. Sloane st. Chelsea
Evans James, *Royal Clarence* P.H. 3 Westbourne pl. Pimlico
Evans James Cook, barrister, 15 Chancery lane
Evans James T. tailor, 17 Lower Phillimore place
Evans Jane (Mrs.), china dealer, 11 Princes st. Westminster
Evans Jane (Mrs.), newsvender & stationer, 37 Up. Berkeley st
Evans Jeremiah, stove grate manufacturer & furnishing ironmonger, 33 King William st. London bridge
Evans John, baker, 16 Southampton st. Camberwell road
Evans John, barrister, 5 New square, Lincoln's inn
Evans John, blackwell hall factor, see Love & Evans
Evans John, bookseller, &c. 20 King's road East, Chelsea
Evans John, bookseller, 9 Portugal st. Lincoln's inn field's
Evans John, bootmaker, 69 Gt. Queen st. Lincoln's inn fields
Evans John, boot & shoe maker, 23 Southampton st. Strand
Evans John, chandler's shop, 58 Cromer st
Evans John, cheesemonger, 234 Shoreditch High st
Evans John, coach trimmer, 1 King's road, Gray's inn la
Evans John, corndealer, 26 Lower st. Islington
Evans John, dairyman, 3 Creed lane, Ludgate st
Evans John, dairyman, 32 Mansion house st. Kennington
Evans John, dairyman, 73 Milton st. Cripplegate
Evans John, ironmonger, 4 Dover place, Old Kent road
Evans John, last maker, 18 Old Compton st. Soho
Evans John, linendraper, 10 & 11 Limehouse causeway
Evans John, linendraper, 56 Union st. Borough
Evans John, merchant, 10 Old change
Evans John, paperhanging manufctr. 2 Pump row, Old st. rd
Evans John, queen's counsel, 11 Crown office row, Temple
Evans John, solicitor, 51 Lincoln's inn fields
Evans & Barns, solicitors, 6 South square, Gray's inn
Evans John, tailor, &c. 57 Long lane, West Smithfield
Evans John, tailor, 3 Gt. Titchfield st. Oxford st
Evans John, water & watch gilder, 70 Banner st. St. Luke's
Evans John, *White Hart* P.H. 46 Kingsland road
Evans John, wholesale stationer, 26 Budge row, Cannon st
Evans John Edward, bookseller, &c. 4 Snowhill
Evans John Edward, teadealer, 134 New Bond st
Evans John Llewellyn, solicitor, see Newbon Ashton & Evans
Evans Joseph, bacon drier, 1 Evans pl. Low. Kennington la
Evans Joseph, boot & shoe ma. 122 Union st. Borough High st
Evans Joseph, boot & shoe maker, 352 Albany rd. Camberwell
Evans Joseph, carpenter, 72 Warren st. Fitzroy square
Evans Joseph, cockfounder, 31 Gee st. Goswell st
Evans Joseph P. surveyor, 1 Mecklenburgh ter. Gray's inn rd
Evans Jsph. S. manfg. statr. & pockt. book ma. 64 Berwk. st. Soho
Evans Joshua, dining rooms, 96 Blackman st. Borough
Evans Josiah, fruiterer, 13 Laurence Pountney hill
Evans Margaret (Miss), outfitter, see Goy & Evans
Evans Mary (Mrs.), bonnet maker, 72 Warren st. Fitzroy sq
Evans Richard, artist, 17 Newman st. Oxford st
Evans Richard, cowkeeper, 28 Widegate st. Bishopsgate
Evans Richard, livery stables, 4 St. John st. Clerkenwell
Evans Richard, farrier, &c. Talbot inn yard, 75 Borough
Evans Robert, carpenter, 14 Doughty mews, Guilford st
Evans Robert, carver & gilder, 61 Ossulston st. Somers town
Evans Robert, hairdresser, 17 Gt. St. Andrew st. 7 Dials

Evans Robert, linendraper, &c. 2 Mount pl. Walworth road
Evans Roger, *Grapes* P.H. 110 Mount st. Berkeley sq
Evans Samuel, carpenter, 40 New Gloucester st. Hoxton
Evans Samuel, cowkeeper, 1 Collingwood st. Blackfriars rd
Evans Samuel, fruiterer, 29 Skinner st. Somers town
Evans Saml. potato dealer, 40 Marchmont st. Brunswick sq
Evans Samuel, sen. baker, 45 Gt. Windmill st. Haymarket
Evans Samuel, jun. baker, 14 Panton st. Haymarket
Evans Sam.Daimond,upholder&ho.agt.7Arabella rw.Pimlico
Evans Septimus, grocer, 7 Cornwall road, Lambeth
Evans Seth Richard,gas meter mak. 97 Chalton st. Somers tn
Evans Susan (Mrs.), grocer, 20 Skinner st. Clerkenwell
Evans Thomas, boot ma. 4 Hopkin's bldgs.Upper st.Islington
Evans Thomas, coal & potato dealer, 134 Houndsditch
Evans Thomas, corn dealer, 4 Aylesbury pl. Old Kent rd
Evans Thomas, curiosity dealer, 17 Maddox st. Regent st
Evans Thomas, dairyman, 36 Castle st. Long acre
Evans Thomas, dairyman, 23 Charing cross
Evans Thomas, fruiterer, 64 Gt. Hall, Hungerford market
Evans Thomas, grocer, 1 Stepney green
Evans Thomas, gun barrel maker, 18 Wells mews,Oxford st. & 3 Bath place, New road
Evans Thomas, marine store dealer, 56 Bermondsey st
Evans Thomas, lodging house,45Up.George st.Bryanstone sq
Evans Thomas, potato salesman, 132 Whitechapel road
Evans Thomas, ready made linen warehouse, & who. stock, brace & shirt collar manufactr. 24 Southampton st. Strand
Evans Thomas, saddler &harn.ma.13 Commrcl. pl.Kentish tn
Evans Thomas Fisher, law institution dormitory, 265 Strand
EvansThomasHy.coachbldr.&pntr.3Longyd.Lamb'sCondt.st
Evans Thos. Henry, laceman, 7 Sydney alley, Leicester sq
Evans Thomas Henry, stockbroker, see Reece &Evans
Evans Timothy, hosier & outfitter, 72 Gracechurch st
Evans Wm. builder & painter, 3 Woburn bldgs. Tavistock sq
Evans Wm. carman, 3½ Butcher row, Ratcliff
Evans Wm. carver & gilder, 18 Silver st. Golden sq
Evans Wm. distiller, see Seager, Evans & Stafford
Evans Wm. fishmonger, &c.High st. Kensington gravel pits
Evans Wm. *Fortune of War* P.H. 22 Upper Thames st
Evans Wm. *Hatchet* P.H. 20 Little Trinity la. Queenhithe
Evans William, linendraper & silk mercer, 29 Piccadilly
Evans Wm. masonic jeweller, 6 Great Newport st
Evans Wm. mathl.&c.instr.mak.9 Squirries st.Bethnal.gr.rd
Evans Wm. mathematical instr. ma. 48 Rosoman st. Clknwl
Evans Wm. milliner, 36 Beckford row, Walworth road
Evans Wm. painter, plumber & glazr. 52 Coppice rw.Clknwl
Evans Wm. paper stainer,173ShoreditchHighst.&William st
Evans Wm. pasteboard maker, see Clifton & Evans
Evans Wm. plumber,1Bray's buildings,Lower road,Islington
Evans Wm. *Queen's Arms* P.H.93 Gt.Guildford st. Borough
Evans Wm. shellfishmonger, 120 Blackfriars road
Evans Wm. silk mercer, see Sewell, Evans, Hubbard & Co
Evans Wm. Carpenter, *Grand hotel*, 43 King st. Covent ga
Evans Wm. David, barrister, 5 New sq. Lincoln's inn
Evans Wm. J. physician, 25 Henrietta st. Cavendish sq
Evans Winifred (Mrs.), dairy, 33 Southwark bridge road
Eve & Phythian, teadlrs.435Strand, & 5 King Wm.st.Strand
Eve, Wolton & Eve, cattle salesmen, 41 West Smithfield
Eve Adam, hairdresser, 66 Lamb's Conduit st. Foundling
Eve George, hairdresser, 4 York pl.Upper st.Islington green
Eve James, printer, 8 Union place, Lower road, Islington
Eve John, watchmaker, 19 New North st. Red Lion square
Eve Sarah (Mrs.), stationer, 19 New North st. Red Lion sq
Eve Thos. ivory&wood turnr.&cabinet ma.86Tottenham ct. rd
Eve Thos. leather seller, 42 Clifton st. Crown st. Finsbury
Eveaux Joseph, boarding house, 139½ Cheapside
Eveleigh Benjamin, grocer, 32 Up. Albany st. Regent's park
Eveleigh John, linendraper,1Frederick pl. Hampstead road
Evenden Thomas, *Swan* P.H.268 Oxford st
Eveness Robert, job master, 17 Shepperton st. Islington
Evening Chronicle newspaper, 332 Strand
Evening Mail newspaper, Printing house sq. Blackfriars
Evens Charles, baker, 61 Paradise row, Chelsea
Evens Charles, bootmaker, 23 Park st. Upper st. Islington
Everall Edward, grocer, 9 Warren st. Fitzroy square
Everall William, *Gordon's hotel*, 1 Albemarle st. Piccadilly
Eveningstar Wolfe, surgeon chiropodist, 82 New Bond st
Everard Catherine (Mrs.), cheesemonger, Kingsland green
Everard John, fruiterer, 2 Eagle place, Jermyn st
Everard Jonathan, baker, 21 Amwell st. Pentonville
Everard Rd. *Sun & Punch Bowl* P.H. 20 Ray st. Clerknwll
Everard Sam. vety. surg. William's mws. Mary st. Rgnt.'s pk
Everard Samuel Wm. butcher, 2 Junction pl. Kentish town
Everard Simon B.*RoyalGeorge* P.H.8 Gt.George st.Bermsy
Everard Thos. *Halfway house* P.H. 29Webber st.Blackfrs.rd
Evered John, carpenter & builder, 1 Coborn road, Mile end
Evered Rd. brassfounder, 10, 11 &12 Charles st. Long acre
Everest Edward, butcher, 6 Temple place, Old Kent road
Everest Felix,*Old Swan* P.H.Old Swan stairs,Up.Thames st
Everest John, carpenter, 51 Gloucester st. Queen sq
Everet Denny, furn. ironmonger, see Schoolings & Everet
Everet Margaret (Mrs.), lodg. ho. 3 Bell's bldgs. Salisbry. sq
Everett J.G. &J. woollen ma. Heytesbury, & 68 Basinghall st
Everett Wm. & Co. premier blacking makrs. 50 & 51 Fetter lane, & 5 King's head court, Holborn hill
Everett Wm.& Son, woolstaplers, Up. Russell st.Bermondsey
Everett Ebenezer, woolstapler, Lamb all. 185 Bermondsey st
Everett Edward John, cheesemonger, 8 King st. Seven dials
Everett Eliz. (Mrs.), milliner & dress ma. 35 Aldenham st
Everett Fred. Pryor, teadlr. 4 Victoria pl. Queen's rd. Dalstn
Everett Henry, barrister, 5 Pump court, Temple
Everett Isaac, coal dealer, 102 Star st. Paddington
Everett Joseph, fruiterer, 6 Chapel st. Bedford row
Everett Robert, newsvender, 15 Gt. Bath st. Clerkenwell
Everett Samuel, cooper, Ferry road west, Poplar
Everett Wm. barrister, 5 Inner Temple lane
Everett Wm. beer retailer, 101 Bermondsey st
Everett Wm. bookslr. & newsm. 14 Finch la. & 17Royal Exch
Everett Wm. newsvender & bookslr. 5 Johnson's ct. Fleet st
Everill, Philip &Whicker(late Savigny,Everill&Co.), cutlers' & surgeons' instrument makers, 67 St.James's st. Pall mall
Everingham Samuel, hosier & glover, 374 Oxford st
Everington Wm. warehouseman, see Ellis, Everington & Co
Everist William Henry, house agent, 45 Theobald's road
Everitt James, grocer, 19 Hamilton row, Bagnigge wells rd
Everitt Samuel, livery stable keeper, 23 Bury st. Bloomsbury
Evernden Phœbe(Mrs.), pat.axletree ma.5 Broadway,Westm
Everett Thomas Edgar, tailor, 287 High Holborn
Evers Arthur, fancy mould turner,29 Ironmonger st. St.Luke
Evers Daniel, *Cart & Horse* P.H. Ashentree ct. Bouverie st
Eversfield & Horne, auctioneers & appraisers, 1 Little Smith st. Westminster,& coal exchange, Lower Thames st
Evershed Thomas, plumber, 9 New Gravel lane, Shadwell
Everson Geo. jun. dyer & calico glaz. 14 Weston pl. King's cr
Everson George, sen. calico dyer, 93 Long alley, Finsbury
Everton Wm. wholes. toy wareh. 70 Bunhill row, St. Lukes
Every George Henry, engraver, 55 Warren st. Fitzroy sq
Eves Alfred, cheesemonger, 3 Nile st. Hoxton new town
Eves Chas.Morgan, *WhiteHart* P.H.72 Bunhill rw.St.Lukes
Eves Wm. Dickens,*Yorkshire Grey* P.H. 4 Park st. Borough
Evill Thomas Ledyard &Co.woollen manfs.6½ Vigo st. Reg. st
Evison Alfred, law stationer, 1 Cook's court, Lincoln's inn
Evison Joseph, law stationer, 1 Temple st. Whitefriars
Evitt Thomas Augustus, solicitor, 40 Haydon square
Evoy Thomas, hat manufacturer, 140 Princes rd. Lambeth
Evrard Jean, surgical instrument maker & manufacturing cutler, 35 Charles st. Middlesex hospital
Ewart and Bell, stockbrokers,3 Copthall chambs.Copthall ct
Ewart, Maccaughey & Delafosse, tea brokers, 4 Copthall ct
Ewart, Taylor & Co. merchants, 1 Crown court, Philpot lane
Ewart Wm. & Co.wine,&c. mers.87Jermyn st.& 19 Swallow st
Ewart Wm. & Son, sewed muslin & cambric manufrs. Belfast (James M'Neill, agent), 3½ Bow lane
Ewart Wm. & David, stockbrokers, 13 Finch lane, Cornhill
Ewart Adam Joseph, undertaker, 3 Brook hill, Clerkenwell
Ewart Francis, barrister, 4 Brick court, Temple
Ewart George, zinc worker, &c. 67 Bridge road,Westminster, & 19 Quickset row, New road
Ewart Henry, tobacconist, 9 Circus st. New road
Ewart Peter,(sec.to *Standard Life Assur. Co.*),82King Wm.st
Ewbank Henry, merchant,6 Idol lane, Tower st
Ewbank Thomas Henry, solicitor, 3 South sq. Gray's inn
Ewbank Wm. C.dep. registrar,5Geo. ter.Crimscott st. Brmsy
Ewell John,*Pitt's Head* P.H.10Northumberland st. New rd
Ewen Edwd. medical plaister manf.106 Jermyn st. St.James's
Ewen Eliza (Mrs.), butcher, 95 Norton st. Portland place
Ewen James, wholesale perfumer, 17 Garlick hill
Ewen Robert, coal merchant, 25 Sutton st.York rd. Lambeth
Ewence Wm. *Lark Hall tavern*, Lark hall lane, Clapham
Ewens Creasy, solicitor, see Sutton, Ewens, Ommaney & Co
Ewens John Samuel, dorset butter & cheese factor, 6 Arthur st. west, London bridge
Ewens Walter, baker, 12 James st. Haymarket
Ewer John J. & Co. importers & publishers of foreign music, 72 Newgate st
Ewer George, butcher, Mare st. Hackney
Ewer John, plumber, 8 Granby st. Waterloo road
Ewer John Jeremiah, baker, 3 Honey lane, Cheapside
Ewer Nelson, butcher, 54 High st. Wapping
Ewer Thomas, fruiterer, 19 Exeter st. Sloane st
Ewin Edward, linendraper & upholsterer, 218 Boro' High st
Ewing Matthew,bookbinder,38St.Andrew's hl.Doctor's com

Ewing Robt. look. glass mak. 34 Gt. Charlotte st. Blckfrs.rd
Ewings Wm. (*manager of the London & Westminster branch bank*), 214 High Holborn
Ewins Danl. John, auctionr.& upholstr. 15 Clark's pl. Islgtn
Ewins James, fishmonger, 7 Ivy lane, Newgate st
Ewstace Mary (Mrs.), dressmak. 12 Gt. Titchfield st. Oxfd. mkt
Examiner weekly newspaper Office, 5 Wellington st. Strand
Examiners Office, Roll's yard, 14 Chancery lane; hours of business, term, 10 to 4; vacation, 11 to 3
Excell Charles, coal dealer, 74 Bunhill row, St. Luke's
Exchequer Bill Office, 2 Whitehall yard
Exchequer Bill Office for the West India Island relief, South Sea house; hours, 10 to 4
Exchequer (Court of), Westminster hall
Exchequer of Pleas Office, 8 & 9 Old square, Lincoln's inn; hours of business, term, 11 to 5; vacation, 11 to 3; long vacation, 11 to 2
Exchequer (Receipt of) Office, 3 Whitehall yard; hours uncertain
Exchequer Rule Office, 10 Symond's inn, Chancery lane; hours, term, 11 to 3 & 6 to 8; vacation, 11 to 3; long vacation, 11 to 2
Exchequer Seal Office, 2 Middle Scotland yd.; hours, 10 to 4
Excise Office, Old Broad st. City; hours of business, 9 to 3; for Commissioners, &c. &c. see "Official Directory"
Excise Export Office, 49 Great Tower st.; hours, 9 to 3
Exeter Hall, 372 Strand
Exham Thomas R. surgeon, 10 Howley pl. villas, Paddington
Exley John, corn & seed factor, Corn market, Mark lane
Exley Rd. grocer & cheesemonger, 1 Onslow pl. Fulham rd
Experience Life Assurance Co. (Thomas Yuille Mardrop, sec.) 58 King William st. City, for directors &c. see page 2024
Exton Hannah (Mrs.), grocer, see Hoystrop & Exton
Exton James, hot presser, 51 Willow walk, Tabernable sq
Exton John, wholesale grocer, 70 Crawford st. Portman sq
Exton Thos. carpenter & builder, 7 Belgrave st. south, Pimlico
Eye Dispensary, 28 Denmark st. Soho
Eyerss Robert, cooper, 5 Brewers green, Westminster
Eyke John, carman & fruiterer, 58 Milton st. Cripplegate
Eykyn John, stock & share broker, 22 Change al. Cornhill
Eyland Samuel, bootmaker, 43 Wigmore st. Cavendish sq
Eyland Sarah (Mrs.), ladies' bootma. 19 Hanway st. Oxford st
Eyles, Evans, Hands & Wells, warehousemen & importers of foreign lace, 5 Ludgate st
Eyles John B. & Rd. S. surgeons, 1 St. Andrews' ct. Holborn hl
Eyles Charles, bed & mattress maker, 9 Shadwell High st
Eyles Charles, surgeon dentist, 11 Brownlow st. Holborn
Eyles Dan. Hen. carpenter, 76 Sun st. Bishopsgate
Eyles William, upholsterer, &c. 11 Brownlow st. Bedford rw
Eynard Louis V. eau de cologne & spt. mer. 5 Yorkter. York rd
Eyre & Godby, who. coffee dealers, 4 Lit. George st. Minories
Eyre & Spottiswoode, bible depository, 189 Fleet st
Eyre & Spottiswoode, Queen's printers, East Harding st. Gough square
Eyre William & Co. hosiers, glovers, &c. 167 Regent st
Eyre Bernel, merchant, see Figgis & Eyre
Eyre Charles, furniture broker, 16 Brick lane, St. Luke's
Eyre Edward, ironmonger, 4 Bowling green st. Kennington
Eyre Frederick Edwin, solicitor, 22 Bryanstone square
Eyre George, carpenter & undertaker, 14 & 15 Coleman st. City
Eyre George John, solicitor, see White & Eyre
Eyre George Lewis P. solicitor, 69 Lincoln's inn fields
Eyre James, potato dealer, 10 Little Bath st. Clerkenwell
Eyre Sir James, physician, 11 Brook st. Grosvenor square
Eyre Joseph, tailor, 7 Gainsford st. Horselydown
Eyre Joshua Hen. law stationer, 20 Carey st. Lincoln's inn
Eyre Matthew, gasfitter, 55 Maze, Tooley st
Eyre Stratford Alfred, surgeon, 3 Fitzroy st. Fitzroy square
Eyre Walpole, attorney, 22 Bryanstone square
Eyre William, solicitor, 1 Bond court, Walbrook, & 16 Bernard st. Russell square
Eyre William Vardy, solicitor, 16 Bernard st. Russell sq
Eyres Wm. & Sons, woollen manufacts. 10 Milk st. Cheapside
Eyres John, coopers' tool ma. 37 Gt. Alie st. Goodman's fields
Eyres William, oil & colorman, 23 Munster st. Regent's park
Eyston George, solicitor, see Barrett & Eystons'
Eyston George Basil, solicitor, see Barrett & Eystons'

FABER Augustus, foreign merchant, 60 Mark lane
Faber Charles Waring, barrister, 23 Chancery lane
Fabian Bentham & Co. manufacturing chemists, 24 Mark la
Fabian William, coal merchant, 9 Bankside, Southwark
Facey Edwd. auctioneer & appraiser, see Sinclair & Facey
Facey Edward Cox, undertaker, 9 Banner st. St. Luke's
Fache Edward, grocer, 2 Millbank st. Westminster
Fachney James, plumber & glazier, 26 Stangate, Lambeth
Faculty Office, 10 Gt. Knightrider st.; hours 9 to 7
Fagan John Henry, stockbroker, 11 Warnford court
Fage & Dring, hydrometer makers, see Dring & Fage
Fage George, butcher, 101 Lambeth walk
Fage Elizabeth (Mrs.), baker, 24 Union st. Bishopsgate
Fagg Robert & Geo. *White Bear* coach office, 221 Piccadilly; *Bell & Crown*, 133 Holborn; & No. 11 Gracechurch st
Fagg Edwin, surgeon, see Ancell & Fagg
Fagg James, butcher, 10 Bermondsey st
Fagg Mary (Mrs.), butcher, 9 Bermondsey st
Fagioli Dominic & Son, barometer ma. 3 Gt. Warner st. Clrknwl
Faiers Henry Howe & Co. jewellers, &c. 34 Ludgate hill
Faiers John, cabinet ma. & upholstr. 43 Broad st. Golden sq
Faija G. artist, 23 Sloane st. Chelsea
Fail Robert Mather, timber dealer, East India rd. Poplar
Faint John, hay salesman, Haymarket, Bridgehouse pl. Boro'
Fair Joseph, fruiterer & greegr. 9½ Tyler st. Regent st
Fair William, baker, 7 Backchurch lane, Whitechapel
Fair William, boot & shoe maker, 100 Fleet st
Fairall John, beer retailer, 8 John's pl. Camberwell New rd
Fairbairn James & Jsh. nursery & seedsmen, Clapham rise
Fairbairn Wm. & Sons, engineers & iron ship builders, Millwall, Poplar
Fairbairn Alex. wine merchant, 33 Clement's la. Lombard st
Fairbairn John, fishmonger, 21 Lime street, & 11 Ship tavern passage, Leadenhall market
Fairbairn Robert, bookbinder, 10 Duke st. Adelphi
Fairbairn William, fishmonger, 281 Bermondsey st
Fairbank Henry, saw, tool & printing press ma. 121 Old st
Fairbank James, surgeon, 13 Leman st. Goodman's Fields
Fairbank John, chemist, 8 Theberton st. Islington
Fairbank Richard David, grocer, 5 Henry st. Gray's inn la
Fairbank Thos. grocer & oilman, 9 Theberton st. Islington
Fairbanks Wm. chandler's shop, 121 Praed st. Paddington
Fairbrass Geo. leather cutter, 1 Richard st. Limeho. fields
Fairbrass James, fruiterer, 44 Great Marylebone st
Fairbridge Robt. carpenter, 18 Ossulston st. Somers town
Fairbrother Benj. S. *Equestrian tavern*, 124 Blackfriars rd
Fairbrother Edmund, cattle salesman, 17 West Smithfield
Fairbrother Geo. pic. frame ma. 18 Thomas st. Stamford st
Fairbrother Hannah (Miss), milliner, 13 Bull & Mouth st
Fairbrother James, cabinet maker, 16 Old st. road
Fairbrother Joseph, file cutter, 24 Short's gardens, Drury la
Fairbrother Saml. *White Horse* P.H. 27 Brook mews. Brkly sq
Fairbrother Sam. Glover, printer, 31 Bow st. Covent garden
Fairbrother Wm. plumber, 22 Silver st. Kensington grvl. pits
Fairburn Geo. woollen & cotton card ma. 59 Compton st. Clkwl
Fairburn Rt. wiredrawer & wire ribbon ma. 25 Old st. St. Luke's
Fairburn Sarah Ann (Mrs.), bookselr. & publishr. 110 Minories
Fairchild Jsph. pianoforte ma. 30 Grafton st. Fitzroy sq
Fairchild Wm. who. & ret. grocer, see White & Fairchild
Fairchild Wm. Henry, goldbeater, 4 Mercer st. Long acre
Faircloth Charles, accountant, 8 Gresham st. City
Faircloth Sarah (Mrs.), lodging ho. 40 Keppel st. Russel sq
Fairclough Ann (Mrs.), lodging house, 5 Trinity sq. Boro'
Fairclough Thos. Morrison, carman, Christian st. St. Geo. ea
Fairey Joseph & Son, opticians, 8 Northumberld. pl. Coml. rd. ea
Fairey Josiah, watch maker, 8 Patriot row, Cambridge rd
Fairey Richard, watch & chronometer maker, 105 Tooley st
Fairfax Benjamin, *Hoop & Grapes* P.H. 29½ Cable st. Wellcls. sq
Fairfax Robt. *Prince of Wales* P.H. 14 Church la. Comml. rd
Fairfoot Hen. Spence, solicitor, 25 Lloyd square, Pentonville
Fairfull Thos. cabinetmaker, 56 Gt. Chart st. & 21 Buttesland st. Hoxton New town
Fairhead James, surgeon, 1 Montague pl. Noal st. Islington
Fairhead Thos. *Horse & Leaping Bar* P.H. 58 Whitchpl. Hgh. st
Fairlam Richard, *Bird in Hand* P.H. 396 Oxford st
Fairlam Rd. Wilcox, goldsmith & watch ma. 33 Ludgate hill
Fairland Chas. Henry, lithographer, 9 Bridgewater square
Fairland Thomas, artist, Pembroke square, Kensington
Fairless Jane E. (Miss), berlin rep. 5 Orange row, Kenngt. rd
Fairlie James, timber merchant, Dockhead, Bermondsey
Fairman Chas. tube drawer, 12 Baker's row, Clerkenwell
Fairman James, [gun maker many years with J. Purday & with the late Wm. Eley], patent wire cartridge, waterproof percussion cap, chemically prepared waddings, gun ammunition & implement warehouse, 68 Jermyn st. (from 36 St. James's st.)
Fairmaner Austin, bootmaker, 112 Bethnal green road
Fairn James, undertaker, 18 Clipstone st. Fitzroy square
Fairn Stephen, *Fleece* P.H. 1 Duke st. Stamford st
Fairrie Brothers & Co. sugar refiners, Church la. Commrcl. rd
Fairs Thomas, painter to her Majesty, & sole proprietor of the transparent ventilator, 22 & 23 Mortimer st. Cavendish square, & 2 Hanover st. Regent st
Fairweather James, chandler's shop, South Lambeth New rd

Faith, Forbes & Co. merchants, 36 Mincing lane, City
Faith George, merchant, 36 Mincing lane
Faith Henry, provision mer.& cheesemgr.168 Shadwell Hh.st
Faith William, ship owner, Lloyd's
Faithfull Charles, *Chapter coffeehouse*, 50 Paternoster row
Faithfull Edward C. solicitor, 5 King's road, Bedford row
Faithfull Jas. Smith, coal mer. Adam's ter. Hampstead rd
Faithfull John, auctioneer, 33 Bouverie st. Fleet st
Faithfull John, carpenter, 5 Adam's terrace, Hampstead rd
Faithorn Stephen, bricklayer, 16 Queen st. King's rd. Chel
Faker John, baker, 3 Church st. Chelsea
Fakes William, wheelwright, 92 Kingsland road
Falcke Hannah & Sons, curiosity dealers, 394 Oxford st
Falcke Wm. crucible potter, Bolingbroke gardens, Battersea
Falcon Henry, attorney, 4 Elm court, Temple
Falconar Christie James, merchant, 71 Cornhill
Falconer Alex. baker & confectioner, 12B, Dean st. Soho
Falconer Forbes, A.M. prof. of lngs. 42 Dorset st. Portman sq
Falconer Geo. Alex. surgeon, 5 Arbour ter. Commercl.rd.east
Falconer Robert, cowkeeper, 18 Salisbury st. New North rd
Falconer Wm. saddler, &c. see Warren & Falconer
Falconer Wm. Rt. furn. undertaker, see Comfort & Falconer
Faldo George, ship carver, 177 Rotherhithe st
Faldo John, haberdasher, 90 St. John st. road
Falera John, baker, 3 Patriot row, Cambridge rd. Mile end
Falkner Charles, greengrocer, 5 Dean st. Westminster
Falkner Edward, linendraper, 26 Gt. Queen st. Linc. inn fields
Falkner George, butcher, 4 King st. Westminster
Falkner Henry, linendraper, 33 Red Lion square, Holborn, & 6 Chalton st. Somers town
Falkner Wm. carpenter, 14 Poplar row, New Kent road
Falkus John, carpenter & undertaker, 45 Adam st. west, Bryanstone sq. & 19 Portsea place, Connaught square
Fallows, Thorpe & Co. ironmongers, 58 Baker st. & 5 King st. Portman square
Fall John, grocer, see Barough & Fall
Fall Thomas, baker, 22 Charles st. Commercial road
Fall Wm. shipping & general accountant, 30 Rood lane
Faller Michel, wooden clock ma. see Camerer, Faller & Co
Fallover William, fruiterer, 70 High st. Camden town
Fallowdown Chas. Selby, solicitor, 2 Paper bldgs. In. Temple
Fallows & Adcock, furnishing ironmongers, & stove grate manufacturers, 4 Halkin st. west, Belgrave square
Fallows Joseph, attorney, 198 Piccadilly
Fallshaw John Fleetwood, fancy box maker, 8 Staining lane
Falltrick Thos. marine store dealer, 18 Emmett st. Poplar
Family Endowment Annuity & Life Assurance Society (William Lewis, actuary), 12 Chatham place, Blackfriars; see page 2027
Famin Peter Edw. wine & brandy mercht. 14 Little Tower st
Famin Léon, imp. of foreign wines & spirits, 27 Mincing lane
Fan William, carman, 9 Church terrace, Pancras road
Fancutt John, fruit salesman, Covent garden fruit market
Fancy & Stebbing, *Blue Anchor* P.H. 1 Limehouse old rd
Fancy Louisa (Miss), *Kent tav.* 1&2 Brownlow st. Bedford rw
Fancy Thos. *Coach & Horses* P.H. 4 Bear yd. Lincoln's inn flds
Fane William Dashwood, barrister, 21 Old sq. Lincoln's inn
Fanner Wm. scale ma. see De Grave, Short & Fanner
Fanshaw Hen. R. india rubber ma. 26 Russell st. Bermondsey
Faraday Robert & Son, brass founders, 114 Wardour st. Soho
Farbridge Geo. brushmaker, 39 Beckford row, Walworth rd
Fardell Thos. carman & liv. stables, Naval row, Blackwall
Fardell Thomas, shipping butcher, 109 Poplar High st
Farebrother Richd. *Rose* P.H. 15 & 16 Gt. Wild st. Drury la
Farebrother, Clark & Lye, land surveyrs. 6 Lancaster pl. Strand
Farebrother Jas. H. S. sailmaker, 31 Millbank st. Westmsr
Farebrother John, furn. broker & mould cutr. 12 Crown st. Soho
Farenden (Misses), ladies' school, 26 Avenue rd. Regent's pk
Farey Benjamin, *Black Boy & Camel* P.H. 9 Leadenhall st
Farey Charles, butcher, 86 King st. Camden town
Farey James, hosier & glover, 172 Regent st
Farey John, civil engineer, 35 Guilford st. Russell square
Farey John, hosier & glover, 19 Newington causeway
Farey Wm. Thos. *Ram inn* coach & waggon office, 78 Smithfld
Farfas Henry & Thomas, mastmakers, 72 Wapping wall
Fargues Francis & Son, engravers & die sink. 47 Berwick st
Fargues John, working jeweller, see Dee & Fargues
Farguson Elizth. (Mrs.), *Barleymow* P.H. 32 Fore st. Limeho
Farina John Maria (of Cologne on the Rhine), manufacturer of genuine eau de cologne, 1 Carpenter's buildings, London wall
Farish James, surgeon, 8 Lancaster place, Waterloo bridge
Farley Henry Thomsett & Co. teadealers & grocers; importers of & dealers in cigars, 5 Little Tower st
Farley & Mills, cabinet makers, 3 Featherstone st. City road
Farley Henry Wm. A. toy & fancy repository, & city conjuring depôt, 31 Fleet st. opposite St. Dunstan's church
Farley James Saml. stonemason, 12 Goswell rd. Clerkenwell
Farley Richd. teacher of navigation, 12 Prince's sq. St. Geo. ea
Farley William, coffee rooms, 28 Water lane, Blackfriars
Farley William, stonemason, 79 Chapel st. Pentonville
Farlow Charles, fishing rod & tackle manufactr. 221 Strand
Farlow Isaac, *King & Queen* P.H. 227 Rotherhithe st
Farlow John King, fishing rod & tackle manufacturer, 5 Crooked lane, City
Farlow Fred. Rice, lighterman & shipping agent, 13 Fountain court, & Duchy wharf, Savoy st. Strand
Farlow Hen. jun. carman, 16 Maiden lane, Covent garden
Farlow John King, ivory & hardwood turner, billiard ball & chess manufacturer, 5 Crooked lane, City
Farlow William, undertaker, 18 Coburg st. Clerkenwell
Farman Henry, fruiterer, 5 Portland row, Camberwell rd
Farmar Robt. Adolph. & Co. oil & italian wa. 41 Mount st. Lambth
Farmer Robert Adolph, chemist, 40 Mount st. Lambeth
Farmer Eliza & Mary, milliners, &c. 41 Ludgate st
Farmer & Gorbell, iron, steel & tin plate mers. ironmongers, metal tool, file & crucible wa. 92 & 93, St. John st. Clerknwl
Farmer & Sanders, milliners, see Sanders & Farmer
Farmer Ben. cabinet & library table ma. 5A, Ivy la. Hoxton
Farmer Benjamin, tailor, 50 Clark st. Stepney
Farmer Chas. iron & steel wareho. 76 Market st. Edgware rd
Farmer Chas. Francis, licensed lighterman, 77 Blackfriars rd
Farmer Daniel, oil & italian warehouse, 28 Aldgate
Farmer David, plumber, &c. 5 Southampton st. Camberwell
Farmer Frederick, wheelwright, 30 Castle st. Long acre
Farmer George, cattle salesman, 41 West Smithfield
Farmer Hannah (Miss), furn. broker, 20 Vine st. Hatton wall
Farmer James, tobacconist, 1 Bloomsbury terr. Com. rd. east
Farmer Joshua, baths, Addington sq. Camberwell rd
Farmer Joshua, newsvender, 11 Hereford pl. Commer. rd. east
Farmer Joshua, jun. stationer, 3 Bloomsbury ter. Comml. rd. ea
Farmer Richard, fruiterer, 1 Prospect pl. Cambridge heath
Farmer Saml. sash ma. & glass cut. 7 Alfred pl. Nwngtn. causwy
Farmer Sarah (Mrs.), cotton wick ma. 82 Curtain rd. Shoreditch
Farmer Thomas, firewood dealer, 4 Upper Belgrave terrace
Farmer Thomas, merchant, City club, 19 Old Broad st. City, & oil of vitriol manufacturer, Kennington common
Farmer Thomas, plumber, 16 South st. King's rd. Chelsea
Farmer Wm. carman, 60 Little College st. Camden town
Farmer Wm. cooper & brewer, Little Chelsea
Farmer Wm. brick merchant, 77 Blackfriars road
Farmer Wm. engine, lathe & tool mak. 33 Gt. Sutton st. Clrknwl
Farmer Wm. mealman, 17 London st. Fenchurch st
Farmer Wm. ornamental carver, 35 Rahere st. York st. City rd
Farmer Wm. tailor, 24 New Quebec st. Portman square
Farmers' Magazine Office, 24 Norfolk st. Strand
Farmilo Peter, fruiterer, 2 Keppel st. Chelsea
Farmiloe George, window glass cutter & lead merchant, 114 St. John st. Smithfield, & 33 James st. Buckingham gate
Farn Edward, solicitor, see Brooksbank & Farn
Farn William, currier, 14 Newcastle st. Strand
Farnan Frank & Sons, silk & woollen dyers, Old Ford
Farncomb Thomas, agent to the Boulby alum works at Whitby, Griffin's wharf, 79 Tooley st
Farncomb Thomas, wharfinger, Griffin's wharf, 79 Tooley st
Farndell Francis Cooper, hatter, 3 Lit. Geo. st. Bermondsey
Farndell Joseph, beer retailer, Blue Anchor rd. Bermondsey
Farndell William, tailor, 93 High st. Portland town
Farnden Edward, linendraper, 44 Long acre, & corn dealer, 16 James st. Covent garden
Farnell Benjamin, bricklayer, 9¼ Upper st. Islington green
Farnell James, printers' ink maker, see Blackwell & Farnell
Farnell Joseph Kirby, linendraper, 21 Finsbury pavement
Farnell William Lewis, *Grange Inn*, 31 Carey st. Linc inn
Farnes Charles, seedsman, 128 St. John st. Smithfield
Farnes Henry, *Sun & Sawyers* P.H. 168 Poplar High st
Farnes Joseph, *Bombay Grab* P.H. High st. Bow
Farnes Wm. Matthew, carpenter & undertak. 88 Poplar High st
Farnham Thomas, cabinet maker, 2 & 3 Mora place, City rd
Farnham W. grocer, 4 Devonshire pl. Walworth common
Farquhar James, proctor, see Sladen, Glennie & Farquhar
Farquhar Thos. N. solicitor, see Johnston, Farquhar & Leech
Farquhar Wm. chronometer & watchma. 6 George st. Tower hill
Farquharson Robert, newsvender, 10 Bloomsbury st
Farr Charles, teadealer & grocer, 5 Lamb st. Spitalfields
Farr Edward, cheesemonger, 55 James st. Oxford st
Farr Francis, cloth dresser, 3 Clifton st. Finsbury
Farr Richd. saddler, 1 Caroline cottage, King's rd. w. Chelsea
Farr Thomas, *Blandford Arms* P.H. 68 Boston pl. Dorset sq
Farr Thomas, tailor, 47 Lower Sloane st. Chelsea
Farr William, cheesemonger, 7 Broadway, Ludgate hill
Farr William, locksmith, 53 Strutton ground, Westminster
Farr William W. barrister, 1 Paper buildings, Temple

Farrance Edward, *Hotel*, 11 Up. Belgrave st. Belgrave sq
Farrance Thomas, confectioner, 66 & 67 Charing cross
Farrand Fredk. builder, 187 Long la. & Long walk, Bermsdy
Farrand Jacob, canteen & plate case ma. 1 Silver st. Wood st
Farrand, Robert, cornfactor, 26 Mark lane
Farrant, George & Son, wheelwrights, High st. Stratford
Farrant Sir George, knt. barrister, 53 Upper Brook st
Farrant George Binstead, barrister, 7 Figtree court, Temple
Farrant John, cutler, 48 Burlington arcade, Piccadilly
Farrant Mary (Mrs.), fruiterer, Borough market
Farrant Richard, dining rooms, 1 Leader st. Chelsea
FarrantWm. plumber&painter,39 Goodge st.Tottenhamct.rd
Farrants Robert Jas. surgeon, 5 Regent terrace, City road
Farrar & Lake, solicitors, 12 Godliman st. Doctors' commons
Farrar & Summers, linendrapers, 25 Gt.Russell st. Cov.gardn
Farrar Edward, surgeon, 48 Guilford st. Russell square
Farrar Elizabeth (Mrs.), milliner, 27 Old Burlington st
Farrar Frederick, solicitor, 12 Godliman st. Doctors' commons, & Halfway house, near Easher, Surrey
Farrar Luke, surgeon,&c. 11Bedford pl.Commercial rd.East
Farrar Richard, general agent, 35 Wood st. City
FarrarWm.stone merch. Red Lion wf.Canal rd.Kingsland rd
Farre Arthur, physician, 22 Curzon st. Mayfair
Farre Frederic John, physician, 35 New Bridge st. Blackfrs
Farre John Richard, barrister, 3 Elm court, Temple
Farre John Richard, physician, 4 Charterhouse square, & 7 Queen's row, Pentonville
Farrell Alice (Mrs.), bookbinder, 4 Bear yd. Lin. inn fields
Farrell Edward, workg. silversmith, 24 Brydges st.Cov.gar
Farrell Garrett, confectioner, 35 Lamb's Conduit st
Farrell James, wine merchant, 50 Lime st
Farrell Ann (Mrs.), coffee rooms, 10 Tavistock row, Cov. gar
Farrell John, surveyor, 18 Rupert st. Haymarket
Farrell Mary A.(Miss), ladies' school, 11 Broad ct.Long acre
Farrell Richard, newsvender, 382 Albany road, Camberwell
Farrell Richard, potato dealer, 13 Lumber court, Seven dials
Farrell Roger, tailor, 30 Great Ormond st. Queen square
Farrell Thomas, coffee house, 58 King's st. Borough
Farren George, barrister, 1 Symond's inn
Farren George, resident director of *Asylum* (*Foreign & Domestic*) *Life Office*, 70 Cornhill,& 5 Waterloo pl. Pallmall
Farren Henry, chemist, &c. 15 Crown row, Walworth road
Farrent Elizab. (Mrs.), fancy repos. 6 Lisson grove north
Farrent Geo. hosier, 27 Church st. Camberwell
Farrer, French & Tatham, proctors & notaries, 26 Great Carter lane, Doctors' commons
Farrer Hen.& Wm. picture dealers & res.14 Wardour st. Soho
Farrer & Parkinson, solicitors, 66 Lincoln's inn fields
Farrer & Penrose, tailors & drapers, 281 High Holborn
Farrer Henry Ward, wine merchant, see Cracklow & Farrer
Farrer James, confectioner, 7 Jerusalem pas. Clerkenwell
Farrer John, cabinet manufacturer,68Curtain rd. Shoreditch
Farrer Mary (Mrs.), boarding house, 32 Dorset square
Farrier Charles Thomas, lighterman, 184 Wapping High st
Farrin John & Son, cattle salesmen, 8 West Smithfield
Farrin & Marshall, cattle salesmen, 8 West Smithfield
Farrin Thomas, cattle salesman, 8 West Smithfield
Farringdon Dispnsry. & Lying-in Hsptl. (Richard Stanning, surgeon), 17 Bartlett's buildings, Holborn
Farrington Joseph, manufacturer of hatbands, galloons, &c. 36 Spital square, Norton folgate
Farrington Richard, fruiterer, 5 Exeter st. Sloane st
Farrington Saml.restor.ofpaintings,52Castle st.Leicester sq
Farrington Wm. baker, 6 Windsor pl. Old Kent road
Farris Richard, baker, 32 Long acre
Farris Robert, *Weavers' Arms* P.H.13 Crown st. Finsbury
Farris Thomas, baker, 27 East st. Manchester square
Farris Wm. paper hanging wa. 18 Cumberland row,Kng's.cr
Farrow Charles, furnish. ironmonger, 18 Gt. Tower st. City
Farrow Daniel, perfumer, see Vickery & Farrow
Farrow David, *New Exchange* coffee rms. 94 Leadenhall st
Farrow Geo. booksell. & newsven.3 Arcade,Hungerford mkt
Farrow George, tailor, 34 New Union st. Lit. Moorfields
Farrow John, potato salesman, 21 Red Lion st. Spitalfields
Farrow John, printer, 32 Pudding lane, Eastcheap
Farrow Joseph, dining rooms, 6 Bermondsey new road
Farrow Richard, plumber, &c. 25 Montagu st. Portman sq
Farrow Thos. cooper, 32 Adam st.&21 Albion st. Rotherhithe
Farrow Wm. beer retailer, 2 Tottenham road, Kingsland
Farrow William, veterinary surgeon, 55 St. George st
Farson Richd. lighterman & coaldlr. 7 Gibson st.Waterloo rd
Farson Stephen E. wax & tallow chandler, 30 Blackfriars rd
Farsyde George James W. barrister, 3 Elm court, Temple
Farthing & Reed, tailors & drapers, 119 Cheapside
Farthing Joshua, tailor & clothier, 64 Goswell st. & 35 Brooke st. Holborn
Farthing John, copying machine manufacturer, dressing case maker & cutler, 42 Cornhill
Farwig Adolphus, tin pl. & wire work, 16 Rupert st.Haymrkt
Farwig Augustus H. wire & tin pl. wa. 1 Salisbury ct.Fleet st
Farwig Chas. Ludwig, tin & japan ware manfr. 63 Watling st
Farwig Fredk. Wm. ironmonger, 12 Henrietta st. Covent gar
Farwig Wm. metal wa. 12 Bridge house pl. Newington cau
Faryon William, *Angel* P.H. 56 Farringdon st
Fase Henry, bookseller & statnr.1 Edwardes ter. Kensington
Fasquel Henry, boot & shoe ma. 3 Piazzas, Covent garden
Fassett Elias De Gruchy, grocer,2 St.Thomas' pl. O. Kent rd
Fatham Joseph, corn dealer, 15 Gray's inn ter. Gray's inn la
Fatharly Thomas, *Mitre* P.H. Palace new road, Lambeth
Fatherly Henry, *Ship* P.H. 299 Rotherhithe st. Rotherhithe
Fatt Frederick, wine mercht. 3 Salters' hall ct. Cannon st
Fatt George, gasfitter, 4 London st. Fitzroy square
Fatt John, oil & italian wa. 19 Liverpool st. Bishopsgate
Faucher Francis, prof. of dancing, 7 Half Moon st.Piccadilly
Faucherre Jules, engraver, 30 Granville sq. Clerkenwell
Fauchon Robert James, butcher, 61 Flagon row, Deptford
Faudel & Phillips, importers of berlin & other wools, & manufacturers of super purse twists, floss, decca & every description of embroidery silks, &c. 39 & 40 Newgate st
Faulconer Harriet (Mrs.), coffee rooms, 91 St.John st.Clknwl
Faulconer Robt. Steph. chemist, see Steedman & Faulconer
Faulconer Thomas, stockbroker, 12 Copthall court, City
Faulding, Stratton & Co. linendrapers by appointment to her Majesty, 13 Coventry st.
Faulkener John, bookbinder & sta. 8 Queen st. Tower hill
Faulkes Stephen, *Rose & Crown* P.H.25 Little Newport st
Faulkner & Johnson, tailors, 36 Gt. Pulteney st. Golden sq
Faulkner Matt.& Jsph.linendr.1 King st. & 120 High Holborn
Faulkner Richd. & Chas. teadealers & oilmen, 44 Jermyn st
Faulkner Alfred, hosier & glover, 107 Regent st
Faulkner Benj. Rawlinson, artist, 23 Newman st. Oxford st
Faulkner Chas. Edw. card mak. 32 Cornwall rd.Stamford st
Faulkner Chas. marine store dlr. 26 Eyre st. hill, Leather la
Faulkner Cope, linendraper, 51 Bermondsey st
Faulkner David, cornchandler, 29 Horseferry rd.Westminstr
Faulkner Edwin, teadealer, 3 William st. Lowndes sq
Faulkner George, *Duke of York* P.H. 17A, Serles pl. Carey st
Faulkner George, hairdresser, 7 Stafford st. Bond st
Faulkner George, sol. see Gregory, Faulkner, Gregory & Co
Faulkner Henry, builder, 51 Jermyn st. St. James's
Faulkner James, builder, 11 York st. St. James's
Faulkner John, ironmonger, 62 St. Martin's le grand
Faulkner John, jun. jeweller, 27 Gt. Castle st. Regent st
Faulkner John, sen. jeweller, 37 Gt. Titchfield st. Oxford st
Faulkner John Alfred, *George* P.H. 108 Old st. St. Luke's
Faulkner John Sharman, who.bootmaker, 5 Wormwood st
Faulkner Lucy (Mrs.), bootmaker, 70 Ossulston st. Somers tn
Faulkner Oliver, bootmaker, 5 Piccadilly
Faulkner Richard, shoemaker, 4 Gt. Alie st. Goodman's fi
Faulkner Robt. grocer, 65 Upper Ground st. Blackfriars
Faulkner Thomas, library, 27 Smith st. King's rd. Chelsea
Faulkner William, jeweller, 13 Lisson grove north
Faulkner Wm. *Weavers' Arms* P.H. 79 Green st. Bethnal gr
Faulkner Wm. wine, spirit & provision mer. 18 Cullum st
Faulks Wm. cheesemonger & butterman, 9 Up. Southwick st
Fauntleroy Robert & Sons, foreign hardwood merchants, Potters' fields, Tooley st. & Clink st. Bankside
Fauntleroy Charles, woolstapler, Russell st. Bermondsey
Fauntleroy John, attorney, 14 Gt. Portland st. Oxford st
Faure (Madame), court dress maker, &c. 2 Little Argyll st
Faure Théodore, french wine & spirit mer. 2 Lit. Argyll st
Faust Geo. bootmaker, 30 Great Marlborough st
Faust George Henry, lithographer, 30 Gt. Marlborough st
Fautley James, fruiterer, Southampton st. Camberwell
Faux William Henry, coal mer. Union wharf, Wilton rd. & lodging house, 18 Manchester buildings, Westminster
Favell, Beddome & Co. warehousemen, 170 Fenchurch st
Favell & Bousfields', wholesale slopsellers, 12 St. Mary Axe
Favell Robert, merchant, see Moberly William, Son & Co
Favell William, tobacconist, 12 Finch lane, Cornhill
Favenc Abraham & G—, silk merchants, Tom's coffee house
Favenc Abraham George, wine mercht. 3 Sherborne la.City
Favenc Geo. exchange & discountbroker, Tom's coffee house
Faver James, oilman, 1 Gt. Carter lane, Doctors' commons
Favre Louis, watch & clock ma. jeweller, &c. 18A, Maddox st
Fawcett Jas. & Co. proprs. of hockley spawaters, 35 Jewin st
Fawcett Joseph & Co. pianoforte mfs. 3 Lower Chester ter
Fawcett Thos. T. & Co. silkma. & corah printers, 12 Trump st
Fawcett William & Co. carpet manufacturers, Kidderminster; & at 59 Skinner st. Snow hill
Fawcett Ann (Miss), milliner, 26 City road, Finsbury
Fawcett Benj. builder, carpenter, &c. 1 Haydon st. Minories

Fawcett Edward, special pleader. 5 Pump court, Temple
Fawcett Frs.Wm.boot tree & last ma. 14 Lisle st. Leicester sq
Fawcett Henry, printseller, 2 Gt.Wild st. Lincoln's inn fields
Fawcett James, cabinet ma. 13 Grenville st. Somers town
Fawcett James, solicitor, 44 Jewin st. Cripplegate
Fawcett James,tailor, 11 Clayton pl.William st.Caledonian rd
Fawcett James, tailor, 28 York st. Kingsland road
Fawcett John, carpet, floor cloth,&c.wa. 2 Angel pl.Islington
Fawcett John, coachbuilder, 118 & 119 St.John st. Smithfield
Fawcett Richard, carpet warehouse, 73 & 74 Whitechapel High st. & 1 Osborne st. Whitechapel
Fawcett Richard, *King's Arms* P.H. 93 St.John st. Smithfld
Fawcett Robert, jun. dyer, 3 Anderson's buildings, City rd
Fawcett Robert, sen. tailor, 26 City road
FawcettSamuelCharles,printer,6Worship st. Norton folgate
Fawcett Thomas, fishmonger, 21 High st. Camberwell
Fawcett Walter Thos. stockbroker, see Hill, Fawcett & Hill
Fawcett Wm. carpenter & builder, 24 Crimscott st. Bermndsy
Fawcitt Horatio, upholsterer, 52 Seymour pl. Bryanstone sq
Fawcus Margaret (Mrs.), chain cable ma. see Pow & Fawcus
Fawdington Wm. confectioner, 98 Upper st. Islington
Fawdon George, newsvendor, 6 Old Compton st. Soho
Fawdon Wm. leather dresser, 1 Swan mead, Brmndsy. nw.rd
Fawkener John, solicitor, see White, Blake, Tylee & Fawkener
Fawkes Alfred Tritton, col. broker, see Maitland's & Fawkes
FawssettCamillus,wool.drap.16&17Gt.May'sbldgs.StMart.la
Fay James, grocer, Church st. Stoke Newington
Fayle Benjamin & Co. merchants, 31 George st. Hanover sq
FayrerJas.&Sons,math.inst.maks.66WhiteLion st.Pentonvlle
Fayrer John, cabinet maker, 36 Nutford place, Bryanstone sq
Feail Thiophinia (Mrs.), coal mer. 2 Gainsford st. Horselydn
Fear Charles, builder, &c. 5 Aston place, Holloway
Fear Henry, market gardener, Battersea
Fear Thomas, gasfitter, 4 Limehouse causeway
Fear Wm. veneer & deal saw mills, 122 Long la. Bermondsey
Fearies Mary (Mrs.), grocer, 115 Portland st. Walworth com
Fearis George, linendraper, 4 & 5 Lambeth walk
Fearnall & Fletcher, ship builder, see Fletcher, Son & Fearnall
Fearnhead Peter, solicitor, 17 Clifford's inn, Fleet st
Fearnley Chas. Thos. grocer, 27 St.George's pl. Knightsbridge
Fearnley Henry, ship chandler, see King & Fearnley
Fearnley Thomas Edward, solicitor, Phœnix pl. Ratcliff cross
Fearns Wm. Jas. ship & ins. broker, 2 Jeffrey's sq. St.Mary Axe
Fearon Hen. *Star & Windmill* P.H. Star corner, Bermondsey
Fearon Hy. B. wine mer. 145 New Bond st. & 94 Holborn hill
Fearon Jhn. Peter, solicitor, 1 Crwn.offi.rw & 8 Figtree ct.Tmpl
Fearon Samuel John, solicitor, see Stevens & Fearon
Feast Thomas, *Bishop Blaize* P.H. 1 New inn yd. Shoreditch
Featham Robert, dyer, 37 Upper st. Islington
Feather Josh. poor rate collctr. 2 Anderson's bldgs. City rd
Feather Robert John, *Fox* P.H. 3 Fox's lane, Shadwell
Feather Thomas, tailor & draper, 113 Bunhill row
Featherstead James, tailor, 5 East st. Red Lion sq
Featherston Thomas, cattle salesman, 8 West Smithfield
Featherstone Francis, watchmaker & jeweller, 75 Fetter la
Featherstone John, bricklayer, see May & Featherstone
Featherstone Richard Daniel, baker, Deptford High st
Featherstone Thomas, stone mason, 7 Chester ter. Boro' rd
Featherstone Wm. dentist, 42 Albemarle st. Piccadilly
Featherstone William, furniture broker, Clare market
Featherstone Wm. painter, 11 Paradise st. Marylebone
Featley Robert, zinc manufacturer, 161 Kingsland road
Featon John, linendraper, 20 Three Colt st. Limehouse
Feaver Thos. propr. of gout embrocation, 5 Connaught terr
Feben Peter, bricklayer, 23 Richmond pl. East st. Walworth
Feddon John, academy, 7 Cleveland st. Fitzroy sq
Fee Farm Rent Office (Wm. Reeves, receiver), 6 Lyon's inn, Strand; hours 11 to 3
Feeny Robert, printer, 26 St. John st. Clerkenwell
Feesey Richd. fruiterer, 1 Francis st. Newington butts
Feetham John & Thos. coal merchants, Norway wf. Millbank st
Feetham Wm. & Mark, stovemakers, furnishing ironmongers to the Queen, 9 Clifford st. Bond st. & 422 Oxford st
Feilder Martha (Mrs.), grocer, 61 King st. Deptford
Feist Herman & Chas.J. wine mers. 16 Gould sq. Crutchd. frs
Feistel Adolphus, wine mer. 192 Wellington ter. Waterloo rd
Felby Fredk. wardrobe dealer, 23 Oakley st. Lambeth
Feldwick Thos. John, coml. boarding ho. 13 Pancras la. City
Felgate Wm. & Co. ship & ins. brokers, & e. i. agts, 15 Birchin la
FelgateChas.grcr.165HoxtonOld town,&Church st.Hackney
Felgate Charles, grocer, 1 Wellington ter. Liverpool rd
Felgate John, builder, 34 Sidney st. Commercial road east
Felgate John Chas. jun. builder, 7 Jubilee pl. south, Coml. rd
Felgate Samuel, grocer & tea dlr. 34 Church st. Shoreditch
Felgate Thos. grocer, 101 Curtain road, Shoreditch
Felgate Wm. *Grapes* P.H. 13 Sandy's row, Bishopsgate

Felkin Robert & Joseph, warehousemen, 52 Old Change
Fell Ann & Jane (Misses), millnrs. 5 Edwardes ter. Kensngtn
Fell John & Samuel, leathersellers, 17 West st. Somers town
Fell Mrs. & Miss, ladies' school, 11 Surrey sq. Old Kent rd
Fell Wm. & Co. wine & barter merchants, 26 Friday st
Fell Wm. Young & Co. waterloo cognac brandy distillery, 84 Waterloo road & 26 Friday st
Fell Alfred, underwriter, shipping agent & auctioneer, 2 Cowper's court, Cornhill
Fell Christopher, coach currier, 159 High Holborn
Fell Frederick James, baker, 18 Paradise row, Chelsea
Fell George, bookseller & stationer, 60 Piccadilly
Fell Geo. jun. leatherseller, 13 Robert ter. King's rd. Chelsea
Fell John, plumber & glazier, 3 North place, Dalston
Fell Mary (Mrs.), grocer, 36 Crown st. Soho
Fell Richard, engineer & plumber, 54 Crown st. Finsbury
Fell Robert. solicitor, 3 Raymond's buildings, Gray's inn
Fell Wm. coal dealer, 22 Foley st. Portland place
Fell Wm. tailor, 107 Snow's fields, Bermondsey
Fell Wm. Halford, carver, gilder & picture frame maker, 7 St. Agnes terrace, Tabernacle walk, Finsbury
Fell Wm. Walker, currier, &c. 15 Warren st. Fitzroy sq
Fella John, carpenter, 6 Carpenter st. Berkeley st
Fellowes Benjamin, bookseller & publisher, 39 Ludgate st
Fellowes John, newsvender, 36 Tottenham court road
Fellowes Joseph, bookseller & tobacconist, 13 Shoe lane
Fellowes RalphThos. *Crown & Sugar Loaf* P.H. 98 & 99 Fleet st
Fellowes Wm. bookbinder, 4 Amen corner, Paternoster row
Fellows & Randell, silk brokers, 63 Old Broad st. City
Fellows Geo. jeweller, 20 Exmouth st. Clerkenwell
Fellows Henry, rag merchant, 15 Queenhithe
Fellows Jemima (Mrs.), grocer, 8 Manchester bldgs. Holwy
Fellows Ann (Mrs.), *King's Head* P.H. 31 Museum st. Blmsbry
Fellows John G. Caledonian nursery, Caledonian rd. Pentnvl
Fellows Margaret (Mrs.), fruiterer, 6 Leicester st. Regnt. st
Fellows Saml. rope mkr. 1 Devonshire st. Newington causew
Fellowship Porters' Hall (George Marten, clerk), 17 St. Mary-at-hill
Fells John, chemist, 185 Church st. Shoreditch
Felstead Noah, teacher of dancing, 8 Goswell road
Feltham John & Co. bankers, 42 Lombard st
Feltham John & Co. discount agents, 42 Lombard st
Feltham James, greengrocer, 1 Tottenham rd. Kingsland
Feltham John, pastrycook, 193 Bermondsey st
Feltham Walter James, grocer, 1 George st. New twn. Deptf
Feltoe Francis & Sons, wharfingers, coal & coke merchants, Belvedere coal wharf, Belvedere road, Lambeth
Feltoe Francis, bookbinder, &c. 24 Church st. Blackfriars rd
Feltoe Francis, wine merchant, 6 Billiter st
Felton George & James, curriers, 184 Brick la. Spitalfields
Felton John, coach & harness mak. 1 Pump row, Old st. rd
Felton Wm John, coachmaker, Halkin st. West, Belgrave sq
Female Orphan Asylum (Miss Sarah Cockburn, matron), Mead place, Westminster road
Female Orphan School, Petersburgh place, Bayswater
Female Penitentiary Asylum, Cumming place, Pentonville
Female Servants' Home Society, 21 Nutford pl. Edgware rd
Fen Office, 6 Serjeants' inn, Fleet st.; hours 10 to 2
Fencock Daniel, dairyman, 35 White Hart st. Drury lane
Fencock John, baker, 10 Vauxhall row
Fencott William, *Angel* P.H. 125 Lambeth walk
Fendall George, butcher, 10 Woodstock st. Oxford st
Fendick Henry, linendraper, 48 Fore st. Cripplegate
Fendt Bernard Simon, musical ins. ma. see Purdy & Fendt
Fenelle George, engineer, Church lane, Whitechapel
Fenge James, boot & shoe maker, 100 Chalton st. Somers tn
Fenn, Kemm & Fenn, wholesale grocers, 32 Botolph lane
Fenn Alex. grocer, 211 Hoxton Old town, & 1 Allerton st. Hoxtn
Fenn Charles, cheesemonger, 1 Suffolk place, Commercial road east, & 27 Frith st. Soho
Fenn Daniel, comb maker, 26 Chapel st. Holywell mount
Fenn George, butcher, 1 Gray's inn lane
Fenn George, tailor, Linden grove, Kensington gravel pits
Fenn John, dlr. in bldg. materials, 34 Regent st. Horsefy rd
Fenn John, merchant & ins. brok. 37 Old Broad st. City, & Lloyd's
Fenn John, watch & clock maker, 63 Bethnal green road
Fenn Joseph, butcher, 15 Sale st. Paddington
Fenn Joseph, mechanical tool, lathe, saw, plane & file manufacturer, & ironmonger & cutler, 105 Newgate st
Fenn Philemon, coach bldr. 2A, New Church st. west, Edgw. rd
Fenn Samuel, baker, 15 South wharf road, Paddington
Fenn Thomas, carver of wood, 14 Little Chapel st. Soho
Fenn Wm. cheesemonger, 35 Marchmont st. Brunswick sq
Fenn William, *Commercial* coffee house, 76 Newgate st
Fenn Wm. locksmith, 2 Gt. Pearl st. Wheeler st. Spitalfields
Fenn William, baker, 1 Robert st. Bedford row

Fenn William, tailor, 28 Gough st. Gray's inn road
Fennell, Child & Kelly, solicitors, 32 Bedford row
Fennell Richard&Co. cotton spinrs.&mfrs. 18 Aldermanbury
Fennell Samuel, merchant, 14 St. Mary Axe
Fennell William, boot maker, 52 Cornwall road, Lambeth
Fenner Hen. & Co.wine mers.Winchester house,OldBroad st
Fenner James, fruiterer, 6 Drake st. Red Lion square
Fenner Joseph, tobacconist, 1 NewChurch st. west, Edgw.rd
Fenner William, general salesman, 7 Skinner st. Somers tn
Fennesay Richard, seedsman, 17 Newington causeway
Fenning & Hale, oilmen & dealers in venison, 5 Poultry
Fenning & Shepard, insurance brokers, 3 King's Arms buildings, Change alley, Cornhill, & Lloyd's
Fenning (Miss), school, 15 Holland st. Kensington
Fenning Richard, boot & shoe ma. 4 Lowndes pl. Holloway
Fenning, Ripley, Brown&Co.e. i. bro. 6LaurencePountney la
Fennings Richard Lawrence & James, granite merchants & contractors, 12 Wellington chambers, London bridge
Fennings' Wharf, Richard Lawrence & James Fennings, 1 Tooley st
Fennings Elizab. (Mrs.),stationr.3Jamaica row, Bermond rd
Fennings Richard, boot & shoe manufr. 112 Curtain road
Fenoulhet James, attorney, 65 Hatton garden
Fenoulhet William, artist, 10 Grafton st. Fitzroy square
Fensham Louis & Co. wine merchants, 38 Dowgate hill
Fensham Louis & Co. merchants & shippers, 38 Dowgate hill
Fensom & Proole, fruiterers, 3 North st. Edgware road
Fensom John, fishmonger, 85 Lower Thames st
Fentiman George,chemist, 2 Clement's inn pas.Clement's inn
Fenton Chas. berlin & fancy repository, 37 Moorgate st
Fenton Chas. painter & glazier, 2 Clement's la. Lombard st
Fenton Charles, plumber, 79 Chancery lane
Fenton Chas. Edwd. proctor, 7Gt. Carterla. Doctors' comms
Fenton Enos, surveyor, 38 West Smithfield
Fenton Francis Henry, *Fenton's hotel*, 63 St. James's st
Fenton Hugh, *Greyhound* P.H. Clapham common
Fenton James, butcher, 51 Davies st. Berkeley square
Fenton Jas. linen bleacher, see Sadler, Fenton & Co
Fenton John, baker & corndealer, 5 Avery row, Grosvenor st
Fenton John, cheesemonger, 6 White Lion st. Pentonville
Fenton John, wine merchant, 79 Mark lane
Fenton Joseph, oilman, 34 Marchmont st. Brunswick sq
Fenton Maria (Miss), dressmaker, 37 Moorgate st
Fenton Perrot, proctor, 5 Godliman st. Doctors' commons
Fenton Samuel, watchmaker, 10 Platt terrace, Somers town
Fenton Thos. baker & cornchandler, 19Davies st. Berkeleysq
Fenton Thos. fishing tackle dlr. 5 Patriot row, Cambridge rd
Fenton Thomas, *Star* coffee rooms, 162 Goswell st
Fenton Thos. Hy. glass, lead & colour mer.26WestSmithfield
Fentum Henry, music seller & publisher, 78 Strand
Fenwick & King, linendrapers, 131 Whitechapel road
Fenwick Ralph, Son, & Laroche, coal factors, ship &insurance agents, 36 St. Mary-at-hill
Fenwick Ralph, artist in fireworks, 25 Regent st. Lambeth
Fenwick Henry, barrister, 6 King's Bench walk, Temple
Fenwick John D. *Three Compasses* P.H. 20 New st. Shadwl
Fenwick Joseph, wine merchant, see Ruck, Son, & Fenwick
Fenwick Thomas, barrister, 1 Hare court, Temple
Fereday John, japanner, 33½ Brick lane, Spitalfields
Ferguson Chas. A. & Thos. mast, oar, block & gun carriage mas. Millwall
Fergusons', Redmayne & Co. cabinet ma. 176 & 177 Oxford st
Ferguson William & Sons, power loom linen factors, 10 Pancras lane, City ; & at Dundee
Ferguson Daniel, paper stainer, &c. 13Stafford st. Lissongro
Ferguson Dan. surg. instr. & truss ma. & cutler, 21 Giltspurst
Ferguson Eliz. (Miss), ladies' school, Mare st. Hackney
Ferguson Geo.childbedlinen wareho. 99 Whitechapel High st
Fergnson Geo. farrier, Sweetapple ct. Bishopsgatest.without
Ferguson George, tailor, 15 Queen st. Golden square
Ferguson James, academy, 23 Minories
Ferguson James, fruiterer, 124 Great Suffolk st. Boro'
Ferguson James, wax work exhibition, 167 High Holborn
Ferguson James William, barrister, 28 Chancery lane
Ferguson John, bookseller, 5 Earl's court, Leicester square
Ferguson John, pilot, 68 Poplar High st
Ferguson Richard, tailor, 3 King's row, Walworth road
Ferguson Robert, physician, 9 Queen st. Mayfair
Fergusson & Bradshaw, woollen drapers, 13 Marylebone st
Fergusson & Forster, wholesale teadealers & spice merchants, 3 St. Mary-at-hill, & 23 Eastcheap
Fergusson Daniel, hairdresser, 35 Liquorpond st
Fergusson James, linendraper, 89 Chapel st. Pentonville
Fergusson John, engraver & printer, 93 Dean st. Soho
Fergusson John, grocer, 22 Boston st. Dorset square
Fergusson John, physician, 21 Cavendish rd. St.John's wood
Fergusson Wm. physician, 21 Grove end rd. St. John's wood
Fergusson William, surgeon, 8 Dover st. Piccadilly
Fermander Jacob, china dealer, 111 Middlesex st. Aldgate
Ferminger John, merchant, 8 Tavistock place, Tavistock sq
Ferne Edw. Haffey, carpentr.&undertkr.23 Swan st.Minories
Ferne Edw. Haffey, *Crown & Anvil* P.H.8 Swan st. Minories
Fernee Rt. butcher, 8 Perseverance ter.Church st.Shoreditch
Fernell Henry, engraver, 6 Clarendon st. Somers town
Ferney Henry, gun maker, 11 Ebenezer pl. Coml.rd.Limeho
Fernie Ebenezer (managing director of *British Commercial Life Insurance Company*), 35 Cornhill
Fernie James, baker, 136 Southwark bridge road
Fernie Thomas, ship builder, 331 Wapping
Fernley George, pork butcher, 1 High st. Kingsland
Ferraby Thomas, upholder, 11 Windmill st. Tottenham ct. rd
Ferraday & Tannen, treacle mks.17Old Montague st.Whtchpl
Ferrand Alexander (Madame), milliner, 2Maddox st. Rgt.st
Ferrari Bernard, looking gl. ma. 23 Northampton st.Clrknwl
Ferraro Peter, carver & gilder, 67 Quadrant, Regent st
Ferrer & Jenkins, foreign wine impts. 12 Cross la. City
Ferrer Prudence (Miss), milliner, 1 Farringdon st
Ferrers Thos. B. stockbroker, 12 Copthall ct. Throgmorton st
Ferrers R. Vincent, upholsterer & bed wa. 10 Marylebone st
Ferrers William Edmund, merchant 25 Bucklersbury
Ferres John, wine cooper & carman, 32 Dowgate hill
Ferrey Benjamin, architect, 7 Bedford st. Bedford square
Ferrie Allen, coppersmith, Thornhill wharf, Caledonian rd
Ferrier William, grocer, &c. 53 Rupert st. Haymarket
Ferrington Henry, fruiterer, 2 Wingrove place, Clerkenwell
Ferris & Buncombe, boot & shoe makers, 106 Tooley st
Ferris Frederick, *Cock & Lion* P.H. Lower East Smithfield
Ferris John, tailor, 3 Melton place, Euston square
Ferris Rich. carpent. & undert. 39 Charles st. Westminster
Ferry Luke, oil & colorman, 1 Ropemakers' fields, Limeho
Fesenmeyer John Ph. silk dealer, 38 Wilkes st. Spitalfields
Fesenmeyer John Fredk.Wm.solicitor, 12 Denmark st.Pntnvl
Fesser Edward, merchant, 3 Austinfriars
Fessey Richard, grocer, &c. 47 Gt. Windmill st. Haymarket
Featherstone Hen.auctionr.estate agt. & valuer, 14Tooley st
Feuillade Geo. R. *Colonnade hotel*, 22 Charles st.St.James's
FevershamJsph.Edwd. cheesemonger,3Grange rd.Bermndsy
Few, Hamilton & Fews', solicitors, 2 Henrietta st.Covnt. gard
FewJames, builder, 123Chancery lane,&16RedLion st.Holbn
Fewell William, hatter, 3 Dover place, Old Kent road
Ffarington Edmund F. barrister, 4 Garden court, Temple
Ffinch Matthew, wine merchant, New King st. Deptford
FfitchCharles (Mrs.), corset & dress ma.50Baker st.Lloyd sq
Fiander John, plumber, painter, &c. 19 Brick st. Park lane
Fickling Robert, marine store dlr. 18 Sidney st. Goswell rd
Fickling Wm. tailor & draper, 84 Bishopsgate st. without
Fiddes Alexander, confectioner, &c. 88 High Holborn
Fiddes Charles, *King's Head* P.H. Church st. Hackney
Fiddey Charles, attorney, see Blakelock & Fiddey
Fidge Henry, butcher, 21 Great Suffolk st. Borough
Fidge John William, grocer, 24 Crosby row, Walworth
Fidge Thomas, butcher, 23 Great Suffolk st. Borough
Fidler Elizabeth (Mrs.), grocer & oil wareh.6Ivy ter.Hoxton
Fidler Joseph, oilman, 22 Smith's place, Hackney road
Fiel George Jacob, cheesemonger, 1 Norton st. Fitzroy sq
Field Benj. & Son, wine & brandy merchants, 4 Botolph la
Field Charles & Co. ale & porter brewers, Wandsworth road
Field & Child, seed merchants, 119 Lower Thames st
Field Edw. & Caleb, stockbrokers, 3 Bartholomew la. Bank
Field Geo. & Co. printing ink mfrs. 11 Red Lion ct. Fleet st
Field Horatio & Co. wadding manfrs.4½ John st. Curtain rd
FieldJames & Son, straw hat mfs. & imptrs.114Fore st. City
Field John Charles & John, wax chandlers, bleachers, oil merchants & dyers, soap makers, 12Wigmore st. 36 Upper Marsh, & 35 Lower Fore st. Lambeth
Field Mary & Geo. Edward, 3 *Compasses* P.H. 67 Bankside
Field Richd. & Co. silk & woollen printers&agts.60 Bread st
Field, Son & Bayley, stockbrokers, 9 Warnford court
FieldThos.Rt.& Jph.Wm.surgeons,2Wilderness rw.Clerknwl
Field, Wardell & Co. wine, spirit & ale merchants, 22 Henrietta st. Covent garden
Field Abraham, tailor, &c. 23 Warwick st. Golden sq
Field Ann Frances (Mrs.), crape dresser, 4 Cambridge road
Field Arthur Bolland, merch. see Pye, Field & Tanqueray
Field Benjamin, solicitor, 4 Lincoln's inn fields
Field Betsy (Mrs.), furniture broker, 161 Tooley st
Field Charles, *Royal Oak* P.H. 1 Princess st. Lisson grove
Field Charles, tallow chandler, 58 Mount st. Lambeth
Field Charles, upholder, 1 Bowling st. Westminster
Field Chas. Dyer, carpen. 44 Castle st. Southwark
Field Edmund, russia merchant, Baltic coffee house
Field Edward, bookbinder, 29 Francis st. Newington butts

Field Edward, *Rose & Crown* P.H. 2 & 7 Oxford st
Field Edwin Wilkins, solicitor, see Sharpe, Field & Jackson
Field Elizb. (Mrs.), linendraper, 1 King st. ter. New North rd
Field George, ale agent, 49 Great Tower st
Field George, beer retailer, 4 Judd st. Brunswick square
Field George, dairyman, 19 Berwick st. Soho
Field George, hop merchant, see Wood, Field & Wood
Field George, leather cutter, 26 Homer st. Marylebone
Field George, *Marlboro' Head* P.H. 97 Bishopsgate within
Field George, oilman & salter, 107 Borough High st
Field George Tatton, wine & spirit merchant, *Pier hotel*, Cheyne walk, Chelsea
Field Hy. ag. to *Licensed Vict. Fire & Life Ass. Co.* 36 O. Jewry
Field Henry, boot & shoe maker, 7 Poppin's court, Fleet st
Field Henry, teadealer, 9 Staverton row, Walworth road
Field Hen. Wm. ormolu frame & case ma. jeweller, &c. 2 Strand
Field Jas. architect & surveyor, 5 Adelaide pl. London bridge
Field James, butcher, 67 Wapping High st
Field James, grocer, &c. 8 Shepherd court, Upper Brook st
Field James, *Horns* P.H. Cuckold's point & 125 Rotherhithe st
Field James, tailor, Church st. Stoke Newington
Field James, wine & spirit broker, 28 Mincing lane
Field John, architect & surveyor, 5 Bennett st. St. James's st
Field John, book & printseller, 65 Quadrant, Regent st
Field John, carman, Port st. Walworth common
Field John, coach spring maker, 98 John st. Fitzroy sq
Field John, gun maker, see Parker, Field & Sons
Field John, hairdresser, 113 Bethnal green road
Field John, profile painter to her Majesty, 2 Strand
Field John, solicitor, 9 Guilford st. Russell square
Field John, tailor, Allan st. Cross st. Islington
Field John, wholesale gun & pistol manufacturer & sword cutler, 3 Union row, Tower hill
Field John Michael, furrier, 2 Rathbone place, Oxford st
Field John Wm. pawnbroker & silversmith, see Reynolds & Field
Field Joseph, hairdresser, 8 Cleveland st. Fitzroy sq
Field Joseph, varnish maker, 1 Edward st. Barnsbury rd
Field Joshua, engineer, see Maudslay, Sons & Field
Field Mary (Mrs.), dressmaker, 4 Strong's pl. Brompton
Field Mary (Mrs.), *Lord Nelson* P.H. 18 Aston pl. Holloway
Field Michael, tobacconist & sta. 29 Ashley crescent, City rd
Field Michael Dyer, hat block maker, 26 Gravel la. Southwk
Field Octavius Adolph. surgeon. 4 Stanhope ter. Hyde park
Field Peter, dyer & scourer, 63 York st. Westminster
Field Peter Wilson, carpenter, 11 Featherstone st. Finsbury
Field Robert, stockbroker, 4 Shorter's ct. & Stock Exchange
Field Samuel, architect & surveyor, 13 Beaufort bdgs. Strand
Field Sarah (Miss), milliner, &c. see Hammond & Field
Field Thomas, furniture broker, 419 Oxford st
Field Thomas, baker, 171 Blackfriars road
Field Thomas, baker, 1 Thurlow place, Hackney road
Field Thomas, gilder, 12 Princes st. Cavendish square
Field Thomas, grocer & teadlr. 116 High st. Marylebone; 7 Adam's row, Hampstead rd.; & 65 Brill row, Somers town
Field Thos. Robt. chemist, 8 Brecknock pl. Camden new town
Field Wm. auctioneer, 2 (corner of) Osnaburgh pl. Regent's pk
Field Wm. bookseller & stationer, see Miller & Field
Field Wm. chemist, 27 Middle Queen's bldgs. Knightsbridge
Field Wm. marblemason, 55 Wilton st. Regent st. Westminster
Field Wm. pastry cook, 2 Thornton st. Dockhead
Field Wm. solicitor, Carlton chambers, 8 Regent st
Field Wm. veterinary surgeon, 224 Oxford st.
Field Wm. wine, spirit & colonial broker, 9 Rood lane
Field Wm. John, pawnbroker, see Reynolds & Field
Fielden John, merchant, Garraway's coffeehouse
Fielder Thos. Edwd. & Geo. proctors, 14 Godliman st. Doc. com
Fielder Edward, cheesemonger, 2 & 85 Fore st. City
Fielder Edward, commercial agent, 25 Crosby hall chambrs
Fielder Henry, agt. to Kent Fire Off. 26 Palace new rd. Lmb
Fielder John, W. lace merchant, 3 Thavies inn, Holborn
Fielder Julius H. carpet bag manfr. 13 Union ct. O. Broad st
Fielder Richard, poulterer, 1 Trinity st. Blackman st. Boro'
Fielder Thomas, baker, 8 Brewer st. Somers town
Fielder Thomas, carver & gilder, 3 Greek st. Soho
Fielder William, *Mail Coach* P.H. 155 Kingsland road
Fielder Wm. watch case maker, 29 Glo'ster st. St. John st. rd
Fieldhouse Charles, grocer, 39 Cleveland st. Fitzroy sq. & 8 Lower st. Islington
Fieldhouse Geo. Jesse, engine turner, 53 Red Lion st. Clrknwl
Fieldhouse Wm. corn dealer, 172 Brick lane, Spitalfields
Fielding Copley, artist, 26 Newman st. Oxford st
Fielding Daniel, butcher, 6 Rosoman st. Clerkenwell
Fielding George, drum & tambourine manufactr. 63 Old st. rd
Fielding Henry, german silver mfr. 16 Thavies inn, Holborn
Fielding James, sheriffs' officer, see Swayne & Fielding
Fielding Robert, newsvender, 33 Old street road
Fielding Simon, tobacconist, 11 Swallow st. Piccadilly
Fielding Thos. who. earthenwa. dlr. 3 Sth. whf. Padgtn. basin
Fielding Thos. wholesale hosier, 50 Wood st. Cheapside
Fielding William, butcher, 9 Aston place, Holloway
Fielding Wm. dyer & scourer, 99 Chalton st. Somers town
Fielding Wm. Edmd. berlinwool rep. 12 Crown st. Walwth. rd
Fields Thomas, stockbroker, 3 Bartholomew lane, Bank
Fieldsend Sarah (Mrs.), boarding house, 5 Thavies inn
Fieldwick Henry, builder, see Garland & Fieldwick
Fife John, mariner, 64 Great George st. Bermondsey
Fife Martha (Mrs.), milliner, 236 Oxford st
Fiford John, carpenter, 20 Coburg st. Clerkenwell
Figdor Bernhard, wool mercht. 79 Basinghall st
Figg George, currier, 112 Britannia st. City road
Figg Elizh. (Mrs.), ladies' school, 88 Bridge rd. Lambeth
Figg John Wilmin, silversmith, 5 Wellington st. Goswell st
Figge John Fredk. merchant, 10 Tokenhouse yard
Figgins Vincent & James, type founds. 17 & 18 West st. Smithfld
Figgins Henry, surgeon, 5 Bayham ter. Camden New tn
Figgins John Burgess, grocer, 4 St. John st. road, Clerknwll
Figgis & Eyre, merchants, 5 Crown court, Philpot la
Figgis Thomas, general merchant, 13 St. Mary Axe
Figgures Harriet (Mrs.), butcher, 5 Green st. Kentish town
Figuls Francisco, imp. of spanish & italian produce & foreign wines, &c. 10 Woburn bldgs. Tavistock sq
Filbey Joseph, tailor, 9 Grove place, Brompton
Filby & Co. ship & insur. brokers, 157 Fenchurch st
Filby Boswell, coach proprietor, Little Chelsea
Filby Charles, chandler's shop, 13 Felix st. Hackney rd
Filby Henry, baker, 95 Harmood st. Hampstead road
Fildas Thos. watchmovementmkr. 32 Wellington st. St. Luke's
Filica Charles, merchant, 30 Throgmorton st
Filkin Richard, physician, 28 Coventry st. Haymarket
Fillans James, sculptor, 82 Baker st. Portman square
Fillery Samuel, butcher, 44 Winchester st. Pentonville
Fillingham Chas. saddler & harness ma. 78 Fenchurch st
Fillingham Elizh. (Mrs.), saddler, 278 Whitechapel road
Filliston Joseph, dairyman, 7 Baltic st. Golden lane
Fillmer Matthew & William, pawnbrokers & silversmiths, 60 South Audley st. & 3 Kent pl. Old Kent road
Fillmer Thomas, pawnbroker, 18 Blackfriars road
Fillmer Wm. pawnbroker, 1 Kennington row. Kenngtn. com
Filmer James, fruiterer, 17 Adam st. west, Bryanstone sq
Filmer Thos. Hen. upholsterer, 28 Berners st. Oxford st
Filmore Egerton, druggist, 15 King st. Holborn
Fimister Ebenezer, bootmaker, 4 Thornton st. Dockhead
Fimister John, boot & shoe maker, 1 Potter's fields, Tooley st
Final Alexr. grocer, 27 Langley pl. Commercial road east
Finan Thos. *Rose & Crown* P.H. 84 Wentworth st. Whitechapel
Finan Thomas, *White Bear* P.H. 1 St. George st
Finch & Robinson, stayma. 5 Parsonage row, Newngtn. butts
Finch John & Son, carpenters, 67 West st. West Smithfield
Finch, Rickman & Co. mustard manufacturers, 5 Queenhithe
Finch Robert & Co. (successors to Mr. Lambert), oil & italian warehouse, 11 Ludgate hill
Finch & Shepheard, solicitors, 21 Old Jewry
Finch & Steel, dressmakers, 1 Hagley place, New Kent rd
Finch Alexr. furn. bro. 23 Ann's pl. Pritchard rd. Hackney rd
Finch Ann (Mrs.), hat manfctr. 10 Harrow alley, Aldgate
Finch Benjn. cheesemonger, 150 Union st. Borough High st
Finch Charles, surgeon, see Philp, Bush & Finch
Finch Edward Hicks, wine mer. 6 Copthall ct. Throgm. st
Finch Frederick, fruiterer, 9 St. Alban's pl. Edgware rd
Finch George, solicitor, 68 Acton st. Gray's inn road
Finch George Wm. solicitor, 57 Lincoln's inn fields
Finch Henry, *George* P.H. 13 Middle row, Holborn
Finch James, beer retailer, 49 Rosoman st. Clerkenwell
Finch James, general cooper, 5 Little Bath st. Clerkenwell
Finch James, straw plait dlr. 26 Cannon st. rd. St. George's east
Finch Jason, cowkeeper, 1 Deptford High st
Finch John, carpenter, 22 Berwick st. Pimlico
Finch John, cattle salesman, 8 West Smithfield
Finch John, shoemaker, 46 Gt. Cambridge st. Hackney rd
Finch John, jun. solicitor, 22 Guilford st. Russell square
Finch Joseph, ham dealer, 104 St. John street road
Finch Michael, chandler's shop, 32 Prospect pl. Cambdg. hth
Finch Minezies, grocer & cheesemgr. 27 East st. Kenngtn. rd
Finch Robert, tobacconist, 2 Stepney rents, Hackney rd
Finch Samuel, *Globe* P.H. 21 King st. Clerkenwell
Finch Samuel, tobacconist, 5 Parsonage row, Newngtn. butts
Finch Sarah (Mrs.), milliner, 119 Shoreditch High st
Finch Stephenson, clockmaker, 8 King square, Goswell rd
Finch Thomas, bootmaker, 5 Blenheim st. Oxford st
Finch Thos. hairdresser, 1 Ambrose pl. Marlboro' rd. Chelsea
Finch Thomas, stonemason, 11 Pierepoint rw. Islington green
Finch Thomas, tallowchandler, 4 High st. Kensington grav. pits

Finch William, *Admiral Keppel* P.H. 100 Hoxton Old town
Finch Wm. baker, 2 Wallington place, Wandsworth road
Finch Wm. cattle salesman, 17 West Smithfield
Finch Wm. prep. boys' school, 7 Denbigh st. Pimlico
Finch Wm. publisher, 95 Hercules buildings, Lambeth
Finch Wm. smith, bellhanger & ironmonger, 25 High st. Bow
Finch Wm. Golding, bear importer, 56 Bishopsgate without
Fincham, Matson & Potts, wh. tea & hop dlr. 3 Martin's la. City
Fincham Wm. & John, butchers, 22 Parker's row, Dockhead
Fincham George, surgeon, 5 Spring gardens
Fincham George, T. physician, 38A, Curzon st. Mayfair
Fincham Hen. who. & ret. tea & spice dlr. 55 Charing cross
Finck Diedrich, tobacconist, 16 East road, City road
Finden & Green, architects & estate agents, 25 Regent st
Finden & Lewis, architects & surveyors, 9 John st. Adelphi
Finden Edwd. engraver, 18 Southampton place, Euston sq
Finden Geo. Fredk. chemist & druggist, see Constable & Finden
Finden John, confectioner, Southampton st. Camberwell
Finden Wm. farrier, 15 Tottenham mews, Middlesex hospital
Finden Wm. historical engra. 49 Camden st. sth. Camden town
Findlay Alex. & Son, map engravs. 4 Quality ct. Chancery la
Findlay Henry, wood mould cutter & composition ornament maker, 60 Gt. Portland st
Findley Edw. *Manchester Arms* P.H. 1 Adam st. east, Man. sq
Findley George, watchmaker, 146 St. George st
Findlow & Rainsley, sable, fitch & camel hair pencil ma. gilders' tips & varnish tool mfs. 29½ Gt. Sutton st. Clknwll
Findon Ann (Miss), milliner, 58 George st. Portman square
Findon James, pat. axletree, coach spring & water closet ma. Black horse yard, 190½ Holborn
Finer Horatio, chronomet. watch & clock ma. 48 High Holbrn
Finer John, corn merchant, see Smith, Finer & Smith
Finer Wm. surgeon, 6 Cambridge pl. Kingsland road
Fines & Recoveries, Office for searching for, Rolls garden, Serjeants' inn, Chancery lane
Fines Charles, chaser, 14 Guildford st. east, Spa fields
Fines John, fruiterer, 44 Lambeth walk
Finey Thomas, bookseller, 22 Gt. Knightrider st
Finigan John, wholesale furrier, 30 Noble st. Cheapside
Fininley Alfred, sur. inst. ma. 2 Surrey pl. Camberwell new road
Fininley David, carpenter, 30 St. George st
Fink Herman, refining powder, Old Ford
Finlason William, barrister, 5 Essex court, Temple
Finlay, Hodgson & Co. merchts. 8 St. Helen's pl. Bishopsgte
Finlay Frederick, architect, 26 Duke st. Westminster
Finlay John, tailor, 29 Fenchurch st
Finlay Thomas, tailor, 14 Laurence Pountney hill
Finlay Wm. M. mast & block ma. Lit. Hermitage st. Wapping
Finlayson David, bohemian glass imptr. Hall of Commerce
Finlaysom Mary A. (Mrs.), human hairma. 25 Wilson st. Fnsby
Finlayson Sarah (Miss), straw hat mfr. 2 John st. wst. Edgw. rd
Finley Lucy (Miss), toy dlr. 4 Waterloo ter. Comrcl. rd. east
Finley Maria L. (Miss), tobacconist, 1 St. Mark's rd. Cambwl
Finley Thomas, tailor, 234 Strand
Finn William, tailor, 71 George st. Portman square
Finnelly William, barrister, 20 Old square, Lincoln's inn
Finney Charles, horsehair ma. 42 Primrose st. Bishopsgate
Finney John, accountant, auctionr. & apprsr. 52 Watling st
Finney John Douglass, attorney, 6 Furnival's inn, Holborn
Finney Stephen, coal mer. 12 Wharf, Paddington basin, Sth. si
Finney William, *Queen's Head* P.H. 237 Poplar High st
Finney Wm. Hen. bread & biscuit baker, 2 Little Tower st
Finnie Jomes, merchant, 20 St. Swithin's lane, City
Finnie Richd. Boyd, spring saddle & harness ma. 70 Piccadilly
Finnimore Henry, coal dealer, 2 Spring st. Marylebone
Finnis Robert & Fred. pilot agents, 3 Lower East Smithfield
Finnis & Fisher, grocers & oilmen, 79 Great Tower st
Finnis Wm. & Co. carv. & gilds. 111 Blackman st. & Gt. Dover rd
Finnis Charles, tobacconist, 18 York pl. Westminster road
Finnis James Richard, lighterman, 10 Globe st. Wapping
Finnis Robert Fitz, attorney, 21 Hart st. Bloomsbury
Finnis Wm. auctioneer, &c. 26 Gt. Russell st. Bloomsbury
Finnis Wm. carver & gilder, 2 St. Thomas pl. Dover rd. Boro'
Finsbury Gen. Benevolent Pension Soc. 13 Providence row
Finsbury Hall of Science (William Bendall, manager), Bell yard, Commercial pl. City road
Finsbury New Central Dispensary (John Wm. Griffith, surgeon), 36 Rosoman st. Clerkenwell
Finsbury Savings' Bank (William N. Wortley, manager), between 18 & 19 Sekforde st. Clerkenwell
Finzi & Williams, wine merchants, 7 Suffolk lane, Cannon st
Finzi Samuel Lion, surg. dentist, &c. 6 Dalby terr. City rd
Firby & Purser, turners & brush ma. 18 Marylebone st. Picd
Fire protective & general building improvement Company (William J. Bray, secretary), 9 Lincoln's inn fields
Firkins Edmund, beer retailer, 46 Stafford st. Lisson grove
Firmin Philip & Samuel, button makers & sword cutlers, 13 Conduit st. Bond st. & 153 Strand
Firmin Charles, boot & shoe maker, 11 Prospect pl. Old Kent rd
Firmin Edwd. Henry, beer retailer, Larkhall lane, Clapham
Firmin Fredk. W. meat salesman, 24 New Newgate st. mkt
Firmin George, manufact. chemist, 18 Great Alie st. & 8 Rupert st. Goodman's fields
Firmin John, carman, 7 Cherubim ct. Glassho. st. Ea. Smithfi
Firmin John, surrey educational instn. 131 Blackfriars road
Firmin Wm. Potto, whitehorse livery stables, Liverpool road
Firminger John, mercht. & insur. broker, 37 Old Broad st. City
Firmstone Jos. iron mer. see Dimmack, Thompson & Co
Firmstone Jos. P. iron mer. 9 Warnford ct. Throgmorton st
Firrell Mark, farrier, Mermaid court, Borough High st
First Lord of the Treasury Office, 10 Downing st. hrs. 10 to 7
Firth & Young, woollen drapers, 1 & 2 Aldgate High st
Firth Chas. M. lithog. engraver & printer, 8 St. Michael's all
Firth Elizabeth (Mrs.), library, 9 Somerset st. Aldgate
Firth James, builder, 24 Gillingham st. Pimlico
Firth John, mustard & sawmills, see Sadler, Firth & Ross
Fischer Augustus & George, merchants, 15 Great St. Helen's
Fischer & Schumann, merchants, 8 Billiter square
Fish Wm. Geo. & Augustine T. pawnbrokrs. Church st. Hackney
Fish Augustine Thos. pawnbro. see Fish Wm. Geo. & Aug. T
Fish Edm. Simmons, *Bear & Ragged Staff*, 67 Up. Ground st
Fish Francis, furniture broker, 12 Cross st. Blackfriars road
Fish Henry, boot & shoe maker, 58 Charles st. Westminster
Fish Henry, plumber, &c. 2 Prince's row, Pimlico
Fish John, fringe manufacturer, 2 Vine place, Old st. road
Fish John, plumber, 1 Trelleck terrace, Vauxhall bridge rd
Fish Joseph, tobacconist, 9 Strutton ground, Westminster
Fish Robert, painter & plumber, 6 Acorn st. Bishopsgate
Fish Samuel Charles Cross, barrister, 2 Hare court, Temple
Fish Thomas, fruiterer, 18 Dartmouth st. Westminster
Fish William Croft, Finsbury bank, 82 St. John st. road
Fishenden George, pastrycook, 3 Brown st. Bryanstone sq
Fishenden Thos. hairdresser, 84 Mount st. Berkeley sq
Fisher & Blundell, surgeon dentists, 49 Frith st. Soho
Fisher & De Jersey, attorneys, 162 Aldersgate st
Fisher & Harland, house painters, 36 Blackman st. Borough
Fisher John & Son, builders, Stratford broadway & Plaistow
Fisher John & Son, tailors, 4 Somerset pl. New rd. Com. rd
Fisher & Ellis, bread & buiscuit bakers, 55 Threadneedle st
Fisher Nicholas & Son, leather & sponge mers. 5 Maze pond
Fisher Robt. & Co. cabinet ma. & upholstrs. 32 Finsbury pl. Nth
Fisher, Son & Co. printers & publishers, Angel st. St. Martin's le Grand, & 9 Bath st. Newgate st
Fisher, Sons, Robinson & Walker, lace manfrs. 12 Watling st
Fisher & Toller, chemists, &c. 18 Conduit st. Regent st
Fisher William & Co. tailors, &c. 31 King William st. City
Fisher Albion, plumber & glazier, 2 Windmill pl. Camberwell
Fisher Alder, surgeon, 11 King st. Snowhill
Fisher Alfred, butcher, 9 Rose st. Newgate market
Fisher Amelia (Miss), dressmaker, see Constance & Fisher
Fisher Benjamin, dairy, 7 Gt. White Lion st. Seven dials
Fisher Benjamin, hairdresser, 4 Church st. Rotherhithe, & 5 Union road, Rotherhithe
Fisher Charles, *Lion & Lamb* P.H. 1 Drummond st. Euston sq
Fisher Charles, gunmaker, 8 Princes st. Leicester square
Fisher Daniel, brushmaker, 16 Panton st. Haymarket
Fisher David, bootmaker, 37½ Clerkenwell green
Fisher David, chemist & druggist, 49 Oakley st. Lambeth
Fisher Eden, stationer & account book maker, 33 Cannon st
Fisher Edward, plate glass factor, 36 Leadenhall st
Fisher Edward, who. milliner & florist, 104 Wood st. & 15 & 16 St. Chads row, Gray's inn road
Fisher Elias Pickwick, cheesemonger, 36 Upper Park place
Fisher Francis, barrister, 4 New sq. Lincoln's inn
Fisher Francis, merchant, 3 Austinfriars
Fisher Frederick, butcher, 16 Noble st. Cheapside
Fisher Fredk. *Old White Bear* P.H. 126 Aldersgate st
Fisher Fredk. straw bonnet ma. 8 Talbot ct. Gracechurch st
Fisher George, hairdresser & perfumer, see Ager & Fisher
Fisher George, poulterer, 23 Duke st. St. James's
Fisher George, tailor, 3 Queen st. Soho
Fisher George, varnish & color ma. 30 Minerva st. Hackney rd
Fisher Geo. Healey, solicitor, 4 Sambrook ct. Basinghall st
Fisher Hannah (Mrs.), fruiterer, 2 Gt. Hall, Hungerford mkt
Fisher Helen (Mrs.), governess ins. 12 Gough sq. Fleet st
Fisher Henry, brush manufacturer, 12 York pl. Kent st. rd
Fisher Henry, coal dealer, 2 Goulstone st. Whitechapel
Fisher Henry, colonial broker, 6 Great Tower st
Fisher Henry, grocer & oilman, 66 Monmouth st. Seven dials
Fisher Henry, plumber, painter & glazr. 18 Air st. Piccadilly
Fisher Hen. Adolphus, rope, line & twine mak. 29 Kent st. Boro'
Fisher Henry Wm. surgeon, 21 Argyll st. Regent st

Fisher Horatio Nelson, solicitor, see Parnther & Fisher
Fisher Isabella (Mrs.), corset ma. 22 Charlotte st. Fitzroy sq
Fisher Isaac, agt. to Cox, Brothers & Co. leadmers. 8 Tooley st
Fisher Ishmael, *Lansdowne Arms* P.H. 10 Paradise row, Isltn
Fisher James, baker, 114 Minories
Fisher James, cutler, &c. 7 Cannon st. road, St. George's east
Fisher James, ship agent, 1 Union row, Tower hill
Fisher James, *Elephant & Castle* P.H. 11 Oxford market
Fisher James Carr, surveyor & estate agent, 4 Austinfriars
Fisher James Wm. bookbinder, 2 Angel ct. Skinner st
Fisher John, baker, 5 Cowcross st. Smithfield
Fisher John, baker, 183 Lambeth walk
Fisher John, baker, 28 Broad st. Bloomsbury
Fisher John, brush manufacturer & carpet broom maker, 3 Exeter place, Gt. Dover road
Fisher John, cabinet maker, 22 Charlotte st. Fitzroy sq
Fisher John, cabinet ma. 10 Tottenham mews, Midlsx. hospt
Fisher John, carpenter, 199 Hoxton Old town
Fisher John, cheesemonger, 5 Union ter. Commercial rd. east
Fisher John, egg salesman, 25 Snow's fields, Bermondsey
Fisher John, fruiterer, 31 Finsbury market
Fisher John, glasscutter, 20 Paddington st. Marylebone
Fisher John, news agent, 1 George's st. Camberwell
Fisher John, R.N. harbour master, office, St. Katharine's stairs
Fisher John, *White Swan* P.H. 57 Rosemary lane
Fisher John A. oil & colorman, 20 Seymour pl. Camden town
Fisher John Cambridge, solicitor, 57 Pratt st. Camden town
Fisher John Philip, grocer & oilman, see Finnis & Fisher
Fisher John Wm. marine store dlr. 3 Leman st. Goodman's fields
Fisher Joseph, art. florist, imprtr. & mnufr. 138 London wall
Fisher Joseph, portrait painter, 36 Leadenhall st
Fisher Joseph, stationer, 5 Throgmorton st
Fisher King, carver & gilder, 16 President st. east, King sq
Fisher Louis Adolph. art. flor. 9 Constitution row, Gray's in. rd
Fisher Luke, coal merchant, 10 York st. Blackfriars road
Fisher Luke, coal merchant, Davies's Palace wharf, Lambth
Fisher Marker, tailor, 19½ Broadwall, Blackfriars
Fisher Nathaniel, bootmaker, 14 Moor st. Soho square
Fisher Richard, attorney, 35 Queen square, Bloomsbury
Fisher Richard Trott, barrister, 3 Stone bldgs. Lincoln's inn
Fisher Robt. Alex. special pleader, 1 Church yd. ct. Temple
Fisher Robert James, chemist & druggist, 76 New Bond st
Fisher Samuel, dressing case manuf. & cutler, 188 Strand
Fisher Samuel, livery stable keeper, 25 Foley place
Fisher Samuel, solicitor, Merchant Tailors' hall
Fisher Sarah (Mrs.), stay ma. 8 Barrossa ter. Cambridge hth
Fisher Sophia (Mrs.), dyer, &c. 55 Grosvenor st
Fisher Thomas, baker, 15 Moor st. Soho
Fisher Thomas, bookbinder, 1 Hanway st. Oxford st
Fisher Thomas, bookseller, &c. 2 Postern row, Tower hill
Fisher Thomas, butcher, 6 Wellington st. Blackfriars road
Fisher Thomas, dealer in fire wood, 44 Albion st. Rotherhithe
Fisher Thomas, fruiterer, 11 St. George's pl. Walworth road
Fisher Thomas, grocer & cheesemonger, & agent to Sun fire office, 261 Poplar High st
Fisher Thomas, shipwright & boat builder, Mill wall, Poplar
Fisher Thomas John, barrister, 1 Church yd. court, Temple
Fisher Thos. Sam. linendraper, 88 Edgware rd. Marylebone
Fisher Timothy, who. tea & coffee dealer, 5 St. Swithin's lane
Fisher Wm. artist, 4 Cork st. Bond st
Fisher Wm. boot & shoemaker, 50 Gt. Carlisle st. Portmn. mkt
Fisher Wm. cab proprietor, 30 Lisson grove north, New rd
Fisher Wm. clerk of the market, 48 Newgate market
Fisher Wm. currier & leatherseller, 16 Dover pl. New Kent rd
Fisher Wm. *Elephant & Castle inn*, Newington butts
Fisher Wm. glass cutter, 5 James st. Oxford st
Fisher Wm. gun & pistol maker, 9 Belvedere road, Lambeth
Fisher Wm. *Portland coffee house*, 1 Little Marylebone st
Fisher Wm. oil & colorman, 7 Love lane, Eastcheap
Fisher Wm. silk broker, 7 Union court, Old Broad st
Fisher Wm. solicitor, 2 Verulam buildings, Gray's inn
Fisher Wm. solicitor to the *Argus Insurance Company*, 19 Doughty st. Mecklenburgh sq
Fisher Wm. *Sun & 13 Cantons* P.H. 21 Great Pulteney st
Fisher Wm. upholsterer, see Taylor & Fisher
Fisher Wm. Alex. timber stave & tar brok. 22 Change alley
Fisher's (Captain) Almshouses (Jacob Herbert, sec.), Mile end road
Fisher Wm. Windsor, solicitor, 3 King st. Cheapside
Fishleigh Geo. *Coach & Horses* P.H. & livery stable keeper, 71 Bartholomew close
Fishmongers' Hall (William Beckwith Towse, clerk), Adelaide place, London bridge
Fishmongers' & Poulterers' Asylum, Committee rooms, 164 Fleet st
ishwick Holdsworth, accountant, 22 Up. Islington ter
Fishwick John, lead merchant, see Champion, Fishwick & Co
Fisk Frederick, boot closer, 90 Bartholomew close
Fisk Hen. fixture dlr. 15 & 16 Chalcroft ter. New cut, Lambeth
Fisk John, back lead point ma. 16 Brittania ter. City road
Fisk John, plumber & glazier, 41 Thanet st. Burton crescent
Fisk John Lee, cheesemonger, 19 Skinner st. Somers town
Fisk Mary Ann (Mrs.), dressma. 10 Providence pl. Kentish tn
Fisk William, artist, 13 Howland st. Fitzroy sq
Fitch Charles, grocer & cheesemon. 33 New Glos'ter st. Hoxton
Fitch Geo. & Son, purveyors of dairy provisions, 66 Bshgt. wthn
Fitch & Morison, plumbers, &c. 35 Carey st. Lincoln's inn
Fitch Augusta (Miss), seminary, 27 Pelham rd. Brompton
Fitch Edwd. *Winchester Arms* P.H. Grove, Gt. Guildford st. Bo
Fitch Fredk. silversmith & jeweller, 18 High st. Marylebone
Fitch George, attorney & solicitor; solicitor & secretary to the metropolitan & provincial legal association, 15 New Bridge st
Fitch George, watchmaker, 18 Redcross st. Cripplegate
Fitch Henry, cooper & dealer in british & foreign plait, 29½ Cannon st. road, St. George's east
Fitch Henry, vellum binder, 58 Watling st
Fitch James, beer seller, 45B, Dean st. Soho
Fitch James, whipmaker, 57 St. Mary axe
Fitch John, builder & bricklayer, 7 Queen st. Golden square
Fitch John, oil & colorman, 54 London wall
Fitch John Henry, solr. & sup. registrar, 17 Union st. Boro'
Fitch John Robert, jeweller & jewel agent, 51 Hatton garden
Fitch Sarah (Miss), ladies' school, 58 Gloucester pl. Prtm. sq
Fitch Wm. carpenter & builder, 11 Michael's grove, Brompton
Fitch Wm. stationer & paper hang. mnfr. see Imray & Fitch
Fitch Wm. undertaker & dep. reg. 48 Carey st. Lincoln's inn
Fitchet David, carpenter, 30 Trinity square, Tower hill
Fitchett Henry, grocer, 110 Eastfield st. Limehouse fields
Fitchett Jacob, *George* IV. P.H. 34 King st. ter. New North rd
Fitchew Joseph, saddler & harness ma. 61 Bridge rd. Lambeth
Fitchew Wm. silversmith & silver worker, 400 Oxford st
Fitkin John, patent truss maker, 72 Old st. road
Fitkin Robert, hat block maker, 16 Bacon st. Bethnal green
Fitkin William, dentist, 108 Fleet st
Fitt George, railway grease ma. Wilmer grdns. Hoxton Old tn
Fitt Jas. sen. lard ma. 4 Wilmer gardens, Hoxton Old town
Fitt Samuel, pipe maker, 4 William st. Whitechapel
Fitter Thos. gasfitter, 10 Ferguson's rents, Snow's fields
Fittis Mary A. (Mrs.), toy wareho. 196 Wellington ter. Wtrlo. rd
Fittock Ellen (Mrs.), grocer, 35 Broomfield place, Deptford
Fitzer John & Wm. Hen. coopers, 6 Foster st. North st. Wtcpl. rd
Fitzer Francis, brassfounder, 9 Clerkenwell close
Fitzgerald Alexr. whitelead & color manufr. 43 Milbank st
Fitzgerald Charles, daguerreotype plate polisher, 5 Newcastle st. Farringdon st
Fitzgerald Daniel, fruiterer, 32 Frederick pl. Hampstead rd
Fitzgerald Edmund, soap maker, 131 Golden lane, St. Luke's
Fitzgerald George, *Crown* P.H. 38 Silver st. Golden square
Fitzgerald George Wm. attorney, 2 Laurence Pountney hill
FitzGerald Henry, coal mercht. Commercial road, Lambeth
Fitzgerald James (Mrs.), corset mak. 16 Newman st. Oxford st
Fitzgerald James, undertaker, 106 Gt. Saffron hill, Hat. gar
Fitz Gerald John, timber mercht. Commercial rd. Lambeth
Fitzgerald John Alley, dyer, 42 Marchmont st. Brunswick sq
Fitzgerald Michael, surveyor, 12 Buckingham st. Strand
Fitzgerald Michael Dillon, M.D. surgeon, 57 High st. St. Giles'
Fitzgerald Stephen Jas. short hand writer, 53 Chancery lane
Fitzgerald Thos. H. D. iron mercht. 9 Laurence Pountney lane
FitzGerald Wm. Rt. S. barrister. Church porch cham. Temple
Fitz Gibbon Thos. grocer & cheesemonger, 16 King st. Boro'
Fitzherbert Edward Herbert, barrister, 1 Paper buildings
Fitzherbert Wm. physician, 1 Paper bldgs. Temple
Fitzhugh Mark, grocer, 25 President st. east, King sq
Fitzmaurice George Lionel, surgeon, 97 Gloucester place
Fitzpatrick Ann & Maria, straw hat makers, 1 Cranbourne st
Fitzpatrick Alice (Miss), milliner, 9 Cranbourne st. Leicester sq
Fitzpatrick Catherine (Mrs.), milliner, 34 Gt. Portland st
Fitzpatrick Francis, surgeon & chemist, 27 Upper Lisson st
Fitzpatrick Henry James, solicitor, 3 Cook's court, Carey st. & 1 Cranbourne st. Leicester square
Fitzpatrick James, barrister, 2 New Temple bdgs. Mitre ct
Fitzpatrick John, bootmaker, 2 Green st. Bethnal green
Fitzpatrick Mary A. (Mrs.), plumasier, 2 Stanhope st. Claremkt
Fitzpatrick Sarah (Mrs.), fruiterer, 113 Gt. Portland st
Fitzpatrick Wm. R. barrister, 1 Elm court, Temple
Fixsen John Fredk. & Co. wholes. grocers, 35 Queen st. City
Flack Abraham, livery stables, 7 Thornton pl. Portman sq
Flack Charlotte (Miss), toy dealer, 2 Sidney pl. Chelsea
Flack Geo. Danl. builder, 6 Bretton ter. King's rd. west, Chelsea
Flack Geo. M. ivoryturn. 1 St. Martin's pl. St. Martin's le grand
Flack Jas. fruiterer, 18 Colonnade, Greville st. Brunswick sq
Flack Jas. oil & colorman, 266 Bethnal Green road

Flack James, *Red Lion* P.H. Church st. Stoke Newington
Flack Jas. Chas. wax & tallow chandler, oilman, &c. 142 Kingsland road, & 6 Wellington pl. Back rd. St. Geo. east
Flack John, butcher, Nelson place, Old Kent road
Flack John, marine store dealer, 32 Broad st. Lambeth
Flack Joseph, *Ben Jonson* P.H. 24 Gt. Wild st. Drury lane
Flack Joseph, grocer, 34 Up. Salisbury pl. Lock's fields
Flack Lydia(Mrs.), furn. bro. 81 Gt. Saffron hill, Hat. gardn
Flack Thomas, builder, Little Chelsea
Flack Westwood, butcher, 183 Up.Whitecross st. St. Luke's
Fladgate, Young & Jacksons', solicitors, 12 Essex st. Strand
Fladgate John, oporto merchant, see Taylor, Fladgate & Co
Fladgate Wm.Mark,solicitor,seeClarke,Fynmore & Fladgate
Flagg Henry, *Greyhound* P.H. 7 New Compton st. Soho
Flagg Robert, *Red Lion* P.H. 4 Houghton st. Clare market
Flaig, Valentine & Co. clockmakers, 39 Kingsland road
Flamant Edmond, commission agent, 7 Red Lion square
Flanagan Wm.&Son, seedsmen & florists, 9 Mansion house st
Flanagan Thomas, slater, 1 Shepperton st. New North road
FlannaganEdw.*GrosvenorArms*P.H. 26George st.Grsvnr.sq
Flandell Thos. grocer & coal merch. 10 James' pl. Hackney rd
Flanders John, baker, 2 Pearson st. Kingsland road
Flanders Thomas, pressmaker, millwright & carpenter, 5 William st. Curtain road, Shoreditch
Flashman & Ford, soda water manufacturers, Halkin wharf, Lower Belgrave place
Flather John, barrister, 24 Old square, Lincoln's inn
Flather Thos. mercht.9 Lady Lake's grove, Mile end turnpike
Flather Thomas, packing case maker, 17 Dowgate hill
Flather Thomas Tertius, oil & italian warehouse, 5 Middle Queen's buildings, Knightsbridge
Flavell James, dyer & scourer, 143 Houndsditch
Flavell Thomas William, solicitor, see Dyson & Flavell
Flavell William, bent timber manuf. 16 Parker st. Drury la
Flawn George, *Phœnix* P.H. 159 Brick lane, Spitalfields
Flaws Alex. gold & silver lace weaver, 28 York st. Westminr
Flaxman & Showell, tailors, 40 Ludgate st
Flaxman John Henry, tailor, 13 Wilson st. Gray's inn road
Flaxman Robert, carpenter & undertaker, 29 Fetter lane
Flaxman Robert, painter, &c. 10 Brooks mews, Davies st
Flawn Charles, beer retailer, 15 Sidney st. Commercial road
Fleay Charles, brush ma. 2 Margaret ter. Paddington green
Fleay John Goss, linendraper, 19 & 20 Deptford broadway
Fleck Andrew, tailor, &c. see Ridler & Fleck
Fleck John, baker, 29 Leigh st. Burton crescent
Fleck Philip, baker, 41 Silver st. Golden square
Fleck William, coffee rooms, 37 Little Queen st. Holborn
FleckneyEliz.(Mrs.), *O.Duke'sHead*P.H. Lr.Fore st. Lmbth
Fleet Brothers, wholesale sugar dealers, 141 Fenchurch st
Fleet Benj. soda water ma. 6½Apollo bdgs.nth.East st.Walwth
Fleet George, dairy, 1 Northampton st. Lower rd. Islington
Fleet John, oil & italian warehouse, 13 Gt. Winchester st
Fleetham Robert, provision mercht. 20 Beer lane, Tower st
Fleetwood Chas. stock & share broker, 3 Bank chambers
Fleetwood George, surgeon, 9 Connaught ter. Edgware rd
Fleetwood George, tailor, 2 William st. Regent's park
Fleetwood Thomas, appraiser, 16 Coldbath sq. Clerkenwell
Flemen Wm. haircutter, &c. 1 Orange row, Kennington rd
Fleming & Drane, boys' school, 3 James pl. Hoxton fields
Fleming MatthiasJ.&Wm.A.carpenters,7Crown ct.Pall mall
Fleming Wm. Hen. & Co.ale&porter brewers,Camberwell grn
Fleming Chas. who. furrier, 4 Knowles ct. Doctors' commons
Fleming David, *Ship* P.H. 46 Old Gravel lane, Wapping
Fleming Elizh. (Miss),school,12 Shepperton pl.NewNorth rd
Fleming George, lighterman, 6 East lane, Bermondsey
Fleming Gilbert, optician, 36 King st. Holborn
Fleming Isabella (Miss), pawnbroker, 78 Farringdon st.; 32 St. Martin's lane; & 1 Lower John st. Golden square
Fleming James, barrister, 25 Old square, Lincoln's inn
Fleming James, painter, &c. 73 Margaret st. Wilmington sq
Fleming James, saddler & harness mak. 261 Tottenham ct.rd
Fleming Jane (Mrs.), dining rooms, 23 Stangate, Lambeth
Fleming John, quadrant, &c. maker, 191 Ratcliff highway
Fleming Joseph,jeweller & pearl worker,5George st. Adelphi
Fleming Joseph Staples, cheesemonger, High st. Deptford
Fleming Matt.Jackson,cabint. mak.2 Back rd.St.George's ea
Fleming Richard, stationer, 71 Freeschool st. Horselydown
Fleming Sam.Hudson,boot & shoema.101 High st.Camden tn
Fleming Thomas Brandon, solicitor, 1 Trinity sq. Borough
Fleming Wm. beer retailer, Southampton st. Camberwell
FlemmingJsph.accountbook mak. 3 Salters'hall ct.Cannon st
Flemyng Robert Stewart, wine merchant, 21 Queen st. City, & 1 New court, St. Swithin's lane
Fletcher, Alexander, & Co. east india agents, 10 King's Arms yard, Moorgate st
Fletcher Hen. & George, army clothiers,&c.128 New Bond st
Fletcher Hen. Son & Fearnall, ship builds. Union dk. Limeho
Fletcher Mary&Son,coopers,11Bread st.hill&10 O.Fish st.hll
Fletcher David & Son, gram. school, Denmark hill, Cambrwl
Fletcher & Phillips, milliners, 18 Wells row, Islington
Fletcher Chas. watch & clock maker, 131 Regent st
Fletcher Chas.E.plumber.18 York st.Charlotte st.Commer.rd
Fletcher Edward, baker, 10 Chalton st. Somers town
Fletcher Edwn. coal & potato dlr. 3 & 4 King's hd. ct. Shoe la
Fletcher Elizabeth (Mrs.), linendraper,21High rd. Knightsbri
Fletcher Ermine S. (Mrs.), statnr. 1 Victoria pl. Dalston
Fletcher Esau, grocer, &c. 62 Albany road, Camberwell
Fletcher George, engineer, 38 Glo'ster st. Oakley st.Lambeth
Fletcher George, hairdresser, 2 Bishop's ct. Chancery lane
Fletcher George, wood dealer, New row, Deptford
Fletcher Hannah(Mrs.),hairdresser,7Lt.Charlot.st.Tot.ct.rd
Fletcher Henry, bookseller, &c. see Relfe & Fletcher
Fletcher Henry, butcher, 7 Thomas st. Oxford st
Fletcher Hugh, carpenter, Hartshorn court, Basing lane
Fletcher Jas. plumber&brassfounder,32 Hart st.Bloomsbury
Fletcher John, baker, 12 Nassau st. Soho
Fletcher John, book auctioneer, 191 Piccadilly
Fletcher John, dairyman, 48 Gt. James st. Lisson grove
Fletcher John, eel pie house, 7 Salisbury st. Lisson grove
Fletcher John, grocer, 27 Thayer st. Manchester square
Fletcher John, hairdresser, 24 Back Church lane
Fletcher John, *King's Arms* P.H. 84 Three Colt st. Limeho
Fletcher John, tailor, 16 Lit. Portland st. Gt. Portland st
Fletcher John, watch & chrono. ma. 27 Davies st.Berkeley sq
Fletcher John B. surgeon dentist, 17 New Burlington st
Fletcher John Dunnington,special pleader,5 Essex ct.Temple
Fletcher Joseph, wharfinger,Wheatsheaf whf. 233 Wapping
Fletcher Lot, carman, 160 Brick lane, Spitalfields
Fletcher Martha (Mrs.), baker, 80 Brewer st. Somers town
Fletcher MaryA.(Miss), seminary, 43 Broomfields,Deptford
Fletcher Richard, law stationer, 51 Bedford row
Fletcher Robert, solicitor, 22 Finsbury square
Fletcher Samuel, pawnbroker, 17 York row, Kennington rd
Fletcher Sarah (Miss), law stationer, 14 Gt. Knightrider st
Fletcher Sarah(Mrs.), milliner, 26 Shoemaker row,Blackfrs
Fletcher Tempest, fruiterer, 35 Bartholomew ter. St. Luke's
Fletcher Thomas, butcher, 177 Kingsland road
Fletcher Thomas, fruiterer, 4 Oxford market, Oxford st
Fletcher Wm. beer retailer, Nine elms, Vauxhall
Fletcher Wm. butcher, 6A, Oxford market, Oxford st
Fletcher Wm. dairyman, 14 Paddington st. Marylebone
Fletcher Wm. fruiterer, 21 Francis st. Tottenham court rd
Fletcher Wm. italian wareho. see Lega,Zumbelli, & Fletcher
Fletcher Wm. lamp maker & bronzist, 51 Hatton garden
Fletcher Wm. linen & woollen draper, hosier, haberdasher, laceman & carpet warehouseman, 168& 169 High Holborn (corner of Museum st)
Fletcher Wm. undertaker, 5 Byde's place, Shoreditch
Fletcher Wm. Cosier, wholesale stationer, see Parsons, Fletcher & Co
Fletcher Wm. Evans, school, see Fletcher, David & Son
Fletcher Wm. Fras. scale maker, 9 Osborn st. Whitechapel
Fleury, Sebastian & Co. egg merchants, 37 Stoney st. Boro'
Fleury Charles, pastry cook, 10 London ter. Hackney rd
Flew William, pianoforte maker, 6 North st. Lambeth
Flexman John, chandler's shop, 15 Sidney st. Goswell road
Flexon Madame, ladies' hairdresser, 13 George st. Portm. sq
Flexton Charles, *Cock* P.H. 72 Tothill st. Westminster
Fley Henry, printer, see Bentley, Wilson & Fley
Flick Eliza & Susan(Misses),lace wa. 136 St.Alb. pl.Edgw.rd
Flick Wm. fancy repository, 3 Clark's pl. High st. Islington
Flies Julian, tailor, 55 Frith st. Soho
Fligh John, boot & shoemaker, 5 Praed st. Paddington
Flight & Barr, royal porcelain works, see Chamberlain & Co
Flight Benjamin & Son, church & chamber organ & self-acting apollonicon builders, 16 King William st. Strand
Flight Charles & Co. tailors & habit makers, 32 Pall mall
Flight Alex. Richd. bookbinder, 20 Chalton st. Somers town
Flight Edward, bootmaker, 12 Salisbury st. Lisson grove
Flight Edward Gill, solicitor, 1 Adam st. Adelphi
Flight Josiah, tailor, 40 Union st. Borough High st
Flight Thomas, merchant, 3 Bond court house, Walbrook
Flight Wm. boot & shoe ma. 62 New Church st. Lisson gr
Flindell Thos. plumber & glazier, 31 Union st. Clarendon sq
Flindt Gustavus & Son, exchange broker, Baltic coffeehouse
Flinley Fredk. beer retailer, 6 Clayton st. Kennington
Flinn Edwd. coal & potato dealer, 39 Laystall st. Liqrpd. st
Flinn James, grosvenor slate works, 14 Belgrave ter. Pimlico
Flinn John Peter, auctioneer, 53 Wigmore st. Cavendish sq
Flinn Robert, beer seller, 11 Old Compton st. Soho
Flint Alfred & Edmund, shoemakers, 46 King st. Snowhill
Flint Algernon L. & Co. manfrs. & warehmn. 35Wood st. City

Flint & Smith, beaver & french hat manufactrs. 11 Castle st Southwark, and 60 Roupell st
Flint & Steel, boot & shoemakers, 311 High Holborn
Flint Abrh. Aug. sec. Birmingham & Manchester Railway Company, 1 Moorgate
Flint Alex. cabinetmaker & spirit mercht. 67 St. Martin's la
Flint Ann (Mrs.), hot & cold baths, 4 Piccadilly
Flint Ann (Mrs.), picture dealer & bookbinder, 4 Piccadilly
Flint Ebenezer, hosier & general outfitter, 48 Ludgate hill
Flint Geo. auctioneer & valuer, 112 Edgware rd. Marylebone
Flint Henry, engraver & door plate maker, 122 Drury lane
Flint Henry, hosier & glover, 120 Leadenhall st
Flint John, baker, 8 Artillery passage, Bishopsgate
Flint Matthew, linendraper & librdshr. 63 Blackfriars road
Flint Thomas, hosier, glover & outfitter, 337 Oxford st
Flint Thomas, lace manufacturer, 40 Friday st
Flintan Wm. Houghton, engine oil & varnish maker, 8 Miles lane, Upper Thames st. & Windmill lane, Camberwell rd
Flintoff Harriet Ann (Mrs.), dressma. 15 Store st. Bedfd. sq
Flintoff James Henry, chemist, 73 Gt. Titchfield st
Flintoff Thomas, surgeon, 73 Gt. Titchfield st. Oxford st
Flitton Elizab. (Mrs.), tobacconist, 13 St. Martin's le grand
Float Jonathan, dairy, 13 Upper area, Hungerford market
Flockhart James, merchant, see Coleman, Flockhart & Co
Flockton Webster & Thos. M. turpentine & tar distillers, & seed crushers, Potter's fields, Horseldn. & Weybridge, Surrey
Flockton George, surgeon, 1 Cambridge ter. Edgware road
Flockton Stephen, russia broker, 1 Hatton court & Baltic
Flood Fanny (Mrs.), seminary, 20 South ter. Alexander sq
Flood Frederick Solly, barrister, 1 Pump court, Temple & St. John's lodge, 8 Alpha road, Regent's park
Flood Henry, tailor, 36 John st. Fitzroy square
Flood James, upholsterer, 11 Charles st. Middlesex hospital
Flood William, dairyman, 5 Everett st. Brunswick sq
Flook James Freek, booksel. & statr. 85 Charlotte st. Fitzroy sq
Flook Silas Freek, law stationer, 14 Cursitor st. Chancery la
Florance Robert, coachmaker, 6 Long acre
Florance Wm. Adams, brewer, 9 Kent place, Old Kent rd
Florence John Hen. colonial & commissn. mercht. 10 Mark lane
Florence John Hen. & Co. distillers, rectifiers, capillaire manufacturers, & importers of dantzic spruce, Bishopsgate distillery, 37 Skinner st. Bishopsgate
Floris Elizbth. (Mrs.), combmaker to her Majesty, 88 Jermyn st
Floud Henry Scott & Co. indigo brokers, 39 Mincing lane
Flower Philip Wm. & Co. new south wales mers. 29 Buckler sb
Flower Alex. engineer & millwright, 4 Holland st. Blkfrs. rd
Flower Ann (Miss), embroiderer to the Queen, 25 Duke st. Grosvenor square
Flower Arthur, auctioneer & estate agent, 5 New Bridge st
Flower Benjamin, fruiterer, 5 Barnsbury st. Islington
Flower Edmund, plumber, &c. 28 Marsham st. Westminster
Flower Edward, solicitor, 69 Chancery lane
Flower George, fishmonger, 88 Harrow road, Paddington
Flower George, hat dyer, 97 Gt. Guildford st. Borough
Flower Hen. district surveyor, 23 Princes sq. St. George's east, & 18 Barge yard chambers, Bucklersbury
Flower James, *Bunch of Grapes* P.H. 100 Fore st. Limehouse
Flower James, *Canterbury Arms* P.H. Lambeth upper marsh
Flower Jane (Mrs.), milliner, 11 Artillery st. Bishopsgate
Flower John, grocer, &c. 32 Upper Jubilee pl. Comml. rd. east
Flower John, merchant, 29 Bucklersbury
Flower John, teadealer & grocer, 22 Fore st. Cripplegate
Flower John Swan, surgeon, 4 Terrace, Camberwell green
Flower John Wickham, solicitor, 61 Bread st. Cheapside
Flower Rachael (Miss), milliner, see Moore & Flower
Flower Samuel, fruiterer, 78 East st. Manchester sq
Flower Thomas, attorney, 96 Hatton garden
Flower Thos. straw bonnet pres. 3 Chapel st. Holywell mount
Flower Thos. who. staym. 4 St. George's st. Albany rd. O. Kent rd
Flower Wm. carman & coal dealer, 22 Cornwall rd Lambeth
Flower William, solicitor, see Gadsden & Flower
Flowerday Jsph. coal dlr. 11 Lit. Chesterfield st. Marybne. st
Flowerday Joseph, pork butcher, 17 Pitfield st. Hoxton
Flowerday Robt. grocer & oilman, 4 Surrey pl. Wandswth rd
Flowerdew William, oilman, 50 Whitmore road, Hoxton
Flowers Farnham & Henry, *New River Head* P.H. Limeh. cut
Flowers Charles, butcher, 77 Church lane, Whitechapel
Flowers Ed. cheesemonger, 2 Claremont row, Barnsbury rd
Flowers Elizh. (Mrs.), chandler's shop, 9 Cheshire st. Bthnl gn
Flowers Farnham, *King's Arms* P.H. 4 High st. Bow
Flowers Frederick, barrister, 2 Elm court, Temple
Flowers Geo. French, bachelor of music, 3 Keppel st. Rusl sq
Flowers Henry, carver & gilder, 74 Tooley st
Flowers James, perfumer, 17 Charles st. Manchester sq
Flowers John B. *Prince of Wales* P.H. 29 Elizabeth st. Eaton sq
Flowers Jonthn. A. *White Hart* P.H. 1 King Edwd. st. Newg. st

Floyd Arthur, bricklayer, 10 George st. Portman square
Floyd Elizabeth (Mrs.), butcher, Church st. Deptford
Floyd Frederick William, hosier, 55 Bishopsgate within
Floyd John, *City Arms* P.H. 10 Garlick hill
Floyd Maria (Mrs.), wardrobe dealer, 10 George st. Portmn. sq
Floyd Robert, coal merchant, 15 Stepney causeway & Ratcliff wharf, Ratcliff cross
Floyd William, van proprietor, 55 Lower George st. Chelsea
Flude Thomas Saville, wine & spirit broker, 60 Mark lane
Fluder George, solicitor, 1 Egremont place, King's cross
Fluister Wm. coffee rooms, 62 Union st. Borough High st
Flynn Daniel, tailor, 7 Addle hill, Doctors' commons
Flynn George, cheesemonger, 144 Kingsland road
Flynn Thomas, tailor, 76 Goswell st
Foa Octave, merchant, 7 Throgmorton st. City
Foale John, sawmaker, 10 Church lane, Whitechapel
Foan Jas. leatherpipe & bucket ma. 158 Alfred pl. Waterloo rd
Foard Edward, *Old Parr's Head* P.H. 1 Cross st. Islington
Foay Hannah (Mrs.), french stay wareho. see Binnie & Foay
Foden Strethill, architect, see Savage and Foden
Fogarty Fred. Wm. M.D. surgeon, 31 Gt. Percy st. Clerkenwell
Fogerty John & Son, coal & coke mers. 34 Charles st. Drury la
Fogg James, *Ben Jonson's Hd.* P.H. Goodman's yd. Minories
Fogg Richard, gold beater, 5 New Church st. west, Edgware rd
Fogg Thos. bldg. material dlr. 137 Edgware rd. Marylebone
Fogg Thomas, rag & bottle dealer, 12 New Compton st. Soho
Foggo David, sec. to *European Life In. Co.* 10 Chatham pl
Foggo Francis Alexander, solicitor, 14 Craven st. Strand
Foggo George, artist, 62 Upper Norton st. Fitzroy square
Folbigg Mary (Mrs.), beer retailer, 99 Bunhill row
Foletti Michael, looking glass, barometer & thermometer manufacturer, 88 Curtain road, Shoreditch
Foley Edward, *Coach & Horses* P.H. Stoke Newington green
Foley Edwd. Alfred, sculptor, 38A, Edward st. Hampstead rd
Foley James Geo. builder, 1 Old Norland ter. Notting hill
Foley John Henry, sculptor, 38A. Edward st. Hampstead rd
Foley Jsph B. ship & ins. brok. Colnl. chbs. 4 John st. Minories
Foley Susan (Miss), milliner & dressmaker, 13 Vere st.
Foley Thaddeus, sec. to *Mar. & Genl. Life Ass.* 5 Arthur st. east
Foligno Edward, silversmith, 12 Bury st. St. Mary Axe
Foligno Isaac, dealer in plate, 16 Finsbury circus
Folkard Richd. & Joseph C. pawnbrokers, 192 Lambeth walk
Folkard Alfred Wm. Harris, pawnbroker, 1 Uptn. pl. Com. rd. ea
Folkard Anthony, *Gen. Graham* P.H. 11 Silver st. Clerknwl
Folkard Baxter, tailor, &c. 69 Jermyn st. St. James
Folkard Charles, seal engraver, 46 Hatton garden
Folkard Edmund, tea dealer, 40 Drury lane
Folkard Frederick, pawnbroker, 160 Blackfriars road
Folkard George, navy agent, see Holmes & Folkard
Folkard James Richman, *City Arms* P.H. 49 West sq. Lambth
Folkard John Cope, pawnbroker, 16 London rd. Southwark
Folkard J. Christmas, pawnbroker, 14 New Bridge st. Vauxhl
Folkard Rd. printer, 22 Devonshire st. Queen sq. Bloomsbury
Folkard Wm. cattle salesman, 17 West Smithfield
Folkard Wm. A. engraver, see Wright and Folkard
Folkes Joseph, butcher, 4 Halfmoon passage, Leadenhl. mkt
Folkes Thomas, baker, 19 Crisp street, East india rd. Poplar
Folkner John, tin plate worker, Mile end rd. near Wades pl
Follenfant John, optician, 6 Fieldgate st. Whitechapel
Follet Armondine (Madame), milliner, 49 Conduit st
Follet Peter N. silk mercer, 49 Conduit st. Regent st
Follett, Hooper & Co. wine merchants, Philpot lane
Follett Brent Spencer, barrister, 22 Old square, Lincoln's inn
Follett John, official assignee, 1 Sambrook court, City
Follett Saml. coffee & dining rooms, 30 Market st. Millbk. st
Follit Frederick, tobacconist, 219 Oxford st
Follit John, publisher & printseller, 22 St. Martin's court
Follit Wm. reposty. of arts, printslr. & publishr. 63 Fleet st
Fonblanque John Wm. Martin, barrister, 30 Chancery lane
Fonseca, Monteiro, Guimaraens & Co. merchts. 42 Crutchedfrs
Fontaine Ferdinand, berlin wa. 18 Mortimer st. Cavendish sq
Fontaine Wm. tallowchandler, soapmaker, & oilman, East st. Hoxton; 37 Chichester place, Gray's inn road; 10 Vere st. Clare market; 12 Lower st. Islington; 28 & 29 Brick lane, St. Luke's; 189 Hoxton old town; 36 Barbican; 2 Church st. Shoreditch; 41 London rd. Bermondsey New town; 1 Elizabeth ter. Hackney road; & 1 Charlotte rw. Walworth rd
Fontanier Joseph, undertaker, 70A, Salisbury st. Lisson grove
Fooks Charles B. estate agent, surveyor & auctioneer, 1 Serle st. Lincoln's inn
Fooks William Cracroft, barrister, 30 Chancery lane
Fooks Woodforde, barrister, 3 Figtree court, Temple
Foord John & Sons, plumbers, 5 Palace new road, Lambeth
Foord Elizh. Mary (Mrs.), carver & gilder, 90 Wardour st. Soho
Foord James, engraver & printer, 7 Little Chapel st. Soho

Foord John Bromley, agent to British & North American royal mail steam ships, 52 Old Broad st. City
Foord Moses, carpenter, 200 Kent st. Borough
Foord Thomas Jennings, solicitor, 7 & 8, Pinner's hall, City
Foot Ann (Mrs.), carman & fruiterer, 29 Windmill st. Finsby.sq
Foot C. (Mrs.), & Co. manuf. chemists, acetous &c. acid & white lead color & varnish, Bolingbroke gdns. Battersea
Foot Joseph & Son, silk manufacturers, 38 Spital square
Foot Edwd. Smith, saddler, 8 Gt. Woodstock st. Marylebone
Foot Elizh. Mary Ann (Mrs.), *Raven & Sun* P.H. Russell st. Berm
Foot George, linendraper, 19 Warwick st. Belgrave road
Foot James Abraham, barrister, 5 Brick court, Temple
Foot John, plumber & glazier, 2 Gt. Woodstock st. Marylebone
Foot Martha (Mrs.), *Tippling Phlphr.* P.H. 40 Liquorpond st
Foot Peter, *Hand & Marigold* P.H. Star corner, Bermondsey
Foot (Mrs.), carman & fruiterer, 29 Windmill st. Finsbury
Foot Robert, fruiterer, Church st. Stoke Newington
Foot Robert, shoemaker, 180 Church st. Shoreditch
Foot William, chemist, 8 Lower Eaton st. Grosvenor pl
Foot William, coal merchant, see Fowler & Foot
Foot William, wig ma. & hair cutter, 12 Finch lane, Cornhill
Foote Edwd. coach painter, 11 Southampton mews, Euston sq
Foote John, surgeon, &c. 36 Tavistock st. Covent garden
Foote Keppel, merchant, 35 Seething lane
Foothead Henry Hugh, wholesale milliner, 16 London wall
Footner & Son, ship & commercial agents, 31 Botolph la
Footner C. (Mrs.), theatrical wig ma. 23 Princes st. Druryla
Foottit Charles, tobacconist, 182 Whitechapel road
Foottit Gervase, color & varnish maker, 138 Rotherhithe st
Forbes, Browne & Young, surgeons, 7 St. George's place, Camberwell, & Camberwell green
Forbes, Chirney & Hutchison, shawl wareho. 40 Friday st
Forbes & Drake, solicitors, 8 Warnford ct. Throgmorton st
Forbes, Forbes & Co. east india agents, 9 King Wm. st. City
Forbes John & James, perfumers, 146 Sloane st. Chelsea
Forbes Andrew, ship broker, see Miller, Forbes & Thomson
Forbes Sir Chas. Fergusson, K.C.H. physician, 23 Argyll st.
Forbes Duncan, prof. of languages, 58 Burton crescent
Forbes Elizh. (Mrs.), chandler's shop, 1 Cook's ter. St. Pancrs
Forbes Henry, cooper, 16 Waterloo st. Camberwell
Forbes Henry, teacher of music, 13 Upper Belgrave place
Forbes John, *Bell* P.H. Bell yard, 5 York st. Westminster
Forbes John, merchant & general agent, 2 Great St. Helen's
Forbes John, physician, 12 Old Burlington st
Forbes John, tailor & draper, 64 High st. Camden town
Forbes John, watchmaker, Hide market Leadenhall market,
Forbes Mary Ann (Miss), dressmaker, 51 South st. Grosvr. sq
Forbes Peter, wine merchant, see Cunningham & Forbes
Forbes Robt. east india agent & ins. brok. 75 O. Broad st. City
Forbes Robert, merchant, see Faith Forbes & Co.
Forbes Robt. jun. ship & ins. bro. & gen. ag. 75 O. Broad st. City
Forbes Wm. grocer, 60 Henry st. east, Avenue road
Forbes William, surgeon, Denmark hill, Camberwell
Force Susannah (Mrs.), tobacconist, 104 Park st. Grosvr. sq
Ford & Gagen, architects & surveyors, 1 Coborn st. Bow rd
Ford Geo. Alex. & Dan. painted table cover mfs. Wilmot sq
Ford Jesse & Thomas, tobacco pipe makers, 15 Wentworth place, Mile end road, & 36 Whitehorse st. Stepney
Ford Saml. & Co. imp. of forn. goods, 14 Tavistock st. Cov. grdn
Ford & Shipway, tailors, 5 Argyll st. Regent st
Ford Geo. John & Sons, printers, 11A, Beech st. Barbican
Ford Thomas & Co. woollen warehousemen, 3 King st. Cheapside, & 31 Ironmonger lane
Ford Wm. Hy. & Son, auctnrs. & uphols. 18 Penton rw. Wal.rd
Ford Alexander, soda water ma. see Flashman & Ford
Ford Andrew, plumber & glazier, 18 Seymour pl. Camden town
Ford Augustus, bootmaker, 4 Gt. Guildford st. Borough
Ford Caroline (Mrs.), *Red Lion* P.H. 20 Gt. Windmill st
Ford Charles, solicitor, 5 Bloomsbury square
Ford Daniel, watch movement ma. 14 Macclesfield st. South
Ford Edward, *Castle* P.H. 3 Portugal st. Lincoln's inn fields
Ford Edward jun, wine mer. & agent, 1 Crooked la. chambers
Ford George, cabinet maker & upholsterer, 22 Clarges st
Ford Geo. Samuel, solicitor, 8 Henrietta st. Covent garden
Ford Henry, architect, 4 Argyle square, New road
Ford Henry, baker, 11 Berwick st. Soho, & 1 Greenland pl. Cromer st
Ford Henry, bootmaker, 2 Water st. Strand
Ford James, architect & surveyor, 4 Argyle sq. New rd
Ford James, baker, 30 Skinner st. Somers town
Ford James, book lock & claspma. 6 Monkwell st. Cripplegate
Ford James, boot & shoe maker, 116 Brook st. Lambeth
Ford James, bricklayer, 24 Baldwin's gardens, Leather lane
Ford James, bricklayer, 8 Britton st. Robert st. Chelsea
Ford James, coffee rooms, 4 Crown st. Walworth road
Ford James, corn & coal dealer, 354 Rotherhithe
Ford Jas. *Ford's hotel*, 13, 14 & 15 Manchester st. Mancher. sq
Ford Jessie Maria (Mrs.), fancy dress ma. 11 Blackfriars rd
Ford Job, dining rooms, 87 Lower Thames st
Ford John, carpenter & builder, 5 St. Alban's st. Lambeth
Ford John, breeches maker & tailor, 29 Surrey st. Strand
Ford John, carpenter & undrtr. 3 Plummer's rw. Whtchpl
Ford John, dairyman, 31 Perceval st. Clerkenwell
Ford John, fruiterer, 7 Roberts pl. Commercial rd. east
Ford John, lamp cotton maker, 4 Milford lane, Strand
Ford John, lodginghouse, 4 & 9 King st. Grosvenor sq
Ford John, patent mastic manufr. 15 Vauxhall bridge road
Ford John, tobacco pipe maker, 28 North st. Pentonville
Ford John, *York* coffee chop ho. & dng rooms, 2 Lawrence la
Ford Joseph, jeweller, 45 Theobald's road, Red Lion square, Holborn
Ford Kanes Jas. bookseller, 6 & 7 Barnsbury pl. Islington
Ford Luke, tobacconist, 45 Chandos st. Covent garden
Ford Matthew, solicitor, see Wharton & Ford
Ford Peter, grocer, 2 Charles st. Grosvenor sq
Ford Richard, plasterer & modeller, Stone ho. Cambridge hth
Ford Richard D. upholsterer, 32 Gt. Carter la. Doctors' com
Ford Robert, oil & italian warehouse, 7 High st. Marylebone
Ford Samuel, grocer, 65½ White Horse st. Commercial road
Ford Simon, carp. & undertaker, 11 Church lane, Whitechpel
Ford Thomas, butcher, 5 Kenton st. Brunswick square
Ford Thos. coachsmith & wheelwright, 18 Wyndham rd. Caml
Ford Thomas, *Crown & Anchor* P.H. St. James's pl. Old Kt. rd
Ford Thomas, plumber, &c. 39 Lambeth walk
Ford Thos. Wm. tobacco pipe ma. 45 Cannon st. Ratcliffe hghwy
Ford William, baker, 49 Old bailey
Ford William, barrister, 1 Essex ct. Temple
Ford Wm. bookbinder, stationer & gum ticket manufacturer, 69 Wood st. Cheapside
Ford Wm. boot & shoe maker, 2 New Bridge st. Vauxhall
Ford Wm. brassfounder, Gun la. Commercial rd. Limehouse
Ford Wm. butcher, 5 Folly, Dockhead, Bermondsey
Ford Wm. card & pill box ma. 9 Oxford Arms pas. Newgate st
Ford Wm. fruiterer, 4 Crawley st. Oakley sq. Somers town
Ford Wm. grocer & teadealer, 29 Chapel st. Holywell mount
Ford Wm. shoemaker, 7 John st. Cambridge heath
Ford Wm. solicitor, see Ranken, Ford, Longbourne & Vickerman
Ford Wm. surgeon, 61 Red Lion st. Holborn
Ford Wm. tailor, 32 Great Carter lane, Doctors' commons
Ford Wm. tailor, 10 Holles st. Cavendish sq
Ford Wm. undertaker, 31 Primrose st. Bishopsgate st
Ford Wm. Augustus, solicitor, 8 Henrietta st. Covent gardn
Ford Wm. Burton, bootmaker, 47 Duke st. Lincoln's inn fi
Ford Wm. Henry, *Duchess of York* P.H. 90 Kingsland road
Ford Wm. Simpson, printseller, &c. 18 Holywell st. Strand
Ford Zechariah, lace manufacturer, 23 Jewin st. Cripplegate
Fordati, Coxhead & Co. merchants 61½ Threadneedle st
Forder Sarah, (Miss), milliner, 34 Grosvenor st. Com. rd. east
Fordham Chas. bricklayer, Cambridge ter. Lr. rd. Islington
Fordham Isaac, emery paper maker, 55 Hatton garden
Fordham James, glass paper ma. 10 Chapel st. Curtain rd
Fordham James, plumber, 11 Jubilee st. Commerl. rd. east
Fordham John, bricklayer, 11½ Merlin place, Spafields
Fordham John, plasterer, 23 Berwick st. Pimlico
Fordham John, wheelwright, Stratford, Essex
Fordham Willam, furniture broker, Well st. Hackney
Foreign Aid Society (Major S. Thorpe, sec.), 10 Exeter hall
Foreign Marriage, Baptism & Burial Reg. 3 Godliman st
Foreign Office, 15, 16 & 17 Downing st
Foreman Ann (Mrs.), fruiterer, 17 Red Lion pass. Red Lion sq
Foreman Frederick, tailor, 76 Long acre
Foreman Geo. *King & Queen* P.H. 25 Chapel st. St. Geo.'s ea
Foreman Geo. whitesmith, 4 Hampstead st. Fitzroy sq
Foreman John, solicitor, 12 Clifford's inn, Fleet st
Foreman Winifred M. (Miss), lace dlr. 47 Bedford st. Cov. gar
Fores (Arthur & Blucher) & Co. publishers, printsellers & frame makers, 41 Piccadilly
Fores Henry Philip, public library, 3 Spur st. Leicester sq
Fores John, auctioneer, 4 King's ter. Commercial rd. east
Fores Mary Ann (Mrs.), lace cleaner, 11 Marylebone st. Gldn. sq
Fores Thomas, cabinet maker, 18 Brokers' row, Redcross st
Forest Robert, slate, stone, cement, lime, brick & tile merchant, Brunswick wharf, Wandsworth road
Forester's Chronicle, 13A, Salisbury sq. Fleet st
Forey William, painter & glazier, 9 North st. Pentonville
Forfar Robt. John, china dealer, 36 Salmon lane, Limehouse
Forgan William & David, bakers, 3 Hatton Garden
Forgart Michael, 3 Thomas st. Oxford st
Forge William, fish salesman, 3 Rood lane, City
Forge Wm. Haggis, fish salesman, 20 Love la. Eastcheap
Forington Mary & Caroline, milliners, 11 Denmk. ter. Pentvl
Forlong Richard, horn & bone button mnfr. 15 Noble st. City

Forman & Hadow, sworn brokers, & gen. agts. 14 Mincing la
Forman David, engraver, 9 Little St. Thomas Apostle
Forman Richard, watchmaker, 35 White's row, Fashion st
Forman Wm. Henry, iron merchant, see Thompson & Forman
Forman Wm. Henry, *Tankard* P.H. 66 Walcot place, East Lambeth, & Brook st. West sq. Lambeth
Forrer Antoine, artist in hair & jewellery to the Queen, 136 Regent st
Forrest George, lamp manufacturer, 12 New st. sq. Fetter la
Forrest James, furniture broker, 1 Brokers alley, Drury lane
Forrest James, tailor, see Kerry & Forrest
Forrest John, jeweller, 5 Pitt st. Fitzroy square
Forrest John, shirtmaker, 26 Gt. Pulteney st. Golden sq
Forrest Richard, nursery & seedsman, Kennington road
Forrest Thomas, lime merchant, wharf, Earl st. Blackfriars
Forrest Thomas, shipowner, 3 Griffin st. Shadwell
Forrest Wm. importer of & dealer in curiosities, 54 Strand
Forrester Charles Robert, notary, 28 Royal Exchange
Forrester George, lath render, Little St. Thomas Apostle
Forrester Henry, glove manuf. see Cresswell & Forrester
Forrester James, baker, 83 Leather lane, Holborn
Forrester John, corndealer, 30 Perceval st. Clerkenwell
Forrester Robt. lodging house, 9 Bell's bldgs. Salisbury sq
Forrester Robt. Miller, hosier & glover, 19 Whitechapel rd
Forrester Thomas M. woollen warehouse, 8 Gresham st. City
Forrester William, baker, 5 Rosoman st. Clerkenwell
Forrester William, jeweller, 32 Marylebone st. Piccadilly
Forrestts Thos. & Wm. boatbuilders, Norway pl. Limehouse
Forrett David, scotch shawl warehouse, see Boyd & Forrett
Forrist Thomas, tobacconist, 8 Temple st. Whitefriars
Forrister Henry, New River turncock, 6 Angel ct. Snowhill
Forrister Joseph, stationer, 184 Wellington ter. Waterloo rd
Forsaith John Smyth, printer, 118 Bethnal green road
Forsaith Josiah, pastry cook, 175 Lambeth walk
Forsaith Thos. engineer & machinist, 53 Paul st. Finsbury
Forsbrey Joseph, meat salesman, 12 Vine court. Spitalfields, & Leadenhall market
Forsbrey Thomas, butcher, 3 Lamb st. Spitalfields
Forscutt Hen. muffin & biscuit baker, 5 George ct. Piccdilly
Forse George, cabinet carver, 18 Tash st. Gray's inn lane
Forse Robert, engraver, 9 Smith st. Somers town
Forsey Charles Wm. carver & gilder, 48 Paul st. Finsbury
Forsey John, cabinet maker, 47 Charles st. Hackney rd
Forshaw Daniel, stationer, see Woollard & Forshaw
Forster & Co. chemists & druggists, 29 Haymarket
Forster, Kennett & Co. wholes. druggists, 29 Haymarket
Forster & Kendrew, cheesemongers, Bow
Forster & Smith, merchants, 5 New city chambers, Bishopsgt
Forster (Matthew) & Co. rice merchants & oil crushers, 5 New city chambers, Bishopsgate within, & Shad Thames
Forster Chas. Fras. undertaker, 19 Devonshire st. Bishopsgate
Forster George, *Duke of Clarence* P.H. 17 Pncrs. pl. Pncrs. rd
Forster Horatio, reed maker, 28 Gun st. Spitalfields
Forster James, coffee rooms, 2 London st. Fenchurch st
Forster James, cowkeeper, 6 Little Pulteney st. Golden st
Forster James A. upholsterer, 9 Gt. Portland st. Oxford st
Forster James Gilson, tailor, 7 Aldgate High st
Forster John, barrister, 58 Lincoln's inn fields
Forster John, beer retailer, 40 Brunswick st. Blackwall
Forster John, merchant, see Sandeman, Forster & Co
Forster John, shipsmith, chain & anchor ma. 63 Low. Shadwell
Forster John, surgeon, 32 Mount st. Lambeth
Forster John, who. tea dealer, see Fergusson & Forster
Forster John Cooper, cabinet maker, 189 Whitechapel road
Forster Martin, solicitor, 3 Laurence Pountney place
Forster Matt. wine mer. & cust. house agent, 5 Beer la. Tower st
Forster Nicholas, chemist & druggist, 105 Holborn hill
Forster Ralph Wm. Elliott, barrister, 4 Stone bdgs. Lin. inn
Forster Robert Edward, artist, 182 Strand
Forster Robert N. accountant, 5 Redman's row, Mile end
Forster Saml. solicitor, see Frere, Forster, Goodford & Co
Forster Simon A. musical instr. ma. 13 Macclesfield st. Soho
Forster Sophia (Mrs.), *Spread Eagle* P.H. Thames bank
Forster Thomas, hairworker, 6 Charlotte st. Fitzroy square
Forster Thomas, mans' mercer, see Brown & Forster
Forster Wm. barrister, 4 Carey st. Lincoln's Inn
Forster Wm. wholesale & ret. teadealer, 5 & 6 Philpot lane
Forsyth Alex. & Co. gunmakers, 8 Leicester st. Leicester sq
Forsyth Andrew, baker, 15 Webber st. Blackfriars road, & 1 Sussex terrace, Hampstead road
Forsyth Elizabeth (Mrs.), orange merc. 121 Lower Thames st
Forsyth George, merchant, 145 Leadenhall st
Forsyth George Robert, *Goldsmiths' Arms* P.H. Goldsmiths' row, Hackney road
Forsyth James, baker, 10 Collingwood st. Blackfriars road
Forsyth John, general commission agent, 8 Gt. Bush lane
Forsyth Osbert, ship & insurance broker, 77 Cornhill
Forsyth Wm. barrister, 1 Paper buildings, Temple
Forsyth Wm. linendraper, 1 Lit. Newport st. Long acre
Forsyth Wm. surgeon & chemist, 455 West Strand
Forsyth Wm. tailor & habit maker, 12 Vere st. Cavendish sq
Fort Brothers & Co. calico printers, 45 Friday st. Cheapside
Fort Gloucester Mills Company, 30 Cornhill
Fort Benjamin, tinman, 5 Copenhagen st. Pentonville
Fort David, appraiser, 39 Booth st. Spitalfields
Fort Harriet (Mrs.), grocer, 1 Marlbro' pl. Kennington cross
Fortens Geo. cooper, turner & toy dlr. 6 Crown row, Mile end rd
Fortescue William & Son, surgeons, 9 Smithfield bars
Fortescue Elizh. (Mrs.), Craven dairy, 46 Queen's rd. Bayswatr
Fortescue James, baker, 5 Grove ter. Queen's rd. Bayswater
Fortescue John, baker, 3A, Charles st. Middlesex hospital, & 2 Brook st. Glo'ster rd. Victoria gate
Fortescue Matthew, barrister, 2 Elm court, Temple
Fortescue Thos. eating house, 7 Lit. Turnstile, High Holborn
Fortescue Wm. surgeon, 64 Hermitage pl. St. John st. road
Forth John Wm. leather seller, 36 Clerkenwell green
Forth & Clyde Navigation Co. (D. Caldwell, sec.), 29 Golden sq
Fortier Magdeleine (Miss), milliner, 9 Bruton st. Bond st
Fortington Elizh. (Mrs.), chandler's shop, 12 Bethnal green
Fortnum, Mason & Co. grocers & teadealers, 182 Piccadilly
Fortune Thos. breeches ma. & tailor, 13 Portugal st. Lin. inn flds
Fortune Thomas, solicitor, 16 Southampton st. Bloomsbury
Forty Daniel, butcher, 1 Drury lane
Forty Mary (Mrs.), pork butcher, 134 Lambeth lower marsh
Forty William, oil & colorman, 56 Tothill st. Westminster
Fortzer George, glass & china dlr. 21 Church st. Kensington
Forward Charles, confectioner, 107 Bishopsgate without
Forward Geo. pat. leather ma. Apple yd. 61 Seward st. Goswl. st
Forward Isaac, coach currier & morocco leather dresser, 3 & 4 Leather lane, Holborn
Forward John, tailor, 11 Weymouth terrace, Hackney road
Forward Thos. stationer & tobacconist, 107 Brick la. Spitalfields
Forward William John, cooper, 10 Princes st. Spitalfields
Forward Wm. oil & colorman & varnish maker, 30 Piccadilly
Forwood Fredk. surgeon, 5 Grosvenor pl. Commercial rd. east
Fosbrooke Leonard, barrister, 12 King's Bench walk, Temple
Fosdick Stephn. *Pickled Egg* P.H. 7 & 8 Crawford pas. Clkwl
Foskett & Neale, wine & spirit merchant, 3 Duke st. Adelphi
Foskett George, meat salesman, 25 Newgate market
Foskett William, leather striper, 133 Long lane, Bermondsey
Foskett James, leather cutter, 4 Friar st. Blackfriars rd
Foss Henry, bookseller, see Payne & Foss
Fossett Charles, hosier & outfitter, 76 Quadrant, Regent st
Fossett John (Mrs.), milliner, 98 Quadrant, Regent st
Fossett Wm. lighterman, 20 Water la. Tower st. & Galley quay
Fossett Selina (Mrs.), stayma. 125 Gt. Portland st. Oxford st
Fossey Wm. & Geo. timber merchs. Batson's wf. Millwl. Poplar
Fossey Chas. pawnbroker, 20 Caroline st. Commrcl. rd. east
Fossey Richard, harp & violin string manufacturer, 5 Gibraltar walk, Bethnal green road
Fossey Thomas, jun. plumber, &c. Ord st. Millwall
Fossick Daniel, solicitor, 1 Angel court, Throgmorton st
Fossick Saml. umbrella manufr. 49 King William st. City
Fossy James, saddler, 69 Skinner st. Bishopsgate
Foster & Braithwaite, stock & share broks. 68 O. Broad st. City
Fosters' & Co. attorneys, 28 John st. Bedford row
Foster Brothers, stockbrokers, 25 Tokenhouse yard
Foster Edwd. & Son, auctioneers, 54 Pall mall, & 14 Greek st
Foster Eleanor & Thos. stationers, 114 Union st. Borough
Foster Harriet & Sarah, milliners, Denmark hill, Cambwll
Foster Henry & Co. who. silk & shawl wareho. 28 Bread st. City
Foster, Hepple & Foster, col. produce agts. 137 Fenchurch st
Foster John & Son, commisn. agts. 4 Barge yd. Bucklersby
Foster & Mansfield, teadealers, 1 Francis pl. New North rd
Foster M. B. & Sons, agents to A. Guinness, Son & Co. dublin; edinburgh, burton & east india pale ale merchants, 53 & 54 Castle st. east, Oxford st
Foster, Porter & Co. who. hosiers, glovers, shawl & ribbon warehousemen, 124 Wood st. & 1 to 3 Goldsmith st. Cheapside
Foster & Rickman, merchants, Lombd. st. chamb. 33 Clement's la
Foster Sarah & Co. cattle salesmen, 8 West Smithfield
Foster, Son & Duncum, art. florists & plumasiers, & art. florists' material dealers, 16 Wigmore st. & 3 Welbeck st. Cavendish square
Foster & West, chemists & druggists, 3 Old Broad st. City
Foster Ann (Mrs.), tin plate workr. 133 Union st. Boro' High st
Foster Archibald, tailor, 72 High st. Shadwell
Foster Benjamin, beer retailer, 5 Upper Duncan pl. City rd
Foster Benjamin, pastrycook, 69 Chiswell st. Finsbury
Foster Benj. Edwd. printing ink, &c. mak. 114 Union st. Boro'
Foster Chas. architect, 1 Willow ter. Canonbury, Islington
Foster Charles, bootmaker, 6 Chapel st. West, Curzon st

Foster Charles Amos, teadealer, 16 Mile end road
Foster Chas.James,barrister, 5 Stone bldgs. Lincoln's inn
Foster David George, iron tool, metal & melting pot wareho. wholesale & retail,23 & 24 St. John's square, Clerkenwell
Foster Edward, undertaker, 5 Marlborough sq. Chelsea
Foster Ellen (Miss), milliner, 13 Henrietta st. Cavendish sq
Foster Elizh. (Mrs.), oil & color wa.2 York ter.Comml. rd ea
Foster Erasmus R. irish comis. merc. 8 Lombard st. chamb
Foster Fanny (Mrs.), potato dlr. 5 Folly, Dockhead,Bermsy
Foster George Holgate, merchant, 40 Moorgate st
Foster Henry, auctioneer, &c. 410 Oxford st
Foster Henry, carpenter, 17 Bartholomew ter. St. Luke's
Foster Henry, wheelwright, 11 Upper Marylebone st. & 28 Upper Ogle st. Fitzroy square
Foster Henton Brown, trunkmaker, 12 Vigo st. Regent st
Foster Israel, boot & shoe maker, 23 Lower st. Islington
Foster James, shawl finisher, 18 Wilson st. Finsbury
Foster James, straw hat maker, 69 Huntingdon st. Hoxton
Foster James, tailor, 106 Gt. Titchfield st. Oxford st
Foster James John, corn & seed factor, 24 Mark lane
Foster John, builder, Church st. Stoke Newington
Foster John, confectioner, 20 East st. Manchester square
Foster John, grocer & oilman, Denmark hill, Camberwell
Foster John, *King's Arms* P.H. 82 Tottenham court road
Foster John, solicitor, 66 Jermyn st. St. James's
Foster John, tripeman, 4 Little Bath st. Clerkenwell
Foster John, undertaker, 56 Featherstone st. City road
Foster John L. coachmak. Northumberland al. Fenchrch. st
Foster John Snowden, tailor, 24 Gt.Crown ct.Lit.Pulteney st
Foster Joseph, *Coopers' Arms* P.H. 24 Tower st. Westmr. rd
Foster Joseph, grocer, 40 Gt. Randolph st. Camden town
Foster Joseph Talwin, copper & tin merchant, British Copper Office, 68 Upper Thames st
Foster Mary Elizh. (Miss), booksel. 24 Aylesbury st. Clknwll
Foster Peter Le Neve, barrister, 92 Chancery lane
Foster Robert, cabinet mak. 19A, Hall park, Edgware road
Foster Samuel, bootmaker, 3 White Horse pl. Mile end rd
Foster Samuel, cheesemonger, 10 NewChurch st.w.Edgw.rd
Foster Samuel, china dealer, 52 Exmouth st. Clerkenwell
Foster Samuel, working jeweller, &c. 1 High st. Marylebone
Foster Sarah(Mrs.),straw hat ma. 2 Crombie's rw.Com.rd.ea
Foster Thos.builder,Wellington foundry,68Charles st.Cityrd
Foster Thomas, carpenter & undertaker, 101 Waterloo rd
Foster Thomas, *Crown* P.H. New st. Deptford
Foster Thomas, *Earl Grey* P.H. 1 Clift st. New North rd
Foster Thomas, grocer, 222 Albany road, Camberwell
Foster Thomas, oil & colorman, 42 New Church st. Lisson gr
Foster Thomas Campbell, special pleader,11Crown office row
Foster Thos. Gregory, barrister, 12 King's benchwlk.Temple
Foster William, clothier, &c. 7 Shadwell High st
Foster William, comb & brushmaker,349 Oxford st
Foster William, fruiterer, North row, Covent garden market
Foster William, grocer, 3 Dockhead, Bermondsey
Foster William, grocer & teadealer, 2 Park st. Borough
Foster William,printer&stereotype fndr.44Primrose st.Bispg
Foster William, publisher, 6 Amen corner, Paternoster row
Foster Wm. stationer, book & printseller, 114 Fenchurch st
Foster William Joseph, pewterer, 202 Kent st. Borough
Foster William M. stockbroker, 6 Barnard's inn Holborn
Foster Wm. Penn, surgeon, Church st. Stoke Newington
Fothergill John, boot & shoe ma. 10 Bear alley, Farringdon st
Fothergill John, fruiterer, 9 Bear alley, Farringdon st
Fothergill Mark,merchant&agricultural ag. 40 Up.Thames st
Fothergill Parkin, *Cock & Lion*P.H.25Wigmore st Caven.sq
Fothergill Thos. jun. stockbroker, 25 Tokenhouse yard
Fothergill Wm. corn factor, 25 Savage gardens, Tower hill
Fotheringham James, lodging ho. 7New North st. RedLion sq
Fotheringham John, baker, 49 Old Compton st. Soho
Fougere James, tailor, 6 Conduit st. Regent st
Foulds Hen. builder & undertak. 20 Queen st. Horselydown
Foulds Henry, jun. builder & undertaker, 39 Gainsford st
Foulds John Harrison, bookbinder, 14 York st. Kingsland rd
Foulger John & Son, color mfrs. Seven star alley, Ratcliff hi
Foulger Samuel & Son, chemists, &c. 133 St. George st
Foulger Thomas & James, tailors, 12 High st. Marylebone
Foulger Charles, solicitor, see Beetham & Foulger
Foulger Henry, upholsterer, 13 Grove terrace, Bayswater
Foulkes George, cheesemonger, 6 Hayfield pl. Mile end rd
Foulkes George, cheesemonger, 59 Minories
Foulkes Griffith, linendraper, 2 & 3 Lit. Russell st. Cov. gar
Foulkes John, ironmonger, 9 St. Dunstan's hill, Gt.Tower st
Foulkes William C. auctioneer, see Beadel & Foulkes
Foulkes William Lennard, barrister, 5 King's Bench walk
Foulsham Chester, *Clayton Arms*P.H.Clayton st. Kenningt
Foulsham Robert, baker, 13 Rufford's bldgs. High st. Islngtn
Foulsham Stephen, beer retailer, 6 Brown's lane, Spitalfields

Founders' Hall (John Gray, jun. clk.), Founders'Hall ct.47 Lothbury
Foundling Hosp.(MorrisLievesley,sec.),Guilfordst.Russellsq
Fountain Elizab. (Mrs.), ivory & bone stainer, 1 Hatton wall
Fountain Henry, bookbinder, 41 Saville st. Fitzroy square
Fountain John, baker, 304 Rotherhithe st
Fountain John, beer retailer, 5 Emanuel pl. Camberwell rd
Fountain James, carpenter, 70 Marylebone lane, Oxford st
Fountain Nath. *Granby* P.H. 38 Percy st. Tottenham ct. rd
Fountain Wm. brass finisher, 13 Cross st. Newington butts
Fountain William, *Hope* P.H. 30 Arthur st.King'srd.Chlsea
Fountain William, wine merchant, 12 Charlotte st. Fitzroy sq
Fountaine T. T. clothier, &c. see Corbett & Fountaine
Fourdrinier Hen. Wm. who.statner.seeHunt,Fourdrinier&Co
Fourdrinier John Coles, solicitor, 1 Scott's yard, Bush lane
Fourmy Jacob, china & glass dealer, 166 Hoxton Old town
Fowell John Digby, wine mercht. 106 New Bond st
Fowke Anthony H. barrister, 6 Stone buildings, Lincoln'sinn
Fowke Frederic, surgeon, 6 Berkeley square
Fowke Frederick Thos. barrister, 7King's Bench walk.Tmpl
Fowke Gustavus W. barrister,6Stone buildings, Lincoln'sinn
Fowke Wm. solicitor, law chambers, 77 Chancery lane
Fowke Wm. Villiers, barrister, law chmbrs. 77 Chancery la
Fowkes Jsph. livery stables, 17 Weymouth mews, Portld. pl
Fowkes Stephen, *Mitre tavern*, 68 St. Martin's lane
Fowle Charles, surveyor, &c. 22 Southwark bridge road
Fowle George Fredk. barrister, 7 King's Bench walk, Temple
Fowle James, oil & italian wa. 4 Stockwell ter. Clapham rd
Fowle John, nurseryman, Holland st. Brixton road
Fowle John, tobacconist, 9 White Hart pl. Kennington lane
Fowle Thomas, tailor, 20 Collingwood st. Blackfriars road
Fowler & Foot, coal merchants, Belvedere road, Lambeth
Fowler & Swift, iron & tinplate works, 73 St. John st. Clkwl
Fowler Ann (Mrs.) wheelwright, 24 Wood st. Westminster
Fowler Benjamin, chair maker, 7 Wood st. Spafields
Fowler Benjamin, hot water apparatus manufacturer, engineer, smith & pump maker, 63 Dorset st. Salisbury sq
Fowler Betty (Mrs.), *Two Brewers* P.H. 10 Lit.Tuftonst.Wr
Fowler Charles, architect, 1 Gordon square
Fowler Charles, pawnbroker, see Warren & Fowler
Fowler Charles, potter, Fox's lane, Shadwell
Fowler Chas. S. mercht. 12 & 13Pinners'hall, Gt. Wnchstr. st
Fowler David, carpenter & builder, 18 Clerkenwell green
Fowler Edward, dealer in horses, 7 South place, Finsbury
Fowler Francis Edmd. Hayman, architect, 28 Sackville st
Fowler Geo. British & for. agency off. 57 Lincoln's inn fields
Fowler Geo. surgeon, 53 Newington place, Kennington road
Fowler George, tailor, 24 Artillery lane, Bishopsgate
Fowler George, tobacconist, 155 Aldersgate st
Fowler Geo. wholes. ironmonger, 45 Red Lion st. Clerkenwell
FowlerHannahAnne(Mrs.),bricklayer,40 Bell yd.Temple bar
Fowler Henry, grocer, 25 Tonbridge st. New road
Fowler James Yates, tobacconist, 31 Up. King st. Bloomsby
Fowler John, baker, 1 Crombie's row, Commercial road east
Fowler John, baker, 94 Lambeth walk
Fowler John, baker, 12 Lit. Trinity lane, Gt. Trinity lane
Fowler John, bricklayer, 94 Gt. George st. Bermondsey
Fowler John,bricklayr. plastr. & bldr. 94 Gt.George st. Brndsy
Fowler John, carpenter, 17 Duke's row, Pancras New road
Fowler John Coke, barrister, 11 Paper buildings, Temple
Fowler John Peter, chemist, 35 Bedford st. Covent garden
Fowler Lucy (Mrs.) china dealer, 5 Duke st. Chelsea
Fowler Mary Ann (Mrs.), pearl stringer, 72 Myddelton st
Fowler Richard, chemist, &c. see Compton & Fowler
Fowler Richard, cowkeeper, 13 Lit. Barlow st. Marylebone
Fowler Saml. *Duke of Sussex* P.H. Grange walk, Bermonds
Fowler Samuel, oil & colorman, 54 Leather lane, Holborn, & 54 High st. Hoxton
Fowler Sarah (Mrs.), straw bonnet ma. 51 Exmouth st.Clknwl
Fowler Scrope, hosier & glover, 294 Oxford st
Fowler Thomas, banker, see Drewett & Fowler
Fowler Thomas, butcher, 22 Granby st. Hampstead road
Fowler Thomas, butcher, 23 High st. Portland town
Fowler Thomas, cabinet maker, 5 Lower Kennington green
Fowler Thomas, cabinet maker, 6 St.James's bldgs.Clerknwl
Fowler Thomas, corndealer, Hawley place, Kentish town
Fowler Thomas, diamond setter, 15 Lock's gardens, Clrknwl
Fowler Thomas, hairdresser, 223 Bermondsey st
Fowler Thomas, marine store dealer, 189 Long la. Brmndsy
Fowler Thomas, wheelwright, 1 Mermaid court, Borough
Fowler Thomas Robert, sec. to Ophthalmic Hospital,19King William st. Strand
Fowler William, artist, 11 Eccleston st. south
Fowler William, beer retailer, 18 Commercial pl. City rd
Fowler William, confectioner, 48 Lower George st. Chelsea
Fowler William, grocer & tea dealer, 45 Old Bailey

Fowler William, surgeon, 9 Mansell st. Goodman's fields
Fowler William, surgeon, 57 Pennyfields, Poplar
Fowler William, surgeon, 130 St George st
Fowlis Thomas, merchant, 19 Abchurch lane, City
Fowls James, butcher, 10 Borough market
Fowls Thomas William, butcher, 176 Lambeth walk
Fowls William, butcher, 245 Bermondsey st
Fownes Brothers, leather dressers & glove manufacturers, 4 Tavistock st. Covent garden; manufactory at Battersea, Surrey
Fownes & Keed, hatters, hosiers & glovers, 6 Coventry st
Fownes Henry, corn & coal dlr. 7 Old Paradise rw. Islington
Fox Brothers, woollen manufacturers, 27 Tokenhouse yard
Fox Charles Henderson & Co. engineers, 24 Fore st. Limeho
Fox Charles&Geo.working silversmiths,139 Old st.St.Luke's
Fox Henderson & Co. enginrs. & machinists, 3 Trafalgar sq
Fox James & Son, barge & boat builders, Limehouse hole
Fox John & Son, surgeon dentists, 21 New Bridge st
Fox & Britten, solicitors, 1 Basinghall st
Fox, Mundell & Fox, proctors, 16 Gt.Knightrider st.Doct.com
Fox, William & Co. merchants, 113 Fenchurch st
Fox Adam, feather purifier, see Booth & Fox
Fox Alfred, furnishing ironmonger, 3 Norfolk pl. Clapham
Fox Augustus, fruiterer, 73 Blackfriars road
Fox Barnet, furrier, 8 Gun st. Spitalfields
Fox Charles, bookseller & publisher, 67 Paternoster row
Fox Charles, glass & china dlr.14Shepperton pl.New North rd
Fox Charles, plumber & glazier, 1 Up. Dorset pl. Clapham rd
Fox Charles, *Red Lion* P.H. 123 Jermyn st. St. James's
Fox Charles J. physician, 30 New Broad st. City
Fox Charles James, real manuf. of the celebrated rouge for polishing gold & silver, potee powders for polishing glass, marble, steel, &c. glossing stuff for watchmak. also emery, black lead & diamond razor strop paste, 111 Gt.Saffron hill
Fox Charles James, furniture dealer, Triangle, Hackney
Fox Charles James, upholsterer, 7 & 8 Eldon st. Finsbury
Fox Daniel, carpenter & builder, 79 Chalton st. Somers town
Fox Ebenezer, oil & colorman, 50 Old Compton st. Soho
Fox Edward, coal dealer & fishmonger, 97½ Shoe la. Fleet st
Fox Edward, silk & velvet manufacturer, see Bailey & Fox
Fox Edward Buckley, merchant, 80 Old Broad st. City
Fox Francis, merchant, see Sanderson, Frys', Fox & Co
Fox Frederick, corn chandler, 75 Goswell road
Fox George, butterman, 2 Broadway, Westminster
Fox Geo. *Carpenters' Arms* P.H. 19 Stafford pl. sth.Pimlico
Fox George, fishmonger, 6 Gt. Chapel st. Westminster
Fox George, grocer, 29 New North st. Finsbury
Fox George, merchant, see Charles & Fox
Fox George T. milkman, 3 Green Dragon ct. St. Saviour's
Fox Henry, grocer & cheesemonger, 34 Brooke st. Holborn
Fox Henry, millwright, 20 St.John st. & 5 & 6 Northampton st
Fox Henry, wine & spirit merchant, 7 Queen's bldgs.Brmptn
Fox Henry Harris, upholsterer, &c.16 Holland pl.Clapham rd
Fox Henry Wilkins, *Portland Arms* P.H.29 New Millman st
Fox Herbert Cole, *Prince Albert* P.H. Hoxton square
Fox James, butcher, 25 Whitechapel road
Fox James, oilman, &c. 192 Hoxton Old town
Fox James, tea, spice & coffee dlr.98&99 Fore st.Cripplegate
Fox Jeremiah, *Sir John Barleycorn* P.H.Thomas st.Whitpl
Fox John, brazier, 3 Bartholomew pl. Bartholomew close
Fox John, appraiser & undertaker, 30 King st. Long acre
Fox John, beer retailer, 1 Middlesex st. Somers town
Fox John, bootmaker, 4 Brandon row, Newington causeway
Fox John, cabinent ma.upholsterer&undertak.14 Newgate st
Fox John, cabinet ma. & upholsterer, 29 Cross st. Blckfrs. rd
Fox John, carpenter, Percy cot.Southside, King's rd.wst.Chlsa
Fox John, *George & Crown* P.H. 12 Broad st. Bloomsbury
Fox John, haircutter & perfumer to H.R.H. Prince Albert, 5 Carlton st. Regent st. (late of the Strand)
Fox John, miniature painter, 77 Cheapside
Fox John, stock & sh. bro 31 Gt.Winchester st.&Stock exchg
Fox John, surgeon, 15 Goswell road
Fox John, tailor & draper, 101 Minories
Fox John, undertaker, 3 New road, St. George's east
Fox John Elliott, solicitor, 40 Finsbury circus
Fox John Gibbs, stationer, 4 High st. Stoke Newington
Fox John W. who. tobacconist, 10 Cross st. Hatton garden
Fox Joseph, grocer & cheesemonger, 1 Lr. Kennington lane
Fox Joseph, hairdresser, 32 & 33 Burlington arcade
Fox Leonard, baker, 20 Rufford's buildings, Islington
Fox Nathan, fruiterer, 10 Londonhouse yard, St. Paul's
Fox Oscar Harger, surgeon, 16 Stepney causeway, Coml.rd.east
Fox Robert, greengrocer & carman, 142 Kingsland road
Fox Samuel, bricklayer, 12 Barnsbury row, Cloudesley sq
Fox Samuel, builder & house agent, Morning lane, Hackney
Fox Samuel, surgeon, 219 Shoreditch High st
Fox Saml.mangr.of Jsph.Gillott's steel pen wa.37 Gracech.st
Fox Samuel, tailor, 4 William st. New Bridge st
Fox Samuel George, academy, 24 Park st. Camden town
Fox Sheffield, shipsmith, 295 Rotherhithe
Fox Thomas, beer retailer, 8 Essex place, Mare st. Hackney
Fox Thomas, cabinet maker, upholsterer & plate glass factor, 93 Bishopsgate within
Fox Thomas, decorative painter & paperhanger, 93 Bishopsgate st. within
Fox Thomas, newsvender, 1 King's row, Cambridge rd. Mile end
Fox Thomas, undertaker, 6 Hawkins st. Sidney st. Mile end
Fox Thomas Henry, wire drawer, worker, weaver & sieve maker, 63 Skinner st. Snowhill, & Wenlock basin
Fox Thomas Manby, artist, 2 Bedford pla. Commrcl. rd. ea
Fox William, carpenter, 15 Powell st. west, King square
Fox William, chemist, 48 Church st. Shoreditch
Fox William, dining rooms, 150 Kingsland road
Fox William, *Hampshire Hog* P.H. 37 Charles st. Westmr
Fox William, *Hungerford Arms* P.H. 19 Villiers st. Strand
Fox William, millwright, engineer & iron founder, 56 Compton st. Clerkenwell
Fox William, *Q. Victoria* P.H. Blue Anchor rd. Bermondsey
Fox Wm. Hunsley, cur. & leath. selr. 199 Up. Whitecross st
Fox William J. butcher, 14 Newport court, Newport market
Foxall Charles, *Sun & Punch Bowl* P.H. 219 High Holborn
Foxall Robt. fishmonger, 4 & 7 Darkhouse la. Billingsgate
Foxell John Allen, haberdasher, 58 Paddington st. Marylebn
Foxhall Edward Martin, architect, & district surveyor to St. George's, Hanover sq. 14B, South st. & 18 South Audley st
Foxley George, plumber & painter, 36 King st. Golden sq
Foxwell Ann (Mrs.), turner & stand mkr. 24 Crown st. Soho
Foxwell Edward, tailor & draper, 13 Lower road, Islington
Foxwell Edwin, draper & haberdash. 26 Judd st.Brunswick sq
Foxwell Francis, tailor, 12 Mount row, Liverpool road
Foxwell George, carman, 8 John st. Dockhead
Foy John, academy, Seymour row, Little Chelsea
Foy Joseph, commission agent, 60 Aldermanbury
Foy Sarah (Mrs.), china dealer, 56 Shoe lane
Foy Wm. cheesemonger, 5 Lit. Crown ct. Princes st. Soho
Foyle George, plate powder ma. &c. 11 Cowper st. City road
Fozard Francis, cowkeeper, 16 Portman pl. Edgware road
Fraas George, tailor, 8 Leicester place, Leicester square
Frackelton Geo. meat slsm. See Pocklington, Frackelton & Jury
Fradelle Henry, artist, 44 Cirencester place, Fitzroy sq
Fradelle Henry Joseph, artist, 9 Percy st. Tottenham ct. rd
Frailey Andrew, oilman, 100 Rosemary lane
Frame William, *Angel* P.H. 61 High st. St. Giles's
Frame William, paper hanger, 17 Parker row, Bermondsey
Framingham Chas. bootmaker, 187 Church st. Shoreditch
Frampton Algernon, physician, 29 New Broad st. City
Frampton Chas. china dealer, 1 Seymour pl. Bryanstone sq
Frampton Daniel Stephen, academy, 19 York pl. Fulham rd
Frampton Eli, grocer&cheesemonger, 45 Perceval st.Clrknwll
Frampton Elizabeth (Mrs.), coffee rooms, 63 Barbican
Frampton Frederick, dancing master, 34 York rd. Lambeth
Frampton James, *Sun* coffee rooms, 30 Long la.Bermondsey
Frampton John, hairdresser, 91 Tottenham court road
Frampton John De Kewer, barrister, 6 Stone bldgs.Linc.inn
Frampton Richard, oilman, 24 Shepherd st. Mayfair
Frampton Wm. carpenter & builder, 12 Earl st. ea.Lisson gr
Frampton Wm. harness maker, 53 Crucifix la. Bermondsey
Frampton Wm. Hamwood, solicitor, 2 South sq. Gray's inn
Framton Thomas, surgeon, 8 High st. Marylebone
France Frederic & Chas. genl. salesmen, 9 Lit. Compton st
France Alfred, stock & share broker, 1 St. Michael's alley
France Eliza Mary (Miss), coal merchant, 22 Stockbridge ter. Pimlico, & Cannon wharf, Cannon row, Westminster
France Frederick, glass engraver, 6 King st. Cloth fair
France Geo. John, genl.salesman, 8½ Ryder's ct.Leicester sq
France Henry, furnishing undertaker, 111 Wardour st. Soho
France John Fredk. surgeon, 88 Cadogan pl. Sloane st
France Robt. Wm. furnish. undertaker, 2 Denmark st. Soho
France Sarah (Mrs.), milliner, 101 Albany st
France Sarah (Mrs.), picture frame ma. 24 Denmark st.Soho
France Thomas, solicitor, see Palmer, France & Palmer
France Thos. timber mer.&wfingr. Bridge wf. Paddington basin
Franchi Anty. G. notary & commn.&cust.ho.agt.16 Savage gdns
Francies Rebecca (Mrs.), *Horns* P.H. 16 Whitechpl. High st
Francillon Jas. barrister, 10 Southampton bldgs. Chancery la
Francis Charles & Son, corn factors, 59 Whitechapel High st. & at Old Corn Exchange, Mark la
Francis Charles & Sons, roman cement & patent mastic manufacturers & lime burners, Nine Elms; Scotland yard; City road basin; Bridge wharf, Kentish town; Old Billingsgate dock, Greenwich; & Liverpool
Francis Henry & Henry D. solicitors, 4 Monument yard

Francis Chas. *Sun* coff. rooms, 32 Fish st. hill, & 127 Lo. Thms. st
Francis Chas. corn dealer & grocer, 2 East st. Kennington rd
Francis Charles, solicitor, 22 Austinfriars
Francis Charles, corn merchant, 188 High st. Borough
Francis David, printer, White horse lane, Stepney
Francis Edmund, shell fishmonger, 8 Bridge road, Lambeth
Francis Frederick John, architect, 2 Cork st. Bond st
Francis Fred. whitesmith & bellhanger, Eaton row, Eaton sq
Francis George, grocer, 10 Cheltenham pl. Westminster rd
Francis George, hatter & glover, 194 Borough High st
Francis Griffith, grocer & teadealer, 89 St. George street
Francis Henry, stockbroker, 57 Threadneedle street
Francis Hugh, teadealer & grocer, 182 Lambeth walk
Francis James Osborne, timber merchant, wharfinger, general commission agent & marble broker, Bridge wharf, & 3 Kemp's row, Pimlico
Francis John, accountant, ho. & estate agt. 53 Chancery la
Francis John, attorney, 1 New Boswell ct. Carey st. Linc. inn
Francis John, bombazine & norwich manufr. 121 Cheapside
Francis John, engraver & die sinker, 10 Hatton garden
Francis John, livery stables, 22 Chapel pl. mws. Belgrave sq
Francis John, sculptor, 56 Albany street, Regent's park
Francis John, tailor & draper, 5 Seabright pl. ea. Hackney rd
Francis Joseph, straw bonnet & fancy wa. 432 Oxford st
Francis Julia (Miss), ladies' school, 11 Devonshire pl. Edgw. rd
Francis Lewis, surgeon dentist, 64 Newman st. Oxford st
Francis Richard, *Crown* P.H. 24 Church street, Lambeth
Francis Richard, printer, 25 Museum street, Bloomsbury
Francis Sarah (Mrs.), milliner, 53 Goswell road
Francis Stephen, cabinet mak. 52 Trafalgar st. Walworth rd
Francis Thomas, baker, 64 Castle st. east, Oxford market
Francis Thomas, baker, 62 New Compton street, Soho
Francis Thomas, sheffield agent, 7 Beaufort bldgs. Strand, & 4 Salisbury st. Strand
Francis Thomas, stockbroker, 5 Angel ct. Throgmorton st
Francis Thomas F. undertaker, 28 Kirby st. Hatton garden
Francis Wm. carman, 4 Ranelagh cot. Commercial rd. south
Francis William, gold watch case ma. 15 King st. Clerknwll
Francis William, *Oxford Arms* P.H. Church st. Deptford
Francis William, plumber, 7 Upper John st. Liverpool road
Francis William, saddler & harness ma. 7½ Great Dover st
Francis William W. upholsterer & cabinet ma. 104 Nw. Bond st
Francis William, wholesale slopseller, 75 Minories
Francis Wm. jun. ho. agent, 33 Up. Seymour st. Portman sq
Francis Wm. Mortimer, painter, 7 Up. John st. Liverpool rd
Francis William Skeggs, auctioneer, 18 St. George street
Franck Frdck. *Storey's gate hotel,* 38 Gt. George st. Westr
Francke William, furrier, 40 Skinner st. Clerkenwell
Francklyn Henry George, merchant, 14 Mincing lane
Franey William, baker, 45 South Audley st
Franghiadi Brothers, merchants, 18 Finsbury circus
Frank Christian, fruiterer, 8 Low. Ranelagh st
Frank John, linendraper & haberdashr. see Coppen & Frank
Frank John, poultry salesm. 6 Ship Tav. pas. Leadenhl. mkt
Frank Livett, artists' colorman, 14 Wellingtn. st. London brge
Frankau Joseph & Co. leech, cigar, &c. import. 22 Gt. Alie st
Frankcom John, *Rodney's Head* P.H. 10 Lit. Suffolk st. Boro'
Frankford Isaac, teadealer, 2 Colett pl. Commercial rd. east
Frankford Isaac, tobacconist, 1 Evaline pl. Comrcl. rd. east
Frankenstein Jacob, shipping & commission agt. 14 Fish st. hill
Frankham & Dixon, solicitors, 79 Basinghall st
Frankham Rd. & Henry, engravrs. 12 Wilson st. Gray's inn rd
Frankland Edwd. (Mrs.), ladies' school, 15 Kennington oval
Frankland Joseph, hatter, Church st. Hackney
Frankland Peter, bootmaker, 19 South st. Manchester sq
Frankland Peter, saddler, 2 Hill st. Finsbury
Frankland Thos. butcher, 37 Langley pl. Commerl. rd. east
Franklin & Woodrow, tailors, 3 Princes st. Hanover sq
Franklin Thos. & Sam. linen drs. & coal mers. 47 Geo. st. Ptm. sq
Franklin Ann (Mrs.), *Feathers* P.H. 8 St. Martin's st. Lestr. sq
Franklin Edmund, coal dealer, 7 Little Essex st. Strand
Franklin Elizh. (Mrs.), fancy repository, Camberwell green
Franklin Ellis A. wholesale & retail grocer, & oil & italian merchant, 20 Vine st. Minories
Franklin Francis M. button wareh. see Chambers & Franklin
Franklin George, butcher, 1 London terrace, Hackney road
Franklin George, hairdresser, 44 North st. Sloane st
Franklin Henry, butcher, 38 King st. Camden town
Franklin Henry, chair caner, 56 Monmouth st. Seven dials
Franklin Henry, shawl cleaner, 35 Berwick st. Pimlico
Franklin James, bottle dealer, 14 Star st. Paddington
Franklin James, silversmith & pawnbroker, 5 Tottenham ct. rd
Franklin John, butcher, 61 Fetter lane, Holborn
Franklin John, butcher, 4 Duncan place, Hackney fields
Franklin John, dairy, 5 Cambridge place, Edgware road
Franklin John, *Coach & Horses* P.H. 1 Norfolk st. Park lane
Franklin Joseph, *Bakers' coffee ho.* 14 Old Quebec st. Prtm. sq
Franklin Lewis, rag & bottle mer. 5 Well st. Wellclose sq
Franklin Matthew, fruiterer, 15 Aylesbury st. Clerkenwell
Franklin Samuel, fruit salesman, Borough market
Franklin Samuel, slipper maker, 24 Church st. Spitalfields
Franklin Sarah (Mrs.), undertaker, 11 Tufton st. Westmstr
Franklin Thomas, *Hoop* P.H. Kensington Gravel pits
Franklin Thos. *King's Arms* P.H. 12 Marylebone st. Picdlly
Franklin Wm. carpenter, 6 Chapel mews, Belgrave square
Franklin Wm. carpenter, 50 Jubilee st. Commercial rd. east
Franklin Wm. Rd. proctor & notary, 8 Godlimanst. Dctrs. com
Frankling Benj. grocer, 25 Hamilton row, Bagnigge wells rd
Frankling Mary (Mrs.), straw bonnet maker, Battersea sq
Frankling Francis, painter, 3 Bridge st. Southwark
Franklyn Arthur, baker & flour fac. 18 Bland ter. Gt. Dover rd
Franklyn Francis B. printer, see Robson, Levey & Franklyn
Franklyn George, silk dyer, 108 Bishopsgate without
Franks & Millard, wholesale tea & coffee dealers & colonial merchants, 14 Little Tower st
Franks & Moore, linendrapers, &c. 36 Crosby row, Walworth
Franks Charles, livery stables, Uxbridge road, Bayswater
Franks George, bookseller, 114 Gray's inn lane
Franks Geo. surgeon & pat. medicine wa. 90 Blackfriars road
Franks Henry, tailor, 6 Windsor place, City road
Franks John, surgeon, 50 Basing place, Waterloo road
Franks John, jun. cattle salesman, 8 West Smithfield
Franks John, sen. cattle salesman, 8 West Smithfield
Franks Martin William, cigar merchant, 127 Blackfriars rd
Franks Peter, plumber, 26 High st. Deptford
Franks William Edward, tea broker, 35 Fenchurch st
Frankum Richard, surgeon, 17 Albemarle st. Piccadilly
Fraser & Lett, accountants, 27 King st. Cheapside
Fraser (Hon. Wm.), Neilson & Co. merchs. 30 Leadenhall st
Fraser Alexander, artist, 65 Upper Seymour st. Euston sq
Fraser Alexander, stockbroker, 5 Bank chambers & Stock ex
Fraser Ann (Mrs.), carpenter, 11 Little Vine st. Piccadilly
Fraser Ann (Mrs.), corset maker, 90 Goswell road
Fraser Donald, surgeon, 1 Oakley square, Somers town
Fraser Hanh. (Mrs.), *Crown & Queen's Arms* P.H. 32 Wapping High st
Fraser James, bookbinder, 90 Long acre
Fraser James, boot & shoe maker, 172 St. George st
Fraser Jane (Mrs.), lodging house, 37 Norfolk st. Strand
Fraser John, boot & shoe maker, 1 Nassau pl. Co ml. rd. east
Fraser John, cabinetmaker, 21 John st. Fitzroy square
Fraser John, merchant & agent, 11 Basing lane, Cheapside
Fraser John, ships' tank & hearth ma. 10 King's pl. Coml. rd. east
Fraser John, solicitor, see Wood & Fraser
Fraser John Farquhar, barrister, 2 Inner Temple lane
Fraser Michael, attorney, 2 Furnival's inn, Holborn
Fraser Patrick, physician, 62 Guilford st. Russell sq
Fraser Robert, baker, 10 Wandsworth road (north side)
Fraser Roderick, surgeon, 15 Harley st
Fraser Susannah (Mrs.), beer retailer, 245 Shadwell
Fraser Thomas, boot & shoemaker, Mile end road
Fraser Wm. Tulloh, east indiamer. 6 Crosby sq. Bishopsgate
Frasi George, engineer & millwright, 158 Goswell st
Frasi George, ironfounder, see Gilbert & Frasi
Frauenknecht Oscar, gen. commission agent, 48 Watling st
Fray John William, farrier, 7 Church st. Westminster
Fraye Peter, foreign importer, 56 Hatton garden
Frazer Alex. beer retailer, 6 St. George's pl. Walworth rd
Frazer James, hairdresser, 7 Leader st. Chelsea
Freak Augustus M. jeweller, 15 St. John's sq. Clerkenwell
Freake Charles James, builder, 37 Eaton square
Freaks Henry, beer retailer, 101 King's pl. Comrcl. road east
Frearson John, haberdasher, 16 Brewer st. Somers town
Frearson Mark, laceman, 14 Hanway st. Oxford st
Freason Joseph Stafford, butcher, 22 Rosoman st. Clerkenwell
Frebout Abraham, silk manufac. 25 Steward st. Spitalfields
Frebout Francis, *Constitution* P.H. 11 Gt. James st. Lisson gr
Frebout Louis, cabinetmaker & upholsterer, 32 Hackney rd
Frederick Emile (Madame), milliner, 40 Albemarle st
Fredericks Wm. & Co. stationers & bookslrs. 25 Motcomb st
Free Robert, accountant, 2 Ingram court, Fenchurch st
Free Thomas, baker, 16 Margaret st. Wilmington sq
Free Thomas, *Nag's Head* P.H. 30 Tothill st. Westminster
Free Church of Scotland, 16 Exeter hall, 372 Strand
Free Trade Club (Edward John Evans, sec.), 27 Regent st
Freebody Ann (Mrs.), milliner, 1 Cottage place, Salmon lane
Freeborne Geo. *Stanhope Arms* P.H. Stafford pl. Glo'ster cresc
Freedom Office, Guildhall; hours of business, 10 to 3
Freegrove Charles, tailor, 10 Tavistock st. Covent garden
Freeland Humphry W. barrister, 42 Chancery lane
Freeland James, grocer, 202 Shoreditch High st
Freeling Chas. Rivers, barrister, 4 New sq. Lincoln's inn

Freelove Thos. & Son, tallow chndlr. 1 Whitehorse st. Stpny
Freem Edward & Mary, bakers, 23 High st. Kensington
Freeman, Bothamley & Benthall, solicitors, 39 Coleman st
Freeman & Horn, drug grinders, 60 Seward st. Goswell st
Freeman John & Co. trimming sellers, 53 St. Martin's lane
FreemanJsph.&Sons,whitelead&co.wrks.Bridgerd.Battersea
Freeman Richd. & Thos. tailors & outfitters, 5 Northumberland place, Commercial road east, & 48 Fenchurch st
Freeman Wm. & John, stone & marble merchants, 27 Millbankst.Wstmnstr.; Canal bsn.Cityrd.&LowGrovest.Deptf
Freeman Abraham, coffee rooms, 13 Blenheim st. Oxford st
Freeman Abraham, wheelwright, 155 Tooley st
Freeman Arthur, agent to the Edinburgh & Leith glassworks, 5 Fenchurch buildings
Freeman Arth. & Son, wine, spirit, &c. mer. 5 Fenchurch bdgs
Freeman Chas. architect & surveyor, 14 Arundel st. Strand
Freeman Chas. Henry, oilman, 16 Brick lane, Spitalfields
Freeman Chas. Wm. oil & colorman, 16 Berwick st. Soho
Freeman David, *Abbey tavern* P.H.Violethill, St. John's wd
Freeman David, umbrella & archery manfr. 126 Oxford st
Freeman Drury, watch key maker, &c. 41 Gee st. Goswell st
Freeman Edw. *Bricklayers' Arms* P.H.31Gresse st.Rathb. pl
Freeman Edward, wax & tallow chandler, & oil merchant to the Queen & the Queen dowager, lamp & chandelier warehouse, manufacturer of fish sauces, & importer of italian stores, 3 Wigmore st. Cavendish square
Freeman Elizabeth (Mrs.), baker, 12 Lombard st. Chelsea
Freeman Eliz. (Mrs.), *Old George* P.H. 1 George ct. Snowhl
Freeman Francis, butcher, 41 Charles st. City road
Freeman George Scott, brewer, George st. Camberwell grn
Freeman GeorgeMoore, grocer, 9 Goldsmith's rw.Hackney rd
Freeman Hen. carpenter & buildr. 75 Cowcross st. Smithfield
Freeman Henry, fruiterer, 19 Fetter lane, Fleet st
Freeman Henry, grocer, 16 Crombie's row, Comrcl. rd. east
Freeman Henry, horticultural builder, Mare st. Hackney
Freeman Henry, tailor, 175 Poplar High st
Freeman Henry, wood broker, 3 Sun court, Cornhill
Freeman Henry Chas. corn dlr. 23 Thayer st. Manchester sq
Freeman Isaac, baker, 8 Lower Smith st. Clerkenwell
Freeman James, *Brown Bear* P.H. 2 Grafton st. Soho
Freeman James, builder, 8 Weybridge pl. Mile end road
Freeman James, caulker, 14 Charlotte row, Rotherhithe st
Freeman James, coffee rooms, 28 James st. Covent garden
Freeman James, grocer, &c. 24 Church row, Pancras road
Freeman James, furn. japanner, 20½ Clipstone st. Fitzroy sq
Freeman James, ironmonger, 189 Church st. Shoreditch
Freeman James, lodging house, 4 Lower Belgrave pl. Pimlico
Freeman James, wholes. cheesemonger, 209 Borough High st
Freeman John, comp. ornament ma.39 Bowling grn. la.Clkwl
Freeman John, & copper comp. Cousin lane, Upp. Thames st
Freeman John, *Fox & Hounds* P.H. 3 Odell pl. LittleChelsea
Freeman John, tailor, see Roth & Freeman
Freeman JohnChas.miller& corn dlr. 20 Grosvenor pl.Cmbrwl
Freeman John, watch mainspring mak.1Galway st. St.Luke's
Freeman John, who.&ret.chemist & annatto ma.13 Blackfrs.rd
Freeman Joseph, agent to the Bowling iron works & the Hallamshire steel works, 8 St. Swithin's lane, City
Freeman Joseph, chemist, 2 Cottage pl. Green st. Kentish tn
Freeman Joseph, cooper, 2 Mayfield pl. High st. Kensington
Freeman Joseph, cowkeeper, 59 London st. Fitzroy sq
Freeman Joseph, lighterman, Battersea square
Freeman Joseph, surgeon, 21 Spring gardens
Freeman Josiah, hairdresser, 17 Stanhope st. Clare market
Freeman Margaret (Mrs.), haberdasher, 8 Bartholomew close
Freeman Matthew, cooper, North st. Poplar
Freeman Richard, *Blenheim hotel*, 94 New Bond st
Freeman Richard, carpenter, 10 Broadway, Southwark, & 6 Mill lane, Tooley st
Freeman Richard, chemist, 5 Clayton pl. Kennington rd
Freeman Richard, clerk of the market, 47 Farringdon mrkt
Freeman Richard, comb mak.17 Smith's bldgs. Long la. Bmsy
Freeman Richd. greengrocer, 63 Tabernacle walk, Finsbury
Freeman Richd. hosier & shirt ma. 22 Edwards st. Portmn. sq
Freeman Richd. Marriott, solicitor, 4 Gt. James st. Bedford rw
Freeman Robert, bricklayer, Layton's grove, Boro' High st
Freeman Robert, chemist & druggist, 38 High st. Kensington
Freeman Sylvester, cooper, Cheyne rw. Cheyne wlk. Chelsea
Freeman Thos. agt. for West's pat. forge back, 21 Bread st. hl
Freeman Thomas, butcher, 24 Gt. Titchfield st. Oxford st
Freeman Thomas, coal merchant, see Edington & Freeman
Freeman Thomas, fringe & trimming seller, 96 Wood st
Freeman Thomas, greengrocer, 5 Union place, Islington
Freeman Thomas, ironmongr.& bellhngr. 10 West st. Golden sq
Freeman Thomas, *Red Lion* P.H. 27 Clarges st. Piccadilly
Freeman Thomas, shell fishmonger, 143 Gt. Suffolk st. Boro'
Freeman Thomas, timber merchant, 1 New walk, Horselydn
Freeman Wm. auctnr. & appraiser, 57 Gt. Coram st. Russell sq
Freeman Wm. bootmaker, 17 Finch lane, Cornhill
Freeman Wm. brush & turnery warehouse, 18 Edgware road
Freeman Wm. coffee rooms, 34 Clerkenwell green
Freeman Wm. fruiterer, 2 Grove terrace, Bayswater
Freeman Wm. fruiterer, 36 Upper Marylebone st
Freeman Wm. grocer, 1 Pont st. Cadogan pl. Chelsea
Freeman Wm. law stationer, 14 Carey st. Lincoln's inn fields
Freeman Wm. mangle ma. & smith, 22 Gt. Saffronhill, Hat. grdn
Freeman Wm. picture frame ma. 11 Barrons pl. Waterloo rd
Freemantle Thomas, *Cock & Crown* P.H. 41 Little Britain
Freemasons' Charity for Female Children (Mrs. Frances Crooks, mistress), Elizabeth pl. Westmtnster rd. Lambeth
Freemasons' Hall, Wm. Henry White, grand secretary, 61 & 63 Great Queen st. Lincoln's inn fields
Freemasons' & General Life Assurance, Loan, Annuity & Reversionary Interest Company (J. Berridge, sec.), 11 Waterloo place; for list of directors, &c. &c. see page 2025
Freemont John Cox, merch.& com.agent, 2 Love la. Eastcheap
Freen Louisa (Miss), watch & clock maker, 30 Fish st. hill
Freen Thomas & Co. cement manfs. Canal rd. Kingsland rd
Freen Thomas & Co. cement manfrs. St. George's st. O. Kent rd
Freer Henry Ashley, *Rose* P.H. 26 Cursitor st. Chancery la
Freese Philip C. exch. disct. & ins. brok. 1 Gt. Winchester st
Freeston Philip, *White Swan* P.H. 68 Chandos st. Cov. gdn
Freestone Edwd. W. straw hat mfr. 152 Shoreditch High st
Freestone Joseph, carman, 16 Commercial road, Pimlico
Freeth Chas. jun. agt. to Sun Fire & Life Office, 65 Welbeck st
Freeth Edwin, cheesemonger, 47 St. John st. Clerkenwell
Freeth George, cheesemonger, 3 Upper Penton st. Pentonvl
Freeth George, solicitor, see Parke & Freeth
Freeth Henry, confectioner, lozenge manufr. & biscuit baker, 52 Bishopsgate st. without
Freeth Thomas Jacob, solicitor, 4 Inner Temple lane
Freeth Wm. linendraper, 58 Lamb's Conduit st. Foundling
Freethy Fredk. mftg. goldsmith, 23 Gt. Sutton st. Clerkenwell
Freethy William, appraiser, 30 Kirby st. Hatton garden
Frego Thomas, bookseller, 6 Charlotte st. Fitzroy sq
Freit Aaron, leech merchant, 4 Little Somerset st. Aldgate
Fremont Ann Amos (Miss), stationer, 30 Brown's la. Spitafields
French Jacob & Sons, goldsmiths, 5 Newcastle pl. Clerkenwell
French & Nephew, cork merchants & manufacturers, & importers of ready made corks, 51 Crutched friars
French & Ogilvie, pawnbrokers, 207 Poplar High st
French & Sadler, chemists & druggists, 18 Norton folgate
French Passport Office, 6 Poland st. Oxford st. 11 to 5
French Protestant Hospital (Richard Howe Giraud, sec.), Bath st. City road
French Protestant Schl. 13A, Windmill st. Tottenham ct rd
French Aaron, breeches maker, see Gobby, Haines & Co
French Benj. tailor, 6 Pitt st. Fitzroy sq
French David, cutler, 24 St. Andrew's road, Horsemonger la
French Edmund, butcher, 5 Grosvenor market
French Elizh. (Miss), school, 18 Up. Montagu st. Montagu sq
French Emma (Mrs.), dairy, 1 Northumberland mews, Maryleb
French Garrett, *Baker & Basket* P.H. 60 Worship st. Finsbury
French George, barrister, 64 Lincoln's inn fields
French George, butcher, 28 Chapel st. New rd. Edgware rd
French George, flute ma. 19 Laystall st. Liquorpond st
French George, plumber & glazier, 17 Fore st. Limehouse
French Geo. Russell, architect, 18 Sussex gardens, Hyde park
French Giles, chandler's shop, 22 Pearson st. Kingsland rd
French James, baker, Bromley
French James, tinman & brazier, Porter's pl. Holloway rd
French James, tobacconist, 31 Princes st. Portman market
French John, bootmaker, 1 New rd. St. George's east
French John, butcher, 12 Artillery passage, Bishopsgate
French John, cattle salesman, 17 West Smithfield
French John, chronometer ma. 80 Cornhill, & 9 Royal Exchange
French John, grocer, 12 Heddon court, Regent st
French John, printer, Gower's walk, Church la. Whitechapel
French John, upholsterer, 2 Clipstone st. Fitzroy square
French John, watch & clock maker, 53 York rd. Lambeth
French John George, surgeon, 41 Great Marlborough st
French John Joseph, oilman, 3 Union pl. Commerl. rd. east
French Joseph, chemist, 1 Palatine pl. Stoke Newington rd
French Newton Henry, butcher, 5 Halfmoon crescent, Pntnvl
French Philip Matthew, proctor, see Farrer, French & Tatham
French Richard, tinman, 4 Baker's row, Whitechapel rd
French Samuel, tailor, 28 Primrose st. Bishopsgate st
French Sarah (Mrs.), staymaker, 73 George st. Portman sq
French Sophia (Mrs.), straw & leghn. hat ma. 226 Oxford st
French Thomas, *Black Horse* P.H. 30 Oxendon st. Haymkt
French Thomas, butcher, 29 Great Quebec st
French Thomas, tailor, 7 Goldsmith's row, Hackney rd
French Thomas, jun. tailor, 232 Bethnal green road

French Wm. *Albion* coffee rooms, 62 Wardour st. Soho
French Wm. carpenter, 5 Richbell place, Lamb's Conduit st
French Wm. dentist, 45 Brick lane, St. Luke's
French Wm. surveyor, 10 John st. Bedford row
French Wm. upholsterer, appraiser & undertaker, 7 Edwards st. Portman square
French Wm. window glass cutter, glass shades, sheet, pipe & white lead merchant, 24 Whitechapel High st
French William Austin, chemist, 309 High Holborn
Frend Alfd. Blackburne, architect, 14 Buckingham st. Adlp
Frend Henry Tyrwhitt, barrister, 28 Southampton buildings
Frere, Forster, Goodford & Cholmeley, solicitors, 6 New sq
Frere Edward, solicitor, 53 Lincoln's inn fields
Fresh & London Bridge Steam Packet wharfs, & Cox & Hammonds' quays, Jackson & Knill, 6 & 7 Low. Thames st
Freshfield James Wm. jun. CharlesK. & Henry R. solicitors, 5 New Bank buildings, Lothbury
Freshwater James & Co. Gt. Western tea mart, 282 Oxford st
Freshwater George, carpenter, &c. 7 Franklin row, Chelsea
Freshwater James, corndealer, 56 Chapel st. Somers town
Freshwater Sam. carp. & undertaker, 19 Park st. Camden town
Freshwater Wm. grocer, 102 Cromer st. Brunswick sq
Freshwater Wm. *Telegraph* P.H. 13 Hawkins st. Mile end rd
Freston George, fruiterer, Church st. Hackney
Fretwell David *Red Lion* P.H. 2 York st. St. James's
Freudemacher Geo. color ma. 54 Church rd. Commer. rd. east
Freudentheil & Hinsch, merchants, 13 Great St. Helen's
Freund Leopold & Co. wool bro. & genl. agts. 76 Basinghall st
Freund Geo. silk hat varnish ma. 5 Hunt st. Pelham st. Brick la
Freund Hen. ironmonger & gold beater, 23 Brick la. Spitalfields
Frew William, baker, 72 High st. Marylebone; & corn & coal merchant, Union wharf, Edward st. Regent's park basin
Frew William, coal merchant, Edward st. Regent's park
Frewer Fras. (Mrs.), cab proprietr. 1 George ter. Neckingr. rd
Frewer Isaac, saddler, &c. 55 Southampton row, Russell sq
Frewer James R. plumber, painter & glazier, 105 Up. Thames st
Frewin William & Edwin, hatters, 10 Tyler st. Golden sq
Frewin Edward, cheesemonger, 32 High Holborn
Frewin James, cabinet ma. 23 Tottenham pl. Tottenham ct. rd
Frewin James, glass & lead merchant, 12 Lisson grove North
Frewin John, greengrocer, 15 Carnaby st. Golden square
Frewin William, wardrobe dealer, 7 East st. Manchester sq
Freyberg Peter, cheesemonger, 49 Warwick st. Golden sq
Fribohn Charles, bootmaker, 57 Rathbone place
Fribourg & Pontet, snuffmakers to the Royal Family, 124 Pall mall
Fribourg & Treyer, purveyors of foreign snuffs to her Majesty & the Royal Family, 34 Haymarket, & 51 Cornhill
Fricke Mary Ann (Miss), milliner, 33 Nutford pl. Bryanstn. sq
Fricker Emily (Miss), ladies' school, 52 Gt. Marlboro' st
Fricker Hen. cap-peak & cockade ma. 2 Albion ter. Kingsland rd
Fricker James, baker, St. John's hill, Wandsworth road
Fricker Keturah (Mrs.), *Ship* P.H. Essex st. Strand
Fricker Robert George, poultry salesman, Leadenhall market
Fricker William, fancy trimming ma. 23 Ashford st. Hoxton
Fricour Augustine, *Fricour's hotel*, 82 & 83 St. Martin's la
Frid Thomas, hop factor, King's Head in yd. 54 Borough
Friday Frances (Mrs.), cowkeeper, 15 Lt. Earl st. Seven dls
Friday John, dairyman, 15 Dean st. Soho
Friedeberg Abrm. furrier & cap ma. 8 King's pl. Com. rd. east
Friedeberg Lionel, genl. mer. & dlr. 10 Miles la. London br
Friedel Adam, lithographic printer, 3 Bloomsbury st. St. Giles'
Friedlander Chas. Martin, physician, Larkhall rise, Clphm
Friedlander Lesser, leech, cigar & goods import. 8 Leman st
Friedlander Lewin Moses, brush ma. see Katz & Friedlander
Friedlander Meyer Wm. & Co. wine merchts. 4 America sq
Friend & Beckwith, wlln. fctrs. & warehmn. 14A, Gresham st
Friend & Boden, sugar refiners, 17 Fieldgate st. Whitechpl
Friend Rd. Prior & John S. timber mers. & bldrs. 42 Banksd
Friend Charles, cowkeeper, 8 Heneage st. Whitechapel
Friend Edward, fruit salesman, 63 Farringdon market
Friend Geo. *Anchor & Hope* P.H. 19 Gt. Charlotte st. Blkfrs. rd
Friend Helen (Miss), beer retailer, 1 Diamond point, Poplar
Friend Henry, grocer, 5 Bouverie st. Edgware road
Friend John S. eng. & for. tmbr. mer. & bldr. see Pryor & Friend
Friend John, *Rose & Crown* P.H. 11 Back Church la. Whitechpl
Friend John Ewer, confectioner, 10 Belmont row, Vauxhall
Friend Joseph, baker, 105 Gt. Portland st. Oxford st
Friend Joshua, ship joiner, 1 Diamond point, Poplar
Friend Martin, fan & skylight manfr. 58 Paul st. Finsbury
Friend Michael, tobacconist, 45 Long acre
Friend Rosanna (Mrs.), teadealer, &c. 13 Cobourg st. Euston sq
Friend Wm. grocer & cheesemonger, 36 Cursitor st
Friend Wm. Henry, zinc worker, 16 Broadway, Westminster
Friendly Societies' Office, 5 Bolton st. Piccadilly
Frier Edmund, tailor, 68 Great Titchfield st. Oxford st
Frier Noah, grocer, 5 Southampton st. Camberwell road
Frieschmann George, teadealer, 152 Upper Whitecross st
Frigout Joseph, tailor, 25 Little Marylebone st
Frinneby Frederick Richard, wholesale painting, general & fancy brush manufacturer, 23 Coppice row, Clerkenwell
Fripp George, artist, 92 Albany st. Regent's park
Frisbee Maria (Mrs.), fruit salesman, 65 Farringdon market
Frisby Charles & Son, wine & brandy merchants, 62 Mark la
Frisby Ann (Mrs.), fishmonger, 2 Darkhouse la. Billingsgate
Frisby Frederic, butcher, 5 Red Lion st. Whitechapel High st
Frisby Louisa (Mrs.), toy wareh. & statnr. 3 Park ter. Camden tn
Fritchley Richd. *Geo. & Dragon* P.H. 1 Northampton pl. Clkwl
Frith Brothers, opticns & powderflash ma. 46 Lisle st. Le'ster sq
Frith, Wallace & Co. mer. & east india agts. 11 Austin friars
Frith Peter & Co. sheffield warehouse, 4 Bolt court, Fleet st
Frith & Smith, silk & satin dressers, Bateman's rw. Curtn. rd
Frith Elizabeth (Mrs.), lodging ho. 26 Thavies inn, Holborn
Frith Frederick, oil & colorman, 1 High st. Newington butts
Frith James, wine & spirit mercht. 89 Bishopsgate without
Frith John, last & boot tree maker, 19A, Princes st. Drury la
Frith William Powell, artist, 31 Charlotte st. Fitzroy sq
Fritz Louis, army clothier, see Krantzcke & Fritz
Frodsham John & Son, chronometer maks. 31 Gracechurch st
Frodsham Charles, chronometer maker, 84 Strand
Frodsham Charles, chronometer ma. see Arnold & Frodsham
Frodsham Wm. Jas. chronometer ma. see Parkinson & Frodsham
Frodsham William James, chronometer watch & clockmaker, 4 Change alley, Cornhill
Froeschlen & Price, tailors, 19 Dover st. Piccadilly
Froggate Benjn. optician, 27 Bridghouse pl. Newngtn. cswy
Froggatt Edwin, optician, 13 Charterhouse st. Charterho. sq
Froggatt George, bootmaker, 75 Coleshill st. Pimlico
Froggatt John, chemist, &c. corner of Grove rd. Mile end rd
Froggatt John, solicitor, 16 Clifford's inn, Fleet st
Froggatt Robert, tailor & draper, 23 Sun st. Bishopsgate
Frohock Mark, chandler's shop, 7 Villiers st. Strand
Froloff Wm. russia merch. 2 Adams ct. Old Broad st. & Baltic
Fromant Charles, woollendraper, 45 Upper Ebury st
Froom William, looking glass manufacturer, 136 Strand
Froomes Henry, tobacconist, 148 Edgware road
Froomes Thos. grocer & cheesemonger, 27 Hall park, Edgw. rd
Frooms Moses, painter, 10 Circus st. New road
Frost John & Co. british lace mnfrs. 11 Wood st. Cheapside
Frost Jsph. & Isaac, brassfounders, 61 to 63 St. John's sq. Clkn
Frost & Norton, turners & brushmakers, 1 York st. St. James's
Frost Robt. & Thos. lace manufs. 4 Goldsmith st. Cheapside
Frost & Sheader, sailmakers & ship chandlers, 320 Wapping
Frost & Vincent, brass & cock founders, 195 Brick la. Sptlfds
Frost Allen, upholsterer, 18 Cirencester place, Fitzroy sq
Frost Benj. Ward, meat salesman, 10 Shambles, Newgate mkt
Frost Charles, engine turner, 27 Myddelton st. Spafields
Frost Chas. Maynard, surgeon, 5 Ladbroke pl. Notting hill
Frost Edmund, bootmaker, 3 Lit. Charles st. Regent's park
Frost Edward, *Grapes* P.H. 1 Bow st. Covent garden
Frost Edward, leather dresser, 21 Greek st
Frost Edwin, grocer, tea dealer, &c. 35 Silver st. Golden sq
Frost Elizth. (Mrs.), *Fountain* P.H. 18A Serle's pl. Carey st
Frost Henry, range & jack maker, 15 Woodstock st. Bond st
Frost James, auctioneer, &c. Wellington ter. Clapham rise
Frost James, fruiterer, 42 New road, St. George's east
Frost James, tailor, 1 Dorset st. Clapham road
Frost James John, rope makr. Sun tavern fields, St. Geo. east
Frost James Morris, *Stirling Castle* P.H. 50 London wall
Frost John, baker, 38 Hindon st. Vauxhall road
Frost John, *Marlboro' Head* P.H. 23 Green walk, Blkfrs. rd
Frost John, oilman, 33 Norfolk st. Middlesex hospital
Frost John Henry, wheelwright, 43 White st. Borough
Frost Joseph, *Marquis of Granby* P.H. 9 High st. Kensington
Frost Louisa (Mrs.), engineer, 86 Union st. Borough
Frost Nicholas, baker, 9 Seabright place east, Hackney rd
Frost Richard, dining rooms, 11 South st. Finsbury market
Frost Robert, butcher, 38 New road, St George's east
Frost Robert, coal dealer, 59 Salisbury st. Lisson grove
Frost Robert, *Ham and Windmill* P.H. 37 Great Windmill st
Frost Robert, livery stables, 93 Park st. Camden town
Frost Robert, haberdasher, 5 St. James's place Bermondsey
Frost Sarah (Mrs.), chandls. shop, 6 Brewer st. nrth, Goswl. rd
Frost Saville Thomas, fixture dealer, 11 Castle st. Long acre
Frost Thomas, coach painter, 22 South Molton st. Bond st.
Frost Thomas, grocer, 117 Fetter lane, Fleet st.
Frost Thomas, grocer & gen. dlr. 60 King st. Westminster
Frost Thomas, grocer, 75 Paradise row, Chelsea
Frost Thomas, printer, & statnr. 45 Marshall st. Golden sq
Frost Thomas Edward, baker, 50 Brook st. Ratcliff
Frost Wm. academy, 29 Vincent square, Westminster
Frost Wm. butcher, 7 Seabright place east, Hackney road

Frost Wm. carpenter, 35 Friday st. Cheapside
Frost Wm. carpenter, 17 Grafton st. Soho
Frost Wm. *Fountain* P.H. 10 New st. Golden square
Frost Wm. fruiterer, &c. 17 King's row Pimlico
Frost Wm. grocer & cheesemonger, 31 Edward st. Stepney
Frost William Edward, artist, 55 Berners st. Oxford st.
Frost William Hales, *Blue Ball* P.H. 4 Boundary st. Shoredtch
Frost Wm. John, linendraper, 118 Brick lane Spitalfields
Frostick Edward, grocer, 1 Bloomsbury ter. Vauxhl. bridge rd
Froud John, builder, 1A, Brewer st. Pimlico
Froud Philip, boot maker, 12 Harp alley, Farringdon st
Frugal Invest. Ass. (Hen. Chas. Barfoot, sec.), 36 Chancery la
Frühling & Göschen, merchants, 2 Crosby sq. Bishopsgate
Fruin Frederick John, house & shipsmith, 41 New Grave la
Fruit Meters' Office (John Hurles, meter), 1 Dean st Tooley st.; hours 6 to 6
Fry & Bennett, fancy cabinet manufacturers, & portable leather desk & dressing case makers, 36 Little Charlotte st. Blackfriars road
Fry, Griffiths & Co. indigo & col. brokers, 130 Fenchurch st
Fry John & Thos. auctioneers & appraisers, 43 Chiswell st
Fry Joseph Storrs & Sons, cocoa ma. 7 Windsor pl. City rd
Fry, Loxley & Fry, solicitors, 80 Cheapside
Fry Thos. & Son, coopers, 6 Shadwell dock st. Lr. Shadwell
Fry Thomas & Son, refined sugar dealers, 77 Cannon st
Fry Alfred Augustus, barrister, 6 Pump court, Temple
Fry Ann (Mrs.), tobacconist, 33 Chancery lane
Fry Cornelius, grocer, 110 Bishopsgate without
Fry Edward, carpenter, 29 Goswell ter. Goswell road
Fry Edward, working jeweller, 14 Litchfield st. Soho
Fry Fredk. house deco. & buildr. King's road west, Chelsea
Fry George, fruiterer, 75 St. John st. Clerkenwell
Fry George, solicitor, see Cattarns & Fry
Fry John, butterman, 6 South st. King's road, Chelsea
Fry John, carpenter & undertaker, Chapel place, Brompton
Fry John, seedsman & florist, Morning lane, Hackney
Fry John Gurney, merchant, see Sanderson, Frys', Fox & Co
Fry Joseph, chairmaker, 1 New inn, Broadway, Shoreditch & 18 Curtain road
Fry Joseph, sealing wax, wafer & ink manufacturer, & importer of india rubber, &c. 14 & 15 Basing lane, Cheapside
Fry Richard Thos. gasfitter, &c. 34 Skinner st. Somers town
Fry Rosalie (Madame), dressma. 15 South st. Grosvenor sq
Fry Samuel, upholsterer, 14 Alfred pl. Newington causeway
Fry Sarah Elizh. (Mrs.), ladies' school, 140 Hoxton High st
Fry Stephen, furniture broker, 6 Aldenham st. Somers town
Fry Thomas, cornchandler, 36 Trafalgar st. Walworth road
Fry Thomas, oilman, 25 Chester st. Kennington cross
Fry Thos. dyer, academy & acctnt. 140 High st. Hoxton Old tn
Fry Thos. Homfray, law stationer, 14 South sq. Gray's inn
Fry William, poulterer, Leadenhall market
Fry Wm. Hubbart, tailor, 20 Pollard's row, Bethnal green
Fry Wm. Robert, timber mercht. 2 Ordnance pl. Circus rd. east
Fryer Wm. & Son, cattle salesmen, 41 West Smithfield
Fryer Charlotte (Miss), lace mnfr. 17 Duke st. Manchstr. sq
Fryer George, teadealer, 1 Surrey place, Grange road
Fryer Henry, boarding house, 27 Great Winchester st
Fryer James Joseph, stock & share broker, 1 Birchin lane
Fryer John, bookseller & stationer, 63 Charing cross
Fryer John, collar maker, 6 Little Stanhope st. Mayfair
Fryer John Cornelius, bootmaker, 4 Penton pl. New road
Fryer Joseph, seedsman, 14 Clarendon ter. Camberwl. nw. rd
Fryer Joseph T. who. stationer, Rupert st. Goodman's fields
Fryer Mary (Mrs.), bonnet ma. 9 Pritchard's pl. Hackney flds
Fryer Richard, linendraper, see Aldwinckle & Fryer
Fryer Richd. washing machine maker, 1 Brown's la. Spitalfi
Fryer Thomas, *Founders' Arms* P.H. 8 Holland st. Blkfrs. rd
Fryer Wm. jeweller, &c. see Jones & Fryer
Fryer Wm. tobacco, snuff & cigar ma. 13 & 14 Smithfield bars
Fryer Wm. watch & case gilder, 37 Wellington st. Goswell st
Fryett John William, pawnbroker, 16 Whitechapel road
Fuce Thos. & Mary E. coal mers. Southwk. br. wf. 11 Bankside
Fudge Absalom, beer retailer, 16 Bouverie st. Paddington
Fudge Chas. manftrng. goldsmith, 45 Seckford st. Clerkenwell
Fudge Dorah (Mrs.), poulterer, 146 Sloane st. Knightsbridge
Fudge James, artist, 111 Sloane st. Knightsbridge
Fuge Robert, coachmaker, see Kipps & Fuge
Fugler Wm. manchester warehouseman, 10 Lawrence lane
Fulcher Geo. & Hen. distillrs. & wine mers. 4 Osborne st. Whtchl
Fulcher George, distiller, 19 Artillery place, Finsbury sq
Fulcher John, linendra. & haberdasher, 111 & 112 Shoreditch
Fulcher Wm. east india agent & ship broker, 78 Cornhill
Fuld Fred. & Co. bankers (Frankfort s. m.), 32 Villiers st. Str
Fulford Henry, cooper, 65 Tothill st. Westminster
Fulford Wm. button & trimming seller, 29 St. Martin's le grand
Fullagar Edwyn, builder, &c. 3 Queenhithe & 10 Gt. Carter la
Fullalove Stephen, glass wa. 300 Oxford st. & 61 Farringdon st
Fullarton Archibald & Co. booksellers, 106 Newgate st
Fullarton Gavin, merchant, 3 Lime st. square
Fullbrook Hen. carpenter, &c. 21 Smith st. King's rd. Chelsea
Fullbrook Joseph, carpenter, 10 & 11 Ormond row, Chelsea
Fuller Augustus E. & Co. merchants, 4 Church ct. Clement's la
Fuller & Hammerton, surgeons, 111 & 112 Piccadilly
Fuller John & Co. hat manufrs. 95 & 96 Long la. Bermondsey
Fuller & Marsh, auctioneers, surveyors & land agents, 2 Charlotte row, Mansion house, & Croydon, Surrey
Fuller & Saltwell, solicitors, Carlton Chambers, 12 Regent st
Fuller Samuel & Joseph, printsellers, publishers, & preparers of superfine water colors, 34 Rathbone place, Oxford st
Fuller & Smith, ship tank makers, Millwall, Poplar
Fullers' & Co. bankers, 66 Moorgate st
Fullers' Almshouses, between 92 & 93 Old st. road
Fuller Abrah. carp. & undertak. 11 Devonshire st. Kennington
Fuller Chas. Wm. hairdresser, 12 Bridge st. Lambeth
Fuller Daniel, meat, poultry & butter sa. 64 Newgate market
Fuller Edmund, greengrocer, 65 George st. Portman sq
Fuller Edw. Ives, coachmaker, 77 & 78 Margaret st. Cvndsh sq
Fuller Francis, land surveyor, 8 Parliament st
Fuller Frederick, solicitor, Carlton chambs. 12 Regent st
Fuller George, baker, 10 Dorset st. Clapham road
Fuller George, ship & insurance ag. 2 Riches ct. Lime st
Fuller George, baker, 33 Lower marsh, Lambeth
Fuller Henry, jeweller & silversmith, 18 Ludgate hill
Fuller Hy. manuftg. stationer & printer, 38 King st. Cheapside
Fuller Hugh P. surgeon, 53 King William st. City
Fuller Jas. baker, 25 Sidney pl. Commercial road east
Fuller Jas. bricklayer, 54 Margaret st. Wilmington sq
Fuller Jas. cattle salesman, 60 West Smithfield
Fuller Jas. furntr. japan. & ho. paint. 29 Hyde st. Bloomsbury
Fuller Jas. plumber, painter, &c. 5 Charles st. Portman sq
Fuller Jas. slater & filter maker, 11 Globe road, Mile end
Fuller Jane (Miss), confectioner, 122 Sloane st. Chelsea
Fuller Jeremiah, assayer, Goldsmiths' hall, Foster lane
Fuller John, barge & boat builder, Millwall, Poplar
Fuller John, chemist, 23 Crosby row, Walworth road
Fuller John, grocer, 12 Lower Porchester st. Edgware road
Fuller John, lodging house, 31 Northumberland st. Marylebo
Fuller John, surgeons' machinist, 239 Whitechapel road
Fuller John, treasr. to the New England Co. 9 Gt. St. Helen's
Fuller John Geo. wine merchant, 28 St. James's st. Pall mall
Fuller Joseph, house & estate agt. 161 Albany st. Regent's pk
Fuller Joseph, who. stationer, 42 Brewer st. Golden square
Fuller Louisa (Mrs.), prof. of music, 26 Up. Baker st. Regent's pk
Fuller Mary (Mrs.), toy dealer, 77 Broad st. Ratcliff
Fuller Richard, fire wood dealer, 39 Union st. Lambeth
Fuller Richd. glass cutter & stopperer, 21 Castle st. Holborn
Fuller Robert, carpenter & bldr. South Island pl. Clapham rd
Fuller Robert, stationer, 16 Bland terrace, Gt. Dover road
Fuller Stephen, carman, Mill st. Lambeth
Fuller Surplis, fruiterer, 27 Borough road
Fuller Thomas, auctioneer & surveyor, 13 Billiter st
Fuller Thomas, chandler's shop, 31 & 32 Sidney st. Somers tn
Fuller Thomas, dining rooms, 5 Lit. Bell alley, Coleman st
Fuller Wm. builder, 16 Brompton grove west, Old Brompton
Fuller Wm. butcher, 104 Snow's fields, Bermondsey
Fuller Wm. carpenter, 18 Gloucester grove west, Brompton
Fuller Wm. corn & coal dealer, 80 Hoxton Old town
Fuller Wm. dairdresser, 25 Long alley, Finsbury
Fuller Wm. ice pail maker, 60 Jermyn st. St. James's
Fuller Wm. lamp manfr. & gasfitt. 36A, Charles st. Hatton gdn
Fuller Wm. rouge manufacturer, 66 West st. West Smithfield
Fuller Wm. wheelwright, Wyndham rd. Camberwell nw. rd
Fuller Wm. Coles (late Batley), portable desk, dressing case, work box & pocket book manufr. 13 Brownlow st. Holborn
Fuller Wm. Cornelius, carman, 21 George st. Grosvenor sq
Fuller Wm. Cornelius, hosier & flannel draper, 157 Oxford st
Fullerton John Chamney, surgeon, 30 Lower st. Islington
Fullford Edmund, law stationer, 3 Serle's pl. Lincoln's inn
Fullford Jacob, fruiterer, 17 West st. Golden square
Fullick, John, baker, 12 Featherstone st. City road
Fullicks Richard, butcher, 4 Princes pl. Commercial rd. east
Fullilove Charles, working cutler, 54 King st. Seven dials
Fulljames Eliz. (Mrs.), *Talbot inn*, Talbot inn yard, 75 Borough High st
Fullmer & Wilkinson, house & sign painters, 1 East st. & 21 Devonshire st. Red Lion sq
Fullstone Henry, chair & sofa ma. 33 Booth st. Spitalfields
Fullstone Thomas, tailor, &c. 18 Park st. Borough
Fullstone Wm. tailor, 43 Turvile st. Church st. Shoreditch
Fulluck Edmund, coffee house, 55 Broad st. Ratcliff cross
Fullwood & Bland, annatto manufacturers & merchants, 24 Somerset place, Hoxton New town
Fullwood James, baker, 63 Blackman st. Borough

Fulton & Green, pat. pepper works, New rd. South Lambeth
Fulton Geo. Alex, gasfitter, Hope cottage, Stepney Old road
Fulton James, tailor & draper, 16 Castle st. East, Oxford st
Fullwell Hannah (Mrs.), stationer, 5 Suffolk pl. Hackney rd
Fundell Joseph, baker, 1 Goldsmith's row, Hackney road
Fundell Joseph, baker, 42 Red Lion st. Holborn
Funge & Bland, *Garraway's coffeehouse*, 3 Change al. Cornhill
Funnell Leggett, baker, 39 York st. City road
Furber Charles, auctioneer, &c. 2 Warwick court, Gray's inn
Furber Charles, *Black Bull* P.H. 17 Lit. Chapel st. Westmr
Furber Chas. David, *Exeter Arms* P.H. 2 Burleigh st. Strand
Furber Henry, violin maker, 50 Britannia row, Islington
Furber James, refiner of gold, &c. see Collins & Furber
Furber John, violin maker, 26 Wellington st. Goswell st
Furber Jonathan, auctioneer, 18 Duke st. Manchester sq
Furby & Stockton, tailors, &c. 35 Sackville st. Piccadilly
Furby Geo. ironmonger & hardwareman, 53 Whitechapel rd
Furby Richard, coachsmith, 10 Castle st. Long acre
Furley Anne & Cath. & Co. goldbeatrs. 8 Gt. Sutton st. Clerknwell
Furley John, manufactr. of hosiery, 1 Lit. Love lane, Wood st
Furley Philip Charles, goldbeater, 26 Long alley, Finsbury
Furley William, gold & silver beater, 45 Gt. Sutton st
Furley William, shopkeeper, Well st. Hackney
Furlonger Chas. Joseph, stokbro. Stock ex. & 10 Throgmorton st
Furnell Wm. Henry, accountant, 29 Ironmonger la. Cheapside
Furner Frederick, solicitor, 42 Southampton buildings, & Eastman place, Old Kent road
Furner Richard, fruit & pea salesman, 62 Farringdon market
Furness Edward, bootmaker, 60 Lamb's Conduit st. Foundling
Furness George, color mnfr. Falcon wf. Maiden la. King's cr
Furness James, pastrycook & biscuit baker, 162 High Holbn
Furness Richd. T. tobaccnst. 40 New Church st. Lisson grove
Furness Robt. greengrocer, 64 Pearson st. Kingsland rd
Furness Rt. oilman, 13 Pearson st. Kingsland rd
Furness Wm. hairdresser, 17 Bermondsey New road
Furnis Samuel, hatter, 112 New Bond st
Furniss Thos. watchmaker & jeweller, 25 Crawford st
Furnivall Charles, *Dolphin* P.H. 16 Long alley, Finsbury
Furnivall James, builder, 22 Harp lane, Tower st
Furnivall John Jas. physician, 3 Weymouth st. Portland pl
Furnivall Thos. 30 Bedford st. Covent garden
FURNIVAL'S INN, 134 Holborn bars
Furr Wm. John, milled lead baker, Honduras st. Old st
Furrell James, law stationer, see Ritchie & Furrell
Furse Ann (Miss), staymaker, 6 South Molton st. Oxford st
Furse John, merchant, see Heath, Furse & Co
Furse Joseph, stay manufacturer, see Roope & Furse
Fursey George, bricklayer, 132 Albany road, Camberwell
Furze John, brewer, see Manners & Furze
Furze John, tailor, 11 Boston st. Park road
Furze Thos. H. wine & brandy merchant, 4 Colonial chambers, John st. Crutched friars
Furze William, bootmaker, 92 Dorset st. Salisbury sq
Fussell Alexander, artist, 29 Argyl st. New road
Fussell Jonathan, currier, 117 Old st. St. Luke's
Fussell Joseph, artist, 20 Sidmouth st. Gray's inn road
Fussell Thomas, oilman, 18 Lr. Chapman st. St. George's ea
Fussell Wm. painter & glass stainer, 5 Augustus st. Reg. pk
Fussey John, tobacconist, 8 Mason's alley, Basinghall st
Futter Charles, jeweller, 6 Johnson's court, Fleet st
Futvoye Charles Francis, dealer in medical glass & earthenware, manufacturers of shopfittings & every description of surgical implements, 58 West Smithfield
Futvoye Edward, solicitor, 23 John st. Bedford row
FutvoyeChas. Fras. teacher of japanning, 3 Lit. James st. Bedf. r
Fyfe Peter, *Princess Victoria* P.H. Earl st. Kensington
Fyfe Thomas, engineer, 26 Tavistock st. Covent garden
Fyffe Edward & Sons, who. teadlrs. 4 Howford bldgs. Fnchrch st
Fyler George, barrister, 4 Pump court, Middle Temple
Fynmore Thos. G. solicitor, see Clarke, Fynmore & Fladgate
Fyson & Curling, solicitors, 3 Frederick's pl. Old Jewry
Fyvie George, baker, 2 Bedford st. Covent garden

GABAIN & Co. merchants, 5 Martin's lane, Cannon st
Gaball Henry, brace & stock ma. 29 Marylebone st. Picdilly
Gaball James, tailor & trimming dealer, 78 Berwick st. Soho
Gabb Frederic, *White Bear* P.H. Bear garden, Southwark
Gabb John, solicitor, 19 Trafalgar st. Walworth road
Gabb John Heatley, butcher, 45 Gt. James st. Lisson grove
Gabell George, hairdresser, 34 Lit. Guildford st. Brunswk. sq
Gaberthuel D. agt. to Morris & Sons needle ma. 48A, Glos'ter pl
Gabetiss Martin, *Old Swan* P.H. 2 Steyman's rw. Holloway rd
Gable Elizabeth (Mrs.), beer retailer, 39 Edward st. Bethn. gn
Gable Isaac, *Red Cross* P.H. 12 Hare st. Bethnal green
Gable Thos. Ebenezer, manufacturer of silk for sieve bottoms, &c. 3 Perseverance ter. Church st. Bethnal green
Gabriel & Newington, solicitors, 44 Lincoln's inn fields
Gabriel Thos. & Sons, timber mers. Commercial rd. Lambeth
Gabriel Benj. Wilmot, manchester wa. 12 Bread st. Cheapside
Gabriel Edmund Nicolas, veterinary surgeon, 15 Rolls buildings, Fetter lane, & Herne hill
Gabriel James Alex. solicitor, see Vincent & Gabriel
Gabriel John Wild, woollen warehouse, 135 Regent st
Gabriel & Newington, solicitors, 44 Lincoln's inn fields
Gaby & Wills, oil & color merchants, indigo, blue & black lead manufacturers, 221 & 222 Shoreditch
Gace Grantham, ship & insu. broker, Lloyd's, Roy. Exchange
Gad & Keningale, copper pl. printrs. 9 Sol's row, Hampstead rd
Gad Sarah (Mrs.), *Old Five Bells* P.H. Bromley, Middlesex
Gadban Elia Paolo, merchant, 9 Finsbury chmbrs. Londn. wall
Gadbury William, coffee rooms, 76 Union st. Boro'
Gadd Charles, chemist, 1 New Bridge st. Vauxhall
Gadd Elizabeth (Mrs.), grocer, 20 Regent st. Lambeth
Gadd John, baker, 79 High st. Camden town
Gadd John, wax & tallow chandler, 13 King st. Holborn
Gaddes David, chair maker, 5 Whiting st. Gt. Waterloo st
Gädechens Diedrich Hinrich, merchant, 2 Crosby square
Gädechens Diod Hiur, merchant, 2 Crosby square
Gadenne Wm. Dan. machine ruler, 1 Moor la. Cripplegate
Gadesden Aug. sugar refiner, see Wainwright & Gadesden
Gadsby Alfred, carpenter, 52 Regent st. Lambeth
Gadsby Wm. carpenter, 12 Charterhouse lane, City
Gadsden & Flower, solicitors, 14 Furnival's inn, Holborn
Gadsden James & Son, sugar refi. 4 Leman st. & 2 Gt. St. Helen's
Gadsden John & Co. who. & retail cheesemongs. 273 Oxford st
Gadsden John & Son, cheesemongers, 30 Ludgate hill
Gadsden David, merchant, 2 Great St. Helen's
Gadsden George, baker, 58 Leather lane, Holborn, & 30 Portpool lane, Gray's inn lane
Gadsden George, butcher, 31 Ernest st. Regent's park
Gadsden Hen. Fras. auctioneer, see Musgrove & Gadsden
Gadsden John, bootmaker, 8 Newcastle place, Edgware rd
Gadsdon Chas. & Benj. coach platers, 22 Union st. Bishopsg
Gadsdon Henry, oil & colorman, 21 Featherstone st. City rd
Gael Samuel Higgs, barrister, 2 Old sq. Lincoln's inn
Gaerth Chas. LL.D. german advocate, 9 Essex st. Strand
Gaffin Edward, sculptor, 63 Quadrant, Regent st
Gage Benjamin, coach builder, 5 New road, Whitechapel rd
Gage Thos. *Three Compasses* P.H. 1 Brick la. Spitalfields
Gage Wm. *Good Samaritan* P.H. 1 Gt. Tower st. Com. rd. ea
Gagen & Ford, architects, see Ford & Gagen
Gagen Geo. architect, &c. 15 Rowland's row, Stepney gr
Gagen Thomas Wm. saddler & harn. mak. 278 Poplar High st
Gagniere Auguste, french silk imptr & manfr. 21 Golden sq
Gahagan Charles, coachmaker, 62A, Edgware road Marylebone, & 27 Queen st. Bryanstone square
Gaimes Charles, hatter & outfitter, 22 Birchin la
Gain David, butcher, 9 Church st. Blackfriars road
Gain Jonathan, butcher, 18 Queen's pl. Kennington road
Gain Joseph, butcher, 2 Virginia pl. Gt. Dover road
Gain Wm. butcher, 2 Brecknock place, Camden New Town
Gaines Wm. & Sarah, seedsmen & herblsts. North rw. Covnt. ga
Gaines Chas. solicitor, 1 Caroline st. Bedford square
Gaines John, market gardener, Battersea
Gaines Nancy (Mrs.), florist, Surrey lane, Battersea
Gaines Mary (Miss), market gardener, Battersea marsh
Gainey Jas. cheesemonger, 46 Charlotte st. Whitechapel
Gains Wm. B. & Co. woollen drapers, 47 Ludgate hill
Gainsford & Goode, drapers & silk mercers, 119 Boro' High st
Gainsford Geo. silk mercer, 9 Paragon, New Kent road
Gairdner Geo. Wm. upholsterer, 80 Tottenham court road
Gairdner Wm. physician, 12 Bolton st. Piccadilly
Gairns James, watch & jewel case ma. 20 Redcross st. Criplg
Gaisford George, baker, 11 Haberdashers' walk, Hoxton
Gaisford George, baker, 179 Kingsland road
Gaisford John, baker, 30 Gravel lane, Southwark
Gaisford Robert, baker, 8 Moor lane, Cripplegate
Gaitskell John & Co. distillers, wine, brandy & liqueur merchants, 229 Bermondsey st
Gaitskell Wm. Senhouse, solicitor, clerk to the trustees of Surrey & Sussex roads, & commissrs. of taxes in 3rd division of East Brixton, 21 Stamford st. Blackfriars road
Gaitt John, plumber & glazier, 59 Edgware road, Marylebone
Gal John Martin, *Rose tavern* P.H. 96 Jermyn st. St. James
Galabin George John, printer, &c. 91 Bartholomew close
Galabin Thomas, stationer, see Harris & Galabin
Galbraith Jas. S. agt. to Arch. Campbell & Co. brewrs. Edinbro, Steel yard, Upper Thames st
Galbraith Robt. cheesemongr. & prov. mer. Commercial rd. ea
Gale, Baker, Warde & Co. who. druggists, Bouverie st. Fleet st
Gale Samuel & Co. ironmongers, 320 Oxford st
Gale Benj. market gardener, Jamaica level, Rotherhithe

Gale Charles James, barrister, 1 Mitre court bldgs. Temple
Gale Fred. cowkeeper, Commercial road, Pimlico
Gale George, *Rose & Crown* P.H. 21 Crucifix lane, Brmndsy
Gale Henry, chemist, 27 Judd place west, New road
Gale Henry, bookbinder & stationer, 16 Goswell road
Gale Jas. grocer, opposite Ferry house, Millwall, Poplar
Gale James, turner, 29 Adam st. Rotherhithe
Gale John, baker, 67 High st. Lambeth
Gale John, chemist, 1 Lower York place, Kentish town
Gale John, tobacconist, 66 Whitechapel High st
Gale John, watch & clock maker, 91 Wheeler st. Spitalflds
Gale John Harry, surgeon, 4 Up. Queen's buildings, Brompton
Gale John Wm. baker, 1 Wood st. north & 15 Ratcliffe ter. Gswl. rd
Gale Joseph, painter, 36 George st. Portland place
Gale Joseph Walter, civil engineer, 9 John st. Adelphi
Gale Mary (Mrs.), german repository, 107 Gt. Portland st
Gale Richard, picture dealer, 47 High Holborn
Gale Samuel, attorney, 70 Basinghall st
Gale Samuel, barrister, 5 Bedford row
Gale Thomas, baker, 11 Chelsea market, Lower Sloane st
Gale Thomas, beer retailer, 7 St. Chad's row, Gray's inn rd
Gale Thomas, cork cutter, 3 Blacknell pl. Walworth commn
Gale William, artist, 44 Berners st. Oxford st
Gale William, fruiterer, 73 Brewer st. Somers town
Gale Wm. timber mercht. 16 Harcourt st. New rd. Marylebone
Gale Wm. watch gilder, 6 Banner st. St. Luke's
Galeari Michael, physician, 6 Walton place, Brompton
Gales Richard Norman, tobacconist, 17 High st. Kensington, & 41 Grosvenor row, Pimlico
Galibert Esprit, french silk shag imp. 9 Bridge st. Southwk
Galiegue John & Co. hat ma. 13 Bartholomew sq. St. Luke's
Galiegue John, hatter, 13 Bartholomew sq. St. Luke's
Galique Sarah (Miss), milliner, 16 Aske terrace, Hoxton
Galilee Anthony, carpent. & builder, 103 High st. Marylebone
Galindo Portia (Miss), academy, see Jardine & Galindo
Gall & Anderson, linendrapers, 67 High st. Camden town
Gall Alexander T. secretary to St. Laurance & Atlantic Railroad Co. 5 Barge yard chambers, Barge yard, Bucklersbury
Gall David, bread baker, 4 High st. Newington butts
Gall Mary (Mrs.), grocer, 1 Circular road, Horsemonger la
Gall Thomas, baker, 55 York st. City road
Gallagher John, artist, 6 Change alley, Cornhill
Galland Francis, ladies' shoema. 2 Brandon st. Walworth
Galland James, coachmaker, 21 Lower Eaton st. Grosvnr. pl
Gallant Susannah Ann (Mrs.), tobacco. 23 James st. Cov. gar
Gallati Pandia Sergio, mer. 8 Finsbury chmbs. London wall
Gallatly George, cheesemonger, 27 Brick lane, Old st
Gallaway & Wilson, ship ins. & cust. house agents, 25 Mincing la
Gallaway George, oilman, 7 Bowling st. Marylebone
Gallaway Henry, tailor, 2 Victoria place, Kentish town
Gallaway Wm. beer retailer, 5 Clarence gdns. Regent's park
Gallemore Isaac, tailor, &c. 4 North row, Grosvenor sq
Galley Geo. Miller, grocer, & cheesem. 1 Oxford st. Mile end
Gallienne Abraham, beer & spirit engine ma. 115 Goswell rd
Gallienne Richard, table knife maker & cutler, 71 Goswell st
Galliers George, chemist & druggist, 221 Tottenham ct. rd
Galliers Geo. jun. fixture dealer, 60 Cable st. Wellclose sq
Gallois Frances (Madame), milliner, 44 New Bond st
Gallon Edward, watch & clock glass man. 34 Leman st
Gallop Benjamin James, *Albert* coffee rooms, 95 Milton st
Gallop John, ironfounder, see Martin & Gallop
Gallop Thomas, chairmaker, 19 Gower place, Euston square
Gallouin John & Co. gen. commis. merchts. 35 St. Swithin's la
Galloway Alex. & Sons, engineers, 19 to 21 West st. Smithfield
Galloway Brothers & Co. merchants, 19 to 21 West st. Smithfield
Galloway David, baker, 1 Gloucester pl. Camden town
Galloway George, tailor, &c. 90 Newman st. Oxford st
Galloway Geo. Robt. brush maker, 75 St. John st. Clerkenwell
Galloway James, baker, 3 Trinity row, Upper st. Islington
Galloway James, furnish. ironmngr. 1 Park st. Dorset sq
Galloway Robert, baker, 30 Millbank st. Westminster
Galloway Robert, potato salesman, 91 Broad st. Ratcliff
Galloway Thos. iron pl. work. & brazier 5 Baker's rw. Clknwl
Galloway Thomas, registrar of the *Corporation of the Amicable Life Assurance So.* 19 Serjeants' inn, & 50 Fleet st
Galley Andrew & Geo. looking gla. mfrs. 166 St. George st
Gally Paul & Peter & Co. barometer, thermometer, & looking glass makers, & general dealers, 50 Exmouth st. Spafields
Gally Pantelione, naturalist, 70 Parsons st. St. George st
Galon Henry & Co. hatters, 418 Strand
Galpin Thomas Carter, professor of drawing, 62 Haymarkt
Galsworthy & Nichols, solicitors, 9 Cook's court, Carey st
Galsworthys' & Watts, solicitors, 19 Ely place, Holborn
Galsworthy Silas, builder, 92 Upper Stamford st. Blackfriars
Galsworthy Wm. solicitor, 19 Ely place, Holborn
Galsworthy Wm. Henry, surgeon, 92 Up. Stamford st. Blkfrs

Galvanized (patent) Iron Company (Samuel Vincent, secretary), 3 Mansionhouse place, City
Gambart, Junin & Co. who. printsels. 25 Berners st. Oxford st
Gambee Wm. upholsterer, &c. Hawley pl. Kentish town
Gambell Geo. shoemaker, 32 John st. west, Edgware rd
Gambell Wm. umbrella maker, 7 Up. Seymour st. Euston sq
Gambell & Davis, who. & export shoe wareh. 45 Fish st. hill
Gamble John & Son (late Donkin, Hall & Gamble, established 1812), original patentee of the new method of preserving all kinds of animal & vegetable food, 78 Cornhill
Gamble Ann (Mrs.), fishmonger, 4 Dean st. Soho
Gamble Charles, cab proprietor, 54 Regent st. Horseferry rd
Gamble Harpur, physician, 7 Duke st. Portland place
Gamble Jas. dairyman, 2 Bailey's pl. Marlboro' rd. Chelsea
Gamble John, *Cat* P.H. 220 Upper Whitecross st. St. Luke's
Gamble Richard, grocer, 24 High road, Knightsbridge
Gamble Thos. *Robin Hood* P.H. 14 Gt. Windmill st. Haymkt
Gamble Thos. Eden, *Mitre* P.H. 90 Broadwall
Gamble William, plumber, &c. 24 Basing lane, Bread st
Gambling Robert, bootmaker, 19 Kingsgate st. Holborn
Game Charles, butcher, 17 Nicholas lane, Lombard st
Game Paul, tobacconist, 31 Brill row, Somers town
Game Saml. oil & italian warehouse, 26 Fish st. hill
Game Wm. fruiterer, 6 Orchard place, Kingsland road
Game Wm. *Swan tavern*, 42 King Wm. st. City, & 25 Fish st. hill
Game Wm. James, *King's Head tavern*, 53 Fenchurch st
Games Ralph Parkinson, solicitor, 3 Trinity st. Bow
Gameson Wm. Henry, cheesemonger, 23 St. John st. road
Gamgee Samuel, hairdresser, 70 Bethnal green road
Gamlen Rt. attorney (firm Poole & Gamlen), 3 Gray's inn sq
Gamlen Thomas, solicitor, see Downes, Gamlen & Scott
Gammage & Mott, cheesemongers, 8 Drury lane, & 30 Broad st. Bloomsbury
Gammage Thos. clockmaker, 8 Wood st. north, Goswell rd
Gammage Thos. *Coopers' Arms* P.H. 5 Green bank, Wapping
Gamman Robert & Son, coal merchts. & wharfingers, Union wharf, 68 Wapping wall, & 7 Wilmot sq. Bethnal green rd
Gammon Chas. carver & gilder, 20 Liverpool st. King's cross
Gammon Henry, ship & custom house agent, 43 Lime st
Gammon James, butcher, Battersea square
Gammon James, harness maker, Abbot st. Kingsland
Gammon Wm. ship broker & customhouse agent, 43 Lime st
Gamson Frederic, chemist & druggist, 77 Hackney road
Gamson Thomas, corn & seed factor, 24 Mark lane
Gamson Thomas B. silversmith, 4 Beauvoir place, Kingsland
Gamson Thomas B. pawnbroker, 5 Manchester bldgs. Hollwy
Gandar Buck Charles, *Hercules tav.* 5 Hercules bldgs. Lambeth
Gandell Geo. stock & share broker, 5 Bank cham. Lothbury
Gandell John, iron merchant, 11 Clement's lane
Gandell Thos. packer, Joiners' hall bdgs. 79 Up. Thames st
Gandell Wm. oil & ital. wa. 31 Charles pl. Hertfd. rd. Kingsland
Gander Henry, *Catherine Wheel inn*, 191 Borough High st
Gander Henry, yeast dealer, Catherine wheel yard, 191 Boro'
Gander Wm. *Old Green Gate* P.H. York place, Hackney road
Gandolfi P. & N. & Co. silk merchants, 30 Throgmorton st
Gandon Clarissa (Mrs.), sugar cooper, 8 Osborne pl. Whtchpl
Gandy Thos. grocer & italian wareh. 36 Lower st. Islington
Gandy Wm. umbrella silk manfr. 16 Princes st. Spitalfields
Gane Edward, upholsterer, 12 Cleveland st. Fitzroy sq
Gane Joseph, cheesemonger, 46 Hoxton Old town
Gange George & Co. pianoforte makrs. 10 Lower Belgrave pl
Gange Nathaniel, grocer, 40 Lower Belgrave place, Pimlico
Gann James & Co. outfitting warehouse, 171 Fenchurch st
Gannaway J. *Carpenters' Arms* P.H. 18 Gray st. Manchestr. sq
Gannaway John, *Crown* P.H. 22 Moor lane, Cripplegate
Gannell Wm. grocer & teadealer, 2 Robert st. Grosvenor sq
Gannell Wm. lodging house, 2 Robert st. Grosvenor square
Gannon John, surgeon, 1 Dean's row, Walworth road
Gannon John Pahie, barrister, 4 Elm court, Temple
Gannon Thomas, grocer, 4 Duke st. Lincoln's inn fields
Gannon William, tailor, 10 Chelsea market, Lower Sloane st
Gant John, zinc manufacturer, 2 Surrey pl. Newington butts
Gant Samuel, zinc manufacturer, 19 Tottenham ct. New road
Gant John Castle, solicitor, 37 Nicholas lane, Lombard st
Ganter Francis, clock maker, 19 Charlotte st. Whitechapel
Ganthony R. Pinfold, watchmaker, 83 Cheapside
Gantlett Thomas, tobacconist, 24 Sloane square, Chelsea
Gantley John, cheesmgr. & bacondrier, 7 Church st. Stk. Newgtn
Gantzman Chas. cabinet maker, see Pervinkler & Gantzman
Gapp Charles Jas. *White Lion* P.H. 12 High st. Pentonville
Gapp John, livery stables, 19 Duke st. Manchester square
Garbanati Joseph, carv. & gilder, 37 Southampton st. Strand
Garbanati Paul, plate glass fac. working carver & gilder & fancy wood picture frame manufacturer, 91 Newman st. Oxford st.; manufactory, Swan yard, St. Martin's lane
Garbut Zachariah, fruiterer, 11 Devonshire st. Lisson gr

Garbutt Robert, bricklayer, 244 Wapping
Garcia A. picture & curiosity imp. 1 Princes st. Hanover sq
Garcia Philip, fruiterer,27&36Poultry,&4 Gt.Turnstile,Holb
Gard (Loveday) & Co. lace warehouse, 83 Oxford st
Gard Charles, fruiterer, 212 Bermondsey st
Gard John, fruiterer, Southampton st. Camberwell
GardWm.Snowdon,for.&brit.lace dr.268Regent circus,Oxf.st
Garde Richard, barrister, 12 Portland place, Clapham road
Garden & Macandrew, comsn. agents, 7 Skinner's pl.Sise la
Garden Alexander, operative chemist, 372 Oxford st
Garden Hugh, army accoutr. mak. & saddler,200 Piccadilly
Garden James, watch & clock maker, 60 Kingsland road
Gardeners' Benevolent Insti.(E.R.Cutler, sec.),97Farring.st
Gardeners' Chronicle Newspaper, 5 Upper Wellington st
Gardeners' GazetteNewspaper Office, 2 Tavistock st.Cov.ga
Gardener Edward S. beer retailer, 4 Artillery la.Bishgsgt.st
Gardener Fred. P. ironmonger & stove maker,30 Newgate st
Gardener James, cooper, 3 Gould's hill, Shadwell
Gardener Samuel, tobacconist, 4 Lombard st. Chelsea
Gardener Tho. M. haberdasher, 2 Red Lion st. Whitechapel
Gardie Francis, horn mercht.Brunton works,Comrcl.rd.east
Gardie Louis, modeller, chaser & water gilder, 8 Percy st
Gardiner John & Son,wine mers.10Crosby hall chmbrs.Bpsgt
Gardiner & Dixon, surgeons, 1 Markham square
Gardiner Sophia & Co. milliners, 121 Whitechapel High st
Gardiner Abraham, picture frame maker, 149 Goswell st
Gardiner Benjamin Webb, stationer, bookseller, printer & publisher of theRoyalBlueBook,20Princes st.Cavendish sq
Gardiner Charles, solicitor, 71 Coleman st. City
Gardiner Daniel, who. & ret. brushma.11Wood st.Spitalfields
Gardiner Edmund, bagatelle board manfr.172 Bethnal gn.rd
Gardiner Ellen C. (Mrs.), outfitter, see Abraham & Gardiner
Gardiner Ezra, grocer, 25 Long la. City,&149Bermondsey st
Gardiner George, fruiterer, 15 Three Colt st. Limehouse
Gardiner Hy. bricklayer & plasterer, 102 East st.Manchr.sq
Gardiner John, beer retailer, 31 William st. Regent's park
Gardiner John, *Cart & Horses* P.H. 18 Upper St.Martin's la
Gardiner John, fruit salesman, Borough market
Gardiner John, *Lass of Gowrie* P.H. 242 Shadwell High st
Gardiner John, solicitor, see Pemberton, Crawley & Gardiner
Gardiner John Bull, architect, 4 Bank chambers, Lothbury
Gardiner Joseph, whosale stationer, see Bowles & Gardiner
Gardiner Matthew,grocer, 16 St. Andrew's hill. Doctors' com
Gardiner Richd. stonemason, 20 Providence bds.New Kent rd
Gardiner Roger Cooper, surgeon, 13 Cheyne walk, Chelsea
Gardiner Samuel, who. & retail grocer, Deptford broadway
Gardiner Saml. Brandon, appraiser, Lark hall la. Clapham
Gardiner Thomas, *Golden Cross hotel*, 452 West Strand
Gardiner Thomas, hat & cap manufr. 12 Up. East Smithfield
Gardiner Thomas, hosier, &c. see Ransom & Gardiner
Gardiner Thomas, milliner, 104 Goswell street
Gardiner Thomas, *Ship* P.H. 7 Finsbury place North
Gardiner Thomas, who. stationer, see Bowles & Gardiner
Gardiner Wm.Jas. surveyor, 29 Southampton row, Russell sq
Gardner Edward & Sons, Oxford warehos. 7Paternoster row
Gardner Hen.&.John,oil refiners & lamp mfrs.453WestStrand
Gardner Henry Wm. & Philip, brewers, 30 St.John st. Clkw
Gardner John & Co. chromo-lithographers, draftsmen, zincographers & printers, 5 Bride court, Bride lane
Gardner John&Son,wine mers.10 Crosby hall chmbs. Bishpgt
Gardner, Nicholl & Co. who. ironmongers, 38 King st. Snowhl
Gardner & Sturm, merchants, 44 Lime street, City
Gardner & Urquhart, east india agents, 11 St. Helen's place, & 4 Narrow st. Ratcliff
Gardner William & Co. carvers & gilders, 6 City road
Gardner Alexander, grocer, 13 New road, St. George's east
Gardner Andrew, *Pilgrim* P.H. 9 Kennington terrace
Gardner Arthur, wig ma. & perfumer, 5 Grocers' hall ct. City
Gardner Benjamin, butcher, 34 Gt. Hall, Hungerford market
Gardner Christopher meat salesman, 54 Aldgate High st
Gardner Denny,desk & dress. case mak. 17 King st.Cheapside
Gardner Edw. bottle merch. 32 Gt. Wild st. Lincoln's inn flds
Gardner Edward, butcher, 15 New King st. Deptford
Gardner Eliza (Mrs.), stay maker, 150 High Holborn
Gardner Francis, horsehair merchant, 14 Vere street, Clare market, & Salisbury, Wilts
Gardner Francis, merchant, 2 John st. Pentonville
Gardner Hannibal, law stationer, 10 Took's ct. Chancery la
Gardner Harriet (Miss), army rag mer,8Gt.Wild st.Drury la
Gardner Harriet (Mrs.), sextoness, 81 Little Britain
Gardner Henry, baker, Church street, Clapham road
Gardner Henry, *Black Bull* P.H. 95 Whitechapel road
Gardner Henry,china&glass dealer,14 Stucley ter.Camden tn
Gardner Henry, harness ma. 37 Liquorpond st. Gray's inn la
Gardner Henry, upholsterer, 30 Paradise st. Rotherhithe
Gardner James, brushmaker, 102 Kent st. Borough
Gardner James, builder, 4 Onslow terrace, Brompton
Gardner James, grocer, 21 Apollo buildings, Walworth
Gardner James, grocer, Lavender hill, Wandsworth road
Gardner James, grocer, &c. 18 St.Andrew's hill, Drs'.commns
Gardner James, map seller, 129 Regent st
Gardner James, naturalist, 427 Oxford st
Gardner Jas.watch case springer, 5 St. James's st. Clkwnl
Gardner Jane(Mrs.),straw bonnet ma. 18Church st.Spitalflds
Gardner John, baker, 74 Mansfield st. Kingsland road
Gardner John, coal mer. & wharfinger, Canal bri. Mile end rd
Gardner John, grocer, 6 Francis st. Golden square
Gardner John, manufacturer of manifold writers, tracing papers, writing fluids & marking ink without preparation, 1 George's place, Old st. road
Gardner John, *Milford Arms* P.H. 47 Milford lane, Strand
Gardner John, surgeon, 49A, Gt. Portland st. Oxford st
Gardner John, tobacconist, 10 London road, Southwark
Gardner John Arthur, barrister, 10 Chancery lane
Gardner John Hen. frame mak. 19 Poppin's court, Fleet st
Gardner John Jsph. carpenter, 36 Mansion ho. st. Kennington
Gardner John J.(Mrs.),fancy repos.36 Mansion ho.st.Kengtn
Gardner John Samuel,worm medicine wareho. 71 Long acre
Gardner John Wm. *Barleymow* P.H.50Long lane,Smithfield
Gardner Joseph, plumber & painter, 2 Fashion st. Dockhead
Gardner Joseph Goodwin, meat salesman,52Aldgate High st
Gardner Louisa (Mrs.),straw hat ma.34Newman st.Oxford st
Gardner Mark, ironmonger, Wandsworth road
Gardner Mary (Mrs.),dairyman, 19 Elizabeth st. sth. Pimlico
Gardner Matthew, *Pied Bull* P.H. 17 Bury st. Bloomsbury
Gardner Rebecca (Mrs.), tobacconist, 63 St. George st
Gardner Richard, *Three Tuns* P.H. 37 Coleman st
Gardner Robert, foreign agent, 109 Fenchurch st
Gardner Rt. *Carpenters' Arms* P.H.11Bridport st. N.Northrd
Gardner Robert, merchant, 46 Lime st
Gardner Robert John, baker & corn dealer, 18 Liquorpond st. & 55 Queen st. Bryanstone sq
Gardner Samuel, shoemaker, 19 Newnham st. Edgware rd
Gardner Samuel C. surgeon, 41 New Church st. Lisson grove
Gardner Sarah T. (Mrs.), herbalist, 44 Clifton st. Finsbury
Gardner Susan (Mrs.), potato dealer, 119 Drury lane
Gardner Thos. bricklayer, 47 Hoxton square
Gardner Thos. hay & straw salesman, Angel, 85 Whitechapel
Gardner Thos. lighterman, Commercial wharf, Mile end rd
Gardner Thos. *New Globe* P.H. Mile end road
Gardner Thos. Hobbs, fruiterer, 70 Charlotte st. Portland pl
Gardner Thos. Philip, surveyor of excise, 28 Gt. Prescot st
Gardner Thos.Wm. brush & comb maker, 255 Regent circus
Gardner Tobiah, butcher, 119 Bethnal green road
Gardner Wm. bootmaker, 4 Gt. Russell st. Bermondsey
Gardner Wm. carver & gilder, 14 Old st. St. Luke's
Gardner William *Duke's Head* P.H. 79 Whitechapel road
Gardner Wm. fishing tackle maker, 58 Noble st. Goswell st
Gardner Wm. furniture brokr. 6&7 Rose & Crown ct. Finsbury
Gardner Wm. hide salesman, 32 Somerset st. Aldersgate
Gardner Wm. tailor, 5 Leadenhall st
Gardner Wm. teadealer, 2 Bridge foot, Vauxhall, 115 Lambeth walk, & High st. Wandsworth
Gardner Wm. turncock, 37 North st. Manchester sq
Gardner William Harry, *George* P.H. 84 Fenchurch st
Gardom Samuel George, solicitor, 37 Threadneedle st
GardonWm.jelly mould maker, 8 Bartholomew sq. St. Luke's
Gare Francis, baker, 17 Southampton st. Camberwell
Gare Susannah (Mrs.), pat. med.wa. 24 Alfred pl. Newntn.ca
Garey Edward Bryant, attorney, 24 Southampton buildings
Garey Geo. plate powder ma. 1 Lit. Barlow st. Marylebone
Garey Geo. Daniel, tailor, 1 Claremont row, Barnsbury rd
Garey John, furniture broker, 6 Globe row, Mile end
GareyElizth.A.(Miss), seminary, 1 Claremont row, Brnsby.rd
Garfield Jesse& Wm.carpenters, 4 Rodney bldgs. New Kent rd
Garford John & Sons, seed crushers, Limehouse hole
Gargrave Ralph Burnop, attorney, 19 Buckingham st. Strand
Garland & Christopher, architects, &c. 11 John st. Adelphi
Garland & Fieldwick, builders, 16 Grosvenor pl. Camberwell
Garland John & Son, *Crown & Anchor* P.H. 43 Leadenhall st. & *Sun* P.H. 7 Sharp's buildings, Minories
Garland John & Sons, wine & spirit merchants, 26 Billiter st
Garland Edward, butcher, 112 Drury lane
Garland Elizabeth (Mrs.), *Bell* P.H. 4 Borough market
Garland Emma (Miss), dress maker, 5 Coles ter. Barnsbry.rd
Garland George, bootmaker, 30 Margaret st. Wilmington sq
Garland Geo. pork butcher, 16 Charles st. Westminster
Garland Henry, surgeon, &c. 1 Barnsbury ter. Liverpool rd
Garland James, pork butcher, 2 Albert pl. Marlboro' rd. Chel
Garland John, porkman, 26 Market place, Oxford market
Garland Joseph, carpenter, 49 Richard st. Commercial rd.ea
Garland Robert, warehouseman, see Darby & Garland

Garland Samuel, linendraper, 12 Exmouth st. Clerkenwell
Garland Thomas, academy, see Robertson & Garland
Garland Thomas, lath render, 36 Belvedere road, Lambeth
Garland Wm. pork butcher, 6 Queen st. Pimlico
Garlant Joseph, sheriffs' officer, 8 Mason's alley, Basinghall st
Garle John, chemist, 12 Terrace, Kensington gravel pits
Garlick John Smith, printer, 23A, Theobald's rd. Red Lion sq
Gariike William, surgeon, &c. 42 Theobald's rd. Red Lion sq
Garling Henry, architect, &c. 27 Bedford row, Bloomsbury
Garman Cornelius E. surgeon, 1 University st. Tott. ct. road
Garman Henry Vincent, surgeon, 1 Coborn terrace, Bow rd
Garman John, baker, 1 Buckingham pl. Marlboro' rd. Chels
Garmeson Joseph, bookseller, 9 Temple st. Whitefriars
Garmonsway Chas. clock & watchmk. 1 Hare st. Bethnal gr
Garn Wm. cheesemonger, 5 Burlington pl. Old Kent road
Garnar William, tailor, 12 Clayton st. Kennington
Garner Sam. & Chas. zinc warehouse, 59 Queen st. Cheapside
Garner Ann (Miss), coffee rooms, 52 Mount st. Berkeley sq
Garner Edwd. spanish leather dresser, 26 John st. Old Kent rd
Garner Edward Samuel, dentist, 29 George st. Portman sq
Garner Geo. stuff manufacturer, 1 Noble st. Cheapside
Garner James, coal dealer, 17 Bear lane, Blackfriars
Garner James, silk & velvet manfr. 22 Princes st. Spitalfields
Garner Jonathan, physcian, 3 Maida hill west
Garner Joseph Samuel, dentist, 49 High st. Kensington
Garner Robert, commercial agent, 44 St. John st. road
Garner Sarah (Mrs.), *Half Moon* P.H. 62 Struttonground, Wmr
Garner Thos. auctioneer & appraiser, 33 St. John st. Clerknwl
Garner Thos. butcher, Little Chelsea
Garner Wm. *Angel & Crown* P.H. 5 Sebbon's bldgs. Islington
Garner Wm. butcher, 5 Villa st. Walworth common
Garner Wm. *Cross Keys* coach office, 15 Gracechurch st
Garner Wm. undertaker, 50 Paul st. Finsbury
Garner Wm. writer & grainr. 20A, wharf, Nth. si. Padngtn. basin
Garners Thomas, dining rooms, 17 Commercial pl. City rd
Garnet & Mowbray, who. druggists, 36 Paternoster row
Garnet Richard, *Bell* P.H. 29 Gt. Bush la. Cannon st
Garnett Anna Maria (Mrs.), hatter, 163 Tooley st
Garnett James Richard, hatter, 3 Duke st. Tooley st
Garnett Jeremiah, oilman, &c. 38 Wigmore st. Cavendish sq
Garnett Robert, cornfactor, see Scott & Garnett
Garnett Robt. Smith, tailor & draper, 30 Ashley cres. City rd
Garnett Thos. E. charcoal dealer, 38 Wigmore st. Cavend. sq
Garnett William, *Gerard's Hall tap*, 2 Basing lane
Garnham Edward, butcher, 75 London rd. Southwark
Garnham Henry, dining rooms, 6 Paradise st. Marylebone
Garnham Jesse, butcher, 1 Halfmoon pass. Leadenhall mrkt
Garnham John, plumber & glazier, 123 Bunhill row
Garnham Rt. *Old Chesterfield Arms* P.H. 11 Shepherd st. Myfr
Garnham Wm. carman, 12 New walk, Shad Thames, Hrslydwn
Garnham Wm. Henry, silk mercer & draper, 30 Red Lion sq
Garnish Thomas, dyer, 7 Dean st. Holborn
Garnish Thomas, plumber, 6 West st. Seven dials
Garrad Benjamin, builder, 12 Goldsmith pl. Hackney road
Garrad Jas. Fred. oil & italian wareh. 7 Charles st. Westminster
Garrard Robert & Sebastian & Co. goldsmiths & silversmiths, 31 Panton st. & 25 Haymarket
Garrard & Rotherham, silk mercers, 7 Leicester square
Garrard John, general salesman, 8 Wade's place, Hackney rd
Garrard John, tailor, 85 Leman st. Goodman's fields
Garrard Stephen, solicitor, 13 Suffolk st. Pall mall east
Garrard Wm. cabinet maker & upholstr. 99 Mary st. Regt's. pk
Garrard Wm. who. pat. waterproof leather & felt hat maker, 1 Loman st. Gravel la. & Neate st. Coburg rd. Old Kent rd
Garratt & Edis, butchers, 4 Farringdon market
Garratt Deborah (Miss), umbrell. ma. 2 Commerce row, Islntn
Garratt Hen. cabinetmaker, 9 Lit. Albany st. Regent's pk
Garratt Hen. John, merchant, see Cunliffe, Garratt & Co
Garratt Hester (Mrs.), chandler's shop, 6 Compton st. Clkwl
Garratt James, beer shop, 40 Perceval st. Clerkenwell
Garratt James, solicitor, 24 Queen st. Cheapside
Garratt Jas. tailor, 17 Wellington pl. East st. Walworth
Garratt John, cattle salesman, 8 West Smithfield
Garratt John, *Copenhagen ho.* P.H. Copenhagen fields
Garratt John, dyer, 15 Pennyfields, Poplar
Garratt John, tailor, 9 Charles st. Grosvenor square
Garratt Joseph, baker, 19 Harrow road
Garratt Sarah (Mrs.), cheesemonger, 6 Whitechapel road
Garratt Thomas, grocer, 15 Dean st. Holborn
Garratt Thomas, sheriff's officer, 109 Chancery lane
Garratt Wm. umbrella manufacturer & depôt for Macintosh's air & waterproof cloths, 70 Cheapside & 19 Cornhill
Garraway Fanny & Ellen, fancy repos. 13 Lit. Queen st. Westmr
Garraway Chas. jeweller, 13 Little Queen st. Westminster
Garraway Wm. brown stone potter, Lower Fore st. Lambeth
Garraway's coffee house, Funge & Bland, 3 Change al. Cornhill

Garrett James & Son, plumbers, 6 Beckford row, Walworth
Garrett Abraham, *William IV.* P.H. 45 Exeter st. Lisson gr
Garrett Alley (Mrs.), grocer, 6 & 7 Wardour st. Soho
Garrett Arthur, linendr. & hosier, 9 Church st. Stoke Nwgtn
Garrett Chas. window glass cutter, 15 Fore st. Limehouse
Garrett Elizh. (Mrs.), rag & phial dealer, 6 Up. Rupert st. Soho
Garrett George, army bootmaker, 130 Jermyn st. St. James's, & 4 Leicester square
Garrett George, surgeon, 41 Union st. Bishopsgate
Garrett George Thos. *Unicorn* P.H. 50 Blackman st. Boro'
Garrett Henry, baker, 21 Warwick st. Pimlico
Garrett Henry, tailor, 2 Blossom st. Norton folgate
Garrett Henry Joseph, dining rooms, 92 Shoe lane
Garrett James, academy, 30 Portland terrace, Regent's park
Garrett Jas. paintr. & plumbr. 3 Liverpool st. Walwrth. com
Garrett John, baker, 23 Borough road, Southwark
Garrett John, *Victory* P.H. near the bridge, Kingsland road
Garrett Mark Brown, surgeon, 3 New road, St. George's east
Garrett Richard, musical instru. mak. 64 King st. Westmnstr
Garrett Samuel, *American wine & spirit stores* & coffee rooms, 56 Oxford st.; & wholesale, 72 Berners st
Garrett Samuel, grocer, Garden row, Deptford New town
Garrett Samuel Silver, conveyancer, Tower of London
Garrett Silas, confectioner, 10 Blackman st. Borough
Garrett Stephen, hide splitter, Page's walk, Bermondsey
Garrett Thomas, *Black Horse* P.H. Kingsland road
Garrett Thomas, grocer, &c. 1 Friendly st. Deptford
Garrett Thomas, porcelain, &c. ma. see Copeland & Garrett
Garrett Wm. bootmaker, 34 Carey st. Lincoln's inn
Garrett Wm. coal & potato dlr. 42 Earl st. East Lisson grove
Garrett Wm. *Fountain* P.H. 14 & 15 Bolingbroke rw. Walwth. rd
Garrett Wm. *King's Arms* P.H. 18 Charles st. City road
Garrett Wm. italian warehouse, sole manufacturer of the royal zest, 36 Great Tower st. City
Garrett Wm *Royal Pavilion* P.H. Howick ter. Vauxhall bdg. rd
Garrett Wm. *Wheatsheaf* P.H. 13 Castle st. Southwark
Garrick Club (Jas. Winston, sec.), 35 King st. Covent gardn
Garrick Theatre, 25 Leman st. Goodman's fields
Garrido Antonio, prof. of languages, 11 St. Bene't's pl. City
Garrit John, lapidary, 6 Red Lion st. Clerkenwell
Garrod Henry John, tailor & habit maker, 65 Poland st
Garrod John, cabinet & chair manfr. 1 Nelson terrace, City rd
Garrod John, grainer, &c. 30 Little Guilford st. Russell sq
Garrod Joseph, general merchant, see Tilbey & Garrod
Garrod Joseph Nich. grocer, 1 Up. Marylebone st. Portland pl
Garrod Samuel, bookbinder, 12 Dorset st. Portman square
Garrod Thomas, *Still* P.H. 6 Barbican
Garrod William, winecooper, 72 Red Lion st. Holborn
Garry William Henry, attorney, 39 Chancery lane
Garset John, tobacconist, 36 High st. Portland town
Garstin Wm. furn. undertaker, 4 Welbeck st. Cavendish sq
Gartenfield John, tailor, 43 Up. Berkeley st. Portman sq
Garth Jonathan, oil & color mnfr. 1 Paradise rw. Rotherhithe
Garth Ralph, *White Lion* P.H. Prince's stairs, Rotherhithe
Garth Thomas Almond, solicitor, see Gatty & Garth
Garthorne Ralph Thomas, manchester agent, 20 Basing lane
Gartland Christphr. imp. of cocoa nut fibre, 34 Sth. Molton st
Garton Wm. & Co. tar & turpentine distillers & ship varnish manufrs. Quebec wharf, Rotherhithe, & at the Baltic
Garton David Price, linendraper, 69 Margaret st. Cavend. sq
Garton Edward, butcher, 179 Tooley st
Garton Henry, linendraper, 85 Great Titchfield st
Garton Josiah, butcher, 187 Tooley st
Garty John, surgeon, 9 Chepstow pl. Camberwell New road
Garwood John, bootmaker, 37 Surrey pl. Old Kent road
Gary Henry George, cheesemonger, 2 Bermondsey New rd
Gascoine William, butcher, 10 Gt. Bell alley, Moorgate st
Gascoyne Elhanan, straw hat ma. 11 London ter. Hckny. rd
Gaselee Binsteed, barrister, 2 New square, Lincoln's inn
Gaselee Chas. surgeon, Cambrwl. gr.; see also Bean, Son & Co
Gaselee Stephen, serjeant at law, 3 Serjts. inn, Chancery la
Gaseltine W. Mary (Mrs.), milliner, 14 Langley pl. Com. rd. e
Gash Thomas & Co. distillers, 26 Aldersgate st
Gash Rd. & Nathan, coachbuilders, King's rd. west, Chelsea
Gash Samuel, furniture broker, 23 Wyndham rd. Camberwll
Gashion Michael, iron dealer, 34 Cowcross st. Smithfield
Gaskarth Harriet (Mrs.), 3 *Stags* P.H. 9 Wolsingham pl. Lmbth
Gaskell & Downs, brewers, 22 White Lion st. Norton folgate
Gaskell Thos. & Fdk. surgeons, 1 Markham sq. King's rd. Chls
Gaskell John Dakin, barrister, 1 Brick court, Temple
Gaskill Lacey T. advertising agent, 53 Moorgate st
Gaskin Isaac, builder, see Cecil & Gaskin
Gaskin John, grocer, 18 Tottenham st. Fitzroy square
Gaskoin George, surgeon, 34 Cambridge terrace, Edgware road, & 7 Up. Southwick st. north, Cambridge terrace
Gaskoin John S. surgeon, 32 Clarges st. Piccadilly

Gas Light & Coke Co.(Thos.V.Barnard,man.), Creek st.Dtfrd
Gaspè Fishery & Coal Mining Company (Charles F. Ellerman, sec.), 2 New Broad st. City
Gasquet Raymond, surgeon, 11 Burton crescent
Gass David & Sons, silversmiths & jewellers, 166 Regent st
Gass John, carpenter & packer, 13 William st. Shoreditch
Gassiot John Peter, sen. wine merchant, 77 Mark lane
Gassiot John Peter, jun. wine merchant, 77 Mark lane
Gasson John, academy, 11 Queen's buildings, Brompton
Gast Charles, muffin baker, 28 Hanway st. Oxford st
Gasting Thos. harness maker, 34 Dorset st. Spitalfields
Gaston Elizh. (Mrs.), tobacconist, 18 Cross st. Newington bts
Gate Alexander Jas. *Red Lion* P.H. Love lane, Shadwell
Gate John, linendraper, 3 Glasshouse st. Regent st
Gatehouse Richard & Co. timber merchants & saw mills, 25 Upper Lisson st. Lisson grove
Gately Stephen, carpenter, 12 Harrow st. Lant st. Borough
Gatenby William, builder, 41 White st. Borough
Gater Charles, dyer, 25 Jewin st. Cripplegate
Gates, Coats, Bartlett & Co. calico printers, 15 Watling st
Gates Frances (Mrs.), grocer, 15 Merlin place, Spafields
Gates George, grocer, 39 Ropemakers' fields, Limehouse
Gates James, 95 Church st. Shoreditch
Gates John, cattle salesman, 41 Smithfield
Gates John Benj. haberdasher, 51 Newington causeway
Gates Sylvanus, saddlers' ironmonger, 37 Great Queen st
GatesThos.goldbeater,24Vine st.Hatton wall&61Old st.St.L.
Gates Thos. Fredk. hairdresser, 5 Upper Eaton st. Pimlico
Gath Emma (Miss), milliner,see Heath & Gath
Gathercole Manning, livery stables, Marah pl. Old Kent rd. & cornchandler, Southampton st. Camberwell
Gathercole Thomas, auctioneer & registrar, Deptford bridge, & Creek rd. Deptford
Gathergood Robt. bricklayer & plasterer, 3 Meard's st. Soho
Gatley Joseph, patent saw mills, Dockhead, Bermondsey
Gatliff Wm. Son & Co. stuff & blanket manufs. 60 Bread st
Gatliff Charles, solicitor, 19 Coleman st
Gatliffe Wm. coal mercht. Middle wharf, Gt. Scotland yard
Gattey Edward John, baker, 23 Paradise row, Chelsea
Gattie & Peirce, perfumers & combmakers, 57 New Bond st
Gattke Julius, furrier & draper, 2 Courtney ter. Kingsland
Gattrell James, painter, glazier, &c. 1 Green st. Grosvenor sq
Gatty & Garth, solicitors, 3 Angel court, Throgmorton st
Gatty & Turner, attorneys, 1 Red Lion square, Holborn
Gatty Woolmer, baker, 22 Rathbone place, Oxford st
Gatward William, tailor, 53 Eagle st. Red Lion square
Gaubert & Kogl, working jewellers, 51 Berwick st. Soho
Gauci Maxime & Sons, lithographs. 9 North cres. Bedford sq
Gauci William, grocer, 60 Great Saffron hill
Gaugain Philip Augustus, artist, 138 Tottenham court road
Gaunt, Wardle & Co. silk manufs. 1 & 2 Huggin la. Wood st
Gaunt James, draper, see Badham & Gaunt
Gaunt John, brassfounder, 22 Sutton st. Goswell road
Gaunt John, porkbutcher&poultr.3Adam's row, Hampstd. rd
Gaunt John, *Rose & Crown* P.H. 66 & 67 Old Broad st. City
Gaunt Thomas Foster, solicitor, 18 Skinner st. Snowhill
Gauntlett James, grocer, High st. Battersea
Gaury Joseph & Co. commission merchants, 80 Watling st
Gausden David, butcher, 121 Poplar High st
Gausden John, butcher, 1 Brunswick st. Blackwall
Gaussen Fredk. Chas. barrister, 2 Harcourt bldngs. Temple
Gaut John, tailor, Mare st. Hackney
Gautery James, carpenter, 26 Little Marylebone st
Gautier Josephine & Co. dyers, &c. 18 Elizabeth st. Eaton sq
Gautier Frederick, french vice consul, 3 Copthall buildings
Gàvêy Rt. Edwin, engravr. &c. 10 St. Benet's pl. Gracech. st
Gavin Edward Alexander, carver, 128 Great Portland st
Gavin Peter & Son, canvas manfrs. Union stairs, Wapping
Gavin Hector, M.D. surgeon, &c. 5 Thurlow pl. Hackney rd
Gawan John, *Duke's Head* P.H. 46 Redcross st. Borough
Gawan Sml*StJohn'sHd.*PH.22Hollnd.st&22JohnstBkfrs.rd
Gawdery John, brush manfr. 13 & 22 Broomfield pl. Deptford
Gawler John, linendraper, 124 High st. Camden town
Gawler Henry, hairdresser, 73 Ossulston st. Somers town
Gawthorn Benj. linendraper, 83 Crawford st. Portman sq
Gawthorp Ben. *Goldsmiths' Arms* P.H.111Wnchstr.pl.Sthwk
Gawthorp Miles, *Portland Arms* P.H. 8 Great Portland st
Gawthorp Saml. wine merchant, 48 Charles st. Westminster
Gawthrop John Chas. tobacconist, 223 Tottenham court rd
Gawtress William, barrister, 161 Fleet st
Gawtrey & Coleman, linendrapers, 3 Lowndes ter. Knightsbr
Gay Jas. & Geo. merchants, 2 Queen's st. pl. Up. Thames st
Gay Charles, jeweller, 13 Kirby st. Hatton garden
Gay Henry, solicitor,7& 8 Barge yd.chambers,Bucklersbury
Gay John, plumber, 6 Grace's alley, Wellclose square
Gay John, surgeon, 1 South st. Finsbury square
Gay John Lewis, engraver, 1 Chester place, Old Kent road
Gay Mary(Mrs.),staymaker, 9 St. James's pl.Bermondsey rd
Gay Richard, theatrical tailor, 9 Mount st. Westminster rd
Gay Robert, grocer & cheesemonger, 29 Old Fish st
Gay Robert, *Spread Eagle* P.H. 137 Upper Whitecross st
Gay Samuel, potato salesman, 64 Castle st. Leicester sq
Gay Samuel William,coal mercht.&greengrocer,30 Fetter la
Gay Thomas, tailor, &c. 4 St. Andrew's hill, Blackfriars
Gay Thos. Aug. law statnr. 16 Southampton bgs.Chancery la
Gay Wm. brush & basket mak. & turner, 113 High Holborn
Gay Wm. fruiterer, 49 Up. Rathbone pl. Middlesex hospital
Gay Wm. mustard manufacturer, 144 Long la. Bermondsey
Gaydon Thomas, hairdresser, 66 Union st. Borough
Gaydor William, tailor, 21 Leather lane, Holborn
Gaye Edward Robert, surgeon,32 Up.George st.Bryanstn.sq
Gayfeyt Jas.&Son, blacking mkrs. 3 BlueAnchor rd.Bermdsy
Gayford Chesterfield & Son, wine merchants, 7 Old Bond st
Gayleard John, sen. habit mak. 56 Beaumont st. Portland pl
Gayleard John, jun. surgeon, 56 Beaumont st. Portland pl
Gayler Henry, leather seller, 38 Eyre st. hill, Leather lane
Gayler James, baker, 6 Constable row, Mile end road
Gayler John, linendraper, 124 High st. Camden town
Gayler John Henry, baker, 140 Shoreditch
Gayler Joseph, currier, 2 Goswell st
Gaylor Thomas,sugar refiner, &c. 40 Webber row,Blackfrs.rd
Gayton Henry,tinplate worker, 65 Tabernacle walk,Finsbury
Gaywood John, lighterman & coal merchant, King & Queen wharf, Rotherhithe, & 229 Rotherhithe st
Gaywood Richard, lighterman, 6 Swan lane, Rotherhithe
Gaze Henry, who. & ret.boot& shoe manufact. 155 Cheapside
Gaze John, collar maker, 32 Hyde st. Bloomsbury
Gaze Saml. Bartholomew, musical & house clock, ship dial & lever clock manufacturer, 26 Princes st. Spitalfields
Geach Henry, gasfitter & plumber, 56 Old Bailey
Geale James, boot&shoe maker, 10 Southampton st.Cambrwl
Geale John, livery stables, New Burlington mews, Regent st
Geany John, greengrocer, 14 Portsea place, Connaught sq
Gear Handel, professor of music, 26 Newman st. Oxford st
Gear John, butcher, 12 Princes st. Fitzroy square
Gear John Wm. artist & lithograph.5 Charlotte st.Fitzroy sq
Gear Joseph, *Britannia* P.H. 36 Fish st. hill
Gear Robt. Eames, linendraper, 19 Seymour pl.Camden town
Gearin Martin, butcher, 24 Flagon row, Deptford
Gearing Edward, shoemaker, 2 Pelham road, Brompton
Gearing James, plumber & painter, 15 Romney ter. Westmr
Gearing Mary(Mrs.),locksmth&bellhgr.22Hollesst.Clre.mkt
Gearing Thomas, carpenter, 19 Newland st. Pimlico
Geary (Maria & Eliza), academy, 74 George st. Euston sq
Geary Wm.&Nephew,reel cotton&brace mfrs.57 Wood st.City
Geary Charles, academy, 18 Green st. Leicester square
Geary Charles, cheesemonger, 237 Bermondsey st
Geary Elizabeth (Mrs.), staymaker, 61 St. James's st
Geary Francis, barrister, 8 Figtree court, Temple
Geary John, fruiterer, 63 Fetter lane
Geary Michael, tailor, 31 Church st. Soho
Geary Stephen, archt. & survey. 10 Hamilton pl.King's cross
Geaussent Stephen, oil & colorman, 63½ Hackney road
Gebhard John, cabinet ma. 1 Barnsbury row, Cloudesley sq
Geddes Andrew, A.R.A. portrait painter, 15 Berners street
Geddes Christopher,*BlueAuchor* P.H. 128 Brook st.Ratcliff
Geddes Geo. merchant & colonial broker, 78 Gt. Tower st
GeddesJohnAlex.*OldCatherine Wheel*P.H.40Bishpsg.witht
Geddes William, baker, 7 Albion place, Hyde park square
Gedge Ann Maria(Miss),baby linen wa.98Bishopsgt.without
Gedge Edward, cigar importer, 28 Up. Marylebone st
Gedge Mark, coffee rooms, 31 Wellington st. Goswell road
Gedge William, wine merchant, 132 Regent st
Gedye James Hichen, *Albion tavern,* 34 Bucklersbury
Gedye Nicholas, solicitor, 14 George st. Mansion house
Gee George, solicitor, 7 Trevor terrace, Knightsbridge
Gee Henry Charles, umbrella maker, 228 Whitechapel road
Gee John, carpenter, 9 Leigh st. Burton crescent
Gee Joseph, butcher, Stratford broadway
Gee Peter, *Morgan's Arms* P.H. Coborn road, Mile end road
Gee William, bootmaker, 52 Charles st. City road
Gee William, boot & shoe maker, 19 Chapel st. Somers town
Gee William, butcher, Stratford broadway
Gee William, calico printer, see Andrews, Sons & Gee
Gee William, tobacconist, 45 Gray's inn lane
Gee Wm.Chas.uphlstr.& bed ma.22Bridgehouse pl. Nwngtn.c
Gee Wm. Samuel, bootmaker,6Old Chapel row,Kentish town
Geer Mary (Mrs.),*Horse & Groom*P.H.19Portugal st.Lin.inn
Geere Hen. *Cape of Good Hope* P.H. 3 St.Ann's pl.Limeho
Geere Henry, timber merchant, East India road, Limehouse
Geere Thomas, timber merchant, Stratford
Geeson John, china & glass dlr. 7 Brunswick st. Blackwall

Geeves Eliza (Mrs.), *Golden Lion* P.H. Wm. st. Caledonian rd
Gefaell Ulrich, clockmaker, 28 Langley pl. Commercl. rd. ea
Geiger Joseph & Co. importers & manufacturers of cigars & snuffs, Halfmoon passage, 18 Whitechapel
Geldart Thomas Charles, barrister, 18 Old sq. Lincoln's inn
Geliot Peter, tin plate work. 14 Heath pl. Cambridge heath
Gell Chas. jun. galvnsd. tinned iron wa. 5 Quickset row, Newrd
Gell Francis Thos. solicitor, Carlton chambers, 8 Regent st
Gell John H. dep. coroner of Westmstr. Lit. Cloisters, Westm
Gell William, grocer, 3 Charles place, East st. Walworth
Gell William, teadealer, &c. 99 Tooley st.
Gellatly Alexander, baker, 4 Ann's terrace, Liverpool road
Gellatly Peter, solicitor & clerk to the Limehouse conjunct trust, 4 Wellington place, Commercial road, Limehouse
Gellatly Thomas, slater, Milton place, High st. Islington
Geller Wm. O. artist, 4 Crescent pl. Mornington crescent
Gem, Pooley & Beisley, solicitors, 1 Lincoln's inn fields
Gemmill John, linendraper, see Kidd, Gemmill & Bemand
Genders Joseph, mariner, 18 Back st. Horselydown
Gen. Advertiser (John Hasler, printer & pub.) 4 Crane ct
Gen. Agt. for the Recruit: Service Office, 80 Pall mall, h. 10 to 3
General Annuity Endowment Association (C. Hewitt, sec.), 40 King William st. City
General Annuity Soc. (Hen. F. Richardson, sec.), 36 Colem. st
General Association of Proprietors of Steam Shipping (Wm. C. Morgan, secretary), 28 St. Swithin's lane
General Benefit Assurance Office, Health, Life & Loan (John Brydie, sec.), 4 Farringdon st
General Dispensary (John Wood, sec.), 36 Aldersgate st
General Dispensary for Children, 16 Queen st. Worship st
Gen. Lying-in Hospital (W. W. Hastings, sec.), York rd. Lmb
General Maritime Assurance Company (Edwey S. Phillips, sec.), 30 Cornhill; for directors, &c. see page 2027
General Mining Association (John Bromley Foord, sec.), 52 Old Broad st. City
General Post Office & Regent's Canal Railway Office (Richard Archd Brooman, sec.), 11 Serjeants' inn, Fleet st
General Post Office Subsorters & Letter Carriers' Provident Soc. (Joseph Harris, sec.), held at the Bell inn, 37 Wood st. City
General Register & Record Office for Seamen, Custom house, Office for issuing Mariners' Tickets, 2 Hammett st Minories.
General Registry Office of Births, Deaths & Marriages, 7&8 Somerset pl. Somerset house; hours of business 10 to 4.
General Reversionary & Investment Company (Wm. B. Hodge, sec.), 5 Whitehall; see page 2026
General Ship Owners' Soc. (N. W. Symonds, sec.), 72 Cornhill
General Steam Navigation Company's Offices (John Wilson, sec.), 69 Lombard st.; 37 Regent circus, Piccadilly; 35 Leadenhall st.; 41 Fish st. hill; Stowage, Deptford; & Brown's wharf, Blackwall stairs.
General Wood cutting Company, sawing & planing mills (John More Douglas, res. director), Belvedere rd. Lambeth
Genet Frederick James, surgeon, 2 Queen's bldgs. Brompton
Genetat Charles, tailor, see Dreyer & Genetat
Genge George, *Three Nuns tap* P.H. 11 Aldgate High st
Genge George Pitman, teadealer & grocer, 72 Chiswell st
Genge Samuel, ship smith, Horseferry road, Limehouse
Genge Thomas, *Kean's Head* P.H. 21 Russell ct. Drury lane
Genna Elijah, linendraper, 36 Edgware rd. Marylebone
Genower John Edw. writer & grainer, 1 Cushion ct. O. Broad st
Gent Charles, general agent, 72 Cheapside
Gent Filby, beer retailer, 11 St. Ann's place, Limehouse
Gent Frank, tailor, 9 Albion bldgs. Bartholomew close
Gent Richard, tailor, 50 Chalton st. Somers town
Gent Sophia (Mrs.), artist, 6 Tavistock st. Bedford sq
Gentry George, haircutter, 111 London wall, City
Gentry Henry, cheesemonger, 61 Snowhill
Gentry John, baker, Broadway, Stratford
Gentry Wm. coffee rooms, 116 St. John st. Smithfield
Geoghegan Michael John & Co. linendrapers, 178 Regent st
Geoghegan Sleater, seal engraver, 7 Palsgrave pl. Temple bar
Geological Society (Leonard Horner, pres.; Rev. W. Buckland, vice pres.; Wm. John Hamilton & Sir Hen. Thos. De la Beche, foreign secs.; John Lewis Prevost, esq. treasurer); Somerset house, Strand
George & Lambert, silk mercers, 192 Regent st
George & Lutwyche, russia merchants, 5 Skinner st. Snowhill
George Charles, cabinet ma. 1 North st. Finsbury mkt
George Clement, leather dresser & seller, 102 Dean st. Soho
George Cornelius, boot ma. 47 Marchmont st. Brunswick sq
George David, shoemaker, 1 Paradise st. Marylebone
George Edward, baker, &c. 42 Park st. Grosvenor sq
George Edward, surgeon, 4 Stucley terrace, Camden town
George Elizabeth (Mrs.), baker, 13 Northampton st. Clkwll
George Elizabeth (Mrs.), dressmaker, 18 Northampton sq
George Fredk. boot & shoe ma. 16 Lit. St. Andrew st. 7 dials
George Fredk. who. stationer, see Morgan, Martyr & George
George George, cattle salesman, 17 West Smithfield
George George, cutler, 20 Crescent st. Euston square, & 15 Park terrace, Camden town
George Henry, builder, 18 Trinity square, Southwark
George Henry, surgeon, 4 Horton villas, Kensington
George James, *Globe* P.H. 43 North Audley st. Grosvenor sq
George James, tailor, 4 Wells st. Gray's inn road, & 2 Parkfield st. Islington
George John, *Falcon* P.H. 5 Pemberton row, Gough sq
George John, leather dresser, see Lutwyche & George
George John, *N. England Lighthouse* P.H. Stone strs. Ratcliff
George John, silk & velvet manufac. 5 Pemberton row, Gough sq
George John, whols. ironmonger, see Higgs & George
George John Nimroide, library, 66 Up. Berkeley st. Portmn. sq
George Joseph, ornamental leather manufr. 81 Dean st. Soho
George Joseph, tobacconist. 13 Quickset row, New road
George Mary (Miss), ladies' school, see Barnett & George
George Peter, tea broker, 38 Fenchurch st
George Philip, dining rooms, 30 Praed st. Paddington
George Rebecca (Mrs.), saddler & leather gilder, 20 Long acre
George Richard, plumber, 14 Wyndham road, Camberwell
George St. John, painter, 22 Clarendon st. Somers town
George Samuel, carman, 14 Kendall's mews, Portman sq
George Samuel, picture dealer, 6 Richmond bldgs. Soho
George Thomas, baker, 12 College st. Chelsea
George Thomas, *Brown Bear* P.H. Deptford High st
George Thomas, farrier, 14 Compton mews, Brunswick sq
George Thos. solicitor, 1 Warnford ct. Throgmorton st
George Wm. carpenter, 27 Gt. Castle st. Regent st
George Wm. cheesemonger, 23 Blandford st. Portman sq
George Wm. grocer, 4 Aldenham st. Somers town
George Wm. grocer, 78 Park st. Limehouse
George Wm. *Maid & Magpie* P.H. 18 Wellington pl. Stepney
George Wm. newsvender, 20 Lit. Chapel st. Westminster
George Wm. printer, 16 Spring st. Portman sq
George Wm. Peter, bricklayer, 3 Sale st. Paddington
Georgiadi Leonidas, merchant, see Chiriaco & Co
Gepp Thomas, cabinetmaker, 20 Crown row, Mile end rd
Geralopulo Constantino, merch. 15 North bldgs. Finsb. circus
Gerard Adam & Co. merchants, 51 Lime st
Gerard & Co. (of Epernay), wine merchants, 12 Clement's lane, Lombard st. (E. S. Polkinghorne & Co. agents)
Gerard Henry, tailor, 13 Hungerford st. Strand
Gerard Joseph, guitar manufacturer, 50 King st. Soho
Gerard Sarah (Miss), ladies' school, 8 Stamford st. Blkfs. rd
Gerardin & Watson, pewterers, 21 Poland st. Oxford st
Gerhold John Harman, baker, 33 William st. Whitechapel
Gerhold John, *Pr. of Orange* P.H. 16 Fieldgate st. Whtchpl
Gerish Francis Wm. ironmonger, smith & founder, patentee of Gerish's hinges & locks, 16 East road, City road
Gerish John, *Crown* beer shop, 18 Lr. Chapman st. St. Geo. east
Germain Elizh. (Mrs.), french dyer, 51 Henry st. east, Avenu. rd
German & Dutch Jews' Hospital (Charles Kerin, sup.), Mile end road
German Mining Company (Thos. Hacket, sec.), 26 Birchin la
German Andrew, jun. solicitor, Maida place, Mile end road
German Samuel, carpenter, 47 York st. Kingsland road
Gerock, Astor & Co. (now Wolf & Figg), pianoforte & musical instrument manufacturers, 20 St. Martin's le grand
Gerrans James Geo. surgeon, 6A, Wyndham pl. Bryanstone sq
Gerrard Edwd. glass & chinaman, 23 High row, Knightsbridge
Gerrard George, juvenile warehouse, 28 Sloane square
Gerrard John Rd. hairdresser, 5 Clement's court, Wood st
Gerrard Mary (Mrs.), fruiterer, 62 Gt. hall, Hungerford mkt
Gerrett Thomas, fancy wareh. 7 Old Cavendish st. Oxford st
Gerry James, builder, 32 Gilbert st. Grosvenor square
Gershon Aaron, cigar manufacturer, 2 Kent pl. Old Kent rd
Gershon Raphael, furn. brok. 36 Northumb. pl. Commercl. rd. e
Gerville & Co. french leather importers, 137 Fenchurch st
Gery John, tobacconist, 7 Manchester buildings, Holloway
Getting John, wine merchant, 46 Lime st.
Gevers Jane (Miss), milliner, 3 Bedford st. Bedford sq
Geyr Henry, importer of foreign goods, 74 Newgate st
Ghrimes Robert, auctioneer, 73 Upper Berkeley st
Ghrimes Samuel, surgeon dentist, 71 Baker st. Portman sq
Gibb (Benaiah) & Son, tailors, &c. 188 St. George st
Gibb Henry, engineer, 12 Cobourg st. Euston square
Gibb Benaiah, general agent, 188 St. George st
Gibb James, hat maker, see Wilson, Gibb & Co
Gibb James, wine & spirit merchant, & dealer in scotch whisky & ale, 43 Bread st. Cheapside
Gibb John, baker, 31A, Upper Seymour st. Portman square
Gibb John, *Crown & Shuttle* P.H. 226 Shoreditch High st

Gibb Richard, coffee rooms, 25 Bridge road, Lambeth
Gibbard Robert, coffee rooms, 376 Oxford st
Gibbens Benj. butcher, 2 Elizabeth st. south, Pimlico
Gibbens George, shipowner, 11 Bedford square east
Gibbens Wm. ship insur. & cus ho. agt. 2 Ingram ct. Fench. st
Gibbens Wm. shipowner, 1 Devonshire pl. Commer. rd. east
Gibbes Thomas, stockbroker, 19 Throgmorton st
Gibbings Thomas, baker, 16 Pollard's row, Bethnal green rd
Gibbings Thos. & Chas. mat. wa. 7 White Horse yd. Colem. st
Gibbins Bros. color & varnish ma. Assembly pl. Mile end rd
Gibbins Jas. & Co. color & varn. mfs. London col. wks. Mile end rd
Gibbins Henry James, hairdresser, &c. 7 King st. St. James's
Gibbins John Nicholson, hosier & draper, 44 Rathbone pl
Gibbins Joseph, carpenter, 1 Newland st. Kensington
Gibbins Mary Ann (Mrs.), *Glo'ster Ar.* P.H. Glo'ster pl. Kenth. t
Gibbins Richard, baker, 17 Clare court, Drury lane
Gibbins Sam. factor, &c. see Leach, Broadbent, Leach & Co
Gibbins Wm. furn. undertaker, 105 Edgware rd. Marylebone
Gibbon Daniel, hosier, glover & shirtmaker, 19 Coventry st
Gibbon Fredk. T. wine merchant, 7 Laurence Pountney hill
Gibbon William Henley, solicitor, see Langley & Gibbon
Gibbons & Miller, ironmongers, 3 Redcross st. Cripplegate
Gibbons & Read, tailors, 4 Clifford st. Bond st
Gibbons & Roe, wholesale stationers, 17 Walbrook
Gibbons S. & Co. hop factors & merchts. St. Andrew's hill
Gibbons, Son, White & Smith, ironmongers, 345 Oxford st
Gibbons Thos. & Co. tailors & outfitters, 18 Up. East Smithfield
Gibbons Abel, bed & mattress ma. 6 Red Lion st. Whitechpl
Gibbons Charles, *Royal Oak* P.H. 41 Elizabeth st. Eaton sq
Gibbons David, special pleader, 1 New court, Temple
Gibbons Eliza (Miss), milliner, Camberwell grove
Gibbons Fredk. cooper, 1 Liverpool st. Walworth common
Gibbons George, cooper, 1 Adelaide pl. Grange rd. Bermdsy
Gibbons George, shipwright, 21 Rotherhithe
Gibbons George, surveyor & estate agt. 20 Old Cavendish st
Gibbons James, coffee rooms, 18 Wentworth place, Mile end
Gibbons James, cooper, 13 East st. Crosby row, Walworth
Gibbons James, ironmonger, 11 Walworth place, Walworth
Gibbons John, brazier, 73 Hill st. Walworth road
Gibbons John, *Ship* P.H. 4 Ratcliff cross
Gibbons John Burdett, wholes. watchma. 45 Hatton garden
Gibbons Joseph, boot & shoe maker, 186 Shoreditch
Gibbons Sills, chandler's shop, 161 Brick lane, Spitalfields
Gibbons Sarah (Mrs.), haberdash. 103 Albany st. Regent's pk
Gibbs Anthony & Sons, merchants, 47 Lime st
Gibbs & Clark, tea urn mfs. & brazs. 22 Gt. Sutton st. Clerkwl
Gibbs David & William, hard, soft & fancy soap manufacturers, 76 Milton st. Cripplegate
Gibbs George & Co. seedsmen, &c. to the Agricultural Society, &c. 26 Down st. Piccadilly
Gibbs Henry Chas. & Chas. solicitors, 58 Old Broad st. City
Gibbs & Hyem, ship & insurance agents & surveyors of shipping, 2 George lane, Botolph lane
Gibbs Richd. & Co. straw hat mfrs. milnrs. &c. 6 Norton folgate
Gibbs Richard & Co. tea brokrs. 2 Whitehart ct. Lombard st
Gibbs Thomas & Co. the seedsmen to the Royal Agricultural Society of England & to the hon. Boards of Agriculture of England & Sweden, 47 Halfmoon st. Piccadilly
Gibbs Thos. D. & Jas. silk mercers, 13 & 14 Plumber's row, Cityrd
Gibbs Dixon, grocer & teadealer, 119 Pall mall
Gibbs Edward, general agt. & comssn. mer. 3 Scots yd. Bush la
Gibbs Geo. livery stables, 32½ & 114 Mount st. Berkeley sq
Gibbs Geo. tailor & draper, 78 King William st. City
Gibbs Geo. vellum & parchment ma. 40 Princes st. Stamford st
Gibbs George, watch & clock maker, 38 Banner st. St. Luke's
Gibbs Hen. carpenter & undertaker, 48 Hampden st. Clarendon square
Gibbs Henry, dorset ale rooms, 76 Holborn hill
Gibbs Hen. gen. salesman, 7 New Church st. west, Lisson gro
Gibbs Henry, grocer, Bridge road, Battersea
Gibbs Henry, printseller, 18 Tichborne st. Haymarket
Gibbs Isaac, woolstapler, Gun alley, 85 Bermondsey st
Gibbs James, attorney, 4 Storeys gate, Westminster
Gibbs James, baker, 5 New Church st. Lisson grove
Gibbs James, baker, 1 Pemberton row, Gough square
Gibbs Job, tombstone letter cutter, 56 Millbank st
Gibbs John, ladies' wardrobe dlr. 9 Earl st. ea. Lissn. grv. nth
Gibbs John, livery stables, 15½ Tichborne st. Haymarket
Gibbs John, nursery & seedsman, Finchley New rd. St. Jhn's. wd
Gibbs John, oven builder & smith, 2 King st. Soho
Gibbs John physician, 6 Baker st. Portman square
Gibbs John, pianoforte ma. 1 Bowyer place, Camberwell rd
Gibbs John, saddler, 22 Whitecross st. Cripplegate
Gibbs John Anderson, baker, 57 Brunswick st. Blackfriars rd
Gibbs John Young, cabinetmaker, &c. 83 Poplar High st
Gibbs Joseph, barrister, 5 Hare court, Temple
Gibbs Joseph, rag & bottle dlr. 4 Gt. Woodstock st. Marylebn
Gibbs Mary (Mrs.), lodging house, 5 Baldwin's ct. Cloak la
Gibbs Mary (Mrs.), milliner, 9 High st. Newington butts
Gibbs Michael, fishmonger, 137 Praed st. Paddington
Gibbs Nathaniel, chandlers' shop, 7 Church rd. Commerl. rd. ea
Gibbs Richard, boot & shoe maker, 27 King st. Camden town
Gibbs Richard, pork butcher, 7 Union st. Lisson grove north
Gibbs Richard, straw hat mfr. 4 William st. Manchester sq
Gibbs Rd. Edwd. ironmonger, 90 to 92 Old Gravel la. Wapping
Gibbs Samuel, coal dealer, 3 King st. Soho
Gibbs Samuel, solicitor, 7 Compton st. east, Brunswick sq
Gibbs Selina Whittaker (Mrs.), oil warehouse, 119 Piccadilly
Gibbs Stephen, livery stables, Crutched friars
Gibbs Thomas, baker, 46 Chichester place, Gray's inn road
Gibbs Thomas, bricklayer, 17 A, Gt. Carlisle st. Portman mrkt
Gibbs Thos. toy-shop, 17A, Gt. Carlisle st. Portman market
Gibbs Thomas Smith, baker, 10 Anthony st. St. George's east
Gibbs William, stock & share broker, 13 Change alley
Gibbs William, solicitor, see Hodson & Gibbs
Giberne Mark & Son, wine, &c. merchs. 55 Old Broad st. City
Giblett John & James, leather merchts. 31 Vere st. Clare mrkt
Giblett John, cattle salesman, see Guerrier & Giblett
Giblett Eliza (Miss), ladies' school, 12 Greville pl. Kilburn
Giblett Richard Henry, butcher, 16 Cross st. Bermondsey
Giblett William, butcher, purveyor to her Majesty, 110 New Bond st
Giblin Edwin, fruiterer, 17 Oxford market
Gibson (John H.) & Nichols (Wm.), notaries, 79 Lombard st
Gibson, Linton & Co. ship & insurance brokers & general agents, 3 Austinfriars & Lloyd's
Gibson Mrs. & Miss, fancy rep. 7 Pantechnicon arc. Belgrv. sq
Gibson & Muir, printers & commission agts. 8 Friday st
Gibson Reginald & Co. who. tea & coffee dlrs. 23 Cullum st
Gibson Robert & Co. saddlers, 1 New Coventry st
Gibson & Todd, oilmen & grocers, 41 Wigmore st. Cavendish sq
Gibson Alexander, cowkeeper, 7 Drury lane
Gibson Alex. genl. commission agt. 4 Brabant ct. Philpot la
Gibson Alexander, linendraper, 8 Frederick pl. Goswell rd
Gibson Alexander, velvet manufacturer, 38 Basinghall st. & shoe mercer, 17 Lisle st. Leicester square
Gibson Alfred, *Lamb tavern* P.H. 44 Lamb's Conduit st
Gibson Ann (Miss), milliner, 12 Pantechnicon arcade, Blgrv. sq
Gibson Chas. grocer & cheesemong. 4 South st. South Audley st
Gibson Chas. writer & gilder, 13 Bevenden st. East rd. City rd
Gibson David, stockbroker, Stock exchange
Gibson Edward, *Savoy Palace* P.H. Savoy st. Strand
Gibson Edward, M.D. surgeon, 1 Hawley ter. Hampstead rd
Gibson George, bookbinder, 108 Drummond st. Euston sq
Gibson George, *Craven Arms* P.H. 38 Marshall st. Golden sq
Gibson Hannah (Mrs.), straw bonnet mkr. 7 Dockhead, Brmdsy
Gibson Henry, fish factor, see Lynn & Gibson
Gibson Henry Gould, wine merchant, 35 Mark lane
Gibson James, baker, 16 Islington High st
Gibson James, baker, 1 Lower Islington terrace
Gibson James, boot & shoe mkr. 16 Lit. Guilford st. Brunswk. sq
Gibson James, *Golden Anchor* P.H. 131 St. John st. Clerknwell
Gibson James, linen yarn mer. & sacking ma. 77 Old st. road
Gibson James, tobacconist, 87 Tooley st
Gibson James, window blind maker, 18 Bath place, New rd
Gibson James Philip, engraver & printer, 9 Alfred terrace, Cambridge heath, & 30 Aldermanbury
Gibson John, accountant, see Webb (C. & W.) & Gibson
Gibson John, solicitor, 5 Bernard st. Brunswick square
Gibson John, beer retailer, 24 Pool st. New North road
Gibson John, mast & block maker, 16 Stoney lane, Tooley st
Gibson John, oil & italian wareho. 20 Motcomb st. Belgrave sq
Gibson John, solicitor, 5 Bernard st. Brunswick square
Gibson John, tailor & milliner, 38 Devonshire st. Portland pl
Gibson John, tobacconist, Stratford broadway
Gibson John Holmes, attorney, 79 Lombard st
Gibson John Robinson, solicitor, 9 Copthall ct. Throgmtn. st
Gibson John Rowland, surgeon, 115 Holborn hill
Gibson John Wm. *The Dark House* P.H. see Bruce & Gibson
Gibson Joseph, architect & surv. 39 Swinton st. Gray's inn rd
Gibson Joseph, coach ironmonger, 120 Long acre
Gibson Joseph, leather seller, 70 Dean st. Soho
Gibson Joseph, shipping butcher, 34 Lower Shadwell
Gibson Leonard, carpenter, 17 Hastings st. Burton crescent
Gibson Sam. provision agent & gen. com. mer. 25 Abchurch la
Gibson Thomas, dairyman, 13 Walbrook row, New North rd
Gibson Thomas, tailor, 8 West st. Golden square
Gibson Thomas Field, silk manufacturer, 22 Spital square
Gibson Wm. *Baker's coffeehouse*, 1 Change alley, Cornhill
Gibson Wm. beer retailer, Jamaica level, Bermondsey
Gibson Wm. bootmaker, 4 Gray's inn passage, Bedford row
Gibson Wm. bootmaker, 42 London wall

Gibson Wm. corn & seed factor, Jack's coffee house, Mark la
Gibson Wm. manchester agent, 16 King st. Cheapside
Gibson Wm. solicitor, see Chisholme, Hall & Gibson
Gibsone Burford, professor of music, 73 Newman st
Gidden Arthur, tanner & currier, 8 Gloucester rw. Walwth. rd
Giddings Jane & Anne, milliners, 5 Edwards st. Portman sq
Giddings James, *Horns* P.H. 68 St. John st. Clerkenwell
Giddins James, horse slaughterer, 31 Green st. Blackfrs. rd
Giddins William, baker, see Bailey & Giddins
Giddins William, *Lion & Lamb* P.H. Deptford green
Giddy John, *Dispatch* coffee rooms, 25 Bride lane, Fleet st
Giddy Osman, chemist, 8 St. James's st. Pall mall
Gideon David, clothes warehouse, 1 Union row, Tower hill
Gideon James, pawnbroker, 18 & 19 Stafford st. Lisson grove
Gidley Bartholomew, shoemaker, 19 Skinner st. Clerkenwell
Gidley Theodore Courtenay, solicitor, 23 Earl st. Blackfriars
Gieseler Ludwig, tailor, 6 Carburton st. Portland road
Giesler Fred. & Co. merchts. & wine mercs. 32 Fenchurch st
Giffard Cha. Moore, grocer, 3 St. George st. Albny. rd. O. Kt. rd
Giffard Francis, solicitor, 47 Vincent square, Westminster
Giffard George Markham, barrister, 26 Chancery lane
Giffard John W. De L. barrister, Hall staircase, Inner Temple
Giffin James, saddler, Church st. Hackney
Giffin Joseph, jewel case maker, 80 Wardour st. Soho
Giffin Thomas, watch & clock maker, 26 Paul st. Finsbury
Gifford & Linder, chemists to his late Majesty, 104 Strand
Gifford Augustus Keppel, who. tobacconist, 121 Holborn hill
Gifford James, coffee rooms, 108 Gray's inn lane
Gifford John, broker, see Price, Gifford & Co.
Gifford John, carpenter, 14 Cumberland st. Middsx. hospital
Gifford Samuel, leather cutter, 1 King st. Kensington
Gifford Samuel, sailcloth & twine warehouse, 72 Mark lane
Gifford Thomas, shoemaker, 13 St. Mark's rd. Camberwell
Gifford William, baker, 11 Windmill st. Finsbury
Gigner Martha (Mrs.), tobacconist, 59 Upper Marylebone st
Gilbank Thomas, attorney, 46A, Coleman st
Gilbart Leggatt, tailor, 99 Oxford st
Gilbart Wm. tailor, 86 Oxford st. & 14 Shoreditch
Gilbert & Cooper, fancy tea chest manfrs. 13 Dorrington st
Gilbert & Frasi, ironfounders & smiths, 55 Golden la. St. Luke's
Gilbert & Goatley, bootmakers, 13 Old Bond st
Gilbert, Hooke, Street & Gutteres, solicitors, 1 Brabant ct
Gilbert & Plater, *Blossoms inn* coach office, 23 Lawrence la
Gilbert & Rivington, printers, 52 St. John's sq. Clerkenwell
Gilbert Wm. & Co. engineers, 4 Milton st. City
Gilbert Wm. & Co. feather merchants, 1 Belle Sauvage yard
Gilbert Wm. & Co. feather purifiers by chemical process, 89 Watling st
Gilbert Alfred, tallow chandler, 20 Silver st. Golden sq
Gilbert Charles Henry, surgeon, 1 Raven row, Spitalfields
Gilbert Ebenezer Thos. cutler, &c. 48 Newington causeway
Gilbert Edmund, hatter, 1 Palatine pl. Commercial rd. east
Gilbert Everett, baker, 4 Henry st. east, Portland town
Gilbert George, book publisher, 24 Seacoal la. Farringdon st
Gilbert George, bricklayer, &c. 16 Benjamin st. Clerkenwell
Gilbert George, tailor, 83 Church st. Rotherhithe
Gilbert George, cotton & rush manufacturer, 79 Old st. road
Gilbert James, baker, 39 Orchard st. Westminster
Gilbert James, coachmaker, 1 David st. Marylebone
Gilbert James (late Gilbert & Grattan), map & book publisher, & map agent by appointment to the Honourable Board of Ordnance, 49 Paternoster row
Gilbert James, *Pine Apple* P.H. 17 Gt. Carlisle st. Portmn. mrkt
Gilbert John, baker, 16 Commercial road, Lambeth
Gilbert John, cowkeeper, 29½ Windmill st. Finsbury
Gilbert John, engineer, 43 Boston st. Hackney road
Gilbert John, *Ferry House* P.H. Mill wall, Poplar
Gilbert John, locksmith, 61 Coppice row, Clerkenwell
Gilbert John, plated wareho. 11 Dyer's buildings, Holborn
Gilbert Joseph Francis, artist, 26 Bennett st. Stamford st
Gilbert Joshua, *Royal Oak* P.H. Plummer's rw. Whitechapl
Gilbert Samuel, wholesale bookseller, 51 & 52 Paternoster rw
Gilbert Samuel Massey, boarding hou. 6 New Basinghall st
Gilbert Stephen, bookseller & news agt. 4 Copthall buildings
Gilbert Thomas, beer retailer, 64 Minories
Gilbert Thomas, bookseller, see Sherwood, Gilbert & Piper
Gilbert Thomas, grocer, 41 Poland st. Oxford st
Gilbert William, builder, 4 Grove, Hackney
Gilbert Wm. butcher, 82 Seymour place, Bryanstone sq
Gilbert Wm. butcher, 8 Vine place, Old st. road
Gilbert Wm. *Globe* coffee rooms, 8 Church la. Whitechapel
Gilbert Wm. printer, 3 Salters' hall court, Cannon st
Gilbert Wm. silk manufacturer, 31 Steward st. Spitalfields
Gilbert Wm. tallowchandler & oilman, 64 Tottenham court road, & 3 Howland st.
Gilbert Wm. who. stay maker, see Coupland & Gilbert

Gilbertson James & Son, coal merchants & wharfingers, Crow & Horseshoe wharf, 6 Upper Thames st
Gilbertson Henry, glass manufacturer, 40 Ludgate hill
Gilbertson Wm. Walker, baker, 52 Judd st. & 32 Hastings st. Brunswick sq
Gilburt & West, silk & velvet manfrs. 4 Russia row, Milk st
Gilby & Scott, ship & ins. brokrs. 4 St. Benet's pl. Gracechurch st
Gilby John, bootmaker, 6 Darby pl. Jermyn st. St James's
Gilby Thomas, livery stable keeper, 2 York road, Lambeth
Gilby Thos. *Woolpack tavern*, 6 St. Peter's alley, Cornhill
Gilchrist James Charles, woollen wareho. 55 Basinghall st
Gilchrist Hugh, china dealer, 6 Gt. Queen st. Lincoln's inn fields
Gilchrist James, tailor, 10 Leathersellers' bldgs. London wall
Gilchrist Sarah (Mrs.), boarding house, 55 Basinghall st
Gilder Geo. John, auctioneer & undrtkr. Kingsland High st
Gilder James, *Lord Nelson* P.H. 17 Pump row, Old st. road
Gilder Wm. Troward, surgeon, 14 Queen Anne st. Cavendish sq
Giles & Bayes, starchmakers, Old Ford
Giles Christopher & Albert, cornfactrs. 8 Catherine ct. Twr. hill
Giles Son & Co. corn factors, 4 Fowke's buildings, Tower st
Giles Ann (Mrs.), baker, 37 Blackfriars road
Giles Bailey, coal merchant, 51 London st. Ratcliff cross
Giles Edmund, plumber, &c. 61 Pennyfields, Poplar
Giles Edward G. wine merchant, 39 Threadneedle st
Giles Francis, civil engineer, 9 Adelphi terrace, Strand
Giles Francis, baker, 5 & 6 Wych st. Strand
Giles Frank, civil engineer, 45 Lincoln's inn fields
Giles George, attorney, 7 Gray's inn square
Giles George, fun. carriage master, 33 Leman st. Goodm. flds
Giles George, grindery dealer, 18 Tower st. Seven dials
Giles George, porkman, 7 Ship Tavern pas. Leadnhll. markt
Giles George King, furrier, 52 Cambridge st. Edgware rd
Giles George Fredk. surgeon, 4 Clifton pl. Cambridge hth
Giles Hanh. (Mrs.), *Devonshire Arms* P.H. Devonsh. st. Gib. rd
Giles James, fish salesman, Billingsgate market
Giles James, furniture broker, 28 Exeter st. Sloane st
Giles James, fish salesman, & commis. agt. 24 St. Mary at hill
Giles James, hatter & tailor, 376 Rotherhithe st
Giles John, baker, 161 Blackfriars road
Giles John, grocer, 13 Bedford st. Bedford sq. Mile end
Giles John, outfitting warehouse, 115 Shoreditch High st
Giles John, surgeon, 27 Butcher row, Ratcliff
Giles John Edward, barrister, 38 Lincoln's inn fields
Giles John West, artist, 27 Stanhope st. Hampstead rd
Giles Joseph, builder & undertaker, 47 Bow la. & Bow, Middlx
Giles Joseph, grocer & cheesemonger, 21 Bayswater terrace
Giles Matthew, grocer & cheesemngr. 16 Philipps st. Kingsld. rd
Giles Netlam, solicitor, 4 Verulam buildings, Gray's inn
Giles Richd. oil & colorman, 49 Gt. Windmill st. Haymarket
Giles Robert, butcher, 35 Theobald's road
Giles Robert Hen. surveyor, 11 Burton st. Burton crescent
Giles Samuel, baker, 27 Church st. Shoreditch
Giles Sarah (Mrs.), baker, 122 Upper Whitecross st
Giles Thomas, dining rooms, 3½ Postern row, Tower hill, & 43 Broad st. St. Giles's
Giles Thomas Hillson, omnibus proprietor, Bow bridge
Giles Wm. baker, 29 Cable st. Wellclose square
Giles Wm. fringe & worsted manfr. 98 Wood st. Cheapside
Giles William, saddler, &c. 41 Great Guildford st. Borough
Giles William, stockbroker, 2 Capel court, & Stock exchange
Giles William, surgeon, 64 London road, Southwark
Gilfillan & Anderson, linen factors, 24 Friday st. Cheapside
Gilford John, cattle salesman, 60 West Smithfield
Gilford Thomas, cattle salesman, 60 West Smithfield
Gilham John, corndealer, 211 Borough High st
Gilham John, solicitor, 24 Bartlet's buildings, Holborn
Gilham William, basket maker, 99 Waterloo road
Gilioli Joseph, physician, 46 Great Marlborough st.
Gilkes Gilbert & Alfred, silk mfrs. 28 Steward st. Spitalfields
Gilkes Joseph, cheesemong. 8 Chichester pl. Gray's inn road
Gilkes Thomas *Red Lion* P.H. 20 Red Lion st. Spitalfields
Gilkes Wm. musical inst. mak. 14 Dartmouth st. Westminster
Gilks Thomas, wood engraver, 1 Crown ct. Threadneedle st
Gill Henry & Co. wine merchants, 37 Crutched friars
Gill & Peppin, chemists, 25 Princes st. Leicester square
Gill William & Thomas, whip makers, 34 West Smithfield
Gill Charles, grocer, 22 Devereux court, Strand
Gill Charles, hairdresser, 249 Wapping High st
Gill Charles, saddler, &c. 35 Duke st. Grosvenor square
Gill David, tailor, 6 Derby st. King's cross
Gill Edmund, artist, 40 Frederick pl. Hampstead road
Gill Francis, plumber, 48 South Molton st. Bond st
Gill Frederick, machine ruler, 66 London wall
Gill George, cider merchant, 5 Hungerford wharf
Gill George, ivory turner, 51 Whiskin st. Clerkenwell
Gill Henry, beer retailer, 24 Doyley st. Sloane square

Gill Henry, pass master for London, 9 Swan la.Up.Thms.st.
Gill Henry John, hook & eye maker, 17 Clerkenwell green
Gill James, hop factor, see Barlow & Gill
Gill James, ivory turner, 63 Regent st. Lambeth
Gill James, pawnbroker, 7 & 8 Wilmot st. Russell square
Gill James, picture cleaner, &c. 13 Rathbone pl. Oxford st
Gill James, tinman, see Roberton (James M.), Son & Gill
Gill James, tailor, 25 Warwick lane, Newgate st
Gill John, carpenter & joiner, 10 Hoxton market
Gill John, corn merchant, New Corn Exchange, Mark lane
Gill John, dyer & scourer, 21 Foley place, Portland place
Gill John, greengrocer, 4 Park st. Islington
Gill John, plumber, 9 Thomas st. Brick lane
Gill John, shoemaker, 9 Lisson grove north
Gill John, tailor, 18 Holles st. Cavendish square
Gill John B. linendraper, 29 Pitfield st. Hoxton
Gill John Carley, cutler, 9 Colonnade, Brunswick square
Gill John William, tobacconist, 52 Theobald's road
Gill Joseph, *George IV.* P.H. 9 George's pl. Old st. road
Gill Maria (Mrs.), lodging house, 10 Cecil st. Strand
Gill Martha (Miss), milliner, 9 Church st. Shoreditch
Gill Martha (Mrs.), lighterman, 1 Calvert st. Wapping
Gill Mary (Mrs.), china warehouse, 15 Bridge st. Westmnstr
Gill Mary (Mrs.), *Cock & Hoop* P.H. 1 Gun st. Bishopsgate
Gill Robert, cheesemonger, 5 Museum st
Gill Robert, lighterman, 8 Addle hill, Doctors' Commons
Gill Robert, tailor & draper, 21 Frith st. Soho
Gill Samuel, *Dun Horse* P.H. 11 Kingsland road
Gill Samuel, furniture broker, 63 Cromer st. Brunswick sq
Gill Samuel, oilman & wax chandler, 149 Regent st
Gill Thos. ale & porter merchant, & agent to Messrs. Thorne & Co. 25 Castle st. Leicester sq. & 47 Gerrard st. Soho
Gill Thos. china & glass man, 14 Brook st. Grosvenor sq
Gill Thomas, coal merchant, 25 Queen's row, Pentonville
Gill Thomas, corn merchant, New Corn Exchange, Mark la
Gill Thomas, merchant, Baltic coffeehouse
Gill Thomas, solicitor, 12 Harrington st. Hampstead rd
Gill Wm. carpntr. & undrtkr, Augustus row, Spa rd. Bermndsy
Gill Wm. hairdresser, 95 London road, Southwark
Gill Wm. ironfounder, 42 Edward st. Limehouse
Gill Wm. ladies' shoemaker, 18 Leonard st. Finsbury
Gill Wm. poulterer & game dealer, Leadenhall market
Gill Wm. sealmaker & jeweller, 10 Low. Smith st. Clerkenwell
Gill Wm. Seth, surgeon, 29 White Lion st. Pentonville
Gillam George, *Brown Bear* P.H. 13 & 14 Seacole la. Skinner st
Gillam George, painter, &c. 258 Tottenham court road
Gillan Wm. Campbell, parliamentary agt. 44 Parliament st
Gillard Ann (Mrs.), *Queen's Head* P.H. 56 Gt. Ormond st. Qu. sq
Gillard Jeremiah, grocer, 28 Norton st. Portland place
Gillard Richard, china dealer, 3 St. Agnes ter. Tabernacle sq
Gillard Wm. portrait painter & modeller, 4 Gower st. north
Gillatt George, auctioneer & surv. 11 King st. Holborn
Gillatt Isaac, wine mer. 204, & 3 *Pigeons* P.H. 205 Piccadilly
Gillatt Samuel, builder, 8 Chapel st. Grosvenor square
Gillbank John, *Bear & Rummer* P.H. 74 Mortimer st. Cvndh. sq
Gillespie Ann & Mary (Misses), stationers, 30 Kingsland cresct
Gillespie Reb. (Miss), haberdshr. 5 Portsea pl. Connaught sq
Gillespies, Moffatt & Co. merchts. 5 Gould sq. Crutchedfriars
Gillespy Rich. & Saml. hairdressers, 163 Tottenham ct. rd
Gillespy Danl. carver & gilder, 43 University st. Tott. ct. rd
Gillespy Thomas, ship & insurance broker, 12 Billiter st. & sailmaker, 334 Wapping High st.
Gillett (Foster) & Co. calico printers, 94 Watling st
Gillett, Lees & Co. plush manufacturers, 36 King st. Cheapsi
Gillett Elizh (Mrs.), baker, 108 Upper Whitecross st. St. Luke's
Gillett Jane (Miss), chandler's shop, 17 Parish st. Horselydn
Gillett John, cabinetmaker, 116 Fetter lane
Gillet John William, dyer, 26 Bidborough st. Burton crescent
Gillet John, plumber & painter, 10 Vinegar yard, Brydges st
Gillett Joseph, baker, 12 Anchor & Hope alley, Wapping
Gillett Robert, oil & colorman, 1 Strutton ground, Westmr
Gillham Charles & Joseph, hatters, 153 Long la. Bermondsey
Gillham Charles, grocer, Park place, Old Kent road
Gillham Charles, hairdresser, 28 Gt. Crown ct. Lit. Pultnyst
Gillham Elizh. (Mrs.), *Moonrakers* P.H. 94 Gt. Suffolk st. Boro'
Gillham Geo. boot & shoe manufacturer, 101 Blackfriars rd
Gillham Joseph, tobacconist, 24 Langley pl. Comm. rd. east
Gillham Maria (Mrs.), strawhat ma. 10 Cleveland st. Mile end
Gillham Samuel, baker, 73 Great Guilford st. Borough, & 212 Blackfriars road
Gillham Wm. *Joe's coffee & chophouse*, 8 Finch la. Cornhill
Gillhome Hannah E. (Mrs.), statnr. 12 Mountter. Nw. rd. Whtcp
Gilliam James, boot & shoe ma. 16 Chapel pl. Liverpool rd
Gilliam John, jeweller, 50 Frith st. Soho
Gilliam John, tobacconist, 8 Compton st. Brunswick square
Gilliat John & Co. merchants, 11 Billiter square
Gillies & Horne, corn factors, 17 Mark lane
Gillies Henry, grocer, 49 Lambeth walk
Gillies John, pastry cook, 144 Tooley st
Gillies Margaret (Miss), artist, 45 Mortimer st. Cavendh. sq
Gilliman James, lodging house, 2 Holywell st. Millbank
Gilling & Clerc, watch case & dial ma. 1 Up. Charles st. Gswl. rd
Gilling Catherine (Miss), dressmaker, 35 Albemarle st
Gilling Hen. S. engineturner, 2 Up. Charles st. Northampton sq
Gilling Leopold, engine turner, 89 Goswell road
Gilling William, ham dealer, 41 Bath st. City road
Gillingham Edward, builder & stonemason, 26 Gough st. Gray's inn road, & 11 Wilson st. Gray's inn road
Gillingham Geo. *Mar. of Camden* P.H. 13 Gt. Collegest. Cam. tn
Gillingham George, veter. surgeon, 61 Church st. Chelsea
Gillingham John, veterinary surgeon, Montagu pl. Stones' end, Borough & 43 Collingwood st. Blackfriars road
Gillingham John, *White Swan* P.H. 18 Farringdon st.
Gillingham Fredk. beer retailer, 1 Wallington pl. Wnswh. rd
Gillingham Moses, builder, 1 Southampton ct. Totnhm. ct. rd
Gillings Wm. & John, cab propietors, 28 Earl st. Horseferryrd
Gillingwater John, hairdresser & perfumer, 148 Holborn bars
Gillingwater William, hairdresser & perfumer, 96 Goswell rd
Gillman Jas. *Square & Compasses* P.H. 62 Tothill st. Westmr
Gillman Joseph Knight, tailor, Stratford broadway
Gillman Robert, merchant, see Clay & Gillman
Gillman Thomas, *Angel* P.H. 85 Whitechapel High st
Gillman William, *Duke's Head* P.H. 16 Mint st. Borough
Gillmore Daniel, tailor, 22 Baldwin st. City road
Gilloch Geo. cabinet maker, 38 Church st. Mile end New twn
Gilloch John, cabinet maker, 38 Holywell lane, Shoreditch
Gilloch Thomas, carver, 28 Holywell lane, Shoreditch
Gillon John & Co. wine & prov. mer. Geo. Jones, agt. 8 Billiter st
Gillot Arthur, surgeon, 45 Haymarket
Gillott George & William Henry, tailors, 36 Strand
Gillott Joseph, steel pen manufacturer to the Queen, wholesale warehouse (Sam. Fox, manager), 37 Gracechurch st
Gillott William, tailor, 22 Northumberland st. Strand
Gillow & Co. merchants & upholders, 176 & 177 Oxford st
Gillyeatt Edward, shoemaker, 1 Claremont pl. Old Kent rd
Gilman Charles, oil & italian warehouse, 267 Oxford st
Gilman John, merchant, 87 Gt. Tower st. City
Gilmore Geo. hairdresser, 36 Church rd. Commerc. rd. east
Gilmore John, shipowner, 3 George yard, Lombard st
Gilmour David, vulcan iron wa. St. Ann's whf. Earl st. Blkfrs
Gilpin Wm. & Co. army clothiers, 1 Northumberland st. Strand
Gilpin Benjamin, straw hat ma. 15 New Church st. Lisson gr
Gilpin Charles, bookseller, 5 Bishopsgate without
Gilpin James, cheesemonger, 66 Charlotte ter. New cut
Gilpin William, warehouseman, see Turner & Gilpin
Gilpin William, woollen draper, 142 Borough High st
Gilruth David, baker, 19 Giltspur st. Newgate st
Gilson & Brown, fishmongs. 3 to 5 Lower area, Hungerford mk
Gilson & Cheeswright, ship & ins. bro. & coml. ag. 62 Lr. Thames st
Gilson George, fishmonger, see Brown & Gilson
Gilson Richard, butcher, 19 North Audley st
Gilson Robert, baker, 50 Millbank st. Westminster
Gilson Samuel, printer & stationer, New grove, Mile end rd
Gilson Thomas, *City of London coffeeho.* 5 & 6 Bucklersbury
Gilson Thomas, fishmonger, 14 New st. Dorset square
Gilson Thomas, jun. fishmonger, 3 Albion pl. Hyde park sq
Giltspur Street Compter (Jas. Raymond Whithair, keeper), 10 Giltspur st. Newgate st
Gilvray Wm. John, hairdresser, 9 Limekiln hill, Limehouse
Gilzean Wm. hairdresser, 10 Liverpool bldgs. Liverpool st
Gimber Henry, music seller, 40 King st. Borough
Gimber James, cheesemonger, see Clare & Gimber
Gimingham Wm. surveyor, 5 Duke st. Adelphi
Gimson Sarah (Miss), confectioner, 64 Crawford st
Ginder Heneage Norton, *Cock* P.H. 3 St. Martin's ct. Ludgate hl
Gingell Edwd. & Son, appraisers, 13 & 14 Barrett's ct. Oxford st
Gingell Edward, upholsterer, 112 Edgware road
Gingell George, hay salesman, 25 West Smithfield
Gingell Harriet (Mrs.), hairdresser, 8 Royal Hospital rw. Chls
Gingell Jas. hay salesman, Kent & Essex yd. 114 Whitechapel
Gingell Wm. lodging house, 107 Mount st. Berkeley sq
Ginger Daniel, *Family hotel*, 1 Bridge st. Westminster
Ginger Geo. vet. surg. Red Lion yd. 9 Lit. Guilfd. st. Brunswk. sq
Ginger Godfree Wm. bookseller, 21 Gt. College st. Westmr
Ginger Thos. *Bull inn & hotel*, 92 Bishopsgate within
Ginger Wm. *Cape of Good Hope* P.H. 39 Albany st. Regent's pk
Gingle Wm. tailor, 1 Johnson st. Somers town
Ginivan Elizabeth (Mrs.), fishmonger, 268 Oxford st
Gintherr & Staple, general agents, 11 Basing lane
Giorgi Peter, teacher of dancing, 31 Smith st. Chelsea
Giovannelli Gregorio, art. florist, 11 Albemarle st. Clerknwl
Gipps Henry Plumptre, barrister, 77 Chancery lane

Gipson Samuel, biscuit baker, 15 Nicholas lane, Lombard st
Girard & Barker, milliners, 21 Bruton st. Bond st
Girard Henry, grocer, 3 Jewry st. Aldgate
Girardet GeorgeAnn(Mrs.), stayma. 15 Gt.Castle st. Regt. st
Girardet James, grocer, 50 Upper George st. Bryanston sq
Giraud Richard Hervè, attorney, 7 Furnival's inn Holborn
Girault Robt. & Co. silk manufactrs. 5 Steward st. Spitlflds
Girdlers' Almshouses, between 42 & 43 Bath st. City road
Girdlers' Hall (Wm. Walton, clerk), 39 Basinghall st
Girdler Thos. Samuel, notary, see Comerford & Girdler
Girdler Wm. russia broker, 60 St. Mary Axe & Baltic
Girdlestone Wm. baker, 4 Brook st. New road
Girdwood & Haviland, surgeons, 177 Prospect pl. Edgwa. rd
Girdwood Gilbert F. surgeon, 1 Southwick cresct. Hyde park
Girerd & Matthes, manftg. jewellers, &c. 36 Newman st. Oxfd. st
Girerd Fanny (Madame), milliner, 36 Newman st. Oxford st
Girle Eliza (Mrs.), grocer, 5 Portland st. Soho
Girling John & Co. clothiers, 37 Hackney road
Girling Henry, carpenter, 35 University st. Tottenham ct. rd
Girling John, carpenter, 5 Alfred ter. Cambridge heath
Girling Thos. bricklayer, 22 Castle st. Long acre
Girling Thos. carpenter, 68 East st. Manchester sq
Girling Wm. wheelwright, 43 Southwark bridge road
Giro James, merchant, 4 Moorgate st. Bank
GirtinThos.Calvert, surgeon, 2 Hornsey row, Upper st Islingtn
Girton John, china & glass warehouse, 98 Edgware road
Gisborne John, merchant, 10 Liverpool st. Bishopsgate
Gissing Geo. *Old King's Head* P.H. 5 Kenngtn. pl. U. Kengtn. la
Gissing Saml. oil wa. 40 Hamilton row, Bagnigge wells road
Gittens William, upholsterer, 112 High st. Camden town
Gittins Richard, tea dealer, 2 Thayer st. Manchester sq
Giubilei Michel (Madame), ct. milliner, 1 Lit. Argyll st. Regt. st
Giuseppi Matthew, surgeon, 103 Milton st. Dorset square
Giustiniani, Castelli & Co. merchants, see Castelli & Co
GivensSarah (Mrs.), *BedfordHd.tav.* 41 Maiden la. Cov. gar
GivryVictor, importer of fancy french mitts, 45 Wood st
Glackner&King, oilmen, 11 Mount row, Livrpl. rd. Islington
Gladdell Charlotte (Miss), staymaker, 286 Regent st
Gladding David&Ben. hearth rug mfrs. 1 James pl. Hoxton flds
Gladding John & David, woollen drapers, 101½ Bishopgt. wt
Gladding John, bookseller, 20 City road, Finsbury square
Gladdish William & Thomas Nunn, lime burners, & blue lias cement manufacturers, Pedlar's acre, Lambeth; Dockhead, Bermondsey; 9 wharf, City road basin; & Danvers wharf, Lombard st. Chelsea
Gladding Robert, bookseller, 97 & 98 Whitechapel road
Gladen John, boot&shoe ma. 5 Parnham pl. Salmon la. Limeho
Gladhill Cornelius, chemist, 22 King David lane, Shadwell
Gladill William S. japanner, 10 Clerkenwell close
Gladman Marianne & Selina, milliners, 17 South Audley st
Gladman Geo. fruit salesman, Covent garden fruit market
Gladman Sarah (Mrs.), coach blind maker, 177 Drury lane
Gladman Wm. J. patten & clog maker, 196 Bethnal gr. rd
Gladstains Robert, grocer, 29 Carnaby st. Golden sq
Gladstone George Joseph, shipbuilder, 10 Brunswick terrace, Brunswick st. & Queen's dock, Blackwall
Gladstone Henry, tobacconist, 1 Postern row, Tower hill
Gladstone Samuel, shipwright, East India road, Poplar
Gladstones James, warehouseman, see Burls & Gladstones
Gladwell Thos. H. carver & gilder, 21 & 87 Gracechurch st
Gladwin Edward, printer, 1 Ship alley, Wellclose square
Gladwin Francis, confectioner, 43 Mount st. Lambeth
Gladwin George, engraver, 8 Charles st. Clarendon sq
Gladwin Thos. George, plumber, painter, &c. 17 Paddington st
Gladwin William, tailor, 3 Francis st. Golden sq
Gladwin William Rowland, smith & crane maker, & machinist, 61 & 62 Watling st
Glaisher Geo. sen. bookbinder, 23 Nassau st. Middlesex hospital
Glaisher Geo. jun. bookslr. & binder, 2 Charlotte st. Fitzroy sq
Glaister Joseph, lathe & tool maker, 36 Seward st
Glaister Richard, sydney merchant, see Ray & Glaister
Glamorgan Iron & Coal Co. (W. Hannay, sec.), 15 Percy st
Glanvill Burgess, architect & surv. 5 Belvedere rd. Lambeth
Glanvill George, *Coach & Horses* P.H. 21 North st. Westminstr
Glanvill John, carpenter, 16 Strutton ground, Westminster
Glanvill Richard, coal dealer, 12 Gough st. Gray's inn road
Glanville Edw. fruiterer, 1 Burton steps, Burton st. Burton cr
Glanville Thomas, tailor, 12 Bell's buildings, Salisbury sq
Glascock Charles, tailor & draper, 163 Fleet st
GlascodineRd. (sec. to Llanelly Rail. & Dock Co.), 1 Old Jewry ch
Glascoe Andrew, bootmaker, 11 Weston st. Borough
Glascott Geo. & Co. copper mers. 5 Gt. Garden st. Whitechpl
GlascottThos.T. copper & metal wa. 20 Brownlow st. Drury la
Glasgow & Garnkirk Railway agency, 57 Moorgate st
Glasgow Life Association, Robt. Mutrie, agent, 93 Watling st. for directors &c. see page 2026
Glasgow & London Shipping Company, 42 Crutched friars
Glasgow, Paisley & Ayr Railway agency, 57 Moorgate st
Glasgow, Paisley, & Greenock Railway agency, 57 Moorgate st
Glasier Jessie (Mrs.), wardrobe purchsr. 20A, Gt. Titchfield st
Glasier Wm. Richd. auctioneer & surveyor, 41 Charing cross
Glass Philip & Son, *Woolpack* P.H. 94 Minories
Glass Alexander, baker, 5 Robert st. Blackfriars road
Glass Alexander, butcher, 3 Hatfield place, Westminster rd
Glass Francis, Blackwell hall factor, 2 Basinghall st
Glass Geo. M. manufacturing chemist, gelatine, color & paper makers' size maker, Brandon st. Walworth
Glass James, coal mer. 6 Queen's Head row, Newington butts
Glass Joseph, chimney sweeping machine mak. 2 Moor lane
Glass Wm. beer retailer, 15 Lit. Guildford st. Brunswick sq
Glass William, butcher, 11 Cornwall road, Lambeth
Glasscock James, baker, 93 Bermondsey st
Glasscock Thos. oil & italian war. 15 Store st. Bedford sq
Glasse Wm. Bulkeley, barrister, 10 New sq. Lincoln's inn
Glasspool John, ladies' boot & shoe maker, 319 Regent st
Glasspool Geo. H. carpenter, 34 Chester pl. Kennington cr
Glazbrook Mary (Mrs.), hatter, Stratford Broadway
Glaze Eliz. (Mrs.), *Turk's Hd.* P.H. 64 Harley st. Cavendish sq
Glazebrook & Co. merchants, 106 Fenchurch st
Glazebrook Henry, coachmaker, 120 Long lane, Bermondsy
Glazebrook John, butcher, 5 William st. Lisson grove
Glazier John, undertaker, 193 Tottenham court road
Glazier John Thos. *Ship* P.H. 14 Artillery la. Bishopsgate
Gleaves Thos. Edmund, *Royal Tent* P.H. 5 Silver st, Golden sq
Gledstanes John H.&Co. merchts. 3 White Lion court, Cornhill
Gledstanes, Coningham&Co. wine mers. 11 Regent st. Pall mall
Gleed Thos. wine cooper & bottle mer. 18 Harp la. Tower st
Gleeson Thos. jeweller, 21 Wilderness row, Clerkenwell
Glegg Jane Harriett (Miss), dressma. 4 Skinner st. Snow hill
Glehn Robert v. mercht. 2 Hercules ct. Threadn. st. & Baltic
Glen Adam, biscuit baker, 106 Regent st
Glen Wm. Cunningham, barrister, 3 Essex court, Temple
Glendining Adam, whfngr. & flourfactor, 21 Bermondsey wall
Glendinning Robert, baker, 98 Charlotte st. Grosvr. square
Glendinning Robert, lodging house, 13 Chapel st. Fitzroy sq
Glenister Sibley, grindery dlr. 17 Stonecutter st. Farringd. st
Glenn John, builder, 3 Liverpool terrace, Islington
Glenn Thos. ginger beer ma. 17 Lit. Earl st. Seven dials
Glennie Adam, coffee rooms, Mare st. Hackney
Glennie John, baker, 6 Beauvoir place, Kingsland
Glennie John Irving, proctor, see Sladen, Glennie & Co
Glenny John, hosier, see Thresher & Glenny
Glenton & Chapman, ironmgrs. & braziers, 147 New Bond st
Glessing John, musical string maker, 10 Bell lane, Spitalfids
Glibbery Wm. boot tree & last maker, 4 Lit. Compton st. Soho
Glindining Sarah (Miss), ladies' school, 6 Queen's bldgs. Brmtn
Glindinning John, silversmith, 192 Sloane st. Knightsbridge
Glinister Edmond, hairdresser, 2 Emmett st. Poplar
Glinister Edmund, grocer, 1 Spring garden pl. Stepney
Glissan James, surgeon, 3 Leonard square, Finsbury
Glitherow Wm. bootmaker, 19 Gt. Sutton st. Clerkenwell
Glitsenstein Joseph, wholesale tortoise shell & ivory comb manufacturer, 29 Mansell st. Goodman's fields
Globe Life & Fire Insurance Office (J. C. Denham, sec.), Cornhill, & 89 Pall mall; see page 2027
Globe & Traveller Newspaper Office, 127 Strand
Glock George, pork butcher, 41 Bermondsey st
Gloucester, Aberystwith & Central Wales Railway Co. (Thos. D. Hawker, sec.), 1 New Broad st
Glover Ths. W&Son, coach, spring&axletree ma. 168 Drury la
Glover Archibald, manchester agent, 3 Queen st, Cheapside
Glover Benjamin, coachsmith, Wood's mews, Grosvenor sq
Glover Charles, cattle salesman, 60 West Smithfield
Glover Chas. livery stable keeper, 19 Eccleston pl. Pimlico
Glover Edward, baker, Old Ford
Glover George, beer retailer, 127 Southwark bridge road
Glover Geo. chem. 19 Goodge st. & 3 Eldon pl. Lr. rd. Islington
Glover George, dyer, 4 Church st. Stoke Newington
Glover George, tailor, 42 Great Suffolk st. Borough
Glover George Augustus, artist, 5 Paddington green
Glover Henry Hubbard, warehouseman, 30 Addle st. City
Glover Jane (Mrs.), milliner, 6 Belgrave road, Pimlico
Glover John, butcher, 3 Russell place, Old Kent road
Glover John, chemist & druggist, 3 Union ter. Comcl. rd. Ea
Glover John, dining rooms, 1 Cowcross st
Glover John, tailor, &c. see Eagleton & Glover
Glover John Herbert, oilman, 194 Bermondsey st
Glover Joseph, accountant, 12 Bucklersbury
Glover Joseph, dyer, Church street, Hackney
Glover Joseph, ironfounder & engineer, see Hendry & Glover
Glover Joseph, pork butcher, 20 Beckford row, Walworth rd
Glover Lawrence, carpenter, 47 Up. George st. Bryanstone sq

Glover Richard, butcher, 57 Bell street, Edgeware road
Glover Samuel, upholsterer, Wood's mews, Grosvenor sq
Glover Sarah (Mrs.), dairy, Eccleston street south, Pimlico
Glover Sarah (Mrs.), stationer, 2 Waterloo ter. Comcl. rd. ea
Glover Thomas, coach smith, Little York mews, Marylebone
Gloyer Thomas, coffee rooms. 3 Little Windmill st
Glover Wm. baker, 79 Friar street, Blackfriars road
Glover Wm. serjeant at law, 2 Serjeant's inn, Chancery lane
Glover Wm. toy dealer, 2 Gloucester pl. King's rd. Chelsea
Glover Wm. Jeffs, ribbon dresser &c. 5 Oat lane, Wood st. & dyer, 16 St. George's place, Camberwell
Gloyne Charles Glynn, chemist, High st. Kensington
Gloyns Richard, academy, 20 Savage gardens, Tower hill
Glyn (Sir Richard Carr, bart.), Hallifax, Mills & Co. bankers, 67 Lombard st
Glynes Randall, solicitor, 8 Crescent, America sq. Minories
Glynn John, plumber, &c. 28 Elizabeth st. south, Pimlico
Glyphographic or Engraved Drawing Office (Henry Geo. Collins, manager), 79 Shoe lane, Fleet st
Goad Martha & Son, undertakers, 38 Great Tower st
Goad & Rigg, hide, fur, skin, tallow, &c. brokers, 17 Markla
Goad Charles, plumber, &c. 2 St. George's pl. High st. Cambwl
Goad George, tailor, 17 Nottingham place, Whitechapel
Goad James, baker, 41 Great Queen st. Lincoln's inn fields
Goad John, plumber & glazier, 32 Smith st. Northampton sq
Goad Martha (Mrs.), wirework & measure ma. 38 Gt. Tower st
Goate John, carver & gilder, 6 Stacey st. St. Giles's
Goater Wm. & Co. grocers & teadealers, 53 Howland st. Ftzry. sq
Goatley Abigail (Mrs.), milliner, 21 Edwards st. Portman sq
Goatley John, grocer, see Salmon & Goatley
Goatley Rebecca (Miss), milliner, 14 Dover st. Piccadilly
Goatley R. (Mrs.), baby linen, &c. rep. 7 New Bridge st. Vauxhall
Goatly Ephraim, bootmaker, see Gilbert & Goatly
Goatly Walter Ephraim, solicitor, 3 Cork st. Bond st
Gobby, Haines & French, trousers & military overall makers, 2 Leicester st. Regent st
Gobby Dominick, furniture broker, 33 Leather la. Holborn
Gobby Joseph, appraiser & undrtkr. 24 Eyre st. hill, Hatn. gn
Gobell William, *Axe* P.H. 25 Milton st. City
Gobey Benedict, law stationer, 12 Cursitor st. Chancery la
Gobey Joseph, straw hat maker, 47 Fleet la. Farringdon st
Goble George & Co. coachmakers, 17 Clarence pl. Claphamrd
Goble Thomas Hinds, hop factor, 259 Borough High st
Goblet Henry Francis, lace manuf. Robin Hood alley, Milkst
Godart Peter, plumber & glazier, 7 Wapping wall
Godart Peter, plumber & glazier, 26 King st. Tower hill
Godber George, commission agent, 31 Lawrence lane
Godbold Edward, grocer, &c. 46 Upper Park st. Islington
Godbold Francis, upholsterer, 34 Francis st. Tottenhm. ct. rd
Godbold John, baker, 1 Manchester terrace, Liverpool road
Godby Hannah (Mrs.), tailor & brace mak. 37 Brooke st. Hlbn
Godby James, grocer, 182 Shadwell High st
Godby James, wholesale coffee dealer, see Eyre & Godby
Godby Robert, currier, &c. 23 Poplar High st
Godchaux I. & Co. merchants, 5 Finsby. chambs. Blomfield st
Goddard & Chambers, grocers & ita. wareho. 49 Adam st. west
Goddard Thos. & Fras. russia brokers, 80 Old Broad st. City
Goddard Alfred, solicitor, 28 King st. Cheapside
Goddard Chas. carman, 27 Gt. Pulteney st. Golden square
Goddard Chas. newsagent, 12 Marylebone lane, Oxford st
Goddard Chas. wheelwright & smith, 36 Rupert st. Hymkt
Goddard Edmund, ham & tongue dealer, 161 Fenchurch st. 103 London wall, & 17 Aldgate
Goddard Edmund, ham & beef dealer, 17 Aldgate
Goddard Edward, stationer & card box manftr. 291 Strand
Goddard Godfrey, solicitor, 101 Wood st. Cheapside
Goddard Hogg Reynolds, fringe mnfr. 11 Newington causeway
Goddard Howell, jun. china dealer & greengrocer, 7 Noble st
Goddard Howell, sen. undertaker, 3 Lillypot lane, Cheapside
Goddard James, ironmonger, 30 Red Lion st. Holborn
Goddard James, machine ma. 5 & 15 Red Lion ct. Spitalfields
Goddard James, tobacconist, 27 Union st. Bishopsgate
Goddard John, wholesale druggist, see Hewlett & Goddard
Goddard John A. customho. foreign coml. & gen. agt. 36 O. Jewry
Goddard Lemuel, iron merchant, 6 Crescent, Minories, & 220 Wapping High street
Goddard Leonard Morse, surgeon, 5 St. John st. road
Goddard Matthew, baker, 354 Albany rd. Camberwell rd. & 2 Dudley place, Clapham road
Goddard Nathaniel, cattle salesman, 37 West Smithfield
Goddard Richard, chemist, &c. 45 Lisson grove north
Goddard Robert, carman, 13 Macclesfield st. south, City rd
Goddard Thomas, general agent & outfitter, 156 Cheapside
Goddard Thos. Ratcliffe, dancing acad. 19 Greville st. Hat. gar
Goddard Wm. baker, 14 Oakley terrace, Old Kent road
Goddard William, beer retailer, 18 Shoreditch High street
Goddard William, dairyman, 20 St. Alban's st. Lambeth
Goddard William, family coal office, 18 Strand
Goddard Wm. furniture dealer, 9 Cross st. Newington butts
Goddard William, grocer, 72 Theobalds row
Godden John & Hen. Jas. solicitors, 3 John st. Bedford row
Godden Benj. *Mulberry Tree* P.H. Mulberry st. Whtchpl
Godden George, tallow chand. 33 Goodge st. Tottenham ct. rd
Godfree Benjamin, baker, 145 Old st. St. Luke's
Godfree John, confectioner, 1 Ray st. Clerkenwell
Godfree Joseph, baker, 1 Charles pl. Hertford rd. Kingsland
Godfree William, baker, Stoke Newington road
Godfree Wm. bootmaker, 19 Upper Ground st. Blackfriars
Godfrees John, eel pie house, 3 Church la. Whtchpl. High st
Godfrey, Barnett & Hancock, boot & shoe makers to the Queen, 3 Conduit st. Regent st
Godfrey & Cooke, chemists, 31 Southampton street, Strand, & 30 Conduit st. Bond st
Godfrey Jas. Chas. & Co. chemists, &c. 31 Edgware road
Godfrey & Soloman, linendrapers, &c. 40 St. John st. Clknwl
Godfrey Chas. furniture broker, 5 Warwick pl. Kingsland rd
Godfrey Charles, jeweller, 15 St James's st. Clerkenwell
Godfrey Charles, lodging house, Bell's bldgs. Salisbury sq
Godfrey Francis Rd. *Queen's Arms* P.H. 37 Dartmouth st. Wmr
Godfrey George, butcher, 8 Oxford market
Godfrey George, grocer, 13 Queen st. Horsleydown
Godfrey George, ham dealer, 63 Paddington st. Marylebone
Godfrey George, tobacconist, 24 High st. Camberwell
Godfrey George, upholsterer, 27 William st. Regent's park
Godfrey Henry, commission agent, 27 Wood st. City
Godfrey John, cattle salesman, 41 West Smithfield
Godfrey John, confectioner, 43 Old st. road
Godfrey John, cabinet maker, 36 Gt. Sutton st. Clerkenwell
Godfrey John, cooper, 25 Widegate st. Bishopsgate
Godfrey John, *Crown & Two Chairmen* P.H. 32 Dean st. Soho
Godfrey John, oil & colorman, 56 Curtain road, Shoreditch
Godfrey John, M.D. surgeon, 3 Mount place, Whitechapel rd
Godfrey Joseph Silvester, barrister, 10 New sq. Lincoln's inn
Godfrey Nathaniel, vinegar mercht. 86 Bankside, Southwark
Godfrey Nicholas, cabinet maker, 26 King st. Clerkenwell
Godfrey Rebecca (Miss), embroiderer, 103 Strand
Godfrey Samuel, jun. willow shape mnfr. 126 Curtain road
Godfrey Thos. sen. egg mercht. 3 Forston st. Shepherdess walk
Godfrey Thos. jun. egg merchant, 37 Britannia row, Islington
Godfrey Wm. marine store dealer, 74 York st. Westminster
Godfrey Wm. *New York tavern*, 2 St. Michael's alley
Godfrey Wm. optical brazier, 72 Noble st. Goswell st
Godfrey Wm. tailor, 3 Somerset terrace, Kensington
Godin Lewis, stockbroker, 27 Tokenhouse yard
Goding & Co. brewers, Belvedere road, Lambeth
Godlee Rickman, barrister, 3 New square, Lincoln's inn
Godlonton Thomas, window blind maker, 162 Kingsland rd
Godly John, *Britannia* P.H. 10 Little Compton st. Soho
Goodman James, confectioner, 27 Seymour st. Euston square
Godrich Francis, surgeon, Little Chelsea, North side
Godsall Henry, gun barrel maker, 86½ Oxford st
Godsalve Thomas, butcher, 9 Charles st. Commercial road
Godsell Fred. & Edmund, wine & spirit brokers, 85 Gt. Tower st
Godsell James, ready made linen warehouse, 64 Oxford st
Godsell Thos. *Bengal Arms tav.* 2 White Lion ct. Birchin la
Godsell Wm. grocer, 1 Edward st. White Horse la. Stepney
Godsell William, solicitor, 6 Furnival's inn, Holborn
Godsmark George, butcher, 16 High st. Camberwell
Godsmark James, grocer, &c. 15 Crosby row, Walworth rd
Godson (Ralph) & Co. drysalters, 25 Fore st. Cripplegate
Godson Edward, ironmonger, 72 Aldersgate st
Godson George, meat salesman, 7 Newgate market & 14 Bowling st. Clerkenwell
Godson Richard, queen's counsel, 11 King's Bench walk, Temple
Godson Stephen Holmes, barrister, 11 King's Bench walk
Godson William, grocer, 1 Edward st. White Horse la. Stpny
Godward Samuel, stone mason, 33 Edward st. Dorset sq
Godward Sarah (Mrs.), goldsmith & jeweller, 89 Boro' High st
Godwin Geo. & Son, architects, 24 Alexander sq. Brompton
Godwin James & Nephew, gold & silversmiths, 304 High Holborn
Godwin Charles, hairdresser, 5 Knightrider ct. Doctrs'. com
Godwin Charles, stock & share bro. 2 Royal Exchange buildings
Godwin Fred. auctioneer, valr. & agent, 3 Halkin ter. Belg. sq
Godwin Henry, trimming warehouse, 62 High st. St. Giles's
Godwin Hen. Morgan, stock & sharebroker, 4 White Lion ct. Cnhl
Godwin Jas. fruit & pea salesman, Covent garden fruit market
Godwin James, *Sloane's Head* P.H. 16 New st. Brompton
Godwin James Thomas, rope & oakum mer. 67 Wapping wall
Godwin John, rope maker, 77 King st. Deptford
Godwin John Henry, paper stainer, see Bowen & Godwin
Godwin Joseph, *Old Vine* P.H. Great Green st. Kentish town

Godwin Joseph, *Plough* P.H. 12 Crown st. Soho
Godwin Louisa (Mrs.), milliner, 8 Cambridge pl. Hackney rd
Godwin Philip, patent wig ma. 7 Greville st. Hatton garden
Godwin Richard, brick & tile mercht. see Hitch & Godwin
Godwin Samuel, news agent, 4 Pitt st. Old Kent road
Godwin Sarah (Miss), milliner, 3 Church lane, Islington
Godwin Thomas, bootmaker, 12 Charlotte st. Whitechapel
Godwin Wm. british plate & picture dealer, 41 Ludgate st
Godwin Wm. dairyman, 111 Albany st. Regent's park
Godwin Wm. jun. artificial flower ma. 13 Derby st. King's crss
Godwin Wm. sen. artfcl. florist, &c. 56 Myddelton st. Clerkenwl
Goetze Noah, stationer & bookseller, 8 Wardour st. Soho
Goez Henry, wool merchant, 72 Basinghall st
Goff Jane & Emma (Misses), milliners, 4 Surrey pl. O. Kent rd
Goff Daniel, tea & coffee dealer, 13 Baker st. Portman sq
Goff George, greengrocer, 43 Regent st. Lambeth walk
Goff Henry, furniture broker, 13 Pleasant row, Pentonville
Goff James, *Old Cherry Tree* P.H. 41 Kingsland road
Goff James, plumber, 2 Salcombe place, Regent's park
Goff James Copeland, upholsterer, 20 Ebury st. Pimlico
Goff Mary (Mrs.), boot & shoe maker, 28 High st. Kensington
Goff Sarah (Mrs.), straw hat ma. 25 Glo'ster row, Grange rd
Gofton Wm. ham & beef wareho. 8 Up. Queen's bldgs. Brmpton
Gogay Saml. silk & cotton dealer, 16½ Church st. Shoreditch
Gogerty Robt. brass turner & inst. ma. 32 King st. Smithfield
Goggins John, *Three Jolly Bakers* P.H. 6 Lit. Chesterfield st
Goggs, Heading & Co. wine merchants, 106 Fenchurch st
Goghan Thomas, baker, 5 Halsey terrace, Cadogan st
Golby Sophia (Miss), fringe & fancy trimmings, canvass, worsteds, &c. for needlework, 14 Coventry st. Haymarket
Gold Henry & Son, wholesale grocers & teadealers, 164 Boro' High st. & Hibernia whf. Montague close, London bridge
Gold & Rogers, outfitters & drapers, 5 Bridge rd. Lambeth
Gold Charles, pocket book maker, 184 Hoxton High st
Gold Frederick Isaac, baker, 5 Wentworth pl. Mile end rd
Gold Isaac, baker, 14 St. John street road
Gold Peter, grocer, 114 & 115 Brick lane, Spitalfields
Gold William, coaldealer & fruiterer, Kingsland green
Goldbourn Wm. Joseph. coal & potato dlr. 10½ Hastings st. Burton crescent
Goldburgh Louis, cap manufacturer, 14 London wall
Goldby Robert, plumber, 15 Princes st. Lit. Queen st. Holbn
Golden Cross coach office, Circus, 33 Regent st
Golden Henry, coffee rooms, 39 North st. Lisson grove
Golden John, coal merchant, 28 Sloane st. Chelsea
Golden Stephen, ladies' shoemaker, 29 Seething la. Tower st
Goldfinch Alfred, tobacconist, 6 Athol place, Pentonville
Goldfinch George, linendraper, Deptford High st
Goldfinch Henry Robert, barrister, 44 Chancery lane
Goldfinch John, carpenter, 2 Shepherd's market, Mayfair
Goldfinch John, fishmonger, 46 Old Bailey, & 21 Charterho. st
Goldfinch Phillis (Mrs.), hatter, 7 Deptford High st
Goldfinch Wm. metal fan light ma. 5 Actonpl. Bagn. wellrd
Goldham Henry, nurseryman, Thornhill road, Islington
Goldie James, carpenter & joiner, Gun lane, Limehouse
Goldin Henry, pork butcher, 10 Hayes ct. Gerrard st. Soho
Golding & Watts, who & ret. bootwar. 3 & 4 Churchst. Shoreditch
Golding Ann (Mrs.), grocer, 5 Kent st. Borough
Golding Bartholemew, grocer, 67 South st. King's rd. Chels
Golding Benjamin, M.D. surgeon, 29 King William st. W. Std
Golding Charles, tailor, 23 Eldon st. Finsbury
Golding Geo. fancy cabinet maker, 9 City terrace, Old st. rd
Golding James, carman, London Dock entrance, & 2 Christian st. St. George's east
Golding James, oil & italian warehouse, 56 Strand
Golding John, basket maker, 4 Boundary st. Shoreditch
Golding John, plumber, 12 Charlton st. Fitzroy square
Golding John H. stockbroker, 10 Warnfordct. Throgmorton st
Golding Joseph, carcase butcher, 73 Aldgate High st
Golding Peter, boot & shoe maker, 33 Ludgate st
Golding Sarah (Miss), *King's Arms* P.H. Bishopsgate ch. yd
Golding Thomas, *Grapes* P.H. 20 Jewin st
Golding Walter, beershop, 3 Westmoreland pl. Walworth com
Golding William, bootmaker, 98 London road, Southwark
Golding William, carman, 24 Spital st. Spitalfields
Golding William, chemist, 42 Up. Albany st. Regent's park
Golding William, fruit & pea salesman, Borough market
Golding William, gunmaker, 27A, Davies st. Berkeley sq
Golding Wm. imp. of wine & spirits, see Barrow, Golding & Co
Golding William, *Red Lion* P.H. 59 Gray's inn lane
Goldingay Barnet Fred. plumber & painter, 275 Wapping
Goldner Stephen, preserved provision man. 137 Houndsditch
Goldney Francis Bennett, lace warehsmn. 4 St. Paul's ch. yd
Goldring Robert, picture dealer, 41 Wardour st. Soho
Goldsborough Edwin, com. agt. 23 Crosby hall cham. Bshpgte
Goldschmidt Solomon Sam. com. merchant, 30 Broad st. bldg
Goldsmid, King & Thompson, agents to the Imperial Brazilian government, 37 Great Winchester st
Goldsmid Aaron, merchant, 10 Warnford ct. Throgmorton st
Goldsmid Andrew, barrister, 10 Crown Office row, Temple
Goldsmid Charles, civil engineer, see Freebody & Goldsmid
Goldsmid Francis Hen. barrister, 5 Stone bldngs. Linc. inn
Goldsmid Fred. David, broker, see Mocatta & Goldsmid
Goldsmid Joseph, birmingham & shef. wa. 56½ Houndsditch
Goldsmid Lamert, fruiterer, 49 Newington causeway
Goldsmid Nathaniel, barrister, 3 Figtree court, Temple
Goldsmid Wm. stockbro. 36 Throgmorton st. Stock exchange
Goldsmith Chas. & Co. scotch & man. warehousemen, 53 Friday st
Goldsmiths' Hall (John Lane, clerk), Foster lane
Goldsmith George, barrister, 9 New square, Lincoln's inn
Goldsmith George, fruiterer, 29 Flagon row, Deptford
Goldsmith James, hairdresser, 4 Spread eagle ct. Finch lane
Goldsmith Jane (Miss), milliner, 42 Great Portland st
Goldsmith John, surgeon, see M'Crea & Goldsmith
Goldsmith John, whipmaker, 67 Blackman st. Borough
Goldsmith John Tanner, carpenter, Southampton st. Cambwl
Goldsmith Joseph, baker, 91 St. George st
Goldsmith Susanna (Mrs.), pastrycook, 6 Bridge ct. Westmr
Goldsmith Thos. boarding ho. 3 George st. Trinity sq. Twr. hil
Goldsmith Thos. wood dealer, Villa st. Walworth road
Goldsmith Thomas, hairdresser, 33 King st. Long acre
Goldsmith Thomas, plumber, 88 Cromer st. Brunswick sq
Goldsmith Wm. glass & chinaman, 42 Judd st. Brunswick sq
Goldsmith Wm. linendraper, 1 Waterloo ter. Commcl. rd. ea
Goldsmith Wm. wine & spirit merchant, 31 Parliament st
Goldsmith Wm. yarmouth ale stores, Market st. Millbank st
Goldson Richd. potato dealer, 31 Langley pl. Comrcl. rd. ea
Goldsworth Wm. china & glass dlr. 11 Portsdown ter. Kilburn
Goldsworthy John, baker, 10 New street, Dorset square
Goldsworthy Robt. bootma. 30½ Portpool lane, Gray's inn la
Goldsworthy Samuel Heath, painter, 9 Essex pl. Mile end rd
Goldsworthy William, plumber, painter, &c. 10 Cowcross st
Goldthorp George, chemist & druggist, 143 Tooley st
Goldthorp Wm. beer retlr. 14 St. Mark's rd. Camberwell new rd
Goldzieher Robert & Co. mercht. & for. agt. 15 Throgmorton st
Gole James & Thomas, solicitors, 49 Lime st
Gole Abraham, colonial agent, Hall of Commerce
Golledge Richard, watchmaker, Stratford broadway
Gollin Bezaleel, watchmaker, 2 Tenter ter. Goodman's fields
Gollings Henry, *Nag's Head* P.H. 3 Postern row, Tower hill
Golton Charles, brazier, 10 Queen st. Ratcliff cross
Gomersal Edwd. Alex. pastrycook, 26 Leman st. Goodman's flds
Gomersall Charlotte (Mrs.), umbrella maker, 3 Theobald's rd
Gomes Francis, physician, 49 George street, Euston square
Gomez Charles, bow maker, 15 Sussex st. Tottenham ct. rd
Gomez Emilie (Mrs.), milliner, &c. &c. 12 Piccadilly
Gomm & Hart, strawhat makers, 257 Regent circus
Gomm Henry, butcher, 38 Charlotte st. Whitechapel
Gomm Henry, pork butcher, 5 Clare court, Drury lane
Gomm Jas. carpenter & undertaker, 23 Bell st. Edgware rd
Gomm John, attorney & scotch agt. 31 Edwards st. Portmn. sq
Gomm Stephen, fishmonger, 20 Tottenham court, New road
Gomme Steph. jun. architect, Arundel chambs. 65 Regent st
Gonne, Lucas & Gribble, merchants, 20 St. Helen's place
Gonner Elizh. (Miss), milliner, 13 Margaret st. Cavendish sq
Gonzales Carlo, LL.D. professor of italian, 33 London street, Fitzroy square
Gonzalez & Dubosc, of Xerez de la Frontera, agent Robt. B. Byass, 1 Langbourn chambers, Fenchurch st
Gooch & Cousens, wharfingers & wareho. keepers, 126 London wall, & Steel yd. Up. Thames st. & Chequer yd. Dowgate hill
Gooch Caroline (Mrs.), *Robin Hood* P.H. 67 Skinner st. Bshpgt
Gooch Edmund, hatter & tailor, 161 Poplar High st
Gooch Edward Frederick, stationer, printer, bookseller & account book manufacturer, 55 King William st. City
Gooch Edward Woodcock, surveyor, 42 Connaught terrace
Gooch Henry, *King's Head* P.H. 178 Tooley st
Gooch James, builder, Hertford rd. Englefield rd. & Mortimer road, Kingsland
Gooch John Vivet, engineer, Railway station, Nine Elms
Gooch Matthew, turner & brush maker, 43 Curzon st. Mayfair
Gooch Samuel, linen ma. 4 Norfolk pl. Lark hall la. Clapham
Gooch Wm. Tovey, stock & share broker, 3 Bartholomew la
Good Daniel & Co. timber merchants, 380 Albany rd. Cmbrwl
Good Hen. & Wm. stationers & accnt. book ma. 60 Moorgate st
Good Susannah & Son, statnrs. & music slrs. 63 Bishpsgt. witht
Good Benjamin, butcher, 9 King David lane, Shadwell
Good Charles, butcher, 25 Newport court, Newport market
Good Charles [late Davidson], rope, net, line & twine manufacturer, 47 & 48 King William st. London bridge
Good Elizh. (Mrs.), pat. medicine wa. 53 Cambridge st. Edg. rd
Good Henry, wine & brandy mercht. 78 Queen st. Cheapside

Good Joseph, *White Horse* P.H. 50 Brick lane, St. Luke's
Good Joseph Hen.jun.architect & surveyor,75 Hatton garden
Good Joseph, cork & spile maker, 3 Eyre st. hill
Good Thomas, chemist & druggist, 47 Minories
Good Sarah (Mrs.), baker, 16 Turnmill st. Clerkenwell
Good Thomas,tailor,teacher of cutting,&reporter of fashions, 6 Conduit st
Good Wm. livery stables, Union yard, 190½ Oxford st
Good Wm. ornamental writer, 62 London road, Southwark
Good William, turner, 27 John st. Fitzroy square
Goodacre Geo.wood turner, Church la.Kensington grvl. pits
Goodacre Joseph, teadealer, 4 Weston st. Somers town
Goodacre Thos. gold wire drawer,2 Cherry Tree ct. Alders. st
Goodale Archibald, baker, 111 Tooley st
Goodall Chas.& Son, card maks.30 Gt. Pulteney st.Golden sq. & manufactory 16 Gt. College st. Camden town
Goodall Chas. broker & apprsr. 24 Henry st. east,Avenue rd
Goodall Charles, chemist, 10Up. Dorset st. Bryanstone sq
Goodall Danl. button & trimming seller, see Carr & Goodall
Goodall Edward, teadlr. &c. 4 York st. Middlesex hospital
Goodall John, *Captain Man of War* P.H.127 PoplarHigh st
Goodall John, surveyor, 10 Panton square, Piccadilly
Goodall Hen. tobacco pipe ma. 18 Rose passage, Golden lane
Goodall Rt. Harley,stock & exchange broker,10 Warnford ct
Goodall William, dyer,&c. 36 Penton st. Pentonville
Goodban John Thos. exchange broker, 4 Angel court
Gooday Edward Wm. solicitor, see Raimondi & Gooday
Goodbarne Thomas, chemist, annatto merchant & manfr. 13 Charles place, Charles square, Hoxton
Goodbehere George Thos. wholesale hardwareman, 9 Wellclose square, & 5 Martin's lane, Cannon st
Goodbody Geo. wine cooper,5New inn, Broadway,Curtain rd
Goodbody Samuel, coach spring & patent axletree maker, 33 Charles st. Drury lane
Goodbody Wm.cabinet maker, 17 New inn yard, Shoreditch
Goodburn Ebenezer, bookseller, &c. 29 Gt. Carter lane
Goodburn Wm. pawnbroker, 63 Ernest st. Regent's park, & 1 Commerce row, Upper st. Islington
Goodby James, saddler, 26 Little Guilford st. Brunswick sq
Goodchap William & Co accountants,&c. 84 Hatton garden
Goodchap George, genl. house agent, see Goold & Goodchap
Goodcheape George, oil & colorman, 76 St. John st. road
Goodcheape John, furnishing undertaker, 115 Aldersgate st. City, & 5 Princess st. Lisson grove
Goodchild James, coffee rooms, 38 Queen st. Cheapside
Goodchild John, carcase butcher, 3 Hanover pl. Old Kent rd
Goodchild Joseph, ham dealer, 239 Shoreditch
Goodchild Joseph, wind. glass & lead mercht. 2 & 3 Tooley st
Goodchild Robert, chemist & druggist, Well st. Hackney
Goodchild Samuel, hosier & glover, 36A, Moorgate st
GoodchildThos. architect & surveyor,70Warren st.Fitzroy sq
Goodchild William, coachmaker, 15 Long acre
Goodday Horatio, surgeon, 48 Baker st. Portman sq
Goode & Allbon, cigar divan & chessrooms, 39 Ludgate hill & 199 Strand
Goode Benj. & Philip, attorneys, 44 Howland st. Fitzroy sq
Goode & Co. [late Wyatt Thos. & Co.] east india & oil merchants, wholesale dealers in sauces, pickles, &c. & for exportation, 102 Leadenhall st
Goode & Lawrence, navy agents, 15 Surrey st. Strand
Goode Benjamin, farrier, 20 Finsbury st. Chiswell st
Goode Charles, draper & mercer, see Gainsford & Goode
Goode Charles, locksmith, 2 Sandys row, Bishopsgate
Goode John, auctioneer & appraiser, 68 Goswell road
Goode John Richard, tailor, 25 Church st. Spitalfields
Goode Joseph, *White Horse* P.H. 50 Brick lane, St. Luke's
Goode Mary (Mrs.),pawnbroker & silversmith,116Goswell st
Goode Philip, solicitor, 43 Howland st. Fitzroy square
Goode Thomas, china & glass warehouse, 15 Mill st. Hanover square, & 19 South Audley st
Goode Thomas, greengrocer, 95 High st. Portland town
Goode Thomas, printer, 8 St. James's walk, Clerkenwell
Goode Thomas, upholsterer, 10 Up. King st. Bloomsbury
Goode Timothy, grocer, 29 Windmill st. Tottenham court rd
Goode Timothy, hairdresser, 27 Windmill st. Tottm. ct. rd
Goode Wm. carpenter, 67 Hill st. Walworth road
Goode Wm. *St. Luke's Head* P.H. 8 King st. Grosvenor sq
Goode Wm. willow sq. & shape m. 8 Birdcage wk. Hackney rd
Goode Wm. Thomas, tailor, 13 Saville place, Mile end road
Gooden Nat. H. confectioner, 8 White Hart pl. L.Kenngtn.la
Gooden William Workman,oil & colorman, 112 Lambeth wk
Goodenough Charles, greengrocer, 6 Portman market
GooderedWm.Henry,wine & spirit merchant,6Hemming's rw
Gooderson Matthew, baker, 1 Green st. Bethnal green
Goodes Geo. & Saml.cigar manufts. 12Princes st. Spitalfields
Goodes William, grocer, 5 Blandford st. Portman square
Goodeve Henry, bottle merchant, 4 Little Bruton st
Goodeve John, attorney, 1 Raymond buildings, Gray's inn
Goodeve Joseph, barrister, 9 Old sq. Lincoln's inn & 41 Kensington square
Goodey Amos, baker, 23 Cowcross st
Goodey Joseph, linendraper, Ring cross, Holloway road
Goodfellow Richard, *Waterman's Arms* P.H. 2 Lr.Shadwell
Goodfellow Wm. Walter, bootma. 5 Newman's row,Lin.inn fi
Goodford Henry, solicitor, see Frere, Forster, Goodford & Cholmeley
Goodge John, lodging house, 16 Arundel st. Panton square
Goodge Selina (Miss), dressmaker, see Brown & Goodge
Goodge Wm.Thomas, grocer, 40 Up. Lisson st. Lisson grove
Goodger Wm. Fredk. surgeon, 13 Bentinck st.Manchester sq
Goodhall Hen. Edmd.merchant,see Smith,Goodhall&Reeves
Goodhall Michael, toothbrush ma.50 Turnmillst.Clerkenwell
Goodhart Emanuel, Son&Patricks,sugar refiners,Horseferry rd. Limehouse, & Hooper square, Goodman's fields
Goodhart Jacob & Sons, sugar refins. 3, 4 & 5 St. George st
Goodhart Alfred H. surgeon, 12 Brecknock cres. Camden tn
Goodhart Emanuel Geo. woolstapler,Up.Russell st. Bermnd
Goodheart James & Wm. desk & dress. case ma.40 Snowhill
GoodhewMaryAnnW.(Miss),ladies'school,25Milnersq.Islgtn
Goodhew William, *Fox* P.H. 58 Princes st. Lambeth
Goodhind Thos. french polisher, 20½ Clipstone st. Fitzroy sq. & 5 Hampstead st. Fitzroy square
Goodhugh Richard, watchmaker, 32 Edward st. Portman sq
Goodhugh Thomas,writing,&c.case ma. 72 Lamb's Conduit st
Goodier John Chas. printer,10 Denmark pl.Well st.Hackney
Goodin Frederick, fishmonger, 2 Park st. Islington
Gooding Edwd. teadealer & grocer, 2 & 161 Hoxton Old town
Gooding Elijah, carpenter, 3 Barking churchyard
Gooding Jane (Mrs.), ladies' school, 34A,Bell st.Edgware rd
Gooding John, french polisher, 21 North st. Whitechapel rd
Gooding Martha(Mrs.),toy&whitewoodmfr.178Totnhm.ct.rd
Gooding Thomas, hatter, 33 Church st. Shoreditch
Goodinge Jas. Boote, engraver & printer,4 Jewin st. Crippleg
Goodinge John, linendraper, 45 Brick lane, St. Luke's
Goodison James, french sax horn trumpet & cornopean ma. 7 Sherrard st. Golden square
Goodison Samuel, who. coffee dealer, see Moore & Goodison
Goodlad Rich. & Co. paper stainers,1 Southampton st.Strand
Goodlad Jas. chemist & druggist, 93 Bunhill row,Chiswell st
Goodlad Jos. Wm. ironmonger,&c. 42 &43RedLion st.Spitafi
Goodlake Wm. Hartley, oil, turpentine & tar broker, 51 Cornhill, & Baltic coffee house
Goodliffs Misses, ladies' school,18 Colebrooke row, Islington
Goodlove Samuel, butcher, 3 Cornwall ter. Camden town
Goodman John&Son,watchma.1NewChapel pl.Kentish town
Goodman Louis & Co. tailors & outfitrs. 227 Tottenham ct. rd
Goodman Richard & Co. mahogany & timber merchants, 41 Compton st.Clerkenwell,&WestIndiaDocks,&79Goswell st
Goodman Saml.&Andw.cowkeepers,26Artillery row,Westmr
Goodman & Taylor, tailors, 38 Great Marlborough st
Goodman Thos.&John,bldg.mat.dlr.25 Hereford pl.Com.rd.e
Goodman Grace (Mrs.), grocer, 8 Coldbath sq. Clerkenwell
Goodman Henry, grocer, 37 Mount st. Lambeth
Goodman Hiller, solicitor, 63 Lincoln's inn fields
Goodman James, butcher, 72 Snow hill
Goodman James, cattle salesman, 17 West Smithfield
Goodman James, *White Swan* P.H. 97 Gt. Portland st
Goodman John, beer retailer, 6 Gt. Sutton st. Clerkenwell
Goodman John, butcher, 20 Skinner st. Somers town
Goodman John, cattle salesman, 60 West Smithfield
Goodman John, leather dyer, 12Amelia rw.Spa rd.Bermndsy
Goodman Richard Alfred, attorney, 3 South sq. Gray's inn
Goodman Samuel, linendraper, High st. Kingsland road
Goodman Saml. wholesale shoe agt. 6 Milton st. Cripplegt
Goodman Samuel, linendraper, 15 Kingsland green
Goodman Thomas, baker, 17 Great Bell alley, Coleman st
Goodman Thomas, corn dealer, Lower road, Rotherhithe
Goodman Thomas, tailor, 35 Earl st. West, Lisson grove
Goodman Thomas, timber merchant, 24 Bedford sq. East
Goodrich Elizabeth(Mrs.),stay & corset maker, 156Oxford st
Goodrich Isaac,tallowchn.& oilman,37 Whitechapel High st
Goodrich William, baker,21 Gt. Ormond st. Queen square
Goodrich Wm. tin plate worker, 3 Club row, Bethnal green
Goodrich Wm. upholsterer, 29 Curtain road, Shoreditch
Goodrick Geo. carpenter, 62 Grosvenor mews, Grosvenor st
Goodrick Horatio Ajax, chemist, 4 Snow's fields, Bermndsy
Goodrick Wm. tin plate worker, 169 Church st. Shoreditch
Goodridge Richard E. & Co. com. mers. 16 Broad st. bldgs
Goodrum Wm. lever watchpallet ma. 25 Perceval st. Clknwl
Goodson Ann (Mrs.), baker, 94 Old st. St. Luke's
Goodson John, merchant, 9 Union court, Old Broad st
Goodson John, plumber & glazier, 3 Royal Oak pl. Eaton sq

Goodson Joseph, dairy, 12 Melton st. Euston square
Goodson Robert, baker, 45 Princess st. Edgware road
Goodson Thomas, frame maker, 20 John st. Fitzroy square
Goodson William, cowkeeper, 25 Gower place, Euston sq
Goodson William, silk manufr. 27 Steward st. Spitalfields
Goodspeed Edwd. venetian blind ma. 126 St. John st. Clknwl
Goodspeed Edwd. jun. window blind ma. 9 Clkenwell. green
Goodspeed Edwd. H. window blind maker, 29 Hatton wall
Goodwill John, engraver & printer, 89 Wardour st. Soho
Goodwin Charles & Co. ship brokers, 102 Fore st. Limehouse
Goodwin, Curling & Co. ship agents, 2 George yard, Lombard st. & at Ramsgate & Deal
Goodwin, Senecal & Banks, silk ma. 15 Steward st. Spitalflds
Goodwin Arnold, plaster of paris & hair ma. 67 Gt. Guildford st
Goodwin Chas. commercial boarding house, 6 Old Fish st
Goodwin Chas. surgeon, 10 Queen's rw. Cambridg. rd. Mile end
Goodwin Edward, bookbinder, 2 Shoe lane, Fleet st
Goodwin Edward, cheesemonger, 18 Great Winchester st
Goodwin Francis, importer of cigars, 171 Bermondsey st
Goodwin George, haircutter, 61 East st. Manchester square
Goodwin George, straw hat mfr. 14 Red Lion st. Clerkenwell
Goodwin Henry, linendraper, Deptford High st
Goodwin Henry, painter & glazier, & potato dealer, 102 Berwick st. Soho
Goodwin James, butcher, 5 Crawley st. Oakley sq. Somers tn
Goodwin James, butcher, 12 Adams row, Hampstead road
Goodwin James, cheesemonger, 38 Upper Ebury st. Pimlico
Goodwin James, chemist & druggist, 7 North Audley st
Goodwin James, corn & coal dealer, 129 Bethnal green rd
Goodwin James, grocer, 18 North st. Sloane st. Chelsea
Goodwin John, baker, 1 Charlton st. Marylebone
Goodwin John, baker, Forest row, Dalston
Goodwin John, carpenter, 48 Liquorpond st. Gray's inn lane
Goodwin John, cheesemonger, 9 Berwick st. Soho, & 150 Lambeth walk
Goodwin John, *Three Crowns* P.H. 97 Up. East Smithfield
Goodwin John, tobacconist & stationer, 6 Hackney rd. cres
Goodwin John, undertaker, 38 Park st. Camden town
Goodwin John, warehouseman, 8 Lawrence lane, Cheapside
Goodwin John Robert, chemist, see Dordoy & Goodwin
Goodwin Martin, bed feather dealer, see Le Geir & Goodwin
Goodwin Mary (Mrs.), grocer, 2 Green st. Theobald's road
Goodwin Mary Ann (Miss), artificial florist, 322 Regent st
Goodwin Richard, beer retailer, 10 Mora pl. City road
Goodwin Richard, coach painter, Hare walk, Hoxton Old tn
Goodwin Rd. coal mer. Sunderland whf. Maiden la. King's crs
Goodwin Richard C. tailor, 34 Chichester pl. Gray's inn rd
Goodwin Robert, *Acorn* P.H. 234 Upper Thames st
Goodwin Ruth (Mrs.), cutler, 19 Porter st. Soho
Goodwin Samuel, livery stables, Little Gray's inn lane
Goodwin Thomas, baker, 33 George st. Portman sq
Goodwin Thomas, butcher, 1 Belmont row, Vauxhall
Goodwin Thomas, grocer, 2 New st. Kennington road
Goodwin Thos. *Hole in the Wall* P.H. 22 Baldwin's gardens
Goodwin Thomas, shell fishmonger, 295 Strand
Goodwin Wm. bookbinder, 48½ Paternoster row
Goodwin Wm. butcher, 6 Orange row, Kennington road
Goodwin Wm. cornchandler, 10 Leman st. Goodman's fields
Goodwin Wm. hardwareman, 16 Eaton lane North, Pimlico
Goodwin Wm. music seller & copyist, 4 Up. Wellington st
Goodwin Wm. plumber, 72 Harrow road, Paddington
Goodwin Wm. J. veterinary surgeon, Queen's mews, Pimlico
Goodwyn George Norfolk, hairdresser, 10 Lamb's Conduit st
Goody Daniel, builder, 1 Ocean row, High st. Stepney
Goody James, tailor, 2 Clifford st. Bond st
Goodyear Thos. & Son, who. chip &c. hat maks. 7 Aldersgate st
Goodyear Frederick (late Smith & Lapoulli), straw plait & foreign warehousemen, 35 St. Paul's churchyd. & 52 O. Chng
Goodyear James, bootmaker, 3 Sermon la. Doctors' commns
Goodyear James, straw bonnet maker, 20 Blackman st. Boro
Goodyear Thomas, hatter, 4 Aldersgate st. City
Goodyer Ann (Mrs.), boarding school, 3 Addingtn pl. Cmbwl. rd
Goodyer Wm. *Talbot* P.H. 2 Lit. Chester st. Grosvenor pl
Googe Thos. *White Bear* P.H. 1 Queen's pl. Kennington rd
Gook Thomas, shoemaker, 20 Little Coram st. Brunswk. sq
Goold & Goodchap, house & general agents, 9 Newgate st
Goold Joseph, rag merchant, 43 King st. Westminster
Goold Joshua, engrav. & printer, 104 Curtain rd. Shoreditch
Goolden Richard Henry, physician, 8 John st. Adelphi
Goole, Doncaster, Sheffield & Manchester Junction Rail. Co's Off. (P. H. Newall, sec.), 26 Bridge st. Westminster
Goole, Doncaster, Sheffield, Ashton, under Lyne & Manchester & Great Grimsby Junction Railway Company (Henry Sctree, sec.), 32 Nicholas lane, Lombard st
Gooze Ann (Mrs.), chair stuffer, 19 Rose & Crown ct. Eldon st
Goozee Thos. carpenter & machinist, 8 Brown's la. Spitalfields
Gorbell John, grocer, &c. 12 New Suffolk st. Comrcl. rd. Ea
Gorbell John, iron & steel merchant, see Farmer & Gorbell
Gorbell Thomas K. stationer, 21 Hereford pl. Comrcl rd. ea
Gorbold William & Son, silk tabaret & coach lining manufacturers, 41 Hoywell lane, Shoreditch
Gorbold Wm. jun. cooper & undertaker, 26 White Lion st. Norton folgate
Gorbold Wm. sen. undertaker, 41 Holywell la. Shoreditch
Gorddard John, beer retailer, 32 Lit. Coram st. Brunswick sq
Gordelier Charles, accountant, 8 Assembly row, Mile end road, & 92 Fenchurch st. City
Gordelier Elizabeth (Mrs.), milliner, &c. 131 London wall
Gordelier Elizabeth (Mrs.), *East London Registry Office for Families & Servants*, 8 Assembly row, Mile end
Gording William, farrier, 106 Edgware road, Marylebone
Gordon Alexander & Son, solicitors, 57 Old Broad st. City
Gordon, Baxter & Co. wholesale manufacturers of pickles, sauces, preserved meats, &c. 46 Botolph lane, City
Gordon-Duff & Co. (of madeira), 138 Leadenhall st
Gordon James Wm. & Co. coopers & merchants, Church row, Limehouse, & Orchard house, Blackwall
Gordon, Knight & Co. distillers, 68 Goswell st
Gordon Thos. Birch & Son, wine merchants, 8 Great Tower st. City, & 8 Princes st. Cavendish square
Gordon, Thomson & Keene, seed & nurserymen, 25 Fenchurch st
Gordon (Webster), Cossart & Co. madeira mrc. 6 Nw. Broad st. Cit
Gordon Alexander, baker, 7 Upper Kennington green
Gordon Alexander, civil & marine engineer, 22 Fludyer st
Gordon Alex. saddler & pat. collar ma. 39 Lisle st. Leicester sq
Gordon Alex. jun. barrister, 6 Quality court, Chancery lane
Gordon Ann (Mrs.), coffee rooms, 7 Romney ter. Horseferry rd
Gordon Arthur, tobacco pipe maker, 34 Easton st. Spafields
Gordon Charles, hairdresser, Surrey pl. Wandsworth road
Gordon Cosmo Wm. produce broker, see Sargant, Gordon & Co
Gordon Cranmer, apothecary, 11 New Gravel la. Shadwell
Gordon Daniel Glassford, merchant, 7 Mortimer st
Gordon David, button manufacturer, 6 Fisher st. Red Lion sq
Gordon Edward, chaser & engraver, 63 Hatton garden
Gordon Edwin, bootmaker, 6A, Princes st. Soho
Gordon Eliza Jane (Mrs.), straw hat ma. 19 Queen st. Towr. hill
Gordon George, lodging house, 16 Chester ter. Eaton sq
Gordon George, tailor, 14 Lower King st. Commercial road
Gordon James, bookslr. statnr. & news vndr. 146 Leadenhall st
Gordon James, farrier, 6 Smart's buildings, Hoxton Old tn
Gordon James Alexander, physician, 71 Grosvenor st
Gordon John, baker, 3 Albion place, Holloway road
Gordon John, special pleader, 10 Paper buildings, Temple
Gordon John, bootmaker, 123 Minories
Gordon John, carpenter, 79 Harrow road
Gordon John, tobacconist, 134 High st. Camden town
Gordon John, *Shakespear's Head* P.H. 88 Waterloo rd. Lmbth
Gordon John G. east india army agent, 6 Gt. Winchester st
Gordon Patrick, solicitor, 3 Symond's inn, Chancery lane
Gordon Peter, tailor, 7 Norway place, Hackney road
Gordon Theodore, physician, 8 Norfolk crescent, Oxford sq
Gordon Thomas, draper, see Walker & Gordon
Gordon Wm. cooper, 24 Bread street hill
Gordon Wm. lodging house, 7 South st. Grosvenor square
Gordon Wm. sail ma. Prince's stairs, 39 Rotherhithe walk
Gordon Wm. wharfinger, 5 Whrf. South side, Paddington basin
Gore John & Co. merchants, 14 Old Jewry
Gore Henry, grocer & cheesemonger, 16 Bridge st. Bermdsy
Gore James, chimney sweep, 27 Chapel st. New road
Gore John Zach. sergeant at mace, 3 Ivy la. Paternoster row
Gore John, haysalesman, 62 West Smithfield, & 12 wf. Paddingtn
Gore John, wharfinger, City wharf, Upper Thames st.; 11 & 12 Wharfs, north side Paddington basin; dust contractor, Rhodeswell road wharf, Limehouse
Gore Samuel, rosin manfr. 18 & 19 Southampton st. Strand
Gore Tho. Hen. pat. medicine agt. 13 Gt. St. Thomas apostle
Gore William, painter, &c. Broadway, Stratford
Goreing Joseph, builder, 15 Philpot st. Commercial road east
Goren James, attorney, 29 South Molton st. Bond st
Gorfin Henry, watchmaker, 90 Albany st. Regent's park
Gorham Francis, watchmaker, High st. Kensington
Gorham James, watchmaker, 5 High st. Kensington
Gorham Richard, grocer, 13 High st. Boro
Gorick Elizth. (Mrs.), lodging ho. 18 Green st. Grosvenor sq
Goring George, stonemason, 142 Regent st. Lambeth
Goring Robt. Hen. boot & shoema. 15 Upper Kennington lane
Goring Thomas, tailor, 11 Blenheim st. Bond st
Goring William, tailor, 14 Pall mall
Gorman, Hamilton & Thorby, wine merchants, 16 Mark lane
Gorman Michael Arthur & Son, stock brokr. 9 Warnford ct. City
Gorman Peter, brazier, 9 Spring street, Marylebone
Gorman Peter, butcher, 30 White Hart st. Drury lane

Gormully Robert, cabinet carver, 47 Gower pl. New road
Gormully Robert, carver, 1 Warren mews, Warren st
Gorrard Wm. merchant, 8 Crown ct. Old Broad st. City
Gorringe Francis John, tailor, 28 City road, Finsbury
Gorrod Thomas, beer retailer, 38 Cumberland market
Gorst Gilpin, wine broker, Old Trinity house, Water lane
Gorton Charles, trunk & packing case maker, 24 Gutter lane Cheapside, & 142 Aldersgate st
Gorton Isaac, butcher, 51 Gt. Windmill st. Haymarket
Gorton John, chemist, & druggist, 131 Middlesex st. Aldgate
Gorton John, dairyman, 1 Notting hill, High st
Gorton Joshua, potato dealer, 44 Brewer st. Golden square
Gorton Thomas, agent to Hartley Bottle Co. Cousin la. City
Gorton Wm. mer. & firewood maker, 18 Wharf road, City road
Gorway Richd. accountant, 47 Adam st. west, Bryanstone sq
Gosbell Henry, stationer & acct. book mak. 116 High Holborn
Gosbell Henry, wholesale straw plait dealer, 61 Chiswell st
Gosch William Henry, tobacconist, 74 Drummond st
Göschen William Hy. merchant, see Frühling & Göschen
Gosden Francis, fishmonger, 11 Gray's place, Fulham road
Gosden John, coffee rooms, 45 Rupert st. Haymarket
Gosden Geo. vet. surg. 10½ Up. Southwark st. nth. Cambdg. ter
Gosden Richard, wine cooper, 17 Northumberland st. Strand
Goslett Alfred, crown, sheet & patent plate glass manufactr. & plate glass polisher & silverer, & composition & carved frame manufacturer, 26 Soho square
Goslett Wm. carver & gilder, 32 South Molton st. Bond st
Goslin Benjamin Thos. brewer, New Richmond road, Fulham
Goslin James, butcher, 16 Clare st. Clare market
Goslin James, carpenter, 117 Bunhill row
Goslings' & Sharpe, bankers, 19 Fleet st
Gosling Ann (Mrs.), tobacconist, 25 Shaftesbury terrace
Gosling Frederick Solly, solicitor, see Clarke & Gosling
Gosling Edward, fruiterer, Centre row, Covent garden mrkt
Gosling Eliza (Miss), ladies' schl. 110 Up. Stamford st. Bkfrs
Gosling Eliza (Mrs.), millinery & lace war. 31 Blackman st
Gosling John, *Eyre Arms tavern*, Grove end rd. St. John's wd
Gosling John, ginger beer maker, 16 High st. St. Giles's
Gosling John, lighterman, 3 Belvedere road, Lambeth
Gosling Mary (Mrs.), oil & colorman, 12 Mile end road
Gosling William, *Swan* P.H. Bridge road, Battersea
Gosling William, chemist & druggist, 3 Gray's pl. Fulham rd
Gosnell John & Co. successors to Price & Gosnell, perfumers & soapmakers, by appointment, to her Majesty & the Royal Family; manufactory, 12 Three King court, Lombard st.; sole patentees of Johnstone's royal patent windsor soap
Gosnold Charles, tailor to the Queen, 26 Ebury st. Pimlico
Goss Jas. & Co. wine merchts. 2 America sq. & 119 Minories
Goss Benj. *Thistle & Crown* P.H. 40A, Thomas st. Grosvenor sq
Goss Elizth. (Mrs.), seminary, 153 Albany rd. Camberwell
Goss James, coffee rooms, 7 Wormwood st. Bishopsgate
Goss Jas. genl. provision merc. & ship chandler, 119 Minories
Goss John, music master, 30 Sloane st. Knightsbridge
Goss John, surgeon, &c. 36 Paternoster row
Goss John Wm. wharfinger & lighterm. Bull wf. Queenhithe
Goss Richd. John, *Three Mariners* P.H. 64 Ropemaker's fields
Gosset Montague, solicitor, 36 Old Jewry
Gossett Montague, surgeon, 40 Broad st. buildings
Gostelow Francis, tobacco & snuff mnfr. 13 Kingsland road
Gostling Wm. T. & Son, proctors, 7 Godliman st. Doctors' cmns
Gostling Augustus, D.C.L. advocate, 9 Great Knightrider st
Gostling Henry, glasscutter, 5 St. Ann's court, Soho
Goswell James, shoemaker, Morning lane, Hackney
Goswell Thomas, 22 Elizabeth ter. Cloudesley square
Gotch John, boot maker, 16 King st. New North road
Goter Wm. H. & Co. fishmongs. 23 & 24 Low. area, Hungerf. mkt
Gotobed Robert, baker, Hawkesbury place, Lock's fields
Gotobed Wm. corn & coal mer. 24 Gt. Portland st. Oxford st
Gott Wm. beer retailer, Church st. Camberwell
Gottheimer Berton, french repos. 61 Gt. Russell st. Blmsby
Gottheimer Peter M. silversmith, 99 Bridge road, Lambeth
Gottlieb Eliza (Mrs.), patent locksmith to the Hon. Board of Excise & Customs, 1 Smith st. Upp. Jubilee pl. Mile end
Gottliebb Hannah (Miss), embroideress, 117 Jermyn st
Gotto Henry (Mrs.), milliner &c. 12 Gt. Russell st. Bloomsby
Gottschalk & Schroder, commission agts. 72 Basinghall st
Gotto John, fringe maker, 6 Union place, Clapham rise
Gotto Wm. fancy trimming manufacturer, 202 Regent st
Goude John Fisher, surgeon, 105 Cheapside
Goudge James, coffee rooms, 13 Little New st. Shoe la
Goudge Wm. bootmaker, 26 Little Bell alley, Coleman st
Goudge Wm. pat. axletree ma. 22 Castle st. East, Oxford st
Goudge Wm. tin plate worker, 81 Up. Whitecross st. St. Luke's
Goudy Elizh. J. (Miss), lodging houses, 14 & 15 Cecil st. Strand
Gougenheim Augustus, translr. of languages, 36 King st. Soho
Gouger Henry, merchant, 6 Great Winchester st
Gouger & Meyer, manfr. warehomen. & agents, 2 Bow la. City
Gough & Roumieu, architects, 10 Lancaster pl. Waterloo brd
Gough Benj. brick & stone mer. & ag. 37 Newington cres
Gough Edward, silk hat maker, 21 Weston st. Somers town
Gough Francis John, attorney, 32 East st. Red Lion sq
Gough Fredk. ale & porter merchant, 1 Gower st. n. New rd
Gough Frederick, wine merchant, 16 Gower st. north, New rd
Gough Harriet (Mrs.), baker, 25 Up. Islington ter. Cloudsly. sq
Gough Jas. *Pr. of Wales* P. H. Eastbourne ter. Paddington
Gough Jas. timber mer. 138 Shoreditch, & 125 Curtain road
Gough Thomas B. coal merchant, Savoy st. Strand
Gough William, silverplater, 75 Hatton garden
Goulborn Wm. Geo. undertaker, 45 King st. Seven dials
Goulburn Edward, S.L. com. of bankruptcy, Basinghall st
Goulburn Fredk. barrister, 12 Downing st
Gould, Dowie & Moore, merchants, 4 Barge yd. Bucklersby
Gould Edwd. Hen. & Thos. oil & colorman, 14 York st. Westm
Gould Robert & Son, hatters, 21 Ludgate hill
Gould Abraham, oil & colorman, 17 Belvoir ter. Vauxhall rd
Gould Charles, boot & shoemaker, 16 New st. Covent gdn
Gould Chas. silkwarehouseman & agt. 6 Gutter la. Cheapside
Gould Eliza (Miss), dining rooms, 15 Henry st. Hampstead rd
Gould Eliza Ann (Miss), milliner, see Belcher & Gould
Gould Elizabeth (Mrs.), baker, 10 Bethnal green, West side
Gould Frances (Mrs.), milliner, 8 Gerard st. Islington
Gould Frederick Joseph, optician, 24 Museum st. Bloomsbury
Gould George, stationer, 5 Star corner, Bermondsey
Gould George, surgeon, &c. 19 Kingsland cres. Kingsland rd
Gould Rev. George Masters, school, Lower rd. Islington
Gould James, fruiterer & greengrocer, 26 Goswell road
Gould John, army & gen. agent, 4 Northumberland st. Strand
Gould John, bootmaker, 4 Albion place, Little Chelsea
Gould John, carman, 31 Holywell row, Shoreditch
Gould John, carpent. & undertaker, 9 Cumming st. Pentonville
Gould John, clothes salesman, 12 & 13 Leader st. Chelsea
Gould John, fishmonger, 1 & 2 Lower area, Hungerford mkt
Gould John, naturalist & bookseller, 20 Broad st. Golden sq
Gould John, nightman & scavenger 5 Worship st. Finsbury
Gould Joseph, fruiterer, 18 Shepherds' market, Mayfair
Gould Mary (Mrs.), milliner, 28 Wigmore st. Cavendish sq
Gould Peter, brokr. & appr. 6 Rowley bldgs. Bermondsey st
Gould Richd. Pendleton, pencil manfr. see Evans & Gould
Gould Robert, beer retailer, Earls court, Old Brompton
Gould Robert, tailor, 14 Gloucester ter. Vauxhall bridge rd
Gould Samuel, lodging house, 5 Carpenter st. Berkley sq
Gould Sarah (Mrs.), milliner, &c. 7A, Manchstr. st. Manchstr. sq
Gould Thomas, fruiterer, &c. 10 Sun ct. Curzon st. Mayfair
Gould Thomas, *Hope* coffee rooms, 32 Villiers st. Strand
Gould Thomas, oilman, 79 Castle st. Leicester sq
Gould Thomas, jun. staymaker, 315 Oxford st
Gould Wm. cabinet maker, 31 New Gloucester st. Hoxton
Gould Wm. patten maker, 126 Up. Whitecross st. St. Luke's
Gould William Ellis, plate glass factor, looking glass & picture frame manuf. carver & gilder, 108 London wall
Gould William W. needle & fishhook manufacturer, 60 Wood st. Cheapside, & at Redditch
Goulden Ann (Mrs.), furniture broker, 25 Vauxhall bridge rd
Goulden Charles, coal merch. & house agent, 123 Bunhill row
Goulden Richard, shoemaker, 99 Long lane, Bermondsey
Goulding John & Sons, upholsterers & general cabinet manufacturers, 1 & 2 Eldon st. Finsbury
Goulding & Ledger, corn merchants, Potters' fields, Tooley st
Goulding Edward, cowkeeper, 11 Edward st. Barnsbury rd
Goulding Hen. boot & shoe ma. 66 Freeschool st. Horselydown
Goulding Hen. Wm. linendraper, 5 Hawley pl. Kentish town
Goulding James, plumber, &c. 34 College st. Chelsea
Goulding Robert, corn factor, see Robinson & Goulding
Goulding Robert, grocer, 3 Margaret ter. Paddington green
Goulding Thomas, fruiterer, 4 New st. Dorset square
Gouldsmith Geo. auctioneer & coal mer. 3 Pont st. Belgrv. sq
Gouldsmith Philip, *Rosemary br. tav.* Shepperton st. N.N. rd
Gouldsmith Woolley, dyer & scourer, 2 Pont st. Belgrave sq
Goulston James, carpet warehouse, 42 Blackman st. Borough
Goulston James, floorcloth manft. Canal bridge, Old Kent rd
Goulston John, wax & wafer ma. 4 Up. Fenton st. Com. rd
Goult Elijah, dining rooms, 28 Whitechapel road
Goulty John, mast, oar & scull maker, 12 Stangate, 37 Bankside, & Grove house, Grove rd. Brixton rd
Gourlay Fred. pewterer & candle mould maker, 27 Hoxton sq
Gout David Ralph, watch & clock maker, 122 Bunhill row
Govaerts Margaret (Mrs.), toywarh. 21 Queen's row, Pimlico
Govan Robert, baker, 177 Tooley st. Borough
Gover Daniel, carpenter, 19 Marquis court, Drury lane
Gover Edward, shoema. Grove passage, Church st. Hackney
Gover Wm. carpenter, White horse lane, Stepney
Government Annuity Office, 19 Old Jewry; hours 10 to 3

Government Victualling yard, East Country Dock yard, Grove st. Deptford
Government Works (Rd. Bayneman), Thames bank, Pimlico
Governor & Co. importers & manufacturers of Frankfort blacks, New North road, corner of Eagle wharf road
Govett Edward, solicitor, 4 Cook's court, Lincoln's inn
Govett Geo. tin plate wkr. & braz. 8 York st.Comcl.rd.Wtcp
Govett John Clement, solicitor, 10 & 22 Lincoln's inn fields
Govett John Jas. tin plate wkr. 27 Mid.Grove st.Comcl.rd.ea
Gow Wm.& Co.shippers of Saunders' ale, 22 Hungerford whf
Gow Charles, artist, 61 Charlotte st. Portland place
Gow Neil, barrister, 1 Gray's inn place
Gow Oliphant, copper plate printer, 65 Fetter lane
Gow Wm. agt.for W. &T. Saunders,brewers.22Hungrfrd.whf
Gowan & Marx, merchants, 7 Copthall ct. Throgmorton st
Gowar & Bennett, surgeons, &c. 1 Kent pl. Old Kent road
Gowar Stephen & Jas. coachmakers, Broadway, Stratford
Gowar Raydon Rd.coach builder, 6Church row, Houndsditch
Gowar Thomas, coach factory, Blackheath road
Gowar Thomas, law stationer, 9 Took's ct. Chancery lane
Gowar Wm.Dean,brush&accoutremt.ma.16Dartmth.st.Wstr
Goward James, *Swan* P.H. 4 Swan st. Shoreditch
Goward Pearson, *Knave of Clubs* P.H.23Club row,Bethnl.gn
Gowen William, razor strop manufact. 9 New inn passage
Gower Abel Anthony, Nephews & Co. merchts.28Coleman st
Gower Abel Lewis, merchant, 31 Finsbury square
GowenCurtis(Mrs.),cabinetmaker,20Gt.James's st.Bdfrd.rw
Gower Edmund, grocer, 16 High st. Kensington, North side
Gower Edmund, umbrella maker, 152 Oxford st
Gower Elzh. (Mrs.), watch spring ma. 5Peerless row, City rd
Gower John, machine ruler, 62½ Cannon st. City
Gower John, warehouseman, 20 Lawrence la. Cheapside
GowerRichd.E.nursery&seedsman,Norland nursery.Notg.hl
Gower Stephen, *George* P.H. 31 Gt. St. Andrew st. Sev.dials
Gowers & Mark, linendrapers, 108 Tottenham court road
Gowers David, seal engraver, 21 King st. Soho
Gowers James Wm. solicitor, 18 King's road, Bedford row
Gowie William, haberdasher, 156 Church st. Shoreditch
Gowing Eloisa (Miss), milliner, 40 Judd st. Brunswick sq
Gowing Joseph, cabinet maker & upholsterer, 2 Cannon row
Gowing Simon, butcher, 27 High st. Notting hill
Gowing Thos. Wm. vet.surg.&farr.1Stucley ter.Camden twn
Gowland James, patent chronometer maker & watch manufacturer, 52 London wall
Gowland Thomas, watchmaker, 5 Leadenhall st
Goy & Evans, outfitters, &c. 25 Cornhill
Goymer Abraham, who. cheesemgr. 145WhitechapelHigh st
Gozar John & Son, house painters, 18 Gt.Trinity la. Bread st
Grabham Thos. cabinet stand, &c. ma. 14 John st. Fitzroy sq
Grabham William Bell, saddler, 32 King st. Westminster
Grace, Yallop & Co. white lead & color manfrs. 122 Old st
Grace Charles, venet.&wireblind ma. 24Middlesexst.Som. tn
Grace Henry, tailor, 135 Praed st. Paddington
Grace Hen.white lead ma. Hollybush gard. Bethnal green rd
Grace James, *Colosseum hotel & baths*, 1 Carburton st. Fitzroy sq.; & Portland road, Regent's park
Grace James, fruiterer, 146 Aldersgate st
Grace James, stationer & toy dlr. 19 High st. Notting hill
Grace John Frederick, surgeon & chemist, 134 Drury lane
Grace Thos. & Co. white lead works, Thames bank, Pimlico
Grace Wm. *Red Lion* P.H. & ship agent, 13 Horselydown la
Grace Wm. Baldwin, silk manufr. 14 Steward st. Spitalfields
Gracey John, butcher, Leadenhall market
Gracie Charles Henry, saddler, 22 Cowcross st
GracieFredk.sealingwax&wafermfr.62Leonard st.Shoreditch
Gracie George, truss maker, 11 Marylebone st. Piccadilly
Gradelle John, jun. bootmaker, 156 Regent st
Gradelle Louchet Louis, bootma. 22 Jermyn st. St.James's
Grady James, *Coachmakers' Arms* P.H.13Rose st.Cov.grdn
Grady James, tailor, 7 Portsmouth st. Lincoln's inn fields
Grady Standish Grove, barrister, 1 Pump ct. Temple
Graeff John George, attorney, 12 Furnival's inn, Holborn
Graf Charles, lithographic & chromo-lithographic printer, 1 Great Castle st. Regent st
Grafer Carsten, scum boiler, 23 Old Montague st. Whtchpl
Graff Charles, merchant, 25½ Crosby hall chambers
Grafftey Sam. & Co. who. perfumers, 26Warwick st.Gldn.sq
Grafton Edward, wholesale watch & clock manufacturer, goldsmith & jeweller, 81 Fleet st
Grafton Henry, machinist&philos.instrum.ma.80Chancery la
Grafton James Jsph. hosier, 8 London terrace, Hackney road
Grafton John, wholesale watch & clock manufacturer & jeweller, 17 Eastcheap
Graggs John, coal&potato dealer, 39Henry st.Hampstead rd
Graham Chas. & Co. merchants, 20 King's Arms yd. & Hull
Graham Geo. & Co.calico prtrs. 11 Cheapside,&49OldChange
Graham & Gray, wine merchants, 62 Bread st. Cheapside
Graham Jas. & Co.corn & seed dress. Merlton's whf. Mill st
Graham John&Co. printers & music sellers, 17 Low.Eaton st
Graham & Murray, manchester warehousemen, 11 & 12 Goldsmith st. Cheapside
Graham Robert &Sons, silk manufacturers, 31 Spital square
Graham, West & Co. engineers & millwrights, 304 Wapping
Graham William & Sons, iron merchants & wholesale ironmongers, Trig lane, Upper Thames st
Graham Andrew, shipowner, 8 Taunton place, Dover road
GrahamAnn(Mrs.),chair& sofa ma.22Clipstone st. Fitzroy sq
Graham Arthur *Duke of York* P.H. Hertford rd. Kingld. rd
Graham Charles, artist, 67 George st. Euston sq
Graham Charles, hosier & shirt maker, 31 New Bond st
Graham Charles, millinery & straw hat wa. 10 London wall
Graham Chas. sec. to Lloyd's register, 2WhiteLion ct.Crnhil
Graham Christopher, grocer, &c. see North, Simpson & Co
Graham Christopher, tailor, 11 Red Lion passage, RedLion sq
Graham Charles Jas. solicitor, 3 Plowden buildings, Temple
Graham David, grocer, 42 Upper Marylebone st
Graham Eliz.(Mrs.),milliner,5Northumberland st.Marylebo
Graham Ellen (Miss), dressma. 46 Berners st. Oxford st
Graham George, tailor, see Henderson & Graham
Graham George John, official assignee, 25 Coleman st
Graham George Christopher, com. agt. Hall of Commerce
Graham Henry, watch manufacturer, 159 St. John st. rd
Graham James, antimony refiner, 13 Calvert st. Wapping
Graham James, baker, 27 Brunswick st. Cromer st
Graham James, furn. ironmonger, 108High st. Camden town
Graham James, rag & bone dealer, Morning lane, Hackney
Graham James John, auctioneer, 12Gt.Queen st.Lin.inn fields
Graham John, coffee rooms, 152 Houndsditch
Graham John, executors of, mer.&shipowner, 13 Birchin lane
Graham John, india shawl & silk warehouse, 10 Ludgate st
Graham John, linendraper, 103 High st. Camden town
Graham John, linendraper, see Hughes & Graham
Graham John (Mrs.), milliner, 5 Holles st. Cavendish sq
Graham John, solicitor, 60 Moorgate st
Graham John, solicitor, 6 Thurloe pl. west, & 60 Moorgate st
Graham John, tailor, 5 Stafford st. Bond st
Graham John, turner, 24 Theobald's road, Lamb's conduit st
Graham John, wharfinger, Brook's wharf, Up. Thames st
Graham Joseph, boot & shoe ma. 45 Ernest st. Regent's pk
Graham Joseph, ready made linen ma. 206 Regent st
Graham Joseph, manuf. chemist, see Crane, Son & Graham
Graham Joseph, who.stationer & leather wa. 2Jewry st.Aldg
Graham Peter, upholsterer, see Jackson & Graham
Graham Robert, colorman & varnish mak. 36 King st. Soho
Graham Robert Hay, physician, 47 Great Portland st
GrahamRobertJames,surgeon&chemist,146HoxtonOld town
Graham Thomas, solicitor, 1 & 3 Mitre ct. chambers, Temple
Graham Thomas, stockbroker, 6 Throgmorton st
Graham William, auctioneer, 27 Church st. Spitalfields
Graham Wm. ivory turner & brush ma.1 Church st.Cambrwl
Graham Wm. turner, 9 Bride lane, Fleet st
Graham Wm. upholsterer, 2 Abchurch yard
Grahame, Moncrieff & Weems, solicitors, 30 Great George st. Westminster
Grain Wm. notary public, 2 King's arms bldgs. Change alley
Grain Wm. jun. notary public, 2 King's arms bldgs.Change al
Grainge Nathaniel, straw & leghorn presser, 68 Banner st
Grainger Abrm. Thos. coal mer. 2 Lr. Belgrave pl. Pimlico
Grainger Frederick Wm. foreign provision broker, see Trimmer & Grainger
Grainger Hen. skinner & furrier, 4 Crosby rw. King's st.Boro'
Grainger Henry, solicitor, see Buchanan & Grainger
Grainger Henry, provision broker, see Trimmer & Grainger
Grainger James, tailor, 55 Pall mall
Grainger Richd. grindery dealr. 11 Holywell la. Shoreditch
Grainger Robert, law stationer, 15 Took's ct. Chancery lane
Graley John & Thos. leather warehouse, 231 Bermondsey st
Grammar Thos. cheesemonger, 13 Union st. Somers town
Grammer Edwd. cheesemonger, 5 Woburn bldgs.Tavistock sq
Grammer Thos. jun. cheesemonger, 69Union st. Somers town
Gramolt Wm. & Co. manufacturers of silk tabourets, furniture damasks, &c. 20 Milk st. Cheapside
Granara Antonio & Co. *Hotel de l'Europe,* 16 Leicester pl. & 3 Duncan place, Leicester square
Grand Junction Canal Company, 14 wharf, south side, Paddington basin; Office, 21 Surrey st. Strand
Grand Junction Canal Company Coal wharf(Rt. Procter, wharfinger), 16 wharf, south side, Paddington basin
Grand Junction Waterworks Office (Wm. M. Coe, sec.), 7 Brook st. Grosvenor sq
Grand Surrey Dock & Canal Comp. (Sam. Travers, sec.), Dock ho. Rotherhithe; & 2 White Lion ct. Cornhill

Grand Trunk Rail.(Sam.Stanway,sec.),3Adelaide pl.Lon.br
Grand Union Canal Offi.(Rd.C.Sale,cl.),20Surrey st.Strnd
Grand Union Rail. (Alfred Beeston, sec.), 78 Cornhill
Grand Western Canal Co.(Edmd. Taverner,sec.),Tokenho.yd
Grane Wm. & Son, solicitors, 23 Bedford row, Bloomsbury
Grange Henry, tailor, 74 Lisson grove north
Grange Sarah(Mrs.),confectioner & fruiterer, 176 Piccadilly
Granger Arthur, *Still & Star* P.H. Harrow alley, Aldgate
Granger Benjamin, solicitor,25 Bucklersbury
Granger Edward, bricklayer, 16 King's row, New road
Granger George Jsph. grocer, 40 Up. North pl.Gray's inn rd
Granger John fruiterer, 11 Bathurst st. Sussex sq. Hyde pk
Granger John, grocer & teadealer, 22 Borough road
Granger Samuel, lighterman & customho. agt. Fresh wharf, Low.Thames st.; Jerusalem coffeeho.Cornhill,&Blackwall
Granger Susannah (Mrs.), plumber, 10Bury st. St. James's
Granger Thos. baker, 22 North st. Lisson grove
GrangerElzh.(Mrs.),*Chmbln's.Arms*P.H.12Noblest.Gswl.st
Granger Thos. Colpitts, barrister, 12 King's Bench walk
Granger Wm. coffee rooms, 16 Pearl cres. Bagnigge wells rd
Granger Wm. plumber, &c. 1 Hall place, Edgware road
Granger Zachariah, butcher, 81 Shadwell High st
Grant Alex. Brothers, stock&shirtma.2Clement's ct.Wood st
Grant, Baldwin & Co. sugar refiners, 17½ St. George's place, St. George's east
Grant Edward & Co. breeches & brace makers,23 Piccadilly
Grant, Grant & Co. merchants, 71 Cheapside
Grant & Griffith, booksellers & publishers, 21 Ludgate st
Grant & Hodgson, tobacco brokers,34 Fenchurch st
Grant John & Co. pawnbrokers, 22 Park side,Knightsbridge
Grant John & James, distillers(Jas.Warren,agt.),4Walbrook
Grant & Kemshead, west india merchants, 46 Lime st
Grant Alexander, dyer & scourer, 14 Green st. Leicester sq
Grant Alexander, west india merchant, 6 Billiter sq
Grant Alexander, shipping butcher, 12 Cock hill, Ratcliff
Grant Alexander Lorent, attorney, see Maltby & Grant
Grant Alexander William, solicitor, seeWalker&Grant & Co
Grant Andrew, pilot, 1 Stebon ter. Philpot st. Commercl. rd
Grant Anne (Mrs.), milliner, 10 Cranbourne st. Leicester sq
Grant Ann(Mrs.), worsted manufr.&berlin wareh.31Oxfrd.st
Grant Charles, attorney, 23 Fitzroy square
Grant Christopher, milliner, 132 Oxford st
Grant Colin, tailor, 2 Union place, Clapham rise
Grant David, merchant, 17½ St. George's pl. St.George's ea
Grant Donald, ventilat. gas offi. 39 Southampton st. Strand
Grant Edward, grease melter, Bow common
Grant Edward, wholesale leather warehouse, 17 Chiswell st. & 142 Tottenham court road
Grant Francis, A.R.A. artist, Sussex place, Regent's park
Grant Francis, haberdasher, Camberwell green
Grant Frederick Allan, solicitor, see Walker, Grant & Co
Grant George, *White Hart* P.H. 64 Leather lane, Holborn
Grant Henry, stockbroker, 3 Shorter's ct. & Stock Exchange
Grant James, special pleader, 2 Plowden buildings, Temple
Grant Jesse, coal mercht. 43A, South st. South Audley st
Grant John, baker, 84 Fetter lane
Grant John, baker, 66 Tothill st. Westminster
Grant John, butcher, 18 King's road east, Chelsea
Grant John, cabinet maker, 10 Cranbourne st. Leicester sq
Grant John, manufacturer of clocks & watches, 75 Fleet st. & pawnbroker & silversmith, 69 & 70 London wall
Grant Joseph, linendraper, 3 Kent place, Old Kent road
Grant JosephHumphrey,solicitor,see Keddell,Baker &Grant
Grant Joshua, tobacconist, 18 Goswell st
Grant John, shell fishmonger& tobacconist,17Gracechurch st
Grant JohnWoodford, furn. broker, 2 to 5 Castle st.Long acre
Grant Klein, physician, 73 St. James's st. Piccadilly
Grant Mary Ann(Mrs.),tailor, 22 Gt. Pulteney st. Golden sq
Grant Nathaniel, physician, 21 Thayer st. Manchester sq
Grant Robert, merchant, see Bell & Grant
Grant Robt. Edmond, physician, 10 Grafton pl. Euston sq
Grant Thomas, fruiterer, 16 Kensington gravel pits
Grant Thomas, linendraper, 7 Barnsbury place, Islington
Grant Thomas M. confectioner, 101 Bishopsgate st. without
Grant William, barrister, 5 Pump court, Temple
Grant William, cattle salesman, 60 West Smithfield
Grant William, fruiterer, 23 Princes st. Westminster
Grant William, grocer, 162 Kent st. Borough
Grant William, smith, 29 Princes st. Lambeth
Grant William, tailor, 3 Blenheim st. New Bond st
Grant William, watchmaker, 126 Jermyn st. St. James's
Grant William, wholesale draper, see Mabyn & Grant
Grant Aug.deVaux Romain, solr. 19 Buckingham st. Strand
Grantham George, butcher, 75 Park st. Camden town
Grantham Joel, carpenter, 5 Princes st. Leicester square
Grantham Rd. Boxall, civil engineer, 2 Robert st. Adelphi
Granville Edward & Co. india rubber manfrs. 132 Cheapside
Granville Augustus Bozzi, physician, 109 Piccadilly
Granville Walter, architect, 109 Piccadilly
Grape James, *Rising Sun* P.H. 24 Blackfriars road
Grapes John, greengrocer, 9 Duke st. Smithfield
Grason Thomas, *Vintners' Arms* P.H. 101 Fetter la. Holborn
Grassby Elisha, boot & shoe ma. 10 Strutton ground, Westmr
Grassby John, bootmaker, 10 Stepney rents, Hackney road
Grater John, pork butcher, 67 Strutton ground, Westminster
Graton Robt. ladies' shoemaker, 3 John st. north, Marylebone
Gratton Joseph, corndealer, 94 Shoreditch
Gratton Martha(Mrs.),strawbonnet ma. 267 Poplar High st
Gratton William, farrier, 6 Devonshire st. Kennington
Gratwick Thomas, grocer, Camberwell green
Grautoff Barnard A. & Co. merchants, 4 Lime st. square
Gravatt Hannah & Son, stationers, &c.8Windmill st. Finsb.sq
Gravatt & Tann, law stationers, 17 Serle's pl. Lincoln's inn
Gravatt Henry, eating house, 15 Tooley st
Gravatt William, civil engineer,34Parliamentst.Westminster
Grave, Lewis & Co. linendrapers, 11 Henriettast. Covent gdn
GraveWinterbourne & Co. linendrapers, 70 & 71 Blackman st
Grave George, grocer & cheesemonger, 2 Old Fish st. hill
Grave George, *Rainbow* P.H. Manchester ter. Liverpool rd
Grave George, watch & clock maker, 271 Whitechapel road
GravellWm.& Son, clock & watchmakers, 29 Charterhouse sq
Gravell John, stationer, 3 Charles st. Berkeley square
Gravell Thomas, carver & gilder, 33&34 Red cross st. Crippleg
Gravenor Charles, surgeon, 36 Ely place, Holborn
Gravenor John, hatter, 5 Perseverance ter. Bethnal green rd
Graves Henry & Co. manfs. of sewing silks, &c. 40 Gutter la
Graves Henry & Co. printsellers & publishers in ordinary to Her Majesty & by special appointment to H.R.H. Prince Albert, 6 Pall mall
Graves Wm. & Geo. L. woollen warehmn. 15 Ironmonger la
Graves & Young, Lowther bazaar, 35 Strand
Graves Ann (Mrs.), *Rose & Crown* P.H. 2 Park la. Piccadil
Graves George, surgeon dentist, 39 Blackman st. Boro'
Graves George C. lighterman, see Phillips & Graves
Graves John Pritchard, auctioneer, &c.8Wigmore st.Cavendish square; & 28 Wellington road, St. John's wood
Graves John Thomas, barrister, 8 Gray's inn square
Graves Joseph, *Phœnix & Crown* P.H. Potter's fields, Boro'
Graves Nathaniel, picture dealer, 11 Russell court, Drury la
Graves Rayner, toyman, 17 Duke st. Manchester sq
Graves Richard, tailor & trousers ma. 313 High Holborn
Graves Richd. Hen. grocer, 7 Well st. Mile end New town
Graves Samuel John, tailor, 7 Belvedere road, Lambeth
Graves Thomas, *Green Dragon* P.H. 198 Poplar High st
Graves Thomas, grocer & cheesemonger, 66 Poplar High st
Graves William, library, 12 Church way, Somers town
Graves William Hen. surgeon, 40 Trinity sq. Tower hill
Gravesend & Rochester Railway, & Thames & Medway Canal Office, 15 New Broad st. City
*Gravesend Steam Packet Diamond Co.*Fresh wf. Lndn. bdg
Gravesend Sons of the Thames Steam Packet Co. (Joseph Davies, sec.), 12 Mark lane, City
Gravesend Star Steam Packet Co. (Wm. Morgan, agent), Railway place, Fenchurch st
Graveson Michael, butcher, 71 Long lane, Bermondsey
Gray, Adams & Hogg, nursery & seedsmen, Kensington rd
Gray BenjaminChas.Thos.&Son,merchants,31 Gt.St.Helen's
Gray & Berry, solicitors, 12 Grove place, Lisson grove
Gray & Bromley, straw hat manfrs.8 Wilsted st.Somers town
Gray Joseph Wace&Co. col.brokers, 11 Commercial sale rms
Gray & Davison, organ builders, 9 & 11 Quickset row, New rd
Gray & MacFarlan, commission merchants, 34 Fenchurch st
Gray Wm. & John, oil & colormen, 10 Bridge road, Lambeth
Gray Abraham, livery stab. 2 Hamilton mews, St. John's wood, & 9 Grove end place, St. John's wood
Gray Alfred, tailor, 32 Duke st. St. James's
Gray Andrew, grocer, &c. 92 Wimpole st. Cavendish square
Gray Andrew, *White Horse* P.H. 113 St. John st. Clerkenwll
Gray Charles, barrister, Devereux chambers, Devereux ct. Strand
Gray Charles, gas apparatus manuf. 6 & 7 NewPark st. Boro'
Gray Daniel R. hairdresser, 242 Whitechapel road
Gray David, attorney, see Clarke, Metcalf & Gray
Gray Donald, drug.drysalt. &ivory brok. 6 Scots yd. Bush la
Gray Douglas, straw bonnet maker, 60 King st. Seven dials
Gray Edward, baker, 1 High st. Notting hill
Gray Edward, bootmaker, 66 Lower George st. Chelsea
Gray Edward, law stationer, 4 Bridge st. Westminster
Gray Elizabeth (Mrs.), picture frame ma. 32 Clerkenwell gr
Gray Frances (Mrs.), milliner & dress ma. Church st. Hackny
Gray Fras. leather slr. & grindery dlr. 249 Whitehapel rd
Gray Fred.Fras.boot & shoe ma.1 LittleRyder st. St.James's

Gray George, cabinet maker, 19 Judd st. Brunswick sq
Gray George, *Bell* P.H. 9 Gt.Carter lane, Doctors' commons
Gray George, goldsmith, jeweller & pawnbroker, 114 Fleet st
Gray George, greengrocer, 195 Kingsland road
Gray George, seedfactor, 23 New Corn Exchange, & Rose cottage, Bow road
Gray Geo.Wm.spirit mer.Chamberlain's whf.11&12Tooley st
Gray George Hebden, accountant, &c. 4 Coleman st. City
Gray George Mounsey, solicitor, 9 Staple inn, Holborn
Gray Harriet (Mrs.), stationer, 2 Theobald's road, Holborn
Gray Henry, butcher, 49 Lower Queen st. Rotherhithe
Gray Henry, engraver, 8 Duke st. West Smithfield
Gray Henry, job master, 4 Earl st.&coachma.17½Blackfrs.rd
Gray Henry, stock & share broker, 13 Throgmorton st
Gray HenryTrimby, ropemaker, 9Grosvenor pl.Comml.rd. ea
Gray Isaac, tobacconist, 114 Drummond st. Euston sq
Gray J. B. surgeon, 3 Sussex terrace, Camden town
Gray James, pilot, 43 White Horse st. Commercl.rd.Stepney
Gray James, saddler & harness mak. 57 West Smithfield
Gray James, tobacconist, 74 Crawford st
Gray James, turner, 24 Old Gravel lane, Wapping
Gray Jane (Mrs.), confectioner, 61 Gray's inn lane
Gray John, artificial eye maker, 7 Goswell road, west side
Gray John, baker, 1 Bethnallgreenrd.&92Churchst.Shoreditch
Gray John, barrister, 8 Crown office row, Temple
Gray John, boot & shoe maker, 44 Wardour st. Soho
Gray John, bricklayer & builder, King st. Old st. road
Gray John, carpenter, 6 Grove lane, Camberwell
Gray John, grocer, 32 Pilgrim st. Walworth common
Gray John, dentist, 25 Old Burlington st
Gray John, furrier, 16 Lower Ranelagh st. Lr. Grosvenor pl
Gray John, hat manufacturer, 1 Short st. New cut, Lambeth
Gray John, *RedLion & SpreadEagle* P.H.94Whtchpl.Highst
Gray John, surgeon, 7 Upper George st. Bryanstone square
Gray John, tailor, 12 Rawstorne st. Brompton
Gray John, tallow chandler, 17 Great Portland st. Oxfordst
Gray John, wholesale silversmith, plater & hardwareman, 5 Billiter square, Fenchurch st
Gray John, wine merchant, see Burdon & Gray
Gray John, jun.solicitor, &clerktoCo.Founders'hall, Lothbury
Gray John Charles, teadealer, see Capper & Gray
Gray John Hunter, shipping butcher, 22 Lower Shadwell
Gray John L. box coat &capemaker, 50Jermynst.St. James's
Gray John Thomas, *Flying Horse* P.H. 2 Oxford st
Gray John Wm. plumber, 10 Warkworth ter. Commercial road east, & 212 Wapping High st
Gray Jonathan, *LordCollingwood* P.H.6Chicksand st.Mile en
Gray Joseph, tailor, 53 George st. Blackfriars road
Gray Joseph Bowers, surgeon, &c. 114 High Holborn
Gray Joshua, D.D. academy, 10 South crescent, Bedford sq
Gray Mary Ann (Miss), preparatory school, 19 Strand
Gray Nutter, coal mer. 8 Cambridge row, Cambridge heath
Gray Owen, solicitor, 25 Great Tower st
Gray Rachel (Mrs.), boarding house, 62 Basinghall st
Gray Reuben, bricklayer, 73 St. George's rd. Borough
Gray Richard, merchant, 5 Adam's court, Broad st
Gray Robert, attorney, 7 New inn, Wych st. Strand
Gray Robert, tailor, 9 Cecil st. Strand
Gray Robert Alex. merchant, see Melhuish, Gray & Co
Gray Robert Wm. coal dealer, 18 & 20 Hollesst.Clare market
Gray Samuel, coffee rooms, 3 Heartley pl. Old Kent road
Gray Sarah (Mrs.), baker, 35 Warwick lane, Newgate st
Gray Thanet(Mrs.), lodging ho.9Marchmont st. Brunswick sq
Gray Thomas, baker, 102 Upper Whitecross st. St. Luke's
Gray Thomas, bottled ale merchant, 35 Pudding lane
Gray Thomas, carpenter, 6 Camberwell grove
Gray Thomas, corn chandler, 8 Bedford pl. Commcl. rd. ea
Gray Thomas, grocer, 14 Fitzroy street, Fitzroy square
Gray Thomas, jobmaster, 119 Mount st. & 52 Brook st
Gray Thomas, oilman, 15 Short's buildings, Clerknwl. close
Gray Thomas, pork butcher, 115 Drury lane
Gray Thomas William, solicitor, 7 John street, Adelphi
Gray Wm. carpenter, 3 Queen Charlotte row, New road
Gray Wm. carpenter & undertaker, Church st. Hackney
Gray Wm. dyer, Church street, Hackney
Gray Wm. greengrocer, 27 East st. Walworth road
Wray Wm. improved artificial leg maker (successor to the late Mr. Potts, of Chelsea, & patronised by the Marquis of Anglesea), 19 Davis street, Berkeley square
Gray Wm. jobmaster, 18 Shepherd st. Oxford st
Gray Wm. jobmaster & horse dealer, 180½ Oxford street, & 38 Somerset street, Portman square
Gray Wm. oilman, &c 5 Church street, Stoke Newington
Gray Wm. plasterer, 28 Platt terrace, Pancras road
Gray Wm. jun. attorney, 21 Flemming st. Kingsland road
Gray Wm. Chas. jun. oilman, 31 Bridge road, Lambeth
Gray Wm. George, stationer, 18 Colvill ter. Chelsea
Gray Wm.Wilson, manifold let. writ. ma. 10 Gt.Winchester st
Grayden Robert, brushmaker, 39 New cut, Lambeth
Graydon Charles, ship chandler, St. Ann's pl. Limehouse
Graygoose John, pawnbroker, 51 Crawford st, Portman sq
Grayhurst, Harvey & Co. goldsmiths & watchmakers, 126 & 128 Regent street (late 64 Strand)
Grayling & Beckett, who. oilmen, 37 London rd. Southwark
Grayling Edward Leggett, baker, 85 Chamber st. Leman st
Gray's inn: entrances, High Holborn; Warwick ct. (39 High Holborn); King's rd. & Gray's inn la.; *Steward's Office & Library*, South sq. hours of attendance, 10 to 3
Grayson Chas. drawing academy, 1 Banner st. St. Luke's
Grayson George, builder, 21 Woodstock street, Oxford st
Grayson Wm. musical instrument ma. 5 Prince's st. Les'tr sq
Grazebrook Michael & William, ironfounders, 10 Wharf, City road basin, & Netherton, near Dudley, Staffordshire
Grazebrook John Worrall, iron agt. 10 Wharf, City rd. basin
Greadey Thomas, *Black Lion tap*, 10 Whitefriars st
Gream Geo. Thompson, surgeon, &c. 42 Hertford st. Mayfair
Grear Robert, wax & tallow chandler, 41 Long acre
Grearson Eizbth. (Mrs.), straw bonnet ma. 10 Bury st. Bmby
Greasley Chas. & Co. woollendrapers, 160 Borough High st
Greasley Francis, corn dealer, 38 Gibson st. Waterloo road
Greasley Martha (Mrs.), oil wa. 17 Cannon st. rd. St. Geo. e
Great Britain Mutual Life Assurance Society (A. R. Irvine, managing director), 14 Waterloo pl. Pall mal
Great European Railway (John Sinnett & Richard Dearmer, secs.), 1A, St. Helens pl. Bishopsgate street
Great Munster Railway (Dudley Byrne, sec.), 63 Moorgate street
Great Northern of France Railway (E. Aimé, sec.), 62 King William street, City
Great Paris & Lyons Railway Offi. (W. Irwin, sec.), 63 Moorgate street
Great Seal Patent Office (Leonard Edmunds, esq. clerk of the Patents), Quality ct. Chancery lane; hours 10 to 4
Great Southern & Western Railway Company (Ireland), (Richd. Stafford, agent), 1 Warnford court
Great Western Railway Office (Charles Alex. Saunders, sec. & chief superintendent), at the London terminus, Paddington; City booking office, 29 Gresham st. City
Gt. Welsh Cen. Rail. Co. (H. Herbert Downman, sec.), 9 Clement's lane
Great Western Railway of Bengal (RobertWolseley, sec.), 147 Leadenhall st
Great Western Railway of Italy, 23 Moorgate st
Great Western Station, Grand Junction road, Paddington
Great Western & Uxbridge Railway (William Henry Wilson, sec.), 449 West Strand
Great Western & Wycombe Railway (William Henry Wilson, sec.), 449 West Strand
Great Wheal Martha Consolidated Mines (Edward J. Cole, sec.), Winchester house, Old Broad st
Greatbach Wm. engraver, 2 Crescent pl. Mornington cresnt
Greatbatch Isaac, agent to Frith Brothers, opticians, 46 Lisle st. Leicester sq. & Arundel st. Sheffield
Greatbatch John, china, glass, &c. mercht. 20 Farringdon st
Greated (Misses), la. school, 4 Up. Gloster st. St. John st. rd
Greathead Hutton, cheesemonger, 108 Lambeth lower marsh
Greathead Jane (Miss), tobacnst. 11 St. Alban's pl. Edgwr. rd
Greathead John, *White Hart* P.H. 12 Lit. Windm.st.Gldn.sq
Greathead Thomas, cheesemonger, 50 Bridge road, Lambeth
Greatorex Jermh. warehsmn. see Bradbury, Greatorex & Co
GreatorexMary(Mrs.), tinpl. wrkr. 7 Southmptn.st.Cambrwl
Greatorex Thomas, dairyman, 122 Albany st. Regent's park
GreatorexWm.Anthony, solicitor, 70 Up. Norton st. Fitzr. sq
GreatrakesJn. *Fishmongers'Arms* P.H.13Holles st.Claremkt
Greaves Chas. Sprengel, barrister, 1 Harcourt bldgs.Temple
Greaves Charles Warren, law stationer, 127 Chancery lane
Greaves Chas. Wm. boat builder, 31 Cheyne walk, Chelsea
Greaves Chris. pawnbroker, 8 Bulstrode st. Manchester sq
GreavesEben.sworn broker&agt.9 King's arms yd.Moorgt.st
Greaves Edwd. chemist, &c. 1Churton st.Vauxhall bridgerd
Greaves George, saddletree maker, 26 Berwick st. Soho
Greaves James, saddletree maker, 31 Crown st. Soho
Greaves John William, tobacconist, 6 Royal Exchange
Greaves Jos. wax & tallow chand. 20 New st. Covent garden
Greaves Joshua, hide & leather seller, 231 Bermondsey st
GreavesRd.blue lias lime&cement mer.2 Whf.Paddngtn.basn
Greaves Richd. stock & sharebroker, see Hodgson & Greaves
Greaves Thomas, carpenter, 32 Lower Queen st. Rotherhithe
Greaves Wm. sen. saddletree mak.11 Portland st.Wardour st
Greaves Wm.jun. saddletree mak. 6 Robert st. Hampstead rd
Greaves Wm. Boker, tobacconist, 16 Gravel la. Southwark
Greayer John Wm.who. irnmngr. & gen. factor, High st. Bow

Greayer Wm. *Barley Mow* P.H. 28 Mount st. Berkeley sq
Gredley John & Co. grocers, &c. 1 James st. Buckingham gate, & at 1 Willow place, Old Kent road
Greed John, tailor, 13 Church st. Blackfriars road
Greedus Charles Philip, porkman, 106 Union st. Borough
Greedy Benjamin, grocer, 8 Vine st. York road, Lambeth
Greely William, grocer, 1 Dockhead, Bermondsey
Green & Banks, wholesale jewellers, 94 Hatton garden
Green Chas. & Son, carpenters, 38 Earl st. west, Edgeware rd
Green & Cobb, plumbs. & paints. &c. 42 Devonsh. st. Queensq
Green & Constable, wholesale & retail ironmongers, & dealers in curriers' tools & stores, 36 King William st. City
Green & Cory, coal merchants, New Barge house wharf, Commercial road, Lambeth
Green Ed. & Co. tailors, 7 Old Burlington st. & 30 Saville row
Green Fred. & Co. ship & insurance brokers, 64 Cornhill
Green & Holme, muslin & counterpane manufacturers, 1 Crown ct. Cheapside, & 3 New Cannon st. bldgs. Manchester
Green Henry & Co. coachbuilders, 1 Snow's fields, Bermdsy
Green John & Geo. linendrapers, 79 Baker st. Portman sq
Green Jsph. G. & Jas. china, glass, &c. ma. 35&36 Up. Thames st
Green & M'Lacklan, chemists & druggists, 42 Whitechapel rd
Green Michael Levy & Co. who. clothiers, 10 Houndsditch
Green & Radmall, who. provision mer. 2 Bishopsgate without
Green Richd. & Henry, shipbuilders, Brunswick st. Blackwall
Green Robert & Co. goldsmiths, &c. 20 Cockspur st. Charing cr
Green & Seager, ladies' school, 5 Portland pl. Clapham rd
Green Abraham, chandler's shop, 28 Collier st. Pentonville
Green Abm. Geo. *Gentleman & Porter* P.H. 30 New st. sq. Shoe l
Green Alexander, secretary to the *Royal Exchange Assurance Corporation*, Royal Exchange, & 29 Pall Mall
Green Ann (Mrs.), baker, 7 Etham place, Kent st. Borough
Green Ann (Mrs.), fruiterer, 18 Gt. James st. Bedford row
Green Benjamin, bldr. & bricklayer, 32 Lower Islington ter
Green Benjamin, tailor, 12 White Lion st. Pentonville
Green Benjamin Richd. artist, 62 Charlotte st. Portland pl
Green Bevis Ellerby, bookseller, see Longman, Brown & Co
Green Catherine (Mrs.), grocer, 11 Clayton st. Kennington
Green Charles, accountant & arbitrator, 7 Cripplegate bldgs
Green Charles, auctioneer, &c. 8 Grove end pl. St. John's wood
Green Charles, butcher, 4 Etham pl. Kent st. Boro'
Green Charles, cabinet mak. 11 Church row, Somers town
Green Charles, corndealer, 13 Radcliffe ter. Goswell road
Green Charles, dyer, 17 Cumberland market, Regent's park
Green Charles, dyer, 25 Park st. Borough
Green Charles, estate agent, 4 Penton row, Walworth road
Green Charles, oil & colorman, 88 St. John st. road
Green Charles, printer, Grove passage, Church st. Hackney
Green Charles, tailor, 52 Berwick st. Soho
Green Charles, tobacconist, 265½ Pickett st. Strand
Green Charles, tripe dealer, 18 Northampton pl. Old Kent rd
Green Charles Dixon, glass cutter, Grove, Great Guildford st. & 42 Primrose hill, Salisbury st. Fleet st
Green Charles Fred. butcher, 26 Grosvenor st. west, Pimlico
Green Charles Morgan, baker, 103 Fetter lane, Holborn
Green Charles Price, barrister, 44 Southampton buildings
Green Charles Richd. cornchandler, 161 High st. Shadwell
Green Christopher, wharfinger, Bush whf. St. Mary Overy's dk
Green Christ. corn & coal mer. 9 Beckford row, Walworth rd
Green Daniel, cheesemonger, &c. 3 Newcastle pl. Edgware rd
Green Edw. baker, 1 Compton st. Clerkenwell
Green Edw. butcher, 12 Upper Seymour st. Euston sq
Green Edw. coal. mer. & wharfinger, 9 Wharf, City rd. basin, & Rutland wharf, Upper Thames st
Green Edw. florist, High st. Battersea
Green Edw. general agent, 38 Walbrook
Green Edw. grocer, 19 Hampton st. Walworth road
Green Edw. S. teacher of music, 4 Mansion ho. pl. Camberwell
Green Edward, tailor & habit maker to the Queen, 8 Clifford st. Bond st
Green Eliz. (Mrs.), juvenile, &c. wareh. 16A, Baker st. Portm. sq
Green Eliza (Mrs.), milliner, 3 Adam st. east, Manchester sq
Green Ezekiel, cowkeeper, 41 Brill row, Somers town
Green Francis, carpenter, &c. 1 Upper James st. Golden sq
Green Francis Gwinnet, surveyor & builder, 18 Portugal st. Lincoln's inn fields, & 45A, Queen Anne st. Cavendish sq
Green Francis Jsph. carpent. & undertak. 35 Berwick st. Soho
Green Frederick, auctioneer, valuer, &c. 17 Upper Southwick st. Cambridge terrace, Edgware road
Green Frederick, solicitor, see Weymouth & Green
Green Frederick Wm. auctioneer & surveyor, 21 Portman st
Green Frederick William, shipowner, 75 Cornhill
Green George, boot & shoe maker, 24 Saville place, Lambeth
Green George, boot & shoe warehouse, 87 Shoreditch
Green George, bootmaker, 191 Albany road, Camberwell
Green George, boot & shoe maker, 26 Grosvenor row, Pimlico
Green George, brushmaker, 136 Kent st. Borough
Green George, carpenter & joiner, 44 Goodge st. Fitzroy sq
Green George, coachmaker, 47 Eagle st. Red Lion square
Green George, furnish. ironmonger, 5 Pitt's pl. Old Kent rd
Green George, grocer & cheesemr. 66 Drummond st. Eust. sq
Green George, official assignee, 18 Aldermanbury
Green George, wheelwright, Rose lane, Ratcliff
Green George Arthur, cheesemonger, 89 Shoe lane, 1 Clare street, & 19 North place, Kingsland road
Green Geo. Fredk. accountant, Hortulan pl. King's rd. w. Chels
Green George Pycock, artist, 27 Lamb's Conduit st
Green George Sewell, grocer, 36 Aylesbury st. Clerkenwell
Green Hannah (Mrs.), rag merchant, 27 Broad st. Lambeth
Green Henry, carpenter & case ma. 5 Arundel st. Haymarket
Green Henry, corn & seed merchant, see West & Green
Green Henry, dairyman, 272 Strand
Green Henry, fruiterer, 3 Denbigh st. Pimlico
Green Henry, grocer, 98 Shadwell High st
Green Henry, marine store dealer, 36 Lambeth High st
Green Henry, oil & colorman, 31 Bartholomew ter. St. Luke's
Green Henry D. cheesemonger, 252 Poplar High st
Green Hy. Thompson, surgeon &c. 2 Ebury st. Pimlico
Green Howe, grocer & cheesm. 29 Halfmoon st. Bishopsgate
Green Isaac, *Five Bells* P.H. Old Ford
Green Isaac, saddlers' ironmonger, bridle cutter, & harness manufacturer, 20 Lisle st. Leicester square
Green James, bead & eye manufactur. 59 Brick la. St. Luke's
Green James, black chain ma. 15 Windsor place, City road
Green James, boat builder, 29 Rotherithe st
Green James, boot & shoe maker, 27 Church st. Camberwell
Green James, bricklayer, 22 Seabright st. Bethnal green rd
Green James, builder, 11 Winckworth buildings, City rd
Green James, butcher, 112 Crawford st. Portman sq
Green James, butcher, 20 Northampton pl. Old Kent rd
Green James, chain cable maker, 14 Bear lane, Blackfriars
Green James, chemist & druggist, 62 Barbican
Green James, coal merchant, Patriot row, Cambridge road
Green James, coffin plate engraver, 109 Gt. Portland st
Green James, grocer, 12 Bermondsey st
Green James, undertaker & coffin furnitr. wa. 37 Kingsland rd
Green James, hairdresser & patent wig maker, 58 Cheapside
Green James, *Little Driver* P.H. Bow
Green James, registrar of births, &c. 96 York rd. Lambeth
Green James, shoe factor & general agent, 58 Barbican
Green James, shuttle maker & turner, 40 Bethnal green rd
Green James, undertaker, 62 Seymour pl. Bryanstone sq
Green James, watchcase maker, 28 Rahere st. Goswell road
Green James, wool dealer & list merchant, 60 Basinghall st
Green James, Wm. cutler & hardwrma. 17 Gough square
Green Jane (Miss), milliner, 36 Queen st. Brompton
Green Job, dairyman, 8 Church terrace, Pancras road
Green John, beer retailer, 130 Holborn hill
Green John, bookseller, 48 Gt. Queen st. Lincoln's inn fields
Green John, building material dealer, Wandsworth road
Green John, butcher, 4 Little Crown court, Soho
Green John, cattle salesman, 17 West Smithfield
Green John, coffee rooms, 104 Leather lane, Holborn
Green John, fruiterer, Long market, Covent garden market
Green John, furnish. ironmonger, locksmith & bellhanger to her Majesty & H.R.H. Prince Albert, 15 Stafford row, Piml
Green John, gold & silver beater, 43B, New Compton st. Soho
Green John, hairdresser, 8 Little Windmill st. Golden sq
Green John, hide & skin salesman, Bermondsey skin market
Green John, imp. of foreign silk, see Oliver & Green
Green John, inventor & maker of the royal seraphine pianoforte & music warehouse, & academy of music on Logier's system, 33 Soho square
Green John, livery stables, Burwood mws. Titchbrn. st. Edg. rd
Green John, oilman, 6 Lit. Crown court, Little Pulteney st
Green John, saddler, 197 Wellington terrace, Waterloo road
Green John, tailor, 14 Denmark st. Pentonville
Green John, tailor, 85 Lower Thames st
Green John, umbrella maker, 72 Monmouth st. Seven dials
Green John, wharfinger, Union wharf, Wapping High st
Green John Alexander, *Golden Lion* P.H. 92 West Smithfield
Green John Edwd. house agt. & appraiser, 46 Whitecross st. City
Green John Evans, undertaker, 7 Paradise st. Lambeth
Green Jn. H. carpenter & bldr 2 Brunswick mews, Portman sq
Green John H. french polisher, 22 Shaftesbury ter. Pimlico
Green John Hugh, dyer, 83 Lisson grove north, Marylebone
Green John Wm. butcher, 23 High st. Camberwell road
Green Jonathan, beer retailer, Ellis st. Sloane st
Green Jonathan, M.D. surgeon & baths, 40 Gt. Marlborough st
Green Joseph, bricklayer, 21 Bennett st. Blackfriars road
Green Joseph, carver & gilder, 14 Charles st. Mddlx. hospital
Green Joshua, jobmaster, Whitehorse yard, Brompton L. gr

Green Laban, wheelwright, 7 Barnet st. Hackney road
Green Lewis Ephraim, wh.clothier, 21 Middx.st. Whitechapel
Green Margaret (Mrs.), chimney swpr. 23 Colonnade, Brswksq
Green Marg. (Mrs.), chinadlr. 28 Mid. Queen's bldgs. Knightsb
Green Marion (Mrs.), artist on velvet, 24 Beaumont pl
Green Nicholas, tailor, 43 Aske st. Hoxton
Green Philip Jas. merchant, 6 Gt. St. Helen's, Bishopsgate
Green Richard, baker, 113 Edgeware road, Marylebone
Green Richard, butcher, 31 Cross st. Islington
Green Richard, corn dealer, 28 Flagon row, Deptford
Green Richard, grocer & cheesemg. 54 Queen st. Brynstn sq
Green Rd. *Hampton Court Palace* P.H. 11 Francis st. Nwgtn
Green Richard, *Hercules Pillars* P.H. 7 Greek st. Soho
Green Richard, ladder maker, 144 Goswell st
Green Richard, ship owner, wharf, Blackwall
Green Richard, tailor, 23 Bevenden st. East road, City road
Green Robert, brush maker, 286 Kent st. Borough
Green Robert, fruiterer, 2 Glasshouse st. Regent st
Green Robert, *George & Phœnix* P.H. 26 Bermondsey st
Green Robert, merchant, 13 Birchin lane
Green Robert, oil & colorman, 32 Lit. Newport st. Long acre
Green Robert, poulterer, 31 Goodge st. Fitzroy sq
Green Robert, stationer, 65 Whitechapel road
Green Robert, tailor, 2 Portland st. Soho
Green Robert Rumble, butcher, 3 Flagon row, Deptford
Green Rowland, oil & colorman, 28 Upper Park pl. Dorset sq
Green Samuel, brace & belt manufacturer, 46 Shoe lane
Green Samuel, chemist, &c. 1 Harleyford place, Kennington
Green Samuel, coffee rooms, 10 Spring st. Portman square
Green Samuel, cowkeeper, 1 York ter. York st. Kingsland rd
Green Sam. corn chandler & carman, 15 Lit. Compton st. Soho
Green Samuel, *Old Fountain* P.H. 3 Baldwin st. City road
Green Saml. watch motion ma. 10 Bartholomew sq. St. Luke's
Green Samuel Buchanan, professor of dancing, 36 Castle st. east, Oxford st
Green Sarah (Mrs.), grocer & teadealer, 40 Crown st. Finsbury
Green Susan (Mrs.), japanner & house pntr. 4 Hollen st. Soho
Green Stephen, brown stone potter, &c. 54 Princes st. Lambeth
Green Susan (Miss), strw. bonnetma. 4 James pl. Holloway rd
Green Thomas, appraiser, 89 & 90 Leather lane
Green Thomas, beer retailer, 93 Kingsland road
Green Thomas, butcher, 3 Little Sussex pl. Hyde park grdns
Green Thomas, cane cot maker, 37 Long alley, Finsbury
Green Thomas, carpenter, &c. 10 Gilbert st. Clare market
Green Thomas, cheesemonger, 11 Munster st. Regent's park
Green Thomas, coaldealer, 3 Backchurch lane, Whitechapel
Green Thomas, dressing & writing case maker, 168 Oxford st
Green Thomas, dyer, 33 Park st. Dorset square
Green Thomas, grocer & cheesmngr. 16 Blenheim st. Oxford st
Green Thomas, hairdresser, 4 Frederick pl. Hampstead road
Green Thomas, hairdresser, 34 James st. Buckingham gate
Green Thomas, *Jacob's Well* P.H. 14 Up. Ground st. Blackfrs
Green Thomas, leather dres. Marigold ct. Star cornr. Bmdsy
Green Thomas, ropemaker, 75 Davies st. Berkeley sq
Green Thomas, tallowchandler, 105 Mount st. Berkeley sq
Green Thomas, who. tallowchnd. & oilman, 89 & 90 Leather lane
Green Thomas, who. grocer & teadealer, 88 Leather la. Holbn
Green Thomas, watchmovementma. 30 Rahere st. Goswell rd
Green Thos. Slater, plumber & painter, 26 Newland st. Kensgton
Green Thomas B. law stationer, 8 Serles pl. Carey st
Green Thos. W. artl. flower imp. 20 Frederick st. Gray's inn rd
Green Wm. artificial florist, 15 Agnes place, Waterloo rd
Green Wm. beer retailer, 152 Waterloo road
Green Wm. boot & shoe maker, 127 Kent st. Borough
Green Wm. brushmaker, 88 Kent st. Borough
Green Wm. butcher, 45 Berwick st. Soho
Green Wm. butcher, 4 Commercial pl. York rd. Lambeth
Green Wm. butcher, 290 Oxford st
Green Wm. carpenter, 30 Baldwin's gardens, Leather lane
Green Wm. chemist & druggist, 11 Tothill st. Westminster
Green Wm. coal merchant, see Williams & Green
Green Wm. commer. board & lodging ho. 17 Gough sq. Fleet st
Green Wm. cowkeeper, 48 Upper Ebury st. Pimlico
Green Wm. dairyman, 4 Pancras st. Tottenham ct. rd
Green Wm. dyer, 24 Earl st. east, Lisson grove
Green Wm. engraver & printer, 40 Wakefield st. Regent sq
Green Wm. fruiterer, 1 Clare court, Drury lane
Green Wm. grocer, 9 Peter st. Great Saffron hill
Green Wm. haberdasher & silk mercer, Church st. Hackney
Green Wm. land agent & surveyor, see Brooks & Green
Green Wm. leather seller, 13 Devonshire st. Lisson grove
Green Wm. mathemat. instrument ma. 14 Fountain pl. City rd
Green Wm. proctor, 1 Bell yard, Doctors' commons
Green Wm. russia mat & bag wareho. 80 Fenchurch st
Green Wm. saddler, 107 Curtain road, Shoreditch
Green Wm. shooting & archery gallery, 4 & 6 Leicester sq
Green Wm. solicitor, 4 Crown court, Cheapside
Green Wm. varnish & color maker, see Cooper & Green
Green Wm. Charles, hairdresser, 4 Ball alley, Lombard st
Green Wm. Henry, attorney, 8 Basinghall st
Greenyard (City) Geo. Martin, keeper, 35¾ Whitecross st
Greenaway Edward, hatter, 38 Bishopsgate within
Greenaway & Wright, engravers on wood, 48 Salisbury sq
Greenaway George, grocer, 9 Flagon row, Deptford
Greenaway Isaac, tailor, Gun lane, Commercial rd. Limeho
Greenaway John, watchmaker, 30 Galway st. St. Luke's
Greenaway Wm. watchmaker, 3 Ashley crescent, City road
Greene Benjamin & Son, west india merchants, 11 Mincing la
Greene & Niner, lamp lustre & cut glass manufrs. 138 Regent st. & 43 Baker st. Portman square
Greene Francis Nath. surgeon, 10 Bernard st. Russell sq
Greene Thomas, M.P. barrister, 19 Duke st. Westminster
Greene Thos. Alex. barrister, 2 Churchyard ct. In. Temple
Greene Thos. Webb, barrister, 9 New square, Lincoln's inn
Greene William, house painter, 14 Tysoe st. Exmouth st
Greener James, hairdresser, Belmont place, Wandsworth rd
Greener Thomas, millwright & engineer, 1 Rose la. Ratcliff
Greenfield Grace (Mrs.), oilman, 49 Brick lane, St. Luke's
Greenfield John, lathe, tool, percussion cap, & tube maker, 10 Broad st. Golden square
Greenfield John, linendraper, 4 High st. Newington butts
Greenfield Mary (Mrs.), coal dealer, 1 Brewer st. Pimlico
Greenfield Wm. bone button mfr. 8 Luntley pl. Chicksand st
Greengrass Alfred, furn. japanner, 7 & 8 Drake st. Red Lion sq
Greengrass Geo. *China Ship* P.H. 4 Lit. Hermitage st. Wapping
Greenhalgh Henry, grocer, 1 Henry st. Hampstead road
Greenhalgh James, surgeon, 5 Southampton st. Camberwell
Greenhalgh Robert, surgeon, 66 Charlotte st. Fitzroy sq
Greenhall Wm. lodging house, 4, 5, & 31 Maddox st. Regent st
Greenham Louisa Ann (Miss), milliner, 38 Ludgate hill
Greenham William, bootmaker, 3 Church la. Commcl. rd. east
Greenhill Benj. John M. scalema. & gas fit. 221 Hoxton old town
Greenhill Charles, manfr. of gilt watch & time-piece keys, steel pipes for gold keys, gold & steel watch hands & seconds, wholesale & retail, 12 Gt. Sutton st. Clerkenwell
Greenhill George & Co. wax chandlers, oil merchants, &c. to the Queen & the Queen Dowager, 7 Bury st. St. James's
Greenhill Frederick, stationer, 8 Gracechurch st
Greenhill Geo. attorney, 11½ Gt. Carter la. Doctors' commons
Greenhill Geo. melter & chandler, 15 St. Ann st. Westminster
Greenhill Geo. treasurer of Stationers' Comp. Stationers' hall
Greenhill Henry, butcher, 7 Henry's pl. Old Kent road
Greenhill Henry, butcher, 6 Orchard place, Blackwall
Greenhill John, manchest. remnant wa. 5 Aylesbury st. Clkwl
Greenhill John, working jeweller, 5 Aylesbury st. Clerkenwl
Greenhill Joseph, prof. & mak. of bugles, 14 Ivy la. Newgate st
Greenhill Thos. stone & coal mer. 23 Portman pl. Edgware road, & 16 Wharf, Paddington basin
Greenhoughs Mary (Mrs.), ladies' school, High st. Bow, Midlx
Greenhow Martha (Mrs.), cheesemngr, 3 Orford row, O. Kent rd
Greenhow Richd. cooper, 1 Walbrook row, New North rd. Hxtn
Greenhow Thomas, brandy distiller, 16 St. John's st. Clknwl
Greening Daniel, straw bonnet mak. 28 Cross st. Islington
Greening Edward, looking glass ma. 7 Peter st. Bishopsgate
Greening Henry, special pleader, 3 Harcourt buildgs. Temple
Greening Henry John, brassfounder, 15 West st. Seven dials
Greening Mary Ann (Mrs.), dyer, &c. Shepherdess wlk. City rd
Greening Richd. James, barrister, 2 Harcourt bldgs. Temple
Greening Wm. carv. & gilder & lookg. glass ma. 79 Coleman st
Greenland Alfred, book & printseller, 4 Old Broad st. City
Greenland Fras. (Mrs.), *Two Brewers* P.H. 189 Up. Whitecrs. st
Greenland George, auctioneer & agent for the sale of pictures, books & other property, 38 Poultry
Greenland James, builder, 11 Elm tree rd. St. John's wood
Greenland Mary Ann (Mrs.), school, 16 Russell st. Lr. Rotherh
Greenland William, poulterer, Leadenhall market
Greenleaf John, grocer, Grove st. Deptford
Greenlee John, hairdresser & wigmaker, 19 Cornhill
Greenley Francis L. pawnbroker, 7 & 8 Broomfield pl. Deptford
Greenshields John Wm. tailor, 11 Lt. Titchfield st. Ptlnd. pl
Greensill Thomas & Son, lamp lustre, & bronze manufacturers to the Royal Family, & oil merchants, 148 Strand
Greensill Francis, special pleader, 3 Essex court, Temple
Greenslade Amos, hop merchant, see Jackson & Greenslade
Greenslade Ann (Mrs.), straw hatma. 20 Richmond pl. Walwth
Greenslade John, dining rooms, 46 Lambeth walk
Greenslade William, dining rooms, 4 Dockhead, Bermondsey
Greensted Edmund, baker, 1 Cleveland st. Mile end road
Greensted Mar. (Mrs.), *Two Brewers* P.H. 23 Geo. st. New Kt. rd
Greensted Sarah (Miss), milliner, 127 Crawford st. Prtmn. sq
Greenstreet Joseph, ship insurance commission, custom house & wine agent, 11 Cullum st

Greenstreet John, hat manufact. 8 Keen's row, Walworth
Greenway Charles, saddler, 11 Kensington High st
Greenway Isaac, locksmith, 13 Lit. Charlotte st. Mdlx. hos
Greenway Thomas, grocer, 37 Cheyne walk, Chelsea
Greenway William, livery stables, 48 Upper Norton st
Greenway William Alexander, baker, 42 Fish street hill
Greenwell Smith, manchester wareh. see White & Greenwell
Greenwell Thomas, coal mer. Red Lion coal wf. 69 Up. Thms. st
Greenwell Thos. ship ins. & gen. com. ag. 10 New Ea. Ind. chambs
Greenwell William, wheelwright, 80 Redcross st. Borough
Greenwich Out Pension Office, War Office, Parliament st
Greenwich Police Court, Greenwich; hours, 10 to 1½
Greenwich Railroad, see "London & Greenwich"
Greenwood A. & S. (Misses), milliners, 11 Cumberld. st. Hkny. rd
Greenwood & Butler, wine & spirit merchts. 110 Fenchurch st
Greenwood & Co. russia merchts. 4 & 5 Rood la. Fenchurch st
Greenwood, Ebbs & Co. general merchants & importers of toys, beads & fancy goods, 14 & 15 Gt. St. Thomas Apostle
Greenwood George & Thomas, linendrapers, 33 Shoreditch
Greenwood Thomas & Co. manchester manufacturers (Wm. Grant Fraser, agent), 88 Watling st
Greenwood Chas. secret springer, 17 St. James's st. Clknwll
Greenwood Charles, turner, 25 Stephen st. Tottenham ct. rd
Greenwood George, work. jeweller, 12 Hanway st. Oxford st
Greenwood Henry, physician, 1 Horselydown la. Southwark
Greenwood John, american clock imp. 6 St. John's sq. Clknwll
Greenwood John, barrister, 3 Pump court, Temple
Greenwood John, carpenter, &c. 10 Arthur st. west, London br
Greenwood John, fruiterer, 2 Gt. Crown ct. Little Pulteney st
Greenwood John, solicitor (sec. to the Borough of Marylebone loyal & constitutional Association), 53 Wigmore st
Greenwood John Beswicke, magistrate, Clrknwell Police Ct
Greenwood Richard, brewer, 35 Old Compton st. Soho
Greenwood Thomas, barrister, 14 Gt. Queen st. Westminster
Greenwood Thomas, bootmaker, 2 Carter st. Walworth rd
Greenwood Thomas, carpenter & builder, 49 Ashford st. Hoxton
Greenwood Wm. *Northumbd. Arms* P.H. Bagnigge wells rd
Greer Chas. cutler & dressing case maker, 44 Newgate st
Greetham Jsph. Wright, chemist, 2 Glebe pl. King's rd. Chelsea
Greey George, linendraper, 36 Upper st. Islington
Gregg Rt. A. Sarsfield, professor of languages & mathematics, Marlboro' place, 37 Drury lane
Gregg Thos. Hen. portrait painter, 8 Grafton st. Fitzroy sq
Gregg Wm. Henry, goldbeater, 37 Poland st. Oxford st
Greggs George & Co. teadealers, 16 Tothill st. Westminster
Grego Chas. & Joseph, looking glass manufs. 27 Leather la
Grego Chas. carver & gilder, 36 Eyre st. hill, Hatton gdn
Grego Gregory, toy dealer, 59 Parson's st. St. George st
Gregoire Jean B. professor of french language, 49 Finsbury sq
Gregory Brothers & Co. ale & beer merchts. 28 St. Mary at hill
Gregory, Collins & Reynolds, engravers on wood, & printers in colors, gold & bronze, 3 Charterhouse square
Gregory, Cubitt & Co. straw hat manufs. 15 Aldermanbury, & at Luton, Beds
Gregory, Faulkner, Gregory & Skirron, solicitors, 1 Bedford row
Gregory Jonas & Thomas, solicitors, 12 & 13 Clement's inn
Gregory, Thomsons & Co. carpet manufact. 52 Little Britain
Gregory & Todd, potato dealers, 17 Duke st. Tooley st
Gregory Abraham, smith, 7 George yard, Hatton wall
Gregory Charles, carpet manufacturer, 212 Regent st
Gregory Charles, shoemaker, 78 Pritchard's rd. Hackney rd
Gregory Edward, carver & gilder, 23 Frith st. Soho
Gregory Edward, plumber, 6 Northumberland st. Marylebone
Gregory Edward jun. solicitor, 13 South square, Gray's inn
Gregory Edward Rogers, chemist, &c. Church st. Hackney
Gregory Elizabth. (Mrs.), fruiterer 119 Lambeth Lwr. marsh
Gregory Geo. carpenter, Orchard row, High st. Camberwl. rd
Gregory Geo. furn. ironmonger, 174 Sloane st. Knightsbridge
Gregory Geo. ham & beef shop, 184 Sloane st. Knightsbridge
Gregory Geo. physician, 31 Weymouth st. Portland pl.
Gregory Geo. Benj. confectioner, 23 Everett st. Brunswck sq
Gregory Geo. Wm. Colley, *Arundel hotel*, 2 Arundel st. Hymkt. & *John o'Groats' tavern*, 61 & 62 Rupert st. Haymarket
Gregory Harriet (Mrs.), bonnet maker, Camberwell green
Gregory Henry, shorthand writer, 77 Chancery lane
Gregory James, chinaman, 21 Shoemaker row Blackfriars
Gregory James, fruiterer, 21 Lower Smith st. Clerkenwell
Gregory James, gun case maker, 3 Castle st. Leicester sq
Gregory James, tailor, Mare st. Hackney
Gregory James, tobacconist, 119 Gt. Portland st. Oxford st
Gregory John, artist, 16 St. James's st. Clerkenwell
Gregory John, baker, 92 Park st. Kennington cross
Gregory John, butcher, 7 Cambridge road, Mile end
Gregory John, cabinetmkr. 2 Suntavern flds. St. George's east
Gregory John, chinaman, 219 Up. Whitecross st. St. Luke's
Gregory John, coffee rooms, 6 Canning place, Old st
Gregory John, oilman, 4 Newington causeway
Gregory John, potato salesman, 40 Crispin st. Spitalfields
Gregory John, teadealer, &c. 19 Princes st. Westminster
Gregory John, upholsterer & undertaker, 97 Old st. St. Luke's
Gregory John Alexander, solicitor, see Kennett & Gregory
Gregory Joseph, boot & shoe maker, 206 Hoxton Old town
Gregory Joseph, smith, 7 Waterloo st. Camberwell
Gregory Joseph, wholesale job warehouse, 34 Minories
Gregory Joshua, law stationer, 7 Cook's court, Carey st
Gregory Mark Henry, sol. Wax Chandlers' Hall, 1 Gresham st
Gregory Reb. (Mrs.), straw hat ma. 4 St. Thos. pl. Gt. Dover rd
Gregory Richard, smith, 78 Turnmill st. Clerkenwell
Gregory Samuel, solicitor, see Carter & Gregory
Gregory Thomas, stationer, 49 Borough road
Gregory Thomas Wm. potato salesman, Spitalfields market
Gregory William, appraiser, 9 Prospect pl. Old Kent road
Gregory William, tailor, 4 Vernon place, Bloomsbury
Gregory William, tailor, 4 St. Agnes terrace, Tabernacle sq
Gregory Wm. (Mrs.), milliner, 3 Carteret st. Westminster
Gregson & Co. east india agents, 14 Austinfriars
Gregson & Kewell, solicitors, 8 Angel court, Throgmorton st
Gregson John, solicitor, 18 Bedford row, Bloomsbury
Gregson William, barrister, 2 Tanfield court, Temple
Greig & Rawlings, timber merchants, Maiden lane, King's cr
Greig William & Co. merchants, 32 City road, Finsbury
Greig Andrew, livery stables, York mews south, Paddington st
Greig Ebenezer, cabinet ma. 27 Farringdon st. & Wheatsheaf yd
Greig James, baker, 1 Blossom place, Holloway
Greig James, corn dealer, 12 Portman place, Edgware road
Greig Robert Reed, solicitor, 13 King's road, Gray's inn
Greig Thomas, carpenter, Ring cross, Holloway
Greig Susannah (Mrs.), baker, 1 St. James's pl. Old Kent road
Greig Woronzow, barrister, 6 King's Bench walk, Temple
Greir John, baker, 10 Alfred row, Spa road, Bermondsey
Greive & Cook, skein silk dyers, 17 Booth st. Spitalfields
Greive & Grellier, marble merchants, Belvedere rd. Lambeth
Greive James, spirit merchant, 34 Bread st. Cheapside
Grellett Brothers & Co. merchants, 7 Lloyd st. Lloyd square
Grellett Frederick, merchant, 22 Austinfriars
Grellier Peter Paul & Co. wine mers. Belvedere rd. Lambeth
Grelliers' & Haines, silk brokers, 67 London wall
Grellier Henry, bookbinder, 23 Gerard st. Soho
Grellier Peter Paul, marble merchant, see Greive & Grellier
Grellier Wm. architect & surv. 20 Wormwood st. Bishopsgt
Grenfell (Pascoe) & Sons, copper office & warehouses, 27 Upper Thames st
Grenside Charles K. barrister, 10 Serle st. Lincoln's inn
Grenwood Thomas, surgeon, 2 Fenchurch buildings
Gresbar Fred. merchant, 5 Jeffrey's sq. St. Mary Axe
Gresham Club (Wm. Best, sec.), 1A, King William st. City
Gresham George, tailor, 16 Somerset pl. Hoxton New town
Gresham Wm. solicitor, 3 Castle st. Holborn
Greswell Henry, beer retailer, 34 Up. Ebury st. Pimlico
Greswold Richard, tailor, 2 Tavistock court, Covent garden
Gretton Henry, tobacconist, 102 Poplar High st
Gretton John, ale stores, see Bass, Ratcliff & Gretton
Greverus Herman Diederich, merct. 3 Whitehart ct. Lomb. st
Greville Benjamin, newsvndr. 62 Gt. Cambridge st. Hackney rd
Greville Charles Wm. chiropodist, 11 Banner st. St. Luke's
Greville George Hen. newsvender, 4 Lamb pl. Kingsland rd
Greville Henry, cabinet carver, 36 Buttesland st. Hoxton
Greville Peniston Grosvenor, solicitor, 42 Lombard st
Grew Henry, seal engraver, 57 Perceval st. Clerkenwell
Grew Samuel, furnishing undertaker, 28 Bethnal green road
Grey & Coles, east india merchants, 4 Gt. Winchester st
Grey George, bootmaker, 91 Leman st. Goodman's fields
Grey Hen. jun. lighterman & cust. ho. agt. 19 Water la. Tower st
Grey James, linendraper, 73 Basing place, Waterloo road
Grey Joseph Thomas, goldsmith, 68 Leadenhall st
Grey Thomas, pawnbroker, Southampton st. Camberwell
Grey Thomas, upholsterer, 16 Eden pl. Old Kent road
Grey Wm. *Ship tavern* P.H. Little Turnstile, Holborn
Grey Wm. Patrick, lead & glass mer. 20 Camomile st. Bshsgt
Grey Wm. Scurfield, barrister, 1 Cloisters, Temple
Grey William Thomas, wine merchant, see Block & Grey
Grey Coat Hospital, Grey Coat place Westminster
Greyell & Bufton (Misses), milliners, 40 Oxford st
Greygoose Edward, oil & ital. wareho. 58 Crawford st. Portm. sq
Gribbel Charles, smith & farrier, Bromley New town
Gribble Henry, solicitor, 3 Raymond's bldgs. Gray's inn
Gribble Thomas, merchant, see Gonne, Lucas & Gribble
Gribble Thos. stockbroker, see Sutton (R.) Gribble & Sutton
Gribble Wm. boot & shoe ma. 11 Old Chapel row, Kentish tn
Gribble William, bricklayer & builder, 27 Boston st. Dorset sq
Gribble William, solicitor, 3 Raymond's bldgs. Gray's inn
Gribble William, jun. solicitor, 80 Lombard st

Grice Isaac, ironmonger, 3 Paragon pl. Lock's fields
Grice John, ironmonger, 18 Cross st. Newington butts
Grice John, jun. coachmaker, 60 Mount st. Lambeth
Grice William, pilot, 8 Brunswick ter. Brunswick st. Blkwl
Gridley Henry, coachmaker, 14 Pied Bull yd. Bloomsbury
Gridley Henry Gillett, solicitor, see Walker & Gridley
Gridley John, tailor, 70 George st. Euston square
Grieg Peter Crawford, greengrocer, 14 East st. Manchester sq
Grierson Geo. smith & ironmon. 1 Lamb's Cond. pass. Red Lion sq
Grierson John, gunmaker, 10 New Bond st
Grierson Thomas, carpet mnfr. see M'Michael & Grierson
Griesbach John H. prof. of music, 3 Carlton villas, Edgw. rd
Griesell Martha Ann (Mrs.), baker, 21 John st. Limehouse flds
Grieve Andrew Reid, artist, 33 Nicholas lane, Lombard st
Grieve David, baker, 10 Ebury st. Pimlico
Grieve James, merchant, 51 Lime st
Grieve John, chemist, &c. 1 John st. Limehouse fields
Grieve Robt. working jeweller, 1 Coldbath sq. Clerkenwell
Grieve William, baker, 1 Dockhead, Bermondsey
Grieve William Royal, ladies' shoemaker, 21 New Bond st
Grieve James & Co. who. cheesemongers, 22 New st. Cov. gar
Grieves Robt. Louis, house & ornam. painter, 12 Church st. Soho
Grieves Sam. printer & stereotype founder, 47 Lambeth wlk
Grieves Samuel, stereotype founder, 6 Red Lion ct. Fleet st
Griff George, *King of Prussia* P.H. Stratford broadway
Griffin Chas. & Geo. & Co. wharfingers, Beal's whf. Tooley st
Griffin John P. & Co. warehousemen, 14 Ironmonger lane
Griffin John & Steph. W. & drug & colonl. broks. 2 Dunster ct
Griffin Thos. & Son, *White Swan* P.H. 196 Shoreditch High st
Griffin & Ward, invalid chair manufacturers to her Majesty & the Queen Dowager, 6 Leicester square
Griffin Alfred, barrister, 1 New square, Lincoln's inn
Griffin Ann (Mrs.), haberdasher, 15 Cambridge rd. Mile end
Griffin Ann (Mrs.), linendraper, 6 & 7 Church st. Camberwell
Griffin Chas. furn. broker, 10 Brook st. New rd. St. Pancras
Griffin Edward, comb maker, 198 Whitechapel road
Griffin Edward, hairdresser & wig maker, 182 Strand
Griffin Emma (Mrs.), cabinet ma. 6 Bowling gn. wk. Pitfld. st
Griffin Francis, escapement mak. 25 Gloster st. St. John st. rd
Griffin Henry, fishmonger, 1 Albemarle st. St. John st
Griffin Henry, hairdresser, 33 Jewin st
Griffin Henry, plumber, 1 Surrey pl. Camberwell New rd
Griffin Henry, tailor, 56, Galway st. St. Luke's
Griffin Henry Horatio, barrister, Hall staircase, Inner Temple
Griffin Isaac, oilman, 9 King's pl. Commercial road east
Geiffin James, woollen warehouse, 13, Basinghall st
Griffin James, house agent & registrar, Battersea square
Griffin John butcher, Clapham road, Kennington common
Griffin John, butcher, 1 Denbigh st. Pimlico
Griffin John, painter, &c. 1 New North st. Finsbury
Griffin John, printer, 34 Friar st. Blackfriars
Griffin John Henry, stationer, 15 Eagle st. City road
Griffin Mary (Miss), lodging house, 3 Norfolk st. Strand
Griffin Nathaniel, barrister, 2 Cloisters, Temple
Griffin Sandiforth, civil engineer, 2 Parliament st
Griffin Thomas, grocer, 47 Red Lion st. Spitalfields
Griffin Thomas, linendraper, 7 Beckford row, Walworth rd
Griffin William, baker, 16 Circus st. New road
Griffin William, carpenter, 48 Cumberland st. Hackney rd
Griffin William, composition ornmt. ma. 39 Charlotte st. Wtch
Griffin William, grocer, 17 High st. Lambeth
Griffin William, silversm. jeweller, & watchma. 73 Cornhill
Griffin William Henry, solicitor, see Horwood & Griffin
Griffin's Wharf, Thos. Farncomb, between 79 & 80 Tooley st
Griffins *Green Man & Still*, Booking Office, 335 Oxford st
Griffis Rodger, marine store dealer, 28 Brill row, Somers tn
Griffith & Densham, builders & carpenters, 8 Sutton st. Soho
Griffith John & Wm. upholsterers & undertakers, 4 Lant st. Boro'
Griffith & Pearson, tailors, 120 New Bond st
Griffith Philip & Thos. & E. wine merchants, 46 Pall mall
Griffith Charles, whipmaker, 322 High Holborn
Griffith Edward, surgeon, see Wright & Griffith
Griffith Edw. Geo. special pleader, 2 Paper bldgs. Temple
Griffith Edward Clavey, solicitor, 19 Lincoln's inn fields
Griffith George, solicitor, 4 Burton crescent
Griffith Henry, barrister, 9 Gray's inn square
Griffith Henry, carpet agent, 57 Basinghall st
Griffith Henry, watch hand maker, 16 Radnor st. St. Luke's
Griffith James, solicitor, 6 Raymond buildings, Gray's inn
Griffith John, architect & surveyor, 16 Finsbury place South
Griffith John, ground glass ma. 32 Gt. Guildford st. Boro'
Griffith John, *King's Arms* P.H. 8 Bridge court, Westminster
Griffith John Michael, house agt. & valuer, 56 King st. Soho
Griffith John Widlake, watchma. 15 Wentworth pl. Mile end rd
Griffith John Wm. architect & surveyor, 9 St. John's sq. Clrkwl
Griffith John Wm. physician, 9 St. John's sq. Clerkenwell
Griffith Joseph, butcher, 2 Adam's row, Hampstead road
Griffith Richard James, surgeon, 287 Bethnal green road
Griffith Samuel Clewin, surgeon, 19 Brunswick sq
Griffith Thomas, steward of Gray's inn, South square
Griffith Walter, surgeon, 1 Bloomsbury pl. Bloomsbury sq
Griffith William, bookseller & stationer, 41 Goswell road
Griffith Wm. bookseller & publisher, see Grant & Griffith
Griffith Wm. surgeon, 31 Lower Belgrave st. Pimlico
Griffith Wm. watch & clock maker, 36 King st. Westminster
Griffith William Pettit, architect, 9 St. John's sq. Clerkenwell
Griffiths Ann & Lydia, milliners, 1 New Burlington st
Griffiths & Bland, chemists, 57 Penton st. Pentonville
Griffiths & Crick, silk mercers to the Queen & the Royal Family, 1 Chandos st. Covent garden
Griffiths Edward Pryce & Co. merchants, 22 Billiter st
Griffiths Eliza & Lucy, milliners, 11 Duke st. Grosvenor sq
Griffiths Geo. & Joel, jun. carvers & gilders, 145 Waterloo rd
Griffiths & Johnson, hatters, 2 Old Bond st
Griffiths & Westmacott, print. in. ma. 33 Compton st. Clrkwl
Griffiths Amelia (Miss), milliner, 3 Canal bridge, Old Kent rd
Griffiths Benjamin, coach maker, 12A, Brewer st. Pimlico
Griffiths Chace Lothrop, printer, 2 Cross st. Islington
Griffiths David, coal dealer, 84 Hare st. Bethnal green
Griffiths David, silk mercer, see Robarts, Griffiths & Crick
Griffiths Edward, fruiterer, &c. 60 Fore st. Cripplegate
Griffiths Edward, saddler, see Douthwaite & Griffiths
Griffiths Edward, 2 *Brewers* P.H. 76 Ewer st. Union st. Boro'
Griffiths Edward P. confectioner, 8 Portland row, Cambwl. rd
Griffiths Elizth. (Mrs.), school, 15 Lr. Ashby st. Northmptn. sq
Griffiths Elizh. (Mrs.), *Norfolk Arms* P.H. 28 Leigh st. Brtn. ct
Griffiths Elliot, hat manufactr. 32 Gray st. Blackfriars road
Griffiths Esther A. (Mrs.), tallowchndlr. 42 Church st. Shored
Griffiths Frederick, printer, 8 Warwick sq. Newgate st
Griffiths Fredk. Wm. solicitor, see Roberts & Griffiths
Griffiths George, coach builder, see Walker & Griffiths
Griffiths Geo. *Rising Sun* P.H. 57 York road, Lambeth
Griffiths Geo. fruiterer, 2 Hosier lane, West Smithfield
Griffiths Geo. *Old Walnut Tree* P.H. Ocean row, Stepney
Griffiths Geo. rag & bottle mer. 40 Robinhood la. Poplar
Griffiths Griffith, carpenter, &c. 28 King st. Golden square
Griffiths Henry, carver & gilder, 27 Drury lane
Griffiths Hugh, turner, 10 Albermarle st. Clerkenwell
Griffiths Isaac, coffee rooms, 4 Marshall st. Golden sq
Griffiths James, beer retailer, Weymouth st. New North rd
Griffiths James, beer retailer, 122 New Gravel lane
Griffiths James, linendraper, 246 Strand
Griffiths James, marine store dealer, 24 Poplar High st
Griffiths James, watch maker, 51 Pearson st. Kingsland rd
Griffiths Jas. Jonathan, ironmonger, 17 Aston pl. Holloway
Griffiths James W. chemist, 7 Melbourne place, Old Kent rd
Griffiths John, chemist & druggist, 41 Clerkenwell green
Griffiths John, *Cross Keys inn*, 103 St. John st. Smithfield
Griffiths John, factor, 27 Gresham st
Griffiths John, linendraper, 27 Pitfield st. Hoxton
Griffiths John, pawnbroker, 7 & 8 Ossulston st. Somers town
Griffiths John, surgeon, &c. 1 Pleasant place, King's cross
Griffiths John I. *Cheshire Cheese* P.H. 5 Lit. Essex st. Strand
Griffiths Joseph, builder, 61 Tabernacle walk
Griffiths Joseph, butcher, 94 High st. Portland town
Griffiths Mary (Mrs.), marine st. dlr. 5 Cumberld. pl. Nwgtn. bts
Griffiths Morris, hair dresser, 44 Barnet st. Hackney rd
Griffiths Nehemiah, ship & ins. brok. 2 White Hart ct. Lomb. st
Griffiths Peter Wm. wine merchant, 36 Surrey st. Strand
Griffiths Rhys B. indigo broker, see Fry, Griffiths & Co
Griffiths Richd. carver & gilder, 30 Bayham st. Camden town
Griffiths Richard, fringe & trimming mnfr. 52 Bow lane
Griffiths Richard, saddler, 102A, Mount st. Berkeley sq
Griffiths Richd. Clewin, surgeon, 10 Gower st. Bedford sq
Griffiths Rd. Stephn. *D. of Sussex* P.H. 12 Gibson st. Waterl. rd
Griffiths Robert, coal merchant, Nine Elms wharf, Vauxhall, & at 12 Belmont pl. Wandsworth rd
Griffiths Robt. J. linendraper, 1A, Grove ter. Qns. rd. Byswtr
Griffiths Thos. *Blue Lion* P.H. 26 Up. North pl. Gray's inn rd
Griffiths Thomas, carpenter, &c. 13 Aston pl. Holloway
Griffiths Thomas, carver & gilder, 107 London rd. Southwk
Griffiths Thomas, coal & coke dealer, 47 Monmouth st. 7 Dials
Griffiths Thomas, cowkeeper, 14 New inn yard, Shoreditch
Griffiths Thomas, glove manf. 32 Whitecross st. Cripplegate
Griffiths Thomas. hardwood turner, 5 Anchor st. Shoreditch
Griffiths Thomas, *Portland Arms* P.H. 54 Gt. Marylebone st
Griffiths Thomas, tobacconist, 97 Praed st. Paddington
Griffiths Thomas, turner, 13 Noble st. Goswell st
Griffiths Walter, grocer, &c. 7 Cloak lane, Queen st. City
Griffiths Wm. builder & surveyor, 16 Edgware rd. Marylebone
Griffiths Wm. china & glass dlr. 15 Providence pl. Kentish tn
Griffiths Wm. coachmaker, 13 Broadley ter. Blandford sq

Griffiths Wm. *Duke of York* P.H. 29½ York st. Portman sq
Griffiths Wm. furniture broker, 32 Old st. road
Griffiths Wm. solicitor, 24 Bucklersbury
Griffiths Wm. working jeweller, 8 Rufford's row, Islington
Griffits Henry, solicitor, 3 Crescent pl. New Bridge st
Grigg Abel, harness maker, Little Chelsea
Grigg George, cheesemonger, 8 Little Turnstile, Holborn
Grigg John, painter, 49 Brill row, Somers town
Grigg Joseph, grocer & oilman, 12 Market st. Mayfair
Grigg John, cheesemonger, 9 Canterbury pl. Old Kent road
Grigg William, engraver, printer & stationer, 183 Regent st
Griggs George, bellhanger, 13 Francis st. Tottenham ct. rd
Griggs James, fruiterer, 80 High st. Marylebone
Griggs Samuel, lighterman, 3 Burr st. East Smithfield
Grignon Peter, chemist & druggist, 174 Regent st
Grignon Wm. italian warehouse, see Taylor & Grignon
Grigson Sarah (Mrs.), tobacconist, 2 Barking Church yard
Grillion Pierre, *Grillion's hotel*, 7 & 27 Albemarle st
Grilleon Francis, *Coburg hotel*, 14 to 16 Charles st. Grosvenr. sq
Grimaldi, Stables & Burn, sols. 1 Copthall ct. Throgmrtn. st
Grimaldi Stacey, translator of records, 1 Copthall court
Grimble Wm. & Co. brandy distillers, Albany st. Regent's pk
Grimble, Podmore & Co. vinegar & acetic acid manufacturs. North pl. Cumberland market & Albany st. Regent's park
Grimble George, baker & grocer, 5 Richard st. Limehouse flds
Grimes Ben. & John, beer engine ma. 2 Osborne st. Whitechpl
Grimes George, *Black Boy* P.H. 9½ Road side, Mile end rd
Grimes John Aug. ironmonger, 9 Kenton st. Brunswick sq
Grimes Robert, tailor, 155 Princes road, Lambeth
Grimley & Co. (Wm. Hooper), herbalists, Centre rw. Cov. gar
Grimmett Samuel, cowkeeper, 42 Cross st. Islington
Grimmond David, baker, 32 Broad st. Golden square
Grimmond Geo. Stevenson, baker, 5 Shepherd's mrkt. Mayfair
Grimoldi Henry, barometer ma. & tobacconist, 24 Greville st
Grimsdale Henry, grocer, 1 & 2 Domingo st. Old st
Grimsdell Henry, *Eagle* P.H. 12 Brecknock pl. Camdn. new tn
Grimsdell Samuel, builder, 2 Sun st. Bishopsgate, & Bell lane, Spitalfields
Grimsey & Line, milliners, 40 High st. Kensington
Grimshaw Wm. & Sons, mechanics' tool wareho. 159 Goswell st
Grimshaw Edmund, barrister, 6 Stone bldgs. Lincoln's inn
Grimshaw George Garnet, stockbroker, 20 John st. Adelphi
Grimshaw James, watch & clock ma. 102 Goswell rd. ea. si
Grimshaw Thomas, armourer, 48 Whiskin st. Clerkenwell
Grimsher John, cheesemonger, 1 New Bridge st. Vauxhall
Grimson John, baker, 11 Kinnerton st, Belgrave square
Grimstone William, foreign & british snuff merchant, tobacco, cigar & snuff manufacturer, inventor of eye snuff made from british herbs only, under the patronage of his late Majesty, H.R.H. the Duchess of Kent, and the Lords of the Treasury; testimonials at 434 Oxford street, & 24 King street, Long acre; manufactory, 434 Oxford street
Grimwade & Thackray, who. stationers, 44 Bread st. City
Grimwood Charles, potato dealer, New King st. Deptford
Grimwood Chas. Ludbrook, bellhanger, 39 Cursitor st
Grimwood James, bricklayer, 44 High st. Poplar
Grimwood Mary (Mrs.), milliner, 44 High st. Poplar
Grimwood Robert, grocer & cheesemonger, 3 North st. Manch. sq
Grimwood Robt. Warner, hosier, 34 Paddington st. Marylebone
Grindlay & Co. east india agents, 16 Cornhill, & 8 St. Martin's place, Charing cross
Grindle George, chemist to her Majesty, 122 Pall mall
Grindley John Collan, grocer, 8 Eaton la. north, Pimlico
Grindon John, bookseller, &c. 16 Dean st. New North road
Grinonneau Alfred, wireworker, 12 Cambridge rd. Mile end
Grinonneau Jas. cagema. & wirewkr. 5 Artichoke rd. Mile e. rd
Grinslade George, *Henry VIII.* P.H. 50 Union st. Southwark
Grinsell Wm. Judson, ale & stout stores, 123 Lwr. Thames st
Grinsted George, hairdresser, 25 Queen st. Ratcliff
Grinsted Henry, stockbroker, see Boughton & Grinsted
Grint John, tailor, 65 New Compton st. Soho
Grint Wm. plumber, painter, &c. 25 Lower East Smithfield
Grinter Thomas, bootmaker, 2 Parker's row, Dockhead
Grinyer Wm. Jas. & Jas. Wilson N. mast maker, 8 Risbie's rope walk
Grisdale George, surgeon, 96 Lambeth walk
Grisdale John, *Elephant & Castle* P.H. 17 Gt. Peter st. Wstmr
Grisdale Jno. Edwin, ticket writer, 4 Bowling gr. wk. Hoxton
Grisdale John Maw, chemist, 216 Tottenham court road
Grisewood George, livery stables, 6 Finsbury place North
Grissell Henry & Martin D. engineers, Regent's canal iron works, Eagle wharf road, New North road, Hoxton
Grissell & Peto, saw mills, Palace new road, & 8 Belvedere road, Lambeth
Grist Charles James, plumber, 12 Gt. Mitchell st. St. Luke's
Grist John, beer retailer, 16 Crown st. Soho
Gristwood Mary Ann (Mrs.), corndlr. 1 Marlborough rd. Chelsea
Gritten Hen. & Sons, picture dlrs. 4 Duncannon st. Charing cr
Gritten Henry Frederick, surveyor, 16 Denbigh st. Pimlico
Gritten Wm. Richd. architect, 6 Bull Head ct. Newgate st
Grix George, library, 47 Featherstone st. City road
Grix Richard, tailor, 49 Featherstone st. City road
Groat Alexander, baker, 18 Dorset st. Portman square
Grobecker Wm. surveyor, estate ag. & auctnr. 8 Mount st. Lmbth
Grocers' Hall (Hen. Bicknell, clk.), Grocers' hall ct. 35 Poultry
Grocers' & Teadealers' benevolent protection Society; Subscription rooms, Commercial sale rooms, Mincing lane (George Garraway, secretary)
Grodeke Chas. tobacconist, 57 Charles st. Westminster
Groffman Ebenezer, cabinet ma. 2 Cannon st. rd. St. Geo. east
Groffman Martha (Miss), straw hatma. 1 Princes pl. Com. rd east
Grogan John, pianoforte tuner, 10 Stockbridge terr. Pimlico
Grogan Micl. floor cloth ma. 7 Cumberland pl. Nwngtn. bts
Grogan Thomas, *White Lion* P.H. 118 Drury lane
Grohe James, watch & clock mak. 7 Wigmore st. Cavend. sq
Gronert John G. *Old Commodore* P.H. 120. Montagu st. Whcpl
Gronow Mary (Miss), umbrella mak. 44 Rufford's blds. Islingt
Groocock Wm. Austin, commission agent, 84 Newgate st
Groom Arthur Philip, attorney, 4 Henrietta st. Cavendish sq
Groom David, confectioner, 16 Fleet st
Groom George, wholesale jeweller, 16 Thavies inn, Holborn
Groom Henry, florist to Her Majesty, Clapham rise, Claphm
Groom James, *Angel & Trumpet* P.H. 23 King st. Holborn
Groom James, wire worker, 2 King st. Kensington
Groom James Foster, official assignee, 12 Abchurch la. City
Groom John, butcher, 1 Hayfield place, Mile end
Groom Mary Ann (Mrs.), baker, 39 Salmon lane, Limehouse
Groom Richard, carpenter, 18 Peerless row, Bath st. City rd
Groom Richard, conveyancer, 3 Henrietta st. Cavendish sq
Groom Richard Charles, gun maker, 108 Cock hill, Ratcliff
Groom Robt. *Bee Hive & Cricketers* P.H. Carter st. Walwth. rd
Groom Rt. lithographic & ornamental drftsmn. 4 Paternstr. rw
Groom Robert, tinplate worker, see Barber & Groom
Groom Thomas, haberdasher, 22 Duke st. Chelsea
Groom Thomas, west india mer. *Jamaica* coffee ho. Cornhill
Groom William, baker, 5 Bermondsey new road
Groom Wm. firewood cut. St. George's wf. Albany rd. O. Knt. rd
Groom William, tailor, 13 Cloth fair, Smithfield
Groom Zechariah, tobacconist, 2 Cumberland row, Islington
Groombridge Rd. & Sons, booksellers & pub. 5 Paternoster rw
Groombridge Edward, baker, 28 White st. Borough
Groombridge Henry, cheesemonger, 46 Grove st. Camden tn
Groombridge John, livery stables, 81½ High Holborn
Groombridge John Wm. carpent. build. &c. 12 Crimscott st
Groome George, builder, 7 Cumming st. north, Pentonville
Groome Robert, tobacconist, 1 Moorhall pl. Up. Kennington la
Grosch George, tobacconist, 3 Chapel st. Tottenham ct. rd
Grosch John, tailor, 5 Francis st. Tottenham court road
Grose John, pawnbroker, 89 Bermondsey st
Grose Delabole Slate Company, 16 Broad st. buildings
Grose John, tailor & slopseller & maker of patent waterproof clothing, 94 Tooley st
Grose Vincent, tailor, 152 Tooley st
Groser George, cab proprietor, 28 Chicester st. Kenningtn. cr
Groser Wm. gold & silver refiner, 27 Red Lion st. Clerkenwell
Grosjean Frederick, inventor of the 6½ & 7 octave harp, & maker & patentee of the crystallized sounding board for all musical stringed instruments, the victoria harp, lyre, wernelin harp, harp support, &c. 11 Soho square
Grosjean Frederick, tailor, 99 Quadrant & 164 Oxford st
Grosrey Celestin, watchmaker, 74 Newgate st
Gross Joseph, railway & mill cart grease maker, oil & colorman, 2 Little Lant. st. Borough
Gross Thomas, bootmaker, 7 Cross st. Blackfriars rd
Grosse Edward, greengrocer, 18 Hertford st. Fitzroy sq
Grosse John, corn & nail operator, 34 Upper Marylebone st
Grosse John, wax & tallow chandler, 34 Upper Marylebone st
Grossmith James, *Red Lion* P.H. 14 Princes st. Drury la
Grossmith John, importer of essences & soap, 24 Cannon st. City
Grossmith Wm. reading soap & tooth powder wa. 135 Strand
Grossmith Wm. Robert, artificial eye, leg, truss & bandage maker, 175 Fleet st
Grosutt John, *Black Bull* P.H. 69 St. John st. Smithfield
Grosvenor Estate Office (Abm. Howard, agent), 9 Davies st. Berkeley square
Grosvenor Place Trust Off. 43 Low. Belgrave pl.; hours 9 to 5
Grosvenor, Chater & Co. wholesale stationers, 11 Cornhill
Grosvenor John, prof. of pianoforte, Liverpool ter. Islington
Grosvenor Samuel, coffee rooms, 2 Up. Duncan pl. City road
Grosvenor Sarah (Miss), toy importer, 53 Burlington arcade
Grosvenor Thos. whip & umbrel. ma. 128 Strnd & 52 Burlngtn. arc
Grottick Saml. John, who. hatter & cloth capm. 18 Fore st. Crp

Groucock, Copestake & Moore, lace & sewed muslin manufacturers, 5 Bow churchyard, & 62 Bread st
Ground George, plumber, 48 Tufton st. Horseferry rd. Wstmr
Grounds David, chemist, 49 Threadneedle st
Grounds George, bootmaker, 57 Lower Sloane st. Chelsea
Grounds Thos. chemist & druggist, Church st. Hackney
Grout & Co. crape & shawl manufrs. 12 Foster la. Cheapside
Grout Geo. silk trimming manufact. 68 Bethnal green rd
Grout John, butcher, 78 Broadwall, Blackfriars
Grout John, potato dealer, 43 Church st. Shoreditch
Grout John, watch maker, 248 Whitechapel road
Grout Susan (Mrs.), coal dealer, 40 East st. Manchester sq
Grout Wm. coffee rooms, 47 Brick lane, Spitalfields
Grove George & Co. cheesemongers, Larkhall la. Clapham
Grove John & Christopher, fishmongers, 150 New Bond st
Grove John Wm. & Son, printers, 5 Trinity st. Blkmn. st. Boro
Grove Ann Isabella (Miss), clothes dealer, 116 Shoreditch
Grove Charles, coffee & chop house, 122 Houndsditch
Grove Charles Houblon, barrister, 49 Chancery lane
Grove Edward, appraiser, &c. 76 Grosvenor terrace, & 12 Regent place, Horseferry road
Grove Edward, clothier, 114 & 115 Edgware road, Marylebone, & 39, 40, 41 & 60 Lower Marsh, Lambeth
Grove Edwd. Richd. corn chandler, 70 Cowcross st. Smithfild
Grove George B. butcher, 13 Dorrington st. Leather lane
Grove James, beer retailer, George st. Camberwell
Grove Jas. boot&shoema. Orchardrow, High st. Camberwellrd
Grove John, irish provision broker, see Reade & Grove
Grove John, tailor & trimming slr. 195 Bethnal green road
Grove John, wheelwright, 6 Marlboro' mews, Gt. Marlboro' st
Grove John Dove, *Spread Eagle* P.H. 56 Broad st. Blmsbry
Grove Richard, carpenter, 20 Old Gloucester st. Hoxton
Grove Sarah (Mrs.), news agent, see Kay & Grove
Grove Thos. fishmonger & venison dealer, 33 Charing cross
Grove Thos. tailor, 39 Cranmer place, Waterloo road
Grove Thos. tailor, 34 Pudding lane, Eastcheap
Grove Thos. watch case ma. 4 Northampton bldgs. Clknwl
Grove Wm. carpenter, 29 Bell st. Edgware road
Grove William, fruiterer & coal dlr. 30 Poppins ct. Fleet st
Grove William John, *Spread Eagle* P.H. 199 Kingsland rd
Grove William Robert, barrister, 4 Hare court, Temple
Grove William, magistrate, Greenwich police court
Grove Wm. Timmins, who. dealer in sugar, 7 Arthur st. west
Grover Chas. confectioner, 13 Stafford rw. & 1 King's rw. Pmlc
Grover Charles, tobacconist, 7 Queen'srw. Stafford rw. Pimlico
Grover George, oilman, 34 Borough High st
Grover George, *Rose & Crown* P. H. Bromley, Middlesex
Grover Henry, wheelwright, 6 Abbey st. Bermondsey
Grover Humphrey, grocer & teadealer, 22 Cannon st
Grover Humphrey, whol. oil & colorman, 161 High Holborn
Grover John, corn chandler, 9 Sidney st. Mile end
Grover John, teadealer, 4 Up Southwick st. nth. Cambdg. ter
Grover John, timber bender, 3 Oxford pl. Westminster road
Grover John Thomas, solicitor, 50 Bedford row, Bloomsbury
Grover Joseph, poulterer, Leadenhall market
Grover Wm. fruit salesman, Fruit market, Covent garden
Grover Wm. grocer, Gibraltar row, Lower road, Deptford
Grover Wm. (Mrs.), clothes salesmn. 5 Thomas st. Oxford st
Grover Wm. grocer, 24 Richmond pl. East st. Walworth rd
Groves Hen.&Geo. mast & blockmks. 1 & 84 Bermondsey wall
Groves & Woolmore, seal & gem engravs. 55 Greek st. Soho
Groves Alfred, butcher, 5 Spring st. Paddington
Groves Edward, *Ship & Whale* P.H. Russell st. Lr. Rotherh
Groves Edw. tailor & clothier, 39 to 41 Lambeth Lwr. marsh
Groves George, baker, 41 Princess st. Lisson grove
Groves James, *Ship* P.H. 16 Tottenham pl. Tottenham ct. rd
Groves James, jun. attorney, 25 Charlotte st. Bedford sq
Groves John, saddler, &c. 58 Bishopsgate without
Groves John, saddler, 243 Blackfriars road
Groves Joseph, baker, 23 Molyneux st. Bryanstone sq
Groves Joseph, butcher, 154 Bishopsgate without
Groves Josiah, farrier, 37 Union st. Kingsland road
Groves Richard Henry, china dealer, &c. 33 Wharf rd. City rd
Groves Saml. tailor & trim. sel. 16 Up. York st. Bryanstone sq
Groves Thomas, butcher, 135 Brick lane, Spitalfields
Groves Thos. lightmn. grany kpr. & whfingr. East la. Bermdsy
Groves Wm. John, tobacconist, 4 Dispensary bdg. Union st
Groves Wm. Walter, hat&cap ma. 10 Panton st. Haymarket
Grubb Edward, barrister, 35 Lincoln's inn fields
Grubb Geo. E. purv. of asses' milk, 27 Kinnerton st. Blgr. sq
Grubb John Eustace, barrister, 19 Old sq. Lincoln's inn
Grubs Steph. teacher of languages, 33 Windmill st. Tott. ct. rd
Grubusch Christian, tailor, 12 Tavistock row, Covent garden
Gruby George, bookseller, 22 High road, Knightsbridge
Grueber Thomas, solicitor, see Dodd, Rowsell & Co.
Grugeon Isaac, corn dealer, 51 Kingsland road

Grumbridge George, linendraper, 99 St. George st
Grumbridge James, turner & stethoscope ma. 47 Poland st
Grummant Thomas, currier, 1 Villa place, Walworth common
Grundy Martha (Mrs.), milliner, 3 Cranbourne pas. Leicest. sq
Grundy Morris, saddlers' ironmonger, &c. see Horton & Grundy
Grundy Thos. bootmaker, 44 St. Martin's la. Charing cross
Grut Nicholas (actuary & secretary of the *Palladium Life Assurance Society*), 7 Waterloo place
Guanziroli Guiseppe & Luigi, artificial florists & plumassiers, importers of french flowers & looking-glass manufctrs. wholesale & for exportation, 106 Hatton garden
Guarantee Society (Thos. Dodgson, sec.), 19 Birchin lane; hours 9 to 4, see page 2028
Guardian Chimney Sweeping Association (Richard Russell, manager), 34 Foley place, Portland place
Guardian Society Asylum (John Gyse Sparks, surgeon, Mrs. Elizth. Dickins, matron), 12 Bethnal green
Guardian Fire & Life Assurance Company (Geo. Keys, sec.), 11 Lombard st. see page 2028
Guards' Club House (Thos. Robinson, sec.), 49 St. James's st
Guazzaroni John B. surgeon, 3 Terrace, Kensington
Gude Richard, jun. solicitor, 9 George yard, Lombard st
Gudge James, appraiser, 16 Denmark st. Pentonville
Gudgen Henry, oil and colorman, see Course & Gudgen
Gudgeon Edward, haberdasher, 113 Whitechapel road
Gudgeon Wm. undertaker, 4 Printing house lane, Blackfrs.
Guedalla Haim, merchant, North & South American Coffee ho
Guedalla Judah, merchant, 12 Finsbury square
Guedalla Moses, merchant, 2 Church court, Clement's la
Guernsey Railway & Pier Co. 11 Tokenhouse yard, City
Guerrier & Giblett, cattle salesmen, 8 West Smithfield
Guerrier Elias, meat salesman, 32 Newgate market
Guerrier Joseph, builder, see Pearse & Guerrier
Guerrier Luke, butcher, 4 Stepney High st
Guerrier Samuel, butcher, 39 Upper st. Islington
Guest Sir John & Co. iron merchants, 42 Lothbury
Guest John & Wm. gilt toy makers, Birmingham (agent George Lyndon, 49 Frith st. Soho)
Guest Edward, surgeon, 19 Whitehead's grove, Chelsea
Guest Edwin, barrister, 4 King's bench walk, Temple
Guest John, upholsterer, 29 Exmouth st. Spafields
Guest Joseph, carpenter, 6 Alfred pl. Holland pl. Kensngtn
Guest Joseph, chandler's shop, 140 Kingsland road
Guest Joseph Mason, teadealer & grocer, 218 Oxford st
Guest Sam. beer retailer, 1 Garden ct. Risbie's rope wlk. Lim
Guest Thomas, *Basing House* P.H. 172 Kingsland road
Gugeri Andrew, barometer, thermometer & looking-glass manufacturer, 16 Charles st. Hatton garden
Gugeri Felix, looking-glass mak. 5 Charles st. Hatton grdn
Gugeri Mary Ann (Mrs.), artif. florist, 24 Middle rw. Holborn
Guggiori & Butti, looking-glass manfrs. 13 Norton folgate
Guibert Joseph, goldsmith, 59 Hatton garden
Guichard Guillaume, french agt. 5 Cherry tree ct. Aldersgt
Guichard Lewis, watch finisher, 32 Whiskin st. Clerkenwell
Guichet Augustus, furniture brk. 1 Commer. pl. Com. rd. east
Guidott William, plumber, 23 East st. Walworth road
Guignard Albert, wine merchant, 25 Saville row, Piccadilly
Guignes Victor, *Hot. du Commerce*, 1 & 2 Lster. st. Lster. sq
Guildhall, Guildhall yd. King st. Cheapsi.; hrs. of bus. 9 to 5
Guildhall Justice room. Magistrates attend from 12 daily
Guilford Thos. *Grosvenor Arms* P.H. 2 Grovr. st. New Bond st
Guillan Mary Ann (Mrs.), baker, 64 Chiswell st. Finsbury
Guilland Ann (Mrs.), baker, 11 Gt. Wild st. Lincoln's inn flds
Guillaume Edward, attorney, 26 Bucklersbury
Guillaume George, watchmak. 16 Myddelton sq. Clerkenwell
Guillaume Jean, combmaker, 41 Gt. Castle st. Regent st
Guillaume Jean Joseph, foreign & english bookseller, & professeur des langues, 36 Elizabeth st. Eaton square
Guillaume Mary F. (Mrs.), milliner, 41 Gt. Castle st. Oxford st
Guilleaume Lion & Co. importers of foreign goods & commission agents, 1 Great Castle st. Regent st
Guillemard John, stockbroker, see Bates & Guillemard
Guillet James, carver & gilder, 42 Bedford pl. Kensington
Guillod Thomas, artist, 11 Cadogan st. Chelsea
Guimaraens Manoel Pedro, merchant, 42 Crutched friars
Guin Daniel, cooper, 7 North place, Kingsland road
Guinness Arthur, Son & Co. dublin porter stores (Sparks Moline, sole consignee), 5 Adelaide place, London bridge
Guinness Richard, teacher of music, 58 East st. Marylebone
Guire Wm. fruit salesman, Boro' mkt. & 4 Taunton pl. Dover rd
Guise Jos. gas fitter & brasswork. 75 Margaret st. Wilmng. sq
Guitard Arend Jacob, notary, &c. 26 Birchin lane, Cornhill
Guitard Chas. Frederick, merchant, see Kops & Co
Guitard Chas. Fredk. notary public, 26 Birchin la. Cornhill
Guiver William, *Pied Bull* P.H. Ring cross, Holloway rd
Gull George, russia broker, 74 Old Broad st. City, & Baltic

Gull Joseph Winney, ship & insurance broker, 4 Brabant ct. Philpot lane, & Baltic coffee house
Gull William Withey, physician, 28 King st. Borough
Gullen Alexander, baker, 220 Poplar High st
Gullett Thomas, carpenter, 10 Gower place, Euston square
Gullick Thomas, boot & shoe mak. 44 Warwick st. Golden sq
Gulliford John Banks, fruiterer, Centre row, Covent garden
Gullivan Patrick, skin dealer, 13 Barnham st. Tooley st
Gulliver Wm. Till, boat builder, 204 Wapping High st
Gully Geo. ladder & hurdle ma. 1 Cock & Castle la. Kingsland
Gumbleton Richard, grocer, 44 Grosvenor row, Pimlico
Gumbrell Peter, gun & ornamen. engraver, 4 Lit. Marlboro' st
Gumersall Hannah (Miss), stay ma. 66 Judd st. Brunswick sq
Gumm Chas. & Co. ship & insurance brokers, 4 King's Arms buildings, Change alley, Cornhill
Gumm John, surgical instrument ma. 7 Whitefriars st
Gummer Thos. *Founders' Arms* P.H. 1 Founders' hall ct. Lothb
Gummow William, smith & engineer, 9 Quickset rw. New rd
Gun & Shot Wharf, Emanuel Silva & Son, between 79 & 80 Tooley st
Gunby John, carpenter, 71 Great Saffron hill
Gundry Richard & Son, shoemakers to the Queen, 1 Soho sq
Gunn Ann (Mrs.), upholsterer, 15 Church st. Camberwell
Gunn Thomas Samuel & Thomas, gen. smiths & bellhangers, 24 Aldermanbury, & 41 Featherstone st. City road
Gunn Eliz. (Mrs.), *Marlboro' Head* P.H. 33 Gt. Marlboro' st
Gunn Geo. tobacconist & newsvend. 28 Mount st. Lambeth
Gunn Isaac, baker, 43 Penny fields, Poplar
Gunn Joseph, butcher, 3 Walker's court, Golden square, & 3 Charles st. Hampstead road
Gunn Thomas, cowkeeper, Hornton st. Kennington
Gunn Thomas, engraver, 7 Green st. Theobald's road
Gunn Volney, america merchant, 28 Noble st
Gunner George, *Old Globe* P.H. 1 Road side, Mile end rd
Gunner George, *Red Lion* P.H. 11 Up. Queen's bldgs. Brompt
Gunner John, lighterman & shipping agent to her Majesty's stationery office, Tower whf. stairs, & 5 Crescent, Minories
Gunner John, wheelwright, 135 Wapping High st
Gunner John, working cutler, 129 Church st. Shoreditch
Gunner Thomas, barrister, 2 Stone buildings, Lincoln's inn
Gunner Thomas, wheelwright, Russell st. Dockhead
Gunner William, dyer, 2 Church la. Kensington gravel pits
Gunning & Quarrell, linenfactors, 25 Gresham st
Gunning Geo. & John, linendraps. 31 Crosby row, Walworth rd
Gunning Alexander T. surgeon 20 New Church st. Lisson gr
Gunning Frederic, barrister, 17 Serjeants' inn, Fleet st
Gunning John, furn. dealr. 6 & 7 St. James' pl. Walworth com
Gunning James, tobacconist, 1 Albert place, City road
Gunning Jsph. W. solicitor & secretary, St. George's hospital
Gunning Thos. Wyatt, barrister, 36 Lincoln's inn fields
Gunnis & Crighton, warehousemen, 28 Milk st. Cheapside
Gunnis Lake Mines (Geo. Wm. Harrison, sec.), 51 Old Broad st
Gunnis Francis, merchant, 11 York place, City road
Gunnis James, woollen warehouseman, 8 Hart st. Cripplegate
Gunnis Elizth. (Miss), drawn bonnet ma. 107 York rd. Lmbth
Gunson Henry, bookslr. statnr. & paperhngr. Stratford, Essex
Gunston John, fruiterer, 32 Featherstone st. City road
Gunston Daniel & Son, cheesemongers, 84 Upper st. Islington, & 110 Goswell st
Gunston Michael, cheesemngr. 31 Featherstone st. City rd
Gunston Michael, optical instrument maker, & Daffy's elixir warehouse, 6 St. James's walk, & 14 Woodbridge st. Clkwl
Gunston Robt. porkman, 28 Liquorpond st. Gray's inn lane
Gunston Robt. sen. porkman, 21 Mount row, Liverpool rd
Gunston Wm. cheesemonger, 38 Exmouth st. Spafields
Gunter Thomas & Co. confectioners, 7 & 8 Berkeley square
Gunter Henry, turtle importer, St. Peter's chmbrs. Cornhill
Gunter Richard, confectioner, 23 Motcomb st. & 15 Lowndes st. Belgrave square
Gunther Henry, pianoforte maker, 7 High st. Camden town
Gunthorpe Geo. John, surgeon, 51 Newington pl. Kenngtn. rd
Gunton & Co. var. & col. ma. Nw. Weston st. St. Thomas' st. Boro'
Gunton & Co. who. druggs. N. Weston st. St. Thomas' st. Boro'
Gunton Dennis, turn. & bird stffr. 10 Anderson's blds. City rd
Gunton Rd. linendraper, silk mer. &c. 25½ Lamb's Conduit st
Gunton Thos. Luther, oilman, 3 Church st. Mile end New twn
Guppy Thomas R. civil & marine engineer, 5 White Lion ct. Cornhill, & Great Western iron ship building & engine work, Bristol
Gurdon William, barrister, 11 Crown office row, Temple
Gurnell Benjamin, greengrocer, 35 Portland st. Soho
Gurner Henry P. wholesale teadealer, 5 Carthusian st
Gurner John, stationer, 9 Wigmore st. Cavendish sq
Gurnett Geo. leather seller, 26 Gt. James st. Lisson grove north
Gurney Joseph & Co. tailors, 56 St. James's st
Gurney & Barton, oil & colormen, 2 Davies st. Berkeley sq
Gurney Geo. & Co. *Red Lion* P.H. Camberwell gate, Walth. rd
Gurney John & Co. brewers, Lambeth walk
Gurney Wm. B. & Sons, shorthand wrs. 26 Abingdon st. Westmr
Gurney & White, oil & colormen, 1 Oakley terrace, Old Kent road, & at Paddington
Gurney Alfred, *Apollo* P.H. 28 Paddington st. Marylebone
Gurney Alfred, wine merchant, 19 Hedge row, Islington
Gurney Arthur, *Two Brewers* P.H. 58 Goswell st
Gurney Arthur, *Brill* P.H. 1 Brewers st Somers town
Gurney Arthur, wine & spirit merchant, 39 High Holborn
Gurney Cath. (Mrs.), *Coachmakers' Arms* P.H. 24 Marylb
Gurney Charles, shorthand writer & translator, Hall of Commerce, Threadneedle st
Gurney Charles, *White Hart* P.H. 1 Mile end road
Gurney Daniel, cattle salesman, 15 West Smithfield
Gurney Daniel, *Northampton Arms* P.H. 24 Goswell road
Gurney Fredk. Kingston, engraver, 6 Blenheim st. Bond st
Gurney George, furniture broker, 24 Old st. St. Luke's
Gurney George, *Masons' Arms* P.H. 51 Upper Berkeley st
Gurney George, *Ship* P.H. 1 Wormwood st. Bishopsgate
Gurney Henry, timber merchant, see Nash & Gurney
Gurney Henry, *Crosby's Head* P.H. 38 Pitfield st. Hoxton
Gurney James, *Hoop & Grapes* P.H. 80 Farringdon st
Gurney Jas. *Mackworth Arms* P.H. 9 Princes pl. Coml. rd. east
Gurney Jason, cattle salesman, 15 West Smithfield
Gurney John, carpenter, Uxbridge road, Bayswater
Gurney John, *City of Hereford* P.H. 10 Charles st. Portman sq
Gurney John, *Oakley Arms* P.H. 27 Oakley st. Mount st. Lmbth
Gurney John, potato salesman, South row, Covent gar. mkt
Gurney Richard, *White Horse* P.H. 8 Little Britain
Gurney Russell, queen's counsel, 2 Inner Temple lane
Gurney Samuel, bill broker, see Overend, Gurney & Co
Gurney Sidney, barrister, 34 Lincoln's inn fields, & 6 Portugal st
Gurney Thomas, baker, &c. 69 Park st. Grosvenor square
Gurney Thomas, butcher, 100 Jermyn st. St. James's
Gurney Thomas Wilshin, oilman, 50 High st. Portland town, & 133 Edgware road, Marylebone
Gurney Warwick Oben, *Britannia tavern*, 33 Little Britain, & 42 Duke st. Smithfield
Gurney Wm. *Coffee House* P.H. 32 Chalton st. Somers town
Gurney William Mollett, stationer, High st. Kingsland
Gurr Charles, linendraper, 3 Norfolk pl. Lower rd. Islington
Gurr Edward, butcher, 8 Little Bath st. Clerkenwell
Gurr Thomas, grocer, 57 Great Hunter st. Dover road
Gurrier Wm. meat salesman, 6 Warwick lane, Newgate st
Gurtice Richard, tailor, 7 Belvoir ter. Vauxhall bridge road
Gushlow Geo. furniture japan. 6 Southampton st. Camberwell
Gustard George Edward, solicitor, 3 Lincoln's inn fields
Gutch George, architect, Bridge house, Harrow road
Gutch John Josh. Wm. pin, needle, &c. ma. see Hall & Gutch
Guthery Thomas D. smith & farrier, 80 New road, Sloane st
Guthrie Alex. printer, 3 Cross ct. Russell ct. Drury lane
Guthrie Alexander, tailor, 54 New Bond st
Guthrie Andrew Wm. writer & grainer, 101 Aldersgate st
Guthrie David Chas. mercht. see Chalmers, Guthrie & Co
Guthrie Elizth (Mrs.), dress ma. 18 Alfred pl. Newington cau
Guthrie George, newspaper agent, 2 Old Jewry
Guthrie George James, surgeon, 4 Berkeley st. Berkeley sq
Guthrie James, baker, 3 Hanover place, Regent's park road, & 4 Blenheim terrace, St. John's wood
Guthrie James, teadealer, 17 Three colt street, Limehouse
Guthrie Phœbe (Mrs.) ladies' school, 34 Earl st. west. Lissn. gr
Guthrie Robert, tailor, see Anstey, Le Gassic & Guthrie
Gutsell & Venis, grocers & cheesemngrs. 32 & 33 Lr. Sloane st
Gutteres Geo. solicitor, see Gilbert, Hooke, Street & Gutteres
Gutteridge James, cooper, 13 Jacob's st. Dockhead
Gutteridge Rachel (Mrs.), fruiterer, 21 Park st. Dorset sq
Gutteridge Thos. merchant, 6 Barge yard, Bucklersbury
Gutteridge Thos. *Prince George* P.H. 16 Up. Albany st. Rgts. pk
Guttridge George, butcher, 7 Gun lane, Limehouse
Guy & Adams, stockbrokers, 5 Change alley, Cornhill
Guy Cornelius, corndealer, 120 Regent st. Lambeth
Guy Edward, jun. watchmaker, 14 Wynyatt st. Goswell rd
Guy Edward, sen. watchmaker, 4 Rahere st. Goswell road
Guy Frederick, fruiterer, 44 Duke st. St. James's
Guy George, boot & shoe maker, 42 Trinity st. Pentonville
Guy George, ironmonger, see Court & Guy
Guy Germain (Mrs.), dress maker, 47 Davies st. Berkeley sq
Guy Henry, surgeon & chemist, 21 Dorset place, Dorset sq
Guy James, saddler & harness ma. 9 Spring st. Crawford st
Guy John, ormolu frame maker, 29 Myddelton st. Clerknwl
Guy John, solicitor, see Addis & Guy
Guy John, surgeon, 30 Bury st. St. James's
Guy Joseph, builder, 20 Vauxhall row, Vauxhall
Guy Mary (Mrs.), milliner, 31 Ludgate hill
Guy Mary (Miss), milliner, &c. 59 Farringdon st

Guy Mary (Mrs.), seedsman & florist, 26 St. John's wood rd
Guy William Augustus, physician, 15 Bloomsbury square
Guyatt John, livery stables, 1 Hannibal rd. Stepney green
Guyaz Rodolph, swiss dairy, 22 Green st. Leicester square
Guyer John, teadealer, 16 Bear lane, Blackfriars
Guynan John, window blind maker, 67 Wells st. Oxford st
Guy's Hospital, between 9 & 11 St. Thomas's street, Boro'
Guyuse Franklin, painter, 3 Bridge st. Southwark
Gwatkin Frederick, solicitor, see Smith, Hunter & Gwatkin
Gwillam John, lodging house, 2 Gt. College st. Westminster
Gwilliams Sam. gardener&nurseryman, 1 Richmond rd. Dlstn
Gwillim Henry, teadealer & grocer, 316 Strand
Gwillim Thos. furntr. broker, 6 Green arbour ct. Old Bailey
Gwilt Joseph & John S. architects, 20 Abingdon st. Westmnr
Gwilt George, architect, 8 Union st. Borough
Gwitham Henry, pastrycook, 197 Church st. Shoreditch
Gwynn Chas. M. linendrap.&house agt. 34½ Comptonst. Clknwl
Gwynn Francis, bootmaker, 1 Crescent st. Euston sq
Gwynn Robert, shoemaker, 43 Union st. Clarendon square
Gwynn William, sailmaker, Pageant stairs, Rotherhithe st
Gwynn Wm. coal dealer, 2 Crispin st. Spitalfields
Gwynn Wm. Chas. bootmaker, 5 Little Turnstile, Holborn
Gwynn Wm. Jas. *Duke of York* P.H. 29 Shadwell High st
Gwynne Robert, fruiterer, 4 Upsdells row, Kingsland rd
Gwynne Sampson, solicitor, Temple chambs. 126 Chancery la
Gwyther John, tailor & draper, 23 Featherstone bldgs. Holbn
Gyde Charles, bookbinder, 8 Red Lion court, Fleet st
Gyde Joseph, engineer, 2 Dutton st. Cromer st
Gyde Wm. engraver & printer, 34 Dean st. Soho
Gyde William, grocer, 96 Cromer st. Brunswick square
Gyde William, jun. grocer, 34 Edmund st. King's cross
Gye Frederick, oil merchant, see Patrick & Gye
Gyett Joseph, *King & Prince of Wales* P.H. 1 Brick st. Park la
Gyfford Samuel, stationer & bookseller, 35 Great Tower st
Gyles Emma & Sarah, seminary, 44 Cross st. Islington
Gyles Daniel, baker, 185 Blackfriars road
Gyles John, surveyor, 16 Regent st. City road
Gyllenship Eliza M. (Mrs.), haberdash. 32 Crosbyrow, Wlwth. rd
Gypp Wm. fruiterer, 4 Trafalgar pl. Walworth com
Gypson Wm. tailor & robe ma. 19 Featherstone bldgs. Holborn

HAACKE Henry, baker, 93 Leonard st. Finsbury
Haarnack Henry, coffee rooms, 50 Newman st
Haase Wm. coach trimmer, 50 Gt. Titchfield st. Oxford st
Habbijam Henry, beer retailer, 1 Cross st. Newington butts
Habbijams George, livery stables, 9½ Newman st. Oxford st
Habell Fred. gold dial finisher, 17 Low. Smith st. Northmptn. sq
Habell John Henry, tailor, 18 Great Pulteney st. Golden sq
Habell Mary (Mrs.), lodging house, 2 Park st. Grosvenor sq
Haberdashers' Alms Houses, Haberdashers' walk, Hoxton
Haberdashers' Foundation Sc. (Geo. Norton, mas.), Bunhillrw
Haberdshrs.' Hall (Wm. N. Beechey, clk.), 8 Gresham st. City
Haberfield Thomas, tailor, 15 Frederick st. Westminster
Habgood Thomas, oil & colorman, 5 Cable st. Wellclose sq
Hachtel John Geo. pork butcher, 13 Nelson pl. Old Kent rd
Hack Eliza R. (Miss), profes. of music, 9 Portland rw. Cambrwl
Hack Elizabeth (Mrs.), fruiterer, 5 Chadwell st. St. John st. rd
Hack Hen. Isaac, pork butcher, 188 Church st. Shoreditch
Hack Richard, fruiterer, 28 Paradise row, Chelsea
Hack Robert, music & musical instrument seller, 174 Fleet st. & 9 Portland road, Camberwell road
Hack Robert, music seller, 174 Fleet st
Hack Robert, music wa. 9 Portland row, Camberwell road
Hack Sarah (Mrs.), milliner, 14 Church st. Soho
Hack William, carpenter, 7 White horse lane, Stepney green
Hackblocks', Clark & Meek, tanners, curriers & leather merchants, Willow walk, Bermondsey
Hacker & Clarkson, tanners, curriers & enamelled leather manufacturers, 7 Church st. Bermondsey
Hacker Ann (Mrs.), dining rooms, 24 Commercial rd. Lambeth
Hacker Edmund Dennis, plumber, 51 Tooley st. Boro'
Hacker Edward, registrar, 1 Moreton villas, Kentish twn. rd
Hacker Elihu, mercht. Jamaica cof. ho. St. Michael's al. Cornh.
Hacker Thomas, ladies' shoemaker, 9 Charlotte st. Fitzroy sq
Hacker Wm. bookselr. & statnr. 53 Margaret st. Wilmington sq
Hacket Charles Andrew, agent & insur. broker, 26 Birchin lane
Hacket Thomas, merchant, 26 Birchin lane
Hackett John & Son, small ware mnfrs. 38 Noble st. Cheapside
Hackett Charles Henry, ship & insurance broker, & insurance & commercial agent, 8 Savage gardens
Hacker James, hatter, 30 Crosby row, Walworth road
Hackett James Thomas, civil engineer, 52 Theobald's road
Hackett Richard Merchant, cabinetma. & upholst. 137 Minories
Hackett Richard M. merchant, 137 Minories
Hackett Sam. baker & pastrycook, 5 Orange st. Red Lion sq
Hackett Wm. linendraper, 5 Black Prince row, Walworth rd
Hackett Wm. marine store dealer, 9 Crown st. Soho
Hackforth Matthew, plumber, 100 Norton st. Portland pl
Hacking Wm. ironmonger, 3 Prospect pl. Cheyne wk. Chelsea
Hackney Carriage Office, 6 Adelphi terrace; 10 to 4
Hackney Parish stoneyard, Hertford rd. Kingsland rd
Hackney Joseph, shoemaker, 42 James st. Oxford st
Hackney Mary Ann (Mrs.), tailor, 12 Printinghouse lane
Hackney Robert, grocer, &c. 8 Cambridge rd. Mile end rd
Hacon Wm. Mackmurdo, solicitor, see Rowland & Hacon
Hackwell Jas. cut glass dlr. 5 Tavistock st. Covent garden
Hackwell John, *Blue Boar* P.H. 55 Aldersgate st
Hackwith John, glasscutter, 32 Wellington mews, Golden sq
Hackwood Wm. Hen. & Co. ship bldrs. King & Queendk. 224 Roth
Haddan Henry, grocer, Denmark hill, Camberwell
Haddan Thomas Henry, barrister. 6 New sq. Lincoln's inn
Hadden Alexander & Sons, worsted spinners, hosiers & carpet manufacturers, 2 Oat lane, Wood st.; & at Aberdeen
Hadden Geo. & Jas. Alex. merchants, 2 King st. Cheapside
Hadden Alex. mercht. & manuf. 12 Pancras la. Bucklrsbury
Hadden Geo. Ernest, architect & surveyor, 8 Furnival's inn, Holborn, & 35 King st. City
Hadden John, civil engineer, 29 Liverpool st. King's cross
Hadden Thomas, baker, 15 Bridge st. Southwark
Hadden Thomas, harness maker, New cross
Haddock George, iron plate worker, 4 Park pl. Walworth
Haddock George Wm. academy, 115 Britannia st. City rd
Haddock Hen. stationer & acct. book maker, 103 Boro' Highst
Haddock Wm. rope & bed sack maker, 42 Oakley st. Lambeth
Haddon James, clothier, 9 King st. Camden town
Haddon John, printer, 24 Castle st. City road
Haddow George, tailor, 12 Cloth fair, West Smithfield
Haddow Joseph, umbrella maker, 57 Leman st. Gdmn's. fields
Hadfield Geo. & Co. varnish & color manf. 25 A, Queen st. City
Hadfield Thos. R. & Joseph R. chemists, &c. 326 High Holborn
Hadfield Thomas, hat & bonnet mfr. 9 Edward st. Blkfrs. rd
Hadingham Mary (Mrs.) & Thos. saddlers, 35 Hosier la. Smfld
Hadkin John (Mrs.), milliner, 92 New Bond st
Hadkiss Thos. file & rasp cutter, 164 Brick la. Spitalfields
Hadgley Edward Richard, *Red Lion* P.H. 5 Wilsonst. Finsbury
Hadland, Shillingford & Esam, manchester warehousemen, 115 & 116 Cheapside
Hadland Henry, cheesemonger, 34 Holborn hill
Hadland James, butcher, 62 Whitechapel road
Hadland John Thos. law & genl. stat. 90 Queen st. City
Hadley Augustus, merchant & agent, 8 Old Jewry
Hadley George, smith, &c. 3 Skinner st. Bishopsgate
Hadley John, baker, 3 Star corner, Bermondsey st
Hadley Nathaniel Layton, solicitor, 8 Gresham st. Wood st
Hadley Thomas, *Queen's Arms* P.H. 28 St. Martin's le grand
Hadlow Henry, surgeon, 32 Jewry st. Aldgate
Hadlow James, greengrocer, Camberwell green
Hadlow Sam. J. governmt. security dealer, Hall of Commerce
Hadlow William, pork butcher, 32 Barbican
Hadnutt George, hosier, &c. 70 Lower marsh, Lambeth
Hadnutt Geo. millinery wareh. 2 Wentworth pl. Mile end
Hadnutt James, antique furniture dlr. 122 Wardour st. Soho
Hadnutt Wm. builder, 5 William st. Lambeth lower marsh
Hadow James E. sworn broker & agent, see Forman & Hadow
Hadow Patrick D. barrister, 5 Essex court, Temple
Hadrell John, *Dolphin* P.H. 44 Red Lion st. Holborn
Hadwen Rd. Sparling, solicitor, 30 George st. Camberwell
Haedy Christr. attorney, Bedford off. Montague st. Blmsbry
Haes & Sons, exchange & stock brokers, 15 Throgmorton st
Haeskell Charles John, tailor, 125 New Bond st
Haffenden John, Son & Co. merchants, 4 Coleman st. bldgs
Haffenden George, milkman, 79 Charlotte st. Portland pl
Hagan Stephen, corset maker, 16 Woodstock st. Oxford st
Hagen Edwd. & Co. sugar refiners, 11 Lit. Alie st. Goodman's fi
Hagen Jacob & Son, merchts. Mill st. Dockhead, Bermondsey
Hagenmeyer Adam, *Horse & Trumpeter* P.H. 1 Crutched frs
Haggard John, D.C.L. advocate, 4 College, Doctors' commns
Haggard John, potato dealer, 64 St. John st. Clerkenwell
Haggart William Henry, wine merchant, 20 Mincing lane
Hagger Henry & Jas. fringe ma. 90 Charlotte st. Fitzroy sq
Hagger Edward, fringe & trimming maker, 178 Oxford st
Hagger Edward, italian wa. 22 Lamb's Conduit st. Foundling
Hagger John, baker, 60 Compton st. Clerkenwell
Hagger John, fringe maker, 15 Southampton row, Russell sq
Hagger Thomas, coffee rooms, 49 Whitcomb st. Haymarket
Haggerstone Savings' Bank (T. L. Burract), 77 Hackney rd
Haggett William, pork butcher, 76 Paradise row, Chelsea
Haghe Louis, lithographer, see Day & Haghe
Hagley Thomas, carpenter, 2 Hatfield pl. & Westminster rd
Hagmaier Anthony, pork butcher, 64 St. George's st
Hagmaier Lewis, pork butcher, 11 Road side, Mile end rd
Hague Hannah (Mrs.), grocer, 4 St. George's rd. Southwark

Hague Sarah (Mrs.), stationer, 8 Newland ter. Kensington
Hague Thomas, architect, &c. 12 King's road, Bedford row
Haig James, barrister, 1 Stone buildings, Lincoln's inn
Haig John, pianoforte mfr. 1 Walworth pl. Walworth rd
Haigh Wm. & Co. wholesale shirt manuf. 9 Huggin lane, Wood street
Haigh Abrhm. hosier, 12 Up. Wellington st. Covent garden
Haigh Francis, leech dealer, 36 St. John st. road
Haigh George, beer retlr. 11 Mount pleasant, Gray's inn la
Haigh George, saddler, 7 Portman place, Edgware road
Haigh Henry, tailors' trimming seller, 79 Drury lane
Haigh Sarah Martha (Mrs.), baker, 9 Spring gdn. pl. Stepney
Haigh William, corkcutter, 14 Church la. Commercial road
Haigh William, merchant, 6 Crosby square, Bishopsgate
Haigh William, warehouseman, 2 New court, Bow lane
Haigs Robert, tobacconist, 10 Crucifix lane, Bermondsey
Haile James, fruiterer, 1 Gresse st. Tottenham court road
Hailes James C. stationer & fancy repos. 27 Leadenhall st
Hailes Nathaniel, bookseller, stationer & juvenile library, 1 William st. Knightsbridge
Hailey Geo. herbalist & leech imp. see Potter & Hailey
Hailing John, tobacconist, 20 Harcourt st. New road
Hailstone Robert, man's mercer, see Lewin & Hailstone
Haime Ann (Mrs.), egg merchant, 8 Borough market
Hain Chas. grocer & cheesemongr. 22 High st. Portland tn
Haines Abm. & Son, who. cheesemongrs. 52 Halfmoon st. City
Haines Edw. W. & Saml. attorneys, 21 Montague st. Russell sq
Haines & Jennings, undertakers, &c. 61 Fore st. City
Haines Alfred, breeches maker, see Gobby, Haines & French
Haines Alfred, wine merchant, see Barnes & Haines
Haines Chas. marine store dlr. 17 Star corner, Bermondsey
Haines Daniel, dairyman, 13 Bury st. Bloomsbury
Haines Elizabeth (Mrs.), corndealer, 5 Clifton st. Finsbury
Haines Geo. auctioneer & estate agt. 7 Park side, Knightsbr. & 9 Grosvenor row, Pimlico
Haines George, bookseller, &c. 8 Rose st. Covent garden
Haines Geo. cheesemonger, 26 Goodge st. Tottenham ct. rd
Haines George, *Mortimer Arms* P.H. 174 Tottenham ct. rd
Haines George, tailor, 8 Great Dover st. Borough
Haines Henry, appraiser, auctioneer, &c. 38 Moorgate st. & 61 Fore st. Cripplegate
Haines Henry, auctioneer, &c. 38 Moorgate st. City
Haines Henry John, silk broker, see Grelliers' & Haines
Haines John, bootmaker, 8 Thornton st. Horselydown
Haines John, dyer, &c. 17 Little Dean st. Soho
Haines John, oil & color & italian warehouse, 22 Lime st
Haines John, *Portman Arms* P.H. 9 Milton st. Dorset sq
Haines John, wine & brandy, &c. mercht. 12 High st. Kensington
Haines Rd. fruiterer, 2 Ship tavern pas. Leadenhall market
Haines Richard, poulterer, 51 New Bond st
Haines Samuel, tailor & draper, 11 High st. Kensington
Haines Sarah (Mrs.), dining rms. 23 Glo'ster ter. Vaux. bdg. rd
Haines Thomas, butcher, 30 Grosvenor row, Pimlico
Haines Walter, butcher, Mare st. Hackney
Haines Wm. biscuit baker, 8 Brick la. Spitalfields
Haines Wm. stationer & news agent, 24 Fetter lane, Fleet st
Hains Henry, curiosity dealer, 1 Robin Hood lane, Poplar
Hains Jane (Miss), milliner, 65 New Bond st
Hains John, butcher, 29 East st. Walworth road
Hains Joshua, butcher, 6 Thornton st. Dockhead
Hains Thomas, butcher, 48 Bermondsey square
Hainstock John, brewer, 4 Tabernacle square, Finsbury
Hainsworth Isaac, *Rose & French Horn* P.H. 58 Wood st City
Hair Powder Office, Stamp Office, Somerset house; hours 10 to 4
Hair George Bush, watch & clock ma. 129 Borough High st
Hair Quintin B. surgeon dentist, 288 Regent st
Hairby Wm. surgeon, 6 Marlborough place, Walworth road
Hairfield Joseph, coffee rooms, 16 Fore st. Limehouse
Hairs George, commission agent, see Webber & Hairs
Haite John Jas. musical instr. slr. 79 Leadenhall st
Hake Wm. Augustus G. barrister, 5 Crown office row, Temple
Hakes William, *Hake's hotel,* 8 Manchester square
Hakewill Edward Chas. architect, 8 Craig's ct. Charing cr
Hakewill John Henry, architect, 8 Craig's ct. Charing cr
Halcombe John, serjeant at law, 3 Serjeants' inn, Chancery l
Haldane Alexander, barrister, 4 Carey st. Lincoln's inn
Haldane George, barrister, 6 Stone buildings, Lincoln's inn
Haldane John, tailor, 18 Old Burlington st
Halden John, shawl manufacturer, 6 Bread st
Halden Mary (Mrs.), fruiterer, 9 Mason's al. Basinghall st
Haldren Joshua (agent to R. Turner & Co.), flannel manufacturers, 3 Sambrook court, Basinghall st
Hale, Boys & Austen, attorneys, 5 & 6 Ely place, Holborn
Hale (Ford) & Sons, wax & tallowchandlers, 7 Cannon st
Hale Lucy & Eliza, ladies' shoema. 1 Charlotte st. Bedford sq
Hale James & William, grocers, 35 Exmouth st. Clerkenwell, & 82 St. John st. Clerkenwell
Hale & Pope, coach ma. 80 Margaret st. Cavendish sq
Hale Chas. tailor & draper, 44 Middleton st. St. John st rd
Hale Edward, *Duke of Wellington* P.H. Wells st. East india rd
Hale Frederick Wm. hairdresser, 87 Fetter lane, Holborn
Hale George, bootmaker, 13 Tavistock st. Covent garden
Hale George, Wheatsheaf brewery, 9 to 12 Redcross st. Crip
Hale George Thos. grocer, 27 Lambeth st. Little Alie st
Hale Henry, grocer, 24 Clifton st. Finsbury
Hale Henry, furniture wareho. 79 Westminster bridge road
Hale Jas. bedding manfr. 12 Green Dragon yd. High Holborn
Hale James, bootmaker, High st. Bow, Middlesex
Hale James, boot & shoe maker, 12 Church st. Stoke Nwgtn
Hale James (Mrs.), court milliner, 261 Regent st
Hale James, law writer, 63 Carey st. Lincoln's inn
Hale Jas. watch motion ma. 17 President st. east, Goswell rd
Hale John, leather cutter, 16 Wood st. Westminster
Hale John, watch motion maker, 22 Galway st. St. Luke's
Hale John, whiting manuf. St. Ann's place, Limehouse
Hale John Richard Westgarth, barrister, 23 Chancery lane
Hale John Wm. average stater, Lloyd's, & 1 White Lion ct. Crnh
Hale Joseph, cheesemonger, 152 Bermondsey st.
Hale Joseph, cheesemonger, 147 Bethnal green road
Hale Marcus, tobacconist, 36 Gresse st. Tottenham ct. rd
Hale Mary Elizabeth (Mrs.), butcher, 80 Gt. Tower st. City
Hale Richard, beer retailer, Little Chelsea
Hale Robert, ale rooms, 32 Norton Folgate
Hale Robert, *Duke of Sussex* P.H. Thrawl st. Brick lane
Hale Rt. John, stationer, 6 Tavistock row, Covent garden
Hale Saline (Mrs.), tobacconist, 91 Berwick st. Soho
Hale Samuel, boot & shoe maker, 31 Clipstone st. Fitzroy sq
Hale Samuel Edward Peacock, oilman, see Fenning & Hale
Hale Stephen, *Waterloo hotel,* see Hanwell & Hale
Hale Thos. brass & metal founder, Pleasant pl. & 29 Broadwall
Hale Thos. carpenter, &c. 58 Southampton st. Pentonville
Hale Thomas, leather cutter, 29 Lambeth walk
Hale Warren Stormes, imp. wax, pat. sperm composite & tallow candle manfr. 21 Gresham st. & 34 Orange st. Southwark
Hale William, dairyman, 14 Southampton st. Fitzroy sq
Hale Wm. soda water, &c. ma. 56 Chandos st. Covent. grdn
Hales John & Co. ale & stout mers. 84 Lower Thames st. & Pudding lane
Hales Henrietta (Mrs.), grocer, &c. 8 Back Church lane
Hales James, appraiser & broker, 90 Gray's inn lane
Hales John, fishmonger, 67 Fetter lane
Hales Joseph, butcher, 102 Crawford st. Portman square
Hales Matthew, pilot, 2 King's terrace, Commercial rd. ea
Hales Thos. brass & copper wire drawer, 117 Fenchurch st
Hales Thomas, fruiterer, 2 Seymour place, Camden town
Hales Wm. boot & shoe maker, 35 Chalton st. Somers tn
Hales Wm. fruiterer, 1 Carthusian st. Charterhouse square
Hales Wm. Jones, appraiser & bro. 29 Gt. St. Andrew st. 7 Dials
Haley James, *Bell & Griffin* P.H. Boss st. Horselydown
Haley Maria (Mrs.), potato dlr. South row, Coventgar. mkt
Halfacre George, corn dealer, 65 New Church st. Lisson gr
Halfhead Robert, cowkeeper, 24 Worship st. Finsbury
Halfhide George, seal engraver, &c. 7 Coventry st
Halfhide Thomas, smith & bellhanger, 231 Upper Thames st
Halfman James, stationer, 6 Quickset row, New road
Halford & Co. navy agents, 41 Norfolk st. Strand
Halford Edward, surgeon, 1 City road, Finsbury square
Halford Henry, jun. butcher, 21 Lower st. Islington
Halford Henry, sen. butcher, 6 Norfolk pl. Low. rd. Islingtn
Halford James, baker, 14 Down st. Piccadilly
Halford John, hatter, 104 St. John st. West Smithfield
Halford John, tailor, 4A, Little Sussex pl. Hyde park
Halford Wm. auctioneer & fur. broker, Church st. Hackney
Halfpenny Joseph, *Bell* P.H. 8 Lit. Titchfield st. Portland pl
Halfpenny Thos. carpenter, &c. 26 St. Ann's ct. Dean st. Soho
Halfpenny William, *Queen's Landing* P.H. 5 Wapping wall
Halfpenny William, upholsterer, 70 Paul st. Finsbury
Haliday Wm. Robt. operative chemist, 37 Leadenhall st
Halifax Wm. *Two Brewers* P.H. 15 Queen's bdgs. Kntsbdge
Halket David, ins. broker, ship & gen. agent, 19 St. Helen's pl
Halksworth Wm. watchmaker, jeweller & engraver, 58 Fleet st
Hall of Information (George Poole, sec.), 8 Fore st. City
Hall & Allan, linendrapers, &c. 69, 70 & 71 St. Paul's churchyd
Hall Benjamin & Son, saddlers, 15 Down st. Piccadilly
Hall & Boyd, sugar refiners, Breezer's hill, St. George's st
Hall Brothers, hat manufactrs. & furriers, 130 London wall
Hall Brothers, merchants & ship broks. 2 Riches ct. Lime st
Hall & Davidson, flour fact. & millers, 16 Langbourn chbs
Hall George & Son, linendrapers, 69 Bishopsgate without
Hall & Gutch, manufacturers of pins, needles & fish hooks, &c. 50 King William st. City, & Gloucester

Hall & Hack, printcutters, 4 Gloucester ter. Old Brompton
Hall Hen.&Cheslyn, solicitors, 16 New Boswell ct. Linc. inn
Hall Henry & Co. hairdressers,&c. 5 Halkin ter.Belgrave sq
Hall Henry & Co. merchants, 147 Leadenhall st
Hall Henry & Co. ship brokers & general agents, 147 Leadenhall st. & Baltic coffee house
Hall Hen. John & Co.merchts.& ship bro.2 Riches ct.Lime st
Hall James T. & Co. sailma. ship chandlers & gen. shipping ironmngrs.17Fore st.Limehouse,lateFairlie, Bonhams'&Co
Hall John & Co. foreign agents, 15 Adam st. Adelphi
Hall John & Co. tea & coffee merchants, 7 George st. Minories
Hall John & Edward, engineers, millwrights & founders, manufactory, Dartford ; office, 23 Lombard st
Hall John & Samuel, hosiers & outfitters, 3 Leadenhall st
Hall John & Son, gunpowder manufacturers, 23 Lombard st
Hall John & Son, trunk case&box ma. undertaks.31Bow lane
Hall Matthew & Co. pannus corium or leather cloth easy boots & shoes for tender feet, also the supporting elastic ankle boots, india rubber goloshes, & portable waterproof dresses for ladies and gentlemen, which can be carried in the pocket, 14 Wellington st. south, Strand
Hall & Mourilyan, attorneys, 2 Verulam bldgs. Gray's inn
Hall & Son, ship & insurance brokers, 6 Circus, Minories
Hall ThomasS.&Wm. J.packers&agts.24Red Lion st. Spitalfi
Hall William John & Co. wharfingers & warehouse keepers, Customhouse & Wool quays, Lower Thames st
Hall of Commerce (Chas.Jas.Ellis, sec.), 62 Threadneedle st
Hall Alexander, wine & spirit merchant, 28 St. Martin's lane
Hall Alfred, linendraper, 29 Princes st. Soho sq
Hall Alfred, solicitor, see Skilbeck & Hall
Hall AmbroseRt. *D. of Clarence* P.H.Cumberld.st.Hckny.rd
Hall Amos plumber, painter, &c. 33 John st. Fitzroy sq
Hall Anne (Miss), grocer, 13 Cornwall cres. CamdenNew tn
Hall Arabella (Mrs.), ladies' shoemaker, 55 Wigmore st
Hall Archibald, baker, 74 Coleshill st. Pimlico
Hall Barton Parkinson, solicitor, 2 & 3 Kensington square
Hall Benj. coffee roaster, 13 King st. Commercial rd. east
Hall Benjamin, cowkeeper, Elm lane, Bayswater
Hall Catherine (Mrs.), millinery wa. 11 Cranbourne st. L. sq
Hall Charles, barrister, 4 Stone buildings, Lincoln's inn
Hall Charles, butcher, 2 Oxford market, Oxford st
Hall Charles, coach carver, Swan yard, 72 St. Martin's lane
Hall Charles, grocer, 7 Little Chester st. Grosvenor pl
Hall Charles, plumber & glaz. 2 Up.George st. Bryanstne. sq
Hall Chas. poulterer, 19 Gt. Hall, Hungerford market
Hall Charles, saddler, 11 Park lane, Piccadilly
Hall Edmund, letterpress printer, 33 Lit.George st.Euston sq
Hall Edward, *George* P.H. 1 Gravel lane, Southwark
Hall Edward, newsagent, 8&9 Fisher st.Red Lion sq.&223Strnd
Hall Edward, surgeon, 16 Bridge st. Southwark
Hall Elizh. (Mrs.), bldg. material dlr. Park pl. Old Kent rd
Hall Elizh. (Mrs.), greengrocer, 21 Gt. Windmill st.Haymkt
Hall Frances (Mrs.), teadealer, 30 Westmoreland pl. City rd
Hall Frances Emma (Mrs.) lace mer.65 Newington causeway
Hall Francis, carver & gilder, 10 Craven buildings, City rd
Hall Fred. bldng. material dlr. 36 Chester st. Kennington la
Hall Frederic, surgeon, 37 Keppel st. Russell square
Hall Fred. A. *Shipwrights' Arms* P. H.35 Friendly st. Deptfd
Hall Frederick James, barrister, 5 Old sq. Lincoln's inn
Hall Geo. accountant, 78 Albany st. Regent's park
Hall George, *Camel* P.H.90 & 91 Philipps st. Kingsland rd
Hall Geo. *Carpenters' Arms* P.H.18 Berry st. Clerkenwell
Hall Geo. cooper, 6 Gt. Cherry garden st. Bermondsey
Hall Geo. corn dealer, 4 Willow walk, Kentish town
Hall Geo. furnishing ironmonger, 185 Fleet st
Hall Geo. hatters' lining cutt.29 Lit. Charlotte st. Blkfrs. rd
Hall Geo. leather seller, 38½ Wilsted st. Somers town
Hall Geo. silkman, 33 Great Winchester st
Hall Geo. solicitor, 11 New Boswell court, Lincoln's inn
Hall Geo. wheelwright, North st. East st. Walworth
Hall Geo. Fredk. pawnbroker, 15 Norfolk st. Middlesex hosp
Hall Geo. Terry, plumber & painter, 327 Rotherhithe st
Hall Geo. Westbury, east india merchant, 43 Lime st. City
Hall Giles, barrister, 3 Elm court, Temple
Hall Giles, solicitor, 6 Barnard's inn, Holborn
Hall Henry, carpenter & undertaker, 59 Redcross st.Cripplgt
Hall Henry, fishmonger, 119 Goswell st
Hall Henry, general agent, Hall of Commerce
Hall Henry, hairdresser, &c. 57 Marchmont st. Brunswick sq
Hall Henry, ham & beef dlr.5 Salmon pl.Grange rd.Bermondsey
Hall Henry, paper manufacturer, 23 Lombard st
Hall Henry, silversmith & jeweller, 284 High Holborn
Hall Henry, solicitor, 20 Great Marlborough st
Hall Henry, stationer, 57 Gt. Coram st. Russell sq
Hall Henry Jas. artificial florist, 26 Eagle st. City road
Hall Henry John, shipowner, 2 Riches court, Lime st
Hall Henry Joseph, coach builder, 99 Long acre
Hall Horatio Wm. solicitor, 23 Rupert st. Haymarket
Hall James, bootmaker, 40 Carey st. Lincoln's inn fields
Hall James, baker, 135 Tottenham court road
Hall James, cheesemonger, 2 Belvoir ter. Vauxhall bdge. rd
Hall James, *Crown & Anchor Arms* P.H.42 Northst.Mnchtr.sq
Hall James, farrier, 212 Borough High st
Hall James, general agent, 17 Princes sq. St. George's east
Hall James, grocer, 23 Robin Hood lane, Poplar
Hall James, hosier & haberdr. 8 Up. Penton st. Pentonville
Hall James, nursery, Harmood place, Hampstead road
Hall James, painter, 25 Cumberland market, Regent's park
Hall James, pawnbroker, 93 High st. Marylebone
Hall James, plumber & painter, 7 St. Ann's pl. Limehouse
Hall James, veterin. surgeon, 15 Theobald's rd. Red Lion sq
Hall James, working cutler, 87 London road, Southwark
Hall James Frederick, tailor, 90 London wall
Hall James Gibs, printer, 12 Hayfield pl. Mile end
Hall James Hen. engrvr.&prntr.Globe yd.56South Molton st
Hall Jane (Mrs.), ironmonger, 2 Port pl. Walworth common
Hall John, beer retailer, Battersea marsh
Hall John, bootmaker, 37 Munster st. Regent's park
Hall John, bow string maker, 4 Harrow alley, Aldgate
Hall John, carpen. & builder, 34 Jubilee st. Commercl.rd.east
Hall John, carpenter, 6 Charles st. Hampstead road
Hall John, coach ironmonger, founder & plater, 5 & 6 Cross lane, Long acre, & 31 Orchard st. Portman sq
Hall John, cutler, 52 Rufford's buildings, Islington
Hall John, dining rooms, 3 Garnault place, Spafields
Hall John, dining rooms, 46 Threadneedle st
Hall John, *Dover Castle* P.H. 36 Commercial rd. Lambeth
Hall John, furniture dealer, 42 Curtain road, Shoreditch
Hall John, hairdresser, 6 King st. Golden square
Hall John, hairdresser, 69 St. John st. Clerkenwell
Hall John, hatter, 12 Castle st. City road
Hall John, hatter, 253 Regent circus, Oxford st
Hall John, hotpresser, 11 Archer st. Gt. Windmill st
Hall John, marine store dealer, 27 Colonnade, Bruns. sq
Hall John, plumber, painter & glazier, 276 Whitechapel rd
Hall John, shipowner, 10 Princes square, St. George's east
Hall John, smith & engineer, 78 Waterloo ter. Waterloo rd
Hall John, surgeon, 23 Paul st. Finsbury
Hall John, tailor, 18 Finch lane, Cornhill
Hall John, wholesale cutler, 56 Old st. St. Luke's
Hall John Charles, solicitor, see Chisholme, Hall & Gibson
Hall John Edw.engrvr.&stationer, 20 George st. Portman sq
Hall John Hancock, barrister, 3 Essex court, Temple
Hall John Orde, solicitor, 1 Brunswick row, Bloomsbury
Hall John Paxton, academy, 9 Adam's pl. King's rd. Chelsea
Hall John Rt. parliamentary agent, see Dyson, Hall & Co
Hall Joseph, beer retailer, 6 Churchway, Somers town
Hall Joseph, currier & leather sell. 22 Symons st. Chelsea
Hall Joseph, currier, &c. 23 Young st. Kensington
Hall Joseph, fruiterer, 27 Green st. Bethnal green
Hall Joseph, fruiterer, 25 Lower Belgrave st. Belgrave sq
Hall Joseph, currier, &c. 8 Broadway, Westminster
Hall Joseph, map engraver, 17 Red Lion square
Hall Joseph Sparkes, elastic bootmaker to the Queen, the Queen of the Belgians, & the Royal Family, 308 Regent st
Hall Josiah, tailor, 13 Yardley st. Exmouth st. Spafields
Hall Knight, bootmaker, 7 Warren st. Camden town
Hall Lieut. C. T. riding academy, 173 Albany st. Regent's pk
Hall Marshall, F.R.S. &c. physician, 14 Manchester square
Hall Mary (Mrs.), chandler's shop, 3 Gilbert st. Clare mkt
Hall Mary (Mrs.), coal dealer, 34 Tufton st. Westminster
Hall Mary Ann (Mrs.), milliner, 9 Amwell ter
Hall Olive, millinery & straw hat wa. 56 St. Paul's churchyd
Hall Richard, hosier & glover, 36 St. George's pl. Kntsbrge
Hall Richard, india rubber golosh manufacturer, 9 Green st. Leicester square, & 97A, Quadrant, Regent st
Hall Richard, law stationer, see Pulfer & Hall
Hall Richard, *Market* coffee house, 4 York st. Boro' market
Hall Richard, draper, tailor & outfitter, 100 Poplar High st
Hall Richard, silk mercer & haberdasher, 29 St. John st
Hall Richard Samuel H. tinman, brazier, &c. to the Hon. Corporation of the City of London, 152 Fenchurch st
Hall Robert, barrister, 1 New court, Temple
Hall Robert, beer retailer, 34 Queen st. King's road, Chelsea
Hall Robert, carpenter & underta. 179 Long la. Bermondsey
Hall Robert, italian warehouse, 63 South Audley st
Hall Robert, shear & scissor manufactory, Plummer's cotton mills, Golden lane, St. Luke's
Hall Robert, ship carver, Princes stairs, 37 Rotherhithe
Hall Robt. Coleman, grocer & teadealr. 70 Wardour st. Soho
Hall Robert Hen. chemist, 6 William's place, Walworth rd
Hall Robert Tapson, carpenter, 37 Paul st. Finsbury

Hall Roger, solicitor, 47 Sutton st. Lr. Goswell st
Hall Samuel, tailor, 33 Paul st. Finsbury
Hall Samuel, wine merchant, see Tidswell & Hall
Hall Samuel, working cutler, 5 Crown st. Finsbury
Hall Samuel Henry, seal maker,48St.James's st. Clerkenwell
Hall Sarah (Miss), milliner, see Harris & Hall
Hall Sidney, engraver, 18 Bury st. Bloomsbury
Hall Sydney, civil engineer, see Sherrard & Hall
Hall Thomas, animal & bird preserver, 7 Mora pl. City rd
Hall Thomas, baker, 9 New Chapel place, Kentish town
Hall Thomas, cabinet maker, 3 East st. Finsbury market
Hall Thomas, carpenter & builder, 237 Whitechapel road, & 7 John st. Sidney sq. Commercial road east
Hall Thomas, coal merchant, 14 Bayswater terrace
Hall Thomas, coal merchant, Union whf. Wilton rd. Pimlico
Hall Thomas, draper, &c. see Spencer & Hall
Hall Thomas, engraver & enameller, 33 Clerkenwell close
Hall Thomas, fishmonger, 3 Clare court, Drury lane
Hall Thomas, fishmonger,31 Gt. Charlotte st.Blackfriars rd
Hall Thomas, linendraper, 103 Bishopsgate without
Hall Thomas, oil wa. 3 Bretten ter. King's rd. west, Chelsea
Hall Thomas, oilman, 32 Lambeth Lower marsh
Hall Thomas, upholsterer, 9 Huntley st. Tottenham ct. rd
Hall Thomas Henry, barrister, 19 Old sq. Lincoln's inn
Hall Thomas Henry, merchant, 48 Finsbury sq
Hall Thomas James, chief magistrate, Bow st. police court
Hall Wm. appraiser & broker, 3 Stucley ter. Camden town
Hall Wm. baker, 160 Lambeth walk
Hall Wm. bradford stuff agent, 130 Wood st. Cheapside
Hall Wm. brushmaker, 28 Thayer st. Manchester sq
Hall Wm.carpentr.&coal merch.2 Clark's pl.Bshopsgt.within
Hall Wm. carpenter & undertkr. 21 Radcliffe ter. Goswell rd
Hall Wm. *Chancellor's Head* P.H. 5 Carey st
Hall Wm. coal dealer, 71 Cable st. Wellclose square
Hall Wm. coffee rooms, 23 Radcliffe terrace, Goswell rd
Hall Wm. crape, paramatta&silk warehsmn. &c.26 Wood st
Hall Wm. engraver, &c. 5 Lascelles pl.Broad st. Bloomsbury
Hall Wm. fishmonger, 4A, Brook st. Gloucester rd
Hall Wm. hairdresser, 8 Princes st. Hanover square
Hall Wm. horse nail ma. 4 Oxford st. Marlboro' rd. Chelsea
Hall Wm. hosier & glover, 277 High Holborn
Hall Wm. law stationer, 5 Hungerford st. Strand
Hall Wm. marine store dealer, 2 Bermondsey wall
Hall Wm. newsman & bookseller, 78 Albany st. Regent's pk
Hall Wm. publisher & bookseller, see Chapman & Hall
Hall Wm. *Rising Sun* P. H. 1 Lombard st. Chelsea
Hall Wm. tailor, 14 George st. Tower hill
Hall Wm. tailor& breeches maker, 113Gt.Russell st.Blmsby
Hall Wm. *Weavers' Arms* P.H. 17 London wall
Hall Wm. wool broker, see Lord & Hall
Hall Wm. writer & painter, 5 Prospect row, Walworth road
Hall Wm. Harry, academy, 90 Mount st. Grosvenor square
Hall Wm. Henry, grocer & cheesemonger, 162 Drury lane
Hall Wm. Hicks, drysalter, 30 Brick lane, Spitalfields
Hall Wm. Jsph. Crow, academy, 6 Chapman pl. Gt.Dover rd
Hallam Edwd. oilman & watchma. 16 Shepperton st. Islingtn
Hallam Isaac, fruiterer, 78 Devonshire st. Lisson grove
Hallam Jas. secret springr. & polishr. 53Gt.Sutton st.Clknwl
Hallam John, lodging & boarding ho. 14 Charterhouse st
Hallam Robert, plumber, Gt. Scotland yard, Charing cross
Hallam Samuel, working goldsmith, see Alstons'& Hallam
Hallam Susannah (Mrs.), oilman, 49 Clerkenwell green
Hallam Wm. newsvender, 29 Liquorpond st. Gray's inn lane
Hallam Wm. H. clo. salesman, 34 & 37 Wilderness row,Clkwl
Hallandal Sarah (Mrs.), staymak. 67 George st. Portman sq
Hallen Samuel, engineer, &c. see Cottam & Hallen
Hallen Samuel, merchant, 52 Stamford st
Hallen Wm. work. jeweller, 6 Richbell pl. Lamb's Condt. st
Haller Bernhard, professor of languages, 100 Fleet st
Haller Clara (Mrs.), miniature painter, 100 Fleet st
Haller John, carpenter, 70 Gt. Prescot st. Goodman's fields
Hallet William, dairyman, 27 Upper Rosoman st
Hallett Bros. linendrapers, 99 Broad st. Ratcliff
Hallett & Davis, ready made linen wa. 2B,Welbeck st.Cav. sq
HallettGeo.&Co.antmy.&albata refiners,52Broadwall,Blkfrs
Hallett Jesse & Alfred, linendrapers, &c. 13 Rotherhithe st
Hallett Rich & Sons, who. slopselrs. 27 & 82 Broad st.Ratcliff
Hallett, Robinson, Maude & Hallett, navy agents, 14 Great George st. Westminster
Hallett, Turner & Co. tailors, 50 South Molton st. Bond st
Hallett Daniel, hairdresser, 7 Edgware road
Hallett Jane (Mrs.), plumber, 10½ John st. west, Edgware rd
Hallett George, grocer, 17 New Quebec st. Portman square
Hallett Henry B. window blind maker, see Snoxell & Hallett
Hallett Henry Hughes, solicitor, 7 Staple inn, Holborn
Hallett John, fishmonger, 16 Homer st. Marylebone
HallettThos.PerhamLuxmoore, barrister, 2 New sq.Linc. inn
Hallett Wm. ivory & hard wood turner, 83 High Holborn
Hallett Wm. solicitor, 38 Clarence gardens, Regent's park
Hallett Wm. Trelawny, barrister, 1 Plowden bldgs. Temple
Halley James, pianoforte maker, 18 Wade's pl. Hackney rd
Halley Richard, beer retailer, 7 Lisson grove north
Halliday Edward&Co.musicsels.&stats.23Bishopsgatewithin
Halliday Ann (Mrs.),boarding ho. 6 Grocers' hall ct.Poultry
Halliday George, wood turner, 10 Drury court, Strand
Halliday John, juvenile hosiery & dress wa. 285 Regent st
Halliday John,mer.&insuranceagt.35Gt.St.Helen's,&Lloyd's
Halliday John, *Stafford Arms* P.H. 29 Stafford pl. Pimlico
Halliday Joseph, turner, 21 Featherstone st. City road
Halliday Michael,parliamentagent,15Buckingham st.Strand
Halliday Richard, coffee rooms, 22 Kingsland road
Halliday Robert, woollen warehouse, 32 Addle st. Wood st
Halliley Anthony & Co.calico printers,2 Bowchyd.Cheapside
Halling,Pearce&Stone,lindpr.2Cockspur st.&15to17Pall m. e
Hallion John Wm. surgeon, 64 Warren st. Fitzroy square
Halliwell Richard, solicitor, see Lovell & Halliwell
Hallmarke, Aldebert & Hallmarke,coachmas.57&58Long acr
Halloway Jonathan, meat salesman, Leadenhall market
Hallowes Wm. solicitor, see Tooke, Son & Hallowes
Hallows George, hairdresser, 28 Lime st
Hallows Wm. Ayscough, chemist, 2 Clark's place, Islington
Hallpike Vincent Hen. pianoforte manufactur. 29 Cromer st
Halls John, braid manufr. 37 New Montague st. Spitalfields
Halls Robert, wholesale coffee dealer, 9 Mincing lane
Hallum Arthur, *Victory* P.H. 75 Albany st. Regent's park
Hallworth &Brewer,carpents.&builders,17LaurencePount.la
Halman Simon, tailor, 35 Southampton st. Strand
Halse & Bandaret,wine merchants,60 St.James's st.Pall mall
Halse Edward Peter&Co.mer.&factors,& imps. of black lead, melting pots & crucibles,&c. 1 Crescent, Jewin st.Criplgte
Halse Ann (Mrs.),carp.& undert. 23Weymouth st.Portld. pl
Halse John, share bro. 15 Finch la. Cornhill, & Stock Exch
Halse Wm. cabinetmaker, 100 Drummond st. Euston sq
Halse Wm. Hooper, galvanist, 5 Pelham cresc. Fulham road
Halsey George, baker, Copperas lane, Deptford
Halsey James Wilson, grocer, 27 Kingsland road
Halsey John, congreve match ma.ValeRoyal,Mdn.la.Kgs. cr
Halsey JohnGosling,*GreenDragonhotel*,86Bishopsgt.within
Halsey Wm. *King's Head* P.H. 29 Old Compton st
Halsey Wm. copper plate printer, 8 Seacoal la. Skinner st
Halson Charles, merchant, 11 South st. Finsbury
Halson Chas.wine mer. & bott.beer exptr.8Cross st. Finsbury
Halstaff&Hannaford,desk&dressing case mkrs.228 Regent st
Halstead Charles, bookseller & statnr. 120 High st. Cmdn. tn
Halstead Chas. hat trimg. ma. 35 Primrose st. Bishpsgt. st
Halstead Mary (Mrs.), lodging house, 8 Arundel st. Strand
Halsted Francis, printseller & bookseller, 108 New Bond st
Halsted Thomas, teadealer & grocer,17 Norton folgate
Halsted William, cheesemonger, 54 Drummond st. Eust. sq
Halton Wm. & Son, tailors, 23 George st. Hanover sq
Halton Wm.Thos. undertaker, 11 Church rw.Upper st.Islng
Halton Wm. Thos. undertak.1½ Portland pl.Lr. road,Islngtn
Ham Chas.tobcnst.&newsagt.6Lamb'sConduitpas.RedLn.sq
Ham Geo. Jas. brassfounder & gasfitter, 77 Little Britain
Ham Thomas, watch & clock maker,Broadway,Ludgatehill
Ham Wm. lastmaker, 72 Cromer st. Brunswick sq
Hamber Wm. sheriffs' officer, 23 Coleman st
Hambidge Martha (Mrs.), pork butcher, 47 Whitechapel rd
Hambidge Rich.meat salesmn.1 White Hart st.Newgte.mkt
Hambidge Robt. remnant war. 16 Clarence pl. Hackney rd
Hambidge SarahM.(Miss),dress ma.18 Portman pl.Edgw.rd
Hambidge Wm.orange mercht. see Woodman & Hambidge
Hambleton Charles, baker, 27 Little Pulteney st. Golden sq
Hambleton Wm. secret springer,&c. 10 King st.Clerkenwell
Hambley Wm.architect,&c.1 Winchest.bldgs.Gt. Winches.st
Hambridge Chas.& Son, coach spring & axletree makers, tire & coach smiths, wheelwrights, &c. 73 Curtain road, Shoreditch; & Milner's mews, Church st. Paddington
HambridgeGeo. pork butcher, 122 Brick la. Spitalfields
Hambro C. J. & Son, merchants, 70 Old Broad st
Hambro' whf. (Wm. James Chaplin & Benjamin Worthy Horne), 68½ Upper Thames st
Hambrook John Major, tobacconist, 105 Tooley st
Hambrook Stephen, builder, 6 Coles terrace, Barnsbury road, & 34 Providence row, Islington
Hamburger,Rogers& Co.gold & silver lacemen&embroiderers to her Majesty & Prince Albert,& army & navy cap & accoutrement manufacturers, 30 King st. Covent garden
Hamer Saml. & Son,coal merchts. Milford wf.near 199 Strand
Hamer David, wine merchant, 18 Fenchurch st
Hamer Henry, silkmerc. linendraper, &c. 59 Blackfriars rd
Hamer James, brass manufacturer, 79 Wardour st. Soho

Hamer Richard, grocer & teadlr.28 Red Lion st. Spitalfields
Hamer Saml. grocer, 3 Cumberland row, King's cross
Hamer Wm. wax, &c. dollmaker, see Douglas & Hamer
Hamerton John, barrister, 2 Essex court, Temple
Hames William, dining rooms, 29 Ship yard, Temple bar
Hames William, tobacconist, 6 St. George's circus
Hamilton, Adams&Co. booksels.&publshs. 33 Paternoster rw
Hamilton, Aplin & Co. wine merchants, 26 Bucklersbury
Hamilton & Bird, booksellers, 21 Hedge row, Islington
Hamilton, Hyde & Co. fringe manufacturers, 127½ Cheapside
Hamilton & Justice, solicitors, 17 Berners st. Oxford st
Hamilton Adam, sheffield agent, 73 Hatton garden
Hamilton Alfred, surgeon, 1 Broad street buildings
Hamilton Alex. bed feather wa. see Blyth, Hamilton & Blyth
Hamilton Andrew, chemist & drugst. 9Broughton pl.Hkny rd
Hamilton Andrew, secretary to the *Alliance fire & life assurance company*, Bartholomew lane
Hamilton Archibald, mercht. see Sinclair, Hamilton & Co
Hamilton Charles Foster, brushmaker, 15 Greek st. Soho
Hamilton De Luk Wm.dentist,12Gt.May'sblds.St.Martin's la
Hamilton Edward, physician, 22 Grafton st. Bond st
Hamilton Fred. artists' colorman, 1 Robert st. Grosvenor sq
Hamilton Geo. hairdresser, 7 Craven buildings, Drury lane
Hamilton Geo. furn. brkr. & carman, 99 Gt. Suffolk st.Boro'
Hamilton Henry, writing master, 18 Francis st. Tott. ct. rd
Hamilton Henry Robt. spectacle maker, 16 Queen st. Clkwll
Hamilton H.Wm.*PearsonArms*P.H.1 Pearson st. Kngsld.rd
Hamilton James, statuary, &c. 80Portland road, Regent'sprk
Hamilton John, carpenter, &c. 4 Exeter st. Strand
Hamilton John, surgeon, 88 Quadrant, Regent st
Hamilton John, wine mer. see Gorman, Hamilton & Thorby
Hamilton John, wine merchant, 2 King st. St. James's
Hamilton John, wine mer. see Knobel, Hamilton & Tuckwell
Hamilton John Q. cotton merchant, 2 Dunster ct. Mincing la
Hamilton John Wm. commercl. ag. 3South gall. Auction mart
Hamilton Lewis Gellie, mercht. see Bruce, Hamilton & Co
Hamilton Mary (Mrs.), artist, 14 Queen sq. Westminster
Hamilton Robert, restaurateur, 41 Princes st. Leicester sq
Hamilton Sydney Douglas, solicitor, 63 Judd st. Brunswk sq
Hamilton Thomas, shoemaker, 59 Marsham st. Westminster
Hamilton Thomas, solicitor, see Few, Hamilton & Few'
Hamilton Wm. glass paper ma. 8½ Rose yd. Rose st. Soho
Hamilton William, merchant, see Laurie, Hamilton & Co
Hamlet Eliza (Miss), milliner, 162 Piccadilly
Hamlet Saml. *Champion* P.H. 14 Radcliffe terr. Goswell rd
Hamlett Wm. plumber, 20 Sutton st. York rd. Lambeth
Hamley William, toy warehouse, 231 High Holborn
Hamlin Henry, registr. of births & deaths, 24 City ter. City rd
Hamlin Isaac, fruit salesman, Square mkt. Covent gdn. mkt
Hamlin John, fruit salesman, Square mkt. Covent gdn.mkt
Hamlin Richard, tailor, 8 Blenheim st. Bond st
Hamling Jonas, scaleboard cut. 55½ Union st. Lambeth wlk
Hamlyn George, *Angel & Crown* P.H. 23 Glos'ter st.Queen sq
Hamlyn Richard, bootmaker, 27 Cross st. Blackfriars road
Hamm Robert, archery wareho. 5 Bedford st. Bedford sq
Hammack, John Geo. architect.&survr.Essex ho.Mile end rd
Hamman Richard, bootmaker, 55 Paradise row, Chelsea
Hammans Anna Maria(Miss),milliner,4Mortimer st.Cav. sq
Hammant&M'Intosh,meat salsmn.4Warwick la.Nwgte.mkt
Hammatt John, comb ma.&library,13LittleWarner st.Clkwl
Hammer Wm. & Son, coachmakers, 272 Whitechapel road
Hammer John, toy warehouse, 35 Seymour st. Euston sq
Hammerton Stephen,ribbon manfr.seeCope,Hammerton&Co
Hammerton Thomas, surgeon, see Fuller & Hammerton
Hammick Sir Stephen Love, bart. surgeon, 35 Cavendish sq
Hammill John B. fire brick, tile & bath brick merchant, & commission agent, Stanton's wharf, Tooley st
Hammon George, livery stables, 30 Whiskin st. Clerkenwell
Hammon Geo. watch case&dial ma.4Skinner st. Clerkenwell
Hammon Henry John, archt. & surveyr. 33 Threadneedle st
Hammon Jas.watch manufacturer, 9Northampton sq.Clrkwl
Hammon Jas. plumber, 99 Great Portland st. Oxford st
Hammon JohnWm. watchcase maker, 11 Sekforde st.Clkwll
Hammon Noah, plumber, 3 Cumberland st. Middlx. hospital
Hammon Rd. statnr. & news agent, 92 Charlotte st.Fitzroy sq
Hammond A——&F——,hosiers& shirtmakers,93Piccadilly
Hammond&Crundall,indigo mers.8Scots yd.Gt.Bush la.City
Hammond Chas.&Wm. breeches, &c. makers, 250 Oxford st
Hammond & Field, milliners & dressmakers, 73 Fleet st
Hammond Richard & Jas. furniture wa. 110 Chancery lane
Hammond Ann (Mrs.), grocer, 9 Temple pl. Old Kent rd
Hammond Charles, stockbroker, see Baily & Hammond
Hammond Cornelius Cook, merchant, 31 Rood lane
Hammond David Hen. broker & furniture dlr. 50 Fleet la
Hammond Edmund, carver & gilder, 18 George st. Baker st
Hammond Edw. baker, 41 Henry st. east, Avenue road
HammondEliza(Mrs.),veterinary surg. 8 South pl. Finsbury
Hammond Francis, staymaker, 8 Leicester square
Hammond Francis, *Crown* coffeerooms, 8 & 9 St.Martin's ct
Hammond Francis F. jeweller, 32 High st. Notting hill
Hammond Francis M. *Churchill Arms* P.H. 9 Peel place, Kensington gravel pits
Hammond Freelove, solicitor, 29 Norfolk st. Strand
Hammond George, builder, 18 King's row, Walworth road
Hammond George, furn. broker, 99 Gt. Suffolk st. Boro'
HammondGeorge,timber agnt.toJ.&G.Mirris,Millwall,Popl
Hammond George,lath rend.47Brandon st.Lockfields,Wlwth
Hammond George,shoemaker,21 Beckford row,Walworth rd
Hammond George, surgeon, 56Gt. Carlisle st.Portmn. markt
Hammond Henry, attorney, 16 Furnival's inn & Hampstead
Hammond Henry, fruiterer, 1 Camberwell grove
Hammond Hen.Erasmus,coal mer.60St.Thomas' pl.Dover rd
Hammond James, bootmaker, 18 Park pl. Kennington cross
Hammond Jas. *City of Norwich* P.H. 2Northrw.Grosvnr.sq
Hammond James, pat. medicine vender, 244 Blackfriars rd
Hammond John, baker, 35 East st. Walworth road
Hammond John, ironmonger,150Up.Whitecross st.&23Old st
Hammond John, livery stables, 4 Portland st. mews, Soho
Hammond John, tailor, 2 Prince's pl. Commercial road east
Hammond John, wool agent, 91 Bermondsey st
Hammond John Bellord, staymaker, 26 Blackfriars road
Hammond Jonathan, fur.brok.&appraisr.1 Green bk.Tooly st
Hammond Joseph, upholsterer, 1 Queen st. Brompton road
Hammond Jsph. *White Hart* P.H.10Portpool la.Gray's inn la
Hammond Munden, advertisement & country newspaper agent, 27 Lombard st. late M. & W. E. Hammond
Hammond Nathan, ship, cust. ho. & gen. agt. 13 Water lane
Hammond Nathaniel, tinman, see Burton & Hammond
Hammond Porter,laceman,11Up.Charles st.Northampton sq
Hammond Richd.tobacconist, 13Woburn bldgs.Tavistock sq
Hammond Rd.Hy.*RisingSun*P.H.1Manchester st.Watrlo.tr
Hammond Robert, cattle salesman, 17 West Smithfield
Hammond Robert, coal merchant, 22 York st. Westminster
Hammond Robert, whip maker, 113 Hoxton Old town
Hammond Simmons, oil refiner, Ordnance wf.133Rotherhithe
Hammond Theodore E. boot tree ma. 40 Broad st. Golden sq
Hammond Thomas,boot&shoe maker,21 Conduit st.Padngtn
Hammond Thomas, grocer, 25 Grosvenor market
Hammond Thomas, tailor, 32 Lisson gr. nth. St. John's wd
Hammond Wm. beer retailer, 1 Southampton st.Camberwell
Hammond Wm. beer retailer, 13 Wades place, Hackney road
Hammond Wm. blind ma. & upholst. 141 High st.Camden tn
Hammond Wm. carpenter, 5 White st. Borough
Hammond Wm. coffee rooms, 130 Edgeware rd. Marylebone
Hammond Wm. corn dealer, 10 Shepherd st. Mayfair
Hammond Wm. decorative house painter, 28 Howland st
Hammond Wm. fruiterer, 87 Long lane, Bermondsey
Hammond Wm. *Hyde Park* coffee rooms, 245 Oxford st
Hammond Wm. merchant, 8 Scot's yard, Gt. Bush lane, City
Hammond Wm. oil & italian wa. 16 Ring cross, Holloway rd
HammondWm.pianoforte maker,1Surrey pl.east,OldKent rd
Hammond Wm. table cover maker, 9 Cleveland st. Fitzroy sq
Hammond Wm. jun. turner, 7 New inn yard, Shoreditch
Hammond Wm. sen. turner, 48 Coppice row, Clerkenwell
Hammond Wm. Henry, auctioneer & estate agt. & carpenter, 28 Chancery lane, & 30 Bell yard, Temple bar
Hamon Peter Gustavus, fencing rooms, 8 James st. Haymrkt
Hamond Charles, oil & colorman, 182 Poplar High st.; 12 Fore st. City; 72 Three Colt st. Limehouse, & 1 York buildings, Bermondsey
Hamond Henry S. ship ins. & genl. com. ag. 70 Lr. Thames st
Hamond Chas. oil & colorman, 72 Three Colt st. Limehouse
Hamond Wm.russia mat & bag wareho. 22Water la. Tower st
Hamp Henry & Co. furn.undertakers,7Phœnix st. Somers tn
Hamper James,col.produce bro.Commercl.cof.ho. Mincing la
Hamper William & Henry, hosiers & glovers, & ready made linen warehouse, 56 Threadneedle st
Hampson Wm. & Sons, watch & clock ma. 79 Theobald's rd
Hampson George, silk, cotton & woollen dyer, 5 Minories
Hampson James, dentist, 7 Dorset square
Hampson James, linendraper, 3 Youls pl. Old Kent road
Hampson Richard,silk mercer & stock maker,49 Holborn hill
Hampson Squire, lathe & tool maker, 99 Lambeth walk
Hampson Wm. bookbndrs'. & stat. press mf. 47 Old Bailey
Hampson Wm. clock & watch ma. 6 Perceval st. Clerknwll
Hampstead Waterworks Office (Thomas Hakewill, secretary), 43 Frederick place, Hampstead road
Hampstead Harriett (Mrs.), *Ram & Magpie* P.H. 1 Fleet st. Bethnal green
Hampton Thomas & John, fruiterers, 9 York pl. Portland tn
Hampton J. W. secretary to *Alfred Home & Foreign Life Assurance Company*, Lothbury

Hampton Daniel, fruiterer, 22 Ivy lane, Newgate st
Hampton Robert, tailor, 66 Banner st. St. Luke's
Hampton Thomas, *Red Lion* P.H. 19 Up. Ebury st. Pimlico
Hampton William, carver & gilder, 18 Mount st. Lambeth
Hampton William, wholesale & retail carpet & general furnishing warehouse, 27 St. Martin's le grand, & 14 Leicester sq
Hampton Wm. Edwd. teadealer, 167 Waterloo road, Lambeth
Hampton Zaccheus, bootma. 48 & 50 Brick la. St. Luke's
Hampton Zaccheus, tobacconist, 50 Brick la. St. Luke's
Hamrock John, artist, 4 Francis st. Tottenham court road
Hamshar James, butcher, 6 Foxton terrace, Thornhill road
Hamshar Richard, butcher, 8 Sidney st. Goswell road
Hamshar Wm. butcher, 6 Brunswick parade, Pentonville
Hamsheir Thomas, bricklayer, 158½ Old Gravel lane
Hamsher Henry, butcher, 7 White Lion st. Pentonville
Hamsher Joseph, glovemaker, 7 Vine place, Old st. road
Hamshere Wm. surveyor, Church st. Stoke Newington
Hamson Jas. ladder maker, 3 Garden row, Camberwell road
Hamston John, furniture broker, 8 Great Earl st. 7 dials
Hanaford Hen. jeweller & engraver, 44 Rahere st. Goswell rd
Hanan Fanny (Mrs.), milliner, 8 Moreton ter. Kentish town
Hanbury Cornelius & Dan. B. chemist, see Allen, Hanbury's & Co
Hanburys' Taylor & Lloyds', bankers, 60 Lombard st
Hanbury Hen. file & saw ma. 1 Downe's pl. Wardour st. Soho
Hanbury Henry, sawmaker, 38 Hart st. Covent garden
Hanbury Samuel, stockbroker, 4 Angel ct. Throgmorton st
Hance & Lock, hatters & army cap makers, 6 St. James's st
Hance Charles, barrister, 1 Harcourt buildings, Temple
Hance Peter, booksel. 14 Upp. Gl'ster pl. King's rd. Chelsea
Hanchet Anna (Miss), corset maker, 26 Hanway st. Oxford st
Hanchet Saml. grocer & cheesemngr. 1 Aldenham terr. Pan. rd
Hancock & Cheese, wholesale druggists, Earl st. Finsbury
Hancock, Rixon & Dunt, chandelier, lamp, & glass manufacturers to her Majesty and the Royal Family, 1 Cockspur st. Pall mall east
Hancock Abraham, printer, 3 Middle row place, Holborn
Hancock Charles, artist, 5 Michael's place, Brompton
Hancock Charles, coal & sand merchant, White Lion wharf, Upper Thames st. & 17 Earl st. Blackfriars
Hancock Charles, merchant, 6 Crosby sq. Bishopsgate
Hancock Charles, printer, 32 Gloucester st. Queen square
Hancock Charles, solicitor, see Yonge & Hancock
Hancock Chas. *Star & Garter* P.H. Parker's ter. Neckinger rd
Hancock Cornelius, fruiterer, 6 Lr. Porchester st. Edgw. rd
Hancock Ebenezer, stayma. 5 High st. Newington butts
Hancock Francis, butcher, 15 Copenhagen st. Pentonville
Hancock George, printer, 55 Aldermanbury
Hancock George, window blind maker, 10 Peerless pl. City rd
Hancock Henry, *Bell* P.H. 40 Great Tower st
Hancock James, baker, 1 Charles st. Queen's elms, Chelsea
Hancock James, *Exeter Arms* P.H. 9 Exeter st. Lisson grove
Hancock James Joseph, chinaman, 77 Princes rd. Lambeth
Hancock Jas. L. ind. rubber hose pipe ma. Goswel. mws. Gswl. rd
Hancock John, dairyman, 12 Upper Porchester st. Oxford terr
Hancock John, grainer, 51 Commercial road, Lambeth
Hancock John, hosier glover & outfitter, 16 Poultry
Hancock John, optician, 30 City road, Finsbury
Hancock John, ship & ins. bro. 17 St. Dunstan hill, & Baltic
Hancock Justinian, *Three Tuns* P.H. 1 Whitechapel High st
Hancock Lewis, poulterer & game dlr. 1 Eagle pl. Jermyn st
Hancock Richard, merchant, Lloyd's
Hancock Sarah (Mrs.), butcher to her Majesty, 64 Park st. Grosvenor square
Hancock Samuel, carpenter, 14 Portland row, Camberwell rd
Hancock Susannah (Mrs.), tinplate wkr. 24 Widegate st. Bpsg
Hancock Thomas, bobbin turner, 33 Thomas st. Brick lane
Hancock Thomas, *Crown* P.H. 14 Stanhope terrace, Hyde pk
Hancock Thomas, grocer, 116 Mount st. Berkely sq
Hancock Thomas, jeweller, 17 New Bond st
Hancock Thos. *White Horse* P.H. 8 Cornwall rd. Lambeth
Hancock Thos. & Jas. who. druggists, 47 Clifton st. Finsbury
Hancock Thomas Wm. teacher of music, 31 Coventry st
Hancock Wm. attorney, 3 Prospect row, Dockhead, Bermndsy
Hancock Wm. commercial agent, 6 Crosby square
Hancock Wm. corn dealer, 6 High st. Deptford
Hancock Wm. dining rooms, 7 Rupert st. Haymarket
Hancock Wm. stone mason, 28 Cambridge pl. Cambridge ter
Hancock Wm. wine, spirit, ale, & porter merchant, 80 Connaught terrace, Edgware road
Hancock Wm. Martin, fishmonger, 5 Dockhead, Bermondsey
Hancorn James Richard, surgeon, 34 Shoreditch
Hancorne Robert, surgeon, 4 Euston square, New road
Hancox Samuel, tailor, 411 Oxford st
Hand in Hand Fire & Life Office (Rt. Steven, sec.), 1 New Bridge st. Blackfriars, for directors, &c. see page 2029
Hand Frederick James, attorney, 89 Chancery lane
Hand Henry, fruiterer, 6 Dock head, Bermondsey
Hand John, hat manufacturer & bootmaker, 84 Cheapside
Hand Mark Walter, ironmonger, 4 Horseferry rd. Wstmr
Hand Thomas, solicitor, 40 Chancery lane
Handasyde Wm. & Co. ironfounders' agents & merchants, 57 Cannon st. City, & Emerson st. Bankside
Handby Rebecca (Mrs.), carpenter, 2 Lit. Vine st. Piccadilly
Handey James, surgeon, 178 Wellington ter. Waterloo road
Handford & Davies, tea dealers, 61 High Holborn
Handford Nath. architect & survey. 16 Cheyne wlk. Chelsea
Handford Thomas, jun. patentee of the waterproof travelling-trunk edged with brass, 6 Strand
Handisyde Charles, upholsterer, 55 Lamb's Conduit st
Handisyde Hen. cabinet ma. 14 John's mews, John st. Bedfd. rw
Handley Edward, *King Wm. IV.* P.H. 6 King Wm. st. Strand
Handley James, who. confectioner, 26 Gt. Earl st. Seven dials
Handley James Hyatt, land agent, 21 Red Lion sq. Holborn
Handley John, brassfounder, 44 Gt. Sutton st. Clerkenwell
Handley John, portrait painter, 5 Redman's row, Mile end
Handley John Wm. lacquer maker, 2 Windsor pl. City road
Handley Joseph, bricklayer, Phœnix yd. Oxford st
Handley Joseph, butcher, 8 King st. Westminster
Handley Mary (Mrs.), *Salisbury Arms* P.H. 9 Salsby. st. Bmsy
Handley Thomas, undertaker, &c. 155 Alfred pl. Waterloo rd
Handley William, confectioner, 58 Chiswell st
Handley Wm. jun. oil & colorman, 23 Up. North st. Whtch. rd
Handley Wm. sen. corndealer, 2 Up. North st. Whitechpl. rd
Handlon Jane (Mrs.), china dealer, 4 Emmett st. Poplar
Hands Decimus, surgeon, 22 Thayer st. Manchester sq
Hands Esther (Mrs.), baker, 4 Myddelton st. Spitalfields
Hands John, dairy & omnibus propr. 4 Irongate wf. Padngtn
Hands John Chickett, wahо. man, see Eyles, Evans, Hands & Co
Hands Joseph, surgeon, 23 Duke st. Grosvenor sq
Hands Joshua, omnibus pro. 24 Wharf (Nth. side), Padgtn. ba
Hands Thomas, cattle salesman, 60 West Smithfield
Hands William, baker, 34 Whitmore road, Hoxton
Hands Wm. calenderer, 13 Tenter st. Little Moorfields
Hands William, cattle salesman, 17 West Smithfield
Handscomb Isaac Henly, haberdasher, 55A, Edgware road
Handy & Stanley, spur makers, 18 Queen st. Seven dials
Handy Benjamin, stationer, Kingsland green
Handy Susannah (Mrs.), copr. brass & bell foundr. 157 Gswl. st
Handy Thomas, law stationer, 11 Cursitor st. Chancery la
Handyside John, baker, 19 Welbeck st. Cavendish sq
Hanfeld John, fur dyer, see Miers & Hanfeld
Hanff Samuel, cap manufr. & furrier, 105 London wall
Hanhart Michael & N. litho. prints. 64 Charlotte st. Fitz. sq
Hanington Thomas, highbury nursery, Holloway road
Hanington Wm. grocer & cheesemonger, 11 Drummond cres
Haniquet Anna (Mdmslle.), milliner, 35 Park st. Grosvenor sq
Hankey (Thomson) & Co. merchants, 7 Mincing lane
Hankeys' & Co. bankers, 7 Fenchurch st
Hankey Wm. A. jun. colonial broker, 14 Mincing lane
Hankie Wm. beer retailer, Dorset st. Clapham road
Hankins George, wine merchant, 14 Queenhithe
Hankins Jesse, window blindmaker, 89 Houndsditch
Hankins John, gen. comsn. agt. & agent for John McMellans' alloa ale, Humphrey's wareho. Montague close, Southwark
Hankins Thomas, surgeon, 1 Windsor terrace, Gt. Dover rd
Hankinson Jas. *Lord Portman* P.H. 14 Up. Dorchester pl
Hankinson Morley, livery stables, Devonshire mews east
Hanks Edwd. Cook, surgeon, 18 Gt. Portland st. Oxford st
Hanks Henry, coachmaker, 40 Rupert st. Haymarket
Hanks John, teadealer, 27 Little Newport st. Long acre
Hanks Maria (Mrs.), beer retailer, 4 Exeter st. Sloane st
Hanks Richard, working jeweller, 11 Duke st. St. James's
Hanks Robert, hatter, 44 Lambeth Lower marsh
Hanks Robert, livery stables, 22 Chester st. Kennington
Hanley Thomas, tailor, 42 Michael's place, Brompton
Hanley Wm. Lucas, solicitor, 11 Angel ct. Throgmorton st. & 34 Wilson st. Finsbury
Hanlon Wm. bootmaker, 2 Queen's square, Aldersgate
Hanly Frances (Mrs.), dining rooms, 26 Liquorpond st
Hanly Laurence, *Gun* P.H. 31 Union st. Bishopsgate
Hanman Ancel, plumber, 2 George st. New Kent road
Hanmer Job Walden, barrister, 3 Old square, Lincoln's inn
Hanmer, Thomas, barrister, 4 Harcourt buildings, Temple
Hann Henry, shipping butcher, 4 Pump yard, Ratcliff cross
Hann James, tailor, 4 Gate st. Lincoln's inn fields
Hann John, tailor & haberdasher, 131 Fetter lane
Hann Reuben, bootmaker, 34 Stangate, Lambeth
Hann Robert, baker, 16½ Stangate st. Lambeth
Hann Wm. butcher, 5 & 6 King David la. Shadwell High st
Hannaford Mary (Mrs.), jeweller, 71 Newman st
Hannaford Thos. C. dressing case ma. see Halstaff & Hannaford
Hannah Adam, baker, 86 East st. Manchester square

Hannah Geo. coal merchant, 21 Norfolk st. Middlesex hosp
Hannah Geo.cabinetmaker,6Tottenham mews,Middlesex hos
Hannah Joseph, hairdresser, 9 Southampton row, Russell sq
Hannah Joseph, wine & brandy mer. 7 Bridge st.Westmnstr
Hannah Robert, oilman, 22 High st. Newington butts
Hannah Walter, oilman, 62 High Holborn
Hannam Edw. tailor, 38 St. John's lane, West Smithfield
Hannan James, bricklayer,&c.6Gt.WhiteLion st.Seven dials
Hannay & Dietrichsen, chemists, druggists, patent medicine dealers, perfumers & enema manfrs. patent garden machine, fire engine & ship pump manufactrs. 63 Oxford st
Hannay's preventive specific wash warehouse, 63 Oxford st
Hanneford Charles, tailor, 33 Hackney road
Hannell Edward, builder, 38 & 39 Lisson grove north
Hannell Edward, grocery & italian wareho. 11 Davies st
Hannen James, baker, Holland st. Brixton road
Hannett Alfred, dyer & scourer, 71 Berwick st. Soho
Hannington Rich. cheesemonger,3 Samson's pl. Bermondsey
Hannis Solomon, shoemaker, 121 Brunswick st. Hackney rd
Hanoverian Consulate, 6 Circus, Minories
Hanrott Henry Augustus, solicitor,29 Queen sq.Bloomsbury
Hanrott Philip Augustus, solicitor, 29Queen sq.Bloomsbury
Hanrott Philip Augustus,jun. solicitor,29 Queen sq.Bloombs
Hansard George, barrister, 22 Old square, Lincoln's inn
Hansard Luke James, printer, 6 Gt. Turnstile, Holborn
Hanscomb Hen. umbrella maker, High st. Stoke Newington
Hanscomb John, corn & coal dlr. 1 Blossom place,Holloway
Hanscomb Robert,grocer&tea dlr.1Frederick place,Mile end
Hanscomb Thomas,wire worker,49 Carlisle st. Lambeth
HanscombeJas.umbrella ma. 4 Prospect row,Bermondsy rd
Hanseatic Consulate, 76 Cornhill
Hansell Wm. cheesemonger, 20 James st. Oxford st
Hansford Benedicta (Mrs.), tobacconist, Deptford High st
Hansford John, dyer, 10 Northumberland st. Marylebone
Hanshaw Wm. butcher, 3 Constitution row, Gray's inn road
Hanslar Henry Stephen, solicitor, 19 Lincoln's inn fields
HanslerGeo.Langley,oilman&tallowchndlr.26Lit.Newport st
Hanslip & Manning, solicitors, 20 Thavies inn, Holborn
Hanson Brothers, merchants, 28 Great Winchester st
Hanson Sam. & Son, imps. of foreign fruit,20& 47Botolph la
Hanson, Smiths' & Stephens, scotch & manchester warehousemen,30 & 31 St. Martin's le grand
Hanson Alfred, barrister, Chapel staircase, Lincoln's inn
Hanson Ann (Mrs.), marine store dlr. 28 Baldwin's gardens
Hanson Benj. meat salesman,26 Shambles,Newgate market
Hanson Harriet (Mrs.), milliner, &c. 20 Rathbone place
Hanson JamesHorn,attorney,9 Blandford st.Manchester sq
Hanson John, oilman, 2 Old road, Limehouse
Hanson John, *Virginia Planter* P.H.Virginia rw.Bthnl.grn
Hanson Joseph,woollen warehouseman,see Hoyle & Hanson
Hanson Matthew, ladies' shoemaker, 5 Princes st.Cavend.sq
Hanson Richard, japanner, 7 Duck lane, Wardour st. Soho
Hanson Samuel, antiquarian upholsterer, 16 John st.Oxfd.st
Hanson Thomas, coal & coke merch. 5Wharf,Wenlock basin
Hanson Walter, seal engraver,22 Took's court,Chancery lane
Hanson William, appraiser, &c.9Blandford st.Manchester sq
Hanson Wm. mason & builder, 65 Mount st. Brkly.sq. Albion wharf, Kensington basin, & 20 Rathbone pl. Oxford st
Hanson William S. hairdresser, 31 High st. Kensington
Hanstock Geo. beer retailer, 7 Lit. Derweston st.Marylebone
Hanton John, bookseller, 9 Museum st. Bloomsbury
Hanwell Geo.&Co. *Waterloo hotel*,85 Jermyn st. St. James's
Hanworth Sarah(Mrs.),marine store dlr.43North st.Sloane st
Hanworth Wm. tobacconist, 26 Shaftesbury ter. Pimlico
Happe Fdk. chandler's shop,23Charles st. St. George's east
Harbar Wm.*DuchessofBrunswick*P.H.Brunswick sq.Dptfd
Harben Chas. Hen. who. cheesemonger, 8 Whitechapel High st. & 40 Goulstone st
Harbert Charles, builder, 20 Clipstone st. Fitzroy square
Harbert Charlt.(Miss),dressma.6Harringtn.st.nh.Hmpstd.rd
Harbert John, oven builder, 16 & 17 Lucretia st. Lambeth
Harbige Wm. tailor, 8 St. Anne's lane, St. Martin's le grand
Harbin & Ward, solicitors, 12 Clement's inn, Strand
Harbin Peter Tait, solicitor, 12 Clement's inn, Strand
Harboard John, bootmaker, 126 Bunhill row, Chiswell st
Harbon James, veterinary sur. 6 Lit. Derweston st. Marylbn
Harbord Charles, bootmaker, 2 Holmes bldgs. Lit.Bell alley
Harbord Henry, grocer, Blue Anchor road, Bermondsey
Harbord Henry, ropemaker, Jamaica level, Rotherhithe
Harborne Saml. ironmonger, 6 Down st. Piccadilly
Harborne Edward, *White Swan tavern*, Mile end road
Harborow, Acock & Co. glove manufacturers to the Queen, hosiers, brace, stock & shirtmakers, 15 Cockspur st
Harborow John, bracemaker & glover,27 Panton st.Haymkt
Harbottell Thomas (Mrs.),corset maker, 70 Oxford st
HarbourMaster'sOffice,St.Katherine's stairs; hours 10 to 4
Harbour William, cork cutter, 3 Ball alley, Lombard st
Harbud Jeremiah,watch movemnt.ma. 22Green ter.Spafields
Harby Thos. & Jas. ropemakers, Bow la. Poplar, nr.the East India Docks; & Jerusalem coffeehouse
Harcourt Thos. surgical inst. ma. 30 Hyde st. Bloomsbury
Hardcastle & Harrison, cheesemongers, 102 St. John st. & 35 Aylesbury st. Clerkenwell
Hardcastle Eliz. (Mrs.), *Hat & Feathers* P.H.164Goswell st
Hardcastle Henry, butcher, 30 King st. Portman square
Hardcastle John Wm. grocer, 11 Corrie place, Old Kent rd
Hardcastle James, beer retailer, 5 Marlboro' st.Blackfrs.rd
Hardcastle Joseph, cheesemonger, 28 Poland st. Oxford st
Hardcastle Samuel, cheesemonger,84 Leman st.Goodms.flds
Hardcastle Susannah (Mrs.),skein cotton dyer,11Lit.Pearl st
Hardcastle Wm. corndealer, 1 Knight's pl. Wandsworth rd
Hardcastle William, insurance broker, Lloyd's
Hardcastle Wm. painter & glazier, 11 Charles st. Comm. rd
Harden Benj. jun. fancy cabinet ma. 36 Coppice row,Clknw
Harden Charles, solicitor, 9 Fleet st
Harden Charlotte (Mrs.), artist in hair, 66 Newman st
Harden Joseph M. stonemason, 1 Bennett st. Blackfriars rd
Harden Philip, west india merchant, 4 Pancras lane
Harden William, goldsmith, 120 Fleet st
Hardie Alexander, cork manufacturer, 59 Goswell road
Hardie Ann (Mrs.), milliner & dress ma. 59 Goswell road
Hardie Hen.pianoforte ma. 3 Glos'ter pl. King's rd. Chelsea
Hardie William C. fancy trimming ma.see Hatton & Hardie
Hardiman John & Son, plumber&glazier, 33 Threadneedle st
Hardiman Samuel, fruiterer, 7 Chapel st. Somers town
Hardin George, linendraper,2Broughton place, Hackney rd
Harding AugustusD.&Co.custom ho.agts 49KingWm.st.city
Harding Brian & Co. coach lace & carpet ma.68 Long acre
Harding, Smith & Co. warehousemen, 82 Pall mall
HardingThos.&Co.imps.ofcigars,wines,&c.12Hartst.Mark la
Harding Thomas & John, bootmakers, 51 St. Martin's lane
Harding Wm.& Son, plate glass factors, 70 Fore st. Cripplgt
Harding Alfred, grocer, 2 Exmouth st. Euston square
Harding Benjamin, greengrocer, 188 Poplar High st
Harding Charles, grocer&cheesemonger,7&8Lit.Gray's inn la
Harding Charles, tailor, 32 East st. Manchester sq
Harding Charles Thos. artist, 37 William st. Hampstead rd
Harding Charles Thomas, florist, 1 Clifford st. Bond st
Harding Daniel, auctioneer, &c. 11 Orchard st. St. Luke's
Harding Daniel, butcher, Southampton st. Camberwell rd
Harding Edwd. beer retailer, 24 Chapel st. Somers town
Harding Frederick, artist, 3 Shorter's ct. Throgmorton st
Harding Frederick, tobacconist, 13 Goswell st
Harding Geo. builder, Surrey wf. Addington sq. Camberwell
Harding George, carpenter, 4 Thomas st. Brick lane
Harding George, grocer, 61 Bunhill row, Chiswell st
Harding George, grocer, 150 New Gravel lane, Shadwell
Harding George, solicitor, see Bray, Warren & Harding
Harding George, tinplate worker, 15 White st. Borough; & 9 Royal Hospital row, Chelsea
Harding Geo. Perfect,artist,69 Hercules buildings, Lambeth
Harding Henry,watch &clockmaker,1Holles st.Cavendish sq
Harding Henry, brass founder, 6 West place,Islington green
Harding James, academy, see Sansbury & Harding
Harding Jas. commercial traveller, 1 Queen st. Stepney
Harding James, straw hat & bonnet ma. 221 Poplar High st
Harding James, tailor, 2 Easton st. Spafields
Harding Jas.window blind ma.35½ Chester pl.Kenngtn.cross
Harding James,window blind maker, 31 Princes rd.Lambth
Harding James Duffield, artist, 4 Gordon square
Harding James Graham, house agent,96 Albany st. Regts.pk
Harding John, auctioneer, 15 Prospect pl. Lw. rd. Deptford
Harding John, carpenter, 15 Edward st. City road
Harding John, *Crown tav. & hotel* 57 Rupert st. Haymarket
Harding John, lacquerer, 38 Chandos st. Covent garden
Harding John, marine store dealer,83 Long la. Bermondsey
Harding John, tailor, 30 Queen st. Horselydown
Harding JohnDorney,D.C.L.advocate,10 College,Doctrs'.com
Harding John Fosse, surgeon, see Brien & Harding
Harding Jonath. watch jewelr. 23 Vineyard gardens, Clkwl
Harding Joseph, farrier, 28 Guildford place, Spafields
Harding Joseph, wine merchant,3 Hungerford wharf, Strand
Harding Mary (Mrs.), dress maker, 182 High Holborn
Harding Mary (Mrs.), shoe peg maker, 21 Great Turner st
Harding Matthew, confectioner, 19 Grafton st. Soho
Harding Peter, carpenter, 22 Park place, Kennington cross
Harding Rachael (Mrs.),cockfoundr.138 St.John st.Smithfld
Harding Richard, bookbinder, 5 New North st. Red Lion sq
Harding Robert, auctioneer, appraiser, undertaker & house agent, 41 Newington causeway
Harding Robert, dyer, 154 St. John st. road
Harding Robert, grocer, 9 North st. Manchester square

Harding Samuel, hairdresser, 41 Dean st. Soho
Harding Stephen, carpenter & bldr. Union rd. Clapham rise
Harding Susannah (Miss), straw bon. ma. 28 Cannon st. Rtclf
Harding Thomas, bookbinder, 3 Broken wf. Up. Thames st
Harding Thomas, builder, 104 Poplar High st
Harding Thomas, marine store dl. 23 Woodland st. Dalston
Harding Thomas, nurseryman, South Island pl. Clapham rd
Harding Thomas, oilman, 67 Marsham st. Westminster
Harding Thomas, undertaker, 6 Shepherd ct. Upp. Brook st
Harding Thos. Elliot, turner, 8 Church pas. Cross st. Islngtn
Harding Walter, *Crown* P.H. 129 Golden lane, St. Luke's
Harding Wm. baker, 90 Gt. Saffron Hill, Hatton wall
Harding Wm. basket maker, 1 Holles st. Cavendish sq
Harding Wm. carpenter&undertaker, 34 Albany rd. Cmbrwl
Harding Wm. fringe & bell rope maker, 192 High Holborn
Harding Wm. grocer, 31 Heath st. Commercial road east
Harding Wm. gun maker, 69 Gt. Queen st. Lincoln's inn flds
Harding Wm. pavior & mason, 5 Johnson st. Westminster, & West wharf, Millbank
Harding Wm. pawnbroker & jeweller, 31 & 32 York st. Westr
Harding Wm. surgeon, &c. 4 Percy st. Bedford sq
Harding Wm. tobacconist, see Croughton & Harding
Harding Wm. jun. dairyman, 25 East st. Manchester sq
Harding Wm. sen. dairy, 13 Up. Dorset st. Bryanstone sq
Harding Wm. sen. brush&basket ma. 33A, Edwards st. Portmn. sq
Hardingham Geo. Gatton, solicitor, 61 Carey st
Hardingham Nath. house agt. &col. 3 Paradise rw. Bethnal gr
Hardingham Samuel, builder & bricklayer, 104 High Holborn
Hardisty Edward B. solicitor, 43 Gt. Marlborough st
Hardman Thomas, pinion maker, 12 Pear Tree st. Goswell st
Hardmans & Iliffes, button manfrs. 16 Gutter la. Cheapside
Hardmeat Charles, fender maker, 22 Budge row, City
Hards Gabriel, fruit & pea salesman, Covent gar. fruit mkt
Hards John, *Dudley Arms* P.H. 47 Dudley grov. Harrow rd
Hardstaff Samuel, grocer, 90 High st. Camden town
Hardwick & Davidson, solrs. Weavers' hall, 22 Basinghall st
Hardwick Joseph & Son, linendrapers, 107 New Bond st
Hardwick Alfred, M.D. surgeon, 28 Lr. Phillimore pl. Kensgtn
Hardwick Edmund, gas fitter, 70 Regent st. Lambeth
Hardwick Edward, boot & shoe ma. 4 College st. Chelsea
Hardwick Jas. dancing academy, 34 Glos'ter ter. Commcl. rd
Hardwick John, glass & china warehouse, 117 St. George st. & 2 Upton place, Commercial road east
Hardwick John, D.C.L. magistrate, Marlborough st. pol. ct
Hardwick John, livery stables, 44 Chenies mews, Bedford sq
Hardwick Joseph, tailor, 23 Middle row, Holborn
Hardwick Philip, R.A. architect & surveyor, 60 Russell sq
Hardwick Thomas, fishmonger, 196 Shadwell High st
Hardwick Thomas, hairdresser, 1 Poplar High st
Hardwick Wm. cabinet maker, 21 Queen st. Pimlico
Hardwicke Wm. surgeon, 12 Lr. Calthorpe st. Gray's inn rd
Hardwicke James, china & glass warehouse, 28 Penny fields, Poplar, & 146 St John st. Smithfield
Hardwidge John, needlemaker to her Majesty, 172 Long lane, Southwark
Hardy Jas. & Sons, playing card maks. 27 St. Paul's church yd
Hardy & Page, cork cutters, 28 Piccadilly
Hardy & Weighton, stationers, 214 Poplar High st
Hardy Wm. Montague & Co. news agents, 136 Fleet st
Hardy Abraham, grocer, 59 Brick lane, Spitalfields
Hardy Benjamin, barrister, 61 Chancery lane
Hardy Benjamin, butcher, 3 Grove terrace, Brompton grove
Hardy Charles N. upholsterer, 5 Grosvenor st. west, Pimlico
Hardy David, plumber, painter, &c. 15 David st. Marylebone
Hardy Edwd. Mitchell, ship & ins. broker, 9 Finch la. Cornhill
Hardy Eliz. (Miss), ladies' school, 7 Artillery ct. Chiswell st
Harle Ezra, surgeon, 109 Chancery lane
Hardy Frances (Mrs.), library, 5 Henry pl. Up. Kenning. la
Hardy Francis, factor, 25 Milk st. Cheapside
Hardy Gathorne, barrister, 4 Inner Temple lane
Hardy George, colonial broker, 27 Mincing lane
Hardy George, ship biscuit ba. see Leftwich, Tousey & Hardy
Hardy Henry, corn dealer, 130 Long acre
Hardy Henry, watchcase mak. 14 Rosoman st. Clerkenwell
Hardy Horatio C.A. *Jerusalem coffee ho.* Cowper's ct. Crnhll
Hardy James, drawing master, 4 Up. Baker st. Regent's pk
Hardy James, plumber, &c. Mason's place, Little Chelsea
Hardy James, watch hand maker, 31 Galway st. St. Luke's
Hardy John, chaser, 24 Coburg st. St. John st
Hardy John, smith & farrier, 47 Holland st. Blackfriars rd
Hardy John, woollendraper, 25 Crawford st. Portman sq
Hardy John Forbes, architect, 23 Rutland gate, Knightsbr
Hardy John, M.P. barrister, 3 Portland place
Hardy John Smart, who. stationer, see Herring, Dewick&Co
Hardy Mitchell Charles, solicitor, 9 Finch lane, Cornhill
Hardy Nathaniel, *Black Lion* P.H. Kilburn
Hardy Peter, actuary to *Mutual LifeAss Soc.* 37 Old Jewry
Hardy Rebecca (Mrs.), milliner, 34 Old Compton st. Soho
Hardy Sam. accountant, 17 Southampton bldgs. Chancery la
Hardy Thos. butcher, 28 Shaftesbury ter. Wilton rd. Pimlico
Hardy Thos. cheesemonger, 15 High st. Kensington So. side
Hardy Thomas, cutler, 70 Three Colt st. Limehouse
Hardy Thos. furniture bro. 26 Union st. Bishopsgate without
Hardy Thos. stationer & printer, 69 Mortimer st. Cavndsh. sq
Hardy Wm. orchill maker, 19 Little George st. Bermondsey
Hardy Wm. professor of music, 41 Gillingham st. Pimlico
Hardy Wm. Langley, hosier, 107 Crawford st. Portman sq
Hardy Wm. Wells, artist & drawing master, 28 Cadogan st
Hardyman Igal, commercl. agent, 7 Fen ct. Fenchurch st
Hardyman Thomas, tailor, 2 King st. Kensington
Hare & Lemon, *Crown* coffee & dining rooms, 35 Drury lane
Hare Wm. & Son, carpet, rug & floorcloth manufacturers, & east india matting importers, 1 King st. Cheapside
Hare Alex. news agent, 92 Sloane st. & 16 North Audley st
Hare Alfred Wm. fancy brush manufr. 11 Alfred st. Islington
Hare Charles, cheesemonger, 45 Up. Marylebone st
Hare Charles John, physician, 9A, Langham place
Hare Edward, *Star & Garter* P.H. 19 Gt. Peter st. Westmnr
Hare George Hy. portrait painter, 33 Up. Berkeley st. west
Hare Jabez, engineering & perspective draughtsman & wood engraver, &c. 10 Nelson square, Blackfriars road
Hare James, linendraper, 2 New st. Dorset square
Hare James, plumbr. painter, &c. 12 Chester st. Kenningtn
Hare John, cus. ho. agt. & ship & ins. bro. Hay's wf. Tooley st
Hare John Wm. barometer & thermtr. ma. see Colomba & Hare
Hare Launcelot, surgeon, 13 Upper Gower st. Bedford sq
Hare Mary (Mrs.), straw hat ma. 37 Charles st. Hatton gdn
Hare Richard, solicitor, 5 South square, Gray's inn
Hare Robert, solicitor, 13 Upper Gower st. Bedford square
Hare Samuel, surgeon, 9A, Langham place
Hare Thos. barrister, 23 Chancery lane
Hare Wm. boarding house, 8 Devonshire sq. Bishopsgate
Hare Wm. coffee & dining rooms, 78 Lombard st
Harenc Chas. Joseph, barrister, 12 King's Bench walk, Temple
Hareshaw Iron Company (Nicholas King, resident London partner), office & warehouse, 14 Fore st. Limehouse
Harford, Rivaz & Co. insurance agents, 75 Old Broad st. City, & Lloyd's
Harford & Bristol Brass Co. (P.S. Ormiston, agt.), 22 Bread st
Harford Henry, tobacconist, 15 Maiden lane, Covent garden
Harford John, nightman & sweep, 17 Adam & Eve ct. Oxford st
Harford Elizh. & Louisa (Misses), milliners, 211 Regent st
Harford Mary Ann (Mrs.), fruiterer, 76 Gracechurch st
Harford Thos. plumber, 10 Stepney rents, Hackney road
Hargrave Bros. flax spinners & ma. of thread & linen by power loom, 1 Crown ct. Cheapside, & Castleton mills, Leeds
Hargrave Brothers, wholesale & export umbrella & parasol & stay manufacturers, 78 Wood st. Cheapside
Hargrave James & Sons, cashmere manufacturers (Edward Upton, agent), 5 Mitre court, Milk st
Hargrave Chas. whalebone manufacturer, 67 Basinghall st
Hargrave John, wholesale & export umbrella manufacturer, &c. dealer in whalebone & well seasoned floorcloths, 6 Bishopsgate without
Hargrave John Fletcher, barrister, 59 Chancery lane
Hargrave Samuel, tailor, 15 Francis st. Tottenham ct. rd
Hargrave Thomas, ironmonger, 82 High st. Shadwell
Hargreave Charles James, barrister, 69 Chancery lane
Hargreave Oliver, barrister, 2 Bloomsbury place
Hargreaves John, bookbinder, 21 Warwick la. Newgate st
Hargrove Robert, hat manfr. 77 New Gravel la. Shadwell
Harker Danl. Rd. undertaker, 3 North bdgs. Finsbury circus
Harker Edw. wax & wafer maker, 37 Fetter la. Fleet st
Harker Geo. spice merchant, 102 & 103 Up. Thames st
Harker John William, jeweller, see Leavers & Harker
Harker Thos. gun maker, 13 Bell st. Vincent sq. Westminster
Harker Wm. coach, harness, &c. currier, 27 Lit. Moorfields
Harkins Charles, wheelwright, 2 Boxtree pl. Grange rd
Harkness Jas. timber merchant, 10 Chapel pl. Long la. Bdsy
Harland Fred. & John, zincman, 3 Cumberland pl. Newington butts
Harland Edmund, cheesemonger, 137 Salisbury ct. Fleet st
Harland Edward, grocer, 4 South Molton st. Oxford st
Harland Richard, wine merchant, 4 Albany st. Regent's pk
Harland Thomas Wm. house painter, see Fisher & Harland
Harle Charles, watchcase maker, 21 Wynyatt st. Goswellrd
Harle Ezra, surgeon, 109 Chancery lane
Harley Benj. musical instr. ma, 1 Summer st. Hatton garden
Harley Elizth. (Mrs.), strawbonnet ma. 1 Lwr. Philmr. pl. Kngtn
Harley Harr. (Mrs.), tobacconist, 296 Albany rd. Camberwell
Harley Henry, saddler, 6 New Union st. Little Moorfields
Harley James, cowkeeper, 10 Charlton st. Fitzroy sq

Harley James, dentist, 23A, Davies st. Berkeley sq
Harley James, engraver, 4 Back Church lane, Whitechapel
Harley Jane E.(Miss), ribbon rosette ma. 6NewUnion st.Fins
Harley John, cabinet inlayer, 8 Robert st. Blackfriars rd
Harley John, marble & colored paper maker, & dealer in bookbindery materials, 5 Racquet ct. Fleet st
Harley John, mar. &colored paper ma. 20St.John's la.Clknwl
Harley John, plumber, &c. 16 Albion pl. Walworth rd
Harley Rd. sec. to *Seamen's Hospital So.*74KingWm.st.City
Harley Thos.bottled ale & porter mercht. 17 Great St.Helen's
Harling Catharine (Mrs.), corn dlr. & seedsman, 2 Dockhead
Harlock Edwd. *Red Lion* P.H. 11 Laystall st. Liquorpondst
Harlock James, watchma. 35 Strutton ground, Westminster
Harlow Frederick, carpenter, 92 Paradise st. Rotherhithe
Harlow John, tobacconist, 9 Leicester square
Harman & Co. merchants, 7 Adam's court, Old Broad st
HarmanThos.Rickman&Son, stockbrokers,14Throgmorton st
Harman Charles, butcher, 151 Shoreditch High st
Harman Charles, veterinary surgeon, 55 Millbank st.Westmr
Harman Chas.Hen. solicitor,4Winckworth buildings,City rd
Harman Dyson, horse dealer, 41 Cross st. Finsbury
Harman George, bootmaker & broker, Deptford High st
Harman James, fruit salesman, Spitalfields market
Harman James, bougie maker, 1 Robert st. Vine st. Blkfrs
Harman James, ironmonger, 13 Chester place, Old Kent rd
Harman John, attorney, 2 Falcon court, Fleet st
Harman John, carpenter, 19 St. James' place, Hampstead rd
Harman Julia (Mrs.), tobacconist, 14 Tabernacle sq. Finsby
Harman Samuel, coachmaker, 100 Gt. Russell st. Bloomsby
Harman Samuel, corndealer, 44 Fore st. Cripplegate
Harman Thomas Henry, linendraper, 116 Gt. Portland st
Harman Wm. farrier, 22 Northampton place, Old Kent road
Harmar & Pearson, distillers, 6 & 7 Redcross st. Cripplegt
Harmden James (Mrs.), milliner, 47 Chapel st. New road
Harmer Chas. china & glass wareho. 40 Lamb's Conduit st
Harmer Chas. Benj. tobacconist, 2 Gt. Turnstile, High Holb
Harmer Henry, beer retailer, Jamaica level, Bermondsey
Harmer John Wm. builder, 59 Aldenham st. Somers town
Harmer Richard, silk manufacturer, see Boyd & Harmer
Harmer Wm. ironmonger, 19 & 7 Horseferry rd. Westminstr
Harms Geo. & Son, waggon wa. Angel inn, 54 Farringdon st
Harms, Son & Brotherton, horsehair manf. 51 Farringdon st
Harms Chas. pastrycook, 12 Spring Garden place, Stepney
Harms Geo. Aubrey, coal merchnt. see Cuthbertson&Harms
Harmsworth Abrm. *White Hart* P.H. 213 Up. Thames st
Harmsworth Henry, *Fox & Hounds* P.H. Stratford
Harmsworth Rich. bootmak. 20 Bartholomew ter. St. Luke's
Harnack Fred. Chas. chinaman, 22 Tottenham st. Fitzroy sq
Harnage Edward, merchant, 37 Gt. Winchester st
Harnden Joseph, bricklayer, 20 Webb st. Bermondsey st
Harness Henry, surgeon, 1 Kimbolton place, Brompton
Harnett William C. & Horatio, merchants, 7 Gt. St. Helen's
Harnett John, dental repository, manufacturer of mineral teeth, & dealer in anatomical preparations, 45 Museum st. Bloomsbury
Harnett Wm. artist in hair & tobacconist, 62 London wall
Harney John, beer retailer, 46 London st. Ratcliff
Harnor William, sen. baker, 82 Snow hill, 45 King st. Snow hill, & 8 Plumber's row, St. Luke's
Harnor William, jun. baker, 10 John's row, St. Luke's
Harnott Henry, plastrs.' hair mftr. Ewer st. Union st. Boro'
Harper & Co.wine, spirit & beer merchts. 2Cowper's ct.Crnhl
Harper Ann (Mrs.), dress & pelisse maker, 20 Coldbath sq
Harper Ann (Mrs.), teadlr, &c. 49 Drummond st.Euston sq
Harper Benjamin, tailor, 64 Cromer st. Brunswick square
Harper Charles, bootmaker, 15 Mercer st. Long acre
Harper Charles, prof. of music,15Compton st.ea.Brunswk.sq
Harper Doyle, tailor, 34 Berwick st. Pimlico
HarperEdw.clog& patten ma. 210 Up.Wh.Cross st.St.Luke's
Harper Edward Norton, agent to Messrs. Bass, Ratcliff & Gretton, brewers, Burton-on-Trent, Jerusalem coffeehouse
Harper Eliza (Mrs.), law stationer, 24 Bell yd. Temple bar
Harper Elizabeth (Mrs.), dairy, 11 Porter st. Soho
Harper Geo. boot & shoe maker, 14 Brown st. Bryanstone sq
Harper Henry, butcher, 193 Shadwell High st
Harper Henry, tailor, 82 Park st. Camden town
Harper Jane (Mrs.), potato dlr. 4 South st. Spitalfields mkt
Harper John, farrier, 1 Bishop's court, Old Bailey
Harper John Alexr.Wm.barrister,13Mitre ct.chamb.Temple
HarperJoseph, *Sun* P.H. 40 Chapel st. Grosvenor place
Harper Robert, surgeon, &c. 2 Conduit st. Hyde park
Harper Saml. glass,china,&c.wareho.13 King's rd. e. Chelsea
Harper Thomas, artist, 23 Alexander sq. Brompton
Harper Thos. lock & cash box ma. 41 Red Lion st. Clerknwll
Harper Thos. jun. prof. of music, 32 Argyle st. New road
HarperThos.sen.prof.of music,19St.Chad's row,Gray's inn rd
Harper William, butcher, 3 John st. Regent's park
Harper William, coach maker,3 George yd. Princes st.Soho
Harper Wm. grocer, 24 Great James st. Lisson grove
Harper Wm. pianoforte maker, 49 Red Lion st. Holborn
Harpham Miles, wholesale fancy cabinet & dressing case maker, 3 Red Lion st. Clerkenwell
Harpur Henry, attorney, 9 Park place, Kennington cross
Harrad Joseph, fruiterer, 27 Nassau pl. Commercial rd. east
Harradence John, *Old Red Lion* P.H. 87 St. John st. rd
Harradence Joseph, butcher, 75 Chiswell st
Harradin Joseph, rag merchant, 33 Dockhead, Bermondsey
Harradine James, beer retailer, 1 Earl st. Blackfriars
Harradine Thomas Saml. tobacconist, 2 Chapel st. New rd
Harral Blagdon, M.D. surgeon, 42 Royal cresc. Notting hill
Harrap Hen.Jsph. boot & shoe maker, 175 Shadwell High st
Harrap Nicholas, bootmaker, Union road, Rotherhithe
Harrap William, carpenter, 65 Paul st. Finsbury
Harratt Chas. colebrookdale iron whfs. 83 Up. Thames st
Harraway John, leather breeches maker, New cross
Harridge Hen. veterinary forge, Pitt's head mews, Mayfair
Harridge Jeremiah, accountant, 13 Colet pl. Commer. rd. e
Harridine Ann (Miss), grocer, 3 White horse st. Piccadilly
Harrigan Peter, tailor, 37 Surrey st. Strand
Harrild Rt.&Sons,printers' matrl.dlrs. compos.rollers & printers' blanket ma. 10, 11 & 12 Gt. Distaff la. & 22 Friday st
Harrild Rt. work. goldsmith, 5 Greneda ter. Commer.rd.east
Harrild Thos. printer, 1 Dudley court, Silver st. Wood st
Harrington & Lucas,wholesale & family teadealers & grocers, 113 Borough High st. & 19 Panton st. Haymarket
Harrington Geo. milliner, 6 Church st. Shoreditch
Harrington Hen. Edw. fruiterer, 15 Barnsbury pl. Islington
Harrington Mary (Mrs.), dressmak.10 NewManor pl.Chelsea
Harrington Richd. law stationer, 5 Serles pl. Lincoln's inn
Harrington Wm. tobacconist, 21 Up. Seymour st. Euston sq
Harrington Wm. Hen. tobacconist, 25 Cloth fair, Smithfield
Harriott James, butcher, Clapham rise
Harris Anthony & Co. coal factors, 17 St. Dunstan's hill
Harris & Baker, meat salesmen, Newgate market
Harris &Billiter,oil mer.6Maze pond,Tooley st.&Mill st.Dkhd
Harris Brothers, manufacturers & importers of wafers & other fancy goods, ormolu & papier machée miniature frames,gilt malls,morocco cases,&c.wholesale silversmiths, 2 New court, Bow lane, Cheapside
Harris Charles & Thomas, shag manufrs. 14 Ironmonger la
Harris & Cumming,worsted spinners & carpet manufacturers, 86 Hatton garden
Harris & Dixon, coal factors & ship agents, 9 Love lane
Harris, Duplex & Harris, surgeons, 13 Fenchurch st
Harris Eliz. (Mrs.), & Son, booksellers, 96 Shadwell High st
Harris & Emary, salt mers. 1 Ferdinand ter. Hampstead rd
Harris & Galabin, stationers, 142 Fenchurch st
Harris George & Sons, stockbrokers, 22 Change alley
Harris & Hall, milliners, 77 Bishopsgate within
Harris & Jacobs, clothes wareh. 35 Marylebone la.Oxford st
Harris John&Richard,potato salesmen,Hay'swharf,Tooley st
Harris John & Thos. herald chasers, 23 OldGlo'ster st.Hxtn
Harris Joseph & Co. discount agents, 29 Lombard st. City
Harris Joseph & George & Co. wholesale tallow chandlers & melters, 72 Broadwall, Blackfriars
Harris & Lilley, soap makers & tallow melters, 5 Gloucester st. Curtain road
Harris (Quarles) & Sons, oporto merchants, 9 Billiter square
Harris & Reece, dairy, 61 King st. Westminster
Harris Ralph & Co. curiosity dlrs. 20 Hanway st. Oxford st
HarrisRd.&Sons, corn&seedfctrs.Salvador ho.200Bishopsg.st
Harris Ruth & Son, furriers & manufrs. 184 Regent st
Harris Samuel & Hen. harness polish ma. 41 Mansell st
Harris Thos. & Son, opticians, 52 Gt. Russell st. Bloomsbury
Harris, Whyting & Co. discount agents & bankers, 29 Lombard st.
Harris Wm. & Son, mathemat. inst. maks. 50 High Holborn
Harris Wm.&Son, carptrs.3Canterbury st.York rd.Lambeth
Harris Aaron, tailor, 1 Hinde st. Manchester sq
Harris Aaron L. operative chemist, &c. 30 Steward st.Bspgt
Harris Abraham, clothes salesman, 31 Chapel st. New rd
Harris Abraham, clothes wareh. 30James st. Buckingham gt
Harris Abraham, navy agent for petty officers & seamen, & clothes warehouse, 1 Sharp's buildings, Tower hill
Harris Alfred, commis. merchant, 23 Jewry st. Aldgate
Harris Ann (Mrs.), *Marquis Granby* P.H.2Pump yd.Ratclff
Harris Anthony, insurance broker, 17 St. Dunstan's hill
Harris Ashur, diamond merchant, 12 Hart st. Bloomsbury
Harris Bartholomew, wholesale stationer, 66 Hatton garden
Harris Cath.(Mrs.), *Robert's Arms* P.H.1Dvnprt.st.Cm.rd.e
Harris Catherine (Mrs.), outfitter, 65 Shadwell High st
Harris Charles, beer retailer, 2 Garden row, Camberwell rd

Harris Charles, carver & gilder, 7 Percy st. Tottenham ct.rd
Harris Charles, teadealer, 91 Borough High st
Harris Charles, *Two Chairmen* P.H. 81 Wardour st. Soho
Harris Charles, working jeweller, 131 Long acre
Harris Christopher, booksl. & news agt. 25 Bow st. Cov. gdn
Harris Cornelius, tool maker, 10 Marylebone la. Oxford st
Harris Cornelius, silk mercer, 77 Bishopsgate within
Harris Danl. cheesemngr. 42 & 43 Bridport pl. NewNorth rd
Harris David, clothes salesman, 27 South st. Manchester sq
Harris David, french polisher, 26 Castle st. east, Oxford st
Harris David, snuff manufactory, 193 Oxford st
Harris Edward, baker, 37 Eastcheap
HarrisEdward,chair & sofa maker, 5 Quickset row, New rd
Harris Edward, *Duke's Head* P.H. 28 Norton folgate
Harris Edward, tobacconist, 85 Crawford st
Harris Edwin, tobacconist, 4 Ray st. Clerkenwell
Harris Eleanor (Mrs.), furrier, 18 Peter st. Saffron hill
HarrisElzth. (Mrs.),chandler's shop, 4 Seymour pl.Cmdn.tn
Harris Elzth. (Mrs.), dyer & scour. 3 Cambridge st.Gldn. sq
Harris Elizabeth (Mrs.),india rubber manufr. 48 Strand
Harris Esther (Miss), carpet shoe ma. 23 St. George st
HarrisFrederic,draftsman & surveyr.14Warwick ct.Holborn
Harris Frederick, haberdashery agent, 4 & 5 Addle st
Harris Frederick, law stationer, 38 Cursitor st. Chancery la
Harris George, barrister, 9 King's Bench walk, Temple
Harris George, boot & shoe ma. 1 Peel pl.Kensgtn. grvl. pits
HarrisGeo.furn. japanner, 10 Cross la. Newton st. Hi. Hlbrn
Harris George, greengrocer, 94 Harmood st. Hampstead rd
Harris George, grocer, &c. 46 Trafalgar st. Walworth
Harris George, medical labeller, 8 Gt. Queen st. Holborn
Harris George, shopkeeper, Mare st. Hackney
Harris George, stonemason, King st. New town, Deptford
Harris George, tailor, &c. 2 Giltspur st. Smithfield
Harris George, writer on glass, 8 Gt. Queen st. Holborn
Harris George James, academy, 58 Westbourne st. Pimlico
Harris Henry, baker, 57 Brewer st. Somers town, & 23 Somers place east, New road
Harris Henry, booksel. & stationer, 18 Bridge st.Westmnstr
Harris Henry, clothes salesman, 5 Holywell st. Strand
Harris Henry, draper, &c. see Murphy & Harris
Harris Henry, fishmonger, 180 Sloane st
Harris Henry, grocer, 1 New st. Horselydown
Harris Henry, hide mercht.2 Union yd.Cole st.Gt. Dover rd
Harris Henry, military outfitter, see Maynard & Harris
Harris Henry, oil & colorman, 12 Dean st. Holborn
Harris Henry, orange merchant, 60 Wilsted st.Somers town
Harris Henry, poulterer, 49 Duke st. Manchester square
Harris Henry, slopseller, 180 High st. Shadwell
Harris Henry, tailor, 1 Gt. Winchester st. Old Broad st
Harris Henry, who. stationer & cigar importer,21 Gt. Alie st
Harris Henry Evans, corndealer, 13 Drury lane, & 53 Broad st. Bloomsbury
Harris Henry Thos.orange mer.&fish salesman,21Botolph la
Harris Hetman Charles, surgeon, 1 Windsor place, City rd
Harris Isaac, oilman, 19 Fenchurch st
Harris Isabelle (Miss), school, 4 Caledonia pl. Caldn. road
Harris Jacob, cowkeeper, 17 Harrow road, Paddington
Harris James, baker, 172 Fenchurch st
Harris James, baker, 62 Roupell st. Cornwall road
Harris James, bootmaker, 12 Rosamon bldgs. Islngtn. grn
Harris James, *Salmon* P.H. 90 Union st. Borough
Harris James, dairyman, 13 Pollen st. Hanover square
Harris James, dyer, 13 Rufford's row, Islington High st
Harris James, linendraper, 8 High st. Bow
Harris James, silk dyer, &c. 8 Kenton st. Brunswick sq
Harris James, tallow chandler, 39 Monkwell st. Cripplegate
Harris James, tea & col. ag. 14 Langbourn cham. Fench. st
Harris Jas.veternry.surgeon, Fox & Goose yd.26London wall
Harris James Edw. auctioneer, 61 Hercules bldgs. Lambeth
Harris James Edw. tea dealer & grocer, 33 Gt. Suffolk st
Harris Jason, *Belgrave Arms* P.H. Queen's road, Dalston
Harris John, artist, 17 Red Lion square
Harris John, artist, 40 Sidmouth st. Gray's inn road
Harris John, baker, 38 Marsham st. Westminster
Harris John, beer retailer, 18 Exeter st. Sloane st
Harris John, booking office, Nag's Head, Borough High st
Harris John, butcher, 250 Bermondsey st
Harris John, butcher, 1 Providence bldgs. New Kent road
Harris John, cabinetmaker, 33 Aldenham st. Somers town
Harris John, carpenter, 15 Adam st. east, Portman square
Harris John, carpenter, 4 Allsop place, Regent's park
Harris John, cheesemonger, 57 Dudley grove, Harrow road, & 230 Oxford st
Harris John, chemist & french polish mfr. 33 Beech st. Brbicn
Harris John, coal merchant, 25 Wapping
Harris John, french warehouse, 133 Cheapside
Harris John, gasfitter & brassfounder, 148 High Holborn
Harris John, mahogany, deal & timber merchant, 33 Wilson st. Finsbury, & at Orange st. Gravel la. Southwark
Harris John, newsvender, 14 Up. Chapman st. St. Geo. east
Harris John, physician, 28A, Albemarle st. Piccadilly
Harris John, silversmith, 27 Nelson st. City road
Harris John, solicitor, 22 Argyll st. Regent st
Harris John, timber merchant, 23 Earl st. Finsbury
Harris John, upholsterer, 231 Tottenham court road
Harris John, watch case maker, 22 Glo'ster st. St.John st. rd
Harris John Greathed, com. of Insolvent Debtors' court
Harris John Jas. watch & clock mak. 11 Up. East Smithfield
Harris John N. tailor & draper, 384 Oxford st
Harris John Rt. silver spoon & fork manufactur. 29 Kirby st
Harris Joseph, baker, 19 Marygold st. Bermondsey
Harris Joseph, furniturebroker, 41 New rd. St.George's st. ea
Harris Joseph, gas fitter, 74 Berwick st. Soho
Harris Joseph, pawnbroker, 80 Hackney road
Harris Joseph, potato salesman, 21 Mill lane, Tooley st. & 183 Shoreditch
Harris Joseph, *Ship* P.H. 13 Carnaby st. Golden square
Harris Joseph, *Ship* P.H. 31 Limekiln hill, Limehouse
Harris Joseph, shipping agent, 67 Lower Thames st
Harris Joseph,*Two Brewers*P.H.129 Bunhill rw.Chiswell st
Harris Langley Hilton, solicitor, 12 Furnival's inn
Harris Laurence, plumber, 127 Edgware road
Harris Lawrence,who. flock dealer,45Brick lane, Spitalfields
Harris Lawrence Beton, foreign warehouseman (agents to Dodfus, Meig & Co. of Paris), 133 Cheapside
Harris Mark Light, cowkeeper, 3 Bouverie st. Paddington
Harris Martha(Mrs.),wardrobe dlr.17Adam st. ea.Portmn.sq
Harris Mary (Miss), grocer, &c. 37 New rd. St. George's east
Harris Mary (Mrs.), confectioner, 7 Church st. Kensington
Harris Mary(Mrs.),*Nag'sHeadInn*, Nag's Head bdgs.Boro'
Harris Mary (Mrs.), stayma.48 Hedge row,High st.Islington
Harris Michael, furrier, 3 Castle st. Houndsditch
Harris Morris, rag merchant, 4 Haddon place, Waterloo rd
Harris Philip, brassfounder, 120 Wardour st. Soho
Harris Philip, tailor, 20 High row, Knightsbridge
Harris Rachel (Mrs.), baker, 12 Aske st. Hoxton
Harris Richard, west india merchant, see Vaux & Harris
Harris Richard Douglas, surgeon, 23 George st. Euston sq
Harris Robert, furniture & bedding manufacturer, 125 High Holborn, & 38 King st. Holborn
Harris Robert, brewer, 34 & 35 Ossulston st. Somers town
Harris Robert, chair & couch maker, 23 Old st. road
Harris Robert, confectioner, 130 Church st. Shoreditch
Harris Robert, *Crooked Billet* P.H. 32 Ratcliff highway
Harris Robert,*Duke of York* P.H.2York ter.Camb. new road
Harris Robert, grocer, 220 Hoxton old town
Harris Robert plumber, &c. 8 Clayton st. Kennington green
Harris Robert, tobacconist, 11 Ann's place, Hoxton
Harris Salem Constable, notary, see Scorer, Withers & Co
Harris Samuel, carpenter & undertaker,22 Noble st.Spafields
Harris Samuel, fishmonger, 15 Langley pl. Comml. road ea
Harris Samuel, *Roebuck* P.H. 37 Park st. Dorset square
Harris Samuel James, whipmaker, 57 St. John st. Smithfield
Harris Silas, color & varnish ma. Grove,Gt.Guildfd. st. Boro
Harris Silvester, egg merch. 10 Railway mews, Drummond st
Harris Simeon John, engraver, 23 Castle st. Leicester sq
Harris Susan (Mrs.), whitesmith, 2Bowling sq.Whitecross st
Harris S.(Mrs.),*Winds.Cast.*P.H.23NwChurch st.w.Egw.rd
Harris Sydney P. portuguese agent, 52 Mount st. Berkly. sq
Harris Thomas, *Bell Sauvage tap* P.H.,B. S. yd.Ludgt. hill
Harris Thomas, *Blue Last* P.H.47 Compton st. Clerkenwell
Harris Thomas, coal merchant, 18 Castle st. east, Oxford st
Harris Thomas, cowkeeper, 7 Bostons t. Dorset square
Harris Thomas, cowkeeper, 11 Lit.Derweston st.Marylebone
Harris Thomas, Eagle brewery, 7 Sol's row, Hampstead rd
Harris Thomas, engine turner, 3 Skinner st. Clerkenwell
Harris Thomas, *Globe* P.H. 22 York bldgs. New rd.Maryleb
Harris Thomas, tailor, 21 Cross st. Islington
Harris Thomas, *White Swan* P.H.1 New st. sq. Shoe lane
Harris Timothy, painter, 6 Blandford mews, Manchester sq
Harris Wm. architect & surveyor, 55 Park st. Grosvenor sq
Harris Wm. attorney, 5 Stone buildings, Lincoln's inn
Harris Wm. baker, 46 South st. South Audley st
Harris Wm. bed & mattress mak.122 Curtain rd. Shoreditch
Harris Wm. beer retailer, 5 Portugal pl. Cambridge road
Harris Wm. *Black Horse* P.H.Low. Thames st. Rotherhithe
Harris Wm. builder, 5 Tavistock ct. Covent garden
Harris Wm. carman & beer retailer, Caledonian rd. Pentonv
Harris Wm. carpenter & builder, 60 Green st. Grosvenor sq
Harris Wm. coal merchant, Irongate wharf, Paddington
Harris Wm. copper plate printer, 26 Phœnix st. Somers tn
Harris Wm. currier, 13 Long lane, Bermondsey

Harris Wm. grocer, 5 Little Peter st. Westminster
Harris Wm. haberdasher, 128 Church st. Shoreditch
Harris Wm. inspector of houses & places for slaughtering horses, 49 Union street, Friar street, Blackfriars road
Harris Wm. ironmonger, 6 Wentworth pl. Mile end road
Harris Wm. *Portman Arms* P.H. 34 Great Quebec st
Harris Wm. *Queen's Head* P.H. 405 Strand
Harris Wm. solicitor, 18 Hart st. Bloomsbury sq
Harris Wm. stationer, 46 St. John st. Clerkenwell
Harris Wm. tailor & draper, 197 Borough High st
Harris Wm. tailor, 4 Barnsbury place, Islington
Harris Wm. tailor, 26 Lamb's Conduit st. Foundling
HarrisWm. timb. mer. York rd. & 32 Palace New rd.Lambth
Harris Wm. Dollond, optician & globe maker, 38 Arundel st
Harris Wm. Gregory, grove brewery, 24 & 25 Lisson grove nt
Harris Wm. Henry, surgeon, 37 Gt. James st. Lisson grove
Harris William Hugh, news agent, 244 Blackfriars road
Harris Wm. Thos. oil, &c. broker, &c. see Aylwin, Bevan&Co
Harris Wintour, surgeon, 1 New Dorset pl. Clapham road
Harris Wolfe, clothes salesman, 133 Rosemary lane
Harrison Arthur & Son, herald painters, &c. 23Gt. Portland st
Harrison & Bell, warehousemen, 9 Milk st. Cheapside
Harrison brothers, notaries, 2 George yd. Lombard st
Harrison & Burn, tailors, 39 Sackville st. Piccadilly
Harrison & Co. stationers, 41 Bedford st. Covent garden
Harrison & Cottle, stockbrokers, 13 Throgmorton st
Harrison & Dobree, attorneys, 22 Hart st. Bloomsbury
Harrison Edward & Chas. solicitors, 19 Bedford row
Harrison Francis & Chas. jewellers, 39 Gt. Marlborough st
Harrison Frederick & Co. london quilting printers, & fancy waiscoat warehousemen, 7 & 8 Bow Church yard
Harrison Harriet & Hen. pawnbrokers, 95 Wardour st. Soho
Harrison John & Wm. painters, &c. 17 Duke st. Grosvenorsq
Harrison Joseph & Sons, tailors, 33 White st. Boro'
Harrison (Layman) & Co. color&varnishma. Stratford, Essex
Harrison Matthew & Sons, stationers & booksel. 82 Cornhill
Harrison&Nichols, ship&ins.agents. 1ThreeKingct. Lombardst
Harrison Robert & Co. merchants, 18 Philpot lane
Harrison Sam. Charles&Co. cheesemngrs, 43MiltonstCriplgt
Harrison Thos.&Colpitts, who. coffee dlrs. 23 Martin's la. City
Harrison Thos. & David, solicitors & irish agts. 5 Walbrook
Harrison Thos. Rd.&Co. printers, 45St. Martin'sla. Charingcrs.
Harrison Wm. & Co. carpenters&tim. mers. Marest. Hackney
HarrisonWm. Henry& Co. commission agts. 150 Fenchurch st
Harrison Winans & Eastwick, merchants, 1 Crooked la. cha
HarrisonAgnes (Mrs.), coal dlr. 1 Lit. Woodstock st. Oxford st
Harrison Alf. Rd. pawnbroker, 1 & 2 Clarendon sq. Somers tn
Harrison Alfred Richard, pawnbroker, 254 Strand
Harrison Anthony, *Golden Anchor* P.H. 9 Park st. Borough
HarrisonAnthy. A. *LordNelson* P.H. 10Manorpl. Nth. Chelsea
HarrisonAugustine, carpenter, 6St. Mark'srd. Cambrwl. nw. rd
Harrison Antonio William Julian, hosiery, millinery, stay, & childbed linen warehouse, 62 Farringdon st
Harrison Caleb Henry, haberdasher, 43 Whitechapel rd
Harrison Chas. *Hero of Maida* P.H 4 Maida hill, Edgw. rd
Harrison Chas. whitesmith, 6 Exeter st. Lisson grove
Harrison Chas. T. teadealer, see Williamson & Harrison
Harrison Daniel, baker, 33 Bridport place, Hoxton
Harrison Daniel, goldsmith, working jeweller & watchmaker, 6 Lowther Arcade, Strand
Harrison Edward, bookseller, 146 Kingsland rd
Harrison Edward Matthew, barrister, 44 Chancery lane
Harrison Edwin, dining rooms, 43 Liverpool st. Bishopsgate
Harrison Edwin, physician, 13 Grove ter. St. John's wood
Harrison Francis, *Pitt's Head* P.H. 98 Broad st. Ratcliff
Harrison Francis, furnishg. ironmonger, 185Tottenham ct. rd
Harrison Fras. John, fellmonger, 40 Crucifix la. Bermondsey
Harrison Frank, solicitor, 3 Verulam buildings, Gray's inn
Harrison Frederick, solicitor, 44 Bloomsbury square
Harrison Frederick, stock&ins. brok. see Hichens'&Harrison
Harrison Fredk. *Tavistock hotel*, Gt. Piazza, Covent garden
Harrison Geo. artist, 15 Foley place, Marylebone
Harrison Geo. brushmaker, 34 Kent st. Borough
Harrison Geo. builder, 16 Carlton terrace, St. James's
Harrison Geo. chandler's shop, 24 Green st. Bethnal green
Harrison Geo. lapidary, 5 Old Compton st. Soho
Harrison Geo. *Montpelier* P.H. 38 Montpelier rw, Bromptn
Harrison George, secretary to the Brighton, Croydon, & Dover Joint station committee, 1 Joiner's st. Tooley st
Harrison Geo. surgeon, 67 Brook st. Hanover square
Harrison George Berkeley, merchent, 24 Gt. Tower st
Harrison George William, merchant, 51 Old Broad st. City
Harrison Harriet (Mrs.), stayma. 1 Saville rw. Walworth rd
Harrison Henry, architect&surveyor, 35Hill st. Berkeley sq
Harrison Henry, beer retailer, 4 Lit. Warner st. Clerkenwell
Harrison Henry, drysalter, 36 Long acre
Harrison Henry, fruiterer, 2 Bermondsey st
Harrison Henry, hairdresser, 2 North Audley st. Grosvnr. sq
Harrison Henry, stationer, 23½ Swan st. Minories
Harrison Henry, surgeon, 8 Egremont place, New road
Harrison Henry, tailor & draper, 10 Leigh st. Red Lion sq
Harrison Henry, wheelwright, George yard, Aldgate
Harrison Isaac, boot & shoe maker, 28 Jewin st. Cripplegate
Harrison James, architect & surveyor, 1 Holford sq. Pentonvil
Harrison James, baker, 41 Pool st. New North road
Harrison James, bootmaker, 10 Lascelles pl. Broad st. St. Giles
Harrison James, builder, 45 & 46 Duke st. Lincoln's inn fields
Harrison James, chemist, &c. Stratford broadway
Harrison James, commissin. agt. & silk printer, 26 Gutter la
Harrison James, hardwaman, 47Guildfordpl. Lr. Kennington l
Harrison James, straw hat presser, 2 Artillery pl. west
Harrison James, tailor & clothes wareho. 37 Hampstead road
Harrison James Park, architect, 11 Chancery lane
Harrison John, accountant, 3 Hagley place, New Kent road
Harrison John, attorney, see Addison & Harrison
Harrison John, bedding wareho. see Bradford & Harrison
Harrison John, boot & shoemaker, 59 Bethnal green road
Harrison John, builder, 15Page's walk, Grangerd. Bermondsy
Harrison John, commisn. agt. for. col. produce, &c. 22Eastcheap
Harrison John, copper plate printer, see Brooker & Harrison
Harrison John, *Earl St. Vincent* P.H. Philpotst. Commerclrd
Harrison John, hatter, 2 Beaufort ter. ea. Kingsrd. we. Chlsea
Harrison John, heel ball manufacturer, 6 Helmet row, Oldst
Harrison John, hop factor, Calvert's bldgs. 241 Boro' High st
Harrison John, lith. & copperplate printer, 46 Museum st
Harrison John, livery stables, 34 Melton st. Euston square, & 28 Euston mews, Melton st
Harrison John, merchant, see Saunders & Harrisons
Harrison John, plasterer, 7 Finsbury st. Chiswell st.
Harrison John, rope & twinemaker, 85Green st. Bethnal green
Harrison John, sawing & planing mills, Swan st. Old Kent rd
Harrison John, sheep salesman, see Martin & Harrison
Harrison John, solicitor, 5 New inn, Wych st. Strand
Harrison John, stockbroker, 7 Hanover pl. Old Kent rd
Harrison John, surgeon, 1 Albany court yard, Piccadilly
Harrison John A. *Ticket Porter* P.H. Arthur st. west, City
Harrison JohnBall, stock brok. 8 Bank chamb. & Stock exch
Harrison John Henry, baker, 274 Strand
Harrison John Joseph, wine merchant, 16 Mincing lane
Harrison John Newman, tobacconist, 15 St. James's st
Harrison John S. solicitor, Rolls chambers, 89 Chancery la
Harrison Joseph, tailor, 8 Lamb place, Kingsland road
Harrison JosephRt. grocer&cheesemn. 31Warren st. Fitzroysq
Harrison Josias Thomas, cooper, &c. 30 Haydon st. Minories
Harrison Leonard, tailor, 121 Gt. Portand st. Marylebone
Harrison Launcelot White, printer, 17 Oxford st
Harrison Margt. (Mrs.), fireiron ma. 34Pear Tree ct. Clrknwl
Harrison Mathew, ironmonger, 2 Hawley pl. Kentish town
Harrison Matthew, smith & bell hangr. 7 Cain pl. Kentish tn
Harrison Pryce Ilbert, barrister, 2 Inner Temple lane
Harrison Ralph, barrister, 6 Old square, Lincoln's inn
Harrison Rueben coach builder, Brook st. New road
Harrison Richard coach lace maker, 90 Drury lane
Harrison Richd. *Peacock* P.H. 16Houghton st. Clare market
Harrison Richd. solicitor, see Tennant, Harrison & Tennant
Harrison Richd. Hopkins, barrister, 3 Tanfield ct. Temple
Harrison Rich. Tarrant, special pleader, 2 Pump ct. Temple
Harrison Robert, dyer & scourer, 84 Queen st. Cheapside
Harrison Robert, silk manf. see Campbell, Harrison & Co
Harrison Robert, stationer, 46 Clipstone st
Harrison Robert L. draper, 89 High st. Portland town
Harrison Samuel, *King's Head* P.H. 14 Earl st. Blackfriars
Harrison Samuel, grocer, &c. 15 Duke st. Portland place
Harrison Saml. locksmith & tinman, 52Stanhope st. Clare mkt
Harrison Sophia (Mrs.), jeweller, 28 St. John's sq. Clerknwl
Harrison Swainston, wine merchant, 37 St. Mary-at-hill
Harrison Thos. apothecary, dispensary, Church row, Islingtn
Harrison Thomas, bricklayer & stenciller, 9Robert st. Hoxton
Harrison Thomas, cattle salesman, 60 West Smithfield
Harrison Thomas, dial enameller, 5 Wynyatt st. Goswell rd
Harrison Thomas, hatter, 8 Little Compton st. Soho
Harrison Thomas, tailor&robema. 21 Brownlow st. Bedford rw
Harrison Thomas, timber mercht. 1 Hudson's ter. Millbank
Harrison Thomas Wm. merchant, 3 Crown ct. Philpot lane
Harrison Wm. auctioneer & valuer, 1 Hanover pl. Old Kent rd
Harrison Wm. average stater, 2 Cowper's court, Cornhill
Harrison Wm. builder, 12 Millbank row, Westminster
Harrison Wm. cheesemonger, see Hardcastle & Harrison
Harrison Wm. cooper, 15 Lambeth walk
Harrison Wm. grocer, 11 York st. Hans place, Sloane st
Harrison Wm. law & general stationer, 116 Chancery lane
Harrison Wm. lodging house, 3 Chapel st. West, Mayfair

Harrison Wm. merchant, see Saddler, Harrison & Co
Harrison Wm. milliner, 21 Bath st. City road
Harrison Wm. painter & glazier, 29 Martin's lane, Cannon st
Harrison Wm. tailor, 1 Ebenezer pl. Commercial rd. Limeho
Harrison Wm. Anthony, surg. dentist, 34 Keppel st. Russell sq
Harrison Wm. George, snuff & cigar manfr. 15 Bucklersbury
Harrison Wm. Hopkins, barrister, 2 New square, Lincoln's inn
Harrison Wm. Russell, surgeon & chem. 2 Marshamst. Westmr
Harriss Robert & Co. ironmongers, Roebuck pl. Gt. Dover rd
Harriss Charles, solicitor, 63 Up. Stamford st. Blackfrs. rd
Harriss James, butcher, 9 Meat market, Leadenhall market
Harriss Robt. Jas. who. shoewareho. 30 Little Bell al. Coleman st
Harriss Sarah (Mrs.), cowkeeper, 129 Goswell st
Harriss Wm. coach builder, George yd. Crowder st. Soho
Harrisson Ludgater Wm. oil & colorman, 269 Whitechapel rd
Harrisson Thomas, *Fleur de Lis* P.H. Fleur de lis st. Nrtn. Flgte
Harrod Charles, tea dealer, 4 Cable st. Wellclose square
Harrod Jas. dairy, 8 Henry st. Cumberland market
Harrod John, grocer, 18 New Quebec st. Portman square
Harrold John, shirtmaker, 102 Whitechapel High st
Harrold Sarah (Mrs.), beer retailer, 1 Bray's place, Islington
Harrold Thomas, carpenter, 8 Cumberland row, Islington
Harrold William, chemist, Church st. Hackney
Harrop Danl. coal mercht. 3 Union whf. South side Paddn. basin
Harrop George, baker, 7 John st. west, Edgware road
Harrop Tabitha (Miss), milliner, 3 Skinner st. Snowhill
Harropp Elijah & Geo. goldsmiths, 5 Lr. Ashby st. Nrthmptn. sq
Harrow Wm. & Son, gasfitters, 14 Portland st. Wardour st
Harrow G. box & case ma. 5 Swallow st. Regt. st. & 38 Old Bond st
Harrow Hannah (Mrs.), carpenter, 34 Brydges st. Covent gar
Harrow Henry, bricklayer, Hatton yard, Hatton wall
Harrower John, beer retailer, 1 Newmarket ter. Cam. heath
Harrowin Ann (Mrs.), ironmonger, Kingsland High st.
Harryman Wm. hopfactor, see Doggett & Harryman
Harsant James Ashley, cane dlr. & man. 20 Norfolk st. Boro'
Harsant Elizth. (Mrs.), carpenter & undertaker, 53 Gt. Tower st
Harsant James Ashley, grocer, 18 Lit. Guildford st. Borough
Harslett Henry, carman, 12 St. Andrew's hill
Harslett Sarah (Mrs.), dairy, 4 Duke st. Grosvenor square
Harston Alfred Dew, surgeon, 22 Trinidad pl. Liverpool rd
Harston Arthur Geo. law stationer, 29 Castle st. Holborn
Hart Aaron & John, who. bootmaks. 62 Leman st. Goodman'fi
Hart & Batten, grocers & teadealers, 39 High st. Deptford
Hart & Crouch, ironmongers & carpet bag frame manufacturers, 45 Drury lane
Hart Fred. & Co. wine imports. 11 Water la. & 64 Lr. Thames st
Hart & Levy, pen & quill manfs. & steel pen agts. 27 Houndsditch
Hart George & Son, hatters, cap makers, & hat lining & leather cutters, & hatters' trimming makers, 205 High Hlbn
Hart & Ingham, linendrapers, see Ingham & Hart
Hart Joseph & Sons, wholesale & retail ironmongers, 53 & 54 Wych st. Strand
Hart Judah & Co. jewellers, silversmiths, &c. 31 Bevis marks
Hart Judah & Co. east & west india merchts. 31 Bevis marks
Hart (Lemon) & Son, wine & spirit importers, 59 Fenchurch st
Hart Michael Hen. & Sons, slopselrs. &c. 83 St. George st
Hart Napthali & Son, wholesale & retail watch, clock & chronometer makers, 5 King street, Finsbury
Hart Aaron Henry, upholsterer & cabinet ma. 356 Oxford st
Hart Abrm. marine store dlr. 20 Grace's alley, Wellclose sq
Hart Abraham Septimus, dentist, 6 Lowndes ter. Knightsbr
Hart Andrew, *Royal Oak* P.H. Haberdashers walk, Hoxton
Hart Ann (Mrs.), teadealer & grocer, 56 West Smithfield
Hart Barnett, clothes salesman, 4 Long lane, Smithfield
Hart Benjamin, hatter, 122 Rosemary lane
Hart Benjamin, tobacconist, 8 Salisbury st. Lisson grove
Hart Charles, grocer, 4 Newington causeway
Hart Chas. stationer & newsvender, 13 Gilbert st. Oxford st
Hart Chas. wine merchant, Ivy cot. Up. Kennington green
Hart Edward, professor of music, 84 Guilford st. Russell sq
Hart Eleazer, rag merchant, 20 White Lion st. Norton folgate
Hart Elizabeth (Miss), baby linen warehouse. 334 Oxford st
Hart Frederick, professor of music, 13 King sq. Goswell rd
Hart George, baker, 23 Seabright st. Bethnal green road
Hart George, butcher, 2 Queen st. Charles sq. Hoxton
Hart George, *Wallace's Head* P.H. 4 Blandford st. Portm. sq
Hart Hannah (Mrs.), *Magpie & Stump* P.H. 56 Fetter lane
Hart Henry, army clothier & tailor, 26 Pall mall
Hart Henry, clothes salesman, 26 Broad st. Bloomsbury
Hart Henry, painter & paperhanger, 4 Knightsbridge terrace
Hart Henry, plumber, 3 Union st. Borough
Hart Henry, solicitor, 2 Portsmouth st. Lincoln's inn fields
Hart Hen. Chas. L. academy, 3 & 4 Old road, Limehouse
Hart James, academy, 10 Gee st. Somers town
Hart James, butcher, 47 Kingsland road
Hart James, commission agent, 6 New Broad st. City
Hart James, shawl warehouse, see Howes & Hart
Hart James, wine merchant, 18 Threadneedle st
Hart Janet (Mrs.), plumber, 53 South Audley st
Hart Joel, draper & mercer, 18 Somerset st. Aldgate
Hart John, baker, 7 Devonshire place, Commercial road
Hart John, clothes salesman, 3 Rosemary lane
Hart John, corn dealer, 16 Rochester ter. Vauxhall bdge. rd
Hart John, lead pencil manufr. 3 Goulstone st. Whitechapel
Hart John, packing case ma. 106 St. John st. Clerkenwell
Hart John, plumber & glazier, 13 Fort st. Spitalfields
Hart John, regimental tailor & masquerade & fancy costume warehouse, 66 Quadrant, Regent st
Hart John, sailmaker, 8 Bird st. London docks, & warehouse 331 Wapping
Hart John, stock maker, 21 Sudeley st. City road
Hart John, veterinary surgeon, 32 Leather lane
Hart John, violin & gun wareho. 14 Princes st. Leicester sq
Hart John, stonemason, 1 Salisbury st. Stepney
Hart John Thos. coachcurrier, &c. 16 Union st. east, Spitalfi
Hart Joseph, baker & corn chandler, 116 Wapping
Hart Joseph, beer retailer, 1 Queen's Head la. Islington
Hart Joseph, music engraver & publisher, & pianoforte maker, 109 Hatton garden
Hart Joseph, plumber, &c. 96 Fenchurch st
Hart Joshua, merchant, Lloyd's
Hart Leah (Mrs.), china dlr. 7 Middlesex st. Aldgate High st
Hart Lewis, clothes salesman, 7 & 26 Holywell st. Strand
Hart Mary (Mrs.), *Feathers tavern*, 1 Hand ct. Holborn
Hart Mary (Mrs.), milliner, &c. 40 Gainsford st. Horselydn
Hart Michael, clothes salesmn. 11 Stepney rents, Hackny. rd
Hart Michael Brannan, coffee rooms, 159 Aldersgate st
Hart Napthali, fruiterer, 6 & 7 Gt. Hall, Hungerford market
Hart Peter, fruiterer, 1 St. Mark's rd. Camberwell New road
Hart Ralph, furniture broker, 31 Gt. Wild st. Lincoln's inn
Hart Richard, solicitor, see Chatfield, Wingate & Hart
Hart Robert, barrister, 2 Middle Temple lane, Temple
Hart Robert, bricklayer, 11 Crosby row. King st. Borough
Hart Robert, engraver, 15 Gloucester st. Queen square
Hart Robert, fancy work repository, 148 New Bond st
Hart Robert, *Guy Earl of Warwick* P.H. 42 St. John st. Clkwl
Hart Samuel, clothier, 3 Barbican
Hart Samuel, hairdresser, 35 Somerset st. Aldgate
Hart Sarah (Mrs.), button & trimming seller, 15 Wych st
Hart Simon, pen & quill manufacturer, 4 Duke st. Aldgate
Hart Solomon Alex. R.A. artist, 22 Charles st. Middsx. hospl
Hart Thomas, *Blue Posts tavern*, 13 Cork st. Bond st
Hart Thomas, fancy stationer, 2 Watt's ter. Old Kent rd
Hart Thomas, hairdresser, 18 Great Marylebone st
Hart Thomas, *Hope* coffee rooms, 8 Sarah pl. Old st. rd
Hart Thomas, merchant, Bridewell whf. William st. Blkfriars
Hart Thomas, provision agent & factor, 2 Seething lane
Hart Wm. baker, 85 Hackney road
Hart Wm. baker, 58 Margaret st. Hackney fields
Hart Wm. baker, 59 Rosemary lane
Hart Wm. carman, 34 Wharf road, City road
Hart Wm. *George & Dragon* P.H. 13 Beech st. Barbican
Hart Wm. grocer & cheesemonger, 170 Union st. Boro' High st
Hart Wm. hat maker, 83 Whitechapel High st
Hart Wm. *Jolly Weavers* P.H. 21 John's row, St. Luke's
Hart Wm. *New Inn* P.H. 9 Bulstrode st. Manchester sq
Hart Wm. merchant, 23 Lombard st
Hart Wm. *White Swan* P.H. 9 Ray st. Clerkenwell
Hart Wm. Benedict, surgeon, see Byles & Hart
Hart Wm. Daniel, ivory turner, 17 Eyre st. hill, Hatton gdn
Harte Roach Dickinson, oil & colorman, 39 Marsham st. Westm
Hartfield Wm. tortoiseshell worker, 134 Long la. Bermondsy
Hartill John, fender & fire iron maker, 89 West Smithfield
Harting Jas. V. & Joseph T. solicitors, 24 Lincoln's inn flds
Hartland Fredk. grocer, 20 Frederick st. Regent's park
Hartley James & Co. (managers of City of Dublin & British & Irish Steam Packet Companies), 137 Leadenhall st.; & 33 Regent Circus, Piccadilly; & Dublin steam wharf, Lower East Smithfield
Hartley James & Co. (John James Kayll, agent), window glass & alkali manufacturers, 43 Upper Thames st
Hartley John & Reed, mast & oar makers, 8 Fore st. Limeho
Hartley's Wharf, Parker & Whitby, Freeman's lane, Back st. Horselydown
Hartley Warwick & Co. engravers & printers, 67 Newgate st
Hartley Bottle Co. (Thomas Gorton, agt.), Cousin lane, Upper Thames st
Hartley Ambrose, potato dealer, 17 Langley pl. Com. rd. east
Hartley Edmund, fruiterer, 10 Down st. Piccadilly
Hartley Edwd. chemist & druggist, 35 Eyre st. hill
Hartley Fountain John, trimming ma. see Chartier & Hartley
Hartley Geo. boot & shoe maker, 41 Charles st. Hampstd. rd

Hartley Hannah (Mrs.), teadealer, 14 Brewer st. Somers tn
Hartley Henry, tailor, 11 Pearson st. Kingsland rd
Hartley James, *Crown* P.H. 356 Oxford st
Hartley James, shipowner, 137 Leadenhall street
Hartley James, solicitor, 27 New Bridge st. Blackfriars
Hartley John, tobacco manufacturer, see Randon & Hartley
Hartley Joseph, pencil & brushma.1 Hampden st. Somers tn
Hartley Joshua, bootmaker, 11 King st. St. James's
Hartley Joseph, tailor, 12 Notting hill High st
Hartley Nathnl. *Axe hotel, tavern & coffee h.* 20 Aldermanbury
Hartley Perceval, barrister, 27 New Bridge st
Hartley Richard, Wm. smith & bell hanger, 13 Crown st. Soho
Hartley Thomas, artist, 109 Stanhope st. Hampstead road
Hartley Thomas, hat manufacturer, 46 Whitechapel road
Hartley Thomas, laceman, 20 Edgware road
Hartley Thomas Robert, hatter, 1 Barbican
Hartley William, shoemaker, 5 Bloomsbury st. Bloomsbury
Hartley William, solicitor, 6 Southampton st. Bloomsbury
Hartnall George, dealer in birds, 2 Edward st. Wardour st
Hartnell Joseph, printer, 5 Red Lion passage, Fleet st
Hartnell Nathaniel, artist, 1 Hagley place, New Kent road
Hartnett Edward, oil & colorman, 50 James st. Oxford st
Harton & Watts, wholesale pewterers, manufacturers of tallowchandlers' candle mould pipes & frames, and music plates & metal inkstands, 61 Shoe lane
Harton James B. lodging house keeper, 11 Charterhouse la
Harton William Hen. attorney, 15 Clifford's inn, Fleet st
Hartree Henry, cooper, Fountain stairs, Bermondsey wall
Hartree William, slopseller, 324 Rotherhithe
Hartridge William, stockbroker, 80 Old Broad st. City
Hartry Thomas & John, dentists, 41 St. Martin's lane
Hartshorn Henry, *Three Kings'* P.H. 9 Orange st. Blmbry
Hartshorn John, cooper, 4 Heneage st. Brick la. Spitalflds
Hartshorn Wm. jun. watch spring ma.4 Heneage st.Sptlflds
Hartshorne Anthony, commisn agt.30 Fashion st.Spitalfields
Hartshorne George, linendraper, 30 Seymour st. Euston sq
Hartshorne Geo. jun. who. ironmongr. 14 Lit. Tower st. City
Harttree Eliza & Geo. embroidery,&c imptrs.11 Edgware rd
Hartwig Isaac, printer, 1 Little St. Mary Axe
Harvard John, inspector of weights & measures, Guildhall
Harvard John, surveyor of weights & measures, 97 Murray st. Hoxton
Harvey, Bartrum & Co. woollen drapers, 73 to 75 Ludgate hill
Harverson John, jun. glass cutt. & lead mer. 42 Hackney rd
Harverson Wm. bldg. material dlr. 171 Church st. Shoreditch
Harvett John, dairy, 26 Elizabeth terrace, Cloudesley sq
Harvey Benj. & Co. linendrapers, 7, 8 & 9 Lowndes ter. Knightsbri
Harvey, Brand & Co. merchants, 9 New Broad st. city
Harvey & Co. goldsmiths & watchmakers, 128 Regent st
Harvey & Darton, booksels. & publishers, 55 Gracechurch st
Harvey Ebenezer & Co. warehousemen, 9 Bow churchyard
Harvey Frederick Lionel & Co. non-blistering block varnish, paint & railway grease manufacturers & wholesale dealers in oil, tallow, cotton, hemp, pitch & tar, 10 Cannon st. St. George's east, & 13 Brook st. Shadwell
Harvey & French, grocers & teadealers, 227 Oxford st
Harvey George & Co. potato salesmen, Mill lane, Tooley st
Harvey Geo. R. & Co. indigo brokers, 35 Mincing lane
Harvey John & Son, silkmercers, linendrapers, hosiers, haberdashers, glovers, &c. 9 Ludgate hill
Harvey Joseph & Co. drapers, &c. 41 to 44 Bridge road, Lambeth
Harvey & Knight, floorcloth manufacturers, 59 Broad st. Bloomsbury, & 13 Upper Marsh, Lambeth
Harvey, Napier & Co. flour, coal & timb. mers. Gd Jnc. wf. Whtfrs
Harvey & Stokes, tailors, &c. 67 Jermyn st. St. James's
Harvey Wm. & Co. wine merchts. 2 New London st. Crutchdfrs
Harvey Wm. & Son, biscuit bakers, 67 Charlotte st. Portland pl
Harvey Wm. & Son, *St. Paul's hotel*, 6 St. Paul's churchyard
Harvey, Williams & Co. tin smelters, see Williams, Harvey & Co
Harvey Alice (Mrs.), undertak. 11 King's row, Cambridge rd
Harvey Benjamin, oil & colorman, 53 Crawford st
Harvey Benjamin, schoolmaster, 19 & 20 Polygon, Somers town
Harvey Bridges, barrister, 19 Old square, Lincoln's inn
Harvey Catherine (Miss), milliner, 5 George st. Hanover sq
Harvey Charles, 3 *Horse Shoes* P.H. 19 Gilbert st. Grosvenr sq
Harvey Charles Cumming, merchant, 24 Friday st
Harvey Christopher, baker, 27 Rochester row, Westmr
Harvey David, carpenter, 10 Corporation row, Clerkenwell
Harvey Edward, who. druggist, see Barron, Harvey & Co
Harvey Edward, *Anglesea hotel & tavern*, 64 Haymarket
Harvey Frances (Mrs.), milliner, 25 Ernest st. Regent's pk
Harvey Frances E. (Mrs.), wheelwright, 16 West st. Smithfd
Harvey Frederick, tobacconist, 8 Vauxhall row
Harvey George, printer, 26 Little Charlotte st. Blackfriars rd
Harvey George, stationer, 30 Chichester pl. Gray's inn road
Harvey George, watch & clock maker, 142 St. George st
Harvey George Luck, wine merchant, 43 Lime st
Harvey George L. wine merchant, 30 Rood lane, Fenchurch st
Harvey Harriet (Mrs.), grocer, &c. 34 Notting hill, High st
Harvey Henry artificial florist, 59 Commercial rd. Lambeth
Harvey Henry, brass founder, 9 Artillery pl. Westminster
Harvey Henry, chairmaker, 11 Artillery st. Bishopsgate
Harvey Henry Martin, solicitor, see Lang & Harvey
Harvey James, trunkmaker, 4 Finsbury market
Harvey James, watchmaker, 27 President st. east, King sq
Harvey Jane (Mrs.), furniture broker, 20 Castle st. Long acre
Harvey John, bootmaker, 18 Little St. Andrew's st. Seven dials
Harvey John, butcher, 9 Cross st. Blackfriars road
Harvey John, carpenter, 15 Worship st. Finsbury sq
Harvey John, grocer, 2 New Gravel lane, Shadwell
Harvey John, ironmonger, see Wright & Harvey
Harvey John, watch motion maker, 35 Seward st. Goswell st
Harvey Joseph, artists' colorman, 15 Catherine st. Strand
Harvey Joseph, builder, St. Mary Axe
Harvey Joseph, coffee rooms, 12 Goodge st. Tott. ct. rd
Harvey Joseph, cowkeeper, 46 Rufford's bldgs. Islington
Harvey Joseph, lamp & glass manftr. 16 King Wm. st. City
Harvey Richard, *Duke of Clarence* P.H. 132 London road
Harvey Richard, plumber, 2 Russell pl. Old Kent road
Harvey Richard, sack maker, 40 Seething la. Gt. Tower st
Harvey Robt. bookseller, 5 Vernon pl. Bagnigge wells rd
Harvey Robert, carman, 17 Fashion st. Dockhead
Harvey Robert, watch jeweller, 1 President st. east, King sq
Harvey Robert, tanner, 19 John st. Dockhead
Harvey Samuel, cabinet maker, 4 Eaton lane north, Pimlico
Harvey Samuel, watch motion maker, 8 King st. Clrknwell
Harvey Susannah (Mrs.), hat box maker, 4 Southwark sq. Boro'
Harvey Thos. baker, 21 High st. Newington
Harvey Thos. curiosity dlr. 16 Cannon st. St. George's east
Harvey Thos. gold & silver beater, 30 Perceval st. Clerknwell
Harvey Wm. fruiterer, 3 Orford pl. Marlborough rd. Chelsea
Harvey Wm. furniture broker, 1 Castle st. Long acre
Harvey Wm. grocer, 1 Cambridge road, Mile end road
Harvey Wm. packingcase maker, see Watson & Harvey
Harvey Wm. surgeon, &c. 48 Lonsdale sq. Islington
Harvey Wm. surgeon, 42 Gt. Queen st. Lincoln's inn fields
Harvey Wm. umbrella & parasol maker, 145 Strand
Harvey Wm. undertaker, 8 Castle st. Falcon sq
Harvey Wm. Edward, academy, 5 Wilmot sq. Bethnal gr. rd
Harvey Wm. G. carpenter & builder, Church st. Hackney
Harvey Wm. Gilmore, gunpowder manf. see Curtis & Harvey
Harwar Henry, law stationer, 2 Furnival's inn, Holborn, & 1 Took's ct. Chancery lane
Harwar Joseph, pianoforte ma. 28 Bloomsbury st. St. Giles's
Harwar Joseph Hen, law stationer, 56 Carey st. Lincoln's inn
Harwar Thomas, law stationer, 4 Serle's pl. Lincoln's inn
Harward Major, secret springer, 9 Waterloo st. St. Luke's
Harwich Railway Company (John Thompson, sec.), 11 Abchurch lane, City
Harwich Railway & Pier Company (Geo. Rusk, sec.), 7 Birchin lane
Harwin James, carpenter, 35 Broad st. Golden square
Harwood & Noble, *Blind Beggar* P.H. 173 Whitechapel rd
Harwood Charles, barrister, 89 Chancery lane
Harwood Chas. corn & coal mercht. 18 Kensington High st
Harwood George, surgeon, &c. 12 Tonbridge pl. New road
Harwood Hen. Fredk. *George* P.H. 43 Thomas st. Horslydn
Harwood John, beer retailer, Battersea
Harwood John, fruiterer, 277 Bethnal green road
Harwood John, house painter, 25 Magdalen st. Bermondsey st
Harwood John, poultry salesman, 61 Newgate market
Harwood John, wholesale stationer & manufacturer of the improved patent metallic memorandum books, steel pens, &c. 26 Fenchurch st
Harwood Joseph Unwin, solicitor, see Shield & Harwood
Harwood Sarah Ann (Miss), oil & ital. wa. 41 Carey st. Linc. inn
Harwood Thomas, bootmaker, 66 Whitechapel High st
Harwood Thomas, engraver, 71 Manchester st. Gray's inn rd
Harwood Thomas, saddler & harness maker, 417 Oxford st
Harwood William, baker, 160 Drury lane
Harwood William, engraver, 10 Pleasant row, Pentonville
Harwood William, nursrymn. Peckham footpath, O. Kent rd
Harwood William, tailor, 53 Piccadilly
Harwood Wm. John, brushma. 3 Portland row, Camberwell
Hase Paul, ladies' shoe wareho. 40 & 41 Burlington arcade
Haselam Sarah (Mrs.), shopkpr. 1 Gibrltr. wk. Bethnl. grn. rd
Haselden Wm. & Co. papier mâché ornament manufacturers, Whitelands, Chelsea, & 26 Wardour st. Soho
Haselden Charles, bookseller, &c. 21 Wigmore st
Haselden Edward, tailor, 23A, King st. St. James's
Haselden William, *Adam & Eve* P.H. 14 Bowling st. Westmnstr
Haseldine Dinah (Mrs.), linendra. 6 Artichoke row, Mile end rd

Haseldine Robt. wardrobe purchsr. 68 Castle st. ea. Oxd. st
Haseldine Wm. tallow chndlr. & oilm. 10 Bell yd. Gracech. st
Haselgrove Joseph, beer retailer, 5 Norfolk pl. Clapham
Haselgrove Thomas, carpenter, 4 Derby st. Gray's inn road & 9 Liverpool st. King's cross
Haselgrove Wm. cheesemonger, 116 Brick lane, Spitalfields
Hasell Samuel, tailor, 15 Finch lane, Cornhill
Hasker Henry, coal & corn mer. 6 Cumberland rw. Walwrth. rd
Haskew James Francis, furniture dlr. 5 St. Benet's pl. City
Haskill John & Wm. cab prop. 3 Upper Church st. Chelsea
Haskins Saml. blind ma. & gasfitter, 55 Brick la. St. Luke's
Haslam & Paddy, linendraps. 21 Southampton rw. Russell sq
Haslam George, confectioner, 183 Bethnal green road
Haslam Henry, confectioner, 32 Goswell st
Haslam Wm. solicitor, 8 Copthall court, Throgmorton st
Haslar George, pork butcher, 27 Cannon st. Ratcliff highw
Haselden Charles, watch hand ma. 21 Waterloo st. St. Luke's
Haselden John, watch hand makr. 31 Galway st. St. Luke's
Haselgrove James, grocer, &c. 228 Francis st. Newington butts
Hasleham Horatio, auctioneer, 3 Jerusalem passage, Clerkenwell, & 10 Oldham place, Bagnigge Wells road
Haslehurst Hen. china & glass, &c. wa. 17 Hereford pl. Com. rd. ea
Haslehurst Sarah (Miss), fancy repository, 41½ Hackney rd
Haslehurst William, refined sugar broker, 12 Mincing lane
Haslem John, artist, 34 Old Bond st
Haslemore Joseph, harness maker, 33 Homer st. Marylebone
Hasler George, cowkeeper, 17 Webb st. Bermondsey
Hasler John, carpenter, 27 Up. Gower mews, Torrington pl
Hasler John, furniture japanner, 5 Hackney road crescent
Hasler John, merchant, 4 Church court, Clement's lane
Hasler John, printer & publisher, 4 Crane court, Fleet st
Hasler Thomas, furnt. japanner, 6 East st. Finsbury market
Haslewood Lewis H. american stock agt. 15 Angel ct. Bank
Haslip Henry, cutler, &c. 11 Southampton row, Russell sq
Haslip James, lighterman, 7 Garford st. Limehouse hole
Haslip Peter, lighterman, 15 Magdalen st. Bermondsey st
Hasloch Geo. ladies' shoemak. 9 Wellington st. north, Strand
Hasluck Sam. gold chain mak. & jeweller, 104 Hatton garden
Hass Angel, tinplate worker, 2 Middlesex st. Aldgate Hi. st
Hassall Arthur H. surgeon, 32 Addison road nth. Notng hill
Hassall John, comb & brush maker, 64 St. Paul's church yard
Hassan Jacob, merchant, 1 Cullum st. Fenchurch st
Hassell & Tarrant, tailors, 3 & 4 Bedford pl. Comml. road east
Hassell Joseph, fruiterer, 19 Park place, Mile end road
Hasset John Blennor, staymaker, 4 John st. Oxford st
Hassett Stephen, brassfounder, 79 Wentworth st. Whitechapel
Hasted John Frederick & Sons, coopers, 12 Pell st. Ratcliff highway, 27 Wellclose sq. & 15 Princes sq. St. George's ea
Hastie Archibald, merchant, 3 West st. Finsbury circus
Hastie Benjamin, baker, 5 Calthorpe place, Gray's inn road
Hastie James, solicitor, 31 Broad st. buildings, City
Hastie Robert, corn factor & east india agent, 305 Wapping
Hastilew Cha. ivory turner & carver, 3 Queen st. Finsbury
Hastings & London Direct Railway, Pier, Harbour & Dock Company (Thomas A. Corbett, sec.), 12 John st. Adelphi
Hastings Rowland & Thos. thimble ma. 31 Gt. Sutton st. Clrknw
Hastings & Watkins, wine merchants, 8 Fenchurch st
Hastings Charl. (Mrs.), milliner, 1 Up. Ashby st. Nrthmptn sq
Hastings Edward, solicitor, 63 Up. Norton st. Fitzroy square
Hastings George, carpenter, 11 James place, Hoxton fields
Hastings George, hatter, 45 Lombard st. City
Hastings Henry, stationer, 9 Whitecross st. Cripplegate
Hastings John, physician, 14 Albemarle st. Piccadilly
Hastings Robt. carpenter, 17 Gt. Titchfield st. Oxford st
Hastings Robt. law bookseller, 13 Carey st. Lincoln's inn
Hastings Robt. tailor & draper, 2 Castle st. Falcon square
Hastings Thos. shipg. cheesemong. 28 Clement's la. Lombard st
Hastings William, linendraper, 72 Houndsditch
Hastings Wm. Warren, solicitor, 3 Harpur st. Red Lion sq
Hastrick Henry, patent flageolet maker, 35 Holborn hill
Hastwell James, glass cutter, 69 Broadwall, Blackfriars
Haswell Ann (Mrs.), chandler's shop, 23 Pearson st. Kngsld rd
Haswell Archbd. & Robt. watch tool mkrs. 12 Up. Ashby st
Haswell David, plumber & glazier, 5 Talbot ct. Gracech. st
Haswell Frederick, ale rooms, 130 Chancery lane
Haswell Robert, plumber, &c. 130 Chancery lane
Hatch James & Wm. builders, 19 Clayton pl. Kennington rd
Hatch Alfred, ham & beef dealer, 8 King st. Snow hill
Hatch Alfred, *Waterloo* coffee rooms, 133 Waterloo road
Hatch John, cheesemonger, 16 Gt. WhiteLion st. Seven dials
Hatch Josiah J. wholesale furrier, 32 Friday st. & 4 Brownlow st. Holborn
Hatch Robert, bread & biscuit baker, 108 Shadwell High st
Hatchard John & Son, booksellers & publishers, 187 Piccadilly
Hatchard Charles, surveyor, 50 Lower Belgrave pl. Pimlico
Hatchard Edward, statuary & mason, 82 Up. Ebury st. Pimlico
Hatchard Hen. Silvanus, undertaker, 47 Crawford st. Prtmn. sq
Hatchard James, sculptor, 37 Lower Belgrave pl. Pimlico
Hatchard John, *Plough Inn*, 52 Notting hill, High st
Hatchard John George, linendraper, 425 Strand
Hatchard William, bookbinder, 24 New st. Brompton
Hatcher Harriet (Miss), milliner, 8 Stockbridge terrace
Hatcher William, butcher, 238 Shoreditch
Hatcher William, eating house, 1A, James st. Oxford st
Hatchett Charles, wholes. & ret. stationer, &c. 34 Moorgate st
Hatchett John, cust. ho. agt. see Taylor, Mousley & Hatchett
Hatchett Thos. emery & sand paper ma. 17 Church st. Splflds
Hatchman Benj & Son, carpentrs. & underta. 17 Pitt st. Fitz. sq
Hatchman Henry, turner, 9 George st. Grosvenor sq
Hatfield Halcomb Wm. & Son, plumbers, &c. Church st. Batsea
Hatfield Benjamin, tailor, Southampton st. Camberwell rd
Hatfield Edward, dyer, 29 Paradise st. Rotherhithe
Hatfield Edward, sheff. pl. war. see Waterhouse, Hatfield & Co
Hatfield Hallows, cotton winder, 7 Wheeler st. Spitalfields
Hatfield Isaac, stationer, 7 Chapel st. Tottenham court rd
Hatfield John, beer retailer, 1 Cumberland pl. Chelsea
Hatfield John, bronzist, 20 Cumberland st. Middlesex hos
Hatfield John, painter & decorator, 60 Albany st. Regt.'s pk
Hatfield John M. plumber & decorator, 32 King st. Golden sq
Hatfield Rd. Parker, physician, 41 Cleveland st. Fitzroy sb
Hatfull Robert & Robert, jun. surgeons, 23 Union st. Deptford
Hatfull George, confectioner, New cross road, Deptford
Hatfull William, smith, Deptford High st
Hathaway John, *Hathaway's hotel*, 7 Brook st
Hatherall Isaac, cheesemonger, 2 Flagon row, Deptford
Hatherell Joseph, cheesemonger, 14 Parker's row, Dockhead
Hatherly John, solicitor, see Pain & Hatherly
Hathersick Walter H. parliamentary agent, 3 Winchester bldgs
Hathorn George & Co. merchants, 6 Broad st. buildings
Hathway Edward, news agent, 4 York st. Westminster
Hathway Henry, newsvender, 16 Royal Exchange
Hatley Frederick, fishmngr. 36 Ridinghouse la. Langham pl
Hatred John Thomas, accountant, agent, &c. 23 Coleman st
Hatsell John, cheesemonger, 95 Crawford st. Portman sq
Hatswell John, bookselr. & publshr. 8 Broadway, Ludgate hl
Hatswill Thomas, baker, 14 William st. Lisson grove
Hatt Thomas, baker, 1 Frederick place, Old Kent road
Hattam James, stationer & toy dlr. Ring cross, Holloway
Hatten Francis, cow keeper, 1 Barrow hill st. Portland town
Hatter John, cow keeper, 21 Moor lane, Cripplegate
Hattersley George, *Blue Coat Boy* P.H. 1 Upper Duncan place, City road
Hattersley John, painter & glazier, 5 Harper st. New Kent rd
Hattersley John, tailor &c. 167 Bishopsgate st. without
Hattersley Wm. botanist & druggist, 137 St. George st
Hattersley Wm. omnibus proprietor, 73 Horseferry road
Hattersley Wm. pianof. ma. & news agt. 43 Regent st. Horsefr. rd
Hattersley Wm. *Rose & Crown* P.H. 62 Tottenham ct. rd
Hatton & Hardie, fancy trimming ma. 6 Wood st. Cheapside
Hatton Thos. & Co. mnfg. chemists, &c. 12 Elder st. Norton fgt
Hatton Edwin, silk mercer, see Williams & Hatton
Hatton Fredk. solicitor, 21 Gt. George st. Westminster
Hatton Henry, bootmaker, 4 Halton pl. Cross st. Islington
Hatton Henry, butcher, 34 York st. Westminster
Hatton James, corndealer, 37 Castle st. east, Oxford st
Hatton James, plumber, &c. 46 Castle st. east, Oxford st
Hatton John, dyer, 12 King's road, Pimlico
Hatton Richard, porkman, 19 Cable st. Wellclose square
Hatton Thomas, cowkeeper, 40 High st. St. Giles's
Hatton Thomas, general & ornamental printer & engraver, 37 King st. & 16 Hart st. Covent garden
Hatton Thomas, meat, &c. salesman, see Dean & Hatton
Hatton Margaret (Mrs.), fruiterer, 187 Bethnal green road
Hatts Robert, coffee rooms, 97 Drury lane
Hatwell Andrew, carman & fruiterer, 2 Leader st. Chelsea
Hatwell Joseph, Hope brewery, Notting hill, High st
Haucock John, greengrocer, 1 Strachan pl. Ball's pond rd
Haucock John Joseph, sheep salesman, 17 West Smithfield
Haughton Moses, artist, 5 Percy st. Tottenham court road
Haughton Wm. linendrap. 13 Black Prince row, Walwth. rd
Haultaufderhyde James, tailor, 3 Bathurst st. Sussex sq
Haurie John Nephew (of Xeres), 106 Fenchurch st
Hava Pierre & Co. merchants, 147 Fenchurch st
Havard Wm. Martin & Co. gasfitters, 59 Brook st. Hanovr. sq
Havard Maria (Mrs.), stayma. 3 Upper Seymour st. Eust. sq
Havart Charles, chemist, 27 High st. Portland town
Havell Mary (Mrs.), bookbinder, 4 Hind court, Fleet st
Havenith Leon H. merchant, 3 Love lane, Eastcheap
Haverfield Henry David, attorney, 29 Bloomsbury st. St. Giles
Havers Thos & Co. tanners, Tyers gateway, 211 Bermonds. st
Havers John, surgeon, 13 York road, Lambeth
Haviland Edwd. surgeon, 1 Southwick crescent, Hyde park

Haviland Edwd. Savage, surgeon, see Girdwood & Haviland
Havill Geo. *Old King's Head* P.H. Green bank, Tooley st
Havinden Jas. grocer & cheesemngr. 4 East India rd. Poplar
Haviside Thos. & Co. ship & insurance brokers, 69 Cornhill
Haw John & Co. tailors, 24 Well st. Jewin st. Cripplegate
Haw John, dairyman, 5 Staple st. Long lane, Bermondsey
Haward & Nixon, builders, 22 Leicester square, & Palace New road, Lambeth
Haward George, merchant, 6 St. Dunstan's hill
Haward Henry, butcher, Robin Hood lane, Poplar
Haward James, butcher, 43 St. John st. Smithfield
Haward Richard, pawnbroker, 39 Princess st. Edgware rd
Haward Rt. *Loadof Hay* P.H. Haverstock hill, Hampstead rd
Haward Thomas, butcher, 7 Pleasant place, Holloway
Hawes & Ottley, hosiers & glovers, 40 & 41 Poultry
Hawes Thos. & Wm. soap & candle ma. Commer. rd. Lambth
Hawes Beatrice (Miss), straw hat ma. 19 Charltte. rw. Wlwth
Hawes James Thomas, pawnbroker, 146 & 147 Whitechapel rd. & 98 Old st. St. Luke's, & 34 & 35 Shadwell High st
Hawes John, brown stone potter, Ferry st. Lambeth
Hawes John, china dealer, 46 White st. Borough
Hawes John Brasier, carpenter, 10 Horsely st. Wlwrth. com
Hawes Jonathan, jun. grocer, 24 Frederick pl. Hampstead rd
Hawes Jonathan, sen. grocer, 23 Pitfield st. Hoxton
Hawes Rd. Brasier, surveyor, 19 Charlotte row, Walworth rd
Hawes Robert, veterin. surgeon, 47 Worship st. Finsbury
Hawes Thomas, butcher, 7 Church st. Cheyne walk, Chelsea
Hawes Wm. mast, oar & scull ma. 46 Up. Fore st. Lambeth
Hawes William, optician, &c. 79 Leadenhall st
Hawes William, poulterer, 38 Paddington st. Marylebone
Hawes William, music seller, 355 Strand
Hawes William, tailor, 7 Gloucester st. Queen square
Hawes William, tailor, 67 Lamb's Conduit st. Foundling
Hawes William H. B. surgeon, 12 King William st. Strand
Hawgood Charles, baker, 13 New Park st. Borough
Hawgood Henry, stationr. & rag mer. 10 Newington causew
Hawgood James, pawnbroker, 9 York place, Kent st. rd
Hawgood Samuel, pawnbroker, 28 Surrey place, Old Kent rd
Hawke John & Wm. builders, 17 Billiter st
Hawke John, hatter, 25 King William st. City
Hawke Johnson, builder, 5 James st. Covent garden
Hawke Wm. fixture dealer, see Ansell & Hawke
Hawken John, builder, 48 Duke st. Lincoln's inn fields
Hawken John Henry, *King's Head* P.H. 31 Long la. Bermnd
Hawken Thos. carpenter, 2 Manor place, Walworth road
Hawker Thos. Drewett, secretary to Gloucester, Aberystwith & Central Wales Railway Company, 21 Soho sq
Hawker Wm. carman, 2 College st. Upper Thames st
Hawkers' & Pedlars' Office, Stamp & Tax Office, Somerset house; hours 10 to 4
Hawkes, Moseley & Co. helmet, army cap, & accoutrement maks. to her Majesty & the royal family, 14 Piccadilly
Hawkes Edward, carver & gilder, 263 High Holborn
Hawkes James, printer, 21 Brunswick place, City road
Hawkes Joseph, baker, 4 Northumberland pl. Commer. rd. east
Hawkes Robert, ironmonger, 106 Long acre
Hawkes Samuel, undertaker, 28 Paul st. Finsbury
Hawkes Sidney Milnes, barrister, 50 Chancery lane
Hawkes Wm. ironmonger, 21 High st. Kensington
Hawkes Wm. *Old Mermaid* P.H. Church st. Hackney
Hawkes Wm. tailor, 19 New st. Kennington road
Hawkesley James, pianoforte ma. 11 Grafton st. Fitzroy sq
Hawkey Wm. H. surgeon, 34 Burton st. Pimlico
Hawkings James, plate, sheet & window glass warehouse, wholesale stationer, &c. 5 Albion place, Blackfriars bridge
Hawkings James, stationer, 5 Albion place, Blackfriars
Hawkings John, upholster, 6 Lisson grove north
Hawkings Wm. furn. broker, 6 Horseferry road, Westminster
Hawkins, Bloxam, Stocker & Bloxam, solicitors, 2 New Boswl. ct
Hawkins Hen. Fk. & C. carvrs. & gildrs. 20½ & 28 Clipstone st
Hawkins & Marsh, liverystables, 78 Gt. Portland st. Oxford st
Hawkins & Strong, plasterers, &c. 36 Paris st. Lambeth
Hawkins Alex. who. & retail ironmonger, 131 London road
Hawkins Ann (Mrs.), mineral water ma. 22 Duke st. St. James'
Hawkins Ann (Mrs.), newsvender, 19 Backchurch la. Whcpl
Hawkins Benj. cheesemonger, 6 Black Prince rw. Walwth. rd
Hawkins Bissett, physician, 30 Golden square
Hawkins Cæsar, surgeon, 26 Grosvenor st
Hawkins Chas. camp equipage & trunk maker, 86 Strand
Hawkins Chas. chair manftr. 1 Hatfield pl. Westminster rd
Hawkins Chas. exors'. admors'. & genl. agt. 5 Bell yd. Drs. cms
Hawkins Charles, surgeon, 2 Albany court yard
Hawkins Charles, teadlr. 146 Brick lane, Spitalfields
Hawkins Chas. Edwd. *Albion* P.H. Horsemonger la. Boro'
Hawkins Chas. Hy. watch case & water gldr. 8 King st. Smthfld
Hawkins Edward, barrister, 2 South sq. Gray's Inn
Hawkins Edward, hat manuftr. 1 Church st. Blackfriars
Hawkins Francis, physician, 18 Bolton st. Piccadilly
Hawkins Fred. carver & gilder, 47 Cirencester pl. Fitzroy sq
Hawkins George, butcher, 64 Exmouth st. Clerkenwell
Hawkins George, butcher, 33 Skinner st. Somers town
Hawkins George, hairdresser, 16 Shepherd's mkt. Mayfair
Hawkins George, oil & color wareho. 88 Bishopsgate without
Hawkins Henry, artist, 5 Gt. Woodstock st. Nottingham pl
Hawkins Henry, baker, 3 Henry st. Portland town
Hawkins Henry, special pleader, 4 Crown office row, Temple
Hawkins Henry J. *Three Compasses*, 15 Salisbury st. Brmndsy
Hawkins James, beer retailer, Battersea fields
Hawkins James, baker, Church st. Clapham road
Hawkins James, bootmaker, 35 South st. Manchester sq
Hawkins James, butcher, 3 Little Ormond st. Queen sq
Hawkins Jas. coffee rooms, 13 Wilderness row, Clerkenwell
Hawkins James, surgeon, 58 Hatton garden
Hawkins James, surgeon, 36 Colet place, Comml. road east
Hawkins James, wine merchant, 20 Up. Kennington green
Hawkins John, blanket & tilting agent, 5 Long la. Smithfield
Hawkins John, cabinet ma. 13 Gt. George st. Bermondsey
Hawkins John, boot & shoe maker, 189 Kingsland road
Hawkins John, carpenter, builder &c. 116 Gray's inn lane
Hawkins John, carpenter, 59 St. Clement's lane, Strand
Hawkins John, carpenter, 5 Sheffield st. Lincoln's inn fields
Hawkins John, riding school, 22 South st. South Audley st
Hawkins John, machine ruler, 26 Little Trinity la. Bread st
Hawkins John, saddler, 26 Francis st. Tottenham court rd
Hawkins John, surgeon, 10 St. James's pl. Old Kent road
Hawkins John, teadealer, 14 Whitechapel High st. & wholesale grocer, Half Moon passage, Whitechapel
Hawkins John, *White Hart* P.H. Deptford green
Hawkins John Isaac, gold pen maker, 26 Judd pl. w. New rd
Hawkins John James, shoemak. 12 Lit. Peter st. Westminster
Hawkins John Vincent, surgeon, 63 George st. Portman sq
Hawkins John Wm. furrier, 8 Hanway st. Oxford st
Hawkins Jonathan, *Red Lion* P.H. Lower road, Rotherhithe
Hawkins Joseph, leather cutter, 133 Kent st. Borough
Hawkins Joseph, tilting forge & tire, nail, axletree & spring manufactory, Up. Ground st. & 1 Hatfield st. Blackfrs. rd
Hawkins Marg. (Mrs.) *Wh. Hart & Fountn.* P.H. 139 Rosema. la
Hawkins Otto, dorset ale & refreshment rooms, 1 Lothbury
Hawkins Phœbe (Mrs.), chandler's shop, 1 Commrl. rd. Lmbt
Hawkins Richard, fruiterer, 8 Steymans row, Holloway rd
Hawkins Richard, grocer, 131 Bethnal green road
Hawkins Robt. Ralph Augustus, barrister, 59 Chancery lane
Hawkins Saml. gen. & cabinet ironmon. 54 Bishopsgt. witht
Hawkins Saml. H. cop. pl. printer, 60 Whitlebury st. Euston sq
Hawkins Thomas, butcher 10 & 11 Oxford market, Oxford st
Hawkins Thomas, cabinet ma. 29 Sidmouth st. Gray's inn rd
Hawkins Thomas, carpenter, 6 Berner st. Commercial rd. east
Hawkins Thomas, cheesemonger, 9 Lit. Earl st. Seven dials
Hawkins Thos. chimney sweep, 25 Cambridge pl. Edgwr. rd
Hawkins Thomas, coffee rooms, 20 Lt. Queen st. Lincns. inn fi
Hawkins Thomas, general agent, 26 Upper Thames st
Hawkins Thomas, *Hawkins hotel*, 26 Dover st. & 29B, Albemarle st. Piccadilly
Hawkins Thos. potato dealer, 12 & 13 Lumber ct. Seven dials
Hawkins Walter, ship. & ins. broker, 2 Fowke's blds. Tower st
Hawkins Wm. accountant, see Horwood & Hawkins
Hawkins Wm. carver & gilder, 5 Glo'ster pl. King's rd. Chels
Hawkins Wm. coal mer. 1 Queen's ter. Marlboro' rd. Chelsea
Hawkins Wm. fruiterer, 5 Marlborough road, Chelsea
Hawkins Wm. ship biscuit baker, 180 Tooley st
Hawkins Wm. tailor, 2 Little Denmark st. Soho
Hawkins Wm. turner, &c. 4 Vigo st. Regent st
Hawkins Wm. H. stockbroker, 5 Angel ct. Throgmorton st
Hawkmoor Mining Company (George William Harrison, secretary), 51 Old Broad, City
Hawkridge Thomas, hairdresser, 105 Old Gravel lane
Hawkridge Thomas, tobacconist, 84 Bunhill row, St. Luke's
Hawks & Crawshay, manufacturers of scrap bar iron, patent chain cables, anchors, &c. Paul's wf. 23 Upper Thames st
Hawks Edw. & Son, shipbldrs. Princes dock, 100 Rotherhithe
Hawks Edward, stereotype founder, see Knight & Hawks
Hawks Emma (Miss), lace wa. 3 Commerce row, Islington
Hawks George, ship broker, Princes dock, Rotherhithe
Hawks John, stationer & account book mak. 181 Shoreditch
Hawks John, trimming slr. 19 White Lion st. Goodman's flds
Hawks Robert Shafto, solicitor, see Piercy & Hawks
Hawksbee Ann (Mrs.), cheesemonger, 106 Up. Whitecross st
Hawksley Geo. house painter, 22 Upper North pl. Gray's inn rd
Hawksley Robert, grocer, 48 Princess st. Edgware road
Hawksley Samuel, grocer, 348 Rotherhithe wall
Hawksley Thomas, surgeon, 57 Margaret st. Cavendish sq
Hawksworth, Eyre & Co. plate dlrs. 16 Devereux ct. Strand

HawksworthJohn S. sheffield wa. see Howard&Hawksworth
Hawley Thos. & Co. goldsmiths & watchma. 123 Regent st
Hawley Wm. & Co. cheesemongers, 5 Clifton pl. Wndsth.rd
Hawley George, cheesemonger, 64 High st. Shadwell
Hawley George, cowkeeper, 18 Theobald's road
Hawley George, grocer, &c. 13 Pitfield st. Hoxton
Hawley John, watchmaker, 56 Frith st. Soho
Hawley John A. cheesemong. 25Brunswk. parade,Brnsby.rd
Hawley Thomas, cheesemonger, 9 Baker's row, Walworth rd
Hawley Thomas, wholesale grocer, 221 Blackfriars rd
Hawley William, grocer, 38 Bridge road, Lambeth
Haworth John & Co. iron founders, Old Manor st. Chelsea
Haworth John, proctor, &c. 20Bennets hill, Doctors'commns
Hawthorn Henry & Co. tea dealers, 74 High Holborn
Hawthorn Josiah & Hen. tea & coffee dlrs.38Tottenham ct.rd
Hawthorn & Shedden, west india merchants, 5 Lime st. sq
Hawthorn John Hugh, surgeon, 2 Hoxton Old town
Hawtin Edward, stationer, 34 Wilson st. Finsbury
Hawtin William, *Albion* P.H. 210 Shadwell High st
Hawtin William, *Duke of Marlboro'* P.H. St. Katherine's
Hawton Eleanor(Mrs.), haberdashr. 27Aylesbury st.Clkwll
Hawton Elizh. (Mrs.), furniture bro. 4 Vine st. Hatton wall
Hawtry William, plumber, painter, builder, &c. 42 Bread st
Hawxby Thomas, chemist, &c. 37 Berners st. Oxford st
Haxell Jas. *Angel* P.H.&wine&spirit mer.14John st.Minories
Hay,Anderson&Sangster,seedsmen,3Surreypl.Nwngtn.butts
Hay Charles & Son, lightermen, 57 Rotherhithe st
Hay Edmund & Hen. tallow melters, 37Carnaby st.Golden sq
Hay Wm. & Co. *Porcupine* P.H. 1 Castle st. Leicester sq
Hay Allan, insurance broker, see Jacks & Hay
Hay Andrew, tailor, 12 Lamb's Conduit passage, Red Lion sq
Hay Charles, lighterman, LowerDeptford road,Rotherhithe
Hay Geo. baker, 2Gloucester terrace, Vauxhall bridge road
Hay George, bootmaker, 181 St. George st
Hay George, shipwright, 333 Wapping
Hay George, trimming manufr. 1 Abbey st. Bethnal green rd
Hay George Gun, solicitor, see Long & Hay
Hay James, cheesemonger, 6 New Gravel lane, Wapping
Hay James, merchant, 4 Austinfriars
Hay James, surgeon, &c. 2 Newgate st
Hay James Gordon, barrister, 2 Figtree court, Temple
Hay John, estate & house agent, 33 Conduit st. Regent st
Hay John, naval & military tailor, 22 Cork st. Bond st
Hay Joseph, tailor, 9 Little Marlborough st. Golden sq
Hay Lucy (Mrs.), *ThreeCompasses* P.H. 7 Lit.Marylebone st
Hay Sarah (Miss), school, 4 Powis place, Haverstock hill
Hay Thomas, oilman, 137 Lambeth walk
Hay William, baker, 6 North Audley st
Hay Wm.medical fixture dlr.25 Lit. Queen st. High Holborn
Hay William, *Gordon Arms* P.H. 262 High Holborn
Hay William, *Grapes* P.H. 14 & 15 Porter st. Soho
Hay William, surgeon, 8 Clifford st. Bond st
Haybittle Frances (Miss), coal mer.Canal bridge,OldKent rd
Haycock Edward, surgeon, 25 Green st. Bethnal green
Haycock Joseph, chemist, &c. 10 Plumber's row, City road
Haycock Valentine, baker, Pomeroy st. Old Kent road
Haycraft Josiah, ironmonger, Broadway, Deptford
Hayday Richard & Co.warehousemen, 22 Milk st. Cheapside
Hayday James, bookbinder, 31 Little Queen st. & George yard, Holborn
Hayday William, bootmaker, 137 Church st. Shoreditch
Hayden Caroline (Miss), milliner, 9 Cornbury pl.Old Kent rd
Hayden Edward, *Angel* P.H. 45 King st. Borough High st
Hayden Fredk. printer, 12 Little College st. Westminster
Hayden Wm. Hen. music sel.& pub. 17 Warwick sq.Newgt.st
Haydon Alfred, linendraper, 3½ Scott's pl. Lr. rd. Islington
Haydon Ben. R. historical painter, 14 Burwood pl. Edgw. rd
Haydon Dennis, chair & sofa maker, 11 St. Ann's court,Soho
Haydon Edward, tripeman, 4 Rochester row, Vauxhall br.rd
Haydon Samuel, cattle salesman, 60 West Smithfield
Haydon Samuel James Bouverie, sculptor, 79 Newman st
Haydon Wm.factor&warehousema.150St.John st.We.Smithfi
Haydon William, smith & farrier, High st. Kingsland
Haydon William Henry, carver, gilder, &c. 66 Kingsland rd
Haye & Ayres, woollen & fancy waistcoat wa. 98 Newgate st
Haye Noel, porkman, 55 Princes st. Leicester sq
Hayer James, pawnbroker, 36 Cheyne walk, Chelsea
Hayes Abraham Thos. jeweller, 4 Compton passage, Clknwl
Hayes Alfred, painter & glazier, 10 Hertford rd. Kingsland
Hayes Charles, newsvender, 1 Suffolk st. Pentonville
HayesChas. Wm.accountant, 17 New Boswell ct.Lincoln's inn
Hayes Christphr. coffee rooms, 36 Warwick la. Newgate st
Hayes Christopher Daniel, jun. floor cloth manufacturer, 166 Fenchurch st. & St. Matthew's place, Hackney road
Hayes George, barrister, 3 Garden court, Temple
Hayes George, calenderer, 20 Lawrence st. Chelsea
Hayes George, printer, 13 Dartmouth st. Westminster
Hayes Hen. dentist, 5Gt. May's bdgs.&12Bedford ct.Cov.gard
Hayes Hen. Wm. pawnbroker, 13 Wilderness row, Clerknwl
Hayes James, chandler's shop, 90 Cromer st. Brunswick sq
Hayes James, pastrycook, 184½ Drury lane
Hayes John, coffee rooms, 1 Love lane, Eastcheap
Hayes John, portrait painter, 1 Frith st. Soho
Hayes Joseph, bottle dealer, 16 & 17 Church st. Camberwell
Hayes Joseph, dentist, 12 Soho square
Hayes Joseph, furn. bro.24Richmond pl. East st.Walworth rd
Hayes Joseph, solicitor, Carlton chambers, 12 Regent st
Hayes Peter, brass & cock founder, 22 St. John st. Clerknwll
Hayes Richard, painter & plumber, 5 Albion pl. Holloway rd
Hayes Robert, solicitor, see Parker & Hayes
Hayes Robert N. general agent, 26 New Bond st
Hayes Stephen, fly proprietor, Edwardes sq. Kensington
Hayes Thomas, surgeon, 50 Southampton st. Pentonville
Hayes Thomas Porrett, solicitor, see Budd & Hayes
Hayes William, barrister, 1 Cloisters, Temple
Hayes Wm. cheesemonger, 1 Artillery passage, Bishopsgate
Hayes Wm. metal sash maker, 1 Pindar place, Gray's inn rd
Hayes Wm. skinner & furrier, 2 Pepper st. Union st. Boro'
Hayes Wm.Chas.auctioneer,&c. 39 Lit.Charlotte st.Blkfrs.rd
Hayes Wm. Fredk. tobacconist, South Lambeth
Hayes Wm. Graves, news agent, 2 Lillypot la. Noble st. City
Hayes Wm. John, cowkeeper, 25 Horseferry rd. Westmnstr
Hayes Wm. S. general salesman, 58 Farringdon st
Hayes Wm. Sumshon, glass & chinaman, 57 Farringdon st
Hayford Henry, watchmaker, 7 Star alley, Fenchurch st
Hayford John, lath render, 52 St. John st. Smithfield
Hayford William, boot & shoe maker, 55 Barbican
Hayhow Richd. nurseryman, 5 St.Mark's rd.Cambrwl.nw.rd
Hayhow Wm. bootma. 88 & 103 St. Geo. st. & 154 Shadwell
Hayle Railway Co. (John MacDonnell, sec.), 35 Broad st.bgs
Hayler Thomas (Mrs.), milliner, 22 Mount st. Berkeley sq
Hayles Henry, herald painter, 8 Union place, New road
Haylett Richard, *Admiral Duncan* P.H. 38 Old Compton st
Haylor William, grocer, 93 Harrison st. Gray's inn road; & 12 Little Guilford st. Russell square
Hayman Wm. & Co. surgeons, 80 Judd st. Brunswick sq
Hayman Hen. corndealer, 28 Stonecutter st. Farringdon st
Hayman James, patentee of the safety ingress & egress omnibus, 27 Mount st. Westminster road, Lambeth
Hayman James Emeny, corndealer, 27 Mount st. Lambeth
Hayman John L. seed mer. Grove, Guildford st. Southwark
Hayman Maria Puttock (Miss), milliner, 8 Southampton rw
Haymarket Office (John Kendall, clerk), 6 Cumberland market, tuesday, thursday & saturday, 9 to 6
Haymarket Theatre, between 7 & 8 Haymarket
Hayne & Co. merchants, manufacturers & wholesale silversmiths, 16 Red Lion st. Clerkenwell
Hayne Chas. upholder & house agt. 54 Museum st. Blmsbry
Hayne George, mahogany & hardwood merchant, 20 Long lane, West Smithfield
Hayne Henry, timber merchant, 129 Old st. St. Luke's
Hayne John, bottle mer.& glass mnfr. 8 Liverpool st.Bishopsg
Haynes Geo.&Co.cottn.&cottn.yrn.& rush mfrs.13Hmpstd.rd
Haynes John & Son, builders, 5 Mount row, Liverpool road
Haynes & Peake, poultry & game salesm. 57 & 58 Newg.mrkt
Haynes Thomas & Sons, coopers, maltsters, ironmongers, brushmakers & turners, 110 & 111 Edgware road
Haynes William & Co. carpenters & builders, 18 Moorgate st.; 64 Coleman st. City; & Wilson st. Finsbury
Haynes Alfred, saddle tree mak. 27 Brownlow st. Long acre
Haynes Ambrose, solicitor, 7 East st. Red Lion square
Haynes Anthony John, *Sun* P.H. 1 Heddon st. Regent st
Haynes Charles, tobacconist, 34 Wilsted st. Somers town
Haynes Edward, grocer, 85 Lambeth lower marsh
Haynes Elizh. (Mrs.), block, &c. ma. Pickleherring, Tooley st
Haynes Edmund, stable keeper, Ridinghouse la. Langham pl
Haynes Esther (Miss), potato dealer, Spitalfields market
Haynes George, french polisher, 1 Fredk. pl. Walworth com
Haynes George, stationer & newsvender, 37 Frith st. Soho
Haynes Henry, carver & gilder, 52 George st. Euston sq. & 16 Great Windmill st. Haymarket
Haynes James, grocer, 76 Edward st. Stepney
Haynes John, dairyman, Well st. Hackney
Haynes John, *Falcon* P.H. 10 Princes st.& 1 Lisle st.Leicstr.sq
Haynes John, grocer, 26 Queen st. Bryanstone square
Haynes John, hairdresser, 4 Mora place, City road
Haynes John, shoemaker, 19 John st. west, Edgware road
Haynes John, tailor, 44 London wall
Haynes Joseph, solicitor, see Carlon & Haynes
Haynes Joseph, watch escapement ma. 51 Charles st. City rd
Haynes Joseph, woollen & stuff wareho. 1 Aldermanbury
Haynes Lucy (Mrs.), grocer, &c. 14 Kinnerton st. Belgrave sq

Haynes Mary (Mrs.), stationer, 1 Union court, Old Broad st
Haynes Mary (Mrs.), tripe dresser, 159 Bethnal green road
Haynes Raymond Levi, surgeon, &c. 8 Ring cross, Holloway rd
Haynes Richard, jun. attorney, 2 Hunter st. Brunswick sq
Haynes Samuel, wheelwright, 61½ Praed st. Paddington
Haynes Sarah (Miss), milliner, see Reddall & Haynes
Haynes Sarah (Mrs.), pork butcher, 15 Langley pl. Com. rd. e
Haynes Thomas, bootmaker, 62 Parson's st. St. George st
Haynes Thomas, dining rooms, 1 Albion pl. Lit. Chelsea
Haynes Thomas, whitesmith, 7 Red Lion ct. Spitalfields
Haynes Thomas Wm. solicitor, 41 Arlington st. Camden twn
Haynes William, cattle salesman, 60 West Smithfield
Haynes William, linendraper, 102 Edgware rd. Marylebone
Haynes William, linendraper, 7 Red Lion st. Holborn
Haynes William, saddle & harness ma. 24 Silver st. Wood st
Haynes William, statuary & mason, 12 Goswell rd. west side
Haynes Wm. trunkmaker, 37 Cannon st. rd. St. George's east
Hayr William, cattle salesman, 60 West Smithfield
Hays Christr. & Jsph. & Albert, Meriton's wf. Mill st. Dckhd
Hays & Newbury, milliners, 6 Colvill ter. King's rd. Chelsea
Hay's Wharf, John Humphery, between 32 & 41 Tooley st
Hays Alfred, fancy stationer, 13 Gt. Castle st. Regent st
Hays Henry, seal & coppr. pl. engr. & jeweller, 168 Regent st
Hays John, basket maker, 65 St. John st. West Smithfield
Hays John, corn & flour factor, 5 Mark lane
Hays Peter, *Fox* P.H. 97 Paul st. Finsbury
Hays Sarah Jane (Mrs.), slopslr. 4 Russell st. Lwr. Rotherhithe
Hays Thomas, baker, 28 Fore st. Cripplegate
Hays William, baker, 37 King st. Borough
Hayslep Charles, woolstapler, 2 Berwick pl. Bermondsey
Hayslep William, oilman, Westmoreland pl. Walworth com
Haysom Frederick, builder, &c. St. Catherine's wharf, Belgrave terrace, Pimlico
Haysom William, statuary, 9 South Island pl. Clapham rd
Hayter & Howell, army packers, 52 Mark lane
Hayter Charles, locksmith, 12 Gt. Chesterfield st. Marylebone
Hayter George, ham & beef dealer, 49 Hackney road
Hayter Sir George, knt. artist, 9 Stratford place, Oxford st
Hayter John, artist, 13 Manchester square
Hayter John, *Southmptn. Arms*, 41 Whittleby. st. Euston sq
Hayter Thos. bed pillar manufact. 6 George's pl. Old st. road
Hayter William, shoemaker, 12 North st. Lisson grove
Hayter William Goodenough, M.P. barrister, patent of precedence, 11 Hyde park terrace
Hayton Thos. Huntsrods, grocer, Jamaica level, Bermondsey
Haytor Granite Co. (W. H. Palmer, sec.), Grosvenor whrf. 1 Millbank row, Westminster
Hayward & Adam, who. booksellers, 48 Paternoster row
Hayward & Chapple, *Castle* P.H. 1 Belinda pl. Canonbry. sq
Hayward Jas. & Co. mercers, drapers, &c. 97 & 98 Tottenhm. ct. rd
Hayward John Pearson & Son, ho. & orn. paints. 88 Newgt. st
Hayward Mary & Son, tailors, 1 Lamb pl. Kingsland road
Hayward Rich. & Sons, sailcloth & twinemak. &c. 93 Minories
Hayward Wm. & John, boatbuilders, Bermondsey wall
Hayward William Turnor & Co. lacemen, 81 Oxford st. & at 37 King's road, Brighton
Hayward Aaron, tailor, 11 Coleshill st. Eaton square
Hayward Ablm. queen's counsel, 11 King's Bench wk. Temp
Hayward Abhm. brazier & shopkeeper, 39 Green st. Bethnl grn
Hayward Chas. coal, potato, &c. dealer, 21 Shadwell High st
Hayward Charles, coffee rooms, 91 Tooley st
Hayward Charles, *King's Arms* P.H. St. George's st. Albany road, Old Kent road
Hayward Charles, oilman, Stratford, Essex
Hayward Edward L. glass & lead mer. see Chater & Hayward
Hayward Eusebia (Mrs.), seminary, Southampton st. Cmbwl
Hayward Ellis, coachmaker, 1 Church row, Pancras rd
Hayward George, baker, 36 London road, Southwark
Hayward George, wholesale stationer, see Barry & Hayward
Hayward Harr. (Mrs.), chandler's shop, 85 Hercules bgs. Lmbh
Hayward Henry, confectioner, 20 Union st. east, Spitalfields
Hayward Henry, cooper, 4 Pitts place, Old Kent road
Hayward Henry, *Mail Coach* P.H. 60 Farringdon st
Hayward Hen. surgeon dentist, 18 Edwards st. Portman sq
Hayward Hen. upholsterer, 14 Chalcroft ter. New cut, Lambth
Hayward James, beer retailer, 3 West st. Walworth rd
Hayward James, carpenter, 2 Old Boswell court, Strand
Hayward Jas. carpenter & builder, 37 George st. Portland pl
Hayward James, ironmonger, 20 St. James walk, Clerkenwl
Hayward James, upholsterer, 8 Borough road
Hayward Jas. Robinson, par. agt. see Dorrington, Hayward & Co
Hayward James Thomas, bootmaker, 21 King st. Snowhill
Hayward John, bookseller, 6 Southampton st. Camberwell
Hayward John, *Green Man* P.H. 57 Berwick st. Soho
Hayward Jno. *Harpur Arms* P.H. 74 Theobalds rd. Red lion sq
Hayward John, solicitor, 2 Adelaide pl. Lon. bdge. & Dartford
Hayward Joseph, *Edinburgh Castle* P.H. 91 Low. East Smithfi
Hayward Louisa (Miss), straw hat ma. 138 High st. Cmdn. tn
Hayward Mark, tailor, 2 Ernest st. Regent's park
Hayward Mary (Mrs.), corn & coal mr. 26 Alfrd. pl. Nwngtn. cau
Hayward Mary (Mrs.), newsvender, 37 Hindon st. Pimlico
Hayward Mary (Mrs.), stonemason, 15 Gt. Guilford st. Boro'
Hayward Philip, solicitor, 13 Furnival inn
Hayward Richd. Edwd. button ma. & cutler, 21 Bouverie st
Hayward Richd. Jas. chandler's shop, 67 Hoxton Old town
Hayward Robert, dining rooms, 14 Up. Park pl. Regent's pk
Hayward Robert, watchmaker, 3 Adelaide pl. Grange rd
Hayward Samuel, fruiterer, 157 Hoxton Old town
Hayward Samuel, *Red Lion* P.H. 34 Spicer st. Spitalfields
Hayward Samuel, stonemason, 52 Whittlebury st. Euston sq
Hayward Spencer, carpenter, South Lambeth New rd
Hayward Thomas, baker, 3 Ropemakers fields, Limehouse
Hayward Thos. brushmaker & turner, 40 High st. Marylebone
Hayward Thos. grocer, &c. 6 Mount Etna pl. Mile end rd
Hayward Thos. *Two Brewers* P.H. 74 Shoe lane, Fleet st
Hayward Thos. Carlyle, sailcloth fac. & mercht. 93 Minories
Hayward Wm. congreve mnfr. 19 Widegate st. Bishopsgate
Hayward Wm. fruit salesman, Covent garden fruit market
Hayward Wm. fruiterer, 20 Holland st. Church st. Kensngtn
Hayward Wm. haberdasher, 6 Bedford pl. Commercial rd. ea
Hayward Wm. marine store dealer, 1 Charles st. Coml. rd
Hayward William, poulterer, 69 Theobald's rd
Hayward Wm. poulterer, 33 Theobald's rd. Red Lion sq
Hayward Wm. Hy. ale agent, Brooks whf. Up. Thames st
Haywood Wm. & Co. america merchants, 9 Rood lane
Haywood Charles H. chemist, 5 St. Martin's ct. St. Mrtn's. la
Haywood Daniel, floorcloth manfr. 37 Newington causeway
Haywood Isaac, merchant, 9 Rood lane, Fenchurch st
Haywood James, haberdasher, 53 Charles st. Westminster
Hayworth Elizth. (Mrs.), shoe wa. 9 Courtenay ter. Kngslnd
Hayworth George, carpenter, 9 Courtenay ter. Kingsland
Hayworth Wm. builder, undtkr. & china wa. Kingsland High st
Hayzen James, upholsterer, 24 Sidney pl. Commercial rd. east
Hayzen Peter, mattress maker, 43 Borough road
Hazard & Worton, stay ma. &c. 8 Trinity row, Upp. st. Islington
Hazard Daniel, wool broker, 19 Basinghall st
Hazard Jane (Mrs.), fruiterer, 43 Jermyn st. St. James's
Hazard John T. paper manfrs'. agent, see Roberts & Hazard
Hazel George, grocer, 23 Snow's fields, Bermondsey
Hazeldine & Matts, coach & van builders, 5 Lant st. Borough
Hazeldine William, dairyman, 2 South Lambeth
Hazell Elizabeth (Mrs.), coffeerooms, 3 Cleveland st. Fitzroy sq
Hazell John, accountant, 9 Gresse st. Tottenham court rd
Hazell John, butcher, 19 Cannon st. Ratcliff highway
Hazell John, butcher, 3 Great Chapel st. Westminster
Hazell Jonathan, manufg. jeweller, 24 Gloucester st. Clerknl
Hazell Louisa (Mrs.), stables, Boar's head yd. Kingst. Westmr
Hazelton Fredk. John, stationer, 10 Salisbury st. Lisson gr
Hazle James, map & printcolorer, 34 Northampton sq Clerkenw
Hazlewood Thos. *Bancroft's Head* P.H. 1 Bancroft's pl. Milend
Hazzard William, plumber, 91 Mary st. New road
Head Alfred, brewer, see Charrington, Head & Co
Head Arthur Jsph. solr. 17 Southampton bldgs. Chanceryla
Head Charles, hairdresser, 7 Bridge st. Southwark
Head Edward, furniture broker, 18 Eaton ln. north, Pimlico
Head Geo. appraiser, house agent, undertaker, plumber, painter & glazier, 7 Upper Baker st. Regent's park
Head Isabella Ann (Mrs.), grocer, 9 Eaton la. north, Pimlico
Head Jas. bricklayer & plasterer, 34 Church st. Soho
Head Robert, bricklayer, 20 Clarence gardens, Regent's park
Head Thomas, shipowner, 3 Howford bldgs. Fenchurch st
Head Walter George, tailor, 36 Percy st. Tottenham ct. rd
Head William, butcher, 29 Penton row, Walworth road
Head Wm. Barnes, ship &c. brkr. 3 Howford bdgs. Fenchurch st
Headde Thomas, grocer, &c. 43 Brick la. St. Lukes
Headen & Co. news agents, 12 Park side, Knightsbridge
Headford Francis, grocer, 163 Long lane, Bermondsey
Heading Francis Wm. wine merchant, see Goggs, Heading & Co
Headlam Thomas Emerson, barrister, 57 Chancery lane
Headland Edward, surgeon, 32 Guilford st. Russell square
Headland Henry T. oil & colorman, 24 Long lane, Smithfield
Headland Thomas H. silversmith & polisher, 13 Gt. Sutton st
Headland Wm. homœpathic chemist, 15 Princes st. Hanoversq
Headland William, tailor, 43 Chapel st. Somers town
Headworth Elizh. (Mrs.), watchma. 55 St. John st. Smithfield
Headworth Thomas, watchma. 80 St. John st. Smithfield
Heagarty James, fishmonger, 1 Oxford market
Heagarty Michael, tailor, 5 West st. Golden square
Heal John Harris & Son, bedding manufacturers, feather dressers & eider down quilt makers, 196 Tottenham ct. rd
Heal William, tailor, 49 Crescent st. Euston square
Heald Richard & Co. 24 Old Change, Cheapside

Heald Edward, projecting letter ma. 8 Holles st. Clare mk
Heald Henry, solicitor, see Hill & Heald
Heale Josiah, barrister, 3 Gray's inn square
Heales Benjamin, secret springer, 44 Ironmonger row
Heales Geo. Saml. proctor, 8 Gt. Carterla. Doctors' commons
Heales John, secret springer, 9 Seward st. Goswell st
Healey John & Co. blacking makers, 7 Vine st. Bloomsbury
Healey Timothy & Co. who. statnrs. & rag mers. bookbinders' cloth makers, mill board makers, 9 Queenhithe
Healey Barnard, *Sir Isaac Newton* P.H. 18 Union st. Middlesex hospital
Healey Edward, printer & publisher, 1 Crane ct. Fleet st
Healey George, *King's Head* P.H. 12 Cumberland mkt. Regt. pk
Healey George, pianoforte mak. 25 Ernest st. Regent's park
Healey John, *King's Arms* P.H. 13 Queenhithe
Healey Jsh. beer retailer, 52 Lit. George st. Hampstead rd
Healey Peter, butcher, 1 Grafton st. Fitzroy square
Healey Thomas Piers, barrister, 3 Elm court, Temple
Healing & Burrows, solicitors, 20 Lawrence lane, Cheapside
Health of Towns Commission (Henry Hobhouse, esq. sec.), Gwydr house, Whitehall
Healy John & Hen. coopers & brush ma. 32 Camden st. Islngtn gr
Healy John & Henry, coopers, 5 West pl. Islington green
Healy Edw. *Drapers' Arms* P.H. 29 Up. Barnsbury st. Islngtn
Healy Francis H. (Bordeaux), wine mer. 38 Crutched friars
Healy James, undertaker, 154 High Holborn
Healy John, law stationer, 3 Westmorland bldgs. Aldersgate
Healy Timothy, orange merchant, 64 Long la. West Smthfld
Healy Wm. ironmonger, &c. see Burbidge & Healy
Hean Wm. jun. cabinet maker, 33 Gt. Russell st. Bloomsbury
Hean Wm. sen. cabinet maker, &c. 30 Gt. Russell st. Bloomsbry
Heaney Francis, *Red Lion* P.H. Red Lion court, Fleet st
Heaney John Henry, *Britannia* P.H. 8 Portland st. Soho
Heaney Thos. Ford, glass & china dlr. 4 Dockhead, Bermndsy
Heap Chas. watch finisher, 3 Gastigny pl. Galway st. City rd
Heap James, umbrella maker, 17 Little Alie st. Goodman's fi
Heap John Camden, solicitor, 13 Millman st. Bedford row
Heaphy John, stockbroker, 39 Lothbury
Heaps John, *Nottingham Castle* P.H. Angel st. St. Martin legr
Heaps John, *Grove tavern* P.H. Grove, Peckham
Heaps Charles Wm. beer retailer, Spring pl. South Lambeth
Heard John & Co. grocers, 59 Brill row, Somers town
Heard Charles, *Windsor Castle* P.H. 10 Regent pl. City rd
Heard Charl. (Mrs.), ladies' school, 15 Southmptn. st. Cambrwl
Heard James, baker, 8 Whitmore place, Hoxton Old town
Heard James Rowe, bootmaker, 8½ Fore st. Cripplegate
Heard Mary Ann (Mrs.), *George* P.H. 6 George row, Bmdsy
Heard William, boot & shoe maker, 9 Cannon st. City
Heard William, *Green Man* P.H. 34 Mansell st. Goodman's flds
Heard William, seedsman & florist, 4 Grange walk, Hoxton
Hearder Joel, who. & retail shoe wareho. 18 Skinner st. City
Hearfield Benj. ostrich feather ma. 1 Orchard pl. Kingsld. rd
Hearl George, bookseller, and dealer in magazines & reviews, 28 Russell court, Brydges st. Covent garden
Hearn John & Co. boot & shoema. 10 Portsdown ter. Kilbn. gate
Hearn & Veary, lace manufacturers, 9 Cheapside
Hearn Geo. soap maker, Short st. Cumberland st. Shoreditch
Hearn John, refiner & sweepwasher, 11 Jerusalem pass. Clknwl
Hearn Joseph, tobacconist, 31 Boston st. Dorset square
Hearn Ralph, gasfitter, 4 Milton st. Cripplegate
Hearn Robert, agent to Sam. Thomas, needle manufacturer, 4 Crown court, Cheapside & Redditch
Hearn Starling S. confectioner, 1 Eliza pl. Sadler's wells
Hearnden Chas. C. *Black Horse* P.H. Cain pl. Kentish town
Hearnden Wm. Hen. linendraper, 58 Marchmont st. Russell sq
Hearne Edmund L. solicitor, 9 Pall mall east
Hearne Henry, fruiterer, 28 Hindon st. Pimlico
Hearne John, bookseller, 81 Strand
Hearne John, merchant, 15 Barge yd. chambers, Bucklersbury
Hearon, Bright, M'Culloch & Co. wholesale druggists, 95 Bishopsgate within
Hearse Wm. Robert, engraver, see Draper, Berry & Hearse
Heasman Francis, pastrycook, 8 Red Lion pas. Holborn
Heasman John, oven builder, 22 Wellington st. Blkfrs. rd
Heartwell Rd. hosier & silk handkercf. dlr. 283 High Holborn
Heath & Barclay, surgeon dentists, 34 Bedford row, Blooms
Heath, Furse & Co. merchants, 31 Old Jewry
Heath & Gath, milliners, 79 Margaret st. Cavendish sq
Heath Geo. & Wm. carpenters, &c. 122 Bishopsgate without
Heath Job & Ebenezer, curriers, &c. 23 Bridge house pl. Boro
Heath, Palmer & Beatson, ea. ind. mer. & agts, 134 Fenchurch st
Heath, Palmer & Beatson, wine merchants, 134 Fenchurch st
Heath Arnold, beer retailer, Park place, Old Kent road
Heath Charles, artist, 6 Seymour place, Euston sq
Heath Charles James, corn & seed factor, 11 Hart st. Mark lane, & 6 New London st
Heath Douglas Denon, barrister, 11 Chancery lane
Heath Edward, fruiterer, 28 Beckford row, Walworth road
Heath Emanuel Barley, carpenter, 5 Monkwell st. Cripplegate
Heath Francis, coach painter, 8 Chapel st. Pentonville
Heath George, serjeant-at-law, 11 Chancery lane, Fleet st
Heath George Frederick, toy & fancy warehouse, 8 Middle row, Holborn
Heath George Thomas, M.D. surgeon, 63 Hoxton Old town
Heath Henry, hatter, 393 Oxford st
Heath Henry B. T. dentist & cupper, 123 Edgware road
Heath Herbert, chop house, 7 King st. Westminster
Heath James, dairyman, Vine yard, Tooley st
Heath John, dentist, 11 Albemarle st. Piccadilly
Heath John, *Duke of Wellington* P.H. 94 Crawford st
Heath John, lodging house, 2 Queen st. Mayfair
Heath John, paperhanger & decorator, 121 Fetter lane
Heath John Carlen, barrister, 1 Pump court, Temple
Heath John Fred. auctioneer & valuer, 27 Bishopsgate wthn
Heath Josiah Marshall, iron master, 2 Winchester bldgs
Heath Mary (Mrs.), baker, 5 Constable row, Mile end road
Heath Peter, livery stables, 1 Tenter st. Little Moorfields
Heath Richard, brassfounder, 2 Three Colt st. Limehouse
Heath Richard, chemist, 2 Princes st. Westminster
Heath Richard, fruiterer, 10 Charles st. Hatton garden
Heath Robert, cheesemonger, 10 Sherbourne pl. Dorset sq
Heath Robert, toy warehouse, 4 Norton st. Fitzroy sq
Heath Samuel, solicitor, 1 Church court, Clement's la. City
Heath Sarah (Miss), milliner, 22 Spencer st. Canonbury sq
Heath Stephen H. who. bootma. 15 & 16 Giltspur st. Smithfld
Heath Thomas, coal merchant, 13 George st. Adelphi
Heath Thomas, dairyman, 11 Ebury st. Pimlico
Heath Thomas, grocer & cheesmgr. 34 Thanet st. Burton cres
Heath William, bookseller, 29½ Lincoln's inn fields
Heath William, builder, &c. 1 Grove, Hackney
Heath William, builder, 13 South Island pl. Clapham road
Heath William, carpent. & builder, 6 Charles st. Horselydown
Heath William, furn. ironmongr. 13 Adam's row, Hampstd. rd
Heath William, jeweller, 62 Mortimer st. Cavendish sq
Heath William, sailmaker, 2 Narrow st. Ratcliff
Heath Wm. solr. Australian chmb. Nag's Head ct. Gracech. st
Heath William, smith & farrier, 4 Pleasant row, Walworth
Heath William, whitesmith, George st. Camberwell
Heathcoat John & Co. lace manufrs. 8 King st. Cheapside
Heathcote John & Co. who. oil & italian wareho. 197, Upper Thames st
Heathcote John E. barrister, 1 King's Bench walk, Temple
Heathcote Robert, solicitor, 2 St. Mildred's ct. Cornhill
Heather Jas. & Co. calenderers & packers, 3 Feathers ct. Milk st
Heather Edw. milliner & straw hat manufr. 5 Crawford st
Heather Geo. copperplate engraver, 13 Charles st. Westm
Heather Geo. glass ca. & cigar box mfr. 83 Sun st. Bishopsg. st
Heather George, muslin warehouseman, 61 Bread st.
Heather Hen. Chas. bootmaker, 18 Charlton st. Fitzroy sq
Heather James, packing case maker, 18 Lamb st. Spital sq
Heather John, conveyancer, 3 Bedford court, Covent garden
Heather John, patten & clog maker, 26 Artillery la. Bshgte
Heather Jonathan E. bootmaker, 4 Huggin lane, Wood st
Heather Wm. bootmaker, 13 Charles st. Westminster
Heather Wm. saddler & harness maker, 63 London wall
Heathfield Richard, lace merchant, 5 Addle st. Wood st
Heathfield Richard, barrister, 1 New square, Lincoln's inn
Heathfield Richard, superintendent to *Metropolitan Life Assurance Society*, 3 Princes st. Bank
Heathfield Wm. solicitor, 8 Featherstone bldgs. Holborn
Heathfield Wm. Eames, experimntl. chemist, Princes sq. Fnsby
Heathorn Joseph L. shipowner, 3 Abchurch lane, City
Heatley Richard & Co. bottle merchants, 2 Bell ct. Mincingla
Heatley Richd. & Son, wine merchants, 2 Bell ct. Mincing la
Heaton Charles & Co. wholesale oil, italian & provision warehouse, 23 & 25 Lime st
Heaton Charles Hord, barrister, 3 Middle Temple la
Heaton Edward, comb makers' agent, 107 Hatton garden
Heaton Geo. booksel. & publisher, 10 New inn passage, Wych st
Heaven Charles, *Geneva Arms* P.H. 3 Hayes ct. Soho
Heaven John, dyer & scourer, 59 Wood st. Cheapside
Heavens Daniel, *Red Lion* P.H. 21 Princes st. Westminster
Heavens Fred. *Pr. of Orange* P.H. 13 Philip st. Ratcliff
Heavens Geo. warehouseman, 6 Powell st. west, Goswell rd
Heavens James, *Mitre & Dove* P.H. 1 King st. Westminster
Heavens James, saddler, 28 South Molton st.
Heavens John, stationer, 7 Ship tav. pass. Leadenhall mrkt
Heaver John, bricklayer, 44 Redcross st. Borough
Heaviside Isabella (Mrs.), *Carpenters' Arms* P.H. 18 Princess st. Portman market
Heaviside Mary Ann (Mrs.), *Gen. Elliott* P.H. 1 Bedfordbury
Hebard Thos. mercht. & agt. Old Trinity House, Water la

Hebard Thomas, *Sun Dial* P.H. 47 Goswell st
Hebberd Mary (Mrs.), ladies'wdrb.dlr.22Clevelandst.Fitz.sq
Hebbert Charles & Co. army clothiers, helmet, army cap & accoutrement makers, 8 Pall mall east
Hebbert Henry, ready made linen & outfit wareh. 187 Strand
Hebbert Isaac, sword cutler & acctremnt ma. 8 Air st. Picdly
Hebblethwaite George, tailor, 4 Lit. Chestr. st. Grosvnr. pl
Hebblewhite Thos. *Bull Inn & Family ho.* 151 Leadenhall st
Hebden James, fruiterer, Mare st. Hackney
HebdenMaryAnn(Mrs.),*Brickla.Arms*P.H.Mrgt.ct.Com.rd
Hebden Richd. W.hosier&glover, 6 Southampton st.Queen sq
Hebditch Geo. bookseller & news agt. 51 Lisson grove north
Hebditch John, grocer, cheesem. &c. 74 Three colt st.Limho
Hebditch Thomas, undertaker, 62 Tabernacle walk, Finsby
Hebdon Ann (Mrs.), marine store dealer, 2 Church st. Minor
Hebdon Thomas, lodging house, 50 Marchmont st
Hebeler (Bernard) & Co. merchants, 106 Fenchurch st
Heberden Charles, barrister, 10 Old square, Lincoln's inn
Heberden Thomas, physician, 11 Upper Brook st
Hebert Elizab. (Mrs.), bookseller & librarian, 88 Cheapside
Hebert Henry, accountant, &c. 14 Serle's place, Lincoln's inn
Hebert John, metal embosser, 9 Short's bldgs.Clerknwl.close
Hebner Jonathan, engraver & printer & label warehouse, 12 Water st. Blackfriars
HebrewCollege(Alx.M'Caul,D.D.pres.) 8Plstne.pl.Cmbdg.rd
Hebting Theodore,watch & clock maker,seeStraub &Hebting
Heck James, fishmonger, Well st. Hackney
Hecker Sam. Hen. T. mercht. 5 Chequer yard, Dowgate hill
Heckinbotham &Knight,undertak.8 Fleur de lis st.Nort.folg
Heckman John Henry, fur & skin dresser, 5 John st. & 32 Chicksand st. Spitalfields
Heckscher Elias Mayer &Co.tobacco mfs. 54Church st.Minor
Hedderley James, writer & grainer, 11 Duke st. Chelsea
Heddon Stone Company, 179 Rotherhithe st
Hederle John, tailor, 4 Francis st. Golden square
Hedge Charles, coal mercant, 2 Falcon wharf, Malden lane, King's cross, & Eaton wharf, Pimlico
Hedge Edward, barrister, 10 King's Bench walk, Temple
Hedge Henry, marine store dealer, 5 Deptford High st
Hedgeland John, architect, 2 Grove place, Lisson grove
Hedger Arthur, custom house agent, Hall of Commerce
Hedger George, diamond mer. 48 Gt. Sutton st. Clerkenwell
Hedger George Fred. watch movement maker & dealer in tools, files & watch materials, wholesale & retail, 10 West place, John's row, St. Luke's
Hedger James, fruiterer, 34 Hayfield pl. Mile end road
Hedger William, land agent & surveyor, 10 New Bond st
Hedges & Butler, italian warehouse, wine merchants & wax chandlers, 155 Regent st. & 62 Piccadilly
Hedges & Smith, hosiers & lacemen, 82 Shoreditch High st
Hedges Harriet (Mrs.), lodging ho. 21 Mount st. Berkeley sq
Hedges, Henry, coal merchant, 4 John st. Battle bridge
Hedges Henry, saddler, 14 Bridge st. Southwark
Hedges James, shoe warehouse, 136 Drury lane
Hedges James, pawnbroker & silversmith, 135 Drury lane
Hedges James, jun. bootmaker, 49 Jermyn st. St. James's
Hedges James, sen. boot & shoe maker, 44 New Bond st
Hedges John, cabinet maker, see Clarke & Hedges
Hedges John, jeweller, 6 Skinner st. Clerkenwell
Hedges John, *Two Chairmen* P.H.Sth.Bruton mws.Brutn.st
Hedges Killingworth, solicitor, see Collier, Hedges & Steel
Hedges Martha (Miss), hosier, 6 Back church lane
Hedges Robert, livery stables, 36 Up. North pl. Gray's inn rd
Hedges Sarah (Mrs.), straw plait dealer, 113 Waterloo rd
Hedges Thomas, carpenter, builder & undertk. High st. Bow
Hedges Wm. harness maker, 109 Edgeware rd. Marylebone
Hedgley John, music seller, 12 Ebury st. Pimlico
Hedgman Cornelius, printer, 12 London wall
Hedgman Jas. national baths, 5 Lit.Queen st. & 218 H. Hlbn
Heditch Wm.Chas.leather pipe ma. 29Charles st.Hatton gdn
Hedley Eliz. M. (Miss), tobacconist, 10 Three Colt st. Limeho
Hedley Jos. consulting gas engineer, 29 Bucklersbury
Hedley Thomas, barrister, 4 Elm court, Temple
Heekes John Bennett, coffee rms. 15 & 16 Church rw. Aldgate
Heeks Isaac, basket maker, 61 White Lion st. Pentonville
Heeley James & Sons, patentees & manufactureas of pens, steel snuffers, cork screws, malleable iron nails, &c. 74 Aldermanbury, &}Mount st. Birmingham
Heeles John B. & Co. estate agts. & auctionrs. 18 Bsnghll. st
Heelis Robert, surgeon, 28 Three Colt st. Limehouse
Heenan James & Co. tobacconists, 24 King William st. City, & 30 Regent st
Heeps Joanna H. (Miss) straw hat mfr. 17 Eldon st. Finsbury
Heeps, John Hen. plumber & glazier, 46 Liverpool st. Bshpgt
Heffer Edmund A. picture frame ma. 57Chalton st. Somers tn
Heffer Edward, carver & gilder, 94 Up.Seymour st. Euston sq
Heffer Hen. coach body ma. &c. 27 Walnut tree wk. Lambeth
Heffer Robert, leather dresser, 5 Russell pl. Bermondsey
Hefferman James, artist, 35 Coleshill st. Eaton sq
Heffill Fisher, teadealer, 16 New Church st. west, Edgware rd. & 79 Salisbury st. Lisson grove
Heffill George, tailor, 14 Chenies st. Bedford sq
Hefford Henry, tobacconist, 60 Great Tower st. City
Hegerty John, smith & ironmonger, 7 Church lane, Commcl.rd
Heges & Smith, linendrapers, 82 Shoreditch
Heginbothom Charles, *Corn Exchange tavern*, Mark lane
Hegley Wm. gunmaker, 57½ Gloucester st. Commercial rd
Heigham Charles Wm. barrister, 19 Old sq. Lincoln's inn
Heigham Thos. Geo. pawnbrokr. 3 to 5 Onslow pl. Fulham rd
Heighington John, barge builder, Battersea fields
Heighington John, wine merchant, 23 Mark lane
Heighway Elizth. (Miss), corset ma. 31 Thayer st. Mnchstr.sq
Heighton Caleb, tobacconist, 85 Cromer st. Brunswick sq
Heighway Thomas, *Crown* P.H. Rupert st. Goodman'sfields
Heilbronn Adolf & Co. essential oil importers, 82 Mark la
Heilbut (S.I.)& Ruben (R.A.), importers of leeches, 3 Princes square, St. George's east
Heilbut, Ruben&Co.merchts.&gen.agts.7 Hart st. Mark lane
Heilbutt Samuel, ship chandler, 14 Limekiln hill, Limeho
Heill George, baker, 210 Bethnal green road
Heimann&Kuper, manufacturers of patent wire ropes, Grand Surrey Canal, Camberwell
Heinemann Frederick, coffee rooms, 2 Nelson pl. Old Kent rd
Heinke Fred.& Son, furn. ironmongers, 103 Great Portland st
Heinrich Johann, tortoiseshell comb manufacturer to the Queen Dowager, 3 York st. Blackfriars road
Heintz Rt. & Son, insurance brokers, 12Copthall ct.&Lloyd's
Heir at Law Society (George Ross, esq. manager), 14 Chatham place, Blackfriars
Heisher Louisa (Mrs.), baker, 8 John st. Limehouse fields
Heisch P——I——, &Co.merchts.1Crown ct.Threadneedle st
Heisch Frederick, merchant, 16 America square, Minories
Heitzman Fidel & Co. wooden clock maks. 40 Norton folgate
HeizmannWilhelm, clockmaker, 15Snow's fields, Bermondsey
Helbert John, stockbroker, 4 Shorter's ct. Throgmorton st
Helder George, solicitor, 17 Clement's inn, Strand
Helder William, solicitor, 10 Lancaster place, Strand
Helion Light Patent Gas Apparatus Manufactory, Aberdeen mews, Marlborough mews, Oxford st. & 18 Charles st. St. James's square
Hellaby Richard, stock, brace, belt & collar maker, 7 Huggin lane, Wood st. & 21 Gutter lane
Hellas William, fruiterer, 2 Queen st. King's road, Chelsea
Hellen Elias, cheesemonger, 161 Kingsland road
Heller (Luis) & Co. merchants, 9 George yard, Lombard st
Hellier Henry, butcher, 24 New st. Dockhead
Hellier Harry, meat salesman, see Moreton & Hellier
Hellier Henry, shoemaker, 57 Brunswick st. Hackney road
Hellier Rd. registrar, 1 George ter. Crimscott st. Bermondsey
Helling Joseph N. wind. glass cuttr. 11 Adams rw. Hmstd.rd
HellingWm.F.glass cuttr.& lead mer.20Adams rw.Hmstd.rd
Hellis Charles, builder, 12 St. James's walk, Clerkenwell
Hellis Dan. carpntr. & undertkr. 9 Northampton st.Clknwll
Hellmers John Fred. & Sons, wine merchts. 27 Mincing lane
Hellwege & Tepper, commission merchts.1 St.Dunstan's hill
Hellyer Frederick & Sons, ship carvers, 25 Rotherhithe
Hellyer John, *Half Moon inn*, 9 Half Moon st. Bishopsgate
Hellyer Wm. Varlo, barrister, 4 King's Bench walk, Temple
Helm Bryan, bricklayer, 4 & 5 Fulwood's rents, High Holborn
Helm Robert, beer engine manufacturer, 25 Branch place, Hoxton & 165 St. John st. road
HelmckenC.(Mrs.), *WhiteSwan*P.H.36 Gt.Alie st.Gdmn's.fi
Helme Chas. carver & gilder, 32 Gt. Sutton st. Clerkenwell
Helme John, attorney, 4 Raymond buildings, Gray's inn
Helme Thos. picture frame maker, 81 Paul st. Finsbury
Helmore & Smith, coal merchants, 151B, Piccadilly & West basin road wharf, Pimlico basin
Helmore Hy.Geo.coal mer.St.Peter's wf. Millbank st. Wstmr
Helms Thos. & Son, tailors & habit ms. 25 Duke st.St.James'
Helms William, baker, 9 Churchway, Somers town
Helps Bryan, menagerie, Elms house, Hammersmith
Helps Charles, tailor, 47 Liquorpond st. Gray's inn lane
Helps Fred. Aug. stock & share broker, 22 Finch la.Cornhill
Helps Jane (Miss), lodging housekeeper, 9 Arundel st.Strand
Helps John, sec. to *Westminster Life Ins. Soc.* 429 Strand
Helps Thos. solicitor, 12 Furnival's inn, Holborn
Helps Thos. Williams, barrister, 3 Plowden bldgs. Temple
Helsdon Isaac & Nath. zinc mnfrs. 20 Lisson grove north
Helsdon John Jas. furn. broker, 36 Gt. Queen st. Linc.inn fi
Helsham Arthur, physician, 16 Constable row, Mile end rd
Helsham Robert, solicitor, 5 Assembly row, Mile end road
Helwig Jacob, tailor & habit maker, 16 Queen st. Pimlico

Hely Michael, coachmaker, 1 Salisbury place, New road
Hemans Bathurst, solicitor, 5 Raymond bldgs. Gray's inn
Hembery Joseph, orange merchant, 41 Watling st
Hembery Joseph Henry, solicitor, 2 Bedford st. Bedford sq
Hemings Miss, ladies' school, 12 Cadogan st
Hemingway Alexander & Walter, chemists, 45 Bryanstonest
Hemingway John, coffee rooms, 16 Old Bailey
Hemingway Thos. corn dealer, 9 Up. Lisson st. Lisson grove
Hemingway Thomas, oilman, 2 Adelaide pl. Stepney green
Hemmens John, upholsterer, Upper John st. Fitzroy sq
Hemment Rhoda (Mrs.), milliner, 16 Guildford pl. Spafields
Hemmin Maria (Mrs.), tailor, 38 Haymarket
Hemming Edward & Son, needle manufacturers (John Sanders, agent), 4 & 5 Addle st. City
Hemming Benjamin, hosier & glover, 35 & 10 Blackfriars rd
Hemming Fred. H. sec. to Londonderry Railway Co. 49 Moorgate street
Hemming Henry, *Café de l'Eurove*, 9 Haymarket
Hemming James, pork butcher, 29 Robinson's row, Kingsland
Hemming James, tailor, 1 Charles st. City road
Hemming Samuel, hosier, 6 Piccadilly
Hemming Thomas, bootmaker, 15 Cross Key sq. Lit. Britain
Hemming Thomas, hairdresser, 2 Crescent st. Euston sq
Hemmings E.&S(Misses), ladies' school, 1 Critchill pl. Hoxton
Hemmings Fortunatus, painter, &c. 15 Brownlow st. Druryla
Hemmings Harriet (Mrs.), beer retailer, 12 Belgravemews ea
Hemmings Michael, *King's Head* P.H. 11 Lit. Woodstock st
Hemmings Samuel, statuary, &c. 40 Regent st. Horseferryrd
Hemmings William, umbrella maker, 2 Broad ct. Bow st
Hemmins Wm. bricklayer, 16 Queen's buildings, Brompton
Hemp William, sheriffs' officer, 19 Serle's pl. Lincoln's inn
HemplemanHenry, greengrocr. 15 Haberdashrs'. walk, Hoxton
Hempson Geo. purvey. of asses' milk, 21 Kinnerton st. Belgr. sq
Hempsted James, corn dealer, 45 Cornwall road, Lambeth
Hems Wm. & Son, cutlers & ironmnrs. 39 & 142 Whitechpl. Hi. st
Hems Benjamin, baker, 1 Lower Chapman st. St. Geo's. east
Hems Hen. furn. ironmongr, cutler, &c. 39 Hedge row, Islington
Hems Thos. baker, 9 Cheshire st. Waterloo town
Hems Thomas, coffee rooms, 7 Bridge court, Westminster
Hems William, butcher, 6 Lower Chapman st. St. Geo's. east
Hemsley Edward, linen, &c. wareh. 4A, Lawrence la. City
Hemsley Henry, optician, 140 St. George st
Hemsley Henry, wine merchant, 7 Tokenhouse yard, Lothbury, & 1 Ebenezer terrace, Kennington common
Hemsley Thomas, optician, 11 King st. Tower hill
Helmsley William, surveyor, 75 Lower Sloane st. Chelsea
Hemsworth, Kibble & Linley, curriers, 80 & 81 St. Martin's la
Henbery Wm. turner, 13 Bridgewater gardens, Barbican
Henbrey Ebenezer, ironmonger, 47 Charlotte ter. New cut
Henbrey Francis, hairdresser, 109 Whitechapel rd
Henckell, Du Buisson & Co. merchts. 18 Laurence Pountney la
Henderson, Arundel & Co. silk mnfrs. 1 Gutter la. Cheapside
Henderson, Dickson & Co. merchants, 16 Bishopsgate st. within
Henderson & Graham, tailors, 11 Great Vine st. Regent st
Henderson John Andrew & Co. nursery & seedsmen, 1 Pineapple place, Edgware road
Henderson & Maughan, silversmiths & jewellers, 17 Poultry
Henderson Robert & John, east india merchants, 7 Mincing la
Henderson Wm. & Co. merchants, 16 Bishopsgate st. within
Henderson Alex. job & postmas. Red Lion yd. 26 Cockspur st
Henderson Alexander, physician, 6 Curzon st. May fair
Henderson Alexander, tailor, 19 Old Burlington st
Henderson Alex. veter. surgeon, Gt. Scotland yd. & 8A, Park la
Henderson David Wilmott, pawnbrkr. 74 Brewer st. Somerstn
Henderson Edward, wine merchant, 166 Piccadilly
Henderson Edw. Geo nursery, &c. Wellington rd. St. John's wd
Henderson George, baker, 1 Mary's place, Kingsland rd
Henderson George, bookseller & stationer, 2 Old Bailey
Henderson George, solicitor, 28 Mansell st. Goodman's flds
Henderson George, tailor, 46 Queen st. Bryanstone sq
Henderson Gilbert, queen's counsel, 2 Harcourt bdgs. Temple
Henderson Hen. silversmith, jeweller & watch ma. 38 Strand
Henderson James, carpenter, 40 Poland st. Oxford st
Henderson Jas. sofa maker, 7 Southampton bdgs. Euston sq
Henderson Jas. stationer, booksel. &c. 7 Grafton st. Fitzroy sq
Henderson James Henry, attorney, 31 Bloomsbury sq
Henderson John, barrister, 4 Hare court, Temple
Henderson John, bootmaker, 6 Hampton st. Walworth rd
Henderson John, carpenter, &c. 1 College pl. Kinnerton st
Henderson John, chairmaker, 42 Windmill st. Tottenham ct. rd
Henderson John, engineer, &c. see Fox, Henderson & Co
Henderson John, fruiterer, 21 Golden lane, Barbican
Henderson John, saddler, &c. 61 East st. Manchester sq
Henderson John, schoolmaster, 72 Newman st. Oxford st
Henderson John, *Shades*, 6 Martin's lane, Cannon st
Henderson John Peter, dentist, 18 Manchester sq
Henderson Mary (Mrs.), baker, 109 Fore st. Cripplegate
Henderson Nicholas, danc. master, 72 Newman st. Oxford st
Henderson Phœbe (Mrs.), baby linen wa. Canal pl. O. Kent rd
Henderson Peter, baker, 14 Pitfield st. Hoxton
Henderson Richard, silver chaser, 6 Glos'ter row, Hoxton
Henderson Robt. dentist, 3 Montagu place, Montagu square, & 36B, Charlotte st. Fitzroy square
Henderson Robert, seedsman, see Beck, Henderson & Co
Henderson Rt. Eason, who. hosiers & flan. fact. 120 Wood st
Henderson Thomas, surgeon, &c. 13 Portman pl. Edgware rd
Henderson Thomas, tailor, 2 Hornton st. Kensington
Henderson Wm. attorney, 10 Lancaster pl. Waterloo bridge
Henderson Wm. baker, 11 Upper Kennington lane
Henderson Wm. tailor, 13 Cherry garden st. Rotherhithe
Henderson Wm. Jas. cabinet ma. 19 Nthumbrlnd. st. New rd
Henderson Wm. Yeats, ship broker, 42 Crutched friars
Hendey Richard, bookseller, 126 Bethnal green road
Hendle Joseph, com. agent, 3 Howford bldgs. Fenchurch st
Hendre Sarah (Mrs.), plumber, 65½ York st. Broadway, Westm
Hendrey Jas. architect & surveyor, 4 Pancras la. Cheapside
Hendrick Daniel, clock ma. 3 Lr. Northampt. st. Clerkenwell
Hendrick Robert, brush ma. 6 Anderson buildings, City rd
Hendrick Thos. John, watchmaker, 7 Westmoreland pl. Cityrd
Hendricks John, confectioner, 2 Church lane, Whitechapel
Hendrie Robt. C. skein silk dyer, 15 Blossom st. Norton fol
Hendrie Robt. who. perfumer, 12 Tichborne st. Haymarket
Hendriks Herman, merchant, 2 Copthall chambers, Copthl. ct
Hendry & Glover, iron founders & engineers, 5 Charles st. Drury lane, & 168 Drury lane
Hendry John, back & vat maker, buyer & valuer of plants, refrigerators, attemporaters, &c. 15 Dorset cres. East r. City r
Hendry John, boot & shoe maker, 8 Chapel st. Edgware road
Hendry Maria (Miss), wardrobe dlr. 106 Gt. Portland st
Hendys William, milliner, 10 Victoria square, Pimlico
Henesey Robert & Sons, mahogany & timber merchants, 189 & 190 High Holborn
Henley Benjamin, fender & fire iron ma, 16 Lisson gro. north
Henley Christiana Ann (Miss), milliner, 29 Beaumont st
Henley Edward, butcher, 3 Folly, Dockhead, Bermondsey
Henley George, *Hat & Plough* P.H. 44 Whitechapel High st
Henley John, china dealer, 2 Bolingbroke row, Walworth rd
Henley Thomas, carpenter, &c. 42 Bell yard, Temple bar
Henley William, bootmaker, 13 Cannon st. Ratcliff highway
Henley William Codner, cider mrcht. 10 Mill la. Tooley st
Henley Wm. Thos. philos. instrumnt. ma. 28 Haydon st. Minris
Henly Robt. furnishing & general ironmonger, 117 Union st. Borough; & 196 Blackfriars road
Henman Charles, architect & surveyor, 12 Clifford's inn
Henman Edward, fishmonger, 18 Basing lane, Bread st
Henman Kezia (Miss), straw bonnet mak. 112 Blackfriars rd
Henman Peter, bed & mattress ma. 18 Frederick pl. Goswell rd
Henman Richard, builder, 10 King's row, Cambridge road
Hennah Joseph Edward, custom ho. agt. 12 Harp la. Tower st
Hennell & Crosby, paperhnging. ma. 1 & 2 Queenst. Sthwk. Br. rd
Hennell Chas. Christian, mercht. 7 Brickhill la. Up. Thames st
Hennell Chas. Tidd, specl. pleader, 1 Harcourt bldgs. Temple
Hennell Robert, silversmith, 14 Northumberland st. Strand
Hennell Robt. Geo. silversmith, &c. 4 Southampton st. Blmbs
Hennen John, physician, 24 Up. Southwick st. Cambridge ter
Hennessey John, cabinet chair & sofa ma. 30 King st. Soho
Hennessy James & Co. merchants, 37 Mark lane
Hennet George, civil engineer, 16 Duke st. Westminster
Henney Charles, undertaker, 119 Chalton st. Somers town
Henney Francis, hosier & haberdashr. 11 Cross st. Newingtn. bts
Henney Thomas, dining rooms, 27 Bridge st. Westminster
Henniker Aldborough, barrister, 70 Chancery lane
Henning Andrew, insurance agent, 6 George yd. Lombard st
Henning John, jun. sculptor, 17 Lr. Belgrave pl. Pimlico
Henning John, surgeon, 13 Coleshill st. Pimlico
Hennings Henry, hardware dealer, 37 Pitfield st. Hoxton
Henningham & Hollis, booksellers & stationers, 5 Mount st
Hennis John Jas. oil & colorman, 7 Dockhead, Bermondsey
Hennis & Whittle, auctioneers, &c. 4 Canning pl. Old st
Henrichsen Henry, sugar refiner, 3 Gt. Prescot st
Henrie & Taylor, milliners, 96 New Bond st
Henriques D. Q. & Co. merchants, 3 Finsbury chambers, Blomfield st. Finsbury
Henriques David N. merchant, 17 Artillery pl. Finsbury
Henriques John Gomes, oil & ital. wa. 13 Park ter. Regt's. pk. rd
Henry & Josephs, merchants, 15 South st. Finsbury
Henry Thomas & Co. wine merchts. 1 Hampstead st. Fitzroy sq
Henry Thos. & Dav. merchts. & sailcloth factors, 44 Mark la
Henry Alexander, M.D. surgeon, 12 Wapping wall
Henry Geo. artificial flower ma. 10 Three King ct. Lombard st
Henry George, merchant & importer of beads & other foreign manufactures, 59 Bread st. Cheapside

Henry Jas. G. linen warehouseman, 3 Laurence Pountney hl
Henry John, fruiterer, 6 Beaufort ter.west, King's rd. Chelsea
Henry John, ropemaker, 7 Cherry garden st. Bermondsey
Henry John Gray, surgeon, 40 Colet pl. Commercial road
Henry John Gray, surgeon, 28 Sidney pl. Commercial rd. east
Henry Mary (Mrs.), corn & coal dlr. & mealman, 85 Holborn hill
Henry Meyer, merchant, 8 Crutched friars
Henry Michael, merchant, 4 South st. Finsbury
Henry Thomas, magistrate, Lambeth st. police court
Henry Thos. John, beer retailer, 18 Brunswick st. Blkfrs. rd
Hensby John, baker, 1 Haddon place, Waterloo road
Henshall Josiah, engraver & coppr. plate printr. 1 Cloudesley ter
Henshall Thos. brass & iron bedstead ma. 58 Compton st. Clkwll
Henshaw Charles, coach maker, see Thrupp, Son & Henshaw
Henshaw Francis, oilman & blacking mkr. 79 Sun st. Bshpsgt
Henshaw Fredk. Henry, artist, 13 Charlotte st. Fitzroy sq
Henshaw John, *Tailors' Arms* P.H. 91 Shad Thames, Southwrk
Henshaw Joseph, baker, 83 Leonard st. Shoreditch
Henshaw Joseph, lace warehouse, 2 Frederick pl. Hmpstd. rd
Henshaw Richard Pitchford, chemist & drugg. 6 Edgware road
Henshaw Thomas, agent to Augier, Freres & Co. of Cognac, 3 Philpot lane, city
Henshaw Thomas, wine & spirit broker, 3 Philpot lane
Hensley James, patent medicine wa. 29 Little Pulteney st
Hensley Lewis, surgeon, &c. 3 Gt. James st. Bedford row
Henslow Stevens Wade, solicitor, see Hughes & Henslow
Hensman Fredk. coal mer. Western wf. George st. Adelphi
Hensman Geo. solicitor, 8 Basing lane, Bread st
Henson Robert & Co. marble, spar & alabaster works, 70 Strand
Henson Henry, bricklayer, 2 Boswell court, Queen square
Henson Martha (Mrs.), coffee rooms, 40 Brown st. Bryans. sq
Henson Thomas, builder, estate & house agent, 3 Park place, Upper Baker st. & 9 Hanover pl. Regent's park road
Henson Thomas, hosier & glover, 51 Tottenham court road
Henton Henry, grocer & cheesemng. 8 Glo'ster pl. Walwth. com
Henton Saml. saddler & harness maker, 7 Bridge st. Lambeth
Hentsch Caspar, furrier, 16 Whitmore place, Hoxton
Hentsch Geo. accountant, 22 Hedge row, High st. Islington
Hentsch George, accountant, 17 New Boswell ct. Carey st
Hentsch Johann Gottfried, furrier, 18 Tavistock st. Cov. garden
Hentsch Mary (Miss), furrier, 22 Hedge row High st. Islington
Hentsch William, surgeon, 23 Laurie ter. St. George's cr. Sthwrk
Henty Elizbth. (Mrs.), stay & corset ma. 172 High Holborn
Henville Wm. woollen draper, &c. see Dibben & Henville
Henville William, law stationer, 14 Took's ct. Chancery lane
Henwood Edw. agt. to the *Yorksh. Insur. Office*, 46 Watling st
Henwood Henry, bricklayer, 7 Wittam's bldgs. Old st. road
Henwood Thomas, carpenter, &c. 7 New Quebec st. Portman sq
Henzell Edward, accountant & agent, 2 Gt. Quebec st
Hepburn John & Thos. leather fact. 5 Bermondsey leather mrkt
Hepburn John & Thomas, tanners, 16 Long la. Bermondsey
Hepburn George, coal dealer, 37 King st. Soho
Hepburn Geo. smith & fire proof box ma. 61 Carey st. Linc. inn
Hepburn Joseph G. attorney, 12 Copthall ct. Throgmorton st
Hepburn Robert, dentist, 8 Davies st. Berkeley square
Heplett George, plumber & glazier, 8 Spring st. Marylebone
Heppel Louisa (Mrs.), fruiterer & confectr. 76 Cornhill
Hepple John, col. produce agent, see Foster, Hepple & Foster
Hepplewhite Thos. *Ship & Star* P.H. 113 High st. Shadwell
Heptinstall William, gunmaker, 18 Swan st. Minories
Heptonstall Richard, *Grapes* P.H. 29 Lit. Earl st. Sev. dials
Hepworth Jsph. & Co. stuff mers. & carpet ag. 23 Ironmonger la
Hepworth Wm. & Co. wine & brandy mr. 2 Laurence Pountney pl
Heralds' Office Bennett's hill, Doctors' comms.; hours 10 to 4
Herald Samuel, shoemaker, 32 John st. north, Marylebone
Herapath's Railway & Commercial Journal Office, 3 Red Lion court, Fleet st.
Herapath Samuel & Co. hatters, 72 Holborn hill
Heraud Jas. A. & Jas. C. law stationers, 25 Bell yd. Temple bar
Heraud Jas. Claudius, ink manufacturer, 25 Bell yd. Temple bar
Herber J. F. & Falck, wine shippers, agent Joseph Greenstreet, 11 Cullum st. Fenchurch st
Herbert John & Son, architectural modellers & artificial stone ornament manufacturers, 42 Parker st. Drury lane
Herbert Alex. tobacconist, 23 Mount pleasant, Gray's inn la
Herbert Alfred, artist, 1 Cumberland buildings, Blackfriars
Herbert Daniel, printer, &c. 2 Brunswick pl. Stk. Nwngtn. rd
Herbert Francis, solicitor, 10 Staple inn & 7 Sloane ter
Herbert Francis George, pawnbroker & silversmith, 81 Farringdon st. & 20 Middle Queen's buildings, Knightsbridge
Herbert George, conveyancer, 9 Old square, Lincoln's inn
Herbert Harriet (Mrs.), corndealer, 196 Up. Thames st
Herbert Henry, cheesemonger, 31 Liverpool st. Bishopsgate
Herbert Henry, *King's Head* P.H. 16 Webb st. Brmndsy. st
Herbert Hen. Wm. chemist & druggist, 22 Langley pl Coml. rd. ea
Herbert James, coffee rooms, 38 Exeter st. Sloane st
Herbert James, grocer, 12 Union st. Somers town
Herbert Jas. B. mnftrng. jeweller, see Mortiboy & Herbert
Herbert John, cabinet maker, 8 Wilmot sq. Bethnal green rd
Herbert John, cutler, 135 Upper st. Islington
Herbert John, draper & haberdash. 36 High st. Marylebone
Herbert John, *Globe* P.H. 5 & 6 Goldsmith's row, Hackney rd
Herbert John, *Globe* P.H. 53 London st. Fitzroy square
Herbert John, linen drap. 13 Brecknock pl. Camden new tn
Herbert John Maurice, barrister, 24 Southampton bldgs
Herbert Joseph, *King's Arms hotel*, 17 Bridge st. & 2 & 3 New Palace yard, Westminster
Herbert Martin, tailor, 63 Davies st. Berkeley sq
Herbert Mary A. (Mrs.), haberdasher, 7 Stepney rents, Hky rd
Herbert Richard, cattle salesman, 60 West Smithfield
Herbert Samuel, rag & bottle mer. 2 Seymour pl. Brynst. sq
Herbert Thomas, enameller, 6½ Wood st. King sq
Herbert Thomas, scalemaker, 39 Cannon st. Ratcliff hway
Herbert Thomas, ship chandler, 88 Tower hill
Herbert William, builder & saw mills, Grosvenor basin, Pimlico, & 15A, King William st. Strand
Herbert William, cowkeeper, 36 James st. Oxford st
Herbert William, fruiterer, North row, Covent garden mrkt
Herbert Wm. gen. mercht. O. Swan brewery, Osborne st. Whtpl
Herbert Wm. grocer & cheesemonger, 1 Boswell ct. Queen sq
Herbert Wm. prof. & pub. of music, 87 Albany st. Regent's pk
Herd Jas. builder, 36 Spring st. Padgtn. & Bathurst mws. Susx. sq
Herd John, mahogany broker, 11 New Park st. Borough
Herdman Mary (Mrs.), grocer, 8 Neptune st. Rotherhithe
Hereford & Merthyr Tydvil Junc. Rail Offi. 1 New Broad st
Hering & Remington, english & foreign book & printsellers, & bookbinders, 137 Regent st
Hering Fred. architect & surveyor, 23 Duke st. Portland pl
Hering George Edward, artist, 4 Southampton st. Fitzr. sq
Hering William, surgeon, 38 Mortimer st. Cavendish sq
Herington & Wells, Britannia brewery, Bath pl. Kensington
Heriot Joseph J. ironmonger, see Huxley & Heriot
Heritage William, hairdresser, 173 Long la. Bermondsey
Herman Ignatz, clockmaker, 13 Compton st. Clerkenwell
Hermen Mary (Mrs.), stayma. 11 Southampton ter. Pentnvl
Hermon Rd. & Son, builders & ho. decors. 22 King st. St. James's & 74A, Margaret st. Cavendish sq
Hern William, grocer, 1 Wellington st. Newington causeway
Hernage Mary Ann (Mrs.), builder, 17 Redcross st. Borough
Herne Bay & Margate Steam Packet Office (George W. Rohrs, secretary), 113 Fenchurch st
Herne Ebenezer, shoe warehouse, see Homan, Herne & Co
Herne Jas. auct. & appraiser, 33 Lombard st. & 172 Shadwell
Hernon John, tailor, &c. 37 Sackville st. Piccadilly
Heron Jacob, babylinen wareh. 25 Bolingbroke row, Walwth
Heron John, builder & surveyor, 14 Carlisle st. Soho sq
Heron Thos. Edwd. cheesemonger, 122 Crawford st. Portman sq
Heron William, sydney agent, 14 Canterbury ter. Dover rd
Herpent Felix, french agent, 20 Sherrard st. Golden sq
Herries, Farquhar, Davidson, Chapman & Co. bankers, 16 St. James's st. Pall mall
Herring Brothers, wholesale druggists, 40 Aldersgate st
Herring, Burness & Co. commer. & insur. agents, 64 Cornhill
Herring, Dewick & Hardy, wholes. stationers, 31 Walbrook
Herring Chas. feather purifier, 14 Kingsgate st. Holborn
Herring Charles, tobacconist, 4 Nelson pl. Old Kent road
Herring Cyrenius, coachmak. 1 Asylum buildings, Westm. rd
Herring Francis, painter, Globe whf. Canal brge. Old Kent rd
Herring Fred. Hen. clothes wareh. 2 Postern row, Tower hill
Herring Geo. ship & insurance broker, 64 Cornhill
Herring James, straw hat maker, 36 Exeter st. Sloane st
Herring John, furn. broker, 13 Baker's row, Whitechapel rd
Herring Robt. Wm. upholsterer & auctioneer, 109 Fleet st
Herring Rowland, coffee rooms, 16 Sun st. Bishopsgate
Herring Wm. grocer & tea dealer, 44 Judd st. Brunswick sq
Herring Wm. menagerie, 21 Quickset row, New road
Herring Wm. surgeon, 74 Sun st. Bishopsgate
Herrman Charles, merchant, 44 Threadneedle st
Herrman Julius D. impt. & dealer in pictures, 4 Greek st. Soho
Herron Geo. Robt. fellmonger, Wild's rents, Bermondsey
Herron James, mining agent, 3 Adams court, Old Broad st
Herschhorn Maurice, dealer in french flowers, feathers & preparations, 31 Gresham st
Hersee Henry, appraiser, Bedford pl. East st. Old Kent rd
Hersey Eliza (Miss), grocer, 31 Star st. Paddington
Hersey James, *George & Dragon* P.H. 91 Long acre
Hersey Wm. chandler's shop, 8 King st. Camden town
Hertslet, Scott & Hertslet, solicitors, 31 Norfolk st. Strand
Hertz, Hartwig & Co. merchants, 113 Fenchurch st
Hertz Bram, sculptor & jeweller, 11 Gt. Marlborough st
Hervé Henry, miniature painter, 12 Cheapside
Hervé Mary Ann (Miss), lace & blond cleaner, 23 Foley pl

Hervey Lord Alfred, barrister, 5 King's Bench walk, Temple
Hervey Wm. tobacconist, 5 Britannia place, Limehouse
Hervieu Auguste, artist, 7 Percy st. Bedford sq
Hescox John, herbalist, &c. 204 Bethnal green road
Heseltine Edward, stockbroker, see Martin & Heseltine
Heseltine Samuel Rd. stockbroker, Stock exchange
Heseltine Wm. dlr. in foreign stocks & shares, Stock exchn
Heseltine Wm. tailor & draper, 15 New st. Dorset sq
Heseltine Wm. Keale, surgeon dentist, 15 Broad st. bldgs
Heselton Clayton Philip, plumber, 3 South st. Manchester sq
Hesketh Robert, architect, 13 Arundel st. Strand
Hesketh Robt. hop&seed factor, Layton's bldgs. Boro' High st
Hesketh Robert, surveyor, 12 Bermondsey square
Heslewood Rt. col. varnish& japan mfr. 16 Cottage rw. Brmsy
Heslop Leonard, cheesemonger, 12 West lane, Bermondsey
Heslop Philip, *Bricklayers' Arms* P.H. 6 New Quebec st
Heslop Wm. univer. dining rooms, 2 Grafton st. Fitzroy sq
Hesse John, cooper, 12 Betts st. Ratcliff highway
Hessendorff Veronica (Mrs.), milliner, 34 Somerset st
Hessin Thos. *Two Chairmen* P.H. 38 Dartmouth st. Westmstr
Hester Joseph, boot & shoemaker, 13 Clement's la. Lombard st
Hester Robert, fishmonger, 8 Church st. Camberwell
Hester Wm. oil & color wa. 15 Pierrepoint row, Islington
Hetherington Joseph & Son, stables, 18 Connaught terrace
Hetherington M— & Co. merchants, 1 Winchester buildings
Hetherington Henry, bookseller, stationer, & news agent, 40 Holywell st. Strand, & 57 Judd st
Hetherington John, tea dealer, 323A, High Holborn
Hetherington Jsph. *Bull & Gate* P.H. New Chapel pl. Kentsh. tn
Hetherington Joseph, lamp ma. & oil refiner, 17 Pall mall
Hetherington Wilson, barrister, 3 New square, Lincoln's inn
Hetley & Co. wholesale glass shade, sheet, crown & patent plate glass warehouse, 35 Soho square
Hett James, pat. self capping gun ma. 21 Conduit st. Bond st
Hettich Clement, clockmaker, 217 Upper Whitecross st
Heudebourck John Leny, druggist, Church st. Hackney
Heuland Henry, mineralogist, 31 Red Lion square, Holborn
Heward Chas. Roope, ironmong. 16 Shaftesbury ter. Pimlico
Heward James Hay, salesman, 72½ Blackman st. Boro'
Heward Robert, news agent, 5 Young st. Kensington
Hewer Charles, butcher, 28 Newgate market
Hewer Thomas, grocer, 2 St. Peter's place, Walworth common
Hewer Thos. Jacob, news ag. & tobacconist, 59 Mount st. Lmbth
Hewer Wm. trimming seller, 22 Warwick st. Golden square
Hewes Jones & Co. tea dealers, 12 Bath place, New road
Hewes George, potato salesman, Spitalfields market
Hewes Thomas, tobacconist, 6 Warwick pl. Kingsland rd
Hewetson Robt. & John, cornfacts. 1 Catherine ct. Tower hill
Hewetson Wm. John & Thomas, upholsterers & bedding manufacturers, 185 Oxford st. 204, 211 & 212 Tottenham court road, & 17 Alfred place, Bedford square
Hewetson Hen. merch. & warehoman. 55 Wood st. Cheapside
Hewetson Henry, merchant, 1 Adelaide pl. London bridge
Hewetson John, artist & cabinet inlayer, 48 Wardour st
Hewetson Thomas, carver, 8 Robert st. Bedford row
Hewetson Thos. *Star* P.H. 108 Wentworth st. Whitechapel
Hewett William & Co. tea agents, 156 Fenchurch st. City
Hewett Charles, bootmaker, 9 Albemarle st. Clerkenwell
Hewett Charles, butcher, 4 Road side, Mile end road
Hewett Charles, coffee rooms, 3 Bird st. Oxford st
Hewett Charles, hydrostatic & perpetual filter maker, 9 King's row, Pentonville New road
Hewett Edward James, confectioner, 188 Regent st
Hewett Edwin Augustus, clothes salesman, 17 Old st. road
Hewett Henry, butcher, 74 Edgware road, Marylebone
Hewett Henry, confectioner, 8 St. George's ter. Hyde park
Hewett John, grocer & cheesemonger, 28 Thomas st. Clerknwl
Hewett John, leather & grindery wa. 2 Lower ter. Islington
Hewett John, straw bonnet mnftr. 9 St. George's ter. Boro' rd
Hewett Maria (Miss), milliner, 326 Regent st
Hewett Prescott Gardner, surgeon, 4 Vigo st. Regent st
Hewett Rich. mattress maker, 5 Union st. east, Spitalfields
Hewett Samuel, dining rooms, 29 Union st. east, Spitalfields
Hewett Samuel, fish salesman, 9 Botolph lane, City
Hewett Thos. *Blue Posts* P.H. 1 Greenhills rents, Smithfield
Hewett Thos. *Coach & Horses* P.H. 49 St. John's sq. Clerknwll
Hewett Wm. silversmith & polisher, 9 Gt. Sutton st. Clknwl
Hewett Wm. teadealer, 86 Goswell road
Hewgill Robert, teadealer & grocer, 163 Shadwell High st
Hewish Jonas, locksmith & bellhangr. 42 Eagle st. Red Lion sq
Hewison Jane & Sarah (Misses), berlin wareho. 18 Radcliffe ter
Hewitson Archibald, grocer, 3 Fox's lane, Shadwell
Hewitt Francis P. & Co. hosiery manfrs. 61 Aldermanbury
Hewitt John & Son, coach body mas. 20 Duck la. Edward st. Soho
Hewitt (Misses), milliners, &c. 77 Charlotte st. Fitzroy sq
Hewitt Wm. & Co. colonial & ea. india brks. 4 Comm. sale rooms
Hewitt Benj. Bradley, solicitor, 4 Pancras lane, City
Hewitt Charles, auctioneer, 21 Warner st. Gt. Dover rd
Hewitt Charles, secretary to *General Annuity Endowment Association*, 40 King William st. City
Hewitt Daniel C. pianoforte & orchestron manufacturer, 16 Hanover st. Hanover sq
Hewitt Edward, cheesefactor, 254 Tooley st. Southwark
Hewitt Frances (Mrs.), tobacconist, 94 Old st. road
Hewitt James, boot & shoe maker, 65 & 66 Tottenham ct. rd
Hewitt James, fishmonger, 1 Prospect row, Walworth road
Hewitt James, *Old Hummums*, Tavistock row, Cov. garden
Hewitt John, chemist & druggist, 5 Cable st. & 1 Well st. Wellclose sq
Hewitt John, *Crown* P.H. 1 Gt. St. Andrew st. Seven dials
Hewitt John, hairdresser, 16 Upper King st. Bloomsbury
Hewitt John, upholsterer, 53 London road, Southwark
Hewitt John Templeman, printer, 27 Boston st. Dorset sq
Hewitt Michael, grocer, 87 King st. Camden town
Hewitt Richd. hop&coal mercht. St. Ann's wf. Earl st. Blkfrs
Hewitt Robert, baker, 77 Theobald's road
Hewitt Robert, tailor, 17 Bateman's row, Shoreditch
Hewitt Samuel, glass rougher, 66 John st. Blackfriars rd
Hewitt Saml. indian war. 11 Arcade, Pantechnicon, Belg. sq
Hewitt Sarah (Mrs.), dressmaker, 88 High Holborn
Hewitt Thomas, chronometer ma. 1 St. Vincent pl. City rd
Hewitt Thomas, coffee rooms, 81 Salisbury st. Lisson grove
Hewitt Thomas, plumber & painter, 24 Cowcross st
Hewitt Thomas, solicitor, see Thompson & Hewitt
Hewitt Wm. *Horse Shoe & Magpie* P.H. 1 Bedford st. Bedford rw
Hewitt Wm. ironmonger, 47 Kingsland road
Hewitt Wm. lamp maker & tin plate worker, 160 Goswell st
Hewitt Wm. muffin baker, 83 Waterloo road
Hewitt William, ribbon dyer, &c. 45 Old Gloucester st. Hoxton
Hewitt William Henry, auctioneer, surveyor & estate agent, clerical agent (successor to G. J. Robinson, deceased), 11 Hart st. Bloomsbury
Hewland John, sailmaker, see Archbell & Hewland
Hewlett & Goddard, who. druggists, 6 Arthur st. west, City
Hewlett Anthony, hairdresser, 5 Burlington arcade
Hewlett Daniel, sculptor, 24 King st. Clerkenwell
Hewlett Elizh. (Mrs.), coach joiner, 31 Thomas st. Grosvnr. sq
Hewlett George, butcher, 26 King st. Clerkenwell
Hewlett Henry, stone mason, Larkhall rise, Clapham
Hewlett Henry Wm. attorney, 34 Great James st. Bedford row
Hewlett Jacob, livery stables, 5 Gt. York mews, Portman sq
Hewlett James, carpenter, 6 Gt. Quebec st. Montagu sq
Hewlett Richd. hairdresser, 42 Duke st. Manchester sq
Hewlett Robt. *White Hart* P.H. 23 Fore st. Limehouse
Hewlett Thomas, currier, 7 Turner square, Hoxton
Hewlett Wm. wholesale druggist, 7 Basing lane, Bread st
Hewlings Mary (Mrs.) herbalist, 13 Union st. east, Spitalfields
Hewlitt John, wine merchant, see Long & Hewlitt
Hewlitt John C. dep. prothonotary, 15 Chancery lane
Hews Thomas, tobacconist, 70c, Salisbury st. Lisson grove
Hewson Anne (Mrs.), butcher, 3 Stockbridge terrace, Pimlico
Hewson James Thomas, hairdresser, 113 Edgware road
Hewson John Jas. birmg. & sheff. wa. 143 Shoreditch High st
Hewson Richd. music seller, 8 Albion pl. King's cross
Hewson Thomas Ansaldo, surgeon, 6 Woburn pl. Russell sq
Hewson William, coffee rooms, 15 Princes st. Westminster
Hewson Wm. Bassett, barrister, 6 King's Bench walk, Temple
Hex Elizabeth (Mrs.), lodgingho. 2 Northumberland ct. Strand
Hexamer Jacob, baker, 5 Oxford market, Oxford st
Hextall Louisa (Mrs.), milliner, 310 Regent st
Hey John, surrey lunatic asylum, Meadow row, New Kent rd
Heybourn Wm. grocer & brit. wine dlr. 23 High st. Kensington
Heydelbach Jonas, wharfinger, Platform wf. 391 Rotherhi. st
Heyden Christian, tailor, 38 Bruton st
Heylin Joseph, silk manufacturer, 25 Fort st. Spitalfields
Heylyn Edward, lodging house keeper, 68 Haymarket
Heyman Simeon, jeweller & hardwareman, 30 Houndsditch
Heyward Richd. who. druggst. see Drew, Hayward & Barron
Heywood Dan & Son, fishmgrs. 1 Billingsgate, & 101 L. Thames st
Heywood Joseph Benj. & Co. fringe mak. 6 Bartlett's bldgs
Heywood Wm. Fredk. grocer, 10 Low. Phillimore pl. Kensingtn
Hezel Edward, hat mnf. 43 Lit. Charlotte st. Blackfriars rd
Hiam Benjamin, tailor, 3 Risbie's rope walk, Limehouse
Hiam John, picture frame ma. 6 New road, Sloane st. Chelsea
Hiam Wm. steel plate mak. 9 Ratcliff row, John's row, City rd
Hibbard Benjamin, dairyman, 20 Hill st. Regent's park road
Hibbard Charles, solicitor, 5 Furnival's inn, Holborn
Hibbard Henry, stationer, 1 Coburg st. Clerkenwell
Hibberd Ann Eliza (Mrs.), stayma. 39 Edgware rd. Marylebo
Hibberd Daniel, carpenter, 20 St. John's wood terrace
Hibbert & Co. west india merchts. 1 Billiter court, Billiter sq
Hibbert Chas. (Mrs.), boarding house, 7 Circus, Minories

Hibbert Edward [successor to John Hibbert], wine, spirit, & porter merchant, 7 Jewry st. Aldgate
Hibbert George, hatter, 180 Lambeth walk
Hibbert Jacob, builder, 1 Albert ter. Queen's rd. St. John's wd
Hibbert John, barrister, 8 New square, Lincoln's inn
Hibbert William, butcher, 64 Whitechapel High st
Hibbert William, horse dealer & contractor, 3 Goswell st
Hibbit Wm. stenographer, 48 Carey st. Lincoln's inn
Hibbitt Frederick James, linen draper, 51 Leather lane
Hibble Chas. Fredk. tailor, 12 Tavistock place, Tavistock sq
Hibble James, oilman, 119 Bishopsgate without
Hibble Thos. oil & colorman, 3 Compton st. Clerkenwell
Hibble William, potato salesman, 24 King st. St. James's
Hibbs John, broom dealer, 28 Wellington pl. Blackfriars rd
Hibbs Thomas, dining rooms, 68 Hoxton Old town
Hibernia Wharf (John Humphrey), Montague close, adjoining London bridge, Borough
Hibernian Mining Company, 6 Austinfriars
Hibon John, chemist & druggist, 12 Down st. Piccadilly
Hibon Thomas, fruiterer, 1 Broker's row, Red cross st. Boro'
Hichens' (R. & W.) & Harrison, stock & share brokers, 18 Threadneedle st
Hickes Francis, insurance broker, 9 Finch lane, Cornhill
Hickes George, cheesemonger, 2 High st. Camberwell rd
Hickes Richard, linendraper, Stratford
Hickford John, grindery dealer, 50 Lambeth High st
Hickinbotham Benjamin, butcher, 79 Aldgate High st
Hickinbotham Joseph, butcher, 77 Aldgate High st
Hickinbotham Wm. pawnbroker, 129 & 130 Kingsland rd
Hickinbottom Wm. grocery dlr. 88 Shaftbry. st. New Nrth. rd
Hickley James, brass box maker, 6 John's row, St. Luke's
Hickley Joseph, tailor, 4 City road, Old st
Hickling Benj. W. wholesale stock, brace, shirt, shirt collar & front manufacturer, 35 Noble st. Cheapside
Hickling Jas. general & furn. ironmonger, 1 Gracechurch st
Hickling John, watchmaker, 122 St. John st. Clerkenwell
Hickling Richard, pianoforte maker, 43 Great Titchfield st
Hickling Samuel, hatter, 12 Bevenden st. City road
Hickman Ann E. & Son, furnishing undertakrs. 1 Cannon st. rd
Hickman Chas. pianoforte tuner, 15 Carburton st. Fitzroy sq
Hickman Edward, surgeon, 10 Southampton row, Russell sq
Hickman George, jun. jeweller, 18 Rawstorne st. Goswell rd
Hickman Geo. sen. pearl worker, 35 Red Lion st. Clerkenwell
Hickman Gregory, brushmaker, 46 Mount st. Lambeth
Hickman Jane (Miss), milliner, 6 Up. Grafton st. Fitzroy sq
Hickman John, *Cobham's Head* P.H. 1 Cobham rw. Clerkwll
Hickman John, saw & tool maker, see Buck & Hickman
Hickman Jos. corndlr. 1 Charles pl. East st. Walworth rd
Hickman Michl. haberdasher, 4 Samson's pl. Grange rd
Hickman Rd. ironmonger, 11 Chapel st. Edgware rd. Maryleb
Hickman Thomas, butcher, 19 Clare court, Drury lane
Hickman William, merchant, Lloyd's coffeehouse
Hickman Wm. Smith, picture dealer, 10 Duke st. St. James's
Hickmott John J. bldg. matl. dlr. 21 Hayfield pl. Mile end rd
Hicks, Baylis & Hicks's, wholesale grocers, 9 Mincing lane
Hicks & Braikenridge, solicitors, 16 Bartlett's bldgs. Holborn
Hicks John & Son, ironmongers, 148 & 149 Borough High st
Hicks Johnson & George, auctioneers, surveyors, & builders, 30 Nicholas lane, & Tooting, Surrey
Hicks & Marris, solicitors, 5 Gray's inn square
Hicks Magnus & John, drysalters, 8 Duke st. Tooley st. Boro'
Hicks Richard & Son, cattle salesmen, 60 West Smithfield
Hicks Richard & Son, meat salesmen, 11 Newgate market
Hicks Alex. Wm. dyer & scourer, 3 New st. Bath st. City rd
Hicks Benjamin, chandler's shop, 36 Fashion st. Spitalfields
Hicks Chas. beer retailer, 53 London st. Fitzroy square
Hicks Chas. charcoal burner, 59 Cowcross st. West Smthfld
Hicks Edward, pork butcher, 34 Cumberland row, King's cro
Hicks Edward Samuel, wharfinger, see Nash & Hicks
Hicks Francis Edwd. surgeon, 7 Henrietta st. Cavendish sq
Hicks Fredk. M.D. surgeon, 119 Stanhope st. Hampstead rd
Hicks George, manufacturer of cylinder pianofortes, 17 Bryant st. Charlotte st. Pentonville
Hicks George, undertaker, 2 St. Andrew's ct. Holborn hill
Hicks Henry, saddler, 119 New Bond st
Hicks Henry, stationer, &c. 130 Tooley st
Hicks James, cabinet maker, 2 Chapel st. Bedford row
Hicks James, *City of Chester* P.H. 62 Bunhill row
Hicks James, surgeon, see Waterworth & Hicks
Hicks John, barrister, 6 South crescent, Bedford square
Hicks John, butcher, 35 Queen's road, Bayswater
Hicks John, chimneysweeper, 2 & 3 Wormwood st. Bishopsgate
Hicks John, corndealer, 50 King st. Seven dials
Hicks John, *Grapes* P.H. 32 Bow lane, Cheapside
Hicks John, grocer, 2 Belinda place, Canonbury square
Hicks John, oil & colorman, 8 Pitt's place, Old Kent road
Hicks John, oil & colorman, 7 Mount place, Walworth road
Hicks Joseph, baker, 18 Coborn road, Mile end road
Hicks Mary Hanh. (Mrs), *Hat & Tun* P.H. 14 Hatn. wl. Hatn. g
Hicks Richard, beer retailer, 14 Ray st. Clerkenwell
Hicks Richard, surgeon, 7 Argyle square, King's cross
Hicks Robert, builder, 13 Palace new road, Lambeth
Hicks Samuel, hairdresser, 98 Cornwall road, Lambeth
Hicks Thomas, solicitor, 10 Clifford's inn, Fleet st
Hicks Wm. customhouse agent, 84 Lower Thames st
Hicks Wm. loom broker, 105 Hare st. Bethnal green
Hicks William, plumber & glazier, 22 Noble st. Cheapside
Hickson Edward & Co. merchants, 8 Lime st
Hickson Sam. & Son. italianwareh. 72 Welbeck st. Cavendsh. sq
Hickson Wm. & Sons, who. boot&shoewa. 20 West Smithfield
Hickson Edward, stationer, account book manufacturer, engraver & printer, 31 King st. & 11 Lawrence lane
Hickson George, water gilder, 8 Lisle st. Leicester square
Hickson John, grocer & teadealer, 7 Exmouth st. Spafields
Hickson William, carpenter, Nine Elms, Vauxhall
Hidden Thos. leather button ma. 5 Richard's pl. Webber st
Hidden Wm. *Hole in the Wall* P.H. 9 Johnst. Davies st. Bkly. sq
Hide Hannah (Mrs.), lodging house, 34 Gerrard st. Soho
Hide John, butcher, 56½ Rosemary lane
Hide John, teadealer & grocer, 26 Queen's row, Pimlico
Hider Joseph, grocer, 4 Church st. Deptford
Hider William, *Britannia* P.H. 30 Moor st. Bryanstone sq
Hides James, farrier, Tavistock mews, Little Coram st
Hidey David, tailor, 4 Earl st. Kensington
Hidey Samuel, tailor, 8 Conduit st. Paddington
Hieatt Wm. orange merchant, Centre rw. Covent gdn. mrkt
Hierokosma & Tailors' Company, 31 Saville row, Piccadilly
Hierons John, grocer, &c. 80 Hill st. Walworth road
Hierons Samuel, *Cross Keys* P.H. 58 Theobald's road
Higbee Robert, grocer, 103 Long lane, Bermondsey
Higgin John, west india merchant, 6 Crosby square
Higgin Robert, leech importer, see Cullen & Higgin
Higginbotham William, hairdresser, 89 Drury lane
Higginbotham Geo. baker, 28 St. Paul's ter. King's rd. Pancras
Higginbotham Hen. ivory & toy dealer, 44 Finsbury market
Higginbotham Matthew, tailor, 36 King st. Holborn
Higgins & De la Fontaine, coach plat. 9 Archer st. Golden sq
Higgins Wm. & Co. hosiers & shirtmakers, 21 Old Bond st
Higgins Cornelius, accountant, 10 New North st. Red Lion sq
Higgins Edwd. Townsend, barrister, 3 Tanfield ct. Temple
Higgins Francis, silver spoon &c. ma. 40 Kirby st. Hattn. gdn
Higgins Hugh, tailor, 2 West st. Golden square
Higgins James, french polisher, 78 Wells st. Oxford st
Higgins James, plumber & glazier, 17 St. James's pl. Hmstd. rd
Higgins Jas. White, architect & surveyor, 15 Furnival's inn
Higgins John, billiard rooms, 76 Cheapside
Higgins John, oil & italian wa. 139 Shoreditch High st
Higgins John, red potter, Princes st.; & *Three Merry Boys* P.H. 15 Upper Fore st. Lambeth
Higgins John, smith & farr. Battle bridge mews, Caledn. rd
Higgins John, tobacconist, 23 Wilderness row, Clerkenwell
Higgins Joseph, chemist, 3 Newland terrace, Kensington
Higgins Richard, bootmaker, 68 Davies st. Berkeley sq
Higgins Richard, *Bricklayers' Arms* P.H. 3 East st. Kngtn
Higgins Richd. *Cart & Horse* P.H. 25 Turnmill st. Clknwl
Higgins Robert, brush manufacturer, 30 Whitechapel rd
Higgins Thomas, coal dealer, 47 Hastings st. Burton cres
Higgins Thomas, painter & glazier, 72 High st. Camden twn
Higgins Wm. cowkeeper & dairyman, 11 North st. Lisson gr
Higgins Wm. *Tiger tavern* P.H. 8 Tower dock, Tower hill
Higgins Wm. watchmaker, 9 Ernest st. Regent's park
Higginson Chas. heraldic painter, 35 Somerset st. Prtmn. sq
Higgs & George, wholesale ironmongers, 179 Boro' High st
Higgs & Son, builders&undertkrs. 59A, Davies st. Berkeley sq
Higgs & Youngman (Misses), ladies' school, 14 Stepney gr
Higgs Alfred, veterinary surgeon, 237 Upper Thames st
Higgs Benjamin, dining rooms, 18 Panton st. Haymarket
Higgs Edward, veterinary surgeon, 23 Bread st. hill
Higgs Frederick, bricklayer, 17 Bacon st. Bethnal green
Higgs James, lighterman, 5 Bickley row, Lwr. Rotherhithe
Higgs James, linendraper, &c. Kingsland green
Higgs John, butcher, 153 Church st. Shoreditch
Higgs John, cheesemonger, 1 Watt's terrace, Old Kent rd
Higgs John, corndealer, 6 High st. Bow
Higgs John, pork butcher, 169 Bethnal green road
Higgs John, plumber, &c. 15 Chester st. Kennington cross
Higgs Robert, butcher, 131 & 140 Brick la. Spitalfields
Higgs Thomas, coroner for the Duchy of Lancaster, residence, Little Cloisters, Westminster
Higgs William, chemist & soda water mnfr. 35 Piccadilly
Higgs Wm. stationer & news agt. 16 Paddington st. Maryleb
Higham & Banner, surgeons, 46 Davies st. Berkeley sq

Higham Mary & Sarah, booksellers, 54 Chiswell st
Higham Ann (Miss), school, 95Shaftesbury st.New North pl
Higham James, grocer, &c. 82 Mary st. New rd. Regent' spk
Higham Samuel, ivory turner, 44 Southampton bldgs.Hobrn
Highatt Charles, gas fitter, 5 Hand court, High Holborn
Highatt Joseph, brush & broom manufacturer, 130 Fetter la
HighBailiff of Southwark Office, Town hall, Boro' High st.; hours 10 to 3
Highbury College, Highbury park north (Joshua Wilson, treasurer; Edwd. Churchyard, sec.), office, 4 Blomfield st. Finsbury; hours 11 to 3
Highett Felix Hen. saddler, &c. 17 Gt. Quebec st. Montagu sq
Highett James, surgeon, 14 City road, South side
Highfield William, watch ma. 17 Denmark st. Pentonville
Highland Society of London (George Bain, esq. hon. sec.), Freemasons' tavern, & 18 Parliament st. Westminster
Highley Samuel, medical bookseller, 32 Fleet st
Highmore Anthony, merchant, Lloyd's
Highmore Rebecca (Mrs.), milliner, 13 Golden square
Higho James Anthony, watchma. 112 Bishopsgate without
Hight John, beer retailer, 3 South st. King's rd. Chelsea
Hight John, tin plate worker, 88 Lambeth lower marsh
Higley Charles, coal & coke merch. 17 Providence row, Finsb
Higly Chas. stationer, &c. 13 Pierrepoint row, Islington green
Higman William Henry & Co. ironmongers & cabinet brass founders, 55 Crown st. Finsbury
Hignet Hen. Jn. toy & turnery wa. 18 Goodge st. Tottenh. ct. rd
Hignett John, *North Briton* P.H. 10 Lincoln place, New North road
Hilbert Solomon, boot & shoe maker, 57 Up. Ebury st. Pimlico
Hildaire Joseph, coffee rooms, 15 South st. Manchester sq
Hilder Edward Augustus, solicitor, see Matthews & Hilder
Hilder Joseph, plumber, 16 Mount row, Liverpool road
Hilder Richard, artist, 25 Stanhope st. Hampstead road
Hildersley John, chairmaker, 5 Hollen st. Soho
Hildersley Thomas, spiral wood turner, 33 Berwick st. Soho
Hildersley Wm. chair & sofa manufr. 18 Hollen st. Soho
Hilditch Geo. Richd. & Jas. silk mercers, 13 Ludgate hill
Hilditch John Fred. attorney, 55 Gower st. Bedford square
Hilditch Richard Henry, artist, 13 Ludgate hill
Hildyard Angelina (Miss), milliner, 9 Charlotte st. Fitzroy sq
Hildyard Christopher J. linendraper, 6 Kennington cross
Hildyard Francis, barrister, 4 Inner Temple lane
Hildyard George, solicitor, 8 Furnival's inn, Holborn
Hildyard Geo. writer & grainer, see Cotton & Hildyard
Hildyard James, *White Hart* P.H. 6 Bell yd. 12 Gracech. st
Hildyard John, barrister, 8 King's Bench walk, Temple
Hildyard Rbt. Chas. queen's counsel, 11 Paper bldgs. Temple
Hile Daniel & Son, boot & shoemakers, 54 Basinghall st
Hiles Charles, baker, 11 Backchurch lane, Commercial rd
Hiles Thomas, bookbinder, 22 Warwick sq. Newgate st
Hiley & Rayment, commercial boarding ho. 18 London wall
Hilhouse & Andrews, tailors, 19 Woodstock st. Oxford st
Hilhouse Rich. & Sons, who. teadealers, 19 Finsbury pl. north
Hilhouse Ann Maria (Mrs.), baby linen wareh. 12 New Bond st
Hilhouse Charles, hatter, &c. 11 New Bond st
Hill, Almon & James, merchants, 10 Austin friars
Hill, Branstone & Wootton, law statrs. 12 Took's ct. Chry. la
Hill Charles & Henry, stockbrokers, 29 Threadneedle st
Hill Charles & Sons, bankers & agents, 17 West Smithfield
Hill & Coulson, bottled malt liquor, cider, perry & spirit merchants, Herbert's passage, Beaufort buildings, Strand
Hill David & Co. brown stone potters, 14 Vauxhall walk
Hill & Davies, jamaica solicitors & west india law agents, 18 Tokenhouse yard, Lothbury
Hill & Dibben, grocers, 2A, Brompton ter. Brompton road
Hill, Fawcett & Hill, stock & share brkrs. 29 Threadneedle st
Hill & Heald, solicitors, 23 Throgmorton st
Hill Henry & Co. brewers, 63 Gray's inn lane
Hill Jas. & Co. irish provision mers. 105 Up. East Smithfield
Hill James & Co. silk manufacturers, 30 Spital square
Hill James & Son, export furn. ironmongers, 94 Goswell rd
Hill James & Sons, russia merchts. 31 Great Winchester sq
Hill John & Son, appraisers & undertakrs. 7 Beech la. Barbican
Hill John & Son, buildrs. 28 Gt. Turner st. Commercial rd. east
Hill & Jones, whol. & export biscuit bakers & confectioners, 62 Bishopsgate within
Hill & King, meat salesmen, 18 & 19 New Newgate market
Hill & Mathews, solicitors, 1 Bury court, St. Mary Axe
Hill, Mills & Co. woollen drapers, &c. 89 St. Martin's lane
Hill & Monkhouse, wharfngrs. Mann's wf. Montague do. Swk
Hill Nathaniel & Son, glovers, 29 Regent st
Hill Richard & Co. ink & varnish manfrs. Old Ford, Middx
Hill Robt. & Jas. tobac. & snuff manfs. 176 & 177 Shoreditch
Hill Rt. & Son, who. & ret. statnrs. & booksels. 71 Boro' High st
Hill & Simms, ship biscuit bakers, 254 Wapping
Hill & Smith, varnish & colorm. 13 Raven row, Mile end
Hill Thomas & Co. warehousemen, 96 Wood st. Cheapside
Hill, Wootton & Branston, law statnrs. 12 Took's ct. Chry. la
Hill's (Rev. R.) Almshouses (G. Downing, treas.), 58 Hill st. Blackfriars road
Hill Abraham, cornchandler & fruiterer, 6 & 7 Whitecross st
Hill Alexr. baker, 8 Great Coram st. Brunswick square
Hill Alf. custom ho. ship & ins. agt. 2 Star ct. Bread st. City
Hill Ann (Mrs.), grocer, 69 Devonshire st. Lisson grove
Hill Ann (Mrs.), milliner, 37 Dorset st. Portman sq
Hill Ann (Mrs.), stables, 9½ Southampton st. Camden town
Hill Ann (Mrs.), tobacconist, 6 Wandsworth road
Hill Arthur Stephen, wholesale druggist, 11 Little Britain
Hill Barney, coalmeter, 48 Dempsey st. Stepney
Hill Benjamin, butcher, 7 Oxford market
Hill Benjamin, lighterman, 1 Copenhagen pl. Limehouse
Hill Charles, cheesemonger, 9 Back Church la. Whitechpl
Hill Charles, cooper, 166 St. John's street road
Hill Charles, tobacconist, 1 Harrison st. Gray's inn road
Hill Charles Hamor, surveyor, 10 Chancery lane, & 4 Brick lane, Spitalfields
Hill Chas. Stephen, attorney, 1 Clement's lane, Lombard st
Hill Christopher, wine & brandy mer. 47 Aldgate High st
Hill Danl. fishmonger, 22 Walbrook, & 18 Budgerow, Cannon st
Hill David, solicitor, 5 John st. Adelphi
Hill Edmund, coal merchant, see Waltham & Hill
Hill Edward, baker, Richmond road, Dalston
Hill Edward, butcher, 8 Marchmont st. Brunswick square
Hill Edward, law stationer, 6 Inner Temple lane
Hill Edward, wholesale staymaker, 95 Whitechapel High st
Hill Edwin, watch manfr. 70 Paradise st. Rotherhithe
Hill Edwin Jas. printer, 48 Northampton st. Clerkenwell
Hill Elizabeth (Mrs.), dock coffee rooms, 84 Old Gravel la
Hill Elizabeth (Mrs.), grocer, 3 Rawstorne st. Goswell rd
Hill Elizabeth (Mrs.), milliner, 171 New Bond st
Hill Elizabeth (Mrs.), stationer, 61 Brook st. Hanover sq
Hill Emma (Miss), *Star* coffee rooms, 230 Hoxton Old town
Hill Frederick, tobacconist, 11 Islington High st. & Penton st. Pentonville
Hill George, bricklayer, 7 Richard st. Commercial rd. east
Hill George, chandler's shop, 126 Hoxton Old town
Hill George, fruiterer, 22 Upper park pl. Regent's park
Hill Geo. *Horse & Groom* P.H. 25 Whetstone pk. Lin. inn flds
Hill George, *Hill's Family hotel*, 22 Spring gardens, & *Ship hotel*, 45 Charing cross
Hill George, potato & coal dealer, 45 Bishopsgate without
Hill George, tinman & ironmonger, Church st. Hackney
Hill George, vet. surgeon, 18 Cumberland row, Islington
Hill George, veterinary surgeon, 1 Robin Hood yd. Leather la
Hill Harriett (Mrs.), milliner, 15 Pickett st. or 260 Strand
Hill Harry, grocer, 19 Boston st. Dorset square
Hill Harry, violin maker, 29 St. George's road, Borough
Hill Henry, barrister, 45 Parliament st
Hill Henry, cabinet maker, 69 Paradise st. Rotherhithe
Hill Henry, cornfactor, 2 New London st. Crutched friars
Hill Henry, furnish. ironmonger, 51 London rd. Southwark
Hill Henry, furniture broker, 14 Circus st. New road
Hill Henry, solicitor, 5 Verulam bldgs. Gray's inn
Hill Henry, solicitor, see Mitchell & Hill
Hill Henry, solicitor, see Williamson & Hill
Hill Henry, tailor, 53 York st. Westminster
Hill Henry Noad, pork butcher, 44 Gt. James st. Lisson gr
Hill Henry Reginald, solicitor, 62 Moorgate st
Hill Henry William, cabinet maker, 27 Pennyfields, Poplar
Hill Hugh, barrister, 1 Inner Temple lane
Hill Hugh, coach maker, Prospect pl. Old Kent road
Hill Humphrey, tailor, 7 Ranelagh grove
Hill Isaac, baker, 2 Dean's bldgs. Commercial rd. Limehouse
Hill James, artist, 58 Newman st
Hill James, barrister, 6 New square, Lincoln's inn
Hill James, beer retailer, 56 York st. City road
Hill James, carpenter, 13 Upper Rosoman st. Clerkenwell
Hill James, furn. ironmonger, 18 Sussex pl. Old Kent road
Hill James, grocer, 28 Henry st. Hampstead road
Hill James, ironmonger, 94 Goswell road
Hill James, poulterer, 1 Grosvenor st. Grosvenor square
Hill James Barton, surgeon, 2 Guilford place, Foundling
Hill James Beech, china dealer, 254 Blackfriars road
Hill Jesse, *Anchor & Hope* P.H. 48 Jamaica st. Com. rd. Stpny
Hill John, bootmaker, 9 Belgrave mews east, Belgrave sq
Hill John, bricklayer, &c. 104 Albany st. Regent's park
Hill John, brush manfr. & turnery dlr. 7 Clement's la. City
Hill John, builder, 45 Upper Albany st. Regent's park
Hill John, carpenter, 18 Macclesfield st. north, City road
Hill John, cattle salesman, 60 West Smithfield
Hill John, coal factor & broker, see Duke & Hill

Hill John, coffee rooms, 188 Lambeth walk
Hill John, coffee & dining rooms, 251 Wapping
Hill John, feather bed & mattress warehouse, 5 Leopard's court, Baldwin's gardens, Leather lane, Holborn
Hill John, chandler's shop, 1 Rochester st. Vincent sq
Hill John, gold & silver beater, 13 Southwark bridge rd
Hill John, *General Abercrombie* P.H. 67 Friar st. Blkfrs. rd
Hill John, grocer, &c. 3 Sun Tavern flds. St. George's east
Hill John, gun & pistol maker, 76 Tooley st
Hill John, haberdasher & man's mercer, 269 & 270 Oxford st
Hill John, ironfounder, 11 King st. Seven dials
Hill John, *Lord Tyrawley* P.H. 71 High st. Marylebone
Hill John, *Old King John* P.H. 14 Holywell la. Shoreditch
Hill John, paperhanger, 59 Westbourne st. Pimlico
Hill John, pin, needle, hook & eye maker, 22 Fish st. hill
Hill John, plasterer, 28 York st. Commercial rd. Whitechapl
Hill John, poulterer, 51 Charles st. Westminster
Hill John, poulterer, 20 Great hall, Hungerford market
Hill John, professor of music, 1 Frederick pl. Goswell rd
Hill John, stock & share broker, see Sims & Hill
Hill John, surgeon, 8 John st. Minories
Hill John, teadealer & grocer, 215 Upper Whitecross st
Hill John, tobacconist, 62½ Aldersgate st
Hill John, trunk & mil. equipage mfr. 97 Quadrant, Regent st
Hill John, watchmaker, 106 Britannia st. City road
Hill John, gold chain ma. & jeweller, 6 St. James's wk. Clknwl
Hill John Brooks, butcher, 11 High st. Kingsland
Hill John Brooks, coachmaker, 20 & 21 Little Moorfields
Hill John Edw. trunk maker, York pl. Upper st. Islington
Hill John Fred. barrister, 5 Inner Temple la. Temple
Hill John Hay, grocer, 5 Ebenezer pl. Neckinger rd
Hill John Moody, solicitor & notary, 6 Gt. Tower street
Hill John R. civil engineer, 28 Up. Stamford st. Blackfriars rd
Hill John Watts, newsvender, 17 Homer st. Marylebone
Hill Joseph, baker, 43 Southampton row, Russell sq
Hill Joseph, beer retailer, 10 Cottage place, City road
Hill Joseph, cook & confectioner, 123 Leadenhall st
Hill Joseph, tooth brush manufr. 11 Castle st. Saffron hill
Hill Joseph, whip maker, 86 Long lane, Smithfield
Hill Joseph Vaughan, who. saw ma. 5 Chichest. pl. Gray's inn rd
Hill Josiah Wm. upholsterer, 15 Cross st. Hatton garden
Hill Lawrence, chemist, 5 Monmouth pl. Old Kent road
Hill Mary (Mrs.), grocer, Cobourg road, Old Kent road
Hill Mary (Mrs.), staymaker, 56 Poplar High st
Hill Mary (Mrs.), *Red Lion* P.H. 31 Poppin's ct. Fleet st
Hill Matthew Davenport, queen's counsel, 44 Chancery lane
Hill Patrick Young, solicitor, 7 Gt. College st. Westminster
Hill Richard, butcher, 24 Maiden lane, Covent garden
Hill Richard, skinner & fur cutter, 34 Mint st. Borough
Hill Richard, wood turner, 85 Long alley, Finsbury
Hill Richd. Morton, oilman, 2 King Edward st. Newgate st
Hill Robert, ale & sandwich rooms, 260 High st. Holborn
Hill Robert, cabinetmaker, 10 Cambridge pl. Edgware rd
Hill Robert, carpenter, 69 Lambeth walk
Hill Samuel, auctioneer & surveyor, 10 Chancery lane
Hill Samuel, hatter, 23 Homer st. Marylebone
Hill Samuel, stockbroker, 1 Angel ct. Bank & Stock exchange
Hill Samuel, watchma. 10 Newton st. New North rd. Islington
Hill Sarah (Mrs.), *Castle* P.H. 26 Castle st. Holborn
Hill Sarah (Mrs.), cornchandler, 14 Road side, Mile end rd
Hill Sarah (Mrs.), dining rooms, 17 Fetter lane, Fleet st
Hill Sarah (Mrs.), rouge ma. 16 St. John's lane, Smithfield
Hill Seymour (Mrs.), chiropodist, 6 York gate, Regent's pk
Hill Sophia (Mrs.), staymaker, 13 Poplar High st
Hill Stephen, tobacconist, 3 James place, Holloway road
Hill Stephen, watch pinion ma. 62 Compton st. Clerkenwell
Hill Susanna (Mrs.), milliner, 98 Piccadilly
Hill Thomas, agt. *Sun Fire offi.* 1 Brooksby st. Liverpool rd
Hill Thomas, baker, 112 Golden lane, St. Luke's
Hill Thomas, engineer, 88 Long lane, Bermondsey
Hill Thomas, gasfitter & brassfounder, 97 Bunhill row
Hill Thomas, *Grave Maurice* P.H. 128 Whitechapel road
Hill Thomas, grocer, 25 High row, Knightsbridge
Hill Thomas, grocer, 3 Manifold pl. Lr. Kennington lane
Hill Thomas, linendraper, Southampton st. Camberwell
Hill Thomas, solicitor, 6 Ingram court, Fenchurch st
Hill Thomas, straw hat warehouse, 29 Beech st. Barbican
Hill Thomas, surgeon, 1A, Sussex ter. Hyde park square
Hill Thomas, tobacconist, 11A, Harper st. New Kent road
Hill Thos. *Weymouth Arms* P.H. 7 Weymouth st. Nw. Kt. rd
Hill Thomas, *York Arms* P.H. 52 Curzon st. Mayfair
Hill Thomas Irving, mining agent, Hall of Commerce
Hill Thos. P. commission agt. 1 Huggin la. Wood st. Cheapside
Hill Townley, operative chemist, 60 Leadenhall st
Hill William, baker, 19 Everett st. Brunswick square
Hill William, baker, 10 Long acre
Hill William, baker, 112 St. John st. road
Hill Wm. biscuit baker & cook, 61 & 62 Bishopsgate within
Hill William, blacksmith, 46 St. Andrew's rd. Borough
Hill William, carpenter, 32 Hatton wall, Hatton garden
Hill William, carver, gilder & looking glass manufacturer, 4 Ironmonger row, St. Luke's, & 122 Fore st. Cripplegate
Hill William, chemist, 64 Bermondsey st
Hill William, coal mercht. White Lion wf. 18 Up. Thames st
Hill William, confectioner, 16 Gt. Turnstile, Holborn
Hill William, grocer, 3 Darby pl. Jermyn st. St. James's
Hill William, grocer, 11 Durham st. Vauxhall
Hill William, grocer, 11 Durham st. Harleyford rd. Kenngtn
Hill William, *King's Head* P.H. 27 Alfred pl. Newington caus
Hill William, medical & chem. agt. 23 St. Swithin's la. City
Hill William, optician, see Watkins & Hill
Hill William, organ builder, 12 Tottenham court New road
Hill William, perfumer & hairdresser, 34 Cheapside
Hill William, sail maker & ship chandler, 77 Wapping wall
Hill William, ship & ins. broker, 2 Muscovy court, Tower hill
Hill William, shoemaker, 8 Carteret st. Westminster
Hill William, silverer & looking glass mnfr. 122 Fore st. City
Hill William, tailor, 8 Jewry st. Aldgate
Hill William Alfred, barrister, 3 Gray's inn square
Hill William Brown, grocer, 20 Liquorpond st
Hill William Isaac, hat manufacturer, 23 King st. Covent garden; manufactory 23 Commercial road, Lambeth
Hill Wm. Matthews, builder, 10 Charlton pl. Islington green
Hill William Rolls, bookbinder, 3 Princes st. Red Lion sq
Hill William, wholesale biscuit baker, see Hill & Jones
Hill William Yevily, brush & basket ma. 27 & 28 Wigmore st
Hillam John C. custom ho. agent, 3 Catherine ct. Tower hill
Hillard John, american merchant, 13 & 14 Bread st. Cheapside
Hillary F. (Mrs.), cornchandler, 27 Horseferry rd. Westmnr
Hillary William, tailor, 6 Gibson st. Waterloo road
Hillas Geo. Leicester, surgeon, 12 Sydney pl. Fulham road
Hilleary Robt. G. A. & Gustavus E. solicitors, 63 Fenchurch st. & Stratford broadway
Hilldrup James, linendraper, 16 Dean st. Westminster
Hillen John, corndealer, 22 Pitfield st. Hoxton
Hiller Edward, butcher, 23 Tyer st. Princes rd. Lambeth
Hillersdon Frederick Edward, solicitor, 2 Stafford st. Bond st. & Barnes, Surrey
Hillery Mary Ann (Mrs.), grocer, 22 Market st. Shepherd'smk
Hilliar James, *Rose Inn*, 57 Old Bailey
Hilliar William, livery stables, Wellington st. Blackfrs. rd
Hilliard Ambrose, strawbon. ma. 32 Somerset pl. Ea. rd. Hoxton
Hilliard Christr. plumber & glazier, 24 St. John st. Westmnr
Hilliard Henry, stationer & mapslr. 9 George yd. Lombard st
Hilliard Rt. grocer & cheesemngr. 2 George's ter. Kentish tn
Hilliard William, plumber, 11 Fair st. Horsleydown
Hilliard Wm. Edwd. solicitor, 2 Raymond bldgs. Gray's inn
Hillier, Lewis & Hillier, attorn. 6 Raymond bldgs. Gray's inn
Hillier's Almshouses (H. Weymouth, sec.), 119 & 120 Curtain rd
Hillier Benjamin, hairdresser, &c. 41 Bucklersbury
Hillier David, coffee rooms, 63 Marylebone la. Oxford st
Hillier Henry, loan office, &c. 17 Cecil ct. St. Martin's la
Hillier Henry Bentinck C. surgeon, 85 Gower st. Bedford sq
Hillier James, beer retailer, 12 Lower Kennington lane
Hillier Jas. N. time glass maker, 10 Fieldgate st. Whitechpl
Hillier Jesse, beer retailer, 33 Green st. Bethnal green
Hillier John, baker, 28 Kent st. Borough
Hillier John, brush, comb, &c. dlr. 48 Gt. Windmill st. Haymkt
Hillier Richard, farrier, see Howe & Hillier
Hillier Thomas, carpenter, 11 Water st. Blackfriars
Hillier William, wheelwright, 2 River lane, Islington
Hilliker Elizabeth (Miss), coffee rooms, 54 Old st
Hillington Ellen (Mrs.), stay & corset maker, 155 Tooley st
Hillman James, nurseryman, 7 Malvern ter. Barnsbury park
Hillman Joseph, boot & shoe maker, Stratford, Essex
Hillman Robert, cabinet ma. 4 Foundling mews, Gray's inn r
Hillman Thomas, tailor, 4 St. George's circus
Hillman Wm. surgeon, 1 Argyll st. Regent st
Hillman Wm. Augustus, surgeon, 1 Argyll st. St. James's
Hills & Alldridge, shipping grocer & provn. mer. 24 Rood la
Hills Hy. & Co. dry yeast manfrs. 4 Freeschool st. Horselydn
Hills & Laport, preservers of fruit, pickles, &c. 93 Gt. Tower st
Hills & Underwood, distillers, vinegar manufs. & imps. of foreign wines & spirits, 25 Eastcheap & 2 St. Mary at hill
Hill's (Rev. R.) Alms Houses (G. Downing, treas.), 58 Hill st. Blackfriars road
Hills Charles, cheesemonger, 89 Bunhill row
Hills Frances (Mrs.), grocer, 47 Royal st. Carlisle st. Lmbth
Hills Frank Clark, manufactg. chemist, Creek st. Deptford
Hills Fredk. confectioner, 42 Harleyford pl. Kennington
Hills George, hatter, 38 Crawford st. Portman square
Hills George, *North Pole* P.H. 387 Oxford st

Hills Henry, grocer & oilman, East India road, Poplar
Hills James Goodwin, linendraper, &c. 139 Lambeth walk
Hills John, cooper, 10 Burlington place, Old Kent road
Hills John, tallow chandler & smelter, High st. Deptford
Hills Mary (Mrs.), butcher, 5 Green st. Bethnal green
Hills Mercy (Mrs.), *Prince George* P.H. Hill st. Walworth rd
Hills Richd. Scrivines, straw hat ma. 26 New Ivy st. Hoxton
Hills Rt. dealer in stocks & shares, 1 St. Michael's al. Cornhill
Hills Robert, surgeon, 1 City terrace, City road
Hills Thomas, *Cheshire Cheese* P.H. Spitalfields market
Hills Thomas Bryant, corndealer, 8 Red Lion st. Holborn
Hills Wm. cornfactor, 4 New London st. Fenchurch st
Hills Wm. oyster merchant, 93 Gt. Tower st. & 5 Idol lane
Hills Wm. pianoforte ma. 5 Harleyford pl. Kennington com
Hills Wm. shoemaker, 123 London road, Southwark
Hillstead Wm. oilman, 104 East st. Manchester square
Hillstead Wm. prof. of music, 104 East st. Manchester sq
Hillstead Wm. jun. flute maker, 104 East st. Manchester sq
Hillum Richard, optician, &c. 109 Bishopsgate within
Hillyard Edward, surgeon, 10 Burton crescent
Hilson James, *Coach & Horses* P.H. 66 Chiswell st
Hilson James, town carman, 1 Victualling office sq. Tower hill
Hilson John, watch jeweller, 48 Perceval st. Clerkenwell
Hilton Adam, stockbroker, 2 Warnford ct. Throgmorton st
Hilton Charles, tailor, 12 Regent st. Horseferry road
Hilton David, news agent, 8 Penton st. Pentonville
Hilton Edward, paper agent, 2 Little Trinity lane
Hilton John, consulting surgeon, 10 New Broad st. City
Hilton Richard, hat dyer, 8 Worcester st. Union st. Borough
Hilton Sam. agent for Manchester goods, 20 Gresham st
Himbury William, corn & coal dealer, 22 Gt. Marylebone st
Himing Geo. who. shoe manufactr. 6 Artillery ct. Chiswell st
Hince James, butcher, 2 Henry st. east, Avenue rd
Hincham Wm. pastry cook, 88 Crown ct. Waterst. Blackfriars
Hinchley James, potato dlr. 3 Nowell's bldgs. Liverpool rd
Hinchliff Nathl. & Co. paperstainers, Whitelands, Chelsea
Hinchliff John E. sculptor, 5 Mornington pl. Hampstead rd
Hinchliff John Jas. engraver, 5 Mornington pl. Hampstead rd
Hinchliffe Jonathan, mason, Canal bdge. Old Kent rd
Hinckley James, coffee rooms, 74 Blackman st
Hincks Charles & Co. who. ironmongers, 221 Boro' High st
Hincks Charles & Co. wholesale dealers in cabinet furniture, 221 Borough High st
Hind Wm. & Son, braid, fringe & fancy trimming manufacturers, 71 Wood st. Cheapside, & 19 Banner st. St. Luke's
Hind Andrew, teadealer, 21 Three Colt st. Limehouse
Hind Francis, tailor, 10 Brewer st. Pimlico
Hind George William, surgeon, 66 Gower st. Bedford sq
Hind James, *Castle* P.H. Goodman's stile, Goodman's fields
Hind James, engraver, 6 Hill st. Finsbury
Hind John, auctioneer, &c. 23 Cannon st. St. George's East
Hind John, plumber & glazier, 24 Duke st. Grosvenor sq
Hind John Thomas, appraiser, 32 Cannon st. road
Hind Peter, *Crown* P.H. 108 Blackfriars road
Hind Samuel, fancy fringe manufr. 19 Banner st. St. Luke's
Hind Thos. *Rising Sun* P.H. 25 Richmond pl. East st. Wlwth
Hinde Benjamin Wm. clockmaker, 13 Banner st. St. Luke's
Hinde Charles, who. chemist & druggist, 98 Fenchurch st
Hinde Edward, straw hat maker, see Wood, Jones & Hinde
Hinde Isaac, cheesemonger, 47 City garden row, City road
Hinde John, brush maker, 3 Sekforde st. Clerkenwell
Hinde Pelley, barrister, 1 Cloisters, Temple
Hinde Sarah (Miss), milliner, 4½ Edwards st. Portman sq
Hinder Mary (Mrs.), dealer in wearingapparel, 15 Harp alley
Hindes Alexr. lighterman, 49 Broad st. London docks
Hindes Ann (Mrs.), dressmaker, 15 Bunhill row, Chiswell st
Hindle Elizabeth (Mrs.), coffee rooms, 2 Cobham rw. Clrknwl
Hindle John, carpenter, 4½ Wharton st. Lloyd sq. Pentonville
Hindley Charles & Sons (successors to Miles & Edwards), furniture printers, upholsterers & cabinet manufacturers, 134 Oxford st.; factory, Red Lion yard, Old Cavendish st
Hindley Wm. & Co. who. & ret. cheesemongers, 14 Gray's inn la
Hindley Hen. hearthrug mfr. 1 & 2 Wenlock cottages, City rd
Hindley Henry, tobacconist, 12 Giltspur st
Hindley Joseph, painter, 51 Edmund st. King's cross
Hindley Samuel, flax spinner, see Maggs, Hindley & Maggs
Hindley Samuel, linen agent, see Maggs, Hindley & Maggs
Hindley Thos. coach builder, 6 Providence blds. New Kent rd
Hindman & Howard, solicitors, 2 Bevis ct. 28½ Basinghall st
Hindmarch Wm. Mathewson, barristr. 7 King's Bnch. wk. Tmpl
Hindmarsh Hen. & Son, solicitors, 7 Jewin crescent, Cripplgt
Hinds Joseph, wax & waferma. 21 Francis st. Tottenham ct. rd
Hindson Margt. (Mrs.), saddler, 10 Charles st. Grosvenor sq
Hine & Co. ham & tongue dealers, 14 Clement's la. Lombd. st
Hine E. & A. (Misses), ladies' school, 10 Allen ter. Kensington
Hine Emma (Mrs.), lodging house, 20 Green st. Grosvenor sq
Hine, Parker & Co. wholesale hosiers, 13 & 14 Milk st. & 3 Gresham st
Hine & Robinson, solicitors, vestry clerks of St. Sepulchre, Middlesex, & clerks to commissioners for paving Goswell st. 32 Charterhouse square
Hine James Samuel, dyer, 9 George st. Blackfriars road
Hine John, *Red Gate* P.H. 34 & 35 Kingsgate st. High Holborn
Hine Joseph, fancy cabinet mfr. 13 Rosoman st. Clerkenwell
Hine Joseph, *Park cof. ho.* 30 Worcester st. Union st. Boro'
Hine Margt. (Mrs.), shipping butcher, 3 Three Colt st. Limeho
Hine Samuel, silk dyer, 1 Cumberland place, Old Kent road
Hines Henry Maken, tailor, 48 Great Portland st. Oxford st
Hines James, shoemaker, 13 Stepney rents, Hackney road
Hines Mary (Mrs.), tobacconist, 4 Colonnade, Brunswick sq
Hinge Thomas, plumber & glazier, 52 Long la. Bermondsey
Hingeston Samuel, barrister, 58 Chancery lane
Hingston Fredk. appraiser, 111 St. John st. Clerkenwell
Hingston Joseph, builder & house ag. 78 Park st. Camden tn
Hingston Philip Wm. carpenter, &c. 38 Hedge row, Islington
Hinkins Charles, butcher, 3 Sarah place, Old st. road
Hinkley Edmond Edward, lighterman, 342 Wapping
Hinkley John, corn & coal dealer, 23 Seething lane, Great Tower st. & 2 Raven row, Spitalfields
Hinks Joseph, coal dealer, 69 Fetter lane, Holborn
Hinks William, smith, Cleveland street, Mile end
Hinksman John, plumber & glazier, 61 Skinner st. Bishopsgt
Hinnem Jonathan, baker & confectnr. 8 Sidney st. Mile end
Hinres & Thompson, millinrs. & haberdash. 31 Gt. Marylebone st
Hinsch Theodore, merchant, see Freudentheil & Hinsch
Hinton Geo. & Son, carpenters, 32 Princes st. Leicester sq
Hinton Archibald, *Crown tavern*, 42 Clerkenwell green
Hinton Edmund, marine store dealer, 28 Thomas st. Oxford st
Hinton Edward, merchant, 28 Clements la. Lombard st. City
Hinton Edward, school, family & clerical agt. 30B, Soho sq
Hinton George, carpenter & builder, 32 Princes st. Leicester sq
Hinton George, glass & china dealer, 1 Pleasant pl. Holloway
Hinton George, sen. dial enameller, 29½ Perceval st. Clerkenwl
Hinton Henry Wm. dial painter, 29½ Perceval st. Clerkenwl
Hinton James, straw & tuscan hat manfr. 56 Theobalds rd
Hinton James Holliday, tailor, 16 Church street, Soho
Hinton Jas. Thos. hairdresser, 7 Three Tuns pass. Newgate st
Hinton John, coffee rooms, 76 Red Lion st. High Holborn
Hinton John, *Highbury Barn Tavern*, Highbury park
Hinton Martha (Mrs.), baby linen wareho. 39 King st. Holborn
Hinton Thomas, tailor, 2 South st. King's road, Chelsea
Hinton William, bricklayer & builder, 17 Pudding lane
Hinton William, carpenter, 10 Mount st. Walworth rd
Hinton William, jeweller, 18 Great Suffolk street, Borough
Hinton William Newport, oilmn. 4 King David la. Shadwl. H. st
Hinton William Samuel, coal merchant, see Petty, Hinton & Son
Hintz Alexander & Co. merchants, 29 Mincing lane
Hinxman John, navy agent, 34 Soho square
Hinxman John D. wine merchant, Kensington High street
Hipkins Russell, carver & gilder, 101 Park st. Camden town
Hipp George, biscuit baker, 3 Bury street, St. James's
Hipp John, school, 96 St. Martin's lane
Hipper James, horsedealer, 51 Cowper street, City road
Hipwell Thomas, linendraper, 69 Piccadilly
Hipwood Joseph H. ship insur. & genl. com. agent, 1 Lime st. sq
Hird Chas. & Son, bootmakers, 8 Arabella row, Pimlico
Hird Chas. & Son, solicitors, 49 Up. Marylebone st. Portlnd. pl
Hird Ann (Mrs.), paper hanger, 119 Drummond st. Euston sq
Hird Francis, surgeon, &c. 12 Cleveland row, St. James's
Hird William, boot & shoe maker, 212 Oxford street
Hirschel David, jeweller, 16 Camomile st. Bishopsgate
Hirschler Samuel, merchant, 8 Basinghall street
Hiscock Charles, wheelwright, 2 Wyndham rd. Camberwell
Hiscock Geo. cheesemongr. 8 New Church st. West, Edgw. rd
Hiscock James, shoemaker, 26 Bell street, Edgware rd
Hiscock John, grocer, 24 New Church st. West, Edgware rd
Hiscock John, ship & house smith, 17 Stoney la. Tooley st
Hiscocks Zachary, watchmak. 7 Lit. Russell st. Covent gar
Hiscox John, who. child-bedlinen wareho. 7 Ernest st. Regt.'s pk
Hisee Ann (Mrs.), grocer & cheesem. 9 Albion st. Rotherhth
Hiskett Elizabeth (Mrs.), plumasier, 35 Frith st. Soho
Hislop & Horton, surgeons, 8 High st. Stepney, & 12 Durham row, Stepney
Hislop Hardy Capt. portuguese agt. 8 Duke st. St. James's
Hislop Richd. chronometer ma. 53 Rosoman st. Clerkenwell
Hislop Thomas & Son, silk manufacturers, 20 Gutter la. Chpsd
Hislop Wm. watch & chronometer maker, 108 St. John st. rd
Hitch & Godwin, brick & tile mers. Lindsey whf. Davis pl. Chels
Hitch Joseph, coachmak. Conant pl. Comrcl. rd. Limehouse
Hitchcock Geo. & Co. silk mercers & linen drapers, 72, 73, & 74 St. Paul's churchyard, & 46 Paternoster row
Hitchcock Harry Wm. & Son, stockbrokers, 2 Copthall ct

Hitchcock & Martyn, solicitors, 38 Davies st. Berkeley sq
Hitchcock Chas. glass & chinaman, 17 Hanway st. Oxford st
Hitchcock Edward, wine mer. ship & ins. broker, 39 Threadneedle st. & Lloyd's
Hitchcock Frederick, barrister, 3 Carey st. Chancery lane
Hitchcock George Charles, merchant, metal agent, & insurance broker, 2 Crosby square, & Lloyd's
Hitchcock Hannah (Mrs.), carman, 11 Well st. Wellclose sq
Hitchcock Henry, greengrocer, 3 White Hart pl. Kenningt. la
Hitchcock John, *Gray's inn coff. ho.* 19 to 22 High Holborn
Hitchcock John, haberdasher, 139 Edgware road, Marylebone
Hitchcock John, turner, 12 Charles st. Blackfriars road
Hitchcock John P. *Rising Sun* P.H. 8 Harper st. Nw. Knt. rd
Hitchcock Robert, woollen warehsmn. see Hocking & Hitchcock
Hitchcock Ts. *Glo'ster Arms tav.* 17 Glo'ster ter. Knsgtn. nw. tn
Hitchcock William, factor & warehouseman, 2 Friday st
Hitchcock Wm. comrl. boarding ho. 13 Bartlett's bldgs. Holbn
Hitchcox Math. *Star & Garter* P.H. 1 Melville ter. Caledn. rd
Hitchen James, bootmaker, 18 Up. Cleveland st. Fitzroy sq
Hitchin John, millinery warehouse, 3 Hanway st. Oxford st
Hitchin Samuel, linendraper, 209 Oxford street
Hitchin Wm. (assistant secretary & accountant of the British & Foreign Bible Society), 10 Earl street, Blackfriars
Hitching John, *Lord Nelson* P.H. 5 Charles st. St. Geo. ea
Hitching Philip, shoe warehouse, 113 Gt. Saffron hill
Hitchins John Bishop, print colorer, map & print mounter & varnisher, 77 Vauxhall st. Lambeth
Hitchins John F. currier, 4 Chichester pl. Gray's inn rd
Hitchinson H. (Mrs), tripe dresser, 88 Brick la. Spitalfields
Hittinger Henry, baker, 37 Cable st. Wellclose sq
Hittinger John, Saml. *Old Star & Crown* P.H. 13 Brdwy Westm
Hix William Poole, baker, 17 Garden row, London road
Hoad Richard, butcher, 31 Gt. Guilford st. Boro'
Hoadley Geo. glass stainer, 6 St. James's pl. Hampstead rd
Hoadly John, butcher, 4 Wyndham road, Camberwell
Hoadly Samuel, auctionr. & apprais. 41 Margaret st. Cav. sq
Hoar Robert Henry & Co. who. cigar dealers, 85 New Bond st
Hoar Charles, mahogany & timber mer. 10 Chester ter. Boro' rd
Hoar Cornelius, accountant, 47 Holywell st. Millbank
Hoar Henry, livery stables, 135 Edgware road, Paddington
Hoar James, saddler, 7 Oldham place, Bagnigge wells road
Hoar Richard, linendraper, 15 John st. Limehouse fields
Hoar Robert, piece broker, 104 Great Suffolk st. Borough
Hoar Thos. livery stab. 3 & 4 Brook mws. Brook st. Glo'ster rd
Hoard Samuel, turner, 56 Ropemakers fields, Limehouse
Hoard Wm. Henry, auctioneer, valuer, surveyor & estate agent, 16 Edwards st. Portman square
Hoare & Cane, linendrapers, 30 Great Marylebone st
Hoare Daniel, bookbinders' tool cutter, 25A, Hatton garden
Hoare Geo. Matthew & Co. brewers, 21 Low. East Smithfield
Hoare Charles, Henry Merrik, Henry Charles, Peter Richard, & Henry, bankers, 37 Fleet st
Hoare Chas. Richard, barrister, 9 New square, Lincoln's inn
Hoare Clotworthy Owen, solicitor, 6 Symond's inn
Hoare Cornelius, clothes salesman, 5 Sparrow corner, Minories
Hoare Edward, butcher, 42 Lisson grove north
Hoare Edward, grocer, 18 Upper Seymour st. Euston square
Hoare Francis Buchanan, solicitor, 30 Lincoln's inn fields
Hoare George, bootmak. 54 Crucifix la. Bermndsy. & 1 Dockhd
Hoare George, cheesemonger, 44 Flagon row, Deptford
Hoare Geo. egg mer. 24 President st. east, King sq. St. Luke's
Hoare Henry Frederick, tailor, 8 Powell st. ea. Goswell rd
Hoare James, carpenter, 16 Poplar High st
Hoare James, grocer, 20 Earl st. West, Lisson grove
Hoare James, grocer & cheesemonger, 64 Westbourne st. Pim
Hoare James, plumber, 44 Compton st. Clerkenwell
Hoare John, cabinet maker, 13 Carburton st. Portland rd
Hoare John, commission agent, see Jacob & Hoare
Hoare Joseph, cheesemonger, 9 Deptford bridge
Hoare Joseph, engraver & printer, see Reeves & Hoare
Hoare Joseph, *Fortune of War* P.H. 4 Giltspur st
Hoare Richard, printseller & frame ma. 18 Gracechurch st
Hoare Thomas, corndealer, 2 Crown st. Walworth rd
Hoare Thomas, corn merchant, 52 Bridge rd. Lambeth
Hoare Thomas, upholsterer, 5 Wardour st. Soho
Hoare Thomas A. turner, 23 Paradise st. Finsbury
Hobbins Margaret (Mrs.), baker, 281 Bethnal green rd
Hobbs Nathaniel & Samuel, building material dealers, Winifred pl. Spa rd. Bermondsey
Hobbs & Reynolds, baby linen wa. 12 St. Martin's ct. Charing cr
Hobbs Charles, carpenter, 5 Chapel st. Suffolk st. Boro'
Hobbs Charles, cheesemonger, 11 Sarah pl. Old st. rd
Hobbs Chas. Hen. grocer, 4 Commercial pl. Kingsland rd
Hobbs Edw. Newman, baker, 20 Wentworth st. Whitechapel
Hobbs George, shoemaker, 57 Bishopsgate within
Hobbs George, *Feathers* P.H. 53 Featherstone st. City rd
Hobbs Henry, corndealer, 3 Lit. Chester st. Grosvenor pl
Hobbs Henry, *Horse & Groom* P.H. 53 Gt. Guildford st. Boro
Hobbs Henry, paper hanger, 11 Church lane, Islington
Hobbs Hezekiah, mast & block maker, 212 Rotherhithe st
Hobbs James, *King's Arms* P.H. 124 Hoxton Old town
Hobbs Jas. jun. *Weymouth Arms* P.H. 34 Weymouth st Port. pl
Hobbs Job *Spanish Patriot* P.H. 14 White Conduit st. Islngtn
Hobbs John, bootmaker, 4 Church st. Horselydown
Hobbs John, cattle salesman, 59 Smithfield
Hobbs John, dairyman, 25 Prior pl. East st. Walworth rd
Hobbs John, hairdresser, 13 London ter. Hackney rd
Hobbs John, shoemaker, 74 Shadwell High st
Hobbs John, surgeon, 35 Southampton row, Russell sq
Hobbs John, tobacco pipe maker, 30 New rd. St. George's east
Hobbs John Thos. cabinet, chair, &c. ma. 25 King's rd. Ea. Chelsea
Hobbs Joseph, brazier, 9 Upper Marylebone st
Hobbs Joseph, wax & tallow chandl. 14 Chapel st. East, Mayfair
Hobbs Sarah (Mrs.), dairyman, 41 Park st. Grosvenor
Hobbs Thomas, butcher, 4 James st. Oxford st
Hobbs Thomas, butcher, George st. Camberwell
Hobbs Thomas, dairyman, 15 Portland st. Soho
Hobbs Wm. boot & shoemaker, 3 Hackney rd
Hobbs Wm. cabinet maker, 1 Sarah pl. Old st. rd
Hobbs Wm. *Castle* P.H. 1 Notting hill terrace, Notting hill
Hobbs Wm. trunk & fancy box ma. 5 Church st. Trinity sq. Boro
Hobbs Wm. fruiterer, 2 Adam st. east, Portman square
Hobbs Wm. H. licensed lighterman & agt. 13 Globe st. Wapping
Hobcraft Wm. sen. rule & mathemat. instrumt ma. 14 Barbican
Hobcraft Wm. jun. optician, 38 Princes st. Leicester square
Hobday Edward, beer retailer, Stucley ter. Camden town
Hobday Maria (Miss), tobacconist, 185 Waterloo road
Hobert John, chandler's shop, 2 Bell yard, Temple bar
Hobhouse Henry, barrister, 9 King's Bench walk, Temple
Hobhouse Thomas Benjamin, barrister, 5 Brick ct. Temple
Hobill Samuel, pawnbroker, 6 White st. Borough
Hobill Thomas, butcher, 11 Rufford's bldgs. Islington
Hobler Francis, solicitor, 26 Bucklersbury
Hoblyn Francis, surgeon, 12 Princes road, Notting hill
Hobman Christopher, carman, 2 Harper st. New Kent road
Hobson, Allfrey & Co. merchants, 34 Great St. Helen's
Hobson & Parrit, grocers, 50 Blackfriars road
Hobson Campbell Wright, solicitor, see Austen & Hobson
Hobson Geo. David & Co. clothiers, 4 Finsbury place south
Hobson Geo. bookseller, 8 Crombie's row, Commercial road east
Hobson Geo. *Red Lion* P.H. 72 High Holborn
Hobson Henry & Son, grocers, 6 Connaught ter. Edgw. rd
Hobson Henry, merchant & cutlery dealer, 68 Houndsditch
Hobson Jesse, wine, spirit, & porter merchant, 45 Leadenhall st
Hobson John, tailor, 14 Clarendon st. Somers town
Hobson Louisa (Mrs.), linen wa. 12 Frederick's pl. O. Kent rd
Hobson Nicholas Geo. surgeon, 5 Great Marylebone st
Hobson Thomas, human hair manufr. 5 West st. Seven dials
Hobson Thomas, boot & shoe maker, 27 Gt. St. Helens
Hobson Thomas, last & boot tree maker, 1 Rose st. Soho
Hoby, Robson & Knowles, upholstrs. trim. ma. 22 Skinner st
Hoby Geo. jun. blacking maker, 48 St. James's st. Piccadilly
Hoby George, boot & shoemaker, 48 St James's st. Piccadilly
Hoch Constantine, wood clock ma. 40 Charles st. Hatton gar
Hockaday Joseph, corkcutter, 32 Cannon st. St. George's east
Hocken Edward Octavius, physician, 13 Bloomsbury sq
Hocken James, tailor, 23 Maddox st. Regent st
Hocken Jane (Miss), milliner & dress ma. 104 London wall
Hockey Abednego, tobacconist, 8 Sol's row, Hampstead rd
Hockin Charles & Co. chemists & druggists, exporters of drugs, perfumery & italian wares, 38 Duke st. Manches-sq. & 1 Bishopsgate st. within
Hockin William, *Angel* P.H. 94 Fenchurch st. City
Hocking & Hitchcock, woollen warehousemn. 47 Old Change
Hocking Samuel, engineer, 4 New Broad st. City
Hockley Danl. brassfinisher, 19 Lit. Carter la. Doctors' coms
Hockley & Beningfield, conveyancrs. 10 Bell yd. Doctors' coms
Hockley Giles, bootmaker, 22 Church st. Blackfriars road
Hockley Geo. *Duke of Sussex* P.H. 55 Kensington High st
Hockley Henry, meat salesman, 35 Newgate market
Hockley Thomas B. *Blue Pump* P.H. 34 Gt. Guildford st. Boro'
Hockly Thos. Allen, oil & lead wa. 23 & 24 Lit. Earl st. 7 dials
Hockly Wm. surgeon, 7 Winckworth place, City road
Hocknell Mary (Mrs.), ladies' shoewa. 12 Tabernacle sq. Finsb
Hodd Rich. ironmngr. 101 Grand Junction ter. Edgware rd
Hodder Chas. *Castle tav.* P.H. Moorgate & 59 Fore st. City
Hodder Fred Aug. gasfitter, & brassfinr. 9 Tottenham ct. rd
Hodder John, cabinet maker, 163 Alfred pl. Waterloo road
Hodder Richard, boot & shoe maker, 97 Dean st. Soho
Hodder Robt. baker, 32 Canterbury place, Old Kent rd
Hodder Wm. cheesemonger, 13 Eden place, Old Kent rd

Hodding Wm. Henry, surgeon, 67 Gloucester pl. Portman sq
Hodge Chas. & Co. iron wks. King's rd. west, Chelsea
Hodge & Home, who. druggists, 102 & 103 Blackman st
Hodge & Lowman, linedrs.& silk mers. 256 to 262Regent st
Hodge Edward, grocer, 44 King st. Camden town
Hodge George, tailor, &c. 10 South Molton st. Oxford st
Hodge Jas. baker, 15 Clifton st. Finsbury
Hodge Jas. tailor, 4 Swallow st. Regent st
Hodge John, grocer, 2 John st. north, Marylebone
Hodge John, merchant, 2 Gt. St. Helen's, Bishopsgate
Hodge John, wholesale stationer, see Spalding & Hodge
Hodge John Watson, stockbrkr. 11 Warnford ct. Thrgmn.st
Hodge Langford Lovell, merchant, 61 Moorgate st
Hodge Mary Ann(Mrs.),milliner,10 Sth. Molton st.Oxford st
Hodge Samuel, engineer, ironfounder, steam boiler & tank manufacturer; foundry, Oak lane, Limehouse
Hodge Wm. bootmaker, 16 Hemming's rw. St. Martin's lane
Hodge Wm. manufacturing stationer, 34 Gt. Marlboro' st
Hodge Wm. veterinary surgeon, Gt. Green st. Kentish town
Hodge W. B. secretary to the *General Reversionary & Investment Company*, 5 Whitehall
Hodges Edward & Co. mrchts.&agts. 7George yd. Lombard st
Hodges Elizabeth & Jane, haberdashers, 1 North st. Lisson gr
Hodges & Johnson, insur.brokers, Lloyd's; & 5 Adams' court
Hodges & Scott, hosiers, glovers & shirt maks. 2 New Bond st
Hodges Abraham, pork butcher, 17 Church rd. Coml. rd. ea
Hodges Benjamin George, distiller, Church st. Lambeth
Hodges Charles, hairdresser, 23A, Princess st. Portman mkt
Hodges Chs. Westcott, tobacconist, &c. 25 Royal Exchange
Hodges Edward, *Royal Oak* P.H. 15 Circus st. New road, & 9 Upper York st. Bryanstone square
Hodges Edward, *White Horse* P.H. 279 Poplar High st
Hodges Edward, jun. ladies' shoemaker, 49 Wigmore st
Hodges George, carpenter, 22 Primrose hill, Salisbury sq
Hodges Geo.H. lithographic printer, 21 Percy st. Tottn.ct.rd
Hodges Geo. *Kentish Arms* P.H. 9 Mabledon pl. Burton crs
Hodges Henry, coach & harness ma. 34 Addington place, & Southampton st. Camberwell road
Hodges Henry, tailor, 3 Warwick st. Regent st
Hodges Hen. Howard, bookseller, 7Compton st. Brunswick sq
Hodges Hezekiah, *Angel & Crown* P.H. 2 Whitechapel road
Hodges James, bootmaker, 43 Wych st. Drury lane
Hodges James, hosier & linendraper, 3 Castle st. Falcon sq
Hodges James, plumber, &c. 35 Felix terrace, Liverpool rd
Hodges Jas. watch ma.&undert. 8 Beauvoir pla. Kingsland rd
Hodges John, cabinet ma. & corn dlr. 6Clarencepl. Hackneyrd
Hodges John, fruiterer, 155 Bethnal green road
Hodges John, furniture broker, 29 Old st. road
Hodges John, silk manufacturer, 21 Steward st. Spitalfields
Hodges John G. hosier & outfitt. 6 Southampton rw. Rssl.sq
Hodges John G. short-hand writer, 61 Millbank st. Westmnr
Hodges John Sam. tailor, 12 Artillery pl. west, Finsbury sq
Hodges Joseph, comb maker, 38 Vauxhall st. Lambeth
Hodges Mary (Mrs.), grocer, 17 Star st. Edgware road
Hodges Philip, *Barley Mow* P.H. 43 Paradise st. Rotherhithe
Hodges Richard, cabinetmaker, &c. 54 Gravel la. Southwark
Hodges Richard, undertaker, 17 Price's st. Gravel la. Boro'
Hodges Richd. Edwd. hairdresser, 47 Warwick st. Golden sq
Hodges Richard Henry, boot & shoe maker, 152 Piccadilly
Hodges Richard John, butcher, 21 Ivy lane, Newgate st
Hodges Thomas, linendraper, 189 Tottenham court road
Hodges Thomas, printer, see Rayner & Hodges
Hodges Thomas, surgeon, 104 Guilford st. Russell square
Hodges Thomas, tobacconist, 68 Park st. Camden town
Hodges Thomas, *Wheatsheaf* P.H. 17 Dorset st. Portman sq
Hodges Thomas Brooks, silk manfr. 20 Steward st. Sptflds
Hodges Wm. blacklead pencil ma. 4 Joiner st. Westminst. rd
Hodges Wm. butcher, 175 Waterloo road
Hodges Wm. barrister, 6 Fig Tree court, Temple
Hodges Wm. clothworker, 13 Kingsgate st. Holborn
Hodges Wm. corkcutter, 15 George st. Princes rd. Lambeth
Hodges Wm. furn. undertaker, 6 Snow's fields, Bermondsey
Hodges Wm. hide & skin salesman, Bermondsey skin market
Hodges Wm. leather dresser, 25 Page's walk, Bermondsey
Hodges Wm. *Skinners' Arms* P.H. 31 Judd st. Brunswick sq
Hodgetts John W. plaster of paris ma. 3 Bedford st. Hat. gar
Hodgkin Thomas, physician, 9 Brook st. Grosvenor sq
Hodgkins Anthony, builder & bricklayer, 14 North row, Park st. Grosvenor sq. & 75 Mount st. Berkeley sq
Hodgkins David, coach harn. smith, 25Brownlow st. Long ac
Hodgkins George, coach smith, 25 Brownlow st. Long acre
Hodgkinson S. & Son, wine & brandy merchants, 54 Upper Seymour st. Portman sq. & Cellars, 15½ Bryanstone st
Hodgkinson Thomas & Co. drug merchants, 86 Snow hill
Hodgkinson Thomas & Co. linendrapers, silk mercers & hosiers to her Majesty, 175 Piccadilly
Hodgkinsons'&Tonge, who.drugs. 21 Lbth. hill&213Up.Thas.st
Hodgkinson Wm. Son & Burnside, who. station. 24 Skinner st
Hodgkinson Edwd. attorney, 10 Godliman st. Doctors' com
Hodgkinson Geo. Edmund, ship ins. broker, 147Leadenhall st
Hodgkinson Henry, paper hanger, 47 Johnson st. Somers tn
Hodgkinson Martha (Mrs.), stationer, 5Courtney ter. Kngsld
Hodgkinson Sampson, wine merchant, 54 Up. Seymour st
Hodgkinson Sarah (Mrs.), milliner, &c. 5Old Nor. st. Red Lion sq
Hodgkinson Walter C. prof. of the flute, 42 Hart st. Bloomsby
Hodgkinson William, solicitor, 56 Burton crescent
Hodgson & Burton, attorneys, 10 Salisbury st. Strand
Hodgson, Concanen & Noyes, solicitors, 5 Lincoln's inn fields
Hodgson, Davies & Co. who. teadealers, 9 & 10 Philpot lane
Hodgson John S. & Co. wine merchants, 1 Well st. Welcls. sq
Hodgson&Greaves, stockbrokers, 3Warnford ct. Thrgmrtn.st
Hodgson & Powis, ship&ins.agents, 13 Change alley, Cornhill
Hodgson Thos. & Co. hat warehouse, 33Bedford st. Covent gar
Hodgson & Walbran, warehousemen, 92 Watling st
Hodgson Wm. Fred.&Co. wine, &c. merchants, 11St. Mary Axe
Hodgson Atkinson, bootmaker, 10 Upper Rupert st. Soho
Hodgson Charles, music seller, see Duff & Hodgson
Hodgson Chas. soda water ma. 24 Bedford st. Covent garden
Hodgson Chas. Francis, printer, 1 Gough square, Fleet st
Hodgson Charles Henry, merchant, 42 Crutched friars
Hodgon Charles James, operative chemist, 406 Strand
Hodgson Christopher, attor.&notary, 3 Gt. Dean's yd. Westm
Hodgson Edmund, auctioneer, 192 Fleet st
Hodgson Edward, solicitor, 35 Abchurch lane, City
Hodgson Elizabeth (Mrs.), dairy, 8 Middle row, Knightsbridge
Hodgson Elizh. Mary (Miss), dress ma. 17 Old Cavendish st
Hodgson Emma (Mrs.), milliner, 113St. Martin's la. Charing cr
Hodgson HenryJohn, barrister, 3 Pump court, Temple
Hodgson Helen (Miss), bookseller, 106 London road
Hodgson Henry Williams, barrister, 59 Chancery lane
Hodgson James, *Hare* P.H. 72 Hoxton Old town
Hodgson James, mercht. & gen.agt. 12 George yd. Lombard st
Hodgson Jas. *Tavistock Arms* P.H. 22 Gt. Russell st. Blooms
Hodgson John, oil & colorman, 27 Union st. east, Spitalfields
Hodgson John, queen's counsel, 4 New square, Lincoln's inn
Hodgson John, solicitor, 8 Gt. Tower st
Hodgson John, sugar refiner, 5 Dock st. Up. East Smithfield
Hodgson John, tobacco broker, see Grant & Hodgson
Hodgson John, turner & patten maker, 17King st. Coml. rd. ea
Hodgson Jonathan, plumber, &c. 51 Amwell st. Pentonville
Hodgson Joseph, surgeon, 1 Norton folgate
Hodgson Joseph, turner, 46 Union st. Whitechapel road
Hodgson Joseph, wood turner, 12 Holywell row, Worship st
Hodgson Mary (Miss), hosier, &c. 12 Jamaica ter. Limehouse
Hodgson Michl. Armstrong, ship broker, 6 Bedford sq. east
Hodgson Philip Brown, chemist, &c. 122 Piccadilly
Hodgson Richard, attorney, 52 Upper Norton st. Fitzroy square, & 10 Salisbury st. Strand
Hodgson Richard, furniture broker, 80 Friar st. Blackfrs. rd
Hodgson Richd. John, surveyor, 13 Frederick st. Gray's inn rd
Hodgson, Robert, solicitor, 32 Broad st. buildings
Hodgson Robert, warehomn. see Oldroyd, Hodgson & Morton
Hodgson Samuel, bookseller & library, 6& 9 Gt. Marylebone st
Hodgson Septimus, cabinet maker, 65Walcot pl. ea. Lambeth
Hodgson Thos. baker, 5 & 6 Windmill row, Kennington green
Hodgson Thos. furn. ironmonger, 8 Chapel st. west, Mayfair
Hodgson Thomas, oil merchant, 5 Carlisle st. Soho sq
Hodgson Thos. publisher, Aldine chams. 13 Paternoster row
Hodgson Thos. sugar refiner, Goodman's stile, Goodm. fields
Hodgson William, attorney, 8A, Red Lion square, Holborn
Hodgson William, currier, 81 Tottenham court road
Hodgson William Edward, tailor, 19 Mary st. New road
Hodgson William Hen. special pleader, 5 Hare ct. Temple
Hodgson Wm. Howard, wheelwright, 30Grosvr. mews, Bond st
Hodgston Allardice D. insurance broker, Lloyd's
Hodgston Allardice, insurance bro. 4Tokenhouse yd. & Lloyd's
Hodgston & Co. merchants, 4 Tokenhouse yard
Hodsdon John Henry, *Crown & Seven Stars* P.H. 47 Rosemary lane
Hodsoll Ambrose F. locksmith, 32 Sclater st. Bethnal green
Hodsoll Thomas, coffee rooms, 15 Chiswell st. Finsbury sq
Hodsoll Wm. beer retailer, 60 St. George st
Hodsoll Wm. watchma. 20 Ratcliff row, John's rw. St. Luke's
Hodson & Gibbs, attorneys, 19 King's road, Bedford row
Hodson & Holmes, child bed linen warehouse, 195 Oxford st
Hodson Daniel, silk machine maker, 27 Gun st. Bishopsgat
Hodson Geo. Alf. *Duke's Arms* & Bwr. sal. P.H. Lambh. Up. mar
Hodson Henry, *Queen's Head* P.H. 412 Oxford st
Hodson Hen. Bateman, architect & survey. 13 NewOrmond st
Hodson James, artist, 3 Amwell st. Pentonville
Hodson James Shirley, bookseller, publisher, law & general stationer & printer, 2 Clifford's inn passage, Fleet st

Hodson James, *Thornhill Arms* P.H. 13 Southamp. ter. Pntnvl
Hodson John, *King's Head* P.H. 2 James st. Covent garden
Hodson Richard, printer, 90½ Holborn hill
Hodson Robert, staymaker, 59 Great Marylebone st
Hodson Saml. importer of wine & spirits, 20 Beer la. Tower st
Hodson S. (Mrs.), coffee rooms, 48 Rufford's bdgs. Islington
Hodson Thomas, baker, 6 Nelson place, Old Kent road
Hodson Thos. coal merchant, 61 Gt. Russell st. Bloomsbury
Hodson Thomas, grocer, Well st. Hackney
Hodson Wm. architect & surveyor, 24 Penton st. Pentonville
Hodson Wm. Robert, dining rooms, 290 Oxford st
Hoe Richard, trunk & case maker & manufacturer of zinc, tin & copper cases, 44 Leadenhall st
Hoeftman Christian, merchant, 3 Walbrook bdgs. Walbrook
Hoerner Louis, pearl worker, 18 Craven st. City road
Hoey Edward, *Anchor & Crown* P.H. 9 King st. Westminster
Hoey Wm. grocer, 19 Page's walk, Bermondsey
Hoffer Robert, grocer, &c. 42 Marylebone lane, Oxford st
Hoffman Ann (Miss), confectioner, 5 Rathbone place
Hoffman Conrad, tailor, 15 Gt. Pulteney st. Golden square
Hoffman Edwd. oilman, 1 Barrossa ter. Cambridge rd
Hoffman Elizabeth (Mrs.), dressmaker, 46 Dean st. Soho
Hoffman Henry, merchant & agent, 10 Tokenhouse yard
Hoffman John Wills, solicitor, 5 Gt. Carter la. Doctors' com
Hoffman Louis, barrister, 11 South square, Gray's inn
Hoffmann Martha & Son, confectioners, wholesale, retail & for exportation, 154 Leadenhall st
Hoffmann Fredk. prof. of music, 6 Gloucester pl. Regent's pk
Hoffmeister Alexander, baker, 130 Gt. Saffron hill, Hattn.wl
Hofford Alfred, tobacconist, 9½ Salmon lane, Limehouse
Hofland Henry, academy, Durham house, Durham pl. Chlse
Hofland James, who. milliner, 88 Chiswell st. Finsbury
Hofman & Schenk, ship agents, 4 Vine st. Minories
Hofman Augustus, auction. & appraiser, 21 Up. St. Martin's la
Hogan & Smith, watch movement maks. 15 King st. Clerkenwl
Hogan John, *Seymour Arms* P.H. 9 Seymour pl. Bryanstone sq
Hogard & Candy, milliners & dressmakers, 105 New Bond st
Hogarth Andrew, ham & beef dealer, 118 Fleet st
Hogarth James, fishfactor, 126 Lower Thames st
Hogarth John, iron merchant, retorts, pipes & country castings, Hartley's wharf, Freeman's lane, Horselydown
Hogarth Joseph, printseller, publshr. & mounter, 5 Haymrkt
Hogden Charles, builder, 2 Union st. Borough road
Hogg & Robinson, oporto merchants, 2 Philpot lane
Hogg Chas. surgeon & vapour baths, 14 Finsbury place south
Hogg Charlotte (Mrs.), stationer & bookseller, 25 Edgware rd
Hogg Edward, tailor, 40 St. James's st. Piccadilly
Hogg Edward Andrew, bootmaker, Church st. Hackney
Hogg George, undertaker, 11 Castle lane, Westminster
Hogg George, undertaker, 89 St. George's road, Southwark
Hogg George, tailor, 32 Old Change
Hogg Georgiana (Mrs.), milliner, 19 Prospect pl. Bermndsy
Hogg Henry, hosier, glover & shirtmaker, 37 Beech st. Cripplegate
Hogg John, barrister, 12 King's Bench walk, Temple
Hogg John, *Lord Nelson* P.H. Dock st. Deptford
Hogg John, M.D. surgeon, 71 Gower st. Bedford square
Hogg Joseph Thompson, who. hosier, see Cox, Horner & Hogg
Hogg Ralph Howden, baker, 5 Newland terrace, Kensingtn
Hogg Robert, chemist & druggist, 104 Borough High st
Hogg Thomas, *Coach & Horses* P.H. 58 York st. Westmnstr
Hogg Thomas, jeweller, 10 Black Prince row, Walworth rd
Hogg Thomas Jefferson, barrister, 3 Plowden bldgs. Temple
Hogg William, cowkeeper, 2 Abdy st. Horselydown
Hogg William, optician & ironmonger, 394 Rotherhithe st
Hogg William, parish clk. & sexton, 6 Park pl. ter. Paddgtn
Hogg William, tailor, 16 Brook st. New road, Marylebone
Hogg William, tailor, 18 Robert st. Hampstead road
Hogg William, wine merchant, 37 Crutched friars
Hogg William, wine merchant, 32 Crutched friars
Hogg William Henry, tailor & draper, 49 Cannon st. road
Hoggart & Norton, auctioneers, 62 Old Broad st. City
Hoggart Arthur, wholesale saddler, 15 Rood lane
Hoggins Christopher A. barrister, 4 Lamb buildings, Temple
Hoggins Sabina (Mrs.), lodging ho. 4 New ct. Farringdon st
Hoghton Alexander A. stockbroker, 4 Austinfriars
Hohnbaum Edith (Mrs.), baker, 1 Clarance pl. Hackney rd
Hoile Edward, chemical & acid ma. Bridge road, Battersea
Hoile John, builder & decorator, 5 Poland st. Oxford st
Hoile Joseph, dyer, 10 Charles st. Charles sq. Hoxton
Hoile William, plumber, Bow High st
Holbeck James & Co. embroiderers, gold lacemn. & army accoutrement ma. to H.R.H. Pr. Albert, 21 Princes st. Hnvr.sq
Holbeck Louis & Son, embroiderers, gold & silver lacemen & army accoutrement makers to H.R.H. Prince Albert & the Royal family, 4 New Bond st
Hoinville George, trimming mnfr. 38 Thomas st. Brick la
Holbein John, commission agnt. 115 Fore st. Cripplegate sq
Holbein Walter, flour factor, 67 Up. Seymour st. Euston sq
Holbird Isaac, estate, &c. agent, 5 Beaufort bldgs. Strand
Holborn Union Register Office (Wm. Roberts James, superintendent registrar), Little Gray's inn lane
Holborn Robert Major & Co. who. teadlrs. 39 Mincing lane
Holborn Wm. accountant & referee, 3 Sun court, Cornhill
Holborow George, cheesemonger, 22 Clare st. Clare market
Holbrook Henry, tailor, 21 Shaftesbury terrace, Pimlico
Holbrook John, french & english hatter, 46 Strand
Holbrook John, plumber, &c. 13 Belvedere road, Lambeth
Holcombe Chas. Thos. refiner of coal tar, spirit, pitch & varnish ma. 10 Broad st. bldgs. & Morden whf. east, Greenwich
Holcombe John, butcher, 78 Crawford st. Portman sq
Holcombe Philip Geo. harpma. 13 Grafton st. east, Tot. ct. rd
Holcombe Walter Augustus, solicitor, 28 Chancery lane
Holdaway Charles, fruiterer, 40 Cheyne walk, Chelsea
Holden Benjamin, wine & spirit mer. 55A, Up. Seymour st. & *Cambridge Coffee House* P.H. 48 Newman st
Holden Charles, tallowchandlr. 48 Cambridge st. Connaught sq
Holden Elias, ironplate worker, 2 St. James' walk, Clerknwll
Holden Hariph, cheesemonger, 43 Judd st. Brunswick sq
Holden Henry, tailor, 8 Gray's inn terrace, Gray's inn lane
Holden John, furniture broker, 95 Cromer st. Brunswick sq
Holden Joseph, market gardener, Bromley, Middlesex
Holden Joseph, tobacconist, 22 Gt. James st. Lisson grove
Holden Robert, pastrycook, 3 Grace's alley, Wellclose sq
Holden Sarah (Mrs.), fruiterer, 211 Poplar High st
Holden Thomas, grocer, 10 Adam st. east, Portman sq
Holden Wm. chandler's shop, 12 Cambridge pl. Cambridge tr
Holden Wm. wholesale jeweller, 3 Commercial place, City rd
Holden Wm. Lloyd, brush, comb, & dressing case ma. fancy basket & gen. wareho. who & ret. 12 Finsbury pavement
Holder Jas. & Sons, bottle mers. 18 & 19 Cumberlnd. rw. Wal. rd
Holder Alfred, *Duke of Clarence* P.H. 19 Wades pl. Hackney rd
Holder Chas. *Rising Sun* P.H. 22 Commercial road, Pimlico
Holder Daniel, livery stables, 31 Claremont mews, Clerkenwl
Holder Edward, glass stainer, 29 St. Chad's row, Gray's inn rd
Holder Edwin, professor of the art of cleaning & restoring damaged paintings, 355 Oxford st
Holder Elizabeth (Mrs.), basket ma. 13 Up. st. Islington
Holder Geo. Thos. smith, 10 Grocers' hall ct. & 4 Huggin lane
Holder James, *Olive Branch* P.H. 6 Thomas st. Oxford st
Holder John, boot & shoemaker, 65 Hare st. Bethnal green
Holder John, cheesemonger, 8 Bermondsey New road
Holder John, *Crown & Thistle* P.H. South Lambeth
Holder Joseph, *Regent's park hotel*, 35 Allsop ter. Newroad
Holder Joseph, tobacconist, 7 Hemmings rw. St. Martin's la
Holder Josiah, brushmaker, 33 New road, St. George's east
Holder Saml. Bateman, manchstr. warehmn. 3 Queen st. City
Holder Thomas, bootmaker, 7 Tottenham pl. Tottenham ct. rd
Holder Thomas, dairyman, 31 Homer st. Marylebone
Holder Thomas Richard, butcher, Canal bridge, Old Kent rd
Holder William, tailor, 27 Whitefriars st. Fleet st
Holder William Thomas, bookseller, 311 Strand
Holderness Edward, pork butcher, 3 Ann's place, Hoxton
Holderness Henry, linendraper, &c. 21 Islington High st. & 114 Whitechapel High st
Holderness Rt. Leonard, piano & harpma. 1 Newmn. st. Oxfd. st
Holdernesse Elizth. (Mrs.), piano ma. 3 Church row, Islington
Holdernesse Geo. Wm. harpmak. 57A, Charlotte st. Fitzroy sq
Holdich George Maydwell, organ builder, 12 Greek st. Soho
Holding Alfred, chairmaker, 11 Bethnal green road
Holding Charles, surgeon & accoucheur, 13 New Bridge st
Holding Isaac, grocer, 19 York st. Locksfields
Holding Richard, splitting mills, Stoney lane, Tooley st
Holding Robert, pastrycook, 16 King's row, New rd. Pentnvl
Holditch Edward D. & Co. blackg. ma. Bear grdn. wf. Banksi
Holditch G. & Sons, cyder, ale & coal merchts. 26 Bankside
Holditch Edward D. coal merchant, 24 Park st. Southwark
Holditch George, coal merchant, 49 Bankside
Holditch John, coal merchant, 49 Bankside
Holdon Richd. hairdresser, 55 Chiswell st. Finsbury
Holdship James Michael, solicitor, 4 Regent square
Holdship John, barrister, 11 Upper Bedford pl. Russell sq
Holdstock Geo. engraver & printer, 4 Bridge st. Southwark
Holdsworth George, butcher, 2 Up. Dorset pl. Clapham rd
Holdsworth Henry, stuff agent, 249 Strand
Holdsworth James, butcher, 2 Wandsworth road
Holdsworth James, *Elephant & Castle* P.H. South Lambeth
Holdsworth James, butcher, Vauxhall gate
Holdsworth John Eastabrook, barrister, 1 Figtree ct. Temple
Holdsworth Peter Thos. potato dealer, 22 Lambeth walk
Holdsworth Philip, chemist & druggist, 116 Whitechapel rd
Holdsworth William, butcher, Kingsland green

Holdsworth Wm. plumber, &c. 5 Portsdown terrace, Kilburn
Hole James, tailor, 15 John st. Horselydown
Hole Joseph, mason & pavior, 231½ Poplar High st
Hole Richard, carpenter, 17 Tottenham st. Fitzroy square
Hole Thomas, carpenter & undertaker, 21 Brick st. Park la
Hole William, bootmaker, 65 Ernest st. Regent's park
Holeborne Wm.Joshua, *Shakespear's Hd.*P.H.1 Lwr.Eaton st
Holebrook Cath.(Miss), ladies'school, 23Devonsh.pl.Edgw.rd
Holebrook Susan(Miss) boys' school, 7Maida hill ea.Edgw.rd
Holesgrove Wm. boot & shoe maker, 66 Burlington arcade
Holford & Co. merchants, 30 Bucklersbury
Holford Thos. Wm. surgeon dentist, 61 South Audley st
Holgate Geo. Roland, china & glass dealer, 5 High Holborn
Holgate John, tobacconist, 1 Millbank st. Westminster
Holibred Stephen, corndealer, 14 John's mews, Bedford row
Holiday Geo. Hen. private teacher, 2 Hampstead st. Fitz. sq
Holiday John, auctioneer, see Bates, Puttock & Holiday
Holker John, fishmonger, 82 Connaught ter. Edgware rd
Holl & Bevan, wharfingers, coal & coke merchants, Milford whf. Milford la. Strand, & Vauxhall whf. Wandsworth rd
Holl Jas. Thos. & Co.wine, spirit,&c.merchts.36Gt.St.Helen's
Holl Henry, *George tap*, 21 Aldermanbury
Holl Jas. Thos. & Co. wine mers. 3 Cross lane,St.Mary at hill
Holl Wm. portrait engraver, 19 Southampton pl. Euston sq
Hollams John, solicitor, see Marten, Thomas & Hollams
Holland & Benwell, merchants, 19 Pinners'hall, O. Broad st
Holland Elizh. & Lucy (Misses), academy, 15 Lwr. Ashby st
Holland Fredk. & Co. merchts.& agts.66 & 68Lwr.Thames st
Holland & Hutchinson, ironmongers, 10Orange rw.Kennigtn
Holland John, jun. & Co.wine &brandy mers.39Fenchurch st
Holland Joseph & Priscilla, bookbinders, 5 Bull & Mouth st
Holland & Kirk, tailors, 43 High st. Marylebone
Holland (Misses), prep. school, 12 Spring ter.Wandswrth.rd
Holland & Watson, wine merchants; 44 Craven st. Strand
Holland William & Sons, cabinet makers & upholsterers, 19 Marylebone st. Piccadilly, & 38 Broad st. Golden sq
Holland Charles, butcher, 1 Church st. St. George's, Boro'
Holland Charles, merchant, 37 Old Broad st. City
Holland Charles, physician, 16 Queen st. Mayfair
Holland Edmund Charles, solicitor, 38 Lincoln's inn fields
Holland Eliza(Mrs.), ladies'school, 37Petersburgh pl.Bsywtr
Holland Eliz.(Mrs.), milliner, 14 Clarendon ter.Cmbwl. N.rd
Holland Frances (Mrs.), hat maker, 199 Bermondsey st
Holland Henry, architect, 11 John st. Adelphi
Holland Henry, coachsmith, 2 Coal yard, Drury lane
Holland Henry, physician, 25 Brook st. Grosvenor sq
Holland Henry, silversmi.&c.13Low.Smith st.Northmptn. sq
Holland James, artist, 11 Osnaburgh st. Regent's park
Holland James, beer retailer, 2 Gt. Guildford st. Borough
Holland James, cheesemonger, 107 Drury lane
Holland James, gunmaker, 44 Gt. Prescot st.Goodman's flds
Holland James, tailor, 74 Park st. Grosvenor sq
Holland James, tobacconist, 58 Borough road
Holland John, boot & shoe maker, see Dare & Holland
Holland John, coachmaker, see Charters, Holland & Newson
Holland John, collar maker, 12 West st. Seven dials
Holland John, engine lathe & tool ma.61 Compton st.Clrknwl
Holland John, tailor, 37 Chapel st. New road
Holland John Harris, tobacconist, 9 King st. Holborn
Holland John P. hosier & glover, 38 Gt. Russell st. Blmsby
Holland John Wm. grocer, 57 Freeschool st. Horselydown
Holland Joseph, beer retailer, 73 Snowhill
Holland Joseph, coachbuilder, see Horne, Thompson & Holland
Holland Josph. Wm. grocer, 78 Lamb's Conduit st.Foundling
Holland Mark, tobacconist, 13 Rawstorne st. Brompton
Holland Philip, coal merchant, 65 Bankside, Southwark
Holland Philip, flour&steammills, Stanleybg. Kgs.rd.w. Chel
Holland Robert, chemist & druggist, 44 Clerkenwell green
Holland Robert George, physician, 44 Clerkenwell green
Holland Saml. patent tinned iron wa. 34 Gracechurch st
Holland Stephen Geo. man's mercer, see East, Landon & Co
Holland Thomas, boot & shoe maker, Jamaica level, Rotherh
Holland Thomas, boot & shoe ma.40 Sth.Audley st.Grosvn.sq
Holland Thomas, butcher, 7 Lower road, Islington
Holland Thomas, tobacco broker, 107 Fenchurch st
Holland Wm. butcher, 5 Snowsfields, Bermondsey
Holland Wm. cheesemonger, 12 James st. Oxford st
Holland Wm. cowkeeper, 19 Dean st. Holborn
Holland Wm. linen draper, 58 & 59 Newington causeway
Holland Wm. nurseryman, 2 Elizabeth st. Hans pl. Chelsea
Holland Wm. teadealer, 127 Oxford st
Holland Wm. Chas. grocer,&c.2 Marchmont st.Brunswick sq
Hollander George, foreign bill agent, 11 Broad st. buildings
Hollands David Fred. & Son, coal merchants, 50 Bermondsey wall, & 1 Grange road, Bermondsey
Hollands Wm. S. architect & surveyor, 37 Bermondsey sq.
Hollaway Henry, baker, 19 High st. St. Giles's
Hollawell Jas.boot&shoema.24 Oakley st.Mount st.Lambeth
Hollebone Wm.J.& Co. vinegar makers, Church st. Millbank
Hollebone Henry, tailor, 20 Duke st. Portland place
Hollell Thos. dairy, 21 Glo'ster ter. Vauxhall bridge road
Hollett William, bootmaker, 7 Hanover pl. Regent's pk. rd
Holley George, furniture broker, 9 Barrett's ct. Oxford st
Holley John, undertaker&appr.62 Charlotte st.Whitechapel
Holleyman John, grocer & cheesemonger, 23 High st. Lambeth
Hollick John, linendraper, 172 & 173 Poplar High st
Holliday & Garner, conference offices, 21½ Sutton st. east
Holliday Cornelius B.watch case mkr. 21 Queen st.ea.Clrknw
Holliday Harriet (Mrs.), boarding house, 28 King st. Cheaps
Holliday John, tailor & draper, 41 Whitechapel road
Holliday Thomas, merchant, 46 Clifton st. Finsbury
Holliday Thomas, tailor, 23 Cross st. Islington
Holliday William, bricklayer, 13 Elm st. Gray's inn lane
Holliday William, *Greenwich Pensioner* P.H. Bow la. Poplar
Holliday Wm. livery stables, Seymour mews, Portman sq
Hollidge Margaret (Mrs.), lodging house, 40 University st
Hollier John, music publisher, &c. see Coventry & Hollier
Hollier Sidney, boot & shoe maker, 25 Penton rw.Walwth.rd
Hollingbury William, horse hair ma. 75 Old st. St. Luke's
Hollingdale Benjamin, carpenter, George st. Camberwell
Hollingdale Edward, linen drap. 20 Parker's row, Dockhead
Hollingdale George, dining rooms, 19 Queen st. Pimlico
Hollingdale George, poulterer & cheesemonger, 31 Red Lion * st. Holborn, & Stratford broadway
Hollings George, stone mason, 100 Green st. Bethnal green
Hollings James, bookbinder, 37 Tavistock st. Covent garden
Hollings Joseph, dairyman, 55 Edward st. Regent's park
Hollingsworth Ann (Mrs.), butcher, 8 Gedling st. Bermondsey
Hollingsworth Chas. wool stapler, Gun alley, Bermondsey st
Hollingsworth Geo. bootmaker, 146 High st. Camden town
Hollingsworth John, baker, 20 Lambeth lower marsh
Hollingsworth John, butcher, So. Island pl. Clapham road
Hollingsworth John, butcher, 113 Edgware road
Hollingsworth John, butcher, 15 Back road, St. George's ea
Hollingsworth John, *Woolpack* P.H. 206 Bermondsey st
Hollingsworth Nathan, saw maker, 147 Poplar High st
Hollingsworth Nathl. solicr.see Stokes, Hollingsworth & Co
Hollingsworth Susanna(Mrs.), bro.3,4&9 Brokers'al. Drury la
Hollingsworth Wm. bootma. 4 Albion pl. east, King's cross
Hollington Thos. tailor, 11 Wentworth place, Mile end road
Hollins John, artist, 47 Berners st. Oxford st
Hollinshed Chas.John, tinpl.work.13Gt.St.Andrew st.7dials
Hollinshed John Wm. gasfitter, 13 Gt. Andrew st. 7 dials
Hollinshed Wm. bedstead maker, 56 King st. 7 dials
Hollinsworth John Wm. coach builder, Denmark hill, Cmbrl
Hollis Charles, pianoforte maker, see Challen & Hollis
Hollis Chas. window blind ma. 26 King's road east, Chelsea
Hollis Geo. Cousin, baker, 3Claremont rw.Barnsby rd. Islgt
Hollis Humphrey, cheesemonger, 94 Norton st. Fitzroy sq
Hollis James, *Paviors' Arms* P.H. St. Margaret's ct. Boro'
Hollis Jane (Miss), milliner, 110 Park st. Camden town
Hollis John, beer retailer, 13 Brook st. New road
Hollis Mark, fishmonger, 17 Adams row, Hampstead road
Hollis Mary (Mrs.), coffee rooms, 23 Elizabeth st. Eaton sq
Hollis Rd.Augustus, grocer&teadealer, 78Judd st.Brunswk.sq
Hollis Thomas, bookseller, &c. see Henningham & Hollis
Hollis Thomas, pork butcher, 283 Oxford st
Hollis Timothy, smith, 11 Ray st. Clerkenwell
Hollocombe Wm. *Bell & Crown* P.H. 43King st.Camdn. tn
Hollot Joshua, hairdresser, 19 Bath st. City road
Holloway & North Islington Dispensary, Francis place, Holloway
Holloway Benjamin, baker, 1 Portland ter. Regent's park
Holloway Chas. flooring works, College wharf, Lambeth
Holloway Edwin, grocer & teadealer, 53 Bridge rd. Lambeth
Holloway Ezekiel, oil warehouse, 36 Poland st. Oxford st
Holloway Henry, *King's Arms tavern*, 87 Snowhill
Holloway James, baker, 79 Lambeth walk
Holloway James, corn dealer & seedsman, 87 Lambeth walk
Holloway James, grocer & oilman, 26 Lant st. Borough
Holloway John, coal agent, 16Wharf sth.side, Paddtn. basin
Holloway John, tailor, 2 Featherstone buildings, Holborn
Holloway Marseille M. printer & pub. 25 Bedford st.Cov.gdn
Holloway Rt. undert. & reg. 2 Up.Southwick st.nth. Edgw.rd
Holloway Robert, union ale brewery, 21 East road, City rd
Holloway Rt. jun. cook & confec. 88 Grand Junc.ter.Edgw.rd
Holloway Stephen Joshua, tailor, 10 Park side, Knightsbrdg
Holloway Thos. cheesemonger, 6 Bridge terrace, Harrow rd
Holloway Thomas, confectioner, 102 Drury lane
Holloway Thos. music & mus. inst.sel.5 Hanway st.Oxford st
Holloway Thomas, patent medicine warehouse, 244 Strand
Holloway William, barrister, 8 New sq. Lincoln's inn

Holloway William, saddler, 36 & 37 Millbank st. Westmnst
Holloway William, american merchant, 49 Lime st
Holloway William George, butcher, Broadway, Deptford
Holloway Wm. Hen. who.& ret. confectioner, 76 Farringdon st
Hollway Joseph Richard, accountant, 50 Moorgate st
Hollyer Elizh. (Mrs.) & Co. plumbers & glaziers, 2 Warwick la
Hollyer Samuel, printseller & pub. 30 Penton st. Pentonville
Hollyman John, tallow chandler, 194 Poplar High st
Hollywell Henry, furniture broker, 3 Windmill st. Finsbury
Hollywell John, hairdresser, 4 Arcade, Hungerford market
Holmaear Mary (Mrs.), scum boiler, 13 Finch st. Whitechpl
Holman Elizh.&Co. wine&coal mer. Phœnix whf. 248 Wapping
Holman Wm. & John, biscuit bakers, 76 Lower Thames st
Holman Andrew, surgeon, 10 John st. Minories
Holman Ann (Mrs.), undertaker, 67 York st. Westminster
Holman Benjamin, *Old Red Cross* P.H. 200 Borough High st
Holman Jas. millwright&engineer, 33 Baalzephon st. Bermsy
Holman Jas. smith, 32 Greenfield st. Whitechapel
Holman James, upholsterer, 30 Hatfield st. Stamford st
Holman Jane (Mrs.), seminary, 12 Stafford st. Lisson grove
Holman John, coal dealer, 68 Wells st. Oxford st
Holman John, wine & coal merchant, 145 Wapping High st
Holman John Baptist, solicitor, 47 Coleman st. City
Holman Patience (Mrs.), haberdasher, 139 Long la. Bermsy
Holman Saml. coach & harness maker, 128 & 129 Long acre
Holman Wm. carpenter, 5 Bidborough st. Burton crescent
Holman Wm. undertaker, 1 Bartholomew square, St. Luke's
Holmbush Copper Mining Company (George William Harrison, sec.), 51 Old Broad st. City
Holmden Jane (Mrs.), butcher, Church st. Hackney
Holmden John Geo. musical clock ma. 53 King sq. Goswell rd
Holme, Loftus & Young, solicitors, 10 New inn, Strand
Holme Wilson, Sewell & Co. distillers, & wine & brandy merchants, 28 Upper Thames st
Holme Hannah (Mrs.), dressma. 60 Hatfield st. Stamford st
Holme Richard, muslin manufacturer, see Green & Holme
Holme Wm. artist, 15 Nassau st. Middlesex hospital
Holmer Wm. & Co. who. ironmongers, 189 Union st. Borough
Holmer George & Son, solicitors, 24 Bridge st. Southwark
Holmer Henry, coach maker, 47 Crispin st. Spitalfields
Holmes & Aubert, paper stainers, 74 Coleman st. & manufactory, 20 Lower st. Islington
Holmes Charles & Son, fishing rod & tackle ma. 123 Fetter la
Holmes & De Hague, stockbrokers, see De Hague & Holmes
Holmes & Folkard, navy agents, 3 Lyon's inn, Strand
Holmes Jsph.&Jas. india shawl wa. 171, 173 & 175 Regent st
Holmes Matthew Steel & Son, watchmakers, 48 Holborn hill
Holmes & Pottle, newsvenders, 14 & 15 Royal Exchange
Holmes Wm. & Robt. booksellers & stationers, 195 Oxford st
Holmes Wm. & Son, solicitors, 25 Gt. James st. Bedford row
Holmes Alexander, carpenter, &c. 27 Wilson st. Finsbury
Holmes Alexander, *King's Head* P.H. 36 Lit. Queen st. Hlbn
Holmes Alfred, statuary & mason, Uxbridge rd. Bayswater
Holmes Allen, tobacconist, 149 Holborn bars
Holmes Benjamin, tobacconist, 22 Coppice row, Clerkenwell
Holmes Charles, butcher, 93 Fore st. Cripplegate
Holmes Charles, lasting warehouse, 35 King st. Cheapside
Holmes Charles, wine merchant, 52 Rathbone place
Holmes Chas. jun. fishingtackle mak. 2 Sydney alley, Leicest. sq
Holmes Charles James, solicitor, 163 Fenchurch st
Holmes Edith (Mrs.), accoucheur & cupper, 118 Crawford st
Holmes Edward, barrister, 5 Raymond buildings, Gray's inn
Holmes Edward, hairdresser, 176 Long lane, Bermondsey
Holmes Edward, tailor, 20 Compton st. Brunswick sq
Holmes Edward Carleton, solicitor, see Allen & Holmes
Holmes Eleanor (Mrs.), childbed linen wa. see Hodson & Holmes
Holmes Elizth. F. (Mrs.), artifi. feather ma. 61 Chrltte. st. Fitzr. sq
Holmes Francis, corndealer, 21 Theobald's road, Red Lion sq
Holmes Fred. ham & beef dealer, 4 Princes st. Leicester sq
Holmes George, furniture broker, 25 Brick lane, Spitalfields
Holmes George, wine & brandy mercht. 49 Lamb's Conduit st
Holmes Hen. hairdrsr.&dresng. casema. 10 Mount st. Brkly. sq
Holmes Henry Grey, bookbinder, 1 New inn buildgs. Strand
Holmes James, artist, 15 Wilton st. Grosvenor place
Holmes James, butcher, 16 John's row, St. Luke's
Holmes James, carpet manufacturer, 36 Castle st. Holborn
Holmes James, carpet manufacturer, 5 New Farringdon st
Holmes James, *Craven's Head* P.H. see Cleveland & Holmes
Holmes James, furnit. broker, 10 Rose & Crown ct. Finsbury
Holmes James, grocer, &c. 24 Wilmot st. Russell square
Holmes James, hairdresser, 2 Elwell pl. Grange rd. Bermnsy
Holmes James, newsvender, 2 Hampstead road
Holmes James, printer, 4 Took's court, Chancery lane
Holmes James, tailor, 9 Gloucester pl. Walworth common
Holmes James Bigg, dressing case maker, 41 Bucklesbury
Holmes Jas. Francis, tallow chandler, 180 Brick la. Spitalfi
Holmes John, boot & shoemaker, 6 Huggin lane, Wood st
Holmes John, bootmaker, 21 Wyndham st. Bryanstone sq
Holmes John, engraver & printer, see Saunders & Holmes
Holmes John, hatter, 4 Union st. Borough
Holmes John, marine store dealer, 18 Friar st. Blackfrs. rd
Holmes John, secret springer, 26 Glo'ster st. St. John st. rd
Holmes John Longmore, tin plate wrkr. 7 Limehouse causwy
Holmes John Shore, plumber, &c. 4 Church pass. Cateaton st
Holmes John William, optician & spectacle makers, 14 Redcross square, Cripplegate
Holmes Joseph F. accountant, 25 Queen's row, Walworth
Holmes Joseph Rd. ale & porter brewer, 213 Poplar High st
Holmes Jos. Foster, accountant, 25 Queen's row, Walworth
Holmes Joseph, *Brave Nelson* P.H. 3 Old Gravel lane
Holmes Lauret, statuary, 1 John st. west, Edgware road
Holmes Lazarus, carpenter, 11 Dorrington st. Leather lane
Holmes Owen Pape, solicitor, 6 Liverpool st. Bishopsgate
Holmes Patrick, teadealer & grocer, 132 Tottenham ct. rd
Holmes Richard, butcher, 14 Lumber court, Seven dials
Holmes Richard, solicitor, 163 Fenchurch st
Holmes Robt. chandler's shop, 16 Canal rd. Mile end road
Holmes Robert, fruiterer, New road, Deptford
Holmes Robert, rag dealer, 1 Up. Bryanstone st. Portm. sq
Holmes Robert, saddler, &c. 47 Cromer st. Brunswick sq
Holmes Robert, stockbroker, Stock Exchange
Holmes Samuel, coffee rooms, 4 Grocers' Hall ct. Poultry
Holmes Samuel, grocer, 1 Prospect pl, Lower rd. Deptford
Holmes Samuel, solicitor, 3 Gt. Knightrider st. Doctor's com
Holmes Sam. Bettison, solicitor, 14 Bucklersbury
Holmes Thomas, bootmaker, 1 Cross st. Golden square
Holmes Thomas, furniture broker, 61 London rd. Southwk
Holmes Thomas, furniture broker, 59 Broad st. Bloomsbury
Holmes Thomas, statuary & mason, 11 Belgrave st. south
Holmes Wm. cheesemonger, 30 Meredith st. St. John st. rd
Holmes Wm. grocer, 18 Charles st. Portman square
Holmes Wm. hairdresser & wigmaker, 3 Old Compton st. Soho
Holmes Wm. hairdresser, 17 Norland road, Notting hill
Holmes William, grocer, 11 Meredith st. Clerkenwell
Holmes Wm. hatter, 7 Hereford pl. Commercial road east
Holmes Wm. mattress mfr. 47 Willow walk, Tabernacle sq
Holmes Wm. tailor, 12 Kenton st. Brunswick square
Holmested Arthur, solicitor, 40 Bedford row, Bloomsbury
Holohan Sarah (Mrs.), braid manfr. 5 Rose st. Covent gardn
Holroyd Edward, com. of bankruptcy, 82 Basinghall st
Holroyd Elizabeth (Mrs.), dining rooms, 60 Old Bailey
Holroyd John Spear, fishing tackle ma. 59 Gracechurch st
Holroyd Sarah (Mrs.), milliner & dressma. 104 Bethnal gr. rd
Holste Henry, merchant, 5 North buildings, Finsbury circus
Holstead John, tailor, 33 Hampstead road
Holstead Susannah (Mrs.), stationer, 58 Ossulston st
Holston James William, tailor, 74 St. Martin's lane
Holsworth Abraham, trimming mfr. 19 Richmond st. St. Luke's
Holsworth Sarah & Ellen, childbed lin. wa. 11 Charles st. Soho
Holt Ascoli & Co. merchants, 55 Old Broad st. City
Holt & Aubin, solicitors, 26 Bucklersbury
Holt John & Wm. S. marine brewery, 39 Broad st. Ratcliff
Holt Thomas & Son, tailors & habit makers, 20 Sackville st
Holt Ann (Mrs.), carpenter & packing case ma. 22 Old Fish st
Holt Barnard W. surgeon, 30 Abingdon st. Westminster
Holt Benjamin, *Grapes* P. H. 15 Crispin st. Spitalfields
Holt Charles, attorney, 14 Guilford st. Russell square
Holt Christopher, *Black Lion* P.H. 10 Whitefriars st
Holt Christopher, *Cooper's hotel*, 15 Bouverie st. Fleet st
Holt Christopher, iron bedstead ma. 16 Tottnhm. ct. New rd
Holt Henry, *Wades Arms* P.H. East India road, Poplar
Holt John, oil & colorman, 31 East st. Manchester sq
Holt John Landfear, baker & pastrycook, 3 Kingsland green
Holt Mary Ann (Mrs.), hosier, 50 Bridge ho. pl. Borough
Holt Nathaniel Jas. W. ea. in. mer. see Mackey, Holt & Co
Holt Raymond B. barrister, 1 Harcourt buildings, Temple
Holt Samuel, carpet & furniture wa. 22 Tottenham ct. road
Holt Thos. coal merchant, 5 Up. Brunswick ter. Barnsby rd
Holt Thos. woollen factor & draper, see Onyon, Holt & Nash
Holt Thos. Jefferson, cook & confec. 63 St. Paul's churchyd
Holt William, barrister, Law chambers, 77 Chancery lane
Holt William, *Bee Hive* P.H. 17 Warner st. New Kent rd
Holt William, carman, 11 Theobald's road, Holborn
Holt William, tailor, 5 North st. Lisson grove
Holt William John, attorney, 13 Chatham place, Blackfriars
Holtham Richd. baker, 1 Cumberland market, Regent's pk
Holtham Thomas, baker, 5 Orchard pl. Kingsland road
Holtham William, bricklayer, 22 Princes sq. Kennington
Holtham William, tailor, Church st. Hackney
Holthouse Carsten, surgeon, 2 Serle st. Lincoln's inn
Holthouse Carsten, sen. sugar brok.&wine mer. 84 Gt. Twr. st
Holthouse Hen. Jas. sp. pleader, 1 Harcourt bdgs. Temple

Holtom John, butcher, 39 Gt. James st. Lisson grove
Holton Francis, butcher, 6 Newport court, Newport market
Holton Henry, tobacconist, 253 Oxford st
Holton Richard, academy, 42 Guildford pl. Lr. Kennington la
Holton Robert, linendraper, 7 Union row, Camberwell
Holton Thomas, blind maker, 2 Dorrington st. Clerkenwell
Holton Ths. Hammond, custm ho. & ship. agent, 15 St. Mary Axe
Holtzapffel & Co. manufs. of engines, lathes, edge tools & cutlery, 64 Charing cross; manufactory, 127 Long acre
Holtzmeyer Henrich H. sugar refin. John st. Church la. Whitch
Holway Thomas, tea urn mfr. & brazier, 1 Allen's ct. Oxfd. st
Holwell Ann (Mrs.), baker, 33 Aldermanbury
Holwell Charles, hatter, 100 Bridge road, Lambeth
Holwell Susanna (Mrs.), who. confect. 11 Crown rw. Walwth rd
Holwell Caroline (Mrs.), lodging ho. 6 Bath st. Newgate st
Holyday Charles, bellhanger, 12 Meard's court, Soho
Holyland James, stuff merchant, 4 Mumford ct. Milk st
Holyman William, nautical & mathematical instrument manufacturer, 27 Sidney place, Commercial road east
Holyoak Robert, cheesemonger, 26 Old Gravel la. Wapping
Holyoake George, needle manufcr. 106 Wood st. Cheapside
Homan, Herne & Co. who. shoe & leather wareh. 25 Skinner st
Homan Danl. chandler's shop, 4 Pritchard's pl. Hackney flds
Homan Daniel, bootmaker, 18 Goldsmith's row, Hackney rd
Homan Samuel, hatter, 79 Shoreditch High st
Home, Eagar & Co. merchants, 25 Rood lane, Fenchurch st
Home Margaret & Mary, seminary, 10 Petersburg pl. Bayswtr
Home & Colonial Infant School Society (John Stuckey Reynolds, hon. sec.), 12 to 14 St. Chad's row, Gray's inn rd
Home Missionary Society, 4 Blomfield st. Finsbury
Home Henry Francis, wholesale druggist, see Hodge & Home
Home James, wine merchant, 20 Dean st. Soho
Home Patrick, merchant, 25 Rood lane, Fenchurch st
Homer Elizth (Mrs.), millnr. 12 Adam st. west, Bryanstone sq
Homer Fredk. *Victory* P.H. 7 Gt. Cambridge st. Hackney rd
Homer John, *Gloucester Arms* P.H. 27 Mason st. Old Kent rd
Homer John James, *Dolphin* P.H. Mare st. Hackney
Homer Wm. drysalter & manufactg. chemist, 8 Billiter st
Homère John George, merchant, 13 Broad st. buildings
Homersham Brothers, woolstaplers, 1 Webb st. Bermondsey
Homersham Arth. Rider, woolstapler, 2 Crimscott st. Bmsy
Homersham Saml. Collett, civil engineer, 20 Lr. Belgrave pl
Homes James, butcher, 16 Silver st. Golden square
Homes James, slaughterman, see Cleveland & Homes
Homes William, bootmaker, 34 Featherstone st. City road
Homeward John, coal dealer, 52 Brick lane, St. Luke's
Homewood Henry, greengrocer, Church st. Hackney
Homewood John, ironmonger, &c. 4 Claremont pl. Old Kent rd
Homeyer Christian, tailor, 4 Mount row, Liverpool road
Homfray Henry Revel, solicitor, 18 Margaret st. Caven. sq
Hone & Loscomb, ladies' school, 21 Brunswick pl. Barnsby. rd
Hone John & Sons, fringe manuft. 43 Newman st. Oxford st
Hone Daniel, hairdresser, Thorney st. Museum st
Hone John, hairdresser, 12 Brown st. Bryanstone square
Hone Wm. grocer, 11 Richmond pl. East st. Walworth rd
Hone William, hairdresser, 36 Earl st. west, Edgware road
Hones Thos. & Co. fishmongers, 11 Colvill ter. King's rd. Chelsea
Honey Ann (Mrs.), *Peacock* P.H. 13 Maiden la. Covent gard
Honey Edward, baker, 4 Adelaide pl. Grange rd. Bermondsey
Honey John, shoemaker, 5 Green st. Bethnal green
Honey William, coffee rooms, 14 Broad st. Bloomsbury
Honeysett A. (Mrs.), *Old George & Dragon* P.H. 81 Leather la
Honeysett Edw. Hen. engrvr. & stationr. 137 High st. Camdn tn
Honeysett Edwd. Hen. stationer, 56 Seymour st. Euston sq
Honeysett Stephen, *Horseshoe & Magpie* P.H. 20 Fetter la
Honeywood James, surgeon, 20 Cannon st. City
Honeywood William, surgeon, 76 Queen st. Cheapside
Honiball James, quilting & valentia wareho. 149 Cheapside
Honiborne Mary (Mrs.), school, Southampton st. Cambrwll
Honniball Wm. butcher, 3 Copenhagen st. Pentonville
Honnor Henry, *Blacksmith's Arms* P.H. 110 Brook st. Ratcliff
Honnor Thomas, tailor, 67 Leadenhall st
Honour James, fruiterer, 3 Shepperton pl. New North road
Honychurch Rich. sen. carpenter, 24 Leonard st. Shoreditch
Honychurch Wm. cooper, 4 Margaret pl. Hackney fields
Honyman George Essex, special pleader, 6 Pump ct. Temple
Hood Robert & Benjamin, linendrapers, Church st. Hackney
Hood Thomas & Charles, iron merchts. 18 Earl st. Blackfriars
Hood, Ward & Hood, ribbon manufrs. 117 Wood st. Cheapside
Hood Arthur, coachmaker, 118 Curtain road, Shoreditch
Hood Charles, *Bull's Head* P.H. 80 Leadenhall st
Hood David, baker, 29 Park terrace, Regent's park road
Hood Edwd. Chas. carman & coal mercht. 1 Alfred ter. Stepney
Hood Edward Theophilus, barrister, 60 Chancery lane
Hood Geo. S. marine decorator, 4 Conant pl. Comml. rd. Limeho
Hood Jacob, tailor, 19 Huntley st. Tottenham court road
Hood James, lace cleaner, 3 Brook st. Hanover square
Hood Jas. Horatio, bookbndr. & statnr. 25 Red Lion sq. Holborn
Hood John, bricklayer, Little Chelsea
Hood Peter, surgeon, 15 Lower Seymour st. Portman sq
Hood Richard, vellum binder, 12 Bartholomew close
Hood Thomas, carver & gilder, 27 Meredith st. Clerkenwell
Hood Thomas, surgeon, 22 Panton st. Haymarket
Hood William, jobmaster, 2 Kinnerton st. Belgrave square
Hood William Hen. iron & brassfounder, see Barnes & Hood
Hoodles Charles, boot & shoe ma. 3 St. Ann's ct. Dean st. Soho
Hook Adam, grocer & cheesemong. 96 Up. East Smithfield
Hook Charles, bootmaker, 9 St. James's st
Hook Charles, linen & woollen dra. 141 St. John st. Smithfld
Hook Frederick, grocer, 28 Amelia st. Walworth road
Hook Frederick, hatter, 79 New Bond st
Hook Henry, *The Number Seven* P.H. 7 Newgate st
Hook James Clarke, artist, 70 Newman st. Oxford st
Hook Jane (Miss), ladies' school, 39 Store st. Bedford sq
Hook John, builder, 54 Welbeck st. Cavendish square
Hook John, carpenter, Southampton st. Camberwell
Hook John, ladies' shoemaker, 66 New Bond st
Hook Joseph, contractor & brick & tile merchant, Nine elms
Hook Mary Ann (Mrs.), lodging ho. 17 Welbeck st. Cavndsh. sq
Hook Richard, tailor, South Island place, Clapham road
Hook St. Pierre B. solicitor, 7 Coleman st. City
Hook Thos. ornament. steel worker, 3 Archer st. Windmill st
Hooke Charles Frederick, baker, 146 Lambeth walk
Hooke Edwd. B. solictr. see Gilbert, Hooke, Street & Gutteres
Hooke Francis, 16 Edward st. Hampstead road
Hooke Francis, baker, 50 Red Lion st. Holborn
Hooke Henry, baker, 93 Fetter lane, Holborn
Hooke James, butcher, 44 Frederick st. Hampstead road
Hooke James Edwin, baker, 85 High st. Camden town
Hooke James, baker, 13 Brick lane, Spitalfields
Hooke John, baker, 38 Upper Barnsbury st. Islington
Hooke John, boot & shoemaker, 24 George st. New road
Hooke Joseph, baker, 48 Beech st. Barbican, & 15 Little Bell alley, Coleman st
Hooke Richard, baker, 75 Shoe lane, Fleet st
Hooke Thomas, confectioner, 80 Charlotte terr. Lambeth
Hooker Benjamin, cheesemonger, 19 Barnsbury pl. Islington
Hooker Charles, cheesemonger, 123 Brick la. Spitalfields
Hooker George, fruiterer, 47 King st. Westminster
Hooker Henry, smith & farrier, Nine elms
Hooker James, attorney, 8 Bartlett's buildings, Holborn
Hooker John, cheesemonger, 18 Brick lane, Spitalfields
Hooker Joseph, hair & flock mer. 20 White's grounds, Brmdsy
Hooker Newman, bootmaker, 121 Church st. Shoreditch
Hooker Peter, lathemaker, 25 John's row, St. Luke's
Hooker Philip, timber merch. Raven row, Whitechapel rd
Hooker Thomas, chemist, 4 Millpond st. Bermondsey
Hooker William, pianoforte maker, 92 Old st
Hookham Thomas, bookseller & publisher, 15 Old Bond st
Hoole Jas. & Co. fender & fire iron wareh. 36 Aldermanbury
Hoole, Lockyer & Parker, metal & tool & steel & iron warehouse, 21 St. James's walk, & 1 Suffolk st. Clerkenwell
Hoole Francis Hen. grocer & teadealer, 205 High st. Boro'
Hoole Henry, teadealer & grocer, 44 London rd. Southwark
Hooman Geo. & James, carpet ma. see Pardoe, Hoomans & Co
Hoon Henry, nurseryman, Harrow road, Paddington
Hooper, Addison & Co. merchants, 23 Laurence Pountney la
Hooper & Avery, colonial brokers, 135 Fenchurch st
Hooper Brothers, annatto & blue makers, & lead grinders, 28 St. John st. Clerkenwell
Hooper Chas. & Co. for. & brit. wine mer. 112 Bishopsgt. within
Hooper C. W. & Benj. leather, hide, & bark factors, 1 Seething lane, & at Leadenhall market
Hooper James Middleton & Co. tea warehouse, 5 Newgt. st
Hooper John & Sons, wholesale confectioners & lozenge manufacturers, 26 & 27 High Holborn
Hooper Rd. & Sons, wine & spirit mercht. 20 & 21 Queenhithe
Hooper Stephen & Geo. statnrs. & parchment dlrs. 45 Fleet st
Hooper Abm. greengrocer, 18 Somerset pl. New rd. Com. rd
Hooper Bartlett, chemist, 43 King William st. City
Hooper Benj. tanner, &c. 2 Alscot pl. Grange rd. Bermondsey
Hooper Charles, surgeon, 9 Clayton pl. Kennington road
Hooper Edmund E. surgeon, 82 Brunswick st. Hackney rd
Hooper Francis Philip, solicitor, see Watkins & Hooper
Hooper George, bricklayer, 4 Eldon st. Finsbury
Hooper George, coachmaker, see Adams & Hooper
Hooper George, wine merchant, see Follett, Hooper & Co
Hooper George Henry, jun. barrister, 8 Old sq. Lincoln's inn
Hooper Harvey Berrow, barrister, 60 Lincoln's inn fields
Hooper James, combmaker, 10 Prospect place, Kingsld. rd
Hooper James, grocer, 70 Lower George st. Chelsea
Hooper James, *King's Arms* P.H. 1 Shepherd's mrkt. Mayfr

Hooper James, merchant, 37 Nicholas lane, Lombard st
Hooper Jeremiah, butcher, 268 Whitechapel road
Hooper John, surgeon, 29 Newington place, Kennington rd
Hooper John Thos. ship & ins. brok. see Sampson & Hooper
Hooper Maria E. (Mrs.), tripedresser, 68 Long la. Smithfield
Hooper Mary (Mrs.), saddle & harn. ma. 5 Gt. Dover st. Boro'
Hooper Nathaniel, solicitor, 5 Pump court, Temple
Hooper Richd. advertising agent, 6 Thavies inn, Holborn
Hooper Richd. needlemaker, see Shrimpton & Hooper
Hooper Robert Little, surgeon, 6 London road, Southwark
Hooper Rowland, linendraper, silk mercer, & haberdasher, family mourning warehouseman, 52 Oxford st
Hooper Rowland (Mrs.), court milliner, 52 Oxford st
Hooper Sam. Francis, tea & colonial broker, 7 Lit. Tower st
Hooper Thomas, butcher, 6 Cannon st. St. George's east
Hooper Thomas, coal & potato dealer, 43 Aldermanbury
Hooper Thomas W. chemist & druggist, 5 Bathurst st. Hyde pk
Hooper Wm. pawnbroker, 31 Dockhead, Bermondsey
Hooper Wm. chemist, &c. 24 Gt. Russell st. Covent garden
Hooper Wm. operative & disp. chemist, 7 Pall mall east
Hooper Wm. timber broker, 13 New City chambers
Hooper Wm. Crockall, wholes. tea dealer, 26 Old Change
Hooppell John, carpenter, 5 Russell st. Bermondsey
Hooton James & William, merchants, 2 Walbrook buildings
Hooton Bembridge, *Sutton's Arms* P.H. 6 Carthusian st
Hopcraft & Broadwater, shipping, &c. agents, 10 Billiter st
Hopcraft Robert, color manufacturer, Stratford, Essex
Hopcraft William, publisher & news agent, 42 Mincing lane
Hopcroft Wm. plumber, &c. 1 Grove pl. Gt. Green st. Kentish tn
Hope Life Assurance Co. (Wm. Bury, sec.), 1 Furnival's inn
Hope Allen F. lodging house, 4 Manchester buildings
Hope Charles, straw hat maker, 54 Princes st. Leicester sq
Hope Charles, tea broker, see Watkins & Hope
Hope D. Egville (Mrs.), profr. of dancing, 23 Prtmn. st. Portn. sq
Hope Geo. liv. stables, Nottingham mews, Marylebn. High st
Hope Geo. Joseph, veterin. surgeon, 66 High st. Marylebone
Hope Hugh, parliament & scotch agt. see Deans, Dunlop & Hope
Hope James Robert, D.C.L. barrister, 3 Paper buildings
Hope Mary Ann (Mrs.), dressmaker, 2 Swan st. Minories
Hopewell Edward & Co. outfitters & clothiers, 24 Leadnhl. st
Hopgood Francis, florist & seedsman, Craven hill nursery, Uxbridge road, Bayswater & 8 St. Agnes villas
Hopgood James, solicitor, 14 King William st. west, Strand
Hopgood Metcalf, jeweller, 202 Bishopsgate without
Hopking Henry Geo. linendraper, 38 Seymour st. Euston sq
Hopkins Daniel & Sons, coachmaks. 36 Davies st. Berkeley sq
Hopkins Frederick Samuel & Co. book & music sellers & stationers, 5 Bishopsgate within
Hopkins & Holdom, oil & clrmn. 14 & 19 Richmond st. Walworth
Hopkins John & Co. linen & carpet wareho. 60 to 63 Shoreditch
Hopkins John & Son, woollen drapers, 31 Shoreditch High st
Hopkins & Purvis, oil & colormen, 20 Greek st. Soho
Hopkins Abram, lamp maker, see Davis & Hopkins
Hopkins Ann G. (Mrs.), seminary, 42 Aldersgate st
Hopkins Catherine C. (Mrs.), haberdash. 27 Long la. Smithfi
Hopkins Charles, tailor, 5 Portman st. Portman sq
Hopkins Chas. A. chemist, 10 Staverton row, Walworth rd
Hopkins Chris. coach maker, 61 & 62 Worship st. Finsbury
Hopkins Edwin, dairy, 21 Charles st. Middlesex hospital
Hopkins Elizh. (Mrs.), grocer, 11 Lit. Guildford st. Brunswk. sq
Hopkins Elizh. (Mrs.), *Three Johns* P.H. 73 Wht. Lion st. Pntvl
Hopkins Fras. clock & wa. spring mak. 52 Noble st. Goswell st
Hopkins Fred. haberdasher, 29 Chapel st. Somers town
Hopkins George, coach plater, 75 Regent st. Lambeth
Hopkins George, dancing & music master, 115 Aldersgate st
Hopkins Henry, tobacconist, 14 Threadneedle st
Hopkins Henry, toothbrush ma. 11 Myddelton st. Spafields
Hopkins Henry Hibbert, stockbroker, 3 Bartholomew lane
Hopkins Henry Jordan, bootmaker, 25 Ebury st. Pimlico
Hopkins James, lodging house, 24 Surrey st. Strand
Hopkins James, tailor, 20 Little Guildford st. Russell square
Hopkins James, tobacconist, 95 Lambeth Lower Marsh
Hopkins James, *White Horse* P.H. 21 Castle st. east, Oxford st
Hopkins John, greengrocer, 102 East st. Manchester square
Hopkins John, grocer, 5 North st. Back Church lane
Hopkins John, pipemaker, 14 Redman's row, Mile end
Hopkins John, shoema. 22 Wyndham rd. Camberwell N. rd
Hopkins John, velvet wire drawer, 36 Bethnal green road
Hopkins John Douglas, architect, 25 Bedford square
Hopkins John Edward, oil & colorman, 87 Blackman st. Boro'
Hopkins John Morgan, physician, 1 Elizabeth st. Eaton sq
Hopkins Joseph, genl. salesman, 16 Lit. Chapel st. Westmnr
Hopkins Manley, average adjuster, 69 Cornhill, City
Hopkins Richard, oil & color. & soap ma. 22 Broadway Deptfrd
Hopkins Robert, lighterman, College wharf, Belvedere road
Hopkins Sarah (Mrs.), gold burnisher, 73 Red Lion st. Clkwl
Hopkins Sarah (Mrs.), hairdresser, North lodge, Albany
Hopkins Thomas, butcher, 18 Mount st. Walworth road
Hopkins Thos. chemist, 21 Union st. Bishopsgate without
Hopkins Thomas, coach fndr. & pltr. 23 White Hart st. Kenngt
Hopkins Thomas, whipmaker, see Shrimpton & Hopkins
Hopkins Thos. Valentine who. stationer, 42 Houndsditch
Hopkins Wm. bootmaker, 6 Lit. Charlotte st. Middlx. hosp
Hopkins Wm. butcher, 88 Farringdon st.
Hopkins Wm. coal dealer, 7 Tower Royal, Watling st
Hopkins Wm. *Hole in the Wall* P.H. St. Dunstan's ct. Fleet st
Hopkins Wm. lighterman, 62 Commercial road, Lambeth
Hopkins Wm. tailor, 18 Brewer st. Somers town
Hopkins Wm. Alexander, sculptor, 25 Bedford square
Hopkinsons' & Burrowes, corn & seed mers. Paul's wf. Thames st
Hopkinson Charles & Co. bankers & army agents, 3 Regent st. Waterloo place
Hopkinson Chris. T. & Co. army clothiers, 64 Pall mall
Hopkinson & Cope, engineers, hydraulic, letter (Albion) press makers, lithographic & copper plate printing & bookbinders' (Albion) arming press manufactrs. 14 New North st. Finsby
Hopkinson George, sawmaker, 22 Curtain road
Hopkinson James, teadealer, 18 Broad st. Bloomsbury
Hopkinson John, boys' school, 1 Portland pl. Wandsworth rd
Hopkinson John, cabinet manufact. 64 Banner st. St. Luke's
Hopkinson Jonathan, west india merchant, 113 Fenchurch st
Hopkinson Joseph, saw & plane ma. 16 Bridge ho. pl. Newing. c
Hopkinson Luke, coach & harness maker, 77 High Holborn
Hopkinson Matthew, coffee rooms, 10 Little Saffron hill, Hatton garden
Hopkinson Thos. tallow chandler, &c. 25 High st. Shadwell
Hopkinson William, tallow chandler & melter, 45 Barbican
Hopley Mary A. (Mrs.), habrdashr. 1 Perseverance. ter. Beth. gr
Hoppe & Boyle, solicitors, 3 Sun court, Cornhill
Hoppe Chas. & Sons, coal & coke merchants, Pig's quay, Bridewell precinct, William st. Blackfriars bridge, City
Hoppe Elizabeth (Mrs.), statnr. & account book ma. 79 Strand
Hoppe Henry, butcher, 1 Baker's row, Whitechapel
Hoppe Ivan, butcher, 20 Langley pl. Commercial road east
Hoppe James, tinman, 2 Sparrow corner, Minories
Hoppe John, who. shoe manufacturer, 3 Bishopsgate without
Hoppe Joseph, grocer & cheesemonger, 65 Minories
Hoppe Wm. John, boot & shoe maker, 77 Fleet st
Hopper Elizabeth (Miss), staymaker, 9 Brompton road
Hopper Jane M. (Mrs.), *White Hart* P.H. 44 Berwick st. Soho
Hopper Thomas, architect, 40 Connaught ter. Edgware road
Hopper Walter Anth. barrister, 3 Stone bdgs. Lincoln's inn
Hopper Mary (Mrs.), carpet & floorcloth wareho. 11 Gt. Queen st
Hopper Wm. tobacconist, 1 Adam's row, Hampstead road
Hopperton Wm. architect & surveyor, 83 Ebury st. Pimlico
Hopps James, of Marsala, wine merchant (Stebbing & Co. agents), 12 Clement's lane, Lombard st
Hopson John, collar & harness ma. 5 Salmon la. Limehouse
Hopson Samuel, turner, 66 & 67 Long lane, West Smithfield
Hopson Thomas, shell fishmonger, 1 King's rd. Bedford row
Hopton Henry, timber bender, 8 Gower st. north, & 8 Upper Tottenham place, Tottenham court road
Hopton's Almshouses, Green walk, Holland st. Blackfriars
Hopwood & Armstrong, copper, brass & iron wire-workers & weavers, & sieve makers, 184 St. George st
Hopwood & Co. fire engine makers, 245 Blackfriars road
Hopwood & Park, wire workers, wire weavers & warehousemen, 23 & 24 Fish st. hill, London bridge
Hopwood John Stephen S. & Son, solicitors, 47 Chancery la
Hopwood James Lomax, grocer, 131 Lambeth walk
Hopwood Joseph, grocer & oilman, 2 Wimpole st. Cavend. sq
Hopwood Josiah, linendraper, 44 Duke st. Manchester sq
Hopwood Owen Thos. umbrella & stayma. 195 Sloane st. Knights
Hopwood Peter, ironmonger. 14 Victoria road, Pimlico
Hopwood Thos. coal mer. Essex wharf, Essex st. Strand
Hopwood Thos. W. S. collector of taxes, 103 Mount st
Hopwood Wm. accountant, 5 Aldine chambrs. 13 Paternst. row
Hopwood Wm. butcher, 102 Whitechapel road
Horace Thos. beer shop, 9 Somerset pl. New rd. Commcl. rd
Horden John, agent to Thomas Salt & Co. brewers, Burton on Trent; 98 Leadenhall st. & 1 & 2 Wharfs, City basin
Horder John Geo. prof. of music, 20 Coles ter. Barnsbury rd
Horder Thos. Wm. wholesale druggist, 19 Fenchurch st
Horder Valentine Thomas, pavior, 221 Upper Thames st
Horder Wm. George, solicitor, 16 Howard st. Strand
Hore John & Henry, merchts. 13 Copthall ct. Throgmorton st
Hore & Son, solicitors, 6 Lincoln's inn fields
Hore Elizabeth (Mrs.), wharfinger, ship agent & booking office keeper, and agent to the Dundee, Perth, & London Steam Shipping Co. Hore's steam wharf, 272 Wapping, Hore's wharf, Hermitage bridge, & booking offices, 18 Strand & 14 Bucklersbury

Hore's wharf, Hermitage, & *Hore's steam wharf* (Mrs. Elizabeth Hore), 272 Wapping
Hore James Fraser, barrister, 24 Old square, Lincoln's inn
Hore Peter, custom ho. & shipping agt. Hore's whf. Wapping
Hore Wm. Rundle, *King's Arms* P.H. 2 Duke st. Grosvenor sq
Horeau Charles (Madame), dressmakr. 54 Mortimer st. Cav. sq
Horine John Wm. baker, 83 Harrison st. Gray's inn road
Horley Edward, baker, 218 Upper Whitecross st
Horlock Christopher, bootmaker, 6 Hatton wall, Hatton gar
Horlock Henry, baker, 122 East st. Kennington cross, & 117 Vauxhall walk, Lambeth
Horlock Hen. carpenter & undertaker, 11 Augustus rw. Spa rd
Horlock James, tailor, High st. Battersea
Horlock John, baker, 1 South st. King's road, Chelsea
Horlock Mk. *Builders' Arms* P.H. 10 Compton st. e. Regnt. sq
Horn, Shirass & Cook, comp. ornmnt. ma. 38 Bedford st. Cov. gar
Horn Charles, jeweller, 24 Leigh st. Burton crescent
Horn Charles, tobacconist, 131 Waterloo road
Horn Charles Aug. tobacconist, 86 Bishopsgate without
Horn George Wm. secretary to Portsmouth, Chichester & Fareham railway company, 5 John st. Adelphi
Horn Henry, barrister, 2 Hare court, Temple
Horn James, engineer, 1 Upper King st. Coml. rd. St. Geo's. ea
Horn John, oilman, 76 Devonshire st. Lisson grove
Horn Richard, baker, 71 Hatton garden
Horn Stephen, fruiterer, 5 Fort pl. Grange rd. Bermondsey
Horn William, drug grinder, see Freeman & Horn
Horn William, sailmaker, 19 Church row, Limehouse
Hornblow Charles, carpenter & undertakr. 1 Webber st. Blkfrs
Hornblower Jethro & Co. wine merchants, 123 Fenchurch st
Hornblower Francis S. who. chemist, see Lowe & Hornblower
Hornblower John Griffice, printer, 77 Myddelton st
Hornblower Joseph, cab builder, 1 Red Lion yd. Gt Warner st
Hornblower Wm. printer & gilder, 1½ Wilderness rw. Clerknwl
Hornby & Towgood, solicitors, 31 St. Swithin's lane, City
Hornby Benjamin, wine merchant, 16 Cannon st. City
Hornby Daniel S. manag. parcels delivery co. 12 Rolls bldgs
Hornby Johannah (Mrs.), wardrobe dealer, 105 Cromer st
Hornby John Stibbins, oil & italian wareho. 35 Houndsditch
Hornby Joseph, straw hat ma. 2 Mary's place, Kingsland rd
Horne & Allen, paperhanging mnfrs. &c. 41 Gracechurch st
Horne Benjamin Worthy & Henry, coach proprietors, *Bolt in Tun*, 64 Fleet st.; *Cross Keys*, 129 Wood st. Cheapside; *George & Blue Boar*, 270 High Holborn; *Golden Cross*, 452 West Strand; & *Branch Office*, 33 Regent circus
Horne & Chaplin, branch coach yd. 63 Drummond st. Euston sq
Horne Christr. & Thomas, poultry salesmen, Leadenhall mrkt
Horne George & Co. booksellers & librarians, 105 Cheapside
Horne Thomas & Neale, coal & coke merchants, 1 Holland st. Blackfriars, & 88 Bankside, Southwark
Horne, Thompson & Holland, coach makers, 254 Oxford st. & 79 Long acre
Horne, Thornthwaite & Wood, opticians, manfrs. of cheml. mathematical, philosophical, & photographic apparatus, hydrometers, saccharometers, barometers, thermometers, &c. 123 Newgate st
Horne Wm. & Jas. jun. coal & coke merchs. Falcon wf. Bankside
Horne Benjamin W. wharfinger, &c. see Chaplin & Horne
Horne Charles, silk warehouse, see Winkworth & Horne
Horne Edgar, auctioneer, see Eversfield & Horne
Horne Edward, teadealer, 2 Frederick place, Old Kent road
Horne Elizabeth (Mrs.), beer retailer, Church st. Hackney
Horne George, cornfactor, see Gillies & Horne
Horne Henry, cooper, 48 St. Mary Axe
Horne Henry, chandler's shop, 10 Bride st. Liverpool road
Horne James, beer retailer, 24 Crown row, Walworth road
Horne Jas. hatter, 111 Tottenham ct. rd. & 1 Wellingtn. st. Lon. br
Horne James, upholsterer, & undertaker, 16 Foley pl. Portld. pl
Horne John, library & newspaper office, 19 Leicester square
Horne Joseph, coal merchant, 28 Barbican
Horne Joseph, painter & paper hanger, 28 Barbican
Horne Mary (Miss), perfumer, 123 Edgware rd. Marylebone
Horne Robert, oil & colorman, 73 Newington causeway
Horne Robert, paper stainer, see Jeffrey, Wise & Horne
Horne Swithin, butcher, 9 Munster st. Regent's park
Horne Thomas, silver, seal, copperplate & wood engraver, & linen manufacturers' stamp cutter, 2 Thanet pl. Strand
Horne Thomas, grocer, 124 Edgware rd. Marylebone
Horne Thomas, hairdresser, 47 Gibson st. Waterloo road
Horne Thomas, tracing paper manufr. 2 Thanet pl. Strand
Horne Wm. builder, 60 Poplar High st
Horne Wm. boot & shoe maker, 8 Richmond st. Leicester sq
Horne Wm. carpenter & undtk. 34 New Montague st. Spitalfi
Horne Wm. plumber, 9 Blossom st. Norton folgate
Horne Wm. watch & clock maker, 114 St. George st
Horne Wm. M. booksllr. & newsagt. 28 Skinner st. Somers town
Horneman Fredk. Edwd. assist. sec. to the Society for Relieving Foreigners in Distress, 10 Finsbury chamb. London wall
Horner & Sons, drug merchants, 20 Bucklersbury
Horner Catherine M. (Mrs.), *Grapes* P.H. 177 Borough High st
Horner Charles, silk plush manufctr. see Reid & Horner
Horner Edwd. *Fountain tav.* P.H. 67 St. George's rd. Southwk
Horner Elizh. (Mrs.), fruiterer, 22 Lit. Guilford st. Bruns. sq
Horner Geo. ornamental painter, &c. 53 Rathbone pl. Oxfd st
Horner Harriet (Mrs.), baker, 110 High st. Camden town
Horner Henry, woollen cloth factor, 32 Banner st. St. Luke's
Horner John, coal merchant, 28 Caroline st. Commerl. rd. east
Horner Michael, leather dresser, Spa road, Bermondsey
Horner Richard, carrier, *Elephant inn*, 112 Fore st. Cripplegt
Horner Robt. *Carpenters' Arms* P.H. 37 John st. Fitzroy sq
Horner Thos. painter & glazier, 15 Hart st. & 6 Bury pl. Bloomsby
Horner Wm. *Rutland Arms* P.H. Rutland st. Hampstead rd
Horner William, *Vauxhall tavern*, Vauxhall
Horner Wm. who. birmingh. & sheffield wa. 4 Copthall bldgs
Horner Wm. wholesale hosier, see Cox, Horner & Hogg
Hornfleck Henry, tailor, 32 Warwick st. Regent st
Horniblow Charles, carpenter, 1 Carlisle st. Lambeth
Horniblow Emma (Miss), tobacconist, 4 Lambeth Up. Marsh
Horniblow Geo. carpenter & undertaker 12½ Kennington cr
Hornidge Samuel Gwinnett, attorney, 16 Bloomsbury sq
Hornidge Thos. surveyor, 10 Mitre ct. chambers, Fleet st
Horning James, lodging house, 4 Torrington square
Horning Wm. Penny, grocer, 19 Queen's pl. Kennington rd
Hornsby James, baker, 1 Lower Belgrave st. Pimlico
Hornsby Jas. coal & corn merch. Ebury whf. Low. Belgrave pl
Hornsby Richard, hairdresser, 46 Chandos st. Strand
Hornzee George, bedstead maker, 2 Colchester st. Whitech
Horrex James, hosier & glover, 59 Albany st. Regent's park
Horrobin Henry, *Magpie* P.H. 12 New st. Bishopsgate
Horrocks John & Co. east india merchts. 9 Bread st. Cheapsi
Horrocks James, beer retailer, 21 Chapel place, Brompton
Horrocks John, undertaker, 7 Eliza place, Sadler's wells
Horrocks Joseph, paperstainer, 9 St. James pl. Hampstd. rd
Horrockses, Miller & Co. cotton manufacturers, 9 Bread st
Horry Sidney Calder, barrister, 126 Chancery lane
Horsburgh Andrew, rout furnisher, see Warder & Horsburgh
Horse Guards, Whitehall, hours of business 10 to 5
Horseley Iron Company (John Gandell, agt.), 11 Clement's lane, Lombard st
Horsey Charles James, staffordshire wareho. 84 Goswell rd
Horsey Henry, brazier & coppersm. 6 Bridge st. Southwark
Horsey Henry, brazier, 6 Bridge st. Southwark
Horsey John, grocer, &c. 4 Hopkins row, Westminster
Horsey Robert, carver & gilder, 6 New North st. Red Lion sq
Horsey Wm. cattle salesman, 8 West Smithfield
Horsfall Geo. dairyman, 32 Earl st. west, Edgware rd
Horsfall Thomas, steel pen maker, see Bishop & Horsfall
Horsfield James C. ironmonger, 131 Tooley st
Horsford Henry, baker, 78 St. George's rd. Southwark
Horsington James, tailor, 3 Marlborough rd. Chelsea
Horsley Charles, attorney, 2 Staple inn, Holborn
Horsley Geo. Sam. jun. baker, 6 King's Head row, O. Brompton
Horsley Geo. Sam. sen. baker, 10 Southampton st. Cambrwl
Horsley Hannah (Mrs.), beer retailer, 13 Flint st. Walworth
Horsley James Francis, baker, 4 Albion pl. Walworth rd
Horsley John, china warehouse, 47 Myddelton st. Clerknwell
Horsley Mary (Mrs.), dairy, 5 Albert pl. Hoxton Old town
Horsley Matthew, cabinet maker, 25 Sloane sq. Chelsea
Horsley Thos. Martin, law stationer & bookslr. 118 Chancery la
Horsley Wm. solicitor, 8 Bank chamb. & Mare st. Hackney
Horsman Ann (Mrs.), straw hat manfr. 38 Wardour st. Soho
Horsman George, tailor, 38 Wardour st. Soho
Horsman Godfrey, who. fishmong. see Sproston & Horsman
Horsman James, bookseller, &c. 9 Brownlow st. Bedford row
Horsman Wm. shoemaker, 16 Grenville st. Somers town
Horstman John, merchant, 26 Finsbury sq
Hort John Kempton, bootmaker, 5 Arbour ter. Commercial road east, & 12 Church la. Whitechapel High st
Horticultural Society (Alex Henderson, M.D. sec.; John Lindley, PH. D. vice sec.), 21 Regent st. Waterloo pl
Horton Elizh & Son, steam eng. boil. mak. 8 New Park st. Boro'
Horton Geo. Melville & Co. who. jewellers, 100 Hatton gdn
Horton & Grundy, curriers & saddlers' ironmongers, 64 Gt. Queen st. Lincoln's inn fields
Horton & Hart, hop & seed facts. Kentish bldgs. 94 Boro' Hi. st
Horton James & Joshua, jewellers, 80 Whitechapel High st
Horton Albert Augustus, tailor, 115 Mount st. Berkeley sq
Horton Benj. wine, spirit & provision mer. 23 Mincing la
Horton Edward, grocer & cheesemonger, Whitehorse la. Stepny
Horton Edward John, attorney, 11 Furnival's inn, Holborn
Horton Emily (Mrs.), milliner, 50 Old Compton st. Soho
Horton John, carpenter & builder, 8 South st. Manchest. sq

Horton John, linendraper, 13 Finsbury pavement
Horton John, painter & glazier, 50 Old Compton st. Soho
Horton John, who. umbrella ma. see Waddington & Horton
Horton Joseph, brush maker & turner, 100 St. John st. rd
Horton Joseph, locksmith & bellhangr.1 Sash ct. Finsbury sq
Horton Joseph, steam engine boiler & gasometer maker, chain cable & iron merchant, 16 Wharf road, Wenlock basin, & at Brierly hill, Staffordshire
Horton Reuben, shell fishmonger, 11 & 17 Tyler st. Regent st
Horton Richard, carpenter, 25 Cumberland st. Hackney rd
Horton Thomas, butcher, 124 Lambeth Lower marsh
Horton Thomas, grocer, 1 Calcutta pl. East India rd. Poplar
Horton Thomas, tailor, &c. 6 Green st. Grosvenor square
Horton Thomas, trunkmaker, 69 Hackney road
Horton Wm. carpenter, 2 Keppel mews north, Russell sq
Horton Wm. beer retailer, 1 Prior pl. East st. Walworth
Horton William, grocer, 51 Charlotte st. Whitechapel
Horton William, harness plater, 7 Lisle st. Leicester sq
Horwell John, cheesemonger, 58 Lambeth Lower marsh
Horwell Wm. cheesemonger, 19 Lambeth Lower marsh
Horwill Abraham, umbrella maker, 36 Mitre st. Aldgate
Horwill Thomas, baker, 11 Silver st. Wood st
Horwitz Morrice, slopseller, 94 Upper East Smithfield
Horwood & Griffin, solicitors, 27 Austinfriars
Horwood & Hawkins, accountants, 31 St. Swithin's lane
Horwood & Watkins, cop.pl.print.115 Up.Seymour st.Eust.sq
Horwood Chas. omnibus prop. High st. Kensington grav. pits
Horwood Charles, tobacconist, High st. Notting hill
Horwood George, bootmaker, 7 Duke st. Lincoln's inn fields
Horwood George, slater, 17 Swan st. Trinity sq. Borough
Horwood Hen. Thos. coffee rms. 7 Up. Penton st. Pentonville
Horwood John, butcher, 23 Chapel st. Somers town
Horwood Martha (Mrs.), meat saleswoman, 1 Newgate mrkt
Horwood Robert, fruiterer, 1 Elizabeth st. south, Pimlico
Horwood Samuel, painter, 4 Upp. Dorset st. Bryanstone sq
Horwood Thomas, conveyancer, 1 New court, Temple
Horwood Thomas, grocer, &c. 69 Newington causeway
Horwood Thos. Alfred, carcase butcher, 26 Newgate market
Horwood Thos. Jas. solicitor, 4 Gt. Winchester st. Old Broad st
Horwood Wm. bookseller & stationer, 36 Ludgate st
Horwood William, grocer, &c. 59 High st. Portland town
Hosack John, barrister, 6 King's Bench walk, Temple
Hose William, oil & colorman, 4 Russell place, Old Kent rd
Hosegood John, tailor, 82 Waterloo road
Hosier Abel, bricklayer, 31 Upp. Cornwall st. St. George's ea
Hosier Edwd. marine store dealer, 4 Charlton st. Somers tn
Hosier John, coffee rooms, 23 Grosvenor mews, Grosvenor st
Hoskin Eliza (Mrs.), ladies' sch. 30 Manchester st. Gr.'s i. rd
Hoskin John, dining rooms, 34 Hampstead road
Hoskin Richd. cook & confectioner, 117 Albany st. Regt. pk
Hosking Eliza (Miss), tobacconist, 49 Bridge road, Lambeth
Hosking John, gen. com. agt. 25 Clement's la. King William st
Hosking John, tailor, 108 Crawford st. Portman square
Hosking John, millwright & engineer, 25 Webber st. New cut
Hosking John, jun, cheesemonger, 109 Crawford st
Hosking Nicholas, trunk maker, 306, 341 & 342 Oxford st
Hosking Richard, boot & shoe maker, 91 Paul st. Finsbury
Hosking William, architect & civil engineer, 23 Woburn sq
Hoskings Charles, baker, 21 Stepney causeway
Hoskings Mary (Mrs.), corset maker, 63 High st. Camden tn
Hosking Geo. Alex. barrister, 9 King's Bench walk, Temple
Hoskins James, grocer, &c. 60 Grove st. Camden town
Hoskins Richard, waggon off. One Swan yard, Bishopsgate
Hoskins Samuel, carpenter, 32 Wych st. Drury lane
Hoskins Samuel, dairy, 9 Old Paradise row, Islington green
Hoskins Thos. *George IV.* P.H. 14 Berner's st. Commerl. rd. ea
Hoskins Williams, coal merchant, see Strong & Hoskins
Hoskins Wm. Hen. tobacconist, 96 Middlx. st. Aldgate Hi. st
Hospital for Consumption & Diseases of the Chest (Osborn P. Cross, sec.), Fulham road, Brompton; Smith st. Chelsea; & 20 Gt. Marlboro' st
Hospital for Diseases of Women (E. Futvoy, sec.) 16 Red Lion sq
Hossack John & Son, mercr. & sail cloth fac. 27 St. Mary at hill
Hotchkin William L. ship & insurance broker & customhouse agent, 3 East India chambers, Leadenhall st
Hotchkiss Jane (Mrs.), beer retailer, 19 St. George st
Hotchkiss John, jun. woollen draper, 48 Blackfriars road
Hotchkiss John, *Running Horses* P.H. 42 Blackfriars rd
Hotson Wm. tailor, &c. 8 Bray's bldgs. Lower rd. Islington
Hottell Thomas, dairy, 21 Gloucester ter. Vauxhall bdg. rd
Hotten John, tailor, 54 St. John st. Smithfield
Hotten Wm. carpent. & undertaker, 45 St. John's sq. Clerknwl
Houbigant Chardin, perfumer & glover, 216 Regent st
Houchin Richd. & Co. engineers & tool ma. 35 Craven st. City rd
Hough Charles B. bootmaker, 7 High st. Newington butts
Hough Eleanor & Maria, coffee rooms, 160 Alfred pl. Watrl. rd
Hough Henry, tailor, 76 Mount st. Berkeley square
Hough James, furn. ironmong. 3 Portsdown ter. Kilburn gate
Hough Samuel, smith & bellhngr. 4 Brownlow mews, Gry's. in. la
Hough Wm. *Anchor & Crown* P.H. 28 Gt. Garden st. Whitech
Hough William, jeweller, 9 George's row, City road
Hough William Rayson, carpenter, 37 Fleet lane, Old Bailey
Houghton, Burnett & Co. merchants, 78 Mark lane
Houghton, Cleveland & Houghton, mers. 41 Threadneedle st
Houghton (Lucas) & Co. fancy stationers, 30 Poultry, & law stationers, 4 Chapel place, Poultry
Houghton, Cleveland & Houghton, merch. 41 Threadneedle st
Houghton Jas. & Son, oil merchants, 27 Bartholomew close
Houghton & Massey, commission agents & warehousemen, 44 Friday st. Cheapside
Houghton Ann (Mrs.), milliner, 4 Bouverie st. Fleet st
Houghton Charles, cabinet brass founder, ironmonger & general nail agent, 44 Farringdon st. & 58 Dudley grove, Paddington green
Houghton George, glass shade & window glass warehouse, 89 High Holborn, see Claudet & Houghton
Houghton Henry, upholsterer, 65 Great Dover road
Houghton James, bookseller & stationer, 98 Jermyn st
Houghton James George, furrier, Mare st. Hackney
Houghton James Robert, surgeon, 2 Earl st. Blackfriars
Houghton John, draper, see Taylor & Houghton
Houghton Joseph, tailor, 27 Low. Smith st. Northampton sq
Houghton Joseph, cheesemonger, 32 Gt. Suffolk st. Borough
Houghton Michael Richd. straw hat ma. 40 Whitechapel rd
Houghton Richard, currier, 3 Tyer's gateway, Bermndsy. st
Houghton Richard, shipwright, 51 Robin Hood la. Poplar
Houghton Thos. boot & shoe maker, 5 Blenheim ter. Chelsea
Houghton Thos. cop. plate printr. 23 Charles st. Hatton grd
Houghton Thos. paper hanger, 32 Marshall st. London road
Houghton Thos. window glass cut. 47 Cannon st. Rtclif. hiway
Houghton Wm. attorney, see Badham, Houghton & Mayhew
Houghton Wm. milliner & haberdasher, 49 Mount st. Lambh
Houghton Wm. stationer, bookseller, &c. 162 New Bond st
Houghton William Harmer, tailor, 20 Lime st. City
Hould & Challis, hatters & outftrs. 18 Change all. Cornhill
Hould Richard, teadealer & grocer, 5 Road side, Mile end rd
Houlder Wm. glass & lead wa. 3 Church st. St. Saviour's, Boro
Houlderness & Morgan, sheep salesmen, 41 West Smithfield
Houldin Chas. ivory turner, 8 Wilson st. Finsbury
Houle Josiah, architect, Warwick court. Holborn
Houlgate Henry, clothes salesman, 81 London road, Sthwk
Houle Daniel & Chas. silversmiths, 24 Red Lion st. Clerknwl
Houliston Alexander, confectioner, 8 Park ter. Regent's park
Houliston James, optician, 33 New Bond st
Houlston & Stoneman, booksel. & publish. 65 Paternoster row
Houlston Ann (Mrs.), fishmonger, 7 Sydney pl. Kg.'s rd. Chels
Houlton Joseph & Son, surgeons, 87 Lisson grove north
Houlton Richd. *Bricklayers' Arms* P.H. Lewisham rd. Dptf
Hounsom Edward, oilman, 22 Cowper st. City road
Housden Jas. brush manfr. 27 & 13 Holles st Cavendish sq
Housden John, carpenter, 44 Freeschool st. Horselydown
Housdon Jas. linendraper & hosier, 6 High st. Camberwell
Hounsell, Schenk & Hounsell, merchants, 4 Vine st. Minories, & St. John's, Newfoundland
House & Clark, skeinsilk dyers, Barbers yd. Brown's la. Spitalfds
House Edwd. carpenter & undertak. 20 Mount st. Lambeth
House Geo. Rd. fancy paper stainer, 31 Fort st. Spitalfields
House Geo. Washington, baby linen wa. 55 St. Paul's ch. yd
House James, cheesemonger, 36 Munster st. Regent's park
House Jas. tailor, 18 Church st. Queen's elms, Chelsea
House John, windowblind mak. 35 Cannon st. St. Geo.'s ea
House Wm. inkstand maker, 1 Victoria ter. Up. Grange rd
House of Lords Committee rooms, 32 Abingdon st. Westminstr
Housego Jacob, butcher, 3 Bathurst st. Sussex sq. Hyde park, & 26 Dudley grove, Harrow road
Housego William, butcher, 4 Broadway, Westminster
Houseless Poor Committee Society (John Sard, secretary), 75 Old Broad st. City, & 58 Westmoreland place, City rd
Houseman Robt. *Horse & Gr.* P.H. 21 St. Martin's st. Leicstr. sq
Houshold Thos. cabinet ma. 14 Crombie's row, Coml. rd. east
Housley Charles, surgeon, see Wadsworth & Housley
Housley Geo. ready made linen wa. see Nicholls & Housley
Housley Samuel, tailor, see Stulz, Housley & Wain
Houson Joseph, attorney, 19 Lincoln's inn fields
Houston Henry, cassimere manfr. see Brittain & Houston
Houston John, coach painter, 31 Cleveland st. Fitzroy sq
Houston Saml. packer & cloth merchant, 15 Gt. St. Helen's
Houston William, plasterer, 18 Praed st. Paddington
Hovell Wm. fruiterer, 12 Clark's pl. Bagnigge wells road
Hovenden John Eykyn, sec. to Tithe Com. 9 Somerset place
Hovenden Robt. who. perfumer, 57 & 58 Crown st. Finsbury
Hover James, paper stainer, 17 Shepherd's market, Mayfair

Hover William, paper stainer,173 Drury lane
Hovey Fdk. Wm. *Three Tuns* P.H. Butcher row, Deptford
Hovil Rd. & Sons, merchts. Colonial chambs. 12 Crutchedfrs
How Thos.& Co. wholes. teadealers, 233 & 234 Boro' High st
How Thomas & Son, tailors, 32 Berwick st. Soho
How Edwd. *Angel & Crown* P.H. 112 Green st. Bethnal gr
How Henry, baker, 2 Bride's pas. & 5 Salisbury ct. Fleet st
How Henry, *Star* P.H. 14 Old Bailey
How John, baker, 35 Leather lane, Holborn
How John Robert, baker, 64 Theobalds road
How Jeremiah, publisher, 132 Fleet st
How Mary Ann (Mrs.), *Queen's Head* P.H.77 HoxtonOld tn
How Thomas, corndealer, 90 St. John st. Clerkenwell
How Thomas, grocer & teadealer, see Brocksopp, How & Co
HowardCharlotte & AnnaS.(Misses),milliners,218 Shoredtch
Howard & Coleman, wholesale druggists, 90 & 91 Cannon st
Howard Edwin B. & Co. merchants & insurance brokers, 3 Abchurch lane, City, & Lloyd's
Howard & Hawksworth, sheffi. pl. war.5 Salisbury st.Strand
HowardJames Peter&Co. drug & colonial brokers, 39 Lime st
Howard John & Saml. C. tailors, 38 Nicholas la. Lombard st
Howard,Ravenhill&Co.King&Queen ironworks,Rotherhithe
Howard Richard & Son,builders, 14 Bridge ho. pl.Newing.ca
Howard Robert & Co. wholesale manufacturers of tin, iron, japanned & copper wares, copper, tinplate & zinc merchants, 115 Old st. St. Luke's
Howard Robert & Co.manfctrs. of patent lamps,& patentees of the improved revolving convex iron safety shutters, revolving perforated blinds, shutter blinds, &c. &c. 115 Old st. St. Luke's
Howard Samuel & Co. engineers, 43 Cornhill
Howard ThomasBurton & Son,solicitors,7Norfolk st.Strand
Howard Wm.&Ann,*Crooked Billet* P.H.37Wych st. Strand
Howard Wm. & Chas. stockbroks. 12 Copthall ct.Throgm.st
Howards' & Kent, manufacturing chemists, Stratford
Howard Abraham, conveyancer, see Boodle & Co
Howard Alfred, solicitor, see Hindman & Howard
HowardAnna(Mrs),*Coach& Horses* P.H. 4 Dover st.Piccadly
Howard Charles, foreign wine merchant, 70 Gt. Tower st
Howard Charles, stockbroker, 6 Barnard's inn, Holborn
Howard Daniel, corn mercht. Whitcombe st. Haymarket
Howard Ebenezer, pastrycook & baker,62 Fore st. Cripplegt
Howard Ebenezer, poultry salesman, Leadenhall market
Howard Eliza(Mrs.),straw bonnet ma.20Panton st.Haymkt
Howard Elizabeth (Mrs.),plumber, &c. 1 Church st.Cmbrwl
Howard Esther (Mrs.), bookseller, 33 Gray's inn lane
Howard Esther(Miss),straw hatma. 40 Chalton st. Somrs.tn
Howard Frederick, pork butcher, 4 Baker's rw.Walworth rd
Howard George, appraiser, 19 Leader st. Chelsea
Howard George, *Roebuck* P.H. 53 Leader st. Chelsea
Howard Geo. Sam. *Salisbury Arms* P.H.9Bear st.Leicstr.sq
Howard George Rayner, *Grapes* P.H. 26 Great Marlboro' st
Howard Henry, R.A. artist, 5 Newman st. Oxford st
Howard Henry, grocer & cheesemngr. 30 Clerkenwell green
Howard Henry, ironmonger, 30 New st. Dorset square
Howard Henry, oil & italian wareh. 25 Bridge st.Westminstr
Howard Henry, plate glass manfr. 4 Railway pl. Fench. st
Howard Henry, tailor, 34 Goswell road, west side
Howard Howard, cheesemonger, 284 Oxford street
Howard James, bookseller, 6 Lamb place, Kingsland road
Howard James,*Jacob's Well* P.H.23Wellst. Mile end,Newtn
Howard James, coffee rooms, 26 Stonecutter st. Shoe lane
Howard James, hat block turner, 17 New Park st. Boro'
Howard John, bootmaker, 14 Keen's row, Walworth road
Howard John, builder, 97 Church st. Shoreditch
Howard John, carman, 2 Russell st. Lower Rotherhithe
Howard John, carpenter & undertaker, 2 Bethnal green rd
Howard John, fishmonger, 34 Threadneedle st
Howard John, fishmonger, 6 Darkhouse lane, Billingsgate
Howard John, porkman, 4 Glo'ster pl. East st. Walworth rd
Howard John, *Queen's Head* P.H.6Darkhouse la.Billingsgt
Howard John William, solicitor, 69 Fenchurch st
Howard Jonathan, solicitor, see Lacey, Howard & Charlton
Howard Joseph, grocer, &c. 4 Upper Park pl. Dorset sq
Howard Joseph, grocer, &c. 66 Castle st. east, Oxford st
Howard Joseph, teadealer, 24 Gower place, Euston square
Howard Peter, butcher, 24 King st. Lower rd. Islington
Howard Richard, appraiser & ho.agt.4Radcliffe ter.Gswl.rd
Howard Richard, bootmaker, 6 Old street road
Howard Richard,*St. Helena tavern*, Lower rd.Rotherhithe
Howard hon. Richard Edwd. barrister, 3 Garden ct. Temple
Howard Robert, plumber, 11 Tysoe st. Spafields
Howard Robert, shoemaker, 5 St. Agnes ter. Tabernacle sq
Howard Robert, surgeon, 6 Upper Gloucester st. Dorset sq
Howard Samuel, manufacturer of artificial flowers, feathers, rouches & mourning collars, &c. 66 Wood st
Howard Samuel, coal merchant, 25 North st. Manchester sq
Howard Samuel, hemp, flax&sacking merchant, 38 Mark la
Howard Samuel, wine cooper, 11 Gilbert st. Grosvenor sq
Howard Sarah (Miss), artist, 5 Newman st. Oxford st
Howard Stanley, jun. stock broker, Stock exchange
Howard Thomas, bricklayer & builder,45 Paddington st
Howard Thomas, furniture brkr. 23&24 Holles st.Clare mk
Howard Thos.civil engin.King&Queen ironwrk.258Rothrhth
Howard Thos. grocer & teadealer, 71 East st. Manchester sq
Howard Thomas, lime & cement merchant, 34 Wharf, City road basin, & at Canal road, Kingsland road
Howard Thomas, registrar, 29 Green st. Bethnal green
Howard Thomas, russia mat & corn mer. 28 Gainsford st
Howard Thomas, surgeon dentist, 52 Fleet st
HowardThomasSaml.butcher,13Bartholomew ter.St.Luke's
Howard Wm.architect & surv.7 Newmarket ter.Cambdg.hth
Howard Wm. brushmaker, 23 Gt. Russell st. Bloomsbury
Howard Wm. carpenter, &c. 48 Bedford st. Covent garden
Howard Wm. *Crooked Billet* P.H. 37 Wych st. Strand
Howard Wm. grocer,62 Paradise row, Chelsea
Howard Wm. *Old King's Head* P.H. Marsham st. & 35 Horseferry road, Westminster
Howard Wm. pocketbook & work box maker,62&63Barbican
Howard Wm. *SekfordeArms* P.H.34|Sekforde st.Clerknwell
Howard Wm. typefounder, Queen's Head yd.73½Gt.Queen st
Howard Wm. Chas. baker, 24 Russell st. Bermondsey
Howard Wm.Hen.baker&confec.14 Prospect pl.Kingsld. rd
Howarth Geo.dlr.inarmycuttings,27 Gt.Sutton st.Clerknwell
Howarth John,chemist,22Mount pleasant, Gray's inn lane
Howchin Wm. *Private hotel*, 10 Dover st. Piccadilly
Howcroft Anthony,mile end nursery, Bow road
Howden Alexander, ship & general agent & insurance broker 102 Leadenhall st
Howden Gidley, inventor & patentee of hot air dispensers & foul air extractors, & furnaces for ovens, 15 Pump row, Old st. road
Howden Wm. fruiterer, 76 Stanhope st. Hampstead rd
Howe & Hillier, farriers, 9 King'sArms yard, Lower Whitecross st. & One Swan yard, Bishopsgate without
Howe & Pigeon, cowkeepers, King st. Rotherhithe wall
Howe & Sons, wine & brandy merchants, 4 St.Dunstan's hill
Howe & Wilcox, law stationers,2 Serle's pl. Carey st
Howe Chas. hat block maker, 81 Redcross st. Borough
Howe Daniel, tailor, 13 Cloak lane,City
Howe Edw. *Horse Shoe & Magpie* P.H. 21 Fetter lane
Howe Elizabeth(Miss),milliner,&c.34 UpperEaton st.Pimlco
Howe Frances (Mrs.),*Globe tavern*,Brunswickst.Blackwall
Howe George, engineer, 119 Great Guildford st. Borough
Howe George, tailor, 24 Seymour st. Euston square
Howe Hannah(Mrs.), potato dealer,South row,Covent gardn
Howe John, bookbinder, 7 Upper Marylebone st.Portland pl
Howe John, bricklayer & plumber, 15 Bridge st. Southwark
Howe John, dentist, 9 Eastcheap
Howe John, grocer, &c. 8 White st. Borough
Howe John, window blind maker, 11 Brompton road
Howe Joseph,chandler's shop,5&6Cross la.Newton st.Holbrn
Howe Richard, florist, 3 Stangate st. Lambeth
Howe Sarah (Mrs.), fishmonger, 2 Penton st. Pentonville
Howe William, coach broker, 32 Cobourg pl. Borough rd
Howe William, shoemaker, 2 Orchard pl. Kingsland rd
Howe Wm. tinplate worker,32 Norfolk st. Middlesex hosptl
Howell & James&Co. warehousemen,9Regent st.Waterloo pl
Howell John & Co. patent malt roasters, Upper Fore st. Lambeth, & Queenhithe wharf, Upper Thames st
Howell John & Son, hosrs.glovrs.&shirtmaks.76Aldergate st
Howell & Panzetta, bootmakers, 141 New Bond st
Howell Wm. & Francis, grocers, 25 East st. Walworth rd
Howell Ann (Mrs.), beer shop, 2 West st. Somers town
Howell Benj. gold lace weav.12Page st.Holywell st.Westmr
Howell Benjamin, butcher, 1 William st. Lisson grove
Howell Charles, surgeon, see Marsh & Howell
Howell Esther(Mrs.),baker,12Church st.Cheyne wk.Chelsea
Howell Geo. slop seller, sou'wester & oiled dress manufacturer, Hermitage stairs, 8 & 9 Wapping
Howell George, tobacconist, 12 Beauchamp st. Holborn
Howell Geo.H.sec.to *VanDieman'sLd.Co.*55O.Broad st.Cty
Howell GeorgeHenry,grocer,5 President st. east,Goswell rd
Howell Harcourt, painter, 7 Howland st. Fitzroy sq
Howell Henry, china warehouse, 11 Norris st. Haymarket
Howell Henry, glass & chinaman, 5 Little New st. Shoe la
Howell Henry, grocer, 28 Carburton st. Fitzroy sq
Howell Henry, plumber, 1 George st. Grosvenor square
Howell Henry, tailor, 49 Marsham st. Westminster
Howell James, architect & surveyor, 1 Vincent sq. Westmr
Howell James, fruiterer, 1 Mount row, Liverpool road
Howell James, grocer, 10 Southampton st. Fitzroy sq

Howell James, pawnbroker, 49 Beech st. Barbican
Howell James, plumber & glazier, 4 Great Tower st. City
Howell James, stationer, 5 Albany st. Regent's park
Howell James, vellum binder, 1 West st. West Smithfield
Howell John, attorney, 24 Bernard st. Russell square
Howell John, attorney, 27 King st. Cheapside
Howell John, grocer, 89 East st. Manchester square
Howell John, *Hand in Hand* P.H. 57 High Holborn
Howell John, *Hope tap*, 23 Ivy lane, Newgate st
Howell John, solicitor, 30 Lincoln's inn fields
Howell John, warehouseman, see Ellis, Everington & Co
Howell Joseph, surgeon, 8 Bridge st. Southwark
Howell Margaret (Mrs.), milliner, 304 Regent st
Howell Matilda (Mrs.), chandler's shop, 8 Collier st. Pentnvle
Howell Mary (Mrs.), butcher, 7 Southampton st. Cambrwl.rd
Howell Richard, haberdasher, 30 South Audley st
Howell Richard, linendraper, 79 Gracechurch st
Howell Robert, marine store dlr. 54 Gt. Guildford st. Boro'
Howell Sarah (Mrs.), brazier, 58 Gt. James st. Lisson grove
Howell Sarah (Mrs.), china & glass seller, &c. 88 Cannon st
Howell Sydney, architect & surveyor, Middle Scotland yard
Howell Thomas, chemist, 41 Dowgate hill
Howell Thos. *Dolly's chop ho.* Queen's hd.pas. Paternos.rw
Howell Thomas, jun. army packer, see Hayter & Howell
Howell Walter, wine & spirit merchant, sole consignee of Jersey brandy, 17 Water lane, Tower st
Howell Wm. cheesemonger, 53 Gt. Windmill st. Haymarket
Howell Wm. coachmaker, 7 Allsop place, Regent's park
Howell Wm. coachsmith, &c. 69 Berwick st. Soho
Howell Wm. *Fleece* P.H. 16 Marsham st. Westminster
Howell Wm. glass & chinaman, 30 Stonecutter st. Shoe lane
Howell Wm. greengrocer, 2 Charles pl. East st. Walworth
Howell Wm. grocer, 25 East st. Walworth road
Howell Wm. potato salesman, 10 Park st. Borough
Howell Wm. stationer, 4 Corbet court, Gracechurch st
Howell Wm. tailor, 5 Carburton st. Portland road
Howell Wm. timbermercht. Bridge wf. Bridge rd. Battersea
Howell Wm. Augustus, ironmonger, 45 Albany st. Regent'spk
Howell Wm. Lockwood, solicitor, vestry clerk of St. George, Middx. & clerk to commis. of pavement, 40 St. George st
Howell William May, colonial broker, 1 Little Tower st
Howells Thos. linendraper, 19 Park place, Kennington cross
Howes & Co. newspaper agents, 7 Thavies inn, Holborn
Howes & Edwards, wine & spirit brokers, 26 Mincing lane
Howes (Groome) & Co. agents to Alexander Hadden & Sons of Aberdeen, carpet manufacturers, worsted spinners & hosiers, 1 Oat lane, Noble st. Wood st. Cheapside
Howes & Hart, india & british shawl warehouse, 60 Fleet st
Howes Edward, barrister, 1 Old square, Lincoln's inn
Howes George, wine merchant, 7 Church st. Paddington
Howes Henry, butcher, 8 Brooke's market, Holborn
Howes Jas. bonnet presser, 54 Brittania rw. Lr. st. Islingtn
Howes James, leather seller, 31 Chiswell st. Finsbury
Howes John, bootmaker, Thornton pl. York st. Portman sq
Howes John, confectioner, 75 Welbeck st. Cavendish sq
Howes John, livery stables, 161 Southwark bridge road
Howes Mary Ann (Mrs.), haberdasher, 49 Whitechapel road
Howes Sarah (Mrs.), linendraper, &c. 2 New King st. Deptford
Howes William, builder, 41 Hart st. Covent garden
Howes Wm. hairdresser, 8 Barking church yard, Gt. Tower st
Howes Wm. Henry, wine & spirit broker, 26 Mincing lane
Howes Wm. S. *Princess Charlotte* P.H. Swallow place, & Princes st. Hanover square
Howett Jsph. Chas. architect, surveyor & valuer, 1 Walbrook
Howgate John, tea dlr. & grocer, 9 Tavistock st. Bedford sq
Howgill Matthew, ship chandler, 173 Tooley st. Borough
Howgrave Francis, grocer, 20 Cirencester pl. Fitzroy sq
Howgrave Mary (Mrs.), coal merchant, Milford wharf, Milford lane, Strand, & 4 Belinda cottages, Canonbury square
Howick Henry, *George* P.H. 23 Stoney st. Borough market
Howie Mary (Mrs.), fruit saleswoman, Spitalfields market
Howis & Masson, oil & italian warehouse, 216 Piccadilly
Howitt, Matthew & Co. warehsemn. 227 to 229 Hi. Holborn
Howitt Benjamin & Co. linendrapers, 111 & 112 Edgware rd
Howitt Enoch D. surgeon, 5 Apollo bdgs. so. East st. Walwth
Howitt Henry, woollen & manchester warehsmn. 87 Snowhill
Howitt John Rt. coal merchant, 19 Wheeler st. Spitalfields
Howitt Robt. charcoal mer. 202 Up. Whitecross st. St. Luke's
Howitt Robt. coal & corn merchant, 95 Aldersgate st
Howitt Robt. undertaker, 71 Leonard st. Shoreditch
Howkins Wm. orange merchant, 10 Botolph lane, Thames st
Howkins Wm. who. fancy stationer, 31 Charles sq. Hoxton
Howland John, baker, 32 Marylebone lane, Oxford st
Howle Joseph, tailor, &c. 8 Conduit st. Regent st
Howlet Henry, attorney, 18 Bartlett's buildings, Holborn
Howlett Elizabeth & Son, printers, 10 Frith st. Soho
Howlett Henry, surgeon, 18 Cambridge ter. Edgware rd
Howlett James, cabinet maker, 6 Saville place, Mile end road
Howlett James Blott, butcher, Church st. Hackney
Howlett John, bricklayer, 28 Brook st. Ratcliff
Howlett Philip G. chemist & druggist, 9 Bruton st. Brkly.sq
Howlett Rd. plumber & ho. agt. 3 Brecknock pl. Camden new tn
Howlett William, carpenter, Cobourgh road, Old Kent road
Howling John, china & glass dealer, 72 Poplar High st
Howling Thomas, bootmaker, 165 Poplar High st
Howorth Mary (Miss), milliner, 68 Hackney road
Howroyd John R. & Co. coachmakers, 36 St. Martin's lane
Howroyd Robert, coffee & chop house, 117 Newgate st
Hows Alfred Coy, pork butcher, 26 Shadwell High st
Hows Edmund Jones, glass & china dlr. Deptford High st
Hows Edmund Jones, porkman, Broadway, Deptford
Hows George, tobacconist, 10 Deptford bridge
Hows William, pawnbroker, 99 Kingsland road
Howse Danl. boot & shoe maker, 92 Redcross st. Borough
Howse George, *Railway hotel*, Nine Elms, Vauxhall
Howse Mary (Mrs.), *Nag's Head* P.H. 80 Gray's inn lane
Howse Robert, grocer & british wine maker, 69½ Strand
Howse Thomas, woollen warhm. see Barber, Howse & Davis
Howse Wm. chemist & sodawater ma. 16 Tichborne st. Haymarkt
Howson Benjamin, stationer & printer, 40 Gresham st
Hoxley Wm. M.D. lunatic asylum, London ho. London la. Hckny
Hoy James, *Maidenhead* P.H. 20 Windmill st. Finsbury
Hoy Joseph, greengrocer, 14 Barnet st. Hackney rd
Hoy Michael, skinner, 4 White st. Borough
Hoy Thomas, plumber, painter, &c. 37 Penton st. Pentonville
Hoyer Jacob, merchant, see Boyson & Hoyer
Hoyland Charles Wm. surgeon, 23 York place, Portman sq
Hoyle & Hanson, woollen warehousemen, 88 Wood st
Hoyle Thomas & Sons, calico printers, 9 Old Jewry
Hoyle Benjamin, staymaker, 1 Camberwell High st
Hoyle David, watchmaker, Pomeroy st. Old Kent rd
Hoystrop & Exton, grocers, 3 New Chapel pl. Kentish town
Hoyte Wm. dairyman, 64 White Lion st. Pentonville
Hozier James, merchant, Nth. & Sth. American coffee house
Hubback John, barrister, 5 New square, Lincoln's inn
Hubback Richard, tallow chandler, 103 Broad st. Ratcliff
Hubbard & Burbidge, land & estate agents, surveyors, auctioneers & valuers, 2 Moorgate st. City
Hubbard John & Co. russia merchts. 3 Newman's ct. Cornhill
Hubbard John A. & Son, merchants, 20 Harp lane, Tower st
Hubbard Alexander, furniture broker, Little Chelsea
Hubbard Ann (Mrs.), stationer, 3 Assembly pl. Kennington
Hubbard Edward, clockmaker, 33 Gibson st. Waterloo rd
Hubbard Edward, hat dyer, 35 Snow's fields, Bermondsey
Hubbard Eliza (Mrs.), straw hat maker, Camberwell green
Hubbard Elizabeth (Miss), staymaker, Church st. Hackney
Hubbard Geo. bonnet shape ma. 86 Devonshire st. Lisson gr
Hubbard Geo. silk mercer, see Sewell, Evans, Hubbard & Co
Hubbard George, tobacconist, 30 Windmill st. Tottenham ct.rd
Hubbard Henry, fruiterer, 28 Windmill st. Tottenham ct. rd
Hubbard Henry, *White Lion* P.H. 14 Fleet la. Farringdon st
Hubbard Henry, plumber, Bow, Middlesex
Hubbard Hen. Saml. *Bull's Head* P.H. 148 Whitechap. High st
Hubbard Jeremiah, tobacconist, 21 Farringdon st
Hubbard John, dyer, Mare st. Hackney
Hubbard John, hop merchant, 120 Borough High st
Hubbard John, plumber, &c. 7 High st. Newington butts
Hubbard John Wm. tobacco, snuff, & cigar manfr. 4 Barbican
Hubbard Joseph John, solicitor, 1 Queen st. pl. Southwark bdg
Hubbard Mary Ann (Mrs.), confetion. 4 Qun's. Hd. rw. New. bts
Hubbard Robert, cowkeeper, 13 Stanhope terr. Hyde park
Hubbard Samuel, *Green Man* P.H. 1 Beaufort st. Chelsea
Hubbard Thomas, tailor, Camberwell green
Hubbard Thomas, watch case ma. 11 Ironmonger st. St. Luke's
Hubbard William, coffee rooms, 56 Castle st. Southwark
Hubbard Wm. confectioner, 1 Upper Dorset pl. Clapham rd
Hubbard Wm. meat salesman, 4 New Newgate market
Hubbard William, pastrycook, 6 Crown st. Finsbury
Hubbert John, tobacconist, 11 Newington causeway
Hubbert John, woolstpr. & mop ma. 18 & 19 Hull st. St. Luke's
Hubbert Samuel, bed & mattrass maker, 68 Old st
Hubble Benjamin, bricklayer, Garden row, Deptford
Hubble Hen. Ephm. *Star & Garter* P.H. 9 Arbour sq. Cmml. rdea
Hubbuck Thomas & Son, lead & color works, oil, pitch & tar merchants, white lead & varnish manufacturers, 115 Upper East Smithfield
Hube John, newsvender, 13 Holland st. Brixton road
Huber Daniel, baker, 158 Whitechapel road
Hubert Charles [from Paris] (successor to Le Saunier), gentlemen & ladies' french boot & shoe maker, 292 Regent st
Hubert James George, barge builder, Nine Elms, Vauxhall
Hubert John Henry, grocer, 4 Port place, Walworth common

Hubert Joseph, law stationer, 6 Cursitor st. Chancery lane
Hubert Julia (Mrs.), grocer, 168 Alfred pl. Waterloo road
Hubert Richard Wm. carpenter, 92 Chalton st. Somers town
Hubert Robt. Geo.W.tobacconist,3 Gt.Alie st. Goodman's fi
Hubert Samuel, builder, Mount gardens, Palace new road, Lambeth, & 23 Crosier st. Lambeth
Hubert Thomas, corn&coal merchant & lighterman,112 High Holborn, & Hungerford wharf,Strand ; office, 1 Great hall
Hubert Thos. Sam. lighterman & coal mer. 53 Millbank st
Hubes William, news agent, 5 Surrey pl. Wandsworth road
Huckell Robt. Whiten, stay & cor. mak. 6 Albert pl. City rd
Hucker Francis, chandler's shop, 7 Berwick st. Soho
Huckett Charles, carpenter, 1 Richmond st. St. Luke's
Huckin John, fishmonger, 93 Upper st. Islington
Huckin Wm. butcher, 39 Foley st. Portland place
Hucklebridge James, chemist, 103 Upper Ebury st.Pimlico
Hucklebridge Miranda (Miss), port.painter, 103Up.Ebury st
Hucks John J. & Co. resin & oil works, Princes st. Lambeth
Hucks George, cooper,37 Old Gravel lane, Wapping
Hucks John, sen. cooper, Princes st. Lambeth, & 8 Paradise st. Rotherhithe
Huckvale Harry,tea & coffee brokr. 9 Commercl. sale rooms
Huckvale Jonathan, butcher, 207 Blackfriars road
Hudd Thos.grocer&teadealer,53 Up. North pl. Gray's inn rd
Hudd Wm.Chas. *King's Arms& Hand*P.H.159Bermondseyst
Huddart Sir Joseph & Co. flat & round ropemakers, sailmakers, & power loom canvass manufacturers, 3 Crosby square, Bishopsgate, & Copenhagen place, Limehouse
Huddleston Jas. chair & cabinet ma. 6 Nassau st.Middlx.hos
Huddleston John Walter, barrister, 5 Inner Temple lane
Huddy Francis, rule manufact. 24 Red Lion st. Holborn
Huddy Mary (Miss), haberdasher, 111 Blackfriars road
Hude Dennis, plumber & glazier, 64 Milton st. Fore st
Hudson, Allen & Co. tailors, see Allen, Hudson & Co
Hudson & Falconer, regimental tailors, 124 New Bond st
Hudson John & Son, importers of leeches, 27 Castle st. Falcon square, & 11 Charlotte st. Hull
Hudson John & Son, porter merchts. 1 Griffin st. Shadwell
Hudson Joseph Hen. & Henry, cabinetma.28 Eldon st. Finsb
Hudson & Peek, pewterers, &c. 41 Fetter lane, Fleet st
Hudson Richd.&Wm.tailors & drapers, 9 Wilson st. Finsbury
Hudson William Bankes & Son, chemists, 27 Haymarket
HudsonWm.&John,who.statnrs.26Lambeth hill,Doctors com
Hudson's Bay Company(Archd.Barclay,sec.),4Fenchurch st
Hudson's Bay fur establishment (Charles Cook, acting proprietor), Argyll rooms, 246 Regent st
Hudson Anth.cheesemong.31 Brunswick Parade,Barnsby rd
Hudson Anthony, grocer & cheesemonger, 24 Bow High st
Hudson Benj. building material dlr. 40 Gt. Peter st.Westmr
Hudson Benjamin, bricklayer, 48 Carlisle st. Lambeth
Hudson Benjamin, *Marquis of Granby* P.H.10& 11Drury la
Hudson Charles, glass painter & stainer in the ancient manner, 12 John st. Pentonville
Hudson Elizth. (Mrs.), fancy repository, Church st. Hackney
Hudson Flavius, teadealer, 6 Baker's row, Walworth road
Hudson Franklin, surgeon, 24 Alexander sq. Brompton
Hudson Frederick, wine mer. 26 Lambeth hill,Up. Thames st
Hudson George, baker, 33 Paddington st. Marylebone
Hudson George Frederick, solicitor, 23 Bucklersbury
Hudson Henry, *Duke of Suffolk*P.H.64Brandon st.Walworth
Hudson Henry, news agent, 74½ Mark lane
Hudson James, butcher, Kensington gravel pits, High st
Hudson Jas.clk. sitter of Poultry Compter, 49 Basinghall st
Hudson John, blind maker, 34 George st. New Kent road
Hudson John, cattle salesman, 17 West Smithfield
Hudson John, clog manufacturer, 23 Featherstone st.City rd
Hudson Jon, house agent, 12 John st. Pentonville
Hudson John, lodging house, 1 Manchester buildings
Hudson John, glass & lead merch. 27 City rd. Finsbury sq
Hudson John, solicitor, 90 Queen st. Cheapside
Hudson John Barthol. coachma. 36 Wyndham st.Bryans. sq
Hudson John Godfrey, barrister, 5 Essex court, Temple
Hudson Joseph, plumber, 22 Abchurch lane, City
Hudson Joseph, smith, 7 Blandford mews, Manchester sq
Hudson Joseph,tobacconist to the royal family,132 Oxford st
Hudson Margaret (Mrs.), grocer,43Gt.Guildford st.Borough
Hudson Mary (Mrs.),boarding house,42 Bow lane,Cheapside
Hudson Mary Ann (Mrs.), butcher, 10 Turnmill st.Clrknwl
Hudson Octavius, draughtsman, 12 John st. Pentonville
Hudson Samuel, baker, 19 Little Earl st. Seven dials, & 113 High st. Marylebone
Hudson Thomas, barrister, 2 New square, Lincoln's inn
Hudson Thomas, chairmaker,21Little Wild st. Linc. inn flds
Hudson Thomas, dining rooms, 1 Shepherds mrkt. Mayfair
Hudson Thomas, human hair manufr. 18 Porter st. Soho
Hudson Thomas, lodging house, 11 South st. Grosvenor sq
Hudson Thomas, music seller, 6 Museum st. Bloomsbury
Hudson Thomas Bentley, solicitor, 4 Old Jewry
Hudson Thomas H. oil & italian wareh. 229 Blackfriars road
Hudson Walter,grocer&italian wa.16Crawford st.Portmn. sq
Hudson Wm. architect & surveyor, 19 Bennett's hill
Hudson Wm. billiard rooms, 43 Watling st. City
Hudson Wm. butcher, 24 Kingsland road
Hudson Wm. butcher, 13 Lower st. Islington
Hudson Wm. fruiterer, 5 Star st. Edgware road
Hudson Wm. *King's Arms* P.H. 61 Lower Thames st
Hudson Wm. ladies' shoemaker, 5 Commercial rd. Lambeth
Hudson Wm. solicitor, 2 Bloomsbury square
Hudson Wm. George, foreign agent, 13 King st. Cheapside
Hudson Wm. Thos. *Duke of Glo'ster* P.H. 79 Seabright st. Bethnal green road
Hudson William Thos. surgeon, &c. 61 South Audley st
Hudswell John, wax & wafer mak.5Three Crown sq. Borough
Hue Clement, physician, 9 Bedford square
Hue Thomas, baker, 2 Pont st. Belgrave square
Huett Noah, bookseller, 37 Princes st. Leicester square
Huffam Timothy& Co. clothiers & tailors, 5 City rd.Finsbury
Huffell Wm. tailor & breeches maker, 10 Grosvenor st
Hugall Elizth. (Mrs.), eating ho. 55 Leather la. Holborn
Hugenia Ann (Mrs.), beer retailer, 15 Charles sq. Hoxton
Huggard Joseph, grocer & oilman, 3 Down st. Piccadilly
Huggard Paris A. chemist, 7 New Church st. Lisson grove
Huggard Joseph, cheesemonger, &c. 28 Down st. Piccadilly
Huggens John, cornfactor, 4 Catherine court, Tower hill, & Jack's coffee house, Mark lane
Huggett & Vaughan (Misses), seminary, 3 Lisson grove nth
Huggett Chas. musical inst.ma.6 Marlborough pl. Kengtn. cr
Huggett George, coffee rooms, 169 Shoreditch High st
Huggett George, parliamentary agt. 49 Essex st. Strand
Huggett Joseph, *King's Head* P.H. Church st. Deptford
Huggett Paulin, *Crown* P.H. 13 Heddon court, Regent st
Huggett Steph. Martin, 3 *Compasses* P.H. Church st. Deptfd
Huggins & Lang, stock & share brokers, 14A, Austin friars
Huggins George, nurseryman, Hill road, St. John's wood
Huggins Isaac, workg. jeweller, 77 Chalton st. Somers town
Huggins John, coffee rooms, 109 Tooley st
Huggins Joseph, fishmonger, 120 Fore st. Cripplegate
Huggins Robert, slater, 2 Little Coram st. Brunswick square
Huggins William, brewer, 8 Richmond buildings, Soho
Huggins William, dried fish mer.25Union st. east,Spitalfields
Huggins William, tallow chandler, 18 Widegate st. Bishopsg
Huggins Wm. Thos. silk mercer & linendr. 97Gracechurch st
Huggitt Thomas, grocer, 3 Exeter st. Strand
Huggonson Edward, *Red Lion* P.H. 19 Charles st. Long acre
Hughes & Beazley,cheesemongrs.& poulterers,79Edgware rd
Hughes & Clark, agents for Yates's patent porcelain projecting letters, 158 Strand
Hughes & Drummond, porkmen, 3 Kennington cross
Hughes Francis & Co. truss & surgical instrument makers & patentees of the elastic spring cravats, 247 High Holborn, & 432 West Strand
Hughes & Graham, linendrapers, 149 Oxford st
Hughes & Henslow, attorneys, 13 Clement's inn, Strand
Hughes John & Co. linendrapers, 22Constable rw.Mile end rd
HughesJohn&Wm.coach ma.28Long acre,&Coal yd.Drury la
Hughes, Kearsey & Masterman, solicitors, 17 Bucklersbury
Hughes & Lancaster, coal mers. 7 Shad Thames,Southwark
Hughes & Lewis, linendrapers, 7 Tothill st. Westminster
Hughes Richard & Thomas, leather hose makers, New cross
Hughes & Smith, blackwell hall factors, 30 Basinghall st
Hughes Sophia & Sons, millstone makers, 8 Gt. Dover st
Hughes & Spence, jewellers, 1 Arlington st. Sadler's wells
Hughes & Strangewayes, linendrapers, 70 & 71 Chiswell st
Hughes Thomas & Co. army, navy, & india outfitters & general clothiers, 203 Regent st. & 76 King William st. City
Hughes Thomas & Son, linenfactors, 3 Queen st. Cheapside
Hughes Ann (Mrs.), butcher, Little Chelsea
Hughes Ann (Mrs.), *Nag's Head* P.H. 10 Whitechapel rd
Hughes Barton Wm. stationer, 5 Gloucester pl. Islington gr
Hughes Benj. basket & turnery deal. 31 London rd.Southwk
Hughes Benjamin, tallow chandlr.6Newland ter.Kensington
Hughes Burton, leathercutter, 14 Hayfield place, Mile end
Hughes Charles, cheesemonger, 82 Crawford st. Bryanstone Hsquare, & 52 High st. Portland town
Hughes Daniel, corndealer, 46 Seymour st. Euston square
Hughes David, *Blue Posts* P.H. 6 Bennett st. St. James's
Hughes David, bookseller & stationer, 8 Park st.Camden tn
Hughes David, solicitor, see Overton & Hughes
Hughes Edward, *Private hotel*, 7 Dover st. Piccadilly
Hughes Elizab. (Mrs.), work. jeweller, 13 Charles st. Wstmr
HughesElizh.Mary(Mrs.),coffeerooms,20Narrow st.Limehse
HughesFredk.Bond,shorthand writer,3Lit.George st.Wstmr

Hughes Gabriel, horsehair sieve ma. 13 Margaret pl. Hckny. fi
Hughes George, artist, 111 St. John st. road
Hughes George, baker, 9 Chapel st. east, Mayfair
Hughes George, *Prince of Hesse* P.H. 30 Fieldgate st. Whtchpl
Hughes George, rule maker, 35 Northampton st, Clerknwll
Hughes Geo. smith & machinist, 16 New inn yd. Shoreditch
Hughes Geo. Hen. writer & grainer, 69 Commercl. rd. Lmbth
Hughes George William, law stationer, 44 Chancery lane
Hughes Harry, cheesemonger, 27 Up. Park pl. Regent's park
Hughes Henry, painter, &c. 8 Marylebone st. Golden sq
Hughes Hen. tar, naptha & varnish ma. Plough rd. Rothrth
Hughes Hen. who. & ret. nautical, &c. inst. ma. 120 Fenchurch st
Hughes Henry Marshall, physician, 14 St. Thomas's st. Boro'
Hughes Henry Pearse, woolbroker, 78 Basinghall st
Hughes Hesketh, patent lace rouche mourning & fancy collar manufacturer, 94 Fore st. City
Hughes Hugh, bookseller & stationer, 15 St. Martin's le grand
Hughes Hugh, *Hope & Anchor* P.H. 8 Glo'ster pl. Camden twn
Hughes James, bricklayer, 13 Lit. Chester st. Grosvenor pl
Hughes James, builder, 11 St. George's pl. Cambrwl. High st
Hughes James, dyer, 105 White Lion st. Pentonville
Hughes James, fruit & pea salesmn. 2 Church st. Boro' markt
Hughes James, ladies' shoemaker, 10 Red Lion st. Holborn
Hughes James, solicitor, 12 Heathcote st. Mecklenburgh sq
Hughes James, watch & clockmaker, 30 Frith st. Soho
Hughes James, whitesmith, Clare market
Hughes Jane (Mrs.), welch flannel factor, 19 King st. Hlbn
Hughes John, bookseller & publisher, see Edwards & Hughes
Hughes John, brewer & beer retailer, 14 Symons st. Chelsea
Hughes John, fruiterer, 8 Suffolk st. Pentonville
Hughes John, herald painter, 84 Greenfield st. Coml. rd. ea
Hughes John, pastrycook, 8 Beauchamp st. Leather lane
Hughes John, solicitor, 10 Chapel st. Bedford row
Hughes John, tobacconist, 68 High st. Portland town
Hughes John Carlyon, wine merchant, see Bell & Hughes
Hughes John George, lamp manufacturer, 158 Strand
Hughes John Langford, tallowchand. 42 Curzon st. Mayfair
Hughes John W. tailor & breeches maker, 77 Cornhill
Hughes Joseph, brassfounder, see Whitfield & Hughes
Hughes Joseph, naut. & optic. inst. ma. 37 & 38 Queen st. Rtclff
Hughes Joseph, tailor, &c. 2 Bury st. St. James's
Hughes Joseph, window blind ma. 33 Featherstone st. City rd
Hughes Mary (Miss), dressmaker, 15 Red cross sq. Cripplgt
Hughes Mary (Mrs.), copper, brass, steel & zinc plate manufacturer, & metal & file warehouse, 107 Shoe lane, Fleet st
Hughes Mary (Mrs.), currier, 6 Moor lane, Cripplegate
Hughes Mary (Mrs.), *Queen's Head inn*, 84 Boro' High st
Hughes Mary (Mrs.), seminary, 119 Albany rd. Camberwell
Hughes Olivia (Mrs.), dressmaker, 16 South row, New road
Hughes Owen Hugh, tailor & hosier, 64 New Bond st
Hughes Richard, account book maker, 28 Addle st. Wood st
Hughes Richard, who. cheesemonger, High st. Deptford
Hughes Richard, stationer, 42 Gilbert st. Grosvenor sq
Hughes Richard, teadealer, see Webb, Hughes & Co
Hughes Richard, wholesale teadealer, 9 Gt. St. Helen's
Hughes Robert, cabinet maker, 24 Long alley, Finsbury
Hughes Robert, grocer & cheesem. 26 Robert st. Hmpstd. rd
Hughes Robert, herald chaser, 52 Clifton st. Finsbury
Hughes Robert, upholsterer & cabinetmaker to H.R.H. the Duke of Cambridge, 115 Piccadilly
Hughes Robt. B. *Prince of Wales* P.H. 23 Chas. st. Queen's Elms
Hughes Rowland, chemist, &c. 3 Burlington pl. Old Kent rd
Hughes Samuel, barrister, 10 Farrar's buildings, Temple
Hughes Samuel, cattle salesman, 8 West Smithfield
Hughes Samuel, civil engineer, 7 & 8 Duke st. Westminster
Hughes Samuel, perfumer & wig maker, 40 Holborn hill
Hughes Sarah (Miss), bookseller, 10 Lit. Turnstile, Holborn
Hughes Seneca, solicitor, 15 Bedford st. Covent garden
Hughes Thos. auctioneer, see Ventom & Hughes
Hughes Thos. cowkeeper, 1 Kingsgate st. Red Lion sq
Hughes Thos. manf. of bookbinding cloth, 51 Bunhill row
Hughes Thos. butcher, 13 Chapel st. ea. Shepherd's market
Hughes Thos. hosier & glover, 61 Marylebone la. Oxford st
Hughes Thos. insr. & exch. broker, 4 Adam's ct. Old Broad st
Hughes Thos. omnibus propritr. 5 Irongate whf. Paddngtn
Hughes Thomas, proprietor of Watson's patent for improvements in draining railways, &c. 51 Bunhill row
Hughes Thos. solicitor, see Day, Hughes & Brown
Hughes Thos. Bird, barrister, 40 Coleman st. City
Hughes Wm. barrister, 9 Old square, Lincoln's inn
Hughes Wm. beer retailer, 8 Little Chapel st. Soho
Hughes Wm. cheesemonger, 9 Colvill ter. King's rd. Chelsea
Hughes Wm. coal mer. & lighterman, 28 Butcher rw. Ratcliff
Hughes Wm. com. boarding ho. 7 Scots yd. Bush la. Cannon st
Hughes Wm. druggist, 197 Bethnal green road
Hughes Wm. *Five Pipes* P.H. Pickleherring, Tooley st
Hughes Wm. fruiterer, 11 New Turnstile, High Holborn
Hughes Wm. jeweller, 117 Borough High st
Hughes Wm. oil & italian wa. 30 Francis st. Tottenham ct. rd
Hughes Wm. painter & glazier, 27 Coldbath sq. Clerkenwell
Hughes Wm. painter & decorator, 85 Albany st. Regent's park
Hughes Wm. plasterer, 9 Rufford's row, Islington High st
Hughes Wm. printer, Cutler's ct. 18 King's head ct. Shoe la
Hughes Wm. solicitor, 35 Northampton square
Hughes Wm. surgeon, 90 High Holborn
Hughes Wm. tailor, 17 Duke st. Adelphi
Hughes Wm. wine cooper, 14 Shepherd's market, May fair
Hughes Wm. Daniel, plasterer, &c. 9 Chapel st. Islington
Hughes Wm. L. surgeon, chemist & drug. 89 Bishopsgt. withn
Hughes Wm. Hughes, barrister, 12 King's bench wlk. Templ
Hughes Wm. Hughes, jun. barrister, 12 King's bench wlk. Templ
Hughes Wm. H. builder, 50 Kensington High st
Hughes Wm. Nightingale, engraver, 4 Castle st. Falcon sq
Hughes Wm. Sevecke, grocer & oilman, 12 King st. St. James
Hughesdon & Ody, wood dealers, New row, Deptford
Hughesdon Andrew, wood dealer, 1 New row, Deptford
Hughesdon Frdk. law stationer, 13 Took's ct. Chancery lane
Hughesdon Joseph, merchant, 41 Mincing lane
Hugill Martha & Rose, ladies' school, 61 Banner st. St. Luke's
Hugman John, currier, 6 Alfred row, Spa road, Bermondsey
Hugman Joseph Wm. candle manfr. 32 Shoemaker rw. Blkfrs
Hugman Wm. C. surgeon, 23 New North st. Red Lion sq
Huguenin Francis, perfumer, 33 Haymarket
Huish Henry, tobacconist, Penton place, Kennington road
Huitson Emma (Miss), ladies' school, 6 Church st. Spitalfields
Hulbert, Layton & Co. tea & colonial brokers, 14 Mincing la
Hulbert Edward, boot & shoe warehouse, 43 Long acre
Hulbert Henry, corn & oatmeal factr. 7 St. Dunstan's alley
Hulbert John, M.D. surgeon, 33 Oxendon st. Haymarket
Hulbert Joseph, butcher, 20 Amwell st. Pentonville
Hulbert Richard, tailor, 30 Bedfordbury, Covent garden
Hulbert Robert, cheesemonger, 5 North Audley st
Hulbert Wm. *Three Kings* P.H. 17 Davies st. Berkeley sq
Hulett David, gasfitter & lamp maker, 54½ High Holborn
Hulford John, boot & shoe maker, 25 Doyley st. Sloane sq
Hulford Thomas, locksmith, &c. 1 Church st. Kensington
Hull Elizh. & Son, spring blind ma. 51 to 53 Bartholomew close
Hull Thos. & Co. wine & spirit merchts. 22 St. Swithin's la
Hull William & Edward, grocers, 74 & 75 Upper Ebury st. Pimlico, & 28 York row, Kennington road
Hull Steam Packets (William John Hall & Co. agents), Customhouse & Wool quays, Thames st
Hull Steam Packets (Edward Abell, agent), 41 Fish st. hill & London bridge wharf
Hull Alonzo, physician, 54 Upper Brook st. Grosvenor sq
Hull Edmund, butcher, 129 Praed st. Paddington
Hull Edward, curiosity dealer, 109 Wardour st. Soho
Hull George, M.D. surgeon, 6 Bath place, Peckham
Hull Hen. *Vernon Arms* P.H. 41 Southampton st. Pentonvl
Hull John, cheesemonger, 4 Upper John st. Golden square
Hull John, coachmaker, Church st. Hackney
Hull John, furniture broker, 9 St. Ann's court, Soho
Hull John, linendraper, 39 Beech st. Barbican
Hull Wm. tailor, 18 Newcastle st. Strand
Hullah Chas. M. biscuit baker & importer of irish provisions, Jamaica coffee house & 97 Wapping
Hullah John, professor of music, 101 St. Martin's lane
Hullah Robert Arnold, auctioneer, 67 Berners st. Oxford st
Hulland Richard, sheriff's officer, 44 Carey st. Lincoln's inn
Hulle Brothers & Co. merchants, 32 Fenchurch st
Hullett Brothers & Co. merchants, 9 New Broad st. City
Hullett Dan. cheesemonger, 187 Wellington ter. Waterloo rd
Hullett Joseph, fur cutter, 15 Union st. Borough
Hullmandel Chas. lithographic printer, 49 Gt. Marlborough st
Hulls Charles, coppersmith, 19 New rd. St. George's east
Hulls Christr. beer retailer, 28 Cromer st. Gray's inn road
Hulls Francis Bailey, beer retailer, 22 Goswell road, west si
Hulm Edwyn St. James, M.D. 1 Tonbridge pl. Burton cres
Hulme Eleanor (Mrs.), *Fox* P.H. 3 Duke st. Bloomsbury
Hulme Eleanor (Miss), *O. Windsor Castle* P.H. 15 Hi. Hlbrn
Hulme Eli, cowkeeper, 24 Colchester st. Whitechapel
Hulme Hanh. (Miss), artist, 19 Brunswick pl. Balls pond rd
Hulme Hen. surgeon dentist, 30 Regent st. Waterloo place
Hulme James, *Clay Hall* P.H. Old Ford, near Bow
Hulme Robert, surgeon dentist, 9 Old Burlington st
Hulse Richd. & Co. druggists & merchants, 14 Little Tower st
Hulse James, basket maker, 29 Red Cross st. Borough
Hulseburg Samuel, tobacconist, &c. 17 & 18 Borough road
Humber & Sanders, auctioneers, 17 King's pl. Comml. rd. east
Humbert & Vencens, italian wa. 13 Panton st. Haymarket
Humbert Francis C. *Hyde Park hotel*, 212 Oxford st
Humble Craster, hop & seed merchant, 82 Borough High st

Humble Wm. Edwd. physician, 6 Manchester ter. Liverpl. rd
Humblestone Clement, butcher, 6 Strong's pl. Fulham road
Humby Charles, bootmaker, 117 Pall mall
Humby Edwin, surgeon, 1 Windsor terrace, Maida hill
Humby George, solicitor, Carlton chambers, 8 Regent st
Humby James, bootmaker, 93 Vauxhall walk, Lambeth
Humby John, surgeon dentist, 18 East road, City road
Humby Wm. dentist, 18 Upp. Wellington st. Covent garden
Humby Wm. Warren, surgeon, 18 Southamptn. st. Fitzry. sq
Hume Chas. & Nath. chemists & druggists, 31 Regent st
Hume Robert & John, solicitors, 43 Lincoln's inn fields
Hume Robt. &Son, carvers & gilders, 65 Berners st. Oxfordst
Hume Robt. M. & John P. solicitors, 44 Lincoln's inn fields
Hume Alexander, baker, 1 Kent st. Borough
Hume Alexander, potato salesman, 51 White st. Borough
Hume Alexander, sole consignee for Lane's Cork stout, dry arch, London bridge, Upper Thames st. City
Hume Archibald, painter, 2 Cobourg st. Clerkenwell
Hume Geo. *Grapes* P.H. 23 & 24 Whitecross st. Cripplegate
Hume Geo. solicitor, 10 Great James st. Bedford row
Hume Hugh, plumber, 69 Great Saffron hill, Hatton garden
Hume James, baker&cornchandler, 11 Michael's pl. Brompton
Hume James, baker, 264 Oxford st
Hume John, fruiterer, 59 Henry st. east, Avenue road
Hume John Robert, physician, 9 Curzon st. Mayfair
Hume Joseph Burnley, barrister, 10 Old sq. Lincoln's inn
Hume Margaret (Mrs.), milliner, 27 King's sq. Goswell road
Hume Matthew, tailor, 3 Beak st. Regent st
Humfrey Charles, soapmaker, 6 Plummer's row, Whitechpl
Humfrey Lebbens Charles, queen's counsel, 5 Brick ct. Templ
Hummel Edmund & Co. hosiers & flannel drap. 29 St. James st
Hummel Henry M. tailor, see Sparding & Hummel
Hummerston Jane M. (Mrs.), prof. of danc. 5 Gt. Smith st. Wstm
Humpage Benjamin, chemist, 51 Judd st. New road
Humpage Henry Job, solicitor, 39 Gt. James st. Bedford row
Humpage Joseph, surgeon, see Dodd & Humpage
Humphrey Chas. dealr. in isinglass, see Simpson & Humphreys
Humphrey Henry, bricklayer, 6 Lit. Charlotte st. Pimlico
Humphrey John, tobacconist, 4 Norfolk pl. Marlborough rd
Humphery John, wharfinger, Hay's wharf, Tooley st. & Kent & Sussex wharf, & Hibernia wharf, Montague close, Boro'
Humphery Jsph. watchmaker, 2 King's cross, Albion pl. east
Humphrey Saml. corndlr. 44 Nelson ter. Stoke Newington rd
Humphrey Thomas, baker, 41 Upper Lisson st. Lisson grove
Humphrey Thos. Bennett, surgeon, 4 Arthur st. east, City
Humphrey William, academy, 56 Clifton st. Finsbury
Humphrey Wm. painter, 5 William st. Hampstead road
Humphrey Wm. Jas. drawing master, 4 York pl. Up. st. Islingtn
Humphreys Thos. & Co. coal & wood mers. Lower rd. Deptford
Humphreys & Wallen, auctioneers, &c. 68 Old Broad st
Humphreys Ann (Mrs.), butcher, 87 Brick lane, Spitalfields
Humphreys Chas. binnacle ma. 136 Pennington st. Rtclf. hwy
Humphreys Chas. grocer, 147 High st. Camden town
Humphreys Chas. auctioneer & surveyor, 61 Leadenhall st
Humphreys Charles, umbrella maker, 64 Kingsland road
Humphreys Daniel, smith & farrier, 2 Horseferry rd. Wstmr
Humphreys David, furn. japanner, 27 Seward st. Goswell st
Humphreys David, wine&beer mercht. 5 Paradise st. Lambeth
Humphreys Edward, boot & shoe maker, 32 Whitechapel rd
Humphreys Edward, builder, 1 Draycott st. Chelsea
Humphreys Edward, solicitor, see Cook & Humphreys
Humphreys Erskine, barrister, 24 Southampton buildings
Humphreys Evan, plumber&glazier, 73 Park st. Grosvenor sq
Humphreys Geo. coal&potato mer. 52 Walnut tree wlk. Lmbth
Humphreys Geo. stock & share broker, 8 Throgmorton st
Humphreys Griffith, haberdasher, 169 Oxford st
Humphreys James Bywater, *Crown* cof. ho. 41 High Holborn
Humphreys John, solicitor, 6 Spital square, Bishopsgate
Humphreys John, tobacconist, 50 Broad st. Bloomsbury
Humphreys John Jas. Hamilton, barrister, 14 Serle st. Lnln's. in
Humphreys Jsph. undertak. & est. agt. 11 Lon. ter. Hkny. rd
Humphreys Louisa (Mrs.), stationer, 12 Spring st. Maryleb
Humphreys Rt. coachsmith, Williams mws. Mary st. Rgt's. pk
Humphreys Samuel, water gilder, 12 Green st. Leicester sq
Humphreys Thomas, attorney, 14 East India chambers
Humphreys Thomas, barrister, 14 Carey st. Lincoln's inn
Humphreys Thomas, gasfitter, brass wrkr. &c. 98 Broad wall
Humphreys Thomas, lodging house, 29 King st. St. James's
Humphreys Thos. toy dlr. 13 Park ter. King's rd. west, Chelsea
Humphreys Wm. fruiterer, 5 St. Dunstan's alley, Tower st
Humphreys Wm. Chas. C. solicitor, 67 Newgate st
Humphreys Wm. Corne, solicitor, 119 Newgate st
Humphreys Wm. Evan, surgeon, 6 Southwick pl. Hyde park
Humphreys Wm. Hy. coal mer. 17 Bennett st. Blackfriars rd
Humphries J. & G. H. wrstd. spin. & carpet m. 47 Skinnr. st. Snowh
Humphries Edw. Lowell, surgeon, 4 Courtney ter. Kingsland
Humphries Francis, solicitor, 17 Green terr. New River head
Humphries Geo. map & puzzle dissector, 3 East st. Hoxton
Humphries Joseph Samuel, tailor, 37 Leicester square
Humphris Edmund, butcher, 1 Maida hill east
Humphris Thomas, ironmonger, 1 Gee's court, Oxford st
Humphry Geo. solicitor, see Wilde, Rees, Humphry & Wilde
Humphry Joseph, barrister, 4 New square, Lincoln's inn
Humphry Joseph Thomas, barrister, 8 Chancery lane
Humphry Richard, tailor, 28 Red Cross st. Cripplegate
Humphry William, artist, 4 Grove terrace, St. John's wood
Humphryes William, *Hotel de Paris*, 58 Haymarket
Humphrys, Keightley & Parkin, solicitors, 43 Chancery lane
Humphrys Harry, solicitor, 12 Gray's inn square
Humphrys Josiah, solicitor, 1 Featherstone blds. Bedford rw
Humphrys Saml. painter, 5 Prior pl. East st. Walworth rd
Humphrys Thos. coach wheelwright, Oxford mews, Edgw. rd
Humpleby John Thos. drysalter & mer. 10 Gould sq. Crthd. frs
Humpris Joseph, butcher, 22 Great Dover st. Borough
Hundley Charles, bootmaker, 64 St. Martin's lane
Hundley Francis, engraver & printer, 64 St. Martin's lane
Hungerford General Steam & Coach Booking Off. 18 Strand
Hungerford & Lambeth Suspension Bridge Co. (Richard Lawrence, sec.), 9 Villiers st. Strand
Hungerford Market Company's Office (Leith And. L. sec.), 9 Villiers st. Strand
Hungerford Wharf, Hungerford Market Company (Thos. Walter, superintendent), Strand
Hunnard John, law stationer. 2 Inner Temple lane
Hunns Thomas, bootmaker, 16 New st. Dorset square
Hunot Emma (Mrs.), haberdasher, 31 East st. Walworth rd
Hunot Samuel Man, chronom. watch ma. 28 Rathbone pl
Hunsdon John Richard, ironmonger, 30 Broad st. Lambeth
Hunt Chas. Edw. & Co. merchts. 6 Pinners' hall, Gt. Winchr. st
Hunt & Collins, tailors & breeches makers, 30 Haymarket
Hunt, Fourdrinier & Co. who. stationers, 12 Sherborne la. City
Hunt Fredk. & Co. waggon & rail carriers, 13 Aldersgate st
Hunt, Hall, Bancks & Sons, card makers to her Majesty the Queen, the Queen Dowager & the royal family, 20 Piccadilly
Hunt John & Co. tin plate workers, 7 Long lane, Bermondsey
Hunt John, Thos. & John, jun. stationers, 34 & 35 Seacoal la
Hunt & Roskell (late Storr, Mortimer & Hunt), jewellers, goldsmiths & silversmiths to her Majesty; manufactory, 26 Harrison st. Gray's inn road, & 156 New Bond st
Hunt & Walley, drapers & silk mercers, 51 & 53 Edgware rd
Hunt Wm. & Ebenezer, mercers & drapers, 182 Shoreditch
Hunt Wm. Ogle & Wm. solicitors, 10 Whitehall
Hunt Wm. Thos. & Co. exporters of drugs, perfumery, &c. 150 Fenchurch st. & 26 Bethnal green, east side
Hunt Abraham, china & glass warehouse, 17 Great Ryder st. St. James's, & 29 Queen's row, Pimlico
Hunt Abraham, stationer, 1 High st. Bow
Hunt Albert, haberdasher, 36 Great Marylebone st
Hunt Allen, *Three Compasses* P.H. 66 Cowcross st
Hunt Ann (Mrs.), livery stables, 10 Courtney ter. Kingsland
Hunt Ann (Mrs.), omnibus prop. Church st. Stoke Newington
Hunt Barringer, *Lord Nelson* P.H. Windmill la. Camberwell
Hunt Benjamin, law & general agent, 24 Upper Stamford st
Hunt Catherine (Miss), milliner, Camberwell green
Hunt Charles, gold cutter, 13 Short's buildings, Clerkenwell
Hunt Charles, merchant, 6 Pinners' hall, Gt. Winchester st
Hunt Charles, plumber, &c. High st. Kensington gravel pits
Hunt Charles Edward, attorney, 2 Barnard's inn, Holborn
Hunt Charles John, billiard rooms, 107 Quadrant, Regent st
Hunt Edmund, glass & chinaman, 104 Crawford st. Portman sq
Hunt Edward, baker, 15 St. Andrew's hill, Doctors' commons
Hunt Edward, hop merchant, Kentish bldgs. Boro' High st
Hunt Edward, slate mercht. & slater, 27 Sale st. Paddington
Hunt Edward Marklew, solicitor, 8 New Boswell ct. Linc. inn
Hunt Edward W. slater, 21 Spring st. Paddington
Hunt Elizh. (Miss), milliner, see Puddiphat, Archer & Hunt
Hunt Frederick, beer retailer, 13 White horse pl. Comm. rd
Hunt Fredk paper hanger & tobact. 14 Salisbury st. Lis. gr
Hunt Fredk. John, bricklayer, 14 Conduit st. Paddington
Hunt George, hairdresser, 50 Freeschool st. Horselydown
Hunt George, livery stables, see Wood & Hunt
Hunt George, plumber & glazier, 1 Kensington High st
Hunt George, tobacconist, 54 Upper Seymour st. Euston sq
Hunt Geo. Alfred, appraiser&broker, 1 Weston pl. King's cr
Hunt George Charles, carman, Lower road, Rotherhithe
Hunt Henry, attorney, 9 St. Mildred's court, Poultry
Hunt Henry, bookbinder, 24 Cullum st. Fenchurch st
Hunt Henry, builder, 2 High st. Notting hill
Hunt Henry, butcher, 15 College st. Chelsea
Hunt Henry, chemist, 1 St. George's terrace, Liverpool road
Hunt Henry, locksmith & bellhanger, 13 Boston pl. Dorset sq
Hunt Henry, *Lord Nelson* P.H. 64 Nelson sq. Blackfriars rd

Hunt Hen. *Physicians' Arms* P.H. 3½ Warwick la. Newgate st
Hunt Henry, pat. garden pot depôt, 29 Queen's row, Pimlico
Hunt Henry, physician, 68 Brook st. Hanover square
Hunt Henry, *Red Lion* P.H. 14 Gt. Wild st. Lincoln's fields
Hunt Henry Arthur, surveyor, 8 York Road, Lambeth
Hunt Henry Prior, school, 14 Lit. Alie st. Goodman's fields
Hunt Holdsworth, barrister, 3 Tanfield court, Temple
Hunt Horatio N. metal & slate billard table maker & tobacconist, 370 Strand
Hunt Isaac, bootmaker, 167 Lambeth walk
Hunt Isaac, grocer & oilman, 10 Hanover pl. Regent's park rd
Hunt Jacob, tailor, 14 Cross st. Bermondsey New town
Hunt James, beer retailer, 3 Johnson's court, Fleet st
Hunt James, builder & brick mer. 75 Horseferry rd. Westmnr
Hunt James, butcher, 64 Charlotte ter. New cut, Lambeth
Hunt James, hairdresser, 89 Waterloo road
Hunt James, house painter & builder, 10 Idol lane, & 10 St. Dunstan's passage, Tower st
Hunt James, contractor, 31 Parliament st
Hunt James, plumber, 61 Gt. Portland st. Oxford st
Hunt James, wine cooper, 18 St. Dunstan's hill
Hunt Jared T. bone mer. & manure ma. Lambeth wf. Up. Fore st
Hunt John, bone boiler, glue & size mnfr. Manor la. Bermondsy
Hunt John, broker, see Keeling & Hunt
Hunt John, butcher, 23 Newport court, Newport market
Hunt John, cheesemonger, 24 Kensington High st
Hunt John, coffee rooms, 100 Old st. road
Hunt John, custom house agent, 150 Fenchurch st
Hunt John, grocer, 1 Albert place, Marlboro' road, Chelsea
Hunt John, lathe & tool maker, 30 Red Lion st. Clerkenwl
Hunt John, soapma. bone crusher, &c. 73 Broad st. Lambeth
Hunt John, tailor & draper, 63 Basinghall st
Hunt John Alexander, grocer, 17 Conduit st. Paddington
Hunt John Atlee, corn dealer, 1 Southampton pl. Camberwl
Hunt John Chas. hearth rug ma. 41 Edward st. Bethnal green
Hunt Joseph, bootmaker, 35 Little Windmill st. Golden sq
Hunt Joseph, carpenter, 13 Redcross square, Cripplegate
Hunt Joseph, straw hat & stay wareho. 16 Kensington High st
Hunt Joseph, surgeon, 9 Little Woodstock st. Marylebone
Hunt Joseph, tobacconist, 24 Kensington High st
Hunt Luke, beer retailer, 1 Weston st. Somers town
Hunt Martha (Mrs.), lace dlr, 1A, Terrace, Kensington High st
Hunt Philip, coal dealer, 34 Salisbury st. Lisson grove
Hunt Ralph, watch tool maker, 10 Helmet row, St. Luke's
Hunt Richd. grocer & tobacconist, 20 Brown st. Bryanstone sq
Hunt Richard Allen, butcher, 55 West Smithfield
Hunt Robert, potato salesman, 33 Clerkenwell green
Hunt Robert, veterinary surgeon, 31½ Gresse st. Tottnhm. ct. rd
Hunt Roger, solicitor, 5 New Bank buildings, Lothbury
Hunt Robt. Hen. printer & engr. 3 New Church st. west, Edgw. rd
Hunt Samuel, baker, 139 Tooley st
Hunt Samuel, tailor, 40 Seymour place, Bryanstone square
Hunt Stephen, *Morland's hotel*, 23 Dean st. Soho
Hunt Stephen, livery stables, 25 Dean st. Soho
Hunt Thomas, baker, 19 Ironmonger lane, Cheapside
Hunt Thomas, baker, 178 Long lane. Bermondsey
Hunt Thomas, cheesemonger, 141 Whitechapel road
Hunt Thomas, fishmonger & poulterer, 2 & 3 Fitzroy market
Hunt Thomas, lecturer on removing stammering, &c. 224 Regent st. & Swanage, Dorset
Hunt Thomas, tailor, 23 New North st. Finsbury
Hunt Thomas, tin plate worker, 11 Printing House la. Blkf
Hunt Thomas, watchmaker & jeweller, 151 Tottenham ct. rd
Hunt Thomas Geo. *Rose & Crown* P.H. 20 Colville ct. Fitzry. sq
Hunt Thomas Joseph, *Fox* P.H. King st. New town, Deptford
Hunt Thomas Rider, undrtkr. 23 Somerset pl. N. rd. Comrcl. rd
Hunt Wm. artist, 62 Stanhope st. Hampstead rd
Hunt Wm. butcher, 3 Bermondsey New road
Hunt Wm. carman, winecooper & bottle mer. 42 Mark lane
Hunt Wm. carpenter, 28 Redcross square, Cripplegate
Hunt Wm. carpentr. & undertkr. 47 Stanhope st. Clare mkt
Hunt Wm. gardener, 12 Peel place, Kensington gravel pits
Hunt Wm. hatter & hosier, 8 Great Ryder st. St. James's
Hunt Wm. ladies' shoemaker, 78 Mount st. Berkeley sq
Hunt Wm. linendra. & silk mercer, 24 Crawford st. Portman sq
Hunt Wm. printer, 16A, Bulstrode st. Manchester square
Hunt Wm. tailor, 7 Philpott ter. Edgware road
Hunt Wm. tailor & undertaker, 31 Upper Stamford st
Hunt Wm. wine merchant, 45 Bedford row, High Holborn
Hunt Wm. Harris, carpentr. & undertr. 8 Church st. Kensingtn
Hunt Wm. Henry, wine merchant, 36 Crutched friars
Hunt Wm. Joseph, tailor, 3 Gainsford st. Horselydown
Hunt Wm. Nathan, statnr. 28 Watling st. & 10 Bow la. Chpsd
Hunt Wm. Thomas, grocer, 23 Lit. Bell alley, Coleman st
Hunter & Coventry, corn fact. 8 Whitehart ct. Lombard st
Hunter & English, millwrights & engineers, Bow High st
Hunter & Edwards, chronometer, watch & clock makers, 43 Cornhill
Hunter James & James, surgeons, 4 Church row, 10 Milner square, & 1 Compton terrace, High st. Islington
Hunter (Z. jun.) & James, leech importers & medical glass dealers, 44 Webber row, Blackfriars road
Hunter Wm. & John R. & Edward, cabinet makers & plate glass factors, upholsterers & timber merchants, 30 Moorgate st. & Bydes' place, 189½ Shoreditch
Hunter Andrew, *Grasshopper* P.H. 15 Charles st. Mile e. nw. tn
Hunter Ann (Mrs.), umbrella mak. 18 Sherrard st. Golden sq
Hunter Anthony, *Earl Cathcart* P.H. 45 Munster st. Rgnt's. pk
Hunter Edward James, stockbroker, 15 Throgmorton st
Hunter Eliza (Miss), staymaker, 117 Upper st. Islington
Hunter George, tailor, 165 Sloane st. Knightsbridge
Hunter Henry, cowkeeper, 22 Upper Clifton st. Finsbury
Hunter Henry, who. confectioner, see Caulfield & Hunter
Hunter James, auctioneer & ho. agt. 30 Orchard st. Portman sq
Hunter James, coach & harness maker, 1 Paul st. Finsbury, & 23 Providence row, Finsbury
Hunter James, surgeon, 10 Milner square, Islington
Hunter James Charles engraver & printer, 57 Houndsditch
Hunter Jameson, merchant, 110 Fenchurch st
Hunter John, baker, 1 Jubilee place south, Commercial rd. ea
Hunter John, baker, 27 Hatton wall
Hunter John, boot & shoe maker, 12 Providence pl. Kentish tn
Hunter John, furniture broker, 212 Bethnal green road
Hunter John, *Magpie & Stump* P.H. 6 Cable st. St. Geo. ea
Hunter John, robe maker & tailor to her Majesty, 26 Chancery lane, & 16 Maddox st. Regent st
Hunter John, surgeon, 4 Church row, Upper st. Islington
Hunter John, surgeon, 83 Gt Tower st. City
Hunter John, surgeon, 11 Hart st. Bloomsbury
Hunter John Charles, surgeon, 30 Wilton place, Belgrave sq
Hunter John Henry, undertaker, 52 Amelia st. Walworth rd
Hunter Mark, merchant, 15 Providence row, Finsbury
Hunter Mark, merchant, 22 Artillery place, Finsbury square
Hunter Mary (Mrs.), *Horse & Groom* P.H. 1 Winsley st. Oxfrd. st
Hunter Mary (Mrs.), milliner, 38 Sloane st. Knightsbridge
Hunter Mary Ann (Mrs.), lodging ho. 38 Gower pl. Euston sq
Hunter Richard, carpet & furniture wa. 148 Tottenham ct. rd
Hunter Richard, french polisher, 33 Portland st. Soho
Hunter Richard, solicitor, see Smith, Hunter & Gwatkin
Hunter Robert, baker, 66 Praed st. Paddington
Hunter Robert, dye wood & indigo mercht. 173 Fenchurch st
Hunter Robert, physician, 6 Great Queen st. Westminster
Hunter Robert, tailor & outfitter, 76 Parsons st. London docks
Hunter Sarah (Mrs.), bookbinder & stationer, 178 High Holborn
Hunter Thomas, *Cavendish hotel*, 81 Jermyn st. St. James's
Hunter Thomas, engraver & printer, 63 Newman st. Oxford st
Hunter Thos. Davis, surgeon, 8 Union ter. Notting hill
Hunter Wm. attorney, 10 Bloomsbury st. Bloomsbury
Hunter Wm. builder, 8 Edward st. Blackfriars road
Hunter Wm. carpenter & undertakr. 55 Three Colt st. Limeho
Hunter Wm. cheesemonger, 132 Upper st. Islington
Hunter Wm. coach builder, 84 Gray's inn lane
Hunter Wm. fish factor, see Starkey & Hunter
Hunter Wm. haberdash. & printer, 21 Chalton st. Somers tn
Hunter Wm. ironfounder, Devonshire pl. Commercial rd. east
Hunter Wm. physician, 86 Sloane st. Chelsea
Hunter Wm. poulterer, 8 Ship tavern pas. Leadenhall markt
Hunter Wm. silversmith, 13 Myrtle st. Hoxton
Hunterian Society (Thos. Mee Daldy, esq. sec.), 4 Blomfield st
Hunting Robert, tailor, 19½ Cumberland st. Hackney road
Huntington John B. & Co. steam excavators, 16 Broad st. bldgs
Huntington Jas. I. greengrcr. & basket ma. 146 Union st. Boro'
Huntley Cath. (Mrs.), stay & corset maker to her Majesty (late of 294 Upper Regent st.), 51 High Holborn
Huntley Eliza (Mrs.), staymaker, 28 Burlington arcade
Huntley Henry, hat manufacturer, 64 Oakley st. Lambeth
Huntley John K. commission merchant (& agent to James Muspratt & Sons, of Liverpool, manufacturers of soda ash, bleaching powder, prussiate of potash, oil of vitriol, oxalic acid, &c. & agent for Liebig's patent manure), 4 John st. Minories, & 216 Wapping
Huntley Matthew, van proprietor, 50 Oakley st. Lambeth
Huntley Reuben Jas. *Wheat Sheaf* P.H. 35 West Smithfld
Huntley Samuel, tailor, 18 East lane, Bermondsey wall
Huntly & Taylor, cloth works. & water proofs. 14 Drury la
Huntly Elizh. (Mrs.), engrav. printr. & stat. 74 New Bond st
Huntly Elizh. (Miss), fancy statnr. 4 Union ter. Notting hill
Hunton Fulleretta & Son, linendrs. Church st. Stoke Newington
Hunton Wm. stationer, 50 Rufford's buildings, Islington
Huntsman Benjamin, baker, 378 Oxford st
Huntsman Benjamin, tool manfr. 4 Lit. Queen st. Holborn
Huntsman Edmund, baker, 155 High Holborn

Huntsman Robert, whol. chemist & soda water mfr. 6 Thrawl st. Spitalfields, & 47 High st. Camden town
Huntsman Wm. slater, 9 Dorrington st. Leather lane
Hunwick John, bootmaker, 17 Mile end rd
Hurcomb Edward, cheesemonger, 51 Union st. Boro'
Hurcomb John, clerk to corn meters' office, 61 Gt. Tower st
Hurford Lewis Wm. & Co. who. tea & coffee dlrs. & patent dandelion coffee manufrs. 32 Walbrook
Hurle Robert, whip maker, New cross
Hurlestone John, butcher, 1 Shepperton pl. New North rd
Hurley Alfred Wm. & Co. wine mers. 65 High st. Camden twn
Hurley & Collinson, upholsterers, 61 Conduit st. Hanover sq
Hurley Archbold, dec. painter, 10 Charlotte st. Fitzroy sq
Hurley Geo. news agt. 3 St. Martin's pl. St. Martin's le grand
Hurley Henry, boot & shoemaker, 3 Swallow st. Piccadilly
Hurley Jas. undertaker, 7 Old Montague st. Whitechapel
Hurley John, attorney, 7 Argyll place, Regent st
Hurley John, cowkeeper, 38 Crispin st. Spitalfields
Hurley Joseph, bootmaker, 13 Avery row, Grosvenor st
Hurlock Philip, apothecary, St. Bartholomew's hospital
Hurlock Philip Thos. chandlr.'s shop, 7 Wyndham rd. Cmbwl
Hurlstone Edwin T. barrister, 7 Crown Office row, Temple
Hurlstone Frederick, artist, 9 Chester st. Belgrave square
Hurly John, furrier, 20 Great Dover st
Hurn Robert, greengrocer, 3 Waterloo st. Camberwell
Hurndull William, boarding house, 37 Burton crescent
Hurnell Wm. *Pewter Platter* P.H. 77 St. John st. Clrknwl
Hurrell & Sheffield, who. potato dlrs. Cotton's whf. 20 Tooley st
Hurrell Charles John, baker, 149 Shoreditch
Hurrell Henry, fruiterer, 26 Seething lane, Tower st
Hurrell Henry, potato salesman, 7 Whitechapel High st
Hurrell John, baker, 65 Richardson st. Long la. Bermondsey
Hurrell John, barrister, 2 Pump court, Temple
Hurrell Joseph H. potato salesman, see Sheffield & Hurrell
Hurrell Mary Ann (Mrs.), back maker, 66 Houndsditch
Hurrell Thomas, cowkeeper, Church st. Battersea
Hurrell Thomas Nich. *Red Lion* P.H. 196 & 197 St. George st
Hurren Brothers, who. slopsellers, 13 Wormwood st
Hurren Benjamin, butcher, 13 Park st. Dorset sq
Hurren Benjamin, *Greyhound inn*, 1 Kensington sq
Hurren Isaac, tailor, 3 Baalzephon st. Bermondsey
Hurren Jacob, grocer, 6 Elizabeth terrace, Hackney road
Hurren James, confectioner, 81 Sun st. Bishopsgate
Hurren Sarah (Mrs.), bookseller, &c. 45 Curtain rd. Shoreditch
Hurry Geo. & Co. bottle merchants, Paul's wf. 25 Up. Thames st
Hurry David, *George & Dragon* P.H. 275 Whitechapel rd
Hurry Edmund, *Star & Woolpack* P.H. 72 Kingsland road
Hurry Herbert, fruiterer, 1 Heddon court, Regent st
Hurry John, grocer & teadler 4 Bury pl. & 12 Bloomsby. mt
Hurry Wm. butcher, 9 Sun ct. Curzon st
Hurry Wm. tobacconist 21 Charlotte row, Walworth rd
Hurst & Jones, glaire mer. 16 Bridport pl. New North rd
Hurst & M'Mullen, seedsmen & florists, 6 Leadenhall st. City; wholesale warehouse, 19 Vine st. Minories
Hurst Carmont, cabinet ma. 10 University st. Tottnhm. ct. rd
Hurst Charles, baker, 87 Curtain road
Hurst Charles, boarding house, 11 Down st. Piccadilly
Hurst Edward, grocer, &c. 17 Princess st. Edgware rd
Hurst James, printer 3 Vauxhall row
Hurst Jas. solicitor, 26 Milk st. Cheapside
Hurst John, tobacco pipe mak. 74 Cowcross st. West Smithfi
Hurst Joseph, academy, 5 Southampton st. Camberwell
Hurst Joseph Sam. academy, 3 Phœnix pl. East st. Walwrth
Hurst Rich. file & saw ma. 8 Greenhill's rents Smithfield
Hurst Rich. glass & china dealer, 18 Old st. St. Luke's
Hurst Richard, ironmonger, 45 Borough High st.
Hurst Rich. *Vernon's Head* P.H. 32 North Audley st
Hurst Robt. H. barrister, 2 Brick court, Temple
Hurst Stephen, carpent. & tobaccon. 28 Seymour pl. Bryanst. sq
Hurst Susanh. (Mrs.), *Ben Jonson* P.H. 27 Gt. Bath st. Clknwl
Hurst Thomas, dairyman, 39 Cambridge st. Edgware road
Hurst Wm. fruiterer, 26 Hosier lane, Smithfield
Hurst Wm. tobacconist, 12 Lit. Knightrider st. Doc. com
Hurst Wm. *Union tavern* P.H. Baker st. Clerkenwell
Hurst Wm. David, tobacco pipe ma. 34 Bowling st. Clerkenwl
Hurst Wm. Joseph, watch maker, 9 Lambeth walk
Hurt Wm. coach & cart wheelwright, Irongate whf. Padngtn
Hurton John, cowkeeper & dairyman, 167½ Drury lane
Husband Hen. & Thos. leather mers. 124 Long la. Bermondsey
Husband & Wyatt, solicitors, 11 Gray's inn square
Husband Robert, straw hat maker, 3 Hayes pl. Kingsland rd
Husband Thomas, beer retailer, 16 John st. Limehouse fields
Husband Thomas Mathew, *Seven Stars* P.H. 22 Rosemary la
Husey Hubert Tuttle, tobacconist, 121 Oxford st
Husey Ralph Allen, merchant, 15 Philpot lane
Husher Chas. *Saddlers' Arms* P.H. 14 Swallow st. Regent st

Husk Charles, meat salesman, see Boyce & Husk
Huskinson Leonard, artist, 39 Penton place, Pentonville
Huskinson Robert, artist, 39 Penton place, Pentonville
Huskisson John & Sl. mfg. chemists, 77 Swinton st. Gray's inn r
Huskisson Francis, baker, 5 Milton st. Cripplegate
Huskisson John, baker, 56 & 147 Whitechapel High st
Huskisson John, butcher, 2 Whitechapel High st
Huskisson Joseph, baker, 200 Up. Whitecross st. St. Luke's
Huskisson Samuel, baker, 1 High st. Kingsland
Husler John, stone merchant, see Cliff & Husler
Huson Edward, surgeon, 6 Church row, Aldgate High st
Huson George John, attorney, 7 Ironmonger lane, Cheapside
Huson Henry, tobacconist, 15 Freeschool st. Horselydown
Huson Nathaniel, china wareh. 120 Gt. Portland st. Oxford st
Hussell James, rush & rod dealer, 1 Redcross court, Borough
Hussey Henry, *Raby Castle* P.H. Winyard st. Kennington
Hussey Elizh. (Mrs.), beer retlr. & timbr. dlr. Park pl. O. Kt. rd
Hussey George William, solicitor, 20 Basing lane, Bread st
Hussey Geo. Wm. solicitor, 85 Queen st. Cheapside
Hussey Gideon, baker, 15 Whitechapel High st
Hussey John Joseph, carpenter, 12 Hertford st. Fitzroy sq
Hussey John Thos. locksmith, &c. 9 Red Lion st. Borough
Hussey Thomas, painter, &c. 10 King's row, Walworth rd
Hussey Thomas, straw bonnet mak. 29 York st. Westminster
Hussey Wm. tailor, 29 Upper John st. Liverpool road
Hussick George, china dealer, Ferry road west, Poplar
Husted Peter, grocer & cheesemonger, 45 North st. Sloane st
Hustler Charles, corndealer, 10 Broadway, Westminster
Hustler James Devereux, surgeon, 53 Park st. Grosvnr. sq
Hustler Orbel James, corn chandler, 2 Sloane sq. Chelsea
Hustler Wm. miller, 1 Lower Felix st. Hackney road
Hustwitt Wm. linendrap. & undertak. 3 Wilson st. Finsbury
Hutchens Jas. *Baker & Basket* P.H. 12 Red Lion st. Whitechpl
Hutcheson Henry, butcher, 20 Warren st. Fitzroy square
Hutchin Sarah (Mrs.), market gardener, Earl's ct. Old Brmptn
Hutchings & Chalker, bootmakers, 16 Shoreditch High st
Hutchings Alf. Attwood, tailor, 49 Dorset st. Manchester sq
Hutchings Edward, carpenter, &c. 16 Castle st. Leicester sq
Hutchings Grace (Mrs.), beer retailer, 13 Swan st. Gt. Dover rd
Hutchings Henry, baker, 42 Long acre
Hutchings Henry, carpenter & undertaker, 19 St. Martin's st
Hutchings Henry, confectioner, 7 Strong's pl. Brompton
Hutchings James, painter & glazier, 22 Castle st. Holborn
Hutchings James, boot & shoemaker, 64 Dean st. Soho
Hutchings Jas. Attwood, woollen draper, 9 West st. Golden sq
Hutchings John, piecebroker, 8 Hop gardens, St. Martin's la
Hutchings John Wm. grocer, 23 Chichester pl. Gray's inn rd
Hutchings Joseph, coal dealer, 16 Marylebone lane
Hutchings Jsph. Peach, *Bird in Hand* P.H. 11 Garden row, London road
Hutchings Major James, *Bull* P.H. Bull court, Tooley st
Hutchings Martha (Miss), chandlr's. shop, 58 Regent st. Wstmr
Hutchings Richd. cabinet maker, 55 Newman st. Oxford st
Hutchings Richd. Payne, *Coach & Horses* P.H. 1 Welbeck st
Hutchings Robert, boot & shoe maker, 50 Leather lane
Hutchings Thomas, shoemaker, 4 Marylebone la. Oxford st
Hutchings Wm. picture dealer, 31 Gt. Pulteney st. Golden sq
Hutchins Ann (Mrs.), rasp & filemak. 8 New inn yd. Tottm. ct. rd
Hutchins Daniel, academy, 12 Wilderness row, Clerkenwell
Hutchins Edward, butcher, 17 Oxford st
Hutchins Geo. collarma. 11 Blandford mws. Baker st. Prtmn. sq
Hutchins Geo. Henry, painter, 1 Park pl. ter. Paddington gr
Hutchins Gilbert, fruiterer, 57 Clark st. Stepney
Hutchins John, chair maker, 54 Foley st. Portland pl
Hutchins John, dyer, 14 Queen's buildings, Knightsbridge
Hutchins John Henry, surgeon, see Smith & Hutchins
Hutchins Thomas, beer retailer, 39 Cold Bath sq. Clerkenwell
Hutchins Thos. warm & cold baths, 25 Cold Bath sq. Clerkenwell
Hutchins Wm. dentist to the late Duke of Sussex, 25 Hanovr. sq
Hutchinson Geo. & Co. gilders, 24 Mortimer st. Cavendish sq
Hutchinson Joshua & Son, stockbrokers, 39 Lothbury
Hutchinson Matthew & Son, hemp & flax dealers, 48 Mark la
Hutchinson Rd. M. & N. carpet & furn. wa. 92 Gnd. Junction ter
Hutchinson Rbt. & Co. merchants & drysalters, 1 Old Swan lane, Upper Thames st. & drug grinders, 11 Bankside
Hutchinson & Smith, ivory & hardwood turners, 67 Wood st
Hutchinson T. & M. & Spiller, carpet warehousemen, 5 Bread st
Hutchinson Tim. & Son, sailma. & shipchandl. 59 Lw. Shadwell
Hutchinson Ann (Miss), ironmgr. see Holland & Hutchinson
Hutchinson Arch. shawl ma. see Forbes, Chirney & Hutchinson
Hutchinson Bury, solicitors, 7 Staple inn, Holborn bars
Hutchinson Catherine (Mrs.), straw hat man. 47 Goodge st
Hutchinson Charles, boatbuilder, Holywell st. Millbank
Hutchinson Elizth. (Mrs.), furrier, 15 St. John st. Clerknwl
Hutchinson Francis, surgeon, &c. 92 Farringdon st
Hutchinson Geo. carver & gilder, 8 Chapel pl. Cavendish sq

HutchinsonGeo.*DukeofClarence*P.H.94Vauxhallst.Lambth
Hutchinson George, grocer, &c. 34 Brandon st. Locks fields
Hutchinson George, grocer, &c. 1 York pl. Fulham rd
Hutchinson Geo. tailor & trim. slr. 54 Charles st. Westmr
Hutchinson George Pierson, teadealer, 7 Crawford st
Hutchinson James, undertaker, 63 Up. Ground st. Blackfrs
Hutchinson John, curiosity dealer, 243 Shadwell High st
Hutchinson John, fruiterer, 36 Theobald's rd. Holborn
Hutchinson John, porkman, 33 South st. Manchester sq
Hutchinson John, surgeon, 105 Milton st. Dorset sq
Hutchinson John, surgeon, 184 Blackfriars rd
Hutchinson John, tailor, 15 St. John st. Clerkenwell
Hutchinson John, *White Hart* P.H. Queen st. Ratcliff
Hutchinson John H. *Duke of Argyle* P.H. 19Lit.Pulteney st
Hutchinson Joseph Benbrick, tailor, 3 Wellclose sq
Hutchinson Mark, carpet ma. & agt. 15 Dalby ter. Islington
Hutchinson Mary(Mrs.),grindery dlr. 2 Leigh st.Red Lion sq
Hutchinson Robert, leather importer, 4 Jewry st. Aldgate
Hutchinson Robert, porkbutcher, 31 Bethnal green rd
Hutchinson Thomas, cheesemonger, 3 Pitfield st. Hoxton
Hutchinson Walter, *Plasterers' Arms* P.H. 157 Tott. ct.rd
Hutchinson Wm. *Barley Mow* P.H. 12 South pl. Islington
Hutchinson Wm. cheesemgr. 112 High st. Marylebone
Hutchinson Wm. *Green Man* P. H. 9 Bucklersbury
Hutchinson Wm. trunk maker, 150 St. George st
Hutchinson Wm.work. jewlr. 21 Up. Rosoman st.Clerknwll
Hutchinson Wm. Barclay, surg. 40 Guilford st. Russell sq
Hutchison Alex. bookseller, 4 Lovell's ct. Paternoster row
Hutchison Andrew Kennedy,solicitor,2Crownct.Threadn. st
Hutchison Chas. pro. of languages, 17 Holland st. Kensngtn
Hutchison George, timber mercht. 16 Palace row, New rd
Hutchison John, surgeon, 8 River ter. north, City rd
Hutchison John, wine merchant, 37 Crutchedfriars
Hutchison Thomas, baker, 123 Crawford st. Portman sq
Hutchison Wm. patentee & inventor of manuel saw frames for cutting marble & stone; & statuary & marble merchant & mason, Salisbury wharf, & 23 Salisbury st. Strand
Hutchons William, builder, 7 Dorset place, Dorset sq
Huth Frederick & Co. merchants, 10 Moorgate st. Bank
Huthwaite & Co. brewers, Bromley, Middlesex
Hutley John, carman, 7 Stephen's mews, Gresse st
Hutley John, wholesale cheesemonger & provision agent, 1 High st. Bloomsbury
Hutson Jane (Mrs.), straw bonnet manfr. 46 King st. 7 dials
Hutson John, solicitor, 20 Upper Clifton st. Finsbury
Hutson Richard butcher, 10 Lombard st. Chelsea
Hutt Henry, hairdresser, 17 Tower st. Seven dials
Hutt John Saml.wine cooper & stout mer.6Skinnerst.Bshpgt
Hutt Richard Thos. fancy stationer, 10 City rd. Finsbury sq
Hutt Thomas Gough, tinman, 208 High st. Shadwell
Huttley John, cabinet maker, 25 Pitt st. Fitzroy sq
Huttley Redgrave Wm. dining rooms, 187 Shadwell High st
Huttly John, bootmaker, 40 Broad st. Bloomsbury
Hutton Js. & Thos. accountants, 5 Jeffrey's sq. St. Mary Axe
Hutton Thos. & Co. importers of berlin wool, patterns, embroideries,&c. manufacturers of fancy silks, canvas, fringes & dress trimmings, 6 Newgate street
Hutton Wm.Barnard & Sons,merchts.& factors,25Watling st
Hutton Benjamin, habit maker, 114 Park st. Grosvenor sq
Hutton Charles, physician, 25 Motcomb st. Belgrave square
Hutton Crompton, special pleader, 3 Churchyd. ct. Temple
Hutton Elizbth. (Mrs.), dining rooms, 90 Long la. Smithfield
Hutton Henry, miller, Nine Elms, Vauxhall
Hutton James, baker, 98 Park street, Grosvenor square
Hutton John, merchant, 11 Warnford court, Throgmorton st
Hutton John, newsvender, 16 Catherine street, Strand
Hutton John, publisher, 56 Mortimer street, Cavendish sq
Hutton Maria (Mrs.), milliner, 127 Upper st. Islington
Hutton Elth.(Mrs.), berlin wa.2Hereford ter. King's rd.Chlse
Hutton Richd. carpet wa. 36 Crawford st. & 7 Wyndham pl
Hux John & Sons, watch manfs. 41 Perceval st. Clerkenwell
Hux John, haberdasher, 23 Bartholomew terrace, Goswell rd
Hux William, pewterer, 7 Wilderness row, Clerkenwell
Huxham John, dairyman, 16 & 82 Shoe lane, Fleet street
Huxley & Heriot, cabinet & general ironmongers, brassfounders & gas fitters, 16, 28 & 29 Castle st. Long acre
Huxley George, tailor & draper, 7 King William st. Strand
Huxley Henry Thomas, barrister, 3 Pump court, Temple
Huxley James, clerk to musician's company, ornamental writer on vellum, & private tutor, 80 Fore st. Cripplegate
Huxley Mary (Mrs.), butcher, 8 St.George's pl.Walwrth.rd
Huxley Richard, china,glass,&c.dealer, 105 Tottenham ct. rd
Huxley Robert, wireworker to her Majesty's honourable board of ordnance, 69 Cannon st. City, & 5 Abchurch yard
Huxley Thomas, solicitor, 3 Pump court, Temple
Huxley Thomas, tobacco & snuff manuf. 13 Whitechapel rd
Huxstable George, tailor, 15 Wine Office court, Fleet st
Huxtable & Appleton, surgeons, Mare st. Hackney
Huxtable Daniel, dyer & scourer, 12 East st. Walworth rd
Huxtable John, chemist & druggist, 104 St.John st. Clknwell
Huxtable Thomas, silk manufactr. 9 Elder st.Norton folgate
Hyam Moses & Simon, clothes manufactrs. & warehousemen, 9 & 10 King st. Cheapside, & Colchester, Essex
Hyam Isaac, painter & glazier, 14 Bevis marks, St.Mary Axe
Hyam Lawrence, tailor, draper & outfit. 36 Gracechurch st
Hyam Levy, clothes dealer, 62 London road, Southwark
Hyam Sumerset, chemist, 151 Brick lane, Spitalfields
Hyams George, tailor & clothier, 17 Holywell st. Strand
Hyams Henry, fishmonger, see Phillips & Hyams
Hyams Henry, furrier & cap maker, 98 St. George st
Hyams Hyam, goldsmith & money changer, 22 & 59 Cornhill
Hyams Joshua, watch manufacturer, 18 Jewry st. Aldgate
Hyams Michael, cigar manuftr. 10 Albert place, City road
Hyams Philip, paper stainer, 198 Borough High st
Hyatt Edwin, printers' joiner, 6 Mortimer market,Tott. ct.rd
Hyatt Eliza (Miss), fringe warehouse, 32 Lamb's Conduit st
Hyde Geo. & Co. paper dealers, manufacturers of sealing wax, envelopes & account books, & the London manifold letter writer, 61 Fleet st
Hyde, Hodge & Co. merchants, 2 Great St. Helen's
Hyde, Lenox & Co. east india merchants, 8 Billiter square
Hyde Arthur Walker, *Clarendon Stores* P.H. 162 Oxford st
Hyde Benjamin, glove manufacturer, 66 Broad st.Blmsbury
Hyde Charles, solicitor, secretary to the London fever hospital, 33 Ely place, Holborn
Hyde Ebenezer Matthias, linendraper, see Smith & Hyde
Hyde Eliz. (Mrs.), *Nag's Head* P.H. Cain pl. Kentish town
Hyde George, cheesemonger, 32 Dockhead
Hyde George, dairyman 11 Sale st. Paddington
Hyde Henry, solicitor, 33 Ely place, Holborn
Hyde James Joseph, beer retailer, 9 South Lambeth place
Hyde James, merchant, 2 Great St. Helen's
Hyde John, fringe manufacturer, see Hamilton, Hyde & Co
Hyde John, shoemaker, 8 Little Chapel st. Westminster
Hyde Martha (Mrs.), cheesemonger, 12 Up. East Smithfield
Hyde Orlando, solicitor, 27 Coleman st. City
Hyde Rd. furniture broker, 1 Cumberland pl. Newington bts
Hyde Rd. whipmaker, 4 Rockingham place, New Kent road
Hyde Robert, tailor, 3 Greyhound court, Strand
Hyde Thos. *St. James's* coffee rms. 12 Swallow st. Piccadilly
Hyde Timothy, fruiterer, 13 Upper East Smithfield
Hyde William, bookseller, 17A Gt. Titchfield st. Oxford st
Hydon Charles, baker, 14 Albion st. Rotherhithe
Hyem & Barber, butchers, 282 High Holborn
HyemGeo.ship&insur.agt.&surv.ofshipping,seeGibbs&Hyem
Hyett Edward, baker, 74 Long alley, Worship st. Finsbury
Hyett James, *Newport Arms* P. H. Newport market
Hyland Henry, butcher, 41 Charlotte ter. New cut, Lambeth
Hyland James, bedsteadmak. 21 Croydon st. Bryanstone sq
Hyland Wm. boot & shoe mak. 10 Hungerford market arcade
Hyland Wm. grocer & teadealer, 8 Union row, Lit. Chelsea
Hyman David, marine store dlr. 1 Cumberld.pl. Newgtn.bts
Hyman William, clothier, 64 King st. Deptford
Hymass John, butcher, 3 Cross st. Hoxton New town
Hyms Solomon, fishmngr.112 Middlesex st.Aldgate High st
Hynam John, mfr.of congreves, magic fusees, blacking, inks, harness & metal polish, annatto, &c. 6 & 7 Princes sq. Finsby
Hynerd Wm. coffee rooms, 15 Marylebone lane, Oxford st
Hyrons En. antq. furniture man, 29 N. North st. Rd.Lion sq
Hyrons James Charles, butcher, 18 Rd. side, Mile end road
Hyslop John, hatter, 22 Narrow st. Limehouse
Hyslop Wm. linendraper, 4 Devonshire bldgs. Gt. Dover rd

I'ANSON Wm.Hy.&Co.tailors&drapers,12Bishopsgatewthn
I'Anson Edw.&Son, archit.&survey.10LaurencePountney la
I'Anson Edwd. upholsterer & cabinet maker, Grosvenor st
I'Anson John & Charles, builders, 4½ Cirencester pl. Fitzroy sq
Ibberson Christph. *Black Boy & Horse Shoe* P.H. 1 Nicholas la
Ibbetson Henry & Son, proctors, 15 Gt. Knightrider st
Ibbetson Fredk. grocer, 10 Brewer st. & 12 Skinner st.Sms.tn
Ibbetson John, grocer, Church st. Hackney
Ibbetson Richard, grocer, 10 Kent place, Old Kent road
Ibbetson Richard, grocer, 143 Church st. Shoreditch
Ibbett Robert Greaves, auctioneer, 167 Fleet st. & appraiser to City of London court of requests, 7 Bridgewater sq
Ibbotson George Augustus, dentist, 66 Brook st. Hanover sq
Ibbotson John, harness maker, 117 Edgware road
Ibbotson John, *Ibbotson's hotel*, 3 & 4 Vere st. Cavendish sq
Ibbotson Thos. who. slopseller, 21 Camomile st. Bishopsgate
Ibbotson Wm. lodging house, 5 Trinity pl. Charing cross
Ibbott James, lighterman, 19 Bond st.Commercial rd. Lambt
Ibbs George, printer, 29 East st. Red Lion square

Ibbs John Christopher, tailor, 16 Bennett st. Blackfriars
Ibetson John, chairma. 18 Lamb's Conduit pas. Red Lion sq
Ibison Geo. furn. broker, 7 Cumberland pl. Newington butts
Icom George, tea dealer, 18 Park ter. Regent's park road
Ide George, coal merchant, 21 Weymouth ter. Hackney road
Iddiols John, straw hat maker, 37 New Compton st. Soho
Idenden Wm. John, outfitter&draper, 2&3 Salmon la. Limeho
Idle Chas.&Sarah (Miss), grocers, 3Falcon pl. Ray st. Clrknwl
Idle Jas. Brougham, stock broker, 1 King's Arms buildings
Idle Jas. Brougham, wine mercht. 6 Talbot ct. Gracechurch st
Ierson Thomas, academy, 72 Manchester st. Gray's inn road
Ierson Thomas Robert, tailor & habit mak. 13 King st. Boro'
Ife Benj. job & postmaster, Market st. Hertford st. Mayfair
Ife Charles, jobmaster, 9 Carrington mews, Mayfair
Ifold William, surveyor, 33 Manchester st. Manchester sq
Igglesden Charles, grocer, 26 King st. Camden town
Iggulden, Puckle & Puckle, proctors, 3 Paul's Bakehouse ct
Ilbery James, bookselr.& statnr. 1 Gt. Titchfield st. Oxford st
Ilbery James, shipping agent, &c. 6 Beer lane, Tower st
Ilderton Henry Decimus, solicitor, 7 Lincoln's inn fields
Iles George, carpenter & blind manfr. 35 Bell yd. Temple bar
Iles George A. tobacconist, 106 St. John st. Smithfield
Iles Hen. iron & tin plate worker, 1 High st. Newn. butts
Iles John, beer retailer, 1 Park ter. King's rd. west, Chelsea
Iles Thos. umbrella stick ma.&horn dlr. 12 Thrawl st. Spitalfi
Iles Thomas, *Three Cranes* P.H. 194 Brick la. Spitalfields
Iles William, carman, 13 Webb st. Bermondsey st
Ilett James, baker, 16 High st. Newington butts
Iley Elizh.(Mrs.), bookseller & stationer, 28Stafford st. Bond st
Iley Thomas, linen & carpet wareh. 115 Whitechapel High st. & 3, 4 & 5 Kent & Essex st.
Iliff James, cattle salesman, 17 West Smithfield
Iliff Joseph, *Windmill inn*, 115 St. John st. Smithfield
Iliff Mathews & Iliff, surgeons, Canterbury row, Newington, & 12 Foxley road, Kennington
Iliff Wm Tiffen, surgeon, 19 Canterbury row, Newington
Iliffe John, solicitor, see Cardale, Cardale & Iliffe
Illidge John, glass & medical wareh. 34 Gt. Dover st. Boro'
Illidge John, stockbroker, Stock Exchange
Illidge John Betts, solicitor, Weaver's hall, 22 Basinghall st
Illidge Thos. Hy. portrait painter, 33 Bruton st. Berkeley sq
Illingworth Jas. tailor & draper, 44 Union st. Bishpsgt. witht
Illingworth Wm. ho.& ship joiner, 9½ Gt. Hermitage st. Wapg
Illingworth Richd. Stonehewer, wine mercht. 11 Waterloo pl
Illingworth Hy. Stanhope, surgeon, see Moore & Illingworth
Illman William, trunk, box & case maker, 33 Noble st. & 11 Westmoreland buildings, Aldersgate st
Illuminated Magazine office, 320 Strand
Illustrated London News office, 198 Strand
Illustration Off. (Journal de Paris), 1 Finch la. Cornhill
Ilott John, surgeon, 28 Cowcross st. St. John st
Ilsley George, brass mounter, 3 Church st. Chelsea
Ilsley Henry, working jeweller, 82 Theobald's road
Ilsley Jeremiah Thos. tire smith, 101 Whitechapel High st
Imber Edmund, beer retailer 19 Walcot pl. West, Lambeth
Imbrie John Edward, shell fish warehouse, 47 Strand
Imbrie John Taylor, tailor, see Sparrow & Imbrie
Imeson Charles, carp. & undertaker, 9 Down st. Piccadilly
Imeson Joseph, builder, 27A, Charles st. Berkeley sq
Imison Samuel, gas fitter, 18 Marquis court, Drury lane
Immhof Nicholaus, clockmaker, 24 Curtain road, Shoreditch
Imperial Baths, Gloucester st. Hackney fields
Imperial Brazilian Mining Ass. 52 Old Broad st
Imperial Coal Company, 450A, West Strand
Imperial Continental Gas Association (Wm. Walton, sec.), 7 Whitehart court, Lombard st
Imperial Fire Insurance Company (P. Milner, accountant), Sun court, Cornhill, & 16 Pall mall; see page 2029
Imperial Gas Light & Coke Company (Alexr. Henry, sec), offices, 33 John st. Bedford row, & 38 Wyndham st. Bryanstone sq.; factories, Maiden lane, King's cross; Great Cambridge st. Haggerston; & King's road, Fulham
Imperial Life Insurance Co. (S. Ingall, actuary), Sun court, Cornhill, & 16 Pall mall; see page 2029
Impey Francis, solicitor, see Clipperton & Impey
Impey William, grocer, &c. 141 Bethnal green road
Imray &Fitch, who. statnrs. & papr hang. mnf. 3 O. Fish st. hl
Imray Eliz. (Mrs.), herbalist, 24 Union st. East, Spitalfields
Imray James, chart publisher, &c. 116 Minories
Imrie James, bread & biscuit baker, 36 Brewer st. Golden sq
Imrie William, surgeon dentist, 16 Saville row, Piccadilly
Im Thurn John C. & Co. merchants, 65 Fenchurch st
Ince Joseph & Son, plasterers, 57 Gt. Saffron hill, Hatton gar
Ince & North, paintrs. &plumbers, 3 Stephen's acre, Blackwll
Ince Edward Brett, publisher of the law journal reports, 5 Quality court, Chancery lane
Ince George, umbrella manufr. 32 Union st. Bishopsgate
Ince James, carman & sand dealer, 23 Whitefriars st
Ince James, furrier, 75 Oxford st
Ince John, surgeon, 3 Lower Grosvenor place
Ince Joseph Murray, artist, 9 George st. Portman sq
Ince Saml. umbrella mak. 12 Old Montague st. Whitechpl
Ince Thomas, wine merchant, 23 New Bond st
Inchbold Thos. Mawson, booksell. & stationer, 7 Ludgate hill
Income & Property Tax offices, see Property & Income Tax offices
Incorporated Law Society of the United Kingdom (R. Maugham, sec.), 106 to 109 Chancery lane
Ind, Coope &Co. ale & porter brewers, Romford, & at the Jerusalem coffee house, Cowpers ct. Cornhill, & 13 Gt. Garden st. Whitechapel
Indemnity Mutual Marine Assurance Co. (Nicholas Chester, sec.), 36 Gt. Winchester st
Independent Gas Light Comp. (Robt. Laing, sec.), office at the works, Haggerston
Indermaur Jacob & Fred. cabinet manufrs. 40 Lant. st. Boro'
Indermaur Fred. cabinet ma. & auctioneer, 71 Union st. Boro'
Indermaur John George, artist, 8 Howland st. Fitzroy sq
Indermaur Herman, dyer & scourer, 51 Wood st. Cheapside, & 29 Finsbury pavement
Inderwick Jno. imp. of meerschaum pipes, 58 Princes st. Leic. sq
India Board, Cannon row, Parliament st
India Insurance Co. 39 Moorgate st. Lothbury
Indian Iron & Chrome Ore Co. 10½ King's Arms yd. Moorgate st
Indian News monthly newspaper, 1 Green arbr. ct. Old Bailey
Indigent Blind Visiting Society (Charles Harman, sec.), 20 Red Lion square, Holborn
Indigent Refuge (Miss Sarah Stephens, matron), 3 Princes st. Bedford row
Infant Orphan Asylum, Wanstead (Rev. P. P. Gilbert, M.A. & Rev. Thomas Stanton, M.A. hon. secs.; Mr. John Buckler, sub. sec.) *office* 2 Winchester bldgs. Old Broad st
Infant School Depository, 19 Cheapside
Infant School Society (J. I. Wathen, sec.), 18 Baldwin's gdns
Infirmary for Asthma, Consumption, and other diseases of the Lungs, (Saml. Amory, sec.), 10 Artillery st. Bpsgate
Infirmary for Diseases of the Skin, & Free Dispensary (John Hastings, surgeon), 1 Blenheim st. Oxford st
Infirmary for Fistula, Piles, & other diseases of the lower Intestine, 38 Charterhouse sq. Tue.& Fri. ½ past 12 to 1
Ing Maria, Agnes, & Mary A. (Misses), *Blue Posts* P.H. 10 Mount Pleasant
Ing Peter, *Essex Head tavern*, 40 Essex st. Strand
Ingall Charles, wine & spirit merchant, 83 Upper Thames st
Ingall Charles, accountant, 6 Bank chambers, Lothbury
Ingall Frederick Blucher, rectifier, 99 Houndsditch
Ingall John Man, merchant, Hall of Commerce
Ingall Samuel, actuary of *Imperial Life Insurance Co.* Sun court, Cornhill, & 16 Pall mall
Ingarfield David, fruiterer, 130 Crawford st. Portman sq
Ingarfield Wm. fishmonger, 36 Paddington st. Marylebone
Ingram & Hart, linendra. & silk mers. 56 Red Lion st. Holborn
Ingham, Stevens & Co. (of Marsala), 16 London st. Fenchurch st
Ingham Edward, boot & shoe ma. 13 East st. Walworth rd
Ingham George, straw hat maker, 46 Banner st. St. Luke's
Ingham James, line&rope ma. South pl. Up. Grange rd. Brmsy
Ingham James, ale merchant, 33 Exmouth st. Clerkenwell
Ingham James Taylor, barrister, 5 Inner Temple lane
Ingham Robert, barrister, 13 King's Bench walk, Temple
Ingle Henry, locksmith & bellhanger, 12 Shoe lane, Fleet st
Ingle James, warehouseman, see Coates, Ingle & Wood
Ingle William, woollendraper & tailor, 91 Shoreditch
Ingledew & Cattley, who. grocers, 68 Upper Thames st
Ingledew & Gandell, tea & col. brokers, 37 Mincing lane
Ingledew Thomas Craike, pea & potato salesman, 35 Lambeth walk, 24 Borough market, & 352 Rotherhithe wall
Ingles David, merchant, 4 Barge yard, Bucklersbury
Inglis & Wakefield, mousseline de laine manufacturers & printers, 20 Friday st. Cheapside
Inglis Adam, clock manufacturer, 39 St. John's sq. Clerknw
Inglis David, watchmaker, 13 Motcomb st. Belgrave sq
Inglis Jas. manager, *Caledonian Insurance Co.* 27 Moorgate st
Inglis John, bookseller & stationer, 13 Tysoe st. Exmouth st
Inglis Malcolm, commission agent, 38 Walbrook
Inglis Mary (Mrs.), leatherseller, 44 Tabernacle wk. Finsbury
Inglis Thomas, coffee rooms, 297 Strand
Inglis Thos. digestive bread baker, 5 New st. Covent garden
Inglis Thomas, *Walnut Tree* P.H. 40 St. Albans st. Lambeth
Inglis William, baker, 14 Lit. Russell st. Bloomsbury
Inglis William, baker, 6 Trinity st. Borough
Inglis William, baker, 60 & 61 John st. Fitzroy sq
Inglis Wm. biscuitbaker & bookg. off. 75 St. Paul's church yd

Inglish Benj. Hanson, proprietor of Scot's pills, 165 Strand
Inglish Chas. watch finisher, 25 Ironmonger st. St. Luke's
Ingolby Fredk. surgeon, see Camplin & Ingolby
Ingoldby Edward, wholesale laceman, 124 Wood st. City
Ingoldsby John, foreign agent, 1 Fowkes bdgs. Gt. Tower st
Ingpen Abel. bookslr. &statnr. 11 Adam'spl. King'srd. Chelsea
Ingram & Cooke, printers, 9 Crane court, Fleet st
Ingram Alexander, baker, 33 Gifford st. Hoxton
Ingram Benj. jun. mahogany & timber mer. 38 Beech st
Ingram Charles, eating house, 46 Borough High st
Ingram Charles, hair dresser, 29 Portland st. Soho
Ingram Edward, poulterer, 18 King David lane, Shadwell
Ingram Edwd. saddletree ma. 24 Earl st. Wilson st. Finsbury
Ingram Edward Russell, solicitor, 1 Lancaster place, Strand
Ingram Emily (Miss), milliner, Albany road, Camberwell
Ingram Hannah (Mrs.), *Ship* P.H. 76 Brunswick st. Blackwll
Ingram Henry, poulterer, 29 Fieldgate st. Whitechapel
Ingram Henry Wm. woollen warehouse, 4 Addle st. Wood st
Ingram James, attorney, see Rooper, Birch & Ingram
Ingram John, hatter, 126 Brunswick st. Hackney road
Ingram John, upholsterer, 29 City road, Finsbury square
Ingram Robt. straw & tuscan manfr. 17 Powell st. east
Ingram Thos. butcher, 12 Bozier's court, Tottenham ct. rd
Ingram Thos. professor of music, 4A, Denbigh st. Pimlico
Ingram William, fishmonger, 14 Clare st. Clare market
Ingram William, watchmaker, 11 Wilderness row
Ings Edward, barrister, 2 Verulam buildings, Gray's inn
Inkpen John, builder & undertaker, 1 Bridge st. Vauxhall
Inkson John, tailor, 10 Little Ryder st. St. James's
Inkson William, linendraper, see Mann & Inkson
Inman John, furnishing undrtkr. 21½, Union rw. NewKent rd
Inman Samuel, undrtak.& veneer cutter, 53 Brick la. St. Lks
Inman William, *Castle tavern*, 31 Mark lane
Inman Thos. auctnr.&farm agt. 22Devonshire pl. Edgwr rd
Inman Wm. Southgate, architect, 5 Upper gore, Kensington
Innell & Cookes, varnish ma. 34 Lit. Queen st. High Holborn
Innell HenryB.&Co. varnish mfrs. BelleIsle, Maidenla. Kgs.cr
Innell (Misses), milliners, &c. 3 Robson's pl. Kennington road
Inner Temple, east of Middle Temple gate, Temple-bar; *Treasurer's Office*, under the hall; hours 10to 4; *Library*, 3 Tanfield court, hours 11 to 4
Innes, Hodge & Co. merchants, 61 Moorgate st
Innes Geo. Archbald, barrister, 2 Plowden buildgs. Temple
Innes George Rose, solicitor & scotch law agt. 20 Billiter st
Innes James, *Queen's Arms hotel*, 76 Cheapside
Innes John, baker, 2 Southampton row, Russell square
Innes John, printer, 61 Wells st. Oxford st
Innes John Jameson, who. cheesemonger, see Jameson & Innes
Innes John Mair, wine merchant, 25 Coleman st
Innes John Rose, merchant, 20 Billiter st
Innes Robert Hugh, merchant, Lloyd's coffee house
Innes William, pianoforte maker, 2 Keppel st. Russell sq
Innholders' Hall (C. Druce, jun. clk.), 6College st. Dowgatehill
Innis & Cooke, surgeons, 29 Fitzroy square
Innis Charles, solicitor, 15 Lincoln's inn fields
Innis William, hairdresser, 29 Whitefriars st
Inman Thomas, house agent, 22 Devonshir pl. Edgeware rd
Innocent Robt. watchma. 11 Ann'spl. Pritchardrd. Hackneyrd
Innocent Thos. grocer, 127 Shadwell High st
Innocent Thomas, tea dealer, see Croft & Innocent
Innot Sarah (Mrs.), undertaker, 9 Weston st. Borough
Innott (Mrs.), bellows & umbrella ma. 302 Kent st. Boro'
Innous Thomas Pettit, coal merchant, 41 Lombard st. City, & Railway wharf, Greenwich road
Inocent John, grocer, 34 White st. Borough
Inrolment Office, Chancery lane; hours 10 to 2 & 6 to 8, during term; & 10 to 3, vacation; David Drew, clerk
Inquirer weekly newspaper, 2 Green arbour ct. Old Bailey
Inskipp Alfred, morocco leath. dres. see Dailey & Inskipp
Inskipp Henry, merchant, North & S. American coffee house
Insley Robert, tailor, 120 Mount st. Berkeley square
Insolv. Debtors' Court Offi. 5 Portugal st. Linc. inn; 10 to 4
Inspector General of Fortifications (Sir John Bourgoyne), 84 Pall mall; 10 to 4
Inspector Tax Account (London dist.) Stamp Off.; hrs. 10to4
Insted Geo. Burgess, fruiterer, 1 Jamaica row, Bermondsy rd
Institution of Civil Engineers (Charles Manby, secretary), 25 Great George st. Westminster
Institution for Diseases of the Ear, 32 Sackville st
Institution for Persons afflicted with Blindness (John Simpson, secretary), 29 Saville row, Old Burlington st
Institution for the Employment & Religious Instruction of the Adult Deaf & Dumb, 26 Red Lion square
Instone Henry, diningrooms, New cross
Invalid Asylum for respectable Females in London & its Vicinity (Mrs. M. Lister), High st. Stoke Newington
Invalid Office, 4 Northumberland st. Strand; hours 10 to 4
Inville John, vestry clerk, 22 Albion pl. Walworth road
Inwards John, fruiterer, 14 Blackmoor st. Drury lane
Inwards Joseph Warren, greengr. 12 Kent pl. Old Kent rd
Inwards Mary (Mrs.), potato saleswoman, Clare market
Inwood Edward, fruiterer, 3 Adam st. west, Bryanstone sq
Inwood James, stationer, 4 Brunswick row, Westminster
Inwood Thomas, baker, 5 East India road, Poplar
Inwood William, carpenter, &c. Stoke Newington green
Ion David, *Mulberry Tree* P.H. Stepney green
I'on John Launcelot, surgeon, 65 Bridge road, Lambeth
Ion Edgar Mortimer, *Warwick Arms* P.H. 14 Gillingham st
Ion John Augustus, baker, 2 Lower Eaton st. Pimlico
Ion John Henry, *Eagle & Wheatsheaf* P.H. 8 Albion pl. Hyde park
Ion Matthew, woollen manufacturer, 6½ Vigo st. Regent st
Ionian Bank (Wm. Kettlewell, sec.), 6 Great Winchester st
Ionides & Co. turkey merchants, 9 Finsbury circus
Ionn Mary Ann (Mrs.), 3 *Compasses* P.H. 1 Freeschool st. Horselydown
Iorns Charles Henry, linendraper, see Austen & Iorns
Ipswich Express, & Essex & Suffolk Mercury 2 Green Arb.ct
Ipswich & Yarmouth Coast Railway Company's Office (Frederick James Bigg), 12 Old Jewry chambers
Irazoqui Miguel, wine merchant, 20 Berners st. Oxford st
Iredale John Hammond, who. teadlr. 75 Charlotte st. Port.pl
Iredell Lestock Wilson, gen. broker, 5 Church ct. Clement's la
Ireland Jane & Son, newsvenders, 6 Lit. Bridge st. Blackfrs
Ireland Charles, *Falcon* P.H. 127 Fetter lane, Holborn
Ireland George, *Golden Fleece* P.H. Mill lane, Deptford
Ireland George, grocer, 2 Bell st. Edgware road
Ireland Geo. *OldDuke Wm.* P.H. 100OldGravel la. Wapping
Ireland James, academy, 7 Russell place, Old Kent road
Ireland James, baker, 86 Theobald's road
Ireland James, bottled ale & stout mer. 8 Hungerford wharf
Ireland James, *Green Dragon* P.H. 102 Fore st. Cripplegate
Ireland John, fruiterer, 1 Baker's row, Walworth road
Ireland John, surgeon, &c. 19 Tabernacle row, Finsbury
Ireland John Jas. surgeon, 17 Marchmont st. Burton cresc
Ireland Peter, carpent. & underta. 33 Augustus st. Rgt's. pk
Iremonger David, carpenter, 58 Gt. Sutton st. Clerkenwell
Ireson John, mason, 49 Vine st. Romney st. Westminster
Irish Evangelical Society (Rev. Thos. James, sec.), 7 Blomfield st. Finsbury
Irish, the Honourable Society of London (John E. Davies, sec.), Irish chambers, Guildhall yard
Irish Henry, saddler, &c. 14 Stockwell terrace, Clapham rd
Irish Land Investment Co. (agents, Messrs. Richard Taylor & Co.) 26 Birchin la. Cornhill; office hours from 10 till 4
Irish North Midland Railway Co. (Philip Pottin Souper, sec.), 5 Barge yard, Bucklersbury
Irish Office, 18 Gt. Queen st. Wesminster; hours 11 to 5
Irish Society (M. E. Conan, sec.), 26 Suffolk st. Pall mall ea
Irish Society of London (Wm. Humphries, sec.), 32 Sackville st
Irish Stamps Sale Off. Stamp off. Somerset ho.; hrs. 10 to 4
Irish Waste Land Improvement Society (Frederick Fry, sec.), 5 St. Mildred's ct. Poultry; hours of attendance 10 to 4 daily
Irish Fredk. carver & gilder, 35 Windmill st. Tottenh. ct. rd
Irish Saml. P. die sinker, &c. 25 Clement's la. Lombard st
Irish Wm. tailor, 2 Short st. Finsbury
Iron Collier Coal Co. (Chs. Barlee, mgr.), 15Duke st. Adelphi
Iron Nathaniel, provision merchant, see Bevan, Iron & Co
Ironmongers' Hall (Simon A Beck, clerk), 118 Fenchurch st
Iron Times Newspaper Office, 112 Fleet st
Irons David, tailor, 56 Market st. Edgware rd Paddington
Irons Ths. floorcloth wa. 12 Princes st. Lecstr.sq.&Lit. Chelsea
Ironside Robt. Duff, provision mer. 1 Bull head ct. Newgate st
Ironside Wm. wine & spirit merchant, 5 Gt. Trinity lane
Irvin Geo. cheesemonger, 8 Artichoke row, Mile end road
Irvine Jas.&Sons, wine, spirit & beer mrchts. 12 Coopers' row
Irvine Elizabeth (Mrs.), optician, 32 Kirby st. Hatton garden
Irvine Alex. Rt. direct. Gt. Britain Life Soc. 14 Waterloo pl
Irvine John, watch movement ma. 34 Spencer st. Goswell rd
Irvine Robert, baker, 73 Cornwall road, Lambeth
Irvine Samuel, grocer, &c. 29 Camden st. Islington green
Irving & Brown, coal merchts. Broken wharf, 224 Wapping
Irving Edward, accountant, 9 Fenchurch buildings
Irving George, boot & shoe maker, 25 Great Saffron hill
Irving James Corbet, solicitor, Roll's cham. 89 Chancery la
Irving John, merchant, see Reid, Irving & Co
Irwin Andrew Wm. plumber & glazier, 7 Bell yd. Temple bar
Irwin Anthony Wellington, solicitor, 11 King's rd. Bedford rw
Irwin George, bootmaker, 160 Shadwell High street
Irwin Henry, surgeon & chemist, 33 Goswell st

Irwin Henry, watch & clock maker, 35 White Lion st. Pentnvil
Irwin John, beer retailer, 1 Charles st. St. George's east
Irwin John, hatmaker, see Wilson, Gibb & Irwin
Irwin John, wigmaker, 18 Berwick st. Soho
Isaac Alexander & Son, curriers, 147 & 148 St. John st. Smthfield
Isaac Alexander, merchant, 148 St. John st. West Smithfield
Isaac Alex. G. import. of beads, 37 Nottingham pl. Whitechapel
Isaac George, bead mercht. 3 Mount ter. New rd. Whitchpl. rd
Isaac Israel, cigar manufacturer, see Allen & Isaac
Isaac John C. curiosity dealer, 12 Wardour st. Soho
Isaac Joseph, pianoforte maker, 75 Lisson grove north
Isaac Joseph, tailor, 119 Middlesex st. Aldgate High st
Isaac Mary (Mrs.), ladies' school, 6 York ter. Kingsland rd
Isaac Philip, mercht. & navy agt. 56 Gt. Prescot st. Goodman's fl
Isaac Wm. auctnr. & appraiser, 5 Seymour pl. York st. Wlwth. rd
Isaac William, whip manufacturer, see Swaine & Isaac
Isaac William Henry, shoemaker, 161 Rotherhithe st
Isaacs Asher & Son, clothes dealers, 11 White st. Houndsditch
Isaacs (Isaac, Henry Freiberg & Lewis), proprietors of the Phils buildings clothes & general mart, Houndsditch
Isaacs Aaron, butcher, 23 Duke st. Aldgate
Isaacs Abraham, clothes salesman, 5 & 6 Rosemary lane
Isaacs Abraham, orange merchant, 11 Lamb st. Spitalfields
Isaacs Benj. *Blue Anchor* P.H. 1 Middlesex st. Whitechapel
Isaacs Elias, solicitor, 6 Jeffrey's square, St. Mary Axe
Isaacs Elizbth. (Miss), dressma. 23 Blackmoor st. Drury la
Isaacs Elizabeth (Mrs.), straw hat maker, 62 King st. Boro'
Isaacs Emanuel, furniture wareho. 134 Aldersgate st
Isaacs Emanuel, furniture dealer, 17 Gt. Charlotte st. Blkfrs
Isaacs Esther (Miss), butcher, 34 Duke st. Aldgate
Isaacs Henry, glass cutter & stopperer, 159 Fenchurch st
Isaacs Hyam, bottle, phial & medical glass merchant, 25 Francis st. Tottenham court road
Isaacs Isaac, appraiser, auctioneer, &c. 8 Houndsditch
Isaacs Isaac, clothes dealer, 112 Houndsditch
Isaacs Isaac, fishmonger, 8 Cullum st. Fenchurch st
Isaacs Isaac, jeweller, 18 Swan st. Minories
Isaacs Isaac, undertaker, 43 Henry st. Hampstead road
Isaacs Joseph, *Black Lion* P.H. 99 Middlesex st. Whitechpl
Isaacs Joseph, pawnbroker, 11 Union st. Bishopsgate
Isaacs Lazarus, fruit merchant, 2 King st. Aldgate
Isaacs Lewis, dealer in jewellery, watches, &c. 66 Leman st
Isaacs Lewis, furniture broker, 25 Chapel st. Somers town
Isaacs Lewis, watchmaker, 23 Houndsditch
Isaacs Michael, imp. of forn. fruits, 7 St. James' pl. Aldgate
Isaacs Morice, furniture broker, 56 Brill row, Somers town
Isaacs Moses, cab proprietor, 20 Bowling green la. Clerkenwl
Isaacs Philip, marine store dealer, 1 New inn passage, & 17 Houghton st. Clare market
Isaacs Phineas, furrier, 12 Norton folgate
Isaacs Rebecca (Mrs.), coal dealer, 27 Liquorpond st
Isaacs Samuel, fruit merchant, 5 & 7 St. James' pl. Aldgate
Isaacs Samuel, orange merchant, 18 Mitre st. Aldgate
Isaacs Solomon, bottle merchant, 18 East st. Manchester sq
Isaacson Isaac, glass warehouse, 222 High st. Shadwell
Isaacson John Frederick, attorney, 40 Norfolk st. Strand
Isaacson Richard, bootmaker, 63 Lit. Albany st. Regt's. pk
Isacke William, bookbinder, 18 Sherborne lane, City
Isbell Isaac, carrier, King st. Battersea
Iselin John James, merchant, 4 Austinfriars, Old Broad st
Iselton Samuel, boot & shoe maker, 33 Gt. Dover st. Boro'
Isern James, lapidary, 16 Upper Union court, Holborn hill
Isherwood Nicholas & Son, house decorators, 35 Ludgate hill
Isherwood James, *Globe* P.H. 53 Regent st. Lambeth
Isherwood John F. painter, &c. 13 Holland pl. Clapham rd
Isherwood Robert, ladies' boot & shoe ma. 17 Ludgate hill
Isherwood Robert, proctor, see Shephard, Isherwood & Co
Isidore Denis M. coiffeur & perfumer, 217 Regent st
Isidore Marchand, hairdresser, 14 Bentinck st. Manchstr. sq
Isitt Charles & John, cattle salesmen, 17 West Smithfield
Isles Joseph, grocer, 8 Broomfields, Deptford
Isley Chas. beer retailer, 41 Wellington st. Goswell st
Islington Dispensary, 1 Church row, Upper st. Islington
Islington Literary & Scientific Society (Chas. Woodward, esq. F.R.S. treas.; Josiah Wilkinson, sec.; Wm. Henry Butterfield, esq. librarian), Wellington st. Upper st. Islngtn
Islington Parish Wharf, 25 Wharf road, City road
Islington Savings' Bk. (N. Clifton, treas.), Mansion ho. Low. st
Islip George, tobacconist, 2 Staverton row, Walworth road
Ismay Joseph, skinner & hatters' furrier, 14 Gt. Guildford st
Ison Wm. baker, 1 New st. Shoemaker row, Blackfriars
Israel Aron, merchant, see Turner, Israel & Co
Israel Henry Ash, carcase butcher, 66 Aldgate High st
Israel Israel, fruiterer, Centre row, Covent garden
Israel John Isaac, butcher, 30 Tower st. Seven dials
Israel Sampson, furn. bro. & statn. 7 Constitn. rw. Gray's in. rd
Israel Sarah (Mrs.), poulterer, 113 Middlesex st. Aldgate
Issel Robert William, shoema. 13 King st. Kensington
Issitt John William, hardwaremn. 50 York st. Westminster
Italian & Austrian Railway Co. (Willam March, sec.), 112 Bishopsgate st. within
Itter Henry, baker, 9 Vere st. Clare market
Ivall David, coach & harness maker, 158 Tottenham court road, & 18½ Cardington st. Hampstead road
Ivatts George, tailor, 6 Great Quebec st. Montagu sq
Ivatts Thomas, *Mason's Arms* P.H. 35 Canterby. pl. Lambeth
Ive Charles Simon, goldsmith & watchmaker, 126 Cheapside
Ive Edward, shipping butcher, 94 Fore st. Limehouse
Ive George Henry, gold & silvrsm. & jwllr. 10 Finsbury pl. nth
Ive William John Alfred, ship builder, Deptford green
Ivens Brothers, merchants, St. Peter's chambers, Cornhill
Ivens Edmund, cattle salesman, 60 West Smithfield
Iverson Edward, tobacconist, 128 Tooley street
Iverson Richard, dining rooms, 42 St. John st. Smithfield
Iverson Thos. plumber & glazier, 21 Church rw. Bethnal green
Ivery James, bell hanger & gasfitter, 4 Pitt st. Fitzroy sq
Ives Jonathan & Co. cheesemongers, 96 Fore st. City
Ives & Swan, booksellers, 14 Paternoster row
Ives Edmund, upholsterer, appraiser, &c. 124 High Holborn
Ives Edward, livery stables, Devonshire rw. mews, Portland pl
Ives George, tailor, 44 Edmund st. King's cross
Ives Henry, turner, 56 Paradise st. Rotherhithe
Ives Henry Stephen, *Globe* P.H. 33 Crutchedfriars
Ives James, furniture broker, 8 Back rd. St. George's east
Ives James, guilder, 1 Nassau st. Middlesex hospital
Ives Jas. Payne, *Old King's Head* P.H. 173 Blackfriars road
Ives John, cattle salesman, 8 West Smithfield
Ives John, clothes salesman, 7 Crucifix lane, Bermondsey
Ives John, varnish manuf. 23 Gt. Queen st. Lincoln's inn fields
Ives John Edwin, grocer, 11 Up. Porchester st. Oxford terrace
Ives Joseph, tailor, 5 Cloth fair, West Smithfield
Ives William, hairdresser, 247 Poplar High st
Ivett James, fruiterer, 25 Newport court, Newport market
Ivey Charles John, fancy trimg. mnfr. 48 Radnor st. St. Luke's
Ivimey John, tailor, Fairfield road, Mile end road
Ivimey Joseph, solicitor & superintendent registrar of births, deaths & marriages for the district of St. Pancras, 26 Chancery lane, & 1 Ampthill square, Hampstead road
Iviny Augustus, chemist, 19 Fashion street, Dockhead
Ivison Fletcher, wine merchant (of Cadiz & Oporto), 35 Crutched friars
Ivison James, carpenter, 3 Bowling green st. Kennington
Ivison Wm. P. accountant, &c. 11 Union ct. O. Broad st. City
Ivory Chas. chimney sweeper, 13 Cross st. King st. Golden sq
Ivory Chas. J. stationer, 23 Coleman st. City
Ivory George, silversmith, 53 Compton st. Clerkenwell
Ivory Thomas, barrister, 25 Old square, Lincoln's inn
Ivory Wm. furniture broker, 23 Broomfields, Deptford
Ivy Edward, coal merchant, 7 Southampton ter. Pentonville
Ivy John, musical instrum. ma. & importer, see Wood & Ivy
Ivyleafe James, hat manufacturer, 139 Regent street
Izant Frederick, dining rooms, 21 Bucklersbury
Izard Isaac, tailor & draper, 47 Gloucester st. Queen sq
Izard John, water gilder, 20 Greenhill's rents, Smithfield bars
Izatt William, boot & shoe maker, 118 Regent st. Lambeth
Izod & Co. dealers in printing materials, compo. roller manufacturers, brass rule cutters, printers' smiths, joiners, space line & metal furniture founders, Wheatsheaf yard, Farringdon street
Izod George, grocer & teadealer, 180 Borough High st
Izod James, auctioneer, 46 Watling st. & 5 Low. Kenningtn. la
Izod James, printers' smith, 2 & 3 Wheatsheaf yd. Farringdon st
Izod James, wine merchant, 18 Cullum st
Izod Wm. ironfdr. & coppersm. Grove, Gt. Guildford st. Boro
Izons Wm. & Co. mfrs. of cast iron kitchen furn. 9 College hill
Izzard James, lodging house, 38 Great Pulteney st
Izzard James, turner in ordinary to her Majesty, bookseller & stationer, 46 Upper Brook st. Grosvenor square
Izzard James, whiting manfr. 14 Heneage st. Whitechapel
Izzard Robert, leather dresser & manufacturer of japan & enamel leather, table covers, &c. 81 Long lane, Borough
Izzard Wm. C. haberdasher, 70B, Salisbury st. Lisson grove

JACCARD David, watchmaker, 26 Perceval st. Clerkenwell
Jack's Coffee House, Old Corn Exchange, Mark lane
Jack Alexander, hardwareman & toy dlr. 78 Fore st. Crippleg
Jack Chas. imprtr. & manfr. of sheet zinc & perforator of all kinds of metal, & mnfr. of zinc window blinds, 80 Upper Thames st. & 8 & 9 Tottenham court, New road
Jack Donald, oil & colorman, 8 Skinner st. Somers town
Jack James, wine, spirit & porter mer. 106 Up. East Smithfl
Jack John, baker, 5 Willow walk, Kentish town

Jack John, coffee rooms, 3 Rupert st. Haymarket
Jack William, tailor, 1 Broad court, Long acre
Jack William, tailor, 88 Wheeler st. Spitalfields
Jackaman Simon, attorney, 1 Bartlett's buildings, Holborn
Jacklin George, tailor & draper, 14 Queen st. Cheapside
Jacklin George, working jeweller, 8 Oakley st. Lambeth
Jacklin Joseph, coppersmith, &c. see Pontifex, Jacklin & Co
Jackman John Whiteman, perfumer, 15 North pl.Knglnd.rd
Jacks & Hay, insurance brokers, 75 Old Broad st. City
Jackson Andrew & Co. woollen warehouse, 81 Queen st.City
Jackson Elizh.Anna&Hannah, juvenile wareho.164 Regent st
Jackson G. L. & Sons, ship & ins.bros. 2 Billiter ct. Billiter sq
Jackson Geo. & Son, surgeons, 30 Church st. Spitalfields
Jackson Geo. & Sons, composition ornament, papier machée & carton pierre manfrs. 49 & 50 Rathbone place, Oxford st
Jackson Geo. & Wm. & Chas. furn. brokers, Little Chelsea
Jackson & Graham, upholsterers, cabinet makers, furniture printers, carpet manufacturers, interior decorators, & house agents, 37 & 38 Oxford st
Jackson & Greenslade, hop & seed mers. 67 Boro' High st
Jackson Henry & Sons, who. boot & shoe mks.65 Leadenhall st
Jackson Henry & Son, wholesale watch manufacturers, 66 Red Lion st. Clerkenwell
Jackson Jas. & Hen. plumbers, &c. 51 Broad st. Golden sq
Jackson Jas. & Son, tailors & habit maks. 5 Cork st.Bond st
Jackson & Jenkyn, solctrs. & irish agts. 11 John st. Adelphi
Jackson Jsph. & Son, merchts.& drysalters, 103 Bermondseyst
Jackson & Knill, wharfingers & warehouse keepers, Cox & Hammond's quays, & Fresh & Londonbridge steam wharfs
Jackson L. & Co. for. stock & railway agts. 11 Pinners' hall
Jackson Richd. & Son, apothecaries, 28 Charlesst.St.James'
Jackson & Smythe, coal mers. Crown wharf, 41 ShadThames
Jackson Thos. Sherriff & Co. linen mfrs. 72 Aldermanbury
Jackson & Walford, bookslrs. & publrs. 18 St. Paul's ch. yd
Jackson Wm. & Co. distilrs. 1 New st. Dockhead, Southwk
Jackson Wm. & Co. wholesale slopsellers, 38 Leadenhall st
Jackson Wm.&Son, wax & tal. chandlrs. 19 Threadneedle st
Jackson & Wilson, wine & spirit merchts. 147 Leadenhall st
Jackson Albert Francis, barrister, 1 Tanfield court, Temple
Jackson Alexander, carpenter, 4 Cleveland st. Fitzroy sq. & 52 Warren st. Fitzroy square
Jackson Alexander, *Princess Amelia* P.H. 181 Oxford st
Jackson Amelia(Mrs.), vellumbinder, 15 Peter's hill, St.Paul's
Jackson Ann(Mrs.), oyster dealer, 12 Tower royal, Watling st
Jackson Ann(Mrs.), haberdasher, 38 Gt.Queen st. Linc.inn flds
Jackson Ann (Mrs.), staymaker, 26 Crosby row, Walw. rd
Jackson Ann (Mrs.), shoemak. 2 Cumberland st. Midlsx.hosp
Jackson Augustus, teadealer, 8 Duke st. Manchester sq
Jackson Benjamin Daydon, stationer, 236 Borough High st
Jackson Catherine (Mrs.), beer retailer, Mill wall, Poplar
Jackson Charles, bedding warehouse, 319 Oxford st
Jackson Charles, bootmaker, 167 Church st. Shoreditch
Jackson Charles, butcher, 34 Farringdon market, & 46 Basing place, Waterloo road
Jackson Charles, carpenter, 5½ Foster st. Bishopsgate
Jackson Chas. copperplate engraver, 8 Red Lion ct. Fleet st
Jackson Charles, dairyman, 100 East st. Manchester sq
Jackson Charles, turner, 4 York st.Church st.Bethnal green
Jackson Charles Robt. Mitchel, barrister, Chapel strs.Lin.inn
Jackson Danl.china & glass wa.51 Margaret st.Wilmingtn. sq
Jackson Diana(Mrs.), tobac.pipema.26 Ewerst.Union st.Boro'
Jackson Edward, cheesemonger, 5 Bath st. City road
Jackson Edwd. *Mourning Bush tav.* 61 St. Martin's legrand
Jackson Edward, wholesale & retail hat manfr. 53 Tooley st
Jackson Edward, woolstapler, 103 Bermondsey st
Jackson Edw. Witherby, button&trim.wa.58 Gracechurch st
Jackson Elizabeth (Mrs.), oilman, 149 Tooley st
Jackson Elizabeth (Mrs.), oil, &c.wa.5 Baker's row, Walw.rd
Jackson Eliz. (Mrs.), tobacconist, 31 High st. Marylebone
Jackson Francis, *Crown* P.H. 25 Marylebone st. Golden sq
Jackson Fred. grocer & oilman, 21 Arlington st. Camden tn
Jackson Geo. carpenter & builder, 25 Dorset st. Spitalfields
Jackson Geo. poultry & pork salesman, 60 Newgate market
Jackson Geo. grindery dealer, 25 Lit. Windmill st. Golden sq
Jackson Geo. oil & colorman, 11 & 12 Purim pl.Cambridge rd
Jackson Geo. professor of music, 25 Brydges st. Covent grdn
Jackson George, solicitor, 23 Finsbury place north
Jackson Geo. umbrella maker, 6 Broad st. Golden sq
Jackson Geo. workinggoldsmith, 82 Charlotte st. Fitzroy sq
Jackson Geo. Abel, block, &c. maker, 5 Stoney lane, Tooley st
Jackson Geo. Bateson, plumber, Grove, Hackney
Jackson Geo. Briant Wheeler, civil engineer, 9 Gray's inn sq
Jackson Geo. Hen. surgeon dentist, 39 High st.Camden town
Jackson Hannah (Mrs.), toy dealer, 29 Farringdon market
Jackson Harriet(Mrs.), medical bookseller, 32 King st. Boro'
Jackson Henry, butcher, 2 Grove Hill ter.Grove la.Cmbrwll
Jackson Henry, stock & share agent, Hall of Commerce, Threadneedle st. & 21 Nelson st. City road
Jackson Henry, carpenter, 9 Lower John st. Golden sq
Jackson Henry, glass manufactr. 6 Princes st. Lit. Queen st
Jackson Henry, hatter, 1 St. Thomas' pl. Old Kent road
Jackson Henry, machinist, 4 Little Compton st. Soho
Jackson Henry, solicitor, 15 St. Helen's place, Bishopsgate
Jackson Henry, upholsterer & house agent, &c.15 Piccadilly
Jackson Henry, whitesmith, 22 Allen st. Goswell st
Jackson Henry Martin, linendraper, see Lester & Jackson
Jackson Herbert, cheesemonger & porkman, 54 Sth.Audley st
Jackson Hugh, solicitor, see Fladgate, Young & Jacksons
Jackson Isabella (Mrs.), ladies' school, 118 Fore st. Cripplgt
Jackson Jacob, genl. factor, 8 Ellison st. Midlx. st. Aldgate
Jackson James, butcher, 39 Upper Marylebone street
Jackson James, chemist & druggist, 107 Union st. Borough
Jackson James, ribbon dresser, 22 Philip lane, London wall
Jackson James, straw hat ma. 25 Price's st.Grav. la.Borough
Jackson James, woollen draper. 11 Clarendon sq. Somers tn
Jackson Jane (Mrs.), grindery dlr. 14 Victoria pl. Hoxton O.tn
Jackson John, bricklayer, 4 Wyndham road, Camberwell
Jackson John, chemist, &c. 47 Southampton row, Russell sq
Jackson John, corn & coal dealer, 22 Broomfields, Deptford
Jackson John, engraver, 12 Hart street, Grosvenor square
Jackson John, file, rasp, &sawmak.20 Gt.Sutton st.Clerkenwell
Jackson John, oil & colorman, 104 Edgware road, Marylebone
Jackson John, plasterer, 33 Marshall street, Golden sq
Jackson John, plumber, &c. 12 Eccleston place, Pimlico
Jackson John, *Royal Oak* P.H. Emmett street, Limehouse
Jackson John, solicitor, see Fladgate, Young & Jacksons
Jackson John, tailor, 51 Bedford row, Bloomsbury
Jackson John, tallowchandler, 130 Upper street, Islington
Jackson John, tobacconist, 7 Meard's court, Soho
Jackson John, watchcase mak. 10 Woodbridge st. Clerkenwl
Jackson John, wood engravr. 12 Cardington st. Hampstd. rd
Jackson John Alex. stationer & pianoforte ma. 32 Greek st
Jackson John Beetham, general agt. 18 Lawrence la. City
Jackson John Hen. booksel. 5 Oddy's row, Islington green
Jackson John Hugh, solicitor, see Fladgate, Young & Co
Jackson John Wm. *Eastnor Castle* P.H.42 Union st.Smrs. tn
Jackson Jsph. accountant, 6 Guildhall chamb. Basinghall st
Jackson Joseph, baker, 55 Foley street, Portland place
Jackson Joseph, boot & shoe makr. 3 Brill row, Somers town
Jackson Joseph, linen & carpet wa. 26 to 29 Shoreditch
Jackson Joseph, marine store dlr. 93 East st. Manchester sq
Jackson Joseph, *Queen's Arms* P.H. 2 Weston st. Borough
Jackson Joseph, spectacle ma. 4 Oldham pl. Wilmington sq
Jackson Joseph D. cabinet maker, 13 Weston st. Bermondsey
Jackson Martin, nurseryman, Edwardes terrace, Kensington
Jackson Mary (Miss), seminary, 7 Lit. New st. Gough sq
Jackson Mason, wood engraver, 12 Cardington st. Hamps. rd
Jackson Paul, surgeon, &c. 18 Thayer st. Manchester sq
Jackson Peter, butcher, 53 Hoxton Old town
Jackson Peter, printer, see Fisher, Son & Jackson
Jackson Peter, silk, &c. wa. see Cheeper, Watson & Jackson
Jackson Ralph, bookseller, 2 Chandos st. Cavendish sq
Jackson Ralph, dlr. in live birds, Gt. Hall, Hungerford mkt
Jackson Richard, candle, soap & oil warehouse, 45 Piccadilly
Jackson Richard, gunmaker, 19 Princess st. Lisson grove
Jackson Rd. *Pitman's Arms* P.H.1 Pitman'sbgs.John'srw.StL
Jackson Richard, solicitor, 14 Craven street, Strand
Jackson Robert, bootmaker, 4 Upper Rupert st. Haymarket
Jackson Robert, coffee rooms, 13 Duke st. Tooley st
Jackson Robert, grocer & teadealer, 21 Goswell street
Jackson Robert, hairdresser, 88 Fenchurch street
Jackson Robert, meat salesman, 11 Warwick la. Newgate st
Jackson Robert, solicitor, see Sharpe, Field & Jackson
Jackson Robinson, upholsterer, &c. see Baily & Jackson
Jackson Samuel, cattle salesman, 8 West Smithfield
Jackson Samuel, engraver, 68 Cheapside
Jackson Saml.sec.to Union Bk.Australia, 38 Old Broad st.City
Jackson Saml. varnish & color ma. Willow wf. 87 Bankside
Jackson Samuel Brown, attorney, 9 New inn, Wych st.Strand
Jackson Sarah (Mrs.), newsvender, 14A, Prospect pl.O.Bromp
Jackson Sarah (Mrs.), *White Swan* P.H. 24 Wapping wall
Jackson Thomas, bootmaker, 4 Princes road, Lambeth
Jackson Thomas, builder & saw mills, Commercial rd. Pimlico
Jackson Thomas, cheesemonger, 9 New street, Dorset sq
Jackson Thomas, earthenware dlr. 178 Church st. Shoreditch
Jackson Thomas, gun & steel cross bow manufacturer, 29 Edwards st. Portman square (late of Upper George st)
Jackson Thos. *Globe tav. & coffee ho.* 37&38 Bowst.Cov.garden
Jackson Thos. livery stables, Pitt's place, Old Kent road
Jackson Thos. music publisher, 21 Orchard st. Portman sq
Jackson Thos. pianoforte maker, 21 Orchard st. Portman sq
Jackson Thos. plumber, 47 Museum st. Bloomsbury

Jackson Thomas Hector, fruiterer, 2 Charlotte st. Portland pl
Jackson Thomas S. linen agent, 72 Aldermanbury
Jackson Walter Edward, *Green Man* P.H. 214 Tooley st
Jackson Wm. baker, 45 Wilsted st. Somers town
Jackson Wm. beer retailer, 5 Queen st. Ratcliff
Jackson Wm. butcher, 11 Clipstone st. Fitzroy sq
Jackson Wm. cheesemonger, 16 Duke st. Lincoln's inn fields
Jackson Wm. chemist & druggist, 93 Cheapside
Jackson Wm. clock & watch ma. 6 Brunswick pl. Brompton
Jackson Wm. furniture dealer, 1 Harp alley, Shoe lane, & 14 Shoe lane, Holborn
Jackson Wm. grocer, 39 Brook st. Lambeth
Jackson Wm. hairdresser, 23 Mercer st. Long acre
Jackson Wm. house decorator, 20 Orchard st. Portman sq
Jackson Wm. metal wareho. 28 Wilson st. Finsbury sq
Jackson Wm. painter, &c. 38 Gt. Queen st. Lincoln's innfields
Jackson Wm. locksm. & bellhange. 14 White's al. Moorgate st
Jackson Wm. *Pawnbrokers' Gazette Office*, 240 Strand
Jackson Wm. plumber & glazier 15 Duke st. Lincoln's inn fi
Jackson Wm. pork butcher, 13 St. Alban's pl. Edgware rd
Jackson Wm. rope, line, twine & cotton waste manufact. for cleaning engines, machines, &c. 152 Blackfriars rd
Jackson Wm. saddler & harness maker, 54 High st. Marylebone, & 15 Park terrace, Regent's park rd
Jackson Wm. smith & fireproof box ma. 11 Serles pl. Linc. inn
Jackson Wm. solicitor, 85 Blackman st
Jackson Wm. tailor, 65 Goswell road
Jackson Wm. watchmaker, 1 Mall, Kensington gravel pits
Jackson Wm. Affleck, solicitor, 11 Staple inn
Jackson Wm. H. tailor, &c. 22 Bartholomew close
Jackson Wm. John, *Eastnor Castle* P.H. Union st. Somers tn
Jackson Wm. Rd. cheesemonger, 17 Crombie's row. Com. rd. east
Jackson Wm. Windale, solicitor, 2 Field ct. Gray's inn
Jackson Wyrill, grocer & cheesemonger, 14 Cambridge rd
Jacob E. & Co. merchants, 8 Lime st. City
Jacob & Hoare, commission agents, 5 Bread st. City
Jacob & Webb, baby linen wa. 13 Carthusian st. Charterho. sq
Jacob Benjamin, coal & corn mer. Creek road, Deptford
Jacob Charles, merch. & australian agt. 6 Ingram ct. Fench. st
Jacob Fred. Wm. dupuytrens pomatum, 59 Gt. Russell st. Blmsy
Jacob John, boot & shoe maker, 160 Poplar High st
Jacob John, rag & bottle dealer, 5 Union st. Bishopsgate
Jacob John, smith & bellhng. 23 Elephant & Castle ct. Whtchpl
Jacob John, surgeon, 3 Goswell rd. West side
Jacob John H. importer of foreign wines, see Carr & Jacob
Jacob Joseph Phelps, carpent. & builder, Camberwell green
Jacob Mary (Mrs.), cornchandler, 65½ Wheeler st. Spitalfi
Jacobi John, shoemaker, 13 Low. King st. Commercial rd. ea
Jacobs Barnard & Emanuel, lamp ma. 12 Up. Marylebone st
Jacobs & Dupuis, ladies' shoe ms. 42 Conduit st. New Bond st
Jacobs John & Sam. curiosity dealers, 8 Brook st. Grosv. sq
Jacobs (Levy & Jonas), grocers, 1 St. James's pl. Aldgate
Jacobs Philip & Son, who. glass wareh. 64 Crown st. Finsbury
Jacobs Sam. & Hen. furniture ware. 56 Princes st. Le'ster sq
Jacobs Abraham, who. glass wareh. 14 & 15 Crown st. Finsbury
Jacobs Abraham Richd. (late Barth), umbrella, cane, whip, fishing tackle & bow & arrow manuf. (wholesale & retail) to the Queen, 32 Cockspur st. & 145 Regent st
Jacobs Benjamin, fruit salesman, 22 Mitre st. Aldgate
Jacobs Chas. fruit salesman, 71 & 72 Farringdon market, & 20 Stonecutter st. Farringdon st
Jacobs Edward, carpenter, 132 Curtain road, Shoreditch
Jacobs Edw. *Duke of Wellington* P.H. Up. North st. Whtchpl. rd
Jacobs Gaskell, orange mercht. Covent garden fruit market
Jacobs Henry, butcher, 27½ Little Duke st. St. Mary Axe
Jacobs Henry, merchant, 35 Surrey st. Strand
Jacobs Henry, pianoforte ma. 24½ Cardington st. Hampstd. rd
Jacobs Henry, turner, 2 Hampshire court, Whitechapel rd
Jacobs Hyam, sponge mercht. 5 Middlesex st. Whitechapel
Jacobs Isaac, bottle wareho. 91 King st. Camden town
Jacobs Isaac Alex. china dealer, see Rosenhaum & Jacobs
Jacobs Israel, fruiterer, 188 Wellington ter. Waterloo road
Jacobs James, coach painter, 4 Union st. Lambeth walk
Jacobs John, artist, 164 Strand
Jacobs John, carpenter, &c. 1 Leman st. Goodman's fields
Jacobs John, clothier, 8 Bury st. St. Mary Axe
Jacobs Joseph, clothes warehouse, see Harris & Jacobs
Jacobs Joseph, file cutter, 46 Grey Eagle st. Spitalfields
Jacobs Joseph, *Freemason's Arms* P.H. 1 Duke st. Whitechpl. rd
Jacobs Joseph, imp. of ancient furniture, 4 Bevis marks
Jacobs Joseph, silversmith, 44 Chichester pl. Gray's inn rd
Jacobs Judah, tailor & clothes salesm. 202 Borough High st
Jacobs Lewis, general salesman, 142 Gt. Saffron hill
Jacobs Lewis, solicitor, 2 Winchester buildings, City
Jacobs Michael, dealer in ancient furniture, paintings, china &c. 66 Gt. Queen st. Lincoln's inn fields
Jacobs Matthew, optician, see Phillips & Jacobs
Jacobs Michael, furrier, 21 Primrose st. Bishopsgate st
Jacobs Moses, cane wareho. 90 Gt. Suffolk st. Borough
Jacobs Moss, cigar manfr. & tobacconist, 26 Houndsditch
Jacobs Moss, merchant, 19 Gt. Alie st. Goodman's fields
Jacobs Samuel, fruit salesman, Farringdon market
Jacobs Samuel, silversmith, 5 Park side, Knightsbridge
Jacobs Samuel, publicans' glass warehouse, 3 Panton st. Haymarket, & 101 Berwick st. Soho
Jacobs Solomon, merchant, 19 Gt. Alie st. Goodman's fields
Jacobs Wm. beer retailer, Hollywood, Little Chelsea
Jacobs Wm. fruit & pea salesman, Covent garden fruit markt
Jacobs Wolfe, spectacle maker, 36 Great Saffron hill
Jacobson Isaac, commission merchant, 46 Lime st
Jacobson Isaac, jeweller & silversmith, 322 & 12 Oxford st
Jacobson Nathaniel, medical agent & valuer, 8 Walbrook
Jacomb Chas. & John D. wool brokers, 2 Basinghall st
Jacomb George, butcher, 39 Great Marylebone st
Jacot Constant, engine turner, 5 Corporation row, Clerknwl
Jacquier Jas. jacquard machine manf. 26 Wood st. Sptlflds
Jacquot John Baptist Paul, french & english basket ma. who. retail & for exportation, 13 Compton st. Burton crescent
Jaffray Charles, wire worker, High st. Deptford
Jaffray John Richmond, america merchant, Lloyd's
Jaffray Rd. mer. 22 Austinfrs. & N. & S. American coffee ho
Jagelman John, soda water ma. 43 Hercules bldgs. Lambeth
Jager Geo. engrav. & watchma. 3 Charles pl. East st. Walw. rd
Jagg Ambrose, bootmaker, 20 Gt. Guildford st. Borough
Jaggars George, shoemaker, 42 Friar st. Blackfriars road
Jagger John, tobacco & snuff manufacturer, 42 Leather lane
Jaggers Robert, undertaker, 60 Union st. Lambeth walk
Jagle Magnus, clockmaker, 31 Up. King st. Bloomsbury
Jago Mahala & Jane, milliners, 8 Courtnay ter. Kingsland rd
Jago Geo. W. S. agt. to Phœnix fire office, 4 York pl. Pimlico
Jago Samuel, glass cutter, 19 Drury court, Strand
Jagoe Brothers & Co. gen. & cmsn. merchants, 74 Gt. Tower st
Jakes Edward, baker, 8 Gt. Cambridge st. Hackney road
Jakins Isaac Negus, surgeon, 32 Osnaburgh st. Regent's pk
Jakman George, tripe dresser, 3 Gravel lane, Southwark
Jalabin M. A. (Mrs.), chand. shop, 5 Stepney rents, Hacky. rd
Jallands William, chemist, 8 New Chapel pl. Kentish town
Jamaica coffeehouse, St. Michael's alley, Cornhill
Jamaica South Midland & Northern Extension Railway (Charles Wright, sec.), 27 Essex st Strand
Jamar Servais, cabinet ma. & upholster. 63 Frith st. Soho sq
James & Allen, oil & colormen, 67 Drury lane
James Charles & Son, boot & shoewa. 138 Whitechapel High st
James & Cubison, milliners & straw bonnet maks. 89 Oxford st
James Geo. & Richd. breeches makers, 21 Clifford st. Bond st
James, Howell & Co. warehousemen, see Howell, James & Co
James & Sargeant, carpenters, 3 Liverpool bdgs. Bishopsgate
James John Hen. & Geo. Joshua, hat manfs. 11 Gravel la. Swk
James John & Sons, corn factors, 1 Great Tower st
James Michael & Co. surgeon dentists, 58 Fleet st
James & Shakspeare, metal brokers, 10 Austinfriars
James Susan & Co. child bed linen warehouse, 104 Oxford st
James & Walker, *Morley's hotel*, 1 & 2 Trafalgar sq. Charing cr
James Wm. & Edward, wine & spirit merchts. 35 Fenchurch st
James W. R. & E. W. solicitors, 23 Ely place, Holborn
James & Wise, chair & sofa makers, 57 Borough road
James Abraham, ironmonger, 16 Grenada ter. Commercial rd
James Alexander, cheesemonger, 140 Aldersgate st
James Alfred, beer retailer, 21 Mansion Ho. st. Kennington
James Ann Dale (Mrs.), ironfounder, Back rd. St. George's ea
James Andrew, shaft & timber bender, 5 Sutton st. Soho
James Benjamin, lath render, 384 Albany road, Camberwell
James Charles, bootmaker, 52 Whitechapel road
James Charles, grocer, 50 Lambeth Lower marsh
James Charles, italian wa. 95 Grand Junction ter. Edgware rd
James Chas. Fras. picture restorer, 9 Upper Berkeley st
James Daniel, baker, 197 Kingsland road
James Daniel, porkman & poulterer, 68 Whitechapel High st
James David, barrister, 3 Old square, Lincoln's inn
James Edmund, coach builder, 13 Alfred pl. Newngtn. causwy
James Edmund, pork butcher, 94 Up. Whitecross st. St Luke's
James Edward, barrister, 2 Elm court, Temple
James Edward Lloyd, paper manf. & agt. 66 Queen st. Cheapsi
James Edwin, barrister, 3 Inner Temple lane
James Francis, boot & shoemaker, 4 Old Jewry, Cheapside
James Francis, solicitor, 51 Lincoln's inn fields
James Francis, tobacconist, Kingsland High st
James Frederick, *Coach & Horses* P.H. 81 High Holborn
James Frederick, confectioner, 20 Mount Pleasant, Grays inn la
James Frederick Charles, carver & gilder, 26 Greek st. Soho
James George, butcher, 3 Whitechapel High st
James George, milliner, 5 Cumberland row, Islington

James George, oilman & tallow chandler, 72 Wardour st. Soho
James George A. chandler's shop, 29 Hyde pl. Bridport pl. Hxtn
James George Fred. grocr. & oilmn. 57 Paddington st. Marylebo
James George Fred. umbrella maker, 3 Paddington st
James Henry, barrister, 6 Old sq. Lincoln's inn
James Henry, calico printers' agt. 6 Dyer's ct. Aldermanbury
James Henry, coffee rooms, 55 Lower marsh, Lambeth
James Henry, *Coach & Horses* P.H. 24 Silver st. Golden sq
James Henry, *Globe* P.H. 9 York st. Borough
James Henry, surgeon, 4 City rd. & 34 Brunswick sq
James Henry, trunk maker, 14 Rathbone pl. Oxford st
James Henry, vet. surg. William's mews, Mary st. Regent's pk
James Henry C. metal broker, 10 Austinfriars, Old Broad st
James Hy. Jas. auctioneer & estate agt. 44 Threadneedle st
James Herbert Geo. weighing crane ma. 44 Fish st. hill
James Hugh [late Story, James & Robinson], tailor, habit, & breeches maker, 55 New Bond st
James Jabez, machinist, smith, bell hanger & brass finisher, York road, Lambeth
James James, auctioneer & appraiser, 60 Hatton garden
James James, filter manufacturer, 25 Poultry
James James, grocer, 32 Addington place, Camberwell road
James James, gun case maker, 8 Bentinck st. Soho
James James, leghorn, straw, &c. bonnet maker, 95 Oxford st
James James, robe maker, 27 Kenton st. Brunswick sq
James James, tailor, 3 Warner st. New Kent road
James Jas. Hen. auctioneer & est. agt. 23 Bartlett's bldgs. Hlbn
James Jane (Miss), milliner, 50 Grosvenor place
James Jane (Mrs.), cowkeeper, 38 William st. Whitechapel
James Jeremiah, combmaker, 11 Addle st. Wood st
James John, academy, 11 Buckingham pl. Fitzroy square
James John, beer retailer, 44 Brick lane, Spitalfields
James John, cheesemonger, 34 College st. Chelsea
James John, oil & colorman, 4 Cambridge pl. Cambridge ter
James John, *Royal Oak* P.H. Lower road, Rotherhithe
James John, solicitor, secondary of London, 5 Basinghall st
James John, *Prince Albert* P.H. James st. Marlbro' rd. Chelsea
James John, tailor, 2 Alfred st. Bedford sq
James John, trunkma. 14 John st. Oxford st. & 102 Oxford st
James John, woollendraper, 9 Southampton st. Strand
James John, jun. solicitor, 58 Lincoln's inn fields
James John Fred. *Bedford Arms* P.H. 1 Grove st. Camden tn
James John Kingston, wine merchant, see Todd & James
James John Wheeler, who. currier, 1 Corbet ct. Gracech. st
James Lewis, custom ho. & gen. agt. 12 Cross la. St. Mary at hill
James Margaret (Mrs.), seminary, 8 Charterhouse st
James Mary (Mrs.), dairy, 83 Cannon st. City
James Morgan, grocer, 16 Park terrace, Camden town
James Peter, baker, 1 Berkeley st. Clerkenwell
James Peter R. *Mitre* P.H. 10 Somers mews, Upp. Southwick st
James Rees, tailor, 15 Conduit st. New Bond st
James Richd. *Alfred's Head* P.H. 6 Alfred pl. Newington ca
James Richard, baker, 45 High st. Notting hill
James Richard, cheesemonger, 8 Victoria road, Pimlico
James Richard, draper & mercer, High st. Stoke Newington
James Richard, leech importer, see Hunter Z. jun. & James
James Richard, *Wheatsheaf* P.H. 139 St. Alban's pl. Edgw. rd
James Richard Wm. pork butcher, 3 Oxford pl. Hackney rd
James Robert, bricklayer & builder, 2 Brewer st. Golden sq
James Rt. rasp & file cutter, 7 Twisters alley, Bunhill row
James Robert, *Rochester Castle* P.H. High st. Stoke Newngtn
James Robert, wine merchant, 17 Store st. Bedford square
James Samuel, baker, Church st. Stoke Newington
James Samuel, barrister, 2 Old square, Lincoln's inn
James Samuel, carpenter, &c. 26 Norfolk st. Middlesex hosp
James Samuel, oilman 92, grocer 93, & cheesemonger & provision merchant 94, Whitechapel road
James Samuel, whitesmith & bellhanger, 5 Saville pl. Mile end
James Samuel James, indigo mercht. & drysalter, 41 Lime st
James Theodore, solicitor, 9 Staple inn, Holborn
James Thomas, barrister, 11 Gray's inn square
James Thomas, boot closer, 37 Brownlow st. Drury lane
James Thomas, bootmaker, 4 Dorset st. Clapham road
James Thomas, bread & biscuit baker, 13 Gt. Portland st
James Thomas, human hair worker, 25 Gt. Sutton st. Clknw
James Thomas, linen draper, see Breeze & James
James Thomas, linendraper, see Moore, James, Tate & Co
James Thomas, linen manufr. &c. see Lewis & James
James Thomas, *Nag's Head* P.H. Wandsworth road
James Thomas, silk manufacturer, 46 Spital square
James Thomas G. builder, 31 Old st. St. Luke's
James Thomas H. tailor & gen. outfitter, 4 Up. East Smithfield
James William, bootmaker, 5 College terrace, Chelsea
James William, cheesemngr. (yard) 3 Swallow pl. Hanover sq
James William, chimney sweeper, 5 Love lane, Eastcheap
James William, coal merchant, 11 South st. Manchester sq
James William, comb manfctr. 58 Vauxhall walk, Lambeth
James William, engraver & enameller, 70 Hatton garden
James William *Gen. Elliott* P.H. 17 Royal Hos. row, Chelsea
James William, grocery dealer, 5 Dorset cres. New North rd
James William, locksmith, 27 Hampstead road
James William, milliner, 29½ Farringdon st
James William, optician, 25 Little Russell st. Bloomsbury
James William, surgeon, 42 Norfolk st. Strand
James William Bosville, wine mer. see Butler, James & Co
James William Boyce, solicitor, 5 Basinghall st
James William Henry, parliamentary agent, 15 New Bridge st. & 2 White Friars st. Blackfriars
James Wm. Milbourne, barrister, 6 Stone bldgs. Linc. inn
James William Reynolds, surgeon, 1 Omega ter. Alpha rd
Jameson & Banks, silk & comn. agts. 4 Honey la. Cheapside
Jameson & Innes, who. cheesemngrs. 27 Rood la. Fenchurch st
Jameson Wm. & Son, merchants, 6 Fen court, Fenchurch st
Jameson Andrew, carpenter, 14 Green st. Bethnal green
Jameson David, tailor, &c. 85 York st. Westminster
Jameson Lessor, quill merchant, 55 Mansell st. Goodman's fi
Jameson Mary (Mrs.), boot & shoema. 6 Seymour pl. Camdn. tn
Jameson Thomas, *Lord Hood* P.H. 6 Rich st. Limehouse
Jameson Wm. painter, plumber, &c. 7 Duke st. Adelphi
Jamieson Brothers & Co. merchants, 33 Gt. Winchester st
Jamieson Alex. actuary of *Reliance Mutual Life Assurance, Loan, &c. Society*, 71 King William st. City
Jamieson Alexander, dentist, 134 Grove st. Camden town
Jamieson George, fruiterer, 9 Walker's ct. Golden sq
Jamieson John, chemist, 16 Amwell st. Pentonville
Jamieson John, sail cloth factor & ins. agt. 27 Crutchedfriars
Janaway James, carman, 8 William st. Manchester sq
James Edwin, *Monmouth Arms* P.H. 10 Singleton st. Hoxton
Janes James & Wm. egg importers, 5 York st. Borough
Janes Jonathan & Geo. bricklayers, 11 Lit. York pl. Marylebne
Janes Elizbth. (Mrs.), window blind ma. 8 Edgware rd. Maryleb
Janes George, *Rose & Crown* P.H. 78 Aldgate High st
Janes Jacob, builder, 15 Alpha road, Regent's park
Janes James, window blind maker, 101 Aldersgate st
Janes Jesse, baker, 27 Queen st. Bryanstone sq
Janes John, potato salesman, 121 Bethnal green rd
Janes John, *Sir John Falstaff* P.H. 15 Brydges st. Covent gdn
Janes John, jun. carpenter, 8 Princess st. Edgware road
Janes Joseph, cattle salesman, 37 West Smithfield
Janes Samuel, boot & shoe maker, 57 North st. Edgware rd
Janes Thomas, window blind maker, 10 Cross st. Finsbury, & 29 Finsbury place north
Jannaway John, grocer & oilmn. 22 & 23 Exeter st. Knightsbge
Jannaway William, pawnbroker, 24 Exeter st. Sloane st
Jannings Henry & Co. wholes. ironmongers, 63 Coleman st
Jannings Chas. hosier, glover & outfitter, 16 Fenchurch st
Jannings Robt. general dealer in manchester & scotch goods, druggets, low woollen cloth, &c. wholesale & for exportation; agent to the Norwich Union fire & life assurance office, & to the General Hail Storm insurance society, 3 Nag's head court, Gracechurch st
Janson Alfred & Co. underwriters, 4 Tokenhouse yard
Janson Fredk. Halsey, sol. see Bayley, Janson & Richardson
Jantzen Gefort, coffee rooms, 208 Sloane st. Knightsbridge
Janvrin Francis, merchant, see De Lisle, Janvrin & De Lisle
Jaquemot John Mark, merchant, 33 Gt. St. Helen's, Bishopsgt
Jaques & Edwards, solicitors, 8 Ely place, Holborn
Jaques & Robinson, printers, 30 Lower Sloane st. Chelsea
Jaques Auguste, watch finisher, 37 Spencer st. Goswell rd
Jaques Charles, printer, 30 Kenton st. Brunswick square
Jaques Frank, skein silk dyer, 95 Hare st. Spitalfields
Jaques George, glass cutter, 77 Tothill st. Westminster
Jaques Henry, watch & escapement maker, 40 Granville sq
Jaques John, brushmaker, 9 Allen st. Clerkenwell
Jaques John, printer, 17 Church pl. Newingt. oppos. the Church
Jaques John, watchmaker, 54 Myddelton square
Jaques John, wholesale ivory & hardwood turner, timber merchant & dealer in ivory & foreign hard woods, & saw mills, 102 Hatton garden, & 33½ Liquorpond st
Jaques Maria (Mrs.), grocer, 7 Bedford st. Mile end road
Jaques Thomas, lodging ho. keeper, 12 Leigh st. Red Lion sq
Jaques Wm. Thos. breeches & trousers maker, 75 Jermyn st
Jaquet Robert John P. *Johnson's tavern*, 21 Clare court, Drury lane, & oil & italian wa. 25 James st. Covent garden
Jaquet Philip, solicitor, see Willoughby & Jaquet
Jaquiery Louisa (Miss), milliner, 36 Mount st. Berkeley sq
Jaquinet Hte. & Co. (of Chalons), wine merchants, Claridge, Day & Co. agents, 21 Pudding lane
Jardell John, dining rooms, 84 Lower Thames st
Jardine & Galindo (Misses), academy, 115 Sloane st
Jardine Charles, woollen warehouseman, 29 Basinghall st
Jardine David, magistrate, Bow st. police court

Jardine James, bootmaker, 46 Old Gloucester st. Hoxton
Jardine James, glass driller, 24 Princes st. Drury lane
Jardine Jas. A. mourning co. master, see Bennicke & Jardine
Jardine James Bell, M.D. surgeon, 44 Drury lane, & 1 Leigh st. Burton crescent
Jardine William, merchant, see Magniac, Jardine & Co
Jarmain Joseph, *Stag* P.H. 29 Dorset st. Portman sq
Jarmain Thomas, bootma. 38 East st. south side, Wlwth. rd
Jarmain Thomas, *Grapes* P.H. 94 Old st. St. Luke's
Jarman Robt. & Son, carpenters & build. 8 Noble st. Cheapside
Jarman Ann (Mrs.), confectioner, 3 Morgan's pl. Liverpl. rd
Jarman Charles, tailor & draper, 40 Duke st. Smithfield
Jarman Eli, academy, 12 Church st. Islington
Jarman Elizth.(Mrs.), paperhanger, 7 Middle row, Knightsbr
Jarman George, bootmaker, 15 Webb st. Bermondsey st
Jarman James, currier, 61 Lambeth walk
Jarman John, tobacco pipe ma. 43 Halfmoon st. Bishopsgate
Jarman Richard, engraver, 8 Bartholomew close
Jarman Thomas, barrister, 3 New square, Lincoln's inn
Jarman Thomas, butcher, 136 Brick lane, Spitalfields
Jarnac Count de, secretary, Hertford ho. 20 Manchester sq
Jarratt Chas. Wm. engraver & printer, 170 St. John st. road
Jarrett Fran. *Plasterers' Arms* P.H. 9 Lit. Marylebone st
Jarrett George, *Sun* P.H. 25 Noel st. Berwick st. Soho
Jarrett George, straw hat manufr. 59 Upper Ebury st. Pimlico
Jarrett Henry, butcher, 78 Broad st. Ratcliff
Jarrett William, butcher, 77 St. George st
Jarrett Wm. law & genl. bookseller, 13 Bell yard, Temple bar
Jarrey William, *Comet* P.H. 7 Christian st. St. George's east
Jarritt & Woodhouse, hatters, 90 New Bond st
Jarrold John, bricklayer, 22 Felix pl. Liverpool rd. Islington
Jarvis & Barry, spice merchants, 6 Turnwheel la. Cannon st
Jarvis & Jones, tailors, 47 Conduit st. Regent st
Jarvis Richard & Son, undertakers, 139 Long acre
Jarvis Wm. & Son, tailors, 9 Gt. Russell st. Bloomsbury
Jarvis Chas. glasscutter, plumber, &c. 38 Gt. Castle st. Reg. st
Jarvis Chas. sen. cheesemonger, 10 Princes pl. Commerl. rd. east
Jarvis Chas. jun. cheesemonger, 180 St. George st
Jarvis Edward, *Silver Cross* P.H. 25 Charing cross
Jarvis Edwd. watrpf. lea. polish ma. 26 Nassau st. Middx. hos
Jarvis Elizabeth (Mrs.), cowkeeper, 69 High st. Marylebone
Jarvis Elizabeth (Mrs.), pork butcher, 20 Foley st. Portld. pl
Jarvis Emily (Miss), milliner, 157 New Bond st
Jarvis Henry, bookbinder, 2 Bartlett's passage, Holborn
Jarvis Henry, egg merchant, 91 Lambeth walk
Jarvis Henry, linendraper, 19 Gt. Smith st. Westminster
Jarvis Henry, surveyor & architect, 32 Trinity sq. Boro'
Jarvis Holman, tailor, 20 Cross st. Islington
Jarvis James, coach maker, Glebe place, King's rd. Chelsea
Jarvis James, lighterman, 42 Commercial road, Lambeth
Jarvis James, painter, 27 Harcourt st. New road
Jarvis James, rag merchant, 14 Etham pl. Dover road
Jarvis James Saxby, *King's Head* P.H. Belvedere rd. Lambeth
Jarvis Jarvis B. chair ma. 4 Cleaver st. Kennington cross
Jarvis John, appraiser & undertaker, 32 Goswell road
Jarvis John, cabinet maker, 31 Chapel st. New road
Jarvis John, cooper, Turk's row, Chelsea
Jarvis John, currier & leather seller, 74 Park st. Camden twn
Jarvis John, surgeon, 13 Hart st. Bloomsbury
Jarvis John, tailor, see Bartle & Jarvis
Jarvis Joseph, dining rooms, 14 Vauxhall Bridge road
Jarvis Robert, tailor, 11 Bell yard, Temple bar
Jarvis Robert, tailor, 9 Steyman's row, Holloway road
Jarvis Sarah (Mrs.), farrier, Chester mews, Grosvenor place
Jarvis Thomas, solicitor, 46 Leicester square
Jarvis Wm. cabinet ma. & upholsterer, 31 Norton Folgate
Jarvis Wm. cheesemonger, 43 Princess st. Lisson grove
Jarvis Wm. hosier & glover, 10 Islington High st
Jarvis Wm. *King's Arms* P.H. 16 Hanway st. Oxford st
Jarvis Wm. tailor, 17 Castle st. east, Oxford st
Jarvis Wm. Isaac, furnit. war. 16 & 17 Melina. pl. Westmins. rd
Jarvis Wm. John, land surveyor, &c. see Rushworth & Jarvis
Jary Edward, baker & confectioner, 110 Up. East Smithfield
Jasper Wm. plasterer, 7 Pelham ter. Pelham rd. Brompton
Jasson Rowe, chocolate manufr. 1 Canal rd. Kingsland rd
Jaulerry & Bourdenx, merchants, 41 Old Broad st. City
Javan Henry, watchmaker, 4 Elizabeth ter. Cloudesley sq
Javan John T. gold wire draw. &c. 14 Market st. St. John st. rd
Javens John, japanner, 13 Coldbath square, Clerkenwell
Jay & Unwin, silk & ribbon agts. & warehousemn. 8 Addle st
Jay Wm. Chickall & Co. mourning ware. 247 & 249 Regent st
Jay Charles, coal factor & shipping agent, see Mills & Jay
Jay Charles fishmonger, 20, 21 & 22 Lr. area, Hungerford mkt
Jay Cyrus, attorney, 15 Serjeants' inn, Fleet st
Jay Edward, surgeon, & reg. of births, 51 Park st. Grosvnr. sq
Jay Elizabeth (Mrs.), butcher, 169 Aldersgate st
Jay George, hairdresser, 24 King st. Camden town
Jay George, solicitor, 27 Bucklersbury
Jay George Batillo, tobacconist, 156 Blackfriars road
Jay Henry, carpenter & joiner, 66 Pratt st. Camden town
Jay Henry, surgeon, 42 Sloane st. Knightsbridge
Jay James, berlin repository, 43 Burlington arcade
Jay James, butcher, 25 Cannon st. Ratcliff highway
Jay John, builder, 65 London wall
Jay Joseph, plumber, 79 Upper Whitecross st. St. Luke's
Jay Joseph, skittle & ball turner, 24 Red Lion st. Hoxton O. tn
Jay Joseph, upholsterer & undertaker, Church st. Hackney
Jay Robert, cowkeeper, 1 Wilks place, Hoxton Old town
Jay Samuel, barrister, 10 Old square, Lincoln's inn
Jay Thomas, boot & shoe maker, 219 Poplar High st
Jaye John, *Hope* coffee rooms, 184 High Holborn
Jaye Wm. bootmaker, 45 Whitechapel road
Jaye Wm. china & glass dealer, 4 Prospect pl. Kingsland rd
Jayne Jas. B. *United States tav.* P.H. 33 Liverpool st. Bshpgt
Jeacock James, nautical instru. mak. 96 Fore st. Limehouse
Jeacote Joseph, cabinet ma. 2 Southampton st. Camberwell
Jeaffreson, Armstrong & Jeaffreson, surgeons, 9 Barnsbury pl
Jeaffreson Henry, physician, 2 Finsbury square
Jeaffreson John Furrance, surgeon, 11 Canonbury sq. Islingtn
Jeaffreson Saml. John, physician, 22 Halfmoon st. Piccadilly
Jeaffreson Wm. surgeon oculist, 21 South Audley st
Jeakes Wm. ironmonger, 51 Gt. Russell st. Bloomsbury
Jeakins John Bishop, tailor, 11 Gt. Ryder st. St. James's
Jeal Charles, bootmaker, 20 Oakley st. Lambeth
Jeal Edward, bootmaker, 14 Princes st. Westminster
Jeal George, baker, 114 London road, Southwark
Jeal John, brassfounder, 21 Old st. St. Luke's
Jeal Richard, *Prince of Wales* P.H. 15 York st. Westmnster
Jeandin Jean Nicholas, importer of french & german baskets & wicker dram bottle manufacturer, 20 Leather la. Holbn
Jeanes John, cabinet ma. & upholstr. see Johnston & Jeanes
Jeanes Robert, livery stables, Russell mews, Keppel st
Jeanes Wm. clothier, 28 Cleveland st. Fitzroy square
Jeanneret Henry, solicitor, see Wright & Jeanneret
Jeannin Alphonse, watchmaker, 10 King st. Covent garden
Jeans Chas. booksel. & station. 90 High st. Portland town
Jeans Francis Henry, chemist & dentist, 87 Whitechapel road
Jeans Isaac, *White Hart* P.H. 63 Myddelton st. Spafields
Jearrad Robert Wm. jun. surveyor & builder, 260 Oxford st
Jeary Elizh. (Mrs.), oil shop, 5 John's pl. Camberwell new rd
Jeavons Thos. engraver, 13 Brunswick parade, Barnsbury rd
Jebb Richard, barrister, 9 New square, Lincoln's inn
Jebson Wm. & Co. merchants, 4 Brabant ct. Philpot lane
Jee Alfred S. civil engineer, 6 John st. Adelphi
Jee Robert, stationer & news vender, 64 Albany rw. Cambwl
Jeeves Thomas, butcher, Broadway, Deptford
Jeeves Wm. plumber, 5 South place, Camberwell new road
Jefferd Wm. wine mercht. see Strongi'th'arm & Jefferd
Jefferies Alfred, bookbinder, 48 Singleton st. Hoxton
Jefferies John, fruiterer, 6 Adam st. west, Bryanstone sq
Jefferies Joseph Chas. beer retailer, 1A, Sudeley st. City rd
Jefferinis John, tobacconist, 2 Myddelton quadrant, Spa fields
Jefferis John & Co. ironfounders, Grove, & 109 Gt. Guildford st
Jefferis Jacob, tooth brush ma. 22 Princess st. Lisson grove
Jefferis John, coffee rooms, 87 Cannon st. City
Jefferiss Thomas & Co. bakers, 37 Great Tower st. City
Jefferiss James Thomas, meat salesman, Leadenhall market
Jefferiss Robert, nursery, 210 Albany road, Camberwell
Jefferiss Thomas, butcher, 39 Old Compton st. Soho
Jefferson Sarah & Rebecca, grocers, 232 Shadwell High st
Jefferson Jas. fancy stationer, 72 Margaret st. Wilmington sq
Jefferson Jane (Mrs.), *British Museum* P.H. 50 Gt. Russell st
Jefferson John, corndealer, 49 Crown st. Finsbury
Jefferson John, smith, 10 Gt. Ormond yard, Queen sq
Jefferson John, tailor, 31 Augustus st. Regent's park
Jefferson Mary (Mrs.), furrier, 69 John st. Fitzroy square
Jefferson Matthew, watchmaker, &c. 236 Shadwell High st
Jefferson Samuel, watchmaker, 36 Bruton st. Bond st
Jeffery Alfred & Co. marine glue ma. Commercial rd. Limeh
Jeffery Edward, beer retailer, 8 East st. south side, Walwth
Jeffery Emanuel, bed & mattress ma. 8 Clayton pl. Kengtn. crss
Jeffery George, butcher, 8 Knightsbridge terrace
Jeffery James, grocer, 20 Long lane, Bermondsey
Jeffery Henry, butcher, 92 Broad st. Ratcliff
Jeffery John, undertak. & ho. agt. 3 Foundling ter. Gray's Inn rd
Jeffery Joshua, bootmaker, 15 Newcastle st. Strand
Jeffery Richard, wine cooper & bottle mer. 6 Gt. St. Helen's
Jeffery Robert, coachmaker, 10 Up. North pl. Gray's inn rd & railway coach ma. Dawson's livery stables, Gray's inn rd
Jeffery Robert, tan dlr. & coal mer. 1 Elwell pl. Grange rd
Jeffery William, butcher, 49 King st. Golden square, & 5 Foubert's place, Regent st

Jeffery Thos. sec. to Vauxhall bri. Co. office, Millbank, Westmtr
Jeffery William, printers' broker, 7 Mark lane
Jeffery Wm. statr. & acct. bookmfr. 7 George yd. Lombard st
Jeffery Wm. tailor, 41 Southampton buildings, Chancery la
Jefferys Benjamin, *Lamb* P.H. 32 Vere st. Clare market
Jefferys Charles, music publisher, 21 A, Soho square
Jefferys Jas. spectacle ma. & optician, 132 St. John st. Smithfd
Jefferys John, cabinetmaker, 17 Coldbath sq. Clerkenwell
Jefferys Michael, shoemaker, 42 Cowcross st. Smithfield
Jefferys Richard James, window blind maker, 428 Oxford st
Jefferys Thomas, dining rooms, 91 Union street, Borough
Jefferys William, corndealer, 85 Bermondsey street
Jefferys Wm. drawing inst. ma. & optician, 26 Wilderness rw
Jeffkins John & Geo. wine & spirit mers. 2 Crosby sq. Bishopsg
Jefford William, painter, glazier, &c. 39 Brooke st. Holborn
Jeffray Andrew Edgar, artist, 11 Bedford st. Bedford sq
Jeffray James, artist, 11 Bedford st. Bedford sq
Jeffree John, engineer, Folly wall, Blackwall
Jeffree John, surgeon, 54 Paradise st. Lambeth
Jeffrey, Wise & Co. paperstainers, Kent & Essex yd. Whtchpl
Jeffrey Han. (Mrs.), chandlr. shop, 33 Hen. st. east, Avenue rd
Jeffrey John, builder, East India road, Poplar
Jeffrey William, wire worker, &c. see Duke & Jeffrey
Jeffreys Elijah, jeweller, 24 Upper Baker st. Regent's park
Jeffreys James, solicitor, 13 Chadwell st. Myddelton sq
Jeffreys Joseph, french polisher, 13 Lamb's Conduit passage
Jeffreys Julius, respirator patentee, wholesale office, 25 Bucklersbury, retail, 148 Regent st
Jeffreys Richd. liverystables, mews, 19½ Devonshire st. Portl. pl
Jeffreys Susanna (Miss), straw hat maker, 60 Edgware rd
Jeffreys Thomas, gold & silver refiner, 30 Hatton garden
Jeffries Esther (Mrs.), stationer, 3 Camberwell New road
Jeffries George, boot & shoe maker, 10 Swan st. Minories
Jeffries Henry, grocer, 35 St. John's lane, West Smithfield
Jeffries Jonathan Charles, dentist, 9 Giltspur st
Jeffries Robert, jeweller, 4 Crown place, Old Kent road
Jeffries William, cabinet maker, 3 East road, City road
Jeffries Wm. fruiterer, 6 Little Sussex pl. Hyde pk. gardens
Jeffryes Edward Trevanion, stationer & bookseller, 14 Sun st
Jeffryes James, furn. undertaker, 54 Church st. Mile end
Jeffs Chas. *Marq. of Cornwallis* P.H. 21 Curtain rd. Shrdtch
Jeffs James, saddler & harness ma. 35 Margaret st. Cavndsh. sq
Jeffs John, boot maker, 28 Hatton wall
Jeffs John, hairdresser, 9 New Bond street
Jeffs John, plumber, &c. Kingsland High street
Jeffs Richard, boot & shoe maker, 13 David st. Marylebone
Jeffs Robert, surgeon, 1 Finsbury square
Jeffs Wm. foreign bookseller & publisher, 15 Burlington arcade
Jeffs William, tailor, 3 Great Sutton street, Clerkenwell
Jeffs Wm. truss & band maker, 14 Weymouth st. New Kent rd
Jeggins Samuel, hosier & slopseller, 241 Shadwell High st
Jegon William, coal merchant & wharfinger, White Lion wharf, 18 Upper Thames street
Jegon William, merchant, 18 Upper Thames st
Jehu David, bootmaker, 8 Jamaica ter. Comrcl. rd. Limehouse
Jekyll Geo. G. grocer & cheesemonger, 38 Lambeth High s
Jekyll Robert, grocer, &c. 12 Bowling st. Westminster
Jelf George, barrister, 13 Great George st. Westminster
Jellicoe & Wix, turkey merchts. 2 Turnwheel la. Cannon st
Jellicoe Chas. act. & sec. of *Protector Life Assoctn.* 35 Old Jewry
Jellicoe Frank, proctor, see Denne & Jellicoe
Jemmett George, coach & harness maker, 137 Long acre
Jencken Ferdinand, physician, Denmark hill, Camberwell
Jenings Chas. & Edmund John, solicitors, 1 Mitre ct. bdgs
Jenkin Charles Lewis, drug broker, agent to the Mulgrave alum works, 3 Clement's lane, Lombard st
Jenkin Ebenezer Alfred, surgeon, 5 Norfolk st. Park lane
Jenkin William, who. milliner, 4 Sidney pl. Comml. rd. ea
Jenkins & Bond, iron & brass founders & manufacturers, Union works, 1 Cherry Garden st. Bermondsey
Jenkins George & Co. wine merchants, 46 Gt. Portland st
Jenkins Wm. & Co. west india merchants, 1 Lime st. sq
Jenkins Wm. & Sons, pianoforte ms. 10 London st. Fitzroy sq
Jenkins Abel, solicitor, see Abbott, Jenkins & Abbott
Jenkins Benjamin, hatter, 131 Drury lane
Jenkins Charles, tailor, 23 Shaftesbury st. New North rd
Jenkins Charles Edward, surgeon, 11 Gt. Prescot st. Goodm. fi
Jenkins David, spectacle ma. 8 Brewer st. north, Goswell rd
Jenkins Edward, auctioneer & appraiser, 2 Exeter st. Strand
Jenkins Edward, *Blue Coat Boy* P.H. 32 Dorset st. Spitalflds
Jenkins Fielder, merchant, Lloyd's
Jenkins Francis, carpenter & builder, 65 Ebury st. Pimlico
Jenkins George, academy, 4 Nassau street, Soho
Jenkins George, grocer, 4 Wentworth place, Mile end
Jenkins George, watchcase maker, 58 Charles st. City road
Jenkins Hannah (Mrs.), haberdasher, 9 Trinity row, Islington
Jenkins Henry, chemist, 8 Barnsbury pl. Up. st. Islington
Jenkins Henry, law stationer, 11 Cook's court, Carey st
Jenkins Henry, undertaker, 47 King st. Snow hill
Jenkins Henry Pust, foreign wine imp. see Ferrer & Jenkins
Jenkins Hilton T. sec. to Oxford & Worcester Extension & Chester Junction Railway, 1 Coleman st. bdgs. Moorgate st
Jenkins James, cowkeeper, 53 West street, Smithfield
Jenkins James, haberdasher, 5 Victoria pl. Queen's rd. Dalston
Jenkins Jemima N. (Miss), cigar mfr. 6 Watt's ter. Old Knt. rd
Jenkins Jeremiah, carpenter, 26 Union row, New Kent road
Jenkins John, baker & grocer, 14 Vauxhall st. Lambeth
Jenkins John, builder, 165 New Bond st
Jenkins John, carpenter, 16 Silver st. Golden square
Jenkins John, coal & timber dlr. 35 Princes st. Rotherhithe
Jenkins John, furnishing undertaker, 2 Liverpool st. Bishopsg
Jenkins John, ironmonger & general agent, patent pump & portable or fixed water closet maker, 138 Houndsditch
Jenkins John, leather cutter, 6 Crown place, Old Kent road
Jenkins John, pork butcher, 49 Liquorpond st
Jenkins John, tobacconist, 53 Bath st. City road
Jenkins John Barrett, upholsterer, 61 Great Prescot st
Jenkins John Hedgcock, cowkeeper, 72 Church st. Rotherhit
Jenkins Joseph B. stockbroker, 13 Angel court, Bank
Jenkins Joseph J. artist, 8 Caroline st. Bedford square
Jenkins Lewis Heather, stationer, 29 Brick la. Spitalfields
Jenkins Margaret (Mrs.), dining rooms, 97 St. John st. Clkw
Jenkins Mary (Mrs.), lodging house, 9 Thavies inn
Jenkins Nicholas, *Leigh Hoy* P.H. Church st. Mile end
Jenkins Philip, beer retailer, 4 Mount ter. Newrd. Whitechpl
Jenkins Richard, beer retailer, 168 Church st. Shoreditch
Jenkins Richard, bricklayer, 22 Lit. Randolph st. Cmdn. tn
Jenkins Rich. Ford, *Catherine Wheel* P.H. Lit. St. James's st
Jenkins Robert, surveyor, 22 Huntley st. Bedford square
Jenkins Thos. baker & corn deal. 10 Whitehorse la. Stepney
Jenkins Thos. chandler's shop, 28 Harrow rd. Paddington
Jenkins Thos. Lowten, barrister, 22 Chancery lane
Jenkins Wm. chandler's shop, 22 Rochester row, Westmintr
Jenkins Wm. cheesemonger, 15 Saville st. Fitzroy sq
Jenkins Wm. grocer, 49 Carnaby st. Golden square
Jenkins Wm. *Royal Duke* P.H. 1 Bloomsbury ter. Com. rd. ea
Jenkins Wm. tailor, 51 Cornhill
Jenkins Wm. jun, architect & surveyor, 20 Bartlett's bldgs
Jenkins Wm. E. pat. of drying ma. see Robinson & Jenkins
Jenkins Wm. E. hairdresser, 41 King William st. City
Jenkins Wm. Saml. gun engraver, 52 Mansell st. Goodman's fi
Jenkinson Chas. Thos. & Alfred, solicitors, 76 Cannon st. City
Jenkinson Alfred, solicitor, 76 Cannon st. City
Jenkinson Fras. bread, &c. baker, 2 Foubert's pl. Regent st
Jenkinson Geo. tailor, 25 Grafton st. east, Tottenham ct. rd
Jenkinson Geo. Matthew, music seller, 12 City road
Jenkinson John, butcher, 297 Albany road, Camberwell
Jenkinson Thomas, ivory turner, 1 Lower Kennington lane
Jenkinson Thos. gold & silver beater, 27½ Compton st. Clrknwl
Jenkinson Thomas North, butcher, 143 Kingsland road
Jenkinson Wm. china dealer, 70 Hackney road
Jenkinson Wm. saddle & harness maker, 44 London wall
Jenkinson Wm. tailor, 21 Adam st. east, Portman square
Jenks James, accountant, 28 Clement's lane, Lombard st
Jenks John, timber mercht. Neal's yd. Queen st. 7 dials
Jenks John Charles, bookbinder, 1 Windsor court, Strand
Jenks Robert Isaac, looking glass & cabinet ma. 55 Bread st
Jenks Thomas, cabinet manfy. 107 Dorset st. Salisbury square
Jenks Thos. who. lookng. glss. & cbnt. man. 107 Dorsetst. Fleet st
Jenkyn James, solicitor, see Jackson & Jenkyn
Jenkyns & Phelps, attorneys, 14 Red Lion sq. Holborn
Jenkyns Francis, merchant, 3 Love lane, Eastcheap
Jennens, Bettridge & Sons, manufrs. of papier maché trays, furniture, fancy articles, &c. to her Majesty, 61 King William st. City, 3 Halkin st. west, Belgrave square, Church st. Chelsea, & Birmingham
Jennens & Dodd (Misses), stayma. 16 North st. Lisson grove
Jennens Thomas, Joseph & William, button, military & naval ornament manfrs. to her Majesty, H.R.H. Prince Albert & the royal family, 56 Conduit st. late 134 Regent st
Jenner, Dyke & Jenner, procts. & notaries, 5 Dean's ct. Doc. com
Jenner Robert & Henry, ale brewers, Crosby rw. King st. Boro'
Jenner Benjamin, boot & shoe maker, 1 Charles st. Hoxton
Jenner Benjamin, fruiterer, 13 Clayton pl. Caledonian rd
Jenner George, artist, 31 Adam st. west
Jenner Henry, coffee rooms, 7 Osborne st. Whitechapel
Jenner Herbert, D.C.L. advocate, 10 College, Doctors' com
Jenner James, academy, 11 Cowley st. Westminster
Jenner Otto, baker, 10 York place, Kent st. road
Jenner Thomas, baker, 59 Regent st. Horseferry road
Jenner Thomas, baker, 42 Rochester row, Westminster
Jenner Thomas, patten ma. 7 Dover pl. west, Kent st. Boro'

Jenner Walter, cabinet maker, 14 Gerrard st. Soho
Jenner William, wharfinger, Phœnix wf. Clink st. Bankside
Jenner William, surgeon, 14 Albany st. Regent's park
Jenner William, undertaker, 43 Foley st. Portland place
Jennett Wm. ivory turnr. 12 Chapel rw. Exmouth st. Clrknwl
Jennings & Cox, proctors & notaries, 18 Bennett's hill
Jennings & Ford, carriers, 23 Lawrence lane, Cheapside
Jennings Jas. & Co. butter & poultry salesman, 23 Newgate st
Jennings Mary & Fras. (Misses), ladies' schl. 108 Camden rd. vil
Jennings & Yeo, birmingham factors, 11 Eldon st. Finsbury, & 11 Edmund st. Birmingham
Jennings Ann (Miss), haberdasher, 36 King st. Borough
Jennings Ann (Mrs.), ladies' school, 52 Gibson sq. Islington
Jennings Christopher, cabinet maker, 4 West st. Hackney
Jennings Daniel, fruiterer, 31 Water lane, Blackfriars
Jennings David, solicitor, 71 Whitechapel road
Jennings Edward, baker, 10 South Island pl. Clapham rd
Jennings Edward, baker, 30 Phœnix st. Somers town
Jennings Edward, solicitor, 16 Chancery lane
Jennings Francis, florist, South Lambeth
Jennings Francis, trimming seller, see Bicknell & Jennings
Jennings George, carpenter, 23 Wellclose sq. Rosemary lane
Jennings George, plumber & builder, 29 Gt. Charlotte st
Jennings George, silk manufacturer, 12 Spital square
Jennings Harrington, painter, &c. 6 University st. Tot. ct. rd.
Jennings James, baker, 14 Charles st. Hampstead road
Jennings James, carver & gilder, 83 John st. Fitzroy sq
Jennings James, grocer, 67 Cornwall rd. Lambeth
Jennings James, laceman, 47 Judd st. Brunswick sq
Jennings James, porkman, 53 Fore st. Limehouse
Jennings John, carpenter, Horseshoe yard, 58 Brook st
Jennings John, coffee rooms, 6 Union st. New Bond st
Jennings John, gassfitter, &c. 4 Charles st. Long acre
Jennings John, goldbeater, 30 Marshall st. London road
Jennings John, grocer, 24 Kent st. Borough
Jennings John, hairdresser, 100 Quadrant, Regent st
Jennings John, pork butcher, 82 Poplar High st
Jennings John Thos. newsvender, 5 Crown st. Finsbury
Jennings Joseph, architect & survey. 14 King st. Portman sq
Jennings Joseph, gasfitter, 8 White Hart st. Drury lane
Jennings Joseph Adam, crape & silk ma. 9 Cobham row, Clknw
Jennings Lewis, *Skinners' Arms* P.H. 10 Skinner st. Bishopsg
Jennings Lydia (Miss), milliner, 3 Queen's terrace, Chelsea
Jennings Robert, publisher, book & print seller, 62 Cheapside
Jennings Samuel, carver & gilder, 8 Goswell st
Jennings Samuel, artist, 1 Poland st. Oxford st
Jennings Samuel, ironmongr. 9 Islington High st. north side
Jennings Sarah (Mrs.), nursery, Park village east, Regent's pk
Jennings Susanna (Mrs.), baker, 22 Tonbridge pl. New rd
Jennings Thomas, blacksmith, 5 King st. Rotherhithe wall
Jennings Thomas, brass manufacturer, plumber & gas fitter, 5 Union st. Whitechapel road
Jennings, Thomas, timber merchant, 131 Rotherhithe st
Jennings Thomas, undertaker, see Haines & Jennings
Jennings Thomas Francis, solicitor, 2 High st. Notting hill
Jennings William, baker, 39 Upper Lisson st. Lisson grove
Jennings Wm. bootmaker, 14 Ann's ter. Cambridge heath
Jennings Wm. butcher, 72 Devonshire st. Lisson grove
Jennings Wm. fruiterer, 56 Clark st. Stepney
Jennings Wm. grocer, 22 Lambeth Lower marsh
Jennings Wm. haberdasher, 55 Bethnal green road
Jennings Wm. tailor, 5 Foregate, St. Clement's, Strand
Jennings Wm. H. smith & mechanst. 7 Grove, Maltby st. Brmdsy
Jennott Charles, grocer, 41 East st. Manchester square
Jenrick & Morgan, engravers, &c. 108 London rd. Southwark
Jenson John, varnish manufacturer, see Kingham & Jenson
Jenson William, *Fir Tree* P.H. Church lane, Whitechapel
Jentzen Henry, dining rooms, 30 Coventry st. Haymarket
Jephs Frederick, fruiterer, 24 Westbourne st. Pimlico
Jephs Frederick, newsvender, 18 Westbourne st. Pimlico
Jephs Samuel, builder, 15 Upper Eaton st. Pimlico
Jepps Manoah, cork manufactr. 3 Duke st. West Smithfield
Jepps Samuel, broker & undertaker, 20 New cut, Lambeth
Jepson Mary (Miss), lad. school, 39 Gt. Pulteney st. Golden sq
Jepson Thomas, gold chain maker & importer of French jewellery, 39 Great Pulteney st. Golden square
Jerard Henry, locksmith & bellhanger, 46 Eastcheap
Jerdein John Inglis, coal merchant, see Lee & Jerdein
Jeremy Henry, magistrate, Greenwich police court
Jerman Martha (Mrs.), furnit. broker, 16 Upper Cleveland st
Jerman William, grindery wareho. 21 Dean st. Fetter lane
Jermy James, butcher, 15 London terrace, Hackney road
Jermy William, butcher, 29 Bethnal green road
Jermyn Geo. Alfred, surveyor, &c. 15 Buckingham st. Strand
Jermyn Harriet (Mrs.), milliner, &c. 78 Margaret st. Cavh. sq
Jermyn Henry, hair cutter, 11 Charles st. Commercial road
Jerningham Edward, manager of the London Joint Stock Bank, Western Branch, 69 Pall mall
Jerom George, carpenter, 41 Princes road, Lambeth
Jerome Ambrosini, artist, 91 Great Russell st. Bloomsbury
Jerome Richard, chimney sweeper, 2 Falconberg ct. Soho
Jerome Thomas, tailor, 5 Oxford market
Jerram John, wholes. teadealer, 14 Fenchurch buildings
Jerrard Paul, zincographic artist, printer & print colorer, 20 Clifton st. Finsbury
Jerrem Samuel, lodging house, 8 Somerset st. Portman sq
Jerrey Samuel, bookseller, 32 Tabernacle walk, Finsbury
Jerrom Thomas, bird dealer, 94 Waterloo road
Jerusalem Coffeehouse, Cowper's court, Cornhill
Jervis Edward, tailor, 54 Brunswick st. Blackfriars road
Jervis Henry Z. solicitor, 18 Laurence Pountney hill
Jervis Jervis John, barrister, 3 New square, Lincoln's inn
Jervis John, Queen's counsel, 3 Essex court, Temple
Jervis John Reginald, carpenter, 13 Low. Kennington green
Jervis Thomas, surgeon, see Bird & Jervis
Jerwood Thomas John, solicitor, 1 Walbrook buildings, & 12 Elm tree road, St. John's wood
Jerwood Thos. J. west india, irish & french agt. 1 Walbrook blds
Jesse & Paddy, linendrapers, 6 Onslow pl. Fulham road
Jessel Joseph Aaron, tobacconist, 45 Lambeth High st
Jessel Zadok Aron, pearl & diamond merchant, 1 Saville row
Jessep John, tailor, 12 Duke st. St. James's
Jessey George, hairdresser, 13 Gt. Windwill st. Haymarket
Jessimey Hervey, *Guy Earl of Warwick* P.H. 9 Gray's inn la
Jesson Chas. *Crown & Sceptre* P.H. 30 Britannia st. City rd
Jesson Elizabeth (Mrs.), fruiterer, 11 Millbank st. Westmstr
Jesson Henry, barrister, 2 Middle Temple lane
Jessop Elizh. & Cath. milliners, 37 Shaftesbury st. Nw. North rd
Jessop Charles, baker, 3 Deptford High st
Jessop Charles, jun. baker, King st. New town, Deptford
Jessop Hannah (Mrs.), milliner, 35 Gibson st. Waterloo rd
Jessop Henry, dairy, 12 St. Alban's place, Edgware road
Jessop John, coffee rooms, 11 Catherine st. Strand
Jessop Wm. furn. brok. & ho. agt. 17 Norfolk st. Middx. hsptl
Jessop Wm. grocer, 1 Meadow pl. South Lambeth
Jessopp Joseph, solicitor, 12 Clifford's inn, Fleet st
Jessup Joseph, coffee rooms, 59 Castle st. east, Oxford st
Jessup William, *Dowgate* coffee rooms, 175 Up. Thames st
Jeudwine George, conveyancer, 10 Gray's inn square
Jeune Rd. & Son, undertakers, 20 Liverpool st. Bishopsgate
Jeune James Thomas, drug & spice broker, 11 Cannon st
Jeves John Job, house & estate agent, 23 Pall mall
Jeves Wm. cabinetmaker & upholsterer, 1 Poplar High st
Jewel Office, Tower; hours 10 to 4
Jewell Ansalem, tailor, 130 Shadwell High st
Jewell Barnard, tailor & outfitter, 79 St. George st
Jewell Joel, furniture broker, 194 Whitechapel road
Jewell Joel, rag & bottle mer. 11 Sheffield st. Linc. inn fields
Jewell John, baker, 2 Virginia row, Bethnal green road
Jewell John, hotpresser & glazer of paper, 22 Bride la. Fleet st
Jewell Thos. fruiterer & coal mer. 17 Charles st. Portman sq
Jewell Wm. carver & gilder, 55 Sloane sq. Chelsea
Jewell Wm. Salmon, *Tiger* P.H. Avebury st. Pool st. Nw. Nth. rd
Jeweller's So. (Wm. Frost, sec.), *Crown & Anchor*, 189 Strand
Jewesbury Hen. Wm. indigo. bro. see Wilkinson & Jewesbury
Jewesson Richard & Co. merchants, 28 Gt. Winchester st
Jewesson Richard, merchant, Hall of Commerce
Jewiss John Thos. & Danl. ship & anch. smiths, 1 Nw. sq. Hrslydn
Jewiss Thomas, *Gun Tavern*, Coal harbour, Blackwall
Jewitt Francis, windowblind spring barrel mak. 14 Gt. Earl st
Jewitt Jas. Watson, solicitor, 14 Southampton st. Bloomsby
Jewish Chronicle Office, 132 Houndsditch
Jews' Orphan Asylum, 22 Leman st. Goodman's fields
Jews' Spanish & Portuguese Almshouses, Heneag. la. Bvis. mks
Jewson Dan. fruiterer & greengrocer, 12 Beer la. Tower st
Jewson Frederick B. R A. professor of music, 60 Berners st. Oxford st
Jewson William, hairdresser, 15 Beer la. Lower Thames st
Jex George, grocer, 4 Odell place, Little Chelsea
Jeyes Francis Ferdinando, solicitor, see Cragg & Jeyes
Jeynes George, chemist, 49 Gt. James st. Lisson grove
Jeynes George Wm. chemist, 42 Princess st. Edgware rd
Jifkins Henry, fruiterer, 2 Lit. Ormond st. Queen sq
Jilks Samuel, carpenter, 34 Hindon st. Pimlico
Jinks George & Co. paper stainers, 45 Skinner st. Snowhill
Jinks Hen. & Co. paperstnrs. & dectr. 19 Up. King st. Bloomsb
Jinks Edward, cowkeeper, Lower King st. Old Kent rd
Jinks John, builder, 2 Thomas st. Back Church lane
Jinks Rich. window blind ma. 20 Up. King st. Bloomsby
Jinnings John T. engineer & ship smith, 46 Wapping Hi. st
Job Brothers & Co. stationers, acct. book ma. paper mounters, tracing paper mnfrs. & japanners. 35 Bread st

Job James, bell pull manf. 22Norfolk st. Low. rd. Islgtn
Job Edwin Hen. tailor & draper, 11 Park ter. Camden town
Job Frederick, watch & clock ma. 17Tichborne st. Haymarkt
Job Robert, watch & clock maker, 1 Gower st. north, New rd
Job Robert, clock & watch maker, 7 Park terr. Camden town
Jobbins Alfred, baker, 1 Victoria grove, Kensngtn. new tn
Jobbins Eleanor (Mrs.), baker, 15 Charles st. Hatton garden
Jobbins George Frederick, baker, 5 Camberwell grove
Jobbins Henry, baker, 5 Brompton terrace
Jobbins John Richard, surveyor, engineering, railway & mechanical draftsman & lithographer, 3 Warwick ct. Hlbrn
Jobbins Thomas, tailor, 5 Adam st. east, Portman sq
Jobbins William, baker, 3 Grove hill ter. Grove la. Cmbrwll
Jobson Christopher, *Apollo* P.H. 191 Tottenham court rd
Jobson Sarah (Mrs.), chandler's shop, High st. StokeNwngtn
Joce Samuel, *White Hart* P.H. 2 Chancery lane, Holborn
Joel Joseph & Co. jewellers, 49 Strand
Joel George, plate glass factor, 23 Acorn st. Bishopsgate
Joel Isaac, appraiser & com. agt. 97 Curtain rd. Shoreditch
Joel Jenkin, tailor, 38 Taberacle walk, Finsbury sq
Joel Mark, broker & appraiser, 2 Primrose st. Bishopsgate
Joel Moss, auctr. surv. & estate agt. 97 Curtain rd. Shoreditch
Joel Sophia (Mrs.), stationer & bookslr. 42 Fore st. Cripplgt
Joel William, tailor, 16 King st. Golden square
Johanning & Co. music sellers, 9 Newman st. Oxford st
John Bull weekly newspaper office, 40 Fleet st
John Thomas, baker, 24 Stangate, Lambeth
Johnes Arth. Jas. barrister, 24 Southmptn. bldgs. Chancery la
Johnes John Hugh, private tutor, 3Up. Spring st. Portman sq
Johns N. & Co. hosiery & ready made linen war. 13&14 Fleet st
Johns Charles, plate glass factor, 7 Kirby st. Hatton garden
Johns Charles, shop & medical fixture dlr. & appraiser, 157 Drury la. & 44 Gt. Queen st. Lincoln's inn fields
Johns Charles, tailor & oakum dealer, 10Ferry rd. west, Poplar
Johns John, coffeerooms, 28 Judd place west, New road
Johns Joseph, cook & confectioner, 29 Grosvenor st. west
Johns Rd. copp. pl. eng. & printer, 7 Gt. St. Andrew st. 7 dials
Johns Thomas, carpenter & undertaker, 3Percivals buildings, & 8 East Mount terrace, Whitechapel road
Johns Susan (Mrs.), leathersell. 39Low. George st. Chelsea
Johns Thos. Coke, printer, 13&14 Wine office ct. &7Gough sq
JohnsWm. Chas. bookbinders' tool cutter, 32Kirby st. Hat. gar
Johnson & Allen, coachmakers, 72 Long acre
Johnson, Atkinson & Co. iron & stl. works, Ranelagh rd. Pimlico
Johnson P. N. & Co. refiners & metallurgists, 79 Hatton garden
Johnson & Core (Mesdames), milliners, 13 Brook st. Grov. sq
Johnson & Day, calenderers & packers, 23 Eldon st. Finsbury
Johnson Dan. T. & Son, tea & hopmers. 2 Aldermary church yd
Johnson Geo. & Co. carpet & manchstr. agents, warehousemen & mourning collar ma. 11 Bow churchyd. & 4 Bow la. Cheaps
Johnson George & Co. carpet agents, 4 Bow lane
Johnson George & Co. tailors, 4 Rolls' buildings, Fetter lane
Johnson George L. & Co. merchnts. 5 Barge yd. Bucklersbury
Johnson Geo. Son & Weatherall, attorneys, 7 King's Bench wk
Johnson Grave & Co. drapers & upholsterers, 25 Blackmn. st
Johnson Hen. Jas. & Hen. Chas. medical school, see Tatum & Johnsons'
Johnson Jas. & Sons, builds. 25 Redcross st. & 43 Monkwell st
Johnson John & Co. printers & publish. 10 Brooke st. Holborn
Johnson John & Co. ship insur. & coml. agents, 68Fenchurch st
Johnson John & Son, military feather & hair plume manufacturers, 4 Great Vine st. Regent st
Johnson John & Sons, assayers of bullion, 6 & 7 Gresham st. Wood st. Cheapside
Johnson John & Wm. ironfounders, 13 Whitecross st. Crplgt
Johnson (Joseph Bulkeley) & Co. wholesale tea dealers, 10 Coleman st. & 63 Paradise st. Liverpool
Johnson, Longden & Co. stockbrokers, 22 Tokenhouse yard
Johnson Lydia & Ann, milliners, 8 South st. South Audley st
Johnson & Maples, coppersmiths, 56 & 57 Charles st. City rd
JohnsonMary (Mrs.), & Co. snuff & tobac. ma. 19Crownst. Finsby
Johnson & Ravey, braziers, &c. 4 Conduit st. Regent st
Johnson & Renny, east india brokers, 57 Fenchurch st
Johnson Richard & Co. hatters to the Queen, 113 Regent st
Johnson Rd. & Son, cabinet ma. 3 Colet pl. Commercial rd. ea
Johnson Richard & Son, wholesale stationers, 46 Coleman st
Johnson Robert & Nephew, warehousemen, 95 &97 Watling st
Johnson & Roffey, emery & bl. lead ma. Edwd. st. Yorkrd. Lambh
Johnson Sam. & Dixon R. house agts. 2 Somerset st. Portman sq
Johnson Sarah & Rose Ann (Misses) ladies' schl. 40 Canonby. sq
Johnson & Simpson, gold & silver lacemen, manufacturers of military & naval accoutrements, gold & silver indian skein thread trimmings & spangles, embroiderers, refiners, wire drawers, & importers of german wire, &c. 10 Little Britain
Johnson, Taber & Johnson, wine mercs. 39 Crutched friars
Johnson & Watson, lamp & lustre ma. 89 Quadrant, Regent st
Johnson & White, who. tea & coffee dealers, 33 Dowgate hll
Johnson Wm. & Co. tailors, 19 Clifford st. Bond st
Johnson Wm. & Co. tallow chand. 174&175 Bishopsgt. without
Johnson Wm. Whittle & Robert, lead, white lead, glass, oil & color manufrs. 8 Brunswick st. Blackwall, & 4 Waterloo pl. Commercial road east, Limehouse
Johnson Aaron, tobacconist, 1 Albion place, Rotherhithe, & Lower road, Rotherhithe
Johnson Adolphus P. insurance broker, 5 Adam's ct. & Lloyd's
Johnson Alexander, carpenter, 14 & 22 Poppin's ct. Fleet st
Johnson Alfred, carpenter, 38 Hosier lane, Smithfield
Johnson Alfred Richard, hatter, see Griffiths & Johnson
Johnson Ann (Mrs.), coal mer. 18Lombard st. Cheyne wk. Chels
Johnson Ann (Mrs.), millin. & haberdash. 7 Tyler st. Regentst
Johnson Anna Maria (Mrs.), *George Inn*, 16West Smithfield
Johnson Benjamin, *Globe* P.H. Ellen st. St. George's east
Johnson Benjamin, plumber, Bromley, Middlesex
Johnson Benjamin, plumber, Bow
Johnson Charles, bootmaker, 4 Palace row, New rd. St. Pancr
Johnson Charles, goldsmith & jeweller, 173 St. John st. road
Johnson Charles, insurance broker, Lloyd's
Johnson Charles, manufacturing cutler & hardwareman, 6 Northumberland place, Commercial road east
Johnson Charles, map & print colorer, 4 Nevill's ct. Fetter la
Johnson Charles, pawnbroker, 25 Providence row, Finsbury
Johnson Charles, ribbon manuf. 1 Little Love la. Wood st
Johnson Charles, shoemaker, 58 Lisson grove north
Johnson Charles, surgeon, 134 Rotherhithe street
Johnson Charles, tailor, see Faulkner & Johnson
Johnson Charles, turner, 30 Southampton Mews, Euston sqre
Johnson Charles James, oil & color wa. 31 Aldgate High st
Johnson Charles Joseph, butcher, 4 Windmill row, Kenngtn
Johnson Chas M. ship & ins. brok. 3 Howford bldgs. Fench. st
Johnson Chas. Polson, academy, 5 Westmoreland st. Maryleb
JohnsonCharlotte (Mrs.), butcher, 74 Compton st. Clerkenwell
Johnson Cuthbert William, barrister, 14 Gray's inn square
JohnsonDanl. chandler's shop, 1, Newcastlest. Whitechpl. Hi. st
Johnson Daniel, manchester agent, 16 Watling st
Johnson Daniel, prof. of dancing, 4 Sermon la. Doctors' comns
Johnson Daniel, tobacconist, 58 Leader st. Chelsea
Johnson David, plumber & painter, 25 Fleet lane, Old Bailey
Johnson Dellawar, bootmaker, 29 West st. New road
Johnson Edward, camp equip. mnfr. & patentee of the metallic folding hinged bedsteads, &c. 160 Piccadilly (late of Leadenhall st)
Johnson Edward, grocer & cheesem. 46Gravel la. Southwark
Johnson Edward, physician, 18 New Burlington st
Johnson Edward, M.D. surgeon, 42 Carnaby st
Johnson Edward, tobacconist, 26 Old Compton st. Soho
Johnson Edward E. corn dlr. & cow kpr. Canal rd. Mile end rd
Johnson Edwin, *South Sea* coffee rooms, 15 St. George st
Johnson Elizh. (Miss), coffee rooms, 9Orange rw. Kenngtn. rd
Johnson Elizh. (Miss), millinery wareho. 78A, Edgware rd
Johnson Elizh. (Mrs.), staymaker, 188 Tottenham court rd
Johnson Ellen (Miss), staymaker, 2 Somerset st. Portman sq
Johnson Emily (Miss), milliner, 61 St. John st. road
Johnson Emma (Mrs.), stationer, 11 Devonsh. bldgs. Dover rd
Johnson Francis, boot & shoe ma. 25Walnut Tree wk. Lmbth
Johnson Francis, chemist, 9 Phœnix st. Somers town
Johnson Francis, corn dealer, 37 Exeter st. Sloane st
Johnson Francis, paper stainer, 2 & 4 New road, Whitechapel
Johnson Francis Arnold, plumber, &c. 30North st. Lisson gr
Johnson Frederic, file, tool & metal wa. see Cotton & Johnson
Johnson Frederick, *Crown* P.H. 7 Essex st. Strand
Johnson Fredk. hairdresser, 6 Gt. Wild st. Linc. inn flds
Johnson Fredk. tobaccon. 9 Gibraltar walk, Bethnal gr. rd
Johnson George, beer retailer, 21 Stephen st. Ttnhm. ct. rd
Johnson George, carpenter, 32 Whitefriars st. Fleet st
Johnson George, furn. broker, Kensington gravel pits
Johnson George, grocer, 43 Princes road, Lambeth
Johnson George, hairdresser, 4½ Northampton row, Holloway
Johnson George, watch hand maker, 7 Queen st. Clerkenwell
Johnson Geo. Atkinson, potato salsmn. Cotton's wf. Tooley st
Johnson Geo. Byng, newsman, &c. 56 Mortimer st. Cavendish sq
Johnson Geo. Richd. platina dlr. 6 & 7 Gresham st. Wood st
Johnson Harriett (Mrs.), straw hat maker, 8 High st. Bow
Johnson Harriette (Miss), milliner, 289 Regent st
Johnson Hen. builder, Woodbridge ho. 16Sekforde st. Clknwl
Johnson Henry, china manufrs'. agent, 107 Hatton garden
Johnson Henry, coal merchant, 13 George st. Adelphi, & Great Scotland yard
Johnson Henry, fruiterer, Spitalfields market
Johnson Henry, grocer, 1 Tunbridge ter. St. Andrew's rd. Boro
Johnson Henry, grocer & teadealr. 156 Bishopsgate st. without
Johnson Henry, hairdresser, 11 South Island pl. Brixton rd
Johnson Henry, printer, 9 Wells st. Oxford st

Johnson Henry, solicitor, 2 New inn, Strand
Johnson Henry, surgeons' inst. maker, 121 Blackfriars road
Johnson Henry, surveyor, see Yallowley & Johnson
Johnson Henry, teadealer & grocer, 231 Blackfriars road
Johnson Henry, east & west india agent, 68 Fenchurch st
Johnson Henry, merchant, 39 Crutched friars
Johnson Henry Charles, surgeon, 6 Saville row, Piccadilly
Johnson Henry C. truss maker, &c. 55 Newington causeway
Johnson Henry James, surgeon, 8 Suffolk pl. Haymarket
Johnson Henry Saml. insurance bro. & underwriter, Lloyd's
Johnson Henry Wm. gold & silver refiner, wire drawer, & gold & silver thread manf. 10 Green ter. St. John st. road
Johnson Hugh, *Fitzroy Arms* P.H. 126 Grove st. Camden tn
Johnson James, beer retailer, 1 Locks sq. York st. Walw. rd
Johnson James, blacking maker, 20 Queen sq. Westminster
Johnson James, boot & shoe ma. 27 Falcon sq. Aldersgate st
Johnson James, boot & shoe manf. 6 Port pl. Walwth. commn
Johnson James, brush maker, 172 Tooley st
Johnson James, coachmaker, 5 Exeter pl. Knightsbridge
Johnson James, dyer, 39 Cannon st. rd. & 49 Triny. st. Rotherh
Johnson James, emery paper maker, & black lead & rotten stone works, 18 Stephen st. Tottenham court road
Johnson James, fruiterer, 10 Union st. Clarendon square
Johnson James, jeweller, 39 Whiskin st. Clerkenwell
Johnson James, leather slr. 20 Langley pl. Commrcl. rd. ea
Johnson James, paperhanging ma. 38 Cannon st. St. George's ea
Johnson James, tailor, 9 North st. Edgware road
Johnson James, tripe dresser, 63 Whitechapel High st
Johnson James, watchmaker, 18 Paddington st. Marylebone
Johnson James, whip maker, Blue boar yard, Aldgate High st
Johnson James Lee, *Fulham Bridge* P.H. 11 Brompton rd
Johnson Jane (Mrs.), grocer, 7 Ann's pl. St. Geo.'s rd. N. Kent rd
Johnson Job, carpet scourer, &c. 98 Hoxton Old town
Johnson John, architect, 9 John st. Adelphi
Johnson John, barrister, 42 Southampton buildings
Johnson John, bedstead maker, 51 Long alley, Finsbury
Johnson John, bootmaker, 4 Canterbury pl. Old Kent road
Johnson John, butcher, 68 Crawford st. Portman square
Johnson John, butcher, 48 St. Martin's lane, Charing cross
Johnson John, butcher, 46 Strutton ground, Westminster
Johnson John, chemist & druggist, 116 Upper st. Islington
Johnson John, coal mer. & wharfingr. New wf. Lit. Abingdon st
Johnson John, coffee rooms, 9 King st. Rotherhithe wall
Johnson John, corn & coal mer. 17 William st. Knightsbridge
Johnson John, east india merchant, 6 Gt. Winchester st
Johnson John, printer, 7 Wellington st. Goswell st
Johnson John, tailor, 8 Strong's pl. Brompton
Johnson John, 3 *Crowns* P.H. 1 Winckworth bldngs. City rd
Johnson John, underta. & registrar, 4 Brunswick st. Hackney rd
Johnson John, warehouseman, see Johnson & Nephew
Johnson John Edw. coach lace & carpet mfr. 44 Gerrard st. Soho
Johnson John Flude, shorthand writer, 2 Charles sq. Hoxton
Johnson John Frederick, plumber, 23 Union ct. Holborn hill
Johnson John How, funl. coachmstr. 4 Tichborne st. Haymkt
Johnson John James, barrister, 10 King's Bench walk, Temple
Johnson John James, solicitor, see Fielder, Johnson & Master
Johnson John James, tailor, 11 Clifford's inn
Johnson John Jarrett, wine merchant, 68 Fenchurch st. & 3 Narrow st. Ratcliffe
Johnson John Morris, engraver, &c. 10 Castle st. Holborn
Johnson Jonathan, billiard rooms, 23 King st. Golden sq
Johnson Joseph, bootma. 17 Tottenham ct. rd. & 78 Longacre
Johnson Joseph, butcher, 143 Brick lane, Spitalfields
Johnson Joseph, corn dealer, 2 Somerset place, Hoxton
Johnson Joseph, dining rooms, 135 Poplar High st
Johnson Joseph, hosier, glover & shirt maker, 323 Oxford st
Johnson Joseph, *Old Sword & Buckler* P.H. 45 Bermndsy st
Johnson Joseph, omnibus proprietor, 12 Church st. Pddngtn
Johnson Joseph, saw, tool, & busk maker 101 Gt. Titchfield st
Johnson Joseph, tobacconist, 3 Assembly pl. Kenngn gr
Johnson Joseph Bulkeley, merchant, 10 Coleman st
Johnson Joseph White, surgeon, 5 Cambridge pl. Regent's pk
Johnson Martha (Miss), artist, 89 Strand
Johnson Martha (Mrs.), tobacconist, 19 Earl st. ea. Lisson gr
Johnson Mary (Mrs.), bookbinder, 13 Leicester st. Regent st
Johnson Mary (Mrs.), coffee rooms, 7 Silver st. Golden sq
Johnson Mary (Mrs.), harpoon & tool ma. 36 Cannon st. rd
Johnson Mary (Mrs.), milliner, 59 Crawford st. Portman sq
Johnson (Mrs.), teacher of music, 13 Queen st. Brompton
Johnson Matthew Walton, statuary, 13 Southampton st. & 27 Buckingham place, Fitzroy square
Johnson Murray Maxwell, solicitor, 7 Gt. Winchester st
Johnson Oliver, oil merchant, &c. see Pinchin & Johnson
Johnson Patrick, official assignee, 20 Basinghall st
Johnson Philip, solicitor, 57 Lincoln's inn fields
Johnson Rebecca (Mrs.), coffee rooms, 157 Hoxton Old town
Johnson Richard, city carman, 6 Bishopsgate buildings
Johnson Richard, wheelwright, French horn yd. 87 High Hlbn
Johnson Richard Green, linendraper, Stratford Broadway
Johnson Robert, builder, 48 Hollywell st. Westminster
Johnson Robert, chemist & druggist, 17 East st. Red Lion sq
Johnson Robert, paint, color, & varnish manufacturer, Stone stairs wharf, Broad st. Ratcliff
Johnson Robt. tailor, 11 Princes st. Bedford row
Johnson Robt. Edw. solicitor, see Baxendale, Tatham & Co.
Johnson Rob. Sparrow, linend. 43 Glo'ster ter. New rd. Com. rd
Johnson Robt. Thos. linendraper, 3 & 4 Broughton pl. Hkny. rd
Johnson Saffery Wm. solicitor, 5 Gray's inn sq. & 2 Verulam buildings, Gray's inn
Johnson Samuel, brass rule cutter, 23 New st. Clothfair
Johnson Samuel, leather seller, 8 Bedford pl. Comml. rd. east
Johnson Samuel, tobacconist, 7 Sidney pl. Commrl. rd. east
Johnson Sarah (Mrs.), *Tyssen Arms* P.H. Dalston
Johnson Sar. A. (Mrs.), *King & Queen* P.H. 258 Rotherhithe st
Johnson Stephen W. bootmaker, 23 New Manor st. Chelsea
Johnson Thomas, academy, 25 Nassau st. Middlesex hospital
Johnson Thomas, appraiser & broker, 59 Old st
Johnson Thomas, auctioneer, 39 Gracechurch st
Johnson Thomas, bootmaker, 20 Bouverie st. Paddington
Johnson Thomas, butcher, 4 Folly, Dockhead, Bermondsey
Johnson Thomas, butcher, 26 Fore st. Cripplegate
Johnson Thomas, butcher, 9 Stepney rents, Hackney road
Johnson Thomas, cabinetmaker, 8 James pl. Hoxton fields
Johnson Thomas, carrier, 24 Devonshire pl. Edgware road
Johnson Thomas, corn & coal merchant, Little Chelsea
Johnson Thomas, currier, see Wallace & Johnson
Johnson Thos. *Devonshire Arms* P.H. 13 Hartland tr. Cmdn. tn
Johnson Thomas, grocer, &c. 47½ City Garden row, City rd
Johnson Thomas, lapidary, 59 King st. Soho
Johnson Thomas, painter & glazier, 18 Gt. Bell al. Moorgate st
Johnson Thos. pat. maltster, 10 New Montague st. Brick la
Johnson Thomas, pawnbroker, 184 Bishopsgate without
Johnson Thomas, picture dealer, 42 Charlotte st. Fitzroy sq
Johnson Thomas, ship & insurance bro. see Seldon & Johnson
Johnson Thomas, tailor, 46 Chiswell st. Finsbury sq
Johnson Thomas, tailor, 8 Norton st. Fitzroy sq
Johnson Thomas Edward, solicitor, 58 Lincoln's inn fields
Johnson Thomas Henry, coal merchant, 5 Spur st. Leicester square, & New wharf, Little Abingdon st
Johnson Thomas Jas. pat. maltster, 19 Booth st. Spitalfields
Johnson Thomas Wm. surgeon, 5 Buckingham pl. Fitzroy sq
Johnson Timothy C. *Mulberry Tree* P.H. Mulberry ct. Finsby
Johnson Wm. appraiser, ho. est. & gen. agt. 54 Red Lion st. Hlbn
Johnson Wm. agt. & receiver, col. of chemistry, 16 Hanover sq
Johnson Wm. barom. & thermom. mak. 34 Hatton garden
Johnson Wm. beer retailer, 3 Conant pl. Comml. rd. Limeho
Johnson Wm. butcher, 4 Little Newport st. Long acre
Johnson Wm. butcher, 12 New st. Brompton
Johnson Wm. cabinetma. & undertak. 16 Barnes pl. Mile end rd
Johnson Wm. chemist & druggist, 254 Borough High st
Johnson Wm. china & glass dealer, 26 Vine st. Hatton garden
Johnson Wm. chronometer, watch & clock maker, 50 Strand
Johnson Wm. coal & potato dealer, 23 Tothill st. Westmstr
Johnson Wm. corndealer, 5 Peerless place, City road
Johnson Wm. cowkeeper, Bow, Middlesex
Johnson Wm. fishmonger & poulterer, 148 Sloane st. Chelsea
Johnson Wm. furn. broker, 5 Clarence pl. Broadway, Deptfd
Johnson Wm. grocer & teadealer, 1 Up. Edmund st. King's cross
Johnson Wm. hatter, 57 King William st. City
Johnson Wm. hop & seed factor, see Simmonds & Johnson
Johnson Wm. oil & colorman, 136 Poplar High street
Johnson Wm. optician, 188 Tottenham court road
Johnson Wm. plasterer & stenciller, 42 Vere st. Clare market
Johnson Wm. plumber, painter, &c. 2 Robert st. Bedford row
Johnson Wm. tailor, 51 Upper Seymour st. Euston square
Johnson Wm. tobacconist, 4 Lowndes terrace, Knightsbridge
Johnson Wm. wine merchant, 36 West Smithfield
Johnson Wm. Coulthard, silk & ribbon agent, 110 Wood st
Johnson Wm. David, stat. & news ag. 33 Garden row, London rd
Johnson Wm. Hen. hairdresser, &c. 12 Crawford st. Portm. sq
Johnson Wm. Hen. solicitor, see Chilton, Burton & Johnson
Johnson Wm. Henry, turner, 147 Aldersgate st
Johnson Wm. John, barrister, 14 Serle st. Lincoln's inn
Johnson Wm. Peter, ladies' shoema. 83 St. John st. Smithfld
Johnson Wm. Spencer, printer & publisher, 60 St. Martin's la
Johnsons, Martin & Fox & Co. engineering surveyors & draughtsmen, 24 Gt. George st. Westminster
Johnston Brothers, brass founders, gasfitters & lamp manufacturers, 9 Cursitor st. Chancery lane
Johnston, Farquhar & Leach, solicitors & parliamentary agents, 65 Moorgate st. & 27 Abingdon st. Westminster

Johnston Elizabeth (Mrs.), & the Misses, dressmakers & milliners to their Majesties the Queen & the Queen Dowager, 16 Dover st. Piccadilly
Johnston Hugh & John & Co. bankers, 15 Gt. Bush lane
Johnston Hugh & John & Co. merchants, 15 Gt. Bush lane
Johnston Jane & Mary (Misses), silversmiths, &c. Cambwll.gn
Johnston John & Jas. fruit merchts. 38 Botolph la. Thames st
Johnston Nathaniel & Sons, wine merchants, 6 Mark lane
Johnston Rt. & Co. who. ironmongers, 63 Gracechurch st
Johnston Alexander, architect, 14 Bernard st. Russell sq
Johnston Alexander, *Black Eagle* P.H. 63 Brick la. Sptlflds
Johnston Alex. sec to Cork & Killarney Railway, 63 Moorgate st
Johnston Alex. Carruthers, iron & hoop merchant, Lloyd's
Johnston Alex. Duguid, barrister, 1 Pump ct. Temple
Johnston Alex. James, barrister, 4 Serjeant's inn, Fleet st
Johnston Andrew, land surveyor, draughtsman & lithographer, 9 Cursitor st. Chancery lane
Johnston Andrew, tailor, 7 Lit. Titchfield st. Portland pl
Johnston Charles, baker, 84 Fore st. Cripplegate
Johnston Charles, baker, Somerset pl. Low. rd. Deptford
Johnston David, baker, 33 King st. Westminster
Johnston Elizh. (Miss), pawnbrkr. 112 Cromer st. Brnswk. sq
Johnston Francis Graydon, surgeon, 4 Beak st. Regent's st
Johnston, Cribb & Maberley, ladies' school, Camberwell rd
Johnston George, furrier, 233 & 248 Regent st
Johnston George, grocer, 231½ Bermondsey st
Johnston George, merchant, 14 Artillery place, Finsbury sq
Johnston George, whitesmith, 7 Norton st. Fitzroy sq
Johnston Hannah (Mrs.), watchma. 2 Elm st. Gray's inn la
Johnston Henry, artist, 64 Warren st. Fitzroy square
Johnston Henry, whalebone broker, see Bowes, Son & Johnston
Johnston James, baker, 8 Dorset pl. Pall mall east
Johnston James, butcher, 17 Clare st. Clare market
Johnston James, solicitor, 100 Chancery lane
Johnston James, sword cutler & belt maker, 68 St. James's st
Johnston John, baker, 4 Eden place, Old Kent road
Johnston John, saddler, see Tate & Johnston
Johnston John, solicitor, see Stokes, Hollingsworth & Co
Johnston John, surgeon, 16 Dover st. Piccadilly
Johnston John, tailor & draper, 16 Up. North pl. Gray's inn rd
Johnston John, jun. carpenter, 7 Red Lion st. Wapping
Johnston Mary (Mrs.), fruiterer, Centre row, Covent garden
Johnston Robert, chemist & soda water mf. 16 Greek st. Soho
Johnston Robert, cigar mnfr. 35 Gloucester st. Comrcl. rd. east
Johnston Robert, coal merchant & wharfinger, Horseshoe wharf, 10 Upper Thames st
Johnston Robert, perfumery, lozenge & genuine patent medicine warehouse, 68 Cornhill
Johnston Robert, plumber & painter, 80 Wells st. Oxford st
Johnston Robert, stockbroker, 5 Shorter's ct. Throgmorton st
Johnston Robert, straw bonnet wa. 10 Church st. Camberwl
Johnston Robert, jun. stockbroker, 5 Angel ct. Throgmrtn. st
Johnston Thomas, baker, 17 King st. Holborn
Johnston Thomas, bookseller, stationer, &c. 53 Moorgate st
Johnston Thomas, coal mer. Horseshoe wf. 10 Up. Thames st
Johnston Thomas Henry, attorney, 16 Cecil st. Strand
Johnston William, baker, 42 Carey st. Lincoln's inn
Johnston Wm. coffee rooms, 54 Red Lion st. Holborn
Johnston William, furrier & skin importer, 441 West Strand
Johnston William, printer, Lit. Red Lion ct. Charterhouse la
Johnston William, surgeon, 51 Mortimer st. Cavendish sq
Johnston William Brown, ship & insur. agt. 85 Lr. Thames st
Johnston William Sheldon, confectioner, 10 Charing cross
Johnstone & Jeanes, cabinet mks. & upholstrs. 67 New Bond st
Johnstone & Marshall, wine & spirit merchts. 44 Gt. Tower st
Johnstone Alex. tobacconist, 19 Crombie's rw. Coml. rd. ea
Johnstone David, lodging house, 10 Chester ter. Eaton sq
Johnstone David Graham, clerk of patents, Patent office, 13 Serle st. Lincoln's inn
Johnstone David G. solicr. see Roy, Blunt, Johnstone & Walton
Johnstone Edward, barrister, 10 Crown office row, Temple
Johnstone Geo. Francis, surgeon, 21 Saville row, Brlngtn. gar
Johnstone James, clerical & schl. agt. 14 Warwick ct. Holborn
Johnstone James, pub. of bankrupt forms, 9 Basinghall st
Johnstone John, *Three Crowns* P.H. 21 Road side, Mile e. rd
Johnstone John B. military tailor, 27 Jermyn st. St. James'
Johnstone Rosina (Miss), lodging ho. 16 Norfolk st. Strand
Joice William, fruiterer, 13 Shepherd's market, May fair
Joiner Wm. coal mercht. Liverpool bldgs. Bishopsgate
Joiners' Hall (Stephen Ponder, sen. clerk), 79 Up. Thames st
Joint Stock Companies' Registry Office, 13 Serjeants' inn
Joliffe Richard, pewterer, 17 Red Lion court, Spitalfields
Jolin Philip, surgeon, 17 St. John's square, Clerkenwell
Jolland George Benjamin & Co. dyers & scourers, 26 Hedge row, Islington, & 8 High st. Newington butts, & 70 Theobald's road, Holborn
Joll Henry, surveyor, 3 Laurie terrace, Westminster rd
Jolley Isabella (Mrs.), bootma. 20 Ryder's ct. Leicester sq
Jolley Richd. plumber & glazier, 17 St. Alban's pl. St. James's
Jolley Thos. umbrella manufr. 1 Harrow road & 112 Edgware rd. Paddington
Jolley Thos. H. fruit mer. 70 Farringdon mkt. & 79 Farringdon st
Jolley William, poulterer, 7 Charing cross
Jolliffe Isaac, wine & brandy mercht. 68 Queen st. Cheapside
Jolliffe Jas. W. *Salmon & Compasses* P.H. 33 Penton st. Pentvle
Jolliffe Wm. Peter, barrister, 6 New square, Lincoln's inn
Jolly Edward, ironmonger, 157 Ratcliff highway
Jolly Hannah (Mrs.), staymaker, 204 Whitechapel road
Jolly John, easy chair ma. 12 Stephen st. Tottenham ct. rd
Jolly John, grocer, 2 Craven court, Craven st. Strand
Jolly John, *Three Cups* P.H. 21 Lower Shadwell
Jolly Mary (Miss), ladies' school, 4 Great Ormond st. Queen sq
Jolly Rebecca (Mrs.), *Angel* P.H. 29 Broad st. Ratcliff
Jolly Richard, fruiterer, 71 Red Lion st. High Holborn
Jolly Richard, shipchandler & sailmaker, 276 Wapping
Jolly Saml. *Anchor & Hope* P.H. Horseferry Branch rd. Rtclf
Jolly Sarah (Mrs.), butcher, 85 St. John st. Clerkenwell
Jolly Thomas, baker, 350 Oxford st
Jolly Thomas, hardware dealer, 213 Shadwell High st
Jolly William, coachmaker, 20 Wilson st. Finsbury
Jolly William, corn & coal merchant, 43 Goswell st
Joly Frederick, merchant, 51 Threadneedle st
Jonas Emanuel & Brothers, cigar & snuff ma. 17 Leman st
Jonas, Simonsen & Co. merchants, 46 Lime st
Jonas Edward, hop merchant, 12 Eastcheap; warehouse, 19 Steel yard, Upper Thames st
Jonas John, artificial florist, 72 Bethnal green road
Jonas John, glass, &c. dealer, 72 Bethnal green road
Jones & Armstrong, hop merchants, 44 Borough High st
Jones Benjamin & Geo. *Duke of Clarence* P.H. 34 Charing cr
Jones & Bevan, curriers, &c. 30 Marylebone st. Piccadilly
Jones & Blaxland, solicitors, 7 Crosby square, Bishopsgate
Jones Brothers, grocers, 150 Bishopsgate without
Jones Brothers, provis. mers. Fishmongers' hall wf. Thames st
Jones & Causton, printers, wholes. & ret. stationers, 47 Eastcheap
Jones & Chalfont, stationers, 10 White Hart pl. Kennington la
Jones Charles James & Son, tailors, 64 Great Dover road
Jones Charles & Son, brassfounders, 36 Monkwell st. Criplgt
Jones Chas. & Sons, harness & shoe curriers, 74 Houndsditch
Jones, Cooke & Green, stock & share agents, 16 Old Broad st
Jones David & Co. sydney merchts. 1 Fen. ct. Fenchurch st
Jones & Dunster, solicitors, 34 Great Marylebone st
Jones Edw. & Co. melters & candle ma. 300 & 301 Kent st. Boro
Jones Edw. Henry & Son, wine & spirit mers. 28 Mark lane
Jones F. & M. (Misses), haberdash. 3 Colvill ter. King's rd. Chlsa
Jones & Fryer, manufacturing jewellers, watch makers, silversmiths & sheffield plated warehouse, 62 Cornhill
Jones George & Co. hat & army cap ma. 80 Borough High st
Jones George & Son, auctioneers & appraisers, 11 & 12 Leicester st. & 5 Princes st. Leicester square
Jones Hannah & Son, cheesemongers, 29 New st. Dorset sq
Jones Henry & Co. gasfitters, &c. 6 Rose st. Covent garden
Jones James & Co. brassfounders, 28 Bow st. Covent garden
Jones John & Co. dealers in pat. malt, 9 Crosby Hall chambs
Jones John & Co. lace manufactrs. 3 Russia row, Milk st
Jones John & Co. *Old Holy Well* P.H. 165 Shoreditch High st
Jones John Perceval & Co. wholesale & retail stationers, 12 Curzon st. Mayfair
Jones John & Ralph, clothiers, 67 St. John st. Clerkenwell
Jones, Loyd & Co. bankers, 43 Lothbury
Jones Michael & Co. grocers, 166 Oxford st
Jones Nathan & Eleazer, boot & shoe wa. 2 Church la. Wtchpl
Jones & Oakes, coal merchants, 10 Coleshill st. Eaton square
Jones Orlando & Co. pat. rice starchma. 10 Osborn st. Whitechpl
Jones & Pain, silk manufacturers, 30 Fort st. Spitalfields
Jones & Radcliffe, surgeons, 51 Strand
Jones Richard & Son, pipe mould ma. 191 Kent st. Borough
Jones Rt. G. & Co. ship & ins. agts. 3 Church ct. Clement's la
Jones Robt. & Son, jewellers, 33 Henrietta st. Covent garden
Jones Robert Philip & Son, corn factors, 8 Mincing lane
Jones, Russell & Co. scotch & manches. warehsmn. 13 Friday st
Jones & Rutherford, law stationers, 15 Serles pl. Lincoln's inn
Jones Samuel & Co. patentees of promethean & lucifer matches & instantaneous lights, patent agents & venders of patent medicines, 201 Strand
Jones, Sells & Co. coal merchants, 55 Bankside, Southwark
Jones & Son, bankers & agts. to cattle salesmn. 41 Smithfield
Jones & Sons (late Blades), cut glass lustre & lamp manufacturers to her Majesty, her royal highness the duchess of Kent, his majesty the Schah of Persia, and east india company, 5 Ludgate hill
Jones & Smith, carvers & gilders, 52 St. George st

Jones & Taunton, bottle merchants, 86 Hatton garden
Jones Theodore & Co. patent wheel wrkrs, 20 Lamb st. Sptl.sq
Jones Thomas & Fras. Wm. Reeve, attorneys, 10 Brunswick sq
Jones Thos. & Co. ostrich feather ma. 39 Union st. Bishopsgte
Jones Thos. & Son, furriers & straw hat mfs. 16 Blackman st
Jones Thos. & Sons, sailmakers & outfitters, 66 Tooley st. & 52 High st. Shadwell
Jones Thos. & Sons, solicitors, 4 Millman pl. Bedford row
Jones, Trinder & Tudway, attorneys, 1 John st. Bedford row
Jones & Walmisley, parliamentary agents, 40 Parliament st
Jones & Waters, tanners, hat leather & cap peak manfrs. 21 St. Andrew's road, Horsemonger lane
Jones Wm. & Co. leather slrs. & stationers, 100 Leadenhall st
Jones Wm. & Co. limeburners, coal & cementmers. 242 Wapping
Jones Wm. Fredk. & Co. sperm refins. Little Vine st. Lambth
Jones Wm. & Griffith, slatewrks. Bangor wf. 2 Union pl. Pimlico
Jones Wm. Henry & Son, curriers & tanners, 173 Borough High st. & Russell place, Bermondsey
Jones Wm. & Samuel, opticians, 30 Holborn hill
Jones Wm. & Sons, tallowchandlers, 15 High st. Pentonville
Jones Wm. & Thos. & Co. oil, color & tallow merchants, Leadenhall bldgs. Gracechurch st.; Robert st. Waterloo road; & New walk, Horselydown
Jones Wm. & Thos. & Co. spermaceti refis. Robert st. Waterloo rd
Jones & Wright, solicitors, 8 St. Swithin's lane
Jones & Yarrell, booksellers & newsmen to her Majesty & the royal family, 34 Bury st. St. James's
Jones Aaron, *Bell* P.H. 2 & 3 Church row, Houndsditch
Jones Abraham Jacob, quill mer. 20 Somerset pl. Nw. rd. Cm. rd
Jones Albert Hatchett, *Golden Anchor* P.H. 139 Golden la
Jones Alexander, carpenter, 3 Bride lane, Fleet st
Jones Alexander, *Ben Jonson* P.H. 27 Pelham st. Spitalfi
Jones Alex. stay & corset ma. 2 Robson's pl. Kennington rd
Jones Alexander, tailor, 2 Old Kent rd. east side
Jones Alexander Henry, butcher, 12 Kent pl. Old Kent rd
Jones Alfred, cooper, turner, &c. 48 Henry st. east, Avenue rd
Jones Alfred, currier & leather seller, 20 Aldgate High st
Jones Alfred, solicitor, 15 Sise lane, Bucklersbury
Jones Alfred, surgeon dentist to the Duchess of Gloucester & the late Princess Augusta, 64 Grosvenor st. Grosvenor sq
Jones Amelia (Miss), ostrich fea. mnf. 9 Queen's head rw. Nwgtn
Jones Amelia Delia (Mrs.), cowkeeper, 110 Goswell rd
Jones Andrew, *Duke of York* P.H. 15 Turk st. Bethnal green
Jones Ann (Mrs.) *Duke of Wellington* P.H. 152 Bishopsgt. with
Jones Anne (Mrs.), *Three Compasses* P.H. 107 Lambeth Lr. mrsh
Jones Arthur Wm. grocer & teadealer, 1 Church st. Minories
Jones Barbara L. (Mrs.), carpent. &c. 41 Gloster st. Coml. rd. east
Jones Bence, physician, 30 Grosvenor st.
Jones Benjamin, cheesemonger 96, & grocer 97, Goswell st
Jones Benjamin, cigar importer, 28 Moorgate st
Jones Benjamin, *Crown & Cushion* P.H 31 Parker st. Drury la
Jones Benjamin, dining rooms, 18 Drummond st. Euston sq
Jones Benjamin, linendraper, &c. 34 City road, Finsbury sq
Jones Brook, cornfactor, Jack's coffee house, Mark lane
Jones Chas. baker, 6 Eccleston st. Chester sq
Jones Chas. beer retailer, 13 York st. Lock's fields, Walwth
Jones Chas. *Bull* P.H. 18 Devonshire st. Bishopsgate
Jones Chas. currier, High st. Stratford, Essex
Jones Chas. goldsmith, 6 Baker st. Lloyd square
Jones Chas. grocer, 12 Gt. White Lion st. Seven Dials
Jones Charles, surgeon, 7B, Manchester square
Jones Chas. tailor, 9 Warner st. New Kent road
Jones Chas. umbrella ma. 15 Windmill st. Tottenham ct. rd
Jones Chas. Chadwicke, serjt.-at-law, 3 Serjt's. inn, Fleet st
Jones Chas. Gwillim, solicitor, 11 Gray's inn square
Jones Chas. James, solicitor, 19 Spital square
Jones Chas. Jas. teacher of music, 9 Whitmore pl. Hoxton
Jones Chas. Robert, grocer, 10 & 11 Shepherd's mkt. Mayfair
Jones Chas. Thos. solicitor, 5 Symond's inn, & 20 East st. Red Lion sq
Jones Charlotte (Miss), milliner, 22 Princes st. Hanover sq
Jones Christopher, grocer, 16 Jubilee pl. Nth. Com. rd. ea
Jones Daniel, goldsmith & jeweller, 8 Glo'ster st. St. Johnst. rd
Jones Dav. actuary of *Univl. Life Assu. Soc.* 1 King Wm. st. City
Jones David, *Adam & Eve* P.H. 52 Jewin st. Cripplegate
Jones David, boot & shoe ma. 23 Lit. George st. Portman sq
Jones David, carpenter, 5 Earl st. east, Lisson grove
Jones David, dairyman, 14 Little Guilford st. Brunswick sq
Jones David, dairyman, 2 Patriot rw. Cambridg. rd. Mileend
Jones David, fruiterer, 40 Wilderness la. Dorset st. Fleet st
Jones David, hairdresser, 184 Drury lane
Jones David, lighterman, & granary keeper, & sack letter, Jackson's wharf, 40 Shad Thames; & Old Rose wharf, Shad Thames
Jones David, oil & colorman, 39 Exmouth st. Spafields
Jones David, oilman, &c. 39 Kensington High st
Jones David, pawnbroker & silversmith, 185 High Holborn
Jones David, tailor, 16 & 17 Hollen st. Wardour st. Soho
Jones David, *Queen's Arms* P.H. 20 & 21 High row, Knightsbridge; & *Three Jolly Gardeners* P.H. 3 Rochester row, Westminster
Jones Davis, cowkeeper, Bingley place, New road
Jones Dinah (Mrs.), *Bird Cage* P.H. Bird Cage wk. Hackney rd
Jones Dinah (Mrs.), wax & tallowchand. 11 Kingst. Portman sq
Jones Dinah (Mrs.), grocer, 38 Princess st. Portman market
Jones Edgate, *Weavers' Arms* P.H. 23 Skinner st. Bishopgt
Jones Edward, bricklayer, 6 Tudor pl. Tottenham court road
Jones Edward, boot & shoemaker, 133 Up. Whitecross st
Jones Edward, carpenter, 4 Charles st. Kensington New tn
Jones Edward, chemist & druggist, 171 High Holborn
Jones Edward, coach currier, 20 & 21 Church st. Blackfrs. rd
Jones Edward, coal mer. Whitefriars New wf. & 34 Penton st
Jones Edward, col. paper & pasteboard mak. 11 & 23 Budge rw
Jones Edward, dairyman, 25 Cloth fair, West Smithfield
Jones Edward, egg merchant, 47 Hampden st. Clarendon sq
Jones Edward, grocer, 68½ Great George st. Bermondsey
Jones Edward, grocer & teadealer, 3 Raven row, Spitalfields
Jones Edward, hatter, 88 Paul st. Finsbury
Jones Edward, hop merchant, 12 Eastcheap, & warehouse, 19 Steel yard, Upper Thames st
Jones Edward, jamaica merchant, 138 Leadenhall st
Jones Edward, linendraper, 29 Marchmont st. Brunswick sq
Jones Edward, merchant, 5 Barge yard, Bucklersbury
Jones Edward, newsvender, 7 Hayes court, Soho square
Jones Edward, silk dyer, 46 Red Lion st. Holborn
Jones Edward, tailor, 2 Hampden st. Clarendon square
Jones Edward, tailor, 7 Queen's Head row, Newington butts
Jones Edward, tailor, 6 Queen st. Ratcliffe
Jones Edward, tailor & draper, 157 Strand
Jones Edward, teadealer, 21 Broad court, Long acre
Jones Edward, watch hand maker, 54 Red Lion st. Clerkwll
Jones Edward, wine & spirit importer, see Chidell & Jones
Jones Edward A. survyr. & decora. 20 Gt. Russell st. Blmsby
Jones Edward Chester, barrister, 4 Stone bldgs. Lincoln's inn
Jones Edward Fenn, tea & genl. merchant, 20 Little Tower st
Jones Edward Watson, *Seven Stars* P.H. Bromley, Middx
Jones Edwin, laceman, 5 Strutton ground, Westminster
Jones Elias Abraham, merchant, 23 Billiter street
Jones Eliza (Miss), artist, 3 Duke st. Portland place
Jones Eliza (Miss), milliner, see Pooley & Jones
Jones Eliza Mira (Miss), riding school, 1 Webber st. Blkfs. rd
Jones Elizh. (Miss), milliner, &c. 3 Broadley ter. Blandfd. sq
Jones Elizabeth (Mrs.), coffee rooms, 26 Gt. Windmill st
Jones Elizabeth (Mrs.), grocer, 381 Albany rd. Camberwell
Jones Elizabeth (Mrs.), lodging ho. 24 Salisbury st. Strand
Jones Elizh. (Mrs.), piece bro. & tailor, 6 Cross st. Golden sq
Jones Elizh. (Mrs.), straw hat ma. 6 Trinity rw. Upp. st. Islgtn
Jones Elizh. M. (Mrs.), fire work ma. 4 Asylum bldgs. Westm. rd
Jones Ellis, welsh flannel fac. 3 Montague pl. Lit. Britain
Jones Enoch, linendraper, 10 & 11 Finsbury terrace, City rd
Jones Evan, boarding house, 1 Northumberland ct. Strand
Jones Evan, carpenter, 11 New North street, Finsbury
Jones Evan, carpenter & builder, 22 Cecil st. Strand
Jones Evan, cooper, 10 Devonshire pl. Up. Kennington lane
Jones Evan, dairy, 17 Allen st. Goswell st
Jones Evan, dairy, 8 Bull & Mouth st. St. Martin's le grand
Jones Evan, grocer & cheesemonger, 8 Marlboro' rd. Chelsea
Jones Evan, livery stables, Pelham road, Brompton
Jones Evan, ship & custom house agent, 11 Idol la. Tower st
Jones Evan Burnell, surgeon, 139 Southwark bridge road
Jones Evan John, furn. undrtak. 12 Church rw. Up. st. Islington
Jones Evan John, undertaker, 7 Church lane, Islington
Jones Even John, oil & colorman, 121 Long lane, Bermondsey
Jones Francis, dining rooms, 45 Rufford's bldgs. Islington
Jones Francis, farrier, 3 Middle row, Knightsbridge
Jones Francis, Scott's sufferance wharf, Dockhead, Brmndsy
Jones Frederick, barrister, 5 Old square, Lincoln's inn
Jones Frederick, feather merch. & hair factor, 43 London wall
Jones Fredk. tailor & piece broker, 15 Prospect row, Walw. rd.
Jones Fredk. Charles, M.D. surgeon, 69 Blackfriars road
Jones Fred. Henry, tea dealer, 69 Boston place, Dorset sq
Jones George, baker, 65 Pearson st. Kingsland road
Jones George, bootmaker, 62 Crawford st. Portman sq
Jones George, carpet manufacturer, see Newcombe & Jones
Jones George, chandler's shop, 35 Bayham st. Camden town
Jones George, coffee rooms, 26 Shaftesbury ter. Pimlico
Jones George, dairy & carman, 7 Drury court, Strand
Jones George, *Dundee Arms* P.H. 16 Bethnal green
Jones George, *Globe* coffee rooms, 167 Union st. Boro'
Jones George, *Fountain* P.H. 4 Clare st. Clare market
Jones George, grocer, 16 Buckingham place, Fitzroy sq
Jones George, grocer, 53 Charlotte ter. New cut, Lambeth

Jones George, grocer, High st. Deptford
Jones George, iron & steel merchant, 27 Old Fish st
Jones George, jeweller, 20 Baker st. Lloyd square
Jones George, nightman, 20 Cambridge road, Mile End road
Jones George, surgeon, 6 Thurloe square, Old Brompton
Jones Geo. wine mer. ship ins. & custom ho. agt. & preserved provision mer. & agt. to John Gillon & Co. Leith, 8 Billiter st
Jones Geo. Harrison, linendrpr. 1 Nowells blds. Liverpool rd
Jones Handfield, physician, 54 Sloane st
Jones Geo. John, cooper, 28 Princes sq. Ratcliff highway & Glasshouse yard, Upper East Smithfield
Jones George John, surgeon, 27 Margaret st. Cavendish sq
Jones George Longfield, paper hanger, 45 London road
Jones Geo. Wm. furrier & straw hat manufr. 101 Oxford st
Jones Grace (Mrs.), lodging ho. 52 & 53 Liverpool st. Bishopsg
Jones Hanbury, conveyancer, 4 Field court, Gray's inn
Jones Hannah (Mrs.), feathermanfr. 1½ Hampton st. Walwth rd
Jones Hannah (Mrs.), silk mercer & milliner, 1 Aldgate High st
Jones Hannah (Mrs.), straw bon. ma. 20 Prospect pl. Cambg. hth
Jones Hannah (Mrs.), tobc. pipe ma. 56 Featherstone st. City rd
Jones Harvey Bowen, solicitor, 22 Austinfriars
Jones Henry, billiard rooms, 17 Giltspur st. Smithfield
Jones Henry, carman, 15 Coopers' row, Crutched friars
Jones Henry, dentist, 22 Seymour st. Euston sq
Jones Henry, grocer, 23 Catherine st. Pimlico
Jones Henry, *Hope & Anchor* P.H. 1 Trinity row, Islington
Jones Henry, oil & colorman, 14 Grosvenor row, Pimlico
Jones Henry, lace warehouse, 54 St. Paul's churchyard
Jones Henry, surgeon dentist, 7 Pall mall
Jones Henry, tailor, &c. 1 Derby st. May fair
Jones Henry, tin plate worker, 44 Old st. St. Luke's
Jones Henry, tobacconist, 3 Ryder's court, Leicester sq
Jones Henry, watch & water gilder, 34 Rahere st. Goswell rd
Jones Henry Ashton, cheesemonger, 162 Blackfriars road
Jones Henry Derviche, surgeon, 23, Soho square
Jones Henry Julius, solicitor, see Coombe & Jones
Jones Henry Pointer, *Royal George* P.H. 20 Carlisle st. Lmbth
Jones Henry Robt. coal mer. Western whf. George st. Adelphi
Jones Henry Tudor, fruiterer, 2 Southampton st. Cambrwll
Jones Henry William, builder, 9 Little Vine st. Piccadilly
Jones Herbert, toy dealer, 5 Henry st. east, Avenue road
Jones Herbt. Geo. serjeant-at-law, 1 Serjeant's inn, Chancy. la
Jones Horace, surveyor, 16 Furnival's inn, Holborn
Jones Hugh, baby linen wareho. 61 & 62 Newington causeway
Jones Hugh, *Cherry Tree* P.H. 8 Backchurch la. Whitechapl
Jones Hugh, house painter, 78 Great Portland st
Jones Hugh, *Lancet* coffeehouse, 56 Bartholomew close
Jones Hugh, shawl fringe ma. 10 Red Cross sq. Cripplegate
Jones Isaac, cabinet maker, 37 Duke st. Aldgate
Jones Isaac, carver & gilder, 2 Albert ter. Queen st. Chelsea
Jones Isaac, pork butcher, 84 East st. Manchester sq
Jones Isaac, shape manufacturer, 17 Peerless row, City road
Jones Isaac, window glass cutter, 17 High row, Knightbridge
Jones Isaiah, surgeon dentist, 129 Strand
Jones Iven Chas. stockbroker, 2 Shorters ct. Throgmorton st
Jones James, accountant, 139A, Cheapside
Jones James, annatto manuftr. 14 New Glo'ster pl. Hoxton
Jones James, baker, 2 Chapel st. Tottenham court road
Jones James, carpenter, packing case ma. & undr. 2 London wall
Jones James, coal & potato dealer, 32 Golden lane, Barbican
Jones James, drug broker, 4 Brabant court, Philpot lane
Jones James, dyer & scourer, 90 Fenchurch st
Jones James, fishing tackle ma. 111 Jermyn st. St. James's
Jones James, grocer & cheesemongr. 4 Freeman's pl. Mile end rd
Jones James, hide & skin salesman, Bermondsey skin market
Jones James, ironfounder, 9 Brick lane, St. Luke's
Jones James, linendraper, 430 Strand
Jones James, optician, 10 Dorrington st. Coldbath fields
Jones James, staymaker, 235 Poplar High st
Jones James, stove maker, 9 Charles st. Long acre
Jones James, surgeon, 69 Berners st. Oxford st
Jones James, surgeon, 70 Judd st. Brunswick square
Jones James, teadealer, see Strange, Jones & Co
Jones James, *Waggon & Horses* P.H. Cumbrlnd. pl. Nwngtn. bts
Jones James Charles, artist, 17 Laurie ter. Bethlem hospital
Jones James David, furn. ironmonger, see Benetfink & Jones
Jones James P. candle, &c. ma. see Pateshall, Brown & Jones
Jones James William, optician, 87 Goswell st
Jones Jane (Miss), milliner, 66 Fore st. Cripplegate
Jones Jenkin, actuary of *National Mercantile Life Assurance Society*, Arthur st. west, London bridge
Jones Jenkin Abel, carpenter, 3 Winchester pl. Kentish tn
Jones Jesse, tobacconist, 33 Cambridge road, Mile end road
Jones John, academy, 45 Carey st. Chancery lane
Jones John, accountant, 1 Trinity terrace, Southwark
Jones John, attorney, 3 Pump court, Temple
Jones John, army clothier, 6 Regent st. Waterloo place, London; & 16 Batchelor's walk, Dublin [& 4 King sq
Jones John, auctioneer & house agent, 56 Bath st. City road,
Jones John, baker, 26 Edmund st. King's cross
Jones John, baker, 6 Norfolk st. King's cross
Jones John, baker, 59 Princess st. Portman market
Jones John, beer retailer, 120 London road
Jones John, blacksmith, King's place, Stones end, Borough
Jones John, bookbinder, 6 Cooper's court, Gt. Windmill st
Jones John, bookseller & binder, 73 Princes st. Leicester sq
Jones John, bootmaker, 7 Reeves' mews, Grosvenor square
Jones John, carpenter, 46 Cloth fair, West Smithfield
Jones John, carpenter, &c. 9 Portland st. mews, Soho
Jones John, carpenter, 76 Great Portland st. Oxford st
Jones John, carpenter & builder, 26 City rd. Finsbury sq
Jones John, cheyne house academy, Up. Cheyne rw. Chelsea
Jones John, city carman, 20 Cooper's row, Crutched friars
Jones John, coffee rooms, 52 Howland st. Fitzroy square
Jones John, coffee rooms, 15 Lit. Chester st. Grosvenor pl
Jones John, cork cutter, 49 King st. Soho
Jones John, cowkeeper, Broad st. & 19 Choppens ct. Old Gravel lane, St. George's east
Jones John, cowkeeper, 25 Dean st. Fetter lane
Jones John, cowkeeper & dairyman, 19 Bull & Mouth st
Jones John, dairyman, 7 Bartholomew close
Jones John, dairyman, 8 Commercial road, Lambeth
Jones John, dairyman, 23 Devonshire st. Queen square
Jones John, dairyman, 1 Lion st. New Kent road
Jones John, dairyman, 9 Nag's head court, Gracechurch st
Jones John, dairyman, 14 Thanet st. Burton crescent
Jones John, *Dog & Duck* P.H. 18 Queen st. Soho
Jones John, dyer & scourer, 23 Hanway st. Oxford st
Jones John, fancy cabinet ma. 16 Union st. east, Spitalfields
Jones John, flax & hemp dlr. & mer. South Sea chambers
Jones John, fruiterer, 111 Brick lane, Spitalfields
Jones John, *George* P.H. George court, Strand
Jones John, glass dealer, 7 Robert st. Grosvenor square
Jones John, *Green Dragon* P.H. 102 Fore st. Cripplegate
Jones John, hairdresser, 4 Opera arcade, Haymarket
Jones John, herbalist, 30 Bowling green lane, Clerkenwell
Jones John, *Hope Arms* P.H. 51 Duke st. Manchester sq
Jones John, hosier & outfitter, 137 Whitechapel High st
Jones John, hotpresser, 1 George yard, Crown st. Soho
Jones John, iron merchant, Iron bridge wharf, & 6 Bankside, Southwark
Jones John, ironmonger, 110 Long alley, Finsbury
Jones John, lodging house, 28 Jermyn st
Jones John, mnftg. goldsmith, 20 Red Lion st. Clerkenwell
Jones John, marine store dealer, 2 Brick la. St Luke's
Jones John, mattress maker, 13 Meard's court, Soho
Jones John, plumber, 43 Redcross st. Borough
Jones John, *Queen's Head* P.H. 3 Albemarle st. Piccadilly
Jones John, rope & rag merchant, 244 & 136 Wapping
Jones John, russia broker, 78 Old Broad st. City
Jones John, *Salutation* P.H. 6 Barton st. Westminster
Jones John, smith, 11 Great Sutton st. Clerkenwell
Jones John, straw hat maker, 7 Freeschool st. Horselydown
Jones John, surgeon, 5 Seymour place, Wandsworth road
Jones John, tailor, &c. 117 Drummond st. Euston square
Jones John, tailor, 18 Little Carter la. Godliman st
Jones John, tailor, 20 Maddox st. Regent st
Jones John, tailor, 21 Ship yard, Temple bar
Jones John, teadealer, 26 Nassau place, Commercial road ea
Jones John, *Three Compasses* P.H. 14 Anchor st. Spitalfields
Jones John, timber dealer, Montague pl. Lower rd. Deptford
Jones John, tinplate worker & packing case ma. 3 Old Fish st
Jones John, tobacconist, 2 James st. Oxford st
Jones John, tobacconist, 9 Pleasant row, Old Kent road
Jones John, umbrella manufacturer, 105 Oxford st
Jones John, veterinary surgeon, 31 Worship st. Norton folgate
Jones John, warehouseman, see Castle, Jones & Wortley
Jones John, watchmaker, 338 Strand
Jones John, *White Lion* P.H. 1 Talbot ct. Gracechurch st
Jones John, wine merchant, 7 Lowndes terrace & *Queen's Arms* P.H. 21 High row, Knightsbridge & *Three Jolly Gardeners* P.H. 3 Rochester row, Westminster
Jones John, jun. wine & bottle merchant, & sole consignee for Barclay, Macdonald & Co. Glenury whiskey, Stonehaven, Scotland; 1 Union place, New road, Marylebone
Jones John A. embroiderer, 21 Rathbone place
Jones John Breeze, linendraper, 105 High st. Marylebone
Jones John C. pianoforte ma. 3 Rutland st. Hampstead road
Jones John Champion, pianoforte ma. 2 Hanway st. Oxford st
Jones John Dalston, surgeon, 1 Queen's road, Dalston
Jones John Edward, civil engineer, A.I.C.E. 8 Cannon row
Jones John Greenstreet, linendraper, 415 Oxford st

Jones John Harper, solicitor, see Armstrong & Jones
Jones John James, *Prince Albert* P.H. 11 Cooper's row, City
Jones John Lee, solicitor, 71 Mark lane
Jones John Morris, bookseller, see Aylott & Jones
Jones John W. tailor, 48 Shoe lane, Holborn
Jones John Wm. fustian manufacturer, 77 Aldermanbury
Jones John Wm. surgeon, 4 Eldon pl. Up. Kennington lane
Jones Joseph, baker, 4 Hope cottages, Wandsworth road
Jones Joseph, bootmaker, 11 Henry st. Gray's inn lane
Jones Joseph, file cutter, 8 Castle st. Saffron hill
Jones Joseph, file & tool wa. 54 Wellington st. Goswell st
Jones Joseph, fruiterer, Borough market
Jones Joseph, pawnbroker, 4 Brown's lane, Spitalfields
Jones Joshua, dairyman, 10 Brazier's blds. Farringdon st
Jones Lewis, *Coach & Horses* P.H. 1 Fan st. Goswell st
Jones Lewis, dairy, 21 Robert st. Grosvenor square
Jones Lewis, tailor, see Jarvis & Jones
Jones Lewis, who.pa.lamp cotton ma. 31 Bridgewater grdns
Jones Louisa (Mrs.), milliner, 5 Crescent pl. Brompton
Jones L. R. sec. to Columbian Mining Association & New Grenada Mining Company, 13 Austinfriars
Jones Magdalen Elizabeth (Mrs.) (successor to Madame Hengler), artist in fireworks, 4 Asylum buildings, Westminster road
Jones Maria (Mrs.), china warehouse, Bow
Jones Maria, grocer & cheesemonger, Wandsworth road
Jones Mark, butcher, 116 Poplar High st
Jones Mary (Mrs.), *Bull's Head* P.H. 94 Wood st. Cheapside
Jones Mary (Mrs.), grocer & teadealer, 97 Rosemary la. Minories
Jones Mary (Mrs.), lodging house, 27 Thavies inn, Holborn
Jones Mary Ann (Miss), milliner & dressma. 41 King's rd. ea. Chlsa
Jones Mary Ann (Miss), oil & col. wa. 69 New Ch. st. Liss. gr
Jones Mary Ann (Mrs.), staymaker, 32 Rathbone pl. Oxford st
Jones Michael, grocer, &c. 48 & 49 Theobald's rd. Red Lion sq
Jones Michael, hatter, 5 Squirries st. Bethnal green road
Jones Morris, fruiterer, New cross
Jones Morris, *Old Parr's Head* P.H. 166 Aldersgate st
Jones Owen, architect, 9 Argyll place, Regent st
Jones Owen, tobacconist, 11 Bowling st. Westminster
Jones Owen G. silk warehouseman, 125 Wood st. City
Jones Peter, operative chemist, 11 Norton folgate
Jones Peter, tailor, 70 Seymour st. Euston square
Jones Phœbe (Miss), milliner, &c. see Kerr & Jones
Jones Philip, merchant, see Lediard, Jones & Mortimer
Jones Rebecca (Mrs.), dressmaker, 9 College ter. Chelsea
Jones Reeves Wm. builder, 78 Colonnade, Brunswick square
Jones Richard, teadealer, see Hewes, Jones & Co
Jones Richard, *Pumpkin* P.H. 21 Seething lane, Tower st
Jones Richard, stay & shoe warehouse, 10½ King st. Soho
Jones Richard, tallow chand. & oilman, 1 & 170 Lambeth walk
Jones Richard, vetery. surgn. 7 Bretten ter. King's rd. w. Chelse
Jones Richard, veterinary surgeon, High st. Battersea
Jones Richard, woollendraper in general, & to the pianoforte trade; manufacturer of the felt hammer & damper cloths, & every description of wool felt for polishing glass, stone, &c.; also the patent woollen & felt concaved elastic as well as every other description of gun wadding; & agent for sale of the patent woollen driving belts, to supersede leather straps for machinery, 27 Bedfordbury, Covent garden
Jones Richd. Brook Holden, glaire mer. see Mansell & Jones
Jones Richd. Brook Holden, glaire mer. see Hurst & Jones
Jones Richd. Lambert, estate & house agt. 40 Lit. Moorfields
Jones Richard Minshull, solicitor, see Peace & Jones
Jones Richard Thos. stonemason, 34 Platt ter. Pancras rd
Jones Robert, bricklayer, 48 Hastings st. Burton crescent
Jones Robert, builder, &c. 106 Ebury st. Pimlico
Jones Robert, builder, 19 Rosoman st. Clerkenwell
Jones Robert, doll maker, 23 Great Mitchell st. St. Luke's
Jones Robert, dyer & cleaner, 12 Boswell court, Queen sq
Jones Rt. granary keep. & lighterm. Pearson's wf. 39 Shad Tham
Jones Robert, grocer & teadealer, 268 Borough High st
Jones Robt. linendraper & haberd. 61 Charlotte ter. New cut
Jones Robert, oilman, &c. 105 Lambeth walk
Jones Robert, *Roebuck* P.H. 72 Union st. Borough
Jones Robert, tailor, 2 Monmouth place, Old Kent road
Jones Robert, who. wood doll ma. 23 Gt. Mitchell st. St. Luke's
Jones Robert, wire worker, 41 Belvedere pl. Borough road
Jones Robert George, heraldic artist, 10 Cirencester place
Jones Robert W. grocer, 12 Mid. Queen's buildings, Kntsbdg
Jones Rowland, grocer, 34 East st. Walworth road
Jones Samuel, artist, 3 Bartholomew lane
Jones Samuel, auctionr. appras. & accntnt. 59 Basinghall st
Jones Samuel, cabinet maker, 88 Old st. St. Luke's
Jones Samuel, clothes salesman, 5 Cumberland pl. Nngtn. bts
Jones Samuel, fruiterer, 24 Leather lane, Holborn
Jones Samuel, jack maker, 25 Goldsmith place, Hackney rd
Jones Samuel, vellum & parchment manufacturer, 22 Cross st Great George st. Bermondsey
Jones Saml. whiting ma. & coal mr. 53 Princes st. Fore st. Lmbth
Jones Sarah (Miss), straw hat ma. see Wood, Jones & Hinde
Jones Sarah Maria (Miss), milliner & dress & court dress maker, 141 Regent st. (from 23 Piccadilly)
Jones Sidney, surgeon & chemist, 49 Davies st. Berkeley sq
Jones Slaney, grocer, &c. 4 & 5 Portland pl. Commercl. rd. east
Jones Stephen, manufacturer of english & foreign sealing wax, wafers & ink, 4 & 5 Talbot court, Gracechurch st. City, & 1 Grange walk, Bermondsey
Jones Stephen, whip maker, 77 Gray's inn lane
Jones Theodore, consulting accountant, & author of various treatises which expose the fallacies of book-keeping as it is usually practised, & bring into immediate notice the defects by which errors & false statements elude detection, point out a simple way to insure perfect correctness in all accounts, & prevent the risk & loss to which commercial houses are exposed, alleviate anxiety of mind, & render perspicuous & simple the labour of the clerks, 38 Nicholas lane, Lombard st
Jones Thomas, boot & shoe maker, 1 Carrington st. Mayfair
Jones Thomas, boot & shoe maker, 57 Seymour st. Euston sq
Jones Thomas, brewer, Turner sq. & 21 Somerset pl. Hoxton
Jones Thomas, builder, 28 Lower Belgrave st
Jones Thomas, carman, 7 Castle ct. Wells st. Oxford st
Jones Thomas, catholic booksel. & publisher, 63 Paternoster rw
Jones Thomas, cheesemonger, 24 York row, Kennington rd
Jones Thomas, *Crown & Anchor* P.H. 29 Ebury st. Pimlico
Jones Thomas, dairyman, 3 Christopher ct. St. Martin's le gd
Jones Thomas, dairyman, 11 Lamb's conduit pas. Red Lion sq
Jones Thomas, dairyman, 2 Little Essex st. Strand
Jones Thomas, draper, &c. see Maund, Jones, Randall & Morris
Jones Thomas, *Duke of Wellington* P.H. 100 Goswell st
Jones Thomas, *George & Guy* P.H. 193 Brick la. Spitalfields
Jones Thomas, *Grapes* P.H. 1 Great Earl st. Seven dials
Jones Thomas, *Grapes* P.H. 3 New Gravel la. Shadwell
Jones Thomas, grocer, 58 Hackney road
Jones Thomas, teadealer & grocer, 111 Tottenham court road
Jones Thomas, hatter, 47 Mount street, Lambeth
Jones Thomas, leather seller, George st. Camberwell
Jones Thomas, medical bookseller, 91 Aldersgate st
Jones Thomas, optician, &c. 62 Charing cross
Jones Thomas, painter & paperhanger, 103 Leadenhall st
Jones Thomas, plasterer, 12 Noel st. Wardour st. Soho
Jones Thomas, razor maker & cutler, 9 Finsbury pl. North
Jones Thomas, *Red Lion* P.H. 22 Portland st. Soho
Jones Thomas, solicitor, 1 King's arms yard, Coleman st
Jones Thomas, special pleader, 6 King's Bench walk, Temple
Jones Thomas, straw & leghorn hat warehouse & milliner, 32 Blackman st. Borough; & 5 Mount place, Walworth
Jones Thomas, tailor, 36 Blackman st. Borough
Jones Thomas, tailor, 15 Charterhouse st
Jones Thomas, tailor & clothier, 25 Colonnade, Russell sq
Jones Thomas, tailor, 23 Devereux court, Strand
Jones Thomas, tailor, 16 Fludyer st. Westminster
Jones Thomas, tailor, 9 Henry st. Cumberland market
Jones Thomas, tailor, 26 Shouldham st. Queen st. Edgware rd
Jones Thomas, *Thatched House* P.H. 9 Red Lion st. Holborn
Jones Thomas, tobacconist, 3 Artichoke row, Mile end
Jones Thomas, tabacconist, 30½ Coventry st
Jones Thomas, warehouseman, 8 Gough sq. Fleet st
Jones Thomas, watchmaker, 23 Harp alley, Farringdon st
Jones Thomas, wheelwright, East India road, Poplar
Jones Thomas, woollen wareho. see Bidgood, Jones & Wilson
Jones Thomas Cheatwood, linendraper, &c. 68 Blackfriars rd
Jones Thomas Evans, linendraper, 5 Knightsbridge terrace
Jones Thos. Geo. bookseller, 30 Gt. Quebec st. Montagu sq
Jones Thomas Jeptha, oil & italian wa. High st. Stk. Newngtn
Jones Thomas Pryce, pawnbroker, 81 Tothill st. Westminster
Jones Thomas Wharton, surgeon, 35 George st. Hanover sq
Jones Thomas Wm. physician, 19 Finsbury pavement
Jones Thomas Williams, merchant, see Woolley & Jones
Jones Tunno, stockbroker, 2 Warnford ct. Throgmorton st
Jones Walter, surgeon, 2 Brunswick pl. Barnsby. rd. Islington
Jones Walter, surgeon dentist, see Alex & Jones
Jones Wm. arbitrator & accountant, 31 Basinghall st
Jones Wm. artist, 27 Clipstone st. Fitzroy square
Jones Wm. beer retailer, 23 Richmond st. East st. Walworth
Jones Wm. boarding house, 46 Leadenhall st
Jones Wm. bootmaker, 103 Crawford st
Jones Wm. bootmaker, 1 Corporation lane, Clerkenwell
Jones William, boot & shoe maker, 103 Crawford st
Jones Wm. boot & shoemaker, 1 Theberton st. Islington
Jones Wm. bootmaker, 84 Crawford st. Portman sq
Jones Wm. bottled beer, ale & cider merchant, 33 Eastcheap

Jones Wm. brasier&coppersmith, 16 Grace's alley, Wellclose sq
Jones Wm. builder, 48 Kensington High st
Jones Wm. butcher, 16 Featherstone st. City road
Jones Wm. butcher, 110 Union st. Borough
Jones Wm. butcher, 23 Westbourne st. Pimlico
Jones Wm. cabinetmaker, 23 Castle st. City road
Jones Wm. chaser, 16 Albion place, Clerkenwell
Jones Wm. chemist, 35 Charing cross
Jones Wm. chemist, 34 Tavistock place, Tavistock square
Jones Wm. coppersmith, &c. 36 & 37 Castle st. Leicester sq
Jones Wm. dairyman, &c. 11 Aske st. Hoxton
Jones Wm. dairyman, 55 Charles st. City road
Jones Wm. dyer, 42 Weymouth st. New Kent road
Jones Wm. farrier, Camberwell new road
Jones Wm. fruiterer, 6 Eaton lane north, Pimlico
Jones Wm. *Goat & Star*, P.H. 7 Swallow st. Piccadilly
Jones Wm. *Grapes* P.H. 4 Albemarle st. Clerkenwell
Jones Wm. grocer, 34 Augustus st. Regent's park
Jones Wm. grocer, 14 Beckford row, Walworth
Jones Wm. grocer, 2 High st. Deptford
Jones Wm. grocer, Stratford broadway
Jones Wm. grocer, Upper North st. Whitechapel road
Jones Wm. hatter, 242 Wapping High st
Jones Wm. *Hope* P.H. 1 Lower Porchester st. Edgware road
Jones Wm. house agent, &c. 72 White Horse st. Ratcliffe
Jones Wm. ironmonger, 1½ Shepperton pl. New North road
Jones Wm. jeweller, see Braithwaite & Jones
Jones Wm. job post master, Camberwell green
Jones Wm. leather cutter, 119 Up. Whitecross st. St. Luke's
Jones Wm. linendraper, 43 Piccadilly [Walworth road
Jones Wm. livery stables & job master, 14 Beckford row,
Jones Wm. oil & colorman, 1 Smith st. Chelsea
Jones Wm. plumber, 43 Rufford's bldgs. High st. Islington
Jones Wm. plumber & glazier, 5 Victoria road, Pimlico
Jones Wm. *Rainbow coffee house*, 3 & 4 King st. Covent gdn
Jones Wm. shoemaker, 42 Princess street, Lisson grove
Jones Wm. silk mercer, &c. 64 Newington causeway
Jones Wm. solicitor, 7 China ter. Kennington road, Lambeth
Jones Wm. solicitor & parliamentary agent, 11 Parliament st
Jones Wm. stockbroker, 2 Shorter's ct. & Stock exchange
Jones Wm. sup. of Relig. Tract Socy. 56 P.N. row&65 St. P.C. yd
Jones Wm. surgeon, 9 Alpha place, Regent's park
Jones Wm. tailor, 17 Brill row, Somers town
Jones Wm. tailor, 6 Cross st. Hatton garden
Jones Wm. tailor, 6 Warren st. Fitzroy square
Jones Wm. tailor & draper, 17 Camden st. Islington green
Jones Wm. teadealer, &c. 8 Norris st. Haymarket
Jones Wm. tobacconist, 12 Sherrard st. Golden square
Jones Wm. *Two Brewers* P.H. 18 Redcross st. Borough
Jones Wm. wax & tallow chandler, 21 Tottenham court road
Jones Wm. wireworker, 179 Whitechapel road
Jones Wm. woollen cloth factor, 61 Basinghall st
Jones Wm. (Mrs.), wheelwright&ironmngr. High st. Battersea
Jones Wm. jun. lapidary, 44 Red Lion st. Clerkenwell
Jones Wm. Anderson, working jeweller, 9A, Leicester sq
Jones Wm. Geo. blind maker, 69 Pritchard's rd. Hackney flds
Jones Wm. Hanbury, conveyancer, 4 Field ct. Gray's inn
Jones Wm. Hen. silversmith, 35 Cranmer place, Waterloo rd
Jones Wm. James, surgeon, 4 Portugal st. Lincoln's inn flds
Jones Wm. John, hatter, 34 Charles st. Middlesex hospital
Jones Wm. Theophilus, merchant, 2 Abchurch lane
Jones Wm. Thomas, printer, 88 Gray's inn lane
Jonson George Cornelius, surgeon, 1 Grosvenor st. west
Jopling Joseph, architect, 29 Wimpole st. Cavendish sq
Jopp James, relieving officer, 18 Seething lane, Gt. Tower st
Jopson William, tailor, 30 Gee st. Goswell st
Jordan Tim. Adams & Co. wheelwrights, 20 Pump row, Old st
Jordan Anthony (of Coblentz), see Deinhard & Jordan
Jordan Benjamin, grocer, 35 Albany road, Camberwell
Jordan Charles Henry, *Crown* P.H. 40 Tufton st. Westmr
Jordan Chas. Jas. custom ho.& genl. agt. Old Trinity ho. Watr. la
Jordan Elizabeth (Mrs.), watchma. 29 Marshall st. Golden sq
Jordan George, baker, 12 Beckford row, Walworth rd
Jordan George John, stone mason, High st. Bow
Jordan George William, newsvender, 282 Strand
Jordan Henry, *Crown & Anchor* P.H. Temple st. Hackney rd
Jordan Henry, tailor, 9 Little Chester st. Grosvenor place
Jordan Henry E. tea, grocery & italian wa. 42 Old Bond st
Jordan Hen. Nathl. carver & gilder, 29 Lwr. Eaton st. Pimlico
Jordan James, plumber, 41 Spring st. Paddington
Jordan John, furnishg. undertaker, 35 John st. Fitzroy sq
Jordan John, *Grosvenor* coffee rooms, 73 Davies st. Berkly. sq
Jordan John, *Shakespear's Head* P.H. 88 Waterloo road
Jordan John, tinplate worker & braz. 42 Wells st. Oxford st
Jordan Joseph, linendraper, 56 London road, Southwark
Jordan Lewis, surgeon, 19 Berners st. Oxford st
Jordan Louisa (Mrs.), ladies' school, 9 Tower royal
Jordan Michael, cheesemonger, 1 Ossulston st. Somers town
Jordan Michael, grocer, 6 Church st. Mile end New town
Jordan Octavius, architect, 12 John st. Adelphi
Jordan Robert, stationer, 25 Shaftesbury ter. Pimlico
Jordan Thomas Joseph, painter & glazier, 6 Fenchurch bldgs
Jordan Thos. Wm. working jeweller, 1 Newcastle st. Clerknwl
Jordan William, tailor, &c. 184 Strand
Jordan Wm. I. wine merchant, 40 St. Mary-at-hill
Jordan Wm. Prue, surgn.& registr. 9 Lo. Belgrave st. Eaton sq
Jorden Walter & Co. coal merchts. 186 Albany rd. Cambrwll
Jorden James, dairyman, 3 Lower Islington terrace
Jorden James, greengrocer & coaldeal. 17 Hart st. Grosv. sq
Jorden Richard, auctioneer, see Pearsall & Jorden
Jordeson & Brown, ship&ins. bro.&com. agts. 2 St. Mary-at-hill
Jordeson Christopher, solicitor, 2 St. Mary-at-hill
Jordon Charles Patrk. breeches maker, 4 St. Ann's ct. Soho
Jorge John, merchant, 46 Clarendon square, Somers town
Jortin — Lee William, solicitor, 43 Lincoln's inn fields
Joscelyne Isaac, tailor & draper, 249 Shoreditch
Joselin Richard, hat manufacturer, 14 Fenchurch st
Joseph (A. & S.), Myers & Co. importers of french, german, swiss & italian manufact. & toy merchts. 144 Leadenhall st
Joseph Brothers, skinners, furriers & wool merchants, 6 Swan st. Gt. Dover road, & Piccadilly, Manchester
Joseph Abraham, imp. of pictures & curiosities, 54 Quadrant
Joseph A. Joseph, stock & share bro. 6 Bank cham. Lothbury
Joseph Edward, surgeon, 15 Great Marylebone st
Joseph Henry, clothes salesman, 21 Minories
Joseph Henry, pencil maker & artists' colorman, 14 Soho sq
Joseph Israel, clothes salesman, 8 Rosemary lane
Joseph James, tobacconist, 8 Weston st. Somers town
Joseph Joseph, fur merchant, 9 Castle st. Houndsditch
Joseph Joseph, orange merchant, 2 St. James's pl. Aldgate
Joseph Joseph, skin mer. see Meyer, Joseph & Meyer
Joseph Joshua, who. boot & shoe wa. 13 Skinner st. Snowhill
Joseph Moss, jeweller & tobacconist, 153 Alfred pl. Waterloo rd
Joseph Reuben, hatter, 4 Houndsditch
Joseph Samuel, sculptor, 41 Charlotte st. Fitzroy square
Joseph Saul, furniture broker, 17 & 11 Brook hill, Clknwll
Joseph Simon Joseph, stock & share broker, 16 Old Broad st
Joseph Solomon, coffee house, 6 St. James's place, Aldgate
Josephs Edwd. share agt. Hall of Commerce, Threadneedle st
Josephs Joseph, tobacco manufactr. 29 Whitechapel High st
Josephs Samuel, orange merchant, 36 Lamb st. Spital sq
Josephs Wm. grocer & cheesemonger, 34 Gresse st. Tot. ct. rd
Joshua David, mer. & com. agent, 28 King st. Cheapside
Joshua Joshua, butcher, 31 Middlesex st. Aldgate High st
Josi Charles, artist, 99 Great Portland st
Josling John, grocer, &c. 63 Praed st. Edgware road
Josling Nathaniel, grocer, 15 Hatton wall, Hatton garden
Josling William, fruit salesman, Borough market
Josolyne John, baker & flour factor, 124 Cockhill, Ratcliff
Joubert Amedée, upholsterer, 8 Maddox st. Hanover sq
Joules & Taylor, butter salesmen, 37 Newgate market
Joules Robert, grocer & teadealer, 27 Brick la. Spitalfields
Jounaux Mary Ann (Mrs.), cane worker, 6 Rose st. Soho
Jourdain F. J. firm Darthez Brothers, 15 Austinfriars
Jourdain Wm. David, silk dyer, 60 Milton st. Cripplegate
Jourdan Edward, stockbroker, 72 Old Broad st. City
Journet Pierre, engineer, 2 Chester terrace, Eaton square
Jowett John, hosier, glover, shirt & stockmaker to H.R.H. Prince Albert, 48 Conduit st
Jowett William, tailor, 14 Shoemaker row, Blackfriars
Joy Alfred, tobacconist, 3 Upper King st. Bloomsbury
Joy Ambrose, boot & shoe maker, 109 Upper st. Islington
Joy Benjamin, plumber & painter, 19 Mount st. Lambeth
Joy Charles, leatherseller, 2 Mount Etna, Mile end road
Joy Edmund Thomas, basket maker, 4 George st. Camberwell
Joy Edward, coal mercht. 7 Southampton ter. Pentonville
Joy Henry, fishing rod & net ma. 6 Opera arcade, Pall mall
Joy James, glover & hosier, 44 Mount st. Lambeth
Joy James, grocer, 22 Villa st. Walworth common
Joy Jessie (Miss), artist, 10 Fitzroy square
Joy John, coal dealer, 5 Beauchamp st. Leather lane
Joy John George, glover & hosier, 35 Newington causeway
Joy John Stanley, solicitor, 1 Staple inn
Joy Mary (Mrs.), nursery, Newland st. Kensington road
Joy Samuel, bootma.&leather selr. 12 Broadway, Limehouse
Joy Thomas M. artist, 4 Russell place, Fitzroy square
Joy William, bookseller & publisher, 44 Paternoster row
Joyce Edw. & Sons, lightrm.&cust. ho. ag. 13 Water la. Tower. st
Joyce & Day, patent stove manufacturers, 113 London wall
Joyce Felix & Co. soap manufrs. 9 King's Arms yard, Moorgate st. & Holly Bush place, Bethnal green road
Joyce Thos. & Son, lamp ma. & oil ref. 43 Bishopt. st. without

Joyce & Parker, grocers, 47A, Manchester st. Manchester sq
Joyce Dinah (Mrs.), stay maker, 10 Essex place, Mare st. Hkny
Joyce Frederick, practical chemist, inventor & sole manufacturer of the anti corrosive percussion gun cap & chemically prepared gun wadding, 55 Bartholomew close, Smithfield
Joyce Isaiah, grocer, 1 Brunswick pl. Barnsbury rd. Islington
Joyce James, corn & coal merchant, 10 Warwick lane
Joyce James, grocer, 22 Marshall st. London road
Joyce James, Old Bell inn waggon office, 30 Warwick lane
Joyce James, tailor, 9 Silver st. Golden square
Joyce James Benj. *Windmill* P.H. 82 Up. Ground st. Blkfriars
Joyce John, coal dealer, 10 Little Windmill st. Golden square
Joyce John, leather, lace & strop cuttr. 6 Middle st. Cloth fair
Joyce John, tailor, 8 Earl st. east, Lisson grove
Joyce Joseph, hatter, 199 Strand
Joyce Joshua, who. ironmonger, 129 Whitechapel High st
Joyce Stephen, patent stove manufactr. 113 London wall
Joyce Thomas, baker, 42 Rupert st. Haymarket
Joyce Thomas, engraver on wood, 6 Well st. Cripplegate
Joyce Thomas, leather dresser & seller, wholesale glove & gaiter manufacturer, 70 Watling st
Joyce Thomas, irondealr. 36 Colonnade, Greville st. Bruns. sq
Joyce Thomas, jun. tailor, 5 Queen st. Golden square
Joyce Thomas, wood type cutter, 7 Stanhope st. Clare market
Joyce Thos. Edwd. ornaml. painter, 2 Hannibal rd. Stepney grn
Joyce William, baker, 18 George row, Bermondsey
Joyce William, baker, 1 Alexander place, Brompton
Joyce William, fruiterer, 18 Lower Sloane st. Chelsea
Joyce William, painter & plumbr. 64 Drummond st. Euston sq
Joyce William, saddler & harness maker, 27 Bow High st
Joyce William, wood engraver, 11 Bolt court, Fleet st
Joyes Alfred Wm. Edwd. linen draper, 1 Broadway, Westmr
Joynes Thomas, coffee rooms, 6 Marshall st. Golden square
Jubb Jane (Mrs.), toy & turnery wareho. 6 Portman pl. Edg. rd
Juby Robert, linendraper & haberdasher, see Thaine & Juby
Juchau Lewis C. featherma. & ivory work, &c. 6 East rd. City rd
Juchau Phillip, fan maker, 78 Fore street, Cripplegate
Juchaw Henry, cheesemonger, 27 Turk st. Bethnal green
Judd William & Son, bootmakers, 245 Regent st
Judd Bartlet, cheesemonger, 10 Sols row, Hampstead road
Judd Charles, fruiterer, 22 Woodland st. Dalston
Judd George, oilman & tallow chand. 10 Webber st. Blkfrs. rd
Judd James, *King's Arms* P.H. Old Chapel row, Kentish tn
Judd John, baker, 82 Kent st. Borough
Judd John, furniture warehouse, 257 & 258 Blackfriars road
Judd John P. wine mercht. (firm N. Johnston & Sons) 6 Mark la
Judd Robert, boot & shoemaker, 9 Beak st. Regent st
Judd Robert, cheesefactor, 6 Ampton st. Gray's inn road
Judd Samuel, cabinet maker & uphlstr. 2 Felix ter. Lvrpl. rd
Judd Thomas, grocer, teadealer, &c. 45 Essex st. Strand
Judd William, boot & shoe maker, 45 Old Bond st
Judd William, printer, see Reding & Judd
Judd William Copeland, barrister, 4 Middle Temple lane
Judd William Henry, surgeon, 9 Maddox st. Bond st
Judge Wm. & Chas. leather button mfrs. 6 East st. Old Kent rd
Judge Advocate General's Offi. 35 Gt. Geo. st. Westm. hrs. 10 to 4
Judge John Edward, *Fox & Anchor* P.H. 18 Charter house la
Judge Joseph, lookng glass frame ma. 3 Wellingtn. st. Gswll. st
Judge Thomas, watch & clock maker, 10 New Quebec st
Judges' Chambers, Rolls' gardens, Serjeants' inn, Chancery la
Judicial Committee of the Privy Council, Whitehall
Judkins Samuel & Co. corn, seed & hop merchants, 71 Tooley st. & Phœnix wharf, Pickle Herring stairs
Judkins Samuel, jun. lighterman, 71 Tooley st. & Phœnix wharf, Pickle Herring stairs
Judkins Elmer, coal merchant, 12 Beaufort buildings, Strand
Judkins Richard, cattle salesman, 15 West Smithfield
Judson & Wilson, merchants & drysalters, 10 Scots yd. Bushla.; & dye wood mills, Gun alley, 85 Bermondsey st
Judson Wm. ironmonger, 30 High st. Kensington
Jukes Coulson & Co. export ironmongers & millwrights, 11 & 12 Clement's la. Lombard st.; & 7 St. Mary's row, Birmingham
Jukes Edward, cheesemonger, Mare st. Hackney
Jukes Henry, carpenter & builder, 12 King st. Portman sq
Jukes Henry, tailor, 45 Leonard st. Finsbury
Jukes John, tailor & clothier, 8 James's place, Hoxton
Jukes Thomas Samson, tailor, 25 Gt. Winchester st
Jukes William, carpenter, 26 Boston st. Dorset sq
Juler Philip, surgeon, 157 High Holborn
Julian George, stationer, 4 Three Colt st. Limehouse
Julien Virginie (Madame), clear starchr. 8 Hanovr. st. Islgtn
Julier George, tobacconist, 11 Cambridge rd. Mile end rd
Julier James, beer retailer, 27 Eastfield st. Limehouse fields
Jullien Louis George, depôt general de musique dansante, 214 Regent st
Jullien Lewis Geo. music publisher, 45 King st. Golden sq
Jullien Susan (Mde.), magasin botanique, 214 Regent st
Julius & Cameron, solicitors, 19 Buckingham st. Strand
Julyan Frederick John, carpenter, 31 King street, Soho
Jumpsen John, smith & farrier, 23 Primrose hill, Salisb. sq
Jung Philip, baker, 110 Drury lane
Jungmichel Charles, merchant, 4 Austin friars
Junior United Service Club (Thomas Hatch, secretary), 11 Charles street, St. James's
Junkison James, leather dresser, 1 Grange road, Bermondsey; & 8 York place, Kent street road
Jupe William, naptha manufactory, Bow common
Jupp Joseph & Son, hatters to the Queen, 222 Regent st
Jupp Saml. & Edwd. B. attorn. Carpenters' hall, Lndn. wll
Jupp Edward, tailor, 12 Great Castle street, Regent street
Jupp Hen. Morgan, archit. & surv. Carpenters' hall, London wl
Jupp John, brass finisher, 10 Long alley, Finsbury
Jupp Joseph, brass founder, 22 Norfolk street, Islington
Jupp Richard, fruiterer, 40 Great James st. Lisson grove
Jurdison Caroli. (Miss), *Caledonian ho.* see Elder & Jurdison
Jurist weekly newspaper Office, 3 Chancery lane, Fleet st
Jury Edmd. meat slsmn. see Pocklington, Frackleton & Jury
Jury Francis, lighterman, 1 Globe st. Wapping
Jury James, auctioneer, estate agent & valuer, 20 King's arms yard; valuer to the Imperial Insurance Company
Jury John, lighterman, 19 Great Hermitage street, Wapping
Jury John C. smith & engineer, 22 Green Dragon yard, Whtchpl
Just George, *Globe* P.H. Highbury vale
Just James, baker, 14 Nassau street, Middlesex hospital
Just Leonard, watch manuf. 19 St. John's sq. Clerkenwell
Justerini & Brooks, foreign liqueur & wine & brandy merchants, 2 Pall mall
Justice of the Peace, weekly legal paper, 136 Fetter lane
Justice John, butcher, 4 George court, Piccadilly
Justice Robert, baker, 1 Holland place, Clapham road
Justice Thomas Francis, solicitor, see Hamilton & Justice
Justins Edward & Son, printers, 48 Mark lane
Jutsum & German, solicitors, 49 Leadenhall st
Jutsum Saml. & Son, meat salesman, 64 & 65 Aldgate High st
Jutsum Chas. Haines, pawnbroker, 65 Whitechapel High st
Juxon Bishop, tinman & brazier, 12 Cobourg st. Euston sq

KAEHLER Henry, sculptor, 85 Norton st. Portland place
Kaehler John, tailor, 45 Leicester square
Kaempf Henry, tailor, &c. 22 South Audley st. Grosvenor sq
Kail William, greengrocer, 73 Fore street, Cripplegate
Kain John, plumber & glazier, 14 Bethnal green, west side
Kain John, plumber, 14 Vittoria pl. Cambridge rd. Mile end
Kaines Francis, bookseller, 9 Fieldgate street, Whitechapel
Kaines James, newsvender, 20 New road, St. George's east
Kairns Eliz. (Mrs.), *Half Moon & 7 Stars* P.H. 119 St. George st
Kaiser Joseph, clockmaker, see Schwearer & Kaiser
Kalber Michael, fur skin dresser, 4 Red Lion st. Clerkenwell
Kalischer Isaac, watch tool wareho. 2 Perceval st. Clerkenwell
Kalman Henry, birmingham & sheffield wholesale warehouse, china & foreign toys, 71 Houndsditch
Kalloway Joseph, *Fleece* P.H. Well court, Queen street, Cheapside, & dining rooms, 8 Queen street, Cheapside
Kaltenback Andrew, watch & clockma. 91 London rd. Sthwk
Kammerer Joseph, clockmaker, 51 King street, Borough
Kampf John, pawnbroker, 22 Holywell lane, Shoreditch
Kaniezki Bartholomew, furrier, 5 Angel ct. Skinner street
Kannegiesser Charles, fur manufacturer, 9 Ryder's court, & 5 Cranbourne street, Leicester square
Karby Edward, plumber, &c. near the Church, Bow
Karby Frances (Mrs.), milliner, 91 Leadenhall street
Karby Geo. mahog. glass frame ma. 21 Chamber st. Goodmn. fi
Karby John Eaton, glazier, &c. 184 Poplar High street
Karby Richard, plumber, &c. 1 Wellington st. Goswell st
Karn Henry, house agent, &c. 37 Hampden st. Clarendon sq
Karr James, fishmonger, Clare market
Karslake & Crealock, solicitors, 4 Regent st. Waterloo place
Kasner Moses, curiosity dealer, 116 Wardour street, Soho
Kates John, hairdresser, 40 Kenton st. Brunswick square
Kates William Henry, gasfitter, 91 Long alley, Finsbury
Katte Stephen, accountant & translator, 50 Threadneedle st. & 416 Strand
Katterns & Warwick, fringe & tassel manufacs. 78 Long acre
Katz Myer, brush manufacturer, 6 New street, Bishopsgate
Kauffman Carl, perfumer & clockma. 12 Princes st. Drury la
Kauffman David, watch & clockma. 28 Marchmont street
Kauth Henry, baker, 25 Chapel street, New road
Kavanaugh Mary A. (Miss), strawbon. ma. 9 Thornton st. Dckhd
Kay & Grove, news agents, 2 Leathersell's. bldgs. London wall
Kay Elizabeth (Miss), milliner, 15 Vere street, Cavendish sq
Kay Elizabeth (Mrs.), lodging house, 38 Norfolk st. Strand
Kay Hildreth, chemist, 3 Upton pl. Commercial rd. east

Kay John, surgeon, 70 Old street, St. Luke's
Kay John, cheesemonger, 23 Goodge st. Tottenham ct. rd
Kay John C. ornamental carver, 4 Clarence pl. Hackney rd
Kay Jonathan, chemist, &c. 7 Prospect pl. Kingsland rd
Kay Joseph, architect & surveyor, 6 Gower st. Bedford sq
Kay Richard, cheesemonger, 47 Seymour pl. Bryanstone sq
Kay Richard B. wine, brandy & cigar mercht. 15 Basinghall st
Kay Susanna (Mrs.), tobacconist, 3 Dean's blds. Com. rd. Limeh
Kay Theresa Ann (Mrs.), milliner, 23 Davies st. Berkeley sq
Kay William, goldsmith, 6 Oxenden st. Haymarket
Kaye Haven, *Fountain tavern*, 39 Redcross st. Cripplegate, & wholesale clothier, 129 Aldersgate st
Kaye James, timber, slate, brick, stone, tile, cement & coal merchant, Bridge wharf, Pimlico
Kaye John, pat. medicine wareho. 13 King William st. City
Kaye Joseph, linendraper, 55 Tottenham court road
Kayes Henry, solicitor, 4 Surrey st. Strand
Kaygill Sarah (Mrs.), earthenware dealer, 2 Cambrwl. grove
Kayler Henry, baker, 10 Bedford st. Bedford row
Kayll John James, agent to Jas. Hartley & Co. window glass & alkali manufs. 43 Upper Thames st
Keable George, cornchandler, 40 James st. Oxford st
Keal John, surgeon, see Rowe & Keal
Kealley Benjamin, chemist, &c. 29 Lit. Newport st. Long acre
Kealy John, grocer, &c. 14 Cumberland pl. King's rd. Chelsea
Kean Anthony, tailor, 113 Goswell st
Kean Peter, stationer & newsman, 39 Bury st. St. James's
Kean Sampson, glass engraver, 6 Cook's court, Carey st
Keane Daniel, solicitor, 36 Lincoln's inn fields
Keane David Deady, barrister, 51 Lincoln's inn fields
Kear Richard, seal skin dresser, 2 Elder walk, Islington
Kear Thomas, grocer, 32 Queen st. Lower road, Islington
Kearney Thos. & Son, boot & shoemaks. 5 Bellyard, Temple bar
Kearney Hen. Wm. teacher of drawing, 6 Thomas st. Horselydn
Kearney Joshua, varnish maker, 32 Albany st. Regent's pk
Kearns John blacking manufr. 19 Little Queen st. Holborn
Kearns John, cutler, 425 Oxford st
Kearns John, shipowner, 9 Catherine court, Tower hill
Kearns William Mosson, solicitor, 5 Red Lion sq. Holborn
Kearse Mary (Mrs.), artist, 48 Foley st. Portland pl
Kearsey Fras. solicitor, see Hughes, Kearsey & Masterman
Keartland Mary & Sons, coach bolt, washer, rivet & nail manufacturers, 14 Mill st. Lambeth
Keartland Sam. cut brad & coach bolt ma. 4 Park pl. Lmbth
Keartland Thomas, brad & burr ma. 31 Chester st. Kenningtn
Kearton William, cheesemonger, 13 & 14 Lamb st. Spital sq
Keasley Thomas, *Fox* P.H. 1 Old Paradise row, Islington
Keast James, builder, &c. 21 Anderson's bldgs. City road
Keast John, grocer, 6 Snow's fields, Bermondsey
Keast John, *Star* P.H. 40 City road, Finsbury square
Keat John Richard, tobacconist, Asylum road, Old Kent rd
Keast Thomas, *Crown* P.H. 16 Lant street, Borough
Keat George, musical instrument maker & music ruler, Black Horse yard, 190½ High Holborn
Keat Jane (Mrs.), rag dealer, 54 Carnaby st. Golden sq
Keat Sophia (Mrs.), watchmaker, 69 Banner st. St. Luke's
Keate Rt. surgeon to the Queen, 15 Albemarle st. Piccadilly
Keates Hugh, coal dealer, 14 Cowcross st. Smithfield
Keates Thomas, beer retailer, 18 Brunswick st. Cromer st
Keates Thomas, meat salesman, 26 New Newgate market
Keates William, military cap ma. 14 Cecil ct. St. Martin's la
Keates William, tailor, 9 Brompton road
Keating Henry Singer, barrister, 1 Paper bldgs. Temple
Keating John, cabinet ma. 22 Grosvenor mews, Grosvenor st
Keating John, tailor, 38 Warwick st. Golden square
Keating Michael, academy, 28 Dartmouth st. Westminster
Keating Philip, hatter, 41 Baalzephon st. Bermondsey
Keating Thos. chemist & druggist, & proprietor of Keating's cough lozenges, 79 St. Paul's church yard
Keating William, barrister, 9 Inner Temple lane
Keating William, cabinet maker, 4 Portland st. Soho
Keatley William Reaves, butcher, 10 Bridge ter. Harrow rd
Keatley John Reaves, carpenter, &c. see Bailey & Keatley
Keats & Ledger, hatters to the late King, 74 Cheapside
Keats Joseph, bookseller & stationer, 142 Sloane st. Chelsea
Keats Joseph, linendraper, 47 Paradise row, Chelsea
Keats Joseph Henry, bookseller, 8 Upper Queen's buildings, Brompton, & 142 Sloane st. Chelsea
Keays William Gamliel, jewel case maker, 4 Hatton wall
Kebbel Shepherd & Co. lead, tin & tinplate merchts. & white lead & shot manfrs. Allhallow's wharf, Upper Thames st
Kebbell George, wig maker, &c. 2 Finch lane, Cornhill
Kebbell James, junr. builder, Richmond road, Dalston
Kebbell Elzbth (Miss), boarding school, 8 Forest row, Dalston
Kebble Henry, spring truss manufr. 19 Warwick st. Regent st
Kebble William, picture frame maker, 3 Dean st. Soho
Keddell, Baker & Grant, solicitors, 34 Lime street, City
Kedge George, grocer & teadealer, 79 Mount st. Berkeley sq
Kedge William, cabinet maker, 12 Prospect pl. Old Kent rd
Kedgley Benjamin, potato salesman, 17 Borough market
Kee Erasmus, straw bonnet maker, 19 Hertford st. Fitzroy sq
Keeble Francis, lodging house, 6 Bateman's bldgs. Soho
Keeble George, grocer, 1 Lower Salisbury pl. Lock's fields
Keeble John, engraver & printer, 27 Poland st. Oxford st
Keech James, chemist, 4 New King street, Deptford
Keed George Franks, ironmonger, see Williams & Keed
Keed William James, hatter, hosier & glover, see Fownes & Keed
Keeford Richard, butcher, 1 King David la. Shadwell
Keeft Thomas, watch case maker, 5 Wilmington st. Spafields
Keegan John, music seller, 3 Burlington arcade
Keel Edward, coffee & chophouse, 3 Lit. St. James's st
Keele James & Co. merchants, 2 Walbrook buildings, City
Keeler James, *Sportsman* P.H. 45 Margaret st. Hackney fields
Keeley Daniel, chandlers' shop, 17 Chester st. Kengtn. cross
Keeley James, *Bull's Head* P.H. 10 Tottenham court road
Keeley John, boot & shoe maker, 8 Russell court, Drury lane
Keeley Thomas, *Noah's Ark* P.H. High st. Deptford
Keeling & Hunt, fruit & general brokers, 2 Monument yard, & 9 Pudding lane
Keeling Abraham, carpenter, 11 Mansion ho. st. Kennington
Keeling Ann (Mrs.), tobacconist, 31 Churchway, Somers tn
Keeling Edward Henry, wine & spirit broker, 11 Gt. Tower st
Keeling & Westmorland, ea. & w. india brokers, 8 Mincing la
Keeling Thomas, baker, 10 Devonshire st. Globe rd. Mile end
Keely Sarah (Mrs.), dairy, 11 Upper Seymour st. west
Keens' & Welch, mustard & blue manfs. 6 Garlick hill
Keen Steph. & Co. ale, &c. brew. 25 John st. & York st. Pntnvl
Keen, Tebbut & Rippin, warehousemen, 122 Wood st
Keen Wm. & Son, estate agents & valuers, 2 Parliament st
Keen Daniel, coach builder, 3 North Audley st
Keen George, coffee rooms, 259 Tottenham court road
Keen George, lighterman, 5 Thomas st. Horselydown
Keen George, wharfinger, Coles Upper wharf, 21 Shad Thames
Keen James, farrier, 16 Lucretia st. Lambeth Lower marsh
Keen Job, gun manufacturer to the Hon. Board of Ordnance & Hon. East India Company, 61 Glo'ster st. Coml. rd. east
Keen John, glove manufacturer, High st. Battersea
Keen John, *Greyhound* P.H. 7 Canning pl. Old st. St. Luke's
Keen John, hairdresser, 22 Addle st. Wood st
Keen Joseph, cheesemonger, 229 Bethnal green road
Keen Stephen Delany, beer retailer, 9 North whf. rd. Padgtn
Keen Richard, boot & shoe mak. 10 Church st. Camberwell
Keen Thos. mason & builder, 15 Shepperton st. New North rd
Keen Thos. surgeon, 15 Manor pl. north, King's rd. Chelsea
Keen Thos. Robins, lighterman, 4 Grange road, Bermondsey
Keene Chas. & Co. india rubber manfctrs. & patentees, 2 Guildford st. 20 York road, & 17 York st. Lambh.; wareh. 13 Goldsmith st. City
Keene Ann (Mrs.), corkcutter, 16 Trafalgar st. Walworth
Keene Frederick Benj. B. tailor, 36 Union st. Clarendon sq
Keene George John, solicitor, 34 Gt. Queen st. Linc. inn fi
Keene Henry, greengrocer, 9 Regent st. Horseferry road
Keene James, cheesemonger, 2 Westbourne st. Pimlico
Keene Mary Martha (Mrs.), *Duke of Kendal* P.H. 20 Upper Berkeley st. west, & 37 Cambridge st. Edgware rd
Keene Rd. Wynn, terracotta works, 124 Vauxhall wk. Lambeth
Keene Samuel T. oil & colorman, 40 South st. Manchester sq
Keene Thomas, coal merchant, 30 Wellington mews, Golden sq
Keene William, seedsman, see Gordon, Thomson & Keene
Keens James, grocer, 2 Pleasant row, Holloway road
Keep James, carpenter & builder, 6 King st. Westminster
Keep Wm. carpenter & builder, 10 King st. Westminster
Keep William, tailor, 13 Little Newport st. Leicester sq
Keer Wm. manchester agent, 34 Friday st. Cheapside
Keevil George, stationer, 8 Northampton row, Holloway
Kefford George, fishmonger, 2 Trinity st. Blackman st
Kefford John, fishmonger, 17 Northampton pl. Old Kent rd
Kehoe Thomas, surgeon, A1 Woburn place, Russell square
Keighley Brothers, stuff warehmen. 5 Priest ct. Foster lane
Keighley & Co. (assignees of), 2 Dunster ct. Mincing lane
Keighley G. W. & S. spinners & stuff mfrs. 42 Gutter la. Cheapsi
Keighley Henry P. stationer, 3 Grenada ter. Com. rd. east
Keighley Thomas Dodd, solicitor, 77 Basinghall st
Keightley Archibald, solcr. & reg. of Charterho. Charterho. sq
Keiley Henrietta (Mrs.), dressmaker, 16 Savage gardens
Keily Richard, merchant, 12 Haymarket
Keith Daniel & Co. silk manufacturers, 124 Wood st
Keith, Prowse & Co. musical instrument manufs. 48 Cheapside
Keith & Shoobridge, silk ma. 124 Wood st. & 13 Goldsmith st
Keith Alexander, surgeon, 195 Piccadilly
Keith Elzbth. (Mrs.), dyer, Savannah pl. Essex st. Kingsland rd
Keith George, baker, 12 Bridge st. Westminster

Keith George, furnish. ironmonger, 46 Brewer st. Golden sq
Keith Geo. John, hay, straw & corndealer, 37 York st. City rd
Keith Henry J. merchant, Baltic coffee house
Keith Henry John, paint brush ma. 94 Long la. Bermondsey
Keith Hester (Mrs.), coffee rooms, 37 Stoney st. Boro' market
Keith John Jas. silversmith, 59 Britannia ter. City road
Keith Thomas Wm. butcher, 14 South pl. Tibberton square
Keith William, plumber &c. 19 Montpelier row, Brompton
Keith Wm. cutler & dressing case ma. 10 Victoriard. Pimlico
Kekewich George Granville, barrister, 3 Paper buildings
Kelday John, pawnbroker, 10 Durham pl. east, Hackney rd
Kele James Wm. beer retailer, 18 Gt. Turnstile, Holborn
Kelham Charles Bird, spice merchant, see Mayor & Kelham
Kelham Wm. engraver & printer, 13 Cullum st. Fenchurchst
Kelk Charles, working silversmith, 20 Denmark st. Soho
Kelk John, builder, see Elger & Kelk
Kelk John, builder, 13 South st. Grosvenor square, & saw mills, Grosvenor basin
Kell & Chaffers, solicitors, 43 Bedford row, Bloomsbury
Kell & Tindley, tallow chandlers, 160 High st. Camden town
Kell George, mast maker, 37 Rotherhithe wall
Kell George, stockbroker, 12 Throgmorton st
Kell Lionell Polhill, surgeon, see Seaton & Kell
Kell Robert, carpenter, 52 Paradise street, Rotherhithe
Kell Robert, wax & tallow chandler to the Queen, 5 Strand
Kell Robert, *White Horse* P.H. 92 Hare st. Bethnal green
Kelland John, city saw mills, 97 Wentworth st. Whitechapl. & 12 Rodney terrace east, Mile end road
Kellaway Geo. ornam. brassworker, 7 Davies st. Berkeley sq
Kellaway Thomas, tailor, 4 Gt. May's bldgs. St. Martin's la
Kelley Joseph, lighterman, Creek road, Deptford
Kelley Sarah (Mrs.), turner, 15 Portugal st. Lincoln's inn flds
Kellow Chas. lithographic printer, 103 Hatton garden
Kelly Wm. & Co. steam machine & general printers, & printers & publishers of the Post Office London Directory 19 & 20 Old Boswell court, Temple bar
Kelly Elizabeth & Son, furnishing ironmngrs. 25 London wl
Kelly John Cookson & Co. printers&statnrs. 32 Houndsditch
Kelly Owen & Co. coal & provision mers. 64 Cannon st. & Dowgate dock, Up. Thames st
Kelly Collan, carpenter, 69 Davies st. Berkeley square
Kelly Chas. coal merchant, 4 Guildford pl. Lr. Kungtn. la
Kelly Edward Robert, M.A. solicitor, 8 Cook's court, Lincoln's inn, & 12 King's parade, Chelsea
Kelly Eleanor (Mrs.), pork butcher, 6 Stepney Old road
Kelly Elizabeth (Miss), staymaker, 2 Minories
Kelly Sir Fitzroy, knt. solicitor general, 8 Figtree ct. Temp
Kelly Frederick, surgeon, 60 Fetter lane, Holborn
Kelly Frederick, trunkmaker, 3 Parkside, Knightsbridge
Kelly George, pork butcher, 2 Heartley place, Old Kent rd
Kelly George, printer, 1 New road, St. George's east
Kelly Geo. writingmaster, 15 University st. Tottenham ct. rd
Kelly Harriet (Miss), ladies' school, 15 University st
Kelly Harriet (Mrs.), ladies'school, 24 Compton st. Brnswk sq
Kelly Hugh, corn chandler, 8 King David lane, Shadwell
Kelly James, coal merchant, 101 Rosemary lane
Kelly James Birch, attorney, 1 Inner Temple lane
Kelly Jane (Mrs.), bookseller &stationer, 2 Vigo st. Regent st
Kelly John, bookbinder, 15 Gower place, Euston square
Kelly John, coach plater & founder, 23 Wells st. Oxford st
Kelly John, greengrocer, 9 Drury lane
Kelly John, hide & skin salesman, 11 Northampton place, Old Kent road, and Skin market, Bermondsey
Kelly Leonard, grocer, &c. 41 Up. Rathbone pl. Oxford st
Kelly Lucius, special pleader, 9 Essex st. Strand
Kelly Martin, stock maker, 40½ Monkwell st. Cripplegate
Kelly Mary Ann (Miss), toy warehouse, 3 Wilderness row
Kelly Matthew, glass stainer, 43 Gerrard st. Soho
Kelly Michael, baker, 6 Buck's row, Whitechapel road
Kelly Michael, carpenter, 3 Joiner st. Westminster road
Kelly Michael, cast iron mercht. contractor for pipes & every description of castings for gas & water works, 30 Bankside
Kelly Owen, coal merchant, Dowgate dock, 83 Up. Thames st
Kelly Philip, grocer and teadealer, 52 St. George st
Kelly Thomas, bookseller & publisher, 16 & 17 Paternoster rw
Kelly Thomas, carpenter, 36 Charles st. Hatton garden
Kelly Thomas W. academy, 24 Compton st. Brunswick sq
Kelly Walter, tailor, 6 South st. Manchester square
Kelly William, grocer, 21 Duke st. Chelsea
Kelly William, painter & glazier, 9 Park st. Dorset sq
Kelly William Henry, bookbinder, 7 Water st. Arundel st
Kelly William Robert, solicitor, see Fennell & Kelly
Kelly Wm. Walter, grocer, 72 Castle st. east, Oxford st
Kelsall Eliz. (Miss), school, Hertford rd. Kingsland
Kelsalls & Co. merchants, 6 Great Winchester street
Kelsey Benjamin, jun. trimming manufr. 97 Hoxton Old town
Kelsey Charles, jeweller, 18 Gloucester st. St. John's st. rd
Kelsey Charles Saml. jun. sculptor, Commercial rd. Lambth
Kelsey James, statuary & mason, Commercial rd. Lambeth
Kelsey John, bricklayer, Paradise row, Rotherhithe
Kelsey John, mason & builder, 72 Paradise st. Rotherhithe
Kelsey Joseph, plumber & glazier, 83 Milton st. Cripplegate
Kelsey Richard, boot & shoemaker, 20 Goodge st. Fitzroy sq
Kelsey Richard, surveyor, 73 Chiswell st. Finsbury
Kelsey Samuel, baker, 61 Gainsford st. Horselydown
Kelsey William Thomas, statuary, Amelia pl. Fulham road
Kelso J. M. (Mrs.), ladies' school, see Midgley & Kelso
Kelson Richard, shipwright, 4 Narrow st. Ratcliff
Kelsy Benj. fancy trimng. mfr. 9 Nichols row, Bethnal grn
Kelting Samuel, umbrella manufr. 84 Bethnal green road
Kelting Thos. chandler's shop, 32 Lambeth st. Goodman's flds
Kelty Susannah (Mrs.), *Castle* P. H. 8 Quaker st. Spitalfids
Kelzey Thomas, bootmaker, 21 Cross st. Blackfriars road
Kemball Hannah (Mrs.), fruiterer, 11 Ashton pl. Holloway
Kemball Thomas, butcher, 92 Lambeth walk
Kember George & Samuel, brass founders & pewterers & plumbers' mould makers, 44 Northampton st. Clerkenwll
Kember Chas. mould ma. brassfounder, &c. 39 King st. Clkwl
Kember Richard John, watch&clock ma. 5 Robert ter. Chelsea
Kembles' & Trower, colonial brokers, 10 Mincing lane
Kemble Celina (Mrs.), lodging house, 14 Panton square
Kemble John, engineer, 20 Greville st. Hatton garden
Kemble John, machinist, lathe & tool ma. 20 Greville st
Kemble John T. sec. to City Club House, 19 Old Broad st. City
Kemble Robert, paper hanger, Stratford broadway
Kemish Henry, grocer, 45 Broad st. London docks
Kemm James, wholesale grocer, see Fenn, Kemm & Fenn
Kemmish Wm. wholesale & retail french & english boot & shoe maker, 16 Lowther arcade
Kemmith Richard, plasterer, 111 Waterloo road
Kemp, Graham & Hall, who. tea & coffee dlrs. 64 Gt. Tower st
Kemp & Hulbert, hay, corn, hop&seedfac. 7 St. Dunstan's pssge
Kemp John & Rd. auctioneers, 37 Judd st. Brunswick sq
Kemp Alfred, tobacconist, 27 Paradise row, Chelsea
Kemp Charles, architect & surveyor, Asylum road, Old Kent rd. office at Calvert's brewery
Kemp Charles, *Queen Elizath.* P.H. Asylum rd. Old Kentrd
Kemp Charles, *King's Head tavern*, P.H. 40 Newgate st
Kemp Charles, office, Calvert's brewery, 39 Up. Thames st
Kemp Christopher, coal dlr. 19 John st. north, Marylebone
Kemp Edward, boot & shoemaker, 19 Great. Titchfield st
Kemp Edward, dyer, 45 Weymouth terrace, Hackney rd
Kemp Edward, solicitor, 9 Trevor square, Brompton
Kemp Eliza (Mrs.), baker, 52 Wilsted st. Somers town
Kemp Elizh. (Mrs.), toy dealer, 25 Grosvenor row, Pimlico
Kemp Francis, fishmonger, 16 Marylebone lane, Oxford st
Kemp George, jeweller, 9 Powell st. west, King square
Kemp George, silk manufacturer, see Stone & Kemp
Kemp George Baring, solicitor, 23 Duke st. Westminster
Kemp Godfrey, cheesemonger, 5 Moreton ter. Kentishtwn. rd
Kemp Godfrey, cattle salesman, 60 West Smithfield
Kemp Henry, corn & seed factor, Jack'scoffee house, Markla
Kemp Henry, cowkeeper, 12 Gilbert st. Clare market
Kemp Henry, varnish maker, Jamaica level, Bermondsey
Kemp James, goldsm.& jeweller, 14 Meredith st. Clerkenwell
Kemp Jesse, oilman, 2 Kenton st. Brunswick square
Kemp John, academy, 18 Buckingham place, Fitzroy square
Kemp John, bricklayer, Pritchard's road, Hackney road
Kemp John, grocer, Bromley, Middlesex
Kemp John Young, conveyancer, 4, Stone bldgs. Linc. inn
Kemp Joseph, gun maker, 31 Duke st. Grosvenor square
Kemp Peter, baker, 107 Princes road, Lambeth
Kemp Richard, chemist, see Botwright & Kemp
Kemp Richard, linendraper, 5 Cambridge pl. Kingsland rd
Kemp Robert, baker, 6 Beak st. Regent st
Kemp Robert, chemist, 2 Queen's place, Holloway
Kemp Robert, skinner & fur cutter, 48 Castle st. Borough
Kemp Samuel, cattle salesman, 8 West Smithfield
Kemp Thomas, foreign wool merchant, 64 Basinghall st
Kemp Thomas, painter & glazier, 10 Short st. New cut
Kemp Thos. surgical instrmt. case ma. 12 Fleet la. Old Bailey
Kemp Thos. Firman, watch maker, 58 Oakley st. Lambeth
Kemp Thos. Reginald, banker&discount agt. 3 Abchurch lane
Kemp William, *Rose & Crown* P.H. 24 Shad Thames
Kemp Wm. veterinary forge, 27 William st. Portland town
Kemper John Hen. grocer, 45 Cannon st. rd. St. George's east
Kemplay James, special pleader, 1 King's Bench wk. Temple
Kemplen Alex. bricklayer & slater, 5 Howland st. Fitzroy sq
Kempshall John, *Star & Garter* P.H. 94 Edgware road
Kempson Geo. S. & Carteret J. solicitors, 31 Abingdon st. Westm
Kempson Samuel, baker, 29 Ray st. Clerkenwell
Kempster Edwin Jas. builder, Grosvenor whf. Addington sq

Kempster John, engraver & printer, 115 London wall
Kempster John, solicitor, 1 Portsmouth pl. Lr. Knningtn. la
Kempster Joseph, coachmaker, 40 Rupert st. Haymarket
Kempton Edward, bootmaker, 66 Three colt st. Limehouse
Kempton Samuel, carpenter, Church st. Waterloo road
Kempton Wm. currier, 1 Phœnix place, Ratcliff cross
Kempshead Mary (Mrs.) & Henry, printers, Low. Knngtn. la
Kemshead Elizabeth (Mrs.) basketmkr. 22 Comptonst. Clrkwl
Kemshead Henry, merchant, 46 Lime st
Kendall Charles Edwin & Son, shoemakers, 27 Barbican; 25 Drury lane; & 107 St. John st. road
Kendall Charles, boot maker, 24 Gt. Saffron hill
Kendall Charles, ship & commercial agent, 7 Fen court, Fenchurch st. & Jamaica coffee house, Cornhill
Kendall Chas. Holland, wine & spirit importer, 59 Mark la
Kendall Edward, organ builder, 16 Young st. Kensington
Kendall George, coffee rooms, 12 Eagle st. City road
Kendall George, blackwell hall factor, 2 Basinghall st
Kendall George, grocer, 2 Upper Copenhagen st. Pentonville
Kendall Harry, blackwell hall factor, 8 Basinghall st
Kendall Henry, merchant, 4 Austinfriars
Kendall Henry Edw. architect, 17 Suffolk st. Pall mall east
Kendall Henry Edw. jun. architect, 33 Brunswick square, & Crown cottage, Haverstock hill, Hampstead
Kendall James, *Canonbury tavern*, Canonbury square
Kendall John, clerk of the market, 6 Cumberland market
Kendall John, hatter & cap maker, 27 New st. Covent garden
Kendall John, merchant & importer of foreign beads, &c. 5 Leadenhall st
Kendall, Joseph, baker, 13 Three colt street, Limehouse
Kendall Moses, *Plough* P.H. St. John's hill, Wandsworth rd
Kendall Richard, turner, 19 Brighton st. Cromer st
Kendall Robt. Oxley, livery stables, Camberwell green
Kendall Samuel, coffee rooms, 31 Hackney road
Kendall Susnh. (Mrs.), whitesmith, 29 Red Lion st. Clerknw
Kendall Thomas, plumber, &c. 21 Gt. Castle st. Regent st
Kendall William, cattle salesman, 60 West Smithfield
Kendall William, machinist, 27 Primrose st. Bishopsgate
Kendall Wm. who. boot ma. 33 Somersetpl. Hoxton New town
Kendel Elias, baker, 13 Allen st. Goswell st
Kendell Frederick W. grocer, 40 Princess st. Lisson Grove
Kender Emma (Mrs.), tallow chandler, 11 Lit. Compton st. Soho
Kendle William, lace manufacturer, 9 Cheapside
Kendon Sarah (Mrs.), beershop, 32 Lit. George st. Bermsy
Kendray George, wine merch. 19 Gt. Queen st. Linc. inn flds
Kendrick Charles, laceman, &c. 244 Tottenham court road
Kendrick Henry, coal mer. 4 Essex st. Noel st. Islington
Kendrick John, bookseller, 4 Charlotte row, Mansion house
Kendrick John, surgeon, 12 Manchester st. Manchester sq
Kendrick Joseph Henry, linendraper, 92 Up. Whitecross st
Kendrick Mathew, A.R.H.A. artist, 28 Grafton st. Fitzry. sq
Kendrick Sarah (Miss), grocer, 110 Lambeth Lower Marsh
Keningale Joseph, cop. plate printer, see Gad & Keningale
Kennaby Brothers, hair merchants & manufacturers, perfumers, & gen. factors, 10 Westmoreland bldgs. Aldersgate st
Kennaby James L. cork cutter, 44 King st. West Smithfield
Kennan Godwin P. *Kennan's hotel*, 3 Crowncourt, Cheapside
Kennard John & Stephen, mers. & ins. brok. 27 Austinfriars
Kennard Rt. Wm. & Co. cast & bar iron & zincwa. 67 Up. Thames st
Kennard Augustus W. cork manufacturer, 117 Minories
Kennard John, wheelwright, 45 Limehouse causeway
Kennard John Orrick, linendraper, 15 Broadway, Deptford
Kennard Samuel, butcher, High st. Bow, Middlesex
Kennard Thomas, baker, 9 Brooksby st. Liverpool road, & 2 Copenhagen st. Pentonville
Kennay Jas. & Co. pianoforte makers, 1 Hackney rd. crescent
Kennedy & Asprey, stationers & dress. case ma. 49 New Bond st
Kennedy & King, perfumers, 13A, Hanway st. Oxford st
Kennedy Thos. & John, livery stables, Larkhall lane, Clapham
Kennedy Alexander, newsvender, 9 Upper Berkeley st
Kennedy Angus, surgeon, Broadway, Stratford
Kennedy Benjamin, stockbroker, Stock Exchange
Kennedy Chas. Rann, barrister, 10 Crown off. row, Temple
Kennedy Daniel, gasfitter, 43 Wells st. Oxford st
Kennedy Denham William, artist, 26 Soho square
Kennedy Geo. carver & gilder, 120 Edgware rd. Paddington
Kennedy Hen. shoem. & grindery dlr. 4 Cecil ct. St. Martin's la
Kennedy James, engineer, 36 Grafton st. east, Tottnhm. ct. rd
Kennedy James, auctioneer & house agent, 46 High st. & 1 Bayham terrace, Camden town
Kennedy James, surgeon, 17 Tavistock square
Kennedy John, bookseller, 35 Portman pl. Edgware road
Kennedy John, bootmaker, 25 Sherrard st. Golden square
Kennedy John, meat salesman, see Duckworth & Kennedy
Kennedy John, tailor, 1 New Quebec st. Portman square
Kennedy Lawrence, pawnbro. 1 Rochest. ter. Stoke Newington
Kennedy Matthew, cocoa matting ma. 18 Kirby st. Httn. grnd
Kennedy Peter, hairdresser, 17 Gwynn's pl. Hackney road
Kennedy Thomas, musical instrument maker, 364 Oxford st
Kennedy Thomas, solicitor, see Maugham & Kennedy
Kennedy Thos. newsvendr. & bookseller, 31 Royal Exchange, 125 Fetter lane, & 9 Upper Berkeley st. Portman sq
Kennedy William, gardener, Jamaica level, Rotherhithe
Kennel Philip, dairyman, 12 Ann's ter. Cambridge heath
Kennell John F. sec. to Blackwall Rail. 60 Fenchurch st
Kennerley & Sang, man's mercers, 7 Marylebone st. Piccadilly
Kennerley Wm. picture cleaner, 7 Howland st. Fitzroy sq
Kennet Wharf, William D. & Frederick White, between 67 & 68 Upper Thames st
Kennet Robt. *Hoop & Grapes* P.H. 14 Broadway, Westmnstr
Kenneth James, jun. fishmonger, 121 New Bond st
Kenneth Robert, fishmonger, 36 Marchmont st. Brunswick sq
Kennett Harriet & M.A. (Misses), dressms. 10 Kingst. Covnt. gdn
Kennett & Reynolds, wax & tal. chands. 25 Lamb st. Spital sq
Kennett Abraham, linendraper, 7 High st. Camberwell
Kennett David, tailor, 37 Chapel st. Belgrave square
Kennett Edward, oilman, 4 Philpot lane
Kennett Edwd. *Coach & Horses* P.H. 35 Whitefrs. st. Fleet st
Kennett Geo. Bagot, who. druggist, see Forster, Kennett & Co
Kennett James, carpenter, 1 Penton st. Walworth road
Kennett John, fishmonger, 48 Chapel st. Somers town
Kennett John, grocer, 20 Shadwell High st
Kennett John, grocer & italian wa. 4 Pont st. Belgrave sq
Kennett Maria (Mrs.), coffee rooms, 2 Clifton st. Finsbury
Kennett Richard Jas. bookseller, 14 York st. Covent garden
Kennett Thos. news agent & printer, 44 Church st. Minories
Kennett Thomas, solicitor, 7 Chatham pl. Blackfriars
Kennett Wm. italian warehouse, 25 Lamb st. Spitalfields
Kennett Wm. watchmaker, 8 Wellington pl. East st. Walwh
Kenney Ephraim, bricklayer, 5 Glo'ster mews ea. Portmn. sq
Kenney Patrick, chandler's shop, 8 Yeates court, Carey st
Kenney Patrick, tailor, 198 Blackfriars road
Kenney Robert, school, 11 Upper Kennington lane
Kenning George Thos. builder & beer retlr. Wandsworth rd
Kennion Robert Winter, barrister, 43 Oxford terrace, & 23 Old square, Lincoln's inn
Kenny James, *Red Lion* P.H. 6 White horse alley, Cowcross
Kenny Mary (Miss), school, 4 Bedford pl. Commercial road
Kenny Michael, fruiterer, &c. 1 Farringdon market
Kenny Wm. Dav. academy, 3 & 4 Wellington pl. St. John's wd
Kenrick Henry, chemist, 21 Gibson st. Waterloo road
Kenrick John, hairdresser, 12 Waterloo st. Camberwell
Kenrick Martin, bookseller, 83 Long lane, Smithfield
Kensal Green Cemetery, office (George William Henry Croft, sec.), 95 Gt. Russell st. Bloomsbury
Kensington & King, wine & spirit merchants, 24 Eastcheap
Kensington, Paines' & Young, colonial brokers, 9 Mincing la
Kensington Dispensary, 13 Holland st. Kensington
Kensington & Brompton Savings' Bank (Chas. Chesterton, sec.), National School ho. Mayfield pl. High st. Kensingtn
Kensington Edward, barrister, 13 Chancery lane
Kensington Edward, merchant, 9 Mincing lane
Kensington Fredk. wine merchant, see King & Kensington
Kensit Henry, jun. solicitor, 29 Bedford row, Bloomsbury
Kensit Thos. Glover, solicitor, Skinners' hall, 8 Dowgate hil
Kent & Bull, linendrapers, 164 New Bond st
Kent John & Co. blackg. ms. South st. Long la. Bermondsey
Kent John Jas. & Co. brushmakers, &c. 11 Gt. Marlboro' st
Kent Mrs. & Miss, ladies' school, 60 Dempsey st. Stepney
Kent Thos. & Co. paint brush ma. & gen. warehomn. 6 & 7 Falcon st
Kent Thos. & Co. horsehair mfs. 28 Southmptn. mews, Euston sq
Kent & Sussex Whf. John Humphery, Montague close, Boro'
Kent Alfred, chemist, 2 Thomas pl. Gravel lane, Borough
Kent Benjn. *Private Family hotel*, 32 Norfolk st. Strand
Kent Caroline (Mrs.), beer retailer, 318 Albany rd. Cambrw
Kent Chas. coal dealer, 43 Tottenham st. Fitzroy square
Kent Edmund Hy. *Prince of Wales* P.H. 10 Church st. Knsngtn
Kent George, blind mak. 14 Constitution row, Gray's inn rd
Kent George, butcher, 22 Upper King st. Bloomsbury
Kent George, gasfitter, 10 Drury court, Drury lane
Kent George, merchant, 122 London wall
Kent James, coach painter, 31 Kenton st. Brunswick square
Kent James, coffee rooms, 19 Strutton ground, Westminster
Kent James, lighterman, 8 Commercial pl. Commercial rd
Kent John, bootmaker, 1 Cottage place, Newington butts
Kent John, fruiterer, 80 Upper Ebury st. Pimlico
Kent John, manufacturing chemist, see Howards' & Kent
Kent John, steel mill maker, 8 Noble st. Goswell st
Kent John King, conveyancer, 28 Essex st. Strand
Kent John Walter, oil & colorman, 4 Stepney Old road
Kent Joseph, tobacco pipe ma. 19 Blue Anchor all. Bunhill rw
Kent Mary (Mrs.), ladies' school, 13 Upper Phillimore place

Kent Robert, grocer, 12 Freeschool st. Horselydown
Kent Robert Thomas, barrister, 15 Serjeants' inn, Fleet st
Kent Samuel Luck, upholsterer, &c. see Luck, Kent & Cumming
Kent Stephen, carpenter, 13 Claremont place, Judd st
Kent Stephen, *Monarch* coffee rooms, 29 Lime st
Kent Thomas, butcher, 99 St. John st. road
Kent Thomas, chemist & druggist, 226 Blackfriars road & 10 St. George's place, Walworth road
Kent Thomas, dining rooms, 23 High road, Knightsbridge
Kent Thomas, teadealer, 54 Fore st. Cripplegate
Kent Thomas Fassett, barrister, 6 Serle st. Lincoln's inn
Kent Wm. bootmaker, 17 Crown court, Pall mall
Kent Wm. saddler & harness maker, 23 Ebury st. Pimlico
Kent Wm. Abbott, silk & velvet manufacturer, 7 Milk st
Kent Wm. Dixon, solicitor, 28 Essex st. Strand
Kent Wm. James, stationer & toy wa. 7 Brewer st. Golden sq
Kent W. T. shell fishmonger, 93 Fenchurch st
Kentish Henry, shoeing smith, 96 Westbourne st. Pimlico
Kentish Sarah (Mrs.), oil & colorwa. 10 Carey st. Linc. inn
Kentish Thomas, academy, 8 Thurlow place, Hackney rd
Kentish Thomas, fruiterer, 29 Rathbone place, Oxford st
Kentish Wm. engraver, see Rowe, Kentish & Osborne
Kentish Wm. greengrocer, 3 Junction place, Kentish town
Kenton Eliz. (Miss), tobacconist, Southampton st. Cmberwell
Kenworthy John & Co. carriers by railway, Axe inn, 20 Aldermanbury, & Railway station, Camden town
Kenyon John Robt. barrister, 11 New square, Lincoln's inn
Kenyon Robert, laceman & glover, 15 Blackfriars road
Kenyon Susnh. (Mrs.), haberd. & hosier, 5 Lit. Nwpt. st. Lg. acre
Kenyon Thomas, patten maker, 6 Haddon pl. Waterloo road
Keogh Dennis, surgeon, 69 Millbank st. Westminster
Keogh Henry, confectioner, 22 Gilbert st. Oxford st
Keogh Thomas, barrister, 20 Orchard st. Portman square
Keohan Thomas, optician, 2 Arbour ter. Commercial rd. east
Keough Jas. tobacconist & carman, 27 Mill lane, Tooley st
Keough Timothy, dairy & carman, 9 Goat st. Horselydown
Kepp Richard & Edward, copper & platina smiths, 40, 41 & 42 Chandos st. Covent garden
Keppell Harriet (Miss), boarding house, 1 Upper Gower st
Ker Alan, barrister, 7 New square, Lincoln's inn
Ker Charles Hen. Bellenden, barrister, 8 Old sq. Lincoln's inn
Ker Thos. agt. to Bell, Rannie & Co. wine mer. 49 Pall mall
Ker Thos. C. solr. & parliamty. agt. 5 Verulam bdgs. Gray's inn
Kerbey Charles, newsvender, 8 Pleasant row, Stepney green
Kerby & Hiscocks, boot & shoe makers, 19 Charles st. & 70 Opera colonnade, Haymarket
Kerby Eleanora (Mrs.), newsvender, 5 Gt. Ryder st. St. James
Kerby John, bookseller & stationer, see Bowdery & Kerby
Kerby John, watch springer & liner, 3 Berkley ct. Clerkenwell
Kerby Wm. oilman & registrar, & agent to the *County* fire office, 40 Leman st. Goodman's fields
Kerley John, fruiterer, 21 Everett st. Brunswick square
Kerley Robert, berlin wa. 10 Marchmont st. Brunswick sq
Kerly Mary Ann & Son, lapidaries, 4½ Clerkenwell close
Kerly & Ware, attorneys, 5 Gray's inn square
Kerly John, baker, 212 Shoreditch High st
Kernan John, seedsman & florist, 4 Gt. Russell st. Cov. gdn
Kernot John, attorney, 7 Welbeck st. Cavendish square
Kerr & Jones, milliners, corset & dress makers, 19 Ludgate hill
Kerr Peter & Son, wire thread manfs. 115 Fore st. Cripplegt
Kerr & Scott, shawl mnfs. & warehousem. 31 St. Paul's ch. yd
Kerr Benjamin, upholsterer, 28 Clifton st. north, Finsbury
Kerr Crawford Davison, merchant, Lloyd's
Kerr Hen. coal mercht. & wharfinger, 13 East road, City rd
Kerr James, baker, 8 Great Cumberland st. Portman sq
Kerr James, chair & sofa manuf. 20½ Clipstone st. Fitzroy sq
Kerr Jas. glass & emery paper ma. 20½ Clipstone st. Fitzroy sq
Kerr James, tailor, 10 Great Vine st. Regent st
Kerr James, potato salesman, Hay's wharf, Tooley st. Boro'
Kerr James, veterinary surgeon, 6 Princes st. Cavendish sq
Kerr John, baker, 1 New st. St. Thomas st. east, Boro'
Kerr Thomas, N. insur. & genl. commission agent, 51 Lime st
Kerr Wm. auctioneer, 51 Little Broad st. London docks
Kerr Wm. H. bookseller, & statnr. 32 Duke st. Manchester sq
Kerr Wm. furniture bro. 51 Anchor & Hope alley, Wapping
Kerr Wm. milliner, 234 Blackfriars road
Kerrell Samuel, cheesemonger, 12 Old st. St. Luke's
Kerrey Peter Philip, fruiterer, 34 Elizabeth st. Eaton sq
Kerrey William, greengrocer, 7 Lower st. Islington
Kerridge David, bricklayer, 8 Great Peter st. Westminster
Kerridge Geo. *Wilton Arms* P.H. 10 Kinnerton st. Belgrave sq
Kerridge James, *Bedford Arms*, P.H. 13 South st. Manches. sq
Kerridge Wm. John, cheesemonger, 10 Artillery pas. Sptflds
Kerrins Michael Joseph, cowkeeper, 20 Lisson grove north
Kerrison John, *Bull Inn tap*, 91 Bishopsgate within
Kerrison Robert Master, physician, 12 New Burlington st
Kerry & Forrest, tailors & habit makers, 20 Cork st. Bond st
Kerry George, linendraper, 21 Bishopsgate without
Kerry Wm. wine & brandy mer. 9 Up. Brook st. Grosvenor sq
Kerschner Fredk. Chas. *Castle* P.H. 1 Albion pl. Holloway rd
Kerschner John, barrister, 4 Middle Temple lane
Kersey Caleb, bricklayer, 20 North Wharf rd. Padgton. basin
Kersey John, conveyancer, 24 Euston square
Kersey Oliver, bricklayer, 6 Hall place, Paddington
Kersey Robert bootmaker, 11 Deptford Broadway
Kersey Robert, bootmaker, 1 Deptford High st.
Kershaw George, ivory, bone & hardwood turner, engine turner, steel pen maker & fanmaker, manufacturer of letter clips, Cowell's clamps & bill files, 17 Wildernessrw. Clknw.
Kerslake Chas. tin plate worker, 1 Tudor pl. Tottenham ct. rd
Kerslake Geo. ladies' shoe maker, 57 Stanhope st. Clare mrkt
Kersting Frances (Mrs.), dressmaker, 66 Mortimer st
Kerswell Wm. straw bonnet ma. 15 Robert st. Grosvenor sq
Kerwin James, stockbroker, 13 Angel court, Throgmorton st
Kerwood John Joseph, coffee rooms, 9 Blenheim st. Oxford st
Kesby John, *Red Lion* P.H. 30 Whitechapel High st
Kesner Isaac, furniture broker, 95 Waterloo road
Kesnor Barnett, tailor, see Moses & Kesnor
Kesten George, tailor & habit maker, 67 Dean st. Soho
Kesten Henry George, tobacconist, 6 Green st. Leicester sq
Kesterton Thomas & Edwin, coach builders, 80 Long acre
Kesterton Richard, lithographic printer, 21 Blackman st
Kesteven (Shepley & Thomas), warehousemen, 21 Milk st
Keston Eliza (Miss), milliner, 67 Old Compton st. Soho
Ketchlee Stephen, tailor & draper, 73 Cornhill
Ketley William, bricklayer, 40 Union st. Whitechapel rd
Kettelty Abraham, tailor, 9 Dean st. Fetter lane
Ketteman Henry, pork butcher, 15 High st. Camberwell rd
Ketteringham Charles, cowkeeper, 10 John's pl. Chelsea
Kettle John & Richard, carriers, Somerset ter. Kensington
Kettle Charles, bookseller, 255 High Holborn
Kettle Fred. paper stainer, 131 St. Alban's pl. Edgw. rd
Kettle George, baker, 216 Upper Thames st
Kettle Henry Fred. surgeon, 16 Calthorpe st. Gray's inn rd
Kettle John, hairdresser, 61 Chalton st. Somers town
Kettle John L. Ross, barrister, 89 Chancery lane
Kettle Rupert, barrister, 8 Mitre ct. chambers, Fleet st
Kettle Wm. bookseller & newsvender, 13 Lit. Queen st. Hlbn
Kettlewell Richard, coal merchant, 65 Bankside, Southwark
Kettlewell Thomas merchant, 15 Angel ct. Throgmorton st
Kettlewell Wm. sec. to Ionian bank, 6 Great Winchester st
Kevan Nathl. plumber & glazier, 4 London ter. Hackney rd
Kevan Peter, slater, 11 Magdalen st. Bermondsey st.
Kew William Henry, wine merchant, 5 Mill st. Hanover sq
Kewell Ann (Miss), outftr. 41 Bridgeho. pl. Newington causy
Kewell William, solicitor, see Gregson & Kewell
Kewney Maria (Mrs.), perfumer, 6 Lower Eaton st. Pimlico
Key Benjamin, oil & colorman, 82 Drury lane
Key Charles Aston, surgeon, 18 St. Helen's pl. Bishopsgate
Key David Alexander, baker, 6 Great Bath st. Clerkenwell
Key Geo. Thos. cheesemonger, 59 New Cut, Lambeth
Key Henry Garrett, merchant, 5 Tokenhouse yard
Key James, bookbinder, 7 Oxford arms pssge. Newgate st
Key James, oil & colorman & blacking ma. 31 Gt. Prescot st
Key James, plumber, 13 Paul st. Finsbury
Key John, cattle salesman, 41 West Smithfield
Key John, cheesemonger, 105 Junction ter. Edgware road
Key John, confectioner, 43 Homer street, Marylebone
Key John, who. slopseller, 21 Lit. Prescot st. Goodman's fi
Key Joseph, uphol. & ho. agent, 18 Brook st. Grosvenor sq
Key Kingsmill Grove, who. statnr. 9 King's arms yd. Colemn. st
Key Louisa (Mrs.), *Old King's Head* P.H. 91 Upp. st. Islgtn
Key Thomas, baker, 10 Melton st. Euston square
Key Thomas, island lead works, Commercial rd Limehouse
Key Thomas, military musical instrument maker to her Majesty, the royal dukes, & the army, 20 Charing cross
Key William, baker, 1 Cardington st. Hampstead road
Key William, cheese agent, 1 & 2 Wharfs, York rd. City rd
Key Wm. stockbroker, 11 Shorter's ct. & 2 Maiden la. Qn. st
Key Wm. Dundas, surgeon, 32 Brudenell pl. New North rd
Key William, warehouseman, 19 New st. square, Fetter la
Keyes Aaron, surgeon, 14 Duke st. Lincoln's inn fields
Keyes George Thomas, builder, 6 Gray st. Manchester sq
Keyes Henry, wine & spirit merchant, 24 Frith st. Soho
Keyes John, *Horse & Groom* P.H. Mare st. Hackney
Keylock Wm. (Mrs.), dressmaker, 30 Old Bond st
Keymer J. & Co. silk printers & com. agts. 11 Wood st. City
Keymer Abraham, *City of Paris* P.H. Old Ford
Keymer Dl. *Norfolk Arms* P.H. Willmst. Hartsla. Bthnl. gr. rd
Keymer John, stationer, engrvr. & printer, 33 Bread st. Chpside
Keynton John, bookbinder, 8 Regent st. City road
Keyton Samuel, fruiterer & coal dlr. 5 Gt. Sutton st. Clkwl

Keys Wm.&Co.linendrapers,6 Roberts pl.Commercl.rd.East
Keys Avis (Mrs.), coffee rooms, 109 Lambeth walk
Keys Geo.sec.of *Guardian Fire & Life Assu.C.*11 Lombard st
Keys John, wine merchant, see Maxwell & Keys
Keys Thomas, gasfitter, 6 Great James st. Lisson grove
Keysell Francis, who.cheesemonger,7 Broad st.Bloomsbury
Keyser Moses S. & Co.whol.boot & shoe agents, 2&3 Aldgate
Keyser Alfred, surgeon, 21 Norfolk crescent, Oxford sq
Keyser Henry, barrister, 1 Plowden buildings, Temple
Keyte Edwin, linen draper, 5 New Gloucester pl. Hoxton
Keyte John, butcher, 1 Ashley terrace, City road
Keyte Joseph, beer retailer, 6 Marlborough road, Chelsea
Keyworth George,cutler & steel worker,19 York st. Westmr
Keyworth James, cutler, 4 Leather lane, Holborn
Kiallmark Geo. Fredk. prof. of music, 29 Percy st.Tott.ct.rd
Kibbell Benjn. butcher, 5 Wallington pl. Wandsworth rd
Kibble Amos, currier, see Hemsworth, Kibble & Lindley
Kibble James, baker, 11 High st. Camberwell
Kibble Wm. coal & potato warehouse, 9 Bloomsbury market
Kibby Elizh.(Mrs.),sailmaker&outfitter,116 Cockhill,Ratlff
Kibler Richd. shoemaker, 4 Jupp's ter. Commercial road
Kid James, wharfinger, King's mills, Rotherhithe
Kidd, Gemmille & Bemand, linendrapers & silk mercers,120 Tottenham court road, & 32 & 33 Grafton st. Fitzroy sq
Kidd (Houston) & Co. scotch whiskey impts. 70 Mark lane
Kidd David, merchant, 70 Mark lane
Kidd George, saddler & harness ma. see Wilkinson & Kidd
Kidd John George, surgeon, 31 Ashley crescent, City road
Kidd Joseph, *Vine* P.H. Vine yard, Tooley st
Kidd Wm.agt.toIsaacCookson&Co.RedBullwfUp.Thamesst
Kidd William, artist, 25 Acton st. Gray's inn lane
Kiddell John, carpenter, 61 Britannia row, Lr.st.Islington
Kidder Arthur, dairyman, 27 Grosvenor row, Pimlico
Kiddle Jane (Mrs.), grocer, 19 Cloth fair, Smithfield
Kiddle John Verender, plumber, 4 Elder st. Norton folgate
Kiddle John Lambert, chemist, 60 Lamb's Conduit st
Kiddle Letitia (Mrs.),coffee rooms,20 Buckingham pl.Fitz.sq
Kiddle Mary (Mrs.), ladies' school, 18 Suffolk pl. Hackn. rd
Kiddy Thos. livery stables, 11 Stanhope ter. Hyde pk. grdns
Kidner George, butcher, 23 Bedford st. Bedford row
Kidner George, *Wheatsheaf* P.H. 4 Upper Marylebone st
Kidner Job, butcher, George st. Deptford New town
Kidner John, shipping butcher, 21 Bermondsey wall
Kidner Samuel, butcher, 10 Millpond st. Bermondsey
Kidston Wm. medical shop fixture ma.4 North st. Mile end rd
Kidwell Emma (Miss),ladies' schl.10 Aldenham ter.Pancrs.rd
Kiernan Francis, surgeon, 20 Manchester st. Manchester sq
Kiff Thomas, ham & beef shop, 22½ Camberwell High st
Kift John, hairdresser, 15A, Hertford st. Fitzroy sq
Kightley Edmd. Fred. cowkeeper, 13 Chester ter. Chester sq
Kightley Edward Saml. cowkeeper, 66 Wilsted st. Somers tn
Kightley Edward Thos. Shorter, solicitor, 8 St. Swithin's la
Kightley Elizabeth (Mrs.), cowkeeper, 5 London st. Fitzroy sq
Kightly Charles, fruit salesman, 6 Borough market
Kightly John, orange merchant, 15 Pudding la. Eastcheap
Kilbee Wm. Thos. beer retailer, 21 New Manor st. Chelsea
Kilbey Henry, cheesemonger, 35 Edwards st. Portman sq
Kilbourn William, fruiterer, Southampton st. Camberwell rd
Kilburn Benjamin, east in.broker, see Norton, Kilburn & Co
Kilburn George, beer retailer, Mill wall, Poplar
Kilburn William, *Crown* P.H. 24 Redcross st. Cripplegate
Kilby Thomas & Co. colonial brokers, 132 & 133 Fenchurch st
Kilby Henry, grocer, 2 Thornton st. Horselydown
Kilby James, carcase butcher, 63 Aldgate High st
Kilby John, smith, 8 Brook hill, Clerkenwell
Kilby Samuel, chandler's shop, 2 Talbot ct. Gracechurch st
Kilby Samuel, coal merchant, 25 Love lane, Eastcheap
Kilby Thomas, undertaker, 2 Talbot court, Gracechurch st
Kilgour Geo. Alex. solicitor, see Burchell, Kilgour & Parson
Kilkenny, Carlow & Wicklow Railway, 449 West Strand
Killbe William, ship agent, 52 Lime st. City
Killby Andrew, meat salesman, Leadenhall market
Killett Eliz. (Mrs.), court dress ma. 16 Percy st. Totnm.ct.rd.
Killhams Geo. furn. undertaker, 44 East st. Walworth rd
Killick & Webb, hardwaremen, 9 Knightsbridge terrace
Killick, Winstanley & Co. stock & share agts.6 Bank chambrs
Killick George, farrier, New cross, Deptford
Killick George, merchant, 2 Brabant court, Philpot lane
Killick Jas.silverm.& jeweller,21 St. George's pl. Knightsbr
Killick John, merchant, 2 Brabant court, Philpot lane
Killick John, warehouseman, 21 New st. square, Fetter lane
Killick Richard, bootmaker, Broadway, Deptford
Killick Richard, coal merchant, 8 Bennet st. Blackfrs. rd
Killwick Wm.haberdasher,19½ Northampton pl. Old Kent rd
Kilner Ellen (Mrs.), stationer, 109 Gt. Russell st. Bloomsby
Kilner Richard, whol. confectioner, 4 Hanway st. Oxford st
Kilner William, cabinet maker, 83 Drury lane
Kilpack Thomas, cigar divan, 42 King st. Covent garden
Kilpatrick John, jeweller, 2 Northampton square
Kilpatrick John, jeweller, 7 King's ter. Bagnigge wells rd
Kilpen Wm. marine store dealer, 8 Star corner, Bermondsey
Kilrush, Dublin & Belfast Junction Railway Company, 14 Pinner's hall, Old Broad st. City
Kilsby Edward, timber merchant, Vauxhall walk, Lambeth
Kilsby Joseph, *Ship & Blue Coat Boy* P.H. 15 Keen'srw. Wlw rd
Kilvington Thos. ham&teadealer, 20 Lit.St. Thomas Apostle
Kilvington Thos. *Rose & Crown* P.H.113 Long la.Bermondsy
Kimbell Ann (Mrs.),furn. broker, 13 & 14 Vine st.Hatton wall
Kimbell Thomas, watchmaker, &c. 214 Tottenham court rd
Kimbell Wm. coal dealer, 6 Church st. Newington
Kimber Edward, bookbinder, see Smith & Kimber
Kimber James & Co. advertising agt. 8 St. Benet's pl. Grach. st
Kimber Robert, butcher, 45 Bell yard, Temple bar
Kimber Stephen, coffee rooms, 15 Cleveland st. Fitzroy sq
Kimber Susan (Mrs.), milliner, 8 Crown st. Finsbury
Kimber Wm. desk & dressing case mak. 5 King st. Holborn
Kimber Wm. Monckton, plumber, 95 Westbourne st. Pimlico
Kimberley Joseph H. baker, 39 St. John's wood terrace
Kimble Robert, shoemaker, 27 Great Marylebone st
Kime Wm. Thos. special pleader, 4 Essex court, Temple
Kimlin John, tailor, 33 High st. Kensington
Kimm Abm. mast, oar, block, pump, &c. maker, 274 Wapping
Kimmins Thos. fruiterer, 10 Great hall, Hungerford market
Kimpton Benjamin, bookseller, 8 Hand court, Holborn
Kimpton Edward, bookseller, 68 Gt. Russell st. Bloomsbury
Kimpton Edward, stationer, see Edgcomb & Kimpton
Kimpton Edward Down, baker, 10 Upper Eaton st. Pimlico
Kimpton Elizth. (Miss), linendra. see Taverner & Kimpton
Kimpton George, *Steelyard* P.H. 88 Upper Thames st
Kimpton Joseph, jun. ship broker, see Barnett & Kimpton
Kimpton Richard, bookseller, 31 Wardour st. Soho
Kimpton Robert, jeweller, 2 Jewin crescent, Cripplegate
Kimpton Thomas, linendraper, 18 High st. Newngtn. butts
Kinahan, Sons & Smyth, *LL* whisky, wine, dublin stout, & ale merchants, 24 & 25 King William st. Strand
Kincaid John W. mercht. & agent, 9 Steel yd. Up. Thames st
Kincaid Sophia (Mrs.) *Simpson's tav. & hot.* Ball ct. 38½ Crnh
Kinchin Wm. lighterman, 28 Great Hermitage st. Wapping
Kinchlow Elizth. (Mrs.), corn dealer, 4 James st. Oxford st
Kind Moses, boot & shoe maker, 3 Snow's flds. Bermondsey
Kindell George, baker, 89 Broad st. Ratcliff
Kinder & Sorrell, solicitors, 25 Jewry st. Aldgate
Kinder William & Son, varnish makers & painters, 14 Avery row, Grosvenor st
Kinder Richard, printer, 2 Green Arbour court, Old Bailey
Kinder Wm. Sidney, solicitor, 23 Southampton buildings
Kinderley, Denton & Kinderley, solicitors, 6 New sq. Linc. inn
Kindersley Rd. Torin, queen's counsel, 3 Stone bldgs. Linc. inn
Kindley Mary A. (Mrs), milliner, 20 Gloster ter. Vauxhl. br. rd
Kindon James, floorcloth manufacturer, see Bathe & Kindon
Kine & Martin, solicitors, 19 Gracechurch st
Kine John, carpenter & undertaker, 14 Sale st. Paddington
King Joseph Curtis & Co. tea deals. 25 South st. Mncstr. sq
King Albert & Co. tea dealers, 98 High st. Borough
King & Attwaters, attorneys, 27 Queen st. Cheapside
King Harriet & Charlotte, fishmgrs. 10 High st. Newington
King & Fearnley, oil merchants, 6 Vine st. Minories
King & Henry, grocers, 13 Providence pl. Kentish town
King Henry & Edward, coach maks. 9 Moor la. Cripplegate
King Henry Samuel & Co. wholesale & retail stationers, printers & engravers, & genl. label ma. 93 Fleet st
King John & Son, leather cutters, 44½ Bedfordbury, & 7 Henrietta st. Manchester sq
King & Kensington, wine & spirit merchants, 24 Eastcheap
King, Melvil & Co. corn factors, 28 Fenchurch st
King (Mrs. & Miss), ladies' school, 47 Old Broad st. City
King Robert & Son, booksellers, 21 Jewin st. Cripplegate
King & Sheath, linen drapers & silk mercers, 264 Regent st
King & Spencer, pawnbrokers, 5 Mary st. Hampstead rd
King Susanna & Co. stay makers, 39 Lamb's Conduit st
King Th.& Son, shipbuilds. Nelson dock, 1 L. Queen st. Rothrh
King Thos. & Wm. merchants, 37 Great Winchester st
King Wm. & Co. builders, 11 Wells row, Upper st. Islington
King Wm. & Henry, coach builders, 119 Shoreditch
King Wm. Read & Son, solicitors, 1 New sq. Lincoln's inn
King William & Thomas K. irish chancery, exchequer & law court commissioners, & for registry of irish deeds, 10 Southampton buildings, Holborn
King Abraham, carpenter & builder, 16 Gt. Winchester st
King Abraham, smith, 5 York st. York road, Lambeth
King Alexr. grocer & oilman, 11 Commercial pl. Kentish tn
King Alfred, oilman, see Glackner & King

King Alfred, M.D. surgeon, 4 Gray's inn lane
King Alice (Mrs.), chair stuffer, 1 New North st. Finsbury
King Ambrose, teadealer, 6 Up. Seymour st. Euston squar
King Ann (Mrs), stock maker, 2 Savoy st. Strand
King Augustus, carpenter, &c. 5 Bowling st. Westminster
King Benjamin, brushmaker, 16 Charles st. Manchester sq
King Benj. cowkeeper, &c. 54 Gt. Windmill st. Haymarket
King Berkeley, lithog. draftsman, 2 Francis st. Bedford sq
King Caroline (Mrs.), dressmaker, 11 Leigh st. Burton cresc
King Chas. architect, 24 University st. Tottenham court rd
King Chas. butcher, 40 Store st. Bedford square
King Chas. chairmaker, 133 Southwark Bridge road
King Chas. statuary & mason, 13 Chenies st. Bedford sq
King Chas. straw bleacher & presser, 1 Oxford market
King Chas. tinman & pewterer, 22 Cock lane, Smithfield
King Chas. undertaker, 21 New Compton st. Soho
King Chas. *White Hart tav.* 276 Oxford st
King Chas. who.mftg.goldsmith, 4 Owen's row, St. John st.rd
King Charles, wholesale & retail agent for Abernethy's pile ointment, "Paul's every man's friend," and Abernethy's pile powders, also every patent medicine of repute, Napier st. Hoxton New town
King Chas. Allen, solicitor, 7 Gray's inn square
King Chas. M. inspect.of Spanish transports, 40 St. Mary Axe
King Chas. Morris, solicitor, 40 St. Mary Axe
King Charles Stafford, solicitor, 15 Serjeants' inn, Fleet st
King Daniel, upholsterer, 16 Ampton st. Gray's inn rd
King David, dyer, 71 High st. Camden town
King David, plumber, painter & glazier, 2 Duke st. Aldgate
King Edward, beer retailer, 27 Denmark st. Soho
King Edward, cheesemonger, 74 Hackney road
King Edward Hen. gen. salesman, 54 Tothill st. Westminster
King Edward T. wine merchant, see Kensington & King
King Eliza (Mrs.), dress & stay ma. 44 North st. Edgware rd
King Elizabeth (Mrs.), dyer & scourer, 44 Essex st. Strand
King Francis, dining rooms, 130 Lambeth walk
King Francis, *Earl of Chatham* P.H. Hughes' fields, Deptd
King Francis, oil & colorman, 56 Wells st. Oxford st
King Francis, tailor, 14 Spencer st. Canonbury square
King Fredk. who. stay & shoe maker, 45 St. John st. Clerknwl
King George, boot & shoe maker, 4 Queen st. King's rd. Chelsea
King George, builder, &c. 6 Cain place, Kentish town
King George, carpenter, 5 Chichester rents, Chancery lane
King George, coffee rooms, 181 Borough High st
King George, dairyman, 17 Marlborough mews, Blenheim st
King George, fishmonger, 92 Lambeth lower marsh
King George, furniture broker, 30 Broomfields, Deptford
King George, floorcloth, carpet, &c. wareho. 31 Goswell rd
King George, oil & colorman, 2 Oxford pl. Westminster road
King George, plumber, 205 Wapping High st
King George, *Red Lion* P.H. 31 Chamber st. Goodman's fi
King George, tallow chandler & melter, 28 Mint st. Borough
King George, undertaker, George st. Camberwell
King George, who. brushmaker, 116 Bunhill row, Chiswell st
King Hannah (Mrs.), grocer, 9 Collier st. Pentonville
King Hannah R. (Miss), lace wareho. 5 Sydney alley, Les'ter sq
King Harriet & Charlotte, fishmgrs. 10 High st. Newington
King Henry, baker, 62 Berners st. Oxford st
King Henry, baker, 106 Great Suffolk st. Borough
King Henry, cheesemonger, Church st. Hackney
King Henry, livery stables, 17 Bathurst mews, Sussex sq
King Henry, meat salesman, 19 New Newgate market
King Henry, oil & colorman, 162 Shadwell High st
King Henry, special pleader, 9 King's Bench walk, Temple
King Isaac, carpenter & builder, 20 St. Mary Axe
King Isabella (Mrs.), *Angel* P.H. 165 Old Gravel la. Wapping
King Jacob, liv. stables & horse dlr. 29 Bridge st. Southwark
King James, brushmaker, 55 Carnaby st. Golden sq
King James, 5 Northampton pl. Canonbury sq
King James, cabinet maker, 18 Beer lane, Tower st
King James, clock maker, &c. 17 King's head ct. Shoreditch
King James, cornfactor, 79 New Corn Exchange, Mark la
King James, engraver, 3 John st. Holland st. Blackfriars rd
King James, grocer, 81 Seymour place, Bryanstone square
King James, lodginghouse keeper, 103 Jermyn st. St. James's
King James, perfumer, see Kennedy & King
King James, wholesale glover, 4 Little Love lane, Wood st
King Jane (Mrs.), boarding house & *Nerot's hotel*, 6 & 15 Clifford st. Bond st
King John, actuary of *Nth. British Ins. Co.* 10 Pall mall east
King John, artist, 21A, Soho square
King John, auctioneer & appraiser, 3 James pl. Hackney rd
King John, beer retailer, 92 Bunhill row
King John, *BlackSwan* P.H. 27 Lit. Carter la. Doctor's com
King John, cabinet maker, 29 Church st. Soho
King John, carpenter, 29 Clarendon st. Somers town
King John, carpenter, 5 Tonbridge st. New road
King John, coachbuilder, 119 Bunhill row, St. Luke's
King John, coach builder, Portland road
King John, conveyancer, 1 Woodland pl. St. John's wood
King John, dairy, 37 Well st. Oxford st
King John, dairyman, 6 Brydges st. Covent garden
King John, fishmonger, 2 York place, Westminster road
King John, fixture dealer, 30 Sidney pl. Commercial rd. east
King John, glass & lead merchant, see Chuck, King & Co
King John, grocer, 8 Everett st. Brunswick square
King John, grocer, 10 Upper Park place, Regent's park
King John, grocer, 13 Mount st. Walworth road
King John, grocer, 29 Neckinger st. Neckinger road
King John, meat salesman, 24 New Newgate Market
King John, music & bookseller, 22½ Crosby row, Walworth rd
King John, optician, 14 Belvedere buildings, Borough road
King John, patent medicine vender, 72 Queen st. Cheapside
King John, pork butcher, 165 Drury lane
King John, printer, 17 College hill, Upper Thames st
King John, *Queen's Head* P.H. 10 Keppel ter. King's rd. Chlse
King John, saddler, &c. 5 Chiswell st
King John, soap maker & tallow chandler, 44 Kingsland rd
King John, surgeon, 10 Portland terrace, Regent's park
King John, teacher of mathematics, 15 Charles sq. Hoxton
King John, upholsterer, 6 Charles st. Grosvenor square
King John, wholesale stationer, see Brown & King
King John B. carpenter & builder, 47 Old Broad st. City
King John Buckton, stockbroker, 3 Bartholomew la. Bank
King John Daniel, barrister, 3 Elm court, Temple
King John Jas. watch & clock ma. 14 Kingsland pl. Kngsld.rd
King John V. herald painter, 7 Beaufort ter. King's rd. Chlse
King John William, artist, 40 Gerrard st. Soho
King Jonathan, tobacconist, 45 Chapel st. Somers town
King Joseph, baker, 18 Vauxhall row, Vauxhall
King Joseph, boat builder, 5 Limekiln hill, Limehouse
King Joseph, coach builder, 26 North Audley st
King Joseph, coach painter, 37 North row, Grosvenor sq
King Joseph, confectioner, 9 Bartholomew close
King Joseph, dairyman, Amwell cot. Amwell ter. Pentonvil
King Joseph, fruiterer, 4 Swallow place, Hanover sq
King Joseph, solicitor, 16 North buildings, Finsbury circus
King Joseph, surgeon, 4 Windmill st. Tottenham court road
King Joseph, tassel mould turnr. 11 Albion bldgs. Barthmw.cl
King Joseph Chas. furn. broker, 1&2 Wellington st. Kingsland
King Joseph Cutis, tea dealer, see Genge & King
King Lucy (Mrs.), newsvender & stationer, 32 Chancery lane, & 14 Great Turnstile
King Maria (Miss), juvenile dressmaker, 15 Aldgate
King Mary (Mrs.), grocer, 19 Up. Berkeley st. west, Edgwr. rd
King Mary (Mrs.), haberdasher, 17 Provinence pl. Kentsh. twn
King Mary Ann (Mrs.), lodging house, 18 Castle st. Falcon sq
King Mary Anne (Mrs.), straw hat ma. 65 Low. Sloane st. Chlse
King Matthew, haberdasher, 9 King's road, St. Pancras
King Matthew, linendraper, see Fenwick & King
King Matthias, tobacconist, 18 Kingsland road
King Nathaniel, *Red Cow* P.H. 13 Old Castle st. Bethnl. grn
King Nathaniel Sadler (secretary to the National Bank of Ireland), 13 Old Broad st. City
King Oliver Waterloo, *Hand & Flower* P.H. 25 Vale st. Kensgtn
King Osmer, surgeon, 37 Bernard st. Russell sq
King Richd. accountant & arbitrator, 30 King st. City
King Richard, chairstuffer & upholsterer, 25 & 26 Old st. road
King Richard, hairdresser, 40 Three Colt st. Limehouse
King Richard, insu. brok. 3 new city chamb. Bishopsgt. within
King Rd. physicn. (sec. to Ethnological So.), 27A, Sackville st
King Richard, umbrella & fishing tackle ma. 75 Cheapside
King Robert, baker, 23 York road, Lambeth
King Robert, east ind. & colonial broker, see Palmer & King
King Robert, herbalist, 153½ Union st. Borough
King Robert, wine merchant, see Gledstanes, King & Co
King Robert Collins, butcher, 54 Lamb's Conduit st
King Robert John, grocer & italian wa. 58 Mortimer st. Cav.sq
King Robert Wm. bookbinder, 32 Lit. Bartholomew close
King Samuel, beer retailer, 8 Calcutta pl. East India rd
King Samuel, bootmaker, 6 Hare court, Aldersgate st
King Samuel, dairy, 11 Collier st. Pentonville
King Samuel, solicitor, 22 Wilmington square, Spafields
King Sarah (Miss), straw hat manfr. 65 Blackfriars road
King Sarah (Mrs.), baker, 10 Wardour st. Soho
King Sarah (Mrs.), gasmeter ma. 21 Cock la. West Smithfield
King Stripling, grocer, 11 Kenton st. Brunswick sq
King Thomas, architect, 9 Burr st. East Smithfield
King Thomas, auctioneer, 11 Coleman st. City
King Thomas, auctioneer, &c. 1 Cottage place, City road
King Thomas, baker, 21 Broomfields, Deptford
King Thomas, baker, 41 Chapel st. Grosvenor place

King Thomas, baker, 24 Little st. Thomas Apostle
King Thomas, bread, &c. baker, 24 Little St. Thomas Apostle
King Thomas, butcher, 12 Paddington st. Marylebone
King Thomas, carrier & tobacconist, 4 Mayfield pl. Kensington
King Thomas, cheesemonger, 5 Charlotte terrace, New cut
King Thomas, currier, 8 York place, Portland town
King Thomas, currier & leathersel. 87 Crawford st. Portman sq
King Thomas, *Feathers* P.H. High st. Notting hill
King Thomas, furn. broker, 8 Weston place, King's cross
King Thomas, furn. broker, 9 Upper Rathbone place
King Thos. grocer & cheesemngr. 10 Robert st. Grosvnr. sq
King Thomas, italian warehouse, 10 Edwards' st. Portman sq
King Thomas, letter founder, 33 Hoxton square
King Thomas, meat salesman, Leadenhall market
King Thomas, *Rose* P.H. 2 Farringdon st. City
King Thomas, toy dealer & stationer, Church st. Hackney
King Thomas, watchmaker, 130 Minories
King Thomas Henry, engraver & zinc plate ma. 2 Smithfield
King Thomas Henry, hairdresser, 268 Bethnal green rd
King Thomas Kirwan, surgeon, 23 Addington pl. Cambrwll. rd
King Thomas Richard, artist, 5 Church row, Islington
King Thomas Wilkinson, surgeon, 36 Bedford sq
King Walter, cheesemonger, High st. Stoke Newington
King Wm. agt. to Imp. Brazilian govnt. see Goldsmid, King & Co
King Wm. baker, 16 Crucifix la. Bermndsy. & 98 Tooley st
King Wm. builder, 21 Manchester terrace, Liverpool road, & 12 Wells row, Islington
King Wm. builder, Stafford cottage, Palace st. Pimlico
King Wm. butcher, 16 Artichoke row, Mile end rd
King Wm. cabinetmaker, &c. 8 Woodstock st
King Wm. carpenter, 8 Up. Chapman st. St. George's east
King Wm. cattle salesman, 60 West Smithfield
King Wm. coach maker, 28 Woburn mews, Woburn pl
King Wm. *Coach Maker's Arms* P.H. Belgrave mews east
King Wm. coffee rooms, 14 Bath st. City rd
King Wm. fishmonger, 118 Drummond st. Euston sq
King Wm. fruiterer, 9 Wilmington pl. Spafields
King Wm. fruiterer, 16 Trafalgar st. Walworth rd
King Wm. furniture broker, 6 Chapel st. New rd
King Wm. furniture broker, 17 Devonshire st. Lisson grove
King Wm. goldsmith & jeweller, 34 Park st. Camden town
King Wm. grocer, see Madderson & King
King Wm. grocer & oilman, 36 & 37 Seymour st. Euston sq
King Wm. manufacturing jeweller, 18 Bridgewater sq
King Wm. meat salesman, 5 Newgate market
King Wm. muslin embroiderer, 32 New Church st. Lisson gro
King Wm. oil & colorman, Kensington gravel pits
King Wm. oil & colorman, 17 Marylebone la. Oxford st
King Wm. oil & italian warehouse, 127 Crawford st.; 100 High st. Camden town, & 98 High st. Notting hill
King Wm. painter & glazier, 78 Chalton st. Somers town
King Wm. pawnbroker & silversmith, 34 High Holborn
King Wm. solicitor, 27 Lincoln's inn fields
King Wm. surgeon, 4 Albion ter. White horse la. Stepney
King Wm. tobacconist, 75 Hoxton old town
King Wm. umbrella, &c. maker, Charlotte st. Portland pl
King Wm. wholesale clothes warehouse, see Sykes & King
King Wm. woollen manufacturer, 17 Gresham st. City
King Wm. Edward, silk mercer to her Majesty, 37 Pall Mall
King Wm. George, *Grapes* P.H. 38 Red Lion st. Holborn
King Wm. Grimwood, surgeon, 7 Thurlow pl. Hackney rd
King Wm. Henry, *Trinity Arms* P.H. Church st. Deptford
King Wm. Henry, *Cadogan Arms* P.H. King's rd. Chelsea
King Wm. Peter, grocer, 1 Spring ter. Wandsworth road
King Wm. Rose, type & stereotype foundr. 13 Newcastle st. Strnd
King Wm. Scott, *Three Mariners* P.H. 26 Bermondsey wall
Kingaby Alexander, lodging house, 3 Falcon st. City
Kingcombe Geo. let. press & cop. pl. printer, 129 High st. Cmdn. tn
Kingdon & Shephard, solicitors, 16 Clifford's inn
Kingdon Thomas K. special pleader, 5 Hare ct. Temple
Kindon William, solicitor, 13 Bedford row
Kingdon William, barrister, 5 Hare court, Temple
Kingdon Wm. surgeon, 2 New Bank buildings, Lothbury
Kinggett John, smith, 23 Little Albany st. Regent's park
Kingham & Jenson, varnish manufacturers, 37 Barbican
Kingham Wm. & Co. varnish ma. & colormen, 37 Barbican
Kingham Mary (Miss), dining rms. 26 Buckingham pl. Fitz. sq
Kingham Thirza (Miss), dressma. 4 Rawstone st. Brompton
Kingham Thomas, jun. baker, 55 St. Martin's lane
Kingham Thomas, sen. baker, 4 Old Fish st. City
Kingham Wm. corn & coal mer. see Burton & Co
Kinghorn John, wine merchant, 25 Philpot lane, City
Kinglake Alexander Wm. barrister, 24 Old sq. Lincoln's inn
Kinglake John Alex. serjt. at law, 3 Brick court, Temple
King's College, 160 Strand
King's College School, 160 Strand
King's College Hospital (Edward C. Stephens, sec.), 7 Portugal st. Lincoln's inn fields
Kings Wm. & Co. coach & harness makers, 100 & 101 Long acre
Kings (Mrs.), sticking plaister maker, see Reid & Kings
Kings William, coach maker, see Scoles & Kings
Kingsbury John, scaleboard cutter, 9 New st. Borough rd
Kingsbury Thomas, cutler & razor maker, 152 Regent st
Kingsbury Wm. shoemaker, 7 Sclater st. Bethnal green
Kingsford & Barnwell, millers, 4 Catherine ct. Tower hill
Kingsford & Lay, cornfactors, 3 Savage grdns. Crutched friars
Kingsford Thomas & Charles, corn & flour factors, 60 Mark lane; flour mills, Church st. Deptford pier; & biscuit bakers, Mill lane, Deptford
Kingsford Edward, manager of the Southwark branch of the London & Westminster bank, 3 Wellington st. Borough
Kingsford Frederick, chemist, 49 High st. Kensington
Kingsford James, solicitor, see Waterman, Wright & Co
Kingshot William, dairyman, 2 Baron st. Pentonville
Kingsland George, chemist, 22 King st. Covent garden
Kingsley & Adnam, wine & spirit merchts. 9 Old Fish st
Kingsman John, gasfitter, 1 Adam's pl. Borough High st
Kingsmill John, bootmaker, 48 Leonard st. Finsbury
Kingsmill Richd. boot & shoemaker, 52 St. John st. Clerkenwell
Kingsmill Thos. copper pl. printer, 26 Kirby st Hatton gard
Kingston John & Co. west india merchants, 3 Lime st. sq
Kingstons', Lambert & Egan, merchts. 14 Liverpool st. Bishpsgt
Kingston Daniel, butcher, 145 Bethnal green road
Kingston Henry, fruiterer, 66 Up. Ground st. Blackfriars
Kingston John, fruiterer, 2 Lisle st. Leicester sq
Kingston Jas. grocer & wax & tallow chan. 37 High st. Knsngtn
Kingston M.A. (Mrs.), *Swan with 2 necks* P.H. 6 Gt. Carter la
Kingston Peter Nugent, physician, 27 Curzon st
Kingston Saml. *Duke of York* P.H. Lark Hall la. Capham
Kingston Valentine, wine & spirit merchant, 9 York st. St. James's, & 11 Argyll place, Regent st
Kingston Wm. linendraper, silk mercer & shawl warehouseman, 21 Bridge road, & 19, 20 & 21 Felix st. Lambeth
Kington Geo. Hen. coal sack ma. 131 Southwark bdge. rd
Kington Mary Ann (Mrs.), lodging ho. 5 Lit. Ryder st. St. Jas's
Kingwell Frederick wheelwright, 17 Phœnix st. Soho
Kinipple John Topliff, *Plough* P.H. 32 Narrow st. Limehouse
Kinloch Henry Archibald, solicitor, 13 New inn, Strand
Kinloch Wm. cheesemong. to her Majesty, 48 Jermyn st. St. Jas's
Kinnear Charles, working jeweller, 16 Gerrard st. Soho
Kinnear George, merchant, see Ellice, Kinnear & Co
Kinner Thomas, *Adam & Eve* P.H. 29 St. John st. road
Kinnier James M.D. surgeon, 28 Dorset crescent
Kinsey James, leather dresser & dyer, 83 Bermondsey st
Kinsey Matthew, bedding warehouseman, 315 Oxford st
Kinsey William, solicitor, 20 Bloomsbury sq
Kinsley Thomas, surgical mechanist, 12 Up. St. Martin's la
Kinton Newbold, grocer & teadealer, 21 Lamb's Conduit st
Kipkins Joseph, bookbinder, 43 Cannon st. Ratcliffe highway
Kipling Jas. & Alfred, iron & steel agents, 22 Dowgate hill
Kipling John & Francis, who. carpet wa. 11 Addle st. Wood st
Kipling John Steward, solicitor, 8 City terrace, City road
Kipling Jonathan, grocer & tallow chandl. Church st. Hacky
Kipling Martha (Mrs.), shirtma. hosier & glovr. 197 Strand
Kipping Thos. gen. com. agt. 14 Pagoda ter. Bermnsdy. New rd
Kippins John, porkman, 129 Shadwell High st
Kippis George, stove maker, 55 Cromer st. Brunswick sq
Kipps & Fuge, coachmakers, 48 & 50 Gt. Marylebone st
Kipps Saml. Martin, painter & grainr. 3 Norfolk st. Mid. hos
Kipps & Walker, paper stainers, 43 Fenchurch st. & 51 Bridgehouse place, Borough, & Greenwich
Kirbey Geo. off. of palace ct. 125 Chnery. la. & 34 Surry st. Str
Kirby, Beard & Co. manufacturers of royal diamond patent & ne plus ultra pins, with perfect solid heads, royal diamond & ne plus ultra drilled eyed needles, and every description of pins, needles & fishhooks, by special appointment to her Majesty Queen Victoria and the Dowager Queen Adelaide, 46 Cannon st. & Gloucester
Kirby & Thwaites, tailors & drapers, 34A, Gt. Russell st. Blm
Kirby Edmund, oilman, 77 Long lane, Bermondsey
Kirby George, lodging house, 34 Surrey st. Strand
Kirby George Goldsmith, conveyancer, 11 Waterloo place
Kirby Jas. Fred. boot & shoe warehouse, 1 Whitechapel road
Kirby James Fredk. general agent, see Smith, Kirby & Co
Kirby Jas. Fredk. Wm. commission agent, 23½ Crosby Hall chambers, Bishopsgate
Kirby John, bootmaker, 17 High road, Knightsbridge
Kirby John, butcher, 14 Old Fish st. City
Kirby John, cabinet maker, 11 Oxford st. Mile end
Kirby John, jeweller, 11 King st. Hatton garden
Kirby John, shoe manufr. 9 Stepney rents, Hackney road
Kirby John, tailor, 39 Keppell st. Russell sq

Kirby John Blake, barrister, 5 Elm court, Temple
Kirby John Johnson, stay maker, 5 Claremont pl. Old Kent rd
Kirby Ralph Smith, booksl. & publishr. 18 Artillery pl. west
Kirby Thos. cheesemngr. & bacon fac. 10 Adam's row. Hampstead road, & 15 Mid. Queen's bldgs. Knightsbridge
Kirby Thomas Freesland, tailor, 13½ Aldersgate st
Kirby William, furniture broker, 5 Penton row, Walworth rd
Kirby William, gas fitter, 8 Grafton st. Soho
Kirby William, upholsterer, 23 York st. Westminster
Kirck Wm. ship agent, 17 London st. Fenchurch st
Kirk & Thompson, cochineal merchants, 20 Gt. St. Helen's
Kirk & Thompson, cochineal merchants, 8 Cross la. Idol lane
Kirk John, engraver, 9 Berkley st. Clerkenwell
Kirk John Joel, chron. engra. & tobact. 31 Clerkenwell gn
Kirk Lucy (Mrs.), dining rooms, 109 Oxford st
Kirk Peter, baker, 49 Tottenham court road
Kirk Thomas, butcher, James's place, Hoxton fields
Kirk Thomas, solicitor, 10 Symond's inn, Chancery lane
Kirk William, law stationer, 38 Carey st
Kirk William, snuff manufacturer, 101 Fleet st
Kirkaldy John & Son, plumbers, painters, &c. 217 Wapping
Kirkaldy Alex. printer & engrav. 1 Fowke's bldgs. Gt. Tower st
Kirkaldy Robert A. printer, 20 Cullum st
Kirkbride Jas. *British Lion* P.H. 34 Redcross st. Borough
Kirkbride John, tailor, 11½ Wellington st. north, Strand
Kirkby Edward, jobmaster, 17½ Adam st. west, Bryanstone sq
Kirkby Samuel, baker, 45 Crawford st. Portman square, & 8 Cumberland row, King's cross
Kirkby Wm. baker, 102 Junction terrace, Edgware road
Kirke Joseph, nursery, Brompton park lane, Old Brompton
Kirke Philip, auctioneer, appraiser, &c. 19 Brompton row
Kirkham Arthur Leech, pawnbrok. & silversmith, 318 Strand
Kirkham John, civil engineer, 3 Tonbridge place, Euston sq
Kirkham Josiah, undertaker, 3 Royal st. Carlisle st. Lambeth
Kirkham Thos. birmingham, &c. agt. 61 King William st. City
Kirkham Wm. grocer, 29 Gt. College st. Camden town
Kirkland Sir John & Co. army agents, 80 Pall mall
Kirkland John, grocer & teadealer, 3 New st. Covent garden
Kirkland Joseph, coffee rooms, 40 St. John st. Smithfield
Kirkman Joseph & Son, pianoforte makers to her Majesty, 3 Soho sq. & 9 Dean st. Soho; manufactory, Dafours pl. Gldn. sq
Kirkham Wm. & Chris. teadlrs. & wine mers. 302 High Holborn
Kirkham Wm. & Co. ea. india col. & metal brok. 2 St. Dunstan's hi
Kirkman Geo. Buchanan, who. statr. see Renshaw & Kirkman
Kirkman Hyde, surveyor, 50 Green st. Grosvenor sq
Kirkman John, solicitor, clerk to the combmakers' company, 27 Laurence Pountney lane
Kirkman (Misses), milliners, 3 Rochester ter. Stoke Newtn
Kirkmann Abraham, barrister, 89 Chancery lane
Kirkness Jas. tinplate worker, 38 Gt. Prescot st. Goodman's fi
Kirkness John, copperplate printer, 26 Tonbridge st. New rd
Kirkpatrick & Cornell, linen drapers, 1 High st. Newington butts, & 3 New Portland place, Wandsworth road
Kirkpatrick Geo. actuary of *Law Life Assu. Soc.* 187 Fleet st
Kirkpatrick John, barrister, 5 King's bench walk, Temple
Kirkpatrick Samuel, teadealer, &c. 91 Queen st. Cheapside
Kirkpatrick Wm. *Geo. Canning* P.H. 1 Grovehill ter. Cambrwl
Kirkup Alfred, surgeon, 7 Vigo st. Regent st
Kirkup John, coal merchant, 47 Rotherhithe st
Kirkwood Alexander, M.D. surgeon, 66 Bridge road, Lambeth
Kirkwood John, surgeon, 12 Aldenham ter. & 77 Brewer st
Kirkwood Thos. pawnbroker, 67 & 68 Brick lane, St. Luke's
Kirlew Wm. jobmaster, 34 Woburn mews, Woburn pl. Tvstk. sq
Kirten Wm currier, 1 Marigold ct. Star corner, Bermondsey
Kirtland John, carpenter & joiner, 25 King sq. Goswell rd
Kirton Thos. Jos. & Co. white lead, col. & vrnsh. ms. 3 Bankside
Kirton James, corndealer, 12 Charles st. Middlesex hospital
Kirton Jas. statnr. & acc. book ma. 1 Gt. Portland st. Oxford st
Kirton Wm. coffee & chop rooms, 3 Peerless place, City road, & 4 Cumberland row, Battle bridge
Kirwan Andrew Valentine, barrister, 9 Inner Temple lane
Kirwood William, tailor, 4 Argyll st. Regent st
Kisch Joseph, surgeon, 2 Circus place, Finsbury circus
Kisch Moses, boot & shoe mak. 189 Bishopsgate st. without
Kisch Simon, tailor, 40 Cranbourn st. Leicester square
Kislingbury William & Co. merchants, 23 High Holborn
Kislingbury William, boot maker, 4 Weybridge pl. Mile end rd
Kiss William Daniel & Son, solicitors, 2 Fen ct. Fenchurch st. & 1 Glo'ster buildings, Walworth
Kiss Samuel, wax & wafer maker, 19 Charles st. Hatton gdn
Kissick John, bookseller & stationer, 10 Tottenham ct. road
Kitcat George & James, bookbinders, 50 Hatton garden
Kitchen & Moore, ironmongers, 23 & 24 High st. St. Giles's
Kitchen Benj. watch & clock ma. 32 Compton st. Brunswk. sq
Kitchen Daniel, gas fitter, 46 Crawford st. Portman sq
Kitchen George, cheesemonger, 92 Leather lane, Holborn
Kitchen John, grocer & cheesemr. 58 Salisbury st. Bermdsy
Kitchen John, lighterman, 8 Beer lane, Great Tower st
Kitchen Robert Bertrum, dyer, 4 Fort place, Grange road
Kitchen Seth, *White Horse* P.H. 16 West st. Golden sq
Kitchen William, butcher, 21 Blandford st. Portman sq
Kitchen William, fruiterer, 112 High st. Marylebone
Kitchener George, seal engraver, 3 Warwick sq. Newgate st
Kitchener James, baker, 1 Craven buildings, City road
Kitchener Thomas, builder, 1 Rodney st. north, Pentonville
Kitchin Joseph & Co. hop merchants, 1 King st. Borough
Kitchin Charles, grocer, 9 Gainsford st. Horselydown
Kitchin Isaac, livery stables, North st. Sloane st
Kitching & Abud, goldsmiths & jewellers to the Queen, 46 Conduit st. Regent st
Kitching Chas. pearl & bead stringer, 13 Richmond blds. Soho
Kitching George, surgeon, 19 Tysoe st. Spafields
Kitchingman Hen. fishing rod ma. 64 Skinner st. Bishopsgt
Kitchner Jas. Bowes, scavenger, 73 Gt. Suffolk st. Borough
Kitchner Peter Chas. coal merch. 83 Gt. George st. Bermondsey
Kite Henry, carpenter, bldr. &c. 24 Cumberland st. Middx. hosp
Kite Jas. lighterman & coal mer. New North rd. bridge, Hoxton
Kither William, butcher, Bow
Kitson Dav. Martin, grocer, &c. 1 John st. Titchfield ter. Reg. pk
Kitson James, wholesale saddler, 154 Fenchurch st
Kitson Thomas, cabinet maker, 96 Hoxton Old town
Kitson Wm. coal merchant, St. Bride's wharf, Whitefriars
Kitson William, soap boiler, 38 White st. Borough
Kitt Arthur, surgeon, 15 Upper Copenhagen st. Pentonville
Kitt Thomas, woollendraper, 30 Cloth fair, West Smithfield
Kitto Charles, coffee rooms, 6 New st. Covent garden
Kittoe Hamilton, surgeon, 2 Chandos st. Cavendish square
Kittrick Thos. ho. & estate agent, 39 Duke st. Grosvenor sq
Kitz Louis, watchmaker, 37 Maddox st. Regent st
Klaftenberger Chas. I. watchma. see Aubert & Klaftenberger
Kleft Mary Ann (Mrs.), oil wareho. 49 Gt. Queen st. Linc. inn fi
Kleft Phillip, cheesemonger, 26 South st. Manchester sq
Klein John Frederick, merchant, 6 George yd. Lombard st
Kleyser & Brothers, clock manufacturers, 4 Goswell st
Kleyser Charles & Co. clockmakers, 4 Broad st. Bloomsbury
Kleyser & Tritschler, clock & watchmakers, 405 Oxford st
Kleyser John, watch & clock ma. & importer, 66 Boro' High st
Klingelhoefer, Francis George, merchant, 75 Old Broad st
Klockmann Adolphus, merchant, 18 Philpot lane & Baltic
Klos John, baker, 55 Great Marlborough st
Klösz Anthony, baker, 47 Cambridge st. Edgware road
Klösz Henry, baker, 3 Moor st. Soho
Klosz Jacob, baker, 2 Tabernacle square, Finsbury
Kluge John Henry, furrier, 49 Gibson st. Waterloo road
Klugh A. E. & M. A. (Misses), milliners, 3 Manchstr. st. Mancr. sq
Klugh & Barratt, milliners, 73 Margaret st. Cavendish sq
Knaggs Henry, surgeon, 3 St. James's terrace, Camden twn
Knaggs William Ridley, oilman, 25 Kensington High st
Knapp Charles, barrister, 2 Brick court, Temple
Knapp Chas. general salesman, 107 Edgware rd. Marylebone
Knapp Geo. silversmith & watchmaker, 14 High st. Islington
Knapp Geo. Jas. jun. bookbinder, 5 Church st. Blkfriars. rd
Knapp Geo. Jas. bookbinder, 10 Green st. Church st. Blkfrs. rd
Knapp Henry, dining rooms, 51 Wardour st. Soho
Knapp Henry, builder, cabinet ma. upholsterer, house agent, general decorator, & original maker of the improved Dr. Arnott's water beds & couches, 40 Cirencester pl. Portland rd
Knapp Jane (Miss), milliner, 32 Paddington st. Marylebone
Knapp John, cabinet maker, 40 Chapel place, Brompton
Knapp John, cheesemonger, 16 Victoria road, Pimlico
Knapp John, mason, Cirencester whf. Augustus st. Regt's. pk
Knapp John, upholsterer & builder, 55 Foley st. Marylebon
Knapp Richard, grocer & brewer, 4 Brick la. Spitalfields
Knapp Thos. cheesemonger, 68 New Church st. Lisson grove
Knapp Wm. upholsterers' trimmg. manfr. 17 Ebury st. Pimlico
Knapton Robt. & Co. billbrokers, 2 Charlotte row, Mansion ho
Knapton James, stonemason, 36 Praed st. Paddington
Knapton Thos. stonemason, 30 Cambridge pl. Cambridge ter
Knapton William, beer retailer, 23 Gower pl. Euston sq
Knell Thomas, timber merchant, 29 Belvedere rd. Lambeth
Knevett Charles, surgeon, 20 Lower Phillimore pl. Kensington
Knevett Henry James, grocer, 7 Gt. Windmill st. Haymarkt
Knevett William, fishmonger, 16 Mount st. Berkeley sq
Knevitt Thos. L. Lieut. R.N. sec. to *Mendicity So.* 13 Red Lion sq
Knewstub William C. wholesale druggist, 95 Minories
Knibbs Francis, *Gun* P.H. Hermitage stairs, Wapping
Knibbs Frederick, livery stables, Newland st. Kensington
Knibbs Lydia (Mrs.), painter, glazier, &c. 99 Praed st. Edgw. rd
Knife John, auctioneer & appraiser, 14 Harp all. Farringdon st
Knight & Barr, engine turners, &c. 4 Newcastle pl. Clrknw.
Knight & Carthew, plumbers & glaziers, 3 York st. St. James's
Knight Charles & Co. publishers, 22 Ludgate st

Knight & Droy, timber merchants, 6 Little Saffron hill
Knight & Foster, retail stationers, 5 Eastcheap
Knight Geo. & Sons, ironmongers, 41&42Foster la. Cheapside
Knight Geo. & Sons, manufacturers of chemical & philosophical apparatus, metallurgists & importers of german black lead & other crucibles, berlin porcelain chemical utensils, only manufacturers of Bakewell's patent soda water machines, &c. 2 Foster lane, Cheapside
Knight Harriet & Emma, milliners, 67 Goswell road
Knight & Hawks, stereotype founders, 13 Clerkenwell close
Knight John & Wm.(lateWrathall & Knight), wine & brandy merchts. storeshippers & biscuit bakers, 77 & 78 Tooley st
Knight & Mason, lime burners, John st. Cambridge heath
Knight & Perry, exotic nursery, King's rd. west, Chelsea
Knight & Poole, locksmiths, 25 Pudding lane, Eastcheap
Knight & Pyne, calico & paper blockms. 16Vineyd.wk.Clrkwl
Knight Richard & Co. carpet warehouse, 273 High Holborn
Knight Richard & Co. cochineal merc.2Martin'sla.Cannonst
Knight Richard & Sons, teadlrs. & grocrs.83 Gracechurch st
Knight Richard & Co. wholesale stationers, 10 Budge row
Knight & Son, secret springers, 81 Westmorland pl. City rd
Knight, Son & Reeves, stock &share broks.14 Tokenhouseyd
Knight Thomas & Stephen, plumbers, 5 Gt. Suffolk st. Boro'
Knight Abraham, butcher & cowkeeper, 118 Poplar High st
Knight Alfred, bootmaker, 22 Cobourg st. Euston sq
Knight Benjn. chandlers' shop, 56 Gt. James st. Lisson grove
Knight Charles, cowkeeper, 1 Mayfield place, Kensington
Knight Chas. plumber, 8 Paradise st. & 225 Rotherhithe st
Knight Charles, upholsterer, 4 Gt. Titchfield st. Oxford st
Knight Charlotte (Mrs.), linendraper, 187 Lambeth walk
Knight Chas. Johnson, builder, 3 Devonshire st. Bishopsgte
Knight Chas. Wm. carpenter & builder, 56 Berners st. Oxford st.; & Harley mews north, Harley st
Knight Cornelius, fruiterer, 52 Up. Baker st. Regent's park
Knight Crabb Wm. house ag. 12Alfred pl. Newington causewy
Knight Danl.statr.&waste paper dlr.40John st. west, Edgw.rd
Knight Elisha, oilman, 77 Charlotte ter. New cut, Lambeth
Knight Fredk. Aug. special pleader, 1Mitre ct. bldgs. Temple
Knight Fred. Wm. genl. engraver, 20 Radcliffe ter. Goswl. rd
Knight George, auctioneer, Crosby hall chbrs. Bishopsgate
Knight George, *Coach & Horses* P.H. 9 Brook hill, Clerknwl
Knight George, coffee rooms & beer retailer, 83 Fetter lane
Knight George, firewood dealer, 30 Albion st. Rotherhithe
Knight George, furniture broker, 16 Whitmore rd. Hoxton
Knight George, grocer, 31 Tyer st. Princes road, Lambeth
Knight Geo.picture framema.11Page's wk.Grange rd.Brmnd
Knight Geo. solicitor, 95 Sloane st
Knight Geo. Charles, tailor, 23 Rathbone place
Knight Geo.Jsph.academy, 2Queen's rw.Cambdg.rd.Mile end
Knight Giles, dairyman, 2 Whitmore st. Hoxton
Knight Henry, corndealer, 2 Bermondsey New road
Knight Henry, linendraper, 27 Exmouth st. Spafields
Knight Henry, solicitor, 17 Basinghall st. City
Knight Henry, solicitor, 16 Bucklersbury
Knight Jacob, tailor, 27 James st. Buckingham gate
Knight Jas. bookbinders' tool cut. 37 Chandos st. Cov. gard
Knight James, bricklayer, 1 Little Portland st
Knight James, coffee rooms, 16 Budge row, Cannon st
Knight James, druggist, 1 Stones' end, Borough
Knight James, marine store dealer, 17 Whitecross st
Knight James, undertaker, 5 New inn yard, Shoreditch
Knight James, watch & clockmaker, 4 White st. Bethnal grn
Knight James B. Wm. printer, 3 King sq. Goswell road
Knight James, wharfinger, &c. see Fetch & Knight
Knight Jasper, floorcloth manufactr. see Harvey & Knight
Knight Jeremiah, coffee rooms, 6 Compton st. Brunswick sq
Knight Jer. hatters' leather cutter, 175 Long la. Bermondsy
Knight John, architect&surveyr.1 UpperGordon st.Euston sq
Knigh John, beer retailer, 2 Gt. Chesterfield st. St. Marylbne
Knight John, carpenter & builder, printers' block maker & paper hanger, 190 Brick lane, Spitalfields
Knight John, carpenter, &c.10 Wallington pl. Wandsworth rd
Knight John, dyer, 4 Blossom st. Norton folgate
Knight John, harness maker, 87 New rd. Sloane st. Chelsea
Knight John, linendraper, &c. 19 Radcliffe ter. Goswell rd
Knight John, muffin baker, 28 Wigmore st
Knight John, soap maker, oil merchant, melter, & tallow chandler, York place, Old Gravel lane, St. George's east
Knight John, statuary & mason, Henry st. Limehouse fields
Knight John, turnery & toy wareho.2 Orchard st. Portman sq
Knight John, wood engraver, see Walker & Knight
Knight John Henry, printer, 16 Warren st. Islington
Knight John Phillip, egg mer. 27 Compton st. Brunswick sq
Knight John Prescott, R.A. artist, 20 James st. Pimlico
Knight Johns, merehant, 61 Moorgate st
Knight Joseph, carpenter, 5Buckingham pl. Marlbro'rd. Chlsa
Knight Joseph, grocer, &c. 11 Maze pond, Tooley st
Knight Joshua, lighterman, 12 Shad Thames& 60Gainsford st
Knight Maria (Miss), haberdasher, 107 London wall
Knight Mary (Mrs.), hairdresser & perfumer, 74 Jermyn st
Knight Mary (Mrs.), lodging house, 38 Maddox st. Regent st
Knight Morrison, surgeon, 47 Dover st. Piccadilly
Knight Peter, coal merchant, 5 Wilton road, Pimlico
Knight Peter, cheesemonger, 2 Prospect pl. Kingsland rd
Knight Phillip, baker, 10 Paradise st. Rotherhithe
Knight Rebecca (Miss), ladies' school, 15 London wall
Knight Richard, plumber & glazier, 35 Bury st. St. James's
Knight Richard, tin plate worker, 11 Fetter la. Fleet st
Knight Robert, dining rooms, 69 Gt. Guildford st. Borough
Knight Robt. lathe tool engine ma. Gt. William st. Pentonville
Knight Robt. Hen. hairdress.&perfumer, 102Bishopsgt. withot
Knight Saml. bookbinders' tool cut. 6 Prujean sq. Old Bailey
Knight Samuel, cheesemonger, 69 Fore st. Cripplegate
Knight Samuel, corn & coal merchant, 57 Gt. Marylebone st
Knight Sam. dairy, 61 Arlington st.&12 Caroline st. Camden tn
Knight Sarah (Mrs.), *Bull & Last* P.H. Grove ter. Kentish tn
Knight Steph. *Ironmongers' Arms* P.H. 7 Lizard st. St. Luke's
Knight Thomas, baker, 4 Spencer ter. Lower rd. Islington
Knight Thomas, fishmonger, 4 Shepherd's market, Mayfair
Knight Thomas, *Admiral Hood* P.H. 103 Tooley st
Knight Thomas, bed & mattress ma. 49Carnaby st. Golden sq
Knight Thomas, butcher, 39 Gilbert st. Oxford st
Knight Thomas *Guy Earl of Warwick* P.H. 37 Warwick la. City
Knight Thomas, hairdresser, 2 Pindar pl. Gray's inn road
Knight Thomas, linendraper, 97 Minories
Knight Thomas, oilman, 11 Newgate st
Knight Thos. wheelwright, 2 Gt. Ormond yd. Queen sq. Blombs
Knight Thos. Clarke, undertaker, see Heckinbotham&Knight
Knight William, baker, 26 Robert st. Chelsea
Knight William, barrister, 9 Inner Temple lane, Temple
Knight Wm. bricklayer, 24 Lit. Windmill st. Golden sq
Knight Wm. builder, 23 Saville place, Lambeth walk
Knight Wm. cheesemonger, 392 Strand
Knight Wm. distiller, see Gordon, Knight & Co
Knight Wm. engraver, see Jackson & Knight
Knight Wm. grindery dealer, 5 Moor lane, Cripplegate
Knight Wm. lodging house, 13 Surrey st. Strand
Knight Wm. oilman, 35 Wilsted st.&22Skinner st. Somers tn
Knight Wm. shell fishmonger, 5 Creed lane, Ludgate st
Knight Wm. shell fishmonger, 357Strand,&26Charing cross
Knight Wm. silversmith, 7Westmoreland blds. Aldersgate st
Knight Wm. Henry, tailor, 26 Stafford place south, Pimlico
Knight Wm. Henry, tailor, 39 Thomas st. Grosvenor sq
Knightbridge Henry, butcher, 71 Margaret st. Wilmington sq
Knightly Peter, carpenter, 5 New inn yard, Shoreditch
Knightly Sam. painter&glazier, 8 New inn yard, Shoreditch
Knightly William, oil & colorman, 29 Duncan pl. London flds
Knightly Wm. plumber & glazier, 51 Bishopsgate st. within
Knighton Giles, tailor, 2 Oxendon st. Haymarket
Knighton John, baker, 119 Great Suffolk st. Borough
Knighton John, carrier, Elephant inn, 112 Fore st. City
Knighton John, grocer, 34 Exeter st. Sloane st
Knighton Wm. junr. tallow chandler, 67 Leather la. Holborn
Knighton Wm. senr. oil & colorman, 67 Leather la. Holborn
Knights Harriet (Miss), berlin wa. Church st. StokeNewington
Knights Henry H. bookbinders' tool cutter, 11 Shoe lane
Knights James, engraver, 34 St. George's road, Southwark
Knights James, pastry cook, 1 East road, City road
Knights Samuel, printseller, 6 Change alley
Knill John & Co. patent soap factory, Wandsworth
Knill Wm. & Co. fruit brokers, 30 Pudding lane, & 35 Botolph lane, Eastcheap
Knill John, wharfinger & wareh. keeper, see Jackson & Knill
Knipe Benjamin, fishmonger, 6 Halfmoon pas. Leadnhll.mkt
Knipe Charlotte (Mrs.), fishmonger, 2 Dove court, Old Jewry
Knipe George, fishmonger, 17 Wormwood st. Bishopsgate
Knobel, Hamilton & Tuckwell, wine mer. 2 King st. St. James'
Knobel William Edward, solicitor, 69 Lincoln's inn fields
Knock Maria Francis (Mrs.), bookbinder, 8 Well st. Cripplg
Knock Richard, coffee roaster, see Wicks & Knock
Knock Richard, *White Hart* P.H. 18 Coal yard, Drury lane
Knock Charles, printer, 75 Myddelton st. Clerkenwell
Knope Wm. painter & glazier, 25 Club row, Bethnal green
Knope Wm. Henry, plumber, &c. 16New Montague st. Spitflds
Knott Charles, butcher, 15 Rawstorne st. Brompton
Knott George, cigar manufacturer, 15 King st. Snow hill
Knott George, grocer, 39 Gt. Queen st. Lincoln's inn fields
Knott Geo. Alex. city insp. weights & measures, Guildhall
Knott James, undertaker, 12 Weston st. Somers town
Knott Jane (Mrs.), statnr. bookseller & binder, 302 Regent st
Knott Job, grocer, 76 Compton st. Clerkenwell
Knott John, general booking office, 33 Fish st. hill

Knott John, tripedresser, 6 Walker's court, Golden square
Knott Robert, *Cross Keys hotel*, 16 Gracechurch st
Knott Rt. Chas. gold worker, &c. 14 St.James's wk.Clkwnwll
Knott Sophia (Miss), wine cooper, 2 Swallow st. Piccadilly
Knott Thomas Baker, builder & coal mer. High st. Deptford
Knott Thomas William, potato salesman, 67 Barbican
Knott William, builder, Creek road, Deptford
Knott William, *Stamford Arms* P.H. 30 Stamford st
Knott William Thomas, potato salesman, 6 York st. Boro'
Knottley Charles, dining rooms, 8 Davies st.Berkeley sq
Know John, *Rose & Rummer* P.H.88 Paradise st.Rotherhithe
Knowelden Wm. engineer & millwri. 65 Gt.Guildford st.Boro'
Knowler Henry, bootmaker, 2 Denmark place, Camberwell
Knowles Chas. James, queen's counsel, 1 Brick ct. Temple
Knowles Edward, chemist & druggist, 74 Hoxton Old town
Knowles Eliz. (Mrs.), *Green Dragon* P.H. Bull's Head passage, Leadenhall market
Knowles Sir Fras. Chas. barrister, 2 Harcourt bldgs. Temple
Knowles Henry Sidney, upholsterer, 107 Wardour st. Soho
Knowles James, lathe & tool manfr. 13 Denmark st. Soho
Knowles James, watchmaker, Royal Hospital row, Chelsea
Knowles Jas.Thos.architect, &c.1 Raymond bldgs.Gray's inn
Knowles John, merchant, 5 Ratcliff cross
Knowles John, oporto merchant, 25 Gt. Tower st
Knowles John, sheffield warehouse, see Walker & Knowles
Knowles John, silk broker, 26 Throgmorton st
Knowles Joseph, watch & clock ma.4 St.George's st.Albany rd
Knowles Lionel Phillips, stockbroker, 1 Bank chambers
Knowles Mary Ann (Mrs.), tea dealer, 6 Cross st. Islington
Knowles Robert, carpet manuf. & agent, 123 Wood st
Knowles Rt. upholstr. trim.ma.see Hoby, Robson & Knowles
Knowles Thos. cabinet carver, 51 Featherstone st. City road
Knowles Thos. chemist & druggist, 61 Seymour st. Euston sq
Knowles Thos. grocer, 72 Chalcroft ter. New cut, Lambeth
Knowles Thos. rag mer. 34 Staple st. Long la. Bermondsey
Knowles Thos.stocking ma.1 Hortulan pl.King's rd.w.Chelsea
Knowles Townley Rigby, barrister, 3 Raymond bds.Gray's inn
Knowles Wm. Henry, tailor, 33 King st. Borough
Knowles William, boot & shoe maker, 209 Bethnal green rd
Knowles William, grocer, 18 New Compton st. Soho
Knowsley Edward, wine merchant, 25 Crutched friars
Knox Alexander, tailor, 17 Charlotte st. Portland place
Knox Andrew, slater, St.Geo.wf.& 8 Clarence pl.Camberwl.rd
Knox Charles George, barrister, 26 Old sq. Lincoln's inn
Knox George, attorney, 4 Bloomsbury square
Knox Geo. Bloomsby.savings bank, 30 Montague st.Russell sq
Knox George, secretary to Shrewsbury, Wolverhampton, Dudley & Birmingham Railway, 3 Moorgate st
Knox George, turner & toy maker, 283 Kent st. Boro'
Knox George Frederick, cupper, 39 Davies st. Berkeley sq
Knox James, carpenter, 31 Gilbert st. Grosvenor square, & 34 New Bond st
Knox Vicesimus, barrister, 3 King's Bench walk, Temple
Knyvett Carey S. army agt. see Hopkinson (Charles) & Co
Kobelt Mary (Mrs.), window blind ma. 17 Cross st. Blkfrs.rd
Kobelt John, *King's Arms* P.H.16 Fieldgate st.Whitechapel
Kobylanski Jacob, earthenware dealer, 18 Gt. Carlisle st
Koch A. A. & A. A. (Misses), ladies' school, 24 Brudenell pl. New North road
Kocher Ernest, tobacconist, 1 Railway pl. Fenchurch st
Koe John Herbert, queen's counsel, 19 Old sq. Lincoln's inn
Koecker Leonard, dentist, 5 Conduit st. Regent st
Koenitzer Wm. merchant, 34 Fenchurch st
Kogl Alois, working jeweller, see Gaubert & Kogl
Kohlbeck George, tailor, 8 Leicester pl. Camberwell new rd
Kohlbeck John, tailor, 50 Castle st. Leicester square
Kohler John D. & Son, furriers, 14 Cheapside
Kohler & Schmidt, tailors, 17 Clifford st. Bond st
Kohler John, horn & trumpet ma. 35 Henrietta st. Cov. gar
Köhler John Conrad, oil & italian warehouse, 8 Stafford row, Pimlico, & 1 Marylebone st. Golden square
Köhler John Conrad, wine & beer merchant, 1 Marylebone st. Piccadilly, & 6 Gt. Newport st. Long acre
Kohler John Wm. pastrycook, 11 King David la. Shadwl.Hi.st
Kohler Wm. lithographic printer, 22 Denmark st. Soho
Köhne Henry, who. staymaker, 16 Laurence Pountney lane
Kohnla Cathn.(Mrs.), chml.laboratory, 3 Orchard st.St.Luke's
Kolle Henry & Son, horsehair manufacturers & merchants, 1 North mews, Little James street, Gray's inn lane
Kolle Charles, horsehair manufr. 10 North pl. Gray's inn la
Kolle Henry Wm. stove grate & range ma. see Pierce & Kolle
Koller James David, news agent, 32 St. James's market
Kollmann's Rail. Loco. Co. (Adol.Wm.Barnes, F.S.A. sec.), 11 Adam st. Adelphi
Konigh & Lemaire, engrav. & enamlr. 4 Bateman's bdg.Soho
Königswarter Brothers, merchants, 8 Copthall court
Kopke Wm. tailor, 23 Union st. Middlesex hospital
Kops, Coussmaker & Guitard, merchts.26 Birchin la.Cornhill
Kopsch & Proby, silk agents, 4 Crown ct. Old Broad st
Korn George, baker, 52 Lambeth walk
Korn Jacob, baker, 24 Gt. Peter st. Westminster
Korner Christopher Henry, bootmaker, 39 Dean st. Soho
Kornherr John Saml. wine merchant & italian warehouse, 35 George st. Portman square
Koster Lewer, spice merchant, Johnson's court, Lambeth st
Kracke Hinrich, *Crown & Leek* P.H. Deal st. Mile end Nw.tn
Kraeutler & Mieville, merchts. 12 Angel ct.Throgmorton st
Krafft Chas. Frederick, fishmonger, 146½ Edgware road
Krantz Julius, chemist, &c. 10 President st. east, King sq
Krantz Theodor, chemist, 165 Tooley st
Krantzcke & Fritz, army clothiers, 25 Bury st. St. James's
Kreeft Christopher, merchant, 9 Billiter square
Krehmer George, consul general for russia, 2 Winchester buildings, & 15 Saville row
Kreisa Francis, tailor, 41 Great Pulteney st. Golden square
Kreps & Co. importers of cigars, 4 Wellington st. Strand
Kronheim Jos.& Co. pat. stereotype founders, 3 Earl st. Blkfrs
Kronheim & Shirving, stamp & diecutters, 32 Paternoster rw
Krotowski Benjamin, fancy cap ma. see Braun & Krotowski
Krüger & Borrett, madeira merchants, 46 Lime st
Kruse & Bull, coal & corn merchants, Old Swan whf. Chelsea
Kuck Jacob, cheesemonger, 26 New road, St. George's east
Kuck Peter, sugar refiner, 5 Christian st. St. George's east
Kuck William, cheesemonger, 33 Munster st. Regent's park
Kuhn Frederick, baker, 222 Oxford st
Kulbach Reinhold, lodging house, 1 Sherrard st. Golden sq
Kuper W. & Co. patent wire rope makers, Grand Surrey Canal, Camberwell
Kurr Lewis, baker, 3 Northumberland ter. Bagnigge wells rd
Kurtz John, cheesemonger, 185 Bethnal green road
Kusel Richard, tobacconist, 20 Nassau pl. Commercl. road ea
Kyan Jas.& Co. varnish & color ma.54 Southampton row, Rus.sq
Kyberd Peter, smoke jack maker, 91 Great Saffron hill
Kybert John, beer retailer, 2 Back hill, Hatton garden
Kyezor Louis, watch, clock & chronom. ma.16 Tottenham ct. rd. & 31 Up. George st. Bryanstone sq.& 46A, Edgware rd
Kyle Henry Stopford, barrister, 2 Old square, Lincoln's inn
Kymer Maximilian, provision merchant, 39 Gt. Tower st
Kynes Chas.& Co. mast & block ma. Randall st. Limehouse
Kynaston Wm. & John, carpet & flannel facts. 4 Gresham st
Kynaston Roger, jun. merchant, 17 St. Helen's pl. Bishopsgate
Kynnersley Edwd. beer retailer, Jamaica level, Bermondsey
Kynnersley Wm. beer retailer, 70 Hill st. Walworth road

LABALESTRIER Mary (Madame), milliner, 15 Brook st
Labalmondière George, merchant, 46 Lime st
Labbett Henry, paperhanger, 12 Bryanstone st. Portman sq
Labdon & Burdge, curriers, 16 Hunter st. Gt. Dover road
La Beaume Michael, galvanist, 11 Argyll st. Regent st
Labern Charles, greengrocer, 39 & 40 Warren st. Fitzroy sq
Labern Henry, manufr. of botanic cream for the hair, by appointment to her Majesty & her Royal Highness the Duchess of Kent, 49 Judd st. Brunswick square
Labern John, tailor, 24½ Wilson st. Finsbury
Labourers' Friend Soc. (John Wood, sec.) Exeter hall, Strnd
Labowitzky, Danl. tobacconist, 140 Praed st. Paddington
Labram Ann (Mrs.), fruiterer, 55 London st. Fitzroy sq
Labram James, shoemaker, 28 & 36 St. Martin's ct. Leicester square, & 130 Tottenham court road
Labrow Ann (Mrs.), coal mercht. 3 Wilmington sq. Spafields
Laby James Thomas, fishfactor, 31 Jewry st. Aldgate
Lacabra Jsph. piano forte ma.41 University st. Totnham.ct.rd
Laccohee Thomas, *Lion & Castle* P.H. 2 Bermondsey wall
Laccohee Wm.M. looking glass frame ma.10 Bartholomew sq
Lacey, Howard & Charlton, solicitors, 28 New Bridge st
Lacey Jesse & Son, willow square manufacturers & timber merchants, 37 Curtain road
Lacey Edward, *Garrick's Head tav.* 27 Bow st. Covent gdn
Lacey Edward, bookseller & publisher, 76 St.Paul's church yd
Lacey Edward, gold & silver chaser, 5 Rolls bdgs. Chancery la
Lacey Edward, livery stables, New yard, Great Queen st
Lacey Esther (Mrs.), bookbinder, 25 Lit.Wild st. Linc. inn fi
Lacey James, brushmaker, 11 Little Earl st. Seven dials
Lacey James Murray, coal merchant, Milford wharf, Milford lane, Strand
Lacey Richard, fringe maker, 177 Tottenham court road
Lacey Wm. tailors' trim. slr. 18 Grace's alley, Wellclose sq
Lachlan's & MacLeod, ship & insurn. brokers, 62 Cornhill
Lack Alfred, saddle & harness ma.12 Stockbridge ter. Pimlico
Lack Frederick Walter Stewart, hosier, see Porter & Lack
Lack John, tailor & draper, 8 Union court, Old Broad st
Lack Thomas, dairyman, 7 Bethnal green, west side

Lack William, poulterer, 215 Shoreditch High st
Lack William, poultry & game salesman, Leadenhall market
Lackersteen Augustus Alex. merchant, 39 Moorgate st
Lackington Henry, baker, 1 George st. Portland place
Lacks Thos. cowkeeper, 7 Victoria pl. Cambridge rd. Mile end
Lacon Charles Gilbert, oilman, &c. 3 New st. Dorset sq
Lacon Frederick Lascelles, tailor, 6 Arundel pl. Coventry st
Lacon Susannah (Mrs.), milliner, 16 Albemarle st. Piccadilly
Lacy & Bridges, attorneys, 19 King's arms yard, Coleman st
Lacy & Reynolds, wholesale gunmakers to the hon. Board of Ordnance, the hon. East India Company, & the shipping trade in general, 21 Great St. Helen's
Lacy Benj. Walker, banker, &c. see Pocklington & Lacy
Lacy Charles, coal mer. Cannon whf. Cannon row, Westmstr
Lacy Francis, milliner & straw hat manufr. 37 Blackman st
Lacy Henry John, butcher, 46 Fetter lane
Lacy Richard, builder, 4 Warwick st. Belgrave road
Lacy Wm. tailor, 20 Lamb's Conduit passage, Red Lion sq
Lacy Wm. tuscan & straw hat ma. 61 Cranbourne st. Le'ster sq
Ladbrook Thomas, *Old Fishing Boat* P.H. Bromley
Ladbury Geo. Herbert, accountant, see Parrinton & Ladbury
Ladbury John Edward, surgeon, 7 Up. Fitzroy st. Fitzroy sq
Ladd Hen. carriage bldr. 3 Windsor ter. Vauxhall bridge rd
Ladd James, hairdresser, 16 Great Titchfield st. Oxford st
Ladd Joseph, fishmonger, 16 Barnsbury place, Islington
Ladd Neat, *Falcon* P.H. Lavender hill, Wandsworth road
Ladd Robert, tailor, 197 Whitechapel road
Ladd Wm. philosophical inst. ma. 10 Cleaver st. Knigntn. cross
Ladds John, builder, 23 Artillery place west, Finsbury sq
Lade John Searles, ivory cutter, 10 Brownlow st. Holborn
Ladensack & Reeve, tailor & linendrapers, 124 & 125 Minories
Ladler & Cope, warehousemen, 72 Newgate st
Ladewig Geo. who. confectioner, 31 North st. Lisson grove
Ladley & Butler, who. brush mfrs. 3A, Clifford st. Bond st
Ladson James, fancy cabinet ma. 25 Primrose st. Bishopsgate
Laffin, Butler & Laffin, tailor, 17 Princes st. Hanover sq
Laffitte, Blount & Co. bankers, 4 Castle court, Birchin lane
Laffitte Jean, foreign goods importer, 31 Addle st. Wood st
Laforest & Co. wine merchants, 21 College hill, Up. Thames st
Lahee Samuel & Son, auctioneers, 65 New Bond st
Lahee Charles, architect, 16 Manor pl. north, King's rd. Chlsa
Lahee Hen. prof. of music, 16 Manor pl. north, King's rd. Chelsea
Laidlaw & Co. merchants & baltic agents, 37 Mincing lane
Laidlaw & Rodwell, bootmakers, 4 Coventry st. Haymarket
Laidler John, chair & sofa ma. 16 Nowell's bldgs. Liverpool rd
Laidler Wm. cheesemonger, 69 & 85 Leather lane, Holborn
Laidman & Cox, law stationers, 119 Chancery lane
Laidman Leonard, receiver of country solicitors' & under sheriffs' accounts, negotiator of law partnerships, practices, &c. 119 Chancery lane
Laight Geo. umbrella ma. 195 Wellington ter. Waterloo rd
Laing & Shand, sailcloth factors, & sack hire warehouse, 5 Pickleherring, Tooley st. & 8 Shad Thames
Laing Allan Stewart, barrister, 3 Tanfield court, Temple
Laing Catherine (Mrs.), baker, 38 Gt. Coram st. Brunswick st
Laing David Gordon, painter, plumber. &c. 2 Villiers st
Laing Geo. Edwd. architect, Carlton chambers, 12 Regent st
Laing John, cork manufacturer, 11 Bedford st. Strand
Laing John, cork merchant & manuf. 11 Bedford st. Strand
Laing John, powerloom linen manufr. 1½ Pancras la. City
Laing Robert, tobacco manufactr. 61 Princes st. Leicester sq
Laing Seton, indigo broker, 39 Mincing lane
Laing Samuel, barrister, 8 King's Bench walk, Temple
Laing William Younger, *Swan* P.H. 49 Mount st. Berkly. sq
Lainson & Aldred, linendrapers, 385, 386 & 387 Rotherhithe
Lainson Henry, linendraper, 14 High st. Deptford
Lainson William, hatter, 42 Coleshill street, Pimlico
Laird John William, stationer & printseller, 1 Leadenhall st
Laird Wm. carpenter & undertaker, 14 North st. Pentonville
Lake & Harrin, mourning & fancy milliners, 175 Oxford st
Lake & Pipe, coal & coke mer. 10 St. Benet's place, Gracechurch st. & Wilton wharf, Grosvenor basin, Pimlico
Lake & Walker, solicitors, 8 New square, Lincoln's inn
Lake John & Henry, solicitors, 10 New sq. Lincoln's inn
Lake Ann (Mrs.), *Peacock* P.H. 11 Addle hill, Doctor's coms
Lake Charles, carpenter & builder, 104 Long lane, Bermondsey
Lake Daniel, *White Horse* P.H. 70 Princes st. Leicester sq
Lake Ephraim, teadealer & grocer, 46 Goswell road
Lake Edward William, attorney, 30 Bury st. St. James's
Lake George, boot closer, 5 Thomas st. Oxford st
Lake George Herbst, solicitor, 19 Great Carter lane
Lake Geo. Wilson, herbalist, 22 Cumberland rw. Walwth. rd
Lake Henry Geo. *British Queen* P.H. Belinda st. Canonbury sq
Lake Isaac, potato salesman, South row, Covent garden
Lake James, woollendraper, 33 Aldgate
Lake James P. barrister, 22 Portugal st. Lincoln's inn fields
Lake James Richard, engraver & printer, 2 Shoe la. Fleet st
Lake John, silk dyer, 10 New road, St. George's east
Lake John, solicitor, Whitmore road, Hoxton
Lake John, tailor, 2 Crown court, Pall mall
Lake John, west india merch. 10 St. Benets' pl. Gracech. st
Lake John James, grocer, 50 Ernest st. Regent's park
Lake Joseph, baker, 76 Hackney road
Lake Joseph, cabinet maker, 24 Borough road
Lake Peter, *Three Herrings* P.H. 15 Bell yard, Temple bar
Lake Richard, hair dresser, 30 Drury lane
Lake Richard, linendraper, 20 Fore street, Cripplegate
Lake Robert, furniture dealer, 3 Nelson place, Old Kent rd
Lake Saml. surveyor & ho. agt. 24 College hill, Up. Thames st
Lake Stephen, bootmaker, 21 King street, Seven dials
Lake Wm. printer, engraver & draughtsman, 170 Fleet st
Lake Wm. *King's Arms* P.H. 20 Crown row, Walworth road
Lake Young Lake, herbalist, 6 Church lane, Whitechapel
Lakeman Edward, bedstead ma. 35 Primrose st. Bishopsgate
Lakeman Geo. cabinet ma. Grove passage, Church st. Hackney
Lakeman Stephen, basket maker, 45 St. George st
Lakeman William, hatter, 47 Broad st. Ratcliff cross
Lakeman William, hatter, 44 Shadwell High st
Laker Edward, currier, 224 Bermondsey st
Laker John, boot & shoe maker, 94 Poplar High st
Lakin Joseph, linendraper, 88 & 89 Crawford st
Lakin William, *Father Red Cap* P.H. Camberwell green
Laking Francis, newsvender, 26 Halfmoon st. Piccadilly
Laking Frederic, surgeon, 12 Marlborough road, Chelsea
Laland John & Co. coal merchants, 25 Bouverie st. Fleet st
Lamacraft Wm. & Co. chemists & druggists, 49 Princes st. Soho
Lamacraft John, bookslr. & statnr. 19 Conduit st. Paddington
Lamacraft Nathaniel, butcher, 2 Lambeth lower marsh
Lamacroft John, porkman, 118 York road, Lambeth
Laman Edward C. pork butcher, 57 Leather lane, Holborn
La Mark Frederick, shipbroker, 9 Water lane, Tower st
Lamb & Axford, baby linen wareho. 85 Upper st. Islington
Lamb James & Son, cattle salesmen, 15 West Smithfield
Lamb Alfred B. wine & mineral water imptr. 149 New Bond st
Lamb Ann (Mrs.), furniture brokr. 3 Brokers' row, Redcross st
Lamb Ann (Mrs.), linendraper, 6 Abbey st. Bermondsey
Lamb Benj. building material dlr. 130 Southwark bridge rd
Lamb Benj. corn & seed dealer, 4 King's pl. Stone's end, Boro'
Lamb Benjamin, painter, &c. 25 Bevenden st. City road
Lamb Charles, solicitor, 24 Queen st. Cheapside
Lamb Christopher, pawnbroker, 196 Sloane st. Chelsea
Lamb Edward, corndealer, 4 Church st. Camberwell
Lamb Edward B. architect & surv. 26 Charlotte st. Prtlnd. pl
Lamb Francis, oilman, 15 & 16 Wells row, Upper st. Islington
Lamb George, goldsmith & jeweller, 69 Cheapside
Lamb George, merchant & agent, 75 Queen st. Cheapside
Lamb Henry, carpenter, &c. 7 St. John st. Smith sq. Westmstr
Lamb James, dealer in paintings, 31 Fleet lane, Old Bailey
Lamb James, east india merchant, 5 Lothbury
Lamb John, coach currier, 1 Cross lane, Long acre
Lamb John, cattle salesman, 60 West Smithfield
Lamb John, custom ho. & shipping agt. 2 Fen ct. Fenchurch st
Lamb John, druggist, 17 Tabernacle square
Lamb John, haberdasher, hosier, &c. 45 Oxford st
Lamb John, linendraper, &c. 6 Newcastle pl. Edgware road
Lamb John, teadealer & grocer, 7 Oxford market
Lamb John, writer & painter, 17 Lit. Saffron hill, Hatton wall
Lamb John Giles, mast & block maker, 93 Fore st. Limeho
Lamb John Stewart, surgeon, 22 Maida hill, Edgware road
Lamb Mary Ann (Mrs.), private hotel & boarding house, 36 & 37 Drummond st. Euston sq
Lamb Richard, jeweller, Stratford broadway
Lamb Roger, wine & brandy & oil & color mercht. 137 Druryla
Lamb Septimus, hairdresser, 5 Poppin's court, Fleet st
Lamb William, butcher, 9 Bethnal green road
Lamb William, surgeon, 55 Earl st. east, Lisson grove
Lamb William, woollendraper, 100 Holborn hill
Lamb William Davis, chemist, 20 Osnaburgh st. Regent's pk
Lambard Thomas, locksmith & bellhanger, Well st. Hackney
Lambard Wm. whitesmith & bellhanger, Morning la. Hckny
Lambden James, bootmaker, 11 Corporation row, Clerknwll
Lambe Jeremiah, hatter, 45 Bridge road, Lambeth
Lambe John, dressing case maker, see Wells & Lambe
Lambe Rich. *William IV.* P.H. 6 Priory pl. Cambwl. new rd
Lambe Rich. Capel, printseller, carver, &c. 96 Gracechurch st
Lambe Robt. com. & chem. agent, & wine imp. 11 Gt. Prescot st
Lambe Wm. customho. agent & lighterm. 66 & 68 Lr. Thames st
Lambe William, surgeon, &c. 1 Bolingbroke row, Walwth. rd
Lambell Catherine (Mrs.), beer retailer, 143 Kingsland road
Lambell John, carpenter, 21 Market row, John st. Oxford st
Lambell John, poulterer, 119 Fore st. Cripplegate
Lambert & Beale, meat salesmen, Leadenhall market

Lambert, Brown & Co. gold lacemen & embroiderers to her Majesty, 236 Regent st
Lambert & Butler, tobacco & snuff manufrs. 142 Drury lane
Lambert Daniel & Sons, wine merchants, 79 Lombard st
Lambert, Donaldson & Co. merchants, see Donaldson, Lambert & Co
Lambert John & Thos. merchs. see Kingston's, Lambert & Co
Lambert & Rawlings, goldsmiths & jewls. 10, 11 & 12 Coventry st
Lambert, Ridley & Co. coal fac. ship & ins. bro. 70 Lr. Thames st
Lambert Thos. & Son, brassfounders, 30 New cut, Lambeth
Lambert & Whitfields, milliners, 3 St. James's st. Pall mall
Lambert Abraham, painter, 5 Barclay st. Clarendon sq
Lambert Burwood, grocer, 16 Drummond crescent, Eustonsq
Lambert Byng, painter, 33 Cumberland markt. Regent's pk
Lambert Charlotte (Mrs.), grocer, 12 Carburton st. Fitzroysq
Lambert Daniel, barrister, Law chambers, 77 Chancery la
Lambert Dan. *King's Head tav.* 26 Ludgate st. & 2 Ave Maria la
Lambert Edward, brewery, Deptford bridge
Lambert Edward, barrister, 4 South square, Gray's inn
Lambert Edward, solicitor, 4 Raymond's buildings, Gray's inn
Lambert Eleanor (Mrs.), tobacco pipe ma. High st. Kingslnd
Lambert Frances (Miss), embroidress to the Queen & repository for decorative needle work, 3 New Burlington st
Lambert Francis, upholsterer, Church st. Hackney
Lambert George, oilman, 80 Old st. St. Luke's
Lambert George F. genl. salesman, 4 Bridge court, Westmr
Lambert George Hall, apothecary, &c. 105 Albany st
Lambert Harry, dentist to the Queen, 24 Marlboro sq. Chelsea
Lambert Henry, *Caledonian Arms* P.H. Caledonian road
Lambert Henry Wm. surgn. 28A, Devonshire st. Portland pl
Lambert James, upholsterer, 1 Dudley place, Clapham road
Lambert John, baker, 1 Bethnal green (west side)
Lambert John, baker, 44 Hart st. Covent garden
Lambert John, baker, 1 Vittoria place, Cambridge road
Lambert John, carver & gilder, 11 Earl st. east, Lisson grove
Lambert John, coach & cabinet carver, 8 Up. Clifton st. Finsb
Lambert John, merchant, 8 Broad st. buildings
Lambert John, silk mercer, see George & Lambert
Lambert John, surgeon, 60 Lisson grove north
Lambert John, tinplate worker & lacquerer, 66 Lambeth walk
Lambert John Wallace, surgeon, 57 Berners st. Oxford st
Lambert Joseph, job master, King's Head yd. Duke st. Linc. inn
Lambert Joseph, timber merchant, see Chapman & Lambert
Lambert Madame, dressmaker, 86 Park st. Grosvenor sq
Lambert Richard, attorney, 32 John st. Bedford row
Lambert Richard, warehouseman, 43 Friday st
Lambert Richard, plumber, 21 Nassau st. Middlesex hospital
Lambert Richd. *Bedford Head tavern* P.H. 15 Bedford st. Bedford square, & 236 Tottenham court road
Lambert Rt. coach proprietor, Brunswick ter. Blackwall
Lambert Samuel, limerick lace manufactr. 77 Aldermanbury
Lambert Samuel, tobacconist, High st. Kingsland
Lambert Samuel, watchmaker, 2 Belinda ter. Canonbury sq
Lambert Sarah (Mrs.), coffee roaster, 2 George yard, Aldgate
Lambert Sarah (Mrs.), *Marylebone Coffeehouse* P.H. 34 East st. Manchester square
Lambert Thos. coach painter, 8 Lit. Woodstock st. Marylbne
Lambert Thos. coal mer. St. George's wf. Up. Belgrave pl. Pmlco
Lambert Thos. pendulum wire ma. 27 Camden st. Islington
Lambert Thos. waxchandler & oil &c. wa. 102 High Holborn
Lambert Thos. Z. G. watch tool dl. 3 Murray st. New North rd
Lambert Wm. baker, George st. Camberwell
Lambert Wm. butcher, 1 Wellington pl. West India docks
Lambert Wm. currier, 20 Bermondsey New road
Lambert Wm. custom house agent, see Nelham & Lambert
Lambert Wm. furniture broker, 39 King st. Seven dials
Lambert Wm. medicine vender, 20 Jermyn st. St. James's
Lambert Wm. teadealer & grocer, 16 Great Titchfield st
Lambert Wm. George, butcher, 16 Abingdon st. Westmnr
Lambert Wm. Robt. saddler & harness maker, 107 Long acre
Lambeth Savings' Bank (Wm. Davies, acty.), Lambeth green
Lambeth Street Police Court, Whitechapel; hours 10 to 5
Lambeth Water Works Co. Office (Wm. Simon Phipps, sec.), 139 Blackfriars road; Works, Belvedere road, Lambeth
Lambeth Chas. bricklayer, Red Lion yd. Warner st. Clerknwl
Lambeth James, coach painter, 12 William st. Shoreditch
Lambley Egbert, tailor, 13 Dean st. Soho square
Lambley Joshua, corndealer, 91 Vauxhall walk, Lambeth
Lambole John, ivory cutter & corn chandler, 35 Foley st
Lambourn Wm. *Ship tavern*, 16 Camden st. Islington green
Lambourne Thomas, greengrocer, 2 New st. Kennington rd
Lambshead Jasper, baker, 36 Ernest st. Regent's park
Lamburn Robert, baker, 107 Cromer st. Brunswick sq
Lamburn William, grocer, 4 Union st. Lisson grove north
Lamford Thos. ironmonger, 18 Chalcroft terrace, Lambeth
Laming Wm. Cotton & Co. merchants, 35 Mark lane
Lammas William, hairdresser, 20 Crown st. Finsbury
Lammin William Henry, solicitor, 5 John st. Adelphi
Lamond Wm. Okey & Alex. & Co. share agts. hall of commerce
Lamont John, clothes salesman, 10 Air st. Piccadilly
Lamont John, mercht. 2 Birchin la. & 24 Broad st. Ratcliff
Lamotte John Lagier, solicitor, 9 Serle st. Lincoln's inn flds
Lampard James, brick mould ma. 54 Church st. Shoreditch
Lampard Mary (Mrs.), pocketbk. ma. 36 Church st. Shoredch
Lampen Joseph, tailor, 9 Elizabeth st. Hans place
Lampen Joseph, tailor, 77 Lisson Grove north, Marylebone
Lampert Wm. printer, 7 Charles st. Queen's Elms, Chelsea
Lamplough & Horsley, ship & ins. agts. 37 Old Broad st. City
Lamplough Henry, chem. & drug. & appraiser, 88 Snowhill
Lamport Richard, butcher, 97 Blackman st. Borough
Lamprell Chas. Fitch, *Dyers' Arms* P.H. 17 Cannon st. City
Lamprell James, fruiterer, 4 Brunswick st. Blackwall
Lamprell Wm. carpenter & builder, 13 Long la. Smithfield
Lampson Curtis M. merchant, 9 Queen st. pl. Upr. Thames st
Lampton Wm. surgeon, 2 Up. Queen's buildings, Brompton
Lamy Charles, grocer & tea dealer, 22 Aylesbury st. Clkwl
Lanaway John, tailor, 4 York place, Kingsland road
Lancaster James & Co. woollen drapers, 12 High Holborn
Lancaster Amelia (Mrs.), furniture brkr. 1 Barrett's ct. Oxford st
Lancaster Benjamin, russia broker, see Wilson & Lancaster
Lancaster Charles, gunmaker, 151 New Bond st
Lancaster Charles, printer, &c. 7 High st. Bow, Middlesex
Lancaster Edmund, baker, 10 Wellington place, Stepney
Lancaster Edward, carpenter, 1 Lit. Bell alley, Moorgate st
Lancaster Edw. R. theatrical agt. 5 Middle New st. Gough sq
Lancaster Geo. *Waterman's Arms* P.H. 93 New park st. Boro'
Lancaster Henry, wine & spirit mer. 3 Cross la. St. Mary at hill
Lancaster James, filter manufactr. 87 Pratt st. Camden town
Lancaster James, tobacconist, 4 Duke st. Chelsea
Lancaster James R. coal merchant, see Hughes & Lancaster
Lancaster John, carpenter & undertak. 5 Goldsmith st. Cheapsid
Lancaster John, linendraper, see Marlow, Lancaster & Co
Lancaster Joseph, chair caner, 19 Rose st. Covent garden
Lancaster Martha (Mrs.), grocer, 14 Earl st. west, Edgw. rd
Lancaster Mary A. (Mrs.), haberdshr. 23 Southmptn st. Cmbwl
Lancaster Thomas Jacomb, merchant, 17 Langbourne chambs
Lancaster William, coffee rooms, 35 St. Mary at hill
Lancaster William, grocer, 68 King st. Golden sq
Lancaster William, jeweller, 14 Regent st. Waterloo pl
Lancaster William, *Ship* P.H. 40 Vine st. Westminster
Lancaster William, undertaker, 387 Albany rd. Camberwell
Lancaster Wm. Jas. insur. brok. St. Peter's chambs. Cornhill
Lance Ann (Miss), artist, 71 Warren st. Fitzroy sq
Lance Ann (Mrs.), pawnbroker, see Perry & Lance
Lance George, artist, 36 Hart st. Bloomsbury
Lance John Henry, barrister, 4 Plowden buildings, Temple
Lance Joseph, dyer & scourer, 7 Brunswick par. Barnsby rd
Lance Richard, silk dyer, 35 High st. Bow
Lance William, hatter, 74 High st. Camden town
Lancefield Alfred & George, butchers, 81 Crawford st
Lancefield Spinning Co. Glasgow, manfrs. shirtgs. stripes, checks, ginghams, &c. (Melliss I. F. & Co. agents), 28 Ironmonger lane, Cheapside
Lancefield Christiana (Mrs.), *George* P.H. 114 Gt. Portland st
Lancefield Henry, carpenter, 30 Devonshire st. Queen square
Lancefield Richard, carpenter, 15 Gt. Chapel st. Oxford st
Lancefield Wm. butcher, Camberwell green
Lancelott Francis, coffee roaster maker, 11 Barbican
Lancet office, 46 Princes st. Soho
Lanchenick Claudius, artist & bookslr. &c. 5 Brompton row
Lanchenick Jane (Mrs.), embroideress, 5 Brompton row
Land & Assessed Taxes Offi. (London) Guildhl. bdgs. hrs. 10 to 4
Land & Assessed Tax Off. for St. George, Hanover square (Edmd. Treberne, clerk), 11 South Molton st
Land Edward, professor of music, 53 Lamb's Conduit st
Land Joseph, trunk maker, 3 Keen's row, Walworth road
Land Wm. hardwareman, 13 Kent pl. Old Kent road
Land Tax Redemption & Regist. Office, Somerset house; 10 to 4
Landell Wm. Wright, lighterman, cornfactor & granary keeper. 41 Thomas st. & 28 Shad Thames & Rotherhithe st
Landells Ebenezer, wood engraver, 6 Bride ct. New Bridge st
Lander Edward, boot & shoe maker, 53 Tottenham court rd
Lander Francis B. brace, belt & garter maker, 408 Strand
Lander John Gilbert, solicitor, 9 Middlesex pl. New road
Landles John Stevenson, fishmonger, 1 Honey lane market
Landmann Col. George, civil engineer, 42 Fish st. hill, City
Landon Thomas & Co. military tailors & army clothiers, 17 Jermyn st. St. James's, & Green's end, Woolwich
Landon Wm. & John, canal carriers, White horse inn, Cripplegate, & 7 Wharf, south side Paddington basin
Landon Arthur John, barrister, 1 Old square, Lincoln's inn
Landon Whittington, fishmonger, 4 South st. Manchester sq

Landon Wm. man's mercer, see East, Landon & Holland
Landragin Martin, shag wire drwr. 86 Seabright st. Bethnl. grn
Lands Richard, cowkeeper, 6 Southampton st. Camberwell
Landsberg David, dlr. in diamonds, 10 George st. Minories
Landseer Chas. A.R.A. artist, 8 Southampton st. Fitzroy sq
Landseer Edwin, R.A. artist, 1 St. John's wood road
Landseer John, engraver, 8 Southampton st. Fitzroy square
Landzelle Wm. Crampten, dentist, 22 Grosvenor st
Lane Bazillai & Son, silk & cotton wa. 7 Church st. Shored
Lane John & Co. ale & porter brewers, 9 Wenlock rd. City rd
Lane Joseph & Son, gold & silver beaters & bronze & varnish makers, 7A, Charles st. Hatton garden
Lane & Prideaux, attorneys, Goldsmiths' hall, Foster lane
Lane Priscilla & Maria, dressmakers, 12 Bedford sq. east
Lane & Raiker, tailors, 26 Saville row, Piccadilly
Lane & Rathbone, medical agents, 13 John street, Adelphi
Lane Ann (Miss), artist, 48 Manchester st. Manchester sq
Lane Arthur, grocer, 20 New Manor st. King's rd. Chelsea
Lane Arthur James, solicitor, 7 Wardrobe ter. Doctors' cmns
Lane Burton, solicitor, 5 Osnaburg terrace, Regent's park
Lane Charles, hairdresser, 17 Bedford st. Bedford row
Lane Charles, undertaker, 10 Hanover st. Walworth road
Lane Denis, tailor, 30 Brooke street, Holborn
Lane Edward, cheesemonger, 58 Cannon st. City
Lane Edward, straw hat manufacturer, 6 Aldersgate st
Lane Geo. coachmaker, 8 Warren mews, Warren st. Fitzroy sq
Lane George, hairdresser, 13 Star street, Paddington
Lane George D. surgeon, &c. 22 Gt. Russell st. Covent grdn
Lane George Henry, merchant, 37 Wharton st. Lloyd sq
Lane Giles, tailor, 100 Dorset st. Salisbury square
Lane Henry, saddle tree maker, 9 Litchfield street, Soho
Lane Hezekiah, *Three Lords* P.H. 27 Minories
Lane James, carpet bag mnfr 5 Cumberland row, Walworth r
Lane James, dining rooms, 8 Cowcross st. Smithfield
Lane Jas. *Lane's Private Hotel*, 1 St. Alban's pl. St. James's
Lane James, solicitor, see Rhodes & Lane
Lane James Hunter, physician, 13 North st. Westminster
Lane Jane (Mrs.), *Joiners' Arms* P.H. Westminster road
Lane John, bootmaker, 5 York st. Westminster
Lane John, *British hotel*, 27 Cockspur st
Lane John, coachmaker, 27 Union st. Middlesex hospital
Lane John, D.C.L. barrister, 10 King's Bench walk, Temple
Lane John, engraver & printer, 291 Albany rd. Camberwell
Lane John, fruiterer, 9 Portsdown terrace, Kilburn
Lane John, grocer, 111 Tyer st. Princes rd. Lambeth
Lane John, lithographer & ornamental writer on vellum, Temple chambers, 126 Chancery lane
Lane John, statuary & mason, 10 Carey st. Vincent sq. Wstm
Lane John, tailor, 17 High st. Marylebone
Lane John, whitesmith & bell han. 40 Lucas st. Com. rd. ea
Lane Joseph & Son, bronzers & varnish manufacturers, 7A, Charles st. Hatton garden (late of Thavies inn)
Lane Joseph, carpent. & undertak. 3 Lit. Tufton st. Wstmr
Lane Joseph, dairyman, 20 Clarges st. Piccadilly
Lane Joshua, grocer, &c. 58 Three Colt st. Limehouse
Lane Louisa (Miss), lace wa. 3 Sydney alley, Leicester sq
Lane Lucy G. (Miss), ready made linen wa. 54 Bishopsg. within
Lane Mary (Mrs.), dairy, 5 Chichester rents, Chancery lane
Lane Mary Ann (Miss), ladies' school, 7 Suffolk pl. Hackney rd
Lane Nathaniel, shoe ma. 10 Horseferry road, Westminster
Lane Richard, furniture broker, 146 Waterloo road
Lane Richard Kirkman, solicitor, 29 Argyll st. Regent st
Lane Saml. *Britannia tavern & saloon*, 188 Hoxton Oldtown
Lane Samuel, orange merchant, 6 York st. Borough
Lane Samuel, portrait painter, 60 Greek st. Soho
Lane Samuel, silk machine maker, 29 Thomas st. Brick lane
Lane Samuel, surgeon, 1 Grosvenor pl. Hyde park corner
Lane Sarah (Miss), grocer, 20 Bride lane, Fleet st
Lane Thos. bedstd. & cornice manf. 6 Providence row. Finsby
Lane Thomas, bootmaker, 70 Wapping
Lane Thomas, dining rooms, 2 Kent st. Borough
Lane Thomas, oil & colorman, 4 Brunswick parade, Pentonville
Lane Thomas, papier machée wareho. 18 Brownlow st. Holbn
Lane Thomas, smoke consuming furnace agent, 28 St. John st
Lane Thomas, undertaker, 15 Crown st. Walworth road
Lane William, dyer, 9 Oxford market
Lane William, solicitor, 4 Bedford place, Russell sq
Lane William, stove mak. & ironmonger, 64 Gt. Titchfield st
Lane William, tailor, 10 Greville st. Hatton garden
Lane William, teadealer, 226 Strand
Lane Wm. Hen. hairdresser, 5 Panton st. Haymarket
Laney Thomas, *Holland Arms* P.H. 18 Symons st. Chelsea
Lanfear Elizbth. (Mrs.), ladies' school, 8 Low. Islington ter
Lanfear Wm. hearth rug mnfr. 2 Herbert bldgs. Waterloo rd
Lang & Harvey, solicitors, 11 Fenchurch buildings
Lang Alfred, architect, &c. 12 Buckingham st. Strand
Lang Charles Evans, architect, 18 Adam st. Adelphi
Lang Charles Von, physician, 32 Bedford sq. Bloomsbury
Lang Elizh. (Mrs.), chandler's shop, 32 Great James st. Hoxtn
Lang Frederick Henry, baker, 22 Lower st. Islington
Lang George Michl. confectioner, 7 St. George's circus, Oblsk
Lang Hugh Boyd, custom ho. & genl. agent, 5 St. Dunstan's hill
Lang James, merchant, 55 Old Broad street, City
Lang John, stock & share broker, see Huggins & Lang
Lang Joseph, gunmaker, 7 Haymarket
Lang Philip, baker, 83 Goswell st
Lang Thomas Hy. hairdresser, 20 Little Earl st. Seven dials
Lang William, hard wood turner, 4 Liquorpond st
Langabeer John, bootmaker, 6 Water st. Bridge st. Blckfrs
Langabeer William, bootmaker, 80 Long lane, Smithfield
Langdale M. Rt. & Son, stockbrkrs. 15 Angel ct. Throgmtn. st
Langdale Wm. Atkinson, solicitor, 7 Gray's inn square
Langdon Augustus, blk. ld. pncl. ma. see Brookman & Langdon
Langdon George, oil & colorman, 24 Bridge road, Lambeth
Langdon James, brushmaker, 62 East street, Manchester sq
Langdon John, dining rooms, 8 Silver st. Golden square
Langdon Lewis, stationer & printer, 135 Cheapside
Langdon Nathaniel, boot & shoemaker, 8 Queen st. Ratcliff
Langdon Robt. cheesemonger, 12 Calthorpe pl. Gray's inn rd
Langdon Robt. ironmonger, 8 John st. Davies st. Berkly. sq
Langdon Wm. saddler & harness mak. 9 Duke st. Manchester sq
Langdon W. B. prop. of chinese collec. 18 St. Geo.'s pl. Kngtsbr
L'Ange & M'Keown, watch & clock makers, 82 Cheapside
Langfield John, greengrocer, 2 Swan st. Great Dover rd
Langford & Bristed, button mnfactrs. & trimming warehomn. agts. to Milner & Morley, silk mfrs. Leek, 9 Gresham st
Langford & Russell, cattle salesmen, 41 West Smithfield
Langford Geo. Wm. law stationer, 2 Portsmouth st. Linc. inn
Langford Jas. cowkeeper & dairyman, 29 Thomas st. Oxfd. st
Langford Joseph, butcher, 177 Drury lane
Langford M. A. (Miss), tobccnist. 15 Colville ter. Kg.'s rd. Chels
Langford Nathl. Geo. spectacle ma. 21 Snows flds. Bermondsey
Langford Richard, cattle salesman, 41 West Smithfield
Langford W. painter, plumber, &c. 43 Devonshire st. Queen sq
Langford Wm. upholsterer, 15 Leonard st. Shoreditch
Langham Jas. G. & Sam. F. solicitors, 10 Bartlett's bldgs. Holbn
Langham Henry, oilman, 1 Darby place, Jermyn st. St. James's
Langham John Mackey, oilman, 4 Red Lion st. Holborn
Langham Thomas, butcher, 86 Connaught ter. Edgware rd. & 1 Oxford terrace, Edgware road
Langhelt Godfrey, rag & bottle wa. 5 North st. Manchester sq
Langhorn Thomas, french polisher, Up. York st. Bryanstne. sq
Langhorn W. R. musical inst. ma. 34 Northampton st. Clkwl
Langley & Gibbon, attorneys, 27 John st. Bedford row
Langley Charles, attorney, 3 Charlotte st. Bedford square
Langley Charles, *Woolpack* P.H. 12 Little Moorfields
Langley David, shoema. 5 Theobald's rd. Kingsgate st. Holbn
Langley Edward, coach carver, 6 Eaton place, Grosvenor sq
Langley Edward, stay maker, 160 Oxford st
Langley Emma (Miss), engraver, 15 Great Dover st
Langley Geo. earthenware dlr. 23 Gt. Crown ct. Lit. Pultny. st
Langley Geo. ironmonger, 46 Tooley st
Langley Geo. stationer, 39 Charlton st. Somers town
Langley Geo. jun. trunkma. 8 Brett's bldgs. Camberwell rd
Langley Geo. sen. trunkmaker, 226 Whitechapel road
Langley Henry, attorney, 3 Charlotte st. Bedford sq
Langley Henry Chas. surgeon, &c. 18 Gwynn's pl. Hackney rd
Langley James, cab proprietor, Page st. Westminster
Langley James, fruiterer, 1 York st. Kingsland road
Langley John, cabinetmaker, 16 Denmark st. Soho
Langley John, coach joiner, 17 & 19 Broad court, Long acre
Langley John, surgeon, 10 Howland st. Fitzroy square
Langley Joseph, coach builder, 50 Foley st. Portland place, & 31 Chenies mews, Bedford square
Langley Rebecca (Mrs.), staymaker, 3 Stone's end, Borough
Langley Richard, *Fox* P.H. 42 Castle street, Southwark
Langley Rich. shopkeeper, Grove pass. Church st. Hackney
Langley Thos. Sinclair, *White Hart* P.H. 66 Welbeck st
Langley Wm. blacking manufctr. 24 Robert st. Grosvenor sq
Langley William, surgeon, 40 Gloucester pl. Portman sq
Langley William T. solicitor, 11 Bedford st. Bedford row
Langlois Claude, artist, 24 Trevor square, Knightsbridge
Langlois Henry, grocer, 32 Manor place, Walworth road
Langlois (Miss), milliner, 45 Park street, Camden town
Langmaid Henry, writing master, 122 Regent street
Langmead Thomas, carpenter, 9 Chenies st. Bedford square
Langmead Wm. builder, 65 Upper North pl. Gray's inn road
Langmore John Chas. surgeon, 15 Upper George st. Brynstn. sq
Langmore William, physician, 40 Finsbury square
Langmore Wm. Butler, surgeon, 4 Christopher st. Fnsby. sq
Langridge Abraham, staffordsh. wareho. 12 Market st. Mayfr
Langridge Charles, staymaker, 45 Hedge row, Islington

Langridge Charles, staymaker, 129 Oxford street
Langridge Jas. cab proptr. 24½ Mount pleasant, Gray's inn la
Langridge James, haberdasher, 5 Leigh st. Burton crescent
Langridge John, tobacconist, 7 Lisson grove north
Langridge Wm. coachma. Black Prince yd. Princes rd. Lmbth
Langrish Mary (Mrs.), grocer, 53 Lower George st. Chelsea
Langslow Robert, barrister, 3 Harcourt buildings, Temple
Langstaff George, surgeon, 2 New Basinghall street
Langstaff William, surgeon, 1 Brown st. Bryanston square
Langstein James, tobacconist, 7½ City road, Old street
Langston William, butcher, 143 Lambeth walk
Langstone Edward, carpenter, 7 Freeman's lane, Horselydn
Langstone John, wireworker, 17 Artillery place, Westminster
Langthon Wm. beer retailer, 18 Little Trinity la. Bread st
Langton Ann E.&C. (Misses), ladies' school, Mare st. Hackny
Langton & Bicknell, sperm oil merchants & spermaceti refiners, 3 High street, Newington butts
Langton Bros.& Scott, who. druggists, 225&226 Up. Thames st
Langton, Langton & Wheatley, wholesale druggists, 15 Laurence Pountney lane; & Arthur st. west, London bridge
Langton & Robinson, timber merchts. Belvedere rd. Lambeth
Langton T.&Son, timber mers. Cementwf. Belvedere rd. Lmbth
Langton Adam, furniture broker, 39 Wellington pl. Stepney
Langton Charles, academy, 36 Southampton st. Camberwell
Langton David, solicitor, Clothwrkrs. hall, 41 Mincing lane
Langton David, jun. solicitor, 7 Furnival's inn, Holborn
Langton Francis, oilman, 145 Up. Whitecross st. St. Luke's
Langton Mary (Mrs.), seminary, 36 Southmptn. st. Cmbrwl
Langton Robt. Thos. *Jews Harp tavern*, Edward st. Regnts. pk
Langwith Samuel, shoemaker, 4 South place, Tibberton sq
Langworthy Jas. Hine, vet. surg. 13 Glo'ster mews Ea. Prtmn. sq
Lanham George, hairdresser, 12 Lower st. Islington
Lanham William, baker, 23 St. George's row, Pimlico
Lanham William, butcher, 1 Upton place, Walworth com
Lankenau John D. merchant, 1 Sambrook ct. Basinghall st
Lankester Henry, butcher, 21 Seymour place, Camden town
Lankester M. A. (Miss), ladies' school, Canal pl. Old Kent rd
Lankester Edwin, physician, 19A, Golden square
Lankester Rt. Laurence, carcase butcher, 2 Whtchpl. High st
Lankester Samuel, harness maker, 35 Broad st. Lambeth
Lankford Edward, egg salesman, 11 Park street, Borough
Lankford Thomas H. egg merchant, 37 Stoney st. Boro' mkt
Lankshear Thos. pocketbookmak. 18 Sekforde st. Clerkenwell
Lankshear William, coffee rooms, 11 Bread street hill
Lankshear William, surgeon, 5 Seymour row, Little Chelsea
Lankstone & Pennington, surveyors, &c. 16 South row, New rd
Lanning Joseph, carver & gilder, 25 Kirby st. Hatton garden
Lanning Thomas, cabinet ma. 43 Theobald's rd. & 14 Green st
Lanon Richard, grocer, 8 Gray's inn lane
Lansdall John, baker, 2, Tottenham court road
Lansdown Daniel, bricklayer, 11 Artillery place, Westminstr
Lansdown Fredk. linendraper & silkmercer, 5 High st. Bow
Lansdown George, carpenter, 35 Earl st. East, Lisson grove
Lansdown Thomas, carcase butcher, 5 Sharp's alley, Cow cross, & 49 Baker street, Clerkenwell
Lansdown Wm. tobacco pipemaker, 52 Essex st. Kingsland rd
Lant Daniel, livery stables, 29 Blackman st. Borough
Lanza Signor George, professor of music, 75 Newman st
Lapeirre Joseph, boot & shoe maker, 50 Brewer st. Golden sq
Lapidge Edward, architect, 2 Derby st. Parliament st. Westmr
Laport Alexr. & John, fruit salesmen, Spitalfields market
Laport Alexander, preserver of fruits, &c. see Hills & Laport
Laporte Geo. Henry, artist, 5 Berkeley place, Connaught sq
Lapoulide P. & Co. merchants, 2 Dunster ct. Mincing lane
Lapoulide Peter, merchant, 2 Dunster ct. Mincing lane
Lapthorn Stephen, builder, 15 Market st. Edgware road
Lapwood Edward, chandlers' shop, Stoke Newington green
Lapworth Alfred & Co. carpet manufacturers to the Queen & the royal family, 19 & 20 Old Bond street
Lapworth Abraham, hatter, 20 Bermondsey square
Lara Phineas Joseph, carpenter, &c. 6 Oxford st. Mile end
Larard James, watchmaker, 9 New Bridge st. Vauxhall
Larard William, bootmaker, 28 Aylesbury st. Clerkenwell
Larbalestier Isabella (Mrs.), who. furrier, 34 Noble st. Chps
Larby Wm. Adams, *Sugar Loaf* P.H. 22 Great St. Helens
Larchin Henry, brewer, see Strong, Larchin & Co
Larcombe John, florist & gardener, 8 Ebury square
Larcombe Wm. boot & shoemakr. 23 N. Henry st. E. Avnue. rd
Larcome Elizabeth (Miss), tobacconist, 18 John st. Blackfrs
Lardner & Fisher, printers, 12 Well st. Cripplegate
Lardner Jas. *Hare & Hounds* P.H. 14 Barnsbury pl. Highst. Isln
Lardner John, muffin baker, 44 Bell yard, Temple bar
Large Edmund, fruiterer, &c. 93 Lambeth walk
Large Hen. cop. & brass plate ma. 2 Gunpowder al. Shoe la
Large James, upholder, 19 Old Cavendish st. Oxford st
Large Mary S. (Mrs.), baker, 3 Walbrook pl. Hoxton New tn
Large William, grocer, 1 Southampton st. Camberwell road
Large William, tripedresser, 93 Shoreditch High st
Large Wm. Collins, coachma. Middle yd. Gt. Queen st. Lin. inn
Large Wm. Henry, professor of music, 140 Sloane st
La Rivière Anthony, lithographer, 18 Clifton st. Finsbury
Lark David, secret springer, 23 Meredith st. Clerkenwell
Lark Henry, watch motion maker, 41 Rabere st. Goswell rd
Lark John, boot & shoemaker, 11 Up. Seymour st. Euston sq
Lark Stephen, bootmaker, 60 Charles st. City road
Larke William, carpenter & builder, 17 Little Moorfields
Larken Wm. plumber & glazier, 9 Charles st. Westminster
Larkin Henry, oil & colorman, 6 Providnce. pl. Up. Kenngtn. la
Larkin James, engraver & printer, 45 Clerkenwell green
Larkin John, cigar importer, 22 Poland st. Oxford st
Larkin John, hatter, 195 St. George st
Larkin Robert Wm. bookbinder, 40 Newman st. Oxford st
Larking William & Sons, wholesale cheesemongers, 13 High st. Whitechapel, & imperial warehouse, Halfmoon passage
Larking Charles, upholsterer, 8 Globe pl. King's rd. Chelsa
Larking Esther (Mrs.), bedstead makr. 36 Queen st. Chelsea
Larking George, glass shade wareho. 12 Broad st. Golden sq
Larking John, van & railway carrier, George yd. Aldermnby
Larking Philip, wheelwright, 36 Queen st. Chelsea
Larkins & Co. merchts. & east india agts. 80 Old Broadst. City
Larkman Thomas, *Dog tavern*, 23 Holywell st. Strand
Larlham Mark, cabinet maker, 30 Gray's inn lane
Larman George, umbrella maker, 64 Bishopsgate without
Larnder George, lighterman, 95 Fore st. Limehouse
Larner Alfred Thomas, watchmaker, 3 Bell's pl. Holloway
Larner Edward, meat salesman, 11 New Newgate market, & 37 St. John street road
Larner Hen. builder &c. 14 Robert ter. King's rd Chelsea
Larner John, builder, 32 Baalzephon st. Long la. Bermonds
Larner Joseph, boot & shoe maker, 60 South Molton st
Larner Sarah (Mrs.), carpenter, 7B Cleveland st. Fitzroy sq
Larner Thomas, beer retailer, 28½ Great James st. Lisson gr
Larner Wm. carpenter & builder, King's rd. West, Chelsea
Larner Wm. carpenter & und. 3 Robert st. King's rd. Chelsea
Laroach George, silk dyer, 19 King st. Golden square
Laroche Bertrand Wm. mercht. & for. agt. 16 Old Broadst. City
Laroche Thos. Wm. coalfac. see Fenwick, Ralph, Son & Laroche
Laroche Thos. Wm. coal & wine mer. 7 Bolton row, Piccadilly
Larrance George, printer, 6½ Dyer's buildings, Holborn
Larrat Henry, *Grapes* P.H. 45 Portpool lane, Gray's inn la
Larronde Edward, wine & brandy merchant, 66 Mark lane
Lart John & Son, wholesale hosiers, 116 Wood st. Cheapside
Larter Wm. coffee rooms, 175 Tottenham court road
Larter Wm. cowkeeper, 4 Ropemaker's street, Finsbury
Larter Wm. rope, line & twine maker, 130 Kent st, Borough
Lasbury Benjamin, butcher, 12 Terrace, Kensington
Lascaridi Antonio, merchant, see Spartali & Lascaridi
Lascelles John, barrister, 4 Brick court, Temple
Lascelles John, cooper & stave mer. see Evans & Lascelles
Lascelles Thomas, butcher, 38 Grosvenor row, Pimlico
La Serre John Geo. stockbroker, 72 Old Broad st
Lash Thomas, wheelwright, Tanner's hill, Newtown, Deptfrd
Lashbrooke John, oilman, 68 Lambeth Lower marsh
Lashman M. (Mrs.), chandler's shop, 37 Earl st. East, Lis. gr
Laskey Samuel, cabinet ma. 30 Leigh st. Burton crescent
Lassam Abraham, beer retailer, 3 Peter's lane, St. John st
Last Samuel & Joseph, trunk makers, 165 New Bond st
Last Elizabeth (Mrs.), butcher, 112 Long alley, Finsbury
Last Joseph, trunk maker, 22 Coventry st
Last Joseph, trunk & dressing case maker, 38 Haymarket
Last Samuel, trunk maker, 256 Oxford st
Last Wm. Cooper, bonnet shape ma. 2 Warwick ct. Gray's inn
Latchford Edward & Benjamin, bridle, bit, stirrup & spur makers to her Majesty, 14 Upper St. Martin's lane
Latchford John, bit & spur maker, 180 Piccadilly
Latchford Wm. Henry, timber merchant, 61 Wardour st. Soho
Latham & Dighton, goldsmiths, &c. 1 Bateman's bldgs. Soho sq
Latham Alfred, merchant, see Arbuthnot & Latham
Latham Charles Wm. chemist, 56 Church st. Bethnal green
Latham Henry, bootmaker, 17 Laurence Pountney hill
Latham James, timber merchant, 5 Hoxton High st. & 41 Bacon st. Bethnal green
Latham John, grocer, 74 Bethnal green road
Latham John, mangle & press maker, 19 Old st. St. Luke's
Latham John Wm. S. physician, 14 Devonshire st. Portland pl
Latham Peter Mere, physician, 36 Grosvenor st. Grosvenor sq
Latham Rt. Gordon, physician, 29 Up. Southwick st. Oxfd. ter
Latham Wm. grocer, 26 New Manor st. Chelsea
Lathbury James, meat salesman, 45 Aldgate High st
Lathbury Robert, *Lamb* P.H. 24 Hertford st. Fitzroy sq
Lathbury Thomas, pork butcher, 34 Chiswell st. Finsbury
Lathwell Wm. pork butcher, 17 Exeter st. Sloane st

Latimer John, hosier & glover, 134 Goswell st
Latimer Sturman, solicitor, 20 King William st. Charg.cross
Latreille Orlando, tailor, 53 South Molton st. Oxford st
La Trobe Rev.Peter (sec.Moravian missions), 33Ely pl. Holb
Latten Robert, perfumer, 4 Grafton st.east, Tottenham ct.rd
Latten Robt. prof. of the flute, 4 Grafton st.ea.Tott.ct. road
Latter, Austen&Sons, hop&seed factors, 9½ Counter st. Boro'
Latter Thomas & Co. plumbers, 14 Duke st. Portland place
LatterArthr.Simon,pawnbkr.20&21Hereford pl.Com.rd.east
Latter Henry, surgeon, 5 Adelphi terrace
Latter Thomas, architect, 16 Grove place, Lisson grove
Latter Wm. lithographic printing press maker, 120 Old st. & 18 Little Moorfields
Lattey Abraham Hely Hutchison, surgeon, 41 Baker st
Lattey Parke Pittar, surgeon, 29 Harley st
Lattie James, currier, 73 Bermondsey st
Lattimore James, wheelwright, 5 New st. Old st
Lauder James, *Constitution* P.H. 32 Bedford st.Covnt.grdn
Lauder Robert Scott, artist, 35 Charlotte st. Fitzroy square
Lauder William, who. leather seller, 122 Long la. Brmndsy
Lauder WilliamPreston, surgeon, 8 Sloane st.Knightsbridge
Lauer Charles, fur skin dyer, 35 Fashion st. Spitalfields
Laughton Andrew, 27 Flagon row, Deptford
Laughton Charles, clothier & outfitter, 28 High Holborn
Laughton James, newsvender, 1 Victoria ter.Horsemongr. la
Laughton James, who. boot & shoe warehouse, 46 Mansell st
Launder James, plumber, painter & glazier, 21 Gray's inn la
Launders John, mercer & tailor,15 Marylebone st. Golden sq
Laundy George & Alfred, law stationers, 28 Castle st. Holb
Laundy H. (Mrs.) & Son, law stationers, 48 Essex st. Strand
Laurence, Cazenove & Pearce, stockbrokers, Auction mart, Bartholomew lane, Bank
Laurence Benjamin, exchange broker, Hall of Commerce
Laurence Benjamin, bill broker, 65 Old Broad st. City
Laurence Charles, brass finisher, 9 Bartholomew square
Laurence George, merchant, 6 Bury court, St. Mary Axe
Laurence George, silk merchant, 4 Union ct. Old Broad st
Laurence John (secretary of *London Fire, Life & Marine Assurance Corporation*), 7 Royal exchange & 10 Regent st
Laurence Thomas,leather fctr.see Streatfield,Laurence & Co
Laurence Thos. jun.leather fac.see Streatfield,Laurence & Co
Laurence Thos. Sam. hosier, glover,&c.160Bishopsg.without
Laurence William, solicitor, 3 Nicholas lane
Laurie Hamilton & Co. merchants, 127 Cheapside
Laurie John & Co. coach builders, Marylebone la.Oxford st
Laurie, Bedford & Rand, saddlers, &c. 296 Oxford st
Laurie & Marner, coach builders, 297 Oxford st
Laurie & Son, trussmakers, 2 Bartholomew close
Laurie & Wilson, warehousemen, 83 Watling street
Laurie Andrew, baker, 89 St. John street road
Laurie Geo. solicitor, see Wimburn, Collett, Laurie & Attree
Laurie Jas. camphine lamp ma. & distiller, 11 Gracech. st
Laurie James, wine merchant, 9 Billiter st
Laurie John, army agent, 10 Charles st. St. James's square
Laurie Joseph, physician, 12 Lr. Berkeley st. Manchester sq
Laurie Peter, barrister, 1 Paper buildings, Temple
Laurie Richard Holmes, map, chart & printseller, 53 Fleet st
Laurie Swinton, dentist, 36 Argyle st. New road
Laurière Richard, jeweller, 62 St. James's st. Pall mall
Lausseure Jules, importer of french wines, 147 Fenchurch st
Laustau John, wine importer, 75 Mark lane, City
Lavanchy Henriette (Madme.) (late L. Payn), milliner & dressmaker to her Royal Highness the Duchess de Nemours (from 22 Old Bond st.), 6 New Burlington st
Lavanchy John Robert, silk mercer, 6 New Burlington st
Lavell & Clowes, wine merchants, 9 Pall Mall east, & 38 Bloomsbury st. St. Giles's
Lavell James, butcher&porkman, 23York row, Kenningtn. rd
Lavell James, *Sun & Horse Shoe* P.H. 101 Gt.Titchfield st
Lavell William, coach carver, 26 Brownlow st. Drury lane
Lavenne Robert, fancy stationer, 6 John st. Oxford st
Lavenu Louis Henry, profsr. of pianoforte, 48 Greek st. Soho
Laver Charles, furrier, &c. 38 Hastings st. Burton crescent
Laver Harriett(Mrs.), pencil ma. 7 Ironmonger st. St. Luke's
Laver Harry, beer retailer, Ferry road west, Poplar
Laver Henry Willis, surgeon, 38Up.Stamford st.Blackfrs. rd
Laver James, stationer & bookseller, 81 Gt. Portland st
Laver James, coppersmith & brazier, 93 Houndsditch
Laver James, *Monarch* coffeehouse, 128 Holborn hill
Laver James, plumber & glazier, 5 Church st. Minories
Laver Robert, cattle salesman, 17 West Smithfield
Laverick William, grocer, 59 Union st. Clarendon sq
Lavers Charlotte (Mrs.), coffee rooms, 69 St. Martin's lane
Lavers Elizabeth(Mrs.), coffeerooms, 12 Marylebn. la.Oxfrd st
Lavers James, bricklayer, 4 George's place, Oxford st. road
Lavers Wm. R. tailor, 54 Carey st. Lincoln's inn fields
Lavey Alfred, music professor, 18 Princes st. Spitalfields
Lavey Haymon, gn. outfit.&shipg. off.19&230ShadwellHigh st
Lavey Solomon Charles, teacher of music & dancing, 16 Wood st. Spitalfields
Lavie Germain, solicitor, see Oliverson, Denby & Lavie
Lavies John, surgeon, 34 Gt. George st. Westminster
Lavis Peter, coal dealer, 18 Caroline st. Commercial rd. east
Lavy Jacob, furrier, 7 Powell st. ea. King sq. Goswell road
Law & Anton, solicitor & parliamentaryagent, 18Fludyer st
Law Edwd. & Wm. gauze dyers & dressers, 37 Monkwell st
Law & Tindal, solicitors, 10 New square, Lincoln's inn
Law Amendment Society (president, Lord Brougham; hon. treasurer, James Stewart, esq.; hon. sec. Wm. Vizard, esq.), 21 Regent st
Law Association for the benefit of widows & families of professional men (John Murray, sec.), 7 Whitehall place
Law Chronicle newspaper office, 8 Warwick sq. Newgate st
Law Dormitory Club ho. (Thos. Fisher Evans, sec.), 265 Strand
Law Gazette newspaper office, 8 Warwick sq. Newgate st
Law Journal Reports office, 5 Quality court, Chancery la
Law Life Assurance Society office (Geo. Kirkpatrick, actuary), next St. Dunstan's church, Fleet st. see page 2030
Law Society (*Incorporated*), of the United Kingdom (Robert Maugham, sec.), 106 to 109 Chancery lane
Law Times weekly newspaper, 29 Essex st. Strand
Law Writers' Provident Institution (Thomas Peters, sec.), Old Ship Tavern, Chichester rents, Chancery lane
Law Charles, grocer & beer retailer, 3 Grange rd. Dalston
Law Charles, surgeon, 3 Artillery place, Finsbury
Law Charles, surgeon, 22 Gloster terrace, New rd. Coml rd
Law Charles, jun. surgeon, 3 Artillery pl. Finsbury
Law Hon. Charles Ewan, queen's counsel, recorder of London, 10 Farrar's buildings, Temple
Law Charles Henry, bookseller, see Souter & Law
Law David, baker, Little Chelsea
Law Edward, lithographer, engr. & printer, see Dean & Law
Law Elizabeth (Mrs.), *Duke's Head* P.H. 236 Rotherhithe st
Law Elizabeth (Mrs.), grocer, &c. 5 East place, Lambeth
Law George Still, barrister, 3 New square, Lincoln's inn
Law Hy. perfume distill.&nursery, Clockho. Kingsrd.west, Ch
Law Henry, Shephard, solicitor, see Vandercom, Cree & Co
Law James, *Blue Last* P.H. 1 Broadway, Ludgate hill
Law James, cheesemonger, 24 Tottenham court road
Law James, linendraper, 96 Mount st. Berkeley square
Law James, potato dealer, 13 Aylesbury st. Clerkenwell
Law Jane (Mrs.), *Queen's Head* P.H. Charlotte st. Whitechpl
Law John, gold & silver beater & gold & silver paper maker, 46 Red Lion st. Spitalfields, &3&4 Bethnal green, nth. side
Law John, *Victoria* P.H. 1 Queen's place, Holloway
Law John Halsey, barrister, 8 New square, Lincoln's inn
Law John Russell, pawnbroker, 94 Blackfriars road
Law Joseph Bradley, surgeon, 90 Blackman st. Borough
Law Robert, copper & brass founder, 107 Brook st. Ratcliff
Law Robert, shoemaker, 23 Great Marylebone st
Law Robert William, linendraper, 81 Bethnal green road
Law Stephen, upholsterer, 102 Great Portland st. Oxford st
Law Thomas, coffee rooms, 117 Drury lane
Law Thomas, insurance broker, see Lister & Law
Law Thomas, tobacconist, 19 King's road, East Chelsea
Law Thomas, tobacconist, 3 Upper Eaton st. Grosvenor pl
Law Thomas Dixon, cheesemonger, 7 Queen's bldgs. Knighbdg
Law William, hair cutter, 20 Carnaby st. Golden square
Law Wm. upholsterer, &c. 48 Devonshire st. Queen square
Law Wm. John, com. of Insolvent Debtors' court
Lawden Caleb, gun & pistol maker, see Tipping & Lawden
Lawder George, cabinet ma.&c.54 Paddington st. Marylebone
Lawder James, upholsterer, 2 Portman st. Portman square
Lawder John, livery stable keeper, 9 Farm st. Berkeley sq
Lawdham John, wheelwright, 9 Stephen mews & 16 Stephen st. Tottenham court road
Lawes James & Co. horsehair seating mnf. 15 James st. Old st
Lawes Robert & Co. bill brokers, 13 Change alley, Cornhill
Lawes Algernon, coal mer. Newcastlewhf. Whf.rd. Hackney rd
Lawes Edward, solicitor, 15 New Milman st. Foundling
Lawes Edward, special pleader, 5 Pump court, Temple
Lawes Edward Hobson Vitruvius, S.L. chief registrar of the Court of Bankruptcy, 82 Basinghall st
Lawes John Bennett, manure factory, Creek rd. Deptford
Lawes Thomas, feather dresser, Prospect pl. Old Kent rd
Lawford Edw. John & Henry S. solicitors, Drapers' hall
Lawford Edward, solicitor to the East India Company, &clerk to the Drapers' Co. Drapers' hall, 27 Throgmorton st
Lawford George, bookseller, 6 Saville pl. New Burlington st
Lawford John Eeles, slate merc. 15 Tottenham court, New rd
Lawford Thos. Acland, stock bro. see Capel, Cuerton & Lawford
Lawford John Lindsey, solicitor, 27 Throgmorton st. City

Lawford Samuel, lighterman, see Redmans & Lawford
Lawford Thomas B. wine merchant, 12George yd. Lombardst
Lawford Wm. upholsterer, 13 Marchmont st. Brunswick sq.
Lawledge Matthias, upholsterer, 26 Weymouth st. Portld pl
Lawler Debh.(Mrs.), fruit saleswoman, Cov.gard. fruit markt
Lawler Ignatius, pewterer, 30 Golden lane, Barbican
Lawler John, hosier&haberdasher, 81 Lambeth Lower marsh
Lawless Patience (Mrs.) circulating library, 13 Philpot lane
Lawley Bernard, who. watch man. 4 Up.Vernon st. Loyd sq
Lawley Sarah (Mrs.), grocer, 154 Old Gravel lane, Wapping
Lawley Richard John, cooper, 18 Red Lion ct. Spitalfields
Lawley Robert, plumber, 23 Whitcomb st. Haymarket
Lawley Wm. pawnbroker, 6 Red Lion st. Borough
Lawman George, wheelwright, 81 East st. Kennington rd
Lawn Benjamin, boot & shoe maker, 30 Bow lane, Cheapside
Lawrance & Brown, meat salesmen, 21Shambles, Newgte.mkt
Lawrance Hen. & Co. blind makers & carpenters, 1 Windmill pl. Camberwell
Lawrance & Plews, solicitors, 32 Bucklersbury
Lawrance Edward, fruiterer, 20 Silver st. Golden sq
Lawrance Frederic (secretary of *Commercial & General Life Assurance Association*), 112 & 113 Cheapside
Lawrance George, watch & clock ma. 1 Chester pl.OldKt.rd
Lawrance Jas. furniture broker, 8 Old st.&28Wilderness row
Lawrance James, hair dresser, 8 Broadway, Deptford
Lawrance John Busley, solicitor, 7 Crosby hall chambers, Bishopsgate
Lawrance Moss Lazarus, merchant, see Lazarus & Lawrance
Lawrance Rebecca (Mrs.), lodg.ho. 2 Bell's blds. Salisby. sq
Lawrance Richard Moore, physician, 27 Arundel st. Strand
Lawrance Wm. grocer, 6 Lowndes terraee, Knightsbridge
Lawrance William, ivory turner, 7 City road, Old st
Lawrance William, upholsterer, 4 Devonshire st. Blomsby
Lawrell William, brush maker, 37 White st. Borough
Lawrence Mary & E. (Misses), milrs.33NewChurch st. Lis. gr
Lawrence& Piercy, grocers & cheesemngrs.27Eagle st.City rd
Lawrence, Pratt & Crowdy, solicitors, 25 Old Fish st
Lawrence Reuben & Son, sashms.26& 27 Tottenham st.Fitz. sq
Lawrence Thomas B. & Co. zinc warehouse, 55 Parliament st. manufactory, 65 Hercules bldgs. & 10 York pl. Lambeth
Lawrence Wm.&Sons, builders, 21 Pitfld.st.Hxtn.&30Bread st
Lawrence Ann (Mrs.), tailor, 28 Penton place, Pentonville
Lawrence Benj. boot & shoe maker, 87 Albany rd. Cambrwll
Lawrence Burton Charles, pastrycook, &c. 93 Strand
Lawrence Charles, builder, 11 Old Montague st. Whitechpl
Lawrence Charles, coal dealer, 38 Brown's la. Spitalfields
Lawrence Chas. custom ho. agt. 27 Ter. Trinity sq.Tower hill
Lawrence Charles, linendraper, 10 Norfolk pl.Lw. rd. Islingtn
Lawrence Charles, oil & colorman, 6 Jewin st. Cripplegate
Lawrence Charles, stock bro. see Mackenzie & Lawrence
Lawrence Chas. Rd. *Marquis of Clanricarde* P.H. 3 Upper Southwick st. north, Cambridge terrace
Lawrence Edward, baker, 5 Bride terrace, Liverpool road
Lawrence Edwd. china dealer, 4 Elliott's row, Islington, & bricklayer, 58 Perceval st. & 25 Whiskin st. Clerkenwell
Lawrence Edward, clothes salesman, 75 Brewer st. Somers town, 1 Royal Hospital row, Chelsea, & 184 Lambeth wk
Lawrence Edward, painter & paperhr. 3 Webber st. Blkfrs.rd
Lawrence Edward, shoemaker, 12 Amelia st. Walworth rd
Lawrence Edward, veterinary surgeon, Bromley, Middlesex
Lawrence Effingham, conveyancer, 44 Chancery lane
Lawrence Eli, woollen draper, 76 & 77 Leadenhall st
Lawrence Eliza (Miss), staymaker, 89 Whitechapel road
Lawrence Erasmus, van proprietor, 63 Curtain rd. Shoreditch
Lawrence Flora (Mrs.), school, 8 Robert st. Hampstead rd
Lawrence Foden, grocer & ironm. 11 Ann's tr. Cambridge hth
Lawrence George, corn dealer, 18 Piccadilly
Lawrence Geo. hardwareman, 23Chalcroft ter. New cut, Lambt
Lawrence Geo. oil & colorman, 21 Rochester row, Westminr
Lawrence Geo. pocket book & dressing case ma.9Nw. Bond st
Lawrence Geo. Joseph, baker, 50 Penton st. Nw. rd. Pentnvl
Lawrence Henry, *Blue Boar's Head* P.H.31Kingst. Westmnst
Lawrence Harry Hanslip, solicitor, 5 South sq. Gray's inn
Lawrence James, carpenter, 3 King st. Kensington
Lawrence, James, coal dealer, 114 Cromer st. Brunswick sq
Lawrence James, commission agent, see Poulton & Lawrence
Lawrence Jas. *Devonsh. Arms* P.H.21 Devonsh.st.Portld pl
Lawrence James, glass & chinaman, 22 Wells st. Oxford st
Lawrence James, grocer, 120 Great Suffolk st. Borough
Lawrence James, lodging house, 24 Euston place
Lawrence Jas. plumber & painter, 1 Back hill, Hatton grdn
Lawrence Jas. upholsterer, 13 Everett st. Brunswick sq
Lawrence John, boot & shoe maker, 88 Whitechapel rd
Lawrence John, boot & shoe maker, 7 Cambridge rd. Mile end
Lawrence John, cheesemonger, 15 Leigh st. Burton crescent
Lawrence John, fishmonger, 2 Motcombe st. Belgrave sq
Lawrence John, linendraper, 46 Chapel st. Somers town
Lawrence John, locksmith, 38 Hart st. Covent garden
Lawrence John, navy agent, see Goode and Lawrence
Lawrence John, solicitor, 29 Lincoln's inn fields
Lawrence Joseph, clothes salesman, 63 Broad st. Bloomsby
Lawrence Joseph, linendraper, 12 Crosby row, Walworth rd
Lawrence Joseph, tailor, 23 Bloomsbury st. St. Giles's
Lawrence Lawrence, grocer, High st. Stoke Newington
Lawrence Margt. (Miss), dress ma.3 Penton pl. New rdPentv
Lawrence Matthew, picture dealear, 86 Berwick st Oxf. st
Lawrence Peter, toy dealer, 110 London rd Southwark
Lawrence Rebecca(Mrs.), cigar box ma.7Boundary st.Shdtch
Lawrence Rich. gen. dealer, 9 Chalcroft ter. Lambeth
Lawrence Robert, fishmonger, 129 Lambeth walk
Lawrence Robt. mathl. inst. ma. 19 Cursitor st. Chancery la
Lawrence Robt. John, painter & glazier, 47 Leadenhall st
Lawrence Samuel, commission stables, 315 Oxford st
Lawrence Saml. dealer in diamonds, watches & jewellery, 14 Bedford st. Covent garden
Lawrence Sophia (Mrs.), baker, 16 Borough road
Lawrence Susannah (Mrs.), *British Tar* P.H. 29 St.Geo. st
Lawrence Thomas, baker, 37 Brook st. Lambeth
Lawrence Thomas, bootmaker, 4 Frederick st. Regent's pk
Lawrence Thomas, builder, 20 Grundy st. East India road
Lawrence Thomas, builder, 16 Roll's buildings, Fetter lane
Lawrence Thomas, carpet broom mnufactry.260Kent st.Boro'
Lawrence Thomas, coach & harness ma.33Wilson st.Finsbury
Lawrence Thomas, plumber, painter, & glazier, 19 Old Change
Lawrence Thomas, wine cooper, 24 Artillery la. Bishopsgate
Lawrence Wm. boot & shoemaker, Bromley, Middlesex
Lawrence Wm. butcher, 23 Richmond pl. East st. Walworth
Lawrence Wm. dng. rooms, 39NewManorst. King'srd.Chelsea
Lawrence Wm. *Grapes* P.H. 21 James st. Covent garden
Lawrence Wm. hairdress. & newsvend. 12 Gt. Trinity la.City
Lawrence Wm. plumber, 10 Church st. Kensington, & 1 Sussex place, New town, Kensington
Lawrence Wm. shell fish shop, 94 London wall
Lawrence Wm. surgeon, 18 Whitehall place
Lawrence Wm. timber merchant, 1 Rodney bldgs. NewKentrd
Lawrence Wm. wholesale glover & manufactr. 12 Gutter la
Lawrence Wm. Craig, confectioner, 158 Oxford st
Lawrie John, naphtha distiller, Union rd. Albany rd. O.Kent rd
Laws Alfred, grocer, 22 Vauxhall st. Lambeth
Laws Henry, grocer & cheesemonger, 1 Grosvenor pl. Boro'rd
Laws James, teadealer & grocer, 53 Broad st. Golden square
Laws Jeremiah, manufacturing chemist, Old Ford
Laws John, baker, 78 Church st. Shoreditch
Laws John, chemist, 9 New Church st. west, Edgware rd
Laws John, ginger beer manufactr. 12 Well st. Cripplegate
Laws Joseph, appraiser & bro. 11 Cloth fair, West Smithfld
Laws Luke, butcher, 8 Newport court, Newport market
Laws Marion (Mrs.), lodging house, 6 Surrey st. Strand
Laws Richard, pawnbroker, 6 Portland row, Camberwell rd
Laws Wm. custom ho. agt. & *K. of Denmark* P.H.24Wapping
Laws William, linendraper, see Turnor & Laws
Lawson & Anderdon, east india & gen. agts. 50 Lime st. City
Lawson David & Co. calico printers, 80 Wood st. Cheapside
Lawson, Spenceley & Brent, chain cable ware. 277 Wapping
Lawson Ann (Miss), music seller, 198 Tottenham ct. road
Lawson Chas. beer retailer, 73 Brunswick st. Blackwall
Lawson Chas. John, clk. of peace for Surrey, 1 North st. Lmbth
Lawson Chrstn. chan.shop & beer ret.19North st.Whtchpl.rd
Lawson Edward, profr. of dancing, 3 Gower st.north, New rd
Lawson Fras. general dealer, 20 Devonshire st. Lisson grove
Lawson Hugh, tailor, 40 Berners st. Middlesex hospital
Lawson James, chair & sofa ma. 20 New inn yard, Shoreditch
Lawson James Hilton, *Hoop & Grapes* P.H.112 St.George st
Lawson John, butcher, 24 Great Guildford st. Borough
Lawson Ann, music seller, 198 Tottenham court road
Lawson Martin, lodging house, 55 Beaumont st. Portland pl
Lawson Peter, beer retailer, 5 Francis pl. Holloway
Lawson Robert, floorcloth & table cov. ma. 10 Watt's bldgs. & 4 Wharf, Canal road, Kingsland road
Lawson Robert, merchant, 39 Gutter lane, Cheapside
Lawson Robert, merchant, 1 Sherborne lane
Lawson Thomas, coach painter, 110 Great Titchfield st
Lawson Thomas, timber merchant, 29 Dover pl. New Kent rd
Lawson Wm. hatter, see Horne & Lawson
Lawson Wm. surgeon, 13 Cleveland st. Fitzroy square
Lawson Wm. trimming seller, 26 Duke st. Grosvenor sq
Lawson Wm. wine, &c. mercht. seeTrower, Lawson & Trower
Lawson Wm. Mears, corn dealer, 2 Langley pl. Coml.rd. east
Lawson Wm. Simpson, grocer, 1 Colet pl. Comml. road east
Lawton Elizabeth (Mrs.), who. confectioner, 8 Rathbone pl
Lawton Philip, pawnbrkr.& silversmth.21 Green st. Leicr.sq
Lawton Rd. surgeon, 20 Albany place, York road, Lambeth

Lawyer Wm. grocer, 1 Devonshire pl. Up. Kennington la
Lax Adolph, importer of foreign silks, 67 Newgate st. City
Laxton Charles, *King's Arms* P.H. 23 Little Moorfields
Laxton Henry, architect & survy. 10 Fludyer st. Westminster
Laxton Henry, architect & surveyor, 145 Strand
Laxton Robert, baker, 120 Upper Whitecross st
Laxton Wm. civil engineer, architect & surveyor, 10 Fludyer st
Lay John, tailor, &c. 24 Bermondsey wall
Lay John, tailor, 4 Swan st. Minories
Lay John Goodhall, cornfactor, see Kingsford & Lay
Lay Robert, clothes salesman, 14 King st. Seven dials
Lay William, butcher, 8 Goldsmith's row, Hackney road
Lay William, fruiterer, 3 Pratt st. Camden town
Lay William, veterinary surgeon, 2 Gun lane, Limehouse
Layborn Thomas, jeweller, 19 Ashley crescent, Wenlock rd
Laybourn & Topham, haberdashers, 37 Wigmore st
Laycock Eliza (Mrs.), grocer, 5 Queen st. Tower hill
Laycock Henry Stainton, barrister, 43 Lincoln's inn fields
Laycock William, beer retailer, 72 Brook st. Lambeth
Laycock Wm. bootmaker, 4 Church lane, Commercial road
Layel James Henry, *Turk's Head* P.H. 71 Aldgate High st
Layfield Richd. cabinet ma. &c. 24 Gt. Pulteney st. Gold. sq
Layland George, engineer, 131 Gt. Suffolk st. Borough
Layland Wm. & Eliza, teachers of dancing, 157 Blackfrs. rd
Layland John, rag merchant, 33 St. Andrew's hill, Blackfrs
Layland Thomas, currier, 108 Shoreditch High st
Layland William, glass cutter, 9 Red Lion court, Fleet st
Layton Charles & Edwin, booksellers, stationers, engravers & printers to the trade, 150 Fleet st
Layton James, tea & colonial broker, see Hulbert, Layton & Co
Layton John, boot & shoe maker, 3 Cumberland row, Islngtn
Layton Mary Ann (Mrs.), *George & Dragon* P.H. 22 Greek st. So
Layton Robert, *Blue Anchor* P.H. 92 York st. Westminster
Layton Robert, boot & shoe ma. 14 Pierepoint row, Islington
Layton Wm. baker, 6 Hemingford terrace west, Islington
Layton William, undertaker, King's road west, Chelsea
Layzell John, shoemaker, 28 Brunswick parade, Barnsby. rd
Layzell Joseph, tobacconist, 14 Hand court, Holborn
Lazarus Hannah & Sons, cap peak ma. 22 Union st. east, Spitfls
Lazarus & Laurance, w. i. merchants, 5 Castle st. Houndsdch
Lazarus & Meyer, importers of foreign wines & spirits, 43 Mansell st. Goodman's fields
Lazarus Aaron, carver & gilder, 28 Whitechapel High st
Lazarus Alfred, pencil maker, 5 Bevis marks, St. Mary Axe
Lazarus Catherine (Mrs.), coal mercht. see Sargent & Lazarus
Lazarus David, furniture dealer, 49 Marylebone la. Oxfd. st
Lazarus Eleazar, engraver, &c. 2 Smith's bldgs. Somerset st. Aldgate
Lazarus Elizabeth (Mrs.), black lead pencil ma. 5 Bevis mks. & 3 Bury st. St. Mary Axe
Lazarus Godfrey, general dlr. 12 Alderson's bldgs. City road
Lazarus Harris, slopseller, 112 Upper East Smithfield
Lazarus Isaac, watchmaker, 13 Oakley st. Mount st. Lambeth
Lazarus Joseph, clothes dealer, 10 Marylebone la. Oxford st
Lazarus Joseph, rag merchant, 146 Shadwell High st
Lazarus Joshua, clothes dealer, 114 Houndsditch
Lazarus Lewis, clothes salesman, 107 Houndsditch
Lazarus Lewis, engraver & printer, 6 Church st. Minories
Lazarus Lewis, fruiterer, 2 Wilson st. Finsbury
Lazarus Lewis, lead merchant, 15 Middlesex st. Aldgate
Lazarus Moses, grocer, 24 Duke st. Aldgate
Lazarus Samuel M. fur coat ma. 1 Magdalen rw. Gt. Prsct. st
Lazarus Samuel, wholesale furrier, 4 Bartholomew close
Lazarus Solomon, west india mer. 21 East India chambers
Lazenby Elizh. & Son, fish sauce ma. 6 Edwards st. Portm. sq
Lazenby Elizh. (Mrs.), oil & italian wa. 56 Lamb's Conduit st
Lazenby John, tailor, 8 Castle st. east, Oxford st
Lazonby Samuel, nurseryman, Little Chelsea
Lea, Bousfield & Co. silk furniture, damask, tabaretts & silk handkerchief manufacturers, 50 Cheapside
Lea & Co. carpet, rug & bombazine mnfs. 34 & 36 Newgate st
Lea Chas. & Co. coal merchs. Beauvoir wf. Kingslandrd. basin
Lea Geo. & Co. coalmers. Ecclestonwf. Up. Belgrave pl. Pmlco
Lea Francis, pocketbook ma. 37 Coppice row, Clerkenwell
Lea Henry Thomas, accountant & agent, 21 Abchurch lane
Lea John, ringma. engraver & enameller 20 Silver st. Wood st
Lea John, gold, coral, & jet cutter, 7 Meredith st. Clerkenwell
Lea Joseph, undertaker, 49 Rahere st. Goswell road
Lea Thomas, coal mer. Northumblnd. wf. Augustus st. Reg. pk
Lea William, engine turner, 35 Skinner st. Clerkenwell
Lea William, *Grapes & Can* P.H. 142 Goswell st
Lea Wm. plumber, grainer, painter & glazier, 14 Hatton gdn
Lea Wm. John, architect & surveyor, 13 Ebury st. Pimlico
Lea Wm. Lyal, architect & survey, 9 Ehrenburghter. Cmdn. tn
Leach, Broadbent, Leach & Co. factr. &c. 1 Castle ct. Lawrence la
Leach & Clark, ship insr. & custom ho. ag. 1 Riches ct. Lime st
Leach Ellen & Car. (Misses), milliners, 54 King st. Golden sq
Leach Benj. tobaccopipe mak. 6 Black Lion yd. Whitechap. rd
Leach Charles, beer retailer, 1 Gt. Carlisle st. Portman mkt
Leach Charles, cooper, Speedy pl. Cromer st. Brunswick sq
Leach Charles, tinman & brazier, 27 Gt. Marlborough st
Leach Edward, beer retailer, 28 East st. Kennington rd
Leach Ellen E. (Mrs.), staymak. 22 Featherstone blds. Holbn
Leach George, butcher, 89 Harrow road
Leach George, music printer, 45 Greek st. Soho
Leach Henry, bricklayer, 197½ Brick lane, Spitalfields
Leach James, accountant, 12 President st. east, Goswell rd
Leach James, surgeon, Bridge st. Vauxhall
Leach Jane (Mrs.), *Gun & Tent* P.H. 9 Fort st. Spitalfields
Leach John, cooper, &c. 10 Stucley terrace, Camden town
Leach John, house agent, 15 Bridge house pl. Newington cwy
Leach John, *Nag's Head* P.H. Battersea
Leach John, leatherseller & grindery dealer, 35 Old st. road
Leach Joseph, plumber, 20 Church st. Camberwell
Leach Joseph, solicitor, 31 Duncan terrace, City road
Leach Matthew, merchant, 4 New London st. City
Leach Richard, watch & clock maker, 5 Great Tower st. City
Leach Robert, plumber, &c. 16 Old Broad st. City
Leach Sam. Forest, jun. bookbind. 8 Orange st. Red Lion sq
Leach Saml. F. sen. classical prof. 34 Glo'ster st. Queen sq
Leach Scott Wm. bootmaker, 4 Bermondsey new road
Leach Susan (Mrs.), bottle dlr. 1 Lit. Coram st. Brunswk. sq
Leach Thomas, barrister, Chapel staircase, Lincoln's inn
Leach Thos. dairyman, 67 Lisson grove north
Leach Thos. watch & clock ma. 2 Limekiln hill, Limehouse
Leach Thos. jun. barrister, Chapel stairs, Lincoln's inn
Leach Thos. P. hairdresser, 4 Ward's pl. Hoxton Old town
Leach Wm. cheesemonger, see Baker & Leach
Leach Wm. hosier, 35 York st. Westminster
Leach Wm. sup. regr. of births, 1 Colet pl. Salmon la. Stepney
Leach Wm. Warren, tailor, 20 Gt. Warner st. Clerkenwell
Leachman F. S. (Miss), ladies' sch. 19 Grosvenor pl. Cmbwl. rd
Leachman Joseph, solicitor, 18 Aldermanbury
Leachman Thomas, solicitor, 41 Basinghall st
Leachman William, silk warehouseman, 5 Gt. Distaff lane
Leacock & Co. merchts. Madeira, & 3 White Lion ct. Cornhill
Lead Company (Chas. Deane, sec.), 9 Martin's la. Cannon st
Leadam Thomas R. surgeon, 65 Tooley st. Borough
Leadbeater John, naturalist, 19 Brewer st. Golden square
Leadbeater John, strong rooms, wrought iron & fire-proof safes, chests, iron doors, &c. manufactr. 125 Aldersgate st
Leadbetter Jas. *Blockmakers' Arms* P.H. 1 Ashley cre. City rd
Leadbetter Wm. *Trafalgar* coffeerooms, 13 King Wm. st. Strnd
Leadbetter Wm. Jas. jeweller, 4 Pollen st. Hanover square
Leadbitter Thomas, solicitor, 7 Staple inn, Holborn
Leader & Cock, music sellers & publishers, & musical instrument warehouse, 63 New Bond st. corner of Brook st
Leader Chas. carpenter & undertaker, 51 Mount st. Lambeth
Leader Charles, lodging house, 16 Manchester buildings
Leader Elizth. (Mrs.), turner, 43 Gt. Russell st. Bloomsby. sq
Leader Henry Francis, grocer, &c. 6 Dove court, Old Jewry
Leader Henry Francis, telescope manufactr. 25 Gt. Percy st
Leader James, butcher, 1 Thornton st. Dockhead
Leader John, tailor, 14 East st. Red Lion square
Leader Robert, tailor, 12 New inn yard, Shoreditch
Leadley Geo. clerk to Thames Police Court, Arbour st. east
Leadley James, wholesale stationer, 7 Duke st. Stamford st
Leadley Miles, bookbinder, 2 Oxford Arms pas. Warwick la
Leaf, Barnett, Scotson & Co. warehousemen, 46, 47 & 48 Wood st
Leaf Christopher & Co. warehousemen, 13 Addle st. Wood st
Leaf, Coles, Smith & Co. warehousemen, 39 Old Change
Leaf Wm. & Co. imp. of chicory, 7 St. Mary st. Whitechapel rd
Leaf Wm. & Co. merchants, 1 Sambrook ct. Basinghall st
Leage Richard Wm. house agent, 16 Nelson st. City road
League Office, 67 Fleet st
Leah George Henry, plumber, &c. 86 Park st. Grosvenor sq
Leah Jno. Dougal, plumber & enginr. 2 Portland rd. Rgnt. pk
Leah Sam. Hen. sen. watch & clock makr. 29 Bath st. City rd
Leahair Abraham, cattle salesman, 60 West Smithfield
Leahy David, barrister, 1 Mitre court buildings, Temple
Leahy Edward Daniel, artist, 13 Berners st. Oxford st
Leak Alex. Piozzi, surgeon, 18 Assembly row, Mile end rd
Leake Frederick & Co. leather hanging office, 52 Regent st
Leake Frederick, surveyor, 52 Regent st
Leake Geo. fruit salesman, 73 Farringdon mkt. & 11 New ct
Leake George, scale maker, 95 Dean st. Soho
Leake James, chandler's shop, 13 Church st. Camberwell
Leake John, gen. agt. & ship ins. brok. 4 Cushion ct. Broad st
Leaker Henry, furn. & general ironmonger, 46 Leadenhall st
Leakey Matthew Henry, hairdresser, &c. 107 Tooley st
Lealand Peter, math. instru. ma. 24 Clarendon st. Somers tn
Leaman & Co. mahogany & rosewood merchts. West India

docks, & counting house, 110 Fenchurch st
Leaman Andrew V. timber merchant, 89 John st. Fitzroy sq
Lean Charles, stockbroker, Auction mart
Lean Joseph, tobacconist, 35 Church st. Lambeth
Lean Vincent Stuckey, barrister, 11 Serle st. Lincoln's inn
Leaning Eliza (Miss), milliner, High st. Deptford
Leapman Isaac, jet manufacturer & bugle worker, 13 East Mount terrace, Whitechapel road
Lear Charles Henry, artist, 35 London st. Fitzroy sq
Lear George Chas. plumber & painter, 16 Sale st. Paddington
Lear Henry, fruiterer, 6 Bozier's ct. Tottenham court road
Lear Henry, painter, 4 James pl. Larkhall la. Clapham
Learmonths' & Roberts, tanners & leather dressers, 24 Bride lane, Fleet st. & Page's walk, Bermondsey
Learmonth Walter & Co. leather merchs. Banbury ct. Long acre
Leary Charlotte (Mrs.), newsvender, 13 Duke st. St. James's
Leary Cornelius, accountant, 29 Lombard st. chambers
Leary Cornelius, mahogany broker, see Skeen & Leary
Leason Joseph, *White Swan* P.H. 82 Park st. Grosvenor sq
Leath James, bookseller & publisher, 5 St. Paul's church yd
Leath James George, physician, 11 Notting hill square
Leath Richard, grocer, 87 Berwick st. Soho
Leathart Charles, who. perfumer, 83 Berwick st. Soho
Leather John, butcher, 2 Chapel st. Somers town
Leather William, warehouseman, 91 London wall
Leatherby John, tailor, 4 Michael's place, Brompton
Leatherdale Henry, builder, 7 Devonshire st. Globe road
Leatherdale John, dining rooms, 40 Shadwell High st
Leathers Edward John, grocer, 71 Tothill st. west, Westmins
Leathers Robert, teadealer, 5 Berwick st. Soho
Leathersellers' Almshouses, Clark's place, Bishopsgate
Leathersellers' Hall (Wm. Vines, clerk), 13½ St. Helen's place
Leathes Thos. Leathes Stanger, mer. see Lovegrove & Leathes
Leathwaite John, booksel. & newsvender, 1 Pope's head alley
Leaver & Shirley, law stationers, 17 Carey st. Linc. inn fields
Leaver Benj. wheelwright, 4 Wharf, Macclesfield st. south
Leaver Harriet (Mrs.), baker, 24 Up. Seymour st. Euston sq
Leaver John, bedsacking maker & door mat manufacturer, 8 Oldham place, Bagnigge wells road
Leaver William, hatter, 45 Aldermanbury
Leavers & Harker, manufctg. jewellers, 2 Duncan pl. City rd
Leavy James, lodging house keeper, 17 Trinity sq. Borough
Leay Thomas, tailor, 9A, Little Titchfield st. Portland place
Le Bean Timothy, oilman, 78 Hackney road
Le Beau Timothy Edm. carman, 33 Sclater st. Bethnal green
Lebenheim Herrman & Co. berlin warehouse, 221 Regent st
Lebentz John, *Red Lion* P.H. 7 Black Lion yard, Whitechpl. rd
Le Blanc & Cook, solicitors, 18 New Bridge st. Blackfriars
Le Blanc Charles, solicitor, 44 Lincoln's inn fields
Le Blond & Co. engravers & designers, bankers & merchants, lithographic, letter press & copperplate printers, 4 Walbk
Le Blond Fras. fancy repository, 41½ Crown row, Mile end
Le Blond Peter, oil & colorman, 3 Mary st. Hampstead rd
Le Breton Francis, merchant, 33 Broad st. buildings
Le Breton Philip Hemery, solicitor, St. Martin's in the fields, register office for births, deaths & marriages, 44 Castle st. Leicester square
Lebrun Alexander, shoe warehouse, 42 Burlington arcade
Lebrun John, cabinetmaker, 7 Lower Kennington green
Lecand Benj. Louis, carver & gilder, 246 Tottenham ct. rd
Lecesne Lewis Celeste, merchant, 11 Fenchurch buildings
Le Chesne Victor, tailor, 56 Lower George st. Chelsea
Le Cheminant John, jeweller, 87 Wimpole st. Cavendish sq
Lechley Anthony, bootmaker, 44 Ernest st. Regent's pk
Lechmere William, solicitor, 22 Southampton st. Bloomsbury
Leck Mary (Mrs.), baker, 41 Gravel lane, Southwark
Leckey Robert, *Waterman's Arms* P.H. 92 Fore st. Limhse
Leckie Patrick Comrie, silk broker, see Waithman & Co
Lecluse Felix, watchmaker, 57 Frith st. Soho
Le Comte John, watchmaker, 7 Duke st. Adelphi
Le Cocq Eliza (Mrs.), glazier, 14 Windmill st. Finsbury
Leconte Edward, appraiser, 6 Norfolk st. Fitzroy square
Le Coq Albert, merchant, 1 Muscovy court, Trinity square
Le Coutre Chas. ship chandler, 21 Russell st. Rotherhithe
Le Cren Jas. painter, plumber & paperhang. 26 Moorgate st
Ledamun James, grocer & cheesemonger, 13 Princes st. Lbth
Ledgar Wm. grocer, 5 Ropemakers' fields, Limehouse
Ledgard Hen. woollen & stuff warehsmn. see Cash & Ledgard
Ledger Edward, hatter, see Keats & Ledger
Ledger George, accountant, arbitrator, &c. 74 Cheapside
Ledger John, tilleting & buckram manufacturer, linen & cotton merchant, Back st. Horselydown
Ledger John, surveyr. of the Surrey new roads, 5 Deptfd. brdg
Ledger Sarah (Mrs.), prof. of music, 2 York buildgs. Chelsea
Ledger Thomas, gasfitter, &c. see Strode & Ledger
Ledger William, baker, 10 Swan lane, Rotherhithe
Ledger Wm. Nathan, grocer, 39 Ironmonger row, Old st
Lediard, Jones & Mortimer, east india merchants, 43 Lime st
Ledsham Charles, baker, 16 Cross st. Hoxton New town
Lee & Bury, architects & surveyors, 20 Golden square
Lee & Coxhead, music publishers, 48 Albemarle st. Piccadilly
Lee Henry & Co. meat salesmen, Leadenhall market
Lee Henry & John, builders, 73 Chiswell st. Finsbury
Lee Henry & Son, butchers, Leadenhall market
Lee Henry & Sons, skinners & furriers, Loman st. Southwark
Lee & Jerdein, coal merchts. 15 Up. Ground st. Blackfriars rd
Lee Mark & Sons, tailors, 50 Munster sq. Regent's pk
Lee Michael & Co. tailors, 29 Duke st. St. James's
Lee (Morris) & Co. cigar manufrs. 15 Bury st. St. Mary Axe
Lee William & Co. wine & spirit mers. 3 Bury pl. Bloomsby
Lee William & Son, bricklayers, 22 King David la. Shadwll
Lee Alexander, M.D. surgeon, 6 Three Crown sq. Borough
Lee Ann (Mrs.), meat saleswoman, 9 Newgate market
Lee Charles, boot & shoe wa. 8 Church st. St. George's, Boro
Lee Charles, nursery, 26 Pelham road, Brompton
Lee Charles, paperhanger & decorator, 16 St. Martin's court, St. Martin's lane
Lee Daniel, straw hat manfr. 45 Myddelton st. Clerkenwell
Lee Daniel James, solicitor, see Coverdale & Lee
Lee David, piece broker, 89 Fore st. Cripplegate
Lee Edward Stephen, solicitor, 43 Lincoln's inn fields
Lee Elizabeth (Mrs.), coffee rooms, 123 Lower Thames st
Lee Francis, carver & gilder, 33 Gt. Marylebone st
Lee Fras. Valentine, barrister, 1 King's Bench walk, Temple
Lee Frederick, butcher, 14 Duke st. Grosvenor sq
Lee Frederick James, beer retailer, 5 Cornwall rd. Lambeth
Lee Frederick Wm. tailor, 41A, Red Lion st. Holborn
Lee Fred. Wm. tailor & draper, 46 Southampton bldgs. Holbn
Lee George, butcher, 11 Cleveland st. Fitzroy square
Lee George, grocer, 17 Sermon lane, Doctors' commons
Lee Geo. merchant & seed crusher, 27 Crutchedfriars
Lee Geo. ship & insurance agent, 27 Crutchedfriars
Lee Geo. registr. of births & deaths, 50 Gt. Queen st. Lin. I.n
Lee Geo. tailor, Bevenden st. 7 Aske terrace, City road
Lee Geo. Laurence, lithograph. writer & print. 245 High Holbn
Lee Geo. Leslie, wine merchant, 75 Old Broad st
Lee Geo. Robert, china warehouse, 39 Cheyne walk, Chelsea
Lee George T. brushmaker, 95 Mount st. Berkeley sq
Lee Henry, butcher, 14 Haberdashers' walk, Hoxton
Lee Henry, meat salesman, see Challis, Harris & Lee
Lee Henry, music publisher, 13 Lisle st. Leicester sq
Lee Henry, oilman, 20 Aldersgate st
Lee Henry, physician, 36 Bloomsbury st. St. Giles's
Lee Henry, surgeon, 13 Dover st. Piccadilly
Lee Isaac John, watchma. 16 Devonshire bldgs. Gt. Dover st
Lee Isaiah, jeweller, hair workr. & optician, 41 Rathbone pl
Lee James, bricklayer, 23 Newton st. Holborn
Lee James, butcher, 53 Farringdon st
Lee James, carpenter, 59 London st. Fitzroy square
Lee James, dyer, 13 Circus st. New road
Lee James, engraver on wood, 97 Princes sq. Kennington
Lee James, grocer, 10 Church st. Chelsea
Lee James, straw hat maker, 6 East road, City road
Lee Jas. Hen. cheesemonger, 1 Gt. Russell st. Covent garden
Lee Jesse, meat salesman, see Stubbing & Lee
Lee John, LL D. advocate, 5 College, Doctors' commons
Lee John, bookseller & publisher, 440 Strand
Lee John, carpenter, 4 Lower Ranelagh st. Pimlico
Lee John, farrier, 254 High Holborn
Lee John, fruiterer, 7 Bedford st. Bedford row
Lee John, fruiterer & bricklayer, 1 Kinnerton st. Belgrave sq
Lee John, grocer & cheesemonger, 8 Old Dorset st. pl. Clphm rd
Lee John, ironmonger, 8 Orchard place, Kingsland road
Lee John, locksmith, 1 Creed lane, Ludgate hill
Lee John, printseller, 102 London wall
Lee John, seedsman & florist, 2 Bray's bldgs. Lr. rd. Islington
Lee John, shoe warehouse, 84 Brick lane, Spitalfields
Lee John, tailor, 8 Grange court, Lincoln's inn fields
Lee John, tailor, 1 Whitefriars st
Lee John, watch finisher, 25 Wellington st. Goswell st
Lee John Benj. attorney, 3 Gt. Dean's yard, Westminster
Lee John Dunkin, sail cloth & sacking wa. 97 Leadenhall st
Lee John Edward, butcher, 59 New Church st. Lisson grove
Lee John Henry, gold piercer, 53 Myddelton st. Spafields
Lee John Joseph, accountant, 1 Devonshire sq. Bishopsgate
Lee John Maclean (Cutler & Co.), wine mercht. 3 Mansion ho. pl
Lee John Would, solicitor, 34 Hunter st. Brunswick sq
Lee Jortin Wm. attorney, 43 Lincoln's inn fields
Lee Joseph, bookseller & news agt. 2 Star alley, Fench ch. st
Lee Joseph, confectioner, 5 Plumber's row, City road
Lee Joseph, paper hanger, 49 Warwick st. Pimlico
Lee Levin, artificial flower & feather ma. 7A Lillypot lane

Lee Margaret (Mrs.), *Half Moon* P.H. 77 West Smithfield
Lee Mark P. tailor, 19 Albemarle st. Clerkenwell
Lee Mary (Miss), milliner & dressmaker, 67 St. James's st
Lee Patrick, bill sticker, 1 Pleydell court, Bouverie st
Lee Philip, crpntr.buildr.&undert.5Windsor tr.Vxhll.bdg.rd
Lee Philip, linendraper, see Walker & Lee
Lee Richard, clothier, 4 Deptford bridge
Lee Richard, confectioner, 26 Aldgate High st
Lee Richard, shoemaker, Battersea square
Lee Richard, arbitrator & accountant, 8 Furnival's inn
Lee Robert, F.R.S. physician, 4 Saville row, Piccadilly
Lee Robt.sen.carpent.&packing case mak.108 St.Martin's la
Lee Sabina (Mrs.), butcher, 32 Portland st. Soho
Lee Samuel, baker, 10 Nag's head court, Gracechurch st
Lee Samuel, curiosity dealer, 57 Gt. Queen st. Linc. inn flds
Lee Samuel, rope merchant, 132 Rosemary lane
Lee Samuel, upholsterer, 2 Crawley st. Oakley sq. Somrs.tn
Lee Samuel, jun. baker, 30 Upper Norton st. Fitzroy sq
Lee Sarah (Mrs.), clog maker, 24 Henrietta st. Manchester sq
Lee Sophia (Mrs.), fruiterer, 18 Shoe lane, Fleet st
Lee Thomas, beer retailer, 1 New Rochester row, Westmr
Lee Thomas, export ironmonger & manufacturer, 5 George yard, Lombard st. & 2 Edmund st. Birmingham
Lee Thomas, cattle salesman, 8 West Smithfield
Lee Thomas, lapidary, 18 Peartree st. Goswell st
Lee Thomas Stafford, surgeon, 2 Upper Gordon st. Euston sq
Lee William, artist, 16 Howland st. Fitzroy square
Lee William, attorney, see Inton-Lee
Lee William, queen's counsel, 58 Chancery lane
Lee William, boot & shoemaker, 1 Abdy st. Horselydown
Lee William, carpenter, 21 East road, City road
Lee William, coachmaker, see Rigby & Lee
Lee William, confectioner, 79 Borough High st
Lee William, *Derby Arms* P.H. 7 Harper st. New Kent rd
Lee William, dining rooms, 134 Church st. Shoreditch
Lee William, fruiterer, 8 Blenheim terrace, St. John's wood
Lee William, furniture broker, 10 Cleveland st. Fitzroy sq
Lee William, furniture broker, 2 & 4 Henrietta st. Manch.sq
Lee William, gardener, Lower road, Rotherhithe
Lee William, hat & cap manufactr. 6 Plumber's row, City road
Lee William, linendraper, 41 Munster st. Regent's park
Lee William, locksmith & bellhanger, 23 Old Fish st. City
Lee William, queen's counsel, 58 Chancery lane
Lee William, whiting manufacturer & lime burner, 16 Upper Ground st. Blackfrs; Wilton rd. Pimlico; & Deptford brdg
Lee William, wh.confectioner, 31 Baldwin's grdns. Leather la
Lee William Henry, cheesemonger, see Rogers & Lee
Lee William Thomas, plumber, 3 South Island pl. Clapham rd
Leech Geo.carpntr.& builder, 8 Thatched house row, Islington
Leech George, toy & fancy wareho. 25 Basing la. Bread st
Leech John, fruiterer, 19 Royal Hospital row, Chelsea
Leech Joseph, solicitor, see Johnston, Farquhar & Leech
Leech Thomas, bootmaker, 5 Chapel st. Somers town
Leech William, wine & spirit merchnt. 34 Gt. St. Helen's
Leeder Elizabeth (Miss), turner, 43 Gt. Russell st. Bloomsby
Leeder Thomas, undertaker, 35 Regent st. Horseferry road
Leeder William, engraver, 22 New Compton st. Soho
Leedham Francis, picture liner, 3 Duck la. Wardour st. Soho
Leedham John, picture liner, 14 Shouldham st. Edgware rd
Leedham John, E.wholes.cheesemonger, see Buss & Leedham
Leeds, Huddersfield, Sheffield & South Staffordshire Railway Co. (R. Shelton Mackenzie, D.C.L. sec.), 1 Moorgate
Leefe Fredk. E. coal mer. 4 Astey's bldgs. Lower rd. Islington
Leefe Jonathan, furrier, 21 Radcliffe ter. Goswell road
Leek Wm. Thos. box & packing case maker & dealer in second hand packing cases, 16½ Lit. Moorfields, & 34 Moorgate st
Leek Wm. Thos. brush & door mat manufacturer, baskets, &c. 34 Moorgate st. City
Leeks Edward Fredk. solicitor, see Dean, Leeks & Dixon
Leeland Benj. coffeerooms, 256 Blackfriars road
Leeland John, baker, 7 Cowcross st. Smithfield
Leeland John, coal & potato dlr. 7 Limekiln hill, Limehouse
Leeming John, bootmaker, 51 Broad st. Ratcliff
Leeming William, bootmaker, 9 Penton st. Pentonville
Leer Christopher & Jas. coachmaks. 69 Bridge rd. Lambeth
Lees George Wyld & Co. linendrapers to her Majesty the Queen, 47 Fleet st
Lees Thomas D. & Co. wine & brandy mercs. 11 & 12 Philpot la
Lees Wm. & Sons, export ironmngrs. 5 Barge yd. Bucklersbury
Lees Diana Ann (Mrs.) news agt. 66 Theobald's rd. Red Lion sq
Lees Edward, jun. cheesemonger, 10 Pitfield st. Hoxton
Lees Edward, sen. cheesemonger, 24 East road, City road
Lees George, tailor, 39 Acton st. Gray's inn road
Lees James, plumber, &c. 19 Garden row, London road
Lees John, cabinet maker, 3 Myrtle st. Hoxton
Lees Robert, plush manufacturer, see Gillett, Lees & Co
Lees Thomas, baker, 124 Lambeth walk
Lees Thomas, grocer, 8 Hackney road crescent
Lees William, wholesale hatter, 46 Lant st. Borough
Leese George Macartney, surgeon, 16 Baker st. Portman sq
Leese Lewis, surgeon, 25 Moorgate st
Leese Richard, carver & gilder, 35 Paul st. Finsbury
Leeson Chas. strawhat manuf. 9 St. John's la. West Smithfield
Leeson John, coal merchant, 41 Davies st. Berkeley sq
Leeson John, surgeon, 4 Finsbury square
Leeson Joseph, surgeon, 6 Edwardes sq. Kensington
Leeson Robert, fruiterer, 20 Back st. Horselydown
Leeson Wm. *White Bear* P.H. 58 St. John st. Smithfield
Leete & Warburton, ironmongers, &c. 146 Tottenham ct. rd
Leete Benjamin, sheep salesman, 41 West Smithfield
Leete Duckett, plasterer, 25 St. George's row, Pimlico
Leete John, ham warehouse, 143 Sloane st. Knightsbridge
Leete John, silversmith & pawnbrok. see Wolsoncroft & Leete
Leete John, solicitor, 10 Foster lane, Cheapside
Leevy Aaron, confectioner, 34 Norton folgate
Lefebvre Henry & Co. for. & british com. agts. 77 Cheapside
Lefebvre Elizth. (Madame), milliner, &c. 57 Gt. Portland st
Lefever Wm. & Son, builders & undertakers, 12 George st. Mansion house, & 1 Plough yard, Shoreditch
Lefever Charles, mathl. inst. ma. 14 Duncan pl. London flds
Lefever Eliza (Mrs.), milliner, 3 York pl. Kingsland rd
Lefever Joseph, grocer, 26 Turk st. Bethnal green
Lefever Wm. Henry, oil & colorman, 28 Kingsland road
Lefevre Henry Shaw, mer. see Thomas John, Son & Lefevre
Lefévre Sir George, physician, 60 Brook st. Bond st
Lefley Samuel, bootmaker, 3 New Turnstile, High Holborn
Lefranceis R. & Co. linseed cake merchants, 48 Mark la
Lefroy George Bentinck, solicitor, 217 Piccadilly
Lefroy Thos. Edwd. Preston, barrister, 5 Pump ct. Temple
Leftwich, Tousey & Hardy, ship biscuit baks. 29 Lw. Shadwell
Leftwich Edwd. cheesemonger, 26 Crown row, Walworth rd
Leftwich George, surveyor, 9 Salisbury st. Strand
Leftwich John, cheesemonger, 12 Bedford pl. Commercl. rd. ea
Leftwich Wm. ice merchant, 43 Cumberland market, & 29 Little Albany st. Regent's park
Lega-Zambelli & Fletcher, italian wareho. 14 Cromer st
Legacy Duty Office, Somerset house; hrs. of business 10 to 4
Legal & Commercial Life Assurance Society (I. C. Hardy, actuary & secretary), 68 Cheapside
Legal & General Life Assurance Society (Thomas Rowe Edmonds, B.A. actuary), 10 Fleet st.; see page 2031
Legal Observer weekly paper, 67 Chancery lane
Le Gassick John, tailor, see Anstey, Le Gassick & Guthrie
Le Gassirk William, tailor, 12 Cork st. Bond st
Le Geir & Goodwin, bed feather dlrs. 76 to 78 Gt. Saffron hill
Legg Samuel & Son, undertakers, 2 Great Knightrider st
Legg Thomas & Son, woolstaplers, 230 Bermondsey st
Legg Charles, grocer, oil & colorm. 17 & 18 Wardour st. Soho
Legg Charles, lodging house, 4 Park st. Grosvenor square
Legg Cyrus, woolstapler, Gun alley, 85 Bermondsey st
Legg George, architect & surveyor, 10 South sq. Gray's inn, & 239 Maida vale, Edgware road
Legg Jane (Mrs.), milliner, 10 Portland row, Camberwell road
Legg John, butcher, 71 Charlotte ter. New cut, Lambeth
Legg John, decorative painter, 1 Caroline st. Pimlico
Legg Jonas, wheelwright, Whetstone park, Lincn's. inn fields
Legg Moses Edward, wholesale glover, 27 Watling st
Legg William, butcher, 25 Britannia st. City road
Legg William, estate & house agent, 13 King st. & 42 Bury st. St. James's
Legg William, furniture broker, 94 Chalton st. Somers town
Legg Wm. Jas. bookbindr. & stnr. 8 Low. Chapman st. St. Geo. ea
Leggatt John & Co. warehousemen, 4 George yd. Lombard st
Leggatt & Neville, print & booksellers, 79 Cornhill
Leggatt Alfred, surgeon, 70 Ebury st. Pimlico
Leggatt Andrew, fruiterer, 67 Wilsted st. Somers town
Leggatt James, umbrella maker, 86 St. John st. road
Legge Henry, cabinet maker, 8 Prospect place, Kingsland rd
Legge Henry, tobacco manufacturer, 143 Old st
Legge John, cabinet maker, 117 Gray's inn lane
Legge William, surgeon, 3 Kingswood pl. South Lambeth
Legge Wm. Geo. acct. wine mer. & gen. agent, 9 Bond ct. Walbrk
Legget David, upholsterer, 16 King st. Covent garden
Leggett Ann (Mrs.), *Adam & Eve* P.H. Eve's pl. Old rd. St. Pcrs
Leggett George, grocer, 15 Albert pl. Bermndsy. New town
Leggett James, cab proprietor, 12 Lamb's bldgs. Bunhill row
Leggett James, shoemaker, 5 Minerva st. Hackney road
Leggett John, baker, 2 Hen & Chicken lane, Walworth com
Leggett Joseph, lodging house, 46 Duke st. St. James's
Leggett William, upholsterer, see Lucas & Leggett
Legh & Bellamy, wine merchants, 95 Quadrant, Regent st
Legleitner Adam, baker, 12 Stepney rents, Hackney road

Le Grand George Wren, grocer, 51 Lambeth walk
Le Grand Wm. british & foreign stock & share broker, 10 Shorter's court, & Stock exchange
Le Gros, Thompson & Bird, crape manfrs. 6 Goldsmith st
Le Grys John, coach builder, 44 Weymouth mews, Portld.pl
Lehocq Charles, french boot & shoe maker, 150 Regent st
Lehrle John, academy, 3 Gt. Turner st. Commercial rd. east
Leidley George, chandler's shop, 13 Heath pl. Cmbdge.heath
Leif John, confectioner, 26 Paul st. Finsbury
Leicester George Ostell, architect, 28 Nelson square
Leifchild John R. sec. to Scottish Prov. Inst. 12 Moorgate st
Leifchild Wm. auctionr.land agt.& surveyor, 62 Moorgate st
Leigh Alfred & Co. manf. chemist, 32 Chicksand st. Whitechl
Leigh Charlotte (Mrs.), stationer, 128 Up. Seymour st. Eustonsq
Leigh-Cliffe (Mrs.), ladies' school, 40 Wharton st. Lloyd sq
Leigh Eliza (Mrs.), straw bonnet ma. High st. Deptford
Leigh Henry Jones, wholesale & retail linendraper & laceman, 76 Leather lane
Leigh Henry Jones, straw hat & bonnet manufr. 74 Leather la
Leigh James Matthew, artist, 13 Fitzroy st. Fitzroy square
Leigh James P. cigar imp. 1 Gt. St. Helen's, Bishopsgate st
Leigh John, gunmaker, 1 Duncan st. Red Lion st. Whitechpl
Leigh Mary (Mrs.), boarding house, 37 Store st. Bedford sq
Leigh Percival, surgeon, 10 Bedford st. Bedford square
Leigh Thomas, solicitor, 16 George st. Mansion house
Leigh William Osborn, surgeon, High st. Deptford
Leighton John & Sons, bookbinders, 40 Brewer st. Golden sq
Leighton & Williams, tobacco brokers, 110 Fenchurch st
Leighton Archb. bookbinder, Lower Ashby st. Northamp. sq
Leighton James, baker, 60 Great Marylebone st
Leighton John, printer, 10 Johnson's court, Fleet st
Leighton John, stationer & bookbinder, 19 High st. Camden tn
Leighton Sarah (Mrs.), *Green Parrot* P.H. 1 Green Arbour ct
Leishman George Robert, tailor, 6 Bury st. St. James's
Leitch John, *King of Prussia* P.H. 5 Dean st. Shadwell
Leitch Richard, jun. artist, 25 Mornington pl. Hampstead rd
Leitch Wm. Leighton, artist, 25 Mornington pl. Hampstead rd
Leith & Glasgow Wharf, Joseph Adams, between 95 & 96 Lower East Smithfield
Leith And. L. sec. to Hungerford market, 9 Villiers st. Strand
Leith James, carver & gilder, 23 Crescent st. Euston square
Leith James, sec. to *Southwark Bridge Co.* 10 Queen st. place
Le Jeune Joseph & Co. improved corset makers, 52 George st. Portman square
Le Keux John Henry, engraver, 10 Belgrave st. King's cross
Le Lievre Henry, skein silk dyer, 8 Cleveland st. Mile end rd
Lemaire Etienne, engraver, see Konigh & Lemaire
Lemaitre Lydia (Mrs.), tobacconist, 23 St. John's la. Clknwl
Lemaitre Wm. Thos. writer on glass & medical labeller, & enameller of specia jars, & fancy wood frame manufacturer, 41 St. John's square, Clerkenwell
Lemale Theodore, surgeon dentist, 62 Chandos st. Cov. gard
Leman & Bryan, wharfingers & shipping agents to all parts of Yorkshire & Lancashire, Commercial wharf & Old Swan pier, 101 Upper Thames st
Leman Henry & James, solicitors, see Vizard & Lemans'
Leman Abraham, *Phœnix* P.H. 21 North st. Lisson grove
Leman Benedictus, goldsm. 10 Gt Prescot st. Goodman's fields
Leman Edward, cheesemonger, 7 Kennington cross
Leman Edward Martin, oil & colorman, 16 Old st. St. Luke's
Leman Lenere (Mrs.) outfitting wa. 10 Gt. Prescot st. Gdmn's.fi
Lemann Charles Morgan, physician, 34 Soho square
Le Mann Fred. Adolphus, biscuit baker, 15 Threadneedle st
Le Mare John & Co. button & trimmings ells. 108 Houndsditch
Le Mare Joshua & Son, silk manufacturers, 27 Spital square
Le Mare Isaac D. galloon manufacturer, 38 Basinghall st
Lemare Wm. T. chandler's shop, 24 Ann's place, Pritchard road, Hackney road
Le Marechal Brothers, silk manufact. 2 Russia row, Milk st
Lemarie James, beer retailer, Well st. Hackney
Lemay Benjamin, tobacconist, 38 Bethnal green road
Lemiere François & Auguste, importers of eggs, 43 Cowcross st. West Smithfield, & 27 Little Earl st. Seven dials
Lemm Edward, potato mercht. 100 St. John st. Clerkenwell
Lemm Edward Weston, trousers maker, & army & navy Ltailor, 33 Northumberland st. Strand
Lemmé John Louis & Co. merchants, 1 Finsbury circus
Lemmon Charles, watchmaker, 45 Gt. Alie st. Goodman's flds
Lemmon Elizabeth (Miss), dressmaker, 84 Fetter lane
Lemmon Geo. carpentr.&builder, 33 Earl st. east, Lisson gr. nth
Lemmon Henry, watchmaker, 6 Up. North pl. Gray's inn rd
Lemmon James, coach painter, 6 Cardington st. Hampstd.rd
Lemoine Henry & Frederick, english & foreign librarians & booksellers, 51 Moorgate st
Le Moine Emma (Mrs), milliner, 192 High Holborn
Lemon Abraham, merchant, 71 Cornhill
Le Moinne Philip L. french barrister & standing counsel in London to the Gt. Luxemberg, Sedan & Dendre Valley, &c. Railways Co. 29 Poultry, & 20 Coventry st. Haymarket
Lemon Abraham, merchant & commis. agent. 71 Cornhill
Lemon Elizth. (Miss), straw bonnet ma. see Verey & Lemon
Lemon James, wine merchant, 1 Palmer ter. Holloway rd
Lemon James, *Crown* P.H. 1 St. Dunstan's alley, Tower st
Lemon Oliver, *Crown* coffee rooms, see Hare & Lemon
Lemon Robert, builder, Stepney green
Lemon Wm. coffee rooms, 14 Up. Wellington st. Covent gard
Lemon Wm. Henry, *St. Paul's Head* P.H. 1 Crispin st Spitlflds
Lemoyne Lydia & Cathn. (Misses), ladies' school, Loudoun rd
Lenard James, undertaker, 76 St. John st. Clerkenwell
Lench Samuel, teacanister, scale, mill manufacturer & japanner, 34 Liverpool st. Bishopsgate
Lendrum John, bookseller & publisher, 7 Warwick square
Le Neve & Sturley, cattle salesman, 41 West Smithfield
Le Neve Chas. *Earl St. Vincent* P.H. Lit. Torrington st. Tor.sq
Le Neve James, butcher, 1 Bridge place, City road
Leney James, beer retailer, Clandon st. Walworth common
Lennaerts John, *One Tun* P.H. 16 Arundel pl. Coventry st
Lennan John, chrono. escapement ma. 15 White Conduit st
Lennard John S. beer retailer, 6 Half Moon cres. Pentonvll
Lennard Geo. Barrett, barrister, 1 Fig tree court, Temple
Lennard Thos. Barrett, disc.&exch.br. see Bennison & Lennard
Lenormand (Madame), milliner, 153 Regent st
Lenox George, iron cable manfr. see Brown, Lenox & Co
Lenox Samuel, custom house agent, 24 Mark lane
Lent James, smith, Glasshouse st. East Smithfield
Lenthall Edmund Henry, solicitor, 10 Staple inn
Lenton Ann (Mrs.), milliner, 22 Bevenden st. East rd. City rd
Lenton Charles Sheppard, surgeon, 33 Leicester sq
Lenton John, butcher, 94 York road, Lambeth
Lenton Wm. Hen. hairdresser, the Cottage, Long la. Smithld
Leo James, fruiterer, Camberwell green
Leo Louis, pro. of music, 2 Watson's cottages, Kingsland rd
Leon George Isaac, watch & clock manufacturer & wholesale jeweller, 23 New Broad st. City
Leon Joseph Isaac, merchant, 10 Warnford ct. Throgmrtn.st
Leon Szymaski, tailor, 47 Rathbone pl. Oxford st
Leonard Charles, surgeon, 13 Surrey place, Old Kent rd
Leonard George, beer retailer, 107 Upper East Smithfield
Leonard George, boatbuilder, Horseferry road, Limehouse
Leonard James, hosier & glover, 251 Regent st
Leonard James, surgeon, 18 Craven st. Strand
Leonard James, butcher, 85 Mount st. Berkeley square
Leonard John, buildr. & appraiser 5 Lowther cot. Liverpool rd
Leonard John Adolphus, baker, 2 Grenville st. Brunswick sq
Leonard Letitia (Mrs.), brace & belt maker, 106 Bunhill rw
Leonard Peter, warehouseman, 71 Wood st. Cheapside
Leonard Samuel, butcher, 28 Brewer st. Golden square
Leonard Thomas, timber merchant, 22 Store st. Bedford sq
Leonard Walter, baker, 416 Strand
Leonard William S. surveyor & land agent, 34 Bedford st. Covent garden, & 3 York place, Fulham road
Leonino Brothers, merchants, 5 Warnford ct. Throgmorton st
Lepage Richard C. bookseller, see Ostell & Lepage
Le Paige Louis, british & for. pat. agt. 22 Change al. Cornhill
Lepard James, baker, 1 Dockhead, Bermondsey
Lepard John, baker, 1 Queen st. Clerkenwell
Lepard John, picture frame maker, see Criswick & Lepard
Lepard Samuel, solicitor, see Thomas, Lepard & Co
Lépée Ed. professor & translator of french & italian languages, 90 Upper Seymour st. Euston sq
Le Parque Eleanor (Mrs.), milliner, 47 Church st. Minories
Lepine Daniel, straw hat mak. 6 Paddington st. Marylebone
Le Plastrier Wm. Louis & Co. watchmakers, 22 Chancery la
Le Plastrier Jane (Madame), milliner, 12 Park ter. Rg.pk. rd
Lepper John, butcher, 12 Newport court, Newport market
Lepper Stephen, cheesemonger, 52 Middlesex st. Somers twn
Le Quesne Mary (Mrs.), staymaker, 4 Poland st. Oxford st
Lequir James, hairdresser, 40 King st. West Smithfield
Lequir James, hairdresser, 1 Upper area, Hungerford mkt
Lerchenfeld Mary Anne (Miss), milliner, 36 Gt. Marylebone st
Lerendu Adele (Mrs.), lodgingho. 6 Somerset st. Portman sq
Lerew Fdk. Harding, surgeon, 17 Edward st. Hampstead rd
Lerew John Midford, chemist, &c. 22 Milton st. Cripplegate
Lerew Wm. Hopeful, surgeon, 41 Up. Norton st. Fitzroy sq
Lerew Wm. Kirby, surgeon, 10 North st. Edgware road
Lerigo David, fruiterer & greengrocer, 25 Greek st. Soho
Lerigo James, fruiterer, 1 Orange st. Red Lion square
Lerminez Julie (Madm.), milliner, 18 Charles st. Mancstr. sq
Le Roy (Mdlle.), professor of the harp, 42 Upper Norton st
Lerro Wm. goldsmith & stayma. 25 Norfolk st. Mddlsx. hosp
Leschallas John, builder, 3 Princes st. Spitalfields
Leschallas Wm. who. stationer, 32 Budge row, Cannon st

Lescher Joseph, Son & Co. starchms.Thomas st.Whitechpl.rd
Lescher Joseph S. who. druggist, see Evans, Lescher & Evans
Lescombe Saml. glass & china wareho. 47 Shoe la. Holborn
Lescot & Mauger, goldsmiths&jew.47 Northampton st.Clknwl
Leserve Fredk. boot & shoe maker, 31 Tothill st. Westmr
Le Seigneur Louis, egg merchant, 6 Kent st. Borough
Lesingham John, painter, Notting hill, Hi.st. Knsgtn.gr.pits
Leslie Lewis & Son, auctioneers, &c. 45 Margaret st. Cav. sq
Leslie Alexander, beer retailer, 6 New King st. Deptford
Leslie Charles R. R.A. artist, 12 Pine Apple pl. Edgware rd
Leslie Chas. M'Murdo, plumber, 31 Gt. Windmill st
Leslie David Alex. surgeon, 9 Brunswick parade, Pentnvlle
Leslie George, carpenter, 58 Poland st. Oxford st
Leslie Geo. Marshall, oil & colorman, 60 Brick la. Sptlfields
Leslie Hugh, cabinet ma. 14 South Molton st. Oxford st
Leslie James, builder, &c. 37 High st. Marylebone
Leslie John, barrister, 7 Mitre ct. chambers, Fleet st
Leslie John, coal merchant, 58 Paradise row, Chelsea
Leslie John, linendraper, 21 Vere st. & 151 Oxford st
Leslie John, tailor & habit maker, 60 Conduit st. Regent st
Leslie John, theological bookselr. 58 Gt. Queen st. Lin.inn fi
Leslie Patrick, merchant, London Institution, Finsbury circus
Leslie Patrick, M.D. surgeon, 27 Wilton place, Belgrave sq
Leslie Robert, merchant, see Cheape & Leslie
Leslie Thos. Chambers, surgeon, 9 Brunswick parade, Pntnvl
Leslie William, granite depôt, see M'Donald & Leslie
Lesslie Frances (Mrs.), stationer, 27 Red Lion st.Spitalfields
Lester Charles & Co. cornfactors, 28 Mark lane
Lester & Jackson, linendrapers, 63 Crown st. Finsbury
Lester Thos. & Sons, silk & velvet manfrs. 1 Aldermanbury
Lester Charles, ship biscuit baker, 75 Wapping wall
Lester Daniel, dining rooms, 50 St. George st
Lester Elias, turner, &c. 73 New Compton st. Soho
Lester George, leather seller, 6 Thornton st. Dockhead
Lester Henry, tobacconist, 122 Aldersgate st
Lester John, builder, 155 Poplar High st
Lester John, dyer & scourer, 20 Church row, Bethnal green
Lester Thomas, bookseller & stationer, 14 Finsbury pl. north
Lester William, coach smith, 4 New rd. Whitechapel rd
Lester William, *Two Brewers* P.H. 27 London wall
Lestourgeon Fredk. Edw. wine & spirit mer. 74 Aldersgate st
Lestourgeon Wm. carver, 3 Fisher ct. Eagle st. Red Lion sq
L'Estrade Alexander, prof. of french, 12 Burton crescent
L'Estrange Francis, surgeon, 28 Euston place, Euston sq. & 12 Gower st. north, New road
L'Estrange Hilard Frederick, barrister, 1 New sq. Lin. inn
L'Estrange Isaac, straw bonnet ma. 27 Harrow rd. Paddngtn
Lesty William, printer, 65 Castle st. Borough
Letche Leonardo, linendraper, 40 Queen st. Bryanstone sq
Letchford Ann (Mrs.), lodging house, 1 Thavies inn, Holborn
Letchford Thomas, coffee rooms, 37 High st. St. Giles's
Letchford William, lodging house, 2 Ely place, Holborn
Lethbridge & Mackrell, solicitors, 25 Abingdon st
Lethbridge Christopher, bootmaker, 47 Mary st. Hmpstd. rd
Lethbridge John Christopher, solicitor, steward to the manor of Old Paris Garden, Christchurch, Surrey, 25 Abingdon st
Lethem, Blyth & Lethem, muslin manufacturers, 3 Friday st
Letford Edward, grocer, 95 Chalton st. Somers town
Lett Stafford, turner, 22 Wilkes st. Spitalfields
Lett Thomas, wharfinger, Lett's whf. Commercial rd. Lambeth
Letts, Son & Co. stationers & mapsellers, 8 Cornhill, & 8 Ryl. Exch
Letts Charles, watch jeweller, 8 Wynyatt st. Goswell rd
Letts George, *Ship* P.H. 49 Marygold st. Bermondsey
Letts John, attorney, 8 Bartlett's buildings, Holborn
Letts Thomas, watch jeweller, 5 Wood st. north, King square
Letts William, watch jeweller, 81 Rahere st. Goswell rd
Leuchars Lucy & Son, dressing case makers, 38 Piccadilly
Leuliette Peter, paris diligence director, 34 & 36 Regent circus
Leuty Henry, carpenter, 36 Great Marylebone st
Levasseur Firmin, watch maker, 2 Frith st. Soho
Leveau Abraham, commrl. traveller, 37 Camomile st. City
Levell Madame, corset maker, 6 Mortimer st. Cavendish sq
Leveque Denis, upholsterer, 8 Charles st. Middx. hospital
Lever John & Joseph, vellum & parchment manufacturers, 13½ Sise lane, City, & Neate st. Coburg rd. Old Kent road
Lever Benjamin, stationer, 19 North st. Lisson grove
Lever Charles, solicitor, 10 King's road, Bedford row
Lever George, surveyor & builder, 1 Bayham st. Camden twn
Lever James, bootmaker, 2 Brompton terrace, Brompton rd
Lever John Chas. W. physician, 12 Wellington st. Borough
Lever Philip, *York* coffee rooms, 1 Swallow pl. Hanover sq
Lever Thomas, boot & shoe maker, 257 Tottenham court road
Leverett Barnett, black pin maker, 229 Kent st. Borough
Leverett Edward, coffee rooms, 5 Warwick st. Golden sq
Leverett Elizabeth (Mrs.), pin maker, 56 King st. Borough
Leverett Henry, chain lighterman, Ferry rd. West Poplar
Leveridge William & Saml. John, wine merchts. 163 Fleet st
Leveroni Jas. comestiles imprtr. 7 Harrison st. Gray's inn rd
Leverton Henry, builder, 26 Hertford st. Fitzroy square
Leverton John, painter, paper hang. &c. 2 Bruton pl. Berkly. sq
Levesque, Edmeades & Co. pianoforte ms. 8 Habrdshr. wk. Hxtn
Levesque James, grocer, 16 Clifton st. Finsbury
Levesque Sarah (Mrs.), tract depository, Church st. Hackney
Levet & Atkins, haberdashers, 38 Princes st. Leicester sq
Levett Rd. & Son, nailms. & ironmongers, 86 Broad st. Ratcliff
Levett Edward, dining rooms, 83 Upper Ground st. Blackfrs
Levett James, picture dealer, 141 Blackfriars road
Levett Mary Ann (Mrs.), tobacconist, 101 Houndsditch
Levey George, printer, see Robson, Levey & Franklyn
Levi Alexander, hebraist, 19 Bury st. St. Mary Axe
Levi Ann (Mrs.), china warehouse, 25 Bermondsey New rd
Levi Humphrey, general broker, 11 South st. Finsbury mkt
Levi Hyam, outfitter, 270 Poplar High st.
Levi John, who. fancy toy dlr. 5 Magdalen row, Gt. Prescot st
Levi Lemin, plate, &c. dealer, 3 St. Mark's st. Goodman's flds
Levi Samuel, clothier, 15 & 17 Gt. James st. Lisson grove
Levi Samuel Mordecai, navy agent, 149 Leadenhall st
Levick & Brothers, merchants, 131 Fenchurch st
Levick Charles, needle manufacturer and sole agent to the solid head pin company, Ravenbour mills, 34 Poultry
Levick Robert, lace manfr. & agent, 41 Gresham st. City
Levick Thos. inspect. of corn returns, 3 Fowkes' bldgs. Tower st
Levien Charles, surv. of taxes, 12 White Lion st. Spitalfields
Levilly Anna (Madm.), milliner & dress ma. 23 Geo. st. Han. sq
Levin Moses & Ephraim, importers of fancy french jewellery, toys, beads, clocks, music boxes, and other foreign manufactures, 16 Great Alie st. Goodman's fields
Levin Henry, boarding house, 24 Bury st. St. Mary Axe
Levin James Henry, merchant, 23 Coleman st. & Baltic
Levin Martin, merchant, 21 Jewry st. Aldgate
Levin Meyer, merchant, 69 Gt. Prescot st. Goodman's fields
Levin Wm. Chas. bill & exchange broker, Baltic coffee ho
Levings John, painter, 6 Robert terrace, Chelsea
Levinson Brothers, brush & comb ma. 46 Bedford st. Cov. grdn
Levinson Isidor, hosier, glover, &c. 61 Charing cross
Levison Samuel, merchant, 12 Copthall ct. Throgmorton st
Levitt Marmaduke, wine & spirit broker, 34 Mark lane
Levitt Thomas, linendraper, 5 Church st. Islington
Levy Augustus Saml. & Co. fruit mers. & gen. com. agts. 20 Botolph la
Levy (Laurence) & Co. sheriff's, officers, 16 Fetter lane & 17 Norfolk st. Strand
Levy Lewis & Co. maccaroni & vermicelli manufacturers, & oil & italian merchants, 35 & 36 Camomile st. Bishopsgate
Levy Mark & Henry, who. stationers, 1 Lit. Duke st. Houndsdtch
Levy Reuben & Co. wholesale watch & clock manufacturers, jewellers, &c. 16 Wilson st. Finsbury
Levy Walter & Co. manufacturers & purveyors of maccaroni & vermicelli to her Majesty, & oil & italian merchants, 2 White's row, near Artillery lane, Bishopsgate without
Levy Aaron, tailor, 38 Warren st. Fitzroy square
Levy Abraham, coal mercht. 43 Gt. Prescot st. Goodman's fl
Levy Abraham, jeweller, 107 Albany st. Regent's park
Levy Abraham, slopseller, see Moses, Levy & Co
Levy Alexander, shipping agent, 20 Cock hill, Ratcliff
Levy Barnett, stone mason, North st. Whitechapel road
Levy Daniel, china & glass dealer, 30 Surrey pl. Old Kent rd
Levy David, fruit merchant, 371 Oxford st. & 77 New Bond st
Levy David, orange merchant, 5 King st. Aldgate
Levy David, outftr. & tailor, 14 Hemming's row, St. Martin's la
Levy Elizh. (Mrs.), agency & commission wareh. 39 Poultry
Levy Elizabeth (Mrs.), glass warehouse, 4 Tyler st. Goldensq
Levy Guldah, naval & milit. wr. 2 Hemming's row, St. Martin's la
Levy Henry, appraiser & furniture bro. 249 Poplar High st
Levy Henry, clothes salesman, 69 Marylebone la. Oxford st
Levy Henry, clothes warehouse, 28 Bevis Marks
Levy Henry, pen & quill manufacturers, see Hart & Levy
Levy Henry, tailor, 59 Marylebone lane
Levy Hyam, clothes dealer, 39½ & 62 London road, Southwk
Levy Hyam, general outfitter, 12 Shadwell High st
Levy Isaac, butcher, 12 West st. Soho
Levy Israel, orange & cokernut mer. 2 Lit. Duke st. Houndsdtch
Levy Jacob, orange merchant, Covent garden, North row
Levy Jacob, scale ma. & who. rag merchant, 14 Drury lane
Levy John, orange merchant, North row, Covent garden mkt
Levy John, who. stationer, & pencil mnf. 83 Aldersgate st
Levy Jonas, merchant, 63 Gt. Prescot st. Goodman's fields
Levy Jonas, turnpike contractor, 29 Aldermanbury
Levy Jonas, watch & clock manufacturer, 6 Wilmington sq
Levy Joseph, clothier, 10 Holywell st. Strand
Levy Laurence, wine merchant, 17 Norfolk st. Strand
Levy Lawrance, clothier, 7 & 19 Upper east Smithfield

Levy Leon, clothes salesman, 314 Strand
Levy Lewis, solicitor, 29 Aldermanbury
Levy Lyon, hatter & clothier, 1 Lambeth Lower marsh
Levy Lyons, clothier, 29 Holywell st. Strand
Levy Martha (Miss), tobacconist, 29 Holywell st. Strand
Levy Morrice, wine mer. 25 Norfolk st. & 6 Howard st. Strand
Levy Moses, clothes salesman, 3 Cottage pl. Newngtn. butts
Levy Moses, fruiterer, 16 Grosvenor st. west, Pimlico
Levy Moses, jeweller, 29 Gt. Prescot st. Goodman's fields
Levy Moses, orange merchant, 17 Mitre st. Aldgate
Levy Moses, rag merchant, 109 Gravel lane, Houndsditch
Levy Nathan, orange merchant, 16 Mitre st. Aldgate
Levy Rudolph, mercht. 3 Crown ct. Threadneedle st. & Baltic
Levy Samuel, naval & military outfitter, portable bedstead & camp furniture manufactory, 28 King William st. Strand
Levy Solomon, furn. broker, 1 & 2 Cumberland pl. Newing. butts
Levy Widow, writer of the course of exchange, 5 Cooper's row, Crutched friars
Levyson Montague, diamond mer. 18 Queen sq. Bloomsbury
Lewellen Fred. *Leopold* coffee & dining rooms, 86 Fenchurch st
Lewellen Fred. tailor, 86 Fenchurch st
Lewellen, Truman & Hitchcock, warehomen. 23 Wood st. City
Lewellin Daniel, attorney, 15 Cook's court, Serle st
Lewen Richard, bootmaker, 4 Mason's alley, Basinghall st
Lewer Henry, bookbinder, 33 Lower Ranelagh st. Pimlico
Lewer James, beer retailer, 13 Chapel st. New road
Lewer John, perfumer, 150 High Holborn
Lewer Wm. Henry, architect, 3 Duke st. Westminster
Lewin & Hailstone, man's mercers, 26 Brewer st. Golden sq
Lewin Charles, cornchandler, 148 Whitechapel road
Lewin Francis Ellicar, coal merchant, 2 Duke st. Portland place, & Salisbury wharf, Salisbury st. Strand
Lewin George Herbert, solicitor, 42 Pall mall
Lewin Henry, solicitor, 8 St. Martin's place, Trafalgar sq
Lewin James, tea dealer, 1 Crawley st. Oakley sq. Somers tn
Lewin Sir Gregory Allnutt, knt. queen's counsel, 1 Elm ct. Temple
Lewin John Thos. stationer & upholstr. 6 Up. Kennington la
Lewin Thomas, barrister, 21 Old square, Lincoln's inn
Lewin Thomas, draper & mercer, see Ash & Lewin
Lewin Thomas Clayton, butcher, 17 Gt. Hall, Hungerfrd. mkt
Lewin Thomas Fox, flour factor, Kennet wf. Up. Thames st
Lewinton Alfred, jun. chemist, &c. 25 Nassau st. Middlx. hos
Lewis & Allenby, silk mercers, 193, 195 & 197 Regent st. & 63 Conduit st
Lewis Arthur & Son, ivory, drug & colon. brokrs. 11 Mincing la
Lewis & Bedwell, tailors, 61 Cheapside
Lewis Brothers, wholesale teadealers, 5 Brabant court, Philpot lane
Lewis Brothers, wine & spirit merchants, 1 Church court, Clement's lane, & 63½ King William st. City
Lewis Charles & Israel, tailors, 20 Cannon st. road
Lewis Horatio & Co. snuff & cigar manf. 206 Bermondsey st
Lewis James & Son, corkcutters, 66 Wells st. Oxford st
Lewis & James, linen manuftrs. & importers, 38 Gutter lane
Lewis & Lewis, attorneys, 10 Ely place, Holborn
Lewis & Lowe, british, foreign & colonial advertisement agents & printers, engravers, lithographers, &c. 3 Castle court, Birchin lane, & 1 Abchurch yard
Lewis Morgan & Son, linendrapers, 87 Oxford street
Lewis & Morland, tailors & habit ma. 31 Maddox st. Regent st
Lewis Richard & Co. printers, 95 Bunhill row, Chiswell st
Lewis Samuel & Co. publishers, 13 Finsbury place south
Lewis Samuel & Co. trimming mnfrs. 57 Wood st. & Coventry
Lewis Wm. & Co. boot & shoe makers, 275 Oxford st
Lewis Wm. & Son, printers & prints. auctions. 21 Finch la. Crnhill
Lewis Abraham, diamond broker, 55 Dempsey st. Stepney
Lewis Alexander, commercial agent, 19 Fenchurch st
Lewis Alfred, grocer, 16 Edward st. Barnsbury road
Lewis Alpha Lewis, book auctioneer, 125 Fleet st
Lewis Ann (Miss), straw bonnet ma. 13 Crescent st. Euston sq
Lewis Ann (Mrs.), bookseller, statnr. & news agt. 34 Mount st
Lewis Arthur James, barrister, 58 Chancery lane
Lewis Benjamin, attorney, 9 Gray's inn square
Lewis Benjamin, baker, 21 Devonshire st. Lisson grove
Lewis Benjamin, furniture broker, 13 St. Ann's court, Soho
Lewis Benjamin, solicitor, 7 Catherine ct. Tower hill
Lewis Caleb, blacking manfr. 4 Princess st. Lisson grove
Lewis Charles, attorney, 9 Grosvenor st. Bond st
Lewis Charles, bookbinder, 35 Duke st. St. James's square
Lewis Charles, dyer & scourer, 28 Oxendon st. Haymarket
Lewis Charles, fruiterer, 16 Little Windmill st. Golden sq
Lewis Charles, manf. & inventor of the omnidirective registered shower bath, 32 Stangate st. Lambeth
Lewis Charles, miller & flour factor, see Vines & Lewis
Lewis Chas. plumbr. paintr. &c. 17 Ordnance rd. St. John's wood
Lewis Chas. Geo. Bone, cabinet carver, 2 Pump row, Old st. rd
Lewis Chas. Vallancey, solicitor, 11 Warwick ct. Gray's inn
Lewis Charlotte A. S. (Miss), mourning millnr. 9 John st. Oxfd. st
Lewis Danl. Edwd. ironmonger, 24 Edward st. Hampstead rd
Lewis David, japanner, 5 Robert's pl. Bowling green lane
Lewis David, linendraper, 40 Harleyford pl. Kennington
Lewis David Thacker, surgeon, 182 Brick la. Spitalfields
Lewis Edward, baker, &c. 28 George st. Grosvenor square
Lewis Edward, bootmaker, 4 Broomfields, Deptford
Lewis Edward, *Flower Pot* P.H. 115 Bishopsgate within
Lewis Edward, italian warehouse, 42 High st. Marylebone
Lewis Edward, solicitor & parlmtry. agt. 7 Adam st. Adelphi
Lewis Edward, tailor, 36 Surrey st. Strand
Lewis Edward Daniel, whitesmith, Augustus st. Regent's pk
Lewis Eliza (Mrs.), fruiterer, 13 North pl. Kingsland road
Lewis Elizbth. (Mrs.), coffee rooms, 1 New wharf, Whitefriars
Lewis Enoch, dairyman, 18 Bermondsey st
Lewis Felix, fruit salesman, Covent garden fruit market
Lewis Francis David, british, foreign & colonial advertisement agent, printer, &c. 3 Castle court, Birchin lane, & 1 Abchurch yard, King William st
Lewis Frederick, carpenter, 2 Foxley rd. Cambwell. new rd
Lewis Fred. Augustus, solicitor, 7 Lyons inn, Strand
Lewis Fred. Christian, artist, 53 Charlotte st. Portland pl
Lewis George, carpenter & builder, 185 Drury lane
Lewis George, gold refiner, 122 Old st. St. Luke's
Lewis George, grocer, 99 East st. Manchester square
Lewis George, grocer, 42 Great Hermitage st. Wapping
Lewis George, merchant & shipowner, 5 Lombard st. chambers
Lewis George Cyrus, ironmonger, 1 Lowndes ter. Knightsbdg
Lewis George Robt. artist, 61 Upper Norton st. Fitzroy sq
Lewis Griffith, painter, plumber, &c. 2 Market st. Oxford st
Lewis Henry, gasfitter, 40 Marsham st. Westminster
Lewis Henry, gold chain maker, 5 Pleasant row, Pentonville
Lewis Henry, gold refiner, 43 Wilderness row, Clerkenwell
Lewis Henry, asiatic tooth powder ma. 35 Norfolk st. Strand
Lewis Henry King, bookseller & news agt. 15 Gower st. north
Lewis Hugh, accountant, 40 Coleman st. City
Lewis Hugh, surgeon, 10 North place, Ball's pond road
Lewis Isaac, baker, 1 Wyndham road, Camberwell
Lewis James, academy, 3 Agnes place, Waterloo road
Lewis James, cowkeeper, 2 Grove ter. Queen's rd. Bayswater
Lewis James, farrier, 22 Long yard, Lamb's Conduit st
Lewis James Henry, printer, 15 Frith st. Soho
Lewis James Henry, writing master, 113 Strand
Lewis James Henry Fredk. solicitor, 28 Essex st. Strand
Lewis Jeremiah, auctioneer, 33 Langley pl. Comrcl. rd. east
Lewis John, ale merchant, 180 Waterloo road
Lewis John, attorney, 7 Arundel st. Strand
Lewis John, bookbinder, 1 Buckingham place, Fitzroy sq
Lewis John, bookbinder, stationer, &c. 9 Gough sq. Fleet st
Lewis John, boot & shoe maker, 1 Gt. Pulteney st. Golden sq
Lewis John, boot & shoe maker, 23A, New st. Covent garden
Lewis John, bricklayer, &c. 12 Brick st. Park lane
Lewis John, carpenter, 34 Warren st. Fitzroy square
Lewis John, chairmaker, 44 Newman st. Oxford st
Lewis John, cheesemonger, 106 Tooley st
Lewis John, music smith, Tottenham mews, Middlesex hosp
Lewis John, surgeon, 4 Haydon square, Minories
Lewis John, tailor, 59 Poland st. Oxford st
Lewis John, wire worker, 4 Cornwall rd. Stamford st. Blkfrs
Lewis John Rugg, solicitor, 2 Field court, Gray's inn
Lewis Levy, tobacconist, 5 Lower st. Islington
Lewis Marcus, merchant, 4 Gt. Prescot st. Goodman's fields
Lewis Mary (Miss), coffee rooms, 26 Marylebone lane
Lewis Maria (Mrs.), *Grey Coat Hospital* P.H. 17 Greycoat st
Lewis Mary Ann (Mrs.), baker, 5 Pleasant row, King's cross
Lewis Matthew, bootma. 31 St. Chad's row, Gray's inn road
Lewis Michael, solicitor, 16 Wilmington square
Lewis Penry, salt & whiting mfr. Hertford road, Kingsland
Lewis Philip, furnshg. ironmonger, 57 Bishopsgate without, & 31 Artillery lane, Bishopsgate
Lewis Rees, cowkeeper & dairyman, 19 Brown's la, Spitalflds
Lewis Richard, cheesemonger, 28 New Milman st. Foundling
Lewis Richard, *One Tun.* P.H. 28 Goodge st. Tottnm. ct. rd
Lewis Richard, stove ma. & locksmith, 57 Curtain rd. Shored
Lewis Richard Jeffreys, artist, 8 Percy st. Tottenham ct. rd
Lewis Robert, cotton broker, 37 Mincing lane
Lewis Robert, dyer, 7 Elizabeth st. Hans place, Sloane st
Lewis Robert, goldsmith & jeweller, 22 Oxford st
Lewis Robert, hairdresser, 7 Windmill row, Kenningtn. grn
Lewis Robert, merchant, 21 Queen st. Cheapside
Lewis Robert, wholesale coffee dealer, 2 Great Tower st
Lewis Roger, cheesemonger, 132 Drury lane
Lewis Samuel, furniture broker, 5 Middle row, Old st
Lewis Samuel, picture dealer, 3 Litchfield st. Soho
Lewis Thomas, artist, 2 Percy st. Tottenham court road

Lewis Thomas, boot&shoema. 9 Up. Dorset pl. Clapham road
Lewis Thomas, coach joiner & trunk maker, 46 Long acre
Lewis Thomas, gold cutter, 2 St. James's st. Clerkenwell
Lewis Thomas, grocer, 1 King st. Lower road, Islington
Lewis Thomas, jewel case maker, 87 Newman st. Oxford st
Lewis Thos. leather cutter, 5 Crombies row, Comcl. rd. east
Lewis Thos. plasterer, 2 Sidney st. Goswell road
Lewis Thos. sec. of *Union Assur. Off.* 81 Cornhill & 70 Baker st
Lewis Thos. solicitor, 25 Clement's lane, Lombard st
Lewis Thos. surgeon, 2 Robert's pl. Commercial road east
Lewis Thos. tailor, 35 Baalzephon st. Bermondsey
Lewis Thos. tallow chandler, 17 Sun st. Bishopsgate
Lewis Thos. undertaker, 21 Yardley st. Spafields
Lewis Thos. warehsmn. & leather import. 62 Basinghall st
Lewis Thos. jun. bootmaker, 11 Bath place, New road
Lewis Thos. Crump, printseller & publisher, 96 Cheapside
Lewis Thos. Hayter, architect, see Finden & Lewis
Lewis Thos. H. jun. architect, 70 Baker st. Portman square
Lewis Thos. Rt. merchant, 16 Gould sq. Crutchedfriars
Lewis Wandford, dairy, 5 Rose & Crown court, Foster lane
Lewis Wm. (actuary to *Family Endowment Society*), 12 Chatham place, Blackfriars
Lewis Wm. bookbinder, 55 Old Bailey
Lewis Wm. booksllr. statnr. & news agent, 47½ Welbeck st
Lewis Wm. bootmaker, 14 Upper st. Islington
Lewis Wm. brass turner & tube drawer, 3 Rose st. Cvnt. gdn
Lewis Wm. butcher, 5 Lime st. passage
Lewis Wm. chemist, 21 Paddington st
Lewis Wm. grocer & cheesemonger, 33 Edward st. Regent's pk
Lewis Wm. haberdasher, 138 Great Suffolk st. Borough
Lewis Wm. horsehair seating manufr. 6 Chapel st. Curtain rd
Lewis Wm. *Rum Puncheon* P.H. 4 Cross la. Newtonst. Hi. Hlbn
Lewis Wm. secret springer, 9 Henry st. St Luke's
Lewis Wm. solicitor, see Hillier, Lewis & Hillier
Lewis Wm. stockbroker, 12 Throgmorton st
Lewis Wm. tailor, 75 George st. Euston square
Lewis Wm. tailor, 82 Theobald's road, Red Lion square
Lewis Wm. trunk maker, 5 Broker's row, Mint st. Borough
Lewis Wm. woolstapler, Tyers gateway, 211 Bermondsey st
Lewis Wm. David, barrister, 3 New square, Lincoln's inn
Lewis Wm. Hen. straw bonnet manufacturer, 34 Ludgate st
Lewis Wm. Jones, surgeon, 7 Spital square
Lewis Wm. Stone, barrister (actuary of *Rock Life Assurance Office*), 14 New Bridge st. Blackfriars
Lewns Mary Ann (Mrs.), who. & retail milliner, 58 Regent st
Lewrington John, grocer & cheesemonger, 32 Kingsgate st
Lewsey James, tailor, 5 Paul's alley, Paternoster row
Lewsey Sophia (Miss), fancy repository, Mare st. Hackney
Lewty Jas. W. & Co. cabinet brass founds. 17 Gt. Queen st. Holb
Lewtas Wm. bottled & bulk beer mer. 4 Fen ct. Fenchurch st
Ley John Henry, clerk to the House of commons
Leykauff John, engraver, 4 Lisle st. Leicester square
Leys, Masson & Co. flax spinners, 12 Pancras la. Bucklersbury
Leyshon William, *Alfred's Head* P.H. 75 Silver st. Stepney
Lialter Isaac, carcase butcher, 67 Aldgate High st
Lias John & Son, silversmiths & silver spoon & fork makers, 8 & 9 Finsbury st. Finsbury sq. & 7 Salisbury ct. Fleet st
Lias Charles, silver spoon & plate manfr. 65 Crown st. Finsbury
Liberty Jonathan, glass cutter, 8 George st. Blackfriars rd
License Office, Stamp Office, Somerset house; hours 10 to 4
Licensed Victuallers' & General Fire & Life Assurance Co. (John Bigg, sec.), 4 Adelaide pl. City, & 444 Strand
Licensed Victuallers' Asylum (George Lawrence Dean, master), Asylum road, Old Kent road
Licensed Victuallers' Protcn. So. (T. Smith, sec.), 3 Nw. Bdg. st
Licensed Victuallers' School, Upper Kennington lane
Lickfold Charles, cheesemonger, 6 Lower st. Islington
Lickfold Henry, fruiterer, 3 Bray's pl. Lower rd. Islington
Lickfold James, straw hat maker, 1 Duke st. Lisson grove
Lickfold William, cheesemonger, 3 Great Quebec st
Lickfold Wm. Edward, tobacco pipe ma. 13 Fox's la. Shadwll
Lidbetter Thomas, windsor chair maker, 4 Bridgehouse pl. Newington causeway, & 28 Boro' road
Liddard Stphn. *Three Tuns* P.H. Portmn. mews so. Portmn. st
Liddell Hon. Adolphus, barrister, 17 Serjeant's inn, Fleet st
Liddell George, tailor, 1 Lower Belgrave place, Pimlico
Liddell Thomas, bootmaker, 1 William st. Whitechapel
Liddell William, barrister, 3 Harcourt buildgs. Temple
Liddiard (Mrs.), lodging ho. 17 Up. Ranelagh st. Pimlico
Lidderdale Charles Henry (actuary to the *Sun Life Assurance So.*), Threadneedle st. Craigs court, & 65 Welbeck st
Lidderdale Halliday, physician, 6 Blandford sq. Dorset sq
Liddiard & Co. calico printers, 61 Friday st
Liddiard Gilbert, manufacturing chemist, 61 Friday street, Cheapside, & Ocean st. Stepney
Liddiard Joseph, baker, 1 Hamilton pl. Deptford High st
Liddiard Thos. coal mercht. 11 St. George's ter. Uxbridge rd
Liddiard Thomas, dairyman, 23 Gt. James st. Bedford row
Liddington Job, pianoforte tuner, 86 Newman st. Oxford st
Liddle George, wine merchant, see Oliveira, Liddle & Co
Liddle John, surgeon, 4 Alie place, Goodman's fields
Liddle John, french polisher, 10 Cross st. Hatton garden
Liddle Walter, corn chandler, 20 Gravel lane, Southwark
Liddon James, bookbinder, 3 Knowles ct. Doctor's commons
Lidgett & Shepherd, ship & insurance brokers, 9 Billiter st
Lidiard George, *Plough* P.H. New grove, Mile End road
Lidiard James Tho. law stationer, 21 Carey st. Lincoln's inn
Lidiard Margaret (Mrs.), grocer, 2 Gt. Hermitage st. Wpng
Lidington John, *Bell & Crown tap*, 133 Holborn hill
Lidington Stephen, *King's Head tavern*, 30 Old Jewry
Lidstone Joseph, builder, 8 Old Bailey
Lidstone Jarvis, butcher, 4 Motcomb st. Belgrave sq
Lidstone Nicholas, butcher, 14 Brewer st. Pimlico
Lidstone Reuben, carpenter, 10 Warren st. Fitzroy sq
Liebrecht Henry, clothes salesman, 137 Bethnal green road
Liepmann Adolph, tailor, &c. 80 Parson's st. London docks
Lifton John, tailor, 19 Bridgewater square, Barbican
Liggins Joseph & Co. west india merchants, 37 Mincing lane
Liggins John, tea dealer, 84 Blackman st. Borough
Liggins John Wheatley, wholesale hosier, 68 Wood st
Light George, coal dealer, 11 Little Chapel st. Westminster
Light Jas. *Queen's Head* P.H. Creechurch la. Leadenhall st
Light John, carman, see North & Light
Light Mary Ann (Mrs.), furn. wareho. 3 Thornton st. Dockhd
Light William, whol. hardwareman & agt. 73½ Queen st. City
Lightbody Absalom Charles, poulterer, 9 Edgware road
Lightbody John, poulterer, 41 Hercules bdgs. Lambeth
Lightfoot, Robson & Lightfoot, attorneys, 26 Castle st. Le'ster sq
Lightfoot Ann (Mrs.), fruiterer, 133 Fetter lane, Fleet st
Lightfoot Edwd. blind mkr. 17 St. George's pl. High st. Cambwl
Lightfoot Henry, upholsterer, 6 Union row, Camberwell
Lightfoot James, beer retailer, 1 Ferdinand st. Hampstead rd
Lightfoot James, *City Arms* P.H. 6 Rose lane, Ratcliff
Lightfoot John, manufacturing goldsmith, Camberwell green
Lightfoot Joseph, hairdresser, 15 Drury court, Drury lane
Lightfoot William, coal dealer, &c. 82 Tooley st
Lightfoot Wm. *Prince Regent* P.H. Salmon lane, Limehou
Lightly & Simon, ship, com. & wine agents, 123 Fenchurch st
Lightly Humphrey Joseph, hairdresser, 7 St. Swithin's lane
Lightup Richard & Geo. vellum binders, 4 Jewry st. Aldgate
Lilby Wm. chandler's shop, 30 Pritchard's rd. Hackney rd
Liles James, bricklayer, 22 Hatton wall, Hatton garden
Liles John, ham & tongue mercht. 9 New st. Covent garden
Liley Edward, tobacconist, 6 Quickset row, New rd
Liley Henry, stables, Swan yard, Queen's bldgs. Knightsbdge
Lill John, grocer, post office, Wandsworth road, Vauxhall
Lill Matthew John, pawnbroker, 7 Blackman st. Borough
Lill Richard, cheesemonger, Deptford broadway
Lilley John & Son, mathematical instrument makers, 7 Jamaica terrace, Commercial road, Limehouse
Lilley Edwd. Wm. soap ma. & tallow melt. see Harris & Lilley
Lilley Charles, sawmaker, 26 Limehouse causeway
Lilley George, mahogany mer. 10 Gun st. Spitalfields
Lilley George, printer, 148 Holborn bars
Lilley John, artist, 19 Newman st. Oxford st
Lilley John, mahog. merch. 3 Canton cot. East Ind. rd. Poplar
Lilley Thomas, boot & shoe maker, 67 King st. Borough, & 2 New Buckenham place, Old Kent road
Lilley Thos. coachsmith, 41 Grosvenor mews, New Bond st
Lilley Wm. wine, spirit & coal mercht. 2 Willow pl. Old Kent rd
Lillie Benj. plumber, painter &c. 70 High st. Marylebone
Lillie Robert, fire wood dealer, Lower road, Rotherhithe
Lillie Susannah (Mrs.), 26 Thayer st. Manchester square
Lillie William, engraver, &c. 65 Margaret st. Cavendish sq
Lillo Thomas & Co. hosiers & outfitters, 323 High Holborn
Lillwall & Moline, wholesale cheesemongers, 42 Lime st
Lillwall & Poole, cheesemongers, 77 Gracechurch st
Lilly James, fruiterer, 4 Buckingham st. Strand
Lilly John, haberdasher, 5 Upper North st. Whitechapel rd
Lilly John, sword cutler & military ornament manufacturer, 13 Archer st. Haymarket, & 23 St. Paul's sq. Birmingham
Lilley Joseph, bookseller, 19 King st. Covent garden
Lilly Joseph, hairdresser, 14 Bethnal green road
Lilly Samuel, barrister, 9 Inner Temple lane
Lilly Thomas, cattle salesman, 8 West Smithfield
Liman Edward, cheesemonger, 28 Lower Sloane st. Chelsea
Limbird John, printer, publisher & stationer, 143 Strand
Limbrick Robert, tailer, 1 Brewer st. Pimlico
Limby Henry, chocolate manuf. see Chambers & Limby
Limebeer Jas. bootmaker, 10 Gt. Queen st. Lincoln's inn flds
Limehouse Savings' Bank (John Inglis, manager), Featherstone bldgs. Salmon lane, Limehouse

Limebeer John, cheesemonger, 108 Albany st. Regent's park
Limer Richard, dairyman, 63½, Compton st. Clerkenwell
Limerick Ann (Mrs.), beer retailer, 25 Brook st. New road
Limperani Joseph, pro. of languages, 7 Albany rd. Camberwell
Limpus John, carman, nightman & sand merchant, Whitefriars st. & Maiden lane, Battle bridge
Lincoln, Bennett & Son, hatters, 2 Sackville st. Piccadilly
Lincolns' Inn; entrances, Lincoln's inn fields; Carey st.; Chancery lane & Serle st
Library, New hall, Lincoln's inn, hours 10 to 4
Steward's Office 15 Old square } hours, term, 10 to 9; vacation, 10 to 5
Lincoln George, shoemaker, 2 Princess st. Edgware rd
Lincoln Henry Cephas, organ builder to her Majesty, 196 High Holborn
Lincoln Joseph, baker, 2 Wellington ter. Kensingtn. gravl. pits
Lincoln Samuel, plumber & glazier, 20 Little Cadogan place
Lincoln William, tailor, 12 Anchor street, Spitalfields
Lincoln Wm. Simpson, bookseller, 3 Cheltenham pl. Wstm. rd
Lind & Rickard, stock brokers, 3 Bank chambers, Lothbury
Lind Wm. Alexr. engraver&printer, 6 Chandos st. Covent gdn
Linda Moses & Co. wholesale cap & carpet bag manufs. 41 Little Charlotte st. Blackfriars road
Lindars James, coal merchant, 22 Austinfriars
Lindars James, commercial agt. & accountant, 22 Austinfriars
Lindars Wm. chemist, 2 Commercial place, Kentish town
Lindenthal Israel Levy (sec. of synagogue), Gt. St. Helen's
Linder Charles, chemist, see Gifford & Linder
Lindfield John, *Duchess of Kent* P.H. 30 Liverpool terrace
Lindfield Thomas, builder, 19 Stanhope st. Hampstead road
Lindfield Wm. builder & bricklayer, 1 Duke st. Bloomsbury
Lindgren Adolphus, merchant, 1 Crown ct. Old Broad st
Lindgren Hans Jonas, ship agent, 13 John st. Minories
Lindley James, bead & bugle manf. 4 Cranbourne st
Lindley Richard, butcher, 15 Newport ct. Newport market
Lindley William, civil engineer, 8 Adelphi terrace
Lindner Frederick, pawnbroker, 8 North pl. Gray's inn lane
Lindo Ephraim&Co. mer. 3 Winchester bldgs. Gt. Winchester st
Lindo David A. merchant, 37 Mansell st. Goodman's fields
Lindo Natheneel, solicitor, 113 Fenchurch street
Lindo Zacharia, surgeon, see Van Oven & Lindo
Lindon John, tailor, Charlotte st. Portland place
Lindon William, merchant, 12 Bucklersbury
Lindop Alfred, toy &bead importer&manufacturer of combs, brushes, &c. 19 Cannon st. City
Lindsay, Bristow & Sparrow, berlin wool, &c. imps. 51 Bread st
Lindsay Geo. & John, merchants, 26 Laurence Pountney la
Lindsay & Matthew, warehousemen, 29 Wood st. City
Lindsay & Mason, solicitors, 26 Gresham street
Lindsay Alexander, painter, 4 St. Dunstan's pas. Thames st
Lindsay Charles, builder, 10½ Addle hill, Doctors' commons
Lindsay Hugh Hamilton, ship & insurance broker, 8 New East India chambers, Leadenhall street
Lindsay John, fringe maker, 7 Grosvenor pl. Coml. rd. east
Lindsay Robert, baker, 7 George's place, Old street road
Lindsay William, baker, 17 Grenada terr. Commercial rd. E
Lindsay Wm. woollen warehouseman, 3 Norton folgate
Lindsay Wm. S. iron & commission mercht. 35 Abchurch la
Lindsay Wm. *Fleece tavern* P.H. Gt. George st. Bermondsey
Lindsell John, barrister, 24 Old square, Lincoln's inn
Lindsell William, solicitor, see Oliver & Lindsell
Lindsey Charles, hardwood turner, 57 Paradise st. Lambeth
Lindsey Elizth. Frances (Mrs.), plumber, 56 Wych st. Strand
Lindsey Henry, coffee rooms, 14 Middle row, Holborn
Lindsey John, baker, 10 Newland terrace, Kensington
Lindsey John, bootmaker, 35 Wapping
Lindsey John, tailor, 90 Drury lane
Lindsey John Thos. goldsmith, &c. 12 Stafford row, Pimlico
Lindsey Joshua, pork butcher, 2 Vere street, Clare market
Lindsey Mark, coal dlr. 9 North st. Sidney st. Commerl. rd. ea
Lindsey Mark, surgical instrument ma. 264 Boro' High st
Lindsey Phœbe (Mrs.), stationer, 10 Commerl. pl. Kentish tn
Lindsey Samuel, teadealer, 63 New cut, Lambeth
Lindsey Samuel, tobaccnst. & newsvndr. Hawley pl. Kentish tn
Lindus Wm. corn chandler, Brompton place, Brompton rd
Lindus Wm. corn chandler, 4 Brompton terrace, Brompton
Line Catherine (Miss), milliner, see Grimsey & Line
Line Mary Ann (Mrs.), milliner, 15 Gt. Newport st. Long acre
Lineham William, butcher, 25 Farringdon market
Linendrapers' &c. Inst. (G. Brace, sec.), 24 Surrey st. Strand
Lines Albert, house agent, 10 Suffolk place, Hackney road
Lines Augustus, hay salesman, 3 Irongate wharf, Paddingtn
Lines Charles, coach builder, 74 Blackfriars road
Lines Ezekiel, butcher, 11 Crown st. Walworth road
Lines James, tailor, Deptford High street
Lines Joseph, beer retailer, 84 Friar st. Blackfriars road
Lines Martha (Mrs.), coal & potato dealr. 9 Lambeth High s
Lines Martha (Miss), straw hat maker, 8 Lamb's Conduit st
Lines Samuel, baker, 14 Friendly street, Deptford
Lines Thomas, french polisher, 13 King st. Golden square
Liney John, iron merchant, 1 Charles st. east, Hampstead rd
Liney William, coffee rooms, 68 High st. Camden town
Linfield James, bricklayer, 25 Market st. Borough road
Linford George, butcher, Deptford bridge
Linford Thomas Lee, beer retailer, 244 Poplar High st
Ling Benj. ship breaker & timbermer. 81&82 Fore st. Limeho
Ling Chas. linendra. 9 &10 Northumberland pl. Commer. rd. ea
Ling James, tailor, 7 Chapel st. west, Mayfair
Ling Robert, private hotel, 4 Suffolk st. Pall mall
Ling Thomas, musical reed mak. 31 Cirencester pl. Fitzroy sq
Ling William, gun & pistol maker, 61 Jermyn st
Lingard James, auctionr. & appras. 36 York st. Commrcl. rd
Lingham Thomas, wine merchant, 35 Great St. Helen's
Lings John Benjamin & Son, wholesale cheesemongers, 1 Spur st. Leicester sq. & 216 Borough High st
Lings Charles, jun. school, 56A, Earl st. east, Lisson gr. nth
Lings William, surgeons' instr. maker & cutler, 1 Jewin st
Liniker William, tailor, 2 Marylebone st. Golden square
Link David, violin string mak. 24 Weaver st. Bethnal green
Linklater John & Jas. Harvie, solicitors, 115 Leadenhall st
Linklater Robt. importer of irish & foreign provisions, & ship chandler, 117 & 269 Wapping
Linley Thomas, agent to Messrs. Naylor, Vickers & Co. file & steel manufacturers, Sheffield, 4 Carter st. Walworth rd
Linley Wm. leather mer. see Hemsworth, Kibble & Linley
Linnæan Society (John Jph. Bennett, secretary), 32 Soho sq
Linnecar Edward Harrison, surgeon, 1 New Basinghall st
Linnegar James, bricklayer, &c. 23 Houghton st. Clare mkt
Linnell John, shipsmith & bellhanger, 53 Rotherhithe
Linnet John, goldsmith & jeweller, 10 Argyll pl. Regent st
Linnett William, baker, 23 Brick lane, St. Luke's
Linney Amos &Son, tailors&armyclthrs. 23 Regnt. st. Waterl. p
Linningdine James, cabinet mak. 13 Featherstone st. City rd
Linnit & Kelly, auctioneers & antq. furn. dlrs. 123 Wardour st
Linom Robert W. teadealer, 22 Whitechapel road
Linsdell Thomas, tobacconist, 1 Youl's pl. Old Kent road
Lindsey Benjamin, agent to Clerical & Medical Life Assurance, office, 4 Upper Dorchester place, Hoxton
Linsey Robert, house agent, 16 City terrace, City road
Linsey Thomas, watch & clock mak. 104 & 172 Shoreditch
Linsley George, cabinet maker, 14 Clarence pl. Hackney rd
Lintil Philip, *Old Swan* P.H. Church st. Battersea
Linton & Clarke, stockbrokers, 4 Shorter's ct. Throgmorton st
Linton Henry, cowkeeper, 11 Allsop place, Regent's park, & 65 Marylebone lane
Linton James, coal merchant, 31 Dudley grove, Harrow rd
Linton Jas. coal mercht. Union wharf, Wilton rd. Pimlico basin
Linton James, teadealer, 11 Melton st. Euston square
Linton James, window glass cutter, 14 Bath pl. New road
Linton John, tailor, 22 Dean st. Soho
Linton Mary (Mrs.), grocr. &cheesemngr. 32 Pratt st. Camdn. tn
Linton Miles, *Star & Garter* P.H. 72 Comptn. st. Clerknwell
Linton Richard, carpenter & builder, Oak lane, Limehouse
Linton William, artist, 7 Lodge place, Regent's park
Linton William James, artist, see Smith & Linton
Lintott James & Son, oil & italian warehouse, 72 Cannon st
Lintott John & Son, cattle salesmen, 41 West Smithfield
Lintott Charles, baker, 3 High st. Notting hill
Lintott Charles, butcher, Bull's head pass. Leadenhall mkt
Lintott Edward, dyer, 54 Ernest st. Regent's park
Lintott James, fruiterer, 6 Moreton terrace, Kentish tn. rd
Lintott Wm. Henry, dentist, 69 Welbeck st. Cavendish sq
Linwood Robert, pawnbroker, 56 St. John st. Clerkenwell
Linwood Wm. merchant, 2 Billiter square, City
Lion Alexander, who. shoe manf. 13 Wood st. Spitalfields
Lions Emanuel & Maeyer, slipper manfr. 16 Union st. Bishspgt
Lions Cornelius, beer retailer, 3 Wapping wall
Lipman Philip & Son, pencil ma. 8 Old Castle st. Whitechapel
Lipman Lewis Philips, pencil ma. 44 Bedford st. Comml. rd
Lipman Lipman, *King of Prussia* P.H. 98 Middlesex st. Aldgt
Lipop Lorenzo, bit & stirrup ma. 3 South Molton la. Brook st
Lippmann Julius, importer of congreves & general agent for foreign fancy goods, 82 Mark lane
Lipscomb Charles, corn & coal mer. 20 Platt ter. Pancras rd
Lipscomb Geo. grocer, 8 Westmoreland bldgs. Aldersgate st
Lipscomb Henry, solicitor, 2 Gresham place, Lombard st
Lipscomb William, carman, 8 Gedling st. Bermondsey
Lipscomb Wm. Hen. waggon office, White Horse yd. Friday st
Lipscombe John & Co. water filter makers, 93 Quadrant
Lipscombe & Knighton, carriers, Elephant inn, Fore st. City
Lipscombe Ann (Mrs.), staymaker, 93 Quadrant, Regent st
Lipscombe Isaac, butcher, 38 Pitfield st. Hoxton

Lipscombe John, tailor, 2 Little Titchfield st. Portland place
Lipsham Chas. tobacconist, Vassall rd. Camberwell New. rd
Liptrot Peter, watch wheel cutter, 54 Gee st. Goswell st
Liquoril William, boot & shoe maker, 94 Hoxton Old town
Liquorish Godfrey Hill, tea dealer, 50 Beech st. Barbican
Liquorish Thomas, *Ship* P.H. 13 Anthony st. St.George's ea
Lisenden John, pork butcher, 130 Borough High st
Lissant John, gun maker, 53 Drummond st. Euston sq
Lisson Joseph, tailor, 1 Upper Grafton st. Fitzroy sq
List Christopher, *Marquis of Anglesea*, P.H. 39 Bow st
List Elizabeth (Mrs.), tripeseller, 175 Drury lane
List Fred. Herbert, printer & bkbndr. 104 Shadwell High st
Lister, Beck & Beck, wine merchants, 5 Tokenhouse yard
Lister & Law, insurance brokers, 31 St. Swithin's lane, City
Lister Christopher, woollen draper, 106 High Holborn
Lister Daniel, solicitor, 23 Berkeley square
Lister Eliz. (Mrs.), cook & confectioner, 65 High st. Marylb
Lister Isaac Solly, merchant, 3 Laurence Pountney hill
Lister John, surgeon, 25 Edward st. Langham place
Lister Nathaniel, physician, 15 Manchester buildings, Wstmr
Lister Tho. *Hole in the Wall* P.H. 1 Glo'ster st. Bloomsbury
Lister Thomas, turner, 11½ Mortimer mkt. Tottenham ct. rd
Lister Thos. watch case joint finishr. 51 Perceval st. Clerknwl
Lister William, blackwell hall factor, 78 Basinghall st
Lister William, jewel case ma. 24 Gt. Queen st. Lincoln's inn fi
Lister William, plumber, 14 King st. Snow hill
Lister William, plumber &c. 3 King Edward st. Newgate st
Liston & Blackwell, engine turners, engra.&c. 51 Wynyatt st
Liston David John, *New Barn* P.H. 12 Pickett st. 258 Strand
Liston Robert, surgeon, 5 Clifford st. Bond st
Litchfield Elijah, attorney, 89 Chancery lane
Litchfield John, beer retailer, 13 Gee st. Goswell st
Litchfield John, builder, 1 Patriot row, Cambrdg rd. Mile end
Litchfield John dining rooms, 18½ Hatton wall
Litchfield Thos. news agent 22 Cannon st. rd St. George's east
Litchfield Vincent, dining rooms, 2 Victoria pl. Hoxton Old tn
Literary Gazette weekly newsp. Office, 7 Wellington st. Strnd
Literary Polish Association (Wm. Ll. Birkbeck, esq. hon. sec.; Lieut. Chas. Szulczewski, resident sec.; Lionel Rodwell, esq. paymaster), 10 Duke st. St. James's
Litherland John, attorney, 22 Brunswick st. Barnsbury rd
Lithgow Francis, market gardener, Battersea
Litman John, hearth rugma. 13 Princes st. Lit. Queen st. Hlbn
Litsenburg Abraham, statuary & mason, 86 Wardour st Soho
Litt & Bushby, mer. & ins. broks. St. Peter's chambs. Cornhl
Littell Lemuel Fredk. tobacconist, 7 Cornbury pl. Old Kt. rd
Littell Thos. carver & gilder, 39 Baalzephon st. Bermondsey
Littig James, bootmaker, 35 Chester pl. Kennington cross
Little George & Co. merchants, 32 Gt. Winchester st. City
Little James & Sons, builders, 1 America square, Minories, & Sise yard, 22 Whitechapel road
Little & Oaksbatt, carpent. & builders, 28 George st. Shoreditch
Little & Sparrow, cloth workers, 7 White hart st. Catherine st
Little Burgess, ironmonger & smith, Broadway, Stratford
Little David, carpenter, 27 Upper Berkeley st. west
Little Edward, cowkeeper, 16 Upper Ranelagh st
Little Edward Cullen, cooper, 14 Camberwell High st
Little Edwd. Cullen, cooper, 4 Wild's rents, Long la. Brmndsy
Little Edward May, cowkeeper, 16 Arabella row, Pimlico
Little Eliza (Mrs.), tobacconist, 5 Duke st. Aldgate
Little Francis, coachmkr. 6 South cresent. mews, Marchmt. st
Little Fras. Ann (Mrs.), station. & books. 34 Henriet. st. Cov. gar
Little George, barrister, 11 New square, Lincoln's inn
Little George, corndealer, 1 Liverpool st. King's cross
Little George, fruiterer, 19 Church row, Somers town
Little Giles, fishing tackle maker, 15 Fetter lane, Fleet st
Little Hen. florist & green grcr. 1 Glostr. pl. King's rd. Chels
Little Jas. Hyatt, prof. of music, 73 Westmoreland pl. City rd
Little Jane (Mrs.), corn & coal dlr. 31 North row, Grosvnr. sq
Little Jeremiah, builder, 2 Omega terrace, Alpha road
Little John, builder & ho. agt. 78 Brunswick st. Hackney rd
Little John, builder & ho. agt. 51 Weymouth ter. Hackney rd
Little John, carpenter & builder, 4 Belton st. Long acre
Little John, dairyman, 27 Elizabeth st. south, Pimlico
Little John, Red Lion stables, 16 Red Lion st. Whitechapel
Little John, sadler, 19 Marshall st. Golden square
Little Joseph, billiard rooms, 5 Picket place, Strand
Little Joseph, builder, 3 Church court, Clement's lane
Little Joseph, cheesemonger, 250 Strand
Little Joseph, timber merchant, 6 Brighton pl. Hackney rd
Little Mary (Mrs.), ladies' school, 1 Rayner pl. Grn's. rw. Clkll
Little Robert, glass & china wareh. 119 Kingsland road
Little Robert, wine merc. 4 Somerset pl. New rd. Commer. rd. e
Little Robt. Ed. stockbroker, 11 Warnford ct. Throgmorton st
Little Thomas, architect, 36 Northumberland st. Marylebone
Little Thomas, lace embroidery, &c. wareho. 43 Oxford st
Little Thomas, potato salesman, Cotton's wharf, Tooley st. & 22 Great George st. Bermondsey
Little Thomas, willow square manufr. 10 Hoxton Old town
Little Walter, scotch whiskey mer. 6 Three King ct. & Baltic
Little William, coal merchant, 15 Earl st. Blackfriars
Little William, coal mercht. Rutland whf. 5 Up. Thames st
Little William, cooper, 2 Little Cross st. Newington butts
Little William Hen. carpenter & builder, 119 Kingsland rd
Little William Henry, builder, 3 Edward's pl. Hackney rd
Little William John, physician, 10 Finsbury square
Littledale Henry Anthony, barrister, 8 King's Bench walk
Littlefield Geo. tailor, 4 Gibraltar row, Lower rd. Deptford
Littlefield James, coal mercht. 2 Goldington st. Somers tn
Littlefield James, potato dealer, 43 Aldgate High st
Littlefield Jane (Mrs.), grocer, 4 James pl. Marlboro' rd. Chels
Littleford John, working jeweller, 6 St. James's st. Clerknwll
Littleford Joseph, coachmaker, 76 High street, Marylebone
Littlejohn Thos. & Son, scotch confectionrs. 77 King Wm. st. City
Littlejohn Alexander, baker, 63 St. George st
Littlejohn Martha (Mrs.), hatter & furrier, 62 Paddington st
Littlejohn Thomas, baker, 129 Brick lane, Spitalfields
Littlepage Richard & William, bakers, Blackwall
Littlewood John & Co. merchants, 115 Wood st. Cheapside
Littlewood Enoch, *King's Arms* P.H. 5 Chapel st. Bedford rw
Littlewood Faulke James, laceman, &c. 34 Blackman st. Boro'
Littlewood John, hosier, 23 New Bond street
Littlewood My. (Mrs.), carriage lamp ma. 32 Up. Kingst. Blsby
Littlewood Samuel, cooper & paper mer. 185 Up. Thames st
Littlewood Sarah (Mrs.), fur bro. 4 Broomfield pl. Deptford
Littlewood Thomas, butcher, 74½ Wells st. Oxford st
Littlewort Charles James, surgeon dentist, 12 New Bridge st
Littlewort William, optician, 7 Ball alley, Lombard st
Littleworth George, watchma. 17 Bridgewater sq. Barbican
Litton James, butcher, 1 Nile st. Hoxton New town
Litton John, chimney sweeper & chimney sweeping machine manufr. 4 Little Grosvenor st. Berkeley sq
Litton John, printer, 6 Church st. Islington
Livemore John, coffee rooms, 1 Poppin's court, Fleet st
Livermore & Tranah, pawnbrokers & general salesmen, 127 Tottenham court road, & 3 Bell st. & 131 Edgware road
Livermore Jas. for. wine & spirit importer, 27 Mincing lane
Livermore Samuel, auctioneer, 32 Beaufort st. Chelsea
Livermore Thomas, coffee rooms, 49 Church st. Shoreditch
Livermore Wm. furnishing ironmonger, 30 Oxford st
Livermore Wm. Chas. bricklayer, 4 Paradise rw. Bethnl. gr. rd
Livesey Joseph, barrister, 42 Sackville st
Living Elizabeth (Mrs.), plumber, 3 Vittoria pl. Cambridge rd
Living Edwin, wax & tallow chndlr. & oilman, 1 Chancery la
Living Elizabeth (Mrs.), plumber, 3 Bethnal grn. west side
Living Robert, poultry salesman, Leadenhall market
Livings John, draw. instrument mak. 63 Rahere st. Goswell rd
Livingston Charles, oil & colorman, 254 Poplar High st
Livingston David, biscuit baker, 114 Bishopgate within
Livingston Jasper, ship ins. & custom ho. agt. 31 Gt. St. Helen's
Livingston Wm. John, sailma. & ship chand. 79 Fore st. Limeh
Livingstone Alex. iron boat builder, Deptford green
Livock James, carpenter, 1 Neville's court, Fetter lane
Lizardi Francis de & Co. merchants, 26 Austinfriars
Lizars Ann (Mrs.), dairy, 27 Maiden lane, Covent garden
Lizarzabura Manuel, merchant, 64 Cornhill
Llanelly Railway & Dock Co. (Rd. Glascodine, sec.) 9 Old Jewry
Llangennech Coal Co. (Chs. A. Gray, sec.), 18 & 19 Crosby hl. cha
Llewellin Edwin, cheesemonger, 17 Crosby row, Walwth. rd
Llewellin Henry, solicitor, 29 Noble st. Cheapside
Llewellin William, cabinet maker, 22 Rupert st. Haymarket
Llewellyn John, gas fit. & brass work. 3 Newman pas. Oxfd. st
Llewellyn John, smith, 2 Newman passage, Oxford st
Llewellyn John (Mrs.), wardrobe purchaser, 1 Newman pas
Llewellyn Thomas, surgeon, 9 Mount pl. Whitechapel road
Llewhellin John, carpenter, 54 Praed st. Paddington
Lloyd David & Co. who. grocers & teadls. 18 Rood la. Fenc. st
Lloyd & Davies, who. perfumers, 7 Rathbone pl. Oxford st
Lloyd Edmund & Co. (Robert Weir, successor), booksellers, publishers, stationers, printers & general newspaper agents, 57 Harley st. Cavendish square
Lloyd Georgiana & Louisa (Misses), staymakers, 79 New Bond st
Lloyd Henry Hugh & Co. tobacconists, 20 Tichborne st
Lloyd & Hobbs, *Rose & Crown* P.H. 168 Goswell st
Lloyd John & Francis, tobacco & snuff manufrs. 77 Snowhill
Lloyd John & Son, glovers, 2 Carlton st. Regent st
Lloyd & Key, stockbrokers, 11 Shorter's ct. Throgmorton st
Lloyd Matheson & Brodribb, tea brokers, 130 Fenchurch st
Lloyd Thos. & Co. grocers & teadealers, 141 Aldersgate st. & 4 Plumber's row, City road
Lloyd Thos. P. & Co. russia merchants, 23 Abchurch lane
Lloyd's Captains' Room, Royal exchange, 9 to 6

Lloyd's Merchants' Rooms, Royal exchange, 9 to 6
Lloyd's List, daily evening paper, 1 Crown ct. Threadndl. st
Lloyd's Register of British & Foreign Shipping (C. Graham, sec.), 2 White Lion court, Cornhill; hours 10 to 5
Lloyd's Subscribers' Room, Royal exchange; hours 10 to 5
Lloyd Benjamin, baker, 27 Bevenden st. Hoxton
Lloyd Bernard Septimus, agent, see Wreford & Lloyd
Lloyd Charles, beer retailer, 25 Flagon row, Deptford
Lloyd Charles, tobacco manufacturer, see Wishart & Lloyd
Lloyd David, coach trimmer, 51 London st. Fitzroy square
Lloyd David, silk manufactr. see Campbell, Harrison & Lloyd
Lloyd Edmund, boot & shoe maker, 57 Houndsditch
Lloyd Edward, bricklayer, 118 Gt. Portland st. Oxford st
Lloyd Edward, printer & publishr. 12 Salisbury sq. Fleet st
Lloyd Edward John, barrister, 9 Old square, Lincoln's inn
Lloyd Eliza (Miss), milliner, 56 Brook st. Grosvenor sq
Lloyd Elizabeth (Miss), haberdasher, 63 Penny fields, Poplar
Lloyd Eusebius Arthur, surgeon, 14 Bedford row, Blomsby
Lloyd Evans, dairyman, 52 London st. Fitzroy square
Lloyd Francis B. physician, 4 Up. Phillimore pl. Kensington
Lloyd Frederick, butcher, 5 Bray's bdgs. Lowr. rd. Islington
Lloyd George John, solicitor, 49 Doughty st. Foundling
Lloyd Hannah (Mrs.), cowkeeper, 18½ Weston st. Somers tn
Lloyd Henry, banker, see Hanbury's, Taylor & Lloyd's
Lloyd Henry, chemist & druggist, 10 Broomfield pl. Deptfrd
Lloyd Henry, *Horseshoe & Magpie* P.H. 5 Gt. Bath st. Clknwl
Lloyd Henry, solicitor, see Bell, Steward & Lloyd
Lloyd Henry Edward Lamkin, engineer & millwright, Paradise row, Gravel lane, Borough, & 33 Nelson sq. Blkfriars
Lloyd Herbert, solicitor, 36 Milk st. Cheapside
Lloyd Hugh, attorney, 34 Gerrard st. Soho
Lloyd James, accountant & arbitrator, 47A, Moorgate st
Lloyd James, cattle salesman, 60 West Smithfield
Lloyd James, hosier & haberdasher, 2 Dockhead, Brmndsy
Lloyd John, advertising agent, 5 Tavistock st. Covent garden
Lloyd John, *Blue Anchor* P.H. 35 Chancery lane
Lloyd John, comb maker, Neate st. Cobourg rd. Old Kent rd
Lloyd John, corn dealer & livery stables, 66 Gray's inn lane
Lloyd John, dining rooms, 3 Church la. Coml. rd. Whitechpl
Lloyd John, glove & brace ma. 1A, Wimpole st. Cavendish sq
Lloyd John, shoe manufctr. 19 Stonecutter st. Farringdon st
Lloyd John, tailor, 9A, Panton square, Haymarket
Lloyd John Horatio, barrister, 1 King's Bench walk, Temple
Lloyd John Hugh, artist, 25 Northumberland st. New road
Lloyd Joseph, fruiterer & oilman, 3 Eagle terrace, City rd
Lloyd Joseph, hat manfctr. 96 Devonshire st. Lisson grove
Lloyd Joshua L. baker, Blue Anchor road, Bermondsey
Lloyd Lydia Perkes (Mrs.), cook & confectioner, 34 Judd st
Lloyd Mary (Mrs.), laundress, 68 Upper Ebury st
Lloyd Mary (Mrs.), tobacconist, 54 Gray's inn lane
Lloyd Maurice, grocer, 1 Broughton place, Hackney road
Lloyd Morgan, barrister, 1 New Temple bldgs. Mitre court
Lloyd Richard, carpenter, &c. Harley mews nth. Harley st
Lloyd Richard, print. sell. & publisher, 8 George yd. Lombard st
Lloyd Richard, tobacco manufacturer, 69 Holborn hill
Lloyd Robert, hatter, 71 Strand
Lloyd Robert, linendraper, 55 Lisson grove north
Lloyd Robert, *Old Coachmakers' Arms* P.H. 97 Long acre
Lloyd Robert John, pawnbroker, 18 Strutton ground, Westmr
Lloyd Samuel, coffee rooms, 11 Duke st. Smithfield
Lloyd Samuel, dyer & scourer, 4 King's pl. Commercial rd. east
Lloyd Samuel, ivory & wood turner, 4 Benjmn. st. Cowcross st
Lloyd Solomon, hairdresser, 1 Foubert's pl. Regent's st
Lloyd Thomas, *Brown Bear* P.H. 30 High row, Knightsbr
Lloyd Thomas, parchment selr. & law statr. 30 Bartlett's bldgs
Lloyd Thomas, surgeon, 5 New Basinghall st
Lloyd Thomas, surveyor, 55 York terrace, Regent's park
Lloyd Thomas, tobacconist, 20 Suffolk pl. Hackney road
Lloyd Thomas, wheelwright, 15 Old st. road, St. Luke's
Lloyd Thomas, wine merchant, 9 Gerrard st. Soho
Lloyd Thomas J. cattle salesman, 17 West Smithfield
Lloyd Thomas Wm. prof. of music & dancing, 97B, Quadrant, & 14 Swallow st. Piccadilly
Lloyd William, bookseller, 36 Chandos st. Covent garden
Lloyd William, bricklayer, see Bennett & Lloyd
Lloyd William, cabinet maker, North st. East st. Walworth
Lloyd William, cabinet maker, 12 Sidney st. Mile end
Lloyd William, dairyman, 36 Felix terrace, Liverpool road
Lloyd William, grocer, &c. 13 King David lane, Shadwell
Lloyd William, hairdresser, 15 Well st. Oxford st
Lloyd William, hatter, 8 Kingsland road
Lloyd William, tailor, 46 Great Suffolk st. Borough
Lloyd William, watchmaker, 6 Britannia row, Hoxton
Lloyd William, *White Horse* P.H. 4 North st. Fitzroy sq
Lloyd Wm. Henry, auctioneer, 5 Hatfield st. Blackfriars rd
Lloyd Wm. Henry, cooper, 4 Hayfield place, Mile end
Lloyd Wm. Watkyn, surgeon, 62 Gt. Russell st. Bloomsbury
Llynvi Iron Company (Fred. Wm. Gibbon, sec.), 21 Moorgate st. City
Load V. C. G. bandanna printer & stock manufactr. 5 Bread st
Loaden William, solicitor, 32 Great James st. Bedford row
Loader Edw. timber mercht. 64 Tabernacle walk, Finsbury
Loader George, butcher, 74 Tottenham court road
Loader Hen. carpentr. & window blind ma. 19 Forest rw. Dlstn
Loader Isaac, timber & rod mercht. 6 Upper Thames st
Loader James, baker, 11 Church st. Camberwell
Loader James, boot & shoe ma. 1 John's pl. Camberwell New rd
Loader John, beer retailer, 23 Back st. Horselydown
Loader John, fruiterer, 16 Nicholas lane, Lombard st
Loader Joseph, wholesale & retail upholsterer, cabinet & plate glass factor, 23 Finsbury pavement
Loader Richard A. C. wholesale & retail upholsterer, cabinet maker & plate glass factor, 24 Finsbury pavement
Loader Sarah (Miss), milliner, 23 Constable rw. Mile end rd
Loader Thos. *Northumberland Arms* P.H. 119 Tottnhm. ct. rd
Loades James, shoemaker, 3 South pl. Camberwell new rd
Loades William, bricklayer, 3 Boot st. Hoxton market
Loadman Wm. Henry, butcher, 39 Paddington st. Marylebone
Loadsman John, dining rooms, 11 Gray's inn lane
Loane John, druggist, 87 Rosemary lane
Loaring Robert (Mrs.), boarding house, 21 Craven st. Strand
Loban Caroline (Mrs.), milliner, 59 Margaret st. Cavendish sq
Lobb Ellis Goode, hosier & glover, 148 Cheapside
Lobb Jas. B. sec. to the *British Salt Co.* 6 Gt. Winchester st
Lobb Thomas, *Grapes* P.H. 22 Tooley st
Lobb William, surgeon, 12 Aldersgate st
Lobley William Jas. undertaker, 4 North st. Backchurch la
Loch William Adam, barrister, 21 Old square, Lincoln's inn
Lochner Chris. Pelley, proctor & notary, 13 Gt. Carter lane
Lochner Wm. Conrad, archit. & survey. Albion pl. London wall
Loch James & George, hatters, 6 St. James's st. Pall mall
Lock Hospital (Benj. Meredith, sec.), Harrow rd. Paddingtn
Lock Alfred, tailor, New King st. Deptford
Lock Dinah (Mrs.), butcher, 32 Boston st. Dorset square
Lock Edward Charles, pianoforte ma. 95 Park st. Camden tn
Lock Francis, coffee rooms, 34 Earl st. west. Edgware road
Lock Henry, butcher, 32 Boston st. Dorset square
Lock Henry, *Feathers* P.H. 50 Duke st. St. James's
Lock James, baker, 158 Drury lane
Lock James, bootmaker, 40 Providence row, Barnsbury row
Lock James, carman, Smith square, Westminster
Lock James, grocer, 39 Charlotte ter. New cut, Lambeth
Lock James, tailor, 6 Cross st. Newington butts
Lock James, timber dlr. & sawyer, 4 Park st. Kennington cr
Lock John, tailor, 57 Milton st. Cripplegate
Lock Lawrence, bootmaker, 94 Drury lane
Lock Leith, tooth fumigator, 363 Oxford st
Lock Richard, beer retailer, 351 Albany road
Lock Robert, ale brewer, *Anchor* brewhouse, 14 Dorset st. Clapham road
Lock Robert, carver & gilder, 27 Cirencester pl. Fitzroy sq
Lock Robert, english wood dealer, 32 Booth st. Spitalfields
Lock Robert, tailor & trimming seller, 187 Hoxton O. town
Lock Robert Fred. solicitor, 8 New inn, Strand
Lock Samuel, dyer, &c. 50 Berners st. Oxford st
Lock Sarah (Mrs.), feather mercht. 24 King st. Cov. garden
Lock Thomas Agland, attorney, 18 Surrey st. Strand
Lock William, bookbinder & stationer, 4 Borough road
Lock William, corndealer & seedsman, 3 King st. Camden tn
Lock William, grocer, 1 Kennington st. Walworth
Lock William, newsagt. & tobcnst. 52 Up. North pl. Gray's inn r
Lock William, painter & grainer, 13 Amwell st. Pentonville
Lock William, plumber & glazier, see Tomlins & Lock
Locke John & Co. lead merchants & white lead manufacturers, St. Peter's chambers, Cornhill, & 7 Shad Thames
Locke & Nesham, builders, 68 Theobald's road, Red Lion square, & Portpool lane, Gray's inn lane
Locke Anthony, warehouseman, 22 Basinghall st
Locke George, builder, 4 East st. Red Lion square
Locke George, straw, &c. bonnet importer, see Way & Locke
Locke Henry Thomas, artist, 322 Albany road, Camberwell
Locke James, surgeon, 25 James st. Buckingham gate
Locke James, plaid & clan tartan wareho. 119 & 127 Regent st
Locke John, barrister, 2 Harcourt buildings, Temple
Locke Joseph, civil engineer, 11 Adam st. Adelphi
Locke Peter, glass warehouse, 32 Hatton garden
Locke Wm. coal mer. New Barge ho. whf. Commrcl. rd. Lamb
Locker Ann & Sarah, grocers, 1 Bedford sq. east, Commrcl. rd
Locker Charles, carpenter, 93 White Lion st. Pentonville
Lockett J. & T. china & earthenware ma. 107 Hatton garden, Henry Johnson, agent
Lockett James, butcher, 55 Hackney road

Lockett Sophia (Mrs.), paperstnr. 13 Bath pl. New rd. Fitzr. sq
Lockey Charles, professor of music, 24 Percy st. Bedford sq
Lockey Richard, warehouseman, 8 Wood st. Cheapside
Lockhart & Duncan, seedsmen & florists, 156 Cheapside
Lockie William, lead manufctr. see Robertson, Lockie & Co
Lockington Thos. K. carpntr. &c. 3 Northumbrld. st. Maryleb
Lockit John, artif. flower manf. 29 Hatfield st. Stamford st
Lockley Samuel, butcher, 8 Cross st. Blackfriars road
Lockley Thomas, physician, 6 St. George's pl. Knightsbride
Locks Wm. mahogany merchant, 1 Leonard st. Curtain rd
Lockton Robt. cheesemonger, 25 Nottingham st. Marylebone
Lockwood, Thackrah & Co. hop mrchts. see Thackrah & Co
Lockwood Caroline (Miss), milliner, 96 Quadrant, Regent st
Lockwood John, auctioneer, surveyor, house & estate agent, undertaker & appraiser, 44 Upper Baker st. Rengent's pk
Lockwood John, builder, house painter, decorator, &c. 44 Upper Baker st. Regent's park
Lockwood John, chandler's shop, 5 Peel pl. Kensngtn. grvl. pts
Lockwood John, escapement maker, 13 Myddleton st. Clerknw
Lockwood John Hawksley, commssn. agt. hall of commerce
Lockwood Joseph, surveyor & ho. agt. 6 Child's pl. Temple bar
Lockwood Paul, chemist, &c. 10 Fieldgate st. Whitechapel
Lockwood Rt. carpenter & joiner, 3 Leicester st. Leicester sq
Lockwood Robert Barrett, notary, 40 St. Mary Axe
Lockwood Wm. boys' school, Well st. Hackney
Lockwood Wm. cheese & butterman, 36 South Audley st
Lockwood Wm. Dav. stationer, bookselr. &c. 75 Nw. Bond st
Lockyer James, architect, 19 Southampton st. Fitzroy sq
Lockyer Jane (Mrs.), *Grosvenor Arms* P.H. 11 Holywll. st. Wmr
Lockyer John, metal & tool wareh. see Hoale, Lockyer & Parker
Lockyer John Richard, perfumer, 48 Park st. Camden town
Lockyer William, baker, 18 King st. Seven Dials
Locock Charles, physician, 26 Hertford st. May fair
Lodder Thos. law stationer, 5 Southampton blds. Chancery la
Loddiges Conrad & Sons, nurserymen, Church st. Hackney
Loddy George, *Bag of Nails* P.H. 1 King's rd. Pimlico
Loder Giles, merchant, 5 Adam's ct. Old Broad st. City
Loder John, professor of music, 165 Albany st. Regent's pk
Loder Richard, who. stationer, see Wiggins, Teape & Loder
Lodge & Cobb, oilmen, 4 Road side, Mile end road
Lodge Thos. & Son, hosiers & outfitters, 53 Oxford st
Lodge Adam, barrister, 5 Brick court, Temple
Lodge Charles, saddler, 21 Redcross st. Borough
Lodge Edward, hosier, glover & outfitter, 13 Strand
Lodge John, hosier, glover & shirt maker, 150 Regent st
Lodge John, oilman, 5 Bloomsbury ter. Commercial rd. east
Lodge Robert, plumber, 2 Chalton st. Somers town
Lodge Robert J. sec. to *Marine Insurance Co.* 27 Cornhill
Lodge William, grocer, 47 Great James st. Lisson grove
Lodwidge George, general broker, 26 Walbrook
Loeber Hannah (Mrs.), tobacnst. 6½ Gt. Windmill st. Haymkt
Loewe Adolph, bookbinder & stationer, 55 Mansell st
Loffill John, carpenter, &c. 34 & 35 Wellington st. Goswell st
Loft George, *Plough* P.H. 40 Rupert st. Haymarket
Loft James, sculptor & plaster cast maker, 29 Clipstone st
Loft Thomas, fruit salesman, Borough market, Southwark
Lofthouse John, grocer, 19 King st. Westminster
Lofthouse Robt. chemist, 1 Lit. St. Andrew st. Seven dials
Lofts David, coffee rooms, 2 Lit. Bruton st. New Bond st
Lofts John, agent for Morison's pills, 368 Strand
Lofts John, stationer, 3 Park pl. Mile end rd. north side
Lofts Richard, ironmonger, 8 Waterloo ter. Commrcl. rd. ea
Loftus Thomas, solicitor, see Holme, Loftus & Young
Loftus Thomas Alex. ale & stout mer. 25 Lamb's Conduit st
Loftus William, solicitor, 10 Devonshire st. Queen sq
Lofty & Potter, solicitors, 36 King st. Cheapside
Logan Walter & Co. merchants, 46 Lime st. City
Logan Cath. (Mrs.), locksmith & bellhanger, 38 Warwick la
Logan Chas. glasscutter, 20 New st. square, Fetter la
Logan Kenneth, tailor, 28 Newman st. Oxford st
Logan Robert, banker & agent, 9 Sise lane, Bucklersbury
Logdon George, *Jolly Sailor* P.H. 182 Ratcliff highway
Logie Hannah (Mrs.), tobacconist, 4 Chalton st. Somers tn
Logie James, potato salesman, 9 Cock hill, Ratcliff
Logie Thomas, hairdresser, 60 Paddington st. Marylebone
Loisel, jun. & Co. italian & french confectionery warehouse, 61 Hatton garden, & 16 Rue Mazagran, Paris
Lokier John, butcher, see Collyer & Lokier
Lomas John, ale rooms, 95 Bridge road, Lambeth
Lomas John, tobacconist, 19 Aldersgate st
Lomas John, tobacconist, 6 Brick lane, Spitalfields
Lomas John Humphrey, butcher, 34 Kensington High st
Lomas Wm. grocer & tea dealer, see Shillcock & Lomas
Lomas Wm. marine store dealer, 110 Snow's fields, Bermndsy
Lomax Edmund, surv. to com. of woods & forests, 10 Fitzroy sq
Lomax M.E. & C.S. (Misses), stationers, 27 Yorkrw. Kenngtn. rd
Lomax Edward, music engraver, 94 Mount st. Grosvenor sq
Lomax Fred. auctnr. & upholsterer, 8 Orchard st. Portmn. sq
Lomax Henry, mariner, 8 Gt. George st. Bermondsey
Lomax Henry, professor of music, 13 Old Quebec st. Oxford st
Lomax James, apothecary, &c. 40 Dorset st. Portman sq
Lomax James, solicitor, 4 Sise lane
Lomax John, turner, 16 Charter house st
Lomer Diedrich C. H. & Co. merchts. 1 London st. Mark la
Lombard John, shoemaker, 2 Great Marylebone st
London Aged Christians' Society (William Humphries, honorary sec), 32 Sackville st
London Annuity Society (Rev. R. H. Shepherd, sec.), 11 Chatham place, Blackfriars
London Association in aid of the Moravian Missions (Robert Webb, sec.), 20 Charles st. Westminster
London Association for the Protection of Trade (Thomas Drewett Hawker, sec.), 21 Soho square
London Assurance Corporation for Fire, Life & Marine Assurance, 7 Royal Exchange, & 10 Regent st.; for directors, &c. see page 2019
London Benevolent Repository, 20 Wigmore st. Cavendish sq
London & Birmingham Railway Office (Richd. Creed, sec.), at the station, Euston square
London & Blackwall Railway Co.'s Office (John Fisher Kennell, sec.), London station, Railway pl. Fenchurch st
London & Brighton Railway Company's Office (Thos. John Buckton, sec.), 2 Joiner st. terminus, Duke st. Tooley st
London & Bristol Railway Co. Gt. Western station, London terminus, Grand Junction road, Paddington
London Cemetery Co. (Chas. Burls, jun. sec.), 15 New Bridge st. & 281 Regent st.; *Cemeteries*, Highgate & Nunhead
London City Mission Office (Rev. Robert Ainslie & Rev. John Garwood, secs.), 20 Red Lion square, Holborn
London Coffee & Eatinghouse Keepers' Society (Samuel Abbott, sec.), Anderton's hotel, 164 Fleet st
London Commissary Registry Office for Wills & Administrations, 16 Gt. Knightrider st.; hours 9 to 4
London Contract Coal Company (George Gordon Cummings, managing director), 10 America square
London Conveyance Company (Robt. Blore, manager), 13 St. Alban's place, Edgware road
London Corn Exchange Company's Office (Wm. W. Wren, sec.), Mark lane; hours 12 to 2
London & County Joint Stock Banking Company (Henry Luard, general manager), 21 Lombard st.; branch 37 West Smithfield; see page 2002
London Diocesan Board of Education (Rev. Richard R. Burgess, hon. sec.), 79 Pall mall; hours 10 to 4
London Dispensary, 21 Church st. Spitalfields
London Dispensary for Diseases of Lungs, 92 Newman st
London Dock Co. (John D. Powles, sec.), 1 New Bank bldgs. Lothbury; *Docks*, near Ratcliff highway
London & Dublin Bank (Sam. W. Perrott, sec.), 46 Piccadilly; see page 2003
London & Dublin Orthodox Journal (Peter Andrews), editors' office, 92 Bartholomew close
London & Durham Coal Co. (Wm. Broady, mgr.), Eastern whf. Adelphi, & 15 whf. Macclesfield st. north, City road
London East Savings Bk. (R.Y. Ellis, acct.) 34 Colet pl. Coml. r
London, Edinburgh & Dublin Life Assurance Co. (Alex. Robertson, manager; John Emerson, sec.), 3 Charlotte row, Mansion house, & 18 Chancery lane; see page 2031
London, Edinburgh & Glasgow Parcels Conveyance Company (R. K. Vorley, manager), 9 Tower royal, Watling st
London & Edinburgh Parcels Delivery Company (George Crouch, man.), 5 Tudor st. & 1 Crown court, Blackfriars
London & Edinburgh Steam Packet Comp. 35 Leadenhall st
London Elocution So. (Hy. Sanders, sec.), 165 Aldersgate st
London Female Mission (Edward Turst Carver & George Groser, secs.), office, 20 Red Lion square; Probation house (Miss Mary Kemp, matron), 57 White Lion st. Pentonville
London Female Penitentiary (James Leech, sec.; Mrs. Harriett Cooper, matron), Cumming place, Pentonville
London Fever Hospital (Stephen Jennings Goodfellow, M.D. resident medical officer), King's cross, St. Pancras old road
London Fire Engine Establishment (James Braidwood, superintendent), 68 Watling st.; see page 2010
London Friendly Institute (Jos. Palmer, sec.), 19 London wall
London Gas Light Company (John R. Hinde, sec.), office, 26 Southampton st. Strand; works, Vauxhall High st
London Gazette (by authority), Cannon row, Westminster; hours of business, Mon. Wed. Thurs. & Sat. 10 to 5; Tues. & Fri. 10 to 3, & for publication, 6 to 7
London & Greenwich Railroad (Henry Adron, sec.), office, 10 Coleman st.; terminus, Duke st. Tooley st
London Hibernian So. (John Brown, sec.), Exeter hall, Stran

London Homœopathic Medical Institution (Paul Francis Curie, M.D. head physician; Edward Charles Chepmell, M.D. resident physician), 17 Hanover square
London Hospital (Wm. B. Bathurst, sec.), Whitechapel rd
London, Hounslow & Western Railway Co. 7 Walbrook
London Infirmary for the Cure of Diseases of the Skin (B. Thornton, esq. sec.), 25 New Bridge st. Blackfriars
London Institution (William Tite, sec. Richd. Thompson & Edwd. Wm. Brayley, librarians), between Nos. 11 & 12 Finsbury circus
London IronCompany (J. Robertson,sec.),109 Fenchurch st
London ItinerantSoc.(Jn.Thos.Read, sec.),8Blmfild.st.Fnsb
London Joint Stock Bank (Geo.Pollard,man.),5Princes st. Bank; Western branch (Edward Jerningham & Henry Robinson, managers), 69 Pall mall; see page 2002
London Journal of Arts Office, 66 Chancery lane
London Journal of Commerce Newsp. Office, 42Mincing la
London Journal & Pioneer, 13A, Salisbury sq. Fleet st
London, Leith, Edinburgh & Glasgow Steam Co. (John Adams, agent), 82 Lombard st. City
London Library (John George Cochrane, sec.), 12 St. James's square
London Life Association (H. J. Brooke, sec.), 81 King William st. City; see page 2032
London & Manchester Direct Railway Company, 29 Moorgate st. Lothbury
London Manure Co. (Edwd. Purser, sec.), 40 NewBridge st
London Marble & Stone Working Company, Esher st. Holywell st. Millbank, Westminster
London Maritime Institutionfor Captains' Widows (Wm. Watson, sec.), Bow common; office, 25 Birchin la.Cornhill
London Mechanics' Inst. (A. M'Farlane,sec.),29Southampton buildings
London Mercantile Journal, 42 Mincing lane
London Mercantile Price Current Off. 9 Liverpool st. City
London Missionary Society(Rev.JohnArundel, home sec.), 8 Bloomfield st. Finsbury
London, Newbury & Bath Direct Railway Co. (G. B. Keeling, esq. sec.), 41 Charing cross
*London Omnibus Conveyance Co.Off.*4Portmanpl.Edgw.rd
London OrphanAsylumOff.(T.P.Rust,sec.),10St.Mary axe
London Oven Coke Works, Vauxhall walk, Vauxhall
London Parcels Delivery Co. 12 Roll's buildings,Fetterlane
London Portsmouth & Chichester Direct Railway Co. (John C. Sommers, sec.), 1A, Adelphi terrace
London Patent Hydraulic Co. Beare's patent pumps & fire engines, 16 Holborn hill
London Philanthropic Soc. (G. E. Stolworthy, sec.), 17 Camomile st
London Provident Institution Savings Bank (Sir T. Baring, bart. president), 1, 2, & 3 Blomfield st. Moorfields
London Reversionary Interest Society (B. & M. Boyd, residt. directs. Hen. T. Thompson, sec.), 4 New Bank bldgs. Lothbury; see page 2032
LondonReli.TractSo.(Thos.Chapman,sec.),1 Aldermanbury
London, Salisbury & Yeovil Junction Railway Office, (Lewis Crombie, esq. sec.), 63 Moorgate st
London Soc. for Promoting Christianity amongst the Jews Revs.J. J.Reynolds&Wm.Ayerst,secs.)3Chathampl.Blkfrs
London Society for the Protection of Young Females & the Prevention of Juvenile Prostitution (James B. Talbot, sec.), Asylum, Tottenham; office, 17Ironmongerla
London Society for Teaching the Blind to Read (Rev. Septimus Ramsey, sec.),38Queen square, Bloomsbury
London & South Western Railway Office (Alfred Morgan, sec.), at the terminus, Nine Elms, Vauxhall
London University College Hospital, Upper Gower st
London, Warwick, Leamington & Kidderminster Railway Co. (Francis E. Davis, accountant), 11 King William st. City
London, Waterford& Chester Shipping Association(Thomas Taylor, secretary), 22 Eastcheap
London & Westminster Bank, Lothbury; *branch banks*, 1 St. James's sq; 213 & 214 High Holborn; 3 Wellington st. Borough; 87 Whitechapel High st.; & 4 Stratford place; see page
London& Westm.CoalCo.(Jph.Shotter,mg.)7John st.Adelphi
London & Westminster Steamboat Co. 9 Villiers st. Strand
London& Windsor Railw.Co.(E.W.H.Bell,sec.)30 Regent st
London Wood Paving Co. [*Perring's Safety Principle*] (John Lee Stevens, man.), 2 Charlotte row, Mansion house
London & York Railway Office (James Ryder Mowatt, secretary), 7 Lothbury, & 3 Park st. Westminster
London Edward, bookbdr. & stationer, 2 Fountain pl.City rd
London Edward, gun & rifle maker, 51 London wall
London Francis, cowkeeper, 1 Clayton st. Kennington
London Fdk. Steph. scale & mill ma. 64 Bishopsgate within
London George, tailor, see Simpson & London
London Jas. chronometer ma. Gt. William st. Caledonian rd
London Jas. patten & clogmaker, 58 Golden la. St. Luke's
London Jas. jun. plumber & painter, 80 Golden la. St. Luke's
London Jemima (Mrs.), china dlr. 62 Golden la. St. Luke's
London John, haberdasher, hosier, &c. 106 Lambeth walk
London John, tire smith, 3 Long yard, Lamb's Conduit st
London Joseph, baker, 16 Goswell st
London Robert, cheesemonger, 9 Up. area, Hungerford mkt
London Thomas, plumber & glazier, 14 Chiswell st
London William, cowkeeper, 3 Brewer st. Pimlico
London William, chandler's shop, Well st. Hackney
London Wm. jun. plumber & glazier, 8 Union st. Bishopsgt
London Willoughby John G. barrister, 23 Old sq. Linc.'s inn
Londonderry & Coleraine & Londonderry & Enniskillen Railw. Off. (Fred. H. Hemming, sec.) 49 Moorgate st. ch
Lone Gyles, *King's Arms* P.H. 5 King st. Borough
Loneragan Jas. cornchandler, 12 Cambridge ter. Islington
Lonergan & Co. merchants, 3 Austinfriars
Loney Mary (Mrs.), lodging house, 61 Gower st. Bedford sq
Loney Thos. Connor, solicitor, 26 Wakefield st. Brunswk. sq
Long Danl. & Son, gun & pistol mnfrs. 8 Old Cavendish st
Long & Cornell, wine & spirit brokers, 65 Mark lane
Long & Hay, solicitors, 44 Lincoln's inn fields
Long & Hewlitt, wine merchants, law chmbrs.77 Chancery la
Long Samuel & Co. woollen manufacturers, 27 Gresham st
Long Alfred, glass cut. & lead mer. 6 Chalcroft ter. New cut
Long Benjamin, fish factor, 97 Lower Thames st
Long Chas. house & ornamental painter, 1 King st. Portm.sq
Long Edward, miller, Old Ford, Bow
Long Frederick Bedford, barrister, 35 Lincoln's inn fields
Long George, magistrate, Marylebone Police Court
Long George, fruiterer, 11 Deptford High st
Long Hannah (Mrs.), corn factor, 29 Parker's row, Dockhead
Long Henry, cheesemonger, 51 King st. Seven dials
Long Henry James Valentine, sworn broker, 65 Mark lane
Long Henry Joseph, tobacconist, 12 Oxford pl.Marlboro' rd
Long Isaac, butcher, 3 Cambridge road, Mile end road
Long James, fishmonger, 20 North Audley st
Long James, fruiterer, 5 King st. Cloth fair, Smithfield
Long Jeremiah, surveyor & estate agent, 190 Shoreditch
Long John, pastrycook, Church st. Hackney
Long John, plumber & glazier, 13 New Church st.Lisson gro
Long John, shoemaker, 109 Upper Seymour st. Euston sq
Long John, solicitor, see Salomon & Long
Long John, solicitor, 56 Clarendon square
Long John, surv.for psh.of Hans Town, 12 Symon st. Chelsea
Long Joseph, mathematical & philosophical instrument ma.; hydrometer, saccharometer, & guaging rule manufacturer, 20 Little Tower st
Long Joseph, wine merchant, 27A, York st. Portman sq
Long Mary (Mrs.), vet.instrument maker, 217 High Holborn
Long Peirce, solicitor, 25 New Millman st. Foundling
Long Richard, plasterer & bricklr. 18 Gutter lane, Cheapside
Long Richard, crapedresser, 30 Gt. Pearl st. Spitalfields
Long Richard, fruiterer, 3 Theberton st. Islington
Long Richard, lucifer match manufr. 30 Gt.Pearl st.Spitalfl
Long Robert Furniss, solicitor, 27 King st. Cheapside
Long Samuel, bootma. 17 Cumberland pl. Newington butts
Long Samuel, *Queen's Head* P.H. 93 High st. Marylebone
Long Thomas, carpenter, 12 New Norfolk st. Lo.rd.Islington
Long Thomas, coal merchant, 15 Old Manor st. Chelsea
Long Thos. *Ld. Monson's Arms* P.H.21 Totnhm.st.Tot.ct.rd
Long Thos. Burt, builder, 48 & 49 Little Britain
Long Wm. fancy bread & biscuit baker, 14 Lamb's Conduit st
Long Wm. fruiterer, 16 Old Gravel lane, Wapping
Long Wm. shell fishmonger & fruiterer, 34 Chancery lane
Long Wm. ship & insurance broker, see Cookes & Long
Long Wm. solicitor, see Staniland & Long
Long Wm. wine merchant, 28 Queen st. Cheapside
Longbourne Wm.Thos.solr.seeRanken, Ford, Longbourne&Co
Longden Geo. Roger, proctor, see Barlow & Longden
Longden Thos. Hayter, stockbr. see Johnson, Longden & Co
Longdill Pynson W. & Co. col. brokers, 36 Crutched friars
Longdon Robert, hosier, glover, &c. 1 Lit. Love la.Wood st
Longdon Wm. Hen. tailor, 13 Eccleston st. south, Pimlico
Longes Richard, plumber & glazier, 11 King st. Borough
Longhurst James & Ephraim, zinc manufrs. 153 Kingsland road, & East road, City road
Longhurst Charles, stables, 23 Gt. York mews, Portman sq
Longhurst Henry, grocer, 14 Brecknock pl.Camden new twn
Longhurst Jas. bricklayer, King st. Battersea
Longhurst Thos. toy dealer, Camberwell green
Longhurst Walter, carpenter, 19 Pelham rd. Brompton
Longhurst W. *Imperial Hotel*, 1 Tavistock row, Cov. grdn

Longland Chas. haberdasher, 1 Gloucester ter. Hoxton
Longland Chas, staymaker, 10 Britannia row, Hoxton
Longley Thomas, toy warehouse, 3 Dorset st. Clapham rd
Longley Wm. carpenter, 1 Eaton pl. Grosvenor sq
Longley Wm. Thomas, paperhanger, 78 Gt. Suffolk st. Boro'
Longman, Brown, Green & Longmans', booksellers & publishers, 39 Paternoster row
Longman Chas. grocer & oilman, 85 Drummond st. Euston sq
Longman Elizabeth (Mrs.), baker, 1 Broad st. Golden sq
Longman Henry, corn dealer, 36 Boston st. Dorset sq
Longmore George, carrier, 9½ Maidstone wharf, Queenhithe
Longmore John, hosier, 13 Red Lion st. Holborn
Longmore John, lodging house, 35 Arundel st. Strand
Longmore Thos. general brass founder, 264 High Holborn, & at 13 St. Mary's row, Birmingham
Longmore Thomas, surgeon, 4 Portland place, Borough road
Longridge & Co. engineers, 8 Wallbrook, Bedlington Iron Works, near Morpeth, & Newcastle-upon-Tyne
Longstaff John & Co. brandydistillers, Back rd. St. George's ea
Longstaff Michael & Co. wool warehousemen, 89 Cheapside
Longstaff Joseph, *Hungfd. hot. & coffee house*, 8 Hungerford st
Longstreeth James, dining rooms, 53 Fetter lane, Holborn
Longuet Gabriel & Son, cognac merchants (agents, R. Sedgwick & Co.), 15 Cannon st
Lonsdale William & Co. hosiers & glovers, 179 Regent st
Lonsdale Christopher (late Birchall & Co.), music seller & publisher, & musical circulating library, 26 Old Bond st
Lonsdale David, linendraper, 29 Aldgate
Lonsdale Edward, paint manfr. see Barsham, Lonsdale & Co
Lonsdale Edward Francis, surgeon, 82 Guilford st. Russell sq
Lonsdale Francis, tea dlr. & grocer, 200 Bermondsey st
Lonsdale Gwalter B. sec. anglo mex. mint co. 5 Broad st. bldgs
Lonsdale Jas. John, barrister, 52 Lincoln's inn fields
Lonsdale Richard, artist, 7 Park cottages, Parkvill. ea. Reg. pk
Lonsdale Richard, grocer, 14 Butcher row, Ratcliff
Lonsdale Richard, solicitor, Temple chambers, Falcon court, Fleet st. & 2 St. Alban's place, Hammersmith
Lonsdale William, barrister, 5 Old square, Lincoln's inn
Looker & Blacker, wardrobe dealers, 25 Wells st. Oxford st
Looker Henry Wm. manufacturing cutler, 42 Leadenhall st
Looker Joseph, library, 2 Southampton st. Camberwell road
Looker Wm. ruby holemaker, 1 Hatton pl. Cross st. Islington
Loom John, corn & coal merchant, 31 Lime st
Loomes John, porkmen, 18 Barnsbury pl. Upper st. Islington
Loomes John, tailor, 10 Lower terrace, Islington
Loomes Joseph & Samuel, porkman, 93 St. John street road
Loomes Samuel, poulterer, 77 St. John street road
Loop Thomas, lapidary, 16 Exmouth st. Spafields
Loose Eleanor (Mrs.), oil & color ware. 7 Sloane sq. Chelsea
Looseley Joseph, parchmt. & vellum ma. Neate st. Cobourg rd
Looseley Thomas, parchment maker, 7 Field's pl. Locks fields
Looseley Charles, butcher, 19 Long alley, Finsbury
Looseley Elizth. Esther (Mrs.), babylin. wa. 20 Princes st. Westr
Looseley Joseph, furniture broker, 49 Crucifix la. Bermndsy
Loosemore Elizabeth (Miss), milliner, 208 Piccadilly
Lopez Lopes Fonséca, foreign warehousemen, 32 Bread st
Lopez Ramon de Bertodano, merchant, 30 Gt. Winchester st
Lopresti Chas. Wm. fish sauce & condiment wa. 199 Piccadilly
Lord & Hall, wool brokers, 8 Basinghall st
Lord George & Co. wine merchts. 3&9 George yd. Lombard st
Lord Hen. W. & Co. east india & colon. brokrs. 38 Mincing lane
Lord & Marlborough, haberdashers, 32 Red Lion st. Holborn
Lord Thomas & Co. east india & forn. agts. 10 Barge yd. chambs
Lord Chamberlain's Offices, Stable yard, St. James's palace
Lord Chancellor's Court, term time, Westminster Hall; vacation, Lincoln's inn hall; residence 25 George st. Hanover square
Lord's Day Observance Society (Rev. John T. Baylee, B.A sec.), 12 Exeter hall, 372 Strand
Lord Great Chamberlain's Office, 2 Abingdon st. Westminster; hours 11 to 5
Lord Mayor's Court Office, 7 Old Jewry; hours 10 to 4
Lord Steward's Pay Office, Gt. ct. St. James's pal. hs. 11to4
Lord Caroline (Mrs.), dressmaker, 6 Church row, Islington
Lord Charles, *Salmon & Ball tavern*, 295 Bethnal green rd
Lord Henry, carpenter & builder, 12 Gt. Ormond yd. Queen sq
Lord Henry, carpenter, &c. 16 New North st. Red Lion sq
Lord James, barrister, 3 Elm court, Temple
Lord James, carpenter, 3 White hart st. Brydges st. Cov. gar
Lord James, coal merchant, 48 Gt. Cambridge st. Hackneyrd
Lord James, coal dealer, 33 Baldwin's gardens, Leather lane
Lord John, glover & hosier, 68 & 69, Burlington arcade
Lord John, *Prince of Wales* P.H. 15 Charlotte st. Portland pl
Lord John, prof. of music, 10 Warwick villas, Harrow road
Lord John, shoemaker, Grange ter. Grange rd. Bermondsey
Lord Mary Ann (Mrs.), grocer, &c. 31 Melton st. Euston sq
Lord Oliver, hair dresser, 125 High st. Camden town
Lord Robert Turner, hair dresser, Church street, Hackney
Lord Thomas, *Crown Tap* P.H. 73 Watling st
Lorden Samuel, hair & glue merchant, dealer in glue pieces, fleshing horns, &c. 7 Butler's buildings, Bermondsey st
Lorimer Geo. cheesemngr. 155 Upper Whitecross st. St. Luke's
Lordonny James, coal merchant, 2 Elizabeth ter. Islington
Lords Robert, farrier, 26 Northumberland mews, Marylebone
Lorimer James, dyer, &c. 1 Lower terrace, Islington
Lorimer Wm. cheesemonger, 6 Perseverance ter. Shoreditch
Lorimier Anthony, bookbinder, 30 Clerkenwell close
Loring Benjamin, stationer, 28 Clift st. New North road
Loriôt John, bootmaker, 16 Brownlow st. Holborn
Lorkin Jerh. & Co. merchs. & blackw. hallfac. 68 Basinghall st
Lorkin John, oil & hop merchant, 23 Aldersgate st
Lorkin Thomas, wine merchant, 12 Rood lane, Fenchurch st
Lorkin Wm. John, bootmaker, 18 Crombie's row, Coml. rd. east
Lorking Wm. coffee rooms, see Robinson & Lorking
Lormier William, watchmaker, 93 Wood st. Cheapside
Losada José R. de, chronometer & watch manufacturer, 20 Woburn buildings, Tavistock square
Losecamp Alfred, egg merchant, 30 Hermes st. Pentonville
Lothian James, bootmaker, 43 Chandos st. Covent garden
Lott George Fredk. musical inst. maker, 23 Princes st. Soho
Lott John, hatter, 83 Tooley st
Lott John Fred. musical instrument ma. 32 King st. Seven dials
Lott Thomas, solicitor, vestry clerk of St. Mary le Bow, City, 43, Bow lane, Cheapside
Lott Wm. confectioner, 11 Bridge st. Lambeth
Louch Brothers, & Thompson, rope ma. Love la. Shadwell
Loudan Mary Ann (Mrs.), watch & clockma. 16 Blackfriars rd
Loudansack & Case, navy agents, 1 James st. Adelphi
Lough Corrib Commission (Jackson Barwise, sec.), 18 Austinfr
Lough Henry, ham & beef dealer, 7 Kent pl. Old Kent rd
Lough John, ham dealer, 181 Brick lane Spitalfields
Lough John Graham, sculptor, 42 Harewood sq. Dorset sq
Lough Joseph, ham dealer, 155 & cheesemong. 156 Shored
Lough Neagh Commission (Jackson Barwise, sec.), 18 Austin fr
Loughborough Thomas, solicitor, 23 Austin friars
Louis Edward, combma. & who. perfumer, 27 Gerrard st. Soho
Louis James, surgeon dentist, 44 Leicester square
Louis John, importer of cigars, 3 Drury court, Drury lane
Louison George, umbrella manufr. 30 Leman st. Goodman'sfld
Lound John, auctioneer, &c. see Nedby & Lound
Loup James, milliner, 2 Flower's buildings, Holloway
Loustau John, wine importer, 20 Mark lane
Louther Wm. & Fred. hosiers & outfitters, 99 Boro' High st
Louvain & Jemeppe Railway (George Dance, sec.), 28 Threadneedle st
Lovat Samuel, barrister, 2 Stone buildings, Lincoln's inn
Love & Evans, blackw. hall fac. & warehmn. 24 Basinghall st
Love Martin & Thomas, corn dealers, 77 New corn exchange, Mark lane, & Stoke Newington High st
Love George, bookseller, stationer, printseller, lithographic printer, & fancy paper maker, 81 Bunhill row
Love James, surgeon & apothecary, 11 Grosvenor row, Piml
Love James, furn. undertaker, 9 Fleur de lis st. Norton folgate
Love John, surgeon, 12 Brook st. Grosvenor sq
Love Kelah, furniture broker, 15 Duke's row, Pancras New rd
Love Philip, painter, 3 Tower st. Westminster road
Love Richard, grocer & teadealer, 51 Brick lane, Spitalfields
Love Thomas, dyer & scourer, 25 Gt. Windmill st. Haymarket
Love Thomas, plumber, glazier, &c. 2 Little Britain
Lovecraft William, tailor, 2 Angel court, Throgmorton st
Loveday Arthur, proctor, 10 Godliman st. Doctors' commons
Loveday Charles Dnl. pawnbroker, 14 St. Albans pl. Edgw rd
Loveday James, bootmaker, 9 King's row, Walworth road
Loveday Samuel, tailor, 8 Church st. Camberwell
Loveday Wm. grocer & cheesem. 27 Chester st. Kennington crs
Lovegrove & Leathes, merchants, 34 Dowgate hill, City
Lovegrove Samuel & Co. *West India Dock tavern*, Blackwll
Lovegrove Samuel & James, *London coffeehouse*, 24 Ludgate hill, & *Brunswick hotel*, Blackwall
Lovegrove Charles, fruiterer, 3 Denmark place, Camberwell
Lovegrove Charles, plumber, 18 New Church st. west, Edgw. rd
Lovegrove Edward, printer, 27 Gee st. Goswell st
Lovegrove James, summerho. bldr. 5&6 Cumbrlnd. row, Kenn. gr
Lovegrove Sarah (Mrs.), berlin wa. 6 King's rd. ea. Chelsea
Lovegrove William, *Fladong's Hotel*, 144 Oxford st
Lovegrove Wm. leather cutter, 5 Broomfields, Deptford
Lovejoy Saml. & Wm. auctioneers, see Warlters, Lovejoy & Son
Lovejoy George, fruiterer, 5 Up. Copenhagen st. Pentonville
Lovejoy Maria Fras. (Mrs.), paperstainer, 4 Long la. Smithfld
Lovejoy Robert, fruiterer, 32 Providence row, Islington
Lovejoy Wm. auctioneer, 25 Up. North pl. Gray's inn road
Lovelace John, leather seller & agt. 18 Greville st. Hatton gdn

Lovelace Marcus, news agt.& statnr.35 King st. Regent st
Loveland & Beckitt, attornies, 64 Lincoln's inn fields, & Shawfield cottage, King's road, Chelsea
Loveland Henry, boat builder, Wapping High st
Loveland John, boot & shoe maker, 102 Waterloo road
Loveland Thomas, cabinet maker, 120 Drummond st. Euston sq
Loveland Wm. china dealer, 17 High st. Portland town
Lovell & Bremridge, auctioneers, surveyors & estate agents, 9 Hatton garden, Holborn
Lovell Charles & Son, plumbers, glaziers & painters, 19 Bow la. Cheapside, & 70 Red Lion st. Holborn
Lovell Chas.W. & Chas.Hen. solicitors, 14 South sq. Gray's inn
Lovell & Halliwell, solicitors, 4 Great Ryder st. St. James's
Lovell Thos. & Co. window glass mers. 53 Red Lion st. Holborn
Lovell Charles, bootmaker, 39 Crescent st. Euston sq
Lovell Elizab. (Mrs.), coffee rooms, 2 Bishop's walk, Lambeth
Lovell Ellen (Miss), dressmaker, 432 West Strand
Lovell Fredk. Geo. chemist, 4 Little Ormond st. Queen sq
Lovell George, plumber & glazier, 1 Brunswk.pl. Balls pnd.rd
Lovell Hanh.M. (Mrs.), leghorn & chip hat dyer, 51 Alders.st
Lovell James, clothworker, 38 Basinghall st
Lovell James, *Job's Castle* P.H. White Lion st. Spitalfields
Lovell John, tax collector, 7 Jewin st. Cripplegate
Lovell John Alphonsus, working jeweller, 44 Barbican
Lovell John Thos. carpenter & builder, 3 Dean st. Shadwell
Lovell Langford, west india merct. 14 New City chambers
Lovell Wm. cattle salesman, 15 West Smithfield
Lovell Wm. jun. architect & surveyor, 20 Swinton st. Gray's inn road, & 45 Church st. Stoke Newington
Loveridge John, dining rooms, 78 Snow hill
Loveridge John Hen. *Yorkshire Grey* P.H. 17 Londn.st. Ftzry.sq
Lovering Geo. Firks, baker, 45 Holywell st. Millbank
Lovesy Conway Whithorne, specl. pleader, 4 Brick ct. Temple
Lovett Charles, coal dealer, 25 Charles st. St. George's east
Lovett Charles, coffee rooms, 5½ Snow hill
Lovett Elizh. (Mrs.), carpenter, 49 East st. Manchester sq
Lovett Giles, carpenter, Kensington gravel pits
Lovett John, carpntr. & undertakr. 33 Dorset st. Portman sq
Lovett John, cheesemonger, 66 High Holborn
Lovett Samuel, surgeon, 23 Clare st. Clare market
Lovett William, fruiterer, 135 Great Suffolk st. Borough
Loveys Andrew Tapper, cooper, 45 Mansell st
Loveys Andrew Tapper, wine & bottle merchant, cooper, &c. 45 Mansell st. Goodman's fields, & 6 Hart st. Mark lane
Lovibond Hen. pat. ale & porter brewer, Wandsworth rd. nth.si
Lovick Thos. surv. of pave. & plmbr. 17 Princes st. Red Ln.sq
Lovick Wm. *Coach & Horses* P.H. 60 Davies st. Berkeley sq
Loving Edward, straw bonnet mnfr. 20 Duke st. Chelsea
Loving Hen. *Northumberld. Arms* P.H. 36 Goodge st. Tot.ct.rd
Lovitt Thomas, carpenter & builder, 35 King sq. Goswell rd
Low Robert & Son, perfumers to her Majesty, & general dealers in combs, brushes, &c. wholes. & retail, 330 Strand
Low Stephen & Son, cattle salesmen, 59 West Smithfield
Low Moor Iron Co. (Morris, Prevost & Co. agts.) Brick hill la
Low Ann (Mrs.), baker, 58 Aldermanbury
Low Archibald M'Arthur, solicitor, 65 Chancery lane
Low Charles, *Rising Sun* P.H. 46 Tottenham court road
Low David, merchant, 6 Nicholas lane, City
Low Dennis, hairdresser, 1 Little Hermitage st. Wapping
Low Edward, baker, 121 Mount st. Berkeley square
Low Elizabeth (Miss), ladies' school, 6 Lit. Ormond st
Low George, baker, 1 Duke st. West Smithfield
Low George, provision agent, Miller's wharf, Lr. Ea.Smithfi
Low Henry, tobacconist, 398 Oxford st
Low James, currier, 17 Portpool lane, Gray's inn lane
Low Jas. ea. india exchnge.broker & agt. 75 Old Broad st. City
Low James, paper manufr. see Pewtress, Low & Pewtress
Low John, bookseller & binder, 14 Little Queen st. Lincoln's inn fi
Low John, cattle salesman, 17 West Smithfield
Low John, dairyman, Oval cottage, Hackney road
Low John, fishmonger, 5 Ship tavern pass. Leadenhall market
Low John, printer, 14 Dorrington st. Leather lane
Low Mark Anthony, undertaker, 12 Union st. east, Spitalflds
Low Robert, baker, 46 Mount st. Berkeley square
Low Robert, *Union Arms* P.H. 26 Panton st. Haymarket
Low Sampson, bookseller & stationer, 42 Lamb's Conduit st
Low Sampson, publishers' circular office, 54 Fleet st
Low Stephen jun. cattle salesman, 37 West Smithfield
Low William, fruiterer, 5 Queen st. Soho
Low William, furn. undertaker, 21 Museum st. Bloomsbury
Low William, painter, 24 King st. Soho
Low William Francis, attorney, 67 Wimpole st
Low William Henry, beer retailer, 210 Shoreditch High st
Low Wm. Shand, stationer & bookseller, 31 Abchurch lane
Lowance Edmund, hairdresser, 2 Hatfield pl. Westminster rd
Lowcock George, razor maker & cutler, 38 Cornhill
Lowcock Richard, who. teadealer, see Miller & Lowcock
London & Weightman, furniture wareho. 112 Edgware rd
Lowden John Dawson, chemist & druggist, 42 Doughty st
Lowe Dan. & Josiah, crape finishers, Wilmers' gardens, Hoxton Old town
Lowe & Farrance (Misses), milnrs. 11 Radcliffe ter. Goswell rd
Lowe & Hornblower, who.& ret. chemist & drugg. 47 Blackfrs rd
Lowe John & William, attorneys, 2 Tanfield court, Temple
Lowe & Oliphant, stationers, account book & copying machine manufacturers, 47 Threadneedle st
Lowe Sapphirus & Co. scotch oatmeal factors, 48 Eastcheap
Lowe Sweeting & Byrne, attorneys, 22 Southampton buildings, Chancery lane
Lowe Anne (Mrs.), straw bonnet mak. 6 Essex pl. Mile end rd
Lowe Catherine (Mrs.), milliner, &c. 4 Oddy's row, Islington
Lowe Charles, chemist & druggist, 23 Little Pulteney st
Lowe Edward, chemist, &c. 15 Up. Glo'ster pl. King's rd. Chelsea
Lowe Edward, printer, 3 Playhouse yard, Blackfriars
Lowe Elizabeth (Mrs.), *Crown* coffee rooms, 29 Eyre st. hill
Lowe Elizabeth (Mrs.), fruiterer, 27 Chapel st. New road
Lowe Francis, engrav.& enamel. 10 Wilderness row, Clrknwll
Lowe George, civil engineer, 39 Finsbury circus
Lowe George, *Queen's Head* P.H. 52 Piccadilly
Lowe George Benj. chandlers' shop, George st. Camberwell
Lowe Henry, greengrocer, 11 Pierrepoint row, Islington
Lowe James, marine store dealer, 2 Odell pl. Little Chelsea
Lowe Jas. *Pagoda* P.H. 7 Pagoda ter. Bermondsey New rd
Lowe Jesse, *East Temple* coffee rooms, 4 Whitefriars st
Lowe John, builder, 6 Little Wild st. Lincoln's inn fields
Lowe John, cabinet maker, 52 Berwick st. Soho
Lowe John, dining rooms, 14 Lit. Crown st. Princes st. Soho
Lowe John, hatter to the Queen, 68 Fleet st
Lowe John Shaw, who. stay manufr. 3 Lit. Carter la. Doct.com
Lowe John William, barrister, 3 Elm court, Temple
Lowe Joseph, law stationer, 27 Bell yard, Temple bar
Lowe Josiah, wholesale clothes warehouse, 3 Minories
Lowe Nathaniel, baker, 79 Hoxton old Town
Lowe Richard, brass turn.& door pl.ma. 16 Porter st. Soho sq
Lowe Richard, *Green Man* P.H. 134 Edgawarerd. Marylebon
Lowe Richard, press tool makr. 26 Meredith st. Clerkenwell
Lowe Robert, bedstead & cabinet mfr. 126 Wardour st. Soho
Lowe Robert Manley, attorney, 2 Tanfield court, Temple
Lowe Samuel, tailor, 26 Barbican
Lowe Thomas, baker, 7 Limehouse Old road
Lowe Thomas, baker, 1 Portland pl. South, Clapham rd
Lowe Thomas, cheesemonger, 57 Up. North pl. Gray's inn rd
Lowe Thomas, marine store dealer, 8 Belvedere bldgs. Boro.rd
Lowe Thomas, minature painter in enamel, 40 Ely place
Lowe Thomas, stamper & die sinker, 55 Museum st. Bloomsbury
Lowe Wm. *One Tun* P.H. 84 Holborn hill
Lowe Wm. printer & statnr. 19 Up. St. Martin's la. Charing cr
Lowe Wm. tailor & draper, 5 Barge yard, Bucklersbury
Lowe Wm. wine coop.& bot.mer. 70 Ossulston st. Somers tn
Lowe Wm. Frederick, bootmaker, 39 Regent st. Horsefy.rd
Lowe Wm. Thomas, surgeon & apothecary, 111 Aldersgate st
Lowell Joseph C. bookseller, see Barthè's & Lowell
Lowen Edward, wine cooper, 39 Steward st. Spitalfields
Lowen John, auctioneer & appraiser, 280 Whitechapel rd
Lower Ed. Wm. architect & surveyor, 23 Park walk, Chelsea
Lowes Edward, sacking, canvass, &c. mfr. 201 Borough High st
Lowes James, carrier, 10 John st. Stoke Newington
Lowis Wm. coffee rooms, 44 Milton st. Cripplegate
Lowless Joseph & Son, solicitors, 2 Hatton ct. Threadneedle st
Lowley Gideon, wine merchant, 15 Gt. St. Helen's Bishopsg
Lowley William, stock manfr. hosier & outfitter, 4 Piccadilly
Lowman Henry, linendraper, see Hodge & Lowman
Lowndes James & William, trunkmakers, 18 Haymarket
Lowndes Thos.& Co. merchants & ship agts. 4 Fenchurch bldgs
Lowndes Wm. & Jas. & Co. scotch warehoumn. 7 Watling st
Lowndes Charles, coffee rooms, 2 Chandos st. Strand
Lowndes John James, barrister, 5 Hare court, Temple
Lowndes Rd. Wm. ship broker & com.agent, 37 Mincing lane
Lowndes William Loftus, queen's counsel, 7 Old sq. Linc.inn
Lownds James & Co. merchants, 83 Upper Thames st
Lownds Barbara C. (Mrs.), oil of vitriol ma. Bridgerd. Battrsea
Lownds Daniel Thos. oil & italian wa. see Collier & Lownds
Lownds Daniel Thos. brushma. 14 High row, Knightsbridge
Lownds John, watchmaker, 36 Nutford place, Edgeware rd
Lowne George Gill, surgeon, 8 King's row, Walworth road
Lowery Thomas, warehouseman, 91 Watlington street
Lowry Edwd. water rate coll. 17 Harrington st. Hampstd. rd
Lowry John linendraper, Lower road, Rotherhithe
Lowry John Philip, cooper, 20 Ropemaker's fields, Limeho
Lowry John Philip, *Two Brewers* P.H. Forc st. Limehouse
Lowson John, baker, 57 Fetter lane
Lowtell Wm. Frederic, coal dealer, 40 Greek st. Soho

Lowther Thos. & Son, clockcase ma. 58 Red Lion st. Clerkenw.
Lowther Charles, tailor, 68 Hermitage pl. St. John st. road
Lowther Elizabeth (Mrs.), *Ship & Star* P.H. 29 Wapping
Lowther John, builder, 8 Queen's row, New road
Lowther Mary (Miss), ladies' school, 22 Thavies inn, Holbn
Lowther Mary (Mrs.), lodging house, 10 Thavies inn, Holbn
Lowther Wm. stationer & acct. book makr. 12 Blackfriars rd
Loxley John solicitor, see Fry, Loxley & Fry
Loxley Thos. Arnold, wine mer. 9 Catherine ct. Tower hill
Loy William, working cutler, 24 King st. Westminster
Loyd James, goldbeater, 12 Craven st. City road
Loyer Fredk. engine turner, 4 Linney court, Museum st
Loynes William, builder, 89 Old st. road
Lozano Manuel Perez, merchant, 36 Crutchedfriars
Luard Henry, gen. manager to *London & County Joint Stock Banking Company*, 21 Lombard st
Lubbock Sir John Wm. & Co. merchants, 1 St. Mildred's ct
Lubbock (Sir John William, bart.), Forster & Co. bankers, 11 Mansion house st
Lubbock Webster, bricklayer, 72 Little Cadogan place
Luby Patrick J. *Nag's Head*, P.H. 137 Houndsditch
Lucas Brothers, who. drugsts. & lozenge ma. 113 Aldersgate st
Lucas Daniel William & Co. hemp & flax dealers, 34 Mark lane; warehouse, 2 Seething lane
Lucas Daniel William & Co. ship & insurance agts. 34 Mark la
Lucas & Harrington, family teadealers & grocers, 19 Panton st. (corner of Princes st. Haymarket), and at their wholesale house, 113 High st. Borough
Lucas Henry & Edward, corn mers. 28 Warwick st. Golden sq
Lucas & Jenner, bottled ale & stout mers. 124 Sloane st
Lucas John & Co. chemists to the Queen, 63 Cheapside
Lucas & Leggett, upholsterers, 35 South Audley st
Lucas Michalls & Co. merchants, 13 New Broad st
Lucas, & Parkinson, attorneys, 9 Argyll st. Regent st
Lucas, Pope & Shaw, lightermen & custom house agents, 21 Water lane, Tower st
Lucas Samuel Hayhurst, & Son, corn factors, 52 Eastcheap
Lucas Ann (Mrs.), farrier, 12 Bread street hill
Lucas Catherine (Mrs.), grocer & cheesem. 21 North st. Sloanest
Lucas Charles, watchmaker, 5 Gutter lane, Cheapside
Lucas Charles Rose, attorney, 5 Arlington st. Camden town
Lucas Christopher, furrier, &c. 59 Quadrant, Regent st
Lucas Daniel, *Crown & Anchor* P.H. 104 Brook st. Ratcliff
Lucas Edmund, coal merchant, 11 Coal exchange, Lower Thames st. & coal mer. & flour fac. 18 Millbank st. Westmr
Lucas Edmund, tailor, 2 Elder st. Norton folgate
Lucas Francis, barrister, 10 New square, Lincoln's inn
Lucas Francis, fancy cabinet ma. 7 Sekforde st. Clrknwl
Lucas Frederick, barrister, 3 Brydges street, Covent garden
Lucas George, chandler's shop, 7 Hoxton old town
Lucas George, dining rooms, 62 Bath st. City road
Lucas George Oakley, surveyor, 23 New Church st. Lisson gr
Lucas Henry, confectioner, 20 Bridge st. Westminster
Lucas Henry, coach joiner, 8 Broad court, Bow st
Lucas Henry, fruiterer, 21 Brewer st. Somers town
Lucas Hubert Henry, barrister, 2 Childs pl. Temple bar
Lucas Jas. builder, 4 Greenland pl. Cromer st. Brunswick sq
Lucas James, fruit salesman, Centre row, Covent garden
Lucas James, lodging house, 8 St. Alban's pl. St. James's
Lucas John, bootmaker, 59 Crawford st. Portman square
Lucas John, confectioner, 41 Kensington High st. & 1 High terrace, Notting hill
Lucas John, fruiterer, 2 Southampton st. Camberwell
Lucas John, *Gower Arms* P.H. 1 Store st. Bedford square
Lucas John, haberdasher, 17 Church st. Shoreditch
Lucas John, ladies' shoemaker, 32 Cowper st. City road
Lucas John, linendraper, 42 Grosvenor row, Pimlico
Lucas John, organ builder, 2 Church lane, Whitechapel
Lucas John, soda water manfr. 5 Well st. Jewin st. Criplgt
Lucas John, straw, leghorn & millnry. wa. 18 Bridge rd. Lmbth
Lucas John, wood carver, 14 Southampton st. Euston sq
Lucas Jonathan, *Three Nuns inn*, 11 Aldgate High st
Lucas Joseph, coal dealer, 22 New Compton st
Lucas Joseph, solicitor, 8 Gray's inn square
Lucas Mary (Mrs.), plumber, 9 King Edward st. Newgate st
Lucas Orton, solicitor, 1 St. Martin's place, Charing cross
Lucas Philip Bennett, surgeon, 8 Manchester st. Mnchtr. sq
Lucas Richd. mfr. of art. flowers, 1 Baches' row, Chas. sq. Cityrd
Lucas Richd. wax chandler, 143 Gt. Suffolk st. Boro'
Lucas Rd. Cockrell, sculptor, 29 Devonshire st. Portland pl
Lucas Robert, merchant, see Gonne, Lucas & Gribble
Lucas Robert, solicitor, 42 Bloomsbury square
Lucas Robert Hood, solicitor, 18 Nottingham st. Marylebone
Lucas Samuel, umbrella maker, Denmark hill, Camberwell
Lucas Saml. Jas. lodging house, 66 Ossulston st. Somers tn
Lucas Sarah (Mrs.), *Anchor & Hope* P.H. 33 Parkst. Knngtn
Lucas Sarah (Mrs.), *Anchor & Hope* P.H. Devonshire st. Kennington lane
Lucas Sarah (Mrs.), dairy, 1 Upper Cleveland st. Fitzroy sq
Lucas Sarah (Mrs.), straw bonnet ma. 11 Broomflds. Deptfd
Lucas Thomas, *Phœnix* P.H. 23 Smith st. King'sroad, Chels
Lucas Thomas, silversmith & jeweller, 9 Crawford st
Lucas Thomas, sugar refiner, see Craven & Lucas
Lucas Wm. brushmaker, 70 Princes road, Lambeth
Lucas Wm. carman, 78 Wells st. & coalmerc. 6 Oxfordmarkt
Lucas Wm. livery stables, Berkeley mews, 74 Up. Berkeleyst
Lucas Wm. proptr. of St. Chad's well, Gray's inn road
Lucas Wm. Owen, surgeon, 8 & 9 Taunton place, Regent'spk
Lucas Wm. Pierre, *Mercers' Arms* P.H. 17 Mercerst. Longacre
Lucchesi Fiordinando, medal ma. 37 Charles st. Hatton gar
Luce John, carpenter & ship joiner, 9½ Thomasst. Shad Thams
Lucena James Lancaster, barrister, 4 Garden court, Temple
Lucena Stephen Lancaster, solicitor, Guildhall chambers, Basinghall st. & Enfield
Lucey Charles, barge builder, 80 Bermondsey wall
Lucey Charles, lighterman & agt. Cox'squay, LowerThamesst
Lucini Francis, looking gl. mkr. 142 Gt. Saffronhill, Htn. gdn
Lucini Provino, picture frame maker, 91 Leather la. Holborn
Luck, Bouch & Coath, warehousemen, 7 & 8 Breadst. Cheapsi
Luck & Croft, linendrapers, 44 York road, Lambeth
Luck, Kent & Cumming, upholsterers & carpet warehouse, 98 Hatton garden, & 4 Regent st
Luck Richd. & Co. worsted, hosiery & carpetmanuf. 49 Watlingst
Luck & Son, cap & silk hat makers, 50 Watling st
Luck Frederick, merchant, see Engstrom, Luck & Co
Luck Geo. timber mercht. 6 Trinity st. Rotherhithe
Luck John William, baker, 160 Rotherhithe st
Luck Peter, fur skin dresser, 18 Bell lane, Spitalfields
Lucker Jane & Isaac, *King's Head* P.H. Earl'sct. O. Brompton
Luckett Henry & Co. sheriffs' officers, 95 Chancery lane
Luckett Henry, coffee rooms, 95 Chancery la. & 42 High Hlbn
Luckett John, coffee rooms, 32 Adam st. west, Portman sq
Luckett Michael, tailor, 8 Great Castle st. Regent st
Luckhurst Thos. grocer & cheesemonger. 1 Barnetst. Hakny. rd
Luckhurst William, stationer, 23 Dalston green, Dalston
Luckie Brthrs. & Co. ship & ins. bro. & mercs. 1 & 2 Fenchch. st
Luckie Alexander, baker, 23 Queen st. Mayfair
Luckie Edward, fishmonger, 23 Lamb's Conduit st. Foundling
Luckie Henry, poulterer, 84 Great Portland st. Oxford st
Luckie Joseph, pork butcher, 35 Upper Marylebone st
Luckie Wm. Edward, fishmonger, 83 Gt. Portland st
Luckin George, boot & shoemaker, 327 High Holborn
Luckin Wm. coach maker, 10 Kennington row
Lucking John, butcher, 34 Walbrook
Lucking Margt. (Mrs.), tobacconist, 4 Richmond st. Leic. sq
Luckins George, millstone manufact. see Weeks & Luckins
Lucquet John Baptiste, dancing mastr. 34 York st. Portmn. sq
Lucraft John, dandy brush mak. 10 Blue Anchor al. Bunhill rw
Lucroft Wm. bootmaker, 4 Queen's head ct. Gt. Windmill st
Lucy Charles, artist, Tudor lodge, Albert st. Morngtn. cres
Lucy Charles, fishmonger, 17 & 99 Lower Thames st
Lucy Wm. fishmonger, 17 & 18 Lower area, Hungerford mar
Lucy Wm. furniture broker, 78 Earl st. east, Lisson grove
Lucy Wm. lighterman, 12 East lane, Bermondsey wall
Ludbrook Samuel, brush manufr. Bancroft's pl. Mile end rd
Luden Frederick, general outfitter, 168 St. George st
Luden John, hosier, &c. 14 Upper East Smithfield
Ludford Geo. furniture japanner, Sash ct. Wilson st. Finsbury
Ludgate & Birt, linendrapers, 2 Carthusian st. Charterhouse sq
Ludlam Jeffery & Co. hosiers & glovers, 174 Piccadilly
Ludlam & Urquhart (Misses), milliners, 115 New Bond st
Ludlam John, working cutler, 1 Bowling st. Marylebone
Ludlow & Mills, hosiery manufactory, 164 Oxford st
Ludlow Armine, butcher, 44 Union st. Somers town
Ludlow Edmund E. east india army agt. 13 Clifford's inn
Ludlow Henry, mourning ring maker, & working goldsmith & jeweller, 6 Goswell road, opposite Spencer st
Ludlow John Malcolm, barrister, 69 Chancery lane
Ludlow Rosetta (Miss), jeweller, 1 Church st. Camberwell
Ludlow Thomas, grocer, 50 Baldwin's gardens, Gray's inn la
Ludlow William, grocer, &c. 24 Paradise row, Chelsea
Ludlow William, working jeweller, Camberwell grove
Luer Charles, coal merchant, 41 Gower place, Euston sq
Luerson John Frederick, beer retailer, West st. Hackney
Luff Elizabeth & Amelia, milliners & dress ma. 35 Bethnal gn. rd
Luff Geo. & Co. pianoforte ma. 103 Gt. Russell st. Bloomsbury
Luff Charles, fruiterer & tobacconist, 23 Well's row, Islington
Luff Henry James, writing engraver, 166 Strand
Luff John, economical coffee house, 34 Brick lane, Spitalfields
Luff Mary Ann Elizabeth (Miss), school, 35 Bethnal gn. rd
Luff Susan (Miss), milliner, 2 Conduit st
Luff William, ham & tongue warehouse, 157 High Holborn

Luff William, pawnbroker, 9 Crown st. Finsbury
Luff William, *Windmill* P.H. 1 Upper Kennington lane
Luff Wm. Miller, dyer & scourer, 26 Warren st. Fitzroy sq
Luffingham John, trimming seller, 14 Tottenham ct. road
Lufkins Chas. stationer & rag dlr. 1 Silver st. Golden sq
Lufkins Wm. rag dealer, 32 Southampton mews, Euston sq
Lugg James, coffee rooms, 2 Marylebone lane, Oxford st
Lugg James, surgeon, 33 Colet place, Commercial rd. east
Lugg William, dairyman, 42 King st. Soho
Luke Abraham North, grocer, 24 Hill st. Walworth road
Luke Ann (Mrs.), boarding ho. 17 & 18 Thavies inn, Holborn
Luke James, surgeon, 39 Broad st. buildings
Luke John, bootmaker, 13 Trinity row, Islington
Luke John, fur skin dresser, 19 & 20 Baldwin's gardens, Lth.la
Luke Joseph, surgeon, 1 St. John st. Clerkenwell
Luke Thomas, grocer, &c. 4 Holloway pl. Holloway
Luke William, cheesemonger, 158 Brick lane, Spitalfields
Luke William, cheesemonger, 170 Church st. Shoreditch
Luker George, bed sacking ma. 71 Charlotte st. Old st. road
Lukey John, boarding house, 78½ Queen st. Cheapside
Lukey Nicholas Veall, coal merchant, Milford wharf, Strand
Lukyn Edward, dentist, 35 New Broad st
Lulham George, *Jolly Caulkers* P.H. Lower rd. Rotherhithe
Lulham Thomas, tailor, 213 Whitechapel road
Lum Thomas, *Duke's Head* P.H. 53 Chamber st. Gdmn.'s flds
Lumb William, bootmaker, 19 Weston st. Pentonville
Lumber Troop (James Scott, sec.), 127 Fetter lane
Lumby Isaac, butcher, 3 Brooke's market, Holborn
Lumby John, butcher, 1 Brooke's market, Holborn
Lumley Ben. solicitor & parliamentary agt. 46 Parliament st
Lumley Edward, bookseller & publisher, 56 Chancery lane
Lumley Henry, artist, 32 Rathbone place
Lumley Isaac, *Lord Wellington* P.H. 31 University st
Lumley John, furniture broker, 14 Queen st. Bryanstone sq
Lumley John Thos. cabinet ma. 13 Lr. Chapman st. St. Geo.ea
Lumley Mary (Mrs.), millwright, smith, &c. 65 Low. Shadwell
Lumley Mary (Mrs.), potato dealer, Spitalfields market
Lumley Mary Ann (Miss), *Windmill* P.H. 55 Rosemary lane
Lumley Robt. coal merchant, Middle wf. Gt. Scotland yard
Lumley Robert, confectioner, 3½ Pleasant row, New road, & 29 Exmouth st. Clerkenwell
Lumley Rt. Wheatley, solicitor, see Oddie, Lumley & Co
Lumley Wm. Geo. assist. sec. to poor law com. Somerset hou
Lumsden George, *King's Head* P.H. 6 Duke st. Linc. inn flds
Lumsden William, baker, 224 Piccadilly
Lunacy Commissioners' Office, 45 Lincoln's inn fields, hrs. 10 to 4
Lunatic Off. (Thos. Cartlege, sec.), Quality court, 10 to 4
Lunatics' Visitors' Offi. (Hen. Enfield, sec.) 45 Lincln's. inn flds
Lund Christopher, teadealer & grocer, 51 Newgate st
Lund Henry, barrister, 6 Figtree court, Temple
Lund John, *Stone Kitchen* P.H. Tower
Lund John Richard, watch, &c. maker, see Barraud & Lund
Lund William, cutler & dressing-case maker, 56 & 57 Cornhill, & 23 & 24 Fleet st
Lund Wm. cutler, dressing-case maker & ivory turner, 23 & 24 Fleet st. City
Lund Wm. upholsts. warehouseman, 10 Marylebone st. Picc
Lundie Hen. (of Madeira), see Murdoch, Shortridge, Lundie & Co
Lundholm John Fredk. & Co. manuf. chemists, 25 Tothill st
Lundy Foot & Co. irish snuff manufs. 51 Skinner st. Snowhill
Lundy Julien, dyer & scourer, 105 Park st. Camden town
Lungley Emma (Miss), ladies' school, 216 Albany rd. Cmbwl
Lunham James & Co. wholesale cheesemongers & provision agents, 231 Boro' High st
Luning Wm. S. exchange broker, Baltic coffee house
Lunn Elizh. (Mrs.), *Lillyput Hall* P.H. 1 Prospect rw. Bermy
Lunn James, fruiterer, 42 Dean st. Soho
Lunn Joseph, sec. to Society for relief of Debtors, 7 Craven st
Lunn Thomas, chemist & druggist, 159 Aldersgate st
Lunn William, wholesale slopseller, 16 St. Mary at hill
Lunnis Thomas, cowkeeper & dairyman, 13 Little Carter la. Doctors' commons, & 15 Old Change
Lunnon Joseph, coffee rooms, 8A, Marylebone lane
Lunson George, dressing-case maker, 2 Charles st. Soho sq
Lunson Mary (Mrs.), jeweller, 27 Aldgate High st
Lunt William, coffee rooms, 1 Myddelton quadrant, Clknwll
Luntley & Dick, printers, 3 New Broad st. court, City
Luntley James Philip, druggist, 16 Bread st. hill
Luntley Josiah John, jun. auctioneer, 42 Bishopsgt. without
Lupton George, painter, 32 George st. Euston sq
Lupton John, livery stables, 16 Alfred mews, Tottnhm. ct. rd
Lupton John, woollen warehouse, 38 Basinghall st
Lupton Priscilla (Mrs.), grocer, 1 Cross st. Hoxton New tn
Lupton Thomas, portrait engraver, 4 Keppel st. Russell sq
Lupton Thomas, insurance broker, Lloyd's
Lusby Charles, grocer, 17 East st. Manchester square
Lusby Robert, cheesemonger, 14 Bridge terrace, Harrow rd
Luscombe John Teed, solicitor, see Bullock & Luscombe
Luscombe Sarah (Miss), toy warh. 40 Cheyne walk, Chelsea
Lush & Merceron, solicitors, 36 Wellclose square
Lush Hen. grindry. wareho. & bootma. 39 Carnaby st. Gldn.sq
Lush John, umbrella maker, 44 St. George st
Lush Joseph, beer retailer, 13 Southampton st. Peckham
Lush Rt. barrister, 4 In. Temple lane, & 34 Mecklenburgh sq
Lush Saml. china wareho. 21 Pierrepoint row, Islington gn
Lush William, beer shop, 243 Borough High st
Lusher James, tailor & draper, see Stone & Lusher
Lushington Henry, barrister, 2 Mitre court buildgs. Temple
Lushington Rt. Hon. Stephen, D.C.L. 8 College, Doctors' com
Lusk, Andrew & Co. shipping grocers, &c. 62 Fenchurch st
Lusty Enoch, pork butcher, 102 Berwick st. Soho
Lütge & Co. who. furriers, 8 King Edward st. Newgate st
Lutostanski Julian, watch engraver, 7 Skinner st. Clknwl
Luther Elias, *Bolt in Tun tap*, Boar's head ct. 65 Fleet st
Luton John, chronometer box maker, 40 Galway st
Lutt Thomas, carpenter, 43 White Lion st. Pentonville
Luttly Beaumont Charles, attorney, Dyer's hall, 3 College st. Dowgate hill
Lutto Joseph, tailor, 120 Houndsditch
Lutto Samuel, tailor, 11 Church lane, Whitechapel
Lutwidge Robert Wilfred S. barrister, 10 Old sq. Linc. inn
Lutwidge Walter, ward rate collector, 116 London wall
Lutwyche & George, leatherdressers & importers of foreign leather, 5 Skinner st. Snowhill
Lutwyche Alfred Jas. P. barrister, 6 Pump court, Temple
Lutwyche William, grocer, 16 Dorset st. Portman square
Lutyens Samuel, exchange & e. i. bill broker, 22 Austinfriars
Lutzemburger Alex. trunk & box manufacturer, 352 Strand
Luxford Thomas, carpenter, 137 Great Suffolk st. Borough
Luxford William, grocer, 17 John st. west, Edgware road
Luxmoore Coryndon Hen. surg. dentist, 21 Keppell st. Russl.sq
Luxmoore Wm. Edward, pawnbroker, 92 St. Martin's lane
Luxton Henry, butcher, 6 Horseferry road, Westminster
Luxton Thomas, butcher, 122 Goswell st
Lyal William, potato salesman, 29 James st. Covent garden, & Cotton's wharf, Tooley st
Lyall Brothers & Co. mercs. & east ind. agts. 6 St. Helen's pl
Lyall John & James Baxter, brewers, Swan walk, Chelsea
Lyall David, craven stables, Great Green st. Kentish town
Lyall Elizh. (Mrs.), *Horseshoe & Magpie* P.H. 25 Mdle. rw. Holb
Lyall George, merchant, Winchester house, Old Broad st. City
Lyall Walter, linendraper, 23 Beckford row, Walworth
Lyas Frederick, coffee rooms, 32 Old Compton st. Soho
Lyas Henry, tailor, 5 Charles st. Westminster road
Lycett & Davies, silk warehousemen, 39 Gutter lane
Lydall Brothers, teadealers, 15 Skinner st. Somers town
Lydall Robert, grocer, 100 Gt. Titchfield st. Oxford st
Lydall Thos. whol. coffee deal. 25 Laurence Pountney lane
Lydamont Sarah (Mrs.), stay maker, High st. Stoke Nwngtn
Lyddon William, solicitor, 24 Carey st. Lincoln's inn fields
Lyddon & Messenger, manchester warehsmn. 39 Gresham st
Lyde George F. hosier & trimming sell. 3 Farringdon st
Lyde William, solicitor, 32 Bucklersbury
Lydekker Gerard Wolfe, barrister, 4 Hare court, Temple
Lye Ann (Mrs.), milliner, 50 Rupert st. Haymarket
Lye John, tailor, 28 Great Pulteney st. Golden sq
Lyel James, cabinet maker, 12 Henrietta st. Manchester sq
Lyell John S. ribbon manufr. see Cornel, Lyell & Webster
Lyell William, boot & shoemaker, 17 Little Britain
Lyes William, grocer, 11 White st. Borough
Lyford Frances (Mrs.), coaldealr. 34 Bedfordbury, Cvnt. gardn
Lyford Richard, shell fishmonger, 63 Tottenham court road
Lygo John, tailor, 9 Grange court, Lincoln's inn fields
Lying-in Institution (Wm. Woolmer sec.), 90 Newman st
Lyle James, purveyor of coffee to the Royal family, 17 Old Bond st. Piccadilly
Lyle James, spirit merchant, 3 Upper Fountain pl. City rd
Lyle Wm. Geo. solicitor, 17 Bloomsbury st. St. Giles's
Lymath Joseph, smith & farrier, 23 High st. Notting hill
Lymath William, farrier, 4 Great York mews, Portman sq
Lyme Regis & Taunton Railway (John Champ, sec.), 23 Finsbury place north
Lynch Alfred, seedsman & florist, Balls pond rd. Islington
Lynch James Hy. artist, 31 Polygon, Clarendon square
Lynch John, cheesemonger, 51 Rosemary lane
Lynch John, tailor, 34 Alfred st. Bedford square
Lynch Jordan Roche, surgeon, 24 Farringdon st
Lynch Mark, coal dealer, 18 George st. Bloomsbury
Lynch Robert, newsvender, 2 Thomas st. Oxford st
Lynch Robert, physician, 15 Somerset st. Portman square
Lyndall John, surgeon, 12 King st. terrace, New North rd
Lyndon George, wholesale jeweller, 49 Frith st. Soho

LyndonCharles,attorney(atMessrs.Raven&Bradley's),2Harcourt buildings, Temple
Lyne Francis, wine & general merchant, 12 Mark lane
Lyne George, silk dyer, &c. 90 Wimpole st. Cavendish sq
Lyne James, *Guinea* P.H. Bruton mews north, Bond st
Lyne John William, brush maker, 61 Aldersgate st
Lyne Lewis Stephens, stockbroker, 29 Threadneedle st
Lyne Sarah Louisa (Mrs.), chandlers' shop, 96 Cornwall rd
Lyne Thomas, tobacconist, 18 Spring st. Portman sq
Lyne Virgil Stephens, merchant, 3 Winchester buildings
Lynes Joseph, tailor, 69 Sun st. Bishopsgate
Lynes Solomon, tailor, 131 Drury lane
Lynes William, warehouseman, 26 Milk st. Cheapside
Lyng George, carpenter, 33 Titchborne st. Edgware rd
Lynn Charles & Co. bootmakers, 297 Kent st. Borough
Lynn & Gibson, fish factors, 106 & 113 Lower Thames st
Lynn John & James, shell fishmongers, 70 Fleet st
Lynn Railway Office (Mark Edward Daniel, secretary), 18 Great George st. Westminster
Lynn Crispus Thos.surgeon dentist, 195 UpperWhitecross st
Lynn Harriet (Miss), ladies'school,56Commrl. rd. Lambeth
Lynn James,*Duke of Wellington*P.H.20Coleshill st.Pimlico
Lynn John, hatter&umbrella manfr.4 Exmouth st. Clrknwll
Lynn William, seedsman, High st. Kingsland
Lynnell Mary (Mrs.), baker, 21 Flagon row, Deptford
Lyon, Barnes & Ellis, solicitors, 7 Spring gardens
Lyon John Andrew & Washington, bleachers, &c.St. Mary-le-Strand place, Old Kent road; *Bull's Head*, Bread st. & *Dolphin*, 318 Oxford st
Lyon John&Thos.&Co.stock&sharebrks.2Birchin.la.Cornhill
Lyon's inn, 27 Newcastle st. Strand
Lyon Alexander, baker, 42 Museum st. Bloomsbury
Lyon Alexander, boot& shoema.13Backchurch la.St.Geo.ea
Lyon Benjn. (sec. to riverDee Co.),9 Mansionhouse st.City
Lyon Elizh. (Mrs.), *WhiteLion* P.H. 13Hemming's row,St. Martin's lane
Lyon FrederickG.pianoforte ma. 22 Nassau st. Middlx. hosp
Lyon Geo.average stater, 29 Crosby hall chambs. Bishopsgt
Lyon George, butcher, 1 Munster st. Regent's park
Lyon George, *Horse Shoe* P.H. Friar st. Doctors' commns
Lyon George William, barrister, 1 Brick court, Temple
Lyon Harriet (Mrs.), french corset maker, 115 Jermyn st
Lyon Hart, merchant, 1 Bury st. St Mary Axe
Lyon Isaac, artificial florist, 20 Westmoreland pl. City road
Lyon Isaac, italian warehouse, 26 Duke st. Aldgate
Lyon John, boot & shoe maker, 45 King William st. City
Lyon John, cattle salesman, 41 West Smithfield
Lyon John Dark, baker, South Lambeth, New road
Lyon Joseph, boarding house, 4 Falcon st. Aldersgate st
Lyon Lewis, watch & clock maker,64 Gray's inn lane
Lyon Thomas, bootmaker, 2 Athol place, Pentonville
Lyon Wm. lighterman & wharfing. Lyon's wf. Up. Thames st
Lyons Abraham & Saul, mercs. Salvador ho. Bishopsgate st
Lyons & Coney, poulterers & buttermen, 32 Windmill st. Fins
Lyons & Avignon Railway Office (E.Aimé, secretary), 62 King William st. City
Lyons Aaron, cabinet maker, 21 Princes sq. St. George's ea
Lyons Emanuel, merchant, 16 South st. Finsbury sq
Lyons Henry, cabinet maker, 21 Princes sq. Ratcliff
Lyons Henry Rt. paperstnr. & decorator, 156 High Holborn
Lyons Jacob, clothier, furrier, fur & cloth cap maker, hatter, macintosh waterproof clothing & carpet bag manufacturer, 10 & 11 Wilson st. Finsbury
Lyons Joseph,gen. salesman,6Cumbrlnd. pl.Newington butts
Lyons Judah, clothes salesman, &c. 27Crown st. Finsbury
Lyons Moss,floorcloth mnf.&paprstnr.6 Dover pl.O. Kent rd
Lyons Samuel, grocer, 39 Middlesex st. Aldgate High st
Lyons Samuel, tailor & draper, 40 Tothill st. Westminster
Lyons Thomas, printing ink maker, see Shackell & Lyons
Lys Nicholas, tailor, 95 Fore st. Cripplegate
Lys William, hatter & coal mer. 5 Road side, Mile end rd
Lysaght, Smithett & Co. east india agents, 6 New Broad st
Lysley William John, barrister, 3 Inner Temple lane
Lysnar George, jeweller, 34 Percy st. Tottenham court rd
Lysons Richard, boot & shoe maker, 44 Cloth fair, Smithfield
Lyster Joseph, tailor, 14 Prospect place, Old Brompton
Lyus Mary Ann(Mrs.), furn. undertaker, 10Tabernacle walk
Lyus Wm. grocer, 15 Albemarle st. Clerkenwell

MAACK & Edwards, merchts, 2 Savage gardens, Tower hill
Mabbett Geo. *Turk's Head* P.H. 8 Charlotte st.Portland pl
Mabbs Robert, dairyman, 139 Upper st. Islington
Maber John Chas. hairdresser, 3 Church lane, Whitechapel
Maber Tim. wine,&c. mer. 12 Clark's pl. High st. Islington
Maberly Geo. coachmaker, 70 Welbeck st. & 8 Marylebo. la
Maberly Joseph & Son, solicitors, 17 King's rd. Bedford row
Mabey Wm. *Lloyd's* coffee house, Royal Exchange,Cornhill
Mabey Wm. tobacconist, 38 Harleyford place, Kennington
Mabin Hen. statnr. & bookbind. 13 Grosvenor row, Pimlico
Mable Thomas, fruit salesman, Borough market
Mabley John, stationer, &c. 9 Wellington st. north, Strand
Mabson George Moulton, potato salesman, 49 High st. St. Giles's; 43 Whitechapel High st.; 4 Whitechapel rd. & Mill lane, Tooley st
Mabyn & Grant, wholesale drapers, 90 Cheapside
M'Adam Alexander, coal & potato dealer, 49 King st. 7 dials
M'Adam Sir James Nicholl, surveyor, 40 Charing cross
M'Alley John, coal & potato dlr. 4 Grosvenor pl. Borough rd
M'Alpin & Nephew, furn. print. & wool wareho. 63 Bread st
M'Andrew William & Sons, merchants, 3 Philpot lane
M'Arthur, Daniel, stationer, 16 Hertford st. Fitzroy sq
M'Arthur Peter, nurseryman, &c. 2 Clarendon pl.Maida hill
M'Auliffe John, fruiterer, 18 James st. Oxford st
M'Bain Alex. Lachlan, umbrella ma. 12 Gt. Smith st. Westr
M'Bean Thos.Alexr. teadealer, 37 Devonshire st. Portland pl
M'Beath William John, solicitor, 2 Duchess st. Portland pl
M'Bride James, tailor, 38 Fleet lane, Farringdon st
M'Bride John, goldsmith & jeweller,41 London st.Fitzroy sq
M'Cabe & Co. chronometer, watch & clock makers, 32 Cornhill, & 19 Royal Exchange
M'Cabe Gilbert, skinner & furrier, 58 Union st. Borough
M'Cabe JamesE.surveyor draughtsman,&c.35Castle st.Hlbn
M'Cabe John, coffee rooms, 12 Park lane, Piccadilly
M'Calla James, auctioneer, 5 Sussex ter. Old Brompton
M'Callan Robert & John, tailors, 40 King st. Covent garden
M'Callum, Worley & Co. ship & insur. brokers, 60 Mark la
M'Calmont Brothers & Co. merchants, 3 Crown ct. Philpot la
M'Cann James, shoe warehouse, 3 Well st. Wellclose sq. 80 Sun st. Bishopsgate, & 46 Cannon st. rd. St. George's east
M'Cann Nicholas, surgeon, 50 Parliament st. Westminster
M'Cardie Philip, baker, 52 Great Windmill st. Haymarket
M'Carthy T. & A. (Misses), ladies' school,19 Trinity sq. Boro'
M'Carthy Callaghan,hairdresser,2 Southampton st.Cambrwl
M'Carthy Chas. skinner, &c. 3 Worcester st. Union st. Boro'
M'Carthy Daniel, *Angel* P.H. 36 City road, Finsbury
M'Carthy Daniel, bootmaker, 4 Oakley st. Lambeth
M'Carthy Felix Joseph, estate office, 3 Fountain pl. City rd
M'Carthy Owen, coal & potato wa.7 Portugal st.Lincoln's inn
M'CartneyWm. James, law stationer, 23 Castle st. Holborn
M'Cash William, baker, Stratford broadway
M'Caskill Janet (Mrs.), millnr.1 Parham pl.Kngs.rd.Chelsea
M'Christie Thomas Young, barrister, 4 Old sq. Lincoln's inn
M'Clarnes Robinson, lighterman, 20 Pudding lane
M'Clary Hen. James, bookselr. & stationer, 32 St. James's st
M'Cleallan Thomas, carpenter, 140 Fetter lane, Fleet st
M'Clean John R. civil engineer, 17 Gt.George st.Westminstr
M'Clellan Kate (Miss), milliner, &c. 280 Regent st
M'Clellan Samuel, watch & clockmaker, Deptford bridge
M'Clise Daniel, R.A. artist, 14 Russell place, Fitzroy sq
M'Cloud Henry, cabinet maker, 5 Quickset row, New road
M'Clure Thomas, manchester agent, 51 Cheapside
M'Coan James, tailor, 4 South Island pl. Clapham road
M'Connell James Luke, tailor, 17 Old Burlington st
M'Cormack James,fruiterer&orange mer.North row,Cov.gar
M'Cormack William, grocer, 18 Hosier lane, West Smithfield
M'Cormick Edward, tailor, 8A, Carlton st. Regent st
M'Cormick Harriet (Mrs.), milliner, 6 Church st. Kensingtn
M'Cormick John, printseller, 36 Haymarket
M'Cormick Owen,*Cannon* P.H.46Cannon st.Ratcliff highwa
M'Cowen Henry, linendraper, 11 Essex pl.Mare st. Hackney
M'Cracken James & Robert, general, foreign & comcl.agents, &agents to S.Stock&Co.wine merchants,of placeVendome, Paris, also agents to the Royal Academy, 7 Old Jewry
M'Craight Charles, engraver, 113 Goswell road
M'Craight Richard, scale maker, 94 Goswell st
M'Craw James, baker, 2 Castle st. Leicester square
M'Crea & Goldsmith, surgeons, 30 Cloudesley ter. Islington
M'Crea Joseph, surgeon, 37 Compton ter. Upper st.Islington
M'Creath Wm. wholesale scotch oatmeal & barley dealer, 11 Burr st. & Hore's Upper wharf, 354 Wapping high st
M'Creight L.H.&A.(Misses),school,8Grosvenor pl.Cambrwl
M'Crerie Alexander, turner, 71 Earl st. east, Lisson grove
M'Crerie Wm. hard wood turner, 6 Earl st. Edgware road
M'Cuiliffe John, greengr. 5 John st. Davies st. Berkly. sq
M'Cullagh, Sons & Co. merchants, 3 New London st
M'Culloch John, bookbinder, 30 St. John's sq. Clerkenwell
M'Culloch Wm. who. druggist, see Hearon, Bright & Co
M'Currey James, builder, Lillington st. Vxhl. rd. Pimlico
M'Cutcheon Ivie, warehouseman,seeM'Dowall&M'Cutcheon
M'Cutcheon John &Wm.merchts.1Wellington st.London bdg
M'Cutcheon John, mer. & shpownr.1Wellington st. Southwrk
M'Danell James, bookseller & news agent, 1 Charterhouse st

M'Dermott Charles, surgeon, 4 Princes sq. Kennington cross
M'Dermott Edwd. potato wa. 5 Church rw. Upper st. Islngtn
M'Dermott George, potato salesman, 1 Counter st. Borough
M'Dermott Henry, *Cock* P.H. Kilburn
M'Dermott John, cowkeeper, 6 Denmark st. Ratcliff highwy
M'Diarmid Hugh, *Belvedere tavern*, 1 Penton st. Pentonville
M'Dona William, printer, 39 Gloucester st. Queen sq
M'Donald Alexander & Co. saltpetre works, Grove, Great Guildford st. Boro', & 3 St. Mildred's court, Poultry
M'Donald Donald & Son, upholsterers & cabinet makers, estate & house agents, appraisers & undertakers, 1 Upper Montagu street, Montagu square
M'Donald & Leslie, aberdeen granite depôt, 1 Quickset row
M'Donald Andrew, cheesemonger, 56 Ray st. Clerkenwell
M'Donald Caleb, teadealer & grocer, 59 Kingsland road
M'Donald Charles Daniel, hairdresser, Well st. Hackney
M'Donald Daniel, greengrocer, 1 Church lane, Islington
M'Donald Donald, carpenter, &c. 122 Aldersgate st
M'Donald Donald, hardwareman, 108 Goswell st
M'Donald Frederick, stationer, 8 Chapel st. Bedford row
M'Donald George, hairdresser, 22 Queen st. Seven dials
M'Donald James, shawl warehouse, 130 Regent st
M'Donald James, linendraper, Silvester rw. Church st. Hkny
M'Donald John, bookseller, 41 Holywell st. Strand
M'Donald John, carpenter, 6 Peter st. Sun st. Bishopsgate
M'Donald Mary Ann (Miss), milliner, 37 Tottenham court rd
M'Donald Richard, toy warehouse, Church st. Hackney
M'Donell George, wine & spirit broker, 16A, Mincing lane
M'Donnell Amelia (Mrs.), cheesemonger, 8 Coborn rd. Mile end
M'Donnell Anthony Jas. tailor, 20 Rathbone pl. Oxford st
M'Donnell Archibald, surgeon, 4 Constitution row, Gray's inn road, & 13 Regent square
M'Donnell Dennis, teadealer, 144 St. John st. road
M'Donnell George, oilman, 32 Sussex st. Bedford sq
M'Donnell John, mining office, 35 Broad st. buildings
M'Donnell Thomas, grocer, 23 Sloane terrace, Chelsea
M'Donold D. & J. cambric collar manufactrs. 19 Cheapside
M'Donough John, *Anchor & Hope* P.H. 62 Brook st. Ratcliff
M'Douall Jane (Mrs.), lodging house, 8 Norfolk st. Park la
M'Dougal, Sambourne & Bell, manufacturers & warehousemen, 30 St. Paul's churchyard
M'Dougall & Upton, solicitors & parliament. ag. 44 Parliament st
M'Dougall Alex. potato & coal dlr. 8 Middle row, Knightsbrid
M'Dougall Archibald, saddler, see Wills & M'Dougall
M'Dougall James, chemist, 19 Old Paradise row, Islington
M'Dougall Lewis, tobacconist, 30 Gt. Titchfield st. Oxford st
M'Dougall Patrick, chemist, 35 Myddelton st. Clerkenwell
M'Dougall Sarah (Mrs.), baker, 26 Up. Marylebone st. Prtld. pl
M'Dowall Ann & C. (Misses), ladies' school, 1 Old Dorset pl. Cm. r
M'Dowall John & Arthur, boot & shoe makers to her Majesty & the Royal Family, 14 Regent st. Pall mall
M'Dowall & M'Cutchan, warehomn. & who. tea dlrs. 27 Friday st
M'Dowall Andrew, saddler, 36 Upper Seymour st. Portmn. sq
M'Dowall Peter, coachbuilder, 36 Up. Seymour st. Portmn. sq
M'Dowall Walter, printer, 3, 4 & 5 Pemberton row, Gough sq
M'Dowall John, tailor, &c. 70 King st. Golden square
M'Duff Charles, solicitor, 37 Castle st. Holborn
M'Euan John, tailor, 29 East st. Red Lion square
M'Evily John, saddler, &c. 26 Gt. Portland st. Oxford st
M'Evoy Thos. coach herald painter, 39 Silver st. Golden sq
M'Ewen Alexander, tailor, 156 Old Gravel lane, Wapping
M'Ewen James, profsr. of music, 178 Albany rd. Camberwell
M'Ewen Peter, biscuit baker, 24 Marchmont st. Brunswk. sq
M'Ewin James, music seller, 20 Charlotte rw. Walworth rd
M'Ewin John, baker, 111 Great Portland st. Oxford st
M'Fadden John, coffee rooms, 7 Cumberland row, Walwth. rd
M'Farlan Mary (Mrs.), *Globe* P.H. 8 Globe st. Wapping, & 58 Wapping High st
M'Farlane Andrew & Sons, bookbinders, 10 Old Bailey
M'Farlane Thomas, glove cleaner, 15 Exeter st. Strand
M'Farline Patrick, boarding house, 111 St. George st
M'Farquhar John L. & Co. ins. broks. 16 George st. Mansion ho
M'Fee James, fishing tackle & archery mfr. 208 High st. Boro
M'Fee Wm. stationer & acct. book mkr. 3 Coleman st. buildgs
M'Gahey John, St. Pancras vestry cl. 1 Gordon st. Gordon sq
M'Geoch Jas. & John, linendrapers, 81½ Greenfield st. Whitec
M'Geoch James, haberdasher, 11 Marshall st. Golden sq
M'Getrick Theodosia (Mrs.), babylin. wa. 117 Tottenham ct. rd
M'Ghie, Page & Smith, ship & ins. brks. 1A, Bishopsgt. wthin
M'Ghie Willoughby, attorney, 2 New inn, Wych st. Strand
M'Gill & Eastman, silk dyers, 85 Connaught terrace, Edgware road, & 2 Windmill st. Tottenham court road
M'Gill & Toms, commission agents, 120 Cheapside
M'Gill James, builder, 44 Woburn mews, Woburn place
M'Gill Jas. *Fellmonger's Arms* P.H. Willow wk. Bermondsey
M'Glashan Alexander, brazier, 16 Long acre
M'Glew & Oldham, wool brokers, 77 Basinghall st
M'Gowan John & Co. printers, 16 Gt. Windmill st. Haymarket
M'Gregor Brice, *Suttling House* P.H. Whitehall
M'Gregor Fergus, baker, 45 Broad st. Bloomsbury
M'Gregor Francis Jas. tobacconist, 25 Princes st. Storey's gate
M'Gregor John, tailor, 17 Charles st. Middlesex hospital
M'Gregor Martha (Mrs.), lodging house, 9 Little Britain
M'Gregor Mary (Miss), lodging house, 15 Harley st
M'Gregor Thomas, woollen warehouse, 150 Cheapside
M'Grigor Chas. Roderick, army agent, 17 Charles st. St. Jas'. sq
M'Guiness Henry Thos. carver, 2 Deal st. Mile end new town
M'Guire Ann (Mrs.), grocer, 47 Cumberland mkt. Regnt's. pk
M'Guire Thomas, hat manufacturer, 424 Strand
M'Guire William E. surgeon & druggist, 29 Cannon st
M'Hale Herbert, *Duke of Ormond* P.H. 17 Princes st. Westr
M'Hugh Michael, coal mer. 1 Gloucester ter. Old Brompton
M'Intosh Alexander, baker, 12 Sussex st. Tottenham ct. rd
M'Intosh Alex. meat salesman, see Hammant & M'Intosh
M'Intosh David, carpenter, 3 Chapel st. New road
M'Intosh David, civil engineer, 39 Bloomsbury square
M'Kardy George, tailor, 17 Warwick st. Golden square
M'Kay William Lewis, commission agent, 27 Fleet lane
M'Kean Hugh, agent, Scottish (Widows' Fund) Life Assurance, 7 Pall mall
M'Kean James, *Lord Belgrave* P.H. 8 Spur st. Leicester sq. & *White Dog* P.H. 32 Widegate st. Bishopsgate
M'Kean Wm. french & irish cambric & handkerchief agent, 4½ Lawrence lane, Cheapside
M'Keand John, linendraper, 21 Gloster ter. New rd. Coml. rd
M'Kellar & Christie, tailors, &c. 11 Old Burlington st. & 27 Saville row
M'Kellar Wm. G. coal mer. White Lion wf. 18 Up. Thames st
M'Kenna James, tailor, 33 George st. Hanover square
M'Kenna Richd. Butler & Co. wine merchants, 49 Mark lane
M'Kenzie, Brown & Co. wine & spirit imp. Exeter st. Strand
M'Kenzie & Ross, tailors, 48 Warwick st. Golden square
M'Kenzie Alex. *East India Arms* P.H. 110 Cock hill, Ratcliff
M'Kenzie Angus, american merch. see Durand & M'Kenzie
M'Kenzie Angus, merchant, 37 Milk st. Cheapside
M'Kenzie Hector, bookbinder, 11 Henry st. Pentonville
M'Kenzie Phœbe (Mrs.), china & glass wa. 8 Crwn. rw. Mile e. rd
M'Kenzie Robert, grocer, 36 Bermondsey sq
M'Kenzie Roderick, wine, &c. mer. 7 Suffolk lane, Cannon st
M'Kenzie Wm. civil engineer, 5 Warwick sq. Belgrave road
M'Kenzies Kenneth, grocer, 60 Park st. Dorset square
M'Kewan Geo. printer & stationer, 9 Gt. Winchester st
M'Key William Lewis, general agent, 27 Fleet lane
M'Kie James & Co. merchants, 4 Pancras la. Bucklersbury
M'Kinnell Charles, wine merchant, 113 Fenchurch street
M'Kinnell John, wine merchant, 18 Mark lane
M'Knight Daniel, painter & grainer, 11 Hayfield pl. Mile end
M'Knight James, berlin wa. 3 Chancery pl. Camberwell new rd
M'Lachlan Hugh, watch & clock ma. 17 Up. East Smithfield
M'Lachlan James, ornamntl. painter, Bedford ter. Clapham rd
M'Lachlan John, printers' auctioneer & valuer, 42 Chiswell st
M'Lachlan William, tailor, 40 Gt. Pulteney st. Golden sq
M'Lacklan James, chemist & drugst. see Green & M'Lachlan
M'Lallan John, black borderer, 18 Artillery la. Bishopsgate
M'Laren Dav. mgr. of South Australian Co. 4 New Broad st. City
M'Laren John, auction. & apprais. 15 Bloomsbury st. St. Giles's
M'Laren Robt. custom ho. agt. 11 Water la. Low. Thames st
M'Laren William, baker, 12 Hartland ter. Camden town
M'Latchie Robt. millwri. & engnr. 3 Cottage la. Com. rd. east
M'Lauchlan Andrew, carver & gilder, 8 Belvedere crescent
M'Lauchlan David Jas. carver & gilder, & plate glass factor, 3 Printing house square
M'Laughlin Andrew, tea urn maker, 42 Gee st. Goswell st
M'Laughlin Edw. horn, hair & glue mer. 138 Long la. Bmdy
M'Laughlin James, publisher, 3 Peterborough ct. Fleet st
M'Laurin Andrew Scott & Co. stuff manufrs. 32 Gutter la
M'Lean Anne (Miss), ladies' school, 15 Acton pl. Kingslnd. rd
M'Lean Chas. who. carver, gildr. & lookg. glass mak. 78 Fleet st
M'Lean Charles, upholsterer, 25 Poland st. Oxford st
M'Lean Donald, yeast merchant, 80 Chalton st. Somers tn
M'Lean Edward, auctioneer & picture dealer, 169 Strand
M'Lean Elizabeth (Mrs.), *Crown* P.H. 22 West Smithfield
M'Lean John, statuary & mason, 26 Sun st. Bishopsgate
M'Lean John, tailor, 135 Fetter lane, Fleet st
M'Lean Norman, *Plume of Feathers* P.H. 24 Low. Shadwell
M'Lean Thomas, lithographer, 70 St. Martin's lane
M'Lean Thomas, printseller & publisher, 26 Haymarket
M'Lean Wm. fruiterer, 5 Hastings st. Burton crescent
M'Leish Sarah (Mrs.), baker, 6 Essex st. Strand
M'Lellan Elizabeth (Miss), milliner, see Roberts & M'Lellan
M'Lellan John, surgic. inst. ma. Gt. Turner st. Commer. rd. East
M'Lellan John Wm. furniture broker, 6 Peel pl. Kensington

M'Lellan Robt. upholsterer, 107 Gt. Russell st. Bloomsbury
M'Leod & Stenning, solicitors, 13 London st. Fenchurch st
M'Leod Donald, tailor, see Thompson & M'Leod
M'Leod George Dean, solicitor, 6 Furnival's inn, Holborn
M'Lerie Thomas, coffee rooms, 26 New Church court, Strand
M'Mahon James, barrister, 11 Paper buildings, Temple
M'Mahon John, file & tool manufacturer, 167 Fenchurch st
M'Manus David, physician, 28 Baker st. Portman sq
M'Manus Felix, cheesemonger, 7 Motcomb st. Belgrave sq
M'Michael & Grierson, carpet manufactrs. 72 Basinghall st
M'Michael Richard, toy dealer, 118 Crawford st. Portman sq
M'Millan Brothers, bootmakers, 105 Jermyn st. St. James's
M'Millan Hugh, *St. Luke's Head* P.H. 10 Little Pulteney st
M'Millan Jas. ladies' shoemaker, 104 Jermyn st. St. James's
M'Millan James, linen draper, 117 St. John st. road
M'Millan Jas. tinman & lamp ma. 33 Brownlow st. Drury la
M'Millan Theodosius, stationer, 17 Wells rw. Upper st. Islingt
M'Mullen John Charles, stockbroker, 13 Change alley
M'Mullen Wm. coffee rooms, 15 Charles st. Middlx. hospital
M'Mullen Wm. Geo. seedsman & florist, see Hurst & M'Mullen
M'Murray Thos. & Co. linen merchants, 2 Milk st. Cheapside
M'Murray Robert, reporter, 18 Clement's inn, Strand
M'Murray William, bookbinder, 2 Lillypot lane, Noble st
M'Murray W. paper maker & who. stationer, 15 Garlick hill
M'Murty Randall, who. cheesemonger, 112 Fore st. City
M'Nab Alexander, chemist, 176 Tottenham court road
M'Nair & Brand, warehousemen, 23 Friday st. Cheapside
M'Nair James, *Southampton Arms* P.H. Nine elms
M'Nally John, vellum binder, 3 Vineyard walk, Clerkenwell
M'Namara Arthur, railway carrier, 38 Shoreditch High st
M'Namara Ewd. wine mer. 10 Rufford's row, Up. st. Islington
M'Naught Daniel, writer & grnr. 11 Hayfield pl. Mile end rd
M'Naughtan & Potters, calico printers (Joseph Aken Chate, agent), 89 Watling st. City
M'Neill F. & Co. mer. & pat. felt mfs. 14 Lamb's blgs. Bunhl. rw
M'Neill F. & Co. merchants, 14 Lamb's buildings, Bunhl. rw
M'Neir James, tailor, &c. 7 South st. South Audley st
M'Nicoll E. & I. (Misses), milliners, 11 Crawford st. Ptm. sq
M'Niel David, jun. stockbroker, 2 Angel court, Throgmtn. st
M'Niell Wm. & Co. patent broom manfr. 60 St. Martin's la
M'Nish Mary Ann (Mrs.), strawbonnetma. 14 Clement's inn pas
M'Omie Thomas, baker, 4 Upper Cleveland st. Fitzroy sq
M'Phail Geo. A. sol. & sup. reg. of births, 17 Wilmington sq
M'Pherson Alfred, grainer, 1 Northampton pl. Canonbury sq
M'Pherson William Bosher, potato salesman, 192 Drury la
M'Queen Wm. Benj. cop. pl. print. 184 Tottenham court rd
M'Quige Thomas, accountant, 3 Staple inn, Holborn
M'Quin Charles, linendraper, 38½ Banner st. St. Luke's
M'Rae & Evans, milliners & lace dealers, 27 Ludgate st
M'Rae John & James, scotch snuff box & cigar case, &c. makers, importers of fancy articles, french warehousemen, miniature & ormolu frame makers, wholesale silversmiths & fancy stationers, wafer importers & manufacturers & importers of tracing paper, 17 Ave Maria lane
M'Rae George, *Blue Last* P.H. 55 Dorset st. Salisbury sq
M'Rae James Layton, solicitor, 1 New inn, Strand
M'Rae John, ribbon manufacturer, 130 Wood st. City
M'Rae Robert, *Horns* P.H. 12 Crucifix lane, Bermondsey
M'Ritchie James, newsvender, 44 Whitcomb st. Pall Mall east
M'Shane Manasses, upholsterer, &c. 32 Foley pl. Portland pl
M'Sparran John, plumber, &c. 1 King Edward st. Wapping, & 1 Honduras terrace, Commercial road
M'Sweeney James, undertaker, 1 Snow's fields, Bermondsey
M'Swiney Eugene, merchant, 150 Fenchurch st
M'Swiney Thomas, statuary & mason, 21 Mount st. Berkely sq
M'Swyny Mary Ann (Miss) lodging house, 2 & 15 Howard st. Strd
M'Whinnie Andrew Melville, surgeon, 5 Crescent, Blackfrs
Macaire Gideon Paul, watch case makr. see Ball & Macaire
Macann Arthur, surgeon, 22 King st. Portman square
Macaranas Joseph, profesr. of languages, 49 Holywell st. Millbk
Macarthur D. & Co. wine mers. 21 Commercial sale rms. Mncg. la
Macartney Henry, hairdresser, 43 Maiden la. Covent garden
Macaulay James, barrister, 28 Chancery lane
Macaulay Kenneth, barrister, 4 Harcourt bldgs. Temple
Macauley Henry, cabinet maker, 25 Curtain road, Shoreditch
Macauley James, barrister, 2 Brick court, Temple
Macauley Thos. gum & naptha mer. 47 Curtain rd. Shoreditch
Macay James, greengrocer, 94 Fetter lane
Macbrayne John Burn, shipping agent, 52 Old Broad st. City
Macbryde Chas. Wilson, imp. of wines & spirits, 45 Watling st
Maccaughey Hugh Wade, teabroker, see Ewart & Co
Macdaniel Charles, razor maker & cutler, 343 Oxford st
Macdermott James, *Albert* P.H. 17 Gray's inn lane
Macdonald Alexander & Co. merchts. 3 St. Mildred's ct. Poultry
Macdonald Donald & Wm. ho. agts. & uphlstrs. 1 Up. Montagu st
Macdonald George, tailor, 22 Dorset st. Portman square
Macdonald J. C. barrister, 3 Churchyard court, Temple
Macdonald Jas. bedstead ma. & undert. 11 Tyssen st. Bthnl. grn
Macdonald James, tobacconist, 29 Stamford st. & 119 Broadwall, Blackfriars
Macdonald Jane (Mrs.), boarding house, 19 Addle st. Wood st
Macdonald John, tailor & clothier, 166 Union st. Borough
Macdonald Mary (Mrs.), boarding ho. 12 Chapel pl. Cavndsh. sq
Macdonald Peter, oil & colorman, 91 Shoe lane, Fleet st
Macdonald Robert, printr. & publshr. 30 Gt. Sutton st. Clerknwl
Macdonald Thomas, shoemaker, 163 Church st. Shoreditch
Macdonald Wm. cabinet maker, 3 Thornton pl. Portman sq
Macdonald Wm. surgeon, 23 Princes st. Cavendish sq
Macdonald Wm. Jas. brass founder & coach plater, 9 Gt. Wild st
Macdonall Wm. newsvender, 94 Dean st. Soho
Macdonnell John, sec. to Hayle Rail. Co. 35 Broad st. bldngs
Macdonnell Patrick, surgeon, 36 Percy st. Bedford sq
MacDowell Patrick, sculptor, 75A, Margaret st. Cavendish sq
MacDowgall Dowgall, bricklr. 7 Charles st. ea. Hampstd. rd
Mace Margaret (Miss), butcher, 142 Poplar High st
Mace Richard, cheesemonger, 24 Langley pl. Coml. road ea
Mace Robert Paul, *White Hart* P.H. 38 Long alley, Finsbury
Mace Thomas, grocer, 46 Broad st Bloomsbury
Mace Wm. floor cloth manufacturer, Old Ford
Mace Wm. Rudd, *Blue Boar* P.H. 17 Sparrow corner, Minories
Macefield John, bookbinder, 26 Myrtle st. Hoxton
Macefield John, gasfitter, 8 Lower Crown st. Westminster
Macefield Joseph, book edge gilder, &c. 22½ Kirby st. Hat. gar
MacEntee John, grocer, 68 High st. Lambeth
Macey Robt. & Son, bricklayr. & buildr. 6 Denzell st. Clare mkt
Macey Robert & Son, builders, 91 Drury lane
Macey John, meat salesman, 13 Rose st. Newgate market
Macey Saml. *Gate House* P.H. 31 Frederick pl. Hampstead rd
Macey Thomas, *British Queen* P.H. 12 White Horse la. Stepny
Macey Uriah, linendraper, 27 Gt. Titchfield st
Macfarlane David, baker, 10 Jewry st. Aldgate
Macfarlane James, west india merchant, 147 Leadenhall st
Macfarlane John, tailor, 35 London st. Fitzroy square
Macfarren George A. professor of music, 73 Berners st
Macgillivray Alex. cabinet ma. see Poole & Macgillivray
Macgregor John, mftg. goldsmith & jeweller, 30 Charterho. sq
MacGregor John James, surgeon, 25 Wood st. Cheapside
MacGregor Joseph Alexr. Jas. solr. 26 Suffolk st. Pall mall
Machaon Daniel, physician, 12 Tavistock pl. Tavistock sq
Mache Joseph, grocer, 6 King st. Cloth fair, Smithfield
Machell George, surgeon, 2 Carlisle st. Soho
Machen Henry, cabinet ma. 4 Myddelton pl. Sadler's wells
Macher David, baker, 5 Commercial place, Kingsland road
Machin George, oilman, 37 City road
Machin Joseph, *Lord Nelson* P.H. 5 Clement's inn passage
Machin Thomas, grocer, Deptford High street
Machu John Henry, fancy trimming, fringe, braid & stay lace manufacturer, 13 Twister's alley, Bunhill row
Macilwain George, surgeon, 3 Albany court yard, Piccadilly
Macilwain Robt. beer retailer, Neate st. Cobourg road
Macintosh Charles & Co. patent india rubber waterproofcloth manufacturers, & sole licensees of Brockedons' patent india rubber stoppers, 46 Cheapside & 58 Charing cross
Macintosh Alexander, printer, 19 & 20 Gt. New st. Fetter la
Macintyre Malcolm, tailor, 17 Frederick st. Hampstead rd
MacIntyre William, physician, 84 Harley street
Mack Henry, carrier, see Deacon, Mack & Co
Mack James, surgeon, 29 King square, Goswell road
Mack Sarah (Miss), milliner, 21 Bidborough st. Burton crst
Mack William, bootmaker, 34 Bell yard, Temple bar
Mack William, market gardener, Blue Anchor rd. Bermond
Mackadem John, copper plate printer, 49 Leman st. Goodm. fi
Mackay & Madew, merchants, 2 Botolph lane, City
Mackay Alex. solicitor & army agt. 28 Charles st. Westmin
Mackay Benjamin, butcher, 189 Lambeth walk
Mackay Donald, jun. west india merchant, 32 Fenchurch st
Mackay Geo. ship & ins. & cus. ho. agt. 25 Gracechurch st
Mackay Hugh, sec. to Bank of Ceylon, 72 Old Broad st. City
Mackay James John, straw hat mnufcr. 31 Broad st. Golden sq
Mackay John, tailor, 20 Green street, Bethnal green
Mackay John, whitesmith, 36 Leman st. Goodman's fields
Mackay Robert, haberdasher, 12 Gray's place, Fulham road
Mackay Robert, nurseryman, Stoke Newington road
Mackay Thomas, tinman, 19 Green street, Bethnal green
Mackelcken Jhn. Hen. *Rose & Crown* P.H. 118 Wapping Hi. st
Macken Jas. & Co. tailors & breeches ma. 42 Conduit st. Bond st
Mackenzie Hunter & Co. merchs. 15 Providence rw. Finsbury
Mackenzie & Lawrence, stock & sharebrokers, 38 Cornhill
Mackenzie (Neil) & Co. manufacturers of fringe, lace, line, tassels, worsted, canvas, superior purse twist, floss decca, tram, sewing & all other kinds of silk, importers of berlin wool & foreign fancy goods, 77 Newgate st. & 17 Bath st

Mackenzie Alex. beer shop, 46 Acton st. Gray's inn road
Mackenzie Alex. wine merchant, 8 Liverpool st. City
Mackenzie Benj. *Regalia* P.H. 11 Augustus sq. Regent's pk
Mackenzie Chas. pianoforte maker, 11 Alfred st. Bedford sq
Mackenzie David, eating house, 4 Francis place, Holloway
Mackenzie Duncan John, wine, brandy & whiskey merchant, manufacturer of british wines, soda water, ginger beer & lemonade, 33 Chamber st. Goodman's fields, Minories
Mackenzie Eneas, printer, publisher & print seller, 111 Fleet st. & 106 London road
Mackenzie Frederick, artist, 1 North place, Hampstead rd
Mackenzie Frederick Wm. M.D. surgeon, 3 Bayswater terrace
Mackenzie Geo. archl. draughtsmn. 3 Claremont row, Islingtn
Mackenzie George, solicitor, see Russell & Mackenzie
Mackenzie Henry, tailor, 30 Wellington st. Goswell road
Mackenzie James, commission agent, 85 Queen st. Cheapside
Mackenzie John, bookbinder, 4 Lower Crown st. Westmnstr
Mackenzie John, tobacco broker, 3 Ingram ct. Fenchurch st
Mackenzie John, wine merchant, 4 Fen court, Fenchurch st
Mackenzie Maria (Mrs.), fruiterer, 6 Water st. Strand
Mackenzie Munro, scotch & linen warehouseman & linen agent, 85 Queen st. Cheapside
Mackenzie Robert, butchers' tailor, 61 West Smithfield
Mackenzie Roderick, east india mer. 3 Bond court, Walbrook
Mackenzie Rowland Hill, physician, 68 Mortimer st. Cvndsh. sq
Mackenzie Stephen, wine & spirit mer. Burleigh st. Strand
Mackenzie Wm. beer retailer, 57 Vauxhall st. Lambeth
Mackenzie Wm. bookseller, 11 Brunswick pl. Barnsbury rd
Mackenzie William, jewel case ma. 19 Norton st. Fitzroy sq
Mackeson Edward, attorney, see Selby & Mackeson
Mackeson Lumsden, barrister, 10 Old sq. Lincoln's inn
Mac Keujie & Lawrence, stock & share brok. 38 Cornhill
Mackey, Holt & Co. merchants & east india agents, & agents to the Phœnix Marine Insurance Company of Calcutta, 20 St. Helen's pl. Bishopsgate
Mackey Alexander, grocer, &c. 38 Gilbert st. Grosvenor sq
Mackey Ann (Mrs.), grocer, &c. 5 Little Stanhope st. Mayfr
Mackey George, *White Hart* P.H. 1 Goswell st
Mackey William, hairdresser, 4 Church lane, Whitechapel
Mackey William, tailor & draper, 13 Cannon st. rd. St. Geo. ea
Mackey William, tailor, Munster square, Regent's pk
Mackie John & Co. merchants, 110 Fenchurch st
Mackie & Meredith, tailors, 14 Southampton rw. Russll. sq
Mackie Geo. watch & clock maker, 31 City road, Finsbury sq
Mackie James, watch & clock maker, 4 White Rose court, Coleman st. & 11 Castle st. City road
Mackie John, bootmaker, 13 Great Marylebone st
Mackie John, lodging house, 3 Eccleston st. Pimlico
Mackie John, shoemaker, 65 East st. Manchester square
Mackie Phœbe (Mrs.), hairdresser, 7 Bell yd. Gracechurch st
Mackie Robert, bookseller & binder, 30 Greek st. Soho
Mackie Robert, merchant, 14 Mitre chbs. 157 Fenchurch st
Mackie Thos. carver & gilder, 13 Cumberland st. Curtain rd
Mackie Thos. *Golden Lion* P.H. 42 Wardour st. Soho
Mackie Wm. surveyor, 12 Lit. Charlotte st. Blackfriars rd
Mackillop James, mercht. see Palmer, Mackillop, Dent & Co
Mackin Peter, baker, 16 Oxford st. Mile end
Mackinder & Co. tallow melters, 2 East st. Portman square
Mackinlay George, chemist & druggist, 52 Edgware road
Mackinlay John, surgeon & druggist, 8 Store st. Bedford sq
Mackinnon Lewis, wharfinger, Miller's whf. Low. Ea. Smithfi
Mackintosh Alex. plumber, 28 Henrietta st. Cavendish sq
Mackintosh Alphonso, *Old Red Lion* P.H. 13 Bridge st. Lamb
Mackintosh Andrew, merchant, 2 Brabant ct. Philpot lane
Mackintosh Donald, tanner, 40 Russell st. Bermondsey
Mackintosh James S. physician, 32 Wilton pl. Knightsbridge
Mackintosh John, wheelwright, 23 Christian st. St. Geo.'s ea
Mackley George, ironmonger, 126 Kingsland road
Mackley Thomas C. wholesale grindery, shoe tip, thread & nail warehouse, heel ball & ink maker, & bees' wax dealer, 6 & 7 New inn yard, Shoreditch
Macklin Robert, tailor, 14 Clifford st. Bond st
Mackmain Fred. ladies' bootmaker, 28 Gt. Portland st. Oxfrd. st
Mackmin John Joseph S. linendraper, 51 Tabernacle walk
Mackmurdo Gilbert W. surgeon, 7 New Broad st. City
Mackness Jackson, baker, 17 Drury lane
Mackness John, baker, Stratford
Mackness Robert, baker, 3 Lambeth walk
Mackness Robert, baker, 43 Milner pl. Lambeth Lower marsh
Mackness Thomas, baker, 209 Shadwell High street, & 45 Three Colt st. Limehouse
Mackrell Wm. Thos. solicitor, see Lethbridge & Mackrell
Mackreth Geo. Edw. who. teadealer, see Tyson & Mackreths
Mackrill Elizh. (Mrs.), grocer, 2 North st. East st. Walworth
Mackrow Isaac, optician, 4 Upper East Smithfield
Maclachlan Peter, baker, 144 Holborn bars
Maclachlan Peter, confectioner & biscuit baker, 6 Birchin la
Maclaran Thos. George & Son, law stationers, 5 Cursitor st
Maclaren James & Son, boot & shoemakers, 55 Cornhill
Maclaran Archbld. united society school, Trinity st. Rotherh
Mac Laren John, bootmaker, 31 New st. Dorset square
Maclaurin Daniel, auditor, accountant, & agent for the purchase & sale of reversionary interests, 83 Lombard st
Maclean, Maris & Co. american merchants, 3 Abchurch lane
Maclean (Moira) & Co. woollen manufrs. 7 Basinghall st
Maclean Alex. ins. broker, 3 Crosby hall chambs. & Lloyd's
Maclean Donald, M.P. barrister, 1 New court, Temple
Maclean James, carpenter & builder, 3 Somerset st. Aldgate
Maclean John, drysalter, see Quiney & Maclean
Maclean John, physician, 29 Up. Montagu st. Montagu sq
Maclean John, wine merchant, 102 Leadenhall st
Macleod George, tailor, 47 Warwick st. Golden square
Macleod Roderick, physician, 1 Low. Seymour st. Portm. sq
Maclintock James, working jeweller, 9 Beech st. Barbican
Maclure Peter, *Bedford Head*, P.H. 5 Up. Kingst. Blmsbury
Maclure Rev. Robt. LL.D. academy, 14 Bulstrodest. Manch. sq
Maclure William, surgeon, 14 Harley st. Cavendish square
MacMahon Patrick, barrister, 10 Farrar's buildings, Temple
Macmeikan John, apothecary, London Hospital, Whtchpl. rd
Macmin John, saddler, 58 King st. Soho
Macmurdo Edward, who. druggist, see Davy, Macmurdo & Co
Macnaghten Steuart, barrister, 4 Old square, Lincoln's inn
Mac Nair John, ale brewer, Leith; & St. Mary Overy's dock
Macnalley George, carpenter, 63 Park st. Camden town
Mac Nally Richard, wine merchant, 60 Mark lane
Macnamara Henry T. J. special pleader, 9 Inner Temple la
Macnaughten & Parry, india & col. brokers, 134 Fenchurchst
Macnaughten Peter, bootmaker, 24 Mount st. Berkeley sq
Macniell Sir John, LL.D. civil engineer, 9 Whitehall place
Macomie Alexr. bookbinder, 6 Percy st. Tottenham ct. rd
Macord Robert, chemist & medical plaster ma. 58 Minories
Macord Robt. Harmer, ironmonger, &c. 63 Low. Thames st
Macpherson Jane (Miss), dressmaker, &c. 29A, Albemarle st
Macpherson William, barrister, 3 Stone buildings, Linc. inn
Macqueen John Fraser, barrister, 7 Old square, Lincoln's inn
Macquillin T.F. *Blakeney's Head*, P.H. 25 Cablest. Wellcls. sq
Mac Rae Charles & Ivie Hare, stockbrokers, 57 Moorgate st
Macrae Edmund, oil & colorman, 119 Whitechapel High st
Macrae Hen. optician & mathematical instrmt. ma. 34 Aldgate
Macron Thomas, furniture broker, 80 St. George st
Macrow Thomas, furniture brok. 3, 4 & 5 Back rd. Shadwell
MacSparran John, plumber, 1 Honduras ter. Commercial rd
Mactaggart Malcolm, *Nag's Head* P.H. 2 Londn. ter. Hckney. rd
Macy Charles, solicitor, 27 Bury st. St. James's
Maddams John, chandler's shop, 4 Cleveland st. Mile end
Maddams Wm. cheesemonger, 1 St. Agnes ter. Tabernacle sq
Madden & Malcolm, oriental booksel. & publish. 8 Leadenhallst
Madden Hen. mnfr. of pat. knife cleaner, 14 George st. Adelphi
Madden Henry, wine mer. York chamb. 13 George st. Adelphi
Madden John, clothes salesman, 17 Wells st. Oxford st
Madden Maria (Mrs.), cupper, 17 Wells st. Oxford st
Madden Owen, *Old Greenland Fishery* P.H. 6 Wappingwall
Madden Wm. last maker & turner, 56 Longla. West Smithfield
Madderson & King, grocers, 6 Sidney place, King's rd. Chelsea
Maddicks Edward, bootmaker, 8 Brunswick st. Cromer st
Maddin Hannah & Son, smiths & toolmakers, 29 Goswell st
Maddin Henry, horse hair manfr. 108 York st. Whitechapel
Maddison James, engineer, 3½ York st. York road, Lambeth
Maddison John, tailor, 38 Upper John st. Fitzroy sq
Maddison Thomas, baker, 189 Shoreditch
Maddock Alfred B. M.D. surgeon, 22 Harley st. Cavendish sq
Maddock Henry Frederick, barrister, 2 Lyon's inn, Strand
Maddock James, baker, 3 Fleet lane, Farringdon st
Maddocks & Cutler, livery stables, 36 Castle st. Leicester sq
Maddocks Francis, dairyman, Canal pl. Old Kent road
Maddocks Joseph, grocer, Bolingbroke gardens, Battersea
Maddox John, grocer, 22 Bermondsey wall
Maddox John, news agt. & bookslr. 10 Up. Albanyst. Regent'spk
Maddox John Wedd, printer & stationer, 3 Dockhead, Bermnd
Maddox John Wm. linendraper, 23 Tavistock st. Covent gar
Maddox Ralph Hen. upholder & ho. agt. 25 Welbeck st. Cav. sq
Maddren Richard, *British Museum* P.H. 50 Gt. Russell st
Maddy John, ginger beer manufacturer, 27 Cannon st road
Maddy Wm. grocer & cheesemonger, 23 Sloane square
Madeley Fred. oil leather dresser, see Dalton & Madeley
Madeley Geo. Edwd. lithogr. printer, 3 Wellington st. Strand
Madgin Rd. carpent. & builder, Fox & Knot ct. King st. Snowh
Madgwick Edward, japanner, see Cooper & Madgwicks'
Madgwick James, japanner, see Cooper & Madgwicks'
Madgwick Thomas, upholsterer, 11 Finsbury pavement
Madle Edward, archery warehouse, 29 Frith st. Soho
Madle Edward, tobacconist, 18 Judd st. Brunswick sq

Madle James, straw hat manufacturer, 31 Park st. Dorset sq
Madley Wm. plumber, painter & glazr. 73 Clarendon st. Smrs. tn
Madlin Joseph, timber merchant, 215 Whitechapel road
Madot Adolphus, prof. of languages, 31 Up. Baker st. Reg. pk
Madox & Wyatt, solicitors, 30 Clement's lane, Lombard st
Madox James Fuller, solicitor, see Madox & Wyatt
Madras Military Fund (Grindley & Co. agents), 16A, Cornhill, hours 11 to 3
Madrid & Valencia Rail. Co. (K. Powell, sec.), 37 Moorgate st
Maers Jacob, tailor, 24 Russell court, Drury lane
Maffey & Walker, shoeing smths. 18 Bruton mews nth. Berk. sq
Magdalen Hospital (J. Brackenbury, sec.), 115 Blackfriars rd
Magee James, hatter, 6 Parker's row, Dockhead
Magenis John, furniture broker, 11 Barrett's ct. Oxford st
Mageniss Peter, surgeon, 29 Chichester pl. Gray's inn road
Maggi & Cave (Misses), milliners, 278 Regent street
Maggioni Manfred, prof. of italian, Portland cot. Portland rd
Maggs, Hindley & Maggs, flax & tow spinners, shoe thread, linen tick, sail cloth, &c. manufacturers, 12 Friday street (late of 7 King's Arms buildings, Wood street), City, & at Bourton, near Wincanton, Somerset
Maggs Felix, tailor, 109 New Bond street
Maggs William, news vender, 19 High road, Knightsbridge
Magnay Bros. who. statnr. 11 College hl. & 181 Up. Thames st
Magnet Agricultural Weekly Newspaper, 299 Strand
Magniac, Jardine & Co. merchants, 3 Lombard st
Magnin Jane (Madame), milliner, 21 Davies st. Berkeley sq
Magnus Nathan & Son, who. boot & shoe ma. 2 Peter st. Bishpgt
Magnus Geo. Eugene, pimlico slate works, Up. Belgrave pl
Magnus Martin L. fur & skin merchant, 3 College hill, City
Magnus Moses, merchant, 20 Gt. Prescot st. Goodman's flds
Magnus Nathaniel, shoe wareho. 13 Fore st. Cripplegate
Magnus Rosetta (Mrs.), who. shoewarehouse, 54 Houndsditch
Magnus Saml. expt. stationr. & acct. book ma. 127 Fenchurch st
Magona Joseph, marine store dlr. 70 Cromer st. Brnswk. sq
Magrath Henry Jesson, bill brokr. see Mathewes & Magrath
Magrath Thos. soda water maker, &c. 5 Maze pond, Tooley st
Magrath William, bootmaker, 5 Francis st. Newington butts
Magrini Romualdo F. prof. of italian, 43 Warren st. Fitzroy sq
Maguire George, barrister, 18 Clement's inn, Strand
Maguire H. Calton, lithogr. & picture dlr. 98 Gt. Russell st
Maguire James, builder, 134 Blackfriars road
Maguire Wm. hosier, Stratford broadway
Magwood Robt. & Co. coal mers. 19 Chadwell st. St. John's st. rd
Maher Maria (Miss), staymaker, 10 Fisher st. Red Lion sq
Mahers & Stevenson, fish factrs. 11 Darkhouse la. Billingsgate
Mahomed Horatio, shampooing surgeon, inventor of the indian medicated vapour & shampooing baths, &c.; baths of all kinds, 7 Little Ryder st. St. James's, from Brighton
Mahon Anthony, tobacconist, 20 Alfred pl. Newingtn. causwy
Mahon Jane (Mrs.), stationer & bookseller, 106 Blackman st
Mahon Thomas, stationer, 90 Waterloo road, Lambeth
Mahoney M. & J. desk & dressg. case ma. 10 Brown's la. Spitflds
Mahony John, surgeon, 72 Paradise row, Chelsea
Mahony Michael John, metal broker, see Short & Mahony
Mahony Wm. tobacconist, 2 Northampton pl. Old Kent rd
Maides Richard, grocer, 1 West st. Hackney
Maides Wm. hay salesman, see Tarling & Maides
Maidlow John, builder & ho. paintr. 11 Warwick ct. Holborn
Maidman George, grocer, 35 Lambeth Lower marsh
Maidment John, grocer, 7 Gloucester ter. Vauxhall brdg. rd
Maidstone Wm. grocer, 10 Gainsford st. Horselydown
Maidwell Chas. corn dlr. 8 Mount ter. New road, Whitechapel
Maielli Fredk. confectioner, 13 Bathurst st. Sussex square
Maile Richard & Son, statuaries & masons, 4 & 5 Keppel row, New road
Mailin George, fruiterer, 14 Rawstorne st. Brompton
Maillard David, greengrocer, 32 Bryanstone st
Maillard Frederick, auctionr. & apprsr. 30 Gt. Dover st. Boro'
Maillet Amelia (Mrs.), lodginghouse, 9 Lit. Ryder st. St. James's
Main, Reed & Co. patent floor cloth manufacturers, Virginia place, Great Dover rd. & 158 Leadenhall st. City
Main Augustus, chemist, 9 Oakley terrace, Old Kent road
Main George, *Old Red Lion* P.H. 46 Coppice rw. Clerknwl
Main John, baker, 24 Grafton st. Fitzroy square
Main John, butcher, 9 Queen's buildings, Knightsbridge
Main Wm. hosier & shirtmaker, 22 Cockspur st. Charing cr
Main Wm. plumber & glazier, 4 Eccleston st. south
Main Wm. Henry, plumber & painter, 34 Water la. Blackfrs
Maine Samuel, currier, 160 Aldersgate st
Mainon Chas. Lewis, french basket ma. 33 Brooke st. Holborn
Mainstone Chas. John, jeweller, 7 Gt. Sutton st. Clerknwl
Mair John, Son & Co. muslin ma. 60 Friday st. Cheapside
Mair George, architect, 18 Charlotte st. Bedford square
Mair George, builder & bricklayer, 256 Bethnal green road
Mair John, warehouseman, 66 Watling street, City
Maire Peter F. merchant, 14 Mark lane
Maire Thomas, tailor & draper, 5 Fountain court, Strand
Mais John Casper, merchant, 7 Savage gardens
Maish Thos. card board box ma. 64 Vauxhall st. Lambeth
Maish Robert, cooper, 12 Russell place, Old Kent road
Maish Sam. *Turf tavern* P.H. Grosvenor pl. Hyde pk. crnr
Maishman William, upholsterer, 1 Regent ter. City road
Maiszner John, grocer, 197 Upper Whitecross st
Maitland & Carr, tailors, 25 Conduit st. Bond st
Maitlands' & Fawkes, colonial brokers, 22 Mincing lane
Maitland & Mitchell, colonial brokers, 37 Mincing lane
Maitland Edward Francis, dyer, 96 High st. Marylebone
Maitland Henry, surgeon dentist, 3 Abchurch yd. Cannon st
Maitland James, hairdresser, 45 Bridge ho. pl. Newing. caus
Maitland John, chemist & druggist, 10 Chester pl. Oxford sq
Maitland John Gorham, barrister, 8 New sq. Lincoln's inn
Maitland Robert, furniture bro. 6 Buckingham pl. Fitzroy sq
Maitland Thomas Fuller, barrister, 6 Pump court, Temple
Maitland Wm. beer retailer, 9 Crosby row, King st. Borough
Maize John, surgeon, 274 Kent street, Borough
Major Ann & Co bottle mers. 8 Allhallows la. Up. Thames st
Major & Gill, manchester mfrs. 23 King st. Cheapside
Major & Wallace, merchants, Cotton's wharf, Tooley st
Major Chas. James, custom house & genl. agt. 21 Billiter st
Major Daniel Bushnel, stockbroker, Stock Exchange & 27 Change alley
Major Henry, furn. ironmonger, 23 St. John st. Clerkenwell
Major James, carpenter, 6 Pell st. Ratcliff highway
Major Thos. *Royal Standard* P.H. 32 Gt. Prescot st. Goodms. fi
Major William M.D. surgeon, 12 Mount pl. Whitechapel rd
Makeham John, tuscan, plait & trim. ma. 15 Queen st. Finsbury
Makeham John P. sup. registrar for Westmr. 10 Dartmouth st
Makeham Sarah (Miss), straw bonnet mfr. 3 Worship sq
Makenzie James Munro, linen factor, 85 Queen st. Cheapside
Makepeace & Walford, goldsmiths, jewellers, silversmiths, & platers, 5 Serle street, Lincoln's inn fields
Makins Joseph, baker, New st. Deptford
Makinson & Sanders, attorneys, 3 Elm court, Temple
Malabre Francis, box maker, 9 Silver st. Wood st. City
Malby Thomas & Co. publishers & manufacturers of the globes of the Society for the diffusion of useful knowledge, 3 Houghton st. Newcastle st. Strand
Malby Thos. varnish ma. 3 Houghton st. Newcastle st. Strand
Malby Thomas, jun. map mounter & colorer, 3 Houghton st. Newcastle st. Strand
Malby Wm. *Blacksmiths' Arms* P.H. 129 Rotherhithe st
Malchar Hugh, *Sun* P.H. Oxford st. & 1 Sidney st. Mile end
Malchar John, beer retailer, 5 Bridge place, City road
Malchar John, *Prince of Wales* P.H. Arbour st. east, Stepy
Malcolm George, surgeon, 1 Globe st. Wapping
Malcolm Hannah (Mrs.), wardrobe dlr. 26 Dorset st. Portm. sq
Malcolm John George, barrister, 4 Lamb buildings, Temple
Malcolm Neill, merchant, 37 Fenchurch st
Malcolm Rt. *Two Chairmen* P.H. 20 Warwick st. Char. cross
Malcolmson Abrm. B. mrcht. Hall of commerce, Thrdndle. st
Malden John Coleman, butcher, 61 Whitechapel High st
Malden Joseph, oilman, 31 Upper Lisson st. Marylebone
Male Christphr. bone brush ma. 20 Rawstorne st. Goswell rd
Male Samuel, law stationer, 12 Gray's inn square
Male Wm. watch & case gilder, 75 Rahere st. Goswell road
Malenoir & Moore, fish salesmen, 110 Lower Thames st
Maleszewski Joseph, engine turner, 18 President st. east
Maley Hy. stone & marble mason, 9 Seymour pl. Camden tn
Maley John, fancy brush manfr. 6 Brooksby st. Liverpool rd
Maley William, cooper, 33 Brill place, Somers town
Maley William, oilman, 71 Brewer st. Somers town
Malfatti Bathlmw. imp. of for. goods, see Bayfield & Malfatti
Malim George, attorney, 11 South square, Gray's inn
Malin Henry Isaac, baker, 46 Brill row, Somers town
Malins & Rawlinsons, iron masters, coal owners & manufacturers of patent galvanized iron, 3 Mansion house place, City, & Millwall, Poplar; Porth Cawl, near Bridgend; Phœnix iron works, West Bromwich
Malins Richard, barrister, 6 Stone buildings, Lincoln's inn
Malkin Charles, grocer, Mason st. Westminster bridge rd
Malkin Geo. *White Swan* P.H. 19 Rufford's bldgs. Islington
Malkin Samuel, artist, 20 Canonbury square, Islington
Mallalieu Wm. & Co. merchts. & gen. agts. 97 Hatton gardn
Mallalieu Alfred, merchant, N. & S. American coffee house
Mallalieu Hen. Martin, underwriter, Lloyd's, & 97 Hatton gdn
Mallalue George, job master, 25½ Wigmore st. & Chandos mews, Chandos st. Cavendish square
Mallam Henry, furniture dealer, 14 Queen's bldgs. Brompton
Mallan Edwd. & Son, surgeon dentists, 155 Oxford st
Mallan James Michael & Sons, surg. dentists, 19 Bouverie st
Mallandain Peter, ebony inkstand ma. 5 James st. St. Luke's

Mallars Edward, general salesman, 129 Drury lane
Mallatt Robt. lighterman, 7 Belvedere cresct. Belvedere rd
Malcott John, statuary & mason, 12 Newgate st. & Granite wharf, 336 Wapping High st
Mallen Chas.D.oil&colorman,6Cannon st.rd.St.George's east
Malleson John, conveyancer, 34A, Charles st. Berkeley sq
Mallett Frederick, short hand writer, 59 Wardour st
Mallett George, tobacconist, 29 High st. Newington butts
Mallett James, plumber & glazier, 85 Long la. Bermondsey
Mallett John, beer retailer, 1 North st. East st. Walworth
Mallett Jonathan, plumber, 13 Back st. Horselydown
Mallett Joseph, printer, 59 Wardour st. Soho
Mallett Rd. herbalist & seedsman, 25 Gt.Charlotte st.Blkfrs
Mallett Thomas, baker, &c. 172 Borough High st
Mallett Wm. blind ma.& undert. 19 Glos'ter ter. Vauxhl.Br.rd
Mallett Wm. Jas. lighterm. 6 College st. Belvedere rd.Lamb
Mallett Wm. Lewis, bricklayer, 23 Carburton st. Portland rd
Mallinson John, wholesale & retail slopseller, 112 Minories
Mallinson Rd. butcher, 6 Albert pl. Marlboro' rd. Chelsea
Mallock Andrew, tarpauling manuf. 60 Millbank st.Westmr
Mallock David, M.A. academy, 60 Millbank st. Westminster
Mallock James, attorney, 8 Southampton st. Bloomsbury sq
Mallory Henry, copperfounder, see Pontifex & Mallory
Mallows John, shoemaker, 18 White st. Borough
Malone Edward, academy, 13 Park st. Islington
Malone Thomas, bootmaker, 79 Long lane, Bermondsey
Malpas Edward, widows' milliner, 31 Finsbury place north
Malpas William, *Falcon* P.H. 84 Upper Thames st
Malpass John, oil & colorman, 110 Houndsditch
Malpass Richard, smith, 128 Long alley, Finsbury
Maltby, Beachcroft&Robinson, solictrs. 34 Old Broad st.City
Maltby & Grant, solicitors, 10 Broad st. buildings
Maltby Thos. Son & Co. lead merchts. 34 Old Broad st. City
Maltby Wm.& Co. manuftg. chemists, Assembly pl.Mile end
Maltby Chas.Fredk.architect&surv.19 Took's ct.Chancery la
Maltby Edward Harvey, magistrate, Marlbro' st. Police ct
Maltby Hy. Bristow, tailor, 13 Westmoreland st. Marylebo
Maltby Hugh, grocer & teadealer, 10 Tabernacle sq.Finsbury
Maltby Jas. tailor & draper, 8 Hanover pl. Regent's pk. rd
Maltby Thomas, grocer & teadealer, 17 Lower st. Islington
Malton & Trollope, solicitors, 60 Carey st. Lincoln's inn
Malton Chas. Jas. A. surgeon, 9 Up. Seymour st. Portman sq
Maltwood M. A. (Mrs.), dressmak. 2 Guildford pl. Lr. Ken. la
Maltwood Richard A. barometer, &c. maker & engraver, 129 Great Saffron hill
Maltwood Thomas, trunk & packing case ma. 29 Oxford st
Maltwood William, imperial trunk maker, 168 Strand
Maltwood Wm. tobacconist, 19 Northampton pl. Old Kent rd
Malyn John, surgeon, 12 James st. Buckingham gate
Malyon Esther (Miss), baker, 107 Poplar High st
Malyon Joseph, *Coopers' Arms* P.H. 12 Miles la. Up. Thames st
Malyon William, bricklayer, 8 Blewitt's bldgs. Fetter lane
Man Mary (Mrs.) & Son, dyers & scourers, 140 Salisbury ct. Fleet st. 118 Albany st. Regt.'s pk. & 86 St. John's wood ter
Man Edward D. colonial broker, 7 Mincing lane
Man George, ironmonger, 36 Broad st. Golden square
Man Henry, wine & spirit broker, 38 Crutchedfriars
Manaton Francis Sampson, heraldic engr. 27 Brooke st. Holbrn
Manby & Ockerby, law stationers, 16 Castle st. Holborn
Manby Wm. Edward, oil & italian warehouse, 230 Strand
Manby Chas. F.G.S. civil engineer, 25 Gt. George st. Westmr
Manby Charles William, hatter, 85 Fleet st
Manby Edward, grocer, 70 Ropemaker's fields, Limehouse
Manby John, law stationer, 29 Castle st. Holborn
Manby Joseph L. civil engineer, 32 Bucklersbury
Mancell Thos. furniture broker, 1 Albion pl. ea. King's cross
Manchee Peter, turner, bdstd. & cornice ma. 129 Curtain rd. Sh
Manchester & Birmingham Continuation & Welsh Junctn. Railway Co. (Wm. Ellis, esq. sec.), 39 Charing cross
Manchester & Birmingham Railway Company (agents in London, Ross & Ash), 32 Great Winchester st
Manchester & Liverpool District Banking Co. see p.
Manchester Life Assurance Offi. (Henry R. Marriott, agt.), 6 Lawrence lane, Cheapside
Manchester Mark, pork butcher, 57 Strutton ground, Westmr
Mandelbaum David, impr. of for. toys, american clocks & fancy goods, wholesale & for exportation, 12 & 13 Minories
Mandeno Wm. tallowchandler & oilman, 162 Shoreditch
Mander Caroline (Mrs.), milliner, 4 Lamb's Conduit passage
Mander George, rule maker, 25 Old Compton st. & 21 Great Crown court, Princes st. Soho
Mander Henry Waterland, barrister, 7 New sq. Lincoln's inn
Mander James, solicitor, 9 New square, Lincoln's inn
Mander John Geo. sydney merchant, 1 Fen ct. Fenchurch st
Mander Thomas, grocer, 38 Brewer st. Somers town
Mandeville Robt. hemp, flax & cane mer. 101 Kent st. Borough
Mandy Henry, meat salesman, 21 Newgate market
Mandy Henry, *Green Man* P.H. 101 New Bond st
Maney & Connor, tailors, 315 High Holborn
Manfield Hannah (Mrs.), wireworker, 6 Red Lion st. Holborn
Manfield William, merchant, Salvador ho. Bishopsgate st
Mangeon James Wm. tobacconist, 90 Quadrant, Regent st
Manger Henry, comml. traveller, 31 Baalzephon st. Brmndsy
Manger Jacob, cheesemonger, 24 Down st. Piccadilly
Manger Wm. tobacconist & snuffmaker, 60 Union st. Borough
Mangles Frederick & Co. sail makers & ship chandlers, 62 Wapping wall, & King's mills, Rotherhithe
Mangles Jas. & Robt. King's flour mills, 292 Rotherhithe st
Mangles & Co. merchants, 8 New Broad st. City
Mangles' Sufferance wharf (James Kid, wharfinger), King's mills, Rotherhithe
Mangold Chas. teacher of pianoforte, 37 Hunter st. Brunsk.sq
Manico Edwd.S. papr.alum, &c. agt. see Coulthard, Manico & Co
Manicom Charles, baker, 36 South Molton st. Bond st
Manington George, tailor, 13 Lisson grove north
Manins John, iron dealer, 1 Samuel st. Mile end New tn
Manistre Henry, confectioner, 60 Tottenham court road
Mankelow Chas. carver & gilder, 22 Mansion house st. Kengtn
Manktelow John, pianoforte maker, 12 Huntley st. Bedford square, & 32 Upper Chenies mews
Manktelow Joseph, fruiterer, 5 Deptford High st
Manktelow William, *Horseshoe* P.H. 10 Grange rd. Bermndsy
Manley Geo.&Co. coal mer. Dye house whf. Clink st. Bankside
Manley Edward, hairdresser, 168 Bethnal green road
Manley James, coal sack & bag maker & patent cloth dresser, 7 Back Church lane, Cable st. St. George's east
Manley Robert, cooper & stave merchant, Potters' fields, & 4 Back st. Horselydown
Manley Wm. coal & broom mer. South st. Long la. Brmndsy
Manly Elizh. (Mrs.), bootma. 70 Strutton ground, Westminster
Manly John Thomas, baker, 194 Upper Thames st
Manly Joseph, baker, 9 Commercial place, Old Kent road
Mann A.& R. bldrs.& iron mers. 28 Glo'ster ter. Vauxhll. br.rd
Mann & Co. varnish & color manufacturers, 65 Gt. Queen st. Lincoln's inn fields
Mann & Inkson, linendrapers, 38 Parliament st. Westminster
Mann James & Son, tailors, 31 Grafton st. Fitzroy sq
Mann James & Sons, albion brewery, 172 Whitechapel road
Mann Wm. Hen. & Co. color merchants & agents for John's patent cement, 5 Maiden lane, Queen st. Cheapside
Mann Andrew, iron dealer, 28 Glo'ster ter. Vauxhall Brdg. rd
Mann Arthur, merchant, 21 Throgmorton st. City
Mann Charles, butcher, 3 Gresham st. City
Mann Charles, stock & sharebroker, 1 Cushion ct. Old Brd st
Mann Charles Fredk. oil & colorman, 35 Aldgate High st
Mann Charles Henry, teadealer, &c. see Banks & Mann
Mann Emily (Mrs.), *Rose & Crown* P.H. 85 Dean st. Soho
Mann George, bookseller & stationer, 39 Cornhill
Mann George, bricklayer, Well st. Hackney
Mann George, jeweller, see Brown & Mann
Mann George Stanley, dining rooms 7 Bucklersbury
Mann James, bootmaker, 23 Green st. Leicester square
Mann James, engineer, 18 Berwick st. Pimlico
Mann James, tailor, 57 South Audley st.
Mann James, tobacconist, 120 Lambeth Lower Marsh
Mann James Hargrave, varnish, &c. ma. see Sargon & Mann
Mann James Steere, auctioneer, 30 Church st. Deptford
Mann John, bootmaker, 43 Haymarket
Mann John, coachmaker, 16 David st. Marylebone
Mann John, custom house agent, 12 Rood lane, City
Mann John, surgeon, 63 Bartholomew close
Mann Jsph. who. biscuit baker, 11 North st. Whitechpl. rd
Mann Mary (Mrs.), milliner, 64 Gt. Carlisle st. Portmn. mkt
Mann Mary Ann (Mrs.), booksel. 36 Langley pl. Com.rd. east
Mann Noah, tallowchandler, 21 Broad st. Bloomsbury
Mann Richard, builder, 13 Paradise row, Chelsea
Mann Robert A. fruiterer, 5 Water lane, Blackfriars
Mann Thos. newsagnt.&bookslr. 3 Princess t. Lit. Queen st. Hlbn
Mann Wm. butcher, 1 Charles st. Commercial road
Mann William, butcher, 65 St. Mary Axe
Mann Wm. cidermerchant, Hibernia wf. Montague close, Boro'
Mann Wm. egg mercht. 2 Sydenham cottgs. Spa rd. Brmndsy
Mann Wm. walking stick manufacturer, 109 Aldersgate st
Mannakay Edwd. buildg. material dlr. 26 Club row, Bethnal gr
Mannell Joseph, cheesemonger, 10 Millpond st. Bermondsey
Mannell Mary (Mrs.), cheesemonger, 124 Church st. Shoredh
Mannell Richard, cheesemonger, 64 Brick lane, Spitalfields
Mannell Wm. cheesemonger, 13 Cable st. Wellclose sq
Mannering David, linendrpr. 6 Up. Penton st. Pentonville
Mannering Ebenezer, tailor, 10 Charles st. Middlesex hosp
Manners & Furze, brewers, Old Castle st. Whitechapel
Manners Thomas, chemist & druggist, 58 Lambeth walk

Manners Thos. *Two Brewers* P.H. 15 New Park st. Boro'
Manners William Henry, miniature painter, 18 Poultry
Manners William Henry, oilman, 76 Lambeth Lower marsh
Mannin (Mrs.), artist, 28 Percy st. Tottenham court road
Mannin Maria (Mrs.), grocer, 18 White Hart st. Low. Kngtn. la
Manning & Anderdon, merchants, 3 New Bank bldgs. Lothbury
Manning Charles & Henry, linendrapers, 2 Holmester. Kntsh. tn
Manning & Cross, milliners, 13 Leicester st. Leicester sq
Manning & Dalston, attorneys, 8A, Hertford st. May fair
Manning Edmd. & Co. draprs & hosrs. 96 Whitechapel High st
Manning Edward & Co. oil refiners & patent opaline candle manufacturers, Manor st. Old Kent rd
Manning & Mason, printers, 12 Ivy lane, Newgate st
Manning Andrew, boot & shoe mak. 2 Jupp's ter. Comrcl. rd. e
Manning Ann E. (Miss), milliner, 25 Church st. Camberwell
Manning Benj. engineer & millwright, 2 Russell st. Blackwl
Manning Edwd. baker, 7 Portugal pl. Cambdg. rw. Mile end
Manning Elizh. (Mrs.), milliner, 7 Norland rd. Notting hill
Manning Frederick John, attorney, coroner for the Queen's household & the verge, 30 Craven st. Strand
Manning George, straw bonnet ma. 97 Bishopsgate without
Manning Geo. wine cooper, 1 Exmouth st. Commercl. rd. ea
Manning Henry, baker, 73 Gray's inn lane
Manning Henry, builder & iron fence ma. 251 & 252 H. Holbn
Manning Henry, linendraper, see White & Manning
Manning James, baker, 3 Gt. Chesterfield st. Marylebone
Manning James, boot & shoemaker, 20 Fashion st. Dockhd
Manning James, *Dial* P.H. 132 Long alley, Finsbury
Manning James, jeweller, 30 Skinner st. Clerkenwell
Manning James, plumber, &c. 3 Marchmont st. Brunswk. sq
Manning James, serjeant-at-law, 3 Serjeant's inn, Chancy. la
Manning James, white hard varnish ma. 8 High Holborn
Manning Jeremiah, beer retailer, 16 Bell st. Edgware road
Manning John, baker, 6 Mason's place, Little Chelsea
Manning John, grocer, &c. 139 Whitechapel High st
Manning Joseph, corndealer, 42 Lambeth lower marsh
Manning Jsph. wine mer. south sea chmbs. 41 Threadneedle st
Manning Maria (Mrs.), oilwarehouse, 2 Plumber st. City rd
Manning Nathaniel, baker, 63 Earl st. east, Lisson grove
Manning Richard, fruiterer & coal dealer, 49 Goodge st
Manning Robert, stockbroker, stock exchange
Manning Robert, toy wareh. 41 Lamb's Conduit st. Foundling
Manning Samuel, carpenter, 23 Pewter platter yd. St. John st
Manning Sarah (Miss), grocer, 44 Aldermanbury
Manning Thomas, carpenter & undertaker, 5 Duke st. Bloomsby
Manning Thomas, dairyman, 14 Lambeth walk
Manning Thos. John, coffeerooms, 3 White Lion ct. Thrgtn. st
Manning Wm. goldcutter, 23 Gloucester st. St. John st. road
Manning Wm. *Robin Hood & Little John* P.H. Whitmr. pl. Hxt
Manning Wm. Oke, merchant, Old Trinity house, Water la
Manning William S. cattle salesman, 17 West Smithfield
Manning Wm. Thos. solicitor, see Hanslip & Manning
Mannoch Edw. marble imitator, 46 Howland st. Fitzroy sq
Mansbridge & Hodges, who. milliners, 36 Aldermanbury
Mansbridge William, fruiterer, 101 Whitechapel road
Mansell & Barnard, wine merchants, 10 Crutched friars
Mansell Geo. Thos. & Co. who. teadealers, 2 Bucklersbury
Mansell Wm & Son, gold watchcase ma. 26 Spencer st. Goswl. rd
Mansell Catherine Bavin (Mrs.), chemist, Mare st. Hackney
Mansell Frederick, engraver & printer, stationer & lithographer, 4 Barnard's inn, Holborn
Mansell George, printer, 3 King st. Borough
Mansell Jacob, carpent. 2 Chapel pl. north, South Audley st
Mansell John, carman, 23 Canterbury place, Old Kent road
Mansell John, toywarehouse, 28 Upp. North pl. Gray's inn rd
Mansell Joseph, who. fancy stationer, 35 Red Lion square
Mansell Richard, cheesemonger, 18 King st. Westminster
Mansell Samuel, chemist, &c. 12 Bermondsey wall
Mansell Thomas, grocer, 38 Devonshire st. Globe road
Mansell Thomas, *Swan & Horse Shoe* P.H. 32 Little Britain
Mansell Wm. furniture dlr. 37 Weston st. Somers town
Mansell Wm. Henry, waggon office, *White Horse*, 29 Friday st
Manser & Ashley, escapement ma. 34 Rosoman st. Clerknwl
Manser Thos. cooper & hoop mfr. 43, & toy dlr. 44 Queen st. Ratclf
Mansfield Jas. & Sons, builders, 11 Lit. James st. Bedford row
Mansfield & Pearce, grocers, 17 Tonbridge st. New road
Mansfield Charles, *Blue Posts* P.H. 32 Old Bond st
Mansfield Charles, *Kentish Waggoner* P.H. 213 Kent st. Boro
Mansfield Charles, plumber, 92 Gray's inn lane
Mansfield George, builder, 12 Henry st. Gray's inn lane
Mansfield George, hairdresser & perfumer, 112 Jermyn st
Mansfield Henry, lighterman, 22 Lambeth High st
Mansfield John, globe coffee rooms, 33 Aldgate High st
Mansfield John, *Oliver's hotel*, 28 Bridge st. Westminster
Mansfield John, ropemaker, 202 Bethnal green road
Mansfield John, zinc worker, 9 Southampton st. Camberwell
Mansfield Mary (Mrs.), boot & shoe ma. 7 Bozier's ct. Tot. ct. rd
Mansfield Richd. Wm. lamp manufacturer, 159 Kingsland rd
Mansfield Robert, beer retailer, 8 Charles st. Coml. rd. ea
Mansfield Robt. grocer, 21 & 22 Southampton st. Camberwell
Mansfield Thomas, tinman & brazier, 5 Bermondsey st
Mansfield Thos. H. painter & paperhanger, 7 Sise lane
Mansfield Wm. pocketbook maker, see Peacock & Mansfield
Mansfield Wm. Christmas, solicitor, 20 John st. Bedford row
Mansfield Thos. tobacconist, 4 St. John's la. West Smithfield
Mansion House Justice Room; magistrates attend from 12
Manson Thos. mercht. & ins. agt. 3 Clement's la. Lombard st
Manson William, auctioneer, see Christie & Manson
Mansse Geo. mercht. & ins. brok. 2 Laurence Pountney lane
Mansse Lewis, merchant, 2 Laurence Pountney lane
Mant Fred. mathematl. & gen. rule makr. 4 Claremont pl. New rd
Mantell Gideon Algernon, surgeon, 19 Chester square
Mantell Lewis, ale & bottle mer. 54 Lit. George st. Hampstd. rd
Mantell Thomas Augustus, brewer, Oxford st. Bloomsbury
Mantica Charles, picture frame ma. 6 Coppice row, Clknwell
Mantle George, wheelwright, Pleasant row, Holloway road
Mantle James, *White Lion* P.H. 4 Green bank, Wapping
Mantle John, grocer, 15 Ship alley, Wellclose square
Mantle Thos. cabinet ma. 101 Devonshire st. Lisson grove
Mantle William, linendraper, see Stagg & Mantle
Manton John & Son, patent gunmakers to the royal family, & by appointment to Prince Albert, 6 Dover st. Piccadilly
Manton William & Co. merchants, 16 New Broad st. City
Manton Edwd. plumbr. & paintr. 33 & 37 New st. sq. Fetter la
Manton George, who. tea & coffee dlr. see Crippin & Manton
Manton Matthew, baker, 2 Elizabeth place, Balls pond road
Manuel William, baker, 1 Boston st. Dorset square
Manvell William, linen factor, see Spencer & Manvell
Manwaring Benjamin, stockbroker, 23 Tokenhouse yard
Manwaring Isaac, saw maker, 44 Rosoman st. Clerkenwell
Manwell George, pro. of pianoforte, 12 Upper Southwick st
Manzy Innocent, looking glass manfr. 35 Cable st. Wellclose sq
Maple & Cook, carpet warehouse, 145 & 147 Tottenham ct. rd.
Maples, Pearse, Stevens & Maples, solicitors, 6 Frederick's place, Old Jewry
Maples Richard, brazier, 32A, Spencer st. Clerkenwell
Maples Richd. Fletcher, grocer, 107 Brick la. Spitalfields
Maples Thomas, statuary & mason, 19A, Paddington green
Mapleson James, solicitor, 25 Essex st. Strand
Mapleson John, cupper to the Queen, 19B, Golden sq
Mapleston George, tailor, 6 Broadley ter. Blandford sq
Maplestone John, tin plate worker, 4 Villiers st. Strand
Mapleton James, leather dresser, see Aitken & Mapleton
Mapley John, cooper, 8 Houghton st. Clare mkt
Mapley Phœbe (Mrs.), staymaker, 6 Houghton st. Clare mkt.
Mapley Wm. glasscutter, 25 Lit. Bell alley, Coleman st
Mapp John, *Duke of Wellington* P.H. 1 Richmnd. ter. Pntvl
Mapp Thos. baker, 1 Brook st. West sq. Lambeth
Mapperley Walter, boot & shoe ma. 20 Meredith st. Clkenwl
Mappin Joseph, wholesale cutlery warehouse, 15 Fore st. City; manufactory, 32 Norfolk st. Sheffield
Mapple Mary A. (Mrs.) staymak. 18 Providence pl. Kentish tn
Mapplethorp John, tailor, 180 Drury lane
Maps Henry, tailor, 4 Cambridge rd. Mile end
Maquet Elizabeth (Mrs.), grocer, 64 Boston pl. Dorset sq
Marabello Maria (Mrs.), *Fleece* P.H. 27 Little Windmill st
March Jas. engraver & printer, 5 Gt. Charlotte st. Blackfriars
March Joseph, hat & capmaker, 74 King William st. City
March Joseph, tailor & draper, 5 India row, E. India rd. Poplar
March Mary (Mrs.), grocer, 162 High st. Camden town
March Saml. furn. ironmonger, 6 Pickett st. or 251 Strand
March Wm. hairdresser, 3 Thatched House rw. Lr. rd. Islgtn
Marcham James, oilman, 53 & 54 York st. City road
Marcham Joseph, ladies' bootmaker, 24 Curzon st. May fair
Marchand Isaac Henry, smith, 13 Folly, Dockhead
Marchand Lucien, manuf. & import. of gold & silver geneva watches, clocks, &c. 2 Red Lion st. Holborn
Marchand, Singer & Co. letter press, copper plate & lithographic printers, 1 Ingram ct. Fenchurch st
Marchant Charles, seal engraver, 15 St. John st. Clkenwell
Marchant Grace (Mrs.), carman, 13 Lit. Welbeck st. Cvndsh. sq
Marchant Henrietta (Miss), toy dealer, 8 Church st. Knsgtn
Marchant Henry, hairdresser, 4 Salmon lane, Limehouse
Marchant Hugh, china & glass wa. 98 Westbourne st. Pimlico
Marchant James, *Sutherland Arms* P.H. 7 Gt. May's bldgs
Marchant John, builder & carpenter, 3 Queen st. Oxford st
Marchant John, printseller & pic. dlr. 28 Frith st. Soho
Marchant John, stay manufacturer, 19 Aldgate High st
Marchant Jonathan, coal merchant, 41 Gerrard st. Soho
Marchant Joseph, baker, 31 Thayer st. Manchester sq
Marchant Richd. plumber & glazier, 19 St. John's la. Clrknwl
Marchant Robert, alton ale rooms, 351 Oxford st

Marchant Thomas, butcher, 12 Portsdown ter. Kilburn gate
Marchant Thos. conveyancer & registrar, Deptford High st
Marchant Wm. cabinet manuf. 23 Gun st. Spital sq
Marchant Wm. wax & tallow chandler, 253 Regent st
Marchant Wm. pawnbroker & jeweller, 438 Oxford st
Marchetti Vincent, figure maker, 1 Leather lane
Marchquick Isaac, chandler's shop, 49 Salisbury st. Lisson gr
Marcooly Wm. tailor, 11 Prospect pl. Old Brompton
Mardall John, wheelwright, 58 Back Church la. Whitechap
Marden Allen, grocer, 70 Lisson grove north, Marylebone, & 4 Pleasant place, King's cross
Marden Henry, *Fox & Goose* P.H. 118 Bermondsey st
Mardling Joel, baker, 100 Long alley, Finsbury
Mardin John, dining rooms, 156 Shadwell High st
Mardon & Prichard, solicitors, 99 Newgate st
Mardon Wm.&Co. pianofortemkrs. 15 Gt. Portland st. Oxford st
Mardon Edward, stationer, 11 Pleasant row, Holloway rd
Mardon Hen. carpntr & undertkr. 20 Devonsh. st. Queen's sq
Mardon John, bookseller & publisher, 7 Farringdon st
Mardon John, carpenter, 18 Lit. Ormond yard, Queen sq
Mare Chas. John, iron ship builder, see Ditchburn & Mare
Maréchal (Fréres), wine merchants, 46 Leicester sq
Mares Wm. & John, upholsterers, 21 Lr. Belgrave st. Belg. sq
Mares Chas. solicitor (at Rankeen, Ford & Co.), 4 South sq. Gra. inn
Mares Thos. basket mak. 23 Widegate st. Bishopgte. without
Marett, Arbouin & Co. (of Cognac), 21 Mark lane
Marett Charles, barrister, 3 Stone buildings, Lincoln's inn
Marfell Richard, linendraper, &c. Church st. Hackney
Margary Thomas G. solicitor & patent agent, Quality ct
Margate & London Steam Packet Office (Wm. P. Boddy, sec.), 33 Fish st. hill
Margerisons' & Co. calico printers, 43 Bread st. Cheapside, & at Manchester
Margerison Cath. (Mrs.), *Prince Wm. Henry* P.H. 230 Blk.f.rd
Margerum John, beer retailer, Clandon st. Walworth cmn
Margery Wm. coal dealer, 98 Bunhill row
Margetson Paul & Co. morocco manufs. New Weston st. & Market st. Bermondsey
Margetson Jas. leather dresser, Wild's rents, Long la. Bermd
Margetson John, stock, brace, &c. ma. see Welch & Margetson
Margetson Parker, surgeon, 3 Adelaide st. West Strand
Margetson Richd. straw hat ma. 165 Tottenham ctourt rd
Margetson Wm. umbrella maker, 47 Church st. Shoreditch
Margetts Edward, solicitor, see Millard & Margetts
Margetts Geo. painter, 12 Lit. Warner st. Clerkenwell
Margetts Richd. fire wood cutter, 12 East road, City rd
Margot David G. tobacconist, 49 Amwell st. Pentonville
Margrave Thos. mercht. City saw mills, Wenlock bas. City rd
Margrave Thos. Jones, merchant, &c. see Esdailes & Margrave
Marillier F. W. H. custom ho. & shipg. agt. 13 Cross lane, St. Mary-at-hill
Marine Insurance Company (Robert John Lodge, sec.), 27 Cornhill, see page 2033
Marine Society (Thos. King, sec.), 54½ Bishopsgate within
Mariners' & General Life Assurance Co. (Thaddeus Foley, F.R.A.S. resident sec.), 5 Arthur st. east, see page 2033
Marion Mary A. (Mrs.), furnishg. ironmngr. 48 Lisson grove n
Maris Andrew, commission mercht. see Maclean, Maris & Co
Maris Andrew, merchant, 45 Burton crescent, New road
Mark Lane Express weeklynewspaper, 24 Norfolk st. Strand
Mark Henry, linendraper, see Gowers & Mark
Mark Henry Richard, stockbroker, stock exchange
Mark John, baker, 1 Chapman place, Dover road
Mark William, fruit salesman, Spitalfields market
Marke Ann (Mrs.), bookseller, 38 Frederick pl. Hmpstd. rd
Markes Thomas, bookseller, &c. 25 Foley st. Portland pl
Markham Arthur Bayley, attorney, 10 Crown office rw. Temple
Markham Francis, milliner, 2 Stones end, Borough
Markham John, chemist & druggist, 11 Gower st. north, New rd
Markham John, plumber, 22 Diamond row, Stepney green
Markham Richard, builder, 9 Union row, Little Chelsea
Markham Richard Jas. tobaccnst. 3 Up. Church st. Chelsea
Markham Robert, shoemaker, 27 Homer st. Marylebone
Markham Thomas, straw hat maker, 13 Up. Marylebone st
Markham William, cowkeeper, 27 Valentine's pl. Blkfrs. rd
Markham Wm. job & postmaster, Chester mews north, Grvnr. pl
Markin Wm. cheesemonger & porkman, 52 Greek st. Soho
Markland Whalley, merchant, 2 Billiter square
Marklew Edward, *Ship tavern*, Talbot court, Eastcheap
Marks & Allen, slatemers. Llanbedrs. wf. Augustus st. Regts. pk
Marks John Isaac & Co. London carriage repository, 19 Langham place, & 107 Great Portland st
Marks Robert & Son, silversmiths & jewellers, 123 Oxford st
Marks Theodore & Simon, paper stain. 59 Princes st. Leic. sq
Marks Aaron, general trimming mak. 23 Silver st. Wood st
Marks Abraham, fruiterer, 201 Oxford st
Marks Alexander, tailor, 83 Chalton st. Somers town
Marks David, quill & pen manufacturer, 55 Houndsditch
Marks Edmund, architect & surveyor, 5 Seymour pl. New rd
Marks Ed. M. grocer & oilman, 3 Blenheim ter. St. John's wood
Marks Francis, furniture broker, 5 Eliza pl. Sadler's wells
Marks Henry, butcher, Clare market
Marks Hen. John, grocer & italian wa. 4 James pl. Hckny. rd
Marks Hyman, carriage broker, 34 London road, Southwark
Marks James, cheesemonger, 78 Brewer st. Somers town
Marks Jas. Hy. *China* coffee rooms, 31 Bishopsgate without
Marks John, coach broker, 54 Bell st. Edgware road
Marks John, plumber, 6 White horse yard, Drury lane
Marks John Lewis, publisher & printer, 91 Long la. Smithfield
Marks Joseph, china & glass dealer, 4 Nelson pl. Old Kent rd
Marks Joseph, rag merchant, 3 Parnham st. Limehouse
Marks Julia (Miss), pen & quill manufr. 265 Boro' High st
Marks Lewis, goldsmith & watchma. 59 Princes st. Leic. sq
Marks Mark, carver & gilder, 93 Blackman st. Borough
Marks Mark, hatter, 30 High st. St. Giles's
Marks Rich. *Lord High Admiral* P.H. 76 Vauxhall brdg. rd
Marks. Rt. *Barley Mow* P.H. 30 Blue Anchor alley, Bunhill rw
Marks Robert, auctioneer, &c. 123 Oxford st
Marks Sarah (Miss), stationer, 20 Charles st. Clarendon sq
Marks Sarah (Mrs.), grocer, 4 James place, Hackney road
Marks Simon, brushma. & sponge mer. 10 Middlesex st. Aldgate
Marks Solomon, quilldrssr. & penma. 8 St. Mark's st. Gdmn'sfds
Marks Solomons, plate glass factor, 55 Houndsditch
Markwell Benjamin, tailor, 7 Kenton st. Brunswick sq
Markwell Isaac, tailor & draper, 7 Pullin's row, Islington
Markwell James William, *Long's hotel*, 16 New Bond st. & *London hotel*, 43 & 44 Albemarle st
Markwell John Thos. booksell. 46 Gt. Titchfield st. Oxford st
Markwell Wm. Jas. wine merchant, *New England & North & South American & Colonial coffee house*, Threadneedle st
Markwick Alfred, surgeon, 19 Langham place, Portland pl
Markwick William, tailor & draper, 22 Mount st. Lambeth
Marlborough college (Albert Gill, sec.), 26 Suffolk st. Pall mall
Marlborough st. Police ct. 21 Gt. Marlboro' st.; hours 10 to 5
Marlborough Edwd. & Co. newspaper agents, 4 Ave Maria la
Marlborough Isabella (Miss), haberd. see Lord & Marlborough
Marler James B. beer retailer, Battersea fields
Marler Jsph. linendraper & haberd. 33 East st. Walworth rd
Marles William, tailor, 10 New Compton st. Soho
Marley Gabriel & Co. linenfactors, 24 to 26 Ironmonger lane
Marley & Clark, curriers & leathersellers, 76 Dean st. Soho
Marley Harcourt Master, silk broker, 36 Old Broad st
Marley James, tailor, 2 Manor pl. Grange rd. Bermondsey
Marley John, *Anchor & Castle* P.H. 167 Tooley st
Marley Miles, surgeon, 11 Cork st. Bond st
Marley Robert, bootmaker, 31 Charles st. Hampstead rd
Marley Thomas, *Clock house* P.H. 21 Castle st. Leicester sq
Marley Wm. Henry, cheesemonger, 87 Gt. Titchfield st
Marlow, Lancaster & Co. lindr. 38 Bridge ho. pl. Newingt. caus
Marlow Edward, cowkeeper, Canal road, Kingsland
Marlow John, baker, 107 Regent st. Lambeth
Marlow John, coal & potato dealer, 7 King st. Seven dials
Marlow Thomas, ironmonger, 63 King st. Seven dials
Marnas Benoit, tailor, 34 Frith st. Soho square
Marner Richard G. coach builder, see Laurie & Marner
Marner Henry, pork butcher, 3 Charles st. Hatton garden
Marnes John, gun maker, 31 Cumberland rw. Walworth rd
Marney John, looking glass manfr. 10 Newman st. Oxford st
Marnham Henry, corndealer, 46 Princess st. Edgware road
Marnham Wm. enameller, 51 Buttesland st. Hoxton New tn
Marnoch Henry, straw hat manufacturer, 102 Goswell st
Marnock Robert, landscape gardener, Inner circle, Regt's. pk
Marns William, rope manfr. 1 Fairfield place, Stepney
Marony John, painter & glazier, 15 Duke st. Tooley st
Marquis Fanny (Miss), booksr. &c. 2 Moreton ter. Kent. tn
Marr Christopher, working jeweller, 112 Wardour st. Soho
Marr David Leach, fruiterer, 25 Park terrace, Regent's park
Marr William, coal merchant, see Neal & Marr
Marr William, patentee & manufacturer of fire proof safes & boxes, the double security detectorlock, &c. 52 Cheapside
Marr Wm. watch hand maker, 6 Albemarle st. Clerkenwell
Marrable Fredk. architect, 1 Lancaster pl. Waterloo bridge
Marrable James, bookbinder, 21 Castle st. City road
Marratt John, optician & spectacle ma. 63 King Wm. st. City
Marriage Ann (Mrs.), stay mak. 23 Hereford pl. Coml. rd. ea
Marriner Joseph, carpet wareh. 9 City road, Finsbury sq
Marriott Hail & Henry, agts. & manch. warhm. 6 Lawrence la
Marriott Thomas & Son, worsted spinners, 11 Basing lane
Marriott A. (Mrs.), opt. trner. 38 New Montague st. Spitalfi
Marriott Benjn. watch & clock ma. 37 Hedge rw. High st. Islntn
Marriott Deborah (Mrs.), wardrobe dealer, 1 Drummond cres
Marriott Edward, watchma. 3 Brooksby st. Liverpool rd

Marriott Francis,cheesemonger&porkman,Church st.Hckney
Marriott George, *Feathers* P.H. 6 Gt. Chapel st. Westmstr
Marriott George E. butterman, &c. 15 Newgate market
Marriott Henry, stove, range, patent dial weighing machine, cooking apparatus & water closet manufacturer, 89 Fleet st. & 74 Old Broad st. City
MarriottHen.Raine,agt. to Manchester life offi.6Lawrence la
Marriott John, builder, 11 George st. Blackfriars road
Marriott John, *Swan* P.H. 52 Skinner st. Snowhill
Marriott Joseph, china dealer, 5 Hatton wall, Hatton garden
Marriott Joseph, oil & italian warehouse, 74 Gracechurch st
Marriott Robert, solicitor, 7 New inn & Colchester
Marriott Valentine Charles, whitesmith, 1 Drummond cres
Marriott Wm. grocer, 9 Seymour st. Euston square
Marriott Wm. hat manufacturer, 33 St. Andrew's rd. Boro'
Marriott Wm. silversmith, &c. 27 Fenchurch st
Marriott Wm. smith, 170 Southwark bridge road
Marriott Wm. tobacconist, 20 Little Charlotte st. Blkfrs. rd
Marriotts Thomas, *Crown* P.H. 36 High st. St. Giles's
Marris William, solicitor, see Hicks & Marris
Marrott William John, wireworker,23 King William st. City
Marrow Luke, bookbinder, 3 Cecil st. Strand
Marryat Joseph & Sons, merchants, 2 Laurence Pountney la
Marryatt Sophia (Miss), fruiterer, Spitalfields market
Mars Victorina (Mrs.), milliner, 33 Duke st. Manchester sq
Mars Wm.leather dres. & dyer,22 Grange walk, Bermondsey
Marschan Adolph. pro. of music, 35 Charlotte st. Portld. pl
Marsden & Shaw, stockbrokers, 1 Angel ct. Throgmorton st
Marsden Thos. & Son, who.druggists, 36 Queen st.Cheapside
Marsden Chas. ornaml. paper mkr. & oilman, Kingsland rd
Marsden George Wm. solicitor, 2 Cloak lane, Queen st. City
Marsden Mark, boot & shoe maker, 4 Lower st. Islington
Marsden Rufus, carpenter, 37 Gilbert st. Grosvenor square
MarsdenWm.cast,wrought iron, & steel mer.Hall of Commce
Marsden William, M.D. surgeon, 65 Lincoln's inn fields
Marsden Wm. Jas. lighterman, bridgho. George rw. Bermnds
Marsh & Edenborough, woolbroks. 200 Bishopsgate without
Marsh Edward & John, watch hand makers, & lancashire movement dealers, 61 Whiskin st. Clerkenwell
Marsh & Godden, haberdashers, 80 Goswell st
Marsh & Howell, surgeons, Stratford, Essex
Marsh Charles, hairdresser, 9 St. George's circus, Obelisk
Marsh Edward, bookseller, 84 Houndsditch
Marsh Frederick, ladies' boot & shoe maker, 148 Oxford st
Marsh George, boot & shoe maker, 1 Old Jewry
Marsh George, linendraper, 32 Carnaby st. Golden square
Marsh George, tailor, 5 Millman place, Bedford row
Marsh Harry, watchmaker, 20 Down st. Piccadilly
Marsh Henry, linendraper, 2 Portsdown ter. Kilburn gate
Marsh Henry Edmund, auctioneer, see Fuller & Marsh
Marsh James, lancashire movement dlr. 22 Tysoe st. Clknwl
Marsh James, army accoutremt. ma. 3BoxTree pl.Grange rd
Marsh John, optician, Balls pond road
Marsh John, poulterer, 11 Red Lion st. Whitechapel High st
Marsh John, sen. poultry & game salesman, Leadenhall mrkt
Marsh John, poultry salesmn. 12Ship tavn.pas. Leadnhll.mkt
Marsh Joseph, baker, 3 Holland place, Kensington
Marsh Joseph, boot & shoe maker, 10 High st. Portland twn
Marsh Joseph, secretary to *National Provident Institution*, 48 Gracechurch st
Marsh Mary (Mrs.), house agent, 46 Park st. Grosvenor sq
Marsh Nicholas, coffee rooms, 1½ Church st. Lisson grove
Marsh Pharoah, ropemaker, 75 Davies st. Berkeley square
Marsh Robert, attorney, Clarence chambers, 12 Haymarket
Marsh Robert, oilman, 6 Charles place, East st. Walworth
Marsh Thomas, cheesemonger, 4 Elwell place, Grange road
Marsh Thomas, grocer&chees. 17 Whitcomb st. Pall mall east
Marsh Thomas, saddler, &c. 1 Charlotte st. Portland place
Marsh Thomas, livery stables, see Hawkins & Marsh
Marsh Thomas, statuary, 20 Quickset row, New road
Marsh Thomas Coxhead, barrister, 2 Harcourt bdgs. Temple
Marsh Wm. baker, 10 Fore st. Limehouse
Marsh Wm. boot & shoe maker, 15 Kingsland pl. Kingsland rd
Marsh Wm. cabinet maker, 3 Edward st. Kingsland road
Marsh Wm. confectioner, 189 Kingsland road
Marsh Wm. grocer & cheesemonger, 28 Mason st. OldKent rd
Marsh Wm. saddler & harness maker, 65 West Smithfield
Marsh Wm. saddler, &c. 49 Long lane, West Smithfield
Marsh Wm. stockbroker, 2 Bank chambers, Lothbury
Marsh Wm. tailor, 3 Gray's inn terrace
Marsh Wm. Watson, bookseller, 24 Old Cavendish st
Marshal & Associate's Office (Exchequer), 5 Child's place, Temple bar; hours, term & sittings after, 11 to 3 & 6 to 8, vacation 11 to 2
Marshal & Clerk at Nisi Prius, Judges' chambers, Serjeants' inn, Chancery lane; hours of business, 11 to 2 & 6 to 8

Marshall Chapman & Co. who. grocers, 179 Upper Thames st
Marshall CharlesHen.&Co. teadealers,52H.KingWm.st.City
Marshall & Dove, tallow melters, stearine manufacturers, & wax & tallow chandlers, 181 High Holborn
Marshall & Edridge, ship & insur. brokers, 34 Fenchurch st
Marshall Frederick & Co. tea dealers, 145 Holborn bars
Marshall, Hutchison & Co. ship & insurance brokers, 1 New City chambers, Bishopsgate within, & Baltic coffee house
Marshall John & Co. general emigration & passenger office, 26 Birchin lane, Cornhill; & at Southampton
Marshall John & Co. ship & insurance brokers & general agents, 26 Birchin lane, Cornhill; & at Southampton
Marshall John & Co. teadealers, 12 Southampton st. Strand
Marshall John & Son, provision agents, Hay's whf. Tooley st
Marshall & Stinton, silk mercers, 11 Vere st. &19 Henrietta st. Cavendish square
Marshall Thos. & Son. crape & bandanna wareh. 15 Cheapside
Marshall William & Co. export ironmongers, 1 Princes st. Commercial road, Lambeth
Marshall William & Co. globe tea warehouse, 20 Strand
Marshall Alex.carv.gild.&printsel.2 Middle rw.Holborn bars
Marshall Alex. window glass cutter, 49 Broad st. Bloomsby
Marshall Alfred, tobacconist, 28 Penton row, Walworth rd
Marshall Ambrose, cattle salesman, see Farrin & Marshall
Marshall B. coppr. plate prntr.2 Meeting ho.ct. Mile'sla.City
Marshall Benjamin, tinman, 22 Marylebone st. Piccadilly
Marshall Charles, artist, 52 Gt. Marlborough st
Marshall Charles, coffee rooms, 17 Catherine st. Strand
Marshall Charles, boot & shoe maker, 208 Oxford st
Marshall Charles fishmonger, 1 Albany pl. Kentish town
Marshall Charles, veterinary surgeon, 76 Church la. Whitech
Marshall Chas. Edwd. chemist, &c. 6 Bedford st. Mile end rd
Marshall Chas. Hen. auctioneer, &c. 18 Duke st. Grosvenr.sq
Marshall Chas. J. ale & porter merchant, 1 Bermondsey ter
Marshall Charles Jeremiah, wine & ale mer. 14 Mark lane
Marshall David, dairyman, 30 Duke st. Grosvenor square; & 24 North st. Manchester square
Marshall David, tailor, 9 Old Boswell court, Strand
Marshall Edmund Smith, goldbeater, 31 John st. Fitzroy sq
Marshall Edward, pewterer, 41 Clifton st. Finsbury
Marshall Edward, jun. working jeweller, Mare st. Hackney
Marshall Edwd.Oliver, coal sack m.&coal.dlr. 5Up.Thames st
Marshall Edward Thomas, hot presser, 6 Wilson st. Finsbury
Marshall Ellen (Miss), hosier, see Parsons & Marshall
Marshall Enoch, plumber & glazier, 32 Lower st. Islington
Marshall Frederick, grocer, 7 Well's row, Upper st. Islington
Marshall Fredk.wine&spirit mercht.seeJohnstone&Marshall
Marshall Geo. architect, 45 Connaught terrace
Marshall Geo. boot & shoe maker, 22 City road, Finsbury
Marshall Geo. bricklayer, 11 Charles st. Clarendon sq
Marshall Geo. coal factor & ship owner, 3 Cross lane, Saint Mary at hill
Marshall Geo. dairyman, 53 Amelia st. Walworth road
Marshall Geo. leather seller, 2 Charles st. Hampstead road
Marshall Geo. provision dealer, 76 Aldgate High st
Marshall Geo. timber mercht. Pageant, 119 Rotherhithe st
Marshall Geo. Lisle, tobacconist, 55 Marchmont st. Brunsw.sq
Marshall Geo. Jas. *Falcon tavern*, Church st. Stk. Newngtn
Marshall Henry, tailor&draper, 12Red Lion pass. RedLion sq
Marshall Henry, tripe dresser, 9 Osborne st. Whitechapel
Marshall Henry Pightling, solicitor, see Clutton, Waller&Co
Marshall Jacob, smith&engineer, 34 Salisbury st. Bermndsy
Marshall James, baker, 14 Hungerford st. Strand
Marshall James, barrister, 27 Southampton bldgs. Chanc. la
Marshall James, boot&shoema. 18 Charles st. Hampstead rd
Marshall James, builder, Rose cottage, Kingsland basin
Marshall James, porkbutcher, 2 King's Arms pl. Com.rd.east
Marshall James, red potter, 71 Princes st. Lambeth
Marshall James, whalebone manuf. 61 Lr. Whitecross st
Marshall Jane (Mrs.), grocer, 72 Brewer st. Somers town
Marshall Jane (Mrs.), grocer, 47 Kennington st. Walworth
Marshall John, baker, 177 Waterloo road, Lambeth
Marshall John, boiler maker, 2 Colchester st Whitechapel
Marshall John, bootmaker, 22 Seething lane, Tower st
Marshall John, bricklayer & slater, 16 Howland st. Fitzroy sq
Marshall John, cheesemonger, 37 Cannon st. & 37 Fish st. hill; & ham & beef dealer, 21 Fish street hill
Marshall John, cheesemonger, 97 Whitechapel High st.; & 105 Whitechapel road
Marshall John, chemist & druggist, 114 Lambeth walk
Marshall John, cowkeeper, 4 Market st. Jermyn st
Marshall John, dantzic mercht. 11 St. Helen's pl. Bishopsgt
Marshall John, *Devonport Arms* P.H. Devnpt. mews, Oxfd. ter
Marshall John, drysalter, 15 Wormwood st. Bishopsgate
Marshall John, fishmonger, Clare market, Drury lane
Marshall John, ham & tongue dealer, 21 Fish st. hill

Marshall John, law stationer, 5 Cook's court, Lincoln's inn
Marshall John, newsvender, 22 High st. St. Giles's
Marshall John, plumber, &c. 13 Cumberland st. Middx. hosp
Marshall John, seal engraver, 65 Banner st. St. Luke's
Marshall John, shippg. & comml. arbitrator, 26 Birchin la
Marshall John, smith & farr. 9 Whf. Nth side, Paddingt. basin
Marshall John, solicitor, see Coe & Marshall
Marshall John, solicitor, 22 Portugal st. Lincoln's inn
Marshall John, staymaker, 10 Baker's row, Walworth road
Marshall John, staymaker, 6 Mount place, Walworth road
Marshall John, surgeon, 8 Crescent place, Hampstead road
Marshall John, upholsterer to the Queen, 31 Soho square
Marshall John H. *Crown & Anchor* P.H. 71 Drumnd. st. Eust. sq
Marshall John H. solicitor, 54 St. John st. road
Marshall Joseph, cheesemonger, 23 Church st. Shoreditch
Marshall Joseph, engravr. & prntr. 11 Henry st. ea. Avenue rd
Marshall Kezia (Mrs.), trunk mak. 5 Duke st. Manchester sq
Marshall Leonard, cabinet mak. 3 James st. Old st. St. Luke's
Marshall Mary Ann (Mrs.), *Cock* P.H. 20 Love la. Eastchp
Marshall Matthew, lighterman, 5 Millpond row, Bermondsey
Marshall Mattw. portable desk ma. 2 Richmond bldgs. Soho
Marshall Matthias, baker, 4 Dean st. Finsbury sq
Marshall Noah, bricklayer, 7 Lit. Guilford st. Brunswk. sq
Marshall Noah, painter & glazier, 5 Cumberland rw. King's cr
Marshall Peter, surgeon & accoucheur, 53 Greek st. Soho
Marshall Philip, engra. & enameller, 52 Rupert st. Haymkt
Marshall Richd. bricklayer, 3 Glo'ster st. Commercial rd. ea
Marshall Richd. beer retailer, Ferry road West, Poplar
Marshall Richard, surgeon, 27 Gt. Charlotte st. Blackfrs. rd
Marshall Robert, baker, 14 Riley st. Chelsea
Marshall Robert, greengrocer, 3 Cleveland st. Fitzroy sq
Marshall Robert, stone mason, New Cross road, Deptford
Marshall Robert, wood carver, &c. 16 Gower pl. Euston sq
Marshall Samuel, shawl, bandanna, &c. warho. 15 Cheapside
Marshall Stephen, russia broker, *Baltic* coffee house
Marshall Susanh. (Mrs.), milliner, 13A, Chester ter. Eaton sq
Marshall Thos. cooper, 8½ Grange road, Bermondsey
Marshall Thos. *D. of Wirtemberg* P.H. 44 Hatfield st. Blkf
Marshall Thos. hosier & shirt maker, 80 Quadrant, Regent st
Marshall Thos. (sec. of *Edin. Life As. Co.*), 11 King Wm. st. City
Marshall Thos. tailor, 6 Wells st. St. James's
Marshall Thos. tallow chandler & oilman, 81 Chancery lane
Marshall Thos. Woolley, boot & shoe maker, 207 Oxford st
Marshall Wm. accountant, 1 Princes st. Stamford st
Marshall Wm. auctioneer, 23 Moorgate st. City
Marshall Wm. cheesemonger, 217 Bethnal green road
Marshall Wm. boot & shoe maker, 23 Wardour st. Soho
Marshall Wm. cheesemonger, 4 Theberton st. Islington
Marshall Wm. dairyman, 6 Copenhagen st. Pentonville
Marshall Wm. *Finsbury* coffee rooms, 1 Short st. Finsbury
Marshall Wm. irish linen mer. 19 Gt. Pulteney st. Golden sq
Marshall Wm. milliner, 15 Grenada ter. Commercial rd. east
Marshall Wm. pianoforte string maker, 19 Gt. Pulteney st
Marshall Wm. potato dealer, 265 Bethnal green road
Marshall Wm. steam engine boiler manufacturer, 9 Sidney st. Mile end gate; & 2 Oxford st. Mile end gate
Marshall Wm. stockbroker, see Mullens & Marshall
Marshall Wm. tailor, see Eddells & Marshall
Marshall Wm. tailor, 6 Camberwell New road
Marshall Wm. tailor & trousers maker, 134 Regent st
Marshall Wm. watch engraver, 22 Bartholomew ter. City rd
Marshall Wm. watch maker, 11 Green ter. New river head
Marshall Wm. Calder, sculptr. A.R.S.A. 6 Up. Belgravepl. Pmlc
Marshall Wm. Forbes, who. grocer & col. agt. 20 Fenchurch st
Marshall Wm. Henry, butcher, 23 Marylebone lane
Marshall Wm. Henry, glover, &c. 1 Parkside, Knightsbridge
Marshall Wm. James, watch maker, 96 Edgware road
Marshall Wm. R. account. & school. 5 Alfredrow, Spard. Bermsy
Marshall Wm. R. jun. printer, 5 Alfred row, Spa rd. Bermsy
Marshall Wm. W. stationer & bookseller, 21 Edgware road
Marshalsea & Palace Courts, Palace place, Great Scotland yard; hours, Fridays 9½
Marshalsea & Palace Court Off. 15 Chancery la.; hrs. 10 to 5
Marsham Charles, beer retailer, 1 Porter's row, Holloway
Marshman Joshua Ryland, barrister, 1 Inner Temple lane
Marsland Geo. engineer, 98 Gt. Guildford st. Southwark
Marsland John, builder, 1 Seymour pl. York st. Walworth rd
Marsom Thos. whip mak. & horse dealer, 1 South pl. Finsbry
Marson Henry, coach & harn. plater, 13 West st. Seven dia
Marson John, fishmonger, 2 Charles st. Middlesex hospital
Marston Joseph Wallis & Co. surgeons, 204 Tooley st. Boro'
Marston James, baker, 13 Union st. Southwark
Marston John, surgeon, 6 Devonshire st. Portland place
Marston John, watch & clock maker, 7 Green st. Leicester sq
Marston Samuel, cooper, 26 Arlington st. Sadler's wells
Marston Thomas, baker, 48 Strutton ground, Westminster
Marston Thomas, cooper & basket mak. 87 Tottenham ct. rd
Marston Thomas, solicitor, 5 Ampthill sq. Hampstead rd
Marston William, baker, 38 Lambeth Lower marsh
Mart Samuel, orange merchant & fruiterer to the Queen & Queen Adelaide, & manufacturer of genuine orange wine, 130 Oxford st. corner of Holles st
Martell & Co. (of Cognac), brandy merchants, 14 Mincing lane, & 72 Great Tower st
Martell Charles, solicitor, 5 Dyers buildings, Holborn
Martelli Charles Hen. Ansley, barrister, 9 Serle st. Linc. inn
Marten, Thomas & Hollams, solicitors, 31 & 35 Coml. sale rms
Marten & Heseltine, stock & share brokers, 9 Finch lane, Cornhill, & Stock Exchange
Marten Denis, furniture broker, 1 Chalton st. Somers town
Marten Geo. clk. to Fellowship Porters' hall, 17 St. Mary-at-hill
Marten George, solicitor, see Marten, Thomas & Hollams
Marten William, watch manufacturer, 20 Bunhill row
Martenhof John, scum boiler, 8 Finch st. Mile end New town
Martens Peter, cabinet maker, 8 Nassau st. Middlesex hospl
Marter Louisa (Miss), ladies' school, Priory, Wandsworth rd
Marter Richard, turner, 38 Cowper st. City road
Marter Samuel, undertaker, 1 Queen st. Pitfield st. Hoxton
Marter William Ingram, solicitor, 5 Furnival's inn
Marthews Isabella (Mrs.), fruiterer, 2 Ambrose pl. Chelsea
Martill Mary (Mrs.), *Bull's Head* P.H. 16 Peter st. Gt. Saffronhl
Martin Casimir & Co. music publishers & importers of the chirogymnast, patentees & sole manufrs. 87 Piccadilly
Martin James & Co. warehousemen, 12 Wood st. Cheapside
Martin Edward & Co. provision agents, 256 Tooley st
Martin & Gallop, iron founders & Redmund's patent hinge manufacturers, 68 Charles st. City road
Martin & Harrison, sheep salesmen, 17 West Smithfield
Martin James & Son, paper hanging manufacturers, 1 Coburg ter. Horseferry road, & 2 Romney st. Westminster
Martin John & Henry, tailors, &c. 186 Sloane street
Martin & Newport, surgeons, 6 Radnor place, Hyde park
Martin, Nottingham & Co. shawl warehsmn. 10 Aldermanbury
Martin Robert & Hugh, tailors, 21 Crown row, Mile end rd
Martin, Stones & Martins, bankers, 68 Lombard st
Martin Thomas & Co. birmingham & sheffield warehousemen, 63 Gracechurch st. & 78 Cornhill
Martin Thomas & Co. printing ink ma. 30 Queen st. Cheapside
Martin Alexander, agent, 106 Newgate st. City
Martin Alfred, grocer, 3 Courthope ter. Bermondsey New rd
Martin Amelia (Mrs.), tobacconist, 30 Gt. Suffolk st. Boro'
Martin Andrew, commsn. mer. 4 New London st. Crutched frs
Martin Ann (Mrs.), saddler, 7 Cumberland row, Battle bdg
Martin Arthur, poulterer & game dealer, 38 Kensington High st. & 5 Lower Eaton st. Pimlico
Martin Benjamin, butcher, 4 Brooke's market, Holborn
Martin Charles, baker, 86 Drury lane
Martin Charles, butcher, 12 King's rd. St. Pancras
Martin Charles, butcher, Treport place, Wandsworth road
Martin Charles, commission agent, &c. see Blogg & Martin
Martin Charles, gold, &c. caster, 21 Gt. Mitchell st. St. Luke's
Martin Charles, solicitor, 17 Salisbury square, Fleet st
Martin Charles, surgeon, Neckinger house, Bermondsey
Martin Chas. Hen. printslr. publisher, &c. 250 Blackfriars rd
Martin Chas. P. glazier, plumber, &c. 37 Brewer st. Gldn. sq
Martin Charlotte (Miss), dressma. 13 Gresse st. Tot. ct. rd
Martin Daniel, tailor, 178 High Holborn
Martin David, orange merchant, 5 East st. Spitalfields
Martin David, silk manufacturer, 6 Prince's st. Spitalfields
Martin David Watson, bookbndr. 1 Prujean sq. Old Bailey
Martin Edward, cabinetmaker, 28 Michael's pl. Brompton
Martin Eli, goldbeater, 14 Fair st. Horselydown
Martin Eliza (Mrs.), book & print seller, 47 Gt. Queen st
Martin Eustace Meredith, spcl. pleader, 10 Crown office row
Martin Francis Offley, barrister, 3 Stone buildings, Linc. inn
Martin Fredk. cabinet ma. uphlstr. & undrtkr. Stratford brdwy
Martin Fredk. gold & silver laceman, 1 Cripplegate buildgs
Martin Fredk. S. timber merchant, Stratford broadway
Martin Fredk. Wm. oil & colorman, 6 Fredrk. pl. Hampstd. rd
Martin Geo. bricklayer, 76 Ropemakers fields, Limehouse
Martin Geo. City greenyard, 35¾ Whitecross st. Cripplegate
Martin Geo. coffeerooms, 3 Bridge st. Lambeth
Martin Geo. copperplate printer, 36 Friday st. City
Martin Geo. french clog maker, 44 Holywell la. Shoreditch
Martin Geo. fruiterer, 5 Salcombe place, Regent's park
Martin Geo. clerk to Fan Makers' Company, City Solicitor's office, Guildhall
Martin Geo. *Sun & Apple Tree* P.H. 32 White Hart st. Drury la
Martin Geo. surveyor, 24 Connaught terrace
Martin Geo. woollen draper, 45 King's road east, Chelsea
Martin Geo. Frederic, fur mnfr. 14 Marchmont st. Burton cr
Martin Geo. Hen. oilman & tallow chandlr. 84 & 85 Cowcross st

Martin Harriet (Miss), milliner, 1 York place, Islington
Martin Henry, baker, 16 John st. north, Marylebone
Martin Henry, butcher, 83 London road, Southwark
Martin Henry, cabinet maker, 21 Lit. Guilford st. Russell sq
Martin Henry, linendraper, 101 Crawford st. Portman sq
Martin Henry Daniel, surveyor, 49 Leadenhall st
Martin Henry Parker, academy, 63 Poplar High st
Martin Hen. Robt. snuff&cigar manfs. 107 Bishopsgate within
Martin Henry Witte, printer, 31 Bartlett's buildings, & 19 Cursitor st. Chancery lane
Martin Isaac, confectioner, 82 Church lane, Whitechapel
Martin Jacob, who. & ret. confectioner, 85 Brick la. Spitlfids
Martin James, bootmaker, 32 Clifton st. Finsbury
Martin James, builder, 17 Back st. Horselydown
Martin James, china dealer & undertaker, 31 Eyre st. hill
Martin James, fruit salesman, Borough market
Martin James, hosier, 11 Mount st. Berkeley square
Martin James, manufacturer of silks, shawls, bandannas, gimps, & fringes, 12 Wood st. Cheapside
Martin James, manufacturer & warehouseman, 38 Gutter la
Martin James, papermaker, 30 Queen st. Cheapside
Martin James, stationer & bookseller, 43 Lisson grove north
Martin James, umbrella mak. 2 Tabernacle walk, Finsbury
Martin James, watch case mak. 48 Wynyatt st. Goswell rd
Martin James, who. slopsel. & warehouseman, 37 Houndsditch
Martin James Ranald, surgeon, 71A, Grosvenor st. Bond st
Martin Jane (Mrs.), coffee rooms, 8 Gt. Russell st. Cov. grdn
Martin Jane (Mrs.), dressmaker, 23 Devereux ct. Strand
Martin John, attorney, 2 New square, Lincoln's inn
Martin John, boot & shoemaker, 49 Pall mall
Martin John, butcher, 120 Upper st. Islington
Martin John, carpenter & underta. 24 Carburton st. Fitzroy sq
Martin John, cheesemonger, 44 High st. Marylebone
Martin John, china clay manufacturer, 12 Clement's lane, Lombard st.; E. S. Polkinghorne & Co. agents
Martin John, corndealer & seedsman, 50 & 51 Minories
Martin John, dairyman, 4 Drake st. Red Lion square
Martin John, farrier, 22 Park st. Kennington cross
Martin John, ham dealer, 56 Edgware road, Marylebone, & 8 Upper King st. Bloomsbury
Martin John, linendraper, see Matthews & Martin
Martin John, *Old Globe* P.H. Mile end road
Martin John, pump maker, 1 Sydney ter. Marlboro' rd Chlsea
Martin John, saddler, 70 Tothill st. Westminster
Martin John, stationer, 9 Chapel st. New road
Martin John, surgeon, 1 Wilmington square
Martin John, tailor, 95 Jermyn st. St. James's
Martin John, tailor, 5 Upper Baker st. Regent's park
Martin John, tailor, 1 York st. Hans place, Chelsea
Martin John, upholsterer, 45 Southampton row, Russell sq
Martin John Benson, lighterman, 26 Thomas st. Horslydown
Martin John Burton, tobacconist, 36 Blackfriars road
Martin John Charles, watchmaker, 20 New st. Bishopsgate
Martin John K. L. artist, 30 Allsop terrace, New rd. Mryleb
Martin John S. carpenter, &c. 16 White Hart st. Low Kngtn. la
Martin John Waller, cheesemonger, 76 Tottenham court rd
Martin Joseph, baker, 88 Mary st. New road, Regent's park
Martin Joseph, beer retailer, 104 Fore st. Limehouse
Martin Joseph, pork butcher, 29 Somerset st. Aldgate
Martin Joseph Job, *Monster* P.H. St. George's row, Pimlico
Martin Joseph Thos. fruiterer, 62 Rahere st. Goswell road
Martin Marcus, barrister, 2 New square, Lincoln's inn, & 40 Bedford place, Russell square
Martin Margaret (Miss), juvenile dressma. 5 Up. Baker st
Martin Martha (Miss), *Martha's* chop ho. 11 Ball al. Lomb. st
Martin Mary (Miss), seminary, Queen's Head la. Islington
Martin Mary (Mrs.), *Acorn* P.H. Lr. Trinity st. Rotherhithe
Martin Mary (Mrs.), *Black Swan* P.H. 7 Ryder's court, Little Newport st
Martin Mary (Mrs.), silk manftr. 29 Fore st. Spitalfields
Martin Mary Ann (Mrs.), milliner, 11 Mount st. Berkeley sq
Martin Matthew, bootmaker, 23 Gt. College st. Westminster
Martin (Misses), milliners, 27 Northumberland st. New road
Martin Nathl. attorney, Vintners' hall, 68½ Up. Thames st
Martin Peter William, stationer, 8 Broadway, Westminster
Martin Richard, blacking manufacturer, see Day & Martin
Martin Richard, bookbinder, 7 Princes st. Barbican
Martin Richard, carpenter, 5 China walk, Lambeth
Martin Richard, corkcutter, 20 Swan st. Minories
Martin Richard, grocer, Chapel place, Balls pond road
Martin Richard, plumber&paintr. 13 Up. Charlton st. Fitzroy sq
Martin Richard Joseph, tobacconist, 7 Princes st. Barbican
Martin Richard Joseph, wholesale sheffield plate & cutlery warehouse, 4 Palsgrave place, Strand
Martin Robert, map & plan draughtsman, lithographic & zincographic printer, 8 Great Newport st. Long acre
Martin Robert, fruiterer, Olive terrace, Camberwell New rd
Martin Robert, fruiterer, 6 Victoria pl. Queen's rd. Dalston
Martin Robert, grocer, &c. Mare st. Hackney
Martin Robt. Buchanan, *Dover Castle* P.H. 7 Broadwy. Dptfrd
Martin Robert Thomas, artist, 43 Old Compton st. Soho
Martin Rubens, grocer & chsmngr. 1 Pomeroy st. Old Knt. rd
Martin Samuel, bootmaker, 6 Great Tower street
Martin Sam. *Cock & Castle* P.H. Robinson's row, Kingsland
Martin Samuel, queen's counsel, 1 Essex court, Temple
Martin Samuel, *Victoria* coffee rooms, 169 Goswell st
Martin Sarah (Mrs.), lodginghouse, 7 Lit. Titchfield st. Portld. pl
Martin Thomas, beast salesman, 17 West Smithfield
Martin Thomas, bookbinder, 14 Fetter lane, Fleet street
Martin Thomas, bootmaker, 10 Blenheim st. Oxford st
Martin Thomas, carpenter, 55 Chapel st. Somers town
Martin Thomas, colored paper ma. 59 & 60 Old st. St. Luke's
Martin Thomas, furn. undertaker, 1 Heartley pl. Old Kent rd
Martin Thomas, wholesale grocer, 44 Eastcheap
Martin Thomas, glass cutter, 45 Rawstorne st. Goswell rd
Martin Thomas, music instrument ma. 22 London st. Fitz. sq
Martin Thomas, pawnbroker, 79 Snowhill & 64 Tooley st
Martin Thomas, pork butcher, 245 Strand
Martin Thomas, solicitor, see Kine & Martin
Martin Thomas, stone merchant, see Scoles & Martin
Martin Thos. *Whittington & Cat* P.H. 35 Whitechpl. High st
Martin Watkin Wm. coal merchant, 1 Baker st. Portman sq
Martin Wm. academy, 76 Three Colt st. Limehouse
Martin Wm. baker, 86 Chancery lane
Martin William, coal merchant, 5 Great Chapel st. Soho
Martin Wm. coal mer. red lion wharf, Canal rd. Kingsland rd
Martin Wm. coffee rooms, 7 Pleasant row, Holloway road
Martin Wm. coffee rooms, 83 Princes road, Lambeth
Martin Wm. *Crown* P.H. Belvedere road, Lambeth
Martin Wm. eating house, 10 Chapel st. St. George's east
Martin Wm. fruiterer, 21 Grosvenor row, Pimlico
Martin Wm. fruiterer, 283 Poplar High st
Martin Wm. grocer, 25 George st. Portland place
Martin Wm. grocer, 10 Skinner st. Somers town
Martin Wm. iron & brass bedstead manfr. stove grate & kitchen range maker, furn. ironmonger, locksmith & bell-hanger, & smith in general, 81 Old st
Martin Wm. mill board maker, 30 Queen st. Cheapside
Martin Wm. oil & colorman, 21 Victoria road, Pimlico
Martin Wm. oilman & cheesemonger, see Miles & Martin
Martin Wm. *Paul's Head* P.H. 104 Paul street, Finsbury
Martin Wm. *Prince Regent* P.H. 4 Walbrook rw. east rd. Hxtn
Martin Wm. *Old Ship tavern*, 6 & 7 Chichester rents
Martin Wm. tailor & draper, 10 Myddelton st. Spafields
Martin Wm. tobacconist, 6 Union place, New road
Martin Wm. watch & clock maker, 50 King st. Westminster
Martin Wm. *World's End* P.H. Ocean row, High st. Stepney
Martin Wm. Beavan, wine merchant, 14 Mark lane, City
Martin Wm. Henry, whip maker, 14 Commercial pl. City rd
Martin Wm. John, grocer, &c. 24 Adam's row, Hampstead rd
Martin Wm. John, grocer, 147 Edgware rd. Marylebone
Martin Wm. Smith, *Bell & Dragon* P.H. 33 Worship st. Nrtn. Fol
Martin Wm. Wilcox, who. cheesemonger, 201 Up. Thames st
Martindale Benjamin, attorney, 19 Cecil st. Strand
Martindale John Wm. bricklayer, 4 New Church st. west, Edg. rd
Martindale Sam. Montagu, barrister, 10 Old sq. Lincoln's inn
Martindale Sophia (Mrs.), boarding house, 75A, Lit. Britain
Martineau Dav. & Sons, sugar refi. Christian st. St. Geo. east
Martineau Peter & Son, sugar refi. 3 Goulstone st. Whitechpl
Martineau Hubert, solicitor, 2 Raymond bldgs. Gray's inn
Martinelli Alfred, barometer mak. 18 Vauxhall st. Lambeth
Martinelli Louis, coach maker, 3 Albany st. Regent's park
Martinez, Gassiot & Co. wine merchants, 77 Mark lane
Martinez Sabastian Gonzalez, wine merchant, 77 Mark lane, & 1 Cumberland terrace, Regent's park
Martini Chas. brandy mer. 14 Mincing la. & 72 Gt. Tower st
Martino Sarah (Mrs.), grocer, 49 Shoe lane, Fleet st
Martins Charles, butcher, 4 Lower Islington terrace
Martins John, cattle salesman, 17 West Smithfield
Martins Thos. ironmonger, 1 Providence pl. York rd. Lmbth
Martinson Wm. wheelwright & stables, 4 Davies st. Berkeley sq
Martius Ernst, tailor, 7 Hanover st. Hanover sq
Martlin Elizabeth (Mrs.), *George* P.H. 1 Little Prescot st
Martorelli Ramon, confectioner, 31 Up. Seymour st. Portmn. sq
Martyn Edward & Hen. woollen drapers, 24 Aldgate High st
Martyn Thos. & Robt. linendrapers, 210 & 212 Whitechapel rd
Martyn Patrick, surgeon, 18 Spring gardens, Charing cross
Martyn William, solicitor, see Hitchcock & Martyn
Martyn William, surgeon, 14 Brompton row
Martyr Charles, who. statr. see Morgan, Martyr, George & Co
Martyr Robt. Smirk, surveyor, 23 Broomfields, Deptford
Martyr Thomas, builder, Albion place, London wall

Marvin Clement, butcher, 27 Farringdon market
Marvin John, butcher, 6 Hope terrace, Notting hill
Marvin Thomas, butcher, 1 Duke st. Manchester square
Marvin Thomas, butcher, 22 Farringdon market
Marvy Fontaine Madame, dressmk. 35 South Audley st
Marvy Jean Augustin, lapidary, 19 Queen st. Golden square
Marwick William, *Red Lion* P.H. 23 Crown court, Pallmall
Marx George, merchant, see Gowan & Marx
Marx Geo. moselle mer. 7 Hartst. Markla.&54 Crutched friars
Marylebone Alms Houses, 77 & 78 St. John's wood terrace
Marylebone Infirmary (Rt. Boyd, M.D. res. physician), N. rd
Marylebone Land & Assessed Tax Office, 160 Oxford st
Marylebone Literary & Scientific Institution (James Bingley, sec.), 17 Edwards st. Portman sq
Marylebone Loyal & Constitutional Association (John Greenwood, secretary), 53 Wigmore st. Cavendish square
Marylebone & Paddington Temperance Hall & Mechanics' Inst. (Daniel Graves, sec.) 65 Gt. Carlislest. Portman markt
Marylebone Police Court, 86 High st. Marylebone, 10 to 5
Maryon Henry, *King's Arms* P.H. Folly, Dockhead
Maryon John, carman, 6 Heneage st. Whitechapel
Maryon John, tailor, 47 Tottenham court road
Maryon Robert, butcher, 93 Old Gravel lane, Wapping
Marzetti John Geo. ship&ins.agt. 9 Cooper's row, Crutchedfrs
Marzetti John Geo. wine mer. 9 Cooper's row, Crutchedfriars
Mascall Francis, jun. special pleader, 7 New sq. Linc. inn
Mase Charles F. dyer, 15 St. George's place, Camberwell
Masey Edward, brass&cockfounder, 3 New st. Horselydown
Masey Hannah (Mrs.), medicl. bottl. wa. 5 Porter st. Nwpt. mkt
Mash Alice (Mrs.), potato dealer, 147 Goswell st
Mash Charles, fruiterer & potato dealer, 288 Oxford st
Mash Elizabeth (Miss), dressmak. 18 Marchmont st. Bnswk. sq
Mash George, potato warehouse, 264 Oxford st
Mash George Wm. potato dealer, 25 Exmouth st. Clerknwll
Mash James, fruiterer, 174 Hoxton Old town
Mash James, potato dealer, 5 Oxford place, Hackney road
Mash Mary Anne (Miss), pastrycook, 117 Fleet st
Mash Thomas, furniture dealer, 102 & 103 Wardour st. Soho
Mash Wm. cowkeeper, 3 Cross st. Westmoreland pl. City rd
Mash Wm. fruiterer, &c. 161 Aldersgate st
Mash Wm. jun. potato mercht. 45 Tottenham st. Fitzroy sq
Mash Wm. sen. potato dealer, 26 Tottenham court road
Masham John, tallow chandler, 12 North pl. Kingsland rd
Mashman William, carpenter, 73 Charlotte st. Portland pl
Maskall Robert Samuel, plasterer, 20 Union pl. Lambeth rd
Maskell George, tailor, 3 Great College st. Westminster
Maskell Henry, butcher, 74 Margaret st. Hackney fields
Maskell John, solicitor, 1 Bank chambers, Lothbury
Maskell Moses, builder, 2 Glo'ster pl. west, Old Brompton
Maskell Osmond, cheesemonger, 29 Upper Marylebone st
Maskell Rd. haberdasher & hosier, 1 Gt. College st. Westmr
Maskell Wm. tailor, 7 Lr. Chapman st. St. George's ea
Maskey James, coffee rooms, 40 Farringdon market
Maskey Wm. scale & mill maker, 125 Golden lane
Masland Wm. pawnbrok. 3 & 4 Melina bdgs. Westminster rd
Maslen John, farrier, Crispin st. Spitalfields
Maslen Joseph, dairyman, 41 Gilbert st. Oxford st
Maslen Stephen, cabinet maker, 89 Charlotte st. Fitzroy sq
Maslin Wm. & Son, coachmks. 22 & 23 Wigmore st. Cavndsh. sq
Maslin Jas. watr. crss. salesmn. 7 Newcastle st. Farringdon st
Maslin Wm. *Tavistock Arms* P.H. 11 Tavistock p. Tavistck. sq
Masol Victor, physician, Denmark hill, Camberwell
Mason, Barlow & Butt, lace manfrs. 118 Wood st. Cheapside
Mason Brothers, merchants, 6 New Broad st. City
Mason & Cattley, merchants, 31 Eastcheap
Mason & Dawson, surgeons, 1 York pl. City road
Mason John Adam & Son, ironmongers, 52 Gt. Marylebone st
Mason & Moore, wholesale cabinet, chair & sofa manufacturers, & dealers in mahogany, 110 Paul st. Finsbury
Mason & Smith, chemists & druggists, 12 Old st. St. Luke's
Mason Thomas & James, livery stables, 240½ Oxford st
Mason Thomas & Maria (Miss), prof. of dancing, 65 Oxford st
Mason Thomas & Son, woollendrapers, 70 High Holborn
Mason & Taylor, town printers & warehsmn. 4 Honey la. Chpsd
Masons' Hall (F. Gwatkin, clerk), 2 Mason's all. Basinghl. st
Mason Abraham John, wood engra. 28 Liverpool st. King's cr
Mason Allen, plumber & glazier, 27 St. John st. Clerkenwell
Mason Alfred R. surveyor, 24 Lime st
Mason Ann (Miss), straw hat ma. 16 Park pl. Kennington cross
Mason Chas. coal & potato dealer, 48 Dorset st. Portman sq
Mason Chas. currier, 6 & 18 Cross st. Bermondsey New town
Mason Chas. livery stables, 129 Piccadilly
Mason Chas. *Royal Standard* P.H. 24 Well st. Wellclose sq
Mason Chas. Alfred, stationer, 24 Broad st. Bloomsbury
Mason Daniel, *Queen's Head* P.H. 63 Fashion st. Spitalfilds
Mason Ebenezer, baker, 4 Victoria pl. Hoxton Old town
Mason Edward, leatherseller, 7 St. George's road, Borough
Mason Edward, lime burner, see Knight & Mason
Mason Edwd. *Triumphant Chariot* P.H. Pembroke mews, Grosvenor place
Mason Edwin, hairdresser, 37 Marylebone lane, Oxford st
Mason Elizh. (Mrs.), poulterer. 5 Chapel st. west, Mayfair
Mason Elizh. Ann (Mrs.), dairy, 14 Gt. Bath st. Clerkenwell
Mason Fanny (Miss), tobacconist, 56 Quadrant, Regent st
Mason Francis, *Wheatsheaf* P.H. 365 Oxford st
Mason Frans. *Olive Branch* P.H. 5 Sidmouth pl. Gray's inn rd
Mason George, baker, 5 College hill, Upper Thames st
Mason George, butcher, 6 Chapel st. Grosvenor place
Mason George, *Globe & Three Pigeons* P.H. 140 Shadwell
Mason George, math. draw. inst. ma. 52 Squirries st. Bthnl. gr. rd
Mason George, stationer & rag merchant, 39 Kingsland rd
Mason George, *Windmill* P.H. Lower road, Deptford
Mason Geo. Bryan, booksel. & statnr. 16 Duke st. Grosvenor sq
Mason Geo. W. W. brewery agent & auctioneer, 33 Bucklersbury
Mason Henry, law stationer, see Trilleo & Mason
Mason Henry, solicitor, see Lindsay & Mason
Mason Henry, whitesmith, 26 Goodman's yard, Minories
Mason Hen. Fred. haberdasher, 40 Clipstone st. Fitzroy sq
Mason Henry R. fancy cabinet mak. 29 Coldbath sq. Clerknwl
Mason Isabella (Mrs.), market gardener, Lower rd. Deptford
Mason Jacob, baker, 6 Torrington place, Torrington square
Mason James, baker, 38 Chapel st. Grosvenor place
Mason James, *Blue Anchor* P.H. 11 Wormwood st. City
Mason James, furniture broker, 19 Lower st. Islington
Mason James, hay & straw salesman, see Brown, Mason & Co
Mason James, *Robin Hood* P.H. 26 Church la. St. Giles's
Mason James, solicitor & notary, 38 Doughty st
Mason James, statuary & mason, 11 Broughton pl. Hackney rd
Mason James, tobacconist, 20 Chapel st. New road
Mason James, tailor & hatter, 10 Kingsland High st
Mason James, watchmaker, 2 Walbrook pl. Hoxton new tn
Mason James Thomas, chemist & druggist, 10 King st. Soho
Mason Jeremiah, cattle salesman, 17 West Smithfield
Mason Jeremiah, tobacconist, 10 Cambridge road
Mason John, *Ben Jonson* P.H. 3 Shoe lane, Fleet st
Mason John, beer retailr. 21 Portsmouth pl. Lr. Kenningtn. la
Mason John, bootmaker, 204 Up. Whitecross st. St. Luke's
Mason John, brushmaker, 28 South st. Manchester square
Mason John, butcher, 2 Shoe lane, Fleet st
Mason John, butcher, 3 Queen st. Chelsea
Mason John, carpenter, 29 London st. Fitzroy square
Mason John, cheesemonger, 38 Clifton st. Finsbury
Mason John, fruiterer & carman, 4 South pl. Up. Kenningtn. la
Mason John, grocer & tea dealer, see Fortnum, Mason & Co
Mason John, painter, plumber & glazier, 2 Cripplegate bldgs
Mason John, ropemaker, 2 Trafalgar row, Walworth common
Mason John, silk manufacturer, 22 Church st. Spitalfields
Mason John, straw pla. wa. 15 Tufton st. Horseferry rd. Westm
Mason John, tailor, 24 Windmill st. Finsbury
Mason John, Wesleyan booksel. 66 Paternoster row, & 14 City rd
Mason John James, veterinary surgeon, 13 Grosvenor st. west
Mason Joseph, grocer, 5 Green st. Leicester square
Mason Joseph Wood, surgeon, &c. 41 Beech st. Barbican
Mason Lumley, potato dealer, 30 Green st. Bethnal green
Mason Maria (Mrs.), grocer, 7 Watts terrace, Old Kent rd
Mason Maria (Mrs.), straw hat ma. 16 Duke st. Grosvenor sq
Mason Matthew, printer, see Manning & Mason
Mason Michael Laurence, surgeon, 5 High st. Newing. butts
Mason Nathaniel, solicitor, see Bridges & Mason
Mason Richd. carpenter & undertaker, 5 Union st. Berkeley sq
Mason Richd. coach build. 24 Grosvenor mews, Grosvenor st
Mason Richard, dyer, 35 Bryanstone st. Bryanstone sq
Mason Richard, *George* P.H. 22 Somerset st. Aldgate
Mason Robert, dyer & scourer, 45 Warwick st. Golden sq
Mason Robert, tailor, 17 Charles st. Hatton garden
Mason Samuel, builder, 1 Charlotte pl. Up. Kennington la
Mason Thos. book & printsel. 2 Gt. Russell st. Bloomsbury
Mason Thos. auctioneer, estate agent, &c. 7 Norton folgate
Mason Thos. brass finisher. 4 Easton st. Spafields
Mason Thos. *Brown Bear* P.H. 31 Worship st. Finsbury
Mason Thos. grocer & tea dealer, 7 Bethnal green road
Mason Thos. *Huntsman & Hounds* P.H. Park pl. Walworth
Mason Thos. lodging house, 14 St. James's pl. St. James's st
Mason Thos. *Marquis of Granby* P.H. 38 Gray's inn lane
Mason Thos. painter & glazier, 30 Charles st. Middlesex hosp
Mason Thos. upholsterer, appraisr. & undrtkr. 21 Panton st
Mason Walter Geo. wood engra. & draughtsman, 135 Fleet st
Mason Wm. attorney, 20 Brownlow st. Holborn
Mason Wm. bootmaker, 21 Bedford st. Bedford row
Mason Wm. fruiterer, 47 Bell yard, Temple bar
Mason Wm. hatter, 2 Carburton st. Fitzroy sq
Mason Wm. *King Harry VIII.* P.H. 38 Road side, Mile end rd

Mason Wm. law stationer, sec. to St. Clement Danes saving's bank, 18 Serle's pl. Lincoln's inn
Mason Wm. lint maker, 3 Globe alley, Fore st. Limehouse
Mason Wm. livery stable keeper, 129 Piccadilly
Mason Wm. market gardener, Grove st. Deptford
Mason Wm. milliner, 95 Shoreditch High st
Mason Wm. printer & publisher, 22 Clerkenwell green
Mason Wm.stationer,5Up.Southwick st.north,Cambridgeter
Mason Wm. tailor, 14 Whitcomb st. Pall mall east
Mason Wm. Ambrose, bookseller, 6 Holywell st. Strand
Mason Wm. Henry, coach builder, Kingsland road
Massa Wm. chemist, 2 Ranelagh terrace, Pimlico road
Massey John & Son, boot, &c. makers, 1 St. Thomas's st. Boro'
Massey Alexander, tailor & draper, 44 Threadneedle st
Massey Benjamin, goldsmith & jeweller, 116 Leadenhall st
Massey Edmund, watch & chronometer maker, 89 Strand
Massey Edward, sen. watch maker & patent log sounding machine maker to the Lords of the Admiralty, 28 King st. Clerkenwell
Massey Edward, watch maker, 3 Tysoe st. Clerkenwell
Massey FrancisJoseph,watchma.17Chadwell st.St.John st.rd
Massey George, hatter, 4 Adam's row, Hampstead road
Massey Henry, stationer, 5 Millbank street, Westminster
Massey John, commission agent, see Houghton & Massey
Massey Rd. house painter, 19 Norfolk st. Middlesex hospital
Massey Robert, wood turner, 13 North st. Fitzroy sq
Massey Sarah (Mrs.), cowkeeper, Lower road, Deptford
Massey Thomas, surgeon, Church st. Camberwell, & Southampton st. Camberwell road
Massey Thomas,watch, chronometer&clock mak.4 Birchin la
Massey William, beer retailer, Matrimony pl. Wndswth. rd
Massey William, boys' school, 89 Bridge road, Lambeth
Massey William, dyer, 1 Odell place, Little Chelsea
Massey William, stationer, 103 Park st. Grosvenor square
Massey William Nathaniel, barrister, 1 Pump court, Temple
Massie Alexander, engineer, Brewhouse la. & 148 Wapping
Massingham Hen. Collier, bootmaker,7 Hackney rd. crescent
Massingham James, haberdaser, 141 Church st. Shoreditch
Massingham Jsph. E. surgeon&chemist,4Green st.Bethnal gn
Massingham Rd. feather, &c. ma. 9 Up. John st. Golden sq
Masson Geo. *Feathers* P.H. 12 Gt.Wild st. Lincoln's inn flds
Masson Henry, cook & confectnr. 10 Tavistock pl. Tvstck. sq
Masson John George, oil & italian wa. see Howis & Masson
Masson Robert, confectioner, 34 Gt. Russell st. Bloomsbury
Masson Thos. confectioner, 53 Gt. Portland st. Oxford st
Master of the Rolls' Secretary's Office, Rolls yard, Chancery lane; hours of business, 10 to 3; long vacation, 11 to 1
Master Mariners' Benevolent Society (William Edward Bates, secretary), 2 Back st. Horselydown
Master George, solicitor, see Johnson, Fielder & Master
Masterman, Peters, Mildred, Masterman & Co. bankers, 35 Nicholas lane, Lombard st
Masterman Thomas & John, brewers, 38 Broad st. Ratcliff
Masterman Hen. solicitor, see Hughes, Kearsey&Masterman
Masterman Matthew, saddler, 116 Piccadilly
Masterman Robert, surgeon, 182 Borough High st
Masterman William Stanley, solicitor, 4A, Wine Office ct. & 6 Hind ct. & 9 Durham place east, Hackney road
Masters Jane & Son, hairdressers, 1 Robert's pl. Comml. rd.e
Masters'inChanceryOffice,25Southampton buildings,Chancery lane; hours, term, 10 to 4; vacat. 11to2; long va.11 to 1
Masters John&Co.wine coopers&bot.mer.11Hare ct.Aldsgt.st
Masters Francis, boot & shoe maker, 52 Aldersgate st
Masters George, hair cutter, 6 King's pl. Commercial rd. ea
Masters George Augustus, undertaker,10 Union st. Deptford
Masters Jane (Mrs.), brushmaker, 18 Harp alley, Shoe lane
Masters John, cheesemonger, 26 Chiswell st. Finsbury
Masters John, clothes dealer, 2 Exeter st. Lisson grove
Masters John, *Duke of Sussex* P.H. 10 Rosemary lane
Masters Jsph. printer, booksel. & stationer, 33 Aldersgate st
Masters Joseph, builder & carpenter, 25 Lower st. Islington
Masters Robert, cattle salesman, 60 West Smithfield
Masters Robert, haberdasher, 17 Clayton pl. Caledonian rd
Masters Thos. confectioner, 16 Little Russell st. Covent garden, & 56 Upper Charlotte st. Fitzroy square
Masters Thos. printer & publisher, 2 New Bridge st. Blckfrs
Masters William, beer retailer, 5 Birdcage wk. Hackney rd
Masters William, brushmaker, 13 Aldersgate st
Masters William, butcher, 116 Long alley, Finsbury
Masters William, pawnbroker, 33 Piccadilly
Masters William, tailor, 26 Great Pulteney st. Golden sq
Masters William Fk.meat slsmn. 11 Shambles, Newgate mkt
Masterson Henry, merchant, *North& Sth. American* coffee ho
Masterson Thomas, muslin manufacturer, 142 Cheapside
Matcham Nelson, barrister, 8 New square, Lincoln's inn
Mate Charles Wm. teacher of music, 13 Cross st. Islington
Mate Elizabeth (Mrs.), midwife, 13 Cross st. Islington
Mate George, printer, 16 Liverpool st. King's cross
Mather Adam & Co. pat. lamp ma. 33 Charles st. Hat. gar
Mather Henry & Co. commission mers. 18 Ironmonger lane
Mather Alex. Andrew builder, 54 King st. Golden square
Mather Anne(Miss),milliner,&c.22Titchborne st.Haymarket
Mather Hume John, perfumer, 12 Edwards st. Portman sq
Mather James, herald chaser, 77 Berwick st. Soho
Mather John, mason, slater, &c. 23 Marshall st. Golden sq
Mather John, surgeon, 63 Bunhill row, Finsbury
Mather Thomas, haberdasher, 1 Shepperton st. Islington
Mather Thos. *RobinHood& LittleJohn* P.H. Church st.Dptfd
Mathers Thomas, cooper, 41 St. John street, Smithfield
Matheson Thos.tea broker, see Lloyd, Matheson&Brodribb
Mathew & Chambers, surgeons, 3Trafalgarpl.ea.Hackneyrd
Mathew Charles, meat salesman, 15 Newgate market
Mathew Geo. wheelwright, 9 Buckle st. Whitechapel
Mathew Geo. Felton tailor&draper, 47 Skinner st.Snowhill, & 4 Warwick square, Newgate st
Mathew Jas. Edwd. surgn.Churchrd.DeBeauvoirsq.Kingsld
Mathew John, butcher, 14 Ivy lane, Newgate st
Mathew John, wine, spirit & insur. broker, 15 Mincing lane
Mathew John Mee, barrister, 4 Gray's inn square
Mathewes & Magrath, bill brokers, 18 Threadneedle st
Mathewman Rd. coal mer. 7 whf. Paddington basin, south si
Mathews & Vaisey, tallow chandls.&oilmn.11 Hungerford st
Mathews Wm. H.&Son, bisc.bakers'tool ma. 22Lant st.Boro
Mathews Charles, bookseller, 55 Penton st. Pentonville
Mathews Chas.ladies'boot&shoe ma.16 Warren st.Fitzroy sq
Mathews Edward, engraver & printer, 46 Berwick st. Soho
Mathews Edward, manchester agent, 2 Bow Church yard
Mathews Edward, upholsterer,5 Homer pl.New rd.Marlybe
Mathews Frederic Thomas, surveyor,1 Edward st.City rd
Mathews George, builder & undertaker,52 Great Titchfield street, Portland place
Mathews George, carpenter, 2½ Cleveland st. Fitzroy sq
Mathews Geo. cooper, yeast & spirit mer. Ratcliff cross whf
Mathews Geo. glass & china dlr. 55 White lion st. Pentonville
Mathews Henry, academy, Northampton ho. Cambwl. green
Mathews Henry, appraiser, 22 Cloak lane
Mathews Henry, linendraper, &c. 204 Oxford st
Mathews James, tailor & outfitter, 13 Deptford High st.
Mathews Jas. windowglass&lead mer. see Smithis&Mathews
Mathews John, dairyman, 3 Upper James st. Golden sq
Mathews John, fruiterer, 5 Westmoreland bdgs. Aldersgate
Mathews John, *Goose& Gridiron* P.H. Londonho.yd.St.Paul's
Mathews John, linendraper, 17 Cable st. Wellclose sq
Mathews John, shoe warehouse, 255 Blackfriars road
Mathews John, solicitor, 1 Mitre court, Temple
Mathews John Hubbersty, barrister, 1 Essex court, Temple
Mathews Joshua, coal merc. Child's Belvedere wf. Lambeth
Mathews Peter, bottle merchant, 18 Charles st. Westminster
Mathews Richard, barrister, 5 Belitha vil. Barnsbury park
Mathews Rich. piano forte ma.6 Homer pl. New rd.Marylebn
Mathews Richard, teadealer & grocer, 47 Albany st. Reg.pk
Mathews Richard Gardner, solicitor, see Hill & Mathews
Mathews Robert, linendraper, 8 Amwell st Pentonville
Mathews Robert N. B. surgeon, see Iliff, Mathews & Iliff
Mathews Sarah (Mrs.), leather cutter, 51 James st. Oxford st
Mathews Sarah (Mrs.), milliner, 22 Broadley ter. Blndfd. sq
Mathews Wilkinson, queen's counsel, 16 Old sq. Lincoln's inn
Mathews Wm. coffee rooms, 7 King st. Tower hill
Mathews Wm. grocer, 6A, Dorset st. Manchester square
Mathews Wm. grocer&italianwareh.27Mountst. Berkeley sq
Mathews Wm. silk dyer, 4 Alsop's bdgs. Gt. Dover rd. Boro'
Mathews Wm. B. who. tin plate, &c. warehouse, 9 Crooked lane, & 28 Martin's lane, Cannon st
Mathias John Edward, surgeon, 13 Up. King st. Bloomsby
Mathieson John, tailor, 82 Bishopsgate within
Mathieson William, tailor, Camberwell green
Mathison Archibald, tailor, 38 Conduit st
Mathison Daniel, tobacconist, 42 Gt. Guildford st. Borough
Matland Wm. teadealer, 10 Nassau pl. Commercial rd. east
Matsell Henry, potato salesman, 44 White st. Borough
Matson Charles, coachmaster, King st. New town, Deptford
Matson Geo. who. teadealer, see Fincham, Matson & Potts
Mattacks William, turner, 38 Grey Eagle st. Spitalfields
Mattam Fred. brewer & livery stables, 18 Brick st. Mayfair
Matterface Abraham, millwright, 46 Granby st.Waterloo rd
Matterface Geo. millwright, 3 Black Lion yd. Whitechpl. rd
Matterface Thomas W. ladies' shoemaker, 15 Buckingham pl
Matthes Herman, manufg. jeweller, &c. seeGirerd&Matthes
Matthew Brothers&Borer, brushma.&ware.106Up.Thames st
Matthew Brothers & Borer, russia mers. 106 Up. Thames st
Matthew George, haircutter, 38 Store st. Bedford square
Matthew Joseph, printer, 16 Glo'ster st. Commercial rd. ea

MatthewMary(Mrs.),dlr.in tuscan&strw.plait,9Wood st.Spfi
Matthew Robert, wharfinger, 257 Wapping High st
Matthew Thomas, grocer, 157 Tooley st. Borough
Matthew Thomas, ropemaker, Jamaica level, Bermondsey
Matthew Thomas, grocer & teaman, 46 Lisson grove north
Matthewman Henry, plumber, painter, &c. 13 Swallow st
Matthews Jsph.&Ann, fruit salesm. 2 Park st.&54 Boro' mkt
Matthews & Martin, linendrap. 50 Chichester pl. King's cross
Matthews Wm.&Richard, wholes.stationers,38HighHolborn
Matthews Abrm.saddler&harn.1 Wellington place,Livpl. rd
Matthews Arthur, ironmonger, 11 Phœnix st.Crown st.Soho
Matthews Benj. hat maker, 6 Haberdasher's walk, Hoxton
Matthews Benjamin, oilman, 40 Cornwall road, Lambeth
Matthews Chas. cutler, 17 & 18 King's Head court, Shoe la
Matthews Chas. dairy, 4 Princess st. Edgware road
Matthews Chas. fruiterer, 188 Bethnal green road
Matthews Chas. turner, 10 Goodge st. Fitzroy square
Matthews ChristianGeo. law statnr.10Warwick ct.Hi.Holbn
Matthews David, *Prince Albert*P.H.21York st. Kingslandrd
Matthews Edmund, saddler, 10 Star corner, Bermondsey st
Matthews Edmund Harley, law stationer, 3 Cursitor st
Matthews Elizabeth(Mrs.),milliner,130 St.Alban's pl.Edg.rd
Matthews Francis, coal mer. 1 Willow st. Vauxhall bdg. rd
Matthews Francis, wheelwright, 51 Holland st. Blackfrs.rd
Matthews George, carcase butcher, 46 Aldgate High st
Matthews George, coffee rooms, 49 Gray's inn lane
Matthews George, tailor, 6 Hamilton pl. Deptford High st
Matthews George, tailor, 11 Pollen st. Hanover square
Matthews George, *White Swan* P.H. 225 Shadwell High st
Matthews Geo.K.bookbinder,&c.20½Warwick la.Newgate st
Matthews Henry, baker, 13 Edgware road, Marylebone
Marthews Henry, furniture broker, 11 High st. Deptford
Matthews Henry, turner in general, 18 Silver st. Wood st
Matthews HughesRobt.surgeon,10Low.Seymour st.Ptmn.sq
Matthews James, beer retailer, Union pl. Clapham road
Matthews James, builder & house agt. 47 Liverpool st. City
Matthews Jas. hairdress. 50 Gt.Queen st.Lincoln's inn fields
Matthews James, meat salesman,12 Warwick la.Newgate st
Matthews James, solicitor, 5 Lant st. Borough
Matthews James, west india merchant, 39 Lime st
Matthews Jas. C. artifl. flower ma. 12 Greenhill's rts. Smthfd
Matthews John, accountant, 1 Bell yard, Doctors' commons
Matthews John, cheesemonger, 17 Bow lane, Cheapside
Matthews John,coalmer.29 Palace new rd.&Medwaywf. Blkfs
Matthews John, french polisher, 1 Cross court, Golden sq
Matthews John, grocer & cheesem. 5 Charles st. Westminr
Matthews John, *King's Arms* P.H. 2 John st. Limeho.fields
Matthews John, linendraper, 3 James pl. Larkhall la. Clphm
Matthews John, pawnbroker, 9 to 11 Princes rd. Lambeth
Matthews John, solicitor, 2 Arthur st. west, London bridge
Matthews John, stout, &c. dealer, 20 Princes st. Fitzroy sq
Matthews John, surgeon, &c. 7 Spencer st. Goswell road
Matthews John, teadealer, 35 Leman st. Goodman's fields
Matthews John, tobacconist, 134 Poplar High st
Matthews John, woollen draper, see Bedward & Matthews
Matthews John Ilott, corn merchant, 198 Shoreditch High st. & steam saw & splitting mills, Plough yard, Shoreditch
Matthews John Pearce, hat manufacturer, 144 Minories
Matthews Joseph, pianoforte ma. 19 Somers pl. east, New rd
Matthews Joseph, stationer, 4 Ocean row, Stepney
Matthews Joseph P. manufg. goldsmith, 29 Gerard st. Soho
Matthews Lucy (Miss), staymaker, 61 Newington causeway
Matthews Marmaduke, auctioneer, 2 Spital square
Matthews Mary (Miss), milliner, 15 Duke st. Manchester sq
Matthews Peter, surgeon dentist, 15 High st. Marylebone
Matthews Richard, barrister, 4 Brick court, Temple
Matthews Richard, cowkeeper, 2 Webb st. Bermondsey st
Matthews Robert, cabinetmaker, 23 Harcourt st. New rd
Matthews Rbt. clothwrkr. & presser, 6 Fitchett's ct. Noble st
Matthews Robert, grocer, 117 Jermyn st. St. James's
Matthews Rt. tanner&moroccomanf.Up.Russell st.Bermonds
Matthews Robert Hughes, surgeon, 10 Lower Seymour st
Matthews Ruth (Miss), ladies' school, 28 Clarendon square
Matthews Samuel, meat salesman, 25 Newgate market
Matthews Stephen, butcher, 32 Munster st. Regent's park
MatthewsStephenLewis,auctioneer,&c.16Unionct.O.Broadst
Matthews Susan (Mrs.),genl.dlr.2Cottage pl.Newingtn.butt
Matthews Thos. *Crown & Cushion* P.H.Pages walk,Bmdsy
Matthews Thos.linendrap.& silk mercer, 18 Aldgate High st
Matthews Thos. saddler, 73 High st. Camden town
Matthews Thos.shawl mfr.see Towler,Campin,Shickle & Co
Matthews Thos. shoemaker, 5 Union st. Middlesex hospital
Matthews Thos. stationer, 40 New North st. Finsbury
Matthews Thos. B. optician, 9 Athol pl.New rd.Pentonville
Matthews Titus, ironmonger & smith, 71½ Poplar High st
Matthews Wm. baker, 9 Parnham place, Brook st. Ratcliff
Matthews Wm. carpenter, 1 Salmon lane, Limehouse
Matthews Wm. embosser, &c. 21 Buckingham st. Strand
Matthews Wm. fruit salesman, Borough market
Matthews Wm. hatter, 27 Chichester place, Gray's inn road
Matthews Wm. japanner, Stratford, Essex
Matthews Wm.plumber,painter,&c.60Aldenham st.Somrs tn
Matthews Wm.pocket book&case ma.3Bartlett's bldgs. Hlbn
Matthews Wm. *Ship* P.H. 1 High st. Stepney
Matthews Wm. surgns.inst.ma.10Portugal st. Lnclns.innfds
Matthews Wm.Henry,cheesemonger, 201 Blackfriars road
Matthews Wm.Hen.statnr.&c.44Up. Seymour st. Euston sq
Matthewson John,engraver&printer,32Cornwall rd.Lambeth
Matthey Alphonso, translator of languages,78 Old Broad st
Matthey John, stockbroker, 78 Old Broad st. City
Matthie JohnChas.ea. in.col. & indigo broker, 38 Mincing la
Matthiessen William & Co. merchants, 12 Coleman st
Mattinson Sarah & Elizth. coffee rooms, 3 West Smithfield
Mattinson James, ham merchant, 4 Leathersellers' bldgs
Mattinson Thomas, ham dealer, 4 Silver st. Wood st. City
Mattison George, wine & sup. rooms, 95 Bridge rd. Lambeth
Mattock Edward, butcher, 54 Marsham st. Westminster
Mattok William, butcher, 59 Lambeth High st
Mattocks George James, appraiser & undertaker, 55 Great Carlisle st. & 31 Circus st. New road, Marylebone
Mattocks Susan (Miss), tobacconist, 109 Gt. Portland st
Mattocks Thomas, dining rooms,79 Brunswick st.Blackwall
Mattocks Wm.bookseller&binder,15Crown row, Mile end rd
Mattress Charles, hairdresser, 84 Fleet st
Matts Thomas, coachspring maker, 85 Charles st. Drury la
Matts Thomas, coach & van builder, see Hazeldine & Matts
Matveicff Gregory, mercht. 2 Adams ct. & Baltic coffee ho
Maubert J.F. & Co.stockbrokers, Stock exchng. Thrgmrtn. st
Maud & Co. coopers & hoop & stave merchants, 128 Wapping
Maud Michael, wool broker, Nun court, 74 Coleman st
Maud Wm. Hen. bootmaker, 17 Lit. Bell alley, Coleman st
Maude J. M. Son & Co. manufacturers of patent portland cement, Upper Ordnance wharf, 143 Rotherhithe st. & 32 Great Winchester st. City
Maude Frederic Philip, special pleader, 3 King's Bench walk
Maude HartwellJohn, navyagt.seeHallett, Robinson&Maude
Maude Henry H. barrister, 6 New sq. Lincoln's inn
Maude James Robinson,wine&brandyimp.seeScaley&Maude
Maude John Milthorp, secretary to the Mexican Company, 32 Great Winchester st
Maude Thomas, plaister spreader, 21 George st. Lambeth
Maudslay, Sons&Field, engineers, Cheltenham pl. Westm. rd
Mauduit John, direc. of messageries royales, 33 Regent circ
Mauger Henry, goldsmith & jeweller, see Lescot & Mauger
Maugham & Kennedy, solicitors, 100 Chancery lane
Maugham Thomas & Co. silk warehousemen, 37 Gutter lane
Maugham Thomas, carman, 12 Snow's fields, Bermondsey
Maughan Edward, traveller, 55 Nelson square
Maughan James, silversmith, &c. see Henderson & Maughan
Maughan John, sta. & tobacconist,3Aldenham ter.Pancras rd
Maughan Nicholas, distillr. 5 Lit. Distaff la. & 12 Old Fish st
Maughan Nicolas, wine, &c. imp. see Sheffield & Maughan
Maughfling Edward, butcher, 2 Union pl. Commercial rd. ea
Maughfling John, butcher, 14 New road, St. George east
Maul John Compton, barrister, 5 Pump court, Temple
Maule & Reynolds, solrs. to Treasury, Gwydir ho. Whitehall
Maule George, barrister, Gwydir house, Whitehall
Maule George Benjamin, barrister, 6 Stone bldgs. Linc. inn
Maule Robert, tobacconist, 95 Broad st. Ratcliff
Maule William, aurist, 7 Gt. George st. Westminster
Maull James, fishmonger, 95 St. John st. road
Maund,Jones,Randall&Morris,woollendrapers,&c.33Cornhill
Maund Chas.music engrav.&print.5Stephen st.Tottnhm.ct.rd
Maund George, artist, 8 Omega terrace, Alpha road
MaunderM&F.(Misses),readyma.linenwa.2Sthmp.ct.Blmsby
Maunder Matthew, market gardnr. Blue Anchor rd. Bermnd
Maunder Robert, baker, 38 Great James st. Lisson grove
Maunder Thomas, baker, 8 South st. King's road, Chelsea
Maunder Wm. baker, 8 Peel place, Kensington gravel pits
Maunsell Wm. Thos. barrister, 1 Pump ct.Temple
Maurenbrecher J. & Co. merchants, 11 Mark lane
Maurice & Co. printers, 4 Howford buildings, Fenchurch st
Mavero Peter, who. brushmaker, 11 Berkley st.Clerkenwell
Mavitta John, fruiterer. 6 Blenheim ter. Bond st. Chelsea
Mavrogordato M. F. & Co. merchants, 29 Broad st. bldgs
Mavrogordato Antonio E. merchant, 18 South st. Finsbury
Mavrogordato Michael Emmanuel, exchange & insurance agent, 14 North buildings, Finsbury circus
Mavrojani Spiridion, merchant, see Ralli & Mavrojani
Mavor Wm. veterinary surgeon & farrier, 4 New Bond st. Belgrave mews, Belgrave square; & 40 Grosvenor mews, Grosvenor st

Maw Charles, *White Lion* P.H. Vauxhall High st
Maw Solomon, surgical instrument mak. dealer in medical glass, earthenware, druggists' fixtures, 11 Aldersgate st
Maw Thomas, *Waterman's Arms* P.H. 61 Bankside
Mawbey Erasmus, *WindsorCastle* P.H. Coopers rd. OldKnt.rd
Mawby & Lloyd, chemists & druggists, 68 Fleet st
Mawby Wm. grocer & teadealer, 14 Aldgate
Mawby Wm. Joseph, shoe wareho. 4 New Bridge st. Vauxhall; & 2 Clifton place, Wandsworth road
Mawdsley John, surgeon, 9 Hanover square
Mawe Thomas Jones, solicitor to the *Norwich Union fire & life Societies*, the *Carron Company*, & the *Norwich Union reversionary Company*, & secretary to her Majesty's Chief Justice in Eyre, 4 New Bridge st. Blackfriars
Mawlam Henry, *Exmouth Arms* P.H. 24 Exmouth st. Commercial rd. east
Mawley Henry, surveyor, 43 Gower st. Bedford sq
Mawley Thos. Robt. marine store dlr. 6 Glo'ster pl. Walw. com
Mawman John, tailor, 11 Bond court, Walbrook
Mawman Thos. tailor, 3 Bury st. Bloomsbury
Mawson John, grocer & cheesemonger, 108 Poplar High st
Mawson Samuel M. picture importer, 3 Berners st. Oxford st
Max John & Co. lithographers, zincographers & engravers by steam power, 2 Royal Exchange; & 33 Nicholas lane, Lombard st; factory, Mansfield st. Boro' rd. Southwark
Maxey James & John, fur. ironmongers, 15 Church la. Whthpl
Maxey John, coffee rooms, 135 Bishopsgate without
Maxey William, cabinet maker, buhl cutter & inlayer, 4 Boot st. Pitfield st. Old st. rd
Maxey William, boarding house, 2 South pl. Finsbury
Maxon Fred. Thomas, solicitor, 6 Lit. Friday st. Cheapside
Maxted John, hat & army cap maker, 7 Carlton st. & 19 St. Alban's place, Regent st
Maxton Ann (Mrs.), baker, 48 Spencer st. Goswell road
Maxwell Alex. & Son, law booksellers, 32 Bell yd. Templ. bar
Maxwell & Keys, wine merchants, 3 James st. Haymarket
Maxwell Wm. & Son, cattle salesman, 60 West Smithfield
Maxwell Charles, dairy, 83 Carlisle st. Lambeth
Maxwell David, *King's Arms* P.H. 140 Houndsditch
Maxwell Elizabeth (Miss), baker, 178 Bethnal greenroad
Maxwell George, tailor, 5 Broadway, Ludgate hill
Maxwell Mary (Mrs.), spur maker, 161 Piccadilly
Maxwell John, *Phœnix* P.H. 16 Upper East Smithfield
Maxwell Peter Benson, equity draftsman & conveyancer, 4 Stone buildings, Lincoln's inn
Maxwell Wm. E. solicitor, see Durrant, Stuart & Maxwell
Maxwell Wm. James, wine merchant, see Shaw & Maxwell
May & Baker, manfg. chemists, Garden wharf, Battersea
May & Bowman, scotch & manchester warehousemen, 3 Wood st. & 34 Milk st. Cheapside
May & Bradley, wine merchants, 16 Jermyn st. St. James's
May & Featherstone, bricklayers, 1 Webber st. Blackfrs. rd
May Richard & Son, tailors, 4 Sackville st. Piccadilly
May & Scarlett, butchers, 48 South Audley st
May Wm. & Son, silk & mohair manufactrs. 4 Bread st. City
May Abraham, butcher, Stratford Broadway
May Andrew, mason, 32 Poplar High st
May Ann (Mrs.), cheesemonger, 8 Gainsford st. Horselydwn
May Chas. gold & silver thimble ma. 8 Curtain rd. Shoreditch
May David, chairmaker, 1 Charles st. Brandon st. Walworth
May Edmund, grocer, 8 Boss st. Horselydown
May Edward, ironmongery wareho. 66, 67 & 370 Oxford st
May Edward Collett, professor of music, 141 Sloane st
May Emanuel, surgeon, 16 Mount place, Whitechapel road
May Francis, blacking maker, see Bryant & May
May George, grocer & teadealer, 2 King's cross
May George, tailor 24 Noel st. Wardour st. Soho
May George, tailor, 12 Compton st. east, Regent sq
May George, undertaker, 9 Eden place, Old Kent road
May Harry, musical repository, see Monro & May
May Henry D. hosier, glover & shirt makr. 5 Moorgate st
May Henry, leatherseller, 37 Baldwin's garden, Leather la
May James, attorney, 2 Princes st. Spitalfields
May James, tailor, 47 Park st. Upper st. Islington
May James Bowen, solicitor, 14 Queen square, Bloomsbury
May John, beer retailer, 29 Pennyfields, Poplar
May John, bricklayer & plasterer, 4, 7 & 8 St. Clement's lane
May John, french polisher, 21 Titchborne st. Edgware rd
May John, gasfitter, 21 Berwick st. Soho
May John, lace manufacturer, 64 Aldermanbury
May John, warehouseman, see Bowman & May
May John Wm. consul genl. for Netherlands, 123 Fenchurch st
May Joseph, cheesemonger, 59 Goswell st
May Joseph, ink manufr. Black Swan alley, 43 London wall
May Joseph Compton, bricklayer, 43 James st. Oxford st
May Leon, surgeon dentist, 32 Gt. Russell st. Bloomsbury
May Lousia (Mrs.), haberdasher, 21 Berwick st. Soho
May Philip, woollen factor & warehouseman, 15 Gresham st
May Richard, cheesemonger, 145 Kingsland road
May Richard, gold & silver mounter, 19 Bury st. Bloomsbury
May Richard, law writer, 6 Cook's court, Lincoln's inn
May Richard Henry, fishmonger, &c. 14 Norris st. Haymarket
May Saml. masquerade repository, 9 Vinegar yd. Drury la
May Sarah (Mrs.), haberdash. 14 Grenada ter. Commer. rd. ea
May Thomas, attorney, 2 Middle Temple lane
May Thomas, dining rooms, 26 Newgate st
May Thomas, livery stables, 3 Crescent, Bridge rd. Southwk
May Thomas, tailor, see Bourne, May & Bourne
May Thomas, tailor, 69 Cheapside
May Thomas, turner, 10 Wilsted st. Somers town
May Thomas Baker, barrister, 35 Lincoln's inn fields
May Thomas Henry, baker & flour factor, 27 Little Britain, & 203½ Upper Thames st
May Thomas Erskine, assistant librarian, House of Commons
May Wm. *Blue Boar* P.H. Stratford, Essex
May Wm. cheesemonger, 17 College st. Chelsea
May Wm. currier, see Chave & May
May Wm. merchant, 123 Fenchurch st
May Wm. supt. registrar, 8 Prospect cottages, Thornhill rd
May Wm. ship & insurance agent, see Dick, Moller & May
May Wm. surgeon, 26 Bow lane, Cheapside
May Wm. tailor, 8 Holles st. Cavendish sq
May Wm. trustee of Dunn's soap patent, Hall of Commerce
May Wm. Christr. carpenter, 13 Salisbury mews, Glo'ster pl
May Wm. S. carrier, 69 Old Bailey
Maybank James, chandler's shop, 23 Gibson st. Waterloo rd
Maybank William, lighterman, Stratford, Essex
Maybery Charles, physician, 3 Earl's court, Old Brompton
Maybin Sam. bedstead maker, 39 Little Queen st. Holborn
Maybury Henry Thos. hairdresser, 11 Shepherd st. Mayfair
Maybury William Augustus, surgeon, 3 Little Tower st
Maycock Hiram, leather slr. 2 Portland st. Walworth comn
Maycock Hiram J. beer retailr. 1 St. George's st. Old Kent rd
Maycock Joseph, *Angel & Sun* P.H. 285 Strand
Maycock Thomas, grocer, 42 Whitecross st. Cripplegate
Mayden Wm. marine store dlr. 48 Salisbury st. Lisson grove
Maydwell Daniel, cattle salesman, 17 West Smithfield
Maydwell Isaac, animal medicine repository, 126 Newgate st
Maydwell James, china warehouse, 185 Lambeth walk
Maydwell Sarah (Miss), ladies' school, 27 Lr. Islington ter
Maydwell Wright, plumber, &c. 4 Alexander place, Brompton
Maye Robert, cider merchant, Griffin's wharf, 79 Tooley st
Mayell Frederick, confectioner, 13 Gt. Marylebone st
Mayen Robert, newsvender, 6 Star st. Paddington
Mayer John Geo. & Co. furriers, 1 Windmill st. Tottnhm. ct. rd
Mayer Charles, cornchandler, 55 & 56 Fore st. Limehouse
Mayer George, umbrella ma. 6 Cannon st. rd. St. George's east
Mayer John George, furrier, 58 Oxford st
Mayer Joseph, french polisher, 27 Kirby st. Hatton garden
Mayers Andrew, cigar manufacturer, 26 St. George st
Mayers Henry, carver, gilder & looking glass & picture frame manfr. 66 Leadenhall st.; & 1 Hanging ditch, Manchester
Mayers John, confectioner, 31 City terrace, City road
Mayers Morris, carver & gilder, 28 Frederick pl. Hmpstd. rd
Mayers Samuel, confectioner, 135 St. Alban's pl. Edgware rd
Mayers Thomas, baker, 1 Elm terrace, Little Chelsea
Mayers Thomas, biscuit baker, 2 Orange row, Kennington rd
Mayers Wm. mahogany & deal mer. 2 Bateman's row, Shordtch
Mayersbach George, plumber, 18 Copenhagen st. Pentnville
Mayes Ambrose, *King's Head* P.H. 24 Fore st. & 1 Three Colt st. Limehouse
Mayes Frederick, tailor, 3 Cleveland st. Mile end road
Mayes Henry, *Blacksmiths' Arms* P.H. 10 Back church la
Mayes John, clock maker, 8 Lower Charles st. Goswell rd
Mayes Robert, beer retailer, 32 High st. Portland town
Mayes William, grocer, 25 Hastings st. Burton crescent
Mayes Wm. Shaw, carpenter, 6 Orange st. Red Lion sq
Mayfield Mary (Mrs.), chandler's shop, 13 Thirza pl. O. Kent rd
Mayger Ann (Miss), stayma. 2 Frederick place, Goswell rd
Mayhead William, fruiterer, 5 Royal Hospital row, Chelsea
Mayhew & Son, solicitors, 26 Carey st. Lincoln's inn
Mayhew Wm. jun. & Co. hat & cap manufacturers, 59 Cheapside
Mayhew Wm. & Co. hat manufacturers, 89 New Bond st. & 128 Union st. Borough
Mayhew Charles, surv. & architect, 14 Argyll st. Regent st
Mayhew Charles, coal & potato dlr. 52 Parker st. Drury la
Mayhew Fredk. solicitor, see Badham, Houghton & Mayhew
Mayhew George, saddler, Camberwell green
Mayhew George, tobacconist, 191 Whitechapel road
Mayhew Jabez, coffee rooms & beer ret. 7 Gt. Chapl. st. Oxfrd. st
Mayhew John, baker, 34 Greek st. Soho
Mayhew John, livery stables, 40 Gt. Ormond yd. Queen sq

Mayhew Robt. academy, 28 Friedenstein ter. Mornington rd
Mayhew Sam. Martin, chemist, 15 High st. Camberwell
Mayhew Thomas, bricklayer & bldr. 6½ Shepperton st. Islgtn
Mayhew Thomas, coffee rooms, 55 Long lane, Smithfield
Mayhew Thomas, glass & china dlr. Mare st. Hackney
Mayhew William, *Anchor* P.H. 1 Bankside, Southwark
Mayhew William, grocer, 5 High st. Camberwell
Maylard John, grocer, 120 Fetter lane
Maylard Martin, silk mercer, 95 Borough High st
Maylin Joseph, fishmonger, 3 Darkhouse lane, Billingsgate, & 21 Pudding lane, Eastcheap
Mayman Jas. & Son, tailors, 38 Munster st. Regent's pk
Mayman Octavius & Co. tailors, 1A, New street, Dorset sq
Mayman Robert, tailor, 20 Edward st. Hampstead rd
Maynard Bros.& Blackburn, merchants, 6 Skinner's pl. Sise la
Maynard & Harris, military & naval outfitters & general agents, 27 Poultry
Maynard Sophia & James, butchers, 42 Paradise row, Chelsea
Maynard Benjamin, smith & farrier, Bromley, Middlesex
Maynard Chas. *Green Dragon* P.H. 21 Paradise row, Chelsea
Maynard Edward, *Bedfrd. Arms* P.H. Bedfrd. ter. Claphm. rise
Maynard Elizth. (Mrs.), butcher, 1A, Royal Hospl. row, Chelsea
Maynard Elizbth. (Mrs.), *Pulteney hotel*, 13 Albemarle st
Maynard Fredk. accountant & ink maker, 24 Bread st. City
Maynard George, *Black Boy & Horse Shoe* P.H. 1 Nicholas la
Maynard George, lighterman, 4 Wallington pl. Wandswrth. rd
Maynard George, stove manufr. 3 Trafalgar st. Walwrth. rd
Maynard Geo. stove grate ma. 17 Young's bldgs. Aldersgt. st
Maynard Henry, baker, 6 Long lane, Bermondsey
Maynard Henry, carpenter, 5 Prospect pl. Old Brompton
Maynard Henry, fruiterer, 10 Pleasant row, Holloway rd
Maynard James, cowkeeper, 8 Commercial pl. Kentish town
Maynard Jonas A. specl. pleader, 2 Mitre ct. bldgs. Temple
Maynard John, pinmaker & music wire drawer, sole agent for Wm. Smith & Co.'s imprvd. steel music wire, 148 Drury la
Maynard Joseph, solicitor, see Crowder & Maynard
Maynard Joseph Starling, furnishing ironm. 50 Lambeth walk
Maynard Peter, carpenter, 10 Lit. Randolph st. Camden tn
Maynard Richard, carpenter, builder, &c. 14 Marshall st
Maynard Riley, linendraper, High st. Kingsland
Maynard Samuel, mathematical & philosophical bookseller, 8 Earl's court, Cranbourn st. Leicester square
Maynard Thomas, butcher, 6 Adam's row, Hampstead road
Maynard Thomas, fancy card & scaleboard box maker, & scaleboard cutter, 95 Curtain road, & 11 Gloucester st
Maynard Thomas, grocer, 7 Belvedere buildings, Borough rd
Maynard William, baker, 52 Upper Lisson st. Lisson grove
Maynard William, butcher, 12 Newport court, Newport mkt
Mayo Newman K. & Herbert, colonial brokers, 17 Mincing la
Mayo & Warmington, manufacturers of mineral ærated waters, & patentees of the syphon vases for all gaseous beverages, 17 Silver st. Wood st. City
Mayo Caroline (Mrs.), *Saracen's Head hotel*, 49 Skinner st
Mayo Fred. Richd. wholes. boot & shoe maker, 99 London wall
Mayo John, blind ma. carp. & undert. 22 Church st. Islington
Mayo John, carpenter & undrtkr. 15 Wyndham rd. Cambwl
Mayo John, printer, & glass & china dlr. 105 Bethnl. green rd
Mayo John, tobacconist, Deptford bridge
Mayo John Ryall, solicitor, 37 Bedford st. Covent garden
Mayo John William, whip mounter, 1 Norway st. St. Luke's
Mayo Thomas, physician, 56 Wimpole st. Cavendish square
Mayo Wm. butcher, 12 Mason st. Westminster bridge road
Mayor Hen. & Co. hop & oil mers. Anchor whf. 9 Up. Thames st
Mayor & Kelham, spice merchants, 2 Little Distaff lane
Mayor George, cabinet maker, 117 Curtain road, Shoreditch
Mayor John, tailor & toydealer, 32 Havering st. Commcl. rd
Mayoss Jane (Miss), art. florist, 11 Cheltenham pl. Westmr. rd
Mayou John, silk mercer, see Challacombe & Mayou
Mayse Sarah (Mrs.), corset maker & milliner, 137 Regent st
Mayson Jonathan, hatter, 59 Freeschool st. Horselydown
Mayston James, corn dlr. 25 Glo'ster ter. Vauxhall bridge rd
Mayston Samuel Rd. tobacconist, 3 Thurlow pl. Hackney rd
Maythorn & Clapton, straw hat makers, Stratford broadwy
Maythorn Eliz. (Miss), straw hat ma. see Clapton & Maythorn
Mazoyer Joseph, poulterer, 15 to 17 Gt. Hall, Hungerford mkt
Mazure Louie, goldchain mak. 8 Lr. Ashby st. Northampton sq
Mazza Vincent, furrier, 13 Norton folgate
Mazzei Giovanni, plaster moulder & figure ma. 23 Gt. Queen st
Mazzinghi Thos. John, barrister, Devereux chambers, Strand
Meabry Charles, grocer & italian wa. 34 Felix ter. Lvrpool. rd
Meacher Sarah (Mrs.), lodging ho. 26 Green st. Grosvenor sq
Meacock James, gas fitter & brass turner, 71 Snow hill
Mead & Bailey, haysalesmen, 5 Whf. south side, Padgtn. basin
Mead George & Co. wine mers. Salvador house, Bishopsgate
Mead & Powell, who. stationers, 93 Whitechapel High st
Mead Alfred, stationer & news agent, 29 Melton st. Euston sq
Mead Charles, baker, 128 Upper st. Islington
Mead Francis, butcher, 2 Bowling st. Marylebone
Mead Henry, tailor, Camberwell green
Mead James, linen factor, 4 Trinity st. Borough
Mead James, upholsterer, 8 Swallow st. Piccadilly
Mead James Whittle, carpenter, &c. 71 Gt. Carlisle st. Edgw. rd
Mead John, gardener, 1 Artichoke row, Mile end road
Mead Joseph, farrier, 41 Old st. St. Luke's
Mead Joseph, beer retailer, 9 Eagle st. Red Lion sq
Mead Joseph, office for *Railway guides*, 10 Gough sq
Mead Joseph, wood engraver, 9 Up. Smith st. Northampton sq
Mead Joseph Choat Sawen, solicitor, 11 Bedford st. Bedford row, & 25 East st. Red Lion sq
Mead Thomas, butcher, 2 Middlesex terrace, Hackney rd
Mead Thomas, grocer & cheesemonger, 4 Trinity st. Boro'
Mead Thomas, tailor, 48 Cornhill
Mead William, engraver & printer, 33 Gt. Queen st. Linc. inn fi
Meade Edw. millwright & engineer, 14 Winter ter. Borough
Meade James, milliner, 55 Grosvenor st. New Bond st
Meade John, silk mercer, 10 South st. South Audley st
Meade Joshua, *Sun* P.H. 16 & 17 Shoemaker row, Blackfrs
Meade Thomas Wm. export porter merchant & dublin stout stores, 131A, Up. Thames st. & 20 Miles la. London bridge
Meaden George, solicitor, see Chamberlayne & Meaden
Meadon John, english & foreign bookseller, 352 Strand
Meader Henry, butcher, 29 King st. Camden town
Meader Thos. Burridge C. *Coach & Horses* P.H. 40 Leather la
Meader William, boot & shoe maker, 3 Harrow road
Meadows Henry, surgeon, 5 Windsor pl. Southwark bridge rd
Meadows James, artist, 5 Hope pl. Mile end rd. north side
Meadows John, carver & gilder, 71 Princes st. Leicester sq
Meadows John, livery stables, 32 Upper Eaton st. Pimlico
Meadows John, seal engra. & die sink. 49 Jewin st. Aldersgt
Meadows John, straw hat ma. 11 Sherborne pl. Blandford sq
Meadows Jonth. Davis, pictr. frame ma. 26 Liverpool st. City
Meadows Thos. baker, 1 Providence pl. Vauxhall bridge road
Meadows Thos. hosier & glover, 98 Crawford st. Portman sq
Meadows Thomas Parker, cooper, 13 Gravel la. Southwark
Meadows William, commercial agent, 25 Bread st
Meads Robert, tobacconist, Asylum road, Old Kent road
Meads Thomas, oilman, 41 Brewer st. Somers town
Meadus Charles, baker, 17 King st. Lower road, Islington
Meadus James, baker, 9 Frederick st. Portland town
Meadway George, sen. butcher, 117 Fore st. Cripplegate
Meadway George, jun. butcher, 2 Stockwell ter. Clapham rd
Meadwell Charles, carpenter & builder, 65 Theobald's road
Meager Thomas, beer retailer, 2 East India road, Poplar
Meager William, wine merchant, 343 Strand
Meagoe Henry, tailor, 9 Brook st. Grosvenor sq
Meahy Michael, working jeweller, 91 Hoxton Old town
Meakin George, grocer, 2 Vernon pl. Bagnigge wells road
Meakin John Forster, upholsterer, 29 Duke st. Grosvenor sq
Meakin William F. architect, 6 Albion pl. Blackfriars road
Meales John, schoolmaster, 7 Charles pl. East st. Walworth
Mean Thomas Charles, tailor, 87 Church st. Shoreditch
Mearis James, butcher, 4 Waterloo ter. Commercial rd. east
Meares John & Co. tailors & drapers, 10 Poultry
Meares Wm. salt merchant, 14 Davies st. Berkeley sq
Meares Wm. bread & biscuit baker, 15 Davies st. Berkeley sq
Meares Wm. cornchandler, 12 & 13 Davies st. Berkeley sq
Meares Wm. stables & job mast. 31 to 33 Grsvnr. mews, Grsvnr st
Mearing John, upholsterer, &c. 98 Gt. Portland st. Oxford st
Mearing Sarah (Mrs.), ham & beef dealer, 1 Water la. Blackfrs
Mears Benjamin, butcher, 9 Hereford pl. Commercl. rd. east
Mears Chas. & Geo. ch. & musicl. bell fndrs. 267 Whitechpl. rd
Mears Charles, undertaker & registrar, 124 Waterloo road
Mears Christopher, butcher, 9 Suffolk st. Pentonville
Mears John, potato dealer, 26 Church st. Shoreditch
Mears Joseph, butcher, 174 Whitechapel road
Mears Joseph, cowkeeper, 160 Bethnal green road
Mears Thomas, butcher, 5 Poplar High st
Mears William, bootmaker, 5 Upper James st. Golden sq
Mears William, brushmaker, 124 Holborn hill
Mears William John, plumber, 14 Up. Ashby st. Northamp. sq
Measam Thos. Chr. soft soap mak. 1 Manifold pl. Kennington la
Measam William, hatter, 12 Aldgate
Measure John, barrister, 4 Serle st. Lincoln's inn
Measures Thos. *New London Bridge* P.H. 20 Maze pond, Boro
Meates Chas. Lowe, italian warehouse, 40 Conduit st. Regnt. st
Meatyard William, upholsterer, 78 Mount st. Berkeley square
Meayers Richard, hatter, 93 Goswell road (West side), & 2 Manchester buildings, Holloway
Meayers Wm. straw hat. mak. 11 Charles pl. Chas. sq. Hoxton
Mecham Joseph, window blind mfr. 14 Warwick pl. Kngsln. rd
Mechanics' Magazine & Patent Office, 166 Fleet st
Mecklenburg Consulate, 9 Billiter square, City

Mechi John Joseph, cutler, dressing case, bagatelle, & magic strop manufacturer, 4 Leadenhall st
Mecklethwaite Frederick N. barrister, 30 Chancery lane
Medbury John, printers' smith, 42 Fleet la. Farringdon st
Medcalf Corns. nurseryman & flor. Beauvoir cresct. Islngton
Medcalf John, watch hand mak. 10 St. John's sq. Clerknwll
Medcalf Mary Ann (Mrs.), *Primrose* P.H. 109 Bishopsgt. witht
Medcalf Robert, solicitor, see Clarke, Medcalf & Gray
Medcalf Stephen, *Green Man* P.H. 10 Cambridge rd. Mile end
Medcalf Thomas, furrier, 18 St. John's lane, Clerkenwell
Medcalf Thomas, harness maker, 34 Worship st. Shoreditch
Medcraft Joseph, jeweller, 5 Lwr. Smith st. Northamptn. sq
Medcraft Joseph, straw hat manufr. 75 Goswell st
Medes George William, stationer, 22 Church st. Camberwell
Medex Mariam (Mrs.), tobacconist, 2 St. George's circ. Oblsk
Medex Simeon, snuff & cigar manufactr. 194 High Holborn
Medgett Thomas, cheesemonger, 6 Bray's buildgs. Islington
Medhurst Edw. John, bootmaker, 3 Prospect row, Bermondsey
Medhurst John, carpenter, 21 Newnham st. Edgware road
Medhurst Thomas, engineer, 1 Denmark st. Soho
Medical Adviser, 421 Strand
Medical Directory Office, 274 Strand
Medical Invalid & General Life Assurance Office (F. G. P. Neison, actuary), 25 Pall Mall
Medical Soc. of London (W. A. Harrison, sec.), 3 Bolt ct. Fleet st
Medical Times newspaper Office, 49 Essex st. Strand
Medicine Licence & Stamp Office, Somerset house; 10 to 4
Medico Botanical Society, 32 Sackville st. Piccadilly
Medland Hen. mfr. of druggsts. sundries see Deane & Medland
Medland Robt. oil & colorman, 6 Brett's bldgs. Camberwll. rd
Medler Henry, carpenter, 8 Wilson st. Finsbury square
Medley Edward, baker, 107 Old st. St. Luke's
Medley Fr. Wm. stock & share broker, 15 Old Broad st.
Medley Sophia (Miss), tobacconist, 8 Silver st. Wood st
Medley Thomas, horse hair manufactr. 102 Bermondsey st
Medlicott Edwd. lime, &c. mercht. see Poynder & Medlicott
Medlicott Edwd. Rd. tallow chandl. 17 Robert st. Grosvenor sq
Medlicott Fanny (Mrs.), toydealer, &c. 6 Dean st. Westminst
Medlicott Samuel, grocer, 33 Ridinghouse la. Langham pl
Medwin & Waylen, engineers, surveyors, & valuers of machinery, 5 Mark la. & Mansfield st. Boro' rd. Southwark
Medwin James, bootma. 23 Gracechurch st. & 118 Regent st
Medwin Matthias, cheesemonger, 2 Crown row, Walworth rd
Medworth John, coppersmith & brazr. 14 Crown st. Walwth rd
Mee Arthur, architect, Carlton Chambers, 12 Regent st
Mee Jas. potato dealer & fruiterer, 38 Chapel st. Pentonville
Meech James, carpenter, 5 Devonshire ter. Globe rd. Mile end
Meed George, soda water manuf. 37 Middle Grove st. Coml. rd
Meehan Thos. coal & potato dlr. 41 Gt. St. Andrew st. 7 dials
Meek John, baker, 69 Lambeth lower marsh
Meek John, cornchandler, 41 Holland st. Blackfriars road
Meek John, ironmonger, 88 Hackney road
Meek John, tanner, see Hackblocks', Clark & Meek
Meek J—. J—. wholesale stationer, rag merchant & manufacturer of mill boards, 44 Tooley st
Meek Mary Ann (Mrs.), music smith, 14 Windmill st. Tot. ct. rd
Meek Peter, fringe maker, 4 Bell's place, Holloway
Meek Robert, tobacconist, 1 Grenville st. Somers town
Meek William, chandler's shop, 35 Brick lane, St. Luke's
Meek William, grocer, 4 Gt. Quebec st. Montague square
Meek William, hairdresser, 7 Leicester st. Regent st
Meeking Charles, woollendraper, 111 Holborn hill
Meeking Charles, linendraper & carpet dealer, 61 & 62 Holborn
Meeking Henry, artificial flower maker, 39 King's rd. e. Chelsea
Meekum Thos. coffee rooms, 8 Margaret ter. Paddingtn. grn
Meeres Cecilia (Miss), chandler's shop, 203 Brick lane, Spflds
Meeres Frederick, stationer, 399 Oxford st
Meeres Jeremiah, cab proprietor, 19 Somerset st. Aldgate, & corn & coal dealer, 10 Little Somerset st. Aldgate
Meeres Thomas, surgeon, &c. 52 Brick lane, Spitalfields
Meers Samuel, *Anchor & Crown* P.H. New st. Deptford
Meeson Thos. & Sons, limeburners & coal merchants, Stratford
Meeson Richard, linendraper, 5 Bedford place, Com. rd. ea
Meeson Roger, barrister, 2 Pump court, Temple
Meffan John, builder, 13 Spring st. Paddington
Mége & Zaehnsdorf, manf. jewelrs. & goldsmiths, 6 Frith st
Meggeson George, chemist & druggist, 61 Cannon st
Meggison, Pringle & Co. solicitors, 3 King's rd. Bedford row
Meggs Elizh. & Ann, berlin wareho. Clifton pl. Wandswth. rd
Megg's Almshouses, 234 Whitechapel
Meggs William, timber merchant, 22 North pl. Kingslnd. rd
Meggy Robert, solicitor & scotch law agent, 15 London street, Fenchurch street, & 33 Trinity square, Borough
Meggy Robert Smith, engraver & printer, 38 Great Tower st
Megnin Charlotte (Mrs.), 3 *Jolly Weavers* P.H. 60 Wheeler st
Megson Christopher, baker, 1 Garden row, Camberwell road
Mehew Perren, beer retailer, Tivoli gardens, Battersea
Meier Ferdinand, wool merchant, 19 Basinghall st
Meikle Robert, lithographer, 145 Aldersgate st
Meikle Wm. engrav. engin. & lathe ma. 14 Panton st. Haymkt
Meikleham Wm. parliamentary agent, 23 Parliament st
Meiklejohn Rt. & Son, ale mer. Three Cranes wf. 69 Up. Thams. st
Meilan Daniel & Co. merchants, 15 New Broad st. City
Meiser Andrew, baker, 3 Up. Lisson st. Lisson grove
Meissner Adolphus, surgeon, 70 Great Tower st. City
Meldola Abraham, chemist, &c. 86 Leman st. Goodman's fields
Meldola Eleazer, surgeon, 6 Great Alie st. Goodman's fields
Meldola Rev. David, 10 Bevis marks
Meldrum & Pyman, brewers, Trafalgar st. Walworth road
Meldrum Robert, baker, 18 Clayton pl. Kennington rd
Melen John Alfred, hairdresser, 214 Shoreditch
Melendez Castaneda & Robertson, merch. 17 St. Helen's pl
Melhuish, Gray & Co. merchants, 29 St. Swithin's lane, City
Melhuish Henry, boot & shoe ma. 17 Sandwich st. Burtn. cres
Melhuish Samuel, bootmaker, 28 Bell yard, Temple bar
Melhuish Thomas Glass, physician, 60 York rd. Lambeth
Melhuish William, plumber, 9 Bedford st. Bedford row
Melladew Thomas, general merchant, 10 Mark lane
Melle William von, merchant, 59 Mark lane
Meller Eliza (Mrs.), day school, 30 Felix ter. Liverpool rd
Meller Henry James, barrister, 10 Clifford's inn, Fleet st
Meller Jas. H. horsehair & flock & bed manf. 63 Lant st. Boro'
Meller Thomas, butcher, Mare street, Hackney
Meller Walter, coachmaker, see Wyburn & Meller
Mellersh Wm. hop & seed mer. King's hd. inn yd. 54 Boro' High st
Mellet Edwin, grocer, &c. 4 Little Chapel st. Westminster
Mellett Thomas, poulterer, 14 Portman market
Melliard George, hat maker, see Berni & Melliard
Mellish Thos. Rt. & Co. cut glass ma. 7 Stafford row, Pimlico
Mellish George, special pleader, 3 Harcourt bldgs. Temple
Mellish Peter, agent, 4 Griffen st. Shadwell
Mellish Peter, silk hose dyer & trim. 72 Banner st. St. Luke's
Mellish Sarah A. (Mrs.), ladies' wardrobe dlr. 7 Stafford row
Mellish Thomas Rt. pat. pencil ma. 7 Stafford row, Pimlico
Melliss James Ferrier & Co. linen & cotton factors, & commission agents, 28 Ironmonger lane, Cheapside
Melliss James Ferrier, merchant, 28 Ironmonger lane
Mello William stockbroker, 80 Old Broad st. City
Mellor James & Co. lace merchants, 49 Bow lane, Cheapside
Mellor Benjamin, fruiterer, 28 Red Lion st. Holborn
Mellor Edward, cheesemonger, 36 Whitechapel road
Mellor John, barrister, 10 Farrar's buildings, Temple
Mellor William, tailor, 29 Union st. Borough road
Mellows James, furniture bro. 89 Salisbury st. Lisson grove
Melluish Robt. button & trim. slr. 57 Red Lion st. Holborn
Melnotte Madame, ladies' shoemaker, 23 Old Bond st
Melson Oliver, tailor, 31 Henry st. east, Avenue road
Melson Eliza (Mrs.), butcher, 201 Brick lane, Spitalfields
Melson Richard, commercial coffee ho. 69 London rd. Boro'
Melton Henry, hatter, 194 Regent st
Melton William solicitor, 6 Bedford row, Bloomsbury
Melvil Robert William, cornfactor, see King, Melvil & Co
Melvill Robt. & Son, watch jewellers, 40 King st. Clerkenwll
Melvill Frederick, coal mer. 40 King st. Northampton sq
Melville David & Co. lace thrd. & cotton mfs. 13 Wood st. City
Melville Geo. pianoforte ma. 14 St. James's pl. Hampstead rd
Melville Helenus, who. stationer, see Batty, Melville & Co
Melville James, sidney mercht. 12½ Bishopsgate st. within
Melville John, merchant, see Cruikshank, Melville & Co
Melville John, pat. handrail manufr. 64 John st. Fitzroy sq
Melvin Wm. Norfolk, auctioneer, 47 Hunter st. Brunswick sq
Memess Robt. chronometer, watch & clock ma. 7 Rosoman st
Menard Julie (Madame), staymaker, 22 South Molton st
Mence Amelia (Miss), milliner, 12 Argyll st. Regent st
Mence Edward, cheesemonger, 2 Sidney pl. Commerl. rd. east
Mence John Chas. boot, &c. maker, 4 Guildford pl. Spafields
Mence William, ham & tongue wareh. 87 Bridge rd. Lambeth
Menday James, chairmaker, 58 Snow's fields, Bermondsey
Mendes Abraham, stockbroker, 12 Copthall court
Mendham Geo. & Co. wine merchts. 1 Red Lion st. Clerkenwell
Mendham Chas. *Green Man* P.H. 39 Union st. Middlesex hos
Mendicity Society (T. L. Knevitt, sec.), 13 Red Lion square
Mendoza Michael, clothes salesman, 1 Rosemary lane, & 3 Sparrow corner, Minories
Menetrier Emile, importer of foreign goods, 57 Friday st.
Menger William, *White Horse* P.H. 30 Friday st
Mennis Mary (Mrs.), dining rooms, 7 Talbot ct. Gracech. st
Mennons Henry Jas. *City Arms* P.H. 15 Hunter st. Gt. Dover rd
Menor Thos. bootmaker, 2A, Royal Hospital row, Chelsea
Menser Louis, cigar manufacturer, 16 Wellclose square
Mensley Wm. shoemaker, 46 Edward st. Regent's park
Mentor James, coffee & cocoa roaster, 7 Rose st. Soho

Menzies Ann (Mrs.), coffee rooms, 6 Pagoda ter. Bermonds
Menzies Robert, carpenter, 12 Goswell road, east side
Menzies Robert, surgeon, 86 Upper Stamford st. Blackfriars
Menzler Lewis, baker, 1 Hayes court, Greek st. Soho
Mercers' Free Grammar School, 20 College hill
Mercers' Hall (James Barnes, clerk), Ironmonger lane
Mercer Horatio Wm. & Co. wine & spirit mer. 92 Lr. Thames st
Mercer Geo. carpenter, 7 Trinity st. Blackman st. Borough
Mercer James, carpenter, see Drewett & Mercer
Mercer Jeremiah, undertaker, 24 Brick lane, Spitalfields
Mercer John, bricklayer, 57 Praed st. Paddington
Mercer Joseph, carpenter, 2 Horsemonger lane, Borough
Mercer Robt. D. raw silk importr. 5 Church pass. Spital sq
Mercer Samuel, market gardener, Blue Anchor rd. Bermndsy
Mercer Thos. carpenter, 2 College terrace, Chelsea
Mercer Thos. oilman, 6 Leigh st. Burton crescent
Mercer Wm. chemist & druggist, 3 Union place, Clapham road, & 5 Lupus st. Belgrave road
Merceron Henry, attorney, see Lush & Merceron
Merchant Seaman's Auxiliary Bible Society (Edward Sutee, sec.), 19 Cheapside
Merchant Seaman's Office, 25 Birchinla. Cornhill ; hours 10 to 4
Merchant Seaman's Orphan Asylum (Wm. Dunn, sec.), Bow road ; office, 98 Gracechurch st
Merchant Tailors' Hall (Samuel Fisher), 30 Threadneedle st
Merchant Tailors' School, 6 Suffolk la. Cannon st
Merchant's, Tradesman's & General Mutual Life Assurance Company, & National Benefit Society (Thomas Musgrave, sec.), 5 Chatham place, Blackfriars
Mercier Francis, stockbroker, see Barclay, Allsop & Mercier
Merck Chas. & Thos. Wm. & Co. tailors, 16 Princes st. Regent st
Meredith Brothers, tea & italian wa. 15 Chandos st. Strand
Meredith & Reeve, solicitors, 8 New square, Lincoln's inn
Meredith Wm. & Sons, chronometer, watch & clock spring manufacturers, & watch glass dealers, 5 Goswell road
Meredith Chas. painter & glazier, 61 Davies st. Berkeley sq
Meredith Edwd. mourning collar manuf. 7 Clifton st. Finsbury
Meredith Edward T. surgeon, 15 Charles st. Westbourne ter
Meredith Eliza (Mrs.), *White Horse* P.H. 21 Wheeler st. Sptlfl
Meredith Fras. (Mrs.), greengrocer, 3 Low. Kennington lane
Meredith Fredk. corn & coal mer. 4 Irongate wf. Padntn. bsn
Meredith Frederick, linendraper, 151 Drury lane
Meredith George, bootmaker, 2 High st. Newington butts
Meredith Henry, bootma. 7 Wellington pl. Back rd. St. Geo. rd
Meredith James, milliner, 39 Burlington arcade
Meredith John, blind maker, 1 Crown court, Finsbury
Meredith John, coal mer. & wharfinger, 10 Whf. Cityrd. basin
Meredith John, livery stables, Kensington Gravel pits
Meredith John, newsvender, 2 Bridge row, Pimlico
Meredith Meredith, who. & retail druggist, 21 Cannon st. rd
Meredith Michael, architect, &c. 6 Blomfield st. Finsbury
Meredith Sophia (Mrs.), grocer, 48 Liverpool st. Bishopsgate
Meredith Thos. corn & coal mer. 108 Edgware road, Marylebo
Meredith Wm. biscuit baker, 21 Low. King st. Com. rd. east
Meredith Wm. fellmonger, 8 Butler's pl. New st. Dockhead
Meredith Wm. fruiterer, 36 Queen st. Bryanstone square
Meredith Wm. *Horse & Groom* P.H. Daggett's ct. Eldon st
Meredith Wm. rag & bottle dealer, 29 East st. Manchester sq
Meredith Wm. tea & italian warehouse, 19 Cannon st. rd
Meredith William, wholesale fancy biscuit baker, 21 King st. Commercial road east
Merewether Henry Alworth, serjeant at law, town clerk, Guildhall
Merewether Hen. Alworth, jun. barrister, 2 Inner Temple la
Merfield Mary A. (Mrs.), engr. & enamel. 5 Radcliffe ter. Gos. rd
Merfield Wm. cutler & optician, 20 Change alley, Cornhill
Merick Ludwik, tailor, 25 Osnaburgh st. Regent's park
Merigan Edward, *Bell & Crown* P.H. 180 Kingsland road
Merigan Michael, cheesemonger, 58 Broad st. Bloomsbury
Merington Geo. & Co. linendraps. & mercers, 154 New Bond st
Meriton Alfred, teadealer, 111 High Holborn
Merivale Herman, barrister, 3 Harcourt buildings, Temple
Merle William, working jeweller, 8 Albert pl. City road
Merlet Peter Fras. prof. of french, 15 Southampton st. Fitzry. sq
Merralls William, cheesemonger, 35 Tottenham court road
Merreck James, tobacconist, 47 Seymour st. Euston square
Merredew Joseph, coach & cart wheelwright, 9 South rw. New rd
Merrell Edward, tailor, 14 Fish st. hill
Merrell Geo. Key, plumber & paintr. 4 Up. Copenhagen st. Petnvl
Merrell Sarah (Mrs.), tinplate worker, 8 New st. Bishopsgate
Merrett, Simes & Merrett, linendrapers & silk mercers, 142 & 144 Regent st
Merrett Jas. fishmonger, 23 Langley pl. Commercial rd. east
Merrett Jas. undertkr. & trunkma. 61 Skinner st. Bishopsgt
Merrett Sarah (Miss), confectioner, 129 Tottenham ct. road
Merrett Thos. newsvender & printer, 7 St. John's sq. Clknwell
Merrett Thomas, *Rose & Crown* P.H. New whf. Whitefriars
Merrett William, butcher, 11 Bozier's ct. Tottenham ct. rd
Merrett William Gwillim, surgeon, 49 Leadenhall st
Merrick John Todd & Co. paper stanrs. Orange ct. Rose st. Soho
Merrick & Wooding, carprs. 1 London pl. London fi. Hackney
Merrick Charles, bootmaker, 52 Exeter st. Lisson grove
Merrick George, carver & gilder, 89 Bridge rd. Lambeth
Merrick John, corn chandler, 60 Church st. Shoreditch
Merrick John, die sinker, 125 Long acre
Merrick John, ginger beer ma. 26 Devonshire st. Lisson gr
Merrick John, ginger beer ma. 1 Salisbury st. Lisson grove
Merrick John, stationer & account book maker, 60 Watling st
Merrick John, turner & shuttle mkr. 3 Sclater st. Bethnl. grn
Merrick John Todd, paper stainer, 15 Lowther arcade, Strand
Merrick Joseph, watchmaker, 34 Paul street, Finsbury
Merrick Rd. desk & dressing case ma. 57 Red Lion st. Clknwl
Merrick Rd. potato dealer, 18 John st. west, Edgware rd
Merrick Rd. secret springer & polish. 10 Banner st. St. Luke's
Merrick Wm. shuttle maker & turner, 67 Church st. Shoredh
Merrifield Geo. ivory turner, 13 Great Turnstile, Holborn
Merrifield Robert, boot & shoe ma. Denmark hill, Cambrwl
Merrill Josiah & Rt. Tomkins, fruit brokers, 28 Pudding la
Merrill Frederick, oilman, 117 Brick lane, Spitalfields
Merrill Henry, grocer, 22 Wheeler st. Spitalfields
Merriman John & Jas. surgeons, 12 & 13 Young st. Kensington
Merriman James, butcher, 31 North Audley street
Merriman Jane (Mrs.), japanner, 31 Charles st. Westminster
Merriman Samuel Benj. solicitor, see Bolton, Merriman & Co
Merriman William, physician, 34 Brook st. Grosvenor sq
Merrin Henry, watchm. 3 Waterloo ter. Comml. rd. east
Merrin John, millwright & engnr. 8 Waterloo ter. Coml. rd. ea
Merriott Amy (Mrs.), stayma. 3A, Wigmore st. Cavendish sq
Merriott Robert, coachmaker, see Duffield & Merriott
Merritt Charles, wholesale glover, 3 Barbican
Merritt Dan. modelr. & composition ornamnt. mkr. 36 Foley st
Merritt Edwin, *Orange Tree* P.H. 16 Palace row, New rd
Merritt Francis, *Crown & Woolpack* P.H. 75 St. John st. rd
Merritt Francis, *Three Tuns* P.H. 39 Turnmill st. Clerknwl
Merritt Mary Ann (Mrs.), haberdasher, 61½ High st. Poplar
Merritt Thomas, *King's Arms* P.H. 128 Bishopsgate without
Merritt Wm. timber merc. 11 Addington st. York rd. Lmbth
Merritt Wm. toyman, 3 Westbourne st. Pimlico
Merry & Nutter, who. cheesemo. 133 & 134 Whitechapel High st
Merry Thos. & Son, drug & drysalters bro. 155 Fenchurch st
Merry Daniel, bootmaker, Church st. Hackney
Merry Edward, cheesemonger, 11 High st. Newington butts
Merry Jas. *Finsbury coffeehouse* P.H. 58 Wilson st. Fnsbry. sq
Merry Richard, jeweller, 41 Goswell st
Merry Thomas, perfumer & toyman, 380 Oxford st
Merryweather Edw. beer retailer, 3 Broadway, Ludgate hill
Merryweather John, corndealer, 231 Poplar High st
Merryweather Moses, pat. fire eng. & pump ma. 63 Long acre
Mersom Thomas, coal merchant, 15 Ernest st. Regent's pk
Merson Thomas, shoemaker, 35 Hackney road
Meryon Charles P. bookseller, &c. see Orger & Meryon
Meryon Edward, surgeon, 4 Bolton st. Piccadilly
Meryweather Francis, jun. pocket book ma. 71 Gt. Prescot st
Meryweather Frans. sen. pocket bk. ma. 42 Bedford st. Comcl. rd
Meryweather Wm. booksel. & statnr. 14 King st. Holborn
Mesnard Emma (Miss), milliner, 12 London st. Fitzroy sq
Mess & Co. merchants, 42 Crutchedfriars
Message William, carpenter, 114 Waterloo road
Messeena John Nathaniel, surgeon, 199 Poplar High st
Messenger John & Son, tripe dressers & pickled tripe warehouse, 1 Borough market, & 45 Farringdon market
Messenger Thos. & Sons, lamp & chandelier manufacturers, 63 Hatton garden
Messenger Ann (Mrs.), tripe dresser, 15 Cowcross st. Smithfld
Messenger Edmund, pork butcher, 98 Lambeth walk
Messenger Edmund, tailor, 4 Southampton st. Camberwell
Messenger Geo. boot & shoe maker, 3 Stepney rents, Hkny. rd
Messenger Henry J. writer on glass, 66 Warren st. Fitzroy sq
Messenger James, carpenter, 3 West st. north, Bermondsey
Messenger John, engraver & printer, 11 South row, New rd
Messenger John, *Marq. Wellington* P.H. 22 Gedlings t. Brmdsy
Messenger Matthew, fruiterer, 36 Dorset st. Portman sq
Messenger Michl. artifl. florist, 39 Gt. Percy st. Clerkenwell
Messengers' Offi. for Insolvent Court, 6 Lyon's inn, Strand
Messent Abraham, baker, 1 Adelaide place, Stepney green
Messent Harriet (Mrs.), milliner, 13 Broadway, Ludgate hill
Messent Samuel, oil & colorman, 42 St. George st
Messent Wm. Thos. shoe warehouse, 13 Broadway, Ludgt. hill
Messer Jas. John, chinaman, 35 Henry st. east, Avenue rd
Messer John, butcher, 12 Brunswick pl. Barnsbury road
Messer John, chemical stopperer, 22 Artillery la. Bishopsgate
Messer John, meat salesman, 12 New Newgate market

Messer Josiah, who. chemist, see Corbyn, Beaumont & Co
Messer Wm. hop factor, Calvert's bldgs. 241 Boro' High st
Messiter Thomas, barrister, 5 New square, Lincoln's inn
Metayer Adele (Madame), milliner, 11 Conduit st. Regent st
Metcalf & Stevens, wholesale teadealers, 74 Mark lane
Metcalf Charles, cabinet maker, 21 Holywell la. Shoreditch
Metcalf George, currier, 94 Wardour st. Soho
Metcalf Henry Francis, seedsman, see Bunyard & Metcalf
Metcalf John, boot & shoe maker, 41 Basinghall st
Metcalf John, cheesemonger, 41 Crown st. Finsbury
Metcalf John, *Coach & Horses* P.H. 140 Whitechapel High st
Metcalf John, seal & copper plate engraver, &c. 8 Pall mall
Metcalf Rebecca (Mrs.), tallow chandler, 7 Gt. Trinity lane
Metcalf Thomas, *Woolpack* P.H. Peter st. Bishopsgate
Metcalf Wm. ginger beer ma. 7 Smart's bldgs. HoxtonO.twn
Metcalf Wm. japanner, 24 Primrose st. Bishopsgate st
Metcalfe Philip & Co. distillers, ThreeMills distillery, Bromley
Metcalfe Jas. & Sons, mnchest. & scotch wa. 29 Gt. Dover st
Metcalfe & Simmons, tailors, 18 Castle st. Falcon square
Metcalfe & Woodhouse, solicitors, 5 New sq. Lincoln's inn
Metcalfe Christopher, teadealer, 16 Southampton row; & oil & italian warehouse, 26 Southampton row, Russell sq
Metcalfe Fred. bookbinder, 5 Marchmont st. Brunswick sq
Metcalfe Frederick, brush & comb maker, 130B, Oxford st
Metcalfe George, coffee rooms, 15 Lisson grove north
Metcalfe George, oil, seed & tallow broker, 18 Pinners' hall
Metcalfe George, tailor, 13 Nicholl square, Aldersgate
Metcalfe James, hop merchant, importer of isinglass & gelatines, & licensed dealer in patent malts, 20 Artillery place, Finsbury square
Metcalfe James Bell, surgeon, &c. Church st. Hackney
Metcalfe Jasper, cabinetma. 6 Clarendon sq. Somers town
Metcalfe John, stockbroker, 2 King's Arms bldgs. Cornhill
Metcalfe John, wharfinger, 5 Burr st. East Smithfield
Metcalfe John, wharfinger, see Watson & Metcalfe
Metcalfe John James, printer, 3 Grocers' hall court, Poultry
Metcalfe Joseph, grocer, 15 South place, Tibberton sq
Metcalfe Joshua, merchant, 29 Broad st. buildings
Metcalfe Mark B. wool dealer, 17 Gresham st. City
Metcalfe Sarah (Mrs.), ladies' schl. 22 Tredegar sq. Mile end
Metcalfe Thomas, carpenter, 4 Princes st. Bedford row
Metcalfe Thos. ginger beer manfr. 2 Church la. Coml. road
Metcalfe Thos. turner & brushma. 22 Elizabeth st. Eaton sq
Metcalfe Tristram Walker, chemist, 16 Crown st. Walwth. rd
Metcalfe Wm. agent to thread manufrs. 130 Wood st
Metcalfe William, barrister, 2 Stone bldgs. Lincoln's inn
Metchim Wm. P. stationer, 5 Red Lion pas. Red Lion sq. Hlbn
Meteyard Horace Wm. B.C.L. resident manager of Agricultural Cattle Insur. Co. 8 Chatham pl
Meteyard Horace Wm. barrister, 4 Gray's inn square
Metherell Jsph. linendraper, 7 Swan st. Trinity sq. Southwk
Methley Willoughby & Thos. Chas. ironmngrs. 51&52 Frith st
Methvin James, baker, 2 Store st. Bedford square
Methven John, baker, 14 Mount ter. New rd. Whitechapel
Metivier Joseph, worsted warehouse, 3 Broad ct. Long acre
Metropolis Chapel Fund Association (Rev. John Robinson, sec.), 4 Blomfield st. Finsbury
Metropolis Churches Fund (Rev. Wm. Dodsworth, sec. George Chas. Silk, assistant sec.), 79 Pallmall; hrs. 10 to 4
Metropolis Improvement Offi. 7 Whitehallyard; hrs. 10 to 4
Metropolitan Anti Corn Law & Parliamentary Registration Association (Sidney Smith, sec.), 2 Whitefriars st
Metropolitan Address Office, 12½ Gough square, Fleet st
Metropolitan Association for improving the Dwellings of the Industrious Classes (C. Gatliff, sec.), 19 Coleman st
Metropolitan Benefit Society's Asylum (W. Baker, sec.), 36 Francis place, Friar st. Southwark
Metropolitan Buildings Off. 3 Trafalgar square; 10 to 4
Metropolitan Commissioners in Lunacy (Edward Du Bois, clerk), 12 Abingdon st. Westminster; hours 10 to 4
Metropolitan Convalescent Institution (John Johnson, sec.), 32 Sackville st
Metropolitan Free Hospital (Edward John Chance, sec.), 29 Carey st. Lincoln's inn fields
Metropolitan Life Assurance Society (Richard Heathfield, superintendent), 3 Prince's st. Bank. See page 2034
Metropolitan Loan Company, 1 Craven st. Strand
Metropolitan (North of Thames) Road Office, 22 Whitehall place; hours of business 10 to 5
Metropolitan Patent Wood Pavement Co. (Wm. Prosser, jun. sec.); mills, Belgrave works, Ranelagh road, Thames bank, Pimlico
Metropolitan Public Carriages Office (Hensleigh Wedgwood, registrar), 6 Adelphi terrace
Metropolitan Railway Junction Office (John Cheese, sec.), 11 Clement's lane, City
Metropolitan Police Office, 4 Whitehall pl.; hours 10 to 4
Metropolitan Servants' Institution & Anti Domestic Fraud Association (J. N. Chapman, mgr.), 1 Lit. Queen st. Holborn
Metropolitan Visiting & Relief Association (William T. Haly, sec.), 4 St. Martin's place, Charing cross
Metropolis Improvement Office, 7 Whitehall yard
Mettam Samuel, coml. academy, 22 Paradise ter. Liverpl. rd
Mettam Wm. british lace mfr. 5 New Gloucester st. Hoxton
Mette, Beeker & Mette, tailors, 14 Sackville st. Piccadilly
Metzgar Sarah (Mrs.), tobacconist, 59 Long lane, Smithfield
Metzler G. & Co. pianforte, seraphine & military musical instrument manufrs. importers of musical instruments & publishers of music, 37 Gt. Marlborough st
Metzler Henry, pharmaceuticalchemist, &c. and die deutsche apotheke, 98 Minories
Meugens Peter Joseph, broker, 23 Mincing lane
Meunier Louis, *Hotel du Prince Albert*, 11 Leicester place
Meux Henry & Co. brewers, 268 Tottenham court road
Mew George, barrister, 12 King's Bench walk, Temple
Mewburn Bowyer, attorney, 9 Great Winchester st. City, & 9 Green terrace, New River head
Mewitt George, tobacconist, 1 Cross st. Hatton garden
Mewkill Robert, paper stainer, 1 Old Fish st. hill
Mewkill Robt. paperhangingma. 12 St. Andrew's hill, Drs.' com
Mews John, jun. hard confectnr. 33 Gt. St. Andrew st. 7 Dials
Mexican Co. (John MilthorpMaude, sec.), 32 Gt. Winchester st
Mexican & South American Company (Schneider Henry William, managing director), 10 New Broad st. mews
Meybruch Gustavus, tailor, 61 Gt. Carlisle st. Portman mkt
Meybruch Priscilla (Mrs.), tailor 45 Up. Berkeley st. Portmn. sq
Meyer & Hanfeld, fur dyers, 2 Queen st. Mile end New town
Meyer Henry & Co. waxchandlers, bleachers & melters & patent elliptic lamp manfs. 126 Piccadilly, & Appleton pl. Walworth
Meyer & Higgs, merchants, 37 Mincing lane
Meyer John & James, tailors, 36 Conduit st. Regent st
Meyer, Joseph & Meyer, skin & fur merchants & wholesale furriers, 21 Bow lane, Cheapside
Meyer Caroline (Mrs.), haberdasher, 34 Goswell st
Meyer Edwd. Benedict, billbro. 13 Angel ct. Throgmorton st
Meyer Edwd. Simeon, armylace, &c. manf. 22 Bedford st. Cov. gn
Meyer Elizh. (Mrs.), ostrichfeatherma. 30 Portland st. Soho
Meyer Frederick, merchant, Baltic coffee house
Meyer Frederick John, artist, 30 Up. North pl. Gray's inn rd
Meyer Henry Myer, wine importer, see Lazarus & Meyer
Meyer Jacob, wholesale job warehouse, 8 Mitre st
Meyer John Adrian, merchant, 37 Mincing lane
Meyer John Charles L. merchant, 38 St. Helen's pl. Bishopsgt
Meyer Joseph Anton, practical chemist, & extirpation of all kinds of vermin office, 69 King William st. City
Meyer Lyon Jacob, merchant, 2 Fenchurch buildings
Meyer Myer Hen. wine&spi.mer. 7 Magdalenrow, Gt. Prescot st
Meyer Nicholas, clock ma. 33 Charlotte st. Whitechapel rd
Meyer Philip Jas. prof. of the harp, 23 Judd pl. west, New rd
Meyer Solomon, merchant, 3 Circus, Minories
Meyer William Andrew, working jeweller, 34 Goswell st
Meyers Barnett, cane mercht. & stick ma. 18 Crutchedfriars
Meyers John Henry, button&trimming slr. 92 Union st. Boro'
Meyers Jsph. Thos. auctioneer, 7 Clark's pl. Islington High st
Meyers Kaufman, umbrella manufctr. 19 Swan st. Minories
Meyers Michael, umbrella ma. 9 Gt. Alie st. Goodman's fields
Meylan Sophia (Madame), court milliner, 6 Old Quebec st
Meymott John C. & Wm. J. solicitors, 86 Blackfriars rd
Meymott Charles, surgeon, 36 Blackfriars road
Meymott Edward, solicitor (secretary to the East Surrey Conservative society), 34 Stamford st. Blkfrs. rd. & Clapham
Meymott Frederic Wm. special pleader, 3 Figtree ct. Temple
Meymott Wm. who. stationer, see Riddle & Meymott
Meyrick Edward Stanton, *Orange* P.H. 33 Queen st. Pimlico
Meyrick Hen. tobacconist, 48 Broad st. & 17 Barrett st. Lambeth
Meyrick Peter Puget, beer retailer, 14 Wesbourne st. Pimlico
Meyrick William, barrister, 7 King's Bench walk, Temple
Meyrick William, solicitor, 2 Furnival's inn, Holborn, & 15 Cambridge terrace, Hyde park
Miall James butcher, 6 Queen's road, Dalston
Michael Jacob, solicitor, 9 Red Lion sq. Holborn
Michael Lyon, who. clothes salesman, 115 & 116 Houndsditch
Michalski Joseph, tobacconist, 19 Ryder's court, Leicester sq
Michau Louis (Madame), prof. of danc. 19 Dover st. Piccadilly
Michaux Walter, color&ital.wa. 5 Constitutionrow, Gray's inn rd
Michel Lecomte, tailor, 286A, Oxford st
Michele John George, surgeon, 23 Russell place, Fitzroy sq
Michell Edmund & Son, boot&shoe manfrs. 11 Aldenham ter
Michell Henry Bath, builder, 4 Northumberland st. Strand
Michell John, house agent, 6 St. Chad's row, Gray's inn rd
Michell John, pocketbook maker, 5 Swan st. Gt. Dover rd
Michell Rd. imp. of french flowers & feathers, 93 Oxford st

Michell Richard, laceman, &c. 94 Oxford st
Michell Sarah (Mrs.), milliner, 79 Quadrant, Regent st
Michell Wm. Henry, manufacturer of ladies' elastic gaiters, & importer of french mitts, 79 Quadrant, Regent st
Michelmore Edw. boot & shoe maker 9 Drake st. Red Lion sq
Michels Frederick, confectioner, 183 Sloane st. Knightsbridge
Michener James, wire worker, 23 St. Ann's court, Soho
Michia John, *Sir John Falstaff* P.H. 126 Old st
Michie Archibald, baker, 33½ Edwards st. Portman square
Michie James, mourning milliner, 111 Regent st
Micklam William Plucknett, tobacconist, 180 Fleet st
Mickle George & Co. house & estate agents & wholesale furniture dealers, 73 Great Russell st. Bloomsbury
Mickle David, architect, 37 Queen square, Bloomsbury
Micklefield Jas. Wm. *Old Red Lion* P.H. 13 Low. Fore st. Lmbh
Micklefield John, toy dealer, 25 King st. Tower hill
Micklefield Joseph, outfitter, 120 St. George st
Micklethwait Fred. Nathaniel, barrister, 30 Chancery la
Micklin Charles, surgeon, Battersea square
Mico Trustees Office (Rev. R. E. Hankinson, secretary), 15 Parliament st. Westminster
Microscopical Society (John Quekett, sec.), 21 Regent st
Micrulachi Emmanuele, merc. see Tamvaco & Micrulachi
Middlebrook Mary (Miss), basket ma. 36 Red Lion st. Spitalfi
Middlebrook Robert, blind ma. 29 Tabernacle wk. Finsbury
Middlebrook Samuel, basket ma. 8 Crispin st. Spitalfields
Middleditch Charles, oil & colorman, 1 Etham pl. Dover rd
Middleditch John, cheesemonger, 12 Clement's inn passage
Middleditch John, watch ma. 111 Shadwell High st
Middleditch Woolfrey, calico printer, 50 Old Change
Middlemiss Jane (Mrs.), baker, 14 Watney st. Commerl. rd.ea
Middlemist Robt. coal mer. Milford whf. Milford la. Strand
Middlesex County Court of Requests, Kingsgt. st. Holbrn.; summonses may be entered every day, except on Saturdays, from 9 to 3; on Saturdays, 9 to 2; Court days, Thursdays, & Fridays
Middlesex County Registration Office, East Temple chambers, 2 Whitefriars st
Middlesex & Essex Road Trust Office (Geo. Dacre, clerk), High st. Bow, Middlesex
Middlesex Hospital (Alexander Shedden, secretary), between 5 & 6 Charles st. Tottenham court road
Middlessex Reform Registration Office (Wm. Henry James, sec.), 15 New Bridge st. Blackfriars, & 2 Whitefriars st. Fleet st
Middle Temple, westward of Midd. Temple gate, Temple bar; *Treasurer's Office*, 1 Plowden buildings; hours 10 to 3; *Library*, Garden court; hours 11 to 4
Middleton Alex. grocer, 4 Up. Dorset place, Clapham road
Middleton Alfred, surgeon, 22 Finsbury pl. nth. Finsbury sq
Middleton Boswell Chas. custom ho. agt. 12 Harp la. Tower st
Middleton Boswell Chas. stationer, 7 Stucley ter. Camden tn
Middleton Charles, *Plough* P.H. 53 Fore st. City
Middleton Charles John, proctor, see Bedford & Middleton
Middleton Edward, grocer, 5 Cardigan pl. Kennington cross
Middleton Edward, warehouseman, 49 Friday st
Middleton George, cooper, 7 Worship st. Norton folgate
Middleton George, fruiterer, 28 Gresse st. Rathbone place
Middleton George, warehouseman, 66 Cheapside
Middleton Henry, trunk & case ma. 20 Plummer's row, Whitech
Middleton Hen. *Doyly Arms* P.H. 11 Orford pl. Mrlbrgh. rd. Chl
Middleton Jacob, pro. of astron. 1A, Ter. High st. Kensington
Middleton James, pencil maker, 7 King William st. City
Middleton James, solicitor, 7 Furnival's inn, Holborn
Middleton James, surgeon, 8 New Basinghall st
Middleton James Goodsell, artist, 76 Newman st. Oxford st
Middleton John, cooper & back mak. 11 Park st. Boro' market
Middleton John, maltster & brewer, Ranelagh rd. Thames bank
Middleton John, pencil maker, 32 Bloomsbury st. Bloomsby
Middleton Joseph, barrister, 4 Essex court, Temple
Middleton Joseph, *Upholders' Arms* P.H. 39 Poland st
Middleton Robert, pianoforte ma. 27 Noel st. Wardour st
Middleton Saffory, coach builder, 40 Long acre
Middleton Thomas, beer retailer, 28 East road, City road
Middleton Thomas, millwright & engineer, 3 Loman st. Boro'
Middleton Wm. Thos. watchma. 10 Grenada ter. Com. rd. east
Middlewood Joshua, adjuster of averages, &c. 11 Great Winchester st. & Lloyd's
Midgley & Kelso, la. school, 19 St. George's ter. Kensgtn. nw. tn
Midgley Thomas, *Twelve Bells* P.H. 21 Bride lane, Fleet st
Midlam John, *Old Plough* P.H. 16 Beaufort bldgs. Strand
Midland Counties coal company, (Saml. Holloway, agt.) 16 Wharf, south side, Paddington basin
Midwinter Thomas, grocer & teadlr. 196 Brick la. Spitalfields
Midwinter Wm. academy, 12 Newland terrace, Kensington
Mier Herman, who. sponge dealer, 49½ Newington causeway
Mier Moris, tailor & draper, 2 Dorset ter. Gt. Dover rd. Boro
Miers Isaac Levy, who. clothier & slop seller, 9 Houndsditch
Miers Samuel, basket ma. 7 Millpond st. Jamaica row, Berm
Miers Thomas, ironmonger, 34 & 75 Whitechapel road
Miers William, miniature frame maker, 8 Greek st. Soho
Miers William John, electrotypist, 8 Greek st
Miersch Charles, tin plate worker, 40 King st. Seven dials
Miesir Andrew, baker, 67 Charlotte ter. New cut, Lambeth
Mieville Andrew Amedée & Co. stock brokers, 11 Angel court
Mieville Jean Louis, merchant, see Kraeutler & Mieville
Migotti Girardo, jeweller, 42 Maiden lane, Covent garden
Miland John, booksel. & stationer, 35 Chapel st. Grosvenor pl
Milbanke Richard Tyler, surgeon, 8 Burwood pl. Edgwarerd
Milborn Robert, tailor, 1 Great Bath st. Clerkenwell
Milbourn James, carman, 2 Boston st. Hackney road
Milbourne James, gilder & looking-glassmaker, 195 Strand
Milburn Robt. & Christopher, warehousemen, 37 Newgate st
Milburn & Son, solicitors, 117 Chancery lane
Mildred & Goyeneche, merchants, 9 New Broad st
Mildred & Watson, for. exch. & ins. brokers, 75 Old Broad st. City
Mileham John, tea dealer, 117 Wardour st. Soho
Milen John, hairdresser, 8 Queen st. Tower hill
Miles & Bellin, army & east india agents, office for transmission of packages overland to India, 69 Cornhill
Miles & Edwards, furniture printers, upholsterers & cabinet manufs. 134 Oxford st. mnfy. Red Lion yard, Old Cavendish st
Miles Elizth. & Thos. bead manufs. 12 Queen st. Finsbury
Miles & Martin, oilmen & cheesem. 4 Gilbert's pas. Clare mrkt
Miles (Misses), academy, 30 Lr. Phillimore pl. Kensington
Miles Misses, professors of music, 31 Baker st. Portman sq
Miles Alfred Webb, army tailor & trousersma. 3 Haymarket
Miles Alfred Wm. bellhanger, engineer, &c. 24 Dowgate hill
Miles Allan, currier, 76 Blackman st. Borough
Miles Charles, architect, 15 St. James's square
Miles Charles, tin plate worker, Stratford broadway
Miles Edmund, jun. merchant, 31 Gt. St. Helen's, Bishopsgte
Miles Edward, bead maker, 61 Long alley, Finsbury
Miles Edward, steel & copperplate printer, 22 Leather lane
Miles Edward, surgeon-dentist, 15 Liverpool st. Bishopsgate
Miles Edwin, saddlers' ironmonger, &c. 43 Bridgeho. pl. Boro'
Miles Elizh. (Mrs.), cheesemong. & eggmer. 17 Broadway, Wstm
Miles Elizth. (Mrs.), manufacturing chemist, Bow common
Miles Felicia (Miss), tobacconist, 4 Narrow st. Limehouse
Miles George, cheesemonger, 29 Upper Ebury st. Pimlico
Miles Geo. *Duke's Head* P.H. 6 Reeve's mews, Grosvenor sq
Miles George Powell, teadealer, 30 Marlborough st. Regent st
Miles Henry, barrister, 2 Raymond's buildings
Miles Henry, cabinet maker, 16 Seabright pl. Hackney rd
Miles Henry, painter, 9 Tufton st. Horseferry rd. Westminster
Miles Henry William, *Red Lion* P.H. 7 Duke st. Manchester sq
Miles James, cheesemonger, 102 Tottenham court road
Miles James, estate, ho. & gen. agent, 3 Brabant ct. Philpot la
Miles James, *Yorkshire Grey* P.H. 24 Woodstock st. Oxford st
Miles James Arthur, wholesale gas furniture, bell crank & key warehouse, 13 Pancras lane, City
Miles Jesse, collar & harness maker, 4 West st. Soho square
Miles John, boot & shoe maker, 2 Theberton st. Islington
Miles John, builder, 23 Dowgate hill
Miles John, cabinet maker & undertaker, 91½ Leather lane
Miles John, chandlers' shop, 22 Somerset st. Aldgate
Miles John, size maker, 41 Crucifix lane, Bermondsey
Miles John, surgeon, 17 Charterhouse square
Miles John, surgeon & chemist, 78 Gracechurch st
Miles John, tailor, 56 Cornwall road, Lambeth
Miles John, tin plate worker, 20 Turk st. Bethnal green
Miles John, wheelwright, Addington square, Camberwell
Miles John Clement, artist, 29 Herbert st. New North road
Miles Sir Jonathan, lunatic asylum, 22 to 34 Hoxton Old tn
Miles Richard, chairmaker, 14 Baker's row, Clerkenwell
Miles Richard, marble & stone merchant, Kingsland basin
Miles Sarah (Mrs.), fruiterer, 7 Whitmore pl. Hoxton Old tn
Miles Septimus, watchmaker, 8 Lit. Carter la. Doctors' com
Miles Thomas, *Bull & Ram* P.H. 114 Old st. St. Luke's
Miles William, boot & shoe maker, 2 Whitmore pl. Hoxton
Miles William, dentist, 27A, Howland st. Fitzroy square
Miles William, lodging house, 8 Providence row, Finsbury
Miles William, oilman, 31 Lamb st. Spitalfields
Miles William Henry, scale maker, 200 Shoreditch
Miles Wm. Henry, tin plate worker, 1 Garden rw. London rd
Mileson Abel Kitching, optician, 23 Emmett st. Poplar
Milestone James, coffee rooms, 2 Cross st. Hatton garden
Milestone Robert, fishmonger, 6 Swallow place, Hanover sq
Miley Miles & Son, trimming wareho. 42 Warwick st. Golden sq
Miley Thomas, cheesemonger, 46 Albany st. Regent's park
Milford Henry, commission merchant, 33 Old Jewry
Milgate Thomas, warehouseman, see Tersey & Milgate

Milgrove William, dining rooms, 23 Liverpool st. Bishopsgt
Mill Jacob, merchant & underwriter, Lloyd's
Mill John, barrister, 1 Plowden buildings, Temple
Mill Thos.surgeonden.10&11 Bridge ho.pl.Newngtn.causewy
Millar & Palmer, wine & spirit brokers, 41 St. Mary at hill
Millar Rd.&Co.who.pickle & sauce ms.5 Princes st.Spitalflds
Millar David, watchmaker, 20 Perceval st. Clerkenwell
Millar George, printer, silk ma. &c. see Gent, Millar & Co
Millar James,coal merchant,4 Wellington rd.St.John's wood
Millar James Cochrane, surgeon, 48 Clifton st. Finsbury
Millar John, grocer, 23 Clipstone st. Fitzroy square
Millar John, surgeon, Bethnal house, Cambridge road
Millar John, who. stay warehouseman, 25 Hatton garden
Millar Joshua, surgeon, 4 Colet pl. Commercial road east
Millar William, merchant & com. agent, 49 Fenchurch st
Millard & Adams, solicitors, 15 Great Distaff lane
Millard Joseph & Sons, spectacle makers & opticians, 24 Coppice row, Clerkenwell
Millard & Margetts, solicitors, 19 Tokenhouse yd. Lothbury
MillardSaml.&Wm.who.tea,coffee, spice dealers,&c 9 Rood la
Millard Alfred, oil & colorman, 24 East st. Walworth
Millard Benjamin, potato salesman, 22 Borough market
Millard Benjamin, plumber, &c. 11 Queen st. Pimlico
Millard Chas. P. tea, coffee & coal agt.seeFranks & Millard
Millard James, bootmaker, 60 High st. St. Giles's
Millard James, pianoforte tuner, 4 Woburn bldgs.Tvstck. sq
Millard James, shoe warehouse, 25 Judd st. Brunswick sq
Millard James, surgeon, 5 Soley terrace, Pentonville
Millard John, chair maker, 8 Cumberland st. Shoreditch
Millard John, optician, 5 York place, Upper st. Islington
Millard John, plumber, painter, &c.24 Margaret st.Cavdh. sq
Millard Thomas, bookseller, 70 Newgate st
Millard Thomas, boot & shoe maker, see Stevens & Millard
Millard Wm. cabinet manuf. 30 Chapel st. Holywell mount
Millard Wm. confectioner, 10 Brecknock pl. Camden N.town
Millard Wm.trunk manufac. 19 Greville st. Hatton garden
Millburn James, carman, 17 Woodbridge st. Clerkenwell
Milledge George, carpenter, Dunsany pl. Wandsworth road
Milledge James, plumber & painter, 82 Albany rd.Cambewl
Milledge Thomas William, tailor, 21 Store st. Bedford sq
Millen David, baker, 7 Crown st. Walworth road
Millen Richard, tool dealer, 69 Cowcross st. Smithfield
Millen Stephen Richd. chemist, 70 Shoe lane, Fleet st
Miller Alexander&Co.general comm.agts. 26 Walbrook,City
Miller & Burgess,glue ma.&bone crushers,Manor la.Bmndsy
Miller & Carr, solicitors, 47 Eastcheap
MillerChas.Taverner & Sons,spermaceti refiners,wax chandlers & oil merchts. 179 Piccadilly, & Dorset whf. Millbank
Miller, Fidel & Co. clockmakers,10 Broad st. Bloomsbury
Miller & Field, booksellers & stationers,6 Bridge rd. Lambeth
Miller, Forbes & Thompson, ship & insurance brokers & general agents, 117 Fenchurch st
Miller,IngleyThomas & Co.brewers,56 Lower Shadwell, & *Crown* brewery, 14 Mary st. New road
Miller & Jones, tailors & woollen drapers, 158 Oxford st
Miller & Lowcock,wh.teadealrs.4 Queen st. pl.Up.Thames st
Miller & M'Mullen, wine merchants, 37 Crutched friars
Miller & Owen (Misses), milliners, 141 New Bond st
Miller & Potter, coal factors, 96 Lower Thames st
Miller, Ravenhill & Co. engineers & iron ship builders,Glasshouse fields, Ratcliff, & the Orchard wharf, Blackwall
Miller & Richard, letter founders, Edinburgh (Thomas Hodgson, agent), Aldine chambers, Paternoster row
Miller Susan & Charlotte, dress ma.16 Duke st.Manchestr.sq
Miller & Thomas, coal dealers, 23 Eagle st. Red Lion sq
Miller Thos.&Co.wh.tea & coffeedlr.13 Camomile st.Bishopsg
Miller Thos. & Son, whols. dealers in quills, 144 Cheapside
Miller Wm. & Co. brandy distillers, Great Scotland yard, & 46 Leicester sq
Miller Wm. P. & Son,carvers & gilders, 81 Gt. Titchfield st
Miller & Williams, surgeons, 1 Claremont ter.Stk.Nwngtn.rd
Miller & Williams, surgeons, 34 Beauvoir ter. Kingsland
Miller Alisan (Mrs.), boarding house, 17½ Watling st
Miller Ann (Mrs.), fruiterer, 18 Wilton st. Westminster
Miller Barnabas, tobacconist, 6 Gt. Suffolk st. Borough
Miller Boyd, merchant, City club house, Old Broad st. City
Miller Catherine (Mrs.), tobacconist, 1 Up. East Smithfield
Miller Charles, stationer, Church st. Stoke Newington
Miller Chas.Bayfield,chemist,dentist,&c. 15 Cheyne wk.Chls
Miller Christian Fredk.porkman, 31 Turnmill st. Clerkenwell
Miller Daniel, repository for toys, silver, ivory, & pearl goods, fancy stationery, turnery, desks, workboxes, combs, brushes, baskets, & fancy articles, 32 Lowndes st. Belgrave sq
Miller David, baker, 27 Down st. Piccadilly
Miller David, oilman & tallow chandler, 80 Bunhill row
Miller Elisha, cheesemonger, 419 Strand
Miller Eliza (Mrs.) linendraper, 72 Goswell road
Miller Elizabeth (Mrs.), boarding ho. 21 Mansell st.Goodm.fi
Miller Elizabeth (Mrs.), coffee rooms, 70 & 71 Farringdon st
Miller Elizabeth (Mrs.), hosier & glover, 132 Minories
Miller Felix Martin, artist, 6 Lower Eaton st. Pimlico
Miller Frederick, baker, 2 Goswell road, 103 Goswell st.; & 32 Pitfield st. Hoxton
Miller Frederick, furniture bro.14 Lit. James st. Bedford rw
Miller Frederick, poulterer, 73 Piccadilly
Miller Geo. baker, 33 Duke st. Grosvenor sq
Miller Geo. baker, 18 Long alley, Finsbury
Miller Geo. cabinetma. 18 Bridgho.pl.&13 Newingt.causewy
Miller Geo. carpenter, 19 Cursitor st. Chancery lane
Miller Geo. commission agent, 42 Gutter la. Cheapside
Miller Geo. furniture broker, 17 Long alley, Finsbury
Miller Geo. furnit. broker, 10 Wittam's buildgs. Old st. rd
Miller Geo. tallowchandlr. & oilman, 19 Whitechapel High st
Miller Hanh. A.(Mrs.),ladies'sch.4 St.Matthew's pl.Hckny.rd
Miller Henry, bread & biscuit baker, 140 Fenchurch st
Miller Henry, *Ben Jonson* P.H. 95 Houndsditch
Miller Henry, *Cumberland Head* P.H. & *Green Gate tavern* P.H. 66 Bath st. City road
Miller Henry, merchant, 12 Fenchurch st
Miller Henry, tinplate worker, 4 Swan yard, Shoreditch
Miller Henry Wm. toy warehouse, 9 Conduit st. Padddington
Miller Ingleby Thos.crown brewery store, 56 Lower Shadwell
Miller Ingleby Thos. jun. solicitor, 3 Abchurch lane, City
Miller James, baker, 4 Drummond st. Euston square
Miller James, basket maker & toy dlr. 5 Bermondsey New rd
Miller James, broker for Turkey produce, 3 Philpot lane
Miller James, butcher, 37 Chiswell st. Finsbury
Miller James, elastic spring maker, 18 Dean st. Fetter lane
Miller James, physician, 40 Welbeck st
Miller James, tooth powder manufacturer, perfumer & stationer, 46 Howland st. Fitzroy square
Miller James, watchmaker, 262 Poplar High st
Miller James, who. cabinet maker, 13 Blackman st. Borough
Miller John, american bookseller, 26 Henrietta st.Covent gar
Miller John, baker, 11 City road, Old st
Miller John, bookseller, 404 Oxford st
Miller John, bootmaker, 9 Holywell st. Strand
Miller John, cabinetmak.&appraiser, 30 Mount st. Lambeth
Miller John, carman, 10 Warren mews, Warren st. Fitzroy sq
Miller John, chandler's shop, 1 Cavendish st. New North rd
Miller John, chemist & druggist, 16 Pitfield st. Hoxton
Miller John, civil engineer, 2 Parliament st
Miller John, corndealer, 47 Lisson grove north
Miller John, lodging house, 30 Essex st. Strand
Miller John, patten maker, 22 Camden st. Walworth
Miller John, ship biscuit baker & grocer, 89 & 90 Tooley st
Miller John, straw bonnet mnfr. 18 Richmond st. St. Luke's
Miller John, tobacconist, 96 Old st. St. Luke's
Miller John Alfred, tailor, 39 Frederick st. Hampstead rd
Miller John Edmund, butcher, 1 Ropemakers' st. Finsbury
Miller John Gale, bricklayer, 18 Blenheim st. Oxford st
Miller John Spittall, warehouseman, see Durie & Miller
Miller John Thomas, butcher, 30 Dorset st. Spitalfields, & Spitalfields market
Miller Joseph, appraiser, &c. 4 Acton pl. Bagnigge wells rd
Miller Joseph, auctioneer, 21½ Blackfriars road
Miller Joseph, carpenter, 80 Harrow road
Miller Joseph, *Cock* P.H. 17 Litchfield st. Soho
Miller Joseph, dairyman, 5 Albion pl. Up. Kennington la
Miller Joseph, dairyman, 39 Seymour place, Bryanstone sq
Miller Joseph, fishmonger, 74 Piccadilly
Miller Joseph, grocer & cheesemonger, 28 New rd. Sloane st
Miller Joseph, lion brewery, 13 Lambeth walk
Miller Joseph, plumber, 49 Whittlebury st. Euston square
Miller Joseph, *Surrey & Sussex hotel*, 246 Blackfriars road
Miller Joseph John, tailor, 13 Mount pl. Whitechapel road
Miller Mark Blowers, attorney, 2 Clifford's inn, Fleet st
Miller Mary (Mrs.), broker, 21 Lr.Ranelagh st.Lr.Grosvr.pl
Miller Richard, oil & colorman, 79 Paradise row, Chelsea
Miller Richard Little, ironmonger, see Gibbons & Miller
Miller Robert, agent to Campbell & Co. brewers, Edinboro', & wine, ale, porter & cider merchant, 6 Cross st.Finsbury pl
Miller Robert, barrister, 32 Essex st. Strand
Miller Robert, carpenter, &c. 2 Newcastle ct. College hill
Miller Robt. gardnr.& florist, 7 Providence pl.Up.Kenngtn.la
Miller Robert, provision mer. & agt. 34 Terrace, Trinity sq
Miller Robert, tailor, 7 Gunpowder alley, Shoe lane
Miller Robert, tailor, 30 Marylebone lane, Oxford st
Miller Robert, watchmaker, 4 Upton pl.Commercial rd.eas
Miller Samuel, barrister, 4 New square, Lincoln's inn
Miller Samuel, butcher, 4 Union st. east, Spitalfields
Miller Samuel Fredk. solicitor, 10 Duke st. St. James's

Miller Sarah (Mrs.), *Queen's Head* P.H. 5 King st. Tower hill
Miller Thomas, artists' color & pencil manufac. 56 Long acre
Miller Thomas, baker, 8 Green st. Leicester square
Miller Thomas, baker, 14 Henrietta st. Manchester sq
Miller Thomas, cheesemonger, 13 Regent st. Horseferry rd
Miller Thomas, cheesemonger, 5 Weybridge pl. Mile end road
Miller Thomas, cotton manfr. see Horrockses, Miller & Co
Miller Thomas, dairyman, 27 Edward st. Regent's park
Miller Thomas, grocer, 1 Commercial place, Kentish town
Miller Thomas, linendraper, 157 Shoreditch High st
Miller Thomas, oil & colorman, 44 Mansell st. Goodman's flds
Miller Thomas, pawnbroker, 15 Kingsland road
Miller Thomas, potato dealer, 145 Brick lane, Spitalfields
Miller Thomas Philbrow, letter press & copper plate printer & engraver, 8 Queen's terrace, Marlboro' road, Chelsea
Miller William, baker, 2 Earl st. Kensington
Miller William, bookbinder, 65 Poland st. Oxford st
Miller William, bookseller, 3 Upper East Smithfield
Miller William, coach builder, 13 Cambridge pl. Rgts. pk
Miller William, engraver, 47 Greek st. Soho
Miller William, plumber, painter, &c. 32 Brewer st. Golden sq
Miller Wm. pianoforte hammer ma. 49 Brewer st. Somers tn
Miller Wm. printer, 5 Drummond st. Euston sq
Miller Wm. ready made linen wa. Kensington gravel pits
Miller Wm. surgeon & chemist, 27 King st. St. James's
Miller Wm. tailor, 27 White Hart pl. Low. Kennington lane
Miller Wm. working jeweller, 3 Mora place, City road
Miller Wm. A. ready made linen wa. 94 High st. Notting hill
Miller's Wharf, Lewis Mac Kinnon, Low. East Smithfield
Millest Samuel, fruiterer & greengrocer, 283 Strand
Millett William, dairyman, 5 Lion st. New Kent road
Millgate Thomas, manchester wareho. see Tarsey & Millgate
Millicent Thos. jun. fur & skin dresser, 24 Noble st. Goswell st
Millidge Benj. Josiah. teadealer, 77 Park st. Camden town
Millidge Thos. workg. jeweller, 33 Wellington st. Goswell st
Millidge William, carpenter, 5 St. Peter's pl. Walworth com
Millidge William, glass & china dealer, 65 Strand
Milligan James & John, corndealers, 64 Portland road
Milligan John & Robert, manufacturers of patent water closets, & plumbers, painters & glaziers (successors to Chambers), 47 Carey st. Lincoln's inn
Milligan Charles, corndealer, Hungerford wharf, Strand
Milligan Charles, umbrella maker, 183 Fleet st
Milligan James, jun. statuary & mason, 64 Portland rd
Milligan Sarah (Mrs.), milliner, 11 Vere st. Oxford st
Milliken William, sec. to bank of Australasia, 2 Moorgate st
Millikin John, surgical instrument maker & cutler, 161 Strand
Millin Simon, butcher, Clare market
Millingen Charles, umbrella & parasol manfr. 5 Spital sq
Millingen P. furrier & feather ma. 6 Dorren's row, Comml. rd
Millington (Crowley) & Co. who. ironmongrs. 151 Up. Thames st
Millington Charles, tobacconist, 54 Charlotte ter. Lambeth
Millington Eleanor S. (Miss), fancy repos. 6 Union pl. Islgtn
Millington John, turner & undertaker, 1 Up. Rathbone pl
Millington Thomas, window glass, & lead, & varnish, & color manufacturer, & merchant, 87 Bishopsgate without
Millis Samuel, beer retailer, 33 Chester pl. Kengtn. cross
Millis Wm. ironmngr. & tin plate wkr. 5 Holles st. Clare mkt
Millis Wm. Fras. *Artichoke* P.H. 20 Clare st. Clare market
Millist Daniel John, tobacconist, 77 Bunhill row
Millman Wm. coal factor & ship & insurance broker, 7 Lower Thames st. see Flint & Millman
Millns Catherine, chandler's shop, 12 York st. Kingsland rd
Millor Wm. & Co. accountants, 30 Rood lane, Fenchurch st
Millross James, plasterer, 15 Cirencester pl. Fitzroy square
Mills Alfred & Charles Samuel, cheesefactors, 21 Tooley street (Wm. Barnes, agent)
Mills Edw. & Hen. artificial florists, 36 North st. Pentonville
Mills James & Co. window glass warehouse, 42 Tooley st
Mills James & Son, brewers, Sussex plate, Old Kent road
Mills & Jay, coal factors & shipping agents, 28 St. Mary at hill, & Northumberland wharf, Blackwall
Mills John & Son, enamelled leather mfs. 17 John st. Old Kent rd
Mills Joseph & Wm. coopers, 6 Hawthorndean pl. Limeho
Mills, Puckle & Co. hop & corn factors, 246 Borough High st
Mills Richard & Son, butchers, 26 Maze, Tooley st
Mills Samuel & Son, printers, 11 Crane court, Fleet st
Mills Thos. & Son, tailors & habit ma. 91 Jermyn st. St. James's
Mills Wm. Hen. & Jas. pawnbrokers, 103 Edgware rd. Maryleb
Mills Alex. *George IV.* P.H. 1 Copenhagen st. Pentonville
Mills Alexr. Wm. law stationer, 2 Carey st. Lincoln's inn
Mills Arthur, barrister, 2 Paper buildings, Temple
Mills Bryan, packer & agent, 9 Union ct. Old Broad st
Mills Catherine (Mrs.), potato saleswoman, 3 Counter st. Boro'
Mills Charles, hosier & glover, 47 Kensington High st
Mills Daniel, boarding house, 18 & 19 Weymouth st. Portland pl
Mills David, baker, 9 Great Peter st. Westminster
Mills Ebenezer, stationer & printseller, 18 Wells st. Oxford st
Mills Edmund, butcher & porkman, 1 Hart st. Crutched friars
Mills Francis, bootmaker, 11 Poland st. Oxford st
Mills Francis, staymaker, 2 Minories
Mills Geo. beer retailer, 13 Aldgate High st
Mills Geo. coach & harness maker, 171 Goswell st
Mills Geo. engrv. & printr. 49 Basinghall st. & 7 James' pl. Hoxtn
Mills Geo. mathematical instrument mak. 82 St. George st
Mills Geo. oil, color & italian wareho. 33 South Molton st
Mills Geo. printer's joiner, 11 Fleet lane, Farringdon st
Mills Geo. undertaker, 28 Gravel lane, Southwark
Mills Geo. Ireland, surgeon, 28 Francis st. Tottenham ct. rd
Mills Henry, barrister, 4 Pump court, Temple
Mills Henry, bunting & stay manufacturer, 18 Gresham st
Mills Henry, grocer, 7 Kensington ter. Kensington gra. pits
Mills Henry, *Mills tavern*, 47 Southampton bldngs. Holborn
Mills Henry, newsvender, 12 Beech st. Barbican
Mills Henry, watchmaker & jeweller, 149 & 171 Oxford st
Mills James, beer retailer, 4 Newgate st
Mills Jas. ale & sandwich rooms, 291 High Holborn
Mills James, boot & shoemaker, 6 Wilmot st. Russell square
Mills James, haberdasher, 28 Grosvenor st. west. Eaton sq
Mills James, milkman, 13 Coal yard, Drury lane
Mills James, pianoforte manuf. 21 William st. Hampstd. rd
Mills James, pin, needle & fish hook warehouse, 7 Eastcheap
Mills James, tailor, 19 Newcastle st. Strand
Mills James, tallow chandler & oilman, Camberwell green
Mills John, *Anchor & Hope* P.H. Ferry road west, Poplar
Mills John, baker, 77 Goswell st
Mills John, *Barking Dogs* P.H. 1 Tabernacle walk, Finsby
Mills John, *Camden Arms* P.H. 1 Gt. Randolph st. Camden tn
Mills John, coach lamp manuf. 38 Primrose st. Bishopsgt. st
Mills John, confectioner, 2 Eldon place, Lower st. Islington
Mills John, corndealer, 5 Fashion st. Dockhead
Mills John, hosier & outfitter, 274 Oxford st
Mills John, land surveyor, auction. & valuer, 24 Poultry
Mills John, solicitor, 3 Brunswick place, City road
Mills John, upholsterer, 7 Dorrington st. Coldbath fields
Mills John Alfred, corndealer, 2 Duke st. Chelsea
Mills John Hillam, barrister, 1 Paper buildings, Temple
Mills Joseph, hosiery manufactory, see Ludlow & Mills
Mills Maria (Mrs.), tobacconist, 5 Stephens acre, Blackwall
Mills Mark, ship & ins. broker, see Douglas & Mills
Mills Martha (Mrs.), tobacconist, 65 Up. North pl. Gray's inn rd
Mills Mary Ann (Miss), grocer, 44 Gravel lane, Southwark
Mills Matthew, grocer, 35 Little Earl st. Seven dials
Mills Michael, silver pl. worker, 17 Ossulston st. Somers tn
Mills Pauline (Mrs.), staymaker, 14 Somerst st. Portman sq
Mills Rebecca (Mrs.), staymaker, 318 Regent st
Mills Richard, *Bird in Hand* P.H. 17 Long acre
Mills Richard (late Birchall & Co.), music seller & publisher, &c. 140 New Bond st
Mills Richard, locksmith & bell hanger, 62 King st. Borough
Mills Rd. printer & stationer, 33 Aylesbury st. Clerkenwell
Mills Richard, shipwright, &c. 335 Wapping High st
Mills Richard Mark, salt merchant, see Tribe, Mills & Co
Mills Robert, grocer & cheesmger. High st. Stoke Newington
Mills Robt. telescope maker, 49 Southampton st. Pentonville
Mills Roger, linendraper, 3 Manor place, Holloway
Mills Samuel, butcher, 26 Seymour pl. Bryanstone square
Mills Samuel, wheelwright, 10 Bett's st. Ratcliff highway
Mills Sarah (Miss), lodging house, 18 Arundel st. Strand
Mills Sarah (Mrs.), rug manfr. Neate st. Cobourg rd. O. Kent rd
Mills Thomas, baker, 159 Poplar High st
Mills Thomas, boat builder, Thames bank, Pimlico
Mills Thomas, builder, Brewers green, Westminster
Mills Thomas, carpenter, 40 Drummond st. Euston sq
Mills Thomas, carpenter, &c. 49 Spencer st. Goswell road
Mills Thomas, dyer & scourer, 30 Charles st. Westminster
Mills Thomas, grocer, 48 Crawford st. Portman square
Mills Thomas, leather cutter, 8 Wheeler st. Spitalfields
Mills Thomas, morocco case ma. 18 Newcastle st. Frngdn. st
Mills Thomas, musician, 2A, Bishop yd. Chas. st. Grosvnr. sq
Mills Thomas, painter, 23 Queen st. Golden square
Mills Thomas, woollen draper, see Hill & Mills
Mills Thomas D. cabinet ma. 11 Frederick place, Goswell rd
Mills Walter, bootmaker, 53 Cheapside, & 28 Newgate st
Mills William, boot & shoe maker, 53 King st. Seven dials
Mills William, cabinet maker, see Farley & Mills
Mills William, coal merchant, 23 Queen's row, Walworth
Mills William, coffee rooms, 23½ Castle st. Holborn
Mills William, furniture broker, 430 Oxford st
Mills William, glove manufacturer, 3 Foster la. Cheapside
Mills William, *Golden Lion* P.H. Stoney st. Boro' market
Mills William, grocer & cheesemonger, 264 Poplar High st

Mills William, house agent, 35 Bridge house pl. Borough
Mills Wm. stove grate maker, 18 Adam st. east, Portman sq
Mills William, stove & range manfr. 1 Princes pl. Kenngtn.cr
Mills William, upholsterer, &c. 430 Oxford st
Mills William, wheelwright, 4 & 15 Berners mews, Berners st
Mills Wm. Dixey, grocer & cheesemonger, 52 Strutton ground
Mills Wm. George, *Three Tuns* P.H. 52 Pennyfields, Poplar
Mills Wm. Hy. wine & spirit mer. & wine cooper, 66 Mark la
Millsom John, farrier, 9 Railway mews, Drummond st
Millson Elizh. (Mrs.), *One Tun* P.H. 59 Chandos st. Cov.gdn
Millsom John, farrier, 9 Railway mews, Drummond st
Millson William Jas. architect, &c. see Wilson & Millson
Millson Wm. chem. & druggist, 8 Diddington pl. Caledonian rd
Millward Elizh. (Mrs.), bedstead ma. 24 Up. Clifton st. Finsbury
Millward Elizh. (Mrs.), brass ma. 29 George st. Grosvenor sq
Millward John, carpenter, 51 Gt. Carlisle st. Portman mkt
Millward John, gun barrel prover, Church la. Whitechapel
Millwood Edwd. mason, &c Kensington pl. Kensgtn. gravl. pits
Millwood John, beer retailer, 15 Camden st. East st. Walw
Millwood John, boot & shoe ma. 23 Nutford pl. Edgeward rd
Millwood Wm. *D. of York* P.H. Kensgtn. pl. Kensgtn. gravl. pits
Millwood Wm. Chas. shoe maker, 35 Dorset st. Portman sq
Milman William, barrister, 11 Paper buildings, Temple
Milne Alex. Geo. & Co. merchants, 10 George yd. Lombard st
Milne, Cruden & Co. thread & linen manufacturers, 18 Bread st. & Aberdeen
Milne, Parry, Milne & Morris, solitrs. 2 Harcourt blds. Temple
Milne Alex. ship & ins. broker, 20 New East India chambers
Milne Alfred, barrister, 4 Garden court, Temple
Milne Elizabeth (Miss), milliner, 4 Drake st. Red Lion sq
Milne George, cutler, 59 Snowsfields, Bermondsey
Milne John, *Flying Horse* P.H. Wilson st. Finsbury
Milne Thos. engraver & printer, 19 Bedford st. Bedford row
Milne William, barrister, 3 Old square, Lincoln's inn
Milner Chas. & Co. tobacco & snuff mfs. 14 & 16 Cannon st. City
Milner & Morley, silk & twist manufacturers, 9 Gresham st. & at Leek; agents, Langford & Bristed
Milner, Morley & Co. silk manufs. 9 Gresham st. City
Milner Thomas & Son, patent portable fire resisting box & safe manufacturers, 47A, Moorgate st. City
Milner Arthur (Mrs.), bootma. 10 Calthorpe pl. Gray's inn rd
Milner Charles, tobacco manufacturer, see Milner & Co
Milner Fras. H. who. oil. & color mer. 48 Crispin st. Spitalfi
Milner George, custom ho. & shipping agent, 1 Cullum st
Milner Henry, furniture broker, 80 Shadwell High st
Milner Jemima Maryanne (Mrs.), milliner, 98 New Bond st
Milner John, stock & share broker, 1 Copthall chambers
Milner John B. muffin baker, 8 Crown court, Pall mall
Milner P. accountant of *Imperial Fire Insurance Comp.* Sun court, Cornhill, & 16 Pall mall
Milner Richard, grocer, 12 Ferry road west, Poplar
Milner Richard, jun. cooper, Millwall, Poplar
Milner Thomas, painter & builder, 13 Gt. Smith st. Westmstr
Milner Wm. *Fishmongers' Arms* P.H. 2 St. George's rd. Boro'
Milnes & Robinson, coal factors, Coal Exchange
Milnes Robert, beer retailer, 27 Gloucester tr. Vauxh. bldg. rd
Milnes Thomas, sculptor, 3 Judd place east, New road
Milns Edward, linendraper, 33 Parliament st. Westminster
Milns Edward, carver, 15 Rosaman st. Clerkenwell
Milo John, tallowchandler, 49 Kingsland road
Milo Theophilus C. imp. of cigars & snuff, 10 Wellington st. Boro
Milo Thos. tobcnst. & imptr. of meerschaum pipes, 402 Strand
Milroy Alexander, & Co. merchants & insurance brokers, 6 Cross lane, St. Mary at hill
Milroy Thomas & Sons, wholesale saddlers, 72 Cornhill
Milroy Gavin, physician, 30 Fitzroy square
Milsom George Page H. surgeon, 70 Tottenham court rd
Milsom Thomas, cowkeeper, 1 Lit. Wild st. Lincoln's innfields
Milson Jane (Mrs.), mop & brush ma. 214 Kent st. Boro
Milsum & Coates, linen & wool. drapers, 112 York rd. Lambth
Milton Agnes (Mrs.), milliner, 5 Cobourg pl. Lr. rd. Rotbrth
Milton David, *Duke of Clarence* P.H. 3 North st. Lisson gr
Milton Edward, tailor, 2 Crescent place, Brompton
Milton George, carman, &c. Elizabeth terrace, Islington
Milton Isaac, bootmaker, 2 New Union st. Lit. Moorfields
Milton James coal dealer, 6 Pierrepoint place, Islington
Milton John, tailor, 46 Poland st. Oxford st
Milton John, teadealer & grocer, 10 Gt. Marylebone st
Milton Mary Ann (Mrs.), lodging ho. 41 Somerset st. Portm. sq
Milton Richard, flexible canvas mnfr. Commercial road east
Milton Thomas Allum, carpenter, 5 Union row, NewKent rd
Milton William, dining rooms, 25 Church st. Shoreditch
Milton William, locksmith, &c. 1 Pierrepoint pl. Islington
Milward John C. *Union* coffee rooms, 2 Cross lane, Long acre
Milward William, chandlers' shop, 30 Mint st. Borough
Mimmack William, butcher, 12 Derby st. Gray's inn road
Mimpriss Thos. Roberts, surgeon, 23 Prospect pl. Wndswth. rd
Mimpriss William, jeweller, &c. 31 Halfmoon st. Piccadilly
Minas Geraes Mining Company (Geo. D. Keogh, sec.), 8 Tokenhouse yard
Minasi Fred. Jas. academy, 3 Colebrooke row, Islington
Minasi Hen. S. sicilian consul genl. 15 Cambridge st. Edgw rd
Minchener Joseph, butcher, 14 Harper st, New Kent road
Minchin James, tailor, 1 White's row, Spitalfields
Minchin William, *Masons' Arms* P.H. 3 Oxford market
Minerva Life Assurance Company (Wm. Thos. Robinson, actuary & sec.), 84 King William st. City; see page 2035
Minden Emanuel, *Horns* P.H. 27 Middlesex st. Aldgate
Mines Royal Copper Co.'s Wareho, (Benj, Joseph Spedding, sec.) Golden heart wharf, Upper Thames st
Mines Louisa Mrs.), shoemaker, 6 York st. Middx. hospital
Mines Philip, tailor, 76 Margaret st. Cavendish square
Minet James Wacker, tobacconist, 2 Stafford st. Lisson gr
Minet Wm. Brissault, solicitor, see Pering, Minet & Smith
Mingay Geo. shipchandler & oilman, 36 Narrow st. Limehouse
Mingay William, tailor, 1 Bingley place, New road
Minier, Adams & Nash, seedsmen, 60 Strand
Minifie Elizabeth (Miss), milliner, 14 Gt. Castle st. Regent st
Minifie William, hairdresser, 398 Oxford st
Mining Journal, Railway & Commercial Gazette, 26 Fleet st
Mining Record Office, 5 Shorter's court, Throgmorton st
Minister Edward & Co. reporters of tailors' fashions, 8 Argyll place, Regent st
Minister Edward & Co. tailors & habit makers, by appointment, to her Majesty, 8 Argyll place, Regent st
Minister John, boarding house, 8 Buckingham st. Strand
Minnett Wm. coal dealer, 9 Queen's ter. Queen's rd. Dalston
Minns James, butcher, 1 Royal Hospital row, Chelsea
Minns Jane (Mrs.), tobacconist, 48 Whitechapel road
Minns John, *George Fourth* P.H. 1 St. Alban's ter. Vauxhl. br. rd
Minns Thomas, *British Queen* P.H. 156 Alfred pl. Waterloo rd
Minor Geo. Thos. haberdasher & hosier, 16 Mount st. Lambeth
Minors Benjamin, brushmaker, 239 Kent st. Borough
Minshaw Samuel, beer retailer, 10 Benjamin st. Cowcross
Minshull & Vanderpant, dentists, 51 Margaret st. Cavendish sq
Minson James, com. boarding house, 18 Peter's hill, Drs'.com
Minster Edwin, fishmonger, 19 Chapel st. New road
Minter Fenn, tailor, 28 Chapel pl. Long la. Bermondsey
Minter George, upholsterer, &c. 33 Gerrard st. Soho
Minter Henry, oil & colorman, 41 Whitefriars st. Fleet st
Minter John, *Horse & Groom* P.H. 60 King st. Borough
Minto Alexander, grocer & teadealer, 74 Wardour st
Minto Thomas, tailor, 1 Goodwin's court, St. Martin's lane
Minton Edwd. *Mitre tavern* P.H. 7 Connaught ter. Edgwr. rd
Minton Henry, tobacconist, 270 Oxford st
Minton Richard, plumber & glazier, 43 St. John st. road
Minton Robt. Joseph, hosier & outfitter, 87 St. George st
Minton Samuel, piecebroker, 50 Duke st. Aldgate
Minton William, cooper, 66 Crawford st. Portman square
Minton William, cowkeeper, 1 Knightsbridge green
Mintorn John, alabaster importer, 36 Soho square
Mintram Charlotte (Mrs.), hairdresser, 7 Burlington arcade
Minty Wm. Hayward, surveyor of taxes, 32 Bloomsbury sq
Mirehouse John, common serjeant, 60 Upper Seymour st
Mirfin John & Co. shawl merchants, 16 Cateaton st
Mirfin George Harvey, attorney, 12 Gray's inn pl. Gray's inn
Misa y Bertemati, wine merchant, 11 Crutched friars
Miskin & Vinen, surgeons, 8 Broad st. Horselydown
Miskin & White, custom ho. agts. 9 Water la. Lr. Thames st
Miskin Nicholas, surgeon, &c. 59 Bridge road, Lambeth
Miskin William, surgeon, 24 Grosvenor pl. Camberwell rd
Mison Charles, locksmith, 7 Clarence place, Deptford
Missen Jsph. *Duke of York* P.H. Ormond yd. York st. St. Jas's
Mist Thomas, wine merchant, 29 Soho square
Mitan Samuel, engraver, 8 Polygon, Clarendon square
Mitcalfe Wm. coal factor, 4 Coal exchange, Low. Thames st
Mitcham John, tobacconist, 54 Kingsland road
Mitchel Peter, tailor, 1 Little Cadogan place, Sloane st
Mitchelhill James, tailor, 20 Argyll st. Regent st
Mitchell & Beynon, metallic hole & steel pen ma. 7A, Falcon square, Aldersgate, & St. Paul's works, Birmingham
Mitchell & Co. wine & brandy merchants, 48 Lime st
Mitchell David & Co. woollendrapers, &c. 40 Cloth fair
Mitchell Geo. Duncan & Co. cornfac. 56 New corn exch. Mark la
Mitchell Geo. & Son, bricklayers, 6 Carlton ter. St. Georg's. rd
Mitchell & Hill, solicitors, 1 Bury court, St. Mary Axe
Mitchell Jas. & Son, charcoal ma. Uxbridge st. Newingtn. cau
Mitchell John & Co. russia merchants, 9 New Broad st. City
Mitchell John & Edw. curriers, &c. 60 Shoreditch High st
Mitchell William & Son, stationers, printers, booksellers & newsvenders, 39 Charing cross
Mitchell Andrew, carpenter & joinr. 1 & 2 Robert st. Limehouse

Mitchell Andrew, tailor, 14 Great Castle st. Regent st
Mitchell Andrew, translator of languages, 27 Tokenhouse yd
Mitchell Ann (Miss), library & undert. 9 New inn yd. Shoredh
Mitchell Ann (Mrs.), grocer, 1 Carrington pl. Down st. Mayfr
Mitchell Archibald, bookseller, 16 Charles st. Middlesex hos
Mitchell Benjamin, tailor, 2 Glo'ster st. St. John's st. road
Mitchell Charles, cowkeeper, &c. 18 Liverpool st. Bishopsgt
Mitchell Charles, *Grapes* P.H. 7 Fore st. Cripplegate
Mitchell Charles, publisher, bookseller & general advertisement agent for all the town & provincial newspapers, proprietor & publisher of the Newspaper press directory, & authorised London agent for Galignani's messenger, Paris, 12 Red Lion court, Fleet st
Mitchell Christian (Mrs.), baker, 9 King st. Westminster
Mitchell Edward, dining rooms, 88 Tooley st
Mitchell Edward, tailor, 6 Guildford st. ea. Wilmington sq
Mitchell Edward, woollen draper, 18 Cloth fair, Smithfield
Mitchell Edward Robt. cabinet carver, 1 Radnor st. St. Luke's
Mitchell Elizabeth (Mrs.), milliner, 12 Litchfield st. Soho
Mitchell Eliz. (Mrs.), butcher, 147 Church st. Shoreditch
Mitchell Emanuel, boot & shoe ma. Vassall rd. Cambrwl. nw. rd
Mitchell Francis Hen. broker, 2 Hammond ct. Mincing lane
Mitchell Fredk. carver & gilder, 4 Holland pl. Kensington
Mitchell Geo. *Boar's Head* livery stables, Counter st. Borough
Mitchell Geo. carpent. & builder, 43 Duke st. Lincoln's inn fi
Mitchell Geo. clockmaker, 8 Woodbridge st. Clerkenwell
Mitchell Geo. comp. ornament ma. Green Dragon yd. Holbn
Mitchell Geo. *Drum* P.H. 63 Snow's fields, Bermondsey
Mitchell Geo. estate & house agt. 21 Motcomb st. Belgrave sq
Mitchell Geo. tobacconist, 35 Gt. Windmill st. Haymarket
Mitchell Geo. whalebone preparer, 45 Cannon st. road
Mitchell Geo. Mich. mgr. London & Westm. Bk. 4 Stratford pl
Mitchell Hen. *Beckford Head* P.H. 38 Old st. St. Luke's
Mitchell Hen. cheesemonger, 51 Rosoman st. Clerkenwell
Mitchell Hen. colonial broker, 12 Commercial sale rooms
Mitchell Hen. melter & tallow chandler, 63 Whitechapel rd
Mitchell Hen. turner, 9 Red Lion passage, Red Lion square
Mitchell Hen. undertaker, 8 Boundary st. Shoreditch
Mitchell Hen. upholsterer, 1 Cadogan row, King's rd. Chelsea
Mitchell Hen. Geo. hairdresser, 2 Ryder's court, Leicester sq
Mitchell James, barrister, 58 Chancery lane
Mitchell Jas. charcoal & old coal burner, 7 Wm. st. Newing. cau
Mitchell James, engineer, see Neilson & Mitchell
Mitchell James, fruiterer, 12 Walker's court, Golden sq
Mitchell James, hosier, glover & shirt maker, 231 Regent st
Mitchell James, livery stables, 32 Upper Montagu st
Mitchell James, tallow chandler, 20 Gt. Wild st. Linc. inn fi
Mitchell James, wire worker, 3 Henry st. St. Luke's
Mitchell James, woollendraper, 57 West Smithfield
Mitchell James Edward, law stationer, 20 Gt. Carter lane
Mitchell Jas. Fras. timber mercht. 2 James st. Cannon st. rd
Mitchell Jas. Peter, scotch ale brewer, 7 Hungerford wharf
Mitchell John, baker, 70 Cadogan pl. Sloane st. Chelsea
Mitchell John, beer retailer, 132 Praed st. Paddington
Mitchell John, beer retailer, 2 Trafalgar st. Walworth rd
Mitchell John, bookseller & publisher to her Majesty, 33 Old Bond st
Mitchell John, bricklayer, 7 New King st. Deptford
Mitchell John, builder, Chester mews, Grosvenor place
Mitchell John, *Cheshire Cheese* P.H. 51 Grosvenor row, Pimlico
Mitchell John, cider merchant, Chamberlain's whf. Tooley st
Mitchell John coffee rooms, 72 London wall
Mitchell John, colonial broker, see Maitland & Mitchell
Mitchell John, confectioner, 360 Rotherhithe
Mitchell John, corn chandler, 33 Shadwell High st
Mitchell John, cutler, 15 President st. east, Goswell road
Mitchell John, engraver & printer, 7 St. James st. Clerkenwell
Mitchell John, feather maker, 26 Exeter st. Sloane st
Mitchell John, livery sta. 74 Grosvenor mews, Grosvenor st
Mitchell John, London & Edinburgh steam packet office, 35 Leadenhall st
Mitchell John, printer, see Walton & Mitchell
Mitchell John, professor of dancing, 4 Portsmouth st
Mitchell John, tailor, 22 Ernest st. Regent's park
Mitchell John Dennison Rose, tobacconist, 4 King's cross
Mitchell John Williamson, dentist, 3 Hanover st. Hanover sq
Mitchell Joseph, baker, 15 Laystall st. Liquorpond st
Mitchell Joseph, cabinet maker, 5 Elizabeth st. Hackney rd
Mitchell Joseph, trunkmaker, 3 Lit. Bell alley, Coleman st
Mitchell Joseph Samuel, tailor, 2 East st. Red Lion square
Mitchell Jos. Theophilus, merchant, see Roberts, Mitchell & Co
Mitchell Joseph Thos. surgeon, 33 Harleyford pl. Kennington
Mitchell Margery (Mrs.), boarding house, 26 Arundel st. Strnd
Mitchell Michael, stables, 39 Keppel mews north, Keppel st
Mitchell Michael, surgeon, 83 Lower Thames st
Mitchell Peter, stockbroker, 1 Copthall ct. Throgmorton st
Mitchell Richard, linendraper, 19 Newington causeway
Mitchell Richard, livery stables, 163 Borough High st
Mitchell Robert, baker, 25 Warner st. New Kent road
Mitchell Robt. linendrap. 19 Middle Queen's bldgs. Knghtsbr
Mitchell Robt. plumber & glazr. 15 Portsea pl. Edgware rd
Mitchell Robert, surgeon, New Cross road, Deptford
Mitchell Robert Geo. baker, 32 Gibson st. Waterloo road
Mitchell Robert G. coal agent, 16 Wharf, Paddington basin
Mitchell Samuel, boot & shoe maker, 21 London wall
Mitchell Samuel, *Crown* P.H. 22 Broad st. Golden sq
Mitchell Samuel, pat. wire blind ma. 9 Old Compton st. Soho
Mitchell Sarah (Mrs.), milliner, 13 Charles st. Grosvenor sq
Mitchell Sophia Ann (Mrs.), milliner, 50 Wigmore st
Mitchell Thomas, accountant, 4 Copthall bldgs. Throgm. st
Mitchell Thomas, bootmaker, 6 Norris st. Haymarket
Mitchell Thomas, builder, 40 Brown's lane, Spitalfields
Mitchell Thomas, clockmaker, 70 Theobald's road
Mitchell Thomas, confectioner, 4 Park pl. Mile end road
Mitchell Thomas, farrier, 23 Berners mews, Berners st
Mitchell Thomas, linendraper, 3 Leadenhall st
Mitchell Thomas, tailor, 261 Oxford st
Mitchell Thomas, tailor, 37 Wyndham st. Bryanstone sq
Mitchell Thos. Francis, cabinetma. 9 Wilson st. Finsbury
Mitchell Viet Chas. black paint ma. Lower Kennington la
Mitchell Wm. bed & mattress maker, 228 Kent st. Borough, & 9 Upper Fitzroy st. Fitzroy sq
Mitchell Wm. butcher, 8 Regent pl. Horseferry road
Mitchell Wm. hairdresser, 35 Boston st. Dorset sq
Mitchell Wm. picture & furn. dlr. 127 London rd. Southwk
Mitchell Wm. tailor, 8 Opera arcade, Pall Mall
Mitchell Wm. tin plate worker, 28 Nicholas la. Lombard st
Mitchell Wm. window glass cutter, 32 Tottenham court rd
Mitchell Wm. C. carpenter & builder, 28 Ebury st. Pimlico
Mitchell Wm. Geo. stock & share broker, 8 Throgmorton st
Mitchelson Henry, *Feathers* P.H. 8 Warren st. Fitzroy sq
Mitchelson Wm. John, printer, 51 Turnmill st. Clrknwll
Mitchener Edwd. A. & Wm. printers, 116 Gt. Russell st. Blmsby
Mitchener Edmund, printer, 5 Brewer st. Somers town
Mitchener Henry, printer, 3 Edward st. Hampstead rd
Mitchener Rich. window blind ma. 39 Gt. Castle st. Regent st
Mitcherson Edwd. *Duke of York* P.H. 9 Royal Hospital rw. Chls
Mitcheson Wm. & Sons, anchor & shipsmiths, & ironmongers, 2 & 3 Garford st. & Emmett st. Limehouse hole, & at Millwall; Chain & Anchor wf. St. Geo. strs. East Country Dock
Mitchiner Wm. tobacconist & printer, 7 Old Chapl. rw. Kntsh. tn
Mitson James, chandler's shop, 19 Broadwall, Blackfrs. rd
Mitton Arthur Henry, oil & italian warehouse, 40 Warwick st. Pimlico, & 3 Glo'ster ter. Vauxhall Bridge rd
Mitton & Nealor, solicitors, 23 Southamptn. bldgs. Chncy. la
Mitton Harriet (Mrs.), milliner, 49 Northampton st. Clknwll
Mivart James Edward, jobmaster, Cock yard, Berkeley sq
Mivart James Edward, *Mivart's hotel*, 41, 42, 43 & 44 Brook st. & 56 Davies st. Grosvenor square
Mixed British & Portuguese Commission (Baron A. T. Valdez, sec.), 3 Delahay st. Westminster
Mizen James, beer retailer, High st. Deptford
Mizen Robert baker & grocer, Uxbridge rd. Bayswater
Moade George, *City Arms* P. H. 6 Blomfield st. Finsbury
Moakes Chas. John, coal merchant, 14 Grey terrace, Great Dover road; & British wharf, 21 Clink st. Bankside
Moase James, saddler & harness maker, Stratford High st
Moat Routledge & Co. wholesale glovers, 115 Wood st
Moat Wm. Crofton, surgeon, 28 Up. Berkeley st. Portm. sq
Moate Charles R. metal & russia broker, 65 Old Broad st
Moates William, accountant, 29 Great St. Helen's
Mobbs & Phillips, linendrapers, 34 Portman pl. Edgware rd
Mobbs Henry, coach joiner, 44 Foley st. Foley place
Mobbs John, workg. jeweller, &c. 10 Lit. Warner st. Clerknwl
Mobbs Samuel, *Prince of Saxe Cobourg* P.H. St. Mary-le-Strand place, Old Kent road
Moberly Wm. Son & Co. mer. & isinglass imp. 28 Gt. Winchestr. st
Mocatta Abraham & Elias, jun. indigo brokers, 39 Mark lane
Mocatta & Goldsmid, brokers in bullion, specie, diamonds & pearls, 53 Threadneedle st. & 1 Old Broad st. City
Mocatta David, architect & surveyor, 32 Brunswick sq
Mocatta Jacob, cochineal, drug & e. i. broker, 10 Lime st. sq
Mocatta John, jun. stockbroker, Stock Exchange, & 3 Copthall chambers
Mockett Wm. cornfactor, Jack's coffeehouse, Mark lane
Mode Adolph, cap maker, 3 Warwick lane, Newgate st
Moet & Chandon, merchants, 123 Fenchurch st
Moffat Alexander, baker, 14 Aylesbury st. Clerkenwell
Moffat David, baker, 126 Up. Seymour st. Euston square
Moffat James, merchant, 1 Bishopsgate st. within
Moffatt & Co. tea agents, 28 Fenchurch st
Moffatt Thomas & Robert, tea brokers, 38 Mincing lane

Moffatt Alexander, brushmaker, 10 King st. Covent garden
Moffatt George, see Gillespies, Moffatt & Co. merchants
Moffatt Harriet (Mrs.), *Admiral Benbow* P.H. 107 Golden la
Moffatt John, coffee rooms, 82 Bethnal green road
Moffatt John Ackers, *One Tun* P.H. 24 Strand
Moffatt John W. music string & military musical instrument manfr. & importer, 29 Minories, & 1 Mansell st. Goodman's fi
Moffatt Wm. Bonython, architect, see Scott & Moffatt
Moffet Elspeth (Mrs.), *Sun* P.H. 104 Upper East Smithfield
Moger Francis Horace, solicitor, 17 Paternoster row, City
Moger Thomas, cheesemonger & poulterer, 113 Holborn hill
Mogford Thomas, artist, 16 Norton st. Portland place
Mogg Edwd. mapslr. & publishr. 14 Gt. Russell st. Covent grdn
Mogge David, *Bell* P.H. 20 Brick lane, Spitalfields
Mogge Christian, sugar refiner, see Briebach & Mogge
Mogge Maria (Mrs.), *Sir Sidney Smith* P.H. Dock st. U. E. Smfi
Moggeridge Henry John, cooper, 16 Cleveland st. Fitzroy sq
Moggridge John, baker, 17 Gt. Suffolk st. Borough
Moggridge Rich. brass cock founder, 44 Turnmill st. Clrknwl
Moggridge Robert, grocer, 160 Kingsland road
Moggridge Robert Jas. newsvender, 7 Brydges st. Covnt. gardn
Moggridge William Henry, dentist, 13 Old Burlington st
Moginie Cornelius, cheese & bacon merchant, 145 Goswell st
Moginie Nathaniel Cranch, solicitor, see Pontifex & Moginie
Moginie Samuel, watchmaker, 17 Brewer st. Pimlico
Mohan Felix Wm. saddler, 15 Nowell's bldgs. Liverpool rd
Mohan John, wine merchant, 13 Great Tower st
Moir David & Son, carpenters & joiners, 38 Cross st. Finsbury
Moir Alexander, baker, 424 Strand
Moir Alex. coal merchant 1 Bromley st. Commercial rd. ea
Moir William, carver & gilder, 54 Paddington st. Marylebn
Moir William, plumber, 20 White Lion st. Norton folgate
Moira Colliery (Ashby de la Zouch), sole London consignee, Arthur Burton, Ranelagh wharf, Commercial rd. Pimlico
Moister Wm. wardrobe purchaser, 3 Fulwood's rents, Holb
Mold Benjamin, boot & shoe maker, 62 North st. Edgwarerd
Mold William, academy, 2 Paulton st. Church st. Chelsea
Mole John, bookseller & bookbinder, 15 Gt. Russell st. Blmsby
Mole John, hairdresser & perfumer, see Dunsby & Mole
Mole Philip, floorcloth ma. 37 Aylesbury st. Clerkenwell
Molero Elizabeth (Mrs.), grocer, 29 Westbourne st. Pimlico
Moles & Robinson, haircutters & wigmaks. 24 High Holborn
Molinara Peter, looking glass mfr. 21 Vine st. Hatton wall
Molinari Andrew, looking glass ma. 4 Greville st. Hattn. gdn
Moline Sparks, sole consignee of Guinness's stout, 5 Adelaide place, London bridge
Molini Charles Fredk. importer of italian books, marble, &c. & general commission agent, 17 King William st. Strand
Moll Jacob, baker, 261 Bethnal green road
Möller Carl, ship & insurance agt. see Dick, Möller & May
Moller Charles C. commisn. merchant, 66 Lower Thames st
Moller Hen. violin & harp string ma. 17 Bell la. Spitalfields
Mollett John, merchant, 1 Austinfriars passage, & Baltic
Mollett Robert, confectioner, 54 Skinner st. Snowhill
Mollindinia Anthony Wm. school, 65 Ossulston st. Somers tn
Molineux Sam. Wm. butcher, 1 Lr. Chapman st. St. Geo. ea
Mollison John, wine & brandy mer. 9 New st. Bishopsgate st
Molloy Charles, solicitor, 8 New square, Lincoln's inn
Molloy Edwd. John, chimney sweeper, 20 Drury ct. Strand
Molloy John Edward, boot & shoe maker, 7 Rose st. Soho
Molloy Mary A. (Mrs.), haberda. 3 Upsdell's row, Kinglnd. rd
Molloy Robert, surgeon, 31 Margaret st. Wilmington sq
Molson Chas. Taylor, oil & colorman, 4 New Park st. Boro'
Molteno Jas. A. ancient & modern printseller, 20 Pall mall
Molyneux Edw. E. barrister, 6 Pump court, Temple
Molyneux Henry, grocer, 11 Essex place, Grange rd. Dalston
Molyneux Robert, patentee, chronometer, astronomical clock & watchmaker, 30 Southampton row, Russell square
Molyneux Samuel E. engineer, millwright, smith, saw mills, &c. scale board cutter, congreve, ink, blacking & annatto manufacturer, 26 City road, Finsbury
Molyneux Thomas, plumber & glaz. 9 George ct. Piccadilly
Mombach Israel L. profr. of music, 5 Castle st. Houndsditch
Mombelli John C. carver & gilder, 22 Vine st. Hatton garden
Moncas John, bookseller, 45 Holywell st. Strand
Monckton Mary (Mrs.), lodging house, 33 Norfolk st. Strand
Monckton William Charles, solicitor, 33 Norfolk st. Strand
Moncreiff Arch. solicitor, &c. see Grahame, Moncreiff & Weems
Moncriefe David, *White Hart* P.H. 36 Exeter st. & 9 Catherine st. Strand
Monds Thos. Wilks, tallow chandler, 53 Glo'str. st. Com. rd
Money James, plumber, 10 Little James st. Bedford row
Money Robert, furniture broker, 18 Cleveland st. Fitzroy sq
Monger John, *Baltic* coffeehouse, 58 Threadneedle st
Monger Robert, grocer, 7 Broad st. Horselydown
Monington Walter, brassfound. & enginr. 5 Fredk. pl. Ham. rd
Monk Sarah (Mrs.) & Son, fruiterers, Borough market
Monk Emily (Mrs.), milliner, 20 Broadley ter. Blandford sq
Monk Fred. carpenter & undertak. 12 & 13 Paradise st. Maryleb
Monk George, painter, &c. 15 Flagon row, Deptford
Monk George, upholsterer, &c. 9A, High st. Portland town
Monk Henry, coal & charcoal merchant, Leader st. Chelsea
Monk Henry, grocer, 28 Rochester row, Westminster
Monk Henry, haberdasher & hosier, 48 Crown st. Finsbury
Monk Henry, porkman, 26 Queen st. Pimlico
Monk John, cattle salesman, 8 West Smithfield
Monk John, grocer, 16 Artillery passage, Bishopsgate
Monk John, linendraper, 4 Little Chelsea, north side
Monk John, nightman, &c. 1 East Mount terrace, Whitechapel
Monk John Wm. general agent, 5 Great Vine st. Golden sq
Monk J. Wm. *Kentish Drovers* P.H. Warlter's bldgs. O. Kent rd
Monk Richard, *Cross Keys inn & hotel*, 128 Wood st
Monk Samuel, cabinet maker, Church st. Hackney
Monk Sarah (Mrs.), *Cricketers* P.H. 4 Orange rw. Kenningt. rd
Monk William, cheesemonger, 1 York st. Borough
Monk William, horseslaughterer, Lit. Nrth. st. Whitechapl. rd
Monk Wm. *Shepherd & Flock* P.H. 11 Lit. Bell. all. Coleman st
Monk Wm. (late Milne & Reid), tailor & habit ma. 8 Grosvenor st
Monkhouse, Johnson & Co. carpet manufacturers, 12 Wood st
Monkhouse Richard & William, timber merchants, St. Peter's wharf, Millbank st. Westminster, & 1 Davies st. Berkeley sq
Monkhouse, Whitfield & Co. carpet & rug ma. 51 Aldermanby
Monkhouse, Winter & Bowman, merchants, 2 Walbrook bdgs
Monkhouse Cyril John, solicitor, 3 Craven st. Strand
Monkhouse Hutton, solicitor, 113 Upper Stamford st
Monkhouse Mary (Mrs.), milliner, 4 Providence pl. Limeh
Monkhouse Wm. Cam, wharfngr. see Hill & Monkhouse
Monkland Canal Agency (Iver H. Mackay, agent), 57 Moorgate st
Monks Francis, shopkeeper, 7 Margaret st. Hackney fields
Monks Henry James, ropemaker, 50 Church st. Shoreditch
Monks Thomas, rope & twine ma. 183 Church st. Shoreditch
Monks Thomas, watchmaker, 3 Church st. Camberwell
Monksfield Fred. & Hannah, grocers, 35 Gt. Marylebone st
Monksfield Charles, oilman, 142 Brick lane, Spitalfields
Monkton Charles, butcher, 27 Holywell row, Shoreditch
Monkton William, butcher, 26 East road, City road
Monmouth & Hereford Railway, 449 West Strand
Monnery Edwd. Josiah & Co. outfitters, &c. 165 Fenchurch st
Monnery John, glove ma. hosier & genl. outfitter, 53 Borough
Monnery John (suc. to Carpenter, Smith & Co.) manuf. of printers' blankets, machine tapes & guts, 53 Boro' High st
Monnery William, glover, 1 Newman's row, Linc. inn fields
Monro & May, musical repository, 11 Holborn bars
Monro Benj. lacquer, varnish & watchmaker, 13 Moor st. Soho
Monro Edward, Thos. physician, 87 Harley st. Cavendish sq
Monro Elizabeth (Mrs.), dressma. 13 Lit. Queen st. Holborn
Monro Robt. bank of British North America, 7 St. Helen's pl
Monro Thomas, coach builder, 29A, William st. Regents pk
Monro Wm. carver & gilder, 68 Cromer st. Brunswick sq
Monson Henry, carpentr. & buildr. 30 East st. Manchester sq
Montagu Basil, queen's counsel, 2 Princes ct. Storey's gate
Montagu Edgar, barrister, 4 New square, Lincoln's inn
Montague Alfred, artist, 61 Frith st. Soho
Montague Geo. glass & china wareho. 17 Park ter. Regent's pk
Montague Henry, boarding house, 8 George st. Minories
Montague John, oil & colorman, 20 Horseferry rd. Westmr
Montague Thomas, fruiterer, 48 Burton st. Burton crescent
Montano Francis, hot presser, 16 Silver st. Golden square
Montebello Alfred de, Mareuil sur aï Champagne (agents, Richard Symonds & Son), 2 Ingram court, Fenchurch st
Montefiore Horatio Joseph, stockbroker, 23 Throgmorton st. & Stock exchange
Montefiore Jacob, mer. Moorgate chambers, 49 Moorgate st
Montefiore John & Son, west india merchts. 147 Leadenhall st
Montefiore Joseph Barrow, mercht. 2 Winchester buildings
Monteith Alex. H. teacher of languages, 13 London wall
Monteith William, barrister, 2 Paper buildings, Temple
Montel Mary (Mrs.), coffee rooms, 20 St. Mary at hill
Monteiro Carlos F. mer. see Fonseca, Monteiro & Guimaraens
Montgomery Japh. velvet wire drawer, 7 Wilkes st, Sptlflds
Montgomery Wm. baker, 16 Bedford pl. Commercial rd. ea
Montoya, Saenz & Co. merchants, 3 Winchester buildings, Great Winchester st
Montresor Thomas, barrister, 36 Lincoln's inn fields
Montugua Charles R. shipping agt. 19 Up. East Smithfield
Moodie Lewis, Highbury nursery, Highbury park
Moody Frederick & Co. woollendrapers, 10 Leicester st. & 1 Sidney alley, Leicester square
Moody John & Co. pewterers, 86 Bermondsey st
Moody Alexander, stockmaker, 46 Gt. Dover st. Borough
Moody Archd. oil & color merchant, 8 Lower Thames st

Moody Charles, plumber, 12 Durham pl. West. Hackney rd
Moody Charles, porkman, 88 Goswell road
Moody Geo. egg mercht. 10 Union st. Hackney rd. Kngslnd. rd
Moody George, law stationer, 98 Chancery lane
Moody James, chemist, 24 Church st. Camberwell
Moody James, grocer, 1 St. Mark's rd. Camberwell New rd
Moody James, grocer, 23 Exmouth st. Spa fields
Moody James, patent lamp ma. 44 Gt. Sutton st. Goswell st
Moody John, boatbuilder, 8 Morgan's lane, Tooley st
Moody John, bootmaker, 6 Flask lane, Pimlico
Moody John, dyer & scourer, 8 Windmill st. Tottenham ct. rd
Moody John, stock, belt & brace maker, 158 Aldersgate st
Moody John, tin plate worker, 35 Freeschool st. Horselydn
Moody John Doble, surgeon, &c. 11 Curzon st. Mayfair
Moody Mary (Miss), tobacconist, 2 Brook st. Ratcliff
Moody Richard, pork butcher, 30 Broomfield pl. Deptford
Moody Richard, tailor, 1 Burton st. Pimlico
Moody Susannah (Mrs.), lace cleaner, 66 Margaret st
Moody Thomas, fruiterer, 37 Little Russell st. Bloomsbury
Moody Thomas, tailor, 29 Robert st. Hampstead road
Moody Thomas, tin plate worker, 19 Star corner, Bermndsy. st
Moody Thos. Neats, surgeon, 33 Bridgehouse place, Boro'
Moody William, barrister, 6 King's Bench walk, Temple
Moody William, basket maker, Broomfield pl. Deptford
Moody William, bootmaker, 25 King st. Golden sq
Moody William, haberdasher, 5 Dorset st. Portman sq
Moody William, tailor & draper, 200 Strand
Moon Ann (Mrs.) & Co. tool manfrs. 4 Lit. Queen st. Holborn
Moon Jonathan & Son, mrchts, 19 Langbourn cham. Fench. st
Moon Elizh. (Mrs.), marine store dlr. 8 Creed la. Ludgate st
Moon Francis Graham, printseller & publisher to her Majesty, bookseller, stationer, &c. 20 Threadneedle st
Moon Charles, tobacconist, 1 Tottenham court road
Moon Chas. Thos. bookslr. stationer & librarian, 12 Regent st
Moon Harriet (Mrs.), babylinen wa. 61 Green st. Grosv. sq
Moon James, architect & surveyor, 1 Millman st. Bedford rw
Moon James, solicitor, 4 Adam st. Adelphi, Strand
Moon John, *Fleece* P.H. 70 Tothill st. Westminster
Moon John, optician, 76 Minories
Moon William, baker, 4 Earl st. Kensington
Moon William, watchmaker & jeweller, 4 Holborn bars
Moone John Thos. coach & herald paint, 8½ Holywell st. Westm
Mooney Francis, printing press ma. 130 Golden la. St. Luke's
Moor James Tate, Tickell & Co. linendrapers & warehousemen, 17 Cheapside & 45½ Old Change
Moor Seth, coach smith, 58 Chester st. Kennington
Moorcraft James, baker, 16 Bermondsey New road
Moorcroft Geo. corn dlr. 9 Church st. St. George's Boro'
Moorcroft Geo. moroc. leath. dres. 1 Tyer's gatew. Bermon. st
Moore Charles & Son, timber merchants, Wilton rd. Pimlico
Moore & Flower (Misses), milliners, 1 Spur st. Leicester sq
Moore Geo. & Wm. tallowchndlrs. & oilmen, 43 High st. St. Giles'
Moore & Goodison, wholesale coffee dealers, 34 Lime st
Moore & Humberstone, pawnbrokers, 11 Leather lane
Moore & Illingworth, surgeons, 1 Arlington st. Piccadilly
Moore James & Co. [late Bicknells' & Moore], hatters, hosiers & army accoutrement makers to her Majesty, Prince Albert, & the royal family, 1 Old Bond st
Moore John & Hen. & Co. pianoforte ma. 138 Bishopsgt. without
Moore John & Sons, church & house clock manufacturers, 38 Clerkenwell close
Moore Wm. & Edward, undertakers, 1 Rathbone pl. Oxford st
Moore & Wilson, wholesale teadealers, 23 Harp la. Tower st
Moore & Woodward, gun makers, 64 St. James's st. Pall mall
Moore's Stock List Office, 61½ Threadneedle st
Moore Adolphus, corn & coal mer. 28 Up. North pl. Gray's inn rd
Moore Alexander, bootmaker, 20 St. John st. road
Moore Ambrose, silk manufacturer, see Wilson, Moore & Co
Moore Amelia (Mrs.), seminary, 89 Shaftesbury st. Nw. Nrth. rd
Moore Andrew, bootmaker, 31 King st. Golden square
Moore Andrew, tailor & draper, 82 Cornhill
Moore Ann (Mrs.), milliner, 29 Broomfields, Deptford
Moore Augustus Henry, solicitor, see Thomas & Moore
Moore Bartholomew, *Marquis Cornwallis* P.H. 28 Warren st. Fitzroy square
Moore Benj. grocer, 5 Hamilton row, Bagnigge wells road
Moore Caleb, comb & brush maker, 13 Barking churchyard
Moore Charles, carver & gilder, 29 St. John st. Clerkenwell
Moore Charles, fruiterer, 6 Robsons place, Kennington road
Moore Charles, linendraper & hosier, 141 Shadwell High st
Moore Charles, publisher, 12 Wellington st. north, Strand
Moore Chas. Caught, auctioneer, &c. 35 Assembly rw. Mile e. rd
Moore Charles Henry, attorney, 36 Lincoln's inn fields
Moore Charles Steph. baker, 1 Grove terrace, Brompton gr
Moore Charlotte (Mrs.), oil & color wa. 13 Green st. Bethnl. gr
Moore Charlotte (Mrs.), *Peele's coffeeho.* 177 & 178 Fleet st
Moore Christopher, sculptor, 22 Howland st. Fitzroy square
Moore David, architect, 11 Upper Ranelagh st. Pimlico
Moore Edmund F. barrister, 11 New sq. Linc. inn, & A9, Albany
Moore Edward, M.D. surgeon, 42 Wards pl. Hoxton Old town, & Thurlow house, Hackney road
Moore Edward Duke, surgeon, 10 Arlington st. Piccadilly
Moore Eliza (Mrs.), coffee & chop ho. 25 Up. Marylebone st
Moore Elizabeth (Mrs.), lodging house, 30 Arundel st. Strand
Moore Elizh. Ching (Mrs.), milliner, 18 Mortimer st. Cavh. sq
Moore Francis, umbrella maker, 33 St. Martin's court
Moore Frederic, watchmaker, 4 Charles st. Hatton garden
Moore Fredk. John, plumber, 21 King st. Covent garden
Moore Fredk. Wm. baker, 49 Dudley grov. Harrow rd. Padntn
Moore George, architect, 64 Lincoln's inn fields
Moore George, carver & gilder, 3 William st. Whitechapel
Moore George, cooper, 5 Star corner, Bermondsey
Moore George, fruiterer, 3 Norland road, Notting hill
Moore George, fruiterer, 26 Bermondsey New road
Moore George, grocer & cheesemonger, 9 White st. Bthnl. grn
Moore George, hatter, see Chapman & Moore
Moore George, lace mfr. see Groucock, Copestake & Moore
Moore George, *Little Bell* P.H. 78 St. John st. Smithfield
Moore George, ornament. confectioner, 19 Lisson grove north
Moore Geo. *Lord Nelson* P.H. 1 Half Nichols st. Bethnal grn
Moore George, soda water ma. 73 Warren st. Tottenham ct. rd
Moore George, timber dlr. Norway whf. & 297 Rotherhithe st
Moore George, watchmaker, 23 Perceval st. Clerkenwell
Moore George, wholesale confectioner, see Murphy & Moore
Moore George Belton, artist, 19 Southampton pl. Euston sq
Moore George F. wholesale italian fish sauce & bottled fruit warehouse, 11 Upper King st. Bloomsbury
Moore George Wm. academy, 5 Watt's bldgs. Kingsland rd
Moore Hannah (Mrs.), tobacc. 12 Up. York st. Bryanstn. sq
Moore Henry, beer retailer, 5 Norton st. Portland pl
Moore Henry, dairyman, Addington square, Camberwell
Moore Henry, linendraper, 22A, Upper Marylebone st
Moore Henry, oil & colorman, manufacturer of German paste & poor man's plaster, 3 & 25 Swan st. Minories
Moore Hen. Arthur, baker, 1 White Lion court, Birchin lane
Moore Henry T. ea. in. agt. & mer. see Mangles' & Co
Moore Isaac Webb, ironmonger, see Kitchen & Moore
Moore Jabez, breeches maker, 136 New Bond st
Moore Jacob, lamp cotton mnfr. 4 St. James's st. Clerkenwl
Moore James, baker, 77 High st. Marylebone
Moore Jas. *Bedford Arms* P.H. 1 Bedford rw. East st. Old Knt. rd
Moore Jas. bookseller, 4 Carthusian st. Aldersgate st
Moore Jas. boot & shoe maker, 5 Stafford st. Lisson grove
Moore Jas. cabinet maker & broker, 68 Old st. St. Luke's
Moore Jas. lighterman, 16 Hatfield st
Moore Jas. linendraper, see Franks & Moore
Moore Jas. razor maker & cutler, 349 Oxford st
Moore Jas. solicitor, 6 South square, Gray's inn
Moore Jas. Rd. *King's Head* P.H. 16 Holywell rw. Shoreditch
Moore Jane (Mrs.), linendraper, 112 Guilford st. Russell sq
Moore Jasper, carriage lamp maker, 1 Cross st. Goswell st
Moore Jemima (Mrs.), tea dealer, 6 Wilsted st. Somers town
Moore John, barrister, 1 New square, Lincoln's inn
Moore John, baths, 4 Tabernacle square, Finsbury
Moore John, beer retailer, Lower road, Rotherhithe
Moore John, boot maker, 45 Goswell rd. & 14 St. John st. rd
Moore John, boot & shoe maker, 11 Marlboro' sq. Chelsea
Moore John, bootmaker, 4 New Park st. Borough
Moore John, brushmaker, 3 Little Charlotte st. Goodge st
Moore John, butcher, 60 Marchmont st. Brunswick square
Moore John, carpenter & builder, 27 Bethnal green road
Moore John, carver & gilder, 1 & 2 West st. Seven dials
Moore John, chandler's shop, 14 Bath st. Hackney road
Moore John, *Duke of York* P.H. 1 Up. York pl. St. John's wd
Moore John, fancy & trimming wareho. 95 Upper st. Islington
Moore John, grocer, 1 Dorchester place, Blandford square
Moore John, jobmaster, 1 John's place, Old Kent road
Moore John, *Rainbow* coffee house, 1 Arthur st. east, Lond. br
Moore John, rag merchant, 108 Bethnal green road
Moore John, salt mer. & drysalter, 8 Paddington bas. south si
Moore John, tailor, 1 Pleasant row, Park road, Regent's pk
Moore John, tailor, 9 Titchborne st. Connaught terrace
Moore John, timber merchant, 12 Upper St. Martin's lane
Moore John, who. & ret. ironmgr. 12 & 13 Lit. Earl st. Seven dials
Moore John Alldin, special pleader, 5 Hare court, Temple
Moore John Ayres, who cabinet manufr. see Mason & Moore
Moore John Thompson, *Red Lion* P.H. 14 King st. Golden sq
Moore John, attorney, 2 Field court, Gray's inn
Moore Joseph, bootmaker, 25 Robert st. Grosvenor square
Moore Joseph, chair & sofa maker, 17 & 18 Wild ct. Gt. Wild st
Moore Joseph, coal dealer, 32 Whitcomb st. Pall mall east
Moore Joseph, physician, 10 Saville row, Piccadilly

Moore Joseph, ship & insurance broker, see Devitt & Moore
Moore Joseph, tailor, 10 West st. Walworth road
Moore Joseph Schroder, barrister, 5 Stone bldgs. Linc. inn
Moore Lewis, bootmaker, 9 Warwick st. Regent st
Moore Louis, carpenter & undertaker, 12 Up. St. Martin's la
Moore Mark, boarding house, 6 Queen st. pl. Up. Thames st
Moore Martin, fruiterer, 5 High st. Portland town
Moore Mary (Mrs.), goldsmith, 7 St. James wall, Clerknwll
Moore Mary (Miss), vegetable ornamt. cut. 40 South Molt. st
Moore Mary Ann (Mrs.), curiositydealer, 25 Tottenham ct. rd
Moore Morris, artist, 27 Grafton st. Fitzroy square
Moore Philip Chas. notary & proctor, 10 Gt. Knightrider st
Moore Ralph, *Queen's Arms* P.H. William st. Portland tn
Moore Regnier Winckley, barrister, 1 Newsq. Lincoln's inn
Moore Richard, carver, 25 Hart st. Bloomsbury
Moore Richard, military tailor, 12 King st. Clerkenwell
Moore Richd. Hanks, fringe manufactr. 12 Bath st. Newgte. st
Moore Robert, *Carlisle Arms* P.H. 2 Queen st. Soho
Moore Robert Jas. bricklayer, 29 Broomfields, Deptford
Moore Robert O. ship & insur. broker, see Ogilby, Moore & Co
Moore Rt. Parker, booksel. statnr. &c. 32 Store st. Bedford sq
Moore Robert W. stockbroker & agent for railway & canal shares, dock stocks, &c. 61 Threadneedle st
Moore Samuel, beer retailer, 1 Stockwell ter. Clapham road
Moore Samuel, perfumer, 24 Gray's bldgs. Duke st. Mnchstr. sq
Moore Samuel, tailor & habit maker, 18 Mortimer st. Cavh. sq
Moore Samuel, who. coffee dealer, 12 Mincing lane
Moore Sarah (Mrs.), fruiterer, 159 High st. Camden town
Moore Sarah (Mrs.), oil & colorman, 129 London road, Boro'
Moore Thomas, bootmaker, 30 Lamb's Conduit st. & 109 High st. Camden town, & 6 Knightsbridge terrace
Moore Thomas, bootmaker, 199 Whitechapel road
Moore Thomas, chemist, see Savory, Moore & Co
Moore Thomas, china wareho. 9A, Munster st. Regent's pk
Moore Thomas, house & estate ag. 1 Holland pl. Kensington
Moore Thomas, *New inn*, 16 Old Change
Moore Thomas, *Pine Apple* P.H. 3 St. George's rd. Boro'
Moore Thomas, rag merchant, 176 Bethnal green road
Moore Thomas, tallow chandler, 36 Cable st. St. George's east
Moore Thomas, trunkmaker, 90 St. Martin's la. Charing cr
Moore Thomas, undertaker, 11 Mortimer mkt. Tottenh. ct. rd
Moore Thomas, wheelwright, Goodman's yard, Minories
Moore Thomas, who. toy warehouse, 26 Rathbone place
Moore Thomas, wine & brandy mer. 23 Basing lane, Bread st
Moore Thomas Ankers, grocer, Stratford broadway
Moore Thornton, statnr. & news agt. 71 Lisson grove north
Moore Wm. baker, 16 Cheltenham pl. Westminster road
Moore Wm. beer retailer, Southampton st. Camberwell
Moore Wm. bootmaker, 15 Up. King st. Bloomsbury
Moore Wm. bottle & stone ware manfr. see Westwood & Moore
Moore Wm. building material dlr. 73 Brandon st. Lock's flds
Moore Wm. cabinetma. 76 Charlotte st. Fitzroy sq
Moore Wm. cutler, 22 Tichborne st. Haymarket
Moore Wm. grocer, 85 Park st. Grosvenor square
Moore Wm. gunmaker, 78 Edgware road, Marylebone
Moore Wm. ivoryturner, 12 Newton st. NewNorth rd. Hoxton
Moore Wm. leatherfactor, 18 Philpot lane, Fenchurch st
Moore Wm. merchant, see Gould, Dowie & Moore
Moore Wm. picture frame maker, carver & gilder, & looking glass manufacturer, 63 Bishopsgate within
Moore Wm. tobacconist, 1 Richmond road, Dalston
Moore Wm. wax & tallow chandler, 3 Great Marylebone st
Moore Wm. wholesale & retail dealer in gold & silver fish, canaries & other birds, 6 Love lane, Eastcheap
Moore Wm. working cutler & razor ma. 220 Tottenham ct. rd
Moore William Henry, teadealer & grocer, 109 Strand
Moorecroft Wm. seal engraver, 5 Roll's buildings, Fetter lane
Moores Chrlte. (Mrs.), tobacconist, 35 East st. Manchstr. sq
Moores Samuel, solicitor, see Amory, Sewell & Moores
Moores William, parchment ma. Wild's rents, Bermondsey
Moorhouse Miles, tailor, 45 Houndsditch
Moorhouse Percival M. stock & share bro. 9 Shorter's court
Moors James, saddle & collar ma. 7 Pitman's bldgs. St. Luke's
Moorton Henry, *George* P.H. 13 Brooke st. Holborn
Mootram Frederick, *Ship* P.H. 36 Wardour st. Soho
Mopsey Thomas N. ginger beer ma. 1 Brighton pl. Waterloo rd
Moracini Giuseppe, dining rooms, 26 Queen st. Golden sq
Moran Hannah (Mrs.), chinawareh. 16 Devonshire st. Lisson gr
Moran Lydia (Mrs.), boardinghouse, 20 Castle st. Falcon sq
Moran Matthew, hosier & glover, 14 Colvill ter. Kg's. rd. Chels
Morant George John, interior decorator & upholsterer by appointment to her Majesty, 91 New Bond st
Morant Henry, house painter, &c. 83 Connaught ter. Edgw. rd
Morant James, grainer, 10 Winchester row, New road
Moravian Missions; secretary, Rev. Peter La Trobé, 33 Ely pl. Holborn; treasurer, Wm. Mallalieu, 97 Hatton garden
Mordan & Hyde, gold pen manufacturers, 6 Goswell rd
Mordan (Sampson) & Co. patentees of the ever-pointed pencils, patent oblique & other steel pens; manufacturers of patent seven guard & improved patent detector locks, cedar drawing pencils of pure cumberland lead, universal & self-adjusting penholders, portable quill pens, correct letter balances, patent & every description of glass & leather inkstands, medicine chests, smelling bottles with the patent spherical stopper, toilets, &c. &c., copying & seal presses & fireproof safes & boxes; manufactory 22 City road, Finsbury square, & at 50 Cheapside
Mordan Edward, manufacturer of engines, lathes, tools, crimping & goffering machines, copperplate printing machines, copying & seal presses, & general machinery; inventor of the hollow bats-wing burner; manufactory 101 Dean st. Soho, & 25 Windmill st. near Lambeth palace
Mordaunt & Lucas, linen factors & manufacturers, 1 Sambrook ct. Basinghall st. & at Dundee & Forfar, N.B
Mordaunt Wm. Hen. & Co. linen factors & manufacturers, 1 Sambrook ct. Basinghall st. & at Dundee & Forfar, N.B
Mordaunt Charles, tailor, 1 Nelson square, Blackfriars rd
Mordaunt Ewer, hatter, 2 Edith pl. Birdcage wlk. Hkny. rd
Mordaunt John, surgeon, Mare st. Hackney
Mordaunt Octavius D. solicitor, 22 Bolton st. Piccadilly
Mordecai Edward, fruiterer, 28 New Church st. Lisson gr. & 1 Portman market
Mordey Thos. Rt. stationer & news agt. 126 Gt. Guildford st
More Alexander, watchmaker, 19 Holywell row, Shoreditch
More Charles Alex. watch & clock ma. 246 Shoreditch High st
More Henry Wm. grocer, 37 Charles st. City road
More John, *Angel & Crown* P.H. Tabernacle sq. Finsbury
More John, merchant, 30 Nicholas lane, City
More John, wholesale harness maker, 5 Market st. Finsbury
More Robert, scottish brewery, 24 Old st. St. Luke's
Moreau Felix & Co. french & eng. cork mfs. 33 ShadThas. Sthwk
Morecraft George, linendraper, &c. 21 New st. Dorset sq
Morehen Edwd. Parker, bookbinder, 12 Finsbury st. Finsby
Morehen Henry, cabinetmaker, 7 Cumberland st. Curtain rd
Morehouse Jas. & Son, dairymn. 28 Lisle st. & 17 Up. St. Mrtn's. la
Moreing Charles, architect, 31 Saville row, Piccadilly
Morel Thomas & Henry, italian warehousemen & wine merchants, 210 & 211 Piccadilly
Morel Dominique, dentist, 1 Langham pl. Portland place
Morel Edward Joseph, coal merchant, 12 Lit. Marylebone st
Moreland John Rd. & Joseph, builders, 18 Old st. St. Luke's
Moreland & Pagden, iron founders, Wenlock road, City rd
Moreland Rd. & Co. millwri. & engineers, 149 Old st. St. Luke's
Morelli Chas. Fras. statnr. & librarian. 227 Hoxton Old town
Moren James, plumber, &c. 24 Blackmoor st. Clare market
Moresby Wm. solicitor, 11 South square, Gray's inn
Moreton & Balfour, ship insu. & gen. agents & agents for preserving provisions, 4 Railway pl. Fenchurch st
Moreton & Foster, who. ironmongers, 12 Clement's la. Lomb. st
Moreton & Hellier, meat salesmen, Leadenhall market
Moreton Ann (Mrs.), white horse stabl. 60 Castle st. Lestr. sq
Moreton Samuel, *Green Dragon tap*, 86 Bishopsgate within
Moreton William, wine merchant, 5 Rood lane
Morewood J. & Co. mach. & lamp oilma. Glassho. yd. E. Smhfi
Morewood & Rogers, patentees of galvanized tinned iron, 9 Steel yard, & 86 Upper Thames st
Morewood John Josph. commsn. mercht. 1 Winchester bldgs
Morey Benj. window blind maker, 2 Chancery pl. Camberwell New road
Morey Harry Edw. shell fishmonger, 201 Bishopsgate without
Morey Henry, butcher, 96 Up. Whitecross st. St. Luke's
Morey Isaac, ivory turner, 27 Allerton st. Hoxton
Morey Jonathan, grocer, 17 Little George st. Westminster
Morey Joseph, *Grapes* P.H. 62 Blackman st. Borough
Morey Wm. Horlock, sawma. & tool dlr. 22 Old st. St. Luke's
Morgan & Bishop, for. commis. agts. 1 Amen corner, Patern. row
Morgan Charles & James Arthur, solicitors, 15 Old Jewry
Morgan David & Son, merchants, Baltic coffeehouse
Morgan John & Co. lace manufrs. 3 Russia row, Milk st
Morgan John & Co. shawl manufacturers, printers, &c. 14 St. Paul's churchyard
Morgan John & Co. tailors, 5 Albemarle st. Piccadilly
Morgan Joseph & Chas. surgeons, 44 & 45 Bedford rw. Blmsby
Morgan, Martyr & George, wholesale stationers & rag merchants, 2 Farringdon st. Ludgate hill
Morgan Thomas & Co. wine merchants, 24 Savage gardens
Morgan Thos. & Son, chandlers & soap ma. 18 Tottenham ct. rd
Morgan Thomas & Son, sailmakers, ship chandlers & ship owners, 10 Thomas st. Horselydown, & Mill lane, Tooley st
Morgan Whittell & Co. woolstaplers, Staple st. Long la. Brmsy
Morgan Wm. & J. *Champion* P.H. 1 Wellingtn. ter. Kens. gra. pts
Morgan Alfred, barrister, 6 Manchester square

Morgan Alfred, blind manufacturer, see Curtis & Morgan
Morgan Arthur, F.R.S. act. of *Equitable Assu. Off.* New Brdg. st
Morgan Ann (Mrs.), dairy, 7 Dorset place, Pall mall east
Morgan Anna (Mrs.), milliner, 6 Princes st. Hanover square
Morgan Arthur, oil & colorman, 11 Pitfield st. Hoxton
Morgan Cadogan, barrister, 3 Plowden buildings, Temple
Morgan Charlotte (Mrs.), *Bull's Head* P.H. 8 Crown st. Soho
Morgan Charlotte (Mrs.), boarding house, 12 Cecil st. Strand
Morgan Christopher, cheesemonger, 96 Leadenhall st
Morgan David, merchant, 4 Crown court, Old Broad st
Morgan Edward, brush ma. 6 New way, St. Thos. st. ea. Boro'
Morgan Edward, coachbuilder, 20A, Up. Lisson st. Lis. grove
Morgan Edward, linendraper, 25 Oxford st
Morgan Edward, shawl mfs. & fur. see Bond & Morgan
Morgan Edward John, printer, 38 New Church st. Lisson grove
Morgan Edward Lloyd, stockbro. 3 Bank chambrs. Lothbury
Morgan Elias, lodging house, 27 Norfolk st. Strand
Morgan Elizabeth (Mrs.), dining rooms, 8 James st. Cov. gar
Morgan Enoch, beer retailer, 141 Praed st. Paddington
Morgan Fras. tailor & piecebroker, 14 Clothfair, Smithfield
Morgan Fredk. tea urn manufr. 17 Wynyatt st. Goswell st
Morgan Fred. Wm. ironmonger, 1 Crown row, Walworth rd
Morgan Geo. *Bricklayers' Arms* P.H. 22 Lit. Clarendon st
Morgan George, carpenter, 29 George st. Portland place
Morgan George, *Glos'ter Arms* P.H. 40 Rochester row, Westm
Morgan George, hairdesser, 6 Broomfields, Deptford
Morgan George J. printer, 33 Acton st. Gray's inn road
Morgan George, tailor, 18 High st. Camden town
Morgan Giles, cattle salesman, 8 West Smithfield
Morgan Harriett (Mrs.), upholsterer, 13 Terrace, Kensington
Morgan Henry, brushmaker, 53 King st. Borough
Morgan Hen. Lloyd, custom ho. agent, 11 Langbourn chambers
Morgan Hugh, hop & seed mer. Talbot inn yd. 75 Boro' High st
Morgan James, cabinet maker, 19 Worship st. Finsbury sq
Morgan James, cheesemonger, Duke st. Chelsea
Morgan Jas. cop. pl. & mus. engrav. 23 Lit. St. Andrew st. 7 dials
Morgan James, dyer, 31 York st. Blackfriars road
Morgan James, engraver, see Jenrick & Morgan
Morgan James, lodging house, 22 Queen st. Golden square
Morgan James, tailor, &c. 52 Southampton row, Russell sq
Morgan Jane (Mrs.), dairy, 9 Lloyd square, Pentonville
Morgan Jane (Mrs.), fruiterer, Covent garden, Long market
Morgan Jeffrey, undertaker, 4 Morgan's place, Liverpool rd
Morgan Jeremiah, whitesmith, 64 Wells st.; & 5 Gt. Titchfld. st
Morgan John, baker, 18 Globe road, Mile end
Morgan John, baker, 6 Cavendish st. New North road
Morgan John, baker, 18 Great Peter st. Westminster
Morgan John, cheesemonger, 9 James st. Covent garden
Morgan John, coffee rooms, 62 Cromer st. Brunswick sq
Morgan John, *Coopers' Arms* P.H. 6 Russell st. Bermondsey
Morgan John, dining rooms, 124 Drury lane
Morgan John, fruiterer, 5 Alexander place, Brompton
Morgan John, oil & italian wa. 207 Sloane st. Knightsbridge
Morgan John, physician, 19 Northampton sq
Morgan John, *Shaftsbury Arms* P.H. 38 Shaftsbury st. Hxtn
Morgan John, statnr. & printsel. 29 Museum st. Bloomsbury
Morgan John, share broker, 2 Copthall court, City
Morgan John, surgeon, see Barker & Morgan
Morgan John, surgeon, 22 Chapel st. Grosvenor place
Morgan John, surgeon, 41 Finsbury square
Morgan John, tailor, 1 Compton mws. Cmptn. st. Burton cres
Morgan John, *Three Cranes* P.H. 57 Watling st
Morgan John, tobacconist, 32 Silver st. Golden square
Morgan John, *White Horse* P.H. 9 Moor lane, Cripplegate
Morgan John Benjamin, proctor, 20 Great Knightrider st
Morgan John Godfrey, wine & spirit mer. 11 York st. Cvnt. gdn
Morgan John Rd. surgeon, 64 Pritchard's rd. Hackney fields
Morgan Joseph, boot & shoe maker, 147 Praed st. Edgware rd
Morgan Joseph, *Grapes* P.H. Little Windmill st
Morgan Joseph Fredk. printer, 47 Whiskin st. Clerkenwell
Morgan Joseph John, plumber, &c. 152 Brick lane, Spitalflds
Morgan Joshua, furniture broker, 7 Old st. St. Luke's
Morgan Mary (Mrs.), paperhanger, 23 Mount st. Lambeth
Morgan Matthew, fishmonger, 1 Wandsworth rd
Morgan Morgan, calenderer, 4 Little Distaff lane, Friday st
Morgan Moses, surgeon, 40 Millbank st. Westminster
Morgan Moses, surgeon, 71 St. Martin's lane, Charing cross
M& 12 Charlotte st. Bedford sq
Morgan Richard, barrister, 4 New square, Lincoln's inn
Morgan Rd. Hy. *Mansfield Arms* P.H. Mansfield pl. Kentishtn
Morgan Robert, carpenter, 18 Woodbridge st. Clerkenwell
Morgan Robert, cattle salesman, 41 West Smithfield
Morgan Robert, cheesefactor, Old George yard, Snow hill
Morgan Robert, oil & colorman, 36 King st. Clerkenwell
Morgan Robt. *Old George inn & tav.* Old George yd. Snw. hill
Morgan Robt. Wm. omnibus propr. 11 Park pl. ter. Padgntn. gr
Morgan Rosalie (Mdme.), milliner, 94 Park st. Grosvenor sq
Morgan Samuel, glover & hosier, 173 Strand
Morgan Samuel, welch ale mer. 16 Old Change, Cheapside
Morgan Susan (Mrs.), fruiterer, &c. Covent gar. Long market
Morgan Susan (Miss), lace warehouse, 24 Shoreditch
Morgan Sidney, hop merchant, Kentish bldgs. 94 Boro' High st
Morgan Thos. *Brazen Serpent* P.H. 49 Richardson st. Bmdsy
Morgan Thomas, italian warehouse, see Cundale & Morgan
Morgan Thomas, hairdresser, 12 Opera arcade, Haymarket
Morgan Thomas, hosier & glover, 11 Albion pl. King's cross
Morgan Thomas, tailor, 66 Berwick st. Soho
Morgan Thomas, wholesale & furnishing ironmonger, 11 Pancras lane, Queen st. Cheapside
Morgan Thomas, plumber & painter, 2 Old Gravel la. Wappng
Morgan Walter, barrister, 16 Old square, Lincoln's inn
Morgan Walter, *Leaping Bar* P.H. 146 Old st. St. Luke's
Morgan Wm. auctnr. & house & estate agt. 115 Aldersgate st
Morgan Wm. baker, 6 Holly st. Dalston
Morgan Wm. brass moulder & undert. 26 Britannia st. City rd
Morgan Wm. cabinet maker, 30 Mansion house st. Kenningn
Morgan Wm. cabinet maker, 24 Union st. Middlesex hosptl
Morgan Wm. carpenter, 30 George st. Portland place
Morgan Wm. carpenter, 10 Limehouse Old road
Morgan Wm. chair manufacturer, 14 Curtain rd. Shoreditch
Morgan Wm. coffee rooms, 4 Commercial place, City road
Morgan Wm. dairyman, 39 Store st. Bedford square
Morgan Wm. dentist & cupper, 1 Finsbury place so uth
Morgan Wm. *Flying Horse* P.H. 19 Crown st. Walworth rd
Morgan Wm. haberdasher, 31 Nicholas st. Hoxton New town
Morgan Wm. hosier, 26 & 27 Middle row, Holborn
Morgan Wm. hosier, 5 Newington causeway
Morgan Wm. hop mer. Queen's head inn yd. 84 Boro' High st
Morgan Wm. looking glass frame mak. 27 Bear la. Blackfrs
Morgan Wm. pill box maker, 10 Vernon pl. Bagnigge wells rd
Morgan Wm. sheep salesman, see Houlderness & Morgan
Morgan Wm. silk mercer, hosier, &c. 94 Park st. Grosven. sq
Morgan Wm. (Mrs.), wheelwright, 1 Chesnut row, Kentish twn
Morgan Wm. B. stockbroker, 14 Angel court, Throgmorton st
Morgan Wm. Hazell, *George* P.H. 166 Bethnal green road
Morgan Wm. Hen. dlr. in ancient china, 17 Hanway st. Oxfd. st
Morgan Wm. P. surgeon, 48 Old st. road
Morgan Wm. Robert, baker, 180 Poplar High st
Morgans Morgan, cowkeeper, 10 York st. Westminster
Morgue George, dancing master, 6 York st. Walworth road
Mori, Lavenu & Co. music sellers & publishers by special appointment to the Queen & H.R.H. the Duchess of Kent, 210 Regent st. & 47 King st
Moriarty Daniel, saddler & harness ma. 34 Berwick st. Soho
Morice James F. ship & insurance broker, 29 Nicholas lane, Lombard st. & Lloyd's
Morice John Charles, stockbroker, 1 Warnford court
Moring Susanna Ann & Jane (Misses), fancy needlework & electrotype apparatus wareho. 8 Blackfriars road
Moring Thomas & Co. carmen, 31 Camomile st. Bishopsgt
Moring Geo. secret springr. & polishr. 20 Galway st. St. Luke's
Moring Thomas, seal engraver, 10 Gate st. Lincoln's inn flds
Moring William, carman, 31 Camomile st. Bishopsgate
Morison, Moat & Co. hygeists, british college of heath, 1 & 2 Hamilton place, King's cross, New road
Morison Sir Alexander, physician, 26 Cavendish square
Morison Alex. Waugh, chemist, 1 Walton pl. Queen st. Brmptn
Morison Geo. west india mer. 21 New City chambs. & Lloyd's
Morison James, baker, Deptford High st
Morison Robert, baker, 49 Drury lane
Morison Thos. Henry, house painter, see Fitch & Morison
Morisse Walter, silversmith, 5 Jewin crescent, Cripplegate
Morland John & Son, umbrella & parasol ma. 50 Eastcheap
Morland Frederick H. tailor, &c. see Lewis & Morland
Morland Joseph, corn & flour dealer, 70 Broad st. Ratcliff
Morland William, ship's boat builder, 29 Rotherhithe
Morland Wm. Kendal, land surveyor, 66 London wall
Morlet John Marie, merchant, 2 Philpot lane, Fenchurch st
Morley Jas. & Wm. manch. warehomn. 4 Carey la. & 36 Gutter la
Morley John & Richard, wholesale haberdashers, hosier, flannel factors, glovers, &c. &c. 18 Wood st. Cheapside
Morley John & Samuel, lace manufacturers, 4 Friday st
Morley L. & Co. umbrella makers, 108 Wood st. Cheapside
Morley, Murray & Co. manch. warhmn. 52 Gracechurch st
Morley, Sorrell & Co. warehousemen, 25 Bread st
Morley Atkinson, *Burlington hotel*, 19 Cork st. Bond st. & 29 & 30 Old Burlington st
Morley Charles Robert, tailor, 9 Bartlett's buildings
Morley Elizabeth (Miss), milliner, see Strong & Morley
Morley George, barrister, 15 Serle st. Lincoln's inn fields
Morley George, music. inst. seller, 80 Whitechapel High st
Morley Henry, picture dealer, 17 Grosvenor st. west

Morley Isaac, appraiser, 1 Sidmouth st. Gray's inn road
Morley James, saddler, 1 Portland pl. Borough road
Morley John, oyster rooms, 27 Bath place, New road
Morley John, pork butcher, 75 Hare st. Bethnal green
Morley John, sewing silk, &c. manf. see Milner, Morley & Co
Morley Joseph, oil & colorman, 21 Houndsditch
Morley Richard, dyer & scourer, 60 Judd st. Brunswick sq
Morley Richard, hairdresser, 37 Surrey st. Strand
Morley Robert, warehouseman, see Capper, Morley & Capper
Morley Samuel, glasscutter, 57 Oakley st. Lambeth
Morley Samuel, tobacconist, 103 Old st. Luke's
Morley Thomas, jeweller & silversmith, 47 Oxford st
Morley Thos. Wm. surgeon, 11 New Cavendish st. Portland pl
Morley Thos. Wilson, hairdresser, 17 Gt. Carter lane
Morley Wm. carpen. & underta. 2 Whitehorse pl. Mile end road
Morley Wm. fruit & potato salesman, 67 & 68 Farringdon markt
Morley Wm. *Mitre* P.H. 61 New Church st. Lisson grove
Morley Wm. *Prince of Wales* P.H. 16 Frederick pl. Hmpstd. rd
Morley Wm. rag merchant, 16 Dacre st. Westminster
Morley Wm. sewing silk, &c. mnf. see Milner, Morley & Co
Morley Wm. Corwell, tailor, 3 Bentinck st. Berwick st. Soho
Morley Wm. Hart, barrister, 15 Serle st. Lincoln's inn
Morley Wm. Hen. pianoforte & music dlr. 6 Clark's pl. Isln
Morley Zachariah, statnr. & newsag. 27 Park ter. Regt. pk. rd
Mornement James, tailor, 36 Galway st. St. Luke's
Morning Advertiser Newspaper Office, 127 Fleet st
Morning Chronicle & Evening Chronicle Office, 332 Strand
Morning Herald Office, 18 Catherine st. Strand, & 103 Shoe la
Morning Post Newspaper Office, Wellington st. north
Morphett Rd. & Co. who. teadealrs. 16 Sise la. Bucklersbury
Morphett Richd. & Geo. hop mercs. 16 Sise la. Bucklersbury
Morphett Nathaniel, solicitor, see Dendy & Morphett
Morrell Edward, engine turner, 37½ King st. Clerkenwell
Morrah James, surgeon, 62 Sloane st. Knightsbridge
Morrell George, builder, 57 George st. Portman square
Morrell George, carpenter, 14 Charles st. Portman square
Morrell George, the civet cat, wholesale perfumer, cutler, portable dressing case maker, importer of foreign fancy merchandise, jewellery, &c. 60 & 61 Burlington arcade, Piccadilly, & 2 Butter market, Reading
Morrell George, cutler & jeweller, see Taylor & Morrell
Morrell Henry, quill warehouse & pencil, sealing wax, wafer, ink, ink powder & printing ink manufctr. 149 Fleet st.; manufactory, 25 Gt. New st. & West Harding st
Morrell Henry, printing ink mfr. 25 Gt. New st. Farringdon st
Morrell James, grainer, 44 Museum st. Bloomsbury
Morrell John, fruiterer, 53 Bethnal green rd
Morrell John, hairdres. 120 Goswell st. & 13 Wells rw. Islng
Morrell Wm. bricklayer, 44 Museum st. Bloomsbury
Morren Rev. John W. ladies' school, 14 Cambridge road
Morren Robt. Wm. & John, woolstaplers, Gun alley, 85 Bermondsey st.; & 1 Russell st. Bermondsey
Morrice John & Geo. timber merchts. 13 South st. Finsbury, & Mill wall, Poplar
Morrice Angelina (Mrs.), hosier, 22 Trinity sq. Tower hill
Morrice George, tailor, 16 Gt. Prescot st. Goodman's fields
Morrice Samuel, cigar manuf. 15 Gt. Prescot st. Goodman's fi
Morris Edw. & Son, tailors, 54 Berwick st. Soho
Morris Francis & Co. builders, 99 Mount st. Berkeley sq
Morris Francis & Thos. wharfingers & coal mers. Rutland whf. & Old Swan, Up. Thames st. & Addington whf. Cmbrwl. rd
Morris King & Gooding, bookbinders' tool cutters, engravers, printers, & brass rule manufacturers, 35 Ludgate st
Morris Joseph & Sons, manfrs. of newly improved drilled needles, D. Gaberthuel, agt. 48A, Gloucester pl. Portmn. sq
Morris, Prevost & Co. merchants, 24A, Gresham st
Morris Samuel B. & Co. lace, sewed muslin, millinery, & flower warehouse, 29 Wood st. City
Morris, Stone & Townson, solicitors, Moorgate st. chambers, 49 Moorgate st.; & 6 Wellclose sq
Morris Thos. & Son, hat manufs. 1 Holland st. Blackfriars rd
Morris Thos. & Wm. Geo. printers, 10 King st. Boro'
Morris Valentine & Son, importers of wines & spirits, 9 St. Mary at hill
Morris Aaron, carpenter, 2 Field pl. Larkhall la. Clapham
Morris Ann (Miss), straw hat mak. 16 Windsor ter. City rd
Morris Anna Maria (Mrs.), undertak. 70 Chalton st. Somerstn
Morris Barnett, cigar manf. 21 Gt. Prescot st. Goodman's flds
Morris Butler Ebenezer, artist, 91 Dean st. Soho sq
Morris Catherine (Mrs.), milliner, 3 Sun st. Bishopsgt. witht
Morris Chas. bookbindrs'. tool cut. 43 Kirby st. Hatton gar
Morris Chas. draper, &c. see Maund, Jones, Randall & Co
Morris David, hat maker, 52 Tabernacle walk, Finsbury
Morris Edward, brushma. 74 Wheeler st. Spitalfields
Morris Edw. ham & beef dealer, 3 Old Jewry
Morris Edward, tailor, &c. 32 Ludgate st
Morris Edward, *India Arms tavern*, 67 Fenchurch st. near the Blackwall Railway terminus
Morris Emanuel, furrier, 44 Mansell st. Goodman's fields
Morris Evan, solicitor, see Milne, Parry, Milne & Morris
Morris Frederick P. barrister, 26 Old square, Lincoln's inn
Morris George, baker, 89 Brick lane, Spitalfields
Morris George, bootmaker, 12 Cumberland st. Middsx. hosptl
Morris George, bricklayer & plasterer, 34 Oakley st. Lambth
Morris George, cabinet maker, 8 Harrow road, Paddington
Morris George, *Coach & Horses* P.H. 11 Upper Wellington st. Covent garden
Morris George, fancy mould turner, 1 Bevenden st. Hoxton
Morris George, ginger beer manfr. 42 Leonard st. Finsbury
Morris George, paper stainer, 13 Frederick's pl. Old Kent rd
Morris George, teadealer, 6 Broadway, Westminster
Morris Grace (Mrs.), *White Hart tav.* 200 Bishopsgate without
Morris Henry, bricklayer, 35 Cirencester pl. Gt. Titchfield st
Morris Henry, furrier & cap maker, 15 Minories
Morris Henry, physician, 26 Sackville st. Piccadilly
Morris Henry, rushmaker, 7 Barbican
Morris Henry, stone mason, South Lambeth, New road
Morris Henry G. hairdresser, 1 Liquorpond st. Gray's inn la
Morris Henry Sutherland, surgeon, 26 Sackville st
Morris Isaac, flannel factor, 7 Princes st. Wilson st. Finsbury
Morris James, breeches maker, 2 Charlotte st. Pimlico
Morris James, butcher, 3 Jubilee st. Commercial road east
Morris James, cabinet maker, 59 Curtain road, Shoreditch
Morris James, hosier, &c. 116 Crawford st. Portman st
Morris James, painter & decorator, 79 Park st. Grosvenor sq
Morris James, sen. plumber, 2 King's Head rw. Old Bromptn
Morris James, solicitor, 12 Crescent, Minories
Morris James (Mrs.), prof. of dancing, 7 Charlte. pl. Up. Kenn. la
Morris Jas. Bagot, tailor & draper, 1 Falcon sq. Aldersgate
Morris James Hen. boot & shoemaker, 29 King st. Portman sq
Morris Jane (Miss), millnr. Box Farm cot. King's rd. Chelsea
Morris John, accountant & agent, 7 Chapel pl. Cavendish sq
Morris John, baker, 28 Lamb st. Spitalfields
Morris John, bread & bis. baker, 49 Cheyne walk, Chelsea
Morris John, bottle warehouse, 29 Marylebone la. Oxford st
Morris John, bricklayer, 3 Crawford passage, Clerkenwell
Morris John, cabinet maker, 6 Gower place, Euston square
Morris John, carpenter, 4 Adam st. east, Portman sq
Morris John, chemist & druggist, 29 Kensington High st
Morris John, cowkeeper, 2 Wells st. St. James's
Morris John, dyer & scourer, 54 Park st. Camden town
Morris John, fruiterer, 21 Northampton pl. Old Kent road
Morris John, house painter & decorator, 234 Oxford st
Morris John, jeweller, 119 Snow's fields, Bermondsey
Morris John, *Leather Bottle* P.H. 1 Charles st. Hatton grdn
Morris John, *Spencer Arms* P.H. 62 Monmouth st. Sevendials
Morris John, surveyor, 58 Fenchurch st. & 4 Trinity terrace, East India road
Morris John, watchmaker, 7 Margaret ter. Paddington green
Morris John, wine cooper, &c. 34 Henry st. east, Avenue rd
Morris John Ball, mer. 15 Barge yd. chambs. Bucklersbury
Morris Joseph, butcher, 39 John st. Limehouse fields
Morris Joseph, stay ma. 15 & 34 St. Martin's ct. Leicester sq
Morris Joseph, tailor, 70 Chalton st. Somers town
Morris Joseph, undertaker, 71 Broadwall, Blackfriars
Morris Joseph, *Red Lion* P.H. 85 Union st. Borough
Morris Lewis, merchant, Tom's coffee house
Morris Mary (Miss), court dress mak. 19 Bolton st. Piccadilly
Morris Mary (Mrs.), patten mak. 4 Compton st. Clerkenwell
Morris Michael, butcher, Glo'ster row, Walworth road
Morris Morris, marine store dlr. 98 Golden lane, St. Luke's
Morris Mowbray, barrister, 2 Stone buildings, Lincoln's inn
Morris Richard, butcher, 18 New road, St. George's east
Morris Richd. *Swedish Flag*, P.H. 2 Princes st. Ratcliff hwy
Morris Robert, baker, Church st. Hackney
Morris Robert, fancy bird dlr. 17 Princess st. Lisson grove
Morris Robert, fruiterer, 1 Prospect place, Kingsland road
Morris Robert, tobacconist, 129 Tooley st
Morris Robert Brudenell, day school, 9 Kingsland green
Morris Samuel, baker, 38 Cleveland st. Fitzroy square
Morris Saml. cheesemonger, 8 Pleasant place, King's cross
Morris Samuel, linendraper, 10 Walker's court, Golden sq
Morris Saml. Ferdinand, butcher, 22 Wormwood st. Bishopsg
Morris Samuel W. law writer, 63 Carey st. Lincoln's inn
Morris Sarah (Mrs.), baker, 11 Edward st. Limehouse
Morris Septimus, stationer, Stratford Broadway
Morris Stephen, butcher, 3 Gloucester pl. Walworth common
Morris Thomas, architect, 58 Warren st. Fitzroy square
Morris Thomas, bricklayer, 22 Queen st. Soho
Morris Thomas, *Coach & Horses* P.H. 45 Brewer st. Golden sq
Morris Thomas, coal mercht. Western wf. George st. Adelphi
Morris Thomas, engineer, 11 Jerusalem ct. St. John st

Morris Thomas, forge & house bellows maker, 7 Drury lane
Morris Thomas, furnishing undertaker, 183 Drury lane
Morris Thomas, glass sta. & bender, 5 Frederick pl. Gosw. rd
Morris Thomas, press & machine maker, 15 Drury lane
Morris Thomas, surgeon, 17 Southampton st. Strand
Morris Wm. cabinet maker, 132 Blackfriars road
Morris Wm. conveyancer, 4 Essex ct. Temple
Morris Wm. fruiterer & coal dlr. 11 Brown st. Bryanstone sq
Morris Wm. grocer, 19 Mount row, Liverpool rd. Islington
Morris Wm. ironfounder, 14 Anchor & Hope alley, Wapping
Morris Wm. oilman, 23 Wellington st. Goswell road
Morris Wm. oil & colorman, 35 Clifton st. Finsbury
Morris Wm. paperstainer, 7 Patriot row, Cmbdge.rd. Mile end
Morris Wm. saddler, &c. 11 Russell st. Mile end road
Morris Wm. smith, 26 Snow's fields, Bermondsey
Morris Wm. stationer, 2 Field place, Larkhall la. Clapham
Morris Wm. surgeon, 8 Bath ter. Camberwell New rd
Morris Wm. *Two Spies* P. H. 47 King st. Seven dials
Morris Wm. wholesale confectioner, 158 St. George st
Morris Wm. Haywood, stables, 2 Paragon mews, New Knt. rd
Morris Wm. Rd. suptdt. Kent water works, Mill la. Deptfrd
Morrish (Gilbert) & Co. chemists, 27 Newcastle st. Strand
Morrish Francis, slater, 3 Chapel st. Pentonville
Morrish James, baker, 1 Sekforde st. Clerkenwell
Morrison Alexander & Co. merchants, 2 Riches ct. Lime st
Morrison, Dillon & Co. warehousemen, 104 to 107 Fore st; & counting house, 32 Milton st. Cripplegate
Morrison Geo. Wm. & Co. coalmerchts. 42, 43 & 47 Forest. Limeho
Morrison James & Co. leather merchts. 2 Crown ct. Philpot la
Morrison, Sons & Co. merchants, 62 Moorgate st
Morrrison Wm. & Co. coopers, Redmead la. Hermitage bdg. Wap
Morrison Wm. & Co. worsted & carpet warehousemen, 4 Star court, Bread st. Cheapside
Morrison Agnes (Miss), ladies school, 2 Adam st. Hampstd. rd
Morrison Geo. lace mfr. (Geo. Boyd, agt.), 15 Staining la
Morrison James, coal factor, 1 Raymond bldgs. Gray's inn
Morrison James, coal factor, 28 St. Mary at hill
Morrison James, surgeon, &c. 121 Edgware rd. Paddington
Morrison John, boot & shoe maker, 6 Marlboro' rd. Chelsea
Morrison John, clock maker, 20 Charles st. City rd
Morrison John, tailor & habit maker, 76 Cheapside
Morrison John, tailor, 15 Craven st. Strand
Morrison John Archib. library, 52 Leman st. Goodman's flds
Morrison Nicholas Careless, oil & colorman, Duke st. Chelsea
Morrison Peter, resident director of *Britannia Life Assurance Company*, 1 Princes st. Bank
Morrison Robert, tailor, 53 St. Paul's churchyard
Morrison Thomas, *Peacock* P.H. 9 Bethnal green
Morrison William, baker, 9 Thirza place, Old Kent rd
Morrison Wm. leather mer. 9 New Leather market, Brmndsy
Morrison Wm. stationer & bookseller, &c. 23 Fenchurch st
Morriss Wm. & Co. machinists, 12 Newington causeway
Morriss Robert, carpenter, 11 George st. Portman sq
Morritt David, grocer, 223 Shoreditch
Morrow John, *Robin Hood & Lit. John* P.H. 33 Tabernacle walk
Morse David & Co. tea & general agents, 133 Fenchurch st
Morse Edward, surgeon, 1 South place, Up. Kennington la
Morse George, greengrocer, 37 William st. Lisson grove
Morse Henry, bookseller & stationer, 68 Leadenhall st
Morse John, fruiterer & greengrocer, Wandsworth road
Morse Joseph, saddle tree maker, 9 Pollen st. Hanover sq
Morse Richard, coffee rooms, 7 Bermondsey New road
Morse Richard, watchmaker, 8 Charing cross
Morse Samuel, optician, 6 Church lane, Whitechapel
Morse William, butcher, 2 Little Newport st. Long acre
Morse Wm. Adams, solicitor, Dyers' hall, College st. City
Morson Thomas N. R. operative chemist, 19 Southampton row, Russell square, & Hornsey road
Morss Saml. watch & clock maker, 2 Green st. Bethnal green
Mortell Philip Henry, tailor, 29 Henrietta st. Brunswick sq
Mortiboy & Herbert, mnftg. jewellers, 8 Newman st. Oxford st
Mortimer Edwd. & Co. stockbrokers, 7 Shorter's ct. Throgm. st
Mortimers' & Gawtry, american merchts, 28 Noble st. City
Mortimer & Hunt, jewellers, goldsmiths & silversmiths to her Majesty, 156 New Bond st. & manufactory 26 Harrison st. Gray's inn road
Mortimer H. H. & Co. wholesale & shipping ironmongers, tin plate & iron merchants, 10 & 25 Great Bush lane
Mortimer & Narey (Misses), court dress makrs. 2 New Bond st
Mortimer Charles, ea. i. mercht. see Lediard, Jones & Mortimer
Mortimer Elizab. (Mrs.), straw bonnet ma. 47 Old Compton st
Mortimer Francis, cabinetmaker, 20 Grove pl. Lisson grove
Mortimer James, coal mrchnt. 1 Lit. Randolph st. Cmdn. tn
Mortimer John, furniture broker, 7 Earl st. Kensington
Mortimer John, farrier, 12 Seymour pl. Bryanstone square
Mortimer John, publisher, 1 Adelaide st. Strand
Mortimer John, solicitor, see Allen & Mortimer
Mortimer John Ellis, cabinet ma. 47 Old Compton st. Soho
Mortimer Lucretia M. (Miss), school, Stafford pl. Vaux. b. rd
Mortimer Robert, tobacconist, 14½ Duke st. Lincn's. inn fl
Mortimer Roger, stockbroker, 35 Throgmorton st. City
Mortimer Samuel, academy, 7 Charles st. east Hampstd. rd
Mortimer Saml. cheesemong. 5 Grove ter. Brompton grove
Mortimer Thomas, attorney, 4 Albany court yard
Mortimer Thomas, *Bell* P.H. 22 East st. Walworth road
Mortimer Thomas Hill, attorney, 4 Albany court yard
Mortimer Wm. coachma. & fruiterer, 4 Marchmont st. Brnsw. sq
Mortimer Wm. *Old King's Arms*, P.H. 37 Short's gardns. Dr. la
Mortimer Wm. Henry, dentist, 12 Harley st. Cavendish sq
Mortimore George, bootmaker, 3 Weston st. Somers town
Mortimore John, dairyman, 24 Little Queen st. Westminster
Mortimore Wm. leather factor, see Boutcher, Mortimore & Co
Mortimore Wm. leather factr. see Streatfield, Laurence & Co
Mortlock Jas. boot & shoe ma. 43 Providence row, Barnsby. row
Mortlock John, china & glass warehouse, 250 Oxford st. & 58 Park st. Grosvenor square
Mortlock Wm. cheesemonger, 20 New road, St. George's east
Mortlock Wm. china & glass warehouse, by special appointment to her Majesty, 18 Regent st. Waterloo place
Morton Chas. E. & Co. Sheffield plate wareho. 61 Fleet st
Morton Jas. & Co. carpet & rug manfrs. 17 Skinner st. Snowhill
Morton John & Geo. *Fitzroy Arms* P.H. 21 Clipstone st. Ftzry. sq
Morton Joseph & George, cutlers, &c. 39 Cheapside
Morton Joseph & George, working cutlers, 2 Craven buildings, Drury lane, & 8 Great Turnstile, Holborn
Morton Joseph & Son, medical fitters, labellers, writers on glass, wood, wire, &c. 8 Francis street, Tottenham court road, & 12 Union terrace, Camden town
Morton Alex. who. haberdasher, 71 Bishopsgate without
Morton Alexander, ship & insurance agent, 20 Great Hermitage st. Wapping, & Baltic coffee house
Morton Andrew, artist, 21B, Soho square
Morton Anthony Knipe, coal merchant, Union wharf, 68 Wapping wall, & Jerusalem coffee house, Cornhill
Morton Charles, hardwareman, Upper East Smithfield
Morton Charles, *St. George* P.H. 4 Belgrave road, Pimlico
Morton David, tobacco pipe ma. 16 North st. East st. Walwrth
Morton Edward, physician, 7 York place, Kentish town
Morton Edward, plumber & glazier, 1 Cleveland st. Fitzroy sq
Morton Edward, shorthand writer, 25 Craven st. Strand
Morton Edward, surgeon, &c. 10 Wood st. Spitalfields
Morton Eliza (Mrs.), babylinen wa. 4 Gt. Russell st. Bloomsby
Morton Eliza (Mrs.), haberdasher, 111 Goswell st
Morton Elizh. (Miss), milliner, 57 Conduit st. Regent st
Morton Fred. Boyce, steam corn mills, see Simmonds & Morton
Morton Gaven, linendraper, 28 Gloster ter. Comrcl. rd. east
Morton Gaven, teadealer, 9 Watney st. Commercl. rd. east
Morton George, chemist, Stratford broadway
Morton George, coal merchant, see Wills, Morton & Morton
Morton George Stevens, tailor, 122½ St. George st. east
Morton Henry, fancy cabinet ma. 13 Colville ct. Fitzroy sq
Morton James, brushma. &c. 5 Quickset row, Newrd. Fitzroy sq
Morton James, warhmn. see Oldroyd, Hodgson & Morton
Morton John, cheesemonger, 15 Grey Coat pl. Westminster
Morton John, coal merchant, see Wills, Morton & Morton
Morton John, *London Apprentice* P.H. 7 Margaret st. Cav. sq
Morton John, marble mercht. & statuary & mason, 2 Southampton st. Strand, & Salisbury wharf, Salisbury st. Strand
Morton John, writer on glass, labeller & general medical sundry dealer, 21 Gt. Charlotte st. Blackfriars road
Morton Mary (Mrs.), cow keeper, 23 Spring st. Portman sq
Morton Mylam, dining rooms, 70 Millbank st. Westminster
Morton Nathaniel, straw hat maker, 162 Tottenham ct. rd
Morton Richard, tallowchandler, 9 North st. Finsbury mkt
Morton Rd. Thos. *Watermans' Arms* P.H. 23 Paris st. Lmbh
Morton Robert, engineer & founder, 240 Wapping
Morton Schell, baker, 5 Tower st. Westminster road
Morton Thomas, butcher, Haverstock hill, Hampstead road
Morton Thomas, grocer, 3 Rawstorne st. Brompton
Morton Thomas, *Sugar Loaf* P.H. 31 Bell yard, Temple bar
Morton Thomas, surgeon, 7 Woburn place, Russell square
Morton Thomas Mylam, butcher, 11 Prospect pl. Kingslnd. rd
Morton Tryphena (Miss), ladies' school, see Boddy & Morton
Morton William, grocer, 3 Charterhouse lane
Morton Wm. *King & Queen* P.H. 3 Gt. Distaff la. Friday st
Morton Wm. *Sun & Punch Bowl* P.H. 60 & 61 Long la. Smthfld
Morttram Edward, hatter, 4 Deptford High st
Mortram Norman, *Horse & Groom* P.H. 19 High st. Nwngtn. btts
Moryoseph Judah, drug & spice mer. 14 Bury st. St. Mary Axe
Moscheles Ignace, profesr. of music, 3 Chester pl. Regt.'s pk
Moscrop Richd. John, *Green Man* P.H. South row, Cov. gar
Mose Thos. wine & spirit mercht. 22 Change alley, Cornhill

Mose Wm. boot & shoe maker, 41 High st. Portland town
Mosedon Benjamin, wholesale clothes warehouse, 7 Minories
Moseley John & Son, manufacturers of planes, lathes, tool chests & mechanical tools of every description, & hardwaremen, 17 & 18 New st. Covent garden
Moseley Alexander, baker, 1 Norfolk st. Commercial rd. east
Moseley Andrew, architect & surveyor, 53 Great Ormond st. & High st. Fulham
Moseley Andrew, architect, 53 Gt. Ormond st. Queen sq
Moseley David, *Union Flag* P.H. 8 Union st. Whitechapel
Moseley Edw. wine, spirit, & por. mer. 1 Up. Glo'ster st. Dorsetsq
Moseley Ellen (Mrs.), plumber, 25 Mincing lane
Moseley Francis, glass & china dealer, Mare st. Hackney
Moseley George, helmet cap ma. see Hawkes, Moseley & Co
Moseley George Robert, oval turner, 16 Memel st. St. Luke
Moseley Henry, artist, 52 Charlotte st. Fitzroy square
Moseley Joseph, barrister, 1 Mitre court buildings, Temple
Moseley Margaret (Miss), silk imp. 5 Hanover st. Hanover sq
Moseley Maria (Mrs.) artist, 52 Charlotte st. Fitzroy sq
Moseley Moss, stationer, 45 Middle Grove st. Commercial rd
Moseley Thomas, hatter, 7 Augustus row, Spa road
Moseley Thomas, solicitor, 13 Bedford st. Covent garden
Moseley Wm. architect, 32 Cumberland ter. Regent's park
Moseley Wm. plane maker, 2 Dorset cres. New North road
Moseley Wm. Samuel, hairdresser, 56 Maze, Tooley st
Mosely Ephraim & Simeon, dentists, 32 Haymarket
Mosely Ephraim, oil & italian warehouse, 48 Leadenhall st
Mosely George, baker, 51 Kensington High st
Mosely Lewin, surgeon dentist, 12 Berners st. Oxford st
Mosely Moses, watchmaker, 26 Bury st. St. Mary Axe
Mosely Simeon, surgeon dentist, 29 Duke st. St. James's
Mosely William, tailor & draper, 17 Whitechapel road
Moser & Co. furnishing ironmongers, &c. 52 Frith st. Soho
Moser Son & Co. iron merchts. & who. ironmgrs. 165 Boro'
Moser Edwd. coal mercht. British whf. Clink st. Bankside
Moser John, lead broker, Baltic coffee house
Moser John, upholsterer, 63 Mortimer st. Cavendish square
Moses Brothers, bristle & brush makers, 58 & 59 Leadenhall st
Moses Brothers, ivory, tortoiseshell & mother of pearl shell merchants, 58 & 59 Leadenhall st
Moses Elias & Son, wholesale & retail clothiers, tailors & outfitters, 154 & 155 Minories, & 83 to 86 Aldgate High st
Moses John & Co. shipchdlrs. & com. agts. 47 Fore st. Limehse
Moses Henry & Edward & Maurice, wholesale slopsellers & merchants, 87 Tower hill
Moses & Kesnor, tailors, 20 Grosvenor row, nth. side, Pimlico
Moses, Levy & Co. who. slopsllrs. & warehsmn. 2 & 3 Aldgate
Moses, Lewis & Co. imprs. of cigars, 27 Russell ct. Drury lane
Moses, Son & Davis, who. slopsellers, 14 & 15 Aldgate High st
Moses Benjamin, curiosity dlr. 6 & 10 Hanway st. Oxford st
Moses Charles Moses, fruiterer, 51 & 60 Mount st. Lambeth
Moses David, fruiterer, 50 London road, Southwark
Moses Elias, china wareh. 104 Up. Whitecross st. St. Luke's
Moses Emanuel, slopseller, 67 Bunhill row, Chiswell st
Moses Henry, slopseller, 3 Lit. St. Mary axe, Houndsditch
Moses Isaac, curiosity dealer, 3 Gray's inn pass. Red Lion sq
Moses Isaac, tailor, 76 St. John st. West Smithfield
Moses John, clothes salesm. 6 Cross ct. Russell ct. Drury la
Moses Joseph, merchant, 23 Finsbury square
Moses Judea, clothes salesman, 3 Russell ct. Drury lane
Moses Maurice, glass & china dealer, 22 Bath st. City road
Moses Michael, dealer in plate, 18 Bury st. St. Mary axe
Moses Michael, fruit merchant, 19 Gracechurch st
Moses Samuel, clothes dealer, 143 Rosemary lane
Moses Solomon, merchant, 4 Little St. Mary axe
Moses Wm. architect, 32 Cumberland ter. Regent's park
Mosley John & Son, gold beaters, 30 Hyde st. Bloomsbury
Mosley Richard & Co. steel pen manufacturers, & birmingham & sheffield warehousemen, 8 Hatton garden
Mosley Robt. & Son, who. jewlrs. & watchmkrs. 113 Fetter la
Mosley Frederick, baker, 27 Robert st. Hampstead road
Mosley Jas. carpenter & builder, 16½ Church st. Spitalfields
Mosley John, carpenter & builder, 6 Davies st. & 17 Davies mews, Berkeley square
Mosley Richard, lapidary, 1 Clerkenwell close
Mosley William, birmingham warehouse, 75 Hatton garden
Mosley William, cutler, 2 St. James's walk, Clerkenwell
Mosly George, baker, 51 Kensington High st. south side
Moss Ambrose & Simeon, upholsterers, High st. Kensington
Moss Chas. & Co. ship & insurance brokers & agent shippers, & agents for Muntz's yellow metal for ships' bottoms, 23 Fenchurch st. & Salmon la. Limehouse, & 4 Baltic buildings, Liverpool
Moss Leah (Mrs.), & Co. cigar mfrs. 1 Liverpool bldgs. Bpsgt
Moss Saul & Co. west india mers. 1 Langbourn chambs. City
Moss Wm. & Edwd. meat salesmen, Leadenhall market
Moss Daniel Luke, stonemason, 4 Fieldgate st. Whitechapel
Moss Edward, solicitor, 4 Queen st. Cheapside
Moss Edwin, surgeon, 71 Wimpole st. Cavendish square
Moss Emanuel, east london plate glass warehouse & looking glass manufactory, 15 Leman st. Goodman's fields, & 57 Paradise st. Liverpool
Moss Emanuel, tobacconist, 61 Quadrant, Regent st
Moss Frances (Mrs.), dressmaker, 21 Wood st. Spitalfields
Moss Frederick, hairdresser, 14 Strutton ground, Westmr
Moss Frederick Wm. veterinary surgeon, 6 Clapham rise
Moss George, bootmaker, 158 Princes road, Lambeth
Moss George, oil & colorman, 124 Edgware road, Paddingtn
Moss Hannah (Mrs.), staymaker, 82 Edgware road; & 12 Middle row, Holborn
Moss Henry, boot & shoe maker, 66 Brill row, Somers town
Moss Hen. custom ho. & shipg. ag. Fishmngs'hll. Up. Thames st
Moss Henry, hairdresser, perfumer, wig maker, & inventor of the metalometer for sharpening razors, 200 Fleet st
Moss Isaac, bootmaker, 21 Vere st. Duke st. Clare market
Moss Isaac, staymaker, 78 Whitechapel High st
Moss James, beer retailer, 1 Grenada place, Old Kent road
Moss James, butcher, 152 Union st. Borough
Moss James, cheesemonger, 5 Shepherd st. Mayfair
Moss James, shoemaker, 32 Thayer st. Manchester square
Moss John, coffee rooms, 5 Belgrave road, Pimlico
Moss John, linendraper, 15 Portman place, Edgware rd
Moss John, merchant, 9 Magdalen row, Gt. Prescott st
Moss Joseph, baker, New cross, Deptford
Moss Joseph, chemist, Stratford
Moss Leah (Mrs.), cigar maker, see Levy & Moss
Moss Matthew, professor of music, 18 Greek st. Soho
Moss Montague, fruiterer, 138 Waterloo road
Moss Richard, brazier, 7 Bartholomew square, St. Luke's
Moss Richard, coachmaker, 4 Little Exeter st. Sloane st
Moss Robert, house painter, &c. 2 Margaret st. Cavendish sq
Moss Robert, pawnbroker, 20 Goswell road, west side
Moss Susanna (Miss), staymaker, 71 Hackney road
Moss Thos. dining rooms, 11 Cambridge pl. Edgware road
Moss Tho. *Royal Standard* P.H. 7 Flemming st. Kingslnd. rd
Moss William, dyer, 29 Little Guildford st. Borough
Moss William, envelope manufacturer, 76 Lisson gr. north
Moss William, *King's Head* P.H. 25 Broad st. Bloomsbury
Moss William, solicitor, 11 Serjeants' inn, Fleet st
Moss William, solicitor, 11 Serjeants' inn, Fleet st
Moss Wm. Selby, upholsterer, 12 Park ter. King's rd. Chelsea
Mossman Chas. & Thos. cattle salesmen, 8 West Smithfield
Mote Edward, fancy cabinet maker, 51 Borough road
Mote Wm. pork butcher, 4 Norfolk pl. Lower road, Islington
Moth George, *Moth's hotel*, 14 New st. Covent garden
Mothersole Thomas, oil & italian wareho. 2 Shoe la. Fleet st
Motion Andrew, *Suffolk Arms* P.H. Boston st. Hackney rd
Motley William, butcher, 23 Warwick st. Pimlico
Mott Daniel, tobacconist, 33 Shoemaker row, Blackfriars
Mott Isaac Hen. Rt. pianoforte mkr. to the Queen, 76 Strand, & 23 Poppin's court, Fleet st
Mott James, cheesemonger, see Gammage & Mott
Mott Rebecca (Mrs.), carwoman, 24 Old Fish st. City
Mott William, bookseller, 6 Weybridge place, Mile end rd
Mott William, silversmith & jeweller, 55 & 36 Cheapside, & 81 & 91 Bishopsgate without
Motte Standish, barrister, 55 Lincoln's inn fields
Mottram Edward & Son, engravers, 4 Little Britain
Mottram John, heraldic & vignette engra. 4 Little Britain
Mottram Rehe & Co. mechlin starch works, Ranelagh road
Mottram William, tailor, 11 Up. Smith st. Northampton sq
Motts Wm. Geo. & Robert, grocers, 46 Whitechapel High st
Mottu Brothers, who. watchmaks. 11 Richmond blds. Soho sq
Mouat Archibald, wine, spirit & ale mer. 13 Creed la. Ludgate st
Mouat Charles, lace, &c. warehouseman, see Watts & Mouat
Mouat John, hatter, 9 Sparrow corner, Minories
Mouatt John, wine merchant & agent for Muir's Edinburgh ale, & importer of whisky, 8 Cooper's row, Crutched friars
Moul James & Sons, tea brokers, 106 Fenchurch st
Moul Wm. coach currier, Blue Anchor yard, 91 York st. Westminster, & tobacconist, 17 York st. Westminster
Mould & Hurst, accountants, 21 Earl st. Blackfriars
Mould Charles, cheesemonger, 47 King st. Snowhill
Mould Henry, wheelwright, Villa st. Walworth common
Mould John, stationer & news agent, 137 St. John st. rd
Mould Thomas, surgeon, 45 Brompton row
Mould William, grocer, 1 Southampton st. Camberwell
Moulden Joseph Eldin, solicitor, 4 St. Thomas's st. Borough
Moulder Elizth. (Mrs.), optical turner, 29 Galway st. St. Luke's
Mouldey Thomas, greengrocer, 6 Lit. Chapel st. Westminster
Moule Thos. & Son, wine merchs. 16 Gould sq. Crutchedfriars
Moule John, coal merchant, 4 Adams court, Old Broad st

Moule John, dyer, 15 Seabright pl. Hackney rd
Moule John Watkins, linendraper, 54 Baker st. Portman sq
Moule Rowland, *Salters' Arms* P.H. 15 Tottenham st. Tot.ct.rd
Moule Wm. insurance agent, 4 Adams court, & Lloyd's
Moules William, fishmonger, 7 Brewer st. Somers town
Moulin Charles, beer retailer, 9 Lit. Coram st. Tavistock sq
Moulinie John Fras. geneva watch ma. 9 Salisbury st. Strnd
Mouls William, *George* P.H. 8 High st. Newington butts
Moulson & Williams, silversmiths, White Hart ct. Le'ster sq
Moult Richard, ginger beer manufactr. &c. 32 Liquorpond st
Moulton Charles, carpenter, 8 Tower royal, Watling st
Moulton Richard, law stationer, 18 Chancery lane, & East gateway, Lincoln's inn
Moulton Wm. tailor, 1 Bidborough st. Burton crescent
Moultrie Edward M. barrister, 1 Alpha place, St. John's wood, & 14 Serle st. Lincoln's inn
Mouncher Charles, tailor, 2 Grove pl. Green st. Kentish town
Mounckfield S. (Miss), ladies' school, Richmond rd. Dalston
Mounsey Grace (Mrs.), *Cock & Woolpack* P.H. 6 Finch la. Cornh
Mount Ch. ag. to W. I. & I. Abbott, lamp ma. 60 Frith st. Soho
Mount Francis Wm. solicitor, 10 Lawrence Pountney lane
Mountague David, roman cement ma. see Turner & Mountague
Mountague James, surveyor of the north district of the City of London, Guildhall
Mountain John, dining rooms, 16 Sherborne lane, City
Mountain Mark, shoemaker, 29 Green st. Bethnal green
Mountain Peter, coach proprietor & carrier by railway, 49 Skinner st
Mountain Richard, printseller, 9 West st. Seven dials
Mountcastle Edward, hatter, 41 King William st. City
Mountcastle George, bookseller, 10 Bedford ct. Covent gard
Mountford Edward, hosier & glover, 47 High st. Notting hill
Mountford John, surgeon, 14 Great Coram st. Russell sq
Mountford Joseph, boiler maker, 33 Wharf road, City rd
Mountfort John, cattle salesman, 41 West Smithfield
Mouque Alfred, artist, 26 Queen's row, Pimlico
Mouque Francis, engraver, 55 Fleet st
Mourilyan & Casey, lithographers, printers, &c. 44 Fleet st
Mourilyan Joseph Noakes, solicitor, see Hall & Mourilyan
Mousell John Wm. seal engraver, 25 Farringdon st
Mousir Geo. hosier, glover & outfitter, 28 High st. Marylebone
Mousley & Co. merchants, 3 Dunster court, Mincing lane
Mousley Andrew, *Crown* P.H. 1 Leigh st. Red Lion sq
Mousley Chas. Hague, cust. ho. agt. see Taylor, Mousley & Co
Mousley Geo. oil & colorman, 13 Up. Cleveland st. Fitzroy sq
Mousley John, *Hope* P.H. 61 Park st. Dorset sq
Mousley John, wine merchant, 26½ New st. Dorset sq
Mousley Wm. Eaton, solicitor, 5 Stone bldgs. Lincoln's inn
Mowatt Robert, cabinet maker, 30 Henry st. Hampstead rd
Mowbray George, wholesale druggist, see Garnet & Mowbray
Mowbray Henry, wine mer. 1 Northumberland st. Strand
Mowbray Wm. Whitby, pilot, Thames st. Lower Rotherhithe
Mower Charles, tailor, 34 Brewer st. Somers town
Mowl Jemima C. M. (Mrs.), bookseller, 264 Bethnal green rd
Mowlem, Freeman & Burt, stone & granite merchants, 8 & 13 Paddington basin, south side; & Twig folly, Bethnal green
Mowtell Joseph, hairdresser, 68 Wardour st. Soho
Moxey James Bennett, baker, 56 Lisson grove north
Moxey Samuel, bricklayer, Battersea
Moxhay Edward, Hall of Commerce, Threadneedle st
Moxhay William, surgeon, 4 Brunswick terrace, Dover rd
Moxley Geo. undertaker, 29 Duke st. Lincoln's inn fields
Moxley Mary Fras. (Mrs.), milliner, 62 Judd st. Brunswick sq
Moxon Charles, house painter & decorator, 33 High st. Marylebone, & 29 Beaumont mews
Moxon Edward, publisher, 44 Dover st. Piccadilly
Moxon Henry, attorney, 2 Tanfield court, Temple
Moxon Thomas, stock & share broker, 69 Old Broad st. City
Moxon William, barrister, 10 New square, Lincoln's inn
Moxon Wm. Parkin, potato salesm. Cotton's whf. Tooley st
Moy John, *Royal Standard* P.H. 32 Stockbridge ter. Pimlico
Moy Robert, plumber, &c. Wandsworth road
Moy William, bricklayer & builder, 1 Rolls bldgs. Fetter la
Moyce John, coal merchant, King st. New town, Deptford
Moyes John, lodging house, 133 Salisbury square
Moyes William & Co. carmen, 24 Cullum st. Lime st
Moyes William, tailor & outfitter, 4 Bozier's ct. Tottm. ct. rd
Moyle Ann (Mrs.), boarding house, 10 Wardrobe place, & 1 Addle hill, Doctors' commons
Moyse Cajetaw, cattle salesman, 59 West Smithfield
Moyse Robt. V. beast & sheep salesman, 59 West Smithfield
Moyse Robert V. corn factor, Jack's coffee house, Mark lane
Moyse Robt. V. hay & straw salesman, 59 West Smithfield
Moyse & Cork, cattle & sheep salesmen, 59 West Smithfield
Moysey John Chaffer, who. tea dlr. 18 Laurence Pountney hl
Moyssi Brothers, merchants, 16 New Broad st
Muckalt & Downing, carpet warehousemen, 107 Shoreditch
Muckarsie George James, dentist, 18 King st. Holborn
Muckell Samuel, beer retailer, 37 Saville st. Foley st
Muckle John, engineer & machinist, 2 Monkwell st. Cripplgt
Muckle John, grocer, 30 Judd st. Brunswick square
Muckleston Paul Davis, brushmaker, 55 Red Lion st. Holborn
Muckley James, seedsman, &c. see Butler & Muckley
Muckley Sarah (Mrs.), beer retailer, 75 Church la. Whtchpl
Mudd James, carpent. & undert. 39 Pritchard's rd. Hackney rd
Mudd James, carpen. & undert. 19 Seabright pl. west, Hckny. rd
Muddell Wm. *Burton coffee ho. & tav.* Freeman's ct. Cheapsi
Muddell Wm. wine & beer mercht. 23 Lit. St. Thomas Apostle
Muddell Wm. upholsterer, &c. 6 Little St. Thomas Apostle
Muddiman Alexr. hairdresser, 55 Davies st. Berkeley square
Muddiman John, shawl cleaner, 27 Aske st. Hoxton
Muddle John, *Pr. Mecklenburgh* P.H. 33 James st. Oxford st
Muddock & Rowland, hosiers & outfitters, 73 Oxford st.
Muddock Emerson G. & Jas. wind. gls. cts. 10 Clerkenwell green
Mudford James & Co. trimming selrs. 177 Shadwell High st
Mudie Thos. & Sons, stationers & news agents, 15 Coventry st
Mudie Charles E. bookseller & librarian, 28 Up. King st. Blmsby
Mudie Christopher, bookseller, 161 Fleet st
Mudie John, baker, 1 Princes st. Wilson st. Finsbury
Mudie Peter, fruiterer, 10 Dorset place, Pall mall
Mudie Peter, fruiterer, 22 St. Martin's st. Leicester sq
Mudry Monsieur, prof. of french, 51 Bernard st. Russell sq
Mudy Thomas, hosiery & glove agent, 26 Philip lane
Muench John, cooper, Denmark st. Ratcliff highway
Muff William, tailor, 22 Davies st. Berkeley square
Muggeridge Henry & Edwd. corn & hop facts. St. Andrew's hill
Muggeridge & Son, stationers & news ag. 38 North Audley st
Muggeridge, Sprague & Co. who. stationers, 61 Queen st. City
Muggeridge Henry, wire drawer, 61 St. John st. Smithfield
Muggeridge Jas. corndealer & coal mer. 85 Tottenham ct. rd
Muggeridge William, corn merchant, 65 York rd. Lambeth
Muggridge Jas. meat salesman, 2 Rose st. Newgate market
Muggridge John, *Blenheim* P.H. 7 Bond st. Chelsea
Muggridge Lucy (Mrs.), butcher, Southampton st. Cambwl
Muggridge Richard, coal dlr. 69 Compton st. Clerkenwell
Mugliston Caroline (Mrs.), chemist, 77 Brewer st. Somers twn
Muhm Michael, sugar refiner, King David lane, Shadwell
Muir Alexander, boot & shoe ma. 18 Up. Berner st. Com. rd. ea
Muir George, staymaker, 40 Barbican
Muir Thos. printer & commission agent, see Gibson & Muir
Muir Wm. hairdresser, 3 George terrace, Commercial rd. ea
Muirhead Robert, carpenter, 37 London st. Fitzroy square
Muirson John Thos. fish. tackle ma. 7 Up. King st. Bloomsb
Mulaney James, dressing case ma. 34 Lisson grove north
Mulcock Thos. Roberts, painter & glazr. 27 High st. Newgtn. bts
Mulder Wm. Joseph, shoemaker, 11 Patriot row, Cambdg. rd
Mules John, baker, 14 William st. Cannon st. road
Mull Henry, pork butcher, 62 Whitechapel High st
Mullen Nicholas Fredk. printer, see Crozier & Mullen
Mullen Samuel, *Mullen's hotel*, 11 Ironmonger lane
Mullens Joseph & Co. surgeons, &c. 52 Leather la. Holbn
Mullens & Marshall, stockbrokers, 3 Lombard st
Mullens James D. mercht. see Perkins, Schlusser & Mullens
Mullens John Jarvis, tobacconist, 24 Fore st. Cripplegate
Mullens Richard (firm, Bush & Mullens), solicitor to the association of London bankers, 7 St. Mildred's court, Poultry
Mullens Wm. buildg. material dealer, 40 Vauxhall wk. Lmbth
Mullens Wm. James, bricklayer, Glster. bldgs. Old Kent rd
Muller (Barnard) & Co. furriers, 4 Redcross st. Cripplegate
Muller Joseph & Co. coach & harness makers, 244 Whtchpl. rd
Muller Frederick, surgeon, 46 Hans place, Sloane st
Muller Hen. statnr. & tobacnst. 7½ Bedford pl. Commercl. rd. e
Muller John, watchmakers' material wa. 40 King st. Soho
Muller John Henry (late Robert Alford), engraver & copperplate, letterpress & gold printer, 13 Bridge st. Southwk
Müller Joseph, curiosity dealer, 31 Castle st. east, Oxford st
Muller Samuel, furrier, &c. 35 Judd st. Brunswick square
Muller Stephen Lunn, surgeon, 1 Devonshire pl. Old Kent rd
Muller William, fur skin dyer, 19 Newcastle st. Whitechapel
Muller Wm. japan hat manuf. see Simpson & Muller
Mullett Fanny (Mrs.), corn dealer, 4 Low. Queen st. Rotherhith
Mullett Fredk. Augs. auctioneer & appr. 8 Blackfriars road
Mullett James, baker, 29 Colonnade, Brunswick square
Mullett Jas. *Edinburgh Castle* P.H. Rhodeswell rd. Limeho
Mullett John, teacher of penmanship, arithmetic, algebra, &c. 3 Allsop terrace, New road
Mullett Joseph, slopseller & grocer, 65 Wapping High st
Mullett Richard Chas. auctnr. & appr. 8 Blackfriars road
Mullett Thos. John, *Red Lion* P.H. 155 Old Gravel la. Wapping
Mullhall Peter, bootmaker, 78 Theobald's road
Mulliens William, auctioneer & appraiser, 57 Leadenhall st
Mullin Nicholas Frederick, printer, 2 Circus st. New road

Mullins, Bros. & Co. smelters, refiners, & assayers & chemical works, Bridge road, Battersea
Mullins Chas.& Geo. silversm. 12 Staverton row, Walwth. rd
Mullins John & Wm. *Red Lion* P.H. 112 Edgware rd. Padngtn
Mullins & Paddison, solrs. & notrs. 1 Gt. James st. Bedfrd. row
Mullins Charles, plate engraver, 46 Regent st
Mullins Chas. worsted & cotton manfr. 15 Charter house la
Mullins Edward, notary, 1 Gt. James st. Bedford row
Mullins Edward, plumber, 50 George st. Blackfriars road
Mullins George, surgeon, 16 Bartholomew pl. Kentish town
Mullins George, tobacconist, 33 Judd st. Brunswick square
Mullins Henry, hairdresser, 8 Old North st. Red Lion sq
Mullins James, fruiterer, 3 Tyler st. Regent st
Mullins James, tinplate & zinc worker, 13 Exmouth st. Clknwll
Mullins John James, bootmaker, 12 Broad court, Long acre
Mullins John William, leather seller, 36 Clerkenwell gn
Mullins Margt. (Mrs.), straw bonnet ma. 13 Green st. Bthnl. gn
Mullins Pat. dairymn. & chsmnger. 31 Bryanstone st. Prtmn. sq
Mullins Thos. grocer & cheesemngr. 33 Eagle st. Red Lion sq
Mullins Wm. umbrella ma. 5 Queen's Hd. ct. Gt. Windmill st
Mullis John, statuary & mason, 95½ Gt. Guildford st. Boro
Mulot Madame, dress, stay & corset ma. 3 Gt. Vine st. Reg. st.
Mulready William, R.A. artist, 1 Linden grove, Bayswater
Mulvey Ann (Miss), ladies' school, 20 Pelham cres. Fulham rd
Mulvey Timothy, tailor, 4 Queen st. Oxford st
Mumford Sl. & Peter, flour & corn fac. 11 Newcastle st. Strand
Mumford Charles, boot & shoe maker, 25 Earl st. Kensington
Mumford George, dairyman, 17 Down st. Piccadilly
Mumford James, coffee rooms, 32 Southwark bridge road
Mumford John, drysalter, 7 Little Bush lane, Cannon st
Mumford John, lace & sewed muslin manfr. 1 Milk st
Mumford John, tailor, 7 London road, Southwark
Mumford Thomas, lodging ho. 36 Halfmoon st. Piccadilly
Mumford Thomas, mattress ma. coach & horses yd. Drury la
Mumm Peter Arnold & Co. (of Rheims), frch. wine imp. 11 Mrk. la
Mumm Peter Arnold, imp. of german wines, 11 Mark la
Mummery George, boot & shoe ma. 67, Gainsford st. Horselydn
Muncaster & Warre, pawnbrokers, 14 Skinner st. Snowhill
Muncaster Robt. watch & case gilder, 9 Cross st. Leonard st
Munday Fredk. & Co. wine mers. 16 Hardwick pl. Coml. rd. ea
Munday John & Wm. pocketbk. & case mks. 4 Red Lion ct. Flt. st
Munday Charles, chemist & druggist, 9 King st. Snowhill
Munday Charles, *Star* P.H. 31 Aldersgate st
Munday Edward, lapidary, 29 Noble st. Goswell st
Munday George, auctioneer, &c. 9 St. Mildred's ct. Poultry
Munday George, plumber, 26 Adam st. west, Bryanstone sq
Munday George, silversmith, 22 Portman pl. Edgware rd
Munday James, builder, 26½ Abchurch lane, City
Munday John, carpenter & builder, 15 Clerkenwell green
Munday John Jackson, tailor, 10 Broadley ter. Blandford sq
Munday Richard, grocer & baker, Cobourg rd. Old Kent rd
Munday Thomas, bricklayer, 21 Back Church lane
Munday Thomas, butcher, 21 Gt. hall, Hungerford market
Munday Thomas, butcher, 47 Old st. road
Munday Thomas, hosiery agent, 26 Philpot la. London wall
Munday William, brass turner, 8 Bridgewater sq
Munday William, solicitor, 61 Carey st. Lincoln's inn
Munday William, tailor, Mare st. Hackney
Mundell John Joseph, proctor, see Fox, Mundell & Fox
Mundell Robert C. brewer, see Broadwood, Mundell & Co
Mundey George, tailor, 1½ Henry st. Gray's inn lane
Mundy Alfred, *Lamb & Lark* P.H. 5 Printing ho. la. Blkfrs
Mundy Edward, saddler, 12 Gloucester mews, Portman sq
Mundy Edward, surgeons' inst. ma. 74 Up. Ground st. Blkfs. rd
Mundy James, coffee rooms, 2 Acton pl. Bagnigge wells rd
Mundy James, umbrella maker, 22 Salisbury st. Lisson gr
Mundy Martha (Mrs.), tailor, 14 Barking ch. yd. Gt. Tower st
Mundy Wm. builder, 3 Philip st. Bck. Chch. la. St. Geo. east
Mundy Wm. carpenter, St. James's rd. Canal br. Old Kent rd
Mundy William, cheesemngr. 46 Up. North pl. Gray's inn rd
Mundy William, dairyman, 21 Henrietta st. Manchester sq
Mungo Airth, *George & Dragon* P.H. 4 St. George's pl. Cambwl
Munk William, physician, 2 Finsbury place south
Munn Aaron, shawl maker & cleaner, 83½ Gt. Portland st. & 5 Gastigney place, Bath st. City road
Munn Alexander, tailor, &c. 23 Chalton st. Somers town
Munn Benjamin, solicitor, 14 Poultry
Munn Edward, corn & coal merchant & dealer in hay & straw, 7 Conduit st. Westbourne terrace, 1 Bathurst mews, Sussex sq. & 13 Stanhope terrace, Hyde park
Munnings (Misses), academy, 31 Hamilton ter. St. John's wood
Munns Richard & Co. upholsterers, &c. 33 & 34 Oxford st
Munns Isaac, carpenter, 10 Glo'ster ter. New. rd. Whitechapel
Munns Joseph Richard, hairdresser, 10 Aldersgate st
Munns William, solicitor, 3 Fenchurch buildings
Munro James, optician, 4 High st. Lambeth
Munro John, portmanteau maker, 8 Stamford st. Blackfriars
Munro Robert P. fruiterer, 2 Old Quebec st. Portman sq
Munro Sarah (Miss), dressmaker, 5 Scarsdale ter. Ksngton
Munro Thomas, cabinet maker, 50 Howland st. Fitzroy sq
Munro William, bootmaker, 5 Temple st. Whitefriars
Munt & Brown, who. straw & leghorn hat manfrs. 40 Wood st
Munt Peter, scourer & dyer, 102 Fenchurch st
Munt Wm. grocer, 21 Bowling Green st. Kennington
Munting James, furniture brokr. 6 Little Turnstile, Holborn
Munting John, carman, 18 Little Moorfields
Munton James, grocer, 30 Robinson's row, Kingsland
Muntz's patent metal for ships' sheathing, 23 Fenchurch st
Murch Joseph & Co. ale & porter merchants, 9 Lime st
Murch Arthur, gardener & florist, 6 Alpha rd. Regent's pk
Murch Henry, fruiterer, 48 Exmouth st. Spafields
Murch Henry, wine & spirit merchant, 63 Canon st. City
Murch James, veterinary surgn. 20 North mews, Burton cresc
Murchie Wm. carpenter & undertakr. 4 & 5 Bird st. Oxford st.
Murchison Simon, surgeon, 21 Holles st. Cavendish square
Murcott Jonathan, coach iron founder & plater, 109 Long acre
Murcott Ann (Mrs.), dressmaker, 4 Litchfield st. Soho
Murcott Wm. H. surgeon, &c. 30 Henrietta st. Covnt. grdn
Murdoch, Shortridge, Lundie & Co. (of Madeira), 17 Mark lane
Murdoch James G. banker, see Bouverie, Norman & Murdoch
Murdoch Robert, cooper, 49 Brunswick st. Blackwall
Murdoch William, M.D. surgeon, 320 Rotherhithe st
Murdock James, patent office, 7 Staple inn
Murdock John, generalwarehouseman, Swan st. Gt. Dover rd
Murdock Wm. gasfitter, 3 Dorchester st. New North rd
Mure James & Co. distillers, three mills, Bromley, Middlesex
Murfey Robert, tobacconist, Little Chelsea, North side
Murgatroyd Adam, trunk ma. & und. 18 Stafford row, Pimlico
Muriel Chas. & Brooke, surgeons, 4 Wellington st. Loudon brdge
Murley Wm. & Chas. fancy waistcoating manufacturers & london quilting printers, 4 Bow church yard, Cheapside
Murley Sylvester, cheesemonger, 178 Lambeth walk
Murley Thos. ham & tongue dealer, 4 Queen's row, Pimlico
Murley Wm. butcher, 5 Shepherd's market, May fair
Murphy & Harris, drapers, &c. 7 & 8 Frederick pl. Hampstead rd
Murphy & Moore, who. confectioners, 116 & 117 Holborn hill
Murphy Robert & Co. merchants, 3 Tooley st. Borough
Murphy Anne (Mrs.), coal merchant, 8 Bouverie st. Fleet st
Murphy Daniel, meat salesman, 21½ New Newgate market
Murphy Dennis, grocer, &c. 1 Wapping wall, Shadwell
Murphy Edw. Wm. physician, 12 Henrietta st. Cavndsh. sq
Murphy Francis Stack, serjt.-at-law, 3 Serjeants' inn, Chancy. la
Murphy Geo. plumber & glazier, 16 Church st. Camberwell
Murphy Hugh, fruiterer, 25 South st. King's road, Chelsea
Murphy James, fruit salesman, Covent garden, fruit market
Murphy Jas. Godfrey, gen. ironmonger, 3 Middle row, Holb
Murphy Jas. pat. turpentine mnf. Stratford & Hall of Commerce
Murphy John, *Lord Exmouth* P.H. 8 Star st. Shadwell
Murphy John P. tailor, 8 Stepney rents, Hackney road
Murphy Lawrence, coach builder, 28 Lit. Queen st. Holborn
Murphy Michael, wood dealer, Garden row, New tn. Deptford
Murphy Miles, bootmaker, 24 White Hart st. Kennington
Murphy Patrick, tea dealer & grocer, 100 Drury lane
Murphy Thomas, bookseller, 10 Denmark terrace, Pentonville
Murphy Thomas, tailor, 23 William st. Regent's park
Murphy William, carpenter, 10 Broomfields, Deptford
Murphy Wm. map & chart slr. 2 Anchor & Hope alley, Wap
Murrall James, leather dresser, &c. Wild's rents, Bermondsy
Murray Adam & Sons, land survyrs. & agts. 35 Craven st. Strand
Murray John & Co. blindmakers to the Queen, 403 Strand
Murray & Newell, milliners, see Newell & Murray
Murray & Paterson, government contractors & hempen cloth sack, bag, &c. manufacturers, 46 Church st. Minories
Murrays, Rymer & Murray, solicitors, 7 Whitehall place
Murray Alexander Elder, printer, see Stewart & Murray
Murray Ann (Mrs.), wine cooper & carman, 4½ Commercial Mroad east, & London dock entrance, Up. East Smithfield
Murray Charles Knight, barrister, 5 Whitehall place
Murray David, stationr. & booksellr. 179 Sloane st. Knightsb
Murray Charles Knight, secretary to the ecclesiastical com-Mmissioners for England & Wales, 5 Whitehall place
Murray Geo. agent for Muir & Co.'s ale, Steel yd. Up. Thames st
Murray George, baker, 74 Whitehorse st. Stepney
Murray Geo. ironmonger & grindery dealer, 13 Leather lane
Murray Grace (Miss), milliner, &c. 35 Rathbone place
Murray Henry, artist, 72 Milton st. Dorset square
Murray Henry Stormont, barrister, 38 Lincoln's inn fields
Murray James, academy & registrar, 8 Suffolk pl. Hackney rd
Murray James, baker, 18 New st. square, Fetter lane
Murray James, bookbinder, 37 Gt. St. Andrew st. Seven dials
Murray James, builder, 36 Great Castle st. Regent st
Murray James, chairmaker, 4 Steward st. Spitalfields

Murray James, chronometer, watch & clock ma. 30 Cornhill
Murray James, *D. of Wellington* P.H. 22 John st. Limeho. flds
Murray James, linendraper, 14 High st. Bow, Middlesex
Murray James, pewterer, 11 Somerset pl. Hoxton new town
Murray James T. pianoforte tuner, 5 Low. James st. Golden sq
Murray John, barrister, 55 Lincoln's inn fields
Murray John, blindmaker, 17 Park side, Knightsbridge
Murray John, bookslr. & statnr. 12 Essex pl. Mare st. Hackny
Murray John, chronometer, watch & clock ma. 33 Wapping Hi. st
Murray John, publisher, 50 Albemarle st. Piccadilly
Murray John, solicitor, see White & Murray
Murray John, upholsterer, 28 Charles st. Middlesex hospital
Murray John, warehouseman, see Morley, Murray & Co
Murray John Jas. warehsmn. see Graham, Coombes & Murray
Murray John Thomas, baker, 12 Southampton ter. Pentnvl!
Murray Jonathan, bookseller, 101 Edgware rd. Marylebone
Murray Mark, bookseller, 2 Grange ter. Grange rd. Bermsy
Murray Mary (Mrs.), boarding house, 45 Gower st. Bdfrd. sq
Murray Mary (Mrs.), dressma. 26 Portman st. Portman sq
Murray Matthew, ostrich feather manufr. 110 London wall
Murray Patrick, webbing slipper ma. 47 Lant st. Bororgh
Murray Robert, locksmith, 7 James st. Haymarket
Murray Richd. Henry, barrister, Devereux court, Strand
Murray Robt. stationer & bookslr. 10 Marshall st. Golden sq
Murray Robert B. window blind mfr. 2 Oxford pl. Watrl. rd
Murray Robert Hamilton, baker, 16 London st. Fitzroy sq
Murray Robert Hepburn, barrister, 5 New sq. Lincoln's inn
Murray Thomas, ironmonger, 13 High st. St. Giles's
Murray Thomas, merchant, 12 Copthall ct. Throgmorton st
Murray Thos. F. engravr. & printr. 91 Charlotte st. Fitzroy sq
Murray William, barrister, 3 Garden court, Temple
Murray William, druggist, 2 Hand court, Bedford row
Murray William, *Market House* P.H. 8 Farringdon st
Murray William, painter, 11 East st. Walworth road
Murray William, refiners' verditer, aquafortis & chemical color manufacturer, 49 Compton st. Clerkenwell
Murray Wm. solicitor, 11 London st. Fenchurch st
Murray William, stationer & bookseller, 57 Oxford st
Murray William Powell, barrister, 59 Chancery lane
Murrell Wm. & Co. drapers & hosrs. 3 & 4 King's road east, Chel
Murrell Charles F. fruiterer, Covent garden fruit market
Murrell Charles W. chemist, 87 Grand Junction ter. Edgw. rd
Murrell Eliz. (Mrs.), fruiterer, 55 Gt. Windmill st. Haymkt
Murrell George, butcher, 4 Halfmoon pass. Leadenhall mkt
Murrell Henry, auctioneer, appraiser, &c. 41 Threadneedle st
Murrell John, cabinet maker, &c. 14 Gibson st. Waterloo rd
Murrell John, optician, 13 Albion place, St. John's lane
Murrell Owen John, fruiterer, 30 Finsbury market, Finsbury
Murrey Robt. smith, &c. 46 Whitcomb st. Pall mall east
Murrieta Cristobal de, merchant, 8 Old Jewry
Murrell Wm. H. lithogrphc. & copper plate printer, 29 Poultry
Murrough John Patrick, solicitor, 7 New inn, Strand
Murry John Money, gen. merchant, 65 Lower Thames st
Murton Chas. booksel. binder & stationer, 12 St. Martin's court
Murton Elizabeth (Mrs.), tobacconist, 62 Gt. Portland st
Murton Robert, dining rooms, 156 St. George st
Murtrie James Taylor, meat salesman, 8 Newgate market
Muruss James, *Black Horse* P.H. 62 York st. Westminster
Murzell Manuel, fruiterer, 10 Charles st. Westborne ter
Muschamp John, tinman, 9 Snow's fields, Bermondsey
Museum of the College of Surgeons, 40 Lincoln's inn fields
Museum of Economic Geology (Sir Henry T. De la Beche, director), 5 & 6 Craig's court, Charing cross
Museum House Free Dispensary & Infirmary (John Hastings, surgeon), 1 Blenheim st. Oxford st
Museum of Pathological Anatomy, 29 Bridgehouse place, Newington causeway
Musgrave Charles, law stationer, 63 Carey st. Lincoln's inn
Musgrave Thomas, sec. to *Merchants, Tradesmans, & Genl. Mutual Life Assurance Company*, 5 Chatham place
Musgrove Wm. & Co. painters, 88 Old Gravel lane, Wapping
Musgrove & Gadsden, auctnrs. & surv. &c. 18 Old Broad st. City
Musgrove Christopher Fred. baker, 4 Belgrave road, Pimlico
Musgrove Mary (Mrs.), pork butcher, 17 Salmon la. Limeho
Musgrove Samuel, fruiterer, New King st. Deptford
Musical Antiquarian Society (Edwd. Fras. Rimbault, LL.D., F.S.A., sec.), Grosvenor cot. 17 Park village east, Regent's pk
Musical Bee Office, 67 Paternoster row
Musical World Office, 60 Dean st. Soho
Muskett Henry, coal mercht. Savoy wharf, Savoy st. Strand
Muskett Mary (Mrs.), coffee rooms, 68 Wilsted st. Somers tn
Muspratt J. & Sons, chemists (J. K. Huntley, agt.), 4 John st. Minories
Muspratt John Petty, merchant & navy agt. 33 Abchurch la
Mussabini Joseph, merchant, 27 Finsbury circus
Mussard Mary (Mrs.), haberdasher, Southampton st. Cmbrwl
Mussell George, chemist & druggist, 7 Church st. Camberwell
Musselwhite Henry, dairyman, 27 Park pl. Kennington cross
Musselwhite Jesse, dairyman, 36 Cornwall road, Lambeth
Musselwhite William, egg mercht. 51 Lambeth lower marsh
Mussett Robt. & James, coal merchants, Creek rd. Deptford
Mussett Henry, confectioner, 12 Barking ch. yd. Gt. Tower st
Mussett Robt. agt. to Hand in Hand fireins. off. Creek rd. Dptfd
Musson & Tymms, saddlers, 1 Arabella row, Pimlico
Musson John, haberdasher, see Clarke & Musson
Must Thomas, hairdresser, 1 Bow churchyard
Must William, hairdresser, 64 Whitechapel High st
Mustart Alexander, shipchandler, 47 Lower Shadwell
Mustill William, potato dealer, 94 Rosemary lane
Muston Chas. watch case maker, 18 Red Lion st. Clerkenwll
Muston George, watchmaker, 18 Red Lion st. Clerkenwell
Muston Jas. feather mer. & who. upholder, 81 Hatton garden
Muston Richard, coffee rooms, 103 Upper East Smithfield
Mustoph George, tobacconist, 189 Shadwell High st.
Muter Robert, merchant, 112 Fore st. Cripplegate
Mutlow James, seal & cop. pl. engraver, 3 York st. Covnt. gdn
Mutrie Robert, agent for manufacturers of fancy silks, printed cottons, bandanocs, & de laines, sole agent for R. F. & J. Alexander, & Co. sewing cotton spinners, Glasgow; also sole agent for Robert M'Clelland & Co. patent linen thread manufacturers, Banbridge, Ireland, 93 Watling st
Mutual Cattle Insurance Co. (Henry Flower, sec.), 301 Strand
Mutual Insurance Benefit Institution (James Bishop, sec.), 51 Threadneedle st
Mutual Life Assurance Society (P. Hardy, actuary), 37 Old Jewry, see page 2032
Muzzell Lewis, coffee & dining rms. 5 Duke st. Stamford st
Myall Joseph, dealer in tobacco, snuff & cigars, 51 Watling st
Myatt Margaret Mary (Miss), milliner, 94 Albany st
Myatt Wm. biscuit baker, 147 Wapping High st
Myatt Wm. foreign china dealer, 22 Primrose st. Bishopsgt
Myatt Wm. solicitor, 35 Throgmorton st. & 7 North crescent, Bedford square
Myers Geo. Day & Co. engr. & printers, 4 Budge row, Cannon st
Myers Lawrence & Co. bristles, ivory, tortoiseshell, russia & whalebone merchts. & comb manufs. 88 Leadenhall st
Myers Lawrence & Co. whalebone cutters, 156 Houndsditch
Myers Abraham, fren. toy mer. see Joseph (A. & S.) Myers & Co
Myers Abrm. who. watch manuf. 79 Leman st. Goodman's fil
Myers Ann (Mrs.), rag mer. 2 White st. Cutler st. Houndsditch
Myers Benjamin, tailor & woollen draper, 72 Oxford st
Myers Benjamin, who. stay manufacturer, 72 Oxford st
Myers David, butcher, 116 Middlesex st. Whitechapel
Myers David, watchmaker, 20 Great Portland st
Myers George, builder, 9 Laurie terrace, St. George's fields
Myers George, butcher, 20 Middlesex st. Aldgate
Myers Henry, surgeon, 94 Milton st. Dorset square
Myers Isaac, butcher, 26 Middlesex st. Aldgate High st
Myers Isaac, watch manufacturer, 5 Ellison st. Aldgate
Myers John, general dealer, 86 St. George st
Myers John, plumber & founder, 273 Kent st. Borough
Myers John, tobacconist, 44 Little Britain
Myers John Frederick, patentee & manuf. of the æolophon & volti subito, 83 Charlotte st. Fitzroy sq
Myers Joseph, bootmaker, 41 Middlesex st. Aldgate High st
Myers Jsh. Cruse, slopslr. & sail maker, 3 Emmett st. Limeh. ho
Myers Laurence, whalebone cutter, 156 Houndsditch
Myers Levi, confectioner, 4 King st. Aldgate
Myers Mendlewitz, fancy repository, 43 London rd. Borough
Myers Michael, fishmonger in ordinary to her Majesty, 1 St. Peter's alley, Cornhill
Myers Michael, glasscutter, 9 Goodman's stile, Whitechapel
Myers Michael, laceman to her Majesty, 60 Brook st
Myers Morris, who. rag mer. 115 Wentworth st. Whitechapl
Myers Moses, jeweller & curiosity dlr. 5 Le'ster pl. Le'ster sq
Myers Moses, tailor & outfitter, 123 Cock hill, Ratcliff
Myers Moses H. prof. of languages, 15 Bury st. St. Mary Axe
Myers Moss, boarding ho. 62 Gt. Prescot st. Goodman's fi
Myers Myer, who. hat, &c. ma. & gen. dlr. 12 Camomile st. City
Myers Phœbe (Mrs.), furniture broker, 137 Tooley st
Myers Rachel (Mrs.), clothes wa. 9 Marylebone la. Oxford st
Myers Raphael, auctioneer, 40 Cannon st. City
Myers Raphael, auctnr. & valuer, 2 Cornbury pl. Old Kent rd
Myers Richard C. agent to John Duffus & Co. engineers & wholesale ironmongers, Aberdeen, & to Forbes & Co. sail makers, 307 Wapping
Myers Robt. Geo. newsv. & tobaccon. 193 van st. Minories
Myers Samuel, enameller, 11 Gloucester st. Curtain road
Myers Thomas, tailor, 32 Goldsmith pl. Hackney road
Myers Wm. printer, 14 Bedford place, & 44 Gloucester ter. Commercial road east

Myers Wm. woollendraper, 14 Gt. May's bldgs. St. Martin's la
Myhill Thomas, grocer, 1 Royal st. Carlisle st. Lambeth
Mylins Wm. academy, 7 Cheyne walk, Chelsea
Mylne James Wm. barrister, 10 Old sq. Lincoln's inn
Mylne Wm. C. civil engineer, New River head, Clerkenwell
Mynn Wm. & Co. hop factors & agents, 75 Borough High st
Myott Ralph, bricklayer, Battersea fields

NADEN Geo. newsvender, 6 Chigwell hill, Ratcliff highway
Naggs Richd. & Thos. bootmakers, 13 Brewer st. Somers town
Naghten Charles, merchant, see Bosanquet & Naghten
Nagle James, *Tower* P.H. 13 & 14 Tower st. 7 dials
Nail Jsph. Henry, auctioneer & ho. agt. 5 Hope ter. Nott. hill
Nail Saml. John, mer. ship & ins. bro. 10 St. Benet's pl. Gracech. st
Nainby Wm. lint manufr. 5 & 6 Bethnal green, north side
Nainton James, plumber, 21 Henry st. east. Avenue rd. Rgts. pk
Nairn Wm. sack, rick cloth & tarpauling manufacturer, linen & canvas factor, 15 Tower royal, Watling st
Nairne Chas. & Edward, stockbrokers, 3 Warnford ct. City
Nairne Charles, surgeon, 8 China terrace, Lambeth
Nairne John, brass & bell founder, 106 Curtain road
Nairne Robert, physician, 44 Charles st. Berkeley square
Naish Wm. & Co. boot & shoe manufact. 37 Moorgate st
Naish Alfred, lodging house, 105 Park st. Grosvenor square
Naish Elizabeth (Mrs.), *St. James' Hotel*, 76 Jermyn st. St. Jas
Naish George S. brushmaker, 10 St. John's la. Clerkenwell
Naish Wm. plumber & builder, 23 Warren st. Fitzroy sq
Nalder Fras. & Son, glove, crape, silk, &c. manfs. 41 Cheapsi
Nalder Francis, hide & tallow bro. see Dyster, Nalder & Roper
Nalder Jas. cloak & millinery wareho. 72 Newington causeway
Nalder John, grocer, 26 Brunswick st. St. John st. road
Nall John, cooper, Villa st. Walworth common
Nalson Emanuel, grocer, &c. 14 North crescent, Bedford sq
Nalson James, grocer, 68 Wheeler st. Spitalfields
Napier John & Francis, engineers, Mill wall, Poplar
Napier David, engineer, Vine st. & 51 York road, Lambeth
Napier Susan (Mrs.), ready made linen wa. 23 Cullum st. City
Napier Thomas, flour, coal & timbr. mer. see Harvey, Napier & Co
Napier Wm. shoe mercer & leather sell. see Sadd & Napier
Napper John, bookbinder, 15 Cross st. Hatton garden
Nappi Paul, engraver on cameo, 31 Newman st. Oxford st
Narbrow Edm. barrelled oyster warehouse & superior ginger beer mkr. established A.D. 1805; 14 Portugal st. Lin. inn flds
Nardin F. & Co. french shoe warehouse, 5 Duke st. Grosv. sq
Nardin Francis, coiffeur de Paris, 5 Duke st. Grosvenor sq
Nardin Pierre, hairdresser, 31 Grosvenor st. Grosvenor sq
Nares John, *Brewers' Arms* P.H. Morgan's la. Tooley st
Narey Maria (Miss), court dressma. see Mortimer & Narey
Nash Andrew John & Co. glass manufacturers, 75 Cornhill
Nash & Ely, woollen factors, 4 King st. Cheapside
Nash & Gurney, timber mer. Globe whf. Globe strs. Rotherh
Nash & Hicks, wharfingers, Pickle Herring, Low wf. Tooley st
Nash Jas. & Richd. barge & boatbuilders, 42 Up. Fore st. Lmbth
Nash, Selmes & Curteis, hop facs. Nag's hd. bdgs. 102 Boro' Hi. st
Nash Thomas & Son, plumbers, builders & decorators, house agts. & uphosterers, 1 Leigh st. & 29 Kenton st. Brunswk. sq
Nash Abraham, carpenter, &c. 18 Everett st. Brunswick sq
Nash Alfred, bookseller, 32 Seymour st. Euston sq
Nash Alfred, wine merchant, 150 Leadenhall st
Nash Andrew, tailor, 13 Coleman st. City
Nash Benj. leathr. cut. & tobacconist, 94 Brick la. Spitalfields
Nash Caroline (Miss), toy dlr. 5 Southampton st. Camberwl
Nash Charles, chemist, 48 Great Marylebone st
Nash Charles, fishmonger, 26 Martin's lane, City
Nash Charles, manchester warehouse, see Delannoy & Nash
Nash Daniel, seedsman, see Minier, Adams & Nash
Nash David, lodging house, 41 Manchester st. Manchester sq
Nash Davyd William, barrister, 3 Essex ct. Temple
Nash Edward, wholesale grocer, see Sewell & Nash
Nash Edward, woollen factor, see Onyon, Holt & Nash
Nash Edwin, architect & surveyor, 53 Moorgate st. Bank
Nash Eliezer, pencil maker, &c. see Wise & Nash
Nash Francis James, who. tea dealer, see Williamson & Nash
Nash Fredk. boot & shoe maker, 9 Prospect pl. Kingsland rd
Nash Geo. Henry, bookseller & stationer, 5 Lyall pl. Eaton sq
Nash Henry, chemist, 31 Sherborne st. Blandford square
Nash Henry, meat salesman, 7 Warwick lane, Newgate st
Nash Hen. Howard, coachmkr. 4 Finsbury pl. nrth. Finsbury sq
Nash Jacob, *Jack of Newbury* P.H. 25 Chiswell st
Nash James, chairmaker, 24 East st. Walworth road
Nash James, *King's Head* P.H. 19 Winchester st. Borough
Nash James, pawnbroker, 27 King st. Borough
Nash James, tobacconist, 11 Stanhope terrace, Hyde park
Nash John, bookbinder, 62 Long lane Bermondsey
Nash John, chandler's shop, 6 Canal place, Old Kent road
Nash John, house painter, 10 Pierrepoint row, Islington grn
Nash John, *King's Head* P.H. 95 Tooley st
Nash John, news agent, 12 Oxford market
Nash John, pawnbroker, 27 Gt. Suffolk st. Borough
Nash John, solicitor, 14 South square, Gray's inn
Nash Johnson Edmd. accountant, 11 New Ormond st. Queen sq
Nash Jonathan, beer retailer, 46 Fore st. Limehouse
Nash Joseph, cheesemonger, 1 Little Ormond st. Queen sq
Nash Joseph, coal merchant, 1 Queen st. Ratcliff cross
Nash Maria (Mrs.), fruiterer, 36 George st. Portman sq
Nash Mary Ann (Mrs.), *Red Lion* P.H. 16 King Edward st
Nash Matthew, british plate manufacturer, 282 Strand
Nash Nathaniel, wheelwright, 13 Upper Kennington lane
Nash Phœbe (Mrs.), bookseller, 16 Parker's row, Dock head
Nash Richard, tailor, 42 Frith st. Soho
Nash Robert, fringe & braid manuf. 47 Wilmington square
Nash Robert, linendraper, 23 Aldgate High st
Nash Samuel, grocer, 13 Limehouse hole
Nash Samuel, *Royal Standard* P.H. 9 Sale st. Paddington
Nash Saml. Alfd. ornmtl. wd. carver, 77 Hercules bldgs. Lmbth
Nash Swan Wedd, ironmonger & smith, see Wright & Nash
Nash Thomas, beer retlr. 6 Jerusalem passage, St. John's sq
Nash Thomas, brushmaker, 1 Devonshr. bldgs. Gt. Dover rd
Nash Thomas, carpenter, 36 Kirby st. Hatton garden
Nash Thomas, grocer, 3 Bedford place, Lower rd. Rotherhithe
Nash Thomas, plumber, 33 Wilsted st. Somers town
Nash Thomas, shoemaker, 14 Cheshire st. Bethnal green
Nash Wm. butcher, 12 Collier st. Pentonville
Nash Wm. carpenter, Bridge road, Battersea
Nash Wm. chairmaker, 45 Gibson st. Waterloo road
Nash Wm. *Cock* P.H. 30 Brook st. New road
Nash Wm. dining rooms, 12 King's pl. Commerl. road east
Nash Wm. greengrocer, 11 Broadley terrace, Blandford sq
Nash Wm. hairdresser, 22 Gt. College st. Westminster
Nash Wm. manchester & woollen warehouse, 41 Noble st. Cheapside, & 18 Gresham st.
Nash Wm. oilman, 44 Exeter st. Lisson grove
Nash Wm. oil & colorman, 77 Earl st. east, Lisson grove
Nash Wm. oil & colorman, 218 Rotherhithe
Nash Wm. painter, 33 Russell st. Lower Rotherhithe
Nash Wm. plumber & glazier, 58 Cannon st. St. George's east
Nash Wm. tobacco mnfr. 118 Up. Whitecross st. St. Luke's
Nash Wm. watch motion maker, 8 Queen st. Clerkenwell
Nash Wm. wheelwright, 54 Edward st. Regent's park
Nash Wm. wine & spirit merchant, see Bull & Nash
Nash Wm. wholesale grocer, Arthur st. west, London bridge
Nasmyth Alex. surgeon dentist, 13A, George st. Hanover sq
Nasmyth George, consulting engineer, arbitrator, valuer & agent for machinery, 9 Barge yard chambers, Bucklersbury
Nason William, chemist & druggist, 128 Fleet st
Natali David, imp. & deal. in for. beads, &c. 10 Lit. St. Mary Axe
Nathan Lewis & Henry, masquerade & fancy costume warehouse, 24 Tichborne st. Haymarket
Nathan Baron, professor of dancing, 10 Kennington cross
Nathan David, furniture dealer, 41 York terrace, Borough rd
Nathan Edward, pawnbroker, 86 Poplar High st
Nathan Edward, slop clothes mak. 1 Heneage st. Whitechpl
Nathan Hannah (Mrs.), fur. brokr. 1 St. George's ter. Boro' rd
Nathan Henry, butcher & salesman, 77 London rd. Southwark
Nathan Hen. lin. dr. & job wareh. 3 & 15 Gt. Garden st. Whitechp
Nathan Henry, merchant, 15 Camomile st. Bishopsgate
Nathan Isaac John, masquerade court & fancy dress maker, 18 Castle st. Leicester sq
Nathan Israel, general salesman, 98 Old st. road
Nathan James, furniture broker, 24 London rd. Southwark
Nathan John, butcher, 45 Middlesex st. Aldgate High st
Nathan Joseph, commission agent, 16 Artillery pl. Finsbury
Nathan Joseph, fancy box maker, 55 Church st. Minories
Nathan Laurence Isaac, sheriff's officer, 103 Chancery lane
Nathan Levy Nathan, carcase butcher, 53 Aldgate High st
Nathan Louis, antique furniture dealer, &c. 35 Wardour st
Nathan Michael, meat salesman, 17 Newgate market
Nathan Moses, slopseller, 192 St. George st
Nathan Nathaniel, carcase butcher, 68 Aldgate High st
Nathan Phineas, watchma. & jew. 44 Caroline mews, Bdfd. sq
Nathan Samuel, butcher, 10 King David lane, Shadwell
Nathan Samuel Walter, custom house & shipping agent, & cane merchant, 2 Muscovy court, Tower hill
Nathan Walter, coal & quill mercht. 2 Muscovy ct. Tower hill
Nathan Wm. pawnbroker, 1 & 2 Three Colt st. Limehouse
Nation Rd. attorney, 23 Somerset st. Portman square, & 4A, Orchard st
Nation Samuel, cabinet maker, 87 Old Gravel la. Wapping
Nation Thomas Wm. boot & shoe maker, 215 Poplar High st
National Animal's Friend Society (Henry May, sec.), 52 Mark lane
Natnl. Assn. for Pol. & Socl. Improvemt. 242A, High Holborn

National Anti Corn Law League (George Wilson, esq. chairman), 67 Fleet st
National Anti Corn Law League Registration of Voters Offices, 2 East Temple chambers, Whitefriars st
National Assurance & Investment Association (Wm. Clark, general actuary), 4 Lancaster place, Strand
National Bank of Ireland (N. S. King, sec.), 13 Old Broad st. City; see page 2004
National Bank of Scotland, see page 2005
National Baths (Wm. Sowter, proprietor), 7½ Mount st. Lambth
National Benevolent Institution (Frederick Latreille, secretary), 56 Southampton row, Russell square
National Brazilian Mining Association, Mocaubas & Cocäes, 26 Throgmorton st
National Debt Office, 19 Old Jewry; hrs. of business, 10 to 3
National Gallery (Lieut. Col. George Saunders Thwaites, secretary), Trafalgar square, Pall mall east
National Guardian Almshouses, Raven row, Mile end road; office, 46 Bedford row, Bloomsbury
National Guardian Institution for Families & Servants (Thomas Butt, secretary), 46 Bedford row
National Life Assurance Society (C. B. Smith, actuary), 2 King William st. City; see page 2035
National Life Insurance Company of Scotland (J. & R Cracken, agents), 7 Old Jewry
National Linen Company (Geo. Pelly Tory, manager), 105 Fleet st. & 98 Farringdon st
National Loan Fund Life Assurance & Deferred Annuity Society (F. F. Camroux, sec.), 26 Cornhill; see page 2036
Nat. Mercantile Life Ass. So. (Jenkin Jones, sec.), Arthur st. w
National Patent Salt Company (Jas. P. Anstice, sec.), 2 Agar st. West Strand
National Provl. Bank of England, 112 Bishopsgate within
National Provident Institution (Joseph Marsh, secretary), 48 Gracechurch st.; see page 2037
National Reversionary Investment Company (Wm. Sim, secretary), 63 Old Broad st. City; see page 2038
National Society for promoting the education of the poor in the principles of the Established Church throughout England & Wales, Sanctuary, Westminster (Ven. Archdeacon Sinclair, treasurer; Rev. Wm. Jas. Kennedy, secretary). For list of schools, see "Schools," in Trades' Directory
National Society's Training Institution, Battersea
National Temperance Society (Theodore Compton, sec.), 39 Moorgate st
National Truss Society (Rd. Harley, hon. sec.), 74 King William st. City
National Vaccine Institution (Clement Hue, physician), 8 Russell place, Fitzroy square
Nartorff Julius, surgeon, 132 Shadwell High st
Natowski Louis & Co. who. stationers, 16 Camomile st. Bishopsgt
Natt Charles, hair cutter & perfumer, 120 York rd. Lambeth
Nattali Michael A. bookseller, 23 Bedford st. Strand
Naturalization of Aliens Off. 3 Winchester bldgs. City
Natusch Frederic & Co. ins. broks. & agts. 13 St. Swithin's la
Natusch Frederic B. Bernard, insurance broker & agent for the assurance companies of Trieste, Havana, &c. 13 St. Swithin's lane, & Lloyd's
Naughton Richard, dairyman, 33 New Compton st. Soho
Nautical Almanac Office, 3 Verulam buildings, Gray's inn
Nautilus Life Preserver Office (Frederick Coventry, resident agent), 12 Wellington st. Strand
Naval & Military Bible Society, 32 Sackville st. Piccadilly
Naval & Military Gazette newspaper, 19 Catherine st. Strand
Navin James, merchant, 4 Langbourn chambers
Navone Dominick, com. merchant, 15 New ea. india chmbs
Nay John, fancy trimming maker, 25 Worship st. Finsbury
Naylor Geo. & Hen. varnish ma. 40A, Whittlebury st. Euston sq
Naylor Mary & Son, varnish makers, 56 & 57 James st. Oxfd. st
Naylor Samuel & Thomas, solicitors, 4 Great Newport st
Naylor Thos. & Sam. attorneys, 4 Gt. Newport st. Long acre
Naylor Elisha, solicitor, 13 Mornington place, Hampstead rd
Naylor Elizabeth (Mrs.), blacking maker, 91 Shadwell High st
Naylor Geo. builder & bldg. matl. dlr. 7 Rochester rw. Westm
Naylor George, engine turner, 9 King st. Clerkenwell
Naylor George Day, linendraper, 7 Hawley pl. Kentish tn
Naylor Henry, elastic bootmaker, 22 Gt. Quebec st. New rd
Naylor James, coal mer. Cherry garden stairs, Bmndsy. wall
Naylor John, farrier, 47 Whitechapel High st
Naylor John, linendraper, 215 Tottenham court road
Naylor John, linendraper, 114 Whitechapel road
Naylor Richard, furn. ironmonger, 16 Red Lion st. Holborn
Naylor Samuel, jun. barrister, 10 New square, Lincoln's inn
Naylor Thomas, linendraper, 22 High st. Marylebone
Naylor Wm. glass & china manfr. 7 Princes st. Cavendish sq
Naylor Wm. locksmith & bellhanger, 31 Broad st. Lambeth
Naylor William B. solicitor, see Venning, Naylor & Robins
Nayman Robert & James, trimming sellers, 38 Munster st
Neairse William, grocer, 41 Edmund st. King's cross
Neal John & Son, coachironmongers & platers, 17 Gt. Queen st
Neal & Marr, coal merchants, old barge ho. whf. Up. Ground st
Neal Alice (Mrs.), shipsmith, 35 Rotherhithe st
Neal Edw. wine merchant, 12A, George st. Hanover sq
Neal Elizbth. (Mrs.), bootma. 40 Up. Berkeley st. Portman sq
Neal Francis, pen maker, 71 Long acre
Neal Geo. cowkeeper, 12 Brewer st. Somers town
Neal George, livery stables, 39 Three Cups yd. Bedford row
Neal George, printer, 7 Fleet lane, Farringdon st
Neal George, tailor, 3 King's Head row, Old Brompton
Neal John, butcher, 9 Canterbury place, Old Kent road
Neal John, gold beater, 87 White Lion st. Pentonville
Neal John, wine & botanic cordial ma. 1 Virginia pl. Dov. rd
Neal Matthew, baker, 7 Fan st. Goswell st
Neal Richard, cheesemonger, 5 Pont st. Belgrave sq
Neal Samuel, solicitor, 5 Austinfriars
Neal Thomas, steel mill mak. 63 St. John st. Clerkenwell
Neal W. *Brown Bear* P.H. 191 Up. Thames st
Neal Wm. silversmith & mounter, 41 Clerkenwell close
Neal Wm. shive turner, 55 Castle st. Borough
Neale John & Edward, oil & colourmen, & ship chandlers, 108 Minories, & 2 Wellington pl. west india docks
Neale Burton, plumber, 40 Baldwin's gardens, Leather la
Neale Edward Vansittart, barrister, 4 New sq. Lincoln's inn
Neale Henry, *Newington Arms* P.H. 18 King st. East st. Walworth
Neale Henry, tobacconist, 2 Rockingham pl. New Kent rd
Neale Jas. cooper, 12 Saville pl. Mile end road
Neale Jas. upholsterer, 3 Knightsbridge ter. Knightsbridge
Neale John, publisher, 112 Fleet st
Neale Jonathan, upholstr. & cab. ma. 45 Gt. Titchfield st
Neale Maria (Mrs.), furrier, 3 Goodwin's ct. St. Martin's la.
Neale Michael, fishmonger, 39 Kent st. Borough
Neale Michael, watch & water gilder, 54 Gt. Sutton st. Clrknwl
Neale Thomas baker, 149 Lambeth walk
Neale Thos. *Three Crowns* P.H. Royal Hospital rw. Chelsea
Neale Wm. Johnson, barrister, 1 Church yd. ct. Temple
Neale Wm. Johnson, barrister, 5 King's Bench walk, Temple
Neale William Michael, surgeon, 8 Sloane square
Neales Geo. furn. undrtak. 39 Baldwin's gardens Leather la
Neall Wm. whip maker, 3 South pl. Up. Kennington la
Nealor Wm. solicitor, see Milton & Nealor
Neat John, *King's Head* P.H. 24 High road, Knightsbridge
Neate Alfred, furniture broker, 85 Waterloo road
Neate Charles, prof. of music, 12 Manchester st. Manchr. sq
Neate Charles Edward, coal & corn merchant & house agt. 20 Notting hill terrace, & Creek wharf, Hammersmith
Neate George, baker, 1 Arthur st. King's road, Chelsea
Neate John Thos. pawnbroker, 40 Duke st. Manchester sq
Neate Richard, beer retailer, Villa st. Walworth common
Neate Rowland, solicitor, 57 Lincoln's inn fields
Neats William, *Grapes* P.H. 109 Drury lane
Neave Richard & Thomas, merchants, 51 Old Broad st. City
Neaves John, plumber, painter, &c. 25 Coles ter. Islington
Neaves William, grocer, 7 Ann's place, Hoxton old town
Neck Robert, attorney, 13 Howard st. Strand
Nedby & Lound, auctioneers & house agents, 15 Southampton buildings, Chancery lane
Needes John Edw. gen. salesman, 97 Edgware rd. Maryleb
Needes Leonard Geo. pawnbroker, 10 Up. Penton st. Pentnvl
Needes Thomas, baker, 12 Regent st. Horseferry road
Needes William, hairdresser, 11 Circus st. New road
Needes Wm. hairdresser, 8 Salisbury st. Lisson grove
Needham William & Co. patent self priming gun & rifle manufacturers, 26 Piccadilly
Needham Alex. boat builder, Paul's whf. 22 Up. Thames st
Needham Ann (Mrs.), wine & spirit mer. 11 Juddpl. east, New rd
Needham Geo. *Hare* P.H. 15 Heath pl. Cambridge heath
Needham Geo. *King's Head* P.H. King's pl. Commrl. rd. ea
Needham Joseph, cattle salesman, 41 West Smithfield
Needham Jsph. *Saracen's Head hotel*, 49 Skinner st. Snowhl
Needham Joseph, special pleader, 11 Paper bldgs. Temple
Needham Joshua, cheesemonger, 191 Shoreditch
Needham Mary (Mrs.), beer retilr. 3 Glo'ster pl. King's rd. Chel
Needham Ralph, linendra. & silk mercer, 105 & 106 Shoreditch
Needham Robert, printer, 9 Ave Maria lane, Ludgate st
Needham Samuel Felix, paper hanging wa. 18 Queen st. City
Needham Samuel Henry, jet ornament ma. 13 Theobald's rd
Needham Thomas, cattle salesman, 60 West Smithfield
Needham William Enne, tailor, 8 King st. Westminster
Needham Wm. Richard, *King's Head* P.H. 7 Brook st. Ratcliff
Needle John, ale, stout & bottle merchant, 3 Crutched friars

NeedleRichard, *WhiteHart*P.H.Hooper's sq.Goodman's flds
Needle Thomas, *Bull'sHead* P.H.5Wellington st.Goswell st
Needle William, carman, 35 Dowgate hill
Neele Margaret (Mrs.), cheesemonger, 36 Broad st. Ratcliff
Neely Wm. bookseller & stationer, 33 St.Swithin's la. City
Neesham Dounton, coffee rooms, 79 Charlotte ter. New cut
Neesham John, cheesemonger, 178 Drury lane
NeesomChas.Hodgson,circultng.library,90Brick la.Sptalflds
Neeves Wm. math. instrument maker, 67 High st. St.Giles's
Negreponte Jas. Constantine, mercht. 27 Finsbury circus
Negretti Henry, glass instrument maker, 19 Leather lane
Negus George Davy, baker, 24 Lamb st. Spitalfields
Negus John,baker,158Bishopsgate without & 34Halfmoon st
Negus Joseph, baker, 4 Little Pulteney st. Golden sq
Negus Thomas, baker, 57 Whitecross st. Cripplegate
Negus Thomas, tailor, 5 Wilson st. Finsbury
Negus William, *Golden Lion* P.H. 35 Fore st. Cripplegate
Neighbour George & Son, oil & italian wa. 127 HighHolborn
Neighbour Thos.&Son,wine mer.&coopers,34King st.Snowhl
Neighbour Edward, coffee rooms, 49 Exmouth st. Clerknwl
Neighbour Edward, tobacconist, 16 Brill row, Somers town
Neill & Waugh,who.sco.oatmeal,&c.dl.20Surrey st.&Corn ex
Neill Thomas, chandler's shop, 36 Brown's lane, Spitalfields
Neill Thomas, tailor, 19 Old Burlington st
Neilson & Mitchell, engineers, millwrights & founders, 15 Wharf road, City road
Neilson Claud, merchant, see Fraser, Neilson & Co
Neilson Ralph, hair cutter & wig ma. 14 Finch la. Cornhill
Neilson Wm. pianoforte maker, 9 Grafton st. Fitzroy square
Neive Wm. baker, 148 St. George st
Nelham & Lambert, custom house agents, baggage warehouse, & London bridge steam packet wharf
Nell Charles, tailor, 3 Sackville st. Piccadilly
NellisRt.Edwd.*Goldn.Horse*P.H.26Theobld's.rd.Rd.Lion sq
Nelmes Mary (Mrs.), staymaker, 55 Glo'ster st. Queen sq
Nelmes Richard, engraver, 19 Whiskin st. Clerkenwell
Nelmes Robert, watchma. 55 Glo'ster st. Queen sq.Blomsby
Nelms Matthew, hearth rug ma.10Back hill, Hatton garden
Nelms Sarah (Mrs.), dairy, 1 George yard, Aldgate
Nelson & Adam,west india mer.14Savage gardens,Tower hill
Nelson & Akerman, linendrapers, 4 Bennett st. Blackfriars rd
Nelson George & Co. patent & general gelatine & isinglass wareho.14 Bucklersbury ; works, Emscote mills, Warwick
Nelson Park & Wm. Benford, solicitors, 11 Essex st. Strand
Nelson S.& E. (Misses),ladies'schl.28Edwards tr.Caledon.rd
Nelson Ann (Mrs.), *Bull Inn*, 25 Aldgate High st
Nelson Chas. Covertry, genl. agent, 11 Langbourn chambers
Nelson Charles Rich, cooper, 23 Church row, Limehouse
Nelson Eleanor (Miss), tobacconist, 20 Upper Marylebone st
Nelson George, dairy, 13 Adam & Eve court, Oxford st
Nelson George, solicitor, 10 New inn, Wych st. Strand
Nelson Henry, carver & gilder, High st. Deptford
Nelson Henry, math. instrum. mak. 2 Glo'ster st. Queen sq
Nelson Horatio, gold chain ma. 18 Rosoman st. Clerkenwell
Nelson John, cheesemonger, 11 Flagon row, Deptford
Nelson John, cheesemonger, 4 New King st. Deptford
Nelson John,coach proprietor, BelleSauvage yd.Ludgate hill
Nelson John, livery stables, 1 Star yard, Carey st
Nelson John, proctor, 17Gt.Knightrider st.Doctors'commons
Nelson John, shopkeeper, 13 High road, Knightsbridge
Nelson John, *Tynemouth Castle* P.H. 192 Wapping
Nelson John, watch & clockmaker, 15 Hayfield pl.Mile end
Nelson Rd. plane & tool ma. 122 Edgware road, Paddington
Nelson Richard Albany, barrister, 25 Old sq. Lincoln's inn
Nelson Robert, *Portland hotel*, 95 Great Portland st
Nelson Sarah (Mrs.), china & glass dlr. 165 Bermondsey st
Nelson Sidney, music seller & publisher, 28 New Bond st
Nelson Thomas, bookseller & publisher, 8 Paternoster row
Nelson Thomas, plane maker, 14 Chapel st. Euston square
Nelson Thomas A. physician, 41 George st. Portman square
Nelson Thomas Marsh, architect, 3 Charles st.St.James's sq
Nelson Thomas Wright, solicitor, 2 Gresham pl. Lombard st
Nelson Wm. cheesemonger, Gibraltar row, Low.rd.Deptford
Nelson Wm. *Neighbour's tavern*, 56 Cannon st. City
Nelson Wm. *Nelson's Head* P.H. Nelson st. Hackney road
Nelson Wm. Bengo, academy, 19 Haberdashers' st. Hoxton
Nelson William Henry, gold beater, 59 Gt. Dover rd. Boro'
Neptune Marine Insurance Co. (Michael Wills, sec.) Freeman's pl.RoyalExchange; for list of directors,&c.see p.2038
Neremburger Paulin (Madame), milliner, 3 Hanway st
Nesbett Crosby Thomas, barrister, 1 Elm court, Temple
Nesbett Samuel, watch gilder, 25 New st. Bishopsgate
Nesbit Anthony & Sons, academy, 38 Lower Kennington la
Nesbit John Collis, pro. of chemistry, 38 Lr. Kennington la
NesbittAlex.&Robt.&Alex.hide&skin broks.149Up.Thamesst
Nesbitt John Alex. & Thos. merchts.1 Dunster ct. Mincing la
Nesbitt James, tailor, 19 Scarsdale terrace, Kensington
Nesbitt William, fancy cabinet maker, 73 Old st. road
Nesham Thomas, builder, see Locke & Nesham
Neslin Robert, pianoforte ma. 28 Everett st. Brunswick sq
Ness Henry, sizemaker, Swan mead, Bermondsey
Ness James, attorney, 4 Dyer's buildings, Holborn
Nestle Andrease & Co. merchants, 37 Crutched friars
Netherclift Joseph, lithographer, 23 King William st.Strand
Netherclift Mary (Mrs.), straw hat ma. 29 Exeter st.Sloane st
Nethercott Fanny (Mrs.), wine cooper, 89 Union st. Boro'
NetherlandsSteamCo(NTempaley,agt),50A,Kg.Wm.st.City
Nethersole Henry, solicitor, 3 New inn, Strand
Nettlefield Richard, cheesemonger, 67 Shoreditch
Nettlefold John S. & Son,ironmongers, &c.54 High Holborn
Nettlefold William, attorney,3Vine st.Smith sq.Westminster
Nettleship Edmond,chemist,24Queen st.&13Curzon st.Mayfr
Nettleship Richard Hutchinson, solicitor, 15 Clifford's inn
Nettleship Thomas, solicitor, see Palmer & Nettleship
Nettleship Wm. fruiterer, 16 Duke st. Manchester sq
Nettleton Joshua, furnishing ironmonger, & patent stove manufacturer to the honorable board of ordnance, 4 Sloane square, Chelsea
Nettleton Sarah (Mrs.), ladies' schl. 9 West ter.Up.Grange rd
Nettleton Thomas, brazier, 75 Farringdon st
Neuens Peter, clock & watch ma.& foreign agent, 32 Bread st
Neumann Lawrence de, merchant, 136 Fenchurch st
Neundorff Frederick, furrier, 18 Aylesbury st. Clerkenwell
Neuth Joseph, *Northumberland Head* P.H.8 Fort st.Sptlfl
Neve William, proctor, 10 Godliman st. Doctors' commons
Nevell & Scott, grocers, 5 Eccleston st. Chester sq. Pimlico
Nevell Nathaniel, bootmaker, 136 St. John st. Smithfield
Nevett Joseph, bookbinder, 1 Johnson's court, Fleet st
Nevill Alfred & Co. wholesale stock & shirt manufacturers 121 Wood st. Cheapside
Nevill (J. B. & W.) & Co. wholesale hosiers, haberdashers, flannel factors, glovers, & shirt ma.11Gresham st.Wood st
Nevill Alfred H.corn chandlr. 17 Chichester pl.Gray's inn rd
Nevill Frederick, glove & hose agent, 3 Falcon square
Nevill Henry, Wm. baker, 17 Sidmouth st. Gray's inn road
Nevill John, hairdresser, 39 Strutton ground, Westminster
Nevill Joseph, beer retailer, Nine elms, Vauxhall
Nevill Thomas, barrister, 8 Duke st. St. James's
Neville & Waistell, french goods imp. 69 Aldermanbury
Neville Benjn. printer & bookseller, see Leggett & Neville
Neville Chas. carpenter,1Carlton cotgs.Brunswick st.Dovr.rd
Neville Henry Stephen,colonial broker, see Evans & Neville
Neville John, tailor, 7 Francis st. Tottenham court road
Neville Samuel, cabinetmaker, 5 Bermondsey New road
Neville Thos. livery stables, 45 Up. North pl. Gray's inn road
Nevin Archibald, *Lowndes Arms* P.H. 3 Lyall pl. Eaton sq
Nevin Barnaby, carpenter & builder, Inwood pl.Kentish twn
Nevins Ann (Mrs.), ladies' school, 45 Canterbury st. York rd
Nevins Robert, merchant, 50 Mark lane
Nevins Robert, painter, see Edwards & Nevins
Nevinson Charles Dalston, physician, 39 Montagu square
Nevinson Edward, barrister, 24 Old square, Lincoln's inn
Nevinson George Henry, solicitor, 2 Elm court, Temple
New Henry John&Co. manufg.chemists, tartaric acid, citric, & oxalic acid, 25 Fieldgate st. & 7 New st. Whitechapel
New Asylum for Infant Orphans, office 32 Poultry (Wm. H. Strudwicke, sec.), Stamford hill
New British Iron Co. (Robt. Smith, sec.), 3 New Broad st
New Brunswick & Nova Scotia Land Co. 5 Copthall court
New Bunhill fields Cemetery, Church st. Islington
New City chambers, 121 Bishopsgate within
New Commercial Steam Co.(JohnBleaden,sec.),17 Fish st.hl
New East India chambers, 23 Leadenhall st
New England coffeehouse, 59 & 60 Threadneedle st
New England Company (John Fuller,treas.),9Gt.St.Helen's
*New FarmersJournal newsp.Off.*7 Wellngtn. st. nth.Strand
New Granada Mining Co. (L. R. Jones, sec.), 13 Austinfrs
New Inn, 20 Wych st. Strand
New London CornExchge.Co.(Wm.W.Wren,clk.), Mark la
New London Genuine Tea Company (Charles Hen. Biaggini, sec.), 25 Coleman st. City
New Model Prison, Caledonian road, Pentonville
New Monthly Belle Assemblée, 24 Norfolk st. Strand
New MonthlyMagazine Office, 13 Gt. Marlborough st
New River Waterworks Office(Fred.Inglis,sec.),Nw.rvr.hd
New Road Omnibus Association, 8 Portman pl.Edgware rd
New Sporting Magazine Office, 24 Norfolk st. Strand
New York Line of Packets, 3 George yard, Lombard st
New Zealand Company (Thos. Cudbert Harington, sec.), 9 Broad st. buildings
New Zealand Journal Office, 1 GreenArbour ct.Old Bailey
New Zealand Packet Office (G. B. Earp), 8 Broad st. bldgs

New Zealand Soc.(J.Watson, chrm.),10Henriettast.Cov.gar
New Charles, china warehouse, 6 Berwick st. Soho
New Elizabeth (Mrs.), grocer, 13 Princes st. Drury lane
New George, grocer, 1 Marlborough road, Chelsea
New Geo. Richd.architect&surv.6Dorchester pl.Blandfrd. sq
New James Randell, dyer & scourer, 9 Gt.Bath st.Clerkenwl
New Joseph, *Red Bull* P.H. 20 St. Ann's ct. Dean st. Soho
New Thomas, surgeon, 4 York pl. Mile end road
NewarkJohn,ladies'shoema.1Queen'sHead rw.Nwngtn.butts
Newbegin Edward, butcher, 1 Holmes bldgs. Lit. Bell alley
Newbegin John, butcher, 227 Bethnal green road
Newberry Charles, builder, 56 Gt. Coram st. Brunswick sq
Newberry Chas. warm&cold baths,56 Gt.Coram st.Bruns.sq
Newberry Robert, tailor & stationer, 20 Mile end road
Newbery Francis & Sons, merchants, 45 St.Paul's church yd
Newbery Jas.&Rd.L.fancy statnrs.2& 3 Hemlock ct.Carey st
Newbery & Terry, newsvenders & printers, 5 Hatton garden
Newbery Chas. vellum binder & mach.ruler, 74 Basinghall st
Newbery Charles, wine merchant, see Raikes & Newbery
Newbery Geo. John, patentee for perforated window blinds, & gen. waterproof manufactory, 3 Church st. Deptford
Newbery John, turner, 33 Crown st. Soho
Newbery JohnRouse,tablecover ma.28Percy st.Tottenh.ct.rd
Newbery Robert, stationer, &c. 20Barnes pl. Mile end road
Newbery Sarah Elizh. (Mrs.), furniture, fringe & trimming manufr. 19 Percy st. Tottenham court road
Newbery Thos. C. galloons, doubles, &c. manuf. 38 Wood st
Newbery Wm. bookseller & publisher, 6 King st. Holborn
Newbery W. tailor, 41 Queen st. Bryanstone square
Newbery Wm. Henry, goldsmith, 49 Greek st. Soho
Newbery Wm. Musson, artist, 23 Charlotte st. Bedford sq
Newbold Ann (Mrs.), milliner, 35 St. John's sq. Clerkenwell
Newbold David, zinc worker, 31 Judd pl. west, New road
Newbold Thomas, cattle salesman, 60 West Smithfield
Newbold William bookbinder, 35 St. John's sq. Clerkenwell
Newbold Wm. pork butcher,148 Up.Whitecross st. St.Luke's
Newbolt Wm. fruiterer, 45 Carnaby st
Newbon Chas. & Son, tailors, 94 Dorset st. Salisbury square
Newbon & Evans, solicitors,1 Wardrobe pl. Doctors' commns
Newbon Wm. map &print colorer, 10 Daggett's ct. Eldon st
Newbury Charlotte (Mrs.), milliner, see Hays & Newbury
Newbury Henry, grocer, 1 Queen's buildings, Brompton
Newby Edgar & Co. warehousemen & agents, & manufacturers of lace & mourning collars, &c. 7 Goldsmith st. Wood st. Cheapside
Newby George, *Grapes* P.H. 86 Fore st. Cripplegate
Newby Henry, butcher, 134 Vauxhall walk, Lambeth
Newby John, cabinet maker, 71 Vauxhall walk
Newby Maria (Mrs.), pawnbroker, 43 Drury lane
Newby Robert, tobacconist, 2 St. James's pl. Bermondsey
Newby Thos. Cantly, publisher, 72Mortimer st.Cavendish sq
NewcastleBrd.& Crown GlassCo.(J.L.Nichol,agt.),Dow.wf
Newcastle & London Steam Packet Co. 35 Leadenhall st
Newcomb & Jones, carpet manufacturers, 19 Skinner st. Snow hill, & Kidderminster
Newcomb Alexander, cabinet ma. 2 Albion pl. Walworth rd
Newcomb Christopher, newsvender, 5 Lillypot la. Noble st
Newcomb John, coffee rooms, 266 Borough High st
Newcomb John, haberdasher, 6 Cumberland rw. Walwth. rd
Newcomb John, *Hertford Arms* P.H. 41 Park st. Grosv. sq
Newcomb Richard, grocer, &c. 5 Pleasant place, Holloway
Newcomb Robt.grocer & cheesemonger, 20 York st.Kgsld.rd
Newcomb Thos. wheelwright, 1 Wright's bldgs. Grange rd
Newcombe & Godfrey, cork cutters, John st. Old Kent road
Newcombe Fredk. ham & beef dlr. 1 Theberton st. Islington
Newcombe Samuel, lithographic printer, 9 Bridgewater sq
Newcome Charles, carpenter, 23 Theobald's road
Newell John & Thomas, butchers, 11 Panton st. Haymarket
Newell & Murray (Mdmes.), milliners, 61 Conduit st
Newell James, fruiterer, 12 Exeter st. Sloane st
Newell Jane (Mrs.), lodging house, 4 Warwick ct. Holborn
Newell John, lighterm.37Thomas st.&9ShadThames,Horslyd
Newell John, upholsterer, undertaker, &c. 45 St. John st.rd
Newell Joseph, fruiterer, 34 Kensington High st
Newell Sarah (Miss), artist, 5 Hanover st. Noel st. Islington
Newell Thomas, boot & shoe maker, 88 Dean st. Soho
Newell William, baker, Church st. Hackney
Newenham Frederick, artist, 14 Kensington square
Newey Benjamin, grocer, 4 Hamilton pl. Deptford High st
Newey Jane (Mrs.), oil & italian wa. 162 Poplar High st
Newey Thomas, butcher, 31 Gt. Turner st. Commercial rd.ea
Newfoundland & B. North American School Society (Rev. J. Haslegrave, M.A. & Major F. Gordon, secretaries), 4 Exeter hall, Strand
Newham James Wm. teadealer, 9 Dean st. Westminster
Newham Robert, cheesemonger, 381 & 382 Rotherhithe
Newhouse Fredk. *Pavilion* P.H. 10 Newcastle st. Strand
Newhouse Thos. *Horse & Groom* P.H. 4 Maiden la. Cov. gar
Newhouse Titus, champagne agent, Hall of Commerce
Newill Thos. & Son, naturalists,12Windsor pl.Southwk.br.rd
Newington William, solicitor, see Gabriel & Newington
NewingtonWm.Peat,grocer&chsmgr.2WhiteHorse ter.Stpny
Newland Francis, butcher, 55 Whitechapel High st
Newland George, coffee rooms, 13 Pollen st. Hanover sq
Newland George, wholesale furrier, 42 Newgate st. & 21 & 22 Greville st. Hatton garden
Newland Henry, hatter, 4 Little Turnstile, Holborn
Newland John, barrister, 3 Tanfield court, Temple
Newland John, undertaker, 6 Back st. Horselydown
Newland Montague, attorney, 1 Stanley terrace, King's road west; & 29 Southampton st. Strand
Newland Sam. Stphn. tobacconist, 29 Nassau pl. Com. rd. ea
Newland Thomas, butcher, 2 Air st. Piccadilly
Newland Thomas, dyer & scourer, 63 Leonard st. Shoreditch
Newland Thomas, hairdresser, 58 North st. Edgware rd
Newling Edward, tailor, 227 Whitechapel road
Newling John, *Lord Nelson* P.H. 100 Mary st. New road
Newling John, tailor & draper, 21 Sidney pl. Commercial rd
Newling William, tailor, 17 Langley pl. Commercial rd. east
Newman Anthony King & Co. booksellrs.32&33Leadenhall st
Newman E.&M.A.(Misses),boys'school,1Church st.Knsngtn
Newman & Barclay, who. statnrs. & engravrs. 48 Watling st
Newman, Hunt & Co. merchants, 12 New Broad st. City
Newman Jemima&K.(Misses),straw bon.ma. 66 Hackney rd
Newman (Misses), ladies' school, 15 King's parade, Chelsea
Newman Saml.&Co.printing ink ma. 1 Poplar rw.N. Kent rd
Newman Thos.C.& Sons,tea agts.9 St. Benet's pl.Gracech. st
Newman Absolom(Mrs.), clothes slsmn.30Thomas st.Oxfd.st
Newman Alfred, architect,&c. 5 Mortimer st. Cavendish sq
Newman Alfred, glove cleaner, &c. 3 Pleasant row,O.Kent rd
Newman Allen, academy, 49 Windsor terrace, City road
Newman AugustaM.(Mrs.),fur. ironmgr.41South st.Manc.sq
Newman Benj. oilman, &c. 74 Welbeck st. Cavendish sq
Newman Charles, carpenter, 1 Carrington mews, Mayfair
Newman Charles, *City Arms* P.H. Ord st. Poplar
Newman Chas. livery stables, 50 York ter. Regent's park
Newman Chas. coppersmith, 6 Plummer's row, Whitechpl
Newman Chas. orange & lemon mercht. Spitalfields market
Newman Daniel, *Bricklayers' Arms* beershop, Millwall
Newman Edward, hairdresser, 4 Yardley st. Clerkenwell
Newman Edwd.oilman & grocer,14½Lt.Bell alley,Coleman st
Newman Edward, printer&statnr. 9 Devonshire st.Bishopgt
Newman George, builder, 6 York place, Portland town
Newman George, butcher, 46 Coleshill st. Pimlico
Newman George, droitwich salt manfr. see Clay & Newman
Newman George, oil & colorman, 99 Cornwall road, Lambeth
Newman George,tailor,1Christopher ct.St.Martin's le grand
Newman Hannah (Mrs.), grocer, 35 Gt. Guildford st. Boro'
Newman Harriet (Mrs.), plumber, 20 Bath st. Hackney rd
Newman Henry, boot & shoe maker, 94 Church st. Chelsea
Newman Henry, linendraper, 3 Lower Eaton st. Pimlico
Newman Henry, *Sun* P.H. 1 Little Sutton st. Clerkenwell
Newman Henry, watch jeweller, 89 Brittannia st. City road
Newman Henry Adams, grocer, 17 Wellington pl. Stepney
Newman James, artists' colorman, 24 Soho square
Newman James, beer retailer, 30 King st. Snowhill
Newman James, bricklayer, 21 Merlin place, Spafields
Newman James,bookseller&dealer in parliamentary reports, papers, &c. 235 High Holborn
Newman James, mnfg. currier, 4&5 Paradise st.Marylebone
Newman James, marine store dlr.147 Long lane,Bermondsey
Newman James, screen handle maker, 4 Ratcliffe row, St. John's row, St. Luke's
Newman Jane (Mrs.), dairy, 24 Bloomsbury st. St. Giles's
Newman John, architect, 32 Tooley st
Newman John, baker, 176 Goswell st
Newman John, bootmaker, 113 Aldersgate st
Newman John,brassworkr.&gas fit.9Bloomsbury st.St.Giles
Newman John, carpenter & porkman, 60 St. John st.Smithfld
Newman John, coachbuilder, 5 Gray st. Manchester square
Newman John, dyer, 1 Strong's place, Brompton
Newman John, grocer, 48 Cornwall road, Lambeth
Newman John, *Horse & Groom* P.H. Church la. Whitechapel
Newman John, philosophical instrument mak. 122 Regent st
Newman John, tobacconist, 7 Queen st. Tower hill
Newman Jsph.R. chandler's shop,25 Mansfield st.Kngsld.rd
Newman Joshua, undertaker&appraiser, 152 Poplar High st
Newman Martha (Mrs.), fruiterer, 4 Swan st.Trinity sq.Boro
Newman Maurice, cigar manufr. 1 Alie pl. Gt. Alie st
Newman (Miss), ladies' school, 7 Victoria gr. Kensgtn.new tn
Newman (Mrs.), ladies' school, Stratford broadway
Newman Peter, grocer, &c. 40 Old Gloucester st. Hoxton

Newman Phillip Robert, shirt maker & outfitter, 120 Oxford st. & 102 & 115 Regent st
Newman Richard, fruiterer, 10 Market st. Mayfair
Newman Richard, tailor, 11 Cirencester pl. Gt. Titchfield st
Newman Richd. tobacconist & sta. 23 Shaftesbury tr. Piml
Newman Robert, grocer, 1 Goldsmith's row, Hackney road
Newman Robert, jobmaster, 20 Swallow st. & 121 Regent st
Newman Saml. bootma. 2 Christopher ct. St. Martin's le gr
Newman Samuel, carpenter, 23 Stockbridge terrace, & 14A, Brewer st. Pimlico
Newman Samuel, cattle salesman, 17 West Smithfield
Newman Samuel, meat salesman, 27 New Newgate market
Newman Sarah (Mrs.), fruiterer, 14 Spring st. Portman sq
Newman Sophia (Miss), straw hat manufacturer & milliner, 182 Oxford st
Newman Thomas, butcher, 7 Theberton st. Islington
Newman Thomas, carman, 76 Fetter lane, Holborn
Newman Thomas, locksmith, 2 Sheffield st. Lincoln's inn flds
Newman Thomas Porter, scale ma. 37 Brick la. Spitalfields
Newman Wm. attorney, 43 Lincoln's inn flds.& Esher, Surrey
Newman Wm. baker, 49 Paradise row, Chelsea
Newman Wm. bookseller, 160 Fenchurch st
Newman Wm. boot & shoe maker, 82 Up. Ebury st. Pimlico
Newman Wm. bricklay. & plasterer, 2 Sheffield st. Linc. inn
Newman Wm. carman, Spital square
Newman Wm. carpenter, 4 Henry st. Cumberland market
Newman Wm. coach & cabproprietor, 17 Hatfield st. Goswl. st
Newman Wm. confectioner, 1 Kingsland High st
Newman Wm. grocer & teadealer to the King of the Belgians, & his Royal Highness the Duke & Prince George of Cambridge, 21 Cockspur st
Newman Wm. staymaker, 163 Goswell st
Newman Wm. staymanfr. 10 Patriot row, Cambrdg. rd. Mile end
Newman Wm. wheelwright, Crooked Billet yd. Kingsland rd
Newman Wm. Rd. engravr. & print. 27 Widegate st. Bishopsgate
Newnam Francis Cha. watch index ma. 19 Skinner st. Clkwl
Newnham Benjamin, tailor, 53 Frith st. Soho
Newnham Henry, baker, 24 King st. Tower hill
Newnham William, grocer, &c. 77 Friar st. Blackfriars road
Newnham Wm. wood dealer, Hughes fields, Deptford
Newport Charlt. (Mrs.). dairy, 5 Foundling mews, Gray's inn rd
Newport Edwin, die sinker & engraver, 13 Upper Ashby st
Newport George, bootmaker, 85 Theobald's road, Red lion sq
Newport George, surgeon, see Martin & Newport
Newport James Garrett, baker, 1 Old Gloucester st. Hoxton
Newport John, ornamental painter, 24 York st. Blackfrs. rd
Newport Lydia (Mrs.), lodging ho. 51 Jewin st. Cripplegate
Newport Richard, fruiterer, 4 Kenton st. Brunswick square
Newport Sarah (Mrs.), trimming seller, 80 Church st. Shored
Newry, Bainbridge & Belfast Junction Railway (James Bryden, sec.), 19 Moorgate st
Newry & Enniskillen Rlwy (Jas. Bryden, sec.), 19 Moorgate st
Newry, Warrenpoint & Rostrum Railway (James Bryden, sec.), 19 Moorgate st
News Exchange, 2 Black Horse court, Fleet st
News of the World weekly newspaper, 299 Strand
Newsam Christr. & Son, haircutters, 6 City road, Finsbury sq
Newsam (Fowler) & Co. merchants, 29 Threadneedle st
Newsham Rchd. plumber, &c. 8 Little Stanhope st. Mayfair
Newsom Joseph & Son, teadealers, 50 Borough High st
Newsom Robert, tobacconist, 12 Coppice row, Clerkenwell
Newsom Tobias, greengrocer, 9 Dover pl. west, Kent road
Newsome Wm. & Benj. woolstaplers, Up. Russell st. Bermondsy
Newsome George, tailor, &c. 20 King st. Clerkenwell
Newson George, bookbinder, 65 Newman st. Oxford st
Newson Geo. Lincoln, prof. of music, 40 Watling st. City
Newson Geo. Wm. cabinet maker, Providence row, Finsbury
Newson Isaac, tailor, 32 Clarence gardens, Regent's park
Newson Jane (Mrs.), fruiterer, 9 Providence st. Walwrth. com
Newson John, builder, timber merchant & lath render, 19 Bloomfield terrace, Pimlico; workshops, 38 Grosvenor mews, Berkeley square; store yard, 50½ Westbourne st. Pimlico; timber yard, Grosvenor row, Pimlico
Newson John, coachmaker, see Charters, Holland & Newson
Newson Jhn. timber mer. & sawyer, 4 Crown ct. Crown st. Finsby
Newson Samuel, cabinet ma. 17 Gt. Barlow st. Marylebone
Newson Thomas, *Cheshire Cheese* P.H. 10 Surrey st. Strand
Newson Wm. furn. ironmonger, 45 Mount st. Berkeley sq
Newstead Benjn. *Queen's Arms* P.H. 1 Up. Kennington lane
Newstead William Henry, solicitor, see Shaw & Newstead
Newth Adrian, tailor & undertaker, 1 King st. Borough
Newth George Elisha, surgeon, &c. 110 Gt. Suffolk st. Boro'
Newth Elijah, glaziers' diamond ma. see Sharratt & Newth
Newton & Appleton, auctioneers & est. agts. 7 Mansion ho. st
Newton & Co. country newspaper office, 2 Warwick square
Newton & Cook, brushmakers, 63 Princes st. Leicester sq
Newton, Gordon & Co. of Madeira, 6 New Broad st. City
Newton Brothers, snuff & cigar manfrs. 37 & 38 Friday st
Newton James & Co. upholsterers, &c. 10 Bruton st. Berkly. sq
Newton Jane & Son, fire brick mers. Falcon dock, 79 Banksi
Newton John & Son, merchants & cork manufacturers, 50 & 51 St. John st. West Smithfield
Newton John & Son, notaries & translators, 10 Birchin lane
Newton Thos. & Sons, timber mers. 14 & 101 Paul st. Finsbry
Newton Wm. & Chas. cabinet makers, 1 Vernon st. Pentonvl
Newton Wm. & Son, british & foreign pat. agts. & appointed draughtsmen to the inrolment office, 66 Chancery lane
Newton & Worssam, millwrights, Comcl. wf. Kingsland rd. bas
Newton Crown Glass Co. (Chas. Morgan, agt.), 5 Savoy st. Stnd
Newton Charles, barrister, 3 Middle Temple lane
Newton Daniel, blacksmith, 7 Vine st. Hatton wall
Newton Edward, surgeon, see Painter & Newton
Newton Francis, publisher, 2 Crown court, Fleet st
Newton George, cabinet ma. Southampton bldgs. Euston sq
Newton George, cattle salesman, 17 West Smithfield
Newton Geo. *Eastern* coffee rooms, 126 Whitechpl. High st
Newton George, house & decorative painter, grainer to the trade, 140 St. John st. West Smithfield
Newton George, tailor, 21 Lit. Randolph st. Camden town
Newton Henry, *King's Arms* P.H. 1 Lawrie ter. Westm. rd
Newton Hen. Chas. artists' colorman, see Windsor & Newton
Newton Henry John, fruiterer, 8 St. James's pl. Bermondsey
Newton Isaac, butcher, 64½ Brick lane, St. Luke's
Newton Isaac, carpenter & builder, 20 London wall
Newton Isaac, quill & pen manufac. 69 Whitechapel High st
Newton James, cork cutter, 55 Marylebone lane
Newton James, grocer, 233A, Tottenham court road
Newton James, lace & child bed linen wa. 85 Up. st. Islington
Newton Jeremiah, cheesemonger, 136 Tottenham ct. road
Newton Jeremiah, cowkeeper, 22 St. John's lane, Clerknwll
Newton John, builder, 1 Terrace, Kensington
Newton John, coal & corn mer. Rosemary branch bdg. Hoxtn
Newton John, grocer & cheesemonger, 17 Up. Rathbone pl
Newton John, printer, 65 Wood st. Cheapside
Newton John, sailmaker, 39 Fore st. Limehouse
Newton John, jun. notary & for. exchange bro. 10 Birchin la
Newton John Price, coml. boarding ho. 32 King st. Cheapside
Newton Joseph, boot & shoemakr. 9 Adam & Eve ct. Oxford st
Newton Joseph Ralph, grocer, 8 Melbourne pl. Old Kent rd
Newton L. van der Veer, physician, 72 Milton st. Dorset sq
Newton Lancelot, warehouseman & agent, 31 Gutter lane
Newton Morris, solicitor, 10 Lancaster place, Strand
Newton Robert, baker, 11 Crescent st. Euston square
Newton Samuel Richard, grocer, 34 Kingsland road
Newton Thomas, shoe agent, 34 Red Lion st. Spitalfields
Newton Thomas Newell, *Red Horse* P.H. 10 Old Bond st
Newton William, confectioner, 127 Curtain road, Shoreditch
Newton William, fruiterer, 1 St. Andrew's road, Borough
Newton William, navy agent, see Pettet & Newton
Newton Wm. silk warehsmn. 4 King's Arms bldgs. Wood st
Newton William, tailor, 7 Maddox st. Bondst.; & 1 Upper Holland st. Kensington
Newton William, tin plate worker, 19 Bartholomew close
Newton Wm. Francis (Mrs.), milliner, 230 Regent st
Newton Wm. James, academy, 41 Brewer st. Golden sq
Newton Sir Wm. John, artist, 6 Argyll st. Regent st
Nex William, carpenter, 4 Pickett place, Strand
Nias Geo. Elmes, printer & engraver, 38 Gracechurch st
Nias Thomas, solicitor, 5 Copthall court, Throgmorton st
Nibbs John, glass cutters' tool ma. 8 King's rw. Walworthrd
Niblett Francis, chemist & druggist, 44 Drury lane
Niblett (Mrs.), ladies' school, 1 High st. Bow
Niblett Philip, tobacconist, 28 Newton st. High Holborn
Niblett Wm. *Three Compasses* P.H. Dalston
Nice Josiah, veter. surgeon, 13 Earl st. Blackfriars
Nichol Anthony & Son, merchts. Dowgate wf. Up. Thames st
Nichol & Miller, bottle merchts. Dowgate wf. Up. Thames st
Nichol George, wine cooper, 33 Haydon st. Minories
Nichol John L. windowglassmanfr. Dowgatewhf. Up. Thamesst
Nicholas Margaret & Son, corndealers, 34 Crispin st. Spitalfi
Nicholas Chas. Thos. pianoforte ma. 2 Chadwell st. St. John st
Nicholas George, merchant, 3 Abchurch lane, City
Nicholas Eugene, carver & gilder, 11 Gt. Titchfield st. Oxford st
Nicholas Henry, carpenter, 15 Duke st. Lisson grove
Nicholas Henry, carpenter, 21 Hardington st. Portman mkt
Nicholas Henry, pork butcher, Stratford broadway
Nicholas James, tobacconist, 6 Church st. Chelsea
Nicholas John, fruiterer, 12 King David lane, Shadwell
Nicholas John, stationer, 13 Upper Jubilee place, Mile end
Nicholas Nathl. bricklayer, &c. 10 Paddington st. Marylebn
Nicholas Samuel, clock & watchmaker, 158 Tooley st
Nicholas Thos. *Camden's Head* P.H. 2 Camden st. Islgtn. gn

Nicholas William, tobacconist, 10 Pickett st. or 255 Strand
Nicholay John Augustus, furrier, by appointment, to their Majesties the Queen & Queen Dowager, & the royal family, 82 Oxford st
Nicholes Henry, confectioner, 71 Piccadilly
Nicholl (Iltid) & Son, proctors, 11 Godliman st. Drs.' coms
Nicholl Geo. Whitlock, barrister, 3 Plowden bldgs. Temple
Nicholl Hen. Iltid, D.C.L. advocate, 5 Gt. Knightrider st
Nicholl John, *Fort* P.H. Fort place, Grange rd. Bermondsey
Nicholl John, lasting, plush, &c. manfctr. 5 Oat la. Wood st
Nicholl Martha (Mrs.), ropemaker, 121 Union st. Borough
Nicholl Wm.Grinsell,sculptor,1 Grafton st. ea.Tottnhm.ct.rd
Nicholl Wm. Lewis, scalemaker, 16 Aldersgate st
Nicholles John, dentist & cupper, 34 Bruton st. Bond st
Nicholls & Doyle, solicitors, 48 Bedford row
Nicholls Francis & Co. merchants, 11 Mark lane
Nicholls & Housley, ready made linen ware. 21 St.James's st
Nicholls & Pellatt, wine merchants (successors to Ann Wooding & Son), 32 King William st. City; & at the *Shades*, Old Swan stairs, Upper Thames st
Nicholls Rd. & Nathl. merchs. & warehousemn. 127Wood st
Nicholls & Whitford, wax bleachers, Battersea
Nicholls William & Charles, breeches makers, 57 Pall mall
Nicholls Ezekiel, carpntr. & buildr. 2 Percy st. Rathbone pl
Nicholls Francis Plumber, tailor, 112 Aldersgate st
Nicholls Fred. printer, 2 Milton st. City, & 105 Kingsland rd
Nicholls Geo. *Sun & Anchor* P.H. 27 St. Dunstan's hill, City
Nicholls Jacob, leech importer, 14 Catherine st. Com. rd. ea
Nicholls James, haircutter, 1 Octagon pl. Kennington comn
Nicholls James, jun. solicitor, 48 Bedford row, Holborn
Nicholls John, Laycock's dairy farm, Park pl. Islington
Nicholls John, beer retailer, Wandsworth road
Nicholls John, chandler's shop, 31 Stangate st. Lambeth
Nicholls John, coal agt. 16wharf, south side, Paddington basin
Nicholls John, farmer, Liverpool road
Nicholls John, fruiterer, 10 Star corner, Bermondsey
Nicholls John, market gardener, Blue anchor road
Nicholls John, tailor & army clothier, 42 Jermyn st.St. Jas's
Nicholls John, tailor, 43 St. Martin's lane, Charing cross
NichollsJsph.rd.contrctr.10whrf.south side,Paddingtonbasin
Nicholls JoshuaJas.coal mercht.OldSwan whf.Up.Thames st
Nicholls Michael,coach cur.37 & 38Lit.Windmill st.Goldn.sq
Nicholls Peter, grocer & oilman, 3 Salcombe pl. Regent's pk
Nicholls Richard, baker, 48 Portland st. Walworth common
Nicholls Richard, fruiterer, 353 Albany rd. Camberwell
Nicholls Robert D. furn. broker, 12 & 13 Brook hill, Clrknwl
Nicholls Thomas, architect & surveyor, 13 Castle st. Holborn
Nicholls Thos. grocer, 1 St. Andrew's rd. Borough
Nicholls Thos. shirt maker, 5 Goldsmith st. Cheapside
Nicholls Thos. tailor, 225 Regent st
Nicholls Thos. jun. architect, &c. 13 Castle st. Holborn
Nicholls Thos. Wilcocks, appraiser & undert. 122 Tooley st
Nicholls Wm. bootmaker, 29 Pool terrace, City road
Nicholls Wm. *Coach & Horses* P.H. 140 St. John st. rd
Nicholls Wm. grocer, 9 Dean st. Commercial rd. east
Nicholls Wm. grocer, 34 St. James terrace, Waterloo rd
Nicholls Wm. printer, 4 East Harding st. Fleet st
Nicholls Wm. Humphrey, brass manufacturer & gas filter, 81 Curtain rd. Shoreditch
Nicholls Wm. road contractor, Adams mews, Edgware rd
Nicholls Wm.Henry, butcher, 5 Foxley rd.Camberwell new rd
Nicholls Wm. Jeremiah, bootmaker, 18 Cable st.Wellclose sq
Nichols John B. & Son, printers, 25 Parliament st. & 46 King st. Westminster
Nichols Joseph & James, bootmakers, 43 Liquorpond st
Nichols Adah(Mrs.), fancy trimm. manufr. 291 Bethnal gn.rd
Nichols Augustus, porkbutcher, 10White Lion st.Goodman'sfi
Nichols Chas. blacksmith, 52 Lower Trinity st. Rotherhithe
Nichols Chas.painter, plumber & glazier, 20 Church st. Soho
Nichols Chas. shawl manuf. 72 Quadrant & Glasgow
Nichols Daniel, butcher, 57 Hindon st. Vauxhall rd
Nichols George, printer, 7 Earl's court, Leicester sq
Nichols Geo.surv.& publisher, 15 Providence bldgs.Nw.Kt.rd
Nichols George Alex. coal merchant 21 Up. Park st. Islgtn
Nichols George Pike, wood engraver, 53 Paternoster row
Nichols Henry, barrister, 2 Stone buildings, Lincoln's inn
Nichols Henry, dining rooms, 97 Brick lane, Spitalfields
Nichols Henry Robert, cabinetmaker, 291 Bethnal green rd
Nichols Jas. *Bricklayers' Arms* P.H. 32 Charles st.Hckny.rd
Nichols James, chemist, 14 Road side, Mile end rd
Nichols James, dairyman, 1 Ernest st. Regent's park
Nichols James, printer, 45 & 46 Hoxton sq
Nichols James, surgeon, 12 Leicester place, Leicester sq
Nichols John, nail & genl. ironmongery wareh. 65 Snow hill
Nichols John, printer & engraver, 9 Chandos st. Cov. garden
Nichols John, silversmith, &c. 38 Castle st. Leicester sq
Nichols John, solicitor, see Galsworthy & Nichols
Nichols John, window glass & lead mer.47 Lambeth Lr.marsh
Nichols Joseph, varnish & japan ma. Bell isle, King's cross
Nichols Joseph Robt. *Fountain* P.H. 1 Fountain pl. City rd
Nichols Joseph West, stationer, 3 Strong's place, Brompton
Nichols Mark, *St. Martin* P.H. 13 Duke st Adelphi
Nichols Richd. bricklayer & builder, 43 Up.Ebury st.Pimlico
Nichols Richard, merchant, see Cole, Nichols & Co
Nichols Robert, cooper, 31 King st. Seven dials
Nichols Thomas, baker, Stratford, Essex
Nichols Thomas, ship & ins. agent, see Harrison & Nichols
Nichols Wm. barrister, 3 Inner Temple lane
Nichols Wm. cheesemonger, 2 John's pl. Camberwell new rd
Nichols Wm.fishmonger, 8 MiddleQueen's bldgs.Knightbrdg
Nichols Wm. glass & china warehouse, 22 King's rw.Pimlico
Nichols Wm. hairdresser, 18 Woburn bldgs. Tavistock sq
Nichols Wm. notary public, see Gibson & Nichols
Nichols Wm. surgeon, 15 Queen st. Bryanstone sq
Nichols Wm.who. shoe wareh. 130 St. John st.West Smithfld
Nicholson Benjamin & Son, masons & builders, 61 Mark lane, & 11 Minories
Nicholson, Besley & Co. wharfingers & warehouse keepers, East India & China wharf, 12 & 14 Lower Thames st
Nicholson & Davis, cabinet, upholstery & carpet manufactory, 318 High Holborn
Nicholson Isaac & Co. merchts. 9 King's arms yd. Moorgate
Nicholson John & Co. tea agents, 15 Fenchurch st
Nicholson John & Wm.& Sons, dstlrs. 114 to120St.Jhn st.Clkw
Nicholson Joseph & Son, coal mer. Phœnix wf.Clink st.Boro'
Nicholson & Mitchell, carpet & linen wa. 30 Aldgate High st
Nicholson & Parker, attorneys, 48 Lime st. City
Nicholson & Parker, solicitors, 48 Lime st. City
Nicholson, Rigg & Co. merchs. & agts. 1 Coleman st. bldgs
Nicholson Rt. & Co. linen & woollen facts. 1 Coleman st. bldgs
Nicholson's Wf. I.I. Nicholson, Besley & Co. 12 & 14 Lr.Thamesst
Nicholson Alex. hoop mercht. & stone agt. 12 Lit. Tower st
Nicholson Charles, linendraper, 26 Pitfield st. Hoxton, & 19 Three Colt st. Limehouse
Nicholson Elizh.(Miss), court dress ma.& milnr. 120 N. Bond st
Nicholson Elizh.(Mrs.), lodging house, 5 Green st. Grosvnr.sq
Nicholson Emily(Miss), artist, 69 Myddelton sq
Nicholson George, solicitor, 21 Abingdon st. Westminster
Nicholson George Henry, barrister, 89 Chancery lane
Nicholson Geo. Jas. attorney, 5 Raymond bldgs. Gray's inn
Nicholson George S. proctor, see Wheeler & Nicholson
Nicholson Henry, *PelhamArms* P.H. Pelham rd. Brompton
Nicholson Henry, rag merchant, 7 Shoreditch
Nicholson Isaac, blacksmith, 33 Wellington st. Blackfrs. rd
Nicholson James, glass & lead warehouse, see Potts & Nicholson
Nicholson James, linendraper, 60 Bishopsgate within
Nicholson James, linendraper, 16 Brecknock place, Camden new town, & 5 & 6 Park terrace, Camden town
Nicholson James, solicitor, 141 New Bond st
Nicholson James, tailor & draper, 7 Mount pl. Whitechapl.rd
Nicholson John, linen draper, 26 Hackney road
Nicholson Joseph, barrister, 28 Chancery lane
Nicholson Joseph, dyer, Snow's fields, Bermondsey
Nicholson Joseph, solicitor, see Seton & Nicholson
Nicholson Matthew, *Jacob's Well* P.H. 65 Milton st.Criplgt
Nicholson Rd.carp.bagma. 1Southampton ct.Southamp.bdgs
Nicholson Rd. wine mer. & agent, 4 Catherine ct. Trinity sq
Nicholson Robt. coppersmith, &c. 7 Bath terrace, Back rd
Nicholson Robt. hat manufr. 16 & 17 John st. west, Blackfrs
Nicholson Robt. linendraper, 6 Wellington terr. Bayswater
Nicholson Robt. jun. brassfounder, 2 Cannon st.Ratcliff hiwy
Nicholson Sam.who.hat ma. 1Winchester pl.Southwarkbr.rd
Nicholson Thos. chandler's shop, 3 Margaret st.Hackney flds
Nicholson Wm. *Craven Arms* P.H. 39Queen's rd.Bayswater
Nicholson Wm. solicitor, 8 Lincoln's inn fields
Nicholson Wm. wine merchant, 70 St. Martin's lane
Nicholson Wm. Morris, grocer, 86 Upper st. Islington
Nicholson Wm. Norris, barrister, 44 Chancery lane
Nickels Christopher, india rubber ma. see Keene & Nickels
Nickels Mary Ann (Miss), grocer, 76 Adam st. Rotherhithe
Nickels Richard, baker, 27 Adam st. Rotherhithe
Nickerson Chas. leatherdresser, 3 Rephidim st. Old Kent rd
Nickinson Thomas, cheesemonger, Battersea square
Nickisson John Chas.manch.& scotch agt. 4 Russia ct. Milk st
Nickisson Geo. Wm. bookseller & publisher, 215 Regent st
Nickisson Sampson, watchmaker, 33 Northampton square
Nickisson Wm. iron mercht.& agent, 21 King's sq.Goswellrd
Nicklen Peter, bootmaker, see Robinson & Nicklen
Nickless Chas. tin plate workr. 49 Collingwood st. Blkfrs. rd
Nickless John, plumber, &c. Wellington pl. West India docks
Nicklin Thomas, chairmaker, &c. 72Gt. Guildford st. Borough
Nickolds (*Mrs.R.*), lodging house, 3Buckingham pl. Fitzroy sq

Nickoll James, oil & seed broker, Hall of Commerce
Nickolls & Shipley, corndealers, 17 Market row, Oxford mkt
Nickolls Joseph, livery stables, Queen's road, Dalston
Nickols John, ship&ins.broker, 33Seething lane, Gt.Tower st
Nickols George, ship smith, Risbie's rope walk, Limehouse
Nickols John, notary, 33 Seething lane, Tower st
Nickols John, solicitor, 16 Queen's row, Pentonville
Nicks Henry, *Cricketers* P.H. 42 London st. Ratcliff
Nicks Thomas, tailor, 30 St. Mary at hill, Lower Thames st
Nicol Elizabeth & Isabella, dressmakers, 69 New Bond st
Nicol James & Co. tea & coffee dlrs. 15Rathbone pl. Oxford st
Nicol Robert&Co. purveyors of coffee, teadealers & grocers to her Majesty&H.R.H. the duchess of Kent, 18 Fenchurch st
Nicol Andrew, baker, 5 Cardigan place, New North road
Nicol Henry, solicitor, see Allen & Nicol
Nicol James Dyce, merchant, 7 Mincing lane
Nicol John, surgeon, Flora cottages, Queen's road, Dalston
Nicol Robert, carpenter & builder, 3 Union st. New Bond st
Nicol Robert, box&packing case maker, 111 Gt. Titchfield st
Nicol Walter, woollendraper, 109 Regent st
Nicol William, shakspeare printing office, 60 Pall mall
Nicolas Alexr. de professor of languages, 34 Sudeley st
Nicolas Sir Harris, G.C.M.G. K.H. barrister, 55Torrington sq
Nicolas John T. surgeon dentist, 7 Conduit st. Regent st
Nicolas-y-Badillo Jose de, mercht. 34Brunswick pl. City road
Nicole & Capt, watchmakers, 80B, Dean st. Soho
Nicole Henry, corn chandler, 19 Old Fish st. City
Nicole Peter Hen. law stationer, 39 Castle st. Holborn
Nicolini Giovanna Battista, foreign goods imp. 17 Harp la
Nicoll & Dewar, cabinet makers, 5 Upper East Smithfield, & scots timber merchants, Fox's lane, Shadwell
Nicoll Henry John & Donald, army & navy clothiers, & patentees of the registered paletot, 114 Regent st
Nicoll Benjamin, hosier & glover, 42 Regent st
Nicoll Benjamin, tailor & habit maker, 36 Moorgate st
Nicoll Fredk. coal agent, 16 whf. south side, Paddgtn. basin
Nicoll John, rope, line & twine ma. Blue Anchor rd. Bermod
Nicoll John, watchmaker, 117 Gt. Portland st. Oxford st
Nicoll Robert, scotch whiskey & provision merchant, 5 Globe st. Wapping
Nicoll Thomas, carver & gilder, 39 Great Titchfield st
Nicoll Thomas, clothworker, 12 Marshall st. Golden sq
Nicoll William, rope maker, 9 New st. Southwark
Nicolls William, bootmaker, 21 Old Gloucester st. Hoxton
Nicolson Rev. Hugh, clerical&school agt. 6 John st. Adelphi
Nicolson Thomas, surgeon, see Barrow & Nicolson
Niell Alexander, surgeon, 150 Bermondsey st
Niell John, M.D. surgeon, 175 Aldersgate st
Niemann John Diedrick, merchant, 33 Gt. Winchester st
NightingaleJoseph&Co. steel&cane reed ma. 2 Wood st. Spitlfl
Nightingale Wm. & Chas. who. feather, horse hair & bedding manfrs. 30 Old Compton st. & 64 Wardour st. Soho, & 16 Newton st. High Holborn
Nightingale Benj. painter & glazier, 74 Princes st. Lambeth
Nightingale Geo. horsehair manf. 18 NewGlo'sterst. Hoxton
Nightingale George, tailor, 13 Charles st. Commercial road
Nightingale Henry, woollen draper, 23 Brewer st. Golden sq
Nightingale John Josiah, bootmaker, 62 Haymarket
Nightingale Samuel, fruiterer, 28 Museum st. Bloomsbury
Nightingale Thos. lkg. glass ma. 20Ravenscroft st. Hackny.rd
Nimmo Edward, butcher, 8 Water lane, Blackfriars
Nind John & Henry, paper hanging ma. 10 Beech st. Barbican
Nind Benj. Wharton, solicitor, 31 Nicholas lane, Lombard st
Nind Charles, paperhanging manufacturer, 7 Little Mitchell st. & 7 Bartholomew square, St. Luke's
Nind Edwd. Lewis, paperhanging manf. Church st. Hackney
Nind John, paper stainer, 1 Bartholomew place, Kingsland
Nind Joseph, paperhanger, 135 Fleet st
Nind Robert, paperhanger, 4 West place, Islington green
Niner Alan Gardener, lamp lustre ma. see Greene & Niner
Niner John, baker & oilman, 47 Shadwell High st
Niner William Thomas, saddler, 229 Oxford st
Ninnis Julia (Mrs.), ladies' school, 30 Surrey sq. Old Kent rd
Ninor John, oilman, 47 Shadwell High st
Ninsel John, merchant, 7 Crescent, Minories
Nippress John, tuscan & straw bonnet ma. 101 Long la. Bmdsy
Nisbert Richard, plumb. painter, &c. 11 Dorset pl. Pall mall
Nisbet James & Co. booksellers & stationers, 21 Berners st. Oxford st
Nisbet Andrew, printer & engraver, 9 Union st. ea. Spitalflds
Nisbet Closs, lighterman, 19½ Bread st. hill, City
Nisbet George R. wine merchant & agent for Dublin stout, & east india ale stores, &c. 11 Jermyn st. St. James's
Nisbet James, hairdresser, &c. 39 Wigmore st. Cavendish sq
Nisbet Mary Ann (Miss), ladies' seminary, 7 Goswell road
Nisbett Frederick, boot & shoe maker, 5 Union st. Bond st
Nisbett George, lighterman, 3 Abdy st. Horselydown
Nisbett Thomas, meat salesman, 8 Newgate market
Nisdall Barkley, livery stables, Church rw. Newington butts
Nisi Prius Office, Judges' chambers, Serjeants' inn, Chancery lane; hours 11 to 2 & 6 to 8
Nissen & Parker, stationers, 68&69 Gt. Tower st. &43Mark la
Nitsch Ferdinand, tailor, 6 Macclesfield st. Soho
Nitsch Ferdinand, tailor, see Roberts & Nitsch
Nivoley Frances Thornton (Mrs.), milliner, 273 Regent st
Nix Susannah & Son, butchers, 282 Bermondsey st
Nix Margaret (Miss), milliner, 69 Mortimer st. Cavendish sq
Nix Waddelow, *Exeter Hall hotel & coffee house*, 375Strand
Nixey Thos. hosier, glover, &c. 80 St. John st. Clerkenwell
Nixey Wm. George, oil & colorman, 22 Moor st. Soho
Nixon Charles & Elizabeth, brushmaks. 51 Gt. Marylebone st
Nixon Edwin & Joseph, upholsterers, 123 Gt. Portland st
Nixon John & Co. cornfactors, 25 Crutched friars
Nixon Frances (Mrs.), lodging house, 22 Green st. Gros. sq
Nixon Fred. harness maker, 111 Gt. Titchfield st. Oxford st
Nixon H. (Mrs.), dress maker, Brompton pl. Brompton rd
Nixon Jas Edw. solicitor, 3 Lyon's inn, Strand
Nixon James Henry, artist, 4 Robert st. Hampstead road
Nixon John, law stationer, 30 Whitefriars st
Nixon John, *Red Lion & Wheatsheaf* P.H. Deptford High st
Nixon John, sailmaker, 265 Wapping
Nixon John, solicitor, 13 Clifford's inn
Nixon Robert, grocer & italia wareho. 2 North st. Edgware rd
Nixon Robert, *Hope* P.H. 63 Banner st. St. Luke's
Nixon Samuel, sculptor, 2 White hart court, Bishopsgate
Nixon Thos. hosier & glover, 88 Piccadilly
Nixon Wm. builder, see Haward & Nixon
Noad Isaac, cooper, 10 New inn yard, Shoreditch
Noad Stephen, silversmith, 23 Charles st. Hatton garden
Noad Stephen J. stock broker, 4 Adams court, Old Broad st
Noah Stephen, coffee rooms, 116 York road Lambeth
Noake Henry, lodging house, 1 King st. Grosvenor sq
Noakes & Goble, hop & seed factrs. 16 ThreeCrown sq. Boro'
Noakes & Pearce, statuaries, 1 South rw. New rd. St. Pancras
Noakes Elias, laceman, 3 New Church st. Lisson grove
Noakes Elizh. & Susan (Misses), milliners, 179 Sloane st
Noakes Robert, who. hardwareman, see Broughton & Noakes
Noakes Wm. fruiterer, 45 Brunswick st. Blackfriars rd
Nobbs Edw. bootma. 6 Leathersellers' bldgs. London wall
Nobbs Wm. carpenter, 47 Crucifix lane, Bermondsey
Nobbs Wm. Mather, chemist, 4 Upper Seymour st. Eustonsq
Noble & Harwood, *Blind Beggar* P.H. 173 Whitechapel rd
Noble & Mee, dairymen, 1 Bartlett's passage, Holborn
Noble Robert & Co. tailors & drapers, 118 Leadenhall st
Noble & Rolls, varnish & color manufacturers, Cornwall rd. Stamford st
Noble Wm. & Co. wine merchts. 8 Onslow pl. Fulham rd
Noble William & John, seed merchants, 152 Fleet st
Noble Abraham, brassfounder, 21 Gt. Sutton st. Clerkenwl
Noble George, dyer, Deptford Broadway
Noble George, russia broker, see Tatchell & Noble
Noble George, wine mer. 80 Londonwall, &9 Lit. Winchester st
Noble Henry, teacher of music, 117 Gt. Russell st. Bloomsby
Noble Henry Thomas, bottle merchant, see Rose & Noble
Noble James, architect & surveyor, 45 Halfmoon st. Piccadilly
Noble James, bookseller & statnr. 1 Freeman's pl. Mile end rd
Noble James, house agent, 33 Great St. Helen's
Noble James, plumber, 5 Down st. Piccadilly, & 21 Ebury st. Pimlico
Noble James, tailor, 18 Sloane square
Noble John, artist, 22 Newman st. Oxford st
Noble John, coffee rooms, 2 St. Martin's ct. Ludgate hill
Noble John, tailor, 9 Star corner, Bermondsey
Noble Joseph, bookseller, 5 New Turnstile, High Holborn
Noble Mark, bookseller, 6 Eliza place, Sadler's wells
Noble Mary (Mrs.), bookseller, 9 King st. Covent garden
Noble Richard, grocer, 40 North st. Lisson grove
Noble Richd. painter, plumbr. & glzr. 9 Clarehall pl. Stpny.gr
Noble Richard Pratchett, artist, 56 Long acre
Noble Samuel, *Blind Beggar* P.H. see Harwood & Noble
Noble Sam. John, pianoforte maker, 13 Abingdon st. & 14 Smith sq. Westminster
Noble Saml. Parker, *Dover Castle* P.H. 1 Mount st. Lambeth
Noble Theophilus, bookseller, 79 Fleet st. & 114 Chancery la
Noble Thomas, carver & gilder, 23 Francis st. Tottnhm. ct. rd
Noble Thomas, ironmonger, 13 Charing cross
Noble Thomas, oil & colorman, 1 Marine cres. Bermondsey rd
Noble William, linendraper, 80 Shoreditch High st
Noble William, tailor, 10 Little Guilford st. Brunswick sq
Noblett John, tanner & coach, saddle, harness & shoe currier, 24 Drury lane, & Wright's buildgs. Grange rd. Bermondsey
Nock & Williams, goldsmiths & jewellers, 18 Frith st. Soho

Nock Samuel & Benjamin, booksellers, 182 High Holborn, & 15 Tottenham court, New road
Nock John, carpenter & undertaker, 72 Richard st. Coml. rd. ea
Nock Joseph, clothier & outfitter, 280 Poplar High st. & tailors' trimming seller, 2 Poplar High st
Nock Samuel, gunmaker, 43 Regent circus, Piccadilly
Nockolds Edmund, coffee rooms, 112 Long acre
Nockolds Thomas, coffee rooms, 20 High st. St. Giles's
Nodder Nicholas, bootmaker, 7 North st. East st. Walworth
Noddings Michael, cabinet maker, 33 Banner st. St. Luke's
Noden Ann (Mrs.), milliner, 1 Mansion ho. pl. Cambrwl. rd
Noden John, hairdresser, 1 Mansion ho. pl. Cambrwl. rd
Noden Stephen, hearth rug ma. 28 Swinton st. Gray's inn rd
Noden Stephen, worsted dyer, 19 Kirby st. Hatton garden
Nodes John & Son, furn. undertak. 62 New Church st. Lisson gr
Nodes Elizh. (Mrs.), livery stables, 41 New Manor st. Chelsea
Nodes George, bookseller & publisher, 194 & 331 Strand
Nodes Henry, undertaker, 22 Robert st. King's rd. Chelsea
Nodes Hy. Oliver, undertaker, 7 Chapel st. Tottenham ct. rd
Nodes James, undertaker, Kensington gravel pits
Nodes Wm. furrier, 18 Norfolk st. Middlesex hospital
Nodes Wm. undertaker, &c. 1 Manchester bldgs. Holloway
Noding John Henry, west india merchant, 15 Mincing lane
Noel George, gold cutter, 25 Low. Smith st. Northampton sq
Noel William, hairdresser, 55 Lambeth walk
Nohill James, tobacconist, 80 Grosvenor st. Grosvenor sq
Nokes George, straw hat manfr. 19 Elizabeth st. Eaton sq
Nokes John, attorney, 74 Guilford st. Russell square
Nokes Samuel, cheesemonger, 65 Cable st. St. George's east
Nokes Samuel, whipmaker, see Pitchford & Nokes
Nolan John Macartney, surgeon, 9 Weymouth pl. New Kent rd
Nolan William, dentist, 32 Southampton st. Covent garden
Noldwritt John S. custom house agt. 4 Custom ho. ct. Beer la
Nolloth Abraham, *Weavers' Arms* P. H. 29 Brown's la. Sptlflds
Nolson William, grocer, 3 Little Bath st. Clerkenwell
Nonconformist Newspaper (weekly), 3 Whitefriars st
Non-Parochial Register Office, Rolls yard, Chancery lane
Noon Elizh. (Mrs.), butcher, 4 Clarence pl. Camberwell rd
Noon Joseph, who. & ret. shoe mfr. 21 Stonecutter st. Shoe la
Noon William Henry, beer retailer, 20 Clark st. Stepney
Nops John Geo. academy, 3 Cambridge ter. Camden nw. tn
Noquet Isaac, *Well & Bucket* P.H. 62 Church st. Shoreditch
Norburn Adolphus Henry, surgeon, 3 Ivy place, Hoxton
Norbury Joseph, coppersmith, 202 Whitechapel road
Norbury Mary Anne (Mrs.), shell fishmonger, 5 Birchin la
Norchi Egisippo, manufacturer & importer of italian marble & alabaster works, 18 King William st. Strand
Norcott William, carpenter, &c. see Ball & Norcott
Norcott William, tobacconist, 32 King st. Camden town
Norcutt Thos. Gascoigne, attorney, 34 Queen sq. Bloomsbury
Norden Richard, *Rock* P.H. 40 Lisson grove north
Nordon Mark Jacob, fruiterer, 27½ Bridge road, Lambeth
Norfor John, pilot, 2 Broad st. London docks
Norgate Fredk. foreign bookseller, see Williams & Norgate
Norie John Wm. & Co. 157 Leadenhall st. see Chas. Wilson
Norie Joseph, undertaker, 37 Hosier lane, West Smithfield
Norland Estate Office, 4 Norland terrace, Notting hill
Norley Sophia (Mrs.), grocer, 8 Bear alley, Farringdon st
Norman Chas. & John, merchants, 6 Railway pl. Fenchurch st
Norman & Duncan, bookbinders, 6 Kirby st. Hatton garden
Norman John & Son, appraisers, 2 Castle ct. Budge row
Norman Phillips & Burton, merchants, 2 New Broad st. City
Norman Abraham John, work. jeweller, 19 Wynyatt st. Gswl. rd
Norman Charles, grocer, 24½ East st. Walworth road
Norman Chr. (Mrs.), ladies' school, Stanhope pl. Hmpstd. rd
Norman Ebenezer, cabinetma. 1 Lit. Turner st. Coml. rd. east
Norman Edmond, *King's Arms* P.H. 10 Windmill st. Finsbury
Norman George, butcher, 153 Up. Whitecross st. St. Luke's
Norman George, outfitter & shirt maker, 54 Charing cross
Norman George, printer, 29 Maiden lane, Covent garden
Norman George, tailor & draper, see Wyatt & Norman
Norman Henry, banker, see Bouverie, Norman & Murdoch
Norman Henry, egg merchant, 70 Drury lane
Norman Henry Burford, surgeon, 3 Duchess st. Portland pl
Norman James, carpenter & fixture dealer, 76 Old st. road, & 19½ Bath street, Tabernacle square
Norman James, poulterer, 93 Bishopsgate without
Norman James Ormond, attorney, 89 Chancery lane
Norman John, baker, 1 Fair st. Horselydown
Norman John, baker, 13 Freeschool st. Horselydown
Norman John, carpenter & builder, 38 Gun st. Bishopsgate
Norman John, hairdresser, 3 West st. Walworth road
Norman John, ship broker & agent, 1 Water lane, Tower st
Norman John, watch jeweller, 55 Wellington st. Goswell st
Norman John Paxton, special pleader, 9 King's bench walk
Norman Joseph, coach plater, 91 Wimpole st. Cavendish sq
Norman Nichls. *Skinners' Arms* P.H. Olive ter. Cmbwl. New rd
Norman Samuel, general agent, 9 Three King ct. Lombard st
Norman Samuel, jeweller, 48 Rahere st. Goswell road
Norman Samuel, tailor, 1 Northampton pl. Canonbury sq
Norman Sarah Cath. (Mrs.), *Dover Castle* P.H. 17 Rotherhithe
Norman Thomas, chandler's shop, 30 Cole Harbour st. Hckny. rd
Norman Thomas, grocer, 19 Peerless row, Bath st. City rd
Norman Thomas, poulterer, 125 St. John street road
Norman Thomas, *Rose & Crown* P.H. 12 Lower Crown st. Westm
Norman Thomas, stationer, 37 Nicholas st. Hoxton New town
Norman Wm. launderer, 99 Hoxton Old town
Norman Wm. coffee rooms, 151 High Holborn
Norman Wm. Henry, baker, 12 Adam's place, King's rd. Chelsea
Norman Wm. Thos. engrv. on wood & printer, 28 Aldermanbury
Norman George Barton, trimming seller, 4 Crown st. Soho
Normandy Alphonse, soapma. & perfumer, 37 Skinner st. Bshpsg
Normansell & Slade, dentists, 1 Gloucester st. Portman sq
Normanton Wm. bootmaker, 2 Cecil court, St. Martin's lane
Norminton Edwin Napoleon, dyer, 23 Kenton st. Brunsw. sq
Norrie Thos. Jas. ship & ins. brok. & gen. agt. Hall of Commerce
Norrington Charles, bread & biscuit baker, 7 Ave Maria lane
Norrington Fred. lace mercht. 69 Hermitage pl. St. John st. rd
Norrington James, *British* coffee rooms, 6 Agar st. Strand
Norrington Mark Edward, machinist & smith, 53 Long alley
Norrington Michael, scale ma. 10 South st. Finsbury market
Norris, Allen & Simpson, attorneys, 19 Bartlett's bldgs. Holbn
Norris & Hearn, ale, stout & porter merchants, 12 John st. Adelphi
Norris Joseph & Son, bricklayers, 4 Gresse st. Totnhm. ct. rd
Norris & Son, engravers, &c. 16 Blomfield st. Finsbury
Norris Thos. & Sons, solicitors, 2 Bedford row, Red Lion sq
Norris Benj. boot & shoe maker, 11 Gt. Chapel st. Soho
Norris Benj. carpenter, &c. 32 Gresse st. Tottenham ct. rd
Norris Benj. Cæsar, bricklayer, 39 George st. New Kent rd
Norris Caleb, surveyor, 10 Lancaster place, Strand
Norris Charles, grocer & cheesemonger, 47 Brook st. Ratcliff
Norris Edward, tobacconist, 52 Broad st. Golden square
Norris Edward Hen. *Rose & Crown* P.H. Fort st. Spitalflds
Norris Frederick, oilman, 30 Gt. Guildford st. Borough
Norris George, butcher, 2 Warwick pl. Kingsland road
Norris George, french polshr. Queen's hd. rw. Newngtn. butts
Norris George, grocer, &c. 8 Sidney pl. King's rd. Chelsea
Norris George, shoemaker, 11 Charlotte st. Old st. road
Norris George, tailor, 41 Rosoman st. Clerkenwell
Norris Henry, beer retailer, 6 Lower st. Islington
Norris Henry, boot & shoemaker, 73 Commercial rd. Lmbth
Norris Jabez, manfg. jeweller, 32 Kirby st. Hatton garden
Norris Jas. booksel. & stationer, 1 St. George's pl. Cmbrwll. rd
Norris James, bricklayer, 7 Thatched House row, Islington
Norris James, who. statnr. & rag mercht. 207 Up. Thames st
Norris John, booksel. stationer & news agent, 58 Fetter lane
Norris John, coach proprietor, 13 Lit. Chapel st. Westmnstr
Norris John, *King's Head* P.H. 20½ Prospect pl. Cambdg. hth
Norris John, plumber, &c. 8 Dartmouth st. Westminster
Norris John Thos. who. stat. & printr. 137 & 138 Aldersgate st
Norris Joseph, commission agent, Hall of Commerce
Norris Joseph, coal merchant, 13 & 14 Middle st. Cloth fair
Norris Mary (Mrs.), milliner, 32 Southampton st. Strand
Norris Nathaniel, plumber, 12 Portland st. Soho
Norris Samuel Edward, currier, leather hose & bucket maker, &c. 58 Shadwell
Norris Sarah (Mrs.), card boxma. 23 Cavendh. st. Nw. North rd
Norris Thos. baker, 21 Pelham st. Spitalfields
Norris Thos. flax & hemp mercht. 1 William st. Newingtn. caus
Norris Thos. hosier & glover, 147½ Oxford st
Norris Thos. tailor, 7½ Boswell court, Queen square
Norris Thos. Edmund, whip ma. 5 Riding house la. Langham pl
Norris Timothy, *Jolly Anglers* P.H. Old Chapel rw. Kentish tn
Norris Whitcomb, wheelwright, 69 Market st. Paddington
Norris William, appraiser, 3 Drinkwater pl. Waterloo rd
Norris William, appraiser & estate agent, 3 Waterloo rd
Norris William, baker, 6 Chapel st. St. George's east
Norris William, builder, Mare st. Hackney
Norris William, carpenter, 12½ Up. North pl. Gray's inn rd
Norris William, carpenter, 49 William st. Regent's park
Norris William, cheesemonger, 25 Strutton ground, Westmr
Norris William, lodging house, 35 Dean st. Soho
Norris Wm. George, grocer, 19 Bolingbroke rw. Walwth. rd
Norrish Robert, baker, 111 Vauxhall st. Lambeth
Norrish William, clothier & hosier, 95 Lambeth walk
North & Bowers, linendrapers, &c. 247 Shoreditch
North & Dixon, blue mnfrs. spice dlrs. & seedsmen, City rd
North, Simpson, Graham & Co. wholesale & retail grocers & teadealers, 36 New Bridge st. Blackfriars, & 190 Fleet st
North Wm. & Geo. slate merchants & slaters, Palace New rd. Lambeth; & at Bangor wharf, Commercial rd. Lambeth

North & Light, carmen, 34 Crutched frs. & Well st. Wellclose sq
North American Colonial Association (Robert Carter, hon. sec.), 11 Leadenhall st
North American Colonial Association of Ireland (James Dewar, sec.), 7 Broad st. buildings
North American Fur Store (Thomas O'Connor, acting proprietor), 230 Regent st
North American Land Agency, 2 New Broad st. City
North American Royal Mail Steam Ships (John Bromley Foord, agent), 52 Old Broad st. City
North British Glass Co. (Cummings, Forth & Co.), works at Gateshead, 10 America square
North British Insurance Co. (B. & M. Boyd, resident directors, H. T. Thomson, sec.), 4 New Bank buildings, Lothbury; & 10 Pall mall east, Trafalgar sq. see page 2048
North Country Coal Company (Thomas Spencer Capel, manager), 42 Lombard st. & 21 Gracechurch st. & Davis's wharf, Potter's fields, Tooley st
North Kent Railway (Charles Fredk. Partington, sec.), 112 Bishopsgate st. within
North Lancashire Steam Navigation Co. 8 St. Swithin's la
North London Depository, for standing & sale of carriages & warehousing furniture, 16½ Chichester pl. King's cross
North London Junction Railway Co. (Harry Burrard Farnall, sec.), 8 Finsbury place south
North London Ophthalmic Institution for Diseases of the Eye (Richard Twining, sec.), 27 Buckingham pl. New rd
North of Scotland Life Assurance Company (secretary, Alex. Edmond), 1 Moorgate st.; see page 2040
North & South American Coffeehouse, 61 Threadneedle st
North Staffordshire Railway Co. (Jonathan Samuda, sec.), office, 1 Old Palace yard, Westminster
North Wales Railway (J. Marriner, sec. pro tem.), 3 Lothbury
North Western Trunk Railway, 3 Bond court, Walbrook
North Charles, carpenter, 16 King st. Soho
North Charles, furn. broker, 1 Queen's hd. ct. Gt. Windmill st
North David, oval turner, 23 Great Windmill st
North Edmund, hairdresser, 12 Little Grosvenor st
North Emma (Miss), milliner, 31 Dorset st. Portman sq
North Ephraim, *Bricklayers' Arms* P.H. 7 Edward st. Soho
North Geo. carman, 10 George st. Southampton st. Pentnvle
North George, painter, &c. see Ince & North
North Henry, oil & colorman, 135 Borough High st
North Horace Augustine, builder, 4 Wood st. Millbank st. Wstm
North James, carpenter & cabinet ma. 1 Flask lane, Pimlico
North James, *Rutland Arms* P.H. 32 Pearson st. Kingsland rd
North James, plumber & glazier, see Ince & North
North John, beer retailer, 142 Vauxhall walk, Lambeth
North John, fruiterer, Church st. Stoke Newington
North John, linendraper, High st. Battersea
North John, surgeon, 18 King st. Portman square
North John, turner, 15 New inn yard, Tottenham court road
North John B. *Golden Fleece* P.H. 6 Scot's pl. Lower rd. Islntn
North John Edwd. *D. of Argyle* P.H. 5 Laystall st. Liqrpond. st
North Joseph, russia tallow & barilla broker, Baltic coffee house, & 8 Artillery place west, Finsbury square
North Joseph James, beer retailer, 19 Spring st. Portman sq
North Thomas, coffee roaster, 188 Long lane, Bermondsey
North Thomas, metal piercer & drawer, maker of zinc window blinds, sash & hand lights with ventilators, zinc wire guards on a new principle, cornice gutters to any moulding ordered, &c. 159 Blackfriars road
North Wm. coal mercht. Sussex wf. Edward st. Regt's. pk. basin
North Wm. soda water maker, 15 Wellclose square
Northcote Stafford & Co. lace merchts. 32 St. Paul's ch. yd
Northcote Charles, ship agent, 16 Water lane, Tower st
Northcote Henry, tailor, 29 Mount st. Berkeley square
Northcote Rd. coachsmith, 33 Robert st. Hampstead road
Northcote Wm. *Brazen Head* P.H. 1 Up. Lisson st. Lisson gr
Northcott Wm. drug, spice & drysaltery broker, 13 Rood la
Northcroft Andrew, law stationer, 96 Chancery lane
Northcroft John, law & general stationer, 97 Chancery lane
Northedge Geo. plumber, 6 Prospect place, Old Brompton
Northen John, coffee rooms, 1 Clifford's inn passage
Northern Counties Railway Coal Co. (Thomas Ellen & R. I. Leeds, managers), 71 Great Russell st. Bloomsbury, & 2 New Farringdon st
Northern Dispensary (J. Casley, sec.), 9 Somers pl. New rd
Northern & Eastern Railway Company (William Bourne, sec.), 41 Shoreditch
Northern Railway Coal Company (Jas. Sydney, manager), 4A, Hanover st. Regent st
Northern & Southern Connection Railway Co. (William Jenkins, sec.), 71 King William st. City
Northern Trunk Railway of France (J. A. Franklin, sec.), 31 Abchurch lane
Northern Abraham, boot & boot top ma. 28 King st. Snowhill
Northey Digory, linendraper, 1 Princes st. Soho
Northfield Chas. stove grate manufr. 50 Hackney road
Northfield Robert, stove range manfac. 61 Kingsland road
Northfield Wm. John, stove manfr. 163 High st. Camden tn
Northumberland & Lancashire Junction Railway Company Office (Thomas M'Quige, sec.), 5 Gresham st. City
Northwood George, solicitor, 22 Dorset st. Portman sq
Northwood Wm. cabinet ma. &c. 5 Margaret st. Cavendish sq
Northwood Wm. dairy, 39 Fore st. City
Norton Daniel & Son, builders, 50 George st. Portman sq
Norton, Kilburn & Co. east india brokers, 16 St. Mary Axe
Norton Matthew & Son, surgeons, 16 Glo'ster pl. New rd. Mylb
Norton & Nethersole (Mesdms.), milliners, 24 Old Bond st
Norton Thomas & Son, wheelwrights, &c. 219 Upper Thames st. & Grange road, Bermondsey
Norton William Jas. & Son, solicitors, 1 New st. Bishopsgate
Norton Wm. & Son, tailors, &c. 1 Williams pl. Walworth rd
Norton Ann (Mrs.), chairmaker, 11 Carnaby st. Golden sq
Norton Ann Elizth. (Mrs.), coal mer. Belmont whf. Nine elms
Norton Arthur, wooll. agent, 7 King st. & 27 Ironmonger lane
Norton Chas. carpenter, 1 Park st. Upper st. Islington
Norton Chas. wheelwright, 5 Tottenham mews, Middx. hos
Norton Daniel, auctioneer, see Hoggart & Norton
Norton Danl. cust. house agent, London st. Fenchurch st
Norton Daniel, timber merchant, 13 Wharf, City road basin, & 23 Wharf road, City road
Norton Edward, surgeon, 29 Upper Baker st. Regent's park
Norton Elizth. (Mrs.), straw hat ma. 24 Ernest st. Regent's pk
Norton Elizth. A. (Mrs.), coalmer. 5 Belgrave pl. Wandswth. rd
Norton Francis, farrier, 9 Farm st. Berkeley square
Norton Francis, turner & brushmaker, see Frost & Norton
Norton Geo. S. law bookseller & publr. see Stevens & Norton
Norton Hon. Geo. Chapple, magistrate, Lambeth st. police ct
Norton Henry Elland, solicitor, see Barker, Rose & Norton
Norton James King, plumber, 26 New st. Brompton
Norton Jason Wilshin, wharfinger, 24 Whf. Paddington basin
Norton John, bootmaker, 10 High st. Kingsland
Norton John, japanner, 25 Vine st. Hatton wall
Norton John, ticket writer & labeller, 41 Aldermanbury
Norton Joseph, plumber & glazier, 13 Jewin st. Cripplegate
Norton Joseph, watchcasemaker, 59 Banner st. St. Luke's
Norton Joseph Emmett, wine merchant, 35 Crutched friars
Norton Louis, attorney, 43 Jewin st. Cripplegate
Norton Louisa F. (Miss), milliner, 16 Brook st. Bond st
Norton Nehemiah, *Dundee Arms* P.H. 48 Charles st. Hrslydn
Norton Rd. livery stabls. 2 College mews, College st. Westmr
Norton Richard, *William the Fourth* P.H. 137 Poplar High st
Norton Robt. tailor, 15 Lit. Charlotte st. Blackfriars road
Norton Robt. wine merchant, 36 Grove end rd. St. John's wood
Norton Robert, surgeon, 11 Oxford terrace, Hyde park
Norton Robert James, tailor, hosier & outfitter, 72 Strand
Norton Robert Jas. (Mrs.), readymade linen wa. 72 Strand
Norton Samuel, farrier, 40 Brewer st. Pimlico
Norton Samuel, umbrella maker, 40 Church st. Shoreditch
Norton Sam. Duncan, *White Swan* P.H. 141 Wapping High st
Norton Sophia (Miss), milliner, 48 Marchmont st. Brunswk. sq
Norton Susannah (Mrs.), milliner, 24 Red Lion st. Holborn
Norton Thomas, *Black Horse & Crown* P.H. 235 Boro' High st
Norton Wm. hosier & laceman, 3 Up. Copenhagen st. Pentonvl
Norton William, merchant, see Rawson, Norton & Co
Norton William, solicitor, 11 South square, Gray's inn
Norton William, tailor, 3 Water st. Blackfriars
Norton William, tobacconist, 219 Whitechapel road
Norton Wm. wine mercht. 3 Walbrook buildings, Walbrook
Norton Wm. Hy. button & trimming seller, 249 Strand
Norvell Chas. Fred. spectacle ma. 8 Maidenhd. ct. Aldrsgt. st
Norvell Henry Nath. tobacnst. & newsvndr. 47½ York st. City rd
Norville William, hat & umbrella manufacturer, 40 Cornhill
Norwich & Brandon Rlwy. Co. (R. Till, mngr.), Guildall. bdgs
Norwich Union Fire & Life Office (Samuel Bignold, sec.), 6 Crescent, New Bridge st. Blackfriars; see page 2039
Norwich Union Insurance Office, 26 Birchin lane, Cornhill
Norwich Union Reversionary Interest Co. (Henry Norris, sec.), 23 Lincoln's inn fields
Norwich & West Norfolk Railway Co. 28 Poultry
Norwood Cemetery Company's Offi. (Griffith Thomas, clk.), 70 King Wm. st. City; cemetery, oppste. St. Luke's ch. Nrwd
Norwood Charles, coffee rooms, 20 Bedford st. Bedford row
Norwood Chas. paperhanging manufr. 13 Bridport pl. New North road, & Beauvoir manufactory, Rosemary brnch. bdg
Norwood John, grocer, 2 Lit. Sussex pl. Hyde pk. gardens
Nosotti Charles Andrew, looking glass ma. 398 Oxford st
Nossoc Alexander, dentist, 26 Percy st. Tottenham ct. rd
Nosworthy & Wells, lithographers in every department of the art, & litho. press manufactrs. 72 Coleman st. Bank

Nosworthy Joseph, bootmaker, 11 Clement's inn pas. Cla. mkt
Nosworthy Thomas L. leather seller, 18 Newton st. Holborn
Notley & Beattie, pawnbrokers, &c. 8 Portman st. Portmn. sq
Notley Mary Ann & Son, carpenters, 12 Creed la. Ludgate st
Notley Edward, coal & potato dlr. 187 Brick la. Spitalfields
Notley Henry, brushmaker, 5 Trump st. Cheapside
Notley John, builder, &c. 9 Old Dorset pl. Clapham road
Notley John, solicitor, 51 Lime st
Notley Joseph, general salesman, 23 Grosvenor row, Pimlico
Notley Thomas, butcher, 59 Robin Hood lane, Poplar
Notman Wm.&Co. who.& ret. teadlrs. 20 Bishopsgate without
Noton Thomas, hosier, &c. 8½ Kennington cross
Nott Edwin, bonnet presser, 56 Drury lane
Nott Francis, clothes salesman, 66 Marylebone la. Oxford st
Nott Geo. builder, apprais. & underta. 23 Cornwall rd. Lmbth
Nott Harriet (Mrs.), milliner, 56 Drury lane
Nott James, hairdresser, 81 Bridge road, Lambeth
Nott Peter, grocer & cheesemonger, 43 Chicksand st. Whitec
Nott Randolph, surveyor, 10 Church st. Camberwell
Nott Thomas, greengrocer, 73 Wardour st. Soho
Nottage Thos. & Wm. *Green Dragon stables*, Worship st. Fnsb
Nottage Mary (Mrs.), *Blue Anchor* P.H. 17 Road side, Mile e. rd
Nottidge William, wool stapler, Russell st. Bermondsey
Notting Sophia (Mrs.), greengrocer, 138 St. John st. road
Nottingham & Boston Railway Off. 14 Birchin la. Cornhill
Nottingham Matthew, custom house & coml. agt. & agt. for patent welded iron tubes for multitubular boilers, gas, &c. & for lamps, chandeliers & gas fittings, 14 Fish st. hill
Nott's patent stove Co. 80 Gt. Queen st. Lincoln's inn fields
Noulton & Wild, boat builders, 63 Lower Fore st. Lambeth
Novelli, Watson & Seaton, merchants, 16 St. Mary Axe
Novello Joseph Alfred, music seller, 69 Dean st. Soho
Novello Robert, bookseller & publisher, 78 Long acre
Novis Benjamin, chemist & druggist, 2 Lower st. Islington
Novis Thomas, chemist, &c. 60 George st. Portman sq
Novra Geo. perfumer & import. of for. goods. 95 Regent st
Nowell John & Co. patent chemical works, Battersea
Nowell Philip & Sons, masons & bldrs. Grosvnr. wf. Wilton rd
Nowell Saml. builder & contractor, Grosvenor wf. Pimlico
Nowell William, tobacconist, 8 Friar st. Blackfriars road
Nowell Wm. Hen. brushma. & bristle mer. 7 Brick la. Sptlfl
Nowland Elizh. (Mrs.), shell fishmonger, 16 Little Carter la
Noy Edward Hampton, solicitor, 59 Fenchurch st
Noyes George Henry, surgeon, see Reynolds & Noyes
Noyes James John, grocer & teadealer, 5 Finsbury pl. north
Noyes John, lodging house, 2 Portsea pl. Connaught sq
Noyes Robert, house agent, painter, &c. 1 Grove terrace, & 1 New Church st. Lisson grove
Noyes Saml. Fred. solicitor, see Hodgson, Concanen & Noyes
Noyes Samuel, ironmonger & smith, 17 Spring st. Paddington
Noyes Thomas, cotton broker, 4 Dunster court, Mincing la
Nugent Edmund Lynch, barrister, 22 Chancery lane
Nugent Jas. biscuit baker & pastrycook, 134 Up. st. Islington
Nugent John, dairyman, 6 St. Thomas pl. Old Kent rd
Nugent Thos. lodging house, 4 Northumberland ct. Strand
Numismatic Society of London (Rev. Henry Christmas, hon. sec.) 41 Tavistock st. Covent garden
Nun William, bootmaker, 18 Duke's court, Bow st
Nunes John, stock & share broker, 33 Clements lane, City
Nunes Raffael, west india mer. 3 Crown ct. Threadneedle st
Nunez David, carpenter & blind ma. 9 Butcher's row, Ratcliff
Nunez Manuel Augustine, merchant, 12 Old Jewry chambrs
Nunn James & Co. straw, leghorn, & chip bonnet manufacturers, milliners, &c. 17 Baker st. Portman sq
Nunn Charles, jun. & Co. linendrapers, 35 Aldersgate st
Nunn Henry Wm. & Co. lace manufs. 21 Lawrence la. Cheaps
Nunn Thos. & Co. cigar & tobac. ma. 5 Rodney bdgs. N. Knt. r
Nunn Thos. & Sons, teadealers, grocers, oil & italian warehousemen & coal merchants, 19 Great James st. Bedford row, & St. Ann's wharf, Earl st. Blackfriars
Nunn Alexander, manufacturer of all articles used in the artificial flower business, 19 Fore st. City
Nunn Edith (Mrs.), bread & biscuit baker, 86 Prattst. Cmdn. tn
Nunn Elizabeth (Mrs.), milliner, 96 Shoreditch High st
Nunn Herbert, straw bonnet wa. 130 Mount st. Berkeley sq
Nunn James, furniture broker, 43 Exeter st. Lisson grove
Nunn Joseph, jobmaster, 2 Deptford High st
Nunn Joshua, boot & shoe maker, 21 Lisson grove, North
Nunn Martin, childbed linen wa. 259 Regent circus, Oxford st
Nunn Richard, goldsmith, &c. 9 President st. east, King sq
Nunn Rd. Coleman, carpntr. & undrt. 7 Providence terrace, Plummer's row
Nunn Samuel, surgeon, 6 Duke st. Westminster
Nunn Thos. Willett, wine mercht. 18 St. John's sq. Clerkenwell
Nunn William, architect & surveyor, 73 Basinghall st
Nunn William, oilman, 20 Hackney road
Nunn William, carver & gilder, Church st. Hackney
Nunn William, fire wood merchant, 17 Arthur st. Chelsea
Nunnery Henry, grocer, 265, & *Half Moon* P.H. 267 Rotherhithe st
Nunney Henry, *Portland Arms* P.H. 2 Long la. Smithfield
Nunney Thos. F. *Duke of York* P.H. 14 Glo'ster st. Clerknw
Nurdin & Peacock, egg merchants, 12 Berwick st. Soho
Nurse & Warren, coachmakers, 43 Crawford st. Portman sq
Nurse David, broker, 31 Chalton st. Somers town
Nurse Edward, plumber, 11 Saville st. Foley st. Fitzroy sq
Nurse Hen. carver & gilder, 10 Old Cavendish st. Oxford st
Nurse Mary (Mrs.), *Essex Serpent* P.H. 42 Charles st. Westm
Nurse Richard, shopkeeper, 10 Gibraltar wk. Bethnl. gr. rd
Nursey Benjn. tallow chandler, 1 Whitehall pl. Kentish town
Nurton George, printer, 48 New Church st. Lisson grove
Nussey & Du Pasquier, apothecaries, 4 Cleveland rw. St. Jas's
Nutchey James, turner, 5 West st. Soho square
Nutkins & Churcher, glass cutters, 6 Marylebone la. Oxford st
Nutkins John, lighterman, 46 Great Hermitage st. Wapping
Nutkins William, butcher, 5½ Gloucester ter. Old Brompton
Nutley Elizh. (Miss), shoemaker, 1 Hardwick pl. Coml. rd. ea
Nutley Thomas, *Broad Arrow* P.H. 88 Milton st. Cripplegate
Nutt David, foreign bookseller, 158 Fleet st
Nutt James, *George & Gate* P.H. 15 Gracechurch st
Nutt John, *Old Bell* P.H. 7 Little Friday st. Cheapside
Nutt Thomas, plumber, painter, paperhanger, &c. 3 Eastcheap
Nutt William, bookbinder, 12 Craven bldgs. Drury lane
Nutt William, turner & bed pillar carver, 15 High st. St. Giles's
Nuttall Samuel & Co. ribbon manufs. 110 Wood st. Cheapside
Nuttall Lawrence, stablekeeper, 4 Adam's mews, Grosvenor sq
Nutter Reymes, cast & bound reed & slay ma. 16 Gun st. Bishpsg
Nutter Richard W. wholesale cheesemgr. see Merry & Nutter
Nutter Whitaker, cheesemonger, 12 Whitechapel High st
Nutting & Wood, pianoforte manfrs. 74 Great Titchfield st
Nutting Henry, who. straw hat ma. 37 Noble st. Cheapside
Nutting John G. button maker, &c. Regent st. Horseferry rd
Nutting Joseph, umbrella maker, 8 Gray's inn passage
Nutting Wm. Jas. seedsmn. 24½ Up Thames st. & 46 Cheapside
Nuttman Benjamin, corndealer, 20 Old Bailey
Nye Edward, boot & shoe maker, 232 Poplar High st
Nye Edwin, stationer & news agent, 8 Orange st. Red Lion sq
Nye James, grocer, 51 Walnutt Tree walk, Lambeth
Nye John, carpenter & builder, 8 Bull court, Tooley st
Nye Jsph. surgical inst. maker, 19 Alfred pl. Newgtn. causwy
Nye Richard, fruit salesman, Spitalfields market
Nye Samuel, surgeons' inst. ma. 16 St. Andrew's rd. Boro'
Nye William, tobacconist, 5 Bermondsey New road
Nye William, wine merchant, 3 New London st. City

OAK Henry, butcher, 36 Kensington High st
Oakden Robert, baker, 31 Union st. Hackney rd
Oakden Robt. *Marquis Granby* P.H. 19 West st. Seven dials
Oakes, Dalgairns & Co. e. i. merchants, 20 Austin Friars
Oakes Robert, *Hour Glass* P.H. 87 Upper Thames st
Oakes Elizh. (Mrs.), strawbonnetma. 3 Orangerow, Kenntn. rd
Oakes Samuel, butcher, New cross
Oakes Thomas, bristle assorter, 8 York place, Pentonville
Oakes Thomas, coal merchant, see Jones & Oakes
Oakes William, boot & shoe maker, 1 Wells row, Islington
Oakeshott Wm. engine turner, 29 St. John st. Clerkenwell
Oakey W. H. & J. hat dyers, Prince's square, Finsbury
Oakey W. H. & J. wholes. hat manufrs. 10 Forest. Cripplegate
Oakey John, emery paper man. 34 Francis st. Newgtn. butts
Oakford John, tailor, 140 Grove st. Camden town
Oakley & Son, tailors & drap. 6 St. Dunstan's pas. Low Thams. st
Oakley Geo. builder, 16 Albion terrace, Wandsworth rd
Oakley Geo. Wm. chemist, &c. 35 Lamb st. Spitalfields
Oakley Henry, cheesemonger, 2 Lamb st. Spitalfields
Oakley Henry, tailor, &c. see Giles & Oakley
Oakley Henry, tailor, 4 Three Crown square, Borough
Oakley John, bootmaker, 36 Berwick st. Soho
Oakley John, engineer, 4 Upper Grange walk, Bermondsey
Oakley John, fender ma. 3 Triangle pl. Camb. rd. Mile end
Oakley John, wine mercht. see Coleman, Flockhart, & Co
Oakley John Allen, shoemaker, Morning lane, Hackney
Oakley Octavius, artist, 3 Bentinck st. Manchester sq
Oakley Richard Ravenhill, stockbroker, 3 Bartholomew la
Oakley Thomas, currier, 31 St. Martin's lane, Charing cross
Oakley Wm. teadealer & grocer, 72 Whitechapel High st
Oakly & Mitchell, engravers, 7 St. James's st. Clerkenwell
Oakshatt James, carpenter, &c. see Little & Oakshatt
Oates Ann (Mrs.), boarding house, 2 Charles st. Commercl. rd
Oates John, tailor, 8 Tavistock row, Covent garden
Oates Parkinson, surgeon, 17 Tavistock pl. Tavistock sq
Oatley Wm. & Sons, plumbers, painters, &c. 25 Aldermanbury
Oats Joseph, cabinet maker & undertaker, 187 Drury lane

Obbard Rt. & Jph. & Co.glass & lead mers. 2 Crescent, Blkfrs
Obbard Wm. Robert, tobacconist, 10 King st. Westminster
Oborne Aaron, carpenter & undertaker, 64 New rd. Sloane st
Oborne Benjamin, philosophical instrument maker, & mechanical modeller, 11 Guildford st. east, Spafields
Oborne Charles, carpenter, 33 Exeter st. Sloane st. Chelsea
Oborne Charles, furniture broker, 31 Exeter st. Sloane st
Oborne Wm. oilman, 7 St. Martin's st. Leicester square
Obre Benj. potato warehouse, 19 Blandford st. Portman sq
Obré Henry, surgeon, 31 Grove place, Lisson grove north
O'Brien, Pearce & Co. printers, 16 Thomas st. Horselydown
O'Brien Francis, tobacconist, 10 Cursitor st. Chancery lane
O'Brien John Waters, lodging ho. 2 Carpenter st. Berkly.sq
O'Brien Martin, water & watch gilder, 2 Allen st. Goswell st
O'Brien Michael William, barrister, 7 Gray's inn place
Observer weekly newspaper Office, 170 Strand
O'Brien Nich. *King's Head* P.H. 7 Cumberland st. Midx.hsptl
Occleston John, haberdasher & hosier, 5 Brook st. Ratcliff
Ocheltree John, farrier, North place, Kingsland road
Ochsé Jacob, stock & hat manufacturer & general agent, 30 Chiswell st. Finsbury
Ockendon William, bootmaker, 90 Poplar High st
Ockerby Horatio, law stationer, see Manby & Ockerby
Ockleford John, locksmith, &c. Blue Anchor rd. Bermondsey
Ocock Wm. chemist & druggist, 36 Judd st. Brunswick sq
O'Connor Edmond, fruiterer, 52 Gt. Peter st. Westminster
O'Connor James, plasterer, 5 Great Trinity lane
O'Connor James, *Rose & Crown* P.H. 16 High rd. Kngtsbdge
O'Connor Jeremiah, *Grapes* P.H. 14 White st. Borough
O'Connor John, coal dealer & greengrocer, 62 Edgware road
O'Connor Michael, stained glass wks. 4 Berners st. Oxford st
O'Connor Wm. surgeon & accoucheur, 21 George st. Portman sq
O'Connor William, surgeon, 18 Hatton wall
Odam John, boot & shoe maker, 37 King's rd. east, Chelsea
Odam John, hairdresser, 2 Samson's pl. Grange rd. Bermondsy
Odam John, tailor & trouser ma. 11 Rupert st. Haymarket
Odam Thomas, fruiterer, 4 Bailey's pl. Marlboro' rd. Chelsea
Oddie, Lumley & Co. solicitors, 18 Carey st. Lincoln's inn
Oddie Richard Harby, barrister, 1 New court, Temple
Oddy James, cheesemonger, 22 James st. Covent garden
Oddy James, *Volunteer* P.H. 1 Rose lane, Commercial road
Oddy Henry Ozias, hairdresser, 31 Fetter lane, Holborn
Oddy Richard, *Queen Adelaide* P.H. 9 Ivy lane, Hoxton
Odell & Atherly, gold lace manufs. 71 & 72 Burlington arcade
Odell Abraham, tailor, 108 Upper st. Islington
Odell Bennett, job master, 42 Keppel mews north, Russell sq
Odell George, letterpress printer, &c. 24 Tavistock st. Cov.gdn
Odell George, printer, 18 Princes st. Cavendish square
Odell Islip, brick maker, Queen's road, Dalston
Odell James, *Saracen's Head Tavern*, 5 Aldgate
Odell Samuel, shipping & custom house agent, 70 Lower Thames st. & Griffin's wharf, Tooley st
Odell Thomas, dairy, 5 Bathurst mews, Bathurst st. Hyde pk
Odell William, dairy, 8 Upper Marylebone st
Odlin Henry, boot & shoe maker, 2 Grange road, Bermondsey
Odling Francis, surgeon, &c. 26 Oxford st
Odling George, surgeon & chemist, 159 Borough High st
O'Donnell Agnes (Mrs.), artificial florist, 47 Monkwell st
O'Donnell John, lathe & tool maker, 1 Peter st. Saffron hill
O'Donnoghue Florence, hat mfr. 9 Cross la. Newton st. Holbn
Ody John & Son, patent truss makers, 292 Strand
Ody George H. plumber & glazier, 10 Poppin's ct. Fleet st
Ody John, patent water closet manufacturer, 292 Strand
Ody Richard, fruiterer, 4 Pleasant place, Holloway
Oelrichs George H. merchant, 46 Commercial sale rooms
Oetzmann & Plumb, pianoforte manufrs. 22 Huntley st
Offen James, carver & gilder, 2 Short st. Finsbury
Offer John, tailor, &c. 3 Shepherd's market, Mayfair
Offer Thomas, poulterer, 44 Lamb's Conduit st
Office for the Registration of Joint Stock Companies (Frederick Rogers, registrar), 11 Serjeants' inn, Fleet st
Office of Mixed "British & Portuguese Commission," 3 Delahay st. Westminster
Office of Works, Guildhall; hours 9 to 5
Office for Patents, William Newton & Son, agents for obtaining patents for inventions in the british dominions & foreign countries, with economy & dispatch, 66 Chancery la
Office for Sailors (Capt. Geo. Pierce, R.N. secretary), 23 Well st. Wellclose square
Office of the Proprietors of Sir Wm. Burnett's patent for the preservation of timber, canvas, cordage, cotton, woollen, &c. from dry rot, mildew, moth, & premature decay (Charles Jackson, sec.), 53 King William st. Lndn.bdg. *Hydraulic apparatus & tanks for the expeditious preparation of the above materials*, at Millwall, Poplar, nearly opposite Greenwich
Office of the Commissioners for the Registration & Regulation of Coal Whippers in the Port of London (Chas. C. Robberd, clerk), King James stairs, Wapping wall; hours from 7 A.M. to 6 P.M
Offley, Webber, Forrester & Co. portugal merchants, 36 New Broad st. City
Offley Chas. Hen. *Offley's tavern*, 23 Henrietta st. Cov. gar
Offley George, attorney, 24 Henrietta st. Covent garden
Offlow Thomas, *Royal George* P.H. New st. Kennington
Offord George, saddler, &c. 71 Sun st. Bishopsgate
Offord Henry, library, 3 Wheeler pl. Haverstck.hl. Hmpstd.rd
Offord Robt. coach & harness maker, 79 Wells st. Oxford st
Offord Sophia (Mrs.), grocer, 101 White Lion st. Pentonville
Ogan William, bootmaker, Church st. Hackney
Ogbourne Wm. W. accountant, &c. 4 Pancras lane, City
Ogden Fredk. last & boot tree ma. 66 Princes st. Leicester sq
Ogden James, goldsmith & jeweller, 11 St. James' wk. Clerknwll
Ogden Wm. Henry, blackwell hall factor, 7 Basinghall st
Ogers Luke B. painter & sew.cott.ma. 11 Brown's la. Spitalfids
Ogg George, baker, 43 Upper North place, Gray's inn road
Ogg George, pro. of languages, 2 Pelham tr. Pelham rd. Bromp
Ogg John Alex. newspaper agent, 4 Lillypot la. Noble st
Ogg (Mrs.), ladies' school, 18 Whitehead's grove, Chelsea
Ogier John C. H. barrister, 46 Carey st. Lincoln's inn
Ogier Peter, barrister, 46 Carey st. Lincoln's inn
Ogilby, Moore & Co. ship & ins. brk. 3 Ingram ct. Fenchurch st
Ogilby Henry, mast maker, Millwall, Poplar
Ogilby William, barrister, 19 Gower st. Bedford square
Ogilvie William, pawnbroker, see French & Ogilvie
Ogilvy John, pomade divine warehouse, 284 Regent st
Ogilvy William, printer, see Wilson & Ogilvy
Ogilwy George, painter & glazier, 5 Judd st. Brunswick sq
Ogilwy Robt. compositn. doll ma. 54 Tabernacle wk. Finsbury
Ogle & Younghusband, solicitors, 4 Great Winchester st
Ogle Charles, tailor, 55 Mount st. Berkeley square
Ogle Edmund, *Pitt's Hd.* P.H. Brnswk.mws. Cmbrld.st. Ptm. s
Ogle Edward, surgeon, 25 South st. Grosvenor square
Ogle John, preparatory school, Loudoun rd. St. John's wood
Ogle Richard, barrister, 2 Paper buildings, Temple
Ogleby Charles & Co. oil merchts. 53 Paradise st. Lambeth
Oglesby Edwd. coffee rooms, 32 Lit. Bell alley, Coleman st
Oglethorpe Mary (Miss), milliner, 33 Edwards st. Prtmn. sq
O'Hara John, bootmaker, 7 Conduit st. Regent st
Ohler Marten, baker, 9 Harleyford st. Kennington common
Ohlson Frederick, teadealer, 56 Albion st. Rotherhithe
Oiley James, wholesa. widows' milliner, 102 Aldersgate st
O'Keefe David, carpenter, 67 New road, Sloane st
O'Keefe Michl. beer retailer, 23 Hamilton row, Bgng.wls.rd
Oke William, builder & furnit. broker, 7 Bloomsbury market
Okey Mary & Son, glass benders, 54 Turnmill st. Clerkenwell
Okey Mary (Mrs.), *Blue Cross* coffeerooms, 20 Newgate mrkt
Okey Nath. Fred. *Hero of Waterloo* P.H. 56 Basing pl. Watrl.rd
Okey Thomas, basket maker & rod merchant, 11 Hart st. Crutched friars, & 16 Quaker st. Spitalfields
Old Corn Market Company (Thos. Levick, sec.), Mark lane
Old Swan Pier, 64 Paradise row, Chelsea
Old David, baker, 19 Old Bailey
Old Thomas T. surgeon, 18 David st. York pl. Marylebone
Old Trenham jun. fish factor, 9 Billingsgate, & Salutation court, Lower Thames st
Oldaker Wm. & Thos. hop & seed merchts. 90 Boro' High st
Oldaker Ann (Mrs.), *King's Head* P.H. 42 Threadneedle st
Oldaker Fitzharding, saddler & harness ma. 16 Finsbury pl. nth
Oldaker Thomas, coach broker, 1 Homer st. Marylebone
Oldbury Thomas, *Hand & Racket* P.H. 21 Whitcomb st
Oldershaw Augustus Piggott, proctor, 11½ Great Carter la
Oldershaw Rt. solicitor, 18 King's Arms yard, & Lr. st. Islngtn
Oldershaw Wm. bricklayer & builder, Brunswick st. Trinity sq
Oldershaw Wm. Watson, solicitor, 7 Tokenhouse yd. Lothbury
Oldfield Frederick H. & Co. wine mer. 14 Dorset st. Porman sq
Oldfield Edmund, barrister, 35 Lincoln's inn fields
Oldfield Elisha, saddler, 1 Motcomb st. Belgrave sq
Oldfield George, wine merchant, 16 Adam st. Adelphi
Oldfield Hen. chemist & druggist, 11 Southamptn. st. Cambwl
Oldfield Jesse, pub. of Cobbett's works, 11 Bolt ct. Fleet st
Oldfield John, butcher, 124 Brick lane, Spitalfields
Oldfield Mary (Mrs.), dairy, Thornhill road, Islington
Oldfield Rich. bellows mak. 68 Cowcross st. West Smithfield
Oldfield Thos. Brame, merchant, 10 George yd. Lombard st
Oldham Elizth. & Son, tallowchndlrs. 33 & 34 Thomas st. Hack.rd
Oldham Benjamin, woolbroker, see M'Glew & Oldham
Oldham George, boot and shoe maker, Camberwell green
Oldham Henry, cutler, 10 High st. St. Giles's
Oldham Henry, surgeon, 13 Devonshire sq. Bishopsgate
Oldham James, silk & stock manfr. 76 Wood st. Cheapside
Oldham John, currier, 36 Long acre

Oldham Wm. (of Cadiz), wine merchant, 3 New London st
Olding Ebenezer, upholsterer & undertaker, 71 Fleet st.
OldingElizth.S.(Mrs.),furn.ironmonger,81 Bishopsgatewithin
Oldis Thomas, plumber, 61 Basinghall st
Oldknow Samuel, solicitor, 1 Chapel st. Bedford row
Oldknow Sarah (Miss), linendraper, 1 Berkeley st. Lambeth
Oldman L.&Co.imp.offor.goods&agts.10LawrencePountnyhl
Oldrey Richard, tobacconist, 3 Wellington ter. Bayswater
Oldrey Thomas cigar manufacturer, 102 St. Martin's lane
Oldridge Cyrus & Alfred, balm of Columbia warehouse, 1 Wellington st. Strand
Oldridge Chas. bookbinder, 3 Flying Horse court, Gresham st
Oldridge Wm. account book maker, 40 New cut, Lambeth
Oldroyd, Hodgson & Morton, warehousemen, 64&65 Bread st
O'Leary James & Co. merchants, 13 Mincing lane
O'Leary Arth.lever watch pallet mak. 12 Powell st.e.King sq
Oliffe Saml. & Co. fishmongers, 49 Gt. Russell st. Bloomsby
Oliphant Jas. army cap & accoutrement mak. 14 Cockspur st
Oliphant George Henry Hewit, barrister, 1 Elm ct. Temple
Oliphant William, watchmaker, 7 Parker's row, Dockhead
Olive Joseph, solicitor, 3 Warwick place, Bedford row
Oliveira, Liddle & Co. wine merchants, 10 Cullum st. & 67 Princes st. Soho
Oliveira John, madeira merchant, 24 Mark lane
Oliveira Joze A. G. mercht. 18 Langbourn chambs. Fench. st
Oliver Worthington&Oliver&Co.warehsemen.7&8Aldrmnbry
Oliver George & Joseph, ironmongers, coppersmiths & tin plate workers, 286 Wapping
Oliver Geo. & Son, accountants, &c. 7 Lawrence la. Cheapsi
Oliver & Goodge, fruiterers, 1 High st. Notting hill
Oliver & Green, importers of for. silks, 18 Cork st.Bond st
Oliver & Green, *Black Horse* P.H. 5 Tichborne st. Haymrkt
Oliver & Lindsell, solicitors, Moorgate st. chambers
Oliver Richard & Co. hatters, 260 Oxford st
Oliver Sam.& Son, silk card design. 12New Montagu st. Sptlfi
Oliver Chas. jun. clock ma.& bellfndr.7&8 Green st.Bthnl gr
Oliver David, *Load of Hay* P.H. 62 Praed st. Paddington
Oliver Ebenezer, boot & shoe ma. 16 Up. Glo'ster pl. Chelsea
Oliver Francis, tobacconist, 70 Wilsted st. Somers town
Oliver Frederick, umbrella maker, 25 Hampstead road
Oliver George, fruiterer, 31 Westbourne st. Pimlico
Oliver George, orange merchant, Centre row, Covent garden
Oliver Henry, painter, 15 & 16 Little Barlow st
Oliver Hen.proctor, 3 Gt.Knightrider st. Doctors' commons
Oliver Isaac, writer & marbler, 52 Up. John st. Fitzroy sq
Oliver James, boot & shoemaker, 118 Bishopsgate without; 3 Newington causeway; 3 Lowndes terrace, Knightsbridge; & 12 Deptford bridge
Oliver James, bootmaker, 102 Borough High st
Oliver James, builder, 8 Osborne st. Whitechapel
Oliver James, carpenter, 15 Christian st. St. George's east
Oliver James, grocer, Battersea
Oliver James, plumber & glazier, 26 Duke st. St. James's
Oliver John, anchorsmith, ironmgr.&brazier, 56 Wapping wall
Oliver John, boot&shoe maker, 7Steyman's row, Holloway rd
Oliver John, cabinet manufacturer, 10 City road, Old st
Oliver John, cabinet maker, 7 Upper Clifton st. Finsbury
Oliver John, fixture dealer, 13 Castle st. Long acre
Oliver John, plumber & glazier, 40 Queen's road, Bayswater
Oliver John, stationer, 234 Poplar High st
Oliver John, wholesale oilman, 33 Whitechapel road
Oliver John, working jeweller, 41 New Glo'ster st. Hoxton
Oliver Jsph. Hanby, who. & ret. grocer, 380 Rotherhithe wall
Oliver Lionel, barrister, 4 Old square, Lincoln's inn
Oliver Michael, mast & block maker, 329 Wapping High st
Oliver Nevil, linendraper, 297 High Holborn
Oliver Nolan, solicitor, 18 Austin friars
Oliver Richd. diamond setter, 3 Woodbridge st. Clerkenwell
Oliver Richd. grocer, 1 Bridge road, Mile end
Oliver Robert, engraver & printer, 56 Rupert st. Haymarket
Oliver Robert, ironmonger, 40 Kensington High st
Oliver Samuel, attorney, 83 Hatton garden
Oliver Samuel, rope manufacturer, 296 Kent st. Borough
Oliver Sarah (Miss), pearl stringer & hair work. 54 Hatton gar
Oliver Susanna (Mrs.), *Portugal hotel*, 155 & 156 Fleet st. & *Tap* P.H. 9 Bolt court, Fleet st
Oliver Thomas, bootmaker, 2 Swan st. Borough
Oliver Thomas, boot & shoe maker, 35 Stafford pl. Pimlico
Oliver Thos. *Drummond Arms tav.* 35 Drummond st
Oliver Thomas, fruiterer & herbalist, 1 Portman market; & 27 New Church st. Lisson grove
Oliver Thomas, saddler & accoutremt. ma. 81 Bermondsey st
Oliver Thomas, solicitor, 36 Old Jewry
Oliver Thomas, tailor, 11 Gt. James st. Hoxton
Oliver Thomas Francis, barrister, 1 Plowden bldgs. Temple
Oliver Wm. artist, 39 Manchester st. Manchester sq
Oliver Wm. butcher, 4 Turnmill st. Clerkenwell
Oliver Wm. cabinet mak. 10 Somers town ter. Clarendon sq
Oliver Wm. *Crown* P.H. Spa road, Bermondsey
Oliver Wm. mahogany & timber merchant, 6 Kingsland rd
Oliver Wm. Cooper, stationer & toy dlr. 90 HoxtonOld town
Oliver Wm. Disney, barrister, 3 Plowden buildings, Temple
Oliver Wm. Elliott, solicitor, 16 New Bridge st. Blackfriars
Oliver Wm.Hy. *Duke of Clarence* P.H. Penton pl. Walworth
Olivers Hannah (Mrs.), grocer, 40 Charles st. Westminster
Oliverson, Denby&Lavie, attorneys, 8Frederick's pl. Old Jewry
Oliverson Richd. & Robt. insurance broks. 5 Warnford ct
Olivey James, bootmaker, 20 East st. Walworth road
Olivier Chas. Hen. merchant & genl. agent, 37 Finsbury sq
Oliviera, Liddle & Co. wine merchants, 10 Cullum st. Fenchurch st. & 67 Princes st. Soho
Olivieri Dominico Andrea, sculptor, 18 Wardour st. Soho
Olley & Bridger, coal merchts. for best coals only, & charcl. brnrs. (late Windle&Co.), Dockhead whf. 52 Shad Thames
Olley George, greengrocer, 60 Union st. Somers town
Olley John, bootmaker, 34 Curtain road, Shoreditch
Olley John, pawnbroker, 43 Poplar High st
Olley John, tailor, 13 Whitmore road, Hoxton
Olley John, vellum binder, 38 Gracechurch st
Olley Philip, beer retailer, 23 Gt. James st. Lisson grove
Olley Thomas, cabinet maker, 21 Buckingham pl. Fitzroy sq
Olley Thomas, coal dealer, 21 Jewin st. Cripplegate
Olley Thomas, *Fishing Smack* P.H. King st. Deptford
Olley Thomas, wine merchant, 2 Brabant ct. Philpot lane
Olley Thos. Geo. cabinet, chair & spiral tur. 98 Norton st
Ollier John & Co. ship & insurance brokers, 9 New East India chambers, Leadenhall st
Olliff Wm. *HarmoodArms* P.H. 29 Harmood st. Hampstead rd
Ollive Edw. Nephew & Co. merchants, 6 West st. Finsbury
Ollive William, earthenwareman, 3 Holland st. Blackfrs. rd
Ollivier Ann & Harriet (Misses), milliners, court dress, corset & linen makers, 54 Pall mall
Ollivier & Brown, tailors, 6 Bolton st. Piccadilly
Ollivier Charles, royal musical repository & circulating musical library, 41 & 42 New Bond st
Ollivier John, bookseller, publisher & stationer, 59 Pall mall
Olman Thomas, furn. broker, 8 Portpool la. Gray's inn lane
Olney Edward, fruiterer, 223 Whitechapel road
Olney Thos. & Co. haberdashers, 139 & 140 Borough High st
Olney Thos. *Silver Cup* P.H. 51 Cromer st. Brunswick sq
Olorenshaw John, baker, 29 Portland st. Soho
Olrod Ann (Mrs.), baker, 24 Bolingbroke row, Walworth rd
Olsen Else (Mrs.), grocer & cheesemgr. 47 College st. Chels
Olyett Robert Wm. carpenter, Deptford green
Olympic Theatre, Wych st. Strand
O'Malley Peter Frederic, barrister, 1 New court, Temple
Omer James, glass cutter, 35 Kirby st. Hatton garden
Omer John, carver & gilder, 18 Howland st. Fitzroy square
Ommanney, Son & Co. navy agents, 22 Norfolk st. Strand
Ommanney Francis, solicitor, see Sutton, Ewins & Co
Omoa Iron Office (Wm. S. Lindsey, agent), 35 Abchurch la
O'Neil Charles, artist, 33 Golden square
O'Neill & Smythe, wine merchants, 30 Crosby hall chambrs
O'Neill Francis, tailor, 29 Upper Park place, Dorset sq
O'Neill Luke, bootmaker, 8 Spread Eagle court, Finch lane
Ongley Edward, blacking ma. 14 Crescent, Southwark bdg. rd
Ongley Thomas, *Cock* P.H. Camberwell green
Onion Stphn.G.&Co. gilt jewel.& brit. plateworker, 50Skinnerst
Onions Aaron, ironfounder, 8½ Coppice row, Clerkenwell
Onions John, working jeweller, 2 Benjamin st. Clerkenwell
Onken Charles, coach builder, 231 Whitechapel road
Onley Thomas, grocer, 14 Lower George st. Chelsea
Onslow Richd. dep. clk. of peace for Surrey, 1 North st. Lamb
Onslow Thos. butcher, Bull's Head pas. Leadenhall market
Onwhyn Joseph, booksel.& news agent, 4 Catherine st. Strand
Onyon, Holt & Nash, woollen facs. & drapers, 15 & 16 Aldgate
Operative Jewish Converts' Institution (Rev. J. Reichardt, master), 13 & 14 Palestine place, Cambridge road
Opthalmic Hospital (Thos. Rt. Fowler, R.N. sec.), 19 King William st. Strand
Oporto Royal Wine Co. agt. T. F. Pinto, 36 Crutchedfriars
Oppenheim Arth.&Co. timb. mer.& lk. gls. ma. 23&24 Yardley st
Oppenheim Brothers, cabinet wa. 17 Mansell st. Goodman's fi
Oppenheim John M. & Co. fur & skin merchants, 18 Bow la
Oppenheim Joseph, optician, 2 Freeman's pl. Mile end road
Oppenheim Morris M. walking stick, cane, looking glass, chair & cabinet mfr. & mahogany & timber mer. 119 Bunhill row
Oppenheim Simeon, merchant, 17 South st. Finsbury
Oram George, strop & dresng. case ma. 25A, Hatton garden
Oram George, tailor, 25 Silver st. Wood st. City
Oram George Jervis, watch mkr. 13 Whiskin st. Clerkenwell
Oram Joseph, wine merchant, 3 Belgrave st. King's cross

Oram Samuel, pearl worker & jeweller, 5 Castle st. Holborn
Oram Walter, baker, 27 Charing cross
Orange John, carpet dealer, 65 Skinner st. Bishopsgate
Orange Joseph, cabinetmaker, 3 Yardley st. Clerkenwell
Orange Joseph, bonnet shape maker, 24 Homer st. Marlebne
Orchard Thomas & Thomas, solicitors, 15 Hatton garden
Orchard William & Co. rick, tent, marquee & tarpauling manufacturers, 5 West Smithfield
Orchard Francis, grocer & ital. wa. 62 Lucas st. Commercial rd. ea
Orchard John, baker, 1 Cambridge ter. Camden New town
Orchard Isabella Eliza (Mrs.), library, 1 Great Woodstock st
Orchard Stephen, butcher, 42 Princes road, Lambeth
Orchard Stephen Chandler, baker, 23 Somers pl. east, New rd
Ord John, russia merchant, 76 Old Broad st. City
Ord John C. jun. cheesemonger, 49 Blackman st. Borough
Ord Margaret Elizth. (Miss), milliner, 40 Conduit st. Bond s
Ord Robert, russia broker, 41 Threadneedle st
Ord William, physician, 9 Warwick st. Belgrave road
Ordish Frederick, architect, 9 John st. Adelphi
Ordish Thos. stationer & bookbdr. 1 Elliott's row, Islington
Ordnance Offi (Civil), Tower; (Military) 86 Pallmall; 10 to 6
Ordoyno Jacob, birch & heath broom ma. 42 Swan pl. O. Kent rd
Ordway Richard, turnery & toy warehouse, 159 Piccadilly
O'Reilly Mary (Mrs.), milliner, Denmark hill, Camberwell
Orford John, draper, silk mercer, &c. 211 Oxford st
Orford Robt. coffee roaster, 10½ King John's ct. Holywell la
Orford Sarah (Mrs.), mat manufr. 1 Villa st. Walworth com
Orford William, baker & corndlr. 23 Gt. Chapel st. Oxford st
Organ John, baker, 65 Harper st. New Kent road
Orgar George, french polisher, 15 Castle st. east, Oxford st
Orgar James, hatter, 63 Seymour place, Bryanstone square
Orger & Meryon, booksels. & stationers, 174 Fenchurch st
Orger Joseph, butcher, 3 Brunswick place, Old Kent road
Orgill Jane (Mrs.), *N. Rum Puncheon* P.H. 4 Rose & Cr. ct. Finsb
Orgill John, *glo'ster wareho.* (coach & waggon offi.) 248 Oxfrd. st
Orgill John James, auctioneer & est. agt. 3 Newman st. Oxford st
Oridge William, custom house agent, 9 Lime st. City
Oriel Charles George C. attorney, 36 Alfred pl. Bedford sq
Oriel Edward, tailor, Deptford High st
Oriel Frederick, surgeon, 21 Alfred place, Bedford square
Oriental Bank, 7 Walbrook, City
Oriental Club House (Fred. A. Sturt, sec.), 18 Hanover sq
Oriental Translation Fund (Earl of Clare, pres. Rev. James Reynolds, sec.), 14 Grafton st. Bond st
Original Steam Packet Co. 9 Villiers st. Strand
Orleans, Tours & Bordeaux Railway Office, 2 Capel court
Orlebar Charles D. solicitor, 127 Great Portland st
Orlebar William, attorney, 6 George st. Hanover sq
Orlemann Peter, pork butcher, 152 Kingsland road
Orme Ann & Sons, dressingcasemfr. 10 Bateman's bulds. Soho
Orme Geo & Chas. distillers & rectifiers, 159 Blackfrs. rd
Orme Francies, solicitor, 54 Chancery lane
Orme Gilbert, linendraper, 12 Little Russell st. Covent gar
Orme Henry, brush & turnery manufacturer, 67 Fore st. City
Orme Henry, dentist, 5 Charles st. Middlesex hospital
Orme John, bedstead & cornice ma. 34 Wheeler st. Spitalflds
Orme Joseph S. dressing case maker, 9 Nassau st. Soho
Orme Malcolm, proctor, 1 Godliman st. Doctors' commons
Orme Robert, haberdasher, 19 Gibson st. Waterloo road
Ormes Samuel, bookseller, stationer, bookbinder & circulating library, 16 City road, Finsbury
Ormiston Francis, *Swan & Sugar Loaf* P.H. 52 Fetter lane
Ormiston Priest Shrubb, agt. to Bristol Brass Co. 22 Bread st
Ormston Ralph, cheesemonger, 34 South ct. Manchester sq
Ormston Robert Walker, cheesemonger, 50 Crawford st
Ormston Wm. cheesemonger, 13 Rufford's bldgs. Islington
Ormston Wm. greengrocer, &c. 31 South st. Manchester sq
Ornithological Society (Tho. Hall, sec.), Lodge, St. James's pk
Ormsby John Edwd. plumber & glazier, 136 St. George st
Orphan Working School (Joseph Soul, sec.), City road
Orphin Edwin, bricklayer & plastr. 9 William st. Regt.'s pk
Orpin Richard, japanner, 59 Monmouth st. Seven dials
Orpwood Edwd. auction. est. agt. &c. 6 Artillery pl. Finsbury
Orpwood Ellen (Mrs.), *George* P.H. Church la. Kensgtn. grvl. pt
Orpwood George, watch & clockmaker, & patent coffee roaster manufacturer, 82 Bishopsgate without
Orpwood Richard, coffee rooms, 24 North row, Grosvenor sq
Orpwood Richard, fruiterer, 26 King st. Snow hill
Orpwood Thomas, coach currier, 17 Bear st. Leicester sq
Orpwood William, stationer & leather cover maker, 43 Warwick st. Golden square
Orr Wm. S. & Co. booksels. & publishers, 2 & 3 Amen corner
Orrell John, chandler's shop, Mill st. Dockhead
Orridge Bros. chemists & druggists, 22 Ludgate hill
Orridge Thos. sen. fruit salesman, 5 Portman market
Orridge Thos. Edward, fruiterer, 26 Gt. Castle st. Regent st
Orris Edmund, butcher, 1 King st. Lower road, Islington
Orritt Charles, corkcutter, 81 Fenchurch st
Orrock James, linendraper, Bow High st
Ortelli Peter, looking glass maker, 3 Leather lane, Holborn
Orthophonic Inst. for Defects of Speech, 32 Sackville st
Ortner Louis, *Coach & Horse tavern* P.H. 16 Conduit st
Orton Charles, greengrocer, 8 Northampton row, Holloway
Orton Elizh. (Mrs.), watch lever escape. ma. 7 Lr. Smith st. Clkw
Orton George, shipping butcher, 69 Wapping
Orton James, perfumer, &c. 4 Queen st. Charles sq. Hoxton
Orton John, bookbinder, 1 Little St. Mary axe
Orton John, fruiterer & greengrocer, 10 Finsbury market
Orton John Chas. escapement ma. 49 Wynyatt st. Goswell st
Orton Thos. cattle salesm. & butcher, 94 Lr. East Smithfield
Orum George, razor strop & dressing case manufacturer, inventor of the canton strop or chinese razor sharpener, & vegetable shaving powder, 25A, Hatton garden
O'Ryan John Wall, irish & foreign provision broker, Jamaica coffee house, St. Michael's alley, Cornhill
Osbaldeston William, solicitor, 6 Furnival's inn
Osborn Hen. Son & Banks, stables, King's mews, Gray's inn la
Osborn William Henry & Co. jewellers, 22 St. James's st
Osborn Alfred (sec. to Equitable Coal Co.), 24 Bishops gt. whn
Osborn And. butcher, 10 Berwick st. & 4 Walker's ct. Golden sq
Osborn Ann (Mrs.), chandler's shop, 19 Charles st. City rd
Osborn Argent, boot & shoemaker, 18 Queen's rw. Cambridge rd
Osborn Charles, baker, 26 Green st. Bethnal green
Osborn Dean, tallowchandler, 12 King st. Rotherhithe
Osborn Eli, boot maker, 2 King's row, Walworth road
Osborn Elizabeth (Mrs.), library, 113 London rd. Southwark
Osborn Geo. butcher, 4 Grosvenor st. Grosvenor square
Osborn Geo. dyer & scourer, 12 Whitmore place, Hoxton
Osborn Geo. newsvender, 46 Baldwin's gardens, Leather la
Osborn Geo. paper hanger & painter, 8½ Gray's pl. Fulham rd
Osborn Geo. porkman, 12 Wentworth place, Mile end road
Osborn Henry, commission stables, 12 Gray's inn terrace
Osborn Henry, china dealer, 20 Aylesbury st. Clerkenwell
Osborn Henry, *Crooked Billet* P.H. 1 King st. Tower hill
Osborn Henry, law stationer, 6 Took's court, Chancery la
Osborn James, butcher, 2 Anglesey pl. Commercial rd. east
Osborn James, cabinet maker, 31 Poplar High st
Osborn John, cabinet maker, 8 Whiskin st. Clerkenwell
Osborn John, coffee rooms, 21 Dean st. High Holborn
Osborn John, estate agent, 23B, Grosvenor st. west, Pimlico
Osborn John, gasfitter, 14 Oxford market
Osborn John, hide & leather factor, Leadenhall market
Osborn John, meat salesman, 7 Whitehart st. Newgate mkt
Osborn John N. oil & colorman, 17 Bolingbroke rw. Walworth rd
Osborn Mary A (Miss), milliner, 10 Clement's in. pa. Clare mkt
Osborn Milcah (Mrs), milliner, 37 Margaret st. Cavendish sq
Osborn Robert, fruiterer, Larkhall lane, Clapham
Osborn Thomas, cowkeeper, 76 Gt. Saffron hill, Hatton wall
Osborn Thomas, butcher, 4 Dorset st. Clapham road
Osborn Thomas, *Grapes* P.H. 52 Haymarket
Osborn Thomas James, chemist & druggist, 130 Brick lane, Spitalfields, & 78 Old st. St. Luke's
Osborn Wm. baker, 114 Poplar High st
Osborn Wm. baker, 23 King st. Covent garden
Osborn Wm. bookseller & stationer, 16 Pitfield st. Hoxton
Osborn Wm. builder & bricklayer, 8 Queen st. Chelsea
Osborn Wm. coal dealer, 27 Brewer st. north, Goswell road
Osborn Wm. engine turner, 59 New Compton st. Soho
Osborn Wm. sen. *Duke of Grafton* P.H. 3 Palace row, New rd
Osborn Wm. jun. *Empress of Russia* P.H. 1 Owen's row, St. John st. rd
Osborne & Watts, plate chest ma. 6 Gt. Newport st. Long acre
Osborne Hen. & Co. coal mers. Stamford bridge, Lit. Chelsea
Osborne Ann (Mrs.), milliner, 49 Russell st. Lr. Rotherhithe
Osborne Charles, confectioner, 33 Bishopsgate without
Osborne Charles Skipp, grocer, 37 Leather lane, Holborn
Osborne Hon. D'Arcy G. spcl. pleader, 12 Paper bldgs. Templ
Osborne George, iron founder, 11 Noble st. Goswell st. & Shaftesbury st. New North road
Osborne George, *York Minster* P.H. 49 Dean st. Soho
Osborne Geo. Alex. bonnet shape ma. 1 Somerset pl. Hoxtn
Osborne Jane (Mrs.), tobacco pipe ma. 130 Bethnal green rd
Osborne John, barrister, 22 Old square, Lincoln's inn
Osborne John, carpenter, 33 Bruton mews north, Bond st
Osborne John, medical lozenge manufacturer, 401 Strand
Osborne John, plate case maker, 14 Leicester st. Leicester sq
Osborne John, ship & insurance broker, 15 Fish st. hill
Osborne Mary (Miss), confectioner, 4 Charles st. Soho sq
Osborne Richard, coffee rooms, 79 East st. Manchester sq
Osborne Richard, engraver, see Rowe, Kentish & Osborne
Osborne Robert, saddler & harness maker, 11 Marylebone la
Osborne Thos. bonnet shape ma. 81 Pearson st. Kingsland rd

Osborne Thos. currier & leather cut. 12 Webber st. Blkfrs.rd
Osborne Thomas, engraver & printer, 27 Lombard st
Osborne Thomas, tool manufacturer, 75 Bunhill row
Osborne Thomas, upholsterer, 14 Eldon st. Finsbury
Osborne William, baker, 23 King st. Covent garden
Osborne William, upholsterer, 232 Whitechapel road
Osbourn Richard, greengrocer, 38 Rawstorne st. Goswell rd
Osbourn William, grocer, 21 Windmill st. Finsbury sq
Osbourne Samuel, coffee rooms, 59 Theobald's road
Oscor Harger Fox, surgeon, 2 Mercers' pl. Commcl. rd. east
Osgood George, solicitor, 3 Raymond bldgs. Gray's inn, & 2 Alexander sq. Brompton
Osland Jas. Hen. woollen dra. & rug manfr. 9 Gun st. Spitlfds
Osler, Follett & Clarkson, glass & lamp dlrs. 44 Oxford st
Osman Henry, plumber & glazier, 94 Park st. Camden town
Osman Rowland Robt. fishmonger, 93 Chapel st. Pentonville
Osman Wm. jun. brewer, Waterloo st. & 4Camberwll.gr.ea.si
Osman William, fruiterer, 22 Warren st. Fitzroy square
Osman William, chandler's shop, 16 Holland st. Blkfrs. rd
Osment John, *Red Lion* P.H. 44 Cow cross st. Clerkenwell
Osment Joseph James, corn & coal dlr. 7 York pl. Kent st. rd
Osment Mary (Miss), dressmaker, 29 Perceval st. Clerknwl
Osmond Brothers, tailors, 3 Sherborne lane, City
Osmond Jas. & Son, cattle salesmen, 8 West Smithfield
Osmond Robert & Samuel, dyers, 99 Leadenhall st
Osmond Samuel & Co. dyers & scourers, 8 Ivy la. Newgate st
Osmond & Seabrook, wine importers, see Seabrook & Osmond
Osmond & Simpson, woollen drapers, 152 New Bond st
Osmond Barbara (Mrs.), ladies' school, 6Gray's inn pas. Hlbrn
OsmondGeo.last&boottree ma.13Gt.May's bldgs.St.Mrtns.la
Osmond James, jeweller, 11 Upper Rosoman st. Clerkenwell
Osmond John, Exeter coffee rooms, 87 Strand
Osmond John, wine merchant, 7 Catherine court, Trinity sq
Osmond Joseph, stationer, &c. 45 Marsham st. Westminster
Osmond Samuel, ladies' shoemaker, 54 Davies st. Berkeley sq
Osmond Samuel, poulterer, 18 Barnsbury place, Islington
Osmond Thomas, upholsterer, 60 London st. Fitzroy sq
Osmond William, beer retailer, 44 James st. Oxford st
Osmond William, builder, 102A, Mount st. Berkeley square
Osmond William, watch case gilder, 4 Hull st. St. Luke's
Ost Elizh. (Mrs.), *Prince Regent* P.H. 20 North st. Wlwrth
Ostell & Lepage, booksel. & ea. india agts. 6 Tudor st. Blkfrs
Ostell William, printer & stationer, 24 Hart st. Bloomsbury
Ostler Jonah, currier, 19 White's grounds, Bermondsey
Ostler Peter, silk dresser, 24 Artillery lane, Bishopsgate
Oswald John, bleacher, see Starey & Oswald
Oswald Wm. irish provision merchant, 22 Birchin lane
Oswell Edward, carpenter, 76 Fetter lane, Holborn
Oswell Edward, solicitor, 52 Lincoln's inn fields
Oswell George, bricklayer, 31 Mason st. Old Kent road
Oswin & Tootal, stock & share bro. 10Angel ct. Throgmortn.st
Otjen James, marine store dlr. 16 Charles st. Hampstead rd
Otley Ann (Mrs.), cornchandler, 266 Tottenham court road
Otley Edward John, library, see Saunders & Otley
Otley Frederick, stock broker, 5 Beak st. Regent st
Otley William, plasterer, 8 Great Warner st. Clerkenwell
Ott William, plumber, 9 Penton row, Walworth road
Otte Gustave, agt. to Didot Frères, publishers, 8Amen corner
Otten James, merchant, *Baltic* coffee house, Threadndl. st
Otter Charles, barrister, 6 King's Bench walk, Temple
Otter John, house agent, 56 Whitehorse st. Stepney
Otter Joseph, army & hunting saddler, 19 Air st. Piccadilly
Ottignon François, foreign basket wareho. 5 Dean st. Soho
Ottley Drewry, surgeon, 5 Bedford place, Bloomsbury
Ottley John, optician, 2 Spring place, Bagnigge Wells road
Ottley Richard, hosier & glover, see Hawes & Ottley
Ottley Warner, west india merchant, 2 Philpot lane
Otto Edward, watchmaker, 53 Cable st. Wellclose square
Ottway John, optician, &c. 11 Devonshire st. Queen square
Ottway Wm. *Camden's Head* P.H. 10 Church la. Limeho
Otty Wm. carpenter, &c. 16 Bedfordbury, Covent garden
Otway Chas. Wm. surgeon, 11 Canterbury rw. Kennington rd
Otway John, solicitor, Stratford broadway
Ouchterlony Margt. (Miss), statnr. 13 Prospect pl. Kngslnd. rd
Oughton Fred. apothecary & chem. 7Southampton st. Cmbwl
Oughton George, turner, 6 Adam's place, Borough High st
Oulds John, tallowchandler, 28 & 135 Tottenham court road, & oil & colorman, 37 Greek st. Soho, &63 Theobald's road, & 21 Cumberland row, King's cross
Oulds Joseph, oil & colorman, 45 Henry st. Hampstead rd
Oulds William, oilman, 28 Peter st. Soho
Oulton John, surgeon, 27 William st. Lisson grove
Ourtz Jacob, engrav. engine turner, 15 Gt. Sutton st. Clknwl
Outhwaite Christopher, accountant, 28 London wall
Outhwaite John, builder & undertaker, 8 Up. East Smithfield
Outhwaite Wm. wood letter cutter & carpenter, 67 Snowhill
Outram Benjamin Fonseca, physician, 1 Hanover square
Outred Thomas, linendraper, Warlter's bldgs. Old Kent rd
Outtram Henry Edward, tailor, 17 Artillery place west
Outtram Jas. baker, 161 & 166 Up. Whitecross st. St. Luke's
Ouvry Frederic, solicitor, see Robinson & Ouvry
Oven John, tailor & breeches maker, 12 Dover st. Piccadilly
Ovenden Christopher, boot & shoe ma. Forest row, Dalston
Ovenden George, surveyor, 1 Roseberry place, Dalston
Ovenden John, oilman, 14 John's row, Brick la. St. Luke's
Ovenden Robt. Thos. engrav. & printer, 45 Carey st. Linc. inn
Ovenden Thomas, undertaker, 20, Shepperton st. Islington
Ovenden Wm. glass & china wareh. 22 Warwick st. Pimlico
Ovens Edward, barrister, 6 Pump court, Temple
Ovens Hen. picture frame ma. 31 Lit. Pulteney st. Golden sq
Ovenston John, upholsterer, 72 Gt. Tichfield st. Oxford st
Over Jas. cheesemonger, 4 Grove ter. Queen's rd. Bayswatr
Overall Frederick Geo. baker, 1 Grange rd. Bermondsey
Overall Samuel, fish factor, 102 Lower Thames st
Overan James, staymaker, 25 St. John st. road
Overbury John & Co. blackwell hall fact. 4Fredk.'s pl. O. Jewry
Overbury Benjamin, blackwell hall factor, 19 Gresham st
Overbury Nathaniel, solicitor, see Dickson & Overbury
Overbury Robt. blackwell hall factor, 17 Basinghall st
Overell William, bellowsmaker, 7 Swan st. Minories
Overend, Gurney & Co. bill brokers, 65 Lombard st
Overend William, barrister, 3 Paper buildings, Temple
Overill William, shopkeeper, 6 Bethnal green, West side
Overitt James, chandler's shop, 19 Hemlock court, Carey st
Overland Parcel & Passenger Office & India Rooms (Waghorn & Co.), 34 Cornhill; 10 to 5
Overman's Almshouses, Montague close, Borough
Overton & Hughes, solicitors, 25 Old Jewry
Overton Benjamin, wholesale milliner, & importer of french models & patterns, 8 Chiswell st
Overton Edward, tailor, &c. 33 Weymouth st. Portland pl
Overton George, hairdresser, 81 Earl st. east, Lisson grove
Overton Henry John, *Three Cups* P.H. High st. Bow
Overton James, coach plater, 17 Queen st. Grosvenor sq
Overton Samuel, bootmaker, 12 Shepherd's market
Overy Charles, stationer, 12 East st. Manchester square
Overy Thomas, brassfounder, 3 Snow's fields, Bermondsey
Ovington, Warwick & Ovington's fancy silk, gauze & chali handkerchief & shawl manufacturers, wove & printed shawls & mixed fabrics for dresses, 137 Cheapside, 46 Gutter lane, & North Exchange buildings, Glasgow
Owden Thomas S. livery stables, 62 Bishopsgate st. without
Owen Hugh & Co. gen. merchs. 3 Bond court house, Walbrook
Owen & Stodart, pianoforte makers, 36 Red Lion sq. Holborn
Owen Abraham, *Grapes* P.H. 110 Fore st. Cripplegate
Owen Arthur, cowkeeper, Church st. Deptford
Owen Arthur, printer, 3 Wine Office court, Fleet st
Owen Charles, cattle salesman, 59 West Smithfield
Owen Charles Spencer, solicitor, 9 Hunter st. Brunswick sq
Owen Charlotte (Mrs.), manf. of pink, blue, purple, mezzotinto, lead saucers, liquid dyes, ronge & carmine, 109 Goswell rd
Owen David, fringe & berlin warehouse, 98 Oxford st
Owen Dorothy (Miss), milliner, 4 Clifford st. Bond st
Owen Edward, brass founder, 121 Shadwell High st
Owen Edwd. Smith, bankrupts' register off. see Austin & Owen
Owen Foster (high constable of Westminster), 15 Chester terrace, Eaton square
Owen Francis, upholsterer, 63 Berners st. Oxford st
Owen George, cheesemonger, 13 New road, St. George's east
Owen George, cooper, 22 Old Boswell court, Lincoln's inn
Owen Henry, chemist, &c. 52 Marchmont st. Brunswick sq
Owen Henry, german repository & fringe manufacturer, 2 Upper Baker st. & 87 Edgware road
Owen Henry, pianoforte maker, 125 St. John st. Clerkenwell
Owen Henry, saddler, 125 Mount st. Berkeley square
Owen Herbert, barrister, 10 King's Bench walk, Temple
Owen Horatio, booksel. & newsvender, 21 Noble st. Cheapsd
Owen Hugh, merchant, 4 Lincoln's inn fields
Owen James, baker, 23 Carnaby st. Golden square
Owen Jesse, hat manufacturer, 31 Ewer st. Borough
Owen John, chair manufacturer, 92 Old street road
Owen John, saddler & harness mak. 7 Lisle st. Leicester sq
Owen John, trunk & packing case maker, 20 Minories
Owen John, wine & spirit merchant, 7 St. Andrew's hill
Owen Joseph, grocer & cheesemonger, 113 Poplar High st
Owen Mary (Mrs.), dairy, 18 Middle st. Cloth fair
Owen Matthew, german repository, 6Wigmore st. Cavndish. sq
Owen Owen, dining rooms, 53 Lower Thames st
Owen Owen, *George* P.H. 45 Castle st. Leicester square
Owen Owen, turkey whetstone manufacturer, 62 Old st. rd
Owen Richard, dairyman, 45 King st. Westminster
Owen Richard, fishmonger, 1 Crown place, Old Kent road

Owen Richard, furniture broker, 93 Shoe lane, Fleet st
Owen Robert, carpenter, 18 Bowling green st. Kennington
Owen Robert, east india warehouse, & importer of sèvre china & curiosities to her Majesty, 95 New Bond street
Owen Robert, french polisher, 6Coe's ter. Charlotte st. Pntnvl
Owen Susan (Miss), milliner, see Miller & Owen
Owen Thomas, gold & silver caster, 28 Red Lion st. Clerkenw
Owen Thomas, hairdresser, 2 Bermondsey New road
Owen Thomas, florist, Blue Anchor road, Bermondsey
Owen Thomas, *Victory* P.H. 27 Edmund st. King's cross
Owen Thomas Owen, surgeon, 19 Guilford st. Russell sq
Owen William, academy, 40 Guildford pl. Lr. Kenningtn. la
Owen William, ironmonger, 14 Robert st. Grosvenor sq
Owen William, silk mercer, see Rumbell & Owen
Owen William Daniel, linendraper, 42, 43 & 44 Gt. Coram st
Owens David, boot & shoe maker, 6Park st. Borough market
Owens David, shopkeeper, 19 Prospect pl. Cambridge heath
Owens Edward, laceman, 6 Halkin terrace, Belgrave sq
Owens George, *Bath* coffee rooms, 36 Lisle st. Leicester sq
Owens John, solicitor, 35 Moorgate st. City
Owens Joseph, *William the Fourth* P.H. 1 Vaughan ter. Cityrd
Owens Luke, *Northamtn. Arms* P.H. 18 pencerter. Lr. rd Islgtn
Owers Ann (Mrs.), ironmonger, 165 Piccadilly
Owers Edward, tobacconist, 13 Gt. James st. Lisson grove
Owers John, butcher, 1 Henry pl. Upper Kennington lane
Owers Wm. beer retailer, 52 York st. Westminster
Owles Esther (Mrs.), plumbers' turner, 9 Earl st. London rd
Owst Robt. & Co. wood & truss hoop merchants, & coopers, Bermondsey wall, near Mill stairs, Dockhead, Bermondsey
Owthwaite & Sinclair, who. tea dealers, 34 Fenchurch st
Owthwaite John, rope & horsehair manufr. 38 Brickla. St. Luke's
Owtram Robert & Co. muslin manufactrs. 13 Watling st
Oxenford Edward, imptr. & dlr. in farina, 70 Lower Thames st
Oxenford John, solicitor, 12 Birchin lane
Oxenham Saml. & Sons, auction. & apprai. 353 & 354 Oxford st
Oxenham George Nutcombe, barrister, 61 Chancery lane
Oxer Shadrack, oilman, 7 Regent st. Horseferry road
Oxford & Cambridge University Club (William George Morris, secretary), 71 Pall mall
Oxford & Rugby Railway, 449 West Strand
Oxford, Witney, Cheltenham & Gloucester Independent Railway (I. Menzies, sec.), 58 Gracechurch st
Oxford & Worcester Extension & Chester Junction Railway (Hilton T. Jenkins, sec.), 1 Coleman st. buildings, Moorgate st
Oxford, Worcester & Wolverhampton Railwy. 449 West Strnd
Oxford Daniel, *Fishing Smack* P.H. Stowage, Deptford
Oxford George, livery stables, 4½ Pratt st. Camden town
Oxford Henry, grocer, 1 Little Smith st. Chelsea
Oxford Joseph, commission merchant, 8 Bury sq. St. Maryaxe
Oxlee Hen. upholsterer & easy chair ma. 27 Friar st. Blkfrs. rd
Oxley John T. & Co. american merchants, 3: Mincing lane
Oxley & Taylor, merchants, 8 George yard, Lombard st
Oxley Edward, butcher, 5 Britannia pl. Wandsworth rd
Oxley Francis, wine merchant, 4 Cross la. St. Mary at hill
Oxley Henry, butcher, 99 St. John st. Clerkenwell
Oxley John Timothy, merchant, 38 Mincing lane
Oxley Thos. bootmaker, 8 Warwick lane, & 23 Warwick sq
Oxman John, grocer & teadealer, 48 East st. Manchester sq
Oyler George, marine store dlr. 4 Suffolk st. Pentonville
Ozanne Jane (Madame), milliner, 2 Brook st. Hanover sq

PACE Brothers & Co. gen. mer. & corn fac. 3 St. Michael's al
Pace Charles, watch & clock maker, 128 Whitechapel High st
Pace Charles, coal merchant, 1 Paddington st. Marylebone
Pace Charles, pastrycook, 5 Paddington st. Marylebone
Pace Charles, wholesale manufacturer of military musical instruments, 49 King st. Westminster
Pace Edmund, metal perforator, see Tylor & Pace
Pace Frederick, wholesale manufacturer of military musical instruments, 15 King st. Westminster
Pace George, boot & shoe maker, 54 Goodge st. Fitzroy sq
Pace Henry, watch manfr. 45A, St. John's sq. Clerkenwell
Pace Jas. locksmith & bellhanger, 36 Charles st. Westminster
Pace John, bookselr. & library, 19 Brecknock pl. Cmdn. nw. tn
Pace Thomas, grocer, 2 Upper Dorset st. Bryanstone square
Pache William, millwright & engnr. 5 Parker's row, Dockhead
Pack Thomas, Wm. carpenter, 37 Trafalgar st. Walworth rd
Packer Chas. jeweller, 78 Quadrant, Regent st
Packer Charles, pianoforte maker, see Towns & Packer
Packer Charles, surgeon, 12 Pitfield st. Hoxton
Packer Elijah, basketmaker, 21 Freeschool st. Horselydown
Packer George, bookseller, 29 Beaumont st. Portland place
Packer James, poulterer, 129 Crawford st. Portman sq
Packer John, shoemaker, 19 Cross st. Hoxton new town
Packer Stephen, basket maker, New cross
Packer Stephen, bootmaker, 12 Thirza pl. Old Kent road
Packer Stephen, cheesemonger, Mare st. Hackney
Packer Thomas, law stationer & lithographer, 30 Chancery la
Packer Thomas, tailor & trimg. seller, 4 Boswell ct. Queen sq
Packer Thomas Scott, butcher, 26 Harcourt st. New road
Packer William, dyer, 2 Notting hill
Packer Wm. *Golden Fleece* P.H. 7 St. John st. road
Packer Wm. statuary & mason, 11 East st. Red Lion square, & Lansdown yard, Guilford st
Packer Wm. David, bootmaker, 36 Red Lion st. Holborn
Packman Wm. *Vine inn & hotel* 70 Bishopsgate within
Packwood John, who. ironmonger, 52 Wood st. Cheapside
Packwood Wm. *Prince of Wales* P.H. 50 Philipps st. Kingsld. rd
Pacy Henry, *Little Coach & Horses* P.H. 29 High Holborn
Padbury Mary (Miss), straw bonnet mkr. 7 Broad st. Gold. sq
Padbury Wm. card board pill box maker, 176 Blackfriars rd
Paddington Eye Infirmary, 8 South whf. rd. Paddington
Paddington Provident Dispensary, 104 Star st. Edgware rd
Paddington Savings' Bank, School house, Harrow road
Paddison Richard, solicitor, see Mullins & Paddison
Paddock Robt. carpenter & builder, 6 Robert st. Davies st
Paddon Charles, clothes salesman, 57 Charlotte ter. New cut
Paddon George, grocer, 15 Munster st. Regent's park
Paddon Henry, grocer, 99 Crawford st. Portman square
Paddon Thomas, carpet warehouse, 128 St. George st
Paddy Richard, linendraper, see Jesse & Paddy
Paddy William, linendraper, see Haslam & Paddy
Pagden Trayton, iron founder, &c. see Moreland & Pagden
Pagden Trayton, wine importer, see Furner & Pagden
Padgett James & Co. wine mer. Pantechnicon, Belgrave sq
Padgett John, artist, 69 Coleshill st. Pimlico
Padgett Wm. coach trimmer, 4 Portsea pl. Connaught sq
Padman John, dining rooms, 55 Chandos st. Covent garden
Pagani & Bonorandi, silk merchs. 5 Crown ct. Old Broad st
Pagden Wm. *Talbot* P.H. 67 Gray's inn lane
Pagden Payton, wine importer, see Furner & Pagden
Page Geo. & Chas. ironmongers, 60 Bridge rd. Lambeth
Page Eleanor & Son, cricket bat ma. 7 Orange rw. Kenngton
Page J. & G. & Co. (late Page & Sons), medallion & general engravers, lithographers, printers, & account book manufacturers, 71 Queen st. Cheapside
Page & Kennedy, pawnbrokers, 16 Low. Eaton st. Pimlico
Page Philip F. & Son, builders, &c. 14 King's rd. Bedford row
Page Samuel & Son, coal merchants, 2 Park st. Dorset sq
Page & Smith, ship & insurance brks. 1A, Bishpsgt. within
Page Wm. & Son, builders, &c. 1 Fitzroy ter. Kentish town
Page Aaron Todd, haircutter & wigmaker, 34 Pall mall
Page Alfred, bootmaker, 55 Fleet st
Page Andrew, gold lapper, 4 Corporation row, Clerkenwell
Page Chas. boot & shoe ma. 15 North Audley st. Grosvnr. sq
Page Charles, cane & cane rib manuf. see Parker & Page
Page Charles, butcher, 158 Hoxton Old town
Page Charles, merchant, 10 Austinfriars
Page Chas. Alfred, oil & colorman, 200 Gt. Dover st. Boro'
Page Chas. Geo. (late Collins), butcher, 5 Dean st. Westmr
Page Elizabeth Mary (Mrs.), *Fountain* P.H. 17 Minories
Page George, baker, 30 Wardour st. Soho
Page George, butcher, 18 Cross st. Hoxton
Page George, ironmonger, Stratford broadway
Page George, teadealer, 25 Parker's row, Dockhead
Page Henry, bootmaker, 7 Paul st. Finsbury
Page Henry, leather merchant, see Clapham & Page
Page Henry, leather seller, 38 Kingsland road
Page Henry, merchant, 10 Austinfriars
Page Henry, patent integument manufr. 114 Kingsland rd
Page Henry, tobacconist, 72 Berwick st. Soho
Page Henry Thos. grocer & teadealer, 141 Minories
Page Henry Thos. tailor, 89 Wimpole st. Cavendish sq
Page James, boot & shoe maker, 18 King st. Borough
Page James, butcher, 6 Gt. Chapel st. Oxford st
Page James, grocer, 1 Beaufort ter. west, King's rd. Chelsea
Page Jann (Mrs.), grocer & cheesem. 116 Regent st. Lambeth
Page John, beer retailer, 4 Newman passage, Newman st
Page John, boot & shoe maker, 5 Adam's row, Hampstead rd
Page John, boot & shoe ma. 7 Brecknock pl. Camden new tn
Page John, builder, 16 South Molton st. Oxford st
Page John, dairyman, 1 Tower royal, Watling st
Page John, fruiterer, 143 Poplar High st
Page John, grocer, Albany road, Barnsbury road
Page John, ivory & hardwood turner, 3 Peter st. Saffron hill
Page John, officer to sheriffs of London, 42 Threadneedle st
Page John, pawnbroker, 1 Glo'ster ter. Vauxhall bridge rd
Page John, potato salesman, South row, Covent garden, & 11 Great Chapel st. Westminster
Page Jonathan, silkshag manufacturer & hatters' trimming manufacturer, 32 Steward st. Spitalfields

Page John George, marbler, 39A, Watling st
Page Joseph Henry, auctioneer & appraiser, estate & house agent, 8 Pancras lane, Cheapside
Page Joseph S. chandler's shop, 69 Park st. Camden town
Page Joshua, tailor, 20 Upper Cleveland st. Fitzroy square
Page Josiah Johnson, ironmonger, 22 Edgware road
Page Philip, baker, 2 Norfolk pl. Larkhall lane, Clapham
Page Philip Flood, architect, 28 Sackville st. Piccadilly
Page Philip Norres, architect, 14 King's road, Bedford row
Page Richard, butcher, 161 Lambeth walk
Page Richard, cheesemonger, 9 Flint st. East st. Walworth
Page Robt. ship & insurance brokr. see M'Ghie, Page & Smith
Page Samuel, broker & agent, see Clarke & Page
Page Saml. Thos. lighterman, 51 Burr st. East Smithfield
Page Selina (Mrs.), grocer, 93 Park st. Kennington cross
Page Simon, potato dealer, 33 Norton folgate
Page Sophia (Miss), perfumer, 14 Gray's place, Fulham road
Page Thomas, brushmaker, 24 Cock lane, West Smithfield
Page Thomas, civil engineer, 2 Middle Scotland yard
Page Thomas, hat, shag, band & galloon manufacturer, 23 White Lion st. Norton folgate
Page Thompson Scott, merchant, see Dean & Page
Page William, artist, 3 Ulster pl. New road
Page Wm. beer retailer, 4 Acton pl. Bagnigge wells road
Page William, bootmaker, see Campbell & Page
Page William, book marbler, 1 Little St. Thomas apostle
Page William, bricklayer, 20 Queen st. Golden square
Page William, butcher, 19 Church st. Shoreditch
Page William, cheesemonger, 12 Harrow road
Page William, coffee rooms, 9 Tower dock, Tower hill
Page William, corkcutter, see Hardy & Page
Page William, corkcutter, 18 Gillingham st. Pimlico
Page William, dancing master, 13 Francis st. Newington
Page William, fire work maker, 22½ Cromer st. Gray's inn rd
Page William, lithographic writer, 8 Castle ct. Budge row
Page William, tobacconist, 13 Union st. Bishopsgate without
Page William, ven. blind maker, 14 Pierrepoint rw. Islngtn. gn
Page William Emmanuel, physician, 43 Curzon st. Mayfair
Pagelsan John, pastrycook, 90 Whitechapel road
Paget Mary N. & Sarah, milliners &c. 10 Brutonst. Brkly. sq
Paget Charles Wm. Stephen, tobacconist, 44 Fetter lane
Paget John, barrister, 3 Middle Temple lane
Paget Robert G. rope & twine manufacturer, 46 West Smithfield, & Westmoreland la. Walworth com
Paget Thomas, oil & colorman, 9 North pl. Ball's pond rd
Paget Wm. surgeons' instrument mak. & cutler, 195 Piccadilly
Pagetts Thos. musical repository, 21 Parkside, Knightsbridg
Pagliano & Nind, *Sabloniere Hotel*, 30 Leicester sq
Paiba Isaac, leather seller, 193 Bethnal green road
Paice Harriet & Sarah Maria, milliners, 27 Georgest. Hnvr. sq
Paice Mary Ann (Miss), & Co. milliners, 17 Princes st. Cav. sq
Paice John, carman, Talbot inn yard, 75 Borough High st
Paice John George, cheesemonger, 13 Fashion st. Dockhead
Paice Thomas, tailor, 3 New Kent road
Paige Charlotte (Miss), milliner, 128 Jermyn st
Pailthorp Rd. tobacconist, 50 Tabernacle walk, Finsbury
Pailthorpe Rd. printseller, 11 Red Lion pass. Red Lion sq
Pain & Hatherly, attorneys, 83 Basinghall st.; & 5 Great Marlborough st
Pain Aaron, marine store dlr. 30 Broad st. Ratcliff cross
Pain Charles, attorney, 17 Surrey st. Strand
Pain George, boot & shoemaker, Canal bridge, Old Kent rd
Pain George, cabinetmaker, 8 Wyndham pl. Bryanstone sq
Pain Geo. potato dealer, 1 Black Prince row, Walworth rd
Pain Henry, butcher, 98 High st. Camden town
Pain James, boot & shoemaker, 1 Temple place, Old Kentrd
Pain James, silk manufacturer, see Jones & Pain
Pain James, silk manufr. 22 Pollard's row, Bethnal green
Pain John, fruiterer, 3 Temple place, Old Kent road
Pain John Brooks, butcher, 4 Fonthill place, Clapham road
Pain John, beer retailer, 4 Frederick place, Goswell road
Pain John Lambert, bricklayer, 6 Church ter. Pancras road
Pain Joseph, meat salesman, 38 Newgate market
Pain Oliver, baker, Broadway, Stratford
Pain Richard, grocer, 11 Brick st. Park lane
Pain Solomon John, attorney, 9 New inn, Wych st. Strand
Pain Thomas, baker, 23 Great Guildford st. Borough
Pain Thomas, *Coach & Horses* P.H. 5 Bruton st. Bond st
Pain Thos. jun. conveyancer, Chapel stairs, Lincoln's inn
Pain Wm. *Angel* P.H. 60 Upper Ground st. Blackfriars
Pain Wm. lodginghouse, 22 Craven st. Strand
Pain Wm. varnish maker & colorman, 36 Liquorpond st
Pain Wm. Gregson, hat manufr. 1 Bishopsgate within
Paine Thos. P. & Son, plumbers & painters, 10 Hornsey row, & 47 Hedge row, High st. Islington
Paine Benjamin, oil & colorman, 8 Church st. Deptford
Paine Cornelius, broker, see Kensington, Paines' & Young
Paine Daniel G. agent to *Norwich Union*, High st. Deptford
Paine Edward, bricklayer, 23 Duke st. Lincoln's inn fields
Paine George, brass finisher, 19 Well st. Cripplegate
Paine George, *Princess Royal* P.H. Warwick st. Pimlico
Paine George Riebau, bookseller, 46 High st. Marylebone
Paine Henry, tailor, 17 Ludgate hill
Paine James, agt. to *Royal Exchange Ass.* Grove la. Dptfd
Paine James, bricklayer, 25 Grove st. Camden town
Paine James, builder, &c. 58 Park st. Camden town
Paine James, music seller, 92 High st. Marylebone
Paine Jas. Benwell, tobacconist, 141 Gt. Suffolk st. Borough
Paine John, fruiterer, 40 Upper Marylebone st
Paine John, *Prince's Head* P.H. 24 Princes st. Westminster
Paine John P. church & turret clock ma. 31 High st. St. Giles'
Paine Leeds, *Bath hotel*, 25 Arlington st. & 156 Piccadilly
Paine Leeds, gen. carrier, Old White Horse cellar, 156 Pcdly
Paine Maria (Mrs.), linendra. 14 Bartholomew sq. St. Luke's
Paine Mary (Mrs.), shell fishmonger, 55 Charles st. Westmr
Paine Rd. auctioneer & survey. 23 Portman st. Portman sq
Paine Samuel, baker & cornchandler, Litt. Chelsea (North side)
Paine Thomas, cheesemonger & grocer, 43 Cloth fair
Paine Thomas Hammond, grocer, 7 Theobald's rd. Red Li. sq
Paine Trayton, chemist, 2 Wellington terrace, Liverpool rd
Paine Walter, oil & italian warehouse, 1 Sherborne lane
Paine William, grocer, see Hawkins & Paine
Paine Wm. D. broker, see Kensington, Paines' & Young
Paine Wm. Henry, plumber, &c. see Paine Thos. Philip & Son
Paine Wm. Stephen, solicitor, 69 Lincoln's inn fields
Painter & Newton, surgeons, 26 Howland st. Fitzroy sq
Painter Chas. Benj. surgeon, 22 Compton st. Brunswick sq
Painter Edward, hairdresser, 8 Gt. College st. Camden town
Painter Edwin, tobacconist, 43 Brewer st. Golden square
Painter George, grocer, 16 St. John st. rd
Painter George, *Ship & Turtle tavern*, 129 Leadenhall st
Painter John, butcher, 10 Pierrepoint row, Islington green
Painter John, potato salesman, 164 Alfred pl. Waterloo rd
Painter Richard, surgeon, &c. 4 Broadway, Westminster
Painter Sarah (Mrs.), cooper, 123 Lambeth Lower marsh
Painter Timothy, tobacconist, 4 Edwards st. Portman sq
Painter Wm. beer retailer, 8 Trafalgar st. Walworth
Painter Wm. china dealer, 86 Regent st. Lambeth
Painter Wm. glover to the Royal Family, 27 Fleet st
Painter Wm. *Horse Shoe & Magpie* P.H. 21 Bridge st. Westm
Painter Wm. Edw. printer & publisher, 342 Strand
Painter Stainers' Hall (P. N. Tomlins, clerk), 9 Lt. Trinity la
Painting Joseph, carpet planner, 5 Cushion ct. Old Broad st
Painton James, butcher, 12 Upper area, Hungerford market
Pairpoint William, water gilder, 7 Green st. Leicester sq
Pakeman Wm. tailor, 107 Hatton garden
Palace Court, Great Scotland yard, sittings every friday; *office*, 15 Chancery lane; hours of business 10 to 5
Paley Christopher, shoemaker, 26 Eagle st. Red Lion sq
Paley Jsph. springer & polisher, 7 Hooper st. Gt. Sutton st
Palfrey Elizth. (Mrs.) cheesemong. 15 Gt. Barlow st. Maryleb
Palfrey William, builder, 3 Flemming st. Kingsland rd
Palgrave Sir Fras. public record off. Rolls' yd. Chancery la
Palin George Fredk. rope, net & twine manufr. 46 Goswell st
Paling Wm. working jeweller, 3 Grove la. Camberwell
Palis Pauline (Madame), dressmaker, 11 Bryanstone st. Portman sq
Palk Charles, cider & perry mercht. 25 Mill lane, Tooley st
Palk Fras. (Miss), chandler's shop, 15 Clarence pl. Hckny. rd
Palladium Life Assurance Society (N. Grut, secretary), 7 Waterloo place; see page 2041
Pallant John, mathem. instru. ma 14 Mercer st. Long acre
Pallant Saml. berlin repository, 4 Pont st. Belgrave sq
Pallet Thomas, scale & weight ma. 2 Sugarloaf ct. Leadnhl. st
Pallett George, *Hereford City* P.H. 5 Litchfield st. Soho
Pallett James, *Black Bull* P.H. 96 Upper Thames st
Pallett James, *Red Cow* P.H. 23 Charterhouse lane
Pallett John, cheesemonger, 4 Chapel st. Somers town
Pallett John, *Feathers* P.H. 50 Hart st. Covent garden
Pallett Robt. *Cock & Bottle* P.H. 30 Cannon st. City
Pallett Wm. manch. warehouse, see Puzey & Co
Palling Charles, blackwell hall factor, 58 Basinghall st
Pallise John, coffee rooms, 15 New Quebec st. Portman sq
Palliser George, saddler, wholesale harness & carriage manufacturer, 8 Finsbury place north, & branch establishment, 4 Bruton st. Bond st
Palliser Richard, saddler & harness mkr. 8 Coleman st
Palm Soren Samuel, tailor & draper, 171 High st. Shadwell
Palmer Chas. & Co. who. brushmaks. &c. 222 Boro' High st
Palmer & Clayton, printers, 3, 4 & 10 Crane court, Fleet st
Palmer, Delafosse & Wathen, who. teadealrs. 22 Fenchurch st
Palmer Edward & Co. woollendrapers, 147 Borough High st

Palmer Ebenezer & Son, theological booksellers, printers, & publishers, 18 Paternoster row
Palmer, France & Palmer, solicitors, 24 Bedford rw. Blmsby
Palmer Fred. & Hen. solicitors, 9 Mitre ct. chambers, Fleet st
Palmer (Geo.), Hope & Co. stockbrokers, 26 Royal Exchange
Palmer & Holt, wire drawers & pin mnfrs. 38 Noble st. City
Palmer Hen. Chas. & Co. hat & cap mnfrs. 51 Blackman st. Boro'
Palmer John & Son, bootmakers, 20 Duke st. West Smithfield
Palmer & King, east ind. & colonial brokers, 14 Mincing la
Palmer, Mackillop, Dent & Co. merchts. 11 King's Arms yard
Palmer Mary Ann & Co. wine mer. 3 Frederick's pl. Old Kent rd
Palmer & Nettleship, attorneys, 4 Trafalgar sq
Palmer Philip & Co. silk mercers, 54 Penton st. Pentonville
Palmer Samuel & James, corn & flour factors, Jack's coffee house, Mark lane, & 44 Comml. sale rooms, Mincing lane
Palmer Samuel & Joseph, theological booksellers & printers, 53 Old Compton st. Soho
Palmer Wm. & Co. pat. candle lamp ma. Lit. Sutton st. Clrkwll
Palmer Anthony, tailor, 26 Little Moorfields
Palmer Arthur, conveyancer, 1 New Square, Lincoln's inn
Palmer Benjamin, baker, 6 Chester place, Bethnal green
Palmer Benjamin, tailor, clerical robe maker, hosier & outfitter, 422 Strand
Palmer Charles, bricklayer, 19 Coppice row, Clerkenwell
Palmer Charles, butcher, 15 Poplar High st
Palmer Charles, stationer, 21 Union st. east, Spitalfields
Palmer Charlotte (Mrs.), habrdshr. 15 Union st. Clarendon sq
Palmer Daniel, farrier, 23 Gravel lane, Southwark
Palmer David, *Nag's Head* P.H. New st. Princes st. Lmbth
Palmer Eliza (Mrs.), ladies' school, 11 Wilmot st. Russell sq
Palmer Elizb. (Miss), milliner, 8 Francis ter. Hampstd. rd
Palmer Emma (Miss), bady linen wa. 35 Surrey pl. Old Kent rd
Palmer Francis, barrister, 8 Old Burlington st
Palmer Francis, greengrocer, 18 Swan st. Minories
Palmer Francis, tailor, 28 Tottenham st. Fitzroy square
Palmer Frederick, baker, 17 Dean st. New North road
Palmer Geo. cheesemonger, 15 Bedfordbury, Covent garden
Palmer Geo. plumber & glazier, 16 Suffolk pl. Hackney rd
Palmer George, printer, 17 Brownlow st. Holborn
Palmer George, teadealer, 6 Old Compton st. Soho
Palmer George Josiah, printer, Savoy st. Strand
Palmer Henry, furniture broker, see Birch & Palmer
Palmer Henry, grocer, 5 Providence buildings, New Kent rd
Palmer Henry, tailor, 2 Grove terrace, Brompton
Palmer Henry, tailor, 29 Gt. Hermitage st. Wapping
Palmer Henry Boswell, woolstapler, see Rayner & Palmer
Palmer Henry Francis, wine merchant, 6 Great St. Helen's
Palmer Henry Geo. dentist, 4 Youl's place, Old Kent road
Palmer James, builder, 72 Upper Whitecross st
Palmer James, carp. & buildr. 2 John st. Church la. Whitechl
Palmer James, chandler's shop, George st. Camberwell
Palmer James, *Five Bells & Bladebone* P.H. 42 Three Colt st
Palmer James, *Grapes* P.H. 3 Old st. road
Palmer James, grocer, 12 Silver st. Golden square
Palmer James, *Lord Chancellor* P.H. 5 North st. Edgware rd
Palmer James, *Mar. of Granby* P.H. 10 Middle rw. Knightsbri
Palmer James, plumber & glazier, 54 Park st. Dorset sq
Palmer James, tailor, 17 Duke st. Smithfield
Palmer James, undertaker, 20 Shaftesbury terrace, Pimlico
Palmer James Barrow, fishfactor, 112 Lower Thames st
Palmer James Barrow, salt merchant, 9 Lower Thames st
Palmer Jarvis, blacking ma. 20 Southampton st. Cambrwl. rd
Palmer John, boot & shoe maker, 81 Goswell st. (east side)
Palmer John, boot & shoe maker, 33 Little Moorfields
Palmer John, bricklayer, 101 Old Gravel lane, Wapping
Palmer John, carpenter, 1 & 2 Artillery place, Westminster
Palmer John, cooper, White st. Bethnal green
Palmer John, *Feathers* P.H. 22 Temple st. Whitefriars
Palmer John, grocer, &c. 11 Brunswick st. Hackney rd
Palmer John, house blind ma. 30A, Thomas st. Grosvenor sq
Palmer John, japanner, 13 Chamber st. Goodman's fields
Palmer John, linendraper, see Sander & Palmer
Palmer John, locksmith, 3 Bath st. Newgate st
Palmer John, picture dealer, 88 Gt. Tower st
Palmer John, stonemason, 38 Gravel lane, Southwark
Palmer John, tailor, 36 Margaret st. Cavendish sq
Palmer John Hinde, barrister, 16 Old square, Lincoln's inn
Palmer John Wm. bootmaker, 14 Lawrence la. Cheapside
Palmer Joseph, baker, 53 Park st. Dorset sq
Palmer Joseph, bricklayer, &c. 41 St. Andrew's hill, Doc. com
Palmer Joseph, plumber & glazier, 24 Minories
Palmer Joseph Moore, wine & spirit bro. see Millar & Palmer
Palmer Mary (Mrs.), milliner, 13 Castle st. Leicester sq
Palmer M.A. (Mrs.), straw bonnet ma. 16 Suffolk pl. Hkny. rd
Palmer Miles, hairdresser, &c. 41 St. John st. road
Palmer Miles Rook, hairdresser, &c. 15 Tottenham court rd
Palmer Nathaniel, barrister, 1 Paper buildings, Temple
Palmer Nathaniel, sculptor, 18 Southampton row, Russell sq
Palmer Nathaniel, toy wareho. 18 Southampton rw. Rssll. sq
Palmer Philip, window glass manfr. 118 St. Martin's lane
Palmer Richard, carp. & build. 32 Little Bartholomew close
Palmer Richard, grocer, 9 Cross st. Golden square
Palmer Robert, chemist, see Decastro, Watson & Palmer
Palmer Robert, ironmonger & gasfitter, 26 St. Mary Axe
Palmer Robert, printer, &c. 13 Providence pl. Up. Knningtn. la
Palmer Robert, tailor, 33 Little Russell st. Bloomsbury
Palmer Robt. jun. watch & clock ma. 24 White hart pl. Kenn. la
Palmer Robert M. baker, 4 King's arms pl. Comr. rd. east
Palmer Roundell, barrister, 11 New square, Lincoln's inn
Palmer Samuel, baker, 21 Gloucester row, Grange road
Palmer Samuel, carpenter, 15 Church st. Camberwell
Palmer Samuel, cowkeeper, 29 Up. Lisson st. Lisson grove
Palmer Samuel, cowkeeper, 3 Ward's pl. Hoxton Old town
Palmer Sophia (Miss), staymaker, 30 Rathbone place
Palmer Stephen, rocking horse maker, 25 Hackney road
Palmer Thomas, jointed clog maker, 3 Milton st. Cripplegate
Palmer Thos. bookbinder & stationer, 18 Princess st. Lissn. gr
Palmer Thos. *Coachmakers' Arms* P.H. Robert st. Blkfrs. rd
Palmer Thomas, corndealer, 17 Counter st. Borough
Palmer Thomas, cornfactor, 30 Shad Thames
Palmer Thos. *Old Red Cow* P.H. 72 Long lane, Smithfield
Palmer Thos. plumber, 11 Kittesford place, Hackney road
Palmer Thos. stock & brace manufacturer, 32 Newgate st
Palmer Thos. translator of latin records, Rolls chapel
Palmer Thos. umbrella & fish. tackle ma. 69 Red Lion st. Hlbrn
Palmer Thos. D. bookbinder, 5 Gt. Chesterfield st. Marylbn
Palmer Thos. Walter, chemist & druggist, 32 Newgate st
Palmer Wm. attorney, 7 Gray's inn square
Palmer Wm. baker, 47 Poplar High st
Palmer Wm. barrister, 6 King's bench walk, Temple
Palmer Wm. beer retailer, 195 Tooley st
Palmer Wm. boarding house, 120 Fore st. Cripplegate
Palmer Wm. bookseller & stationer, 7 New Bridge st. Vauxhall
Palmer Wm. bricklayer, 5 Tyer st. Princes road, Lambeth
Palmer Wm. *Bull* P.H. Great Dover road, & livery stables, Warner st. Dover road
Palmer Wm. coffee rooms, 8 Back st. Horselydown
Palmer Wm. *Duchess of Oldenburgh* P.H. 38 Goswell road
Palmer Wm. fruiterer, 37 High st. Notting hill
Palmer Wm. fruiterer, 57 Park st. Dorset sq
Palmer Wm. hop & seed merchant, 17 Mark lane
Palmer Wm. hosier & outfitter, 399 Strand
Palmer Wm. (late John Fletcher), laceman, 61 St. Paul's churchyard, & milliner, 16 Clark's place, Islington
Palmer Wm. parthenium lecture rooms, 72 St. Martin's lane
Palmer Wm. slater, Stratford, Essex
Palmer Wm. tallow chandler, 16 White hart st. Drury lane
Palmer Wm. tobacconist, 37 Garden row, London rd. Boro'
Palmer Wm. tool dealer, 72 Wheeler st. Spitalfields
Palmer Wm. trimming seller, 18 Aldgate
Palmer Wm. Francis, builder, 1 Christopher st. Hatton gdn
Palmer Wm. Henry, mercht. see Heath, Palmer & Beatson
Palmer Wm. James, hairdresser, 29 Newcastle st. Strand
Palmer Wm. James, tailor & robe maker, 25 Grosvenor st
Palmer Wm. Shrubsole, oil & italian wareho. 143 St. George st
Palmer Wm. Vaughan, electrotypist, 42 Gloucestr st. Queen sq
Palmer's Almshouses & School, Palmer's pas. Westminster
Palser Edward, oil & colorman, 111 Kingsland road
Palser Henry, printseller, 366 Strand
Palser James, rocking horse maker, 122 Waterloo road
Palser Thos. sen. ancient & modern printseller, 183 Strand
Pamment Henry, cheesemonger, 43 Penton st. Pentonville
Pamment Henry, fruiterer, Judd cottage, Judd st. Brnswk. sq
Pamphillion Fredk. cheesemonger, 76 Castle st. Leicester sq
Pamphilon James, coffee rooms, 27 Brydges st
Pamplin Wm. botanical bookseller, 45 Frith st. Soho
Pancras & N. W. London Savings' Bank (John M'Murton, secretary), 50 Charlotte st. Fitzroy square
Panchard George, jeweller, 15 Arlington st. Sadler's wells
Pangborn James, grocer, 22 Milton st. Dorset square
Pank John & Son, tailors, 25 John st. Holland st. Blackfriars
Pank James, shopkeeper, 2 Coal Harbour st. Hackney rd
Pank Thomas, surveyor, 123 Praed st. Paddington
Pankhurst Dillnott, fruit salesman, Fruit mkt. Covent gardn
Pankhurst Geo. carpenter & packing ca. mak. 77 Coleman st
Pankhurst John, wheelwright, Battle bdg. mws. Caledonian rd
Pankhurst Thos. fruit salesma. Covent garden fruit market
Panklibanon Iron Works Company, 58 Baker st. & 5 King st. Portman square
Pannell Chas. jun. shipping butcher, 12 Lit. Hermitage st
Pannell Chas. sen. shipping butcher, 26 Russell st. Rotherhi
Pannell Henry, cheesemonger, 2 Myddelton st. Clerkenwell

Pannell Joseph, butcher, High st. Battersea
Pannell Joshua, bootmaker, 12 Sherborne pl. Blandford sq
Pannell Mary (Mrs.), grocer&cheesem. 32 Robin Hood la. Poplar
Pannell Michael, jun. leather seller, manufacturer of gold & silver leathers, door & library leathers, & table cover manufacturer, 4 Skinner st. Snowhill
Pannell Wm. grocer & cheesemonger, 93 Poplar High st
Panormo Edwd. violin & guitar ma. 12 Richmond st. Le'str. sq
Panormo Louis, guitar ma. & music sel. 46 High st. St. Giles's
Panormo Matilda (Miss), milliner, 52 High st. Marylebone
Pantechnicon (Seth Smith, proprietor), Halkin st. west, & Motcomb st. Belgrave square
Panter John Edward, barrister, 58 Chancery lane
Pantheon Bazaar & Picture Gallery, 359 Oxford st. & 8 Great Marlborough st
Panther Samuel, ham dealer, 17 High st. Newington butts
Panther Samuel, ham&beef shop, 21 Triangle, Kenngtn. crs
Pantin & Turner, wholesale brushmakers, stationers&warehousemen, 87 & 88 West Smithfield
Panting Thomas, carman, canterbury whf. Belvedr. rd. Lmbth
Pantlin William, tailor, 7 York st. Westminster
Panton Elizh. (Mrs.), baker, 12 Elizabeth st. Sloane st
Panton James, general commission merchant&sworn brok. for the sale of ships, &c. 1A, Bishopsgate within
Panton James, sailcloth, canvass, tarpaulin & twine factor, 237 Wapping
Panton James, sworn broker, 1A, Bishopsgate st. within
Panton Wm. James, baker, 3 Ranelagh road, Thames bank
Panzetta George, gasfitter, 19 Gt. Chapel st. Oxford st
Panzetta William, bootmaker, see Howell & Panzetta
Pape (Simpson Goy) & Co. tailors, 17 Hanover st. Hanover sq
Pape Edward, surgeon, 1 Princes st. Stamford st. Blackfrs
Pape Henri, pianoforte maker, 75 Grosvenor st
Pape Wm. carpenter & builder, 47 Webber row, Blackfriars
Pape Wm. clock case maker, 12 Helmet row, St. Luke's
Pape Wm. working cutler, 84 Vauxhall walk, Lambeth
Papes Henry, pianoforte manufacturer, 75 Grosvenor st
Papineau Wm. & Co. chemical mfrs. Albion wharf, Old Ford, & High st. Bromley, Middlesex
Papineau John, ink maker, Vine st. Minories
Papineau John, stationer & printer, 19 Mark lane
Papineau Richard, carpenter, 8 Gilbert's bldgs. Westmr. rd
Papon Elise (Madame), dressmaker, 23 Grosvenor st
Papprill Joseph, tailor, 3 Featherstone buildings, Holborn
Papp Harry, whip maker, 11 Middle row, Knightsbridge
Papps George, boot & shoe mfr. 11 Church la. Whitechapel
Papwell Thomas, bedstead maker, 38 Ray st. Clerkenwell
Papworth John B. architect, &c. 10 Caroline st. Bedford sq
Papworth John Woody, artist, 10 Caroline st. Bedford sq
Papworth Wyatt Andrew, artist, 10 Caroline st. Bedford sq
Paqualin George, shipbroker, 5 Water lane, Gt. Tower st
Paradise Benj. who. & manufg. stationer, 40 Watling st
Paragreen Robert, baker, 37 Upper Ebury st. Pimlico
Paravagna & Casella, coral manufacturers & merchants, 3 Brabant court, Philpot lane, Fenchurch st
Paravagna Joseph, coral mercht. 3 Brabant ct. Philpot lane
Paravicini Jas. Prior, stock broker, Stock exchange
Parbery Samuel, plumber& glazier, 10 Wells mews, Jermyn st
Parbury, Thacker & Co. east ind. agts.& merchts. 46 Lime st
Parcell Mary & Ellen (Misses), milliners, 62 Conduit st
Parcell Edward, plumber, &c. 16 Sandwich st. Burton cres
Parden James, bricklayer, 53 Freeschool st. Horselydown
Pardoe, Hoomans & Co. carpet manufacturers & worsted spinners, 20 Skinner st. Snowhill, & Kidderminster
Pardoe George, physician, 22 Cavendish square
Pardon Benjamin, printer, see Blackburn & Pardon
Pardon Benjamin, *Rose & Crown* P.H. 1 Little Pulteney st
Pardon William, printer, 7 Bennett st. Blackfriars
Pardow James, needle & fish hook manufr. 44 Basinghall st
Pardy Mary (Mrs.), dressmaker, 27 New st. Brompton
Pardy William & George, *Lamb Tavern*, Leadenhall market
Pare John, *Barley Mow* P.H. 135 Salisbury ct. Fleet st
Pare William, railway traffic statist, 11 John st. Adelphi
Parent Peter, tailor, 60 Frith st. Soho
Parfelt Thomas, engraver, 57 Myddelton st
Parfitt Benjamin, stone mason, 3 Artillery st. Horselydown
Parfitt Edward, watch hand mak. 9 Jerusalem pas. Clerknwl
Parfitt Thomas, engraver, 20 Woodbridge st. Clerkenwell
Parfrey Philip, beer retailer, Ferry, Thames bank, Pimlico
Parfrey Youngs, wheelwright, see Smith & Parfrey
Parham James, pork butcher, 9 Broadway, Westminster
Parham William, pork butcher, 3 Crown st. Soho
Pariente Joshua, merchant, 18 Coleman st
Paris Chas. S. & Rt. T. mer. Salvador ho. Bishopsg. st. & Baltic
Paris Peter & Son, acid manufacturers, Battersea fields
Paris Thomas & Sons, windsor soap makers, 139 Strand
Paris & Lyons Railway Co. (*Ganneron's Company*), (Villaboisnet & Filder, secs.), Tokenhouse yard
Paris & Lyons Rlway. Co. (G. Byam, sec.), 19 King's Arms yd
Paris & Lyons Rlwy. Office (E. Aimé, sec.), 62 King Wm. st. City
Paris & Rouen Rlwy. Co. (Easthope&Son, agts.), 38 Throgmorton st. City
Paris & St. Quentin Railway Co. 20 King's Arms yard
Paris & Strasburg Railway Co. 11 Old Jewry
Paris Hugh, marine store dealr. 4 Prospect row, Walworth rd
Paris John, horse dealer, 35 Ray st. Clerkenwell
Paris John Ayrton, physician, 27 Dover st. Piccadilly
Paris Louis, chaser, 57 Britannia terrace, City road
Paris Peter, artificial florist, 10 Denmark st. Soho
Paris Robt. cabinetma. & upholst. 32 Bouverie st. Fleet st
Paris Thomas, brewer, 23 to 27 Laystall st. Liquorpond st
Paris Thomas, windsor soap maker, 139 Strand
Parish Clerks' Hall (Joseph Wheeler, clerk), 83 Wood st
Parish Charles, architect, Carlton chambers, 12 Regent st
Parish Geo. E. who. soap & candle wareho. 57 Up. Thames st
Parish Hannah (Mrs.), wooll. draper, 25 White Horse yd. Dry. la
Parish James, *Spotted Dog* P.H. 8 Strand la. Strand
Parish John, hardwareman, 6 Northampton ter. City road
Parish Jonathan, furniture dlr. 7 Union pl. Lisson grove nth
Parish Samuel, shoemaker, 13 Chichester rents, Chancery la
Parish Thos. *White Horse* P.H. 6 Fan st. Goswell st
Park Lewis & Chas. sewed muslin manufrs. 13 Cheapside
Park & Thornbory, haberdashers&hosiers. 186 High Holborn
Park Alexander Atherton, Master of Court of Com. Pleas, Common Pleas Office, Chancery lane
Park Arch. Alex. engraver & publisher, 47 Leonard st. Fins
Park John, hat manufactr. 9 Lemon st. Loman's pond, Boro'
Park John, waterproof cloth manfr. see Spill & Park
Park John Cornelius, builder, Battersea marsh
Park Mungo, surgeon, 100 Old st
Park Patrick, sculptor, 13 Bruton st. Berkeley square
Park Thomas, cowkeeper, 4 George's terrace, Kentish town
Park Thomas, tailor, 41 Bury st. St. James's
Park Thomas, wine merchant, 5 Cushion court, Old Broad st
Park William, cowkeeper, 1½ Brewer st. north, Goswell rd
Park William, wire worker, see Hopwood & Park
Parke & Freeth, solicitors, 63 Lincoln's inn fields
Parke George, engaver, 38 Bridport place, New North road
Parken Ann (Mrs.), toy warehouse, 4 Charlotte st. Whitech
Parken John Palmer, solicitor, 13 New Boswell ct. Linc. inn
Parken Wm. Palmer, barrister, 13 New Boswell ct. Linc. inn
Parker, Field & Sons, gun makers, &c. to her Majesty's hon. Board of Ordnance, the hon. E. I. Company, the Hudson's Bay Company, & armourers to the police, 233 High holborn
Parker, Furnivall & Parker, military publishers & booksellers, 30 Charing cross
Parker, Hayes, Barnwell & Twisden, solicitors, 1 Linc. in. flds
Parker John & David, warehousemen, 96 Minories
Parker & Lings, tailors, 35 Warwick st. Regent st
Parker & Page, cane & cane rib ma. 10 Bacon st. Bethnal gr
Parker & Pepper, milliners, 75 Lower George st. Chelsea
Parker Philip & Peter, booksellers, 181 Long la. Bermondsey
Parker Richard & Co. carriers, New inn, Old Bailey
Parker, Son & Pritchett, teabrokers, 131 Fenchurch st
Parker & Scrutton, stock & share brokers, 81 Old Broad st
Parker, Taylor & Rooke, attorneys, 3 Raymond bldgs. Gray's inn
Parker & Trendall, drapers, 7 Shepperton pl. New North rd
Parker & Upton, coal merchants, Beaufort wharf, Strand, & 54 Marshall st. Golden square
Parker & Whitby, sufferance & general wharfingers, Hartley's wharf, Freeman's lane, Back st. Horselydown
Parker Wm. Augustus & Co. mer. 1 Three King ct. Lombd. st
Parker Wm. & Saml. B. color & tar mers. Creek st. Deptford
Parker Abraham, ho. ag. & appraiser, 11 Gower st. & 42 Keppel st
Parker Society (Wm. Thomas, sec.), 33 Southmptn. st. Strand
Parker Benjamin, carpenter & undertaker, 22 Drury lane
Parker Chas. archit. & surv. 16 Tavistock st. Bedford sq
Parker Chas. cowkeeper, 1 Tudor place, Tottenham ct. rd
Parker Chas. tailor, 7 Upper Albany st. Regent's park
Parker Christr. J. wholesale hosier, see Hine, Parker & Co
Parker Daniel, carpenter, 1 St. James's market
Parker Danl. furn. brok. 20 & 21 Laystall st. Liquorpond st
Parker Edward, baker, 2 Marlborough road, Chelsea
Parker Edward, tailor, 4 Gravel lane, Southwark
Parker Eleanor (Miss), academy, 2 King st. Finsbury
Parker Emma (Miss), china wa. 43 Hedge row, Islngtn. High st
Parker Frederic John, brit. metal goods ma. 7 Lit. Compton st
Parker Frederick, animal charcoal manufacturer, Bow common, & 138 New Gravel lane, Shadwell
Parker Fred. wood engraver, 10 Southampton st. Strand
Parker Fred Hen. surgeon, 82A, Mount st. & 11 Portugal st
Parker George, baker, Church st. Hackney

Parker George, cabinet ma. 36 Grafton st. east, Tottm. ct. rd
Parker George, carpenter, 15 Saville place, Mile end road
Parker George, chemist, 74 St. Martin's lane, & 1 Long acre
Parker Geo. furn. ironmonger, 22 New rd. St. George's east
Parker Geo. Chas. *Devonshire Arms* P.H. 17 Queen st. Goldn. sq
Parker George Russell, silk broker, 16 St. Mary axe
Parker Henry, baker, 20 Lower st. Islington
Parker Hy. Walter, assistant poor law com. Somerset house
Parker Henry, fruiterer, Centre row, Covent garden market
Parker Henry, lamp manufacturer, 22 Plough ct. Fetter la
Parker Henry, wire worker, 156 Kingsland road
Parker Isaac, beer retailer, New road, South Lambeth
Parker James, beer retailer, 10 Gainsford st. Horselydown
Parker James, boot & shoe ma. 48 Barclay st. Somers town
Parker James, boot & shoe ma. 30 Camden st. Islington green
Parker James, corn factor, 4 Catherine court, Tower hill
Parker James, glass bender, 5 Little St. Mary Axe
Parker James, queen's counsel, 2 New square, Lincoln's inn
Parker James, shawl agent, 9 Great Distaff lane
Parker James, watchcase joint finisher, 17 King st. Clerknwll
Parker James, working optician, 33 Gr. Ormond st
Parker James Rawes, pocket book ma. 5 Little Distaff lane
Parker Jane (Mrs.), livery stables, 20½ West Smithfield, & 26 Hosier lane, West Smithfield
Parker John, *Barleymow* P.H. 8 Dorset st. Portman sq
Parker John, bootmaker, 6 Bridge court, Westminster
Parker John, boot & shoe maker, 6 Bridge st. Lambeth
Parker John, carpenter, 28 Upper Edmund st. King's cross
Parker John, cooper, 88 Broadwall, Blackfriars
Parker John, corkcutter, 36 Houndsditch
Parker John, fruiterer, 2 Bell yard, Gracechurch st
Parker John, jet worker & jeweller, 30 Up. King st. Blmsby
Parker John, oilman & grocer, 1 Glo'ster ter. New rd. Whtchl
Parker John, statuary, 17 Salisbury st. Lisson grove
Parker John, surgeon, 20 Great Dover road
Parker John, tailor, 12 Webb st. Bermondsey st
Parker John Chawner, cheesemonger, 5 King st. St. James's
Parker John H. railway carrier, King's Arms inn, Snowhill
Parker John Joseph, coal merchant, see Burrows & Parker
Parker John Thomas, potato merchant, 148 Shoreditch
Parker John W. undertakr. & fur. bro. 10 Norway pl. Hckny. rd
Parker John William, publisher, 445 West Srand
Parker Joseph, tailor, 44 Upper Berkeley st. west
Parker Joseph Wm. secret springer, 9 Up. Smith st. Nthmptn sq
Parker Kenyon Stevens, queen's counsel, 13 New sq. Linc. inn
Parker Martha (Miss), dress ma. 50 Gt. Russell st. Bloomsbury
Parker Martha (Mrs.), dress ma. 29 Up. Berkeley st. west
Parker Mary (Mrs.), *White Horse* P.H. 8 Castle st. Long acre
Parker Michael, china, &c. mender & wareho. 3 New Quebec st
Parker Nath. Eastaugh, *Three Tuns* P.H. 84 West Smithfield
Parker Noah, butcher, 37 East st. Manchester sq
Parker Paul, grocer, 14 Tottenham pl. Tottenham court rd
Parker Richard, bootmaker, 34 Fetter lane, Fleet st
Parker Richard, grocer, 7 White Hart pl. Lr. Kennington la
Parker Richard (Mrs.), milliner, 263 Regent st
Parker Richd. *Newcastle on Tyne* P.H. 7 Cambridge st. Gold. sq
Parker Robert, florist & seedsman, Mayfield road, Dalston
Parker Robert, potato salesman, Scovell's wharf, Tooley st. & 135 & 138 Shoreditch
Parker Robert, *Wheatsheaf* P.H. 37 Kenton st. Brunswick sq
Parker Robert, woollendraper, 96 High Holborn
Parker Samuel, builder, Tanners hill, New town, Deptford
Parker Samuel, grocer, &c. 43 Sloane square, Chelsea
Parker Samuel, hatter, 58 & 59 Marylebone la. Oxford st
Parker Tamery (Mrs.), jeweller, 13 Edwards st. Portman sq
Parker Thomas, barrister, 6 Old square, Lincoln's inn
Parker Thomas, jun. barrister, 6 Old square, Lincoln's inn
Parker Thomas, builder, 38 Keppel st. & Torrington place
Parker Thomas, butcher, 2 Honey lane market, Cheapside
Parker Thomas, *Castle* P. H. 6 Bullin cout, 407 Strand
Parker Thomas, cornchandler, 30 Compton st. Brunswick sq
Parker Thomas, hatter, 40 Crawford st. Portman square
Parker Thomas, paper stainer, see Townsend, Parker & Co
Parker Thomas, solicitor, 6 Lincoln's inn fields
Parker Thomas, solicitor, 18 St. Paul's churchyard
Parker Thomas, *Three Tuns*, P.H. 22 Gt. New st. Fetter la
Parker Thomas B. brush & toy dealer, 37 Lr. Islington ter
Parker Thomas Hen. printseller, 42 Princes st. Leicester sq
Parker Thos. Jas. auctioneer, &c. High st. Stoke Newington
Parker Thomas Madgshon, attorney, 3 New inn, Strand, & Deptford High st
Parker Wm. academy, 7 Artillery st. Bishopsgate
Parker Wm. bricklayer, 18 Vine ct. Wheeler st. Spitalfields
Parker Wm. cabinet maker, &c. 5 Queen st. Worship st
Parker Wm. chess board manufr. 10 Wilmot sq. Bethnal gr. rd
Parker Wm. glass & china man, 22 Judd st. Brunswick sq
Parker Wm. grocer, 2 Noel st. Wardour st. Soho
Parker Wm. oil & colorman, 10 & 11 Houghton st. Clare mkt
Parker Wm. pork butcher, 223 Borough High st
Parker Wm. surgeon, 5 Parker's row, Dockhead
Parker Wm. wheelwright, coach & horses yard, Drury la
Parker Wm. Dorrell, potato dealer, 13 Cowcross st. Smithfield
Parker Wm. Garner, jeweller, 30 Glo'ster st. St. John st. rd
Parker Wm. James, tailor, 15 Carlisle st. Soho
Parker Wm. Phillips, solicitor, see Nicholson & Parker
Parker Wilmot, barrister, 36 Carey st. Lincoln's inn
Parkes, Smith & Co. solicitors, 12 Bedford row
Parkes Thos. & Joseph, hop & seed factors, 7 Counter st. Boro'
Parkes Chas. Hen. parliamentary agt. see Dyson, Hall & Parkes
Parkes Dan. button mould & counter turner, 7 King st. Clkwn
Parkes Ebenezer, printers' joiner & rule cutter, 142 Fetter lane, & 33 Thomas st. Stamford st
Parkes Hy. Wm. patent lock 5 & 7 guards, fire proof iron door, deed & cash box manufacturer, 268 Strand
Parkes John, commission merchant, 37 Fenchurch st
Parkes John, ironmonger, 24 High st. Marylebone
Parkes John, ironmonger, 41 High st. Notting hill
Parkes John, lapidary, 21 Grafton st. Soho
Parkes Joseph, solicitor to the charity commission suits, & parliamentary agent, 21 Great George st. Westminster
Parkes Josiah, civil engineer, 11 Gt. College st. Westminster
Parkes Mary (Mrs.), printseller & publisher, 22 Golden sq
Parkes Wm. Barney, physician, 31 Gt. Marlborough st
Parkes Thomas Wm. solicitor, see Parks, Smith & Co
Parkhouse Henry, linendraper, 8 North pl. Ball's Pond road
Parkhouse John, dining rooms, 3 Gt. Windmill st. Haymarket
Parkhouse Thomas, dining rooms, 38 High st. St. Giles's
Parkhurst Wm. ostrich feather manufr. 41 Broad st. Golden sq
Parkin Charlt. (Miss), umbrella ma. 18 Phœnix st. Somers tn
Parkin John, surgeon, 20 Whitehead's grove, Chelsea
Parkin Mary (Mrs.), coal merchant, Copperas la. Deptford
Parkin Peter Spurr, solicitor, 3 Clifford's inn
Parkin Richard, confectioner, 33 Little Earl st. Seven dials
Parkin Richd. grocer & teadealer, 31 High st. Kensington
Parkin Thomas, gun barrel maker, 5 Meard's court, Soho
Parkin Wm. solicitor, see Humphrys, Keightley & Parkin
Parkins James & Co. tobacconists, 101 Holborn
Parkins George Hall, *Princess Royal* P.H. 71 Paul st. Finsb
Parkins James, auctioneer & valuer to the woollen trade, & house agent, 85 Cheapside
Parkins James, baker, 49 Upper George st. Bryanstone sq
Parkins James, wine & spirit mer. 17 Bishopsgate within
Parkins John, bookseller & binder, 2 Church st. Westminster
Parkins William, stationer, 11 Hanway st. Oxford st
Parkinson & Frodsham, chronometer, &c. maks. 4 Change alley
Parkinson Geo. & Son, surgeon dentists, 1 Racquet ct. Fleet st
Parkinson John & Thos. wax bleachers, 21 Skinner st
Parkinson Wm. H. & Jas. merchs. 15 Union ct. Old Broad st
Parkinson Fred. Kidman, solicitor, 4 Raymond bdgs. Gray's inn
Parkinson George, tailor & draper, 32 Wapping wall
Parkinson Hen. chronom. & watchma. 65 Red Lion st. Clrknw
Parkinson James, chronometer ma. 53 Red Lion st. Clrknwl
Parkinson Jas. Hicks, shipping grocer, 5 & 6 Pump yd. Ratcliff
Parkinson James Ullett, linendraper, 7 High st. Stepney
Parkinson John, architect & survey. 20 Rahere st. Goswell rd
Parkinson John, plumber & glazier, 10 Union ter. Notting hill
Parkinson John, solicitor, see Lucas & Parkinson
Parkinson John, solicitor, see Farrer & Parkinson
Parkinson John Herring, surgeon dentist, 36 Sackville st
Parkinson John Jas. windowblind ma. 7 Blue Cross st. Le'str. sq
Parkinson John L. sheep salesman, 37 West Smithfield
Parkinson Joseph, architect, 41 Sackville st. Piccadilly
Parkinson Richard, tailor, 13 Beauchamp st. Brooke st. Hlbn
Parkinson Robert Hen. furnish. ironmonger, &c. 79 Oxford st
Parkinson Thomas, carpenter, &c. 23 Clarges st. Piccadilly
Parkinson Thos. plumber & glazier, 26 King st. Bloomsbury
Parkinson Thos. tailor, 24 Little St. Andrew st. Seven dials
Parkisson John, fruiterer, 23 Lower Eaton st. Grosvenor pl
Parkman Joseph, watch maker, 9 Wellington st. Goswell rd
Parks Alfred, plumber, 47 Wimbourne st. New North rd
Parks Amos, baker, 43 Up. Salisbury place, Lock's fields
Parks Charles C. tailor, 14 Three Crown square, Borough
Parks Edgar, ironmonger, 140 Fleet st
Parks Edward, butcher, 9 New King st. Deptford
Parks Edward, butcher, 50 Flagon row, Deptford
Parks Frederick, tailor & draper, 57 King William st. City
Parks Hen. coal mercht. & grocer, High st. Kingsland
Parks Joseph, baker, 21 York st. Westminster
Parks Thomas, dairy, 4 George's terrace, Kentish town
Parkyn Mary, Amelia & Harriet (Mesdames), millnrs. 92 Qdrnt
Parkyn Robt. & Fredk. shawl wareho. 84A, Quadrant, Regt. st
Parkyn Francis, carpenter & bldr. 2 Bedford st. Bedford row

Parkyn Robert, laceman, 82 Quadrant, Regent st
Parlby John, carp. builder & undertk.49 Foley st.Portland pl
Parlett & Smith, chair makers, 12 Francis st. Tottnm. ct. rd
Parlett Wm. shoemaker, 35 Webber st. Blackfriars rd
Parliament Office, House of Lords, Old Palace yard
Parliamentary Journal Office, 43 Parliament st.Westmtr
Parliamentary Papers' Sale Offices, 6 Gt. Turnstile, Holborn, & 11 Bridge st. Westminster ; hours 9 to 8
Parlour Isaac, stone mer.DeBeauvoirwf.Canal rd.Kingsld.rd
Parlour Richard, *Prince Albert* P.H. Queen's road, Dalston
Parman George, furniture broker, 57 Old st. St. Luke's
Parman James, windsor chairmaker, 67 Old st. St. Luke's
Parman Wm. John, chairmaker, 18 Featherstone st. City rd
Parmenter Eliz.(Mrs.), horse slaughterer,1 Maiden la.Kgs.cr
Parmenter Geo. nurseryman,1Holmes terrace,Kentish town
Parmenter John, umbrella maker, 39 Hackney road
Parmenter Samuel, lithographic printer, 304 Strand
Parminter Wm. painter & glazier, 4 Queen st. Ratcliff
Parnall Wm. & Co. clothiers & hosiers, 219 Blackfriars rd
Parnall Henry, hosier & outfitter, 100 Bishopsgate without
Parnell & Banner, ship & ins. brokers, 57 Gracechurch st
Parnell & Smith, surgeons, 7 Bennett st. St. James's st
Parnell & Tanqueray, attorneys, 34 New Broad st. City
Parnell Gervas, brewer, see Baverstock & Parnell
Parnell Henry, auctioneer & valuer, Moorgate st. chambers
Parnell Jane (Mrs.), stationer, 39 High st. Marylebone
Parnell John Jessopp, solicitor, 12 Clifford's inn, Fleet st
Parnell Michael, ironmonger, 32 Little Queen st. Holborn
Parnell Paul, barrister, 3 Hare court, Temple
Parnell Robert Thomas, orange merchant, 15 Eastcheap
Parnell Thomas, cabinet ma. 18 Shepperton st. NewNorth rd
Parnell Thomas,optician & chart seller, 2 Lr.East Smithfield
Parnell Thomas, tailor, 11 Eyre st. hill
Parnell Thomas, watchmaker, 32 High st. Bow
Parnell William, butcher, 4 Patriot row, Cambridge road
Parnell William, hosier, 1 Wilderness row, Clerkenwell
Parnell William, ship & insur. broker, 57 Gracechurch st
Parnther & Fisher, attorneys, 50 Fenchurch st
Parr Ann (Mrs.) & Nthl. *King's Head* P.H. 186 Church st. Shoreditch
Parr Ann Cluff (Miss), servants' registry office,103 Holborn
Parr Edward, watchmaker, see Plumbly & Parr
Parr Francis, registrar, 22 Bridge st. Southwark
Parr George, stationer & bookseller, 19 Broad ct. Long acre
Parr Henry, grocer, 10 Grosvenor row, Pimlico
Parr Henry, grocer & cheesemonger, 9 St. John st. road
Parr Henry, tobacconist, 7 Pierrepont row, Islington
Parr James Ebenezer, butcher, 7 Agar st. Strand
Parr John, coal agent, 16 Wharf, so. side, Paddington basin
Parr John, cooper, 19 Seething lane, Tower st
Parr John, teadealer, 200 Blackfriars road
Parr John Edward, barrister, 11 Paper buildings, Temple
Parr Thos. hat block ma.& undertaker,20 Gravel la. Borough
Parr Thomas, tobacco pipe maker, 4 Finch st. Whitechapel
Parr William, *Green Man* P.H. 7 Green st. Grosvenor sq
Parratt & Walmisley, parliamentary agents,House of Lords
Parratt Charles, butcher, 13 Skinner's pl. Leadenhall mrkt
Parratt Edward,advertising agent,3Up.Wellington st.Strnd
Parratt James, surgeon & chemist, 18 Mount st. Berkeley sq
Parratt James, tailor, &c. 6 New Bridge st. Vauxhall
Parratt John, carman, 40 Betts st. Ratcliff highway
Parratt Wm. cheesemonger, 69 Margaret st. Wilmington sq
Parrell William, solicitor, 25 New North st. Red Lion sq
Parrett Benjamin, furn. broker, 81 Cromer st. Brunswick sq
Parrett Daniel, grocer & oilman, 45 Little Britain
Parrinton & Ladbury, accountants, 16 King st. Cheapside
Parris Edm.T.artist to theQueen dowgr.17Grafton st.Bond st
Parris Mary (Mrs.), straw hat ma. Southamptn. st. Cmbrwl
Parris Richd. engineer & modeller, 25 Up. St. Martin's lane
Parris Robert, architect, &c see Willshire &Parris
Parrish Ann (Mrs.), lodging house, 16 Carlisle st. Soho sq
Parrish John Thomas, plumber, &c. 43 North st. Edgw. rd
Parrish MaryA. (Mrs.), confectioner, 41 Earl st. e.Lisson gr
Parrish Philippa (Mrs.), boot & shoe maker,168Kingsland rd
Parrish William, *Union* P.H. 73 Jermyn st. Haymarket
Parrit Edward, grocer, see Hobson & Parrit
Parritt John, plumber, 13B,Windmill st.Tottenham court rd
Parron John, tailor, 5 Bentinck pl. High st. Portland town
Parrott John & Son, hat lining cutters, 130 Union st. Boro'
Parrott Charles, warehouseman, 1 Little Love lane,Wood st
Parrott George, builder, 22½ Diamond row, Stepney green
Parrott John, carman, 37 Seething lane, Gt. Tower st
Parrott John, who. & retail confectioner, 134 Boro' High st
Parrott Richard, chairmaker, 3 Charles st. St. George's ea
Parrott Wm.Geo.ironmong. 7 Clement's inn pass. Clare mkt
Parrott Wm. Joseph, furnish. ironmong. 61 Union st. Boro'

Parry & Baseley, wholesale cheesemongers, 87 Holborn hill
Parry John & Thomas, linendrapers, &c. 10 Ludgate hill
Parry & Sons, tallow chandlers, melters, & manufacturers of patent grease for carriage wheels & railway machinery, & colormen, 15 Fleur de lis court, Spitalfields
Parry Thomas & Son, coal & coke merchants, Islington wharf, 21 Macclesfield st. north, City road
Parry Anna (Mrs.), servants' registry office, 15 Blandford st
Parry Arthur, accountant, 22 Northampton sq. Clerkenwell
Parry Daniel, paper stainer, 84 Hackney road
Parry David,coal mer.Child's Belvedere wf.Belved.rd.Lmbth
Parry David, tobacconist, 51 Beech st. Barbican
Parry David, wholesale grocer, 36 Bread st. Cheapside
Parry Edwd. ironfndr. & smith, 105 Golden lane, Barbican
Parry Edward Lewis, woollendraper, 10 Tothill st. Westmr
Parry Geo. J. coffee roaster, 20 Colchester st. Whitechapel
Parry George John, solicitor, 12 George st. Mansion house
Parry Henrietta (Miss), who. milliner, 70 Watling st
Parry Henry, carpenter & builder, see Vandersteen & Parry
Parry Hen.german hone imp. & strop ma. 8 Brooke st. Holbn
Parry Henry, hat manufacturer, 20 St. John sq.Clerkenwell
Parry Henry, solicitor, Deptford High st
Parry Hen. Aldridge, india brok. see Macnaughtan & Parry
Parry Jabez, undertaker, 46 Paddington st. Marylebone
Parry James, picture cleaner, 5 Lisle st. Leicester square
Parry James, children's shoema. 31 Union rw. New Kent rd
Parry Jane (Mrs.), butcher, 16 Oxford market
Parry Jane (Miss), fishmonger, 42 Union st. Borough
Parry Joel, builder, 24 Houghton st. Clare market
Parry John, chandler's shop, 80 York st. Westminster
Parry John, *Hanover* coffee rooms, 1 Pollen st. Hanover sq
Parry John, insurance brok. 3 Warnford ct. Throgmorton st
Parry John, jun. prof. of music, 17 Tavistock st. Bedford sq
Parry John Billingsly, queen's counsel,9New sq.Lincoln's inn
Parry John H. barrister, 35 Southamptn. bldgs. Chancery la
Parry Joseph, cheesemonger, 22 Flagon row, Deptford
Parry Louisa (Miss), milliner, &c. 81 Margaret st.Cavdsh. sq
Parry Louisa (Mrs.), hosier&laceman, 1 Albion pl. King's cr
Parry Mary (Mrs.), milliner, 49 Wigmore st. Cavendish sq
Parry Richd. chandler's shop,9St.Mark's rd.Cambrwl.Nw.rd
Parry Richard, pawnbroker, 20 Flagon row, Deptford
Parry Richard, surgeon, 14 Church row, Newington butts
Parry Robert, beer retailer, see Cheyne & Parry
Parry Samuel, butcher, 12 Norway place, Hackney road
Parry Stephen, coffee rooms, 18 Ivy lane, Newgate st
Parry Susannah (Mrs.),grocer,29White Horse st.Coml.rd.ea
Parry Thomas, dairy, 3 Low.Porchester st. Edgware road
Parry Thomas, hop & seed mercht. 75 Borough High st
Parry Thomas Sparke, coal merchant, 23Wharf,Harrow rd. & Islington wharf, 21 Macclesfield st. north, City road
Parry Thomas William, optician, 24 Holywell st. Strand
Parry William, file cutter, 33 Chenies mews, Bedford sq
Parry William, grocer, 12 Neptune st. Rotherhithe
Parry William, solicitor, see Milne, Parry, Milne & Morris
Parsall Wm. Henry, cornfactor, 26 Mark lane
Parsey Arthur, artist, 2 Spur st. Leicester square
Parsley Wm. *Green Dragon* P.H. 30 Belvedere rd.Lambeth
Parslow & Bates, sack collectors, 10 Loman st. Borough
Parslow Wm. flour & sack wareh. 44 North row, Grosv. sq
Parson John, solicitor, see Burchell, Kilgour & Parson
Parson John, solicitor, see Baker & Parson
Parson Thos.Edgcombe,solicitor,see Blower,Vizard & Parson
Parsonage Abraham, butcher, 8 King's pl. Comcl. rd. east
Parsons Arthur W. J. & Co. merchants, 75 Coleman st
Parsons, Fletcher & Co. printing ink manufacturers, wholesale stationers,&sole wholesale agents forTarling's metallic writing ink, 22 Bread st
Parsons & Marshall, hosiers & glovers, 33 City rd. Finsbury
Parsons Charles, attorney, Temple chambers, Fleet st
Parsons Charles, baker, 240 Poplar High st
Parsons Charles, oil & italian warehouse, 210 Oxford st
Parsons Edw. grocer & cheesemonger, 62 Regent st. Westmr
Parsons Fredk. who. druggist, 10 Camomile st. Bishopsgate
Parsons Fredk. wholesale druggist, 19 King st. Finsbury
Parsons George, *Baldfaced Stag* P.H. 38 Upper Clifton st. & Worship square, Finsbury
Parsons George, solicitor, 4 Manchester bldgs. Westminster
Parsons George, wheelwright, 9 Goswell road
Parsons James,coach & livery lace manufacturer,39Long acre
Parsons James, dyer, 8 Great Chapel st Oxford st
Parsons James, *Green Man* P.H. 37 Newcastle st. Whtchpl
Parsons James,grocer&cheesemongr.30 Marsham st.Westmr
Parsons James, mathematical divider, 50 RedLion st. Clknwl
Parsons James H. merchant, 75 Coleman st
Parsons James Henry, modeller, &c. 7 Brownlow st. Bedford row, & 100 High Holborn

Parsons John, baker, 1 Medway st. Horseferry road
Parsons John, baker, 18 Mount Pleasant, Gray's inn lane
Parsons John, beer retailer, 6 Lit. Cadogan pl. Belgrave sq
Parsons John, cheesemonger, 136 High st. Camden town
Parsons John, button & trim. seller, 29A, South st. Manch.sq
Parsons John, engineer, 75 Bankside
Parsons John, fruiterer, 17 South place, Tibberton square
Parsons John, *North Country Sailor* P.H. 109 Wapping High st
Parsons John, *Thistle & Crown* P.H. 109 Wapping High st
Parsons John Meeson, stockbroker, 6 Raymond buildings, & stock exchange
Parsons (Mrs.), ladies' school, 5 Brooksby st. Liverpool rd
Parsons Moses, hosier, glover, & shirtma. 268 Regent circus
Parsons Richard, baker & grocer, 7 Limehouse causeway
Parsons Richard, beer retailer, King's road west, Chelsea
Parsons Richard, butcher, 72 Leather lane, Holborn
Parsons Robert, baker, 1 Upper North pl. Gray's inn road
Parsons Robert, chemist & druggist, 98 York st. Westminster
Parsons Samuel, organ builder, 2 Lit. Russell st. Bloomsbury
Parsons Sarah (Mrs.), builder, Battersea rise, Wandsworth rd
Parsons Sedwell (Mrs.), fruiterer, 224 Tottenham court road
Parsons Stephen, fruiterer, 11 Michael's grove, Brompton
Parsons Thomas, barrister, 24 Old square, Lincoln's inn
Parsons Thomas Fulham, chemist & druggist, 125 Edgware rd
Parsons Wm. cheesemonger, 41 Three Colt st. Limehouse
Parsons Wm. ironmong. & engineer, Vine st. York rd. Lambeth
Parsons Wm. *Man in the Moon* P.H. Colchester st. Whitechpl
Parsons Wm. poulterer, 49 South Audley st
Parsons Wm. poulterer & game dealer, 11 Sun ct. Curzon st
Parsons Wm. solicitor, 34 Halfmoon st. Piccadilly
Parsons Wm. teadealer, 19 Gt. Turner st. Commercl. rd. east
Parsons Wm. teadealer, 165 Lambeth walk
Parsons Wm. timber mercht. Camberwell wf. Addington pl
Parsons Wm. tobacconist, 2 College st. Chelsea
Parsons Wm. tobacconist, 6 Spur st. Leicester square
Parsons Wm. *Two Brewers* P.H. 36 Jermyn st. St. James's
Parsons Wm. umbrella mnfr. 43 Margaret st. Wilmington sq
Parsson Wm. Nehmh. millwright & engnr. 34 Gravel la. Southk
Part James, surgeon, 2 Cambridge ter. Camden new town
Part Thomas, grocer, 38 East st. Kennington road
Parthenon Club House (Jas. Hall Daly, sec.), 16 Regent st
Partington Edward, butcher, 116 High st. Camden town
Partington Edward, conveyancer, see Boodle & Co
Partington Joseph, confectioner, 190 Strand & Cambrwl. gr
Partington Richard, beer retailer, 42 Marshall st. Golden sq
Partington Wm. watch & clock mkr. 52 Paddington st. Maryleb
Partis David Rich. *Three Compasses* P.H. 200 Rotherhithe
Partis John, confectioner, 2 Baker's row, Walworth road
Partis William, locksmith, 8 Rose & Crown ct. Finsbury
Parton John, linendraper & hosier, 3 Queen's row, Pimlico
Partoon William, coffee rooms, 3 North place, Lambeth
Partrick Elizh. Mary & Son, coffin furnit. ma. 199 Boro' High st
Partridge Charlotte & Ellen, artists, 2 York pl. Portman sq
Partridge & Price, calico printers, 16 Cheapside
Partridge Christr. watchmak. 13 Wentworth pl. Mile end rd
Partridge Francis, coal merch. Red Lion wharf, 4 Bankside
Partridge Jas. boot & shoemaker, 7 North pl. Balls Pond rd
Partridge Jas. furniture broker, 43 Old st. St. Luke's
Partridge Jas. herbalist, 40 Chapel st. Somers town
Partridge Jas. *Victoria tav.* Lit. Sussex pl. Hyde pk. gardens
Partridge Jane (Mrs.), cheesemonger, 201 Sloane st
Partridge John, artist, 21 Brook st. Grosvenor sq
Partridge John, carpenter & blindmaker, 15 City road
Partridge John, wholesale stationer, 128 Chancery lane
Partridge Joseph, stockbroker, 5 Bank chambrs. Lothbury
Partridge Michl. boot & shoe ma. 9 Northampton rw. Hollowy
Partridge Rd. professor of anatomy, 17 New st. Spring gdns
Partridge Roger, saddler, &c. 30 Thayer st. Manchester sq
Partridge Samuel, oil & colorman, 82 Three Colt st. Limeho
Partridge Samuel, shoemaker, 49 Queen st. New cut
Partridge Samuel John, barrister, 3 Elm court, Temple
Partridge Samuel Thos. physician, 2 York place, Portman sq
Partridge Saml. Wm. news agt. 2 Lovell's ct. Paternoster rw
Partridge Thomas, jeweller, 26 Woodbridge st. Clerkenwell
Partridge Walter, commission agent, 75 Aldermanbury
Partridge Wm. barrister, 10 Farrar's buildings, Temple
Partridge Wm. coffee roaster, 16 Whitecross st. Cripplegate
Partridge Wm. herald painter, &c. 122 Gt. Portland st
Partridge Wm. Henry, grocer, &c. 4 Pitfield st. Hoxton
Pascall Wm. L. surgeon, 17 Charlotte st. Fitzroy sq
Pascoe Charles, glass, &c. dealer, 28 Broomfields, Deptford
Pascoe Hen. ready made linen wa. 23 Old Compton st. Soho
Pascoe James, tailor, 63 Rupert st. Haymarket
Pascoe John Thos. mineralogist, 30 Heneage st. Whitechapel
Pascoe William, potato dealer, 34 Ridinghouse lane
Pasfield George, pork butcher, 33 Gt. Carter la. Doctors' coms
Pasfield Joseph, linendraper, 92 Minories
Pasfield William, bricklayer, 2 Paddington st
Pash Joseph Allworth, wholesale shoe manufacturer, 7 & 8 Frederick's place, Old Kent road
Pashen John, keyed bugle & trumpet mak. 139 Aldersgate st
Pashler John B. butcher, 2 Brett's bldngs. Camberwell road
Pashley Robert, barrister, 12 King's Bench walk
Pask John, musical inst. manuf. 8 Lowther arcade, Strand
Pask Oliver, stationer, 87 Old st. St. Luke's
Paskell Wm. carver & gilder, 7 Park ter. Regent's park
Paskins Daniel, coachsmith, 19 Brownlow st. Drury lane
Pasley & Sharpe, glass & bottle merchants, 51 Curtain road
Pasley George, shop fixture dealer, 67 Old st. road
Pasmore Daniel, artist, 2 Gower place, Euston square
Pasmore John Frederic, artist, 2 Gower place, Euston sq
Pasmore Robt. cider merchant, Chamberlain's whf. Tooley st
Pasmore William, bookbinder, 17 Manor pl. Walworth rd
Pass Michael & Co. lime merchants, Battersea fields
Pass Charles, oilman, 20 Tottenham court, New road
Pass David, butcher, 38 Duke st. Aldgate
Pass Henry, surgeon dentist, 45 Cambridge terrace
Pass John Henry, engraver, 43 Sekforde st. Clerkenwell
Pass Michael, lime merchant, 3 Belmont pl. Wandsworth rd
Passenger Robert, potter & glassman, 94 & 95 Union st. Boro'
Passenger Wm. artifi. florist, 13 Somers town ter. Clarendon sq
Passfield William, dining rooms, 9 Bridge st. Lambeth
Passingham George, merchant, & ship & insurance agent, 136 Fenchurch street
Passingham Geo. wine & spirit merchant, 106 Fenchurch st
Passingham Richard, *Adam & Eve* P.H. 209 Hoxton Old twn
Passmore Elizh. (Mrs.), potato salesman, Limekiln hill, Lmhse
Passmore Emanuel, *Queen Victoria* P.H. 25 King st. Snowhill
Passmore Francis, printer, 45 Borough road
Passmore George, tailor, 7 Great Ryder st. St. James's
Passmore Geo. tobacconist, 23 John st. west, Edgware road
Passmore Hen. boot & shoemaker, 65 Westbourne st. Pimlico
Passmore Hen. P. plumber & paint. 8 Prospect pl. Old Kent rd
Passmore Joseph, tailor, 6 Vernon pl. Bagnigge wells road
Passmore Sarah (Mrs.), fruiterer, 17 Addle st. Wood st
Passmore Wm. saddler, 12 Compton st. Brunswick square
Passover Bread Association (M. Hart, sec.), 27 Goulstone sq
PASSPORT OFFICES, *See General Index*
Pasteur Adolphus, colonial broker, see Patry & Pasteur
Pastorelli Antonio, barometerma. &c. 4 Cross st. Hattongarden
Patch Charles, builder, 20 Queen's ter. Queen's rd. Bayswater
Patch John, barrister, 2 Pump court, Temple
Patching Robt. Wm. grocer, 20 Calthorpe pl. Gray's inn rd
Pate James, nurseryman, Well st. Hackney
Pateman Wm. Slater D. publisher, 4A, Wine Office ct. Fleet st
Patent Concentrated Tea Co. (W. H. Bellamy, sec.), 2 Moorgate st
Patent & Design Register Office, 166 Fleet st
Patent Fuel Co. (W. N. De Mattos, sec.), 15 St. Mary Axe
Patent Kamptulicon Elastic Pavement Co. (Geo. Walter, mang. trustee); office 42 Lombard st.; works, Greenwich road, Greenwich
Patent Woollen Cloth Co. (R. R. Friend, sec.), 8 Love lane, Aldermanbury
Patent Office (her Majesty's), 13 Serle st. Linc. inn; hrs. 10 to 4
Patent Oropholite Co. (P. F. Page & Son, secs.), 14 King's road, Bedford row
Patent Ramoneur Association, 30 Upper Seymour st. Portm. sq.; branch offices, 192 High Holborn, & 21 Allen st. Marsh gate, Lambeth
Patent Safety Cab Com. (Hen. Webber, manager), 9½ King st. Portman square
Patent Wood Carving Com. 5 Henrietta st. Covent garden; manufactory, Ranelagh road, Thames bank
Pater John, solicitor, 16 Gt. Randolph st. Camden town
Pater William, surgeon, 1 Marine pl. Commercial rd. east
Paternoster George, chemist, &c. 7 Windsor pl. Old Kent rd
Paternoster John, surgeon, 30 Norfolk st. Strand
Paternoster Richard, barrister, 2 Essex court, Temple
Paternoster Thos. coach lace ma. 13 Charlotte st. Fitzroy sq
Paterson Alexander, sck. bag & matwa. see Murray & Paterson
Paterson Edward, solicitor, see Burrell & Paterson
Paterson Edward, solicitor, 23 Throgmorton st
Paterson Henry, stables, Old Norland terrace, Notting hill
Paterson James, cabinet maker, 15 Rupert st. Haymarket
Paterson John, baker, 10 Green st.; 46 Castle st. & 72 Princes st. Leicester square
Paterson John, solicitor, 29 Colebrooke row, Islington, & 57 Cannon st. City
Paterson John, stock, collar, shirt & brace ma. 104 Wood st
Paterson Peter, jun. bootmaker, 79 Chiswell st. Finsbury
Paterson Richd. for. stock bro. 2 Exchange bldgs. Capel court

Paterson Wm. barrister, 1 New Mitre ct. buildings, Temple
Paterson Wm. coal merchant, 24 Orchard st. Portman sq
Paterson Wm. fruiterer, 94 Westbourne st. Pimlico
Paterson Wm. shoemaker, 2 Broadway, Westminster
Paterson Wm. solicitor, 68 Old Broad st. City
Paterson Wm. stationer, 60A, White horse st. Stepney
Paterson Wm. Richd. general salesman, 1 Broadway, Westm
Paterson Wm. Simpson, solicitor, 7 Bouverie st. Fleet st
Pates Joseph, baker, 1 Manor pl. south, King's rd. Chelsea
Pates Richard, baker, 22 Little Marylebone st
Pateshall, Brown & Jones, candle & soap ma. 112 Fench. st
Patey William & Co. wholesale perfumers, 37 Lombard st
Patey Robt. liverystbls. Rose & Crownyd. 26 Kingst. St. James'
Patience Wm. carpenter & builder, 17 Gt. Bathst. Clerkenwell
Patient & Sheffield, coal & slate merchants, 20 Throgmorton st. & Union wharf, Kingsland road
Patient George, tailor, 168 Sloane st. Knightsbridge
Patient James, tanner, Swan mead, Bermondsey New road
Patient John, stockbroker, 20 Throgmorton st
Patient Wm. Francis, tanner, see Smith & Patient
Patison & Turner, tartan & tweed manufacturers, 3 Star court, Bread st. & 62 Queen st. Glasgow
Patison James & Co. flax spinners & thread manufacturers, Johnstone mills, Renfrewshire; warehouses, 62 Queen st. Glasgow, & 3 Star court, Bread st.
Patman Emma & Ann (Misses), milliners, 4 Brompton place
Patman Francis, baker, 265 Albany road, Camberwell
Patmore Sarah (Mrs.), *Woolpack* P.H. 32 Gravel la. Southwrk
Paton & Charles, soap makers, 148 & 240 Wapping High st
Paton & Hay (successors to Paul Beardsley), manufacturing goldsmiths, 9 Upper Charles st. Northampton square
Paton & Stewart, american merchants, 28 Noble st. Cheapside
Paton George, barrister, 4 New square, Lincoln's inn
Paton Wm. cabinet maker, 48 Berwick st. Soho
Paton William, merchant & ship agent, see Unonius & Paton
Patrick & Gye, oil merchants, 94 Newgate st
Patrick Alexander, *French Horn* P.H. 113 Lambeth walk
Patrick Clement T. *Ship & Camel* P.H. 12 Fashion st. Dkhead
Patrick James, bricklayer, 56 Backchurch la. Whitechapel
Patrick John Agnew, tithe agent, 1 Furnival's inn
Patrick Mark, builder, 37 Belvedere road, Lambeth
Patrick Thos. gold lace manufr. &c. see Bullmore & Patrick
Patrick Wm. sugar refiner, see Goodhart, Son & Patrick
Patrickson Joseph, academy, 1 Barnsbury park
Patriot Newspaper Office, 5 Bolt court, Fleet st
Patriotic Fund Office, 37 Old Broad st. City; hours 10 to 4
Patry & Pasteur, east india & colonial brokers, 38 Mincing la
Patston Samuel, scale maker, 1 Gibraltar wk. Bethnal gr. rd
Pattemore Henry, grocer, 83 Paul st. Finsbury
Patten Edward Hen. & Co. merchants, 3 Great Tower st
Patten Wm. & Co. window glass & color mers. 20 Old Fish st
Patten Edward, engraver, 14 Derby st. Gray's inn road
Patten Edw. Hen. cust. ho. & commerl. agent, 3 Gt. Tower st
Patten George, A.R.A. artist, 50 Berners st. Oxford st
Patten James, attorney, 41 Ely place, Holborn
Patten John, plumber & glasscutter, 24 Constable rw. Mile e. rd
Patten Jonathan, naval architect & surveyor, 26 Birchin la
Patten Joseph, east india merc. & agt. Hall of Commerce
Patten Sarah (Mrs.), ladies' school, 33 Beaufort st. Chelsea
Patten Thomas, wine merchant, 3 Ingram ct. Fenchurch st
Patten William Vandyke, artist, 27 Howland st. Fitzroy sq
Pattenden & Smith, hop & seed factors, 247 Borough High st
Pattenden Joseph, bootmaker, 33 Leonard st. Shoreditch
Pattenden Wm. agent to Phœnix office, 171 Poplar High st
Patterson & Beeston (Misses), dressmaks. 37 North Audley st
Patterson Edward & Co. chemical paste makers, 57 Gower st
Patterson Albert, appraiser, 8 Lyon's inn, Strand
Patterson Elizabeth (Miss), haberdasher, Church st. Hackney
Patterson George, academy, 1 Montague pl. Kentish town
Patterson Henry, livery stables, 16 Whitcomb st
Patterson James, *Wills Coffee ho.* 7 Searle st. Leicester sq
Patterson John, coffee rooms, 22 Duke st. Smithfield
Patterson John, bread & bisc. bak. 22 Princes st. Cavendish sq
Patterson John Miles, rope, line, &c. maker, Old Ford
Patterson Joseph, tailor, 5 Swallow place, Hanover sq
Patterson Joshua, professor of music, 3 Myrtle st. Hoxton
Patterson Mercy (Miss), dressmaker & milliner, 80 Fleet st
Patterson Mervyn, surgeon, 5 Norfolk st. Park lane
Patterson Ralph, *Patterson's hotel*, 48 Brook st
Patterson Richard, beer retailer, 47 Bath st. City road
Patterson Robt. *Old Green Man & Still* P.H. 122 Oxford st
Patterson Robt. tailor, 10 Little Chapel st. Westminster
Patterson Wm. beer retailer, 29 Compton st. Brunswick sq
Patterson Wm. clock, &c. case mkr. 29 Easton st. Spafields
Patterson Wm. cooper, 4 Elm st. Gray's inn lane
Patterson Wm. grocer & corndealer, 46 Cross st. Islington

Pattie David, bookseller, 10 St. Alban's place, Edgware rd
Pattinson Joseph, warehouseman, 60 Bread st. Cheapside
Pattison & Harding, tailors & drapers, 80 Cornhill
Pattison Jas. & Sons, silk & genl. merchts. 57½ Old Broad st
Pattison Edward, ladies' boot & shoe maker, 74 Oxford st
Pattison Henry, livery stable keeper & jobmaster, White Horse yard, Stratford mews, & Hindemews, Marylebone la
Pattison James, bootmkr. 12 Orford pl. Marlbro' rd Chelsea
Pattison James, livery stable keeper & job master, 1 Stratford mews, & Mill hill mews, Welbeck st
Pattison Joseph, coach master, 2 Warren mews, Warren st
Pattison Martha (Mrs.), lodgingho. 30 Nw. North st. Red Lion sq
Pattison Mary (Mrs.), baker, 13 Little Windmill st. Golden sq
Pattison Thomas S. drug dealer, 42 Crutched friars
Pattison Timothy, cheesemong. 3 Northumberland pl. Com. rd
Pattison Wm. carpenter, 6 Snow's fields, Bermondsey
Pattle Daniel, *Hunter's Arms* P.H. 11 Comptonst. Brnswk. sq
Patton Mary Ann & Harriet, seminary, 64 Trinity sq. Boro'
Patton James, *Junction Arms* P.H. 4 Praed st. Paddington
Patton Robert, chandler's shop, 31 Pool st. New North road
Pattrick Joseph, oil & colorman, 51 Whitechapel High st
Pattyn Joseph, hairdresser, 6½ Gt. Titchfield st
Pattyn Sophi (Mdme.), dressma. 6½ Gt. Titchfield st. Oxford st
Paul & Burrows, soda water ma. 5 Bow st. Covent garden
Paul de Vere & Co. vegetable & spice essence manufacturers (George Raphael, proprietor), 22 Abchurch la. & at Dalston
Paul Sir John D. bt. & Jn. D. jun. bankers, see Strahan, Paul & Co
Paul & Smith, tailors & drapers, 36 Bucklersbury
Paul Thomas & Co. cabinetmakers, upholsterers, & carpet manfrs. 10 Mansion house st
Paul Andrew, surgeon, &c. 8 Green st. Grosvenor sq
Paul Chas. printer & publr. 18 Gt. St. Andrew st. Seven dials
Paul Edward, cattle salesman, 15 West Smithfield
Paul Edwin, silk dyer, see Ashwell & Paul
Paul Edwin, solicitor, see Bennett & Paul
Paul Frederick, gas fitter, 47 York st. Westminster
Paul George, engra. & printer, 50 Margaret st. Wilmingt. sq
Paul George, hairdresser & perfumer, 174 Goswell st
Paul James, baker, 162 Church st. Shoreditch
Paul James, bookseller, &c. 1 Chapter House ct. St. Paul's chyd
Paul James, surgeon, &c. 20 Prospect row, Bermondsey rd
Paul John, accountant, 29 Surrey place, Old Kent road
Paul John, asst. clerk to the City of London Union, & registrar of marriages for the City of London, 35 Cannon st
Paul John, cabinet maker, 5 Upper Rathbone place
Paul John, cabinet maker, 16 Gt. Titchfield st. Oxford st
Paul John, printing press maker, 129 Great Saffron hill
Paul John A. surgeons' instrum. ma. 4 Little Russell st. Cov. gar
Paul John Hayball, surgeon, 29 King William st. City
Paul Joseph Thos. auctioneer, &c. 151 Sloane st. Knightsb
Paul Maria (Mrs.), furniture broker. 70 York st. Westminster
Paul Mary (Mrs.), grocer, 30 Gt. Saffron hill, Hatton garden
Paul Sarah (Mrs.), work box manufa. 71 St. John st. Clerknwl
Paul Thomas, *Antelope* P.H. 10 White Hart st. Drury lane
Paul Thomas, merchant, 3 Summers ct. Bishopsgate st
Paul Thomas, potato salesman, see Sheen & Paul
Paul William, fruiterer, Well st. Hackney
Paul William, printer, 129 Gt. Saffron hill
Pauli Emilius, merchant, 4 Chequer yard, Dowgate hill
Paull Archibald & Co. merchants, 147 Leadenhall st
Paull Edward, hatter, 15 Cheapside
Paull Rev. Henry Andrew, academy, 15 Foley pl. Portland pl
Paull Stephenson, cornfactor, 1 Portland row, Camberwell
Paull Thomas, lithographer, 34 Kirby st. Hatton garden
Paull Wm. groat manufacturer, 6 Baldwin's court, Cloak la
Paull Wm. Warr, carpenter & builder, 4½ Exeterpl. Gt. Dover rd
Paulson Eliezer, chemist & druggist, 88 Chancery lane
Paulson John, egg mer. 11 Ship Tavern pass. Leadnhl. mrkt
Paulton John, stonemason, 2 High st. Portland town
Pauncefort Alway, engraver, 1 Newcastle st. Farringdon st
Pause Francis, dairyman, 57 Carnaby st. Golden sq
Pausey Robert, bookseller & news agent, 27 Exeter st. Knightsbridge, & 10 Brompton road
Pavey John & Son, newsvenders, 47 Holywell st. Strand
Pavey Edward L. paper stainer, 127 Tooley st. Borough
Pavey Henry, paper stainer, 84 St. George's rd. Southwark
Pavey Henry, surgeon, 4 Newcastle place, Edgware road
Pavey James, bootmaker, 16 Deptford High st
Pavey John Baldwin, tailor, 11 Swallow st. Piccadilly
Pavey John Rugman, account. 189 Wellington ter. Wtrloo. rd
Pavey William, florist, King's road, Chelsea
Pavey Wm. painter & paperhang. 22 White Hart pl. Kenningtn
Pavia Philip, commission agent & mer. 18 Cullum st
Paviour Thomas, stonemason, 71½ Basing place, Waterloo rd
Pavis John, *King's Arms* P.H. 84 Three Colt st. Limehouse
Pavis John, *Portsmouth Arms* P.H. 4 Shepherd st. Oxfrd. st.

Pavis Philip, tin ware dealer, 48 New Compton st. Soho
Pavit George, grocer & cheesemonger, 8 Upper Rathbone pl
Pavitt Wm. & Co. millers, 247 Wapping, & 24 Mark lane
Pavitt George, solicitor, 2 Gray's inn square
Pavyer Benjamin, letter founder, 31 Bartholomew close
Pawle Francis, stockbroker, 4 Old Broad st. City
Pawley Robert, fruiterer, 118 Chalton st. Somers town
Pawley Wm. tobacconist, 182 Wellington ter. Waterloo rd
Pawley Wm. manufacturing jeweller, 22 Red Lion st. Clrkwl
Pawnbrokers' Gazette Office, 240 Strand
Pawnbrokers' Licence Office, Somerset house; hours 10 to 4
Pawsey William, butcher, 6 High st. Marylebone
Pawson John F. & Co. warehousemen, 8, 9, 10 & 11 St. Paul's churchyd. & 22, 23 & 24 Gt. Carter lane, Doctors' commons
Pawson Thos. & Son, woollen manfs. 27 King st. & 16 Lawrence la
Paxman Wm. sen. silk dyer, 10 Wheeler st. Spitalfields
Paxman Wm. James, dyer, 57 Elizabeth st. Hackney road
Paxon Francis, solicitor, 18 Featherstone buildings, Holborn
Paxon William, attorney, 9 Gray's inn terrace
Paxon Wm. stationer & vellum binder, 7 Skinner st. Snowhl
Paxton & Co. wine merchants, 5 Pall mall ea. & 2 Dorset pl
Paxton Eliz. (Mrs.), baker, 56 High st. Kensgtn. south side
Paxton Henry, cheesemonger, 18 Jermyn st. St. James's
Paxton Jas. currier & japan leath. dress. 36 Russell st. Brmdy
Paxton Richard, chemical works, Bow common
Paxton Thomas, artist, 5 James st. Covent garden
Pay Geo. & Son, wine merchts. 8 Rodney bldgs. NewKent rd
Paymaster General's Office, Whitehall; hours 10 to 4
Payne John, stationer & newsvender, 73 Blackman st. Boro'
Payne & Daniels, iron, &c. merchants, see Daniels & Payne
Payne Edward & Son, coach & livery lace & fringe makers, 60 Great Queen st. Lincoln's inn fields
Payne & Foss, booksellers, 81 Pall mall
Payne Geo. & Son, grocers, 46 Mortimer st. & 328 Regent st
Payne & Loder, Payne's patent for the preservation of wood & other vegetable substances, Whitehall wharf, Cannon row, Westminster; Fleetwood on Wyre, Lancashire; Wisbeach, Cambridgeshire; Guildford, Surrey; & Southampton
Payne Mary Ann & Co. coach lace & fringe manufacturers, 25 Great Queen st. Lincoln's inn fields
Payne Randolph & Sons, wine merchants, 61 St. James's st
Payne Robt. & Co. soda water ma. 11 Salisbury pl. New rd
Payne & Slee, vinegar makers, Church st. Horselydown
Payne Wm. & Son, imp. of foreign toys, baskets & dealers in writing desks, work boxes & fancy articles, 16 & 17 High Hlbn
Payne Anthony, boot & shoe ma. 3 Orange row, Kenngtn. rd
Payne Benjamin, chemist, King st. Battersea
Payne Charles, *Bricklayers' Arms* P.H. 29 Eagle st. Red Lion sq
Payne Charles, grocer, Battersea square
Payne Charles, ironmonger, 56 King st. Westminster
Payne Charles, miller, see Day & Payne
Payne Charles, patent meat salter, 2 Crescent road, Millbank
Payne David, vegetable salesman, Borough market
Payne Douglas, linendraper, 14 Devonshire bldgs. Dover rd
Payne Edward Wood, grocer, 20 Conduit st. Paddington
Payne Edward Wood, *Hope* coffee rooms, 41 Haymarket
Payne Eliza (Miss), milliner, 36 Wigmore st. Cavendish sq
Payne George, baker, 1 Middlesex ter. Hackney road
Payne George, fishmonger, 6 Etham pl. Kent st. Borough
Payne George, greengrocer, 1 Lit. Guilford st. Brunswick sq
Payne George, tailor, 7 Little St. James's st. St. James's
Payne George, jun. registrar of births, &c. 10 Bath st. Nwgt. st
Payne George Burton, surgeon, 4 Gray Coat pl. Westmnstr
Payne George David, tailor, 19 Conduit st. Bond st
Payne Henry, cattle salesman, 60 West Smithfield
Payne Henry Edw. whipmaker, 2 Pleasant row, Old Kent rd
Payne Henry James, *Rose & Crown* P.H. 17 Queen st. Tower hill
Payne James, brazier, 3 Windmill row, Kennington green
Payne James, butcher, 75 Snowhill
Payne James, coffee rooms, 26 Dowgate hill
Payne James, fruiterer, 12 Oxford market
Payne James, fruiterer, 7 East st. Spitalfields
Payne James, fruit & pea salesman, Borough market
Payne James, grocer, 1 King's terrace, Bagnigge Wells rd
Payne John, brassfounder & figure caster, file, tube, & gas apparatus warehouse, 62 & 63 Shoe lane, Holborn
Payne John, cowkeeper & dairyman, 19 Shepherd's market
Payne John, fruiterer, 1A, Everett st. Brunswick sq
Payne John, fruiterer, &c. 18 Shepherd's market, May fair
Payne John, grocer, 53 Brewer st. Golden sq
Payne John, law stationer, 3 Cursitor st. Chancery lane
Payne John, *Rose* P.H. 12 Monkwell st. Cripplegate
Payne John, tailor, 28 Bowling st. Westminster
Payne John, whol. stationer, see Rock Brothers & Payne
Payne John Thos. bookbinder, 31 Tabernacle walk, Finsbury
Payne John Thos. tailor, &c. 27 Grosvenor st. west, Eaton sq
Payne Joseph, barrister, 1 Churchyard court, Temple
Payne Joseph, bootma. 36 Road side, Mile end road
Payne Joshua, engraver & printer, 1 Hare place, Fleet st
Payne Julian, parliamentary agent, 1 Clifford's inn
Payne Martha (Mrs.), *Berwick Arms* P.H. 69 Castle st. ea. Ox. st
Payne Mary Ann (Mrs.), *Brunswick hotel*, 52 Jermyn st
Payne Paul, plumber, 8 Ratcliffe row, John's row, City road
Payne Philip, butcher, 3 Orchard place, Kingsland road
Payne Richard, bricklayer, High st. Bow, Middlesex
Payne Robt. Chas. *King's Head* P.H. Canon alley, 63 St. Paul's churchyard
Payne Robert H. west india merchant, 2 Philpot lane, City
Payne Sarah (Mrs.), fruiterer, 54 Baalzephon st. Bermdsey
Payne Thomas, beast salesman, 60 West Smithfield
Payne Thomas, *Red Lion* P.H. 1 Union st. Berkeley sq
Payne Thomas B. shower bath manufer. 95 High st Maryleb
Payne Wm. baker, 142 Whitechapel road
Payne Wm. *Barleymow* P.H. 210 Up. Thames st
Payne Wm. barrister, 1 Churchyard court, Temple
Payne Wm. blacksmith, 16 Colchester st. Whitechapel
Payne Wm. blind maker, 1 Paragon mews, New Kent road
Payne Wm. brass & german silv. founder, 119 Waterloo rd
Payne Wm. bricklayer, 32 High st. Bow
Payne Wm. butcher, 18 & 19 Oxford market
Payne Wm. butcher, 14 Southampton terrace, Pentonville
Payne Wm. coach smith, 72 St. George's rd. Southwark
Payne Wm. coffee rooms, 24 Lower st. Islington
Payne Wm. coroner of Lond. & Southwk. 1 Churchyd. ct. Temple
Payne Wm. fruiterer, Borough market
Payne Wm. hairdresser, 1 Warwick lane, Newgate st
Payne Wm. news agt. & statnr. 82 Gt. Titchfield st. Oxford st
Payne Wm. shoemaker, 2 Globe road, Mile end
Payne Wm. watch & pedometer ma. 62 & 163 New Bond st
Paynter Francis, carpntr. & packg. case ma. 20 Gt. Trinity la
Paynter Thomas, magistrate, Hammersmith police court
Paynter Francis Edwd. solicitor, 2 Gt. James st. Bedford rw
Paynter John, merchant, 64 Coleman st
Paynter Joseph Wm. waterpr. boot ma. 2 Marylebone st. Picca
Paynter Wm. carman, 3 Alfred mews, Tottenham court rd
Pays Thomas, fruiterer, 190 Long lane, Bermondsey
Payze Timothy, hornbeam timber mer. 2 Salmon la. Limeho
Pea Harriet (Mrs.), milliner, 31 Windmill st. Finsbury
Pea Samuel, painter, 31 Windmill st. Finsbury
Peabody, Riggs & Co. merchts. 6 Warnford ct. Thrgmtn. st
Peabody George, mercht. 6 Warnford ct. Throgmorton st
Peace & Jones, solicitors, 190 Tooley st. Borough
Peace Society (Alex. Brockway, asst. sec), 19 New Broad st
Peacey Thomas, tallow chandler, 14 Glo'ster row, Grange rd
Peach Wm. & Co. cigar wareho. 9 Lit St. Thomas Apostle
Peach John, cattle salesman, 8 West Smithfield
Peach John, rag mercht. 21 Alfred pl. Newington causeway
Peach Joseph, upholsterer, 13 Henrietta st. Manchester sq
Peach Lucy (Mrs.), grocer, 19 Back st. Horselydown
Peach Thos. (sec. to *Commer. Travellers' So.*), 38 Ludgate hill
Peach Wm. coffee rooms, 2 Queen's Head ct. Gt. Windmill st
Peache Clement, lighterman, Belvedere rd. Lambeth
Peache Jas. Courthorpe, timber mer. Belvedere rd. Lambeth
Peachey Francis, attorney, 4 George st. Hanover sq
Peachey George, pianoforte maker, 73 Bishopsgate within
Peachey James, pawnbroker & silversmith, 38 Goswell st
Peachey James, solicitor, 17 Salisbury square, Fleet st
Peachey John, smith & japanner, 69 Quadrant, Regent st
Peachey Joseph, silversmith & jeweller, 7 Athol pl. Pentonvil
Peachey William, butcher, 100 Tooley st
Peacock & Mansfield, pocketbook makers & publishers, booksellers, stationers, &c. 18 Salisbury square, Fleet st
Peacock Stephen & Son, leathersels. 18 Salisbury sq. Fleet st
Peacock Alex. silk manufacturer, 12 Steward st. Spitalflds
Peacock Anthony, accountant, 4 Bridge place, City road
Peacock Barnes, barrister, 1 Harcourt buildings, Temple
Peacock Charles, haberdasher, 4 Star corner, Bermondsey
Peacock Edward, grocer, 17 Rufford's buildings, Islington
Peacock Edward James, tailor, 12 Upper Eaton st. Pimlico
Peacock George, commission agent, 32 King st. Cheapside
Peacock Hamerton Richd. chemist, &c. 170 High st. Poplar
Peacock James, baker, 39 White st. Borough
Peacock James, butcher, 14 Strachan place, Ball's pond rd
Peacock James, fruiterer, 10 Gt. Cherrygarden st. Bermdsy
Peacock James, potato salesman, 40 White st. Borough
Peacock James, who. linen mercht. see Bank, Peacock & Co
Peacock James G. who. glue dealer, &c. 8 Lower Thames st
Peacock Jesse, ladies' shoemaker, 12 George st. Portman sq
Peacock John, *Archduke Charles* P.H. White Hart st. Kenngtn
Peacock John, carpentr. & ship joinr. 124 High st. Shadwell
Peacock John, *Three Compasses* P.H. 15 Lit. Guildford st. Boro'

Peacock John D. tailor, 40 Upper John st. Fitzroy square
Peacock John Hisiop, *Globe* P.H. 58 New Compton st. Soho
Peacock Lewis, solicitor, 43 Lincoln's inn fields
Peacock Mark Beauchamp, solicitor to the post office, General Post Office, St. Martin's le grand
Peacock Mary Ann (Miss), milliner, 12 George st. Portman sq
Peacock Richard Watts, *Wheatsheaf* P.H. 15 Star st. Shadwell
Peacock Robert, shoemaker, 95 Up. Whitecross st. St. Luke's
Peacock Robert Thos. shoemaker, 37 Lambeth Lower marsh
Peacock Thomas, *Bull tap* P.H. Bull inn yd. Aldgate High st
Peacock Thomas, carpenter, &c. 32 Beckford row, Walworth
Peacock Thomas, chimney sweeper, 20 Burton st. Pimlico
Peacock Thomas Bevel, physician, 7 Finsbury pavement
Peacock Thomas Henry, butcher, 4 Cannon st. City
Peacock Walter Anderson, baker, 161 Bishopsgate without
Peacock Wm. dairyman & fruiterer, 104 Mount st. Berkeley sq
Pead Leonard, wine merchant, 25 Coleman st. City
Pead Robert Geo. cheesemonger, 4 Honey lane market, City
Peadle Thomas, livery stables, 27 Fitzroy mews, Fitzroy sq
Peak Edward, carver & gilder, 85 Goswell st
Peak James, artificial flower manufr. 17 Hoxton square
Peak James, furniture & fixture dealer, 61 Old st. road
Peak James, grocer, 59 Lower George st. Chelsea
Peak Thomas, hosier & outfitter, 29 Whitechapel road
Peak William, pianoforte maker, 94 Princes rd. Lambeth
Peake Richard & Son, cattle salesmen, 15 West Smithfield
Peake Rt. & Son, coachm. 5 Lisle st. & 11 Princes st. Le'ster. sq
Peake Agnes (Mrs.), *Queen's Head* P.H. 19 Gt. Tower st. City
Peake Elizth. (Mrs.), *Royal Mortqr* P.H. 21 London rd. Sthwk
Peake Henry, bricklayer, 13 Rosamon buildings, Islington
Peake Jane (Mrs.), milliner, 13 Rosamon buildings, Islington
Peake Joseph, builder, 4 Fair st. Horselydown
Peake Michl. Hordon, drysalter & cheml. agt. 8 Billiter st
Peake Robert, engh. & for. stock brokr. 3 Bartholomew la
Peake Robert William, solicitor, see Edwards & Peake
Peake Thomas, butcher, 49 Bedford st. Covent garden
Peake Thomas (manufacturer, Tunstall, Staffordshire), terro metallic blue tiles for all parts of roofs, blue & red for floors, &c. also pipes for drains & conduits, London depôt, 22 Whitefriars st. Fleet st
Peake Thomas, plate case maker, 3 Windsor ct. Monkwell st
Peake Thomas, poultry salesman, see Haynes & Peake
Peake Wm. china & glass war. 2 Knightsbridge terrace
Peakome William, saddler, 7 Princes st. Cavendish square
Peal Chas. building material dealer, 16 & 24 Crown st. Soho
Peal Cornelius, tobacconist, 16 Princes st. Little Queen st
Peal Nathaniel, waterproof boot & shoe maker, 11 Duke st. Grosvenor square
Pear John, haircutter, perfumer & wigmaker, 32 Poultry
Pearce & Burrows, work. silversmiths, 12 Banner st. St. Luke's
Pearce & Conran, safety letter box ma. 41 King William st
Pearce & Countze, coach, &c. mak. 7 Cross la. & 102 & 103 Lng. ac
Pearce, Phillips & Winckworth, solicitors, 10 St. Swithin's la
Pearce & Thynne, land agents, 11 Gt. George st. Westminster
Pearce Benjamin, builder, 8 White st. Bethnal green
Pearce Caleb, bootmaker, 8 Compton st. Clerkenwell
Pearce Charles, pastrycook, 7 Great Suffolk st. Boro'
Pearce Charles, who. shirtmaker, 1 Gresham st. Wood st
Pearce Charles, tailor, 20 Crown court, Pall mall
Pearce Chas. T. stockbro. see Laurence, Cazenove & Pearce
Pearce Diana (Mrs.), leather cutt. 27 Lit. Guilford st. Brunsk. sq
Pearce Edward, statuary, see Noakes & Pearce
Pearce Edward Hooper, slopseller, 2 High st. Deptford
Pearce Eliza, grocer, see Mansfield & Pearce
Pearce Elizabeth (Mrs.), cooper & turner, 3 South Lambeth
Pearce Elizab. Ann (Mrs.), *Ship* P.H. 23 Walcot pl. Lambeth
Pearce Francis, silversmith, &c. 9 Newington causeway
Pearce Frederick, bottle wareho. 19 Crown ct. Pall mall
Pearce Frederick, cheesemonger, 7 Deptford High st
Pearce Frederick, tailor, 6 Sackville st. Piccadilly
Pearce Frederick, tobacconist, 87 Chiswell st
Pearce George, back maker, Charles st. City road
Pearce George, fruiterer, 5 Crescent st. Euston square
Pearce Geo. mer. & insurance bro. 2 Bank chmbrs. 39 Lothbury
Pearce George, plumb. & glazier, 11 Plumber's row, City rd
Pearce Hen. art. florist, 8 Nottingham pl. Eagle wf. rd. N w. N. rd
Pearce Henry, beer retailer, 87 Fenchurch st
Pearce Henry, tailor, 32 Riley st. King's road, Chelsea
Pearce Henry F. Johnston, *Norfolk Arms* P.H. 288 Strand
Pearce Isabella (Mrs.), 1½ Stanhope st. Hampstead road
Pearce James, baker, 18 Ashley terrace, City road
Pearce James, beer retailer, 11 Gt. St. Anne st. Westminster
Pearce James, bricklayer, 26 New rd. Sloane st. Chelsea
Pearce James, carman, 47 Praed st. Paddington
Pearce James, cheesemonger, 68 Bunhill row
Pearce James, fruiterer, 256 Tottenham ct. rd. & 34 Edgware rd
Pearce James, hairdresser, 31 Well st. Oxford st
Peace James, mason, 50 London st. Ratcliff
Pearce James, tripe dresser, 239 Bermondsey st. & 85 Bethnal green road
Pearce Jeremiah, oven & house builder, 184 Drury lane
Pearce John, brush maker, 34 Duke st. Grosvenor square
Pearce John, dairyman, 7 King st. Portman sq
Pearce John, linendraper, see Halling, Pearce & Stone
Pearce John, painter & glazier, 102 Gt. Titchfield st
Pearce John, watch & clock maker, 101 Gt. Peter st. Westm
Pearce John James, classical academy, 50 Hoxton Old town
Pearce Joseph, black borderer, 41 Duke st. Aldgate
Pearce Joseph R. papier maché & dressing ca. wa. 77 Cornhill
Pearce Josiah, jeweller, 45 Mount st. Lambeth
Pearce Mary (Miss), dressmaker, 16 Old Cavendish st
Pearce Mary A. (Mrs.), grocer, 9 Coe's ter. Charlt. st. Pntnvl
Pearce Matthew John, wholesale & retail teadlr. 7 Philpot lane
Pearce Nichls. inspr. of detective police, 2 Cowley st. Westmr
Pearce Richard, *Cloudesley Arms* P.H. Cloudesley st. Islingtn
Pearce Richard, porkman & cheesemongr. 50 Crown st. Finsby
Pearce Richard, sawmaker, 92 Paul st. Finsbury
Pearce Richd. Alex. coal & potato dlr. 84 Golden la. St. Luke's
Pearce Robert, carpenter, 25 Marlborough sq. Chelsea
Pearce Robert, dairy, 3 Little Guilford st. Brunswick sq
Pearce Robert, fruiterer, 5 Hope terrace, Notting hill
Pearce Rt. impt. of tous-les-mois, 11 Palace new rd. Lambeth
Pearce Robert, leather breeches & professed trousers & gaiter ma. 23 Edwards st. Portman sq. (nephew & suc. to Foster)
Pearce Robert, plumber, 9 East road, City road
Pearce Robert, tailor, 3 Howard st. Strand
Pearce Samuel, boot & shoe maker, 86 Lambeth Low. marsh, & 2 Assembly place, Kennington common
Pearce Samuel, plumber & glazier, 19 Bell yard, Temple bar
Pearce Samuel, surgeon, &c. 135 Bethnal green road
Pearce Samuel, surgeon, 253 Bethnal green road
Pearce Sarah (Mrs.), appraiser, 13 Red Lion pas. Red Lion sq
Pearce Thomas, bricklayer, 18 Exeter st. Lisson grove
Pearce Thomas, fishmonger, 3 Henry st. Hampstead road
Pearce Thomas, fruiterer & greengrocer, 7 Queen st. Pimlico
Pearce Thomas, *Hand & Shears* P.H. 1 King st. Clothfair
Pearce Thomas, lamp & lustre manufr. 23 Ludgate hill
Pearce Thomas, jun. house painter & writer, 46 King st. Boro'
Pearce Thos. Wm. boys' school, 16 Peel pl. Kensingtn. grav. pts
Pearce William, bricklayer & plasterer, 9 Old Fish st. City
Pearce William, fruiterer, 8 Chelsea market, Low. Sloane st
Pearce William, gasfitter, 30 Hatton wall, Hatton garden
Pearce William, goldsmith & jeweller, 1 Durham st. Strand
Pearce William, grocer & teadealer, 18 Clare st. Clare markt
Pearce William, vitriol works, Bow common
Pearcey John, mast maker, 75 Church st. Rotherhithe
Pearcy Geo. naval architectl. modlr. 15 Tonbridge pl. New rd
Pearcy James, *White Horse* P.H. 17 St. George's pl. Knightsbr
Pearcy Robert, last & patten ma. 79 St. John st. Smithfield
Pearcy Thomas, coachsmith, &c. 23½ York st. Commercl. rd. ea
Pearkes George, oyster rooms, 13 Vinegar yard, Drury lane
Pearl Jas. Wilson, horse dealer, 8½ Milton st. Dorset sq
Pearl Joseph, fruiterer, 7 Church st. Stoke Newington
Pearl Robt. Jas. dyer & scourer, 56 Queen st. Bryanstone sq
Pearless Charlotte (Mrs.), livery sta. 33 Tonbridge st. New rd
Pearmain James, grocer, Maiden lane, Battle bridge
Pearman John, music printer, 13 Castle st. east, Oxford st
Pearman Philip, saddler, 41 Duke st. Grosvenor square
Pearman William, hairdresser, 33 Grosvenor row, Pimlico
Pearmine George Edward, mast & block ma. 50 Low. Shadwell
Pearpoint Maria (Mrs.), glass cutter, 4A, Took's ct. Chncry. la
Pearrett Thomas, ostrich feather ma. 6 Whitmore rd. Hoxton
Pears Andw. & Fras. who. & ret. perfumers, 55 Wells st. Oxford st
Pearsall & Jorden, auctioneers, &c. 1 Bernard st. Russell sq
Pearsall Esther (Miss), strawhat ma. 41 Northampton st. Clkw
Pearsall James, clk. of the market & register, 7 Coal exchnge
Pearsall James, jun. silkman, 145 Cheapside
Pearse & Child, west india merchts. 8 Finsbury place south
Pearse & Guerrier, builders, 261 High Holborn
Pearse John & Brice & Co. blackwell hall factors, 22 Moorgate st. & army clothiers, 8 Craig's court, & 98 Long acre
Pearse Wm. Chancey & Co. stationers & engrs. 2 Queen st. Chpsd
Pearse David Wm. surgeon, 20 Colet pl. Commercial rd. east
Pearse Francis, baker, 22 Goodge st. Tottenham ct. rd
Pearse Francis, sack ma. & coal dlr. 40 Holland st. Blackfrs. rd
Pearse George, surgeon & registrar, 46 Marsham st. & 5 Regent st. Westminster
Pearse Hannah (Mrs.), milliner, &c. 283 Regent st
Pearse Harriet (Mrs.), lodging house, 9 Norfolk st. Strand
Pearse Henry, cork cutter, 69 Curtain road, Shoreditch
Pearse James, butcher, 2 Dockhead, Bermondsey
Pearse James Frodsham, butcher, 3 Wilson st. Finsbury

Pearse John, chemist & druggist, Larkhall lane, Clapham
Pearse Joseph, chinaman, 22 South st. Manchester square
Pearse Mary Ann (Mrs.), fruiterer, 2 Leather lane, Holborn
Pearse Nathl. Summers, hairdresser, 8 King st. Borough
Pearse Peter John T. solr. see Maples, Pearse, Stevens & Co
Pearse Wm. ironmonger & gasfitter, 239 Tottenham court rd. & 16 Cumberland market, Albany st. Regent's park
Pearsey Mary Ann (Mrs.), bookseller, 23 Porter st. Soho
Pearson Alfred, coal & wine merchant, 5 Mark lane
Pearson Ann (Mrs.), printer, 11 White Lion st. Norton folgate
Pearson Charles, butcher, 14 Tabernacle walk, Finsbury
Pearson Charles, city solicitor, & solicitor to the honble. the Irish society, Guildhall yard, City, & Lord Mayor's court office, 7 Old Jewry
Pearson Charles, paintr. & papr. hangr. 92 High st. Portld. tn
Pearson Charles, ship & custom ho. agt. 27 Crutched friars
Pearson Charles Hill, solicitor, see Sandys & Pearson
Pearson Cornelius, engraver, 7 Castle st. Holborn
Pearson Elizabeth (Mrs.), dressmaker, 57 Oxford st
Pearson Emanuel, wesleyan association book room, 5 Horse shoe court, Ludgate hill
Pearson George, bootmaker, 3 Arabella row, Pimlico
Pearson George, confectioner, 22 St. George's place, & 25 Queen's buildings, Brompton
Pearson George, surgeon, 14 Beaumont st. Portland place
Pearson Harriett (Mrs.), *Waterloo tavern*, 69 Haymarket
Pearson Henry, coach maker, 14 Wilmot st. Russell sq
Pearson Henry, fruiterer, 26 Brunswick parade, Barnsbury rd
Pearson Henry, barrister, 5 Brick court, Temple
Pearson Henry, china, &c. dealer, 95 White Lion st. Pentonville
Pearson James, cheesemonger, 75 East st. Manchester sq
Pearson James, china dealer, 6 Amwell st. Pentonville
Pearson James, grocer, 55 Bridge road, Lambeth
Pearson James, eschol nursery, Caroline pl. Hampstead rd
Pearson James, tobacconist, 9 Hoxton old town
Pearson John, barrister, 3 New square, Lincoln's inn
Pearson John, boot & shoe maker, 208 Tottenham ct. road
Pearson John, *Cleveland Arms* P.H. 23 Montagu st. Portmn. sq
Pearson John, *George* P.H. Morgan's lane, Tooley st
Pearson John, teadealer & grocer, 81 Hackney road
Pearson John, upholsterer, 20 Old st. road
Pearson John, wine, spirit & beer merchant, 6 Cross lane, St. Mary at hill
Pearson John Loughborough, architect, 31 Keppel st
Pearson Mary Ann (Mrs.), clothes dlr. George st. Camberwell
Pearson Michael, distiller, see Harmar & Pearson
Pearson Peter, fruiterer, 110 Lambeth walk
Pearson Philip, tailor, see Griffith & Pearson
Pearson Rebecca (Mrs.), tobacconist, 5 Newcastle st. Strand
Pearson Robert, bootmaker, 5 Dorrington st. Leather lane
Pearson Robert, dyer, 21 Galway st. St. Luke's
Pearson Robert, merchant, 13 Birchin lane, Cornhill
Pearson Robt. wharfinger, Stanton's wf. Stoney la. Tooley st
Pearson Stephen, clothier, 2 Lamb's Conduit st. Foundling
Pearson Thomas, attorney, 22 Essex st. Strand
Pearson Thomas, ironmonger, 18 Calthorpe pl. Gray's inn rd
Pearson Thomas, *Mitre tavern*, 125 Chancery lane
Pearson Thomas, wine merchant, 3 Darlington pl. Vauxhall
Pearson William, attorney, 17 White Conduit st. Islington
Pearson William, bootmaker, 4 Eliza place, Sadler's wells
Pearson William, furniture broker, 3 Old st. St. Luke's
Pearson Wm. plate glass silverer, 10 Robinhood ct. Shoe la
Pearson William, tailor, 50 Devonshire st. Queen sq. Blomsby
Pearson William, tailor, 1 Glebe place, King's road, Chelsea
Pearson William, who. & ret. stationr. 36 Bishopsgate within
Pearson William, teadealer, 36 Frith st. Soho
Pearson William Charles, tailor, 14 London wall
Peart & Dossetor, hosiers & glovers, 12 & 13 Poultry
Peart William & Co. printers, 163 St. John st. road
Peart Henry B. who. cheesemonger, 17 Broadway, Deptford
Peascod John, custom ho. & shipg. agt. 12 Harp la. Lr. Thms. st
Pease Wm. Hen. & Co. wine merchts. 2 Ingram ct. Fenchurch st
Peat Henry & Thomas, saddlers to her Majesty's cavalry, harness makers, &c. 167 Piccadilly
Peat Charles, hairdresser, 1 Port place, Walworth common
Peat James, straw hat manufacturer, 13 Wardour st. Soho
Peat John, grocer, 39 York road, Lambeth
Peat Samuel, coffee rooms, 3 King's cross
Peate Joseph, bootmaker, 97 St. George st
Peaten John, ironmonger, 44 Paddington st. Marylebone
Peatfield John, fencing master, see Winterbottom & Co
Peatie James, mast & block maker, 163 Wapping
Pechell Augustus, barrister, 4 Harcourt buildings, Temple
Peck Benjamin, dairy, 4 Belinda pl. Canonbury sq. Islington
Peck Elizabeth (Mrs.), day school, 11 Bethnal gn. ea. side
Peck John, tea dealer & grocer, 75 Fore st. Cripplegate
Peck John, music seller & publisher, 44 Newgate st
Peck Richard, *Swan* P.H. Old Brompton
Peck Samuel, carpenter, 64 Ossulston st. Somers town
Peck Samuel Burdett, shirt maker, 1 Brompton rd. Kngtsbdg
Peck Thomas, bookbinder, 52 Hoxton sq
Peck Thomas, coachmaker, 5 City road, Old st
Peck William, bricklayer, 23 Baldwin st. City rd
Peck Wm. Henry, builder, 28 Aldenham st. Somers town
Peckett Charles, solicitor, 25 Barnsbury park, Islington
Peckham Thomas G. [late W. Patten & Co.], seed & hop factor, 3 Three Crown square, Borough
Peckham Wm. Scott, barrister, 3 New Boswell ct. Lin. inn
Peckover Chas. brushmaker, 3 Lansdown ter. Caledonian rd
Peckover Edmund, tailor, see Russell & Peckover
Pecqueur Louis, upholsterer, 9 Paddington st. Marylebone
Peculiars' Register Offi. 5½ Bell yd. Doc. com.; hours 9 to 7
Pedden Mary (Mrs.), milliner, 14 Seymour pl. Camden tn
Pedder William, bookseller, 17 Holywell st. Strand
Peden John, goldsmith, &c. 33 Kenton st. Brunswick sq
Peden Thomas, coachmaker, 9 Duke st. Portland place
Pedler John & Co. tailors & drapers, 38 Ludgate st
Pedler Geo. Stanbury, who. & retail druggists, 199 Fleet st
Pedley Thos. & Co. wool merchants, 3 Barge yd. Bucklersbury
Pedley Henry, solicitor, 59 Fenchurch st
Pedler Robt. H. *Red Lion & Ball* P.H. 62 & 63 Red Lion st. Holbn
Pedley Wm. Hen. tinplate worker, 5 Southampton st. Cmbwl
Pedretti Peter, *Salmon & Compass* P.H. 13 Dorrington st
Pedee Ambrose, druggist, 45 Liquorpond st. Gray's inn la
Pedee Ambrose, surgeon, 6 Burton st. Burton crescent
Peek Brothers & Co. importers & wholesale tea, coffee & spice dlrs. 21 Eastcheap; 31 Love la. & 4 St. Mary at hill
Peek George, butcher, Kingsland High st
Peek Jeremiah, pewterer, see Hudson & Peek
Peek Thomas, bricklayer, &c. 27 Rawstorne st. Goswell rd
Peek Thomas, machine ruler, see Ward & Peek
Peeke Roger, ludgate cloth hall, 1 Ludgate st
Peeke Saml. grocr. & undrtakr. 8 Up. Edmund st. King's cross
Peel, Allan & Co. calico printers & warehn. 126 Wood st. City
Peel Edmund & Co. cotton manufacturers, 64 Aldermanbury
Peel John S. & Co. publshrs. of tailors' fashions, 37 Leicester sq
Peel Robert & Thomas, calico printers, 1 Star ct. Bread st
Peel Wm. & Co. stuff manfrs. & merchts. 5 Carey la. Gutter la
Peel James, artist, 4 Barton st. Westminster
Peel John picture liner & restorer, 17 & 18 Golden square
Peel John W. printer, 74 Charlotte terr. New cut, Lambeth
Peel Jonathan, barrister, 2 Elm court, Temple
Peel Robert, potato dealer, 2 East st. Spitalfields
Peel William, grocer, 2 Portman place, Globe rd. Mile end
Peeling Benjamin, *Rose & Crown* P.H. 23 Charles st. Stepney
Peeling Samuel, *Victoria* P.H. Stoke Newington road
Peell Edmnd. cooper & brushma. 12 Marchmont st. Brunswk. sq
Peell Edmund, potato dealer, 60 Brick lane, St. Luke's
Peers Geo. T. plumber, painter, &c. 18 Ironmonger la. Cheapside
Peers James, hairdresser, 171 Kingsland road
Peet Jas. & Chas. S. silk & ribbon manuf. 26 Philip la. Wood st
Peet Edwd. cowkeeper, 5 North mews, Burton crescent
Peet Samuel, corkcutter, 4 Barnet place, Hackney road
Peet Samuel, *Wilmington Arms* P.H. 20 Yardley st. Clrknwl
Peet Thomas, agent for french goods, 5 Gutter la. Cheapside
Peet William, shoemaker, 36 Gt. James st. Lisson grove
Pegg Nathaniel, coal & coke merchant, Phœnix wharf, Clink st. Bankside
Pegg Samuel, iron merchant, see Bailey, Pegg & Co
Pegg William, baker, 3 Coburg place, Bayswater, & 4 Ladbroke grove, Notting hill
Pegg William, wholesale stationer & rag merchant, 90 Upper Ground st. Blackfriars, & 14 Shoe lane, Fleet st
Pegge Charles, grocer & teadealer, 31 Bath st. City road
Peggram James, grocer, 8 High st. Kingsland road
Pegington Wm. city carman, 114 Long alley, Moorfields
Pegler Brothers, merchants, 46 Lime st
Pegler Frederick, chemist, 38 Ebury st. Pimlico
Pegler Geo. Hen. engraver & enamelr. 23 Woodbridge st. Clerkwl
Pegler Samuel, *Ship* P.H. 14 Phœnix alley, Long acre
Pegler Thos. *Duke's Head* P.H. 37 St. Martin's st. Le'ster sq
Pegler Wm. Haskett, agent, see Richardson & Pegler
Pegram James, jun. carpenter & undertakr. 1 Holly st. Dalston
Pegram Jas. sen. builder, Shrubland grove, Queen's rd. Dalstn
Pegram John, linendraper, Kingsland green
Pegrum Samuel, meat salesman, 13 New Newgate market
Peil & Blaylock, ribbon importers, 72 Newgate st
Peile Alfred, music seller, King's road west, Chelsea
Peile Solomon, brandy merchant, 5 Idol lane, Tower st
Peile Thomas Hanson, solicitor, 6 Great Winchester st
Peirce Chas. J. architect, 5 Madeley vil. Kensington new tn
Peirce Clement Anthony, perfumer, &c. see Gattie & Peirce

Peirce George, printer, 310 Strand
Peirce Jas. agent & warehouseman, 45 Fore st. Cripplegate
Peircey George, builder, 27 New st. Bishopsgate
Peircey John, coal dust&blacking ma. 24Duke st.Stamford st
Peircey Sarah (Mrs.), tobacconist, 5 Church row, Aldgate
Peirse John, leather enameller & japanr. 59 HoxtonOld town
Peirse Wm. Jas. *Greyhound* P.H. Up. Grange rd. OldKt.rd
Peirson John & Son, furn. ironmongers, 1 Sun st.Bishopsgate
Peirson Geo. Carr, barrister, 35 Southampton blds.Chanc.la
Peirson James, solicitor, 11 Furnival's inn, Holborn
Peirson Robert, bookbinder, 23 Great Winchester st. City
Peirson Stephen, carpenter, Old Brompton, Middlesex
Peirson Thomas, who. straw hat manuf. 2Russia row, Milk st
Peirson Wm. butcher, 8 New Manor st.King's road, Chelsea
Peirson Wm. tailor & piece broker, 7 Weston st.Somers twn
Peisley DavidThos.who.colormn.&tallowch.58Juddst.Newrd
Pelerin Wm. Gustavus, naturalist, 65 Lamb's Conduit st
Pelham Jabez, attorney, 28 Arbour sq. Commercial road
Pelican Life Insurance Comp. (R. Tucker, secretary), 70 Lombard st. & 57 Charing cross; see page 2040
Pell Bennett, distiller, &c. see Bishop & Pell
Pell John, tobacco & snuff manufacr. 137 Borough High st
Pellatt Apsley [late Pellatt & Green], glass manufacturer to her Majesty; patentee of the glass illuminators & incrustations; manufacturer of improved vials, new renaissance chandeliers, & dealer in tea table & desert china, Falcon glass works, Holland st. Blackfriars road, & Bazaar, 58 Baker st. & 5 King st. Portman square
Pellatt Henry, attorney, 64 Dorset st. Salisbury square
Pellatt Mill, wine merchant, see Nichols & Pellatt
Pellatt Thomas, shoemaker, 2 Carrington pl. Down st
Pelle John, ladies' shoemaker, 2 Wigmore st. Cavendish sq
Pelletier Augustus, artist, 46 Howland st. Fitzroy square
Pelling George, builder, &c. 14 Sidney st. Goswell road
Pelling George, grocer, 13 Monmouth place, Old Kent rd
Pelling James, carpenter, &c. 5 Holloway pl. Holloway
Pelling John, carpenter, 11 White Conduit terr. Pentonville
Pelling John, painter, 1 James place, Holloway
Pells Cornelius, tailor, 11 Princes road, Notting hill
Pelly Sir John Hen. bt.merch. 1 Winchester bldgs.Gt.Win.st
Pelly John, tailor, Well st. Hackney
Pelly John Hen. merchant, 1 Winchester bldgs.Gt.Winch.st
Pelly Raymond, merchant, 26 Austin friars
Pelton Charles, baker, 3 Princes st. Westminster
Pelton James, engineer, pump maker, beer engine maker, cock founder, brazier & pewterer, 6 West st. Soho
Pember John, cheesemonger, 53 Crutchedfriars
Pember John Edward, stockbroker, Stock exchange
Pember Matthew, plumber, 8 Brandon rw. Newington causew
Pemberton, Crawley & Gardiner, solicitors, 20 Whitehall pl
Pemberton & Price, carpenters, 36 Horseferry rd.Westminstr
PembertonWm.&Co.mercts.4 Alderman'swalk.NewBroad st
Pemberton Charles, solicitor, 4 Symond's inn, Chancery lane
Pemberton Joseph, hairdresser, Bridge road, Battersea
Pemberton Rd.Nock, engra.&printer, seeTrimlet&Pemberton
Pemberton Thos. plumber & glazr.66Regent st.Horseferry rd
Pemberton Wm.Augustus S.solicitor, seeWalter&Pemberton
Pemble Edwd. glass & china warho.7 White horse st. Stepney
Pembridge Thomas, grocer, 23 Hertford st. Fitzroy square
Pembroke William, butcher, High st. Deptford
Pemell William, special pleader, 1 Elm court, Temple
Pemeller Francis Henry, undertaker, 4 Shoe lane, Fleet st
Pemeller Thomas, coal merchant, 31 Tysoe st. Spafields
Pendered John, ironmonger, 1 Bridge st. Lambeth
Pendrigh Alex. *Royal Yacht* P.H.49 Stanhope st.Clare mkt
Pendrill Thomas, bookseller, 14 Union st. Bishopsgate
Pendry Henry, *Red Cross* P.H. 19 Newgate market
Penfold Marchant, haberdasher, 6 Orford pl. Marlboro' road
Penfold Oliver, druggist, 4 Blackmoor st. Drury lane
Penfold Stephen, coal merchant, 3 New ct. St. Swithin's la
Penfold Thomas Edwd. attorney, 42 Mecklenburgh square
Penhey Henry, wax & tallow chandler, 2NewBridge st.Vaxll
Peninsular & Oriental Steam Navign. Co. (James Allan, sec.), 51 St. Mary axe
Penistan Benjn. hosier, 29 Sidney pl. Commercial rd. east
Penistan Rich. haberdasher, 11 Staverton row, Walworth rd
Penkivil Wm. Jones, solicitor, West st. Finsbury circus
Penlington Thomas & Co. merchants, 22Change alley, Cornhill
Penman John, cabinet maker, 177 Kent st. Borough
Penman William, wire worker, 17 Snowsfields, Bermondsey
Penn John & Son, engineers & steam engine manufacturers, Greenwich & Deptford pier
Penn Edward, attorney, 22 Essex st. Strand
Penn Eliza (Mrs.), juvenile warehouse, 5Baker st.Portman sq
Penn George, *Horselydown* P.H. 1 Fair st. Horselydown
Penn George Jas. tea dlr.11 Warkworth ter.Comcl.rd.Limho
Penn Jacob, tobacconist, 92 St. George st
Penn John, wheelwright, 6 Love lane, Brook st. Ratcliff
Penn John, *Union* coffee rooms, 82 Bunhill row
Penn John Camp, boot & shoe maker, 143 Holborn bars, & 97 Crawford st. Portman square
Penn Mary Ann (Mrs.), linendraper, 18 Ferry rd.wst. Poplar
Penn Richard, butcher, 18 Lambeth walk
Penn Thomas, grocer, 4 Stepney rents, Hackney road
Penn Thomas, law, comcl. & genl. agent, &c. 11 Water lane
Penn Thomas, tobacconist, 208 Borough High st
Penn William, coffee rooms, 50 Marylebone lane
Penn William, engraver & printer, 31 Great Bush lane
Penn William, stationer & pocketbook ma. 23 Cannon st.City
Pennack Wm. fruiterer, &c. 16 King's road east, Chelsea
Pennell John Wilson C. surgeon, 6 Princes st. Hanover sq
Pennell William, official assignee, 31 Basinghall st
Pennethorne James, architect, 7 Whitehall yard
Penny Wm. & Co. varnish & japan manufs, 251 Tottenm.ct.rd
Penny Richard, painter & glazier, 27 Porter st. Soho
Penny Thos. tailor & hosier, 43 Goodge st. Tottenham ct. rd
Penny Wm. mathemat. inst. maker, 25 Broad st. Ratcliff
Pennicott Edward, plumber, 44 Skinner st. Clerkenwell
Penniket Elizth. (Mrs.), cab proprietor, 6 Silver st. Blmsby
Penniket Henry, dining rooms, 72 Sun st. Bishopsgate
Pennington John F. & Co. ostrich feather mers. 9 Walbrook
Pennington Robt.& Son, chrono. ma.11 Portland rw.Cmbrwl
Pennington Andrew, dairy, 1 Trevor ter. Knightsbridge
Pennington Christopher, baker, 135 Vauxhall walk
Pennington Henry, cheesemonger, 4 Beech st. Barbican
Pennington John, average stater, 4 Austinfriars
Pennington Wm. George, solicitor, see Wade & Pennington
Pennington Robert Reney, physician, 15 Portman square
Pennington Thomas, furniture broker, 19 New st. Goldn. sq
Pennington William, surgeon, 21 Montague pl. Russell sq
Penny Charles & Sons, wholesale stationers, &c. 37 Bow lane
Penny Joshua & Co. wine merchs. 5Queen st.pl.Up.Thames st
Penny Alfred, coal merchant, 12 Newcastle wharf, City road basin, 20 & 21 wharfs, Wenlock basin
Penny Benjamin, bootmaker, Deptford High st
Penny Edward, *William IV.* P.H. 45 Golden la. St. Luke's
Penny Henry, bootmaker, 44 Chapel st. Pentonville, & 1 Mount row, Liverpool road
Penny Henry, stationer, vellum binder & metallic book manufacturer, agt.forDickinson's printing cards, 11 Old bailey
Penny Henry George, lighterman, 11 Lucas st. Rotherhithe
Penny Jane (Mrs.), *Waterman's Arms* P.H. 289Rotherhth.st
Penny John, tailor, &c. 27 Princes st.Stamford st. Lambeth
Penny Joseph, *India Arms* P.H. 48 Trinity st.Rotherhithe
Penny Rebecca(Mrs.), corsetmaker, &c.113Longacre, Cov.gar
Penny Richard, coal & potato dealer, 6 Litchfield st. Soho
Penny Rowland, tailor, 57 George st. Euston square
Penny Thomas, boot & shoe maker, 10 Union rw. Lit.Chelsea
Penny Thomas, house painter, &c.5 Berkeley pl. Edgware rd
Penny Thomas, *Vine* P.H. 84 Broad st. Ratcliff
Pennycad Henry, bricklayer, 7 Southampton st. Euston sq
Pennycad John, teadealer, 63 Strutton ground, Westminster
Pennycad Wm. grocer & cheesemonger, 48 WappingHigh st
Pennyfeather Henry, cabinet ma. 2 Lit.Warner st. Clrknwll
Penrice John, oil & colorman, 3 Thornton st. Dockhead
Penrose Arthur W. chemist, 5 Amwell st. Pentonville
Penrose Sarah(Mrs.), chandler's shop, 48Russell st.L.Rothrh
Penrose Thomas, tailor, &c. see Farrar & Penrose
Penry Henry, greengrocer & coal dealer, 23 Hackney road
Penry Wm.Jas.beerret.&coff.rooms, 16&17RedLion st.Sptlfds
Penryn Thomas, working jeweller, 44 Robert st. Hoxton
Pensa Margt. (Mrs.), barometer ma. 25 Charles st. Hat.gdn
Penson George, wholesale cheesemonger, 43 Newgate st. & 270 Bermondsey st
Penson Thomas, bookseller, 3 Pitt's place, Old Kent road
Penston Sarah (Miss), ironmonger, 21Penton rw.Walworthrd
Penstone Giles, linendraper, 1 Leicester pl. Cambrwl. Nw.rd
Pentecost Wm. Thos. dairyman, 319 Albany rd. Cambrwl
Penton Edwin & Stephen, bakers, 3 Lupus st. Belgrave rd
Penton Charles, caneworker, 29 Norfolk st. Middlesex hosp
Penton David, currier & leatherseller, 14 Marylebone lane
Penton Edward, currier, 78 Charlotte st. Fitzroy square
Pen-y-bryn & Moel-Tryfan Slate Co. (Joseph Hedley, manager), 20 Bucklersbury
Peowrie Charles, grocer, 15 Sparrow corner, Minories
Pepler William, bricklayer, 24 Circus st. New road
Peploe James, butcher, 2 East st. Walworth
Peplor Richard, coachpainter, Wyndham road, Camberwell
Peplow Joseph, surgeon, &c. 13 Tottenham court road
Pepper & Reeves, manufacturing chemists, 18 Lewisham st. Westminster, & 29 Wharf, City road
Pepper Elizabeth (Miss), ironmonger, High st. Bow

Pepper James, tobacconist, 22 Villiers st. Strand
Pepper John, bootmaker, 39 Castle st. east, Oxford st
Pepper John, solicitor, 10 Upper Ranelagh st
Pepper Mary (Mrs.), bootmaker, 68 Walnut Tree wk. Lmbth
Pepper Thomas, *Red Lion inn*, 109 Aldersgate st
Pepper Wm. oil & colorman, 13 Middlesex st. Aldgate
Peppercorn George, butcher, Deptford Broadway
Peppercorn Joseph, cheesemonger, 9 & 10 Deptford Broadw
Peppercorn Thos. grocer, &c. Church st. Stoke Newington
Peppercorne Jas. W. & Chas. stockbrokers, 2 Old Broad st
Peppercorne Francis, surgeon, 3 Delahay st. Westminster
PeppinJane&Charlotte, coal merc.4NewNorth st.RedLion sq
Peppen Sydenham Henry, chemist, see Gill & Peppin
Peppin Thomas, wine, brandy & coal merchant, 1 Mason's alley, & 14 Basinghall st
Pepys & Williams, surgical instrmt.maks.&cutlrs.22Poultry
Perceval Ann (Miss), milliner, 1 Halkin terrace, Belgrave sq
Percival, Smythe&Smythe,coalmrc.seeSmythe,Percival&Co
Percival Daniel, boot & shoe maker, 4 Castle ct. Birchin la
Percival Jas. oilman & provisn. mer.1Valentine pl.Blkfrs.rd
Percival James, soap maker, 13 Beaumont square, Mile end
Percival Joseph, oil & colorman, see Smythe & Percival
Percival Joseph, cart grease manufr. 14 Green st. Blackfrs
Percival Mary (Mrs.), milliner, 9 Holywell st. Millbank
Percival Samuel, shipbroker, see Wilkin & Percival
Percival Thomas, hairdresser, 6 Mayfield pl. Kensington
Percival Thomas, silkman & throwster, 24 Austinfriars
Percival Thos. wind musical instrum. mak. 89 St. James's st
Percival William, merchant, 1 Fen court, Fenchurch st
Percival William, veterinary surgeon, 22 Montpelier square
Percy Charles, draper & tailor, 8 Charles st. Hatton garden
Percy Francis, leather seller, 3 Port place, Walworth comm
Bercy James, lath render, 79 Devonshire st. Kennington la
Percy John, jun. builder, 54 Regent st. Horseferry road
Percy John, sen. builder, 56 Regent st. Westminster
Percy John Thomas, *Fox* P.H. 1 White st. Borough
Percy Joseph, *Nag's Head* P.H. 31 New Compton st. Soho
Percy Sidney Richard, artist, 11 Johnson st. Somers town
Percy Thomas, architect & surv. 1 Alfred pl. Bedford sq
Percy Thomas, mason, 2 Church st. Newington
Peregrine John Pryor, surgeon, 3 Halfmoon st. Piccadilly
Peregrine Thomas, surgeon, 17 Mount st. Grosvenor sq
Pereira David Lopez, merchant, 15 King st. Finsbury
Pereira Ebenezer, auctioneer, 35 Tottenham rd. Kingsland
Pereira Henry, plumber, & oil & colorman, 216 Bethnal gr. rd
Pereira Jonathan, physician, 47 Finsbury square
Pereira Sylvano F. L. wine & genrl. mercht. 91 Gt. Tower st
Perez Brothers & Capdepon, of Port St. Mary, 36 Crutchfrs
Perez Sixto, professor of music, 20 Great Marylebone st
Perez-Lozano Manuel, merchant, 36 Crutchedfriars
Perfect Alfred, dentist, 40 Brook st. Grosvenor st
Perfitt Samuel, hatter, 7 Albion place, Battle bridge, & 31 Skinner st. Somers town
Perigal & Brady, merchants, 3 Clement's lane, Lombard st
Perigal George, merchant, 3 Clement's lane, Lombard st
Pering, Minet & Smith, solicitors, 5 Laurence Pountney pl
Pering Allen, solicitor, 41 Mincing la. & 5 Laurenc. Pountny. pl
Perkes George, silk warehouseman, 12 Addle st. Wood st
Perkin & Stones, linendrapers, 37 Parliament st
Perkin Benjamin, *Black Horse* P.H. 114 Aldersgate st
Perkin Geo. Fowler, carpenter, &c. 3 King David la. Shadwell
Perkin James, *Bricklayers' Arms* P.H. 34 King st. Regent st
Perkin Richard Thornton, pawnbroker, 357 Rotherhithe, 12 King's road east, Chelsea, & 2 Albion pl. Battle bridge
Perkin Thomas, *Hope* P.H. 84 John st. Fitzroy square
Perkins, Bacon & Petch, bank note engravers, 69 Fleet st
Perkins James & Son, boot & shoe makers, 42 Dowgate hill
Perkins Rd. & Ed. ladies' shoemakers, 47 Red Lion st. Holborn
Perkins S. E. & E. (Misses), ladies' sch. 2 Kittesford pl. Hcky. rd
Perkins, Schlusser & Mullens, merchants, 67 Mark lane
Perkins & Sharpus, who. tin plate workrs 6 Bell ct. Cannon st
Perkins Abraham, livery stables, 14 Lit. Russell st. Covent gdn
Perkins Angier March, engineer & patent hot water apparatus manufactory, 6 Francis st. Regent sq. Gray's inn rd
Perkins Charles, gold cutter, 37 Gt. Sutton st. Clerkenwell
Perkins Charles, wine merchant, 67 Mark lane, Fenchurch st
Perkins Eizh. (Mrs.), italian wa. 1 Brecknock pl. Camdn. new tn
Perkins Helen (Mrs.), *Rose & Crown* P.H. 57 Drury lane
Perkins Henry, brewer, see Barclay, Perkins & Co
Perkins Henry, carman, 23 Drummond crescent, Euston sq
Perkins Henry John, surgeon dentist, 31 York pl. City road
Perkins Houghton, consulting surgeon, 25 Mortimer st
Perkins James, baker, 6 Bartholomew pl. Kentish town
Perkins James, cheesemonger, 26 Minories
Perkins Jas. *Mqs. Wellington* P.H. 40 Up. Cornwall st. St. Geo. e
Perkins Jas. Dillon, grocer, 1 North side, Grosvenor rw. Piml
Perkins John, cork manfr. Heath pl. Commercial road east
Perkins John, plumber, &c. 6 Northampton row, Holloway
Perkins John, working goldsmith & silver filligree worker, 7 North place, Gray's inn lane
Perkins John, jun. cork merchant, 7 Church la. Whitechapel
Perkins John G. jun. stock agent, 11 Warnford ct. Throgmtn. st
Perkins John Thos. pasteboard ma. 39 Monmouth st. 7 Dials
Perkins Joseph, engraver & printer, 68 Coleman st
Perkins Joseph Rd. gold cutter, 46 Lit. Sutton st. Clerknwl
Perkins Richard, dentist, 19 Park square, Regent's park
Perkins Richard, solicitor, 15 Regent square, Gray's inn road
Perkins Robert, ladies' shoemaker, 37 Bell yard, Temple bar
Perkins Samuel, potato salesman, 13 & 14 Red Lion st. Spitalfi
Perkins Samuel, ship owner, 16 Princes sq. St. George's east
Perkins Sarah (Mrs.), *Pr. of Wales* P.H. 8 Princes sq. Kennigtn
Perkins Thomas, carpenter, 6 Dowgate hill
Perkins Thos. coal mer. Clarence wf. Addington sq. Camberwl
Perkins Thomas, dining rooms, 6 Panton st. Haymarket
Perkins Thos. portable baths, Red Lion yd. 4½ O. Cavndsh. st
Perkins Wm. carpenter & undertaker, 223 Hoxton Old town
Perkins Wm. dentist, 8A, North st. Edgware road
Perkins Wm. furniture broker, 27 Vine st. Hatton garden
Perkins Wm. gold cutter, 47 Clerkenwell close
Perkins Wm. plumber & tobacconist, 26 Hanway st. Oxford st
Perkins Wm. straw hat maker, 7 Prospect row, Walworth rd
Perkins Wm. trimming maker, 61 Curtain road, Shoreditch
Perkins Wm. umbrella maker, 75 Union st. Borough
Perkins Wm. varnish & japan maker, 12 Clerkenwell green
Perko John, furrier, 44 Cross st. Islington
Perks John Brownjohn & Thomas Henry, millers, Cherry garden stairs, Bermondsey wall
Perks Charles, stationer & bookseller, 110 St. Martin's lane
Perks Edward, patentee of the New patent Helix drilled eyed needles, pin, needle & fish hook manufacturer, Redditch & Stoke mills, Worcestershire, & 34 Poultry
Perks Robert, rule maker, 36 Cannon st. St George's east
Perks William Larkin, newspaper agent, 111 St. Martin's la
Perks Zachariah Walker, coffee rooms, 148 Aldersgate st
Perown William, tailor & habit maker, 1 Maze pond, Boro'
Perram Geo. boot & shoe maker, 8 Southampton st. Cmbrwl
Perram James, wholesale teadealer, 10 Austinfriars
Perren Edward, wheelwright, 2 & 3 Lit. Grove st. Lisson grove
Perren George, turkey coffee rooms, 3 Brewer st. Golden sq
Perren George Mark, *Red Lion* P.H. 103 Whitechapel rd
Perren James, fire stone mer. Hen & Chicken la. Walwth. com
Perren John, carpenter & builder, 37 Aldermanbury
Perren Joseph, coffee rooms, 118 Houndsditch
Perren Joseph, oilman, colorman & varnish manufacturer, 40 George st. East st. Walworth
Perrett John, shoe warehouse, 10 Paddington st
Perrett John, tailor, 34 Howland st. Fitzroy square
Perriam Abraham, *Albion* coffee rooms, 188 Wapping High st
Perriam Charles, grocer, 17 Portland st. Soho
Perrier Jouet & Co. wine mer. (A. Boursot, agent), 9 Hart st. Crutched friars
Perrier Ulysse, watch ma. 5 Wilmington st. Wilmington sq
Perrin David, oil & colorman, 21 Carlisle st. Lambeth
Perrin Elizabeth M. (Mrs.), oil wareh. 33 Chalton st. Somers tn
Perrin George, bricklayer & plasterer, 1 Stepney Old road
Perrin James, silk dyer, see Stevens & Perrin
Perrin James, wool broker, 38 Walbrook
Perrin John, baker, 14 Weston st. Borough
Perrin John, stockbroker, Stock exchange
Perrin Thomas, carpenter & bldr. 11 Kent pl. Old Kent road
Perrin William, baker & flour factor, 55 Leadenhall st
Perring Claude, barrister, 19 Lincoln's inn fields
Perring Henry, jeweller & watch ma. 8 City rd. Finsbury sq
Perring John, billiard rooms, 251 Regent st
Perring John, hatter, 85 Strand, & 251 Regent st
Perrott, Watts & Perrott, calenderers, glazers & packers, 24 Tenter st. Little Moorfields
Perrott Richard, commission agent, see Taylor & Perrott
Perrott Richard, boot & shoe maker, 34 Ernest st. Regent pk
Perrott Samuel W. (sec. to London & Dublin Bk.), 46 Piccadilly
Perrott Thomas, chairmaker, 28 Church st. Mile end new tn
Perrott Wm. beer retailer, 1 Devonshire st. Kennington
Porrottet Louis, manufacturer of mother of pearl, parasol furniture & other fancy articles, 4 North cres. Bedford sq
Perry & Brown, carpenters, 18½ Symons st. Chelsea
Perry & Co. glass & lustre manufacterers to her Majesty, 72 New Bond st
Perry James & Co. patent pen, inkstand & ink manufacturers, booksellers & stationers, 37 Red Lion square, Holborn
Perry James & James R. law stationers, 62 Carey st. Linc. inn
Perry James & Saml. bootmakers, 8 Francis pl. Hertford rd
Perry John A. & Son, who. ironmongers, 7 Bishopsgate without

Perry Joseph & Son, musicians, 14 Bury st. Bloomsbury
Perry & Lance, pawnbrokers, 51 Old Compton st. Soho
Perry Matthew & John, carp. & builders, Laurence st. Chelsea
Perry Wm. & James, statuaries & masons, Church st. Hckny
Perry Alexander, baker, 15 Cable st. Wellclose square
Perry Ann (Miss), grocer, 8 Whitehorse lane, Stepney
Perry Charlotte (Miss), bookseller, 9 Lit. Bell al. Coleman st
Perry Ebenezer, architect & surv. 39 Spencer st. Goswell rd
Perry Edward, boot & shoe maker, 5 High st. Stoke Nwngtn
Perry Edward, professor of music, 41 Gibson sq. Islington
Perry Eliza (Miss), beer retailer, 3 Graham st. west, Pimlico
Perry Francis, russia broker, Baltic coffee house
Perry Francis, jun. merchant & russia broker, 5 Austinfriars
Perry Frederick, printer, 93 Great Tower st. City
Perry George, baker, 11 Lower st. Islington
Perry George, biscuit baker, 64 Stone's end, Borough
Perry George, grocer, 36 George st. Lambeth
Perry G. M. surgeon, 11 Union st. Deptford
Perry Henry, furniture broker, 10 Lit. St. Andrew st. 7 dials
Perry Henry, hairdresser, 12 & 13 Burlington arcade
Perry Hen. perfumer & bohemn. glass wa. 59 Burlington arc
Perry Henry, surgns. instrmt. ma. 15 Up. Seymr. st. Euston sq
Perry Henry James, barrister, 6 Gt. James st. Bedford row
Perry Isaac, baker, 6 Britannia st. Bagnigge Wells road
Perry James, baker, 11 Wellington pl. Back rd. St. George's ea
Perry James, fancy steel manufctr. 16 Thavies inn, Holborn
Perry James, fruiterer, 13 Exeter st. Sloane st
Perry John, barrister, 2 Gray's inn place
Perry John, beer retailer, 19 Up. Lisson st. Lisson grove
Perry John, builder, see Brown & Perry
Perry John, corndealer & brewer, 92 St. George's rd. Borough
Perry John, corndealer, 73 Tothill st. Westminster
Perry John, farrier, Lower terrace, Islington
Perry John, fishmonger, 17 Mount row, Liverpool road
Perry John, furn. broker, 9 Portsmouth st. Lincoln's inn fields
Perry John, grocer, 8 Narrow st. Limehouse
Perry John, grocer, 4 Southampton terrace, Pentonville
Perry John, meat salesman, 15 Newgate market
Perry John, sec. *Canada Company*, 13 St. Helen's place
Perry John, smith, Bromley, Middlesex
Perry John, surgeon, 4 Eaton square, Pimlico
Perry John, tailor, 13 Carteret st. Westminster
Perry John, teadealer, 13 Portland row, 13 High st. Cmbrwl
Perry John, upholsterer, appr. & undertakr. 61 London wall
Perry John, watchmaker & jeweller, 40 Oxford st
Perry John, wood & ivory turner, 7 Weston pl. King's cross
Perry John, jun. oil & color wa. 12 Portland row, Camberwell
Perry John Whitby, statuary, &c. Triangle, Hackney
Perry John William, carman, 8 Moor lane, Cripplegate
Perry Joseph, drysalter, 27 Wheeler st. Spitalfields
Perry Joseph, *Duchess of York* P.H. York st. Locks fields
Perry Louis, surgeon, 19 Berners st. Oxford st
Perry Lydia (Mrs.), hatter, 32 Eyre st. hill, Hatton garden
Perry Margaret (Miss), staymaker, 1 Bishopsgate st. witht
Perry Maria (Miss), straw bonnt. ma. 12 Pollards rw. Bthnl. gr
Perry Mary (Mrs.), oilman, 114 Albany st. Regent's park
Perry Richard, barrister, 7 Old square, Lincoln's inn
Perry Robert, *Cutler's Arms* P.H. 3 Cutler st. Houndsditch
Perry Robert, tailor, 8 Wardour st. Soho
Perry Samuel, dining rooms, 42 King st. Westminster
Perry Sarah (Mrs.) grocer & cheesemgr. 1 Sidney st. Coml. rd
Perry Sarah (Mrs.), stove maker, 5 Gt. Earl st. Seven Dials
Perry Thomas, carpenter, 44 Upper Rosoman st. Clerkenwell
Perry Thos. *Bankrupts' Registry off.* King's arms bldgs. Crnhl
Perry Thomas, fruiterer, 3 Broker's row, Red cross st
Perry Thomas, grocer, 43 George st. Euston square
Perry Thomas, smith & bellhanger, 56 Eagle st. Red Lion sq
Perry Thomas, wholesale confectioner, 203 Borough High st
Perry Thomas, working jeweller & cutler, 131 Oxford st
Perry Walter, bootmaker, 10 Low. Porchester st. Edgware rd
Perry William, baker, 28 Limehouse causeway
Perry William, bootmaker, 82 Friar st. Blackfriars road
Perry William, bricklayer, 3 Ropemakers' st. Finsbury
Perry William, chairmaker, 38 Booth st. Spitalfields
Perry William, coach broker, 22 Frederick pl. Hampstd. rd
Perry William, confectioner, 60 Oxford st
Perry William, confectioner, 8 Goldsmith's row, Hackney rd
Perry William, fruiterer, 28 Wimbourne st. New North road
Perry William, hosiery agent, 17½ Addle st
Perry William, law stationer, 1 Bream's bldgs. Chancery la
Perry Wm. who. & retail glover, 19 Crown row, Walworth rd
Perry Wm. Alexr. silk dresser, see Archer, Perry & Archer
Perry Wm. John, printer, 17 Devonshire square
Perryman Charles, carver & gilder, 52 Berwick st. Soho
Perryman James, *Hope* coffee rooms, 190 Drury lane
Perryman Margt. (Mrs.), last maker, 11 Thornton st. Dockhd
Perschky Jesse, newsvender, 14 Union st. Kingsland road
Perton William, plumber & glazier, 3 Young st. Kensington
Perugea Anthony, furniture broker, 25 York st. Westminster
Peruzzi Henry, tailor, &c. 16 Grosvenor st. west, Eaton sq
Pervinkler & Gantzman, cabinetmakrs. 3 Brown's la. Spitflds
Pescodd George, baker, 1 Hollond st. Kensington
Pescott Geo. & Wm. carriers by railway, George yd. Aldrmnby
Pescud George, beer retailer, 10 Thirza place, Old Kent rd
Pesley Fredk. Chas. barrister, 4 Southampton bldgs
Pesman John, slopseller, 47 Wapping
Pesman Lewis & Son, printers, &c. 15 Lamb st. Spitalfields
Pestell Hen. haberdasher, 3 Clement's inn pas. Clare market
Petch Henry, engraver, see Perkins, Bacon & Petch
Petch & Knight, wharfngs. & coal mers. 56 Shad Thames
Petch Isaac Hill, umbrella mak. 3 St. John st. Clerkenwell
Petch John, coal merchant, Phœnix wf. Bridge st. Vauxhall
Petchell John, oilman, 31 Liquorpond st
Petchell Charlotte (Mrs.), oil & colorman, 101 Whitecross st
Peter Alexander, merchant, see Davidson & Peter
Peter Daniel, cheesemonger, 1 Vauxhall row
Peter John Thomas Henry, barrister, 4 Inner Temple lane
Peter Robert, baker, 53 Amwell st. Pentonville
Peterken Hen. Jas. printer & bookseller, 208 Poplar High st
Peterken Thomas, baker, 10 Robin Hood lane, Poplar
Peterken Thomas, baker, 25 Grundy st. East India road
Peterkin Charles, cooper, 15 Vinegar lane, Commercial rd
Peterkin John, watchmaker, 25 Cleveland st. Fitzroy sq
Peters & Banbury, ribbon manufrs. 45 Wood st. Cheapside
Peters John & Daniel, cotton dyers, 13 New Ivy st. Hoxton
Peters John F. & W. tobacconists, 127 Drury lane
Peters Thomas & Sons, coach & harness makers, 95 & 96 Park st. Grosvenor sq. & 11 Upper George st. Bryanstone sq
Peters & Underwood, linendrapers, 33 Sloane sq. Chelsea
Peters Ann (Miss), *New York* coffee rooms, 120 Minories
Peters Ann (Miss), stay & corset ma. 5 Arabella row, Pimlico
Peters Chas. straw & tuscan hat ma. 19 Plumbers' st. City rd
Peters Edwin, *Princess Royal* P.H. 36 Johnson st. Comml. rd
Peters Henry, butcher, 88 Tottenham court road
Peters James, straw hat manufacturer, 442 West Strand
Peters Jane (Mrs.), milliner, art. florist, &c. 442 West Strand
Peters John, carpenter, 7 Eli st. Pearson st. Kingsland rd
Peters Rd. Thos. *Geo. & Blue Boar hotel*, 270 High Holborn
Peters Robt. linendraper, 19 Hereford pl. Commercl. rd. east
Peters Thomas, coachmaker, 20 Adam st. west, Edgware rd
Peters Thomas, law stationer, 13 Serle's place, Lincoln's inn
Peters Wm. bricklayer & plasterer, 5 Primrose st. Bishopsgt
Peters Wm. glazier, &c. 5 Mount ter. New rd. Whitechapel rd
Peters William, tailor, 7 Castle st. Falcon square
Petersdorff Charles, barrister, 1 Tanfield court, Temple
Petersdorff Edward, special pleader, 1 Tanfield court, Temple
Peterson William & Son, bootmakers, 33 Poultry
Peterson Andw. Thos. Turton, barrister, 1 Essex ct. Temple
Peterson John, ladies' shoemaker, 48 Mount st. Lambeth
Peterson Matilda (Miss), boarding house, 69 Pall mall
Peterson Thomas, coffee rooms, 18 Robert st. Grosvenor sq
Pether Harry, artist, 2 Spring terrace, Wandsworth road
Pether Stephen, stables, 10 Lit. Derweston st. Marylebone
Pether Wm. cooper & brushmkr. 93 Gt. Titchfield st. Oxford st
Petheram John, bookseller & publisher, 71 Chancery lane
Petheram Mary Ann (Miss), milliner, 7 Albion pl. Hollowy. rd
Petherbridge Wm. linen & woollen draper, 25 Hatton gardn
Pethick Edward, smith, 46 Millbank st. Westminster
Pethick Margaret (Mrs.), stay & corset ma. 2 Islington pl
Petit John, watchmaker, 125 Bethnal green road
Petit Jules, ladies' french boot & shoe war. 124 Regent st
Petit Louis Hayes, barrister, 9 New sq. Lincoln's inn
Petit Louis Peter, barrister, 7 New square, Lincoln's inn
Petitt Samuel, *Bull's Head* P.H. 3 Bread st. City
Petley Thomas, lighterman, 7 Gt. Hermitage st. Wapping
Peto Samuel Morton, builder, see Grissell & Peto
Petre Elizabeth (Mrs.), grocer, 8 London, ter. Hackney rd
Petre Joseph, teadealer, 2 Grosvenor pl. Commercial rd. east
Petrie Alexr. S. & Co. merchants, 7 Ironmonger lane
Petrie Alexr. sackclothmnfr. 9 St. Martin's pl. St. Martin's le Gd
Petrie Henry, carpenter, 13 Sir Wm. Warren's sq. Wapping
Petrie John, india rubber golosh maker, 34 Berners st
Petriken Ja. yeast mercht. 6 Castle st. ea. & 12 Berners mws
Petrocochino Alex. Pandia, merchant, 9 Finsbury pavement
Pett James, carpenter, &c. 18 Caroline pl. Hampstead road
Pett James, perfumer, comb & brush maker, 243 Regent st
Pett Richard, coal dealer, 22 Bell st. Edgware road
Pettepher Richard, butcher, 3 Phœnix st. Somers town
Petter John B. & C. H. *Crown & Dolphin* P.H. 29 Cannon st. St. George's east
Petter Geo. *Chapman Arms* P.H. 25 Lr. Chapman st. St. Geo's. e
Petter George Edwd. bookseller & stationer, 102 Cheapside

Pettet John & Son, ironmongers, 17 Brook st. St. Pancras
Pettet & Newton, navy agts. 10 Lancaster pl. Waterloo brdg
Pettet John, insurance & commission agt. 29 Bucklersbury
Pettet Mark, carpenter, 14 Church st. Islington
Pettet Thomas, confectioner, 39 City road, Finsbury square
Pettett Geo. house painter, 2 Up. Montagu st. Montagu sq
Pettifer William, baker, 42 Munster st. Regent's park
Pettigrew Robert, tailor, &c. see Bingley & Pettigrew
Pettigrew Thos. Joseph, surgeon, 8 Saville row, Piccadilly
Pettigrew William Henry, surgeon, 200 Tooley st
Pettigrew William V. M.D. surgeon, 30 Chester st. Grsvnr. pl
Pettingell William Parrish, tailor, 31 North Audley st
Pettipher Thomas, saddler, 110 Shadwell High st
Pettit Charles, silver chaser, 7 Thanet place, Temple bar
Pettit Geo. auctioneer & appraiser, 48 Brewer st. Golden sq
Pettit Geo. dairyman, 8 South Island place, Clapham road
Pettit James, bookseller, 5 Goswell st
Pettit James, grocer, &c. 60 Robinhood lane, Poplar
Pettit John, bootmaker, 47 Molyneux st. Bryanstone sq
Pettit Joseph, tea & coffee rooms, 27 King st. Portman sq
Pettit Louisa (Mrs.), dressmaker, 13 Tavistock st. Cov. gar
Pettit Mary A. (Mrs.), straw hat ma. 3 Aldenham st. Somers tn
Pettit Philip, fruiterer & dairyman, 4 Grove la. Camberwell
Pettit Richd. *Captain Cook* P.H. 27 Marman st. Coml. rd. ea
Pettit Thos. undertaker, 3 Aldenham st. Somers town
Pettit Walter, grocer, 14 Turnmill st. Clerkenwell
Pettit William, cattle salesman, 60 West Smithfield
Pettitt Raymond, engraver & printer, 4 Brewer st. Golden sq
Pettitt Thos. H. statnr. & acct. bk. ma. 1 Old Compton st. Soho
Petty Bag & Cursitor's Office, Rolls yd. Chancery la.; 10 to 6; in long vacation from 10 to 4
Petty, Hinton & Son, coal merchants & wharfingers, Royal George wharf, 88 Bankside
Petty, Wood & Tomlin, grocers & oilmen, 53 Threadneedle st
Petty Edward, hairdresser, 22 Rotherhithe
Petty Richard, machine ruler, 28 Old Jewry
Petty Thomas, baker, 21 Boston st. Dorset square
Petty Wm. plumber, 18 Crown row, Walworth road
Peverall John, linendraper, 54 Cromer st. Gray's inn road
Peverett Wm. grocer & teadlr. 30 Church st. Camberwell
Pew Jane (Mrs.), furniture dlr. 3 Lit. Cross st. Newington bts
Pew John, furniture broker, 6 Surrey place, Walworth rd
Pew John, furniture broker, 7 Staverton row, Walworth rd
Pewterers' Hall (Wm. Dadley, clerk), 17 Lime st
Pewters George, brush maker, 58 Goswell road
Pewtress, Low & Pewtress, paper manfrs. 30 Gracechurch st
Pewtress & Son, wholes. stationers, 67 Newington causeway
Peyton & Aikin, surveyors, &c. 10 Cook's court, Lincoln's inn
Peyton & Harlow, pat. metallic bedstead ma. 12 Panton sq
Peyton Joseph, bootmaker, 82 Cheapside
Pfaff Anthony & Co. clock makers, 67 Coleman st. City
Pfeil Adolph Leopold & Co. who. irnmngrs. 5 & 6 Broad st. Blms
Pfeil & Hammond, ladies' school, 27 Low. Belgrave pl. Pimlico
Pfeil Mary (Mrs.), baker, 3 Brook st. Ratcliff
Pfisterer George, baker, 32 Hare st. Bethnal green
Pfleger Christopher, broker, see Bowring & Pfleger
Phair Joseph, printer, 67 Great Peter st. Westminster
Phairs William, hat manufacturer, 11 Union st. Borough rd
Phare Geo. & Co. bottle merchants, Hungerford whf. Strand
Pharmaceutical Society (Geo. W. Smith, sec.), 17 Bloomby. sq
Pharoah John, butcher, 2 Tabernacle walk, Finsbury
Pharoah William, fruiterer, 17½ Cross st. Newington butts
Pheasant William, gasfitter, 76 Curtain rd. Shoreditch
Phelps & Co. wine merchts. (from Billiter st.), 5 Rood lane
Phelps Joseph & Son, stationers, 44 Paternoster row
Phelps Geo. Hen. vellum binder, 27 Martin's la. Cannon st
Phelps James, optician, 5 City terrace, Old st. road
Phelps James Clement, corn dlr. 7 Glo'ster pl. Walw. com
Phelps John, tobacconist, 14 Church st. Kensington
Phelps John, who. grocer, see Conway, Phelps & Hayward
Phelps Josiah, mason, 9 Pierrepoint row, Islington green
Phelps Peter, beer retailer, 13 Westmoreland pl. Wlwth. com
Phelps Richard, coal merchant, 22 Spring st. Portman sq
Phelps Thomas, optician, 6 Southampton st. Camberwell
Phelps Wm. madeira merchant, 5 Rood lane, Fenchurch st
Phelps Wm. *Royal Mail* P.H. 124 Upper st. Islington
Phelps Wm. solicitor, see Jenkyns & Phelps
Phelps Wm. stationer, 7 Vauxhall st. Lambeth
Phelps Wm. tobacconist, 10 Clement's inn passage
Phenés & Williamson, upholsterers, 86 London wall, & New Broad st. City
Phibbs George, wine merchant, 37 Crutchedfriars
Philanthropic Society for Children of Convicts (Chas. A. Dodd, sec.), 15 London road
Philcox George & Co. chronometer makers, 104 Fenchurch st. & 247 Borough High st

Philip William & Son, tailors, 14 Oxendon st. Haymarket
Philipe George Peter De Rhe, solicitor, 9 Gray's inn sq
Philippe Achille, champagne agent, Hall of Commerce, & 55 Trinity sq. Borough
Philipps Henry, solicitor, 4 Sise lane, Bucklersbury
Philipps Lewis, coffee & reading rooms, 49 Tooley st
Philipps Robt. Nathan, barrister, 9 King's Bench wk. Templ
Philipps Vincent, seal, die & copper plate engraver, & steel stamp cutter, 30 Sun st. Bishopsgate
Philips Chas. F. solicitor, Albion chmbs. 11 Adam st. Adelphi
Philips Esther (Mrs.), dressmaker, 7 Gt. Quebec st. New rd
Philips Joseph, special pleader, 1 New Temple bldgs. Mitre ct
Philips Sarah (Mrs.), fruiterer, 1A, Gray's inn lane
Phillimore John George, barrister, 6 Pump court, Temple
Phillimore Joseph, D.C.L. advocate, 15 College, Doctors' com
Phillimore Phineas, bottle mer. 3 Broomfield pl. Deptford
Phillimore Robt. J. D.C.L. advocate, 15 College, Doctors' com
Phillip Thomas, oilman, 21 Coleshill st. Eaton square
Phillipe John, wardrobe dealer, 40 Gibson st. Waterloo rd
Phillippo James, dealer in horses, 43 Cross st. Finsbury
Phillipps & Graves, lightermen & cus. house agts. 11 Rood la
Phillipps, Rowell & Lowther, custom house & comm. agents, 5 St. Dunstan's hill
Phillipps & Tiplady, ship & ins. brokrs. 3 George yd. Lombd. st
Phillipps Chas. S. March, barrister, 3 Stone bldgs. Linc. inn
Phillipps Jeremiah S. stone & steel seal engraver, 14½ Old st
Phillipps Leonard, arborist, &c. Wandsworth road
Phillipps Philip, cane dealer, 32 Sun st. Bishopsgate
Phillipps William Phillipps, stock & share broker, Auction mart, Bartholomew lane, or Stock exchange
Phillips, Allcard & Co. imperial saw mills, Wenlock road
Phillips & Beesley, upholsterers, cabinet makers & plate glass factors, 18 Finsbury place south
Phillips Brothers, watchmakers & goldsmiths, 31 Cockspur st
Phillips & Burton, merchants, 2 New Broad st. City
Phillips Christopher & James, fresh butter & pork salesmen, 68 Newgate market
Phillips (Coleman Lyon) & Co. comb makers & horn & bone mers. 17 John st. Minories, & 9½ Gould sq. Crutchedfriars
Phillips Edmund & Co. merchants & importers of american, irish & hamburgh provisions, 8 London st. Fenchurch st
Phillips & Eldred, linen factors, 22 Milk st. Cheapside
Phillips George & Fredk. tailors, 1 Thornton st. Dockhead
Phillips & Hyams, fishmongers, 10 Gt. Suffolk st. Borough
Phillips Jas. & Son, solicitors, 28 Laurence Pountney lane
Phillips John & Geo. fancy plaid & linen wa. 198 Regent st
Phillips & Jacobs, opticians, 231 Tottenham court road
Phillips John S. & John H. dentists, 96 Charlotte st. Fitzroy sq
Phillips, King & Co. merchants, 8 Fowkes' buildings, Tower st
Phillips (Laurence) & Sons, merchants & east india agents, 16 George st. Mansion house
Phillips & Relfe, milliners, 21 Conduit st. Regent st
Phillips & Samson, tailors, 68 Lamb's Conduit st. Foundling
Phillips Samuel & Co. merchants & east india agents, Levant house, St. Helen's place, Bishopsgate
Phillips Thomas & Co. wholesale grocers, 45 Eastcheap
Phillips Thomas & Chas. corn mer. 32 Wilton pl. Knightsbdg
Phillips Widow & Son, watch manufacturers, & dealers in second hand plate & watches, 10 Bury st. St. Mary Axe
Phillips Abraham, tailor, 42 Shadwell High st
Phillips Abraham, tobacconist, 64 Bath st. City road
Phillips Alfred, florist, Jamaica level, Rotherhithe
Phillips Ann (Mrs.), circul. library, 46 James st. Oxford st
Phillips Barnet, clothes salesman, 2 Sharp's bldgs. Minories
Phillips Barnett, jeweller, 8 Castle st. Houndsditch
Phillips Benjamin, beer retailer, 123 Vauxhall walk
Phillips Benjamin, boot & shoe ma. 48 High st. Notting hill
Phillips Benjamin, F.R.S. surgeon, 17 Wimpole st
Phillips Benjamin, tailor & draper, 106 Tottenham court rd
Phillips Benjamin, undertaker, 166 Bermondsey st
Phillips Benj. Samuel, berlin wool wa. see Faudel & Phillips
Phillips Chas. boot & shoe maker, 98 St. John st. road
Phillips Chas. boot maker, 5 Mortimer market, Totten. ct. rd
Phillips Chas. ivory & bone brush maker, 20 King st. Soho
Phillips Chas. paper stainer & hanger, 9 Totton st. Stepney
Phillips Chas. patent wig maker, 4 Sutton pl. Crown st. Soho
Phillips Chas. tailor, 48A, Moorgate st. City
Phillips Chas. watchmaker, 41 Upper Rosoman st
Phillips Chas. Hen. engraver & printer, 19 Gracechurch st
Phillips Chas. Hen. surgeon, 11 Cleveland row, St. James's sq
Phillips Chas. John, steam flat. mills, 28 Parker st. Drury la
Phillips Charlotte (Mrs.), grocer, 8 St. Thomas pl. Gt. Dov. rd
Phillips Cornelius, cabinetmaker, 5 Angel place, Islington
Phillips Daniel, cheesemonger, Church st. Hackney
Phillips David, billiard rooms, 99 Regent st
Phillips David, silver spoon, &c. ma. 12 Wilson st. Finsbury

Phillips David, slopseller, 206 Shoreditch High st
Phillips Edmund, merchant, 8 London st. City
Phillips Edmund, law stationer, 25A, Bedford row
Phillips Edmund John, *Golden Ball* P.H.41 King st. Snow hill
Phillips Edward, beer retailer, 2 Mansell pass. Haydon sq
Phillips Edward, agent to Bass, Ratcliff & Gretton, india ale stores, 67 Lower Thames st
Phillips Edward, wine, spirit & beer mer. 67 Lr. Thames st
Phillips Edward Fox, attorney, 5 Great Tower st
Phillips Edward Rd. attorney, 76 Gt. Titchfield st. Oxford st
Phillips Edwy Stanley (sec. to *Gen. Marit. Ass. Co.*), 30 Cornhill
Phillips Emanuel, marine str. dlr. 15 Lit. Coram st. Brnswk. sq
Phillips Francis H. timber mer. 5 Cumberland ter. Lloyd sq
Phillips George, bookbinder, 104 High Holborn
Phillips George, furniture broker & carpenter, Battersea sq
Phillips George, linendraper, 153 Bermondsey st
Phillips George, locksmith & bellhang. 172 Bishopsgate without
Phillips George, watch case maker, 26 Radnor st. St. Luke's
Phillips Geo. Bridges C. dentist, Denmark hill, Camberwell
Phillips George Richard, grocer, 37 & 38 Aldersgate st. 47 Monkwell st. & 57 Crawford st. Portman square
Phillips Geo. Wm. linendraper, 4 Bridge st. Borough
Phillips Hannah (Mrs.), *George* P.H. 25 Old Bailey
Phillips Henry, artichect & surveyor, Moira chambers, 17 Ironmonger lane, & 5 Bermondsey square
Phillips Henry, baker, 44 Middlesex st. Aldgate High st
Phillips Henry, bookseller, 264 Oxford st
Phillips Henry, bootmaker, 13 Princes st. Leicester sq
Phillips Henry, fishmonger, 1 Cumberland pl. Newington bts
Phillips Henry, law writer, see Butler & Phillips
Phillips Henry, leech merchant, 3 Shadwell High st
Phillips Henry, linendraper, see Mobbs & Phillips
Phillips Henry, potato dealer, 2 Brewer st. Somers town
Phillips Henry, tailor, 19 David st. Marylebone
Phillips Henry, tobacconist, 45 New Compton st. Soho
Phillips Henry, whalebone cutter, 20 Milton st. Cripplegate
Phillips Henry Wyndham, artist, 8 George st. Hanover sq
Phillips Henry W. engineer, 15 Hart st. Bloomsbury square
Phillips Hugh, haberdasher, 82 Tothill st. Westminster
Phillips Jas. coach & house spring curtain ma. 30 Drury la
Phillips Jas. calendr. & packer, 9 King's Arms yd. Moorgate st
Phillips James, *Dun Cow* P.H. Northampton pl. Old Kent rd
Phillips James, fruit salesman, 69 Farringdon market, & fruiterer, 8 Holborn bars
Phillips James, glass cutter, see Welch & Phillips
Phillips James, lodging house, 41 Beaumont st. Portland pl
Phillips James, plasterer, &c. 11 London wall
Phillips James, plumber & painter, 71 Princes st. Le'ster. sq
Phillips James, shopkeeper, Well st. Hackney
Phillips James, smith, &c. 6 Queen's Head ct. Gt. Windmill st
Phillips James, surgeon, Bethnal house, Cambridge road
Phillips James, tailor, 58 Margaret st. Cavendish square
Phillips James, twine manufacturer, 47 Union st. Borough
Phillips James, watchmaker, 45A, Hedge row, Islington
Phillips James, *White Horse* P.H. 23 Lr. Queen st. Rotherhithe
Phillips James Lawrence, sheriff's officer, 75 Basinghall st
Phillips James Percy, solicitor, see Pearce, Phillips & Co
Phillips Jesse, glass warehouse, 27 City terrace, City road
Phillips John, beer retailer, 5 East st. Old Kent road
Phillips John, bricklayer, 8 St. Alban's ter. Vauxhl. bdge. rd
Phillips John, carpenter & undertaker, 101 Old st. St. Luke's
Phillips John, dairyman, 90½ Regent st. Lambeth
Phillips John, feather manufacturer, 4 Savoy st. Strand
Phillips John, fruiterer, 1 Cottage pl. Green st. Kentish town
Phillips John, grocer & cheesemongr. 10 Hall pl. Edgware rd
Phillips John, grocer, 10 William st. Lisson grove
Phillips John, land surveyor & fruiterer, 5 Torrington place
Phillips John, law stationer, 17 Chancery lane
Phillips John, shipchandlr. & rigger, 5 Stephens acre, Blkwll
Phillips John, tailor, 70 Chancery lane
Phillips John, tailor, 1 Pinner's ct. Old Broad st
Phillips John, translator of latin records, 17 Chancery lane
Phillips John, wine importer, 6 Bloomsbury pl. Bloomsbury
Phillips John Aldam, merchant, 2 Riches court, Lime st
Phillips John Geo. work. jeweller, 4 Cobham row, Clerknwll
Phillips John R. *Plasterers' Arms* P.H. 77 Seymour st. Eustn. sq
Phillips John Robert, tailor, 15 St. John sq. Clerkenwell
Phillips John Rouse, *Virginia tavern*, 4 Newman's ct. Crnhll
Phillips John Samuel, stationer, see Reed & Phillips
Phillips Jonathan, chinaman, 358 & 359 Oxford st
Phillips Joseph, carpenter & joiner, 15 Queen st. Oxford st
Phillips Joseph, dyer, 2 Pool st. New North road
Phillips Joseph, jeweller, &c. 26 Bevis marks
Phillips Joseph, tea urn cock ma. 5 St. James' bdgs. Clerknwl
Phillips Joseph, wine & sp. mer. 8 Black raven ct. Tower st
Phillips Josiah, tailor, 2 Friar st. Blackfriars road
Phillips Lawrence, army & navy clothier, sword cutler & accoutrement maker, military hat & cap maker, hosier, shirt maker, outfitter & portable camp & cabin furniture manufacturer, 28 Strand
Phillips Lewis, clothes salesman, 57 Marylebone lane
Phillips Lucy (Mrs.), chinadealer, 19 Henrietta st. Brunsw. sq
Phillips Mark, tailor, 1½ Somerset pl. New rd. Whitechapel
Phillips Martha (Mrs.), lodging house, 35 Jermyn st
Phillips Mary (Miss), lodging house, 26 Norfolk st. Strand
Phillips Mary (Mrs.), milliner, 2 Theberton st. Islington
Phillips Mary Ann (Mrs.), milliner, 91 Crawford st
Phillips Moss, *King's Arms* P.H. Hayfield pl. Mile end rd
Phillips Nathaniel, umbrella ma. 24 King's rd. east, Chelsea
Phillips Nuthall Lenox, *Boot* P.H. 47 Wells st. Oxford st
Phillips Paul, carpentr. & undertakr. 17½ Addle st. Wood st
Phillips Philip, fruit merchant, 21 King st. Aldgate, & 5 Cree Church lane
Phillips Philip, trunkmaker, 30 St. Martin's la. Charing cr
Phillips Philip, watchmaker, 3 Steward st. Spitalfields
Phillips Philip John, milliner, see Fletcher & Phillips
Phillips Philip John, plumber, &c. 18 Wells row, Islington
Phillips Philip Saunders, pawnbroker, Stratford, Essex
Phillips Philip S. sponge mer. 23 Wormwood st. Bishopsgt
Phillips Rachael (Mrs.), saddler, 38 Worship st. Nortn. folgt
Phillips Revell, barrister, 3 Harcourt buildings, Temple
Phillips Richard, auctioneer & valuer, 24 Chiswell st
Phillips Richard, cupper, 7 Cross st. Newington butts
Phillips Richard, jun. dairyman, 48 High st. Portland town
Phillips Richard, fishmonger, 30 Silver st. Golden sq
Phillips Richard, grocer, 48 High st. Portland town
Phillips Rich. *Old Will Somers* P.H. 6 Lamb st. Spital sq
Phillips Richd. upholsterer, &c. 5 Marylebone st. Piccadilly
Phillips Richard, wheelwright, 17 Addle hill, Doctors' commons, & 171 Upper Thames st
Phillips Richard Matthew, grocer, 4 Grove ter. Brompton
Phillips Robt. bleacher & blocker, 46 Up. North pl. Grs. inn rd
Phillips Robert, music seller, 205 Whitechapel road
Phillips Samuel, carpenter, &c. 13 Cecil ct. St. Martin's la
Phillips Samuel, clothier, 15 Tyler st. Regent st
Phillips Samuel, *Dog & Duck* P.H. 13 Princes st. Bedford rw
Phillips Samuel, greengrocer, 5 Odell pl. Little Chelsea
Phillips Samuel, mer. & horse hair mfr. 4 Water la. Tower st
Phillips Samuel, dantzic spruce imp. 13 Princes st. Bedfd. rw
Phillips Samuel, saddletree manufacturer, 65 Bunhill row
Phillips Samuel, scale maker, 18 Vine st. Hatton garden
Phillips Samuel, tailor, 6 Duke st. Aldgate
Phillips Samuel, watchma. & working jewelr. 2 Paddington st
Phillips Sidney J. commisn. agt. 19 Lombard st. chambers
Phillips Simon, furrier & cap mak. 26 Cutler st. Houndsditch
Phillips Solomon, cigar manufacturer, 165 High Holborn
Phillips Stephen, jun. merchant tailor, see Challis & Phillips
Phillips Thomas, bookbinder, 12 Plumber st. City road
Phillips Thomas, butcher, 31 Rosoman st. Clerkenwell
Phillips Thomas, carpenter, box maker, &c. 145 Fleet st
Phillips Thomas, cheesemonger, 18 King's pl. Commrcl. rd. e
Phillips Thos. custom. ho. agt. & lighterman, Hall of Commerce
Phillips Thomas, naphtha lamp manufacturer, 145 Fleet st
Phillips Thomas, pewterer, 86 West Smithfield
Phillips Thomas, plumber, Church st. Hackney
Phillips Thomas, plumber, New cross
Phillips Thomas, plumber, 4 Temple place, Old Kent road
Phillips Thomas, silk manufacturer, see Casey & Phillips
Phillips Thomas, tin plate wor. 14 Gastigny pl. Bath st. City r
Phillips Thomas Grace, surgeon, 44 Albion st. Hyde park
Phillips Thomas James, *Red Lion* P.H. 66 Old st. St. Luke's
Phillips Thomas Joddrell, barrister, 7 New sq. Linc. inn
Phillips Walter Thos. *Old Red Cock* P.H. 18 Mill la. Tooley st
Phillips Walter Thos. ship & custm. ho. agt. 18 Mill la. Tooley st
Phillips Wm. auctioneer & estate agent, 73 New Bond st
Phillips Wm. baker, 1 Spring garden place, Stepney
Phillips Wm. cattle slaesman, 15 West Smithfield
Phillips Wm. corn & coal dealer, 148 Bethnal green road
Phillips Wm. haberdasher, 2 Ossulston st. Somers town
Phillips Wm. linendraper, 9 Norland road, Notting hill
Phillips Wm. oilman, &c. 50 & 51 Strutton ground, Westmr
Phillips Wm. pewterer, 25 Borough road
Phillips Wm. *Queen Charlotte* P.H. 1 Millpond st. Bermondsey
Phillips Wm. quill merchant, &c. see Cooper & Phillips
Phillips Wm. saddler & harn. mak. 26 Sherrard st. Golden sq
Phillips Wm. steel letter cutter, 16 St. James's blds. Clerknw
Phillips Wm. tobacconist, 2 Deptford Broadway
Phillips Wm. who. brushma. 143 Minories, & 1 Lit. George st
Phillips Wm. Thos. tobacconist, 43 Lambeth High st
Phillipson Montague & Co. chemists & exporting druggists, 1 Budge row & 17 Tower royal
Phillipson Beerend Jacob, cheesemonger, 55 Leman st

Phillipson Chas. surgeon dentist, 34 Up. Montagu st. Mntg. sq
Phillipson Edward, chemist, 116 Tottenham court road
Phillipson John, teadealer & grocer, 60 & 61 Goswell st
Phillott Arthur, surgeon, 4 Wimpole st. Cavendish sq
Phillpot Rd. & Co. sheriff's officer, 13 Gt. Bell all. Moorgt. st
Phillpotts John, barrister, M.P. Reform Club, 104 Pall mall
Phillpotts Thos. Griffin, solicitor, 8 Earl st. Blackfriars
Philo George, undertaker, 15 Susannah st. Poplar
Philo James, working jeweller, 12 Red Lion st. Clerkenwell
Philological School Soc. (Edwin Abbott, head master & secretary), 38 Gloucester place, New road, Marylebone
Philosophical Institution (John Owen, librarian), 32 to 37 Beaumont square, Mile end
Philp, Bush & Finch, Kensington ho. lunatic asylum, Knsgn. rd
Philp John & Co. bootmakers, 3 Haymarket
Philp John & Son, printers, 33 Warner st. Dover road
Philp & Whicker (late Savigny & Co.), cutlers & surgeons instrument makers, 67 St. James's st, Pall mall
Philp David, grocer & bri. wine dlr. Southampton st. Cmbwl. rd
Philp Francis Rd. physician, 28 Grosvenor st. Grosvenor sq
Philp James, cutler, &c. see Everill, Philp & Whicker
Philp Thomas, butcher, 5 High st. Marylebone
Philp William, attorney & solicitor, 27 King st. Holborn
Philp Wm. smith & bellhanger, 6 Knightrider ct. Doct. com
Philpot George, fishmonger, 18 Bishopsgate without
Philpot Henry, chemist & druggist, 32 Praed st. Edgware rd
Philpot John, cheesemonger, 118 Gt. Suffolk st. Borough
Philpot John, jun. attorney, 3 Southampton st. Bloomsbury
Philpot Nathl. grocer & cheesemgr. Southampton st. Cmbwl
Philpot Thomas, tobacconist, 18 Whitechapel road
Philpot Thomas G. ship & insur. agt. 33 Gracechurch st
Philpot William, stockbroker, 7 Tokenhouse yard
Philpot William, tobacconist, 7 Emmett st. Poplar
Philpott & Bullivant, who. tea & coffee dealers, 1 Abchurch yd
Philpott David, tailor, 48 Gainsford st. Horselydown
Philpott Henry Wm. lodging house, 14 Up. North pl. Grs. inn rd
Philpott James, beer retailer, 5 Union st. Lisson grove
Philpott James, cheesemonger, 2 Church row, Aldgate High st
Philpott James Whatman, silk hat ma. 28 Cutler st. Hounds
Philps Robert & Co. linendrapers, 51 & 52 Poplar High st
Phinn Edward Thomas, *Lamb & Flag* P.H. 23 Clerkenwell grn
Phinn Thomas, barrister, 1 New court, Temple
Phipos James, stationer & library, 88 Hackney road
Phippard Moses, mason, 11 Berner st. Commercial rd. east
Phipps John & Co. wholes. stationers, 176 Upper Thames st
Phipps Hon. Edmund, barrister, 6 Figtree court, Temple
Phipps Harriet (Mrs.), school, 3 Chesterfield st. King's cross
Phipps John, architect, 3 Palace place, Gt. Scotland yard
Phipps Richard, bookseller, 2 Church st. Camberwell
Phipps Samuel, butcher, 36 Lower Belgrave st. Eaton sq
Phipps Samuel, grocer, 15 Nassau place, Commerl. rd. east
Phipps Thomas, coal dealer, 2 Fair st. Horselydown
Phipps Thomas, saddler, 243 High Holborn
Phipps Thomas, wholesale stationer, 2 Old Fish st. hill
Phipps Wm. straw hat manufr. 8 Church st. Stoke Newington
Phipps Wm. Downs, ladies' shoemaker, see Buddell & Phipps
Phipson Weatherley, barrister, 1 Hare court, Temple
Phœnix Fire Office (Thomas Richter, esq. sec.), 19 Lombard st. & 57 Charing cross
Phœnix Gas Light & Coke Company Office, 64 Bankside, Southwark; works, 50 Wellington st. Blackfriars road, & 64, 73 & 86 Bankside; Charles Pridden, sec
Phœnix Marine Insurance Company of Calcutta (Mackey, Holt & Co. agents), 20 St. Helen's pl. Bishopsgate
Physical Society (John Birkett, sec.), Guy's Hosptl. Boro'
Physick Edward G. jun. sculptor, 20 Up. Glo'ster pl. Dorset sq
Phythian Thomas, grocer, see Eve & Phythian
Piarce Thomas, grocer, 35 Forston st. Ashley cres. City rd
Picard Francis, artist, 35 Robert st. Hampstead road
Picard Isaac, tobacconist, 191 Piccadilly
Picciotto, Mongredien & Co. merchants, 8 Crosby square
Pick Ratcliffe, dining rooms, 66 Minories
Pickard & Green, silk & ribbon dyers, calenderers, embossers, waterers & printers, 9 Fitchet's court, Noble st. Cheapside
Pickard Henry, haberdasher, 43 Cannon st. rd. St. George's ea
Pickard Jane (Mrs.), tobacconist, 4 Paradise row, Chelsea
Pickard Joseph, brass, ivory & wood turner, & wholesale turnery & toy warehouse, 17 Broad st. Bloomsbury
Pickard Thomas Spiller, hatter, 66 Sun st. Bishopsgate
Pickard Wm. grocer & cheesemon. 2 Holland pl. Kensington
Picken Andrew, artist, 32 Friedenstein ter. Mornington rd
Picken George, linendra. &c. 29 Crosby row, Walworth rd
Pickering Samuel & John, drug broks. 33 Gt. St. Helen's
Pickering, Smith, Thompson & Pickering, solicitors, 4 Stone buildings, Lincoln's inn
Pickering Edwin F. hatter, 183 Wellington ter. Waterloo rd
Pickering John, land agent, 7 Whitehall place
Pickering John, plumber & glazier, 39 Little Moorfields
Pickering Johnathan, engraver on wood, 18 Shoe lane
Pickering Jonathan, ship smith, Thames place, Limehouse ho
Pickering Percival A. barrister, 2 Paper buildings, Temple
Pickering Robert, turner, 5 Well st. Mile end New town
Pickering Samuel, corn merch. St. Ann's wf. Earl st. Blkfrs
Pickering Thos. math. instrum. ma. 36 Regent st. Lambeth
Pickering Thos. undertaker & window blind manufacturer, 3 Providence row, Finsbury square
Pickering Thos. N. ironmonger, 19 Princes st. Stamford st
Pickering Thos. W. crown glass & lead mer. 186 Kingsland rd
Pickering Wm. bookseller & publisher, 177 Piccadilly
Pickering Wm. grocer, 3 Clarence pl. Camberwell road
Pickering Wm. B. surgeon, 1 Brook st. Glo'ster rd. Hyde pk
Pickernell Brothers, ship & insu. broks. 38 Fenchurch st
Pickersgill Sarah (Miss), tobacconist, 33 Gt. Quebec st
Pickersgill Fredk. Richd. artist, 8 Leigh st. Burton crescent
Pickersgill Henry William, R.A. artist, 18 Soho square
Pickersgill John, merchant, 4½ Warnford court, City
Pickett Joseph & Co. pianoforte ma. 58 Up. Marylebone st
Pickett George, cheesemonger, 17 High st. Newington butts
Pickett George, silversmith & jeweller, 265 Oxford st
Pickett Gilbert Jesser, engraver, 15 Princes st. Barbican
Pickett James, boot & shoe ma. 12 Grenville st. Brunswick sq
Pickett Joseph, cowkeeper, 29 Everett st. Brunswick sq
Pickett Louisa (Miss), milliner, 7 Gt. Marlborough st
Pickett Thomas, cowkeeper, 4 Calthorpe pl. Gray's inn rd
Pickett Wm. coal dealer, 25 Weston st. Somers town
Pickett Wm. dairy, 28 Gt. Marlborough st
Pickett William Tillott, dyer, Bridge st. Vauxhall
Pickford & Co. general carriers by railway & canal, Castle inn, Wood st. & Gresham st. City; 158 Regent st.; 395 Oxford st.; & 1 & 2 Wharfs, City road; & warehouses, Oval road, Camden town; Railway station, London bridge; & Bricklayers' Arms station
Pickford & Roberts, pawnbrokers, 13 Wittam's bldgs. Old st. rd
Pickford Thos. & Son, wine, ale & porter mers 14 New st. Bishopsgt
Pickford Fras. M. (Miss), corset ma. 86 Charlotte st. Fitzr. sq
Pickford Henry, furniture broker, 8 East road, City road
Pickford James, builder, 15 Queen's head lane, Islington
Pickford James, carpenter & undertakr 6 Bartholomew close
Pickford James, shoemaker, 191 Up. Whitecross st
Pickford Thomas, butcher, 35 Baldwin st. City rd
Pickford Wm. carpenter & builder, 4 Orford row, Old Kent rd
Picking John, coppersmith, 4 Hoxton Old town
Pickle Herring Lower Wharf, Nash & Hicks, Stoney lane, between 95 & 96 Tooley st
Pickle Herring Upper Wharf F. M. Beresford, Stoney lane, between 95 & 99 Tooley st
Pickles Thos. *Horse Shoe & Magpie* P.H. 55 Fenchurch st
Pickman Andrew, hairdresser, 23 Eyre st. hill
Pickman James, grocer, 2 Newcastle pl. Edgware rd
Pickrell James, *Duke of York* P.H. Henry st. Gray's inn lane
Pickstock John Luce & Co. honduras mers. 39 Clement's la. City
Pickstock John (Mrs.), milliner, 17 Holles st. Cavendish sq
Pickup Edmund, currier & leather cutter, 174 Lambeth wlk
Pickworth Henry, butcher, 8 Corporation row, Clerkenwell
Pickworth James, coffee rooms, 37 Throgmorton st. City
Pickworth John, butcher, 6 Gilbert st. Grosvenor sq
Pickworth Thomas, butcher, 1 Norfolk st. Middlesex hospital
Pico Juan José, wine merchant, 6 Mark lane
Picot Philip Hy. *Yorkshire Grey* P.H. 30 Hart st. Bloomsbury
Pictor Stephen, statuary & mason, 20 Princes rd. Notting hl
Pictorial Times Office, 351 Strand
Pidding Jas. & Co. who. tea dealers, 1 Talbot yd. 75 Boro'
Pidding John Rhodes, tea mer. & com. agt. 22 College hl. City
Pidding Mary (Mrs.), confectioner, 24 Store st. Bedford sq
Piddington Peter, carpenter, 89 Mount street, Berkeley sq
Piddington Wm. smith & ironmonger, 15 Earl st. Blackfriars
Piddock Wm. glasscutter & seller, 17 Maiden la. Covent gar
Pidduck Isaac, physician, 22 Montague st. Russell sq
Pidgeon Jonathan S. stock & share broker, 10 Warnford ct
Pidgeon Matthew, corn dealer, Bow
Pidgeon Robert, tailor, 44 Henry st. east, Avenue rd
Pidgeon Thomas, tailor, 54 Long acre
Pierce & Kolle, stove, grate & range ma. 5 Jermyn st. St. Jas
Pierce Edwd. glass cutter, 4 Britannia row, Islington
Pierce Elizbth. (Mrs.), fruiterer, 4 Queen's hd. pas. Newgate st
Pierce John, agent for Gover's window sashes, 289 Strand
Pierce Robert, stone agent, 17 Warwick sq. Newgate st
Pierce Thomas H. furn. & gen. ironmngr. & cutlr. Church st. Hkny
Pierce Wm. bookseller & binder, 31 Singleton st. Hoxton
Pierce Wm. carpenter & sash maker, 21 Gt. Maze pond, Boro'
Pierce Wm. *Dolphin* P.H. 73 Red cross st. Borough
Piercy & Hawks, solicitors, 15 Three Crown square, Boro'

Pierce JohnRd.&Geo. jewellers, 7 Stephen st. Tottenh. ct. rd
Piercy Catherine (Mrs.), *Hanover hotel*, 3 Hanover square
Piercy Elizbth. (Mrs.), boarding house, 40 Craven st. Strand
Piercy George, tobacconist, 5 Chapel place, Liverpool rd
Piercy Robert, baker, 12 York st. Westminster
Piercy Robert James, grocer & cheesemonger, 73 Goswell st
Piercy Thomas, baker, 13 York st. Westminster
Piercy Thomas H.B. wine cooper & bottle dlr. 58 Fenchrch.st
Piercy William, grocer, 30 Stephen st. Tottenham court rd
Pierotti Henry, wax modeller, [13] Manchester st. Gray's inn rd
Pierotti John, plaster figure maker, 21 Gower pl. Euston sq
Pierpoint C. (Mrs.), *Pontefract Castle* P.H. 36 Edward st
Pierpoint Thomas, bricklayer, 2 Margaret st. Commercial rd
Pierpoint Wm. Robt. paperhanger, 18Crombie'srw.Com.rd.ea
Pierssene Wm. copper plate printer, 19 Vere st. Clare mrkt
Piffard John Guerard, stockbroker, Stock exchange
Pige Hen. Peter, pawnbroker, 13 Vittoria pl. Cambridge rd
Pige Henry Peter, pawnbroker, [13 Bethnal green, west side
Pige Peter, pawnbroker, 155 Church st. Shoreditch
Pigeon Henry & Alfred S. distillers, 158 Borough High st
Pigeon Rich. H. & Son, who. druggists, 31 Throgmorton st
Pigeon John, cowkeeper, see Howe & Pigeon
Piggot Ann (Mrs.), chandler's shop, 12 Church st. Lambeth
Piggot Samuel, whiting manuf. Pleasant row, Old Kent rd
Piggott George, baker, 31 White Hart st. Kennington lane
Piggott Jacob, *White Swan* P.H. Kennington common
Piggott John, baker, 3 Charles st. Grosvenor square
Piggott John, carpenter, 8 Matrimony pl. Wandsworth rd
Piggott John, cheesemonger, 4½ Green st. Bethnal green
Piggott Jonth. Walter, hosiery agt. & manf. 24 Addle st. City
Piggott Simon Fraser, barrister, 10 Old square, Lincoln's inn
Piggott Thomas, kitchen screen maker, 34 John st. Fitzroy sq
Piggott William, army clothier, marquee, tent, rick cloth & tarpaulin manufacturer, 115 Fore st. Cripplegate
Piggott Wm. fishmonger, 65 Brick lane, St. Luke's
Piggott Wm. Peter, mathl. inst. mkr. 11 Wardrobe pl. Doc. cms
Pigot Juliet (Mrs.), teadealer & grocer, 152 Lambeth walk
Pigott David, Wray & Co. button manufact. 8 Gresham st
Pigott Abijah, bookseller, 39 Harleyford pl. Kenington com
Pigott Augusta (Miss), grocer, 56 St. George's rd. Southwark
Pigott David, beer retailer, 23 New Compton st. Soho
Pigott Gillery, barrister, 3 Pump court, Temple
Pigott Thos. meat & poultry salesman, 63 Newgate market, & 34 West Smithfield
Pigous & Wilks, gunpowder ma. Dartford, & 34 Throgmorton st
Pigram Thomas Richd. tailor, 27 Theobald's rd. Red Lion sq
Piguet Abram Elisha, watchcase ma. 4 Richmond bdgs. Soho
Pike Henry & James, ironmongers, 14 Brydges st. Covt. gdn
Pike Ann (Mrs.), clasp maker, 8 Oxford arms pas. Warwk. la
Pike Charles, grocer, 8 Denmark terrace, Pentonville
Pike Chas. sen. carpent. & pack. case ma. 109 St. John st. Smthfld
Pike Chas. jun. carpenter & packingcase ma. 25 Duke st. Smthfld
Pike Chas. Andrew, solicitor, 1 Cursitor st. Chancery lane
Pike Dinah (Mrs.), linendraper, 7 King st. Covent garden
Pike Edward, china wareh. 2 South Island pl. Clapham rd
Pike Esther (Miss), stay maker, 95 Bridge road, Lambeth
Pike Francis Wm. solicitor, 26 Bedford row, Bloomsbury
Pike Frederick, hairdresser, 32 Church st. Shoreditch
Pike Fredk. wax & tallow chandler, 77 Borough High st
Pike George, *Grapes* P.H. 93 Borough High st
Pike George, *Mitre* P.H. Mitre court, Hatton garden
Pike Henry, grocer, 9 Cumberland row, Islington
Pike Jabez, oilman, 66 Harper st. New Kent road
Pike James, ironmonger, 1 Little Dean st. Westminster
Pike James, tailor, 5 Belgrave st. south, Pimlico
Pike John, baker, 179 Church st. Shoreditch
Pike John, baker, 22 High row, Knightsbridge
Pike John, haberdasher, 63 Brill row, Somers town
Pike John, hop mercht. impr. of isinglass, irish & scotch whisky & dublin patent brown malt, 228 Borough High st
Pike John, shell fishmonger, 6 King st. Snow hill
Pike John, solicitor, 26 Old Burlington st
Pike John Henry Robert, custom house, ship & commercial agent, 10 Water lane, Tower st
Pike Joseph, bootmaker, 66 Snow's fields, Bermondsey
Pike Luke, breeches maker, 14 St. James's st. Pall mall
Pike Paul, tobacconist, 36 New Manor st. King's rd. Chelsea
Pike Philip, baker, 81 Shoe lane, 1 Royal Hospital row, Chelsea, & Church st. Hackney
Pike Robert, house ag. & upholsterer, 23 Mary st. Regent's pk.
Pike Samuel, auctioneer, 15 Wilderness rw. Clerkenwell
Pike Sarah (Mrs.), fancy brushmaker, 5 Coburg st. Clrknwl
Pike Walter, hatter, 3 Bermondsey new road
Pike Warburton, special pleader, 12 King's Benchwlk. Temple
Pike William, baker, 3 George st. Camberwell
Pike Wm. milliner, 4 Saville row, Walworth road

Pilbeam Thomas, coachsmith, spring, axletree maker & wheelwright, 36 Parker st. Drury la. & 10 Phœnix alley, Long acre
Pilbrough Henry, carpenter, Millman mews, Guilford st
Pilbrow's Atmospheric Railway & Canal Propulsion Co. (Charles Collins, sec.), 6 King William st. City
Pilcher John & Edw. corn & flour factrs. Jack's coff. ho. Mark la
Pilcher John G. & Jeremiah & Sons, lead & color works, oil, pitch & tar merchants, white lead & varnish manufacturers, Morgan's lane, Tooley st. & 71 Cornhill
Pilcher Charles, *St. George's* P.H. 23 Lambeth road
Pilcher George, surgeon, 7 Gt. George st. Westminster
Pilcher Thomas Morris, vet. surgeon, 14 Hawley crescent, Kentish town road
Pilcher Wm. hairdresser, 36 Surry place, Old Kent road
Pilcher Wm. organ builder, 23 Up. Belgrave pl. Pimlico
Pilcher Wm. tobacconist, 71 Gray's inn lane
Pilcher Wm. Humphery, solicitor, 18 New Broad st
Pile George, tailor, 33 Newman st. Oxford st
Pile George, wine merchant, Salvador house, Bishopsgate
Pile James, baker, 11 East st. Walworth road
Pile Joseph, statuary & mason, Mare st. Hackney
Pile Robt. fruiterer, 28 Weymouth st. Portland place
Pile Simon, solicitor, 93 Hatton gar. & 41 Castle st. Holborn
Pile Wm. *Anchor & Hope* P.H. 54 Lr. Thames st
Pilgrim James, solicitor, see Atkinson & Pilgrim
Pilgrim Joseph, *Barleymow* P.H. New gravel lane
Pilkington Benjamin & Son, gold chain makers, & manufacturing jewellers, 39 Perceval st. Clerkenwell
Pilkington Geo. & Son, teadealers, 113 St. John st. road
Pilkington Benj. jun. gold chain mak. 31 King st. Clerknwl
Pilkington Geo. telescope, microscope & camera maker, optical glass grinder, & spectacle manuf. 14 Clarence place, Pentonville
Pilkington Wm. surveyor, 1 Vincent sq. Westminster
Pilkinton Saml. gasfitter, 44 North st. Manchester sq
Pill Alfred, pastrycook & confectioner, 51 Cheapside
Pillans James, jun. mer. 8 Old Jewry, City
Pilleau Wm. solicitor, 25 Bucklersbury
Pillivant Wm. soda & seidlitz case, chip & cardboard fancy box manufacturer, 69 Noble st. Goswell st
Pillow John, printer, 8 Horselydown lane
Pillow Thomas, lighterman, Symon's whf. 79 Tooley st
Pilon Wm. *Castle tavern*, 271 Regent st
Pilsworth Wm. stationer & vellum binder, 18 Pudding lane
Pilton William Henry, brick agent, Jerusalem coffeehouse
Pim Jesse linendraper, High st. Stoke Newington
Pim Jesse, linendraper, 57 Barbican
Pim John, agent to life & fire insurance, loans, annuities, &c. &c. 72 Basinghall st
Pim John, carpenter & builder, 6 White hart pl. Kenningtn. la
Pimm Charles, birmingham agent, 11 Thavies inn
Pimm George, chemist, &c. 12 Keen's row, Walworth road
Pimm Henry, greengroc. & carman, 1 Francis st. Westminster
Pimm Henry, plumber, 5 Barking churchyard, Gt. Tower st
Pimm James, confectioner, 77 Cheapside
Pimm James, oyster warehouse, 3 Poultry
Pincherle David, merch. 6 Finsbury chambrs. London wall
Pinches Wm. & Son, academy, 2 East pl. Walcot pl. Lambeth
Pinches Ths. R. medallist, die sinkr. & seal engrvr. 62 Newman st
Pinches Wm. *King's Head* P.H. 1 Lr. Ranelagh st. Pimlico
Pinchin Geo. & Co. old bath ale stores, 23 Hungerford whrf
Pinchin Harry & George, tanners, Grange, Bermondsey
Pinchin & Johnson, oil merchants & color manufacturers, 10 St. George st. & New road, St. George's east, & 39 Colet place, Commercial road east
Pinchin William, oilman, 193 Church st. Shoreditch
Pinckard George H. (actuary to the Clerical & General life Assurance Society), 78 Gt. Russell st. Bloomsbury
Pinckard Henry, mercht. 2 Hatton ct. Threadneedle st
Pinckard Richard, physician, 11 Bloomsbury square
Pinckney James, hatter, 85 Poplar High st
Pincombe Charles, linendraper, 89 Tottenham court road
Pincombe George, cowkeeper, 17 Broadley ter. Blandford sq
Pinder Edward, chemist, 123 High st. Camden town
Pinder Edward, saddler, 4 Up. Spring st. Portman square
Pinder John, cheesemonger, 10 Spring st. Paddington
Pinder John, seed & hop factr. King's hd. inn yd. 54 Boro' Hi. st
Pinder Richard, jun. wine merchant, 8 Fenchurch st
Pinder Samuel, copperplate printer, 17 Ashley cr. City road
Pinder Thomas, plumber, 1 Graham st. Macclesfield st. north
Pinder William, plumber & painter, 4 Cottage pl. City road
Pine William, baker, 13 Old Montague st. Whitechapel
Pine Richard, haberdasher, 3 Provost st. City road
Piner Susannah (Mrs.), lodging house, 124 Mount st. Brkly. sq
Pinero John Danl. solicitor, 16 Lr. Calthorpe st. Gray's inn rd

Pinet, Castillon & Co.(of Cognac),agency, Bell ct.Mincing la
Pinfold Joseph, school slate mak. 5 Adam's pl. Boro' High st
Pinfold Thomas, carpenter, &c. 6 George st. Portman square
Ping Joseph, eating house keeper, 21 Carnaby st. Golden sq
Pinheiro Charlt. (Mrs.), tobacconist, 143 Whitechapel Hi. st
Pini Joseph, carver & gilder, 23 Brooke st. Holborn
Pink George & Co. waggon masters, Van inn, 18 Giltspur st
Pink Chas. *WhiteHorse & Half Moon* P.H. 141 Boro'High st
Pink George, builder, 44 Regent st. Horseferry road
Pink John, builder & architect, 15 Blomfield rd. Maida hill
Pink Thomas, plasterer, 8 Duke st. Bishopsgate
Pink Wm. moulder& figure maker, 31 Mary st. Hampstead rd
Pinkerton Fredk. Wm. grocer & coal mercht. 30 Rathbone pl
Pinkerton John, genl. agent, 15 Philpot lane, City
Pinkerton John, glass cutter & china dealer, 3 Great Dover st. & Grove, Great Guildford st. Southwark
Pinkerton Mark, merchant, 15 Philpot lane, City
Pinkerton Robert, watch & clock mak. 2Charlotte st. Pentnvl
Pinkney Richard, bootmaker, 46 Church st. Shoreditch
Pinkney Thomas Francis, solicitor, 41 Chiswell st
Pinn & Atkinson, tailors & breeches makers, 54 Brook st
Pinn Edward, baker, 9 Union st. Bishopsgate
Pinn Francis, baker, 12 Middle Queen's bldgs. Knightsbridge
Pinn John, cheesemonger, 96 East st. Manchester sq
Pinnell Geo. Fred. silversmith, 18 Redcross sq. Cripplegate
Pinnell John, oil& colorman, 214 Whitechapel rd.&33 Minories
Pinnell Hannah (Miss), grocer, Mare st. Hackney
Pinnell Richard, *Freemasons' Arms* P.H. 81 Long acre
Pinnell Thomas, zinc worker, 5 Warren st. Camden town
Pinner Benjamin, appraiser & house agent, 55 Goodge st
Pinner David, printers' press maker, 34 Crown st. Finsbury
Pinner John, undertaker, 2 Regent pl. Globe rd. Mile end
Pinner William, cooper, 23 Wilson st. Finsbury square
Pinniger & Westmacott, solicitors, 28 John st. Bedford row
Pinnock John, coach broker, 1 Castle st. Long acre
Pinnock Joseph, ornmtl. leather gildr. 25Cirncestr. pl. Fitz.sq
Pinnock William, coal, &c. dealer, 76 Hoxton Old town
Pinnock William, hatter, 54 Threadneedle st
Pinnock Wm. umbrella ma. 10 Mount pleasant, Gray's inn la
Pinsent Savery, solicitor, 16 Bucklersbury
Pinto Henry & Co. cigar manufs. 62 Shoreditch High st
Pinto, Perez&Co. merchants&wine merchts. 36Crutchedfriars
Pinto Theodore Ferreira, agent to the royal Oporto wine company, 36 Crutchedfriars
Pinwill John Morgan, solicitor, 68 Gt. Suffolk st. Borough
Pipe John, cooper, 3 Circular road, Horsemonger lane
Pipe Jonas, bricklayer, 25 Queen square, Westminster
Pipe Michael, baker, 21 Foley st. Portland place
Pipe William, coal & coke merchant, see Lake & Pipe
Piper Thos. & Wm. builds. 74Gt. Tower st.&173Bshps. without
Piper Elizh. (Mrs.), timber & deal yard, 189 Bethnal green rd
Piper George, baker, 24 Cumberland market, Regent's park
Piper George, tobacconist, 18 Shadwell High st
Piper Henry, collector of taxes, 85 Aldersgate st
Piper Henry Hunt, plumber, painter & decorator, 42 Eastcheap, Green Dragon yard, Halfmoon st. Bishopsgate st
Piper James, smith, 19 Barnsbury rw. Cloudesley sq. Islntn
Piper John, butcher, 46 Grosvenor row, Pimlico
Piper John, cork cutter, 98 Broadwall, Blackfriars
Piper John, hairdresser, 30 Museum st. Bloomsbury
Piper John, ironmonger & tin plate worker, 92 Shoreditch
Piper Joseph, beer retailer, 17 Hertford road, Kingsland
Piper Joseph, cowkeeper, New st. Kennington
Piper Mary (Mrs.), confectioner, 84 Union st. Borough
Piper Mary (Mrs.), grocer, 10 Prospect place, Old Kent road
Piper Thomas, dining rooms, 2 Dean st. Soho
Piper Thomas Foot, who. stay & corset ma. 4 Bishopsgate wtht
Piper William, bookseller, see Sherwood, Gilbert & Piper
Piper William, composition ornament mnfr. seeCook & Piper
Piper William, dairyman, Box cottage, King's road, Chelsea
Piper William, *Duke of York* P.H. York terrace, Borough rd
Piper William, potato dealer, 48 Queen st. Bryanstone sq
Pippett George, fruiterer, 10 Park ter. Regent's park road
Pippett Stephen, fruiterer, &c. 64 East st. Manchester sq
Pirie Alexr. & Sons, paper mnfrs. 43 Watling st. & Aberdeen
Pirie John & Co. ship brokers, 71 Cornhill
Pirie William, barrister, 7 New square, Lincoln's inn
Pirkis James, oil & colorman, 7 Stepney rents, Hackney rd
Pissey Frederick Miles, tailor, 123 Leadenhall st
Pistell Wm. statuary, 10 Quickset row, New rd. Fitzroy sq
Pistor Henry Edwd. imp. of foreign toys, &c. 94 Houndsditch
Pitcairn John, merchant & ins. broker, 27 Broad st. buildings
Pitcher Augustus Edward, solicitor, 89 Guildford st
Pitcher Chas. *Portm. Arms* P.H. 2 Up. Berkeley st. Portm.sq
Pitcher George, baker, 18 Gravel lane, Southwark
Pitcher George, builder, &c. 11 Walnut Tree walk, Lambeth
Pitcher HenryJ. proctor&notary, 11 Godliman st. Doctrs.'com
Pitcher William, fruiterer, 3 William st. Manchester square
Pitcher William, ship builder, Canal dock, Blackwall
Pitchford John & Co. manufacturing chemists, Stratford
Pitchford & Nokes, whipmaks. 1 & 5 Marylebonela. Oxford st
Pite Henry Danford, printer, 37 Cheyne walk, Chelsea
Pite William, pastrycook & fruiterer, 40 Kingsland road
Pither Har. (Mrs.), boarding house, 15 Alfred pl. Bedford sq
Pither Edward, tobacconist, 2 Harrow road, Paddington
Pither Thomas, stationer, 34 Dorset st. Portman sq
Pither William, *King's Arms* P.H. 1 Ranelagh rd. Pimlico
Pithey Wm. merchant, 18 Austinfriars
Pithouse Joseph, nail & bracket tinner, 18 Rose st. St. Luke's
Pitkeathly James, carpenter, 6 Up. Maryleb. st. Portland st
Pitkin John, hat lining cutter, 11 WhiteLionst. Norton folgt
Pitkins James, bonnet shape ma. 57 Edward st. Bethnal gr
Pitman Edward Dix, barrister, 3 New square, Lincoln's inn
Pitman Esther (Mrs.), spanish boarding ho. 14 Finsbury sq
Pitman George, fishmonger, 83 Broadwall, Blackfriars
Pitman Hen. Alfred, physician, 28 Montague pl. Russell sq
Pitman James, piecebroker, 26 Cloth fair, West Smithfield
PitmanRobt. working jewlr.&corn dealr. 19Garnault pl. Spafi
Pitman William, wine merchant, 150 Fenchurch st
Pitney Edmund, grocer, 1 Pembroke ter. Caledonian road
Pitney Elizabeth (Mrs.), grocer, 2 Halfmoon cres. Pentnvl
Pitsch William, tailor, 42 Sackville st. Piccadilly
Pitt James & Co. hatters & cap makers to her Majesty, 8 Piccadilly
Pitt Wm.&Co. soda water mnfrs. Fox&Knox ct. Kingst. Snowh
Pitt Wm. Henry & Co. hot water & steam apparatus maks. 9 York place, Pentonville
Pitt Ann (Miss), milliner, 43 St. James's pl. St. James's
Pitt Benj. carpenter & builder, 5 Islington pl. Cloudesley sq. & 1 Upper Copenhagen st. Pentonville
Pitt Benj. smith & bellhanger, 1 Lit. George st. Westminster
Pitt Charles, stay & corsetmaker, 13 Shoreditch
Pitt Charles, watchmaker, 3 Duke st. Manchester sq
Pitt Edward, tailor, 5 Wyndham road, Camberwell
Pitt Eliz. (Mrs.), china&glass wa. 72 Up. Berkeley st. Port.sq
Pitt George, furn. ironmongr. 3& 4Gt. Portland st. Oxford st
Pitt George, registrar, 23 Paradise row, Rotherhithe
Pitt Henry, shipping butcher, 10 Wapping wall
Pitt James, chinaman, 17 Lower Ranelagh st. Pimlico
Pitt James, hat manufacturer, 17 Stafford row, Pimlico
Pitt James, window blind maker, 62 Wells st. Oxford st
Pitt John, grocer & cheesemonger, 27 East st. Walworth rd
Pitt John, hatter, 17 Nelson st. Hackney road
Pitt John, watchmaker, 36 Crown st. Finsbury
Pitt John, watch & chronometer maker, 47 Kingsland rd
Pitt Jonas, carpenter, 8 Blandford mews, Manchester sq
Pitt Mark, law stationer, 53 Chancery lane
Pitt Rich. hairdresser & perfumer, 26 Gt. Smith st. Westmi
Pitt Richard, *Pitt's Head* P.H. 27 Henry st. Portland town
Pitt Uriah, fruiterer, 2 Hall place, Lower Kennington la
Pitt Wm. auctioneer, apprais.& ho. agt. 25 New Broad st. City
Pitt William, baker, 20 Park st. Camden town
Pitt William, brassfounder, 39 Monmouth st. Seven dials
Pitt Wm. butcher, 3 Skinner's pl. Leadenhall market
Pitt William, cheesemonger, 2 Church st. Mile end New tn
Pitt William, fruit salesman, 15 Hart st. Covent garden
Pitt William, haberdasher & hosier, 145 Sloane st. Chelsea
Pittar & Co. diamond & jewel merchants, 10 John st. Adelphi
Pittar Parke, european & oriental agt. 14 George st. Adelphi
Pittard James, bookbinder, 15 Little New st. Shoe lane
Pittard James, grocer, 24 George st. New Kent road
Pittendreigh Saml. John, solctr. see Ensor & Pittendreigh
Pittman Herbert & Robert, bricklayers, 16 HoxtonOld town, & Crooked Billet yard, Kingsland road
Pittman Mary Ann & Son, booksel.&prntrs. 5 &20Warwick sq
Pittman Eliza (Miss), milliner, 64 Gt. Portland st. Oxford st
Pittman Francis, orange merchant, 24 Botolph lane
Pittman George, farrier, 13 Princes st. Upper Stamford st
Pittman George, fruiterer, 110 Albany st. Regent's park
Pittman Jas. fishmonger, 14 Skinner's pl. Leadenhall market
Pittman James, lodging house, 25 Thavies inn, Holborn
Pittman John, chinaman, 32 Lamb's Conduit st. Foundling
Pittman John, who. haberdasher, see Carlisles', Pittman &Co
Pittman John Russell, potato dealer, 41Broad st. Bloomsbury
Pittman Richd. solicitor for the parish, 31 Paddington green
Pittman Robt. who. haberdasher, seeCarlisles', Pittman & Co
Pittman Thomas, greengrocer, 30 University st. Tot. ct. rd
Pittman Thomas, solicitor, 18 Charlotte st. Portland place
Pittock James, pastrycook, 109 St. George st
Pitts Henry & Co. manfg. chemists, 19 Claremont pl. Judd st
Pitts William & Son, coach builders, 42 Hercules buildings, & Oakley st. Lambeth

Pitts Charles, tailor, 27 Tavistock st. Covent garden
Pitts James, fruiterer, 8 Kingsland road, Dalston
Pitts Samuel, saddler & harness maker, 2 Bentinck st. Soho
Pitts Saml. Taylor, haberdasher & stayma.136 Lambeth wlk
Pitts Thomas, linendraper, 3 Up. Gloucester pl. Dorset sq
Pitts William Charles, grocer, 213 Bethnal green road
Pittway John,desk & dressing ca. ma. 4Kirby st.Hatton gdn
Pitty David, linendraper, 13 Mount ter. New rd. Whtchpl.rd
Pitz (the Misses), stationers, 13 Lamb's Conduit st. Foundlg
Pixley William, ropemaker, see Curling, Pixley & Co
Pizzala Augustus, optician, 7 Charles st. Hatton garden
Pizzala Charles, looking glsss maker, 84 Leather lane
Pizzala Peter, italian alabaster & glass shade warehouse,91 Quadrant, Regent st.
Pizzey Samuel, grocer, 3 High st. Kingsland
Pizzey Thomas, cabinet & blind maker, 81 Old street road
Pizzie Caleb, willow square maker, 2 Windsor ter. City rd
Place & Carbery, tailors, 16 Charing cross
Place & Wood,manfrs.of sewingsilks,twists,&c.10Gresham st
Place John Thomas, grocer, 37 Gt. Porland st. Oxford st
Place Matth. berlin fancy repository, 103 Upperst.Islington
Plackett Richd. *White Lion* P.H. 44 Vere st. Clare market
Plaisted John, wine & spirit imp. see Vickers, Plaisted & Co
Plaisterers' Hall, Addle st. Wood st. (John Conquest, clerk), 53 Moorgate st
Plane John, window blind maker, 46 Hackney road
Plank Andrew, beer retailer, Wandsworth road
Plank George, publisher, Old Trinityho.Water la. Tower st
Plant Edward, jun. *French Horn* P.H. 26 Crutched friars
Plant Jonathan, bricklayer, 4 & 42 White Lion st. Pentnvle
Plant Richard, grocer, 1 Trinity ter. East India rd. Poplar
Plant Robert, hosier, glover & shirt maker, 6 Gracechurch st
Plant Thomas, chandler's shop, 28 & 29 James st. Oxford st
Plant Thomas, painter, &c. 1 Amelia place, Fulham road
Plant Wm. enameller, 24 Meredith st. Clerkenwell
Plante Peter, hosier, see Pope & Plante
Plasket Thos. Hen. & Son, wine & brandy merchants, 24½ Old Burlington st
Plaskett & Shilton, builders, Robert st. Vine st. Waterloo rd
Plaskett Reuben, watchmaker, 31 Raven st. Whitechapel rd
Plastow James, fruiterer, 7 Prospect pl. Kingsland road
Plater Eli & Co. linendrapers, 33 East st. Manchester sq
Plater John, Blossoms inn coach&waggon offi.23Lawrence la
Plater Thomas, fishmonger, 48 King st. Westminster
Plater William Chas. butcher, 33 Cable st. Wellclose sq
Platford John, linendraper & hosier, 26 Crown st. Finsbury
Platow (Morritz), & Co. [late Vardy & Co.], gas fitting manufacturers, & patentees & manufacturers of the double cone gas burner, the gas moderator, Platow's automaton coffee urn & Platow's beer engine, 55 High Holborn
Platt Benjamin, chairmaker, 11 Clarence pl. Hackney road
Platt Edward, barrister, 3 Hare court, Temple
Platt George, bootmaker, 2 Maddox st. Bond st
Platt James, builder & bricklayer, 32 John st. Fitzroy sq
Platt James, secret springer & polshr. 30 Clerkenwell close
Platt James, stationer, 13 Shepperton pl. New North road
Platt John, house painter&paperhanger,3 John st.Oxford st
Platt John, solicitor, 5 Church court, Clement's lane
Platt Robert, painter, 11 Star st. Edgware road
Platt Samuel, barrister, 10 Hyde park gardens
Platt Thomas, barrister, 4 Stone buildings, Lincoln's inn
Platt Thomas, tobacconist, 5 Albert place, City road
Platt William, upholsterer & broker, 270 Whitechapel road
Platten Thomas, blacking maker, 20 Russell st. Mile end
Platts Fredk. engrv. & stationr. 53 New Church st. Lisson gr
Platts Isaac, pawnbroker,21 Upper York st. Bryanstone sq
Platts Joseph,stock,bit&toolmaker,13LittlePeter st.Westmr
Platts Sophia (Mrs.), tobacconist, 2 Blackmoor st. Drury la
Plaw Thos, beer retailer, 18 Green st. Paddington
Plaw Thos.*Greyhound* chop,&c.house, 18 Paddington green
Plaw William, carpenter & builder, King's rd. west, Chelsea
Plaxton Wm.Wells,ref.sugar bro. Com. coffee ho. Mincing la
Player Geo.C.housedecorator,5NewChurch st.west,Edgw.rd
Player Horatio,watchmaker,2 North place, Gray's inn lane
Player William, carpenter, 11½ High st. Camberwell
Playfair Thos. house agt.& appraiser,15 Portman st.Ptmn.sq
Playll John James, bootmaker, 165 Bishopsgate without
Playne Peter P. & Chas. woollen manfrs. 9 Ironmonger lane
Playne Wm. & Co. woollen cloth manuftrs. 22 Basinghall st
Playsted Hen. carpenter & undertakr.14Heddon st.Regent st
Pleasant Edmund, builder, 14 Coburg st. Clerkenwell
Pledge Henry, grocer, 5 Flagon row, Deptford
Pledge James, mattress maker,2 Rodney bldgs.New Kent rd
Pledge William Edward, carpenter, 11 South Lambeth
Pledger Ben. John, tailor, 34 Up.York st. Bryanstone square
Pienderleath Robert, furniture dealer, 17 Praed st. Edgw. rd
Plested James, tobacconist, 122 St. George st
Plester William, carpenter, 9 Bevenden st. Hoxton
Plews John, builder, &c. Millwall, Poplar
Plews John, timber merchant, 7 Store st. Bedford sq
Plews Robert, hosier, glover & outfitter, 129 Strand
Plews Thomas, solicitor, see Lawrence & Plews
Pleydell John Cleeve, wine merchant, 46 Lime st. City
Pleydell Thomas, confectioner, 35 Bishopsgate without
Plimmer Henry, beer retailer, 11 Jamaica row, Bermondsey
Plimmer John, anchor brewery, Russell st. Chelsea
Plimmer Wm. bricklayer, 12 Shepperton pl. east. Islington
Plimpton Alexander, cornfactor, 13 Bankside, Southwark
Plimpton Alex. jun. corn & seed factor, 33 Gracechurch st
Plimpton James, merchant,44 Cross st. Finsbury
Plimpton Michael, confectioner, 34 Barbican
Plimpton Sam. corn, seed & hop factor Kentish bdgs. Boro'
Plimsoll Thomas, furrier & berlin wool warh. 156 Oxford st
Plomer James, boot & shoemaker, 14 College st. Chelsea
Plow Henry Anthony, F.S.A.,F.R.A.S. academy, Claphamrise
Plowes John & Co. merchants, 64 Old Broad st. City
Plowman Harkles,*RedLion*P.H.21York row, Kennington rd
Plowman James, baker, 17 Hatton wall
Plowman James, collar maker, 41 North row, Grosvenor sq
Plowman James, chandler's shop, 49 Salisbury st. Lisson gr
Plowman John, bootmaker, 9 Agar st. Strand
Plowman John, *Three Compasses* P.H. Wandsworth road
Plowman Joseph, trimming warehouse, 107 Fetter lane
Plowman Richard, solicitor, see Roche, Plowman & Roche
Plowman Solomon, bricklayer, 95 Broadwall, Blackfriars
Plowright John, *Greyhound* P.H. 9 Henrietta st.Brunswksq
Plucknett & Roberts, solicitors, 17 Lincoln's inn fields
Plucknett George, surveyor, 19½ Frederick st. Gray's inn rd
Plucknett Ann (Mrs.), fish. linema.54Amelia st.Walworthrd
Pluckrose William, muffin baker, 65 Drummond st.Euston sq
Plum George, cutler, 17 Pickett st. or 262 Strand
Plum Thos. Wm. architect & registrar, 21 Addington sq
Plum William, baker, 8 Eyre st. hill, Leather lane
Plumb David, straw plait dealer, 17 Jubilee st. Coml. rd. ea
Plumb Edwd. *George & Ball* P.H. 67 Orchard st. Westmstr
Plumb Henry, bootmaker, 33 King st. Covent garden
Plumb John, tailor, 5 Little Queen st. Westminster
Plumb John, umbrella maker, 64 Burlington arcade
Plumb John, silversmith & jeweller, 194 Oxford st
Plumbe Ann S.(Mrs.),agt. for south sea arrow root, 3 Alie pl
Plumber Sarah & Co.who.staymakers,29King st. Tower hill
Plumbers' Hall (JohnBeckwith Towse,clerk), 12 Gt. Bushla
Plumbly & Parr, watchma.16 New Cavendish st. Portland pl
Plumbridge John, orange merchant, 22 Botolph lane
Plumer Thomas Hall, barrister, Examiner's office, Roll's yd
Plumley Geo. buhl cutter,35 Winchester st. Pentonville
Plumley Peter, iron mer. 42 New Park st.Boro',&5 Bankside
Plumley Peter, solicitor, see Vincent & Plumley
Plummer EdmundH.coal&potatodlr.17Bland ter.Gt.Dovr. st
Plummer John, cotton manufacturer, see Wilson& Plummer
Plummer John, printer, 29 Pudding lane, Eastcheap
Plummer Saml. *RockinghamArms*P.H.31Hosierla.Smthfld
Plummer Sarah (Mrs.), printer, 178 Upper Thames st
Plummer Wm. bookseller & news agent,46 Theobald's road
Plumpton Robert, tailor, 19 Newgate st
Plumpton Susan (Mrs.), staymaker, 14 High st. Deptford
Plumpton Wm. linen&woollen draper, 68 &69 Whitechapel rd
Plumtre Chas. John, barrister, 3 Churchyard ct. Temple
Plumptre Edward Hallows, attorney, 4 Lamb bldg. Temple
Plunkett Henry, *Goat* P.H. 41 Tash st. Gray's inn lane
Plunkett Randal, manufacturer of patent malt, 84 Mark la
Plym Lydia(Mrs.),booksel.2Bretten ter. King's rd.w.Chelsea
Plymouth, Falmouth, Exeter, Dublin & Belfast Steam Packet Company (James Hartley & Co. managers), 137 Leadenhall st. 33 Regent st. Piccadilly; & Dublin, Cork, Leith & Berwick wharf, Lower East Smithfield
Poarch Ann (Mrs.), school, 39 St. Mary axe
Pockett Daniel, fish salesman, 3 Giltspur st.West Smithfield
Pocklington, Frackelton & Jury,meat slsmn. 8 Newgate mkt
Pocklington & Lacy, bankers, & agents to cattle salesmen, 60 West Smithfield
Pocklington John, cattle salesman, 60 West Smithfield
Pocklington Joseph Pain, meat salesman, 19 Newgate st
Pocklington JosephPain, meat salesman, 6 Rose st. Newgt.st
Pocklington Robert Thomas, butcher, 31 Old Change
Pocknell Harriet (Mrs.), milliner, 11 Artillery place west
Pocock Arthur Wm. & Co. fancy bread & biscuit bakers, & makers of the indian bread, 27 & 28 Old Jewry
Pocock & Marston, solicitors, 10 Norfolk st. Strand
Pocock & Sons, coal merchts. St. Bride's wharf, Whitefriars
Pocock Chas. plumber, painter, &c. 51Goodge st. Tott. ct.rd
Pocock Edward, dining rooms, 206 Blackfriars road

Pocock George, boot & shoe maker, 8 Peerless pl. City road
Pocock James, carpenter & undertaker, 10 Castle st. City rd
Pocock James, *Fox* P.H. Back road, Kingsland
Pocock John Carne, solicitor, 27 Lincoln's inn fields
Pocock John Innes, solicitor, 27 Lincoln's inn fields
Pocock Markland G. child's shoe ma. 69Church st. Shordtch
Pocock Mary (Mrs.), grocer, 39 Princess st. Lisson grove
Pocock Thomas, boot & shoe wareh. 5 Duke st. Tooley st
Pocock Thomas, leather & shoe factory, 3 Queen's buildings, Knightsbridge; 20, 21 & 22 Southwark bridge road; 5 Gray's place, Fulham road; 143 Edgware road; 5 Duke st. London bridge, & 18 Newington causeway
Pocock Thomas, shoe mart, 140 Lower marsh, Lambeth
Pocock Thomas, solicitor, 58 Bartholomew close, City
Pocock Thos. Wm. lithographer & printer, 129 Gt. Saffron hill
Pocock Thos. Willmer, surgeon, 4 Brompton row
Pocock Wm. baker, 38 Palace st. Pimlico
Pocock Wm. plumber & glazier, 8 Manchester st. Manch. sq
Pocock Wm. shell fishmonger, 67 Old Bailey
Pocock Wm. surgeon, &c. 2 Charterhouse square
Pocock Wm. Fuller, architect, 10 Trevor ter. Knightsbridge
Pocock Wm. Thos. tailor, 3 St. Michael's alley, Cornhill
Pocock Wm. Willmer, architect, 2 Halkin ter. Belgrave sq
Podger Joseph, grocer, 10 Henry st. Cumberland market
Podmore Geo. & Hen. stockbrokers, 4 Cushion ct. O. Brd. st
Podmore Charles, vinegar mfr. see Grimble, Podmore & Co
Podmore Isaac, tobacco pipe maker, 57 Carlisle st. Lambeth
Podmore Robt. stockbroker, 1 Hatton ct. Threadneedle st
Podmore Thomas, birmingh. warhsmn. see Twells & Podmore
Podmore Thomas, die sinker, seal & general engraver, & medallist, 29 Bedford st. Covent garden
Poett Geo. Joseph, surgeon, 3 University st. Tottenham ct. rd
Pogmore Joseph, who. brushma. &c. 5 David st. Marylebone
Poile Geo. marine store dlr. 10 Bartholomew close, Lit. Brit
Poile George, pawnbroker, 26 Bridge road, Lambeth
Poile Thomas, pawnbroker, 168 Borough High st
Point Sarah (Mrs.), china wareho. 12 Harp alley, Shoe lane
Pointer Geo. Augustus, surgeon, 132 Drummond st. Euston sq
Pointer Rd. *Prince & Princess* P.H. 3Gravel la. Southwark
Pointer Thomas, biscuit baker, 18 Carburton st. Fitzroy sq
Pointing Edward, dairyman, 10 Gt. Pulteney st. Golden sq
Pointing Joshua James, com. wool agent, 228 Bermondsey st
Points Ann & Son, barge builders, Upper Fore st. Lambeth
Poittevin Joseph Henry Jerome, patent & highly concentrated manure manufr. Queen st. Church st. Mile end new town
Polack Lipman, tailor, 86 Leman st. Goodman's fields
Poland Peter & Co. whol. furriers, 52 Bread st. Cheapside
Poland P—, R. & Son, fur & skin mers. 4 Cloak lane, City
Poland George, furrier, 90 Oxford st
Poland John, who. furrier, 5 Mount place, Whitechapel rd
Poland Joshua A. fish salesman, 5 Mount pl. Whitechapel rd
Polden & Lafargue, ship & insurance agents, 10 Gould sq
Polden Eliza (Miss), grocer, 19 King st. Borough High st
Polden James, booking office, Catherine wheel yd. Borough
Pole Brothers, merchants, 21 Billiter st. City
Pole William, barrister, 8 New sq. Lincoln's inn
Pole Wm. Edmund, barrister, 1 New square, Lincoln's inn
Polglase Richard, ironfounder, 230 Poplar High st
Polhill Richard Cowley, wine & spirit merchant, 2 Walbrook buildings, & 3 Bond court, Walbrook
Police Gazette (Monday, Wednesday & Friday), Bow st. Cov. ga
Polish Refugees' Office (John S. Tebbs, secretary), 2 Middle Scotland yard; hours 2 P.M. to 6 P.M.
Political Scientific Institution (David Cater, sec.), 1 Turnagain lane, Skinner st. Snowhill
Polkinghorne Edwin S. & Co. merchants, 12 Clement's lane
Polkinghorne Edwin S. wine mer. 3Nag's Head ct. Clement's la
Pollack John, tailor, 5 Great Alie st. Goodman's fields
Pollard Charlotte & Co. art. florists, 8 Warwick st. Golden sq
Pollard Edward William & Charles, surgeons, 1 Brompton square, Fulham road
Pollard John & Co. warehousemen, 12 Coleman st
Pollard Charles Fredk. surgeon, 26 Brompton crescent
Pollard Geo. man. to London Joint Stock Bk. 5 Princes st. Bank
Pollard James, baker, 12 Pleasant row, Stepney green
Pollard James, *Red Lion* P.H. 5 Redcross sq. Cripplegate
Pollard James, tailor, 9 Redcross square, Cripplegate
Pollard John D. solicitor, 9 Little Abingdon st. Westminster
Pollard Mary (Mrs.), bookseller, 5 William's pl. Walworth rd
Pollard Richard, grocer, 14 Union st. east, Spitalfields
Pollard Samuel, grocer, 23 Cross st. Islington
Pollard Sarah (Mrs.), boarding ho. 17 Bedford pl. Russell sq
Pollard Thomas, lace warehouseman, see Webb & Pollard
Pollard William, butcher, 27 Doyley st. Sloane sq. Chelsea
Pollard William, cheesemonger, 1Glebe pl. King's rd. Chelsea
Pollards Martha (Miss), ladies' school, 97 Park st. Camdn. tn
Pollett Geo. E. & Son, cattle salesmen, 8 West Smithfield
Pollett Hugh, accountant, &c. 1 Furnival's inn
Pollett Montague, linendraper, 1 Ann's ter. Old Kent road
Polletty John, bricklayer, 5 Queen's terrace, Chelsea
Polletty William, bricklayer, 5 Queen's terrace, Chelsea
Polley Thomas, bed sacking maker, 4 Webber st. Blackfrs. rd
Pollock Geo. K. & Chs. M. I. solicitors, 19 Gt. George st. Westm
Pollock & Turner, surgeons, 7 Bath place, Kensington
Pollock Alex. boot & shoe maker, 7½ Providence pl. Kentish tn
Pollock David, Q.C. com. of Insolvent Debtors' court
Pollock George, carpet warehouseman, 12 Wood st. City
Pollock George Fredk. barrister, 2 Brick court, Temple
Pollock Isaac, manchester warehouse, see Adams & Pollock
Pollock John, agent for the Scottish Provident Life Insurance Company, 12 Great St. Thomas Apostle
Pollock John, agent to paper makers, 12Gt. St. Thomas Apostle
Pollock Thomas, chemist & druggist, 129 Fenchurch st
Pollock Timothy, surgeon, 26 Hatton garden
Pollock William Frederick, barrister, 1 King's Bench walk
Pollon Francis Thomas, pegged boot ma. 27 Lombard st
Pollon Frederick, bootmaker, 80 Watling st
Pollon John, french boot maker, 98 Cheapside
Polonceau's Bitumen Pavement, manufactory, Bow common, Middlesex; office, 15 Wharf rd. City rd. (John Pilkington, sec.)
Polwarth Robert, bookbinder, &c. 8 Queen's row, Pimlico
Polwin Christopher, teadealer, 3 Pollen st. Hanover square
Polyblank George, hosier, 97 St. John st. road
Polyblank Jas. Elliott, linendraper, 2 Barnsbury pl. Islington
Pomeroy William, wood busk maker, 10 Gee st. Goswell st
Pomfrett Robt. Wm. cork cutter, 105 London rd. Southwark
Pomroy & Roberts, umbrella ma. 8 Mansionhouse pl. Cmbwl rd
Poncy Abraham, watchmaker, 47 Gt. Russell st. Bloomsby
Poncy John, commission agent, 47 Gt. Russell st. Bloomsby
Pond Hen. coal & potato dlr. 44 Cannon st. rd. St. George's east
Pond James, dyer & scourer, 9 Orange st. Red Lion sq
Pond John, brushmaker & turner, 2 Tyler st. Golden square
Pond John, grocer, 1 Trafalgar st. Walworth road
Pond John, hair cutter, 43 Theobald's road
Pond John, shipping & general agent, 11 Water la. Tower st
Pond Robert, cutler, 29 Bell st. Edgware road
Pond William, chandler's shop, 6 Fashion st. Dockhead
Ponder James, baker, 158 Upper Thames st
Ponder Richard, army tailor, 37 Duke st. St. James's
Ponder Thomas, cigar manufacturer, 16 Chiswell st. Finsbury
Ponder William, baker, 67 High st. Portland town
Ponder William, surgeon, 54 Redcross st. Cripplegate
Ponler John & Son, tim. mers. 18 St. George's pl. St. Geo. east
Pons Mary (Madame), milliner & straw hat ma. 37Sackville st
Ponsford & Painter, milliners, 8 Gt. Pulteney st. Golden sq
Ponsford George, butcher, 46 Blackfriars road
Ponsford Henry, solicitor, 8 New inn, Wych st. Strand
Ponsford James, buildr. & archtct. 9 South side, Pddngtn. basin
Ponsford James, publisher, 122 Fleet st
Ponsford John, artist, 17 Grove terrace, St. John's wood
Ponsford John, woollen merchant, see Southall & Ponsford
Ponsford Lionel, builder, 10 Porchester terrace
Ponsford William, builder, 39 Gloucester, road, Hyde park
Ponsonby hon. Fred. Geo. Brabazon, barrister, 10 Farrar's buildings, Temple, & 3 Cavendish square
Ponsonby Thomas, plate glass & cannabic ornament warehouse, carver & gilder to the Queen, 32 Regent circus
Pontecorboli Angelo, foreign wareo. 15 Broad st. Golden sq
Ponten & Bean, makers of the cuirass shirt, 95 Cheapside
Ponten Joseph B. *Charlotte tav.* 32 Bucklersbury & 15 Poultry
Ponten Wm. Elton, surgeon, &c. 22 Ludgate hill
Pontet Edward, snuff maker, 124 Pall mall
Pontet Francis, jun. snuff mak. & importer, 60 Charing cross
Pontifex & Barnett, brass founders, 4 Gt. Dover st. Borough
Pontifex (Edmund & William) & Wood, farringdon copper, brass, lead & engine works, Shoe lane, Holborn
Pontifex (E. & W.) & Wood, manufrs. of dye extract, white lead, colors, varnishes, &c. Millwall, Poplar, & Shoe lane
Pontifex, Jacklin & Pontifex, coppersmiths, back & vat makers, millwrights & engineers, 54 & 55 Shoe lane, Holborn hill
Pontifex & Mallory, copperfoundrs. &c. 15 & 16 Up. St. Martin's la
Pontifex & Moginie, solicitors, 5 St. Andrew's court, Holborn
Pontifex Sydney, builder, 8 Bloomfield terrace, Pimlico
Ponting David, grocer & cheesemonger, 53 Hill st. Wlwth. rd
Ponting Dorothea (Miss), charcoal ma. 20 Lloyd's rw. St. John st
Ponting Richard Thos. tailor, 35 Beauvoir ter. Kingsland rd
Pontop & South Shields Rail. Co. (Rd. Till mgr.), Guildhl. bds
Ponzini John, carver, gilder & looking glass manufacturer, 22 Hatton garden
Ponza Chas. railway share agt. 11 Angel ct. Throgmorton st
Pook William, painter, 4 Harris terrace, St. George st

Pooke William, grindery dealer, 14 Fisher st. Red Lion sq
Pool & Boulton, solicitors, 1 Walbrook buildings
Pool John, coal dealer, 19 Grey Eagle st. Spitalfields
Pool John, dairy, 9 Norwich court, Fetter lane
Pool John, teadealer, 22 St. Swithin's lane
Pool Joseph, bookbinder, 26 Bartholomew close
Pool Joseph, gold beater, 1 Cleaver st. Kennington cross
Pool Wm. cabinet maker, 15 Brewer st. north, Goswell road
Poole & Carpmael, patent agents; patents procured, & all business relating thereto conducted at the patent office, 4 Old square, Lincoln's inn
Poole & Gamlen, solicitors, 3 Gray's inn square
Poole Hugh & Son, carvers&gild. 9 Birdcage walk, Hckny.rd
Poole James & Son, tailors & drapers, 4 Old Burlington st. & 32 Saville row, Piccadilly
Poole John & Co. mer. & ins. brokers, 1 Crown ct. Philpot la
Poole John & Son, curriers, Wellington pl. Walworth common
Poole & Knight, whitesmiths, 25 Pudding lane, Eastcheap
Poole & Macgillivray (late James Oliver), cabinet makers, &c. 25 Princes st. Cavendish square
Poole & Mattock, butter, meat, &c. salesmen, 22 Newgate mkt
Poole Benj. *Old Whitmore's Head* P.H. 1 Hoxton old town
Poole Benjamin, *Poole's hotel*, 28 Fish st. hill, & 128 Lower Thames st
Poole Benjamin, *Steam Packet hotel*, 28 Fish st. hill
Poole Burnet Minifie, solr. 16 Goulden terr. Barnsbury rd
Poole Caroline (Mrs.), academy, 15 Lowthercottages, Liverpl.rd
Poole Clement jun. willow square manuf. 19 Whitecross st
Poole Elizh. (Miss), dressma. 88 Harrison st. Gray's inn rd
Poole George, watchcase maker, 4 Wood st. north, King sq
Poole George Schultz, printer, 5 White st. Bethnal green
Poole Henry, cabinet maker, 182 Hoxton Old town
Poole Henry, statuary & mason, 11 Great Smith st. Westm
Poole James, builder & bricklayer, 16 Quaker st. Spitalfields
Poole James, haberdasher, 30 Tabernacle walk, Finsbury
Poole James, house agt. & builder, 7 Blossom st. Norton folgate
Poole James, milliner, 3 High st. Deptford
Poole James, watch escapement maker, 21 Lr. Chadwell st
Poole John, accountant & auctioneer, 9 Spital square
Poole John, cheesemonger, see Lillwall & Poole
Poole John, chronometer ma. 7 Brunswick ter. Commer.rd.ea
Poole John, doll maker, 8 Twister's alley, Bunhill row
Poole John, pewterer, 124 Wardour st. Soho
Poole John, silk manufacturer, 9 Goldsmith's st. Cheapside
Poole John, soap maker, &c. 8 Union place, Clapham road
Poole Joseph, butcher, 32 Goodge st. Tottenham court road
Poole Joseph, currier, 23 Broad st. Bloomsbury
Poole Joshua T. grocer&cheesemonger, Southamptonst.Camb
Poole Matthew, foreman to New River Co. 2 Broken wharf, 41 Upper Thames st
Poole Matthew, brush maker, 15 Hill st. Regent's Park rd
Poole Moses, clk. of inventions, 13 Searle st.&4Oldsq.Linc.inn
Poole Richard, *Mitre tavern*, Mitre court, 44 Fleet st
Poole Robert, boot & shoe maker, 9 Chester pl. Old Kent rd
Poole Robert, *Green Man* P.H. Stratford
Poole Samuel, boot & shoe maker, 7 Red Lion pas. Holborn
Poole Thomas, fruiterer, North row, Covent garden market
Poole Thomas, solicitor, 6 South sq. Gray's inn, & Holloway
Poole Thomas Evered, solicitor, 43 Carey st
Poole Wm. coffee rooms, 242 Tottenham court road
Poole Wm. goldsmith & jeweller, 56 Wynyatt st. Goswell rd
Poole Wm. livery stables, 14 Wells mews, Wells st. Oxford st
Poole Wm. oil & colorman, 26 Hertford st. Fitzroy sq
Poole Wm. solicitor, 36 Great Ormond st. Queen square
Poole Wm. tailor, 47 Paradise st. Lambeth
Poole Wm. H. solicitor, 10 Gray's inn place, Gray's inn
Pooles & Stopfords', hat manfrs. 35 Stamford st. Blackfrs. rd
Pooles Wm. bootmaker, 27 Exmouth st. Commercl. rd. east
Pooley Hen. & Son, weighg. machine mfrs. 9 Earl st. Blkfrs
Pooley (Mrs.), & Jones (Miss), millinrs. 23 Holles st. Cavend. sq
Pooley James, solicitor, see Gem, Pooley & Beisley
Pooley Martha (Mrs.), chndlr'sshop, 23 Margart.st. Wilmgn.sq
Pooley Wm. haberdasher, see Debenham, Pooley & Smith
Poolley Ann (Mrs.), *Shakspear's Hd.* P.H. 38 Shakspear's wk
Poor Law Commissioners (England & Wales), 1&2 Somerset place, Somerset house, Strand; hours of business 10 to 5
Poore Charles, *Star & Garter* P.H. 110 Whitechapel road
Poore Charles, *Sun & Last* P.H. 18 Newgate market
Poore John, dyer & scourer, 23 Union st. Bishopsgate
Poore Samuel, shoemaker, 70 Cable st. Wellclose square
Poore Wm. Dyke, barrister, 2 Child's place, Temple bar
Poovey Samuel, grocer, 2 Etham place, Gt. Dover road
Pope Charles Lee, solicitor, see Bennett, Bolding & Pope
Pope John B. & Co. coalfactors & ship & insurance brokers, 8 Lower Thames st. & Goole, Yorkshire
Pope & Plante, hosiers, 4 Waterloo place, Pall mall
Pope Thos. & Co. blacking ma. 16 Compton st. Clerkenwell
Pope George, solicitor, 12 Gray's inn square
Pope George, butcher, 68 St. George's road, Southwark
Pope Henry, carpenter, 5 Eldon st. Finsbury
Pope Henry, wholesale stationer & pattern card maker, 22 Budge row; manufactory 36½ Percy st. Bagnigge wells rd
Pope Henry Alexr. gas fitter & brass finisher, 5 Eldon st
Pope Henry George, herbalist, 217 Kent st. Borough
Pope James, bookseller & binder, 12 Church st. Hackney
Pope John, coachmaker, see Hale & Pope
Pope John, engraver, 26 Great Bath st. Clerkenwell
Pope John, *George IV.* P.H. 5 Leicester st. Regent st
Pope John, *King's Arms* P.H. 1 Park place, Liverpool rd
Pope John, wholesale stationer, 10 Basing lane, Bread st
Pope John Robinson, surgeon, 3 Manchester sq
Pope Joseph, dressing case&pocket book,&c.mf.186Blkfrs.rd
Pope Joseph, undertaker, 31 Gerrard st. Soho
Pope Mary (Mrs.), *Red Lion inn*, Kilburn
Pope Matthias, draper, 46 Nelson ter. Stoke Newington rd
Pope Richard, tailor, 59 King William st. City
Pope Robert, attorney, 2 Raymond buildings, Gray's inn
Pope Roof, tailor, 13 Hatton garden
Pope Samuel, *Crown inn*, Paul's alley, St. Paul's churchyard
Pope Samuel, furn. ironmonger, 119 Crawford st. Portman sq
Pope Samuel, scotch & manchester agent, 62 Bread st
Pope Samuel, tailor, 2 Well st. Cripplegate
Pope Sam. Richd. pianoforte ma. 72 Great Russell st. Blmsby
Pope Sophia (Miss), tobacconist, 37 Mary st. Hampstead rd
Pope Thomas, butcher, 8 Kennington cross, Lambeth
Pope Thomas, coal merchant, 34 Cockspur st; Billingsgate wharf; Church st. Greenwich; Railway wharf, Deptford; & York & Augustus wharfs, Augustus st. Regent's park basin
Pope Thomas, tailor, 26 Jermyn st. St. James's
Pope Wm. coal dealer, 17 Exeter st. Lisson grove
Pope Wm. engraver, 50½ Red Lion st. Holborn
Pope Wm. furn. ironmonger, 80 & 81 Edgware rd. Marylebne
Pope Wm. lighterman, &c. see Lucas, Pope & Shaw
Pope Wm. lodging house, 6 Palsgrave place, Strand
Pope Wm. tailor, 13 Harcourt st. New road
Pope Wm. Clayton, teadealer & grocer, 26 Finsbury pavemt
Popham James, dlr. in tambour work, 13 Church st. Shoredit
Popham Wm. surgeon, 5 Queen's Head row, Newingtonbutts
Popkin Alfred Eude, stationer, 15 Walbrook
Poplar Gas Light Co. (Wm. Smith, sec.), Ferry rd. west, Poplar
Poplar Lit. & Sci. Insti. (T. E. Bowkett, sec.), 67½ Poplar Hh.st
Poplar Savings' Bank (Rt. Dixon, sec.), Townhall Poplar Hh.st
Pople John, *Duke of Gloucester* P.H. 21 Glo'ster rw. Walwth
Pople Leonard, coffee rooms, Pickett place, Strand
Poplett John, printer, 43 Beech st. Barbican
Poppe Frederick & Co. merchants, 3 New London st
Popple George, *Coach & Horses* P.H. 43 Carnaby st. Golden sq
Poppleton Richd. leather factor, 4 Bermondsey, Leather mkt
Popplewell Peter, button & trim. wa. 2 Church pssge. Gldhll
Poppy Thos. silk mercer & draper, 285 & 286 High Holborn
Porcas Charles Hall, cornchandler, 13 Ocean row, Stepney
Porch Isabella (Mrs.), ale agt. & carrier, *India Arms*, 44 Lime st
Porret Louis, tailor, 31 Duke st. St. James's
Porrett David, carpenter 14 & 15 Woburn bldgs. Tavistock sq
Porritt Isaac, printer, &c. Deptford High st
Porsonage Frederick, butcher, 13 Salmon lane, Limehouse
Port Charles, grocer, 34 Whitefriars st. Fleet st
Port Eglington Spinning Company, worsted spinners & carpet manufacturers, 105 Wood st. & at Glasgow
Port of London & Thames Assurance Association (Captain Bathurst Symes, resident director & secretary), 65 Lower Thames st
Portable Bath Company, 71½ Oxford st
Portal Rd. B. & Bernrd. B. wine mer. see Dingwall, Portal & Co
Portal Wm. Anderson, attorney, 10 Clifford's inn, Fleet st
Portbury Edward, historical engr. 12 Claremont rw. Islington
Portbury Joseph, tobacconist, 38 London road, Southwark
Portch Daniel, cheesemonger, 50 Goodge st. Tottenham ct. rd
Portch James, manufacturer of screens & handles, card racks, white wood articles, varnishing, &c. leather goods, canvas for embroidery, fans made & repaired, miniature cases, frames & matt flatts, drawings & prints mounted or varnished, 26 Princes st. Cavendish square
Porch Joseph, cheesemonger, 1 Fisher's alley, Whitefriars
Portch Sarah (Mrs.), hat box & trunk ma. 3 Pitts pl. O. Kent rd
Porteous & Gregson, linendra. 17 & 18 Beckford row. Walwth.rd
Porter & Lack, stock & shirt makers & hosiers, 94 Strand
Porter & Robertson, cigar & snuff ma. 7 Cross la. St. Mary at hill
Porter Wm. Hen. & Co. patent anchor ma. 149 Cheapside
Porter Catherine (Mrs.), seal engraver & medallist, 3 Perceval st. Northampton square

Porter Wm. & John, ropemakers, Jamaica level, Rotherhithe
Porter Charles, fancy cabinet & toy wa. 38 Marchmont st
Porter Charles, watch & clock maker, 227 Bermondsey st
Porter Christopher, bricklayer, 22 Glo'ster st. Queen square
Porter Daniel D. merchant, N. & S. American coffee house
Porter Daniel Greenaway, wine merchant, 81 Gt. Tower st
Porter Edward, auctionr. & house agt. 6 Regent pl. Globe rd
Porter Francis oil&italian wa. 32 Elizabeth st. Eaton square
Porter Geo. architect and surv. Fort pl. Grange rd. Bermonds. & 10½ Kennington row, Kennington common
Porter Geo. fruiterer & coal dealer, 62 Wapping High st
Porter Geo. professor of music, 32 St. James's pl. OldKent rd
Porter Geo. smith & bellhanger, 48 Gt. Alie st. Goodman's fi
Porter Henry, lodging house, 38 Regent circus, Piccadilly
Porter Henry Edward, butcher, 2 NewQuebec st. Portman sq
Porter James, baker, Ford's buildings, Battersea
Porter James, bottle jack maker, 30 Newcastle st. Strand
Porter James, cabinet maker, 9 Sarah pl. Old st. road
Porter James, carpenter, 31 Shaftesbury pl. Aldersgate st
Porter James, fringe maker, 130 London wall
Porter Jas. upholst. & undertaker, 166 High st. Camden tn
Porter John, solicitor, 22 Lincoln's inn fields
Porter John, cabinet maker, Hertford road, Kingsland
Porter John, cheesemonger, 79 Crawford st. Portman sq
Porter John, coffee rooms, 34 Liquorpond st. Gray's inn la
Porter John, fruiterer, 2 Elliott's row, Lower st. Islington
Porter John, chandler's shop, 25 Somerset st. Aldgate
Porter John hairdresser, 13 Bear st. Leicester sq
Porter John, improved iron fence, hurdle, galvanized corrugated iron roof & building manufacturer, Grove iron works, Gt. Guildford st. & Bridge pl. Bridge st. Southwark
Porter John, shoe mercer, 58 Sun st. Bishopsgate without
Porter Joseph, fruiterer, &c. 99 Goswell road
Porter Joseph, trimming seller, 17 Bedfordbury, Cov. gardn
Porter Joseph Long, bookseller & stationer, 43 Sloane st
Porter Marquis, printer, 28 Melton st. Euston sq
Porter Mary (Miss), ready made linen & general equipment warehouse, 56 Charing cross
Porter Mary (Mrs.), *John of Jerusalem* P.H. 1 Rosoman st
Porter MaryAnn(Mrs.), shoemfr. 38 Monyersst. HoxtonNw.tn
Porter Richard, hosier, see Foster, Porter & Co
Porter Robert, baker, 30 New Church st. Lisson grove
Porter Robert, cornchandler, 47 Freeschool st. Horselydown
Porter Samuel, tailor, 10 Francis st. Newington butts
Porter Thomas, architect & surveyor, 19 City ter. City rd
Porter Thomas, bootmaker, 17 Henrietta st. Manchester sq
Porter Thomas, chair & couchmaker, Sash court, Wilson st Finsbury, & 7 Beauvoir place, Kingsland road
Porter Thomas, surgeon, 145 Bishopsgate without
Porter Thomas, surgeon & apothecary, 32 Euston sq. New rd
Porter Thomas, jun. surveyor, 19 City terrace, City road
Porter Wm. british & foreign fruit dealer, 109 Goswell st
Porter Wm. carver & gilder, 28 New cut, Lambeth
Porter Wm, coffee rooms, 13 Up Wellington st. Cov. gardn
Porter Wm. leather&grindery dealer, 18 Star st. Paddington
Porter Wm. nightman, 8 Eaton lane North, Pimlico
Porter Wm. wine&spirit mer. 27 Shaftesbury ter. Wilton rd
Porter Wm. Chas. grocer & dairym. 5 Oxenden st. Haymakt
Porteus Edgar, die sinker, engraver & printer, 331 Strand
Porthouse Thos. watch & chronom. ma. 10 Northampton sq
Portington Harriet (Mrs.), linendraper, 43 Paddington st
Portland Club House(John Wm. Walsh, sec.), 1 Stratford pl
Portland Railway Comp. Office,3 Westrn. whrf. Abingdon st
Portlock Mary (Mrs.), milliner, &c. 21 Swan st. Minories
Portor Geo. architect, 6 Fort pl. Grange rd. Bermondsey
Portsmouth, Chichester, & Fareham Railway Company (George Wm. Horn, sec.), 5 John st. Adelphi
Portsmouth & Chatham Direct Railway Company, (John C. Somers, sec.), 1A, Adelphi terrace
Portsmouth&LangstonDockCo.(G.N. White, sec.), Moorgtst
Portuguese Government Agency, 14 Finsbury chambers, London wall; hours of business, 11 to 3
PortugueseJewsOrphans'So.(A.H. Salom, sec.) 10 BevisMks
Portuguese & Spanish Jews' Hospital (Almosnino Soloman, sec.), Mile end road
Portwine Catherine (Mrs.), butcher, 9 Lumber ct. Seven dials
Portwine William, cap maker, 77 Hoxton Old town
Posno Maurice Joseph, merchant, 19 Finsbury circus
Post Magazine Almanac Offi. 4A, Wine Office ct. Fleet st
POST OFFICE—(General) St. Martin's-le-grand
For list of Post Office Receiving Houses throughout the metropolis, and full information as to the details of Post arrangements, see "POSTAL DIRECTORY."—And for the Officers of the Establishment, see "OFFICIAL DIRECTORY."
Post Wm. Henry, beer retailer, 1 Charles st. St. George's east
Post Office London Directory Offices, 19 & 20 Old Boswell court, Temple bar
Postan Thos. Geo. auctionr. estate & ho. agt. 48 Aldersgate st
Postill Charles, grocer, 38 Snowsfields, Bermondsey
Postill Thomas, boot & shoe maker, 38 George st. Portman sq
Potier Wm. bow string & gut manufr. 33 Green st. Blackfrs. rd
Pothipher Henry, carver & gilder, 1 Warwick pl. Kingsld. rd
Pott Chas. Arthur & Wm. vinegar makers, Bridge st. Southwk
Pott Emma (Miss), ladies' school, 20 Brooksby st. Liverpl. rd
Pott Francis Swaine, smith & ironmonger, see Burt & Potts
Pott Fred. Wm. proctor, 13 Godliman st. Doctors' commons
Pott Stephen, china, &c. wareho. 3 Barnsbury st. Liverpool rd
Pott Thomas Alfred, accountant, see Grand & Pott
Pott Wm. Holiday, smith & ironmonger, see Burt & Potts'
Potten John, beer retailer, 30 North st. Edgware road
Potter Charles H. & Edwin, paper stainers, 29 Budge row
Potter & Collingridge, attorneys, 5 Basinghall st
Potter & Hailey, importers of leeches, herbalists & seedsmen, 66 Farringdon market
Potter Henry & Sons, smiths, 3 Porter st. Soho
Potter John & Co. dyers & scourers, 121 Gray's inn lane
PotterAnn(Mrs.), fancy repostry. 4 Northmton. rw. Hollwy. rd
Potter Catherine (Mrs.), *Peacock* P.H. Francis st. Wstmtr. rd
PotterChas. bookbinder & printer, 16 Warwick pl. Kingslnd. rd
Potter Edmund, hairdresser, 6 Frederick's pl. Old Kent rd
Potter Edward, carpenter, &c. 19 Windmill st. Tottn. ct. rd
Potter Edward, cooper, 37 St. George st
PotterGeo. *Sir Wm. Walworth* P.H. 10 Beckford rw. Wlwth. rd
Potter George, smith, 1 Lit. Vine st. Waterloo rd. Lambeth
Potter George Augustus, tobacconist, 53 Piccadilly
Potter George Wm. K. solicitor & secondary of London, 5 Basinghall st
Potter Henry, butcher, 3 Grove ter. Queen's rd. Bayswater
Potter Henry, manufactr. of spruce, 6 Wood st. Westminster
Potter Hy. musical instrmnt. makr. 2 Bridge st. Westminster
Potter Henry, library, 1 Chester place, Old Kent road
Potter James, beer retailer, 34 Wharf rd. City road
Potter James, fruiterer, &c. 40 Park st. Grosvenor sq
Potter James, *Leopard* coffee rooms, 65 WhitechapelHigh st
Potter James, *Ship* P.H. 10 Hunt st. Pelham st. Spitalfields
Potter James, tailor, 4 Theobald's road, Red Lion square
Potter James, *White Horse* P.H. 64 Shoreditch
Potter John, scale maker, 90 Britannia st. City road
Potter John, secret springer, 23 Rahere st. Goswell road
Potter John Dell, stockbkr. Exchange, & 6 Throgmorton st
Potter John Sudaby, dyer & scourer, 14 Goodge st. Tot. ct. rd
Potter Rd. Henry, architect, 11 Henrietta st. Brunswick sq
Potter Rt. livery stables, Eclipse yd. Up. George st. Bryanst. sq
Potter Robert, *Norfolk Arms* P.H. Halfmoon cres. Pentnvl
Potter Robert, stockbroker, 6 Throgmorton st. & Stock exchge
Potter Samuel, baker, 3 Lombard terrace, Chelsea
Potter Samuel, fishmonger, 1 Drury court, Drury lane
Potter Samuel, solicitor, see Lofty & Potter
Potter Samuel, jun. solicitor, 36 King st. Cheapside
Potter Sarah (Mrs.), teadealer, 32 High st. St. Giles's
Potter Thomas, *Blue Ball* P.H. Horse Shoe alley, Wilson st
Potter Thomas, city carman, 56 Halfmoon st. Bishopsgate
Potter Thos. furn. ironmonger, 44 South Molton st. Bond st
Potter Thomas, working jeweller, 26 Newcastle st. Strand
Potter Thomas, tallowchandler, 73 Crawford st. Portman sq
Potter Thomas Henry, merchant, 22 East India chambers
Potter Wm. bookseller, 12 Bear st. Leicester square
Potter Wm. boot & shoe maker, 129 St. George st
Potter Wm. bricklayer, 37 Gt. Pulteney st. Golden sq
Potter Wm. city carman, 14 Halfmoon st. Bishopsgate
Potter Wm. cooper, 3 Vauxhall st. Lambeth
Potter Wm. dining rooms, 230 Tottenham court road
Potter Wm. furniture broker, 10 Lit. Shire lane, Temple bar
Potter Wm. hairdresser, 3 Wandsworth road
Potter Wm. *HourGlass* P.H. Trafalgar pl. Walworth common
PotterWm. importer of wines & spirits, 87 Aldgate High st
Potter Wm. silversmith & plater, 17 Craven st. Strand
Potter Wm. toydealer, 21 New Church st. west, Edgware rd
Potter Wm. Simpson, coal factor, see Miller & Potter
Pottier Geo. Lewis, corn dealer, 54 Church st. Shoreditch
PottingerWm.&Co. tailors, drapers&hattrs, 64 Kg. Wm. st. City
PottingerMary(Mrs.), *Crown & Dolphin* P.H. 5 High st. Stepny
Pottinger Thomas, *Civet Cat* P.H. 14 Church st. Kensingtn
Pottinger Thomas, tailor & hatter, 9 Eastcheap
Pottle Lucy & M. milit. featherma. 25A, Rupert st. Haymarkt
Pottle John, newsvender, see Holmes & Pottle
Pottle John Rowland, surgeon, 20 Bath st. City road
Potto Ellen (Miss), milliner, 64 Mortimer st. Cavendish sq
Potton William, haberdasher, 34 Lamb st. Spital sq
Potts Edward & William, solicitors, 8 Serjeant's inn, Fleet st
Potts Frances (Mrs.), & Son, lace warehouse, 28 Pall mall

Potts & Nicholson, glass & white lead wa. 63 Queen st. City
Potts Robt. Ullock & John, chemists, &c. 55 South Audley st
Potts Chas. treasurer, Foundling hospital, Guilford st
Potts Fanny (Mrs.), boarding & lodging house, 29 Watling st
Potts Frederick Wm. Proctor, 18 John st. Bedford row
Potts George B. artist, 28 Pall mall
Potts John, basket maker, 11 Crispin st. Spitalfields
Potts John, who. teadealer, see Fincham, Matson & Potts
Potts Lawrence Holker, physician, 9 Buckingham st. Strand
Potts Matthew, pocket book & case ma. 18 Brooke st. Holborn
Potts Robert, confectioner, 28 Brick lane, Spitalfields
Potts Sarah (Mrs.), jewlr. & perfr. box ma. 11 Brooke st. Hlbn
Potts Stephen, japanner, 44 Wynyatt st. Goswell road
Potts Thomas, fruiterer, 9 Southampton st. Camberwell
Potts Thomas, gun maker to her Majesty's hon. Board of Ordnance, & the hon. East India Co. wholesale gun, pistol & rifle maker, & sword cutler, Haydon sq. Minories
Potts Wm. surgeon, 27 South Audley st
Potts William, tallow chandler, 89 Farringdon st
Poucher Richard, alamode beef house, see Edwards & Poucher
Pouget Francis, architect & surveyor, 52 Trinity sq. Borough
Poulain James, coffee rooms, 2 City road, Old st
Poulden Chas. John, ho. & estate ag. 24 Cumberland st. Portm. sq
Poulden George, barrister, 1 Figtree court, Temple
Poulson Benjamin, tailor, 51A, Mortimer st. Cavendish sq
Poulson Benjamin, tailor, 94 Quadrant, Regent st
Poulson Jabez, japan & varnish ma. 5 Church lane, Whitechapel, & Bow common
Poulter & Cooper, wholesale stationers, 3 Great St. Helen's
Poulson Jsph. window glass cutter, 9 Portman pl. Edgware rd
Poulter Charles, *Hope* P.H. 82 High holborn
Poulter Charlotte (Mrs.), dining rooms, 9 Edward st. Soho
Poulter Edward, *Hope* P.H. Duke's Head pass. Newgate mkt
Poulter Edward Jas. shoe wa. 1 Colvill ter. King's rd. Chlsa
Poulter Geo. plumber & painter, 20 Blenheim st. Bond st. Chlsa
Poulter John, printer, 1 Great Chesterfield st. Marylebone
Poulter John Sayer, barrister, 5 King's Bench walk, Temple
Poulter John, plumber & glazier, 1 Anns row, Stepney green
Poulter Wm. *Duke of Sussex* P.H. 18 Pierrepont row, Islngtn
Poultney Wm. hatmaker, 17 Crosby row, Borough
Poulton Charles & George, carpet wareho. 67 Blackfriars rd
Poulton & Elms, carpenters & undertakers, 13 Vauxhall walk
Poulton & Lawrence, commission agents, 119 Cheapside
Poulton Christr. fishmonger & venison dealer, 62 Jermyn st
Poulton George, wholes. & retail cheesemonger, 52 Tooley st
Poulton George, dining rooms, 7 Star corner, Bermondsey
Poulton Henry, butcher, 10 New Turnstile, Holborn
Poulton James, butcher, 2 Folly, Dockhead, Bermondsey
Poulton James, draper, 5 Blackmoor st. Drury lane
Poulton John, ham & tongue mer. 32 Nicholas la. Lombard st
Poulton Joseph, grocer, &c. 7 Devonshire, terrace, Globe rd
Poulton Rt. watchmaker, 2 Mayfield pl. High st. Kensington
Poulton Sarah (Mrs.), grocer & teadlr. Triangle, Hackney
Poulton Wm. butcher, 31 Paradise st. Rotherhithe
Poulton Wm. *Shakspere* coffee rooms, 7 Chandos st. Cov. gn
Poultry & Giltspur Street Compter office, Whitecross st. prison; hours of business, 11 to 3, & 5 to 7
Pounce James Hen. china ware. 33 Edwards st. Portman sq
Pouncy John W. & Sons, wholesale stationers, 65 Long acre
Pound & Tasker, trunkms. & underts. 64 & 81 Leadenhall st
Pound John, hatter, &c. 121 Bishopsgate without
Pound Matthew, chemist & druggist, 198 Oxford st
Pound Samuel, tailor, 9 Red Lion st. Wapping
Pound William, hatter, 5 Sidney place, Commercial rd. east
Pounds Joseph, *Green Man* P.H. 83 Bermondsey wall
Pounsford Robert, *Bull's Head* P.H. Camberwell green
Pountain Thos. & Geo. saddlers & harness ms. 66 Dean st. Soho
Pountney Geo. Fred. comb mnfr. 3 Patriot row, Cambridge rd
Pountney Wm. comb ma. 6 Dorchester pl. New Nth. rd. Hoxton
Poupard Abraham, scalema. 5 King's pl. Commercial rd. east
Poupard Charles, scalemaker, 39 Brown's lane, Spitalfields
Poupard Edwin, scalemaker, 74 Red Lion st. High Holborn
Poupard John, tobacco & snuff manufactr. 45 Goodge st
Poupard William, scalemaker, 30 Wych st. Strand
Poupart John, market gardener, Little Chelsea
Poupart Wm. market gardener, Blue Anchor yd. Bermondsey
Pout George, surgeon, 65 Borough High st
Pout William Charles, stationer, &c. 19 Blackman st. Boro'
Povah John, butcher, 6 Up. Southwick st. Nth. Cambrg. ter
Povall Matilda (Miss), bootmaker, 45 King's rd. east, Chlsea
Povey Chas. Richd. coffee rooms, 2 Redcross st. Cripplegate
Povey William, cab proprietor, 10 Saville pl. Lambeth walk
Povoas Amelia (Miss), milliner, 1 High st. Stoke Newington
Pow & Fawcus, patent purchase for ships' windlass, chain cable & anchor manufacturers, 49 Lower Shadwell
Pow John, *Tower Shades* P.H. 35 Terrace, Trinity sq. Towr. hl
Pow Thomas, pork butcher, 69 Three Colt st. Limehouse
Powdich Geo. spice mer. & drysalter, 26 College st. Dowg. hl
Powditch Thomas, brewer, Wild's rents, Long la. Bermondsey
Powe Jeremiah, plumber, 16 Mount st. Walworth road
Powel Edwin, baker, 6 Neckinger road, Bermondsey
Powell Broderip (F. & W.) & Wilde, sols. 9 New sq. Linc. inn
Powell Bros. & Co. bristol bottle co. 22 Steel yd. Up. Thames st
Powell Edward & Wm. fancy paper stainers, 10 Wilson st. Finsbury, & 4 Cross st. Finsbury
Powell Henry & Son, who. oilmen & irish & foreign provision merchants, 28 Fenchurch st. & St. Katherine's, Tower
Powell Henry & Son, wholesale oilmen, 28 Fenchurch st
Powell Henry & William H. coachbuilders, 43 Old Bond st
Powell Jas. & Sons, wine merchts. 60 Carey st. Lincoln's inn
Powell Jas. & Sons, glass makers, & patentees of flowered quarries & ornamented panes for windows, 16 Temple st. Whitefriars
Powell John & Co. snuff & cigar manufacturers, 4 Clark's terrace, Cannon st. road, St. George's east
Powell & Kertland, tobac. & snuff ms. 3 King's pl. Com. rd. ea
Powell & Lealand, opticians, 24 Clarendon st. Somers town
Powell Mary Ann & Grace, dressmakers, &c. 66 New Bond st
Powell Sarah & Maria (Misses), haberdashers, 53 Hackney rd
Powell Thos. Jas. & Thos. leather & hidefactors, 36 Lime st
Powell Townsend & Co. merchants, 80 Watling st
Powell & Williams, coal merchants, 22 Wharf road, City rd
Powell Ann (Miss), milliner, 13 Gloucester st. Queen sq
Powell Caleb Edw. ass. sol. to the Mint, 5 Raymond bdgs. Graysin
Powell Charles, baker, 45 Bermondsey square
Powell Charles, livery stables, 1 Holland st. Clapham rd
Powell Charles, painter, 3 Castle st. Saffron hill
Powell Charles, tailor & draper, 93 St. George st
Powell Daniel, silk manufacturer, 5 Russia row, Milk st
Powell David, merchant, see Cotesworth, Powell & Pryor
Powell David, surgeon, 21 Garnault place, Clerkenwell
Powell Edw. J. ass. sol. to the Mint, 5 Raymond bldgs. Grays inn
Powell Edwin S. chemist, 13 Jamaica ter. Comrcl. rd. Limeho
Powell Elizabeth (Mrs.), bootmaker, 187 Drury lane, & 147 & 148 Great Saffron hill
Powell Elizh. (Mrs.), whipma. 33 Bryanstone st. Bryanst. sq
Powell Geo. lithographic artist, 2 Paul's court, Huggin lane, Wood st. & 17 Upper Rosoman st. Clerkenwell
Powell Geo. solicitor, see Springall, Thompson & Powell
Powell Geo. stockbroker, 1 Warnford ct. & Stock Exchange
Powell Geo. surveyor, 8 Beaufort buildings, Strand
Powell Geo. tailor, 44 York st. City road
Powell Geo. undertak. carpntr. &c. 6 Knightrider ct. Doc. com
Powell Rev. Giles, B.A. clerical agt. 6 Warwick ct. Grays inn
Powell Hector, linendraper, 70 Blackfriars road
Powell Henry, booksel. & newsvend. 17 Bartholomew close
Powell Henry, china wareh. 13 King's pl. Coml. rd. east
Powell Henry, farrier, 2 Smith's buildings, Leadenhall st
Powell Henry, inventor & patentee of the templer caps, 102 New Bond st
Powell Henry (late Keene & Powell), outfitter, hosier, draper, & glover, 102 New Bond st
Powell Henry, surgeon, see Saner & Powell
Powell Henry, M.D. surgeon, &c. 36 Finsbury square
Powell Henry, tin plate worker, 1 Fisher st. Red Lion sq
Powell Isabella (Mrs.), tobacco. 1 Lit. Cross st. Newgtn. bts
Powell James, bookseller, 19 Wyndham st. Bryanstone sq
Powell James, hatter & outfitter, 66 High st. Portland twn
Powell James, paperstainer, 12 Camden st. Walworth
Powell James, surgeon, 16 Gt. Coram st. Brunswick sq
Powell James, umbrella maker, 63 Tothill st. Westminster
Powell James Chas. chair ma. 65 Shaftesbury st. New Nth. rd
Powell James Chase, surgeon, 47 Chiswell st. Finsbury sq
Powell Jas. John, surgeon, 2 New Portland pl. Wandswth. rd
Powell James White, surgeon, 9 Parker's row, Dockhead
Powell John, accountant, 4 Angel court, Throgmorton st
Powell John, baker, 15 New st. Golden square
Powell John, carpentr. & builder, 15 Gt. George st. Bermdsy
Powell John, grocer, 10 Oakley st. Mount st. Lambeth
Powell John (late Scwartz & Powell), harp & violin string maker, wholesale & for exportation, 3 White's row, Sptflds
Powell John, *Lion* P.H. 22 Lion st. New Kent road
Powell John, needle manufacturer, 6 Brook st. New road
Powell John, oil & colorman, 10 Lower road, Islington
Powell John, *Rising Sun* P.H. Spa road, Bermondsey
Powell John, *Spencer's Arms* P.H. 1 Silver st. Clerkenwell
Powell John, stone mason, High row, Silver st. Kensington
Powell John, trunk & military equipage manufacturer, 36 Pall mall, & 59 Paddington st. Marylebone
Powell John, undertaker, 31 Little Britain
Powell John, wood turner, 50 Bethnal green road
Powell John Clarke, merchant, between 16 & 17 St. Helen's pl

Powell John Wm. book binders'tool ma.8Up.Smithst.Clrkwl
Powell Jonathan, cornchandler, 15 Upper Marylebone st
Powell Joseph, basket maker, 21 Water lane, Tower st
Powel Joseph, beer retailer, 1 Canal bridge, Old Kent road
Powell Joseph, *Fish & Bell* P.H. 9 Charles st. Soho square
Powell Joseph, grocer, &c. 56 Leather lane, Holborn
Powell Joseph, locksmith & bellhanger, 142 Lambeth walk
Powell Lewis, M.D. surgeon, 12John st. Berkeley sq
Powell Lucy (Miss), cupper, 16 Water st. Blackfriars
Powell Maria (Miss), tobacconist, 164 Oxford st
Powell (Mrs.), ladies' boarding school, 3 King Edward ter
Powell Nathaniel James, who. stationer, see Mead & Powell
Powell Rd. gas fitter & brass finisher, 59 Sun st. Bishopsgate
Powell Robert, solicitor, 13 Beaufort buildings, Strand
Powell Sam. cowkeeper, 2B, Hall pl. Edgware rd. Paddingtn
Powell Sarah G. (Miss), seminary, 11 Cloudesley sq. Islntn
Powell Sidney, optician, 112 Gray's inn lane
Powell Thos. *Artichoke* P.H. 34 Farringdon st
Powell Thos. baker, 45 Grosvenor row, Pimlico
Powell Thos. cabinet maker, 24 Gt. James st. Bedford row
Powell Thos. haberdasher, 16 Nottingham st. Marylebone
Powell Thos. foreign wines & spirits importer, 72 Mark lane
Powell Thos. hairdresser, 9 Brompton road
Powell Thos. oil & colorman, 42 Crescent st. Euston sq
Powell Thos. oven build. & ironfoundr. 49 Lisle st. Leicester sq
Powell Thos. patent medicine vender, 5½ Blackfriars road
Powell Thos. phial dealer, 37 Crown st. Soho
Powell Thos. undertaker, 148 Tooley st. Borough
Powell Virgil Jas. tobacconist, 12 Haberdashers' walk
Powell Virgel James, tobacco manufacturer, 3 King's place, Commercial rd. east, & 2 Pleasant row, Regent's park
Powell Walter, corn dealer, 48 Leather lane, Holborn
Powell Whiston, genl. agent, 12 Copthall ct. Throgmorton st
Powell Wm. baker, 15 King st. Soho
Powell Wm. bedstead ma. 3 Cumberland pl. Newgtn. butts
Powell Wm. lock, clasp, edging & corner manufacturer for account books, 4 Wardrobe place, Doctors' commons
Powell Wm. bookseller & statnr. 2 Newman's rw. Linc. inn fl
Powell Wm. engraver & enameller, 3 Rahere st. Goswell rd
Powell Wm. fellmonger & leather dresser, 4 Alfred rw. Spa rd
Powell Wm. grocer, 11 Rose & Crown ct. Eldon st. Finsbury
Powell Wm. pewterer, &c. 11 Church st. Shoreditch
Powell Wm. veterinary surgeon, 19½ Webb st. Bermondsy. st
Powell Wm. woolstapler, Russell st. Bermondsey
Powell Wm. Henry, pawnbroker, 16 Up. Park pl. Dorset sq
Power Alfred, bootmaker, 20 High st. Newington butts
Power David, barrister, 1 Cloisters, Temple
Power George, *Pitt's Head* P.H. Lucas st. Bethnal grn. rd
Power James, merchant, see Reis, Power & Co
Power John, physician, 9 Gt. Queen st. Westminster
Power John Arthur, physician, 37 Nelson square
Power John Hen. chemist & druggist, Denmark hl. Cmbrwl
Power John, stock & share broker, 1Copthall chambers, City
Power Mary (Mrs.), chemist & druggist, 56 Hackney road
Power Michael, *DukeofKent* P.H.2Peterst.Southwk.bdge.rd
Power Robert Francis, physician, 11 Queen st. Mayfair
Power Timothy Francis, merchant, 9 Hart st. Bloomsbury
Power Wm. *Victoria* P.H. Pomeroy st. Old Kent road
Power Wm. Henry, surgeon, 1 Tillotson place, Waterloo rd
Powers Chas. tailor & breeches ma. 5 Maddox st. Regent st
Powers Geo. stove range ma. 3 Louth's bldgs. Up. Ea. Smithfd
Powis John, mer. com. a. & in. brok. Lloyd's, & 3 Crooked la
Powis Littleton T. fruit meter, 19 Crimscott st. Bermondsey
Powis Thos. livery stables, 29 Grosvenor mews, Bond st
Powis Wm. barrister, 4 Carey st. Lincoln's inn
Powis Wm. carpenter & undertaker, 93 Drury lane
Powis Wm. ship & insurance agt. see Hodgson & Powis
Powis Wm. staymaker, 5 Lamb's Conduit st. Foundling
Powl Joseph, furniture broker, 13 Hatton wall
Powle Bevan, tea & coffee dealer, see Wyatt & Powle
Powles Brothers & Co. merchants, 13 Austinfriars
Powles George, hosier & outfitter, 44 Fleet st
Powles James, livery stable keeper, 34 East st. Red Lion sq
Powles James, *Three Tuns* P.H. 12 Cross st. Hatton garden
Powley Robert, dairyman, 1 Market st. Bloomsbury
Pownall & Cross, solicitors, 8 & 9 Staple inn, Holborn
Pownall Chas. Edw. solicitor, 28 Nicholas la. Lombard st
Pownall George, architect, &c. see Wigg & Pownall
Pownall George, fringe maker, 1 Stephen st. Tottenhm. ct. rd
Pownall George Hall, coal merchant, Dowgate wharf
Pownall George Hall, westind. mercht. 2 Adelaidepl. Lndn. bdg
Pownall John Fish, barrister, 19 Old square, Lincoln's inn
Pownall Robert Edward, proctor, 6 Great Knightrider st
Pownceby Henry, printer, 7 & 50 Cannon st. St. George st
Pownceby Jas. wholesale stationer, &c. 194 High st. Shadwell
Pownceby John, bookseller & binder, 277 Whitechapel road
Powneys Sarah (Mrs.), ladies' school, 7 Banner st. St. Luke's
Powsey Richard, *New Star & Crown* P.H. 3 Broadway, Westminster
Powter & Wright, coffee rooms, 7 Belmont row, Vauxhall
Powys Bransby Wm. solicitor, 8 Staple inn, Holborn
Powys Philip Lybbe, barrister, 2 Harcourt bldgs. Temple
Poynder (Thos.) & Medlicott (Edward), lime, tile & cement merchants, 18 Earl st. Blackfriars; Great Scotland yard; 7 north side, Paddington basin; Dockhead, Southwark; Grosvenor basin, Pimlico; & Cambridge heath, Hackney
Poynder Thos. Henry Allen, barrister, 13 New sq. Lincoln's inn
Poynter Ambrose, architect, 1 Poet's corner, Westminster
Poynter Chas. flourfactor, 30 Webb's Country tr. New Kent rd
Poynter John, coach builder, 18 Little Ormond yd. Queen sq
Poynter Thomas, meat salesman, 62 Aldgate High st
Poynter William, pallet jeweller, 28 King st. Goswell st
Poynter William, solicitor, 2 South square, Gray's inn
Poyntington John, dairyman, 26 Leather lane, Holborn
Poynton James, builder, Jamaica level, Bermondsey
Praed, Fane, Praed, & Johnston, bankers, 189 Fleet st
Pragh Joseph Van, straw & tuscan bonnet mr. 42 Gt. Alie st
Pragnell Ann E. (Mrs.), brass finisher, 98 Long la. Bermndsy
Prain David, fruiterer, 9 Cambridge place, Cambridge ter
Prall Thomas Willis, *King's Arms* P.H. 108 Edgware road
Prance Miles Hammett, barrister, 3 Gray's inn square
Prangnall Archibald Edwin, oil brok. 4 Union ct. Old Broad st
Prangnell Hannah (Mrs.), coffee rooms, 1 Hatton garden
Prangnell Moses, baker, 31 Westbourne st. Pimlico
Prangnell William, baker, 5 Little Chester st. Belgrave sq
Pratchell John Hall, linendpr. 1 Sydneypl. King's rd. Chelsea
Prater Charles & Co. army clothiers, cap & accoutrement makers, 2 Charing cross
Prater Joseph, grocer, 53 Long alley, Finsbury
Pratt Chas. T. & Son, desk & dress. case ma. 4 Vineyd. wlk. Clrkw
Pratt Saml. & Co. pat. wood carving works, Eccleston pl. Pmlc
Pratt & Stanbrough, wine & brandy merchts. 13 Berner's st
Pratt Ann (Mrs.), straw bonnet maker, 118 Tottenham ct. rd
Pratt Benjamin, coffee rooms, 5 Scott's place, Islington
Pratt Charles, butterman, 7 Upper Area, Hungerford mkt
Pratt Charles, fringe maker, 1 Knightsbridge terrace
Pratt Charles, watch & clock maker, 22 Lower st. Islington
Pratt Charlotte (Mrs.), haberdasher, 38 Chalton st. Somers tn
Pratt David, solicitor, 6 Raymond buildings, Gray's inn
Pratt David, solicitor, see Lawrence, Pratt & Crowdy
Pratt Edward, chemist, 25 Coventry st. Haymarket
Pratt Edward, decorator, 118 New Bond st
Pratt Eusebius, boot maker, 2 Up. North pl. Gray's inn road
Pratt Francis, boot maker, 28 Queen st. Chelsea
Pratt Frederic Thos. D.C.L. advocate, 2 College, Doctors' com
Pratt George, agent to John & W. Taylor, cotton spinners, Leicester, 4 Bow churchyard
Pratt George, bricklayer, 5 King's row, Knightsbridge
Pratt George, mason & slater, Stratford broadway
Pratt Henry, baker, Ford's buildings, Battersea
Pratt Henry, trunk & portmanteau manufr. 123 New Bond st
Pratt Hen. Wm. plumbr. & bldr. 2 South pl. Up. Kennington la
Pratt Jabez, ham & beef dealer, 76 Borough High st
Pratt John, bed sacking manufr. 1 Orchard st. St. Luke's
Pratt John, cattle salesman, 15 West Smithfield
Pratt John, dealer in crape, 12 Baldwin st. City road
Pratt John, harpist, 29 Beaumont st. Marylebone
Pratt John, merchant, see Rucker & Pratt
Pratt John, surgeon, Southampton st. Camberwell
Pratt John, tailor, 3 Redcross square, Cripplegate
Pratt John Adey, tailor, 8 Grey terrace, Great Dover road
Pratt John Tidd, barrister for savings' banks, friendly societies, &c. 5 Bolton st. Piccadilly
Pratt Jonas, chandler's shop, 12 Virginia row, Bethnal grn
Pratt Joseph, bootmaker, 74 Castle st. Southwark
Pratt Joseph, cheesemngr. 5 Wellington ter. Knsngtn. gl. pts
Pratt Michael, haircutter, 24 Cross st. Blackfriars rd
Pratt Newman, cheesemonger, 6 Eccleston st. South, Pimlico
Pratt Richard, baker, 29 Camden st. East st. Walworth rd
Pratt Rich. *Crown & Anchor* P.H. Cheshire st. Waterloo tn
Pratt Richard, pavior & nightman, 39 Gray's inn lane
Pratt Robert, beer retailer, 3 Crescent place, Brompton
Pratt Samuel, jun. cabinet maker, upholsterer & imp. of ancient furniture, armour, &c. 47 New Bond st. & 3 Grosvenor st
Pratt Samuel, sen. camp equipage manufactory, & patentee of the new patent compendium for travelling, 19 Cockspur street, Charing cross
Pratt Sarah (Mrs.), milliner, 18 Davies st. Berkeley sq
Pratt Thomas, army agent, 29 Parliament st
Pratt Thomas, carpent. & underta. 2 Mount rw. Liverpool rd
Pratt Thomas, fringe manufr. 13 Gt. Pulteney st. Golden sq
Pratt Thomas, grocer, 22 Ship yard

Pratt Thomas, ham dealer, 25 Beckford row, Walworth rd
Pratt Thomas, shoemaker, 43 Clipstone st. Fitzroy square
Pratt Wm. beer retailer, 14 William st. New Kent road
Pratt Wm. cheesemonger, 2 Victoria pl. Queen's rd. Dalston
Pratt Wm. grocer, 33 Marchmont st. Brunswick square
Pratt Wm. ham & beef dealer, 183 Borough High st
Pratt Wm. physician, 34 Southampton bldngs. Chancery la
Pratt Wm. *Rose & Crown* P.H. 15 Crown st. Soho
Pratt Wm. K. *White Horse* P.H. 59 Baldwins gardens
Prayer Book & Homily Society (Rev. Francis Dollman, sec. Thomas Seaward, visiting secretary & agent), 1 Exeter hall, 372 Strand
Preater Alfred, hairdresser, 4 College terrace, Chelsea
Prebble Charles, perfumer, 14 New Church st. Lisson grove
Prebble Edward, coffee rooms, 2 Bridge st. Southwark
Prebble Elgar, meat salesman, 11 Newgate market
Prebble Thos. deputy registrar, Camberwell grove
Prebble Wm. grocer, 25 Elizabeth ter. Cloudesley sq
Preddy Wm. beer retailer, 1 Lansdowne ter. Caledonian rd
Preece Caleb, tobacconist, 4 Glo'ster ter. Vauxhall bdge. rd
Preece Richard, *Grapes* P.H. 31 Gt. Suffolk st. Borough
Preece Richard, *Windsor Castle* P.H. 114 Gt. Suffolk st. Boro'
Preece Wm. *Hole in the Wall* P.H. 45 Chancery lane
Preedy Charles, builder, 10 Hare walk, Hoxton Old town
Preedy Charles James, surgeon, 18 St. John st. road
Preedy John, hatter, 2 Fleet st
Prehn Thos. merchant, 4 Brabant court Philpot lane
Preist Saml. & Henry, poulterers, 11 Gt. Marylebone st
Preist John, razor maker & cutler, 253 Oxford st
Preist John, tailor, 48 Goswell st
Preist Robert, cowkeeper, 1 Hill road, St. John's wood
Preist Wm. trunk manufacturer, 3 King's row, Pimlico
Preller Charles Aug. iron & tin plate mercht. 14 Eastcheap
Prendergast Harris, barrister, 4 Old sq. Lincoln's inn
Prendergast Michael, barrister, 32 Castle st. Holborn
Prenter Wm. baker, 27 York st. Portman square
Prentice Samuel & Co. hemp, linen & yarn mers. 9 Mincing la
Prentice Charles, bootmaker, 74 Charlotte st. Portland pl
Prentice George, butcher, 5 Knightsbridge green
Prentice John, confectioner, 12 Cheapside
Prentice John, jun. confectioner, 28 Hedge row, Islington
Prentice Saml. attorney, 13 Bedford sq. Commercial rd. east
Prentice Samuel, barrister, 4 Essex court, Temple
Prentice Wm. Jee, meat & butter slsmn. 24, 25 & 2 Newgate mkt
Prentis Chas. pork butcher, 177 Bermondsey st
Prentis Frank, teadealer & grocer, 1 Folly, Dockhead
Prentis Henry Ward, cheesemonger, Deptford Broadway
Prerogative Court Office, College sq. Doctors' commons; hours 10 to 4
Prerogative (Will) Office, 6 Great Knightrider st.; hours of busines, Feb. Mar. April, May, June, July, Aug. & Sept. 9 to 4; Oct. Nov. Dec. & Jan 9 to 3
Presbury George, artist, 19 Rodney st. Pentonville
Presentation Office Quality ct. Chancery lane (Jos. L. Bolton, esq. dep. clerk); hours 10 to 4
Prescott, Grote, Ames & Cave, bankers, 62 Threadneedle st
Prescott Ann (Mrs.), chandler's shop, 83 Cromer st. Bruns. sq
Prescott Henry, painter, 11 Upper Spring st. Marylebone
Prescott Henry James, merchant, see Rew, Prescott & Co
Prescott John, printer, 8 Turnagain lane, Farringdon st
Prescott Stephen, leatherseller, 11 Keen's row, Walworth rd
Preserver Fire & Life Office (John Widowson, sec.), 3 Bond court, Walbrook
Presidy Alfred & Co. importers of french silks, blonds, lace, shawls &c. 10 Huggin lane, Wood st. Cheapside
Presland Saml. & Co. manchester wa. 5 Castle ct. Lawrence la
Presland John, bootmaker, Stratford broadway
Presland John, hat lining cutter & hat & cap trimming warehouse, 42 Lit. Charlotte st. Blackfriars road
Presland John, *Three Crowns* P.H. 3 Well st. St. James's
Presland Samuel, hatter & cockade ma. 48 College st. Chelsea
Presland Wm. tailor & draper, 201 Tottenham court road
Presley William, wine cooper, &c. 94 John st. Fitzroy sq
Press Dinah (Miss), stock ma. 76 Manchester st. Gray's inn rd
Press James, cowkeeper, 43 Drummond crescent, Euston sq
Press Thomas Richard, grocer, 1 Broomfields, Deptford
Press William, *Duke of Richmond* P.H. Queen's rd. Dalston
Pressler Mary (Mrs.), dyer, 98 Pread st. Edgware rd
Pressley Timothy, herbalist, 25 Triangle, Kennington cross
Prestage Charlt. (Mrs.), strawbont. ma. 21 Brnswk. st. Hkny. rd
Prestage John Thos. lock maker, see Bramah, Prestage & Co
Prested Fred. Osmond, *Monmouth Hd* P.H. 40 Castle st. Lei. sq
Prestige Sarah (Mrs.), tobacconist, 5½ Scotts pl. Lr. rd. Islngtn
Prestige Thomas, linen & woollen draper, 111 Long acre
Preston Hen. & Son, who. druggists, 94 St. John st. Smithfield
Preston Ann (Mrs.), wireworker, 113 Snow's fields, Bermondsy
Preston William & John, leather breeches makers & tailors, by appointment, to her Majesty's household, & H. R. H Prince Albert, 126 New Bond st
Preston Barthlmw. cooper, 21 Church st. Newtown, Mile end
Preston Benj. work. silversmith, 41 Coppice row, Clerkenwell
Preston Charles, furniture dealer, appraiser & house agent, 1 Wych st. Strand
Preston Edward, artist, 31 Burlington arcade
Preston George, saddler, 2 Grove lane, Camberwell
Preston Grant, nautical brazier & manufctr. of patent cabin stoves, ventilating deck lights, binnacles, & improved side scuttles, &c. compass maker to her Majesty & the Royal yacht squadron, &c. 2 Union row, Minories
Preston Henry John, solicitor, see Elmslie & Preston
Preston Hen. Mark, tea dealer & grocer, 106 Goswell st
Preston Jabez, hop & seed factor, 10 & 11 Counter st. Boro'
Preston James, italian warehouse, 88 Oxford st
Preston James, earthenware dlr. 4 Grove lane, Camberwell
Preston John, chandler's shop, Southampton st. Camberwl
Preston John, indigo broker, 4 Fen court, Fenchurch st
Preston John, solicitor, 12 Tokenhouse yard
Preston John Kerrison, surgeon, 8 Osnaburgh st. Regent's pk
Preston Ralph, book edge gilder, 28 Maiden la. Covent garden
Preston Richard, oriental pickle depôt, 38 Leicester square
Preston Samuel, dairyman, 13 John st. Liverpool road
Preston Samuel Tolver, barrister, 12 New Boswell ct. Carey st
Preston Samuel Waterhouse, chemist, 48 Cross st. Islington
Preston Sarah (Mrs.), baker, 16 South Lambeth
Preston Thomas, *Coborn Arms* P.H. 4 Coborn rd. Mile end rd
Preston Thomas, herbalist, 141 Union st. Borough High st
Preston William, grocer, 48 Burton st. Burton crescent
Preston Wm. Stephen, appraiser, &c. 2 Rupert st. Haymarket
Preston Wm. Thomas, barrister, 2 Figtree court, Temple
Prestwell Thomas, bootmaker, 44 William st. Regent's park
Prestwich Joseph, jun. & Co. wine & spirit merchts. 20 Mark la
Prestwidge Samuel, grocer, &c. 13 Belton st. Long acre
Preswell Thos. carpenter, 6 Lit. Albany st. Regent's park
Preteer Catherine (Mrs.), clothes dlr. 29 Churchway, Som. tn
Pretious Thomas Mason, hatter, 3 Piccadilly
Prettejohn Edward, cider mer. 3 Morgan's la.; 79 Tooley st
Pretty Daniel, tailor, 39 Margaret st. Cavendish square
Pretty Dan. trimg. sell. & piece br. 17 Brewer st. Golden sq.
Pretty Geo. W. surgeon, &c. 14 Manchester ter. Liverpool rd
Pretty John, *Cornwall Arms* P.H. 76 Cornwall rd. Lambeth
Pretty Thomas, fruiterer, 10 Chapel st. Somers town
Pretty Thomas, potato dealer, 47 Cross st. Islington, & 10 Chapel st. Somers town
Pretty William, surgeon, Maude cottage, Mornington road
Pretty Walter Brown, linendraper, 4 Thurlow pl. Hackney rd
Prettyman Robert S. *Saracen's Head* inn, 7 Camomile st
Pretyman & Rixon, booksellers & stationers, 29 Poultry
Pretyman Sarah (Mrs.), milliner, 25 Holles st. Cavendish sq
Pretyman Daniel Green, merchant, see Bartrum & Pretyman
Previtali Luigi, lodging house, 15 Arundel st. Panton sq
Prevo Mark, wig maker, 100 St. Martin's lane, Charing cross
Prevo Mark, jun. hairdresser, 416 Strand
Prevost George, vice-consl. for Switzerland, 24A, Gresham st
Prevost James, merchant, 29 St. Swithin's lane
Prevost James L. wadding & cotton ma. 43 Lisle st. Leicester sq
Prevost John Lewis, agent & consul general for Switzerland, 24A, Gresham st
Prevost Louis A. teacher of languages, 122 Crawford st
Prew Benjamin, tailor & outfitter, 36 & 37 Aldgate High st. & 295 High Holborn
Pribble Friend James, butcher, 70 Leather lane, Holborn
Price & Bolton, attorneys, 1 New square, Lincoln's inn
Price Brothers, merchants, 52 & 53 St. Mary Axe
Price & Brown, stock & share brokers, 4 Change alley
Price Sir Chas. bart. Marryat & Co. bankers, 3 King Wm. st. City
Price Chas. & Co. merchants; turpentine, rosin, pitch & tar manufactrs. William st. Blackfriars; oil merchants & seed crushers, Milwall, Poplar
Price Chas. & Co. pin manufs. 37 Edmund pl. Aldersgate st
Price Charlotte & Son, cheesemongers, 124 Bishopsgate wtht
Price & Co. perfumers to the royal family, 28 Lombard st
Price David & Co. woollen warehousemn. 3 Huggin la. Wood st
Price Danl. Kerl & Co. patentees of the white leghorns, imprs. of french blonds, & all kinds of fancy goods, 33 Ludgate st
Price Edwd. & Co. patent candle mfy. Belmont, Vauxhall
Price Edw. & Philip, mattress ma. 15 Printer's pl. Bermndsy
Price, Gifford & Co. colonial & east india brokers, 5 Mincing la
Price & Gosnell (now John Gosnell & Co.), manufacturing perfumers & soap makers; sole patentees of Johnstone's royal pat. windsor soap, 12 Three King court, Lombard st
Price Joseph & Co. coffin furniture ma. 12 King st. Snowhill

Price John Blount & Edward Flower, corn & coal merchants & granary keepers, 6 Macclesfield st. north, City road
Price Wm. F. & Son, army agents, 34 Craven st. Strand
Price Current Office(London Mercantile),9Liverpl.st.City
Price Current Office(London New),42Mincing la.Fench.st
Price Current Office (Prince's),42 Mincing la. Fench. st
Price Allen Ford, surgeon, Deptford High st
Price Ann (Mrs.), *Duke of York* P.H. 202 Blackfriars road
Price Ann (Mrs.), earthenware dealer, 5 Boro' market
Price Ann (Mrs.), *Griffin* P.H. 9 Leonard st. Finsbury
Price Benj. solicitor, 17 Ironmonger lane
Price Charles, butcher, 6 Gilbert's passage, Clare market
Price Charles, coal dealer, 25 Earl st. east, Lisson gr. north
Price Charles, dining rooms, 16 Drury lane
Price Charles, glass bender, 20 Clerkenwell green
Price Charles, ship smith, 2 Stephen's acre, Blackwall
Price Charles Berbage, jeweller, 34 Duke st. Manchester sq
Price Charles John, manufacturing chemist, Battersea
Price Daniel, tobacconist, 162 Bishopsgate st
Price Daniel, sen. pat. of the white leghorns, imp. of french flowers, fancy gds.& ostrich feath.ma. 6 Pilgrim st.Ldgt.st
Price David, dairyman, 12 Conduit st. Paddington
Price David, tailor, see Davies & Price
Price Edward, fruiterer, 7 Mason's alley, Basinghall st
Price Edward, furniture broker, 91 Golden lane, St. Luke's
Price Edward, grocer, 2 Brett terrace, Hampstead road
Price Edward Eastman, baker, 81 Upper Ebury st. Pimlico
Price Edw. John, emery & gl. paper ma.8 Church st. Spitalfl
Price Edwin Plumer, barrister, 2 Inner Temple lane
Brice Edwd. Wm. blackwell hall factor, 28 Basinghall st
Price Fras. furniture brkr. 9 Westmorland bdgs. Aldersgate st
Price Frederick, grocer, 10 Blackmoor st. Clare market
Price Frederick, tea dealer, 51 Bishopsgate without
Price Frederick Jsph. watch & clock ma.24 Queen st. Gldn. sq
Price George, bird stuffer, 42 Cannon st. St. George's east
Price George, builder, see Dennis & Price
Price George, cheesemonger, 108 Praed st. Paddington
Price George, grocer, 35 Gt. Titchfield st. Oxford st
Price George, solicitor, 6 Throgmorton st
Price George, tailor, 44 Castle st. east, Oxford st
Price George, teadealer, 39 Upper Berkeley st. Portman sq
Price George Wm. wine merchant, see White & Price
Price Hannah (Mrs.), haberdasher, 51 Houndsditch
Price Henry, *African Chief* P.H. 37 Wilsted st. Somers tn
Price Henry, mathemat. instrument ma. 58 Brook st. Lmbh
Price Henry, soapmaker, 23 Princes sq. Ratcliff highway
Price Henry C. engineer & patentee of ventilating & warming apparatus, 2 Derby street, Parliament st
Price James, sheffield agent, 4 Bolt court, Fleet st
Price James, baker, 149½ Tottenham court road
Price James, bookbinder & stationer, 21 Chiswell st
Price James, coffee rooms, 10 Adam st. west, Bryanstone sq
Price James, enameller&writer on glass,7 Bridge rd. Lambeth
Price James, *Green Dragon* P.H. 3 Villiers st. Strand
Price James, *King's Head* P.H. Wells mews, Wells st. Oxford st
Price James, linendraper, 33 Gt. Queen st. Lincoln's inn flds
Price James, *Stag tavern*, Portland terr. Wandsworth road
Price James, writer on glass, 2 Manchester bldgs. Westmr
Price Jane (Mrs.), grocer, 6 David st. Marylebone
Price Jane (Mrs.), grocer, &c. 5 Holland st. Kensington
Price John, appraiser & furniture dlr. 100 Whitechapel road
Price John, bedstead maker, 21 Brooke st. Holborn
Price John, *Belle Sauvage hotel*, Belle Sauv. yd. 38 Ludgate hl
Price John, boot & shoe maker, 2 Lime st. passage
Price John, butcher, 10 Lucas pl.&3 King's Arms pl. Com.rd.east
Price John, carpenter, see Pemberton & Price
Price John, grocer, 122 Shadwell High st
Price John, pork butcher, 11 King pl. Commercial road east
Price John, *Queen's Head* P.H. 20 Pitfield st. Hoxton
Price John, smith & bell hanger, 46 Praed st. Paddington
Price John, teadealer & grocer, 21 Cotton st. Poplar
Price John, *Three Mackerel* P.H. Hope place, Mile end rd
Price John Dutton, solicitor, 4 King's road, Bedford row
Price John Hen. brass mfr. 24 Wyndham st. Bryanstone sq
Price Joseph, butcher, 1 Brandon row, Newington causeway
Price Joseph, cabinet maker, 59 Crown st. Finsbury
Price Joseph, machine ruler, 11 Bullin court, 408 Strand
Price Joseph, tailor, 10 Church st. Camberwell
Price Joseph, thimble manufr. 49 Red Lion st. Clerkenwell
Price Lewis, fishmonger, 26 Strutton ground, Westminster
Price Mary (Mrs.), dairy, 33 Cursitor st. Chancery lane
Price Mary (Mrs.), dining rooms, 79 Broad st. Ratcliff cross
Price Nehemiah S. accountant & coml.agt. 9 Liverpool st. City
Price Owen, boot & shoe maker, 1 Earl st. Kensington
Price Ralph, treasurer, Bridewell hospital, 14 New Bridge st
Price Rees, cheesemonger, 18 Conduit st. Paddington
Price Rees, merchant, 39 Clement's lane, Lombard st
Price Richard, Alexander, barrister, 3 Brick court, Temple
Price Robert, calico printer, see Partridge & Price
Price Robert, watchmaker, 36 Pitfield st. Hoxton
Price Robert Alexander, attorney, 14 John st. Adelphi
Price Sarah (Miss), grocer, 11 King's road, St. Pancras
Price Sarah (Mrs.), chandler's shop, 10 Charles st. St. Geo's. ea
Price Selina (Miss), millinr. &c. 65 Conduit st. New Bond st
Price Simon, tailor, see Froeschlen & Price
Price Thomas, beer retailer, Blue Anchor rd. Bermondsey
Price Thomas, butcher, 29 Langley pl. Commercial rd. east
Price Thomas, butcher, 20 Kingsgate st. Holborn
Price Thomas, dairyman, 7 Bride lane, Fleet st
Price Thomas, *Flying Horse* P.H. 53 Milton st. Cripplegate
Price Thomas, furniture broker, 17 Gt. Wild st. Drury lane
Price Dr. Thomas (sec. of *Dissenters & Gen. Life & Fire Insurance Co.*), 62 King William st. City
Price Thomas, veterinary surgeon, 99 Park st. Kengtn. cross
Price Thomas Elliott, auctioneer, 48 Chancery lane
Price Vincent, straw hat maker, inventor & manufacturer of the italonian pressing machine, rewarded by the Society of Arts, & inventor of the new manumotive carriage, 33 Wardour st
Price Walter, tailor, 9 Alfred st. Bedford sq
Price Wm. appraiser & undertaker, 5 New Park st. Boro'
Price Wm. artist, 46 Warren st. Fitzroy sq
Price Wm. boot & shoe maker, 46 Gt. Prescot st. Goodman's fi
Price Wm. butcher, 36 James st. Buckngham gate
Price Wm. coffee rooms, 14 Poland st. Oxford st
Price Wm. dairyman, 25 Croydon st. Bryanstone sq
Price Wm. east india agt. & mer. see Mangles, Price & Moore
Price Wm. fruiterer, 4 Hawley place, Kentish town
Price Wm. lodging house, 2 Manchester blds. Westminster
Price Wm. oilman, Albion pl. east, Battle bridge
Price Wm. pork butcher, 2 Gloucester pl. Walworth common
Price Wm. tallow chandler, 31 Great Saffron hill
Price Wm. Archer, working jellewer, 122 London wall
Price Wm. Lillwall, statnr. & bkslr. 16 Conduit st. Paddngtn
Price Wm. Thomas, solicitor, 36 Up. George st. Edgware rd
Prichard & Collette, attorneys, 57 Lincoln's inn fields
Prichard Henry & Son, brush makers, 15 & 35 Newgate st
Prichard Charles, furniture bro. 3 Crescent st. Euston sq
Prichard Daniel, coal merchant, Great Scotland yard
Prichard George Berry, solicitor, 4 Gt. Winchester st. City
Prichard Henry, commission agent, 81 Watling st
Prichard John, upholsterer, &c. 23 Cleveland st. Fitzroy sq
Prichard John, upholsterer, 11 Providence row, Finsbury
Prichard Wm. chemist (& baths), 23 King st. Westminster
Prichard Wm. shoemak. 16 William st. Charlotte st. Blkfrs
Prichard Wm. B. civil engineer, 24 & 27 Wilmington sq. & 15 St. John's wood road, Regent's park
Prichard Wm. Davis, oilman & grocer, 4 Lyall pl. Eaton sq. & 36 Devonshire st. Portland pl
Prichard Wm. Taylor, solicitor, see Mardon & Prichard
Prickett Fredk. auctioneer& valr. 14 Wandsworth rd. Vauxhll
Prickett Geo. surveyor, &c. 12 Southampton blds. Chancery la
Prickett Geo. jun. auctioneer & surveyor, 14 Lincoln's inn fields, & 12 Southampton buildings, Chancery lane
Prickett Thomas, butcher, 2 Pomeroy st. Old Kent road
Prickett Warren, butcher, 34 Old Gravel lane, Wapping
Prictor Wm. cabinetmaker, 3 Waterloo ter. Commercial rd
Priday Wm. turner & stationer, 4 King st. Holborn
Pridden John, grocer, 2 Sol's row, Hampstead road
Priddey Mary Ann (Mrs.), chndlr's. shop, 54 Salisbury st. Liss. gr
Priddle Benj. boot & shoe ma. 7 Gt. Carlisle st. Portmn. mkt
Priddle Benjamin, boot & shoe maker, 149 Edgware rd
Priddle Edward, coffee rooms, 35 Wych st. Strand
Priddle James, tailor, 3 Wilson st. Gray's inn rd
Priddle Robert, shoemaker, 47 Leather lane, Holborn
Priddle Thos. jun. carpenter & buildr. 28 Cross st. Islington
Priddle Wm. *Phœnix* P.H. 1 Palace st. Pimlico
Priddy Johanna & Son, cheesemongrs. 7 Dockhead, Brmsy
Pride Alexander, potato agent, Hay's wharf, Tooley st
Pride Robert, fruiterer, 4 Leigh st. Burton crescent
Prideaux Charles Greville, barrister, 2 Elm court, Temple
Prideaux Frederick, barrister, 28 Chancery lane
Prideaux H. (Mrs.), veterinary surgeon, Phœnix yd. Oxford st
Prideaux Peter, carpenter, 64 Chamber st. Leman st
Prideaux Walter, solicitor, see Lane & Prideaux
Prideaux W. sec. to the Assam Company, 57 Old Broad st. City
Pridgeon Augustus Fredk. bootma. 44 Gt. St. Andrew st. 7 dials
Pridmore Joseph, academy, 13 Windmill pl. Camberwell rd
Prier James, grocer, 5 Leicester pl. Camberwell New road
Priest & Scott, linendrapers, 42 & 43 Goswell road
Priest Benjamin, chemist, &c. 14 Parliament st. Westminster
Priest Frederick, pawnbroker, 141 & 142 Long acre

Priest John, furniture broker, 6 Angel pl. New rd. Pentonville
Priest John, jun. coffee&dining rooms, 30 Gibson st. Lambeth
Priest Right John, last ma. &c. 1 White Lion st. Norton Folgt
Priest Wm. uphlstr. & auctnr. 17&24 Water st. New Bridge st
Priest William, upholsterer, see Prichard & Priest
Priestley John, wax chandler, see Timberlake & Priestley
Priestley Sarah (Mrs.), city carman, 38 Glo'ster st. Coml. rd
Priestley Thomas Potter, importer of dutch rushes. & chair manufacturer, & city carman, 3 & 4 Market st. Finsbury
Priestman Wm. butcher, 22 Newport court, Newport mkt
Priestnall Edward, trimming seller, 64 Red cross st. Boro'
Prime Benjamin, teadealer, 4 Bishopsgate without
Prime Cornelius, builder, 40 Alfred st. City road
Prime David, bricklayer, 10 King's row, New rd. Pentonville
Prime David, bricklayer, 61 St. John st. Clerkenwell
Prime Jsph. cheese factor & provision mercht. 34 Eastcheap
Prime Joseph, tobacconist, 40 Fore st. Cripplegate
Prime Samuel, cabinet maker, 14 Lower road, Islington
Prime Thos. plater on british plate, 49 Salisbury square
Prime William, baker, 24 Alfred st. City road
Prime William, builder, 8 Brunswick st. Hackney road
Prin & Surridge, coach builders, 30 Church st. Camberwell
Prince & Co. who. clothrs. outftrs. & slopslrs. 11 Leadenhl. st
Prince Alexander, office for procuring patents of invention, & for registration of designs, 14 Lincoln's inn fields
Prince Azariah, *White Horse* P.H. 3 Grove, Church st. Hkny
Prince George, lodging house, 8 & 9 New Palace yard, Westmr
Prince George, turner, 50 Holland st. Blackfriars road
Prince James, tailor, 26 Change alley, Cornhill
Prince John, brush & toy wareho. 16 Southampton rw. Newrd
Prince John, grocer, 8 Prince's place, Commercial rd. east
Prince John, plumber & glazier, 16 Southampton row, New rd
Prince John, wholesale stationer, 27 Bread st. Cheapside
Prince Mary (Mrs.), livery stables, 5 Gower mews, Bedfd. sq
Prince Richard, baker, 24 Henry st. Portland town
Prince S. Augusta (Miss), prof. of dncing. 27 Edwards st. Ptm. sq
Prince Thomas, cabinet ma. 13 Leathersellers' bldgs. Lndn. wl
Prince Thomas, carman, 59 Bermondsey st
Prince Thomas, cheesemonger, 68 Newington causeway
Prince William, tailor, 10 Short's buildings, Clerkenwell
Prince William, drum battledore m. 28 York st. Kingslnd. rd
Princess's Theatre, 73 Oxford st
Pring John, baker, 25 Brooke st. Holborn
Pring John, plumber, Battersea fields
Pring Susannah (Mrs.), butcher, 17 Blackmoor st. Clare mkt
Pring Thos. Jas. architect & surv. 33 Bouverie st. Fleet st
Pring William, *Blue Last* P.H. 7 Gt. Distaff la. Friday st
Pring William, boot maker, 4 Francis st. Golden square
Pringle Ed. G. *Bank of Friendship* P.H. Bagcrofts pl. Mile ed
Pringle Eleanor (Mrs.), *White Horse* P.H. 69 Wapping wall
Pringle Isabel (Mrs.), lace wa. 4 Hertford ter. King's rd. Chls
Pringle James, engraver & chaser, 9 President st. west
Pringle John, grocer & teadealer, 77 Bishopsgate without
Pringle John, pastrycook, 8 St. Agnes ter. Tabernacle sq
Pringle Robert, baker, Regent place, Globe road, Mile end
Pringle Wm. solicitor, see Meggison, Pringle & Co
Pringuer William H. butcher, 27 King st. Tower hill
Prior, Turner & Co. merchts. 42 Com. sale rooms, Mincing la
Prior Asher, ironmonger, 51 Marchmont st. Brunswick sq. & 2 King's row, Pimlico
Prior Charles, hairdresser, 13 Little Bell alley, Moorgate st
Prior Cornelius Winter, oilman, &c. Camberwell green
Prior Edward, outfitter & hosier, 13 Finsbury place north
Prior Frederick, coffee rooms, 24 Market st. May fair
Prior Henry, linendraper, 72 Hackney road
Prior Jas. confectnr. & tobaccon. 2 Park side, Knightsbrdg
Prior John Venn, barrister, 9 Old square, Lincoln's inn
Prior John Wm. silversmith & jeweller, 67 Newngtn. causeway
Prior Jonathan Charles, coal merchant, 153 Up. Thames st
Prior Richard, surgeon, 9 Marlborough pl. Walworth road
Prior Richard Arber, builder, 33 Newman st
Prior Samuel, tailor, High st. Kingsland
Prior Stephen, silk & worsted dlr. 10 Broad ct. Long acre
Prior Thomas, boot & shoe ma. 8 St. John's la. West Smithfield
Prior Thomas, coal dealer, 81½ Drury lane
Prior Thomas R. coal mercht. Union whf. Kingsland rd. basin
Prior Thomas Young, barrister, 1 Elm court, Temple
Prior Wm. bootmaker, 25 Little Moorfields
Prior Wm. bootmaker, 32 Wilderness row, Clerkenwell
Prior Wm. carver & gilder, 14 South row, New road
Prior Wm. confectioner, 105 Blackfriars rd. & 119 Newgate st
Pritchard Edward & Co. cigar manufrs. 54 Bartholomew close
Pritchard Henry & North, hatmaks. 31 Stamford st. Blckfrs. rd
Pritchard & Son, proctors, 18 Gt. Knightrider st. Docrs. coms
Pritchard Brothers (T. N. & R.), importers & manufacturers of tobacco, snuff & cigars, 100 London wall
Pritchard Andrew, optician, 162 Fleet st
Pritchard Benjamin, *Talbot* P.H. Mortimer rd. Kingsland
Pritchard Charles, tobacconist, 4 Rufford's bldgs. Islington
Pritchard Chas. plumber, &c. 4 East pl. Walcot pl. Lambeth
Pritchard Charles Edward, hatter, 12 Rotherhithe
Pritchard Daniel, coal dealer, 9 South st. South Audley st
Pritchard Ebenezer, law stationer, 6 Symond's inn
Pritchard Edward, attorney, 9 Staple inn, Holborn
Pritchard Edward, attorney, 35 Tavistock pl. Tavistock sq
Pritchard Edward, carpenter & builder, 15 Warwick lane, & 1 St. John's court, King st. Snowhill
Pritchard George, stationer, 14 Sherrard st. Golden sq
Pritchard George, tailor, 20 Palace st. Pimlico
Pritchard George, turner, 87 Earl st. east, Lisson grove
Pritchard Henry, bootmaker, 46 Collingwood st. Blkfrs. rd
Pritchard Henry, *Percy* livery stables, 41 Percy st. Tott. ct. rd
Pritchard James, butcher, 17 Seymour place, Camden town
Pritchard James, fruiterer, 4 John st. west, Edgware rd
Pritchard James, tailor & draper, 6 Deptford Broadway
Pritchard James, tailor, 36 Mary st. New road
Pritchard Jane (Mrs.), builder, &c. 29 Steward st. Spitalfields
Pritchard John, barrister, 52 Lincoln's inn fields
Pritchard John, *Black Lion* P.H. 6 Bishopsgate within
Pritchard, John, carver & gilder, 23 Exeter st. Lisson grove
Pritchard John, cheesemonger, 4 Norris st. Haymarket
Pritchard John, *Dock House* P.H. 4 East India road, Poplar
Pritchard John (Mrs.), fruiterer, 52 Gt. Portland st. Oxford st
Pritchard Joseph, tailor, 12 South row, New road
Pritchard Mary Elizth. (Miss), dressma. 25 Davies st. Brkly. sq
Pritchard Moses, *Fountain* P.H. 9 King st. Seven dials
Pritchard Peter, hair cutter, 18 Coppice row, Clerkenwell
Pritchard Robert Thos. tailor, 9 Jermyn st. St. James's
Pritchard Samuel, butcher, 70 Park st. Camden town
Pritchard Sarah (Mrs.), fruiterer, 22 Adams rw. Hampstead rd
Pritchard Thomas, fruiterer, 30 Guildford place, Spitalfields
Pritchard Thomas, *Independent* P.H. 24 Brewer st. Somers tn
Pritchard Thomas, oil & hop merchant, 30 West Smithfield
Pritchard Thos. K. surgeon, 20 Manchester st. Manchester sq
Pritchard Wm. proctor, high bailiff of Southwark, 18 Great Knightrider st. & 6 College, Doc. com. & Town hall, Sthwk
Pritchett Charles, surgeon, 6 Limekiln hill, Limehouse
Pritchett Chas. Evans, ready made linen wareh. 443 Stand
Pritchett Edward, hosier & outfitter, 26 Strand
Pritchett Humphrey, stock & share brok. 74 Old Broad st
Pritchett John Thos. tea brok. see Parker, Son & Pritchett
Pritchett Martha (Mrs.), academy, 20 Parker's ter. Ncknger. rd
Pritchett Rd. Ellis, gun manf. 59 Chamber st. Goodman's flds
Pritchett Thomas, stationer, &c. 5 Windsor pl. Old Kent rd
Pritchett William, furniture warehouse, 204 High Holborn
Pritchitt James, jun. brush maker, 79 Kent st. Borough
Pritchitt John, sen. brush maker, 220 Kent st. Borough
Pritt George, solicitor, see Burke, Pritt, Venables & Co
Private Bill Office, House of Commons, 2 Parliament st
Privy Council Office, Downing st.; hours, 11 to 4
Privy Seal & Signet Office, 28 Abingdon st.; hours, 10 to 3
Prizeman Thos. teadealer, &c. 12 Cross st. Hoxton new town
Prizeman Thomas, grocer & teadealer, 27 East road, City rd
Prizer Wolfe, clothes salesman, 102 Chalton st. Somers town
Probart Robt. Henry, brassfounder, 49 Seward st. Goswell st
Probert Edward, butcher, 16 Great Bath st. Clerkenwell
Probin John, gun & pistol maker, 11 Agar st. Strand
Probin Thos. Foy, tallow chandlr. 17 Cross st. Newngtn. butts
Probutt John, butcher, 19 Shepherd's ct. Shepherd's market
Probyn Thomas, *Black Horse & Swan* P.H. 9 Blackman st. Boro.'; & *Three Compasses* P.H. 146 High Holborn
Probyn Wm. oil & italian warehouse, 35 Lower Belgrave st
Prockter Elizh. (Mrs.), painter & glazier, 13 Ivy la. Newgt. st
Prockter Charles, beer retailer, Battersea fields
Prockter Geo. *Catherine Wheel* P.H. 10&11 Union st. Boro'
Prockter Henry, *Britannia* P.H. Grove st. Deptford
Prockter Henry, turner, &c. 12 Dean st. Westminster
Prockter James Simpson, glue maker, Fort place, Bermondsy
Procktor William, poulterer, Frederick place, Mile end road
Procter Joseph & Percy, tobacco mfrs. 197 Bishopsgt. witho
Procter Bryan Waller, barrister, 4 Gray's inn square
Procter Christopher solicitor, see Tatham & Procter
Procter Elizabeth (Miss), lodging house, 10 Pall mall east
Procter Elizabeth (Mrs.), plumber, 59 Shoe lane, Fleet st
Procter Henry, butcher, 77 Goswell road
Procter John, cheesemonger, 94 Tottenham court road
Procter John, furniture printer, see Curling & Procters
Procter John, *White Swan* P.H. 7 Temple st. Whitefriars
Procter Joseph, furniture printer, see Curling & Procters
Procter Robert, cheesemonger, see Todd & Procter
Procter Robert, wharfinr. 16 Whf. South side, Paddington ba
Procter William, bootmaker, 17 Exeter st. Strand

Procter William, cheesemonger, 19 Comrc. pl. Old Kent rd
Proctor Francis, omnibus proprietor, 28 Lisson grove north
Proctor Henry, upholsterer, 27 Newman st. Oxford st
Proctor James, cheesemonger, 51 Up. Lisson st. Lisson grove
Proctor James, plumber, &c. 1 Sherborne pl. Blandford sq
Proctor John, physician, 17 Whitehead's grove, Chelsea
Proctor Joseph, beer retailer, 84 Aldersgate st
Proctor Richard, butcher, 79 St. John st. Clerkenwell
Proctor Robert, alderney dairy, 9 Perceval st. Clerkenwell
Proctor Samuel, M.D. surgeon, 7 Norland place, Notting hill
Proctor Sarah (Mrs.), fruit saleswoman, Borough market
Proctor Thos. Benj. M.D. surgeon, 6 Clarence pl. Clamp rd
Professional & Commercial Detector Association (John Simpson, secretary), 25 Moorgate st
Proger Maria (Mrs.), lodging ho. 9 Sussex st. Tottcn. ct. rd
Prohowsky Jacob, tailor & outfitter, 101 Up. EastSmithfield
Prole Scales & Co. merchants, 3 Dunster court, Mincing la
Promoter Life Assurance & Annuity Company (M. Saward, sec.), 9 Chatham place, Blackfriars; see page 2042
Properjohn John, butcher, 49 Charlotte terrace, New cut
Properjohn William, butcher, 170 Drury lane
Propert John, brushmak. mnfr. of breeches paste, boot top powder, blacking, &imp. of french varnish, 22 Sth. Audley st
Propert John, surgeon, 6 New Cavendish st. Portland place
Property & Income Tax Special Commissioners' Office, 9 Lancaster place, Waterloo bridge; hours 10 to 4
Property & Income Tax Office, Somerset house
Property & Income Tax Office for the city of London, 36 Basinghall st.; hours 9 to 6
Prophit William, surgeon, 2 Church lane, Whitechapel
Prosser Hannah & Ann (Misses), milliners, &c. 57 NewBondst
Prosser Stephen & John, shell fishmongers, 6 High Holborn, & 17 Great Turnstile
Prosser Amelia (Mrs.), grocer, 12 John st. west, Edgware rd
Prosser Edward, turkey carpet warehouse, 32 Lawrence la
Prosser Henry, shell fishmonger, 202 Fleet st
Prosser Isaac, town traveller, 19 Virginia ter. Gt. Dover rd
Prosser James, fruiterer, 8 Upper Berkeley st. Portman sq
Prosser James, gen. dealer, 13 Canterbury pl. Old Kent rd
Prosser John, goldsmith, jeweller & watchmk. 61 Piccadilly
Prosser John, army cap & accoutrement mak. 9 Charing cr
Prosser John, saddler, 35 South Molton st
Prosser Robt. *Barleymow brewery*, 9 King's pl. Coml. rd. ea
Prosser Thomas, grocer, 14 Golden lane, Barbican
Prosser Thomas, linendraper, hosier, &c. 179 Shoreditch
Prosser Thomas, secretary to Waterford & Kilkenny Railway, 34 Broad st. buildings
Prosser Thos. boot & shoemaker, 54 Marylebone la. Oxford st
Prosser Thos. jun. muffin baker, 54 Marylebone la. Oxford st
Prosser Wm. fishmonger, 1 Kingsland green
Prosser Wm. grocer, 14 Charlton st. Fitzroy square
Prosser Wm. wine, ale & porter merchant, 98 Leadenhall st. & Mitre court, Milk st. Cheapside
Prosser Wm. Howard, organ bldr. 14 New st. Horseferry rd
Prosser's *Patent RailwayGuideWheelCom.* (Geo. Hadley, sec.), 36 New Broad st. City
Protection from Swindlers Offi. (Perry's), King's Arms building, Cornhill
ProtectionfromSwindlersOffi. (T.S.Morgan, sec) 101 Woodst
Protector Life Association (C. Jellicoe, secretary), 35 Old Jewry; see page 2043
ProtestantAssn. (Rev. Jas. Lord, sec.), 11 Exeterhall, 372 Stnd
Protestant Dissenting Ministers' Society, for the relief of widows & children, 2 Adelaide pl. London bridge
ProtestantUnion Soc. (Rev. John Hunt, sec.), 7 Blomfield st
Prothero John, mat. instrument ma. see Claxton & Prothero
Prothero Thomas, solicitor, 4 Furnival's inn, Holborn
Prothero John, jun. metal broker, 1 St. Michael's alley
Prothonotary's Office, Town hall, Boro' Highst.; hrs. 10 to 2
Proudfoot Edward, tailor, 3 Pinner's court, Old Broad st
Proudfoot Edward, tailor, 7 Spread Eagle court, Finch lane
Proudfoot Thomas L. bookbinder, 73 George st. Euston sq
Proudman Edward, *Grapes* P.H. 18 Counter st. Borough
Proudman Francis, *Hand & Flower* P.H. 6 Kensington gore
Proudman Joseph, sad. & harness ma. 29 Red Lion st. Spitflds
Prout James, hairdresser, &c. 2 Castle court, Birchin lane
Prout John William, barrister, 57 Chancery lane
Prout Peter, currier, 34 Lit. Pulteney st. Golden square
Prout Thomas, pat. medicine vender & perfumer, 229 Strand
Prout William, physician, 40 Sackville st. Piccadilly
Provident Clerks' Life Assurance & Benevolent Friend Association (F. Mullinder, LL.D., F.S.S. sec.), 42 Moorgate st
Provident Dispensary, 6 Charlotte st. Portland place
Provident Institution (Edwd. Boodle, sec.), 5 St. Martin's pl
Provident Life Office (John A. Beaumont, manag. director), 50 Regent st
Provident Savings' Bank (Edward Boodle, act.), 5 St. Martin's place
Provincial Bank of Ireland (Thomas Hewat, sec.), 42 Old Broad st. City; see page 2000
Provincl. Medical & Surgl. Journal, 46 Princes st. Le'ster sq
Provis Wm. Alex. civil engineer, 24 Abingdon st. Westminster
Provisional Protection So. & Servants' Home, &c. (Chas. Gordelier, sec), 8 Assembly rw. Mile ed. rd.; offi. 92 Fench. st
Prowett Robert, dentist, 16 Berkeley square
Prowett Septimus, picture dealer, 107 Regent st
Prowse John, engine turner, 5 Corporation la. Clerkenwell
Prowse John, furnishing ironmonger, 21 Red Lion st. Holborn
Prowse John Sparke, ship broker & notary, 28 Clement's la
Prowse Thomas, sole manufacturer of C. Nicholson's flutes, pianofortes, & musical instruments in general; music publisher, &c. 13 Hanway st. Oxford st
Prowse Wm. musical instrument ma. see Keith, Prowse & Co
Proye Peter, butcher, 7 Broadway, Westminster
Pruce John, lighterman, 13 New Park st. Borough
Prudence William, solicitor, see Sutton, Ewens & Co
Prudence El. (Mrs.), *Swan's Nest* P.H. 11 Gt. Swanal. Moorgt. st
Prujean Francis, solicitor, 5 Staple inn, Holborn
Prust Wm. *Horn of Plenty* P.H. 5 Lit. Guilford st. Russ. sq
Pryce Elijah & Co. drysalters, 1 Cullum st
Pryce John Seys, tailor, 7 Augustus st. Regent's park
Pryce Thomas Eastman, oilman, 1 York terrace, & 12 Northampton place, Old Kent rd.; & 37 Crosby row, Walwth. rd
Pryce Richard, shell fishmonger, 413 Strand
Pryer John, carpenter & builder, 8 Regent st. Horseferry rd
Pryce John, dairyman, 3 Craven yard, Drury lane
Pryer Thomas, solicitor, 17 Finsbury pavement
Pryke Richd. *Lord Nelson* P.H. 18 Up. Charton st. Fitzroy sq
Pryke Charles Alexander, baker, 15 Old st. St. Luke's
Pryor & Friend, eng. & for. timber mer. & blders. 42 Bankside
Pryor Samuel & Henry, umbrella manufact. 43 Holborn hill
Pryor Charles, auctioneer & surveyor, 24 Mark lane
Pryor John, chandler's shop, 2 Newington cres. Ball's pond
Pryor Marlborough, merchant, see Cotesworth, Powell & Co
Pryor Robert, barrister, 7 Old square, Lincoln's inn
Pryor Robert, watchmaker, 254 Tottenham court road
Pryor Thos. surgeons' instrument mak. 23 King st. Tower hill
Public Dispensary for the relief of the sick poor at their own homes (J. S. Phillips, sec.), 4 Bishop's ct. Lincoln's inn
Public Ledger daily newspaper, 1 St. Dunstan's hill
Public Record Offices; Head office, Rolls' yard, Chancery lane: Branch offices, Rolls' chapel, Tower; Chapter house; Poet's corner, & Carlton ride; hours of attendance, from 10 till 4
Public Works Loan Office, South Sea house; hours 10 to 4
Publishers' Circular Office, 54 Fleet st
Puckle Edwd. [late Colnaghi & Puckle], publisher & printseller to Her Majesty & Royal Family, 23 Cockspur st. Charing cross
Puckle James & Robt. manchester warehousemen, 8 Milk st
Puckle George, hop & corn factor, see Mills, Puckle & Co
Puckle Henry, proctor, see Iggulden, Puckle & Puckle
Puckle Thos. Broadhurst, proctor, see Iggulden, Puckle & Co
Puckridge Alfred John, watchmaker, 7 Orange st. Bloomsb
Puckridge Ann (Mrs.), academy, 4 Goldsmith st. Gough sq
Puckridge Benjamin, coachmaker, 166 Kingsland road
Puckridge Francis Lambreach, sole manufacturer of Liston's transparent membrane plaister, plain membrane & gauze lessc & others, 3 Dobson's ter. New st. Kennington rd
Puckridge Frederick, beer retailer, 148 Hoxton Old town
Puckridge Jonathan, tea dealer, 2 Duke st. Manchester sq
Puckridge Wm. sign carver, 17 Hosier lane, West Smithfield
Puddick John E. & Co. winemers. Albionchbrs. 11 Adamst. Adelp
Puddick Richard, dining rooms, 81 West Smithfield
Puddick William, dining rooms, 4 Smithfield bars
Puddicomb Joseph, straw hat maker, 14 Pitt st. Old Kent rd
Puddicomb Thos. news agent, 24 Bridgehouse pl. Newingtn. ca
Puddicombe Edw. Dunsterville, solicitor, 3 Furnival's inn
Puddicombe Thos. chandler's shop, 28 Devonshire st. Lsn. gr
Puddiphat, Archer & Hunt, milliners, 55 Rathbone place
Puddy Elisha, baker, 1 Sidney st. City rd
Puddy George, bootmaker, 24 Little Windmill st. Golden sq
Puddy Matthew, china dealer, 120 Albany st. Regent's pk
Puest & Wicke, sugar refins. Gower's wk. Church la. Whitechpl
Puget, Bainbridge's & Co. bankers, 12 St. Paul's churchyd
Pugh Robert & Son, coal merchants, Salisbury wharf, Strand
Pugh Thos. & Co. wholes. ironmongers, 13 King st. Snowhill
Pugh William & Charles, upholsterers, auctioneers & undertakers, 6 Blackman st. Borough
Pugh Wm. & Son, sugar brokers & coopers, 71 Gt. Tower st
Pugh Ann Julia (Mrs.), straw hat maker, Well st. Hackney
Pugh Charles, rectifier, see Vincent & Pugh

Pugh Charles, solicitor, 13 King's road, Gray's inn
Pugh Cornelius, teadealer & grocer, 8 King William st. City
Pugh David, barrister, 5 King's Bench walk, Temple
Pugh David, dairyman, 1 Bartholomew close
Pugh Edwd. sen. soapma. & oilman, 8 Barking ch. yd. Gt. Tower st
Pugh Edward, tanner, Willow walk, Bermondsey
Pugh Elizabeth (Mrs.), milliner, 40 Clifton st. Finsbury
Pugh George, fruiterer, 119 & 120 Cromer st. Brunswick sq
Pugh Henry Robert, library, 25 Bath st. City road
Pugh James, *Ship* P.H. 14 Berkley st. Clerkenwell
Pugh James, *Peacock* P.H. 34 Whitecross st. Cripplegate
Pugh John, oilman, &c. 12 Queen st. Cheapside
Pugh John, weelwright, 85 Gt. Suffolk st. Borough
Pugh John Walter, mourning establishment, 163 Regent st
Pugh Joseph, carpenter, 11 Southampton ter. Pentonville
Pugh Lewis, *Rising Sun* P.H. 12 Henry's place, Old Kent rd
Pugh Mary (Mrs.), dressmaker, 1A, High st. Portland town
Pugh Richard Harris, haberdasher, see Wreford & Pugh
Pugh Robert Henry, gas fitter, 58 Brick lane, St. Luke's
Pugh Thomas, carman, 17 Hill st. Finsbury
Pugh Thomas, cowkeeper, 26 Carnaby st. Golden square
Pugh Thomas, dairyman, 12 Bride st. Liverpool road
Pugh Thomas, grocer, 26 Sidney pl. Commercial road east
Pugh Thomas, hairdresser, 7 Colvill ter. King's rd. Chelsea
Pugh Thos. saddlers' ironm. & bridle cutter, 66 Gt. Queen st
Pugh Thomas Bless, solicitor, 10 Langbourn chambers
Pugh, Thos. Edwd. cheesemonger, 1 Theobald's rd, Red Lion sq
Pugh Walter, hairdresser, 14 Colville ct. John st. Fitzroy sq
Pugh William, tailor, &c. 315 Regent st
Pulbrook Lot, fishmonger, 46 Blackfriars road
Pulbrook Lot, bootmaker, 61 Blackfriars road
Pulbrook Hen. Rt. grocer, oil & colorman, 96 Blackfriars rd
Pulbrook George, shoemaker, Clarence pl. Clapham road
Puleston Thomas & Son, cheesemongers, 21 North Audley st
Pulfer & Hall, law stationers, 6 Serle's place, Lincoln's inn
Pulfer George William, bootmaker, 8 George's pl. Old st. rd
Pulford Robert & Sons, tailors, 65 St. James's st, Pall mall
Pulford Richard, surveyor, 58 Clarendon square
Pulham Robert Benj. carpenter, 5 Bury place, & 4 Pied Bull yard, Bury st. Bloomsbury
Pulham Samuel, livery stables, 9 Harpur mews, Red Lion sq
Pull Susannah (Mrs.), milliner & dressma. 60 Fetter lane
Pullan Ann (Mrs.), confectioner, 197 & 198 Fleet st
Pullan John, billiard table manufactory, 198 Fleet st
Pullan Thomas, tobacconist, 89 Blackman st. Borough
Pullar Tedrack Fink, leather cutter, 100 North st. Walworth
Pullein Walter, warehousm. & agent, 34 St. Paul's churchyd
Pulleine James, barrister, 1 King's Bench walk, Temple
Pullen John & Saml. bookbinders, 55 Redcross st. City
Pullen Joseph & Son, auctioneers, 80 Fore st. Cripplegate
Pullen Wm. & Son, fruit slsmen. 76 Farringdon mkt. & Cov. gdn
Pullen Chas. stationer & tobacconist, 6 Red Lion pas. Holbn
Pullen Daniel, potato dealer, 2 Eyre st. hill, Leather lane
Pullen James, furniture broker, 62 Eagle st. Red Lion sq
Pullen James, fruiterer, 15 Little Bell alley, Coleman st
Pullen James Thomas, solicitor, 14 Basinghall st
Pullen John, solicitor, 21 Bedford st. Covent garden
Pullen Mary (Mrs), dyer & scourer, 13 Little Moorfields
Pullen Richard, fruiterer, 45 Lamb's Conduit st. Foundling
Pullen Thomas, tailor, 41 Stanhope st. Clare market
Pullen William, cabinet maker, 3 Robert st. Grosvenor sq
Pullen William, fruiterer, Covent garden long market
Pullenger Geo. tobacco pipe maker, 56 Bell st. Edgware rd
Pulley Brothers, stockbrokers, 8 Shorter's ct. Throgmorton st
Pulley Charles Horton, solicitor, 28 Gt. Winchester st
Pulley Frederick, confectioner, 89 Lambeth lower marsh
Pulley John, plumber, 111 Paul st. Finsbury
Pulley John, proctor, 15 Gt. Carter la. Doctors' commons
Pulley John, wholesale confectioner, 147 Lambeth walk
Pulley Joseph Knollys, porkman, 66 Lambeth Lower marsh
Pulley Rachl. (Mrs.), ladies' shoema. 3 Road side, Mile end rd
Pulley Samuel, bootmaker, 60 Ernest st. Regent's park
Pulley Wm. Mills, proctor, 15 Gt. Carter la. Doctors' comns
Pullin Ann (Mrs.), baker, 23 Castle st. east, Oxford st
Pullin George, baker, 7 Church row, St. Pancras road
Pullin George, baker, 256 Strand
Pullin George, bootmaker, 16 Whitcomb st. Pall mall
Pullin James, locksmith, 56 Tabernacle walk, Finsbury
Pullin John, *Salisbury Arms* P.H. 111 Eastfield st. Limeho. flds
Pullin Mary (Mrs.), lodging house, 3 Mabledon pl. New rd
Pullin Thomas, grindery dealer, 7 Clare court, Drury lane
Pulling Alexander, barrister, 6 Crown office row, Temple
Pulling Charles, potato salesman, Hay's wharf, Tooley st
Pulling Frederick Leopold, M.D. surgeon, 21 Old Fish st. City
Pullinger John, *Gregorian Arms* P.H. St. James's pl. Brmds. rd
Pullman Robt. Wm. & John, leather sellers, 17 Greek st. Soho
Pullum William, milliner, 13 Hyde place, Hoxton
Pulman James, F.S.A. registrar, Herald's college, Doctors' cmns
Pulman Jno. barrister, 4 Elm ct. Temple, & Shore ho. Hackney
Pulsford Samuel & Son, tailors, 71 Lamb's Conduit st
Pulsford Edward, engraver, 13 William st. Caledonian road
Pulsford John, bootmaker, 5 Dockhead, Bermondsey
Pulsford Wm. carpent. & bldr. 11 & 12 St. Martin's st. Leicester sq
Pulsford Wm. tailor & waterproofer, 4 King st. St. James's
Pummell Henry, fishmonger, 35 Crosby row, Walworth road
Pummell Samuel, fishmonger, 25 High st. Kensington
Pummell Samuel, jobmaster, 25 King st. Kensington
Pummell Samuel Adams, fishmonger, 3 Old Kent road
Pumphrey John, fruiterer, 9 John's pl. Camberwell New rd
Punch weekly periodical Office, 92 Fleet st
Punchard Alfred, tailor, 11 Short's bldgs. Clerkenwell close
Punchard John, rag merchant, 10 Bread street hill
unnett David, grocer, see Smith & Punnett
Punt Jesse, *Green Man & Still* P.H. 173 Upper Whitecross st
Punter Henry, poulterer & porkman, 8 Newington causeway
Punter John, carman, Northumberland alley, Fenchurch st
Punter John, tailor, 3 Homer pl. New rd. Marylebone
Punton James Archibald Bodfield, stationer, 13 Piccadilly
Punyer James, beer retailer, 13 Cain pl. Kentish town
Purbrook Charles, grocer, 75 Earl st. east, Lisson grove
Purcell Ann (Mrs), grocer. 85 Hoxton Old town
Purcell David, dining & coffee rooms, 109 Up. East Smithfield
Purcell Edward, *King's Arms* P.H. 47 Up. Ebury st. Pimlico
Purcell Richd. Harris, barrister, 6 Cambridge st. Edgwr. rd
Purchas Elizb. (Mrs.), saddle tree ma. 10 Archer st. Golden sq
Purchase Charles, farrier, 1 Brunswick mews, Wilmot st.
Purches Wm. & Ch. shoe mercers, 22 Up. Seymour st. Euston sq
Purday Thomas Edward, music seller & publisher, & musi-Pcal instrument maker, 50 St. Paul's churchyard
Purday Zenas Trivett, music publisher, 45 High Holborn
Purdey James, gun manufacturer, 314½ Oxford st
Purdon George, grocer, 9 St. Andrew's hill, Blackfriars
Purdon Thomas, carver, 65 John st. Holland st. Blackfriars
Purdue & Twiddy, cheesemongers, 152 Borough High street
Purdue Henry, house agt. 19 Edward st. Star cor. Bermondsy
Purdue Thomas, surveyor of taxes, 20 Sherrard st. Golden sq
Purdy & Fendt, musical instrument makers, 3 Oxenden st
Purdy Wm. & Son, bootmakers, 9 Calthorpe pl. Gray's inn rd
Purdy Abraham, baker, 263 Poplar High st
Purdy George, professor of music, 9 Rood lane
Purdy James, wheelwright, Nine Elms, Vauxhall
Purdy Thomas, stationer, &c. 49 Poplar High st
Purfurst Wm. french bootmaker, 2 Philpott ter. Edgware rd
Purkess Geo. publisher, bookseller & stationr. 60 Dean st. Soho
Purkin accountant, see Dashwood & Purkin
Purkins Wm. plumber & glazier, 16 Barrett's ct. Oxford st
Purkis John, brush maker, 1 Weymouth terrace, Hackney rd
Purkis John, tailor, 13 Goldsmith place, Hackney rd
Purkis Susannah (Mrs.), horse hair manfr. 56 Crown st. Finsby
Purkiss John & Son, house painters, 29 Old change, City
Purkiss John & Son, house painters, 5 Gt. Distaff la. Friday st
Purkiss Devorix, shoemaker, 8 New Church st. Lisson grove
Purkiss Jane (Mrs.), *Bell* P.H. 12 Millpond st. Bermondsey
Purkiss Jabez, hairdresser, 256 Borough High st
Purkiss Mary A. (Miss), fruiterer, 11 & 58 Gt. Hall, Hungfd. mkt
Purkiss William, bricklayer, 29 Hampden st. Clarendon sq
Purkiss William, tallow chandler, 29 Crown st. Finsbury; 1 Gt. Trinity lane, Bread st.; & 29 Bread st. hill
Purland Theodosius, surgeon dentist, 59 Mortimer st
Purle Jas. bow & arrow ma. 15 Stephen st. Tottenham ct. rd
Purle William, archery warehouse, 34 Berners st
Purnchard Isaac, greengrocer, 4 Commercial pl. Kentish twn
Purnell Charlotte (Mrs.), grocer, 93 Drummond st. Euston sq
Purnell George, fruiterer, 67 Lower George st. Chelsea
Purnell George, turner, carver & cabinet ma. 78 Curtain rd
Purnell Henry, marine store dlr. 19 Bear alley, Farringdon st
Purnell John, watch & clock ma. 43 Seymour st. Euston sq
Purnell John Jas. consulting surgeon, 34 Charterhouse sq
Purnell John P. hosier, 66 Shoreditch
Purnell Joseph, carpenter, 21 Cumberland st. Middlesx. hosp
Purnell Samuel, tailor, 6 Greville st. Hatton garden
Purnell William, merchant, see Guest & Co
Purney Geo. Hen. plumber & glazier, 13 Spring st. Portmn. sq
Purrett Lucy (Mrs.), grocer, 90 Gt. Peter st. Westminster
Purrier & Wright, solicitors, 35 New Broad st. City
Pursell Fras. Jonathan, *White Hart* P.H. 25 Botolph la
Pursell Lawrence, oilman, 77 Lamb's Conduit st. Foundling
Pursell Samuel, tool & hardware house, 420 Strand
Pursell Thomas, pork butcher, 5 Lumber court, Seven dials
Purser Caroline (Mrs.), pawnb. 1 Jamaica ter. Coml. rd. Limeho
Purser Edward, wholesale & retail chemist, 40 New Bridge st
Purser Robert, turner & brush maker, see Firby & Purser

Pursey Benj. & Son, carp. & builds. 33 Gt.Castle st.Regent st
Pursey Chas. Christopher, whitesmith,28Somersetst.Aldgate
Pursey Thomas, coachsmith, 62 Market st. Edgware rd
Pursey Wm. Henry, fruiterer & tailor, 14 Spring st. Paddgtn
Purshouse John Wm. enameller,22Wilderness rw.Clerknwell
Purslow John, tailor, 6 Upper King st. Bloomsbury
Purslow Joseph, carpenter, 15 Wenlock road, City rd
Purssell James, biscuit baker, 78 Cornhill
Purssell William, baker, 10 Hart st. Crutchedfriars
Purssey Edmund, butcher, 5 New Bridge st. Vauxhall
Purssey John, butcher, 50 Mount st. Lambeth
Purssord Fredk. Jas. cheesemonger, 148 Bermondsey st
Purssord Robert,cheesemonger, 6 Theobald's rd.Red Lion sq
Purssord William, cheesemonger, Kingsland High st
Purt George, soda water manufacturer, 13 St. Mary at hill
Purt Thomas, dairyman, 13 St. Mary at hill
Purton Wm.&Jas.brass workers, 2Arlington st. Sadler's well
Purton Edward, *BedfordArms* P.H.7 Bedford st. Commrl.rd
Purvis Peter & John, bootmakers, 37 Whitechapel rd
Purvis Alexander, watchmaker, 4 North Audley st
Purvis C. Henry, oil & colorman, see Hopkins & Purvis
Purvis James, boot & shoe maker, 145 Shadwell High st
Purvis John, mason, 39 Hampden st. Clarendon sq
Purvis Margaret(Mrs.),bootma.6 Grosvenor pl.Comcl.rd.east
Purvis Peter, boot & shoe maker, 18 Charles st. Comrcl. rd
Purvis Peter Pringle, shoemaker, 9 London ter. Hackney rd
Purvis Robert, straw hat ma. 37 Charlesst. Hampstead rd
Purvis Thomas, queen's counsel, 2 Stone buildings, Linc. inn
Purvis Thomas, boot & shoe maker, 10 Deptford High st
Purvis Thomas, grocer, 14 Red Lion st. Holborn
Purvis William, baker, 199 Blackfriars road
Purvis William, livery stables, Somerset ter. Kensington
Putland & Woods, wholesale saddlers, saddlers' & harness makers' ironmongers & manufacturers of Read's patent reins, 60 Crown st. Finsbury
Putland Hy. *King Wm. IV.*P.H.St.Andrew'srd.Hrsmngr.la
Putley Francis, watch & clock makr. 40 Newington causewy
Putley George, butcher, 184 Borough High st
Putley Isaac, manufacturing cutler, 114 Borough High st
Putnam Geo. Palmer, american publishr. seeWiley&Putnam
Putnam William, fruiterer, 1 Little Bruton st
Putnano Wm. Alfred, silversmith & jeweller, 5 Union st.Boro
Puttick James, grocer, 48 King st. Seven dials
Puttick Robert, hairdresser, 21 Fish st. hill
Puttman George, tailor, 38 Little Pulteney st. Golden sq
Puttman Jonathan, baker, 27 North st. Lambeth
Puttock Charles, bookseller & stationer, 26 Grafton st. Soho
Puttock James, poulterer, 38 High st. Marylebone
Puttock John, butcher, 72 Gray's inn lane
Puttock Robert, gold cutter, 20 Whiskin st. Clerkenwell
Puxley Francis, haircutter, &c. 12 Ireland row, Mile end
PuxonWm.bacon drier, Black Bull yd. Peter's la. St. John sq
PuxonsMaryA. &Isabella(Misses),ladies'schl.10Charterho.sq
Puzey & Pallett, manchester warehousemen, 58 Bread st
Puzey Eleanor (Mrs.), *Grapes tav.* 9 Three Tuns pass.Ivyla
Puzey Henry, linendraper, 72 Lisson gr. north, Marylebonec
Puzey William, hatter, 76 Wardour st. Soho
Pyall Charlotte (Mrs.), artist, 115 London road
PyattWm. Brymer, gen. salesmn. 7 Langley pl. Comrcl. rd
Pybus Hen.buttr.& poultry salesmn.see Jennings,Pybus & Co
Pybus Mary Ann (Mrs.), milliner,36 Sandwichst.Burtoncrest
PybusThos. Wm. grocer&teadealer,3NewBridgest.Vauxhall
Pye, Field & Tanqueray, merchants, 25 Mark lane
Pye George, coach plater, 3 Langley st. Long acre
Pye George, tin agt. & insurance brokr. 9 New Broad st.City
Pye John, dining rooms, 3 Church place, Piccadilly
Pye John, glass engraver, 9 Russell court, Drury lane
Pye Thos. timber mercht. & steam saw mills,King's rd.Chels
Pye William, dining rooms, 73 St. John's st. Smithfield
Pye William, optician, 20 Albion bldgs. Bartholomew close
Pye William, eagle saw mills, Old Brompton
Pyk John, carrier to London, 34 Broomfield pl. Deptford
Pyke Alexander, cooper, 20 Gt.Turner st.Commercial rd.ea
Pyke George, solicitor, 43 Lincoln's inn fields
Pyke John Leon & Saml.statrs.& sponge mers.52 Mansell st
Pyke Hugh, law, clerical & comml. agent, 87 Chancery la
Pyke Henry Hugh, barrister, 87 Chancery lane
Pyke Mary (Miss), slopseller, 21 Well st. Wellclose sq
Pyke Saml.black lead pencil ma.52Gt.Prescot st.Goodm.flds
Pyle Philip, *Coopers' Arms* P.H. 4 Old Fish street hill
Pym John, merchant, 81 Old Broad st. & Hall of Commerce
Pyman & Bird, chemists,&c.43 Castle st.east,Oxford market
Pyman John, brewer, see Meldrum & Pyman
Pyman Samuel, receiv. of fee farm rents, see Bell & Pyman
Pymm George, bookbinder, 14 Up. Crown st. Westminster
Pymm Philip,glass&staffordshire war.97Fore st.Cripplegate
Pyne Daniel & Joseph, staymakers, 53 Long la.Bermondsey
Pyne George, registrar of births,&c.43 Henry st.Pentonville
Pyne George H. surgeon, 1A, Middlesex pl. New rd.Marylbn
Pyne Henry, barrister, 12 Porchester place, Oxford square
Pyne Henry, haberdasher, 161 Bethnal green road
Pyne John, beer retailer, 115 Long alley, Finsbury
Pyne Mary (Mrs.), ladies' school, 1 Highbury park west
Pyne Richard, *Old Bell* P.H. 6 Wellington st.north, Strand
Pyne Robert, painter & glazier, 9 St. Andrew's road, Boro'
Pyne Samuel, chaser, 54 Newman st. Oxford st
Pyne Thomas, jun. plumber, 14 Swan st. Great Dover road
Pyne William, attorney, 4 Inner Temple lane
Pyne William, harness maker, 20 Friar st. Blackfriars rd
Pyne Wm. Darling, oilman & tallow chandler,44Hackney rd
Pynock Jas. pianoforte manuf. 38 Museum st. Bloomsbury
Pyott Thomas, stationer,29 Brunswick parade,Barnsbury rd
PyrkeJ. S. & Sons, tea urn ma. 4 & 5 Dorrington st. Cdbth.sq
Pyrke Martin Robert Lazarus, printer, 7 Church st. Dptfd
Pyrke Thos. King, bookseller & statnr.6 High st.Notting hill
Pywell Wm. & Co. hatters, 69 Long la. Bermondsey
Pywell William, ladies' school, 3 Berwick pl. Grange road

QUADRI Giuseppe, looking glass ma.5 St.John's la. Smithfi
Quain John Richard, special pleader, 2 Essex court, Temple
Quain Richard, surgeon, 23 Keppel st. Russell square
QuaintrellHn. *FiveInkHorns*P.H.34NewNicholsst.Bthnl.gr
Quaintrell Wm. bone mer.crusher,&c.3 Buck's row,Whitech
Quallett Geo.Watts, auctioneer, 39 Clement's la.Lombard st
Quance Catherine (Mrs.), grocer, 71 Seymour st.Euston sq
Quance James, plumber & painter, 2 Elm ter. Lit Chelsea
Quantrell Geo. antique cabinet ma.28½ Henry st.Hmpstd.rd
Quarell Saml. linen factor, see Gunning & Quarell
Quarier Elizabeth (Mrs.), stationer,48 Up.John st.Fitzroy sq
Quarles William, solicitor, 21 Red Lion square
Quarny Joseph, grocer, 22 Mary st. Hampstead road
Quarrel Fanny (Mrs.), butcher, Church st. Hackney
Quarrell David, butcher, Church st. Hackney
Quarrell Elizabeth (Mrs.), butcher, 5 West st. Hackney
Quarrell Francis, merchant, 67 Aldermanbury
Quarry Thomas, *Victory* P.H. John st. Cambridge heath
Quarter Master General's Office, Horseguards; hrs. 10 to 5
Quartermaine Joseph, upholder, 39 George st. Portman sq
Quartermaine Thomas, *York hotel*, 39 New Bridge st. Blackfriars; & *Crown & Sceptre tavern*, Greenwich
Quarterman Ann (Mrs.), *Red Lion* P.H.7City rd.Finsbury sq
Quarterman Edward, carpenter, 2 Millpond st. Bermondsey
Quarterman Edward, tobacconist, 4 King st. Borough
Quarterman William, coffee rooms, 3 King st. Borough
Quartly Henry, grocer, 73 Hoxton Old town
Quay Joseph, ornamental painter, 10 Pritchard's pl.Hckny.fi
Queen Ann's Bounty Office, Dean's yard, Westminster; hours of business, *Treasurer's department*, 10 to 2; *Secretary's department*, 10 to 4
Queen Charlotte's Lying-in-Hospital, Homer pl. New rd
Queen Square Police Court, Westminster; hours, 11 to 5
Queen's Bench (Court of), Westminster Hall & Guildhall
Queen's Bench Office, King's bench walk, Temple; hours of business, term, 11 to 5; vacation, 11 to 3
Queen's Bench Master's Office, 2 Mitre court buildings, King's bench walk; hours, term, 11 to 5; vacation, 11 to 3
Queen's Concert rooms, 4 Hanover square
Queen's Printing Office, Printers' st.Shoe la.&9E.Harding st
Queen's Prison, Belvedere place, Southwark bridge road
Queen's Remembrancer's Office, 22 Duke st. Westminster; hours, 10 to 4
Quekett Edwin John, surgeon, 50 Wellclose square
Quekett John, sec. to the Microscopical Soc. 21 Regent st
Quelch Henry, printer, 40 Lit. Charlotte st. Blackfriars rd
Quelch James, *Dick's* coffee house, 8 Fleet st
Quelch Thomas, fishmonger, 17 York pl. Kent st. road
Quelle Christopher, retail furrier, 19 Ludgate hill
Quennell William, builder, Lower Kennington lane
Querini Jemima (Mrs.), milliner, 22 Clarges st
Quested Richard, *Laurel Tree* P.H. 185 Brick la. Spitalfi
Quested Samuel, corndealer, &c. 77 Harrow rd. Paddington
Quick John & Co. hatters, 21 King's row, Pimlico
Quick John &Sons, paperstnrs. 2 North st. mews, Fitzroy sq. & 70 Great Titchfield st
Quick James Carthew, who. coffee dealer, 148 Fenchurch st
Quick John, baker, Stratford broadway
Quick JohnJas.plumber & glazier,31 Park ter.Regent's pk.rd
Quick John V. printer & tobacconist,5 Weston pl. King's cro
Quick Walter Cross, baker, 17 Bouverie st. Edgware road
Quiddington Nathaniel, tailor, 5 Albemarle st. Piccadilly
Quigley John, bookseller, 44 Duke st. Lincoln's inn fields
Quilter, Ball, Jay & Crosbie, accountants, 57 Coleman st.City

Quilter John Wm.& Co. grocers, 126½ Brick lane, Spitalflds
Quilter & Taylor, attorneys, 7 Gray's inn square
Quilter George, oilman, 20 Melton st. Euston square
Quilter Saml. sign writer, 2 Paul's ct. Huggin lane, Wood st
Quin Charles, gold & silver beater, 122 Fetter lane
Quin Frederick, foreign agt. 3 Up. Wellington st. Strand
Quin Fredk. Foster, physician, 4 Arlington st. Piccadilly
Quin Maria (Miss), dressmaker, 26 Gt. Ormond st. Queen sq
Quin Thomas, painter, &c. 1 Sussex ter. Camden New town
Quin Thomas, *Silver Lion* P.H. 42 Pennyfields, Poplar
Quin Thos. Dolby, clock & watchmaker, 18A, Gt. Titchfield st
Quince Samuel, coffee rooms, 35 George st. Grosvenor sq
Quincey Richard, merchant, 7 Basing la. Bread st. Cheapside
Quiney & Maclean, drysalters, 24 Commercial sale rooms
Quinlan Joseph, ship chndlr & provision mer. 33 Trinity sq
Quinlan Mary Ann (Mrs.), dressmaker, 3 Mercer st. Long acre
Quinlan Thos. *Howard Arms* P.H. 32 Arundel st. Strand
Quinn James, fishmonger, 9 Mill st. Hanover sq
Quinn James, shell fishmonger, 40 Haymarket
Quinn James, wine cooper, 23 Grosvenor market, Davies st
Quinney Isaac, teadealer, 2 Lombard terrace, Chelsea
Quinton Ishmael, *Jolly Farmers* P.H. 58 Cumberland market
Quinton Jeremiah, coach bldr. 13 Cottage place, City rd
Quinton John, baker, 19 Bermondsey New road
Quinton John, dining rooms, 6 Sarah pl. Old st. road
Quinton John, whitesmith, 11 Park st. Dorset square
Quinton Joseph, grocer, 46 Baalzephon st. Bermondsey
Quinton Mary (Mrs.), cabinet ma. 6 Garden row, London rd
Quinton Mary Ann (Mrs.), chandler's shop, 61 Raherest. Gswl. rd
Quinton Saml. lock & whitesmith, 23 Broadley ter. Bldfd. sq
Quinton William, butcher, 86 Leather lane

RABACHE Charles, agent for J. Lausseure's french wines' 9 Opera arcade, Pall mall
Rabbeth John, cheesemonger, 18 Red Lion st. Holborn
Rabbeth John, cheesemonger, 9 Up. Glo'ster pl. King's rd. Che
Rabbeth William, solicitor, 6 Clements inn, Strand
Rabbiotti Lewis, chandler's shop, 14 Laystall st. Lqrpnd. st
Rabbits Edward Harris, leather seller, 20 Sloane square
Rabson Thomas, hop & seed factor, 4 Three crown sq. Boro'
Raby John, turner, 3 Wellington pl. Back rd. St. George's ea
Raby Lewis, baker, 1 Church lane, Whitechapel
Raby Robt. Wm. tailor, 12 Devonshire bldgs. Gt. Dover st
Raby Thos. Victor, blond & lace cleaner, mender, joiner & dyer, 40 Wigmore st
Racine Jas. & Wm. Hen. silk dyers, 14 St. John st. Bethnal grn
Racine Geo. (agt. to Atlas Fire Off.), 19 London ter. Hackney rd
Racing Calender Newspaper, 6 Old Burlington st
Rackett Sarah (Mrs.), deed & fire proof box manufacturer to the hon. society of Lincoln's inn, & locksmith, 18 Bell yard, Temple bar
Rackett William, sen. deed & fire proof box manufacturer, locksmith & bell hanger, 10 Bell yard, Temple bar
Rackham James, cabinetmaker, 9 Judd st. Brunswick sq
Rackham Joseph, bootmaker, 3 Emanuel pl. Camberwell rd
Rackham Peter, merchant, 10 Sise lane, Bucklersbury
Rackham Willoughby B. S. solicitor, 46 Lincoln's inn fields
Rackstraw Saml. & Son, fishmongers, 41 Lamb's Conduit st
Rackstraw James, fishmonger, 37 George st. Portman sq
Rackstraw William, baker, 4 Arabella row, Pimlico
Rackstraw William, *Gun Tavern*, 12 Stafford row, Pimlico
Rackwitz Charles, baker, 13 Charterhouse lane, St. John st
Racster Martin, stock & share broker, 1 Birchin lane
Radcliff & Butterworth, grocers, 10 Ann's ter. Old Kent rd
Radcliffe Augustus, jun. glaziers' diamond manufr. & window glass & lead mercht. 32 Chichester pl. Gray's inn rd
Radcliffe Augustus, sen. patent glaziers' & artists' diamond manufacturers, 67 Hermitage place, St. John st. road
Radcliffe Charles, engraver & printer, 38 Maiden la. Cov. gar
Radcliffe Derwentwater, surgeon, see Jones & Radcliffe
Radcliffe Jas. tailor, 4 Brown st. Bryanstone square
Radcliffe John, corn dealer, 18 Tysoe st. Exmouth st
Radcliffe John Thos. chandler's shop, 11 Henry's pl. O. Kent rd
Radclyffe Edw. carver, gilder & picture frame dealer, liner, restorer & importer, 237 High Holborn
Radclyffe Hen. working silversmith, 58 Frith st. Soho
Radclyffe John N. coach plat. & founder, 9 Queen st. Grosv. sq
Radclyffe Leopold H. manf. goldsmith, 5 Nassau st. Soho
Radclyffe Robt. Bolton, picture liner, 28 York rd. Lambeth
Raddall & Haynes (Misses), milliners, 95 Grand Junction ter
Radden Jas. J. locksmith & bellhanger, 32 St. Swithin's la
Raddon Richd. beer retailer, 21 Britannia st. City road
Raddon Robert, painter, 21 Hatton wall, Hatton garden
Radenhurst Charles B. mercht. see Turnbull & Radenhurst
Radenhurst Edw. brushm. 3 Manor pl. south, King's rd. Chelsea
Radermacher Peter Michael, tailor, 15 Queen st. Soho
Radford John, auctioneer & house agent, &c. 77 Chancery la
Radford John, tobacconist, 146 Fleet st
Radford Robert, fruiterer, 79 Cromer st. Brunswick sq
Radford Wm. baker, 30 Gt. College st. Camden town
Radford Wm. physician, 21 Suffolk st. Pall mall east
Radford Wm. stone merchant, 14 Fore st. Limehouse
Radiger Charles Nicholas, barrister, 1 Churchyard ct. Temple
Radley George, *Radley's hotel*, 10 New Bridge st
Radmall John, who. provision mercht. see Green & Radmall
Radmall Thomas, alton ale stores, 39 Bath st. City rd
Radmall Wm. wholes. bonnet shapemak. 55 Brick la. Spitalfl
Radway Emanuel, baker, 24 Tottenham st. Tottenham ct. rd
Rae Edmund Horsfall, law stationer, 7 Cook's ct. Lincoln's inn
Rae George, bone boiler, 34 Green st. Friar st. Blackfrs. rd
Rae John, coffee rooms, 73 Cable st. Wellclose square
Rae Joseph John, solicitor, 4 Bedford row
Rae William, *Bell tavern & chop house*, 95 Fleet st
Raffe Mary (Mrs.), *Needlma. Arms* P.H. 23 Dalgleish st. Cml. rd
Raffell James, furniture broker, 44 Eagle st. Red Lion sq
Raffen George, fruiterer, North row, Covent garden market
Raffen Geo. jun. fruiterer, North row, Covent garden mkt
Raffles Thomas Stamford, barrister, 3 Hare court, Temple
Raftery John, tobacconist, 27 St. John st. Clerkenwell
Ragg George, butcher, 2 William st. Manchester square
Ragg Robert, paper agent, 43 Watling st
Raggett Geo. P. surveyor, 38 University st. Tottenham ct. rd
Raggett Henry, wine mer. 37 & 38 St. James's st. & 59 Jermyn st
Raggett Robert, cheesemonger, 1 Up. King st. Bloomsbury
Ragland Henry Miller, foreign agent, 12 Eastcheap
Ragless Thomas, pastrycook, 39 Paradise row, Chelsea
Ragsdale & Elks, shirt makers, hosiers & glovers, 34 Strand
Rahill Thos. H. statnr. & acct. book ma. 3 Red Lion st. Hlbn
Rahles John, furrier & cloth cap maker, 332 Oxford st
Rahn George, sworn broker, 52 Mark lane
Raikes & Newbery, wine merchants, 3 Mincing lane
Railly John, cheesemonger, 4 Upper Penton st. Pentonville
Railton James, stockbroker, 56 Threadneedle st
Railton Jane (Mrs.), grocer, 2 Queen st. Lower rd. Islington
Railton Joseph, linendraper, 22 Paradise row, Chelsea
Railton Robert, plumber, 4 Brewer st. Pimlico
Railton William, architect, Carlton chambers, 13 Regent st
Railway Advertiser, 1 Crane court, Fleet st
Railway Chronicle, 14 Wellington st. north, Strand
Railway Clearing house, 111 Drummond st. Euston sq
Railway Exchange Club Chambers & Goods Depôt 28 St. Swithin's lane, & Guilhall coffeehouse
Railway Express, 11 Wellington st. north
Railway Herald newspaper Office, 9 St. Michael's all. Cornh
Railway Mail newspaper Office, 27 Coleman st
Railway Record newspaper Office, 153 Fleet st
Railway Times newspaper Office, 122 Fleet st
Railway World, Jos. Duncan, publisher, 2 Crane ct. Fleet st
Raim Henry, bricklayer, 15 Princes st. Red Lion square
Raiman Thomas Henry, bootmaker, High st. Deptford
Raimbach David M. artist, 99 Stanhope st. Hampstead rd
Raimondi & Gooday, solicitors, 14 South sq. Gray's inn
Raimondi John Ferdinand, attorney, 36 Lincoln's inn fields
Raimondi Willoughby, solicitor & clerk to the managers of the St. Clement's Danes Holborn estate charities, 23 Surrey st. Strand
Rainbird Robert, grocer, 38 Kenton st. Brunswick sq
Rainbow Sarah (Mrs.), grocer, 38 New Manor st. Chelsea
Raine John, *Anchor & Hope* P.H. 198 Wapping High st
Raine John, tailor, 4 Belgrave st. south, Pimlico
Raine Thos. cheesemonger, 28 Houndsditch; & at Clapham
Raines William, barrister, 1 New court, Temple
Rainey, Bruce & Co. west india mers. 1 Bell court, Mincing la
Rainger Eliza (Mrs.) straw hat manfr. 2 Down st. Piccadilly
Rains Brothers, forn. warehouse, 4 Crescent, New Bridge st
Rains Henry & Sons, paper mill board, & sheet lead mills, Mill st. Dockhead, & Bermondsey wall
Rains & Son, whole. stationers, 4 Crescent, New Bridge st
Rains Eliz. (Mrs.), fruit saleswoman, Covent gardn. fruit mkt
Rains Geo. Wm. bootmaker, 34 Up. Jubilee pl. Mile end
Rains John, fruiterer, Centre row, Covent garden
Rains Rupert, solicitor & notary, 15 Fish st. hill
Rains Samuel, grocer & teadealer, 8 Chapel st. Somers town
Rains William, fruiterer, 67 Gt. hall, Hungerford market
Rainsford Henry, butcher, 54 Great James st. Lisson grove
Rainsford John, butcher, 83 Park st. Grosvenor square
Rainsford Octavius, booksel. 17 Camden st. south, Camd. tn
Reinsley Thos. camel hair pencil ma. see Findlow & Rainsley
Rainy Alexander, land & estate agent, 14 Regent st
Raistrick Alfred G. dyer & scourer, 6 Park ter. Regnt's. pk. rd
Rait David, baker, 1 Mount ter. New rd. Whitechapel rd
Rait George, tailor & draper, 25 Moorgate st. Bank

Rake James, grocer, &c. Camberwell green, west side
Rake Richard, teadealer, &c. 25 Gt. Suffolk st. Borough
Rake Thomas, carman, 138 Curtain road, Shoreditch
Rakes Geo. prof. of music, 4 Forston st. Ashley ter. City rd
Rakes John, tailor, 13 North st. Fitzroy square
Ralli Antonio & Co. merchants, 42 Albion pl. London wall
Ralli Brothers, merchants, 25 Finsbury circus
Ralli Carati & Co. merchants, 8 Blomfield st. Finsbury
Ralli & Mavrojani, merchants, 1 Jeffrey's sq. St. Mary Axe
Ralli Pantia, greek consul, 25 Finsbury circus
Ralli Pandia Theodore, merchant, 30 Finsbury circus
Ralph Charles & Co. genl. furn. ironmongers, 54 Cheapside
Ralph James & Son, tailors, 150 Strand
Ralph Fras. Hen. apprsr & ho. agt. 4 Greystoke pl. Fetter la
Ralph James, shipping butcher, 18 Wapping wall
Ralph John, staymaker, 21 Crown st. Finsbury
Ralph John, mast, oar & scull maker, 50 Lr. Fore st. Lambeth
Ralph Peter, carpenter, 24 Vale place, Hammersmith road
Ralph Thomas Sharman, surgeon, &c. 8 Charlotte st. Fitzroy sq
Ralph Wm. bootmaker, 14 Warren st. Tottenham court rd
Ralph Wm. dairy, 14 Lower Whitecross st. Cripplegate
Ralph Wm. tailor, 59 Southmolton st. Bond st
Ralphs Edward, fan. ribbon manuf. 5½ Wood st. City, & Coventry
Ralston A. & G. & Co. merchants, 21 Tokenhouse yard
Ramadge Francis Hopkins, physician, 24 Ely pl. Holborn
Ramage George, *India House tavern*, Blackwall stairs
Ramage Peter, *Ship* P.H. 170 Long lane, Bermondsey
Ramage Wm. builder & surv. 10 & 11 Lit. Portland st. Regent st
Ramage Wm. Thos. *Duke of Clarence* P.H. 302 Rotherhithe
Ramazzotti Giacinto, dlr. in fancy articles, 59 Frith st. Soho
Rampling Horace, butcher, 30 Gt. Hall, Hungerford markt
Rampling John, goldbeater, 13 New inn st. Shoreditch
Ramsay Chas. plumber & painter, 35 Gt. Prescott st. Goodms. fl
Ramsay James, artist, 12 Newman st. Oxford st
Ramsay James, boot & shoe maker, 32 Brownlow st. Drury la
Ramsay P. braid & trimming manfr. 53 Wood st. Cheapside
Ramsay Thomas Goulding, wine merchant, 9 Billiter square
Ramsay William, baker, 93 Cannon st. City
Ramsay William, wine merchant, 9 Circus, Minories
Ramsbotham Charles Wheen, merchant & importer of foreign wines, 3 Dunster court, Mincing lane
Ramsbotham Fras. Henry, physician, 14 New Broad st. City
Ramsbotham Joseph M. surgeon, 15 Amwell st. Pentonville
Ramsdale & Butler, fruit salesman, Borough market
Ramsdale George, engraver, 7 Ball alley, Lombard st
Ramsdale Joseph, fruit salesman, 6 Church st. Boro' mrkt
Ramsdale Mary Ann (Mrs.), staymaker, 15 Norton folgate
Ramsden Geo. & Edwd. color works, 96 Whitechapel road
Ramsden John & Co. merchants, 16 Hyde st. Bloomsbury
Ramsden Richard & Son, sugar refiners, capillaire makers, rum & brandy coloring manufrs. 7 Brooke st. Holborn
Ramsden John George, barrister, 7 New sq. Lincoln's inn
Ramsden Richard, general merchant, 33 Abchurch lane
Ramsden Robert, engineer, ironfounder, & coppersmith, 100 Kingsland road
Ramsey Henry & Isaac, auctionrs. & timbermrs. 61 Poplr. Highst
Ramsey Joshua & Son, builders, 36 Walbrook
Ramsey Abdy, auction & estate agt. 21 Percy st. Tott. ct. rd
Ramsey Ann (Miss), lodging house, 3 Adam st. Adelphi
Ramsey Elizabeth (Mrs.), straw hat ma. 84 Poplar High st
Ramsey John, jeweller, 51 Red Lion st. Clerkenwell
Ramsey Wm. drug & seed agent, 21 Great Winchester st. City, & 1 Salisbury lane, Bermondsey wall
Ramsey Wm. plumber, painter, &c. 13 Bermondsey wall
Ramshaw James, engraver & printer, 33 Fetter lane
Ramshay Wm. barrister, 2 Hare court, Temple
Ramuz Alexander, upholsterer, cabinetmaker & patent billiard table maker, 17 Frith st. Soho
Rance Henry, butcher, 63 Gainsford st. Horselydown
Rance James, *Bull & Anchor* P.H. 92 High Holborn
Rance Josiah, *Woodman* P.H. 11 Doyley st. Sloane square
Rand John, artist, 37 Howland st. Fitzroy square
Rand John, cheesemonger, 113 Gt. Suffolk st. Borough
Rand Joseph Howard, glass & chinawar. 20 Bridge rd. Lmbth
Rand Richard John, boot & shoe ma. 184 Long la. Bermnds
Rand Samuel, hairdresser, 1 Gt. Suffolk st. Borough
Rand Thos. saddler, see Laurie, Bedford & Rand
Rand Wm. china & glass dlr. 12 Lower Kennington green
Randall John L. architect, 2 Providence pl. Up. Kenngtn. la
Randal Wm. fishmonger, Camberwell green
Randall Sophia & Son, bricklrs. 108 White Horse st. Com. rd
Randall & Vincent, solicitors, 8 Castle st. Holborn
Randall Alfred Mayor, surgeon, 43 Finsbury square
Randall Ann (Mrs.), *Ship on Launch* P.H. Limekiln dock
Randall Benjamin, baker, 60 Chandos st. Covent garden
Randall Chadd Ragedale, solicitor, 14 Tokenhouse yard
Randall Charlotte (Mrs.), wardrobe dlr. 5 Bridge ct. Westr
Randall Edmund Geo. solicitor, 56 Welbeck st. Cavendish sq
Randall Fred. Gould, law stationer, 10 Staple inn, Holborn
Randall Geo. Thos. *Old Bunch of Grapes* P.H. 108 Bermondsey
Randall Jas. commercial boarding house, 7 King st. Cheapside
Randall James, greengrocer, 33 Gt. Guildford st. Borough
Randall John, coachbuilder, 273 & 274 Whitechapel road
Randall John, coachmaker, wheelwright, spring maker & tire smith, 32 Regent st. Horseferry road, Westminster
Randall John, french polisher, 15 Shoe lane, Fleet st
Randall John, coffee rooms, 73 Berwick st. Soho
Randall John, solic. see Brundrett, Randall, Simmons & Brown
Randall John, venetian blind ma. 25 Lambeth road, Obelisk
Randall Joseph, carpenter, 8 Gt. James st. Lisson grove
Randall Nathl. T. architect & survyr. Harleyford rd. Vaxhl
Randall Richard, draper, see Maund, Jones, Randall & Morris
Randall Richard, tailor, 14 Conduit st. Bond st
Randall Samson, tailor, 8 Bouverie st. Paddington
Randall Stephen, *King's Head* P.H. 1 Orchard pl. Kingslandrd
Randall Thos. butcher, 21 Silver st. Golden square
Randall Thos. melter & bone mer. 15 Gt. Peter st. Westminster
Randall Thos. pork butcher, 78 & 79 London road, Southwark
Randall Thomas Henry, *Lord Holland* P.H. Holland st. Brixton road
Randall Wm. baker, 6 Glo'ster place, King's road, Chelsea
Randall Wm. tailor, 6 Charlotte st. Pimlico
Randel Nathan, hair & lime manufr. 59 Princes st. Lambeth
Randell, Howell & Randell, malt factors, coal merchants & lightermen, 12 Queenhithe
Randell Ebenezer Kemp, solicitor, 23 Birchin lane
Randell George, brick & tile maker, Maiden lane, King's cross, & Union terrace, Bagnigge Wells road
Randell George, *General Wolfe* P.H. Little Gray's inn lane
Randell Henry, barrister, 11 New square, Lincoln's inn
Randell James Saunders, railway carrier, *White Horse*, Cripplegate buildings, & 136 London wall
Randell John, silk broker, see Fellows & Randell
Randell John Wm. builder, &c. 15 Lower King st. Coml. rd. east
Randell Jim, *Two Brewers* P.H. 22 Brick st. Park lane
Randell Richd. plumber & glazier, 27 Norton st. Fitzroy sq
Randfield Thomas, brushmaker, 13 Oxford mkt. Oxford st
Randle Elizabeth (Mrs.), straw hat ma. 36 Cirencester place
Randle James, cork manufacturer, 4 Hackney road
Randle Wm. *Queen's Head* P.H. Pageant's stairs, 120 Rothrhte
Randoll & Shinn, army agents, 4 Northumberland st. Strand
Randoll Thomas, aqua fortis & blue verditer maker, East road, City road
Randolph John, surgeon, 55 Marsham st. Westminster
Randolph John James, barrister, 24 Old sq. Lincoln'n inn
Rands George, china warehouse, 8 White Lion st. Pentonvl
Ranelagh Suspension Bridge Co. 5 Robert st. Adelphi
Ranford Edward, chandler's shop, 79 Broadwall, Blackfriars
Ranford Wm. measure & brush ma. 37 Gt Guildford st. Sthwk
Ranger Joseph, greengrocer, 18 Freeschool st. Horselydown
Ranger Robt. Apsley, engineering surv. 15 Duke st. Adelphi
Ranger Wm. civil engineer, 13 Pelham place, Fulham road, & College, Putney
Ranger Wm. ironmong. & turner, 4 Church rw. Up. st. Islngtn
Ranken, Ford, Longbourne & Vickerman, solicitors, 4 South square, Gray's inn
Ranken John S & Co. commission agts. 2 Honey la. Cheapside
Rankin Benjamin, stock broker, 23 Tokenhouse yard
Rankine William, bootmaker, 94 Cheapside
Ranking John & Henry & Co. merchants, 11 St. Helen's pl
Rankley James, cheesemonger, 43 Union st. Middlesex hospital
Rannie John, baker, 35 Berners st. Oxford st
Ransby Mary Ann (Mrs.) milliner, 37 Providence rw. Brnsby. rw
Ransdale George, cheesemonger, 43 Up. Lisson st. Lis. grove
Ransford Edwin, music seller, 13 Charles st. Soho
Ransley William, rule & tool maker, 20 Stangate, Lambeth
Ransom & Co. bankers, 1 Pall mall east
Ransom & Gardiner, silk mercers, 41 Hedge row, Islington
Ransom Dennis, working jeweller, 7 Gerrard st. Soho
Ransom John, 3 *Swedish Crowns* P.H. 25 Old Gravel la. Wapg
Ransom Wm. mast ma. Hanover stairs, 298 Rotherhithe st
Ranson Edward, dairyman, 34 George st. Grosvenor square
Ranson Shearman, saddler, 76 Harrow road, Paddington
Ranson Wm. cowkepr. & dairyman, 43 North st. Manchest. sq
Ranwell Adam, linendraper, 9 Norton folgate
Ranyard William, attorney, 6 South square, Gray's inn
Raper's Waterproofing Co. 5 Rodney bldngs, New Kent rd
Raper John & Co. tailors & drapers, 9 Bridge road, Lambeth
Kaper George Wayt, leather cutter, 92 London wall
Raper William, porkman, 8 Tichborne st. Haymarket
Raphael Raphael & Sons, merchants, 2 Crescent, Minories, & 5 Shorter's court, Throgmorton st

Raphael Barnet, slopseller, 3 Postern row, Tower hill
Raphael Geo. proprietor of Paul de Vere & Co's vegetable essences&spice,22Abchurchla.City,&Richmond rd.Dalston
Raphael Ralph Philip, cigar manufacturer & furniture broker, 53 Leman st. Goodman's fields, & at Liverpool
Rapkin Elizabeth (Mrs.), bootmak. 6 Union pl. Blackman st
Rapkin John, engraver, 3 Warwick la. & 31 North st. Pntnvll
Rapley & Welchman, manufactg. jewellers, 72 Dean st. Soho
Rapley Benj. beer retailer, Southampton st. Camberwell
Rapley John, corn & coal dlr. Southampton st. Camberwell
Rapley James William, jeweller, 41 Skinner st. Clerkenwell
Rapley William, goldsmith, &c. 33 Northampton st. Clknwll
Rapp John Lewis, *Rapp's Family hotel*, 23 Golden square
Rapson Jacob, veterinary surgeon, see Eldridge & Rapson
Rapson John Bartlett, appraiser & undertaker, 36 Grosvenor row, Pimlico, & 64 Upper Ebury st. Pimlico
Rasch Arthur A. insurance broker & underwriter, Lloyd's
Rasch Frederic Carne, barrister, 4 Old square, Lincoln's inn
Rasch John Peter, underwriter, Lloyd's
Rasch Oswald, solicitor, 1 Staple inn, Holborn bars
Rashbrooke Elish.&Susan(Misses), milliners, 44Sloane square
Rashleigh John, lath render, 19Charles st, Kensington new tn
Rassell George, fishmonger, 3 Albert pl.Marlbro' rd.Chelsea
Rastall James, butcher, 14 Chelsea market, Low. Sloane st
Rastall John, chandler's shop, 59 Squirries st. Bthnl. gn. rd
Rastall Thomas, stationer, &c. 24 Ebury st. Pimlico
Rastrick John U. civil engineer, 454 Strand, 46 Eaton square & 1 Robert st. Adelphi
Ratcliff John & Charles, lamp wareho. 103 Hatton garden
Ratcliff Gas Light & Coke Company (John Gill, secretary), 189 Wapping High st. & 4 Johnson st. St. George's east
Ratcliffe George, fishmonger, 8 Billingsgate
Ratcliff John Burton, baker, Ferry road west, Poplar
Ratcliff Matthew, coffee rooms, 11 St. George's circus
Ratcliff Thomas, baker, 34 Brook st. Ratcliff
Ratcliff Thomas, jun. baker, 6 Lit. Newport st. Long acre
Ratcliffe James Thomas & Henry, wholes. & ret. stationers & farmers' rag merchants, Harrow st. Lant st. Borough
Ratcliffe James, chinaman, 2 Heath pl. Commercial rd. ea
Ratcliffe John Bond, porkman, 83 Blackman st. Borough
Ratcliffe Maria (Mrs.), baker, 9 South Molton st. Bond st
Ratcliffe Robert, corndealer, 139 Hoxton Old town
Ratcliffe Robert, tailor, 24 Lower Sloane st. Chelsea
Ratcliffe Thomas, *Swan* P.H. Uxbridge road, Bayswater
Ratcliffe Wm. bookseller, 15 Green st. Leicester sq
Rate Lachlan Mackintosh, consul general of Texas, 15 Bishopsgate within
Rateau (Latour) & Co. glove cleaners, 130 New Bond st
Ratford Isaac, market gardener, Bromley, Middlesex
Rathbone Bernard, corn mer. 2 New Corn Exchnge.Mark la
Rathbone Edward, corn merchant, 2 Newington causeway
Rathbone Geo. comb & brush mak. 33 Berners st. Oxford st
Rathbone George V. outfitter, see Christian & Rathbone
Rathbone John, medical agent, see Lane & Rathbone
Rathbone John, surgeon, &c. 1Webb's County ter. NewKent rd
Rathbone Richard, pastrycook, 2 Hayes court, Soho
Rathbone Wm. barrister, 4 King's Bench walk, Temple
Rathbone Wm. carpenter & builder, 12 Clifton st. Finsbury
Rathbone Wm. corn mercht. Trig wharf, Upper Thames st
Rathbone Wm. leather cutter, Kingsland High st
Ratheram Chas. silver plater, 29 Bartlett's bldgs. Holborn
Ratley James, *Bell* P.H. 11 Church st. Lambeth
Ratliff John & Cleophas, ribbon manfrs. 78Wood st. Cheapside
Ratliffs & Co. silk manufacturers, 78 Wood st. Cheapside
Ratray Wm. (actuary & secretary of *Victoria Life Assurance & Loan Company*), 18 King William st. City
Ratcliffe James, tailor, 4 Brown st. Bryanstone sq
Rattee George, butcher, 15 Hertford road, Kingsland
Rattenbury Henry, Chas. hatter, 21 South Molton st. Bond st
Rattenbury John, sack wareho. 54 Snow's fields, Bermndsy
Rattenbury Nicholas, *Halfway House* P.H. Blue anchor rd
Ratton Joseph, stockbroker, 1 Crown ct. Threadneedle st
Ratton Lewis, attorney, 2 Pinner's court, Old Broad st
Rattray Alexander, baker, 109 Bishopsgate st. within
Rattray Alexander, baker, 3 Panyer alley, Newgate st
Rattray Alex. ironmgr. 18Bedford pl.&7Portld.pl.Coml.rd.ea
Rattray Charles, baker, 27 Bell st. Edgware road
Rattray John, tin plate worker, 23 Butcher row, Ratcliffe
Ratty Wm. surgeon, 6 Chester st. Kennington
Rausch & Corpe, tailors, 15 King st. St. James's
Rausch Wm. Engleherd, merchant, 23 Cullum st
Raven & Bradley, solicitors, 2 Harcourt buildings, Temple
Raven Andrew, grocer & cheesemonger, 26 Little Coram st
Raven Henry Taylor, solicitor, see Derby & Raven
Raven Henry, surgeon, 18 Hunter st. Brunswick sq
Raven James, *Crown & Cushion* P.H. 73 London wall
Raven John, sealingwax&wafer ma. stationr.&c. 46Fish st. hill
Raven Samuel, jun. solicitor, 6 Northampton pl. Islington
Raven Richard, solicitor, 2 King's Bench walk, Temple
Ravenhill George, mer. see Borradaile Wm. Sons & Ravenhill
Ravenhill Henry, see Howard, Ravenhill & Co
Ravenhill Newell Pat. tailor, 30 Gt. Windmill st. Haymrket
Ravenhill Richard, engineer, see Miller, Ravenhill & Co
Ravenhill Wm. linen & carpet wa. 34 & 35 Beech st. Barbican
Ravenor George, pawnbroker & silversmith, 19 Tothill st. Westminster, & 18 Middle Queen's bldgs. Knightsbridge
Ravens Thomas, bedstead maker, 135 Goswell st
Ravenscroft Thos. & Sons, tailors, 1&2 Warwick st. Charing cr
Ravenscroft Amelia (Mrs.), confectioner, 15 High st. Bow
Ravenscroft Burton, patent forensic wig maker, 3 Serle st
Ravenscroft Chas. Thos. carpenter, &c. 12Maiden la. Cov. gar
Ravenscroft Hen. Wm. attorney, 21 Guilford st. Russell sq
Ravenscroft Samuel, bookbindr, 3Greenhill's rents, Smithfield
Ravenshear John, cheesemonger, 2 Berwick st. Soho
Ravey Charles, brazier, see Johnson & Ravey
Raw Joseph & Son, wholesale grocers, 4 Eastcheap
Raw James, turner, 70 Golden lane, St. Luke's
Raw Joseph, solicitor, 5 Furnival's inn, Holborn
Rawbone & Hawks, scotch ale brewers, Holywood brewery, Little Chelsea
Rawbone George, surgeon, 17 Manor pl. King's rd. Chelsea
Rawbone Thos. oil & colorman, 1 High st. Newington butts
Rawbone William, grocer, 23 Devonshire st. Lisson grove
Rawcliffe Robert, tailor, 26 Charlotte st. Fitzroy square
Rawding John, tailor, 8 Holywell lane, Shoreditch
Rawes Martha (Mrs.), linendraper, 11 Wenlock rd. City rd
Rawles William, currier & leather cutter, 133 Drury lane
Rawley Joseph, plumber & painter, 10 Rosoman st. Clerknwl
Rawley Samuel Thomas, oilman, 17 Church st. Shoreditch
Rawlin Robert, tailor, 2 Cross st. Hoxton New town
Rawling John, tailor, 27 Mount st. Berkeley square
Rawling Joseph, ormolu frame ma. 32 Edward st. Hmpstd. rd
Rawlings Chas. & Edmond, lacquerers, 21 Drury ct. Strand
Rawlings & Seddens, corset makers, 14 Gilbert st. Oxford st
Rawlings & Summers, workg. goldsmiths, 10Gt. Marlboro' st
Rawlings Benjn. Wm. solicitor, 5CrosbyHall ch. Bishopsgate
Rawlings Charles, cabinet & chair manufacturer, upholsterer & undertaker, 55 Upper Marylebone st
Rawlings Charlt. (Miss), ladies' schl. 19 Colet pl. Coml. rd. ea
Rawlings Dan. manufacturer of fine cloths, 3 Lothbury
Rawlings John, butcher, 102 High st. Camden town
Rawlings John, china & glass wa. High st. Stoke Newingtn
Rawlings John, ginger beer ma. 2 Nassau st. Middlesex hosp
Rawlings John, linendraper, 3 Field pl. Larkhall la. Claph
Rawlings John Edw. bookslr.&tobacnst. 170Tottenham ct. rd
Rawlings Joseph, barrister, 1 Inner Temple lane
Rawlings Wm. goldsmith & jeweller, see Lambert & Rawlings
Rawlings William, hairdresser, 98 Fetter lane
Rawlings Wm. timber merchant, see Greig & Rawlings
Rawlins John & Co. coach builders, 38 Portland pl. Foley pl
Rawlins Alexr. dealer in building materials, 39 Curtain rd
Rawlins Hen. Armstrong, surgeon, 1 Francis ter. Kentish tn
Rawlins John, linenfactor & warehouseman, 133 Oxford st
Rawlins John, smith & bell hanger, 16 Ebury square
Rawlins Mary (Mrs.), pianist, 5 River st. Lr. rd. Islington
Rawlins Nicholas, hairdresser, 75 Leather lane, Holborn
Rawlins Robert, boys' school, Clifton st. Wandsworth rd
Rawlins Samuel, furniture broker, 3 Margaret pl. Hackney fi
Rawlins Samuel George, solicitor, 15 Salisbury st. Strand
Rawlins Thomas, fishmonger, 31 King st. Portman sq
Rawlins Thomas Griffin, stationer, 13 Gerrard st. Soho
Rawlins Wm. physician, Church cot. York ga. Regent's pk
Rawlins Wm. Waller, lime & coal whf. King's rd. St. Pancras
Rawlinson & Coatsworth, staymakers, 7 John st. Oxford st
Rawlinson Geo. & Co. silk & lace manfrs. 34 King st. City
Rawlinson Charles, iron master, see Malins & Rawlinson
Rawlinson Christopher, barrister, 1 Essex court, Temple
Rawlinson Edw. A. surgeon, 24 Glo'ster crescent, Regt. pk
Rawlinson John, magistrate, Marylebone st. police court
Rawlinson John, city carman, 50 Bread st
Rawlinson Mark, van proprietor, 66 Shoe lane, Fleet st
Rawlinson Stephen, painter, 4 Tichborne court, Holborn
Rawlinson Thos. livery stables, 2 Lit. Distaff la. Friday st
Rawlinson Thos. who. teadlr.& grocer, 16 Skinner st. Snowhill
Rawlinson Wm. butcher, 61 Lisson grove north, Marylebone
Rawlinson Wm. linendraper, 153 Minories
Rawlinson Wm. wine merchant, 4 George st. Minories
Rawll George, tailor, 56 St. Mary Axe
Rawnsley Henry Chas. civil engineer, 5 Robert st. Adelphi
Rawnsley Robert, boot & shoe ma. 40 Princess st. Edgw. rd
Rawson, Barker & Co. white lead manufacturers at Sheffield (agent, Thomas Dunnage), 3 Laurence Pountney place

Rawson, Norton & Co. east india merchts. 62 Moorgate st
Rawson Geo. coffee rooms, Halfmoon pas. Leadenhall markt
Rawson Margt. (Mrs.), confectnr. 91 Crown ct. Water st. Blkfrs
Ray E. & S. (Misses), seminary, 39 Hart st. Bloomsbury
Ray Geo. & Co. manufacturers of silk hosiery, 41 Gutter la
Ray & Glaister, sydney merchants, 8 Old Jewry
Ray Charles, surgeon, 7 Elizabeth st. Eaton square
Ray Charles, surgeon, 82 Gracechurch st
Ray Charlotte (Mrs.), plumber, 1 Canterbury pl. Old Kent rd
Ray David, cheesemonger, 8 King st. Portman square
Ray Edwd. Wm. baker, 25 Aldenham terrace, Pancras road
Ray Frederick, grocer, 1 Weston st. Borough
Ray George, coal dealer, 18 High st. Kensington
Ray George, lath render, 76 Vauxhall walk, Lambeth
Ray George, soda water manfr. 23 Artillery row, Westmnstr
Ray Henry Belward, chief master, Comn. pleas, Chancery la
Ray James, curiosity dealer, 1 King st. Poplar
Ray Jeremiah Jas. ironmonger, tin, zinc & general metal merchant, wirewkr. wire drawer, &c. 42 Broad st. Golden sq
Ray Joel & Co. ship & insur. brokers, 39 Botolph la. Thames st
Ray John, coal merchant, 3 Narrow st. Ratcliff, & 27 Church st. Rotherhithe
Ray John, shoemaker, 9 Bray's bldgs. Lower rd. Islington
Ray Joseph, map & print colorer, 31 Belvedere rd. Lambeth
Ray Mary C. (Mrs.), teacher of piano, 52 Up. Marylebone st
Ray Richd. fruiterer, 9 Princes st. Little Queen st. Holborn
Ray Samuel, jeweller, 35 Great Castle st. Regent st
Ray Stuart, bookbinder, 43 Duke st. St. James's
Ray Walter John, surv. & land agt. 23 Lincoln's inn fields
Ray William, cheesemonger, 26 Coventry st. Haymarket
Ray William, pianoforte tuner, 19 Gillingham st. Pimlico
Ray William, pin & needle wa. 2 Fieldgate st. Whitechapel
Ray William, teadealer, &c. 96 White Horse st. Stepney
Raybould Benj. coffee rooms, 41 Tothill st. Westminster
Raybould James, upholsterer, 40 Augustus st. Regent's pk
Raybould Wm. umbrella ma. 2 Church pas. Cross st. Islngtn
Rayden William Harris, merchant, 3 Sun court, Cornhill
Rayley John, stockbroker, 2 Hercules ct. Threadneedle st
Rayley Richard, barrister, 8 Old square, Lincoln's inn
Raymen John, tinplate worker, 35 Brill row, Somers town
Rayment James & Sons, wharfingers & coal merchants, 4 & 5 Broken wharf, & Winckworth wharf, Upper Thames st
Rayment Chas. lighterman, 180 & Broken wf. 41 Up. Thames st
Rayment Jeremiah, carman, 5 Parhnam place, Ratcliff
Rayment John, chimney sweeper, &c. 2 Norwich ct. Fetter la
Rayment John, timber merch. 14 Hanover st. Walworth rd
Rayment Joseph, fishmonger, 162 Lambeth walk
Rayment Mary (Mrs.), straw hat presser, 24 Cowper st. City rd
Rayment Samuel, butcher, 27 Cable st. Wellclose sq
Rayment Wm. commercial boarding ho. see Hiley & Rayment
Raymint Martha (Mrs.), coffee rooms, 11 Peerless pl. City rd
Raymond John & Son, lightermen, wharfingers & granary keepers, Horseshoe Sufferance wf. Clink st. Southwark
Raymond, Mead & Co. boat & barge builders, wharfingers & lightermen, Raymond's wharf, 50 Rotherhithe st
Raymond Cuthbert, cheesemonger, 3 Finsbury place north
Raymond John, lightmn. &c. 15 St. Saviour's churchyard, Boro'
Raymond John, special pleader, 9 King's Bench wlk. Temple
Raymond John Alex. interprt. & genl. agt. 5 Princes sq. Ratcliff
Raymond Thomas, tobacconist, 125 Cheapside
Raymond William, plumber, painter & glazier, 109 Minories
Rayner & Andrew, russia & oil brkrs. 10½ Old Broad st. City
Rayner & Hodges, printers, 109 Fetter lane, Fleet st
Rayner & Palmer, woolstaplers & seed mer. 2 Russell st. Bermsy
Rayner & Rayner, chemists, &c. 1 Cambridge pl. Hackney rd
Rayner Barnabas, printer, 1 Goldsmith st. Gough square
Rayner Charles, dining rooms, 13 Seymour st. Euston sq
Rayner Edmond B. *Penton Arms* P.H. 1 Claremont pl. New rd
Rayner Edw. Purton, *Black Horse* P.H. 109 High st. Marylb
Rayner George, turner, Southampton st. Camberwell
Rayner John, coffee rooms, 72 Great Queen st. Lincoln's inn, & 13 Old Compton st
Rayner John, surgeon, Queen's rd. Dalston
Rayner Mary (Mrs.), tailor, 104 London wall
Rayner Richard, butcher, Wandsworth road
Rayner Richard, cabinet maker, see Barnwell & Rayner
Rayner Thomas James, butcher, 114 Gt. Suffolk st. Borough
Rayner Thos. Ottrey, M.D. surgeon, 1 St. Matthew's pl. Hcknyrd
Rayner William, auctioneer & sec. to the Haggerstone, Dalston & Beauvoir town, Holborn & West London, Finsbury & Moorfields, & Westminster road Mutual Benefit Investment Association, 29 Upper Stamford st. Lambeth
Rayner Wm. teadealer, &c. 3 St. Peter st. Hackney road
Rayner Wm. sen. builder, &c. 23 John st. Cambridge heath
Rayner Wm. Edwd. builder, 17 Suffolk place, Hackney rd
Raynes Augustus, surgeon, 20 Church st. Shoreditch
Raynham Richd. bookseller & statnr. 21 Brownlow st. Holborn
Rayson Alexander, merch. & gen. agent, 1 Riches ct. Lime st
Rea Robert & Co. Irish provision agents & wholesale cheesemongers, 95 Upper Thames st. & Essex st. Whitechapel
Rea Edw. chemist & varnish manf. 115 Wardour st. Soho
Rea Edw. coal dealer, 1 Croydon st. Bryanstone sq
Rea Geo. coffee rooms, 1 George ter. Commercial road east
Rea James, hairdresser, 25 New road, St. George's east
Rea Thos. coach smith, Ridinghouse lane, Langham pl
Rea Wm. wax, &c. chandler, 115 Park st. Kennington cross
Read Benjamin & Co. tailors, 12 Hart st. Bloomsbury
Read Henry & Co. silk brokers, 27 Austinfriars
Read John & Co. chemical & mineral agts. 57 Cannon st. City
Read Mary & Co. engravers & printers, 16 Hart st. Covnt. gdn
Read Septimus & Son, surgeons, 41 Jewin st
Read Chas. grocer, 41 Up. Albany st. Regent's park
Read Chas. grocer & cheesemonger, 25 New Manor st. Chelsea
Read Chas. statnr. 28 Lowr. Ranelagh st. Lowr. Grosvenor pl
Read Daniel, coffee rooms, 71 Fetter lane, Holborn
Read Edward, tailor, 59 Great Marylebone st
Read Elizb. (Mrs.), beer retailer, 41 Up. Salisbury rd. Walwth
Read Elizb. (Miss), ladies' school, Hollywood, Lit. Chelsea
Read Elizabeth (Mrs.), pork butcher, 68 Up. Whitecross st
Read Emma (Mrs.), *King's Arms* P.H. Craven bldgs. City rd
Read Francis, builder, & marble & stone saw mills, Upper Belgrave pl. Pimlico
Read Geo. coal dealer, 36 Whiskin st. Clerkenwell
Read Geo. hosier, shirt & stock maker, 15 Pall mall
Read Geo. linendraper, 207 Bethnal green road
Read Geo. linendraper, Mare st. Hackney
Read Geo. tailor, 11 Northumberland pl. Commercial road
Read Geo. jun. butcher, 8 High Holborn
Read Geo. sen. butcher, 284 Strand
Read Harriet (Mrs.), boarding house, 49 Gloucester place
Read Jas. brassfndr. & gun metal ma. 30 Brownlow st. Longacre
Read James, chandler's shop, 21 Union st. Kingsland road
Read James, paperhanger, 19 Cumberland row, King's cross
Read James, jun. carpenter, 14 Wyndham st. Bryanstone sq
Read James, tobacconist & china wa. 4 Osnaburgh pl. New rd
Read James, sen. carpenter, 32 Wyndham st. Bryanstone sq
Read Jefferson Hen. glover &c. 133 St. Alban's pl. Edgw. rd
Read John, appraiser, house & general business agent, & law agent, 34½ Bell yard, Temple bar
Read John, builder, see Smith & Read
Read John, builder, 12 Crutchedfriars
Read John, carpenter, see Smith & Read
Read John, carpenter, builder & packing case maker, 35 Whitecross st. Cripplegate
Read John, furniture broker & appraiser, 71 London wall
Read John, grocer, 3 Artillery terrace, Westminster
Read John, pork butcher, 43 Lambeth walk
Read John, solicitor, 22 Stamford st
Read John, surgical instrument maker to the late King, & the Hon. East India Company, patentee of the stomach pump & enema fountain, 35 Regent circus, Piccadilly
Read John, tailor, 5 Little Argyll st. Regent st
Read John, tailor, 11 Upper Brook st. Grosvenor square
Read John Wm. shoemaker, 100 Shoreditch High st
Read John W. *Original Red Cow* P.H. 22 Long la. Smithfield
Read Joseph, whitesmith, 13 Shepherd st. Oxford st
Read Joseph Stephen, rope, net, & mat ma. 14 St. Mary-at-hill
Read Mary (Mrs.), chandler's shop, 20 John st. Cannon st. rd
Read Philip, fruiterer, 34 Compton st. Brunswick sq
Read Reginald, surgeon, 22 St. John's square, Clerkenwell
Read Richard, coal merchant, 50 Park st. Grosvenor square
Read Samuel, account book ma. & stationr. 95 London wall
Read Sam. coopers' tool ma. 5 St. George's pl. St. George's ea
Read Steph. engineer & machinist, 51 Paradise st. Rotherhith
Read Thomas, chandler's shop, 17 Wilmot st. Bethnal gr. rd
Read Thomas, fruiterer, 37 Up. Lisson st. Lisson grove
Read Thomas, grindery warehouse, 53 Carnaby st. Golden sq
Read Thomas, hairdresser & perfumer, 19 New st. Dorset sq
Read Thomas, *King's Arms* P.H. 33 Princes st. Lambeth
Read Thomas, linendraper, 9 & 10 Sidney pl. Commercil. rd. east
Read Thomas, working jeweller, 75 George st. Portman sq
Read Thomas Peter, surgeon, 18 Hornton st. Kensington
Read Wm. boot & shoemaker, 6 North place, Dalston
Read Wm. butcher, 36 Greek st. Soho
Read Wm. coffee rooms, 1 Beak st. Regent st
Read Wm. cooper, Creek road, Deptford
Read Wm. cowkeeper, 103 Great Titchfield st. Oxford st
Read Wm. grocer, 51 South st. King's road, Chelsea
Read Wm. grocer, 18 Arthur st. King's rd. Chelsea
Read Wm. reed maker, 45 Crispin st. Spitalfields
Read Wm. tailor, 7 Kingsland row, Dalston
Read Wm. tailor, see Gibbons & Read

Read Wm. wheelwright, 106 Hoxton Old town
Read Wm. working jeweller, &c. 77 Jermyn st. St. James's
Readdy Jas. & Son, coopers, 10 Back Church la. Whitechapl
Readdy Joseph, currier, 12 Church la. Whitechapel High st
Reade & Grove, provision merchants, 3 Tooley st
Reader Sarah & Elizabeth (Misses), dressmakers, 29 Bell yard, Temple bar, & 214 Oxford st
Reader Charles, law bookseller, 29 Bell yard, Temple bar
Reader Elizh. (Mrs.), haberdasher, 3 Howard's pl. Hackney rd
Reader Geo. carpent. & build. 18 Grundy st. East India rd
Reader James, hatter, 45 Great hall, Hungerford market
Reader John, *Crown tavern*, 7 Bow lane, Cheapside
Reader Joseph, fruiterer, 6 Cobourg st. Clerkenwell
Reader Wm. locksmith & bellhanger, 17 Cullum st. Fench. st
Readford Joseph, chair & sofa ma. 86 Earl st. east, Lisson gro
Reading Henry, coach smith, 14 Ridinghouse la. Langham pl
Reading Jas. potato dealer, 5 Princes pl. Commercl rd. ea
Reading Moses, baker, 8 Staverton row, Walworth road
Reading Richard, platers' agent, 21 Salisbury st. Strand
Reading Wm. coachmaker, 9 Mortimer st. Cavendish sq.; factory, 101 Gt. Titchfield st
Readman Henry, cattle salesman, 17 West Smithfield
Ready Charles, wine cooper, 6 Mitre st. Aldgate
Ready Henry, oilman, 2 Weybridge place, Mile end road
Ready James Walker, *Dolphin* P.H. 135 Old st. St. Luke's
Real del Monte Min. Co. (Jno. Phillips, sec), 2 Duke st. Adlph
Reaman Christian, baker, 88 Bethnal green road
Rearden Dennis Jas. estate land agt. 9 Panton sq. Haymarkt
Reardon Denis, *Ship* P.H. 92 Great Saffron hill
Reardon John, coffee rooms, 3 Bishop's ct. Chancery lane
Reardon John, optical glass grinder, 42 Easton st. Spafields
Reason Thos. painter, &c. 1 Prospect place, Old Brompton
Reaveley Ann (Mrs.), grocer, 42 Paddington st. Marylebone
Reaveley John, wholesale stationer & rag merchant, Hammond's wharf, Queenhithe
Reavell Wm. gun maker, 30 Southampton st. Strand
Reay John, jun. & Reay Henry, wine merchants, corner of Hart st. 64 Mark lane
Rebbeck Arthur, *Distillers' Arms* P.H. 11 Gt. Saffron hill
Rebbeck Benj. oilman, 2 Cambridge road, Mile end road
Rebbeck Catherine (Mrs.), *Coopers' Arms* P.H. 121 Gt. Saf. hl
Rebbeck Wm. *Golden Anchor* P.H. 59 Gt. Saffron hill
Rebecca John B. architect, 8 Duke st. St. James's
Rebello Francis, merchant, 26 Mark lane
Rebello Francisco, portuguese vice consul, 16 Up. Woburn pl
Receipt Stamp Office, Somerset house; hours 10 to 4
Receiver of Corn Returns Office (George Joyce, receiver), Board of Trade, & 52 Parliament st
Receiver Gen. of Crown Rents for Mdlx. 80 Pall mall; 11 to 3
Receiver Gen. of Droits of Admiralty, 10 Lancaster place
Receiver General's Office for Stamps, Somerset ho.; 10 to 4
Reckless Joseph, lace, thread, &c. manufr. 72 Aldermanbury
Reckless Mary Ann (Miss), milliner, 304 Regent st
Recknell Saml. custom house agent, 11 Water lane, Tower st
Recknell Samuel, law agent, 11 Water lane, Tower st
Record Newspaper Office, 54 Fleet st
Record Offices—see OFFICIAL DIRECTORY
Record Thomas, butcher, 28 Lower Queen st. Rotherhithe
Record Thomas Hen. *Swallow Galley* P.H. 143 Rotherhithe st
Recruiting Office, 17 & 25 Duke st. Westmr.; hours 11 to 5
Redaway James, copper & steel plate eng. 5 Maida hill west
Reddall & Haynes (Misses), milliners, 94 Grand junction ter
Reddall John, carpenter & builder, 11 Type st. Chiswell st
Reddell Cook, patent truss maker, 400 Strand
Redden John, wheelwright, 34 Gravel lane, Southwark
Reddey John, carpet planner, 51 Marshall st. Golden square
Reddin Michl. & Edmund, contractors & carmen, 3 Castle yd Holland st. Blackfriars, & Windsor wharf, 42 Bankside
Redding John, grocer & cheesemgr. 4 Wells row, Islington
Redding Joseph, cheesemonger, &c. 1 Oddy's row, Islington gn
Reddish Ann Eliza (Mrs.), baker, 78 Little Britain
Reddington Philip, painter, 2 Colet pl. Commercial rd. east
Reddock Ralph, inspector of New River Company, 6 Broken wharf, Upper Thames st
Redfern Thos. & Son, sacking mkrs. 68 Turnmill st. Clknwell
Redfern George, hosier, 13½ Newington causeway
Redfern Thos. corn dlr. & beer retlr. 2 Coburg pl. Old Kent rd
Redfern Wm. tallow chandler, 115 Curtain road, Shoreditch
Redford Arthur & Son, printers, 96 London road, Southwark
Redford Arthur, jun. printer, 24 Albion pl. Walworth rd
Redford George, surgeon, 32 Golden square
Redford Samuel, carpenter, 11 Brill row, Somers town
Redgley Benjamin, potato salesman, Boro' market
Redgrave Amelia (Mrs.), milliner, Foster ct. 23½ Gt. Queen st
Redgrave James Fraser, artist, 95 Albany st. Regent's park
Redgrave Thomas, watch ma. jeweller, &c. 7 Palace row, Nw. rd
Redgrave Wm. plater & brass fnd. 22 Gt. Queen st. Linc. inn flds
Redhead Laurence, ship broker, 59 Mark lane
Redhead Benjamin, hide & skin salesman, Bermondsey sk. mkt
Redhead Nath. breeches ma. &c. 6 Bedford pl. Vauxhl. bdg. rd
Redhouse Thos. ship & insur. broker, 3 Crooked la. Cannon st
Reding & Judd, printers, 4 Horse Shoe court, Ludgate hill
Redish James, ivory turner, 5 Goldsmith pl. Hackney rd
Redley John, plumber, 20 John st. north, Marylebone
Redman Geo. C. & Co. shipchndls. 9 Ebenezer pl. Com. rd. Limeh
Redman Henry, cooper, 1 Young st. Kensington
Redman Henry, hairdresser, 80 Myddelton st. Spafields
Redman James, boot ma. 46 Russell st. Lower Rotherhithe
Redman Jane (Mrs.), baker, 9 Well st. Mile end New town
Redman John, bricklayer, 48 Church st. Deptford
Redman John Baldry, civil engineer & surveyor, 5 Cable st. Wellclose sq. & 5 New palace yard, Westminster
Redman Joshua, ivory & bone brushma. 10 Norman st. St. Luke's
Redman William, broker & appraiser, King st. Kensington
Redmans & Lawford, lightermen & granary keepers, 36 Mark lane, & Mill st. Dockhead
Redmayne Giles, silk mercer, laceman, &c. 20 New Bond st
Redmayne Leonard, cabinetma. see Fergusons', Redmayne & Co
Redmond Francis, *Swiss Cottage tavern*, Finchley New rd
Redmond John Boldery, civil engineer, 5 New Palace yard
Redmond (Miss), milliner, 64 Conduit st, Regent st
Redmond Thomas, beer retailer, 96 Britannia st. City rd
Redpath Christopher Jas. ironfounder, see Brown & Redpath
Redpath Henry Syme, solicitor, 13 St. Swithin's lane
Redrup Ann & Son, bricklayers & plasters. 11 Lit. Moorfields
Redshaw & Bowman, furn. broks. 7 Baynes row, Coldbath fi
Redulius John, *King & Queen* P.H. 24 Three Colt st. Limeho
Redwin Richd. tobacco pipe maker, 16 Lit. Clarendon st
Redwood Edwd. chandler's shop, Southampton st. Cambrwll
Redwood Edwd. chinaman, 31 Up. King st. Bloomsbury
Redwood Henry, china & glass dealer, 170 Sloane st
Redwood Wm. undertaker, 27 Up. York st. Bryanstone sq
Redwood Wm. watchmaker, 100 Park st. Camden town
Ree Henry Paul, surgeon, 11 Union place, City road
Reece & Evans, stockbrokers, 39 Lothbury
Reece George & Co. chemists (Medical Hall), 168 Piccadilly
Reece Elizabeth (Mrs.), dairy, see Harris & Reece
Reece George, surgeon, 45 Sussex gardens, Hyde park
Reece John, bookseller, 32 Clement's lane, Lombard st
Reece John, teadealer & grocer, 248 Shoreditch
Reece Richd. Marsden, attorney, 2 Furnival's inn, Holborn
Reece Thomas, tobacco & snuff manuf. 113 Shoreditch
Reece Thomas Edmonds, linendraper, 39 & 40 Blackfriars rd
Reed Benj. & Son, architects & surveyors, 64 O. Broad st. City
Reed & Curtis, shaft benders, 5 George st. Old Montague st. Whitechapel
Reed & Knight, ship & fancy biscuit bakers, 97 Goswell rd. & Jamaica coffee house, St. Michael's alley, Cornhill
Reed & Louch Brothers & Thompson, ropema. Love la. Shdwl
Reed & Phillips, law stationers, 5 Bishop's ct. Chancery la
Reed Robert & Co. surveyors & valuers, 2 Robert st. Adelphi
Reed & Robinson, solicitors, 31 Moorgate st
Reed Sarah & Elizh. (Misses), grocers, &c. 58 Lucas st. Coml. rd
Reed & Shaw, attorneys, 59 Friday st. Cheapside
Reed Thomas & Sons, music wareho. 44 Hedge row, Islington
Reed & Thwaites, clockmakers, see Thwaites & Reed
Reed Archibald, gun & pistol maker, 5 Fountain pl. City rd
Reed Charles, printer, see Tyler & Reed
Reed Digory, tailor, see Farthing & Reed
Reed Edward, baker, 32 Northampton st. Clerkenwell
Reed Edwd. *Black Lion* P.H. 31 Nw. Montague st. Brk. la. Sptlfl
Reed George, carpenter, 6 Wellington place, Stepney
Reed George, fishmonger, 15 Bedford court, Covent garden
Reed Hayter Thornton, corn & coal mer. Mill st. Dockhead
Reed Henry, corn dealer, 172 Church st. Shoreditch
Reed Henry, fruiterer & greengrocer, 6 Crown ct. Pall mall
Reed Henry, tailor, see Cutler & Reed
Reed Jacob, tailor, 10 Leather lane, Holborn
Reed Janet (Mrs.), milliner, 45 Church st. Minories
Reed John, cornchandler, 119 Brick la. Spitalfields
Reed John, greengrocer, 80 Church la. Whitechapel High st
Reed John, grocer, 43 Oxford st. Stepney
Reed John Fredk. coffeehouse, 5 White Hart st. Newgt. mkt
Reed Joseph, cutler & carman, 167 Long lane, Bermondsey
Reed Joseph, fish salesman, 20 Love lane, Eastcheap
Reed Mary (Mrs.), milliner, 51 Broad st. Golden square
Reed Robert, ale stores, Brook's wharf, Upper Thames st
Reed Robt. *Anchor & Hope* P.H. 35 Sthmptn. st. Cmbrwl
Reed Robert, tailor, 6 Great Pulteney st. Golden square
Reed Samuel, goldsmith & jeweller, 38 Fetter la. Fleet st
Reed Sarah (Mrs.), fruiterer, 1 Earl st. ea. Lisson grov. nth
Reed Thomas, floorcloth maker, see Main, Reed & Co

Reed Thomas, greengrocer, 4 Church st. Minories
Reed Thomas, newsvender, 18 John st. Oxford st
Reed Thomas, straw hat maker, 22 NewQuebec st. Portmn.sq
Reed Wm. coffee rooms, 10 Shadwell High st
Reed Wm. grocer, 1 Brooksby st. Liverpool road
Reed Wm. grocer, 37 Edward st. Regent's park
Reed Wm. linendraper, 1 Church st. Rotherhithe
Reed Wm. undertaker, 5 Upper Ashby st. Clerkenwell
Reed Wm. wood dealer, Union road, Rotherhithe
Reeder Fulcher, furniture dealer, 49 Bethnal green road
Reeder Rd. *Goat* P.H. 9 Queen st. Horselydown
Reedman John, fruiterer, 8 Rufford's buildings, Islington
ReesEdm.&Edwin, hairdresr.&wigmks.6Edgware rd.Marylb
Rees David, physician, 8 Craven st. Strand
Rees Elizabeth (Mrs.), jeweller, 7 Hanway st. Oxford st
Rees George, linendraper, 18 Gt. Russell st. Covent garden
Rees George Augustus, surgeon, 5 Artillery pl. Finsbury
Rees George Owen, physician, 59 Guilford st. Russell sq
Rees Henry, dairyman, 12 King st. Bartholomew close
Rees Henry, surgeon, 45 Finsbury square
Rees John, solicitor, see Wilde, Rees, Humphry & Wilde
Rees Josiah, merchant, 8 Lime st
Rees Mary (Mrs.), dairywoman, 6 Ivy lane, Newgate st
Rees Rees, tailor, 36 Banner st. St. Luke's
Rees Richard, bootmaker, 32 Duke st. St. James's
Rees Richard, general agent, 55 Crown st. Finsbury
Rees Richard James, cutler, 45 George st. Portman square
Rees Samuel, eating house, Wellington pl. West India dock
Rees Sophia (Mrs.), milliner, 1Southampton row, Russell sq
Rees Thomas, cheesemonger, 80 Old st. St. Luke's
Rees Thomas, tailor & habit ma. 33 Queen st. Cheapside
Reeve Anna & B. (Misses), pawnbro. 13 Red Cross st.Criplg
Reeve Bros.] lithographers, let. press printers & pubs. of illustrated scientific works, 8 King William st. Strand.
Reeve Daniel & Co. linendrapers & outfitters, 144 & 145 Saint George st
Reeve William & Richard, chintz furniture printers, &c. to her Majesty, 163 Piccadilly, opposite Bond st
Reeve Alfred, lamp mfr. & gas fitr. Egyptian hall, 170 Pcdly
Reeve Ann (Mrs.), straw bonnet ma. 12 Church st. Cambwl
Reeve Daniel, tailor & linendraper, see Ladensack & Reeve
Reeve Edwin, tailor, 5 Lowther arcade, & 389 Strand
Reeve Elizabeth (Mrs.), milliner, 15 Carthusian street
Reeve Ellis, stockbroker, 7 Pope's head alley, Cornhill
Reeve Emma (Miss), childbed, &c.warehouse, 160 Oxford st
Reeve Henry, boot & shoe maker, 6&57 Princes st.Leicester sq
Reeve Henry, chandler's shop, 30 Green st. Bethnal green
Reeve Henry, clerk of appeals, Privy Council Office
Reeve Henry Philip, baker, 1 Theberton st. west, Liverpool rd
Reeve James, boot & shoema. 34 White Hart st. Drury lane
Reeve John, beer retailer, Albany road, Barnsbury park
Reeve John, boot & shoe ma. 39 Margaret st. Wilmington sq
Reeve John, dairyman, 41 Lower Belgrave place
Reeve John, *Mitre* P.H. 7 Deptford bridge
Reeve John, oilman, 43 Green st. Bethnal green
Reeve John Forster, surgeon, 34 Great Ormond st. Queen sq
Reeve John William, *Bell inn*, Newgate market
Reeve Joseph, wire worker, iron & brass bedstead manufactr. 8 Quickset row, New rd. Fitzroy sq
Reeve Joseph, tailor, 20 Warwick st. Golden square
Reeve Philip, solicitor, see Meredith & Reeve
Reeve Richard Nelson, woollen wareho.1Skinner st.Snowhill
Reeve Robert, newsvender & stationer, Gray's inn gateway
Reeve Samuel, tailor, 3 High st. Deptford
Reeve Sarah(Mrs.), spring & axletree ma. 6Market st.Finsby
Reeve Thomas, apothecary, 17 Calthorpe pl. Gray's inn rd
Reeve Thomas, *Rising Sun* P.H. Castle st. Long acre
Reeve Thomas, carver & gilder, 45 Green st. Bethnal green
Reeve Thomas, pawnbroker, 19 & 20 Gray's inn lane
Reeve Wm. beer retailer, 1 Globe road, Mile end
Reeve Wm. bootmaker, 13 & 14 Gt. Russell st. Bloomsbury
Reeve Wm. John, coal mer. 35 Halfmoon st. Piccadilly, & Beaufort wharf, Beaufort buildings, Strand
Reeve Wm. Thomas, oil & colorman, 118 Fetter la. Holborn
Reeves & Hoare, engravs. & printers, 15 Warwick ct. Holborn
Reeves & Sons, manfrs. of artists' colors, &c. 113 Cheapside
Reeves Benj. window blind ma. 1 Upsdell's rw. Kingsland rd
Reeves Charles, dining rooms, 58 Gray's inn lane
Reeves Charles, wheelwright, Cock yard, Tothill st. Westmr
Reeves Edward, bed sacking manfr. 2 George's pl. Old st. rd
Reeves Edward, grocer, 10 Pancras st. Tottenham ct. rd
Reeves Elizth.Mary (Mrs.), clock & watch ma. 208 Shoreditch
Reeves Geo. *Hercules tavern*, 119 Leadenhall st
Reeves Geo. silver turner, 12 Bridgewater gardens, Barbican
Reeves Geo. upholsterer, 25 New Union st. Little Moorfields
Reeves Geo. *White Hart* P.H. 89 Whitechapel High st
Reeves Geo. jun. silver turner, 20 Bridgewater pl. Fan st
Reeves Hen. insp.of weights&measures, 15Stacey st.St.Giles'
Reeves Hen. teadr. 6 Gt.Chapel st.Westmr. & 25Gt.Smith st
Reeves James, merchant, see Smith, Goodhall & Reeves
Reeves James, *Orchard House* P.H. Orchard pl. Blackwall
Reeves James, straw hat maker, 8 Cranbourne st
Reeves Jane (Miss), straw hat ma. 21 New Churchst.Lis.gro
Reeves John, refiner & sweep washer, 137 Goswell st
Reeves John David, butcher, 38 Church rd. Commercl. rd.ea
Reeves John Russell, mercht. 11 King's Arms yd.Moorgate st
Reeves Joseph, cowkeeper, 16 Bidborough st. Burton cresn
Reeves Richard, bricklayer, 76 Shaftesbury st. New Nth. rd
Reeves Robert Wm. boot&shoe ma. 8 Henry's pl. Old Kent rd
Reeves Richmond, butcher, 16 Whitefriars st. Fleet st
Reeves Samuel, printer, 23 Henry st. Pentonville
Reeves Samuel, *World's End* P.H. King's rd. west, Chelsea
Reeves Thomas, stock&share broker, see Knight, Son&Reeves
Reeves William, bookseller, 4 Cowley st. Westminster
Reeves William, jun. bricklayer, 109 Britannia st. City road
Reeves William, sen. bricklayer, &c. 26 Somerset pl. Hoxton
Reeves William, dining rooms, Stafford pl. Regent's pk
Reeves William, fee farm rent office, 6 Lyon's inn, Strand
Reeves William, live stock dlr. Horseferry branch rd.Limeho
Reeves William, smith & farrier, Nag's Head yd. Leather la
Reeves William, tailor, 20 North st. Manchester square
Reeves William, teadealer, 27 Church way, Somers town
Reeves William Geo. cowkeeper, 30 Queen st. Brompton rd
Reeves William, watch & clock ma. 51 Newington causeway
Reffell Henry, booksell. bind. & statnr. 14 Gt. Portland st
Reffold John, potato dealer, South row, Covent garden mrkt
Refford Hen.Wm. chandler's shop, 40&50Chandos st.Cov.gar
Reform Club (William Henry Bond, sec.), 104 Pall mall
Reform Registration Association City of London (George Wansey, hon. sec.), 9 King's Arm's yard, Moorgate st
Refuge for the Destitute (Rev W. Ford Vance, M.A. chaplain&secretary), female establishment (Mrs.Sarah Francis, superintendent), 52 Hackney road; male establishment (James Searl, superintendent), 1 Hoxton Old town
Refuge for the Westend Houseless Poor, 60 Marketst.Edgw.rd
Regent's Canal Dock Office (John Bigg, dock master), 29 Queen st. Ratcliff cross
Regent's Canal Office (Edmund Leonard Snee, sec.), 20 Wharf, City road basin
Regent's Canal Railway, 3 Park st. Westminster
Register Office (peculiar for wills), 5½ Bell yard, Doctors' commons; hours of business 9 to 7
Registrar of Metropolitan Buildings Off. 3 Trafalgar sq
Registrars' Office for Chancery, Chancery lane
Registrar's Offi. for Judgments in the Equity, Common Law & Bankruptcy Courts; Terrace, Serjeants' inn, Chancery lane; hours, term, 11 to 5; vacation, 11 to 3; 10 Aug. to 24 Oct. 11 to 2
Registry Office of the Dean & Chapter of St. Paul's, 5 Dean's court, Doctors' commons; hours 10 to 4
Registry of Deeds for Middlx. 23 Bellyd.Templebar; hrs.10to3
Registry of Designs' Office, 35 Lincoln's inn fields; hrs.10to4
Regless, Sherrett & Co. woollen drapers, 109 St. Martin's la
Regnart Wm. butcher, 21 Felix terrace, Liverpool road
Regnier Alexandre, hairdresser, 25 South Audley st
Rehbein Henry, *Leopard* coffee rooms, 39 Warwick la. City
Rehorn John, fruiterer, 20 Ernest st. Regent's park
Rehsif Ablett & Co. outfitters, 27 King William st. City
Reichell Charles, fishmonger, see Brasier & Reichell
Reichenbach Wm. gas fitter, 33 Borough road
Reichle Anton, clockmaker, 25 Brill row, Somers town
Reichloser Reinfett, tailor, 15 Lamb's Conduit passage
Reickers Herman, fruiterer, 32 Margaret st. Wilmington sq
Reid & Hornor, silk, plush, velvet, &c. manfrs. 21 Spital sq
Reid, Irving & Co. merchants, 16 Tokenhouse yard
Reid John & Wm. grocers, wine, spirit & provision merchts. 66 Fenchurch st
Reid & Kings, sticking plaster ma.2Cumming st.Pentonville
Reid (Neville) & Thomson, wine mers. 2 Suffolk la. Cannon st
Reid Thos.W. & Sons, alum agts. Hambro'whf.Up.Thames st
Reid Wm. & Co. brewers of porter & stout, Liquorpond st
Reid Wm & Fredk.linendrapers & trimming wa.51Conduit st
Reid Alexander, general factor, 70 Lower Thames st
Reid Ann(Mrs.), dressg.case silver mntr. 22 Dean st.Fetter la
Reid Charles, coal dealer, 20 Duke's court, Bow st
Reid Charles Joseph, engraver, 5 Charles st. Bridgwtr. gdns
Reid David, bread & biscuit baker, 10 Leadenhall st
Reid David Alex. bootmaker, 70 Sun st. Bishopsgate
Reid Frederick, M.D. surgeon, 25 Duke st.Westminster
Reid George, coal mercht. Dowgate dock, 83 Up. Thames st
Reid George, furniture dealer, 30 Exeter st. Sloane st
Reid George, merchant, 147 Leadenhall st

Reid James, dining rooms, 125 Fenchurch st
Reid James, fish salesman, 20 Love lane, Eastcheap
Reid James, greengrocer, 24 Drury court, Drury lane
Reid James, physician, 10 Bloomsbury square
Reid James, silk manufacturer, see Sanderson & Reid
Reid James, undertaker,53 Goodge st. Tottenham court rd
Reid John, bootmaker, 31 New North st. Red Lion sq
Reid John, corn & coal merchant, 4 King's row, Pimlico
Reid John, grocer, 8 Green bank, Wapping
Reid John, who. ladies' bootma.18Lit.Charlotte st.Blkfrs.rd
Reid John, liendraper, 121 High Holborn
Reid John, pianoforte tuner, 29 Queen st. Golden sq
Reid Joseph, merchant, 3 Sun court, Cornhill
Reid Maria (Mrs.), jun. fruiterer,Covent gdn.mkt.North row
Reid Mary Ann (Mrs.), fruiterer, Covent gdn.mkt.West end
Reid Robert, auctioneer, see Cafe, Son & Reid
Reid Robert, bread & biscuit baker, 52 Bernard st.Russell sq
Reid Robert, fruiterer&greengrocer,6Wormwood st.Bishpgt
Reid Robert, silk mercer, 1 Gt. Russell st. Bloomsbury
Reid Sarah (Mrs.), staymaker, 17 Charles st.Middlesex hos
Reid Thomas, baker, 24 Old Compton st. Soho
Reid Thomas, basket maker, 9 Wheeler st. Spitalfields
Reid Thos.*Bricklayers' Arms* P.H. 63 Charlotte st.Old st.rd
Reid Thomas,ship&ins.brok.39Wilson st.Finsbury,& Lloyd's
Reid William, baker, 12 Little Vine st. Piccadilly
Reid William, oil & colorman, 6 Bedford pl.Commrcl.rd.east
Reid William, shoemaker, 9 Gt. Cambridge st. Hackney rd
Reid Wm. engineer & machinist, 25 University st. Tot. ct.rd
Reid William, tobacconist, 38 Rochester row, Westminster
Reid William, tobacconist, 2 Silver st. Golden sq
Reid William Henry, architectural, engineering & scientific bookseller, publisher & stationer, 15 Charing cross
Reid Wm.Ker,golds.& silv.plate ma.5Bream'sbdgs.Chanc.la
Reid Wm. M. baker, Princes road, Notting hill
Reilly John, carpenter & builder, 5 Lit. Warner st. Clknwll
Reilly John, *King's Head* P.H. 35 Crown st. Soho
Reilly Joseph Charles, gunmaker, 316 High Holborn
Reilly Mary (Mrs.),dressma. 10 Southampton rw.Russell sq
Reilly Michael, *Blue Post's* P.H. 5 Tottenham court road
Reilly Miles John, varnish manufr. 19 Old st. Luke's
Reilly William, cabinet portable desk, rosewood & russia leather dressing-case manufr. 8 Finsbury terrace, City rd
Reily & Storer, silver plate manufrs. 6 Carey lane, Gutter la
Reily James, baker, 90 Bunhill row
Rein F. Charles, accoustic instrument maker, 340 Strand
Reis, Power & Co. merchants, 34 Fenchurch st
Reisner Adam,accordion mnfr. 45 Burlington arcade,Picdly
Reiser Benedict, skin merchant, 6 Falcon st. Aldersgate
Reisner Adam, accordion maker, 10 Lowther arcade,Strand
Reitze John, baker, 203 Bethnal green road
Relfe & Fletcher, booksellers & stationers, 15 Cloak la. City
Relfe Jane (Miss), milliner, see Phillips & Relfe
Relfe John, grocer, 4 Gracechurch st
Reliance Mutual Life Assurance Society (Alex. Jamieson, LL.D. actuary), 71 King William st. City; for the list of directors, &c. see page 2050
Religious & Charitable Institution (William Dunstan Skinner, secretary), 32 Sackville st. Piccadilly
Religious Tract Soc. (William Jones, superintendent), 56 Paternoster row, & 65 St. Paul's Church yard
Religious Tract Soc. depôt (Mrs. S. Levesque),Chch.st.Hkny
Relph Isaiah Hill, *George IV.* P.H. Edward st.Regent's pk
Relph Joseph, silk manufr. & agent, 6 Mitre ct. Milk st
Remington David R. stockbroker, 76 Old Broad st. City
Remington George, civil engineer, 18 Adam st. Adelphi
Remington Henry, bookseller, see Hering & Remington
Remmett Robt. special pleader, 1 Paper buildings, Temple
Remmie Elizh.(Mrs.),confectnr. 20 NewOrmond st.Queen sq
Remnant & Edmonds,bkbindrs. 8 to 12Lovells ct.Paternr.rw
Remnant Frederick, corn dealer, 65 Aldersgate st
Remnant Frederick William, solicitor, 75 Cheapside
Remnant James, *Grapes* P.H. 30 Thomas st. Horselydown
Remy George & Co. merchants, 2 Gt. St. Helen's
Renals James, hosiery agent, 30 Addle st. Wood st
Renaud Charles, *Limmer's Hotel*, 1 George st. Hanover sq
Renaud Peter Thomas,coal merchant, 13 George st.Adelphi
Rendall Charles, surgeon,41 York st. Westminster
Rendall Simon, solicitor, 16 Clement's inn
Rendel Jas. Meadows, civil engineer,8 Gt.George st. Westm
Rendell Geo. tailor,&c. 15 Shepherd's ct.Shepherd's market
Rendell Henry, butcher, 279 Oxford st
Rendell John, butcher, 1 Queen st. Grosvenor square
Rendell William,carrier,LittleChelsea,near the *Goat & Boots*
Rendell Wm.cheesemonger, 26 Bolingbroke row, Walwth.rd
Rendell Wm. fishmonger, 3 Princess st. Edgware road
Rendell William, fruiterer, Little Chelsea
Rendle Fras.&Son, ironfounds. Ray st.&12Clerkenwell close
Rendle Samuel, linendraper, 49 Ernest st. Regent's park
Rendle William, surgeon, 81 Blackman st. Borough
Rendle Wm. teadealer, 7 Cumberland place, Old Kent road
Renell Robt. P. & Co. merchts. 12 Mark la. Fenchurch st
Renn William, fishmonger, 14 New st. Brompton
Rennalls William Rodon, barrister, 1 Elm court, Temple
Rennell Charles John, barrister, 2 Plowden bldgs. Temple
RennickFrancis&Co.mfrs.ofchina,earthnwre.&c.9Toknho.yd
Rennie George & Sir John, civil engineers, 6 Holland st. Blackfriars road, & Deptford green
Renninson John, *Prince Albert* P.H.5Conduit st. Paddngtn
Renninson Thos. *Sir Is. Newton* P.H.54High st.Portland tn
Renno Bamfield,coach harness smith, 37 King st.Drury lane
Renno Thomas Hurven, bed screw, curtain pulley, bed rod, & iron & brass bedstead maker, 2 Langley st. Long acre
Rennoldson Chas.*Coach & Horses* P.H. 29 Ray st. Clknwell
Rennoldson Isaac,math. inst.ma.5Cambridge pl.Hackney rd
Rennoles Thos.watch ma. 21 Northampton st. Clerkenwell
Renny David Henry, east india broker,seeJohnson & Renny
Renny James Henderson, merchant, 1 Sun court, Cornhill
Renshaw James & Co.merchants,3WhiteHart ct.Lombard st
Renshaw & Kirkman, wholesale stationers, 12 Budge row
Renshaw Charles, spectacle case maker,14Oakley st.Lmbth
Renshaw Edmund, color manufac. 28 Laurence st. Chelsea
Renshaw Henry, medical bookseller & publisher, 356 Strand
Renshaw Joseph, land surv.&agt.8Union ct.Old Broad st
Renshaw Thos. Chas. barrister, 5 Stone bldgs. Lincoln's inn
Rentell Elizabeth (Mrs.), milliner, 5 Garden row, Camberw
Rentell Henry C. plumber, 20 High st. Camberwell
Rentell John, oil & colorman, 194 Shoreditch High st
Renton & Blair,saddlers,&har.maks.30Brewer st. Golden sq
Renton Alexander, accountant, 2 Coleshill st. Pimlico
Renton Jacob, seal engraver, 8 Frith st. Soho
Renton John, artist, 2 West st. Finsbury circus
Renton William, lampmaker, 3 Union st. New Bond st
Renton Wm.soap ma. & tallowcha.5& 6 Park pl.Wlwth.com
Rentzsch Sigismund, watch,&c.ma.2George st.St.James's sq
Renwick Charles, *Angel* P.H. Stratford broadway
Renwick James, spirit bubble ma. 2 Booth's pl. Turnmill st
Renwick Robert, surgeon, 3 Henry's place, Old Kent rd
Renwick Thomas, merchant, Brook's wharf, Upp.Thames st
Renwick Wm. *Spread Eagle* P.H. 13 Limehouse causeway
Repingon Adolphe,mercht. 33 Nag's head ct. Gracechurch st
Report Office, Chancery lane
Repton Paul, bootmaker, 18 Stonecutter st. Farringdon st
Repuke John, musician, 72 John st. Tottenham court road
Resker Robt. Root, coffee rooms, 82 St. John st. Smithfield
Respirator (wholesale) Office, 25 Bucklersbury
Restall Robt. carpen.&builder,30York blds. Newrd. Maryleb
Restell Chas. brush, basket & turnery war. 36 Goswell road
Retallick Joseph, beer retailer, 1 Salmon lane, Limehouse
Retzbach John, porkman, 8 Cable st. Wellclose square
Reuter Simon,woolmerch.Moorgatest.chmbrs.49Moorgatest
Revel Charles, baker, 6 Whitefriar's st
Revell John, grocer,&c. 24 Elizabeth st. South Pimlico
Revell Robert S. bkslr. & statnr. 21 Penton row, Wlwth. rd
Revell Samuel, hatters' trimming seller, 3 Little Prescot st
Revenue Enquiry Commissioners' Offi. Gwydirho. Whitehall
Reversionary Interest Society (Chas. Geo. Christmas sec.), 17 King's Arms yard, Coleman st.; see page 2044
Reversionary Property Agency Office, 83 Lombard st
Revett Thomas, laceman, 155 Whitechapel road
Revill William Thomas, tailor, 13 Brunswick pl. Bnsby. rd
Rew, Prescott & Co. merchants, 55 Old Broad st. City
Rew Geo. Crawford,merch.&ins.bro. 3Bank cham. & Lloyd's
Rew Wm. Andrew, barrister, 3 Tanfield court, Temple
Rew William Pell, merchant, Lloyd's
Rexom William, pianoforte tuner, 29 Queen st. Golden sq
Rexter Fras. hairdress mufr. & perfum. 8 Crown ct.Chanc. la
Rexworthy George, billiard rooms, 53 Piccadilly
RexworthySarah(Mrs.),lodginghouse,2Trinitypl. Charing cr
Reybaud Pierre Jean, wine merchant, 15 Fish st. hill
Reyem Henry, tobacconist, 75 Chapel st. Pentonville
Reynal Geo. T. R. solicitor,Ld. Mayor's ct. office, OldJewry
Reynardson Hen. Birch, barrister, 5 King's bench walk,Tmpl
Reynell & Weight, printers, 16 Lit. Pulteney st. Golden sq
Reynell Fras. Adolphus, academy3Harleyford pl.Kngtn.com
Reynell George, office for London Gazette & town & country newspaper advertisements, 42 Chancery lane
Reynell James, general merchant, 7 Bread st. hill
Reynell John Griffiths, solicitor, 42 Chancery lane
Reynolds & Brett, surgeons, High st. Stoke Newington
Reynolds Chas. & Co. coal mercs. Rutland whf. Up.Thames st
Reynolds (Fras.&John) & Richards & Co. hatters,125 Strand
Reynolds & Field, pawnbro. & silversm. 4 Stones' end, Boro'

Reynolds Geo. & Stephen, corn chdlrs 94 Salisbury st. Lis.gr
Reynolds James & Son, silk dyers, Temple st. & Durham house, Hackney road
Reynolds John & Chas. wiredrwrs.& wkrs. 57 New Compton st
Reynolds John & Co. merchants, 24 New City chambers
Reynolds Joseph & Sons, mnfs. of playing & message cards, drawing boards, &c. hotpressers & glazers of paper, 27 to 30 Vere st. Lincoln's inn fields
Reynolds & Noyes, surgeons, 42 Moorgate st
Reynolds Sam. & G. iron&zinc plate wrkrs. 23 Grafton st. Soho
Reynolds Scutt & Co. wharfingers & insurance brokers, St. Andrew's wharf, 316 Wapping
Reynolds Thos. & Son, merchants, 16 John st. Crutched friars
Reynolds Wm. & Son, fishmongs. 9 Lower area, Hungerford mk
Reynolds Abrhm. Edwd. pawnbroker, 19 Rd. side, Mile end rd
Reynolds Adam, coachbuilder, 14 Elm st. Gray's inn lane
Reynolds Ann (Mrs.), grocer, 2 Nowell's bdgs. Liverpool rd.
Reynolds Charles, cooper, 17 White's row, Whitechapel rd
Reynolds Chas. saddler&harness ma. 18 High rd. Knghtsbdg
Reynolds Chas. Joseph, printseller, 28 Denmark st Soho
Reynolds Edm. Hy. plumbr.&paprhngr 17 Peerless pl. City rd
Reynolds Edward, cowkeeper, 77 East st. Manchester sq
Reynolds Elizh. (Miss), dress maker, 17 Grafton st. east
Reynolds Fred. genl. engrav.&die sink. 15 Old Broad st. City
Reynolds Fred. genl. outfitter & hosier, 12 Charing Cross
Reynolds George, butcher, 6 Salisbury court, Fleet st
Reynolds George, cattle salesman, 15 West Smithfield
Reynolds George, chemist & registrar, 271 Bethnal green rd
Reynolds George, tailor, 3 Upper Baker st
Reynolds Geo. wheelwright, 2 Foundling mews, Gray's inn rd
Reynolds Geo. Fred. tailor & draper, 53 Mansell st. Goodmn. fl
Reynolds Geo. Wm. coal mer. Londn. wf. Pritchard's rd. Hkny
Reynolds Harriet (Mrs.), baby linen wa. see Hobbs & Reynolds
Reynolds Henry, cabinet ma. & upholstr. 153 Hoxton Old tn
Reynolds Henry, cheesemonger, 50 Whitechapel High st
Reynolds Henry Revell, jun. joint sol. to treasury, Whitehall
Reynolds Henry Revell, sen. chief com. insvnt. debtor's ct
Reynolds James, baker, 22 Redcross st. Borough
Reynolds James, coal dealer, 5 Lion st. New Kent rd
Reynolds James, cowkeeper, 27 Bedford st. Commercial rd
Reynolds James, gold, silver & tinsel lace&thread manufacturer & embroiderer, 62 West st. West Smithfield
Reynolds James, gunmaker, see Lacy & Reynolds
Reynolds James, copperpl. printer & bookseller, 174 Strand
Reynolds John, academy, 23 Chadwell st. Myddelton sq
Reynolds John, booksell. & library, 11 Church row, Aldgate
Reynolds John, cheesemonger, 16 Charterhouse lane
Reynolds John, painter & glazier, 16 Redcross sq. Cripplegt
Reynolds John, staymaker, 7 Cross ct. Russell ct. Drury la
Reynolds John, button & trimming seller, 124 London road
Reynolds John, oilman, 18 Fashion st. Dockhead
Reynolds John Hammon, tall. chndlr. see Kennett & Reynolds
Reynolds John Hamilton, attorney, 77 Chancery lane
Reynolds Joseph Wm. button maker, see Boggett & Reynolds
Reynolds Joshua, teacher of music, 21 Powell st. ea. King sq
Reynolds Mary (Mrs.) linendraper, 159 Hoxton High st
Reynolds Patrick, fruiterer, 9 Tower dock, Tower hill
Reynolds Reuben Joshua, oilman, 18 Constable row, Mile end rd
Reynolds Rd. chaser&china mounter, 16 Polygon, Somers twn
Reynolds Rd. east india & colonl. brok. 25 Commerc. sale rooms
Reynolds Robert, stationer, engraver & printer, 115 Fleet st
Reynolds Samuel, attorney, 28A, Howland st. Fitzroy square
Reynolds Samuel, sailmaker & ship chandler, 29 Shad Thames
Reynolds Samuel, solicitor, 22 Haverstock hill
Reynolds Sarah (Mrs.), furn. broker, 105 Gt. Suffolk st. Boro'
Reynolds Sarah (Mrs.), stationer, 13 George st. Euston sq
Reynolds Stephen, corn dealer, 67 Crawford st
Reynolds Susannah (Mrs.), *Magpie & Pewter Platter* P.H. 107 Wood st
Reynolds Thomas, boot & shoe ma. 8 Providence rw. Finsby
Reynolds Thomas, cheesemonger, 6 Cowcross st. St. John st
Reynolds Thomas, furrier, 21 Singleton st. Hoxton New town
Reynolds Thomas, ham merchant, 176 Waterloo road, Lmbth
Reynolds Thomas, inspr. of weights, &c. 208 Brick la. Spitalfl
Reynolds Thomas, oil warehouse, 3 Coppice row, Clerkenwll
Reynolds Thomas, provision merchant, 16 King st. Tower hl
Reynolds Thomas, tailor, 162 Fleet st
Reynolds Thomas, tailor, 35 Gt. Pulteney st. Golden sq
Reynolds Thomas, jun. merchant, 31 Great St. Helen's
Reynolds Wm. bookbinder & seller, 6 Eldon st. Finsbury
Reynolds Wm. brazier, see Temple & Reynolds
Reynolds Wm. builder, Knsngtn. pk. & 2 Eagle Whf. rd. City rd
Reynolds Wm. builder, 1 Clarendon terrace, Notting hill
Reynolds Wm. cheesemonger, 24 Old st. St. Luke's
Reynolds Wm. coach spring ma. 1 Green Dragon yd. Holborn
Reynolds Wm. fishmong. 15 Dean st. Westr. & Hungrfd. mkt
Reynolds Wm. millinery & bonnet wa. 39 Bishopsgate without
Reynolds Wm. oilman, 30 Paul st. Finsbury
Reynolds Wm. *Royal Standard* P.H. 13 Frederick st. Hmpsd. r
Reynolds Wm. wine merchant, 13 Skinner pl. Sise lane
Reynolds Wm. Walter, baker, 3 Chadwell st. St. John st. rd
Reynoldson John, cattle salesman, 41 West Smithfield
Reyroux & Bromehead, solicitors, 35 Old Broad st. City
Rheam Edward, currier, 2 Abbey st. Bermondsey
Rheinlander & Collins, mnfs. prntrs.& manch. agts. 82 Watlng. st
Rheinlander Henry, baker, 15 Green st. Bethnal green
Rheinlander Philip A. *Albion* P.H. Albion st. Rotherhithe
Rhind James, tailor, 121 Up. Seymour st. Euston sq
Rhind Jane (Mrs.), statnr. 7 Lit. Sussex pl. Hyde park gardens
Rhind Wm. laceman, &c. 189 Sloane st. Knightsbridge
Rhoades Richard, *Westminster hotel*, 1 Bridge ct. Westmr
Rhoades & Williams, funeral & mourning warehousemen, 11 Wood st. Cheapside
Rhoads Thos. Sons & Co. merchants, 1 Vine st. Minories
Rhoads Thomas & Sons, ebony inkstand manufacturers to her Majesty's stationery office, New square, Minories
Rhoads John, *Bell & Horns* P.H. Alexander pl. Brompton
Rhodes & Crucknell, woollen warehousemen, 6 Gresham st
Rhodes & Lane, attorneys, 63 Chancery lane
Rhodes John & Co. pianoforte ma. 50 Seymour st. Euston sq
Rhodes Thos. Wm. & Alfred, brickmakers, Balls pond rd
Rhodes Christopher, calico printer, see Bradshaw, Rhodes & Co
Rhodes George, coffee & dining rooms, 45 Coleman st. City
Rhodes Hannah (Mrs.), dressmaker, 4 Hornton st. Kensngtn
Rhodes Hen. architect & surv. 26 Margaret st. Cavendish sq
Rhodes Henry, bricklayer, 30 Newland st. Kensington
Rhodes Henry, oil & colorman, 1 Charlotte st. Pimlico
Rhodes James, builder, Queen's Head lane, Islington
Rhodes James, dairy, Southampton st. Camberwell rd
Rhodes John, R.A. artist, 2 Maddox st. New Bond st
Rhodes John, boot & shoe maker, 43 Duke st. Manchester sq
Rhodes John, *Cole Hole tavern*, Fountain court, Strand
Rhodes John, hop & seed mer. Calvert's bdgs. 241 Boro' High st
Rhodes John, tobacnst.& pianoforte mkr. 3 King st. Westmnstr
Rhodes Jsph. carpent.& sash ma. 4 Cumberlnd. pl. Nwngtn. btts
Rhodes Joseph H. oil&colorman, 7 Claremont pl. Old Kent rd
Rhodes Richard, soapmaker, 1 Carlisle st. Lambeth
Rhodes Richard, dairyman, St. George's st. Albany rd
Rhodes Thomas, solicitor, 9 Davies st. Berkeley square
Rhodes Wm. *Cider Cellar* P.H. 20 Maiden la. Covent garden
Rhodes Wm. pot&tile maker, between 77 & 78 Hackney rd
Rhodes William, teadealer, 77 Aldersgate st
Rhymney Iron Co. (T. E. Scudamore, sec.), 7 Laurence Pountney hill
Riach & Main & Co. merchants, 7 West st. Finsbury circus
Riach James, merchant, 7 West st. Finsbury circus
Riadore Evans, physician, 73 Harley st. Cavendish square
Ricardo J. & S. & Co. merchants, 11 Angel court, Bank
Ricardo & Wilkinson, stockbrokers, 56 Threadneedle st
Rice Charles, bookseller, 123 Mount st. Berkeley sq
Rice Charles, flock & hair manufctr. 219 Bermondsey st
Rice Charles, horse hair manufr. 25 Friar st. Blackfriars rd
Rice Elinor (Miss), french corset maker, 274 Regent st
Rice George, cabinet maker, 51 Marshall st. Golden sq
Rice George, tallow chandlr. 25 Up. Salisbury pl. Lock's flds
Rice Griffiths, bottled ale & stout mer. 29 Rathbone place
Rice Henry, attorney, 39 Jermyn st
Rice Henry, cheesemonger & pork butcher, 81 Goswell road
Rice James, grocer & cheesem. 58 Brook st. West sq. Lambth
Rice James, hairdresser, 14 Mortimer st. Cavendish sq
Rice John, cowkeeper, 48 Paddington st. Marylebone
Rice John, dairy, 5 Finsbury st. Chiswell st
Rice John, *Norfolk* coffee rooms, 64 High st. St. Giles's
Rice John, jun. butcher, 10 Upper Queen's bldgs. Brompton
Rice John George, butcher, Lr. Brompton grove, Brompton
Rice Joseph, fruiterer, 1 Phœnix st. Somers town
Rice Margaret (Miss), academy, see Swaine & Rice
Rice Mary (Mrs.), bottle jack maker, 5 Helmet row, St. Luke's
Rice Mary (Mrs.), lodging house, 4 Chester ter. Eaton sq
Rice Mary Ann (Mrs.), gold&silver beatr. 33 Hosier la. W. Smthfl
Rice Philip, *Archery tavern* P.H. 4 Bathurst st. Hyde pk
Rice Robert, oilman, Lambeth lower marsh
Rice Samuel, woollen warehousemn. 16 Addle st. Wood st
Rice Thomas, coffee rooms, 37 St. Martin's lane
Rice Thomas, leather dresser, 62 Snow's fields, Bermondsey
Rice Thomas H. stationer, 14 Charles st. St. James's sq
Rice William, tailor, 16 Addle st. Wood st
Rich Geo. & Son, venison dlrs.& pastrycooks, 2 Ludgate hill
Rich Charles, engineer, 10 Palace row, New road
Rich Charles, solicitor, 7 Regent ter. Commercl. rd. Ratcliff
Rich Chas. who.& retail tobacconist, 43 Shadwell, & 77 Cable st
Rich Chas. *Windmill inn* P.H. 10 Wyndham rd. Camberwll

Rich George, *Harp & Crown* P.H.50 Warwick st.Golden sq. & 1 Glasshouse st. Regant st
Rich George, bar iron warehouse, see Winter & Rich
Rich Henry William, wine & spirt merchant, 79 Upper Thames st. & 1 Joiners' Hall buildings
Rich Mary Ann (Mrs.), meat salesman, 3 New Newgate mkt
Rich Matthew, tallow chandler, see Cotterell & Rich
Rich Obadiah, american agent, 12 Red Lion square, Holborn
Rich Wm. vellumbinder, 8 Christopher ct. St. Martin's le grand
Richard Edwd. Wm. surgeon, 18 Gt. Newport st. Long acre
Richard John, boarding house, 8 King st. Finsbury
Richards, Clarke & Clarke, solicitors, 9 Chapel st. Bedford row
Richards & Co. flaxspinners, bleachers, & linen manufacturers, Aberdeen, Montrose, Dundee & Manchester, 45 Bread st. City
Richards Evans & Co. hopmers. Calvert's bdgs. 241 Boro' Highst
Richards & Goodbody, linendraders, 163 Kingsland road
Richards John & Sons, bottle mers. 5,6,&7 Raven row, Spitalfi
Richards Richard & Son, wholesale ironmongers & stone saw manufacturers, 95 New Park st. Borough
Richards Thos. S. & Co. export ironmongers & iron merchants, &c. 117 & 118 Bishopsgate within, & at Birmingham
Richards & Taylor, flock & saw mills, Lr. Salisbury pl. Walw
Richards Ann (Mrs.), dairy, 25 Newcastle st. Strand
Richards Ann (Mrs.), milliner, 7 Adelaide ter. Islington
Richards Augustus, coffee rooms, 274 Bethnal green rd
Richards Charles, farrier, 16 Hill st. Finsbury
Richards Charles, printer, 100 St. Martin's lane, Charing cross
Richards Chas. B. toilet & smelling bottle ma. 29 Thavies inn
Richards David, baker, 241 Strand
Richards Edward, pork butcher, 11 Exeter st. Sloane st
Richards Edward Lewis, barrister, 4 Essex court, Temple
Richards Elizabeth (Miss), ladies' school, 31 Park st. Islgton
Richards Francis, engineer & smith, 5 Princes st. Lambeth
Richards Frederick, pocket book manuftr. 17 Woodstock st
Richards Geo. auctioneer, 43 Rathbone place, Oxford st
Richards Geo. pork butcher, 47 Grosvenor row, Pimlico
Richards George, shoemaker, Southampton st. Camberwell
Richards George J. silversmith, 26½ Sekforde st. Clerkenwell
Richards Hannah (Mrs.), grocer, 1 Purbeck place, Lambeth
Richards Henry, chemist, 55 St. James's st. Pall mall
Richards Henry, solicitor, 7 Chandos st. Cavendish sq
Richards Henry, tailor, 15 Avery row, New Bond st
Richards Jacob, upholst. & cabinet mak. 122 High Holborn
Richards Jas. beer retailer, 3 Hastings st. Burton crescent
Richards Jas. hosier & trimng. sel. 16 Little Bell al. Coleman st
Richards Jas. tobacconist, 70 Union st. Borough
Richards Jas. Rt. roasting jack maker, 8 Bethnal green rd
Richards Jane (Miss), ladies' school, 19 Gt. Coramst. Brunswk. sq
Richards Jane (Miss), milliner, 12 Cranbourne st. Leicester sq
Richards Joel, carpent. 2 Sussex pl. Kensington new town
Richards John, agent to Phœnix Fire Offi. 13 Clarendon st
Richards John, broker in metal, &c. 12 George yd. Lomb. st
Richards John, carpenter, &c. 28 New North st. Red Lion sq
Richards John, china warehouse, 87 Mount st. Berkeley sq
Richards John, china dlr. 3 Black Prince row, Walworth rd
Richards John, dairyman, 97 Up. Whitecross st. St. Luke's
Richards John, livery stables, Beaumont mews, Marylebone
Richards John, musical instmt. ma. 25 Cromer st. Gray's inn rd
Richards John, paper hanger, 4 Winchester pl. Sthwk. br. rd
Richards John, pawnbroker, &c. 102 Bridge road, Lambeth
Richards John, *Red Lion* P.H. 3 Green st. Theobald's road
Richards John, rope & twine ma. Wandsworth rd. North side
Richards John (sec. of *Sun Fire Office*), 63 Threadneedle st. 3 Craig's ct. Charing cross, & 65 Welbeck st. Cavndsh. sq
Richards John, *Ship* P.H. 27 Lime st
Richards John, whipmaker, 76 Bermondsey st
Richards Jonathan, baker, 1 York place, Portland town
Richards Joseph, confectioner, 10 Hereford pl. Coml. rd. ea
Richards Joseph, cook & confectioner, 55 Goswell road
Richards Joseph, surgeon, 28 Newcastle st. Strand
Richards Mary Ann (Mrs.), beer retlr. South Lambeth, New rd
Richards Mary A. (Mrs.), smith & pumpma. 3 Bargeho. st. Bkfs
Richards Nicholas, carp. & build. 30 Camomile st. Bishopsgt
Richards Oliver, solicitor, 16 Warwick st. Regent st
Richards Owen, law bookseller & publisher, 194 Fleet st
Richards Priscilla (Miss), lace dealer, glover, &c. 153 Cheapside
Richards Robt. house agent, 21 Southampton st. Somers town
Richards Robert Samuel, barrister, 1 Churchyard ct. Temple
Richards Samuel, chemist, 7 Brett's bldgs. Camberwell road
Richards Samuel, surgeon, 39A, Bedford square
Richards Susannah (Mrs.), baker, 8 Hall park, Edgware rd
Richards Susannah (Mrs.), butcher, 3 Horseferry rd. Westr
Richards Thos. carpenter & builder, 20 Salisbury st. Strand
Richards Thos. carpenter & builder, Salisbury wf. Strand
Richards Thos. gas fitr. & brass mfr. 17 New Compton st. Soho
Richards Thos. grocer & cheesem. 13 Keen's row, Walworth rd
Richards Thos. law stationer, 11 Took's ct. Chancery lane
Richards Thos. A. surgeon, 2 Terrace, Camberwell green
Richards Thos. B. *King's Arms* P.H. 8 Green bank, Wapping
Richards Thos Jas. secret springer, 6 Orchard st. St. Luke's
Richards Wm. average adjuster, 10,11 & 12 New City chambrs
Richards Wm. bookbinder, 21 Old change, Cheapside
Richards Wm. brewery, 73 Bunhill row, & 58 Old st. St. Luke's
Richards Wm. carpenter & builder, 37 Exeter st. Lisson gr
Richards Wm. coffee roaster, 37 Middle Grove st. Coml. rd. ea
Richards Wm. coffee rooms, 211 Tooley st
Richards Wm. gold & silver assayer, 6 Staining la. Wood st
Richards Wm. haberdasher, 8 Blackmoor st. Clare market
Richards Wm. milkman, 25 Newton st. Holborn
Richards William, jeweller, 34 Dean st. Soho
Richards Wm. stationer & bookslr. 6 High st. Newington butts
Richards Wm. tin plate work. 29 Frederick st. Portland tn
Richards Wm. John, solicitor, 26 Gt. College st. Camden town
Richards William Joseph, *The Hoy* P.H. Creek rd. Deptfrd
Richards Wm. Parry, wine merchant, see Chalie & Richards
Richards Wm. Saml. corn dlr. 1 Britannia pl. Wndswrth. rd
Richardson Brothers, merchants & saltpetre refiners, 72 Cornhill, & 11 East road, City road
Richardson & Connell, solrs. & parlmntry. agts. 21 Fludyer st
Richardson & Digman, solicitors, 1 Walbrook
Richardson Edmund & Jas. bookbinders, 14 St. Swithin's la
Richardson Fred. Geo. & Co. bonding yd. & whrf. Risbies' rope walk, Limehouse
Richardson George & Co. (late Stratton & Co.) patent stove & range manufacturers, gas fitters, bell hangers, zinc & brass plate makers & engravers, furnishing ironmongers & general smiths, 133 Cheapside, & 2 Gutter lane, City
Richardson J. & Co. irish linen bleachers & manufacturers, 1 2 & 3 Watling st. & 34 Old Change, City
Richardson James & Sons, slop sellers, 72 Wapping
Richardson John & Thomas & Co. cambric manufacturers, 8 Ironmonger la. Cheapside & Springfield, Lurgan, Ireland
Richardson Mary & Lucy, school, 1 Colebrook row, Islingtn
Richardson & Pegler, agts. & accnts. 16 Warwick st. Golden sq
Richardson Smith & Sadler, solicitors, 28 Golden square
Richardson & Son, ropemakrs. & ship chandlrs. 170 Tooley st
Richardson & Talbot, solicitors, 47 Bedford row, Bloomsbry
Richardson Thomas & Son, booksellrs. & publishers, 172 Fleet st
Richardson Tim. & Sons, hop & seed mrs. 2 Wellingtn. cha. Boro
Richardson & Tucker, dining rooms, 308 High Holborn
Richardson & Turner, haberdashers, Southampton st. Cambrwl
Richardson William Hayden, Benjamin & Jonathan, flint glass manufacturers, 3 Dyer's buildings, Holborn
Richardson Alexander, baker, Deptford broadway
Richardson Alice (Mrs.), chandler's shop, 23 North st. Man. sq
Richardson Ann (Mrs.), tobacconist, 9 Rufford's bdgs. Islingtn
Richardson Ann (Mrs.), fishmngr. 70 New Church st. Lisson gr
Richardson Archibald, british wine manfctr. Old Ford, Bow
Richardson Benj. solicitor, 13 Suffolk st. Pall mall east
Richardson Benj. Fox, chemist, 4 Park ter. Camden town
Richardson Bernard, silk manufacturer, 1 Milk st. Chpside
Richardson Chas. Jas. architect, 22 Brompton cres. Brmptn
Richdardson Chas. coal merchant, 9 Bankside, & 6 Copthall ct
Richardson Chas. haberdashr. & hosier, 46 Tothill st. Westmr
Richardson Chas. norland estate offi. 4 Norland ter. Nottg. hl
Richardson Chas. tailor, 45 Gloucester st. Queen sq. Blmsby
Richardson Chas. Geo. barrister, 3 Tanfield court, Temple
Richardson Chas. James, architect & surveyor, 22 Brompton crescent
Richardson David Wm. grocer, 28 & 43 Wellclose square
Richardson Ed. hay & straw salesman, see Brown, Mason & Co
Richardson Edward, ship & ins. brokr. 2 Cowper's ct. Cornhill
Richardson Edward John, wine & spirit mercht. 16 Giltspur st
Richardson Edward, surgeon, 18 Gt. Newport st
Richardson Elizth. (Mrs.), lodging house, 12 Arundel st. Strand
Richardson Elizth. (Miss), straw hat ma. 55 Gt. Portland st
Richardson Emma (Mrs.), pro. of mus. 13 Barrossa tr. Cmbg. rd
Richardson Eve (Mrs.), dining rooms, 175 Whitechapel rd
Richardson Francis, *Crown* P.H. 119 Long acre
Richardson Francis, wirewkr. fendr. &c. ma. 11 Sun st. Bishpsgt
Richardson George, carpenter, 30 St. Andrew's rd. Boro'
Richardson George, chemist, &c. 12 Norland pl. Notting hill
Richardson George, cutler, Mayfield pl. High st. Kensingtn
Richardson George, merchant, 2 Gt. St. Helen's, Bishopsgate
Richardson George, saddler, 225 Oxford st
Richardson George, wndw. blind ma. 25 Whitehorse st. Stepney
Richardson Haigh, *Grapes* P.H. 27 London road, Southwark
Richardson Harriet Ann (Mrs.), *Jolly Miller* P.H. 41 Webber row, Blackfriars road
Richardson Henry, picture dlr. 68 Newman st. Oxford st
Richardson Henry, tailor & outfitter, 66 & 67 Pennyflds. Poplr
Richardson Henry, packing case ma. 102 John st. Fitzroy sq

Richardson Henry, *Ship* P.H. 3 Hart st.Crutchedfriars
Richardson Hen. Beckley, F.S.A. architect, &c.9Gray's inn sq
Richardson Henry Francis, solicitor to the worshiptul company of joiners, to the city of london general pension so. & to the general annuity society, 36 Coleman st
Richardson Henry N. chandler's shop, 1 Felix st. Hackneyrd
Richardson Jas. *Adml. Vernon* P.H.8NewNichols st. Bethl.gr
Richardson James, baker, 4 Vine st. Westminster
Richardson James, bootmaker, 42 Cloth fair, Smithfield
Richardson James, coal dealer, 2 George st. Blackfriars rd
Richardson James, coffee rooms, 66 Whitechapel road
Richardson Jas. glass & china dlr. 40 Union st. Bishopsgate
RichardsonJas. *Pr.of Wales* P.H. Gt.Hermitage st. Wapping
Richardson Jas. share & stk. bro.1 Three King's ct. Lombd. st
Richardson Jas. M. bookseller, stock broker, & east india agent, 23 Cornhill
Richardson James Smith, tailor, see Binnie & Richardson
Richardson Jane (Miss), stay ma. 1 Duke st. Grosvenor sq
Richardson John, architect, &c. 7 Up. North pl.Gray's inn rd
Richardson John, beer retailer, 97 Green st. Bethnal green
Richardson John, boot & shoe maker, 37 Fish st. hill
Richardson John, butcher, 2 Kingsland row, Dalston
Richardson John, butcher, 6 Sharp's buildings, Minories
Richardson John, carpenter & builder, 19 Great Trinity lane
Richardson John, carpenter, 2 Prujean square, Old Bailey
Richardson John, cheesemonger, 41 Old Bond st
Richardson John, coalmerchant, 22 Millbank st. Westminster
Richardson John, ironmonger, 62 Edgware rd. Marylebone
Richardson John, leather dresser, 114 Hoxton Old town
Richardson John, portrait painter, 1 Colebrooke row, Islngtn
Richardson John, printers' broker, 55 Gt. Sutton st. Clrknwl
Richardson John, saw & tool maker, 16 Leather lane
Richardson John, tailor & draper, 10 Billiter st
Richardson John Town, fruiterer, 28 Wigmore st
Richardson Joseph, bricklayer, 115 Praed st. Paddington
Richardson Joseph, professor of flute, 35London st. Fitzroy sq
Richardson Joseph, tailor, 35 Goodge st. Tottenham ct. rd.
Richardson Mary (Mrs.), confectioner, 19 Duke st.Smithfield
Richardson Mary A.S.(Mrs.), ladies'school, Church rd.Kngsld
Richardson Matthew Danby, grocer, 269 Bermondsey st
Richardson Pelham, bookseller, printer & stationer, 23 Cornhill
Pichardson Philetus, solicitor, see Bayley, Janson & Co.
Richardson Reuben, baker, 37 Strutton ground, Westminster
Richardson Rd. bookselr. & statr. 21 St. John st. Clerkenwell
Richardson Rd. builder & bricklayer, 50 Queen st. Brynstn.sq
Richardson Rd. *Rose & Three Tuns* P.H. 14 Lit. Earl st. 7 dials
Richardson Robert net, marquee & rick cloth maker, 21 Tonbridge pl. New road, & 41 Judd st. Brunswick square
Richardson Robert, chain cable manufactr. &c. 252 Wapping
Richardson Robert, physician, 19 Gordon st. Gordon square
Richardson Robert, ropemaker, Jamaica level, Rotherhithe
Richardson Rowld.S. bootma. 17 New Church st.west, Edg.rd
Richardson Samuel *Bee Hive* P.H.4 Steven's pl.NewNorthrd
Richardson Saml. earthenware dlr.19 Lumber ct.Seven dials
Richardson Saml. sheep salesman, 41 West Smithfield
Richardson Saml. surgeon & chemist, 1 West pl. Islington gr
Richardson Saml. tailor, 67 Compton st. Clerkenwell
Richardson Thos.boot & shoe ma. 32 Kingsland cr.Kingsld.rd
Richardson Thomas, cheesemonger, 83A, London rd. Southwark, & ale & porter merchant, 17 Holborn
Richardson Thos. currier & leather cut. 33 Somerset st. Aldg
Richardson Thos. fruiterer, 11 Ellis st. Sloane st
Richardson Thos. merchant, 72 Cornhill
Richardson Thos. pawnbroker, 12 Henry st. Portland town
Richardson Thos. stayma. 21 Asylum ter. King's rd. Chels
Richardson Thos. stone cutter, 10 Chapel st.Tottenham ct. rd
Richardson Thos. wine cooper, 24 Goodman's yd. Minories
Richardson Walter, upholsterer, 117 Upper Seymour st. Euston sq
Richardson Walter, wine merchant, 1 Union ter. Notting hill
Richardson Wm. artist, 38A, Edward st. Hampstead rd
Richardson Wm. baker, 196 Poplar High st
Richardson Wm. coal dlr. 39 Lit. Pulteney st. Golden sq
Richardson Wm. coal & coke & toy warehouse, 80 Shoe la. & toy warehouse, 3 Cobham row, Coldbath sq
Richardson Wm. commission merchant, 10 Mark lane
Richardson Wm. furn. undertaker, 8 Orange rw.Kenngtn.rd
Richardson Wm. *Gibraltar* P.H.11Gibraltarwk. Bethnl.gr.rd
Richardson Wm. *Hope* P.H. 90 St. John st. West Smithfield
Richardson Wm. lithographer, 6 Bond court, Walbrook
Richardson Wm. machine ruler, 20 Goulstone st. Whitechapl
Richardson Wm. solicitor, 4 Lyon's inn, Strand
Richardson Wm. surgeon, 19 Oxford terrace, Edgware road
Richardson Wm. tobacconist, 1 Prospect pl.Qn's. rd. Dalston
Richardson Wm. willow square mfr. 71 Leonard st. Finsbury
Richardson Wm. Burbidge, solicitor, Guildhall
RichardsonWm.C. *Prince of Wales* P.H.13Holywll. la.Shdch
Richardson Wm. Stephens, barrister, 3 Tanfield ct. Temple
Richbell Francis, furn. broker, 4 Charlton st. Fitzroy sq
Richbell Wm. carman, Whitehart yd. Brooke st. Holborn
Richens Wm. Thomas, hosier, 363 Oxford st
Richer Wm. *Red Lion* P.H. 81 Paradise st. Rotherhithe
Riches & Deering, law stationers, 19 Carey st. Lincoln's inn
Riches Benjamin, cooper, 4 Gt. Wild st. Lincoln's inn fields
Riches Edwd. cheesemonger, 36 & 37 Salisbury st.Bermndsy
Riches Hannah (Mrs.), milliner, 8 Lt. Charlotte st. Blkfrs. rd
Riches Henry, grocer, 2 Road side, Mile end road
Riches John, fruiterer, 7 East st. Old Kent road
Riches Jonathan, builder, 3 Burwood place, Connaught terr
Riches Louisa (Miss), lodging house, 79 Up. Stamford st
Riches Richd.brush mak.& turner, 18 Lowr. Eaton st.Pimlico
Riches Robert, teadealer, 37 Salisbury st. Bermondsey
Riches Saml. H. dairyman, 38 & 39 Marylebone la. Oxford st
Riches Wm. potato salesman, 132 Whitechapel rd
RichesWm.Ambrose, oilman&grocer, 3Up.Charlesst.Westmr
Richings James, tailor, 32 New North st. Red Lion sq
Richins Richard, grocer, 24 Princes sq. Kennington cross
Richman Edmund Charles, surveyor, 2 Farm st. Berkeley sq
Richman Francis, builder, Regent st. Horseferry rd
Richmond Robt.K.& ArthurJ.surgeons, 4 Star corner, Bermsy
Richmond Son & Co. coopers & stave, yeast & beer merchants, 14 Millbank row, Westminster
Richmond Railway (Richard Meade, sec.), 3 Moorgate st
RichmondAlfred, mercht.N.&S.American cof.ho.Thrdneedl.st
Richmond George, artist, 10 York st. Portman sq
Richmond George, bookbinder, 53 Skinner st. Snow hill
Richmond George, tailor, 13 Jewin crescent, City
Richmond George, tailor, 33 Pitfield st. Hoxton
Richmond John, livery stables, 2 Glasshouse yd. & fruiterer, 5 Broadway, Blackfriars
Richmond Lewis, tailor, 35 Gower place, Euston sq
Richmond Matthew, carman, 148 Kingsland rd
Richmond Robert, barrister, 10 King's Bench walk, Temple
Richmond Robert, cattle salesman, 60 West Smithfield
Richmond Robt. Milburn, plumber, 18 Whitefriars st.Fleet st
Richmond Samuel, glass & china dlr.44 York st.Westminster
Richmond Thomas, artist, 16 Beaumont st. Portland place
Richmond William, news agent, 15 Arundel pl. Coventry st
Richmond William, coal merchant, Great Scotland yard
Richnell Mary (Mrs.), tobacconist, 1 Williams pl.Walwth.rd
Ritcher Charles Saml. furrier, 2 St. Vincent place, City rd
Ritcher Henry, lodging house, 86 Lisson grove north
Ritcher Thos. sec. to *Phœnix Fire Office*, 19 Lombard st
Rickard John, plumber, 87 St. George's road, Southwark
Rickard William, stockbroker, 3 Bank chambers, Lothbury
Rickards & Campkin, law stationers, 33 Castle st. Holborn
Rickards George & Son, solicitors, 62 Old Broad st. City
Rickards George & Sons, distillers, 207 Piccadilly
Rickards, Little & Co. east india agents & merchants, 15 Bishopsgate within
Rickards & Walker, solicitors, 29 Lincoln's inn fields
Rickards Frederick, artist, 6 Union st. Clarendon square
Rickards George Kettilby, barrister, 4 Elm court, Temple
Rickards Henry, ivory turner, 26 Goswell ter. Goswell rd
Rickards John, livery stables, Unicorn yard, 106½ Oxford st
Rickards Jonathan, baker, 1 York place, Portland town
Rickards Jonathan, baker, 23 New st. Dorset square
Rickards Joseph, hardwood turner&dealr.35Gun st.Bshpsga
Rickards Robert, carpet warehouse, 1 Chiswell st
Rickatson Thos. saddle currier, 57& 58 St.Clement's la.Strnd
Rickehaus John Henry, colonial mer. 52 Lower Thames st
Rickerby Joseph, printer & publisher, 15 Sherborne lane
Ricket Henry, *Hope* P.H. Field st. Bagnigge wells road
Rickets Chas. gas stove maker & fitter, also registered proprietor & manufacturer of the smoke elevation for curing smoky chimneys, 5 Agar st. Strand
Rickets John, butcher, 64½ Leather lane
Rickett George, hosier, glover & outfitter, 220 Strand
Rickett Henry, beer retailer, 14 Spencer st.Northampton sq
Rickett Jas. coach spg. ma. 1 Charles st. east, Hampstd. rd
Rickett Thos. coal & coke mer. Bridge whf. Cambridge hth
Rickett Wm. brace & stock manf. 4 Amwell ter.Clerkenwell
Ricketts, Boutcher & Co. merchants, 38 Gracechurch st
Ricketts, James & Co. merchants, 8 Moorgate st
Ricketts Benjamin, coffee rooms, 47 Whitechapel High st
Ricketts David, grocer, 8 Gt. Chesterfield st. Marylebone
Ricketts Edward, shoemaker, 188 Union st. Borough
Ricketts Edward, staymaker, 188 Union st. Borough
Ricketts Hannah (Miss), milliner, 1 Conduit st. Bond st
Ricketts James, butcher, 11 Skinner st. Somers town
Ricketts James, coachsmith, 1 Charles mews, Drummond st

Ricketts James, combmaker, 21 Nassau pl. Comcl. rd. east
Ricketts James, coffee rooms, 4 & 5 Church la. Whitechapel
Ricketts Thos. bricklayer, &c. 98 Broadwall, Blackfriars
Rickford George, tobacconist, 2 Cambridge rd. Mile end
Rickford Mary (Mrs.), stationer, 32 Limekiln hill, Limehous
Rickit James, haberdasher, 64 Earl st. east, Lisson grove
Rickman James, bottle merchant, 9 & 10 Hungerford wharf, Strand, & 4 Holland st. Blackfriars road
Rickman James, coal mer. Western wf. George st. Adelphi
Rickman Jas. mustard manuf. see Finch, Rickman & Co
Rickman Samuel Philip, merchant, 11 George yd. Lombard st
Rickman Wm. potato dealer, 31 James st. Covent garden
Ricks Isabella (Miss), milliner, 19 Mount st. Berkeley sq
Rickwood Caroline E. (Mrs.), la. school, 4 Terrace, O. Kent rd
Riddall James, shell cleaner, 163 Old Gravel lane, Wapping
Riddall William, grocer, 56 King st. Deptford
Riddell David, architectl. modeller, see Bernasconi & Riddell
Riddell Francis Henry, barrister, 19 Old square, Lincoln's inn
Riddell Henry Matthias, barrister, 8 New sq. Lincoln's inn
Riddell Robert, *Old George* P.H. 47 Drury lane
Riddell Sir Walter Buchanan, bart. barrister, 13 Old square
Riddell William, sailmaker & shipchandler, 204 Wapg. High st
Riddick John, baker, 12 Lambeth walk
Riddick Thos. baker, 60 East st. Manchester square
Ridding Richd. china & glass warehouse, 61 Paddington st
Ridding Thomas, printer, 6 Marylebone lane
Riddington Thomas, fruiterer, 1 Somerset ter. Kensington
Riddle Jas. & Thos. cabinet makers, 54 Wells st. Oxford st
Riddle & Meymott, wholesale stationers, 25 Paternoster row
Riddle Gabriel, mechanist & mnfr. of pat. ever pointed pencils & leads, & cumberland lead drawing & writing pencils, penholders, & quill & steel portable pens; revolving top, fountain & duplex inkstands; self-adjusting letter balances, pat. hemispherical stoppered bottles, pat. locks, iron safes, fire proof boxes, &c. 172 Blackfriars road
Riddle Henry, window blind maker, 2 Bedford pl. Coml. rd
Riddle Walter, grocer, 79 Gloucester pl. Kentish town
Riddlesdale Daniel, butcher, 25 Newport ct. Newport mkt
Riddy James, *Britannia* coffee rooms, 63 Tooley st
Ride John, corn dealer, 80 High Holborn
Rideal Titus & Son, wine merchts. 143 & 144 Union st. Boro'
Rideal Sarah (Mrs.), lodging house, 17 Manchester bldgs
Ridenton Samuel, machinist, 4 Vine st. Hatton wall
Rider Brothers, leather dressers, hat, leather trimming & patent composition hat tip manufrs. 61 Redcross st. Boro'
Rider Thomas & Son, carpenters & builders, 3 Great Tower st. City; & 121 Union st. Borough
Rider Francis, beer retailer, 9 Marine st. Bermondsey
Rider Geo. *Hope* coffee rooms, 5 William st. New Bridge st
Rider Henry, teadealer & grocer, 98 New Park st. Borough, & 23 Great Guildford st. Borough
Rider Jacob, harness maker, 1 Parker's row, Dockhead
Rider John, printer & stereotyper, 14 Bartholomew close
Rider John, watchmaker, Camberwell green
Rider Richard, potato dealer, 45 Cross st. Islington
Rider Robert, basket maker, 9 Crispin st. Spitalfields
Rider Thomas, beer retailer, 19 Compton st. Clerkenwell
Rider Thomas, butcher, 4 Waterloo st. Camberwell
Rider Thos. I. bent timber manfr. 19 Compton st. Clerkenwell
Rider Wm. tailor, 15 Meard's court, Soho
Rider Wm. official seal engraver, 10 Pickett st. or 255 Strand
Rider Wm. *Rider's hotel*, 46 Salisbury square, Fleet st
Rider Wm. livery stables, 35 Queen st. Cheapside
Ridge Benjamin, birmingham agt. 3 Artillery ct. Chiswell st
Ridge Francis L. court plaister & tinted goldbeaters' skin manufacturer, 3 Dobson's terrace, Kennington road
Ridge Geo. Hen. cheesemonger, 12 Grosvenor row, Pimlico
Ridge John, brickma. Bethnal grn. whf. Bonner's hall fields
Ridge John, tailor, 7 Grosvenor st. Grosvenor square
Ridge Joseph, physician, 37 Cavendish square
Ridge Michael, cheesemonger, 2 Norfolk pl. Lr. rd. Islington
Ridge Samuel, stockbroker, 72 Old Broad st
Ridge Stephen, corn dealer, 3 Borough road
Ridge Wm. carpenter, 15 Gresse st. Tottenham court road
Ridge Wm. corn, flour & seed mer. 15 Grosvenor row, Pimlico
Ridge Wm. solicitor & parliam. agent, 36 Cross st. Islington
Ridge Wm. who. tea & coffee dealer, see Young, Ridge & Co
Ridgway & Co. tea dealers, 4 & 5 King William st. City
Ridgway Alexander F. general agent, 42 Leicester square
Ridgway Edw. gold turner, 11½ Northampton st. Clerkenwll
Ridgway James, bookseller & publisher, 169 Piccadilly
Ridgway John, carpenter & builder, Kensington High st
Ridgway Richard B. infant school depôt, 22 Chichester pl
Ridgway Richard Bowling H. accountant, 4 Trafalgar sq
Ridgwell James, dairy, 18 Charlotte st. Fitzroy square
Ridgyard William, marine store dlr. 29 Gibson st. Waterloo rd
Riding Roger, physician, 36 Euston square
Ridington Thomas, bootmaker, 15 Finsbury place north
Ridler George, beer retailer, Frederick st. Portland town
Ridler Henry, *Crown & Anchor* P. H. 9 Brewer st. Golden sq
Ridler Richard, *Duke of York* P.H. 59 Regent st. Horseferry rd
Ridler Valentine, *Bell & Crown tav. & hotel*, 133 Holborn hill
Ridler William, bootmaker, 28 Queen st. Golden square
Ridley & Fleck, tailors, &c. 54 Great Marlborough st
Ridley Mary & Ann (Misses), milliners, 37 Jewin st
Ridley, Son & Ellington, upholsterers' warehousemen, fringe, floor cloth & table baize manufacturers & floor cloth makers, 46 & 47 Newgate st. & Lower road, Islington
Ridley & Bayley, shipbrokers, see Bayley & Ridley
Ridley Charles, surgeon, &c. 14 Bedford st. Bedford square
Ridley Esther (Miss), milliner, &c. 139½ Hoxton Old town
Ridley Fred. Hen. ladies' shoemaker, 52 St. Paul's churchyd
Ridley George, barrister, 5 Pump court, Temple
Ridley George, wine & spirit merchant, 52 Crutched friars, & 2 Chester place, Old Kent road
Ridley John, coal fac. ship & ins. bro. see Lambert, Ridley & Co
Ridley John, tobacconist, 27 Finsbury pavement
Ridley John, workbox, &c. manfr. 37 Jewin st. Cripplegate
Ridley Mary Ann (Mrs.), straw bonnet ma. 139½ Hoxton O. tn
Ridley Stephen Hen. surveyor, 8 Little Tufton st. Westminster
Ridley Thomas, watch & clock mkr. 6 Gt. Charlotte st. Blkfrs
Ridley Thomas Benj. *Thistle & Crown* P.H. 39 St. Martin's la
Ridley William, furrier & hatter, 44 Warwick st. Regent st
Ridout John, surgeon, 10 Montague st. Russell square
Ridpath Alexr. & Son, tailors, 3 Maddox st. Regent st
Ridpath Alexander, tailor, 6 Upper Baker st. New road
Ridpath Thos. pawnbroker, 25 & 26 Up. Seymour st. Euston sq
Ridsdale Benj. bookbinder, 12 South st. Finsbury market
Ridsdale Fras. Jas. solictr. see Wiglesworth, Ridsdale & Co
Ridsdale Geo. surgeon, 1 Gower place, Euston square
Ridsdale Thomas, brass finisher & gasfitter, 54 Minories
Riekie James, baker, 409 Strand
Riekie Margaret (Mrs.), baker, 111 Old st. St. Luke's
Rielly Thos. revolving chair ma. 18 Quicksett row, New rd
Ries Samuel, grand cigar divan, 101 & 102 Strand
Rietiker Jacob, tailor, 61 Berwick st. Soho
Rigby Edward & Charles, brushmakers, 80 Gracechurch st
Rigby Joseph & Charles, builders & saw mills, 23 Holywell st. Millbank
Rigby & Lee, coachmakers, 7 Park lane, Piccadilly
Rigby Edward, physician, 23 New st. Spring gardens
Rigby James, nurseryman, 16 Gloucester rd. Old Brompton
Rigby Jeremiah, tobacconist, 6 Ireland row, Mile end road
Rigby John, hat manufr. 6 Essex st. Gravel la. Southwark
Rigby Martha (Mrs.), bookbinder, 41 George st. Blackfrs. rd
Rigby Thomas, boot & shoe mak. 13 Little Compton st. Soho
Rigby William, *Red Lion* P.H. 4 Maze, Tooley st
Rigg Charles Merit, physician, 22 York place, Portman sq
Rigg George, grocer, 15 Pleasant row, Stepney green
Rigg James, merchant, see Nicholson, Rigg & Co.
Rigg Jonathan, broker in hides, skins, &c. see Goad & Rigg
Rigg Thomas, coal merchant, 37 Paradise st. Rotherhithe
Rigg William, stationer, 16 Chalton st. Somers town
Rigge, Brockbank & Rigge, perfumers to her Majesty & the Royal Family, 35 New Bond st. & 5 East st. Brighton
Rigge Thomas H. & Co. perfumers & cutlers, 65 Cheapside
Rigge John S. merchant, see Sanderson, Frys', Fox & Co
Riggline Geo. grocer, &c. 14 South wharf road, Paddington
Riggs John, builder, 41 York st. St. Luke's
Riggs Joseph, grocer & cheesemngr. 32 College st. Chelsea
Righy William, solicitor, 7 John st. Adelphi
Rigley Henry Adolphus, solicitor, see Collins & Rigley
Rignall Mary (Mrs.), tobacconist, 59 Richard st. Comcl. rd. east
Riles Saml. woollendraper & trimg. slr. 17 Bishopsgt. st. witht
Riley Benjamin, cheesemonger, 18 Islington High st
Riley Benj. velvet & silk hat plush manufactr. 118 Wood st
Riley Charles, bookbinder, 2 St. Andrew's hill, Doctors' com
Riley Charles, hosier & outfitter, 67½ Blackman st
Riley Daniel, tailor, 24 Bowling green lane, Clerkenwell
Riley Francis, *Ship & Whale* P.H. 19 Wapping wall
Riley George, bookbinder, 18 Warwick sq. Newgate st
Riley George, woollendraper, 257 Borough High st
Riley Horatio, bookbinder, 29 & 30 Greenhill's rents, Smithfield
Riley Hugh, couch & easy chair mak. 5 Welmer grdns. Hoxton
Riley James, cheesemonger, 3 Mount pl. Walworth road
Riley James, *Green Man & Still* P.H. 5 Coppice row, Clerknw
Riley James, oilman, 34 Pitfield st. Hoxton
Riley James tailor, 8 Church st. Trinity sq. Borough
Riley Jahn, *Hole in the Wall* P.H. 8 Gate st. Lincoln's inn flds
Riley John, lighterman, 66 & 68 Lower Thames st
Riley Joseph, tin plate worker, 31 Whitmore road, Hoxton
Riley Peter, hat manufactr. 24 Cannon st. St. George's east

Riley Richard, livery stables, 1 Railway mews, Drummond st
Riley Richard, tailor, 88 London road, Southwark
Riley Roland, tailor, 19 Basinghall st
Riley Shaw, upholsterer, Wandsworth road, north side
Riley Thomas, fruiterer, 1 Clifton place, Wandsworth rd
Riley Thomas, printer, 3 Hind court, Fleet st
Riley Wm. coal dlr. 31 Windsor st. Lower rd. Islington
Riley William, *Rose & Crown* P.H. 1 Star st. Shadwell
Rilot Elizth. (Mrs.), staymaker, 8 Gt. Titchfield st. Oxford st
Rily Chapman Wm. & Co. ship stores' merchants, 9 Princes sq. & 21 Albert sq. Commercial road [east
Rimbault Edw. prof. of music, Grosvenor cot. 17 Park village
Rimell Henry, livery stables, 56 New Bond st
Rimell Thomas, beer retailer, 6 Chapel place, Brompton
Rimmel Hyacinthe, wholes. perfumer, 39 Gerard st. Soho
Rimmer Ann (Mrs.), trimm. seller, 9 Lit. Chapel st. Soho
Rimmer Charles, woollendraper, see Williams & Rimmer
Ring & Conquest, who. tin plate workers, 27 Old Change
Ring Charles, proctor, 3 Gt. Knightrider st. Doctors' commons
Ring David Babington, barrister, 3 Brick court, Temple
Ring Frederick, solicitor, 26 Queen st. Cheapside
Ring James, grocer, 19 New King st. Deptford
Ring James, tobacconist, & hard confectioner, 48 Shadwell
Ring John Thomas, carpntr. bldr. & undtkr. 3 Grange rd. Brmsy
Ring Mary Ann (Miss), milliner, 16 Margaret st. Cavend. sq
Ringer John, *William the Fourth* P.H. 12 Ship yd. Tmpl. bar
Ringham James, loding house, 21 Portsea pl. Connaught sq
Ringrose John, bookseller, &c. 11 Sherrard st. Golden sq
Ringshaw Geo. furniture broker, 42 Waterloo st. Camberwell
Rintoul Ann (Mrs.), artists' repos. 33 Southamptn. st. Strand
Rintoul Robert, printer, 3 Clarence place, Stepney green
Rintoul William, drawing master, 33 Southamptn. st. Strand
Riordon Patrick, feather merchant, 9 Cross st. Hatton grdn
Ripkey John, child's chaise maker, 1 Coal yard, Drury lane
Ripley, Brown & Co. east india brokers, 6 Laurence Pountney lane, & 14 Mincing lane
Ripley Lucy (Mrs.), grocer, 8 Chapel st. Tottenham ct. rd
Ripley Robert, by appointment to her Majesty's forces, sole agent for Marder's waterproof jet blacking, Hooker's ct. 26 Nicholas lane
Ripley Robert, salt merchant, Hooker's ct. Nicholas lane
Ripley William Richard, solicitor, 7 Whitehall place
Ripper Wm. carpenter, &c. 10 Thornton st. Dockhead
Rippin Benjamin, academy, 9 Brunswick st. Blackwall
Rippin William, *Black Horse* P.H. 400 Oxford st
Rippingham & Rose, solicitors, 17 Gt. Prescot st. Goodman's fi
Rippington John & Charles, butchers, 24 Up. Marylebone st
Rippington Edwin, butcher, 63 George st. Euston sq
Rippon & Burton, general furnishing ironmongers, makers of nickel silver & patentees of the chunk & vesta stove, 39 Oxford st. corner of Newman st
Rippon Abrm. Crofton, tobacco ma. see Crofton & Rippon
Rippon Charles, attorney, 190 Blackfriars road
Rippon Henry, baker, 13½ Bethnal green, west side
Rippon Thomas, bootmaker, 34 Coldbath sq. Clerkenwell
Rippon William, carpenter & builder, 22 Charterhouse lane
Rippon's Almshouses (Sam. Gale. esq. tr.), New Park st. Boro'
Ripsher (Swan) & Co. linendrapers, 18 Lisle st. Leicester sq
Risdon John, stockbroker, Stock Exchange
Risley Shuckburgh, solicitor, 14 Furnival's inn, Holborn
Risso Alexander, merchant, 1 Cullum st. Fenchurch st
Risson Henry, bootmaker, 47 Penton st. Pentonville
Rist Alfred, baker, 1 Collier st. Pentonville
Rist Chas. surveyor, appraiser, &c. 24 Seething la. Tower st
Ritchie Brothers, merchants, 117 Bishopsgate within
Ritchie & Furrell, law stationers, 8 Chancery lane
Ritchie Alfred, coal mercht. & wharfinger, Deptford bridge
Ritchie Ann (Mrs.), *George* P.H. 113 Cock hill, Ratcliff
Ritchie Arthur M. special pleader, 3 Church yd. ct. Temple
Ritchie Charles, jeweller, &c. 120 Oxford st
Ritchie Charles Robt. dyer, 76 Park st. Grosvenor square
Ritchie David, tobacconist, 43 William st. Regent's park
Ritchie Fredk. baker, 39 Weymouth st. New Kent road
Ritchie Geo. comm. mer. 45 Skinner st. & 31 St. Mary at hill
Ritchie James, baker, 8 Chester place, Old Kent road
Ritchie James, *Brown Bear* P.H. 30 Eldon st. Finsbury
Ritchie James Wm. baker, 11 Lr. Salisbury pl. Locksfields
Ritchie John, baker, 12 Cannon st. City
Ritchie John, merchant, Garraway's coffeeho. 'Change alley
Ritchie Thomas, chandler's shop, William st. Caledonian rd
Ritchie Thomas, printer, see Compton & Ritchie
Ritherdon & Carr, ship bro. & sur. of shipping, 16 Billiter st
Rittener & Saxby, foreign porcelain wareho. 41 Albemarle st
Rittman Frederick, tailor, 4 Warwick pl. Kingsland rd
Ritson Thos. printer, 12 Northampton st. Lwr. rd. Islington
Rivaz Alex. Hugonin, insurance agt. see Harford, Rivaz & Co
River Dee Comp. Off. (Benj. Lyon, sec.), 9 Mansionhouse st
River Fergus Drainage & Embankment Co. (Jackson Barwise, sec.), 18 Austinfriars
Rivers Charles, broker, Garraway's coffee house
Rivers Chas. colonial bro. O. Trinity ho. 5 Water la. Tower st
Rivers Francis, bonnet shape warehouse, 3 Paul st. Finsbury
Rivers George, tailor, 11 Gower place, Euston square
Rivers James, oil & colorm. 2 Paragon pl. Locksflds. Walw
Rivers James Horatio, *Wheatsheaf* P.H. 18 Borough market
Rivers James Kemp, tailor, 2 Paul st. Finsbury
Rivers John Henry, *Fox & Hounds* P.H. Lit. Guildford st. Boro'
Rivett Wm. & Sons, upholsterers, 50 Crown st. Finsbury
Rivett James, house agent, Stratford
Rivett Samuel, hairdresser, 8 Prospect pl. Kingsland road
Riviere Daniel Valentine, artist, 8 Cirencester pl. Fitzroy sq
Riviere Henry P. artist, 13 North crescent, Bedford square
Riviere Isaac, gunmaker, 315 Oxford st
Riviere Robt. bookbinder, 28 Gt. Queen st. Lincoln's inn flds
Riviere William, artist, 46 Cirencester pl. Fitzroy square
Rivington Francis & John, booksellers & publishers, 62 St. Paul's churchyard, & 3 Waterloo place, Pall mall
Rivington Charles, solicitor & clerk to the Stationers' Company, 1 Fenchurch buildings
Rivington Wm. printer, see Gilbert & Rivington
Rivolta Anthony, merchant, 21 Lower Calthorpe st
Rivolta Dominico Antonio, solicitor, 44 Bloomsbury sq
Rix John & Nathaniel, ironmongers, 224 Shadwell High st. & 384 Platform, Rotherhithe
Rix Cecil, coal merchant, 3 Gt. Alie st. Goodman's fields
Rix Henry, coal mer. Albany whf. Albany rd. Old Kent rd
Rix Henry, cork merchant, 33 Pudding lane
Rix John, butcher, Well st. Hackney
Rix John, merchant & com. agent, 3 George yd. Lombard st
Rix Mary (Mrs.), plumber, &c. 11 Penton st. Pentonville
Rix Nathaniel, ironmonger, 12 Arbour sq. Commercial rd. ea
Rixen James, tailor, 9 Broadway, Blackfriars
Rixon Wm. & Son, solicitors, 20 Jewry st. Aldgate
Rixon Adolphus, bookseller, see Pretyman & Rixon
Rixon Frederick, lamp & glass ma. see Hancock, Rixon & Dunt
Rixon Wm. chief bailiff, Stepney manor, 20 Jewry st. Aldgate
Roach Chas. fruiterer, 40 Warwick st. Golden sq
Roach John, bricklayer, 3 Paradise row, Chelsea
Roach Mary Sh. (Mrs.), granarykepr. Pickleherring, Tooley st
Roach Pope, chemist & druggist, 210 Borough High st
Roach Richard, grocer & tea dealer, 103 Fenchurch st
Roach Wm. carpenter, New yard, Gt. Queen st. Lincoln's inn fields
Road & Street Cleansing Co. 62 Charing cross
Road Francis, china & glass wa. 101 Lambeth Low. marsh
Roadnight Joseph, coal mer. Middle wf. Gt. Scotland yd
Roads Charles, oil & colorman, 55 Goswell st. & 11 Black Prince row, Walworth
Roads Joseph, tallow chandler, 5 Greek st. Soho
Roads Joseph, omnibus propr. 27 New Church st. Edgw. rd
Roake & Varty, booksellers & stationers, 31 Strand
Roake Edmund, cattle salesman, 8 West Smithfield
Roake Henry, tea dealer, 1 Constable row, Mile end road
Roake John George, engraver, 386 Oxford st
Roan George, trunkmaker, 9 York place, Westminster rd
Roan Wm. calico printer, see Strachan & Roan
Robarts, Curtis & Co. bankers, 15 Lombard st
Robarts, Griffith & Crick, silk mercers, 1 Chandos st
Robarts Frederick, proctor, see Townsend & Robarts
Robarts George, stationer, 8 Constitution row, Gray's inn rd
Robarts Henry, woollendraper, 62 Conduit st. Regent st
Robarts Hen. Pratt, surgeon, &c. 11 Gt. Coram st. Brunswk. sq
Robarts Nathaniel, proctor & notary, 4 Dean's court, & 27 Great Carter lane, Doctors' commons
Robb Alexander, biscuit maker, 95, & oil & colorman, 96 St. Martin's lane
Robb Peter, surgeon, 33 St. Martin's le grand
Robbie James, chandler's shop, 6 Fort pl. Grange rd. Bermdsy
Robbins Chas. carpenter & undertaker, 1 Abbey st. Bermdsy
Robbins Edward, gilder, 194 Wellington ter. Waterloo road
Robbins Edward, tailor, 4 Rose lane, Ratcliff
Robbins George, stationer, 2 Moreton pl. Kentish town
Robbins Henry, beer retailer, Bridge road, Battersea
Robbins James, beer retailer, 106 Poplar High st
Robbins James, silk dyer, 4 Seabright st. Bethnal green road
Robbins James, stationer & news agt. 45 Up. Baker st. New rd
Robbins James, *Two Angels & Crown* P.H. 10 Up. St. Mrtn's. la
Robbins John, *Artichoke* P.H. 71 Kent st. Borough
Robbins Joseph, watchmaker, 24 Perceval st. Clerkenwell
Robbins Kinneard, clerical & law wig maker, 46 Carey st
Robbins Mary (Mrs.), milliner, 45 Great Marylebone st
Robbins Rich. damp & drop lake mfr. 1 Deal st. Mile end Nw. tn

Robbins Samuel, *Brickla. Arms* P.H. 12 Parker's row, Dk.hd
Robbins Thomas, furn. undertaker, 11 Etham pl. Dover rd
Robbins Wm. grocer, 52 Hindon st. Pimlico
Robbins Wm. old ship timber dealer, &c. Battersea fields
Roberson Chas. & Co. artists' colormen, lead & hair pencil, varnish & color makers & stationers, 51 Long acre
Robert Thomas & Co. hatters, 68 Barbican
Robert James, embroiderer, 10 Richmond buildings, Soho
Roberton Jas. Matthew, Son & Gill, tinmen, 63 Fore st. Limeho
Roberton Jas. Matthew, plumber, 3 Providence pl. Com. rd. ea
Roberts & Adlard, slate merchants, Potter's fields, Tooley st. & Mill st. Dockhead, Bermondsey
Roberts Charles & Co. eupodistic boot & shoe makers, 36 High Holborn, & 151 Strand.
Roberts Charles & Co. warehousemen, 17 St. Paul's chyd.
Roberts Emily & Fras. (Misses), dressmaker, 71 Welbeck st
Roberts George Wintle & Co. accountants, 73 Basinghall st
Roberts & Griffiths, attorneys, 25 Tokenhouse yard
Roberts Harriet & Charlotte, school, 28 Penton st. Pentonvil
Roberts & Hazard, paper manufacturers' agents, 9 College hill
Roberts Henry Edwd. & Co. tea dealers, 13 Lower Seymour st
Roberts & M'Lellan, milliners, 89 New Bond st
Roberts Michael & Edward, mast, block & pump makers, 159 Rotherhithe st. & Lower York st. Rotherhithe
Roberts, Mitchell & Co. east ind. merchs. 15 Old Jewry chmbs
Roberts Robert & Co. woollen drapers, 4 & 5 Aldgate High st
Roberts & Nitsch, tailors, 100 Mount st. Berkeley square
Roberts & Roby, auctioneers, &c. 24 Moorgate st. City
Roberts Samuel, Angel & Co. silversmiths, 5 Bridgewater sq
Roberts Samuel & Son, livery stables, 242A, Oxford st
Roberts & Son, cork merchants & manufacturers, & importers of foreign corks, 10 Eastcheap, & 5 Botolph lane
Roberts, Smith & Co. sheffield plate wareho. 8 Duke st. Adelphi
Roberts Thos. & Co. pro. of Parr's life pills, 8 Crane ct. Fleet st
Roberts Thomas & Joseph, soapmakers, 99 York st. Westmr
Roberts Ann (Mrs.), baker, 1 Grange rd. sth. side Bermndsy
Roberts Ann (Mrs.), brushmaker, 110 Great, Portland st
Roberts Anne (Mrs.), tobacconist, 17 Francis st. Totnhm. ct. rd
Roberts Ann (Mrs.), tobacconist, 14 Pennyfields, Poplar
Roberts Benjamin, grocer, 20 St. James' market, Haymarket
Roberts Benoni Benjamin, bootma. 62 Flagon row, Deptford
Roberts Cath. (Miss), umbrella ma. see Pomroy & Roberts
Roberts Charles, bootmaker, 36 High Holborn
Roberts Charles, blindmaker, 48 North st. Edgware road
Roberts Charles, builder, 2 Dudley court, Silver st. Falcon sq
Roberts Charles, drug broker, 38 Mincing lane, City.
Roberts Charles, wax & tallow chandler to the royal family, 37 to 39 Chandos st. Covent garden
Roberts Charles Julius, physician, 31 New Bridge st. Blackfriars
Roberts Daniel, bootmaker, 27 Marylebone st. Picadilly
Roberts Daniel, leather dresser, see Learmonths' & Roberts
Roberts David, bookbind. & stat. 7 Grange pl. Hoxton New tn
Roberts David, R.A. artist, 7 Fitzroy st. Fitzroy square
Roberts Edward, ham merchant, 85 Farringdon st
Roberts Edward, livery stables, 12 Whitmore road, Hoxton
Roberts Edm. Austin, grocer & oilman, 13 Hackney rd. cresc
Roberts Edward, butcher, 8 Gt. Chapel st. Westminster
Roberts Edward, tailor, 3 Mead's court, Old Bond st
Roberts Edward Boyd, hatter & furrier, 32 Moorgate st. Bank, & 239 Regent st
Roberts Edward James, porkman, 4 Glo'ster pl. Old Kent rd
Roberts Geo. baker, 96 Milton st. Finsbury
Roberts Geo. butcher, 63 Exmouth st. Clerkenwell
Roberts Geo. carpenter & builder, 5 Ebury square
Roberts Geo. cowkeeper, 77 Milton st. Dorset square
Roberts Geo. estate & commission agent, Hall of Commerce, & 13 City road
Roberts Geo. laceman, ladies' hosiery & stay ware. 183 Oxford st
Roberts Geo. springwind. blind ma. 29 Brownlow st. Drury la
Roberts Geo. stationer, 4 Brewer st. Somers town
Roberts Geo. Fras. stationer, 161 Union st. Boro' High st
Roberts Hannah (Mrs.), tobacconist, 81 Mary st. New rd
Roberts Henry, architect, 13 Suffolk st. Pall mall east
Roberts Henry, baker, 24 High st. Shadwell
Roberts Henry, cabinet maker, 8 Queen st. Hoxton
Roberts Henry, carver & gilder, 58 Windsor st. Islington
Roberts Henry, cigar imp. 2 Winchester buildings, City
Roberts Henry, grocer, &c. 119 Lambeth walk
Roberts Henry, painter & glazier, 6 Foley st. Portland pl
Roberts Henry, pawnbroker, see Pickford & Roberts
Roberts Henry, perfumer, 11 Gt. Russell st. Bloomsbury
Roberts Henry, rag & bottle dlr. 23 Cecil court, St. Martin's la
Roberts Henry, tailor, 3 Clipstone st. Fitzroy square
Roberts Henry, tailor, 16 Young st. Kensington
Roberts Henry Boydon, solicitor, 36 Friar st. Blackfriars rd. & 10 Church st. Trinity square, Borough
Roberts Henry, tailor, solicitor, 2 Bride ct. New Bridge st
Roberts Henry Thos. pork butcher, 2 Melbourne pl. O. Kent rd
Roberts James, butcher, 10 Gt. Cherry garden st. Bermndsy
Roberts James, cattle salesman, 37 West Smithfield
Roberts James, engraver & printer, 3 New st. Bishopsgate
Roberts James, glazier, 3 Porter's place, Holloway
Roberts James, mahogany merchant, 9 Billiter st
Roberts James, registrar of births, &c. 38 Duke st. St. James
Roberts James, *Rodney's Head* P.H. 4 Old st
Roberts James, jun. paper box maker, 6 London wall
Roberts James, sen. paper box maker, 137 London wall
Roberts James Henry, printer, 41 Tabernacle walk, Finsbury
Roberts John, academy, 103 Hoxton old town
Roberts John, *Artichoke tavern*, see Brendel & Roberts
Roberts John, baker, 76 Pratt st. Camden town
Roberts John, boat builder, 6 Bishop's walk, Lambeth
Roberts John, bootmaker, 34 Chester st. Kennington
Roberts John, bootmaker, 191 Hoxton Old town
Roberts John, butcher, 26 Green st. Bethnal green
Roberts John, cane & stick maker, 91 West Smithfield
Roberts John, china & glass dealer, Deptford broadway
Roberts John, coal merchant, 3 Brunswick place, Balls pd. rd
Roberts John, conveyancer, 2 Inner Temple lane
Roberts John, grocer, 2 Hickman's folly, Dockhd. Bermdsy
Roberts John, harness maker, 14 Regent st. Horseferry rd
Roberts John, hide splitter, 25 Long lane, Bermondsey
Roberts John, linendraper, 6 Cook's terrace, St. Pancras
Roberts John, merchant, 3 Crosby square
Roberts John, oil & colorman, 3 Exmouth st. Spafields
Roberts John, pawnbroker, 42 York st. Westminster
Roberts John, printer & ticket writer, 8 Cannon st. road
Roberts John, shive turner, 57 Castle st. Southwark
Roberts John, soda water manfr. 50½ Blackman st. Borough
Roberts John, *Sol's Arms* P.H. 1 Sol's row, Hampstead rd
Roberts John, surgeon, &c. 34 Finsbury circus
Roberts John, tailor, Little Chelsea, near Stamford Bridge
Roberts John, tobacco & snuff ma. 126 & 127 Whitechapel rd. & 115 & 116 High st. Borough
Roberts John, wholesale spice dealer, 34 Eastcheap
Roberts John, winecooper, 1 Mansell pas. Haydon sq. Minories
Roberts John A. oil & colorman, 8 Flagon row, Deptford
Roberts John Hy. surg. Norfolk villa, Finchly. nw. rd. St. John's w
Roberts Joseph, auctioneer, surveyor & valr. 7 Old Jewry
Roberts Joseph, bookseller, &c. 2 Arabella row, Pimlico
Roberts Joseph, grocer & cheesemonger, 89 Lambeth walk
Roberts Joseph Michael, engrav. & print. see Baily & Roberts
Roberts Keturah (Miss), perfumer, 110 St. Martin's lane
Roberts Maria (Mrs.), herald chaser, 75 Upper Berkeley st
Roberts Mary (Mrs.), clothes' salesman, 74 New Compton st
Roberts Mary (Mrs.), dressma. 52 Up. Seymour st. Ptmn. sq
Roberts Mary (Mrs.), market gardener, High st. Deptford
Roberts Mary (Mrs.), *Woolpack* P.H. Morning lane, Hackney
Roberts Mary Ann (Miss), milliner, 132 New Bond st
Roberts Michael, butcher, 1 Horseferry road, Westminster
Roberts Mitchell Wm. wholesale grocer, 3 Botolph lane
Roberts Moses, linendraper, 200 Oxford st
Roberts Onesiphorous, woollendra. 9 Marylebone st. Piccadilly
Roberts Percy, cheesemonger, 22 New st. Covent garden
Roberts Philip, solicitor, 28 Carey st. Lincoln's inn
Roberts Rathbone Bartlett, barrister, 7 New sq. Lincoln's inn
Roberts Richard, builder, 13 Kennington row, Kenningtonrd
Roberts Richard John, solicitor, see Plucknett & Roberts
Roberts Robert, carpenter, Globe road, Mile end
Roberts Robert, cheesemonger, 75 Rosemary lane, Minories
Roberts Robert, fish factor, 118 Lower Thames st
Roberts Robert, fruiterer, 6 Crucifix lane, Bermondsey
Roberts Robert, linenfactor, 39 Gt. Tower st
Roberts Robert, tobacco & snuff manufacturer, 54 St. John st. Clerkenwell, & 4 High st. Newington butts
Roberts Robert Jas. undertaker, 14 Robert st. Bedford row
Roberts Rt. Wm. sec. to White Knight's estate Co. 15 Portman st
Roberts Roger, watchmaker, 116A, Gt. Titchfield st
Roberts Rowland, capillaire ma. 3 Britannia row, Islngn
Roberts Rowland Wm. wine & spirit mer. 44 Cross st. Finsbury
Roberts Samuel, tobacconist, 38 St. John st. Clerkenwell
Roberts Stephen, tailor, see Corss & Roberts
Roberts Thomas, baker, 6 Cross st. Wenlock road
Roberts Thomas, carman, 3 Cousin lane, Up. Thames st
Roberts Thomas, carpenter, 12 New Nelson st. Commercl. rd
Roberts Thomas, fruiterer, 6 Charles st. east, Hampstead rd
Roberts Thomas, *Globe* coffee rooms, 72 Fore st. City
Roberts Thomas, haberdasher, 30 Wigmore st. Cavendish st
Roberts Thomas, linendraper, 17 Blackman st. Borough
Roberts Thomas, linendraper, 17 Hardwick pl. Comml. rd. east
Roberts Thomas, linendraper, 32 Marchmont st. Brunswick sq
Roberts Thomas, linendraper, 6 Waterloo pl. Comml. rd. east

Roberts Thomas, mahogany broker, 9 Billiter st
Roberts Thomas, mason, Bolingbroke gardens, Battersea
Roberts Thomas, steel mill maker, 3 Union st. Bishopsgate
Roberts Thomas, solicitor, 17 Spring gardens
Roberts Thomas, umbrella maker, 98 Goswell st
Roberts Thomas Alex. boat builder, Bishop's walk, Lambeth
Roberts Thomas Alexr. grocer, 28 Foley place, Portland pl
Roberts Thomas Robt. wharfinger, 13 Wharf road, City rd
Roberts Wm. baker, 55 Curtain road, Shoreditch
Roberts Wm. boot & shoe maker, 5 London rd. Southwark
Roberts Wm. builder, 6 Warren st. Camden town
Roberts Wm. butcher, 3 Fore st. Cripplegate
Roberts Wm. comb & brush maker, 18 St. Martin's court
Roberts Wm. engraver & printer, see Baily & Roberts
Roberts Wm. engraver, 7 Fan st. Goswell st
Roberts Wm. general salesman, 5 Park st. Borough market
Roberts Wm. grocer & cheesemonger, 80 Princes rd. Lambeth
Roberts Wm. grocer & oilman, 25 Lower Sloane st. Chelsea
Roberts Wm. hairdresser, 198 Bethnal green road
Roberts Wm. leather factor, 8 Billiter st
Roberts Wm. linen draper, 69 Paul st. Finsbury
Roberts Wm. potato dealer, 44 Three Colt st. Limehouse
Roberts Wm. potato salesman, 2 New road, St. George's east
Roberts Wm. ruby pen maker, 15 Exmouth st. Spafields
Roberts Wm. surveyor & land agent, 68 Chancery lane
Roberts Wm. tailor, Lancelot place, Trevor square
Roberts Wm. tailor, 28 Maze, Tooley st
Roberts Wm. tobacconist, 178 Poplar High st
Roberts Wm. George, bandanna warehouse, 62 Bread st
Roberts Wm. George (Mrs.), ladies' school, 21 Granville sq
Roberts Wm. Henry, barrister, Inner Temple hall staircase
Roberts Wm. Henry, *Dolphin* P.H. 318 Oxford st
Roberts Wm. Owen, shoemaker, 4 Tabernacle row, City road
Roberts Wm. Prowting, solicitor, 2 Robert st. Adelphi
Robertshaw Geo. Morris, shirt ma. & hosier, 100 Oxford st
Robertson Divie & Son, wine merchts. &c. 17 Villiers st. Strand
Robertson & Garland, boarding school, Mare st. Hackney
Robertson Geo. & Co. merchants, 28 Gt. Winchester st
Robertson Geo. & Son, tailors, 47 Albemarle st. Piccadilly
Robertson James & Co. iron merchants, & gas & waterpipe merchants, sun chambers, 61½ Threadneedle st. & 67½ Up. Thames st. & at Glasgow
Robertson J. C. & Co. east india army agents & military equipment depôt, 116 Jermyn st. St. James's
Robertson John & Son, bookbinders, 18 Roll's bldgs. Fetter la
Robertson, Lockie & Co. window glass & lead manufacturers, Old swan wharf, Upper Thames st
Robertson (Misses), ladies' school, 1 Gresham ter. Dalston
Robertson & Nicholson, wine merchts. 17 Villiers st. Strand
Robertson Robert Henderson & Co. flax spinners & linen manufacturers, Dunfermline; warehouses, York st. Manchester, & 10 Watling st
Robertson Alexr. coml. boarding house, 158 Aldersgate st
Robertson Alexr. dairyman, 31 Jermyn st. St. James's
Robertson Alexr. lodging house, 16 Bury st. St. James's
Robertson Alexr. manager of the *London, Edinburgh & Dublin Life Assurance Co.* 3 Charlotte row, Mansion house, & 18 Chancery lane
Robertson Alexr. merchant, 38 Broad st. buildings
Robertson Andrew, baker, 142 Oxford st
Robertson Andrew, law bookseller, 5 Gt. Turnstile, Holborn
Robertson Benjamin, button maker, see Carr & Robertson
Robertson Christiana (Mrs.), artist, 6 Bentinck st. Man. sq
Robertson Daniel, general manager to *National Provincial Bank of England*, 112 Bishopsgate st
Robertson David, bellows maker, 32 Drury lane
Robertson David, conveyancer, see Spottiswoode & Robertson
Robertson Donald, dairyman, 15 Sherrard st. Golden square
Robertson Douglas, baker, 1 Heath place, Cambridge heath
Robertson Erasmus Robert G. barrister, 9 Serle st. Linc. inn
Robertson George, baker, 31 Addington pl. Camberwell road
Robertson George, baker, 4 Macclesfield st. Soho
Robertson George, beer retailer, 54 Long lane, Smithfield
Robertson George, beer retailer, 107 Goswell st
Robertson George, cigar & snuff ma. see Porter & Robertson
Robertson George, shipchandler, &c. St. Ann's pl. Limehouse
Robertson George, teadealer & grocer, 198 Piccadilly
Robertson James, *Adam & Eve* P.H. Swan lane, Rotherhithe
Robertson James, baker, 2 New Bridge st. Vauxhall
Robertson James, baker, 2 Somerset pl. Kennington common
Robertson James, cabinetma. &c. 8 Nottingham st. Marylebone
Robertson James, engineer, 12 Gt. Ryder st. St. James's
Robertson James, furniture broker, 5 Hayes court, Soho
Robertson James, solicitor, 44 Southampton bdgs. Holborn
Robertson James, surgeon, 11 Melcombe pl. Dorset sq
Robertson James Thomas, baker, 3 Salmon lane, Limehouse
Robertson John, *Appletree & Mitre* P.H. 30 Cursitor st. Chan. la
Robertson John, baker, 19 Calthorpe pl. Gray's inn road
Robertson John, baker, 9 Princes st. Mile end New town
Robertson John, *British Oak* P.H. 1 Oxford st. Mile end
Robertson John, comisn. mer. & gen. pro. agt. 70½ Lr. Thames st
Robertson John, fish factor & prvsn. agt. 70½ Lwr. Thames st
Robertson John, hairdresser, 196 Church st. Shoreditch
Robertson John, lithographer, 9 Hatton garden
Robertson John, merchant, 109 Fenchurch st
Robertson John, *New Inn* P.H. 186 Tottenham court road
Robertson John, *Queen Catherine* P.H. 4 Brook st. Ratcliff
Robertson John, ropemaker & proprietor of Rapson's patent slide tiller, Limehouse hole, & 1 Emmett st. Limehouse
Robertson John, supervisor of excise, 6 ullin's row, Islingtn
Robertson John, writing master, 3 Coventry st. Haymarket
Robertson John, *York Minster* P.H. 17 Foley st. Portld. pl
Robertson John E. P. D.C.L. advocate, 16 College, Drs'. Com
Robertson Joseph Clinton, civil engineer, 11 Serjts.' inn
Robertson Joseph Clinton, patent & registration of designs office, 166 Fleet st
Robertson Richd. Hopkins, surgeon, 36 Albemarle st. Picdly
Robertson Robt. cheesemonger, 49 Paddington st. Marylebn
Robertson Samuel, baker, Miles lane, Upper Thames st
Robertson Samuel, confectioner, 35 King William st. City
Robertson Thomas, baker, 38 Featherstone st. City rd
Robertson Thomas, surgeon, 12 Cross st. Islington
Robertson Thomas James, pawnbroker, 1 New Park st. Boro
Robertson Thos. Storm, surgeon, 36 Assembly rw. Mile end rd
Robertson William, artist, 5 Blandford pl. Regent's park
Robertson William, baker, 130 Aldersgate st
Robertson William, baker, 67½ St. James's st
Robertson William, barrister, 3 New sq. Lincoln's inn
Robertson William, cattle salesman, 8 West Smithfield
Robertson Wm. confectioner, 38 Paradise row, Chelsea
Robertson William, ironmonger, Church st. Hackney
Robertson Wm. mercht. & general agent, 38 Crutched friars
Robertson Wm. *Queen's Head* P.H. 5 Caroline pl. City rd
Robertsonian Institution (A.H. Monteith dir.), 13 Londonwl
Robeson Louisa (Miss), tch. of music, 15 Paradise rw. Islgtn
Robeson John M. *Pulpit Office*, Glasshouse yard, Blackfrs
Robeson Richd. coffee rooms, 24 Liverpool st. Bishopgate
Robeson Thos. plaster of paris ma. Mnt. Pleasant, Gray's in. la
Robey Joseph William, grocer & cheesemonger, Bow High st
Robey Wm. sailma. Leith & Glasgow wf. Low. East Smithfield
Robieson George, carpenter, &c. 19 Denmark st. Soho
Robillard Emanuel, prof. of french, 19 Rathbone place
Robins John & Sons, cap & cap peak mfrs. 139 Houndsditch
Robins John & Wm. stationers, account book manufacturs. printers, booksellers, bookbinders, & paperhangers, 57 & 58 Tooley st
Robins's Patent Royal Water Filter Warehouse, 88 Quadrant
Robins Alfred, printer, 7 Southampton st. Strand
Robins Edward, coffee rooms, 25 Chapel st. New road
Robins George, auctioneer, 10 Piazzas, Covent Garden
Robins George, surgeon, 31 Bedford st. Covent Garden
Robins Isaac, carpenter, 28 Broadley ter. Blandford sq
Robins James, bootmaker, 385 Oxford st
Robins James, boot & shoemaker, 73 Drury lane
Robins James, boot & shoemaker, 20 Tothill st. Westminster
Robins James, mattress maker, 24 Tottenham st. Fitzroy sq
Robins John, cheesemonger, 63 Wardour st. Soho
Robins John, tailor, 14 Opera arcade, Haymarket
Robins John, wheelwright, Ham yard, Great Windmill st
Robins John, jun. cap peak & hat case mak. 20 Houndsditch
Robins John Wm. stockbroker, 29 Threadneedle st
Robins Joseph, book & print pub. 116 Upper Stamford st
Robins Joseph, composition doll manf. 6 Tabernacle walk
Robins Joshua, stonemason, Bow
Robins Peter, carpenter, 49 Molyneux st. Bryanstone sq
Robins Samuel, grocer & cheesemonger, 29 Lion st. New Kent rd
Robins Thos. boot & shoemaker, 27 Pratt st. Church st. Lambth
Robins Thos. plumber, 7 Upper Boston st. Blandford sq
Robins Thos. Fras. solicitor, see Venning, Naylor & Robins
Robins Wm. grocer, 39 Marshall st. Golden sq
Robins Wm. stationer, 21 Crimscott st. Bermondsey
Robins Wm. surgeon, 16 Upper Southwick st. Oxford terrace
Robins Wm. timber dealer, Wandsworth road, north side
Robins Wm. Lewin Tugwell, attorney, 36 Bury st. St. James's
Robins Wm. Robert, brass founder, 17 Crown st. Soho
Robinson & Austin, wine & spirit mers. 34 King st. Holborn
Robinson & Aumonier, gold & silversmiths, 153 Leadenhall st
Robinson & Barlow, solicitors, 26 Essex st. Strand
Robinson & Barrow, (from 38 Devonshire st.) mathematical & optical instrument makers, 26 Oxendon st. Haymarket
Robinson & Belville, teadealers, grocers & sole proprietors of the patent barley & patent groats, 64 Red Lion st. Holborn

Robinson & Brooking, merchants, 2 Alderman's walk
Robinson & Cook, coach builders in ordinary to her Majesty, 12 Mount st. Berkeley square & Mount row
Robinson & Cuff, haberdashrs.&gen. cmn. agts.37Gresham st
Robinson Edward Hen. & Co. cutlers, 53 Bishopsgate within
Robinson & Escombe,wine merchants, 74 Gt. Tower st. no
Robinson & Goulding, corn factors, 10 Trinity sq. Tower hill
Robinson Mary & Frances, girls' school, 23 High st. Mrylbn
Robinson Jas. & Chas. F. solicitors,7Queen st.pl.Up.Thms.st
Robinson James & Co. pianoforte manufrs. 43 Moorgate st
Robinson Jas. & Co. woollen mers. 6&7Addle st. & Huddersfi
Robinson Jas. & Son, music sellers, 71 Wardour st. Soho
Robinson Jas.&Wm. silk&velvetmnfrs.3&4Milk st.Cheapside
Robinson & Jenkins, manufacturers of Robinson's patent drying machine for drying all articles of wool, cotton, & other fibrous materials in the manufactured & unmanufactured state, 27 Charles st. Middlesex Hospital
Robinson John & Co. outfitters, 3to5 Nassau pl.Comrl.rd.east
Robinson John & Son, artificial leg & hand makers, 35 Northumberland st. & 10 Northumberland court, Strand
Robinson John & Sons, merchts.&ins.broks.8Geo.yd.Lmbd.st
Robinson John & Thos. silk manufs. 21&23 Fort st.Spitalflds
Robinson John C. & Co. cheesefactors, 206 Tooley st
Robinson & Lorking, coffee rooms, 13 Grafton st. Soho
Robinson & Nicklen, bootmakers,36 Marylebone la.Oxfrd.st
Robinson & Ouvry, solicitors, 13 Tokenhouse yard
Robinson&Robson,upholdrs.undertaks.auctionrs.&appraisrs. 68 Welbeck st. Cavendish sq. & 13 Shepherd st. Oxford st
Robinson, Sanford & Co. silk & velvet manfctrs. 30 Milk st
Robinson & Son, boys' school, 4 Broomfield pl. Deptford
Robinson Vincent & Co.india mat wa. 38 Welbeck st.Cav. sq
Robinson Wm. H. & Thos. grocers & teadealers,44 Piccadilly
Robinson Wm. R. & Co. merchants, 28 Great Winchester st
Robinson Abraham,plumber&glazier,3 Ann's ter.Livrpool.rd
Robinson Alfred, attorney, 17 Orchard st. Portman sq
Robinson Alfred, coffee rooms, 1 Britannia st. City road
Robinson Alfred H. machine ruler, 16 Green st. Leicester sq
Robinson Ann(Mrs.),coppersmh.22 Lit.St.Andrw.'sst.7Dials
Robinson Ann(Mrs.),glass & china dlr. 3 Kingslnd.row,Dlstn
Robinson Ann(Miss),tobacconist,2 Russell pl.Old Kent road
Robinson Anna S.(Mrs.),shipg. butcher,105 Brook st.Ratclf
Robinson Anthony Geo. ship. & insur. agent,11 Geo. yd.City
Robinson Aug. Octavius,oporto mer. see Hogg & Robinson
Robinson Benj.(auctioneer), repository for the sale of horses, carriages, harness, &c. by auction, 29 Little Britain, City, & 23 Sekforde st. Clerkenwell
Robinson Benj. tailor, 40 Gloucester st. Queen square
Robinson Benj. Coulson, barrister, 3 Inner Temple lane
Robinson Benj. James, tailor, see Wheeler & Robinson
Robinson Camilla (Miss), stay maker,see Finch & Robinson
Robinson Cath. Anne (Mrs.), cigar ma. 20 Beer la. Tower st
Robinson Cath.(Mrs.),tinplate work.40 Old Compton st.Soho
Robinson Charles, appraiser, 1 Church lane, Islington
Robinson Charles, barrister, 2 Essex court, Temple
Robinson Charles, coach joiner, 53 Gt. Queen st.Linc. inn fi
Robinson Charles (late Bramah & Robinson), engineer,millwright, founder, &c. Pimlico road
Robinson Chas. *Falcon & Keys* P.H.39 Gt.Russell st.Blmsby
Robinson Charles, linendraper, 105 & 106 Upper st. Islington
Robinson Charles, locksmith, 6 Greenland pl. Cromer st
Robinson Charles, surgeon, 6 Dorset place, Dorset square
Robinson Charles,writing & dressing case ma. 53 Gt.Queen st
Robinson Chas. B. estate agent, 7 Oxford ct. Cannon st
Robinson Christian James, solicitor, see Reed & Robinson
Robinson Christopher, pork butcher, 218 Blackfriars road
Robinson Christr. pork butcher,35Ridinghouse la.Lnghm.pl
Robinson Claxton Baldock, dining rooms, 8 Bucklersbury
Robinson Daniel, brushma. 43 Gt. Queen st. Lincoln's inn fi
Robinson Daniel, merchant, 4 St. Mildred's court, Poultry
Robinson David, bootmaker, 1 South row, New road
Robinson David, coffee rooms,24 Bath place, New road
Robinson Edward, merchant, 117 Cheapside
Robinson Edward, merchant, 9 George yard, Lombard st
Robinson Edward, *Thistle & Crown* P.H. 42 Wapping
Robinson Edwd. Breese, solicitor, 4 Savage grdns. Tower hill
Robinson Edwin, bar wigma.21Aldgate& 59Carey st.Linc.inn
Robinson Elias, *Hanover sq.* P.H.1 St. George's ter. Hyde pk
Robinson Eliza (Miss),stay,&c.wareh.23High st.Marylebone
Robinson Elizabeth (Mrs.), baker, 100 Whitechapel High st
Robinson Elizh. (Mrs.), hbrdshr. 8Up.Cleveland st.Fitzry.sq
Robinson Elizh. (Mrs.), plumber 39½ Vine st.Westminster
Robinson Elizh. (Mrs.), tobacconist, 47 Up. Rathbone place
Robinson Ericus, calenderer, see Wilkinson & Robinson
Robinson Francis, grocer, 15 Shoreditch High st
Robinson Francis, solicitor, 36 Jermyn st
Robinson Frederick, barrister, 11 Crown office row, Temple
Robinson Frederick, butcher, 22 Cumberland row, New road
Robinson Fred.Wm. professor of music, 30 Windmill st. Fins
Robinson George, auctioneer, 53 Wigmore st. Cavendish sq
Robinson George, *Laurel Tree* P.H.34 Bayham st.Cmdn. tn
Robinson George, pork butcher, 21 Lower st. Islington
Robinson George, sheep salesman, 41 West Smithfield
Robinson George, stationer, 7 Wellington ter. Clapham rd
Robinson George, surgeon, 24 City road, Finsbury square
Robinson George, tailor, 16 Bow lane, Cheapside
Robinson George, toy wareho. 3 William st. Regent's park
Robinson Geo. trunk & portmanteau mkr. 131 Holborn hill
Robinson Henry, accountant,4 Cambridge st. Golden sq
Robinson Henry, carver & gilder, 37 Clifton st. Finsbury
Robinson Henry, fruiterer, 2 Bolingbroke row,Walworth rd
Robinson Henry, japanner & papier machée manufacturer, 59 Carey st. Lincoln's inn
Robinson Henry, linendraper, 49 Notting hill High st
Robinson Henry, manager of the London Joint Stock Bank, western branch, 69 Pall mall
Robinson Henry, reg. of births, &c. 4Cambridge st.Golden sq
Robinson Henry, surgeon, 17 Savage gardens, Tower hill
Robinson Henry,wharfinger & sawmills,Belvedere rd.Lmbth
Robinson Henry Chas. surgeon, 2 Caledonian pl. Cal. rd
Robinson Henry George, attorney,6 Halfmoon st. Piccadilly
Robinson Henry Wm. turner, &c. 25 Crosby row, Walworth
Robinson Horatio, perfumer, &c. 131 Oxford st.
Robinson Isabella(Mrs.),*Griffin* P.H.28 Half moon st.Picdly
Robinson Jacob, *Magpie & Punchbowl* P.H.58 Bshpsgt.wthn
Robinson James baker, 53 Coppice row, Clerkenwell
Robinson James, baker 13 Queen st. Tower hill
Robinson James, dentist, &c. 7 Gower st. Bedford square
Robinson Jas. com.agent & curiosity dealer, 45 New Bond st
Robinson James, grocer, 109 Curtain road, Shoreditch
Robinson James, hair cutter, see Moles & Robinson
Robinson James, livery stable keeper, 7 Lit. Bruton st
Robinson James, plumber & glazier, 41 Upper Ebury st
Robinson James, solicitor, 29 Ironmoner lane, City
Robinson James, tailor, see Simons & Robinson
Robinson James Wilson, military tailor, 25 Aldersgate st
Robinson John, appraiser, 14 & 15 Pleasant row,Pentonville
Robinson John, baker, 1 Clayton place, Kennington road
Robinson John, billiard rooms, 64 South Molton st
Robinson John, biscuit baker, 2 Aldenham ter. Pancras road
Robinson John, bricklayer, &c. 32 Cleveland st. Fitzroy sq
Robinson John, coal factor, see Milnes & Robinson
Robinson John, dining rooms, 16 Great Tower st. City
Robinson John, fruit & pea salesman, Covent gdn. fruit mkt
Robinson John, fruiterer, 3 Warwick pl. Kingsland road
Robinson John, grocer, 1 Fuller's terrace, Pimlico
Robinson John, lodginghouse keeper, 21 Bury st. St.James's
Robinson John, *Mariners' Arms* P.H. 119 Gray's inn lane
Robinson John, sen. pork butcher, 46 Brick lane, St. Luke's
Robinson John, shoemaker, 10 Walworth pl. Walworth rd
Robinson John, tailor, 58 St. Paul's church yard
Robinson John, tailor, 62 Seymour st. Euston square
Robinson John, wine importer, 38 Jewin st. Cripplegate
Robinson John Foster, painter, plumber, &c. 19 Low.Eaton st
Robinson John Francis, artist, 12 Oxford st. Mile end
Robinson John Rayner, saddlr. & tobnst. 20 Wells rw. Is'gtn
Robinson John W. shiphearth&tank ma.106Broad st.Ratcliff
Robinson John W. wine merchant, 35 Mark lane
Robinson Jonathan, surgeon, 19 Brick lane, Spitalfields
Robinson Joseph, beer retailer, 50 Broad st. Ratcliff cross
Robinson Joseph, bookseller, 40 High Holborn
Robinson Joseph, *St. Alban's hotel*, 12 Charles st. St. James
Robinson Joseph P. whfngr.Southwk.steam wf.Montague clo
Robinson Joseph S. jun. cabinet ma.&upholsterer,395Oxfd.st
Robinson Joseph, sen. auct. &appraiser&ho.agt.395 Oxford st
Robinson Lawson, grocer & teadealer, 66 St. George st
Robinson Marmaduke,navy agent,see Hallett,Robinson &Co
Robinson Martha(Mrs.),ladies'school,21Somerset pl. Com.rd
Robinson Martha (Mrs.), court milliner, 45 New Bond st
Robinson Martin, watch & case gilder, 16 Baltic st. Golden la
Robinson Mary Ann(Mrs.),lodging house,9 Manchester blds
Robinson Nathl. baker, 11 Bretten ter.Kg's. rd.west,Chelsea
Robinson Newman, *Hog in the Pound* P.H. 294 Oxford st
Robinson Peter, harness maker, 7 Manchester st. Waterloo tn
Robinson Peter, haberdasher, draper, &c. 103 Oxford st
Robinson Peter, laceman, &c. 107 Oxford st
Robinson Rachael (Mrs.), oilman, 120 Brick lane, Spitalfids
Robinson Rebecca (Mrs.), milliner, 43 Dorset st. Portman sq
Robinson Reuben, *St. Paul's* P.H.56 Chiswell st
Robinson Richard, coal merchant, 458 West Strand
Robinson Richard, fishmonger, 16 Norland rd. Notting hill
Robinson Richard, grocer, 9 Dorset crescent, New North rd
Robinson Richd. Radford, surgeon, Camden row, Camberwl

Robinson Robert, currier, 99 Dean st. Soho
Robinson Robert, greengrocer, 48 Praed st. Paddington
Robinson Samuel, solicitor, 12 Great Marlborough st
Robinson Samuel, coal dealer, 29 Crown st. Soho
Robinson Samuel, coffee rooms, 119 Blackfriars road
Robinson Samuel Thomas, *Bell* P.H. 12 Basinghall st
Robinson Sarah (Mrs.), baker, 2 East st. West sq. Lambeth
Robinson Sarah (Mrs.), *Lady Owen's Arms* P.H. 63 Goswll. rd
Robinson Sarah (Mrs.), loding. ho. 12 Took's ct. Chancery la.
Robinson Scipio, sen. porkman, 4 Lit. St. Andrew st. 7 Dials
Robinson Scipio, jun. porkman, 90 Salisbury st. Lisson grove, & 14 Cumberland row, King's cross
Robinson Skeffington, west india merch. 1 Crown ct. Philpot la.
Robinson Stephen Thomas, *George* P.H. 207 Shoreditch
Robinson Susannah (Mrs.), lodging house, 8 Manchester bldgs.
Robinson Susannah Mary, (Mrs.), truss ma. 19 Kingsland rd
Robinson Thomas, academy, 1 Whiting st. Gt. Waterloo st
Robinson Thomas, baker, 19 Barbican; 45 Judd st. New rd.; 40 Exmouth st. Spafields; & 14 Goswell st
Robinson Thomas, butcher, Church st. Hackney
Robinson Thos. corkcutter, 48 Sidney st. Mile end
Robinson Thos. chandler's shop, 10 Praed st. Paddington
Robinson Thos. pawnbroker, 1 Mortimer st. Cavendish sq
Robinson Thos. pork butcher, 9 High st. Portland town
Robinson Thos. tailor, 52 Acton st. Gray's inn road
Robinson Thos. tea-lead & chest dr. 6 White Horse yd. Coleman st
Robinson Thos. W. sewing cotton & trim. ma. 132 Bunhill row
Robinson Wm. D.C.L. advocate, 7 College, Doctors' commons
Robinson Wm. baker, 96 Union st. Borough
Robinson Wm. baker, 38 Ironmonger row, Old st
Robinson Wm. baker, 27 Lambeth wlk. & 29 Lambth. lwr. msh
Robinson Wm. boys' school, 22 Chichester pl. Wandsworth rd
Robinson Wm. builder, 8 St. John's wood terrace
Robinson Wm. butcher, Broadway, Stratford
Robinson Wm. cabinetmaker, 4 Green st. Blackfriars road
Robinson Wm. dairyman, 25 Seymour st. Euston sq
Robinson Wm. fan & skylight mak. 59 Eagle st. Red Lion sq
Robinson Wm. shoemak. 14 Jamaica st. Commercl. rd. Stpny
Robinson Wm. solicitor, see Hine & Robinson
Robinson Wm. tailor, 16 Gt. Piazza, Covent garden
Robinson Wm. Cowper, whole. ironmonger, 6 Cannon st. City
Robinson Wm. J. cigar imp. 5 Paul's alley, St. Paul's chrch. yd
Robinson W. T. ac. & sec. *Minerva Life Assu. Co.* 84 King Wm. st
Robinson Wm. Tooke, solicitor, see Maltby, Beachcroft & Co
Robinson Wm. Walker, bookseller & pub. 69 Fleet st
Robison John, manufacturer of shirt collars, fronts, stocks, & braces, 2 Gresham st. Wood st. City
Robison Sarah (Miss), milliner & dressma. 7 Hanover st. Havr. sq
Roblow Thos. Hen. fishing tackle ma. 30 Up. Marylebone st
Robon John William, cooper, 12 Whitmore road, Hoxton
Robottom Henry, chaser, 10 St. John st. road
Robottom Peter, fruiterer, 1 Montpelier st. Brompton
Robson & Jones, house decorators, 214 Piccadilly
Robson James & Co. fringe manufacturers, 125 Newgate st
Robson John & Co. coach & harness makers, by appointment, to her Majesty, 19 South st. & 67 South Audley st.
Robson, Levey & Franklyn, printers, 23 Gt. New st. Fetter la
Robson Saml. & Co. portmanteau, trunk, carpet bag & coach imperial manufacturers, 35 Crawford st. Bryanstone sq
Robson Thos. & Nephew, marble mers. Western wf. Abingdon st
Robson Charles, builder, 16 Finsbury st. Chiswell st
Robson Charles, wine mercht. 4 Crown ct. Threadneedle st
Robson Charles Oswald, builder, 17 Abchurch lane, & 16 Finsbury st
Robson Christopher, attorney, 13 Clifford's inn, Fleet st
Robson Edward, tailor, 15 Cloth fair, Smithfield
Robson Edward, trimming ma. see Hoby, Robson & Knowles
Robson Geo. coach, sadd. & hrnss. currier, 33 Lisle st. Lstr. sq
Robson George, lozenge & liquorice maker & wholesale confectioner, 1A, St. Thomas's place, Great Dover road
Robson George, wheelwright, 86 Redcross st. Borough
Robson George Young, barrister, 49 Chancery lane
Robson John, solicitor, see Lightfoot, Robson & Lightfoot
Robson John, stockbroker, 80 Old Broad st. City
Robson John, upholder, see Robinson & Robson
Robson John, wheelwright, 56 Mount st. & 19 South st. Brkly. sq
Robson Mary (Mrs.), dressmaker, 11 Elm st. Gray's inn la
Robson Monro Wm. scotch whisky mer. & com. agt. 28 Bread st
Robson Nathaniel, spring boot manufactr. 68 New Bond st
Robson Richard Cheesman, solicitor, 26 Bucklersbury
Robson Richard, solicitor, 17 Margaret st. Cavendish sq
Robson Ridley, merchant, 4 New East India chambers
Robson Thomas, coach wheelwright, 4½ Marshall st. Golden sq.; 29½ Liquorpond st. & 41 Laystall st. Hatton garden
Robson Thos. fixture dealer, 6 Wittam's bldgs. & 49 Old st. rd
Robson Thos. hairdresser, 53 Lt. George st. Hampstead road
Robson Thos. sewed muslin manufacturer, 7 Wood st
Robson Thos. Joseph Fred. organ builder, 101 St. Martin's la
Robson Wm. bricklayer, Church st. Stoke Newington
Robson Wm. bricklayer, 5 Cobourg st. Euston square
Robson Wm. grocer, 87 High st. Camden town
Robson Wm. Evans, stock & share broker, 37 Threadneedle st
Robson Wm. Froggatt, solicitor, 10 Lancaster place, Strand
Roby Alfred, baker, 8 Gt. Russell st. Bloomsbury
Roby Andrew, baker, 10 Tavistock st. Bloomsbury
Roby Charles, auctioneer, see Roberts & Roby
Roby Reuben, tailor, see Wray & Roby
Roca Joseph M. merchant, 20 Fenchurch st
Rochard Francis Theodore, artist, 40 Foley pl. Portland pl
Rochard Simon Jaques, artist, 281 Regent st
Rochas Henry & Son, stockbrokers, 6 Bank chambs. Lothbry
Rochat Jn. D. *Greenland Fishery* P.H. 30 Redman's rw. M. e. rd
Rochat Jules, watch ma. 2 Cornwall cr. Camden New town
Roche, Plowman & Roche, solicitors, 2 Up. Wellington st
Roche John, *Two Brewers* P.H. 27 George st. Bloomsbury
Roche John, wire worker, 15 Smith's buildings, City road
Roche Thomas, printer, 25 Hoxton square
Rochfort Ann (Mrs.), glover & stockmaker, 10 Opera arcade
Rochfort Frank, pawnbroker, 34 & 35 Brewer st. Golden sq
Rock Life Assurance Office on Lives & Survivorships (Wm. S. Lewis, actuary), 14 New Bridge st. Blackfriars; see page 2043
Rock, Brothers & Payne, cardmakers & wholesale & export manufacturing stationers, 11 Walbrook, City
Rock Charles, clock maker, 94 Fetter lane, Holborn
Rock John Dennis, tin & tinpl. agt. 2 Whitehart ct. Lombard st
Rock John Frederick, grocer & teadealer, 64 Hackney rd
Rock Wm. printer & engraver, 5 Cumberland row, Walworth rd
Rockall William, fruiterer, 54 Gloucester st. Queen sq
Rocke James, furn. brkr. 1 & 2 Lit. Crown ct. Princes st. Soho
Rockell Thos. corn dlr. 16 Richmond pl. East st. Walworth
Rockhill Frederick, straw bonnet wa. 208 Tottenham ct. rd
Rockley John, *New Hummums tavern & hotel*, Tavistock row, Covent garden
Rodborne Thos. ostrich feather manufr. 7 Chiswell st. Finsbury
Rodborne Michael, coal dealer, 32 Homer st. Marylebone
Rodd Horatio, picture dealer, 9 Gt. Newport st. Long acre
Rodd Thos. booksel. & publisher, 9 Gt. Newport st. Long acre
Rodd Wm. grocer & cheesemr. 24 Montpelier rw. Brompton
Rodda Richard Burrows, gun maker, see Brown & Rodda
Rodden Edward, beer retailer, 1 Portland st. Walworth com
Rodden Edward, cooper & beer retlr. Webb st. Walwth com
Roddis James, baker, 29 Gray's inn lane
Roddrick David, beer retailer, 157 Union st. Borough
Roden Edward, *Boar's Head* P.H. 19 Exeter st. Strand
Roden John, enginr. & millwright, 22 New rd. St. George's ea
Rodger & Rhind, tailors, 10½ Gt. Pulteney st. Golden sq
Rodgers Edmund & Co. (late Kipling), hosiers & outfitters, &c. 29 New st. Covent garden
Rodgers Edmund & Co. tailors & clothiers, 156 & 157 Fleet st
Rodgers John & Son, clothiers, hosiers, brace & silk purse ma. & patentees of the lever buckles, & spring hooks & eyes, 39 & 40 Chiswell st. Finsbury, & Broad st. Birmingham
Rodgers George, dairyman, 5 Easton st. Spafields
Rodgers George, ladies' wardrobe dlr. 44 South st. Grosv. sq
Rodgers Julian Edward Disbrowe, surgeon, 2 Up. Ebury st
Rodgers Thomas, solicitor, 37 King st. Cheapside
Rodick & Daukes, stout agents, see Daukes & Rodick
Rodick Edward L. & Henry, silkmen, 52 Old Broad st. City
Rodick George, coal merchant, Rutland wharf, Upper Thames st. & 3 Exeter st. Strand
Rodin Sarah (Mrs.), fruiterer, 3 Surrey pl. Kennington com
Rodman George, china & glass dealer, Little Chelsea
Rodman Stephen, who. old iron dealer, 10 Vauxhall bridge rd
Rodman Wm. tallowchandl. & melter, 25 King st. Long acre
Rodocanachi, Sons & Co. merchants, 26 Finsbury circus
Rodocanachi Giovanni M. mer. 9 Finsbury cham. London wall
Rodrigues Henry, bookseller & stationer, 21 Piccadilly
Rodrigues Isaac & Robt. John, butchers, 29 Norton folgate
Rodway Elizabeth (Miss), milliner, 1 Long lane, Bermondsey
Rodway Henry Baron, patent horse shoe mnfr. 297½ Oxford st
Rodway Jane (Mrs.), glass & china dealer, 4 Grafton st. Soho
Rodwell George, merchant, 157 Fenchurch street
Rodwell Henry, silk broker, 6 Gt. Winchester st
Rodwell Hunter, barrister, 1 New court, Temple
Rodwell John, bookseller, 46 New Bond st
Rodwell John, butcher, 19 Richmond pl. East st. Walwth. rd
Rodwell Rt. bookseller & tobacconist, 2 Surrey pl. Kennington
Rodwell Saml. Rushworth, bootmkr. see Laidlaw & Rodwell
Rodwell Wm. stockbroker, 22 Throgmorton st. & Stock exch
Roe Ann (Mrs.), japanner, 78 Bunhill row, Chiswell st
Roe Charles, bookseller, 16 Vere st. Clare market

Roe Charles, bookseller & library, 3 Leigh st. Red Lion sq
Roe Edmund, currier & leather strap ma. 9 Air st. Piccadilly
Roe Edward, surgeon, 1 Albion pl. Belinda st. Canonbury sq
Roe Edward Thos. tobacconist, 2 St. Mark's rd. Cambwl. N. rd
Roe Freeman, plumber & pntr. & alabaster imp. 69A, & 70 Strand
Roe George Hamilton, physician, 6 Hanover square
Roe James, brushmaker, 8 Up. Ashby st. Northampton sq
Roe John, professor of music, 18 Gower place, Euston sq
Roe Peter, physician, 1 Porteus ter. Park pl. Paddington
Roe Thomas, solicitor, Temple chambers, Falcon ct. Fleet st
Roe Thomas, wholesale stationer, see Gibbons & Roe
Roe Wm. tailor & breeches maker, 7 Warwick st. Golden sq
Roe William David, tobacconist, 121½ Blackfriars road
Roebuck John Arthur, queen's counsel, 3 Essex ct. Temple
Roeder Charles, baker, 143 Bethnal green road
Roelants Louise (Mdlle.), dressmaker, 33 Argyll st. Oxford st
Roessler Fredk. teacher & accountant, 16 Bird st. Wapping
Rofe William, ironmonger, 125 Albany road, Camberwell
Roff Edmund L. & Henry L. fishmongers, 10 Billingsgate
Roff Phœbe (Mrs.), baker, 214 Hoxton Old town
Roffe Joseph, silversmith, 1 Bolingbroke row, Walworth rd
Roffe William, brushmaker, 37 High st. Portland town
Roffee John, cornchandler, 5 George st. Camberwell
Roffey Wm. & Son, coal & corn mers. Old barge house wharf, Upper Ground st. & 21 Walcot pl. east, Lambeth
Roffey Edward, emery paper maker, see Johnson & Roffey
Roffey Edward, wheelwright, High st. Camberwell
Roffey George, baker, 21 Paradise st. Rotherhithe
Roffey Richard, bricklayer, 3 Smith's bldgs. Long la. Brmnds
Roffey Thomas, attorney, 20 Walcot pl. east, Lambeth
Roffway James, painter, 15 Baches row, City road
Roffway John, house decorator, &c. 9 Huggin lane, Wood st
Rogers Brothers, provision merchants, 61 Grey Eagle st
Rogers Charlotte & Son, tin plate workers, 38 Bedfordbury
Rogers & Dear, upholders, 23 & 24 St. George's pl. Knightsbrdg
Rogers George & Alfred, linendrapers, 3 Up. Marylebone st
Rogers James & Charles, solicitors, 22 Manchester buildings, Westminster, & 12 Cannon row, Westminster
Rogers John & Co. wholes. hosiers, 103½ Wood st. Cheapside
Rogers John, Nephew & Co. warehousemen, 91 Watling st
Rogers John & Son, tobacco & snuff manufrs. 392 Oxford st
Rogers Joseph & Sons, manufacturing cutlers (Adam Hamilton, agent), 73 Hatton garden
Rogers & Knaggs, surgns. 70 Mortimer st. & 1 Mornington cr
Rogers & Lee, who. & retail cheesemongers, 48 Farringdon st
Rogers, Olding & Co. bankers, 29 Clement's la. Lombard st
Rogers Robert & Co. gold lace manufacturers & embroiderers to her Majesty & Prince Albert, & army & navy cap & accoutrement makers, 30 King st. Covent garden
Rogers Rt. & Hy. glass paper ma. 12 & 13 Prospect rw. Walw. rd
Rogers Simon & Son, fancy warehm. 15 Sackville st. Piccadilly
Rogers Thomas & Co. shirt makers, 20 Addle st. Wood st
Rogers' Almshouses, 2 Hart st. Wood st. City
Rogers Alfred Josias, veterinary surgeon, Knightsbridge gn
Rogers Alfred Chas. fruiterer, 12 Belmont pl. Wandsworth rd
Rogers Ann (Mrs.), ladies' school, 5 Alfred st. Bedford sq
Rogers Arnold, M.R.C.S. dentist, 296 Regent st
Rogers Benj. bricklayer, Great Green st. Kentish town
Rogers Benj. plumber & glazier, 31 George st. Portman sq
Rogers Caroline (Miss), dressma. 11 Blandford st. Portmn. sq
Rogers Charles, bootmaker, 33 Artillery row, Westminster
Rogers Charles, cheesemonger, 27 Fore st. City
Rogers Charles, dentist, 2 Cork st. Bond st
Rogers Charles, plumber, &c. 18 Devonshire st. Queen sq
Rogers Chas. saddler & harness ma. 43 Bishopsgate within
Rogers Colin, physician, 29 Dorset square
Rogers David, baker, 117 Chancery lane
Rogers Edward, cooper, Kingsland green
Rogers Edward, dairyman, 8 Field place, St. John st. rd
Rogers Francis Newman James, Q.C. 4 Inner Temple la
Rogers Fred. reg. joint stock co. 13 Serjt.'s inn, Fleet st
Rogers Frederick Wm. dentist, see Clark & Rogers
Rogers Geo. carpent. & undertak. 17 Greenfield st. Whitechpl
Rogers Geo. coal merchant, 17 Lit. George st. Bermondsey
Rogers Geo. comp. ornament maker, see Buxton & Rogers
Rogers Geo. corn chandler, 16 Smithfield bars
Rogers Geo. confectioner, 269 Bethnal green road
Rogers Geo. grocer, 1 Globe road, Mile end
Rogers Geo. tailor, 11 Queen st. Hoxton market
Rogers Geo. tobacconist & snuff maker, 58 High st. St. Giles's
Rogers Geo. John, *Newcastle coffeerooms*, 21 St. Mary at hil
Rogers Geo. William, manufacturing furrier, 30 Fleet st
Rogers George Williamson, *Ivy House* P.H. Ivy pl. Hoxton
Rogers Henry, baker, 4 Fox's lane, Shadwell
Rogers Henry, butcher, 115 Goswell st
Rogers Henry, portrait painter, 2 Finsbury terrace, City r l
Rogers Henry, mineralogist & dealer in curiosities, 9 Bell yard, Temple bar, & 64 Carey st
Rogers Henry Alex. glass engraver, 6 Furnival's inn pl. Hlbn
Rogers Henry Jsph. auctionr. & apprais. 9 Fleet la. Farringd. st
Rogers Israel, coach builder, 1 Beaumont st. Marylebone
Rogers James, grocer, 32 Windmill st. Tottenham ct. road
Rogers James, grocer & oilman, 17 Clarendon square
Rogers James, hairdresser, 101 Shoreditch
Rogers James, italian warehouse, 451 Strand
Rogers James, menagerie, 17 City terrace, City road
Rogers James, outfitter & draper, see Gold & Rogers
Rogers James, tobacconist, 23 Lambeth lower marsh
Rogers James, jun. bricklayer, 4 New North st. Red Lion sq
Rogers James, sen. builder, &c. 24 Gloucester st. Queen sq
Rogers Jane (Mrs.), chandler's shop, 43 Weymth. st. N. w. Kt. rd
Rogers John, baker, 1 Charles st. Hampstead road
Rogers John, beer retailer, 95 Cornwall road, Lambeth
Rogers John, bootmaker, 23 St. Martin's st. Leicester sq
Rogers John, boot & shoe maker, 1 College terrace, Chelsea
Rogers John, farrier, 7 Canterbury place, Old Kent road
Rogers John, *Fortune of War* P.H. Belle isle, Battle bridge
Rogers John, grocer, &c. 14 Goldsmith's row, Hackney road
Rogers John, hat manufacturer, 89 Broadwall, Blackfriars
Rogers John, painter & glazier, 31 Marylebone la. Oxford st
Rogers John, plumber & painter, Church st. Deptford
Rogers John, ship & insurance broker & commercial agent, 2 White Hart court, Lombard st
Rogers John, solicitor, see Smedley & Rogers
Rogers John, tailor, 6 Three King court, Lombard st
Rogers John B. cheesemonger, 7 Aylesbury st. Clerkenwell
Rogers John Jope, barrister, 11 King's Bench walk, Temple
Rogers Joseph, carver & gilder, 24 Duke st. Bloomsbury
Rogers Joseph, grocer, 35 Hackney road
Rogers Joseph, haberdasher, 34 Worship st. Finsbury sq
Rogers Joseph, surgeon, 53 Wardour st. Soho
Rogers Joseph, tobacconist, 13 Dean st. Soho
Rogers Joseph G. corn & coal mer. High st. Stoke Newngtn
Rogers Joshua, artist's colorman, 133 Bunhill row
Rogers Joshua, chandler's shop, 38 Salmon la. Limeho. flds
Rogers Josiah Frederick, staymaker, see Brown & Rogers
Rogers Maria A. (Mrs.), ladies' sch. 7 Bedford pl. Lr. rd. Rothrh
Rogers Philip, coffee rooms, 34 Brewer st. Golden sq
Rogers Richard, bookseller, Stratford
Rogers Richard, fruiterer, 14 James st. Haymarket
Rogers Richard, fruiterer, 96 Poplar High st
Rogers Richard, plumber, 18 Chapel st. Somers town
Rogers Richard, turner, 9 Fair st. Horselydown
Rogers Robt. plumber, painter, &c. 50 Gt. Alie st. Goodman's fi
Rogers Robert, solicitor, 16 Union court, Old Broad st
Rogers Samuel, attorney, 2 Bank chambers, Lothbury
Rogers Samuel, who. & retail cheesemonger, 26 Kingsland rd
Rogers Sarah (Mrs.), grocer, 15 Royal Hospital row, Chelsea
Rogers Stephen, timber merch. 7A, Cleveland st. Fitzroy sq
Rogers Thomas, coffee rooms, 93 York st. Westminster
Rogers Thomas, *Duke of York* P.H. 1 Up. Rathbone pl. Midx. hos
Rogers Thomas, grocer, 5 Howard's place, Hackney road
Rogers Thomas, modeller & plasterer, 31 John st. west, Edgware road, & 16 Winchester row, New road
Rogers Thomas, smith & bellhanger, 10 South row, New rd
Rogers Thomas, tobacconist, 15 Strachan pl. Ball's Pond rd
Rogers Thomas Lovell, grocer, 12 Bedfordbury
Rogers Wm. architect, 20 Pratt st. Lambeth
Rogers Wm. *Ashby Castle* P.H. 10 Up. Ashby st. Nrthmptn. sq
Rogers Wm. barrister, 2 Stone buildings, Lincoln's inn
Rogers Wm. boot & shoe maker, 43 Tothill st. Westminster
Rogers Wm. builder, 24 Bow st. Covent garden
Rogers Wm. cabinet maker, 12 Up. Cleveland st. Fitzroy sq
Rogers Wm. *Camden Head* P.H. 241 Bethnal green road
Rogers Wm. commission merchant, 23 East india chambers
Rogers Wm. grocer, &c. 9 Anchor & Hope alley, Wapping
Rogers Wm. grocer, 4 King's row, Walworth road
Rogers Wm. *Green Man* P.H. 6 Lit. George st. Westminster
Rogers Wm. *Horse & Groom* P.H. 8 John st. ws. Edgware rd
Rogers Wm. *King's Arms* P. H. 13 Newgate market
Rogers Wm. *Lion & Lamb* P.H. 14 Margaret st. Wlmngtn. sq
Rogers Wm. plasterer, 10 Chapel st. Curtain road
Rogers Wm. shawl & silk warehouse, 9 Addle st. City
Rogers Wm. smith, 10 New inn yard, Tottenham ct. road
Rogers Wm. surgeon, see Knaggs & Rogers
Rogers William, veterinary surgeon, 218 Whitechapel road
Rogers Wm. watchmaker, 2 Tower st. Westminster road
Rogers Wm. *White Hart* P.H. 191 Drury lane
Rogers Wm. wine merchant, 1 Skinner st. Snow hill
Rogers Wm. Gibbs, carver & gilder, & collector of ancient carvings, 3 Gt. Newport st. Long acre
Rogerson John, solicitor, 50 Lincoln's inn fields

Rogers Wm. Edward, grocer, 9 Dockhead, Bermondsey
Rogerson John, stone mer. Victoria wf. 1 Union pl. Pimlico
Rogerson John, surgeon, 2 Back road, St George's east
Rogerson Joseph, cattle salesman, 8 West Smithfield
Rogerson Joseph, printer, 24 Norfolk st. Strand
Roget Peter Mark, physician, 18 Up. Bedford pl. Russell sq
Rohde & Carter, coal merchants & coal agents, 15 South whf. Paddington basin, Claycross & Snibston whf. Caledonian rd. & at the Railway station, Kilburn bridge
Rohde George, nurseryman, Caledonian road
Rohde Samuel, accountant, 3 Crosby sq. Bishopsgate
Rohrs George W. (sec. to *Herne Bay & Margate Steam Packet Company*), 113 Fenchurch st
Rohrweger Julius C. merchant, 62 Mark lane
Rokes & Webster, furnishing undertakers, 58 Lant st. Boro'
Roland Daniel, tailor & habit ma. 9 Panton st. Haymarket
Rolandi Peter, foreign bookseller, 20 Berners st. Oxford st
Roles John, greengrocer, 6 Little Compton st. Soho
Roles John, *White Hart* P.H. Battersea
Roles Joseph, *Wheatsheaf* P.H. South Lambeth
Rolfe & Edmunds, solicitors, 12 South square, Gray's inn
Rolfe Francis & Co, tailors, &c. 35 Gt. Marlborough st
Rolfe William & Sons, patent pianoforte makers; warehouse, 61 Cheapside; manufactory, 31 & 32 London wall
Rolfe Daniel, coffee rooms, 4 White Horse st. Piccadilly
Rolfe George, carpenter & builder, 13 Coleman st. buildings
Rolfe George, drapers' agency off. 2 Church pas. Gresham st
Rolfe Henry Wm. school, 252 Bethnal green road
Rolfe James Burdett, currier, &c. 13 Marlborough sq. Chelsea
Rolfe John, tailor & habit maker, 110 Leadenhall st
Rolfe Robert, clock manufr. 42 Coppice row, Clerkenwell
Rolfe Thomas, jun. wine mer. wine fining ma. wine cooper & bottle merchant, & agent for Smeed's concrete marin. 6 & 34 Gt. St. Helen's
Rolfe Wm. Hen. wine merchant, 3 & 9 George yd. Lombard st
Rolfes Henry A. dealer in cigars, 8 Fenchurch buildings
Rolfes Wm. George, tobacco broker, 8 Fenchurch buildings
Roll Edward Chas. engrav. & printer, Dunning's alley, Bishopgt
Rolland Oliver, parisian corset maker, 20 Mount st. Berkly. sq
Roller Fredk. Wm. & Co. merchants, 15 Union ct. Old Broad st
Rolleston Ar. Rt. *Old Swan* P.H. 63 Paradise row, Chelsea
Rollings Thos. grocer, 29 Lower Ranelagh st. Pimlico
Rollinson John, awl blade mfr. 16 Norman's bldgs. St. Luke's
Rolls Court: Term time, Westminster hall, up stairs; Vacation hall adjoining Rolls chapel, Rolls yard, Chancery lane; hours 10 to 4
Rolls James & Co. plumbers & glaziers, 89 Cannon st. City
Rolls Brothers, varnish maks. St. James's rd. Old Kent rd
Rolls Edmd. Thos. school, 6 A, Featherstone bldgs. Holborn
Rolls James, floor cloth & table cotton manufacturer, & oil cloth painter & japanner of silk & linen, Lower Kennington la. late of the Canal bridge, St. James' rd. O. Kent rd
Rolls James, varnish, &c. manufacturer, see Noble & Rolls
Rolls John, *Marlborough Head* P.H. 24 North Audley st
Rolls Josiah, manufacturer, by appointment, to her Majesty, of floor cloth & table covers & japanned, oiled, painted silks, linens, &c. for the army & navy, St. James's rd. Kent rd
Rolls Thomas, plumber, glazier, & painter, 98 Wapping
Rolls William, boot & shoema. 94 Union st. Lambeth walk
Rolph Thomas, builder, &c. 5 Shepherd ct. Up. Brook st
Rolt John, barrister, 6 Stone buildings & 52 Harley st
Rolt Peter, timber merchant, see Brockelbank & Rolt
Romaine William Govet, barrister, 4 Harcourt bldgs. Temple
Romanis Robert, hosier & glover, 33 Cheapside
Romans Thomas, potato salesman, Cotton's whf. Tooley st
Rombauts Peter Jn. & Co. human hair imps. 25 Red Lion st. Holb
Römcke Fredc. Herman, merchant, see Berles, Römcke & Co
Rome Thos. corn, &c. measure mkr. 54 Featherstone st. City rd
Romer Frank, prof. of music, 11 Harrington st. Hampstd. rd
Romer Wm. Kimber, watch jeweller, 28 Tysoe st. Exmouth st
Romilly John, queen's counsel, 6 New square, Lincoln's inn
Ronald Robt. farrier, 19 Gt. Pearl st. Wheeler st. Spitalfields
Ronalds Charles, attorney, 1 Verulam buildings, Gray's inn
Ronalds Edmund, wholesale cheesemngr. 109 Up. Thames st
Ronaldson John James, wine merchant, 6 New Broad st. City
Rondeau Saml. steel & coppr. plte. mkr. 73 Noble st. Goswell st
Ronketti John George Harris, optician, 19 Leather lane
Rood John Yeoman & Co. who. bedding, horsehair, wool & flock ware. 29 Old Compton st. & feathr. dres. 9 Maiden la. King's cs
Roods Henry C. surgeon, 67 Gt. Russell st. Bloomsbury
Roods Thomas, artist, 67 Gt. Russell st. Bloomsbury
Roof Job, umbrella & stick maker, 119 Long alley, Finsbury
Rook Edward, tobacconist & library, 21 Edward st. City rd
Rook John, tailor, 52 Queen st. Bryanstone square
Rook Thomas, town carman & contractor, 6 Gibraltar walk, Bethnal green, & Little Hill st
Rookby Ann (Mrs.), saddler, 76 Gray's inn lane
Rooke, Son & Burge, trimmingms. 6 Critchill pl. New North rd
Rooke & Tautz, tailor, 11 Thayer st. Manchester square
Rooke Ann (Mrs.), milliner, 13 Thayer st. Manchester sq
Rooke Edward, accountant, 5 Brunswick place, City road
Rooke Frederick, tailor, &c. 50 Wellington st. Goswell st
Rooke George, *Pied Horse* P.H. 3 Chiswell st. Finsbury
Rooke George, pork butcher & poulterer, 60 London st
Rooke George, tailor, 14 Gt. Queen st. Lincoln's inn fields
Rooke Peter, tailor, 13 Thayer st. Manchester square
Rooke Peter Henry, barrister, 9 Serle st. Lincoln's inn fields
Rooke Thomas, grocer, 10 Great Swan alley, Moorgate st
Rooke Thos. James, solicitor, see Parker, Taylor & Rooke
Rooke Wm. professor of music, 74 Newman st. Oxford st
Rooker George, butcher, 28 Seymour st. Euston square
Rooker John, butcher, 82 Chalton st. Somers town
Rooker John, divider & engraver of mathematical instruments, 26 East st. Lamb's Conduit st
Rooks Thos. statuary & mason, 19 Marlboro' pl. Kennington cr
Rookwood Jesse, carpenter, 36 Great Ormond yard, Queen sq
Room Henry, artist, 4 York cottages, Old Brompton
Room Henry, portrait painter, 23 Charles st. Berners st
Roome James, corndealer, 83 East st. Manchester sq
Roome Thomas, organ metal pipe ma. 67 John st. Totnh. ct. rd
Rooney Robt. Alex. genl. brush ma. 27 & 28 Bishopsgate without
Roope & Furse, stay manufacturers, 69 Pennyfields, Poplar
Roope Cabel, oporto merchant, 12 New Broad st. City
Roope Charles, linendraper, 144 Sloane st. & 17 Sloane square, Chelsea
Roope William G. madeira wine merchant, 14 Mark lane
Rooper, Birch & Ingram, attorneys, 68 Lincoln's inn fields
Roose Mary (Mrs.), coffeerooms, 21 Judd st. Brunswick sq
Roots Augustus, barrister, 1 Tanfield court, Temple
Roots George, barrister, 1 Tanfield court, Temple
Roots Henry Shuckburgh, physician, 2 Russell square
Roots Thomas, veterinary surgeon, 13 Winchester st. Boro'
Rootsey George, pork butcher, 15 Brick lane, Spitalfields
Rootsey Margaret (Mrs.), saddler, 129 Mount st. Berkeley sq
Rootsey Richard, baker, 20 Aldersgate st
Rope John William, confectioner to her Majesty & the Duchess of Kent, 31 Lamb's Conduit st
Rope Robert, carpenter, 6 York st. Sloane st. Chelsea
Rope Richard, working jeweller, 8 Edwards st. Portman sq
Roper Joseph & Son, tea urn manufrs. braziers & patent plate warmer manufrs. 68 Snow hill
Roper Thomas & Co. who. druggists, 6 Falcon sq. Aldersgate
Roper Benj. *Somers Arms* P.H. 69 Wilstead st. St. Pancras
Roper Catherine (Mrs.), cowkeeper, 16 Britannia st. City rd
Roper Charles, coffin maker, 2 Cannon place, Whitechapl. rd
Roper Charles R. concentrated jelly manufr. 31 Poultry
Roper Charles Robert, chemist, Church st. Hackney
Roper David Riddall, surveyor, 11 Stamford st. Blackfriars rd
Roper Edmund, undertaker, 6 Goldsmith pl. Hackney road
Roper Francis, barrister, 5 Mitre ct. chambers, Fleet st
Roper Freeman C. S. hide broker, see Dyster, Nalder & Roper
Roper George Fyson, milliner, 37 Rathbone place, Oxford st
Roper Giles Symonds, surgeon, 5 Ossulston st. Somers town
Roper Henry, furniture broker, 38 Broad st. Lambeth
Roper Henry, insurance broker, Lloyd's
Roper John, beer retailer, 23 Easton st. Spafields
Roper John Hy. west india merch. see Trecothick, Roper & Son
Roper Joshua, attorney, 1 Staple inn, Holborn
Roper Mary (Mrs.), engraver & printer, 13 New st. sq. Shoe la
Roper Robert, *Earl Grey* P.H. Mile end, by the turnpike
Roper Samuel, plumber & glazier, 121 Wardour st. Soho
Roper Thomas Henry, barrister, 26 Chancery lane
Roper Wm. bricklayer & builder, 166 Shadwell High st
Roques Alexander, professor of french, 56 High Holborn
Rorke John, wood letter manuf. 3 Bishop's walk, Lambeth
Roschone John, carver & gilder, 16 Crescent, Southwark br. rd
Roscoe James, upholsterer, 6 Baker's row, Whitechapel
Roscoe Richard, surgeon, 16 Millman st. Bedford row
Roscoe William, ink manufacturer, 22 Basing lane
Rose & Arnett, silver engravers, 28 Marylebone st. Golden sq
Rose Henry & James, dentists, 48 Gower place, Euston sq
Rose John & Co. porcelain manuftrs. 4 Newcastle st. Strand
Rose John & Son, carpenters, 60 King st. Boro' High st
Rose John & Son, dyers & scourers, 29 Poland st. Oxford st
Rose Jonathan & George, writers & gilders, 56 Gray's inn la
Rose & Noble, bottle merchants, wine coopers & agents for dublin stout, india, pale, scotch & other ales, Salisbury wharf, Salisbury st. Strand
Rose Thomas & Wm. linendrapers, 121 St. George st
Rose Amelia (Mrs.), *Batt's hotel*, 41 to 43 Dover st. Picadil
Rose Arthur, color merchant, 65 Trinity square, Borough
Rose Benjamin Robt. oil warehouse, 39 Noble st. Cheapside

Rose Catherine (Mrs.), milliner, 19 Francis st. Tottnhm. ct. rd
Rose Charles, surgeon, 10 Barnes place, Mile end rd
Rose Chas. upholsterer, &c. 50 Southampton rw. Bloomsby
Rose Elizabeth (Mrs.), lace dlr. 26 Lower Sloane st. Chelsea
Rose Fredrk. hop & seed mer. Calvert's bldgs. 241 Boro' Highst
Rose George, attorney, 43 Lincoln's inn fields
Rose George, fruiterer, 13 Great Bath st. Clerkenwell
Rose George, grocer, 11 Regent st. Horseferry rd
Rose George, plumber & glazier, 6 Duke st. Smithfield
Rose George James, solicitor, 6 New inn, Strand
Rose Hemming L. wine mer. Salisbury whf. Salisbury st.
Rose Hen. architect & surveyor, 100 Gt. Guildford st. Boro'
Rose Isaac, jeweller & salesman, 45 Tooley st
Rose Isaac, shumac merchant, 11 Grange rd. Bermondsey
Rose James, cabinet maker, 108 Hoxton Old town
Rose James, watch jeweller, 1 Up. Chadwell st. Pentonville
Rose James, solicitor, see Bebb & Rose
Rose Jemima Amelia (Miss), fancy rep. 112 Up. st. Islington
Rose John, cooper & brewer, 37 High st. Bow
Rose John, flute manufacturer, see Rudall & Rose
Rose John, teadealer, 143 Whitechapel rd. 213 Borough High st. & 178 Shoreditch
Rose John, solicitor, Filacer's office, Qn's. Bench office, Temp.
Rose John, surgeon, 1 Trinidad place, Liverpool rd
Rose John, teadealer, 23 Union st. east, Spitalfields
Rose John, undertaker, 55 Poplar High st
Rose John, *Watermans' Arms* P.H. 11 Dockhead, Bermndsy
Rose John Benson Coles, barrister, 43 Parliament st
Rose John Burrows, *Adml. Vernon* P.H. Up. Groundst. Blkfrs
Rose John Mitchell, flute maker, see Rudall & Rose
Rose Joseph, grocer, 149 Brick lane, Spitalfields
Rose Joseph, smith & farrier, 12 Wallington pl. Wandswth. rd
Rose Joseph Franklin, surg. 60 Stamford st. & 16½ Blkfrs. rd
Rose Joseph M. teadealer & grocer, 352 Oxford st
Rose Louisa (Miss), milliner, 14 Canterbury pl. Old Kent rd
Rose Mary (Miss), ladies' school, 18 College st. Chelsea
Rose Mary (Mrs.), boarding house, 2 Montague st. Russell sq
Rose Mary Ann (Mrs.), jeweller, 96 Farringdon st
Rose Philip, solicitor, see Barker, Rose & Norton
Rose Samuel, merchant, 30 Nicholas lane
Rose Samuel, news vender, 139 Waterloo road
Rose Samuel, wheelwright, 15 Bowling green la. Clknwll
Rose Thomas, cattle salesman, 15 Smithfield
Rose Thomas, green grocer, 32 Maze, Tooley st. Borough
Rose Thomas Wm. wholesale furrier, 13 Wood st. Cheapside
Rose Wm. anchor, chain & ship smith, see Barrick & Rose
Rose Wm. barrister, 1 Hare court, Temple
Rose Wm. cattle salesman, 8 West Smithfield
Rose Wm. grocer, 5 Kent place, Old Kent road
Rose Wm. grocer, 26 Whitefriars st. Fleet st
Rose Wm. hairdresser, 32 St. Andrew's hill, Blackfriars
Rose Wm. locksmith, 132 Cornwall road, Lambeth
Rose Wm. solicitor, see Rippingham & Rose
Rose Wm. A. white lead, color & varnish mer. 23 Queenh
Rose Wm. Grant, parliamentary agent, 43 Parliament st
Roseblade Joseph, *Perseverance* P.H. 9 Weston st. Somers tn
Rosenberg Adolph, rag mer. 46 Bedfordbury, Covent garden
Rosenbrock Claus, *Crown* P.H. 39 New rd. St. George's ea
Rosenhaum & Jacobs, china warehouse, 240 Whitechapel rd
Rosenthal Ludwig, merchant, 81 Mark lane
Rosewell Wm. carpenter, 34 Windmill st. Tottenham ct. rd
Rosher Henry & Geo. & Edward, lime & cement merchants, 28 to 30 Limekiln hill, Limehouse; Montague close, Boro'; Kingsland basin; & 21 Milbank st. Westminster
Rosier Jas. stockbroker, 2 Adam's ct. Old Broad st & Stock exc
Rosier John, *Crown & Anchor* P.H. 129 Waterloo road
Rosier Joseph Nunwick, pawnbroker, 140 Tooley st. & 42 Turnmill st. Clerkenwell
Rosier Richd. insur. & com. agt. 28 Broad st. bldgs. & Baltic
Rosinbloom Joseph, slipper ma. 15 Devonshire st. Bishopsgt
Roskell Joseph Kaye, solicitor, 3 Cork st. Burlington gar
Roskell Robert, jeweller, see Hunt & Roskell
Rosling & Watson, cornfactors, New Corn Exchange, Mark lane, & Bull stairs wharf, 18 Up. Ground st. Blackfriars
Rosling Alfred, timber merchant, & saw & planing mills, 16 Bankside, & Old Bargehouse wharf, Up. Ground st. Blckfrs
Rosoman Elizabeth (Mrs.), piece broker, 52 Curtain road
Ross Alex. & Sons, pat. peruke ms. 119 & 120 Bispgt. within
Ross & Ash, merchant & insur. brokers, 32 Gt. Winchst. st
Ross Caroline & Charlotte, seminary, 8 Giltspur st
Ross Alexander, army accoutrement maker, & contractor to Her Majesty's Hon. Board of Ordnance, & the Hon. East India Company, Grange mills, Bermondsey
Ross Alexander, shoemaker, 11 Fleur de lis court, Fleet st
Ross Alexander, wine & spirit merchant, 42 St. Mary axe
Ross Andrew, general agent, 15 Tower Royal, Watling st
Ross Andrew, optician, 21 Featherstone buildings, Holborn
Ross Benjamin, pocket book maker, 68 Aldersgate st
Ross Car. J. (Mrs.), *Caledonian tav.* 8 Claremont ter. Stoke New. road
Ross Daniel, surgeon, 56 Shadwell High st
Ross Daniel, wholesale grocer, see Tompsett, Ross & Co
Ross Elizabeth (Mrs.), butcher, 106 Long alley, Finsbury
Ross Elizabeth (Mrs.), tool maker, see Dredge & Ross
Ross George, colonial broker, 28 Mincing lane
Ross George, surgeon, 2 Leicester pl. Camberwell New rd
Ross Harriott (Mrs.) baby linen wa. 2 Caledonia ter. Caledo. rd
Ross Hen. professor of music, 14 Brunswick pl. Barnsby. rd
Ross Hen. solicitor, 15 Wine office court, Fleet st
Ross Hen. (Mrs.), newsvender, 18 Lit. Carter la. Doctors' Coms
Ross Hugh, artist, 24 Russell place, Fitzroy sq
Ross Hugh, barrister, 13 Chancery lane
Ross James, boat builder, New Cut, Limehouse
Ross James, grocer & teadealer, 56 Gt. Tower st
Ross John, ballast agent, 21 Caroline st. Commercial rd. ea
Ross John, cabinet maker, 48 Worship st. Finsbury
Ross John, fishmonger, 19 George st. Portland place
Ross John, oil & colorman, 44 Goswell rd
Ross John, soda water manufr. 2 Bream's bdgs. Chancery la
Ross Maria (Mrs.), milliner, 15 Prospect pl. Kingsland rd
Ross Matilda C. (Mrs.), school, 15 Young st. Kensington
Ross Peter, china & glass wareho. 18 New st. Dorset sq
Ross Rickman, oil, mustard & sawmills, see Sadler, Firth & Ross
Ross Thos. engraver & printer, 8 Giltspur st. Smithfield
Ross Thos. frankfort black maker, 8 Giltspur st
Ross Thos. steel & copper plate printer, see Dixon & Ross
Ross Thomas, tailor, see M'Kenzie & Ross
Ross Wm. tailor & breeches maker, 29 Robert st. Grosvenor sq
Ross Sir Wm. Chas. knt. R.A. miniature painter to the Queen, 38 Fitzroy square
Rosselli Asdrubale & Emanuel, merchants, 23 Mincing lane
Rosselli Jacob, merchant, 18 Trinity sq. Tower hill
Rosselloty & Evors, accountants & general commission agts. 3 Warwick st. Charing cross
Rosser Archibald Richard F. solicitor, 63 Lincoln's inn fields
Rosser Richard, attorney, 36 Southampton row, Bloomsbry
Rosser Wm. Henry, solicitor, 2 Dyer's buildings, Holborn
Rossetti Blase, coach maker, 29 Drury lane
Rossi Louis, hairdresser & perfumer, 254 Regent st
Rossi Ralph, importer of & dealer in wines & spirits; shipper of Barclay & Co.'s porter & pale ale, 16 Little Tower st
Rossi Ralph, licensed custom house agent, 16 Lit. Tower st
Rossini Gasparrino, coal dealer, 7 Amelia st. Walworth rd
Rossiter Wm. & John, woollen manufs. 78 Basinghall st
Rossiter Chas. *Perseverance* P.H. 22 Gt. St. Andrew st. 7 Dials
Rossiter Charles, plumber & painter, 59 Chenies mews, Bedf. sq
Rossiter Fred. carp. & builder, 14 Nicholas lane, Lombard st
Rossiter Jas. wholesale portmanteau & trunk manufacturer for exportation, 15 Greville st. Hatton garden
Rossiter Nicholas, tailor, 242 Blackfriars road
Rosson John, solicitor, 6 St. Martin's st. Leicester square
Roswell Henry George, cooper, 5 Cross st. Islington
Rotch Benjamin, barrister, 1 Furnival's inn, Holborn
Roth & Freeman, tailors to H.R.H. Prince Albert, 4 Old Bond st. Piccadilly
Rotherford Rt. *Brownlow Arms* P.H. 13 Brownlow st. Druryla
Rotherham & Co. *Bricklayers Arms* P.H. 43 Mountst. Berklysq
Rotherham Foundry Company (Samuel & Thomas Currington, proprietors), 50 Upper Thames st
Rotherham Chas. *D. of Wellington* P.H. 28 Princes st. Leic. sq
Rotherham Henry, *George* P.H. 23 Crown st. Soho
Rotherham Jeremiah, haberdasher, &c. 83 & 84 Shoreditch
Rotherham John, wine & spirit mer. 13 Silver st. Golden sq
Rotherhithe Grammar School (Rev. Wm. B. Hutchinson & Cornelius Felix Zurhorst, masters), Lower rd. Rotherhithe
Rothery Wm. & Hen. C. proctors & nots. 12 Gt. Knightrider st
Rothery Joseph, carpet agent, 11 Addle st. Wood st
Rothery William, barrister, 10 Stratford place, Oxford st
Rothery Wm. proctor & notary, 12 Great Knightrider st
Rothon Jonth. chimney sweeper, 69 Ropemakers flds. Limho
Rothschild N. M. & Sons, merchts. 3 New ct. St. Swithin's la
Rothschild Louis Meyer, diamond mer. 71 Gt. Queen st
Rothschild L. N. de, austrian consul general, 3 New court, St. Swithin's lane
Rothwell P. & Son, china, &c. dealers, 21 Cleveland st. Fitzroy sq
Rothwell Samuel & Son, printers, 6 Cross la. St. Mary at hill
Rothwell Richard, artist, 31 Devonshire st. Portland place
Rothwell Wm. grocer, 214 Shadwell High st
Rothwell Wm. mathe. inst. divider, 74 Westmoreland pl. City rd
Rotterdam Steam Packet office (Nicholas Temperley, agent), 50A, King William st. City

Rotton Robert, coach & harness plater, 5 Baltic st. Golden la
Rotton Wm. Henry, jeweller, 4 Bentinck st. Berwick st. Soho
Rouch Charles, chinaman, 4 Folly, Dockhead
Rouch Frederick, cheesemonger, 18 Up. King st. Bloomsbury
Rouch Wm. cheesemonger, 12 Clayton pl. Caledonian rd
Roudhloff Dominic & Arnould, guitar & guitar string manufs. & artist's colormen, 81 Charlotte st. Fitzroy sq
Rouen & Havre Railway Company, 38 Throgmorton st
Rouge John, professor of music, 54 Rathbone place
Rougemont Brothers, merchants, 14 Broad st. buildings
Rouget Jean Baptiste, *Giraud's hotel*, 61 Castle st. Leic. sq
Rough William Henry, barrister, 1 Paper buildings, Temple
Rought Thomas, picture dealer, &c. 17 Regent st
Rougier Pierre M.A. jacquard mach. ma. 15 Princes st. Sptlfs
Roumieu John, solicitor, see Whitmore, Roumieu & Walters
Roumieu Robert Lewis, architect, see Gough & Roumieu
Round Edmund, special pleader, 4 Harcourt buildings, Temple
Round Fred. Willding, ship & ins. agt. see Symons & Round
Round Henry, clothes salesman, 35 Lit. Windmill st. Golden sq
Round Joseph, tailor, 16 Brewer st. Pimlico
Round Martin, bookbinder, 129 Fetter lane
Round Oliver Stephen, barrister, 36 Lincoln's inn fields
Round Whinfield Stephen, barrister, 36 Lincoln's inn fields
Rountree Edward, *Weaver's Arms* P.H. 3 Bakers row, Whitchp
Rountree Fredk. *Crown & Sceptre* P.H. 24 Woolmore st. Poplar
Roupell Charles Morris, barrister, 13 Old sq. Lincoln's inn
Roupell George Leith, physician, 15 Welbeck st
Roupell John Stuart, barrister, 5 New sq. Lincoln's inn
Roupell Rd. Palmer, lead ash smelter, 16 Cross st. Blackfrs. & smith & engineer, Bear la. George st. Blackfriars road
Roupell Rd. Palmer leadsmltr. Dyer's blgs. Gravel la. Sthwk
Roupell Robt. Prioleau, queen's counsel, 5 New sq. Linco's.in
Rous John, fish salesman, 3 Billingsgate
Rous John, hairdresser, &c. 22 St. Mary at hill
Rouse Benj. R.C. chemist, 9 Wellington st. Lond. bdge. Boro'
Rouse Edward, baker, 6 Jamaica row, Bermondsey rd
Rouse John, grocer, 1 Ebenezer pl. Neckinger rd. Bermondsy
Rouse John, oil & colorman, 145 Hoxton Old town
Rouse Joseph, undertaker, 54 Brunswick st. Hackney rd
Rouse Patrick, bootma. 13 Opera arcade, Haymarket
Rouse Richard, *White Conduit Ho. tav.* Penton pl. Pentvl
Rouse Robert, chemist & drugst. 1 Wigmore st. Cavendish sq
Rouse Thomas, *Eagle tavern*, Shepherdess wlk. City rd
Rouse William, bottle merchant, 6 Gun lane, Limehouse
Rouse William, furniture broker, 89 High st. Poplar
Rouse Wm. camp stool manufacturer, 252 Kent st. Boro'
Rouse Wm. Chas. painter & ho. agt. 2 Stucley ter. Camden tn
Roussel Lewis, merchant, Baltic
Rout John, manchester warehouseman, 8 Little Moorfields
Rout Sarah (Mrs.), teadealer, 3 High st. Newington butts
Rout Thomas, *Crown tavern* P.H. 12A, Old Cavendish st
Routen Fredk. hairdresser, 36 Windmill st. Finsbury
Routh Elizh. (Mrs.), lodging ho. 21 Manchester bldgs. Westm
Routh Jas. groc. & cheesemgr. 18 White Hart st. Drury lane
Routh John, merchant, 9 Austinfriars
Routh John, jun. merchant, 9 Austinfriars
Routh Randolph, merchant, 9 Austinfriars
Routh Robert Alfred, solicitor, 53 Lincoln's inn fields
Routh Wm. R. grocer & teadealer, 25 King st. Clothfair
Routledge & Co. pat. saw mills, 5 Holland st. Blackfriars rd
Routledge Frdk. J. & Felix J. for. mers. 11 Addle st. Wood st
Routledge George, bookseller & publisher, 36 Soho square
Routledge John, currier, 10 Old Fish st. hill
Routledge Thomas, brandy agent, 89 Gt. Tower st
Routledge William, linendraper, 30 Bridge road, Lambeth
Rouw George, dairyman, 6 Pleasant row, Holloway road
Rouw Peter, sculptor, &c. 80 Norton st. Fitzroy square
Row William, sen. Son & Co. hide, fur & skin brokers & warehousekeepers, &c. 23 Little St. Thomas Apostle
Row Benjamin, plumber, 1 Earl st. Kensington
Row Chas. John, carver, gilder, &c. Little Bridge st. Blkfrs
Row George, boot & shoe maker, 31 Kingsland road
Row George, fishmonger, 12 London terrace, Hackney road
Row John, fishmonger, 214 Bethnal green road
Row Mary (Miss), seminary, 7 River terrace north, City rd
Row Mary (Mrs.), stationer, &c. 28 Marlboro' st. Regent st
Row Thomas, *Golden Key* P.H. 19 Bell st. Edgware rd
Row William, butcher, 142 Union st. Borough
Row Wm. Robert, boot & shoe maker, 115 Crawford st
Rowbotham John, sup. reg. of births, 55 Queen's rw. Wlwrth
Rowbotham Joseph, bookbinder, 70 Castle st. east, Oxford st
Rowcliff Matthew, bricklayer, 23 Crown st. Soho
Rowcliffe Charles, *Nag's Head* P.H. 39 Leather lane
Rowcliffe Geo. auctioneer, valuer & furniture broker, 8 Newington causeway, & 4 Cumberland pl. Newington butts
Rowdon Fredk. & Alfred, wholesale grocers, 9 Mincing lane
Rowdon Fras. stationer & tobacconist, 2 Brown st. Bryanst. sq
Rowdon Hen. Mortimer, surgeon, 24 Bayham ter. Camden tn
Rowdon Philip, bootmaker, 16 Kingsgate st. Holborn
Rowe & Keal, surgeons, 24 Woburn pl. & 6 Up. Woburn pl
Rowe, Kentish & Osborne, security bankers, cheque & bank note engravers, stationers & printers, 16 Change al. Cornhll
Rowe, Lawrence & Son, merchants, Baltic coffeehouse
Rowe Alfred, academy, 2 Addison road north, Notting hill
Rowe Ann (Mrs.), confectioner, 176 Strand
Rowe Benjamin, woollendraper, see Woollett, Rowe & Clay
Rowe Catherine (Mrs.), berlin wool rep. 101 Milton st. Dorst sq
Rowe Charles, upholster, 61 Mount st. Berkeley square
Rowe Chas. Geo. prof. of music & singing, 8 Up. ter. Islingtn
Rowe Chas. Wm. dairyman, 56 Gt. Coram st. Brunswick sq
Rowe Charlt. (Mrs.), oil & colormn. 6 Ann's ter. Cambridge hth
Rowe George Robert, physician, 2 Golden square
Rowe Hartnoll, ironmonger & smith, 12 Upper Kennington la
Rowe James, corndealer, 1A, Charles st. Ea. Hampstead rd
Rowe James, vet. surgeon, 13 Crescent, Bridge rd. Southwk
Rowe James, furn. ironmonger, 7 Blandford st. Portman sq
Rowe James William, tailor, 1A, Little Ryder st. St. James's
Rowe John, appra. & auctnr. 9 Rotherfield st. north, Islington
Rowe John, beerretailer, Westmoreland pl. Walworth com
Rowe John, grocer & cheesemonger, 14 Market st. May fair
Rowe John, shipsmith, East india road, Poplar
Rowe Joseph, iron & tin plate worker, 5 Lr. Kennington la
Rowe Richard, carpenter, 59 Clarence gardens, Regent's pk
Rowe Joseph *Pembroke Arms* P.H. 50 Pembroke sq. Kensingtn
Rowe Richard, wholesale teadealer, see Clarke & Rowe
Rowe Thomas, bedstead maker, 13 High rd. Knightsbridge
Rowe Thomas, coffee rooms, 11 Blackmoor st. Drury lane
Rowe William, dyer, 3 Bedford row, East st. Walworth rd
Rowe Wm. builder, &c. 7 Glo'ster pl. Glo'ster cres. Reg. prk
Rowe Wm. haberdasher, 16 Bridge st. Westminster
Rowe William Carpenter, barrister, 2 Pump court, Temple
Rowed Chas. timber mercht. 33 Charles st. Hampstead rd
Rowed John, pianoforte maker, 7 Frederick pl. Hampstd. rd
Rowed Richard, fishmonger, 22 Devonshire st. Portland place, & 43 Beaumont st
Rowell Edwd. custom ho. agt. see Phillipps, Rowell & Lowther
Rowell James, butcher, 8 Webber st. Blackfriars road
Rowell John, butcher, 9 Surrey place, Wandsworth road
Rowland Alexander & Son, sole proprietors of the original macassar oil & kalydor, 20 Hatton garden
Rowland & Hacon, solicitors, 38 Threadneedle st
Rowland Christopher Rd. chemist, &c. 260 Tottenham ct. rd
Rowland James, fishmonger, 18 Munster st. Regent's pk
Rowland James, tailor, 54 Long acre
Rowland John, fruiterer, 17 Young st. Kensington
Rowland John, lodging house, 4 Cecil st. Strand
Rowland John, watch cap maker, 9 Woodbridge st. Clerkwll
Rowland Jonathan, cheesemonger, Earl's ct. Old Brompton
Rowland Joseph, dealer in paintings, &c. 8 St. Mary Axe
Rowland Maria (Mrs.), ladies' school, 30 Brewer st. Goldn. sq
Rowland Richard, cowkeeper, 1 Queen st. Tower hill
Rowland Richard, physician, 39 Queen sq. Bloomsbury
Rowland Richard, physician, 9 Woburn pl. Russell sq
Rowland Sarah (Mrs.), plumber, 3 Broad st. Golden square
Rowland Thomas, hairdresser, 5 Sheffield st. Linc. inn fields
Rowland Wm. tin plate worker, 48 Gt. Guildford st. Borough
Rowlands Christopher & Son, goldsmiths, 146 Regent st
Rowlands Robt. watch case & dial mak. 35 Meredith st. Clkw
Rowlands Wm. engraver, 46 Wellington st. Goswell rd
Rowlands Wm. goldsmith, 33 Low. Smith st. Northampton sq
Rowlandson & Atkinson, manufacturers & calico printers, 19 & 20 King st. Cheapside, & 12 & 13 Cateaton st
Rowlandson Henry, paper hanger, 10 York st. Kingsland rd
Rowlandson Lancelot, carpet & furn. wa. 83 Whitechapel rd
Rowlatt Samuel, solicitor, 43 Lamb's Conduit st
Rowles John, dyer, 71 London road, & 8 Blackman st. Boro'
Rowles Wm. cheesemgr. & butcher, 33 Clifton st. Finsbury
Rowlett John, coal & potato dealer, 6 Robert st. Oxford st
Rowley & Banbury, milliners, 10 South pl. Camberwell Newrd
Rowley Edward, tobacconist, 12 Vauxhall bridge rd
Rowley John, baker, 55 London road, Southwark
Rowley John, optician, 26 Edgware road, Marylebone
Rowley John George, bookbinder, 108 Hatton garden
Rowley John R. dining rooms, Belvedere road, Lambeth
Rowley Jonas, baker, 38 Paradise st. Rotherhithe
Rowley Joseph, butcher, 33 Up. Lisson st. Lisson grove
Rowley Mark, working optician, 56 Goswell road, west side
Rowley Richd. painter & glazier, 34 Skinner st. Clerkenwell
Rowley Robt. physician accoucher, 37 King William st. City
Rowley Thomas, coach builder, see Cook, Rowley & Co
Rowley Thomas, tailor, 87 John st. Fitzroy square
Rowley Thomas, teadealer, see Stenins, Rowley & Co

Rowling James, boot & shoemaker, 2 Wyndham rd. Cambrwll
Rowling John, tobacconist, 54 Brook st. Lambeth
Rowling Joseph, bootmaker, 5 Wyndham road, Camberwell
Rowney, Dillon & Rowney, artists' colormen, 51 Rathbone pl
Rowuson & Drew, wholesale ironmongers & dealers in malleable zinc, 11 Bennett's hill; 217 Up. Thames st. & Paul's wf
Rowntree Henry, tailor, 22 Sidmouth st. Gray's inn road
Roworth Charles & sons, printers, 38 Bell yard, Temple bar
Roworth John, coffee rooms, 6 Wade's place Hackney rd
Rowse Charles, coffee rooms, 55 Crawford st. Portman sq
Rowse William, rag merchant, 2 Wheeler st. Spitalfields
Rowse William, smith, 2 Dacre st. Westminster
Rowsell Charles John, accountant, 4 Dowgate hill
Rowsell Chas. John, accountant, Skinner's hall, Dowgate hill
Rowsell John Thos. solicitor, firm Dodd, Rowsell, Grueber, & Dodd; clerk to the city of London union, & superintendent registrar of births, deaths, & marriages for the City of London, 35 Cannon st.; hours 10 to 4
Rowsell Saml. Wm. ruled account book wareh. 31 Cheapside
Roxberry Charlotte, perfumer, see Arnold & Roxberry
Roxborough Alex. jun. farrier, 9 Alfred mews, Tottm. ct. rd
Roxburgh Francis, barrister, Rolls chmbrs. 89 Chancery la
Roxburgh Wm. physician, 38 Gloucester place, Portman sq
Roxby Esther (Mrs.), grocer & cheesemngr. 10 New st. Horslydn
Roxby Henry, ship insurance broker, 46 Lime st
Roy, Blunt & Johnstone, attorneys, 42 Lothbury
Roy Robt. & Co. coal mers. Sunderland whf. Maidenla. King's cr
Roy Charles, plumber, 45 Robert st. Hoxton
Roy James, impervious tar paint manufactory, 47 Bankside
Roy Richard, solicitor, 37 Great George st. Westminster
Roy Sarah (Mrs.), ladies' school, 69 Dean st. Soho
Roy William, bread & biscuit baker, 68 St. Mary Axe
Royal Academy of Arts (Henry Howard, R.A. secretary), Trafalgar square, Pall mall East
Royal Academy of Music (Rev. Fredk. Hamilton, supnt.; Joseph Gimson, sec.), 4 Tenterden st. Hanover sq
Royal Adelaide Gallery of Practical Science, 13 Lowther arcade, & 7 Adelaide st. West Strand
Royal Adelaide Lying-in Hospital (Wm. Henry Yell, surgeon), 10 Queen st. Golden sq
Royal Agricultural Society of England (James Hudson, secretary), 12 Hanover square
Royal Asiatic Society (Rd. Clarke, sec.), 14 Grafton st. Bond st
Royal Astronomical So. (Capt. W. H. Smyth, R.N. presdt.; & Rev. Robt. Main & Wm. Rutherford, esq. secs.; Rev. R. Sheepshanks, foreign sec.; Richard Harris, esq. assist. sec.; Geo. Bishop, esq. treasurer), Somerset house, Strand
Royal Asylum for destitute Females, Manor Hall, Lit. Chelsea
Royal Bank of Australia (Benj. Wood, sec.), Austin friars, see page 2009
Royal Botanic So. of London, Inner circle, Regent's park
Royal College of Surgeons, 40, 41 & 42 Lincoln's inn fields
Royal Dis. for Diseases of the Ear, 10 Dean st Soho, 9 to 12
Royal Engineers' Office, London district (Major Lewis Alexander Hall, commanding royal engineer), 11 James st. Buckingham gate; hours 10 to 4
Royal Exchange Assurance Corporation (A. Green, sec.), 29 Pall mall, & Royal Exchange; see page 2042
Royal Farmers' Life & Fire Insurance Office (John Hanson, managing director), 346A, Strand
Royal Free Hospital (Rev. Robert Collier Packman, sec.), Calthorpe place, Gray's inn road
Royal General Dispensary (W. James, surgeon), 26 Burton crescent
Royal Geographical Society (Lord Colchester, pres.; Col. Jackson, sec.; Rev. G. C. Renouard, foreign sec.; John Shillinglaw, esq. asst. sec.), 3 Waterloo place, Pall mall
Royal Harbour of Ramsgate Office, 22 Austinfriars, 11 to 4
Royal Highland Schl. Soc. (Js. Thomson, sec.), 25 Fenchurch st
Royal Humane Soc. (Joseph Charlier, sec.), 3 Trafalgar sq
Royal Infirm. for Diseases of the Eye, Cork st. mws. Bond st
Royal Institute of British Architects (Charles Fowler & George Bailey, hon. secs.), 16 Grosvenor st
Royal Institution (Rev. John Barlow, sec.), 21 Albemarle st
Royal Jennerian & London Vaccine Insti. (Chas. Chantry, sec.), 18 Providence row, Finsbury sq. & 3 Union ct. Hlbn. hill
Royal Kent Dispensary (A. Burridge, surgeon), Deptford broadway
Royal Literary Fund (Octavian Blewitt, sec.), 73 Great Russell st. Bloomsbury
Royal London Militia Quarters, 23 Euston square
Royal London Ophthalmic Hospital (Thomas S. Heward, house surgeon), Blomfield st. Finsbury
Royal London Welch Dispensary (Edw. Wm. Richards, surgeon), 18 Great Newport st. Soho
Royal Marines Office, 22 New st. Spring grdns; hours 10 to 5
Royal Mail Steam Packet Office (Edward Chappell, Capt. R.N. sec.), 55 Moorgate st.; hours 10 to 5
Royal Masonic Institute for Boys (Augustus Union Thiselton, sec.), 7 Bloomsbury place, Bloomsbury
Royal Maternity Lying-in Charity (Francis Wilson, sec.), 17 Little Knightrider st
Royal Medical & Chirurgical Society (Wm. Fred. Chambers, M.D. F.R.S. pres.; George Crusham, M.D. & T. B. Curling, secs.), 53 Berners st. Oxford st
Royal Military Asylum (Capt. Wm. Siborn, sec.), King's road, Chelsea
Royal Mines of Cobre Association, 26 Austinfriars
Royal Mint, Little Tower hill; hours of business 10 to 4
Royal National Institution for the Preservation of Lives from Shipwreck (Thomas Edwards, sec.), 20 Austinfriars
Royal Naval Benevolent Society (Commander Dickson, sec.), 18 Adams st. Adelphi
Royal Naval Annuitant Society, 3 Clifford's inn, Fleet st
Royal Naval Club House (David Foggo, sec.), 160 Nw. Bond st
Royal Naval Female School (Arthur Ellis, sec.), office, 32 Sackville st. Piccadilly; school, Richmond, Surrey
Royal Naval, Military & East India Company Life Assurance Society Offices (Joseph C. Brettell, sec.), 13 Waterloo place, see page 2042
Royal Naval School (Rev. T. Chambers, M.A. head master), New cross, Deptford
Royal Orthopœdic Institution for Club Feet (H. G. Gridley, hon. sec.) 6 Bloomsbury square
Royal Polytechnic Institution for the advancement of the arts & practical science (R. I. Longbottom, sec.), 309 Regent st. & 5 Cavendish square
Royal & St. Peter's Dispensary (Stevens Nicholas Henry, dispenser), 13 Lower Belgrave place, Belgrave road
Royal Santiago Mining Company, 38 Broad st. buildings
Royal Sea Bathing Infirmary (John Paul, sec.) 35 Cannon st
Royal Society (Dr. Roget, secretary), Somerset house
Royal Society of Literature (Rev. Richard Cattermole, sec.), 4 St. Martin's place, Charing cross
Royal Society of Musicians (John A. Wood, sec.), 12 Lisle st
Royal Society for the Prevention of Cruelty to Animals (Henry Thomas, sec.), 12 Pall mall
Royal South London Dispensary (Wm. Hentsch, surgeon), 23 Laurie terrace, Westminster road
Royal Universal Infirmary for Children (Edwd. Hoare, sec.), 180 Wellington terrace, Waterloo road
Royal Veterinary College (William Sewell, professor & secretary), College st. Camden town
Royal James, japanner, 22 York st. Blackfriars road
Royce James, butcher, 269 Rotherhithe
Royce John, carpenter, 19 Marlborough mews, Blenheim st
Royce John Robert, grocer, 75 Albany st. Regent's park
Roycroft John, builder, 42 Trafalgar st. Walworth road
Royer Charles, plumasier & furrier, 45 Poland st. Oxford st
Royer William Henry, appraiser, 17 Old st. St. Luke's
Royle George, bookbindr.'s toolcutter, 20 Ivy la. Newgate st
Royle John, plumber, &c. 1 New st. Princes st. Lambeth
Royle John Forbes, physician, 4 Bulstrode st. Manchester sq
Royle Eliza (Miss), ladies' school, 67 Judd st. Brunswick sq
Royle Sarah (Mrs.), plumber, painter, &c. 8 Kennington row
Royle William Richard, writing engraver, 251 High Holborn
Royou William, wine cooper, 35 Eastcheap
Royston & Brown, booksellers, printers, general stationers, & letter copying machinemanfctrs. &c. 40 & 41 Old Broad st. City
Royston Jas. & Co. wire drwrs. & card maks. 9 Aldermanbury
Royston John, currier, 32 Chapel st. Somers town
Rozenbaum Abraham, french comml. agent, 126 Goswell st
Rozier Charles, undertaker, 6 Bentinck st. Soho
Rubbi Luigi D. vocal academy, 25 Gt. Pulteney st. Golden sq
Ruben Ruben Abraham, leech importer, see Heilbut & Ruben
Rubergall John, cowkeeper, Little Chelsea, north side
Rubergall Thomas, optician to their Majesties, 24 Coventry st. Haymarket
Rubergall Wm. wharfinger, Bull wf. Paradise row, Chelsea
Rubery Edward, pawnbroker, 283 Bethnal green road
Rubidge Jas. Chs. coachbldr. 10 Foundling mews, Gray's inn rd
Rubidge Susan (Mrs.), strawbonnet ma. 2 Mecklenburgh ter
Ruck John & Cornelius, wholesale cheesemongers & provision merchts. Topping's whf. & 8 Duke st. London br. Boro'
Ruck John & William D. wholesale cheesemongers & provision merchants, Scovell's wharf, Tooley st
Ruck, Son & Fenwick, wine & brandy mers. 19 St. Dunstan's hill
Ruck William, solicitor, 14 Mincing lane
Rucker (I. A.) & Bencraft, colonial broks. 26 Comcl. sale rooms
Rucker & Pratt, merchants, 13 Mincing lane
Rucker Sigismund & Sons, e. & w. india brks. 12 Gt. Tower st
Rudall & Rose, flute manfrs. 1 Tavistock st. Covent garden

Rudall John, barrister, 4 Stone buildings, Lincoln's inn
Rudall John Henry, merchant, 8 Gould sq. Crutched friars
Rudall William, barrister, 50 Chancery lane
Rudd Stanley G.& Co.pianoforte ms.25 Tavistock st.Cvnt.gn
Rudd & Tyler, milliners, 75 New Bond st
Rudd Adelaide R.(Miss),girls' school,34Clipstone st. Fitz. sq
Rudd Eric, barrister, 29 Lincoln's inn fields
Rudd George, bricklayer, 10 Holland st. Brixton rd
Rudd George, poulterer, 1 Clarence place, Regent's park
Rudd Henry, merchant, 13 Tokenhouse yard
Rudd John, pianoforte maker, 4 Circus st. New rd. Maryleb
Rudd Richard, jun. plumber, Denmark hill, Camberwell
Rudd Samuel, dealer in live birds, 47 Kingsland road
Rudd Thomas, fruiterer, 20 Weymouth st. Portland place
Rudd William, *Castle* P.H.35 Shouldham st. Edgeware rd
Ruddell Elizab.(Mrs.),lodging house, 32½ Mount st.Grvnr.sq
Ruddell Richard, bootmaker, 58 Amelia st. Walworth road
Rudderforth Henry (Mrs.), staymak.42Newington causeway
Rudderforth John, tailor, 36 Cleveland st. Fitzroy sq
Rudderforth John Thos. staymaker,52Newington causeway
Rudderforth Thos. jun. stayma. 13 Parkside, Knightsbridge
Ruddiman John, hairdresser, 9 Bermondsey st
Ruddock Samuel, goldsmith, 7 Denmark st. Soho
Ruddock Wm. grocer & oilman, 41 Basing pl. Waterloo rd
Rudduck Samuel, stay haberdasher & horsehair manufacturer, 20 Anchor st. Shoreditch
Rudelhoff Henry John, pork butcher, 28 Redcross st. Boro'
Rudge Joseph, tobacconist, 20 Portugal st. Linc. inn fields
Ruding John Clement&Sons, cornfacs. Salvador ho.Bishopsg
Ruding Rogers, merchant, Baltic coffee house, & Salvador house, 200 Bishopsgate
Rudkin Chas. Thos. *Salutation & Cat* P.H.17 Newgate st
Rudkin F. W. coal merchant, Milford wharf, Strand
Rudkin Henry, carpenter, 8 Paddington st. Marylebone
Rudland & Broad, brushmakers, &c. 164 Shoreditch
Rudland Charles, dining rooms, 4 Up.Lisson st.Lisson grove
Rudler Geo. ladies' boot&shoe mak. 11 Foley st. Portland pl
Rudram John, shoemaker, Waterloo st. Camberwell
Ruegg Henry, furniture broker, Deptford bridge
Ruel Hugh Wm. gold & silver refiner, 175 High Holborn
Ruff Edward & Co. map mounters, &c. 2 Hind ct.147Fleet st
Ruff Harvey, *Bell* P.H. 5 Bell yard, Gracechurch st
Ruff Robert, carpenter & builder, 37 King st. Golden square
Ruffell Daniel, beer retailer, 302 Albany road, Camberwell
Ruffell John C. butcher, 50 Hercules buildings, Lambeth
Ruffell John Johnson, writer & grainer, 24 Church st. Soho
Ruffell Joseph, wood turner, 5 Up. Clifton st. Finsbury
Ruffle Josiah, baker, 1 Thomas st. Back Church la.St.Geo.ea
Ruffle Elizabeth (Mrs.), hairworker, 53 Poland st
Ruffle George, fruit, spice & general agts. see Sandle&Ruffle
Ruffle Geo. bricklayer & plasterer, 21 Princes rd. Lambeth
Ruffle Elizabeth (Mrs.), baker, 121 Rosemary lane
Ruffle Rt.cabinet ma. & upholst.34Gt.Queen st.Linc.inn flds
Ruffy Jacob, merchant, 25 Crutched friars
Ruffy Wm.Daniel,undtkr.&c.sec.to the United Patriots Argus Burial Benefit Soc. 13Tottenham ct. New rd. St. Pancras
RuggJames&Son,buildrs.&shipjoiners,23Limekilnhill,Limho
Rugg John&Co. timber mrchts. Conant pl.Comml.rd.Limeho
Rugg Henry Hodson, surgeon, 15 Broadley ter.Blandford sq
Rugg James, tailor & trimming sell. 52½ Beech st. Barbican
Rugg John, builder, Conant pl. Commercial rd. Limehouse
Rugless Hen.bootmak.4Crombie's row,Commercial rd. east
Rugless Thos. watch & clock ma. 3 Cannon st.rd. St.Geo.east
Rule Edward & Alfred, ship & ins. broks. 102 Leadenhall st
Rule Benj. shell fishmonger, 38 Maiden lane, Covent garden
Rule George, baker, 20 Charles st. St. George's east
Rule George, linendraper, Deptford High st
Rule William, ornamental painter & grainer, 45 Chiswell st
Ruler's Office (William Hall, ruler),Narrow st.Ratclff. cross
Rumbal Daniel, dairyman, Morning lane, Hackney
Rumball Henry, grocer & cheesem. 3Spencer ter.Lr.rd.Islgtn
Rumball William Samuel, coachmaker, 37 Long acre
Rumbell & Owen, silk mercers, 78 Oxford st
Rumbelow Wm. surgeon, 8 Devonshire st. Queen sq. Blmsby
Rumble & Sadgrove, architects & surveyors, 61 Mark lane, & Reading, Berks
Rumble Henry, pastrycook, 196 Kingsland road
Rumble Richard, tailor, 7 Leathersellers' bldgs. London wall
Rumbol George, oven builder, 18 Vine st. Lambeth
RumboldCharlt.(Mrs.),chandlr's.shop,1 RoyalOakpl.Eatn.sq
Rumbold Thomas, wheelwright, Back road, St.George's east
Rumfitt John Wm. bookbinder, 33 Castle st. Leicester sq
Ruming David, *Duke's Head* P.H. 1 Queen st. Chelsea
Rumley John, engraver, 12 Brooke st. Holborn bars
Rumley Wm. beer retailer, 5½ St. John's lane, Clerkenwell
Rumley Wm. bricklayer, 105 Gt. Saffron hill, Hatton garden
Rummens Joseph, greengrocer, 71 Little Britain
Rummer Ebenezer, carpenter, 85 Britannia st. City road
Rummey George, cowkeeper, 8King's Head row,OldBromptn
Rumney Thomas, undertaker, 15 Trafalgar st. Walworth rd
Rumsey Arthur, wine merchant, 37 Old Bond st
Rumsey Charles, wholesale druggist, 18 Bread st. hill
Rumsey Francis, smith & farrier, Mare st. Hackney
RumseyH.A.*ThreeKingdoms tav.&choph.*P.H.Harp la.City
Rumsey John, horn, hair & bone mercht. Dean st. Shadwell
Rumsey John, *Ship & Rising Sun* P.H. 134 Shadwell High st
Rumsey John, tripe dresser, 83 Fore st. City; 115 Whitechapel road; 97 Shadwell, & 1 Tabernacle square
Rumsey Robert Crook, solicitor, 2 Arthur st. Gray's inn rd
Rumsey William, coffee rooms, 2 Smithfield bars
Rumsey William, general salesman, 25 Lambeth walk
Rumsey Wm. Sentance, who. chemist,&c. 3 Queen st. place
Runchman Matthew, corn dealer, 5 York pl. Kingsland road
Runchman Saml.John,corndealer,44 Paradise st.Rotherhith
Runciman Charles, artist, 18 Oxford terrace, Hyde park
Runciman Patrick, bootmaker, 4 Rupert st. Haymarket
Rundall Jas.east in.& new zealand agt. 17 Throgmorton st
Rundle Thos. china & glass wa. 13 Chalton st. Somers town
RundleWm.*MarquisofGranby*P.H.Orangest.Gravl.la.Boro
Runey Chas. beer retailr.13 Durham st.Harleyfd.rd.Kengtn
Runey Charles, beer retailer, 15 Durham st. Vauxhall
Runham Elizabeth (Mrs.), *Dog&Bell*P.H.Dock st.Deptford
Runnington John, grocer, 151 Bermondsey st
Runnington John, grocer, 67 Tooley st. Borough
Rusby Jas. liv. stables, French horn yd. 26 Crutchedfriars
Rusby William, *Ship tavern*, 15 Water lane, Tower st
Rusby William, stone merchant, see Brown, Rusby & Booth
Ruscoe Thomas, law stationer, 8 Quality court,Chancery la
Rush Francis, beer retailer, 14 Mount row, Liverpool road
Rush George, tailor, 6 Bridge st. Westminster
Rush John Roger, solicitor, 18 Austin friars
Rush Joseph John, tailor, 8 Providence pl. Kentish town
Rush Wm. insp. of gasworks,61 Grosvenor ter. Horsefrry.rd
Rush William, wine merchant, 43 Mark lane
Rushall George, basket maker, 45 Webber row, Blackfriars
Rushall James, *Rose & Crown*P.H.38Brunswick st.Blkfrs.rd
Rushbrook Charles, tailor, 79 Leather lane
Rushbrook George, hairdresser, 15 Paradise st. Marylebone
Rushbrook George, tailor & draper, 19 High st. Marylebone
Rushbrook James, tailor, 75 Little Britain
Rushbrook John, tailor, 8 Exmouth st. Clerkenwell
Rushbrook Robert,hairdresser,14 NewNorth st.Red Lion sq
Rushbury Henry Duncalfe, solicitor, 3 Mitre ct.Ely pl.Hlbn
Rushforth Richard, surgeon, 40 Howland st. Fitzroy sq
Rushton George,who.grocer & teadlr.34 St.John st.Clrknwll
Rushton Henry, hairdresser, 1 Princes st. Little Queen st
Rushton James,furniture bro.13 Northampton pl.OldKentrd
Rushton Levy, tailor, 3 Upper Yardley st. Clerkenwell
Rushton William, tailor,35 Fair st. Horselydown
Rushworth Geo.A.&Chas. H. attorneys,10 Staple inn,Holbrn
Rushworth & Jarvis, land surveyors & auctioneers, Saville row, Piccadilly, & 19 Change alley, Cornhill
Rushworth James,cowkeeper, 20 Up. Charlton st.Fitzroy sq
Rushworth William, butcher, 144 Brick lane, Spitalfields
Rushworth William,cabinet maker, 130 Waterloo rd
Rusk John James, boot & shoe maker, 53 High Holborn
Rusk Wm. Rushton,clothier, &c.1 Lit.Chapel st.Westminst
Ruskin, Telford & Co. merchants, 7 Billiter st
Russ Isaac, tailor, 31 Gerrard st. Soho
Russ James, plumber & glazier, 36 Princes's st.Portmn mkt
Russ Thomas, cheesemonger, 1 Etham pl. Kent st. Borough
Russ Walter John, dyer & scourer, 104 Goswell st
Russell & Gottlieb, dressmakers, 117 Jermyn st
Russell Jas. & Sons, patent iron, locomotive, marine & gas tube manufrs. 81 Upper Ground st. Blackfriars
Russell John & Robt. leather dressers, 8 Gt. Winchester st
Russell Joseph & Co. mnchstr.warehsmn.&agts.33O.Change
Russell Joseph & Co.wine mers.1&2 WhiteHartct.Lombrd.st
Russell & Mackenzie, solicitors, 82 Borough High st
Russell Matilda&Mary A.straw hat makers,20East rd.Cityrd
Russell & Peckover, tailors, 6 Maddox st. Regent st
Russell Thos. & Co. carriers, Blossoms inn, Lawrence la.City
Russell Thos. & Co. grocers & teadlrs. 72 Borough High st
Russell Thos.&Co. hop & seed factors, 262 Borough High st
Russell Wm. & James, *Red Lion* P.H. 339 Strand
Russell Instit. (E. W. Brayley, F.S.A. sec.), 55 Gt.Coram st
Russell Alexander, ivory cutter, 2 Newman st. Oxford st
Russell Alexander Dakers, baker, 14 Gt. Tower st. City
Russell Archibald C. pawnbroker, 172 Bermondsey st
Russell Charles,bricklayer,32South cres.mews, Marchmnt.st
Russell Charles, fishmonger, 38 Gresham st. City
Russell Charles, florist, &c. Bridge road, Battersea

Russell Charles, *Sharp's Private hotel*, 30 Albemarle st
Russell Chas. Jas. Wm. surveyor, Stratford broadway
Russell Edward, butcher, 148 Lambeth walk
Russell Edward, *Dolphin* P.H. 15 Hyde st. Bloomsbury
Russell Edwd. easy chair & sofa manufacturer, 9 Old st. rd
Russell Elizh. (Mrs.), lodging house, 28 Arundel st. Strand
Russell Elizh. (Mrs.), news agent, 32 Wigmore st
Russell Elizh. (Mrs.), tobacconist, 2 Windmill st. Lambeth
Russell Emma (Miss), milliner, 93 Park st. Grosvenor sq
Russell Francis, barrister, 2 Figtree court, Temple
Russell Fdk. leather seller, 11 Lit. Chapel st. Westminster
Russell Geo. boot & shoe maker, 52 Fenchurch st
Russell Geo. bricklayer & plasterer, 6 Bride lane, Fleet st
Russell Geo. cabinetmaker & upholsterer, 14 Goswell road
Russell Geo. furnishing undertaker, 100 Queen st. Chelsea
Russell Geo. hop & seed factor, 227 Borough High st
Russell Geo. pianoforte maker, 18 Bath place, New road
Russell Geo. rope & twine ma. 47 Gt. St. Andrew st. 7 Dials
Russell Geo. tobacconist, 6 Arcade, Hungerford market
Russell Geo. Lake, barrister, 21 Old sq. Lincoln's inn
Russell Harriet (Mrs.), dressmaker, 15 Holywell st. Milbnk
Russell Henry, cabinet maker, 120 Curtain rd. Shoreditch
Russell Henry, hosier, 77 Lambeth walk
Russell Henry, plumber, &c. 2 Shepherd st. May fair
Russell Henshaw S. solicitor, 1 & 3 Mitre ct. chambs. Temple
Russell Hugh, linen & cotton factor, 5 Sise lane, City
Russell Israel, curiosity dealer, 31 King st. Covent garden
Russell Jacob, pawnbroker, 43 Fore st. Cripplegate; & 10 Shoreditch; & 14 & 15 Frederick's place, Old Kent road
Russell James, baker, 4 Broad st. Lambeth
Russell James, butcher, 29 Jewin st. Cripplegate
Russell James, cork cutter, 7 Lit. May's bldgs. St. Martin's l
Russell James, queen's counsel, 6 Old sq. Lincoln's inn
Russell Jas. stationer, &c. 79 & 80 Aldersgate st
Russell Jas. surgeon, 24 Goulden terrace, Barnsbury road
Russell Jas. Thos. solicitor, 37 Percy st. Tottenham ct. rd
Russell John, hairdresser, 13 Gt. Bell alley, Coleman st
Russell John, grocer, 1 York terr. Camberwell New road
Russell John, newsvender, 43 Store st. Bedford sq
Russell John, Archibald, barrister, 1 Child's pl. Temple bar
Russell John Edw. watchmaker, 4 Bedford st. Cvnt. gardn
Russell John Henry Cromwell, solicitor, 8 Gray's inn sq. & 20 Wharton st
Russell Joseph, beer retailer, George st. Camberwell
Russell Mary (Mrs.), court milliner & dressmaker to her Majesty, 41 Pall mall
Russell Mary (Mrs.), grocer, Gt. Green st. Kentish town
Russell Matilda (Miss), straw hat ma. 20 East road, City rd
Russell Matt. Hen. plumber & glazier, 135 Union st. Boro'
Russell Nancy (Miss), staymaker, 8 Aldgate High st
Russell Richard, butcher, 81 Castle st. Leicester sq
Russell Richard, haberdasher & hosier, &c. 135 Oxford st
Russell Richard, scotch warehousem. see Jones, Russell & Co
Russell Richard Thos. surgeon, 12 Thornton st. Horsleydn
Russell Richard Tyler, general salesman, 176 Tooley st
Russell Robert, butcher, 82 Cowcross st. Smithfield
Russell Samuel, engraver, 15 Chester terrace, Borough rd
Russell Simon, linendraper, 8 Grove terrace, Bayswater
Russell Stephen John, printer, 3 Lovell's ct. Paternoster row
Russell Thos. cooper & backmaker, 90 West Smithfield
Russell Thomas, law stationer, 8 Serle's pl. Linc. inn fields
Russell Thos. watch, jewel & miniature case, leather pen & pencil case manufacturer, 50 Gt. Sutton st. Clerkenwell
Russell Thomas Innocent, corn dealer, 38 & 39 King st. Boro'
Russell Thomas James, dining rooms, 175 Tooley st
Russell Timothy, organ builder, 2 Gray's inn terrace
Russell Wm. blacking manufr. see Warren, Russell & Wright
Russell Wm. butcher, 11 Church st. Kensington
Russell Wm. butcher, 177 Upper Whitecross st. St. Luke's
Russell Wm. butcher, 8 Windmill row, Kennington green
Russell Wm. cabinetmaker & builder, 14 James st. Oxford st
Russell Wm. coffee rooms, 18 Cheltenham pl. Westminster rd
Russell Wm. fish salesman, 10 Darkhouse lane, Billingsgate
Russell Wm. grocer, 40 William st. Regent's park
Russell Wm. pro. of mathema. & lang. 180 Prospect pl. Edgw. rd
Russell Wm. zinc broker, Grove st. Deptford
Russell Wm. Farrer, cattle salesman, see Langford & Russell
Russell Wm. Moyart, collector of city dues, 8 Coal Exchange
Russia Company (Thos. Cope, sec.), 25 Birchin lane
Russian & Canadian Fur Company, 214 Regent st
Rust Elizabeth (Mrs.), milliner, 16 Golden square
Rust Jeremiah, watchmaker, 1 Ladbroke grove, Notting hill
Rust Thomas, oilman, 10 Crown st. Walworth road
Ruston Thomas & Son, corn & seed factors, 25 Mark lane
Ruston Wm. City corn office, Catherine court, Tower hill
Rutherford, Drury & Co. wine merchants, 20 Billiter st
Rutherford Grace & J. (Misses), dressmakers, 40 Pall mall
Rutherford, Grant & Co. madeira merchants, 20 Billiter st
Rutherford George, solicitor, 13 Lombard st
Rutherford Geo. B. law stationer, see Jones & Rutherford
Rutherford Geo. Shaw, physician, 23 Devonshire st. Portland pl
Rutherford James, baker, 23 Barbican
Rutherford James, tailor, 7 Great Marlborough st
Rutherford Samuel, surgeon, 132 St. George st
Rutherford Thomas, brassfounder, 23 Hart st. Covent gardn
Rutherford Thomas, oilman, &c. 27 Gt. James st. Lisson grove
Rutland & Ball, wine & brandy merchts. 5 Water la. Tower st
Rutland Charles, coachmaker, Ham yard, Gt. Windmill st
Rutland Geo. Norris, hosier & glover, 229 Tottenham ct. rd
Rutland James, baker, 20 Old Burlington st
Rutland James William, hosier & glover, 145 Oxford st
Rutland Joshua, linendraper, 255 Poplar High st
Rutland Samuel Philip, oil & colorman, 74 Hackney road
Rutland Thos. leather cutter, 1 South Island pl. Clapham rd
Rutland Thos. leather seller, 2 Lit. Mount st. Walworth rd
Rutland Wm. saddler, &c. 199 Sloane st. Knightsbridge
Rutlidge Arnold, tobacconist, 2 Duncan pl. Hackney fields
Rutley T. B. & Co. railway carriers, George yd. Aldermanby
Rutley James Francis, seedsman, see Batt & Rutley
Rutley Mary (Mrs.), linendraper, Bromley, Middlesex
Rutley Mary (Mrs.), picture dlr. 5 Gt. Newport st. Long acre
Rutley Samuel, builder & undertaker, Bromley, Middlesex
Rutlidge Edward, linendraper, 10 Colvill ter. King's rd. Chls
Rutson Edward, solicitor, 6 Webb's County ter. New Kent rd
Rutt Charles, coffee rooms, 19 Charles st. Westminster
Rutt Samuel, timber merchant, 1 Bear lane, Blackfriars rd
Rutter John & Wm. umbrella makers, &c. 122 Cheapside
Rutter & Trotter, solicitors, 4 Ely place
Rutter Ann (Mrs.), bookseller & stationer, 6 Kingsland road
Rutter John, *Ship Defiance* P.H. Grove st. Deptford
Rutter John, stationer & bookseller, 17 William st. Regt.'s pk
Rutter Richard, ironmonger, 32 Rodney st. Pentonville
Rutter Samuel, *Prince of Wales* P.H. 64 Blackman st. Boro'
Rutter Spencer, lithographer, 5 Adam's ct. Old Broad st
Rutter Valentine, meat salesman, 27 Newgate market
Rutter Wm. furn. ironmonger, 22 Radcliffe ter. Goswell rd
Rutter Wm. gunmaker, 48 Aldenham st. Somers town
Rutter Wm. jeweller, 3 Nassau st. Soho
Rutter Wm. saw maker, 37 Cannon st. rd. St. George's east
Rutter Wm. surgeon, 1 Albert st. Mornington crescent
Rutterford John, pianoforte maker, 4 Brewer st. Pimlico
Ruttledge James, physician, 15 Hanover st. Hanover sq
Rutty John, linendraper, see Dudley & Rutty
Rutty John, timber, brick & coal merchant, & bent timber manuf. 108 Edgware rd. & 2 South side, Paddington basin
Rutty Samuel, pavior, Elder st. Norton Folgate
Ryall Hen. T. historical & gen. engraver, 1 Robert st. Adelphi
Ryall Nathaniel, *King's Head* P.H. 44 Eastcheap
Ryalls Sa. (Mrs.), hardw. dlr. 45 & 46 Fleet la. Farringdn. st
Ryan & Dale, merchants & insur. broks. 65 Old Broad st. City
Ryan Charles, wireworker, 4 Garden row, Camberwell road
Ryan Cornelius Jas. *Duchess of Cornwall* P.H. 75 Cornwll. rd
Ryan James, fruiterer, Battersea square
Ryan James, physician, 28 Somerset st. Portman square
Ryan James Joseph, carver & gilder, 13 & 14 Long acre
Ryan John, coffee rooms, 6 Temple st. Whitefriars
Ryan John, dyer, calenderer, &c. 28 North Audley st
Ryan John, surgeon, 14 Liverpool st. Bishopsgate
Ryan John, undertaker, 22 Wood st. Spitalfields
Ryan Martin, undertaker, 7½ Douglas st. Vincent square
Ryan Michael, carpenter & joiner, 13 Hollen st. Soho
Ryan Phillip, straw bonnet maker, 16 Swan st. Minories
Ryan William, surgeon, 15 Shaftesbury terrace, Pimlico
Ryde, Curteis & Whitworth, who. grocers, 83 Up. Thames st
Ryder Martha & Sons, tobacco & snuff manufs. 28 Chiswell st
Ryder Thos. & Co. east india merchs. & com. agts. 7 Jeffery sq
Ryder John, carpenter, 18 Ernest st. Regent's park
Ryder John, chemist, 6 Hereford ter. King's rd. Chelsea
Ryder Joseph, tobacco manufacturer, 86 High Holborn
Ryder Richard, tobacco pipe ma. 1 Upper Fore st. Lambeth
Ryder Samuel, wheelwright, 3 Swan st. Gt. Dover road
Rydon Thomas, carpenter, &c. 18 Wynyatt st. Goswell st
Rye & Thomas, mine, share, & gen. agent, 80 Old Broad st
Rye Edward, solicitor, 16 Golden square
Ryland Archer, barrister, 36 Carey st. Lincoln's inn
Rayland John Collet, moreton ho. academy, Kentish town rd
Ryland William, corn factor, 19 Jewry st. Crutchedfriars
Ryland William, tallow chandler, 2 Gray's inn lane
Ryle Ann (Mrs.) & Co. printers, 2 & 3 Monmouth ct. 7 dials
Ryle Ann (Mrs.), printer, see Paul & Ryle
Ryle John Atkinson, law stationer, 24 Castle st. Holborn
Ryley Edward Charles, barrister, 3 Inner Temple lane

Ryley Edward, secretary of *Australasian, Colonial & Genl. Life Assurance & Annuity Com.* 126 Bishopsgate within
Ryley Robert Ralph, barrister, 3 Inner Temple lane
Ryley Rowland, fishmonger, 3 Orange st. Bloomsbury square
Ryman Charles, greengrocer, 174 Waterloo road
Rymer Alfred, currier & grindery dealer, 10 Nassau st. Soho
Rymer Charles (late Dudgeon), corn dealer & importer of scotch oatmeal gritts, 18 Bedford st. Strand
Rymer Duncan, printseller, 19 Princes st. Wardour st. Soho
Rymer George, tallow chandler, 21 Batty st. Commercial rd
Rymer John, tailor, 27 Shoemaker row, Blackfriars
Rymer John Snaith, solicitor, see Murray, Rymer & Murray
Rymer Leonard, saddler & harness makr. 6 Bruton st. Bond st
Rymer Wm. Hen. solicitor, 59 Chancery lane
Rymill Robert, grocer & teadealer, 6 Brompton row
Ryton Wm. fancy brushmaker, 25 Ossulston st. Somers town

SAALFELD A. I. & Co. stuff mer. (Jsph. A. Chase, agt.), 89 Watling st
Sabberton James, tailor, 38 Golden square
Sabel & Co. merchants, 25 Broad st. buildings, City
Sabey Joseph, china dealer, 22 Brunswick parade, Pentonvl
Sabin Edward Lamb, barrister, 4 South square, Gray's inn
Sabine Wm. & Son, architect & surv. Winchesterho. O. Broadst
Sabine Edward, perfume warehouse, 1 Pilgrim st. Ludgatehill
Sabine Edward, stationer, Denmark hill, Camberwell
Sabine Henry Robert, playing & message card, & drawing board maker, 1 Lovell's court, Paternoster row
Saby Simon, coffee rooms, 1 North st. Ropemaker's st
Sachs Christian, hat wareho. 20 Princes st. Leicester sq
Sachs Thos. working jeweller, 1A, St. George's ter. Hyde pk
Sack, Bremer & Co. shipagts. & ins. brokers, 19 London st. City
Sack Charles, butcher, 3 South pl. Tibberton sq. Islington
Sack Frederick William, merchant, 19 London st. City
Sack William, butcher, 155 Upper Whitecross st
Sacker John, tailor, 7 Epping place, Mile end road
Sacker Joseph, *Black Horse & Windmill* P.H. 5 Fieldgate st
Sacker Wm. Hen. tin & zinc manuf. 29 Hayfield pl. Mile end
Sackett & Ruscoe, law stationers, 8 Quality ct. Chancery la
Sacred Harmonic Society (Thos. Brewer, secretary), Exeter Hall, 372 Strand
Sadd & Napier, shoemercers & leathersellers, 40 Lisle st. & 9 Leicester place, Leicester square
Sadd James, *Marshal Keate* P.H. Preston rd. Poplar
Sadd John, paper stainer, 4 Trinity st. Blackman st. Boro'
Sadd Joseph, diamond worker, 29 Wilmington square
Sadd Robert, bricklayer, &c. 18 South Lambeth
Saddington Samuel & Co. shoe thread manufacturers, & wholesale grindery warehouse, 129 St. John st. Smithfield, & Grove Flax mills, Southwark
Saddington Samuel & William D. brush, searse, & sieve makers, turners, &c. 63 Wood st. Cheapside
Saddler John, coffee rooms, Camberwell green
Saddler Stephen, cheesemonger, 1 Frederick st. Regent's pk
Saddler's Hall (Giles Clarke, clerk), 143 Cheapside
Sadgrove William & Alfred, upholsterers & cabinet makers, 18, 20 & 21 Eldon st. Finsbury circus
Sadgrove Fredk. surv. & agt. Cowley cottages, Wandsworth rd
Sadgrove Thomas, architect & surv. see Rumble & Sadgrove
Sadgrove William Harry, solicitor, 52 Mark lane
Saddler, Fenton & Co. irish linen bleachers & warehousemen, Edward Prior, agent, 6 Watling st. & at Belfast
Saddler, Firth & Ross, oil, mustard & saw mills, 87 Great Guildford st. Borough, & Crown wharf, 57 Bankside
Sadler, Harrison & Co. merchants, 17 Austinfriars
Sadler Samuel & Co. linen factors, 11 Ironmonger lane
Sadler Charles, tobacconist, 11 Bath st. City road
Sadler Edward, solicitor, 3 Lincoln's inn fields
Sadler Elizabeth (Mrs.), cowkeeper, 17 David st. Marylebo
Sadler Francis, furn. undertaker, 1 Fore st. Cripplegate
Sadler Francis A. insurance brkr. Lloyd's, Royal exchange
Sadler Geo. cheesemong. & dairy. 2 Denbigh st. Belgrave rd
Sadler George, ham dealer, 16 London house yard, St. Paul's
Sadler George, tailor, 20 Hanover st. Hanover square
Sadler Hannah (Miss), bookselr. 81 Church st. Shoreditch
Sadler Henry, baker, Grundy st. East India road
Sadler Henry, livery stables, 137½ New Bond st
Sadler James, tallowchandler, 35 Vere st. Clare market
Sadler John, lamp black mft. Jamaica level, Bermondsey
Sadler Joseph, butcher, 9 Green st. Bethnal green
Sadler Robert R. solicitor, see Richardson, Smith & Sadler
Sadler Samuel, boot & shoe maker, 39 Stafford pl. Pimlico
Sadler Simeon, chaser, 6½ Wood st. north, King sq. Goswell st
Sadler Solomon, school, 8A, Church st. Edgware road
Sadler Thos. chemist, see Bennett & Sadler
Sadler Thos. chemist & druggist, see French & Sadler
Sadler Thos. meat salesman, 12 Newgate market
Sadler Thos. pork dealer, 82 Fore st. Cripplegate
Sadler Thos. *Waterman's Arms* P.H. 21 Old Castle st. Bethnl. gr
Sadler Wm. *Duke Wellington* P.H. 16 South st. Kingsrd Chels
Sadler Wm. Flint & Co. insu. agents, 7 Pope's head alley, Cornhl
Sadler Wm. F. millwright, engineer, &c. 96 Tooley st
Saenz José Maria, merchant, see Montoya, Saenz & Co
Saenz José Maria, New Granadian & Mexican consulate, 3 Winchester buildings, Gt Winchester st
Saers John Wm. *Albion* coffe rooms, 7 Foregate, Clement's inn
Saffell Hen. W. auctioneer & accountant, 5 Eastcheap, City
Saffell John Richard, proprietor of Dr. Sibly's medicines, 34 Newington crescent, Kennington road
Saffery Mary A. (Mrs.), furniture brok. High st. Stoke Nwngtn
Sage Courtney, plumber, 186 Wellington ter. Waterloo rd
Sage David, beer retailer, 10 Copenhagen st. Barnsbury rd
Sage Elizh. W. (Mrs.), lighterman, 66 Mark lane
Sage Elizh. Winter (Mrs.), milliner, 6 Finsbury place south
Sage James, bookseller, 4 Newman's row, Lincoln's inn flds
Sage Jeremiah, haberdasher, 66 Up. Whitecross st. St. Luke's
Sage John, fruiterer, 3 Portman market
Sage William, tailor, 2 Devonshire bldgs. Gt. Dover road
Sage Wm. Carrington, butcher, 3 Charles st. Comm. rd. east
Saggers Geo. birch & alder dealer, 16 Great Dover st
Saggers Joseph, grocer, 77 Brook st. Ratcliff
Saggers Thomas, chandler's shop, 22 Whitmore road, Hoxton
Sahler Jacob, baker, 5 Little St. Andrew st. Seven dials
Saich Matthew, carpenter & bldr. 25 Up. Berkeley st. west, & Albion mews east, Albion st. Hyde park
Sailmakers' Almshouses, Mile end road
Sailors' Female Orphans' Home (Rev. Charles Hyatt, hon. sec.), 66 Great Prescot st. Goodman's fields
Sailors' Home, or Brunswick Maritime Establishment (Capt. Geo. Pierce, R.N. sec.), 23 Well st. London docks
Sailors' Home Institution (William Medland, superintendent), East India road, Poplar
Sailors' Magazine Office, 12 Wellington st. south, Strand
Sainsbury Joseph, cabinet ma. & upholstr. 167 Tottenham ct. rd
Sainsbury Mary (Mrs.), china & glass wa. 30 High st. Maryleb
Sainsbury Rd. watchma. 9 Wingrove pl. St. John st. Clrknwl
Sainsbury Samuel, chemist & soda water manufr. 177 Strand
Sainsbury Wm. Henry, hotpresseser, 2 Apollo ct. Templebar
St. Andrew's Wharf, S. Reynolds & Co. 316 Wapping High st
St. Ann's Society Schools, offices, 2 Charlotte row, Mansion house; schools, 4 St. Ann's lane, G.P.O.; & Brixton hill
St. Bartholomew's Hospital, between 41 & 54 West Smithfield
St Clement Danes Savings' Bank (William Mason, secretary), Vestry hall, 264 Strand
St Columbus College Ireland Office (Rev. Nugent Wade, hon. sec.), 79 Pall mall; college, Stackallan, co. of Meath
St. George's Chess Club (Geo. Walker, sec.), 5 Cavendish sq
St. George's Hanover sq. Visiting Association (Rev. Allen Cooper, & Thomson Hankey, jun. secs.), 18 Grosvenor mews, Grosvenor st
St. George's Hospital, Hyde park corner
St. George's & St. James's Dispensary, 60 King st. Golden sq
St. Ives Junction Rlwy. (J. MacDonnell, sec.), 35 Broadst. bdgs
St. James's Chronicle newspaper Office, 38 New Bridge st
St. James's Club House (Wm. Simmonds, sec.), 50 St. James's st
St. James's Paving Office (Jehoshaphat York, clerk), 16 Marshall st. Golden square
St. James's Picture Gallery, Josh. Taylor, prop. 58 Pall mall
St. James's Wine Establishment (Crockford & Co.), 10 St. James's st
St John del Rey Mining Co. (G. D. Keogh, sec.), 8 Tokenho. yd.
St. Katharine Dock Company (Sir John Hall, K.C.H. sec.), Tower hill; Docks, near the Tower, east india department, Cutler st. Houndsditch
St. Katharine Dock Company's Steam Packet Wharf (J. Clippingdale, superintendent), St. Katharine's
St. Lawrence & Atlantic Railroad Co. 4 Barge yard, City
St. Leonard Shoreditch Savings' Bank Parochial School (Robt. Davies, treas., Wm. Smith Forsaith, act.), 2 Kingsland road
St. Luke's Hospital for Lunatics, Old st. City road
St. Mark's College, near Holleywood, Little Chelsea
St. Martin's Public Subscription Library (Edwin Chas. Prince, sec. & librarian), 42 Castle st. Leicester square
St. Marylebone General Dispensary, 77 Welbeck st
St. Marylebone Savings' Bank (Douglass Finney, manager), 76 Welbeck st
St. Pancras (South Western District) Paving Office, 30 Howland st
St. Patrick's Catholic Schools, Hampstead heath, & 8 Tudor place, Tottenham court road

St. Paul's Covent Garden Savings' Bank (W. Cribb, sec.), 15 Gt. Russell st
St. Petersburgh Steam Ship Co. (Anthony George Robinson, agent), 11 George yard, Lombard st
St. Thomas's Hospital, St. Thomas's st. Borough
St. André Durant, consul general for France, 3 Copthall buildings, & 44 Montagu square
St. Aubyn James Pearse, architect, 5 Furnival's inn
St. Barbe John, custom house agt. 15 Philpot la. & Lloyd's
St. Bauzel Henry, prof. of music & french, 56 High Holborn
St. John Rd. building material dlr. 10 Belton st. Long acre
St. John Robt. *Perseverance* P.H. 20 William st. Hampstd. rd
St. Julien Chas. Baker, carver, &c. 6 Windmill st. Tot. ct. rd
St. Lawrence & Co. imperial peg boot manufrs. 44 Regent st
St. Ledger Wm. stationer, 42 King's rd. east, Chelsea
St. Leon Eliza (Miss), milliner, 15 Church st. Camberwell
St. Losky Jacob, cigar manufr. 9 Bishopsgate without
St. Paul Sir Horace, mrcht. coal owner, Wenlock basin, City rd
Saker George & William, bricklayers, 15 Russell st. Bermondsey, & 6 Upper Fort place, Grange road
Saker Ann (Mrs.), grocer, 4 Fair st. Horselydown
Saker George, jun. bricklayer, 13 Prospect row, Bermsy. rd
Saker Saml. *Queen's Head* P.H. 41 Acton st. Gray's inn rd
Saker Thomas, bricklayer, 2 Barnham st. Tooley st
Saker Wm. tobacconist, 2 Thomas st. Whitechapel rd
Salaman Isaac, ostrich feather manfr. 69 Lamb's Conduit st
Salaman Simeon K. tailor & habit maker, 19 Charing cross
Sale Jas. & Robt. bakers, 13 Union terrace, Notting hill
Sale Ann (Mrs.), haberdasher, 8 Cumberland row, Walwth. rd
Sale Charles Frederick, currier, Gun alley, 85 Bermondsey st
Sale David, grocer, 10 Drake st. Red Lion square
Sale John, carpenter, 9 Lock's square, York st. Walworth rd
Sale Jn. Bernard, organist to the Queen, 25 Holywell st. Mllbnk
Sale Thos. bootma. 1 St. George's st. Albany rd. Old Kent rd
Salembier Henry & Co. merchants, 28 Mincing lane
Sales, Pollard & Co. snuff & tobacco manufs. 57 Redcross st
Salignac George (of Cognac), 48 Mark lane
Salisbury & Baleman, printers, 2 Red Lion ct. White Hart st
Salisbury Frederick, printer, &c. 109 Chalton st. Somers twn
Salisbury George, tailor, 1 Queen st. Lower rd. Islington
Salisbury George, *Webb's hotel*, 220 Piccadilly
Salisbury Henry John, *Hope* P.H. 2 Wilmot st. Russell sq
Salisbury Isaac, fruiterer, 3 Ellis st. Sloane st
Salisbury John, tailor, 7 Manchester bldgs. Holloway rd
Salisbury John Crew, surgeon, 25 City terrace, City road
Salisbury Thomas, carver & gilder, 2 Brokers' alley, Drury la
Salisbury William, lookg. glass frame ma. 84 Kingsland rd
Salkeld John & Thos. woollen & manch. wa. 23 Aldermanbury
Salkeld John, engineer, see Miller, Ravenhill & Co
Sallnow George, hatter, 33 Limekiln hill, Limehouse
Salmon Brothers, cork merchts. & cutters, 86 Piccadilly
Salmon John & Co. teadealers, 69 Tottenham court road & 8 Stucley terrace, Camden town, & 57 High st. Portland twn
Salmon, Ody & Co. patent truss manufacturers, 292 Strand
Salmon & Goatley, teadealers, 91 Edgware rd. Marylebone
Salmon Wm. & Jas. & Co. upholsterers, 42 Gt. James st. Bedford r
Salmon Alfred, watch & clock maker, 24 Queen st. Pimlico
Salmon Amos, brushmaker, 1 Paddington green
Salmon Chas. clothes salesman, 11 Stepney rents, Hackny. rd
Salmon Daniel, tailor, 49 Bridgehouse place, Borough
Salmon Edward, barrister, 4 King's Bench walk, Temple
Salmon Edwin, provision dealer, 5 Lower East Smithfield
Salmon Francis, baker, 345 Rotherhithe
Salmon Frederick, surgeon, 12 Old Broad st. City
Salmon George, baker, 10 Compton st. Brunswick sq
Salmon George, carpenter, 52 Praed st. Paddington
Salmon Harriet (Miss), stay warehouse, 82 Lisson grove north
Salmon Horatio John, commission agent, 3 Webb st. Bermdsey
Salmon John, carpenter, 32 North st. Lisson grove
Salmon John, foreign & english fruiterer, 86 Piccadilly
Salmon John, fruit importer, 86 Piccadilly
Salmon John, *King John's Head* P.H. 8 Albemarle st
Salmon Joseph, baker, 126 St. George st
Salmon Joseph, baker, 5 Upper Seymour st. Euston sq
Salmon Moses, orange merchant, 66 Blackman st. Borough
Salmon Nathaniel, ticket writer, 8 Red Lion ct. Fleet st
Salmon Richard Wm. dairyman, 18 Hampton st. Walworth rd
Salmon Robert, *King's Arms* P.H. Little Chelsea
Salmon Salmon, watchmaker, 3 Gt. Turnstile, Holborn
Salmon Sarah (Mrs.), midwife, 4 Southampton st. Camberwell
Salmon Sophia (Miss), milliner, 3 Argyll st. Regent st
Salmon Thos. boot & shoe maker, 12 Bridgewater st. Somerstn
Salmon Thomas, coffee rooms, 44 St. George st
Salmon Thomas Deere, barrister, 123 Chancery lane
Salmon Wm. cheesemonger, 3 Essex pl. Mare st. Hackney
Salmon Wm. fruiterer, 1 Grange road, Bermondsey
Salmon Wm. grocer, 110 Brandon st. Lock's fields, Wlwth
Salmon Wm. linendraper, 22 Red Lion st. Holborn
Salmon Wm. tailor, 62 Theobald's road, Red Lion square
Salmon Wm. J. optcn. & telescope mkr. 254 Whitechapel rd
Salomon & Long, solicitors, 7 Windmill st. Tottenham ct. rd
Salomon Moses, snuff manufacturer, &c. 67 Haymarket
Salomons (Barrent) & Sons, fancy wareh. 42 Old Change
Salomons David & Joseph, merchants, 1 Shorter's court
Solomonson Simon Geo. solicitor, 12 Clement's lane, City
Salsbury Edmund, tailor, 71 Holborn hill
Salsbury Maria (Mrs.), carriage lamp maker, 133 Long acre
Salt Offices (Worcester & Cheshire), 1 Leadenhall st
Salt Thos. & Co. pale india ale stores, 98 Leadenhall st
Salt Henry, engraver, 9 Great Turnstile, Holborn
Salt Isaac, cutler, &c. 45 Edgware road
Salt Isaac, *Snow Shoes* P.H. 21 Royal Hospital rw. Chelsea
Salt John, physician, 53 Hamilton terrace, St. John's wood
Salt Joseph, builder, 1 Montague place, Millwall, Poplar
Salt Mary (Mrs.), grocer, 16 Foley st. Foley place
Salt Robert, bookseller & statnr. 43 Cleveland st. Fitzroy sq
Salt Thos. Clutton, lamp manufacturer, 75 Hatton garden
Salt Wm. cutler, 118 Piccadilly
Salter Ephraim & Co. carriers, 190 Bishopsgate without
Salter John & Co. who. & ret. hatters, 101 Blackman st. Boro'
Salter, Unwin & Co. hatters, 130 Whitechapel High st
Salters' Hall (Edward Thompson, clerk), St. Swithin's la
Salter Ann (Mrs.), marine store dlr. 28 Lambeth Up. marsh
Salter Charles, tailor, 25 Upper King st. Bloomsbury
Salter George, livery stables, Hobart place, Eaton square
Salter Henry, auctioneer & estate agt. 29 Gracechurch st
Salter Henry, bootmaker, 29 Charing cross
Salter Henry, boot & shoe maker, 29 Charing cross
Salter Isaac, grocer, 53 St. Clement's lane, Strand
Salter Jas. box & packg. case mk. 35 Nw. Nichol's st. Bthnl. gn
Salter John, boot & shoe maker, 56 Tower st. Westminster rd
Salter John, horsehair manufr. 12 Union st. Kingsland road
Salter John, silk manufacturer, 22 Steward st. Spitalfields
Salter John, tailor, 74 Chalton st. Somers town
Salter John, *White Lion* P.H. 153 Old Gravel la. Wapping
Salter Mary (Mrs.), artist, 47 Charing cross
Salter Richd. F. surgeon, 8 Park pl. villas, Paddington
Salter Robert, china wareho. 42 William st. Regent's park
Salter Robert, ship & insurance broker, 75 Old Broad st. City
Salter Thos. corn & flour fact. 42 Horselydn. la. & Nw. Corn ex
Salter Thomas, porkman, 139 Salisbury court, Fleet st
Salter Thomas, *Russell coff. ho. & tav.* 17 Piazza, Cov. gdn. & *Old Red Lion* P.H. Piazza, & 12 Gt. Russell st. Cov. gdn
Salter Thos. Fredk. hatter, 10 Bshpgt. witht. & 24 Aldgate
Salter William, academy, 56 Chalton st. Somers town
Salter William, artist, 51 Pall mall
Salter William, bookseller & stationer, 17 New st. Dorset sq
Salter William, boot & shoe maker, 47 London wall
Salter William, coal dealer, 1 Eaton lane north, Pimlico
Salteri Jas. & Co. brit. & foreign looking glass wa. 374 Strand
Saltmarsh Robert, *Crown & Thistle* P.H. 11 Billiter st
Saltmarsh Sam. watch case mak. 74 Myddelton st. Spafields
Saltmarsh Thos. Wm. lodging house, 57 Dorset st. Salisby. sq
Saltmer Fred. G. bootmaker, 22 Cleveland st. Fitzroy square
Saltwell William, solicitor, see Fuller & Saltwell
Salvador House, 200 Bishopsgate without
Salvi Giovanni Battista, wine mer. 10 Duke st. Portland pl
Salvin Anthony, architect, &c. 21B, Saville row, Piccadilly
Salway Joseph Eisdell, surveyor, 117 Sloane st
Sambourne & Bell, warehousemen, see M'Dougal & Co
Sambre & Meuse Rail. (Sydney Cumberland, sec.) 61 Moorgt. st
Sambrook Rd. Thos. *Bricklayers' Arms* P.H. corner Old Kent rd
Sambrook Thos. G. coal mercht. Arundel wf. Water st. Strand
Samler Henry, attorney, 6 Little Friday st
Samler Wellington, solicitor, 3 Raymond buildings, Gray's inn
Sammell John, wholesale boot, shoe & leather warehouse, 13 Ironmonger lane, Cheapside
Sammes Wm. carp. & undert. 35 Lambeth sq. Lower marsh
Sammons Thomas, oil & colorman, 5 Green st. Bethnal green
Samms James, *King & Queen* P.H. 11 High st. Kensington
Sampson, Batard & Co. merchts. 9 Copthall ct. Throgm. st
Sampson & Hooper, ship & insurance broker, 2 Dunster ct
Sampson George, *Globe* coffee ho. 71 Compton st. Clerkenwell
Sampson George, surgeon, 12 Chester st. Grosvenor place
Sampson Henry, coffee rooms, 35 Bow st. Covent garden
Sampson Isaac, tailor, 206 Brick lane, Spitalfields
Sampson John, baker, 61 Tooley st
Sampson John, printer, &c. 4 York place, Hackney road
Sampson John, undertaker, 1 Earl st. London rd. Borough
Sampson Joseph, jun. baker, 6 Neptune st. Rotherhithe
Sampson Levi, manchester warehouse, 40 Friday st. City
Sampson Mary (Mrs.), dressmaker, 20 Brighton st. Cromer st

Sampson Peter, coffee rooms, Wharf rise, Kingsland road
Sampson Peter Smith, grocer, 51 & 52 Hoxton Old town
Sampson Peter Smyth, grocer, 40 Star st. Edgeware road
Sampson Richard, *Jolly Waterman* P.H. 23 Rotherhithe st
Sampson Richard, tailor & draper, 325 Oxford st
Sampson Robert, tailor & draper, 2 Princes st. Leicester sq
Sampson Sampson, manchester warehsmn. 9 Union st. Boro'
Sampson Samuel, barrister, 10 King's Bench walk, Temple
Sampson Samuel, tea broker, 4 New London st. Crutchdfrs
Sampson Thomas, artist, 2 Percy st. Bedford square
Sampson Thos. shipbro. 21 Bedford sq. ea. & 2 Dunster ct. City
Sampson Thos. timber & deal yard, 14 Wade's pl. Hackney rd
Sampson Wm. inventor & manufacturer of the patent door mat, ropes, line twines, &c. near canal, Kingsland rd
Sams Geo. & Co. Hercules brewery, Mansfield pl. Kentish tn
Sams Chas. coalmerchant, Wiltonwhf. Grosvnr. basin, Pimlico
Sams Henry, fancy cabinet mk. 4 Hanover pl. Regent'spk. rd
Sams James, dairy & butterman, 34 Chapel st. Grosvenor sq
Sams James, *Greyhound* P.H. 28 Brooke st. Holborn
Sams John, bedstead & bed pillar manufacturer, 5 Chapel st. Holywell mount
Smas John, italian warehouseman, see Sherborn & Sams
Sams John, *Sun* P.H. 50 Lamb's Conduit st
Sams Joseph, antiquarian, 56 Gt. Queen st. Lincoln's inn flds
Sams Samuel, *Roebuck* P.H. 16 Cannon st. rd. St. George's ea
Sams William, furniture broker, 44 Carlisle st. Lambeth
Sams Wm. Brown, tailor & woollendraper, 24 Barbican
Sams Wm. R. agent to Guardian fire & life ass. 1 St. James's st
Sams Wm. Raymond, bookslr. to her Majesty, 1 St. James's st
Sampson Antonio Benj. & Aug. jewellers, 11 Denmarkst. Soho
Samson Blum, toy & french fancy dealer, wholesale & retail, 3 & 4 & 20, 21 & 24 Lowther arcade, Strand
Samson John, fancy cabinet manufr. 21 South row, New rd
Samson Lazarus, who. jewlr. & hardwrmn. 56 Houndsditch
Samson Lazarus Heiman, gen. outfitter, 100 Up. ea. Smithfld
Samson Louis, stockbroker, 11 Warnford ct. Throgmortn. st
Samson RobertWm. coal mercht. Essex wf. Essex st. Strand
Samson Simeon, tailor, see Phillips & Samson
Samson Theresa (Mrs.), milliner, 4 Duke st. Grovenor sq
Samter Jsph. com. agt. & musical inst. imp. 1 George st. Min
Samuda Abraham, colonial broker, 1 Bury st. St. Mary Axe, & 2 South st. Finsbury
Samuda Brothers, engineers, & patentees of the atmospheric railway, Orchard pl. Blackwl. office, 10 London st. Fen. st
Samuda David, merchant, 1 Bury st. St. Mary Axe, & 2 River terrace, North Islington
Samuda Jonathan, merchant, 11 Angel ct. Throgmorton st
Samuel Abraham & Son, watchma. 13 Lit. Alie st. Goodman's fl
Samuel Brothers, tailors & outfitters, 29 Ludgate hill
Samuel & Phillips, merchants, 1 Austinfriars
Samuel Bunford, merchant, 11 Poultry
Samuel Daniel, baker, 6 & 32 Middlesex st. Aldgate High st
Samuel Henry, surgeon, 39 Mansell st. Goodman's fields
Samuel Isaac, artificial florist, 20 Sekforde st. Clerkenwell
Samuel James, beer retailer, 85 London road, Southwark
Samuel James, bootmaker, 12 East road, City road
Samuel James, bootmaker, 1 Ireland row, Mile end
Samuel John, circ. library, 41 Gt. Randolph st. Camden tn
Samuel Joseph C. linendraper, 2 New Bridge st. Vauxhall
Samuel Lewin, glasscutter, 9 Church lane, Whitechapel
Samuel Lyon, goldsmith & jeweller, 13 Bury st. St. MaryAxe
Samuel Mendal, slopseller, 95 St. George st
Samuel Michael, tailor, 40 King William st. City
Samuel Moses, clothier, 33 Strutton ground, Westminster
Samuel Moses, linendraper, 31 Mansell st. Goodman's fields
Samuel Ralph, watch & clock ma. 55 Compton st. Clerknwl
Samuel Sampson, solicitor, 11 North bldgs. Finsbury circus
Samuel Samuel, cane dealer, 4 Sun st. Bishopsgate
Samuel Samuel, merchant, 11 Poultry
Samuel Samuel, watchmaker, 162 Brick lane, Spitalfields
Samuel Simon, clothes salesman, 48 Marylebone la. Oxford st
Samuel Simon, east india & africa merchant, 6 Adam's ct
Samuel S. M. merchant, 23 Finch lane, Cornhill
Samuell Robert, ham & tongue wa. 61 Up. Nth. pl. Gry's innrd
Samuell Thomas, ham & beef warehouse, 66, & diningrooms, 66 Castle st. Leicester square, & 19 Leigh st. Burton cres
Samuels Emanl. I. & Co. lapidars. & optcns. 73 Gt. Prescot st
Samuels George, paperhanging mfr. 2 Conant pl. Coml. rd
Samuels Marcus. curiositydl . 13 Up. East Smithfiel
Samuels Henry & Co. watch ma. & slopsllr. 135 Sahdl. High st
Samuels Isaac, clothes dlr. 3 Prospect row, Walworth rd
Samuels Samuel, fancy cabinet ma. 1 Hosier la. WestSmthfld
Samways Joseph, *Cooper's Arms* P.H. 13 Silver st. Wood st
Samwell Edwin, linendraper, 10 Haberdasher's walk, Hoxtn
Samwell Francis, surgeon, 52 Margaret st. Cavendish sq
Sancton Philip, merchant, see Todhunter & Sancton
Sandall Richd. F. furn. undertaker, 50 Mount st. Berkeley sq
Sandaver John, cabinet maker, 12 Kenton st. Brunswick sq
Sandbrook Michael, cheesemonger, 62 St. Mary Axe
Sandeford John, butcher, 4 Sidney pl. King's rd. Chelsea
Sandeford John, tailor, 20 Robert st. King's road, Chelsea
Sandell & Smith, booksellers, 12 Peerless place, City road
Sandell David, wholesale stationer, 14 Sherborne lane
Sandell George, *Phœnix* P.H. 11 & 12 Harrow st. Liston grove
Sandell George, *Phœnix* P.H. 12 Union st. Lisson grove
Sandell Joseph, mahogany merchant, 148 Waterloo road
Sandell Wm. coal & potato dealer, 91 Church st. Shoreditch
Sandell Wm. confectioner, 58 Wimpole st
SandemanAlex. & Co. accountants & agts. 30 King st. Cheapside
Sandeman, Forster & Co. merchants, 20 St. Swithin's lane
Sandeman Geo. & Co. general ironmongers, 2 York st. Boro'
Sandeman & Knight, cattle salesmen, 59 West Smithfield
Sandeman Alexander M. accountant, 30 King st. Cheapside
Sandeman Hugh Fraser, stockbroker, 27 Tokenhouse yard
Sandeman Jas. engin. & millwright, 9 Princes sq. St. Geo.'s ea
Sander James & Geo. chinamen, 319 & 320 High Holborn
Sander John & Co. linendrapers, 127 St. George st
Sander & Palmer, linendrapers, 215 & 216 Shadwell High st
Sander Joseph, hosier, &c. 5 Little Pulteney st. Golden sq
Sander Joseph, milliner, 40 Burlington arcade
Sanders & Farmer, milliners & straw hat mak. 117 Piccadily
Sanders & M'Crindle, ladies' school, Eden place, O. Kent rd
Sanders Joseph & Co. appraisers, 41 Allen st. Goswell st
Sanders Benjamin, pork butcher, 156 Poplar High st
Sanders Charles, refiner & sweepwasher, 3 St. John's sq. Clkwl
Sanders Charles, coal agent, 16 Wharf, Paddington basin
Sanders Charles, sugar manufactory, Stratford
Sanders David, *Raven* P.H. Battersea square, Surrey
Sanders Edward, coffeehouse, 13 Marshall st. Golden square
Sanders Edward, locksmith & bellhanger, 63 Lambeth walk
Sanders Edward Albert, attorney, 66 Basinghall st
Sanders Elizh. (Mrs.) diningrooms, 3 Bolingbrok. rw. Wlwth. rd
Sanders Frederic, coal merchant, 1A, Upper Albany st
Sanders Frederic, equitable funeral co. western branch, for furnishing funerals at stated charges, 1 Upper Albany st
Sanders Geo. artist, 25 Allsop ter. New road, Marylebone
Sanders George, painter & glazier, 35 Cleveland st. Fitzroy sq
Sanders Geo. Williams, barrister, Rolls yard, Chancery la
Sanders HannahE. (Mrs.), law sta. 1 Lit. Charlotte st. Blkfrs
Sanders Harriot (Mrs.), grocer, 13 New King st. Deptford
Sanders Henry, painter & glazier, 14 London st. Fitzroy sq
Sanders Henry Alexander, wholesale & export envelope manufacturer, 7 Red Lion court, Fleet st
Sanders Hugh, bootmaker, 1 Wimpole st. & 11 Edwards' st. Portman square
Sanders James, butcher, 102 Long lane, Bermondsey
Sanders James, fruiterer, 6 Crutchedfriars
Sanders JamesChristopher, sign painter, 233 Bethnal grn. rd
Sanders James Hodges, grocer, 5 Maida hill east
Sanders John, baker, 13 Cooper's row, Crutchedfriars
Sanders John, coachmaker, 91 York st. Westminster
Sanders John, grocer, 38 Wells st. Oxford st
Sanders John, needle & hook & eye mak. 4 & 5 Addle st. City
Sanders John, tailor, 9 Conduit court, Long acre
Sanders John, jun. shoemaker, Morning lane, Hackney
Sanders John, sen. shoemaker, Morning lane, Hackney
Sanders John Jas. statuary & mason, 6 Keppel row, New rd
Sanders John Thos. solicitor, 11 Gray's inn square
Sanders Joseph, bookbinder, see Smith & Sanders
Sanders Joseph, city dining rooms, 209 Upper Thames st
Sanders Jsph. silk mercer & drapr. 101 Gt. Russell st. Blmsby
Sanders Jsph. John, china dlr. 11 Paradise row, Rotherhithe
Sanders Nathnl. clothes salesman, 2 & 53 Holywell st. Strand
Sanders Richard, carpen. & builder, 12 Leigh st. Burton cresc
Sanders Richard, confectioner, 6 Field's pl. Lock's fields
Sanders Richard, *Ship* P.H. 29 Skinner st. Bishopsgate
Sanders Robert Bradfield, solicitor, see Cook & Sanders
Sanders Samuel, toyman, 33 Queen st. Bryanstone square
Sanders Thomas, barrister, 10 Crown Office row, Temple, & 37 Guildford st. Russell square
Sanders Thomas, carpenter, 56 Gt. Portland st. Oxford st
Sanders Thomas, grocer, 3 Cowcross st. Smithfield
Sanders Thomas, hatter, 84 High Holborn
Sanders Thomas, law stationer, 48 Carey st. Lincoln's Inn
Sanders Thomas, *Pilgrim* P.H. 35 Queen's row, Walworth
Sanders Thomas, *Rose* P.H. 88 Wimpole st. Cavendish sq
Sanders Thomas, solicitor, see Makinson & Sanders
Sanders William, china wareho. 38 Freeschool st. Horselydown
Sanders William, corn & coal dlr. 2 Frederick pl. Hampstead rd
Sanders William, crown coffee rooms, 91 Harrow road
Sanders William, merchant, 19 Mincing lane
Sanders William, sheep salesman, 59 West Smithfield

Sanders William, tinplate worker, 192 Brick la. Spitalfields
Sanders William John, *White Horse* P.H. 1 Union st. Boro'
Sanders William Oats, baker, 49 Lant st. Borough
Sanderson Chas. Jas. & Co. cigar manufctrs.11 Basinghall st
Sanderson, Frys, Fox & Co. merchants, 14 St. Helen's place
Sanderson & Murray, bottld. beer mers.Steel yd.Up.Thams.st
Sanderson & Poole, merchts.& ins. broks.1Crownct.Philpot la
Sanderson & Reid, silk manufacturers, 41 Gresham st
Sanderson Richd. & Co. disct. broks. 83 King William st.City
Sanderson Chas. stockbroker,3White Lion ct.Throgmorton st
Sanderson Edwin, cigar manufr. 56 St. John st. Smithfield
Sanderson Emily (Miss), milliner, see Bloxam & Sanderson
Sanderson Francis, oilman, 17 Seymour st. Euston sq
Sanderson George, baker, 7 Lit. Knightrider st. Doc. com
Sanderson John, coal dealer, 6 Archer st. Gt. Windmill st
Sanderson John, oil & colorman, 65 Poplar High st
Sanderson John, umbrella & fishg. tack. mfr. 26 Blackfrs. rd
Sanderson John Rd. tin plate worker, 12 Sun st. Bishopsgate
Sanderson Joseph, butcher, 99 Wardour st. Soho
Sanderson Joseph, tailor, 19 New Bond st
Sanderson Margt. (Mrs.), stationer, 3 Richmond pl. Wlwth.rd
Sanderson Mary Ann (Mrs.), dentist, 9 Howland st. Fitzroy sq
Sanderson Morgan, stationer, East street, Walworth
Sanderson Richd. smelling bottle ma. 9 Brooke st. Holborn
Sanderson Robert, tailor, 15 Lower Eaton st. Pimlico
Sanderson Stephen, ironmonger, 86 Chalton st. Somers town
Sanderson Theop. *Southampton tav.* 21 Southampton bldgs
Sanderson Thos. bookseller, 1 Crooked la. King William st
Sanderson Thomas, shoemaker, 62 Paul st. Finsbury
Sanderson Wm. *Blue Anchor* P.H. 9 Clare st. Clare market
Sanderson Wm. cheesemonger, 82 Hackney road
Sanderson Wm. tobacconist, 9 Newgate st.&52½ High Holborn
Sanderson Wm. S. plumber, 49 Broad st. Lambeth
Sanderson Wm. Walton, baker, 7 Gt. Russell st. Covent gar
Sandford Henry & Co. grocers, 16 Providence pl. Kentish tn
Sandford Edwd. barrister, Law chambers, 77 Chancery la
Sandford Geo. Webb, chemist, see Blake, Sandford & Blake
Sandford Isaac, bootmaker, 1 Flagon row, Deptford
Sandford James, music seller, 10 Wentworth pl. Mile end rd
Sandford Richd. chemist, 17 White horse la. Stepney
Sandham Elijah, grocer, &c. 3 Steven's pl. New North rd
Sandham Hannah (Mrs.), grocer & tea dlr. 249 Bermondsey st
Sandieson Wm. cap maker, 23 London road, Southwark
Sandifer Rt. tallowchandler, 13 Artillery pass. Bishopsgate
Sandilands John, jeweller, 31 Sudely st. City rd
Sandilands John, tailor, 12 Conduit st. Regent st
Sandison Geo. *Crown & Sceptre* P.H. 9 Cumberld.st e. Regt pk
Sandison Jas. carpenter & underta. 3 Bedford st. Covent gar
Sandison Wm. ironmoger, 36 Southampton st. Strand, & 6 & 7 Maiden lane, Covent garden
Sandland & Crane, hosiers & shirt makers, & inventers & makers of the belt band drawers, 55 Quadrant, Regent st
Sandland Wm. general agent, 82 Hatton garden
Sandle & Roffle, fruit, spice, & gen. agents, 29 Pudding la
Sandoe Anthony, fancy cabinet & white wood ornament ma. ornamental stationer & varnisher, 24 King st. Holborn
Sandom Jane (Miss), confectioner, 116 Gt. Suffolk st. Boro'
Sandom Wm.S. solicitor, 57 Gracechurch st.& Deptford High st
Sandon Fredk. surgeon dentist, 14 Orchard st. Portman sq
Sandon Nathaniel, coffee rooms, 19 Gt. Russell st. Cov. gdn
Sandon Sarah (Mrs.), grocer, 9 Gt. Warner st. Clerkenwell
Sands Chas. *Prince Regent* P.H. 37 Felix ter. Liverpool rd
Sands Christopher, straw hat ma. 10 Church st. Spitalfields
Sands James, tailor, &c. 3 Radcliffe terrace, Goswell rd
Sands Mary (Mrs.), ladies' school. 7 Shepprtn. st. New Nth.rd
Sands Mary (Mrs.), midwife, 47 King st. Borough
Sands Robt. engrav.& mapcolorer, 9 Southampton tr. Pentnvl
Sands Samuel, tailor & draper, 8 David st. Marylebone
Sands Thomas, rule maker, 164 Church st. Shoreditch
Sands Wm. chandler's shop, 1 Cambridge road, Mile end
Sands Wm. picture frame ma. 24 Gt. Arthur st. Goswell st
Sands Wm. tailor & habit ma. 6 Little Argyle st. Regent st
Sandwell James, tobacconist, George st. Camberwell
Sandwell Richard, *Windmill* P.H. 44 High st. Lambeth
Sandwell William, baker, 5 Paradise st. Rotherhithe
Sandwich William & Co. perfumers, 19 Church st. Soho
Sandy James, *Green Dragon* P.H. 38 King st. Golden sq
Sandy Samuel, fret cutter, 8 Up. Smith st. Northampton sq
Sandys, Carne & Vivian, engineers, &c. 4 New Broad st. City
Sandys & Pearson, solicitors, 5 Serjeants' inn, Fleet st
Sandys Richard Hill, barrister, 89 Chancery lane
Sandys Samuel, surgeon, 4 Francis terrace, Kentish town
Saner & Powell, surgeons, 36 Finsbury sq. & 36 Wilson st
Sanford Feake, solicitor, 20 John st. Adelphi
Sanford Henry, wholesale ironmonger, 180 Bishpsgt. without
Sanford John, who. & ret. stationer, see Bowen & Sanford
Sanford Wm. book edge, &c. marbler, 40 Maiden la. Cov.gdn
Sanford Wm. silk & velvet mfr. see Robinson, Sanford & Co
Sang William, man's mercer, see Kennerley & Sang
Sanger Charles, brush manufacturer, 123 Lambeth walk
Sanger Daniel, linendraper, Camberwell green
Sanger John, patent medicine warehouse, 150 Oxford st
Sanger John, tobacconist, 238 Shadwell High st
Sanger Nathaniel, oilman, 2 Mount st. Lambeth
Sanger William, attorney, 4 Essex court, Temple, & 23 Seymour place north, Euston square
Sangiovanni Benedetto, artist, 23 Nassau st. Middlsx. Hosp
Sangster John & Co. granary keepers, 90 Shad Thames
Sangster William & John, whip, cane & umbrella makers, 10 Royal Exchange, 94 Fleet st. & 140 Regent st
Sangster Frederick, seed merchant, 252 Whitechapel road
Sangster John, commission agent, 14 Philpot lane
Sangster John, seedsman, see Hay, Anderson & Sangster
Sangster Martin, solicitor, 31 St. Swithin's lane, City
Sanguine John, carpenter, 13 Market st. St John's st. rd
Sanguinetti Francisco Bernardo, tailor, 53 New Bond st
Sangwin William, carpenter, 21 Mary st. New road
Sangwine Thomas, fur manufactr. 5 Richmond bldgs. Soho
Sankey & Cundy, civil engineers, 12 John st. Adelphi
Sans Benjamin, furniture broker, 31 Long alley, Finsbury
Sansbury Thomas, academy, 9 Rose st. Soho
Sansbury Maria (Miss), ladies' school, 10 Stk. Newington gn
Sansom Geo. mason & buildr. 12 Alfred st. Vauxhall brdg. road
Sansom John, hosier & stocking manf. 21 Brick la. Spitalfilds
Sansom Micah Hy. grocer, &c. 5 Brunswick parade, Pentvl
Sansom Thos. sheffield pla. wa. see Waterhouse, Hatfield & Co
Sansum Charles, tobacconist, 60 Gt. Guildford st. Boro'
Sansum Frederick, dyer & scourer, 21 Threadneedle st
Sansum James (Mrs.), ladies' school, Lr. Kennington lane
Sant James, artist, 19 Soho square
Santer Jane & H. straw hat ma. 31 Devonsh. bldgs. Gt. Dvr. st
Santer Charles, cattle salesman, 59 West Smithfield
Santy Ann (Mrs.), milliner, 131 Fleet st
Saphin Peter, watch & clock ma. 43 Whitcomb st. Pall mall
Sapsford Benjamin, Camberwell dairy, 3 Grove, Camberwell
Sapsford Frederick, grocer, 39 Queen Ann st. Cavendish sq
Sapsford Keats Silvester, baker, 20 Queen Ann st. Cav. sq
Sapsworth Saml. oil & colorman, 33 White Lion st. Pentonvl
Sapte, Banbury, Muspratt & Co. bankers, 77 Lombard st
Sapwell Benjamin, grocer, &c. 86 Dean st. Soho
Sapwell John, plumber, 9 Shepherd st. Mayfair
Sapwell Thomas, confectioner, 90 Gracechurch st
Saraiva Francisco, wine mercht. 13 Marylebone la. Oxford st
Sarbourg Leonhard, gold laceman, embroiderer & importer of foreign wires, tinsel, laces, &c. 10 Adelaide st. Strand
Sard John, sec. *Houseless Poor Com. Soc.* 75 Old Broad st. City
Sard Samuel, who. teadealer, 34 George st. Blackfrs. road
Sard Sarah (Mrs.), rope, line & twine spin. 2 Church st. Hrslydn
Sarel John, baker, 7 Exeter st. Sloane st
Sarfas Henry & Thos. mast & blockmakers, 72 Wapping wall
Sargant Brothers, manufs. of muskets, fowling pieces, pistols, swords, matchets, bayonets & gun barrels (manufactories, 74 Edmund st. & Charlotte st. Birmingham), 2 Coleman st. buildings
Sargant, Gordon & Co. produce brokers, 38 Mincing lane
Sargeant & Lazarus, coal merch. New crane wrf. Wappingwall
Sargeant Durham, tailor, 142 Shadwell High st
Sargeant George, cheesemonger, 84 High st. Marylebone
Sargeant Isaiah, tinplate worker, 49 Tothill st. Westminster
Sargeant John, cooper, 52 & 109 Snow's fields, Bermondsey
Sargeant Joseph, milliner & laceman, 62 Poplar High st
Sargeant Richard, solicitor, 10 Norfolk st. Strand
Sargeant Wm. beer retailer, 76 Devonshire st. Kennington
Sargenson William S. wine merchant, 5 Pall mall
Sargent & Lazarus, coal mers. 43 Mansell st. Goodman's flds
Sargent Allen, optician, 17 Ryder's court, Leicester square
Sargent George Fredk. artist, 5 Bouverie st. Fleet st
Sargent Henry, dairyman, 11 Leigh st. Red Lion square
Sargent James, hairdresser, 10 Church st. Stoke Newington
Sargood & Cocks, house decorators, paper hangers, glaziers & plumbers, 98 London wall
Sargood Jsph. carver & gilder, 21 Cumberland row, Walwth rd
Sarjeant William Thomas, merchant, 1 King st. Finsbury
Sarjent George Reid, artist, 3 Charlotte st. Fitzroy square
Sarjent John, *King's & Key* P.H. 142 Fleet st
Sarjent John, muffin & crumpet baker, 1 York st. Westminster
Sarl John & Sons, gold & silversmiths, watchmakers & jewellers, 18 Cornhill & 18 Poultry
Sarrell E. (Miss), ladies' schl. 58 Westbourne grv. Bayswtr
Sarson Ann (Miss), coffee rooms, 5 St. Martin's ct. Ludgate hl
Sarson James Thos. ink, mustard & vinegar ma. City road
Sarson Michael, *Windsor Castle* P.H. 33 Park ter. Rgt's. pk

Sartain Edward, tailor, 7 West st. Golden square
Sarvent Geo. brokr. & cabinet ma. 100 Devonshire st. Lisn. gr
Sarvis John, pianoforte tuner, 28 Upper Ebury st. Pimlico
Sass Henry, artist, 25 Henrietta st. Brunswick square
Sasse Charles Samuel, baker, 26 High st. Portland town
Sasse Frederick, baker, 43 Princes st. Leicester square
Sasse George Henry, baker, 33 High st. Kensington
Sasse John, baker, 18 Ryder's court, Leicester square
Sasse Wm. Edwd. baker, 22 Weymouth st. Portland place
Satchell, Timothy & Co. hat manufacturers, 158 Fenchurch st. & 12 Rood lane
Satchell John, solicitor, see Stevens & Satchell
Satchill Richard, dairyman, 6 Winsley st. Oxford st
Satirist Newspaper Office, 334 Strand
Satow David & Co. merchants, 3 Love lane, Eastcheap
Satterley Thomas, tailor, 7 Weston st. Bermondsey
Satterthwaite Clement, stock & share bro. 38 Throgmorton st
Satterwaite Jas. cowkeeper, 20 Cumberland st. Middx. hosp
Sauerbrey Chas. Rt. ship & insur. broker, 106 Fenchurch st
Saul Elzh. & Richard, meat salesmen, 8 New Newgate market
Saul Saul & Son, carcase butchers, 57 Aldgate High st
Saul Abraham, carcase butcher, 56 Aldgate High st
Saul David, *Shipwright's Arms* P.H. Emmett st. Limehouse
Saul Edward, carcase butcher, 59 Aldgate High st
Saul Henry, butcher, Ferry road west, Poplar
Saul James, butcher, 73 Three Colt st. Limehouse
Saul John, fruiterer, 15 Union st. Middlesex hospital
Saul John, smith, 21 Hertford st. Fitzroy square
Saul Moses, appraiser & ho. agt. 63 Albany rd. Camberwell
Saul William, butcher, 59 Aldgate High st
Saul William, ironmonger, 61 Crawford st
Saull Wm. D. & Co. wine & brandy merchts. 15 Aldersgate st
Saull William, cooper, 14½ Tottenham court New road
Saundby Robert, hat trimming seller, 20 Castle st. Borough
Saundby Thomas, clothier, 10 Albion place, Battle bridge
Saunder William, carpenter, 10 Eaton lane north, Pimlico
Saunder Wm. Deacle, surgeon dentist, 33 Baker st. Portm. sq
Saunderian Institution (Robert Farre Dalrymple, sec.), Blomfield st. London wall
Saunders & Carr, milliners, 34 Maddox st. Regent st
Saunders & Evans, silk mercers, 6 Ludgate st
Saunders Geo. & Co. gasfitters, 2 Drummond st. Euston sq. & 17 Moreton terrace, Kentish town
Saunders & Harrisons, merchants & seed crushers, Brooks wharf, Upper Thames st
Saunders & Holmes, engravers & printers, 18 Long acre
Saunders John & Edward, who. stationers, 60 Queen st. City
Saunders Joshua & Wm. insurance brokrs. 13 Copthall court
Saunders Mary & M. A. statnrs. 63 St. Thomas's pl. Gt. Dover st
Saunders & Otley, publishers, 50 Conduit st. Regent st
Saunder Wm. & Thos. burton & pale ale stores, Hung. whrf
Saunders Alexander, paper hanging manufacturer & decorator to her Majesty; upholsterer, cabinet maker, gilder, house agent, &c. 170 Regent st
Saunders Benj. tin plate worker, 10 John's row, St. Luke's
Saunders Benj. Wm. baker, 70 Gt. Suffolk st. Borough
Saunders Charles, barrister, 3 Hare court, Temple
Saunders Chas. Alex. sec. to Gt. West. railway, 29 Gresham st. & Paddington
Saunders Chas. Walter, grocer, 19 Shoemaker row, Blkfrs
Saunders Daniel, furn. brok. Camberwell grove, Camberwell
Saunders Daniel, watchmaker, 13 Park side, Knightsbridge, & 8 Gloucester ter. Vauxhall bridge road
Saunders David, pork butcher, 7 Queen st. Ratcliff
Saunders Edward, beer retailer, Battersea fields
Saunders Edwin, dentist, 16 Argyll st. Regent st
Saunders Eliza (Mrs.), bootma. 19 Gt. May's bldgs. St. Martin's la
Saunders Emanuel, grocer, 59 Dorset st. Fleet st
Saunders Evelyn John, *Fox* P.H. Denmark hill, Camberwell
Saunders Evelyn W. *Grove House tavern*, Camberwell grove
Saunders Francis, baker & corndealer, High st. Vauxhall
Saunders Francis, cowkeeper, 63 Market st. Edgware road, & 55 Queen st. Edgware road
Saunders George, bottle merchant, wine cooper, soda & mineral water & ginger beer ma. Clarendon grove, Somers tn. & 7 Moreton terrace, Kentish town
Saunders Geo. dairyman, 1 Wyndham rd. Cambrwll. New rd
Saunders George, grocer, 39 Marchmont st. Brunswick sq
Saunders George, grocer, 77 Paradise row, Chelsea
Saunders George, grocer, Wharf road, King's cross
Saunders Henry, ale & porter brewer, 84 Paul st. Finsbury
Saunders Henry, carpenter, 23 & 24 Goswell st
Saunders Henry, tailor, 11 Gt. Ryder st. St. James's
Saunders Henry A. linendraper, &c. 5 King's rd. Ea. Chelsea
Saunders Isaac, *Old George* P.H. 5 Strong's pl. Fulham rd
Saunders Jacob, porkman, 366 Rotherhithe st
Saunders James, bacon drier, Valentine pl. Blackfriars road
Saunders James, baker, 18 Bell st. Edgware road
Saunders James, beer retailer, 6 Pleasant pl. King's cross
Saunders James, bootmaker, 2 Hart st. Crutched friars
Saunders James, coffee rooms, 17 Circus st. New road
Saunders James, horsedealer, Sweet Apple ct. Bishopsgate
Saunders James, tin pl. worker, 4 Clare hall pl. Stepney grn
Saunders James Ebenezer, fish factor, 7 Lower Thames st
Saunders John, cheesemonger, 35 King's road east, Chelsea
Saunders John, cheesemonger, 6 Up. Park pl. Regent's pk
Saunders John, coffee rooms, Battersea
Saunders John, dining rooms, 123 Bethnal green road
Saunders John, dining rooms, 35 Church st. Shoreditch
Saunders John, hairdresser, 20 Gt. James st. Lisson gr. north
Saunders John, hatter, 10 Union st. Borough road
Saunders John, hoop bender, Narrow st. Ratcliff cross
Saunders John, *Lamb & Flag* P.H. 6 James st. Oxford st
Saunders John, picture importer & dealer, 114 Holborn hill
Saunders John, rag & bottle mer. 17 Old Gravel la. Wapping
Saunders John, ready made linen wa. 37 Mansion ho. st. Ken
Saunders John, timber merchant, 28 St. John's la. Clerknwll
Saunders John, *York hotel*, 40 Basing pl. Waterloo road
Saunders John Coleman, fishmonger, 258 Oxford st
Saunders John L. chandler's shop, George st. Camberwell
Saunders Joseph, boarding house, 79 Little Britain
Saunders Jos. *Green Man & French Horn* P.H. 54 St. Martin's la
Saunders Joseph, hat manufacturer, 59 Whitechapel road
Saunders Joseph, horn presser & horn hoof & bone mercht. 117 Bermondsey st. & 47 Britannia st. Bagnigge wells rd
Saunders Joseph, oil & colorman, 3 Shadwell High st
Saunders Josiah, ironmonger, 2 St. Agnes ter. Tabernacle sq
Saunders Martha (Mrs.), marine store dlr. 18 Fair st. Hrslydn
Saunders Richard, carver & gilder, 31 Foley st. Portland pl
Saunders Richard, lapland rug ma. 39 Long la. Bermondsey
Saunders Richd. plumber & painter, 28 Gt. Guildford st. Boro'
Saunders Richard, woollen draper, 56 Leadenhall st
Saunders Robert Wm. furniture broker, 151 Whitechapel rd
Saunders Samson, picture frame ma. 27 Penton st. Walwrth. rd
Saunders Samuel, barrister, 3 Middle Temple lane
Saunders Samuel, linen draper, 1 Bermondsey New road
Saunders Samuel, tailor, 5 Edward st. Blackfriars road
Saunders Stephen, grocer, 21 Bryanstone st. Bryanstone sq
Saunders Susan (Mrs.), boarding house, 6 Golden square
Saunders Thos. carpenter, 13 Gt. Queen st. Lincoln's inn fields
Saunders Thos. carpenter & undertk. 1 Printing ho. la. Blkfrs
Saunders Thos. carver & gilder, 10 David st. York pl. Marylbn
Saunders Thos. carver & gilder, 31 Newman st. Oxford st
Saunders Thos. who. confectioner, 43 St. John st. Clerkenwell
Saunders Thos. *White Horse* P.H. King's Head yd. Linc. inn fi
Saunders Thos. Bush, barrister, 19 Lincoln's inn fields
Saunders Thos. H. bank note paper maker, 8 Cloak la. City
Saunders Thos. J. surgeon, 31 Maddox st. Regent st
Saunders Thos. William, barrister, 1 Cloisters, Temple
Saunders Trelawney Wm. map selr. & publishr. 6 Charing cross
Saunders Wm. baker, 10 Chester st. Kennington cross
Saunders Wm. boot & shoe ma. 13 Prospect pl. Old Brompton
Saunders Wm. butcher, 43 Brick lane, Spitalfields
Saunders Wm. coffee rooms, 27 Bow lane, Cheapside
Saunders Wm. dairyman, 13 Queen st. King st. Seven dials
Saunders Wm. grocer, 26 Doyley st. Sloane square
Saunders Wm. hatter, 30 Shadwell High st
Saunders Wm. hosier, glover & outfitter, 164 Strand
Saunders Wm. music seller, 6 Wellington ter. Clapham rd
Saunders Wm. oilman, 8 Charlotte st. Whitechapel
Saunders Wm. turner & loom broker, 26 Sclater st. Bethnal gr
Saunders Wm. Hen. grocer, 5 Bennett st. Fitzroy square
Saunderson & Murray, bottled beer mers. Steelyd. Up. Thames st
Saunderson Chas. plumber & glazier, 26 Charles st. Westmr
Saunderson George, tobacconist, 13 Crown st. Walworth rd
Saunderson Henry, artificial florist, 28 Aldermanbury
Saunderson James, dining rooms, 16 Angel ct. Throgmorton st
Saunderson John, custom house agent, 6 Beer lane, Tower st
Saunderson John, hatter, 92 Bridge road, Lambeth
Saunderson John, tailor, Southampton st. Camberwell
Sauvarin Rd. Chas. hairdresser, 12 Abbey st. Bermondsey
Sauze James, stationer, &c. 47 Aldermanbury
Savage & Foden, architects & surveyors, 31 Essex st. Strand
Savage Alfred, steeled mill ma. & machinist, 43 Eastcheap
Savage Ann L. (Miss), livery stable keeper, 111 Fetter lane
Savage Astley, cheesemonger, 5 Queen's road, Dalston
Savage Benj. comb maker, 12 Haberdashers' pl. west, Hoxton
Savage Charles, dining rooms, 60 Snowhill
Savage Edgar, tinplate worker, 6 Hanover pl. Regent's pk. rd
Savage Eliza A. (Miss), milliner, &c. 3 Holles st. Cavendish sq
Savage Elizh. (Mrs.), cheesemongr. 50 Grosvenor rw. Pimlico
Savage George, tobacconist, 15 Beauchamp st. Holborn

Savage Henry, house agent, 6 Devonshire bldgs. Gt. Dover rd
Savage Henry, surgeon, 34 Dorset place, Dorset sq
Savage James, carpenter & undertaker, 7 Gray's inn terrace
Savage James, cheesemonger, 6 Emanuel pl. Camberwell rd
Savage James, cooper, 24 Hosier lane, West Smithfield
Savage James, dyer, 4 Dean st. Westminster
Savage John, baker, 14 Gt. Titchfield st. Oxford st
Savage John, bricklayer, 6 Newnham st. Edgware road
Savage John, *Grapes* P.H. 21 Old Compton st. Soho
Savage John, grocer, 5 Old Chapel row, Kentish town
Savage John, pawnbroker, 73 Whitechapel road
Savage John, *Rising Sun* P.H. 12 Somers pl. east, New rd
Savage John M. copperplate printer, 51 Foley st. Portland pl
Savage Joseph, carpenter, 13 Barnsbury row, Cloudesley sq
Savage Margaret (Mrs.), dressma. 15 Compton st. Brunsk. sq
Savage Mary (Mrs.), grocer, 107 Brandon st. Walworth
Savage Phœbe (Miss), dressmaker, 55 Mortimer st. Cav. sq
Savage Richd. human hair manufr. 21 Gt. Chapel st. Oxford st
Savage Robert, cornchandler, 39 Brick lane; & appraiser, furniture broker & undertaker, 14 Church ct. Spitalfields
Savage Robert, greengrocer & coaldlr. 20 Kinnerton st. Belg. sq
Savage Robt. tobaccont. 23 Glo'ster row, Grange rd. Brmdy
Savage Samuel, painter, 13 Middleton bldgs. Portland pl
Savage Thomas, carver & gilder, 15 Hereford pl. Comrl. rd. e
Savage Thomas, haberdasher, 213 Tottenham court road
Savage Thomas, law wig maker, 1 Cloisters, Temple
Savage Thomas, pawnbroker, 55 Paradise st. Lambeth
Savage Thomas (Mrs.), strawhat ma. 6 Up. Dorset pl. Clphm. rd
Savage Thomas, watchmaker, 21 Sidney st. Goswell road
Savage William, *King's Arms* P.H. Davis place, Chelsea
Savage William, solicitor, 12 Furnival's inn
Savage William, tinplate worker, 89 Chalton st. Somers town
Savell Thos. chandler's shop, 27 Woodland st. Dalston
Savell Thos. Hen. watch motion ma. 8 Peerless row, City rd
Savery Theophilus, chemist, 10 Moreton ter. Kentish town rd
Savery Thomas, butcher, 2 Wellington st. Newington causewy
Savidge John, blind maker, 6 Melville pl. Caledonian road
Savigny & Co. cutlers' & surgeons' instrument makers, 67 St. James's st. Pall mall
Savile Ann (Mrs.), tobacconist, 37 High Holborn
Savill Charles Lambert, tailor, 15 West st. Golden sq
Savill Thos. Choate, printer, 4 Chandos st. Covent garden
Saville John & Co. cheesemonger, 2 Broadway, Blackfriars
Saville John, coffee rooms, 17 High st. St. Giles's
Saville James, tobacconist, 4 Weston place, King's cross
Savin Charles (Mrs.), milliner & dressma. 33 South Audley st
Savings' Bank Circular, 1 Green Arbour court, Old Bailey
Savings' Bank Office, 5 Bolton st. Piccadilly; hours 10 to 4. (For list of Metropolitan Savings' Banks, see TRADES DIRECTORY)
Savory A. B. & Sons, watchmakers & jewellers, 9 Cornhill; manufacturing silversmiths & dealers in foreign coin & bullion, 14 Cornhill; manufactory, 5 Finsbury pl. south
Savory, Moore & Co. chemists to the Queen, 143 New Bond st. & 220 Regent st
Savory Sarah & Son, pewterers, &c. 4 Church st. Shoreditch
Savory Bellamy, stationer & dressing case mak. 46 Cornhill
Savory Hen. Bladon, *Three Crowns* P.H. 3 Dowgate hill, City
Savory John, baker, 63 Brewer st. Somers town
Savory John, plumber & glazier, 66 Parson's st. St. George st
Savory Thomas Cox, watch & clockmaker, 54 Cornhill; & silversmith, 47 Cornhill
Saw John, cheesemonger, 43 Bath st. City road
Saw William, bookbinder, 37 Vere st. Clare market
Saward John & Chas. linendraps. 5 & 6 Hereford pl. Com. rd. ea
Saward James Townsend, barrister, 4 Hare court, Temple
Saward John, linendraper & silk mer. 15 Newrd. St. Geo.'s east
Saward Michael, sec. to *Promoter Life Assurance & Annuity Company*, 9 Chatham place, Blackfriars
Sawer Thomas, surgeon, 1 Lyon terrace, Edgware road
Sawkins Edward, fruiterer, 71 St. George st
Sawkins Thomas, fancy brushmaker, 66 Hoxton Old town
Sawkins William, builder, 5 Queen st. King's road, Chelsea
Sawman John, bootmaker, 21 Webber st. Blackfriars road
Sawtell Francis, butcher, 43 New Church st. Lisson grove
Sawtell Richard, butcher, 2 North place, Balls pond road
Sawtell Walter, grocer & cheesemngr. 1 North pl. Balls pond rd
Sawyer & Brettell, solicitors, 2 Staple inn, Holborn
Sawyer Rich. & Son, engravers & printers, 38 Frith st. Soho
Sawyer Charles, livery stables, 7 Park st. Kennington cross
Sawyer Edmund, barrister, 2 Pump court, Temple
Sawyer Elisha, hairdresser, 1 Glo'ster st. Comrcl. road east
Sawyer George, surgeon, 73 Myddelton sq. Clerkenwell
Sawyer Henry, coal merchant, Union wharf, Kingsland basin, & 30 Kingsland road
Sawyer James, livery stables, 71 Curtain road, Shoreditch
Sawyer James, tailor, 5 North street, Sloane street
Sawyer John, plumber & glazier, 17A, King's row, Pimlico
Sawyer John James, surgeon, 101 Park st. Grosvenor sq
Sawyer John T. builder, 27A, George st. Portman sq
Sawyer Jonathan, coal mer. 2 St. Alban's ter. Vaux. bdg. rd
Sawyer Joseph, *Grapes tavern*, 13 Church row, Aldgate
Sawyer Mary (Mrs.), lodging house, 8 Surrey st. Strand
Sawyer Mary Jane (Mrs.), linendraper, 30 Goswell road
Sawyer Richard, copperplate printer, 17 Church st. Soho
Sawyer Robert, dealer in hardware, 75 Charlotte tr. New cut
Sawyer Thomas, news agent, 5 Pope's Head alley, Cornhill
Sawyer Thomas, tobacconist, 125 Long alley, Finsbury
Sawyer William, fruiterer, 8 Beckford row, Walworth road
Sawyer William, tin plate worker, 24 Market st. Borough rd
Sawyer William, jun. potato merchant, 74 London rd. Southwk
Sawyer Wm. Edwd. bookslr. & statnr. 4 Amelia pl. Walwth. rd
Saxby Thomas, undertaker, 22 New Ormond st
Saxby William, porcelain warehouse, see Rittener & Saxby
Saxe Charles & Co. tailors, 25 Conduit st. Bond st
Saxelby Sarah (Mrs.), milliner, 72 New Bond st
Saxon Consulate, 76 Cornhill
Saxton Edward, solicitor, 75 Cornhill
Saxton Joseph, tinplate worker, 15 Earl st. London road
Saxton Nathl. mahogany mer. Blkfrs. brdg. wf. Up. Ground st
Saxton (Misses), ladies' school, 4 Edward's pl. Hackney rd
Say Edmund, builder, New cross
Say Frederick Richard, artist, 18 Harley st
Say John, currier, 8 Laxon court, Long lane, Bermondsey
Sayce Joseph, tailor & habit maker, 53 Cornhill
Sayce Susan (Miss), dressmaker, 193 Piccadilly
Sayce William, wine cooper, 17 Northumberland st. Strand
Sayer Jas. & Son, plumbers, &c. 5 Beauvoir pl. Kingsland
Sayer Augustin, physician, 28 Up. Seymour st. Portman sq
Sayer Benjamin, *George* P.H. 29 Brewer st. Golden sq
Sayer Charles, bedstead maker, 18 Swan yard, Shoreditch
Sayer Edw. comssion. agt. 3 Gt. Knightrider st. Doctors' com
Sayer Henry, bedstead & cabinet ma. 27 Long al. Finsbury
Sayer Henry, commercial saw mills, Commercial road east
Sayer Jas. pawnbroker, 68 & 116 Drury lane
Sayer James, *Red Lion* P.H. 27 Up. King st. Bloomsbury
Sayer John, saddler, Stratford
Sayer John, shoemaker, 8 Union st. Middlesex hospital
Sayer Joseph, bedstead maker, 32 Crispin st. Spitalfields
Sayer Robert, beer retailer, 24 New st. Covent garden
Sayer Thos. H. fringe ma. 1 Church row, Up. st. Islington
Sayer Wm. H. teadealer, &c. 11 Orchard st. Portman sq
Sayers Charles, artists' brush manf. 27 Theobald's rd. Holbn
Sayers Hen. *Pewter Platter* P.H. 40 Charles st. Hatton gar
Sayers Robert, fishmonger, 29 Crawford st. Portman sq
Sayers Thos. carpenter, &c. 14 Lamb's Condt. pas. Rd. Ln. sq
Sayers Wm. appraiser, &c. 67 East st. Manchester sq
Saynes James, hatters' furrier, 56 Great Dover road
Saysell John & Co. linendrapers, 157 Waterloo road
Saywell George, carpenter, 20 Colchester st. Whitechapel
Saywell Rd. bookslr. & statnr. 24 Featherstone bldgs. Holbn
Saywell Robert, solicitor, Temple chambers, Fleet st
Scace Robert, surveyor, 26 New Church st. west, Edgware rd
Scace Susan (Miss), dressmaker, 22 Harcourt st. New rd
Scadding Benjamin, lodging house, 24 Bartholomew close
Scadding Edwin Ward & Son, solctrs. 2 & 3 Gordon st. Gordn. sq
Schacht George, skin merchant, 37 Queen st. Cheapside
Scales Geo. & Sons, linen manufacturers, 19 Milk st. & Newark upon Trent
Scales Wm. & Edw. meat salesmen, 44 Aldgate High st
Scales Chas. grocer, &c. 85 Old st. St. Luke's
Scales Edw. solicitor, 12 Copthall ct. City
Scales James, furniture broker, 16 Lucas st. Rotherhithe
Scales Jas. B. auction. & appraiser, 5 Jamaica row, Bermondsey
Scales John, picture cleaner, 6 Duke st. Chelsea
Scales Jonathan, butcher, 23 Penton row, Walworth road
Scales Samuel, carpenter, &c. 1 Albion st. Rotherhithe
Scales Wm. butcher, 29 Limehouse causeway
Scales William, linendraper, 84 Old st. St. Luke's
Scales Wm. Finlayson, news agt. & bookseller, 195 Shoredch
Scaley & Maude, wine & brandy importers, 69 Mark lane
Scambler Thomas, fruiterer, 61 North st. Edgware road
Scamell Geo. & Benj. who. ironmongs. 73 & 74 West Smithfield
Scammell Joseph, silversmith, 53 Edmund st. King's cross
Scammell Thos. collar & harness ma. 30 Lisson grove north
Scanavi Demetreo Alexander, mercht. 9 New Broad st. City
Scanes J. Hooper, *Old George* P.H. 58 Stanhope st. Claremkt
Scanlan David, watchmaker, 20 Bell yard, Temple bar
Scanlan Edward, surgeon, 18 Park pl. villas, Paddington
Scanlan Louisa (Mrs.), lodging ho. 10 Thayer st. Manches. sq
Scanlan Robert, artist, 63 Burton crescent, Russell square
Scannell Daniel, surgeon, 6 Upper Ranelagh st. Pimlico

Scantlebury John, beer retailer, 8 Market st. Edgware rd
Scantlebury Wm. builder, 30 Eastbourne ter. Paddington
Scarborough John, conveyancer, 19 Tokenhouse yard
Scarborough John, warehouseman, 50 Bow lane, Cheapside
ScarboroughJohnRoyston,mer.&wine imp.8Crosby hl.chamb
Scarborough Thos. coal merchant, see Ward & Scarborough
Scarbrow Frederick, corn dealer, 166 Alfred pl. Waterloo rd
Scarbrow Stephen, cheesemonger, 91 High st. Portland twn
Scarbrow William, corn dealer, 38 Wilsted st. Somers town
Scard John, attorney, 2 North crescent, Bedford square
Scarfe Claxon, timber merchant, 3 Osnaburgh pl. New road
Scarfe Edward, *White Bear* P.H. 100 Berwick st. Soho
Scarfe Turrell Jas. watch & clock maker, 59 Dean st. Soho
Scarff Thos. carpenter, 21 Gloucester st. Comrcl. rd. east
Scargill John, solicitor, 2 Hatton court, Threadneedle st
Scarlefield Thos. gold size mak. 4 Monmouth ct. Seven dials
Scarlett James, butcher, 77 Warren st. Fitzroy square
ScarlettJohn,coachma.&wheelwr.8Hargraveter.Berm.Nw.rd
Scarlett Joseph, plumber, 18 Henrietta st. Brunswick sq
Scarlett Robert, butcher, 17 Goswell road
Scarlett Thos. ham & beef shop, 26 King William st. City
Scarlett Wm. woollendraper, 4 Marylebone st. Piccadilly
Scarman Hannah (Mrs.), corset maker, 17 Maddox st
Scarman William, dentist, 10 George st. Hanover sq
Scarnell Thos. & Co. hatmakers, 3 Tothill st. Westminster
Scarnell Thos. clothes salesman, 17 Grosvenor row, Pimlico
Scarnell Wm. Henry, wine merchant, 58 Lombard st
Scarratt & Partington, woollen warehomn. 7 Queen st. City
Scarratt James, wholesale button, trimming, & manchester warehouseman, 12 Milk st. Cheapside
Scarrott Thomas, engraver, see Collins & Scarrott
Scarvell George, tobacconist, 97 Westbourne st. Pimlico
Scates Joseph, concertina manufacturer, 40 Frith st. Soho
ScatliffJohn Parr, surgeon, 48 Sloane square, Chelsea
Scears Edward, bootmaker, 3 Drury lane
Sceley John Fran. boot& sh.ma.31Lit.Guilford st.Russell sq
Schacht Charles, tailor, 13 Sackville st. Piccadilly
Schacht George, skin merchant, 37 Queen st. Cheapside
Schacht Theodore, merchant, 3 New London st. City
Schade Andrew Fredk. cabinet maker, 2 Harriet st. & 1 Cottage place, Sloane st
Schaezler & Co. merchants, 11 Bury court, St. Mary Axe
Schaezler Adolphus Fredk. bavarian consul gen. 11 Bury ct
Schaezler Adolphus Frederick, merchant, 11 Bury court
Schäfer Chas. baker, 5 Kensington ter. Kensngtn.gravel pts
Schäfer Christian Hen.baker,83 Up.Whitecrss. st.St.Luke's
Schäfer James William Henry, merchant, 48 Fenchurch st
Schäfer Philip, saddler, 44 Brewer st. Golden sq
Schafer William, baker, 49 James st. Oxford st
Schaffer John, engine turner, 37 Spencer st. Goswell rd
Schaller Joseph, ladies' shoe & clog maker, 19 Charles st. Middlesex hospital
Schambers Joseph, cabinet maker,15 Panton st. Haymarket
Scharf George, artist, 14 Francis st. Tottenham ct. road
Scharff George, comb maker, 24 Lant st. Borough
Scheer Frederick, mercht. 3Adam's ct.Old Broad st.&Baltic
Schenck G. C. of Kelsterbach, near Frankfort, wine mercht. (E. S. Polkinghorne & Co. agents), 12 Clement's lane
Schenck John Jacob&Co.merchts.4 Pancras la.Bucklersbury
Schenck John Theodore, ladies' shoemaker, 29 Conduit st
Schenk Brothers, ship agents, see Hofman & Schenk
Schenk William, merchant, see Hounsell, Schenk & Co
Schere Hen. auctioneer & estate agt. 84 St. John's Wood terr
Scherer Geo. Fredk. watch & clock maker, 227 Regent st
Scherzinger Constantine, clock mak.77 Church la. Whitchpl
Scheurer Elizabeth (Mrs.), baker, 48 St. George st
Scheydt Peter, french wine merchant, 151 Fenchurch st
Schild Chrisr. J. baker, 9 Bridghouse pl. Newngtn.causway
Schilizzi John M. & Co. merchants, 3 Circus pl. London wall
Schilling James, tobacconist, 136 Fenchurch st
Schilsky Joseph Henry, wholesale jeweller, watch & clock manufacturer, birmingham & sheffield warehouseman, & dealer in watch materials & importer of foreign merchandise, 90 Houndsditch
Schimtt John, baker, 17 White Hart place, Kennington la
Schioer Henry, coffee rooms, 5 Langley pl. Commercl. rd. ea
Schlarb Charles, baker, 64 Cornwall rd. Lambeth
Schleicher A— F. merchant, 7 Fen court, Fenchurch st
Schleiermacher Chas. wool mer. 3 Wor'ster pl. Up. Thames st
Schlencker MaryAnn&M.(Misses),dress ma.112 NewBond st
Schlencker Jacob, oil & colorman, 30 Goswell st
Schlencker Thos. sugar refiner, Denmark st. Ratcliff highway
Schlesinger Joseph & Co. engineers, patentees & mnfrs. of the pat. letter clips, hydraulic inkstands & selfadjusting rules, 4 Water la. Tower st. & 18 Easy row, Birmingham
Schlusser Alexander, mercht. see Perkins, Schlusser & Co
Schlesinger Martin Samuel, commission agent, 34 King st. Holborn; & Hall of Commerce, Threadneedle st
Schlutow Theodor, ship brok. see Castendieck & Schlutow
Schmae Edw. & Wm. confectioners, 23 Vale pl. Kensington
Schmaeck Moritz, merchant, &c. 9 Scot'syd. Bushla.&Lloyd's
Schmelzer Christopher & Jsph. bootma. 1 Rupert st. Haymkt
Schmidt Elizabeth (Mrs.), bookbinder, 12 Tavistock row, Covent garden
Schmidt Henry, merchant, 24 Lime st
Schmidt Henry, tailor, see Kohler & Schmidt
Schmitt Casper, *King of Prussia* P.H. 82 Lambeth st. Little Alie st
Schmitzberger Wenzeslaus, glass engraver, 77 Long acre
Schmollinger Wm. *Grasshopper tavern*, 13 Gracechurch st
Schmonsees John, *Two Brewers* P.H. 10 Spital st. Spital fi
Schnackenberg Han.(Mrs.), *BrunswickArms*P.H. Hooper sq
Schneider John & Co. merchants, 10 New Broad st. mews
Schneider Peter, baker, 4 High st. Camberwell
Schnelle Henry, merchant, Baltic coffee house
Schnibben Wm. engraver on wood, 9Westmoreland pl.City rd
Schofield George, hairdresser & perfumer, 276 Regent st
Schofield James, agent & printer of bandannas, india & brit. corah shawls, mousseline de laines, &c. 12 Bread st. City
Schofield James, grocer & teadealer, 21 Holborn hill
Schofield John, curiosity dealer, 42 Old Compton st. Soho
Schofield Joseph, tailor, 12 Magdalen st. Bermondsey st
Schofield Thos. custom ho. & com. agent, 52 Low. Thames st
Schofield Wm. curiosity dlr. 19 Whitcomb st. Pall mall east
Schofield Wm. Edwd. board & lodging ho. 93 Bartholomew cl
Scholefield Joshua & Sons, hardware merchants, 52 Eastcheap, & at Birmingham (G. Smythe, agent)
Scholefield Frances (Mrs.), George inn yard, 70 Boro' High st
Scholefield George, merchant, 3 Austinfriars
Scholefield Joseph, cutler & dressing case ma.124Cheapside
Scholes John, *Elephant inn*, & carman, 112 Fore st. Cripplegt
Scholey George & Son, tobacco brokers, 24 Mark lane
Scholey George, confectioner, 14 Shadwell High st
Scholey JohnB.spice mer. & who. coffee dlr.33St.Mary at hill
Scholey Thos. engineer, 36 Baalzephon st. Bermondsey
Scholl John, engineer & gasfitter, 41 Berwick st. Soho
Schollar Samuel, dairyman, 27 Gt. Castle st. Regent st
Schomberg Joseph Trigg, barrister, 40 Chancery lane
Schomberg Louis, lithographer. 20 John st. Pentonville
Schomborg Wm. coal dealer, 2 Leman st. Goodman's fields
Schönlank Brothrs.& Co. merchants, 9 Bury sq. St. Mary axe
School for the Indigent Blind (Robert Sharp, sup.), St. George's circus, Southwark
School of Design (Walter R. Deverell, sec.), Somerset house
School of the London Society for promoting Christianity among the Jews (Rev. J. B. Cartwright, chaplain), 12 Palestine place, Cambridge road
Schooling Henry & Charles, merchants & importers of french & foreign perfumery, fruits, confectionary, chemicals, &c. 3 Barge yard, Bucklersbury
Schooling Sapphira (Mrs.), bootmaker, 47 Wardour st. Soho
Schoolings & Everet, wholesale furnishing ironmongers, 14 Great Garden st. Whitechapel
Schorch John, baker, 17 Brick lane, Spitalfields
Schorse Hen. Geo. tarpauling ma. 5 Lit. George st. Bermnd
Schott Fred. ladies' french shoe ma. 15 Pantechnicon arcade
Schottlaender Wm.Edwd.mer.&com.agt. 8Geo.la.Botolph la
Schottler Clement Aug. *Ship& PunchBowl*P.H.55Wapping
Schrader Hen. C. coffee rooms, 4 Bull'sHead pas.Grachch st
Schrader John, cheesemonger, 49½ Lambeth walk
Schrampie Adolph, commis.agent, see Weismann&Schramme
Schrebeir Geo. bread & biscuit baker, 44 Hoxton High st
Schrier Samuel, rope maker, 1 Wade's place, Mile end road
Schrimshaw Wm. lodging house, 3 Portsea pl. Connaught sq
Schroder, Hincken & Co. sugar refins. 7Christian st. St. Geo.e
Schroder John Henry & Co. merchants, 102 Leadenhall st
Schroder Ludolf Balthazar&Co.merchs.48Comml.sale rooms
Schroder John, bootmaker, 4 William st. Cannon st. road
Schroeder Richard, pro. of music, 333Albany rd. Camberwell
Schubaeh Joseph, general agent, 7 Laurence Pountney la
Schuler Matt. & John, clock maks. 16 Commercial pl. City rd
Schuller Konrad, tailor, 1 Surrey place, Wandsworth rd
Schultz Christopher F. bootmaker, 24 Limehouse causeway
Schultz Henry, marine store dealer, 8 Fair st. Horselydown
Schultz Henry, oilman, 12 Philpot st. Commercial road east
Schultz Johann R. profes. of german, 20 Princes st. Caven.sq
Schulze Dorothy & Son, printers, 13 Poland st. Oxford st
Schumann Richard, merchant, see Fischer & Schumann
Schunck, Souchay & Co. merchants, 8 Tokenhouse yard
Schunter Gottlieb, baker, 23 Liquorpond st. Gray's inn lane
Schwabe Salis & Co. calico printers (Richard Birdsall, agent), 6 Bow church yard

Schwabacher Leopold, imptr. foreign wines, 49 Haymarket
Schwar & Saum, clock manufactrs. 19 East st. Walworth rd
Schwartz Andrew, vinegar & spirit coloring manufacturer to her Majesty's revenue, 3 White's row, Spitalfields
Schwartz Gottlieb S. potato salesm. 14 Hereford pl. Comml. rd
Schwartz Henry Wm. merchant, 1 Gt. St. Helen's, Bishopsgate
Schwarz William, baker, 49 Green st. Bethnal green
Schwarzschild A. & Co. genl. agents, 1 Plough ct. Lombard st
Schwearer & Kaiser, watch & clock ma. 30 Park ter. Reg.'s pk
Schweitzer Leonard, gun & plate case ma. 7 Broad ct. Long acre
Schweppe Jacob & Co. wine merchants, & soda, lemonade & mineral water manufacturers by special appointment to her Majesty, H.R.H. Prince Albert, the Duchess of Kent, the Duchess of Gloucester, & all the royal family, 51 Berners st. Oxford st.; & at Liverpool, Bristol & Derby
Schwind John, baker, Bromley, Middlesex
Sciiaz John Peter, coffee rooms, 34 Vere st. Clare market
Scoffern John, physician, 10 Henry st. east, Avenue rd
Scofield Abraham, *George* P.H. 22 Great Chapel st. Oxford st
Scofield George, bookbinder, 74 Gt. Suffolk st. Borough
Scolaro Joseph, imp. of forn. fancy goods, 10 Charles st. Soho sq
Scoles Joseph & Son, tailors, 45 Great Marlborough st
Scoles & Kings, coachmakers, 100 & 101 Long acre
Scoles & Martin, stone mers. Market wf. North pl. Regent's pk
Scoles Joseph John, architect, 11 Argyll place, Regent st
Scoltock John, engineer, 203 Wapping High st
Scoones Edward, fruiterer, 39 Chapel st. Grosvenor place
Scoones Francis, pawnbroker, 4 Perseverance ter. Bethnal gn
Scoones Henry, fruit salesman, Borough market
Scoones Richard, jun. bootmaker, 47 Moorgate st. Bank
Scoones Richard, bootmaker, 255 Borough High st
Scoones Wm. Lidwell, carcase butcher, 60 Aldgate High st
Scorah John, china dealer, 2 Portman market, Marylebone
Score Charles, solicitor, 43 Carey st
Score George, dairyman, 4 Priory pl. Camberwell new rd
Scorer, Withers & Harris, notaries, 24 Royal Exchange
Scorrar William, harpoon maker, 31 Narrow st. Limehouse
Scotcher Charles, pianoforte mak. 17 Norton st. Fitzroy sq
Scotcher Thomas, furnishing undertaker, 56 St. George st
Scotcher Thos. pianoforte ma. 122 Drummond st. Euston sq
Scotchman Edward, *Crown* P.H. 7 Henry st. Portland town
Scotchmer James Thos. hairdrsr. 19A, Compton st. Brunwk. sq
Scothrup Chas. carpent. & undtk. 4 Margaret st. Cavendish sq
Scotland, Lord Advocate's Office (Rt. Hon. Duncan M'Neill, M.P. lord advocate; Donald Robertson, sec.), Gwydir house, Whitehall
Scotland Andrew, baker, Deptford High st
Scotland Colley Harman, barrister, 1 Pump ct. Temple
Scots Fusileer Guards' Hospital (Wm. Henry Judd, surgeon), Lillington st. Vauxhall bridge road
Scotney Sarah (Mrs.), milliner, 90 New Bond st
Scott Abraham & Co. wholes. jewellers, 60 Red lion st. Holbor
Scott Anthony & Co. earthenware manufrs. 249 Wapping
Scott, Bell & Co. east india agents & general merchants, 2 Alderman's walk, New Broad st
Scott Brothers, merchants (Naples), 37 Old Broad st. City
Scott & Browne (Misses), boardg. school, 4 Kingsland green
Scott Charles & Co. sewed muslin manufrs. 9 Lawrence lane
Scott & Combs, solicitors, 6 St. Mildreds court, Poultry
Scott Charles James & John, ship biscuit bakers & irish & foreign provision merchants, 282 Wapping High st. & Jamaica coffeehouse, Cornhill
Scott, Cawthorn & Scott, stockbrokers, 16 Throgmorton st. & Stock exchange
Scott, Eden & Co. patent fuel factory, the Stowage, Deptford
Scott Fredk. & Co. coal & coke merch. & com. agts. 57 Cannon st
Scott E. & J. & H. & L. (Misses), school, 12 Trelleck ter. Vauxhl. rd
Scott Elizh. & Ann (Misses), seminary, 3 Brett's buildings, Camberwell road
Scott & Garnett, cornfactors, 2 Moorgate st. & granaries, 242 Rotherhithe
Scott James & Co. manufactrs. & warehousemen, 59 Friday st
Scott Jas. & Son, bootma. 2 Southampton bldgs. Chancery la
Scott (Misses), ladies' school, 12 Trellick ter. Vauxhall rd
Scott & Moffatt, architects, 20 Spring gardens
Scott Peter & Son, bakers & corn dlrs. 15 Gt. Moore pl. Lmbth
Scott Saml. F. & Co. paperstains. 49 Lw. Belgrave pl. Pimlico
Scott Sir Claude, bart. & Co. bankers, 1 Cavendish square
Scott & Tahourdin, solicitors, 25 Lincoln's inn fields
Scott & Thorpe, teadealers & grocers, 72 Bishopsgate within
Scott & Watson, printers' smiths, &c. 25 Tysoe st. Exmouth st
Scott Wm. & Co. turners, 23 Baker's row, Clerkenwell
Scott Wm. Hugh & Andrew, merchants, 37 Old Broad st. City
Scott Wm. & Jas. & Geo. printsellers, 20 Henrietta st. Cov. gar
Scott Wm. & Son, bootma. 10 Francis st. Tottenham ct. rd
Scott Wm. & Son, meat salesmen, 30 & 31 Newgate maket
Scott Wm. & Son, stock & share brokers, 20 Throgmorton st
Scott, Wing & Co. manufacturers of clocks, watches & wholesale jewellers, 59 & 60 Red Lion st. Holborn
Scott & Wright, man's mercers, 6 Glasshouse st. Regent st
Scott Abraham, *Sugar Loaf* P.H. 34 Betts st. Ratcliff hiway
Scott Adam, publisher, 36 Charterhouse square
Scott Alexr. bill sticker & van adv. 8 Church st. Waterloo rd
Scott Alexr. carpenter, 8 Lime st. & Culver ct. Fenchurch st
Scott Alexr. coffee rooms, Hide market, Leadenhall
Scott Alexr. commission agent, 3 Howford bldgs. Fench. st
Scott Anthony, carman, Christian st. St. George's east
Scott Catherine (Mrs.), basketma. & turner, 5 Panton st. Hymkt
Scott Charles, cheesemonger, 187 Kingsland road
Scott Charles, grocer, 206 Poplar High st
Scott Charles, linendraper, 52 Kingsland road
Scott Charles, old roman baths, 5 Strand lane, Strand
Scott Charles, sen. harness maker, 103 Leather lane, Holborn
Scott Charles, silk mercer, 3 Plumber's row, City road
Scott Chas. Davison, solicitor, see Downes, Gamlen & Scott
Scott Charles Gustavus, tobacconist, 36 Bath st. City rd
Scott Christiana (Miss), academy, 17 Broad st. Golden sq
Scott David, baker, 20 Fish st. hill, & 100 Lower Thames st
Scott David, carpenter & builder, 4 New rd. Sloane st. Chelsea
Scott David, hairdresser & wigma. 8 Bowling st. Marylebone
Scott David, hat manufacturer, 83 Holborn bridge
Scott David, 3 *Bucks tavern*, 22 Old Jewry, & 23 Gresham st
Scott Dyster Wm. oil & colorman, 14 Chester pl. Old Kent rd
Scott Edward, oil & colorman, 6 Marlborough rd. Chelsea
Scott Edward, timber merchant, see Stivenson & Scott
Scott Elizabeth (Mrs.), seminary, 3 Queen st. Brompton
Scott Emily (Miss), artist, 14 Maddox st. Regent st
Scott Emily A. (Miss), artist, Sussex cot. Park vil. ea. Rgt. pk
Scott Francis, agent to Ruinart Pere et Fils (of Rheims), 13 London st. Fenchurch st
Scott Geo. engineer & millwright, 5 & 6 King st. Commer. rd. ea
Scott Geo. engineer, &c. 3 Essex st. & 5 Bouverie st. Fleet st
Scott Geo. farrier, 49 Halfmoon st. Bishopsgate
Scott Geo. greengrocer, Richmond pl. East st. Walworth rd
Scott Geo. livery stables, 42 Weymouth mews, Weymouth st. & White Horse yard, New Cavendish st
Scott Geo. pork butcher, 14 Princes st. Lambeth
Scott Geo. tailor, see Edwards & Scott
Scott Geo. tailor, 86 Queen st. Cheapside
Scott Geo. watch case maker, 19 Radnor st. St. Luke's
Scott Geo. Rd. auctioneer & share agt. 8 Carey st. Linc. inn
Scott Geo. Walter, stock broker, see Aston & Scott
Scott Harriet (Mrs.). milliner & dressma. 124 Bethnal gr. rd
Scott Henry, *Cock* P.H. 27 Old st. St. Luke's
Scott Henry, tailor, &c. 9 Tottenham court, New road
Scott Humphrey, timber dealer, Morning lane, Hackney
Scott Isabella (Mrs.), baker, 2 & 13 King st. Portman square
Scott James, auctioneer & apprisr. 6 Cambridge st. Golden sq
Scott James, beer retailer, 3 Lower terrace, Islington
Scott James, beer retailer, 1 Park place, Mile end road
Scott James, butcher, 5 Prospect place, Kingsland road
Scott James, chair maker, 31 Fuller st. Bethnal green
Scott James, fancy repository, Camberwell green
Scott James, furniture broker, 15 Gt. Earl st. Seven dials
Scott James, hemp & flax mercht. 11 Trinity sq. Tower hill
Scott James, linendraper, 35 Mount st. Lambeth
Scott James, merchant, 5 Nicholas lane, Lombard st
Scott James, physician, 37 Grove end road, St. John's wood
Scott James, physician, 369 Strand
Scott James, pork butcher, 63 Leather lane, Holborn
Scott James, ship & insurance broker, see Gilby & Scott
Scott James, wine merchant, 7 Oxford court, Cannon st
Scott James Cole, woollen warehn. see Willott, Scott & Day
Scott James G. matheml. instrument ma. 17 Bermondsey wall
Scott James John, barrister, 1 Cloisters, Temple
Scott Jas. Wm. P. solicitor, 2 Southmptn. bldgs. Chancery la
Scott John, bookseller, 5 King's row, Walworth road
Scott John, cigar maker, 13 Upper Clifton st. Finsbury
Scott John, comm. merchant, 8 Devonshire sq. Bishpsgte st
Scott John, drysalter & color mer. Brook's whf. Up. Thames st
Scott John, fire brick & coke agt. Hermitage bdge. wf. Wppng
Scott John, fruiterer, 12 & 57 Gt. Hall, Hungerford market
Scott John, grocer & oilman, 4 Spring st. Paddington
Scott John, hairdresser, &c. 61 Three Colt st. Limehouse
Scott John, locksmith & bellhanger, 26 St. John st. road
Scott John, physician, 12 Bedford square
Scott John, pianoforte maker, 26 Sloane st. Chelsea
Scott John, solicitor, 8 Chancery lane, Fleet st
Scott John, special pleader, 9 Clifford's inn, Fleet st
Scott John, stationer, 8 Stockwell terrace, Clapham road
Scott John, stockbroker, Stock excha. & 5 Bank chambers
Scott John, surgeon, 53 High st. Camdenta

Scott John, surgeon, 17 Park lane, Piccadilly
Scott John, furniture printer, 315 Oxford st
Scott John, wheelwright, 73 Horseferry road, Westminster
Scott John, wholesale teadealer, see Downes & Scott
Scott John Edmund, solicitor, 6 St. Mildred's ct. Poultry
Scott John Guillum, stockbroker, see Hammond, Scott & Co
Scott John Wray, stock & sharebroker, 3 Bartholomew la
Scott Jonathan, tailor, &c. 8 Bennett st. St. James's st
Scott Joseph, artist, 62 Charing cross
Scott Joseph, *Exchequer hotel & tavern*, 1 New Palace yd. 14 Bridge st. & 32 Parliament st
Scott Louisa (Mrs.), wardrobe dealer, 12 Chalton st. Somrs tn
Scott Martha (Mrs.), coffee rooms, 264 Whitechapel road
Scott Mary Ann (Mrs.), stationer, 10 South pl. Camberwl. rd
Scott Mary E. (Miss), milliner & dressma. Camberwell grn
Scott Matthew Richard, mercht. &c. Lombard st. chambers
Scott Montagu, solicitor, Grecn. chmbrs. 19 Devereaux ct. Strd
Scott Nicholas, trunk maker, 149 High Holborn
Scott Percival, *Lord Nelson* P.H. 20 Fair st. Horselydown
Scott Peter, lighterman, 20 Windsor pl. Southwark bdge. rd
Scott Philip David, tailor, 17 Bury st. St. James's
Scott Richard, baker, 34 Crosby row, Walworth road
Scott Richard, carpenter, Church la. Kensington gravel pits
Scott Richard, who. confectioner, 7½ Crown row, Walwth. rd
Scott Rd. Minty, *Princess of Wales* P.H. Grove la. Deptford
Scott Rd. Thos. tobacconist, 18 Chichester pl. Gray's inn rd
Scott Robert, breeches maker, 19 Old Compton st. Soho
Scott Robert, *Bricklayers' Arms* P.H. 12 Earl st. Blackfriars
Scott Robert, chemist, 2 Mornington rd. Camden town
Scott Robert, grocer & teadealer, 44 Fetter lane
Scott Robert, hatter, 121 Regent st
Scott Robert, musical instrument ma. 5 Upper Albany st
Scott Robert, surgeon, &c. 9 Up. Barnsbury st. Islington
Scott Robert, tailor, 5 Orchard st. Portman square
Scott Samuel, silkman, 4 Pinners' hall, Old Broad st. City
Scott Sophia (Mrs.), grocer, 10 Exmouth st. Euston sq
Scott Susannah (Mrs.), basketmaker, 43 Old Compton st. Soho
Scott Thomas grocer, & cheesemonger, 61 Bethnal green rd
Scott Thomas, manchester agent, 19 Broad street buildings
Scott Thomas, ship & anchorsmith, Bell whf. 42 Low. Shadwell
Scott Thomas, tailor, 58 Upper John st. Fitzroy square
Scott Thomas, tailor, 37 Howland st. Fitzroy square
Scott Thomas, *Two Brewers* P.H. 84 Bankside
Scott Thomas, who. druggist, see Langton, Brothers & Scott
Scott Walter, hosier, glover, &c. see Hodges & Scott
Scott Wm. artist, Sussex cot. 11 Park village east, Regent's pk
Scott Wm. baker, 74 Seymour st. Euston square
Scott Wm. brick mkr. Shepherd's Bush la. Hammersmith
Scott Wm. butcher, 12 East st. Walworth road
Scott Wm. coffee broker, 87 Gt Tower st. City
Scott Wm. dentist, 4 Golden square, Regent st
Scott Wm. glass toy manufact. 34 Theobald's st. New Kent rd
Scott Wm. gun & pistol ma. 27 Leman st. Goodman's fields
Scott Wm. lighterman & coal dealer, 22 Mill lane, Tooley st
Scott Wm. lighterman, 263 Rotherhithe st
Scott Wm. locksmith & bellhanger, 31 Leather lane
Scott Wm. printer, 11 & 12 Little New st. Shoe lane
Scott Wm. stationer, 5 Gibraltar row, Deptford
Scott Wm. west india & col. broker, see Simpson, Scott & Co
Scott Wm. wine merchant, 4 Adam st. Adelphi
Scott Wm. wine merchant, 1 Church row, Limehouse
Scott Wm. wine merchant, 1 Dunster court, Mincing lane
Scott Wm. Pulteney, solicitor, see Hertslet, Scott & Hertslet
Scotten Francis Benjn. straw hat manufctr. 136 Goswell st
Scottish Amicable Mutual Life Ass. (Wm. Jones Penkivil, agent), West st. Finsbury circus
Scottish Episcopal Church Society (Rev. Thomas Bowdler, A. J. C. Laurie, hon secs.), 79 Pall mall
Scottish Equitable Life Assurance Society (William Cook, agent), 61A, Moorgate st.; for directors, &c. see page 2045
Scottish Hospital & Kinloch Bequest (James Adair, sec.), 7 Crane court, Fleet st. & 17 Fetter lane, Fleet st
Scottish Mercantile Institution, 29 Poultry
Scottish Prov. Inst. (John R. Leifchild, sec.), 12 Moorgate st
Scottish Provident Life Insurance Co. (John Pollock, agent), 12 Great St. Thomas Apostle
Scottish Union Fire & Life Insur. Co. (Fred. Garle Smith, sec.), 37 Cornhill, City; see page 2044
Scottish (Widows' Fund) Life Insurance Society (H. M'Kean, agent), 7 Pall mall; see page 2050
Scoular Wm. sculptor & plaster cast mak. 92 Dean st. Soho
Scouler & Cull, tailors, &c. 1 Pennyfields, Poplar
Scouler James, tailor, 2 Wellington pl. West India docks
Scouse John, *Hare* P.H. 109 Brick lane, Spitalfields
Scovell John Henry & George, wharfingers, Topping's, Cotton's, & Depôt & Symon's wharfs, Tooley st
Scovell John Henry & Geo. agts. to the Loftus alum works, & exporters of flanders bricks, Topping's wharf, Tooley st
Scovell Geo. gold & silver thread manf. 29 Clerkenwell close
Scoven John, plumber, Wyndham road, Camberwell
Scowen Robert, bricklayer, 7 Copenhagen st. Pentonville
Scowen Wm. hairdresser, 6 Lisle st. Leicester square
Scrace Wm. baker, 1 St. Mark's road, Camberwell New rd
Scrimgeour Robert Shedden & John Shedden, stockbrokers, 41 Threadneedle st
Scrimgeour Wm. W. general manager of the Union Bank of London, 2 Princes st. Mansion house
Scrimshaw William, tailor, Battersea square
Scripps Wm. A. & Son, news agents, 13 South Molton st. Bond st
Scripture Readers' Society for Ireland (Rt. Hon. Thomas Lefroy, M.P. sec.), 32 Sackville st. Piccadilly
Scripture Readers' Society (Rev. John Hampden Gurney, sec.), 4 Trafalgar square
Scriven James & Son, auctioneers & surveyors, 21 Barbican
Scriven Henry William, tailor, 1 Margaret st. Cavendish sq
Scriven John, barrister, 2 Elm court, Temple
Scrivener Ambrose, haberdasher, 272 Bermondsey st
Scrivener Fras. (Mrs.), milliner, 29 Addington pl. Cambrwl
Scrivener Hayter, corn dealer, 339 Wapping High st
Scrivener John T. corn dealer, 1 Church lane, Whitechapel
Scrivener Samuel, beer retailer, 1 Francis pl. Holloway
Scrivener Thomas, butcher, Clare market
Scrivener Thos. corn dlr. 38 White Horse st. Comrcl. rd. Stpny
Scrivener Thomas, plumber, 2 Park lane, Liverpool road
Scrivener William, *Royal Oak* P.H. 8 Cross st. Bermondsey
Scrivens James, accountant, 15 Millbank row, Westminster
Scrivens Samuel, skinner, see Doherty, Scrivens & Co
Scrivens William, veterinary surgeon, 19 Giltspur st
Scroxton Joseph Hy. tin plate worker & ornamental japanner, manufacturer of tea canisters, fancy boxes, bowls, &c. tobacco jars & scoops, cash, deed & biscuit boxes, 137 Bishopsgate without
Scruby John, tailor, 17 Susannah st. East India rd. Poplar
Scruton (Mrs.), dressma. 16 Brunswick parade, Barnsbury rd
Scrutton Alexr. stockbroker, see Parker & Scrutton
Scrutton Jas. stationer & acct. book mkr. 111 Fore st. Cripplet
Scrutton John, furniture broker, 1 King st. Deptford
Scrutton Thos. ship broker, see Urquhart & Scrutton
Scudamore Ann (Mrs.), fruiterer, 11 Abbey st. Bermondsey
Scudamore Capel, undertaker, 11 Bull & Mouth st
Scudamore Edmd. Mark, tobacconist, 15 Bridge rd. Lambth
Scudamore Mary K. (Miss), haberdasher, 3 Wells rw. Islingtn
Scudamore Sir Chas. physician, 6 Wimpole st. Cavendish sq
Scudamore Wm. fruiterer, &c. 34 Bow lane, Cheapside
Scudder Charles, chaser, 31½ Clerkenwell close
Scull John, *Duke of York* P.H. 45 Queen st. Bryanstone sq
Scull Wm. *Bricklayers' Arms* P.H. 54 Park st. Grosvnr. sq
Scully Daniel, *Cross Keys* P.H. 125 Wentworth st. Whitechapel
Scully Edward Thos. silk dyer, 15 Eden pl. Old Kent road
Scully Francis, barrister, 44 Lincoln's inn fields
Scully John, cheesemonger, 1 Chapel st. Somers town
Scully John, provision dealer, 130 Upper Thames st
Sculthorp John, colorman, 4 Brickhill lane, Up. Thames st
Sculthorpe Richd. bookseller, 99 Gt. Peter st. Westminster
Scurfield Robert, coal factor, see Smith, Scurfield & Co
Scurlock John T. proctor & notary, 6 Bell yd. Doctors' cms
Scurr Jas. jun. tin & iron pl. wkr. 9 Norfolk pl. East st. Wlwth. rd
Scurr Michael, plumber & painter, 146 Wapping
Scurr Thos. Fras. *George IV.* P.H. Richard st. Limehouse fl
Scurr Wm. tin plate worker, 132 Brick lane, Spitalfields
Scutchey Mary Ann (Mrs.), baker, 56 Pearson st. Kingsld. rd
Scutt John, dining rooms, 49 Wells st. Oxford st
Scutt Thos. Benjamin, attorney, 11 Tokenhouse yard
Sea Coal Meters Off. (Wm. Wright, clk.), 5 Coalex. Lr. Thms. st
Sea Policy Stamp Office, 3 New Bank bdgs. Loth.; hrs. 10 to 4
Seaborn Elizh. (Mrs.), *White Bear* P.H. 30 Park st. Gros. sq
Seaborn Geo. cheesemong. & tripe dres. 97 Shadwell High st
Seaborn George, cheesemonger, 67 Whitehorse st. Stepney
Seaborne Thos. rag merchant, 18 Grafton st. Soho
Seaborne Wm. bootma. 1 Britannia pl. Commercial rd. east
Seaborne Wm. wheelwright, 3 New road, Whitechapel road
Seabrook & Osmond, importers of wines & spirits, 60 Fenchurch st
Seabrook Wm. & Sons, musicians, 14 Lambeth road
Seabrook Alfred John, greengrocer, 27 Deptford High st
Seabrook Arthur, *Bee Hive* P.H. Cobourg rd. Old Kent road
Seabrook Christ. *Lads of the Village* P.H. New King st. Dptfd
Seabrook Dbrh. (Mrs.), *Barleymow* P.H. 40 Duke st. Grvnr. sq
Seabrook Elizabeth (Miss), trunkmaker, 5 Cheapside
Seabrook Isaac, surveyor, 43 Regent square, Gray's inn rd
Seabrook John, ironmonger, 39 Bell st. Edgware road
Seabrook John, livery stables, 4 Theberton st. Islington

Seabrook John, wine merc. 32 Northampton sq. Clerkenwell
Seabrook Reuben, straw hat maker, 100 Gt. Titchfield st
Seabrook William James, *Rose inn* P.H. New cross
Seadon Baker, bootmaker, 6 King st. St. James's square
Seagar George, artificial flower mfr. 24 Noble st. Wood st
Seage Charles, fruiterer, 6 Upper York st. Bryanstone sq
Seager, Evans & Stafford, distillers, 19&20 Millbank rw. Westm
Seager Ebenezer, tobacconist, 67 Upper Whitecross st
Seager Edward, tobacconist, 6 Lit. Smith st. Westminster
Seager George, tailor & draper, 5 King st. Cheapside
Seager John, wine merchant, 4 Hungerford wharf, Strand
Seager Julia (Miss), ladies' school, see Green & Seager
Seager Saml. oil & italian warehouse, 4 Noble st. Cheapside
Seager Sarah (Mrs.), ironmonger, 2 Lit. James st. Bedford rw
Seager Wm. watch glass maker, 8 Berkley st. Clerkenwell
Seagood Frederick, jeweller, 56 Red Lion st. Clerkenwell
Seagrave John, hairdresser, 249 Tottenham court road
Seagrave Wm. surgeon, &c. 16 St. George's rd. New Kent rd
Seakins Ann (Mrs.), brushmaker, 100 Kent st. Borough
Seakins John, brush manfr. 3 Laurel pl. Queen's rd. Dalston
Seal Office, 28 Abingdon st.; hours of business 10 to 3
Seal Office (Exch.), 2 Middle Scotland yard; hours 10 to 4
Seal Geo. sheriffs' officer, 193 Blackfriars road
Seal George, china & glass warehouse, 2 Blackfriars road
Seal George, livery stables, 69 Worship st. Norton folgate
Seal George, milliner & hosier, 19 Pitfield st. Hoxton
Seal Joseph, butcher, 1 Walker's court, Lit. Pulteney st
Seal Samuel, china & glass wa. 2 Gt. Queen st. Linc. inn fi
Seal William, beer retailer, 36 Lower George st. Chelsea
Seal William, boot & shoemaker, 8 Union row, Camberwell
Seal William, plumber, &c. 11 Queen st. King's road, Chelsea
Seal William, wholesale clothes warehouse, 3 Houndsditch
Seale Edward Jas. fishmonger & oyster rooms, 127 Wardour st
Seale William, tobacconist, 24 South row, New road
Seales Samuel, tobacconist, 9 Featherstone st. City road
Sealey James, corndealer, 17 John st. north, Marylebone
Sealey John, carman, 18 Marine st. Bermondsey
Sealey John, potato dealer, 19 King David lane, Shadwell
Sealy Charles, cabinetma. 3 Francis st. Newington butts
Sealy Edward Forward, solicitor, 11 Lincoln's inn fields
Sealy James, ornamental painter, 7 York ter. Kingsland
Sealy John, linendraper, 13 Stucley ter. Camden town
Seaman's Hosptl. Soc. Ship 'Dreadnought,' off Greenwich; (Richard Harley, secretary), office, 74 King William st. City
Seaman's Registry & Pay Office, 7 Waterloo terrace, Commercial road east; hours of business 10 to 5
Seaman Charles, silk manufacturer, see Wilson, Seaman & Co
Seaman Edw. Cleveland, solicitor, 12 Pancras la. Bucklersby
Seaman Joseph, pork butcher, 43 Munster st. Regent's pk
Seaman Robert, baker, 94 Britannia st. City road
Seaman Sarah (Mrs.), baths, 9 Suffolk place, Pall mall east
Seaman Wm. coachma. 3 Windmill st. Tottenham ct. road
Seaman's Registry & Savings Bank, 12 Circus, Minories
Seamark John, *Surrey Arms* P.H. Thomas st. Kennington com
Seamer Thomas, silk manufacturer, see Cockin & Seamer
Sear Joseph, cheesemonger, 15 London terrace, Hackney rd
Sear Joseph, grocer & cheesemonger, 12 East st. Walwth rd
Sear Joseph, plumber, 35 Mount st. Berkeley square
Search Francis & Co. bed & mattress war. 48 Clerkenwell grn
Search John, butcher, 1 Mount place, Walworth road
Search John, fruiterer, Long market, Covent garden
Search Thomas, coachsmith, 14 Coal yard, Drury lane
Search Stephen, corn & coal merchant, Church st. Chelsea
Seare Sam. & Co. engravs. & bookbinds.' tool cut. 44 High Holb
Seare John, china warehouse, 90 Blackman st. Borough
Seare Thomas, barrister, 2 South square, Gray's inn
Seares Saml. ham & beef dealer, 84 High st. Camden town
Seares William, linendraper, 22 Featherstone st. City rd
Seares Wm. R. *D. of Wellington* P.H. 15 Brnswk. st. Hkny. rd
Searl James, Refuge for the Destitute, Hoxton Old town
Searl John Remnant, carpenter, 19 Church st. Camberwell
Searl William, coffee rooms, 27 Ray st. Clerkenwell
Searle Geo. & Sons, boatbuilders, 10&11 Stangate, Lambeth; & private boathouse, 5 Bishop's walk, Lambeth
Searle Henry & Co. upholsterers, 25 & 26 Bishopsgate witho
Searle Astley, upholder, auctioneer, ho. agt. &c. Camberwl. gr
Searle George, clockmaker, 15 Wellington st. Goswell st
Searle George, fruiterer, 40 Paddington st. Marylebone
Searle George, furniture broker, 2 Union st. Deptford
Searle George, surgeon, 42 Cumming st. Pentonville
Searle Henry, eau de cologne importer, 169 Blackfriars rd
Searle Henry S. surgeon, 13 Queen's place, Kennington rd
Searle James, baker, 5 Haberdasher's walk, Hoxton
Searle John Pollard, tailor, 7 President st. west, King sq
Searle Rd. grocer & oilman, 54 Burr st. Lower East Smithfld
Searle Richard, *Hoy & Helmet* P.H. Lower East Smithfield
Searle Samuel, *Salisbury Arms* P.H. 1 Durham st. Strand
Searle Thos. John, stone mer. Portland whf. 47 Wapping wl
Searle Wm. bookbinder, 19 Frith st. Soho
Searle Wm. haberdasher, Denmark hill, Camberwell
Searles Thos. boot & hat mak. 13 & 14 Bedford pl. Coml. rd. ea
Searles Thomas, boot & shoe maker, 168 Shoreditch
Searles Thomas, boot & shoe manfr. 139 Whitechapel road
Searles Thos. hatter, 14 Bedford pl. Commercial road east
Searles Wm. harness maker, 50 Whitcomb st. Haymarket
Searratt George, hairdresser, 33 King st. Westminster
Sears John, tinplate worker, 59 Seymour st. Euston sq
Sears Robt. tinplate worker, 2 York st. Middlesex hospital
Sears Wm. Jsph. letterpress printer, 3 & 4 Ivy la. Newgate st
Searson George, undertaker, 14 Platt terrace, Pancras road
Searson Luke, cheesemonger, 29 St. George st
Searson Robert, window blind maker, 28 Gower pl. Euston sq
Seaton & Kell, surgeons, 8 Bridge st. Westminster
Seaton Charles, cowkeeper, 20 Upper Rathbone place
Seaton Edward, surgeon, 77 Sloane st. Knightsbridge
Seaton John Fox, merchant, see Novelli, Watson & Seaton
Seaton Joseph, coalmercht. 13 George st. Adelphi & Richmond
Seaton Joseph, butcher, 88 Bermondsey st
Seaton Louis John, carpet wareho. 3 Frederick pl. Hampstd. rd
Seaton Robert, *Coach & Horses* P.H. 17 Lit. Compton st. Soho
Seaton Robert, *Dublin Castle* P.H. 18 Park st. Camden town
Seaward & Capel, enginrs. Canal iron works, Millwall, Poplar
Seaward David, leathercutter, 26 Exeter st. Lisson grove
Seaward William, carman, 37 Dowgate hill
Seaward William, hardwareman, Deptford High st
Seaward William, undertaker, 21 Ironmonger st. Old st
Sebeille Francis, omnibus propri. Bowling gr. st. Kensington
Secker George, pawnbroker, 26 John's row, St. Luke's
Secker Isaac Onslow, barrister, 5 Pump court, Temple
Secker Richard, watchmaker, 25 Meredith st. Clerkenwell
Secombe Roger, saddle & harness ma. 23 Long la. Smithfield
Secondaries' Office to the Sheriffs of London, 5 Basinghall st.; hours of business 10 to 7
Secretan & Capper, stock & sharebrokers, Change alley
Secretan Francis Lewis Philip, insur. broker, 21 Austinfriars
Secretan Fred. *Alliance Marine Assur. Co.* Capel ct. Bank
Secretary's (Rolls) Office, Rolls yard, Chancerylane; hours 10 to 3, long vacation 11 to 1; except Saturdays & red letter days
Secretary of State's Office (Colonial Department), 14 Downing st.; (*Foreign Department*) 16 Downing st.; & (*Home Department*, hours of business, 9 to 7), Whitehall
Sedcole James, chaise saddler, 11 Brownlow st. Drury la
Seddens Anna (Miss), corset maker, see Rawlings & Seddens
Seddon James, gun & pistol ma. 78 Low. Sloane st. Chelsea
Seddon Jsph. who. & ret. grocer & teadlr. 26 Whitechapel High st
Seddon Peter John, rag & bottlewa. 149 Unionst. Boro' High st
Seddon Robert, *Fox & Hounds* P.H. 264 Tottenham ct. rd
Seddon Samuel, merchant, 4 Pancras lane, Bucklersbury
Seddon Thomas, house agent, undertaker, upholsterer & cabinet manufr. to her Majesty, Calthorpe pl. Gray's inn rd
Seddon Wm. bread & biscuit baker, 1 Baker st. Lloyd sq
Sedgley Henry, tobacconist, Camberwell green
Sedgwick Robert & Co. ship & general agents, 15 Cannon st
Sedgwick & Taylor, pat. lamp, lustre & cut glass mfrs. & oil mers. patentees of the diaphanous reflector, 186 Piccadilly
Sedgwick Francis, sack & bag manufacturer, 9 Clothfair
Sedgwick George, shorthand writer, 8 Furnival's inn
Sedgwick George, tailor & habit maker, 2 Beak st. Regt st
Sedgwick Jas. grocer & cheesemonger, 20 Well st. Oxford st
Sedgwick John Bell, sec. to Coll. of Physicians, Pall mall ea
Sedgwick Leonard Wm. wholesale teadealer, 15 Cannon st
Sedgwick Rd. potato salesman, 8 Munster st. Regent's pk
Sedgwick Rd. coffee rooms, 245 Shoreditch & 1 King's Hd. ct
Sedgwick Robert, custom house agent, 15 Cannon st
Sedgwick Samuel, physician, 19 Pembroke sq
Sedgwick Thomas, oilman, 97 Mount st. Berkeley sq
Sedgwick Thomas L. ironmonger, 41 Mark lane
Seear George, pianoforte maker, 75 Castle st. east, Oxfd. st
Seear Henry, grocer, 6 Prospect place, Kingsland road
Seear James, grocer & cheesemongr. 5 Prospect pl. Kingsld. rd
Seeger George, fur skin dresser, 3 Union buildings, Leatherla
Seeger Godfrey A. merchant, 13 Idol lane, Tower st
Seekel Myer, watchmaker, 19 Duke st. Aldgate
Seekings William Hen. butcher, 34 Lisle st. Leicester sq
Seelenmeyer George, boot & shoe mak. 39 Frith st. Soho
Seeley, Burnside & Seeley, booksells. & publishs. 54 & 169 Fleetst
Seeley John, artificial stone mfr. 1, 2, 3 & 4 Keppel row, New rd
Seeley John, butcher, 81 Fore st. Cripplegate
Seeley Mary (Mrs.), *Spread Eagle* P.H. 6 Charles st. Midx. hos
Seeley William, bricklayer, &c. 1 Cloudesley st. Islington
Seelie Joseph, wine & brandy mercht. see Atkinson & Seelie

Seely John, beer retailer, 41 Curtain road, Shoreditch
Seex John, cabinet maker, 9 Kennington row
Segalla Jacob, merchant, 46 Lime st
Segary Sam. Treslove, *George & Dragon* P.H. Vauxhll. Hi. st
Segrott Anne (Mrs.), baker, 10 Lit. Peter st. Westminster
Seguier Wm. & John, picture cleaners, 3 Russell ct, St. James's
Seguin Wm. Henry, prof. of singing, 43 Curzon st. Mayfair
Segura Hilary de Ramon, merchant, 2 Copthall buildings
Seidler Charles, merchant, 66 Mark lane
Seigenberg John, black lead pencil mak. 202 Brick la. Spitalfi
Seignette Louis Elizee, wine mercht. see Currie & Seignette
Seiler & Bockhorn, violin & harp stg. ma. 3. Sharp's all. Cow cr
Selane Fred. stovemaker, 26 Gloucester ter. Vauxhall br. rd
Selby & Mackeson, solicitors, 16 Serjeants' inn, Fleet st
Selby Thomas & Sons, japanners, Brownlw. mews, Gray's in. la
Selby Caroline (Miss), tobacconist, 45 Lamb's Conduit st
Selby David, oil & color warehouse, 38 Blackfriars road, & 16 York row, Kennington road
Selby Edward, undertaker, 52 Leonard st. Tabernacle walk
Selby Emanuel, plumber & painter, Camberwell green
Selby George, sen. solicitor, 12 St. John st. road
Selby George, jun. solicitor, 12 St. John st. road
Selby Harriet (Mrs.), confectioner, 7 Green st. Bethnal gr
Selby James William, merchant, 8 Fenchurch st
Selby Robert, wine & spirit merchant, 3 Burleigh st. Strand
Seldon & Johnson, ship & ins. brokers, 148 Leadenhall st
Seldon Robert, ship & commission agent, 23 Cullum st
Self Wm. & Son, auction. & valuers, 51 Crown st. Finsbury sq
Self Charles, appraiser & furnitr. broker, 139 Poplar High st
Self Charles, ornamental painter, &c. 15 Sun st. Bishopsgate
Self James, cooper, 207 Wapping High st
Self James, ship agent, Orchard house wharf, Blackwall
Self John, preserver of birds, French horn yd. 87 High Holb.
Self John, teadealer & grocer, 3 Store st. Bedford square
Self Justina (Mrs.), *Blue Boar tap* P.H. Aldgate High st
Self Wm. surgeon, 8 Lucas pl. west, Commercial road east
Selfe Henry Selfe, barrister, 12 King's Bench walk, Temple
Selfe Thomas, fruiterer, 32 Watling st
Selfe Wm. watchmaker, 4 Corthope ter. Bermondsey New rd
Selig Solomon, chair & sofa manufacturer, 17 Barbican
Selim, Dean & Co. foreign money exchangers, 9 Coventry st
Selkirk & Miller, glass & china wa. 6 Spring st. Paddington
Selkirk James, cut glass manufacturer, 145 High Holborn
Sell Jas. gold &c. wire drawer, 11 Greville st. Hatton gar
Sellar Frederick, grocer, Nine elms, Vauxhall
Sellar George, grocer & coal dlr. 7 Queen st. York st. Wlwrth
Selle Edward Fredk. grocer, the coffee pot, 7 Northumberland place, Commercial road east
Sellen William, butcher, 10 Chapel st. Curtain road
Sellers Ann (Mrs.), grocer & cheesemonger, 25 Coal yd. Drury la
Sellers Leonard, chem. & druggist, 3 Broad st. Bloomsbury
Sellers Thos. Josph. beer retailer, 77 Ossulston st. Somers tn
Sellis William, greengrocer, 11 College st. Chelsea
Sellman Robt. & Son, tallowchands. 13 Broad st. Bloomsbury
Sellman Geo. ginger beer ma. 6 Welmer gardens, Hoxton Old tn
Sellman Wm. carpenter, 3 Douglas st. Vincent square
Sells Charles, general salesman, 193 Tooley st
Sells Edward Perronett, coal merchant, see Jones, Sells & Co
Sellwood George, jobmaster, see Blake & Sellwood
Sellwood Henry, fruiterer, 9½ Gt. Woodstock st. Marylebone
Sellwood John *Royal Exchange*, P.H. 26 Sale st. Paddington
Sellwood William, grocer, 79 Bunhill row, Chiswell st.
Selman Geo. confec. & gingerbeer ma. 72 Strutton grd. Westm
Selmes Frederick, hop factor, see Nash, Selmes & Curteis
Selmes Jeremiah, butcher, Deptford High st
Selson George, wine merchant, 42 Great Tower street, City
Selth Robert, poulterer, 27 Tottenham court road
Selves Samuel & Geo. shoemakers, 92 Wheeler st. Spitalflds
Selvin William, hardware dealer, 29 Crown st. Soho
Selway Enoch, teadealer, 33 Bryanstone st. Portman sq
Selwood Ann Phillippa (Mrs.), poulterer, 2 Pavedal. Newgt. mk
Selwyn Charles Jasper, barrister, 7 Old sq. Lincoln's inn
Selwyn William, queen's counsel, 7 Old sq. Lincoln's inn
Semark John, *Hops* coffee rooms, 52 Gt. Alie st Gdmn's. fields
Semken John, carpenter & timber merch. 18 Sclater st. Bethnl. gr
Semon Edward, boys' school, 16A, Chichester pl. Gray's inn rd
Semon Elizabeth (Mrs.), ladies' school, 16A, Chichester pl
Semple Robert, surgeon, 2 Rufford's row, Upper st. Islingt
Semple Robert Hunter, surgeon, 3 Sands bldgs. Islington
Semple William, surgeon, 38 Upper st. Islington
Senington & Cox, farriers, 25 St. John's la. West Smithfield
Senior Jas. & Co. grocers & tea. dlrs. 44 King's rd. ea. Chelsea
Senior George, *Weavers' Arms* P.H. 5 Edward st. Kingsld. rd
Senior Robert, grocer, 12 Hoxton Old town, east side
Senior Thomas, locksmith, 100 Broadwall, Blackfriars
Senior United Service Club (T. H. Wills, sec.), 116 Pall mall
Senior Wm. Morgan, who. shipping ironmgr. 52 Eastcheap
Sennett Christopher, skinner, 114 Snow's fields, Bermondsey
Sentance Valentine & Son, tea dealers, 2 Clare st. Clare mkt
Sentance Wm. grocer & tea dealer, 52 Blackman st. Borough
Sentinel Weekly Newspaper Office, 7½ Wellington st. north
Senyard Robert, painter, 87 Stanhope st. Hampstead road
Sequeira James, apothecary & chemist, 38 Jewry st. Aldgate
Serbutt John, boot & shoe ma. South Island pl. Clapham rd
Sercombe John C. & George, general merchants, 66 Mark la
Sercombe Mary (Mrs.), ladies' seminary, 10 Curtain road
Sercombe Rupert Clampitt, commission agent, 66 Mark la
Serfaty Solomon Moses, leech merchant, 111 Houndsditch
Sergeant Elizh. (Mrs.), ladies' school, 9 John st. we. Edgw. rd
Sergeant E. B. (Mrs.) ladies' schl. 18 Grosvenor pl. Cmbrwl. rd
Sergeant Frederick Thos. barrister, 2 New sq. Lincoln's inn
Sergeant John, satin dresser, 64 Buttesland st. Hoxton
Sergeant Thomas, law stationer, see White & Sergeant
Sergeant Trumpeters' Licence Office, 34 Mount st. Berkly. sq
Serjeant Cornelius, grocer, 31 Clerkenwell close
Serjeant Hannah (Mrs.), bookbinder, 11 Staining la. Wood st
Serjeant Susannah (Mrs.), grocer, 95 St. John st. Smithfld
Serjeant John, boot & shoe maker, 11 Gutter lane, Cheapside
Serjeant John F. solicitor, 10 Crosskey sq. Lit. Britain
Serjeant Joseph, wharfinger, &c. see Denton & Serjeant
Serjent George, news agt. 7 Christopher ct. St. Martin's le gr
Serle Frederick, builder, 13 Somerset st. Aldgate
Serle Thomas, bricklayer & carpenter, 50 St. Mary Axe
Serny John B. physician, 8 Nottingham terrace, New rd
Serquet Emanuel, patent harp ma. 20 Charles st. Middsx. hosp
Serrell Dalton Haskoll, solicitor, 3 South sq. Gray's inn
Serrell Frances (Mrs.), milliner, 55 Poland st
Servant Saml. gilder & picture frame ma. 7 Leather lane
Servante Samuel, furnishg. undertaker, 232 High Holborn
Servants' Institution (Geo. Webb, hon. sec.), 42 Gt. Maryleb. st
Servants' Registry Office, 110 Hatton garden
Sessions House for Middlesex (Charles Wright, keeper), Clerkenwell green; hours 9 to 8
Sessions House, Old Bailey; hours 10 to 5
Sessions House for Surrey, Newington causeway
Sessions House for Tower Liberty, 33 Wellclose square
Sessions Ho. for Westminster, New Court House, Guildhall
Sessions Wm. stationer, 2 Charles st. Manchester sq
Sesston George, grocer, Clapham rise, north side
Setchel John Fredk. bookseller, 23 King st. Covent garden
Seton & Nicholson, attorneys, 12 George st. Adelphi
Setzer Charles, pork butcher, 127 Hoxton Old town
Sevecke Mary (Miss), ladies' school, 6 Windsor ter. Maida hill
Sevel James, fruiterer, 8 Motcomb st. Belgrave sq
Severn John Percy, barrister, 2 Inner Temple lane
Severn Joseph, historical painter, 21 James st. Buckinghm. gt
Severn Thos. H. professor of music, 2 Bury pl. Bloomsbury
Severn William, optician, 1 Walbrook pl. Hoxton New town
Severne Chas. proctor & notary, 2 Godliman st. Doctrs.' com
Severs Thomas, blackwell hall factor, 18 Basinghall st
Sevett Wm. Christopher, coffee rooms, 82 Whitechapel rd
Seward Henry, bed & mattress maker, 15 Blackman st. Boro'
Seward John (Mrs.), ladies' school, 60 Brompton sq
Sewell Benjamin & Sons, merchs. 1 Chatham pl. Blackfriars
Sewell, Evans, Hubbard & Bacon, silk mercers & linendrapers, 44 & 45 Old Compton st. & 46 & 47 Frith st. Soho
Sewell, Daun & Co. distlrs. & wine mers. 28 & 215 Up. Thames st
Sewell & Hyatt, ladies' school, 4 Up. Cheyne row, Chelsea
Sewell John & Son, importers of french, german & italian manufacturers, 49 Fore st. Cripplegate, & 123 London wall
Sewell & Nash, wholesale grocers, 40 King William st. City
Sewell, Norman & Sewell, merchs. 1 Chatham pl. Blackfrs
Sewell Sarah & Mary A. fancy rpstry. 3 Northmptn. pl O. Kent rd
Sewell & Son, tailors, 5 Hawthorndean pl. Comrcl. rd. Limeho
Sewell Charles, plumber, 18 Winchester row, New rd
Sewell Charles, seed & hop mers. 13 Three Crowns sq. Boro'
Sewell Charles Brodie, M.D. surgeon, 27 Walbrook
Sewell Clara (Mrs.), furniture broker, 47 Gray's inn lane
Sewell Edward, hairdresser, 110 High st. Camden town
Sewell Edward, hat & army cap maker, 40 Old Bond st
Sewell Edward, *Ship & Pilot* P H. 27 Wapping
Sewell Fredk. Jsph. veterinary surgeon, Eaton row, Eaton sq
Sewell Geo. carpenter & builder, 18 Winchester row, New rd
Sewell George, distiller, see Holme, Wilson, Sewell & Co
Sewell George Edward, builder, &c. 20 Lisson grove north
Sewell Henry, solr. 13 Gray's inn sq. & Newport (I. of Wight)
Sewell Isaac, solicitor, see Amory, Sewell & Moores
Sewell John, builder, 7½ Church st. Paddington
Sewell John, corn dealer, 65 Brewer st Somers town
Sewell John, furniture brkr. 2 Rockingham pl. New Kent rd
Sewell John, plumber, &c. 8 Charterhouse sq. & 57 Aldersgate st
Sewell John, surgeon, 59 Lambeth Lower marsh

Sewell John, tailor, 2 Queen st. Ratcliff
Sewell Joseph, grocer, 47 Upper Seymour st. Euston sq
Sewell Joseph, veterinary surgeon, 10 Water st. & 313 Strand, & 58 Wych st
Sewell Margaret (Mrs.), lodging house, 57 Aldersgate st
Sewell Mary (Mrs.), grocer, 34 Wapping High st
Sewell Richard, confectioner, 6 Tichborne st. Haymarket
Sewell Robert, pork butcher, 18 Up. York st. Bryanstone sq
Sewell Thomas, hairdresser, Ferry road west, Poplar
Sewell Thomas, shoemaker, 17 Rochester row, Westminster
Sewell Wm. butcher, 3 High st. Portland town
Sewell Wm. cowkeeper, 37 Gt. James st. Hoxton
Sewell Wm. livery stables, Princes row, Pimlico
Sewell Wm. stationer, 5 Waterloo pl. Commercial road east
Sewell Wm. tailor, 14 Baldwin st. City road
Sewell Wm. wheelwright & smith, 124 Praed st. Edgware rd
Sewell Wm. B. merchant, 9 Mincing lane
Sewell Wm. Geo. *Three Compasses* P.H. 6 White Hart st. Drury lane
SEWERS:—of the Metropolis & Environs—Offices for:—
Holborn & Finsbury (Messrs. Stable & Lush, clerks), Court House, 7 Hatton garden; hours 10 to 4
London, City of (Joseph Daw, principal clerk), Guildhall; hours 10 to 4
Poplar & Blackwall (William Baker, jun. clerk), 4 Albion terrace, Limehouse; hours 9 to 4
Regent street (Wm. Adams), Office of Woods, Whitehall place; hours 10 to 4
St. Katherine's, near the Tower (John Virgo, clerk), 34 Essex st. Strand; hours 10 to 4
Surrey & Kent (Beria Drew, clerk), 185 Bermondsey st.; hours 10 to 8
Tower Hamlets (John Wm. Unwin, clerk), office 15 Great Alie st.; hours 11 to 3
Westminster & part of Middlesex (Lewis Cooke Hertslet, clerk), Court house, 1 Greek st. Soho sq.; hrs. 9 to 4
Sewers Ann (Miss), milliner, 11 Princes st. Hanover square
Sex Edward, stockbroker, 3 Bartholomew lane, Bank
Sex George, job master, 24 & 25 Stonecutter st. Farringdon st
Sexton (Misses), milliners, 3 Clifton pl. Wandsworth road
Sexton & Warren, tea dealers, &c. 5 High st. Newington butts
Sexton George, carver, 81 Berwick st. Soho
Sexton Humphrey, silk reel mfr. 12 New Gloucester st. Hoxtn
Sexton Mary Ann (Mrs.), brace & belt manufac. 130 Fetter la
Sexton Richard, appraiser & furniture brok. 21 Old st. St. Luke's
Sexton Sarah (Miss), dressmaker, 55 Hoxton square
Sexton Sarah (Mrs.), carver, 9 Up. Charlton st. Fitzroy sq
Sexton Thomas, furniture broker, 36 Chalcroft ter. New cut
Sexton William, tobacconist, 164 Bermondsey st
Seyd William & Co. general agents, 32 Bucklersbury
Seyfang Charles, pork butcher, 66 Hatfield st. Stamford st
Seyfang Christopher Frederick, printer, 57 Farringdon st
Seyffert George, curiosity dealer, 77 Wardour st. Soho
Seyfried Ann (Mrs.), poulterer, 19 Sidney pl. Coml. rd. east
Seyler & Co. merchants, 36 St. Mary at hill
Seymour Edmd. & Jas. engravers & enamellers, 40 Gerard st
Seymour William & Son, gold & silver beaters & bronze powder manufacturers, 38 Long acre
Seymour William & Sons, merchants, 24 Lime st
Seymour Ann (Mrs.), milliner & dressma. 1 Brompton road
Seymour Chas. ironmonger, 1 St. James's walk, Clerkenwell
Seymour Edward, potato salesman, 40 York road, Lambeth
Seymour Edward J. physician, 13 Charles st. Berkeley sq
Seymour Edward Thomas, *Old Hicks* P.H. 55 King st. Soho
Seymour Eliza (Miss), tobacconist, 14 Newington causeway
Seymour Francis, butcher, 125 Jermyn st. St. James's
Seymour James S. twine & shoe thread mfr. 24 Pudding la
Seymour John, saddler, 3 Hosier lane, Smithfield
Seymour William, bootmaker, 8 Bermondsey new road
Seymour William, builder, 7 Upper Church st. Chelsea
Seymour William, stone mason, 91 Kingsland road
Seymour William Digby, merchant, 32 Fenchurch st
Seyssel Asphalte Company, "Claridge's Patent" (John Farrell, sec.), 15 Stangate, Lambeth
Shaboe George, cork cutter, 3½ Well st. Wellclose square
Shackel Edward, teadealer, 73 Mark lane
Shackel Frederick, livery stable keeper, 233 Oxford st
Shackel William, bacon merchant, 2 Canning pl. Old st
Shackell & Lyons, printing ink ms. 35 Coppice row, Clrknw
Shackell William, coal dealer, 64 Ernest st. Regent's park
Shackelton C. & Co. wax & tallow chandler to her Majesty, 15 Poland st. Oxford st
Shackleton John, rag & phial dlr. 50 Carnaby st. Golden sq
Shadbolt Chas. jun. & Co. mahogany merchts. 2 Lime st. sq
Shadbolt George, ostrich feather merchant, & funeral feather warehouse, 9 Walbrook, & 15 Church st. Soho
Shaddocks George, academy, 7 King's row, Walworth road
Shade George, engraver & printer, 76 Charlotte st. Fitzroy sq
Shadford George, cabinet ma. 14 Club row, Bethnal green
Shadforth John B. upholsterer, 7 Seymour pl. Bryanstone sq
Shadrack Philip, butcher, 44 Seymour pl. Bryanstone sq
Shadrake Thomas, *Green Man* P.H. 27 Poplar High st
Shadrake Thomas, *Prince of Wales* P.H. Naval row, Blackwall
Shadwell Caley, barrister, Serle's chambers, 4 Carey st
Shadwell Charles, solicitor, 4 South square, Gray's inn
Shadwell Lancelot, barrister, 4 Old square, Lincoln's inn
Shadwell Louis Henrie, spec. pleader, 3 K. Bench wk. Temple
Shadwell Thomas M. secretary to the trustees of the Royal Harbour of Ramsgate, 22 Austinfriars
Shafe James, tobacconist, 52 Bishopsgate within
Shafe John, tin plate worker, 4 Stepney rents, Hackney rd
Shailer Henry, nursery & seedsman, & nursery appraiser, Battersea fields
Shailer Wm. tobacconist, 22 Royal Hospital row, Chelsea
Shain John W. *Old Kg. John's Hd.* P.H. 49 Mansfield st. Kgsl. rd
Shakel Edward, carriers' agent & booking office, 69 Old Bailey
Shakel James, dining rooms, 3 Church st. Deptford
Shakeshaft Ann (Miss), milliner, 14 High Holborn
Shakeshaft Thomas, leather dresser, 18 Chalton st. Smrs. tn
Shakespeare Harriet (Miss), dressma. 38 High st. Marylebn
Shakespeare Hen. iron gas tube ma. 25 Gt. Mitchell st. St. Luk
Shakespeare Jane (Miss), dress & corset ma. 357 Oxford st
Shakspeare Wm. wire & tin pl. wa. see James & Shakspeare
Shalders Richd. builder, 18 Grosvenor st. Commercl. rd. east
Shalders Richd. *Grosvenor Arms* P.H. 18 Grosvenor st. Com. rd
Shales John, tailor, Stratford
Shales John, watch case maker, 42 York st. City road
Shales Sarah (Mrs.), tailor, Stratford broadway
Shallard Wm. & Ben. painters & gls. 70 Up. Seymour st. Eustn. sq
Shallard Marianne (Mrs.), grocer, 29 Robert st. Bedford row
Shallcross Robert, boot & shoema. 50 York road, Lambeth
Shallis James & Son, bleachers, 14 Bride ter. Liverpool rd
Shand Alexander, printer, 20 Peter st. Sun st. Bishopsgate
Shand Geo. Long, sail & tarpauling maker, see Laing & Shand
Shand Helen (Mrs.), baker, 21 Little Knightrider st
Shand Thos. hairdresser, 48 Marchmont st. Brunswick sq
Shand Wm. baker, 77 George st. Portman square
Shand Wm. patent artf. leg maker, 6 Buckingham st. Strand
Shands Margaret (Mrs.), baker, 32 Old Change
Shands Thomas, coachmaker, 12 Pump row, Old st. road
Shankey James, teadealer, &c. 43 Houndsditch
Shanks Ann (Mrs.), leather seller, 75 Bermondsey st
Shanks Robt. coach & harns. ma. 4, 70 & 71 Gt. Queen st. Linc. in. fi
Shankster Charles, poulterer, 21 North Audley st
Shankster Charles, tobacconist, 307 Oxford st
Shanley Francis, printer, 3 Morris pl. Southwark bridge rd
Shanly Francis, printer, 7 Red Cross square, Cripplegate
Shannaw Francis, door plate mnfr. 22 Sekforde st. Clknwl
Shannon Daniel, corn chandler, 1 Well st. Mile end New town
Shannon Esther (Miss), boarding ho. 24 Artillery pl. Finsbury
Shannon John, boot & shoe maker, 9 Lambeth Lower marsh
Shannon John, coffee rooms, 84 Church st. Shoreditch
Shannon Morris, sheriff's off. 2 Red lion passage, Red lion sq
Shapcott Chas. J. bootmaker, 8 Portugal st. Lincoln's inn
Shapcott Alexander, boot & shoemaker, 413 Oxford st
Shapland John, grocer, 9 Limehouse causeway
Shapland Joseph, barrister, 4 Pump court, Temple
Shapter Charles Rayner, *Feathers* P.H. Hungerford wharf
Shapter Henry Droyer, solicitor, 5 Verulam bldgs. Gray's inn
Shapter John, barrister, 8 New square, Lincoln's inn
Shardelow James, oil cloth ma. 33 Red Lion st. Spitalfields
Shareholder newspaper, 302 Strand
Sharland Thos. & Co. silk mercers, 39 Bishopsgate within
Sharland James, paper hanger, 17 Sale st. Paddington
Sharland Sarah (Miss), milliner, 57 Bishopsgate within
Sharman Alfred, beer retailer, 31 Strutton ground
Sharman John, carpntr. & undertakr. 29 Brooke st. Holborn
Sharman Thos. carpenter & undertaker, 136 Drummond st
Sharman Wm. shawl & parasol fringer, 135 London wall
Sharod Henry, bootmaker, 108 Kingsland road
Sharod Sarah (Mrs.), staymaker, 108 Kingsland road
Sharps' & Wilkins, bullion & jewel brokers, 31 Gt. Winchester st
Sharp Fred. & Co. fringe & lace manufacturers, 37 Wood st. & 5 Little Love lane
Sharp Geo. & Sml. stonemasons, 30 Commercial rd. Lambeth
Sharp James & John, slate merchants, slate masons, cistern manufs. & slaters, 181 Tooley st. & Stanton's lower wharf
Sharp John & Thomas, gunpowder makers, 8 Birchin lane, Cornhill, & Guildford
Sharp, Sturt & Co. warehousemen, see Ward, Sturt & Sharp
Sharp & Whitbourn, millers, 8 Birchin lane; & at Barking
Sharp & Wright, law stationers, 7 Cursitor st. Chancery lane

Sharp Allen, greengrocer, 29 Gt. James st. Lisson grove
Sharp Andrew, bootmaker, 12 Great Winchester st
Sharp Benj. *North Briton* P.H. Bedford square east
Sharp Chas. saddle & harns. ma. 4 Blenheim ter. Bond st. Chels
Sharp Clement, auctioneer & accountant, 35 Abchurch lane
Sharp Colin, muslin manufacturer, see Brown, Sharps & Co
Sharp Daniel Thos. butcher, 65 Paddington st. Marylebone
Sharp David, rope & twine dealer, 14 White st. Bethnal gr
Sharp Edmund, solicitor, 2 Devonshire ter. High st. Marylb
Sharp Edw. bricklayer, 1 Bishop yd. Charles st. Grosvenor sq
Sharp George, beer retailer, 42 William st. Whitechapel
Sharp George, butcher, 51 Albany st. Regent's park
Sharp Geo. Jesse, tailor & draper, 16 Duke st. Tooley st
Sharp Harriet (Miss), lace dlr. 194 Sloane st. Knightsbridge
Sharp Henry, manchester warehouse, 49 Aldermanbury
Sharp Henry, tallow melter, 6 Deptford High st
Sharp Henry, watch finisher, 16 Brewer st. North, Goswell rd
Sharp Henry Lockyer, surgeon, 39 Porchester ter. Bayswater
Sharp James, coal merchant, Oak lane, Limehouse
Sharp James, coal mer. & carman, Risbies rope wf. Limeho
Sharp James, confectioner, 54 Broad st. Bloomsbury
Sharp James, muslin manufactr. see Brown, Sharps & Co
Sharp James, shawl cleaner, 6 Haberdashers' pl. west, Hoxtn
Sharp James, surgeon, 21 Grosvenor st. west, Pimlico
Sharp Joseph, pawnbroker, Broadway, Deptford
Sharp John, printer, 30 Kent st. Borough
Sharp John, tailor, 8 Gt. Vine st. Regent st
Sharp John, tailor, 18 Green st. Bethnal green
Sharp John, tobacconist, 71 Paradise row, Chelsea
Sharp John Geo. window glass cutter, 21 Bermondsey new rd
Sharp Joseph, boot & shoe ma. 25 Henrietta st. Covent gar
Sharp Joseph, butcher, 194 Hoxton Old town
Sharp Joseph, currier, Gun alley, & 4 Russell st. Bermondsey
Sharp Josiah, deputy warden, Goldsmiths' hall, Foster la
Sharp Mary (Mrs.), librarian, bookseller, &c. 4 Berkeley sq
Sharp Philip H. butcher, 3 Portugal pl. Cambridge rd. Mile end
Sharp Richd. bricklayer, Cock yd. Davies st. Berkeley sq
Sharp Robert, bootmaker, 192 Church st. Shoreditch
Sharp Samuel, bricklayer, 9 Gt. James st. Lisson gro. north
Sharp Samuel, optician, 16 Church row, Pancras road
Sharp Samuel, solicitor, 37 Ely place, Holborn
Sharp Stephen, baker, 27 Chalton st. Somers town
Sharp Thomas, baker & corn dealer, Well st. Hackney
Sharp Thomas, carpenter, 1 Sussex pl. Kensington New town
Sharp Thomas, indigo blue maker, 96 Newgate st
Sharp Thomas, tailor, 120 Bethnal green road
Sharp Thomas S. glass cutter, 8 York st. Blackfriars road
Sharp Timothy, statuary & mason, 13 St. Clement's la. Strand
Sharp William, blackwell hall factor, 17 Basinghall st
Sharp William, carpenter, 24 Titchborne st. Edgware rd
Sharp William, coal merchant, see Smith & Sharp
Sharp William, gunmaker, 7 Little Alie st. Goodman's fields
Sharp William, jeweller, see Wright & Sharp
Sharp William, solicitor, 2 Verulam buildings, Gray's inn
Sharp William, tailor, 48 George st. Portman square
Sharp William, tobacconist & perfumer, 2 Gt. Russell st. By
Sharp William Thomas, bookseller, 97 Upper st Islingston
Sharpe Anna (Mrs.) & Co. haircutters, &c. 65 Haymarket
Sharpe, Field & Jackson, solicitors, 41 Bedford row
Sharpe Henry & Daniel, merchants, 26 Broad st. buildings
Sharpe Jas. & Son, sashma. & glaziers, 30 White Lion st. Spitalfl
Sharpe John & Richd. table knife manuf. 5 Gough sq. Fleet st
Sharpe John & Son, orange merchants, 114 Lower Thames st
Sharpe Joseph & Sons, glass & lamp manfctrs. 59 Old bailey
Sharpe Richard S. & Son, teadealers, &c. 56 Fenchurch st
Sharpe Alfred, booksel. & engraver, 17 St. Martin's ct. Les'tr. sq
Sharpe Edward, dairyman, 30 Bear lane, Blackfriars road
Sharpe Eliz. (Mrs.), linendr. 3 Leicester pl. Camberwell Nw. rd
Sharpe Geo. Young, chemist, &c. 9 Glos'ter pl. Islington green
Sharpe Henry, plumber & glazier, 10 Old Compton st. Soho
Sharpe Henry, teadealer & grocer, 44 Bishopsgate within
Sharpe James, glass & bottle mercht. see Pasley & Sharpe
Sharpe James Sybery, grocer, 34 Green st. Stepney
Sharpe John, trunk & portmanteau ma. 60 Borough High st
Sharpe Joseph, greengrocer, 119 Wardour st. Soho
Sharpe Joseph, notary, Faculty Office, 10 Gt. Knightrider st
Sharpe Richard, cutler, 4 Gough square
Sharpe Robert, commercial & genl. agent, 23 Budge row, City
Sharpe Robert, iron steel & tin plate mer. 23 Budge row, City
Sharpe Thomas, tailor & outfitter, 136 Whitechapel High st
Sharpe Thomas, grocer, &c. 1 Titchfield st. Dean st. Soho
Sharpe Thomas B. bookselr. & statr. 15 Skinner st. Snowhl
Sharpe Wm. coalmercht. New Bargehouse whf. Coml. rd. Lmbth
Sharpe William, grocer, see Clarkson & Sharpe
Sharpe William, stockbroker, 1 Bank chambers, Lothbury
Sharpe Wm. stockbroker, 1 Prospect pl. Cheyne wlk. Chelsea
Sharpe William Edward, solicitor, 2 Gt. Knightrider st
Sharpe Wm. Prentice, staymak. 36 John st. Holland st. Blkfrs
Sharpen John, coffee rooms, 3 Lit. May's bldgs. Bedfordbury
Sharpey Wm. physician, 35 Glo'ster crescent, Regent's pk
Sharpin Wm. Robert, hotel keeper, see Tyssen & Sharpin
Sharpless Thomas. *King's Arms* P.H. 42 Sclater st. Bethnal gr
Sharpus & Cullum, china & glass manfrs. 13 Cockspur st
Sharpus Fredk. W. tin plate worker, see Perkins & Sharpus
Sharratt & Newth, glaziers' patent diamond & lead vice manufacturers, 44 Perceval st. Clerkenwell
Sharwood Edward, wine merchant, 48 Lime st
Sharwood James Allen, druggist, 55 Bishopsgate without, & 98 Fenchurch st
Sharwood Langton, architect & surveyor, 16 Furnivals inn
Sharwood Sam. pawnbkr. & jeweller, 105 & 106 St. John st. rd.
Sharwoods Sam. & Ths. typefounders, &c. see Wood & Sharwoods
Shattock George Fredk. *Wheatsheaf* P.H. 359 Rotherhithe
Shattock James, boot & shoe maker, 115 Tottenham court rd
Shattock William, butcher, 9 Diddington pl. Caledonian rd
Shave Charles, *Turk's Head* P.H. 20 Bird st. Wapping
Shave David, furnit. broker, 1 Fieldgate st. Whitechapel rd
Shave Jehu, winemer. 4 Smith's bdgs. Mansell st. Goodman's flds
Shave John, cook & confectioner, 51 Curzon st. Mayfair
Shave William, *White Horse* P.H. 21 Finsbury st. Finsbury
Shaw & Attridge, tea agents, 18 Little Tower st
Shaw & Caffary, merchants, 12 St. Helen's pl. Bishopsgate
Shaw & Day, copper plate printers, 9 Robert st. Bedford row
Shaw & Dowling, army clothiers, 3 Streatham st. Blomsby
Shaw Francis & Co. cabinet ma. 21 & 22 Shoreditch High st
Shaw Jane & Co. biscuit bakers, 225 Borough High st
Shaw John & Sons, bookslrs. print. & publ. 136 to 138 Fetter la
Shaw, Maxwell & Co. wine merchants, 7 Salisbury st. Strand
Shaw & Newstead, solicitors, 18 Ely place, Holborn
Shaw Thos. Sant & Co. canal carriers, Bull whf. Queenhithe
Shaw Alexander, cloth worker, presser, packer, waterproof, & drill shrinker, 18 Little Portland st. Gt. Portland st
Shaw Alexander, furn. broker, 27 Strutton ground, Wstmr
Shaw Alexander, surgeon, 23 Henrietta st. Cavendish sq
Shaw Andrew, baker, 10 Webb st. Bermondsey st
Shaw Ann (Mrs.), tailor, 96 Bermondsey st
Shaw Anthony, coal dealer, 11 Bloomsbury market
Shaw Benjamin, engraver, 79 King William st. City
Shaw Benjamin, painter & glazier, 16 Abchurch lane, City
Shaw Catherine (Miss), seminary, 43 Bedford pl. Kensingtn
Shaw Charles, attorney, 47 Fish st. hill
Shaw Charles, baker, 18 Charles st. Horselydown
Shaw Charles, silversmith & plater, 5 Hind ct. Fleet st
Shaw Charles, stockbroker, see Marsden & Shaw
Shaw Chas. Alfred, vellum binder, 13A, Serle's pl. Linc. inn
Shaw Dorothy (Mrs.) grocer, 27 Esher st. Up. Kennington la
Shaw Duncan, bread & biscuit baker, 2 Clare hall, Stpny. gr
Shaw Elizabeth (Mrs), glaziers' diamond ma. 82 Goswell rd
Shaw Edmund, export stationer & paper mr. 124 Fenchurch st
Shaw Fras. (Mrs.), *Waggon & Horses* P.H. Hertfrd. rd. Kgsld. rd
Shaw Francis, linen & carpet wareh. 92 Bishopsgate without
Shaw Frederick, carpenter & builder, 60 London wall
Shaw George, boot & shoe maker, 33 John st. west, Edgw. rd
Shaw George, hosier, 19 Windmill st. Finsbury sq.
Shaw George, surgeon, King st. Battersea
Shaw George John, solicitor, 8 Furnival's inn
Shaw George Ledger, solicitor, see Reed & Shaw
Shaw Harriet (Mrs.), chandler's shop, 3 Barnet st. Hackney rd
Shaw Henry, agent to Messrs. Gammon & Son, Belmont glass works, Birmingham, 2 Gerrard st. Islington
Shaw Henry, artist, 37 Southampton row, Bloomsbury
Shaw Henry, boot & shoe maker, 253 Poplar High st
Shaw Henry, commission agent, 2 Gerrard st. Islington
Shaw Henry, surgeon & chemist, 142 Bishopsgate without
Shaw James, commission agent, 19 Cheapside
Shaw James, cowkeeper, 11 Wells st. Oxford st
Shaw James, *Jacob's Well* P.H. 1 Jacob's well pas. Barbican
Shaw James, *Queen's Arms* P.H. Spa road, Bermondsey
Shaw James, whosesale stationer & printer, 41 Tooley st. & 180 Tottenham court road
Shaw Jas. Veitch, law stationer, 3 Gt. Knightrider st. Doc. com
Shaw John, architect, 23 Montague st. Russell square, & Christ's hospital
Shaw John, attorney, 85 Queen st. Cheapside
Shaw John, builder, 39 Cardington st. Hampstead road
Shaw John, coach builder, Vine yard, 100 Aldersgate st
Shaw John, dining rooms, 113 Drury lane
Shaw John, engraver, 78 Cornhill
Shaw John, hairdresser, &c. 6 Cardigan pl. Kennington cross
Shaw John, horse dealer, 5 Osnaburgh st. Regent's park
Shaw John, lighterman, see Lucas, Pope & Shaw
Shaw John, *Mitre* P.H. 14 Duke st. & 242 Tooley st

Shaw John, solicitor, see Bailey, Shaw & Smith
Shaw John, undertaker, 24 Gloucester st. Commercial rd. ea
Shaw John, yeast manufr. 21 Cannon st. rd. St. George's ea
Shaw John F. bookseller, &c. 27 Southampton rw. Russell sq
Shaw Joseph, baker, 7 Coburgh place, Up. Kennington lane
Shaw Joseph, cheesemonger, 198 Bermondsey st
Shaw Joseph, earthenware dealer, 18 Chapel st. Edgware rd
Shaw Joseph P. upholsterer & ho. agt. 47 Mortimer st. Cavn. sq
Shaw Richard, army, navy, livery & foreign button manufacturer, 11 Opera arcade, Pall mall
Shaw Richd. linen & carpet warehouse, 201 Borough High st
Shaw Robert, boot & shoemaker, 62 Lisson grove north
Shaw Robert, prop. of Gowland's lotion, 137 Fetter lane
Shaw Robert, *Tower* P.H. 10 Gilbert's bldgs. Westminster rd
Shaw Robert Benjamin, printer, 2 Cornbury pl. Old Kent rd
Shaw Rowland Pritchard, teadealer, 68 Holborn hill
Shaw Sarah (Mrs.), tobacconist, Church st. Hackney
Shaw Silvester, cop. plate printer, 46 Gower pl. Euston sq
Shaw Stephen, bookbinder, 22 Old Boswell court, Carey st
Shaw Susannah (Mrs.), bread, &c. baker, 50 Charles st. Wstm
Shaw Thomas, carpenter, 23 Plumber st. City road
Shaw Thomas, builder, 39 Southampton mews, Euston sq
Shaw Thomas, linendraper & carpet wareho. 239 & 240 Boro'
Shaw Wm. army clothier, see Dickey, Shaw & Co
Shaw Wm. builder, 39 Cardington st. Hampstead road
Shaw Wm. furniture broker, 1 Castle st. Long acre
Shaw Wm. harness maker, 12 Adam st. west, Bryanstone sq
Shaw Wm pewterer, 17 King st. Borough
Shaw Wm. jun. fur. ironmonger, 39 Newington causeway
Shaw Wm. sen. who. furnish. ironmonger, 253 Blackfriars rd
Shaw Wm. Robert, coach, harness & shoe currier, leather dresser & seller, Wild's rents, Long lane, Bermondsey
Shayer Isaac, tailor, 86½ Berwick st. Soho
Shayer Wm. hosier, glover & gen. outfitter, 229 Piccadilly
Shayler James, furrier, 35 Whiskin st. Clerkenwell
Shayler James, fur & skin dyer, 21 Little Saffron hill
Shaylor George, tailor, &c. 29 Norton st. Fitzroy square
Shaylor John, tailor, 19 Bear yard, Lincoln's inn fields
Shea John, surgeon, 33 Gt. Charlotte st. Blackfriars rd
Shea John, woollen warehouseman, 59 Aldermanbury
Shead Elizh. (Miss), & Co. fancy biscuit bakers, 114 Cheapside
Shead William, egg merchant, 1 & 2 Claremont st. Hackney rd
Sheader Joseph, sailmaker, &c. see Frost & Sheader
Sheaf Stephen, hairdresser, 33 Tufton st. Westminster
Shean Wm. baker, 85 Bermondsey st
Shear Andrew & Nephew, tailors, 31 Craven st. Strand
Sheard Henry, tailor, draper & outfitter, 166 Strand
Sheard Wm. Luke, tea & coffee dlr. 8 Glos'ter pl. Old Kent rd
Sheard Wm. Luke, grocer, 6 Queen's bldgs. Knightsbridge
Shearer James, watchmaker, 2 Wakefield st. Brunswick sq
Shearing Richard, decorative house painter, paper hanger, plumber, glazier & undertaker, 12 Rupert st. Haymarket
Shearing Robert, agent to Wilders & Co. ale & porter merchants, 16 Laurence Pountney lane
Shearing Samuel, working jeweller, 43 Berwick st. Soho
Shearman & Day, carpenters, 4 Prospect pl. Kingsland rd
Shearman & Evans, solicitors, 2 Gray's inn square
Shearman John Hen. & Co. merchants & agts. 11 Clement's la
Shearman & Slater, solicitors, 23 Great Tower st
Shearman Ann (Mrs.), building material & shop fixture dealer, 126 Curtain road, Shoreditch
Shearman Edward, booking office, 122 Oxford st
Shearman John, baby linen warehouse, 5 Finsbury pavem
Shearman Montague, solicitor, 1 Trinity pl. Charing cross
Shearman Thos. bootmaker, 27 King st. Seven dials
Shearman Wm. carpenter, 2 York ter. Camberwell new road
Shearman Wm. physician, 30 Northampton sq. Clerkenwell
Shearmur Jas. pill box maker, 18 Newcastle st. Farringdon st
Shearmur Thos. grocer, 11 Amelia st. Walworth road
Shears James & Sons, copper merchants & dealers in Muntz's patent yellow metal sheating, 27 Bankside
Shears James & Sons, coppersmiths, brass & bell founders & pewter worm makers, 27 Bankside
Shears James & Sons, engineers & manufactures of vacuum pans & apparatus for sugar works & refineries, 27 Bankside
Shears David, beer retailer, 17 Featherstone st. City road
Shears Samuel, smith & bell hanger, 6 Hoxton Old town
Shears Ambrose, boot & shoe maker 5 Edward's st. Portman sq
Shearsmith Robert, watchmaker, 26 Brydges st. Covent grdn
Shearwood George, east india mercht. 1 Riches ct. Lime st
Sheasby John, baker, 6 Henry st. St. Luke's
Sheasby Wm. hairdresser, 4 Green walk, Blackfriars road
Sheath Wm. linendraper, &c. see King & Sheath
Shebbeare Charles John, barrister, 5 New sq. Lincoln's inn
Shedden Robert & Sons, merchants, 6 Bedford square
Shedden Wm. Geo. merchant, see Hawthorn & Shedden
Shee Martin Archer, barrister, 63 Chancery lane
Shee Wm. serjeant-at-law, 2 Serjeants' inn, Chancery lane
Sheehan Fred. *Hoop & Grapes* P.H. 29 Cross st. Hatton gdn
Sheehan John, barrister, 4 Hare court, Temple
Sheel Robert, teadealer, 36 Wilsted st. Somers town
Shee Thos. grocer, 18½ Skinner st. Somers town
Sheen & Paul, potato salesmen, Cotton's wharf, Tooley st
Sheen Abram. *Feathers* P.H. 1 High Timber st. Up. Thames st
Sheen Ann (Mrs.), tobacconist, Southampton st. Camberwll
Sheen James Richard, chemist, &c. 4 New Bridge st. Vauxhall
Sheen Meshack, potato salesman, 3 Chapel pl. Long la. Brmsy
Sheen Oliphant S. gas lantern ma. & fitter, 91½ Holborn hill
Sheen Samuel, undertaker, 13 Church lane, Commercial rd
Sheerman John, *Cooper's Arms* P.H 25 Trinity sq. Tower hill
Sheerman John, grocer & teadealer, 15 Goodge st. Fitzroy sq
Sheerman William, picture liner, 144 Waterloo road
Sheffield Hen. & Edwd. timber mer. 12 Church la. Whitechapl
Sheffield & Hurrell, potato salesmen, 10 & 11 Union st. east, Spitalfields; 75 Farringdon market, & Cotton's wharf, Tooley st
Sheffield Isaac & Wm. solicitors, 63 Old Broad st
Sheffield & Maughan, imprs. of wines & spirits, 12 Old Fish st
Sheffield, Nottingham & London Direct Railway Co. (Henry Frederic Alston, sec.), 1 Moorgate
Sheffield Benj. bookbinder & stationer, 46 Banner st. St. Luke's
Sheffield Edmund, timber mercht. 3 New rd. St. George's east
Sheffield Henry, coal merchant, see Patient & Sheffield
Sheffield Isaac, dentist, 12 Wigmore st
Sheffield John, barrister, 23 Old square, Lincoln's inn
Sheffield John, smith, Old Ford
Sheffield John, tea dealer, 67 Whitechapel road
Sheffield Joseph James, ironmonger, 183 Ratcliff highway
Sheffield Thos. timber mer. see Cheswright, Sheffield & Co
Sheffield William, tobacconist, 59 Gt. Sutton st. Clerkenwell
Sheil James, organ builder, 20 Seymour crescent, Euston sq
Sheilds Joseph, tailor, 43 Aldenham st. Somers town
Sheilds Mark, clothes salesman, 13 Charlton st. Fitzroy sq
Sheill Charles, tailor, 18 Arundel st. Haymarket
Shelbourne William, *Blue Posts* P.H. 1 St. Ann's place, West India dock road
Shelbourne Wm. *Blue Posts* P.H. Commercl. rd. Limehouse
Shelden John, butcher & pork butcher, 5 North st. Whtchpl. rd
Sheldon David, fruiterer, 10 Steyman's row, Holloway road
Sheldon Edwd. jun. customho. & shipping agt. 19 Fenchurch st
Sheldon Henry, baker & grocer, 5 Little Grosvenor st
Sheldon James, merchant, 72 Old Broad st
Sheldon James, hairdresser, 139 St. John st. road
Sheldon John, oil & colorman, 10 Smithfield bars
Sheldon John, chemist & dentist, 72 Euston square
Sheldon Joseph, fruiterer, 1 White Lion st. Pentonville
Sheldrake, Bigg & Co. anatomical machinists, 29 Leicester sq
Sheldrick Bennett & Geo. builders, 3 Dalston ter. Dalston
Sheldrick, Dawson & Lockwood, fustian, velvet, &c. manufacturers (H. J. Collett, agent), 39 Friday st
Sheldrick James, chandler's shop, 2 Tyssen place, Dalston
Sheldrick Richard Henry, baker, 4 Howard's pl. Hackney rd
Sheldrick Thomas, tailor, 20 High st. Portland town
Sheldricke James, timb. mercht. & lightm. 27 Low. Shadwell
Shelford Leonard, barrister, 3 Brick court, Temple
Shell Frederick, hairdresser, 130 Goswell road
Shellard Henry William, chemist & druggist, 235 Strand
Shellard Joseph, tailor, 41 Stafford place, Pimlico
Shelley Charles, wheelwright, Church st. Camberwell
Shelley Joseph, leather dyer & seller, 101 Shoe lane, Fleet st
Shelley Robt. smith & farrier, 4 Tenter st. Little Moorfields
Shelley Thomas, tailor, 29 Redcross square, Cripplegate
Shelmerdine John, grocer, 22 Castle ct. Fulwd's. rents, Holbn
Shelton James, butcher, 86 Shoreditch
Shelton Job, cattle salesman, 17 West Smithfield
Shelton Richard, plumber & glazier, 8 Draycott st. Chelsea
Shenston James T. scale, weighing machine, mill & enamel weight manufacturer to her Majesty, 395 Strand
Shenton Edwd. & Wm. livery stables, 18 Green st. Grosv. sq
Shenton John, livery stables, William mews, Adam st. west
Shenton John, plumber & glazr. 2 Wynyatt st. Goswell road
Shenton Thomas, grocer, 255 Bethnal green road
Shenton Wm. beer retailer, St. John's hill, Walworth
Sheowring Wm. Hen. rug ma. 6 Gt. Cambridge st. Hackney rd
Shepard John, butcher, 7 Limehouse causeway
Shepard John, seedsman & florist, see Turner & Shepard
Shepard Robert Howard, insur. brok. see Fenning & Shepard
Shepard Stephen, grocer, 37 Frederick pl. Hampstead road
Shepard Thos. shoemakr. 15 Purim pl. Cambridge rd. Mile end
Shepcutt John, cheesemonger, 2 Lower st. Islington
Shephard, Isherwood & Shephard, proctors, bishop of London's registry, 3 Godliman st. Doctors' commons

Shephard James & Sons, stationers,25Shoemaker row,Blkfrs
Shephard Mary & Co. brassfounders, 21 Hatton garden
Shephard Fred. auctioneer, 32 Up. York st. Bryanstone sq
Shephard Fred. glass warehouse, 1 Pierrepoint rw. Islngtn
Shephard Fred. printer, Milton pl. High st. Islington
Shephard George, oil & colorman, 15 Water st. Blackfriars
Shephard Jas. chemical glass stopperer, 11Summer st.Clrkw
Shephard Jas. Valentine, baker, 16 Aston pl. Holloway
Shephard Mary (Mrs.), dressmaker, 140 Drury lane
Shephard Mark, solicitor, see Kingdon & Shephard
Shephard Thomas, turner, 21 William st. St. George's east
Shepheard Charles, solicitor, see Finch & Shepheard
Shepheard Edward, ivory turner,31 Gt. Chart st. Hoxton
Shepheard Geo. hat mnfr. Bailey's bldgs. Pepper st. Boro'
Shepheard G. Wallwyn, artist, 34 Gt. James st. Bedford row
Shepheard Hughes John, pawn brk.16 Plumber's rw. Cty. rd
Shepheard Lewis Henry, artist, 100 Guildford st. Russell sq
Shepheard Ralph (Mrs.), straw hat manufactr.106 Oxford st
Shepheard Wm. butcher, 2 U. Gloster pl. King's rd.Chelsea
Shepheard Wm. coal agt. 21 whf. Paddington basin, n. side
Shepheard Wm. straw bonnet & hat maker, 110 Oxford st.
Shepherd & Co. roman cement manufacturers, Cousin lane, Up. Thames st. & Gt. Scotland yard, Westminster
Shepherd & Colman, hotpressers, 5 Red Lion ct. Fleet st
Shepherd Jane E. & C. (Misses), china dlrs. 5 Goodge st
Shepherd John & Co. white lead manufacturers, 52½ Great Guildford st. Borough & Love lane, Bankside
Shepherd & Sutton, pat. stereotype fndrs. 3 Earl st. Blkfrs
Shepherd Wm.&Co.breeches mkrs. & tailors,39So. Audley st
Shepherd Aaron, pianoforte maker,30Sloane square Chelsea
Shepherd Alex. Murray, haberdasher, 12 Deptford High st
Shepherd Ann (Mrs.), confectioner, 176 Fleet st
Shepherd Benjamin, coffee rooms, 19 James st. Covent grdn
Shepherd Caleb, china & glassman, 119 Whitechapel road; & at 3 & 4, Spectacle alley, Whitechapel
Shepherd Charles, chronom. & watchmkr. 53 Leadenhall st.
Shepherd Mrs. & Miss, ladies' school, 9 City ter. City rd
Shepherd Chas. hotpresser,30St.Martin's st.Leicester square
Shepherd Charles, painter & glazier, 3 Sloane square Chelsea
Shepherd Edw. timber merchant, Wenlock basin, City rd
Shepherd George, baker, 46 Kensington High st
Shepherd George, fruiterer,8 Church st. Cheyne wk.Chelsea
Shepherd George, *Hampshire Hog* P.H. 410 Strand
Shepherd George, ship smith, 6 Gedling st. Bermondsey
Shepherd Henry, working jeweller,34Davies st. Berkeley sq
Shepherd Isaac, livery stables, 54 Whitcomb st.Leicester sq
Shepherd James, baker, 132 Union st. Borough
Shepherd James, *Bell* P.H. 18 Cecil ct. St. Martin's lane
Shepherd Jas. *Fr. Horn & ½ Moon tav.* East hill,Wandswth
Shepherd James, glass grinder, 40 Ewer st. Union st. Boro'
Shepherd James, grocer, 9 John st. Limehouse fields
Shepherd James, medicated lozenge manfr. 12 Crane ct
Shepherd James, ship owner, 1 Lime st. square
Shepherd James, watch cap maker, 41 York st. St. Luke's
Shepherd Jane (Mrs.) coach prop. 15 Church st. Camberwell
Shepherd Jane (Mrs.), newsvender, 17 Carnaby st. Goldn.sq
Shepherd John, grocer, 113 Brook st. Ratcliff
Shepherd John, hairdresser, 4 Nowell's bldgs. Liverpool rd
Shepherd John, plumasier, 56 South Molton st
Shepherd John, plumber, 3 Cross lane, Long acre
Shepherd John, solicitor, see Wright, Smith & Shepherd
Shepherd John, trunk ma. & undertak.90 Bishopsgate within
Shepherd John, wood turner, 90 Gt. Titchfield st. Oxford st
Shepherd John, sen. watch cap maker, 15 King sq.Goswellrd
Shepherd John Anthy.*Sidney Arms*P.H.8Charles st.Stepney
Shepherd John Bax, architect & surv. 2 Tufnell pl. Islington
Shepherd John Henry, farrier, White Hart Inn yd. 62 Boro'
Shepherd Joseph, *Anchor* brewery, 9 Star corner, Bermndsy
Shepherd Joseph, boot & shoe ma.8 Chester st.Kenningtn. cr
Shepherd Joseph, grocer, 1 Baucroft's place, Mile end road
Shepherd Joseph, oil & colorman, 28 King st. Camden town
Shepherd Joseph, oil & colorman, 12 Rufford's bldgs. Islgtn
Shepherd Joseph, ship & ins. broker, see Lidgett & Shepherd
Shepherd Joseph,watch cap ma.9Presidentst. east,Goswell rd
Shepherd Meldrum, baker, 412 Oxford st
Shepherd Peter, baker & confectioner, 23Blackman st.Boro'
Shepherd Richard, cooper, St. James's place, Garlick hill
Shepherd Richard, *Surrey Coal Hole* P.H.123 Blackfriars rd
Shepherd Robt. trunk ma. & undert.8 Alfredpl. Newgtn.caus
Shepherd Sarah B.(Miss),straw hat ma.&millinr.37O.Bondst
Shepherd Samuel, cement manufacturer, Cousin lane wharf, Upper Thames st. & Great Scotland yard
Shepherd Samuel, printer, 9 Primrose st. Bishopsgate st
Shepherd Theophilus, chinaman,29 Guildford pl. Spafields
Shepherd Thomas, barrister, 6 New square, Lincoln's Inn
Shepherd Thomas butcher, Clare market
Shepherd Thos. silversmith & jewlr. 58 Conduit st. Regt. st
Shepherd Wm. cane worker, 13 Woodland st. Dalston
Shepherd Wm. china dlr. 4 Goldsmith's row, Hackney road
Shepherd Wm. coffee rooms, 11 Wallington pl. Wandswth.rd
Shepherd Wm. fruiterer, 23 Garden row, London road
Shepherd Wm. upholsterer, &c. 20 Moorgate st
Shepherd Wm. George, surgeon, 103 & 104 Goswell road
Shepherd Wm. Jas. watch cap maker, 53 Rahere st. Goswl.rd
Sheppard Ann & Co. birmingham, manchester, sheffield & staffordshire warehouse, & wholesale haberdashers, 132 Kent st. Borough, & 63 New Compton st. Soho
Sheppard Geo. Wm. B. & Geo. woollen manufacturers, 7 King st. Cheapside, & 27 Ironmonger lane
Sheppard & Son, stock brokers, 28 Threadneedle st
Sheppard Abraham jun. market gdnr.Jamaica level, Bmdsy
Sheppard Alfred B. solicitor, 18 Lincoln's inn fields
Sheppard Anthony, nursery&seedsmn,16Sherrard st.Gldn.sq
Sheppard Benj.carpent.& undertak. 3 Up. John st. Golden sq
Sheppard Charles, coal dealer, 11 Turnmill st. Clerkenwell
Sheppard Chas. Halford, barrister, 3 Plowden bldgs.Temple
Sheppard Edw.baker & corn dealer,28 Robinson's rw.Kigsld
Sheppard Edw. butcher, 106 Lambeth lower marsh
Sheppard Edw. Harmer, surgeon,4 Wyndham pl.Bryanst.sq
Sheppard Emma (Miss),ladies'shoema.3 Crown st.Wlwth.rd
Sheppard Frances(Mrs.),butcher, 5 Harp alley, Shoe lane
Sheppard Frederick Sampson Wm. solicitor, 22 Grosvenor st. & 24 Holywell st. Milbank
Sheppard Gabriel, plumber & glazier, 14 Bury st.Bloomsbv
Sheppard George, attorney, 15 Cook's court, Carey st
Sheppard Hen. brushmaker, 10 President st. west, King sq
Sheppard Henry, market gardener, Prosp.pl.Lower rd.Dpfd
Sheppard Henry, pork butcher, 94 High st. Camden town
Sheppard Henry Joseph, grocer, 7 Union ter. Notting hill
Sheppard James jun. cornfactor, see Coventry & Sheppard
Sheppard James, gas fitter, 13 Dorrington st. Leather lane
Sheppard James, whitesmith, 27 Goldsmith pl. Hackney rd
Sheppard John, fruiterer, 20 Colville ter. King's rd.Chelsea
Sheppard John, haberdasher, 2 Laurel pl. Queen's rd.Dalstn
Sheppard John, porkman, 98 Shoreditch
Sheppard John, wax chandler, 39 Maddox st. Regent st
Sheppard Maria (Mrs.), *King & Queen* P.H. 11 High st. Newington butts
Sheppard Mary (Mrs.), lodging house, 7 Arundel st. Strand
Sheppard Samuel, jeweller to the Queen & Royal Family,63 Brook st. Hanover sq. (late 17 Hanover st)
Sheppard Samuel tailor, 12 Tabernacle row, Finsbury
Sheppard Thomas, cheesemonger, 88 Borough High st
Sheppard Thomas, furn. broker, 6 Harp alley, Farringdon st
Sheppard Thomas, poulterer, 17 High st. Notting hill
Sheppard Thomas, tailor, 22 Grosvenor st. Grosvenor sq
Sheppard Thomas, tripe dealer, 66 Fetter lane
Sheppard Wm. butcher, Ring cross Holloway road
Sheppard Wm. carpenter, 3 Warwick square, Newgate st
Sheppard Wm. *King's Arms* P.H. Kennington road
Sheppard Wm. pork butcher, 18 Skinner st. Somerstown
Sheppard Wm. Hy.gasfitter & bell hanger, 10 Bucklersbury
Sheppeard John Helson, plasterer, 9 Vine st. York rd
Shepperd Alfred, fishmngr. 1 Bolingbroke rw. Walworth rd
Shepperd Francis, brazier, Albion pl. St. John's la.Clerknwl
Shepperd James, builder, 8 Cadogan terrace, Sloane st
Shepperd William,*King's Head*P.H.St.George'srow,Pimlico
Shepperson Job, soapmaker, 44 Baalzephon st. Bermondsey
Shepperson Matthew, artist, 19 Victoria road, Pimlico
Shepperson Thos. manch. & woollen warehmn. 27 Cheapside
Sheraton Thomas, artist, 4 Camberwell new road
Sherborn & Sams, oil & italian warehousemen, 173 Piccadilly
Sherborn Chas. upholder & undertkr. 10 King st. St. James's
Sherborn Edward, hosier & woollen draper, 185 Strand
Sherborn John, oil & colorman, 321 Oxford st
Sherborn Wm. gaiter & brace mak.65 Princes st. Leicester sq
Sherborne Francis, baker, 54 Gt. Peter st. Westminster
Sherburd William, linendraper, 2 Globe road, Mile end road
Sherer, Waugh & Co.wine & spirit merchants,3 St. Mary Axe
Sherer Charles, custom ho. agt. & lighterman, 12 Rood lane
Sherer Peter, pat. wig ma. 22 Cumberland st. Middlsx.hosp
Sherer Robt.sack&twine mfr.11 Broadway, St.Thomas',Boro
Shergold John, baker, 176 Hoxton Old town
Sheridan John, tin,iron &japan ware mfr.Cross st.Com.rd.ea
Sheriff of Essex Office, 2 Gresham pl. Lombard st.; hours, term 10 to 5, vacation 11 to 3, 10th Aug. to 24th Oct. 11 to 2
Sheriff of Kent Office, 24 Bedford row; hours of business, term 11 to 5, vacation 11 to 3, 10 Aug. to 24th Oct. 11 to 2
Sheriff of Middlesex Office, 24 Red Lion square; hours of business, term 11 to 5, vacation 11 to 3, from 10th Aug. to 24th Oct. 11 to 2
Sheriff of Surrey Office, 8 New Inn, Strand; hours, term

11 to 5, vacation 11 to 3, 10th Aug. to 24th Oct. 11 to 2
Sheriff Richard, carpenter, 6 Duke st. Lisson grove
Sheriff of Sussex Office, 24 Bedford row; term 11 to 5, vacation 10th Aug. to 24th Oct. 11 to 2
Sheriffs of London Office, 5 Basinghall st.; hours 10 to 7
Sheriffs Court Office (London), Whitecross street prison; hours of business 11 to 3 & 5 to 7
Sherley George, butcher, 4 Upper King st. Bloomsbury
Sherlock Thos. & Co. button manufact.15King st.Covent gdn
Sherlock Charles, butcher, 9 Queen st. Pimlico
Sherlock Mary Elizh. (Mrs.), milliner, 7 St. Mary at hill
Sherlock Thomas, brushmaker, 32 Rosoman st. Clerkenwell
Sherlock Thos. furniture broker, 15 Castle st. Long acre
Sherman Daniel, builder, &c. 1 Paradise rw. Bethnal green rd
Sherman Edward, *Bull & Mouth & General Post Office hotel*, St. Martin's le grand
Sherman Edward, *Oxford Arms inn*, Warwick lane
Sherman Elizth. (Mrs.), lighterman, 110 ShadThames, Sthwk
Sherman George, *Horns* P.H. 35 Bermondsey sq. Grange rd
Sherman John, carpenter, Mare st. Hackney
Sherman John, *Crown* P.H. 23 West st. West Smithfield
Sherman Michael, coffee rooms, 24 Crispin st. Spitalfields
Sherman Samuel, tailor & draper, 17 Earl st. Finsbury
Sherrard Richard, surgeon, 8 New Bond st
Sherrard & Hall, civil engineers, 2 Gt. George st. Westmr
Sherrard & Winterton, trimming ware. 240 Tottenham ct. rd
Sherrard Charlotte (Mrs.), prof. of music, 35 Eastst. Red lion sq
Sherrard Edward, tailor, 36 Hart st. Bloomsbury
Sherrard John, tailor & habit maker, 240 Tottenham ct. rd
Sherrard Joseph, tailor, 7 Southampton row, Russell square
Sherratt Thos. Hen. solicitor, 47 Mornington pl. Hmpstd. rd
Sherrell Jas. hairdresser, 2 Blenheim ter. Bond st. Chelsea
Sherren John, *Cock & Crown* P.H. 29 St. Andrew's hl. Drs'cmns
Sherrett Fredk. woollendraper, see Regless, Sherrett & Co
Sherriff Fredk. & Co. linendrprs. 6 Stockwell ter. Clapham rd
Sherriff Henry, straw hat maker, see Whiddington & Sherriff
Sherriff John, painter, 2 Castle st. Long acre
Sherriff John Wm. stationer & acct. book ma. 11 Ludgate st
Sherriff Wm. bricklayer, &c. 3 Chesnut row, Kentish town
Sherrin Christn. (Mrs.) & Co. plumasiers, 15 Church st. Soho
Sherrin Thos. artificial florist, 7 Printinghouse sq. Blackfrs
Sherrin Thos. butcher, 35 Duke st. Manchester square
Sherring Jas. harness mkr. 2 Church st. Cheyne wlk. Chlsa
Sherring Stephen John, furn. ironmonger, locksmith & bellhanger, 20 George st. & 42 Duke st. Grosvenor square
Sherrington Fras. confectioner, 45 Salisbury st. Lisson grove
Sherry Jas. grocer & italian wareho. 3 Sloane st. Knightsbg
Sherry John, leather seller & currier, 5 Clerkenwell green
Sherston Mary Ann (Mrs.), livery stables, 26 St. Martin's st. Leicester square; 23½ Whitcomb st.; & 68 Haymarket
Sherwell Wm. & Son, coachmaks. 1 Prospect rw. Mile end rd
Sherwin, Cope & Co. imperial printing press manufacturers & engineers, 5 Cumberland st. Shoreditch
Sherwin Frank, surgeon dentist, 14 Bruton st. Bond st
Sherwin Joseph, ironfounder, see Evans & Sherwin
Sherwin Thomas, backgammon table, chessboard, men, &c. manufacturer, 67 Gt. Queen st. Lincoln's inn fields
Sherwin William, brushma. 15 Stockwell terr. Clapham rd
Sherwin Wm. Atkinson, comb manufr. see Drane & Sherwin
Sherwin Wm. H. restaurateur, 26 Clement's lane, City
Sherwin Wm. Keene, oil & colorman, 4 Inwood pl. Kentish tn
Sherwood (Bailey & Newman), contractors, builders & brick makers, Belvedere road, Lambeth
Sherwood, Gilbert & Piper, booksel. & publ. 23 Paternoster row
Sherwood John & Fredk. who. & ret. cheesemngrs 29 Newgatest
Sherwood John & Thos. solicitors, see Vincent & Sherwood's
Sherwood Edward, grocer, 12 Gt. James st. Lisson grove
Sherwood James, clothier, 7 Peel pl. Kensington gravel pits
Sherwood James, gun & cannon lock maker, 12 Wellclose sq
Sherwood John, cheesemonger, 4 New Bridge st. Vauxhall
Sherwood John, dining rooms, 9 Adelaide st. Strand
Sherwood Joseph, parliamentary agent, 44 Parliament st
Sherwood Robt. fur brokr. 2 Brokers'row, Redcross st. Boro
Sherwood Samuel, grocer, 12 Horselydown lane, Borough
Sherwood Thomas, coffee rooms, 9 Cable st. Wellclose sq
Sherwood Thomas, wool stapler, 239 Bermondsey st
Sherwood Wm. carpentr. & undert. 1 Belvedere cres. Lambeth
Sherwood Wm. toy dealer, 4 St. George's ter. Borough rd
Shether Danl. pocket book ma. 23 Edmund pl. Aldersgate st
Shetland Fishery Co. (A. Anderson, managr.), 15 St. Maryaxe
Shevill Wm. C. jun. auctioneer, &c. 258 Bethnal green rd
Shew Geo. upholstr. auctioneer & surveyor, 41 Cross st. Islingtn
Shew William, dentist, 13 Upper Marylebone st. Portland pl
Sheward Samuel, horsedealer, 19 Green st. Grosvenor sq
Shewell John & Son, stockbrokers, 25 Tokenhouse yard
Shewell Joseph Talwin, draper, Deptford High st
Shick Frederick, fuzee chain ma. 58 Rahere st. Goswell rd
Shick James, wheel & fuzee cutter, 22 Rahere st. Goswell rd
Shickle Chas. Wm. shawl manuf. see Towler, Campin & Co
Shicknell Chas. fishmonger, 16 Rufford's bldgs. Islington
Shield & Harwood, solicitors, 26 Queen st. Cheapside
Shield Peter, tailor & draper, 3 Shoreditch
Shield Wm. surgeon, 118 Park st. Camden town
Shields G. (Mrs.), straw bonnet ma. 39 Stanhope st. Clare mkt
Shields George Oscue, warehouseman, 69 Wood st
Shields Henry Charles, furn. broker, 19 Boston st. Dorset sq
Shields James, gasfitter & ironmonger, 3 Lambeth Lr. Marsh
Shields John, boot & shoe maker, 6 Horseferry rd. Westmtr
Shields John, doll manufacturer, 65 Oakley st. Lambeth
Shiels John S. ale agt. & wine mer. Three Cranes wf. Up. Ths. st
Shiers James, bricklayer, 81 Chalton st. Somers town
Shiers John, clog maker, 23 Hayfield place, Mile end
Shiers John C. patten & french clog ma. 68 Union st. Borough
Shiers William, clog & patten ma. 92 Brick la. Spitalfields
Shilcock Henry, plumber, &c. 28 Cambridge pl. Edgware rd
Shilcock Joseph, cattle salesman, 41 West Smithfield
Shilcock William, cattle salesman, 41 West Smithfield
Shildrick John, tobacconist, 33 Up. Albany st. Regent's pk
Shillam Rt. C. *Crown & Anchor* P.H. 6 Low. George st. Chlsea
Shillcock & Lomas, grocers & tea dlrs. 37 Gt. Dover st. Boro'
Shillibeer George, patent funeral carriage proprietor, 1 & 2 Commercial pl. City road, Finsbury; & 136 Union st. Soutwk
Shillingford Benj. fruiterer, 7 Low. Smith st. Northmptn. sq
Shillingford Richard (Thomas Hoyle & Sons), calico printers, 9 Old Jewry chambers
Shillingford Rd. warehmn. see Hadland, Shillingford & Esam
Shillinglaw John, librarian, Royal Geogra. So. 3 Waterloo pl
Shillito Brothers, wholesale grocers, 145 Upper Thames st
Shillito John, beer retailer, 9 Wyndham rd. Cambrwll. Nw. rd
Shillito Richard, *Swan & Hoop* P.H. 28 Pavement, Finsbury
Shillito Stephen, bootmaker, 18 Charterhouse st
Shillito Wm. H. drug & rag brok. 6 Langbourn cham. Fench. st
Shilston Joseph, carpenter, 1 Huntley st, Bedford square, & 1 Upper Chenies mews, Bedford sq
Shilton Joseph, grocer & cheesemr. 2 & 3 Stepney High st
Shilton Thomas, builder, see Plaskett & Shilton
Shimwell Thomas, tailor, 19 Union st. east, Spitalfields
Shine George Lamb, surgeon & chemist, 100 Aldersgate st
Shingfield Adam, carpntr. & joiner, 53 Jubilee st. Com. rd. ea
Shinkwin Rt. irish newspaper offi. 21 Little Queen st. Wstmr
Shinn Benjamin Hardwick, army agent, see Randoll & Shinn
Shinn George, umbrella manufr. 29 Paradise row, Chelsea
Shinn George, coffee rooms, 58 Bethnal green rd
Shinn John, cabinet manufacturer, 9 St. John st. rd
Shiplee Elizh. (Mrs.), grocer & cheesemr. 3 Lion st. Nw. Kt. rd
Shipley Henry Jas. paperhanger, 2 Printers' pl. Bermondsey
Shipley John, saddler & harness maker, 181 Regent st
Shipley John Geo. jun. saddler & harness ma. 24 Jermyn st
Shipley Joseph, *Nag's Head* P.H. 74 St. John st
Shipley Wm. brassfounder, 1 Braziers' bldgs. Farringdon st
Shipley Wm. corndealer, see Nickolls & Shipley
Shipley Wm. *Yorkshire Grey* P.H. 85 Bermondsey st
Shipman James, upholst. & undertaker, 29 Gracechurch st
Shipman John, coal dealer, 27 Somerset st. Aldgate
Shipman Richard, tripe dresser, 5 Whitechapel High st
Shipowners' Towing Company (William Beare Caulfield, sec.), 102 Leadenhall st. & 5 Fox's lane, Shadwell
Shipping Mercantile Gazette ev. newsp. 54 Gracechurch st
Shipston Francis, builder, Stratford, Essex
Shipton James & Co. carriers, Elephant inn, Fore st. City, & 10 wharf, Macclesfield st. north, City road
Shipton James, spring & axle ma. 1 Cardigan pl. Kenningtn
Shipton John, linendraper, 24 & 25 Islington High st
Shipton John, locksmith & bellhanger, 74 Watling st
Shipton Joseph, french polisher, 7 Earl st. ea. Lisson grove
Shipton Thomas, *Sun & Sportsman* P.H. 64 High st. Marylebn
Shipwash & Co. english & foreign mineral water warehouse, 7 Bury st. St. James's
Shipway Catherine (Mrs.), tobaccopipe ma. 27 John st. Dckhd
Shipway James, hatter, 89 Upper st. Islington
Shipway John, trunk mkr. & undertaker, 34 Blackfriars rd
Shipway William, tailor, see Ford & Shipway
Shipwrecked Fishermen & Mariners' Benevolent Society (Francis Lean, secretary), 26 Bucklersbury; hours 10 to 5
Shirafs Wm. comp. ornament, &c. ma. see Horne Shirafs & Cook
Shirley Arkel, baker, 34 Aylesbury st. Clerkenwell
Shirley Benjn. boot & shoe warehouse, 17 Blackfriars rd
Shirley George, printseller, 37 Goswell st
Shirley John, chemist, 97 High st. Marylebone
Shirley John, goldbeater, 24 Wilderness row, St. Luke's
Shirley Samuel, blackwell hall factor, 8 Basinghall st

Shirley Sarah (Mrs.), milliner, 49 Salisbury sq. Fleet st
Shirley Stephen, perfumer, 22 Princess st. Portman market
Shirley Thos. bootma. 27 Appleby st. Pearson st. Kngslnd. rd
Shirley Thos. butcher, 42 North Audley st
Shirley Thos. grocer & teadealer, Kingsland green
Shirley Thos. livery stables, 16 Whitehorse st. Stepney
Shirley Wm. Hy. Sheriff, law stationer, see Leaver & Shirley
Shirreff Charles Ireland, solicitor, 7 Lincoln's inn fields
Shirreff James Hale, surgeon, Deptford High st
Shirress James, surgeon, 48 Chapel st. Pentonville
Shirt Wm. & Co. who. coffee dealers, 10 Arthur st. west
Shirt John, cheesemonger, 4 Brett's buildgs. Camberwell rd
Shirt John, grocer, &c. 41 & 42 Broad st. Lambeth butts
Shirt William, watchmaker, 10 Peerless pl. City rd
Shirtliff Edward Dickinson, chemist, &c. 90 Chiswell st
Shirvill John, bootmaker, 65 Chapel st. Pentonville
Shoberl Frederick, jun. printer to his Royal Highness Prince Albert, 51 Rupert st. Haymarket
Shoebridge George, fruiterer, 58 Freeschool st. Horselydwn
Shoebridge Wm. grocer & teadealer, 53 East st. Manchestr. sq
Shoebridge Wm. Fredk. surgeon, 5 Northampton pl. O. Kent rd
Shole Simeon, watchmaker, 5 Church st. Deptford
Sholl James, oil & colorman, 33 Lamb st. Spitalfields
Shoner John Fredk. biscuit baker, 101 Princes rd. Lambeth
Shoobert Broths. wine coopers, 5 Two Swan yd. Bshpsg. wtho
Shoobert John, cooper & ship chandler, 5 Low. East Smithfield
Shoobert John Conrad, undertaker, 16 Cleveland st. Mile end
Shoobert Thomas, undertaker, 18 Cleveland st. Mile end rd
Shoobridge Thomas, silk manfr. see Keith & Shoobridge
Shoolbred, Cook & Co. linen & woollen drapers, silk mercers, hosiers, haberdashers & carpet warehousemen, 154, 155 & 156 Tottenham ct. rd. & 37, 38, 43 & 44 Grafton st. east
Shoolbred John & Co. tailors & surgical bandage makers, 34 Jermyn st. St. James's
Shoolbred Archibald, tailor & woollen draper, 3 Budge row
Shoosmith Matthew, ironmonger, 6 Gt. Dover st. Borough
Shoppee Peter, linendraper, 14 Judd st. Brunswick sq
Shord Henry, tailor, 54 Northampton st. Clerkenwell
Shore Abraham, carpet, linen & furnishing warehouse, 90 Whitechapel High st
Shore Charles, carpenter, 47 St. John st. Clerkenwell
Shore Geo. beer retailer, 2 Salmon pl. Grange rd. Bermondsey
Shore William, jeweller, 45 Liverpool st. Bishopsgate
Shores John Hen. & Co. tailors & outfitters, 193 Shoreditch
Shorey Ebenezer, scalema. & gasfitter, 94 Bethnal green rd
Shorman John, engraver & printer, 6 Gt. Pulteney st
Shorpin Robert, fruiterer, Camberwell green
Short & Mahony, metal brokers, 1 Newman's ct. Cornhill
Short Robert & Charles, buff & chamois leather sellers, & army accoutrement makers, 37 Lisle st. Leicester sq
Short Andrew, coffee rooms, 14 Red Lion st. Whitch. High st
Short Arthur, physician, 59 Clarendon sq. Somers town
Short Charles, dining rooms, 38 Cannon st. City
Short Chas. Henry, law stationer, 9 Took's ct. Chacy. la
Short Henry, plumber, &c. 18 Old Chapel row, Kentish town
Short Henry, shoemaker, 69 Bethnal green road
Short Henry, watch & clock ma. 3 Seymour pl. Camden twn
Short James, builder, 13 New Henry st. east, Avenue road
Short James, *Northumbrlnd. Arms* P.H. 13 Holland st. Blkfrs
Short John, butcher, 79 Bethnal green road
Short John, fishmonger, 238 Strand
Short John, haberdasher, 9 Norfolk st. King's cross
Short John, *Strand hotel & tavern*, 333 Strand
Short John, who. hardwareman & silversmith, 15 Lime st
Short John James, stockbroker, Stock exchange
Short Joseph, beer retailer, 10 Cheshire st. Bethnal green
Short Robert, boot & shoe maker, Stratford broadway
Short Samuel R. scale maker, see De Grave, Short & Fanner
Short Thomas, straw bonnet warehouse, 192 Tooley st
Short William, butcher, 18½ Sidney pl. Commercial rd. east
Short William, cabinet maker, 13 Cadogan st
Short William, emery paper ma. 45 St. John st. Smithfield
Short William John, surgeon, 19 Little Moorfields
Shorter Hannah (Mrs.), tobacconist, 44 Myddelton st. Clrkwll
Shorter James, baker, 6 Manifold pl. Lr. Kennington lane
Shorter John, china & glass dealer, 36 Crispin st. Spitalfields
Shorter John, wine merchant, see Bailey & Shorter & Co
Shorter Richard Miller, *Bull coach & waggon office*, livery stable keeper & city carman, 92 Bishopsgate within
Shorter Richard Miller, corn & coal merch. 34 Camomile st
Shorter Thos. Edw. tobacconist, 1 Margaret ter. Paddingt. gn
Shorter Wm. *Prince of Wales* P.H. 25 St. George's rd. Southw
Shorthose David, *Cock & Bottle* P.H. 21 Bedfordbury, Cov. gdn
Shorthose David, *Three Horse Shoes* P.H. 19 Gilbert st. Grov. sq
Shortridge John, merchant, see Yuille, Shortridge & Co
Shott Wm. corn merchant & wharfinger, 34 Shad Thames
Shott Wm. cornfactor, 2 Thomas st. Horselydown
Shotten Geo. *Marquis of Wellington* P.H. 12 New st. Dockhd
Shotten Robert, confectioner, 15 Barton st. Westminster
Shotter John Strother, cheesemonger, 9 Oxford market
Shotter Joseph, who. stationer, engraver, &c. 38 Eastcheap
Shotter Thomas, army clothier, laceman, &c. 12 Jermyn st
Shotton, Bouts & Shotton, wholesale grocers, 9 Mincing lane
Shoubridge & Bramley, solicitors, 3 Bedford row
Shouls Richard, plumbr. paintr. &c. 7 Leman st. Goodman's fls
Shouls Thomas, plumber, 12 Norfolk st. Commercial rd. east
Shoults George, carpenter, 14 Webb st. Bermondsey st
Shoults Elizh. M.A. (Mrs.), harness ma. 20 Webb st. Brmdsy. st
Shoults Wm. carpenter & builder, 27 Maze, Tooley st
Shout (Misses), milliners, 14 North Audley st
Shove Charles, straw hat manufr. 3 George st. Blackfrs. rd
Shove George, corn factor, Deptford broadway
Shoveller Wm. & Son, curriers, 8 Brompton road
Shoveller John, jun. wine merchant & agent for Allsopp's Burton & India pale ale, 33 Finsbury place north
Shoveller Wm. jun. currier, 2 Bridgehouse pl. Newington cau
Shoveller Wm. sen. currier, &c. 21 Lisle st. Leicester sq
Showel James, stationer, Broadway, Stratford
Showell Chas. stationer, 15 Union st. Bishopsgate without
Showell John Storer, tailor, see Flaxman & Showell
Showell Wm. James, beer retailer, 8 Salmon la. Limehouse
Showler Amelia (Miss), *White Bear* P.H. Up. Fore st. Lambth
Showler Robert & Son, law stationers, 8 Cursitor st. Chancy. la
Showler Sophia & Charlt. lace dealers, 63 Bridge rd. Lambth
Showler John, surveyor, 2 Bowling green la. King st. Boro'
Shram John Fred. wholesale glass dealer, 121 Shoreditch
Shreeve Robert, upholsterer, 54 Seymour pl. Bryanstone sq
Shreve Wm. tobacconist, 18 Fair st. Horselydown
Shrewsbury, Wolverhampton, Dudley & Birmingham Railway (G. Knox, sec.), 3 Moorgate st
Shrewsbury Mary (Mrs.), tobacconist, 59 London rd. Southw
Shrimpton & Hooper, needle makers, 18 King square, Goswell road, & at Studley, Warwickshire
Shrimpton & Hopkins, whipmakers, 11 Wilson st. Finsbury
Shrimpton Charles, saddler, 64 Gt. Saffron hill, Hatton grdn
Shrimpton John, bread & biscuit bak. 23 Broad st. Lambeth
Shrimpton Thos. *Good Man* P.H. 75 Norton st. Fitzroy sq
Shrimpton Thos. M. wheelwright & smith, 35 Curtain road
Shripton Henry, greengrocer & coal dlr. 2 David st. Marylbn
Shrosbree Wm. naturalist, 87 Shaftesbury st. New North rd
Shubrook Francis, tailor, 78 New Bond st
Shuckford Jas. & John, brewers, Clifton st. Wandsworth rd
Shuckford Jas. sen. carpenter, Clifton st. Wandsworth rd
Shuffle John, hairdresser, 15 Middle st. Cloth fair
Shufflebottom Geo. coach ma. Williams mws. Mary st. Rgts. pk
Shuffrey William Henry, upholsterer, 161 Strand
Shuker Timothy, dairyman, 5½ John st. Berkeley sq
Shum Ralph, pork butcher, 15 Houghton st. Clare market
Shum Robert, solicitor, see Meggison, Pringle & Manisty
Shum Wm. pork butcher, 37 Bath st. City road
Shurey John, glass cutter, 31 St. Andrew's hill, Doctors' com
Shurly Thomas Lester, tailor, 34 Upper Park pl. Dorset sq
Shurvell Thomas, *Noah's Ark* P.H. 313 Oxford st
Shury Jas. (Mrs.) & C. & J. royal york baths, 54 York tr. Rgt's pk
Shury John, engraver, printer & stationer, 12 Gt. Carter la
Shury Richard, scale maker, 77 Chamber st. Leman st
Shute & Faulke, lace & muslin warehmn. see Faulke & Shute
Shute Fredk. G. & Co. lace & embrod. muslin wareho. 64 Friday st
Shute Robert, surgeon, 27 Mecklenburgh square
Shute Theodore, M.D. surgeon, 21 Wellingtn rd. St. John's wood
Shute Thos. engineer & tool ma. 40 Cannon st. Ratcliff highwy
Shute William, machine ruler, 10 Old Fish st. Old Change
Shuter Richard & Wm. fringe ma. 21 St. Martin's ct. Leicester sq
Shuter Thomas Allen & Co. coopers & hoop merchants, Shad Thames, & 82 Upper Thames st
Shuter James, fruiterer, 1 Dean st. Shadwell
Shuter Jas. lighterman & potato mer. 1 Gould's hill, Shadwell
Shuter John David, solicitor, 67 Millbank st. Westminster
Shuter Joseph, bootmaker, 1 Sugar loaf ct. Leadenhall st
Shuter Joseph, fruiterer, 54 Leadenhall st
Shuter William, painter & glazier, 58 St. Mary axe
Shuter William, tobacconist, 66 Ernest st. Regent's park
Shutt William & Bros. timber sawyers, Church row, Limeho
Shutt Mary (Mrs.), plumber, 35 Three Colt st. Limehouse
Shutt Thomas, artificial florist & plumasier, 119 Long acre
Shuttleworth George Edm. & Sons, auctioneers, &c. 28 Poultry
Shuttleworth John Bradley & Co. who. tea dlrs. 33 Eastcheap
Shuttleworth & Stamper, chemists, &c. 140 Leadenhall st
Shuttleworth Wm. Sewell & Co. tea agents, 151 Fenchurch st
Shuttleworth Geo. M. undertaker, 2 Penton row, Walworth
Shuttleworth John S. lithographic & letter press printer to her Majesty, 3 Chapel place, & 28 Poultry

Shuttleworth Thos. watch & clock maker, 48 Carthusian st
Sibert Henry, tailor, 41 Fleet st
Sibeth John Nicholas, merchant, see Suse & Sibeth
Sibley Charles, artist, 6 Russell place, Fitzroy square
Sibley Chas. bandana & fancy wareho. 3 Huggin la. Wood st
Sibley Elizabeth (Mrs.), tobacconist, 12 Tottenham ct. road
Sibley Eliza A. (Miss), music&mus.ins. sell. 42 Whitcomb st
Sibley Frances (Mrs.), fruiterer & news agent, 92Chancery la
Sibley George, tobacconist, 10 Sarah pl. Old st. road
Sibley Henry, solicitor, 5 Wharton st. Lloyd sq. Clerkenwell
Sibley Henry, tailor, 21 Bethnal green road
Sibley James, grocer, 7 Salmon lane, Limehouse
Sibley John, plumber, Foxton terrace, Thornhill road
Sibley Martha (Mrs.), baker, 2 High st. Kingsland
Sibley Mary J. (Mrs.), *Three Tuns* P.H. 2 Kensington High st
Sibley Rd. silversmith, 10 Dufour's pl. Broad st. Golden sq
Sibley Robt. architect & survey. 39 Gt. Ormond st. Queen sq
Sibley Robert, tobacconist, 1 Bloomfield ter. Pimlico
Sibley Sarah (Mrs.), carver & gilder, 45 Broad st. Golden sq
Sibley William, baker, 14 Strachan place, Balls pond road
Sibley William, coal merchant, Milford lane, Strand
Sibon Robert, shell fishmonger, 40 Little Queen st. Holborn
Siccama Abel, B.A. prof. of languages, 15 Finsbury pavement
Sice Charles, fruiterer, 2 Cambridge st. Golden square
Sichart John Godfrey, merchant, 7 Arthur st. west
Sick & Maimed Seaman's Office, Admiralty, Somerset house; hours of business, 10 to 4
Sicklen Wm. brushmaker & stationer, 24 South Audley st
Siday Richard, fruiterer, 19 York st. Westminster
Siddall Charles, cutler, 8 Kent place, Old Kent road
Sidden Henry, surgeon, 78 Blackfriars road
Siddle John, merchant, 58 Lombard st
Sidebotham Samuel, agent, see Escombe & Sidebotham
Sidebottom Alexr. Radclyffe, barrister, 2 New sq. Linc. inn
Sidebottom Edward Venner, barrister, 4 New sq. Linc. inn
Sidey Henry, cabinet carver, 10 Peerless row, City road
Sidey Elias, sofa maker, 1 Richmond st. St. Luke's
Sidey Isaac, brassfounder, 24 Poland st. Oxford st
Sidey Samuel, gold beater, 30 Baldwin st. City road
Sidle Robert, tobacconist, 14 Up. Gloucester st. Dorset sq
Sidney Algernon, parl. agt. &solicitor, 58 High st. Camden tn
Sidney George, solicitor, 13 South square, Gray's inn
Sidney Henry, grocer, 9 Vernon place, Bagnigge wells road
Sidney John Apsley, attorney, 53 Beaumont st. Portland pl
Sidney Philip Joseph Marlow, solicitor, 4 Mitre ct. Temple
Sidney Thomas, teadealer, 8 Ludgate hill, & 3 Lit. Bridge st
Sidney Thomas, tea importer, 8 Ludgate hill, also of the following establishments: at Leeds, Sidney & Stables, 167 Briggate; Manchester, Sidney & Horsman, 2 Market st.; Hull, Sidney & Hall, 31 Market place; Norwich, Sidney & Ladyman, 6 Gentleman's walk
Sidwell Fredk. Wm. stationer, 14 Grenada pl. Old Kent rd
Sidwell Thomas, bricklayer, 73 Harrow road, Paddington
Siebe Augustus, engineer, 5 Denmark st. Soho
Siebert John, baker, 22 Duke st. Lincoln's inn fields
Sieling John, harp&violin string ma. 3 Bowling st. Clrkn wll
Siers Eliza (Mrs.), lodging house, 38 Bury st. St. James's
Sieveking Edward &Son, merchants, 3Skinner's pl. Sise lane
Sievier Robert Wm. sculptor, 12A, Henrietta st. Cavendishsq
Siffken Henry Jacob, merchant, 57&58 Commercl. sale rooms
Siggers Charles, fruiterer, 2 Prospect pl. Old Brompton
Siggers Geo. *Hercules* P.H. 14 Devonshire st. Lisson grove
Siggers Isaac, tailor, 7 Brownlow st. Drury lane
Siggers James, breeches maker, 6 Newcastle st. Strand
Siggs Charles, dairyman, 1 Blenheim ter. Bond st. Chelsea
Siggs John, cheesemonger, 150 Hoxton Old town
Sigismund Sutro, physician, 3 Great Marlboro' st
Sigmond George Gabriel, physician, 31 Baker st. Portman sq
Sigmund Andrew, baker, 12 Kingsland road
Sigsworth Frederic Parker, grocer, 23 Bread st. Cheapside
Silberrad Richard, custom house agent, 79 Low. Thames st
Silby Seth, tailor, 30 Exmouth st. Clerkenwell
Silby Thomas, boot & shoe maker, 115 Bishopsgate without
Silcock John Cook, tailor, 51 Brewer st. Somers town
Silcock Robert, carpenter, 12 Homer st. Marylebone
Silcock Simon, *Carpentrs' Arms* P.H. Actonpl. Bagnigge wl. rd
Silcock Simon, *Cross Keys* P.H. 1 Blackfriars road
Silcock William, *Duke of York* P.H. 22 Phœnix st. Somers tn
Silcox Henry, grindery dealer, 41 James st. Oxford st
Silcox William, *Russell Tavern* P.H. 6 Crawley st. Somerstn
Silenne Alexis, coffee rooms, 4 Bridge st. Westminster
Silk & Brown, coachmakers, 8 & 9 Long acre
Silk John, porkman, 202 Shadwell High st
Silk John Alexander, solicitor, 2 Brunswick square
Silk Robert, porkman, 17 Skinner st. Somers town
Silk Thomas, gilt metal worker, 53 King st. Soho
Silk Wm. Banks, *Cathedral hotel*, 48 St. Paul's church yard, & 50 Old Change
Sillem Herman, merchant, 2 Crosby square
Silley Abraham, painter, &c. 14 Seymour pl. Bryanstone sq
Sillitoe Robert, fishmonger, 3 Market st. Oxford st
Sills James, grocer, 1 Old Boswell court, Strand
Sills Joseph, gold chain mak. 8 Bowling gn. la. Coppice row
Silva Bruno & Son, merchants, 35 Crutchedfriars
Silva Emanuel & Son, wharfingers, Gun&Shot whf. Tooley st
Silva Moses Gomes, west india merc. 19East India chambers
Silva Samuel, boot maker, 6 Church row, Aldgate High st
Silver Stephen Winckworth & Co. clothiers, ready made linen & outfitting warehouse, 10 & 66 & 67 Cornhill; 4½ Bishopsgate within; workshops, 33 & 34 Nassau place, Commercial road east; & 10 & 11 St. George's crescent, Liverpool
Silver Edward David, M.D. surgeon, 30 Berners st
Silver Frederick Joseph, leather factor, 111 Tyer's gateway, 211 Bermondsey st.; & Hide market, Leadenhall
Silver William, barrister, 3 Elm court, Temple
Silverlock Henry, engraver, & copperplate, letterpress & lithograpic printer, & medical label warehouse, 3 Wardrobe terrace, Doctors' commons
Silverlock John, teadealer, 132 Leadenhall st
Silverside Giles&Stephn. N. meat salesmen, 6 Newgate mrkt
Silverside Giles, butcher, 31 Paternoster row
Silverside Sarah (Miss), shoe ma. 25 Gt. Bath st. Clerkenwl
Silverthorn Wm. brewer, Portland place, Peckham road
Silverthorne Stephen, beer retailer, 1 Peerless place, City rd
Silverton William, beer retailer, 1 Chapel pl. Ball's Pond rd
Silvester & Warrington, seal & copperplate engravers & printers to her Majesty, 27 Strand
Silvester Henry Richd. solicitor, 19 Gt. Dover st. Borough
Silvester James, fruit salesman, Long market, Covent gardn
Silvester John, carcase butcher, 51 Aldgate High st
Silvester John, livery stables, 4 Paultons tr. King's rd. Chlsa
Silvester John, *Qn's. Railway tav.* 8 Charles st. Westbn. ter
Silvester Joseph, coal mer. 34 Church st. Cheyne wlk. Chels
Silvester Peter, iron plate worker, 42 Gt. St. Andrew st
Silvester Thomas, printer, 1 Chesterfield st. King's cross
Silveston Jacob, jeweller, 36 Duke st. Aldgate
Silveston Mark, baker, 36 Duke st. Aldgate
Silvey Ann (Mrs.), billiard rooms, 57 Greek st. Soho
Sim George, baker, Church st. Stoke Newington
Sim George, jun. baker, 34 Carnaby st. Golden square
Sim George, sen. baker, 1 Pitfield st. Hoxton
Sim James, builder, 8 Little Torrington st. Torrington sq.; & 11 Bedford place, Hampstead road
Sim James, statuary & builder, Johnstone pl. Mile end road
Sim John, wood broker, see Churchill & Sim
Sim Wm. accountant & referee, 63 Old Broad st. City
Sim Wm. builder, surveyor & agent, 11 Lamb's Conduit st
Sim Wm. solicitor, 8 King's Bench walk, Temple
Simco Charles, chronometer ma. 37 Rahere st. Goswell rd
Simco Thomas, grocer, 48 Bath st. City road
Simco Thomas, tinplate worker, 62 Goswell st
Simcock Thomas, *Eight Bells* P.H. Church st. Hackney
Simcocks Jonathan, baker, 13 Broadwall, Stamford st
Simes John Thomas & Co. wool brokers, 58 Coleman st
Simes Ebenezer, carpenter, &c. 59 White Lion st. Pentonville
Simes John, fruiterer, 3 Cross st. Blackfriars road
Simes John, paperhanger, 22 Chalton st. Somers town
Simes Robert, dining rooms, 1 Duke's Head pas. Nwgt. mkt
Simes Wm. carpenter & undertaker, 2 Ellis st. Sloane st.; & 4 Cadogan terrace, Chelsea
Simes Wm. Frederick, fruiterer, 3 Henry st. Hampstead rd
Siminton Robert, linendraper, 19 Moor st. Soho
Simkin & Buck, wholesale grocers, 88 Leadenhall st
Simkin Edward, chemist, &c. 2 New Cavendish st. Portland pl
Simkin Wm. Smith, who. & export. ironmong. 81 London wall
Simkins Edward, meat salesman, 3 White Hart st. Nwgt. mkt
Simkins Edmund, butcher, 10 Essex st. Noel st. Islington
Simkins Francis, coffee rooms, 41 Seymour pl. Bryanstone sq
Simkins George, boot & shoe m. 123 Up. Seymour st. Euston sq
Simkins Thomas, baker, 24 Whitefriars st. Fleet st
Simmonds Hannah & J. (Misses), dress ma. 19 Clifton st. Finsbry
Simmonds John & Oliver William, goldsmiths, silversmiths, jewellers, furnishers of plate & other requisites for routs, dinners, &c. on hire, 3 Southampton row, Russell sq
Simmonds & Morton, steam corn mills, Belvedere rd. Lambeth
Simmonds & Ward, commer. & for. news agents, 18 Cornhill
Simmonds Dennis, grocer, 1 Duke's row, Saint Pancras
Simmonds Eve (Mrs.), clothier, High st. Newington butts
Simmonds Geo. hat manuf. 6 John st. west, Blackfriars rd
Simmonds Geo. H. survyr of pavements, 7 Gt. Alie st. Whtechpl
Simmonds Hannah (Mrs.), milliner & dress ma. 306 Regent st
Simmonds Henry, tobacconist, 2 High st. Newington butts

Simmonds Henry, jun. hop & seed factor, 239 Boro' High st
Simmonds Isaac, veterinary surgeon, 15 Up. East Smithfield
Simmonds James, carpenter, 10 Horseshoe yd. Brook st
Simmonds Jeremiah, hatter, 155 Union st. Borough
Simmonds John, bootmaker, 144 Long acre
Simmonds John Daniel, builder, 11 Bear yd. Lincoln's inn fi
Simmonds Peter Lund, commission merchant, foreign newspaper, advertising & general agent, 6 Barge yard
Simmonds Rd. bedstead ma. 61 Gt. Cambridge st. Hackny.rd
Simmonds Richd. whalebone cutter, see Smith & Simmonds
Simmonds William, grocer, 3 Printing house la. Blackfriars
Simmonett Joseph, machinist, 12½ Adam's pl. Borough
Simmons Hannah (Mrs.) & Son, 46 Judd st
Simmons Isaac&Co.typefounds.14Newcastle st.Farringdon st
Simmons John & Co. who. & genl. stationers, 59 Bishopsgate without, & 27 Artillery lane
Simmons Margaret & Ann (Misses), milliners, 15 Wigmore st
SimmonsAbrm. *SheridanKnowles*P.H.12Brydges st.Cov.gn
Simmons David, tinman, 9 Sharp's buildings, Minories
Simmons Ebenezer Leadbeater, watchmaker, 26 Coleman st
Simmons Edwd. watch & clock ma. High st. Stoke Newngtn
Simmons Edward Robert, barrister, 13 Clifford's inn
Simmons Fredk. letterpress print. 7 Up.Rosoman st. Clkwll
Simmons George, academy, 122 Brunswick st. Hackney rd
Simmons George, bookseller, &c. 63 Edgware road
Simmons George, bootmaker, 29 Up. York st. New road
Simmons Geo. furrier & genl. cap manufacturer, 13 Langley pl. Com. rd. Whitechapel, & 29 Redcross st. Cripplegate
Simmons George, sack collector & whfinger.203Up.Thames st
Simmons George, surgeon, 13 Judd st. Brunswick square
Simmons Henry, engineer, 127 Cornwall road, Lambeth
Simmons Hen.Wm. engraver, 42 Mornington pl. Hampstd.rd
Simmons Jas. congreve match ma. 12 Windmill st. New cut
Simmons John, fancy ball & court dress maker, &masquerade warehouse, 7 Tavistock st, Covent garden
Simmons John, marine store dlr. 25 Charles st. Hatton gardn
Simmons John, roman cement mfr. 5 Portland pl. Borough rd
Simmons John, straw hat wareho. 20 King William st. City
Simmons John, surgeon, 156 Tooley st. Borough
Simmons John, tailor, 5 Buttesland st. Hoxton
Simmons Joseph, chemist & druggist, 38 Lambeth walk
Simmons Mary (Mrs.), *Wh.Hart* P.H.1Wh.Hartst.Ngt.mkt
Simmons Morrice, watch manfr.40Gt.Prescot st.Goodman's fi
Simmons Moses, tinman & brazier, 100 Upper Whitecross st
Simmons Nicholas Fras. surgeon, 5 Hatcham ter. New cross
Simmons Peter, stationer, &c. 34 St. Mary axe
Simmons Richard, emery paper ma. 12 Short st. Tabrncle. sq
Simmons Richard, fruiterer, 15 Norfolk pl. Walworth rd
Simmons Richard, upholsterer, 20 New North st.Red Lion sq
Simmons Robert, bookbinder, 23 Goswell ter. Goswell road
Simmons Robert, warehouseman, 49 Bow lane, City
Simmons Sarah (Mrs.), enginr.&ironfound.25 Stoney st.Boro'
Simmons Simeon, masquerade wareho.13 Holywell st.Strand
Simmons Simeon, tinplate worker, 7 Pitfield st. Hoxton
Simmons Simon, clothier, 24 Chapel st. Edgware road
Simmons Susannah (Mrs.), glass & china wa.49Aldersgate st
Simmons Thomas, bookbinder, 19 Middle st. Cloth fair
Simmons Thomas, carpenter, 9 River st. Islington
Simmons Thomas, chandelier&lustre ma.31 Southampton row
Simmons Thomas, tailor, see Metcalfe & Simmons
Simmons Thomas Charles, wine & spirit mercht. 48 Mark la
Simmons Valentine, ornamental painter, 26 High st. Marylebn
Simmons Wm. bricklayer & builder, 61 St. Martin's lane
Simmons Wm. carpenter, 9 Prospect pl. Cambridge heath
Simmons Wm. cowkeeper & corndealer, 63 Cowcross st
Simmons Wm. *Crown & Anchor* P.H. 28 Farringdon st
Simmons Wm. *DurhamArms* P.H. Harleyford rd. Vauxhall
Simmons Wm. pawnbroker, 3 Hackney road crescent
Simmons Wm. rag & phial dlr. 41 Bedfordbury, Covent grdn
Simmons Wm. solicitor, see Brundrett, Randall & Co
Simms Jas. & Geo. compass ma.9Greville st. Hatton garden
Simms & M'Intyre, booksellers, 13 Paternoster row
Simms Henry, optician, 14 Camden cottages, Camden town
Simms John, agent for iron & brass bedsteads, 141 Fleet st
Simms John, camp equipage manufr. see Winfield & Simms
Simms John, cooper, 185 Long lane, Bermondsey
Simms Joseph, beer retailer, 42 Brill row, Somers town
Simms Wm. mathematical inst mak. see Troughton & Simms
Simms William Hen. ship biscuit baker, see Hill & Simms
Simnitt Geo. Jas. bootmaker, 6 Lit. Alie st. Goodman's flds
Simnitt John, bootmaker, 18 Bishopsgate within
Simon George, ship & commer. agent, see Lightly & Simon
Simon George Philipps, chemist, 18 Finch lane, Cornhill
Simon Henry Andrews, barrister, 2 Middle Temple lane
Simon John, barrister, 3 Brick court, Temple
Simon John, surgeon, 11 Wellington st. Strand
Simon-leon Joseph, artifl. florist, 20 Princes st. Hanover sq
Simon Louis M. stockbroker, 7 Warnford ct. Throgmorton st
Simon Siegfried, enamelled sealskin ma.66Shaftesburyst.Hxn
Simonds Jas. Beart, vet. surgeon, 9 Gt. College st. Camd. tn
Simonds (Mrs.), lodging house, 71 Connaught terrace
Simonds Richard, coal merchant, 7 Wilmington sq. Spafields
Simonds Samuel, library, 23 Chester st. Kennington cross
Simonds William May, russia broker, 75 Old Broad st. City
Simonett Joseph, machinist, 12½ Adam's pl. Redcross st. Boro'
Simonett Wm. ivory combmak. 23 Park pl. Kennington cross
Simons & Hands, tobacconists, 73 High Holborn
Simons & Robinson, tailors, 30 Store st. Bedford square
Simons Ann M. (Mrs.), child bed linen wa. 1 New st. Cov.grdn
Simons Eleazer Jacobs, mer. 11 Leman st. Goodman's fields
Simons George, watch manufacturer, 49 King sq. Goswell rd
Simons John, tobacconist, 9 Hand court, High Holborn
Simons John, sen. coal mercht. Camden wharf, Camden tn
Simons John, jun. coal mercht. Bridge wharf, Camden town
Simons John James, tool & melting pot warehouse, 47 Clerkenwell green, & furn. undertaker, 4 Clerkenwell gr
Simons Nicholas, barrister, 11 New square, Lincoln's inn
Simons Richard, wine & spirit merchant, 27 Mincing lane
Simons Wm. builder, 6 Artillery terrace, Westminster
Simons Wm. butcher, 76 East st. Manchester square
Simons Wm. butcher, 33 Upper Park place, Dorset square
Simons Wm. grocer, 29 Church st. Lambeth
Simons Wm. paper hanging mfr. 26 Gt. Winchester st. City
Simons Wm. sen. silk mercer, 10 & 11 Leicester square
Simons Wm. jun. silk mercer & lace, &c.wa. 312 High Holborn
Simons Wm. Phipps, lace warehouse, 1New st. Covent garden
Simper Robert, tobacconist, 17 Palace row, New road
Simpkin, Marshall &Co.booksell.&publish.4Stationers'hall ct
Simpkin Charles, farrier, 2 Church st. Blackfriars road
Simpkin Joseph, plumber, &c. 11 Portman st. Portman sq
Simpkin Richard, plumber, 74 Seymour pl. Bryanstone sq
Simpkin Wm. tax collector, 7 Marlborough sq. Chelsea
Simpkins Hen. printer, 46 Up.Johnst.Fitzroysq.& 70½ Strand
Simpkins John, engraver, 4 Clement's inn, Strand
Simpkinson JohnAug.F. queen's counsel, 8 Old sq. Lincn's.inn
Simpson & Cobb, solicitors, 63 Moorgate st. Bank
Simpson & Dimond, solicitors, 10 Henrietta st. Cavendish sq
Simpson Frederic & Co. (late Paine & Simpson), who. comb & brush mfrs. hardwaremen & cutlers, writing desk, dressing case & workbox makers, birmingham & sheffield general agents, 57 Borough High st
Simpson John & Jas. furniture printers, &c. 53 Skinner st
Simpson & London, tailors, 103 Quadrant, Regent st
Simpson & Muller, silk hat manufacturers & japann'd hat& cap makers, Farnham place, Gravel lane, Boro'
Simpson (Pinder) & Sons, land agents, 29 Saville row
Simpson, Scott & Co. west india & col. broks. 73 Gt. Tower st
Simpson, Shepherd & Co. cheesemongers & butter salesmen, 44 Warwick lane, & 261 Oxford st
Simpson & Starkey, mftg. goldsmiths & jewlrs.29 Hattongdn
Simpson & Stevenson, curriers, 1½ Artillery pl we.Chiswl. st
Simpson S. & Co. cutler & surgical instrument ma. 55 Strand
Simpson Thos. & Co. merchts. 9 King's Arms yd. Moorgate st
Simpson Thomas & Co. tailors, 13 Finch lane, late of 6 Sweeting's alley
Simpson Thomas, jun. & Co.[successors to Paine & Simpson], comb & brush manufactrs. hardwaremen & cutlers, dressing case, writing desk & workbox maks. 156 Leadenhall st
Simpson Thos. Bridge & Co. merchants, 156 Leadenhall st
Simpson W—— & Co. engineers, Belgrave road, Pimlico
Simpson Wm. & Henry, tailors & drapers, 139 Leadenhall st
Simpson & Young, calico printers, 47 St. Paul's Churchyard & at Manchester
Simpson Zephaniah & Thos. linendraps.49 & 50 Farringdon st
Simpson Alfred, butcher, 90 Shadwell High st
Simpson Alfred, hat manf. 6 Lit. Charlotte st. Blackfriars rd
Simpson Ann (Miss), ladies' school, 70 Hatton garden
Simpson Carrington, builder, 3 Saville place, Lambeth ; & furnishing undertaker, Canterbury place, Lambeth
Simpson Charles, grocer, 10 Chapel st. New rd. Marylebone
Simpson Charles, grocer, 13 Kingsland road
Simpson Charles, landscape painter, 10 Carlisle st. Soho sq
Simpson Charles, oil and colorman, 4 Pratt st. Lambeth
Simpson Chas. stationer, 4 Providence buildgs. New Kent rd
Simpson Charles, saddler, 57 Gt. Portland st. Oxford st
Simpson Charles, stockbroker, 21 Tokenhouse yard
Simpson Charles, surgeon, 12 Cambridge st. Golden square
Simpson Charles, M.D. surgeon, 5 Eccleston st. south, Pimlico
Simpson Crawford, colonial broker, see Wood & Simpson
Simpson David, biscuit & bread baker, 46 Old Bond st
Simpson David, venetian blind ma. 81 Whitechapel High st
Simpson Edward, *George* P.H. 53 South st. Grosvenor sq

Simpson Edward, linendraper, 80 Ossulston st. Somers tn
Simpson Eliza (Mrs.), baker, 7 Buckingham pl. Fitzroy sq
Simpson Elizabeth (Mrs.), linendraper, 89 Gray's inn lane
Simpson Elizabeth (Mrs.), milliner, 30 Budge row, City
Simpson Elizabeth (Mrs.),staymaker&milliner,129Oxford st
Simpson Emma (Miss), lodging ho. 1 Chapel st. Bedford rw
Simpson Francis, chinaman, 2 & 3 Queen's Hd.rw.Nwgtn.bu
Simpson Geo. baker, 24 New road, St. George's east
Simpson Geo. barrister, 19 Old square, Lincoln's inn
Simpson Geo. beer retailer, 79 Lower Thames st
Simpson Geo. bookbinder, 25 Bread st. hill, City
Simpson Geo. bricklayer, 2 St. Mark's rd. Camberwll nw. rd
Simpson Geo. cabinet manufacturer, 12 Eldon st. Finsbury
Simpson Geo. chemist, 1 Robson's place, Kennington road
Simpson Geo. chinaman, 1 Ship tavern pas. Leadenhall mkt
Simpson Geo. plumber, &c. 2 Cleveland st. Fitzroy sq
Simpson Geo. *Secretary to the Cheesemongers' Benevolent Institution*, 8 Bath st. Newgate st
Simpson Geo. station. & bookbind. 21 Adams row, Hampst.rd
Simpson Geo. surgeon, 6 Bedford st. Bedford square
Simpson Geo. tinfoil manufacturer, see Elmslie & Simpson
Simpson Geo. Oakley, perfumer, 20 Rolls bdgs. Fetter lane
Simpson Godwin, blind ma. 6 Lucas pl. Commercial rd. east
Simpson Henry, cheesemonger, 58 Chapel st. Somers town
Simpson Henry, merchant, 6 Union court, Old Broad st
Simpson Henry Charles, hair dresser, 49 Old st. road
Simpson Isaac, corndealer, 28 Skinner st. Somers town
Simpson Isaac, gold & silver laceman, see Johnson&Simpson
Simpson Isaac, *Sir R. Abercrombie* P.H.13Chas.st.Hattn.gdn
Simpson James, beer retailer, 21 King William st. City
Simpson James, civil engineer, Chelsea waterworks, Thames bank, & 33 Gt. George st. Westminster
Simpson James, ho. painter&gilder, 104 High st.Marylebone
Simpson James, linendraper, 3 Lucas pl. Commercl. rd. east
Simpson James, patent medicine vendor, 286 Strand
Simpson James, plasterer & bricklayer, 9 College st.Chelsea
Simpson James plumber & painter, 52 High st. Kensington
Simpson James, surgeon, 21 King st. Camden town
Simpson James Gilson, *Three Tuns* P.H. 11 Billingsgate
Simpson Jane (Mrs.), lace mender, 20 Portland st. Soho
Simpson John, *Blue Posts* P.H.23Grosvenor mews,Grosvr. st
Simpson John, cheesemngr. 9 Margaret ter. Paddington grn
Simpson John, coffee rooms, 21 Old Bailey
Simpson John, conveyancer,29Savillerow,Burlington gardens
Simpson John, flute & flageolet maker, 266 Regent st
Simpson John, grocer, 99 Golden lane, St. Luke's
Simpson John, ins. brok. & gen. agent, see Suart & Simpson
Simpson John, mercantile agency office, 25 Moorgate st
Simpson John, portrait painter, 10 Carlisle st. Soho sq
Simpson John, *Sec. to the Profsnl. & Comrcl. Detector Association*, 25 Moorgate st. City
Simpson John, warehouseman, 78 Basinghall st. from No.18
Simpson John, *William Fourth* P.H. 10Beauchamp st.Holbn
Simpson John, wine merchant, 35 Mincing lane
Simpson John Henry, oil & colorman, 54 London rd. Borough
Simpson John Woodhouse, barrister, 3 Church yd. ct. Temple
Simpson Joseph, ladies'shoema.3Hopkinsbdgs.Up.st.Islingtn
Simpson Joseph, potato dlr. 3 Langley pl. Commercial rd. ea
Simpson Margt. (Mrs.), potato dlr. 45 Charles st. St. Geo. ea
Simpson Mary (Mrs.), chandler's shop, 21 Prosp.pl.Camb.hea
Simpson Mary (Mrs.), marine store dlr.134Cornwall rd.Lam
Simpson Miles, galloon&double mfr. 6 Dyers' ct. Aldermanby
Simpson Palgrave, solicitor, see Norris, Allen & Simpson
Simpson Percy, special pleader, 5 Mitre ct. chambers,Temple
Simpson Peter, coffee rooms, 174 Kingsland road
Simpson Pinder, conveyancer, 29 Saville row, Piccadilly
Simpson Reuben, boot & shoe maker, Church st. Hackney
Simpson Richard, grocer & italian wa. 17 Gt. Marylebone st
Simpson Robert, baker, 3 Knight's pl. Wandsworth road
Simpson Robert, coal & coke dealer, 81 Mount st.Berkeley sq
Simpson Robert, stock & sharebroker, 23 Tokenhouse yard
Simpson Robert, tobacconist, 5 North pl. Hampstead road
Simpson Sarah (Mrs.), hosier & glov.12New st.Covent gardn
Simpson Thomas, builder, 5 Lit. St. James's st. St. James's
Simpson Thos. *Cheshire Cheese* P.H.16Mount plsnt.Gr.in.la
Simpson Thomas, grocer, 8 Rosoman st. Clerkenwell
Simpson Thomas, silk merchant, 11 Laurence Pountney hill
Simpson Thomas, tailor, 40 Dean st. Soho
Simpson Thomas, watchmaker, 129 Oxford st
Simpson Thos.B. *Albion tavern*, 26 Gt.Russell st.Cov.garden
Simpson Thomas Jas. cabinet maker, 20 Wilson st. Finsbury
Simpson Wm. civil engineer, Belgrave road, Pimlico
Simpson Wm. corn dealer, Southampton st. Camberwell
Simpson Wm. grocer, 19 Gt. Windmill st. Haymarket
Simpson Wm. grocer, 3 Octagon pl. Kennington common
Simpson Wm. surgeon, 4 High st. Bloomsbury
Simpson Wm. military tailor, 21 Portland st. Soho
Simpson Wm. oil & colorman, 1 Portman pl. Edgware road
Simpson Wm. whipmaker, 25 Hosier lane, West Smithfield
Simpson Wm. Butler, house decorator, &c. 456 West Strand
Simpson Wm. Heddon, auctioneer, estate agt. & undertaker, 58 Gt.Tower st.; sale rooms,11 Bedford pl.Commrcl. rd.ea
Simpson Wm. Henry, french & english baker, 391 Strand
Simpson Wm. Henry, woollendraper, see Osmond & Simpson
Simpson Wm. Robert, solicitor, 8 Red Lion st. Clerkenwell
Simpson Wm. Warre, russia brok. Baltic, & 65 Old Broad st
Simpson Wm. Wooley, auctioneer & appraiser of estates, breweries, & church property, 18 Bucklersbury
Sims & Hill, stock & share brokers, 3 Bartholomew lane
Sims & Smith, stationers & news agents, 92 Goswell st
Sims Wm. & Jacob, merchants, 8 George yard, Lombard st
Sims, Willyams, Nevill, Druce & Co. copper merchants, Steelyard wharf, Upper Thames st
Sims & Miller, staymakers, 34 Hackney road
Sims Alfred, *Clown* P.H. 62 St. John st. road
Sims Francis, stay manufacturer, 83 Bishopsgate without
Sims George, tailor, 2 Fair st. Horselydown
Sims James, tailor, 4 Union st. Charles st. Berkeley sq
Sims John, carpenter, 13 Queen st. Golden square
Sims John, stone mason, 61 Praed st. Paddington
Sims John, stone mason, Uxbridge road, Bayswater
Sims John, upholsterer, 2 Cleveland st. Fitzroy square
Sims John, wardrobe dealer, 1 Union st. Middlesex hospital
Sims Joseph, *White Hart* P.H. 21 Park side, Knightsbridge
Sims Juliana (Miss), stationer, 44 Silver st. Golden sq
Sims Robert, grocer, 1 Whitmore place, Hoxton
Sims Robert, looking glass manufactr. 150 Aldersgate st
Sims Robert, writer & gilder, 28 Friar st. Blackfriars road
Sims Sarah (Miss), ladies' boot & shoe ma.9Jewin st. Crippgt
Sims Sarah(Mrs.),hairdresser,4King'sHd.ct.St.Martin's le gr
Sims Thomas, baker, 8 Southampton st. Camberwell road
Sims Thomas, *Earl of Effingham* P.H. 235 Whitechapel rd
Sims Thomas, linendraper, 28 Park terrace, Regent's pk. rd
Sims Thomas, wheelwright, 22 Gt. York mews, Portman sq
Sims Wm. coach & harness mak. 51 Gt. Queen st. Linc. inn fi
Sims William, coffee rooms, 241 Blackfriars road
Sims William, tailor, 20 George st. Euston square
Sims William, warehouseman, 8 Johnson's ct. Fleet st
Simson Thos. & John, timber brs. 5 King's arms bldgs. Cornhl
Simson Alexander, mahogany broker, 75 Old Broad st. City
Simson Fras. Webb, uphold. & cabinet ma. 26 Bow st.Cov.gar
Simson George, pasteboard box maker, 15 Hoxton square
Simson John, merchant& consul for baden,1Riches ct.Lime st
Simson Thomas Benjamin, academy, 39 St. Mary axe
Simson William, cabinet maker, 39 Up. John st. Fitzroy sq
Sinclair & Facey, auctions. & apprais. 4 Finsbury ter. City rd
Sinclair, Hamilton & Co. merchants, 16 Gould sq. Crutched friars (late Sinclair Alexander)
Sinclair John & Co. distillers, Princes st. Lambeth
Sinclair Benjamin, teadealer, see Owthwaite & Sinclair
Sinclair Charles, manufacturer of glass chandeliers, lustres, lamps, &c. watch & clock glasses, china, glass, & staffordshire warehouse, 69 Old st. St. Luke's
Sinclair Donald, physician, 38 Bruton st. Berkeley square
Sinclair Duncan, *Durham Arms* P.H.Durhm.pl.ea.Hckny.rd
Sinclair Duncan, *Olive Branch* P.H.64Lambeth lower marsh
Sinclair Duncan, *Pear Tree* P.H. 65 Lambeth lower marsh
Sinclair Duncan, *Skinners' Arms* P.H.127Gt.Suffolk st.Boro'
Sinclair George, herald chaser, 4 Finsbury ter. City road
Sinclair James, fruiterer, 1 Kennington cross
Sinclair Jeremiah, hairdresser, 19 Holles st. Clare market
Sinclair John, distiller, Princes st. Lambeth
Sinclair John, *D. of Clarence* P.H. 14 Langley pl. Com. rd.e
Sinclair John, fruiterer, 8 Wallington pl.Wandsworth road
Sinclair John, *Rockingham Arms* P.H.1Newingtoncauseway, & 1 Rockingham place, New Kent road
Sinclair John Jas. hot presser, 21 Norman's bldgs. St.Luke's
Sinclair Joseph, *Blk. Boy & Apple Tree* P.H.49St.Martin's la
Sinclair Robt. shoemaker, 172 Up.Whitecross st. St. Luke's
Sinclair Thos. watch & clock glass ma.20 Old st. St. Luke's
Sinclair Wm. dentist, 42 Gerrard st. Soho
Sinderby Elizh.W. (Mrs.),watchmaker, 18 Bull & Mouth st
Sinfield Thos. undertaker, 13 Bride st. Liverpool road
Singer Alf. & Co. brown stone & chemical potters, Vauxhall
Singer Chrlt. (Mrs.),3*Neats' Tongues* P.H.3Gt.Pearl st.Sptlf
Singer George, printer, see Marchant, Singer & Co
Singer Julius, tailor, 9 Tenter ter. Tenter gd. Goodman's flds
Single Thos. auctioneer & surveyor, 34 Coleman st
Singleton Benjamin, lodging house, 28 Upper Belgrave pl
Singleton Cuthbert, attorney, 21 Gt. James st. Bedford row
Sinkins George, painter, 2 Tower st. Seven dials
Sinkins John, linendraper, 11 Broad st. Golden square

Sinkins Joseph, linendraper, 9 Upp. Queen's bldgs. Bromptn
Sinkler Edward, pork butcher, 2 King's road east, Sloane sq
Sinkler Robt. pork butcher, 11 Mid. Queen's bdgs. Knightsb
Sinnock & Park, carpenters & packing case makers, 83 Farringdon st. & 5 Greystoke pl. Fetter lane
Sinnott Jas. scavenger, 6 King John court, Holywell lane, Shoreditch, & Old Gravel lane
Sinnott Wm. jun. scavenger, 41 Belvedere road, Lambeth
Sinton George, nurseryman & florist, Hampstead road
Sintzenich Edwd. R. land & est. agt. 31 Grosvenor st. Gros. sq
Sintzenich Gustavus E. artist, 3 Princes st. Fitzroy sq
Sion College & Library (Rev. Henry Christmas, M.A. librarian & secretary), London wall
Siordet, Meyer & Co. general merchts. 3 St. Helen's place
Siordet John James, merchant, 3 St. Helen's pl. Bishopsgate
Siordet Robert Lewis, merchant, 3 St. Helen's pl. Bishopsgate
Sired Ambrose, fruiterer, 22 Seymour place, Camden town
Sired Wm. bootmaker, 22½ Rodney st. Pentonville
Sirett Charles, tailor, 1 West pl. St. George's rd. Southwark
Sirrell Thos. Charles, gold & silver refiner, 54 Barbican
Sisley Thos. & Chas. imptr. of french goods, 79½ Watling st
Sisley Thos. baker & confectioner, 5 Lamb pl. Kingsland rd
Sison Edward, surgeon & chemist, 19 Goswell st
Sissens Thomas, bricklayer, 30 Charles st. Hampstead road
Sisson James, paperhanger, 268 Rotherhithe st
Sisson Thomas, hair dresser, 46 Burlington arcade
Sisson William, parliamentary agent, 46 Leicester sq
Sissons Rt. carpent. & undertak. 101 Whitehorse st. Stepney
Sisterson Walter H. smith & engineer, 1 Morris pl. Southwk. b. rd
Sitch Benj. french watch gilder, 35 Gt. Queen st. Lin. inn flds
Sitch Samuel, water gilder, 17 Oxford st
Sitton Frederick Wm. coffee rooms, 51 Chiswell st
Sivil William, carpenter, 77 Law chambers, Chancery lane
Sizeland Wm. *Marlborough tavern*, Abbey rd. St. John's wd
Sizer Sarah (Mrs.), lace warehouse, 9 Newington causeway
Sizer Wm. Paul, *Robin Hood* P. H. 1 Duke st. Westminster
Skae Peter, surveyor, 52 Hart st. Covent garden
Skan Wm. linendraper & hosier, 6 Union ter. Notting hill
Skardon John, dentist, 11 Victoria road, Pimlico
Skarratt Rd. Thos. newsagt. 1 Union ter. Bagnigge wells rd
Skeags John, oil & colorman, &c. 5 Star alley, Fenchurch st
Skeats Joseph, cooper, 12 Gt. Crown ct. Little Pulteney st
Skeats William, cooper, 37 Marshall st. Golden sq
Skeel David & Thos. surgeons, 42 Norfolk st. Strand
Skeen & Leary, mahogany brokers, 75 Old Broad st. City
Skeen Drusile (Miss), dressmaker, 34 Bedford st. Comrcl. rd
Skeen Edwin Allen, mahogany & timber merchant, 24 New Montague st. Spitalfields
Skeere Thomas, beer retailer, 17 New st. Kennington road
Skeet Charles, accountant, 4 Dorset st. Portman sq
Skeet James, carrot salesman, North row, Cov. garden mkt
Skeet Mary A. (Mrs.), cowkeeper, 4 Fortunate pl. Bluegate flds
Skeet Richard, tailor, 36 Lisson grove north, St. John's wood
Skeffington Thomas, cattle salesman, 60 West Smithfield
Skeffington Wm. booksellr. & stat. 3 Oddy's row, Islington gr
Skegg Robt. surgeon & accoucheur, 2 St. Martin's pl. Charing cr
Skegg Edwd. & Joseph, chair & couch maks. 7 John st. Curtain rd
Skegg Wm. Harper, solicitor & registrar of births, &c. 39 Brudenell place, Hoxton
Skelding Thomas, surgeon, 11 Euston square
Skelt Martin & Benj. prints. & publishs. 11 Swan st. Minories
Skelton Benj. valuer & appraiser, 83 High st. Marylebone
Skelton Geo. pianoforte mak. 55 Up. John st. Fitzroy sq
Skelton George, tailor, 315 Albany road, Camberwell
Skelton James, scagliola mfr. 51 William st. Regent's park
Skelton James, tailor, 15 Cheapside
Skelton John, *Ship* P.H. 12 Lower Shadwell
Skelton John, tinman & brazier, 61 Wych st. Strand
Skelton Margaret (Miss), professor of music, 15 Cheapside
Skelton Mary Elizh. (Miss), artist, 32 London st. Fitzroy sq
Skelton Robert, engraver & printer, 1 Savoy st. Strand
Skelton Thos. butcher, 15 Lit. Charlotte st. Middx. hospital
Skelton Tom, hairdresser & perfumer, see Honey & Skelton
Skelton Wm. *Duke of York* P.H. 13 Great Marylebone st
Skelton Wm. teadealer & grocer, 49 Bishopsgate within
Skerratt James, tailor, 147 Grove st. Camden town
Skerritt Anne Eliza (Miss), fancy statr. 79 St. John st. road
Skerritt James, baker, 1 Royal Hospital row, Chelsea
Skerry Charles, academy, 19 Castle st. Holborn
Skerry Wm. watchmaker, 9 Dartmouth st. Westminster
Skey Fred. Carpenter, surgeon, 13 Grosvenor st. Bond st
Skidmore Thos. Robt. medical & gen. glass war. 19 Haymarket
Skilbeck & Hall, solicitors, 19 Southampton buildings
Skilbeck Joseph & John, drysalters & mers. 202 Up. Thames st
Skillett Stephen, stationer, 3 Ebenezr. pl. Comml. rd. Limeho
Skiller Richard, cornchandler, 80 Drury lane
Skiller William, *Ship* P.H. 123 Poplar High st
Skillman Hy. law & general statnr. 51 King st. Westminster
Skimer William, jun. wholesale clothier, 18 Minories
Skingle John, baker, 6 Henry st. Hampstead road
Skingley Agnes (Mrs.), straw hat & bon. ma. 210 Poplar High st
Skinner Henry & Son, tobacconists, 243 Strand
Skinner Jas. & John & Son, whipmkrs. 11 Finsbury pl. north
Skinner Allan Maclean, barrister, 1 Pump court, Temple
Skinner Ann (Mrs.), grocer, 17 Pembroke pl. Vauxhall br. rd
Skinner Charles, cider mercht. Hiberniawhf. Montague close
Skinner Charles, clockmaker, 23 Pool terrace, City road
Skinner Chas. Coe, ladies' boot & shoe maker, 97 Oxford st
Skinner Edwd. fruiterer, 19 Great Bland st. Dover road
Skinner Daniel, grocer, 8 Portland st. Walworth common
Skinner Daniel, stonemason, Orchard row, High st. Cambrwl
Skinner Fitzowen, barrister, 1 New square, Lincoln's inn
Skinner Frederick, wheelwright, Union rd. Rotherhithe
Skinner George, dyer, 69 Crawford st
Skinner George Thos. stockbroker, 5 Angel court, Bank
Skinner Henry, scalemaker, see Webb & Skinner
Skinner Harriet (Mrs.), milliner, 27 Exeter st. Sloane st
Skinner Hen. John, tobacconist, 3 St. Martin's ct. Le'ster sq
Skinner James, *Brown Bear* P.H. 65 Broad st. Bloomsbury
Skinner James, builder, 10½ Stanhope st. Glo'ster gt. Regt's pk
Skinner James, clothes salesman, 1 Clarence grds. Regts. pk
Skinner James, tailor, 38 Brewer st. Golden square
Skinner James, timber merchant, Butcher row, Ratcliff
Skinner John, boarding house, 18½ Little Knightrider st
Skinner John, bootmaker, 9 Blenheim st. Bond st
Skinner John, builder, 4 King st. Finsbury
Skinner John, chinaman, 15 Star corner, Bermondsey st
Skinner John, coalmerchant & lighterman, Narrow st. Ratclff
Skinner John, *Red Lion* P.H. 5 Gt. Warner st. Clerkenwell
Skinner John Henry, tobacconist, 67 Holborn hill
Skinner John Thos. undertkr. 18 Cardingtn. st. Hampstead rd
Skinner Richard, baker, Garden row, Deptford New town
Skinner Robert, cheesemonger, 103 Curtain road, Shoreditch
Skinner Sophia (Mrs.), saddler & hrrness maker, Camberwell green, & Dulwich, Surrey
Skinner Thomas, boot & shoemaker, 162 Tooley st
Skinner Thomas, coach builder, 52 Gray's inn lane
Skinner Thomas, fruit salesman, Covent garden fruit market
Skinner Thomas, russia broker, Baltic coffe house
Skinner Wm. baker, Alfred place, Sidney st. Mile end
Skinner Wm. beer retailer, 245 Bethnal green road
Skinner Wm. boot & shoe maker, Stratford, Essex
Skinner Wm. fruiterer, 29 Upper King st. Bloomsbury
Skinner Wm. ironmonger, 9 Mount row, Liverpool road
Skinner Wm. tailor, 50 Jermyn st. St. James's
Skinner Wm. tailor, 11 St. Martin's court, St. Martin's lane
Skinner Wm. David, tobacconist, 5 Crown row, Walworth rd
Skinners' Alms Houses, 37 Gt. St. Helens, & Mile end road
Skinners' Hall (Thomas Glover Kensit, clerk), 8 Dowgate hill
Skinsley Archer, fish salesman, 19 St. Mary at hill
Skipper & East, stationers & printers, 1 St. Dunstan's hill
Skipper Henry, beer retailer, 46 Dorchester st. New North rd
Skipper Henry, *Black Bull* P.H. 60 Gray's inn lane
Skipper Henry, corn factor, 19 Jewry st. Crutchedfriars
Skipper Peter Thomas, merchant, 180 Upper Thames st
Skipper Rt. *Horns & Horseshoe* P.H. 3 Cable st. Wellclose sq
Skipsey John & Co. house painters, 25 Carey st. Lincoln's inn
Skipworth George Borman, barrister, 8 New sq. Lncln's. inn
Shipwith Lionel, proctor, 20 Gt. Knightridger st. Doct. com
Skirll Mary (Mrs.), pork butcher, 41 St. John st. Clerkenwell
Skirrow Charles Francis, solicitor, see Gregory Faulkner & Co
Skirrow Walker, jun. special pleader, 3 Pump ct. Temple
Skirrow Wm. copper, brass, zinc, tin, tinplate & general metal agent & dealer, 198 Upper Thames street
Skirving John, engraver, &c. see Kronheim & Skirving
Skitt John & Co. white lead & color mers. 5 Union st. Boro'
Skoles Elizabeth (Mrs.), cowkeeper, 14 North st. Fitzroy sq
Skone John, *Bird in Hand* P.H. 2 Northampton st. Clrknwl
Skoulding Edw. R. milliner, 11 New Church st. Lisson grove
Skowing John, watch engraver, 43 St. John's sq. Clerkenwell
Skudder George, wheelwright, 27 Broomfields, Deptford
Skudder Henry, wheelwright, 9 Broomfields, Deptford
Skudder John, grocer, 22 Back st. Horselydown
Skudder William, potato dealer, 28 Broad st. Lambeth
Skuse Benjamin, dairyman, 2 Brill row, Somers town
Skuse John, comb manufacturer, 6 Heath pl. Cambridge heath
Skynner Henry, solicitor, 46 Gt. Portland st
Skynner Robert, conveyancer, 42 Mortimer st. Cavendish sq
Skinner William Henry, sen. solicitor, 75 Gt. Titchfield st
Skyring William Henry, surveyor, 21 Old Jewry
Slack Joseph & Son, hatters & hosiers, 62 South Audley st
Slack Richard & John, furnishing ironmongers, 336 Strand

Slack Henry James, wool broker, see Buxton & Slack
Slack James, hairdresser & perfumer, 4B, Sloane st
Slack Wm. Gilliam, solicitor,10 Union st.Hill st.Berkeley sq
Slade & Wadeson, proctors & notaries, 20 Bennett's hill
Slade Aaron, fruiterer, 73 Park st. Camden town
Slade Catherine (Mrs.), corset ma.2 Corporation row,Clkwl
Slade Chas.china & glass warehouse, 2 Walker's ct.Golden sq
Slade Frederic William, barrister, 2 Pump ct. Temple
Slade Hen. carpenter & packing case ma. 17 Charterhouse st
Slade James, bricklayer, 5 Munster st. Regent's park
Slade John, bone button ma.7Tilley st.Tenter ground,Spitalfi
Slade John, china & glass wa. 9 Clement's inn pas.Clare mrkt
Slade John, coffee rooms, 31 New Church st. Lisson grove
Slade John, law stationer, 16 Carey st. Lincoln's inn
Slade John, ship & insur. bro. & color merch.69 Up.Thames st
Slade Joseph, coffee rooms,45 Grafton st.ea.Tottenham ct. rd
Slade Laura (Mrs.), milliner, 86 Leadenhall st
Slade Philip, carpenter, 12 Sale st. Paddington
Slade Richard Greville, dentist, see Normansell & Slade
Slade Robert, *Bull* P.H. Milford lane, Strand
Slade Samuel, baker, 17 Warwick place, Kingsland road
Slade Wm. bricklayer, 49 Chenies mews
Slade Wm. coachmaker, 102 St. John st. road
Slade Wm. tailor & trimming seller, 12 Little Saffron hill
Slade Wm. tailor, 8 Thomas st. Shad Thames
Slade Wm. Bushnell, surgeon,&c. 2 Foregate, Clement's inn
Sladen, Glennie, Farquhar & Sladen, procts.19 Bennett's hill
Sladen St. Barbe, solicitor, 6 South terrace, Brompton, & 14 Parliament st
Slaney & Jelly, colonial agents, 12 Little Tower st
Slaney Goddard & Co. tea brokers, 157 Fenchurch st
Slaney George, fruiterer, 7 Carpenter st. Berkeley sq
Slaney John, cabinet maker, 37 Skinner st. Bishopsgate st
Slaney Richard, *DevonshireArms* P.H.20Duke st.Manchr.sq
Slaney Simion Sutton, linendraper, 38A, Lamb's Conduit st
Slaney Wm. Henry, attorney, 13 Gray's inn square
Slape Henry, bookseller, 21 Brecknock pl. Camden new tn
Slark Wm. & Son, furnishing ironmongers, 10 Cheapside
Slark Ann (Mrs.),chemic.stopperer,2Goldsmith st.Gough sq
Slark Robert, baker, 2 Warwick st. Belgrave rd
Slark Thomas, hairdresser, 7 Little Ormond st. Queen sq
Slark Wm. coach,van & wag. offi. 13 High rw.Knightsbridge
Slark Wm. ironmonger, &c. see Dare & Slark
Slark Wm. whip & umbrella maker, 67 Burlington arcade
Slate Thomas, bookbinder, 2 & 18 King's head ct. Holborn
Slater Ann (Mrs.), tobacconist, 234 Whitechapel rd
Slater Samuel & Son, tailors, 45 Albemarle st. Piccadilly
Slater David, brushmaker, 29 Windsor terrace, City rd
Slater Francis, solicitor, see Shearman & Slater
Slater Henry, livery stables, 9 Clay st. Marylebone
Slater Henry, upholsterer, Sidney pl. King's rd. Chelsea
Slater James, gasfitter, 23 Denmark st. Soho
Slater James, printer, 13 St.George's pl. Back rd. St.Geo. ea
Slater James John, chandler's shop, 24Maze,Tooley st.Boro'
Slater Joel, butcher, 42 Lower Belgrave pl. Pimlico
Slater John, bootma. 126 Union st. Boro',&135Lambth.Lr.ma
Slater John, butcher, South Lambeth pl. South Lambeth
Slater John, cattle salesman, 60 West Smithfield
Slater John, tailor, 2 King st. Regent st
Slater Joseph, carpenter, Knightsbridge green
Slater John (Mrs.), ladies' school, 5 Hall pl. St. John's wood
Slater Robert, plumber & painter, Deptford High st
Slater Sarah (Miss), ladies' school, 25 Grove pl.Lisson gr.nth
Slater Thomas, butcher, 9 & 10 High st. Kensington, & 47 Jermyn st. St. James's
Slater Thomas, hairdresser & perfumer, 10 Lowther arcade
Slater Thomas, varnish maker, 4 New inn yd. Shoreditch
Slater Ward, tea dealer, 4 & 5 Camberwell grove
Slater Ward, tea dealer, 76 Drury lane
Slater William, watchmaker, 193 St. George st
Slater Wilson, patent copper powder barrel maker & gunpowder office, 332 Wapping
Slatford Henry, bootmaker, 7 North buildings, Finsbury cir
Slatter Eliz. (Mrs.), lace cleaner, 10 Euston place, Euston sq
Slatter Geo. wine & brandy mercht. 22 Cullum st. Fench. st
Slatter Jas. coach lace maker, 12 Charles st. Blackfriars rd
Slatter Thomas, coach builder, 98 John st. Fitzroy sq
Slatter Thomas, coach & harness maker, 134 Long acre
Slatter Thomas W. academy, 3 Smith st. King's rd. Chelsea
Slatter Walter Wm. haircutter, 24 Marylebone st. Piccadilly
Slatyer James, tailor, 1 Aylesbury st. Clerkenwell
Slatyer Joseph, tailor, 1 Upper Charles st. Northampton sq
Slaughter Alfred, linendraper, 13 Bedford ct. Covent garden
Slaughter Edward, solicitor, 5 Duchess st. Portland place
Slaughter Jas. currier & leather cutter, 92 Poplar High st
Slaughter Mihill, coal mercht. Bridewell whf. Wm. st. Blckfs
Slaymaker Thos. fruiterer & fruit sales. Centre rw.Covnt. gdn
Slaytor James Henry, brush maker, 8 Leather lane
Sleap Francis, tailor, 32 Plumbers' st. City road
Sleap John G. merchant & insur. brok. 69 Old Broad st. City
Sleap Jonathan Thomas, attorney, 2 Middle Temple lane
Sleap Thomas, tailor, 16 Worship st. Finsbury
Sleath William, mourning milliner, 56 Bunhill row
Sledmar Ann (Mrs.), cheesemonger, Highbury vale
Slee Edward & Co. diet drink manufs. 92 Borough High st
Slee Edward Richardson, vinegar maker, see Payne & Slee
Slee T. P. & C. B. mustard & blue makers, Russell pl. Bermsy
Slee George, bootmaker, 12 Warwick st. Belgrave road
Slee Robert, solicitor & superintendent registrar of births, deaths & marriages for the Union of St. Olave's, Southwark, & vestry clerk for St. John's parish, 1 Parish st. St. John's, Southwark
Sleeman John, chemist & drug. 14 Windsor pl. Sthwk.bdg.rd
Sleeman M. A. (Mrs.), *OldCommodore* P.H.183PoplarHigh st
Sleet Jas. boot & shoe ma. 4 Strewan pl. King's rd. Chelsea
Sleet Jas. boot & shoe maker, 36 York st. Kingsland rd
Sleigh & Wooley, sewing silk & twist ma. 74 Aldermanbury
Sleigh John, artist, 25 Mary st. Hampstead road
Sleight Charlotte (Miss), dressma. 18 High st. Camberwell
Sleight Thomas, gasfitter, 4 Duke st. Westminster
Sleight W. H. *Goldsmiths' Arms* P.H. 17 Lit. Sutton st.Clkwl
Slemmon Thos. mathl. inst. mak. 3 Brandon rw. Newing. cau
Slight Elizh. (Mrs.), marine store dlr. 29 Brook st. St. Pncrs
Sligo & Shannon Railway Co. (Abrm. Gole, sec.), Winchester house, Old Broad st
Slim Edward, grocer, 133 Upper st. Islington
Slim Henry, dairyman, 1 North st. Sloane st
Slim James, silk manufacturer, 17 Spital square
Slim Joseph, cowkeeper, 18 Ernest st. Regent's park
Slim Thomas, boot & shoe maker, 97 Fetter lane, Holborn
Slingsby Eliz. (Mrs.), haberdasher, 40 Gt. Titchfield st
Slinn Charles, boot & shoe maker, 29 Chancery lane
Slinn Joseph, plumber, 1 Bloomsbury court, High Holborn
Slipper Benjamin, miller, Blue Anchor rd. Bermondsey
Slipper James, chemist & druggist, 87 Leather lane
Slipper John, butcher, 1 Acton pl. Bagnigge wells road
Slipper Thos. surgeon, 6 Beckford pl. Kennington common
Sloan John, tailor & trimming seller, 198 Sloane st
Sloan Thomas, law stationer, see Stevenson & Sloan
Sloane John & Co. cheesemongers, 114 St. Martin's lane
Sloane George, special pleader, 6 Pump court, Temple
Slocomb Thomas, grocer, 24 Sudeley st. City road
Slocombe John, baker, 3 Britannia place, Wandsworth road
Slocombe Robt. tallow chandler, 9 Charlotte st. Portland pl
Slocombe William, laceman, 53 Newington causeway
Slodden Isaac & Co. annatto ma. 46 Weymouth ter. Hcky.rd
Slodden Sarah (Mrs.), lodging house, 8 Norfolk st. Strand
Slograve Chas. *White Horse* P.H. 37 Rupert st. Haymarket
Sloman Ben. furniture broker, 52 Old Compton st. Soho
Sloman Samuel, outfitting warehouse, 19 King st. Tower hill
Sloman Samuel, upholsterer & easy chair ma. 45 Wardour st
Sloman William, cabinetmaker, 22 Gower pl. Euston sq
Slope Thomas, linendraper, 55 Piccadilly
Sloper Alfred, rule maker, 14 Wellington st. Blackfriars rd
Sloper James, stationer & bookbinder, 47 Holborn hill
Sloper John Dobbs, boot & shoe maker to her Majesty, 19 Store st. Bedford sq
Sloper John William, solicitor, 6 Vernon pl. Bloomsbury
Sloper Joseph, painter & paprhngr. 106 High st. Marylebn
Sloper Thomas, bookseller, 31 Beaumont sq. Mile end
Sloper Thos. rule maker, 28 Freeschool st. Horselydown
Slous Joseph Gideon, grocer, New cross
Slouse Gideon, artist, 1 Oval road, Regent's park
Slow John, carpenter&undertaker,1Gedling ter. Bermondsey
Slow Joseph, beer retailer, 1 Beauvoir pl. Kingsland rd
Slow Rt. Jas. *Prince Wm. Henry* P.H. 111 Bermondsey st
Slowburn Hen. cheesemonger, &c. 30 Lambeth Lowr. marsh
Slowman Abraham, sheriff's officer for Middlesex, 90 Chancery lane, & 4 Cursitor st
Slowman Ben. wine & spirit merchant, 32 St. Mary at hill
Sluce Wm. watch & clock mak. 22 Church row, Bethnl. grn
Sly Bannister, *King Wm. 4th* P.H. 49 Flagon row, Walwth
Sly Elizabeth (Mrs.), straw hat maker, 7 Jewry st. Aldgate
Sly Hen. John Lee, *King's Arms* P.H.Gt.College st. Westm
Sly John, leather cutter, 34 Gt. St. Andrew st. Seven dials
Sly Stephen, engraver on wood, 11 Bouverie st. Fleet st
Slyfield George, boarding house, 5 Norfolk st. Strand
Slyth Joseph, stationer, 68 South Audley st
Smaggasgale Wm. tin platework.16Holywell row,Worshp.st
Smale George, boot & shoe maker, 59½ Newington causeway
Smale George, wheelwright, 35Southamptn.mews,Euston sq
Smale Henry, mechanical dentist, 187 High Holborn

Smale Henry Lewis, proctor, 3 Dean's ct. Doctors' commons
Smale James, boot & shoemaker, 74Seymour pl. Bryanstn.sq
Smale John, barrister, 1 New square, Lincoln's inn
Smale Thomas, dealer in sea horse, sea cow, natural & manufacturer of improved mineral teeth, 187 High Holborn
Smale Thos. jun. manfr. of mineral teeth, 187 High Holborn
Smale Wm. Adderley, solicitor, 30 Arundel st. Strand
Smales Thos. Wm. engraver & printer, 2 Manners st. York rd
Small & Co. merchants & east india agents, 8 Old Jewry
Small Pox Hospital (James Frederick Marson, resident surgeon), King's cross, St. Pancras Old road
Small Elizh. S. (Mrs.), plumber, &c.6Fonthill pl. Clapham rd
Small Harriet (Mrs.), fruiterer, 6 South Molton st
Small James, cheesemonger, 116 Aldersgate st
Small James, milliner & laceman, 2 Norton folgate
Small Mark, jeweller, 36 New Compton st. Soho
Small Thomas, working jeweller, 3 Dacre st. Westminster
Small William, painter & glazier, 3 SouthMolton st. Bond st
Smallbone Alexander, bootmaker, 8 Dean st. Holborn
Smallbone John, bedstead ma.23Cumberland st. Middlx.hosp
Smallbone William, stock broker, Stock exchange
Smallcomb Jn. *Rose & Crown* P.H. 8London ho. yd. St. Paul's
Smalley Overton, laceman, 2 Barnsbury pl. Islington
Smallhorn John, carver & gilder, 9 Cleveland st. Fitzroy sq
Smallman Joseph, builder, 1 Chester st. Grosvenor pl
Smallridge Wm. saddler to the Queen, 4 Holles st. Cavendh.sq
Smallridge Wm.Jas.saddler, 13Devonshire bldgs. Gt. Doverrd
Smallwood Thos. Downes, fringema.5Princes st. Lit. Queen st
SmallwoodWm.bdg.material dlr. Rockingham ho. Nw. Kentrd
Smallwood Wm. Thos. brass founder, 12½ London st. Ratcliff
Smart & Buller, solicitors, 56 Lincoln's inn fields
Smart (Denham) & Co. cornfactors, 29 Fenchurch st
Smart Edwd.&Hen. picture dealers, 10 Tichborne st. Haymkt
Smart James & Son, corn & coal merchants, 33 Chiswell st
Smart Walter & Co. lithographic draughtsmen & printers in colors, 10 Leather lane
Smart Alexander, watch & clock ma. 32 Chapel st. Grosv.sq
Smart Ann (Mrs.), boot & shoe maker, 1 Stoney la. Tooley st
Smart Benj. H. tea. of elocution, 55Connaught ter. Edgw. rd
Smart Charles, furniture broker, 30 Chapel st. Somers town
Smart Chas. agricultural implement maker & ironfounder, 369 Oxford st. & Phœnix foundry, Coldbath fields
Smart Edward, picture dealer, 2 Smith st. King's rd. Chelsea
Smart Emma (Mrs.), ironmonger, 14 High st. Kensington
Smart George, grocer & cheesemonger, 42 Duke st. St. James's
Smart George, professor of dancing, 29 Leman st
Smart George, saw mills, York road, Westminster road
Smart Henry, locksmith, &c. 1 Drury court, Strand
Smart James, accountant, 3 Furnival's inn, Holborn
Smart James Durant, brushmaker, 54Judd st. Brunswick sq
Smart John, silk manufacturer, 37 Union st. Bishopsgate
Smart John, smith, 5 Princes st. Leicester square
Smart John, tailor, 28 New Church court, Strand
Smart Joseph, watch&chronometer ma.10King st. Tower hill
Smart Kneller, refiner, &c. 60 Princes st. Leicester square
Smart Mary Ann (Mrs.), boot & shoe ma. 183 Whitechapel rd
Smart Nevill, whiting mnfr. Canal wf. Canal bdg. OldKent rd
Smart Robt. leather dresser, 31 Richardson st. Longla. Brmdsy
Smart Thomas, tailor, 54 James st. Oxford st
Smart Walter, watch maker, 5 Hand court, High Holborn
Smart William, attorney, 2 Figtree court, Inner Temple
Smart William, coal merchant, see Brames & Smart
Smart Wm. composition ornament mfr. 18Crown st. Finsbury
Smart Wm. engraver, 3 Brunswick st. St. John st. road
Smart Wm. solicitor, 19 Austinfriars
Smart Wm. writing master, &c. 7 New st. Covent garden
Smartt Chas. Henry, coal merchant, 25 Sun st. Bishopsgate, & Milford wharf, Milford lane, Strand
Smartt Thomas Lifford, attorney, 25 Sun st. Bishopsgate
Smeaton David, baker, 3 Chapel st. Somers town
Smedley & Rogers, solicitors, 40 Jermyn st
Smee Wm. & Son, wholesale cabinet makers & upholsterers, 6 Finsbury pavement, & 34 Little Moorfields
Smee Alfred, surgeon, 7 Finsbury circus
Smee Jas. jewelr. silversmith & hardwareman, &c. 1 Minories
Smee Robt. grocer, 15 Henry st. Pentonville
Smeed Edward, general dealer, 1 North st. Mile end
Smeed George, dairyman, 2½ St. Andrew's hill, Doctors'com
Smeed George, *Lord Clive* P.H. 36 Duke st. Manchester sq
Smeed John, baker, 35 Drummond crescent, Euston sq
Smeed Richard, baker, 87 Up. Seymour st. Euston sq
Smeed Thomas, tailor, 32 Garden row, London road, Boro'
Smeed Wm. *Crown & Sceptre* P.H. 28 Brmptn.rw. Brmptn
Smeeton James, cattle salesman, 41 West Smithfield
Smeeton John, butcher, 5 Ann's terrace, Cambridge heath
SmeetonSamuel, butcher, 69 Goswell st
Smellie Geo. pawnbroker & salesman, 184 Shadwell High st
Smellie James, surgeon, 42 Brewer st. Somers town
Smellie Thos. Geo. copper pl. printer, 4 Bedford ct. Cov.gar
Smellie William, tripe dresser, 244 Shadwell High st. & 24 Nassau place, Commercial road
Smellie Wm. James, *Black Dog* P.H. 32 Crown st. Finsbury
Smerdon John Robert, academy, 20 Lower Islington ter
Smerdon Mary Ann (Mrs.), straw hat ma.95Bishopsgte.witht
Smerdon Wm. Fullwood, boys'school, 10Wt. Conduitter. Ptnvl
Smethurst James, lamp mak. & oil mer. 138 New Bond st
Smethurst John, surgeon, 18 Mornington pl. Hampstead rd
Smily Wm. Robt. manufacturing silversmith, wedding ring maker & silver snuff box maker, 9 Camomile st. Bshpsgt
Smirke Edward, barrister, 3 North, King's Bench walk
Smirke Sidney, architect & surveyor, 24 Berkeley sq
Smith Alfd. & Co. Falcon brwy. Greenwlk. Holland st. Blkfrs
Smith A. & Co. pastrycooks, 26 Poultry
Smith & Agace, blind ma. 3 Castle la. Southwark bridge road
Smith & Allistons', solicitors, 4 Warnford ct. Throgmorton st
Smith & Anderson, muslin warehousemen, 130 Cheapside
Smith Alexander & Son, grocers, 27 Michael's pl. Brompton
Smith Andrew & Robert, provision mer. 2 New st. Bishopgte
Smith Andrew & Son, sheep salesmen, 17 West Smithfield
Smith Ann (Mrs.) & Co. who. confectnrs. 4&5 Fell st. Woodst
Smith Ann & Sons, jewellers, 4 Carlisle st. Soho
Smith & Atkins, solicitors, 12 Serjeants' inn, Fleet st
Smith & Attwood, window glass manfrs. see Attwood & Smith
Smith & Baber, floorcloth manfrs. South pl. Knightsbridge
Smith & Bannister, coachmks. 8 Lit. Marlboro' st. Regent st
Smith Benjamin & Son, corn & coal merchants, 90 Fore st. Cripplegate, & 8 London wall
Smith Benjamin & Son, corn merchants, 29 Upper Thames st
Smith Benj. & Thos. Wantner, manufacturing chemists & color manufacturers, 12 Church st. Mile end, & 14 Corbet court, Brown's lane, Spitalfields
Smith & Bosbery, linendrapers, 208 Regent st
Smith & Brodribb, soap makers, 2 Bermondsey New rd
Smith & Brookes, ladies' academy, 14 Finsbury circus
Smith Brothers & Co. merchant tailors, &c. 223 Regent st
Smith & Campion, potato salesmen, 39 Stoney st. Boro'mkt
Smith & Carrington, corn distillers, Thames bank, Pimlico
SmithCharlesFox&Co. lamp manfrs. & oil merchts. 281 Strand
Smith Charles & James, painters, &c. 55 Gt. Marylebone st
Smith Chas. & Saml. gunmakers, 64 Princes st. Leicester sq
Smith Charles & Son, map & globe sellers, 172 Strand
Smith Charlotte & Son, potato dealers, 15 Red Lion st. Spitalfields, & 139 Church st. Bethnal green
Smith & Clark, straw hat makr. & artifl. florists, 32 Addle st
Smith C. S. & J. W. teamen & grocers, 52Princes st. Leistr.sq
Smith & Cooper, bristol toymakers, importers & dealers in foreign & british toys, wholesale & for exportation, 12 & 13 Chiswell st. Finsbury
Smith Chas. D. & Co. nurserymen, Elizabeth st. south, Pimlico
Smith & Cook, *Crown & Anchor* P.H. 9Gt. Guildford st. Boro'
Smith & Cooper, insur. ship & cus. ho. agts. 12 Harp la. Tower st
Smith Daniel & Son, surveyors, auctioners & land agents, 10 Waterloo place, Pall mall
Smith & Dawes, carriers, 69 Old Bailey
Smith & Dewey, lace manufacturers, 9 Wood st. Cheapside
Smith & Ebbs, stationers & printers, 5 Postern row, Tower hill
Smith Edmund & Walter, jewellers, 30 Maddox st. Regent st
Smith Edward & Co. stone merchts. 36Alfred st. & 5 Wharf, City road
Smith Edward & Co. tailors, 60 Old Broad st. City
Smith, Elder & Co. booksellers & stationers, 65 Cornhill
Smith Elizh. (Miss), & Co. strw. bont. mas. 95Tottenham ct. rd
Smith & Erichsen, merchants, 110 Fenchurch st
Smith, Finer & Smith, corn merchts. lightermen & granary keepers, Wheatsheaf wharf, 3 Upper Thames st
SmithFrancis&Abraham, nurserymn. Cambridge hth. Hckny
Smith & Fry, warehousemen, 57 Friday st. Cheapside
Smith Geo.&Co. casting pot & fire brick ms. 25Gt. Mitchell st
Smith George & Co. malt distillers, Whitechapel rd. & Eagle wharf, 270 Wapping High st
Smith George & Co. warehouse for Bentick & Pelham's washing & bleaching compound, 13 King William st. City
Smith George & Compton, solicitors, 5 Southampton bldgs
Smith George & Son, leather sellers & dealers in grindery, 12 Upper Chapman st. Cannon st. rd
Smith Geo. & Sons, who. furriers, 13 to 16 Gough sq. Fleet st
Smith, Goodhall & Reeves, merchts. 4 Laurence Pountney pl
Smith Henry Bates & Co. wine mers. 4 St. Paul's churchyd
Smith, Hunter & Gwatkin, attorneys, 9 New sq. Lincoln's inn
Smith & Hill, varnish & color manfrs. 13 Raven rw. Mile end
Smith & Hyde, linendrapers, 5 Canning place, Old st
Smith Jas. Bogle & Co. west india mers. 15 Tokenhouse y.

Smith Jas. & Co. linendrapers,&c. 58 & 59 South Audley st
Smith James & Co.wine & brandy mers.2 Crescent pl. Blkfrs
Smith Jas. Herbert & Co.tanners, Wild's rents,Bermondsey
Smith James & Robert, oven builders, 23 York st. York rd
Smith Jas. Dimmock&Co.prntrs.7 East Harding st.Gough sq
Smith James & Son, tanners & leatherdressers, 5 Little Britain, & 9 Bermondsey New road
Smith James Scott & Co. rectifiers, Whitechapel road
Smith Jas. Wilson & Son, button & trim. sels.39Bedfordbury
SmithJeremh.&Son,mers.& cotton yarn mfrs.77Queen st.City
Smith John Bland & Co. woollen cloth waterproofers, 38 Basinghall st. & 18 St. Martin's court
Smith John & Co.artists' colormen,34 Marylebone st.Picca
Smith John Neve & Co. linendrapers, 197 High Holborn
Smith John & Co. silk dyers, Eagle house, Mile end road
Smith John & Co. teadealers, 12 Grafton st. Soho
Smith John & James, *Angel inn*, 1 High st. Islington
Smith John M. & Saml. M. carvers & gilds. 137 NewBond st
Smith John Passam & Co. tea dealers, 1 Coventry st.Haymkt
Smith John & Sidney, warehousemen, 73 Aldermanbury
Smith John & Son,gun & pistol manufactory, 4 Thavies inn
Smith John & Son, tailors,103PoplarHigh st.&36 Bucklsbry
Smith John & Sons, wholesale clock & clock case makers, & manufacturers of clock & watch and timepiece glasses, 2 & 18 St. John's square, Clerkenwell
Smith John & Stephen,*King'sHead*P.H.15 Broad st.Blmsby
Smith & Linton, engravers on wood, 85 Hatton garden
Smith & Lowe (Misses),milliners&dressmks.seeLowe&Smith
Smith Martha & Harriet, teadlrs. 28 Crescent st. Euston sq
Smith & Mirfin, solicitors, 12 Gray's inn place
Smith & Nephew, perfumers in ordinary to her Majesty & royal family, 1 Princes st. Cavendish square
Smith & Parfrey, Pimlico wheel works, 33 Up. Belgrave pl
Smith & Patient, tanners, Queen st. Bermondsey New rd
Smith, Payne & Smiths', bankers, 1 Lombard st
Smith & Punnett, grocers, 129 Shoreditch High st
Smith & Read, carpenters, 5 Whitechapel High st
Smith Richard Tew & Co. carriers, New inn yard, O.Bailey, & Birmingham
Smith Robt.& Co. umbrella makers, 5 Holborn bars
Smith Robt.&John,who.tea dealers,8LaurencePountney hill
Smith RoddamA.&Son,corndlrs.12 Dover pl.west,Kent st.rd
Smith Samuel& Benj. truss&surgl.inst.mks.1 High Holborn
Smith Samuel & James, land agents, 2 Gray's inn square
Smith Samuel & Son, insurance brokers, 6 Bank chambers, Lothbury
Smith & Sanders, bookbinders, 2 Ivy lane, Newgate st
Smith & Sargeant, straw bonnet ma.9 John st.west.Edgw.rd
Smith, Scurfield & Co.coal factors,3 Cross la. St.Mary at hill
Smith (Sebastian) & Co.wine merchants,21Queen st.Chpsde
Smith & Sharp, coal mers. coke burners & whrfigrs. Hermitage whf. 343 Wapping; Oak whf. 11 City rd. basin; Times whf. New North rd.; & Savoy & Waterloo whfs. Strand
Smith & Shilstone, carpenters, 6 Canterbury pl. O. Kent rd
Smith & Simmonds, whalebone cutters, whale fin merchants, & importers of rattans, 11 Fell st. Cripplegate
Smith & Steer, stockbrokers, 77 Old Broad st. City
Smith & Stephens, drapers, 24 Upper King st. Holborn
Smith, Sundius & Co. ship & general agents & insurance brokers, 76 Cornhill, & Baltic coffee house
Smith Susannah & Son, plumbers, 3 Bread st. hill
Smith & Taylor, solicitors, 3 Basinghall st
Smith Thos. & Co. coal factors &ship ins. broks.11Waterlane
Smith Thos. & Edw. pawnbrokers, 17South st.Manchester sq
Smith Thomas John & Joseph, quill merchants, pen, ink, & wax manufacturers, & makers of the improved metallic paper memorandum books, 3 Pilgrim st. Ludgate hill
Smith Thos. & Walter, corah printers & silk mfs. 35 Poultry
Smith Thos. & Wm. ship owners & e. i. agents, 78 Cornhill
Sm th Thomas Woodroffe & Co.merchants,29 Gt.St.Helen's
Smith & Thompson, silk manufacturers, 56 Friday st
Smith (Turberville) & Co. carpet & rug mfs. 9Gt.Marlbro' st
Smith & Tyers, liquid sugar refiners, 203 Up. Thames st
Smith & Watkins, linendrapers, 133 & 134 Tottenham ct. rd
Smith & Weaver, surgeons, 1 Stockwell villas, Clapham rd
Smith,Weedon & Co.wholesale stationers, 22 Paternoster rw
Smith Wm. & Co. agents & dealers in tea, 46 Fenchurch st
SmithWm.&Co.imps.of cigars,12King'sArms yd.Moorgate st
Smith Wm.&Co.scale&weigh. machine ma.238 Boro'High st
Smith Wm.&George, printsellers, 24 Lisle st. Leicester sq
Smith Wm.& Jas.*Fountain&Grapes* P.H. 112Blackman st
Smith Wm.Lepard&Co.who.stationers,32 James st Cov. gar
Smith Wm.&Son, linendrapers,16to20Shaftesbury ter. Pimli
Smith Wm. Henry & Son, stationers, newsmen, & *Bombay Times* agents, & pocket book makers, 192 Strand
SmithWm.&Wm.Wyke,attorneys,16Southamptn.st.Blmsby
Smith's Patent Ship Propeller Co. 25 Finsbury pavement
Smith Abel,*NewCrown&Cushion*P.H.55Mount st.Lambeth
Smith Abraham, baker,11 Upper Park place,Dorset square
Smith Abraham, tailor, 62 King st. Westminster
Smith Albert, M.R.C.S. dentist, 14 Percy st.Tottenham ct.rd
Smith Alexander, butcher, Leadenhall market
Smith Alexander,corn&coal mer. 40 Aldenham st. Somers tn
Smith Alexander, fruiterer, Denmark hill, Camberwell
Smith Alex.work.silversmith,3Bedfordbury, Covent garden
Smith Alfred, carpenter & bldr.85 White Lion st. Pntnville
Smith Alfred, cut glass manuftr.27 Everett st.Brunswick sq
Smith Alfred, stock ma. 10Charles st.City rd.& 108Wood st
Smith Alfred, *White Horse*P.H.50Gt.Saffron hill,Hattonwl
Smith Alfred Bucknell,tobccnst.&bookbind.60 St. John st.rd
Smith Alfred Wm. solicitor, see Weir & Smith
Smith Ambrose, poulterer, 1 Adam st. east, Portman sq
Smith Andrew, boot ma.16Clayton pl.William st.Caledon.rd
Smith Andrew, carman, 34 Maze, Tooley st
Smith Andrew, engineer, millwright, & manufacturer of patent wire rope, Millwall, Poplar; 2 Whitelion ct. Cornhill, & 69 Princes st. Leicester square
Smith Andrew, physician, 7 Pelham crescent, Brompton
Smith Ann (Mrs.), furniture brkr.1 Mount Etna,Mile end rd
Smith Ann (Mrs.), hardware dealer,1 Russell pl.OldKent rd
Smith Ann (Mrs.), newsagent, 11 James st. Oxford st
Smith Ann (Mrs.), oil, color & varnish ma. 121 Fore st.Cripl
Smith Ann (Miss), milliner, 24 Southampton rw. Bloomsbry
Smith Ann (Miss), cutler, 72 King William st. City
Smith Ann (Mrs.), *Three Cups hotel*, 88 Aldersgate st
Smith Ann Diana (Mrs.), timber carter, 62 Cornwall road
Smith Anne (Mrs.), milliner, &c. 6 Maddox st. Bond st
Smith Archibald, barrister, 25 Old square, Lincoln's inn
Smith Arthur, solicitor, 58 Lincoln's inn fields
Smith Ashton, carman, 12 Archer st. Golden square
Smith Attwood Henry, solicitor,108 Dorset st. Salisbury sq & 8 Park place, Maida hill, west
Smith Augustus, brush manufctr. 8 Osborne st.Whitechapel
Smith Augustus, hosier & glover, 173 Waterloo road
Smith AugustusB. hothouse bldr. Glebe pl.King's rd.Chelsea
Smith Baker Peter, solicitor, 77 Basinghall st
Smith Benjamin, brewer, Canal bridge, Old Kent road
Smith Benjamin, butcher, Deptford High st
Smith Benjamin, butcher, 8 Orange st. Bloomsbury
Smith Benjamin, farrier, 6 Three Cups yard, Bedford row
Smith Benjamin, *King's Arms* P.H. 43 Narrow st. Limehse
Smith Benjamin, oil & colorman, 107 Fleet st
Smith Benjamin, printing ink maker, 7 Wine Office court, Fleet st. & Old Ford, near Bow
Smith Benjamin,silversmith, 12 Duke st. Lincoln's inn fields
Smith Benjamin, stone mason,Albion wharf,Deptford bridge
Smith Benjamin, straw hat mfr. 93 Gt. Peter st.Westminstr
Smith Benjamin, tailor, 25 Henry st. Pentonville
Smith Bernard,warehouseman,seeHanson,Smiths'&Stephens
Smith Bridget (Mrs.), school,33 Hamilton ter. St.John's wd
Smith Browning, physician, 7 Bedford place, Kensington
Smith Caroline (Miss), milliner, 13 Old Cavendish st
Smith Caroline (Mrs.),coffee rooms,1 Church st.Shoreditch
Smith C. (Mrs.), *Perseverance*P.H.32Marshall st.Golden sq
Smith Casper, shoemaker, 83 Leman st. Goodman's fields
Smith Catherine(Mrs.),mnfr.&imp.of cigars,20Sun st.Bhpsg
Smith Charles, Albion coffee rooms, 64 Wood st. Cheapside
Smith Charles, baker, 26 Broad st. Ratcliff cross
Smith Charles, barrister,6 Middle Temple lane
Smith Charles, coal merchant, see Helmore & Smith
Smith Charles, corndealer, 14 James st. Covent garden
Smith Charles, dairy, 1 Abbey st. Bethnal green
Smith Charles, fruiterer, 71 Crawford st. Marylebone
Smith Charles, fruiterer, 7 Southampton st. Camberwell
Smith Charles, furn. broker, 4 Henrietta st. Manchester sq
Smith Charles,*Glaziers'Arms*P.H.29Water la.Earl st.Blkfs
Smith Charles, glover, 27 Red Cross st. Cripplegate
Smith Charles, gold laceman, &c. 12 Piccadilly
Smith Charles, grocer, 39 East st. Walworth road
Smith Charles, grocer, 78 Paradise st. Rotherhithe
Smith Charles, grocer, 14 Westmorland pl. Walworth com.
Smith Charles, linendraper, 16 Newington causeway
Smith Charles, *Marlboro'Arms*P.H. 19Alfred st.Bedford sq
Smith Chas. pianoforte ma. 5 Pritchard's pl. Hackney fields
Smith Charles, pocket book maker, 13 Noble st. Cheapside
Smith Charles, printer & stationer, 6 Hart st. Mark lane
Smith Charles, *Royal Mail tavern*, 17 Noble st. Cheapside
Smith Charles, slate & metal billiard & bagatelle table manufacturer, 2 & 3 Market st. Hart st. Bloomsbury
Smith Charles, surgeon, 17 Nottingham st. Manchester sq
Smith Charles, surgeon, 1 Up. Craven pl. Kentish town
Smith Charles, tailor, 105 Gt. Titchfield st. Oxford market

Smith Charles, tailor, Sion pl. East st. Walworth road
Smith Charles, tailor, 30 Surrey place, Old Kent road
Smith Charles, tin plate worker, 2 Lion st. New Kent road
Smith Charles, wire worker, 10 Princes st. Drury lane
Smith C.B.actuary to *Nat.LifeAssr.Soc*.2 KingWm.st.City
Smith Charles C. teadealer, 60NewChurch st.Bermndsy.wal
Smith Charles Dowton, artist, 5 Terrace, Gray's inn lane
Smith Charles D. nursery & seedsman, Bridge rd. Battersea
Smith Charles Fredk. birmingham manuf. Jerusalem coff.ho
Smith Charles Frederick, brewer, see Ind & Smith
Smith Charles H. sculptor, &c. 29 Clipstone st. Fitzroy sq
Smith Charles Henry, grocer, 25 Edwards st. Portman sq
Smith Charles Hen. (lateFielder,Johnson & Smith),solicitor, 13 Duke st. Manchester sq. & 2 York bldgs. New road
Smith Charles Hick, ironmonger, lamp & stove manufacturer, 25 Pavement, Finsbury
Smith Charles James, patent gun, pistol & rifle maker, 61 King William st. City, & 28 Whittall st. Birmingham
Smith Charles James, picture dealer, 92 Wardour st
Smith Charles James, solicitor, 2 King's arms yd.Coleman st
Smith Chas. Manley, attorney, 61 Lincoln's inn fields
Smith Charles Reymond, sculptor, 37 Glos'ter pl. New road
Smith Chas. Roach, chemist, &c. 5 Liverpool st. Bishopsgate
Smith Charles Saml. tailor & clothier, 79 Tottenham ct. rd
Smith Christiana (Miss), umbrella mfr. 7 Tottenham ct. rd
Smith Clement, pawnbroker, 9 & 10 Bath st. City road
Smith Clement, stockbro. 3 Bartholomew la. & Stock exch
Smith Const.(Mrs.),3 *Pigeons&Star*,16 Hatfield st.Goswl.rd
Smith Cornelius, surgeon, 56 Gracechurch st
Smith Cornelius Hen.upholsterer,10 Bowyer pl.Cambrwll.rd
Smith Daniel Edward, builder, 15 Webber st. Blackfriars rd
Smith Daniel Omer, bookbinder, 7 Church st.Blackfriars rd
Smith David, accountant, 7 Mabledon pl. Burton crescent
Smith David, *Bell Inn* P.H. 87 Wood st. Cheapside
Smith David, boot & shoemaker, 27 Red Lion st. Holborn
Smith David, boot & shoemaker, 49 St. Mary Axe
Smith David,*LordNelson*P.H.16Duke'srw.Newrd.St.Pncrs
Smith David, tailor, &c. 40 Coleman st. Bank
Smith Ebenezer, surgeon, 7 Billiter square
Smith Edgar Edward, beer retailer, 19 Wilsted st. Somers tn
Smith Edmund, coal & potato dealer, 21 Lumber ct. 7 dials
Smith Edmund J. land agent, 14 Parliament st. (late 25)
Smith Edmund, linendraper, see Higes & Smith
Smith Edward, auctioneer & house & estate agent, 13 George st. Mansion house
Smith Edward, beer retalr. 9 Cheltenham pl.Westminstr. rd
Smith Edw.*Brickla.Arms*P.H.14Elizbth. st.South, Pimlico
Smith Edward, chandler's shop, 10 Duke st. Lisson grove
Smith Edward, cheesemonger, 294 Oxford st
Smith Edward, draper & tailor, 47 & 48 Houndsditch
Smith Edward, furniture broker, 5 Robert st. Grosvenor sq
Smith Edward, hot presser, 4 Chapel place, Spitalfields
Smith Edward, mathematicl. inst.ma.11 Exmth.st.Coml.rd.e
Smith Edward, *NewCross* P.H. New cross, Deptford
Smith Edward,solicitor,5Chancerylane,&9Tyndale pl.Isligtn
Smith Edward, tobacconist, 1 Gower st. north, New road
Smith Edward, varnish manufacturer, 17 Finsbury market
Smith Edward, wholesale linendraper, see Allan & Smith
Smith Edward, worsted & carpet wa. 83 Queen st.Cheapside
Smith Edward Francis, barrister, 42 Chancery lane
Smith Edward Osborne (sec. to the Reliance Mutual Life Assurance Society), 71 King William st. City
Smith Edwin, solicitor, 12 Gray's inn place, Gray's inn
Smith Edwin Dalton, artist, 7 Hertford st. Mayfair
Smith Elisha, grocer, 2 Deptford High st
Smith Eliza (Mrs.), bookinder, 5 Ivy lane, Newgate st
Smith Eliza (Mrs.), cowkeeper, 20 George st. Bloomsbury
Smith Eliza (Mrs.), dairy, 2 Drury lane
Smith Eliza (Mrs.), piece broker, 3 Duke st. Aldgate
Smith Elizabeth (Miss), dressmkr. 16 Powel st. ea.Goswel.rd
Smith Elizabeth (Mrs.),dressmaker,10 Lit. Chapel st. Westr
Smith Elizabeth (Mrs.),baker, 23Up. York st. Bryanstone sq
Smith Elizabeth (Mrs.), clock spring mkr. 8 Rawstone st
Smith Elizabeth (Mrs.), fruiterer, confectioner & purveyor to their Majesties & the royal family, 72 St. James's st
Smith Elizabeth (Mrs.), general chandler, 20 Gt. Bush lane
Smith Elizabeth(Mrs.),milliner&ct.dress mkr.22 Hanover sq
Smith Elizabeth (Mrs.), silk dyer, 65 Cannon st. City
Smith Elizabeth (Miss), stationer, 40 Berwick st. Soho
Smith Elizabeth (Mrs.), tobacconist, 46 Fore st. City
Smith Ellen (Mrs.), lodging house, 5 Thayer st. Manchtr.sq
Smith Elliott, baker, 33 Gt. Windmill st. Haymarket
Smith Emma (Mrs.), straw bonnet mkr. 64 Bethnal green rd
Smith Eusebius, wholesale leather seller, 35 Camomile st
Smith Evan, plater, see Roberts, Smith & Co
Smith FannyE.(Mrs.),*SugarLoaf*P.H.41Church st.Mileend
Smith Frances, (Mrs.), dairy, 23President st. East, King sq
Smith Francis (Mrs.), straw bonnet ma. 23 Coml.rd.Lambh
Smith Frances Mary (Mrs.), fruiterer, 20 Welbeck st.Cav.sq
Smith Francis, tobacconist, 61 Redcross st. Barbican
Smith Francis Redhead, attorney, 6 Barnard's inn
Smith Francis, stay warehouse, 85 Edgware rd.Marylebone
Smith Frederick, *Albion* P.H. 259 Blackfriars road
Smith Frederick, confectioner, 17 City rd. Finsbury
Smith Frederick, hosier, 5 High st. Newington butts
Smith Frederick,plumber,painter&glazier,34Cannon st.City
Smith Frederick, russia broker, 5 Adam's ct. Old Broad st
Smith Frederick, tailor, 14 Noble st. Cheapside
Smith Frederick A. seal engraver,40 Cursitor st.Chanceryla
Smith Frederick Geo. law stationer, 11 Cooks ct. Linc.inn
Smith Frd.G. sec.to*Scottish UnionFire& LifeOffice*,73Cornl
Smith Frederick Harris, undertaker, 5 Savage gardens
Smith Frederick James, barrister, 1 New court, Temple
Smith Frederick Wickins, solicitor, see Whiteside & Smith
Smith Fredk.Wm.linendrpr.hosier,&c.1 Junction pl.Kntshtn
Smith Geo. architect, &c. 5 Frederick's pl. Old Jury
Smith Geo. baker, 42 Whitechapel High st
Smith Geo. beer retailer, 52 Marylebone lane, Oxford st
Smith Geo. bookbinder, 24 Duke st. West Smithfield
Smith Geo. boot & shoe maker, 51 Gt. Alie st.Goodman's fls
Smith Geo. bootmaker, 15 St. Martin's st. Leicester sq
Smith Geo. brazier & tinman, 4 Seymour row, Lit. Chelsea
Smith Geo. builder, see Armstrong & Smith
Smith Geo. builder, 1 Wilton mews, Grosvenor place
Smith Geo. carpenter&undertaker,53 New Compton st.Soho
Smith Geo. cheesemonger, 143 Hoxton Old town
Smith Geo. china,glass&ea rthenware warehouse, 57Conduit st. Regent st
Smith Geo. coach lace maker, 9 Winkworth bldgs. City rd
SmithGeo.coach builder,8Park pl.&5&6Park st.Knningtn.cr
Smith Geo. corn dealer, 41 Red Lion st. Spitalfields
Smith Geo. corn dealer, Warlter's buildings, Old Kent rd
Smith Geo. dairy, 28 Gt. Wild st. Lincoln's inn fields
Smith Geo. dyer & scourer, 98 Mount st. Berkeley sq
Smith Geo. enameller, 3 Francis ct. Berkeley st.Clerknwell
Smith Geo. fishmonger, 50 White st. Borough
Smith Geo. fruiterer, 9 Theobald's road
Smith Geo. furnishing undertaker & funeral featherman, 4 John st. Oxford st
Smith Geo. furniture wareh.22A, Frederick st. Gray's inn rd
Smith Geo. greengrocer, 85 Berwick st. Soho
Smith Geo. grocer, 22 Glo'ster ter. Vauxhall bridge road
Smith Geo. hop&seed mer.NewPark st.Boro',&22Emerson st
Smith Geo. hosier, glover & shirtmaker, 178 Strand
Smith Geo. ladies' shoemaker, 87 Friar st. Blackfriars rd
Smith Geo. nursery,11Manchestr. ter. Livpl.rd.Barnsbury rd
Smith Geo. oil & italian wareh. 55 Drummond st.Euston sq
Smith Geo. oil & italian warehouse, 87 London wall
Smith Geo. oilman, 11 High st. Stepney
Smith Geo. *Old Geo.* P.H. 59 Anchor & Hope alley,Wapping
Smith Geo. shawl & silk warehouse, 32 Ludgate hill
Smith Geo. ship modeller, 208 Rotherhithe
Smith Geo. smith, 22 Apollo buildings, East st. Walworth
Smith Geo. solicitor, 24 Golden square
Smith Geo. solicitor, see Pickering Smith & Co.
Smith Geo. *Star & Garter* P.H. 26 Sloane square, Chelsea
Smith Geo. surgeon, see Parnell & Smith
Smith Geo. surgeon, 3 Bennett st. St. James's
Smith Geo. surveyor, 5 Frederick place, Old Jewry
Smith Geo. tailor, Belle Sauvage yard, Ludgate hill
Smith Geo. tailor, &c. 2 Argyll st. Regent st.
Smith Geo. teadealer& grocer, Stockwell place,Clapham rd
Smith Geo. upholsterer, appraiser, &c. 24 Conduit st
Smith Geo. watch enameller, 41 Gt.Sutton st. Clerkenwell
Smith Geo.whiting manufacturer,11& 62 Lr.Fore st.Lambeth
Smith Geo. wine cooper, 1 Steel yard, Upper Thames st
Smith Geo. Alletheus, builder, 50 Old Bailey
Smith Geo. Fred. solicitor, see Wright, Smith & Shepherd
Smith Geo. Henry, *Red Cow* P.H. 69 King st. Deptford
Smith Geo. Hines, linendraper, &c. 38 Kingsland road
Smith Geo. Jas. P. barrister, 1 King's Bench walk, Temple
Smith Geo. M. solicitor, see Richardson, Smith & Saddler
Smith Geo. Richard, beer retailer, 138 Holborn bars
Smith Geo. Spencer, surveyor, 85 Baker st. Portman sq
Smith Gilbert, potato dealer, Church st. Deptford
Smith Hannah (Mrs.),beer machine ma.49 Strutton gr.Wstm
Smith Hannah (Mrs.),coffin furn. ma.1 Osborne st.Whitechpl
Smith Hannah (Miss), water gilder, 7 Staining la. Wood st
Smith Hannah W.(Mrs.),clock spring ma.5 Queen st.Clknwl
Smith Harriet (Miss), milliner, 3 John's pl. Cambrwll. nw. rd
Smith Harriet(Mrs.),straw bonnet ma.6Tyler's ct.Carnaby st
Smith Henry, academy, 4 Northampton pl. Canonbury sq

Smith Henry, baby linen wareho. 23 Shoreditch High st
Smith Henry, beer retailer, 106 & 107 Goswell road
Smith Henry, bookslr. & stationr. 4½ Edwards st. Portman sq
Smith Henry, butcher, 23 Leather lane, Holborn
Smith Henry, clock & watch spring maker, 31 Percival st
Smith Henry, coffee rooms, 86 St. John st. Smithfield
Smith Henry, confectioner, 135 Goswell st
Smith Henry, flour factor, 53 Trinity square, Borough
Smith Henry, fruiterer, 28 Upper John st. Liverpool road
Smith Henry, fruit salesman, 2 Borough market
Smith Henry, grocer & teadealer, 23 Bermondsey st
Smith Henry, grocer & teadealer, 37 Lamb's Conduit st
Smith Henry, hairdresser, 3 Sidney pl. Commercial rd. east
Smith Henry, hairdresser, 82 Tooley st
Smith Henry, harness maker, 50 Baalzephon st. Bermondsey
Smith Henry, *King's Arms* P.H. 1 Abbey st. Bethnal green
Smith Henry, lamp ma. 12 Rufford's row, Upper st. Islington
Smith Henry, linendraper, 2 Upper Seymour st. Euston sq
Smith Henry, oil & colorman, 146 Shoreditch
Smith Henry, silk mercer, 22 Hanover square
Smith Henry, smith & farrier, Bull yd. Milford la. Strand
Smith Henry, solicitor, 2 Portsmouth st
Smith Henry, statuary & mason, Downham road, Kingsland
Smith Henry, surgeon, 67 Torrington square
Smith Henry, surgeon, 17 Henrietta st. Cavendish square
Smith Henry, tobacconist, 17 Cheltenham pl. Westminster rd
Smith Henry Alonzo, modeller, 42 Up. Norton st. Fitzroy sq
Smith Henry Bedwell, grocer, 1 Scott's pl. Lower rd. Islington
Smith Henry Benj. boot & shoe mak. 2 Star corn. Bermndsy. st
Smith Henry Dekar, floor cloth manufacturer, 165 Strand
Smith Henry Dixon, engraver, &c. 3 Gough sq. Fleet st
Smith Henry Porter, actuary to the *Eagle Life Assurance Company*, 3 Crescent, Blackfriars
Smith Henry Smith, artist & picture dealer, 80 New Bond st
Smith Henry Tilden, hop & seed fact. see Pattenden & Smith
Smith Hen. V. acct. to *Com. & Gen. Life Assur. Co.* 37 Golden sq
Smith Herbert, artist, 2 Sloane terrace, Chelsea
Smith Horatio, watchmaker, 20 Critchell pl. New North rd
Smith Hugh, architect, 3 Bedford row, Holborn
Smith Hugh Wallis, barrister, 19 Old sq. Lincoln's inn
Smith Isaac, builder, 11 Took's court, Chancery lane
Smith Isaac, grocer, 14 Carnaby st. Golden sqare
Smith Isaac, *Half Moon* P.H. 23 Duke st. West Smithfield
Smith Isaac, linendraper, 55 Wardour st. Oxford st
Smith Isaac, livery stables, 1 Cornwall ter. mews, Rgt's. pk
Smith Isaac, metal & steel polisher, Saffron pl. Saffron hill
Smith Isaac Geo. fancy cabinet ma. 10 Perceval st. Clerknwl
Smith Jacob, baker, 87 Kingsland road
Smith Jacob, china & glass dealer, 123 Upper st. Islington
Smith James, academy, 16 Camden terrace, Camden New town
Smith James, baker, 35 Hereford st. Lisson grove
Smith James, baker, Howard's place, Cambridge heath
Smith James, baker, 5 Narrow st. Limehouse
Smith James, baker, 243 Shoreditch High st
Smith James, baker, 121 Snow's fields, Bermondsey
Smith James, baker, Up. North st. Whitechapel rd
Smith James, beer retailer, Neate st. Cobourg rd
Smith James, beer retailer, 28 White Lion st. Norton folgate
Smith James, bookbinder, 13 Rolls' buildings, Fetter lane
Smith James, bootmaker, 11 Norfolk place, Islington
Smith James, boot & shoe factor, 6 Somerset place, Hoxton
Smith James, bricklayer, King st. New town, Deptford
Smith James, bricklayer, 8 North st. Sloane st. Chelsea
Smith James, bricklayer, 37 Sekforde st. Clerkenwell
Smith James, butcher, 1 Amelia st. Walworth road
Smith James, butcher, 29 Aylesbury st. Clerkenwell
Smith James, butcher, Camberwell green, East side
Smith James, cabinet ma. 25 Alfred pl. Newington causeway
Smith James, *Carpenters' Arms* P.H. 131 Kingsland road
Smith James, carpenter & joiner, 5 Queen st. Chas. sq. Hoxton
Smith James, carpenter, 1 Marah place, Old Kent road
Smith James, carver & gilder, 4 Lit. Queen st. Westminster
Smith James, chaser, 6 Paradise st. Finsbury
Smith James, cheesemonger, High st. Stoke Newington
Smith James, chemist & druggist, 59 Barbican
Smith James, coal & potato dealer, 98 Lambeth Lower marsh
Smith James, *Cock* P.H. 20 Bow lane, Cheapside
Smith James, coffee rooms, 4 Little Ryder st. St. James's
Smith James, commis. agent, 1 Smith's bldgs. Goodman's flds
Smith James, confectioner, 184 Church st. Shoreditch
Smith James, dairyman, 71 George st. New road
Smith James, engineer, 27 Denmark st. Seven dials
Smith James, engraver & printer, 10 King st. Snow hill
Smith James, engraver & jeweller, 101 Regent st
Smith James, farrier, 7 Denmark place, Camberwell
Smith James, fruiterer, 25 Brown st. Bryanstone square
Smith James, furniture dealer, 6 Amelia place, Fulham rd
Smith James, gasfitter & brass finisher, 8 Charterhouse lane
Smith James, grocer, Church st. Deptford
Smith James, grocer & cheesemonger, 9 Exeter st. Sloane st
Smith James, indigo & drysaltery broker, 43 Lime st
Smith James, ironmonger, 25 London road, Southwark
Smith James, leather cutter, 30 Strutton ground, Westmnstr
Smith James, linendraper, 3 Commerce row, Up. st. Islington
Smith James, linendraper, 19 Lambeth walk
Smith James, linendraper, 6 New Bridge st. Vauxhall
Smith James, marble mer. Black Lion wf. Lr. East Smithfield
Smith James, market gardener, St. George's row, Pimlico
Smith James, oilman, 110 York road, Lambeth
Smith James, optician, 50 Ironmonger row, Old st
Smith James, *Plough* P.H. 31 Kingsgate st. Holborn
Smith James, printers' press maker, 24 Denmark st. Soho
Smith James, *Rosemary Branch* P.H. Southmptn. st. Cmbrwl
Smith James, saddler & harness maker, 5 Wigmore st
Smith James, school, 42 Great Cambridge st. Hackney road
Smith James, scotch law agent, 14 Soho square
Smith James, secretary to the Catholic Institute, 14 Soho sq
Smith James, *Sheer Hulk* P.H. New King st. Deptford
Smith James, dyer, silk & satin dresser, see Frith & Smith
Smith James, skinner & furrier, 9 Pump row, Old st. road
Smith James, solicitor, 3 Great Knightrider st
Smith James, straw hat presser, 44 Gt. Alie st. Goodman's fi
Smith James, *Swan & Sugar Loaf* P.H. 4 Folly, Dockhead
Smith James, tailor, 64 King st. Golden square
Smith James, timber merchant, Mansfield st. Borough road
Smith James, tobacconist, 12 Vernon pl. Bagnigge wells rd
Smith James, tobacconist, 203 Rotherhithe st
Smith James, undertaker, 7 Laurence Pountney hill
Smith James, *White Lion* P.H. 125 Edgware rd. Paddington
Smith James, *Windsor Castle* P.H. Harrow road
Smith James, sen. sheep salesman, 41 West Smithfield
Smith James, jun. sheep salesman, 41 West Smithfield
Smith James Allpress, manchester agent, 27 Milk st. City
Smith James Ansell, corndealer & livery stable keeper, 16 Princes st. Westminster
Smith James Bonaventure, artist, 7 Cleveland st. Fitzroy sq
Smith James Frederick, barrister, 1 New court, Temple
Smith James Geo. cattle salesman, 59 West Smithfield
Smith James Herbert, tanner, Grange, Bermondsey
Smith Jas. John, newsvender & library, 20 Broad ct. Long acre
Smith James Mark, surgeon, 1 John st. London fields, Hckny
Smith James Pearce, tailor & draper, 450 Strand
Smith Jas. T. coal mer. & lime & coke burner, sun whf. Deptford
Smith James William, accountant, 48 Lincoln's inn fields
Smith Jane (Mrs.), brushmak. & turner, 3 Earl st. east, Lisson gr
Smith Jane (Mrs.), grocer, 36 Drummond crescent, Euston sq
Smith Jane (Mrs.), plumber, 38 Wellclose square
Smith Jane (Mrs.), tailor, 33 Throgmorton st
Smith Jeremiah, fancy stationer & black borderer, 42 Rathbne. pl
Smith Jesse, cheesemonger, 185 Borough High st
Smith Job, blind maker, 16 Kennington row, Kennington rd
Smith Job, builder, 28 Worship st. Finsbury
Smith Job, cattle salesman, 8 West Smithfield
Smith Job, summer house builder, nr. the Horns, Kennington
Smith John, *Albion* P.H. 7 Beak st. Regent st
Smith John, *Angel* P.H. 1 Webber st. Blackfriars road
Smith John, baker, 121 Brick lane, Spitalfields
Smith John, baker, 13 Clare st. Clare market
Smith John, baker, 46 High st. Lambeth
Smith John, baker, 3 Lamb's Conduit st. Foundling
Smith John, baker, 56 Mount st. Lambeth
Smith John, baker, 22 Oxford st. Mile end
Smith John, baker, 321 Strand
Smith John, barrister, 11 King's Bench walk, Temple
Smith John, beer retailer, 1 Lion st. New Kent road
Smith John, bootmaker, 9 Exmouth st. Clerkenwell
Smith John, bootmaker, 41 Flagon row, Deptford
Smith John, boot & shoe maker, 3 Church st. Stoke Newington
Smith John, bricklayer, 10 Coal yard, Drury lane
Smith John, broom dlr. 15 King's Bench wk. Wllngtn. st. Blkfr
Smith John, butcher, 277 Bermondsey st
Smith John, butcher, 214 Blackfriars road
Smith John, butcher, 71 Cornwall road, Lambeth
Smith John, butcher, Warlter's buildings, Old Kent road
Smith John, carman, London dock entrance
Smith John, carpenter, 20 Hosier lane, West Smithfield
Smith John, carpenter, 23 Old Fish st. Old Change
Smith John, carpenter & builder, 8 Orange st. Gravel la. Boro'
Smith John, cheesemonger, 6 South pl. Tibberton sq. Islingtn
Smith John, chemist & druggist, 83 Leader st. Chelsea
Smith John, clockmaker, 70 Charlotte st. Fitzroy square
Smith John, coal, &c. mercht. 11 Anderson's bldgs. City rd

Smith John, coal merchant, Child's wharf, Belvedere road
Smith John, coal & potato warehouse, 4 Mount Etna, Mile end
Smith John, cooper, 1 Waterloo st. Walworth common
Smith John, cooper, Ring cross, Holloway road
Smith John, *Crown* P.H. 23 Vere st. Clare market
Smith John, *Crown & Horseshoe* P.H. 50 Holborn hill
Smith John, dining rooms, 31 Kent st. Borough
Smith John, doorspring & hingema. 50 Lit. Bartholomew close
Smith John, fancy trimming ma. 29 Wilkes st. Spitalfields
Smith John, farrier, 20 Carburton st
Smith John, furniture broker, 25 Circus st. New road
Smith John, *Globe* P.H. 88 Holborn hill
Smith John, grocer, 12 Brewer st. Golden square
Smith John, grocer, 9 King st. Commercial road east
Smith John, grocer & tea dealer, 85 Fetter lane
Smith John, haberdasher, see Debenham, Pooley & Smith
Smith John, haberdasher, 125 London road, Southwark
Smith John, hairdresser, 4 Charles st. Westminster
Smith John, hairdresser, 3 Grosvenor place, Borough road
Smith John, hatter, 2 Deptford bridge
Smith John, *Lamb & Flag* P.H. 33 Rose st. Long acre
Smith John, leather seller, 8 Brunswick parade, Barnsbury rd
Smith John, leather seller, 7 Clayton st. Kennington
Smith John, leather seller, 7 Warren st. Fitzroy square
Smith John, linendraper, 65 Exmouth st. Clerkenwell
Smith John, livery stables, 9 Caroline mews, Bedford square
Smith John, livery stables, 31 High st. Bow
Smith John, nurseryman & florist, Dalston, & Covent garden
Smith John, oilman, 132 Lambeth lower marsh
Smith John, *Old Three Tuns* P.H. 1 Broadway, Westminstr
Smith John, painter & glazier, 10 Little College st. Westmnstr
Smith John, perfumer, 17 Ernest st. Regent's park
Smith John, pianoforte maker, 2 Oval road, Regent's park
Smith John, piece broker, 40 Duke st. Aldgate
Smith John, plumber & glazier, 78 Hoxton Old town
Smith John, pork butcher, 33 Northumberland st. Marylebon
Smith John, poulterer & game dlr. 89 Shadwell High st
Smith John, *Queen's Head* P.H. 12 Whitecross st. Cripplegt
Smith John, rope & twine maker, 49 Long acre, & Old Ford
Smith John, russia merchant, 5 Austinfriars
Smith John, sheep salesman, 41 West Smithfield
Smith John (of Brigstock), sheep salesman, 41 West Smithfield
Smith John, *Ship* P.H. 94 Shad Thames, Horselydown
Smith John, ship. butcher, 53 Anchor & Hope alley, Wppng
Smith John, shipwright, see West & Smith
Smith John, smith & brazier, 16 Ship yard, Temple bar
Smith John, smith & gasfitt. 4 Marlboro. mews, Blenheim st
Smith John, smoke jack ma. & irnmngr. 6 High st. St. Giles's
Smith John, solicitor; clerk & superintendent registrar of births, deaths, & marriages, for the Whitechapel Union, 23 Leman st. Goodman's fields
Smith John, solicitor, 1 Field court, Gray's inn
Smith John, stationer, vellum manufr. & tanner, 49 Long acre, & printer & bookseller, 52 Long acre
Smith John, stock broker, 3 Shorters court, Throgmorton st. & Stock exchange
Smith John, surgeon, 40 Banner st. St. Luke's
Smith John, surgeon, 72 Freeschool st. Horselydown
Smith John, surgeon, 1 South place, Finsbury
Smith John, surgeon, 13 North st. Poplar
Smith John, tailor, 6 Newcastle st. Farringdon st
Smith John, tailor, 51 Poland st. Oxford st
Smith John, tailor, 17 Tavistock st. Covent garden
Smith John, tailor, see Paul & Smith
Smith John, tanner, 3 Ascot pl. Grange rd. Bermondsey
Smith John, timber mer. Southampton st. Camberwell rd
Smith John, tinman, 20 Fitzroy market, Tottenham ct. rd
Smith John, tobacco pipe maker, 24 Green bank, Wapping
Smith John, underta. 3 Chatsworth bldgs. Low. rd. Deptfd
Smith John, undertaker, 11 Upper Clifton st. Finsbury
Smith John, vellum manufr. Gloucester rw. Walworth rd
Smith John, *Victoria tea gardens*, Uxbridge rd. Bayswater
Smith John, *White Hart* P.H. 2 White Hart st. Drury la
Smith John, *White Horse* P.H. 50 South Audley st
Smith John, *White Swan* P.H. 181 Upper Thames st
Smith John, wholesale Sheffield wareho. 3 Jewin crescent
Smith John, who. windsor chair ma. 23 Old st. St. Luke's
Smith John, window glass wa. 30 Princes st. Leicester sq
Smith John Adam, coach builder, 22 South rw. New rd. Pancra
Smith John Alexander, accountant, 8 Basinghall st
Smith John Bell, artist, 10 Sackville st. Piccadilly
Smith John Bland, linendraper, 22 Felix ter. Liverpool rd
Smith John Buchanan, portmanteau, trunk, packing case, & mop & broom stave maker, 6 Adam's pl. Borough
Smith John Challis, *Blk. Horse* P.H. 23 Old Boswell ct. Carey st
Smith John D. merchant, 2 Adams court, Old Broad st
Smith John Harcourt, house agent, see Anderson & Smith
Smith John Hetherington, solicitor, 1 Blandford st. Portman sq
Smith John Hood, wine & spirit merc. 1 Bell ct. Mincing la
Smith John Huson, warehouseman, 57 Friday st. Cheapside
Smith John James, fruiterer, 3 Spectacle alley, Whitechapel
Smith John James, tailor, 25 Halfmoon st. Piccadilly
Smith John James, tobacconist, 9 High st. Bow, Middlesex
Smith John (Mrs.), milliner, &c. 3 Blenheim st. New Bond st
Smith John Rd. plasterer, 13 Christian st. St. George's east
Smith John Robt. fancy cabinet ma. 1 Guildford st. east, Spafi
Smith John Russell, bookseller, 4 Old Compton st. Soho
Smith John Samuel, cooper, 111 Golden lane, St. Luke's
Smith John Simm, surgeon, 17 Trinity square, Tower hill
Smith John Sydney, butcher, 91 Gt. Titchfield st. Oxford st
Smith John Thos. fruiterer, 17 Motcomb st. Belgrave sq
Smith John Wilfred, *Crown* P.H. 2 Thorney st. Bloomsbury
Smith John Wm. baker, 25 Langley pl. Commercial rd. east
Smith John Wm. barrister, 2 Mitre ct. buildings, Temple
Smith John Willoughby Lacy, plumber, 30 Dorset st. Prtmn.sq
Smith Jonah, corn & hay dealer, &c. 4 Upper Kennington la
Smith Jonathan, grocer, &c. 11 Hart st. Grosvenor square
Smith Joseph, academy, 9 Chapel row, Exmouth st
Smith Joseph, baker, 16 Limekiln hill, Limehouse
Smith Joseph, baker, 9 St. George's road, Borough
Smith Joseph, barrister, 1 Field court, Gray's inn
Smith Joseph, bookbinder, 15 Albion blgs. Bartholomew close
Smith Joseph, booksel. publisher, & printer, 193 High Holborn
Smith Joseph, boot & shoe maker to her Majesty, 7 Crown row, Walworth road
Smith Joseph, boot & shoe ma. 4 High st. Portland town
Smith Joseph, bricklayer, Bow lane, Poplar
Smith Joseph, carpenter, 49 Lower Trinity st. Rotherhithe
Smith Joseph, carpenter, 48 Worship st. Shoreditch
Smith Joseph, dairyman, 66 Coleshill st. Pimlico
Smith Joseph, *County terrace tavern*, 31 Webb's county terrace, New Kent road
Smith Joseph, dairyman, 32 Little Earl st. Seven dials
Smith Joseph, gold & silver beater, 10 Union pl. City road
Smith Joseph, hairdresser, 3 Bruton st. Bond st
Smith Joseph, iron merchant, 29 Broad st. Lambeth
Smith Joseph, ironmonger, 6 Gt. Titchfield st. Oxford st
Smith Joseph, ironmonger, smith, &c. Prospect pl. Knglsd.rd
Smith Joseph, *Jolly Gardeners* P.H. St. George's row, Pimlico
Smith Joseph, mast maker, 103 Fore st. Limehouse
Smith Joseph, newsvender, 4 Staining lane, Wood st
Smith Joseph, optician, 15 Palace row, New rd. St. Pancras
Smith Joseph, plumber & glazier, 22 Woodstock st. Oxford st
Smith Joseph, saw maker, 27 Crown st. Soho
Smith Joseph, smith, 20 Norfolk st. Borough
Smith Joseph, solicitor & superintendent registrar of births, deaths & marriages for the district of St. Luke's, 6 Finsbury ter. City rd
Smith Joseph, stationer, see Sims & Smith
Smith Joseph, statuary & mason, 7 Snow's fields, Bermondsey
Smith Joseph, tobacconist, 25 Strand
Smith Joseph, straw hat manfr. 9 Mansion house pl. Cmbwll
Smith Joseph, surgeon, 38 Clapham road place
Smith Joseph, tailor, 10 Little Russell st. Bloomsbury
Smith Joseph, warehouseman, see Hanson, Smiths' & Stephens
Smith Joseph, watchmaker, 18 Bride lane, Fleet st
Smith Joseph, woollen draper, 12 Marshall st. Golden sq
Smith Joseph Samuel, pinmaker, 15 Gt. Dover st. Borough
Smith Joseph Wontner, stove & range maker, smith & engineer, gas fitter & lamp ma. fitter of hot water apparatus & warm baths, 21 Tenter st. Lit. Moorfields
Smith Joshua, bed pillar maker, 12 John st. Holywell mount
Smith Josiah, agt. for Estcourt's india blue, 28 Hatton grdn
Smith Josiah, chemist, 1 Westbourne st. Pimlico
Smith Josiah, mahogany & rosewood mer. 28 Hatton garden
Smith Josiah William, barrister, 8 Old square, Lincoln's inn
Smith Junius, american mercht. 4 Fen court, Fenchurch st
Smith Leny D. crape mnfr. waterer, &c. 1 Lit. Knightrider st
Smith Leonard, grocer, 18 Beauvoir ter. Kingsland road
Smith Louisa (Miss), prof. of music, 23 Fredenstein terrace
Smith Louisa (Mrs.), grocer & cheesem. 37½ Poplar High st
Smith Margaret (Mrs.), *Queen's Head* P.H. 67 Broad st. Radclff
Smith Maria (Miss), milliner, 33A, Edwards st. Portman sq
Smith Margt. (Mrs.), coal & coke deal. 22 Whitefriars st
Smith Margt. (Mrs.), saddler & harness ma. 65 Cornwall rd
Smith Margt. (Mrs.), stay & bonnet ma. 34 Crawford st. Portm.sq
Smith Margt. (Mrs.), tobacconist, 5 Church st. Stoke Newngtn
Smith Martha (Mrs.), dress maker, 8 Gerrard st. Soho
Smith Martha (Mrs.), window blind ma. 4 Hanover st. Long ac
Smith Mary (Mrs.), books. 4 Laurel pl. Queen's rd. Dalston
Smith Mary (Mrs.), boot & shoe maker, 90 Goswell st
Smith Mary (Mrs.), chenille mnf. 3 Abbey st. Bethnal gr. rd

Smith Mary (Mrs.), *Coach & Horses* P.H. 199 Shadwell High st
Smith Mary (Mrs.), confectioner, 9 Homer place, New road
Smith Mary (Mrs), dealer in rags, 25 Fleet lane, Old Bailey
Smith Mary (Mrs.), fruit sales. Covent garden fruit market
Smith Mary (Mrs.), furn. broker, 8 Vine st. Hatton garden
Smith Mary (Miss), milliner, 19 St. James's st. Pall mall
Smith Mary (Mrs.), straw hat manufr. 4 Wilmot st. Russel sq
Smith Mary (Mrs.), wardrobe dealer, 95 High st. Marylebone
Smith Mary Ann (Mrs.), governess agt. 30 Alfred pl. Bedf. sq
Smith Matilda (Mrs.), fruiterer, 23 Swan st. Minories
Smith Matthew, boot & shoe ma. 21 Cromer st. Brunswick sq
Smith Matt. confectioner, 88 High st. Camden town
Smith Michael, baker, 21 Moor st. Soho
Smith Michael, bootmaker, 15 Fair st. Horselydown
Smith Michael, solicitor, see Bailey, Shaw & Smith
Smith Montague Edward, barrister, 3 Paper bldgs. Temple
Smith Moses, fruiterer, 32 Upper King st. Bloomsbury
Smith Nathaniel, ale & stout house, 10 Foley place
Smith Nathaniel, carpenter & builder, 132 Blackfriars road
Smith Noyce, auctioneer, estate & house agent, 302 Regent street, & 1 Hanover place, Regent's park road
Smith Ormond, ship chandler, 46 Rotherhithe st
Smith Oscar, ivory turner, 16 Ryder's court, Leicester sq
Smith Owen George, grocer, 32 Paddington st. Marylebone
Smith Peter, bricklayer, 19 Berkley st. Clerkenwell
Smith Peter Hen. saddler & cover ma. 10 Beak st. Regent st
Smith Pierce, baker, 6 Queen st. Pimlico
Smith Pillett, artist, 5 Gray's inn terrace
Smith Protheroe, surgeon, 15 John st. Bedford row
Smith Reuben, cowkeeper, 65 Praed st. Paddington
Smith Richard, carver &c. 16 Bennett st. Blackfriars road
Smith Richard, cowkeeper, 33 Easton st. Spafields
Smith Richard, dairyman, 15 Oxford market, Oxford st
Smith Richard, dairyman, 29 Praed st. Paddington
Smith Richard, glass & china warehouse, 196 Regent st
Smith Richard, grocer & teadealer, 39 Exeter st. Sloane st
Smith Richard, grocer, &c. 6 Harmood place, Hampstead rd
Smith Richard, grocer, &c. Stratford broadway
Smith Richard, house agent, 29 Baker st. Clerkenwell
Smith Richard, potter & hardwaremn. 1 Rl. hospital rw. Chlsa
Smith Richard, russia broker, Baltic coffeehouse
Smith Richard, shoemaker, 1 Charles st. City road
Smith Rd. solicitor, 67 Chancery la. & 12 Harpur st. Red Lion sq
Smith Richd. tailor & habit mkr. 22 Montagu st. Portman sq
Smith Richd. vet. surgeon, 15 Rufford's bdgs. Hi. st. Islngtn
Smith Richard, wine & spirit merchant, King's rd. Chelsea
Smith Rd. Carpenter, solicitor, 26 Bridge st. Southwark
Smith Richd. Collins, ship & insur. brok. see Page & Smith
Smith Richard Moore, sculptor, Glebe pl. King's rd. Chelsea
Smith Rigby Davies, bootmaker, 74 London wall
Smith Robert, baker, 41 Old Compton st. & 46 Dean st. Soho
Smith Robert, baker, 148 Poplar High st
Smith Robert, bootmaker, 15 Long alley, Finsbury
Smith Robert, bricklayer, 19 Wyndham road, Camberwell
Smith Robert, butcher, 29 High st. Bow
Smith Robert, chemist, 18 Thornton st. Horselydown
Smith Robert, cornchandler, 4 & 5 Gloucester place, King's road, & 13 College st. Chelsea
Smith Robert, furniture broker, 18 Brook st. New road
Smith Robert, ironmonger, 13 Gutter lane, Cheapside
Smith Robert, oil & colorman, 1 Beauvoir ter. Kingsland rd
Smith Robert, plumber, 20 East road, City road
Smith Robert, sec. to new British iron co. 3 New Broad st. City
Smith Robert, ship & insurance broker, see Brook & Smith
Smith Robert, tailor, 16 King's row, Walworth road
Smith Robert, tobacconist, 3 Queen st. Ratcliff
Smith Robert, wine cooper, 16 North mews, Burton crescent
Smith Rt. Arthur, house painter, 10 Northampton pl. Old Kent road, & 22 Charlotte row, Walworth road
Smith Robt. B. *Bricklayers' Arms* P.H. Southmptn. st. Cmbw
Smith Robert Davis, general mercantile & commission agent, importer of foreign toys & merchandize, original manufacturer & proprietor of Robert Smith's metropolitan shaving soap, damascus cream, &c. &c. 1 Laurence Pountney pl. Cannon st
Smith Robert George, solicitor, 5 New inn, Wych st. Strand
Smith Rt. Hen. baker, 3 Belinda pl. Canonbury sq. Islington
Smith Rt. Walker, grocer, 1 Gordon st. City road
Smith Rosser, corndealer, 275 Bermondsey st
Smith Saddler, carman, 26 Holywell row, Shoreditch
Smith Samuel, baker, 41 Clipstone st. Fitzroy sq
Smith Samuel, blind maker, 29 Garden rw. London rd. Boro'
Smith Samuel, *Blue Posts* P.H. 14 Rupert st. Haymarket
Smith Samuel, *Coach & Horses* P.H. 1 Gt. Marlboro' st
Smith Samuel, coach carver, 33 Ham yd. Gt. Windmill st
Smith Samuel, coal mer. Waterloo wf. Strand, & 7 Fountain ct
Smith Samuel, confectioner, 191 Poplar High st
Smith Samuel, confectioner, 3 Salmon lane, Limehouse
Smith Samuel, *Druid's Head* P.H. 6 Church st. Deptford
Smith Samuel, *Europa* P.H. Church st. Rotherhithe
Smith Samuel, fruit salesman, Spitalfields market
Smith Samuel, grocer & cheesemonger, Battersea square
Smith Samuel, gun lock maker, 6 Newcastle st. Whitechapel
Smith Samuel, lodging house, 40 Southampton buildings
Smith Samuel, oil & italian warehouse, 16 Mark lane
Smith Samuel, porkman, 7 Princes st. Leicester square
Smith Samuel, stationer & printer, see Ebbs & Smith
Smith Samuel, straw hat wareh. 77 Sun st. Bishopsgate
Smith Samuel, surgeon, 114 Blackfriars road
Smith Samuel, tailor, 71 Commercial rd. Lambeth
Smith Samuel, timber agent, 23 Pump row, Old st. road
Smith Samuel, watch jeweller, 148 St. John st. road
Smith Samuel, working jeweller, 5 Arundel pl. Coventry st
Smith Samuel Augustus, shipping agent, 24 Billiter st
Smith Samuel Mountjoy, merchant, 14 Watling st. City
Smith Sarah (Mrs.), *Chequers* P.H. 55 Tothill st. Westminster
Smith Sarah (Mrs.), livery stables, 1 Up. George st. Sloane sq
Smith Sarah (Mrs.), trim. sel. 16 Stonecutter st. Farringdn. st
Smith Seth, builder, 33 Eaton sq. & Belgrave rd. Pimlico
Smith Sidney, hosier & shirtmaker, 34 Burlington arcade
Smith Sidney, secretary to the *City of London League registration committee*, 15, 16, 17 & 18 East Temple chambers, Whitefriars st. Fleet st
Smith Sidney, sec. to *Met. Anti Corn Law Ass.* 3 Whitefriars st
Smith Sidney, solicitor, 8 Barnard's inn, Holborn
Smith Sophia (Miss), grocer, &c. 17 Brown st. Bryanstone sq
Smith Spencer, general smith, 11 West st. Soho
Smith Stephen, sen. coffee rooms, 26½ Lamb st. Spital square
Smith Stephen, jun. coffee rooms, 5 Beech st. Barbican
Smith Stephen, fruiterer & coal dlr. 10 Swallow st. Piccadilly
Smith Sydney, solicitor, 68 St. John's wood terrace
Smith Talbot, *Lincoln hotel*, 7½ Manchester st. & 20 South st. Manchester square
Smith Thomas, army agent, see Barron & Smith
Smith Thomas, artificial florist & milliner, 66 St. Paul's ch. yd
Smith Thomas, baker, 55 Chiswell st. Finsbury
Smith Thomas, baker, 47 Redcross st. Borough
Smith Thomas, barge builder, 30 Upper Fore st. Lambeth
Smith Thomas, basket maker, 10 Conduit court, Long acre
Smith Thomas, beer retailer, 5 Charles st. Hampstead road
Smith Thomas, beer retailer, 10 Sandwich st. Burton crescent
Smith Thomas, blackwell hall factor, see Hughes & Smith
Smith Thomas, bookseller, 20 Brewer st. Golden square
Smith Thomas, bootmaker, 23 Burlington arcade
Smith Thomas, boot & shoe maker, 7 Stepney old road
Smith Thomas, brass founder, 51 Castle st. east, Oxford st
Smith Thomas, brassworker, 14 Queen st. Oxford st
Smith Thomas, brown stone pottery, 72 Princes st. Lambeth
Smith Thomas, butcher, 38 Monkwell st. Cripplegate
Smith Thomas, carpenter & builder, 3 Dockhead, Bermondsey
Smith Thomas, carpenter, 29 Wellington st. Blackfriars road
Smith Thomas, carver & gilder, 23 Denmark st. Soho
Smith Thomas, cattle salesman, 17 West Smithfield
Smith Thomas, cheesemonger, 3 Felix ter. Liverpool road
Smith Thomas, cheesemonger, 173 Hoxton old town
Smith Thomas, estate agent, 19 King's Arms yard
Smith Thomas, furn. broker & chinaman, 4 Crucifix la. Brmdsy
Smith Thomas, coal dealer, 19 Theobald's road, Red Lion sq
Smith Thomas, cork manufacturer, 49 Eastcheap
Smith Thomas, currier, 186 Bethnal green road
Smith Thomas, dyer, 74 Chapel st. Pentonville
Smith Thomas, estate agent, &c. 15 Redman's row, Mile end
Smith Thomas, farrier, Burwood mews, Titchbrn. st. Edgwr. rd
Smith Thomas, fishmonger, 7 Portman market
Smith Thomas, flour factor, 12 Seymour st. Euston square
Smith Thomas, furniture designer, 36 Thayer st. Manches sq
Smith Thomas, *George* P.H. 234 Kent st. Borough
Smith Thomas, glass & china warehouse, Wandsworth road
Smith Thomas, grocer, 11 Howard's place, Hackney road
Smith Thomas, grocer, Little Chelsea
Smith Thomas, grocer, 33 Southampton st. Camberwell road
Smith Thomas, gunmaker, 288 High Holborn
Smith Thomas, hairdr. & perfumr. 16 Gt. Russell st. Bloomsby
Smith Thomas, *Hope* P.H. 16 Blackmoor st. Drury lane
Smith Thomas, house painter, 15 Up. Berkeley st. west
Smith Thomas, imp. of foreign goods, 60 Freeschool st
Smith Thomas, livery stables, 5 Cambridge pl. Edgware rd
Smith Thomas, livery stables, 13½ Gt. Windmill st. Haymkt
Smith Thomas, livery stables, 7 Southwick mews, Cambr. ter
Smith Thomas (Mrs.), stay maker, 30 New Bond st
Smith Thomas, music pin maker, 3 Pump ct. Union st. Boro'
Smith Thomas, *Old Rose* P.H. 51 St. George st

Smith Thomas,organ bldr.5 Union st.Walcot pl.Lambth.wlk
Smith Thomas,pawnbro. 98&99Grand Junction ter.Edgw.rd
Smith Thomas, pawnbroker, &c. 2 Pitfield st. Hoxton
Smith Thomas, plumber, 1 Artillery st. Bishopsgate
Smith Thomas, potato dealer, 6 Butcher row, Ratcliff
Smith Thomas, printer, 43 Mincing lane
Smith Thomas, sailmaker, 37 Prince's st. Rotherhithe
Smith Thomas, sculptor, 10 Wellington st. Strand
Smith Thomas, sheep salesman, 59 West Smithfield
Smith Thomas, ship carver, 224 Rotherhithe st
Smith Thomas, *Ship* P.H. 10 High st. Newington butts
Smith Thomas, smith&farrier,Lawrence st.Cheyne wk.Chels
Smith Thomas, solicitor, 15 Furnival's inn, Holborn
Smith Thomas, surgeon, 14 Bow lane, Cheapside
Smith Thomas, tanner, 4 Alscott place, Grange road,& Hide market, Leadenhall market
Smith Thomas, teadealer, 17 Cambridge st. Edgware road
Smith Thomas, tobacconist, 1 Cambridge rd.Mile end
Smith Thomas, tobacconist, 12 Tyler st. St. James's
Smith Thomas, varnish & color manf. see Hill & Smith
Smith Thomas,watch movement maker, see Hogan & Smith
Smith Thomas, wheelwright,5 Alfred mews,Tottenham ct.rd
Smith Thomas, wholesale coffee dealer, 13 Mincing lane
Smith Thomas, wool & hair mattress ma. 10 Silver st. City
Smith Thos. Bishop, tailor, 1 Southampton pl. Vauxhall
Smith Thos. Bruce, upholsterer, 41 Brompton row
Smith Thos. Chaloner, barrister, 5 King's Bench walk
Smith Thos. Early, who. slopseller, see Early & Smith
Smith Thos. Edward, *Red House* P.H. 35 College st. Chels
Smith Thos. Fry, *Black Horse* P.H. Lower rd. Rotherhithe
Smith Thos. George, stationer, 22 Down st. Piccadilly
Smith Thos. George, stock broker, 2 Warnford court
Smith Thos. Grey, sec. to the Equivalent Co. 7 Dowgate hill
Smith Thos. Henry, attorney, 7A, Milton st. Dorset square
Smith Thos. Henry, ho.& estate agt.9 Liverpool st.King's crs
Smith Thos. James, wholesale hosier, 26 Phillip la.Wood st
Smith Thos. John, wine cooper, Green's row, Camberwell rd
Smith Thos. M. civil engineer, Chapel pl. Duke st. Westmnr
Smith Thos. Pickford, surgeon,31 Brick lane, Spitalfields
Smith Thos. P. goldsmith & jeweller, see Barber & Smith
Smith Thos. Sidney, carpenter & packing case maker, & dealer in laths & scantling for wine cellars, prepared by Payne's patent process for resisting dry rot, 15 Gt.Tower st
Smith Thos. Southwood, physician, 38 Finsbury square
Smith Thos. Wicks, coffee & ale rooms, 120 Aldersgate st
Smith Timothy, linendraper & hosier, 100 Edgware rd
Smith Timothy, news agent, 2 Bell yard, Temple bar
Smith Toulmin, solicitor, 12 King's bench walk
Smith Toulmin Joseph, barrister, 1 Hare court, Temple
Smith Valentine, dlr. in tea & british wines,53 Aldersgate st
Smith Vincent, barrister, 5 Stone buildings, Lincoln's inn
Smith W. secretary to Paddington Provident Dispensary, 104 Star st. Edgware road
Smith Walter, academy, 9 Dufour's pl. Broad st. Golden sq
Smith Walter, grocer & cheesemonger, 10 Poplar High st
Smith Walter, solicitor, 9 St. Mildred's court, Poultry
Smith Walter Samuel, bootma. 19 Lower Smith st.Clrknwll
Smith Warner, tailor, 49 Bridport place, New north rd
Smith Wm. *Artichoke* P.H. 18 Cambridge road, Mile end
Smith Wm. baker, Guildford st. Walworth common
Smith Wm. baker, 36 Old st. St. Luke's
Smith Wm. baker, 14 Russell st. Lower Rotherhithe
Smith Wm. baker, 2 Young st. Kensington
Smith Wm. baker, 17 St. George st
Smith Wm. bookbinder, 15 St. John's lane, Clerkenwell
Smith Wm. bookbinder, see Bull & Smith
Smith Wm. bookseller & publisher, 113 Fleet st
Smith Wm. boot & shoe maker, 33 Gresse st. Rathbone pl
Smith Wm. boot & shoe maker, 9 Park terrace, Regent's pk
Smith Wm. breeches ma.&tailor, 25 Sherrard st.Golden sq
Smith Wm. builder, &c. 22 Tabernacle row, City road
Smith Wm. builder, 39 Tavistock mews, Bedford sq
Smith Wm. butcher, 16 Eastcheap, Gracechurch st
Smith Wm. butcher, 18 Old Gravel lane, Wapping
Smith Wm. button & trimming seller, 33 Wardour st. Soho
Smith Wm. carpenter & builder, 5 Cambridge st. Golden sq
Smith Wm. carpenter & builder, 29 St. Mary at hill
Smith Wm. carpenter& builder, 66 Park st. Camden town
Smith Wm. carpenter & builder, 253 Tottenham court road
Smith Wm. carpenter &wheelrt.19 Marigld.ct.Star cr.Bmdy
Smith Wm. cheesemonger, 12 Blackmoor st. Clare market
Smith Wm. cheesemonger, 112 Brook st. Ratcliff
Smith Wm. cheesemonger, 1 Marsham st. Westminster
Smith Wm. chimney sweeper, 1 Rose & Crown ct. Foster la
Smith Wm. china dealer, 13 Peel pl. Kensington gravel pits
Smith Wm. coach smith, 47 High st. Marylebone
Smith Wm. coal merchant, 10 Lower King st.Commercialrd
Smith Wm. coal &potato wa.30Grove st.Commercial rd east
Smith Wm. coffee rooms, 2 Litchfield st. Soho
Smith Wm. commission agent, 9 Gresham st. Wood st
Smith Wm.cooper&stave ma.13John's rw.Brick l.St. Luke's
Smith Wm. corkcutter, 6 Little Tower st. City
Smith Wm. corn dealer, 39 Broad st. Lambeth
Smith Wm. cowkeeper, 17 Benjamin st. Cowcross st
Smith Wm. cowkeeper & dairyman, 90 White Lion st. Pentnl
Smith Wm. *Dolphin* P.H. 6 Tonbridge st. New road
Smith Wm. egg merchant, 26 Riley st. Chelsea
Smith Wm. engraver & printer, 40 Aldermanbury
Smith Wm. *Friend at Hand* P.H. 1 Elizth.st.Hans.pl.Slon.st
Smith Wm. fruiterer, 39 Fish st. hill
Smith Wm. fruiterer, 2 Yardley st. Clerkenwell
Smith Wm. furn. broker & prof. of music, 105 Tooley st
Smith Wm. gas meter manufacturer, 66 Snow hill
Smith Wm. grocer, 2 Ropemakers fields, Limehouse
Smith Wm. grocer, 16 Paradise row, Chelsea
Smith Wm. grocer, 9 Three colt st. Limehouse
Smith Wm. grocer, 14 Westmorland pl. Walworth common
Smith Wm. grocer & cheesemonger, 276 Poplar High st
Smith Wm. grocer&cheesemonger,62William st. Regent's pk
Smith Wm. gun maker, 13 Crown ct. Wardour st. Soho
Smith Wm. hairdresser, &c. 17 Red Lion st. Whitechapel
Smith Wm. hatter, see Flint & Smith
Smith Wm. hat maker, 21 Coventry st. Haymarket
Smith Wm. horn presser, 5 Star corner, Bermondsey st
Smith Wm. hosier & glover, 3 Ludgate st
Smith Wm. kitchen range & stove mnftr. 70 Snowhill
Smith Wm. linendraper, see Dickins, Smith & Stevens
Smith Wm. linendraper, 3 Salmon lane, Limehouse
Smith Wm. livery stables, 8 Arthur st. west, London bridge
Smith Wm. livery stables, Bristow st. Earl st. Blackfriars
Smith Wm. map & print colorer, 21 Woodbridge st. Clknwll
Smith Wm. mason, 10 East st. Hoxton Old town
Smith Wm. military cap & belt maker, 7 Litchfield st. Soho
Smith Wm. music seller, 37 Charles st. Horselydown
Smith Wm. newsman, 3 Saville pl. New Burlington st
Smith Wm. newsvender, 10 Kittesford pl. Hackney road
Smith Wm. newsvender & stationer, 25 Silver st. Golden sq
Smith Wm. oil & colorman, 82 Leman st. Goodman's fields
Smith Wm. paper hanger & house agent, 2 Hackney road
Smith Wm. paperhanger &c. 79 Margaret st. Cavendish sq
Smith Wm. pawnbroker, 1 Clark's pl. High st. Islington
Smith Wm. pawnbroker, 3 & 4 Lower st. Islington
Smith Wm. piece broker, 7 South row, Golden square
Smith W plaining & moulding factory, 12 Wharf rd. City rd
Smith Wm. plumbr.& glaz. 12Union cr. Union st.Kingsld.rd
Smith Wm. porkman& poulterer, 6 Prospect pl. Kingslnd.rd
Smith Wm. potato salesman, Mill lane, Tooley st
Smith Wm. *Rose & Crown* P.H. 32 Allen st. Goswell st
Smith Wm. potato salesman, 166 Shoreditch High st
Smith Wm. *Red Lion* P.H. 52 Basinghall st
Smith Wm. rope maker, New Church st. Bermondsey wall
Smith Wm.*RoyalSovereign*P.H. 11 Bluegate flds.St.Geo's.ea
Smith Wm. *Royal Standard* P.H. 227 Piccadilly
Smith Wm. *Royal* wine shades, 5 Leicester square
Smith Wm. sack & bag maker, 55 Snow's fields, Bermondsey
Smith Wm. scotch box maker, 46 Lisle st. Leicester sq.
Smith Wm. sheffield plate wareho.3 St.Michael's al.Cornhill
Smith Wm. smith & ironmonger, 70 Snow hill
Smith Wm. solicitor, 2 Francis st. Golden square
Smith Wm. solicitor, 16 Wilmington square
Smith Wm. stockbroker, 27 Tokenhouse yard, Lothbury
Smith Wm. surgeon, 28 Artillery place west, Finsbury
Smith Wm. surgeon, 21 Charlotte st. Fitzroy square
Smith Wm. surgeon, 2 Dowgate hill
Smith Wm. surgeon, Southampton st. Camberwell
Smith Wm. surgical instrument & truss maker, 2 New st. St. Thomas's st. Borough
Smith Wm. tailor, 17 Cross st. Hatton garden
Smith Wm. tailor, Church st. Hackney
Smith Wm. tailor, 5 North st. Fitzroy square
Smith Wm. tailor, 5 Upper John st. Golden square
Smith Wm. timber merchant, 97 Curtain road, Shoreditch
Smith Wm. tobacconist, 39½ Strutton ground, Westminster
Smith Wm. turner, 3 Winchester pl. Southwark bridge road
Smith Wm. upholsterer, 94 York st. Westminster
Smith Wm. warehouseman, 2 Star court, Bread st. City
Smith Wm. warehouseman, see Leaf, Coles, Smith & Co
Smith Wm. who. boot&shoe wareho. 105 St.John st.Smithfld
Smith Wm. wine merchant, see Bellamy & Smith
Smith Wm. jun.engraver&printer,25Warwick la.Newgate st
Smith Wm. sen. veranda bldr. 8Northampton pl.Old Kent rd
Smith Wm. Alex. wh. glovemanufr. 36 Lower Whitecross st

Smith Wm. Arnet, *King'sArms* P.H.52 Beech st. Barbican
Smith Wm. Castle, solicitor, see Pering, Minet & Smith
Smith Wm.Chas.cordage & sail cloth fac.&mer. 43 Trinity sq
Smith Wm.Chas. plumber & painter, 9 Spring st. Paddington
Smith Wm.Clifford,carp.&builder,11 Exeter pl.Knightsbridg
Smith Wm. Glaygorn, furniture brkr.141 Waterloo rd. Lmbth
Smith Wm. Henry, LL.D. barrister, 5 New sq. Lincoln's inn
Smith Wm. Henry, civil engineer, 10 Adam st. Adelphi
Smith Wm.Henry,coal merchant,Crownwhf.Creekrd.Deptfd
Smith Wm. Henry, coal merchant, &c. 3Wenlock rd. City rd
Smith Wm. Henry, hotpresser, 46 Basinghall st
Smith Wm. Henry, linendraper, 11 Spring st. Paddington
Smith Wm. Hen. *RoyalMint* P.H.30 South wharf rd. Paddtn
Smith Wm. Henry, solicitor, 12 Bedford row, Bloomsbury
Smith Wm. Henry, surgeon, 6 Clarence place, Clapham rd
Smith Wm. Hen. upholder& undertak. 72 Old Broad st. City
Smith Wm.Hornsby, solicitor, 2 Adelaide pl. London bridge
Smith William Hunt, wine & spirit merchant, & agent for Messrs. Deinhard & Jordan, of Coblentz,13 Little Tower st
Smith Wm. James, architect, 7 Whitehall yard
Smith Wm. John, auctioneer, 8 Orange row, Kennington rd
Smith Wm.John,engraver&printer,14 Lit.Moorfields,Finsbry
Smith Wm. Marten, warehouseman & general agent, Cross lane, St. Dunstan's hill, & Harp lane, Tower st
Smith Wm. Richard,newsagent,77 Crawford st.Portman sq
Smith William Robert, gasfitter, brass finisher & lamp manufacturer, 53 London wall
Smith William Samuel, *Red Cow* P.H.4 King st. Snowhill
Smith Wm. Sladon, ladies' school, Wright's la. Kensington
Smith Wm. Waterhouse,corn&coal mer.nr.Battersea church
Smith Wm. Welby,grocer&cheesemonger,Camberwell green
Smith Wm. Wright,lodgingho.3Carpenter'sbldgs.Lndn.wall
Smith Zachariah, *Windsor Castle* P.H.60 Albany st
Smithe Wm. Forster, barrister, 46 Lincoln's inn fields
Smither Elizabeth (Mrs.), coffee rooms, Camberwell green
Smither Henry, carman, 22 Christian st. St. George's east, & 110 Upper East Smithfield
Smither John, carman, 1 Well st. Wellclose sq. & London Dock entrance
Smither Wm. grocer & teadealer, 28 Gracechurch st
Smithers & Co. mers.&genl.agts.2 Adelaide pl.London bridge
Smithers Charles, fishmonger, 1 Duke's st. Tooley st
Smythers George,coal & potato dlr.55 Amelia st.Walwth.rd
Smythers John, tobacconist, 105 East st. Manchester sq
Smithett W.Pascall,ea.india ag.see Lysaght,Smithett & Co.
Smithfield Agency & Banking Co. 59 West Smithfield
Smithies Jas. prof. of music, 10 Glo'ster ter. Vauxhl. br. rd
Smithis & Mathews, window glass & lead mers.7 Gt.Dover st
Smithson & Straker, milliners, 17 Sackville st. Piccadilly
Smithson Cecilia (Miss), milliner, 32 Gt. Marylebone st
Smithson James, grocer & tea dealer, 59 Leather lane
Smithson Steven, pork butcher, 41 Paddington st
Smithson Thomas, tea dealer, 29 Fore st. Cripplegate
Smithson William, porkman, 13 Gt. Newport st. Long acre
Smithson Wm.Stphn.carver & gilder, 8 James st. Oxford st
Smithwaite Hen. firewood dealer, Belvedere rd. Lambeth
Smout Joseph, butcher, 56 Up. North pl. Gray's inn rd
Smowton Jas. undertaker, 74 Golden lane, St. Luke's
Smyrk Edwd. fringe & bell rope maker, 9 Hill st. Finsbury
Smyrk John, sen. builder, 1 Brook's row, Bagnigge wells rd
Smyth & Nephew,perfumerstotheQueen,116&117 NewBond st
Smyth Edward, artist, 85 Newman st. Oxford st
Smyth Frank, pianoforte maker, 15 Park st. Camden town
Smyth Frederick John, haircutter, 7 Bray's bldgs. Islington
Smyth George, surgeon, 43 Sackville st. Piccadilly
Smyth Geo. Lewis, parliamentary agt. 2 Derby st. Westmr
Smyth Geo. Wm. marble turner,38 William st. Regent's pk
Smyth James Richd. physician, 43 Sackville st
Smyth John Alex. Thompson, wine mer. see Allan & Smyth
Smyth John Edward, surgeon, 166 Lambeth wk
Smyth Leigh C. solicitor, 6 Ehrenburg ter. Regent's park
Smyth Philip, surgeon, Bromley, Middlesex
Smyth Richard Henry, colonial agent, Hall of Commerce
Smyth Robert Maclean, merchant, 11 Parliament st
Smyth Sarah (Mrs.), dressma. 20 Gt. Castle st. Regent st
Smyth Susanna (Mrs.), grocer, 15 Duke st. Grosvenor sq
Smyth Wm. Grey, surgeon, &c. 59 Vauxhall walk, Lambeth
Smythe & Perceval, oil & colormen, 137 Borough High st
Smythe & Percival,soapms.&c.14Greenst.Wellingtn.st.Blkfs
Smythe, Percival &Smythe,coal mers.Red Lionwhf.Bankside
Smythe George, general agent, 52 Eastcheap
Smythe Thomas, accountant, 14 Ashley terrace, City rd
Smythe Thomas, barrister, 49 Chancery lane
Smythe Wm. solicitor, 22 John st. Bedford rw
Smythies John Kinnersley, barrister, 35 Southampton bldgs
Snaith Temple John, tailor, 25 North st. Lisson grove
Snaith Thos. *Freemasons' Arms* P.H.19 Suffolk st.wt.Kngs.cs
Snape George, *Castle* P.H. 17 Gt. Chapel st. Westminster
Snape Isaac, butcher, 48 Fore st. Limehouse
Snape Joseph, nurseryman, Union gardens, New North road
Snape Robert James, special pleader, 12 Paper buildings
Snart Neariah (Miss), mathml. inst. ma. 35 King st. Boro'
Snead Henry, boot & shoe maker, 38 & 39 Tothill st. Westminster, & 7 New st. Covent garden
Snead Maria (Miss), boot & shoe wareho. 12 Kent st. Boro'
Snead Ralph, bootmaker, 184 Union st. Borough, & 71 Lambeth Lower marsh
Snead Wm. haberdasher, 17 Portland st. Walworth common
Snee John Adolphus, navy agent, see Collier & Snee
Sneed James, cheesemonger, 36 Sun st. Bishopsgate
Sneed John, oilman, 15 Margaret st. Wilmington sq
Sneezum Thos. carpenter & builder, 6 Rupert st. Haymarket
Sneezum William, carpenter, Well st. Hackney
Snelgar Joseph, *WaterlooArms* P.H. 50 High st. Marylebone
Snelgar Thomas Yallowley, stationer, 16 Basinghall st
Snelgar Wm. wine mercht. see Burleigh, Snelgar & Burleigh
Snelgrove James, lodging ho. 12 Park st. Grosvenor sq
Snell William & Edward, upholsterers & house agents, 27 Albemarle st. & 1 Belgrave road, Pimlico
Snell Cuthbert, tailor, 9 Princes st. Cavendish square
Snell Frances (Mrs.), fruiterer, 3 Shoe lane, Fleet st
Snell George Blagrave, shorthand writer, 36 Chancery lane, & 14 Abingdon st. Westminster
Snell Henry, cart wheelwright, 1 Dean st. Soho
Snell James, butcher, 44 Margaret st. Wilmington square
Snell James, linendraper, 130 Lower marsh, Lambeth
Snell James, tailor, 51 New Compton st. Soho
Snell James, tailor, 55 Radnor st. St. Luke's
Snell James P. commission agent, 43 Friday st. Cheapside
Snell John, beer retailer, 34 Gt. Carter la. Doctors' comns
Snell John, carpenter & builder, 16 Dorset st. Clapham rd
Snell John, coal & coke dealer, 16 & 17 Harp al. Farringdon st
Snell John, grocer & cheesemonger, 4 Dorset st. Clapham rd
Snell Samuel, foreign wine, liqueur & brandy mer. by appointment to her Majesty & royal family, 12 Haymarket
Snell Thomas, confectioner, 31 Mount st. Lambeth
Snell William, printer, 5A, Newcastle pl. Edgware road
Snell Wm. Philip, solicitor, Carlton chambers, 8 Regent st
Snellgrove Showell & Co. vellum binders, 23 Camomile st
Snellgrove John, butcher, 1 Cambridge rd. Mile end road
Snellgrove William, tailor, 89 Hackney road
Snelling George & John, pork butchers, 55 Minories
Snelling Benjamin, baker, 288 Kent st. Borough
Snelling Benj. ironmonger, 13 Hereford pl. Commercialrd.ea
Snelling Benjamin, tailor, 5 Brewer st. Golden square
Snelling Chas. hairdresser, & perfumer, 20 Gracechurch st
Snelling John, fishmonger, see Dutch & Snelling
Snelling John, *NewRedLion* P.H. Harrow road, Paddington
Snelling Joseph, lodging house, 2 King st. Grosvenor square
Snelling Joseph, poulterer, 18 Gt. hall, Hungerford market
Snelling Thomas, oil & italian wareho. 30 Fenchurch st
Snelling Thomas, oilman, 29 Shoemaker row, Blackfriars
Snelling Thomas, oilman, 66 Great Tower st
Snelling Wm. baker, 13 & 22 Mint st. Borough
Snelling Wm. clothes salesman, 1 Dockhead, Bermondsey
Snelson Thomas, beer retailer, 127 Curtain rd. Shoreditch
Snew William, cheesemonger, 3 Parker's row, Dockhead
Snewin Charles, timber merchant, 11 Back hill, Hatton gdn
Snewing Chas. *HarcourtArms* P.H.32 Harcourt st. Marylebn
Snewing Wm. *Northumberland Arms* P.H. 77 Wells st
Sneyd Sarah (Mrs.), corset maker, Church st. Hackney
Snitch Chas. James, surgeon, 33 Brydges st. Covent garden
Snodin Wm. &Co. tallow chandlers, 41 Red lion st. Holborn, & 30 Theobald's road
Snook Frederick, tailor, 67 Marylebone lane, Oxford st
Snook Jas. shell fishmonger & fruiterer, 10 Finch la. Cornhill
Snook Thos. Edwd. shipbuilder, Regent dock, Millwall, Poplr
Snosswell Wm. watch & musical clock ma. 1 Farringdon st
Snow Anthony, carriage manufactr. 3 Bridge st. Vauxhall
Snow Edward, teadealer, 55 High st. St. Giles's
Snow Geo. colored gold chaser, 30 Spencer st. Goswell rd
Snow James, tailor, Stratford
Snow James Thos. butcher, 12 Pollen st. Hanover square
Snow John, bookseller & publisher, 35 Paternoster row
Snow John, hairdresser, 38 Silver st. Golden square
Snow John, surgeon, 54 Frith st. Soho
Snow John Wright, auction. & app.56 Dorset st. Salisbury sq
Snow Joseph Durbin, baker, 13 High st. Deptford
Snow Matthew, grocer&cheesemongr. 23 Towr. st. Wstmr. rd
Snow Nathan, coffee rooms, 3 & 4 Sherrard st. Golden sq
Snow Peter, *St.John'stav.* Lord's cricket gd. St.Jn's. wd. rd
Snow Wm. tailor, &c.41 Windmill st. Tottenham court road

Snow Wm. wheelwright, Holland st. Clapham road
Snow Wm. Ephraim, surgeon, 26 Tredegar sq. Mile end road
Snowden Chas. dyer & scourer, 1 Yorkter. Commercialrd.east
Snowden George, cabinet & chair ma. 5 Crown row, Mile end
Snowden Henry, dining rooms, 11 Maiden la. Covent gardn
Snowden James, linendraper, 2 Lower st. Islington
Snowden Robert, teadealer, 7 Plumber's row, City road
Snowden Susan (Mrs.), cowkeeper, 15 Star st. Paddington
Snowden Wm. mangle maker, 32 St. Chad's row, Gray's inn rd
Snowdon Geo. Wrangham, chemist & druggist, 2 Haymarket
Snowdon John Porker, leather seller, 68 Devonshire st. Lisson grove, & 15 Chapel st. Edgware road
Snowdon Wm. brass founder, 24 Church row, Newington butts
Snowley Wm. *King & Queen* P.H. 50 Hare st. Bethnal green
Snowling John, grocer, William st. Caledonian road
Snowshill John, balance wheel & fusee cuttr. 55 Lit. Sutton st
Snoxell & Hallett, window blind ma. 84 & 85 Dorset st. Salisby. sq
Snoxell Wm. transpa. blind ma. 96 Regt. st. & 131 Chancery la
Snuggs Charles, auctioneer, 18 Anderson's bdgs. City road
Snuggs Charles, auctioneer, 16½ Smithfield bars
Snuggs John, turner, 182 Long lane, Bermondsey
Snuggs John, jun. toy whip manufr. 116 Long la. Bermdsey
Soady Robert Williams, barrister, 5 New square, Lincoln's inn
Soame James, builder, &c. 20 Cecil court, St. Martin's lane
Soames Hen. A. & E. russia brokers, 76 Old Broad st. City
Soames & Wilkie, soapmakers, 65 Wheeler st. Spitalfields
Soames Joseph, solicitor, 38z, Park st. Grosvenor square
Soames Jonathan, pianoforte mkr. 26 Cleveland st. Fitzry. sq
Soames Nicholas, russia brok. 80 Old Broad st. City, & Baltic
Soane Museum (Geo. Bailey, curator), 13 Lincoln's inn fields
Soane James, china & glass warehouse, 278 Oxford st
Soane John, cowkeeper, 61 York st. Westminster
Soanes John & Son, rope, line & twine manufacturers, 13 Cockhill, Ratcliff, & Bow common lane
Soanes Geo. linseed oil & whalebone brok. 5 Austinfriars
Soanes James, potato dealer, 5 Boswell court, Queen square
Soaper Fred. confectioner, 52 Lisson grove north, Marylebone
Soar Geo. Atkins, plumber & glazier, 20 Gt. Marylebone st
Soar James, watchmaker, 5 Paradise st. Finsbury
Soar Richd. cabinet & chairmaker, &c. 67 & 68 Kingsland rd
Soares Manoel Joaquim, merchant, 34 Great Tower st
Social, Literary & Scientific Institution (Edward Trulove, sec.), 23 John st. Fitzroy square
Society of Antiquaries (Sir Henry Ellis Nicholas Carlisle, sec.), Somerset house, Strand
Society of Apothecaries of London (Robt. B. Upton, clerk), Water lane, Blackfriars
Society of Arts (Francis Wishaw & John Scott Russell, joint secs.), 19 John st. Adelphi
Society for the Diffusion of Useful Knowledge (Thomas Coates, secretary), 42 Bedford square
Society for the Discharge & Relief of Persons imprisoned for Small Debts (Joseph Lunn, sec.), 7 Craven st. Strand
Society for the Emancipation of Industry (Benjamin Clarke, secretary), 15 Exeter hall
Society of Guardians for the Protection of Trade (Edwd. Fred. Leeks, sec), 2 Charlotte row, Mansion house
Society of Painters in Water Colors (John W. Wright, sec), 5 Pall mall east
Society (New) of Painters in Water Colors (James Fahey, sec.), 53 Pall mall
Society for Promoting Christian Knowledge, 67 Lincoln's inn fields & 4 Royal exchange
Society for Promoting Female Education in the East (Edward Suter, sec.), 19 Cheapside
Society for Promoting the Enlargement, Building & Repairing of Churches & Chapels (Rev. Thomas Bowdler, sec.), 4 St. Martin's place, Charing cross
Society for the Propagation of the Gospel in Foreign Parts (Rev. E. Hawkins, B.D. sec.; Rev. G. H. Fagan, M.A. assist. sec.), 79 Pall mall; City Branch (Rev. V. Knox Child, M.A. hon. sec.), 51 Liverpool st. Bishopsg.; hrs. 10 to 4
Society for Providing an Asylum & Relief for Aged & Infirm Fishmongers & Poulterers, Anderton's hotel, 164 Fleet st. third Thursday in every month, at 7 o'clock
Society for Relieving Foreigners in Distress (Charles Murray, hon. sec. F.E. Horneman, assist. sec.), 10 Finsbury chambers, London wall
Society for the Relief of Necessitous Widows & Children of Protestant Dissenting Ministers (Henry K. Smithers, sec.), 2 Adelaide pl. London bridge
Society for the Relief of Poor Pious Clergy (Samuel Tomkins, treasurer), 76 Lombard st
Society for Relief of Widows & Orphans of Medical Men in London & its Vicinity (Charles R. Walsh, sec.), 42 Halfmoon st
Society for the Relief of Widows (Joseph Fincher, sec.), 32 Sackville st
Society for the Suppression of Vice (Henry Prichard, sec.), 57 Lincoln's inn fields
Society of Schoolmasters (Octavian Blewitt, F.G.S. sec.), 73 Great Russell st. Bloomsbury
Sockett & Roberts, dairymen, 3 Mitre square, Aldgate
Socquet Joseph, table cover printer, 57 Eagle st. Red Lion sq
Soddy Wm. corndealer, 115 High st. Camden town
Soden & Iliffe, ribbon & trimming mks. 15 Noble st. Chpside
Soden James, stationer & library, 50 Stamford st. Blackfrs
Soden John Ross, stockbroker, Stock Exchange
Soden Jonathan, furn. undertaker, 16 Upper Marylebone
Soden Wm. builder & bricklayer, 5 Earl st. London road
Sodo James, chandler's shop, 11 Up. North st. Whitechapel rd
Soelman Wm. commercial academy, 59 Greek st. Soho
Soesman Abraham, *King George* P.H. Burr st. Lr. E. Smfld
Softlaw Joseph, *Bridgehouse hotel*, Wellington st. London br. & *Adelaide hotel & shades*, 7 Adelaide place London bdge
Softly Edward, cheesemonger, 12 Stucley ter. Camden tn
Sohnge Christian, *King of Prussia* P.H. 8 Blue Anchor rd. Bermondsey
Soho Bazaar, 4, 5, 6, 7 Soho sq. & 6, 7 & 8 Dean st. Soho
Soho Plate Company, 16 Salisbury sq. Fleet st
Soilleux Albert, weavers' cutler, 47 Sclater st. Bethnal gr
Sola Alfred, professor of singing, 21 Charlotte st. Fitzroy sq
Sola Chas. M. professor of music, 21 Charlotte st. Fitzroy sq
Solari Angelo, merchant, 25 St. Swithin's lane
Soldi John B. for. silk imp. 7 Windsor pl. Southwark bridge rd
Soles (Hen. Wm. & Wm. Chas.) & Turner, sols. 68 Aldrmnbry
Sole George, brewer, 35 Chenies mews, Bedford square
Solicitor General's Office, 8 Figtree court, Temple
Solicitor's Register Office (weekly pub.), 44 Carey st. Lincoln's inn
Solis David, fruiterer, 47 Borough road
Solita Felix Lewis, tailor, 12 St. George's pl. Camberwellrd
Solloway Major, chandler's shop, 22 Bermondsey New rd
Solly Isaac & Son, merchants, 5 Jeffrey's sq. St. Mary axe
Solly Joseph, wholesale hosier, &c. see Allen & Solly
Solly Samuel, surgeon, 1 St. Helen's place, Bishopsgate
Solly Stephen Fras. druggist, 3 St. George's circus, Obelisk
Solome David, refiner & goldsmith, 2 Bridge st. Lambeth
Solomon A. & Son, leghorn & chip, hat manufacturers, & embossers of silk, paper hangings & bookbinders' cloth, &c. 2 & 3 Sandys st. Widegate st. Bishopsgate
Solomon Henry & Co. wholesale watch manufacturers, hardwaremen & importers of foreign merchandise & musical instruments, 31 Houndsditch, & 60 Tothill st. Westminster
Solomon Abraham, artist, 18 Threadneedle st. City
Solomon Abraham, furniture dealer, 59 Gt. Queen st. & 23 Little Queen st. Holborn
Solomon Alexander, hosier & glover, 1 King's road, Pimlico
Solomon Benjamin, tailor, &c. 10 White Horse st. Piccadilly
Solomon David, furniture broker, 21 Chalcroft ter. New cut
Solomon Eve (Mrs.), eating house, 14 Lisson grove north
Solomon Henry, furniture broker, 45 & 46 Holborn hill
Solomon Henry, shipping agent, 95 Upper East Smithfield
Solomon Henry, stencil cutter, 6 Well st. Mile end New town
Solomon Henry, tobacconist, 25 Wentworth st. Whitechapel
Solomon Israel, furrier, 12 King st. Seven dials
Solomon Joel Woolf, portrait painter, 1 Strand
Solomon John, butcher, 6 Bedford pl. Lower rd. Rotherhithe
Solomon Jonas, butcher, 109 Middlesex st. Aldgate
Solomon Joseph, fruiterer, North row, Covent garden mkt
Solomon Joseph, oilman, 13 Broadway, Deptford
Solomon Levy, lead pencil makr. 106 Gravel la. Houndsditch
Solomon Lewis, fruit salesman, Centre row, Covent garden
Solomon Lewis, furniture broker, 19 Temple st. Whitefriars, & 4 Pilgrim st. Ludgate hill
Solomon Lewis, tailor, 6 Trump st. Cheapside
Solomon Mary (Mrs.), clothes dealer, 140 Rosemary lane
Solomon Michael, shoe mfr. 21 Union st. Bishopsgate without
Solomon Morris, tailor & draper, 51 Long la. West Smithfild
Solomon Moses, sen. clothes salesman, 6 Vinegar yd. Cov. gar
Solomon Phineas, watch manfr. 26 Mansell st. Goodman's fi
Solomon Rosetta (Mrs.), dressmaker, 45 Spital square
Solomon Samuel, clothes dealer, 39 Kensington High st
Solomon Saml. fruiterer, Centre row, Covent garden market
Solomon Saml. lamp glass wareho. 63 Poland st. Oxford st
Solomon Saml. prof. of hebrew, french, &c. 2 Bevis Marks
Solomon Saul, tailor, 53 Long lane, Smithfield
Solomon Silvester, tailor, 35 Cloth fair, Smithfield
Solomon Solomon, furniture broker, 12 Chapel st. New rd
Solomon Solomon, tailor, 1 Strand
Solomon Wm. grocer & cheesemonger, 147 Union st. Boro'
Solomon Zimlor, picture dealer, 15 Duke st. Manchester sq

Solomons & Jacobs, clothes salesmen, 61 Sun st. Bishopsgate
Solomons Saml. & Benjn. opticians & aurists, 39 Albemarle st
Solomons Abraham, mercht. & warehomn. 26 Basinghall st
Solomons Alexr. sen. covered hat m. 59 NewGravel la. Shdwll
Solomons Charles, chemist & druggist, 196 Tooley st
Solomons Elias, patentee of spectacles, & inventor of apparatus for deafness, 36 Old Bond st. Piccadilly
Solomons Henry, ship agent, 1 Shorter st. St. George's east
Solomons Henry, timber mercht. York st. York rd. Lambeth
Solomons Isaac, *Fishmongers' Arms* P.H. 4 St. James's pl. Ald
Solomons John, skinner & furrier, 7 Fishmongers alley, Boro
Solomons John, timber merchant, Byde's pl. Shoreditch
Solomons Joseph, tailor & slop seller, 74 St. George st
Solomons Michael, upholsterer, 1 Sloane st. Chelsea
Solomons Moses, who. furrier & imp. of skins, 3 Little Britain
Solomons Samuel, slop seller, 52 Houndsditch
Soltau Geo. & Wm. & Co. merchts. 15 St. Helen's pl. Bishops
Somalvico Joseph & Co. opticians, barometer & thermometer & hydrometer manufacturers, 2 Hatton garden
Somerby John, grocer, 13 Victoria pl. Hoxton Old town
Somerfield Hen. ivory turner, 67 Marylebone la. Oxford st
Somers Susan (Mrs.) & Co. corn merchts. 22 North Audley st
Somers Alfred Wm. butcher, 56 Cambridge st. Edgware rd
Somers George, boot & shoe maker, 63 High st. Portland tn
Somers Hannah (Miss), milliner, 18 Charles st. Clarendon sq
Somers Isaac, jeweller, 5 Bevis marks
Somers James, butcher, 9 King's road, Victoria rd. Pimlico
Somers Judah George, stationer, 67 Houndsditch
Somers Sarah (Mrs.), tobacconist, Henry st. ea. Avenue rd
SOMERSET HOUSE, 151 Strand
Somerset Arthur Edward, barrister, 3 Pump court, Temple
Somersetshire Midland Railway, 9 Tokenhouse yard
Somerton Joseph, cheesemonger, 19 Stafford row, Pimlico
Somerton Maria (Mrs.), toywareho. 112 Edgware rd. Padgtn
Somervail Charles R. merchant, 147 Leadenhall st
Somervell Wm. foreign & eng. leather wa. 3 Little Love la
Somerville James Curtis, barrister, 11 Lincoln's inn fields
Somes Joseph & Frederic, shipowners, 35 Broad st. Ratcliff, & Lloyds
Somes Major & Edwin, pawnbrkrs. 33 Paradise row, Chelsea
Somes Francis, pawnbroker, 200 Brick lane, Spitalfields, & 1 Green st. Bethnal green
Somes (exrs. of the late) Joseph, shipowner, 35 Broad st. Rtcff
Sommers Benjamin, cheesemonger, 22 Gutter la. Cheapside
Sommers Edward, baker, 3 Motcomb st. Belgrave sq
Sones Thomas, tobacconist, 43 St. George st
Songhurst Gideon, carpenter, 53 Stanhope st. Clare market
Songi Elizth. (Madame), dressma. 22 Gt. Castle st. Regnt. st
Sons of the Thames, Gravesend Steam Packet Company (Joseph Davies, sec.), 12 Mark lane
Sooby John Jenner, *Bacchus* P.H. 160 Hoxton Old town
Soper John & Sons, bldrs. & undrtkrs. 8 Meadow rw. Nw. Kentrd
Soper Ann (Miss), milliner & dress maker, 35 Albemarle st
Soper Ebenezer, furniture printer, 15 Cheapside
Soper Elizh. (Mrs.), cheesemonger, 1 Gt. Bland st. Dover rd
Soper Henry silk manufacturer, 32 Spital sq
Soper James, broker & agent, 81 Mark lane
Soper Jane (Mrs.), sash line ma. 4 Blossom st. Norton Folgate
Soper John, beer retailer, 8 Meadow row, New Kent rd
Soper Wm. boot & shoe maker, 31 Gower place, Euston sq
Soppet John Wharton, linendraper, 3 High st. Marylebone
Sore Hen. plumber & glazier, 25 Foxley rd. Cambrwl. nw. rd
Sore Henry, plumber, 9 Hill st. Walworth rd
Sorel & Banes, leathersellers, 50 Bishopsgate within
Soresby James & Wm. carriers to Derby, 27 Whf. rd. City rd
Sorg Chas. watch & clock ma. 16 Frederick pl. Old Kent rd
Sorrell John, patent axletree maker, High st. Bow
Sorrell Geo. & Thos. pat. axletree, lathe & pen makrs. Old Ford
Sorrell Harry Robt. hosier & outfitter & glover, 88 Strand
Sorrell Elizth. Jane (Mrs.), milliner, 17 Eldon st. Finsbury
Sorrell John, baker, 20 Snow's fields, Bermondsey
Sorrell John, solicitor, 1 Gwynn's place, Hackney rd
Sorrell John, solicitor, see Kinder & Sorrell
Sorrell Joseph, tailor, 36 High st. Bow
Sorrey Sarah (Miss), fruiterer, 1 Maidenhead ct. Aldsgt. st
Sosson Alexander, french repostry. 106 Park st. Camden tn
Sotheby (Leigh) & Co. auctioneers of literary property & works of art, 3 Wellington st. Strand
Sotheran Thos. & Son, statnrs. & booksellers, 10 Lit. Tower st
Sotheran Chas. filter & wine cooler maker, 12 Little Britain
Souchay, Schunck & Co. merchts. see Schunck, Souchay & Co
Soughton John, beer retailer, 17 Goswell rd. east side
Soughton John, carpenter, 14 Powell st. east, King sq
Soul Caleb, grocer & cheesemngr. 120 Long alley, Finsbury
Soul Eli, bookbinder & seller, 26 Tabernacle walk, Finsbury
Soul Joseph, sec. to Orphan Working School, City rd
Soul Matthew, bookbinder, 5 Hall pl. Lr. Kennington la
Soul Wm. silk dyer, 48 York st. Westminster
Soulby John & Co. sail makers, ship chandlers, & mathematical instrument makers, New stairs, 126 Wapping
Soulier & Ward, tobacco & snuff makrs. 4 Burlington arcade
Soulsby John & Co. coal merchants, Milford lane, Strand
Soundy Chas. barge builder, 8 Little Abingdon st. Westmr
Soundy George Fredk. grocer, 12 Union ter. Notting hill
Soundy John, tobacconist, 3 Dover pl. west, Kent st. rd
Soundy Joseph, grocer & tea dlr. 13 Brown st. Bryanstone sq
Sounes Wm. & Co. adhesive seal wafer manfr. 46 Rupert st
Souper Thos. E. sec. to Thames Plate Glass Co. 3 Savoy st. Strand
Souter & Law, schl. bookselrs. publishrs. & statnrs. 131 Fleet st
Souter & Symons, builders, 3 Exeter st. Sloane st. Knightsbr
Souter Fredk. baker & corn dlr. 8 York st. Boro' market
Souter Isaac, bookbinder, 11 Bell's buildings, Salisbury sq
Souter William, general agent, 7 Silver st. Wood st
Soutter Wm. copper smith, Newmarket st. Birmingham, & at 21 Red Lion st. Clerkenwell, James Standley, agent
South Australian Banking Co. 54 Old Broad st. City, see p. 2009
South Australian Colonization Commission, 9 Park st. Westminster; hours 11 to 5
South Australian Company (David M'Laren, manager), 4 New Broad st. City
South Australian Society (Jn. H. Croucher, jun. sec.), 27 Leadenhall st
South-Eastern & Continental Steam Packet Company (Captn. Wm. O'Brien, sec.), 4 Joiner st. Tooley st
South-Eastern & Dover Railw. Off. (Capt. Wm. O'Brien, sec), terminus, Duke st. London Bridge, Capt. Charlewood, R.N. superintendent; *Transfer Off.* 4 Joiner st. Tooley st
South Metropolitan Cemetery Co.'s Off. (Griffith Thomas, clerk), 70 King Wm. st. City; cemetery opposite St. Luke's church, Norwood
South Midland & North Union Railway (Geo. Jackson, sec.), 23 Finsbury place north
South Metropolitan Gas & Coke Co. (Thomas Livesey, sec.), Canal bridge, Old Kent road
South Sea Company (C. F. Gibson, sec.), South Sea House, Threadneedle st.; hours of business 9 to 3
South Wales Railw. Co. (N. Armstrong, sec.), 449 W. Strand
South-Western Railway, see "Londn. & South Westn. Railwy"
South Yorkshire Railway Co. 3 Park st. Westminster
South George & Son, furniture brokers, 172 Lambeth walk
South George, cowkeeper, Portland pl. Lower rd. Islington
South James, oil & colorman, 241 Tooley st
South Saml. Thos. beer machine ma. 21 George st. Blkfrs. rd
South Thomas, silk mercer, 15 Leicester square
South Thos. surgeon, 8 Judd st. & 6½ Hunter st. Brunswick sq
Southall & Ponsford, woollen & stuff merchants, 13 & 14 King st. Cheapside
Southall Benj. *Lord Nelson* P.H. 15 Oakley ter. O. Kent rd
Southall Charles, paper stainer, 105 Bunhill row, St. Luke's
Southall William, water gilder, 4 Canning place, Old st
Southam Henry (successor to M. Muir), patentee for preparing floor boards & match boarding, &c. saw mills, Gillingham st. Grosvenor basin, Pimlico
Southam James, curiosity dealer, 19 Green st. Leicester sq
Southampton Dock Co. (Geo. Saintsbury, sec.), 19 Bishpsg. wbn
Southampton Estate Office, 1 Southampton st. Fitzroy square; hours of business 9 to 5
Southampton Paving Trust Commissioners (J. Arnell, sec.), Edward st. Hampstead road
Southampton & Great Western Junction Railway (Wm. Bevan, solicitor), 6 Old Jewry
Southan George A. stationer & library, Mare st. Hackney
Southan John, fruiterer, Stratford broadway
Southard Chas. cork cutter, 7 Gate st. Lincoln's inn fields, & 11 Arcade, Hungerford market
Southbrook Sophia (Miss), straw hat ma. 18 Store st. Bedf. sq
Southby Joseph, firework mak. 14 Saville pl. Lambeth walk
Southby Thomas Edwd. hat manufact. 128 & 129 London wall
Southcomb Hen. *Duke of Cumberland* P.H. 20 Bryanstone st
Southcott Wm. grocer & cheesemong. 30 Lit. Coram st. Russ. sq
Southcott Wm. Henderson, beer ret. 4 Church row, Somers tn
Southee John, music seller, 9 Rathbone place
Southee Robert, solicitor, 16 Ely place, Holborn
Southern Edwin, teadealer, &c. 291 Oxford st
Southern Counties Union, & Bristol, Bath & Dover Direct Railway (Rt. Hope Gadesden, sec.), 70 King William st. City
Southern George, *London Apprentice* P.H. 12 Old st. rd
Southern Isabella (Mrs.), dairy, 7 Bretten ter. west, Chelsea
Southey Geo. & Co. who. curriers, 1 Chenies st. Bedford sq
Southey Thomas & Son, wool brokers, 23 Coleman st
Southey Wm. & Co. tailors & breeches ma. 5 Bury st. St. James
Southey Alfred, printer, see Cuthbert & Southey

Southey Geo. cook & confectioner, 81 Judd st. Brunswick sq
Southey Henry Herbert, physician, 1 Harley st
Southey James, auctioneer & appraiser, 191 Tooley st
Southey James, sworn broker, 191 Tooley st
Southey John, berlin wool & fancy reposit. 67 Hackney rd
Southey John, hat manufr. 8 Gt. Charlotte st. Blackfriars rd
Southey John, fruiterer, 38 Freeschool st. Horselydown
Southey Wm. japanner & bedstead ma. 2 Pancras st. Tot. ct. rd
Southey Wm. Couzens, cabinet ma. 15 Nw. Glo'ster pl. Hoxtn
Southgate John & Son, trunk & packing case manufacturers, 76 & 77 Watling st. & 3 George yard, Bow lane
Southgate Francis Thomas, solicitor, 10 Gray's inn place
Southgate George, fishmonger, 45½ Rosoman st. Clerkenwell
Southgate Henry, auctioneer of literary property, 22 Fleet st
Southgate Jas. Webb, floorcloth manufacturer, 26 London rd
Southgate James W. jun. floorcloth ma. 147 Blackfriars road
Southgate John, packer & calendr. Crown ct. & 23 Old Change
Southgate John, jun. trunk maker, Crown ct. Old Change
Southgate Samuel, builder, 16 Gate st. Lincoln's inn fields
Southgate Thomas, barrister, 89 Chancery lane
Southgate Thomas, bricklayer, 9 Old North st. Red Lion sq
Southgate William, painter, 5 St. Chad's row, Gray's inn rd
Southin William, baker, 14 Cleveland st. Fitzroy sq
Southland Wm. teadealer, 2 King's pl. Commercial rd. east
Southon George, gasfitter, 33 Hampstead road
Southon John, coal dealer, 30 Upper Lisson st. Lisson grove
Southward James, tailor, 21 Brewer st. Golden square
Southwark Bridge Office (James Leith, sec.), 10 Queen st. place, Upper Thames st.; hours 10 to 4
Southwark Court of Record, Prothonotary's office, Town hall, Borough High st.; hours 10 to 2
Southwark Court of Requests, Swan st. Trinity st. Stone's end; office hours 9 to 2; Court days, Tuesdays & Fridays
Southwark Fund for Schools & Churches (William T. Haly, sec.), 4 St. Martin's place, Trafalgar square
Southwark Literary Institution (Charles Mackie, sec.), 8 Portland place, Southwark bridge road
Southwark Police Court, Blackman st. Borough
Southwark Savings' Bank (Thomas Day, sec.), 9 Three Crown square, Borough
Southwark Steam Wharf, J. P. Robinson, Montague close, adjoining London Bridge, Borough
Southwark Water Works Office (James Rossiter, sec.), Sumner st. Southwark; works, Battersea fields
Southwell James Callis, booksell. 2 Blandford st. Portman sq
Southwell Edward Joseph (sec. to *Mutual Building Association*), 80 Jubilee st. Stepney
Southwell Mary (Mrs.), grocer, 16 Moor st. Soho
Southwell Valentine, writer & painter, Park pl. East st. Walw
Southwell Wm. pianoforte ma. 12 St. James's pl. Hampstd. rd
Southwells & Co. carpet manufacturers, 24 Basing lane, Bread st. & Bridgenorth, Salop
Southwood James, bricklayer, 73 Market st. Paddington
Southwood John, cooper, 15 Richard st. Commercl. rd. east
Southwood Joshua, gold trimming maker, 46 Aldermanbury
Southwood Joshua, surgeon, 9 Fore st. Cripplegate
Southwood Thomas, chemist, 11 Bridge terrace, Harrow rd
Southwood Walter, solicitor, see Bartley & Southwood
Southwood William, linendraper, see Wallis & Southwood
Soutten Frank, meat salesman, 24 Newgate market
Soutter Richard & Robert, ship chandlers, sailmakers, & packing tarpaulin manufacturers, 49 Lower Shadwell
Soutter Samuel & Christian, ship chandlers, sailmakers, & wharfingers, Bell wharf, 44 Lower Shadwell
Soutter John, leather cutter, 17 & 18 New st. Dockhead
Soutter Wm. pastrycook & confectioner, 2 Shoreditch
Sovereign Life Assurance Office (George Cumming, sec.), 5 St. James st. Piccadilly
Soward John & Son, statuaries & builders, 241 Tottnhm. ct. rd
Soward George Jas. plumber, glazier, & painter, 3 Huntley st. & 3 Upper Chenies mews, Bedford square
Soward John, button & trimming seller, 77 Drury lane
Sowden John, tailor, 6 Great Woodstock st. Marylebone
Sowdon Henry, upholsterer, carpenter & cabinet warehouseman, 1 & 2 Commercial place, Old Kent road
Sowerbutts Thos. wholesale & export mfr. of fancy walking & umbrella sticks & canes, 12 Duke st. Bishopsgate
Sowerby Dickenson, pawnbroker, 49 Brick lane, Spitalfields
Sowerby George B. naturalist, 50 Gt. Russell st. Bloomsby
Sowerby James, table cover, &c. agt. 46 Berners st. Oxford st
Sowerby Jane (Mrs.), pawnbroker, 81 Cable st. Wellclose sq
Sowerby John, *Green Dragon* P.H. 188 Bishopsgate without
Sowerby John, perfumer, 226 Borough High st
Sowerby Joseph, corkcutter, 149 & 150 Shadwell High st
Sowerby Joseph, linendraper, see Williams & Sowerby
Sowerby Judith (Mrs.), booksell. 3 Mead pl. Westminster rd
Sowerby Thomas Benn, pawnbroker, 78 Chiswell st.; 3 & 4 Grosvenor row, Pimlico; & 156 Hoxton Old Town
Sowerby William, dyer, 112 Broadwall, Blackfriars
Sowter Isaac, wharfinger & carrier, 27 Wharf rd. City rd
Sowter William, butcher, 26 Greenhill's rents, Smithfield
Sowter William, national baths, 7½ Mount st. Lambeth
Sowton George, corndealer, 7 Monmouth pl. Old Kent rd
Sowton James, solicitor, 27 Great James st. Bedford row
Sowton William March, barrister, 6 King's Bench walk, Tem
Spademan John, pianoforte mak. 31 William st. Hampstead rd
Spaeth Chas. Benjamin, merchant, 4 Brabant court, & Baltic
Spaiham Henry Mills, solicitor, 123 Chancery lane
Spain Martha (Mrs.), butcher, 9 Old Quebec st. Portman sq
Spalding & Hodge, who. stationers, 145, 146 & 147 Drury la
Spalding John, druggist, 27 Eldon st. Finsbury
Spalding Simon, bootmaker, 14 Gt. Pulteney st. Golden sq.
Spanish Consulate Office, 37 Old Broad st. City
Spanish Financial Commission, 7 Tokenhouse yd. Lothbry
Spankhurst Matthew, fruiterer, Borough market
Spanswick David, carpenter, 2 Camberwell new road
Spanton John, blacksmith, 3 York pl. Hackney road
Sparding Henry & Son, military tailors, 7 Hanover square
Spark Mary (Mrs.), cowkeeper, 19 New rd. Sloane st. Chelsea
Sparke Reuben, potato merchant, 33 Farringdon st. & 55, 57, & 59 Farringdon market
Sparke Ezra, cheesemonger, 252 Oxford st
Sparke George Yarde, solicitor, 11 Warwick ct. Gray's inn
Sparke John, livery stables, 95 Lit. Cadogan pl. Belgrve. sq
Sparke John Guyse, surgeon, 15 Finsbury place south
Sparkes Ann (Mrs.), straw bon. mkr. 1 Harleyford st. Ken. com
Sparkes Anna H. & P. & M. (Misses), bonnet mkrs. 76 Houndsd
Sparkes & Clark, stockbrokers, 3 Bartholomew lane, Bank
Sparkhall Edward, printer, 142 Cheapside
Sparkhall Edward, tailor, 142 Cheapside
Sparks & Co. distillers' chemists, 134 St. John st. Smithfield
Sparks Jonathan & Co. surgical bandage mkrs. 28 Conduit st
Sparks Elizb. (Mrs.), milliner & dress ma. 201 Whitechpl rd
Sparks Elizb. (Mrs.), servants' office, 34 Princes st. Le'ster. sq
Sparks George, carpenter & builder, 12 King st. Tower hill, & Glasshouse st. East Smithfield
Sparks Geo. sack & russia mat wareh. 21 Swan st. Minories
Sparks Robert, *Cape of Good Hope* P.H. 8 Lime st. City
Sparks Thos. bootmaker, 3 Gilbert st. Grosvenor square
Sparks Thos. bootmaker, 25 Whitefriars st. Fleet st
Sparks Thos. tailor, 2 Raven st. Whitechapel road
Sparks Thos. Edward, bootmaker, 3 Tower royal
Sparks Wm. James, pianoforte tuner, 44 George st. Euston sq
Sparks Wm. John, dining rooms, 49 Henry st. east, Avenue rd
Sparling Wm. barrister, 19 Old square, Lincoln's inn
Sparrey Arthur, glass & bottle wa. 4 Jerusalem pas. Clknwll
Sparrey Jas. straw hat mak. 27 Hedge row, High st. Islingtn
Sparrey John, butcher, 17 Rosoman st. Clerkenwell
Sparrow & Imbrie, tailors, &c., 34 Newington causeway
Sparrow Fred. & Co. teadlrs. & wine merchts. 8 New Bridge st
Sparrow Samuel Thos. J. & Sons, pearl workers, 11 New North st. Red Lion square
Sparrow Thos. & Son, strawcleaners, 98 Cromer st. Brunswk. sq
Sparrow Anthy. brln. wool imp. see Lindsay, Bristow & Sparrow
Sparrow Charles, goldsmith, 11 New North st. Red Lion sq
Sparrow Frederick, teadealer & grocer, 31 Charing cross
Sparrow Harry, coffee rooms, 112 St. John's st. Clerkenwell
Sparrow Henry, confectioner, 28 Kensington High st
Sparrow Henry, wholesale & retail teadealer & grocer, 95 High Holborn; wareho. entrance, 22 Dean st. High Hlbrn
Sparrow John Coggins, potato dealr. 4 High st. Marylebone
Sparrow Joseph, millinery wareho. 1 Brompton ter. Brmptn
Sparrow Joseph S. clothworker, see Little & Sparrow
Sparrow Mary (Miss), grocer, 54 Vauxhall st. Lambeth
Sparrow Mary (Mrs.), stables, 35 & 36 Grosvnr. mws. Bond st
Sparrow Robert, bellhanger, 3 St. Mark's rd. Cambrwll. New rd
Sparrow Thomas, brushmaker, 28 Stamford st. Blackfrs. rd
Sparrow Wm. building matl. dlr. 31 John st. north, Marylebone
Sparrow Wm. hairdresser, 66 Seymour st. Euston square
Sparrow Wm. tailor, 10 Millman st. Bedford row
Sparrow Wm. tobacconist, 65 Farringdon st
Sparry John James, butcher, 52 Penton st. Pentonville
Spartali & Rascaridi, merchants, 8 New Broad st. City
Spaul John, imp. of beads & foreign manufacts. 19 Beer lane
Spaul John, wine mer. & for. goods imp. 19 Beer lane, Tower st
Spaull Benjamin, shoemaker, 39 Henry st. east, Avenue road
Spaull Richard, tailor, see Ellis & Spaull
Spavin William, wholesale teadealer, see Cock, Spavin & Co
Spawforth & Sons, wine & brandy mers. 3 Castle ct. Budge row
Spawforth Sophia (Mrs.), coffeehouse, 9 Carnaby st. Golden sq
Speake & Tipper, grocers & cheesemongers, 126 London rd
Spear Jacob, musical clock ma. 5 Halton st. Cross st. Islingtn

Spear John Henry, *Axe tap* P.H. Three Nuns ct. Aldermnbury
Spear Mary (Mrs.), cutler, 2 Well st. Wellclose square
Spearay Job, chandler's shop, 3 Tottenham rd. Kingsland rd
Spearing George, dyer & scourer, 29 Leadenhall st
Spearing Holly Richard, cooper, 6 Fulwood's rents, Holborn
Spearman Fredk. Cleobury Mortimer, auctioneer & surveyor, 77 Old Broad st. City; & Stoke Newington road
Spearman John, gunmaker & gun stock manufacturer, 25&26 Chamber st. London; & Steelhouse lane, Birmingham
Spearpoint James Henry, confectioner, 7 Abbey st. Bermndsy
Spectator weekly newspaper, 9 Wellington st. Strand
Spedding Thos. zinc worker & furn. bro. 14 High rd. Kntsbrdg
Speechley Edw. Campion, tailor & draper, 98 Union st. Boro'
Speechley John, bricklayer, 11 William st. Charlotte st. Blkfrs
Speechly William, livery stables, Swan inn yd. Gt. Dover st
Speechly William, *Swan inn*, 8 Great Dover st
Speed George Henry, *Green Man* P.H. 19 New st. Cov. gdn
Speed James, poulterer, 13 New st. Covent garden
Speed Peter, grocer, 47A, Carnaby st. Golden square
Speed Rowlnd, *White Hart* P.H. 12 Black Prince rw. Watloo. rd
Speed William, barrister, 9 New square, Lincoln's inn
Speedy George, *Green Man* P.H. Balls pond road
Speedy Henry, *Boot* P.H. 117 Cromer st. Brunswick square
Speer George, tooth brush maker, 3 White st. Bethnal grn
Speering Mary (Mrs.), *Globe* P.H. Broomfield pl. Deptford
Speet John, button & trimming wa. 5 Marlboro' rd. Chelsea
Speight Geo. furniture broker, 14 & 20 Castle st. Long acre
Speir William, merchant, 6 Gt. Winchester st. Old Broad st
Speller Edward, grocer, &c. 36 Berners st. Oxford st
Speller George, furn. broker, 12 Prospect pl. Kingsland rd
Speller Jas. bricklyr. & furn. brok. 12 Copenhagen st. Pntnvl
Speller John, cheesemonger, 57 Goswell st
Speller Richard, *Hope* coffee rooms, 52 Lime st
Speller Robert, *Union* P.H. 21 Essex st. King's cross
Speller Wm. builder & carpenter, 30A, Up. Berkeley st. West
Speller Wm. iron pl. work. & pump ma. 14 York st. Blkfrs. rd
Spelman Sam. boot & shoemaker, 36 Gt. Prescot st. Goodm's fl
Spelzini John, baromtr. ma. 11 Beauchamp st. Brooke st. Holbn
Spence, Baggallay & Son, wholesale haberdashers & silk mercers, 4, 5 & 6, Love lane, Wood st. Cheapside
Spence, Brothers & Co. general brokers, 59 Fenchurch st
Spence James & Sons, merchants, 59 Fenchurch st
Spence Daniel, carman, 163 Bermondsey st
Spence George, queen's counsel, 2 Stone bldgs. Lincoln's inn
Spence James, jeweller, see Hughes & Spence
Spence John, baker, 26 Clipstone st. Fitzroy square
Spence John, china dealer, 1 Queen st. Charles sq. Hoxton
Spence John Clarke, ship bldr. see Tebbutt, Stoneman & Co
Spence Joseph, hatter, 38 King's road east, Chelsea
Spence Martha (Miss), straw hat ma. 1 Chadwell st. Pentvl
Spence Peter Andrew, importer of sherry & port wines, 28 Crosby hall chambers
Spence Robert, *Masons' Arms* P.H. Horsemonger la. Boro'
Spence Thos. carvr. & bed pillr. ma. 39½ Curtain rd. Shoredtch
Spence Thomas, tailor, 8 Throgmorton st
Spence Wm. agent for british & foreign patents & registration of designs, mechanical draftsmen, &c. 43 Cornhill
Spence Wm. tobacconist, 6 Shepperton pl. New North road
Spenceley Fred. *King's Hd. & 8 Bells* P.H. 45 Cheyne wk. Chel
Spenceley Richd. chain cable ma. see Lawson, Spencely & Co
Spenceley Wm. *Swan* P.H. 4 Sloane st. Knightsbridge
Spencely Jas. oil & colorman, 24 Goodge st. Tottenham ct. rd
Spencely James, wind. glass & lead mer. 281 Whitechapel rd
Spencer & Asher, perfumers, 29 Nottingham pl. Whitechapel
Spencer, Browning & Co. mathematical & optical inst. maks. & wholes. dealers in bunting for ships' colors, 111 Minories
Spencer & Cartwright, plumbers, 53&54 Princess st. Ptmn. mkt
Spencer & Cooke, clerical agents, 16 Gt. James st. Bedford row
Spencer Edward & Co. carpenters & joiners, cabinet case & trunk makers & timber merchants, 18 Billiter st
Spencer Eliza & L. (Misses), school, Cmbdg. rw. Cambdg. bth
Spencer Geo. H. & Jas. fur manfs. 5 Pilgrim st. Ludgate hill
Spencer & Hall, linendrapers, 53 Lisson Grove, north, Marylebone, & 85 High st. Portland town
Spencer & Hewitt, linendrapers, 180 Oxford st
Spencer Jas. & Son, saddle tree ms. 25 Gt. Warner st. Clrknwl
Spencer Josiah & Co. wharfngrs. Liddard's whf. Shad Thames
Spencer & Manvell, linen factors, 12 Bow churchyard
Spencer & Taylor, surgeons, 59 St. John st. road
Spencer & Wood, rubbish carters, &c. 78 Goswell st
Spencer Anne (Mrs.), chandlers' shop, 16 Cambdge pl. Edgw. rd
Spencer Charles Child, prof. of music, Mare st. Hackney
Spencer David, button & trim. sel. 23 Stanhope st. Clare mkt
Spencer David, jun. tailor, 23 Stanhope st. Clare market
Spencer Ebenezer, willow manufac. 230 Shoreditch High st
Spencer Edward, fruiterer, 26 York row, Kennington road
Spencer Edwd. solicitor, 11 Brunswick parade, Barnsbury rd
Spencer Edwd. John, beer retlr. 4 Stephen's acre, Blackwall
Spencer Edwd. W. engraver, 12 Gt. Windmill st. Haymarket
Spencer George, chemist, 30 Marchmont st. Brunswick sq
Spencer George, mattress & bedding ma. 11 Tottenham ct. rd
Spencer George, surveyor, 217 Albany road, Old Kent road
Spencer George, tailor, 33 Walnut Tree walk, Lambeth
Spencer Geo. English, solicitor, 110 Chalton st. Somers town
Spencer George English, solicitor, 6 Lincoln's inn fields
Spencer Henry, boot & shoemaker, 157 Houndsditch
Spencer Henry, fruiterer, 7 Dean st. Westminster
Spencer Henry, meat salesman, 14 New Newgate market
Spencer Henry, plumber & painter, 2 Charles st. Portman sq
Spencer Henry, solicitor, 69 Westmoreland place, City road
Spencer Henry, surveyor, 3 Everett st. Brunswick sq
Spencer James, butcher, 9 Wellington place, Stepney
Spencer James, clothier, 5 Albion place, east, King's cross
Spencer James, comb maker, 7 Meard's st. Soho
Spencer James, *Cricketers* P.H. 50 Cheyne walk, Chelsea
Spencer James, iron & bone dealer, 66 East st. Marylebone
Spencer John, beer retlr. 14&15 Vittoria pl. Stoke Nwngtn. rd
Spencer John, cooper, 22 Tabernacle walk, Finsbury
Spencer John, corkcutter, 20 Princes sq. Ratcliff highway
Spencer John, *Folly House* P.H. Folly wall, Blackwall
Spencer John, fruiterer, 27 Granby st. Hampstead road
Spencer John, grocer, 136 Hoxton Old town
Spencer John, newsvender, 97 Cromer st. Brunswick sq
Spencer John, porkman, 49 Fetter lane
Spencer John, stationer & library, 18 Bouverie st. Paddington
Spencer John, surgeon, &c. Lark Hall lane, Clapham
Spencer John, M.D. surgeon, 28 Upper Albany st
Spencer John, tobacconist, 32 King's st. Snow hill
Spencer John H. wine & spirit merchant, 48 Fenchurch st
Spencer John Wm. feather bed manufacturer, 15 Oxford st
Spencer Joseph, chemist & druggist, 38 Lamb's Conduit st
Spencer Josiah, general merchant, 6 Bengal pl. New Kent rd
Spencer Lee, pawnbroker, see King & Spencer
Spencer Maria Fenton (Miss), milliner, 62 Gt. Russell st. Bloombs
Spencer Pearey, cowkeeper, 5 Orange row, Kennington rd
Spencer Richard, attorney, 1 Verulam buildings, Gray's inn
Spencer Richd. booksell. stat. & librarian, 314 High Holborn
Spencer Robt. auctioneer & appraiser, 6 Bedford st. Bedford rw
Spencer Robert, bookbinder, 16 Bridgewater sq. Barbican
Spencer Robert, currier, 10 Lambeth lower marsh
Spencer Robert, market gardener, Battersea marsh
Spencer Robert, tailor, 16 Lisle st. Leicester sq
Spencer Robert, tailor & draper, 3 Vernon pl. Bloomsbury sq
Spencer Rt. wood & papiermachée japanner, 6 Newyd. Gt. Qn. st
Spencer Robert Cress, butcher, 20 Somerset st. Aldgate
Spencer Samuel, grocer, 7 Smart's buildings, High Holborn
Spencer Thomas, linendraper, see Warren & Spencer
Spencer Thomas, naturalist, 7 Gt. Portland st. Portland pl
Spencer Thomas, surgeon, 31 Myddelton sq. Clerkenwell
Spencer Thomas, tailor, 195 Hoxton Old town
Spencer Thomas, who. comb manufact. 9 Worship sq. Finsbury
Spencer T. Hall, mesmerist, 59 Pall mall
Spencer William, corn dealer, 23 Compton st. Brunswick sq
Spencer William, general salesman, 64 Whitechapel road
Spencer William, grocer, 8 John st. Limehouse fields
Spencer William, linendraper, 19 Cumberland row, Isln. Hi. st
Spencer William, oilman, 110 Chalton st. Somers town
Spencer William, tobacconist, 4 Saville pl. New Burlington st
Spender James, picture liner, 55 Gt. Queen st. Lincoln's inn fi
Spensley Wm. & Co. silk mers. & agts. 8 Little Winchester st
Spensley William, cheesemonger, 5 Horseferry rd. Westmstr
Spering Wm. haberdash. &c. 3 Victoria pl. Hoxton Old twn
Sperring Jas. *British Lion* P.H. Cavendish st. New nrth. rd
Sperry James, boot & shoe maker, 83 Hoxton Old town
Speth Geo. Wm. & Co. general merchants, 1 John st. Minories
Spettigue Edmund, lodging house, 1 Cottage rd. Eaton sq
Spettigue Edmund, printer & law bookseller, 67 Chancery la
Spettigue Edmunds, lodging house, 1 Cottage rd. Eaton sq
Speyer John, tailor & draper, 52 High Holborn
Spice & Bennet, livery stables, 2 Market st. Mayfair
Spice Charles, baker, 1 Jubillee place, Chelsea
Spice Richd. Geo. ham & beef dlr. 21 Gt. Russell st. Covnt. gar
Spicer Wm. livery stables, 20 Northumberland mews, Marylb
Spicer John Edw. & Sons, who. stationers, 18½ New Bridge st
Spicer Henry, chemist, Stockwell place, Clapham road
Spicer Lewis, cabinet maker, 6 Garnault place, Spa fields
Spicer William (agent Worthington, Robinson, brewers, Burton on Trent), 3 Cross st. Finsbury
Spicer Joseph Betsworth, plasterer, 5 Basing lane, Bread st
Spicer William, grocer, 19 Little Guilford st. Brunswick sq
Spicer Thomas G. professor of languages, 26 Gerrard st. Soho
Spiegelhalter Geo. wood clock ma. 6 Mount pl. Whitechapel rd

Spielman Adam & Co. foreign money exchange office, importers of russia copper coin, & genl. merchants, 10 Lmbrd.st
Spiers Benjamin, ladies' boot & shoe maker, 402 Oxford st
Spiers Charles, silk ma. hatters trim. hat band, &c. 10 Spital sq
Spiers John, stuffmelter, Belle isle, Maiden la. King's cross
Spiers Robert, carman, 10 Swan st. Trinity sq. Borough
Spiers Walter, printer & publisher, 17 North Audley st
Spike Henry & Co. ship chandlers & sailmakers, 310 Wapping
Spike Edward, solicitor, 15 Clifford's inn, Fleet st. & 77 Upper Ebury st. Pimlico
Spiking Wm. baker, 5 Dover st. Piccadilly
Spikins John, carpenter & builder, 20 Dartmth. row, Wstmnstr
Spill & Park, waterproof cloth ma. 63 St. George st. Ratcliff
Spillane Mary Ann (Mrs.), grocer, 15 Friendly st. Deptford
Spillane Paul, boot & shoe ma. 77 Vauxhall walk, Lambeth
Spiller Abraham, bottle dealer, &c. 35 North row, Grosvnr. sq
Spiller Chas. Wm. undertaker, 26 Upper Ebury st. Pimlico
Spiller Christain Clark, general stationer, 102 Holborn hill
Spiller Edmund Pim, oil & italian wareho. 98 Holborn hill
Spiller Frederick Tremlett, attorney, 5 Gray's inn square
Spiller Joel, engineer & machinist, Battersea
Spiller John, carpent. & undertak. 23 Whiskin st. Clerkenwll
Spiller John, slater & lath render, 17 Harcourt st. New rd
Spiller John Horatio, *Grapes* P.H. 96 Holborn hill
Spiller John Jubilee, solicitor, 38 Camomile st. Bishopsgate
Spiller Thomas, painter & glazier, 26 Bedfordbury, Covent gdn
Spiller William, *White Lion* P.H. 19 Upper Thames st
Spiller Wm. Hy. carpet warehm. see Hutchisons' & Spiller
Spilling George, tailor, 31 Upper Park place, Dorset sq
Spilling Thomas, newsvender, 58 St. John st. rd
Spillman Edmund, bootmaker, 12 Bloomsbury st. Bloomsby
Spillman George, *Lyceum tavern*, 354 Strand
Spillman Thos. *Gent. & Porter* P.H. 16 Nicholl sq. Aldersgt
Spilsbury & Downes, who. button warehouse, 1 & 2 Huggin la
Spilsbury Henry, patent antiscorbutic drops warehouse, 15 Soho square
Spilsbury Robert, goldsmith & jewel. 8 Poland st. Oxford st
Spincer Robert, cattle salesman, 15 West Smithfield
Spindler Barnard, leather dresser, White's grounds, Bermond
Spindler Sarah (Mrs.), *Star* P.H. 38 St. John's wood terrace
Spink Marshall & Son, goldsmiths, 2 Gracechurch st
Spink Henry, ironmonger, smith & gasfitter & stove maker, 54 Lisson grove north
Spink John, butcher, 3 Up. York st. Bryanstone square
Spink Walter, dining rooms, 36 Whitechapel High st
Spink Wm. butcher, 13 Salisbury st. Lisson grove
Spinks Ann (Mrs.), fruiterer, 5 Jerusalem passage, Clerknwl
Spinks Frederick Lowton, barrister, 2 Churchyard ct. Temple
Spinks Geo. building matrl. dlr. 128 Cornwall rd. Lambeth
Spinks Jemima (Mrs.), laundress, 4 Grove lane, Camberwell
Spinks John, solicitor, 27 Gt. James st. Bedford row
Spinner Wm. greengrocer, 20 King's row, Pimlico
Spire Joseph, tobacconist, 81 Quadrant, Regent st
Spires Nehemiah, dyer & scourer, 182 Drury lane
Spires Richard, saddler, 29 Cumberland market, Regent's pk
Spring Edward Wm. *Acton Arms* P.H. Acton pl. Kingld. rd
Spirit George, fruiterer, North row, Covent garden market
Spitalfields Benevolent Institution for relieving Sick and Lying-in Women (Jph. Percival, sec.), 21 Church st. Sptflds
Spitalfields Benev. Soc. (Edwd. Sutee, sec.), 19 Cheapside
Spittle Henry, ornamental engraver, 29 Dean st. Soho
Spittle James, baker, 45 Whitecross st. Cripplegate
Spittle Thomas, furniture broker, 9 Whitmore row, Hoxton
Splatt Francis, upholsterer, 34 Sloane st. Knightsbridge
Spode & Copeland, see Copeland & Garrett
Spofford James, floor cloth manufactr. 50 Skinner st. Snow hill
Spofford James, house painter, 2 Chichester pl. Gray's inn rd
Spokes James, bookseller, 122 London road, Southwark, & 1 Crown st. Walworth road
Spokes William, bed sacking ma. 34 Union st. Kingsland rd
Spon Edward & Francis, booksels. 6 Crombie's row, Com. rd. ea
Spon Edward, jun. bookseller, 15 Queen st. Cheapside
Spong Charles, tailor, 223 Tottenham court road
Spong Chas. Henry, registrar, 7 Mornington pl. Hmpstd. rd
Spong George, teadealer, 4 Chapel st. Tottenham court road
Spong James, *Chequers* P.H. 36 Wapping wall
Spong John, chandler's shop, 25 Lower George st. Chelsea
Spong Joseph, japanner, 7 Brook st. New road, Marylebone
Spong Martha (Mrs.), beer retailer, Wandsworth road
Spong Thomas Nash, solicitor, 9 King Edward st. Lambeth
Spooner, Attwoods & Co. bankers, 27 Gracechurch st
Spooner & Phillips, linendrapers, 6 Glo'ster ter. New rd. Coml. rd
Spooner Samuel & Son, lath renders, 10 Thomas st. Brick la
Spooner (Thos.), Leggatt & Co. warehmn. 4 Geo. yd. Lombard st
Spooner William & Co. plate war. 49 Salisbury sq. Fleet st
Spooner Geo. ornamental confectioner, 102 Whitech. High st
Spooner Henry, turner & machinist, 5 Whitecross st. Crippleg
Spooner Isaac, barrister, 2 Old square, Lincoln's inn
Spooner James, baker, 13 Philip st. St. George's east
Spooner Mary (Mrs.), boarding ho. 15 America sq. Minories
Spooner Michael, tailor, 3 Talbot court, Eastcheap
Spooner Ralph Carr, oil & colorman, 33 Bath st. City road
Spooner Robert, *Princes' Head* P.H. 2 Buckingham st. Strand
Spooner William, barrister, 4 Elm court, Temple
Spooner William, print & bookseller, 377 Strand
Spooner William, butcher, 54 Bridport place, New North rd
Sporle Wm. sailma. Cherry garden stairs, Bermondsey wall
Sporting Magazine Office (monthly), 5 Warwick sq. Newgt. st
Sporting Review Office, 24 Norfolk st. Strand
Sportsman Office (monthly), 24 Norfolk st. Strand
Spottiswoode & Robertson, convey. & parl. agts. 27 Gt. Geo. st
Spottiswoode Andrew, bible depôt, see Eyre & Spottiswoode
Spottiswoode Andrew, printer, New st. square, Fetter lane
Spradbery Jas. *Hambro' hotel & coffee ho.* 6 & 7 Water la. Tow. st
Spragg Edward, printer, 2 Tavistock row, Covent garden
Spragg George, law stationer, 1 Took's court, Chancery lane
Spragg John, fruiterer, 8 Charles street, Grosvenor square
Spragg Thomas, beer retailer, 8 Church st. Blackfriars rd
Sprague Daniel, tailor, 39 Old Bond street
Sprague Thos. who. stationer, see Muggeridge, Sprague & Co
Sprague Thos. stationer, 4 College hill, Upper Thames st
Sprague William, musical instrument maker, 7 Finsbury pavement, & 20 Little Moorfields
Sprange Daniel, academy, 5 Lonsdale square, Islington
Sprang William Henry, auctioneer, 11 Kennington cross
Sprat Robert, bootmaker, 15 King's road, Pimlico
Spratley Michael, oil warehouse, 11 Up. Kennington green
Spratley Thomas, saddler & harness maker, 2 Wandsworth rd
Spratswill William, tailor & draper, 36 Holborn hill
Spratt Mrs. & Miss Julia, teachers of drawing, 3 Chester terrace, Eaton square
Spratt Henry, china warehouse, 4 Ranelagh ter. Pimlico
Spratt Isaac, brush & toy dealer, 1 Brook st. Hanover square
Spratt Isaac, tobacconist, 58 Brewer st. Somers town
Spratt John, coach & harness maker, 4 New rd. Sloane st
Spratt John, stationer, manifold writer ma. & manfcr. of ink, sealing wax, wafers, &c. 137 Tottenham court road
Spratt Robert, boot & shoe maker, 15 King's road, Pimlico
Spratt William, beer retailer, 69 Newgate st
Spratt William, builder, Vassall road, Camberwell New road
Spratt William, coach builder, 2 Upper George st. Chelsea
Spratt Wm. *Whiteferryhouse* P.H. Commercial rd. Pimlico
Spreadberry Wm. blacking & ink ma. 17 Hare st. Bethnal gr
Spreadbrow Robt. tobacconist, 20 High road, Knightsbridge
Spreadbury Jno. *Lord Wellington* P.H. Pleasant rw. O. Kt. rd
Spreck John, tailor, 27 Henrietta st. Covent garden
Spreckley Edward, butcher, 51 Albemarle st. Piccadilly
Spredbury John, grocer, 30 White Hart pl. Lr. Kennington la
Sprigens & Surman, poultry & game salesmen, Leadnhl. mkt
Sprigg Richd. archtl. bookseller, 106 Gt. Russell st. Bloomsby
Sprigge John, solicitor, 18 Up. North pl. Gray's inn road
Spriggins James, bricklayer, &c. 9 Rosoman st. Clerkenwell
Spriggs Fras. picture frame ma. 50 John st. Holland st. Blkfrs
Spriggs John, cattle salesman, 60 West Smithfield
Spriggs William, grocer, &c. 12 Aston place, Holloway
Spring Francis, hosier, &c. 23 King's road east, Chelsea
Spring George, dairyman, 39 Star st. Edgware road
Springall, Thompson & Powell, attorn 3 Raym. blds. Gray's in
Springall George, engineer, 14 Wych st. Strand
Springall Jane (Mrs.), baker, 90 Bishopsgate without
Springall John, pat. axletree maker, Bow
Springall William, baker, 199 Shoreditch High st
Springall William, tobacconist, 42 Liquorpond st
Springate William, blacksmith, 1 Limehouse causeway
Springbett Brothers, wine & beer merchants, 11 Leadenhall st. & 3 Charlotte row, Walworth road
Springer William, tailor, 12 Broadley ter. Blandford sq
Springfield, Son & Nephew, silk merchants, 66 Coleman st
Springsguth Matthew, grocer, 6 Claremont ter. Stk. Nwngtn. rd
Springthorp John, tobacconist & printer, 130 London road
Springuth James, bootmaker, 53½ Chiswell st
Springweiler & Thomson, medicine chest, dressing case, sample case, chemical chest, fancy & general cabinet manufacturers, 2 Duke st. West Smithfield
Sproston & Horsman, who. fishmongers, 24 Love la. Eastcheap
Sprules Elizabeth (Miss), staymaker, 139 Minories
Sprules John William, cooper, Blue Anchor rd. Bermondsey
Sprunt & Parry, pawnbrokers, 80 Paradise st. Rotherhithe
Spry James, baker, 15 West lane, Bermondsey wall
Spry John, lodging house, 4 & 5 Lower Grosvenor place
Spry William, artist, 54 Warren st. Fitzroy square
Spurge William, hairdresser, 6 Cumberland row, Islington

Spurden, Woolley & Co. straw hat mfs. & imp. 42 Friday st
Spurgeon John, printer, 28 Sudeley st. City road
Spurgeon Jonathan, french polisher, 25 Wilson st. Finsbury
Spurgeon Michael, cheesemonger, 75 Paradise st. Rotherhithe
Spurgeon Wm. wheelwright, 13 Cross st. Hatton garden
Spurgin Daniel, *Feathers* P.H. Dockhead, Bermondsey
Spurgin Isaac, linendraper, 13 Park terrace, Camden town
Spurgin James, wheelwright, 59½ Gray's inn lane
Spurgin Job, *Old Justice* P.H. 21 Mint st. Borough
Spurgin John, physician, 38 Guildford st. Russell square
Spurgin Thomas, *Royal Oak* P.H. 282 Kent st. Borough
Spurging Thos. *George & Dragon* P.H. 192 Shadwell
Spurling John Henry & Son, stockbrokers, 12 Copthall court
Spurling John, tobacconist, 46 Chester st. Kennington cross
Spurr Joseph, chandler's shop, 3 Lit. Warner st. Clerkenwell
Spurr Strafford, solicitor, 3 Copthall buildings
Spurrel James, carpenter, 3 Cannon st. rd. St. George's east
Spurrel John, herald painter, 17 Vine terrace, Lambeth
Spurrier John William, barrister, 25 Old sq. Lincoln's inn
Spurrier Wm. Jubber, wine merchant, 181 Regent st
Spurway Frederick John & William George, decorators & paper stainers, 173 Bishopsgate st. without
Spurway Ann (Miss), milliner, 24 Shaftesbury ter. Pimlico
Spurway Fredk. J. B. barrister, 1 Warwick court, Holborn
Spyer John, merchant, 30 Broad st. buildings
Spyer Jones, solicitor, 30 Broad st. buildings
Spyer Laurence, hosier & glover, 26 Leadenhall st
Squance Barry Parr, solicitor, see Tilson & Squance
Square John Henry, solicitor, see Clayton & Square
Square Robt. furn. ironmonger, 12 Pirepoint row, Islington
Squibb George James, surgeon, 6 Orchard st. Portman sq
Squibb Wm. tobacconist, 47 Princess st. Portman market
Squier Danl. carcase butcher & salesman, 75 Aldgate High st
Squire & Wells, floorcloth manuf. Windmill lane, Camberwll
Squire Charles, carver & gilder, 38 Lisle st. Soho
Squire George, baker, see Baber & Squire
Squire George, greengrocer & coaldealer, 27 Finsbury market
Squire James, greengro. & coal dealer, 23 Finsbury market
Squire James, tailor, 122 High st. Camden town
Squire James, tailor, 5 South pl. Tibberton sq. Islington
Squire John, butcher, 14 Pearson st. Kingsland road
Squire John, printseller, &c. 41 Worship st. Finsbury
Squire Jonathan, fishmonger & carman, 5 Cleveland st
Squire Mary Ann (Mrs.), needle & sail tool ma. 173 Shadwell
Squire Peter, chemist (upon the establishment) of the Queen & H.R.H. the Prince Albert, 277 Oxford st
Squire Rd. carriage lamp mkr. 16 South st. Manchester sq
Squire Robert, house agent, 3 Smith's bldgs. Gray's inn rd
Squire Wm. pianoforte maker, 294 High Holborn
Squire Wm. surgeon, 6 Up. Portland pl. Wandsworth road
Squire Wm. tobacconist, 28 Leather lane, Holborn
Squire Wm. pork butcher, 124 Tottenham court road
Squirel Jonah, boot & shoe ma. High rw. Silver st. Kensngtn
Squires Ann (Mrs.), fruiterer, 23 East st. Manchester square
Squires Charles, plumber, 23 Spencer st. Canonbury sq
Squires George Ashby, bootmaker, 12 Newcastle st. Strand
Squires Hen. *Bricklayers' Arms* P.H. 20 Glo'ster st. Com. rd. ea
Squires Jeremiah, plumber, &c. 12 Emmett st. Limehouse
Squires John, gun barrel mak. 12 Newcastle st. Whitechapel
Squires John, ironmonger, 111 Lambeth lower marsh
Squires John, straw hat ma. 36 Seymour pl. Bryanstone sq
Squires Margt. (Mrs.), stay & corset ma. 12 Emmett st. Poplar
Squires Wm. marine store dealer, 52 Chamber st. Leman st
Squirrell John, stay & surg. belt ma. 47 Margaret st. Cav. sq
Sray Alfred, bootmaker, 47 Edgware road, Marylebone
Stabb Ewen, merchant, 48 Lombard st
Stabb John, lodging house, 24 & 25 Old Fish st
Stable Saml. linendraper, 28 St. John st. Clerkenwell
Stableford John, carpenter, 11 North st. Fitzroy square
Stableford William, carpenter, 37 Clipstone st. Fitzroy sq
Stables Hen. Edw. solicitor, see Grimaldi, Stables & Burn
Stace Jane (Miss), dressmaker, 20 Charles st. Middlesex hos
Stacey Geo. whol. druggist, see Corbyn, Beaumont & Co
Stacey Henry Alfred, boot & shoe maker, 6 High st. Newington butts, & 156 Lambeth walk
Stacey Isaac, tailor, &c. 17 Tichborne st. Haymarket
Stacey Isaac, *Three Compasses* P.H. 28 Bermondsey New rd
Stacey James, china dealer, 15 Clare court, Drury lane
Stacey James, *Duke of Clarence* P.H. 56 Tooley st
Stacey John, tailor, 3 Bridge court, Westminster
Stacey John, tailor, &c. 5 Everett st. Russell sq
Stacey John Wm. boot & shoemak. 48 Grosvenor row, Pimlico
Stacey Wm. pork butcher, 89 Goswell st
Stacey Wm, who. cap manuf. 20 St. Andrew's road Borough
Stacpoole Frederick, artist, 2 Calthorp st
Stacy Wm. & Ben. diamond jewellers, 35 Tavistk st. st. Cov. gar
Stacy Geo. jeweller, &c. 17 St. Alban's pl. Edgware road
Stacy James, boot & shoe maker, 184 Kingsland road
Stacy John, lodging house, 33 Arundel st. Strand
Stacy Robt. ornam. paper mak. 3 New inn yard, Shoreditch
Stadden Thomas, cattle salesman, see Dimbleby & Stadden
Staddon John, surgeon, &c. 12 Union st. Borough
Staddon William, farrier, 1 Cock lane, Smithfield
Staff Wm. & Son, tarpaulin & rope man. 2 Lawson st. Dov. rd
Staff Charles, surgeon, 39 Roebuck place, Gt. Dover rd
Staff George, boot & shoe maker, 18 Tothill st. Westminste
Stafford Sarah & Ann, milliners, 5 Barnsbury pl. Islington
Stafford Charles, Edw. carpenter, 9 Queen's pl. Gt. Queen st
Stafford James, cowkeeper, 28 Hermes st. Henry st. Pentnvl
Stafford John, fruit salesman, Borough market
Stafford John, jun. tailor & draper, 29 Holborn hill
Stafford John, sen. tailor & draper, 66 West Smithfield
Stafford Richard, railway agent, 62 Moorgate st
Stafford Richard A. surgeon, 28 Old Burlington st
Stafford Robert, cabinet mkr. 19 Adam st. east, Portman sq
Stafford Robert, distiller, see Seager, Evans & Stafford
Stafford Sarah (Miss), ready made linen wa. 17 Fore st. City
Stafford Thomas Wm. school, 340 Albany road, Camberwell
Stafford Timothy, watch mak. 8 South st. Kings rd. Chelsea
Stafford Wm. solicitor, 13 Buckingham street, Strand
Stafford Wm. upholsterer, 5 Theobald st. New Kent road
Stag Thomas, corn chandler, 7 York pl. Portland town
Stage Coach Duty Office, Somerset house; hours 10 to 4
Stagg & Mantle, linendrapers, 1, 2 & 3 Leicester sq
Stagg Charles, boot & shoe ma. 4 Belgrave mews ea. Blgr. sq
Stagg George, lodging house, 4 Church st. Soho sq
Stagg James, tanner, Richardson st. Long lane, Bermondsey
Stagg John, secret springer, 61 Wellington st. Goswell st
Stagg Mary (Mrs.), rag & bottle dlr. 18 Lit. Coram st. Brunsw. sq
Stagg Thomas Emanuel, baker, 1 St. Peter's pl. Walwth. com
Stagg Wm. brass manufacturer, 59 Coppice row, Clerkenwell
Stagg William, linendraper, 5 Newington causeway
Stahl Emanuel & Co. leather sellers & importers of foreign leathers, 32 Villiers st. Strand
Stahlschmidt Fredk. agent, see Drolenvaux & Stahlschmidt
Stahlschmidt Henry George, coal & coke merchant, Clarence wharf, Addington sq. Camberwell
Staig John, statuary & mason, 5 Rodney bldgs. New Kent rd
Staight Danl. pa. veneer & ivory sawmills, 35 Charles st. Hat. gdn
Staight George, ivory turner, 9 Skinner st. Snowhill
Staight Thos. wholesale ivory worker & turner, 12 Walbrook
Stainbank Chris. & Son, mers. ship & ins. agts. 147 Leadenhall st
Stainburn & Baugh, hat manufacturers, 31 Gresham st. & Southwark square, Borough
Stainer William, registrar, 2 Broadway, Southwark
Staines & Richmond Junction Railway (John C. Govett, sec.), 32 Moorgate st
Stains Benjn. *Fountain* P.H. Artichoke row, Mile end road
Stains Edward, teacher of mathematics, fortification, & military drawing, 9 Salisbury place, New road
Staines James, tailor, 7 Bowling st. Westminster
Staines Richard, surgeon, Stratford broadway
Stains Robert, historical engraver, 33 Alfred st. Bedford sq
Staines Wm. carpent. buildr. & undertaker, 18 Gt. St. Helen's
Staines Wm. fruiterer & greeng. 7 Vernon pl. Bagnge. wls. rd
Stainforth John, *Angel* P.H. 150 Poplar High st
Stains Rd. Yorkshire Stingo brewery, New rd. Marylebone
Stainsbury Jas. T. beer retailer, 2 Old Montague st. Whtchpl
Stainton Henry, agent for the Carron Co. 15 Up. Thames st
Stainton Robt. John, ironplate wor. 31 Red Lion st. Sptlfds
Stainton Septimus, omnibus proprietor, Highbury park
Stainton Zaccheus, tailor, 42 Russell st. Lower Rotherhithe
Stalain Henry, ironplate smith, 3 Turnagain la. Farringdon st
Stalder George, turner, 4 David st. Marylebone
Staley Edw. linendraper, &c. 136 Waterloo rd. & 67 New cut
Staley George, grocer, 167 Poplar High st
Stalker Mary Ann (Mrs.), tobacns. 30 Elizabeth st. sth. Piml
Stallard William Henry, banker, 76 West Smithfield
Stallebrass Thos. timber mer. 9 Manchester st. Waterloo town
Stallibrass John & Son, cattle salesmen, 17 West Smithfield
Stallybrass Martha L. (Miss), milliner, 150 Leadenhall st
Stalman Geo. button & trimming seller, 37 South Molton st
Stalman Henry, barrister, 23 Old square, Lincoln's inn
Stalman John, tailor, 18 Hatton garden
Stalman John Whitmore, teaman & grocer, 4 Jermyn st
Stalon John, carver, 42 Berwick st. Soho
Stamford Lydia (Miss), milliner, &c. 18 & 19 Burlington arca
Stammer Thos. grocer & italian war. 19 Tichborne st. Haymk
Stammers Ann (Mrs.), *Waterman's Arms* P.H. Bermdsy. wl
Stammers Edward, silversmith & cutler, 99 & 100 Strand
Stammers Fred. hosier & glover, 3 Bridge st. Westminster
Stammers John, brush maker, 103 Mount st. Berkeley sq

Stammers Joseph, barrister, 6 Chancery lane
Stammers Saml. *Kent & Essex* P.H. Kent & Essex yard, Whitechapel High st
Stamp Office, Somerset house; hours of business 10 to 4
Stamp Edward, baker, 11 Duke st. Lisson grove
Stamp Geo. french polisher, 10 Charlotte st. Curtain rd
Stamp John, cheesemonger, 30 Mount st. Berkeley sq
Stamp Samuel, baker, 6 Union road, Horsemonger lane
Stamp William, baker, 42 Regent st. Horseferry road
Stamp William, wine cooper, 2 Three Oak lane, Dockhead
Stamp Wm. Chas. bath mnfr. brazier, &c. 46 Red Lion st. Clknwl
Stamper Ralph, chemist, see Shuttleworth & Stamper
Stamper Wm. zinc manf. 15 Quickset row, New rd. Fitz. sq
Stamwitz Ernest, tailor, 24 Gt. Pulteney st. Golden square
Stanborough Saml. & Son, bricklayers, Kingsland green
Stanborough Jas. beershop & bricklayer, 5 & 6 Ann's pl. Hoxtn
Stanborough James, coffee rooms, 141 Goswell st
Stanbridge Henry, commission mer. 150 Fenchurch st
Stanbridge Thos. B. satindresser, Hrberdshrs'. pl. west, Hoxtn
Stanbrough Thos. Chas wine mer. see Pratt & Stanbrough
Stanbury Benj. carrying agt. Talbot inn yd. 75 Boro' High st
Stanbury George, printing ink manufacturer, dealer in lithographic materials & paris black, 4 Dean st. Fetter la
Stanbury James, grocer, 2 Portman pl. Edgware road
Stanbury James, grocer & teadlr. 103 St. John st. Clkenwell
Stanbury Joseph, school, 5 St. Matthew's pl. Hackney rd
Stanbury Martha (Mrs.), carriers' agt. George yd. Aldermanby
Standard evening newspaper, 38 New Bridge st. Blackfrs
Standard Life Assurance Company (Peter Ewart, resident secretary), 82 King William st. City; see page 2046
Standbrook Saml. jobmaster, 9 Hamilton mws. St. John's wd. rd
Standen Charles, shoemaker, 19 Harcourt st. New road
Standen Edwd. shetland & shawl warehouse, 112 Jermyn st
Standen James (Mrs.), livery stables, 38½ King st. Golden sq
Standen Matthew, butcher, 1 North st. Edgware rd
Standen William, cheesemonger, 102 Park st. Grosvenor sq
Standerwick James, commission merchant & importer of wines & cigars, 30 London wall
Standeven Richard, grocer, 36 Sudeley st. Islington
Standfast Hen. Taylor, news agent, see Brown & Standfast
Standfast John, cheesemonger, 347 Rotherhithe st
Standfast Wm. carpntr. & undertakr. 88 East st. Manch. sq
Standfast Wm. Geo. artist, Temple chmbs. Falcon ct. Fleet st
Standfield John Thos. stationer, &c. 33 Carey st. Linc. inn
Standidge Wm. & Co. lithographers & artists, 77 Cornhill
Standing Samuel, ironfounder, 9 Osborne st. Whitechapel
Standish Joseph, print colorer, 40 Lower Kennington lane
Standley Jas. coppersmiths' agent, 21 Red Lion st. Clerknwl
Standley John, brassfounder, Heneage st. Brick lane
Standley Miles, undertaker, 41 Noble st. Goswell st
Standly Edw. & Richd. scotch warehousemen, 67 Cheapside
Standring Benj. & Son, wine, spirit & porter mer. 152 Minories
Staner Maria (Mrs.), baker, 16 Hinde st. Manchester sq
Stanes Hen. & Wm. lin. & wooln. draprs. 11 Gilbert st. Oxfd. st
Stanes James, china & cut glass warehouse, 115 Minories, & 5 America square
Stanes John, fruiterer, 7 Coborn road, Mile end road
Stanfield Clarkson, R.A. artist, 48 Mornington pl. Hampst. rd
Stanfield George Clarkson, jun. artist, 48 Mornington pl
Stanfield William, baker, 2 Earl st. London road
Stanford George, baker, 83 Albany road, Camberwell
Stanford Samuel, baker, 8 Lambeth Upper marsh
Stanford Thomas, tailor, 8 Brownlow st. Bedford row
Stanger Henry, grocer, Stratford Broadway
Stanger Hugh Fisher, watchmaker & jeweller, 46 Old st. rd
Stanger Joseph, stove & range mafr. 165 Southwark bdg. rd
Stanger Samuel, grocer, 12 Devonshire st. Kennington
Stangroom Joanna (Mrs.), basket maker, 11 St. Mary at hill
Stangroom Margaret (Mrs.), glass stainr. 30 Percevl. st. Clkw
Stanham R. & Son, builders & undrtkrs. 3 Edwardes ter. Knsngtn
Stanham George, builder, &c. 20 Vale pl. Hammersmith rd
Staniforth William & John, teadealers, 138 Oxford st
Staniland & Long, attorneys, 9 Bouverie st. Fleet st
Stanley Caleb R. artist, 25 Maddox st. Regent st
Stanley Edward, linendraper, 67 Lambeth Lower marsh
Stanley Edward, spur maker, see Handy & Stanley
Stanley Edward, surgeon, 23A, Brook st. Grosvenor sq
Stanley Elizabeth Mary (Mrs.), hatter, 7 Clark's pl. Islingtn
Stanley George, auctioneer, 21 Old Bond st. Piccadilly
Stanley Geo. Hen. carpenter, 24 Cannon st. rd. St. George's ea
Stanley Gervase, ironmonger, 227 Blackfriars rd
Stanley Harold, solicitor, 3 Bedford row
Stanley Henry, hairdresser, 4 Albion place, Rotherhithe
Stanley James Wm. coffee rooms, 66 Gt. Carlisle st. Ptm. mk
Stanley John, butcher, 175 Hoxton Old town
Stanley John, carpenter, &c. 24 Wells row, Up. st. Islington
Stanley John, coffee rooms, 39 High st. St. Giles's
Stanley John Blackett, shipchandler, 18 Up. East Smithfield
Stanley Phœbe (Miss), confectioner, 8 Huggin la. Wood st
Stanley Richard, *Marquis Granby* P.H. 33 Castle st. east
Stanley Robt. harness ma. 35 Mansion house st. Kenngtn
Stanley Thomas, general dlr. & broker, 49 Gt. Saffron hill
Stanley Thos. furniture broker, 84 Cromer st. Brunswick sq
Stanley William, linendraper, 88 Crawford st. & 16 Middle Queen's buildings, Knightsbridge
Stanley William, *Marlbro' Arms* P.H. 10 College st. Chlsea
Stanley William, wine merchant, 15 Cockspur st. Charing cr
Stanley Zachariah, tobacconist, 36 Gray's inn lane
Stannah Samyntas & Co. distillers, 23 White st. Lit. Moorflds
Stannard & England, plumbers, painters, house agents, &c. 7 Mill st. Hanover sq.; & 2 Ladbroke grove, Notting hill; & Craven cottage, Queen's road, Bayswater
Stannard Wm. & Son, carvers & gilders, 18 Broad st. Golden sq
Stannard William & Co. lithographic printers, & printers in gold & colors, &c. 7 Poland st. Oxford st
Stannard Alfred, haberdasher, 26 Langley pl. Commerl. rd
Stannard Erasmus, upholsterer, 1 Vine pl. Old st. rd
Stannard George, ivory turner, 16 Woodbridge st. Clerkenwl
Stannard Henry, *Three Compasses* P.H. 77 Mount st. Brkly. sq
Stannard Jas. stationer & bookbindr. 12 Nassau pl. Comcl. rd. ea
Stannard John, carver & gilder, 40 Lisle st. Leicester sq
Stannard John, general dealer, 2 Old Fish st. hill
Stannard Joseph, pic. fr. ma. 19 Whitecross st. Cripplegate
Stannard Richard, tailor, 3 Red Lion st. Whitechapel
Stannard Robert, plumber, &c. 8 Ryder's court, Leicester sq
Stannard Wm. *York coffee house & hotel*, 1 Upper Wellington st. & 11 York st. Covent garden
Stannard William, tailor, 14 Hosier lane, West Smithfield
Stannard Wm. John, lithographer, &c. 6 Warwick ct. Gray's inn
Stanner Ann (Mrs.), *Old Bell* P.H. 1 Dacre st. Westminster
Stansby George, wharfinger, 9 Paddington basin, North side
Stansell John James, fancy box manufctr. 34 Albermanbury
Stansfeld George, toy & brush wareho. 16 Up. Baker st. New rd
Stanton's Wharf, Robert Pearson, Stoney lane, Tooley st
Stanton's Lower Wharf, Geo. Wheeler, Stoney la. Tooley st
Stanton Brothers, telescope manufacturers & tube drawers, metal tube, wire, file, tin & tinplate wareho. &c. 73 Shoe la. Holb
Stanton John & Sons, wholesale teadealers, 78 Cannon st
Stanton Charles, chandlers' shop, 80 Hare st. Bethnal green
Stanton Henry Richard, *Victory* P.H. 167 Oxford st
Stanton James, pewterer & beer engine maker, 4 Coppice row
Stanton James, shoe manufacturer, 8 Crown st. Soho
Stanton Prudence (Mrs.), beer engine mak. 42 Little Britain
Stanton Thomas, manufacturer of bronze & or-molu, 42 Grosvenor mews
Stanton William, dairyman, 34 Clarence gardens, Regt's. pk
Stanton William, plumber, 46 Radnor st. St. Luke's
Stanway William, glass bottle mer. 9 Cousin la. Up. Thames st
Stanynought Lucy (Mrs.), booksl. 84 Connaught ter. Edgw. rd
Stanyon John, bookseller, 90 London road, Southwark
Staple Harriet (Miss), library, 10 Keen's row, Walworth rd
STAPLE INN, 2 Holborn bars
Staples John & Thomas, *Albion Tavern*, & purveyors of turtle to her Majesty, 153 Aldersgate st
Staples Edward, oil & italian warehouse, 5 Gutter lane
Staples George, working jeweller, 8 Craven bldgs. Drury la
Staples Henry, butcher, 9 St. George st
Staples John Adeney, law writer, 6 Cook's ct. Lincoln's inn
Staples John N. law stationer, 15 Serles' pl. Lincoln's inn
Staples Mary Ann (Mrs.), *Shovel* P.H. 27 Nw. rd. St. George's ea
Staples Moses Wm. attorney, 5 South square, Gray's inn
Staples Saml. architect & surveyor, 69 Newman st. Oxford st
Staples Thos. bookbinders' tool cutter, 30 Castle st. Holborn
Staples Thos. chair maker, Cumberland place, & Cross st. Newington butts
Staples Thos. haircutter & perfum. 137 Shoreditch High st
Stapleton & Thorn, brick, coal & ash merchants, & wharfingers, 8, 15 & 16 wharf, Paddington basin, North side, & Middlesex wharf, Maiden lane, King's cross, & Whitefriars wharf
Stapleton Fossett, tin & iron pl. mfr. 1 White horse la. Stpny
Stapleton Henry Fossett, ironmonger, 5 Park pl. Mile end rd
Stapleton Maria E. (Miss), hosier & glover, 10 & 11 Burlin. arcd
Stapleton Robert, livery stables, New Broad st mews
Stapleton Stephen Edwd. ironmonger, 10 Roadside, Mile end rd
Stapleton Thos. W. ship & cust. ho. agt. 12 Crutched friars
Stapley Charles, painter, 2 Strewan pl. King's rd. W. Chels
Stapylton Robert George, barrister, 3 New sq. Lincoln's inn
Stapp John & Son, wholesale cheesemongers, 85 Snowhill
Stapp Richard, gun maker, 2 Goldsmith place, Hackney rd
Star & Benstead, plumbers, painters & glaziers, 17 Hamilton mews, St. John's wood road

Star Gravesend Steam Packet Offi. (Wm. Morgan, agent), Blackwall terminus, Railway place, Fenchurch st
Star Life Assurance Co. (William Edward Hillman, sec.), 44 Moorgate st.; see page 2046
Starbuck Edward F. engineer & iron merchant, 2 Walbrook
Starck John, musical instrumt. mkr. 35 Green st. Bethnal gr
Stares James, baker, 17 Old Paradise row, Islington High st
Starey & Oswald, bleachers, 10 Bow la. Cheapside & Croydon
Starey Richard, linen factor, 26 Watling st. City
Starey Thomas, coal merchant & accountant, 10 Bow la. City
Starie Henry, stationer, &c. 23 Tichbourne st. Haymarket
Starie John Joseph, furnishing ironmonger, 10 King st. 7 Dials
Starie Joseph H. printer & publisher, 166 High Holborn
Stark Chas. bread & biscuit baker, 17 Kensington High st
Stark David, baker, 6 North st. Manchester sq
Stark Wm. butcher, 7 Beaufort ter. west, King's rd. Chelsea
Stark Wm. tobacconist, 112 Drummond st. Euston sq
Starke Edward, grocer, 1 Queen st. Lower road, Islington
Starke Hannah (Mrs.), tallowchnd. 2 Goodman's yd. Minories
Starke Hugh, fruiterer & coal mercht. 4 Bury st. St. James's
Starke (Mrs. Wm.), stay wareh. 16 Woburn bldgs. Tavistock sq
Starkey & Hunter, fish factors, 10 Billingsgate
Starkey Joseph & Co. merchants, 6 Skinners' pl. Sise lane
Starkey Chas. carman & scavenger, 7 & 8 Maiden la. King's cr.
Starkey Edward, goldsmith, &c. see Simpson & Starkey
Starkey Fanny (Mrs.), fruiterer, 47 Little Britain
Starkey James, carpenter & builder, 46 Old st. St. Luke's
Starkey John, hairdresser, 15 Swan st. Minories
Starkey Joseph, laceman & embroiderer, 5 Old Bond st
Starkey Samuel, ring mak. & jeweller, 18 King st. Clerknwl
Starkey Susan (Miss), grocer, 51 Wilsted st. Somers town
Starkey Wm. commission merchant, 2 Pancras lane, City
Starkey Wm. sheep salesman, see Whitbread & Starkey
Starkey William Rd. fish factor, Billingsgate & 7 Bury sq. St. Mary Axe
Starkey Wm. Rd. who. stationer, &c. see Cripps, Son & Starkey
Starkie James, chemist & druggist, 4 Strand
Starkie Thomas, queen's counsel, 1 Hare court, Temple
Starling Cath. (Mrs.), *Portland Arms* P.H. Portland place, 10 Clapham road
Starling Edward, attorney, 7 Sackville st. Piccadilly
Starling George Augustus, conveyancer, 40 Leicester sq
Starling Henry, chemist, 117 York road, Lambeth
Starling Henry P. engraver, 8 Adelaide terrace, Islington
Starling James, plumber, 1 Windsor pl. Southwark br. rd
Starling James Kearsley, bookseller, 87 Upper st. Islington
Starling John, grocer, 17 Upper York st. Bryanstone sq
Starling John, *Trinity Arms* P.H. 1 Swan st. Borough
Starling Joseph, stock broker, Stock exchange
Starling Joseph, wine importer, 81 Old Broad st
Starling Parlett, dep. registrar, 8 Adelaide ter. Islington
Starling Samuel, outfitter, &c. 75 Gracechurch st
Starling Wm. carver & gilder, 35 Phœnix st. Somers town
Starling Wm. coal mercht. 12 Wharf, Wenlock basin, City rd
Starling William Dulerson, agent, Hall of Commerce
Starmer Lucy (Mrs.), baker, 9 Orchard st. Portman sq
Starmer William, straw hat maker, 65 Lambeth walk
Starr Ann (Mrs.), coffee rooms, 52 Sloane square, Chelsea
Starr Robert, oil & colorman, 151 Bethnal green road
Starr Thomas, barrister, 3 Garden court, Temple
Starr William, watchmaker, 1 Park side, Knightsbridge
Starr William Edward, hatter, 12 Bermondsey New road
Start Ebenezer, warehouseman, 123 Wood st
Starters William, carpenter, 24 Hatton wall, Hatton garden
Startin George, sugar & colonial agent, 150 Fenchurch st
Startin James, surgeon, 3 Finsbury place south
Startup Amelia (Miss), strawhatmfr. 5 South st. King's rd. Chel
Startup Henry, baker, 9 Rochester row, Westminster
State Paper Office, 12 Duke st. Westminster; hours 11 to 4
Stater James, grocer, 21 Coborn road, Mile end road
States Edward, bootmaker, 41 Kenton st. Brunswick sq
Statham Rev. Fras. F. academy, 23½ High st. Newington butts
Statham Hugh, surgeon, 8 Knight's place, Wandsworth rd
Statham Richard George, *Albion* coffee rooms, 67 Watling st
Statham William, surgeon, 9 Gt. Chapel st. Westminster
Stationers' Hall (Chas. Rivington, clerk), Stationers' hall ct
Stationery Office, James st. Buckingham gate; hours 10 to 4
Statistical Society (Richard King, M.D. sec.), 11 Regent st
Staton Henry, fishmonger, 4 Tyler's court, Golden square
Staton Hen. writer & grainer, 33 Haberdashers' st. Hoxton
Stauch Jacob, baker, 18 Bedfordbury, Govent garden
Stauffer Robert, Son & Co. watch manufacturers (from Chaux de fonds & Geneva), 43 Skinner st. Snowhill
Stauffer Julius, merchant, 2 Chatham place, Blackfriars
Staunton, Comer & Co. gen. & commisn. mers. 32 Gt. St. Helen's
Staunton Michael & Sons, stationers & booksellers, 9 Strand
Staunton Edward, solicitor, 10 Norfolk st. Strand
Stavley Wm. veterinary surg. 7 Steyman's row, Holloway rd
Stawte Charles, glass cutter, 68 Gt. Peter st. Westminster
Stayner John, jun. builder, 21 Mile end road
Stayner Joseph, ship & insurance broker, 110 Fenchurch st
Steabben Joseph, cheesemonger, 33 Seymour st. Euston sq
Stead Ann (Mrs.), dressmaker, 115 Fetter lane, Fleet st
Stead Arnold, gold & silv. laceman, 18 Marquis ct. Drury la
Stead David, pat. wood paving office, 5 Barge yd. Bucklersbry
Stead Francis, engraver in general, 31 Dean st. Soho
Stead Jas. wood paving works, Norway whf. 125 Rotherh. st
Stead John Henry, grocer, 1 Pleasant row, King's cross
Stead Samuel, baker, 56 Lant st. Borough
Stead Thomas, surveyor, 25 Glo'ster st. Queen sq. Bloomsbury
Stead William, *Gibraltar* P.H. 16 St. George's rd. Southwark
Stead William, jun. *Sportsman* P.H. 11 Southwark bridge rd
Steadman Francis, hatter, 71 Bishopsgate st. within
Steadman Geo. Thomas, solicitor, 4 Crosby hall chambers
Steadman James, linendraper, 44 Bedford st. Covent garden
Steadman John, engineer, 20 Hayfield place, Mile end
Steadman Martha (Mrs.), grocer, 21 Doyley st. Sloane sq
Steadman William, carman, 57 Cornwall road, Lambeth
Steains, Rowley & Co. wholesale teadealers, 75 Cannon st
Steains Chas. hosier, 4 Victoria gro. Kensington New town
Steains Henry, coal mercht. 3 Dorchester pl. New North rd
Steam Baths' Company, 11 St. James's place, St. James's
Steam Shipowners' Association (W. C. Morgan, sec.), 28 St. Swithin's lane
Steane Charles, boot & shoe ma. 59 Chapel st. Somers town
Steane Joseph, oil & color warehouse, 159 Lambeth walk
Stearman William, builder, 4 Broadway, Westminster
Stearn Edward, upholsterer, Stratford broadway
Stearns John, baker, High row, Silver st. Kensington
Stearns Joseph, jun. stockbroker, 2 Hercules ct. Threadn. st
Steart James, cheesemonger, 12 Borough road
Steavenson John, solicitor, see Tucker & Steavenson
Stebbing Jas. & Son, undertakrs. 98½ White horse st. Stepney
Stebbing Thomas & Co. merchants, 12 Clement's lane
Stebbing Charles, carpenter, &c. 2 Heath pl. Cambridge hth
Stebbing Edward, billiard rooms, 17 Sherborne lane, & 11 Cannon st. City
Stebbing Frederick, woollen draper, 15 Holborn hill
Stebbing Thos. *Blue Anchor* P.H. see Fancy & Stebbing
Stebbing Thomas, wine merchant, 12 Clement's la. & 20 Cloak la
Stebbings James, butcher, 88 Rosemary lane, Minories
Stechert Louis, tailor, 15 Argyll st. Regent st
Stedman Charles Henry, solicitor, 18 Aldermanbury
Stedman James Edmund, baker, 9 Prospect row, Walworth rd
Stedman John, barrister, 11 New square, Lincoln's inn
Stedman Phillis (Miss), grocer, 56 Brandon st. Walworth
Stedman Phillis (Mrs.), baker, 42 Brandon st. Lock's flds. Wlth
Stedman Rd. poultry salesman, 14 Ship tavern pas. Leadnhl. mkt
Stedman Sarah Ann (Mrs.), tobacconist, 7 Wade's pl. Hackny rd
Stedman Silas, surgeon, 60 Guilford st. Russell square
Stedman Stephen, carpenter, builder, &c. King st. Battersea
Stedman Wm. Chas. surgeon, 31 Manchester st. Manchester sq
Steed James, dairyman, 1 Norris st. Haymarket
Steed John, beer retailer, High st. Stoke Newington
Steed Joseph, carpenter, 7 Liverpool st. King's cross
Steed Thos. *Man in the Moon* P.H. 23 Park ter. King's rd. Chel
Steeden Samuel, potato salesman, 4 & 7 Portman market
Steeden Thomas, fruiterer, 2 & 3 Portman market, Marylebone
Steedman & Faulconer, chemists, &c. 5 & 6 Keen's row, Walwrth
Steedman Charles, japanner, 35 Charles st. Hampstead road
Steedman James, japanner & tinman, 7 Belton st. Long acre
Steel Arthur Chas. & Thos. mercers, 51 & 52 Borough High st
Steel John F. & Co. ironfounders, 5 Marlboro' mews, Blenheim st
Steel Thomas & Son, lightermen, 3 Trinity st. Rotherhithe
Steel Alfred, boot & shoe maker, 85A, Edgeware road
Steel Barnabas, flour factor, see Waters & Steel
Steel Chas. tailors' trimmer & straw bon. ma. 81 Gray's inn la
Steel David, newspaper agent, 2 Spring gardens
Steel Edward, plasterer, bricklayer, &c. 15 Dorset st. Claph. rd
Steel Ellen (Mrs.), cheesemonger, 14 Gt. White lion st. 7 Dials
Steel Enoch, glass & chinaman, 15 Princes st. Soho
Steel Geo. baker, 9 Woodstock st. Oxford st
Steel Geo. lighterman, 128 Rotherhithe st
Steel Geo. pattern ma. for cast iron, 26 St. John's sq. Clerknwl
Steel Geo. solicitor, see Collier, Hedges & Steel
Steel Henry, tailor, 23 Bennett st. Blackfriars
Steel James, lighterman, 1 Trinity st. Rotherhithe
Steel John, lighterman, 2 Bickley row, Lower Rotherhithe
Steel John, pewterer, 12 Cowper st. City road
Steel John, beer retailer, 4 Queen's row, Cambridge road
Steel John, tinman, 25 Bacon st. Bethnal green
Steel John, turner & spin. wheel ma. 11 Sclater st. Bethnal gr

Steel Joseph, *Union* P.H. 2 Mint st. Borough
Steel Margaret (Mrs.), baker, 57 Cambridge st.Edgware rd
Steel Margaret (Mrs.), baker, 18 Gt. Titchfield st.Oxford st
Steel Matilda (Mrs.), dressmaker, see Finch & Steel
Steel Richd. carpent.&furn.brok.52 Glo'ster st.Com.rd. east
Steel Samuel, baker, 28 Fetter lane, Fleet st
Steel Thomas, boot & shoe maker, 258 & 259 Strand; 65 High Holborn; 203 Oxford st.; & 84 Edgware road
Steel Thomas, boot & shoe maker, see Flint & Steel
Steel Thomas, lighterman, 3 Trinity st. Rotherhithe
Steel Thomas Rice, law stationer, 12 Chancery lane
Steel Wm. carpenter, 21 Duke st. Lisson grove north
Steel Wm. tailor, &c. 168 Fenchurch st
Steel Wm. tobacconist, 93 Park st. Camden town
Steele Adam Rivers, solicitor, 1 Lincoln's inn fields
Steele Alexander, baker, 61 Bath st. City road
Steele Amias, tallow chandler, 49 Dorset st. Portman sq
Steele Francis, cowkeeper, 34 Haydon st. Minories
Steele Martin, tailor, 24 Charles st. Westminster
Steele Samuel, wood turner, 34 Gt. Titchfield st. Oxford st
Steer Francis, tin plate worker & brazier, 8 East rd. City rd
Steer Frederick, haberdasher, 155 Lambeth walk
Steer George, plumber & glazier, 22Munster st. Regent's pk
Steer George John, stockbroker, see Smith & Steer
Steer James, dairyman, 19 Bride lane, Fleet st
Steer John, engraver, 21 Coventry st. Haymarket
Steer John, writer & grainer, 6 Windsor st. City road
Steer Philip Richardson, chemist, 20 New st. Dorset sq
Steer Samuel, *Ship* P.H. 17 Ivy lane, Newgate st
Steer Thomas, working cutler, 69 Oxford st
Steer William, fishmonger, 28 Carnaby st. Golden square
Steere William, barrister, 92 Chancery lane
Steet George Carrick, surgeon, 119 St. John st. road
Steet Martha (Mrs.), plumber, 33 Gt. Titchfield st. Oxfordst
Steet William Robert, chemist, 119 St. John st. road
Steevens Francis Jas. *Blade Bone* P.H.83 Church st.Shdtch
Steff William, bricklayer, 9 Queen st. Chelsea
Steffenoni Joseph, upholstr.& cabinet mfr. 142Holborn bars
Steggall John, physician, 2 Southampton st. Bloomsbury
Steggals Henry, grocer, 14 Gifford st. Hoxton Old town
Steggle Cornelius, plumber & glazr. 11 Crown row, Mile end
Stehn Christian, merchant, 25 Crutched friars
Steib Richard, shoemaker & registrar, Church st. Hackney
Steib Richard, jun. boot & shoe maker, Mare st. Hackney
Steill Benjamin, bookseller & publisher, 20 Paternoster row
Stein Fredk. Wm. agent & imp. of for. goods, 70 Newgate st
Stein George, merchant, Brewhouse lane, Wapping
Stein George, merchant, 31 Copenhagen place, Limehouse
Stein Henry Ferdinand, merchant, Brewhouse la. Wapping
Steinberg Esther (Mrs.), milliner, &c.65Judd st.Brunswk.sq
Steinitz Charles Francis& Co. manufacturers of inlaid wood for flooring, 10 Berner st. Commercial road east
Steinmann Daniel, watch & clock maker, 29 North Audley st
Steirly Christian R. stationer, 6 Lit. Grosvenor st. Grosv. sq
Stelfox Wm. smith & lithogra. press ma. 25Baldwin's grdns
Stelling Wm. carpenter & builder, 11 New inn yd.Shoreditch
Stembridge Charles, tailor, see Blackwell & Stembridge
Stembridge Elizabeth (Mrs.), cooper, 28 Goswell st
Stembridge Robert, tailor, 12 Bartholomew ter. City road
Stemson Henry, law stationer, 15 Carey st. Lincoln's inn
Stemson Robert, tailor, 27 Marlborough st. Regent st
Stening James, hairdresser, 62 Whiskin st. Clerkenwell
Stenlake William, tailor, 2 Cowcross st
Stennett William, *George IV.* P.H. 156 Goswell st
Stennett William, wharfinger, see Wilkinson & Stennett
Stennett Wm. wharfinger, 34 Trinity square, Tower hill
Stenning & Church, solicitors, 39 Long lane, Bermondsey
Stenning Benjamin, solicitor, see M'Leod & Stenning
Stennings James, confectioner, 87 Long acre
Stenson John, bookseller, 1 Glo'ster pl. King's rd. Chelsea
Stent William & Son, butchers, 52 Charles st. Westminster
Stent William, coal dealer, 21 Little Earl st. Seven dials
Stent William, hosier & shirt maker, 261 Oxford st
Stephen Alexander, ironmonger, 60 Gt. Russell st.Bloomsby
Stephen Sir George, solicitor, 3 Furnival's inn, Holborn
Stephen Margaret (Miss), milliner, 11 Dover st. Piccadilly
Stephens G. O. & Co.genl.mrchts.St.Michael chambs.Crnhll
Stephens Thos. & Co. merchants & ins. brokers, 4 Lime st.sq
Stephens Allison, milliner, &c. 64 Quadrant, Regent st
Stephens Andrew, miniature painter, 107 Hatton garden
Stephens Archibald John, barrister, 61 Chancery lane
Stephens Benj.goldsmith & starmaker, 7 Serle's pl.Linc.inn
Stephens Benj. plumber, 49 Up. John st. Fitzroy sq
Stephens David, chaser, 30 Up. Park place, Dorset square
Stephens Edward, hairdresser, 19 Wellington place, Stepney
Stephens Edwd. Bowring, artist, 27 Up. Belgrave pl. Pmlco
Stephens Eliza (Mrs.), milliner, 128 Waterloo road
Stephens Elizb. (Miss), artist, 19 Peters hill, Doctors' Coms
Stephens Geo. coach & house smith, 17Brownlow st.Drury la
Stephens Geo. law stationer, 11 Carey st
Stephens Gilbert, solicitor, 30 Chapel st.Grosvenor place, & 13 Northumberland st. Strand
Stephens Harriot (Mrs.), army & navy clothier & contractor for naval & military stores, Paul's wharf, 24 Upper Thames st
Stephens Henry, inventor of writing fluids, 54 Stamford st
Stephens Henry, watch & clock maker, 4 High st.Marylbne
Stephens James, chemist, 4 Wharf rise, Kingsland road
Stephens James, furniture broker, 9 Newcastle st. Strand
Stephens James, grocer & oilman, 16 King's row, Pimlico
Stephens James, grocer, &c. 31 Kingsland cresc.Kingslnd.rd
Stephens James, plasterer, 22 Grafton st. Fitzroy square
Stephens John, barrister, 1 Elm court, Temple
Stephens John, brushmaker, 48 Up. North pl. Gray's inn rd
Stephens John, butcher, 43 George st. Blackfriars road
Stephens John, currier, 2 Rephidim st. Old Kent road
Stephens John, linendraper, Camberwell green
Stephens John, teadealer, 118 St. George st
Stephens John, writer, 3 Denmark st. Ratcliff highway
Stephens John Ruding, insurance broker, Lloyd's
Stephens Joseph, *Rising Sun* P.H. 20 Hackney rd. crescent
Stephens Joseph, bootmaker, 4 Cadogan rw. King's rd.Chels
Stephens Mary (Miss), *Rose & Crown* P.H.172 Union st.Boro'
Stephens Mary Ann (Mrs.), carpentr.12 Bullin ct.408Strand
Stephens Richd. (of Marsala), mer. 16 London st. Fench. st
Stephens Richd. tripe dresser, 155 Church st. Shoreditch
Stephens Robert, baker, 75 Tottenham court rd
Stephens Samuel, turner, 142 Church st. Shoreditch
Stephens Samuel Fox, bill broker, 58 Lombard st
Stephens Sam. Josiah, surv.&build.4 & 5Charlotte st.Port.pl
Stephens Sophia Ann(Mrs.), hosier, 2Burlington pl.O.Kentrd
Stephens Susan F.(Mrs.), stationer, 121 Albany st.Regent's pk
Stephens Thomas, *Blue Cross* P.H. 69 Wardour st. Soho
Stephens Thomas, bookseller, 14 London road, Southwark
Stephens Thomas, boot & shoe ma. 30 William st. Lisson gr
Stephens Thomas, carpenter, 17 Union st. east, Spitalfields
Stephens Thos. 3 *Jolly Gardeners* P.H. 151 Union st. Boro
Stephens Thos. pawnbroker, &c. 82 & 83 Wardour st. Soho
Stephens Timothy, umbrella manufr. 66 Newgate st
Stephens Wm. bootmaker, 69 York road, Lambeth
Stephens Wm. plumber & glazier, 18 Gilbert st. Oxford st
Stephens Wm. solicitor, 30 Bedford row, Bloomsbury
Stephens Wm. stationer, 35 Throgmorton st
Stephens Wm.warehousemen, see Hanson, Smiths' & Stephens
Stephenson Chas. & Co. export & whol. ironmongers, engineers, millwrights, smiths & gasfitters, manufacturers of iron fencing & hot water apparatus, steam kitchens, &c. 61 Gracechurch st. & 17 New Park st. Southwark
Stephenson (G. & R.) & Bidder, civ.engineers, 24 Gt.George st
Stephenson, Mager&Co.bluema.drug grds.Madn.la.King's cr
Stephenson Robt. & Co. engineers, 2 Walbrook, & at Newcastle on Tyne; Edward F. Starbuck, agent
Stephenson Ann (Mrs.), dairy, 3 Boyle st. Saville row
Stephenson Augustus, wine & spirit merchant, 2 Sise lane
Stephenson Edward Simon, solicitor, 12 Gt.Queen st.Westm
Stephenson Elger, news agt. 9A, Billiter sq. Fenchurch st
Stephenson George, plumber, 10 Grove ter. Bayswater
Stephenson George, undertaker, 34 Hampden st.Clarndn. sq
Stephenson James, barrister, 42 Southampton buildings
Stephenson James, carpenter, 3 Red Lion pass. Hoxtn.Oldtn
Stephenson James, linendraper, 4 Arbour ter.Comml. rd. ea
Stephenson James, upholsterer, 17 Winchester row, New rd
Stephenson John, linendraper, 27 Frederick pl.Hampstead rd
Stephenson John Denmore, fishmonger, 82 Blackman st
Stephenson John J. e.&w.i. produce dealer, 10 St.Mary at hill
Stephenson John James, coal merchant, 10 St. Mary at hill
Stephenson Joseph, cowkeeper, 23 Whitefriars st. Fleet st
Stephenson Matthew, lodging house, 16 Emmett st. Poplar
Stephenson Robert, biscuit baker, irish & foreign provision merchant, 285 Wapping & Jamaica coffee house
Stephenson Robert, engineer in chief of the London & Birmingham railway; Robert B. Dockray, resident engineer; office, Euston station
Stephenson Robert, surgeon, 6 Low.Southwick st. Oxford sq
Stephenson Sarah (Mrs.), baker, 17 Brunswick st. Blackwall
Stephenson Simon, attorney, 12 Gt. Queen st. Westminster
Stephenson Thomas, dairy, 7 Shepherd ct. Upper Brook st
Stephenson Thomas, merchant, see Cattley & Stephenson
Stephenson Thomas, stationer, 70 Oxford st
Stephenson Thomas, tailor, 15 Harrington st. Hampstead rd
Stephenson Timothy, linendraper, 22 Conduit st. Paddingtn
Stephenson Wm. booksel. & newsvender, 12&13Parliament st

Stephenson Wm. carpet, bed & cabinet war. 4 Blackfriars rd
Stephenson Wm. grocer & teadealer, 86 Tooley st
Stephenson Wm. nurseryman, &c. Maida vale, Edgware rd
Stephenson Wm. painter, &c. 2 Martha st. Cambridge hth. rd
Stepney Meeting Almshouses (Thos. Freelove, sec.), Salmon la
Stepple Jonathan, hosier & glover, 145 Shoreditch High st
Stepto William, butcher, 18 Newport ct. Newport market
Steptoe Geo. musical instru. tuner, 30 Beaumont st. Port.pl
Steptoe William, herbalist, Covent garden fruit market
Stericker Wm. & Co. wholesale teadealers, 49 Fenchurch st
Sterland William, hat manufr. 7 Union st. Bishopsgate
Sterling Henry, gold cutter, 19 Woodbridge st. Clerkenwell
Stermer Joseph, furniture broker, 3 Haddon pl. Waterloo rd
Stern Brothers, merchants, 4 Angel court, Throgmorton st
Stern Robert, farrier, 10 Gun lane, Limehouse
Sternberg Heber, fr. polisher, 15 Colville ct. John st. Fitzroy sq
Sterry Joseph & Sons, oil & colormen, 156 Borough High st
Sterry, Sterry & Co. oilmen & drysalters, 143 Boro' High st
Sterry Henry, commission merchant, 21 Basinghall st
Sterry Henry, merchant, 38 Trinity square, Tower hill
Sterry Henry, jun. surgeon, 10 Grange road, Bermondsey
Sterry Samuel Henry, surgeon, 1 Alscot place, Grange road
Stert Arthur & Co. wine merchants, 20 Clifford st. Bond st
Sterzel Mary (Mrs.), straw hat mnfr. 231 Bethnal green rd
Steven Robert, secretary to *Hand in Hand Fire & Life Office*, 1 New Bridge st. Blackfriars
Stevens & Alexander, architects, 6 Clement's inn
Stevens Ambrose & Co. who. coffee dealers, 39 Gt. Tower st
Stevens & Fearon, attorneys, 1 Gray's inn square
Stevens Geo. & Joseph, timber merchants, Kingsland rd. canal
Stevens John & Son, gas engineers, brass founders & gasfitters, manufacturers of steam, gas & chemical apparatus, Darlington works, 19 Southwark bridge rd
Stevens John Crace & Saml. auctioneers, 38 King st. Covent gdn
Stevens John R. & Co. dorset ale str. Old Barge wf. Up. Ground st
Stevens & Millard, boot & shoe manufacturers, 194 Tooley st. & 373 Rotherhithe st
Stevens (V. & R.) & Norton, law booksellers & publishers, (successors to the late J. & W. T. Clarke, of Portugal st.), 26 & 39 Bell yard, Lincoln's inn
Stevens & Perrin, silk dyers, 5 Myrtle st. Hoxton Old town
Stevens Thos. & Son, patentees & mnfrs. of Martin's cement, plaster of paris & roman cement works, 186 Drury lane
Stevens & Satchell, solicitors, 6 Queen st. Cheapside
Stevens Alfred, teadealer, see Metcalf & Stevens
Stevens Benjamin, coffee rooms, 35 Holywell la. Shoreditch
Stevens Caroline (Mrs.), lodging ho. 22 Harleyfd. pl. Ken.com
Stevens Catherine (Mrs.), fruiterer, 62 Castle st. ea. Oxford st
Stevens Charles, carver, gilder & looking-glass manufacterer to the trade, 40 Holywell lane, Shoreditch
Stevens Charles, greengrocer, 64 Regent st. Horseferry rd
Stevens Charles, registrar, 3 St. George's st. Albany rd
Stevens Charles, saddler, 2 Clifton st. north, Finsbury
Stevens Charles, solicitor, 20 Mabledon pl. Burton cres
Stevens Charles, solicitor, see Maples, Pearse & Co
Stevens Charles, *Unicorn* P.H. 84 Hoxton Old town
Stevens David, hay compresser, live stock dlr. North st. E.i.rd
Stevens Edward Cephas, secretary to *King's College Hospital*, 7 Portugal st. Lincoln's inn
Stevens Edwin, butcher, 15 Gt. Chapel st. Westminster
Stevens Eliza (Mrs.), tobacconist, 155 Upper Thames st
Stevens Elizh. (Mrs.), china dealer, 101 High st. Marylebone
Stevens Elizh. (Mrs.), straw hat maker, 77 Kingsland rd
Stevens Fredk. Wm. *Goldsmiths' Arms tav.* 23 Gutter la
Stevens George, carver & gilder, 44 Whitcomb st
Stevens George, engraver, &c. 11 Castle st. Long acre
Stevens George, grocer, 39 King st. Deptford
Stevens George, importer of foreign lace, cambrics, &c. & manufacturer of british lace, 218 Regent st
Stevens George, leatherseller, Well st. Hackney
Stevens George, plumber & glazier, 153 Bermondsey st
Stevens George, *Rose & Crown* P.H. 25 Little Britain
Stevens George, stationer, 55 Hoxton Old town
Stevens George, surveyor, 26 Paddington basin, north side
Stevens George, tailor, 13 Denbigh st. Belgrave rd. Pimlico
Stevens George Thomas, butcher, 67 Cannon st. City
Stevens Henry, barrister, Chancery chambers, 30 Chancery la
Stevens Henry, chemist & druggist, High st. Stoke Newington
Stevens Henry, com. agent, 15 Dorchester pl. New North rd
Stevens Henry, hairdresser, 6 Edward st. Wardour st. Soho
Stevens Henry, tallowchand. 41 Seabright st. Bethnal gr. rd
Stevens Hen. John, lett. pr. & copp. pl. printer, 8 Philpot la
Stevens Isaac Thos. watch escapemt. ma. 34 Ironmonger st
Stevens James, boot & shoe maker, 295 Oxford st
Stevens James, brush maker, 2 Hamilton pl. High st. Dptfrd
Stevens James, carpenter, 19 Denmark st. Ratcliff highway
Stevens James, milliner, 140 Gt. Suffolk st. Borough
Stevens James, surgical inst. ma. 10 Gower st. north, New rd
Stevens James, watch engraver, 45 Brick lane, St. Luke's
Stevens James S. engineer, Claremont cot. Park pl. Padngtn
Stevens John, carver & gilder, 15A, Cleveland st. Fitzroy sq
Stevens John, city surveyor, Guildhall & 6 Clement's inn
Stevens John, grocer, 6 Cleveland st. Fitzroy square
Stevens John, plumber, 7 Hall place, Lr. Kennington lane
Stevens John, safety light manufacturer, 18 Worthington place, Bethnal green Old road
Stevens John, *King of Pruss.* P.H. 30 Lit. Charlotte st. Bkfrs
Stevens John, scavenger, Horseferry branch rd. Limehouse
Stevens John, soap manufactur. 9 St. Mary st. Whitechapel rd
Stevens John, surveyor, 260 Oxford st
Stevens John, tailor, 9 & 10 Bear yard, Lincoln's inn fields
Stevens John, wine merchant, 48 Lime st
Stevens John Henry, engraver & brass & zinc plate manufacturer, 5 Great Wild st. Lincoln's inn fields
Stevens John, jun. dairyman, 4 Lower Kennington lane
Stevens John Lee, consulting engineer, 2 Charlotte row, Mansion house, & 2 King Edward st. St. George's, Borough
Stevens John M. job, &c. master, 8 Belgrave mws. ea. Belgrv. sq
Stevens John Robert, for. exch. broker, see Crole & Stevens
Stevens Joseph, frame maker, 35 Charles st. City road
Stevens Joseph, ironmonger, 10 High st. Camberwell
Stevens Joseph, linendraper, see Dickins, Smith & Stevens
Stevens Joseph, upholsterer, 33 Goswell road, west
Stevens Margaret (Miss), saddler, 18 Queen st. Golden sq
Stevens Mark, watchmaker, 37 King st. ter. New North rd
Stevens Matthew, dealer in medicines, 13 New st. Old st
Stevens Mercy (Mrs.), ladies' shoema. 17 Lit. Titchfield st
Stevens Mirian (Mrs.), baker, 30 Cumberland rw. Islingtn
Stevens Nicholas, timber merchant, 42 Old st. St. Luke's
Stevens Richard, *Fountain* P.H. Deptford broadway
Stevens Richard, jun. ivory turner, 120 Waterloo rd
Stevens Robert, *Carpenters' Arms* P.H. 32 Burton st
Stevens Robert, china dealer, 32 Chalcroft ter. New cut
Stevens Robert, ivory turner & carver, 9 Greek st. Soho
Stevens Samuel, oilman, 344 Rotherhithe st
Stevens Saml. pawnbroker, &c. 1 High st. Newington butts
Stevens Samuel Gloster, dyer, 1 Fashion st. Dockhead
Stevens Simon, glass & china wareho. 45 Coleshill st. Pimlico
Stevens Stephen, wheelwright, 15 Perry st. St. Pancras
Stevens Thos. academy, 14 Mansell st. Goodman's fields
Stevens Thos. barrister, 12 New Boswell court, Carey st
Stevens Thos. brazier & tinman, 9 Paradise st. Marylebone
Stevens Thos. carpenter & buildr. 31 Leman st. Goodmn's. flds
Stevens Thos. cheesemonger, 26 Fetter lane, Fleet st
Stevens Thos. fancy cabinetma. 60 Wellington st. Goswell st
Stevens Thos. french clog ma. 12 Holywell la. Shoreditch
Stevens Thos. fruiterer, 11 Foley place, Portland place
Stevens Thos. greengrocer, &c. 66 King st. Golden square
Stevens Thos. grocer, 6 Portland ter. Wandsworth road
Stevens Thos. *Horse & Groom* P.H. 89 Curtain road
Stevens Thos. stationer, &c. 19 Marylebone lane, Oxford st
Stevens Thos. soap manufr. Dock st. Up. East Smithfield
Stevens Thos. tallow chandler, 65 Rosemary lane
Stevens Thomas John, coppersmith, brazier, plant & fixture dealer, 113 & 114 Golden lane
Stevens Timothy, grocer & british wine dl. 2 Nursery pl. O.Kt.rd
Stevens Wm. agent for (Bass & Co.) ale stores, 49 Great Tower st. City, & 3 York road, City road
Stevens Wm. baker, 80 Theobald's road, Red Lion square
Stevens Wm. beer retailer, 74 Bridport pl. New North rd
Stevens Wm. boot & shoe maker, 16 Carnaby st. Golden sq
Stevens Wm. butcher, 17 Crucifix lane, Bermondsey
Stevens Wm. cattle salesman, 8 West Smithfield
Stevens Wm. coffee rooms, 131 Praed st. Paddington
Stevens Wm. *Fox* P.H. 133 Great Suffolk st. Borough
Stevens Wm. fruiterer, 41 Albany st. Regent's park
Stevens Wm. *Hand & Flower* P.H. 1 Gravel la. Southwark
Stevens Wm. printer, 37 Bell yard, Temple bar
Stevens Wm. printer, 43 Castle st. Holborn
Stevens Wm. *Rose inn*, 80 West Smithfield
Stevens Wm. stationer, pub. & news vend. 42 Tottnhm. ct. rd
Stevens Wm. watchmaker, 14 Bartholomew sq. St. Luke's
Stevens Wm. water gilder, 12 King's head court, Shoe lane
Stevens Wm. wax & tallow chandler, 222 Tottenham ct. rd
Stevens Wm. wine & brandy mer. 78 & 80 Bishopsgt. within
Stevens Wm. Gregson, watchma. 57 Wellington st. Goswl. st
Stevens Wm. Henry, boat builder, 43 Rotherhithe wall
Stevens Wm. Henry, butcher, 95 New Gravel lane
Stevens Wm. Henry, *Torbay* P.H. 40 Rotherhithe
Stevenson Geo. & Sons, mercs. 9 King's arms yd. Moorgate st
Stevenson, Salt & Sons, bankers, 20 Lombard st
Stevenson & Sloan, law stationers, Mitre court, Fleet st

Stevenson Joseph & John, manufacturers of french shell & horn combs, & britannia metal spoons, 9 Cripplegate buildings; manufactory at Sheffield
Stevenson Brian, baker, 3 Little New st. Shoe lane
Stevenson Brian, grocer, 17 Little New st. Shoe lane
Stevenson Caroline (Mrs.), school, 5 Mornington road
Stevenson Chas. builder, 14½ Osnaburgh st. Regent's park
Stevenson Chas. carman & dairy, 14 Patriot rw, Cambridge rd
Stevenson Curtis, egg mercht. 12 Bridport pl. New North rd
Stevenson Elizth. (Mrs.), coal dlr. 85 East st. Manchester sq
Stevenson Frederick, wine merchant, 26 Tokenhouse yard
Stevenson George, jun. baker, 8 Essex st. Strand
Stevenson Geo. sen. baker, 1 Burlington place, Old Kent rd
Stevenson George, fishfactor, see Mahers & Stevenson
Stevenson George, grocer, 159 Up. Whitecross st. St. Luke's
Stevenson James, tobacconist, 11 George court, Piccadilly
Stevenson Jane (Mrs.), chandler's shop, Larkhall la. Clapham
Stevenson Jane S. (Mrs.), american boarding ho. 8 America sq
Stevenson John, fruiterer, Mare st. Hackney
Stevenson John, grocer, 21 Hackney road
Stevenson John, solicitor, see Meggison, Pringle & Co
Stevenson John Mackeness, solicitor, 3 Cork st. Bond st
Stevenson Leader, merchant, 9 King's arms yd. Moorgate
Stevenson Lewis, shoemaker, 7 St. George's ter. Borough rd
Stevenson R. earthenware manufacturer, George Smythe, agent, 52 Eastcheap
Stevenson Richard, fruiterer, 35 Devonshire st. Portland pl
Stevenson Richard Jas. watch & clock ma. 234 Bethnal gn.rd
Stevenson Soph. (Mrs.), fishmong. 7 Wallington pl. Wndswth.rd
Stevenson Thomas, leatherseller, Park place, Walworth
Stevenson Thomas, surgeon, 24 Edgware road, Marylebone
Stevenson Thomas, M.D. surgeon, 37 Upper Grosvenor st
Stevenson Thomas Godfrey, bootmaker, Well st. Hackney
Stevenson Wm. carpenter & frame ma. 5 Lit. Chapel st. Soho
Stevenson Wm. carpet warehouse, 8 King st. Covent garden
Stevenson Wm. merchant, 101 Up. Thames st.; & 22 Milner sq
Steventon Richard, beer retailer, 7 Little Coram st
Steverson John, muffin baker, 22 Earl st. ea. Lisson gr. north
Steward Elizh. (Mrs.), tobacconist, 16 Lit. Earl st. Sev. dials
Steward Elizabeth B. (Mrs.), dairy, 40 Old Bond st
Steward John, coffee rooms, 60 London road, Southwark
Steward John, dentist, 20 Mortimer st. Cavendish square
Steward Robert, *King of Prussia* P.H. 4 Wych st. Strand
Steward Samuel, carman, Church st. Deptford
Steward Samuel, solicitor, see Bell, Steward & Lloyd
Steward Sophia (Miss), dressmak. 12 Davies st. Berkeley sq
Steward Thomas, hatter, 11 Rosoman st. Clerkenwell
Steward Thomas B. corndealer, 58 Regent st. Horseferry rd
Stewards & Co. stone merchants, Western wharf, Abingdon st
Stewardson Edward, tailor, 33 St. Andrew's hill, Drs.comms
Stewardson Henry, *BlueCoat Boy* P.H. 42 Lant st. Borough
Stewart A. & Westmorland, merchs. Winchester ho. O. Broad st
Stewart David & Rt. land surveyors, 94 Gt. Russell st. Blmsby
Stewart Henry & Son, surgeons, &c. 1A, Weymouth st. Prtlnd pl
Stewart Jas. & Co. for. wareh. & oil merchs. 11 Old Broad st. City
Stewart & Maclaren, surgeons & chemists, 43 Aldersgate st
Stewart & Murray, printers, &c. 1 Green arbour ct. Old Bailey
Stewart Robert & Son, hat makers, 20 Shoreditch
Stewart & Tracey, hide & leather factors, 30 London wall
Stewart Wm. & Thomas, builders, Rhodeswell rd. Limehouse
Stewart, Alexander, academy, 4 Gt. College st. Camden town
Stewart Alexander, baker, 57 Tothill st. Westminster
Stewart Alexander, merchant, Winchestr. ho. Old Broad st. City
Stewart Alexander, watchmaker, 38 Perceval st. Clerkenwell
Stewart Alexander Patrick, physician, 130 Mount st
Stewart Alexander W. *Yarmouth Town* P.H. 168 Old Gravel la
Stewart Charles, barrister, 2 Paper buildings, Temple
Stewart Charles, zinc worker, 40 Bell st. Edgware road
Stewart Chas. theolog. booksel. 11 King William st. Strand
Stewart David, merchant, see Paton & Stewart
Stewart Donald, ivory turner & dealer, 349 Oxford st
Stewart Duncan, yeast dealer, 39 Gray's inn lane
Stewart Edward, *Haunch of Venison* P.H. 4 Brook st
Stewart Eliza (Miss), lodging house, 39 Brewer st. Golden sq
Stewart Fred. tallowchandler, 167 Sloane st. Knightsbridge
Stewart George Charles, accountant, 2 Philpot lane
Stewart Henry, hairdresser, 16 Parkside, Knightsbridge
Stewart Henry Charles, surgeon, 1 St. John's Wood grove
Stewart James, baker, 6 Bridge st. Borough
Stewart James, baker, 11 Cross st. Blackfriars road
Stewart James, barrister, 4 Old square, Lincoln's inn
Stewart James, calico, &c. printer, 3 Lit. Friday st. & Glasgow
Stewart James, grocer, 5 Chapel st. Belgrave square
Stewart James, *St. George's hotel*, 32, 33 & 34 Albemarle st
Stewart Jane (Mrs.), brushmaker, 21 King st. Commrl. rd. east
Stewart John, artist, 6, Cirencester pl. Fitzroy square
Stewart John, baker, 23 Granby street, Hampstead road
Stewart John, engineer, 290 Rotherhithe st
Stewart John, grocer, 10 Church lane, Saint Giles's
Stewart John, hatter, 106 & 107, St. George st
Stewart John, tailor & draper, 68 Cheapside
Stewart John, tailor, 68 Seymour place, Bryanstone sq
Stewart John, teadealer, 31 Hampton st. Walworth rd
Stewart John, tin plate worker, 3A, Davies st. Berkeley sq
Stewart Joseph, sugar & colonial broker, Commercial coffee house, Mincing lane, & 1 Cullum st
Stewart Lawrence Robertson, commission agent, sole agent for H.S. Fitchie, umbrella gingham mnfr. 7 New Basinghall st
Stewart Leonard, physician, 28 Keppel st. Russell sq
Stewart Mary (Mrs.), court milliner, 15 Baker st. Portman sq
Stewart Mary Ann (Mrs.), grocer, &c. Union rd. Clapham rise
Stewart Pat. Maxwell, west india merchant, 17 Finsbury circus
Stewart Robt. Wm. miscellaneous dlr. 116 Blackfriars road
Stewart Thomas, *Crown* P.H. Rhodeswell road, Limehouse
Stewart William, dairyman, 4 Curzon st. Mayfair
Stewart William, fruiterer, 5 Fairfield terrace, Stepney
Stewart Wm. ladies' boot & shoemaker, 9 Gt. Ryder st. St. James
Stewart Wm. silkman, 173 Church st. Shoreditch
Stewart Wm. Christie, worsted & fringe ma. 1 Noble st. City
Stewart Wm. George, pawnbroker, 7 Notting hill High st
Stewart Zachariah John, hatter, 249 High Holborn
Stibbard Geo. Davey, wine mer. see Vincent & Stibbard
Stibbard John Davey, customho & ship agt. 8 Geo. la. Botolph la
Stibbs Edward C. bookseller, 25 Holywell st. Strand
Stichbury James, *Fountain* P.H. 16 Virginia row, Bethn.gr.rd
Stickland Edward, tailor, 273 Strand
Stickland Michael, dairyman, 36 Upper Albany st
Stickland Robert, grocer, 58 Leman st. Goodman's fields
Stickland Wm. carpenter, 30 Michael's place, Brompton
Stickley Henry, boot & shoema. 7 Stockwell ter. Clapham rd
Sticdwood Robert, beer retailer, 20 Bermondsey New rd
Stickwood Wm. ding. roms, 63 Crawford st. & 30 Chapel st. N w.rd
Stiebel Brothers, merchants, 8 Crosby square
Stiebel Siegmund M. & Co. merchants, 8 Lime st. City
Stiff James, baker & coal dlr. 27 Trafalgar st. Walworth rd
Stiff James, brown stone potter chemical apparatus & water filter maker, 39 High st. Lambeth
Stiff John, butcher, 1 Windsor place, Old Kent road
Stiff Richard, linendraper, 67 Old st. St. Luke's
Stiff Thomas, livery stables, 5A, Quebec mews, Portman sq
Stiffel & Cartier, merchants, 36 Old Jewry
Stileman Thomas, baker, 61 Freeschool st. Horsleydown
Stiles John, ginger beer manuf. 52 Wells st. Oxford st
Stiles Chas. oil & colorman, 9 Tavistock st. Covent garden
Stiles Jas. watch joint finisher, 52 Perceval st. Clerkenwell
Stiles Joseph, boot & shoe maker, 31 High st. Notting hill
Stiles Joseph Davis, upholsterer, 27 Stamford st. Blackfriars
Stiles Robert, *Golden Lion* P.H. 42 Gravel lane, Southwark
Stiles Stephen, builder, 5 Edward st. Kingsland road
Stiles Susan (Mrs.), timberyd. 55 Green st. Wellington st. Blkfrs
Stiles Wm. coppersmith, plate maker, &c. 23 Lisle st. Leic.sq
Stiles Wm. fruiterer, 13 Boswell court, Queen square
Stiles Wm. philosoph. instru. ma. 29 Seward st. Goswell st
Stiles Wm. statuary & mason, 2 Edward st. Kingsland road, & Eagle wharf road, City road
Still William & Charles, cattle salesmen, 17 West Smithfield
Still Adam, tailor, 158 Poplar High st
Still John, *Burlington Arms* P.H. 21 Old Burlington st
Still John, coach & harness mak. 11 Smith's blds. City rd
Still John, law stationer, 25 Castle st. Holborn
Still John, potato salesman, 106 Bermondsey st
Still Robert, solicitor, 5 New square, Lincoln's inn
Still Robert George, tailor, &c. 209 Poplar High st
Still Wm. accountant, 63 Coleman st. City
Stillwell, Edward, wire drawer, see Atherly & Stillwell
Stillwell, Jas. silk mnfr. 7 White Lion st. Norton folgate
Stillwell John, butcher, 21 Lambeth lower marsh
Stillwell Samuel, tobacconist, Park place, Old Kent road
Stilwell Thomas & Sons, navy agents, 22 Arundel st. Strand
Stilwell Absalom, *Salmon & Ball* P.H. 32 Lamb st. Spitlfids
Stilwell Chas. surgeon, 1 Charlotte row, Bermondsey
Stilwell Richard, oil & color & salt merchant, 73 Shoreditch
Stilwell Rd. watch & case gilder, 50 Whiskin st. Clerkenwell
Stimpson H. (Mrs.), milliner & dress maker, 13 Trevor square
Stimpson Henry, tailor, 2 Arthur st. Knightsbridge
Stimpson James, confectioner, 7 High st. St. Giles
Stimpson Thomas, carpenter, 13 Trevor sq. Knightsbridge
Stimpson Wm. ironfounder, 18 Crosby row, Walworth road
Stimpson William, *White Horse* P.H. Old Ford
Stimpson Wm. *Williams'* dining rooms, 4, 5, 6 & 7 Old Bailey
Stinchcombe Thomas & Co. woollen drprs. 27 & 28 Cloth fair
Stinn Charles, boot maker, 103 Holborn

Stinson Henry, boot & shoemkr. Southampton st. Camberwell
Stinton John, silk mercer, see Marshall & Stinton
Stinton Joseph, barrister, 5 New square, Lincoln's inn
Stirling Wm. & Walter, cotton spinners & manfs 5 Bow ch. yd
Stirling Thos. & Wm. slaters, Bow bridge, Stratford, & 7 St. Ann's place, Commercial road, Limehouse
Stirling John, coal merchant, 68 Lambeth walk
Stirling John William, chemist, 86 Whitechapel High st
Stirling Thos. slate merchant & slater, & inventor of the patent slab slating, far exceeding lead in appearance and durability, Belvedere wharf, Belvedere road
Stitfold Eliz. (Mrs.), hairdresser, 199 Brick la. Spitalfields
Stivens John & Co. british wine makers, 3 Budge row, City
Stivenson & Scott, timber merchts. 47 Princes st. Leicester sq
Stoakes Stephen, hop mer. 3 Bowling gr. la. King st. Boro'
Stoate Henry, carpet & furnishing wareho. 39 Crawford st.
Stoatt Thos. *Builders' Arms* P.H. 1 Charles st. Kensgtn. Nw. tn
Stobbes John, statuary, Cambridge wharf, Wilton rd. Pimlico
Stobbs Caroline (Mrs.), staymaker, 433 Strand
Stoby James, boot & shoe maker, 48 Church st. Minories
Stock Robert & Son, tailors & habit ms. 1 Maddox st. Regt. st
Stock Anna R. (Mrs.), coffee rooms, 95 Fenchurch st
STOCK EXCHANGE, Capel court, Bank
Stock Exchange Express, Commercial & Railway Reporter, Office 170 Fleet st
Stock Edward, boarding house, Poplar High st
Stock Edward, boys' school, Poplar house, Poplar High st
Stock Frederick, japanner, 36 Monmouth st. Seven dials
Stock John, hairdresser & cap ma. 37A, Princess st. Lei'ster sq
Stock John Shapland, barrister, 2 Plowden bldgs. Temple
Stock Philip, plumber & glazier, 38 Gray's inn lane
Stock Susan (Miss), stayma. 29 James st. Buckingham gate
Stock Thomas, currier, 68 Bermondsey st
Stock Thomas, tailor, Coleman cotts. Coleman cr. Bermondsy
Stock Thomas, baker, 87 Shaftesbury st. New North road
Stock Thomas, jun. woolstapler, 224 Bermondsey st
Stock Thomas, sen. baker, 53 Whitmore road, Hoxton
Stock Wm. Tomlin, baker, 14 Charlton crescent, Islingtongreen
Stockall James, naturalist, 115 Gt. Titchfield st
Stockbridge Ann (Mrs.), tailor, 3 Cumbld. rw. Kengtn. green
Stockbridge Geo. tobacconist, 35 Gt. Wild st. Lincoln's inn fi
Stocken Alfred, coach builder, 34 St. George's pl. Knightsbdg
Stocken Chas. bookseller & stationer, 53 Quadrant, Regent st
Stocken Fred. coach & harness ma. Halkin st. Grosvenor pl
Stocken Fred. coach bldr. Old Barrack yd. St. George's pl
Stocken James Julius, tobacco mfr. see Beynon & Stocken
Stocken Thos. prof. of music & singing, 37 Albany st. Regt pk
Stocken Wm. furnishing undertak. 1 Parkside, Knightsbridge
Stocken & Curtis, hydraulic enginrs. 71 Red Lion st. Clkwl
Stocker & Nodes, furn. undertaker, 90 Park st. Camden tn
Stocker Elizabeth (Mrs.), painter, 11 Lit. Chester st. Grosv. pl
Stocker George, ale rooms, 417 Strand
Stocker Henry, baker, 181 Wapping High st
Stocker John, plasterer, 27 Rodney st. Pentonville
Stocker John, P. solicitor, see Hawkins, Bloxam, Stocker & Co
Stocker Peter, baker, 14 Cornwall road, Stamford st
Stocker Richard, surgeon, see Willmer & Stocker
Stocker Samuel, *Rising Sun* P.H. 78 Gray's inn lane
Stocker Thos. Bliss, art. flowerma. 28 Marchmont st. Burton cr
Stockford James & Son, hairdressers, 28 Cannon st. City
Stockham Edward, baker, 17 Great Winchester st
Stockham John, fruiterer, Vassall rd. Camberwell Newrd
Stockham (Mrs.), dressing case ma. 19 Grove pl. Lisson grov
Stockham William, baker, 144 St. John st. West Smithfield
Stockil Rebecca (Mrs.), teadealer, 31 Charles st. Horselydwn
Stocking Henry, bookseller, &c. 36 Red Lion st. Holborn
Stocking James, china warehouse, 9 Rotherhithe wall
Stocking Samuel, grocer, 3 Water st. Strand
Stockings Edward, carpenter, 43 King st. Clerkenwell
Stockins William, saddler, 39 Worship st. Finsbury
Stockley George, butcher, 4 Bath st. City road
Stockley Gilkes, bookseller & stationer, 31 Charles st. Berners st. & 11 Clarence place, Camberwell road
Stockley Richd. carpet & floor cloth wa. 173 Ratcliff highw
Stockley Sam. cop. pl. engr. & print. 13 Gt. Russell st. Cov. gar
Stockley Thomas, grocer, 178 Sloane st. Knightsbridge
Stockley Thomas, potato dealer, 6 Bath st. City road
Stockman Benj. medcl. plaister ma. 11 Gt. White Lion st. 7 Dials
Stockman Edward, tobacconist, 5 Hopkins row, Westmnstr
Stockman Henry, plasterer, 41 Molyneux st. Bryanston sq
Stockman John, outfitter, 66 Bridge road, Lambeth
Stockman Thomas, tobacconist, 2 Besom pl. Old Gravel lane
Stocks Edward, lighterman, 4½ College hill, City
Stocks Joseph, french polisher, 54 St. Clement's la. Strand
Stocks Joseph, glass cutt. & *Castle* P.H. 20 Holland st. Blackfs
Stockton Samuel & Co. linendrapers, Church st. Hackney
Stockton John, tailor, &c. see Furby & Stockton
Stockton Joseph, wine cooper, &c. 1 John's mews, Bedford row
Stockton Samuel, wine cooper, 4 Long yard, Lamb's Conduit st
Stockton Saml. Radness, muffin bkr. 65 Cromer st. Brunswk. sq
Stockwell Benj. Jas. live stock dlr. Montague pl. Mill wall
Stockwell Samuel, bootmaker, see Cockerell & Stockwell
Stockwell Stephen, cabinet maker, 54 Long alley, Finsbury
Stockwell Thomas, undertaker, 49 Aldenham st. St. Pancras
Stockwell Wm. Hen. furnishing undertkr. 31 Hampstead rd
Stodart Wm. & Son, grand pianoforte makers, 1 Golden sq. & 57 Wells st. Oxford st
Stodart Alfred, pianoforte maker, see Owen & Stodart
Stoddart & Carley, who. watch ma. 61 Red Lion st. Clrkwl
Stoddart & Co. of Madeira, 11 Bread st. Neil, Black & Co. agt
Stoddart John Wm. ivory turner, 4 Edith pl. Hackney rd
Stoddart Robt. watch & chron. ma. 13 Red Lion st. Clerknwl
Stodgell William, *Red Cross* P.H. 10 Up. East Smithfield
Stodhart Elizth. & Sons, ironmngs. 18 & 19 High st. Camberwell
Stodhart Ebenezer, ironmgr. see Stodhart Elizth. & Sons
Stodhart Thomas, ironmgr. see Stodhart Elizth. & Sons
Stoffell William, toy dealer, 10 Dockhead, Bermondsey
Stoger George, tobacconist, 12 Chandos st. Covent garden
Stohwasser Joseph, tailor, 39 Conduit st. Bond st
Stoker George, hatter, 9 Hayes court, Soho
Stokes & Dalton, stockbrokers, 5 Tokenhouse yard
Stokes Francis & Co. brandy distillers, 99 Holborn hill
Stokes Francis & Son, grocers, 3 Windsor pl. Old Kent rd
Stokes Henry & Co. national cognac brandy distillery, 18 King st. Snow hill
Stokes, Hollingsworth, Tyerman & Johnson, solicitors, 24 Gresham st
Stokes Thos. & Chas. barge & boat builders, 52 Rotherhithe st
Stokes Charles, currier, &c. 11 Gloucester row, Walworth
Stokes Charles, stockbroker, 28 Threadneedle st
Stokes Charles, surgeon dentist, 65 Brook st. Hanover sq
Stokes Charles Rosser, law stationer, 40 Cursitor st
Stokes Edward, hatter, 52 Cheapside
Stokes Edward, jeweller, 2 Corporation row, Clerkenwell
Stokes Elizabeth (Mrs.), meat saleswoman, 3 Newgate market
Stokes Francis, teadealer & grocer, dealer in foreign & british wines, & manfr. of french portable jelly, 175 Strand, & 3 Windsor place, Old Kent road
Stokes George, builder, 11 Westbourne mews, Victoria gate
Stokes Henry Graham, proctor, see Dyke & Stokes
Stokes Hy. Joseph, teapot handle ma. 13 Hosier la W. Smithfld
Stokes Isaac, straw hat maker, 125 Wardour st. Soho
Stokes John, bookseller, 6 Portsea pl. Connaught sq
Stokes John, corn dealer, 169 Ratcliff highway
Stokes John, dining rooms, 2 Commercial pl. York rd. Lamb
Stokes John, hardwareman, 49 Kent st. Borough
Stokes John, tailor, 3 Markham st. King's rd. Chelsea
Stokes Joseph, hairdresser, 13 Perceval st. Clerkenwell
Stokes Joseph, tailor, see Harvey & Stokes
Stokes Mary (Mrs.), teapot handle ma. 1 Hart ct. Bdgwtr. grdns
Stokes Naomi (Mrs.), shoemaker, 21 Church st. Shoreditch
Stokes Robert, brass chaser, 10 Dean st. Fetter lane
Stokes Robert, cheesemonger, North st. Poplar
Stokes Samuel, cheesemonger, 3 Hamilton pl. High st. Deptfd
Stokes Samuel, oilman, 13 Salmon lane, Limehouse
Stokes Sarah (Mrs.), calenderer, 24 & 27 Grosvenor market
Stokes Thomas, cheesemonger, 3 Clayton pl. Kennington rd
Stokes Thomas N. lace wareho. 13 Up. Glo'ster pl. King's rd. Chl
Stokes Thomas, merchant, 28 Threadneedle st
Stokes Thomas, shoemaker, 177 Bethnal green road
Stokey Thomas, bridle cutter, 2 North st. Ropemaker st
Stokey Thomas, lamp manufacturer, 11 Union pl. New rd
Stole William, tailor, &c. 2 Shepherd ct. Upper Brook st
Stollard Elizh. (Mrs.), grocer, 9 Londonhouse yd. St. Paul's
Stollard Richard, grocer, 51 Notting hill, High st
Stollard Wm. grocer & cheesemonger, 58 Chandos st. Cov. gdn
Stollé John, vinegar maker, 9 Christian st. St. George's east
Stollmeyer Conrad Frederic, merchant, 266 Strand
Stolterfoht Herman, merchant, see Collman & Stolterfoht
Stonall Isaac, tailor, 34 Ebury st. Pimlico
Stonar Mary (Mrs.), *Queen's Hd.* P.H. 74 Gt. Guildford st. Boro'
Stonard Mary (Mrs.), oil & color wareho. 179 Hoxton Old tn
Stone Brothers, who. chemists & druggists, 24 Garlick hill
Stone & Bryer, haberdashers, 44 King William street, & Arthur street east, London bridge
Stone & Everett, lace manufacturers, 12 Wood st. City
Stone Elizabeth (Mrs.) & Co. staymakers, 15 Lamb's Conduit st
Stone James & Son, tailors, 40 Bishopsgate within
Stone John & Son, livery stables, 44 Upper Marylebone st
Stone & Kemp, silk manufacturers, 34 & 35 Spital square
Stone & Lusher, tailors & drapers, 9 Skinner st. Snowhill
Stone Rt. & Son, coal mer. 18 Wharf, Millbank st. Westmnster

Stone Sarah&MaryAnn, dressmkr. 1 Up.Fountain pl. City rd
Stone & Turner, solicitors, 57 Jermyn st. St. James's
Stone Wm. Harris&Co.lace&muslin manfrs.&c.3Lawrence la
Stone & Williamson,coal mer. 9 Bankside &145Leadenhall st
Stone Ann (Miss), grocer, 45 Union st. Clarendon square
Stone Benjamin, linendraper, see Perkin & Stone
Stone Charles, builder, 20 Bennett st. Stamford st
Stone Charles, oilman, 21 Mount pleasant, Gray's inn road
Stone Cornelius, baker, Preston road, Poplar
Stone David Henry, solicitor, see Cox & Stone
Stone Edward, linendraper, see Halling, Pearce & Stone
Stone Edward, news agent, Clifton st. Wandsworth road
Stone Edward, stay manufacturer, 9 Middle row, Holborn; 1 Hanway st. Oxford st; & 33 Crawford st. Bryanstone sq
Stone Edwd. *Waterloo* P.H. 16 Samuel st. Cannon st. road
Stone Edwd.who. & retail grocer, 11 Dockhead, Bermondsey
Stone Edwin, *GreenMan& frenchhorn* P.H. 96Dean st.Soho
Stone Elden Edwd. auctioneer, appraiser & undertaker, 83 St. John st. Clerkenwell
Stone Elizabeth (Mrs.), *Globe* P.H. 24 Gt. Chart st. Hoxton
Stone Emma(Mrs.),plumber,12Chichester rents,Chanceryla
Stone Francis, biscuit baker, 69 Blackman st. Borough
Stone Francis, tobacco pipe ma. 7 Nowell's bldgs. Liverpl. rd
Stone Frank, artist, Tavistock house, Tavistock square
Stone George, appraiser & undertaker, 20 Golden la. Barbican
Stone George, baker, 1 York bldgs. Millpond st. Bermondsey
Stone George, banker, see Martin, Stones & Martins'
Stone George, butcher, 1 Cherry garden st. Rotherhithe
Stone George, tailor, 13 Brewer st. Golden square
Stone Henry Blackler, baker, 42 Liverpool st. Bishopsgate
Stone Henry Chas. accountant, 4 Howley pl. Belvedere rd
Stone Henry Dormer, egg merchant, 188 Bermondsey st
Stone Jacob, *Five Bells* P.H. 28 Little Moorfields
Stone James, carpenter, 18 Princes st. Drury lane
Stone James, grocer & registrar, 3 Elm terrace, Brompton
Stone James, ham & beef shop, 2½ Road side, Mile end road
Stone James, harness maker, 33 Earl st.west, Edgware rd
Stone James, oilman, 19 Gt.Wild st. Drury lane
Stone James, *Queen's Head tav.* 14 St. Martin's le grand
Stone John, boot & shoe maker, 22 Goswell st
Stone John, butcher, 44 Portland st. Walworth common
Stone John, cheesemonger, 23 Windmill st. Finsbury
Stone John, cook & confectioner, 16 Ebury st. Pimlico
Stone John, corkcutter, 3 Old Montague st. Whitechapel
Stone John, dairy, 17 Carthusian st. Charterhouse sq
Stone John, fruiterer, 10 Kingsland row, Dalston
Stone John, gold chain maker & jeweller, 7 Myddelton st
Stone John, leather dresser, 20 New st. Dockhead
Stone John, livery stables, 51 Great Titchfield st. Oxford st
Stone John, tailor, 11 Rosamon buildings, Islington green
Stone John Chas. brace, belt & garter manfr. 9 Goldsmith st
Stone John Jefferies, east india merchant&agt.19Austinfriars
Stone Josiah, brassfounder & finisher, & copper nail & rivet manufactr. 11 Dowgate hill & Deptford railway station
Stone Josiah, butcher, 8 Chapel place, Liverpool road
Stone Lewis, merchant, 44 Threadneedle st
Stone Nicholas, teadealer & grocer, 5 Aldermanbury
Stone Richard, proctor, 11 Gt. Carter la. Doctors' commons
Stone Richard, *Ship* P.H. 20 Farmer st. Shadwell
Stone Richd. jun. oil & colorman, 11 Gibson st. Waterloo rd
Stone Richd. sen. tallow chand.27&28Buckingham st.Strand
Stone Richard, town carman, London dock entr.Up.E.Smthfi
Stone Robert, livery stables, 107 & 108 High st. Marylebone
Stone Samuel, grocer, 40 Turnmill st. Clerkenwell
Stone Samuel, silk broker, 7 Austinfriars
Stone Sarah (Mrs.), hairdresser, 3 Dove court, Old Jewry
Stone Thomas, cooper & turner, Clapham rise
Stone Thomas, general dealer in hardware, 6 Bermondsey st
Stone Thomas, leather seller, 20 Chiswell st
Stone Thomas, solicitor (firm Morris, Stone & Townson), clerk to the guardians, & superintendent registrar of births, deaths & marriages for the parish of St. George in the East, 6 Wellclose sq. & 7 Shorter st
Stone Thomas, surgeon, apothecary, Christ's Hospital, 1 Windmill court, Giltspur st
Stone Thomas Arthur, physician, 16 Curzon st. May fair
Stone Thomas Arthur, surgeon, 16 Curzon st. May fair
Stone William, baker, 8 Portugal st. Lincoln's inn
Stone Wm. copperplate printer, 6 East Harding st. Gough sq
Stone Wm. *Grapes* P.H. & wine mer. 23 Panton st. Haymkt
Stone Wm. tobacconist, 130 Edgware road, Marylebone
Stone Wm. upholsterer, 53 Foley st. Portland place
Stone Wm. *Woodman* P.H. 20 Woodland st. Dalston
Stone Wm. James, tailor, 2 Union road, Rotherhithe
Stonebridge Thos. greengrocer & coal dealer, 71 Cromer st
Stoneham Eliza (Miss), shoemaker, 251 High Holborn
Stoneham Wm. butcher, 3Millpond st.Jamaica rw.Bermndsy
Stoneham Wm. saddler, 1 St. James's pl. Hampstead road
Stonehouse Chas. artist, 44 Upper Norton st. Portland pl
Stonelake James, tailor, 14 Frederick place, Goswell rd
Stoneman George, ship builder, see Tebbutt, Stoneman & Co
Stoneman John, bookseller, &c. see Houlston & Stoneman
Stoneman Mary (Mrs.), tobacconist, 63 Hackney road
Stoner Alfred, carpenter, 73 Hercules buildings, Lambeth
Stoner Joseph, coal agent, 14 Water st. Blackfriars
Stoner Samuel, herbalist, 71 Brick lane, St. Luke's
Stones Wm.B.&Son, manchesterwarehousemen, 13 Warwick st
Stonestreet Fetherston, barrister, 35 Gower st. Bedford sq
Stonhill Thos.Ingram, cabinet ma. 2 Up. Spring st.Portmn.sq
Stonhold Zachariah, bootmaker, 90 Mary st. Hampstead rd
Stonor Henry, barrister, 4 Serle st. Lincoln's inn
Stooke Letitia (Mrs.), butcher, 2 Camomile st. Bishopsgate
Stooks Thomas, merchant, see Elmslie & Stooks
Stopfords' Adam & Elisha, hat ma. see Pooles' & Stopfords'
Stopford William, butcher, 133 Poplar High st
Stopher Thomas, carpenter, 50 Warwick st. Pimlico
Stoppani Francis, looking glass mfr.&c.25 Red Lion st. Holbn
Storar W. S. & T. & Co. warehousemen, 138 Cheapside
Storar Julia (Mrs.), tobacconist, 86 Bridge road, Lambeth
Storer George, silverplate manufacturer, see Reily & Storer
Storer James, tobacconist & stationer, 27 St. John st. road
Storer Joseph, bone brush ma. 107 Portland st. Walw. com
Storer Joseph, grocer, 2 Portland place south, Clapham rd
Storer Sarah (Mrs.), locksmith, Church st. Stoke Newington
Storer William, umbrella maker, 94 St. George st
Storey Andrew, attorney, 5 Gray's inn place
Storey Ann (Mrs.), dressmaker, 3 Davies terrace, Davies st
Storey Frances S. (Mrs.), coffee rooms, 116 Fore st. City
Storey James, goldsmith & jeweller, 176 Regent st
Storey James, shoemaker, 106 Waterloo road, Lambeth
Storey John, cheesemonger, 165 Alfred place, Waterloo rd
Storey John, dairyman, Lower road, Rotherhithe
Storey Joseph, grocer, 1 Bride st. Liverpool road
Storey Thomas, carpenter & builder, 23 New st. Brompton
Storey Thomas, glasscutter & staffordshire warehouseman, 19 King William st. City, & 55 Cannon st
Storks Henry, serjeant at law, 3 Serjeants' inn, Chancery la
Storks Robert Reeve, surgeon, 44 Gower st. Bedford square
Storr Edw. Timson, plumber, painter, &c. 4 Lit. St. James st
Storr Paul, wine, hop & seed merchant, see Storey & Storr
Storr Solomon Robert, painter, 10 Grafton st. Fitzroy sq
Storr William, dairyman, 3 Westmorland st. Marylebone
Storr Wm. Brumfitt, auctioneer, see Debenham & Storr
Storrar John, physician, 6 Holles st. Cavendish square
Storrar Robert, baker, 2 Bathurst st. Sussex sq. Hyde park
Storrs & Beard, platers & silversmiths, 106 Cheapside
Storton John, hairdresser, 54 Aldersgate st
Story & Browne, tailors, 157 New Bond st
Story & Storr, wine & brandy & hop & seed merchants, 15 John st. Crutchedfriars
Story Andrew Cooper, tailor, 160 Tottenham court road
Story Benjamin, chandler's shop, 17 Cook's ter. St. Pancras
Story Christopher, hat manufacturer, 38 High st. Bow, & Stratford, Essex
Story George, scale, weighing machine & mill manufacturer, 2 Church lane, Commercial road east
Story Henry, coal merchant, 7 Charterhouse lane
Story James Hamilton, barrister, 17 Bryanstone square
Story John, surgeon, One mile stone, Mile end
Story Sophia (Miss), stationer, 10 Warwick st. Belgrave rd
Story William, tailor, 62 Fleet st. & 1 Bouverie st
Stote Charles, coal dealer, 19 Little Warner st. Clerkenwell
Stotesbury Robert, wood turner, 30Heath st. Comml. rd. east
Stothard George & James, sailmakers, 72 Wapping wall
Stothard Alfred J. medal engraver, 34 Up. Park st. Islington
Stott Chas. Jeremiah & Sam. woollen ma. 4 Silver st. Wood st
Stott Walker, brick mercht. Horse Shoe whf. 10Up.Thames st
Stotter Samuel U. boot& shoe ma. 34Mansion ho. st.Kenngtn
Stout Hannah (Mrs.), painter, &c. 22 Shepperton st. Islington
Stout Robert, *NewPierHouse* P.H. 34Cheyne walk, Chelsea
Stout Wm. mahogany mer. 73 Mortimer st. Cavendish sq
Stout Wm. tobacconist, 1 Victoria pl. Comrcl. rd. Limehouse
Stovel Joseph, military tailor, 1 Suffolk place, Pall mall east
Stovell & Brown, ship brokers & agents, 157 Fenchurch st
Stovell Samuel (Mrs.), straw hat mnfr. 59 Oxford st
Stovin William, solicitor, 2 Duchess st. Portland place
Stow Edw. corn & coal dlr. 9 Wells row, Upper st. Islington
Stow George, oil & colorman, 18 Marchmont st. Burton cresc
Stow Wm. *Golden Last* P.H. 4 Counter st. Borough
Stow Wm. *Red Lion* P.H. 21 Basing lane, Bread st
Stow Wm. Crawford, surveyor, 1 Camden pl. Camberwell
Stow Wm.Thos. toy wareho 22 New Church st. west, Edgw.rd

Stowe Henry, meat salesman, see Dodds & Stowe
Stowell Francis W. *City Arms* P.H. 31 Great Tower st
Stowell James De F. straw bonnet ma. 8 Glo'ster pl. Islingtn
Stower James, carpenter, 10 Glo'ster mews east, Portman sq
Stower Wm. cheesemonger, 15 Lit. Carter lane, Godliman st
Stowers Chas. Hen. law & genl. statnr. 7 Warwick ct. Holborn
Stowers Nowell, surgeon, 26 Albion st. Hyde park
Stowers Nowell, surgeon, 5 York row, Kennington road
Stowers Thomas, painter & glazier, 22 Charterhouse square
Stowton Wm. *Globe* P.H. 11 Derby st. Gray's inn road
Stracey Sparks, plumber, &c. 4 Mount row, New Kent road, & 225 Bermondsey st
Strachan & Roan, calico prints. & warehousmn. 56 Friday st
Strachan Robert Alexander & Charles Henry (late Wilkinson Joshua Richard), anticorrision paint, frankfort black & varnish manufacturers, 54 Watling st. Cheapside
Strachan Wm. & Co. merchants, 6 Copthall ct. Throgmtn. st
Strachan Archibald, butcher, 57 Albany st. Regent's park
Strachan Chas. Hen. printers' ink mkr. 17 King's rd. Camdentn
Strachan David, saddler & harness maker, 100 New Bond st
Strachan Janet (Mrs.), boarding ho. 25 Gt. Trinity la. City
Strachan John, whiskey store, 3 Dean st. Westminster
Strachan Josiah G. factor, see Chamberlain & Strachan
Strachan Samuel, butcher, Church st. Hackney
Strachan Walter H. chemist, Sidney pl. King's rd. Chelsea
Stracy Rebecca (Miss), stationer, 2 Hanover pl. Regt. pk. rd
Stradley Benj. poulterer, 3 Ship tavern pas. Leadenhall mkt
Stradling John, tailor, 41 Great Windmill st. Haymarket
Strahan (Wm.) Paul (Sir John D. bart.), Paul (John D.) & Bates (Robert M.), bankers, Temple bar without, 217 Strnd
Strahan Ann (Miss), coffee rooms, 19½ Lower st. Islington
Strahan Dan. Hen. bookbinder, &c. 5 Tyler's ct. Carnaby st
Straight Robert M. deputy clerk of assize for Home circuit, 1 Middle Temple lane
Strains Edward James, bootmaker, 44 Seward st. Goswell st
Straith John, indigo & colonial bro. 27 & 28 Commer. sale rms
Straiton Alex. watchmaker, 15 Lit. Knightrider st. Doct. com
Straker Daniel, tobacconist, 14 Aldersgate st
Straker Ellen (Miss), milliner, see Smithson & Straker
Straker John, ivory worker, 11 Redcross square, Cripplegate
Straker Sam. lithograph. & press ma. 80 Bishopsgate wthn
Straker Sam. Lawrence, tobacconist, 9 St. Geo's pl. Walwth rd
Straker Wm. theological bookseller, 3 Adelaide st. Strand
Straker Wm. Robert, bookbinder, 35 Monkwell st. Cripplegate
Strand Loan & Discount Office, 302 Strand
Strand Theatre, between 168 & 169 Strand
Strand George, confectioner, 27 Edgware road, Marylebone
Strand James, coffee rooms, 12 Water lane, Blackfriars
Strand Union Office (Jas. Corder, clerk), 6 Bow st. Covnt. gar
Stranders David Joseph, merchant, 31 Broad st. buildings
Strandeven Thomas Dodge, coal dlr. 5 Richmond st. Lei'ster sq
Strange Brothers & Co. wholesale grocers, 65 Houndsditch
Strange Geo. Fred. & Co. ivory deasl. 20 Charles st. Hatt. gar
Strange Char. (Mrs.), *Golden Lions* P.H. 36 Britannia st. Gr. in. r
Strange George, biscuit baker, 53 Chiswell st. Finsbury
Strange George, surgeon, 20 Charles st. Hatton garden
Strange Henry, grocer, 14 Turk st. Bethnal green
Strange James, chemist & druggist, 20 Queen's row, Pimlico
Strange John, cattle salesman, 8 West Smithfield
Strange Thomas, baker, 14 New Manor st. Chelsea
Strange William, bookseller & publisher, 21 Paternoster row
Strange Wm. grocer & cheesemonger, 46 Cheyne walk, Chelsea
Strange William Heath, cheesemonger, 14 Broadway, & 12 Great Chapel st. Westminster
Strangers' Friend Society (James Hiley, sec.), 7 Exeter hall
Strangward John Davis, baker, 35 Union st. Bishopsgate wt
Strangwayes D'Arcy, solicitor, 4 Barnard's inn, Holborn
Strangwayes Richd. draper, see Hughes & Strangewayes
Strangways Thos. Hen. solicitor, 11 King's rd. Bedford row
Strapps Samuel, shoemaker, 5 Gibralter wlk. Bthnl. gr. rd
Stratford David, baker, 13 Cherry Garden st. Rotherhithe
Stratford Henry, fruiterer, 7 Bridge ter. Harrow road
Stratford Jas. artist in fireworks, 24 Union ct. Holborn hill
Stratford James, butcher, 11 King st. Cloth fair
Stratford James, shorthand writer, 3 Lit. George st. Westmr
Stratford John, printer, 2 Nassau place, Commercial road
Stratford Richard, *White Hart* P.H. Old Ford
Stratford Stephen, carpenter, 35 North st. Lisson grove
Stratford Thomas, wheelwright, 66 York st. Lambeth
Stratford William, bootmaker, 8 Moor st. Soho
Stratford Wm. Saml. nautical almanack off. 3 Verulam bldgs
Stratham Thomas, pianoforte maker, 22 Sidney st. City road
Strathearn David, hairdresser, 23 Marylebone lane, Oxford st
Strathearn Thomas, hairdresser, &c. 44 Albany st. Regt's. pk
Strathern Alexander, baker, 14 Denmark st. Soho
Stratton John & Co. veneer saw mills, 6 Midford pl. Tot. ct. rd
Stratton Anthony, commission agt. 2 Philpot la. Fench. st
Stratton George, butcher, 4 Silver st. Golden square
Stratton John Wm. chocolate maker, 15 Regent st. Lambeth
Stratton Joseph, butcher, 74 Devonshire st. Lisson grove
Stratton Joseph, chronom. & watchmaker, 1 Grove pass. Hckny
Stratton Joseph, *Red Cow* P.H. 5 High st. Deptford
Stratton Richard, coal dealer, 1 South wharf rd. Paddington
Stratton Richd. linendraper, see Faulding, Stratton & Co
Stratton Samuel, solicitor, 27 Lincoln's inn fields
Stratton Stephen, tailor, 34 Albion st. Hyde park
Stratton Thomas, barrister, 2 Old square, Lincoln's inn
Stratton William, tobacconist, 179 Lambeth walk
Straub & Hebting, watch & clock makers, 77 Blackman st
Straub Joseph, watch & clock maker, see Brugger & Straub
Straub Michael, clock maker, 53½ Chiswell st
Straughan John, 3 *Crowns* P.H. 9 Richmond st. Leicester sq
Straus Abraham, foreign seedsman, 46 Hungerford market
Straw Alexander, sawmaker, 1 Poplar row, New Kent road
Straw Wm. saw & toolmak. 18 White Lion st. Goodman's fields
Strawson John, wheelwright, 34 Marylebone la. Oxford st
Stray Charles, house & estate agt. 31 Portman pl. Edgware rd
Stray Charles, jun. bootmaker, 43 Kensington High st
Stray Charles, sen. bootmaker, 210 Tottenham court road
Stray Frederick, tailor & trousers maker, 39 Haymarket
Stray George, bootmaker, 3 Crawford st. Portman sq
Stray Wm. Henry, hat maker, 41 Lambeth walk, & 4 Harrow rd
Streat John, beer retailer, Copperas lane, Deptford
Streatfeild, Laurence & Mortimore, leather & hide factors, Leadenhall hide market, & 3 St. Mary Axe
Streather Joseph, bootmaker, 11 Broad st. Bloomsbury
Strebling Wm. carpenter, 3 George yd. Duke st. Grosvnr. sq
Stredder Sophia (Miss), milliner, 21 Sherborne st. Blndfd. sq
Stredder Thomas, carpenter, &c. 9 Union ter. Notting hill
Streek James, tailor, 2 Francis st. Newington butts
Streek John, grocer, 5 North row, Grosvenor sq
Streek Thomas James, paper hanger, 18 High st. St. Giles'
Street Francis & Son, curiosity deals. 21 Brewer st. Golden sq
Street Sophia & Son, watch case gilders, 44 Gee st. Goswell st
Street Arthur, chandler's shop, 14 Pitt st. Fitzroy sq
Street Benjamin, veterinary surgeon, 5 Brick st. Park lane, & 4 Streets buildings, Mount st
Street Betsy (Mrs.), newsvender, 18 Temple st. Whitefriars
Street Geo. house ag. 111 Goswell rd east, & Northfleet
Street Geo. Horatio, news agent, 11 Serle st. Lincoln's inn
Street Henry Cooch, *Elephant & Castle* P.H. King's road, St. Pancras
Street James, livery stables, 3 Robinhood yard, Leather lane
Street John, painter, 9 White Conduit terrace, Pentonville
Street Louis, hairdresser, 5 Suffolk pl. Commer. rd. east
Street Richard, nurseryman, Well st. Hackney
Street Samuel, shoemaker, 6 Bear yard, Lincoln's inn fields
Street Thomas, optician, 39 Commercial road, Lambeth
Street Thos. H. sol. see Gilbert, Hooke, Street & Gutteres
Street Wm. plumber, 3 Crescent place, Hampstead road
Street Wm. vellum binder, Bird in hand court, 76 Cheapside
Street Wm. Henry, builder & undertak. Church st. Deptford
Street Wm. H. oil & colorman, 41 King st. Borough
Street Wm. Jesse, solicitor, 69 Lincoln's inn fields
Streeten Fras. Towers, barrister, 5 Quality ct. Chancery lane
Streeter Edwin, linendraper, 2 Grosvenor row, Pimlico
Streeter John Soper, surgeon, &c. 20 Harpur st. Red Lion sq
Streeter Robert, cattle salesman, 59 West Smithfield
Streeter Thomas, linendraper, 61 High st. Camden town
Streeter Wm. *Welch Harp* P.H. 47 Chandos st. Covent gar
Streeting George, hairdresser, 27 Great Titchfield st
Streeton John, market gardener, London fields, Hackney
Streeton Wm. brassfounder, 4 Midddlesex ter. Hackney rd
Streets Jacob, *Horse & Dolphin* P.H. 25 St. Martin's st. Leicester square
Stretten John, general hardware dealer, 7 Duke's ct. Bow st
Stretton Chas. Marston, solicitor, 18 Southampton bldgs
Stretton Francis, grocer, 16 Gravel lane, Southwark
Stretton John, porkbutcher, 55 Charlotte ter. Newcut, Lambth
Stretton Wm. coffee rooms, 14 Oxford st
Stretton Wm. watch finisher, 16 Ratcliffe row, City road
Strevens Edw. S *Safe Harbour* P.H. Arbour st. West, Stepny
Strevens Henry B. chemist, 142 St. John st. road
Strevett Mary (Miss), staymaker, 9 Up. King st. Bloomsbury
Strevett Richard, beer retailer, 11 Cromer st
Stribblehill Joseph, coppersmith, 78 Shoe lane, Fleet st
Strick Edward, solicitor, 10 Doughty st. Mecklenburgh sq
Strickett Mark, ropemanufctur. Maiden lane, Battle bridge
Strickland Chas. & Rd. chocolate ma. 15 Gibson st. Waterloo rd
Strickland Charles, carpenter, 3 Church pass. Chancery la
Strickland Fredk. Wm. wine merchant, 22 Chancery lane, & 8 Symond's inn

Strickland Fred.Wm.coalmer.Western wf.Georgest.Adelphi
Strickland Michael, dairy, 48 Cumberland mkt. Regent's pk
Strickland Rd.Wm. tailor&habit ma. 22 Lt.Queen st.Wesmr
Strickland Robt.carpenter&c.6Westmoreland bldgs.Aldrsgt
Strickland Thos. ivory turner & carver, 18 Cowper st.City rd
Strickland Wm. furn. brok. 6 Gt. Crown ct. Lit. Pulteney st
Strickland Wm. tailor, &c. 8 Broadway, Ludgate hill
Strickland Wm. tailor, 8 New Bond st
StricklandWm. *Wheatsheaf* P.H.12Up.Chapman st.St.Geo.e
Stride Edward, coffee & dining rooms, 6 St. Swithin's lane
Stride James, parliamentary agent, 13 Fludyer st. Westmr
Stride John, merchant, 7 Tokenhouse yard
Strike Peter, *Hat & Feathers* P.H. 45 Gravel la. Southwk
Stringer & Booty, oil mers. 34 Leadenhall st. & Billiter st
Stringer Frances (Miss), undertaker, see Biers & Stringer
Stringer Francis, *Shepherd&Flock* P.H. 27 High st.Marylbn
Stringer James, custom house, ship & commercial agent, & consignee of dantzic spruce, & importer of foreign produce, 83 Lower Thames st
Stringer John, furniture broker, 7 Chalcroft ter. New cut
Stringer Samuel, solicitor, 1 Trinity st. Blackman st. Boro'
Stringer Step. coach ironmgr. 20 Northumberland st. New rd
Stringer Thomas, baker, 3 New st. Kennington rd
Stringer Thos. druggist, 18 Marlboro' pl. Kennington cross
Stringer William, confectioner, 43 Old st. road
Stringer William, grocer, 20 Charterhouse lane
Stringer Wm. gun manufr. 104 White Lion st. Pentonville
Stringfield George, butcher, 32 Duke st. Bloomsbury
Stringle John, gas lantern manufr. 77 Broadwall, Blackfrs
Stripling George, tailor, 21 East st. Red Lion square
Stripling Geo. William, tailor, 14 New North st. Red Li. sq
Stripling Thomas, coffee rooms, 20 Gt. Titchfield st
Strobel George, baker, 33 Brick lane, Spitalfields
Strode & Ledger, gasfitters, &c. 4 Huggin la. & 8 Allen st
Strode Frances (Miss), tobacconist, 213 Tottenham court rd
Strofton & Carter, wine merchants, 65 South Molton st
Strohm Wm. baker, 1 Canning place, Old st
Strong Alfred & Fred.varnish & japan makers, 117 Long acre
Strong & Hoskins, coal merchants, Dyehouse whf. Clink st
Strong John & Thomas, stereotype founders, Crown court, Chancery lane, & 17 St. John's lane, Clerkenwell
Strong, Larchin & Co. brewers, 8 Pump yard, Ratcliff
Strong & Morley, milliners, 14 Park pl. ter. Paddington gn
Strong Elizabeth (Mrs.), baker, 37 Poplar High st
Strong Henry Linwood, barrister, 5 Brick court, Temple
Strong John, furnishing ironmonger, 15½ Judd place west, New road, & 38 Skinner st. Somers town
Strong John, *Reform* P.H. 68 Long lane, Bermondsey
Strong Jsph. wine mercht. & provision agt. 84 Up. Thames st
Strong Lucy (Mrs.), milliner, 18 Theobald's road
Strong Rd. saddler, 52 Goswell st. & 12 Macclesfield st.north
Strong Sidney, cigar manufacturer, 64 & 65 Watling st
Strong Valentine, coal mer. 10 Church st. St. Saviour's dock
Strong William, bricklayer, 49 York st. Broadway, Westmr
Strong William, hatter, 125 Great Suffolk st. Borough
Strong William, hatter, 37 Sloane square, Chelsea
Strong William Fredk. chemist & druggist, Deptford High st
Strong William Oswald, hatter, 2 Old Bond st
Strongi'th'arm & Jefferd, wine mers. 71 Quadrant, Regent st
Strongi'th'arm Charlot.(Mrs.),millinr.90East st.Manchstr.sq
Strongi'th'arm John, seal engraver, 1 Waterloo pl. Pall Mall
Strother Betsey (Mrs.), artificial florist, 42 South Audley st
Strother Joseph & Son, coal merchs.3 Hornton st.Kensingtn
Strother John James, cheesemngr.2Mason's al.Basinghall st
Stroud & Johns, picture dealers, 2 Wardour st. Soho
Stroud David, bookseller, 163 Blackfriars road
Stroud David, hosier & glover, 89 Edgware road
Stroud Eliz. (Mrs.), dressmaker, 11 Tichborne st. Haymarket
Stroud Jas. brickmaker, 1 Liverpool ter. Liverpool rd. Islngtn
Stroud John, linendraper, 19 Edgware road, Marylebone
Stroud John, *Queen's Head* P.H.10Lit.Charlotte st. Blckfs.rd
Stroud Louisa Mrs. dressmaker, 6 New Bridge st. Vauxhall
Stroud Micah, hosier & glover, 99 Tottenham court road
Stroud Michael W. grocer, 27 Providence row, Finsbury
Stroud Richard,nurseryman,35Mornington pl. Hampstead rd
Stroud Robert, cheesemonger, 8 Minories
Stroud Susannah (Mrs.), tobacconist, Larkhall la. Clapham
Stroud Thomas, *Brewers' Arms* P.H. 26 Aldenham terrace, Somers town
Stroud Thomas,wrkng.goldsmith, 14 Craven bldgs. Drury la
Stroud William, boot & shoemaker, 4 Clifton st. Finsbury
Stroud William, physician, 20 Gt. Coram st. Brunswick sq
Stroughill Charles, solicitor, 7 Coleman st. City
Stroulger Timothy, tailor, 53 Sloane square
Strowker Wm. haberdasher, &c. Foxley ter. Thornhill road
Strudwick — (Mrs.), lodging ho. 46 Lr. Belgrave pl. Pimlico
Strudwick Thos. cutler & drssng. case mkr. 14 New Bond st
Strudwick William, grocer, 11 Chichester pl. Wandsworth rd
Strugnell Abraham C. & Co. tea dealers, 221 Oxford st
Strugnell Abraham C. grocer, 9 Adam's row, Hampstead rd
Strugnell Chas. E. fancy cabinet mrk. 63 West st. Smithfield
Strugnell Frederick Wells, grocer, &c. 109 Edgware road
Strugnell James, desk & dress.case mkr.14Cross st. Hatn.gdn
Struthers William, slate merchant, 28 Parliament st. & 57 Millbank st. Westminster
Strutt William George & Joseph, cotton spinners, 45 Fore st. Cripplegate
Strutt Charles Edward, surgeon, 4 Adelaide st. Strand
Strutt George, ironmonger, 5 St. George's st. Albany rd
Strutt John, solicitor, 18 Buckingham st. Adelphi
Strutt Joseph, bookbinder, 1 Streatham st. Bloomsbury
Strutton Jane (Mrs.), straw bonnet mfr. High st. Stk. Nwgton
Strutton Charles, lighterman, 33 Commercial rd. Lambeth
Strutton Louis, lighterman, 32 Commercial road, Lambeth
Strutton Wm. timber mercht. & survyr. 32 Com. rd. Lmbth
Strutz Wm. coal dealer, 11 Cannon st. Ratcliff highway
Stuart George & Co. merchants, 6 Nicholas lane
Stuart Jsph. & Son, irish & for. prov. agts. 43 K. Wm. st. City
Stuart Wm. Forbes&Co.merchts.&fishfctrs.104Lwr.Thames st
Stuart Archibald, *Feathers* P.H. Church st. Deptford
Stuart Abel, physician, West cot. South bank, Regent's pk
Stuart David, baker, 6 Stockbridge terrace, Pimlico
Stuart David, tailor, 9 Finch lane, Cornhill
Stuart Fras. morocco leather dresser, 10½ Kent pl. Old Kent rd
Stuart Geo. brush maker&turner, 12 Primrose st. Bishopsgate
Stuart George, printer, 38 Rupert st. Haymarket
Stuart D. barrister, 1 Brick ct. Temple
Stuart James, tailor, 3 West st. Golden square
Stuart John, solicitor, 49 Russell square
Stuart Hen. warehouseman,10Constitution rw. Gray's inn rd
Stuart John, queen's counsel, 12 Old square, Lincoln's inn
Stuart John, solicitor, see Capes & Stuart
Stuart John, tailor & draper, 8 Church st. Soho square
Stuart John Arch, solicitor, 6 New inn, Strand
Stuart Samuel, colonial broker, 21 Gt. Tower st. City
Stuart Sarah (Miss), milliner, 19 Conduit st. Regent st
Stuart Stephen, tailor to her Majesty's household, 36 Great Marlborough st
Stuart Wm. attorney, see Durrant, Stewart & Maxwell
Stuart Wm. woollen manufacturer, see Bevan & Stuart
Stuart Wm. Backhouse, tailor & draper, 4 Wilson st. Finsby
Stubbens Edwin, egg & butter mer. 115 Regent st. Lambeth
Stubbing & Lee, meat salesmen, Leadenhall market
Stubbing Ann (Miss), butcher, 17 Charing cross
Stubbing Benjamin, cattle salesman, 17 West Smithfield
Stubbing John, tobacconist, 262 Tottenham court road
Stubbings Hannah (Mrs.), milliner, 69 Judd st. Brunswick sq
Stubbings John, chandler's shop, 6 Alfred ter. Cambridge hth
Stubbings Thos. poulterer, 9 Lr. Ranelagh st. Lr. Grosvenor pl
Stubbins Wm. basket maker, 7 Crispin st. Spitalfields
Stubbington George, leather sell. 11 Mercer st. Long acre
Stubbington John, collar maker, 12 Castle st. & 10 Mercer st. Long acre
Stubbs & Absolom, who. grocers & tea dealers, 23 Rood lane
Stubbs Charles, colonial broker, 23 Great Tower st
Stubbs Daniel, linendraper, Church st. Hackney
Stubbs Eliz. (Mrs.), toydealer, 1 Courtney ter. Kingsland rd
Stubbs Frederick, *Fleur de Lis* P.H. 70 Houndsditch
Stubbs George, bent timber merchant, 139 Goswell st
Stubbs James, bookseller & stationer, 10 Upper Baker st
Stubbs James, grocer, Blue Anchor road, Bermondsey
Stubbs John, fruiterer, &c. 163 Lambeth walk
Stubbs John, working jewl. 7 Dufour's pl. Broad st. Golden sq
Stubbs John Holt Eikes, M.D. surgeon, 22 Old Burlington st
Stubbs John Morris, grocer & teadealer, 140 Edgware rd
Stubbs John Wm. wine cooper, 72 Mark lane
Stubbs Peter, cork cutter, 17 Queen st. Grosvenor square
Stubbs Sarah (Mrs.), berlinwareh. 11 Gt. College st. Cmdn. tw
Stubbs William Edward, solicitor, 15 Furnival's inn, Holborn
Stubington Joseph, fruiterer, 1A, Frederick st. Regent's pk
Stubs Edward, furrier & milliner, 29 Ludgate st
Stuchbury Geo. Thos. lighterman, 37 Seething la. Gt. Tower st
Stuchbury Samuel, oilman, &c. 26 Wapping high st
Stuchfield Edward, horse dealer, 7A, Paddington green
Stuchfield John, harness mkr. 33 John st. North, Marylbn
Stuck John, dentist, 166 Grove st. Camden town
Stuck Wm. butcher, 114 Upper Whitecross st. St. Luke's
Stucké, Cuthbertson & Stucké, tailors, 13 Argyll st. Oxfd. st
Stuckey, Reynolds & Co. bankers' agents, 51 Lombard st. City
Stuckey George, outfitting & baby lin. wa. 68 Gracechurch st
Stuckey Robert, tobacconist, 2 Pitt's place, Old Kent road
Stuckey Wm. ship agent, 13 Mitre Chambers & 157 Fench. st

Studd Wm. Keable, builder, 7 Trinity st. Liverpool road
Studer Matthew, watchmaker, 4 Seward st. Goswell st
Studley James, cheesemonger, 8 Pierepoint row, Islington
Stukely John, dairyman, 8 Brydges st. Covent garden
Stultz, Housley & Wain, tailors, 10 Clifford st. Bond st
Stumbke Thos. tailor & habit maker, see Theaker & Stumbke
Stump Samuel John, artist, 7 Cork st. Bond st
Stumpff John Andrew, harp ma. 44 Gt. Portland st. Oxford st
Stunell Charles, tailor, 1 Waterloo st. Camberwell
Stunt Charles, watch manufacturer, 182 Oxford st
Stunt George, iron merchant, 11 Holland st Blackfriars rd
Stunt Henry, saddletree maker, 9 Brownlow st. Drury lane
Stunt Edward, bootmaker, 57 Strand
Stunt Robert, watch manufactr. 19 Spencer st. Goswell rd
Stunt Thos. Patey, auctioneer, 28 New Church st. west, Edgw. rd
Sturch John, butcher, 30 & 4 Churchway, Somers town
Sturch Joseph Gwillim & Co. teadealers, 6 High st. Nwngtn btts
Sturch Wm. carver & gilder 16 Lit. Coram st. Brunswick sq
Sturdee Mary Ann (Mrs.), school, 7 Broomfield pl. Deptford
Sturdy Ann (Mrs.), grocer, 7 Charles pl. Charles sq. Hoxton
Sturge Thos. & Son, oilmen & spermaceti refiners, 6 N. Kent rd
Sturge Danl. coal & stone mer. 35 Bridge whrf. City rd. basin
Sturge Henry J. oil & colorman, 1 Staverton rw. Walworth rd
Sturgeon Charles, barrister, 8 Southampton bldgs. Chanc. la
Sturgeon Jas. portable & medic. baths, 3 New Basinghall st
Sturgeon Edwd. *Coach & Horses* P.H. 36 Crown row, Mile end rd
Sturgeon John, herald chaser, 161 High Holborn
Sturgeon (Mrs.), seminary, 5 Eldon pl. Up. Kennington lane
Sturgeon Thomas Bennett, farmer & dealer in live stock, South Ocendon hall, Essex; & Jerusalem coffee house, Cowper's court, Cornhill
Sturgeon Wm. plumber & ho. decorator, 2 Up. Park pl. Dorset sq
Sturges John, corndealer, 12 Heath pl. Cambridge heath
Sturges John, corn merchant, 23 Orchard st. Portman sq
Sturges Wm. *Bk. of England* P.H. 29 South wf. road, Pdgtn
Sturkey Mary Ann (Miss), grocer, 14 John st. North, Marylb
Sturland Thomas, railway & canal carrier, 126 London wall, & 18 Wharf, City road (Wm. Woolley, agent)
Sturley Thomas, cattle salesman, see Le Neve & Sturley
Sturm Charles, merchant, see Gardner & Sturm
Sturman Benjamin, gunmaker, 42 Kingsland road
Sturman George, gun & pistol maker, 25 East rd. City rd
Sturmy Herbert, solicitor, 8 Wellington st. London bridge Boro'
Sturrock Alexander, baker, 6 Webber st. Blackfriars road
Sturt & Sharp, warehousemen, 91 Wood st. Cheapside
Sturt, Sharp & Ward, who. hosiers, see Ward, Sturt, Sharp & Co
Sturt Edward, butcher, 79 Paul st. Finsbury
Sturt Richard, coachsmith, 12 Lit. Ormond yard, Queen sq
Sturt Robert, *Golden Lion* P.H. Camberwell green
Sturtevant & Co. electrogilders, 3 Newcastle pl. Clerknwl. close
Sturtevant Rd. Lawrence, soap mak. 3 Newcastle pl. Clknwl. cl
Sturtridge Chas. tuscan & straw plait wa. 1 Union st. Bishpsgt
Sturz John James, merchant, Nth. & Sth. American coffee ho
Stutchbury Henry, bookseller & naturalist, 47 Theobald's rd
Stutchbury James, lighterman, 38 Seething lane & Galley-quay, Lower Thames st
Stutchbury Samuel, oilman, 26 Wapping High st
Stutchbury William, beer retailer, Gt. College st. Camden tn
Stutchfield John, fruiterer, 15 New Church st. we. Edgw. rd
Stutely Martin, goods' depository, Chichester pl. Gray's inn rd
Stutely Martin Joseph, architect, &c. 2 Gower st. Bedford sq
Stutfield Chas. & Sons, wine & brandy mers. 139 St George st
Stutter Joel, cutler, 184 Shoreditch High st
Stutter John, hop mer. Kentish buildings, 94 Borough High st
Stutter Thos. printer, 3 & 4 Church row, Bethnal green rd
Styan Thos. Wm. & Thos. & Co. tea & col. brokers, 12 Lit. Tower st
Styant James, plumber, painter, &c. 1 Lr. Sloane st. Chelsea
Styche & Shepherd, grainers, 6 Fountain place, City road
Styche Benjamin, grocer, 40 Stafford place, Pimlico
Style Henry, *Sir John Falstaff* P.H. 46 Houndsditch
Styles Charles, cabinet maker, 80 Paul st. Finsbury
Styles George, baker, 19 Upper Marylebone st. Portland pl
Styles Charlotte (Mrs.), tobacconist, 8 New Bond st
Styles Sarah (Mrs.), milliner, 101 Tooley st
Styles Thomas, cabinet mkr. & paper hanger, 61 Lr. Sloane st
Styles Wm. carpentr. & builder, 5 Barnsbury pl. Upper st. Islgtn
Styles William, *Union Flag & Punch Bowl* P.H. 64 Wapping
Styring Wm. A. camel hair pencil ma. 23 Cross st. Hatton gar
Suart & Simpson, insurance brokers & genl. agts. 13 Birchin la
Subpœna Office, Rolls yard, Chancery lane; hours, term, 10 to 4; vacation, 11 to 1
Such Edwin, chemist, surgeon, &c. 3 Goswell road
Such George, physician, 27 New st. Dorset square
Such John, printer, 29 Budge row, Cannon st
Such Joseph Jas. auctioneer, 20 Bolingbroke row, Walworth rd
Such Thos. carpentr. & undertak. 20 Bowling st. Clerkenwell
Such Thos. Wm. carpenter & bldr. 6 Foundling ter. Gray's inn rd
Such Wm. last & boot tree maker, 86 Long alley, Finsbury
Suchwell Thomas, library, 27 Crescent st. Euston square
Suckley Sam. coal & corn measure ma. 10 Robert st. Blkfrs. rd
Suckling George Fuller, carpenter, 11 Coleman st. buildings
Suckling James, lodging house, 25 Orchard st. Portman sq
Suckling Nathaniel, leather seller, 36 Chapel st. Pentonville
Sudbury Wm. & Co. hat manufacturers, 3 Oxendon st. Haymkt
Sudbury Elizh. (Miss), child bed linen wa. 14 Hanway st
Sudbury Mary Chapman (Miss), lace baby linen wa. 89 Oxford st
Sudbury Henry, coach builder, 21 Queen st. Golden sq
Sudbury Robert, builder, 13 Quickset row, New road
Sudlow & Kingdon, solicitors, 6 N. Palace yd. Westminster
Sudlow, Sons & Torr, solicitors, 20 Chancery lane
Sudlow John, engraver & printer, 134 Aldersgate st
Suffell Charles, mathematical instrument ma. 132 Long acre
Suffolk James Christie, tobacconist, 20 White Hart st. Drury la
Sugar James, corn & coal dealer, 191 Kingsland road
Sugden & Borras, warehousemen, 16 Aldermanbury
Sugden John, statuary, 1 Hargrave ter. Bermondsey New rd. & 3 Coburg rd. Old Kent rd
Sugden Lewis, pianoforte maker, 20 Crawford st. Portman sq
Sugden Robert, boarding school, Camden place, Peckham
Sugden Wm. statuary & mason, 3 Thomas pl. Gravel la. Sthwk
Sugg & Hatchard, furnish. undertakers, 95 York st. Westmr
Sugg Thos. gasfitter & meter maker, 168 Hoxton Old town
Sugg William, gasmeter & apparatus manufacturer, brass-founder, gasfitter & engineer, 19 & 20 Marsham st. Westmr
Suggate William, *Rose & Crown* P.H. 83 Bunhill row
Suggett Samuel, baker, 85 Margaret st. Cavendish sq
Sulley Thos. jeweller, 21 Red Lion yd. Red Lion st. Clrknwl
Sullivan Christopher, optician, 22 Charles st. Hatton garden
Sullivan Dennis, bootmak. & grocer, 9 Little Knightrider st
Sullivan Dennis, hairdresser, 53 James st. Oxford st
Sullivan Henry, marine store dlr. 2 Edward st. Barnsbury rd
Sullivan Jas. lithographer, 22 Chancery la. & Symond's inn
Sullivan John, carpenter, 25 James st. Oxford st
Sullivan John, surgeon, 101 Guilford st. Russell square
Sullivan Michael C. printer, 22 Chancery la. & 7 Symond's in
Sullivan M. Wogan, dentist, 9 Alfred place, Bedford square
Sullivan Richard, beer retailer & jeweller, 4 Deptford bridge
Sullman Richard, baker, 108 Drury lane
Sully Charles, boot & shoe maker, 149 Fenchurch st
Sully Geo. composition ornament mak. 16 Clerkenwell green
Sully Jph. *Whittington & Cat* P.H. 11 Church rw. Beth. gr. rd
Sulman Joseph, plumber & glazier, 7 Brunswick st. Hckny. rd
Sulman Richard, baker, 44 Up. North place, Gray's inn road
Sulman Thomas, springer, liner & polisher, 15 King Edward st. Islington, & 3 King st. Clerkenwell
Sumeran Bartholomew, lookgl. mak. 27 Lisle st. Leicester sq
Sumersell John, bootmak. 21 East st. Crosby row, Walworth
Summer Wm. crape dresser & lace dyer, 63 Worship st. Finsbry
Summerfield Joseph, pocketbk. mak. 26 Noble st. Cheapside
Summerlin James, butcher, 50 Aldersgate st
Summerlin Thomas, fishmonger, 37 Silver st. Golden sq
Summers Hy. & Jas. linendrprs. 6 Commercial pl. Kingsld. rd
Summers Thos. & Son, gold & silver beaters, 19 Little Britain & 89 London wall
Summers Elizabeth Ann (Miss), milliner, 5 Brompton road
Summers Charles, surgeon, 60 Euston square
Summers Edgar Edward, grocer, 1 Chapel pl. Liverpool rd
Summers George, butcher, 15 Gravel lane, Southwark
Summers Hen. grocer & cheesemg. 6 Holmes ter. Kentish tn
Summers James, linendraper, see Farrar & Summers
Summers James, linendraper, 139 Kingsland road
Summers John, carpenter & builder, 21 King st. Soho
Summers Matilda (Mrs.), gold & silver beater, 105 Shoe lane
Summers Philip, late Summers & Smith, manufacturer of linen bands, morocco & fancy papers generally, engraver & printer in gold, embosser of paper hangings, &c. 12 Tabernacle walk, Finsbury
Summers Robert, pawnbroker, 27 & 28 Bath st. City rd
Summers Robert, veterinarian, 6 Spring st. Portman sq
Summers Samuel, chandler's shop, Morning lane, Hackney
Summers Samuel, chemist, 5 Hamilton pl. Deptford High st
Summers Thomas, chandler's shop, 16 Temple st. Hackney rd
Summers Thos. Sedgwick, granary keeper, Bermondsey wall
Summers Wm. black lead pencil manufacturer, 8 Calthorpe place, Gray's inn road
Summers Wm. coppersm. & brazier, 7 Haddon pl. Waterloo rd
Summers Wm. tobacconist, 6 Back st. Horselydown
Summers Wm. who. coffee dealer, 38 Fenchurch st
Summers Wm. workg. goldsmith, see Rawlings & Summers
Summers Wm. Henry, solicitor, 66 Princes st. Leicester sq
Summersby Elizabeth (Mrs.), *Feathers* P.H. 336 Oxford st
Summersby Wm. shoemaker, 65 Strutton ground, Westmnstr

Sumner Chas. special pleader, 10 Farrars bldgs. Temple
Sumner Charles, gasfitter, 9 John st. Tysoe st. Spafields
Sumner Edward, fishmonger, 8 Dockhead, Bermondsey
Sumner Francis, carpenter, 2 Park place, Highbury vale
Sumner George, oilman, plumber, &c. 5 Salmon la. Limeho
Sumner John, jun. engraver, 10 Queen st. Soho
Sumner Mary (Mrs.), workg. jeweller, 1 Churchrw. Houndsdch
Sumner M.A. (Miss), stay&corsetma. 64 Up. Nth. pl. Gray's i. rd
Sumner Rhoda (Miss), milliner, 26 High st. Marylebone
Sumpter Henry, butcher, 6 Francis place, Holloway
Sumpter Henry, engraver, 44 Haymarket
Sumpter Joseph, butcher, 30 Farringdon market
Sumpter Joseph Saml. statuary, 21 Whitmore road, Hoxton
Sumpter Wm. Thos. statuary, &c. 51 Brudenell pl. New North rd
Sumption John, city carman, 7 Clark's bldgs. Snowhill
Sun Evening Newspaper Office, 112 Strand
Sun Fire Office (J. Richards, secretary), 63 Threadneedle st.; 3 Craig's court, Charing cross, & 65 Welbeck st. Cavendish square; see page 2047
Sun Life Assurance Soc. (Chas. Henry Lidderdale, actuary), 63 Threadneedle st.; 3 Craig's court; & 65 Welbeck st.; see page 2047
Sunday School Society (Joseph Eke, hon. sec. Wm. Henry Bruce, asst. sec.), 1 Trump st. Cheapside
Sunday School Society for Ireland (John Johnson, secretary), 32 Sackville st
Sunday School Union (W. H. Watson, P. Jackson, R. Latter, W. Groser, secretaries), 60 Paternoster row
Sunday Times weekly newspaper office, 103 Fleet st
Sunderland Glass Co. (John Watson, agt.), 74 Lwr. Thames st
Sunderland, Dolans' & Co. army clothiers, 97 St. Martin's la
Sunderland Wm. lampblk. &blk. leadma. Canal basin, Hertfd. rd
Sundon Charles, fruiterer, 154 Drury lane
Sunley, Barugh & Co. wine mers. & shippers, 13 St. George st
Sunley John, ship & custom house agent, 11 Water la. Twr. st
Sunley John Maltby, ship & insurance broker, 71 Cornhill
Sunley Robert, grocer & teadealer, 40 Goswell road
Sunman William, tailor, 10 Little Queen st. Westminster
Sunter Elizh. (Mrs.), ironmngr. &gen. smith, 65 Carlislest. Lmth
Sunter John, ironmonger, &c. 4 Elizabeth pl. Westmnstr. rd
Supple John, boot & shoe ma. 56 Freeschool st. Horselydown
Surgey Wm. Palmer, ins. & gen. ag. 13 Langbourn chambers, Fenchurch st
Surman John, poultry salesman, see Sprigens & Surman
Surman Thos. nursery & seedsman, Lavender hill, Wandsw. rd
Surman William Harry, solicitor, 11 New sq. Lincoln's inn
Surmon David, plumber & glazier, 93 Aldersgate st
Surmon Henry, veterinary surgeon, 9 Long lane, West Smithfield, & 70 Bartholomew close
Surmon John, window blind maker, 29 Clothfair, Smithfield
Surr Jane (Miss), boarding house, 25 Friday st. Cheapside
Surr Joseph, sewing silk & twist ma. 12 King st. Cheapside
Surr Timothy, attorney & notary, 80 Lombard st
Surrage John, barrister, Law chambers, 77 Chancery lane
Surrey County Gaol, John Keene, governor, Horsemonger lane, Borough
Surrey Dispensary, 6 Great Dover road, Borough
Surrey Lunatic Asylum, Meadow row, New Kent road
Surridge James, coach builder, see Prin & Surridge
Surridge Henry, *Dolphin* P.H. 60 Coleman st. City
Surridge Wm. wholesale cheesemonger, 21 West Smithfield
Surtees Frederic Richd. barrister, 3 Plowden bldgs. Temple
Surtees William Edw. barrister, 3 Plowden buildings, Temple
Surveyor of Crown Lands Office, 8 Richmond terrace, 10 to 6
Surveyor's Office of the Port of London, 19 Austinfriars; hours of business, 10 to 4
Surveyor of Taxes for the City of London & Inns of Court, 16 Old Jewry; hours of business, 10 to 4
Suse & Sibeth, merchants, 35 Lime st
Sutch John, bootmaker, 28 Marylebone lane
Sutcher John, bootmaker, 28B, Marylebone lane
Sutcliff Jsph. grocer & teadlr. 28 Gt. College st. Westminster
Sutcliff William, chemist & druggist, Camberwell green
Sutcliffe Henry, *Gold Chain* P.H. Tower
Sutcliffe John (Mrs.) ladies' school, 14 Granville sq
Sutcliffe John Knapp, solicitor, 5 New Bridge st. Blackfriars
Sutcliffe Robert F. gold & silver refiner, sweep washer, & dealer in jewellery & second hand plate, 19 Long acre
Sutcliffe Thomas, tailor, 52 Charlotte ter. New cut, Lambeth
Sutcliffe Wm. woollen & stuff manufctr. 20 Lawrence lane
Suter Alfred & Co. auctioneers & general agts. 65 Fenchurch st
Suter Alfred & Co. wine, ale & stoutmerchs. 65 Fenchurch st
Suter Edward, stationer & bookseller, & agent for Patrick Ritchie's patent copying presses, 19 Cheapside
Suter George, bricklayer & plastr. 64 Park st. Camden town
Suter Rich. architect, 28 Fenchurch st. & 62 St. Paul's chyd
Suter Thomas, butcher, 1 Jones st. Davies st. Berkeley sq
Sutherland Charles & Co. colonial brokers, 24 Mincing lane
Sutherland Geo. & Son, corn&coal mers. 3 Grsvnr. pl. Com. rd. e
Sutherland James & Co. merchants, 5 Fen court, Fenchurch st
Sutherland James & Thomas, merchants, 5 Fen ct. Fnch. st
Sutherland Alexander John, physician, 1 Parliament st
Sutherland Alex. John F.G.S. physician, 1 Parliament st
Sutherland Alex. Rt. F.R.S., F.G.S. physician, 1 Parliament st. & Silver hill, Torquay
Sutherland Elizh. (Mrs.), nursery, Maida vale, Edgware rd
Sutherland John, tailor, 10 Upper Fitzroy st. Fitzroy sq
Sutherland William, oilman, 55 Gainsford st. Horselydown
Suthers William, tobacconist, 11 Eagle st. City road
Suthery Harriet (Miss), milliner, &c. 344 Strand
Sutro Bernhard, teacher of languages, 94 London wall
Suttaby Robt. A. & Co. booksellers&publshrs. 1&2 Stationers' ct
Suttie William, glass cutter & stopperer, 12 Gt. Wild st
Suttle James, coal dealer, 15 Bell st. Edgware road
Suttly Joseph, bookbinder, 4 Cross st. Bermondsey, New tn
Sutton, Ewens, Ommanney & Prudence, solicitors to Waterloo Bridge Company, National Loan Fund Society, & London & Brighton Railway Company, 6 Basinghall st
Sutton (R.) Gribble & Sutton, stockbrokers, 22 Royal Excha
Sutton J. & Co. carriers, *Beehive*, 33 Whitecross st. Criplgat
Sutton Joseph & William, sailmakers, 43 Bankside, Southwark
Sutton Wm. & Co. patent medicine ware. 10 Bow church yd
Sutton Estate Off. (J. Tidd Pratt), 5 Bolton st. Piccadil. 11 to 3
Sutton Chas. *Union Arms* P.H. Union road, Clapham rise
Sutton Elizabeth (Mrs.), coffee rooms, 4 High st. Shadwell
Sutton Ellen, dressmaker, 16 Grosvenor st. west
Sutton Ellice Price, solicitor, 40 Gt. Ormond street
Sutton Francis, optician, 3 Gt. May's bldgs. St. Martin's la
Sutton George, butcher, 9 Kingsland row, Dalston
Sutton George, coal dealer, 3 Broad st. Lambeth
Sutton George, optician, 16 Bridge road, Lambeth
Sutton George, tobacconist, 1 Broad court, Long acre
Sutton Henry, baker, 2 Well st. Mile end new town
Sutton Hen. tallow chandler & oilman, 23 Whitechapel road
Sutton Jas. wine mer. & com. agt. 3 Budge row, Watling st
Sutton John, beer retailer, 34 Charles st. Commercial road
Sutton John, boot & shoemaker, 13 Frith st. Soho
Sutton John, bricklayer, 8 Little Brook st. New road
Sutton John, cheesemonger, 3 Lit. St. Andrew st. Seven dials
Sutton John, grocer, 14 Crown row, Walworth road
Sutton John, hairdresser, 21 Park terrace, Regent's park rd
Sutton John, leather dresser, 20 New st. Abbey st. Bermondsey
Sutton John, stockbroker, 5 Angel court, Throgmorton st
Sutton John, surgeon, 1 Crown st. Finsbury
Sutton John, tailor & breeches ma. 48 Old Broad st. City
Sutton Lewis, corn dealer, 13 Shadwell High st
Sutton Martin, furniture bro. 38 Wellington pl. Stepney
Sutton Samuel, chairmaker, 15 North row, Grosvenor square
Sutton Samuel, cutler & jeweller, 68 Old Bailey
Sutton Stephen, oil & italianwa. 7 Cardigan pl. Kenngtn. cross
Sutton Thos. *Bricklayers' Arms* P.H. 201 Up. Whitecross st
Sutton Thos. brushmaker, 15 Gt. Crown ct. Lit. Pulteney st
Sutton Thos. powder flask & shot pouch ma. 58 Berwick st
Sutton William, bricklayer & plasterer, 46 Gee st. Goswell st
Sutton William, butcher, 8 Featherstone st. City road
Sutton William, butcher, 3 Gt. Chapel st. Westminster
Sutton William, cutler & hardwareman, 144 Fleet st
Suvardi Gaetano, fancy bird cage ma. 42 St. George st
Swabey Henry B. proctor & notary, 2 Paul's bakehouse ct
Swaffield Joseph, tin, iron & zinc worker, 20 Fieldgate st
Swain Job, tailors, &c. to the Queen, 379 Oxford st
Swain & Rice (Misses), academy, Wright's la. Kensington
Swain Daniel, beer retailer, 40 Praed st. Paddington
Swain Henry Charles, cowkeeper, 21 John st. Dockhead
Swain Jane (Mrs.), millinery & lacewa. 38A, Lamb's Conduit st
Swain James, book & printseller, 14 Gt. Marylebone st
Swain Jane (Mrs.), millinery&lace wa. 38A, Lamb's Conduit st
Swain John, who. comb manufactr. 25 Warren st. Fitzroy sq
Swain Joseph, engraver on wood, 18 Elder st. Norton folgate
Swain Richard Thos. trimming seller, 41 High st. St. Giles'
Swain Sarah (Mrs.), corn chndlr. 16 South st. Grosvenor sq
Swain Thos. music&musicl. instm. sellr. 53 Up. Baker st. Nw. rd
Swain Wm. linendraper, &c. 21 Cleveland st. Fitzroy sq
Swain Wm. John, pianoforte tuner, 43 Michael's pl. Bromptn
Swaine, Boord & Co. distillers & wine mers. Bartholomew clo
Swaine Hen. J. & Joseph, hop & seed mers. 9½ Counter st. Boro'
Swaine & Isaac, whip manufacturers to the Queen, Prince Albert & the royal family, sponge importers & general warehousemen, 185 Piccadilly
Swaine (Misses), ladies' school, 22 Surrey sq. Old Kent rd
Swaine Benj. tinman & brazier, Montevideo pl. Kentish tn
Swaine Henry, tin plate worker, 14 York pl. Westminster rd

Swaine John, engraver, 28 Great Pulteney st. Golden sq
Swaine John, linendrapers, 40 Chapel st. Edgware rd
Swaine Richd. Hinds & Wm.curriers,1Coppice rw. Clerknwll
Swaine Wm. Edward, physician, 41 Foley place
Swainland George, dairy, 97 Poplar High st
Swainsbury Samuel, cabinet turner, 7 Finsbury market
Swainson Charles & Co. calico printers, 87 Watling st
Swainson & Gould, cotton & wadding mfrs. 60,61&62Wood st
Swainson Geo.watch &chrnmtr.ma.13Clayton st.Kensington
Swainson Wm. fringe & worsted manufr. & importer of berlin wool,&c. 72 Wood st. City
Swainson John, *Peacock Inn*, 6 Islington High st
Swainston Richard, *Queen's Head* P.H.23Gt. Bath st.Clkwl
Swale Ralph&Wm.Hen.booksellers,21 Gt.Russell st. Blmsby
Swale James, tailor, 23 Cross st. Blackfriars road
Swale John Wm. linendraper, see Wilson & Swale
Swale William, tailor, 50 Coppice row, Clerkenwell
Swallow Benjamin, bookseller, 17 Holywell st. Strand
Swallow Fred. statnr. & newsvendr. 63 Pratt st. Camden twn
Swallow Martin, stationer, 7 Marchmont st. Brunswick sq
Swallow Rd. L. *York Minster* P.H. Philpot st. Com. rd. ea
Swallow Wm. marine store dlr. 21 Earl st. ea. Lisson gr. Nth
Swan & Edgar, silk mercers, haberdashers, linendrapers, hosiers & furriers, &c. 39, 41, 45, 47, 49 & 51 Quadrant, Regent st. & 9, 10 & 11 Piccadilly
Swan, Pearce & Co. warehousemen, 29 St. Paul's churchyd
Swan River News & Western Australian Chronicle, monthly newspaper, 17 Fenchurch st
Swan Charles, hard soap maker, 72 Paul st. Finsbury
Swan E— H—(Mrs.), pattern designer,34 Gt. Percy st.Clkwl
Swan George, soap maker, 94 St. John st. Clerkenwell
Swan Henry, solicitor, 2 Gt. Knightrider st. Doctors' com
Swan Hugh, laceman, 15 Hanway st. Oxford st
Swan Hugh, straw bonnet wareh. 59 High st. Camden town
Swan John, bookseller, see Ives & Swan
Swan John, straw bonnet maker, 35 Windmill st. Tot. ct. rd
Swan Joseph, carpenter & undertaker, 9 Hoxton market
Swan MaryAnn(Mrs.)*Adam & Eve*P.H.1 Paradise ter. Islngtn
Swan Robert, meat salesman, 12 New Newgate market
Swan Robert, solicitor, 4 Serjeant's inn, Fleet st
Swan Samuel, bed & mattress maker, 146 St. John st. rd
Swan Samuel, linendraper, 85 Albany road, Camberwell
Swan Sarah (Mrs.), chandler's shop, 28 Plumber st. City rd
Swan Susan(Mrs.),bread baker,&c. 194 Bishopsgate without
Swan Wm. *Peacock* P.H. 41 Minories
Swancott John, dairy, 24 Kirby st. Hatton garden
Swann Charles, barrister, 1 Hare court, Temple
Swann David Leonard, dyer, &c. 51 Upper North pl. Gray's inn rd. & 34 Myddelton st. Clerkenwell
Swann Henry Thomas, fishmonger, 1 Portman st. Portm. sq
Swann John, cart grease mfr. 4 Hodson st. Newington butts
Swann John Howes, linendrap. 3 Crombie's row, Coml. rd. e
Swann Joseph, furn. broker, 10 Baynes row, Coldbath fields
Swann Mary (Mrs.), lodging house, 10 Southampton bldgs
Swann Moses, plumber, &c. 44 Theobald's road, Red Lion sq
Swann Richard, butcher, 1 & 2 Cross st. Blackfriars road
Swann Robert, grocer, 7 Cambridge place, Edgware road
Swann Robert, working goldsmith, 33 York st. Westminster
Swann Sophia (Mrs.), lodging ho. 43 Southampton buildings
Swann Wm. butcher, 1 Salmon pl. Grange rd. Bermondsey
Swannell James, butcher, 4 Goldsmith place, Hackney rd
Swannell John, butcher, 41 Southampton st. Pentonville
Swannell Sarah(Mrs.),chandl's.shp.71 Margaret st. Hkny.flds
Swannell Thos. butcher, 5 Woodland pl. St. John's wood
Swanston Clement Tudway, queen's counsel, 51&52 Chancery la
Swanston Thos. plumber, &c. 52 South st. South Audley st
Swanton Ann (Mrs.) & Son, meat salesmen, 51 Shambles, & 16 Newgate market
Swanton Wm. butcher, 12 Lambeth lower marsh
Swatman Thomas, brush ma.& turner, 17 Charles st. Grosv. sq
Swatton Henry, Thos. dutch rush importer, 3 Dean st. Soho
Swayne & Bovill, guano importers & dlrs. bonded warehouse, Millwall, Poplar, & 19 Abchurch lane
Swayne & Bovill, patent railway wheel makers & engineers, Millwall, Poplar, & 19 Abchurch lane
Swayne John & Co. saw mills, 9 Mermaid ct. 119 Boro' High st
Swayne George, wine merchant, 19 Abchurch lane, City
Swayne Herbert Wigan, surgeon, 25 Goswell road
Swears & Sons, hosiers, glovers, shirt makers & flannel factors, & lilliputian warehouse, 2 New st. Covent garden
Swedish & Norwegian Consulate, 2 Crosby sq
Sweeny Chas. Stewart, physician, 11 Chester pl. Hyde pk. sq
Sweet & Bailey, teadealers, 38 South Audley st
Sweet Alfred, corndealer, 18 Leather lane, Holborn
Sweet Andrew, ironmonger, 20 St. James's pl. Hampstead rd
Sweet George, barrister, 60 Chancery lane
Sweet John, builder, 59 Wilsted st. Somers town
Sweet John, hairdresser, 4 Steyman's row, Holloway road
Sweet Stephen, law bookseller, 1 & 3 Chancery lane, Fleet st
Sweet Thomas, butcher, Church st. Stoke Newington
Sweet Thomas, carver & gilder, 9 Rathbone place, Oxford st
Sweet Wm. carver & gilder, 38 Chancery lane
Sweeting Alfred, printer, 15 Bartlett's buildings, Holborn
Sweeting Charles, solicitor, see Lowe, Sweeting & Byrne
Sweeting George Waters, ship owner & builder, 3 Paradise row, Clyde dock, Rotherhithe
Sweeting John S. fish & oyster merchant, 159 Cheapside
Sweeting Robinson, hay salesman, Angel, 85 Whitechapel
Sweetland John, cowkeeper, 2 Alfred mews, Tottenham ct. rd
Sweetland John Park, solicitor, 3 Union court, Old Broad st
Sweetland Michael, baker, 32 St. John st. road
Sweetland Stephen Haymon, baker, 1 Portsdown ter. Kilburn
Sweetland Wm. Frost, cowkeeper, 64 Jermyn st. St. James's
Sweetman Geo. furn. japanner, 4 White Lion ct. Seven dials
Sweetman Joseph, bread & bis. baker, 9A, Lit. Chapel st. Westmr
Sweetman Wm. grocer, 11 Baldwin's gardens, Leather lane
Sweetman Michael, surgeon, 47 St. John's st. Clerkenwell
Sweetzer Mary A. (Mrs.), school, 3, Halton pl. Cross st. Islingtn
Swendall Richard, turner, 41 Thomas st. Brick lane
Swepson Wm. furnishing ironmonger, 68 Cannon st
Swepstone Martha (Mrs.), la. school, 1 St. Geog's. pl. St. Geo. st
Swift John & Chas. Wm. printers, 1 Glo'ster pl. East st. Wwth
Swift Abel, corn dealer, 41 Somerset place, Hoxton
Swift Algernon H. iron mer. 21 Crosby Hall chambers
Swift Chas. stove manufacturer, 10 Addle st. Wood st
Swift Cordall S. tobacconist, 128 Gt. Saffron hill, Hatn. gdn
Swift George, cabinet maker, 35 Store st. Bedford sq
Swift Isaac, job master, 1 Gower mews, Torrington pl
Swift James, bookseller, 4 Little Queen st. Westminster
Swift John, shoe agent, see Belcher & Swift
Swift Owen, *Horseshoe* P.H. 25 Tichborne st. Haymarket
Swift Richard Levinge, barrister, 89 Chancery lane
Swift Richard, iron & tinplate worker, see Fowler & Swift
Swift Richard, wholesale & export shoe manufacturer & agent for the northamptonshire shoe manuftrs. 87 Hatton grdn
Swift Stephen, engraver, 41 Sekforde st. Clerkenwell
Swift Wm. Henry, tailor & draper, 29 Aldgate High st
Swifte Edmund Lenthal, keeper of the jewel house, Tower
Swimming Society (J. Strachan, treas.), 3 Dean st. Westmtr
Swinborn John, coal & corn dealer, 1 Hales ter. Commrcl. rd
Swinbourn Wm. *Cross Keys* booking off. 108 St. John st. Smthfl
Swinburn George, commercial boarding house, 7 Falcon sq
Swinburn Hen. mrcht. & drysalter, 22 Gt. Bush la. Cannon st
Swinburn Robert, stone mason, 57 White Horse st. Stepney
Swinburn Samuel, varnish manuftr. 34 Spring st. Paddington
Swinburn William, carman, 49 Bell st. Edgware road
Swinburne R. W. & Co. manfrs. of plate polished patent crown, sheet & cylinder glass (Wm. Kidd, agt.), Red Bull wharf, Up. Thames st.; manftry. South Shields & Newcastle-upon-Tyne
Swinburne Thomas, barrister, 11 South square, Gray's inn
Swinburne Wm. engineer, Bridge st. Surrey side Westmr. brdg
Swindell Thos. springer & liner, 14 Berkley ct. Clerkenwell
Swindells James, secret springer, 51 Perceval st. Clerkenwell
Swindells Thomas, upholsterer, 118 Aldersgate st
Swinden Charles, coffee rooms, 41 Gibson st. Waterloo rd
Swindley Joseph, baker, 10 Church lane, Kensngtn. grvl. pits
Swiney Bryan, skein silk dyer, 7 Elder st. Norton folgate
Swinford Wm. & James, lithographic printers, 276 Strand
Swinford John, cornfactor, Jack's coffee house, Mark lane
Swingler Rebecca (Mrs.), flourfactor, 144 Tottenham ct. rd
Swinnerton Rd. chinaman, 6 Cumberland row, King's cross
Swinnock William, painter, 44 Monkwell st. Falcon sq
Swinscow Wm. & Rd. B. hat mfrs. 64&65 Hatfield st. Stamfd. st
Swinstead Bernard, straw hat warehouseman, 32 Oxford st
Swinstead Charles, milliner, 15 Ludgate hill
Swinstead John, milliner, 4 Sydney alley, Leicester sq
Swinstead John, straw hat ma. 28 & 30 Blackman st. Borough
Swinstead William, milliner, 4 Norton folgate
Swinstead Wm. milliner & straw hat manfctr. 84 Oxford st
Swinton Wm. & Co. commission merchants, 49 Moorgate st
Swinyard Thos. G. tobac. pipema. 16 Gardiner's la. Yk. st. Wstmr
Swire Roger, chemist & druggist, 14 Edgware rd. Marylebone
Swonnel Saml. & Son, pat. maltsters, Comcl. cof. ho. Mincing la
Swygart Jsph. mathematicl. inst. ma. 43 Edmund st. Kngs crss
Sydenham Soc. (James R. Bennett, M. D. sec.), 45 Frith st. Soho
Sydenham Wm. bootma. & saddler, 54 Rathbone place
Sydenham Wm. *Harp* P.H. 13&14 Little Russell st. Covnt. grdn
Sydenham William, jeweller, 17 Dean st. Fetter lane
Syder Mingay, physician, 61 Upper Stamford st
Sydney Edward Isaac, solicitor, 7 Liverpool st. Bishopsgate
Sydney Sydney Isaac, solicitor, 27 Bevis marks, St. Mary axe

Syeds Agnes(Mrs.),compass & math. inst. ma.379Rotherhithe
Syeds John Ramsey, tobacconist, 378 Rotherhithe st
Syer Jas. I. & Co. auctioneers&surv.29A,New Bridge st.Blkfs
Syer Edmund, cabinet maker, 3 New North st. Finsbury
Syer Jas. Joseph, architect & surv. 29 New Bridge st. Blkfrs
Syer John, baker, 3 Hamilton row, Bagnigge wells road
Syer Wm. cabinet maker, &c. 12 South st. Finsbury market
Syers Chas. fishmonger, &c. 20 Sidney pl. Commercial rd. ea
Syers Morris R. gen.mercht.&shipping agt. 147 Fenchurch st
Sykes John & Co. tobacco manufs. 5 Redcross st. Cripplegate
Sykes John & Son, patent powder flask makers (Alfred Binyon, agent), 40 Tavistock st. Covent garden
Sykes & King, who. clothes warehouse, 84 & 85 Tower hill
Sykes Richd. & Joseph & Co. tobacco manfs. 6 Bread st. hill
Sykes Edward, special pleader, 2 Inner Temple lane
Sykes James, box maker, 4 Holywell row, Worship st
Sykes John, tobacco & snuff ma. 157 Bishopsgate without
Sykes John, wholesale clothes wareho. 84 & 85 Tower hill
Sykes John,winecooper & bottle mer.7Oliveter.Cmbwl.Nw.rd
Sykes John, wine & spirit merchant, 2 Chancery lane
Sykes Joseph, tailor, &c. 6 Star alley, Fenchurch st
Sykes Thomas, cloth cap ma. 23 Lit. Windmill st. Golden sq
Sykes Thomas, hosier, 9 Upper st. Islington
Sykes William, dealer & timber merchant, 11 Osborne st. Whitechapel; & 14½ Palace row, New road, St. Pancras
SykesWm.wax & tallow chand.7 York st. Middlesex hospital
Sylvester John, butcher, 10 Lower st. Islington
Sylvester John, butcher, 34 New Manor st. Chelsea
Sylvester John, civil engineer, 96 Gt. Russell st. Bloomsbury
Sylvester Nathaniel, merchant, licensed custom house, commercial & foreign agent, 65 Lower Thames st. corresponding with Messrs. Denis, of Paris
Sylvester Peter, tinplate worker, 75 Strutton ground
Sylvester William, butcher, 84 & 85 Chancery lane
Sym Andrew, stock & share broker, 9 Tokenhouse yard
Syme William, printer, Blackhorse yard, Rathbone place
Symes Capt. Bathurst, resident director of *Port of London & Thames Assurance Association*, 65 Lower Thames st
Symes Edmund Sheppard, surgeon, 77 Grosvenor st. Bond st
Symes John C. solctr.see Teesdale, Symes, Weston & Teesdale
Symes Joseph, cheesmgr. 6 Middle Queen bdgs. Knightsbdg
Symes Joseph Henry, general salesman, 70 Kingsland road
Symes Louisa (Mrs.), grocer, 2 Royal Hospital row, Chelsea
Symes Rebecca(Mrs.),clock,&c.ma.15Anderson'sbdgs.Cityrd
Symes Robert, dining rooms, 7 Water lane, Blackfriars
Symes William, surgeon, 3 Tavistock square
Symes William, teadealer, 19 Victoria road, Pimlico
Symm Joseph, mercht.&coml. agt. 2 Turnwheel la. Cannon st
Symmonds Mary (Miss), *Crown* coffee rooms, 37 Carey st
Symmonds Robert, teadealer, 20 Marchmont st. Brunswk. sq
Symmonds Wm. hairdresser, 119 Gt. Titchfield st. Oxford st
Symmons Levy, glass & chinaman, 31 Duke st. Aldgate
Symmons Samuel, glass cutter, 30 Duke st. Aldgate
Symmons Sophia (Miss), ladies' school, 11 Paddington green
Symonds & Duff, accountants, 29 Poultry
Symonds Geo.&Co.wine & spirit mers. 2 Hammet st.Minories
Symonds Jas. & John, cattle salesmen, 60 West Smithfield
Symonds Jas. C. & Nathl. pawnbrokers, 38 Baldwin's grdns
Symonds Rd. & Son,madeira & gen. mers.& agts. for the Duc de Montebellos champagnes, 2 Ingram ct. Fenchurch st
SYMOND'S INN, 22 Chancery lane
Symonds Andrew, market gardener, Lombard st. Battersea
Symonds Arthur, registrar of metropolitan buildings, 3 Trafalgar square, Charing cross
Symonds Edward, butcher, 6 Lamb st. Spital square
Symonds Erasmus,*Star* P.H.4 Nag'sHead ct.Gracechurch st
Symonds Henry, carpenter, 2 John st. Davies st. Berkeley sq
Symonds Horatio, tailor, 15 Great Winchester st
Symonds John, hairdresser, 2 Sherborne lane, City
Symonds John, *Ipswich Arms inn*, 3 Cullum st. Fenchurch st
Symonds John, ironmonger, 91 Goswell road
Symonds John, *Saracen's Head inn*, waggon office, 5 Aldgt
Symonds John, tailor, 1 Sand's buildings, Islington
Symonds Nathl. W. sec. to gen. ship owners soc. 72 Cornhill
Symonds Price Chas. surgeon, 15 Alfred pl. Newington cswy
Symonds Robert, cabinet ma. 6 John's pl. Camberwell new rd
Symonds Thomas, meat salesman, Leadenhall market
Symondson Philip, musical bell ma. 32Wellesly st.Somers tn
SymondsonWm.mercht.&ins.broker,15Unionct.OldBroad st
Symonds & Round, ship & ins. & cust. house agts. 17 Mark la
Symon's Wharf, John Henry & George Scovell, Morgan's lane, between 79 & 80 Tooley st
Symons Andrew, engineer, 17 Lombard st. Southwark bdg. rd
SymonsArthur,chandler'sshop,106Shaftesburyst.Nw.Nth.rd
Symons Chas. plate chest ma. & joiner, 1 Princes st. Fiztroy sq
Symons Elias Octavius, builder, see Souter & Symons
Symons Edwd. Wm. clk. Thames Police ct. Arbour st. east
Symons Geo. carpenter & builder, 8 Rawstorne st. Brompton
Symons Henry, bottle dealer, 82 East st. Manchester sq
Symons Hen.Sam. milliner, &c. 8Oddy's row, Islington green
Symons Jellinger C. barrister, 1 Harcourt buildgs. Temple
Symons John, cider merchant, 12 Hungerford whf. Strand
Symons John, clerk to Guardians of Poplar, 1Kerby st. E.I.rd
Symons John, dyer, Stratford, Essex
Symons John, general dealer, 38½ Cowper st. City road
Symons John, solicitor, 33 Old Jewry
Symons Joseph, grocer, &c. 28 Queen's row, Pimlico
Sympson Joseph Dyer,solicitor, see A'Beckett,Son&Sympson
Symons Thomas, bookseller & news agent, 11 Brompton row
Symons Thomas, currier & lea. sell. 6 Cornwall rd. Lambeth
Symons Wm. *Albion* coffee rooms, 99 OldGravel la.Wapping
Symons Wm. M. printer & bookseller, Bridge st. Vauxhall
Sympson Betsey (Mrs.), broker, 4 Queen st. Pimlico
Syms Benj. umbrella maker, 14 Tichborne st. Haymarket
Syms Brown John, lighterman, 8 Parish st. Tooley st
Syms Thomas, lighterman, 49 Gainsford st. Horselydown
Synnot Robert, M.D. surgeon, 8 Westbourne pl. Sloane sq
Syred Daniel, nurseryman, &c. Blomfield road, Maida hill
Syrett Henry, laceman, 18 York row, Kennington road
Syrett Thomas, carman, Redmead la. Hermitage, Wapping
Syrett Wm. carpenter, 10 Walbrook row, New North road
Syrrett Frederick, stationer, 72 Old Broad st
Szlumper Albert, tailor, 45 Gerrard st. Soho

TAAFFE James, lodging house, 14 Duke st. St. James's
Taaffe John, stationer, 128 Crawford st
Tabb Henry, tobacconist, 44 Munster st. Regent's park
Tabb James, coffee rooms, 34 Seymour pl. Bryanstone sq
Tabb John, teadealer & grocer, 2 Up. Eaton st. Pimlico
Taber James, bricklayer, 29 Lit. Albany st. Regent's park
Taber John, wine merchant, see Johnson, Taber & Johnson
Taber Robert Wilkins, plumber, 10 Low. James st. Golden sq
Tabernacle Almshouses(Edwd. Selby, sec.), Tabernacle row, City road
Tablet Weekly newspaper, 3 Brydges st. Covent garden
Tabor John Joseph, fishmong.Bull's head pas. Leadenhl. mkt
Tabor Wm. varnish & japan maker, 21 Gt. Trinity lane
Tabor Wm. wholesale druggist & perfumer, 21 Gt.Trinity la
Tabraham John, rag merchant, 51 Fore st. Limehouse
Tabrum Charles, brush manuf. 2 Weston pl. King's cross
Tabrum Hen.hop & seed fac. 84 Queen's Head inn yard, Boro'
Tabrum Horace, gold beater, 17 Nassau st. Middlesex hospl
Tabrum William, stuff warehouse, 95 Wood st. City
Tacey John C. school stationer, 18 City road, Finsbury
Tackle Porters' Station, 3 Green Arbour court, Old bailey
Tackle Richard, baker, Creek road, Deptford
Tackley Edward, cutler, 9 Chalton st. Somers town
Tackley Edward, tailor, 6 Manchester bldgs. Holloway road
Tackley Wm. jun. tailor, 88 Upper st. Islington
Tackley Wm. sen. tailor, 19 Bartholomew terrace, St. Luke's
Taddy & Co.manufacturers of,&wholesale dealers in tobacco, snuff & cigars, 45 Minories
Tadloo David, butcher, 11 Diamond row, Stepney green
Tadloo James, butcher, 21 Plumber st. City road
Tadloo Joseph, scale maker, &c. 75 Sun st. Bishopsgate
Tadman Thos. patten & clog maker, 276 Kent st. Borough
Taft John, stone mer. & bldr. 2 Irongate wf. Paddington basin
Tagart Chas. Fortescue,solicitor,1 Raymond bldgs.Gray's inn
Tagg Thos. & Son, fur. undertkrs. 166 Bishopsgate st.without
Tagg Adah (Mrs.), fancy brush manuf. 29 Mary st. New rd
Tagg Ann (Mrs.), grocer & teadealr. 12Norris st.Haymarket
Tagg Elizabeth (Miss), jeweller, 17 Middle row, Holborn
Tagg John, fruiterer, 15 Grace's alley, Wellclose square
Tagg Peter, slopseller, 75 Tooley st
Tagg Wm. furn. undertaker, 49 Chichester pl. Gray's inn rd
Tagliabue C. optician, &c. see Casella & Tagliabue
Tagliabue Angelo, barometer mak.3 Charles st.Hatton gdn
Tagliabue Anthony, barometer mak. 31 Brook st. Holborn
Tagliabue John, barometer maker, 11 Brook st. Holborn
Tahourdin Charles, attorney, see Scott & Tahourdin
Tailby William, tailor, 8 Adam st. west, Bryanstone sq
Tailor Nathaniel, boot maker, 20 Old Compton st. Soho
Tailors' Benevolent Institution (William Hall, secretary), 32 Sackville st. Piccadilly
Tait Adam, beer retailer, 1 Back st. Horselydown
Tait Henry, tailor, 11 Gt. Chesterfield st. Marylebone
Tait Jas. *Rose & Crown* P.H. 12 Hart st. Duke st. Grosv. sq
Tait James, tin plate worker, 15 Fashion st. Dockhead
Tait William, merchant, 4 Gt. Winchester st
Taite James, tailor & trimming seller, 5 Gt. Portland st
Taite John, jun. tailor, 228 Oxford st
Täkle Christian, tailor, 28 Upper North pl. Gray's inn rd

Taitson Frances (Mrs.), milliner, 2 Providence pl. Lambeth
Talbot George & Henry & Sons, bombazeen & carpet manufacturers (H. Griffith, agent), 57 Basinghall st
Talbot Rd. & Edwd. barge blds. 26 Church st. Rotherhithe
Talbot Robert & Sons, barge builders, 282 Rotherhithe
Talbot Charles, stationer & printer, 174 Tooley st
Talbot Frederic, solicitor, see Richardson & Talbot
Talbot Hon. John Chetwynd, queen's counsel, 1 New ct. Temple
Talbot James Beard, secretary to the London Society for the Protection of Young Females, 17 Ironmonger lane, & Asylum, Tottenham
Talbot Thomas, shoemaker, 32 Charles st. Commercial road
Talbot Wm. iron plate manufacturer & brazier, & wholesale kitchen furniture tinner, 104 Gt. Titchfield st
Talbot Wm. Henry, boot maker, 25 Fore st. Limehouse
Talboys William, tailor, 8 Talbot ct. Gracechurch st
Taleur Mary Ann (Miss), ladies' school, 4 Beak st. Regent st
Talfourd Field, artist, 86 Newman st
Talfourd Thos. Noon, serjt.-at-law, 3 Serj. inn, Chancery la
Tall John & Co. turpentine rectifiers, 103 Hatton garden
Tall Robert, fruiterer, 76 Castle st. East, Oxford st
Tallack John, plasterer, 6 Stanhope st. Hampstead rd
Tallemach Richard, attorney, 13 Serle st. Lincoln's inn
Tallerman Elias, cap & shoe ma. 20 Christian st. St. Geo. Ea
Tallerman Harris, shoe ma. 6 Liverpool bldgs. Liverpool st
Tallibart Louis, watchmaker, 48 Rathbone place
Tallis John & Fredk. publishers, 3 Jewin st. Cripplegate
Tallowchandlers' Hall (John Curtis, clerk), 5 Dowgate hill
Talmadge John T. & Co. tea agts. & who. dlrs. 61 King William st
Talmadge William, barrister, 1 Cloisters, Temple
Talmadge Hen. dyer & scourer, 134 Fetter lane, Fleet st
Talmedge Charles, boot manufr. 3 Wentworth pl. Mile end rd
Talmedge Daniel, grocer, &c. 144 Poplar High st
Tame Henry, scavenger, 14, 17 & 18 Whf. north st. Padngtn. ba
Tame John, law stationer, 5 Took's court, Chancery lane
Tamlyn John, barrister, 44 Chancery lane
Tamlyn John, ham dealer, 25 Blackfriars road
Tammadge Hen. grocer & cheesemo. 6 Margaret st. Wilmgtn. sq
Tamplin George, solicitor, see Blake & Tamplin
Tamplin Rd. Wm. surgeon, 29 Gt. Queen st. Lincoln's inn fields
Tamvacho & Micrulachi, merchants, 18 South st. Finsbury
Tancred Charles, solicitor, 1 Furnival's inn, Holborn
Tancred Henry Wm. queen's counsel, Reform club, 104 Pall mall
Tandy John, brush & toy wareh. 14 Montcomb st. Belgrave sq
Tann Edward & Sons, patentees & manfs. of the double lever guarded reliance lock, latch & double bodied fire proof safes, doors, iron rooms, improved & panneled safe door chest, & of every description of doors for party walls, 2 Minerva terrace; manufactory, 1 Hope st. Hackney rd
Tann Edw. jun. corn merchant, 10 Broughton pl. Hackney rd
Tann Geo. fire proof room & safe ma. 18 Hope st. Hackney rd
Tann James, law stationer, see Gravatt & Tann
Tanner & Raven, milliners, 41 Homer st. & 22 Molyneux st
Tanner & Ward, leather factors, Leadenhall place, Leadenhall market, & 98 Leadenhall st
Tanner Alfred Octavius, solicitor, 4 New Basinghall st
Tanner Benj. lime & cemt. mer. Dowgate wf. Canal rd. Kingsld. ba
Tanner Charles, grocer, 8 Mansell st. Goodman's fields
Tanner Charles William, coal & corn merchant, Stratford
Tanner Geo. auctioneer & appraiser, 2 Elizabeth st. Hackney rd
Tanner George, grocer, 355 Albany road, Camberwell
Tanner George, tailor, 89 Praed st. Paddington
Tanner Geo. Tho. fruiterer, 2 Ann's terrace, Liverpool road
Tanner Henry, tobacconist, 263 Bethnal green road
Tanner James, biscuit baker, 58 Brick lane, Spitalfields
Tanner James, coal dealer, 23 Clift st. New North road
Tanner James, hair dresser, 208 Fleet st
Tanner Jas. Jones, leather & glove wa. 8 Well ct. Queen st. City
Tanner John, cabinetmaker, 73 Minories
Tanner John, carpenter, 37 Wellesley st. Euston square
Tanner John Joseph, solicitor, 53 Moorgate st. Bank
Tanner Joseph, plumber, 162 Bethnal green road
Tanner Jsph. Steph. surveyr. of pavmts. &c. 6 Cross st. Hoxton
Tanner Mary Ann (Mrs.), *Dog & Partridge* P.H. Bow
Tanner Matilda (Miss), treacle ma. see Ferraday & Tanner
Tanner Richard, gold, zinc, steel & platina pen manufactr. to the most eminent mercantile establishments of London & Westminster, &c. 16 Artillery pl. west, Finsbury
Tanner Robert, greengrocer, 19 Sidney st. Goswell rd
Tanner Robert, surgeon, 56 Manchester st. Manchester sq
Tanner Thomas, milliner, 7 Cranborne st. Leicester sq
Tanner William, cheesemonger, 22 Cable st. Wellclose sq
Tanner William, *Swan* P.H. 1 Provost st. City rd
Tanner William, tallow chandler, 1 Beresford st. Walworth
Tanner Wm. watch & clock maker, 3 Church row, Islington
Tanner Wm. Peter, chemist & druggist, 5 Flagon row, Deptford
Tannock James, artist, 16 Newman st. Oxford st
Tanqueray Brothers, wine merchants, 5½ Pall mall
Tanqueray Chas. & Co. rectifiers, Vine st. Bloomsbury
Tanqueray & Wrottesley, wine merchants, 5½ Pall mall
Tanqueray Aveling, merchant, see Pye, Field & Tanqueray
Tanqueray Thomas Butts, solicitor, see Parnell & Tanqueray
Tansley Peter, who. straw hat ma. 122 St. John st. Smithfield
Tansley Samuel, glassman, 11 Dorset st. Portman sq
Tanswell John, solicitor, 5 King's Bench walk, Temple
Tanton George Jsph. vet. forge, 45 Up. North pl. Gray's inn rd
Tanton Thomas, coffee rooms, 163 Drury lane
Taperell Charles, carpenter, 14 Smith's buildings, City rd
Taphouse Wm. engine & mach. smith, 26 Gt. Guildford st. Boro'
Tapiscott William Hogg, carpenter & undertaker, 35 Lisle st. Leicester sq. & Falconberg court, Crown st. Soho
Taplay James, biscuit baker, 1 Prospect row, Mile end rd
Taplay William, cooper, 12 Seymour pl. Camden town
Tapley James, *Crown* P.H. 27 Chalcroft ter. New cut, Lmbth
Tapley John & Son, man. silversm. 40 Roupell st. Cornwall rd
Tapley Francis, fishfactor, 109 Lower Thames st
Tapley Wm. grocer & cheesemonger, 9 Regent st. Westmin
Taplin Christopher, tailor, 265 High Holborn
Taplin George, *Horns* P.H. 1 Hackney rd
Taplin Samuel, fruiterer, 28 Star st. Edgware rd
Taplin Thos. *Rising Sun* P.H. 12 Printer's pl. Bermondsey
Taplin Thos. russian mat & sack warehouse, 8 Queenhithe
Taplin Thos. Jas. outfitting warehouse, 32 Aldgate High st
Taplin William, tobacconist, 10 Hayfield pl. Mile end rd
Tapling, Brothers & Co. carpet warehousemen, worsted & yarn agents, 105 Wood st
Tapling George, wine merchant, 32 Aldermanbury
Tapner Joseph, bricklayer, 30 Arlington st. Sadler's wells
Tapp James, boot & shoemaker, 8 Pleasant row, Holloway rd
Tapp James, haberdasher, 34 Broad st. Bloomsbury
Tapp William, tailor, 63 Harrison st. Gray's inn road
Tappenden Edwd. bricklayer, 3 Arbour st. west. Com. rd. east
Tappenden Thos. tailor, 3 Friendly place, Old Kent road
Tappenden Wm. grocer, 51 Grundy st. East India road
Tapper Charles, draper, 73 Theobald's road
Tapper John Henry, woollendraper, 7 Sun st. Bishopsgate
Tappin Thomas T. *Red Lion* P.H. 41 Hoxton Old town
Tappin William, butcher, 51 Princess st. Edgware road
Tapping George, newsvender, 66 Compton st. Clerkenwell
Tapping Thos. special pleader, 8 Mitre ct. chambers, Fleet st
Tappolet David Lewis & Co. gold, silver & tinsel lace & spangle manufacturers, embroiderers, sword cutlers, &c. 6 Little Britain, & 41 Lombard st
Tappren William, dairyman, 9 Arcade, Hungerford market
Taprell, Holland & Sons, cabinet makers, see Holland & Sons
Taprell William, barrister, 1 Hare court, Temple
Tapscott William Hogg, carpenter & joiner, 35 Lisle st. Lestr. sq
Tapsell Thomas, grocer, &c. 72 Park st. Grosvenor square
Tapson Edmund, lath render, 73 Lower George st. Chelsea
Tapson Joseph, *White Horse* P.H. South row, Covent grdn
Tapster John, *Eastey's hotel*, see Tarbar & Tapster
Tapster Stephen Edwd. *Craven hotel*, 45 & 46 Craven st. Strand
Tarbar & Tapster, *Eastey's hotel*, 27 Southampton st. Strand
Tarbath George, *Castle* P.H. 94 Long alley, Finsbury
Tarbox Edwd. stationer, 13 Cranbourne st. Leicester sq
Tarbutt John, basket maker, 4 Grenada place, Old Kent rd
Targett Edwd. oilman, 10 Cross st. Hoxton New town
Targett Joseph, wheelwright, 9½ Church st. Edgware road
Targett Robert, glass dealer, 25 Windmill st. Finsbury
Targett William, undertaker, 168 Tottenham court road, & 34 New Compton st. Soho
Tarling & Maides, hay & straw salesmen, 28 St. John st. Clkw
Tarling Charles, clothes salesman, 20 Goswell st
Tarling Henry James, inkmaker, 28 St. John st. Clerkenwell
Tarlton James, rope, line & twine manfr. 113 Gray's inn lane
Tarn Thomas, carpet agt. & carpet bag manfr. 5 Goldsmith st
Tarn William, linendraper, 2 Newington causeway
Tarner Geo. Ensor, stationer & news ag. 16 High st. Marylebone
Taroni Andw. & Co. looking-glass ma. 4 Back hill, Hatt. gar
Tarplee John, boot & shoe maker, 101 Old st. St. Luke's, & 107 Blackman st. Borough
Tarr John, coal merchant, Beaufort wharf, Strand, & 8 Brunswick place, City road
Tarrant Alfred, bookbinder, 16 Gt. Queen st. Lincoln's inn
Tarrant George, grocer, 81 Albany road, Camberwell
Tarrant Joseph, carpenter, 33 Union row, New Kent road
Tarrant Walter, silversmith, see Clothier & Tarrant
Tarrant Wm. carpenter & undertak. Southampton st. Cambwl
Tarrant Wm. pawnbroker, 30 Gt. Charlotte st. Blackfriars
Tarrant Wm. Barnes, solicitor, see Bristow & Tarrant
Tarratt Thos. Walter, hosier & glover, 9 Finsbury pavement
Tarring John, architect & surveyor, 23 Charles st. Middlesex hos

Tarris Jane (Mrs.), coffee rooms, 11 Orange st. Red Lion sq
Terry Charles, baker, 25 Penton pl. Pentonville
Tarry James, cheesemonger, 12 St. George's pl. Walworth rd
Tarry John, chandler's shop, 28 Essex st. King's cross
Tarry Samuel, baker, 47 Hackney road
Tarry Wm. pianoforte maker, 4 Theberton st. Islington
Tarsey & Millgate, manchester warehousemen, 3 Gresham st
Tarte William, plumber, 17 Tothill st. Westminster
Tarver Georgina & Son, ship break. & timber mer. Battersea
Tarver John, pastrycook, 27 Coventry st. Haymarket
Tasker & Pound, trunk ma. & undertkrs. 64 & 81 Leadenhall st
Tasker Geo. watchmaker, 13 Back Church la. Whitechapel
Tasker John, cheesemonger, 105 St. John st. Clerkenwell
Tasker Joseph, cheesemonger, 77 Chapel st. Pentonville
Tasker Thomas, wine & brandy merchant, 8 Idol la. Tower st
Tasker Thos. Jas. linen draper, 37 New Church st Lisson gr.
Tasker William, bootmaker, 11 Bartholemew close, City
Tasker William, boot & shoe maker, 112 Goswell st
Tasker Wm. wine & brandy merchant, 7 Idol lane, Tower st
Tasman Thos. & Son, trunkmakers, 11 Grocers' hall ct. Poultry
Tasman Henry, tobacconist, 7 Plumber's row, City road
Tassell Geo. Albert, corndealer, 3 Up. Area, Hungerford mkt
Tassell John, cornchandler, 128 Gt. Suffolk st. Borough
Tassell John, corndealer, 91 Great Suffolk st. Borough
Tassell Samuel, hosier, 22 Holborn
Tassell William, wardrobe dealer, 91 Wardour st. Soho
Tastet Fermin de & Co. merchants, Bishopsgate churchyard
Tatchell & Blunt, newsvenders, 12 Staining lane, Wood st
Tatchell & Noble, russia brokers, 9 George yard, Lombard street, & Baltic coffee house
Tate Ann & Son, goldsmiths, 204 Regent st
Tate & Johnson, saddlers, 92 Park st. Grosvenor square
Tate, Morrison & Co. coal & coke mers. 46 Bankside, Sthwrk
Tate Frederick, carver & gilder, 18 Percy st. Bedford sq
Tate George James, nurseryman, Wandsworth road
Tate James, bootmaker, 6 Holles st. Cavendish square
Tate John, wholesale cheesemonger, 3 Oxford st
Tate James, *Red Lion* P.H. 145 Fenchurch st
Tate Peter Turnbull, pawnbroker, 1 Cambridge st. Golden sq
Tate Richard, seedsman & florist, 15 Upper ter. Upper st. Islgtn
Tate Robert, baker, 58 High Holborn
Tate William, commercial teacher & account. 5 Warnford ct
Tate William, corn dealer, High st. Kingsland
Tate Wm. linendraper, see Moore, James, Tate, Tickell & Co
Tate William, solicitor, 10 Basinghall st
Tate Wm. Blamire, writing ink ma. 9 Artillery st. Bishopsgt
Tatham & Gray, surgeons, 193 High st. Poplar
Tatham & Procter, solicitors, 10 New square, Lincoln's inn
Tatham Thomas Trevor & Son, attorneys, 11 Staple inn, Hlbn
Tatham Thos. Jas. & Son, land agents, 27 Bedford pl. Russell sq
Tatham Alfred Chas. solicitor, 11 Staple inn, & Highgate
Tatham Charles, army cap & accoutrement maker, 37 Charing cross
Tatham Frederick, artist, 17 Newman st. Oxford st
Tatham George, cabinet maker, 115 High Holborn
Tatham Henry, gun, pistol & rifle maker; manufacturer of the patent truss, 37 Charing cross
Tatham Hen. tin plate work. 26 New Montague st Spitalfields
Tatham Hen. wine merchant, 7 Frederick's pl. Old Jewry
Tatham John Lawrence, barrister, 6 New sq. Lincoln's inn
Tatham Joseph, tin plate worker, 22 Ratcliffe highway
Tatham Meaburn, solicitor, see Baxendale, Tatham & Co
Tatham Montagu John, proctor, see Farrer, French, & Tatham
Tatham Robt. Chas. tin plate worker, 37 Brown's la. Sptflds
Tatham Thomas Christopher, merchant, 32 Fenchurch st
Tatham William, solicitor, 22 Throgmorton st
Tatler James, dairyman, 36 King st. Camden town
Tatler Susan (Mrs.), beer retailer, 2 Bingley pl. New road
Tatlock & Bevis, silk brokers, 69 Basinghall st
Tatlock & Love, manufacturers of sewing & mending cotton, cotton waste, &c. lamp & candlewicks, 52 Coleman st
Tatman Elizabeth (Mrs.), baker, Church st. Deptford
Tatman William, general dealer, 13 Wilson st. Finsbury
Tatnell Harry & Co. melting pot & crucible & earthen stove back makers, Whitecross st. Borough
Tatnell Henry, silver plate wareho. 49 Salisbury sq. Fleet st
Tatten David, umbrella mak. 20 Albemarle st. Clerkenwell
Tatten John, oilman, 14 Rotherhithe st. West lane
Tattersall Rd. & Edm. & Son, auctioneers, Grosvenor place
Tattersall George, saddler, 52 Davies st. Berkeley sq
Tattersall Geo. survey. auct. & land agent, 42 Pall mall
Tattersall Geo. agt. for hosiery, gloves, &c. 40 Noble st. City
Tattersall John, wine merchant, 61 Ebury st. Pimlico
Tattersall John, wine & spirit broker, 23 Mark lane
Tattersall Thomas, hairdresser, 3 Maddox st. Bond st
Tattershall Edward B. attorney, 9 Gt. James st. Bedford row
Tatton Jane (Mrs.), *Thomas' hotel*, 25 Berkeley square
Tatum & Johnson, medical school, Kinnerton st. Belgrave sq
Tatum Thomas, surgeon, 3 George st. Hanover square
Tatum William, lithographic printer, Crooked la. chambers
Tatum William, sen. printer, 32 Primrose st. Bishopsgate
Taunton & Bush, stock & share brokers, 26 Austin friars
Taunton Charles, bottle merchant, see Jones & Taunton
Taunton Fredk. Adolps. telescope maker, &c. 22 Norfolk st. Islington, & Brown's cottage, Canonbury sq
Taunton Henry, *Alfred's Head* P.H. 33 Alfred ter. Stepney
Taunton John Colley, surgeon, 48 Hatton garden
Taunton Joseph, *Royal Oak* P.H. Stepney green
Taunton Thomas, surgeon, 14 Devonport st. Oxford terrace
Taunton William Doidge, solicitor, 3 South sq. Gray's inn
Tavender John Geo. calico glazier & dyer, 14 Pool ter. Cityrd
Taverner & Kimpton, linendrapers, 28 Oxford st
Tavener James, grocer, 79 Arthur st. King's rd. Chelsea
Taverner Joseph & Sons, wire drawers & workers, 33 St. John's lane, Clerkenwell, & 141 & 142 Old st. St. Luke's
Taverner Benj. saddler & harness ma. 9 Bowling st. Marylebone
Taverner Edmund, solicitor, 9 New Broad st. City
Taverner Henry, *Mitre* P.H. 3 Mitre st. Aldgate
Taverner Jonathan, *Queen's Head* P.H. 7 Pump yard, Ratcliff, & *Royal Crown* P.H. 131 St. George st
Taverner Joseph, paper stainer, see Archer & Taverner
Taverner Joseph, *Swan tavern* P.H. 5 Mansell st. Goodman's fi
Taverner Lewin, barrister, 9 Gray's inn square
Taverner Stephen, *King William IV.* P.H. Nw. Gravel la Shd
Taverner Thomas, tobacconist, 152 Church st. Shoreditch
Taverner Wm. *Salisbury Arms* P.H. 22 Camomile st. Bishpgte
Taw Abraham, commission agent, 72 Houndsditch
Taw Abraham, writing & copying fluid maker, 72 Houndsditch
Taw Abraham, agent for Huntley & Palmer, wholesale confectioners, makers of the celebrated Reading biscuits, 72 Houndsditch
Taw Abraham, wholesale agent for Reckitt's patent soluble starch, 72 Houndsditch
Tawner Thomas, cigar merchant, 13 Wellclose square
Tawney James Dodsley, attorney, 36 King st. City; and 21 Regent square, Gray's inn road
Tax office, Somerset house; hours of business, 10 to 4
Taxing Masters in Chancery offices, 12 Staple inn, Holborn; hours of attendance from 10 till 4
Tayler Ann (Mrs.), hairdresser, 1 Craven court, Craven st
Tayler Caleb, surgeon, High st. Deptford
Tayler Fanny (Miss), straw hat wa. 4 Frederick pl. Old Kent rd
Tayler George, coal merchant, see Dalgleish & Tayler
Tayler Henry, grocer, &c. 112 & 113 Tooley st
Tayler Henry, solicitor, 15 Church st. Spitalfields
Tayler James, mealman & baker, 65 South Audley st
Tayler James, uphols. house agt. &c. 3 Lower Seymour st
Tayler Joseph, hairdresser, 27 Crispin st. Spitalfields
Tayler Joseph, tailor, 54 Whittlebury st. Euston square
Tayler Lewis, picture cleaner, 20 Cloak lane, City
Tayler Lewis, picture cleaner, 2 Fisher's all. Water la. Fleet st
Tayler Mary (Mrs.), brush & toy dlr. 1 Denmark hill, Cambwl
Tayler Thomas, baker, High st. Bow
Tayler Wm. builder, Brown's buildings, Kensington High st
Tayler Wm. conveyancer, 17 Park st. Grosvenor sq
Tayler Wm. *Malpas Arms* P.H. 7 Charles st. Grosvenor sq
Tayler Wm. oilman, 4 White Hart pl. Low. Kennington la
Tayler Wm. solicitor, New Cross road, Deptford
Tayler Wm. tailor, &c. 75 Wimpole st. Cavendish sq
Tayler Wm. Henry, cheesemonger, 10 Lit. Bell al. Colemanst
Tayler Wm. Jas. barrister, 6 Stone buildings, Lincoln's inn
Tayleure John, book & printseller, 2 Adelaide st. West Strand
Taylor & Aburrow, druggists & drysalters, Idol lane
Taylor & Ball, wine merch'ts. 26 Nicholas lane, Lombard st
Taylor Benjamin & Sons, cabinetmakers, upholsterers, plate glass factors, bedding manufacturers, decorators & steam packet furnishers, 6, 7 & 8 Roebuck pl. Gt. Dover st
Taylor & Black, brush & turnery mnfrs. 50 Gracechurch st
Taylor & Booth, solicitors, 12 Clement's lane, City
Taylor & Bowley, Dowie's patent elastic ladies' & gentlemen's boot & shoe makers, 53 Charing cross, & 25 Spring grdns
Taylor Brothers, chocolate & mustard manfrs. 211 Brick la
Taylor & Brown, law stationers, 5 Serle's pl. Carey st
Taylor & Collison, solicitors, 28 Gt. James st. Bedford row
Taylor David & Sons, merchants, 46 Cross st. Finsbury
Taylor & Doggett, bootma. 35 Davies st. Berkeley sq
Taylor Ebenezer & Son, jewellers, 25 Bartlett's bldgs. Holborn
Taylor E. & S. (Misses) shopkeepers, 15 Church st. Camberwell
Taylor & Fisher, upholst. & undertakers, 110 Fenchurch st
Taylor, Fladgate & Yeatman, oporto mercs. 34 Fenchurch st
Taylor Geo. & Bros. piano fret cutters, 50 Tottenham ct. rd

Taylor & Grignon, italian wa.&wine mr.2 Suffolk st.Pall ml.e
Taylor H. L. & Co. wholesale cast iron fender & fire iron warehouse, 10 Queen st. & 10 Well court, Cheapside
Taylor & Houghton, drapers, 90 & 91 GrandJunct.ter.Edg.rd
Taylor Hugh & John F. coal factors, 36 St. Mary at hill
Taylor Humphrey & Co. rectifiers, King's road, Chelsea
Taylor Jas. & Co. vinegar works, 67½ Long lane, Bermndsy
Taylor John & Co. lightermen, Fresh wharf,2Low.Thames st
Taylor John & Henry, colonial brokers,88 Gt. Tower st. & 16 Mincing lane
Taylor John & Son, emery & flock mills, 11½Redcross st. Boro'
Taylor John & William, anatomical machinists, 37 Strand
Taylor John & William, cotton spinners, Leicester, & 4 Bow churchyard (George Pratt, agent)
Taylor Joseph & Co. linen mer. & bleachers,85Queen st.City
Taylor Joshua & Co. meat salesmen, 45 Newgate market
Taylor & Morrell, cutlers, jewelrs. & perfumers, 101 Oxford st
Taylor, Mouseley&Hatchett, cus.ho.ag.6Savage gdns.Twr.hl
Taylor & Perrott, commission agents, 14 Gresham st
Taylor Richard & Co. merchants, 26 Birchin lane, Cornhill
Taylor Richard & John Edward, printers, Red Lion court, Fleet st. & 3 Robinhood court, Shoe lane
Taylor & Smith, engineers, medallists, die sinkers & seal engravers, 33 Little Queen st. Holborn
Taylor & Son, perfume distil. to the Queen, King's rd. Chelsea
Taylor Thos. & Son, plain&fancy drill & linen manufacturers, 1½ Pancras lane, Bucklersbury; Barnsley & at Manchester
Taylor, Walker & Co. brewers, 37 to 43 Fore st. Limehouse
Taylor & Walton, booksellers & publishers to University college, 28 Upper Gower st. Bedford square
Taylor & Wickings, solicitors, 3 Finsbury trrace, City road
Taylor Wm. & Co. booksellers, 40 Goodge st. Fitzroy sq
Taylor William & Co. curriers, 15 Lisle st. Leicester sq
Taylor Wm. & W. H. coachbldrs. &c. 5 Brook st. Grosvnr. sq
Taylor Abraham, surgeon, 4 Spur st. Leicester square
Taylor Adolphus, fishmonger, 22 London road, Southwark
Taylor Alfred, fruiterer, 32 Queen's road, Bayswater
Taylor Alfred Henry, artist, 72 Charlotte st. Fitzroy sq
Taylor Andrew, crape ma.seeCourtauld, Taylors'&Courtauld
Taylor Ann (Mrs.), seminary, 6 Ashford st. Hoxton
Taylor Anne E. (Mrs.), babylinen wa. see Weale & Taylor
Taylor Anthony, tea dealer, 62 Dean st. Soho
Taylor Arthur, printer, 39 Coleman st
Taylor Augustus, grocer, 1 Park st. Limehouse
Taylor AugustusBanks, custom house agt.26Nicholas la.City
Taylor Benj. conjuring trick ma. 17 Theberton st. Islington
Taylor Benj. grocer & tea dealer, 31 Barbican
Taylor Benj. locksmith, 47 John st. Holland st. Blackfrs. rd
Taylor Catherine (Mrs.), cheesemonger, 92 Rosemary lane
Taylor Charles, baker, 40 Beckford row, Walworth road
Taylor Charles, cabinetmaker, 20 Portsea pl. Connaught sq
Taylor Charles, farrier, 11 Frederick st. Portland town
Taylor Charles, locksmith & bellhanger, 7 Wood st.Spafields
Taylor Chas. plumber & glazier, 43 Barnet st. Hackney rd
Taylor Charles, surgeon, 18 Holland pl. Clapham road
Taylor Charles, tailor, 4 Charles st. Sloane terrace
Taylor Charles, tailor, 3 Cross st. Islington
Taylor Charles, tailor, see Goodman & Taylor
Taylor Charles Alfred, artist, 42 Duke st. St. James'
Taylor Charles Benjamin, oilman, 96 Rosemary lane
Taylor Chas. F. *Grafton Arms* P.H.21Grafton st.Fitzroy sq
Taylor Charles Richard, dealer in ancient coins & medals, 10 Tavistock st. Covent garden
Taylor Chas. Thos. ref. sugar bro. 6 Commercial sale rooms
Taylor Christina (Miss), milliner, &c. see Henrie & Taylor
Taylor Daniel, dyer & scourer, 7 Stepney High st
Taylor Daniel, wine & spirit merchant, 146 Borough High st
Taylor Daniel, upholsterer, 67 Albany road, Camberwell
Taylor David, builder, 11 Charles st.Westminster
Taylor David, fruiterer, 31 Carburton st. Portland road
Taylor David, surgeon, 37 Harleyford pl. Kennington com
Taylor David, watchmaker, 20 Tysoe st. Spafields
Taylor Edmond, cowkeeper, 9 White Horse lane, Stepney
Taylor Edward, baker, 2 Holloway place, Holloway
Taylor Edward, builder, 2 Rodney buildings, New Kent road
Taylor Edward, dairyman, 10 Wilmot st. Russell square
Taylor Edward, fruiterer, 11 Beech st. Barbican
Taylor Edward, ladies' shoemaker, 34 & 62 Lamb'sConduit st
Taylor Edward, tailor, &c. 11 Crosby row, Walworth road
Taylor Edward, teadealer, 89 Upper Whitecross st
Taylor Edward, *Thistle& Crown* P.H.84 Gt.Peter st.Westm
Taylor Edward Abel, auctioneer, 26 Brydges st. Covent gdn
Taylor Edward Bryan, engraver, 2 Macclesfield st. Soho
Taylor Edwin C. stationer & toymr.2 Connaught ter.Edgw.rd
Taylor Elizh. (Mrs.), liqueur rectifr. 18 Marlboro' sq.Chelsea
Taylor Elizh. (Mrs.), *Crown* P.H. 1 Crown court, Fleet st

Taylor Elliot Bower, stationer, 3 Coventry st. Haymarket
Taylor Francis, baker, 66 Bethnal green road
Taylor Francis, builder & undertaker, 43 South Molton st
Taylor Francis, pork butcher, 9 Dockhead, Bermondsey
Taylor Fred. wax & tallow chandler, 3 Orange st. Red Lion sq
Taylor Fred. wholesale teadealer, 104 Upper Thames st
Taylor Gaius Alfred, oilman, 3 Mount Etna, Mile end road
Taylor George, baker, 1 Charlotte row, Holloway road
Taylor George, baker, 7 Seymour place, Camden town
Taylor George, beer retailr.3 Glo'ster pl.East st.Walworth rd
Taylor George, beer ret. 20 Richmond pl.East st.Walwrth rd
Taylor George, bookseller & statnr. 5 Wells row, Islington
Taylor George, cabinet carver, 4 Bacon st. Bethnal green
Taylor George, cabinet maker, 227 Shoreditch
Taylor George, carpenter, &c. 1 George st. Adelphi
Taylor Geo. cloth worker & waterproof. see Huntly & Taylor
Taylor Geo.envelope ma.Fox&Hounds yd.Swallowpl.Hnvr.sq
Taylor George, grocer & italian wa. 8 George st.Portman sq
Taylor George, hairdresser, 35 Brydges st. Covent garden
Taylor George, hatter, 7 Tichborne st. Haymarket
Taylor George, house & estate agent, 62York ter.Regent's pk
Taylor George, linendraper, 78 Bishopsgate without
Taylor George, locksm. & bellhanger, Uxbridge rd. Bayswtr
Taylor George, porkman, 157 Whitechapel road
Taylor George, printer, 7 Little James st. Bedford row
Taylor George, chandler's shop, 56 Castle st. Leicester sq
Taylor George, tailor, 7 Britannia ter. King's rd. west, Chlsa
Taylor George, tailor & habit maker, 151 Regent st
Taylor George, tailor & habit maker, 6 New Bond st
Taylor George, tobacconist, 19 Stafford row, Pimlico
Taylor George, tobacconist & snuff ma.8 Bridge st. Lambeth
Taylor George, warehouseman, see Mason & Taylor
Taylor George, who. & ret. grocer, 53 Bishopsgate without
Taylor George, working jeweller, 28 John's row, St. Luke's
Taylor George Frederick, plumber, Well st. Hackney road
Taylor George Frederick, solicitor, see Smith & Taylor
Taylor George Hayward, house painter & plumber, 54 Upper Norton st. & end of Portland road, New road
Taylor George Henry, solicitor, 23 Lincoln's inn fields
Taylor George Henry, solicitor, 5 Nicholas lane, Lombard st
Taylor George L. architect, 3 Trafalgar sq. Charing cross
Taylor George Robert, hairdresser, see Cormie & Taylor
Taylor George Thos. tailor, 40 Bridgehouse place, Boro'
Taylor Gustavus Thos. attorney, 18 Featherstone bldgs. Holb
Taylor Henry, bed & cornice ma. 1 Peter st.Sun st.Bishopsgt
Taylor Henry, *Blue Anchor* P.H. Bell ct. 163 Fenchurch st
Taylor Henry, carptr. 12 Salisbury mews, New rd. Marylbn
Taylor Henry, chemist, 10 Foster lane, & 10 Pall mall
Taylor Henry, customho.&ship agent, 7NewEastIndia chamb
Taylor Henry, dairyman, 3 Harcourt st. New road
Taylor Henry, french polisher, 39 Newman st. Oxford st
Taylor Henry, hair dresser, 37 Broad st. Bloomsbury
Taylor Henry, hosier & glover, 114 Gt. Russell st. Blmsbry
Taylor Henry, iron founder & grate mak.46 Crown st.Finsbry
Taylor Henry, linendraper & carpet warehouse, 23 Oxford st
Taylor Henry, patent lamp manfr. see Sedgwick & Taylor
Taylor Henry, ship agent & broker, Jamaica coffee house
Taylor Henry, zinc manufacturer, 5 Sun st. Bishopsgate
Taylor Henry Villiers de B.barrister, 3 New sq. Lincoln's inn
Taylor Hugh, hairdresser, 1 Vaughan place, City road
Taylor Isaac Cleaver, tailor, 27 Change alley, Cornhill
Taylor James, agent to Armitage Brothers, 49 Moorgate st
Taylor James, attorney, 15 Furnival's inn, Holborn
Taylor James, baker, 15 Victoria ter. Brunswick st.Dover rd
Taylor James, baker, 15 Victoria terrace, Horsemonger la
Taylor James, boot & shoe maker, 4 Ellis st. Sloane st
Taylor James, banker, see Hanburys', Taylor & Lloyds'
Taylor James, birmingham wa.6Wilderness row, Clerkenwell
Taylor James, carpenter, 14 Boston st. Dorset square
Taylor James, confectioner, 17 Stangate, Lambeth
Taylor James, engraver, 25 Wakefield st. Regent square
Taylor James, fishmonger, 43 Lombard st
Taylor James, *George* P.H. 19 West lane, Bermondsey wall
Taylor James, glover & hosier, 13 Cornhill
Taylor James, hat & cap manufacturer, 45 Farringdon st
Taylor James, lock & printers' smith, 31Tabernacle rw.Cityrd
Taylor James, maltster, Bromley, Middlesex
Taylor James, merchant, 3 George yard, Lombard st
Taylor James, painter & glazier, 48 St. Alban's st. Lambeth
Taylor James, plumber, 7 St. Ann's la. St. Martin's le grand
Taylor James, printer, 344 Strand
Taylor James, printers' smith, 31 Tabernacle row, City rd
Taylor James, rocking horse mkr.2 Shoemaker's row, Blkfrs
Taylor James, shipping butcher, 63 Minories
Taylor James, *Sun* P.H. 7 London wall
Taylor James, velvet & silk weaver, 3 Lit. Love la. Wood st

Taylor James, woollen agent, 49 Moorgate st. City
Taylor James, working jeweller, 48 Baldwin st. City road
Taylor JamesGeo. carpenter, Portland pl. south, Clapham rd
Taylor JamesMolyneux, attorney, 11 Furnival's inn, Holborn
Taylor Janet (Mrs.), navigation warehouse, 104 Minories
Taylor Jasper H. tailor, hosier & outfitter, 38 Old Bond st
Taylor Jasper Wilson, accountant, 62 Coleshill st. Eaton sq
Taylor Jessett John, dealer in english timber, 95 Brick lane, Spitalfields
Taylor John, attorney, 2 Castle st. Holborn
Taylor John, baker, 210 Brick lane, Spitalfields
Taylor John, baker, Camberwell green
Taylor John, baker, 3 Church st. Clapham road
Taylor John, baker, 55 Union st. Borough
Taylor John, basket maker, 125 Whitechapel High st
Taylor John, booksell. & publisher, 10 Broad st. Bloomsbury
Taylor John, boot & shoe maker, 69 High st. Camden town
Taylor John, bootmaker, 53 Lime st
Taylor John, *Britannia* P.H. 29 Golden lane, Barbican
Taylor John, *Bull's Head* P.H. 20 Little Windmill st
Taylor John, butcher, 23 Brown's lane, Spitalfields
Taylor John, card&pasteboard manuf. 11 John's row, St. Luke's
Taylor John, carpenter, 41 Brown st. Bryanstone square
Taylor John, carpenter & undertak. 15 Marine st. Bermondsy
Taylor John, carpenter, 8 Princess st. Lisson grove
Taylor John, carpet & upholstery wa. 91 & 92 St. John st. rd
Taylor John, carver & gilder, &c. 9 Norfolk st. Middlx. hospl
Taylor John, cheesemonger, 5 Jewin st. Cripplegate
Taylor John, cheesemonger, 35 Lit. Pulteney st. Golden sq
Taylor John, china dealer, 126 Church st. Shoreditch
Taylor John, civil engineer, 2 Duke st. Adelphi
Taylor John, dairyman, Bridge road, Battersea
Taylor John, dealer in foreign animals, 218 Poplar High st
Taylor John, dining rooms, 15 Moorgate st. Bank
Taylor John, fancy stationer, 7 London ter. Hackney road
Taylor John, *Feathers* P.H. 13 Stoney st. Borough market
Taylor John, fruiterer, 17 Kenton st. Brunswick square
Taylor John, fruiterer, 4 Munster st. Regent's park
Taylor John, gasfitter & lamp maker, 10 Exeter st. Strand
Taylor John, general dealer, 5 Gt. Carlisle st. Portman mkt
Taylor John, greengrocer, 111 High st. Camden town
Taylor John, grindery dealer, 16 New Compton st. Soho
Taylor John, grocer, 41 Brown st. Bryanstone square
Taylor John, grocer, teadealer & fruit importer, 44 Poultry
Taylor John, hairdresser, 89 St. John st. Clerkenwell
Taylor John, hat manufr. 12 Lit. Charlotte st. Blackfriars rd
Taylor John, ivory worker, 12 Arlington st. Sadler's wells
Taylor John, *King's Head* P.H. King st. mews, Park st
Taylor John, manchester warehouseman, 5 Pancras lane
Taylor John, oil & italian warehouse, 30 Jermyn st
Taylor John, physician, 18 Keppel st. Russell square
Taylor John, poulterer, 2 Tyler's court, Golden square
Taylor John, shoemaker, 9 Staining lane, Wood st
Taylor John, smith & ironmong. 6 Acton pl. Bagnigge wells rd
Taylor John, solicitor, 110 Fenchurch st
Taylor John, solicitor, see Quilter & Taylor
Taylor John, *SpreadEagle* P.H. 7 Old North st. Red Lion sq
Taylor John, surgeon, 4 Ely place, Holborn
Taylor John, surgeon, 16 Surrey place, Old Kent road
Taylor John, tailor, 26 Duke st. Piccadilly
Taylor John, tobacconist, 64 Piccadilly
Taylor John, tobacconist, 139 Rotherhithe st
Taylor John, tobacco pipe manfactr. 11 Wood st. Cromer st
Taylor John, umbrella maker, 22 Old st. St. Luke's
Taylor John, watch & clock ma. Glo'ster pl. Cambrwll. Nw. rd
Taylor John, watch glass mak. 12 Charles st. Hatton garden
Taylor John, whitesmith, 53 Old st. road
Taylor John, wine brok. & mercht. Coml. coff. room, Mincing la
Taylor John, jun. surgeon, 64 Queen's road, Bayswater
Taylor John Gent, baker, 22 Blackmoor st. Clare market
Taylor John Henry, architect & district surveyor, 22 Parliament st. Westminster; 22 Queen st. Cheapside; & Warner's terrace, Tottenham high cross
Taylor John Henry, solicitor, 10 South pl. Finsbury sq
Taylor John Hockley, barrister, 13 Old sq. Lincoln's inn
Taylor John James, coal mercht. Vauxhall whf. Wandswth. rd
Taylor John Joseph, tobacconist, 208 Tooley st
Taylor John Mercer, soda water ma. Portland ter. Wal. com
Taylor John Pitt, barrister, 1 Plowden buildings, Temple
Taylor John Robert, law stationer; 34 Parliament st.; 33 Southampton buildings; 54 Chancery lane; 16 Cannon row, Westminster, & 3 Arthur st. east, City
Taylor John Skardon, solicitor, Guy's hospital, Southwark
Taylor Jonathan, confectioner, 32 Surrey pl. Old Kent road
Taylor Joseph, boot maker, 18 Carnaby st. Golden sq
Taylor Joseph, bricklayer, 8 High st. Deptford
Taylor Joseph, brush manufacturer, 228 Blackfriars road
Taylor Joseph, builder, Albion hall, Albion pl. London wall
Taylor Joseph, carpenter, 55 Southampton st. Pentonville
Taylor Joseph, corndealer, 12 Southampton st. Camberwell rd
Taylor Joseph, dining rooms, 9 Minories
Taylor Joseph, grocer, 15 Spring st. Portman square
Taylor Joseph, grocer, 39 Wellington place, Stepney
Taylor Joseph, grocer & coal mercht. 20 & 21 Broad st. Lambeth
Taylor Joseph, pianoforte key mak. 82 Albany st. Regnt's. pk
Taylor Joseph, plumbr. & glazr. 10 Clement's la. & 44 Eastchp
Taylor Joseph, saw manufacturer, 27 Thomas st. Grosvenor sq
Taylor Joseph, surgeon, 9 New Bridge st. Blackfriars
Taylor Joseph, working silversmith, 65 King st. Soho
Taylor Joseph William, *White Hart* P.H. 81 Theobald's rd
Taylor Joshua, linendraper, 10 Gwinn's pl. Holloway road
Taylor Joshua, upholsterer & government contractor, 42 Haydon square, Minories
Taylor Josiah, prop. St. James's gallery, 58 Pall mall
Taylor Lewis, ironmonger, 26 Bowling green la. Clerkenwell
Taylor Lydia (Mrs.), milliner, 37 King st. Holborn
Taylor Maria (Miss), ladies' school, Glo'ster pl. Cambl. N. rd
Taylor Martha (Miss), school, see Tonks & Taylor
Taylor Mary (Miss), haberdashr. 5 St. Mark's rd. Cambwl. N. rd
Taylor Mary (Mrs.), *Coachmakers' Arms* P.H. 29 Bryanstone st
Taylor Mary (Mrs.), fruit & oyster wareho. 8 Bear st. Leicest sq
Taylor Mary Ann (Mrs.), lodging house, 48 Jewin st
Taylor Martin, bookseller & publisher, 1 Wellington st. Strand
Taylor Matthew, currier, 6 Union st. Middlesex hospital
Taylor Minett, corn chandler, 1 Southwick mews, Camb. ter
Taylor Peter, grocer, 86 Brick lane, Spitalfields
Taylor Peter Alfred, crape ma. see Courtauld, Taylors' & Co
Taylor Philip, oil & color warehouse, 148 Houndsditch
Taylor Priscilla (Miss), stationer, 86 Kingsland road
Taylor Richd. *Berkeley Castle* P.H. 17 Rahere st. Goswell rd
Taylor Richard, boatbuilder. 17 Church row, Limehouse
Taylor Richard, butcher, 4 Goldsmith's row, Hackney road
Taylor Richard, chemist, 5 Port place, Walworth common
Taylor Richard, drysalter, &c. 57 Sun st. Bishopsgate
Taylor Richard, fruiterer, 8 Bury st. Bloomsbury
Taylor Richard, grocer & cheesemngr. 83 Earl st. ea. Liss. gr
Taylor Richard, tailor, 24 Great Marlborough st
Taylor Richard, tailor, 46 London st. Fitzroy square
Taylor Richard, tailor & habit maker, 65 St. Martin's lane
Taylor Richard, warehouseman, 62 Bread st. Cheapside
Taylor Richard B. trimming manufr. 140 Bethnal grn. road
Taylor Richard H. wine merchant, Jamaica coffee house
Taylor Rich. T. account book ma. 17 Devonshire st. Queen sq
Taylor Robert, baker, 5 Watt's terrace, Old Kent road
Taylor Robert, *Black Horse* P.H. 172 Kent st. Borough
Taylor Robert, bricklayer, 4 Spencer st. Canonbury sq
Taylor Robert, farrier, Lower road, Rotherhithe
Taylor Robert, linendraper, 27 Brunswick par. Pentonville
Taylor Robert, haberdash. 2 Little St. Andrew st. Seven dials
Taylor Robert, livery & com. stables, Draycott pl. Chelsea
Taylor Robert, oilman, &c. 3 Elliott's rw. Lower st. Islingtn
Taylor Robert, stationer, 49 Newman st. Oxford st
Taylor Robert, watchmaker, 43 Albany st. Regent's park
Taylor Robert Charles, plumber, &c. 197 Shadwell High st
Taylor Samuel, boys' school, 18 Low. Ashby st. Northmptn. sq
Taylor Samuel, coachmaker, 5 Gt. Windmill st. Haymarket
Taylor Samuel, farrier, 180 Bethnal green road
Taylor Samuel, linendraper, 1 Wentworth place, Mile end
Taylor Samuel, printer, George yard, 92 Drury lane
Taylor Samuel, shoe & shirt wareho. 180 Bethnal green rd
Taylor Samuel, tailor, 9 Jamaica ter. Comml. rd. Limehouse
Taylor Samuel, *Union* coffee rooms, 26 Bevenden st. City rd
Taylor Samuel Guy, auction & estate agent, 3 Grosvenor st
Taylor Sarah (Miss), dress ma. 5 Took's ct. Cursitor st
Taylor Sarah (Mrs.), grocer, 1 Portland pl. Walworth com
Taylor Sarah (Mrs.), omnibus propr. 70 Gt. Carlisle st. Ptm. mt
Taylor Sidney, tobacconist, 4 King William st. Strand
Taylor Silas Badger, merchant, see Oxley & Taylor
Taylor Stephen, baker, 97 London wall
Taylor Steph. *Crooked Billet* P.H. 6 Portsmouth st. Lin. inn fi
Taylor Stephen, hairdresser & perfumer, 92 Strand
Taylor Stephen, shoemaker, 164 Rotherhithe st
Taylor Stephen Chas. wine & porter merc. 21 Savage gardens
Taylor Susan (Mrs.), butter salesman, see Joules & Taylor
Taylor Susannah (Mrs.), linendraper, 247 Bethnal green rd
Taylor Thomas, artist, 40 Hastings st. Burton crescent
Taylor Thomas, artist, 1A. Adelphi terrace
Taylor Thomas baker, 12 Gracechurch st
Taylor Thomas, baker, 25 Plumber st. City road
Taylor Thomas, bookbinder, 9 Huggin lane, Wood st
Taylor Thomas, butcher, 19 Silver st. Golden square
Taylor Thos. carpntr. & undertak. 8 Princes sq. Kenningtn

Taylor Thomas, cheesemonger, 108 York road, Lambeth
Taylor Thomas, coal mercht. 28 Gt. James st. Bedford row
Taylor Thomas, grocer, &c. Highbury park
Taylor Thomas, ham factor & cheese agent, Topping's wharf, & 12 Duke st. Tooley st
Taylor Thomas, ham & tongue warehouse, 81 Chiswell st
Taylor Thomas, library, 9 New church st. west, Edgware rd
Taylor Thomas, meat salesman, 12 Rose st. Newgate mkt
Taylor Thomas, oilman, 66 Great Titchfield st
Taylor Thomas, painter & glazier, 28 Nelson st. City road
Taylor Thomas, secretary to the London, Waterford, & Chester Shipping Association, 22 Eastcheap
Taylor Thomas, *Seven Stars* P.H. 53 Carey st. Linc. inn flds
Taylor Thomas, surgeon, &c. 289 Bethnal green road
Taylor Thomas, surgeon, 9 New Bridge st. Blackfriars
Taylor Thomas, surgeon, 21 Gt. Titchfield st. Oxford st
Taylor Thomas, tailor & draper, 24 Parker's rw. Bermondsy
Taylor Thomas, tailor & draper, 238 Tottenham court rd
Taylor Thomas, tobacco pipe ma. 45 Holywell la. Shoreditch
Taylor Thomas, *Two Sawyers* P.H. Palace New rd. Lambeth
Taylor Thomas, umbrella maker, Clapham rise
Taylor Thomas, working jeweller, 29 Trinity st. Liverpl. rd
Taylor Thomas, writer & grainer, 12 Denmark st. Soho
Taylor Thos. Dd. solicitor, 12 North bldgs. Finsbury circus
Taylor Thomas E. painter, 3 Bell yard, Gracechurch st
Taylor Thomas Hamlet, solicitor, 7 South square, Gray's inn
Taylor Thomas J. grocer, Palatine ho. Stoke Newington rd
Taylor Thomas Parker, milliner, 6 Hayes court, Soho
Taylor Thos. Stephen, *Green Man & Bell* P.H. 1 Dark ho. la
Taylor Walter, baker, 25 High road, Knightsbridge
Taylor Well, artist, 13 Foley place, Gt. Portland st
Taylor Wm. basket maker, 54 Leman st. Goodman's fields
Taylor Wm. boot & shoe maker, 41c, Park st. Grosvenor sq
Taylor Wm. butcher, 9 Skinner's place, Leadenhall market
Taylor Wm. cabinet maker, 6 Odell place, Little Chelsea
Taylor Wm. carpenter, 9 Field pl. Lark hall lane, Clapham
Taylor Wm. carpntr. & straw bont. ma. 5 Lower st. Islington
Taylor Wm. coachma. &c. 18 Providence bldgs. New Kent rd
Taylor Wm. fishmonger, 63 Castle st. east
Taylor Wm. fruiterer, 18 Shoemaker row, Blackfriars
Taylor Wm. furniture broker, 30 Long alley, Finsbury
Taylor Wm glover, &c. see Adshead & Taylor
Taylor Wm. grocer, 102 Cornwall road, Lambeth
Taylor Wm. hairdresser, 172 Waterloo road, Lambeth
Taylor Wm. hosier, glover, &c. 110 High Holborn
Taylor Wm. house agent, East India road, Poplar
Taylor Wm. linendraper, 29 Lamb's Conduit st. Foundling
Taylor Wm. locksmith, 22 High st. Deptford
Taylor Wm. manchester & wool agt. 6 Crosby sq. Bishopsgate
Taylor Wm. oil & colorman, 26 Drury lane
Taylor Wm. poulterer, 52 Albemarle st. Piccadilly
Taylor Wm. saw mills, see Richards & Taylor
Taylor Wm. smith & bellhanger, 27 Glo'ster st. Queen sq
Taylor Wm. surgeon, 88 Church st. Shoreditch
Taylor Wm. surgeon, see Spencer & Taylor
Taylor Wm. surgeon, 80 York road, Lambeth
Taylor Wm. tailor, 1 Dove court, Old Jewry
Taylor Wm. tailor, 21 Old Cavendish st
Taylor Wm. tailor & clothier, 4 Ringcross, Holloway road
Taylor Wm. teadealer & grocer, 117 Regent st
Taylor Wm. tobacconist, 6 Melbourne pl. Old Kent road
Taylor Wm. undertaker, 114 Gt. Russell st. Bloomsbury
Taylor Wm. whipmaker, 54 Coppice row, Clerkenwell
Taylor Wm. zinc works, Marsh lane, Battersea
Taylor Wm. Fowler, leather gilder, table, mat & musical instrument cover maker, 11 Trinity st. Liverpool road
Taylor Wm. Gardner, india, linen, &c. brok. 14 Geo. st. Mans. ho
Taylor Wm. George, grocer & italian wa. 82 High st. Cam. tn
Taylor Wm. Grimwood, solicitor, 14 John st. Bedford row
Taylor Wm. Henry, confectioner, 13 Arcade, Hungerfd. ma
Taylor Wm. Henry, pawnbroker, 184 Bethnal green road
Taylor Wm. Hen. quill & pen merchant, 49 Borough High st
Taylor Wm. Jackson, stock broker, 13 Gt. Carter lane; 2 & 3 Capel court, & Stock exchange
Taylor Wm. John, newsvender, 31 Seymour pl. Bryanstone sq
Taynton Henry, surgeon, 7 Bedford pl. Commercial rd. east
Teague Charles Brooks, solicitor, 5 Crown court, Cheapside
Teague Frederick, statuary & mason, 144 High st. Camden tn
Teague James Alexander, solicitor, chief clerk to the magistrates at Guildhall; ward clerk of Cripplegate within, & clerk to tackle house & ticket porters' society, 18 Aldermbry
Teakle George, fruiterer, 19 Bethnal green road
Teale John, general dealer, 376 Strand
Teape Henry & Son, printers, George st. Tower hill
Teape Hannaniah, stationer, see Wiggins, Teape & Loder
Teare John, work. silversmith, 86 Crown ct. Tudor st. Blkfrs

Teasdale Eliza, James & Co. merchants & importers of leeches, 5 Water st. Bridewell precinct, Blackfriars
Teasdale Michael, ironmonger, 3 Ranelagh ter. Pimlico rd
Teasdale Robt. surv. of pavements, 10 Phœnix st. Somers tn
Teasdale Thomas, printseller, 20 Lisson grove north, New rd
Teasdale Wm. *Cat & Salutation tap* P.H. 3 Rose st. Newgt. mkt
Teasdale Wm. confectioner, 3 Lit. Queen st. Westminster
Tebbey John, boot maker, 10 White Lion st. Pentonville
Tebbitt Robert, surgeon, 240 Blackfriars road
Tebbs Henry V. & Charles, proctors, 21 Gt. Knightrider st
Tebbs William, solicitor, 24 Essex st. Strand
Tebbut, Stoneman & Spence, ship builders, &c. Limekiln dock, Limehouse; & at New Crane dock, Shadwell
Tebbutt John, solicitor, 29 Austinfriars
Tebbutt Julius, fruiterer, 3 Victoria gr. Kensingtn. New tn
Tebbutt Marshall, grocer, 6 New Church st. west, Edgware rd
Tebbutt Thomas, coffee rooms, 4 James st. Haymarket
Tebworth Thomas, chandler's shop, Mary's pl. Kingsland
Tedder Wm. Hen. grocer, 2 Victoria gro. Newtown, Kensgtn
Teed George, shoemaker, 21 John st. Holland st. Blackfriars
Teed George, solicitor, 40 Chancery lane
Teed John Godfrey, queen's counsel, 3 New sq. Lincoln's inn
Teed Rt. Gibson, *Naked Boy & Woolpack* P.H. 23 Parish st
Teede & Bishop, who. grocers, 1 Crown court, Philpot lane
Teede George, attorney, 5 Sloane terrace, Chelsea
Teede John, who. grocer & teadealer, 85 Bishopsgate without
Teel Wm. fruiterer, 3 William's place, Walworth road
Teesdale Hy. & Co. map publishers, 2 Brunswick row, Queen sq
Teesdale John & Sons, tea & coffee dealers, 21 Cannon st
Teesdale, Symes, Weston & Teesdale, sols. 31 Fenchurch st
Teetgen Augustus, teadealer, 154 Whitechapel road
Teetgen John, comb & brush ma. 10 Bishopsgate without
Teevan James, surgeon, 30 Chesham st. Belgrave square
Teevan William, surgeon, 23 Bryanstone square
Tegart Edward & Co. apothecaries, 39 Pall mall
Tegg Thomas, bookseller, 73 Cheapside
Teighe & Smith, ship & insurance brokers 14 Birchin lane
Teil Geo. & Co. ea. india merchs. & agts. 9 Old Jewry chambs
Tekell Thomas, engraver, 2 Wood st. Spitalfields
Tekuch Samuel, furrier, 83 New Bond st
Tekusch Saml. & Co. furriers, 17 Southampton st. Fitzroy sq
Telfer Adam, smith & engineer, 127 Praed st. Edgware road
Telfer Alexr. pianoforte mak. 18 Woburn bldgs. Tavistock sq
Telfer Charles, glass cutter, 13 Ireland row, Mile end road
Telfer George, coal merchant, Stoke Newington green
Telfer James, pawnbroker, 70 Up. Whitecross st. St. Luke's
Telfer James Geo. glass cutter, 14 Red Lion court, Spitalfids
Telfer John, hosier, glover & outfitter, 46 High Holborn
Telfer Richd. Hudson, hosier & glover, 10 New st. Covt. gdn
Telfer Somerville, pawnbroker, 178 St. George st
Telford Charles, stock & share broker, 11 Throgmorton st
Telford Henry, merchant, see Ruskin, Telford & Co.
Telling James, bread & biscuit baker, 8 Backchurch lane
Telling Wm. baker, 4 Churton st. Vauxhall bridge road
Tempany Thomas & Co. paper stainers, 94 Farringdon st
Tempany Andrew John, accountant, 94 Farringdon st
Tempany Edmund, corndealer, 41 Crawford st. Portman sq
Tempany Wm. James, tobacconist, 11 Long acre
Temperance Provident Ins. (T. Compton, sec.) 39 Moorgate st
Temperley Nicholas, coal agent & coal merchant, 50a, King William st. City, & Whiting's wharf, Broad st. Ratcliff cr
Templar Jacob, bricklayer, 27 Little Guildford st. Borough
Temple & Bonner, solicitors, 16 Furnival's inn, Holborn
Temple & Reynolds, braziers, 10 Princes st. Cavendish sq
TEMPLE (The), near Temple bar
Temple Charles, *Cock* P.H. 62 Chalton st. Somers town
Temple Christopher, queen's counsel, 22 Old sq. Lincoln's inn
Temple Henry, solicitor, 3 Elm court, Temple
Temple John, broker & appraiser, 16 Exeter st. Sloane st
Temple Joseph, tailor, 71 Charlotte st. Portland place
Temple Leofric, barrister, 1 Essex court, Temple
Temple Richard *White Bear* P.H. 78 Aldersgate st
Temple Robert, staymaker, 25 Margaret st. Cavendish sq
Temple Robert, turner, 80 Poplar High st
Temple Stephen, barrister, 3 Hare ct. Temple
Temple Wm. beer retailer, 109 Cornwall road, Lambeth
Temple Wm. brush & turnery wa. 26 Motcomb st. Belgrave sq
Temple Wm. wax & wafer maker, 18 Artillery st. Bishopsgt
Temple Wm. Woods, solicitor, 4 Blomfield st. Finsbury circus
Templeman Joseph R. & Co. merchants, 2 St. Helen's place
Templeman Charlotte (Mrs.), bookseller, 6 Gt. Portland st
Templeman James, academy, 73 Mount st. Berkeley sq
Templeman John, bottle dealer, 106 Star st. Paddington
Templeman John, corn lighterman, 47 Gainsford st. Horselyd
Templer John C. special pleader, 10 Farrar's bldgs. Temple
Templeton Allan, paper manfr. agt. 15 Lit. St. Thomas Apostle

Templeton James & Co. glasgow patent carpet & rug manufacturers, 26 Skinner st. Snow hill, & at Glasgow
Templeton Patrick Stuart, school, 10 Poland st
Tempney George Richard, tailor, 16B, Old Cavendish st
Ten Broeke William, merchant, 18 Throgmorton st
Ten George, paper stainer, 22 Lowther arcade, Strand, & 2 Clayton place, Kennington road
Tennant Charles, Sons & Co. manufacturers of bleaching powders, oil of vitriol, soda & soap, & commission merchants, 101 Upper Thames st
Tennant & Co. attorneys, 2 Gray's Inn square
Tennant Henry D. & Co. ship chndls. 13 Emmett st. Poplar
Tennant & Webster, straw hat manufs. 6 North st. Edgware rd
Tennant Edwd. beer retlr. 25 White Hart pl. Low. Kenningtn. la
Tennant Edward, currier, 1 Mason st. Old Kent road
Tennant Elizabeth (Miss), glass & china dealer, 62 St. John st
Tennant George, special pleader, 12 Paper bldgs. Temple
Tennant Geo. *Westminster Arms* P.H. 14 Market st. Westmr
Tennant Henry, barrister, 5 New sq. Lincoln's inn
Tennant James, carpenter, 19 Robert st. Hoxton
Tennant James, mineralogist to her Majesty, importer of shells, minerals & ornamental works of art, maufr. of derbyshire spar, & marble ornaments, 149 Strand
Tennant James, shawl fringer, 2 Silver st. Wood st
Tennant Richard, *Punch Bowl* P.H. 1 Hemlock ct. Carey st
Tennant Wm. carpenter, 13 Cumberland pl. King's rd. Chelsea
Tennant Wm. fishing tackle maker, 3 Broadway, Ludgate hill
Tennant William, tailor, 17 Aske st. Hoxton
Tennant Wm. H. locksmith & bellhang. 1 Moreton pl. Kentish tn
Tennants & Woodbridge, wine mers. 6 Trinity sq. Tower hill
Tennison John, tailor & draper, 20 Haymarket
Tennison Joseph, dispensing chemist, 11 Silver st. Golden sq
Tennison Joseph, surgeon, 8 Broughton place, Hackney rd
Tent William, hosier, glover, shirtmaker & outfitter, 21 Royal exchange, North east corner
Tenth's Office, Dean's yard, Westminster; hours 10 to 2
Tepper George, carpenter & joiner, 1 Chapel st. Grosvenr sq
Tepper Hen. Fredk. Leopold, mercht. see Hellwege & Tepper
Tepper John, bookbinder, 166 High Holborn
Tepper Richard, bootmaker, 1 Chapel st. Grosvenor square
Terdrey Charles, currier, 4 Camden st. Walworth
Ternan Charles & Son, builders, 4 Polygon, Clarendon square
Terni Vito, merchant, 1 Cushion court, Old Broad st
Ternouth John, sculptor, 9 Lower Belgrave place, Pimlico
Terratt Jas. *Rose & Crown* P.H. Salisbury la. Bermondsey wall
Terrell Hull, solicitor, 30 Basinghall st
Terrell Robert Hull, solicitor, 14 Gray's inn square
Terrell Thomas Hull, barrister, 10 New sq. Lincoln's inn
Terrell William Hull, barrister, 4 Stone blgs. Lincoln's inn
Terrett Joseph, upholsterer & underta. 11 Gt. Suffolk st. Boro'
Terrey John Edward & Co. silversmiths, 31 Hatton garden
Terrington Wm. Walmsley, winemer. & ins. bro. 5 Gt Winches. st
Terry John & Son, carps. & packingcase mas. 5 Bread st. hill
Terry Ann (Mrs.) tailor, 22 Holiday yard, Creed lane
Terry Benjamin, baker, 36 Hatton wall
Terry Charles, *Blue Boar* P.H. 111 Gt. Russell st. Bloomsb
Terry Charles, boot & shoe maker, 18 Well st. Wellclose sq
Terry Chas. ea. in. mer. 11 New east india chamb. Leadenhll st
Terry Chas. linendraper & silk mercer, 76 & 77 Chiswell st. & carpet warehouse, 1 Finsbury st. Chiswell st
Terry Clara (Mrs.), milliner & dressma. 12 Hanover pl Rgts. pk. rd
Terry Edmund, ancient furniture dealer, 15 Wardour st. Soho
Terry Edward, grocer, 5 Chapter st. Westminster
Terry Elizb. (Mrs.), milliner, 50 Manchester st. Manchstr. sq
Terry George, cook & confectioner, 74 Leadenhall st. & 23 New Broad st. City
Terry George, grocer, Bolingbroke gardens, Battersea
Terry Henry merchant, 8 Old Jewry
Terry Isaac, watchmaker, 36 Princes st. Leicester square
Terry James, basket maker, 42 Chalton st. Somers town
Terry Jas. cabinet & fur. ironmong. 78 & 79 Long la. Smithfield
Terry James, fishmonger, 28 Little Earl st. Seven dials
Terry James, plain & cut glass manf. 25 St. John st. Clrknwl
Terry James, marine store dealer, 22 Bermondsey st
Terry James, teadealer, &c. 23 Shoemaker row, Blackfriars
Terry James Wm. gun maker, 24 Gt. Prescot st. Goodman's fld
Terry John, *Apple Tree* P.H. 1 Dorrington st. Clerkenwell
Terry John, fruiterer, 4 Bouverie st. Paddington
Terry John, tailor, 3 Cheltenham pl. Westminster bridge rd
Terry John, tailor, 43 Curtain road, Shoreditch
Terry John, tailor, 66 Oakley st. Lambeth
Terry Joseph, meat salesman, Leadenhall market
Terry Joseph, tailor, 21 Church st. Soho
Terry Moses, baker, 1 Paragon pl. Locks fields, Walworth
Terry Peter, newsman & printer, see Newbery & Terry
Terry Robert, plumber, &c. 50 Manchester st. Manchester sq
Terry Thomas, pork butcher, 73 Strutton ground, Westmr
Terry Thomas, beer retailer, 18 Bath place, New road
Terry William, painter, 7 Gloucester place, New road
Terry Wm. surgeon, 45 Southampton buildings, Chancery la
Terry Wm. John, dining rooms, 111 Upper East Smithfield
Terry & Milgate, warehousemen, 3 Gresham st. City
Teschemacher Ed. Fred. chemist, Commercl. coff. ho. Mincing la
Tesner John, beer retailer, Bedford row, East st. Walw. rd
Tesseyman Charles, bookbinder, 5 Broad court, Long acre
Tessier Louis & Sons, goldsmiths & jewellers, 32 South Audley st
Tessier Prosser Hen. *Anchor & Hope* P.H. 108 Up. Ea. Smithfield
Testar Henry & Co. sewing silk manufrs. 16 Gutter la. Cheapside
Testar George, sen. *Red Lion* P.H. 30 St. John st. road
Testar John, tailor, &c. 81 South Audley st
Tester James, coal merchant, 5 Bartlett's buildings
Tester Richd. tire smith & spring ma. 1 Asylum blds. Westm. rd
Tetley James Rimington & Son, cotton brokers, 19 Commercial sale rooms
Tetley Wm. tilt & tarpaulin manufacturer, 63 Kingsland rd
Tett Charles, painter & paperhanger, 38 Dean st. Soho
Tett Samuel, paperhanger, 2 Greuville st. Somers town
Tett William, plumasier & art. florist, 23 Hanway st. Oxford st
Tett Wm. Francis, carver, 14 Molyneux st. Bryanstone sq
Teulon S. & W.H. hop merchants, 6 Cooper's rw. Crutchedfrs
Teulon John, printer, 57 Cheapside
Teulon Peter, solicitor, 22 Queen st. Golden sq
Teulon Samuel S. architect, 18 Millman st. Bedford row
Teulon Thos. corndealer, 41 Upper Berkeley st. Portman sq
Teuten Charles, news agent, 20 Upper Cleveland st. Fitzroy square, & 5 College st. Chelsea
Teversham Mark, cheesemonger, 36 Ludgate hill
Tewart Brothers, Wheeler & Co. woollen factors, 4 Ludgate st
Tewkesbury Amos, greengrocer, 62 Exmouth st. Clerkenwell
Teychenue F. & Co. feather purifiers, 32 Redcross sq. Crippl
Thacker Anthony, coal mer. & custom ho. agt. 1 Gt. St. Helen's
Thacker Chas. *Red Lion & Punch Bowl* P.H. 51 St. John st. Clkw
Thacker Thomas, trunk maker, 1 Connaught terrace
Thacker Thomas Doe, tailor, 32 Tysoe st. Exmouth st
Thacker Wm. cooper, 27 Page's walk, Bermondsey
Thackrah, Lockwood & Co. hop & seed mer. 9 Duke st. Tooley st
Thackray Wm. who. stationer, see Grimwade & Thackray
Thackthwaite Robert, attorney, 24 Essex st. Strand
Thackway Wm. tailor, 12 Union place, New road
Thain John, stay & corset maker, 28 Lower st. Islington
Thain John, staymaker, 11 Stayman's row, Holloway road
Thaine & Juby, linendra. & haberdash. 41 & 42 Exmouth st. Spafi
Thaine Richard Robert, *Ship inn*, 54 Blackman st
Thames Embankment office, 2 Mid. Scotland yard, 10 to 4
Thames & Medway Canal office, 15 New Broad st. City
Thames Plate Glass Co. (Thos. E. Souper, sec.), Savoy wf. Savoy st. Strand; manufact. Bow creek, Blackwall
Thames Police Station, Arbour st. east, Stepney; hours 10 to 5
Thames Police Station, (Wm. Isbester, inspc.) Follywall, Blkw
Thames Steam Towing Co. (John Waters, man.), 306 Wapping
Thames Tunnel Company office (Joseph B. Blundell, sec.), 5 Tunnel rd. Rotherhithe; works, 332 Rotherhithe st
Thames Tunnel wharf, 51 Rotherhithe st
Thane William, artist, 16 Russell place, Fitzroy sq
Tharp John, silk manufactr. 8 White Lion st. Norton folgate
Tharp Thomas, *Royal Oak* P.H. 154 Wapping High st
Thatcher John & Son, seedsman, 33 Hedge rw. High st. Islington
Thatcher Anthony, bottle wareho. Albion pl. London wall
Thatcher Anthony (Mrs.), milliner, 27 New st. Dorset sq
Thatcher Benj. goldsmith & jeweller, 11 St. John's sq. Clkwl
Thatcher Daniel, fruiterer, 65 Gt. hall, Hungerford market
Thatcher Henry, furniture broker, 5 Folly, Dockhead
Thatcher John Thomas (late Perrins & Taylor), coach currier, 40 Parker st. Drury lane
Thatcher Thomas, tailor, 8 Thomas st. Oxford st
Thatcher William, grocer, 9 Newland terrace, Kensington
THAVIES INN, 57 Holborn hill
Thayer Joseph, tobacconist, 55 Fetter lane
Theaker & Stumbke, tailors, 19 Oxendon st. Haymarket
Theakstone Geo. Humphrey, solicitor, 27 Alsopp ter. New rd
The Govenor & Company of Copper Miners in England, copper & tin smelters, tin plate manufacturers, & merchants, 57½ Old Broad st.; Castle Baynard, & 12 to 14 Upper Thames st
Thelwall William, paperhanger, 9 East st. Manchester sq
Themans Jacob, cigar importer, 187 St. George st
Theobald Charles, hairdresser, 17 Charles st. Westminster
Theobald Daniel, bootmaker, 11 Chapel st. east, Curzon st
Theobald George, bootmaker, 20 Cowcross st. Smithfield
Theobald George, who. milliner, 10 Crown st. Finsbury
Theobald James, butcher, 32 Robinson's row, Kingsland
Theobald John, hosier, 11 Skinner st. Snowhill

Theobald John Peter, solicitor, 16 Furnival's inn, Holborn
Theobald Robert, bookseller, 89 Bartholomew close
Theobald William, shoemaker, 19 High st. Kensington
Theobalds William, pianoforte maker, 314 Oxford st
Theroulde Samuel, silk manufr. 5 Wilkes st. Spitalfields
Thesiger Sir Frederic, attorney general, 2 King's Bench walk, Temple
Thibou Malcolm Danl. carpenter, 8 Union pl. Blackman st
Thick Charles, solicitor, 8 Union ct. Old Broad st
Thicke Charles James (resident sec. to the *British Mutual Life Assurance Society*), 17 New Bridge st
Thick Robert, carver, 35 Clipstone st. Fitzroy square
Thickbroom T.&W. coal & mahog. mer. Norway wf. Milbk.st
Thickbroom Alf. watch case maker, 10 Galway st. St. Luke's
Thickbroom Jas. watch case ma. 12 Skinner st. Clerkenwell
Thicke Charlotte & Elizbth. artists, 17 Duke st. Portland pl
Thicthener William, watchmaker, 36 Shadwell High st
Thielcke Frederick, merchant, Capel court
Thielcke Frederick, merchant, Baltic coffee house
Thierry Nicola, french boot & shoe maker, 70 Regent st
Thies Anthony Fredk. confectioner, 84 Edgware road
Thies Edward, baker, 2 Amelia place, Walworth road
Thies Fred. Anthy. baker, 10 Up. Southwick st. Edgware rd
Thies James Charles, bread & biscuit baker, 30 Wapping
Thies John, bread & biscuit baker, 61 Old Broad st. City, and 4 Long alley, Finsbury
Thies Wm. Ernest, baker & flour factor, 2 Great Trinity lane, & 3 City road, Finsbury square
Thilthorp John, bricklayer, 19 China walk, Lambeth
Thimbleby Joseph, leather seller, 23 Long alley, Finsbury
Thimbleby Richard, butcher, Camberwell green
Thimbleby Rd. leather cut. 24 Bevenden st. Hoxton New tn
Thimbleby Robert Lane, butcher, 7 Camberwell grove
Thin Jas. agt. for MacNair's Leith ales, St. Mary Overy's dock
Thirion Peter, skin dresser, 1 Hitt's pl. Ray st. Clerkenwell
Thirkettle Henry, engine turner, 34 Wynyatt st. Goswell st
Thirlway Mary (Mrs.), grocer & cheesemonger, 53 Milbank st
Thirst Edward, *Moore Arms* P.H. 1 Halsey ter. Cadogan st
Thirst John, builder, 56 North st. Edgware road
Thiselton John, painter & paperhang. 7 King's rd. ea. Chelsea
Thiselton Octavius Young, undertaker, 14 Somers pl. east
Thistleton Augustus, printer, 37 Goodge st. Tottenham ct. rd
Thistlewood John, solicitor, 16½ Lawrence lane
Thitchener Thos. C. watchmaker, 18 High row, Knightsbridge
Thodey Winwood, glover, 4 Poultry
Thöl John Phillip, merchant, 28 Mark lane
Thomas & Chapman, merchants, 9 New Broad st. City
Thomas Edwd. & John, printers & pub. 26 Russell ct. Drury la
Thomas Elizh. & Son, builders, 1 Circus rd. ea. St. John's wd
Thomas Ferdinand & Co. glass & china dlrs. 9 Tichborne st
Thomas F. Lewis & John Wm. goldsmiths, 153 New Bond st
Thomas George & Son, last & patten mkrs. 33 Cannon st. Ratcliff
Thomas & Green, commisn. agts. 6 Clement's ct. Milk st
Thomas Israel & Sons, stationers & ledger ware. 20 Cornhill
Thomas John & Co. upholsterers, 10 Chalcroft ter. New cut
Thomas John, Son & Lefevre, merchants, 21 Austinfriars
Thomas, Lepard & Williams, solicitors, 9 Cloak lane
Thomas & Moore, solicitors, 7 South square, Gray's inn
Thomas Philip Wm. & Sons, stockbrokers, 50 Threadneedle st
Thomas Rd. & Co. wine mercts. & merchts. 63½ King Wm. st. City
Thomas Richd. & Son, solicitors, 3 Fen court, Fenchurch st
Thomas Robert & Son, boot & shoe makers, 36 St. James's st
Thomas William & Brothers, wholesale stay, shoe & clothing manufacturers, & patentees of the corset werley & carpet bag fastenings, 128 & 129 Cheapside
Thomas William & Son, dining rooms, 203 Shoreditch High st
Thomas Alex. silver planisher, 31 Kirby st. Hatton garden
Thomas Ann (Mrs.), cowkeeper, 212 Bermondsey st
Thomas Archibald, shopkeeper, 8 Temple st. Hackney rd
Thomas Benjamin, cowkeeper, 25 Gt. Carlisle st. Portman mk
Thomas Benjamin, tailor, 9 Southampton st. Camberwell
Thomas Bridget (Mrs.), stay & corset ma. 2 Beech st. Barbican
Thomas Cath. (Mrs.), *Phœnix* P.H. 12 Stacey st. St. Giles's
Thomas Charles, bottle dealer, 5 Charlton st. Fitzroy sq
Thomas Charles, fruiterer, 10 Frederick st. Vincent square
Thomas Charles Augustus, last maker, 6 Wells st. Oxford st
Thomas Charles Evan, solicitor, 11 Jermyn st. St. James'
Thomas Charles Smith, proctor & notary, 11 Gt. Carter la
Thomas Charlotte (Mrs.), *Marquis of Granby* P.H. New cross
Thomas Daniel, tailor, 9 Wallington pl. Wandsworth road
Thomas David, tallowmelter, 111 Bethnal green road
Thomas Edward, boot & shoe maker, 130 London wall
Thomas Edward, lapidary, 31 Low. Smith st. Northampton sq
Thomas Edward, linendraper, 75 High st. Whitechapel
Thomas Edward, livery stables, 11 Kendall's mews, Portman sq
Thomas Edward, tailor, 32 Aldermanbury
Thomas Edward, tailor, 10 Henry st. Gray's inn lane
Thomas Edward, writing & dressing case ma. 54 Hatton grdn
Thomas Ed. John, windw. blind ma. 5 Essex pl. Mare st. Hkny
Thomas Elizbh. (Mrs.), bookseller, 23 Trinity sq. Tower hill
Thomas Emily (Mrs.), stationer, 3 Victoria pl. Commercl. rd
Thomas Evan, linendraper, 116 Aldersgate st
Thomas Frank, dentist, 4 Upper North pl. Gray's inn road
Thomas Fredk. grocer & oilman, 1 Pullam ter. King's rd. Chel
Thomas Fredk. physician, 3 Park village east, Regent's park
Thomas Fredk. *Victoria* P.H. 18 Three colt st. Limehouse
Thomas Frederick S. law & mine agent, 14 Poultry
Thomas Fredk. Wm. auctioneer, 3 Union court, Old Broad st. City, 10 Barnsbury place & 11 Rufford's row, Islington
Thomas George, coal merchant, Salisbury st. wharf, & 68 Strand
Thomas George, tea & coffee warehouse, 110 Shoreditch
Thomas George Evan, solicitor, 3 St. James's sq. south side
Thomas Griffith, clerk & registrar to south metropolitan cemetery company office, 10 King William st. City
Thomas Griffith, solicitor, see Marten, Thomas & Hollams
Thomas Griffith, surgeon, 4 Claremont square, Pentonville
Thomas Harley, manchester agent, 9 Gresham st. City
Thomas Henry, attorney, 35 Lincoln's inn fields
Thomas Henry, mining agent, 8 George yard, Lombard st
Thomas Henry, potato dealer, 68 Leather lane, Holborn
Thomas Henry, surgeon, 11 Glo'ster terr. Vauxhall bridge rd
Thomas Hugh, boot & shoe maker, 76½ Wardour st. Soho
Thomas James, baker, 65 Regent st. Horseferry rd. Wesm
Thomas James, cabinet maker, 57 Bath st. City road
Thomas James, fruiterer, 3 Salmon pl. Grange rd. Bermndsy
Thomas James, plumber, &c. 13 John st. Holywell mount
Thomas James Beaumont, tobacco mfr. 115 St. George st
Thomas Jane (Mrs.), grocer, 3 Providence pl. Vauxhall br. rd
Thomas Jane (Mrs.), shoemaker, 21 Lambeth walk
Thomas John, builder & upholder, 9 Lit. Stanhope st. Mayfair
Thomas John, butcher, 106 Drury lane
Thomas John, chemist, &c. 34 Devonshire st. Portland pl
Thomas John, coach plater, 33 Eagle st. Red Lion sq
Thomas John, coal dealer, see Miller & Thomas
Thomas John, coal merchant, 9 Dover st. Piccadilly
Thomas John, cowkeeper, 21 Palace st. Pimlico
Thomas John, dairy, 10 Elder st. Norton folgate
Thomas John, dairyman, 4 Green st. Leicester sq
Thomas John, dairyman, 49 Crutchedfriars, & 9 Botolph all
Thomas John, fancy repository, 11 Wilderness row
Thomas John, feather dresser, see Blakeley & Thomas
Thomas John, fruiterer, 92 Bermondsey st
Thomas John, greengrocer, 102 Tooley st
Thomas John, grocer & teadealer, 4 Hungerford st. Strand
Thomas John, grocer & teadealer, 290 Kent st. Borough
Thomas John, haberdasher, 48 & 49 Charlotte st. Whitechpl
Thomas John, jeweller, 15 Warwick pl. Kingsland road
Thomas John, linendraper, 57 St. Martin's la. Charing cross
Thomas John, painter & glazier, 19 Sussex st. Tottenham ct. rd
Thomas John, potato merchant, 85 St. George st
Thomas John, *Warwick Arms* P.H. Warwick road, Kensington
Thomas John, watchmkr. 2 Jealous row, New rd. St. Geo. east
Thomas John, wireworker, 9 Hall place, Edgware road
Thomas John Alexious, tailor & hatter, High st. Kingsland
Thomas John Evans, F.S.A. sculptor, 7 Lr. Belgrave pl. Pimlico
Thomas Joseph, newspaper & advertising agent, office of the *Courrier de l'Europe & L'Illustration*, & of the *Railway Advertiser*, 1 Finch lane, Cornhill
Thomas Joseph, carpenter, see Cowell & Thomas
Thomas Joseph, *Fountain* P.H. 19 Lower Sloane st. Chelsea
Thomas Joseph, shoemaker, 29 Shouldham st. Edgware road
Thomas Mary (Mrs.), artificial florist, 55 Burlington arcade
Thomas Mary Ann (Mrs.), tobacconist, 199 Upper Thames st
Thomas Maurice, solicitor, 6 New Boswell ct. Lincoln's inn
Thomas Ophelia (Miss), dressmaker, 8 Old Cavendish st
Thomas Ralph, barrister, 16 Chancery lane, & Grove cottage, Chiswick
Thomas Ralph, solicr. to Scottish hospital, 7 South sq. Gray's inn
Thomas Richard, collar maker, 27 Glo'ster st. Coml. rd. east
Thomas Richard, haberdasher, 53 Grosvenor row, Pimlico
Thomas Richard, oil & italian wareho. 102 Bishopsgate within
Thomas Richard, sharebroker, 8 George yard, Lombard st
Thomas Richard, solicitor (firm R. Thomas & Son), clerk to the Glovers' Company, solicitor to the Mines Royal Company, vestry clerk to St. Gabriel Fenchurch, & secretary to the Langbourn ward charity schools; & Frederick Richard Thomas, 3 Fen court, Fenchurch st
Thomas Richard, *White Hart* P.H. 1 Kennington cross
Thomas Robert, cheesemonger, 7 Bartholomew ter. City rd
Thomas Robert, engraver & printer, 21 Chancery lane
Thomas Robert R. plumber, &c. 23 Church rw. Newingtn. btts

Thomas Rowland, teadealer, 107 Upper Whitecross st. St. Luke's, & 6 Regent terrace, City road
ThomasSamuel,accountant,27Austinfriars(from9Finch lane)
Thomas Samuel, *Fish* P.H. 12½ Fisher st. Red Lion square
Thomas Samuel,plumbr.&glazr.2 Mansion ho. st.Kennington
Thomas Samuel, refiner & dealer in foreign coins & bullion merchant, 21 Cornhill
Thomas Samuel, cigar importer, 133 Regent st
Thomas Samuel John, surgeon, 68 London road, Southwark
Thomas Sarah (Mrs.), british wine ma.69Queen st.Cheapside
Thomas Sophia (Mrs.), bootma. 57 New Church st.Lisson gr
Thomas Thos. carpenter, 14 Exmouth st. Euston square
Thomas Thos. *Hatchett's hotel, & New White Horse cellar* P.H. 67 Piccadilly, & 1 Dover st
Thomas Thos. linendraper, 8 & 9 Tabernacle walk, Finsbury
Thomas Thos. plumber & glazier, 12 Everett st. Brunswick sq
Thomas Thos. surgeon & dentist, 64 Berners st
Thomas Thos.blowg.machinema.11Hamilton st.Wndswth.rd
Thomas Thos. Lane, coal mer.4 King's parade,King's rd.Chel
Thomas Tom. fruiterer, 136 Edgware road
Thomas Wm. advertisement agent, 20 Catherine st. Strand
Thomas Wm. attorney, 3 Ely place, Holborn
Thomas Wm. boot & shoe maker, 80 Little Britain
Thomas Wm. boot & shoe maker, 48 Lower Sloane st.Chelsea
Thomas Wm. bricklayer, see Wigzell & Thomas
Thomas Wm. bricklayer, 41 Princes st. Stamford st
Thomas Wm. builder, 14 Upper King st. Bloomsbury
Thomas Wm. carpenter, 19 Camden st. East st. Walworth rd
Thomas Wm. china & glass dealer, High st. Kingsland
Thomas Wm. coal merchant, Salisbury st. wharf, Strand
Thomas Wm. dairyman, 16 Backchurch lane,Whitechapel
Thomas Wm. decorator, painter, &c. 39 London st.Fitzroy sq
Thomas Wm. dining rooms, 5 Sidney pl. King's rd. Chelsea
Thomas Wm. goldsmith,watchmaker & jeweller, 10 Strand
Thomas Wm. greengrocer, 22 Alfred pl. Newington causw
Thomas Wm. greengrocer, 31 Whitefriars st
Thomas Wm. hat & cap maker, 53 Rufford's bldgs. Islington
Thomas Wm. hatter, 38 Wilderness row, Clerkenwell
Thomas Wm. patten & clog maker, 29 Great Saffron hill
Thomas Wm. poultry salesman,6Three tun pas.Newgate mkt
ThomasWm. veterinaryforge,2 Charles mews, Drummond st
Thomas Wm. who. hatmanfr.10Princes st.MileendNewtown
Thomas Wm. Francis, tailor, 10 Gt. Castle st. Regent st
Thomas William Henry, merchant, see Boyd & Thomas
Thomas Wm. Penn, pilot, 4 Hawthorndean pl. Limehouse
Thomason George Thos. printer,&c. 75 Nicholas st. Hoxton
Thomason Marianne (Mrs.), straw hat maker, & straw plait dealer, 75 Nicholas st. Hoxton
Thomason James, Phœnix saw mills & mahogany & deal yard, 18 New Montague st. Spitalfields
Thomasset Theodore, merchant,2 Gt. St. Helen's, Bishopsgt
Thomel & Carrand, importers of silk, 67 Newgate st
Thomel Madame, milliner & court dress ma. 180 Regent st
Thomerson William, builder, 5 London st. Hackney road
Thompson Chas. & Fred. coal mers. 54 Dorset st. Salisbury sq
Thompson David & Chas. genl. salesmn.11 Up. St.Martin'sla
Thompson Elizh. & Martha, wire workers, 38 Myddleton st
Thompson & Debenham,solicitors, Salter's hl. St.Swithin's la
Thompson & Forman, iron mers.Dyers' hallwf.Up.Thames st
Thompson Geo. & Sons, engineers, machinists, millwrights, founders, pump makers, well sinkers & improved leather pipe & bucket makers, Eccleston st. east, Pimlico
ThompsonGeo. B.&Co.ironmongers&bellhangs.390 Oxford st
Thompson Geo. & R. curriers & leather sellers, 10 Fan st
Thompson Henry & Co. ship & insurance brokers, & overland agts. 2 Cowper's ct. Cornhill, & at 84 High st. Southmptn
Thompson & Gilbert,boot makers,12 Gt.Windmillst.Hymkt
Thompson & Hewitt, attorneys, 2 Bucklesbury
Thompson Jas. John&Chas.Hen. coal mer.252Wppng.High st
Thompson Lawrence&Co. printers&booksellers,19Gt.St.Hlns
Thompson Peter & Co. army clothiers, tailors & habit makers to her Majesty, his royal highness Prince Albert & the royal Family, 12 Frith st. Soho
Thompson & Smith, dentists, 22 George st. Hanover square
ThompsonWm. & Co. brushma. & turners, 307 High Holborn
ThompsonWm. & Co. wine &spirit mers.15Cooper's row,City
Thompson Wm. & Co. sheriffs' officers, 31 Chancery lane
ThompsonWm. Jas. &Sons, tea & col. broks. 38 Mincing lane
ThompsonAgnes (Mrs.), lodging house kpr. 10 Mabledon pl. New road
Thompson Alex. beer retailer, 58 Anchor & Hope al.Wapping
Thompson Alex. *Blackamoor's Head* P. H. 3 Cartwright st. Rosemary lane
ThompsonAlex.paint.&paprhngr.46Stanhope st.Hampstd.rd
Thompson Alex. saw & tool manufacturer, 99 Old st. rd
Thompson Alfred, undertaker, 7 Purim place, Cambridge rd
Thompson Amelia (Miss), prepa. school, 26A, Grove end rd
Thompson Andrew, cardbd.box mak.5Lit.St.ThomasApostle
Thompson Ann (Miss), oil wareho. 1 Henry st. St. Luke's
Thompson Ann (Miss),straw bonnet ma.65Bethnal green rd
Thompson Ann (Mrs.), tripedealer, 46 York st Westminster
Thompson Anna (Miss), ladies' school,35 Lisson groveNorth
Thompson Anthony,marine store dlr. 8 Club rw. Bethnal grn
Thompson Anthony, merchant, Lloyd's
Thompson Benjamin, wax chandler, 22 Brewer st.Golden sq
Thompson Betsy (Mrs.), painter, 33 Lime st. City
Thompson Chas. haberdasher, 26 High row, Knightsbridge
Thompson Chas. pawnbroker, 15 King's pl. Coml. rd. East
Thompson Chas. statuary, 1 Osnaburg st. Regent's park
Thompson Chas. tailor, see Daniels & Thompson
Thompson Charles J. dentist, 22 George st. Hanover sq.
Thompson Charlt. (Miss) ladies' school,9 Stafford st.Liss.gr
Thompson Clarke, *Bell* P.H. 157 Wapping High st
Thompson Clementia, fruiterer, 61 Gt. hall, Hungerford mkt
Thompson Daniel, coffee rooms, 62 Long lane, Smithfield
Thompson Darius, surgeon dentist, 128 Strand
Thompson David, baker, 21 St. James's pl. Hampstead rd
Thompson Ebenezer, watchma. 181 Sloane st. Knightsbridge
Thompson Edw. cornmeas.&coal shovel ma.82St.John st.Clk
Thompson Edw. watchmaker,26 Upper King st.Bloomsbury
Thompson Edw. wool merchant, 60 Basinghall street
Thompson Edw. John,glass&hand wa.59Welngtn st.Goswl.rd
Thompson Eleanor (Mrs.), printer, 1 Camden st. Islington
Thompson Francis, barrister, 12 King's Bench walk
Thompson Francis,firewood dealer,35NewChurch st.Brmdsy
Thompson Francis, tailor, 11 Conduit st. Regent st.
Thompson Frederic, barrister, 5 Brick ct. Temple
Thompson Fredk. surveyor,19 Robert ter.King's rd.Chelsea
Thompson Fredk. trimming sellr. 10 Cross st.Newngtn butts
Thompson Fredk. E. solicitor, see Springall, Thompson & Co
Thompson George, cabinet maker, 14 King st. Borough
Thompson George, confectioner, 88 York st. Westminster
Thompson Geo. *Coronation* P.H.125U.Seymour st.Euston sq
Thompson George,meat salesman,5&6NewNewgate market
Thompson, George, solicitor, 8 Earl st. Blackfriars
Thompson George, tailor, 2 Eaton terrace, Eaton square
Thompson George, tailor, High st. Bow, Middlesex
Thompson Geo. Beeston & Co.leather pipe ms. 389 Oxford st
Thompson Geo. Jas. pilot, 14 Warkworth ter. Commercl. rd
Thompson Hannah (Miss), school, 21 Kirby st. Hatton grdn
Thompson Hannah (Mrs.), grocer, 21 Fair st. Horselydown
Thompson Henry, dairyman, 19 Devonshire st. Lisson grove
Thompson Henry, hatter, 65 Great Suffolk st. Borough
Thompson Henry, ship & ins. broker, 2 Cowper's ct. Cornhill
Thompson Henry, stockbroker, Stock exchange, Capel court
Thompson Henry E. travelling equipage ma. to the Queen, & patentee for the metallic military bedstead, 116 Long acre
Thompson Hugh, *Cheshire Cheese* P.H. Marquis ct.Drury la
Thompson Isaac, pewterer, 65 Bethnal green road
Thompson Isaac, tailor & draper, 32 Minories
Thompson James, baker, 64 Sun st. Bishopsgate
Thompson James, bricklayer, 49 Portpool la. Gray's inn la
Thompson James, *City Arms tavern*, 4 Pope's Head alley
Thompson James, ship biscuit baker, 353 Wapping
Thompson James, boot & shoe ma. 34 Cloth fair, Smithfield
Thompson James, cattle salesman, 17 West Smithfield
Thompson James, cheesemonger, 27 Lamb st. Spital square
Thompson James, coal merchant, 8 Fountain court, Strand
Thompson James, cochineal merchant, see Kirk & Thompson
Thompson James, fishmonger, 32 Little Marylebone st
Thompson James, grocer, &c.1Up.Southampton st. Pentonvl
Thompson James,grocer & cheesemongr.68West st.Smithfield
Thompson James, hide & skin salesman, Bermndsy. skin mkt
Thompson James, linen & manchester wareho. 21 Watling st
Thompson James, *Queen's Arms* P.H. 381 Oxford st
Thompson James, tailor, 11 Chichester rents, Chancery lane
Thompson James, veterinary surgeon, 3 Penton st. Pentonvl
Thompson James F. pawnbroker, 74 East st. Manchester sq
Thompson Job, coachmaker, 4 & 5 Little Grove st. Lisson gr
Thompson John, attorney, see Beaumont & Thompson
Thompson John, baker, 20 Harp alley, Shoe lane
Thompson John, baker, 5 Orford pl.Marlborough rd.Chelsea
Thompson John, baker, 16 Paradise row, Rotherhithe
Thompson John,builder,&steam saw mills,Camberwell green
Thompson John, coach joiner, 9 Up. Spring st. Marylebone
Thompson John, cochineal merchant, see Kirk & Thompson
Thompson John, coffee rooms, 14 Wellclose square
Thompson John, *Crown & Anch.* P.H.10 King'sHd.ct.Shoe la
Thompson John, dairyman, 46 Newman st. Oxford st
Thompson, John, engraver, 19 Red Lion st. Clerkenwell
Thompson John, furn. broker, 5 Broker's alley, Drury lane
Thompson John,iron&tin pl.mr.see DimmackThompson&Co.

Thompson John, ironmonger, 34 South Molton st. Bond st.
Thompson John, machine ruler & vellum binder, George yd. & 15 Craven buildings, Drury lane
Thompson John, merchant, 11 Abchurch lane, City
Thompson John, *Rising Sun* P.H. 38 Clothfair, Smithfield
Thompson John, rope mak. see Reed, Louch Bros. & Thompson
Thompson John, special pleader, 1 Middle Temple lane
Thompson John, stationer, 203 Poplar High st
Thompson John, statuary & mason, 13 Wells row, Islington
Thompson John, surgical instrument ma. 38 Gt. Windmill st
Thompson John, tailor & outfitr. 64 & 65 Pennyfields, Poplar
Thompson John, tailor, 27 Silver st. Wood st
Thompson John, tailor, 2 White Lion st. Norton folgate
Thompson John, tailor, 27 Wakefield st. Regent square
Thompson John, tripe dresser, 157 Aldersgate st. & 2 Rosoman st. Clerkenwell
Thompson John, window blind ma. 48 Whitcomb st. Pall mall
Thompson John, woodcutter, 1 Russel st. Low. Rotherhithe
Thompson John, jun. coal mer. Union wf. 68 Wapping wall
Thompson John Carby, silk manufr. see Smith & Thompson
Thompson John Danl. *Northbd. Arms* P.H. 18 Nrthumlnd. st
Thompson John G. D. law stationr. 7 Palsgrave pl. Temple bar
Thompson John J. boat bldr. Horseferry stairs, Rotherhth. st
Thompson John J. oil & colorman & melter, 25 Old Gravel lane
Thompson John M. solicitor & scotch law agt. 33 Bucklersbury
Thompson John S. trimmg. selr. & haberdshr. 106 Holborn hill
Thompson John V. serjt. at law, 4 Up. Belgrave st. Belgrv. sq.
Thompson John W. stocking trimmer & silk dyer, 135 Strand
Thompson Jonathan, paper stainer & decorator, 120 Cheapside; manufactory 1 York place, Walworth road
Thompson Joseph, grocer, 2 Staverton row, Walworth rd
Thompson Joseph, human hair mnfr. 16 Kirby st. Hatton gar
Thompson Joseph, linendraper, 3 Ter. Kensington High st
Thompson Joseph Berry, mathemat. instr. ma. 36 Wapping
Thompson Joseph Eyles, undertaker, 59 York st. Westminr
Thompson Joshua, oil & colorman, 28 Gt. Titchfield st.
Thompson Juliana (Mrs.), dressmkr. 7 Bydes pl. Shoreditch
Thompson Julius H. ship & ins. brok. see Aubert & Thompson
Thompson Lewes, *Bartholomew* coffee ho. 39 We. Smithfield
Thompson Marshall, *Thompson's hotel*, 28 & 29 Cavendish sq
Thompson Mary (Miss), chndl's. shop, 11 Russell pl. Old Kent rd
Thompson Mary (Mrs.), *Talbot hotel*, 39 & 40 Greenst. Gros. sq
Thompson Mary Ann (Mrs.), milliner, 107 Drummond st
Thompson Pearson, cheltenham salt wa. 7 Throgmorton st
Thompson Matthew Jas. *Crown* P.H. 3 Green st. Leicester st
Thompson Peter, export builder, Commercial road, east
Thompson Richard, baker, 22 Prospect pl. Cambridge heath
Thompson Richard, beer retailer, Millwall, Poplar
Thompson Richard, chemist, 12 Albert place, City road
Thompson Richard, shoemaker, 16 Bedford ct. Covent gardn
Thompson Richard, solicitor, 40 Coppice row, Clerkenwell
Thompson Richard, tailor, 6 Charles st. Manchester square
Thompson Richard, umbrella mfr. 7 Keen's row, Walworth rd
Thompson Rd. Brickwood, grocer, 2 Park ter. Camden town
Thompson Robert, printer, 12 Henry st. Pentonville
Thompson Robert, printer, 1 Little James st. Gray's inn la
Thompson Robert, tailor, 8 Bateman's buildings, Soho sq
Thompson Sam. birmingh. wa. & boarding ho. 103 Hatton gar
Thompson Samuel, cheesemonger, 70 Gt. Guildford st. Boro'
Thompson Samuel, coal & coke mer. 103 Hatton garden
Thompson Samuel, tailor & draper & outfitter, 19 St. Mary-at-hill, & 39 Eastcheap
Thompson Saml. Richd. tailors' trimg. slr. 8 High st. Shrdtch
Thompson Sarah (Miss), ladies' school, 14 Union st. Deptford
Thompson Seth, physician, 19 Brook st. Grosvenor square
Thompson Stephen, dairyman, 59 Gt. Portland st. Oxford st
Thompson Susan (Mrs.), milliner, &c. 18 St. Geo.'s pl. Cambwl
Thompson Theophilus, physician, 3 Bedford square
Thompson Thomas, bootmak. 24 St. Martin's st. Leicester sq
Thompson Thomas, carpenter, 30 Church row, Pancras road
Thompson Thomas (late Johnson), lint manufacturer, &c. 86 Long lane, Bermondsey
Thompson Thomas, *Duke of York* P.H. 35 Munster st. Rgt's pk
Thompson Thomas, solicitor, 109 Chancery lane
Thompson Thomas, solicitor, 5 Devonshire st. Queen sq
Thompson Thomas, watch maker, 6 Oakley st. Lambeth
Thompson Thomas, wheelwright, 10 Little Welbeck st
Thompson Thomas, *White Hart* P.H. 75 Gt. Tower st. City
Thompson Thos. Charles, barrister, 6 Pump court, Temple
Thompson Thos. Clement, R.H.A. artist, 76 Welbeck st
Thompson Thos. Kirkby, coln. produce agt. 32 Fenchurch st
Thompson Thos. Perronet, Edwd. barrister, 21 Old sq. Linc. inn
Thompson Thos. Willet, plumber, Essex place, Mile end rd
Thompson Thos. Wilmot, news agent, 2 Palsgrave pl. Strand
Thompson Wm. agent, see Goldsmid, King & Thompson
Thompson Wm. architect & survr. 2 Conduit st. west, Hyde pk
Thompson Wm. baker, 37 Church st. Shoreditch
Thompson Wm. baker, 46 Great James st. Lisson grove
Thompson Wm. baker, 30 Seymour place, Bryanstone sq
Thompson Wm. cabinetma. 22 Clubrow, Church st. Bethnal grn
Thompson Wm. cabinetma. 26½ Lit Guildford st. Bloomsbury
Thompson Wm. coachbuilder, see Horne, Thompson & Holland
Thompson Wm. *Globe & Friends* P.H. 13 Morganst. Coml. rd. ea
Thompson Wm. grocer, 1 Orford st. Marlboro' rd. Chelsea
Thompson Wm. grocer & cheesemonger, 87 Park st. Camden tn
Thompson Wm. ironmonger, 6 Boundary st. Shoreditch
Thompson Wm. lighterman & timber mer. 7 Romney st. Westmr
Thompson Wm. livery stables, Southampton row, Russell sq
Thompson Wm. *Old Parr's Head* P.H. 166 Aldersgate st
Thompson Wm. sail maker, 11 Cooper's row, City
Thompson Wm. solicitor, 44 Burton st. Burton crescent
Thompson Wm. surgeon, 6 Lambeth walk
Thompson Wm. surgeon, &c. 4 Lower Kennington green
Thompson Wm. tailor, 45 Dorset st. Manchester sq
Thompson Wm. tailor, 34 Gower place, Euston sq
Thompson Wm. timber merchant, 33 King st. Clerkenwell
Thompson Wm. tobacconist, 134 Praed st. Paddington
Thompson Wm. tobac. pipe ma. 4 Artichoke row, Mile end rd
Thompson Wm. *Western* coffee rooms, 39 Drury lane
Thompson Wm. who. brush ma. 15 Up. North pl. Gray's inn rd
Thompson Wm. Alfred, fruiterer, 30 Fore st. Cripplegate
Thompson Wm. George, grocer & wine dealer & agent to Phœnix Fire Office, 11 St. George's st. & 1 Neate st. Albany road, Old Kent rd
Thompson Wm. Hen. *Sun* P.H. Mason st. Westminstr. bdg. rd
Thompson Wm. Ths. cheesemonger, 4 Goldsmith rw. Hackny. rd
Thompson Wm. Thos. tobacconist, 40 Freeschool st. Horslydn
Thoms Peter Perring, printer & stereotye founder, 12 Warwick square, City
Thoms Robert, baker, 64 Lisson grove north, Marylebone
Thoms Wm. baker, 22 St. Andrew's road, Borough
Thoms Wm. operative chemist, see Burrows & Thoms
Thoms Wm. watch & case gilder, 51 Northampton st. Clerkw
Thomsett Jas. engine smith, 36 Chambrlns. yd. Belvedere rd
Thomson, Bonar & Co. merchants, 57½ Old Broad st. City
Thomson Brothers, wine & spirit mers. Old Trinity ho. Water la
Thomson Brothers & Sons, calico printers, &c. 2 Bow ch. yd
Thomson James & Co. ship & insurance brokers, 6 Billiter sq
Thomson John Mason & Sons, law stationers, 9 Chancery la
Thomson & M'Leod, tailors, 19 Princes st. Hanover sq
Thomson & Stephens, ship & ins. brok. St. Michael's chamb. City
Thomson Adam, baker, 3 Coborn road, Mile end road
Thomson Adam, clock & watch maker, 25 New Bond st
Thomson Alexander, *Sir George Osborne's Head* P.H. 28 Princes st, Mile end new town
Thomson Alex. wharfinger, Down's wharf, Lower East Smthfld
Thomson Andrew, *Anchor & Hope* P.H. 53 Edward st. Stepney
Thomson Anne (Miss), lodging house, 32 Surrey st. Strand
Thomson Anthony Todd, physician, 30 Welbeck st. Cavdsh. sq
Thomson Charles, surgeon, 3 King's terr. Bagnigge wells rd
Thomson David, baker, 27 Upper Berkeley st. Portman sq
Thomson Elizh. (Mrs.), confectioner, 65 London road, Sthwk
Thomson Francis, pawnbroker, Old Chapel rw. Kentish tn
Thomson Francis, pawnbroker, 25 Eyre st. hill
Thomson Frederick, cabinet maker, 10 Charterhouse st
Thomson Fredk. medicine chest ma. see Springweiler & Thomson
Thomson Frederick Hale, consulting surgeon, 48 Berners st
Thomson George, baker, 26 Castle st. Falcon sq
Thomson George, egg merch. 18 Croydon st. Bryanstone sq
Thomson George, general agent, 12 Bucklersbury, City
Thomson George, *Marq. Cornwallis* P.H. 22 Dyer st. Southwk
Thomson George, pawnbroker, 17 Frederick pl. Hampstead rd
Thomson Greig, dentist, 29 Grosvenor st. Grosvenor sq
Thomson Henry Urmston, physician, 123 Piccadilly
Thomson Henry T. sec. to the North British insurance company & London Reversionary interest society, 4 New Bank buildings
Thomson James, architect, 57 Devonshire st. Portland place
Thomson James, artist, 97 Albany st. Regent's park
Thomson James, baker, 7 Newcastle st. Strand
Thomson James, chemist, 15 Globe road, Mile end
Thomson James, potato merchant, 152 Wapping High st
Thomson Jas. seed & nurseryman, see Gordon, Thomson & Co
Thomson James Richard, solicitor, 9 George st. Minories
Thomson Jane (Mrs.), *Shad Dock House* P.H. Shadwell dock st
Thomson John, boot & shoe maker, 3 Red Lion pass. Fleet st
Thomson John, physician, 80 Coleman st. City
Thomson John, ship, &c. broker, see Miller, Forbes & Thomson
Thomson John, straw hat manfr. 13 Gt. Union st. Newington
Thomson John, wine merchant, see Reid (Nevile) & Thomson
Thomson John Duffin, attorney, see Walsh & Thomson
Thomson John Mason, law stationer, 6 Symond's inn

Thomson John Robt. merchant, St. Peter's chamb. Cornhill
Thomson John Scarlett, solicitor, 17 John st. Bedford row
Thomson Lawrence, baker, 28 Elizabeth st. Eaton square
Thomson Mary (Mrs.), artist, 25 New Bond st
Thomson Mary (Mrs.), *Bird in Hand* P.H. Bow
Thomson Mary Ann (Miss), straw bonnet ma. 241 Whitechp. rd
Thomson Matthew, watchma. 4 Barnsbury villas, Liverpl. rd
Thomson Peter, *George* P.H. 9 Gt. Queen st. Lincoln's inn flds
Thomson Robert, baker, 14 Arlington st. Camden town
Thomson Robert, baker, Kingswood place, South Lambeth
Thomson Robt. egg mercht. 7 Adelphi wf. Durham st. Strand
Thomson Robert, grocer, 4 Burlington place, Old Kent road
Thomson Robert Wm. civil engineer, 18 Adam st. Adelphi
Thomson Susah. (Mrs.), haberdasher, 22 Cannon st. St. Geo.'s e
Thomson Thomas, fruiterer, 7 Samson's place, Grange road
Thompson Thomas D. bookseller, 13 Upper King st. Bloomsby
Thomson Wm. coachmaker, 33 Mortimer st. Cavendish sq
Thomson Wm. orange merchant, 111 Lower Thames st
Thomson Wm. M.D. surgeon, 51 Charlotte st. Fitzroy sq
Thomson Wm. Archibald, auctioneer, 326 Oxford st
Thomson Wm. Dalrymple, bookslr. & statr. 138 Up. st. Islngtn
Thonger Robert, leather seller, Southampton st. Camberwell
Thorborn Walter, grocer & cheesemong. 5 Lit. Compton, Soho
Thorburn George, merchant, 21 Haydon square, Minories
Thorburn John, bookbinder, 2 Pleydell st. Fleet st
Thorburn Richard, bookseller, 31 Newcastle st. Strand
Thorburn Robert, artist, 77 Up. Berkeley st. Portman sq
Thorby Thomas, wine mercht. see Gorman, Hamilton & Thorby
Thorley Joseph, cabinet maker, &c. 10 Newman st. Oxford st
Thorman Edward, plumber, Stratford broadway
Thorman Thos. & Co. who. teadls. 2 Maiden la. Queen st. Cheaps
Thorman Robert, plumber, Bromley, Middlesex
Thorn Alexander, oil & italian wareho. proprietor of the tally ho sauce & potted yarmouth bloaters, 223 High Holborn
Thorn Edward, butcher, 16 Portman market, Marylebone
Thorn Edward, dining rooms, 24 Tothill st. Westminster
Thorn Fred. Wm. hat mfr. 46 Hatfield st. Stamford st. Blkfrs
Thorn George, baker, 205 Poplar High st
Thorn Grace (Mrs.) farrier, 4 Marlboro' mews, Blenheim st
Thorn Henry *George* P.H. 14 Bury st. St. James's
Thorn Henry, hosier & merino manufacturer, 23 Ludgate st
Thorn John, builder, 3 Little Stanhope street, Mayfair
Thorn John, carman, 5 Little Albany st. Regent's park
Thorn John, cheesemonger, 198 Brick lane, Spitalfields
Thorn Joseph, carpenter, 11 Barnet st. Hackney road
Thorn Peter, bottled stout merchant, and manuf. of pat. apparatus for bottling wines, 40 Castle st. Leicester sq
Thorn Peter, whip maker to her Majesty, 185 Regent st
Thorn Reuben Tredcein, bookbinder, 59 Basinghall st
Thorn Richd. Lawrence, surgeon, 31 Upper Belgrave place
Thorn Robert, fishmonger, 121 Cornwall road, Lambeth
Thorn Thomas, dining rooms, 3 & 4 Bucklersbury
Thorn Wm. brick, coal & ash merch. see Stapleton & Thorn
Thorn Wm. coachmaker, 98 New Bond st. & 10 John st. Oxfd. st
Thorn Wm. *Crown* P.H. Back hill, Hatton garden
Thorn Wm. *Duke of Wellington* P.H. 13 Brighton st. Cromer st
Thorn Wm. *Middleton Arms* P.H. 7 Mansfield st. Kingslandrd
Thornborough Wm. wheelwr. 5 Compton mews, Brunswick sq
Thornborrow Wm. general agt. 8 King's Arms bldgs. Cornhill
Thornborrow Wm. underwriter, 34 Trinity square, Borough
Thornbory Jane (Miss) haberdasher, see Park & Thornbory
Thornbury Thos. boot & shoe ma. 3 Lt. Crown ct. Princes st. Soho
Thornby Hammon (exors. of) *King's Arms* P.H. 106 Bishopsgate within
Thorndike Andrew Snape, attorney, 11 Staple inn, Holborn
Thorndike Wm. mathematical inst. mkr. 2 Eaglest. City road
Thorne John Mills & Son, ale &c. brew. Nine Elms, & 6 Mark la
Thorne Rd. & John, carpenters, Pembroke mews, Grosvenor pl
Thorne Timothy & Son, westminster brewery, Earl st. Horseferry road, & Market st. Millbank st. Westminster
Thorne Charles, malster, Commercial road, Pimlico
Thorne George, gasfitter, 19 Fore st. Cripplegate
Thorne Jeremiah, tailor, 1 Portsmouth st. Lincoln's inn fields
Thorne John, builder, 11 Caroline st. Pimlico
Thorne John, *Dolphin* P.H. 50 Whitechapel road
Thorne John, surgeon, 4 Mylne st. Claremont sq. Pentonvill
Thorne Joseph, carpenter, Southampton st. Camberwell rd
Thorne Robert, dyer, &c. 31 Somerset place, Hoxton
Thorne Samuel, miller, Millwall, Poplar
Thorne Theop. (Mrs.), dress ma. 10 Scarsdale ter. Kensingtn
Thorne Thos. coffee rooms, 28 Lit. Carter la. Doctors' com
Thorne Wm. linendraper, 9 Crawley st. Somers town
Thornett Charles, water cress dealer, 25 Queen st. Seven dials
Thornewell James, grocer & cheesemonger, Camberwell grove
Thornhill John Jas. & Co. cutlers to the Queen, 144 New Bond st
Thornhill Edward & Son, flour factors & coal mer. 24 Mark la
Thornhill Geo. & Co. colonial newspaper office, 3 Staining la
Thornhill Henry T. woollen agent, 3 Sherborne lane, City
Thornhill James, baker, 33 Tottenham court road
Thornhill Jas. plumber & painter, 6 Garden row, Camberwell
Thornhill William, ship & insurance agent, 24 Mark lane
Thornthwaite Wm. Hen. optician, see Horne, Thornthwaite & Co
Thornton Edwd. Norton & Son, undertakers, 174 Boro' High st
Thornton & Son, auctioneers, valuers, land & estate agents, 58 Fenchurch st. & Stratford & Brentwood, Essex
Thorntons' (R. & R.) & West, east india merchants, Old Swan wharf, Upper Thames st
Thornton Alex. *Bricklayers' Arms* P.H. 8 Up. Dorchr. pl. Hxtn
Thornton Benj. surgeon, 4 Shepperton pl. New North road
Thornton Chas. Dry, carriage repository, Little Chelsea
Thornton Ebenezer, commission agt. 25 Clement's lane, City
Thornton Edward, conveyancer, 4 Stone bldgs. Lincoln's inn
Thornton Edward, plumber & glazier, 24 Coleman st
Thornton Edward Lane, hosier, &c. 7 Ludgate hill
Thornton Elizh. (Mrs.), beer retailer, 4 Heath pl. Hackney rd
Thornton Frances (Mrs.), milliner, &c. 273 Regent st
Thornton John, baker, 17 Union st. Borough
Thornton John, house painter, &c. 4 Wilson st. Finsbury
Thornton John, whiting manufacturer & limeburner, Nine Elms, Vauxhall
Thornton John, hairdresser, &c. 77 Red Lion st. Holborn
Thornton John, ornamental painter, 2 Lit. Woodstock st
Thornton John, tailor, 110 Drummond st. Euston square
Thornton Joseph, cabinetma. 2 Hale's ter. Commrcl. rd. east
Thornton Mary (Mrs.), umbrella ma. 8 Church rw. Ald. High st
Thornton Philip, surgeon, 3 Museum st. Bloomsbury
Thornton Robert, *King's Arms* P.H. 1 Claremont rw. Islngtn
Thornton Robert, tailor, 14 Seabright pl. west, Hackney rd
Thornton Thomas, baker, Church st. Deptford
Thornton Thomas, *Brompton* coffee rooms, 7 Brompton road
Thornton Thomas, house & ornam. painter, 31 Gt. Carter la
Thornton Thomas, jeweller, 35 Dean st. Soho
Thornton Thomas, *Pine Apple* P.H. 30 Westbourne st. Pimlico
Thornton Thomas, upholsterer, &c. 22 Cross st. Islington
Thornton Wm. butcher, 66 Regent st. Horseferry road
Thornton Wm. carpenter, 105 Little Cadogan pl. Sloane st
Thornton Wm. furnishing undertaker, 18 Little Pulteney st
Thornton Wm. rickcloth & tarpaulin maker, 90 Harrow road
Thornton Wm. tobaccopipe ma. 36 Gt. James st. Hoxton Old tn
Thornton William Henry Scott, auctioneer, Stratford
Thorogate James John, carman, 13 Norwich court, Fetter la
Thorogood James, cab proprietor, 18 Cobourg st. Euston sq
Thorogood John, *Blue Boar inn*, 30 Aldgate High st
Thorogood Samuel, *Assembly House* P.H. Kentish town
Thorogood Sam. *Swan* P.H. 6 High st. Kensington Gravel pits
Thorowgood & Besley, typefounders, 2 Fan st. Aldersgate st
Thorowgood John, grocer, 8 King st. Camden town
Thorowgood John, grocer, 1 Stringer's row, Lr. rd. Rotherh
Thorowgood Saml. bootmaker, see Dutton & Thorowgood
Thorowgood George, stonemason, 24 Canal rd. Kingsland rd
Thorp Charles, butcher, 31 St. John st. road
Thorp Chas. *Running Horse* P.H. 32 Duke st. Grosvenor sq
Thorp George, baker, 45 Bath st. City road
Thorp George, baker, 4 Marlborough road, Chelsea
Thorp George, linendraper, Surrey house, Clapham rd
Thorp Henry, broker & undertaker, 48 James st. Oxford st
Thorp Hen. Edwin, beer retailer, 105 Bishopsgate st. within
Thorp John Jarman, watchmaker, see Matthews & Thorp
Thorp Jonathan, silk manufacturer, 30 King st. Cheapside
Thorp Nicholas, chairmaker, 67 Worship st. Norton Folgate
Thorp Thos. cheesemonger, 18A, Compton st. Brunswick sq
Thorp William, retail brewer & corn dealer, 27 & 28 Chapel st. Curtain road, Shoreditch
Thorp William, tailor, 24 Little Pulteney st. Golden sq
Thorpe Francis & Co. thread manfrs. 130 Wood st. Cheapside
Thorpe Chas. grocer & undertaker, 1 Prospect pl. Stepney gn
Thorpe George, *Robin Hood tavern*, 281 High Holborn
Thorpe George, sen. cowkeeper, Glasshouse fields, Ratcliff
Thorpe George, jun. cowkeeper, 52 Queen st. Ratcliff
Thorpe Henry, boot & shoema. 8 Britannia pl. Wandsworth rd
Thorpe Henry, grocer & teadlr. 29 Chapel st. Edgware road
Thorpe Henry, tobacconist, 3 Frederick st. Regent's park
Thorpe John, artist, 22 Rutland st. Hampstead road
Thorpe John, bricklayer, 4 New Church st. West, Edgware rd
Thorpe John, painter & paper hngr. Southampton st. Cambrwl
Thorpe John, teadealer, see Scott & Thorpe
Thorpe Joseph Thomas, cheesemonger, 24 Rupert st
Thorpe Nicholas, tailor & clothier, 28 St. Mary at hill
Thorpe Richd. cabinetmaker, 10 Up. Charlton st. Fitzroy sq
Thorpe Rd. Wray, *Prince Albert* P.H. 16 Alfred st. City rd
Thorpe Thomas, bookseller, 178 Piccadilly
Thorpe Thomas, haircutter, 87 Bunhill row

Thorpe Thomas, hairdresser, 47 James st. Oxford st
Thorpe Wm. fruit salesman, Covent garden fruit market
Thorpe Wm. Beck, butcher, 30 Aylesbury st. Clerkenwell
Thorpe Wm. James, barrister, 7 New sq. Lincoln's inn
Thorrington John, fruiterer, 34 St. Andrew's hill, Blackfrs
Thredder John & Co. hatters, 74 Fleet st
Thredder Robert, hatmaker, 26 Blackman st. Borough
Three Cranes Wharf, William Todd & Son, between 69 & 78 Upper Thames st
Threlkeld Hen. accountant&auctioneer,35King st.Cheapside
Thresher & Glenny,hosiers,outfitters,& shirtmaks.152Strand
Thresher Edward, hatter, 22 Kensington High st
Thresher William, grocer, 39 Carlisle st. Lambeth
Thring Henry, barrister, 30 Lincoln's inn fields
Thring Joseph, tailor, 20 Brooke st. Holborn
Thring Samuel, trunkmaker, 68 Marylebone la. Oxford st
Thring Theodore, barrister, 8 King's Bench walk, Temple
Throssell Charles, coffee rooms, 245 Borough High st
Throssell Charles, herbalist, 13 Harp alley, Shoe lane
Thrower Edward, potato dealer, 8 Lumber ct. Seven dials
Thrower John, whitesmith, Melbourne pl. Old Kent rd
Thrower Thomas, farrier, Melbourne pl. Old Kent rd
Thrupp Charles & Co. coachmakers, 269 Oxford st. & 33 George st. Grosvenor square
Thrupp, Son & Henshaw,coachmks.53George st.Portman sq
Thrupp Frederic, sculptor, 30 Gloucester place, New road
Thrupp Hen.Jsph.coach spg.&axletree mak.5Geo.st.Gros.sq
Thrupp John, solicitor, 2 Winchester bldngs.Gt.Winchestr.st
Thrupp JosephWm.solicitor,see Burgoynes, Thrupp & Clark
Thrupp William Henry, coal merchant, 8 St. Thomas' st. east, & Crown wharf, Shad Thames
Thurburn & Co. merchants & east india agents,5 Crosby sq. Bishopsgate within
Thurgar Abraham, carpenter, 17 Charles st. City road
Thurgood God. baker, 92 & grocer, 94 Gt. Titchfield st
Thurgood Godfrey Goodwin, baker, 34 Crown st. Soho
Thurgood William, *Black Horse* P.H. 47 Barbican
Thurgood Wm.grocer& oilman, 13 Theobald's rd.Red Lion sq
Thurkle Benj. sword cutler & belt maker, 104 High Holborn
Thurland John, tracing paper ma. see Gardner & Thurland
Thurlby Sarah(Mrs.),*Two Black Boys*P.H.Well st.Hackney
Thurley Henry, grocer, &c. 121 Brook st. Ratcliff
Thurley James Samuel, undertaker, 50 Shadwell High st
Thurling Hen. William, firewood dlr. 5 New whf. Whitefriars
Thurling Thomas, butcher, 29 Red Lion street, Holborn
Thurlow Edward, carpenter, 21 Hoxton square
Thurlow Robert, *New Grapes* P.H. 242 Bermondsey st
Thurlow Thomas Edward, cheesemonger, 99 Rosemary lane
Thurlow Jeremiah, carpenter, 20 New Millman st. Foundling
Thurmim John C. & Co. merchants, 65 Fenchurch st
Thurman Wm. & Co. who. hosiers, 50 Wood st. Cheapside
Thurman Joseph, goldcaster, 3 Kirby st. Hatton garden
Thurmott William, coal merchant, 29 Bedford st. Covent garden, & Great Scotland yard, Charing cross
Thurnell Wm. Giles, plumber, 17 & 18 Parker's rw. Dockhead
Thursfield Edmund, oil & italian warehouse, 21 Oxford st
Thurston Harriet (Mrs.), seminary, 246 Albany rd. Cambrwl
Thurston John, billiard & bagatelle table manufacturer, by appointment, to her Majesty, also of the improved revolving lamp, 14 Catherine st. Strand
Thurston John, stockbroker, 7 Tokenhouse yard
Thurston Simon, surveyor, 9 Southampton st. Bloomsbury
Thurston William, tailor, 13 Clark's place, Islington
Thurtell Emily (Miss), boarding house, 137 Leadenhall st
Thwaites & Reed, clockmakers, 4 Rosamon st. Clerkenwell
Thwaites Charlotte (Miss), milliner, 40 Gracechurch st
Thwaites John, saddler&harness ma.159 Bishopsgate without
Thwaites John, woollen draper, 18 Blackman st. Borough, & 388 Oxford st
Thwaites Peter, fruit salesman, North row, Covent garden
Thwaites Samuel, sen. fruiterer, North row, Covent garden
Thwaites Thomas, tailor & draper, see Kirby & Thwaites
Thwaites Thomas Smith, tailor, 2 Hampton st. Walworth rd
Thwaites William G. solicitor, 4 Lyon's inn, Strand
Thyer James, grocer, 4 Westbourne st. Pimlico
Thynne Fredk. land agent, see Pearce & Thynne
Tiarks Henry Frederick, merchant, 48 Fenchurch st
Tibbatt Robert, lodging house, 7 King st. Grosvenor sq
Tibbatts Horace Nelson, surgeon, 14 Old Paradise rw. Islngtn
Tibbatts John, stove grate maker, 44 Bishopsgate without
Tibbatts Wm. featherdressr. & mattrass ma. 76 Hackney rd
Tibbee John, fruiterer, 25 Compton st. Brunswick sq
Tibbetts Caleb, plumber, 11 Great Ormond st. Queen sq
Tibbetts Jeremiah, builder, 14 Commercial pl. Kentish town
Tibbey Edward, diamond merchant, 22 Frith st. Soho
Tibbitt Saml. dressing case ma. 9 Queen's head la. Islingtn
Tibbitts Elizabeth (Mrs.), butcher, 7 Lambeth walk
Tibbitts John, who. stationer, 5 Budge row, Cannon st
Tibbles Wm. *Ship & Sailor* P.H. Effingham place, Deptford
Tibbs Josiah Hawkins & Co. grocers, 36 Wigmore st
Tibbs Henry, working jeweller, 27 Berwick st. Soho
Tibbs John, cooper, 2 Barbican
Tibbs John E. russia broker, 4 Cushion ct. & Baltic coff. ho
Tibbs Joseph, locksmith, 5 Princes st. Bedford row
Tibbs Joseph E. jun. russia broker, Baltic coffee house
Tibbs Josiah, importer of foreign wines, 17 Gt. Tower st
Tibbs Josiah H. grocer & tea dealer, 294 Oxford st
Tibbs Richd. Wm. dentist, 4 Gloucester st. Queen sq
Tibbs Thomas Cooper, 3 Francis place, Holloway
Tibbutt Esau, whip manufacturer, 180 Whitechapel road
Tibenham Eliza (Mrs.),shoemak. 32 Charles st.Middlx. hsptl
Tibson Arthur, surgeon, 1 Spring st. Paddington
Tichener John, stationer, Bridge road, Battersea
Tickell George, cheesemonger, 2 Broad st. Golden square
Tickell Hen. linendraper, see Moore, James, Tate, Tickell & Co
Tickell Richard, painter, Battersea
TicknerHen.*StJohnofJerusalem*P.H.28St.John st.Clerknwl
Tickner Samuel, furn. broker, 299 Albany rd. Camberwell
Tidbury Robert, hatter, 73 Long acre, & 38 South st. Manch.sq
Tidd James, eating house, 8 High st. Portland town
Tidd John Lester, stationer & tobacconist, 57 Goswell road
Tidd William, barrister, 59 Walcot place east, Lambeth
Tiddeman Fredk. Aug. & Co. iron merchts. Earl st. Blackfrs
Tidder Jos. umbrella & parasol mkr. 8 Lit. Alie st. Gdmn's. fi
Tidey Alfred, artist, 29 Edwards st. Portman square
Tidman Thos. Wm. paper hanger, 130 Cornwall rd. Lambeth
Tidman William, who. druggist, 10 Wormwood st. Bishopsgt
Tidmarsh & Brown, staffordsh. wareho. 4 Rosemary la. Minories
Tidmarsh Chas. & Son, carpenters, &c. 2 Compton pl. Nw. Nh. rd
Tidmarsh James, wholesale cutler, steel pen & comb warehouse, 13 Eyre st. hill, Hatton garden
Tidmarsh Richard, tobacconist, 10 Duke st. Smithfield
Tidmarsh Saml. Hen. prof. of music, 5 Taunton pl. Park rd
Tidmarsh Wm. carver & gilder, 24 Park st. Up. st. Islington
Tidswell & Hall, wine merchants, 28 Budge row, Cannon st
Tidswell Elizh. (Mrs.), shopkepr. 41 Gt. Cambridge st. Hckny. rd
Tidy George, *King's Head* P.H. Old Mint, Tower
Tidy Wm. Callender, surgeon, Cambridge heath, Hackney rd
Tielens John Anthony, merchant, 8 London st. Fenchurch st
Tierney Wm. pianoforte tuner, 10 Rolls buildings, Fetter la
Tietjen Martin, cowkeeper, 8 William st. Curtain road
Tiffin Chas. uphol. & bug destroyer, 17 Somers pl. e. New rd
Tiffin James B. printseller, &c. 79 Wardour st
Tiffin John, bootmaker, 17 Portsea place, Connaught sq
Tiffin Robert, tobacconist, 73 Borough High st
Tiffin Walter Benj. ancient & modern printseller, 434 Strand
Tighe Chas. stay & bonnet shape wa. 15 Etham pl. Kent st. Boro'
Tighe John, pawnbroker, Broadway, Deptford
Tigwell Joseph, grocer, 1 Spring Garden place, Stepney
Tijou Henry, carver & gilder, 8 Vauxhall Bridge road
Tijou Thomas, carver & gilder, 73 Union st. Borough
Tilbrook Frank, grocer, 3 Market st. Jermyn st
Tilbury Edwd. & Co. storerooms for warehousing goods, &c. 35 & 49 High st. Marylebone; & Blandford pl. Regent's pk
Tilbury, Son & Clarke, coachmakers, 35 Glo'ster pl. New rd
Tilbury Edmund, plumber, painter, &c. 6 Nottingham st
Tilbury John, jobmaster, 48 Mount st. Berkeley square
Tilby John, butcher, 38 Carnaby st. Golden square
Tilby John, tailor, 2 East st. Old Kent road
Tildesley Samuel, sawing, &c. mills, see Buddle & Tildesley
Tiley Edward, dairyman, 28 Saville st. Fitzroy square
Tiley Thomas, butcher, 48 Kennington st. Walworth
Tilke Joel, *Bedford* coffee ho. 9 Warwick lane, Newgate st
Tilke Saml. W. medical botanist, 8 Thayer st. Manchester sq
Till Geo. & Co. eng. & for. stock & sharedlrs. 27 Lombard st. City
Till John, coach proprietor, 75 Connaught ter. Edgware rd
Till Richard, land tax rooms, Guildhall buildings
Till Wm. *Flying Horse* P.H. 63 Lambeth st. Whitechapel
Till Wm. *Plumbers' Arms* P.H. Low. Belgrave st. Pimlico
Till Wm. Thomas, tobacco broker, see Bremner & Till
Tilleard John & Son, solicitors, 34 Old Jewry
Tilleard John, oil & colorman, 28 Gt. Suffolk st. Borough
Tiller Thomas, baker, 5 Field pl. Larkhall lane, Clapham
Tillet Alex. & John, saltpetre refins. 4 Yorkter. Yorkrd. Lamth
Tillett Elizabeth (Mrs.), chair & sofa stuffer, 42 Old st. rd
Tillett George, commisn. agent, Hall of Commerce, City
Tillett Jas. engineer & millwright, 7 Marygold st. Bermondsy
Tillett Joseph, currier, 53 Marshall st. Golden square
Tillett Samuel, special pleader, 4 Inner Temple lane
Tilley & Garrod, bronze powdr. mfrs. & gen. mer. 45 Newgate st
Tilley Henry, tobacconist, 91 Piccadilly
Tilley John, coach painter, 13 Weymouth mews, Portland pl

Tilley John, *Roebuck* P.H. 1 Edward's place, Hackney rd
Tilley John, tailor, 7 New road, St. George's east
Tilley Joseph, hat dyer, see Dunn & Tilley
Tilley Joseph, pawnbroker, 1 Road side, Mile end road
Tilley Richard, lodging house, 15 Cloak lane, City
Tilley Samuel, surgeon, 27 Paradise row, Rotherhithe
Tilley Sarah (Miss), artificial flower ma. see Wilson & Tilley
Tilley Thomas, carpenter, 78 Praed st. Paddington
Tilley Thomas, gasfitter, 4 Edward st. Kingsland road
Tilley Thomas, wire weaver, 1 Edward st. York road, & 14 & 15 Stangate mews, Lambeth
Tilley William, baker, 40 Albany st. Regent's park
Tilley Wm. Joshua, fire engine maker, 245 Blackfriars road
Tilley Wm. Joshua, leathr. pipe & bucket ma. 245 Blackfrs.rd
Tilley Wm. Joshua, pump & engine maker, 245 Blackfrs. rd
Tilling James, dairyman, 80 Earl st. east, Lisson grove
Tilling Robt. cheesemonger, 84 Earl st. east, Lisson grove
Tilling Robert, van proprietor, 33 Charles st. Middsx. hosp
Tilling Wm. appraiser, 30 New Manor st. King's rd. Chelsea
Tilling Wm. jun. brush ma. 13 Adams pl. King's rd. Chelsea
Tillingham Wm. chair maker, 64 Princes road, Lambeth
Tillman Wm. & George, tailors, 3 Osborne st. Whitechapel
Tillman George, coach lamp maker, 14 King st. St. Luke's
Tillman James Edward, tailor & tobacconist, 4 Aldgate
Tillman Thomas, tailor, 200 Whitechapel road
Tillotson John, *Grapes* P.H. 69 St. George st
Tillotson William, barrister, 2 Stone buildings, Lincoln's inn
Tillott Edwin, chandler's shop, 2 Albert pl. Hoxton Old tn
Tillott James, carpenter, 33 Upper Clifton st. Finsbury
Tills Charles, carpenter, 30 King st. Clerkenwell
Tilly Alfred, painter & glazier, 14 Pollen st. Hanover sq
Tilly Charles Watkins, surgeon, 4 Church st. Camberwell
Tilly George, coffee rooms, 11 Gt. James st. Lisson grove
Tilly John, cornchandler, 6 Cross st. Blackfriars road
Tilly Wm. carpenter & undertaker, 14 Pollen st. Hanover sq
Tillyard John, cowkeeper, 18 Bear yd. Lincoln's inn fields
Tilson & Squance, attorneys, 29 Coleman st
Tilson Edward, smith & bellhngr. 9 North ea. pass. Wellclose sq
Tilson George, mahogany merchant, 2 Lime st. square
Tilstone Chas. F. manager, Bastenne Asphalte, or Bitumen Co. 31 Poultry & Millwall
Tilstone Isabella (Mrs.), haberdasher, 78 York st. Westminster
Tilstone Wm. Hen. merchant, 1 Crown ct. Threadneedle st
Tilt Benjamin, butcher, 77 York st. Westminster
Tilt Charles, coachmaker, 3½ Suffolk place, Hackney road
Tilt Edward Wm. physician, 10 Norfolk st. Park lane
Tilt Joseph, custom house agent, 150 Fenchurch st
Tiltman Thos. & Son, fruit salesmen, Long mkt. Covnt. gdn
Tiltman George, oil & colorman, Kensington gravel pits
Tiltman George, oil & colorman, 93 High st. Notting hill
Tily William Grayall, baker, 19 Earl st. Horseferry road
Timberlake & Priestley, wax & tallow chandls. 311 Oxford st
Timberlake Chas. *Queen's Head* P.H. 15 Albany st Rgt's.pk
Timberlake James, *Brown Bear* P.H. 21 Bear la. Blackfrs.rd
Timberlake Thomas, hat block maker, New st. Southwark
Timbrell Andrw. *Goldsmith's Arms* P.H. 1 Albionbgs. Brthol.cl
Timbrell Jane (Mrs.), teadealer, 14 Leigh st. Burton crescent
Timbrell Samuel, carver & gilder, 2 Seymour row, Lit. Chelsea
Timbrell Thos. temple dining rooms, 41 Bell yd. Temple bar
Timbury Chas. & Son, eng. & bkbnds' tool cuts, 44 Paternostr. row
Timbury Frederick, bookbinders' tool cutter, 104 Fetter la
The Times & Evening Mail Office, Printing house sq. Blackfrs
Times Henry G. chemist & druggist, 4 Thayer st. Manch. sq
Timewell Jas. corndl. 96 Grand Junction ter. Edgware road
Timewell John, army tailor, 24 Duke st. St. James's
Timewell Wm. builder, 1 Hanover st. Noel st. Islington
Timm George, marine store dealer, 108 Hoxton Old town
Timm Joseph, solicitor, stamp & tax office, Somerset house
Timms Arthur James, confectioner, 104 Norton st. Fitzroy sq
Timms John, *Fox & Grapes* P.H. 18 Primrose st. Bishopsgate
Timms Wm. fruiterer, 11 St. Alban's place, Haymarket
Timms Wm. Hy. wine & spirit merc. 32 Northumberland st
Timms Wm. Robert, glover & stock mak. 124 Aldersgate st
Timothy David, bed feather merc. upholder, &c. 31 Barbican
Timothy Edmund, bedding manfr. 12 Corrie pl. Old Kent rd
Timothy John, coal & potato dlr. 22 Marylebone la. Oxford st
Timothy Wm. carpet & bedding wareho. 12 Shoreditch High st
Timperon & Dobinson, west india merchants, 26 Philpot lane
Timpson Abel, tobacconist, 121 Chalton st. Somers town
Timpson Mortimore, builder, Stanhope pl. Hampstead road
Tims Thos. cabinet ma. & house ag. 63 Charlotte st. Fitzroy sq
Timson John, baker, 21 Sidney st. Commercial road
Tindal Arthur, newsagent, 2 Lovell's court, Paternoster row
Tindal Charles John, barrister, 36 Lincoln's inn fields
Tindal Thomas, solicitor, see Law & Tindal
Tindal William, barrister, 2 Tanfield court, Temple
Tindale Ebenezer, tobacco & snuff ma. 14 Cock hill, Ratcliff
Tindale Elizth. (Mrs.), tobacconist, 56 Brick lane, Spitalfields
Tindale Henry, chemist, 105A, Crawford st. Portman square
Tindale Henry, surgeon, 26 Upper Montagu st
Tindale Michael F. auctn. & undert. 1 Portland pl. Com. rd. ea
Tindall Edwd. coal & coke mer. 85 Church st. Rotherhithe
Tindall Geo. & Co. ship & insur. agents, 2 Riches ct. Lime st
Tindall Geo. coal mer. 36 Charles st. Commercial road east
Tindall Wm. merchant & shipowner, importer & manufacturer of cocoa nut oil, 34 Cornhill; manfy. Millwall, Poplar
Tindall William, potato salesman, 68 Wapping High st
Tindley John Wm. tallow chandler, see Kell & Tindley
Tingey Samuel & Son, cattle salesmen, 8 West Smithfield
Tingey Geo. Thompson, undertaker, 258 Kent st. Borough
Tingey William, pawnbroker, 10 & 11 Greek st. Soho
Tingley Benj. coal & potato dlr. 15 Northampton rw. Hllwy. rd
Tink John, grocer & teadealer, 67 Union st. Clarendon sq
Tinkler Geo. Wm. custom ho. & comm. agt. 13 Harp la. City
Tinkler John, dyer & scourer, 10 Lit. Carter la. Drs'. commons
Tinley Edward, linendraper, 5 Pownall ter. Kennington road
Tinney William Henry, queen's counsel, 9 Old sq. Lincoln's inn
Tinning John, whip thong maker, 9 New Compton st. Soho
Tinslay James, tailor, 94 Curtain road, Shoreditch
Tinslay John, solicitor, 2 Rolls buildings, Chancery lane
Tinslay Joseph, confectioner, 11 Providence pl. Kentish tn
Tinsley James, plumber, 4 Russell ct. Brydges st. Cov. grdn
Tinson George, butcher, 6 Little Bath st. Clerkenwell
Tinson Henry, butcher, 2 Chelsea market, Lower Sloane st
Tinson William, *Two Brewers* P.H. 164 High Holborn
Tiplady John, merchant, 5 Barge yard, Bucklersbury
Tiplady William Henry, shipbroker, see Phillipps & Tiplady
Tipper & Belgrave, who. tea dlrs. & grocers, 20 Cullum st
Tipper Samuel & Co. who. stationers, 42 Upper Thames st
Tipper Alfred, china & glass warehouse, Clare market
Tipper Benjamin, wholes. stationer, 10 Maiden lane, Queen st
Tipper Edgar, tailor, 8 Stanhope st. Clare market
Tipper Hen. butcher, 6 & 7 Spectacle alley, Whitechapl. High st
Tipper Henry, grocer, 3 Kirby st. Hatton garden
Tipper John, butcher, 5 Spectacle alley, Whitechapel High st
Tipper John, conveyancer, 5 Newmarket ter. Cambridge hth
Tipper Thomas, timber merchant, 28 Gravel la. Borough
Tippett Benjamin Matthew, druggist, 3 Sloane st
Tippett George, builder, 14 Russell st. Bermondsey
Tippett James, baker, 10 Aylesbury st. Clerkenwell
Tippett James, coffee rooms, 9 Black Prince row, Walw. rd
Tippett Thos. Knight, oilman, 3 Stringer's row, Rotherhithe
Tippetts Jas. Berriman, solicitor, 6 Pancras la. Bucklersbury
Tippin Ralph, tin & zinc worker, 23 Eldon st. Finsbury
Tipping & Lawden, gun & pistol ma. 20 Bartlett's bldgs. Hlbn
Tipping James, french polisher, 72 New Compton st. Soho
Tippins Saml. hairdresser, 3 & 4 New Montague st. Sptalflds
Tipple Sarah (Mrs.), teadealer, 50 Gower place, Euston sq
Tipple Woodward, fruiterer, 55 Amwell st. Pentonville
Tippler Robert, colonial broker, 89 Great Tower st. City
Tipton Abraham James, pat. lint mnfr. 8 Etham pl. Old Kent rd
Tipton Charlotte (Mrs.), *Britannia* P.H. Little Britain & 42 Duke st. Smithfield
Tirebuck Joseph & Isaac, printers, 24 Queen st. Cheapside
Tirhoot Company (Henry Gouger, sec.), 6 Gt. Winchester st
Tirkin James, *Castle* P.H. 24 Carnaby st. Golden sq
Tirrell Joseph, baker, 21½ Bowling green st. Keningtn. com
Tisdall Charles, saddle tree maker, 34 Broad st. Golden sq
Tisdall Edmund, dyer & scourer, 36 Duke st. Grosvenor square; & 5 Church st. Kensington
Tisdall Sarah (Mrs.), calenderer, hotpresser & silk waterer, 19 Coal yard, Drury lane
Tisdall Thos. G. banker & agt. to cattle salesmn. 15 West Smthfi
Tisdell Thomas, *Rose & Crown* P.H. 17 Love la. Eastcheap
Titchbourne Susan (Mrs.), stationer, 56 Paddington st
Titchiner John, *Britannia* P.H. Britannia pl. Bishopsgate
Titchmarsh Thos. fruiterer & oyster dealer, 280 Bermondsey st
Titcomb Ralph, butcher, 6 Surrey place, Kennington comm
Tite Benj. Michael & Son, oil & italian wareho. 86 Holborn hill
Tite Joseph, grocer, 26 Union st. Borough road
Tite Thomas, tobacconist, 16 Lambeth walk
Tite William, architect, 17 St. Helen's place, Bishopsgate st
Titford Chas. button & trimming warehouse, 26 Aldgate
Titford Richard Vandome & Co. scale, weight, weighing machine & measure makers, 117 Leadenhall st
Titford Chas. french polisher, 13 Constitution rw. Gray's inn rd
Titford Henry, engravr. & printr. 5 St. James' walk, Clerkenwell
Tithe Commissnrs (England & Wales), 9 Somerset pl. hrs. 9 to 6
Titley John & Co. woollen drapers, 194 High st. Boro'
Titley John, greengrocer, 5 Brick lane, Spitalfields
Titley Susannah (Mrs.), grocer, 4 Church st. Cheyne wk. Chels
Titmuss & Dowding, meat salesmen, 5 Warwick la. Newgate st

Titmuss Daniel, butcher, 8 Henry st. Pentonville
Titmuss Thomas, hairdresser, 70 Long lane, WestSmithfield
Titt, Sansom & Co.jelly ma. Broughton ho.White Conduit fi
Titt Noyce (Miss), corset ma.8 St. James's pl.St. James's st
Tittensor Mary (Mrs.), glass & china dealer, 189 Drury lane
Titterton Alfred John, who.oil &colormn.seeHay & Titterton
Titterton George, brushmaker, 70 Margaret st.Cavendish sq
Titterton Geo. stationer & printer, 12 George yd. Lombd. st
Titterton George, *New Tariff* P.H. 42 Old st. road
Titterton George Penn, writer & grainer, 41 Upper North pl
Titterton Richd. A.S. law stationer, 30 Castle st. Holborn
Tiver John James, law stationer, 1 Cursitor st. Chancery la
Tobacco Customs' Office, Pennington st. Ratcliff highway; hours of business, from, March 1st to October 31st, 8 to 4; from Nov. 1st. to Feb. 28th, 9 to 4
Tobias James, tailor, 27 Jewry st. Aldgate
Tobias Joseph, capmaker, 31 Friar st. Blackfriars road
Tobias Morris, chronometer, watch & clockmak. 31 Minoriss
Tobin Marg. (Mrs.), catholic bookseller, 11 St.George's circus
Toby Henry & Son, hotho. bldr. 3 Glebe pl. King's rd.Chelsea
Toby Abraham, baker, 20 William st. Whitechapel
Toby John, who. ladies' bootmaker, 41 Wellingtonst.Borough
Toby Wm. bookseller, Beaufort ter. King's rd. west, Chelsea
Tod David & Wm. surgeons, 5 Sol's row, Hampstead road
Tod James, builder, 11 Walcot place West, Lambeth
Todd A. M. & Co. merchants, 28 Clement's lane, Lombard st
Todd Anthony & Wm. cheesemongers, 5 High st. Pentonville
Todd & Barreyman, babylinenwa.2 Northampton pl. Cnby.sq
Todd Brothers, west india merchants, 110 Fenchurch st
Todd Henry John & Co. warehousemen, 4 Bow churchyard
Todd & James, wine merchants, 11 John st. Adelphi
Todd & Procter, cheesemongers, 78 St. Paul's church yard
Todd & Woodman, straw bonnet wareho. 25 Ludgate hill
Todd & Wright, cheesemongers, 16 Camberwell High st
Todd Wm. & Co. bootmakers, 4 Barnsbury place, Islington
Todd William & Son, wharfingers, merchants & agents, Red Lion & Three cranes wharfs, 69 Upper Thames st
Todd Alexander, potato dealer, see Gregory & Todd
Todd Benjamin, linendraper, 5 Great Russell st. Bloomsbury
Todd Bruce Beveridge, baker, Mare st. Hackney
Todd Charles John, oilman & grocer, see Gibson & Todd
Todd Christopher, statuary & mason, 32 College st. Chelsea
Todd David, baker, 33 Water lane, Blackfriars
Todd Esther (Mrs.), cheesemonger, 55 Ossulston st. Somers tn
Todd George, builder, 10 Orford pl. Marlboro' rd. Chelsea
Todd George, *Builders' Arms* P.H. 16 Russell st. Chelsea
Todd George, tailor, 2 Charles st. Portman square
Todd George Michael, surgeon, 4 Watt's ter. Old Kent rd
Todd Henry F. west india mer. 4 Barge yd. Bucklersbury
Todd Isaac, fruiterer, 1 Church st. Shoreditch
Todd Isaac, fruiterer, 178 Kingsland road
Todd James, cheesemonger, 1 Somerset pl. Kennington com
Todd James, *Union tavern* P.H. 191 Oxford st
Todd John, baker, 7 Hereford terrace, King's road, Chelsea
Todd John, barrister, 1 Elm court, Temple
Todd John, haberdasher, 9 Camberwell High st
Todd John, haberdasher & laceman, 7 Middle row, Holborn
Todd John, ironmonger, 7 Bury st. Bloomsbury
Todd John, solicitor, 23 Thavies inn, Holborn
Todd John, cheesemonger, 36 Kensington High st
Todd John, chemist, 2 York terrace, Kent st. road
Todd John, surgeon, 1 Exeter place, Great Dover road
Todd John, jun.coal fact.&ship&insr.brok.65 Low.Thames st
Todd John Cattley, ship chandler, 112 Cock hill, Ratcliff
Todd John Waterloo, surgeon, 6 Devonshire ter. Globe road
Todd Michael, rag & bottle mer. 9 Houghton st. Clare mkt
Todd Parker, butcher, 70 Fetter lane
Todd Ralph, stockbroker, 1 Capel court
Todd Richard, tailor, 15 Fort st. Spitalfields
Todd Robt. Bentley, F.R.S. physician, 26 Parliament st
Todd Sarah (Mrs.), stay & corset maker, 14 Hanway st
Todd Thomas, cheesemonger, 10 Queen's row, Pimlico
Todd Wm. baker, 1 Greville st. Hatton garden
Todd Wm. builder, 13 Wellington road, St. John's wood
Todd Wm. coal merchant, 34 Nelson square, Blackfriars rd. & Red Lion wharf, 69 Upper Thames st
Todd Wm. hairdresser, 96 Brick lane, Spitalfields
Todd Wm. hairdresser & perfumer, 154 Oxford st
Todd Wm. linendraper, 10 Wells row, Islington
Todd Wm. tailor, 33 Francis st. Newington butts
Todd Wm. J. linendraper, &c. 4 Lowndes ter. Knightsbridge
Todhunter & Sancton, indigo merchants, 31 Eastcheap
Todman Henry, *Griffin* P.H.30 Villiers st.&19 Duke st.Adlph
Todman Henry, *Union* coffee rooms, 204 Blackfriars road
Toe John, corn & hay dlr. 18 Marsham st.&Smith sq.Westm
Toesland Edwd.carman&coal mer.2Marlboro' mws.Oxford st
Tofft George, manfg. jeweller, 8 Bell's bldgs. Salisbury sq
Tofield Wm. carpenter, 1 Southampton st. Camberwell
Toghill John, iron plate wareho. Swan yd.Ferry st.Lambeth
Toker Phillip Champion, proctor, 14 Gt. Knightrider st
Tolcher Robert Hooper, shorthand writer, 59 Chancery la
Toleman James, hook & eye manufactr. 11 Tabernacle walk
Toleman James, paper stainer, 170 Goswell st
Toley Mary Ann (Mrs.), ladies' school, 8 Fonthill pl.Clphm.rd
Tolfree Henry, tailor, 33 Gibson st. Waterloo road
Tolfree John, tailor, 33 Oakley st. Lambeth
Tolfree Robert, grocer, 4 Orford pl. Marlboro' rd. Chelsea
Tolfree Thos. confectioner, 4 Wilderness row, Clerkenwell
Tolhurst John, baker, 79 Lambeth lower marsh
Tolhurst John, lead, oil & color merchant, 60 Tooley st
Tolhurst Stephen, shoemaker, 59 Gt. Carlisle st.
Tolkien Henry, music seller, 28 King William st. City
Toll Louisa Leonora (Mrs.), fancy repo. 121 Up. st.Islington
Tollady John, marine store dealer, High st. Kingsland
Toller Edward & Sons, proctors, 4 Gt. Knightrider st
Toller John, chemist, see Fisher & Toller
Toller Samuel Bush, barrister, 23 Old square, Lincoln's inn
Toller Thomas, attorney, 6 Gray's inn square
Tollervey Horatio, paper stainer, 92 Hercules buildings
Tolleth Alexr. bootmaker, 41 Gt. Russell st. Bloomsbury
Tolleth Andrew, boot&shoe maker, 18 Rathbone pl.Oxford st
Tolley Edward, spectacle maker, 32 Henrietta st. Cov. gdn
Tolley Henry James, grocer, Old Ford
Tolley Templeman, bricklayer, 37 Lamb st. Spital sq
Tollitt John, livery & job stables, 156½ Oxford st
Tolman James, cooper, 10 Barnsbury row, Islington
Tolman John Sheppard, grocer & cheesem. 169 Rotherhithe
Tolman Simon, perfumer, &c. 35 Somerset place, Hoxton
Tolman Thos. *King & Queen* P.H.1 Foley st.Gt.Titchfieldst
Tolman William, grocer, 45 Russell st. Lower Rotherhithe
Tolman William, tailor, 21 White Conduit st. Islington
Tolman William Gibbs, grocer, 303 Rotherhithe
Tolosano Harriet (Mrs.), dressmaker, 7 Page st. Millbank
Tolworthy John, bricklayer, 47 Brick lane, St. Luke's
Tomalin George, baker, 1 Essex st. King's cross
Tomalin Joseph, coal dealer, 36 North st. Lisson grove
Tombes James, coffee rooms, 3 Church st. Shoreditch
Tombleson Thomas, builder, 4 Warwick st. Golden sq
Tomes James, porkman, 30 Boston st. Dorset square
Tomes James, tobacconist, 3 Boston st. Dorset square
Tomes John, surgeon dentist, 41 Mortimer st. Cavendish sq
Tomkins Benjamin, malt factor, 12 Queenhithe
Tomkins Benjamin, papr. hger. 39 Up.Yorkst.Bryanstonesq
Tomkins Benjamin A. woollendraper, seeBlackett&Tomkins
Tomkins Charles, artists' tool & hair pencil manufacturer, wholesale & retail, 24 Little Queen st. Holborn
Tomkins Charles, butcher, 7 Newport ct. Newport market
Tomkins Edmund, stockbroker, 3 Bartholomew lane, Bank
Tomkins Edward, tailor, &c. 20 King st. Holborn
Tomkins Fredk. linendraper, 3 Charles st. Middlesex hospital
Tomkins John, horse hair manfr. 43 Clifton st. Finsbury
Tomkins John, solicitor, 11 Gray's inn square
Tomkins John, *Peacock* P.H. 25 Gray's inn lane
Tomkins John Newton, resident surgeon, National vaccine establishment, 8 Russell place, Fitzroy square
Tomkins Lewis Wm. plumber, paintr. & glazr. 53 Dean st.Soho
Tomkins Thomas, cowkeeper, 1 White Conduit ter. Islington
Tomkins Wm. bread, &c. baker, 1 Gillingham st. Pimlico
Tomkins Wm. gold & silver piercer, 12 Rahere st. Goswell rd
Tomkins Wm. painter, 21 Rupert st. Haymarket
Tomkinson Saml. F. W. confectioner, 1 Beckford row, Walw.rd
Tomkison Jas. hairdresser, 5 Gt. White Lion st. Seven dials
Tomkison Thomas, pianoforte maker, 77 Dean st. Soho
Tomlin James & Co. e. i. mer. & agts. 26 Birchin la. Cornhill
Tomlin Edward, butcher, 1 Queen's road, Bayswater
Tomlin Elizh. (Mrs.), tobacconist, 11 Hanover pl. Park road
Tomlin George, linendraper, 47 Lamb's Conduit st
Tomlin James, cheesemonger, 144 Church st. Shoreditch
Tomlin James, fruiterer, 4 Bermondsey New road
Tomlin James, linendraper, 20 Kensington High st
Tomlin John, *Bowl & Pin* P.H. 5 Little Mitchell st.St. Luke's
Tomlin John, ironmonger, &c. 16 Tabernacle square
Tomlin Joseph, cutler, scissors, shears & razor maker (late of 36 Leather lane), 9 Market st. Newport market
Tomlin Mary (Mrs.), cowkeeper, 20 Bayswater ter. Bayswater
Tomlin Sackett, grocer & oilman, see Petty, Wood & Tomlin
Tomlin Wm. carpet & floor cloth manufact. 32 Charing cross
Tomlin Wm. coal merchant, 1 Green st. Bethnal green road, & Twigfolly bridge, Bethnal green
Tomlin Wm. dairyman, 33 Drummond st. Euston square
Tomlin Wm. parchment maker, Pleasant row, Old Kent road
Tomlin Wm. jun. worsted wa. 32 Charing cross & Gt.Scotld.yd

Tomlins & Lock, plumbers, &c. 46 Henry st. ea. Avenue rd
Tomlins Philip Nelson, solicitor, 9 Little Trinity lane
Tomlinson Charles & Co. who. & retail linendrapers,33Bow la
Tomlinson Chas. bricklayer, 6 Laura pl. Holland pl. Knsgtn
Tomlinson Charles, oilman, 36 Featherstone st. City road
Tomlinson Hannah (Mrs.), boarding house, 3 Pancras lane
Tomlinson Henry, builder, 1 Kingsland green
Tomlinson John, artist, 10 Maddox st. Regent st
Tomlinson John, steel plate printer, 10Frederick pl.Goswellrd
Tomlinson John, grocer, 2 Fort pl. Grange rd. Bermondsey
Tomlinson John, wholesale laceman, 3 Pancras lane
Tomlinson Joseph, accountant, 34 Henrietta st. Cov. garden
Tomlinson Joseph, grocer & teadealer, 10 Tower royal
Tomlinson Margt.(Mrs.),coal mer.21 Marylebone st.Goldn.sq
Tomlinson Sarah (Mrs.), lodging ho. 21 Green st.&47Park st
Tomlinson Thomas, barrister, 3 (North) King's Bench walk
TomlinsonWm.Benj.pawnbro.11&12Up.Geo.st.Bryanstonesq
TomlinsonWm. Rt. leather dresser,8 Charlotte st. Fitzroy sq
Tommey Henry, carpet bag mnfr. 22 Marsham st. Westmr
Tompion John, brush manufacturer, 97 Upper st. Islington
Tompkins George, harness maker, 32 Chapel st. New road
Tompkins Humphrey,coal dl. 9 Gt. Windmill st. Haymarket
Tompkins John, carpenter, 18 Granby st. Hampstead road
Tompkins Thomas, coal&potato dlr.25 High st. Camden town
Tompkins Thomas, fruiterer, 2 Queen's rd. Notting hill
Tompkins Wm. boot & shoe maker, 1 Swan st. Gt. Dover rd
Tompsett, Ross & Co. wholesale grocers, 8 Billiter st
Tompsett Joseph, saddler & harness mkr. 205 Hoxton Old tn
Tompson & Wilson, surgeons, 15 Tavistock st. Covent gdn
Tompson Edward, brassfounder, 11 Waterloo road, Obelisk
Tompson Edward, solicitor, see Pickering, Smith & Co
Tompson James, plumber & painter,3 Blandford pl.Dorset sq
Tompson James, tobacconist & hairdresser, 50 Goswell rd
Tompson Joseph, watchmaker, 9 Hooper st. Clerkenwell
Tom's coffeehouse, Cowper's court, Cornhill
Toms Saml. Rogers & Co. wine&spirit mer. 103 Fenchurch st
Toms Aaron, cheesemonger, 23 Cloth fair, West Smithfield
Toms Charles, coffee rooms, 1 Skinner's pl. Leadenhall mkt
Toms Edwd. Geo. stockbrok.7 Bnk. chamb.&StockExchange
Toms Joseph, toy & fancy repository, Kensington High st
Toms Richd. Thos. com. agent, see M'Gill & Toms
Toms Robert, tripeman, 146 Edgware road, Marylebone
Toms Thomas, potato dealer, 132 Golden lane, St. Luke's
Toms William, butcher, 25 Bow lane, Cheapside
Tomsett John, fruiterer, 42 Charlotte terrace, New cut
Tomsey Mary (Mrs.), lodging house, 13 Arundel st. Strand
Tomson James, ribbon dresser, 16 Moor lane, Cripplegate
Tomson John, fruiterer, 11 Norway place, Hackney road
Toner John, agent to calico printers, 39 Friday st
Tong Wm. ladies' shoemaker, 20 Norton st. Fitzroy sq
Tonge George, who. druggist, see Hodgkinsons' & Tonge
Tongue John, cabinetmaker, 76 Paul st. Finsbury
Tongue John Wm. packing case mak.70&71St.John st.Smfld
Tonkin Ebenezer, plumber & glazier,10 Terrace, Kensington
Tonkin Henry, coachmaker, 24 Park pl. Kennington cross
Tonkin James, iron bedstead maker, 315 Oxford st
Tonkins & Ladley, brush ma. & turners,24 Old Burlington st
TonkinsonJohn,*KingAlfred*P.H.11Lisson grve.north,Nw rd
Tonks & Taylor, ladies' school, Bridge road, Battersea
Tons Richard, blood dryer, Bow common
Tonson William, tailor, Southampton st. Camberwell
Toogood Henry, solicitor, 22 Parliament st
Toogood Henry & Wm. solicitors, 18 Charles st. St. James's
Toogood James, grocer, 27 Elizabeth st. South, Pimlico
Toogood Thomas, glass&bottle mer.37 Mount st.Berkeley sq
Tooke, Son&Hallowes, solicitors, 39 Bedford row, Bloomsby
Tooke Geo. Theodore, cabinetmak. 23 Judd st. Brunswick sq
Tooke Robert, hairdresser, 6 Gt. Windmill st. Haymarket
Tooke Samuel, market gardener, Grange road, Dalston
Tookey Wm. undertaker & parish clk.48 High st.Marylebone
Toole James, teadealer, 17 Devonshire st. Bishopsgate
Toole Richard, bricklayer, 10 Robinhood lane, Poplar
Tooley Abraham,sugar refiners' iron mld.ma.8Betts st.Ratcl
Tooley Jeremiah, grocer, 6 Trafalgar place, Clapham rd
Tooley John, fruiterer & potato dealer, 67 Tottenham ct. rd. & salesman, Covent garden fruit market
Toombes Charles, scale maker, 35 Gee st. Goswell st
Toomer Charles, livery stables, 26 Lower st. Islington
Toomer Thomas, grocer & teadealer, 41 Monkwell st. Crplgt
Toomer Wm. carpenter,&c. 42 Up. John st.Tottenham ct. rd
Toone Wm. cooper & back maker,121 St. John st. Smithfield
Toovey James, bookseller & publisher, 192 Piccadilly
Toovey Thomas, coffin maker, furnishing undertaker & appraiser, 215 High Holborn
Toovey Thomas,law stat.32 Southampton bldgs.Chancery la
Topcoate Joseph, carpenter, &c. 13 Norris st. Haymarket
Topham & Fawcett, hosiery manfr. 1 Huggin lane, Wood st
Topham O. & Son, engineers & millwr. 157 Up.Whitecross st
Topham William, barrister, 7 Figtree court, Temple
Topliff Robert, professor of music, 51A, Trinity sq. Boro'
Topliff William, upholsterer, 27 Lit. Queen st. Holborn
Toplis Edward & Son, tobacco & snuff manufs. 71 Shoreditch
Toplis James & Son, actioneers, appraisers & surveyors, & to the Sun Fire Office, 16 St. Paul's churchyard
Toplis George, tobacconist, 19 Grosvenor row, Pimlico
Toplis Henry, brewer, 8 Frederick st. Hampstead road
Toplis James, surveyor, 30 New Bridge st. Blackfriars
Toplis James, tobacco manufacturer, 57 Minories
Toplis Richard, oil & colorman, 155 Goswell st
Toplis Saml.Slater, upholsterer & cabinet mak.9 Berner's st
Toplis Wm. tailor, 16 Westbourne st. Pimlico
Topper Samuel, hoop bender, 27 White st. Borough
Topping Charles M. preparer of microscope objects, 1 York place, Pentonville hill
Topping's wharf (John H. & G. Scovell), 3 to 11 Tooley st
Tops Nicholas P. shell fish wa. 3 Up. Cleveland st. Fitzroy sq
Torey John & Son, curriers, japanners,& cap peak manufacturers, 8 White's row, Spitalfields
Torkington John, oil & colorman,25 Lower Eaton st.Pimlico
Torkington Ossgood, cheesemong. & grocer, 93 Chancery la
Torkington Percival Thomas, attorney, 3 Chester terrace, Borough road, & 22 New Bridge st
Torond Henry, pattern drawer & designer for every description of needlework, 1 Providence row, Finsbury square
Torr Richd. & Son, animal charcoal & ivory black manufrs. chemical works, Deptford, & Lower rd. Rotherhithe
Torr John, baker, 61 Leman st. Goodman's fields
Torr John Smale, solicitor, see Sudlow, Sons & Torr
Torr Maria L.(Mrs.),ready made lin.wa.9Rufford's rw.Islgtn
Torrance Joseph, agent for Guinness' extra stout, scotch & burton ales, & Bass's pale ale, 8 Hastings st. Burton cres
Torre John, solicitor, 15 Bernard st. Russell square
Torriano Wm. Harcourt, barrister, 6 Stone bldgs. Linc. inn
Torry Alexr. who. ivory turner, 18Vineyd. gdns.Clerkenwell
Torry David, hairdresser, 32 Leigh st. Burton crescent
Torry David, hairdresser, 4 Amwell st. Pentonville
Torry James, carpenter, 12 Queen st. Pitfield st. Hoxton
Tosar Bros. shippers of sherry wines, 29 St. Dunstan's hill
Tossell Edward, breeches maker, 29 Old Bond st
Tosswill Charles S. & Co. commission merchants, importers & manufacturers of cigars, 21 Budge row
Tosswill Chas. Speare &Co. engrvs. & printers, 24 Budge row
Tosswill John & Robert, tanners, hair manufacturers,& hair felt manufacturers, 1 Neckinger rd. & Spa rd. Bermondsey
Tosswill Chas. Speare, chemist,8Torrington pl. Torrington sq
Tothill Fredk. Disting, surgeon, 8 Charles st. St. James's sq
Totman Thos. tobacconist, 39 Warren st. Fitzroy sq
Tottem George, watch & clock ma. 4 Crescent pl. Brompton
Tottey John, ham shop, 71 Chapple st. Pentonville
Tottie Charles & Son, merchants, 2 Crosby square
Tottie Charles, consul gen. for Sweden & Norway,2Crosby sq
Tottie John Wm. agent, 29 Gresham st
Tottie Wm.vice consul for Sweden &Norway,2 Crosby sq
Tottidge Samuel, carpenter,Whitmore place, Hoxton
Tough Thos. academy, Great Green st. Kentish town
Toulmin Henry & Calvert, ship & insurance sworn brokers, & general agents, 31 Great St. Helen's
Toulmin Abraham, physician, 76 King William st. City
Toulmin Augustus, wine merchant, 31 Great St. Helen's
Toulmin Chas. liv. stables, 6 South Island pl. Clapham rd
Toulmin Joseph, surgeon, Mare st. Hackney
Toulmin Robert, attorney, see Chester, Toulmin & Chester
Tounsend James, baker, 122 Wentworth pl.Whitechapel
Tourell Lewis, coal & potato dlr. 6 Church la. Commercial rd
Tourle John Joseph, solicitor, 13 Southampton buildings
Tours& NantesRailway (DeRaigecourt Co.),13 Broad st.bldgs
Tours& NantesRailway Offi. (Lefebvres Co.),9 New Broad st
Toussy Wm. ship biscuit bakr. see Leftwich,Tousey&Hardy
Toussaint Joseph, wax chandler, &c. 45 Pall mall
Toussaint Thos. Chas.ornaml. pntr. 18 Sherrard st. Golden sq
Toussant Francis, bootmaker, 15 Frith st. Soho
Tout Jacob, leather dresser, 28 Long lane, Bermondsey
Tout John, builder, 44 Medway st. Horseferry road
Tout Thos. *Dorset Arms* P.H. 15 Old Dorset pl.Clapham rd
Tovey Jane (Miss), milliner & dress maker, 81 Albany st
Tovey Henry Lacock, surgeon, 162 Bermondsey st
Tow John, bath maker, 14 Harcourt st. New rd. Marylebone
Tow James, lunatic asylum, Battersea
Tow Peter, baker & confectioner, Bridge road, Battersea
Towell Charles, fishmonger, 43 Bedford st. Covent garden, & 7 & 8 Lower area, Hungerford market
Towell Henry, horse slaughterer, 1 Bowling st. Clerkenwell

Towell Thos. painter, glazier & paper hanger, 18 New Park st. Borough, & 5 Brunswick place, Old Kent road
Tower Hamlets' Court of Requests, 30 Osborne st. Whitechpl. 10 to 3; Court days, Tuesday & Friday at 11
Tower Hamlets' Dispensary (Valentine Edwards, medical resident), 40 Colet place, Commercial road east
Tower Edwin A. corn & coal merchant, 1 Lime st. passage
Tower James, upholsterer, 9 Baron st. Pentonville
Tower Thos. barrister, 4 King's Bench walk, Temple
Towers & Newton, milliners & gen. dra. 26 Lit. Pulteney st
Towers James, *Spread Eagle* P.H. 49 Rotherhithe st
Towers John, general dealer, 6 Commercial rd. Lambeth
Towers Wm. butcher, 17½ Tottenham court, New road
Towers Wm. Crawford, merchant, 3 Hungerford wharf, Strand
Towerzey Alfred, chemist, 20 Marylebone st. Piccadilly
Towgood Henry & George, stockbrokers, 33 Throgmorton st
Towgood John, barrister, 64 Chancery lane
Towgood Samuel, solicitor, see Hornby & Towgood
Towill Edward, boot & shoe maker, 237 Borough High st
Towle Fredk. Wm. surgeon, 190 Sloane st. Knightsbridge
Towler, Campin & Matthews, shawl manufacturers, 46 Friday st. Cheapside; manufact. Elm hill, Norwich
Towler Char. (Mrs.), *Queen's Head* P.H. 1 Fleet st. Bethnan gn
Towler Jas. brush ma. turner & winecooper, 8 Up. Eaton st. Pim
Towler James, tailor, Mare st. Hackney
Town Charles, artist, 103 Now Bond st
Town Clerk's (City) Office, Guildhall; hours 10 to 4
Town Hall, between 247 & 253 Borough High st
Town Missionary & Scripture Reader's Society (John Blanchard, secretary), 20 Red Lion square
Town & Emanuel, importers & manufacturers of buhl, marquetrie, resner & carved furniture, by appointment to the Queen, 103 New Bond st
Town Henry William, hairdresser, 59 Union st. Borough
Town Joseph, chemist, 7 Carthusian st. Charterhouse sq
Town Philip, cheesemonger, 11 Goswell st
Town Robert, greengrocer, 4 Flagon row, Deptford
Towndrow, Wm. N. chemist, 5 Courthopeter, Bermondsy. nw. rd
Towne Alexander, surgeon, 29 Kingsland crest. Kingsland rd
Towne Jireh, chocolate mills, George st. Wentworth st. Whitchp
Towne Josiah, solicitor, 9 William st. Knightsbridge
Towne Richard, ship & insurance broker, & commercial & custom house agent, 114 Fenchurch st
Towne William, cabinet maker, 7 Lion st. New Kent road
Townend William & Co. merchants, 3 Brabant ct. Philpot la
Townend Simeon, worsted heald yard mfr. 20 London wall
Townend Thomas, hatter, 16 & 18 Lime st
Townend William, hatmaker, 190 Regent st. & 20 Bread st
Towner Edward, coal dealer, 47 Crescent st. Euston sq
Townes John & Son, saddelry & harn. makers, 141 Cheapside
Townes Hen. Geo. oil & italian wa. 21 Munster st. Regent's pk
Townes John Rd. S. grocer, &c. 21 Shaftesbury ter. Pimlico
Townley James, attorney, 21 Coleman st. City
Townley James, general commn. agent, 34 Throgmorton st
Townley James, surgeon, 7 Marlboro' pl. Kennington cross
Townley John, furnishing undertaker, 25 Cowper st. City rd
Townley Rd. artist in hair & manfr. jeweller, 317 Regent st
Towns & Packer, pianoforte makers, 20 Oxford st
Towns Wm. backmaker, 16 King st. Commercial road east
Townsend Mary A. & M. ladies' school, 61 Gibson sq. Islgton
Townsend Parker & Co. paper stainers, 131 & 132 Goswell st
Townsend & Roberts, proctors & notaries, 15 Godliman st
Townsend Edmd. fishmonger, 6 Lower area, Hungerford mkt
Townsend Elizh. (Mrs.), baker, Montague pl. Lower rd. Deptfd
Townsend Frances (Mrs.), plumber, 74 Paradise row, Chelsea
Townsend Geo. Bell, accntnt. & ho. agent, 49 Leadenhall st
Townsend Geo. Richard, grocer, 20 Salisbury st. Lisson gr
Townsend Hannah (Miss), confectnr. 58 Bridge rd. Lambeth
Townsend Harriet (Mrs.), poulterer, 16 Charles st. St. James'sq
Townsend Hen. Meredith, surgeon, 75 Newington causeway
Townsend Hen. Norman, accntnt. 8 Fenchurch bgs. Fench. st
Townsend James, bootmaker, 25 Featherstone st. City rd
Townsend James, coal dealer, 6 Gt. Carlisle st. Portman mkt
Townsend James, dairyman, 2 Union terrace, Notting hill
Townsend John, butcher, 47 Friar st. Blackfriars road
Townsend John, butcher, 56 York road, Lambeth
Townsend John, butcher, 111 York road, Lambeth
Townsend John, butcher, 10 Upper area, Hungerford mkt
Townsend John, china dlr. 2 Upper area, Hungerford mkt
Townsend John, poulterer, porkman, &c. 70 Queen st. Cheapsl
Townsend John Adam, surgeon, 48 Finsbury circus
Townsend John T. carcase butcher & meat sa. 9 Deal st. Mile en
Townsend Joseph, tobacconist, 42 Crown st. Finsbury
Townsend Joseph Thomas, furniture & bedding warehouse, 18 & 19 Rufford's buildings, Islington
Townsend Samuel, surgeon, 5 Wilmot st. Brunswick sq
Townsend Sarah (Miss), ladies' school, 45 Nelson sq. Blkfrs. rd
Townsend Theodore, pawnbroker, 4 Bengal pl. Old Kent rd
Townsend Thomas, dyer & scourer, 16 Sloane sq. Chelsea
Townsend Thomas, fruiterer, 28 St. John st. road
Townsend Thomas Willis, shirt ma. & hosier, 121 Piccadilly
Townsend Wm. baker, Battersea High st
Townsend Wm. haberdasher, &c. see Early, Townsend & Co
Townsend Wm. hatter, 76 Lamb's Conduit st
Townsend Wm. proctor & notary, 20 Gt. Knightrider st
Townsend Wm. Charles, barrister, 3 Figtree court, Temple
Townshend Edmund, teadealer, 8 Walworth pl. Walworth rd
Townshend Edmund, wine mer. 12 Waterloo pl. Pall mall
Townshend George, coachmaker, 37 New st. mews, Dorset sq
Townshend John, solicitor, 17 Howland st. Fitzroy sq
Townsend Mary Ann (Mrs.), upholsterer, &c. 59 Judd st
Townson Charles, coal merchant, King st. New twn. Deptfrd
Townson John, tobacconist, 44 Lr. George st. Chelsea
Townson Richard, solicitor, see Morris, Stone & Townson
Towse Charlt. (Mrs.), ladies' school, 4 Walworth pl. Walw. rd
Towse John Beckwith, clerk & solicitor to Cooks' & Plumbers' Company; ward clerk of Bridge within, & vestry clerk of St. Michael, Crooked lane, 24 Laurence Pountney lane
Towse Robert Beckwith, solicitor, 24 Laurence Pountney lane, & clothworkers' hall, Mincing lane
Towse Wm. Beckwith, clerk to the Fishmongers' Company, Fishmongers' hall, Adelaide place, London bridge
Towsey Elizabeth M. (Mrs.), stationer, 24 Foxley road, Camberwell new road
Toxopholite Society, Inner circle, Regent's park
Toy & Hanson, manufacturers of plumbers' brass work, water closets, pumps, lamps, chandeliers & gas fittings generally, patentees of the universal candle lamps, glass & lead mers. 28 Leicester sq. (late of Castle st. Holborn)
Toy Thomas, tailor, &c., 147 Fenchurch st
Toy Wm. *King's Arms* P.H. 22 King st. Camden town
Toynbee Joseph, F.R.S. surgeon, 12 Argyll place, Regent st
Toyne George, hosier, 65 Shoreditch High st
Toyne Henry, linendraper, 56 Shoreditch High st
Toyne Robert, boot & shoe maker, 8 Up. East Smithfield
Tozer Henry & Son, who. tin plate workers, 3 Dean st. Soho
Tozer Eliza (Miss), milliner, 3 Wardour st. Soho
Tozer Jane (Mrs.), lodging house, 44 Bedford st. Coventgar
Tozer John, barrister, 2 Church yard court, Temple
Tozer John, boot & shoe mak. 9 Northumberland st. Marylb
Tozer John, grocer & cheesemr. 18 West pl. Bath st. City rd
Tozer John, toy & brush wareho. 20A Paddington st. Marylb
Tozer John, *Castle* P.H. 19 City road, Finsbury sq
Tozer Mary Ann (Mrs.), fashionable millinery, mourning, straw & tuscan warehouse, 3 Cranbourne st. Leicester sq
Tozer Thomas, carpenter, &c. Old Barrack yd. Knightsbridge
Tozer Thos. cheesemonger, 2 Granby st. Mornington crescent
Tozer Thos. furnishing ironmonger, 55 Dean st. Soho
Tozer Wm. wholesale & retail boot & shoe maker, 40 Gracechurch st. & 6 Royal Colonnade, Brighton
Tozer Wm. oil, lead, &c. merchant, 13 Halfmoon st. Bishopsgate
Tracey Geo. Matthew, surgeon, 8 St. Ann's villas, Acacia rd
Tracey Isaae, violin string maker, 12 Sharp's alley, Cowcross
Tract depôt, 1 Warwick sq. Newgate st
Tracy John Wise, surgeon, 54 New Church st. Lisson grove
Tracy Thomas, ivory turner, 19 John st. Holland st. Blkfrs. rd
Tracy Wm. M. surgeon, 13 Hill st. Berkely sq
Trade List Newspaper, Old Trinity ho. Water la. Tower st
Trader & Walton, fancy repostry. 23 Park ter. Regent's pk
Trahern Robt. coffee rooms, 9 Dirkhouse lane, Billingsgate
Trail, Chasmore & Co. patent sail maks. 3 Walbrook bldgs
Trail David, pawnbroker, &c. 14 Amwell st. Pentonville
Trail David, pawnbroker, 17 New Church st. Lisson grove
Trail Edwin, watch & clock maker, 145 Edgware rd. Marylb
Trail James, pawnbroker, 6 Stucley terrace, Camden town
Traill James, magistrate, Union hall police court
Trail John, solicitor, 4 Hare court, Temple
Trail William, pawnbroker, 14 Chapel st. New road
Trail William, watchmaker, 18 Duke st. Lisson grove
Trailes James, tin plate worker, 10 Notting hill High st
Tranah John, bookbinder, 6 Fitchet's court, Noble st
Tranah William, pawnbroker, see Livermore & Tranah
Transfield Thomas, saddler, &c. 50 Robin Hood lane, Poplar
Transport Office, Admiralty, Somerset house; hours 10 to 4
Tranter & Lines, dressmakrs. 28 Liverpool ter. Liverpool rd
Tranter Charles, *Angel & Trumpet* P.H. 1 Stepney High st
Tranter Thomas, *Three Tuns* P.H. 20 Rupert st. Haymarket
Tranter William, musician, 50 Bath st. City road
Trantum Richard, cabinet ma. 2 North st. Finsbury market
Trapp John & Co. printers & engravers, 31 Budge row
Trapp Thos. Pierson, tallowmltr. &c. 1 Church st. St. Saviour's
Trappitt Henry, engraver, 26 King st. Commercial rd. east

Trass Robert, tailor, 9 Trinity row, Upper st. Islington
Tratt & Attfield, upholsterers, 19 Brook st. Grosvenor sq
Tratt Henry, boot & shoe mak. 82 Drummond st. Euston sq
Travellers' Club House (Wm. Browne, sec.), 106 Pall mall
Travers Joseph & Sons, wholes. grocers, 19 St. Swithin's la
Travers Benjamin, F.R.S. surgeon, 12 Bruton st. Bond st
Travers Benjamin, jun. surgeon, 6 St. Thomas's st. Borough
Travers James, chemist, 367 Rotherhithe st
Travers John T. veterinary surgeon, 11 Belvedere rd. Lambeth, & 7 Mayfield place, High st. Kensington
Travers Saml. *Grand Surrey Canal Office*, 290 Rotherhithe
Travis William, insurance broker, Lloyd's
Traxton Joseph, lithog. draughtsman, 13 Cross st. Hatn. gn
Trayler Joseph, carpenter, 26 Duke st. Bloomsbury
Traynor Pat. Augstn. hair & feather mer. 3 & 20 King st. St. Luke's
Treacher Edwd. & Co. art. flo. material dlrs. 16 Gibson st
Treacher, Osborn & Hall, who. druggs. 28 Wilson st. Finsbury
Treacher Georgiana Louisa (Mrs.), milliner, 57 Regent st
Treacher Joseph, dining rooms, 29 Gt. Tower st
Treacher Joseph, fruiterer, 31 Castle st. Leicester square
Treacher Wm. butcher, 21 Backchurch lane, Whitechapel
Treacher William, furrier, 57 Regent st
Treadaway George, tailor & draper, 29 & 30 Harrow road
Treadaway Richard, butcher, 15 Portman market, & 6 New Church st. Lisson grove
Treadgold Wm. tobacconist, 26 Hamilton rw. Bagnig. wells rd
Treadwell Francis, fruit salesman, Borough market
Treadwell John, ladies' boot & shoe ma. 16 Adam st. ea. Manc. sq
Treadwell Wm. locksmith & bell hanger, 6 George st. Blkfrs. rd
Treadwell Wm. wine & provsn. mer. 3 Nag's Hd. ct. Grch. st
Treadwell Wm. jun. short hand writer, 14 Nelson sq. Shwk
Treasure Edward, tailor, 30 Cleveland st. Fitzroy square
Treasure Geo. Walter, woollendraper, see Wild & Treasure
Treasurer for County of Middlesex Office, Sessions house, Clerkenwell green; hours 11 to 3
Treasury Office, Whitehall; hours of business 10 to 4
Treays Andrew, grocer, 21 King st. Deptford
Treays William, bootmaker, 1 Caroline place, Goswell st
Treble Harriet Elzh. (Miss), seminary, 1 Park pl. Mile end rd
Treble John, linendraper & haberdasher, 409 Oxford st
Treble Thomas, hairdresser, 129 Jermyn st. St. James's
Treby John, tailor, 84 Kennington st. Walworth
Trecothick, Roper & Son, west india mers. 126 Fenchurch st
Tredgold Jemima (Miss), hosier, see Urquhart & Tredgold
Tredinnick Richard, mine & share agent, 16 Cornhill
Tree Louisa & Emily, haberdashers, New rd. South Lambth
Tree Benjamin, whip maker, 4 Angel ct. Gt. Windmill st
Tree Emily (Mrs.), rule mak. 22 Lit. Charlotte st. Blkfrs. rd
Tree James, working jeweller, 3 Hunter st. Gt. Dover road
Treeby Joseph, slater, 3 Princes st. Red Lion square
Treeby Thomas, builder, &c. 107 Milton st. Dorset square, & 18 York st. Portman square
Treffry Henry William, engineer, millwright, founder, & boiler maker, 23 Walnut tree walk, Lambeth
Tregear Henry, carpenter, 14 Vine terrace, Waterloo road
Treggon Henry & Co. zinc manufacturers & plumbers, 22 Jewin st. & 57 Gracechurch st
Trego John, builder, 5 Coleman st. City
Trego William, plumber, painter, &c. 30 Jewry st. Aldgate
Tregunno Mary (Mrs.), *Neptune* P.H. Creek st. Deptford
Treharne William, bricklayer & builder, 41 Drury lane
Trehern & White, solrs. 13 Barge yard chambs. Bucklersby
Trehern Wm. baker, 10 Gt. College st. Camden town
Treherne David, *Giraudiers htl.* 48 Hymkt. & 133 Jermyn st
Treherne Edmund, land & assessed tax offi. 11 South Molton st
Treibmann Christian Henry, merchant, 23 Coleman st
Treibner Timothy F. russia broker, 81 Old Broad st
Treleigh Consolidated Copper Mines Off. 57 Old Broad st
Treloar Thomas, cocoa nut fibre warehouse, 42 Ludgate hill
Treluddra Mary (Miss), turnery & toy wareh. 206 Piccadilly
Tremain George, hat manufr. 34 Southampton rw. Russell sq
Tremain Rob. haircutter & tobacconist, 23 White st. Boro'
Tremain Wm. commission salesman, 52 Edward st. Regt's pk
Tremenheere John Henry, barrister, 1 New sq. Lincoln's inn
Tremere William, painter, 26 Upper York st. Bryanstone sq
Tremlett Edwd. oil & colorman, 12 King st. Low. rd. Islngtn
Tremlett Elias, tanner, 45 Long lane, Bermondsey
Trendell Thomas, boot & shoe ma. 109 Edgware rd. Paddngtn
Trender John James, bookbinder, 23 Well st. Cripplegate
Trender Robert, walking stick maker, 13 Barbican
Trenerry John, foreign wines, imp. & agt. 1 Fen ct. Fench. st
Trenery Thomas, surgeon, 4 Salisbury st. Lisson grove
Trenery Wm. jun. mine agt. & share brok. 50 Threadneedle st
Trenholm Thos. butcher, 7 Claremont ter. Stoke Newngtn. rd
Trenklee Michael, engraver, 32 Whitehart st. Kennington
Trent Edwin, linendraper, 16 Etham place, Gt. Dover road
Trent Geo. grazier, Albany wharf, Edward st. Regent's park
Trent James, butcher, 3 Ferdinand st. Hampstead road
Trent John, fur. broker, 5 Cumberland pl. Newington butts
Trent Joseph, oilman, 92 Long alley, Finsbury
Trentham Geo. *George the Fourth* P.H. 3 Duke st. Lisson gr
Treppass Chas. coke burner, see Wilkinson & Treppass
Tress Charles, cheesemonger, 22 Marlboro' st. Regent st
Tress Francis, coal merchant, 39 Portman pl. Edgware rd
Tress Richd. architect & surveyor, 23 Lit. St. Thomas Apostle
Tress Wm. architect & surveyor, 1 Princes st. Wilson st. Finsby
Tressidder John, bootmaker, 15 Arundel pl. Coventry st
Treuter John, baker, 14 Duke st. Chelsea
Trevallion Jsph. cabriol. chair ma. 3 New Glo'ster st. Hoxton
Trevenon James, merchant, 8 Moorgate st. Lothbury
Trevers & Wilson, tailors, 1 Gloucester pl. Old Kent rd
Trevers John & Son, builders, 1 Gloucester pl. Old Kent rd
Trevers John & Son, builders, Priors pl. East st. Walwth. rd
Treverton Hender & Son, fancy box & case maker, 49 York st. City rd. & 12½ Macclesfield st. south, City rd
Trevethan Jsph. upholsterer, &c. 11 Stanhope st. Glo'ster gate
Trevett Thos. bootmaker, 85 Salisbury st. Lisson grove
Trevillion Thos. gold & silver beater, 39 Wynyatt st. Clknwll
Trevillion Wm. painter & glazier, 14 Wynyatt st. Goswell st
Trevor (Mrs.), ladies' school, 24 Alpha road, Regent's park
Trew George, dyer, 33 Plumber st. City road
Trew Wm. surgeon, 19 Woburn place
Trewby Wm. coal merchant, Millbank wharf, Westminster
Treweek Caleb, trimming seller, 27 Gibson st. Waterloo rd
Trewheela Wm. surveyor, Hall of commerce, Threadneedle st
Trewinnard Ann (Mrs.), milliner, 13 Kingsland pl. Kingsld. rd
Trewinnard Joseph, watchmaker, 16 Bermondsey wall
Treyer Gotlieb Augustus, snuffmaker, see Fribourg & Treyer
Trezevant Theodore M. coal mercht. 13 George st. Adelphi
Trezies James, watchmaker, 21 Lit. Russell st. Bloomsbury
Tribble Wm. F. builder & house agent, 76 Lucas st. Coml. rd. ea
Tribe & Mills, salt merchants, 18 Mill lane, Tooley st
Tribe Ann (Mrs.), chairmaker, 93 Old st. St. Luke's
Tribe Edward, attorney, 6 Barge yd. Bucklrsby. & 34 Foley pl
Tribe James, plumber, 75 Drummond st. Euston square
Tribe Wm. tailor & outfitter, 34 Foley pl. Portland pl
Trice Wm. carpenter, 38 Brewer st. Pimlico
Tricker Abraham, grocer, 12 Crawley st. Somers town
Tricker Zechariah, builder, 4 Pitt st. Old Kent road
Trickett George, bookbinder, 24 Gt. Smith st. Westminster
Trickett Richard, grocer, &c. 34 Church st. Deptford
Trickey George, *Two Mariners* P.H. Vinegar la. Coml. rd. ea
Triebner Timothy Fredk. russia broker, 81 Old Broad st. City, & Baltic coffee house, Threadneedle st
Trier Thedor & Co. merchants, 14 Fenchurch st
Triffitt John, *Coach & Horses* P.H. 11 Maddox st. Regent st
Trig Wharf, Wm. Rathbone, between 29 & 35 Upr. Thames st
Trigg Arthur John, tobacconist, 113 Crawford st
Trigg Edward, greengrocer, High row, Silver st. Kensingtn
Trigg James, dairy, Earl's court, Old Brompton
Trigg John F. liv. stables, 8 & 9 Brook mws. Glo'ster rd. Hyde pk
Triggs Alex. ivory & bone brushmak. 13 Wilmingn. pl. Clkwl
Triggs Herbert, ladies' shoe ma. 17 Hunter st. Brunswick sq
Triggs Jonathan, builder, 22 Buckingham pl. Fitzroy square
Triggs Richard, tailor, 28 Gt. St. Helen's, Bishopsgate st
Trigs John, tailor, 60 Back Church lane, Whitechapel
Trill & Jennens, bottled ale merchts. 40 Mark lane
Trilleo & Mason, law stationers, 7 Carey st. Lincoln's inn
Trilleo Thomas, *Portman Arms* P.H. 33 Portman pl. Edgw. rd
Trimbey Geo. merchant & head imp. sole agent for Foster's parama waterproof clothing, &c. 39 Queen st. Cheapside
Trimbey George, sadlrs.' wooln. fact. 39 Queen st. Cheapside
Trimbey James, merchant, 39 Queen st. Cheaside
Trimby Thomas & Son, paperhangers, 35 Bow la. Cheapside
Trimby John, *Duke of Wellington* P.H. 92 Drury lane
Trimen Andrew, architect & surveyor, 9 Adam st. Adelphi
Trimen James, law stationer, 11 Portugal st. Lincoln's inn
Trimlet, Cole & Henderson, engrs. & printrs. 15 Oxendon st. Haym
Trimmer & Grainger, for. provis. brok. 17 Pudding la. Eastchp
Trimmer Charles, tobacconist, 2 Road side, Mile end
Trimmer Jas. T. merchant, 18 New City chambers, Bshpsgt. st
Trimmer John, stationer, 11 Brecknock pl. Camden New tn
Trimmer Wm. grocer, &c. 1 Torrington pl. Torrington sq
Trimming Edwin L. attorney, 6 Barnard's inn, Holborn
Trimnell Edw. fringe & carpet manufact. 252 Regent st
Trimnell Michael, butcher, 4 Wardour st. Soho
Trimnell Samuel, booking office, 6 Tottenham court road
Trinder Henry, merchant, 72 Watling st
Trinder Jabez, undertaker & painter, 5 George st. Blackfrs. rd
Trinder Jas. coal & potato dealer, 14 Lit. St. Andrews st. 7 Dials
Trinder James, grocer, 21 Richmond st. Lisson grove
Trinder Thos. job master, 9 St. Ann's vil. Acacia rd. St. Jn's. wd

Trinder Wm. auctioneer & appraiser, 23 Princes st. Soho
Trinder Wm. who.shoe wa.23 Wilderness la.Dorset st.Fleet st
Trinder William Henry, solicitor, see Jones, Trinder & Co
Tring, Reading & Basingstoke Railway Company, 1 New Broad st
Tring, Reading, &c. Railway Offices, 26 New Broad st.City
Tring Samuel, hosier, 133 Borough High st
Tringham Joseph & Son, sugar refiners, 116 Holborn hill, & 17 Coppice row, Clerkenwell
Tringham George, watchmaker, 15 Golden lane, Barbi can
Tringham George, working goldsmith, 2 Priest ct. Foster la
Trinidad Great Eastern & South Western Railway Co. (Henry L. Bristow, sec.), 29 Nicholas lane, Lombard st
Trinitarian Bible Society (William Hen. Johnson, sec.), 4 Crescent, New Bridge st
Trinity Alms Houses, Mile end road
Trinity Buoy Wharf (Captain Poulter, superintendent), Orchard place, Blackwall
Trinity House, Trinity square, Tower hill
Trinity Light Dues Office, Trinity house: hours 10 to 4
Trinnick John, grocer & cheesemonger, 1 Elm st. Gray's inn la
Tripe John, surgeon&chemist, 7 King's pl.Commercial rd.east
Tripe Wm. ship & ins. broker, 3 Nag's Head ct. Gracechurch st
Triphook Rt.Wm. carver & picture dlr. 13 Grosvenor st.west
Tripp Charles, oil & colorman, 25 Rosemary lane
Tripp Richard Stevens, barrister, 24 Old sq. Lincoln's inn
Tripp Samuel Sommers, tailor, 9 South st. Manchester sq
Tripp Stevens, solicitor, 2 Adelaide pl. London bridge, & 34 Cumming st. Pentonville
Tripp Thomas, *Old Ivy House* P. H. 84 Goswell st
Tripp Thomas, pork butcher, 18 York st. Broadway, Westmr
Tripp William, appraiser, 38 York st. Westminster
Tripp Wm. locksmith & ironmonger, 59 St. Mary Axe
Tripp Wm. *Rising Sun* P.H. 78 Gray's inn lane
Trist George, auctioneer & appraiser, 80 Old Broad st. City
Triston John Hovell, solicitor, 40 Southampton buildings
Tristram Henry, merchant, 12 Bankside, Southwark
Tritsch Joseph, boot&shoe manfr. 72 Gt. Russell st. Blmsby
Tritschler Jph. & Co. clock maks. 91 East st. Manchester sq
Tritschler Joseph & Co.german clock mks. 191 High Holborn
Tritschler John, clock maker, see Kleyser & Tritschler
Tritton Frederick, solicitor, 11 Three Crown square, Boro'
Tritton Robert, *Nag's Head* P.H. 343 Oxford st
Tritton Thomas, tailor, 7 Norris st. Haymarket
Tritton Wm. *Crown & Sceptre* P.H. 57 ShadThames, Sthwk
Tritton Wm. Thomas, *Dog & Stile* P.H. Earl st. London rd
Trivass Frances (Mrs.), ladies' school, 14 Munster sq.Rgnts.pk
Troake Nathan, saddler, 69 Britannia terrace, City road
Trodd John, carpenter, 14 Noble st. Goswell st
Trokes Charles & Co. *City of Quebec* P.H. 237 Oxford st
Troll William, jun. baker, 9 Gt.Carlisle st. Portman market
Troll William, sen. baker, 5 Davies st. Berkeley square
Trollope George&Sons, house decorators to her Majesty, upholders & house agents, 15 & 17 Parliament st. & 3 Prince s st. Westminster
Trollope Edward, solicitor, see Malton & Trollope
Trollope John, colonial agent, 151 Fenchurch st
Trollope John, tea & coffee dealer, 13 Eastcheap
Trollope Thomas, fruit salesman, Fruit market, Covent gardn
Trorey William, *Crown* P.H. 15 Brewer st. Golden sq
Trory Wm. beer retailer, Abbot st. Kingsland
Trotman M.&C.(Misses), milliners, 4 Somerset ter. Kensington
Trotman Ebenezer, architect & surveyor, 14 Furnival's inn
Trotman Ebenezer, pork butcher, 28 Edward st. Limehouse
Trotman Mary (Mrs.), haberdasher, 16 Skinner st. Somrs. tn
Trotman Richd. bone boiler, 30 Green st. Blackfriars road
Trotman Saunders, hairdresser, 2 Newland ter. Kensington
Trotman Thomas, cheesemonger, 96 High st. Camden town
Trotman Wm. cheesemonger, 9 Lower road, Islington
Trotman Wm.stm. eng.&range boiler ma. Whitecross st. Boro'
Trott Charlotte & Son, school slate ma. 23 Union st. Boro'rd
Trott John, ironmonger & shoeing smith, Battersea square
Trott Joseph, bricklayer, &c. 13 Poplar row, New Kent rd
Trott Thomas, builder, 7 Primrose st. Bishopsgate
Trott Thomas, straw hat manfr. 24 Bartholomew ter. City rd
Trott William, solicitor, 1 Crown court, Threadneedle st
Trott William, straw hat maker, 72 Red Lion st. Clerkenwl
Trotter Elizth. (Mrs.), *Mitre* P.H. 104 Upper st. Islington
Trotter Frederick, barrister, 16 Old square, Lincoln's inn
Trotter James Charles, undertaker, 1 Kirby st.Hatton grdn
Trotter Thos. Dixon Marr, solicitor, see Rutter & Trotter
Trotter William, lighterman, 24 Emerson st. Bankside
Troughton & Simms, mathematical inst. maks. 138 Fleet st
Troughton Edwd. watch case joint finish. 17 Kingst. Clrknwll
Troughton George, butcher, 35 Fish st. hill
Troup John, watch manfr. & who. jeweller, 36 Hatton garden
Trouse & Turner, farriers, George yd. Leather la. Holborn
Trout John, fruiterer, 7 Church way, Somers town
Trovell John & Co. coach platers, 38 Castle st. ea. Oxford st
Trowbridge Hen. smith & gas fitt. High st. Stoke Newington
Trowell Thomas, teadealer, &c. 93 St. Martin's lane
Trower & Bridgen, hop & seed mer. WhiteHartinnyd. 62 Boro'
Trower, Lawson & Trower, wine&sp.mers. 39 St. Mary at hill
Trower Francis Charles, barrister, 6 New sq. Lincoln's inn
Trower Frederick, colonial broker, see Kembles' & Trower
Trower James, corn dealer, 15 Portland road
Trower James, corn dealer, 23 Upper Marylebone st. Portland place; & 15 Portland road, Regent's park
Trower Joseph, smith & farrier, Little Chelsea
Trower Robert, carpenter, 29 Crown st. Soho
Trousdale John, merchant, Brook's wharf, Upper Thames st
Troy (Damas) & Co. merchants, 14 Philpot lane, City
Troy John, bootmaker, 376 Strand
Troy Richard, cheesemonger, 48 Redcross st. Borough
Truby Thomas, warm, cold & vapour baths, 34 St. Mary axe
Trudgett John, rope, line & rope mat. ma. Lee st. Kingslandrd
True John Wm. tobacconist, 31 Little Bell alley, City
True Wm. chandler's shop, 21 Copenhagen st. Pentonville
Truefitt Francis, hairdresser & perfumer, 1 New Bond st
Truefitt Paul, court head dresser, 25 & 26 Burlington arcade
Truefitt Peter, hairdresser, &c. 20 & 21 Burlington arcade
Truefitt Thomas, brush & turnery wareh. Camberwell green
Truelove John, butcher, 26 Chapel st. Somers town
Trueman Chas. & Co. merchants, 1 New Broad street court
Trueman & Cook, general brokers, 40 Mincing lane
Trueman Joseph & Co. general agents, 40 Mincing lane
Trueman Charles, who. tea dealer & grocer, 25 Coleman st
Trueman George, bootmaker, 6 Carlton st. Regent st
Trueman Robert, fringe manufacturer, 57 Fore st. City
Trueman Robert, tailor, 44 Brewer st. Somers town
Trueman Thomas, berlin warehouse, 7 Victoria rd. Pimlico
Trulock Francis, potato dealer, 1 Gilbert st. Grosvenor sq
Truman, Hanbury, Buxton & Co. brewers, 174 Brick la. Sptlfl
Truman Charles, wig maker, 13 Princes st. Cavendish sq
Truman Christopher, warehsmn. see Lewellin, Truman & Co
Truman Edwin, dentist, 40A, Haymarket
Truman George Frederick, oilman & corn dlr. 8 Mlpnd.st.Ber
Truman John, ham & beef shop, 17 Goodge st. Fitzroy sq
Truman Mary (Mrs.), oil warehouse, 25 Crown st. Finsbury
Truman Matthew, surgeon, 44 Gloucester pl. Kentish town
Truman Thomas, bookseller & registrar, 23 Vine st. Hattn.gn
Trumpler & Rouquette, merchants, 5 Lime st. square
Trumpler Charles, merchant, 5 Lime st. square
Trundell Gregory, last & boot tree maker, 33 Houndsditch
Trundle Wm. bootmaker, 32 Freeschool st. Horselydown
Truscoat Geo. gold, &c. wire drawer, 10 Berkleyct. Clerknwl
Truscott Henry, furniture dlr. 10 Commercial pl. Old Kent rd
Truscott James, manchester agent, 6 Dyer's ct. Aldermanbury
Truscott Thomas, wholesale & export stationer, general printer, & account book manufacturer, &c. 24 Nelson square, Blackfriars road
Truss John Nelson, watch manfr. 59 Myddelton st. Clerknwll
Truss Jonathan, grocer, 27 Hindon st. Pimlico
Truste Daniel, brace maker, 38 Whitecross st. Cripplegate
Truwhitt Geo. solicitor, 2 Cook's ct. Cary st. & at Finchley
Try Eliza (Miss), *Grapes* P.H. 45 Strand
Try Thos. machinist & brassworker, 4 Poland st. Oxford st
Trye James Henry, merchant, Stock exchng.&10 Wrnford.ct
Tuach Francis & Son, woolstaplers, 232 Bermondsey st
Tuach Wm. Alexander, surgeon, 24B, Davies st. Berkeley sq
Tuall George, fishmonger, 1 Felix cott. Liverpool road
Tubb & Son, leathersellers, 16 Plumber's st. City rd
Tubb Henry, baker, 313 Regent st
Tubb Henry, general dealer, 17 Chalcroft terrace, New cut
Tubb John Bersemen, cheesemonger, 22 Lower Eaton st
Tubb Mary (Miss), grocery & oil wa. 2 Prospect row, Berm.rd
Tubb Thomas, dairy, 6 Palace row, New road
Tubb William, *Castle* brewery, 10 St.George's rd. Southwark
Tubb William, painter&paperhngr. 77 Charlotte st. Fitzroy sq
Tubbs Francis, sail maker, Horseferry branch rd. Ratcliff
Tubbs John, bedstead maker, 5 Haddon pl. Waterloo road
Tubbs John, brush manufacturer, 14 Berwick st. Soho
Tubbs Richard, bootmaker, 19 Felix ter. Liverpool road
Tubbs Richd.Thos. warehouseman & silk agent, 74 Aldrmnbry
Tubbs Thomas, linendraper, 2 Thurlow pl. Hackney rd
Tubbs Thomas, violin bow maker, 31 Carlisle st. Lambeth
Tubby Joseph, shell fishmonger, 8 Change alley, Cornhill
Tuck Thos.&Co. pianoforte makers, 33 Hyde st. Bloomsbury
Tuck Alfred, sheep salesman, 59 West Smithfield
Tuck Cather. (Mrs.), tin plate wrkr. 40 OldCompton st. Soho
Tuck Edmund, improved electro plater, 22 George st. Adelphi
Tuck Francis, oil & colorman, 138 St. Alban's pl. Edgware rd

Tuck Henry, butcher, 38 Cheyne walk, Chelsea
Tuck Jabez, bookseller, 2 Albion ter. Wandsworth road
Tuck Jas. H. coal & corn mer. Durham whf. Lr. Belgrave pl
Tuck James Hunter, nurseryman & florist, Sloane st
Tuck John, phitheon academy, 171 St. John st. road
Tuck Major, butcher, 23 Ring cross, Holloway road
Tuck Mark, tailor & dining rooms, 5 Mayfield pl. Hi.st. Kngstn
Tuck Thos. Jas. baker, &c. bunhouse, Duncan pl. Lond. flds
Tuck William, confectioner, Church st. Hackney
Tuck Wm. Henry, chemist & druggist, 1 Grove st. Mile end rd
Tucker, Barnett & Co. stockbrokers, 11 Birchin la. Cornhill
Tucker Francis & Co. melters & wax & tallow chandlers, & oil merchants to her Majesty & the royal family, 18 South Molton st. Bond st.; & High st. Kensington
Tucker John & Jas. pressers & packers, 10 Noble st. Cheapsi
Tucker Richard & Sons, shoe thread & twine manufacturers, 1 Wellington st. London bridge
Tucker & Steavenson, solictrs. Sun ch. 61½ Threadneedle st
Tucker Chas. oilman, 4 Field pl. Larkhall lane, Clapham
Tucker Chas. Wm. grocer & italian wareho. 42 Essex st. Strand
Tucker Edward, discount & money agt. 24 Spring gardens
Tucker Edwd. *P. George of Cumberl.* P.H. 25 Fred. st. Porld. tn
Tucker Eliza (Miss), babylinen wareh. 11 Store st. Bedford sq
Tucker Flower, gold & silver beater & manufacturer of gold beaters' skin, 8 Fleet lane, Farringdon st
Tucker Francis, dining rooms, see Richardson & Tucker
Tucker Fredk. plane & tool manufr. 10 Bath place, New rd
Tucker Fredk. John, solicitor, 6 Raymond bldgs. Gray's inn
Tucker George, upholsterer, 20 College st. Westminster
Tucker Geo. C. confectioner, 13 Russell court, Covent gard
Tucker Harriet (Miss), ladies' school, 57 Holborn hill
Tucker Isaac, carpenter, 5 William st. Hampstead rd
Tucker James, bookbinder, 7 Lit. Warner st. Clerkenwell
Tucker James, boot & shoe maker, High st. Battersea
Tucker James, fruiterer, 17 Upper Seymour st. Euston sq
Tucker James, tailor, 25 Charles st. Westminster
Tucker Jedidah Stephens, barrister, 5 Pump court, Temple
Tucker Jervis, solicitor, 35 John st. Bedford row
Tucker John, fishmonger, 8 Black Prince rw. Walworth rd
Tucker John, hairdresser, 2 Heddon court, Regent st
Tucker John, silk printer, 10 Trump st. & West Ham, Essex
Tucker John Hodges, surgeon, 38 Berner's st. Oxford st
Tucker Joseph, lighterman, 60 York st. York rd. Lambeth
Tucker Joseph, stock & sharebrok. 8 Bank Chamb. Lothbury
Tucker Joseph, woollendraper, 27 Sun st. Bishopsgate
Tucker Joseph E. sail cloth, twine, webs, &c. ma. 47 Fish st. hill
Tucker Joseph Vincent, plane manuf. &c. 31 Sun st. Bishopsgt
Tucker R. secretary to *Pelican Life Insurance Office*, 70 Lombard st. & 57 Charing cross
Tucker Richard, butcher, 54½ Long acre
Tucker Richd. livery & bait stables, 44½ Hart st. Cov. garden
Tucker Richd. vet. surgeon & farrier, 46 Tufton st. Westm
Tucker Sarah (Mrs.), tobacconist, 10 Dockhead, Bermondsy
Tucker Silas, plumber & paperhanger, 44 Cannon st. rd
Tucker Thamar (Mrs.) *John of Gaunt* P.H. 5 Dukest. Lin. in. fi
Tucker Thomas, *Bull* P.H. 7 Little College st. Westminster
Tucker Thos. coachmaker, &c. 7 Pump row, Old st. rd
Tucker Thos. dairyman, 72 Drummond st. Euston sq
Tucker Thos. lamp manufr. & oil merchant, 269 Strand
Tucker Thos. painter, 7 Weston st. Pentonville
Tucker Thos. stationer & bookseller, Camberwell green
Tucker Thos. staymaker, 20 Mount rw. Liverpool rd. Islingtn
Tucker Walter, carpenter, 19 King st. Commercial rd. east
Tucker Wm. builder, 59 Warren st. Fitzroy sq
Tucker Wm. curiosity dealer, naturalist, 83 Quadrant
Tucker Wm. plumber, 4 Shorter st. St. George's east
Tucker Wm. poulterer & cheesemonger, 287 Strand
Tucker Wm. surgeon, Oxford pl. Marlboro' rd. Chelsea
Tucker Wm. surgeon, 28 South Molton st
Tucker Wm. tobacconist, 11 Wandsworth road
Tucker Wm. Edwd. chemist & druggist, 118 Londonrd. Borough
Tucker William Henry, windowglasswareho. 127 High Holborn
Tuckett Charles, bookbinder, 20 Lit. Russell st. Bloomsbury
Tuckett Charles, boot & shoe warehouse, 263 Boro' High st
Tuckey John W. & Co. linendrapers, 47 Dukest. Manchestersq
Tuckey Henry, italian warehouse, 43 George st. Portman sq
Tuckey Thomas, builder, 1 Victoria square, Pimlico
Tuckfield George, tobacconist, 97 Broad st. Ratcliff
Tuckfield Joseph, watch & clock manufr. 127 Shoreditch
Tuckwell John, wine mer. see Knobel, Hamilton & Tuckwell
Tuckwell Samuel, grocer, Deptford High st
Tuckwood John, chinaman, 22 Homer st. Marylebone
Tudor Sam. & Wm. white lead ma. 166 & 167 Up. Thames st
Tudor Geo. brush & sieve maker, 123 Long alley, Finsbury
Tudor Henry, stockbroker, 3 Hatton court, Threadneedle st
Tudor John, dairy, 14 Charles st. Hatton garden
Tudor Owen Davies, barrister, 30 Chancery lane
Tudor Samuel, wholesale druggist, 166 & 167 Up. Thames st
Tudway Clement, solicitor, see Jones, Trinder & Tudway
Tuely Chas. & Co. mahogany merchants, 35 Bridge wharf, City road basin, & 8 Regent terrace, City road
Tuff James, academy, 28 Jewry st. Aldgate
Tuffield Thomas, tallow chandler, &c. 89 Hoxton Old town
Tuffin William, bootmaker, 19 Snow's fields, Bermondsey
Tuggs John, marine store dlr. 1 Portland pl. Walworth com
Tugwell Charles, silver chaser, 10 King's sq. Goswell road
Tuke Francis, oporto merchant, 25 Crutchedfriars
Tuke George Howen, billiard rooms, 34 Red Lion st. Holborn
Tuke Wm. Epworth, sworn wine broker, &c. 25 Gt. Tower st
Tulk John, carpentr. & undertkr. 16 Shepherd's ct. Shpd's. mkt
Tull John, grocer & cheesemonger, 4 Botolph alley
Tull Saml. net, rope, line & twine ma. 153 Fenchurch st
Tullett Alfred, who. stationer, 117 Whitechapel High st
Tullett Hen. Wm. 3 *Brewers* P.H. 1 Norfolkpl. Low. rd. Islngn
Tullett Wm. hardwareman, 47 Chapel st. Somers town
Tullett John Thos. *Talbot* P.H. 1 Goodge st. Tottenham ct. rd
Tulley Charles & Sons, opticians, 7 Church row, Islington
Tulley Alfred, grocer, Church st. Hackney
Tulley William & Son, egg merchants, 5 Mint st. Borough
Tulloch John & James, merchants, 11 Lombard st
Tulloch Donald, coal merchant, Great Scotland yard
Tulloh James, surgeon, 3 Agar st. Strand
Tully Joseph, carpenter, 23 Appleby st. Pearson st. Kngsld. rd
Tunbridge John, baker, 9 Salmon lane, Limehouse; & Ferry road west, Poplar
Tune Chas. bootmaker, 50 Charlotte ter. New cut, Lambeth
Tune Henry, boot & shoe warehouse, 102 Blackfriars road
Tune Henry, boot & shoe maker, 92 High st. Notting hill
Tungatt Edward, tailor, 1 Princes square, Ratcliff highway
Tungatt John, sailma. wine & beer mer. 76 to 78 Fore st. Limho
Tungay Wm. *Geo. & Dragon* P.H. 18 Princes st. Leicester sq
Tunks Thomas, builder, 8 Terrace, Kensington
Tunley Wm. & Co. general carriers, by canal & railway, 17 Old change, 1 Wharf, Praed st. Paddington basin, & Camden town station
Tunnacliffe Wm. Henry, who. brushma. 5 Princes st. Westm
Tunnicliff Wm. Geo. *Blakeney's Hd.* 40 Rufford's blds. Islngtn
Tunstall Edwd. greengrocer, 5 Winbourne st. New North rd
Tunstall Jonathan, tailor, 4 Webb st. Bermondsey st
Tupman Geo. & Hen. watch & clock ma. 31 Gt. Russell st. Blmsby
Tupp John, confectioner, 8 Tottenham court road
Tupper Geo. Fred. lithographer, 25 Clement's la. Lombard st
Tupper Heathfield, surgeon, 1 Warwick square, Kensington
Tupper John, grocer, 61 Dorset st. Salisbury square
Tupper Martin, jun. surgeon, 5 New Burlington st
Tupper William, dealer in hams & tongues, 33 Up. Marylbn. st
Tur Eliza (Mrs.), lace cleaner & mender, 24 Haymarket
Turbill Edward, cheesemngr. 34 Gt. James st. Lisson grove
Turbyfield Wm. umbrella maker, 8 Hayfield pl. Mile end rd
Turffrey John, fur skin dresser, 4 Little Suffolk st. Borough
Turffrey Joseph, skin dresser, 2 Butler's pl. New st. Dockhd
Turffrey Thomas, manure dealer, 3 Russell st. Dockhead
Turk (Miss), ladies' school, Clayton pl. Kennington road
Turk Rd. N. *Dolphin tavern*, Lower area, Hungerford mrkt
Turk William, meat salesman, 21 New Newgate market
Turle James, organist of Westmr. Abbey, Cloisters, Westmr
Turley Richard, beer retailer, 60 Cromer st. Brunswick sq
Turley William, carpenter, 76 Seymour pl. Bryanstone sq
Turmine Daniel, brush manfr. 15 Wade's pl. Hackney road
Turnage Robert, hairdresser, 12 Northumberland st. New rd
Turnage Thomas Sparrow, cooper, 20 Robert st. Grosvnr. sq
Turnbull James L. & John, card ma. & hot pres. Holywell mt
Turnbull John & Son, carpenters & bldrs. 4 Suffolk la. City
Turnbull, Maxwell & Co. sewed muslin mnfrs. 2 Bow chrchyd
Turnbull Alexander, physician, 48 Russell square
Turnbull Alexander, tanner, Blue Anchor road
Turnbull Francis, baker, 10 Park ter. King's rd. Chelsea
Turnbull Francis, seal engraver, 32 Red Lion st. Clerkenwell
Turnbull George, bread & biscuit baker, 41 Lambeth High st
Turnbull George, grocer, 36 Charles st. Middlesex hospital
Turnbull Hector, commission agent at Messrs. Hodgston & Co. 4 Tokenhouse yard
Turnbull James, baker, 93 Dorset st. Salisbury square
Turnbull John, fishmonger, 27 Montagu st. Portman square
Turnbull John, saddler, &c. 21 Macclesfield st. south, City rd
Turnbull Robert, baker, Church st. Deptford
Turnbull Stephen, saddler, &c. 64 Up. North pl. Gray's inn rd
Turnbull Thomas, artist, 47 Clarendon sq. Somers town
Turnbull Thomas, teadealer, Church st. Deptford
Turnbull Thos. timber mer. & saw mills, 33 Wm. st. Portland tn
Turnell Wm. *Old Pitt's Head* P.H. 17 Tyssen st. Bethnal gn
Turner Alfred & William, attorneys, 32 Red Lion sq. Holborn

Turner & Arney, undertakers & auctioneers, 61 Shoreditch
Turner & Billson, wholesale coffee dealers, 29 Mark lane
Turner & Clark, livery stables, 127 St. John st. Smithfield
Turner & Cubley, color manufs. 120 Princes road, Lambeth
Turner Edward & Co. tallow chandlers, 203 Whitechapel rd
Turner Elizh. & Fras. linendrapers, 7 Surrey pl. Kngtn. com
Turner Geo. & Son, builders, 1 & 25 White st. Lit. Moorfields
Turner & Gilpin, warehousemen, 1 Northumberland st.Strnd
Turner (Hammond) & Sons, button makers, 130 Cheapside
Turner Henry & John, surgeons, 10 Bedford pl. Russell sq
Turner Hy. N. & Co. paper stnrs. Elizabeth st. south, Pimlico
Turner Israel & Co. merchants, 11 Gt. Tower st
Turner James & Son, coach & harness makers, 113 Long acre
Turner James & Thomas, horse infirmary, 311 Regent st
Turner John & Thomas, goldsmiths & jewellers to the Queen, 58 & 59 New Bond st
Turner Mary S.&C. (Misses), school, 78 Westmrlnd.pl.City rd
Turner & Montague, cement makers, 6 Wharf, Paddington basin, Falcon wharf, 80 Bankside; Stratford & Blackwall
Turner Ralph & Co. flannel & baize manfrs. 3Sambrook court
Turner Richard & Co. wine importers, 75 Mark lane
Turner Robt. & Son, brewers, Church st. Clapham rd. Kngtn
Turner Samuel & Co. importers & distillers of tar, turpentine & naptha, manufacturers of pitch, rosins, varnishes & lamp black, & refiners of coal tar, Orchard place, East India docks; & Jerusalem coffee house
Turner & Shepard, seedsmen & florists, 99 New Bond st
Turner Thomas & Son (late Barrow & Turner), engineers & smiths, manufacturers of Barrow's patent sashes, iron revolving shutters & hot water apparatus for conservatories & buildings generally, 38 East st. Manchester square
Turner Thos. & Sons, paperstainers, 4 Williams pl. Walwth.rd
Turner Wm. & Co. button makers & warehomn. 6&8 Bow la
Turner Wm. & Co. hat manufacturers, 2 Bread st. Cheapside
Turner William & Sons, refiners, 48 Barbican
Turner Alfred, beer retailer, 27 King st. Islington
Turner Alfred, custom house agt. Jerusalem coffee house
Turner Alfred, tailor, Bromley, Middlesex
Turner Amelia (Miss), artist, 8 Singleton st. Hoxton
Turner Ann (Mrs.), milliner, &c. 66 George st. Portman sq
Turner Augustus H. *Duke of Wellington* P.H. 50 Wellington street, Newington causeway
Turner Benj. B. waxchandler, see Brecknell, Turner & Sons
Turner Brooke, solicitor, see Gatty & Turner
Turner C. A. (Miss), haberdasher, see Richardson & Turner
Turner Caleb, booksel. stati. & printer, Church st. Hackney
Turner Chas. A.R.A. engraver, 50 Warren st. Fitzroy sq
Turner Charles, *Grapes* P.H. Fisher's alley, Whitefriars; & 24 Primrose hill, Salisbury square
Turner Charles, leather seller, 14 Church st. Shoreditch
Turner Chas. Frederick, china warehouseman, 9 Oxford st
Turner Chas. *Tailors' Arms* P.H. 20 St. Clement's la. Strand
Turner Chas. varnish & color ma. 8 & 9 Broad st. Bloomsbury
Turner Charles Robert, master of court of Queen's Bench, Queen's Bench office, Temple
Turner Charlotte (Mrs.), grocer, 16 Salisbury st. Lisson grove
Turner Daniel, boot&shoe maker, 64 Wilsted st. Somers town
Turner Daniel, fruiterer, 1 Lyall place, Eaton square
Turner David, strawhat maker, 1 Crawford st. Portman sq
Turner Edward, beer retailer, 1 Charlotte st. Bagnge.wells rd
Turner Edward, chemist, 33 Oxenden st. Haymarket
Turner Edward, hairdresser, 4 Church st. Stoke Newington
Turner Edward, hairdresser, 15 Homer st. Marylebone
Turner Edward, sen. hairdresser, 141 Edgware road
Turner Edward Charles, cutler, 44 St. John st. Smithfield
Turner Edwd. Wm. pawnbroker, 17 Crown row, Walworth rd
Turner Elizh. (Mrs.), butcher, 24 Fitzroy mkt. Tottenhm.ct.rd
Turner Elizh. (Mrs.), cooper, 37 Gt. Prescot st. Goodman's fields
Turner Elizabeth (Mrs.), corn dealer, 112 Union st. Borough
Turner Elizh. (Mrs.), oil wareho. 1 Lit. James st. Bedford row
Turner Elizh. (Mrs.), stationer, 15 Hardwick pl. Comml.rd. ea
Turner Emanuel, *Rising Sun* P.H. 27 Brooksby st. Livpl. rd
Turner Francis, artist, 86 Newman st. Oxford st
Turner Francis, baker, 5 Clarence place, Clapham road
Turner Francis, barrister, 7 New square, Lincoln's inn
Turner Fred. clock dial silverer, 7 St. James's walk, Clknwll
Turner Frederick, coal dealer, 7 Stangate, Lambeth
Turner Frederick, solicitor, see Sole, Sole & Turner
Turner Frederick John, barrister, 7 New sq. Lincoln's inn
Turner Geo. baker, 111 Borough High st
Turner Geo. cowkeeper, 7 Keppel st. Chelsea
Turner Geo. fruiterer, 42 Store st. Bedford square
Turner Geo. furnish. ironmngr. 17 Bridgehouse pl. New. caus
Turner Geo. ironmonger, 12 Kingsgate st. Holborn
Turner Geo. solicitor, 30 Charles st. City road
Turner Geo. solicitor, see Hughes & Turner
Turner Geo. tailor, 74 Poplar High st
Turner Geo. trimming seller, 56 St. Martin's la. Charing crs
Turner Geo. James, queen's counsel, 11 New sq. Lincoln's inn; & 6 Harley st. Cavendish sq
Turner Geo. Snape, dairy, 1 Brunswick place, Brompton
Turner Henry, fishmonger, 1 Lit. Sussex pl. Hyde Park gdns
Turner Henry, fishmonger, 8 Coventry st. Haymarket
Turner Henry, furniture broker, 6 Weston pl. King's cross
Turner Henry, grocer, 8 South place, Tibberton square
Turner Henry, jeweller, 38 Great Sutton st. Clerkenwell
Turner Henry, linendraper, 27 Crawford st. Portman sq
Turner Henry, merchant, 29 Mark lane
Turner Henry, who. & ret. haberdasher, 40 Beech st. Barbican
Turner Henry John, solicitor, 27 Percy st. Tottenham ct. rd
Turner Henry Wall, barrister, 10 Crown office row, Temple
Turner Hewitt Fysh, floor cloth, table cover & patent blind manufacturer, 46 Myddelton st. & 46 Berners st. Oxford st
Turner Henry Scott, solicitor, see Stone & Turner
Turner Isaac, saddler & harness maker, 38 Wych st. Strand
Turner James, beer retailer, 15 Orchard st. St. Luke's
Turner James, biscuit baker & confec. 4 Queen's rd. Dalston
Turner James, bread & biscuit baker, 67 Bishopgate within
Turner James, bookseller, 23 Russell court, Drury lane
Turner James, bricklayer, Pedlar's orchard, Stepney
Turner James, butcher, 64 Aldersgate st
Turner James, butcher, 75 Whitehorse st. Stepney
Turner James, cabinet maker, Whitmore row, Hoxton
Turner James, coach & cart builder, 7 Waterloo road
Turner James, cabinet maker, Honduras ho. Grange pl. Hxtn
Turner James, *Crown* P.H. 46 Tabernacle walk, Finsbury
Turner James, dairyman, 71 Regent st. Lambeth
Turner James, linendraper, 35 Hedge row, Islingtn. High st
Turner James, plumber, 15 Bermondsey New road
Turner James, professor of singing, 17 King st. Finsbury
Turner James, printer, 20 Cross st. Hatton garden
Turner James, surgeon, see Pollock & Turner
Turner James, tailor, 32 Dorset st. Portman sq
Turner James, tailor, 13 Flagon row, Deptford
Turner James, tobacconist, 45 Plumber's st. City road
Turner James Thomas, coffee rooms, 48 Bridge rd. Lambeth
Turner Jeffery, tobacconist, 16 Eyre st. hill
Turner John, baker, 38 King st. Seven dials
Turner John, barrister, 2 North bank, Regent's park
Turner John, beer retailer, 19 Lower Ranelagh st. Pimlico
Turner John, beer retailer, 7 Oxford st
Turner John, beer retailer, Strachan place, Balls pond road
Turner John, *Blue Anchor* P.H. 102 Bunhill row
Turner John, brewer, 2 Heneage st. Whitechapel
Turner John, chairmaker, &c. 25 Skinner st. Bishopsgate
Turner John, coal merchant, 38 South Molton st. Oxford st
Turner John, *Elephant* P.H. 26 Robinson's rw. Hi.st. Kingsld
Turner John, fruiterer, 66 Bermondsey st
Turner John, fruiterer, 4 Brick lane, St. Luke's
Turner John, fruiterer, 2 Princes st. Lt. Queen st. Holborn
Turner John, furn. broker, 21 John st. west, Blackfriars rd
Turner John, grocer, &c. 13 Collier st. Pentonville
Turner John, naturalist, & importer of oriental porcelain & curiosities, 21 Wellclose sq
Turner John, pianoforte & music warehouse, 84 Leadenhall st
Turner John (late Cook), printers' smith, brass rule cutter, & general dealer, 24 Brooke st. Holborn
Turner John, saw & truss ma. 14 Gt. St. Andrew st. Sevendials
Turner John, scale maker, 34 Crown st. Soho
Turner John, *Ship* P.H. 5 Boundary st. Shoreditch
Turner John, surveyor, 43 Lower Belgrave place, Pimlico
Turner John, tailor, 13 Kenton st. Brunswick square
Turner John, tailor, &c. 4 Market st. Mayfair
Turner John, whip maker, 1 Caroline mews, Bedford sq
Turner John, working cutler, 50 Tothill st. Westminster
Turner John Alvey, pianoforte ma. & music selr. 19 Poultry
Turner John G. coffee rooms, 235 Shadwell High st
Turner Jonathan, dining & coffee rooms, 6 Mill st. Hanover sq
Turner Jonathan, upholsterer, 6 Nassau st. Soho
Turner Joseph, china, glass, &c. wareh. 139 Praed st. Edgw.rd
Turner Joseph, confectioner, 20 Great Titchfield st
Turner Joseph, fruiterer, 4 Church st. Mile end New town
Turner Joseph, coffee rooms, 3 Richmond st. Leicester sq
Turner Joseph, furnishing undertaker, 1 Farringdon st
Turner Joseph, hairdresser, Charlotte st. Portland place
Turner Joseph, sheffield plate warehouse, gold & silversmith, & jeweller, 43 Ludgate hill
Turner Joseph, silversmith & pawnbroker, 170 Waterloo rd
Turner Joseph, solicitor, 63 Boro' road, Southwark
Turner Joseph Holden, solicitor, 8 Chancery lane
Turner Joseph Mallord Wm. R.A. artist, 47 Queen Anne st
Turner Maj. Wm. agt. to Bengal milit. orphan soc. 69 Cornhill

Turner Maria (Mrs.), paper stain. 2 Parsonage rw. Nwn. butts
Turner Marshal, solicitor, see Yates & Turner
Turner Mary (Mrs.), court dress ma. 12 Baker st. Portman sq
Turner Mary (Mrs.), milliner, &c. 4 Market st. Oxford st
Turner Nicholas, fruiterer, 3 Union st. east, Spitalfields
Turner Peter, dairy, 8 Dorrington st. Cold bath fields
Turner Peter Bruce, bill broker, 12 Bucklersbury
Turner Rachael (Mrs.), milliner, 3 York st. Westminster
Turner Richard, baker, 7 Heartley place, Old Kent road
Turner Richard Charles, carpntr. & builder, 119 Houndsditch
Turner Richard Edwd. special pleader, 2 Tanfield ct. Temple
Turner Richard Valentine, stockbroker, 18 Throgmorton st. & Stock exchange
Turner Robert, beer retailer, 39 Brick lane, St. Luke's
Turner Robert, blacking makr. 59 Three Colt st. Limehouse
Turner Robert, mourning warehouse, 16 Ludgate hill
Turner Robert, plumber, &c. 17 Blandford st. Portman sq
Turner Robert, tailor, 5 New Quebec st. Portman sq
Turner Robert, working cutler, 11 Phœnix st. Somers town
Turner Robert Henry, baker, 11 Crescent pl. Burton crescent
Turner Rowland, tailor, 2 Old Cavendish st
Turner Samuel, baker, 185 Bishopsgate st. without
Turner Samuel, barrister, 9 Gray's inn square
Turner Samuel, bookbinder, 4 Bond court, Walbrook
Turner Samuel, bootmaker, 6 Goodwin's ct. St. Martin's la
Turner Samuel, carpenter & undertaker, 26 Walbrook
Turner Samuel, cattle salesman, 15 Smithfield
Turner Samuel, dancing academy, 5 Blomfield st. Finsbury
Turner Samuel, grocer, 26 Wormwood st. Bishopsgate
Turner Samuel, *Marquis Cornwallis* P.H. 89 Bethnal gr. rd
Turner Samuel, tobacconist, 11 Aylesbury st. Clerkenwell
Turner Thomas, barrister, 7 Old square, Lincoln's inn
Turner Thomas, basket maker, 11 Gt. Pulteney st. Golden sq
Turner Thomas, brazier, 20 Young st. Kensington
Turner Thomas, builder & material dlr. Clandon st. Walw. com
Turner Thomas, carpent. & builder, Clandon st. Walworth com
Turner Thomas, *Crown* P.H. 38 Gt. Ormond yard, Queen sq
Turner Thos. draughtsman & lithographer, 76 Little Britain
Turner Thomas, hairdresser, 60 Gt. Carlisle st. Portmn. mkt
Turner Thomas, pawnbroker, 79 York place, Waterloo rd
Turner Thomas, physician, 31 Curzon st. Mayfair
Turner Thomas, smith, &c. see Barrow & Turner
Turner Thomas, stonemason, 4 Somerset pl. New rd. Comml. rd
Turner Thomas, tobacconist, 7 John's pl. Camberwell New rd
Turner Thomas, upholsterer to her Majesty & the Queen Dowager, 139 New Bond st
Turner Thomas, who. brushmaker, see Pantin & Turner
Turner Thomas B. human hair ma. & perfumer, 71 Snowhill
Turner Thos. Peregrine, solicitor, 2 Field court, Gray's inn
Turner Wm. basket maker, 5 Queen st. Grosvenor square
Turner Wm. bookseller, 46 Squirries st. Bethnal green rd
Turner Wm. beer retailer, 64 Regent st. Westminster
Turner Wm. brass manf. & gasfitter, 47 Rupert st. Haymarket
Turner Wm. brewer, 4 Hull terrace, St. Luke's
Turner Elizabeth, butcher, 24 Fitzroy market
Turner Wm. cabinet maker, 52 Ossulston st. Somers town
Turner Wm. carpenter, 5 Harrow road, Paddington
Turner Wm. carpenter, 16 Keen's row, Walworth road
Turner Wm. china dealer, 1 Denmark pl. Camberwell
Turner Wm. feather & flower maker, 74 Judd st. Brunswick sq
Turner Wm. *Fox & Knot* P.H. Fox & Knot ct. King st. Snow hl
Turner Wm. fruiterer, 15 Berwick st. Soho
Turner Wm. gasfitter, 5 Robert st. Lower marsh, Lambeth
Turner Wm. grocer, 7 Henry st. east, Portland town
Turner Wm. ironmonger, 4 Queen's road, Dalston
Turner Wm. jeweller, 43 Myddelton st. Clerkenwell
Turner Wm. mangle maker, 15 Vine st. Hatton garden
Turner Wm. professor of dancing, 7 Nelson sq. Blackfrs. rd
Turner Wm. rope & twine maker, 6 Union st. ea. Spitalfields
Turner Wm. shoemaker, 8 Seabright pl. east, Hackney road
Turner Wm. tailor, 11 George st. Hanover square
Turner Wm. tailor, see Hallett, Turner & Co
Turner Wm. tobacconist, 2 Bridge court, Westminster
Turner Wm. turner, 10 Grange road, Bermondsey
Turner Wm. Hall, surgeon, see Castle & Turner
Turner Wm. Henry, solicitor, 8 Mount pl. Whitechapel road
Turner Wm. John, corndealer, 9 Brecknock pl. Camden New tn
Turner Wm. John, corndealer, 5 John st. Titchfield. ter. Rgt's pk
Turner Wingfield Ashton, saddler, 12 Edgware road
Turney Alexander, brewer, Addington sq. Camberwell
Turney Catherine (Miss), milliner, 279 Regent st
Turney George, grocer, 3 Wyndham road, Camberwell
Turney George Leonard, needle, pin, & hook & eye manufacturer, 106 Wood st. City
Turney Robt. milliner & straw hat mak. 50 Fore st. Cripplega
Turney Wm. dairyman, 75 Mary st. Regent's park
Turnham John, baker, 35 Mansell st. Goodman's fields
Turnley Brothers, lightermen & agents, 22 Savage gardens
Turnley James Wm. lighterman & agent, 19 Harp la. Tow. st
Turnley Wm. Saml. & Co. mahogany & rosewood importers, 21 New Bridge st
Turnor Edward & Co. coopers & hoop benders, 39 Wapping
Turnor & Laws, linendrapers, Church st. Hackney
Turnstill Wm. coal & wood dealer, 64 Charlotte st. Old st. rd
Turpie Andrew, baker, 37 Queen's road, Bayswater
Turpin Geo. turner & hard wood dlr. 34 Booth st. Spitalfields
Turpin Hen. fishing tackle ma. 124 St. John st. road
Turpin Joseph, coffee rooms, 2 Gilbert st. Grosvenor square
Turpin Joseph, grocer, 24 Wellington st. Goswell st
Turpin Richard, cutler & dressing case instrument maker, 25 Eyre st. hill, Leather lane
Turpin Susannah (Mrs.), watchmakr. 62 Banner st. St. Luke's
Turpin Wm. *Old Essex Serpent* P.H. 6 King st. Covent gar
Turquand Samuel Jas. linendraper, 23 Church st. Camberwl
Turquand William, official assignee, 13 Old Jewry
Turrell Ann (Mrs.), chandler's shop, 1 Virginia rw. Bethnal gr
Turrell Edwin, straw hat & millinery wareho. 28 Oxford st
Turrell James, carpenter, 21 Warren st. Fitzroy sq
Turrill John & Co. writing & dressing case ma. 250 Regent st
Turrill Richard & Son, coachmakers, 22 & 23 Long Acre
Turrill Owen, *Bull & Bell* P.H. 19 Ropemakers' st. Finsbury
Turrill William, shoemaker, 3 Pollard's row, Bethnal green
Turtill Robert, saddler, 221 High Holborn
Turtle Thomas & Wm. butchers, 37 Alfred st. Bedford sq
Turtle John, carver & gilder, 22 Upper st. Martin's lane
Turtle Meshach, fruiterer, 3 Upper Dorset pl. Clapham rd
Turtle William, butcher, 78½ Tottenham court road
Turtley Philip, cyder mer. Carpenter Smith's whf. Tooley st
Turvey Henry, butcher, Cobourg road, Old Kent road
Turvey Jesse Wm. tailor, 7 Goswell terrace, Goswell road
Turvey John, naturalist, 4 Cambridge rd. Mile end road
Turvey Joseph, butcher, 24 Bath st. City road
Tuson Edward William, surgeon, 10 Russell pl. Fitzroy sq
Tuson Henry, printer, 38 Narrow st. Limehouse
Tuson William, ropemaker & ship chandler, 37 Narrow st. Limehouse, & 9 & 10 Risbies rope walk, Limehouse
Tussaud (Madame) & Sons, exhibition, 58 Baker st. Portm. sq
Tustian Thos. & Co. rule maks. 18 Princes sq. Ratcliff highw
Tustin & Barlow, attorneys, 4 New Bridge st
Tustin Thomas, eating house, 132 Shoreditch
Tutin Thomas, glass & china dealer, 1 Whitmore rd. Hoxton
Tutin William, boot & shoe maker, Camberwell green
Tuting Wm. hairdresser & perfumer, 89 Queen st. Cheapside
Tutt Edward, stationer, 115 High st. Marylebone
Tutt Willoughby D. bootmaker, Warlters' bdgs. Old Kent rd
Tuttiett & Broad, surgeons, 1 Spencer's ter. Westminster
Tutton Robert, farrier, 4 Lansdowne mews, Guilford st
Tutton John, coachbuilder & harness mak. 20 South Audley s
Tutton Joseph, beer retailer, 137 New road, Sloane st
Tutton Lucy (Miss), glass, &c. dealer, 19 Down st. Piccadilly
Tutton Sarah (Miss), lodging house, 9 Craven st. Strand
Twaites James, bootmaker, 7 Saville place, Lambeth walk
Tweddell John, solicitor, 3 Mitre ct. Ely place, Holborn
Tweed John James, jun. surgeon, 9 Gilbert st. Grosvenor sq
Tweed John James, sen. surgeon, 4 Alfred place, Bedford sq
Tweed Robert, chemist & druggist, 101 London wall
Tweedale Jacob & Sons, flannel, baize & blanket manufacturers, 56 Wood st. Cheapside
Tweeddale Francis, baker, 14 Bloomsbury st
Tweeddale James Dunbar, physician, 87 St. Martin's lane
Tweeddale Robert, baker, 2 James st. Buckingham gate
Tweedie Alexr. F.R.S. physician, 30 Montague pl. Russell sq
Tweedy William, tailor, 22 Upper Ebury st. Pimlico
Twelftree Jane (Mrs.), *King's Head tav.* King's Head ct. St. Pl's
Twells & Podmore, metal wareh. 2 Brownlow st. Drury la
Twells Philip, barrister, 1 New square, Lincoln's inn
Twemlow Thomas F. barrister, 2 Stone bldgs. Lincoln's inn
Twentyman Laurence & Son, mers. 12 George yd. Lombard st
Twentyman Richard, silk agent, see Bennoch & Twentyman
Twigg William, shoemaker, Stratford Broadway
Twight Wm. surveyor & ho. agt. 29 Up. Jubilee pl. Mile end rd
Twilley Wm. carver & gilder, 6 Stepney rents, Hackney rd
Twinberrow William, chemist, 2 Edwards st. Portm sq
Twine William, boot & shoe maker, 179 Oxford st
Twining Richard, George, John A. Richard, Samuel H. & William B. bankers, 215 Strand
Twining Richard & Co. teamen to the Queen, importers, tea merchants, & wholesale & retail tea dealers, 216 Strand
Twining Aldred, solicitor, see Wing & Twining
Twining William, physician, 13 Bedford pl. Russell square
Twinn Edward Henry, cheesemonger, 128 Shadwell High st
Twisden Thos. Edwd. solicitor, 5 Verulam buildings

Twiss & Brownings', merchants, 37 Mark lane
Twiss Horace, queen's counsel, 54 Chancery lane
Twiss Richard, solicitor, 39 Cambridge terrace, Hyde park
Twiss Travers, D.C.L. advocate, 15 Gt. Knightrider st
Twitchin Wm. carriers' agent, Greyhound inn, King st. Smthfld
Twitchings George, watch dial maker, 25 Galway st. St. Luke's
Twoart George, carrier to Chelsea, 19 Sloane sq. Chelsea
Twopeny William, barrister, 4 Lamb building, Temple
Twyford David, beer retailer, 253 Borough High st
Twyford Samuel, magistrate, Bow st. police court
Twyman Stephen, coffee rooms, 2 Water lane, Blackfriars
Twyman William, bootmaker, 8 Church st. Deptford
Twyman Wm. Sidney, tobacconist, 178 Goswell st
Tyack Joseph, butcher, 6 Weston st. Somers town
Tyars Maria Anna (Miss), juv. clothing wa. 6 Charles st. Soho
Tyars William Salmon & Co. linendrapers, 113 Minories
Tyars John, linendraper, 7 Charles st. Soho square
Tyas Isaac H. & Richard, attorneys, 13 Beaufort bldgs. Strand
Tye Edward, *Geo. the Fourth* P.H. 25 Montpelier sq. Brompton
Tye Edward, painter & glazier, Downham road, Kingsland
Tye John, druggist, 1 Lower Queen's row, Pentonville
Tye Thomas, house painter, 147 Waterloo road
Tye William, cattle salesman, 41 West Smithfield
Tyerman Charles Richard, solicitor, see Stokes & Co
Tyerman Thomas, architect & surveyor, 6 Chancery lane, & 12 Queen's buildings, Brompton
Tyers R. J. & Co. fish sauce wa. 58 Boro', & 203 Up. Thames st
Tyers Robert John, sugar refiner, see Smith & Tyers
Tyffee Geo. Henry, tobacconist, Deptford High st
Tylee Edward, solicitor, see White, Blake, Tylee & Fawkener
Tyler Geo. & Rich. law stationers, 38 & 49 Carey st. Linc. inn fi
Tyler Hayward & Co. cast iron warehse. 85 Up. Whitecross st
Tyler Hayward & Co. engineers, &c. manufacturers of soda-water engines, hydraulic presses, &c. 85 Up. Whitecross st
Tyler Hayward & Co. plumbers' & ironmongers' brass founders, braziers, & manufacturers of lift pumps, water closets, &c. 85 Upper Whitecross st
Tyler John & Son, hat manufacturers, 80 Union st. Borough
Tyler & Reed, printers, 5 Bolt court, Fleet st
Tyler & Rogers, gold lacemen, 26 Bedford st. Covent garden
Tyler, Venables & Wilson, stationers, see Venables, Wilson & Co
Tyler Ann (Miss), embroiderer, 61 South Molton st. Bond st
Tyler Charles, jeweller, 169 Brick lane, Spitalfields
Tyler Edward, beer retailer, Colvill ter. King's rd. Chelsea
Tyler Elizabeth (Miss), milliner, see Rudd & Tyler
Tyler George, butcher, Leadenhall market
Tyler George, jeweller, 15 Holywell st. Strand
Tyler Henry, bricklayer, 63 Long lane, Bermondsey
Tyler Henry, fruiterer, Prospect place, Kingsland road
Tyler Henry Frederick, solicitor, 47 Bedford row
Tyler James, butcher, 10 Sherrard st. Golden sq
Tyler James, oil & colorman, 11 Leonard st. Finsbury
Tyler James, thermometer maker, 5 Charles st. Hatton gdn
Tyler James Thomas, butcher, Well st. Hackney rd
Tyler John, cabinet maker, 63 Gt. Cambridge st. Hackney rd
Tyler John, fish factor, 11 Cross lane, St. Mary at hill
Tyler John, *Rose & Crown* P.H. 39 Bartholomew close
Tyler John, solicitor, 3 Staple inn, Holborn
Tyler John H. *Watermen's Arms* P.H. Pickle herring, Tooley st
Tyler Joseph, chair & sofa ma. 59½ Broad st. Bloomsbury
Tyler Joseph, dairyman, 1 Norwich court, Fetter lane
Tyler Joseph, solicitor, 7 South square, Gray's inn
Tyler Rich. *Valiant Trooper* P.H. 9 Goodge st. Tott. ct. rd
Tyler Robert, carpenter & builder, 30 Castle st. Leicester sq
Tyler Robert, smith & farrier, 3 Long lane, Bermondsey
Tyler Samuel, *Fountain & Star* P.H. 3 Castle ct. Lawrence la
Tyler Thos. G. cooper & waste paper dr. 8 Gt. Trinity la. City
Tyler Thomas, stationer & bookseller, 164 Tottenham ct. rd
Tyler William, butcher, 91 Bishopsgate within
Tyler William, dairyman, 2 Queen st. Seven dials
Tyler William, *Grapes* P.H. 14 Dowgate hill
Tyler William, oilman, 1 Field terrace, King's cross
Tyler William, pro. of Zoological grd. Penton pl. Walworth
Tyler William, tailor, 3 South row, Golden square
Tyler Wm. Henry, ladies' shoe ma. 2 Knight's pl. Wndswrth. rd
Tyler Wm. Watt, engraver, 10 Haberdasher's pl. West, Hoxtn
Tylor & Essex, manufacturers of cocoa & chocolate, steam mills, 5 Flower & Dean st. Brick lane, Whitechapel
Tylor Joseph & Son, lamp ma. Coll. of Physicians, Warwick la
Tylor Joseph & Son, braziers, brass founders, tea urn, lamp, & soda wtr. mchine. manfrs. Coll. of Physicians, Warwick la
Tylor & Pace, metal perforators, envelope manufacturers, &c. 11, 12, 13 & 14, John st. London fields, Hackney
Tylor John Joseph, chemist & druggist, 164 Piccadilly
Tylor Joseph Savory, surgeon, 32 Charterhouse square
Tymms Thomas, saddler, see Musson & Tymms

Tyndale John Warre, barrister, 11 Lincoln's inn fields
Tyne Elizabeth (Mrs.), glass, &c. dealer, 18 Kensingt. High st
Type Matthew, japanr. & tea tray ma. 31 Coppice row. Clknw
Tyrell William, hairdresser, 22 Windmill st. Finsbury
Tyrer Henry James, watchmaker, 9 Red Lion st. Clerkenwell
Tyrie John, baker, 10 Park st. Borough
Tyrie John Garnett, merchant, 1 Crown court, Old Broad st
Tyrrell Edward, city remembrancer, Guildhall
Tyrrell Elizabeth (Mrs.), lodging house, 111 Strand
Tyrrell George, builder, 26 Marlborough sq. Chelsea
Tyrrell John, confectioner, 19 Arthur st. King's rd. Chelsea
Tyrrell John, goldbeater, 2 Greek st. Soho
Tyrrell Joseph, cheesemonger, 2 Church st. Horselydown
Tyrrell Joseph, furniture broker, 262 Whitechapel road
Tyrrell Louisa (Mrs.), fancy stationer, 2 Greek st. Soho
Tyrrell Richard, bolt & rivet iron works, Deptford pier
Tyrrell Richard, wine & spirit merchant, 39 Gt. Tower st
Tyrrell Timothy, solicitor, Guildhall
Tyrrell William, *Plough* P.H. 23 Carey st. Lincoln's inn
Tyrwhitt Robert Phillip, barrister, 4 Brick court, Temple
Tyser George, fruiterer, 10 Ann's ter. Cambridge heath
Tyser Richd. B. commission agt. 3 Railway pl. Fenchurch st
Tyser Richd. B. manchester agt. 6 Railway pl. Fenchurch st
Tyson & Mackreth, wholesale teadealers, 39 Cannon st. City
Tyson Benjamin, butcher, 1 Pont st. Cadogan pl. Chelsea
Tyson Joseph, boot & shoe maker, 107 Waterloo road
Tyson William, *Hay Field* P.H. Hayfield place, Mile end
Tyssen & Sharpin, *Victoria & Euston hotels*, Euston sq
Tyssen John R.D. solicitor, 1 Winchester bldgs. Gt. Winch. st
Tytheridge John, *Black Swan*, P.H. High st. Bow
Tytherleigh Thomas, butcher, 57 Castle st. Leicester sq
Tytherleigh Wm. glover, &c. 11 Gt. Russell st. Bloomsbury
Tyzack, Dobinson & Co. patent windlass, chain, cable, & anchor manufacturers, & ship smiths, cast iron founders & forgemen (John Joseph Hedley, agent), 264 Wapping, & North Shields

UBEE James, spectacle maker, 13 Crown st. Soho
Ubsdell Charles & Co. Great Western Emporium, drapers & tailors, 1 & 2 Oxford st
Udall Edward, mechanical tool dealer, 27 Sloane sq. Chelsea
Udall Henry, barrister, 3 Fig Tree court, Temple
Udall Jas. Geo. laceman, 20 Barnsbury pl. Upper st. Islngtn
Udall John, *Queen's Head* P.H. 13 Lit. Pulteney st. Golden sq
Udell William, bedstead maker, 37 Skinner st. Bishopsgate
Uffell James, tailor, 39 Kenton st. Brunswick square
Uffindell Charles, butcher, 40 Salmon lane, Limehouse
Uffindell Joseph, grocer, 16 South pl. Tibberton sq. Islington
Ufford John George, Highbury brewery, Holloway
Ullathorne William & Co. manufacturers of shoe thread & tow yarns, & wholesale grindery warehousemen, 12 Gate st. Lincoln's inn fields, & flax mills, Barnard Castle
Ullathorne William, russia merchant, Baltic coffee house
Ullmer Edwin & Wm. printing press makers & printing material manufacturers, 110 Fetter lane
Ullmer & Watts, printers' brokers, manufacturers of printers' materials, & dealers in new & second-hand presses & type, 76 Little Britain
Ullmer Henry, baker, 1 Pump yard, Ratcliff
Ulph Ann & Son, tailors, 56 Upper Marylebone st
Ulph Hen. butcher & cattle salesmn. 40 Up. Albany st. Regt's pk
Ulph John William, tailor, 40 Frederick pl. Hampstead rd
Ulster Canal Company, 6 Austinfriars
Umney Richard, furnish. undertaker, 100 Broad st. Ratcliff
Umpelby Hen. boot ma. 68 Charlotte ter. New cut, Lambeth
Umpelby Thomas, boot & shoe maker, 120 Lambeth walk
Umphelby John, rice & spice mer. 2 Love lane, Eastcheap
Umpleby Geo. Wm. woollen draper, 112 Holborn hill
Umppelby Emma (Mrs.), tobacconist, 105 Cornwall rd. Lmbth
Underdown Caroline Matilda (Mrs.), hatter, 203 Strand
Underdown Robert, hatter, 73 Quadrant, Regent st
Underdown Wm. plumber & paintr. 7 Platt ter. Pancras road
Underhay Wm. auctioneer, appraiser, house & estate agent, undertaker, & life & fire insurance agent, 9 Up. Baker st
Underhay Wm. plumber, painter, & decorator, 9 Up. Baker st
Underhill Hen. & Robt. glass cutters & chemical stopperers, smelling bottle & toilet ma. 18 Cross st. Hatton garden
Underhill Charles, general smith, 3 Back st. Horselydown
Underhill Mary Ann (Miss), ladies' school, 16 Everett st
Underhill Wm. galloon manufactr. 12 Wine office ct. Fleet st
Underhill Wm. *Queen's Head* P.H. 3 Water lane, Blackfrs
Underton Geo. musical tube ma. 13 Museum st. Bloomsbury
Underton Micah, carpenter, 35 Great Chart st. Hoxton
Underton Philip, carpenter, 2 Winckworth place, City road
Underton Thos. oil & colorman, 86 Church st. Shoreditch
Underton Thos. plumber & glazier, 65 Old st. road

Underwood Adam & John, cattle salesmen, 17 West Smithfield
Underwood Brothers, chasers, 114 Goswell road
Underwood Brothers, grocers, 8 New st. Covent garden
Underwood William & Son, woollen warehouse & clothiers, 1 Vere st. & 151A, Oxford st
Underwood Alfred, butcher, 5 Kinnerton st. Belgrave sq
Underwood Charles, butcher, 56 Regent st. Horseferry road
Underwood Charles, solicitor, see Bull & Underwood
Underwood Charles, teadealer, 11 James st. Covent garden
Underwood Edward, teadealer, &c. 3 Barnsbury pl. Islington
Underwood Francis, cattle salesman, 60 West Smithfield
Underwood Frederick, teadealer, 41 Blackfriars road
Underwood George, medical agent, 1 James st. Adelphi
Underwood Henry Thos. cutler, & *General Steam Packet Office*, 56 Haymarket
Underwood James, baker, Mile end, Mile end road
Underwood James, fruiterer, 3 Penton st. Pentonville
Underwood James, general salesman, 34 Lambeth walk
Underwood James, goldsmith, 57 Great Chart st. Hoxton
Underwood James, *Grapes* P.H. 356 Rotherhithe
Underwood Jas. manchester manufctr. 4 Bow church yard
Underwood James, tailor, 13 Lit. Russell st. Bloomsbury
Underwood James, tailor, 10 Warwick st. Belgrave road
Underwood John, butcher, 4 Providence row, Islington
Underwood John, livery stables, Albion mews, ea. Albion st
Underwood Joseph, distiller, see Hills & Underwood
Underwood Lewis, fishmonger, 44 Adam st. west, Portman sq
Underwood Mary (Mrs.), toydlr. 3 Ladbroke grove, Nottinghill
Underwood Thomas, dentist, 45 Gt. Marlborough st
Underwood Thomas, carpenter, 5 Clarendon st. Somers town
Underwood Thomas, linendraper, see Peters & Underwood
Underwood William, butcher, 20 Queen's road, Bayswater
Underwood William, tailor, 44 Frith st. Soho
Undey Chas. Hen. coal & coke mercht. 36 Surrey st. Strand
Undey George Edward, *Spotted Dog* P.H. 46 Poplar High st
Undrell Samuel, spectacle dlr. 53 Wellington st. Goswell st
Unett Eliza & Emma (Misses), straw hat wa. 22 Lisson grove n
Unett John, house agent, &c. 45 Chapel st. Edgware rd
Unger John Andrew, merchant, 7 Fen court, Fenchurch st
Union Assurance Office (Thomas Lewis, sec.), 81 Cornhill, & 70 Baker st.; see page 2045
Union Bank of Australia (Samuel Jackson, sec.), 38 Old Broad st. City; see page 2008
Union Bank of London (Wm. W. Scrimgeour, gen. manager), 2 Princes st. Bank
Regent st. Branch (Hy. T. Clack, manager), Argyll pl
Charing cross branch (Alex. Wight, manager), 4 Pall mall east; see page 2001
Union Club House (John Mackenzie, sec.), Trafalgar sq
Union Hall Police Court, 190 Union st. Borough
Union Insurance Society (*of Canton*), Fred. Wm. Appach, agent, 18 Tokenhouse yard
Union Plate Glass Company, plate glass manufacturers (works, Pocket Nook, St. Helen's, Lancashire), 26 Soho square, Alfred Goslett, agent
Unite Jas. & John, tarpaulin, &c. ma. 18 St. Alban's pl. Edgw. rd
Unite George, silversmith, 16 Thavies inn, Holborn
United General Gas Company, 6 Austinfriars
United Hills' Mine Company, 5 Adam's court, Old Broad st
United Kingdom Life Assurance Company (Edward Boyd, esq. resident director; E. Lennox Boyd, esq. assist. do.), 8 & 9 Waterloo place, Pall mall, for directors, &c. see page 2047
United Law Clerks' Society (Harry George Rogers, secretary), Crown & Anchor tavern, 189 Strand
United Mexican Mining Association (J. Mather, sec.), 8 Gt. Winchester st
United Peninsular Railway Office (Thomas Samuel Cutbill, sec.), 1 Royal Exchange buildings
United Service Club Ho. (Thos. He. Willis, sec.), 116 Pall mall
United Service Gazette, Chas. Evans, publish. 351 Strand
United Service Magazine office, 13 Gt. Marlborough st
United Service Museum, Middle Scotland yard
United University Club House (Wm. Hoys, sec.), Pall mall east
Unitt William, warehouseman, 1 Little Love lane, Wood st
Universal Corn Reporter Office, 42 Mincing lane
Universal Life Assurance Society (M. E. Impey, sec.), 1 King William st. City, see page 2048
Universal Salvage Co. (Walter Raymond, sec.), 12 Old Jewry chambers, Old Jewry
University College & Hospital (Charles Atkinson, sec.), Upper Gower st. north, New road
University Life Assurance Society (Charles M. Willich, secretary & actuary), 24 Suffolk st. Pall mall east
University of London Off. Somerset ho. Strand; hrs. 10 to 4
Unnett Peter William, beer retailer, 225 Strand
Unorius & Paton, merchants & ship agents, 16 Gt. St. Helen's
Unsworth William & George (late Baldock's), foreign china & antique furniture warehouse, 1 Hanway st. Oxford st
Unsworth James, turner, 24A, Henry st. Portland town
Unsworth Jerh. for. china dealer, 10 Princes st. Bedford row
Unthank Anthony & Co. tailors, 34 Gt. Pulteney st. Golden sq
Unthank Charles, patten & clog maker, 4 Old street road
Unthank John, barrister, 3 King's Bench walk, Temple
Unwin & Albert, hairdressers & perfumers, 24 Piccadilly
Unwin Benjamin, cowkeeper, 62 Berwick st. Soho
Unwin Charles, grocer, 165 Bethnal green road
Unwin Edward, hatter, see Salter, Unwin & Co
Unwin Henry, hairdresser, 47 St. George st. St. George's east
Unwin Henry, stockbroker, 8 Bank chambers, Lothbury
Unwin Isaac, builder & undrtkr. 30 & 31 Poland st. Oxford st
Unwin Jacob, printer & stationer, 31 Bucklersbury, City
Unwin James, dyer & scourer, 13 Church row, Pancras rd
Unwin John Wm. attorney, 15 Gt. Alie st. Goodman's fields
Unwin Mark, bricklayer, 11 Crosby row, Borough
Unwin Samuel, ready made linen wareh. 57 & 58 Lombard st
Unwin William, baker, 16 Penton place, Walworth
Unwin Wm. builder, 90 Milton st. Dorset sq
Unwin Wm. shopkeeper, 1 Pollard's row, Bethnal green
Unwin Wm. Scales, baker & coal merchant, Battersea
Upcott Joseph, wheelwright, Steven's mews, 80 Hoxton old tn
Upcroft John M. attorney, 4 Salisbury pl. New rd. Marylebo
Upfold Wm. bookbinder, 17 City road, Finsbury
Upham Hugh N. chaise saddler, 10 Brownlow st. Drury la
Upham Samuel, tailor, Morning lane, Hackney
Upjohn & Bright, watchmanfrs. &c. 15 King William st. Strand
Upper Canada Clergy Society (Rev. Septimus Ramsey, secretary), 103 St. Martin's lane
Upperton Samuel, *Bell Inn* P.H. Kilburn
Upsall Robert, pawnbroker, 10 Barbican
Upsall Thomas, butcher, 7 Weybridge place, Mile end rd
Upsher Wm. fishmonger, Borough market
Upton Wm. & Co. leather dressers, wholesale curriers & foreign importers & shoe mercers, 1 & 2 Gerard st. Soho
Upton Walter & Co. oilmen & lamp manufs. 66 Basinghall st
Upton Archer Thos. solr. see Baxendale, Tatham, Upton & Co
Upton Edward, artist, 17 Euston place, Euston sq
Upton Edwd. coal & coke mer. Horse shoe wf. 10 Upper Thms. st
Upton Georgiana (Mrs.), butcher, 7 Three Colt st. Limeho
Upton Henry, dining rooms, 228 Strand
Upton John Alfred, tobacconist, &c. Mare st. Hackney
Upton Richard, pro. of dancing, 11 London st. Fitzroy sq
Upton Robt. Brotherson, solicitor, see M'Dougal & Upton
Upton Thomas, carpenter, 23 Wilmot st. Russell sq
Upton Thomas, coal merchant, see Parker & Upton
Upton Thomas, dairyman, Bond st. Vauxhall
Upton Thomas, stock broker, 11 Warnford court
Upton William, dining rooms, 91 Strand
Upton Wm. fruiterer, 4 Mansion house st. Kenningtn. cross
Upton William, tailor, 28 Henrietta st. Covent garden
Upton William, tailor, 48 Tabernacle walk, Finsbury
Upward John, bricklayer, &c. 51 South Molton st. Bond st
Upward John W. stock & sharebroker, 15 Throgmorton st
Urch Henry, saddler, 84 Long acre
Ure Alexander, surgeon, 13 Charlotte st Bedford sq
Ure Andrew, M.D., F.R.S., analytical chemist, 13 Charlotte st. Bedford sq
Uren Stephen, bootmaker, 11 Park side, Knightsbridge
Urie James, haircutter, 10 Chiswell st. Finsbury
Urling Geo. Fred. & Co. lacemen to the Queen, 224 Regent st
Urlwin Philip, corn dealer & coal mercht. Camberwell green
Urquhart & Scrutton, ship & ins. brokrs. 7 St. Michael's alley
Urquhart & Tredgold, hosiers, 18 Devonshire bdgs. Gt. Dover st
Urquhart Alexander, baker, 9 Bridge ter. Harrow road
Urquhart Alexander, e. india agent, see Gardner & Urquhart
Urquhart Freeman, cooper, &c. 17 Wapping wall, & 205 Wapping High st
Urquhart Helen (Miss), milliner, see Ludlam & Urquhart
Urquhart James, cornfactor & ship biscuit baker, 60 Wapping wall, & 58 New corn exchange, Mark lane
Urquhart John, timber merchant, 336 Oxford st
Urquhart Walter Alexander, wine & general merchant, 7 Great Tower st
Urquhart William, baker, 94 Tyer st. Prince's road, Lambeth
Urry John C. baker, 60 Charlotte ter. New cut, Lambeth
Urry Richard, baker, Deptford broadway
Urry William, baker, 13 Bowling st. Westminster, & 19 Langley pl. Commercial rd. east
Urwick Rd. & Benj. wine & liqueur mers. 11 Foster la. Cheapsde
Usborne Thomas & Son, malt & corn factors, & insurance brokers, 5 New London st. Crutchedfriars, Old Corn exchange, & Sharp's wharf, 239 Wapping

Urwick Thos.Son& Dent,wine & brandy mers. 84 Gt.Tower st
Usher Andrew & Co. wine & spirit merchants, 1 Northumberland street, Strand, & at Edinburgh
Usher George, tailor, 8 St. Ann's court, Soho
Usher Mary (Mrs.), boot & shoe mkr.11 Ring cross, Holloway
Usher Phœbe Hester (Mrs.), cloakma.26 Warwick st.Rgnt.st
UsherThos.Dixon,*Mould'shotel*,15&16Suffolk st.Pall mall ea
Usher Thomas James, coach lace manfr.73 Long la. Smithfld
Usherwood William, silversmith & jeweller, 400 Strand
Uster Henry L. T. von, professor of languages,3 Berkeley sq
Ustonson Maria (Mrs.), fishing rod, tackle & net manufactr. to her Majesty, 48 Bell yard, Temple bar
Utley Henry, tailor, 14 Lit. Carter la. Doctors' commons
Utton William, oil & italian wareho. 26 Gower pl. Euston sq
Uzielli Theodosius, stock & sharebroker, 75Old Broad st.City

VACCINE Dispensary, at St. John's vestry hall, Fair st. Horsleydown
Vacher Thomas & Sons, stationers & law stationers, 29 Parliament st
Vachette Lousia (Mrs.), staymaker, 12 King st. Portman sq
Vade John Knox, physician, 8 Upper Seymour st
Vagts Peter, *Chequers* P.H. 13 Providence row, Finsbury
Vaile Joseph, auctioneer & ho. & estate agt. 315 Hi. Holborn
Vaile Samuel, laceman, 13 Crown row, Walworth road
Vailes John, tailor, 13 Ailington st. Pimlico
Vaizey John, solicitor, 2 South square, Gray's inn
Valder John, hairdresser, 140 High st. Camden town
Valdez Antonio Travassos, sec. to the mixed British & Portuguese Commission,& first attaché in London to her most faithful Majesty, 3 Delahay st. Westminster
ValeJno.Hy.&Co.Bordeauxmer.(A.&C.Cock,agt)3Dunsterct
Vale John, butcher, Leadenhall market
Vale John, dealer in berlin wool, &c. 115 York rd. Lambeth
Vale John, machinist, 35 Union st. Lambeth walk
Vale Robert, *Old Black Bull* P.H. Stratford Broadway
Vale Samuel, fruiterer, North row, Covent garden market
Vale Thos. coal dlr. & carpentr. 33 Bridgewaterst.Somers tn
Vale William, musical clock maker, 32 Paul st. Finsbury
Valente Jose Maria Rebello & Thos. Archer, of Oporto (agency, Wm. & Robt. Christie & Co.), 5 Fenchurch buildgs
Valentine Daniel, cabinet maker, 4 New inn yd. Shoreditch
Valentine Elias, drysalter, 6 Shoreditch High st
Valentine Francis, malt factor, 24 Mark lane
Valentine John, furnishing ironmonger, 397 Oxford st
Valentine Joseph, furn. broker, 10 Whitmore row, Hoxton
Valentine Saul, refiner, 3 Sandy's row, Bishopsgate
Valentiny John, tailor & trimming sel.9Maiden la.Cov. gard
Valintine George Edwd. architect, &c. 1 Southampton st
Vallance & Beioley, attorneys, 9 Old Jewry chambers
Vallance Henry & John, solicitors, 20 Essex st. Strand
Vallance James, solicitor, 4 King's Bench walk, Temple
Vallance James Thomas, surgeon, Stratford broadway
Vallance Robert, carpenter, &c. 12 Star corner, Bermondsey
Vallas John, baker, East India road, Poplar
Vallé Frederick, italian warehouse, 21 Haymarket
Vallentine Benjamin, importer of beads, toys & foreign manufactures, general commission agent, 70 Leadenhall st. & 62 Edgbaston st. Birmingham
Vallentine Jacob & Son, gen. outfitters, 60 Wych st. Strand
Vallet Ernest, prof. of languages,2Beckford pl.Kenngtn.com
Vallings Frederic, solicitor, see Young, Vallins & Young
Vallis Robert, boot & shoe maker, 9 Mayfield pl. Kensington
Valloton James, haberdasher, &c. 1 Eldon pl. Low. st. Islgtn
Vallogne Charles, watch & clock maker, 10 Church st. Soho
Van Thos. & Sons, marquee, tent, flag, rick cloth, improved tarpaulin,rope,line,&c. makers & ship chandlrs. 17Tooley st
Van Butchell Edwin Martin, surgeon, 14 Broad st.Golden sq
Van Butchell Sidney Job, surgeon, 27 Baker st. Portman sq
Vance Adam, carpenter & blind ma.7Edmund st.King's cross
Vance John, barrister, 12 Serle st. Lincoln's inn
Vance Thomas, barrister, 2 Hare court, Temple
Vandenbergh Algernon Sidney, surgeon, 39 Bethnal green rd
Vandenbergh John, chemist, 4 Queen's road, Dalston
Vanden Ende Peter, wool merchant, 14 Broad st. buildings
Vandercom, Cree, Law&Comyn, attorneys, 23Gt.Bush la.City
Vander Gucht Charles, silk mercer, 286 Regent st
Vandergucht Edwin, *Grove's Private hotel*, 48&49Albem. st
Vanderlinden Chas. jelly mould mkr.3 Devonsh st.Queen's sq
Vanderlyn Joseph, tailor, 105 Houndsditch
Vandermark Miss, ladies' school, 76 Kingsland road
VandermeulenEliz.(Mrs.),marinestr.dlr.8Cmbld.pl.Ngtn.bts
Vanderpant Hy. Cressy, dentist, see Minshull & Vanderpant
Vanderplank Samuel, cloth wrkr. 54 Lit. Bartholomew close
Vanderpool Parnell, refiner, 11 Hatton garden
Vandersteen Charles, *Two Bells* P.H. 7 Whitechapel road
Vandersteen Charles, carpenter & builder, 33 Bethnal green road, & 5 Church row Bethnal green
Vandersteen, Chas. jun. horsehair ma. 3 Osborne pl.Brick la
Vandersteen Chas.sen.*FryingPan* P.H.207 Black la.Spitalfi
Vandersteen James, horn & hoop mer. 207 Brick la. Spitalfields, & 3 Osborne place, Whitechapel
Vandersteen Wm.*Black Dog* P.H. 45 Church st.Shoreditch
Vandersteen Wm. house agt. & rent col. 33 Bethnal green rd
Vandersteen Wm. John, silk manfr. 33 Bethnal green road
Vander Vyver Peter F. A. corn & seed factor, general merchant & commission agent, 17 London st. City
Vandewall & Tippler, colonial brokers, 89 Gt. Tower st
Van de Wall Philip, black ma. 14 Chapel st. Curtain road
Vandrant Chas. stationer & berlin warehouse, Stratford
Van Diemen'sLand Company'sOffice (George H. Howell, secretary), 55 Old Broad st. City
Vane George, house agent, 29 Henrietta st. Brunswick sq
Vane Henry, ship rigger, Turner's wharf, Narrow st.Ratcliff
Vane Henry M. attorney, Carlton chambers, 12 Regent st
Van Goor Ezkiel, steel pen & fluid ma.7Duke st. Bishopsgate
VanhamWilliam, ivory, tortoise & turtleshell worker, 5Thanet place, Temple bar
Vanheems William Henry, tailor, 38 Dorset st. Portman sq
Van Heythuysen Richard Edward, solicitor to the Foundling Hospital, 31 John st. Bedford row
Vanhouse Jas. & Son, west & east india brokers, 37 Mincing la
Vanier Stephen *Carved Lion*P.H.30South st.Sth. Audley st
Van Houten GerrittJan. Danl. merchant, 12 Copthall court
Van Kempen Peter, accountant, 1 Cottage grove, Mile end rd
Van Meegen Gilles Johannes, tobacconist, 18 Fish st. hill
Van Neck Gerard & Joshua & Co. merchants, 2 Austinfriars
Vann Edward, solicitor, 16 Providence rw.Worshp.st.Finsby
Vann John, butcher, 22 Norton folgate, & meat salesman, Leadenhall market
Vanner John, silk manufacturer, 15 Spital square
Vanner Richd. plasterer & stencl. 1 Cole st. Gt. Dover road
Van Notten Peter & Charles & Co.merchts.21 & 22 Billiter st
Van Notten Peter & Charles & Co. merchants, 24 Lime st
Van Oven & Lindo, surgeons, &c. 30 Bishopsgate without
Van Oven Barnard, surgeon, 30 Gower st. Bedford square
Van Praagh Lammert, umbrella maker, 1 Postern row
Van Praagh Morris, wholesale jeweller, 57 Gt. Prescot st
Van Putten James, commissn. merch.& agent 47 Mark lane
Van Sandau Andrew, solicitor, 27 King st. Cheapside
Van Scolina George, chemist, 27 Dudley grove, Paddington
Van Scolina Richd. J. jun. watch jeweller, 113 Goswell rd
Van Scolina Rd. sen. watchmak. 70 Charlotte ter. New cut
Van Sommer James, stockbroker, Stock Exchange
Vanveer Fras. chandler's shop, 7 Buckingham pl. Marlbro'rd
Van Voorst John, bookseller & publisher, 1 Paternoster row
Van Zeller Francis Ignatius, Portuguese consul general, 5 Jeffery square, St. Mary Axe
Van Zeller Fras. Ignatius, mer. 5 Jeffrey sq. St. Mary Axe
Varden Wm.Hen. bookseller & stationer, 154Borough High st
Vardon John & Son, wholesale ironmongers, 3 Gracechurch st. & Corbet court, Gracechurch st
Vardon & Son, stockbrokers, Stock Exchange
Vardy Lambert Joshua, surgeon, 53 Stamford st. Blackfriars
Vardy Wm. Stoughton, solicitor, 18 Finsbury place north
Varicas Robert A. surgeon, 29 Woburn place, Tavistock sq
Varley & Son, seal & copperplate engravers, jewellers & dealer in articles of vertu, 80 Fleet st
Varley Cornelius, artist, 1 Charles st. Clarendon square
Varley Hen. G. silk dyer, 7 South st. Manchester square
Varley John, tailor, 127 Edgware road, Marylebone
Varley Samuel, boot & shoe maker, 159 Fenchurch st
Varley Samuel, ready made clothes warehouse, 64 Drury la
Varnam Chas. grocer & tea dlr. 1 Myddelton st. Clerkenwell
Varnam James, grocer, 136 High st. Shoreditch
Varney Christopher, baker, Grove lane, Deptford
Varney John, baker, 20 Brill row, Somers town
Varney John, carman, 36 Upper Rosoman st
Varney John, grocer, 10 Clement's inn passage, Clare market
Varney Lucy (Mrs.), dining rooms, 16 Newcastle st. Strand
Varney William, dairyman, 46 Bell yard, Temple bar
Varnham Arthur, stationer & account book mafr. 61 Strand
Varnish Henry, silk manufacturer, 10 Gresham st
Varty Wm. N. & John, linendrapers, 47 Bishopsgate within
Varty Edward, printer, 27 Camomile st. Bishopsgate
Varty John, shawl manufactr. &c. 14 St. Paul's churchyard
Varty Thomas, stationer, bookseller & publisher, 31 Strand
Vasey George, engraver, 27 Clarendon square
Vasey John, tin & iron plate worker, 68 King st. Soho
Vaucher's pat. woven hose offi. 1 Three King ct. Lombard st
Vaudeau Brothers, gen. agents, importers & manufacturer of artificial flowers, 11 Nicholl square, Aldersgate street

Vaudeau Louis Jean Baptiste, art. flower ma. 11 Nicholl sq
Vaughan & Cotterell, silvrsmths. & pawnbrks. 39 & 40 Strand
Vaughan & Sheldon, honduras merchants, 26 Austinfriars
Vaughan Samuel & Son, merchants, 70 Fenchurch st
Vaughan Charles, saddler, Little Chelsea
Vaughan Chas. tailor & draper, 31 Charles st. Middlsx. hosp
Vaughan David, boot & shoe maker, 1 Brown's la. Spitalflds
Vaughan Elizh. (Mrs.), lace joiner, 26 Great Titchfield st
Vaughan Evan, cooper & turner, 15 Cross st. Newington bts
Vaughan Henry, butcher, Clare market
Vaughan Hen. Halford, barrister, Devereux chambrs. Strnd
Vaughan James, butcher, 275 Bethnal green road
Vaughan James, packer, see Bowyer & Vaughan
Vaughan Jane (Miss), academy, see Huggett & Vaughan
Vaughan John, carpenter, 16 Avery row, Grosvenor st
Vaughan John, linendraper, 141 Whitechapel High st
Vaughan John, sen. tailor, 33 Thayer st. Manchester sq
Vaughan John B. oil & colorman, 56 Blackman st. Borough
Vaughan John, artificial stone work, 6 Portland pl. Boro' rd
Vaughan John Herbert, butcher, 17 Lamb st. Spital sq
Vaughan Martha (Miss), milliner, 8 Pantechnicon arcade
Vaughan Mary Ann (Mrs.), who. widows' cap.ma. 26 Banner st
Vaughan Petty, merchant, 70 Fenchurch st.
Vaughan Richard, butcher, 95 Praed st. Paddington
Vaughan Robert, butcher, 2 Goldsmith's row, Hackney rd
Vaughan Samuel Bradford, solicitor, 16 Argyle st. New rd
Vaughan William, merchant, 70 Fenchurch st
Vaughan William, poultry salesman, Leadenhall market
Vaughan Wm. A. haberdasher & linendraper, 19 & 20 Aldgate
Vause Martha (Mrs.), butcher, 6 Little Bell alley, Coleman st
Vaux & Harris, mers. & ins. bro. 13 Gt. St. Helen's, & Lloyd's
Vaux John Jas. Frs. cornchndlr. 10 Lr. Salisbury pl. Lock's fi
Vauxhall Bridge Co. (Thos. Jeffery, sec.), Millbank, Wstmr
Vauxhall Waterworks (Wm. Butterworth, sec.), Upper Kennington lane
Vavasseur James, silk manufr. see Carter, Vavasseur & Rix
Vawser Charlotte (Miss), artist, 35 Graham st. Pimlico
Vawser George Richard, sen. artist, 35 Graham st. Pimlico
Vawser George Richard, jun. artist, 35 Graham st. Pimlico
Vawser M. A. cattle salesman, 60 West Smithfield
Veal James & Son, solicitors, 19 Abingdon st. Westminster
Veal George, wheelwright, 2 Plough yard, Shoreditch
Veal John, plate chest maker, 21 Wardour st. Soho
Veal Samuel, oil & colorman, 103 Junction ter. Edgware rd
Veale Wm. & George, dairymen, St. John's wd. farm, Acacia rd
Veale Edward, appraiser, 5 St. Thomas's pl. Old Kent road
Veale George, goldsmith, &c. see Widdowson & Veale
Veale Geo. *Montagu Arms* P.H. 3 Up. Montagu st. Montagu sq
Veale Mary (Miss), milliner, 49 Gt. Titchfield st. Oxford st
Veale Richard, tailor, 49 Great Titchfield st. Oxford st
Vear William North, lithographic printer, 26 Gt. St. Helen's
Vearey William, baker, 97 Lambeth walk
Vears Robert, academy, 19 Cole st. Great Dover st
Veary Joseph, lace manufacturer, see Hearn & Veary
Vedy Louis George, stationer, Battersea square
Veitch Alex. & Son, wire wrks. & fender ma. 111 St. John st
Veitch Andrew, patent pianoforte maker, 17 Everett st
Veitch James, ale brewer, Canal, St. George's st. Albany road
Veitch James, physician, 33 Kensington square
Veitch Robert, carpenter, 25 Mary st. Hampstead road
Venables Thomas & John, linen & woollen drapers, 103 Whitechapel High st. & 34 Aldgate High st
Venables, Wilson & Tyler, wholesale stationers & paper manufacturers, 17 Queenhithe
Venables Adolphus, artist, 74 Newman st. Oxford st
Venables Benjamin, meat salesman, 4 Newgate market, & 30 Paved alley
Venables Emily Rose (Miss), artist, 13 Nottingham terrace
Venables Geo. Stovin, barrister, 2 Mitre ct. bldgs. Temple
Venables James, butcher, 234 Tottenham court road
Venables James, livery stables, 4 Lodge pl. St. John's wood
Venables John, meat salesman, 30 Paved alley, Newgate mkt
Venables Joseph, cap maker, 109 Wood st
Venables Robert, physician, 5 St. Vincent pl. City road
Venables Rowland Jones, parl. agent, see Burke & Venables
Vencens Margrt. (Mrs.), italian wa. see Humbert & Vencens
Veness & Baily, printers, 14 Deptford High st
Veness James, boat bldr. College st. Belvedere rd. Lambeth
Veness Thomas, butcher, 2 Deptford High st
Vengan Mary (Mrs.), dining rooms, 9 Wandsworth road
Venis Samuel, grocer, 2 Surrey place, Wandsworth road
Venn John & Sons, notaries & translators, 2 Pope's head all
Venn Benj. perfumer, 4 Commerce row, Upper st. Islington
Venn Daniel, baker, 4 Black Prince rw. & 16 Crosby rw. Walwth
Venn Francis, baker, 48 St. John st. Clerkenwell
Venn Henry, chemist & druggist, 25 Warwick st. Golden sq
Venn James, tobacconist, 5 Lisson grove north
Venn Samuel, baker, 26 Middle Queen's buildings, Knightsbridge, & 16 Northampton row, Holloway
Venn Thos. Wm. porkman, 2 Bull's head pas. Gracechurch st
Venn William, baker, 4 Eldon place, Lower st. Islington
Vennel Charles, tailor, 6 St. Martin's pl. St. Martin's le grand
Vennell Josiah Godfrey, tailor, 4 Clement's court, Wood st
Venner Robert, dining rooms, 1 New Compton st. Soho
Venner Thos. solicitor, 62 George st. Euston square
Venning, Naylor & Robins, solicitors, 9 Tokenhouse yard
Venning William & Co. merchs. 12 Pancras la. Bucklersbury
Venning Francis, trimming seller, 17 Mortimer st. Cavend. sq
Venning William, carver & gilder, 13 Rathbone pl. Oxford st
Venour Stephen Chas. solicitor, see Butterfield & Venour
Ventom & Hughes, auctioneers, 7½ Angel ct. Throgmorton st
Ventris Edward, stationer, 3 Hawley pl. Kentish town
Ventris Ellis John, confectioner, 141 Tooley st
Ventura Isaac de Joseph, merchant, 3 White hart ct. Bishpgt
Venus John Henry, butcher, 24½ Yardley st. Clerkenwell
Venzano Nicholas, merchant, 20 Austinfriars
Vercoe Charles, grocer, 19 Sandwich st. Burton crescent
Verdera Rafael, wine merchant, 126 Jermyn st. St. James's
Verdier John Francis, grocer, New cross
Verdin & Shipwright, working jewellers, 65 Frith st. Soho
Verdin John, coffee rooms, 117 Chalton st. Somers town
Vere Thomas, fruiterer, 3 Edward st. Barnsbury road
Verebay William, clog maker, 5 Cambridge road Mile end
Verey & Lemon, hosiers & straw hat makers, 293 Regent st
Verey William & George, brewers & maltsters, Kilburn
Verey George, *Wheatsheaf* P.H. 23 Church row, Somers tn
Verey James, *Duke of Clarence* P.H. 19 Munster st Regt.'s pk
Verey Thos. *Richmond Arms* P.H. 48 Richmond st. Edgw. rd
Vergara (B.) & Dickison, importers of wines, 18 Little Tower st
Verge Benjamin, baker, 82 Holborn hill
Verge Wm. cowkeeper, 22 Baldwin's gardens, Leather lane
Verily Samuel, furn. broker, 18 Devonshire st. Lisson grove
Verinder Henry, working cutler, 79 St. Paul's church yard
Verity Benj. brass founder & gasfitter, 17 Bedford ct. Cov. gn
Verity James, boot & shoe maker, 19 Leicester st. Regent st
Vermeir & Champion, gen. merchants, 147 Fenchurch st
Vernall Saml. Thos. builder, 6 Albany st. Regent's park
Vernell John, silk manufactory, 18 Steward st. Spitalfields
Verney Henry, stationer, 1 Orford pl. Marlboro' rd. Chelsea
Verney Susannah (Mrs.), toy dlr. 15 Stucley ter. Camden tn
Vernier Eleanor C. (Mrs.), paper ruler, 264 High Holborn
Vernon Catherine (Mrs.), milliner, 11 Sloane sq. Chelsea
Vernon Geo. secret springer & polisher, 2 Lower Ashby street, Clerkenwell
Vernon Henry Louis, tobacconist, 16 King's rd. Bedford row
Vernon Norton, jeweller, 17 Crown st. Soho
Vernon Richard, coal merchant, Essex whf. Essex st. Strand
Vernon Thomas, basket maker, 9 Garter court, Barbican
Vernon Wm. army clothier, &c. 1 Bloomsbury square
Vernon Wm. *Coach & Horses* P.H. Northumberland all. Fenc. st
Verrall John, registrar, Charles st. Old Gravel la. St. George's
Verrall Richard, coachmaker, 7 Old Dorset pl. Clapham rd
Verralls John, hat manufr. 34 St. George's pl. Hyde prk. crnr
Verrey Charles, confectioner, 229 Regent st
Verrey Louis, confectioner, 3 Pall mall
Verrey William, plumber, painter & glazier, 1 Cullum st
Verring James, *Bedford Arms* P.H. 21 Charlotte st. Bedfd. sq
Verron Thomas, tailor, Layton's bldgs. 143 Boro' High st
Verry John, hairdresser & artist in hair, 18 Eastcheap
Verry William, plumber & glazier, 31 Seething lane, Tower st
Vertue George & Co. saw mills, Canada whf. 130 Rotherhithe st
Vertue Stephen & Son, corn & seed factors, 31 Gt. St. Helen's
Vertue Arthur Leopold, merch. 31 Gt. St. Helen's, Bishopsgt
Vertue Chas. insurance broker & ship agent, 21 Austinfriars
Vertue Thomas, corn & seed factor, 20 Mark lane & 14 New Corn Exchange, Mark lane
Verulam Society, 29 Essex st
Very Martha & Sarah, stationers, 32 New Glo'ster st. Hoxtn
Vesper Thomas, pawnbroker, 13 Sidney pl. Commer. rd. east
Vesper Thomas, watchma. 5 Wellington pl. Commer. rd. east
Vesper Wm. watchmaker, &c. 12 Sidney pl. Coml. rd. east
Vestey Mary (Mrs.), city car. 3 Samuel st. Mile end New tn
Veterinary College (Wm. Sewell, professor & sec.), College st. Camden town
Vette Hannah (Mrs.), straw bonnet ma. 10 Charles st. Westm
Vevers James, woollen warehouse, 149 Cheapside
Vey John, baker, 25 Half moon crescent, Pentonville
Vezey Joseph & Jas. wax & tallow chandlrs. 122 Edgware rd
Vezey Edward, oil & colorman, 1 Gray st. Manchester sq
Vezey Peter, carcase butcher, Fox & Knot yard, Snowhill
Vezey Peter, *Lock & Key* P.H. 62 West Smithfield
Vialls Benjamin, silk dyer & scourer, 18 Oxford st

Vialls Edmund, *Hope* coffee rooms, 41 Fore st. Cripplegate
Vialls John Palmer, glass manufactr. 2 George st. Adelphi
Vials John, *Victoria* P.H. 106 Chalton st. Somers town
Vialou Isaac, painter & glaz. 4 King's Head ct. Fish st. hill
Vicar General's & Peculiar Offices of the Archbishop of Canterbury, 5½ Bell yard, Doctors' commons; hours 9 to 7
Vicary Mary Ann (Mrs.), wheelwrt. 9 Lit. Grove st. Lisson gr
Vicat James, linendraper, 49 Blackfriars road
Vicat James, woollen warehouseman, 27 Wood st. City
Vice Chancellors' Courts, term time, Westminster hall; vacation, Lincoln's inn (near the Hall)
Vice Harriet (Miss), oil & italian warehouse, 105 Goswell rd
Vice Henry James, oil & colorman, 3 Abbey st. Bermondsey
Vice Wm. cop. plate printer, 19 Newcastle st. Farringdon st
Vickerman Cha.R.solicitor,see Ranken,Ford,Longbourne&Co
Vickerman David, tailor, 3 Manor place, Walworth road
Vickerman John, tobacconist, 81 Tooley st
Vickers Joseph & John & Co. distillers, rectifiers & importers of foreign wines & spirits, 28 Stoney st. Borough market
Vickers, Plaisted & Co. import.of wine,10 Cooper's rw.Towr.hl
Vickers Zach. Jas. & Alf. brushma. 30 Queen's row, Walworth
Vickers Ann (Mrs.), oil & italian ware. 43 Coleshill st.Pimlico
Vickers Charles, stock & sharebroker, 12 Cornhill
Vickers Elizb. Ann (Mrs.), librarian, 11 Barton st. Westmr
Vickers Francis, preserved provision merchant, 35 Great hall, Hungerford market
Vickers George, publisher, 28 Holywell st. Strand
Vickers Henry, plumber, painter, &c. 16 Barton st. Westmr
Vickers Hen. Wm. butcher, 2 Worship st. Shoreditch
Vickers James, coffee rooms, 77 Houndsditch
Vickers Jas. isinglass & distlrs'.chem. 6 Devonshire sq. Bishpg
Vickers James, merchant, 24 Mark lane & Lloyd's
Vickers John, baker, 19 Park side, Knightsbridge
Vickers John, butcher, 28 Rosoman st. Clerkenwell
Vickers John, cowkeeper, 4 Graham st. west, Pimlico
Vickers John, *Life Guardsman* P.H.28 High row,Knightsbg
Vickers Joseph, butcher, 3 Scott's pl. Lower rd. Islington
Vickers Thomas, bootmaker, 9 Queen st. Ratcliff cross
Vickers Thomas, builder, 24 Sidney st. City road
Vickers Thos. sen. carpenter & undert. 46 Penton pl. Pentonv
Vickers Thomas, painter, 18 Sidmouth st. Gray's inn road
Vickers Wm. Henry, butcher, 26 St. Mary at hill
Vickers Wm. Randall, surgeon, 32 Baker st. Portman sq
Vickerstaff George, fruiterer, 6 Ryder's ct. Leicester sq
Vickery & Farrow, patent wig makers & perfumers, 6 Tavistock st. Covent garden
Vickery Charles, china warehouse, 37 Gt. Marylebone st
Vickery Chas. Jas. ladies' boot ma.39 Tottenham st.Tot.ct.rd
Vickery James, tailor, 10 Lower Sloane st. Chelsea
Vickery Joseph, *Lamb & Hare* P.H. Portsmouth pl. Lr. Keng
Vickery Lawrance, tailor, 4 Arundel st. Haymarket
Vickery Richard, lodging ho. 5 Warwick st. Charing cross
Vickery Robert, grocer & teadealer, 27, & confectioner, 29 Bedford row, Walworth
Vickery Samuel, coal merchant, 20 Chiswell st
Vickery Thomas Munnings, solicitor, 25 Lincoln's inn fields
Vickery William, *White Hart* P.H. 6 Milbank st. Westmstr
Vickress Thomas & Son, *Grapes* P.H. 45 Aldersgate st
Vickress James, *Black Boy* P.H. 162 Upper Whitecross st
Vickress Mar.C.(Mrs.), *Angel & Crown* P.H.31 Union st.e.Spls
Vickress William, *Rodney*, P.H. 11 Bridge row, Lambeth
Vickridge Jas. &Son,glass & chinaman,5 New Bridgest.Vxhll
Vickridge Frederick James, linendraper, Camberwell green
Victoire (Madame), milliner, 4 Baker st. Portman sq
Victor Isaac, tobacconist, 3 Holborn bars
Victoria Life Assurance & Loan Company (Wm. Ratray, secretary), 18 King William st. City
Victorine Caroline (Mad.),millinr.23 Bentinck st.Manchstr.sq
Victualling Office, Somerset house; hours, 10 to 4
Videon Geo. nurseryman & florist, 1 Clarendon pl. Maida hill
Vidler Charles, *Three Tuns* P.H. 4 Bridgewater gardens
Vidler Elhanan Winchester, cabinet ma. 8 Hoxton market
Vidler Geo. *Turk's Head* P.H. 10 Motcombe st. Belgrave sq
Vidler John Wm. coal merch. 15 Kingsland cres. Kingsld.rd
Vie William, dining rooms, 64 St. Mary axe
Viel Geo. Hypolite, watch & clock maker, 33 Frith st. Soho
Viel Jethro, sen. 3 *Loggerheads* P.H. 1 Virginia rw.Bthl.gr
Viel Jethro, jun. *Cock & Hoop* P.H. Church st.Mile end n.tn
Vieyres Anthony, watch & clock maker, 40 Pall mall
Vigar John, coffee rooms, 8 Nowell's bldgs. Liverpool road
Vigers Edward & Co. furn. undertaks. 1 Broadway, Westm
Vigers Edw. jun. saw & planing mills, Church st. Clapham rd
Vigers Edward, sen. timber merchant, Clapham road
Vigers Francis, auctioneer, see Davis & Vigers
Vigers Francis William, carpenter & builder, 13 New wharf Whitefriars, 31 Lawrence lane, Cheapside
Vigne Henry & Sons, stockbrokers, 7½ Tokenhouse yard
Vignoles Charles, civil engineer, 4 Trafalgar square
Vigurs Louis & Co. merchants, 57½ Old Broad st.
Vile Alfred, beer retailer, 1 Fulwood's rents, Holborn
Vile George, *Box Tree* P.H. 5 Gravel lane, Houndsditch
Vile Oliver, mang.of London & Westminster bk.1 St.James's sq
Vile Robt. furnt. broker, 64 Snow's fields, Bermondsey
Vile Thomas, stockbroker, 1 Shorter's ct. Throgmorton st
Viles George, grocer, 47 Charles st. Horsleydown
Viles Henry Andrew, grocer, 303 Kent st. Borough
Villamil Juan Santos & Co. merchs.3 Copthall chambs.City
Villiers & Son, tailors, 14 Arlington st. Myddleton square
Villiers Hon. Chas. Pelham, barrister, Rolls yd. Chanceryla
Villiers John Fitzpatrick, equity draughtsman & conveyancer, 7 New square, Lincoln's inn
Vinall George, tailor, 99 High Holborn
Vinall John, barrister, 1 Churchyard court, Temple
Vinall Wm. *Adelaide tavern*, Haverstock hill, Hampstead
Vince Chas. S. picture frame mak. 16 Tavistock st. Cov. gar
Vince Eliza (Miss), haberdasher, 55 Henry st. ea. Avenue rd
Vince George Watts, timber merchant, Rose lane, Ratcliff
Vince Joseph, boot&shoe ma. 32 Frederick st. Hampstead rd
Vince Richard, carpenter, 6 Thornhill road, Islington
Vince Thomas, livery stables, 36 New st. mews, Dorset sq
Vince William, beer retailer, Newland st. Kensington
Vince Wm. *Grundy Arms* P.H. 20 Grundy st. East India rd
Vincent, Aley & Co. bit & spur makers, 159 Regent st
Vincent & Bedford, solicitors, 2 Dartmouth st. Westminster
Vincent & Gabriel, solicitors, 4 Inner Temple la. Temple
Vincent & Plumley, attorneys, 22 Moorgate st. City
Vincent & Pugh, rectifiers, &c. 16 New Park st. Borough
Vincent & Pugh, wine & brandy merchants, 10 Rood lane
Vincent & Sherwood's, solicitors,9 King's Benchwalk,Temple
Vincent & Stibbard, wine & spirit importers, 46 Lime st
Vincent Edward, surgeon, Stratford, Essex
Vincent George, surgeon, 109 Sloane st. Chelsea
Vincent Geo. Giles, conveyancer,3 Broad Sanctuary, Westm
Vincent Henry, *Ship* P.H. 243 Wapping High st
Vincent Isaac, stationer, pasteboard maker & hot presser, 5 Little St. Thomas Apostle
Vincent Jacob, attorney, 10 South square, Gray's inn
Vincent James, boot & shoe maker, 63 Great Saffron hill
Vincent James, *Butler's Head* P.H.12 Gt.Bell al.Coleman st
Vincent James, grocer & cheesemonger, 14 High st. Lambeth
Vincent James, solicitor, 31 Paddington green
Vincent John, baker, 3 Broomfield place, Deptford
Vincent John, farrier, 14½ Macclesfield st. south, City rd
Vincent John, tailor, 123 Union st. Borough
Vincent John Painter, surgeon, 16 Lincoln's inn fields
Vincent Joseph, butcher, 3 St. Chad's row, Gray's inn rd
Vincent Philip, newsvender, 118 Blackfriars road
Vincent Robt. ironmngr.&scalema. 5 St.George's pl.Cambrwl
Vincent Saml. sec. *Pat. Galvanized Iron Co.*3 Mansion ho.pl
Vincent Thos. baker, 18 Edward st. Star corner, Bermondsey
Vincent Thomas, flour factor, 3 Muscovy ct. Tower hill
Vincent Thos. *Sun & Half Moon* P.H. 36 Broad st. Lon.docks
Vincent Wm. bootcloser, 26 James st. Oxford st
Vincent Wm. brass & cock founder, 29 Church st. Spitalfds
Vincent Wm. boot & shoe ma. 3A, Grove ter. Qun's rd. Baysw
Vincent Wm. coffee rooms, 27 Thomas st. Grosvenor sq
Vincent Wm. Chas. architectural carver,8 Chalton st.New rd
Vincent Wm.S.watchmaker,2 Caroline cottage,King's rd.west
Vincer Martha & Son, boot&shoe ma. 22 Bolingbrok.rw.Wlw
Vincer Edward, *Dover Castle* P.H. 30 Church rd. Coml.rd.ea
Vincer Edward, smith, 10 New st. Brompton
Vincer Sarah (Mrs.), locksm. &bellhngr.2 North st. Sloane st
Vincett Saml. *Three Cups* P.H. 22 Bedford st. Bedford row
Vindin James, bookseller, 4 Charles pl. York rd. Lambeth
Vine Adam, tailor, 22 Northampton sq. Clerkenwell
Vine Alfrd. Hen.agt.to *Coml.& Gen. Life Ass. Co.* 17 Sekforde st
Vine Elizb. (Mrs.), stationer, 3 Tabernacle walk, Finsbury
Vine Fredk. fruiterer, 41 & 42 Union st. Middlesex hospital
Vine Hen. plumber & painter, 48 Gt. Russell st. Bloomsbury
Vine James, brushmak.&toy wa. 7 Gloucester pl. Islington gn
Vine Thomas, baker, 19 Stockbridge terrace, Pimlico
Vine Thomas Walter, carpenter, 20 Peerless row, City rd
Vine Wm. carpenter, 13 Magdalen st. Bermondsey st
Vind Wm. Chas. surveyor, 4 Spring ter. Wandsworth rd
Vinen Edward Hart, surgeon, &c. 164 Blackfriars road
Vinen James Northcote, surgeon, see Miskin & Vinen
Viner Charles, beer retailer, 8 Ordnance rd. St. John's wood
Viner Charles Edward, watchmaker, 82 Old Broad st. City, & 235 Regent st
Viner Hen. Lewis, who.&ret. perfum.4 Maddox st.Nw.Bnd.st
Vines & Lewis, millers & flour factors, 35 Crutched friars
Vines Caleb, attorney, 28 Canonbury square, Islington

Vines Jabez, miller, Creek's mills, Battersea
Vines Richard, chemist & druggist, 75 Aldersgate st
Vines Richd. consulting vet. surg. 13Gt.College st.Camdn.tn
Vines W. clerk to the Brewers' Co. Brewers' hall, Addle st. Wood st
Viney John & Co. builders, &c. 6 Pollen st. Hanover square
Viney Edward Wm. blind maker, 52 Borough road
Viney James, grocer & cheesemonger, Bromley, Middlesex
Viney John, carpenter & builder, 31 New st. mews, Dorset sq
Viney John, trunkmaker & undertaker, 48 Cornhill
Viney Temperance (Mrs.), coaldlr. 16 Lit. Wild st. Linc. inn. fl
Viney Wm. paper stainer, 100 High st. Marylebone
Vineyard Proprietors' Campany, 48 Mark lane, City
Vining Richard, cutler & dressing case maker, 125 Regent st
Vinn Benj. artists' pencil mak. 3 Northampton st. Clerkenwell
Vink Frederick, ship chandler & sailmaker, 328 Wapping
Vink John, merchant, 4 Crescent, Minories
Vinnicombe Richard, tailor, 8 Howland st. Fitzroy square
Vinson Henry, hairdresser & perfumer, 124 Leadenhall st
Vinsun John, carpenter&underta. 12 Catherine st. Coml. rd. ea
Vinten John, bootmaker, 17 Stafford pl. Pimlico
Vinter John, grocer, 206 High Holborn
Vinter Wm. tailor, 3 Old North st. Red Lion square
Vintners' Alms Houses, 21&22 Constable row, Mile end road
Vintners' Hall (Charles Martin, clerk), 68½ Up. Thames st
Vintners' Porters' Office, 2 Botolph lane; hours 10 to 4
Vintner William, dairyman, 5 Windmill st. Tottenham ct. rd
Vinton Jas. engrav. & print. &c. 2 Cardigan st. Hampstd. rd
Violett Joseph, newsvender, 5 Charles st. Blackfriars road
Vipan Edward James, solicitor, 50 Jermyn st. St. James's
Vipond John, wholesale cheesemonger, 6 Old Fish st. City
Viret John, hosier, 17 Edgware road, Marylebone
Virgo John, attorney, 34 Essex st. Strand
Virtue George, bookseller & publisher, 24, 25 & 26 Ivy lane, Newgate st. & printer, 65 Bartholomew close
Virtue Hannah (Mrs.), milliner, 4 Henry st. Cumberland mrkt
Virtue James, bookseller, 3 Water st. Blackfriars
Virtue John, carpenter, 13 Alfred mews, Tottenham ct. rd
Virtue John, uphlstr. carpen. & bldr. 58 Newman st. Oxford st
Vitta Agostino, foreign warehouse, 14 St. Swithin's lane, & 5 Charles st. Grosvenor sq
Vitty Christopher, beer retalr. 5 Aylesbury pl. Old Kent rd
Vivian & Sons, copper smelters, Paul's wf. 25 Up. Thames st
Vivian James, *Blue Anchor* P.H. 47 Farringdon st
Vivian John, *Globe* P.H. 65 Lisson grove, north
Vivian Sarah (Mrs.), milliner, 25 New Church st. west, Edgware road
Vivian Wm. manchester agent, 1 Star court, Bread st. City
Vizard & Lemans', solicitors, 51 Lincoln's inn fields
Vizard William, solicitor, see Blower, Vizard & Parson
Vizard William, jun. barrister, 51 Lincoln's inn fields
Vizard William, jun. solicitor, see Blower, Vizard & Parson
Vize James, poultry salesman, 6 Three Tuns passage
Vizer William, attorney, 48A, Moorgate st. Bank
Vizetelly Brothers & Co. printers & engravers, 8 Peterborough court, 135 Fleet st
Vizard Wm. lodging house, 100 Park st. Grosvenor sq
Voce Thomas, baker, 25 Hayfield place, Mile end road
Voelcker Geo. & Co. merchs. 1 Carpenter's bldgs. London wl
VoganJas. & Son, corn merchants, 1 Maze, Tooley st. Southwk
Vogel & Co. merchants, 4 Pancras lane, Queen st. City
Vogel Ann (Mrs.), printer, 1 St. George's pl. Camberwell rd
Vogiebcim Francis, sodawater mak. 13 Craven blds. City rd
Vogt Charles & Frederick, clockmakers, 30 Wigmore st. & 57 Gt. James st. Lisson grove
Vogt Anthony, watch & clock maker, 17 Carburton st
Vohman George Henry, baker, 4 Broadway, Ludgate hill
Vohman Leonard, baker, 7 Charles court, Strand
Vohman Wm. *St. Paul's* P.H. St. Paul's pl. Walworth com
Vohman Wm. Christian, *Black Boy* P.H. 124 Wapping High st
Vokins John & Wm. carvers & gilders, 5 John st. Oxford st
Vokins Chas. coal merchant, Pimlico whf. Wilton rd. Pimlico
Vokins Thomas, fruiterer & corn dlr. 74 Well st. Oxford st
Volckman John & Sons, wholesale & retail confectioners, 101 Bishopsgate within, & High st. Stratford, Essex
Volckman Francis, confectioner, High st. Stoke Newington
Volk Plazi, clockmaker, 38 Goodge st. Tottenham ct. rd
Vollam Edward, boot & shoe wareho. 76 Bishopsgate without
Vollar Charles, coffee rooms, 156 Wapping High st
Voller Henry, coal dealer, 43 Princess st. Edgware rd
Voller James, beer retailer, 15 Crombies row, Comml. rd. ea
Voller John, *White Hart* P.H. 49 St. Clement's la. Strand
Voller William, cooper, 36 Gt. Bush lane, & 8 Martin's lane, Cannon st. & 10 City road
Vollum Henry, appraiser & upholsterer, 79 Goswell road
Vollum John, carpet warehouse, 80 Goswell road
Vol Carnap Geo. & Co. foreign agents, 18 Queen st. Cheapside
Von Dadelszen Geo. Michael, merchant, 23 Mincing lane
Von der Heyde John, tobacco & snuff manf. 80 Low. Thames st
Vonhollen Ann (Mrs.), grocer, 51 Seymour pl. Bryanstone sq
Von Mallen John Henry, bootmaker, 41 Wellclose square
Von Melle William, merchant, 59 Mark lane
Vonstein Mathew, tailor, 3 Hanover st. Hanover sqnare
Vooght John, butcher, Larkhall lane, Clapham
Vooght Thomas, *Blue Posts* P.H. 7 Holborn bars
Vooght William, baker, 28 Union st east, Spitalfields
Voqade Joseph, *Albion* P.H. 210 & 211 Shadwell High st
Vorley William & Edward, wholes. chemists, 8 Old Swan la
Vorley William & Edward, candle rush ma. Old Swan la
Vorley John, fishmonger, 57 Albany st. Regent's park
Vorley Robert Knight, chemical agent, 9 Tower Royal
Vorley William, cattle salesman, 41 West Smithfield
Vos Abraham, cigar mnfr. 25 Gt. Prescott st. Goodman's fields
Vos Solomon, grocer, 11 St. George st. St. George's east
Voss David, lighterman & cust. ho. agt. 1 Pudding la. Eastch
Vote James Kent, builder, 9 King st. Clerkenwell
Vouillon & Laure (late Maradan, Carson & Co.), milliners & dressmakers to her Majesty, 12 Princes st. Hanover square
Voules Wm. James, barrister, 9 Inner Temple lane, Temple
Vousley Hen. John, *Kg. of Denmark* P.H. 9 Denmark ter. Pntv
Vousley John, *Simon the Tanner* P.H. 19 Long la. Bermdsy
Vowells Alfred, grocer, &c. 28 High st. Portland town
Voysey Samuel, grocer, 1 Back road, St. George's east
Voysey Thos. egg merchant, 42 Red cross st. Union st. Boro'
Voysey Thomas, grocer, 34 Sidmouth st. Regent square
Vulcan Iron warehouse St. Ann's wharf, Earl st. Blackfrs
Vulliamy Benj. L. watch&clock maker to her Majesty; to the Office of Woods; the Ordnance, & the Post Office, 68 Pall mall
Vulliamy Lewis, architect, 13 Savile row, Piccadilly
Vyse Chas. brit. & foreign straw manufacturer, 30 Ludgate st
Vyse Thos. & Sons, merchants, & straw hat manufacturers, 3 Cripplegate buildings; Luton, Beds.; Florence, New York

WACE Alexander, butcher, 46 George st. Portman square
Wace Charles, meat salesman, 1 Rose st. Newgate st
Wace Mary Ann (Mrs.), butcher, 11 Ivy lane, Newgate st
Wace Thomas, butcher, 3 Old Paradise row, Islington green
Wacey Edward, carpenter, &c. 29 Goldsmith pl. Hackney rd
Wacey Jonathan, for. & eng. bookseller, &c. 29 Old Jewry
Wacey Robert, carpenter, 2 Canal bridge, Cambridge heath
Wack William, tailor, 57 Upper John st. Fitzroy square
Wackerbarths & Colling, sugar refi. 45 Parson's st. St. George st
Wackett Eliza (Mrs.), cowkeepr. 11 Ridinghouse la. Langhm. pl
Wadd Thomas Milner, surgeon, Bevis ct. 28 Basinghall st
Waddams Thomas, hairdresser, 54 Broad st. Bloomsbury
Waddell John, grocer, 79 Seymour st. Bryanstone sq
Waddell Joseph, baker, 3 Park st. Borough market
Waddilove Alf. D.C.L. advocate, 17 College, College sq. D.com
Waddilove Henry Jesse, proctor, 3 Great Knightrider st
Waddingham Edwd. John, china dealer, 28 High st. Bow
Waddington, Horton & Co. wholesale umbrella & parasol manufacturers, 1 Coleman st. City
Waddington Horatio, barrister, 3 King's Bench walk, Temple
Waddington Mary (Mrs.), lodgingho. 6 Wardrobe ter. Doc. com
Waddington Robert, carpenter, 9 George st. New Kent rd
Waddy Cadwallader, parliamentaryag. 13 Fludyer st. Wstmr
Wade Brothers, linendrapers, 9 Clarence pl. Camberwell
Wade Charles & Brothers, silkmercers, Deptford High st
Wade John & Son, tailors & drapers, 57 Holborn hill
Wade & Pennington, solicitors, 1½ Frederick's pl. Old Jewry
Wade Thomas & Son, cotton brokers, 116 Fenchurch st
Wade Alfred, grocer & cheesemonger, 20 Old Gravel lane
Wade Benjamin, tailor, &c. 111 Strand
Wade Charles, baker, 8 Goodge st. Tottenham court rd
Wade Charles, grainer & writer, 14 Hill st. Finsbury
Wade Charles, linendraper, see Wade Brothers
Wade Charles Jsph. special pleader, 3 Church yd. ct. Temple
Wade Elizh. (Mrs.), shopkeeper, 12 Bacon st. Bethnal green
Wade Field, house painter, 5 Gt. Distaff lane, Friday st
Wade George, grocer, &c. 4 Deptford High st
Wade Golding, butcher, 9 Marygold st. Bermondsey
Wade Henry, baker, 22 Tothill st. Westminster
Wade James, baker, 1 Lower King st. Commercial rd
Wade James, surgeon, 16 Stockbridge terrace, Pimlico
Wade John, blacksmith, 1 Britton st. Robert st. Chelsea
Wade John, builder, 43 Broomfield place, Deptford
Wade John, cloth agent, 32 Lambeth square
Wade John, gasfitter, 48 Fetter lane
Wade John, grocer, 39 Cornwall road, Lambeth
Wade John C. inspector of weights & measures, 1 Crescent, Southwark bridge road
Wade Joseph, chemist & druggist, 30 East st. Walworth rd

Wade Josiah, baker, 42 York st. Broadway, Westminster
Wade Mark, butcher, 6 Crown st. Walworth road
Wade Mary Ann (Miss), dressmak. 42 Duke st. Manchtr. sq
Wade Orlando, ship smith, 1 Nutkin's corner, Bermond.wall, & Nightingale lane, Upper East Smithfield
Wade Richard, builder, 3 Albany ter. New rd. Regent's pk
Wade Richard, carrier, White horse inn, Cripplegate
Wade Richard, tailor & clothier, 89 Cheapside
Wade Robert, carpenter, 113 Crawford st. Portman sq
Wade Robert, surgeon, 68 Dean st. Soho
Wade Robert F. congreve rocket manfr. and ordnance stores manfr. West Ham, & 14 London st. Fenchurch st
Wade Robert F. ship & insurance broker, & commercial agent, 14 London st. Fenchurch st
Wade Thos. grocer & cheesemngr. 19Greenhill's rents, Smthfld
Wade Thomas, stationer, 13 Kensington High st
Wade Thos. Jas. chandler's shop, 80 Chamber st. Goodm. flds
Wade William, baker, 21 Fetter lane
Wade William, baker, 99 White horse st. Stepney, & 6 Suffolk place, Commercial road east
Wade William, farrier, 4 Barron's place, Waterloo road
Wade William, grocer, Jamaica level, Bermondsey
Wade William, teadealer, 7 Clarendon square, Somers town
Wade Wm. John, carvr.gild.& pic. frame ma.86Leadenhall st
Wade's London Review Office, 1 Whitefriars st
Wadeson Edwd. Weyman, proctor&notary, seeSlade& Wadeson
Wadeson Robert, oil & colorman, 171 Upper Whitecross st
Wadeson Robert Spiller, solicitor, 11 Austinfriars
Wadey Edward, fishmonger, 5 Bury st. Bloomsbury
Wadey John, bricklayer, 93 St. George's road, Southwark
Wadey Peter, carpenter, 158 Southwark bridge road
Wadge Jonathan, wine, spirit & liqueur merc. 71 Haymarket
Wadham William, grocer, 2 Brewer's green, Westminster
Wadhams Chas. carpent. & under. 40Charlotte st. Portland pl
Wadland Philip, hairdresser, 2 Tothill st. Westminster
Wadley Geo. *King's Arms* P.H. 19 Frederick st. Regent's pk
Wadsworth & Housley, surgeons, 28 Broad st. Golden sq. & 2 Great Marlborough st
Wadsworth Arthur John, truss & surgical instrument maker, 8 Bell yard, Gracechurch st
Wadsworth John Ivey, stockbroker, 3 Bartholomew lane
Wadsworth Drissel (Mrs.), dairy, 17 Upper King st. Blmsby
Wadsworth Mary (Mrs.), straw hat ma.38Beckford rw. Wlwth
Wadsworth William, baker, 37 Cambridge road, Mile end rd
Waeick John, baker, 23 Bermondsey wall
Wageman Michael Angelo, artist, 25 Mount st. Berkeley sq
Wageman Thos. artist, 25 Mount st. Berkeley square
Wagener John, sugar refiner, 3 Mansell st. Goodman's flds
Wagg Frederick, furniture broker, 140 Whitechapel road
Wagg Wm. upholsterer & broker, 270 Whitechapel road
Waggett James, physician, 1 Norland square, Notting hill
Waggett Wm. tailor, 4 Argyll st. Oxford st
Waggstaff Robert, potato salesman, Spitalfields market
Waghorn & Co. agents for passengers, parcels, &c. overland to India, 34 Cornhill
Waghorn Fredk.&Co.ale& stout merchts.4 Water la. Tower st
Waghorn John, butcher, 6 Dorset place, Pall mall east
Wagland James, grocer, 1 Love la. Brook st. Shadwell
Wagner Charles, baker, 75 Crawford st. Portman square
Wagner Chas. F. agent to PhœnixOff. 19Charlotte st. Fitz.sq
Wagstaff Chas. Eden, portrait engr. 30 Argyle st. King's crs
Wagstaff Geo. carptr. & builder, 15 Bartlett's pass. Holborn
Wagstaff James, architect, &c. 1 Albion ter. Canonbury sq
Wagstaff James, plumber, 39 Little Bartholomew close
Wagstaff James, tinman, 39 Squirries st. Bethnal green rd
Wagstaff James, watchma. 179 Brick lane, Spitalfields
Wagstaff Joseph, japanner, 76 Monmouth st. Seven dials
Wagstaff Martha (Mrs.), milliner, 4 Bethnal green road
Wagstaff Mary (Mrs.), lodginghouse, 12 Charlotte st. Pimlico
Wagstaff Thos. china wareh. 11 London house yd. St. Paul's
Wagstaff Thos. flock, list dealer, & rag merchant, 9 Providence place, & 26 New North st. Finsbury
Wagstaff Wm. builder & undertaker, 11 Clay st. Marylebone
Wagstaff Wm. coal merchant, see West & Wagstaff
Wagstaffe Matthew French, surgeon, 10Walcot pl. Lambeth
Wagstaffe Wm. Conghan T. surgeon, 117 Long la. Bermnds
Waigh Robert, beer retailer, 228 Bethnal green road
Waight Alfred Hen. beer retailer, 20 Berkeley st. Lambeth
Waight Robert, machine & gen. smith, 16 Gelding st. Brmdsy
Waight Wm. watchmaker, 14 Gray's place, Fulham road
Waight Wm. jun meat salesman, 11 Warwick lane, City
Wailes George, special pleader, 1 Cloisters, Temple
Wain Geo. grocer & brit.wine dealer, 1 King's rd. east, Chelsea
Wain Richard, tailor, see Stulz, Housley & Wain
Wainewright Robt. Arnold, solicitor, 7 Angel ct. Throgm. st
Wainewright Wm. liverpool office, 20 Fludyer st. Westminstr
Wainwright Brothers, plate glass & cabinet wa.44 Conduit st
Wainwright & Gadesden, jun. sugar refiners, Christian st. St. George's east
Wainwright Chas. plasterer, 5 Sherborne st. Blandfd.square
Wainwright Henry Wm. brush maker, 84 Whitechapel road
Wainwright Jas. grease manf. 10 Thornton st. Horselydown
Wainwright Jas. herald painter, 10 Kirby st. Hatton garden
Wainwright Jas. plasterer, 15 Harcourt st. New road
Wainwright Jas. plasterer, 4 Sherborne st. Blandford sq
Wainwright John, comp.ornament ma.8Rose yd. Rose st. Soho
Wainwright John, oilman, 33 Freeschool st. Horselydown
Wainwright Jordan, wind music inst.ma.27 Greenhill's rents
Wainwright Walter Clarke, tobacconist, 58 Fore st. City
Wainwright William, butcher, 170 Upper Whitecross st
Wainwright William, gold beater, 11 George row, Bermdsy
Wainwright William, loan office, 58 Fore st. City
Waistell Geo. Rudd, french goods imp. seeNeville& Waistell
Wait Charlotte (Mrs.), boot maker, High st. Bow
Wait George, ironmonger, 23 Lit. Guilford st. Brunswick sq
Wait Harriet (Mrs.), boot&shoe wa. 82 Whitechapel High st
Wait Joseph, boot & shoe maker, 30 Lower Eaton st. Pimlico
Wait Wm. cloth cap maker, 15 Dartmouth st. Westminster
Waite Benjamin, oil & colorman, 5Eldon pl. Low.st. Islington
Waite Benj. Redhead, butcher, 24 Wormwood st. Bishopsgt
Waite Charles, physician, 3 Old Burlington st
Waite Elizabeth (Mrs.), city carman, Queen st. King st. Boro
Waite Enoch, tobacconist, 226 Bethnal green road
Waite George, surgeon dentist, 2 Old Burlington st
Waite John, attorney, 8 Welbeck st. Cavendish square
Waite John, butcher, 6 Lr. Salisbury pl. Lock's flds. Walwrth
Waite John, butcher, 123 Bishopsgate without
Waite John, dentist, 12 Sackville st. Piccadilly
Waite John, tailors' trimming seller, 4 West st. Golden sq
Waite John, *White Lion* P.H. 36 Church st. Lambeth
Waite John George, wholesale seed mer. 1 & 4 Eyre st. hill
Waite John George, *William IV.* P.H. 1 Eyre st. hill
Waite Richard, tailor, 74 New Bond st
Waite Wm. grocer&cheesemonger, 7Glo'ster pl. Walwrth.com
Waites James, marinestore dealer, 40 Exeter st. Lisson grove
Waithman Henry & Co. silk brokers, 52 Old Broad st. City
Wake Sarah&Hen. slate manufr. 16 Lombard st. Lant st. Boro
Wake Charles, plumber & glazier, 26 King st. Westminster
Wake Hannah (Mrs.), bricklayer, 32St. Martin's st. Leicstr.sq
Wake Hannah (Mrs.), warm & cold baths, 32 St. Martin's st. Leicester square
Wake John, baker, 52 Bermondsey st.
Wake John, bricklayer & plasterer, 3 Richmond bldgs. Soho
Wake Wm. sen. bricklayer, 10 Totford pl. Neckinger rd
Wake Wm. jun. builder&bricklayer, 1 Printer's pl. Bermndsy
Wakefield Geo. W. &J. linen drapers, 8 Sun st. Bishopsgate st
Wakefield Daniel, queen's counsel, 12 New sq. Lincoln's inn
Wakefield Geo. surgeon, 27 Ossulston st. Somers town
Wakefield Henry, surgeon, &c. 6Albion place, Battle bridge
Wakefield Henry, surgeon, 1 Lansdowne pl. Brunswick sq
Wakefield John, watchmaker, 48 South st. South Audley st
Wakefield John, working silversmith, 38King st. Clerkenwell
Wakefield Jos. Colen, de laine manfr. see Inglis& Wakefield
Wakefield Mary Ann (Mrs.), milliner, 93 New Bond st
Wakefield Richard, teadealer, 35 Crown st. Finsbury
Wakefield Reuben, bricklayer, 8 Gastigney pl. Bath st. City rd
Wakefield Thomas, egg salesman, 180 Drury lane
Wakefield Thomas, surgeon, 16 Judd pl. West, New rd
Wakefield Wm. linendraper, 1 Vernon pl. BagniggeWells rd
Wakelin James, coal merchant, 2 Stafford pl. Pimlico, & Union wharf, Wilton rd. Pimlico
Wakelin John, locksmith, &c. 11 Chapel st. Tottenham ct. rd
Wakeling Giles & Son, upholsterers, 36 Gerrard st. Soho
Wakeling Bridget (Mrs.), tobacnst. 17B, Great Carlisle st
Wakeling Elizh. (Miss), turner, 28&29 Silver st. Regent st
Wakeling Henry Beverley, solicitor & vestry clerk of Clerkenwell, 5 St. John's sq. Clerkenwell
Wakeling John Kearse, china wa. 35 Lower Kennington la
Wakeling Wm. soda water mfr. 72Tower st. Westminster rd
Wakeman, Brashier & Francio, straw bon. wa. 56 High st. Camden town
Wakenell Charles, carpenter, 226 Albany rd. Camberwell
Wakley Thomas, M.P. coroner for Middlesex, 35 Bedford sq
Walbancke Frederick, sheriffs' officer, 23 Coleman street
Walbancke Geo. working goldsmith, 16 Devereux ct. Strand
Walbran John, warehouseman, see Hodgson & Walbran
Walburn John, grocer, 3 Upper East Smithfield
Walby Eliz. & Ellen (Misses), seminary, Mare st. Hackney
Walby George, ironmonger, 4 Pleasant row, Holloway rd
Walby James, boiler & gas apparatus ma. 59 Greek st. Soho
Walby Thomas, coal merchant, 11 Princes st. Drury lane
Walcot Thomas, solicitor, 1 Churchyard court, Temple

Waldegrave Richard, surgeon, 34 Sun st. Bishopsgate
Walden Charles, floor cloth manfr. see Clarke & Walden
Walden Daniel, butcher, Church st. Hackney
Walden Hen. Edw. basket mak. & turner, 71 Shoe la. Fleet st
Walden Joshua, pork butcher, 64 Golden lane, St. Luke's
Walden Martha (Miss), straw hat ma. 68 Freeschool st. Hslydn
Walden Mary (Mrs.), basket ma. 43 Fleet la. Farringdon st
Walden Samuel, basket maker, rod dealer & brush & turnery wa. 32 Farringdon st. & Grand Junction st. Whitefriars
Walden Sarah (Mrs.), straw hat ma. 41 Seething la. Tower st
Waldie George, coal factor, 28 St. Mary at hill
Waldie Hannah (Mrs.), *Don Saltero's coff. ho.* 18 Chyn. wk. Chls
Waldie Jas. *White Horse & Bower* P.H. 1 Romney terrace
Waldon John, straw bonnet maker, 4 Crown st. Soho
Waldron Edward, *Ten Bells* P.H. 34 Church st. Spitalfields
Waldron James, basket rod mer. Dowgate dock, 82 Up. Thms. st
Waldron Thomas, saddler, 8 Henrietta st. Manchester sq
Walduck Charlotte (Miss), milliner, 273 Bethnal green rd
Walduck John, chemist & druggist, 86 New Bond st
Walduck Sherwin, merchant, 5 Windsor place, City road
Walduck Thos. Hen. lodging house, 5 Warwick ct. Holborn
Walduck Wm. Knowles, trimming manfr. 273 Bethnal green rd
Waldvogel Anthony, clockmaker, 82 St. George st
Wale Betsey (Mrs.), leather cutter, 30 Camden st. Walworth
Wale John, cabinet maker, 5 Up. Spring st. Portman sq
Wale Wm. *Bayswater tav. & tea gards.* Elm la. Bayswater
Walenn & Allchin, teadealers, 36 Gt. Portland st. Oxford st
Wales George Richard, auctioneer, see Ellis & Wales
Wales Henry, glove manufacturer, 2 Castle st. Finsbury
Wales James, tin plate worker, 33 Poplar High st
Wales Oliver Wm. archery ware. 101 Tyer st. Princs. rd. Lmbth
Wales Peter, *Crooked Billet* P.H. 198 Hoxton Old town
Wales Richard, fancy stationer, High st. Stoke Newington
Walesby Francis Pearson, barrister, 10 Farrar's bgs. Temple
Waley Jacob, barrister, 69 Chancery lane
Waley S. Jacob, stock broker, Stock Exchange, & 20 Throgmorton st
Walford Thos. & Arthur & Fred. H. solicitors, 27 Bolton st
Walford Charles, chair ma. 16 & 17 Stangate mews, Lambeth
Walford Edward, teadealer & grocer, 2 Gt. Trinity lane, City
Walford Edward Vernon, booksel. see Jackson & Walford
Walford Edwin, tailor, &c. 24 Drummond st. Euston sq
Walford Fras. Joseph Gourdez, barrister, 1 New sq. Linc. inn
Walford Fred. special pleader, 4 King's Bench walk, Temple
Walford Geo. attorney, 8 Grafton st. Bond st
Walford Geo. Eastfield, surgeon, 4 Commerl. ter. Com. rd. east
Walford Geo. Hen. Jas. goldsmith, see Makepeace & Walford
Walford John, shoemaker, 99 York st. Westminster
Walford Joseph Green, barrister, Custom house
Walford Rich. bandanna printer & silk ma. 27 Laurence la
Walford Walter S. *Duchess of Clarence* P.H. 1 Belvoir ter
Walford Weston Styleman, barrister, 2 Plowden bds. Temple
Walford Wm. plumber, 15 East st. Manchester sq
Walkden John & Sons, flannel, baize, blanket, drugget, dimity, & table cover warehousemen, 26 Lawrence lane
Walkden Thomas, butcher, 18 Rufford's builds, Islington
Walker Abhm. & Co. drapers, army clothiers, &c. 346 Strand
Walker Alfred & William, foreign wine & champagne merchants, & britishwine manufacturers, 6 Com. pl. City rd
Walker & Bridgett, saw mills, 8 Lr. Queen st. Rotherhithe
Walker Brothers & Co. merchants, 63 Fenchurch st
Walker & Brown, silversmiths & pawnbrokers, 38 Whitechapel rd. & goldsmiths & jewlrs. 92 Whitechapel High st
Walker & Burges, civil engineers, 23 Gt. George st. Westmr
Walker & Cole, breeches makers, 5 New Bond st
Walker Edward & Son, general tool, metal & crucible warehouse for watch & clock makers, jewellers, &c. 55 Red Lion st. Clerkenwell
Walker Geo. F. & Co. sawmills, Collegewf. Belvedere rd. Lambth
Walker Geo. & Son, publishers of music, 17 Soho square
Walker Geo. & Son, anchorsmiths, sailmakers & ship chandlers, 165, 166 & 222 Wapping High st
Walker & Gordon, linendrapers, 128 & 129 Blackfriars rd
Walker, Grant & Co. solicitors, 13 King's row, Bedford row
Walker & Gridley, attorneys, 5 Southampton st. Bloomsby
Walker & Griffiths, coach bldrs. 5 Charles pl. Westbrne. ter
Walker John & Chas. geographers & engra. 9 Castle st. Holb
Walker John & Co. iron plate workers, 46 St. John's sq. Clkwl
Walker Joseph & Co. cabinet ma. & upholstrs. 65 Holborn hl
Walker & Knight, wood engravers, 10 Guilford pl. Spafields
Walker & Knowles, sheffield ware. 7 Beaufort bldgs. Strand
Walker & Lee, linendrapers, 165 Oxford st
Walker Mary & Ann (Mesdames), milliners, 33 Pall mall
Walker Nicholas & Co. fruiterers, 9 Queen's ter. Marlbro' rd
Walker Richard & John, patent corrugated iron factory, Upper Fort place, Grange road, Bermondsey
Walker Richd. & John, carpents. & undertak. Fort pl. Grange rd
Walker Robert & S. pawnbroks. 9 Waterloo ter. Coml. rd. e
Walker Step. & Sam. & Co. printers' joiners, 45 Lit. Barthlmw. cl
Walker & Walton, british wine manfs. 21 New Farringdon st
Walker Wm. & Son, woollen warehmn. 9 Gresham st. & Leeds
Walkers' & Co. worsted spinners, Bradford, Yorkshire (Thomas Walker, agent), 90 Bermondsey st
Walkers', Parker & Co. lead merch. shot, & white lead ma. Lambeth lead wks. Belvedere rd. Lambeth, & 27 Abchurch la
Walker Adam Lawson, grocer, 4 & 5 Union pl. Clapham rise
Walker Alex. chemist, &c. 10 Ireland row, Mile end road
Walker Ann (Mrs.), butcher, 43 Barbican
Walker Benjamin, cattle salesman, 17 West Smithfield
Walker Benjamin, stationer, 191 Hoxton Old town
Walker Benj. Ed. *Goat & Compasses* P.H. 8 Up. Fitzry. st. Fitz. sq
Walker Caleb, grocer, &c. 12 Spring st. Paddington
Walker Charles, beer retailer, 117 London rd. Southwark
Walker Charles, dairyman, 25 Exeter st. Sloane st
Walker Chas. smith & engineer, 21 Lit. Sutton st. Clerknwl
Walker Charles, linendraper, 11 King's pl. Comml. rd. east
Walker Charles, solicitor, 5 New inn, Wych st. Strand
Walker Charles, tailor, &c. 38 Sackville st. Piccadilly
Walker Chas. Edmund, teadealer, 102 London rd. Southwark
Walker Chas. Page, reel cotton mnfr. 8 Draycott pl. Chelsea
Walker Charlotte (Mrs.), tobacconist, 83 Long lane, Smithfld
Walker Daniel, painter, 11 Stafford st. Lisson grove
Walker Deane F. lecturer, 7 Camden rd. villas, Camden tn
Walker Edmund, bootmak. 7 Glo'ster ter. New rd. Whcbpl
Walker Edmund, master of Exchequer of Pleas, 8 Old sq
Walker Edward, auctioneer, &c. 53½ Southampton row
Walker Edwd. *Bull's Head* P.H. 2 Newmarket st. Wapping
Walker Edwd. *Queen's Head* P.H. 50 Theobald's rd. Bloomsb
Walker Edwd. solicitor, see Lake & Walker
Walker Edward, upholsterer, 53½ Southampton row
Walker Edwd. wirework & sieve ma. 6 Cardington st. Hmpst. rd
Walker Eliza (Mrs.), ladies' school, 8 Red Lion sq. Holborn
Walker Elizh. (Mrs.), library, 3 Bedford st. Mile end
Walker Francis, optician, 17 Wapping wall
Walker Francis, medicine vndr. 4 Up. Southampton st. Pntnvil
Walker Fras. Wm. lodging house, 30 Weymouth st. Portland pl
Walker Frederick, watchmaker, 93 Broad st. Ratcliff
Walker Frederick Fras. engraver, 48 Union st. Clarendon sq
Walker George, anchorsmith, 222 Wapping High st
Walker George, chaser, 17 Albemarle st. Clerkenwell
Walker George, dairyman, 42 Charles st. Hampstead road
Walker George, farrier, 7 Manifold pl. Low. Kennington la
Walker George, lodging ho. 7 Northumberland st. Strand
Walker George, newsvender, 26 Maddox st. Regent st
Walker George, tailor, 33 St. James's st. Pall mall
Walker George, tinplate & iron mer. 5 Pinners' hall, Gt. Winch. st
Walker George Alfred, surgeon & apothecary, 101 Drury lane, & bath proprietor, 11 St. James's pl. St. James's
Walker Giovanni, musical librarian & copyist, 19 Marshall st. Golden square
Walker Greaves, attorney, 11 Beaufort buildings, Strand
Walker Henry, bootmaker, 9 Upper Marylebone st
Walker Henry, bread & biscuit baker, 14 Weston st. Borough
Walker Henry, builder, Ferry road west, Poplar
Walker Henry, chemist, 59 St. John st. Clerkenwell
Walker Henry, chem. & druggist, 35 Skinner st. Somers town
Walker Henry, grocer & teadealer, 33 Coleman st
Walker Henry, manufacturer to the Queen, of needles, fish hooks, steel pens, hooks & eyes, &c. 1, late 20, Maiden lane (now called Gresham st.), New Post Office, Wood st
Walker Henry, *Morley's Hotel*, see James & Walker
Walker Hen. Guilder, coachma. 16 White Lion st. Norton folgt
Walker Holden, solicitor, 13 Furnival's inn, Holborn
Walker Isaac, silk manufacturer, see Bartholomew & Walker
Walker James, baker, 19 Seymour st. Euston square
Walker James, bootmaker, 19 Hatton wall, Hatton garden
Walker James, cabinet maker, 115 Jermyn st. St. James's
Walker James, fruiterer, 8 East st. Spitalfields
Walker James, paper stainer, see Kipps & Walker
Walker James, smith & smoke jack ma. 26 Harp al. Shoe la
Walker James, tailor, 9 Frederick st. Regent's park
Walker James Hurry, berlin repository, 9 Vere st. Cav. sq
Walker James Hurry, coal mer. Feltoe's whf. Belvedere rd
Walker Jane (Mrs.), pawnbro. & upholsterer, 41 York rd. Lambth
Walker Joel, tailor, 59 Jermyn st. St. James's
Walker John, auctioneer & appraiser, 16 Wardour st. Soho
Walker John, baker, 42 King st. Camden town
Walker John, butcher, 1 Britannia row, Hoxton
Walker John, butcher, 52 Kensington High st
Walker John, carpenter & builder, 38 Charles st. City road
Walker John, chronometer maker, 40 Princes st. Leicester sq
Walker John, drug broker, 60 Gracechurch st

Walker John, drysalter, 90 Wheeler st. Spitalfields
Walker John, *Eagle* dining rooms, 5 Eagle terrace, City rd
Walker John, fruiterer, 18 Up. Ashby st. Northampton sq
Walker John, *George* P.H. 8 New road, St. George's east
Walker John, grocer, 3 Andrew's pl. St. Andrew's rd. Boro'
Walker John, lacemanfr. see Fisher, Sons, Robinson & Walker
Walker John, livery stables, 1 Tenterden st. Hanover square
Walker John, lodging house, 8 Howard st. Strand
Walker John, oven builder, 3 Allen st. Lambeth
Walker John, physician, 11 Chester st. Grosvenor sq
Walker John, patentee & manufr. of the hydraulic engine & air-proof water closets, 3 Jewry st. Aldgate, & 1 Crooked la
Walker John (Mrs.), painter & glazr. 74 Mount st. Berkely. sq
Walker John, *Pitt's Head* P.H. 150 Old st. St. Luke's
Walker John, queen's counsel, 3 Old square, Lincoln's inn
Walker John, tailor, 8 Camden st. Walworth
Walker John, tailor, 6 Trafalgar place west, Hackney rd
Walker John, tinplate worker, 19 Cow cross st. Smithfield
Walker John, undertaker, 47 Bridge ho. pl. Newington cans
Walker John, jun. rus. broker, 75 Old Broad st. City, & Baltic
Walker John Thomas, barrister, 14 Serle st. Lincoln's inn
Walker John William, scale maker, 8 Newcastle st. Strand
Walker Jonathan, scale & machine mak. 5 Bridge st. Southwk
Walker Joseph, carpenter & builder, 10 Wood st. Westmstr
Walker Joseph, cattle salesman, 41 West Smithfield
Walker Joseph, dairyman, 72 George st. Portman sq
Walker Joseph, fishmonger, 3 Shoemaker row, Blackfriars
Walker Joseph, ironfounders' agent, 52 Alfred st. City rd
Walker Joseph, printers' joiner, &c. 65 Hoxton Old town
Walker Joseph W. organbuilder, 27 Francis st. Tottenhm. ct. rd
Walker Joshua, dyer, 5 Sun Tavern fields, St. George's east
Walker Joshua, livery stables, 13 Princes st. Hanover sq
Walker Josiah W. surgeon, 16 Glo'ster tr. New rd. Comml. rd
Walker Julia (Mrs.), baker, 150 Sloane st. Chelsea
Walker Margt. T. (Mrs.) *Olive B.* P.H. 1 Minerva st. Hckny rd
Walker Mary (Miss), straw bonnet maker, 85 Aldersgate st
Walker Mary Ann (Mrs.), corn dlr. 32 Gt. Quebec st. Montg. sq
Walker Mary Ann (Mrs.), *One Swan* P.H. One Swan yd. Bishp
Walker Mary M. (Mrs.), *Flower Pot* P.H. 144 Church st. Shrdth
Walker Matthew, carpenter, 7 Macclesfield st. sth. City rd
Walker Nicholas, *Barleymow* P.H. 111 Drury lane
Walker Philip, tailor, &c. 8 & 9 South crescent, Bedford sq
Walker Ralph, anchorsmith, &c. Church pas. 344 Rotherhithe
Walker Richard, stock & share agent, 20 Throgmorton st
Walker Richd. tailor, 13 Clarendon ter. Camberwell new rd
Walker Rd. T. pianoforte m. 6 Portsmouth pl. Lw. Kenngtn. la
Walker Robert, cabinet maker, 82 Margaret st. Cavendish sq
Walker Robert, pawnbroker, 5 St. John st. Clerkenwell
Walker Samuel, beer retailer, 111 Cromer st. Brunswick sq
Walker Samuel, *Cock & Neptune* P.H. 72 Parsons st. St. George st.; *Bull's Head* P.H. 44 Carnaby st. Golden sq.; & *Duke of Cambridge* P.H. 177 Whitechapel road
Walker Samuel, fruiterer, 38 Berwick st. Soho
Walker Samuel, smith & engineer, 44 Noble st. Goswell st
Walker Samuel, solicitor, see Rickards & Walker
Walker Samuel Rose, pawnbroker, see Alton & Walker
Walker Samuel Wiltshire, hatter, 133 Leadenhall st
Walker Sarah (Miss), school, 29 Laurence Pountney lane
Walker Sarah (Mrs.), undertaker, 29 Laurence Pountney la
Walker Sarah (Mrs.), watchglass ma. 6 Castle st. Houndsditch
Walker Snowball Wm. wedding cake maker, 49 Pall mall
Walker Sophia (Mrs.), bookselr. & stationr. 4 Carthusian st
Walker Steph. *Bricklayers' Arms* P.H. 40 Strutton gd. West
Walker Steph. *Coach & Horses* P.H. 4 Royal Hospitl. row. Chels
Walker Scott (agent to Joseph Cliffe, fire brick maker, Wortley, near Leeds), 10 Upper Thames st
Walker Thomas, carpenter, 23 King st. Soho
Walker Thomas, stove maker, 302 Oxford st
Walker Thomas, chemist, &c. 48 Tooley st
Walker Thomas, fruiterer, 84 Albany road, Camberwell
Walker Thomas, fruiterer, 19 Carnaby st. Golden sq
Walker Thomas, grocer, 2 Half Nichols st. Bethnal green
Walker Thomas, grocer, 3 York pl. Millpond st. Bermondsey
Walker Thos. hatter, 49 Crawford st. & 8 Grosvenor row, Pmlco
Walker Thos. jeweller & whip mount. 37 Buttesland st. Hoxton
Walker Thomas, shoeing smith, see Maffey & Walker
Walker Thomas, solicitor, 12 Furnival's inn, Holborn
Walker Thomas, watch & cloth ma. 29 Glo'ster st. Queen sq
Walker Thomas, wholesale grocer, see Collins & Walker
Walker Thomas Chas. pink saucer ma. 23 Alfred st. City rd
Walker Thomas Henry, bricklayer, 25 New st. Brompton
Walker Thomas Longridge, chain cable & anchor manufacturer, rope & sail maker & ship chandler & agent for Trail's patent storm sails, 341 Wapping
Walker Walter, grocer, 6 New Church st. Lisson grove
Walker Wm. army agent, 5 St. James's square (south side)
Walker Wm. barrister, 1 King's Bench walk, Temple
Walker Wm. bell hanger, 19 Harper st. New Kent road
Walker Wm. bookseller, 9 Leatherseller's bldgs. London wll
Walker Wm. cabinetmaker, 4 Westmoreland st. Marylebone
Walker Wm. chemist, 42 Tothill st. Westminster
Walker Wm. chemist & druggist, 2 White horse st. Stepney
Walker Wm. clothier, 40 Radnor st. St. Luke's
Walker Wm. coach spring ma. 3 George yd. Crown st. Soho
Walker Wm. fruit salesman, Covent garden fruit market
Walker Wm. *Golden Eagle* P.H. 234 Shadwell High st
Walker Wm. hairdresser, 10 Ellis st. Sloane st
Walker Wm. herald painter, 10 Crescent, Bridge rd. Southwk
Walker Wm. hist. engraver, &c. 64 Margaret st. Cavendish sq
Walker Wm. *King of Prussia* P.H. Union st. Deptford
Walker Wm. law & genl. bookseller & stationer, 196 Strand
Walker Wm. *Lion & French Horn* P.H. 5 Pollen st. Hanover sq
Walker Wm. livery stable keeper, 2 Coleman st
Walker Wm. lodging house, 7 Manchester buildings
Walker Wm. *Old Crown & Cushion* P.H. 63 Mount st. Lambth
Walker Wm. oven builder, 40 Royal st. Carlisle st. Lambeth
Walker Wm. plumber, &c. 27 Cowcross st. West Smithfield
Walker Wm. stationer, &c. 5 Melton st. Euston square
Walker Wm. surgeon, 51 St. John st. Clerkenwell
Walker Wm. tailor, 2 Jones st. Berkeley square
Walker Wm. *Walker's hotel*, 33 Dean st. Soho
Walker Wm. wholesale & retail fishmonger, 175 Goswell st
Walker Wm. worsted spinner, see Wood & Walker
Walker Wm. Adam, grocer & oilman, Little Chelsea
Walker Wm. Falconar, solicitor, 3 South square, Gray's inn
Walker Wm. Geo. pewterer, 15 Brown's lane, Spitalfields
Walker Wm. Geo. tobaccopipe ma. 38 Wheeler st. Spitalfields
Walker Wm. Joseph, grocer, 68 Whitehorse st. Stepney
Walker Wm. Josiah, boot & shoemaker, 123 Whitechapel road, & 304 Oxford st
Walker Wm. P. law stationer, 19 Castle st. Holborn
Walker Willoughby N. solicitor, 28 Gt. Ormond st. Queen sq
Walkers Wm. Henry, working jeweller, 90 Gt. Titchfield st
Walkington Rt. whole. cheesemonger, &c. 8 High st. Bloomsb
Walkington Rt. upholst. & cabin. ma. 45 Rathbone pl. Oxfd. st
Walkley Stephen, grindery warehouse, 58 King st. Sevendials
Walkley Wm. *King's Head* P.H. 4 James st. Buckingham gate
Walko Martin, furrier, 5 Angell ct. Skinner st. Snow hill
Walkom John Alexander, straw hat warehouse, 36 Oxford st
Walls Patent Protection of Metals Office, 25 Gt. Tower st
Wall Ann (Miss), milliner, 2 Theberton st. west, Liverpool rd
Wall Ann (Mrs.), chndlrs. shop, 1 Mountpleasant, Gray's inn la
Wall Ann E. (Mrs.), *Britannia* P.H. 19 St. George's pl. Back rd
Wall Benjamin, *Woodstock tav.* P.H. 11 Woodstock st. Oxf. st
Wall Elizabeth (Mrs.), linendraper, 7 Pitt's pl. Old Kent rd
Wall Francis, coal dealer, 5 Church lane, Whitechapel
Wall George, carpenter, Church st. Deptford
Wall Henry, baker, 56 Strutton ground, Westminster
Wall Henry, tailor & draper, 31 Tabernacle walk, Finsbury
Wall James, baker, Bow
Wall James, hairdresser, 6 Ring cross, Holloway road
Wall James, printer, 7 High st. Bow
Wall John, tailor, 9 Tabernacle row, City road
Wall John Prichard, surgeon, &c. 6 Mount st. Berkeley sq
Wall Joseph, artist, Addison road south, Kensington
Wall Priscilla (Mrs.), brassfndr. 5 Exeter pl. Gt. Dover rd
Wall Robert, saddler & harness maker, 425 Piccadilly
Wall Thomas, dining rooms, 9 Artillery passage, Bishopsgate
Wall Thomas, pork butcher, 113 Jermyn st. St. James's
Wall Thomas, sen. corndealer, 132 Edgware rd. Marylebone
Wall Thomas Collier, baker, 24 Victoria road, Pimlico
Wall Wm. butcher, 25 Carnaby st. Golden square
Wall Wm. fruit salesman, Covent garden fruit market
Wall Wm. grocer, 12 Clipstone st. Fitzroy square
Wall Wm. potato salesman, 23 Red Lion st. Spitalfields
Wall Wm. tripe dresser, 2 Market st. Jermyn st
Wall Wm. wine & brandy merchant 2 Gt. Prescot st. Goodm. flds
Wallace & Johnson, curriers, Wild's rents, Bermondsey
Wallace Caroline M. (Mrs.), boarding ho. 8 Adam st. Adelphi
Wallace David, stationer, 3 Southampton st. Camberwell
Wallace Edward James, barrister, 57 Chancery lane
Wallace Emma (Mrs.), tobacconist, 18 Brunswick st. Hckny rd
Wallace George, barrister, 10 New square, Lincoln's inn
Wallace James, hatter, 17 Chapel st. New road
Wallace James, merchant, see Major & Wallace
Wallace John, *Eight Bells* P.H. 20 Collingwood st. Blkfrs. rd
Wallace John, fruiterer, High st. Kingsland
Wallace John Andrew, surgeon, 7 Savile row, Mile end road
Wallace Martin, *Gloucester tavern* P.H. 187 Sloane st
Wallace Richard, surgeon, &c. 9 John's terrace, Hackney rd
Wallace Robert, architect, 41 Parliament st. Westminster
Wallace Robert, cheesemonger, 26 Henry st. east, Avenuerd

Wallace Robert, fruiterer, 111 Cock hill, Ratcliff
Wallace Thomas, butcher, 39 Old Bond st
Wallan William, carpenter, 1 Arnold pl. Walworth road
Wallas Gilbert Innes, barrister, 10 Crown office row, Temple
Wallas Thomas, madeira merchant, 48 Fenchurch st
Wallby Benjamin, butcher, 2 Bray's pl. Lower rd. Islington
Wallen Wm. & Son, architects&surveyors, 1 Circus pl. Fnsbry
Wallen John, architect, &c. 11 Spital sq. & 68 Aldermanbury
Wallen John, auctioneer, see Humphreys & Wallen
Wallen Joseph, timber merchant, 1 Salmon la. Limehouse
Waller Benjamin & Son, coach builders, 80 Long acre
Waller Charles & Co. ironmongs. 3 Roebuck pl. Gt. Dover rd
Waller & Coleman, electro platers & gilders, 20 Hatton gdn
Waller William & Son, booksellers & dealers in autographs, 188 Fleet st
Waller Ann (Mrs.), dress maker, 5 Duke st. Portland pl
Waller Arthur, jun. chemist, 237 Tottenham court road
Waller Augustus, surgeon, 1 St. Mary Abbotts ter. Kensington
Waller Charles, cheesemonger, 176 Bermondsey st
Waller Charles, physician, 9 Finsbury square
Waller Elizth. (Miss), ladies' school, 13 Stoke Newington gr
Waller Frederick, stationer, 49 Fleet st
Waller Fredk. wine cooper, 3 Bailey's pl. Marlbro' rd. Chlsa
Waller George, butcher, 93 Golden lane, St. Luke's
Waller George, grocer, 78 Tottenham court road
Waller George, leather dlr. 4 Union pl. Lower rd. Islington
Waller George, undertaker, 1 Queen st. Horselydown
Waller George, upholsterer, 37 Assembly row, Mile end
Waller George, jun. solicitor, 24 Finsbury circus
Waller James, fruiterer, Nelson place, Old Kent road
Waller James William, lighterman, 52 Lower Thames st
Waller John, builder, 3 Belgrave road, Pimlico
Waller John, cowkeeper, 17 Ferry st. Lambeth
Waller John Green, artist, 20 Charles st. Middlesex hospital
Waller Joseph, hatter, 6 John st. Holland st. Blackfriars
Waller Joseph Henry, teadealer, 3 Queen's road, Dalston
Waller Judith (Mrs.), silk mercer, 76 Houndsditch
Waller Lewis, bricklayer, 19 White Hart st. Drury lane
Waller Rachael (Mrs.), dressmak. 13 Half Moon st. Piccadil
Waller Rd. Thos. brass mfr.&gasfit. 6 Goodman's stile, Goodmfi
Waller Robert, grocer, &c. 42 King st. Seven dials
Waller Samuel, carman, 3 Colet pl. Salmon lane, Limehouse
Waller Thomas, fruiterer, 33 Chapel st. Grosvenor sq
Waller Thomas, fruiterer, 27 Gower place, Euston square
Waller Thomas, livery stables, 43 Chenies mews, Bedford sq
Waller Thomas, solicitor, 2 Churchyard court, Temple
Waller Thomas, staymaker, 9 Duke st. Grosvenor square
Waller Thomas, straw & tuscan manufr. 103 Wood st; manufactories at Luton, Florence, St. Alban's&Cranfield; warehouses at Pearl st. New York, & Market st. Philadelphia
Waller Thomas, tailor, 17 Nassau st. Middlesex hospital
Waller Thomas George, solicitor, 1 Essex court, Temple
Waller Timothy Truman, newsman, 3 Staining lane, Wood st. & oilman, &c. Kingsland green
Waller Wm. attorney, 5 Clement's inn, & 53 Up. Seymour st
Waller William, fishmonger, 32 James st. Buckingham gate
Waller William, fruiterer, 5 Foxton ter. Thornhill road
Waller William, grocer, 48 Dudley gr. Harrow rd. Padngtn
Waller William, grocer, 7 Walker's court, Golden square
Wallers Catherine (Miss), ladies' school, 17 York pl. Fulham rd
Walles Jas. *George & Vulture* P.H. 36 Haberdasher st. Hoxtn
Walley Thomas, draper, &c. see Hunt & Walley
Wallford William, bootmak. 31 Marchmont st. Burton crest
Wallinger Arnold, barrister, 3 Inner Temple lane
Wallington Benjamin, solicitor, 3 Crown ct. Threadneedle st
Wallington Charles, corn dealer, 25 Old st. St. Luke's
Wallington Joseph, baker, 118 Old st. St. Luke's
Wallington Leonard, cabinet & mattress ma. 4 Gray's inn ter
Wallington Rd. confectioner, 21 Rosoman st. Clerkenwell
Wallington Septimus, surveyor, &c. 3 Crown ct. Threadndl. st
Wallis Geo. & Thomas, varnish & color makers, 64 Long acre
Wallis Harriet (Miss), & Co. hosiers, &c. 84 Whtchpl. Hi. st
Wallis John & Co. wine & beer merchants, 64 Millbank st
Wallis & Southwood, linendrs. 35 & 36 Parliament st. Westm
Wallis Thomas & Son, tailors & drapers, 17 Poultry
Wallis Ann (Miss), millnr. & dressma. 45 Tufton st. Westmr
Wallis Ann (Mrs.), milliner, 22 Low. Smith st. Northmptn sq
Wallis Benjamin, ornamental painter, 11 Union st. Deptford
Wallis Benjamin, ship builder, &c. Orchard pl. Blackwall
Wallis Charles, saddler, 62 Cannon st. Ratcliff highway
Wallis Chas. ship ins. & custom agt. 13 Change al. Cornhill
Wallis Charles Edward, dentist, 44 Gt. Marlborough st
Wallis Charles William, solicitor, see Aston & Wallis
Wallis Edward, dissected map manufacturer & publisher, 42 Skinner st. Snowhill; fancy repository, 32 High st. Islngtn.; english timber yard, 56 Lit. Sutton st. Clerkenwell
Wallis Edward, dressing case ma. 9 Gt. Turnstile, High Hlbn
Wallis Edward (Mrs.), poulterer, 2 Swallow pl. Hanover sq
Wallis Francis, meat salesman, 51 Newgate market
Wallis Frederick, baker, 46 William st. Regent's park
Wallis Frederick, painter, 19 Trafalgar st. Walworth rd
Wallis George, baker, 1 Salisbury st. Bermondsey
Wallis George, coffee rooms, 30 Crispin st. Spitalfields
Wallis George, marine store dlr. 1 Charles st. Blackfrs. rd
Wallis George, veterinary surgeon, 13 Edward st. City road
Wallis George Starkins, livery stables, 279 Whitechapel rd
Wallis George Wm. baker, 8 Pleasant row, Old Kent rd
Wallis James, gasfitter & scalemakr. 74 Oakley st. Lambeth
Wallis John, grocer, 3 Woolmore st. Ea. India rd. Poplar
Wallis John, ironmonger, 36 Fore st. Cripplegate
Wallis John, law stationer, 3 Cursitor st. Chancery lane
Wallis John, tailor, 19 Eden place, Old Kent road
Wallis John Charles, surgeon, 45 Sidney st. Mile end
Wallis John, coal merchant, 42 New Gloster st. Hoxton
Wallis Joseph, porter merchant, 154 Fenchurch st
Wallis Joseph, *Rodney's Head* P.H. 23 Robert st. Grosv. sq
Wallis Luke, tailor, 4 Darby pl. Jermyn st. Piccadilly
Wallis Mary Ann (Mrs.), confectnr. 3 Mill Pond st. Bermsy
Wallis Richd. *Adam & Eve* P.H. 20 Bath place, New rd
Wallis Richard, baker, 40 Red Lion st. Clerkenwell
Wallis Robert, shipwright, Horseferry branch rd. Ratcliff
Wallis Rosalie (Mrs.), milliner, 6 George st. Minories
Wallis Stephen, bread & bis. baker, 7 Union pl. Clapham rise
Wallis Thos. cattle salesman, 15 West Smithfield
Wallis Thos. *London Bridge tav.* 2 Wellington st. Borough
Wallis Thos. plumber, painter, &c. 74 Harrow road
Wallis Thos. woollendraper, 141 Oxford st
Wallis Wm. baker, 1 Brunswick parade, Islington
Wallis Wm. ironmonger, 6 Hart st. Duke st. Grosvenor sq
Wallis Wm. carpenter, 71 Harrow road, Paddington
Wallis Wm. pork butcher, 172 Hoxton Old town
Wallis Wm. woollendraper, 70 Whitechapel High st
Wallis Wm. George, discount agent, &c. 40 St. Mary Axe
Walliss Robt. silver spoon & fork ma. 6 President st. east
Wallroth Charles, merchant, 2 Crosby square, Bishopsgate
Walls John & Wm. Albert, attorneys, 44 Bloomsbury square
Walls Edward, cowkeeper, &c. 51 Gt. James st. Lisson grove
Walls James, baker, 2 Commerce row, Upper st. Islington
Walls James Walter, surgeon, 9 Windmill st. Finsbury sq
Walls John, tailor, 10 Brunswick ter. Commercial rd. east, & 59 Fenchurch st
Wallwork Harriet (Mrs.), lodging ho. 21 Northumberland st
Walmesley Richard, barrister, 14 Serle st. Lincoln's inn
Walmesley Richard, wine merch. 33 Mount st. Berkeley sq
Walmisley G. A. & Co. wine & beer mer. 2 Ingram ct. Fench. st
Walmisley Edward, solicitor, 68 Chancery lane
Walmisley John Angus, parl. agent, see Jones & Walmisley
Walmisley John Richard Lambert, sol. 12 North st. Westmstr
Walmisley Frederick, artist, 18 Cowley st. Westminster
Walmisley Thos. Forbes, prof. of music, 18 Cowley st. Westmr
Walmisley William, parl. agent, see Parratt & Walmisley
Walmsley & Co. iron merchants, 3 Upper Thames st
Walmsley George, Edward Batten, & Wm. pawnbrokers, 155 Borough High st
Walmsley Henry B. patent maltster, 24 New road, Mile end
Walmsley Edward, hatter, 138 Union st. Borough
Walmsley Jas. worsted & fringe manfr. 12 King st. Cheapside
Walmsley John Watson, solicitor, 100 Chancery lane
Walmsley Thomas, barrister, 6 Figtree court, Temple
Walne Daniel Henry, surgeon, 72 Guilford st. Russell sq
Walpole Eliza (Mrs.), milliner, &c. 11 Rufford's row, Islngtn
Walpole John, *Crown* P.H. 39 Lower Islington terrace
Walpole Spencer Horatio, barrister, 6 Serle st. Lincoln's inn
Walrond William James, solicitor, 13½ Sise lane, City
Walsby Chas. carpenter, 8 Gibraltar walk, Bethnal gr. rd
Walsh & Thompson, solicitors, 68 Lincoln's inn fields
Walsh Wm. Serrant & Co. mers. & wine im. 56 Berwick st. Soho
Walsh Charles Robert, surgeon, 42 Halfmoon st. Piccadilly
Walsh Finey Nicholas, short hand writer, 9 Parliament st
Walsh George, tailor, 13 Church st. Soho
Walsh Hugh, hair dresser, 200 St. George st. St. George's ea
Walsh James, carpenter, 2 Green st. Theobald's road
Walsh James, wholesale & export hat & cap manufacturer, 50 Old Change
Walsh James (Mrs.), stay & corset ma. 91 Mount st. Berkeley sq
Walsh John, chemist, 5 Brunswick st. Blackwall
Walsh John, *White Swan* P.H. 109 Bunhill row
Walsh Jonathan Rogers, bougie ma. 12 Bartholomew sq
Walsh Joseph Valentine, *White Horse tav.* 100 High Holborn
Walsh Mary (Mrs.), *Valiant Trooper* P.H. 257 Oxford st
Walsh Richard, tobacconist, 14 Bermondsey st
Walsh Wm. picture cleaner, 15 Leicester st. Leicester sq

Walsh Wm. Henry, attorney, 4 Copthall buildings
Walsham Jesse & Son, cattle salesmen, 8 West Smithfield
Walsham Wm. H. build. & bricklayer, 26 Chapel st. Pentonv
Walsham Wm. Henry, *Gun* P.H. 117 Shoreditch High st
Walshe Walter Hayle, physician, 47 Charlotte st. Fitzroy sq
Walter & Jones, milliners, 2 Queen's road, Bayswater
Walter & Pemberton, solicitors, 4 Symond's inn, Chancery la
Walter & Whitehurst, coachmakers, 313 Oxford st
Walter Abel, fruiterer, 33 Thomas st. Oxford st
Walter Arthur Antoine, solicitor, 72 Lombard st
Walter Chas. & Son, glass cutters, 16 Amelia st. Walworth rd
Walter Caroline (Mrs.), *Bull & Mouth* P.H. 31 Hart st. Blmsb
Walter Chas. bootma. 2 Beaufort ter. west, King rd. Chelsea
Walter Chas. *George IV.* P.H. 12 Portsmouth st. Lincoln's inn fields, & 8 Gilbert's passage, Clare market
Walter Chas. pawnbroker, 6 High st. Marylebone
Walter Chas. *Wheatsheaf* P.H. 53 Kensington High st
Walter Chas. David, newsvender, &c. 36 Bell yd. Temple bar
Walter Chas. David, booksel. & newsvend. 13 East rd. City rd
Walter Edward, coaldealer, 42 Marylebone lane, Oxford st
Walter George, *Blue Post* P.H. 10 Shoe lane
Walter George, bootmaker, 29 Chalton st. Somers town
Walter Geo. manager & trustee of the Patent Kamptulicon & Elastic Pavement Co. 42 Lombard st. & Greenwich rd
Walter Henry, steam flour mills, Canal bridge, Old Kent rd
Walter James, cowkeeper, 31 New road, Sloane st. Chelsea
Walter James, oil & italian wa. 23 Up. King st. Bloomsbury
Walter James, pawnbroker, 15 Thornton st. Dockhead
Walter James, surgeon, 26 Burton crescent
Walter John, boot & shoe maker, 21 Kent st. Borough
Walter John, *King's Head* P.H. 13 Gt. Ryder st. St. James's
Walter John, pawnbroker, 106 Aldersgate st. & 48 Goswell rd
Walter John Frederick, M.D. surgeon, 23 New Bridge st. Blackf
Walter John Kent, cheesemonger, 34 Lower Belgrave st
Walter Lazarus, tailor, 12 Church st. Spitalfields
Walter Michael, who. hardwrmn. 21 Fleet la. Farringdon st
Walter Richard, *King's Head tavern*, 25 Poultry
Walter Robert, brass founder, 118 Church st. Shoreditch
Walter Samuel, baker, Gibraltar row, Lower rd. Deptford
Walter Stephen, tobacconist, 2 Ridinghouse la. Langham pl
Walter Theophilus, picture dealer, 131 Curtain rd. Shoreditch
Walter Thomas, grocer, 39 Holland st. Blackfriars road
Walter Thomas, *Mitre tavern*, 38 Fish st. hill
Walter Thomas, patent nailwareh. & ironmong. 24 Walbrook
Walter Thomas Beck, pawnbroker, 17 Victoria rd. Pimlico
Walter Thomas John, grocer, 6 Turnmill st. Clerkenwell
Walter Wm. boot & shoe maker, 12 Norfolk st. Middlsx. hosp
Walter Wm. cabinet maker, 29 Tufton st. Westminster
Walter Wm. clothwkr. & packr. 56 Fore st. & 120 & 121 Lond. wll
Walter Wm. fruiterer, 32 Poland st. Oxford st
Walter Wm. *Royal Standard* P.H. 75 Drury lane
Walters Joseph & Co. machinists & trussmakers, 82 London wall & 16 Moorgate st. City
Walters Stephen & Sons, silk & velvet mnfs. 15 Wilson st. Finsbry
Walters Ann (Mrs.), midwife, 7 Lisson grove, north
Walters Daniel, silk manufacturer, 14 Wilson st. Finsbury
Walters Fredk. B. ham & beef dlr. 8 Bishopsgate st. without
Walters George, gunmaker, 7 Guildford place, Spafields
Walters Henry, bridle cutter, 3 Type st. Finsbury
Walters James, wine merchant, & *Guildhall hotel*, 32 Gresham st. & 22 King st. Cheapside
Walters John Eldad, solr. see Whitmore, Roumieu & Walters
Walters James, *Grapes* P.H. Brompton Lower grove
Walters Margaret (Mrs.), lodging house, 4 Lr. Southwick st
Walters Maurice, bootmaker, 2 Oxford st. Sydney st. Stepney
Walters Patrick Clement, tailor, 96 Gt. Portland st
Walters Stephen, solicitor, 36 Basinghall st
Walters Thomas, irish linen factor, 1 Church pas. Gresham st
Walters Walter, dairyman, 34 Northumberland st. Strand
Walters Wm. grocer, 19 Salisbury st. Lisson grove
Walters Wm. Hen. trimming manufactr. 11 Greenhill's rents
Waltham & Hill, coal mer. 19 Macclesfield st. north, City rd. & 27 Noel st. Islington
Waltham John, oilman, 5 Edward st. Wardour st. Soho
Waltham William, tailor, 9 Mercer st. Long acre
Walther & de Vos, merchants, 15 Angel ct. Throgmorton st
Walther David, bookseller, 42 Piccadilly
Walther Ferdinand E. mercht. & agt. 5 Barge yd. Bucklersbry
Walthew Fred. James & Richard, attorneys, 5 Furnival's inn
Walton Forbes & Drake, solicitors, 8 Warnford court
Walton Isaac & Co. wine & spirit merchants, 15 Mark lane
Walton & Mitchel, printers, 24 Wardour st. Soho
Walton Charles, british wine manf. see Walker & Walton
Walton Charles, grocer, 16 Rotherhithe wall
Walton Charles, ship & insur. brok. 3 Newman's ct. Cornhill
Walton Chas. solicitor, 34 Coleman st
Walton Christopher, goldsmith & jeweller, 24 Ludgate st
Walton Denys, teadealer & grocer, 51 Broad st. Bloomsbury
Walton Edmund, coach & harness mak. Duncan pl. City road
Walton Francis, shipchandler & sailmaker, 283 Wapping
Walton George, grocer, 140 Goswell st
Walton Geo. plumber & gasfitter, 5 George ter. Coml. rd. east
Walton Henry, surgeon, &c. 74 Long acre
Walton Henry H. surgeon, 6 Bernard st. Russell square, & Central London Ophthalmic Institution, 7 Everett st
Walton Henry M. importer of german & french toys & fancy goods, 191 Bishopsgate without
Walton James, bookseller, see Taylor & Walton
Walton James, grainer, 3 Russell st. Bermondsey
Walton James, grocer & tallow chandlr. 31 Pitfield st. Hoxton
Walton James, teadealer & grocer, 129 Bishopsgate without; 57 Whitechapel High st.; & 230 Poplar High st.; & Stratford broadway
Walton James, teadealer, 128 Upper Whitecross st
Walton Jas. timb. mer. Old Jamaica wf. Up. Ground st. Blkfrs
Walton John, tailor, 9 High st. Bow, Middlesex
Walton John, *Westmorland Arms* P.H. 15 Westmld. pl. City rd
Walton John Charles, engraver & printer, 4 Deptford bridge
Walton John Edridge, candle ma. 11 Duke st. Manchester sq
Walton John Whitehead, artist, 27A, Old Bond st
Walton Joseph, woollendraper, 17 Gerard st. Soho
Walton Mathias, bricklayer, Well st. Hackney
Walton Mathias, *Two Brewers & Magpie* P.H. 11 Shoreditch
Walton Philip, builder & bricklayr. 75 Cable st. St. George's ea
Walton Richard, hosier & glover, 1 Birchin lane
Walton Robert, shorthand writer, 15 Chancery lane
Walton Thomas, academy, Commercial pl. Old Kent road
Walton Thomas, shipwright & barge bldr. 2 Bermondsey wall
Walton Wm. attorney, Girdlers' hall, 39 Basinghall st
Walton Wm. beer retailer, 6 Britannia pl. Wandsworth road
Walton Wm. hop & oil merchant, see Yates, Walton & Turner
Walton Wm. imp. of foreign fancy merchandise, 160 Fleet st
Walton Wm. mason, 24 Pitt st. Fitzroy square
Walton Wm. oil & color wa. 7 King st. Lower rd. Islington
Walton Wm. solicitor, &c. 97 Wapping
Walton Wm. teadealer, &c. 72 & 73 St. George st. east
Walton Wm. Henry, master of Exchequer of Pleas, 8 Old sq
Walworth James, currier, 17 Lambeth lower marsh
Walworth Literary & Scientific Institution (John S. Noldwritt, hon. sec.), 21 Manor place, Walworth
Walwyn Richard, printer, 22 Kirby st. Hatton garden
Wand James, *Flying Horse* P.H. Mare st. Hackney
Wand Wm. tin plate worker, 181 Whitechapel road
Wandsworth Police Court, Love la. Wandsworth; hrs. 10 to 1
Wangemann Frederick, baker, 23 West Smithfield
Wanger Wm. cowkeeper, 12 Shepperton st. Islington
Wanhill John, baker, 82 Vauxhall st. Lambeth
Wanhill Wm. baker, 49 Regent st. Lambeth
Wanlace Eliz. (Mrs.), porkbut. 19 Marchmont st. Brnswk. sq
Wanlace Joseph, solicitor, 15 Colet pl. Commercial rd. east
Wanless Wm. Hen. snuff & cigar dealer, 15 Queen st. Cheapside
Wanostrocht Nicholas, portrait painter, 29 Nicholas lane
Wannell Wm. Thos. *King's Arms* P.H. 34 Surrey rw. Blkfrs. rd
Wansborough John, carver, 24 Warren st. Fitzroy sq
Wansbrough Thos. Wm. surgeon, King's rd. west, Chelsea
Wansey George, solicitor, 30 Ely pl. & 3 Moorgate st
Wansey Wm. indigo & genl. merchant, 1 Riches ct. Lime st
Want Thos. & Son, builders, King's road, St. Pancras
Want George, bricklayer, stenciller, &c. 15 Little Moorfields
Want Thos. *Bricklayers' Arms* P.H. 19 Narrow st. Limeho
Waples Elizabeth & Grace, milliners, 7 Great Portland st
Wapshott Ellen (Miss), milliner, 39 Hunter st. Brunsk. sq
Waraker Mary (Miss), stationer, 49 Albany st. Regent's pk
Waraker Thos. law stationer, 50 Chancery lane, & 35 King st. Westminster
War Office, Horse Guards; hours of business 10 to 4
Warburg John & Sons, cigar impors. & mftrs. 54 Mansell st
Warburg Marcus & Co. merchants, 4 Water la. Tower st
Warburg Carl. physician, 3 Warwick square, Kensington
Warburton Gideon & Co. ironmongers, 146 Tottenham ct. rd
Warburton Amelia (Miss), dressma. 51 Hatfield st. Blkfrs
Warburton James, stuff mfr. 3 Flying Horse ct. Gresham st
Warburton John, lunatic asylum, Bethnal house, Cambridge road, Mile end; & Whitmore road, Hoxton
Warburton Jonathan, hat manufr. 11 Castle st. Southwark
Warburton Thos. Acton, barrister, 10 Serle st. Lincoln's inn
Warcup John Barnard, ironmonger, 3 Deptford broadway
Warcup Wm. Willis, bookseller, &c. 4 Deptford broadway
Ward & Angell, leather hide & glue facs. 118 Bishopsgate st
Ward Brothers, merchants, 24 Broad st. buildings
Ward & Chambers, block & mast makers, 240 Rotherhithe
Ward Chas. & Fred. academy, 63 Gt. Titchfield st. Oxford st

Ward Elizh. & Son, cutlers, 16 Artillery st. Bishopsgate
Ward Geo. Haly & Co.printers,16 Bear alley,Farringdon st
Ward Jas. Cl. & Co.india rubber, manufrs.33 Gt. St.Helens
Ward James & Thomas, builders 11 & 12 Jewin st.; 52 Redcross st. & 198 Upper Whitecross st. St. Lukes
Ward John & Edward, cornfactors, Old Corn Exch.Mark la
Ward John & Son, builders & bricklayers, 94 Aldersgate st
Ward Nathaniel Bagshaw & Son, surgeons, 7 Wellclose sq
Ward & Peek, machine rulers, 17 Nicholl sq. Aldersgate st
Ward Rd. & Co. coach,&c. curriers,23 Brownlow st.Drury la
Ward Samuel & Co. oil, lead & color mer. 44 Up, Thames st
Ward & Scarborough,coal mers. Honduras whf.74 Bankside
Ward & Soulier,tobacco & snuff makers, see Soulier &Ward
Ward, Sturt, Sharp, &Ward,wholesale hosiers,haberdashers, & flannel men,89Wood st.Cheapside; manufactory Belper, Derbyshire
Ward Thos. & Co. booksel. & publishers, 27 Paternoster row
Ward Wm. & Joseph whipmakers,1St.George's rd.Southwk
Ward Ann (Mrs.), dining rooms, 3 Silver st Wood st
Ward Catherine(Mrs.),fancy wa.12Low.Belgravepl.Pimlico
Ward Charles, coach ironmonger, 164 Drury lane
Ward Charles, fruiterer & greengrocer, 190 Lambeth walk
Ward Charles, manufacturer of bent timber, & dealer in lancewood spars, 54 Parker st. Drury lane
Ward Charles, surgeon, 19 Newgate st
Ward Charles, tailor, 3 Snow's fields, Bermondsey
Ward Charles, tobacconist, 2 Gt.Russell st. Covent Garden & 146 Leadenhall st
Ward Charles, wine merchant, 1 Chapel st.west, Mayfair
Ward Charles, jun. coach lace ma. 53 Parker st. Drury la
Ward Chas.S. bricklayer, &c.96 & 97Philipps st.Kingslndrd
Ward Chas.Wm.*Rose& Punch Bowl*,P.H.4Redm.row Ml.ed
Ward Clement T. painter & glazier, 32 Tavistock st.Cov.gar
Ward Cornelius, musical instrument maker, & patentee of the newly invented flute, & patentee of the newly invented drums, 36 Great Titchfield st. Oxford st
Ward Ebenezer, academy, 12 Upper Barnsbury st.Islington
Ward Ebenezer, academy, 20 Cloudesley sq. Islington
Ward Elizabeth (Mrs.), butcher, 26 Borough road
Ward Elizabeth (Mrs.), oil & color wareho. 152 Goswell st
Ward Essington, gold swivel, earring-joint & wire maker, 10 Lower Charles st. Northampton sq
Ward Francis, chemist, 14 Grosvenor st. west, Eaton sq
Ward Fs.*White Hart tav.* 17Up. Glos'ter pl.King's rd.Chels
Ward Francis, *Masons' Arms* P.H. 18 Maddox st. Regent st
Ward Fred. H. oil & colorman, 3 Arbour ter. Commer. rd. ea
Ward Fred. Wm. surgeons' inst. maker, 3 Athol pl. New rd
Ward George, boot & shoe maker, 5 Long lane, Smithfield
Ward George, butcher, 23 Jubilee place, Chelsea
Ward George, cabinet ma.9 Gibraltar walk,Bethnal green rd
Ward George, fruiterer, 7 Windmill st. Finsbury
Ward George, glass & china dealer, 54 Fore st. Limehouse
Ward George, lighterman, 67 Lower Thames st
Ward George, oil & italian wareho. 4 Store st. Bedford sq
Ward George James, oilman, 49 Myddelton st. Clerkenwell
Ward George Raphael, artist, 31 Fitzroy sq
Ward Hanh. (Mrs.), meat salesw. 10 Rose st. Newgate mkt
Ward Harriet (Mrs.), tobacconist, 69 Theobald's road
Ward Henry, attorney, 51 Lincoln's inn fields
Ward Henry, fish salesman, 31 St. Mary at hill
Ward Henry, printer, 8 Upper Dorset place, Clapham rd
Ward Henry, tailor, 62 Castle st. Leicester sq
Ward Henry, tailor, 68 Princes st. Leicester sq
Ward Henry Frederick, tailor, 100 Long lane, Bermondsey
Ward Henry Pilkington, chemist, 44 Marshall st. Golden sq
Ward Henry Wm. wine, spirit, & beer mer. 36 Seething la
Ward Isaac, chocolate maker, New court, Old Bailey
Ward Isaac, oilman, 17 Richmond place, East st.Walworth
Ward James, R.A. artist, 6 Newman st. Oxford st
Ward James, boot & shoe maker, 14 Brick la. Spitalfields
Ward James, cabinet maker, 3 Albert place, City road
Ward James, coachmak. 31 Southampton mews, Euston sq
Ward James, *George* P.H. 1 George st. Blackfriars rd
Ward James, glass & lead mercht. 49 London rd. Southwk
Ward James, grocer, &c. 25 Great Chart st. Hoxton
Ward James, grocer, 48 Trinity st. Rotherhithe
Ward James, grocer, &c. 35 Worship st. Finsbury
Ward James, hearthstone & bath brick ma.New whf.Whitefrs
Ward James, lapidary, 1 Wardour st. Soho
Ward James, meat salesman, 4 Newgate market
Ward James, potato salesman, 99 Golden lane, St. Luke's
Ward James, solicitor, 39 Essex st. Strand
Ward James, staffordshire warehouse, 337 Rotherhithe st
Ward James, wax & tallow chandler, 2 Oxford market
Ward James, workg.tinman & gasfitter,80High st.Camden tn
Ward Joan (Mrs.), ladies' school, King's row, Knightsbridge
Ward John, bellows maker, Upper North st. Whitechapel rd
Ward John, bootmaker, 12 St. James's walk, Clerkenwell
Ward John, butcher, 82 Aldersgate st
Ward John, coffee rooms, 2 Upper Rupert st. Soho
Ward John, corndealer, &c. 1 Vere st. Clare market
Ward John, fruiterer, 12 Grosvenor market
Ward John, grocer & cheesem. 22 Queen st. Low. rd. Islingtn
Ward John, hairdresser, 58 Kingsland road
Ward John, leather factor, see Tanner & Ward
Ward John, operative chemist & druggist, manufacturer of matheml. electri. & philosoph. apparts. 79 Bishopsg.within
Ward John, shipsmith, 6 Lower east Smithfield
Ward John, staymaker, 2 Cambridge road, Mile end
Ward John, tailor, 14 Devonshire place, Edgware road
Ward John, tallow chandler, 14 Wilsted st. Somers town
Ward John, upholsterer, &c. 2 Saville row, Walworth road
Ward John Brocks, solicitor, 185 Bishopsgate without
Ward John Leveson Gower, barrister, 22 Lincoln's inn fields, & 10 New square, Lincoln's inn
Ward John Wallis, furniture brok. 26 Penton row, Walw. rd
Ward Jonathan (Mrs.), milliner, 17 Mount st. Lambeth
Ward Joseph, butcher, see Bryan & Ward
Ward Joseph, fishmonger, 18 Eyre st. hill, Hatton garden
Ward Joseph, miller, 12 Mark lane
Ward Joseph, shoemaker, 57 Chapel st. Pentonville
Ward Kyrle, refiner&dlr.in gilders'mats.2Lit.Comptn.st.Soho
Ward Lenton, butcher, 87 Drummond st. Euston square
Ward Martha (Miss), ladies' school, 21 & 22 Trinity sq. Sthwk
Ward Martin, merchant, 142 Cheapside
Ward Mary (Mrs.), boarding house, 7 Somerset st. Aldgate
Ward Mary (Mrs.), butcher, 21 East st. Walworth rd
Ward Mary (Mrs.), ladies' school, 16 Bethnal green, ea. side
Ward Mary (Mrs.), toydlr. 3 Foxley rd. Camberwell new rd
Ward Ogier, surgeon, 21 Lower Phillimore pl. Kensington
Ward Page, laceman, 61 Piccadilly
Ward Philip, newsvender, 4 Denmark place, Camberwell
Ward Richard, grocer, 88 New road, Sloane st
Ward Richard, iron mer. Union whf. 44 Narrow st.Limehous
Ward Richard, ribbon manufactr. see Hood, Ward & Hood
Ward Richard, shoemaker, 19 High st. Newington butts
Ward Richard, watchmaker, 27 Banner st. St. Luke's
Ward Richard, wholesale & for exportation, saddler, &c. 29 Queen st. Cheapside
Ward Richard, *Yorkshire Grey* P.H. 1 Gray's inn terrace
Ward Richard Danvers, solicitor, 12 Clement's inn
Ward Richard George, meat salesman, 14 Newgate market
Ward Robert, bricklayer, 7 Woolmore st. East India road
Ward Robert, fringemaker, 10 Windmill st.Tottenham ct.rd
Ward Robert, timber merchant, 8 Oxford st. & Western wharf, Edward st. Regent's park
Ward Robt. J. *Britannia* P.H. 135 Southwark bridge road
Ward Sam. boot & shoe makr. 29 Grenville st. Somers town
Ward Sam. carpent. & undertak.22 Lit. Alie st.Goodman's fi
Ward Sam. lasting & shalloon manufacturer, 7 Lillypot lane
Ward Sam. warehouse for hardware, cutlery, british plate & britannia metal, glass & cabinet wk. 18 Lowther arcade
Ward Stephen, chandler's shop, 29 Church rd. Comrcl. rd. ea
Ward Stephen, letterpress printer, 88 Wardour st. Soho
Ward Stephen Hen. surgeon, 35 Finsbury circus
Ward Susan (Mrs.), furn. broker, 25 Barrett's ct. Oxford st
Ward Thos. architect & surveyor, 95 Kingsland rd. west side
Ward Thomas, button & trimming seller, 386 Oxford st
Ward Thomas, glass stainer, 67 Frith st. Soho
Ward Thomas, importer of french prints, 103 Strand
Ward Thomas, importer of cigars, &c. 16 John st. Minories
Ward Thomas, mercht. 25 New City chambers, Bishopsgate
Ward Thomas, pork butcher, 136 Union st. Borough
Ward Thomas, *Royal Oak* P.H. 1 Regent st. Horseferry rd
Ward Thomas, shipowner, 2 Cock hill, Ratcliff
Ward Thomas, stock & shirt collar ma.62Bread st.Cheapside
Ward Thomas, turner, &c. 34 Wellington place, Stepney
Ward Thomas, writer & grainer, 48 Bedford st. Covent grdn
Ward Tryman, fishmonger, 87 Leather lane, Holborn
Ward Wm. ale & porter merchant, see Crimp & Ward
Ward Wm. baker, 10 Horsley st. Walworth common
Ward Wm. baker, 10 St. Alban's terrace, Vauxhall bridge rd
Ward Wm. barrister, 1 Plowden builbings, Temple
Ward Wm. beer retailer, 43 East st. Walworth
Ward Wm. boot & shoe maker, Grove st. Deptford
Ward Wm. bootmaker, 1 New st. Kennington road
Ward Wm. bottle warehouse, 1 Church row, Aldgate
Ward Wm. builder & undertaker, 35 Red Lion st. Holborn
Ward Wm. butcher, 3 Foregate, Clement's inn, Strand
Ward Wm. dyer & scourer, 8 Queen st. Golden square
Ward Wm. fruiterer, 23 North Audley st
Ward Wm. grocer, 169 Lambeth walk

Ward Wm. grocer, 40 Henry st. east, Avenue road
Ward Wm. hairdresser, 48 Bethnal green road
Ward Wm. hemp, flax & cane mer. 25 Lit. Guildford st. Boro'
Ward Wm. house painter, &c. 29 Duke st. Stamford st
Ward Wm. japanner, 40 Garden row, London road, Borough
Ward Wm. jobmaster, 3 Blenheim mews, Blenheim st. Oxfd st
Ward Wm. *Jolly Sailor* P.H. 7 Cobourg pl. Low. rd. Rotherhithe
Ward Wm. land aurveyor, 46 Leicester square
Ward Wm. pipemaker, Davis place, Chelsea
Ward Wm. pork butcher, 5 Broomfield place, Deptford
Ward Wm. printing ink maker, 25 Gt. New st. Fetter lane
Ward Wm. *Queen Charlotte* P.H. Church st. Deptford
Ward Wm. shirt and stock maker, 10 Bishopsgate within
Ward Wm. who. shoe & clog manufr. 161 Church st. Shoreditch
Ward Wm. stove & range ma. 14 Tottenham st. Tottenh. ct. rd
Ward Wm. tobacco pipema. 1 Brewer's court, Bedfordbury
Ward Wm. turner, 29 Paradise st. Finsbury
Ward Wm. wharfinger, imp. & shipper of all kinds of fire & bldg. bricks, tiles & cmt. &c. Honduras wharf, 74 Bankside
Ward Wm. window blind maker, 21 Amelia st. Walworth
Wardale Geo. Harriott & Co. italian wareho. 38 St. Mary axe
Warde Ambrose, who. druggist, see Gale, Baker, Warde & Co
Wardell John Lloyd & Co. wine & gen. merchts. 7 Billiter st
Wardell George, *Swan tavern*, Clapham road, Stockwell
Wardell John, grocer & store shipper, 9 Wapping wall
Wardell Joseph, shoemaker, see Cooper & Wardell
Wardell Joseph, cab proprietor, 35 Hindon st. Pimlico
Wardell Robert, cooper, 16 Theobald's road, Red Lion sq.
Wardell Wm. wine, spirit & ale mer. see Field, Wardell & Co
Wardell Wm. W. architect & surveyor, 27 Bishopsgate within
Warden Elizabeth (Mrs.), coffee rooms, 18 Carlisle st. Soho
Warden James, butcher, 26 Exmouth st. Spafields
Warden William, coffee rooms, 5 Broad st. Golden sq
Warder & Horsburg, rout furnishers, 62 Gt. Marylebone st
Warder Robert, fruiterer, 2 Grove terrace, Brompton road
Warder William, fruiterer, 61 Great Marylebone st
Wardlaw James, baker, 2 South pl. Camberwell New road
Wardle Henry & Thos. silk manufacturers, 121 Cheapside
Ward's patent washing & cleansing powder, supplied wholesale by Abraham Taw, 72 Houndsditch
Wardman Thos. Jas. *Geo. IV.* P.H. Brunswick st. Hackney rd
Wardrop & Ewart, madeira merchs. 33 Clement's la. City
Wardrop James, surgeon, 2 Charles st. St. James's square
Wardroper William, surgeon, 45 Welbeck st. Cavendish sq
Ware Elizabeth & Co. outfitters, 26 Davies st. Berkeley sq
Ware John & Thomas, attorneys, 98 Kingsland road
Ware Benjamin, chemist, 10 Dorset st. Portman square
Ware Bethel, straw bonnet warehouse, 217 Tottenham ct. rd
Ware Bethel, straw & tuscan manufr. see Wilson, Ware & Co
Ware Edward, tailor, 17 Holland st. Brixton road
Ware George, solicitor, 33 Blackman st. Borough
Ware James, grocer & cheesemonger, 102 Union st. Borough
Ware John, baker, 20 Ivy la. & 6 Torrington pl. Torrington sq
Ware John, *Lord Duncan* P.H. New cross road, Deptford
Ware John, vestry clerk of Shoreditch, 97 Kingsland road
Ware John, wheelwright, 14 Glasshouse yd. Aldersgate st
Ware Joseph, painter, 45 King st. Soho
Ware Martin, oculist & surgeon, 51 Russell square
Ware Patrick John, *Three Kings* P.H. Clerkenwell close
Ware Samuel, solicitor, see Kerly & Ware
Ware Sarah (Mrs.), commercial coffee rooms, 42 Minories
Ware Sarah (Mrs.), tobacconist, 8 Cumberld. pl. Nwngtn. bts
Ware Thomas, painter & glazier, 33 Lit. Gulfrd. st. Brunswk. sq
Ware Thos. super. registr. Shoreditch dist. 98 Kingsland road
Ware William, corn chandler, 2 Lambeth walk
Ware William, fruiterer, 11 North pl. Balls pond road
Wareham Joseph, painter, 32 Baldwin's gardens leather la
Wareham Laurence, pianoforte silker, &c. 38 Up. Rathbone pl
Warfolk Mary (Mrs.), lodging house, 30 Duke st. St. James's
Warin James, chemist & druggist, 41 Blackman st. Boro'
Waring Charles, coffee rooms, 188 Upper Thames st
Waring Jasper, merchant, see Williams & Waring
Waring John, prof. of music, 7 Gt. Charlotte st. Blackfrs. rd
Waring Peter, who. wire worker, 15 Little Chapel st. Soho
Waring Thomas, corn & coal merch. 8 Blandford st. Portman sq
Waring Thomas Albert, architect, 20 Pratt st. Lambeth
Warkminster Hermann, coffee rooms, 178 Shadwell High st
Warland, Condron & Co. crape & silk manuf. 17 Gutter lane
Warlters, Lovejoy & Son, auctioneers, 55 Chancery lane
Warlters John, auctioneer, 13 Claremont row, Barnsbury rd
Warman George, butcher, 1 St. George's market, Borough
Warman George, teadealer, 60 Commercial rd. Lambeth
Warman James, fruiterer, 33 Clark st. Stepney
Warman John, upholsterer, 4 Gt. St. Thomas Apostle
Warman Robert, map colorer, 4 New st. Bishopsgate
Warman William, stationer, &c. 21 Cross st. Islington
Warmington Edward, grocer, &c. 24 Regent st. Horsefry. rd
Warmington Henry, tailor, Hill st. Walworth road
Warmington Jas. hide & skin salesmn. Bermondsey skin mkt
Warmington John grocer, 10 Bridge st. Southwark
Warmington Joseph, butcher, Leadenhall market
Warmisham Elizh. (Mrs.), straw hat ma. 12 Fort st. Spital sq
Warmisham Samuel, scale maker, 11 Fort st. Spital square
Warmisham William, tailor, 35 Up. Edmund st. King's cross
Warmsley Thomas, corn chandler, 3 Hayfield pl. Mile end
Warmsley William, baker, 12 Diamond row, Stepney green
Warnar Henry, dining & coffee rooms, 30 North Audley st
Warne Ann (Mrs.), carpen. & builder, 8 Mill st. Hanover sq.
Warne Edmund, builder, 41 & 42 Lisle st. Leicester sq
Warne Edmund, jun. plumber, painter, &c. 5 Gerrard st. Soho
Warne James, beer retailer, 16 Manor place, Walworth rd
Warne Samuel, soda water manufr. 122 Blackfriars road
Warne Thomas, army & navy contractor, 9 Henrietta st. Covent garden, & 165 New Bond st
Warne Thos. beer engine maker, 113 Blackfriars road
Warne Thomas, boot & shoe maker, 3 & 4 Leather lane
Warne Thomas, silk dyer, 32 Great Sutton st. Clerkenwell
Warneford Richard, solicitor, 6 Symond's inn, Chancery la
Warner & Barclay, family & dispensing chemists & wholesale druggists, 55 Fore st. City
Warner John & Son, brush, & combmakers, 52 Tottenham ct. rd
Warner John & Sons, brassfounders, 8 Jewin crescent
Warner & Warner, seedsmen & florists, 28 Cornhill; warehouse, 3 & 4 Laurence Pountney lane, Cannon st
Warner Alfred F. tinplate worker, 25 Union st. Bishopsgate
Warner Ann (Mrs.), *Bedford Hotel*, Gt. Piazza, Covent gdn
Warner Ben. Jno. secret springer, 28 Wynyatt st. Goswell rd
Warner Charles, gasfitter, 2 Artillery st. Bishopsgate
Warner Chas. *Coachmakers' Arms* P.H. 8 Belgrv. mws. Blgr. sq
Warner Chas. *Sawyers' Arms* P.H. 20 Marylebone lane
Warner Chas. tobacconist, 127 Brick lane, Spitalfields
Warner Daniel, bookslr. & stanr. 9 Shepperton pl. New northrd
Warner Edward, patent lamp ma. & gasfitter, 142 Minories
Warner George, oilman, 51 Cornwall road Lambeth
Warner Hannah (Mrs.), bookseller, 43 Chapel st. Pentonville
Warner Henry fruiterer, 27 Jewin st. Cripplegate
Warner Jas. baker, 49 Castle st. Leicester square
Warner James, carpenter & undertaker, 6 Ivy lane, Hoxton
Warner James, law stationer, 9 Cusitor st. Chancery lane
Warner James, tailor, 6 Market st. Fitzroy market
Warner John, barrister, 11 King's Bench walk, Temple
Warner John, cart grease ma. Belle isle, Maiden la. King's cr
Warner John, livery stables, 7 Lit. Torrington st. Torrington sq
Warner John, surgeon, Hertford road, Kingsland
Warner Lawrance, grocer, 76 St. George's road, Southwark
Warner Mary (Miss), milliner, 272 Strand
Warner Mary (Mrs.), basket ma. 10 Tavistock rw. Cov. grdn
Warner Patience (Mrs.), china & glass ware. 3 Chelsea mrkt
Warner Rebecca (Mrs.), *Grapes* P.H. 4 Rose st. Covent grdn
Warner Richard, potato salesman, Scovell's wf. Tooley st
Warner Robert, house agent, 17 Park place, Mile end
Warner Robert, wheelwright, 5 West st. Commercl. rd. Pimlico
Warner Sarah (Mrs.), milliner, &c. 59 Margaret st. Cavendish sq
Warner Stephen, bookseller, 6 Shepherdess walk, City rd
Warner Thomas, cutler, 25 Sackville st. Piccadilly
Warner Thomas, grocer &c. Stratford, Essex
Warner Wm. basket maker, 7 Leg alley, Long acre
Warner Wm. *Cock* P.H. Church st. Hackney
Warner Wm. painter, 22 Brook st. New road
Warner Wm. seal engraver, 22 New North st. Red Lion sq
Warner Wm. tailor, 59 Margaret st. Cavendish sq
Warner Wm. tailor, 28 Upper Seymour st. Euston sq
Warner Wm. Robt. seal engraver, 55 Rupert st. Haymarket
Warnett John, bricklayer, 15 Cornwall road, Lambeth
Warr Francis, stationer & printer, 63 High Holborn, & letter press printer, 3 Red Lion passage, Red Lion square
Warr Henry Wm. bricklayer, &c. 12 Ring cross, Holloway
Warr John, cattle salesman, 37 West Smithfield
Warr Thomas, baker, 165 Hoxton Old town
Warr Thomas, china & glass dlr. 31 Surrey pl. Old Kent rd
Warr Wm. coal, &c. dealer, 34 Lower Sloane st. Chelsea
Warran Robert, french polisher, 2 City ter. Old st. road
Warrand Alexander, solicitor, 6 Skinner st. Snow hill
Warre Brothers, merchants, 32 Fenchurch st
Warre James & Co. insurancer brokers, 32 Fenchurch st
Warre Wm. Henry, pawnbroker, see Muncaster & Warre
Warren Dan. & Thos. I. india agts. & mer. 75 Old Broad st. City
Warren Caroline E. & M. A. locksmiths, &c. 8 Marshall st. Gldn. sq
Warren & Falconer, saddlers & harness maks. 54 Sloane sq
Warren & Fowler, pawnbrokers, 76 Old st. St. Luke's
Warren & Leachman, sugar brokers, 15 Commcl. sale rooms
Warren & Spencer, linendrapers, 7 Commercial pl. Old Kent rd

Warren, Russell & Wright, proprietors of the original & celebrated ROBT.WARREN's japan liquid blacking; also manufacturers of writing inks & harness blacking, 30 Strand
Warren & Withers, who. grocers, &c. 96 Houndsditch
Warren Adolphus, solicitor, 106 Shoe lane, Fleet st
Warren Ambrose Wm. jun. printer, 16 Arabella row, Pimlico
Warren Augustus, solicitor, see Bray, Warren & Harding
Warren Chas. grocer & cheesmgr. 24 Chalton st. Somers town
Warren Edward, coal merchant, 13 George st. Adelphi
Warren Edward, grocer, 4 Dean's buildings Commrcl. road
Warren Edwin, plumber, &c. 58 Henry st. east, Avenue road
Warren Eleanor (Mrs.), fan. repository, 8 Albion pl. Hollowy. rd
Warren Elizh. (Mrs.), berlin wa. 2 Manor pl. Holloway
Warren Esther (Mrs.), coffee rooms, 21 Seymour st. Euston sq
Warren Geo. fan. stationer & perfumer, 12 Lamb's Condt. st
Warren Geo. pianoforte ma. 23 Chichester pl. Wandsworth rd
Warren Francis, wine merchant, see Chapman & Warren
Warren Henry, stationer & news agt. 18 London st. Fitzroy sq
Warren James, agent to J.&J. Grant, distillers, 4 Walbrook
Warren James, carpenter, 4 Bartholomew ter. York st. City rd
Warren James, com. agt. & scotch whiskey impr. 4 Walbrook
Warren James, carver, 20 Sussex st. Tottenham court road
Warren James, grocer, 15 Princes road, Notting hill
Warren James, hairdresser, 7 Cumberland rw. Walworth rd
Warren James, optician, 335 Oxford st
Warren Jane (Miss), ladies' school, 5 Deptford High st
Warren John, carpenter, 9 Arundel pl. Coventry st
Warren John, cattle salesman, 37 Smithfield st
Warren John, dentist, 32 George st. Hanover square
Warren John, *General Townshend* P.H. 231 Oxford st
Warren John, pianoforte ma. 1 Liverpool st. Bishopsgate
Warren John, tailor, 10 Up. Southampton st. Pentonville
Warren John, *White Horse & Cross Keys* P.H. 72 Goswell st
Warren John William, packing case maker, 8 Stationers' ct
Warren Joseph, job master, South end, Kensington New town
Warren Peter John, boot & shoe maker, 110 Poplar High st
Warren Richard, *Union tavern* P.H. 11 John st. Oxford st
Warren Robert, coachmaker, see Nurse & Warren
Warren Samuel, barrister, 12 King's Bench walk, Temple
Warren Samuel, grocer, &c. 1 Dean st. south, Borough
Warren Samuel, tailor, 35 George st. Portland place
Warren Stephen, ham & beef shop, 3 Albion place, King's crs
Warren Thomas, appraiser, 77 Oxford st
Warren Thomas, builder, 11 Cross st. Newington
Warren Thomas, dining rooms, 11 Grove terrace, Bayswater
Warren Thomas, grocer, &c. 3 Commercial pl. Kentish town
Warren Thomas, tailor, 36 Arundel st. Strand
Warren Thomas, upholstr. cabinet ma. & undtr. 77 Oxford st
Warren William, blind ma. 11 Chapel st. Church st. Islington
Warren William, coffee rooms, 77 Charlotte st. Portland pl
Warren William, gas fitter, 2 Windmill row, Kennington gr
Warren William, tailor, 62 South Molton st. Bond st
Warren William, jun. butcher, 16 Down st. Piccadilly
Warren Willam, sen. butcher, 404 Strand
Warren William Joseph, *Warren's hotel*, 1 Regent st
Warren Zachariah, carpenter & builder, 7 Wilson st. Finsbury
Warrick John & Son, drug merchants, &c. 3 Garlick hill
Warrier Joseph, wireworker & bird dlr. 14 London rd. Boro'
Warriner Robert, upholsterer, 9 Whitmore road, Hoxton
Warriner Wm. miniature frame ma. 16 Charlotte st. Fitzroy sq
Warrington Edwd. Dore, timber broker, 15 New city chambrs
Warrington John, *Hope & Anchor* P.H. 14 Hereford st. Lisson gr
Warrington Michael, surgeon, 15 Blackmoor st. Drury lane
Warrington Thos. fruit salesman, Covent garden fruit market
Warrington William, glass stainer, 42 Upp. Berkeley st. west
Warrington William, plumber, Deptford green
Warrington William, seal & copper plate engraver & printer to her Majesty, 27 Strand
Warry George, solicitor, 7 New inn, Strand
Warry Robert, fruiterer, 2 Dean st. Holborn
Warry Wm. Keen, musical inst. mak. 18 Up. John st. Liverpl. rd
Warter Joseph & Sons, who. cheesemongers, 105 Boro' High st
Warter Henry De Grey, solicitor, 1 Carey st. Lincoln's inn
Warth Charles, teadealer & grocer, 1 North place, Lambeth
Warth Joseph, teadealer & grocer, 3 Baker's row, Walwth. rd
Warth Wm. W. linendraper, silk mercer & hosier, 166 Oxford st
Wartnaby Joseph, ins. agt. 2 Adam's ct. Old Broad st. & Lloyd's
Warton Charles, auctioneer & surveyor, 38 Threadneedle st
Warton Matthew, district surveyor, 29 Spital square
Warton Richard, plumber, &c. 13 Belmont ter. Wandswth. rd
Warton Robert, deputy district surveyor, 64 Old st. road
Warton Robt. surveyor, 6 Collingwood pl. Broad st. Ratcliff
Warton Wm. Henry, solicitor, 3 Crown ct. Threadneedle st
Warwick & Cheltenham Railway (Henry Cassin, sec.), 3 Church court, Old Jewry
Warwick Ann (Mrs.), *Queen's Head* P.H. 199½ Bermondsey st
Warwick Benj. goldsmith, jeweller & engrav. 124 Regent st
Warwick Chas. gauze mfr. see Ovington, Warwick & Ovingtons'
Warwick Christopher, bookbinder, 19 Roll's bdg. Fetter lane
Warwick George, engrav. & printer, see Hartley, Warwick & Co
Warwick James, academy, 27 Hampton st. Walworth rd
Warwick John, grocer & teadealer, 22 Chapel st. Somers tn
Warwick John, merchant, 10 Carpenter's bldgs. London wall
Warwick Jn. Edington, naturalist, 23 New st. Kenningtn. rd
Warwick Joseph, fringe manufr. see Katterns & Warwick
Warwick Mary Ann (Mrs.), fruiterer, 8 Gilbert st. Clare market, & potato saleswoman, Clare market
Warwick Robt. Erlam, grocer, &c. 6 Broadway, Ludgatehill
Warwick Stephen, sealma. & jeweller, 1 Northamptn sq. Clkwl
Warwick Thomas, dairyman, 10 Church row, Aldgate
Warwick Thomas, grocer, 15 Cross st. Newington butts
Warwick Thomas, hairdresser, 11 Motcomb st. Belgrave sq
Warwick Thomas, saddler, 5 James pl. Holloway rd
Wase William, butcher, 177 Goswell st
Washbourne Hen. bookseller, 18 New Bridge st. Blackfriars
Washington & Daviss, silk manufs. 14 Milk st. Cheapside
Washington Charlotte (Mrs.), grocer, 136 Golden la. St. Luke's
Washington George, oilman, 122 Whitechapel rd
Washington George, who. tea & coffee dlr. 3 Howford bldgs
Washington Jas. oil & colorman, 3 Clare st. Clare market
Washington John Power, *Black Bull* P.H. 6 Thomas st. Brick la
Wasmuth Elizh. (Mrs.), *Waterman's Arms* P.H. 261 Wappg
Wasp John, bootmaker, 20 St. Martin's ct. St. Martin's lane
Wass Charles W. artist, 1A, Adelphi terrace
Wass Robert, manufacturer of the celebrated white almond soap, 51 King William st. City
Wassell Joseph, pawnbroker, &c. 9 Pickett st
Wastall Wm. tailor, 11 Michael's grove, Brompton
Wastell Joseph, silver piercer, 2 Gee st. Goswell st
Wastell Wm. *White Lion*, P. H. 37 Fashion st. Spitalfields
Wastie Henry, surgeon & chemist, 2 Kennington cross
Wastie James, butcher, 26 Beckford row, Walworth rd
Watchman newspaper office, 161 Fleet st
Watchhorn H. J. *Coach & Horses* P.H. High st. Kensington
Watchhorn Jn. Hn. *New Dover Cstl.* P.H. 53 A, Brdg. rd. Lbth
Watchorn Francis, paintr. & decoratr. 6 Brunswk. ter. Dovr. rd
Waterfall Charles, umbrella maker, 47 Newington causeway
Waterfield Wm. mat maker, 42 Tabernacle walk, Finsbury
Waterford & Kilkenny Railway Company (T. Prosser, sec.), 34 Broad street buildings
Waterford, Wexford, Wicklow & Dublin Railway, 449 Strand
Waterford Robert Wm. gen. dlr. 18 Fredrck. pl. Newingtn. butts
Waterhouse, Hatfield & Sansom, Sheffield plate warehouse, 4 Bolt court, Fleet st
Waterhouse George, watch & clock manufacturer & importer of geneva lunette glasses, 55 Rupert st. Haymarket; & at 4 Rue Kleberg, Geneva
Waterhouse Jacob, butcher, 36 George st. New Kent road
Waterhouse John, law stationer, 12 Carey st. Lincoln's inn
Waterhouse Joseph, cabinet maker, 83 White Lion st. Pentvl
Waterhouse Richard, baker, 4 King's road east, Chelsea
Waterhouse Thomas, painter, 1 & 2 Star st. Edgware road
Waterloo & Atlas Omnibus Off. 19 Nw. Church st. w. Edgw. rd
Waterloo Bridge Co. (Geo. Powell, clerk), 8 Beaufort bldgs
Waterloo Subscription Office, see National Debt off.; 10 to 3
Waterlow James & Sons, law stationers, letter press & lithographic printers, 24 Birchin lane, 66 London wall, & 49 Parliament st
Waterlow Charles William, builder & manufactr. of sashes, doors & shopfronts to the trade, 121 Bunhill row
Waterlow James, law stationer, see Culsha & Waterlow
Waterlow Sydney, merchant, 7 King st. Finsbury
Waterlow Thomas, fruit salesman, Spitalfields market
Waterlow Walter, law stationer, 7 Cutchill pl. Hoxton
Waterman's Hall (John Banyon, clerk), 18 St. Mary at hill
Waterman's Steam Packet Co. Adelphi pier, Geo. st. Adelphi
Waterman, Ellerby & Co. hop merchants & importers of isinglass, 10 & 11 Wellington chambers, London bridge
Waterman, Wright & Kingsford, solicitors, 23 Essex st. Strand
Waterman Charles, cutler, 34 Meredith st. Clerkenwell
Waterman James, builder, 3 Winsley st. Oxford st
Waterman Jas. builder & ho. agent. 8 Edward st. Hmpstd. rd
Waterman James, hosier, glover, &c. 59 Threadneedle st
Waterman John, ladies' shoemaker, 54 Wardour st. Soho
Waterman J. lcksm. & bellh. Williams mews, Mary st. Rgts. pk
Waterman Richard, turner, 79 Leonard st. Shoreditch
Waterman Wm. bricklayer, &c. 8 Mansion ho. st. Kenningtn. rd
Waters Henry & George, grocers, 2 Southampton pl. Nine Elms
Waters John & Edwin, yarn spinners, 57 Wood st. & Manchstr
Waters Jonas & Sons, wine coopers & wine merchants, 1 & 2 Arthur st. west, London bridge

Waters Samuel Reeve & Son, tailors,5 Coventry st.Haymkt
Waters & Steel,whrfngrs.& flour factors,8 Holland st.Blckfrs
Waters Thos. Methold & Co.wine & gen. mrchts. 106 Fench.st
Waters Ann M.(Mrs.),servants'reg.off.9 Park st.Up st.Islgtn
Waters Charles, coal dealer,14 Stephen st.Tottenham ct. rd
Waters Charles Henry, picture dealer,26 Queen's rw.Pmlco
Waters David, ironmong. 17 Colonnade, Brunswick square
Waters Edmund Thos.jun.stockbro.1 Warnford ct.& stock ex
Waters Frederick, cheesemonger & porkman, 274 High Holborn, & 60½ Goswell road
Waters George, grocer, Hughes fields, Deptford
Waters George Wm. tanner, see Jones & Waters
Waters Henry, shirt maker, see Capper & Waters
Waters James, linendraper see Collins & Waters
Waters James, lithographer, 5 Sambrook court
Waters James, lodging house, 11 Craven st. Strand
Waters John, accordion dealer, 4 Saville place, Lambeth
Waters John, physician, 2 South crescent, Bedford square
Waters John, sail cloth fact. 2 Sampson's gardens, Wapping
Waters John, shipping butcher, 85 Wapping wall
Waters Margt.(Mrs.),*King's Arms* P.H.43Parker st.Drury la
Waters Martha (Mrs.) lace & millinery wareho. 3 Ebury st
Waters Robert, baker, 197 Sloane st. Knightsbridge
Waters Robert, gasfitter, 51 Baldwin's gardens, Leather lane
Waters Thomas, tea & coffee dealer, see Baldwin & Waters
Waters William, baker, 16 Tysoe st. Exmouth st
Waters William, cattle salesman, 17 West Smithfield
Waters Wm. carpenter & undertaker, 12 Bridge st. Southwk
Waters William Richd. artist, 67 Castle st. east, Oxford st
Waters Joseph John, tobacconist,233 Poplar High st
Waterston Wm. accountant & actuary, 37 Moorgate st
Waterson Wm. cabinetmaker,2A, Norfolk st.Middlesex hosp
Waterworth Geo.& Wm. comb manuf. 2 Bishopsgate within
Waterworth & Hicks, surgeons, 4 High st. Newington butts
Waterworth Charles, surgeon, 5 Bengal pl. New Kent road
Waterworth John, plumber, 171 Bishopsgate without
Waterworth David, bootmaker, 6 Stepney rents, Hackney rd
Waterworth Wm. plumber, &c. 16 Wormwood st. Bishopsgt
Watford Edward, plasterer, 5 West place, City road
Watford John, butcher, 26 Windmill st. Finsbury
Wathen George Henry, architect, 12 Regent st
Wathen John Beardmore, solicitor, 28 St. Swithin's lane
Wathen Josiah Iles, solicitor, 47 Bedford square
Watherston & Brogden, who. jewellers,16Henrta. st.Cov.gar
Watherston James Henderson (exor. of John R. Cassell), pawnbroker, 155 Brick lane, Spitalfields
Watkin Mary (Mrs.), dairy, 4 Sugar loaf ct. Leadenhall st
Watkin Robert, carrot salesman, Borough market
Watkins & Hill, opticians & philosophical instrument makers, 5 Charing cross
Watkins & Hooper, attorneys, 11 Sackville st. Piccadilly
Watkins & Hope, tea brokers, 133 Fenchurch st
Watkins Sarah & Co. tailors, 17 Cork st. Bond st
Watkins Thomas & Son, button & trimming sellers, 133 Regent st
Watkins Wm. & Elizh.bootmakers,17Thornton st. Dockhead
Watkins & Williams, fishmongers, 99 Jermyn st
Watkins Alexander, surgeon, &c. 34 High st. Marylebone
Watkins Alfred, watch maker, 120 St. John st. road
Watkins Benjamin, dairy, 26 Gt. Crown ct. Little Pulteny st
Watkins Benjamin, lodging house, 14 Queen st. Soho
Watkins Catherine (Mrs.), haberdasher,12 Lower rd.Islngtn
Watkins Charles, beer retailer, Orchard place, Blackwall
Watkins Christr. Thomas, pewterer,69 Freeschool st.Hrslydn
Watkins Daniel, copper pl. printer, see Horwood & Watkins
Watkins Daniel, surgeon, 6 John st. Titchfield ter. Regt's. pk
Watkins David James, coffee rooms, 130 Shoreditch High st
Watkins Edmund, butcher, 1 Cumberland st. Middx. hosp
Watkins Edward, oilman, 2 Octagon pl. Kennington com
Watkins Edward, racket maker & oilman,122Vauxhall walk
Watkins Edward, saw maker, 28 Church st. Shoreditch
Watkins Edwd. sen. bldg. mat.dlr.18 Belvedere bldgs.Boro'rd
Watkins Eleanor (Mrs.),chair spring ma. 14 Crown st. Soho
Watkins Elizabeth (Mrs.), hosier & shirt ma. 308 Oxford st
Watkins Evan, building material dealer, 36 Lant st. Boro'
Watkins Fowell, wine merchant, see Hastings & Watkins
Watkins FrankGeo.locksmth.& bellhgr.3 Claytn.st.Kenngtn
Watkins Frederick, oilman, 3 Munster st. Regent's park
Watkins George, boot & shoe ma. 222 Albany rd. Camberwll
Watkins Geo. Wm. oil & italian warehouse, 308 Oxford st
Watkins Henry,stables,5Cumberland mews nth.Bryanstn.sq
Watkins Henry Geo. drawing master, 13 Lwr. Islington ter
Watkins Henry John, oil & colorman, 6 Crown st. Soho
Watkins James, academy, Eden place, Old Kent road
Watkins Jas.diamond & pearl set. 7 Albemarle st. Clerknwl
Watkins James, fruiterer, 21 Trinity square, Tower hill
Watkins James, *Two Brewers* P.H.Glasshouse st. ea.Smthfld
Watkins James, upholsterer, &c. 57 Lamb's Conduit st
Watkins John, chemist, &c. Broadway, Stratford
Watkins John, cupper, 21A, Saville row, Piccadilly
Watkins John, fishmonger, 31 Princes st. Leicester sq
Watkins John, surgeon, &c. 2 Falcon sq. & 92 Newgate st
Watkins John,tan dealer, 4 Samson's pl.Grange rd.Bermndsy
Watkins John, *Three Goats' Heads* P.H. Wandsworth road
Watkins John Henry, carpenter,45 Union st. Lambeth walk
Watkins John Roger, shipowner, Pier head, Shadwell
Watkins Joseph, linendraper, see Smith & Watkins
Watkins LoriniaM.(Miss),bookbind.47St.John's sq.Clerknwl
Watkins Maria (Mrs.),court milliner, 7 Baker st.Portman sq
Watkins Richard, fishmonger, 8 Norton folgate
Watkins Richard, upholsterer, 115 New Bond st
Watkins Richard, jun. tailor, 4 Maddox st. Regent st
Watkins Richd. whitesmith, 16 Lower Belgrave pl. Pimlico
Watkins Robert, *Imperial Crown* P.H. Bromley, Middlesex
Watkins Robert,indigo blue ma.8 Trafalgar pl. w.Hackney rd
Watkins Robert, watch jeweller, 29 Tysoe st. Spafields
Watkins Samuel, baker, 14 Southampton st. Camberwell
Watkins Sarah (Miss), *George* P.H. 2 St. Mary axe
Watkins Stephen, brickmaker, 1 Irongate wf. Paddington, & 29 Dudley grove, Harrow road
Watkins Thomas, baker & builder,15Cross st.Brmdsy.Nw.tn
Watkins Thomas, *King of Denmark* P.H. 18 Old Bailey
Watkins Thomas, *Poulterers' Arms* P.H.Leadenhall market
Watkins Thomas, who. quill & pen. manuf. 1 & 2 Cannon st
Watkins Timothy,razor strop man.18 Globe road, Mile end
Watkins Wm. dyer, scourer,&c. 5 London ter. Hackney rd
Watkins Wm. engraver, 36 Granville sq. Bagnigge wells rd
Watkins Wm. locksmith, 10 Museum st. Bloomsbury
Watkins Wm.painter&glaz.8Chalcroft ter.New cut,Lambeth
Watkins Wm. tailor, 7 Little Argyll st. Regent st
Watkins Wm. porkman, 13 Great Trinity lane, City
Watkins Wm. Henry, cattle salesman, 15 West Smithfield
Watkins Zachariah, button & trimming seller,108 Regent st
Watkinson Alfred, scale maker, &c. 2 Lower Kennington la
Watkinson Edward, painter, &c. 2 White Horse la. Stepney
Watkinson George, haberdasher, 15 Ann's ter. Cambrdg hth
Watkinson Jas. hot press. & ribbon waterer, 26 Monkwell st
Watkinson Thomas, builder, 62 York terrace, Regent's park, & 30 Watling st
Watkinson Wm. house agt.&appras.56 Bishopsgate st.within
Watkinson Wm. slopseller, 10 Rotherhithe wall
Watkis Thomas, pork butcher, 181 Poplar High st
Watkiss Aaron A. *Princess Alice* P.H.13Murray st.New Nth.rd
Watley Wm. smith & bellhanger, 11 Lit. Grove st.Lisson gr
Watlin Marrain (Mrs.), butcher, 3Lit.Newport st. Long acre
Watling Arthur & Co. agents to the Roslin gunpowder mills, 146 Leadenhall st
Watling Elizabeth (Miss), news agent, 409 Strand
Watling Hen. Godard, butcher, 21 Marchmont st.Brunsw.sq
Watling Hen.Goddard, *Wrekin tavern* P.H.22Broad ct.Bowst
Watling Hen. Richd. *Navy Arms* P.H. NewKing st.Deptfrd
Watling John Emanuel, plumber, & *Union* coffee rooms, 15 Hemming's row, St. Martin's lane
Watling Lionel, cattle salesman, 59 West Smithfield
Watling Philip, fishmngr.& poulterer, 105High st.Camdn.tn
Watling Thomas, fruiterer, 6 Goldsmith's row, Hackney rd
Watling Wm. *Pimlico* dining rooms, 13 King's road,Pimlico
Watmore Charlotte (Miss), bonnet wareho. 15 Cranbourne st
Watmore James, builder, 5 Fisher st. Red Lion st
Watmore James, confectioner, 7 Lower st. Islington
Watmore James, who. confectioner, 19 Brownlow st. Bedf. rw
Watmough George,coal merch. Edward st. Regent's pk.basin
Watney Daniel, distiller, Wandsworth
Watney John, corn & seed factor, 72 Great Tower st
Watson, Broughton & Son, solicitors, 5 Falcon square
Watson&Chambers,ship&ins.brok.10 Commercial sale rooms
Watson & Cooper, silversmiths & platers,29 King st. Soho
Watson & Cuell, mining agnts.&sharebro.1St.Michael's alley
Watson Eliza J. & Ann, *Angel Inn*, St. Clement's, Strand
Watson & Flindt, share brokers,75 Old Broad st
Watson George & Henry, silversmiths,31 Duke st. Oxford st
Watson&Harvey, packing case ma. 44Wood st.&33Mnkwl.st
Watson John & Co. furniture printers, 56 Holborn hill
Watson John & Co. furniture printers, 55 & 56 Holborn hill
Watson John & Joseph, sawmills, Battersea bridge road
Watson John & Son, carpet manufrs. 88 Wood st.Cheapside
Watson John & Son, manufacturers of silver plated goods (Richard Reading, agent), 21 Salisbury st. Strand
Watson John & Wm. linendrapers, 5 Crosby row, Walworth
Watson & Marchant, smiths, Earl's court, Old Brompton
Watson Samuel & Sons, attorneys, 12 Bouverie st. Fleet st. & at Hammersmith

Watson &Metcalfe, wharfingers, Brown's quay, 352Wapping
Watson & Son, carpet manufacturers, 88 Wood st.Cheapside
Watson Thomas & Wm. hosiers & glovers, 20 Milk st
WatsonWm.Geo.&Co.colorma.27Poultry,&16Narrowst.Lim
Watson Wm.Geo.&Jas. bakers, 1NewChurch st.Bermondsey
Watson, Wood & Bell, carpet manufacturers & importers of turkey carpets, 35 & 36 Old Bond st
Watson Abraham, *Britannia* P.H. St. Ann's pl. Limehouse
Watson Adam, scotch agent, 7 Ironmonger lane
Watson Alexander, dentist, 13 Church st. Soho
Watson Andrew James, bedstead maker, 5 Marylebone lane
Watson Andrew Kippis, barrister, 2 Plowden bldgs. Temple
Watson Ann (Mrs.),stationer,10Diddington pl.Caledonian rd
WatsonAnnW.(Mrs.),milliner,9St.Agnew's ter.Tabernacle sq
WatsonBarclay Farquharson, attorney, 36 Lincoln's inn fields
Watson Carrol, barrister, 4 Pump court, Temple
Watson Charles, fancy cabinet ma. 8Gt.Arthurst.Goswell st
Watson Charles, fringe manufacturer, 68 Fore st. City
Watson Charles, grocer, 62 Shadwell High st
Watson Charles, jeweller, silversmith, hardwareman, paper tea tray maker, & sole inventor of the new albata plate, &c. 41 & 42 Barbican, & 16 Norton Folgate
Watson Charles, stockbroker, 32 Royal exchange
Watson Christopher, grocer, 4 Lit.Torrington st.Torrngtn sq
Watson Daniel, solicitor, 8 Gray's inn square
Watson David, tobacconist & snuff maker, 59 Boro' High st
Watson Edmond George, butcher, 52 Church st. Shoreditch
Watson Edmund B. linendraper & hosier, 24 Greek st. Soho
Watson Edmund Temple, cornfactor, see Rosling & Watson
Watson Edward, watchmaker, &c. 6 King st. Cheapside
Watson Edward Francis, carver & gilder, 201 Piccadilly
Watson Edward Thos. painter & glazier,13 John st.Minories
Watson Edwin George, coal & charcoal dealer, 106 Fetter la
Watson Elias, patent sash line maker,4Wilkes st.Spitalfields
Watson Elizabeth (Mrs.), baker, 7 Knightsbridge terrace
Watson Elizabeth (Mrs.), milliner, 30George st.Hanover sq
Watson Elizh.C.(Mrs.),ladies' sch.10 Virginia pl.Gt.Dover rd
Watson Ellis,saddler & harness ma. 10Gt.Windmillst.Hymkt
Watson Francis Pagett, accountant, 8 Thavies inn, Holborn
Watson George, butcher, 14 Deptford High st
Watson Geo. cabinet maker, 19 Mansell st. Goodman's fields
Watson George, cabinet maker, 42 Spring st. Paddington
Watson Geo. furn. broker,&c. 46 Portugal st. Linc. inn fields
Watson Geo. lamp & lustre manuf. see Johnson & Watson
Watson Geo. linendraper, 1 & 2 Up. Seymour st. Euston sq
Watson Geo. printer, 5 Kirby st. Hatton garden
Watson Geo. prof. of music, 42 Mansell st. Goodman's fields
Watson George Frederick, butcher, Deptford High st
Watson Geo. Henry, surgeon, 14 Brighton place, NewKent rd
Watson Harris, stove & range manufacturer, 35 Whitecross place, & 19 Wilson st. Finsbury square
Watson Henry, grocer, 39 Dorchester st. New North road
Watson Henry, hairdresser, 12 Cowcross st. Smithfield
Watson Henry, surgeon, 4 Half Moon st. Piccadilly
Watson Henry Sparkes, mercht. seeNovelli,Watson&Seaton
Watson HenryWm.grnr.&pain.7Sionpl.O.Knt.rd.&4 N.Kt.rd
Watson Humble, baker,19 Bedford place, Commercial road
Watson James, *Angel* P.H. 7 Gt. Chapel st. Westminster
Watson James, baker, 167 Fleet st.
Watson James, barrister, 2 Cursitor st. Chancery lane
Watson James, bookbinder, 53 Long acre
Watson James, bookseller, 5 Paul's alley, Paternoster row
Watson James, fruiterer, 9 Middle Queen's bldgs. Knightsbr
Watson James, patent sash line maker, 66 King st. Soho
Watson James, stockbroker, 32 Royal exchange
Watson James, tailor, 83 Edgware rd. Marylebone
Watson James, tailor, 81 Whitechapel High st
Watson Jas. wax & wafer ma.11Gt.Cambridgest.Hackney rd
Watson Jane (Miss), milliner, &c. 29Edward st. Portman sq
Watson Jesse, bread & biscuit baker, 39 Whitechapel rd
Watson John, accountant, 5 Cumberland mkt. Regent's prk
Watson John, baker, 54 Haymarket
Watson John, braid machine mkr. 11 Crown st.&Hoxton sq
Watson John, *Brunswick hotel*, 10Hanover sq.&13Princes st
Watson John, cabinet maker, &c. 52 Bethnal green rd
Watson John, clothier, Deptford bridge
Watson John, coalfactor, &c. see Charleton & Watson
Watson John, confectioner, 138 Minories
Watson John, confectioner, 4 Suffolk pl. Lower rd. Islington
Watson John, cooper, 14 Allen st. Goswell st
Watson John, grocer & teadealer, 18 Goswell road
Watson John, ham dealer, 68 Seymour st. Euston sq
Watson John, oil & colorman, 80Up.Whitcross st. St. Luke's
Watson John, pianoforte maker, 28 Dover pl. New Kent rd
Watson John, smith, Canal road, Kingsland
Watson John, solicitor, 27 Worship st. Finsbury
Watson John, sunderland bottle wareho. 74 LowerThames st
Watson John, surgeon, 5 Red Lion st. Holborn
Watson John, surgeon, 13 Southampton st. Bloomsbury
Watson John, tailor, 35 East st. Manchester sq
Watson John, *Two Chairmen* P.H. 24Davies st.Berkeley sq
Watson John, sen. attorney, 10 Henrietta st. Covent garden
Watson John, jun. solicitor, 10 Henrietta st. Covent garden
Watson John Aston, ironmonger, 28 Judd st. Brunswick sq
Watson John Burgess, architect, 39Manchester st.Manch. sq
Watson John Chas. hairdresser, 10Prospect pl. Old Bromptn
Watson John G. confectioner, 11Up.Seymour st. Portman sq
Watson John Leuis, *Castle* P.H. 98 Kent st. Borough
Watson Jonathan, printselr. & publishr. 7 Vere st. Oxford st
Watson Joseph, cabinet ma.&c.15Gt.Quebec st. Montague sq
Watson Joseph, painter, 16 Sussex st. Tottenham court rd
Watson Joseph, silk wa. see Cheeper, Watson & Jackson
Watson Joseph, tailor, 41 Broad st. Golden sq
Watson Joseph Heapy, solicitor, 2 Winchester buildings
Watson Keturah (Mrs.), straw hat manufacturer, 13 Aldgate
Watson Louis, coal mer. Cannon whf.1Cannon row, Westmr
Watson Lucy (Mrs.), *Ropemakers' Arms* P.H.New st.Dptfd
Watson Mary (Mrs.), boarding ho. 31 Arundel st. Strand
Watson Mary (Mrs.), comp. ornamnt. ma. 6 Lit.Pulteney st
Watson Mary (Miss), confectioner, 6 Upper Kennington lane
Watson Mary(Miss), dressma.5Chancery pl.Cambrwl.New rd
Watson Michael, shipowner, 340 Wapping High st
Watson Mich. jun. stationer, book& chart seller, 340Wapping
Watson Mulgrave L. sculptor, 13 Upp. Glo'ster st.Dorset sq
Watson Richard, jun. brass founder, 16 Cloth fair, Smithfield
Watson Robert, chemist, see Decastro, Watson & Palmer
Watson Robert, coach builder, 57 King st. Golden sq
Watson Robt.Hen.manfg.chemist,38WalnutTree wlk.Lmbth
Watson Samuel, greengrocer, 121 Cock hill, Ratcliff
Watson Seth Benjamin, physician, 16 Norfolk st. Park lane
Watson Stewart, portrait painter, 91 Dean st. Soho
Watson Thomas, coachmaker, 33 High st. Kensington
Watson Thomas, dentist, 42 Park st. Grosvenor square
Watson Thomas, linendraper, 7 Up. Dorset pl. Clapham rd
Watson Thomas, oil & colorman, 229 Shadwell High st
Watson Thomas, pewterer, see Gerardin & Watson
Watson Thomas, physician, 16 Henrietta st. Cavendish sq
Watson Thomas, wine mer. & cooper, 4Primrose st.Bishopsgt
Watson Thomas Anthony, pen & quill mercht. 52 Lime st
Watson Wm. artist, 40 London st. Tottenham court road
Watson Wm. baker, 233 Rotherhithe
Watson Wm. butcher, 259 Bethnal green road
Watson Wm. cattle salesman, 8 West Smithfield
Watson Wm. china dealer, 3 Claremont place, Old Kent rd
Watson Wm. currier, Richardson st. Long lane, Bermondsey
Watson Wm. *Eight Bells* P.H. 18 Ironmonger row, Old st
Watson Wm. general salesman, 12 City road, Old st
Watson Wm. grocer, 78 Earl st. east, Lisson grove north
Watson Wm. ironmonger, 5 Commercial pl. Kentish town
Watson Wm. merchant, 20 Duncan terrace, Islington
Watson Wm. *Nell Gwynne* P.H. 1 Grosvenor row, Pimlico
Watson Wm. printers' smith, &c. see Scott & Watson
Watson Wm. stationer, 3 St. Ann's la. St. Martin's le grand
Watson Wm. undertaker, 27 Tabernacle walk, Finsbury
Watson Wm. watch & clock maker, 25 North Audley st
Watson Wm. *White Horse* P.H. 3 Stafford row, Pimlico
Watson Wm. who. clothes salesmn. 5 Philes bldgs. Hndsditch
Watson Wm. wine merchant, see Holland & Watson
Watson Wm. Dance, wine, ale& porter mer.73Gt. Russell st
Watson Wm. Davy, barrister, 10 Crown Office row, Temple
Watson Wm. Edwd. *Swan* P.H. 5 Lit. Ormond st.Queen sq
Watson Wm. Geo. watch & case gilder, 7 James st.St.Luke's
Watson Wm. Hen. painter, 7 Sion pl. East st. Walworth rd
Watson Wm. Hen.M.P.queen's counsel,3King'sBen.wk.Temp
Watson Wm. Henry, locksmith, 5 Brill row, Somers town
Watson Wm. Webster, barrister, Pumpcourt, Temple
Watt Euphemia &F.(Misses),dlrs.in pickles,&c.44Coleman st
Watt George & Co. linen & cotton factors, 8 Old Jewry
Watt Robert & Co. west india merchants, 44 Coleman st
Watt Charles, baker, 39 Southampton st. Pentonville
Watt David, ivory turner, 15 Market row, Oxford market
Watt Elizabeth (Mrs.), dairy, Bartholomew pl. Kentish town
Watt Isaac, land agent & surveyor, 11North pl.Gray's inn la
Watt James, engineer, see Boulton, Watt & Co
Watt James, *Horse & Groom* P.H. 301 Oxford st
Watt James, law stationer, 29 Wych st. Strand
Watt Robert, agent for Lea & Perrin's sauce, 44 Coleman st
Watt Robert, general commission agent, 44 Coleman st
Watt Robert, pawnbroker, 14 Exmouth st. Spa fields
Watt Thomas, tobacconist, 31 Bow st. Covent garden
Watt Wm. oil & colorman, 30 Brunswick parade, Barnsbury road, & Park terrace, Liverpool road, Islington

Watt Wm. *Lion & Key* P.H. 55 Lower Thames st
Watteen & Fearns, proprietors of Watteen's patent for preventing incrustation in steam boilers & steam generators, 2 Jeffrey's square, St. Mary axe
Watters John Nichol, surgeon, 25 Bedfordbury, Covent grdn
Watters Roger, barrister, 10 New square, Lincoln's inn
Watton George Hastings, tobacconist, 23 New Bond st
Watts & Harton, wholesale pewterers & manufacturers of tallow chandlers' candle mould pipes & frames, & music plates & metal inkstands, 61 Shoe lane, Holborn hill
Watts Henry & Co. wine & spirit mer. 63 Lincoln's inn fields
Watts Joshua&Thos.peerless pool baths, 51 Baldwin st.City rd
Watts & Mouat, lace, &c. warehousemen, 3 Russia row, Milk st
Watts Anthony A. solicitor, King's Arms buildings, Cornhill
Watts Benjamin, *Admiral Keppel* P.H. Marlboro' rd. Chelsea
Watts Cassandra (Mrs.), *Owen Glendower* P.H. 163 Aldergt. st
Watts Chas. grocer &cheesemonger, Bridge pl. Old Kent rd
Watts Charles, hairdresser, 83 York st. Westminster
Watts Daniel, confectioner, 18 Ship alley, Wellclose sq
Watts David R. *Pontefract Castle* P.H. 1 Chapel st. Marylebone, & 1 Southampton row, New road
Watts Edward, coal dealer, 47A, Harrison st. Gray's inn rd
Watts Edward, lampmaker, 31 Harcourt st. New road
Watts Elizabeth (Mrs.), lodging house, 6 Norfolk st. Strand, & 4 Arundel st. Strand
Watts Frederick, billiard table ma. see Burroughs & Watt
Watts Frederick, oil & colorman, 118 Shoreditch High st
Watts George, gardener, 7 Grove lane, Camberwell
Watts George, grocer&cheesemongr. 2 Jubilee st. Comml. rd. ea
Watts George, grocer, 2 Green st. Paddington
Watts George, grocer, &c. 35 King st. Long acre
Watts George, confectioner, 5 Church la. Commercial road
Watts George, plumber & painter, 38 Mount st. Berkeley sq
Watts George, wine & spirit mer. 32 Seething la. Tower st
Watts Geo. Edwd. gold&silv. wiredrawer, 8 Kirby st. Hat. gar
Watts George Frederick, chemist, perfumer, chemical fire box, match, fusee & writing fluid ink maker, 17 Strand
Watts George Taylor, *King's Head* P.H. Grove la. Deptford
Watts Go. Wm. zinc. work&furn. bro. 3 St. George's pl. Cmbl. rd
Watts Hannah (Mrs.), plumasier, 4 Roebuck pl. Gt. Dover rd
Watts Henry, corndealer, 4 Upper Bryanstone st
Watte Henry, fancy cabinet maker, 118 Bunhill row
Watts Henry, printers' broker, see Ulmer & Watts
Watts Henry, *Golden Fleece* P.H. 3 Lit. Knightrider st. City
Watts Henry, record keeper, 5½ Bell yard, Doctor's comms
Watts Henry, tobacconist, Mare st. Hackney
Watts Henry, tobacconist, Well st. Hackney
Watts Isaac, iron founder, see Eustice & Watts
Watts Isaac, smith & farrier, White Lion st. Chelsea
Watts James, boot & shoe maker, 99 Westbourne st. Pimlico
Watts James, coal merchant, 63 Lincoln's inn fields, & Essex wharf, Essex st. Strand
Watts James, fringe manufacturer, 10 Great Portland st
Watts James, fruiterer, 6 Duke st. Adelphi
Watts James, fruiterer, 49 Hedge row, High st. Islington
Watts James, grocer, &c. 88 Monmouth st. Seven dials
Watts James, sash maker & horticultural builder, 8 Claremont place, Old Kent road
Watts John, artificial florist, 31 Rodney st. Pentonville
Watts John, bootmaker, 54 Threadneedle st
Watts John, brown stone potter, &c. see Doulton & Watts
Watts John, chemist, &c. 106 Junction ter. Edgware road
Watts John, circulating library, 56 Bethnal green road
Watts John, cooper, 108 Shoe lane, Fleet st
Watts John, dairyman, 12 Carlton st. Regent st
Watts John, gold & silver laceman, 21A, Frith st. Soho
Watts John, *Hope coffee house*, 7 Air st. Piccadilly
Watts John, registrar, 2 Albion place, Thornhill road
Watts John, tailor, 34 Museum st. Bloomsbury
Watts John, tailor, 9 Swan yard, Shoreditch
Watts John Henry, cheesemonger, 7 Grosvenor row, Pimlico
Watts Joseph, tailor & army clothier, 2 St. James's st
Watts Joshua Jas. wholes. pewterer, see Harton & Watts
Watts Lucy (Mrs.), grocer, 12 Croydon st. Bryanstone sq
Watts Mary (Mrs.), dairy, 22 Frederick st. Hampstead rd
Watts Mary Ann (Mrs.), furrier & strawhat ma. 13 Tichbne. st
Watts Philip, baker, 40 Grove lane, Deptford
Watts Reading, builder, 17 Eaton place west, & 6 Motcomb st. Belgrave square
Watts Richard, corndealer, 24 Brunswick st. Cromer st
Watts Richard, straw hat wareho. 2 Youl's pl. Old Kent rd
Watts Robert, tailor, 6 Youl's place, Old Kent road
Watts Sarah J. (Miss), confectr. 1 Queen's Hd. row, Newgtn. btts
Watts Septimus, surgeon, 3 Northampton row, Holloway rd
Watts Thomas, beer retailer, St. Ann's place, Limehouse
atts Thomas, builder, &c. 2 South st. South Audley st
Watts Thomas, butcher, 71 Praed st. Paddington
Watts Thomas, butcher, 212 Upper Thames st
Watts Thomas, calenderer, see Perrott, Watts & Perrott
Watts Thomas, carpenter, 38 Gt. Titchfield st. Oxford st
Watts Thomas, carpenter, 27 University st. Tottenham ct. rd
Watts Thomas, cheesemonger, 49 Munster st. Regent's pk
Watts Thomas, currier, 8 Old Paradise row, Islington green
Watts Thomas, farrier, John st. Cambridge heath, Hackney
Watts Thomas, fishmonger, 8 London road, Southwark
Watts Thomas, ladies' shoemaker, 15 Lit. Marylebone st
Watts Thomas, nursery & seedsman, Camden pl. Peckham
Watts Thomas, solicitor, 8 Coleman st
Watts Thomas, solicitor, see Ashley & Watts
Watts Thomas, tailor, 41 East st. Walworth road
Watts Thomas, *White Swan* P.H. Waterloo ter. Coml. rd. ea
Watts Thomas, zinc worker, 7 Burlington pl. Old Kent rd
Watts Thomas Smith, *White Swan* P.H. Commercial rd. ea
Watts Walter, solicitor, 20 Bedford row, Holborn
Watts Wm. accountant & coal merchant, 16 New Quebec st
Watts Wm. baker, 36 St. George st. east
Watts Wm. chinaman, 28 Davies st. Berkeley square, & 1 Kensington terrace, Kensington gravel pits
Watts Wm. coal dealer, 9 Salisbury st. Lisson grove
Watts Wm. *Duke of York* P.H. 13 Grove la. Low. rd. Deptford
Watts Wm. linendraper, 4 Deptford High st
Watts Wm. lodging house, 46 Trinity square, Southwark
Watts Wm. printer, 12 Crown court, Pickett st. Strand
Watts Wm. nurseryman, Stoke Newington road
Watts Wm. outfitter, 3 Limekiln hill, Limehouse
Watts Wm. tailor, 48 Castle st. east, Oxford st
Watts Wm. tobacconist, 43 Threadneedle st. City
Watts Wm. George, solicitor, 231 Bermondsey st
Wattson Thomas, tinman & brazier, 9 St. Ann's pl. Limehouse
Waud Chas. confectioner to the Queen, 38 New Bond st
Waud Edwd. coal merchant, Regent's canal dock, Limehouse; & Marston wharf, Old St. Pancras road
Waud Elizabeth (Mrs.), ostrich feather ma. 84 St. John st. rd
Waud Nelson, *Bull & Pump* P.H. 72 Shoreditch High st
Waude John, coach builder, corner of New & Old Kent roads
Waugh George & Co. chemists to the Queen, 177 Regent st
Waugh & Son, carpet manufs. 3 & 4 Goodge st. Tottenhm. ct. rd
Waugh Andrew, tailor & piece broker, 3 Cloth fair
Waugh Charles, butcher, 4 Guildford st. east, Spafields
Waugh Edgar Achilles, carpet wareho. 4 Dyers' bdgs. Holborn
Waugh George, solicitor, 5 Gt. James st. Bedford row
Waugh John, chemist & druggist, 60 High st. Camden town
Waugh Joseph, wine merchant, see Sherer, Waugh & Co
Waugh Margaret (Miss), millin. &haberdash. 26 Whitechapel rd
Waugh Wm. scotch oatmeal dealer, see Neill & Waugh
Waugh Wm. Robt. tinplateworker, 43 Tottenham st. Fitzroy sq
Waveneyvalley & Gt. Yarmouth Railway Co. 2 Nicholas la
Wawn Geo. Henzell & John Twizell, coal fac. Coal Exchange
Waxchandlers' Hall (Mark Hy. Gregory, clerk), Gresham st
Way James & Co. teadealers, &c. 272 Oxford st
Way & Locke, importers & manufs. of tuscan, leghorn, & straw hats, 8 Goldsmith st. & 10 Gutter lane, Cheapside
Way Wm. & Son, butchers, 6 Duke st. Manchester sq
Way Benjamin, bookseller&stationer, 75 York st. Westmnstr
Way Edward Milgate, tailor, 19 Holland st. Kensington
Way Elizabeth Ann (Miss), grocer, 6 Borough road
Way George, coffee rooms, South row, Covent garden market
Way George, locksmith, 25 Hatton wall, Hatton garden
Way Job, *Zetland Arms* P.H. Princes road, Notting hill
Way John, jack ma. 24 John's row, Brick lane, St. Luke's
Way Robert, upholder & cabinet maker, 6 Sun st. Bishopsgate
Way Samuel A. Barrow, surgeon & herbalist, 3 Park st. Boro'
Way Thomas, cooper, Hollywood, Little Chelsea
Way Thomas Benjamin, butcher, 29 Wigmore st. Cavendish sq
Way Wm. hairdresser & perfumer, 22 Lit. Queen st. Westr
Way William, surgeon, 8 Boyne terrace, Notting hill
Way Wm. stove & grate manufr. 11 Old Compton st. Soho sq
Waygood Richard, agricul. imp. ma. 39 Bridgeho. pl. Boro'
Wayland Henry & James, watchmakers, Stratford broadway
Wayland Charles, pork butcher, 17 Chapel st. Somers town
Wayland Edward, painter, 18 White Lion st. Pentonville
Wayland Thomas, florist, King st. Battersea
Waylat Robert, chemist & druggist, 4 Pavement, Finsbury
Waylen Alfred, patent steam plate manfr. 12 Mark lane
Waylen Robert, cabinet maker, 44 Great Windmill st
Waylett Harriet (Miss), millin. & ladies' shoema. 23 Cannon st
Waylett James, bootmaker, 23 Cannon st. City
Waylett Richard S. jeweller, 233 Oxford st
Wayman Daniel, farrier & wheelwt. 16 Vauxhall wlk. Lmbth
Wayman Robert, wire weaver, see Bacon & Wayman
Waymark Francis, *Horse Shoe inn*, 66 Stones' end, Borough
Wayre William, furrier, 41 Oxford st

Wayre Joseph & Co. french dyers, &c. 74 Lamb's Conduitst. & 29 & 160 Oxford st
Wayt Charles, fishmonger, Little Chelsea
Wayte Henry, confectioner, inventor & sole vender of the soupe de galles, 5 Gracechurch st
Weaber Henry & Co. working opticians, 129 Oxford st
Weaber Henry, spectacle maker, 15 Carlisle st. Soho sq
Weack Thomas, hairdresser, 191 Brick la. Spitalfields
Weaklen William, carpenter, 8 Northampton st. Clerkenwl
Weakley Cha. bone&ivorybrush ma. 1 Newton st.N.North rd
Weaklin Fred. stat. & acct. book maker, 91 Farringdon st
Weale & Taylor, babylinen warehouse, 314 Regent st
Weale David, baker, 16 Old Fish st
Weale John, bookseller & publisher, 59 High Holborn
Weale Thomas, gun maker, 9 Keppel st. Chelsea
Weale Thomas, *White Hart* P.H. 15 St.Thomas's st. e.Boro'
Weall & Berkeley, solicitors, 20 Margaret st. Cavendish sq. & 2 Falcon court, Fleet st
Wealthy Richard, fruiterer, 18 Lower st. Islington
Wealthy Thos. jun. tobacconist, 27 Warren st. Fitzroy sq
Wear Edward, baker, 35 Manor place, Walworth road
WearHannah(Mrs.),broker,1Brokers'rw.Redcross st.Sthwk
Wear John, provision dlr. 23 Alfred pl. Newington causeway
Weare Jas. printer, bookseller & stationer, 96 St. John st. rd
Weare Sarah (Mrs.), tobacconist, 8 Bethnal green, west side
Wearing Edward Bird, appraiser, &c. 80 Bethnal green rd
Wearing Henry, furniture broker, 2 Brick lane, Spitalfields
Wearing William Alfred, barrister, 28 Chancery lane
Weatherall Edwd. solicitor, see Johnson, Son & Weatherall
Weatherall John, carpenter, 2 Princes st. Drury lane
Weatherby Chas. &Jas. *RacingCal.* publs. 6 OldBurlington st
Weatherby Charles, confectioner, 63 Park st. Camden tn
Weatherhead Hen. & Son, watergilds. 1 Newcastle pl. Clerkw
Weatherhead George, tool warehouse, 33 St. George st
Weatherhead Geo. Hume, physician, 63 Guilford st. Rusl.sq
Weatherhead John, tailor, 31 Spencer st. Goswell road
Weatherhead Thurston, law stationer, 7 Quality court
Weatherill Wm. kid glove mfr. 5 Tower Royal ct. Watling st
Weatherley Charles, confectioner, 3 Moreton pl. Kentish tn
Weatherley George, confectioner, Camberwell green
Weatherley Henry, confectnr.&lozenge mer. 54 Theobld's rd
Weatherley Wm. confectioner, 24A, Marchmnt.st.Burtn.cres
Weatherly John, grocer, 6 Grove lane, Camberwell
Weathers George, surgeon, 41 High st. Camden town
Weatherstone Thomas, cabinet maker, 81 Union st. Boro'
Weavers' hall (Benj. Hardwick, clerk), 22 Basinghall st
Weaver Alfrd. carver, gilder&curiositydlr. 46 Wardourst. Soho
Weaver Amos, grocer, 32 Vauxhall st. Lambeth
Weaver Francis, fishmonger, 22 Lower st. Islington
Weaver Francis, tobacconist, 23 Lower st. Islington
Weaver James, fruit & pea salesman, Borough market
Weaver John, dining rooms, 253 High Holborn
Weaver John, fruit salesman, Covent garden fruit market
Weaver John, lodging house, 17 Arundel st. Haymarket
Weaver Joseph, pawnbro. 25 Richmond pl. East. st. Walw. rd
Weaver Levant, surgeon, 2 Dowgate hill
Weaver Loraine, surgeon, see Smith & Weaver
Weaver Mary (Mrs.), butchr. 2 Fuller'ster. Wooden br. Pimlico
Weaver Richard, outfitter, 189 Poplar High st
Weaver Thos. carpenter & undertak. 31 North row, Grosv. sq
Weaver Thomas, meat salesman, 23 New Newgate market
Weaver Wm. acadmy. 15 St. George's pl. Back rd. St. George's e
Weaver Wm. appraiser, 81 Park st. Camden town
Weaver Wm. coach carver, 9 Upper Clifton st. Finsbury
Weaver Wm. coal & lime wharf, Battle bridge wf. King's cross
Webb Chas.&John &Co. woollen warehousemn. 17 Coleman st
Webb (C. & W.)&Gibson, accountants, 9 Friar st. Blkfriars.rd
Webb Elizh.& Susannah (Misses), school, 13 Park pl. Lvrpl.rd
Webb Emma & Sarah Ann, milliners, 5 Church st. Camberwell
Webb Geo. & Co. lithographic & zincographic printers, 8 Farringdon st. & 54½ Moorgate st. City
Webb George & Archibald Tunno, wine & spirit merchants, 31 Great St. Helen's
Webb Hen.&Jsph. watch case & dial ma. 8 Skinner st. Clknwell
Webb Henry & Orlando, solicitors, 22 Sackville st. Piccadilly
Webb, Hughes & Gye, who. teadlrs. 2½ Laurence Pountney hill
Webb Mary & Sarah, straw hat makers, 186 Oxford st
Webb & Pollard, lace & sewed muslin wareho. 96 Watling st
Webb Rt. & Wm. brickma. Coach & Ho. la. Stoke Newgn. grn
Webb & Skinner, scale makers, 119 Union st. Borough
Webb, Thompson & Co. cheesemongrs. 109 Tottenham ct. rd
Webb & Williams, wholesale tea dealers, 4 Pancras lane
Webb Wm.&Sons, wine&brandymers 37 KingWilliam st. City
Webb Anna (Mrs.), bricklayer & plasterer, 64 Old st. road
Webb Benjn. wheelwright, 10 Addle hill, Doctors' commons
Webb Browne, cheesemonger, 208 Blackfriars road
Webb Chas. gold laceman, 23 Old Bond st
Webb Charles, surgeon, 86 Great Titchfield st
Webb Charles James, cheesemonger, 440 Oxford st
Webb Charles John, pianoforte maker, 142 Leadenhall st
Webb David, boot & shoe maker, 33 Broad st. Lambeth
Webb Conrade Manger, cheesemonger, 119 & 138 Edgware rd
Webb Daniel, beer retailer, St. Ann's place, Limehouse
Webb Ebenezer, statnr. &bookslr. 3 Commercial pl. Kingsldrd
Webb Edmund, oil & italian wareho. 63 Fore st. City
Webb Elisha, china warehouse, 1 Freeschool st. Horselydown
Webb Eliza. (Miss), french florist, 49 Burlington arcade
Webb Elizabeth (Miss), baby linen wa. see Jacob & Webb
Webb Elizh. (Miss), ladies' school, 20 Bowling gr. st. Kenngtn
Webb Elizabeth (Mrs.), boot ma. 83 Union st. Boro' High st
Webb Frank, wine & spirit mer. 4 Cooper's row, Crutchedfrs
Webb Frederick, grocer, 203 Blackfriars road
Webb Frederick P. wine & spirit mer. 1 RoyalExchangebldgs
Webb Frederick, stationer, 2 Upper Marylebone st
Webb Gabriel Gregory, woollendraper, 82 Cheapside
Webb George, *Albion* coffeerooms, 17 Cleveland st. Fitzroy sq
Webb George, bootmaker, 15 Grenada pl. Old Kent road
Webb George, bricklayer, 36 Eagle st. Red Lion square
Webb George, brickmaker, Green lane, Stoke Newington gr
Webb George, builder, Gower's walk, Church la. Whitechpl
Webb George, butcher, 53 Curtain road, Shoreditch
Webb George, carpenter, 7 South st. King's road, Chelsea
Webb George, cheesemonger, 19 Bridge road, Lambeth
Webb George, cheesemonger, 140 Lambeth walk
Webb George, cheesemonger, 38 Surrey place, Old Kent rd
Webb George, cooper, 16 Cross st.& 99 Broadwall, Blackfrs
Webb George, flour factor & coal mer. 11 Water la. Tower st
Webb George, hardwareman, see Killick & Webb
WebbGeo. lacerouche, mourng. collar, &ar. flwr. ma. 75 Wood st
Webb George, pawnbroker, 35 High st. Kensington
Webb George, printcutter, Lower Felix st. Hackney rd
Webb George, *Seven Stars* P.H. 111 Whitechapel High st
Webb George, silversmith, &c. 36 Gt. Russell st. Bloomsbry
Webb George, stockbroker, Stock exchange
Webb George, tobacconist, 41 Friar st. Blackfriars rd
Webb George A. ticket writer, Pickett st. chambers, Strand
Webb George B. architect, 3 Mortimer st. Cavendish sq
Webb Hannah (Mrs.), hatter, Stratford, Essex
Webb Henry, furrier, 3 Caroline st. Commercial rd. east
Webb Henry, haberdasher, 132 Church st. Shoreditch
Webb Henry, hair cutter & wig maker, 29 Marylebone la
Webb Horatio, cheesemonger, 131 Tottenham court rd
Webb Horatio, cheesemonger, 5 Lowndes' ter. Knightsbridge
Webb Isaac, boarding house, 5 Artillery court, Chiswell st
Webb James, baker, 310 High Holborn, & 10 RedLi. st. Holbrn
Webb James, barge builder, 90 & 91 Fore st. Limehouse
Webb James, boot & shoe ma. 31 Church st. Shoreditch
Webb James, chinaman, 12 Skinner's pl. Leadenhall market, & White Hart inn yard, 62 Borough High st
Webb James, *George* P.H. Goodman's yard, Minories
Webb James, dining rooms, 92 Hoxton Old town
Webb James, silk hat manufactr. 34 Bethnal green rd
Webb James, theatrical ornament ma. 75 Brick la. St. Luke's
Webb James, tobacco pipe maker, 9 Portland st. Wardour st
Webb John, baker, 13 Widegate st. Bishopsgate without
Webb John, butcher, 13 Strutton ground, Westminster
Webb John, cabinet maker, 13 Smith's buildings, City rd
Webb John, calf & sheep salesman, 41 West Smithfield
Webb John, carman, 38 Wilson st. Finsbury sq
Webb John, hemp & flax hackle maker, 18 Goswell st
Webb John, kid leather dyer, 145 Long lane, Bermondsey
Webb John, optician, 28 Francis st. Tottenham court rd
Webb John, soda & mineral water ma. Rosamn. bgs. Islngtn. gr
Webb John, tailor, 40 Davies st. Berkeley sq
Webb John, upholsterer & cabinet maker, 8 Old Bond st
Webb John Charles, engraver & stationer, 34 Cursitor st
Webb John Hen. woollen ma. 68 Basinghall st. & Trowbridge
Webb John Maximilian, wholesale cheesemonger, 215 Blackfriars road, & 13 Collingwood st. Blackfriars road
Webb John Whiteman, surgeon, 25 Wardour st. Soho
Webb Joseph, tailor, 9 Belgrave mews east, Belgrave sq
Webb Joseph, toymaker, 5 Bacon st. Spitalfields
Web Joseph Benj. brass turner, 42 York st. City road
Webb Mary (Miss), milliner, 27 Newman st. Oxford st
Webb Matthew, woollen draper, 137 St. Alban's pl. Edgwr. rd
Webb NicholasWalter, *Peacock* P.H. 52 Holland st. Blkfrs. rd
Webb Obadiah, bricklayer, 35 Redman's row, Mile end
Webb Richard, butcher, 62 High st. Portland town
Webb Richard Francis, shipchandler, 4 King st. Tower hill
Webb Richard Wm. scalemaker, 10 High st. Marylebone
Webb Richard Wm. solicitor, 16 Austinfriars
Webb Robert, blacksmith, The mall, Kensington gravel pits

Webb Robert, jeweller, 1 Macclesfield st. Soho
Webb Robert, *King's Arms* P.H.53 Rawstorne st.Goswell st
Webb Robert, *King's Arms* P.H. 41 Rotherhithe wall
Webb Robert, seal engraver & printer, see Evans & Webb
Webb Robert, shipwright, Elephant stairs, 336 Rotherhithe
Webb Robert, surgeon, 266 Poplar High st
Webb Sarah (Mrs.),prof.of dancing, 28 Edwards st.Prtmn.sq
Webb Simeon, leathersellr.21 Colville ct.John st.Fitzroy sq
Webb Stephen, cheesemonger, 28 London road, Southwark
Webb Thomas, butcher, 5 Newport court, Newport market
Webb Thomas, cheesemonger, 257 Bethnal green road
Webb Thomas, egg importer, 186 Lambeth walk
Webb Thomas, hairdresser, 3 Perceval st. Clerkenwell
Webb Thomas, hairdresser, 51 Ropemakers' fields, Limeho
Webb Thomas, livery stables, 13 Red Lion st. Whitechapel
Webb Thomas,machinist&lathe ma.7Portland st.Wardour st
Webb Thomas, porkman, 54 Bridge road, Lambeth
Webb Thomas, silk dyer, &c. 56 Wigmore st. Cavendish sq
Webb Thomas Geo. veterinary forge,Nelson st.Whitechapel
Webb Thomas Robert,surgeon,18Wyndham st.Bryanstone sq
Webb Valentine Baker, civil engineer, 14 Duke st. Adelphi
Webb Wm. baker, Clifton st. Wandsworth road
Webb Wm. butcher, 26 Newport court, Soho
Webb Wm. carpenter, Mare st. Hackney
Webb Wm. chelsea academy, 9 Lower Sloane st. Chelsea
Webb Wm.*City of Canterbury* P.H.13Well st.Mile end N.tn
Webb Wm.engraver& printer,21 Lambeth hill,Up.Thames st
Webb Wm. gold & silver lace maker, 48 Piccadilly
Webb Wm. land agent, see Chapman, Webb & Chapman
Webb Wm. livery stables, 60 Gray's inn lane
Webb William, lodging house, Bath place, New road
Webb Wm. *Lord Liverpool* P.H. 9 Clark st. Stepney
Webb Wm. oil & colorman, 22 Widegate st. Bishopsgate st
Webb Wm. oil & italian warehouse, 98 Bishopsgate within
Webb Wm. packing case maker, 4 Gt. Distaff lane
Webb Wm. paper hanging warehouse, 20 King st. Islington
Webb Wm.pewterer&candle mould fr.ma.28President st.east
Webb Wm. saddle tree maker, 8 Ropemakers' st. Finsbury
Webb Wm. surveyor, 63 Lincoln's inn fields
Webb Wm. undertaker, 5 Green terrace, New river head
Webb Wm. wine & brandy merchant, see Austwick & Webb
Webb Wm. sen.watchma.2 Northampton ter.York st.City rd
Webb Wm. jun. watchmaker, 5 Sudeley st. City road
Webb Wm. C. tobacconist, widows'milliner,&c.49Goswell st
Webb Wm. Frederick, tailor, 12 Three Oak lane, Dockhead
Webb Wm. Stammers, dairy, 5 Sherrard st. Golden sq
Webber Alex. & Co.wine merchants, 8 Davies st.Berkeley sq
Webber & Hairs, commission agents, 131 Cheapside
Webber Henry, jun. & Co.wine merchants,15St.Dunstan's hi
Webber Cha. G. portgl.mer.seeOffley,Webber,Forrester&Co
Webber George, baker, 236 Bermondsey st
Webber George, baker, 2 Grenada place, Old Kent road
Webber Henry, wine merchant, 58 Brook st. Grosvenor sq
Webber Hen. Incledon, tobacconist, 86 Whitechapel road
Webber James, *Carlisle Arms* P.H. 43 Carlisle st. Lambeth
Webber James C. saddler, 29 Litchfield st.& 10West st.Soho
Webber John, baker, 29 Salisbury st. Lisson grove
Webber John, ivory turner, 33 Charles st. City road
Webber John, jun. cheesemonger, 45 Silver st. Golden sq
Webber John, sen. cheesemonger, 1 Brewer st. Golden sq
Webber John Huish, attorney, 3 Caroline st. Bedford sq
Webber Michael Jas. fruiterer, Centre row, Cov.gar.market
Webber Richard, cooper, 47 Brunswick st. Blackwall
Webber Richard, organ builder & pianoforte maker, 39 Drummond st. & 40 Whittlebury st. Euston square
Webber Sam.G.watchcap&indexma.17Northamptonst.Clkw
Webber Sarah(Mrs.),chandler'sshop,9Copenhagn.st.Pntnvl
Webber Thomas, bread & biscuit baker, 81 Lombard st
Webber Thomas, butcher, 90 High st. Marylebone
Webber Wm. fellmonger, 2 Rephidim st.Hunter st.Dover rd
Webber Wm. *Geo. the Fourth* P.H. East India road,Poplar
Webber Wm. teadealer, &c. 89 High st. Marylebone
Webber Wm. Robert, *Lamb* P.H. 9 New turnstile, Holborn
Webbon James, rubbish carter,Red Lion row,Walworth com
Weber Chas. Fred. mer. 3 Winchester bldgs.Winchester st
Weber Frederic, physician, 8 Grosvenor st. Bond st
Weber Henry, working optician, 129 Oxford st
Webley John, coffee house, 9 Carnaby st. Golden square
Webling Henry, butcher, 26 Park terrace, Regent's park
Webster Geo. &Thos.prliamntry.agts.26Gt.George st.Wstmr
Webster John & Co. warehousemen, 19 Aldermanbury
Webster Richard, Son & Co. chronometer mkrs.to the Lords of the Admiralty, the East India Company, & watch & clock manufacturers, 74 Cornhill
Webster Alex. ribbon manuf. see Cornell, Lyell & Webster
Webster Andrew, carver & gilder, 18 Port st.Newport mrket
Webster Ann (Mrs.), lodg.ho.& pat.medicine vend.29Store st
Webster Ben. *Rose & Crown* P.H.112 & 113East st.Kngtn. rd
Webster Ben. theatrical publisher, 19 Suffolk st. Pall mall e
Webster Chas. barrister, 13 New Boswell ct. Lincoln's inn
Webster Charles, bed pillar, bedstead & cornice manfr. 2 & 22 New inn, Broadway, Shoreditch
Webster Charles, watch & clock ma. 24 Red Lion st. Holbn
Webster Daniel, plumber, &c. 15 Isabella st. Broadwall
Webster David, stationer, 9 Regent place, Horseferry road
Webster Edward, barrister, 3 Old sq. Lincoln's inn
Webster Edwin, tailor, 24 Panton st. Haymarket
Webster Eliza (Mrs.), size manufr. Bridge rd. Battersea
Webster George, cabinet maker, 2 Linden place, Bayswater
Webster George, grocer, 21 Lit.Windmill st. Golden sq
Webster George, hairdresser, 29 Fleet la. Farringdon st
Webster George, *Star & Garter* P.H. 43 Hedge row,Islington
Webster George, surgeon, 78 Connaught ter. Edgware rd
Webster George, *Union* P.H. 4 Union st. New Bridge st
Webster Hannah (Mrs.), fruiterer, 11 George st. Mansion ho
Webster Henry, barometer ma. 3 Vineyard walk, Clerkenwl
Webster Henry, dairyman, 58 Princes st. Portman market
Webster Henry (successor to the late H. Berry, patentee), sole manufacturer of Berry's patent portable inkstands & instantaneous lights,with indian rubber stoppers, importer of french wax taper matches, &c.&c. 21 Long acre (late of 134 Drury lane, & 21 Bedford st. Covent garden)
Webster James, tailor, &c. 11 Air st. Regent st
Webster John, bread & biscuit baker, 58 Coleman st. City
Webster John, cooper, 28 Charles st. Hampstead
Webster John, physician, 24 Brook st. Grosvenor sq
Webster John, readymade lin.wa. 41 St. James's st. St. Jas's
Webster John, saddler, &c. 120 & 121 Gt. Guildford st. Boro'
Webster John,whiskey mer. 11 Rodney bldgs. New Kt. rd
Webster John Wm. gold & silver caster, 2 Porter st. Soho
Webster Mary Ann (Mrs.), lodging house, 25 St. James's st
Webster (Mrs.),prof. of music, 10 Southmp. rw. New rd
Webster Mary (Mrs.),oil shop, 16 Brunswick st. Brnswk. sq
Webster Michael, builder, 102½ Mary st. New road, & 50 Upper Albany st. Regent's park
Webster Philip, oil & colorman, 3Guildford st. east,Spafields
Webster Ridley M. accountant, 1 River ter. north, City rd
Webster Robert, *King's Arms* P.H. 39 Brook st. Ratcliffe
Webster Saml. sackmaker, Pleasant pl. Broadwall, Blackfrs
Webster Thos. solicitor, 25 Queen st. Cheapside
Webster Thos. special pleader, 2 Pump court, Temple
Webster Thos. surgeon, 22 Langley pl. Commercial rd. east
Webster Thos. tobacconist, 77 Edgware road
Webster Wm. coach brokr.& repositry.77Market st.Edgw.rd
Webster Wm. fancy biscuit baker, 11 Moorgate st. Bank
Webster Wm. gl. & emery paper ma. 28 Charles st.Hamps.rd
Webster Wm. hardwareman, 13 Chelsea market
Webster Wm. medallist & coin dlr. 17 Gt. Russell st.Cov. gar
Webster Wm. undertaker, 58 Lant st. Borough
Webster Wm. Maule, solicitor, 15 New Boswell court
Wedd Absalom, livery stables,Wallis yd. 29 Queen's rw.Piml
Wedd George, corn & flour factor, 17London st.Fenchurch st
Wedd Mary (Miss), ladies' school, 4 Agar st. Strand
Weddell & Atkinson, coal mers.Cannon wf.Cann. rw.Westmr
Weddell Thos. accountant, Camberwell green
Wedge Charles, linendraper, 73 Sun st. Bishopsgate
Wedge James, turner & brokr. 1 Trafalgar rw. Walwth cmn
Wedgwood Ralph, manufacturer of patent manifold writers & nectographs, 4 Rathbone place, Oxford st
Wedgwood Thos. dealer in china, glass & earthenware, who. retail & for exportation, 5, 6 & 7 Crispin st. Spitalfields
Wedlake Edward, china wareho. 17 Brewer st. Somers town
Wedlake Henry B. solicitor, see Clowes,Wedlake & Clowes
Wedlake Mary (Mrs.), (widow of the late Thos. Wedlake) agricultural implement maker, engineer & machinist, 118 Fenchurch st.; manufactory, Hornchurch, Essex
Wedlake Wm. gold chaser, 29 Lit. Sutton st. Clerkenwell
Weeden Edward, fruiterer, 270 Bethnal green road
Weeden Elizabeth (Mrs.), oil & color wareho.115Edgware rd
Weeden Jas. Fred. engrav. & print. 8 Hatfield st.Stamford st
Weeden John, engraver, 50 Charles st. City road
Weeden Jonathan, cut glass ma. 28 Wormwood st. Bishopsgt
Weeden Thos. butcher, 16 Stucley ter. Camden town
Weeden Wm. fruiterer, 25 Wilmot st. Russell sq
Weeding Thos. e. i. mercht. & agent, 6 Gt.Winchester st
Weedon Francis & Co. british & for. lace ma. 13 Goldsmith .
Weedon Edwin, artist, Temple chambs. Falcon ct. Fleet st
Weedon George, butcher, 45 Henry st. east, Avenue road
Weedon Henry, *Rising Sun* P.H. 128 Kent st. Borough
Weedon James, law stationer, 21 Cursitor st. Chancery lane
Weedon Matthias, shoemaker, 94 Devonshire st. Lisson gr
Weedon Thos. surgeons' instru. ma. 41 Hart st. Bloomsbury

Weedon Thos. teadealer, 14 Pleasant row, Holloway road
Weedon Thos. wholesale station. see Smith, Weedon & Co.
Weedon Wm. upholsterer & undert. 75 Wells st. Oxford st
Weedon Wm. butcher, 8 City road, Old st
Weeds Mary Ann (Mrs.), tobacconist, 1 Portland pl. Boro' rd
Weekes Amos, saddle & harness ma.24Brownlow st.Long acre
Weekes Henry, sculptor, 29 Lower Belgrave place, Pimlico
Weekes Thomas, gold chaser, 86 Dean st. Soho
Weekly Chronicle newspaper Office, 337 Strand
Weekly Dispatch newspaper Office, 139 Fleet st
Weekly Evangelist Office, 2 Pemberton row, Gough square
Weekly John, coal & potato dlr. 9 Sheffield st. Lincoln's inn fi
Weeks & Day, hothouse bldrs. Glo'ster.pl. King's rd. Chelsea
Weeks Chas. (from Coventry st.), mechanist, 202 Piccadilly
Weeks Edw. sen. horticult. build. Hortulan pl. King's rd. Chlsa
Weeks Elizabeth (Mrs.), confectioner, Church st. Hackney
Weeks Henry, carpenter, 26 King st. Soho
Weeks Henry, solicitor, 12 Cook's court, Lincoln's inn
Weeks James, furniture broker, 71 Wardour st. Soho
Weeks James, grocer & cheesemonger, 1 Gedling st.Bermdsy
Weeks John, boot & shoe maker, 74A, Well st. Oxford st
Weeks John, currier & grindery dealer, 260 Whitechapel rd
Weeks John, grocer & tobacconist, 220 Shadwell High st
Weeks John, leather cutter, 51 Cannon st. St. George's east
Weeks John William, woolstapler, 106 Bermondsey st
Weeks Stephen, oilman, 31 James st. Buckingham gate
Weeks Thomas, solicitor, 10 Tokenhouse yard, & Tottenham
Weems Robert, solicitor, see Graham, Moncreiff & Weems
Weemys & Lorck, bookbinders, 13 Charles st.Hatton garden
Weetch Jonathan, turner, 105 Poplar High st
Wegg William, physician, 5 Maddox st. Bond st
Wehnert Edward Henry, artist, 23 Charlotte st. Bedford sq
Wehnert Nicholas, solicitor, 23 Charlotte st. Bedford sq
Weibel & Wilkin, yeast imps. 4 Spread Eagle ct. Finch lane
Weible William, clothes salesman, 120 Gray's inn lane
Weichbrodt John, general agent, 13 Angel court, Bank
Weidner Andrew, pork butcher, 148 Goswell st
Weigner John Michael, pork butcher, 6 Duke st. Chelsea
Weigall Charles Henry, artist, 13 Michael's pl. Brompton
Weigall Henry, engraver & printer, 3 St. James's st
Weights & Measures Office, 3 Whitehall yd.; hours 10 to 4
Weight Charles, printer, see Reynell & Wright
Weight George, cowkeeper, 11 Earl st. London road
Weight John, upholst. & cabinet mak.12Macclesfield st. Soho
Weight Joseph, baker, 3 Waterloo st. Camberwell
Weight Julius, saddler & harness ma.29 Sun st. Bishopsgate
Weight Thos. coach spring mak. King's pl. Stones' end, Boro'
Weight Wm. plumber & glazier, 124 Southwark bridge road
Weightman Fred. bonnet block & stand ma. 58 Long la. City
Weightman Hugh, barrister, 1 Paper buildings, Temple
Weightman James M. solicitor, 1 Warwick court, Holborn
Weightman Walter, *Three Compasses* P.H. 1 King st.Golden sq
Weighton Edward, stationer, see Hardy & Weighton
Weinert John Geo. Fred. pork butcher, 7 Orchard pl. Knglnd. rd
Weippert John, harpist, &c. to her Majesty, 21B, Soho sq
Weippert Wm. professor of music, 24 Ernest st. Regent's pk
Weir Maria & Son, plumbers. 17 Gainsford st. Horselydown
Weir Matt. & John, drapers, 42 Glo'ster ter. New rd.Whtchpl
Weir & Smith, solicitors to Coopers' Co. 71 Basinghall st
Weir Robert, bookseller, 67 Harley st. Cavendish square
Weise John James, hatter, 73 Tooley st. Borough
Weismann & Schramme, commis.agents, 7 Finsbury chambers
Weiss John & Son, surgns'. cutlers & bath maks. 62 Strand
Weitzel Ehrhardt Anton, baker, 80 Crawford st
Weitzel Frederick, baker, 5 Margaret ter. Paddington green
Welbank Richard, newsvender, 21 Sloane square, Chelsea
Welbank Richard, surgeon, 102 Chancery lane
Welborne Joseph Widdowson, silk mercer, 38 Albemarle st
Welbrock Harman, *Black Horse* P.H. 4 Well st.Wellclose sq
Welch John & Son, straw hat manufactrs. 12 Aldermanbury
Welch & Margetson, stock, brace, &c. manufrs.134Cheapside
Welch & Phillips, win. glass merchs. 116Bishopsgate without
Welch Mary & Eliza (Misses), milliners, 35 Edward st
Welch Arthur Henry, barrister, 4 Stone bldgs. Lincoln's inn
Welch & Sidgwick, color & varnish manufacturers, 15 Gt. Trinity lane, Cheapside, & Bankside
Welch Benjamin, glass merchant, 4 White Hart ct.Bishpgte
Welch Charles, coal merchant, see Barraud & Welch
Welch Edward, builder, 17 Kinnerton st. Belgrave square
Welch Edward, chemist, 111 Guilford st. Russell square
Welch Edward, floorcloth manuf. 1 Chapel st. New road
Welch Edward, tobacconist, 15 Whitecross st. Cripplegate
Welch George, boot & shoemaker, 22 Davies st. Berkeley sq
Welch George, butcher, 21 Suffolk place, Hackney road
Welch George, coffee rooms, 155 St.George's st.St.George's ea
Welch George, *Fox* P.H. Russell st. Mile end gate
Welch George, stationer, 136 Salisbury court, Fleet st
Welch Henry, baker, 48 Hampden st. Somers town
Welch Henry, dairy, 5 Brecknock place, Camden new town
Welch James, chandler's shop, Morning lane, Hackney
Welch James, *White Horse* P.H.67Theobald's rd.Red Lion sq
Welch John, special pleader, 3 King's Bench walk, Temple
Welch John White, merchant, 9 New Broad st. City
Welch Joseph, cattle salesman, 8 West Smithfield
Welch Joseph S. printseller & publisher, 24 St. James's st
Welch Joshua, jun. glass, lead & colr. mer. 12 Panton st. Haymkt
Welch Montagu Suart, barrister, 7 King's Bench wlk.Temple
Welch Patrick Robert, barrister, 2 Churchyard ct. Temple
Welch Thos. oil & italian wareho. 181 Bishopsgate without
Welch Wm. bread & biscuit baker, 3 James st.Covent garden
Welch William, cattle salesman, 60 West Smithfield
Welch William, coffee rooms, 6 Lime st. passage
Welch William, cowkeeper, 6 Tyler st. Golden square
Welch William, dairyman, 19 Silver st. Wood st
Welch William, fruiterer, 6 Gloucester pl. Old Kent road
Welch William, job master, 18 Gloucester ter.Vauxhl. br. rd
Welch William George, surgeon, 390 Strand
Welch William Keen, button & trim.slr.6 Marylebn.st.Gold.sq
Welchman Elizh. (Mrs.), chinawa. 41 Marchmont st.Brunsw.sq
Welchman Mary Ann (Mrs.), ostrich feather dlr.15 Hanway st
Welchman Richard, jeweller, see Rapley & Welchman
Weld Charles Rd. asst. sec. Royal Society, Somerset house
Weldhen Reuben, baker, Little Chelsea
Weldon John & Sons, cattle salesmen, 41 West Smithfield
Weldon Bowker, chemist, &c. 6 Portsdown ter. Kilburn gate
Weldon Henry Wm. grocer, High row, Silver st.Kensington
Weldon James, feather mercht. 13 New Millman st. Bedfd. row
Weldon William, *Oliver's Mount* P.H. 7 Mount row, Berkly.sq
Welfare Henry, furrier & fancy capma. 58 Castle st. Southw
Welford Richard Griffiths, barrister, 6 Chancery lane
Wellam George, mechanist, 6 Curtain road, Shoreditch
Wellard William, baker, 67 Welbeck st. Cavendish sq
Wellbeloved William, butcher, 7 Deptford High st
Wellborne Charles, solicitor, 31 Tooley st. Southwark
Wellborne Henry Pelling, saddler & har. mak. 210 Tooley st
Wellby John, gold & silver refiner, 57 King st. Soho
Wellby John, undertaker, 40 Princes st. Rotherhithe
Welldon William, butcher, 246 Poplar High st
Wellen Nicholas, lighterman, 22 Dempsey st. Stepney
Weller George, solicitor, 8 King's road, Bedford row
Weller Geo. toy warehouse, 31 Hasting st. Burton crescent
Weller Isaac, grocer, 9 Vauxhall row, Vauxhall
Weller James, hay salesman, Battersea
Weller John, lighterman, 55 John st. Holland st. Blackfriars
Weller Maria (Mrs.), grocer, 8 Crown st. Walworth road
Weller Samuel, fishmonger, 99 Bishopsgate within
Weller Samuel, furn. broker, 22 Tavistock st. Covent gardn
Weller Thomas, wheelwright, 8 New st. Borough road
Weller William, butcher, Corrie place, Old Kent road
Weller William, butcher, 2 Whitmore road, Hoxton
Weller William, cheesemonger, 87 Farringdon st
Weller William, *Fountain* P.H. 24 Newcastle st. Strand
Welley John, boot tree maker, 10 Stanhope st. Clare market
Welling William, oil & colorman, 1 Amelia pl. Walworth rd
Wellington Charles, *Cock* P.H. North st. Sloane st
Wellington John, cheesemonger, 2 Newland pl. Kensington
Wellman George, oil & colorman, 21 Lit. Coram st. Brnswk.sq
Wellman John, tailor, 10 Maddox st
Wells Henry & Son, saddlers, 20 Percy st. Tottenham ct. rd
Wells Hesketh D. & Rt. Ths. wood mers. Canal wf. Lr. rd Deptfd
Wells John & Son, jewellrs. & pawnbro. 6 & 7 High st. Knsgtn
Wells & Lambe, desk & dressing case makers, 29 Cockspur st
Wells Mary & Son, corkcutters, 20 Budge row, Cannon st
Wells Westrop & Prinse, stock & sharebro. 75 O. Broad st.City
Wells Wm. & Benj. bricklayers, 4 Russell st. Bermondsey st
Wells & Winn, commer. & custom ho. agts. 3 Love la. Eastcheap
Wells Augustus, dining rooms, 2 Eastcheap
Wells Benj. Weston, floor cloth manufr. see Squire & Wells
Wells Charles, basket maker, Piazza, Covent garden
Wells Charles, prepd. wood for engravg. dlr. 6 Bouverie st
Wells Christopher, *Crown* P.H. 60 Shadwell High st
Wells Daniel, tobacconist, 35 Regent st. Horseferry road
Wells David, bootmaker, 2 Weston st. Somers town
Wells Edw. jun. *Hugh Myddleton tav.* 10 Myddltn. pl. Sadlr. wls
Wells Edward, sen. *London Spa* P.H. 1 Exmouth st. Spaflds
Wells Edw. window blind manufacty. 99 London rd. Southwk
Wells Edw. wire worker, 13 South Island place, Clapham rd
Wells Frances (Miss), coal mer. 22 wf. & 59 Harrow rd. Padgn
Wells Fred. A. cabinet maker, &c. 30 Gresse st. Tot. ct. rd
Wells Geo. attorney, 1 Brunswick ter. Commercial rd. east
Wells George, grocer, Southampton st. Camberwell
Wells Hardy, civ. engineer & sur. 6 Serjeants' inn, Fleet st

Wells Henry, ale & porter brewer, Larkhall lane, Clapham
Wells Henry, baker, 34 King st. Deptford
Wells Henry, brewer, see Herington & Wells
Wells Henry, coal & corn dealer, 228 Shoreditch
Wells Henry, grocer, 89 Vauxhall walk, Lambeth
Wells Henry, surgeon, 31 London st. Fitzroy square
Wells Henry Tomkins, saddler, 100 Albany st. Regent's pk
Wells James, auctioneer & ho. agt.15 Suffolk pl. Hackney rd
Wells James, basket maker, 3 Blackmore st. Drury lane
Wells James, cabinet ma. 4 Raven row, Whitechapel road
Wells James, coffee rooms, 13 Church lane, Commercial rd
Wells James, draper & trimming seller, 6 St. Ann's lane
Wells James, hairdresser, 27 Stonecutter st. Farringdon st
Wells James, newsvender & stationer, 3 Leigh st. Burton cres
Wells James, scaleboard maker, 24 Ewer st. Union st. Boro'
Wells John, brush & toy warehouse, 6 Portman market
Wells John, butcher, 47 Borough High st
Wells John, cabinet maker & undertaker, 210 Regent st
Wells John, coal dealer, 20 White Horse alley, Cow cross st
Wells John, fender maker, 36 Gee st. Goswell st
Wells John, hairdresser, 12 Ryder's court, Leicester sq
Wells John, livery stables, 41½ & 240 Blackfriars road
Wells John, nurseryman, 275 Albany road, Old Kent road
Wells John, pawnbroker, 52 Broad st. Bloomsbury
Wells John, plumber, 74 Waterloo terrace, Waterloo road
Wells John, pork butcher, 97 Lambeth Lower marsh
Wells John, solicr. & reg. of births, 23 Percy st. Bedford sq
Wells John, tailor & draper, 12 Caroline st. Bedford square
Wells John, *Three Cranes* P.H. 1 Park place, Mile end rd
Wells John, watch case maker, 42 Perceval st. Clerkenwell
Wells John, working jeweller, 43 Museum st. Bloomsbury
Wells John, sen. fringe & tassel manufr. 16 Rathbone place
Wells John Deane, solicitor, 13 George st. Mansion house
Wells John James, tobacconist, 12 Bury st. St. James's
Wells John James, wine merchant, 12 Villiers st. Strand
Wells John Robinson, surgeon, 11 Charlotte st. Fitzroy sq
Wells John Wm. blindma. 8 Somers pl. west, New rd. St. Panc
Wells Joseph T. perfumer, 7 Little Charlotte st. Blkfrs. rd
Wells Maria (Mrs.), haberdasher, 15 Rotherhithe wall
Wells Martha (Mrs.), *Yarmouth Arms* P.H.88 Lr. Thames st
Wells Mary (Mrs.), baker, 32 Gt. James st. Lisson grove
Wells Mary (Mrs.), cabinet ma. 4 Ridinghouse la. Langhm. pl
Wells Mary Ann (Mrs.), prof. of danc. 3 Tavistock st. Cov. gar
Wells Mordaunt L. barrister, 6 Serjeants' inn
Wells Richard, blind maker, 98 Trafalgar st. Walworth rd
Wells Richard, *Rose & Crown* P.H. Church st. Stoke Nwngtn
Wells Richard, *White Horse* P.H. 9 Pitfield st. Hoxton
Wells Richard Forester, surgeon, 1 Steward st. Spitalfields
Wells Robert, butcher, 27 Skinner st. Somers town
Wells Robert, warehouseman, see Eyles, Evans, Hand & Wells
Wells Samuel, barrister, 6 Serjeants' inn, Fleet st
Wells Samuel, bricklayer, 21 Great George st. Bermondsey
Wells Samuel, cabinet ironmonger, 13 Old st. rd. Shoreditch
Wells Simon, furniture broker, 87 Salisbury st. Lisson gr
Wells Thos. *Carpenters' Arms* P.H.26 Pritchard's rd Hckny. rd
Wells Thos. cheesemonger, 97 New Park st. Borough
Wells Thos. dairyman, 33 Edmund st. King's cross
Wells Thomas, grocer, 1 Brett's buildings, Camberwell road
Wells Thos. *Ld. H. Admiral* P.H.29 New Church st. Lisson gr
Wells Thos. oil & italian warehouse, 4 Vauxhall bridge foot
Wells Thomas, *Red Cow tavern*, Dalston
Wells Thomas, shop fixture dealer, 183 High Holborn
Wells Thos. *White Hind* P.H.6 Broadway, St. Thomas st. Boro'
Wells Thos. wine merchant, 13 Mincing lane
Wells Thos. writing desk, work box, &c. ma. 9 Holborn bars
Wells Wm. appraiser & house agent, 12 Hackney rd. crescent
Wells Wm. carpenter, 2 Fan court, Miles lane, Up. Thames st
Wells & Claxton, coal mers. Victoria whf. Bankside, Southwk
Wells Wm. corn merchant, White Lion wharf, 18 Upper Thames st. & New Corn Exchange
Wells Wm. dyer & scourer, 1 William st. Shoreditch
Wells Wm. furniture broker, 16 Drury court, Strand
Wells Wm. fruiterer, Holland st. Brixton road
Wells Wm. jeweller, 8 Dean st. Fetter lane
Wells Wm. *Middleton Arms* P.H. Queen's road, Dalston
Wells Wm. *Spotted Dog* P.H. 298 Strand
Wells Wm. surg. inst. ma. 5 Alfred ter. Whitehorse la. Stepney
Wells Wm. tailor, 93 New Bond st
Wells Wm. tobacconist, 12 Kingsland place, Kingsland road
Wells Wm. Hen. sofa mfr. 4 Charles st. Mile end New town
Wells Wm. John, cabinet ma. 99 Devonshire st. Lisson grove
Wells Wm. Richd. chemist, &c. 31 London st. Fitzroy sq
Wells Wilson Henry, pump maker, 18 Bermondsey New rd
Wellsman Mary (Mrs.), stationer, 1 Devonshire st. Lisn. gr
Wellspring John, chemist & druggist, 3 Chandos st. Strand
Wellstead John, upholsterer & house agt.32 Mount st. Brkly. sq
Wellsted James, upholder, 12 & 13 Molyneux st. Bryanstone sq.; 30 Shouldham st. & Wellsted yard, Seymour pl
Wellsted Joseph, builder & house agt.103 St. John's wood ter
Wellsted William, builder, 21 High st. Portland town
Wellum Sophia (Mrs.), tobacconist, 12 Northmbrlnd. st. Nw. rd
Welsby William Newland, barrister, 2 Elm court, Temple
Welsford Joseph & Co. auctioneers, 8 & 9 Palace rw. New rd
Welsford George, grocer, 28 South wharf road, Paddington
Welsford Henry, comb maker, 170 Ratcliff highway
Welsford Robert, tailor, 46 Essex st. Strand
Welsh Charity School (Frederick Lacey, secretary), Calthorpe place, Gray's inn road
Welsh Slate Company (Wm. Hodgson Bowes Barwis, sec.), 1 New Boswell court, Lincoln's inn
Welsh Alfred, carpenter, 31 High st. Marylebone
Welsh Edward, barrister, surveyor of taxes, 16 Old Jewry, Cty
Welsh George, ham & beef shop, 163 Bethnal green road
Welsh John, boot & shoe ma. 2 Thatch'd ho. rw. Lr. rd. Islngtn
Welsh Patrick, bootmaker, 54 Lambeth walk
Welsh Richard, *Blue Anchor* P.H.4 Lit. Anchor st. Bthnl. grn
Welsh Thos. *Prince of Brunswick* P.H.58 Brunswk. st. Blkfrs
Welsman Edward, baker, 6 Albert ter. Queen st. Chelsea
Welsman William, boot & shoe maker, 12 Eyre st. hill
Welstead Charles, solicitor, 66 Berners st. Oxford st
Welton Richard, upholsterer, 33 Up. Seymour st. Portman sq
Wenborn Charles, tailor, Deptford High st
Wenborn Josiah, cabinet maker, 154 Goswell st
Wenborn Robert, scale maker, 172 High Holborn
Wenborn Thomas, boot & shoe ma. 101 Quadrant, Regent st
Wenborn Thomas, scale ma. 1 Charles pl. York rd. Lambeth
Wenden Geo. *Four Swans tav. & hotel*, 83 Bishopsgt. within
Wenden Thomas, grocer, 10 Susannah st. Poplar
Wendt Fred. & Co. ship & insurance agents, 51 Lime st. City
Wenham Eliza (Miss), milliner & dress ma. 3 Caledonian rd
Wenham Wm. carpenter & house agt. Rotherhithe pl. Strtfrd
Wenham Lake Ice Company, 164A, Strand
Wenman John, uphols. 26 Whitehart pl. Low. Kennington la
Wensley Richd. *Three Wheatsheaves* P.H.53 Edge rw. Islgtn
Went James, *Millerof Mansfield* P.H.1 Snow's flds. Bermond
Wentworth Edwd. floorcloth & table cover ma. 160 Whitechapel rd.; Cambridge pl. Hackney rd.; & 19 Gracechurch st
Wentworth Thomas, dairyman, 3 Wyndham road, Cambrwl 1
Wentworth Wm. fruiterer, 31 Devonshire st. Queen sq
Wentworth Wm. hide & skin salesm. Bermondsey skin mrkt
Wentzell & Cownden, boat buildrs. 59 Low. Fore st. Lambeth
Wentzell & Cownden, *Ship* P.H. Lower Fore st. Lambeth
Were E. (Mrs.), artist in wax flowers, 5 York tr. Cmbwl. New rd
Were James, butter & cheesemonger, 8 Cambridge st. Golden square, & 33 North Audley st
Were Wm. gen. commn. ship & prov. agt. 44 Botolph la. Thas. st
Werndly Hen. glass stainer, 1 Chapter st. Regt. st. Westmsr
Werner John G. & Son, wholesale furriers, 12 Little Britain
Wernham Isaac, jeweller, 60 Charlotte st. Fitzroy sq
Wernham Joseph, baker, 151 Houndsditch
Wertheim Benj. bookseller & publisher, 13 Paternoster row
Wertheimer John & Co. eng. & for. printrs. 1 Circus pl. Lon. wall
Wertheimer Samson, bronzist, 35 Greek st. Soho
Wesbey William & Co. tailors, 14 Princes st. Hanover sq
Wescot Joseph, baker, 9 Road side, Mile end
Weslake John, watchmaker, 21 Bridge st. Southwark
Wesleyan Book room, 5 Horseshoe court, Ludgate hill
Wesleyan Centenary hall & Mission house, 17 Bshpsg. within
Wesleyan Chronicle newspaper, 13 Wellington st. north
Wesleyan Conference Offices (John Mason, sec.), 14 City road, Finsbury square, & 2 Castle st. Finsbury; hours 9 to 7
Wesleyan Female Orphn. Asylm. 8 Royl. hl. Queen's rd. Baysw
Wesleyan Mission So. 17 Bishopsgate within
Wesleyan Office, 1 Crane court, Fleet st
Wesleyan Weekly newspaper, 13 Wellington st. Nth. Strand
Wessel Christian R. pub. of foreign music, 67 Frith st. Soho
Wessell Elizh. (Mrs.), grocer, 14 Grove lane, Deptford
Wessels Hen. Wm. gen. agt. & com. mer. see Brocklesby & Wessels
Wesson John, *Green Man* P.H. 127 Hoxton Old town
West Edwd. & Co. ship & insur. agts. 5 St. Benet's pl. Gracech. st
West John & Henry, mast, oar, block, pump, & gun carriage, &c. makers, Mill wall, Poplar; 19 Mill lane, Tooley st. & Commercial dock, Russell st. Lower Rotherhithe
West & Green, corn & seed mer. Rutland wf. Up. Thames st
West Harriet & Maria, school, 22 Hanover st. Walworth rd
West James Wm. & Caroline, brewers, 1 Union ter. Comml. rd. e
West Maria & Anna, prep. school, 25 Lr. Belgrave pl. Pimlico
West & Smith, shipwrights, 31 Shad Thames, & 36 Thomas st
West & Wagstaff, coal & cokemer. Coml. whf. Coml. rd. Lambeth
West Wm. & Danl. civil engineers, 16 & 17 Egremont pl. New rd
West Wm. John & Co. merchants, 36 Crutched friars
West Wm. & Nehemiah, curriers, 68 New Compton st. Soho

West Cornwall Rlwy.(J.MacDonnell,sec.),35Broad st.bldgs
West EndCoalCo.(JohnCapel,manager),20St.Geo.pl.Hd.pk
West of England Fire & Life Insurance Company,20 New Bridge st.; for list of directors, &c. see page 2050
West FlandersRlwy.Co.(Wm.Jesse,sec.),11King William st
West India Club (Thos. Ellis, sec.), 60 St. James's st
West India Planters& Merchants, Standing Committee of (Geo. Saintsbury, sec.), 12 Old Jewry
West India Dock Co. see "East & West India Dock Co"
West Kent Wharf, Montague close, nr. St. Savr.'s ch. Boro'
*WestLondonMedicat.VapourBathIns.*3Gt.Castlest.Reg.st
West of London & Westminster Cemetery Company's Office (John H. Ruddock, secretary), 153 Piccadilly; cemetery, Fulham road, Brompton
WestLondonRailwayCo.(J.Thompson,sec.),11 Abchurch la
West London Savings' Bank, 27 Farringdon st
West Middlesex Waterworks(Matthias K.Knight,sec.),offi. 20 Nottingham pl. New rd.; & 37 North st. Manchester sq
West Wheal Jewel Mining Association, 75 Old Broad st
West Alexander, dining rooms, 81 Church lane, Whitechapl
West Andrew Wood, undertaker, 24 Banner st. St. Luke's
West Benjamin, bookbinder, 2 St. James's walk,Clerkenwell
West Benjamin, jeweller, 23 Marchmont st. Brunswick sq
West Benjamin Mills, academy, 17 Red Lion st. Clerkenwell
West Byatt, dentist, 3 Old Broad st. City, & 1 Rodney terrace east, Mile end road
West Chas.advertising agent,1Lamb'sConduitpas.RedLionsq
West Charles, chemist, 5 Bridge st. Westminster
West Charles, physician, 37 Charterhouse square
West Cornelius,boot&shoe mak.5 Steyman's rw. Hollowy. rd
West Edward, fruiterer, Church st. Hackney
West Edward, marine store dealer, 31 Whitechapel road
West Edward(Mrs.),milliner,&c.68Margaretst.Cavendish sq
West Edward, professor of music, 3 Robert ter. Chelsea
West Edward, wine merchant, 7 Upper Berkeley st. west
West EdwardChas.chandlerss'hop,1 Brunswk.st.Hackney rd
West Elijah, coal merchant, 5 Nichols sq. Hackney road
West Elizabeth(Mrs.),china&glass dlr.27 Crosby rw.Wlw.rd
West Ellis Henry, slate mer. 1 Irongate wf.Paddington basin
West Fitzmaurice, cutler & dressing case manufacturer to the Royal Family, 1 St. James's st
West Francis, optician & electrotyp. 83 Fleetst.& 41 Strand
West George, grocer, 1 Carpenter st. Berkeley sq
West George, mast, oar & block maker, 265 Wapping
West George, stonemason, 12 Cannon st. road, St. George's east; stone yard, 225 Wapping High st
West George,surgeonapothecary,2Hackney rd.cres.Hack.rd
West George, tailor & draper, 162 Union st. Borough
West George, tobacconist, 92 Gt. Russell st. Bloomsbury
West Harriet(Mrs.),iron&wirewk.mfr.17Quickset rw.Newrd
West Henry, baker, 27 Bridge road, Lambeth
West Henry, french boot & shoe importer,19 Lowther arcade
West Henry, turner, 9 Clarence place, Hackney road
West Horace, hairdresser, 2 Albemarle st. Clerkenwell
West James, haberdasher, 76 & 77 Shoreditch High st
West James, sealing wax & wafer maker,27Lombard st.City
West Jas. sto. & share bro.6 SpreadEagle ct.Threadneedle st
West James, tailor & habit maker, 52 Gt. Marlborough st
West Job Henry, retail brewer & maltster, 87 Hackney rd
West John, brushmaker, 12 Great Marylebone st
West John, coffee rooms, 2 South Wharf road, Paddington
West John, gasfitter & general brass manfr. manfr.of lamps & chandeliers, 27 Church st. Lambeth
West John, plumber & painter, 73 Goswell road
West John, teadealer & grocer, 3 Carlisle st. Soho sq
West John Charles, printer, 14 Wells st. Oxford st
West John Jas. land surveyor,25 Low. Belgrave pl. Pimlico
West Joseph, bookbinder, 28 Hosier lane, Smithfield
West Joseph, boot & shoe maker, 16 Gt. Guildford st. Boro'
West Joseph, butcher, 1 Bedford place, Commercial rd. ea
West Joseph, carpenter & builder, 7 Redcross sq.Cripplegt
West Joseph, fruit salesman, Covent garden fruit market
West Joseph, grocer, 6 Bedford pl. Commercial road east
West Martin, furnish. undertaker, 46 Hercules bldgs.Lmbth
West Richard,coalmer.&carman,10St.James's pl.Hmpstd.rd
West Richard, engraver, 18 Devonshire place, Edgware rd
West Richard, hardwareman & ironmonger, 48 Chiswell st
West Richard, hopfactor, 1 Three Crown sq. Borough
West Robert James, tobacconist, 13 Thornton st. Dockhead
West Samuel, artist, 78 Newman st. Oxford st
West Samuel, carman, 6 Lady Lake's grove, Mile end road
West Saml. *Masons' Arms*P.H.18Titchbornest.Edgware rd
West Sarah (Mrs.), shoemaker, 1 Lit. Coram st. Brunswk. sq
West Stephen, appraiser, 9 Bowyer place, Camberwell road
West Thomas, coffee rooms, 56 Bridge road, Lambeth
West Thomas, cutler, 8 Artillery place, Westminster
West Thomas, goldsmith & jeweller, 18 Ludgate st
West Thos. grocer&brit.wine mer.3Calthorpe pl.Gray's inn rd
West Thomas, oilman & tallowchandler,Broadway, Stratford
West Thomas, solicitor, 15 Connaught square
West Walter Thos. smith in general, 8 Clifton st. Finsbury
West Wm. beer retailer, 109 Star st. Paddington
West Wm. boot & shoe maker, 5 Theberton st. Islington
West Wm. brassfounder, 58 Backchurch lane, Whitechapel
West Wm. carpenter & bottle dealer, 3 David st. Marylebne
West Wm. cigar manufacturer, 3 Steyman's row, Holloway
West Wm. cook & confectioner, 2 Up. Baker st. Regent's pk
West Wm. linendraper, 6 London terrace, Hackney road
West Wm. plumber & glaz. 5 Lower Seymour st. Portman sq
West Wm. pork butcher, 22 Chapel st. New road
West Wm. soda water fountain, 27 Lombard st
West Wm. solicitor, 38 Ely place, Holborn
West Wm. stockbroker, 1 Capel ct. Bartholomew la. City
West Wm. tailor & piece broker, 56 Carnaby st. Golden sq
West Wm. theatrical printseller, 56 Wych st. Strand
West Wm. trunk & box maker, 21 Barnet st. Hackney road
West Wm. zinc ware. 13 White hart pl. Lower Kennington la
West Wm. Charles, painter, 69 New Compton st. Soho
West Wm. Hen. ruby pin ma. 40 Wellington st. Goswell st
Westacott Geo. plumber, painter & glazier, 45 St. Mary axe
Westacott John, plumber, Three Falcon ct. 145 Fleet st
Westall Thos. & Co. fancy & manchstr. warhm. 26 Gresham st
Westall Wm. & Co.whalebone ma.& fin.mers. 69Aldersgate st
Westall Richard, salt merchant, see Weston & Westall
Westall Thomas, woollendraper, 26 Gresham st
Westan Wm. umbrella ma. 8 Grace's alley, Wellclose sq
Westaway David, tailor, see Huffam & Westaway
Westbrook Jno.& Andw. *Poulter.Arms*P.H.Freemans'ct.Chs
Westbrook John, bootmaker, 1 Bride lane, Fleet st
Westbrook John, chemist, &c. High st. Stoke Newington
Westbrook Thomas, shipbuilder, Folly wall, Blackwall
Westbrook Wm. chandler's shop, Orchard pl. Kingsland rd
Westbrook Wm. coal dealer, 34 Gt. Windmill st. Coventry st
Westbrook Zach. coal mer.& wfgr. Sun wf. Narrow st.Ratlf.cr
Westbury William, beer retailer, 5 Emmett st. Poplar
Westbury William, lithographic printer, 29 Walbrook
Westby August. Geo. carver & gilder, 9George st.Portman sq
Westcott George, bootmaker, 16 Princes st. Red Lion sq
Westcott John, potato warehouse, 10 Sharp's bdgs. Minories
Westcott John, *Tiger* P.H. Camberwell green
Westcott John M. *BridgeHouse*P.H.28Whitmore rd.Hoxtn
Westcott Samuel, beer retailer, 26 Bath st. City road
Westcott Wm. dairy & porkman, 9 Upper Baker st.Lloyd sq
Westell Jane (Mrs.),bookseller,5Bozier's ct.Tottenham ct.rd
Wester Peter, coffee & dining rooms, 54 St. George st
Westerdale John, van proprietor, 68 Shoe lane, Fleet st
Westerdale Wm. potato dealer, 33 & 35 Farringdon market
Westerman Robert, hairdresser, 81 Harrow rd. Paddington
Western Annuity Society, 38 St. Mary Axe, & Exeter, (George Harriott Wardale, agent)
Western Australian Land Co. (B. Roller, sec.), 33 Old Broad st
Western Direct Railway Company, 20 Poultry
Western Dispensary (Wm. Henry Firth, surgeon), 23 Charles st. Westminster
Western Exchange Bazaar, 10 Old Bond st.
Western Gas Light Co. (John T. Tidd, sec.), 11 Poultry
Western General Dispensary, 9 Lisson grove south, New rd
Western Grammar School (Rev. John Robert Crawford, head master), North terrace, Alexander sq. Brompton
Western Life Assurance Society, 3 Parliament st. (Edwd. Thomas Richardson, actuary & sec.); see page 2049
Western Literary Institution (James D. Malcolm, sec.), 47 Leicester square
Western Jas. & Sons, solicitors, 7 Gt. James st. Bedford row
Western Abraham, registrar of births, 5 Clerkenwell close
Western Charles Francis, solicitor,7Gt.James st.Bedford row
Western John, combmaker, 27 Upper Jubilee pl. Mile end rd
Western Thomas, glass stainer, 39 Brewer st. Somers town
Western Thomas George, conveyancer, 52Lincoln's inn fields
Western Wm. *Merlin'sCave*P.H.3Margaret st.Cavendish sq
Western Wm. wheelwright, North wharf rd. Paddington
Westerton Charles, bookseller, 15 Park side, Knightsbridge
Westerton Saml. cheesemonger, 48 Castle st. Leicester sq
Westerton Wm. accountant & actuary, 8 Austinfriars
Westgarth Wm. organ builder, 14 Quickset row, New rd
Westhorp Isaac, merchant, 9 George yard, Lombard st
Westhorp Theophilus, rigger, see Wright & Westhorp
West India Planters' & Merchants' standing Committee, 12 Old Jewry
Westin Louisa (Miss), dining rooms, 11 Finch la. Cornhill
Westlake Charles, butcher, 2Newport ct. Newport mkt. Soho

Westlake James, grocer, 1 Bartholomew ter. York st. City rd
Westlake Thomas, grocer, 2 Union st. New Bond st
Westlake Wm. ironmonger, &c. 45 Brunswick st. Blackwall
Westley's & Clark, bookbinds. & embosrs. Friarst. Doctors'com
Westley Francis (Mrs.), baker, 12 South st. Manchester sq
Westley Fred. C. bookseller & news agent, 163 Strand
Westley George, professor of music, 17 Throgmorton st
Westley John, grocer, 21 Huntworth ter. Portman market
Westley Joseph, plumber, 14 Wood st. Spafields
Westley Margt. (Mrs.), oil wa. 34 Southampton st. Camberwell
Westley Thomas, lodging house, 34 Albany st. Regent's park
Westley Wm. bookbinder, 8 Warwick square, Newgate st
Westley William, carver & gilder, 13 Exeter pl. Knightsbridge
Westley William, optician, see Carpenter & Westley
Westley William, shoe agent, 23 Bartlett's bldgs. Holborn
Westmacott Charles, cabinet of art, 107 Gt. Russell st. Bmby
Westmacott Hn. Seymour, solicitor, see Forster's & Westmacott
Westmacott Sir Richard, R.A. sculptor, 14 South Audley st
Westmacott Richd. jun. sculptor, 21 Wilton pl. Belgrave sq
Westmacott Stewart, artist, 17 Nottingham st. Marylebone
Westmacott William, architect, Council Office, Whitehall
Westmacott Wm. print. ink ma. see Griffiths & Westmacott
Westmarland Joseph, cheesemonger, 21 Chapel st. Somes. tn
Westminster Court, Guildhall, Westminster
Westminster Court of Requests (Christhr. Cuff, chief clerk), 29½ Castle st. Leicester sq.; hours 10 to 1
Westminster Fire Office (William Meredith Browne, secretary), 27 King st. Covent garden
Westminster General Dispensary (Thos. P. Tarrant, surgeon, John Wills, sec.), 9 Gerrard st. Soho
Westminster & General Life Assurance Association (W. M. Browne, actuary), at the Westminster Fire Office, 27 King st. Covent garden; see page 2051
Westminster Hospital, (J. Wilson, sec.), Broad sanctuary, Westminster
Westminster Literary, Scientific & Mechanics' Institution (William Hen. John Traice, sec.), 6 & 7 Gt. Smithst. Westminstr
Westminster Loan Offi. (Jn. Coombs, sec.) 20 Mercr. st. Longacr
Westminster Marble Factory (T. H. Hartley, manager), Westminster, 1 Earl st
Westminster Medical Society (Dr. Chune, sec.), 32 Sackville st
Westminster Penitent Female Asylum (Joseph Keep Kilpin, hon. sec.; Mrs. Martha Martin, matron), 1 Meards st. Soho
Westminster Savings' Bank, City of (Henry Poole, actuary), Sessions house, Broad sanctuary
Westminster Society (John Helps, sec.), 429 Strand; see page 2051
Westmoreland Elizabeth Jane (Mrs.), *Wheatsheaf* P.H. 24 High st. Camden town
Westmoreland Society (Jas. Burra, sec.), 18 Bread st. City
Westmoreland Isaac, mer. see Stewart A. & Westmoreland
Westmoreland John, e. india bro. see Keeling & Westmoreland
Westoby Wm. Amos S. barrister, 5 Old sq. Lincoln's inn
Weston Warwick & Co. wool, &c. fact. & mer. 73 Gracechurch st
Weston & Westall, salt merchants, 115 Lower Thames st. & 29 Wharf, City road basin
Weston & Young, bankers, 6 Wellington st. London bridge
Weston Benjamin, butcher, 36 Up. Lisson st. Lisson grove
Weston Charles, butcher, 6 Wells row, Islington
Weston Charles, grocer, 9 Blenheim ter. Bond st. Chelsea
Weston Charles Hen. barrister, 3 Harcourt bldgs. Temple
Weston Daniel, linendraper, 89 Minories
Weston Edwd. John, jun. bricklayr. 54 John st. Blackfrs. rd
Weston Edward John, builder, 60 Brunswick st. Blkfrs. rd
Weston Fedk. *Crown tav.* 22 King Edward st. Newgate st
Weston George, barrister, 7 New square, Lincoln's inn
Weston George, builder, 4 Arthur st. King's rd. Chelsea
Weston George, *Cock & Magpie* P.H. Wilson st. Finsbury
Weston Geo. hop & seed fac. Queen's hd. inn yd. 84 Boro' High st
Weston George, rag dealer, Southampton st. Camberwell
Weston Geo. wholesale tobacconist, 17 Lit. Queen st. Holbrn
Weston Hen. bottle ale & beer stores, 242A, High Holborn
Weston Henry, merchant, 31 St. Swithin's lane
Weston Hen. printer & stationer, 40 Rathbone pl. Oxford st
Weston Hen. *Six Cans & Punchbowl* P.H. 242 High Holbrn
Weston Henry Wm. gen. agent & account. 17 Ironmonger la
Weston James, butcher, 43 Gravel lane, Southwark
Weston James, cement & plaster maker, St. Andrew's wharf, Earl st. Blackfriars; Middle wharf, Great Scotland yard; Tide Mill wharf, Deptford, & Millwall, Poplar
Weston James, hat manufr. 18 Bishopsgate st. within
Weston James, *King's Arms* P.H. 2 Houghton st. Clare mrkt
Weston James, solr. see Teesdale, Symes, Weston & Teesdale
Weston John, accountant, Queen st. chambs. Queen st. City
Weston John, chocolate manufr. 1 Portland rd. Portland pl
Weston John, merchant, 32 Fenchurch st
Weston John, undertaker, 12 East st. Hoxton
Weston John, watch pendant maker, 3 King st. Clerkenwell
Weston Jno. Skerratt, warehousemn. 31 Lawrence la. Cheapsid
Weston Joseph, cane worker, 1 Cavendish st. New North rd
Weston Judith (Mrs.), packing case ma. 11 St. Andrew's hill
Weston Richard, *Surrey* coffee rooms, 18 Union st. Boro'
Weston Richard, goldsmith & jeweller, 11 Rose st. Soho
Weston Richard Henry, jun. shipwright, anchor & ship smith, Gun dock, 280 Wapping
Weston Thomas, coal & charcoal dlr. 8 Gt. Bell al. Coleman st
Weston Thomas, straw hat maker, 166 Tottenham court, rd
Weston Thomas, surgeon, 47 Hoxton Old town
Weston Thomas Eyre, solicitor, 43 Lincoln's inn fields
Weston Thomas S. bricklayer & bldr. 69 Shoe lane, Fleet st
Weston Thomas Stephen, bricklayer, 32 Noble st. Cheapside
Weston William, *Bell* P.H. Lower road, Rotherhithe
Weston William, builder, 1 Somers mews, Somers st. Pdngtn
Weston William, grocer, 11 Leader st. Chelsea
Weston William, plasterer, 20 Graham st. Pimlico
Weston William, shirt & collar manufacturer, 73 Wood st
Westover Richard, leather seller, 3 Theberton st. Islington
Westron & Dignam, warhusmen. 8 Watling st. & 21 Gt. Distaff la
Westron Hen. *Elephant & Castle* P.H. 23 Whitchp. High st
Westrop Hen. profsr. of music, 19 Gt. Percy st. Pentonville
Westrop John King, silks, gloves, &c. agent, 16 Staining la
Westrup Walter & Co. ship bis. bakers, 194 Wapping High st
Westwood Robert & Sons, chemist & druggist, 16 Newgate st
Westwood & Moore, glass bottle & stone ware manufacturers, 10 Wharf, north side, Paddington basin
Westwood & Wrights, ironfounders, Canal rd. Kingsland rd
Westwood Daniel, fruiterer, 56 Snows fields, Borough
Westwood Daniel, wireworker, 3 Mount row, New Kent rd
Westwood John, coffee rooms, 53 Judd st. Brunswick sq
Westwood John, gardener, New road, South Lambeth
Westwood Mary Ann (Mrs.), hatter, 7 Beech st. Barbican
Westwood Sarah (Mrs.), corkcutter, 17 Baker's row, Whtcp
Westwood Wm. shipping butcher, 4 High st. Stepney
Westwood Wm. solicitor, see Chauntler & Westwood
Wetenhall George & Co. sharebrokers, & proprietors of the *Share Guide*, 1A Angel court, Bank
Wetenhall James, stockbroker, 13 Copthall court
Wetenhall John, stockbroker, 1 Angel ct. Throgmorton st
Wetherall James, *Red Hart* P.H. 111 Fetter lane
Wetherell Sir Chas. knt. queen's counsel, 5 Stone bldgs. Lin. inn
Wetherell John, coffee rooms, 24 Charing cross
Wetherell Jsph. *Duke of Wellington* P.H. 8 Cannon st. St. Geo. ea
Wetherell Mary (Mrs.), cowkeeper, 11 Lit. Marylebone st
Wetherell Nathan, barrister, 3 Old square, Lincoln's inn
Wetherhead Thomas, surgeon, 13 Up. Baker st. Regent's pk
Wetherhead Thos. surgeon, see Palethorpe & Wetherhead
Wetherfield Wm. & Hen. fruit salesmen, Covent gard. fruit mkt
Wetherfield John, surgeon, 1 Henrietta st. Covent garden
Wetherilt Charles, smith & brazier 11 Sun ct. Curzon st
Wetherilt Elizabeth (Mrs.), baker, 11 Carlisle st. Lambeth
Wetten & Ellis, attorneys, 48 Conduit st. Hanover sq
Wetten Mary (Mrs.), coffee rooms, 29 Coventry st. Haymarkt
Wetten Rt. Gunter, architct. & survyr. 6 Gt. College st. Westm
Wettig Sophia, (Mrs.), tailor, 37 Foley pl. Gt. Portland st
Wetton George, baker, 6 Felix terrace, Liverpool road, & 19 Lower road, Islington
Wetton James, baker, 3 Road side, Mile end road
Wetton William Edward, baker, 106 Brick lane, Spitalfields
Wever William, poulterer, Camberwell green
Wevill John, tobacconist, 4 Surrey pl. Newington butts
Wey John, tobacconist, 72 Bridport pl. New North road
Weybret Henry, shoemaker, 12 Green st Bethnal green
Weybret John, boot & shoe maker, 212 Whitechapel road
Weyl Simon, merchant, 3 Copthall buildings
Weymouth & Green, solicitors, 10 Angel ct. Bank
Weymouth Jonathan, solicitor, 89 Chancery lane
Whale Andrew Reid, teadealer, 209 High Holborn
Whale Geo. grocer, &c. Patriot row, Cambrdg. rd. Mile end
Whale Henry, grocer, 13 Hawkins st. Sidney st. Mileend
Whale Joseph, cattle salesman, 8 Smithfield
Whale Samuel, tailor, 1 Great Titchfield st
Whale Mary A. (Mrs.), *Cherry Tree* P.H. 12 Gt. Cherry garden st. Bermondsey
Whale Wm. *Fountain* tea gardens, Jamaica level, Rother
Whalebone George, coach plater, 5 Duke st. Bishopsgate
Whales John, tailor, 5 Gresse st. Tottenham court road
Whaley John, carpenter, 17 Brewer st. north, Goswell rd
Whaley John, watch & clockmaker, 14 Mount st. Lambeth
Whaley Wm. pewterers' cabinet ma. 64 Rahere st. Goswell rd
Whalley Geo. Hammond, barrister, 4 Serjeant's inn, Fleet st
Whalley Joseph, w. i. mercht. 7 Gt. Prescot st. Goodman's fi
Whalley Richard, provision agt. & merch. 25 Pudding la

Whalley William, attorney, 14 Gray's inn square
Wharram Wm. & Son, funl.carriage masters,25 Bridge ho. pl
Wharton & Ford, solicitors, 8 Lincoln's inn fields
Wharton Hen. & John & Chas. pawnbrokers, 20 Crosby row, Walworth road, & 243 Bermondsey st. Borough
WhartonWm.&Co.who.milliners&child bedlinenwa.191Strnd
Wharton Geo. Odell, pawnbroker, 36 Mount st. Lambeth
Wharton James,news agent,&c. 20½ Charlotte rw.Walwth.rd
Wharton John, beer retailer, Camden st. south, Camden twn
Wharton John Jane Smith, solicitor, 36 Lincoln's inn fields
Wharton Joseph, woolstapler, 60 Bermondsey st
Wharton Robert, barrister, 1 Tanfield court, Temple
Wharton Robert, surveyor,Collingwd. ho.6 Broad st.Ratcliff
Whateley Wm. queen's counsel, 3 Tanfield ct. Temple
Whateley Saml.&Co.grcrs.&cheesemgrs.10William st.Liss.gr
Whateley Edward, dairy, 51 Church road, Commercial rd.ea
Whateley James, cheesemonger,10James st. Cannon st. road
Whateley Thos. Denman, barrister, 8 New sq. Lincoln's inn
Whatmore Ann (Mrs.),*NewInn*P.H.5Edgware rd.Marylebn
Whatmore Henry,china & glass seller, 76 Tothill st. Westm
WhatmoughMary(Mrs.),straw hat ma.35St.John's la.Smthfl
Whayman Wm.coal & coke mer.35 Jubilee st.Commcerl.rd.ea
Wheal Ann (Mrs.), grocer, 11 Bury st. Bloomsbury
Whealler John A.oilcake & seed mer. & com. agt. 34 Mark la
Wheatcroft (German) & Sons, canal & rail. carriers, 126 London wall; & Wharf, 4 South side, Paddington basin
Wheatcroft Wm. brassfounder, 18 Berkley st. Clerkenwell
Wheater James, *Walter Arms* P.H. Flood st. Deptford
Wheater Saml. lathe maker & smith, 104Golden la.St.Luke's
Wheatland George,chairmaker,17Northumberland st.Nw.rd
Wheatley James Thos. & Co. lightermen & sailing barge owners, Waterloo dock, & 31 Commercial road, Lambeth
Wheatley Benj. Robt. bookseller, 42 Maiden la. Covent gdn
Wheatley Charles Francis, bootma. 28 Duke st. Bloomsbhry
Wheatley Geo. S. *London Hospital*P.H.207Whitechapel rd
Wheatley Henry,pro. of music,5Up.Queen's bldgs,Brompton
Wheatley James, turner, 78 Long alley, Finsbury
Wheatley James F. lighterman & barge owner, Waterloo dock, & 3 Commercial rd. Lambeth, & at Kensington basin
Wheatley John, coach master, 12 Park la. Kennington cross
Wheatley Joseph Sherwood, solicitor, 34 Walbrook
Wheatley Richd. painter & glazier, 7 William st. Shoreditch
Wheatley Robt. Benj. solicitor, see Abbott & Wheatley
Wheatley Wm. druggist, see Laagton, Langton & Wheatley
Wheatley Wm. fruiterer, 64 Lower Sloane st. Chelsea
Wheatley Wm. prof. of dancing, 5 Up.Queen's bldgs. Brmpt
Wheatley Wm. shoemaker, 39 Gt. Portland st. Oxford st
Wheatley Wm. wharfing. Waterloo dock, Comm. rd. Lmbth
WheatleyWm.Hen. registrar, 33 Esher st. Up.Kennington la
Wheatly Jane (Miss), bookseller, 50 Amwell st. Pentnvlle
Wheatly Robt. Hen. solicitor, 1 New inn, Wych st
Wheaton James, chemist, 11 Sol's row, Hampstead road
Wheatsheaf wharf, Joseph Fletcher, 233 Wapping High st
Wheatstone Charles & William, patentees of the concertina, & music & musical inst. maks. 20 Conduit st. Regent st
Wheeldon John, clothes salesman,157&159 ShadwellHigh st
Wheeler & Ablett, ready made linen warehouse, 23 Poultry
Wheeler & Brockwell (executors of the late John Wheeler), cut glass manufacturers & mounters, 80 Leather lane
Wheeler & Co. stockbrokers, Stock exchange,&3 Hercules ct
Wheeler & Cronin, manufacturers of gold,silver,&giltjewellery, 28 Bartlett's buildings, Holborn
Wheeler Edmd.John&Co.com.mers.&col. agts. 52 O.Broad st
Wheeler & Nicholson, proctors & notaries, 6 Godliman st.
Wheeler & Robinson, tailors, 9 Princes st. Hanover square
Wheeler Ann (Miss), milliner, 44 Burlington arcade
Wheeler Benj. builder & surveyor, Cornwall cres. Camdn. tn
Wheeler Charles, gun ma. 41 Royal st. Carlisle st. Lambeth
Wheeler Cornelius, auctioneer & appraiser,28 Leadenhall st
WheelerEdmd.J.mgr.ofS.AustralianBk.Co.54O.Broadst.Cy
Wheeler Eliz. Sarah(Mrs.),booksel.15Montcomb st.Belgr.sq
Wheeler Fredk. Wm. bookseller, 84 St. John st. road
Wheeler George, baker, 439 Oxford st
Wheeler Geo. grocer&cheesemnger.Portlandter.Wlwrth.com
Wheeler George, surgeon, 56 Queen's road, Bayswater
Wheeler George, wharfinger, Stanton's lower wharf, Stoney lane, 96 Tooley st., &Wheeler's wf.27Churchst.Rotherhith
Wheeler Geo. Rt. tobacco pipe maker,12 Newton st. Holborn
Wheeler Gervase, manuf. jeweller, 28 Bartlett's buildings
Wheeler Hen.card & pasteboard ma. 14 Coppice rw. Clrknwl
Wheeler Hen. carpenter, 17 Bell yard Fleet st
Wheeler Homer, boot & shoe maker, 46 Little Britain
Wheeler James, cheesemonger, 3 Union ter. Notting hill
Wheeler James, teadealer, 9 North row, Grosvenor square
Wheeler Jemima (Miss), grocer, 8 Field place, Lock's fields
Wheeler John, tailor, 77 Gt. Tichfield st
Wheeler John B. hosier, see Ablett & Wheeler
Wheeler John Buchan, chemist, 57 Charlotte st. Fitzroy sq
Wheeler Joseph, brass & cock founder, engine pump, water closet&beermach. ma.92Tottenham ct. rd.&Howland mews
Wheeler Joseph, clerk to parish clerks's company,at the hall, 83 Wood st. Cheapside, & 9 Jamaica row, Bermondsey
Wheeler Joseph, dairy, 6 Camomile st. Bishopsgate
Wheeler Joseph, tailor, Denmark hill, Camberwell
Wheeler Mark, japanned furn.manuft. 8 Newton st.Holborn
Wheeler Mary Ann (Mrs.), *Harrow* P.H.25 Borough markt
Wheeler Richard,coal mercht. St.Ann's whf.Earl st.Blackfrs
Wheeler Robert, cheesemonger, 29 Frederick pl.Hampstd rd
Wheeler Robert, tailor, 27 Park st. Dorset square
Wheeler Saml.carpenter & case mak.53Castle st.Leicester sq
Wheeler Sarah (Mrs.), coffee rms. 32 Lt.Charlotte st.Blkf.rd
Wheeler Thomas, bead manfr. 37 King st. Clerkenwell
Wheeler Thomas, hairdresser, 25 Nassau pl. Comcrl. rd. ea
Wheeler Thomas, surgeon, 61 Gracechurch st
Wheeler William,coach maker,Alfred mews,Tottenham ct.rd
Wheeler William, coal & potato dealer, 95 Berwick st.Soho
Wheeler Wm. map mounter&colorer,9Wine office ct.Fleet st
Wheeler William Henry, baker, 94 Golden lane, St. Luke's
Wheeler William Henry, oil & colorman, 91 Bethnal gr. rd
Wheeler William Henry, tailor, 24 King st. Portman square
Wheeler Wm.Sidney,wool fact.seeTewart Bros.Wheeler&Co
Wheelhouse Geo. distiller & rectifier, 6 Deptford br.Deptford
Wheelhouse Wm.composition doll ma.1Sandy'srw.Bishopsgt
Wheelock Joseph, attorney, 10 Chancery lane
Wheelton, Brewer & Buckland, packer's, 4Bath st.Newgt.st
Wheen Richard & John, soap makers, 78 St. George st
Whelan James, ironmonger, Church st. Hackney
Whelan James, jun.gasfitter&gasfitting manufacturer to the trade, & brass finisher in general, 10 Pump row, Old st.rd
Whelan T. Peter, coin & medal dealer, 202 High Holborn
Wheldon John, bookseller, 4 Paternoster row
Wheldon Joseph, coffee rooms, 1 Russell st. Blackwall
Wheldon Joshua, hatter, 5 Union pl. Lisson grove north
Whelham George, fruiterer, &c. 5 Surrey place, Kennington
Whelham George, jun. shoe wareho. 4 Surrey pl.Kennington
Whellan James, baker, 23 Great Wild st. Drury lane
Wheller James Geo.*Horse& Groom* P.H. 240½ Blackfriars rd
Whellock Arthur, lighterman,52 L.Thames st.&Galley quay
WhelpdaleHenry,*OldDrurytavern*,23Bridgesst.Cov.gardn
Whelpdale Wm. Stephen, *King's Head* P.H. 12 Smithfield
Whenman Charles, trunk ma.22 Frederick pl.Hampstead rd
Whenmouth Gartrall Chas. brass turner, 8 Lit. College st
Whetham Stephen & Sons, merchants,sail cloth, shoe thread nets, twine & web manufacturers,38 Gracechurch st
Whetstone James, carpenter, &c. 9 High st. Notting hill
Whettam Frederick, grocer, 3 Wharf rise, Kingsland road
Whewell Henry, chemist, 29 Borough road, Southwark
Whibley Ambrose, fruiterer, 45 Red Lion st. Holborn
Whichello Rowland, teadealer, 22 Castle st. Leicester sq
Whichelo Fredk. Wiedenbach, *Edinbro' Castle* P.H. Mornington rd. & Stanhope st. Gloucester gate, Regent's park
Whichelo Henry, brass founder, 113 Fore st. Cripplegate
Whichelo John, artist, 26 Charles st. St. James's square
Whichelo Mary Ann (Mrs.), furrier, 2 Church st.Camberwell
Whicheloe Holland Thos. grocer, 5 Gt. George st., Bermndsy
Whichelow Thomas, baker, 17 Cross st. Newington butts
Whicher Charles,greengrocer,14Church row,AldgateHigh st
Whicker & Philp (late Savigny & Co.), cutlers' & surgeons' instrument makers, 67 St. James's st. Pall mall
Whicker George, cutler, see Everill, Philip & Whicker
Whidborne George F. surgeon, 28 Queen square, Bloomsbury
Whiddington & Sherriff,str.hat ma.63NewChurch st.Lsn.gro
Whiddington Richard, tailor, 46½ Princes st. Lisson grove
Whiddon Mary (Mrs.), plasterer, 54 Clarendon st. Somers tn
Whiddon Sarah (Mrs.), dining rooms, 17 Cursitor st
Whiddon Thomas,plasterer&modlr.51Aldenham st.Somrs.tn
Whiffen David, baker, 145 St. John st. road
Whiffen George, ropemaker, Tanner's hill,New town,Dptfrd
Whiffen Edward H.surgeon,104 Grand Junction ter.Edgw.rd
Whiffen Henry, chemist, 80 Albany st. Regent's park
Whiffen James, tailor, 345 Albany road, Camberwell
Whiffen John, saddler, Broadway, Deptford
Whiffen William, carman, the Stowage, Deptford
Whiffin Frederick, butcher, 10 Ellen st. Back Church lane
Whiffin Henry, butcher,30 Somerst st. Aldgate
Whigham James, barrister, 5 Plowden buildings, Temple
Whildon Samuel, gasfitter, 118¼Waterloo road
Whiley James, cheesemonger, 123 Upper White cross st
Whiley Mary(Mrs.),hat box maker,4Cambridge rd.Mile end
Whiley Samuel Burr, shoemaker,2 Webber st.Blackfriars rd
Whiley Wm. Milword,cheesemgr.123Up.Whitecrs.st.St.Lk's
Whillier George, dyer, 18 Aske st. Hoxton

Whimper JosiahWood,wood engrav.20Canterbury pl.Lmbth
Whindley Jas. picture frame ma. 5 Wellington st. Blkfrs. rd
Whinney Thomas, job master & livery stable keeper, 28 Shepherd's market, May fair
Whipham Theodore Wm. special pleader,10King'sBench wk
Whipham Wm.yeast dlr.13Baker's mews,Baker st.Portm.sq
Whipp Samuel, tanner, currier & leather seller, Spa road
Whipple Geo. watch oil manufact. 22 Garnault pl. Clrknwl
Whipple John, wholesale & retail staymaker, 53 Barbican
Whipps James, beer retailer, Church st. Hackney
Whippy & Co. saddlers, &c. 35 & 36 North Audley st
Whishaw Chas. J. & Hen. attorneys, 1 South sq. Gray's inn
Whishaw Fras.civilengnr.sec.to Soc.of Arts,19 Johnst.Adlphi
Whishaw James, barrister, 1 Southampton row, Russell sq
Whiskard JamesAugustus,pawnbroker,9 Sun st.Bishopsgate
Whisker Joseph, carman, 25 North st. Sloane st. Chelsea
Whiskin James Fuller, wine mercht. 4 Carlton st. Regent st
Whisler John&Co.woollen warehousemen,31 Lawrencela.City
Whisson Nath. *Crown & Anchor* P.H.32Judd pl.Wst.New rd
Whistler Frederick & Co. merchants, 16 Sise la.Bucklersbury
Whistler Frederick & Co. winemerchants,16 Sisela.Bcklrsbry
Whistler Edward (from the late C. Vaughan's), silversmith & pawnbroker, & dealer in secondhand plate, jewellery, guns, pistols & rifles, 11 Strand
Whistler Edwd.Webster, colonial produce agt.9Fenchurch st
Whitaker Chs.&J. mould trnrs.16Whitehorse alley,Cowcross
Whitaker & Jerrand, sole proprietor of W. Little's patent indian corn starch, 25A, & 69 Hatton garden
WhitakerJohnH.&Co.printers,22Chanceryla.&7Symond'sinn
Whitaker John & Joseph, turners, 51 Rawstorne st. & at 10 Brewer st. north, Goswell road
Whitaker & Wolff, surgeons & apothecaries, 225 Shoreditch
Whitaker Alfred H. conveyancer, 4 Field court, Gray's inn
Whitaker Charles James, coffee rooms, 5 Houndsditch
Whitaker James, prof. of music,36 Prichard's rd.Hackneyrd
Whitaker Edward Thomas, solicitor, 12 Lincoln's inn fields
Whitaker Emily (Miss), lawstatnr. Serlest. gatewy.Linc.inn
Whitaker John, beer retailer, 9 Carburton st. Fitzroy square
Whitaker John, beer retailer, 19 Robert st. Hampstead road
Whitaker John, professor of music, 24 Thavies inn
Whitaker John, dealer in iron safes, 28 Water la. Blckfrs
Whitaker John, stationer & gen. slsman. 109 Bethnal grn. rd
Whitaker Joseph, solicitor, 7 Furnival's inn, Holborn
Whitaker Joseph, french polisher, 11 Chester ter. Boro' road
Whitaker Joseph, tassel mould turner, 36 Farringdon st
Whitaker Joseph Wm.*Noah'sArk*P.H. 3 New Park st. Boro'
Whitaker Richard, sen. tinplate wkr. 62 St. John st. Smithfl
Whitaker Robert, card maker, 13 Little Britain
Whitaker Robert, chair maker, 10 Nelson place, City rd
Whitaker Stephen, pawnbroker,12 Long la.West Smithfield
Whitaker Thomas,*ChesterArms*,P.H.1Chester ter.Eaton sq
Whitaker Thomas,*HampshireHog*,P.H.90Berwick st.Soho
Whitaker Thomas, linendraper, 83High st. Portland town
Whitaker Thos. wholesale & retail stationer, 10 Walbrook
Whitaker William, turner, 4 Denmark st. Soho
Whitaker Wm. watch & clock maker, 8High st. Camberwell
Whitbourn Francis, merchant, 8 Birchin lane
Whitbourn Francis, miller, see Sharp & Whitbourn
Whitbourn John,chair & cabinet maker, 29 Park st.Dorset sq
Whitbread & Co. brewers, Chiswell st. &26Wharf rd.City rd
Whitbread & Starkey, sheep salesmen, 60 West Smithfield
Whitbread Edward, baker, 1 Brett terrace, Hampstead rd
Whitbread Gordon, barrister, 8 New sq. Lincoln's inn
Whitby Stone Comp.(Wm.Radford, agt.), 14 Forest. Limeh
Whitby Edward, wharfinger, see Parker & Whitby
Whitby John Burridge, cowkeeper,34Woodland st. Dalston
Whitby Luke, builder, 11 Poultry
Whitby Wm.skin mer.& commis.agt.13Lit.St.ThomasApostl
Whitchurch James, bacon drier, 118 Goswell st
Whitchurch Thos.grocer & italian wa.26High st. Kensington
Whitcomb & Barton, metal brokers, 75 Old Broad st. City
Whitcombe Arthur, look. gl. mfr. 23Coventry st.Haymarket
Whitcombe George, tobacconist, 191 Church st. Shoreditch
Whitcombe John, wine merchant, 1 Park st. Grosvenor sq
Whitcombe Nathaniel Jas. solicitor,12Bedford st.Bedford sq
White Alex. & Son,brass manfrs.40 Tabernacle walk,Finsby
White,Blake,Tylee&Fawkener,solicitors,14 Essex st. Strand
White & Borrett, solicitors, 35 Lincoln's inn fields
White Chas. G. & Co. anchorsmiths, ironfounders, &c. 5 George yard, Lombard st.; & Emmett st. Limehouse
White Eustace & John Wm. solicitors, 37Old Broad st.City
White, Eyre &White, solicitors, 11Bedford row,Bloomsbury
White & Fairchild, teadealers, 63 Borough High st
White George & Henry, butchers, 123 Edgware rd.Paddgtn
White, Greenwell & Co. carpet warehouse, 78 Watling st
White, Greenwell & Co. linendrapers, 53, 54&55 Blackfrs. rd
White&Greenwell,manchst.&silk wareho.107&108 Cheapside
White Henry & Co. wine & spirit brokers, 16 Mincing lane
White Jas. & Son, auctioneers, &c.14 Union ct. Old Broad st
White John Bazley & Sons, roman & portland cement manufacturers, brickmakers & marble merchants, & patentees of Keene's marble cement, 17 Millbank st. Westminster; Earl st. Blackfriars; Albion wharf, Deptford bridge; C. Bell's wharf, South wharf rd. Paddington; & Druce's wharf, Paradise row, Chelsea; depôt, 36 Seel st. Liverpool; manufactory, Swanscombe, Kent
White John&Chas.&Co.wine &brandy merchants,10Lime st
White JohnChas.&Son,merchs.15Barge yd.Chamb.Bucklsb
White John & Robert, ship smiths, &c. 95 Lr. East Smithfi
White Joseph & Co. tailors, 11 Wade's pl. Hackney rd
White Louisa (Mrs.) & J. B. cutlers, 8 Gt. St. Andrew st
White, Lewis & Co. grocers & oilmen, 52 Crown st. Finsby
White, Lupton & Co. manchester warehousemen & linen merchants, 53 Bread st. & 79 Watling st
White Martha Hawkes&Co.shoewa.15Juddst.Brunswicksq
White & Murray, solicitors, 7 Whitehall place
White Patrick & Co. commission agent, 5 Gt.Trinity lane
White & Price, wine & brandy merchants, 45 Mark lane
White Richard James & Co. feather dressers, 33 Rodney st Pentonville & 2 Russia row, Milk st. Cheapside
White Richd. Saml. & Son,solicitors, 11 Lincoln's inn fields
White Saml. H.&Co.gen.&for.merchts.16St. Albanspl.StJas'
White & Sergeant, law stationers, 14 Serles pl. Lincoln'sinn
White & Syer, oil & colormen, window glass & lead merchants & paper stainers. 195 Whitechapel rd
White Thos. & Co. coal merchants, Bell wharf, Mile end rd
White Thos. Hen. & John,tobacco manufacts,213 Shoreditch
White ThomasReynolds& Alfred, aquafortis manufacturers & chemists, 10 Castle st. Saffron hill
White Thomas & Son, bootmakers, 1 Charles st.Westminstr
White Thomas Nickalls&Son,coachmakers,29&30 Longacre
White William & Co. furriers, 42 Wigmore st. Cavendish sq
White Wm. D.&Fred.G.wharfingrs.Kennet wf.U.Thames st
White Wm.& Hen. carvers&gilders,23 Barnetst.Hackneyrd
White William & Son, hatters, 68 Cheapside
White's ClubHouse(HenryRaggett,prop.)37&38St.James' st
White Abraham, butcher, 5 Middlesex st. Aldgate High st
White Alexander, bread & biscuit baker, 249 Oxford st
White Andrew, baker, 208 Bermondsey st
White Andrew, board & lodging ho. 11 America sq.Minories
White Andrew, commission agent, 11 America sq.Minories
White Andw.M.D.dep.insp.gen.ofhospls.14Hertford st.Mayfr
White Ann(Mrs.),babylinenwarh.17Woburn bldgs.Tavstk.sq
White Ann (Mrs.), hotpresser,1 Princes sq.Wilson st.Finsby
White Anthony, surgeon, 5 Parliament st. Westminster
White Anthony R. tea, coffee & col.produce agt.8Eastcheap
White Arthur James, hatter & hat manufr. 19 Regent st
White Barnard, butcher, 93 Lower marsh, Lambeth
White Benjamin, corndealer, 28 Red Lion st. Whitechapel
White Benjamin, hardware & fancy wareho.79 Houndsditch
White Benjn. horse slaughterer,12Thomas st.Whitechapelrd
White Benjamin, house agent, 24 Lime st
White Benjamin, shopkeeper, 26 Hereford st. Lisson grove
White Catherine (Mrs.), stationer, 5 Cleveland st. Fitzroy sq
White Chas. beer retailer, Southampton st. Camberwell
White Chas. boot & shoe maker, 80 East st. Manchester sq
White Chas. coachmaker, 14 Cheltenham pl. Westminster rd
White Chas. cornchandler, &c. 5 Up. Grafton st. Fitzroy sq
White Chas. *Royal Standard* P.H.17Harper st. NewKent rd
White Chas. window glass & lead dealer, 193 Whitechapel rd
White Chas. wine merchant, 4 Paragon, New Kent road
White Chas. G. oilman, 13 High st. Camberwell
White Charlotte (Mrs.), potato dealer, 1 Park st. Borough
White Charlotte M.(Mrs.), baker, 47Wentworth st. Whtchpl
White Clement, tailor & draper, 36 King st. Covent garden
White Daniel, chemist, 19 Park terrace, Regent's park road
White David, boat & barge builder, 85 Bankside, Southwark
White David, bootmaker, 8 Gt. Crown court, Lit.Pulteney st
White David, chandler's shop, 21Charles st. St. George's east
White David, cheesemonger, 19 Copenhagen st. Pentonville
White David, smith, 24 Berwick st. Pimlico
White David, tailor, 5 Gt. Pulteney st. & 8 Gt. Crown court
White David, *Turk's Head* P.H. 75 Turnmill st. Clerkenwell
White David Thos. drawing & picture dealer, 28 Maddox st. Regent st. & 29 Gt. James st. Bedford row
White Edlin, wholes. tea & coffee dealr. see Johnson & White
White Edwd. basket & brush maker, turner, &c. 27 Cannon st
White Edward, gunmaker, 3 Worcester st. Old Gravel lane
White Edward, solicitor, 12 Gt. Marlborough st
White Edward, surgeon, 73 Lamb's Conduit st. Foundling
White Edward, wine merchant, 50 Mark lane
White Edward Gillam, barrister, 1 New sq. Lincoln's inn

White Edwin, bedstead & bed. pillar mak. 57 Old st. St. Luke's
White Elisha, baker, 2 Flagon row, Deptford
White Elizh. (Mrs.), baker, 6 Little Carter la. Godliman st
White Elizh. (Mrs.), baker, 1 Tyssen st. Bethnal green
White Elizh. (Mrs.), coffee rooms, 1 St. Andrew's hill, Doc.com
White Elizh. (Mrs.), *Lebeck's Head* P.H. 75 Shadwell High st
White Elizh. (Mrs.), straw hat ma. 18 Market row, Oxford mkt
White Ellen (Madame), french milliner, 56 Quadrant, Reg. st
White Francis, cooper, Canal bridge, Old Kent road
White Francis, grocer & oilman, 2 Goldsmiths row, Hackney rd
White Francis, hairdresser, 2 Portland place, Borough road
White Francis, newsvender, 2 Carnaby st. Golden square
White Fras. E. (Mrs.), lodg. ho. 3 Northumberland ct. Strand
White Fras. G. surgeon, 45 Glo'ster ter. New rd. Commercl. rd
White Frederick, brewer, 13 North st. Sloane st
White Frederick, hairdresser, 3 Charlton st. Fitzroy sq
White Fred. leather cutter, 9 Henrietta st. Manchester sq
White Fred. *Old Parr's Head* P.H. 4 Little Knightrider st
White Fred. Thomas, barrister, 6 Stone bldgs. Lincoln's inn
White George, attorney, 12 Hatton garden
White George, bottle & rag merc. 22 Robt. st. Grosvenor sq
White George, bricklayer, 5 Hampstead street, Fitzroy sq
White George, carp. & undertak. 16 Tufton st. Westminster
White George, carpenter, 3 Stafford pl. south, Pimlico
White George, carver, &c. 39 Vauxhall bridge road
White George, *Crown* P.H. Mayfield pl. Kensington High st
White George, *Crown & Sugar Loaf* P.H. 14 Garlick hill
White George, dealer in birds, &c. 11 High row, Knightsbdg
White George, grocer, 279 Albany road, Camberwell
White George, grocer, 10 Old Chapel row, Kentish town
White George, haircutter & stationer, 12 Charles st. Portman sq
White George, hosier & glover, 3 Rockingham rw. New Kent rd
White George, oil & colorman, 32 North st. Edgware rd
White George, smith, 15 Lock's sq. York st. Walworth road
White George, tailor, 205 Regent st
White Geo. *White Hart* P.H. 10 Vine ct. Wheeler st. Sptlflds
White Geo. Arden, *White Lion* P.H. 6 Brick la. St. Luke's
White Geo. Bailey, grocer, 147 Shoreditch High st
White Geo. Francis, surgeon, &c. 8 Haymarket
White Geo. Francis, surgeon, &c. Langley pl. Coml. rd. east
White Geo. Harton, artist, 69 Dean st. Soho
White Geo. Henry, merchant, 1 Birchin lane, Cornhill
White Geo. Towry, barrister, 25 Old sq. Lincoln's inn
White Geo. W. upholsterer, 13 Cheltenham pl. Westminst. rd
White Harriot (Miss), coffee rooms, 8 Rosamond bldgs. Islgtn
White Heloise (Madame), milliner, 269 Regent st
White Henry, book & music seller, 350A, Oxford st
White Henry, brass finisher, 11 Guildford pl. Spa fields
White Henry, coal dealer, 52 Chapel st. Somers town
White Henry, linendraper, 7 Hamilton pl. Deptford High st
White Henry, *Masons' Arms* P.H. 37 Watney st. Coml. rd. east
White Henry, painter, glazier, &c. 25 Frith st. Soho
White Henry, plumber, 8 Carburton st. Fitzroy sq
White Henry, *Red Cross* P.H. 33 Barbican
White Henry, tailor & draper, 53 Great Marlborough st
White Henry, *Victory* P.H. 27 Nelson st. Bethnal gr
White Henry, wharfinger, Carron whf. 87 Low. East Smithfield
White Henry Cornelius, confectioner, 121 Goswell st
White Henry Hopley, barrister, 13 Old sq. Lincoln's inn
White Henry John, merchant, 76 Old Broad st. City
White Henry William, potato dealer, 101 Bethnal green rd
White Isaac, tailor, &c. 28 Tabernacle walk, Finsbury
White Isabella A. (Mrs.), hosiery, glove & shirt wa. 146 Strand
White James, bricklayer, 29 John st. west, Edgware rd
White James, builder, 36 East st. Red Lion sq
White James, cabinet maker, 15 Vere st. Clare market
White James, chemical manfrs. agt. Dowgate wf. Up. Thas. st
White James, *Crown* P.H. Lambeth road, Obelisk
White James, furniture broker, 19 St. Clement's la. Strand
White James, gardener, 32 Chapel st. Pentonville
White James, grocer, 13 New North st. Finsbury
White James, hairdresser, Stratford broadway
White James, livery stables, 5 Devonport mews, Oxford ter
White James, marine store dealer, 14 Emmett st. Poplar
White James, millmaker, 266 High Holborn
White James, *Portsmouth Arms* P.H. 4 Shepherd st. Oxford st
White James, *Spread Eagle* P.H. 303 Oxford st
White James Henry, shoe ma. 33 Pritchard's rd. Hackney rd
White James P. *Globe* P.H. King's road wst. (so. side) Chelsea
White James Wm. lath & timberyard, 10 Church st. Shoreditch
White Jane (Mrs.), butcher, 15 Regent st. Horseferry road
White John, agt. to the Sun Fire offi. 7 Gt. Russell st. Blmsby
White John, architect, 1 Devonshire pl. north, New road, & Westbourn green, Harrow road
White John, bookseller & stationer, 2 Devereux ct. Strand
White John, butcher, 205 Shadwell High st
White John, cheesemonger, 38 Mount st. Lambeth
White John, chemist to her majesty, 228 Piccadilly
White John, *Crown & Cushion* P.H. 9 Little Russell st. Covent garden
White John, earthenware dealer, 4 Neptune st. Rotherhithe
White John, general turner, 5 Whitehart st. Drury lane
White John, grindery dealer, 6 Gt. St. Andrew st. Sevendials
White John, grocer & cheesemonger, 59 Cotton st. Poplar
White John, grocer & cheesemonger, Nine Elms, Vauxhall
White John, livery stables, 5 Lit. Cadogan pl. Sloane st. Chels
White John, *Phœnix* P.H. 19 Princes st. Cavendish sq
White John, plumber, 28 Mid. Grove st. Commercial rd. east
White John, plumber, 55 Paul st. Finsbury
White John, registrar of births, 15 Gt. Charlotte st. Blkfrs. rd
White John, solicitor, see Trehern & White
White John, surgeon, &c. 1 Princes st. Westminster
White John, tailor, 28 Gerrard st. Soho
White John, tailor, 29 Mount st. Lambeth
White John, tailor, 21 Warren st. Fitzroy square
White John, timber merchant, White Horse lane, Stepney
White John, tobacconist, 5 Hackney road
White John, wine merchant, 7 St. Benet's pl. Gracechurch st
White John Joseph, insurance broker, Lloyd's
White John Wm. baker, 32 Charles st. Westminster
White John Wm. proctor & notary, 10 Godliman st. Doc. coms
White Joseph, architect, 68 Lamb's Conduit st
White Joseph, chimney sweep, 12 North row, Grosvenor sq
White Joseph, china & glass manufacturer, 210 Regent st
White Joseph, herbalist, Covent garden fruit market
White Joseph, house painter, paper hang. &c. 22 Coleman st
White Joseph, insurance broker, Lloyds
White Joseph, *King of Prussia* P.H. 7 Low. John st. Gldn. sq
White Joseph, *Sir Sidney Smith* P.H. 26 Chester st. Kengtn. cr
White Joseph, tobacconist, 25 Clare st. Clare market
White Joseph, turner, 4 Cross st. Golden square
White Joseph, waste paper dealer, 113 Broadwall, Blkfrs. rd
White Levi, grocer, 1 Churchway, Somers town
White Mary (Mrs.), baker, 18 Finsbury pavement
White Mary (Mrs.), dining rooms, 7 James st. Oxford st
White Mary E. (Miss), hosier & shirt maker, 248 High Holborn
White (Miss), ladies' school, 32 Kensington square
White Nathaniel, *White Lion* P.H. 51 Brook st. Grosvenor sq
White Peirce, plumber, 2 Paradise row, Chelsea
White Peter, billiard table maker, 26 Broad st. Golden sq
White Rebecca (Mrs.), tobacconist, see Brampton & White
White Richard, boot & shoe maker, 193 Drury lane
White Richard, livery stablekeeper, York st. Walworth rd
White Richard, teadealer & grocer, 149 Princes rd Lambeth
White Richard, union dairy, 5 Union st. New Bond st
White Richard, wine & spirit merchant, 34 Long acre
White Richard James, feather mer. 33 Rodney st. Pentonville
White Richard Saml. barrister, 22 Old sq. Lincoln's inn
White Robert, baker, 56 Wardour st. Soho
White Robert, custom house agent, see Miskin & White
White Robert, dairyman, 11 Lr. Porchester st. Edgware rd
White Robt. locksmith & bellhngr. 35 Betts st. Ratcliff hgwy
White Robert, locksmith & bellhanger, 12 Queen st. Pimlico
White Robert, pat. leather dresser, Devonshire st. Globe rd
White Rt. Faulder, gen. advertisement off. see Barker & White
White Saml. cheesemonger, 15 & 16 St. Alban's pl. St. James's
White Samuel, furnishing undertaker, 50 Borough road
White Samuel, piece broker, 30 Broad st. Golden square
White Samuel, shoemaker, 4 Gt. Carlisle st. Portman markt
White Samuel Geo. solicitor, 4 Sion college gardens, Aldrmnby
White Samuel White, merchant, Garraway's coffee house
White Sarah (Mrs.), *Black Bull* P.H. 296 Rotherhithe wall
White Sarah (Mrs.), cheesemonger, 34 Aldersgate st
White Sarah (Mrs.), cheesemonger, 5 Lombard st. Chelsea
White Sarah (Mrs.), coffee rooms, 4 Lower Thames st
White Stephen, butcher, 17 Limehouse causeway
White Stephen, surgeon, 1 Lamb's Conduit st. Foundling
White Stephen Prescott, barrister, 2 Old sq. Lincoln's inn
White Thomas, *Artichoke Inn*, 21 Newington causeway
White Thomas, *Bell* P.H. 11 Noble st. Cheapside
White Thomas, beer retailer, 152 Shadwell High st
White Thomas, butcher, 3 Crown st. Walworth road
White Thomas, chairmaker, 7 Joiner st. Westminster road
White Thomas, chemist & medicine chest depôt, 24 Cornhill
White Thomas, coal mercht. Dowgate wharf, Up. Thames st
White Thomas, corn & coal merchant, Globe wf. 330 Wapping
White Thomas, farrier, New yd. Gt. Queen st. Lincoln's inn flds
White Thos. grocer & cheesemonger, 25 Ferry rd. wst. Poplar
White Thomas, hairdresser, Southampton st. Camberwell
White Thomas, *Moor's Arms* P.H. Bromley New town
White Thomas, *Salutation* P.H. 21 Princes st. Stamford st
White Thomas, ship agent, 83 Lower Thames st

White Thomas, tobacconist, 55 Old st. St. Luke's
White Thomas, window blind maker, 201 Poplar High st
White Thos. Henry, curiosity dealer, 12 Cross st. Newington
White Thos. Hewson, upholsterer, &c. 28 Store st. Bedford sq
White Walter, oil & colorman, 63 St. Mary Axe
White Walter, solicitor, 6 Chancery lane
White Wm. baker, Ferry road west, Poplar
White Wm. baker, 23 Park st. Dorset square
White Wm. bookseller, 24 Pall mall
White William, cheesemonger, 42 Chapel st. Grosvenor pl
White Wm. cheesemonger, 52 Chapel st. Pentonville
White Wm. cheesemonger, 2 George row, Bermondsey
White Wm. chemist to her Majesty, 8 Haymarket
White Wm. cowkeeper, 14 Sandwich st. Burton crescent
White Wm. fruiterer, 4 Brill row, Somers town
White Wm. fruiterer, 61 Salisbury st. Lisson grove
White Wm. grocer, 108 Goswell st
White Wm. *Guilford Arms* P.H. 83 Guilford st. Russell sq
White Wm. hat manufact. 9 Crescent, Southwark bridge rd
White Wm. *Horse & Groom* P.H. 4 Geo. yd. Duke st. Grovnr. sq
White Wm. livery stable keeper, 21 Beckford rw. Walwth. rd
White Wm. printer, 79 Gt. Queen st. Lincoln's inn fields
White Wm. surgeon, 21 Aldersgate st
White Wm. tailor, 3 Chichester rents, Chancery lane
White Wm. tailor, 74 Leman st. Goodman's fields
White Wm. tobacconist, 103 Strand
White Wm. *University Hotel*, 29 Grafton st. east
White Wm. wholesale shirt maker, 70 Wood st. Cheapside
White Wm. B. printslr. & picture dlr. 14 Brownlow st. Bdfd. row
White Wm. Denton, *Globe* P.H. 118 High Holborn
White Wm. Fredk. D.C.L. advocate, 15 Regent st. & 1 College, Doctors' commons
White Wm. Hen. printr. & paper stain. 22 Crown rw. Mile en. rd
White Wm. Raine, grocer, 55 Strutton ground, Westminster
White Wm. Thomas, baker, &c. 22 Gt. Ormond st. Queen sq
Whitebrooke William, cooper, 39 Borough road
Whitechapel & Tower Hamlets' Savings' Bank (Jeremiah Thomas Ilsley, sec.), 6 Osborne st. Whitechapel
Whitechurch Edward, coach & harness maker, 82 Long acre
Whitechurch George, hosier, 59 Bishopsgate st. within
Whitechurch Rd. buildr. 89 Chancery la. & 2 Star yd. Carey st
Whitechurch Wm. grocer, 9 Bedford pl. Comml. road east
Whitehall James, ship chandler, 61 Wapping wall
Whitehead & Anderson, tailors & outfitters, 72 Fore st. Lmhs
Whitehead & Brothers, manufacturers of the patent woollen driving belts to supersede leather straps for machinery (agent, Richard Jones), 27 Bedfordbury, Covent garden
Whitehead Alicia (Mrs.), haberdasher, 44 Bath st. City rd
Whitehead Benjn. currier, Dean's mws. Holywell la. Shrdth
Whitehead Edward, tailor & outfitter, 258 Poplar High st
Whitehead Emma (Miss), ladies' school, 7 Blomfield st. City
Whitehead Frances (Mrs.), baker, 56 Brick la. Spitalfields
Whitehead George, conveyancer, 2 Boyle st. Saville row
Whitehead Henry, attorney, 7 Whitehead's grove, Chelsea
Whitehead James, grocer, 17 Ray st. Clerkenwell
Whitehead James, mast & block ma. 75 Fore st. Limehouse
Whitehead James Saml. pork butcher, 28 Low. marsh, Lmbth
Whitehead James Samuel, pork butcher, 192 Shoreditch
Whitehead John, stockbroker, see Carden & Whitehead
Whitehead Lyttleton, appraiser & brok. 3 Moor la. Cripgt
Whitehead Philip, tailor, 43 Upper York st. Bryanstone sq
Whitehead Robert, *Rum Puncheon* P.H. 98 Up. Whitecross st
Whitehead Thomas, appraiser, 39 Aldermanbury
Whitehead Thos. *Bricklayers' Arms* P.H. 11 Chapel ct. Boro'
Whitehead Thomas, fruiterer, 3 York pl. Hackney road
Whitehead Thomas, working gun ma. 117 Dorset st. Fleet st
Whitehead Thomas H. french polisher, 93 John st. Fitzroy sq
Whitehead Thomas M. solicitor, 2 Gt. James st. Bedford rw
Whitehead Wm. chimney sweeper, 49 Gt. Alie st. Goodman's fi
Whitehead Wm. grocer, 1 Weybridge place, Mile end road
Whitehead Wm. Miller, printer, 27 Polygon, Clarendon sq
Whitehead Wm. Hen. registr. of Bankruptcy, 82 Basinghall st
Whitehorn Caleb, grocer & tea dlr. 34 Sloane sq. Chelsea
Whitehorn Elizabeth (Mrs.), carman, 1 New rd. St. George's
Whitehorn James, lime merchant, Nine elms, Vauxhall
Whitehorn James, whiting manufr. 33 Wharf rd. City rd
Whitehorn John, jeweller, 20 Featherstone bldgs. Holborn
Whitehorn Wm. *Rodney's Head* P.H. 22 Rodney st. Pentonvl
Whitehouse Jas. & Co. needle manfs. 2 Nottingham pl. City rd
Whitehouse John & James, opticians, 10 Tottenham court rd
Whitehouse John & Sons, wharfingers & canal carriers, *Greyhound* yard, Milton st. Fore st.; & 17 Wharf, City rd. basin
Whitehouse Benj. boiler maker, 2 Nottingham pl. City road
Whitehouse David, clock dial enamlr. 4 Wilmington st. Spafl
Whitehouse Henry, modelr. & chaser, 22 Wynyatt st. Goswl. rd
Whitehouse James, grocer, 31 Featherstone st. City road
Whitehouse John, coach ironmong. & plater, & carriage lamp, spring & axletree ma. 5 Mead place, Westminster road
Whitehouse John, furrier, 153 Oxford st
Whitehouse John, straw bonnet & lace wareh. 154 Oxford st
Whitehouse John Hen. optician, 29 William st. Hampstead rd
Whitehouse Joseph, solicitor, 1 Francis st. Bedford square
Whitehouse Joseph, solicitor, 36 Lincoln's inn fields
Whitehouse Joseph, spectacle ma. 3 Wilmington st. Spafields
Whitehouse Nathaniel, optician, 1 Castle st. Leicester square
Whitehouse Richard, poulterer, Church st. Hackney
Whitehouse Richard, solicitor, 7 Chancery lane
Whitehurst Charles, commsn. agt. 1 George yd. Aldermanbury
Whitehurst Chas. Howard, queen's counsel, 1 Brick ct. Temple
Whitehurst Wm. coachmaker, see Walter & Whitehurst
Whitelaw James & Son, carpenters & builders, 25 Litchfield st. Soho, & 25 Store st. Bedford square
Whitelaw George, bookbinder, 189 Fleet st
Whitelaw James, statuary, &c. 5 Bath pl. New rd. Fitzroy sq
Whitelaw Mary (Miss), milliner, 202 Oxford st
Whitelaw Scott, cabinet maker, Holly st. Dalston
Whiteley George, barrister, 3 Middle Temple lane
Whiteley James, undertaker, 24 Brook st. New road
Whiteley John, *Blue Bell* P.H. 116 St. George street
Whiteley John, coal merchant, 13 Harper st. Red Lion sq
Whiteley John, tailor, 41 St. James's pl. St. James's st
Whitell Robt. appraiser, 1 Bedford pl. Commercial rd. east
Whitell Robt. furni. brok. 8 Devonshire pl. Comrcl. rd. east
Whitelock Henry, clothes salesman, 65 Compton st. Clkwl
Whitelock Henry, marine store dlr. 10 Brunswick st. Blkwll
Whitelock John, attorney of Sheriffs' ct. 70 Aldermanbury
Whitelock Wm. work. jeweller, 46 Northampton st. Clerkwl
Whitelock Wm. E. haberdasher, hosier & shirt ma. 166 Strnd
Whitelocke Wm. W. linendraper, &c. 3 Prospect row, Mile end r
Whiteman Fredk. haberdasher, 8 Portland pl. Cambridge rd
Whiteman George F. picture dlr. 19 Swinton st. Gray's inn rd
Whiteman Hen. Jas. french & engh. stay manuf. 34 Old st. rd
Whiteman John Henry, engraver, 97 Wardour st. Soho
Whiteman Robert, tobacconist, Little Chelsea
Whiten Francis, cooper, 97 Great Peter st. Westminster
Whiter William, beer retailer, 105 Brick lane, Spitalfields
Whiteside & Smith, solicitors, 63 Lincoln's inn fields
Whiteside James, coal merchant, Cannon rw. wf. Westmnr
Whiteside John, *Cooper's Arms* P.H. 16 West st. Smithfield
Whiteside Joseph, watchmaker, see Cousens & Whiteside
Whiteside Robert Butler, draper & tailor, 32 Aldgate
Whiteway John Hayman, solicitor, see Edwards & Whiteway
Whitfield & Hughes, brassfounders, lamp manufacturers & gasfitters, 32, New st. square, Shoe lane
Whitfield John & Geo. Jas. cheesemong. 16 Lamb's Cond. st
Whitfield Thomas & Son, grocers, 210 Sloane st. Knightsbdg
Whitfield Alfred, coal mer. 27 Bermondsey wall, Bermondsy
Whitfield Benjamin, fruiterer, 4 Lower terrace, Islington
Whitfield E. (Mrs.), carpet & rug ma. 38 Bishpsg. within
Whitfield Elizh. (Mrs.), egg mer. 2 Church rd. Commercl. rd
Whitfield Elizabeth (Mrs.), linen draper, 12 King st. Westm
Whitfield Geo. carpet & rugma. see Monkhouse, Whitfield & Co
Whitfield Jackson, coffee rooms, 65 King st. Westminster
Whitfield Jackson, lodging house, 25 Cecil st. Strand
Whitfield Sam. jun. brass founder, 38 Oxford st. Birmingham, & at 21 Red Lion st. Clerkenwell; James Standley, agent
Whitfield William, butterman, 44 Old Bond st
Whitfield William, surgical instrument ma. 104 High Holbn
Whitfield William Benson, surgeon, 64 Lamb's Conduit st
Whitfields Fanny (Miss), milliner, see Lambert & Whitfields
Whitford George, watchmaker & jeweller, 1 Smithfield bars
Whitford Samuel, working silversmith, 4 Porter st. Soho
Whitford Thomas, wax bleacher, see Nicholls & Whitford
Whiting Charles, merchant & gen. agent, 7 St. Michael's alley
Whiting Fras. & Co. patent felt mfrs. 5 Barge yd. & Old Ford la
Whiting Matthew & Francis, merchants, Whiting's wharf, 75 & 76 Broad st. Ratcliff, & 5 Barge yard, Bucklersbury
Whiting & Nicholls, cattle salesmen, 37 Smithfield west
Whiting Chas. letter cutter, 29 Charles st. Hampstead rd
Whiting Chas. printer, Beaufort ho. Beaufort bdgs. Strand
Whiting Charles, chemist, 58 Upper Ebury st. Pimlico
Whiting Elizabeth (Mrs.), lodging house, 4 Craven st. Strnd
Whiting Frederic, solicitor, see Brunton & Whiting
Whiting James, *Atlas Newspaper Office*, 6 Southampton st
Whiting James, grocer, &c. 43 Castle st. east, Oxford st
Whiting John, boot & shoe maker, 5 Charlton pl. Islington
Whiting John, butcher, 18 King David lane, Shadwell
Whiting John, wood turner, 35 George st. Shoreditch
Whiting Joseph, circulating lib. 7 Hosier la. West Smithfield
Whiting Joseph, coach smith, 14 Polygon, Clarendon sq
Whiting Jsph. coach spring ma. 19 & 20 Up. Chenies mws. Bd. sq
Whiting Mary (Mrs.), grocer, 1 Norfolk pl. Larkhall la. Clphm

Whiting Richd. *Southampton Arms* P.H.141Tottenhm.ct.rd
Whiting Thomas, bookbinder,7Oxford Arms pas. Newgate st
Whiting Thos. teadlr.& grocer, 8 Chapel st. Grosvenor pl
Whiting Thos. Edwd. fur skin dresser, 15 Kirby st. Hat. gar
Whiting Wm. coffee rooms, 6 Vauxhall bridge foot
Whiting Wm. fruiterer, 4 Southampton st. Camberwell
Whiting Wm. surgical machinist&med.books.15Kingst.Boro'
Whitlam Richd. potato salesman, South row, Covent garden
Whitlaw Charles, patent medicated vapour baths, 30 Argyll st. & 3 Great Castle st. Regent st
Whitley Nathan & Son, ironfoundrs.66 Gt.Guildford st. Boro'
Whitley John, lodging house, 8 Lower James st. Golden sq
Whitling Edmund, wine merchant, 3 Bartholomew lane
Whitelock & Moultrie, solicitors, 70 Aldermanbury
Whitelock John, solicitor, see Moultrie & Whitelock
Whitlock James, *White Swan* P.H.160 Old Gravel lane
Whitlock Mary (Mrs.), chemical works,4Apple yd.Seward st
Whitlock Robert, cheesemonger, 80 Castle st. Leicester sq
Whitlock Robert, cheesemonger, 19 Drury lane
Whitlock Robert, fruiterer, 4 Melbourne pl. Old Kent rd
Whitlock Thos. coach ma. 1 Holland lodge, Addison rd.Kens
Whitlock Thos. coachmaker, 6 Edwardes ter. Kensington rd
Whitlock Wm. chairmaker & turner, 30 Church st. Lambeth
Whitlock William, cheesemonger, 21 Tower st. Seven dials
Whitly William, tailor, 1 Drake st. Red Lion sq
Whitman Thos. architectural carver, 8 Gt. College st.Westmr
Whitmarsh Dan.&Co.lampglassdepôt,10Princes st.Bedfd.rw
Whitmarsh David & Co. glass dealers, 26 Silver st. Goldensq
Whitmarsh Francis, queen's counsel, 3 Serle st. Linc. inn
Whitmarsh Francis, jun. barrister, 8 New Boswell court
Whitmarsh Hen. furn. broker, 54 Westbourne st. Pimlico
Whitmarsh John G. engraver, lithographer, copperplate & letterpress printer, 15 Ironmonger st. St. Luke's
WhitmarshT.H.*George& Vulturetav.&ho.*6Georgeyd Lmbd st
Whitmee Benjamin, farrier, Southampton st. Camberwell
Whitmee John, steel mill & smoke jack maker, 18 Fenchurch buildings; 70 St. John st. Clerkenwell, & 2 Brunswick mews, Brunswick square
Whitmee William, baker, Union road, Clapham road
Whitmee William, coffee rooms, 34 Gt. Castle st. Regent st
Whitmill Elizh.(Mrs.),fruiterer,1Gray'sbldgs.Manchester sq
Whitmore, Roumieu & Walters, solicitors,9New sq.Linc. inn
Whitmore & Sons, stock & share brokers, 17 Change alley
Whitmore Chas. Shapland, barrister, 12 King's Bench walk
Whitmore George, underwriter & ins. broker, 17 Austinfriars
Whitmore John, chemist & surgeon, 125 Oxford st
Whitmore Thomas, fruiterer, 45 Charles st. Westminster
Whitmore Wm. official assignee, 2 Basinghall st
Whitnall Thomas, butcher, 46 Dorset st. Portman square
Whitney Edw. oilman&tallow chandlr. 62 Fetter la. Holborn
Whitney Wm. Wilberforce, butcher, 17 Skinner st. Somers tn
Whitney Wm.U.surgeon&accoucheur,12Gt.College st. Wstm
Whitroe Chas. furniture brok. 7 Regent st. Horseferry road
Whitsey Joseph, engraver, 8 Alfred row, Spa rd.Bermondsey
Whitt John, cooper, Great Woodstock st. Marylebone
Whittaker & Co. booksells. & publishs. 13 to 16 Ave Maria la
Whittaker Edwd. bookbinder, 27 Skinner st. Bishopgate st
Whittaker George, stonesaw maker, Bath st. Tabernacle sq
Whittaker John, builder, 18 Newland st. Pimlico
Whittaker Joseph, grainer, 26 Brown st. Bryanstone square
Whittaker Richd. furn. brok. 8 Lit. Chester st. Grosvenor pl
Whittaker Thos. sheriffs' officer, see Davis (P.) & Whittaker
Whittaker Wm. builder, 18½ Crosby row, Walworth road
Whittaker Wm. tinplateworker,13Laystall st. Liquorpond st
Whittel Samuel Uppum,undertaker,1Staple st.Long la.Boro'
Whittell Samuel Henry, tailor, 31 Dean st. Soho
Whittem William & Co. coach curriers, &c. 30 Parker st. & 16 Little Queen st. Holborn
Whittemore William, bookseller, 44 Paternoster row
Whitten John, corndealer, 2 White Hart pl. Kennington la
Whitten Wm. rubbish carter, 15 Devonsh.pl.Up.Kenningt.la
Whittenbury Chas. baker.16 Hereford pl. Commercial rd.ea
Whittet George, baker, 27 Little Bell alley, Coleman st
Whittet Sarah (Mrs.), tea dlr. 70 Margaret st.Wilmington sq
Whittey John, oil & colorman, 12 Mortimer rd. Kingsland
Whittey Robert, hairdresser, 93 Brook st. Lambeth
Whitting James, plumber, painter, &c. 7 Union st. Deptford
Whittingham Geo. Robt. & Hannah, grocers, 39 Piccadilly
Whittingham & Wilkin, lace, &c. ma. 27 Mercer st. Long acre
Whittingham Charles, printer, 21 Took's court, Chancery la
Whittingham John, hairdres.31 Goodge st. Tottenham ct. rd
Whittingham Matthew, grocer & teadealer, 375 Oxford st
Whittingham Thos. hairdresser, 120 Chalton st. Somers twn
Whittington Benjamin, solicitor, 2 Dean st. Finsbury sq
Whittle & Hildyard, serjeants at mace, 11 Tokenhouse yd
Whittle Alfred, cheesemonger, 63 Lower marsh, Lambeth
Whittle Bramley, surgeon, 43 Norfolk st. Strand
Whittle George, auctioneer, see Hennis & Whittle
Whittle John, coachbuilder, Bow
Whitton Frances (Mrs.), boarding house, 47 Jewin st
Whitwell John, fruiterer, 78 Warren st. Fitzroy square
Whitwell Samuel, tailor, 23 Stonecutter st. Farringdon st
Whitwell Wm. confectioner, 1 Rufford's buildings, Islington
WhitwhamJames, *ThreeCompasses*P.H.3 Silver st.Golden sq
Whitworth Joseph & Co. engineers & proprietors of "Road & street cleaning Co." 62 Charing cross
Whitworth John B. who. grocer, see Ryde, Curteis & Co
Whitworth Joseph, tailor, 7 Leonard st. Finsbury
Whitworth Robert, barrister, 5 New square, Lincoln's inn
WholesaleDrapers'& Grocers' Soc.(Augustus Henry Cooper, sec.), Moira chambers, 17 Ironmonger lane, Cheapside
Wholey Frances (Mrs.), grocer, 85 Westbourne st. Pimlico
Whorlow Giles George, carrier, *India Arms*, 44 Lime st
Whowall John Wm. gasfitter, 80 Long lane, Bermondsey
Whowall Rt.Wm. brassfounder & gasfitter, 12 King st. Boro'
Whur Robert, tailor, 15 Queen's road, Bayswater
Whybrow George, wholesale shipping oilman, 4 Minories
Whyle Charlotte (Miss), haberdash. 18 Richmond pl.Walwth
Whyle Sarah (Mrs.), jeweller, 15 Perceval st. Clerkenwell
Whyman Joseph, perfumer, 2 Vere st. Cavendish square
Whytall Thomas, upholsterer, &c. 41 Upper st. Islington
Whyte John, cooper, 8 Limekiln hill, Limehouse hole
Whyte John, wine, spirit & colonial broker, 9A, Mincing la
Whyte John Ballingall, provision mercht. 10 Up.E.Smithfld
Whyte Mark Beresford, barrister, 4 Garden court, Temple
Whyte Rob. who. hardware & fancy ware. 22 Houndsditch
Whyte William John, solicitor, 61 Russell square
Whytock R. & Co. carpet manufacs. 5 New Farringdon st
Whytock Andrew, grocer, 30 Kingsgate st. Holborn
Wiber Chas. grocer & cheesemonger, Green st. Kentish town
Wibberley Susan (Mrs.), china dealer, 14 Store st. Bedford sq
Wibberley Thomas, coal dealer, 31 Windmill st. Totten.ct.rd
Wibrow Horatio, soap maker, Southampton st. Camberwell
Wich John Gerard, merchant, 11 Bury ct. St. Mary axe
Wiche Robert, hatter, 5 New King st. Deptford
Wichelow Thos. coal merchant, 48 Charles st. Westminster
Wick John, pork butcher, 252 Bermondsey st
Wicke John, sugar refiner, see Puest & Wicke
Wicken Charles, *Old Justice* P.H. Bermondsey wall
Wickenden Thos. tallowchandler, 65 King William st. City
Wickenden William, fruiterer, 4 Gt. Carter la. Doctors' com
Wickens George & Son, hop & seed facts. 247 Boro' High st
Wickens Edwin, cheesemonger, 26 Beckford row, Walwth.rd
Wickens George, carman, Queen'sHd.inn yd.84 Boro'High st
Wickens Henry, solicitor, 23 Old Burlington st
Wickens James, jun. solicitor, 1 Chandos st. Cavendish sq
Wickens Jas. Stephn. conveyancer, 1 Chandos st.Cavend. sq
Wickens John, barrister, 7 New square, Lincoln's inn
Wickens John, stationer, 128 Old st
Wickens Saml. *Prince of Wales* P.H. 52 Banner st.St.Luke's
Wickens William, beer retailer, 16 Lower st. Islington
Wicker Ann (Mrs.), milliner, 9 Lamb place, Kingsland road
Wicker AnnDarling(Mrs.), *King'sArms*P.H.Mill wl.Poplar
Wicker John Thos. bricklayer, 45 Three Colt st. Limehouse
Wicker Richard, *Cock* P.H. 125 & 126 Cock hill, Ratcliff
Wickes Alfred Nelson, watch & clock maker, 8 Clement's la
Wickes Geo. Augustus, tailor, 29 Chester st. Kennington
Wickes Henry, shipping butcher, 177 Poplar High st
Wickes Thos. ivory turner, 69 Long acre
Wickes Thos. undertaker & house agt. 16 Sussex pl.O.Kentrd
Wickes Valentine, watch enameller, 53 Gt. Sutton st
Wickham Edgar, surgeon, 23 East road, City road
Wickham Edward, surgeon, 7 Lowndes place, Holloway
Wickham Henry, solicitor, see Wood & Wickham
Wickham Henry Fisher, who. dlr. in leeches, 9 Ossulston st
Wickham John George, grocer, 71 Pratt st. Camden tn
Wickham John Hedge, picture dealer, 21 Wardour st. Soho
Wickham Thomas, carman & contractor, Trinity arms yard, Swan st. Borough
Wickham William, beer retailer, 170 Blackfriars road
Wicking Benjamin, pianoforte maker, 48 Kingsland road
Wicking James, *Half Moon Inn* P.H. 132Borough High st
Wicking Mary (Mrs.), undertaker, 24Cumberland st.Shrdch
Wickins Robert, dyer, 6 York place, Westminster road
Wicks & Knock, coffeeroasters, 2George yd.Coal yd.Drury la
Wicks Hannah (Mrs.), fruiterer, 3 Edward st. Wardour st
Wicks Harriet (Mrs.), milliner, &c. 19 Kenton st. Brnswk.sq
Wicks Henry, plumber & painter, 19 Kenton st. Brnswk.sq
Wicks James, glove leather stainer, see Dudfeild & Wicks
Wicks M. (Mrs.), *DoverCas.*P.H.43Weymh.mws.Weymth st
Wicks Robert, *King's Arms* P.H. Kingsland green
Wicks Samuel, greengrocer, 110 Wardour st. Soho

Wicks William, builder, 33 Brown st. Bryanstone sq
Wicks William, carpenter, 5 Millman rw. King's rd. Chelsea
Wickson James, butcher, Canal bridge, Old Kent road
WicksteeJAlfd. manufg. chemist, Bolingbrokegrds. Battersea
Wicksteed Edward, painter, 15 Canterbury pl. Old Kent rd
Wicksteed Charles Frederick, seal engraver, 271 Strand
Wicksteed Geo. upholsterer & cabinet wa. 3 Wardour st
Wicksteed Hen. John, seal engraver, 40 Theobald's road
Wicksteed Thomas, civil engineer, Old Ford, Bow
Wickwar John, manf. station. & binder, 6 Poland st. Oxford st
Widdeson Darcy H. who. ironmong. 31 Terrace, Trin. sq. Twr. hl
Widdicombe John, *Three Tuns tavern*, 36 Jewry st. Aldgate
Widdows Thomas, builder, Church st. Stoke Newington
Widdowson & Veale, goldsmiths & sword cutlers, 73 Strand
Widdowson William, tobacconist, 161 Goswell st
Widdrington Ann (Mrs.), ho. pntr. &c. 7 South Moltn. st. Bond st
Widenham Richard, chronometer, watch & clock maker to the hon. Board of Admiralty, 13 Lombard st
Widger John Austin, linendraper, 1 Surrey place, Kengtn. cr
Widnall Geo. Fred. who. statr. 118 Edgware rd. & 6 Harrow rd
Widnell Eliza & Mary A. (Misses), milliners, 317 High Holbn
Widnell Mary Ann (Mrs.), milliner, 33 Southampton row
Widows' Friend & Benevolent Society (Henry Mathews, sec.), 22 Cloak lane, City
Widows' National & General Life Annuity & Assurance Society, 3 Adelaide place, London bridge
Widows Charles, chandler's shop, 2 Barnet st. Hackney rd
Wiebelitz Thos. Hen. baker, 4 York pl. Millpond st. Brmnsy
Wiebkin Henry, bootmaker, 19 Oxford st. Mile end
Wieland Robt. Geo. & Wm. Thos. watchmks. 1 Lr. st. Islngtn
Wieland Chas. chronometer ma. 12 Warkworth ter. Coml. rd. ea
Wieland Fredk. watch & clock ma. 14 Crosby row, Walwrth
Wier Sarah (Mrs.), tobacconist, 89 Aldersgate st
Weiss Joseph, M.D. professor of hydropathy, 28 Sackville st
Wigan Edward & Co. hop merchants, 4 Duke st. Tooley st
Wigan Edward, isinglass merchant, 8 Fenchurch st
Wigan Geo. surgeon, 42 Somerset st. & 3 Duke st. Mnchstr. sq
Wigg & Pownall, architects & surveys. 7 Bedford rw. Bloomsby
Wigg Robt. plumber, painter, &c. 64 Gt. Cambridge st. Hac. rd
Wigg Robert, shoemaker, 11 Lamb place, Kingsland road
Wigg Smith Spencer, barrister, 12 South square, Gray's inn
Wiggett Boaz, dining rooms, 16 Castle st. east, Oxford st
Wiggett Harriet (Mrs.), dairy, 5 Thatched ho. rw. Low. rd. Islng
Wiggett James, brushmaker & turner, 138 Drury lane
Wiggin Timothy & Co. american merchants, 21 Tokenho. yd
Wiggin Thomas, beer retailer, 169 Hoxton Old town
Wiggins, Teape & Loder, whols. stationers, 10 & 11 Aldgate
Wiggins Fredk. horse dealer, Little Bridge st. Blackfriars
Wiggins James, hairdresser, 161 Old Gravel lane, Wapping
Wiggins Job, machine ruler, Smith's bldgs. Leadenhall st
Wiggins John, boot tree ma. 22 North st. East st. Walworth
Wiggins Joseph, picture dealer, 10 Brown st. Bryanstone sq
Wiggins Samuel, appraiser, 8 Lyon's inn, Strand
Wiggins Saml. auctioneer & agt. 27 Craven st. & Lyon's inn
Wiggins Thos. undertak. & sexton, Kennington oval
Wiggins Wm. bed & mattress ma. 21 Mid. Grove st. Com. rd. ea
Wiggins Wm. grocer & cheesemngr. 1 Dorset st. Clapham rd
Wiggins Wm. Henry, corn chandler, 63 High st. St. Giles
Wigginton James, scale maker, 19 Union st. Kingsland rd
Wigginton Thos. jet work. & jeweller, 4 Corporation la. Clkwl
Wiggs Wm. & Co. sweeps, 6 King's head ct. St. Martin's le gr
Wiggs Francis, slop seller, 236 Poplar High st
Wiggs William, bricklayer, Bromley, Middlesex
Wight Jas. & Thos. who. hat. manuft. 158 Shadwell High st
Wight Alex. mangr. of Union Bank of London, 4 Pall mall ea
Wight Alex. surgeon, 6 St. Mary le Strand pl. Old Kent rd
Wight George John, solicitor, 56 Gt. Marylebone st
Wight James, watchmaker, 181 Union st. Borough High st
Wight Robert, lodging house, 1 Howard st. Strand
Wight Thomas, solicitor, 25 Percy st. Tottenham court road
Wight William, tailor, 10 Stepney causeway
Wightman David, bread & biscuit baker, 26 Cannon st. City
Wightman Mark, sailcloth & linen factor, & agt. for Wm. Ferguson & Sons, power loom linen factors (Dundee), 10 Pancras lane
Wightman Saml. ink & acct. book mnfr. 17 & 18 Douglas st. Wstm
Wighton Peter, baker, 20 Coventry st. & 1 Gt. Windmill st
Wighton William, baker, 6 Kemp's row, Pimlico
Wiginton Edmund & Son, undertakers, 110 Old st. St. Luke's
Wiglesworth, Ridsdale & Craddock, solicitors, 5 Gray's inn sq
Wigley Benj. beer retailer, 4 & 5 Trevor ter. Knightsbridge
Wiglesworth Thos. & Joseph, accountants, 7 Ironmonger la
Wigley Benj. ironmonger, 3 Brunswick parade, Pentonville
Wigley Charles, leather pipe maker, 103 High Holborn
Wigley John, bottle dealer, 29 Lit. Guilford st. Russell sq
Wigley Wm. coffee rooms, 4 Grocer's hall court, Poultry
Wigmore Wm. jeweller, 3 Compton pass. Compton st. Clknwl
Wignell Wm. John, butcher, 106 Albany st. Regent's park
Wigram Money & Henry Loftus, ship owners & ship builders, 98 Gracechurch st., & Brunswick street, Blackwall
Wigram Loftus Tottenham, queen's counsel, 4 Stone bldgs
Wigzell & Thomas, bricklayers, 12 Green st. Theobald's road
Wigzell Jane (Mrs.), coffee house, 26 Paddington st. Marylb
Wilbourn Henry, *Ship & Shears* P.H. 16 Lower Shadwell
Wilbourn Wm. *Horns & Two Brewers* P.H. Grange rd. Brmdsy
Wilbraham Edward, queen's counsel, 11 Old sq. Linc. inn
Wilbraham Isaac, boys' school, 42 Aske street, Hoxton
Wilby John, *Three Tuns* P.H. 2 Moor st. Grafton st. Soho
Wilby Robert, wine merchant, 51 Lime street
Wilby Thomas, jun. renter, St. Bartholomew's hospital
Wilce James, cheesemonger, 10 Vigo st. Regent st.
Wilch James, furrier, 3 Great Suffolk st. Borough
Wilcher Lewis & Son, tallow chandlrs. 39 Crucifix la. Brmdsy
Wilcock Oliver, wholesale tea & spicedealer, 33½ Lime st
Wilcocke, Hen. Ray, pianoforte dealer & music seller, 61 London rd., & dancing master, 88 St. George's rd. Southwk
Wilcocks Joseph, pork butcher, 10 Lit. Charlotte st. Fitzroy sq
Wilcocks Thomas, pork butcher, 77 Tottenham court road
Wilcockson Wm. printer, 13 Rolls buildings, Fetter lane
Wilcox Francis, meat salesman, 1 Newgate market
Wilcox George, wire worker, 7 Silver st. Clerkenwell
Wilcox Henry, hair dresser, 33 Marylebone st. Regent st
Wilcox Isaac, tailor, 10 Little Bell alley, Coleman st
Wilcox James, *King's Head* P.H. 79 Gt. Portland st. Portlnd. pl
Wilcox James, law stationer, see Howe & Wilcox
Wilcox John, beer retailer, 63 Rahere st. Goswell road
Wilcox John, professor of music, 86 Great Titchfield st
Wilcox John Henry, builder, 4 Upsdall row, Kingsland rd
Wilcox Joseph, tailor, 28 Little Bell alley, Coleman st
Wilcox Mark, butcher, 29 Liverpool terrace, Liverpool rd
Wilcox Owen James, linendraper, 58 Poplar High st
Wilcox Thos. *Bear & Ragged Staff* P.H. 11 Bear st. Leicst. sq
Wilcox Thomas, tailor, 25 Argyll street, Regent st
Wilcox William, tailor, 6 Lower John st. Golden square
Wilcoxon Arthur & Robt. plate glass manufacturers, wholesale cabinet makers & paper stainers, 1 Monument yard
Wilcoxon & Sons, plate glass manufacturers, wholesale cabinet manufacturers & paper stainers, 1 Monument yard
Wilcoxon Ralph, boot & shoe warehouses, 1 Howland st.; 93 Tottenham court road; wholesale, 60 King William st. City; 99 Regent's quadrant; 5 Walker's court, Golden square; 289 & 303 Oxford st. & 11 Islington High st
Wild John & Sons, wine & spirit bro. 7 Martin's la. Cannon st
Wild Thos. & Co. soap ma. 10 Gloucester ter. New rd. Coml. rd
Wild & Treasure, woollen drapers, 17 Marylebone st. Piccadilly
Wild Alfred, plumber, 7 Bowling green lane, Clerkenwell
Wild Edward, boat builder, see Noulton & Wild
Wild Edward, coffee rooms, 3 Rufford's buildings, Islington
Wild Edward, newsvender, 48 Marshall st
Wild George, cooper, 17 Prince's st. Mile end New town
Wild George, grocer, 55 Oxford st
Wild Harry, chemist, 5 Norfolk pl. Lower rd. Islington
Wild Henry, wine & spirit merchant, 98 St. Martin's lane
Wild Henry Wm. colored gold chaser, 14 Queen st. Clerknwl
Wild James, coal dealer, 4 Britannia st. Bagnigge wells rd
Wild James William, architect, 9 Argyle place, Regent st
Wild John R. undertaker & cemetery agt. 197 Blackfriars rd
Wild Joseph, goldbeater, 28 Hyde place, Hoxton
Wild Joseph, grocer, 22 King st. Holborn
Wild Launcelot, newsagent & publisher, 13 Catherine st. Strnd
Wild Robert, wholesale slopseller, 45 Houndsditch
Wild Thomas, shoemaker, 8 Strutton ground, Westminster
Wild Wm. cabinet maker, 40 Cannon st. rd. St. George's Ea
Wildbore Daniel Peacock, surgeon, 105 Old st. St. Luke's
Wildbore Frederic, surgeon, &c. 180 Shoreditch High st
Wildbore Saml. surgeon, 6 Kensington ter. Kensington gr. pts
Wilde Jas. & Co. flock merchants, 15 Whitecross st. Cripplgt
Wilde, Rees, Humphry & Wilde, soltrs. 21 College hl. Up. Th. st
Wilde Chas. Rt. Claude, barrister, 9 Serjeants' inn, Fleet st
Wilde George, solicitor, see Powell, Broderips' & Wilde
Wilde Hen. Sedgwick, barrister, 3 Serjeants' inn, Fleet st
Wilde Jas. Plaisted, barrister, 1 Serjeants' inn, Chancery la
Wilde Robert, upholsterer, 14 Old st. road
Wilde Sam. Fras. Thos. barrister, 10 Serjeants' inn, Fleet st
Wilde Sir Thos. kt. queen's serjeant, 9 Serjeants' inn, Fleet st
Wilde Thos. Montague Carrington, barrister, 9 Serjts. in. Fleet st
Wilde William, sugar broker, 3 Commercial sale rooms
Wildee Philip, *Marqs. Wellesley* P.H. 89 Cromer st. Brnswk. sq
Wilden Charles, flour factor, 6 Mark lane
Wilden Jas. cheesemong. 13 Up. Chapman st. St. George's ea
Wilder Rowland, butcher, 121 Edgware rd. & 4 Conduit st. Pdgtn
Wilders William, wine merchant, see Bellchambers & Wilders

Wilders & Co. ale & porter merchants, Robert Shearing, agent, 16 Laurence Pountney lane
Wildes Ann (Mrs.), coffee rooms, 29 Triangle, Kennington cross
Wildes George, armerica merchant, 4½ Warnford court
Wildey Wm. & Co. cocoa nut fibre mnfs. 7 Holland st. Blkrs
Wildey Chas. coach sprg.mr. Fogerty's bdgs. Chas.st. Drury la
Wildey Henry, cabinet & bedstead mak. 84 Berwick st. Soho
Wildgoose William, surgeon, 8 Sherborne st. Blandford sq
Wildin Thomas, printer, 79 Cowcross st. Smithfield
Wilding George, grocer, 2 Church way, Somers town
Wilding Wm. carpenter, 4 Mason st. Old Kent rd
Wilding Wm. *Pendennis Castle* P.H. 7 Lamb st. Spital sq
Wildman Richard, barrister, 1 New court, Temple
Wildsmith Jane (Mrs.), *Green Dragon* P.H. Well st. Hckny
Wildy Mary & Son, law & general booksllrs. 90 Chancery la
Wildy Alfred, hat maker, 266 Oxford st
Wildy George, plasterer, 43 Swan place, Old Kent road
Wileman Hen. who. staffordshire wa. Irongate wf. Paddingtn
Wileman Henry, jun. china & glass wareho. 90 Edgware rd
Wiles John Wooten, hosier, 96 Fleet st
Wiles William, ironmonger, Stratford, Essex
Wiley & Putnam, american literary agency, importers of american books, & purchasers of english books for exportation, No. 6 Waterloo place, Pall mall
Wiley Charlotte (Miss), lace, millinery, haberdashery, hosiery, child bed & ready made linen wareh. 206 Oxford st
Wiley George, locksmith, 5 Windmill st. Finsbury
Wiley John, academy, 3 Christopher st. Finsbury
Wiley John, chandler's shop, 21 Cecil court, St. Martin's la
Wiley Mary (Mrs.), smith, &c. Tyndale pl. Upper st. Islington
Wiley Sarah (Mrs.), fruiterer, 17 Panton st. Haymaket
Wiley Elizabeth (Mrs.), oil & italianwa. 5 Windmill st. Finsbury
Wilford Chas. boot ma. 7 & 8 Gracechurchst. & 22 Kg. Wm. City
Wilford George, *Star & Garter* P.H. 125 Shoreditch
Wilgoss James, furnishing ironmonger, 4 North st. Lisson gr
Wilgoss John Wm. stationer 38 High st. Portland town
Wilkenson Alfred, tobacconist, 9 Charles st. Hatton garden
Wilkerson John, fruiterer, 28 Little Britain
Wilkes Francis, auctioneer & picture gallery, 53 Southampton row, Russell square
Wilkes Francis, bricklayer & plasterer, 23 St. Mary axe
Wilkes George, bottle merchant, 6 Lit. Torrington st
Wilkes George V. chemist & druggist, 1 Hayfield pl. Mile end rd
Wilkes John, direct. of the author's inst. 28 Surrey st. Strand
Wilkes John Collins, bookseller, 20 Bridge st. Southwark
Wilkes Joseph Roberts, coffee rooms, 46 Ray st. Clerkenwell
Wilkes Peter, painter & glazier, 5 Little Torrington st
Wilkes Peter, tobacconist, 167 High st. Camden town
Wilkes Robt. Stanhope, gen. bookseller, 16 Craven st. Strand
Wilkes Thomas, brassfounder, 87 York st. Westminster
Wilkes Thomas, grocer & chsmngr. 40 Edward st. Regt's pk
Wilkes Wm. ham & beef shop, 4 Aldenham ter. Pancras rd
Wilkey John, grindery wareho. 28 Shouldham st. Edgwr. rd
Wilkie & Crokat, merchants, 4 Fen court, Fenchurch st
Wilkie & Soames, soapmakers, 65 Wheeler st. Spitalfields
Wilkie Alexander, bread & biscuit baker, 42 Aldersgate st
Wilkie Frederick, plumber, &c. 11 Blenheim st. Oxford st
Wilkie James, pianoforte maker, 67 Warren st. Fitzroy sq
Wilkie John, cabinet maker, 20 Nassau st. Middlesex hospl
Wilkie John, *Crown* P.H. 14 Gt. Crown ct. Princes st. Soho
Wilkie Wm. pianoforte tuner, 11 Southampton pl. New rd
Wilkin & Percival, ship brokers, 18 Austin friars
Wilkin David, yeast importer, see Weibel & Wilkin
Wilkin George, barrister, 3 Essex court, Temple
Wilkin George, tailor, 64 Frith st. Soho
Wilkin Henry, miniature painter, 20 Newman st. Oxford st
Wilkin James, laceman, 33 Blackfriars road
Wilkin James, solicitor, 217 Piccadilly
Wilkin Thomas Martin, solicitor, 3 Furnival's inn, Holborn
Wilkin Simon, lace maker, see Whittingham & Wilkin
Wilkins Charles & Co. woollen manufactrs. 1 Basinghall st
Wilkins Edw. & John, who. confectioners, 57 & 58 St. John st
Wilkins Jane & Mary Ann, pat. stay makers, &c. 8 Berners st
Wilkins Samuel & Son, &c. marble & stone masons, 29 Judd place west, New road, & 35 Platt terrace, Pancras road
Wilkins & Son (late Robinson, Wilkins & Son), lighthouse & patent lamp manufacturers, 24 & 25 Long acre
Wilkins Ann (Mrs.), furn. ironmong. 18 Grosvenor row, Pimlico
Wilkins Blanchard, brush mnfr. 16 Pleasant row, Stepney gr
Wilkins Charles, barrister, 8 King's Bench walk, Temple
Wilkins Charles, beer retailer, 41 Philips st. Kingsland rd
Wilkins Ebenezer, butcher, 38 Britannia rw. Low. st. Islingtn
Wilkins Elizh. (Miss), beer retailer, 12 Pierrepoint rw. Islingtn
Wilkins Gastrill, solicitor, 34 Gracechurch st
Wilkins George, baker, 41 Lant st. Borough
Wilkins Harriet (Miss), haberdasher, 22 Park ter. Chelsea
Wilkins Hen. Webb, statuary & mason, 21 Barclay st. Som. tn
Wilkins Henry, wine merchant, 14A, St. Helen's place
Wilkins Ignatius, surgeon, 10 Sloan ter. Chelsea
Wilkins James, chandler's shop, 5 Brown's lane, Spitalfields
Wilkins James, tobacconist, 22 Hayfield pl. Mile end rd
Wilkins John, *Blue Anchor* P.H. Russell st. Bermondsey
Wilkins John, cheesemonger, 24 Elizabeth st. Eaton sq
Wilkins John, carcase butcher, 24 Princes sq. Ratcliff highway
Wilkins John, fellmonger, Russell pl. Bermondsey
Wilkins John, newsvender & tobac. 47 Rosoman st. Clkwll
Wilkins John Thos. oil & colorman, 6 & 7 Gray's pl. Fulham rd
Wilkins John W. surv. of pavements, 10 Edward st. Hampstd. rd
Wilkins Jonathan, grocer, 17 Kingsland road, Shoreditch
Wilkins Joseph, springer & polisher, 37 Skinner st. Clknwll
Wilkins Matthew, watchmaker, 15 Radnor st. St. Luke's
Wilkins Rd. Haighton, stockbrok. 4 Bank chambs. Lothbury
Wilkins Robert, cheesemonger, 153 Drury lane
Wilkins Robert, chandler's shop, 17 Ravenscroft st. Hack. rd
Wilkins Sarah (Mrs.), perfumer, 3 Carburton st. Fitzroy sq
Wilkins Solomon, cowkeeper, Albion mews east, Albion st. Hyde park
Wilkins Thos. corn mer. 52 New corn exchange, Mark la
Wilkins Thos. *Shakspear's Head* P.H. 33 Up. Jubilee pl. Mi.e. rd
Wilkins Thomas, shoemaker, Morning lane, Hackney
Wilkins Wm. beer retailer, Bolingbroke gdns. Battersea
Wilkins Wm. bricklayer, 5 Exmouth st. Euston sq
Wilkins Wm. engineer, 11 Newton st. High Holborn
Wilkins Wm. Bushby, barrister, 89 Chancery lane
Wilkins Wm. Geo. russian agt. 3 Pinners ct. & *Baltic* coff. ho
Wilkins Wm. James, boot & shoe maker, 75 Poplar High st
Wilkins Wm. Pickford, coppersmith, 10 Old st. St. Luke's
Wilkinson & Cobbold, solicitors, 7 Lincoln's inn fields
Wilkinson & Dobson, silversmiths & jewellers, 32 Piccadilly
Wilkinson Hen. & Co. hatters, 30 Cockspur st. Charing cross
Wilkinson, Heywood & Co. varnish, &c. makers, Caledonia place, Battle bridge, & Bell isle, Maiden lane
Wilkinson Jas. & Son, gun makers to the Queen, 27 Pall mall
Wilkinson & Jewesbury, indigo & gen. bros. 138 Leadenhall st
Wilkinson Joseph & Co. bill brokrs. & agts. 8 St. Mildred's ct
Wilkinson & Kidd, saddlers & harness makers, 257 Oxford st
Wilkinson Mary Ann & Sons, law stationers, 49 Coleman st
Wilkinson Philip & Son, brassfounders, 8 Tottenham mews
Wilkinson & Treppass, coke burners, 157 Fenchurch st
Wilkinson & Robinson, calenders & packers, 15 Hill st. Finsby
Wilkinson & Stennett, wharfingers, Botolph wf. Lr. Thames st
Wilkinson Wm. & Chas. interior decorators, cabinet makers, upholsterers, auctioneers, appraisers, & house agents, 14 Ludgate hill
Wilkinson Abraham, prof. of music, 21 Sandwich st. Brtn. cres
Wilkinson Amelia (Mrs.), dressmaker, 20 Grosvenor st
Wilkinson Arthur O. merchant, 3 Winchester bldgs. City
Wilkinson Benjamin, baker, 50 Essex st. Kingsland road
Wilkinson C. commercial agent, 62 Lower Thames st
Wilkinson Charles, cheesemonger, 1 Thornton st. Dockhead
Wilkinson Charles, physician, 27 Liverpool ter. Islington
Wilkinson Charles, tallowchandler, 88 Houndsditch
Wilkinson Edwin John, coppersmith, 13 Golden la. Barbican
Wilkinson Eleanor (Mrs.), fruiterer, 8½ Up. Baker st. Lloyd sq
Wilkinson Eliza (Miss), confectioner, 6 Cobourg pl. Bayswtr
Wilkinson Emma (Mrs.), staymaker, High st. Kingsland rd
Wilkinson Francis, haberdasher, 8 Stepney rents, Hackny rd
Wilkinson Frederick, barrister, 1 Stone bldgs. Lincoln's inn
Wilkinson Frederic B. coppersmith, 100 London rd. Sthwk
Wilkinson George, oil & colorman, 241 Bermondsey st
Wilkinson Geo. silver plated wa. 41 Tavistock st. Cov. gard
Wilkinson Geo. Edwd. machine ruler, 114 Fetter la. Fleet st
Wilkinson George Horatio, timber merchant, 139 Curtain rd
Wilkinson Henry, copper pl. printer, 1 Prujean sq. Old Baily
Wilkinson Henry, gun maker, 56 Mansell st. Goodman's flds
Wilkinson Henry, warehouseman, 70 Aldermanbury
Wilkinson Husting, lodging house, 15 Manchester bldgs
Wilkinson James, fishmonger, 44 Coleshill st. Pimlico
Wilkinson James, lapidary, 3 Charles st. Hatton garden
Wilkinson James, wholesale jeweller, 18 Castle st. Holborn
Wilkinson James John, special pleader, 1 Pump ct. Temple
Wilkinson James J.G. surgeon, 13 Store st. Bedford sq
Wilkinson John, accountant, 9 Copthall ct. Throgmorton st
Wilkinson John, bootmaker, 53 Gloucester st. Queen sq
Wilkinson John, butcher, Church st. Hackney
Wilkinson John, carpenter & builder, 4 East st. Finsbury mkt
Wilkinson John, engraver, &c. 6 Tysoe st. Wilmington sq
Wilkinson John, engraver & printer, 2 Skinner st. Clerknwl
Wilkinson John, painter, see Fullmer & Wilkinson
Wilkinson John, writer & grainer, 20 Gloster rw. Grange rd
Wilkinson John B. french flower imp. 53 Wharton st. Lloyd sq
Wilkinson Jonathan, tailor, 11 Park place, St. James's

Wilkinson Joseph, engineer & machinist, 31 St. George's rd
Wilkinson Joseph, jeweller, 5 New Bridge st. Vauxhall
Wilkinson Joseph, liv. stables, George inn, Aldermanbury
Wilkinson Joseph, merchant, 8 St. Mildred's court, Poultry
Wilkinson Joseph, stuff agent, 6 Dyer's ct. Aldermanbury
Wilkinson Joseph, wheelwright, 19 Huntingdon st. Hoxton
Wilkinson Josiah, solicitor, 2 Nicholas lane, City
Wilkinson Josiah, tailor & habit ma. 9 Sherrard st. Golden sq
Wilkinson Joshua Richard, anticorrosion paint manufacturer to the Queen & most public bodies (now R. & C. Strachan), 54 Watling st. near Queen st. Cheapside
Wilkinson Mary (Mrs.), cheesemonger, 58 St. George st
Wilkinson Mary (Mrs.), *King's Arms* P.H. 3 Philip la. Lond. wl
Wilkinson Mary (Mrs.), lodginghouse, 14 Thavies inn, Holborn
Wilkinson Mary Ann (Mrs.), currier, 22 Silver st. Golden sq
Wilkinson Michl. wax & tallow chandler, 21 Old Cavendish st
Wilkinson Michl. E. solicitor, 4 River st. Myddelton sq
Wilkinson Paul, hatter, Gresham house, 38 Moorgate st
Wilkinson Peter Richd. who. stationer, 38 Queen st. City
Wilkinson Richard, bricklayer, 2 Mary st. New road
Wilkinson Richd. S. stockbroker, 8 St. Mildred's ct. Poultry
Wilkinson Robert, brass moulder, 33 Whitecross pl. Finsbury
Wilkinson Robert, chandler's shop, 22 Chicksand st. Whtchpl
Wilkinson Robert Hindley, barrister, 25 Old sq. Lincoln's inn
Wilkinson Sam. carpenter, 2 Christopher st. Hatton garden
Wilkinson Sam. Jas. cigar import. 7 Jeffrey's sq. St. Mary axe
Wilkinson Sam. laceman & hosier, 4 Queen's bdgs. Knightsbr
Wilkinson Thomas, bootma. 4 Southampton row, Russell sq
Wilkinson Thomas, coal mer. Union whf. Wilton rd. Pimlico
Wilkinson Thomas, coffee rooms, 6 Blandford st. Portman sq
Wilkinson Thos. coffee rms. 45 Chichester pl. Gray's inn rd
Wilkinson Thos. fancy leathr. case ma. 33 Bedford st. Covnt gn
Wilkinson Thomas, ironmonger, 77 Quadrant, Regent st; & 9 Bathurst st. Sussex square
Wilkinson Thomas, patent mangle & agricultural repository, 309 Oxford st. near Bond st
Wilkinson Thos. C. *Grapes* P.H. 17 Duke st. Lic. inn fields
Wilkinson Wm. chemist, &c. 3 Pickett st. or 248 Strand
Wilkinson Wm. dining rooms, 64 Gracechurch st
Wilkinson Wm. grocer, 127 Grove st. Camden town
Wilkinson Wm. merchant, 9 Water lane, Tower st
Wilkinson Wm. merchant, 54 Old Broad st. City
Wilkinson Wm. painter & glazier, 5 East st. Finsbury mrkt
Wilkinson Wm. plumber, &c. 8 York st. Hans pl. Chelsea
Wilkinson Wm. surgeon, Bridge ho. Caledonian rd. Pntonvl
Wilkinson Wm. tailor, 7 Seymour row, Little Chelsea
Wilkinson Wm. tallow chandler, 67 Bethnal green road
Wilkinson Wm. wheelwright, 36 Old Gravel lane, Wapping
Wilkinson Wm. whip mnfr. 51 New Church st. Lisson grove
Wilkinson Wm. Arthur, stockbrokr. see Ricardo & Wilkinson
Wilkinson Wm. Henry, hatter, 80 Strand
Wilkinson Wm. Martin, solic. & pat. agt. 44 Lincoln's inn fields
Wilks John & Richard, merchants, 4 Spital square
Wilks Eliza (Mrs.), strawhat ma. 60 Theobald's rd. Red Lion sq
Wilks Geo. August. Fred. physician, 19 Hart st. Bloomsbury
Wilks James, coach beader & maker of spring curtain rollers, 140 Drury lane
Wilks Jonas, linen & welch flannel warehmn. 79 & 80 Watling st
Wilks Joseph, importer of woollen yarns, 186 Regent st
Wilks Robert, gunpowder maker, see Pigous' & Wilks
Wilks Sam. watercress salesman, Long market, Cov. garden
Wilks Thomas, undertaker, 60 Theobald's road
Wilmott Charles, stationer & bookseller, 251 Oxford st
Will James, baker, 70 Brewer st. Somers town
Willament Simon, *Cock* P.H. 21 Wells row, Islington
Willan Edward, solicitor, 35 Bedford row
Willan S. (Miss), court milliner & dress ma. 28 Manchester st
Willan Thomas, surgeon, 38 Albany st. Regent's park
Willans Peter & Sons, woollen mnfrs. 21 & 22 Ironmonger la
Willans Wm. accountant & grot mnfr. 1 Bridge st. Southwark
Willard Geo. cheesemonger & poulterer, Triangle, Hackney
Willard Geo. Edward, *Albion* P.H. 30 Low. East Smithfield
Willard Henry, *Crown* P.H. 12 King's rw. New rd. Pentonvll
Willard Wm. poulterer, 20 Union st. Bishopsgate
Willats Thos. & Rd. opticians, mnfrs. of cheml. mathematical & philosophical inst. & photographic apparatus, hydrometer, saccharometer, barometer & thermom. maks. 98 Cheapside
Willcock & Bennett, builders, 1 Bridge terrace, & 4 & 5 Porteus road, Harrow road
Willcock John, butcher, 61 King st. Borough
Willcock John Wm. barrister, 6 Stone bldgs. Lincoln's inn
Willcock Stephen, carpt. & builder, 76 Gt. Chart st. Hoxton
Wilcocks John, cheesemonger, 30 Rosoman st. Clerkenwell
Willcocks Wm. greengrocer, 10 Lit. Charlotte st. Goodge st
Willcox Brodie, jun. ship bro. & cust. ho. ag. 15 St. Mary axe
Willcox Henry, baker, 26 Hart st. Bloomsbury
Willcox John, fruiterer, 25 Leigh st. Burton crescent
Willcox Thos. last, patten & boot tree maker, 1 Lant st. Boro'
Willder George, *Falcon* P.H. 3 Sutton st. Soho
Willder John & Son, linendrapers, 2 Church st. Kensington
Willder Wm. *Fox under the hill* P.H. Eastern wf. or 75 Strand
Willement Thomas, artist in stained glass to the Queen, 25 Green st. Grosvenor square
Willemite George, *Bull's Head* P.H. 1 Shadwell High st
Willes Irwin Lewis, solicitor, 4 Maddox st. Regent st
Willes James Shaw, barrister, 3 Inner Temple lane
Willes Wm. guano imp. & agrcltrl. agt. see Clarance & Willes
Willes Wm. Green, wine & spirit mer. 28 Martin's la. Cannon st
Willett, Poynter & Dyneler, proctors, 1 Paul's Bakehouse ct
Willett Edward & Nephew, shawl manfs. 63 Friday st
Willett Thos. Wm. & Fras. drapers, 8 Grosvenor pl. Commer. rd. e
Willett Benjamin, baker, 179 Bethnal green road
Willett Charles, genl. commission agent, 88 Fleet st
Willett Charles, sole licensee for the sale & manufacture of Hancock's patent flexible back brushes, 88 Fleet st
Willett Charles, sole agent for Jardine's indian condiments, curry paste, chutney sauce, curry powder, &c. &c. 88 Fleet st
Willett James, dentist, 20 York bldgs. New road, Marylebn
Willett John, grocer & teadealer, 6 North pl. Balls pond rd
Willett Richard, cheesemonger, 5 Up. Dorset pl. Clapham rd
Willett Sarah (Mrs.), coffee rooms, 18½ Bridge ho. pl. Boro'
Willetts Richard, biscuit baker, 7 Old st. road
Willey Richard & Co. silk mercers, 15 & 16 Ludgate st
Willey Cornelius, tailor, 53 Davies st. Berkeley square
Willey Jas. accountant & referee, 15 Beaufort bldgs. Strand
Willey Robt. Turner, cheesemong. & poultr. 54 Tottenham ct. rd
Willey Thomas, fruiterer, 108 Brandon st. Lock's flds. Wlwth
Willey Wm. coach & harness maker, High st. Kingsland
Willey Wm. cutler, 113 St. George's st
Willgoss John, bricklayer, 7 Northumberland st. Marylebn
William John, beer retailer, 5 Lower George st. Chelsea
Williams Ann & Hen. ironmongers, 20 Park pl. Kennington cr
Williams & Beardmore, hatters, 60 New Bond st
Williams & Blake, coffee brokers, 11 Mincing lane, City
Williams & Edwards, academy, 8 Edward's ter. Caledonian rd
Williams Chevin & Co. stock & share bro. 30 Bucklersbury
Williams & Clapham, goldsmiths & jewellers, 14 Strand
Williams, Coopers, Boyle & Co. who. stationers, 85 Smithfield
Williams, Deacon, Labouchere, Thornton & Co. bankers, 20 Birchin lane, Cornhill
Williams Edmund Morgan & Co. flanl. facts. 1 Star ct. Bread st
Williams Elizabeth & Jane (Misses), school, 1 Haverstck. hill
Williams, Foster & Co. copper smelters & merchants, british copper office, 68 Upper Thames st
Williams Edmund & Hamerton, stock & share agts. Stock exch
Williams & Green, coal mers. Union wf. Grosvenor basin, Pimlc
Williams, Harvey & Co. tin smelters & mers. 68 Up. Thames st
Williams & Hatton, silk mercers, shawl & cloak manufacturers, linendrapers, haberdashers, lacemen, & general warehousemen, 111 Oxford st. & 272 & 274 Regent circus
Williams Hugh & Sons, tailors, 54 West Smithfield
Williams James & Co. painters & glaziers, 2 Fell st. Cripplegate
Williams John & Co. patent ledger warehouse & stationers, & proprietors of the paging machine, 29 Bucklersbury
Williams John & Co. tailors & habit makers, 43 Conduit st
Williams John D. & Co. stock & share broks. 3 Copthall cham
Williams John & Robt. *Cock* P.H. 45 Whitechapel High st
Williams John & Samuel, leather warehouse, 26 Lime st
Williams John & Son, carpents. 9 Commercial rd. Lambeth
Williams John & Son, soap maks. 28 Compton st. Clerkenwell
Williams & Jones, woollen warehousemen, 28 Basinghall st
Williams Jsph. & Co. ale & port. mer. Old swan, Up. Thms. st
Williams Joseph R & Co. ship & insurance brokers, 3 Clement's la
Williams & Keed, ironmongers, 100 Crawford st. Marylebone
Williams Lewis & Son, stationers & printers, 25 Walbrook
Williams & Norgate, for. bookselrs. 14 Henrietta st. Cvnt. gn
Williams Rd. John & Co. chemists, 8 Halkin st. west, Belgrave sq
Williams Richd. & Son, wine merchants, 2 Moorgate st. City
Williams & Rimmer, woollen drapers, 44 Blackfriars road
Williams & Sowerby, linendrapers, &c. &c. 61 & 62 Oxford st. & 3, 4 & 5 Wells st. Oxford st
Williams Stephen & John H. solrs. see Winter, Williams & Co
Williams & Waring, merchants, 116 Fenchurch st
Williams Wm. & Co. silversmiths & jewellers, 223 Oxford st
Williams Wm. & John, oil & colourmen, 232 Tottenham ct. rd
Williams Wm. & Son, shipwrights, Fountain dk. & Bermondsy. wl
Williams Adam, tailor, 10 Hop garden, St. Martin's lane
Williams Albert, solicitor, 38 Lincoln's inn fields
Williams Alex. locksmith, 15 Seething lane, Great Tower st
Williams Alfred, butcher, 131 Church st. Shoreditch
Williams Alfred, custom house & coml. agt. 66 Lr. Thames st
Williams Allen, surgeon, 11 St. Thomas's st. Borough

Williams Ann (Mrs.), lighterman, 2 Beer la. Tower st
Williams Ann (Mrs.), dressmaker, 7 Holland st. Kensington
Williams Ann (Mrs.), teadealer, 2 Stockbridge ter. Pimlico
Williams Ann (Mrs.), *Granby's Head* P.H. 8 Villiers st. Strand
Williams Anthony, printer, 1 Crown ct. Threadneedle st
Williams Benjn. iron plate worker, 30 Redcross st. Borough
Williams Benjn. music printer & publisher, Fountain ct.; 30 Cheapside, & 2 Alsop's buildings, Great Dover road
Williams Benjamin Walker, ropemaker, Stapel st. Boro'
Williams Benjn. wholesale tea & coffee dealer, 35 Jewry st. Aldgate, & 34 Little George st. Minories
Williams Benjamin Bacon, stockbroker, Stock exchange
Williams Car. (Miss), fancy repos. 8 Norland rd. Notting.hl
Williams Cath. (Mrs.), ladies' school, 6 John's ter. Hackney rd
Williams Chas. baker, 14 Baldwin's gardens, Leather lane
Williams Chas. *Bricklayers' Arms* P.H. 46 Southmoulton st
Williams Charles, coal factor, 12 Coal exchange
Williams Charles, coal merchant, see Powell & Williams
Williams Charles, haberdasher & men's mercer, 22 Walbrook
Williams Charles, jeweller, see Catchpole & Williams
Williams Charles, lapidary, 15 Benjamin st. Cowcross st
Williams Charles, wholesale coffee dealer, 38 Fenchurch st
Williams Chas. C. general com. agt. see Blackwell & Williams
Williams Chas. Clark, pawnbroker, 89 New crane, Shadwell
Williams Chas. F. boys' school, 17 Portman pl. Edgware rd
Williams Chas. H. brougham house school, 3 Blenheim pl. Wellington road, St. John's wood
Williams Chas. Jas. B. F.R.S. physician, 7 Holles st. Cavdh. sq
Williams Chas. Jsph. M.A. academy, 38 Charles st. Westminster
Williams Charles Reynolds, solicitor, see Cox & Williams
Williams Charlotte (Miss), lodging house, 41 Leicester sq
Williams Christopher, grocer, 33 Gt. James st. Lisson grove
Williams Daniel, ancient booksel. 44 Holywell st. Strand
Williams Daniel H. solicitor, 2 Copthall ct. Throgmorton st
Williams David, boot & shoe maker, 9 Albion pl. Battle bridge
Williams David, coffee rooms, 9 Upper East Smithfield
Williams David, copper plate printer, 30 Cheapside
Williams David, earthenware dealer, 100 Gt. Suffolk st. Boro'
Williams David, fruiterer, 21 Great Winchester st
Williams David, ginger beer ma. 41 Church rd. Coml. rd. ea
Williams David, potato dlr. & cowkpr. 24 Rose & Cr. ct. Finsb
Williams David, solicitor, see Thomas, Lepard & Williams
Williams Edward, butcher, 134 Lambeth walk
Williams Edward, fringe manfr. 12 Wilkes st. Spitalfields
Williams Edwd. linendraper, 40 King's road east, Sloane sq
Williams Edward, mercht. & factor, 60 Queen st. Cheapside
Williams Edward, tailor, 43 Gower place, Euston square
Williams Edward, undertaker, 7 Beresford st. Walworth rd
Williams Edward H. surveyor, 2 Whitefriars st. Fleet st
Williams Edward P. bookseller, 5 New Bridge st. Blackfriars
Williams Edward Vaughan, barrister, 2 Inner Temple lane
Williams Edwin Morrett, wood engraver, 144 Fleet st
Williams Eleanor (Mrs.), milliner, 191 Sloane st. Knightsbdg
Williams Elizabeth (Mrs.), milliner, 20 London st. Fitzroy sq
Williams Elizh. (Mrs.), saddler, 9 Middle row, Knightsbdg
Williams Eleanor (Mrs.), linendraper, 32 & 33 Lambeth walk
Williams Ellice, mourning warehou. see Rhoades & Williams
Williams Emily (Mrs.), stationer, South Lambeth
Williams Francis, artist, 13 Newman st. Oxford st
Williams Francis, hairdresser, 6 Great Dover st. Boro'
Williams Francis, miscellaneous dealer, 190 High Holborn
Williams Frederick, cook, &c. 9 Manchester st. Manch. sq
Williams Frederick, professor of music, 4 Eden pl. Old Kt. rd
Williams Frederick, shorthand writer, 88 Chancery lane
Williams Fredk. Fras. *Green Man* P.H. Keppel rw. New rd
Williams Frederick Sims, barrister, 53 Chancery lane
Williams George, builder & coal mer. Church st. Hackney
Williams George, builder, 3 Union road, Rotherhithe
Williams George, butcher, 1 Edward st. Wardour st. Soho
Williams George, cabinet maker, 33 Duke st. St. James's
Williams George, carpenter, 22 East pl. Walcot pl. Lambth
Williams George, cowkeeper, 28 Up. Cleveland st. Fitzroy st
Williams George, commission agent, 2 Crooked la. Cannon st
Williams George, for. water mer. see Dessoulavy & Williams
Williams George, ironmonger, 8 Nassau st. Soho
Williams George, linendraper, 158 Hoxton Old town
Williams George, plumber, 33 Frederick st. Portland town
Williams George, shipchandler, 19 Rotherhithe wall
Williams George, surgeon, 9 Granby st. Hampstead road
Williams George, tailor, 4 Gt. Marlborough st
Williams George, tailor, see Cook, Williams & Cook
Williams Geo. Beard, awlblade ma. 17 Norman's bldgs. St. Luk's
Williams George G. *Williams' hotel*, 4 Albemarle st
Williams George Grey, pawnbroker, 4 Stepney High st
Williams Geo. Hen. porter dlr. 26 Basinghall st. & 4 Sambk. ct
Williams Geo. Hen. solicitor, 12 New North st. Red Lion sq
Williams Geo. Jas. oval & round turner, 60 Sun st. Bishopsgt
Williams Geo. Thos. barrister, 4 King's Bench wk. Temple
Williams Hamerton John, commission agent for sale of stock, shares, &c. Stock exchange & 80 Old Broad st. City
Williams Harriet (Mrs.), staymaker, 220 Tottenham ct. rd
Williams Harry, upholsterer, 26 Berners st. Oxford st
Williams Helena (Mrs.), milliner, 191 Sloane st. Knightsbdg
Williams Henry, chairmaker, 53 Union st. Borough
Williams Henry, dining rooms, 65 Broad st. Ratcliff
Williams Henry, fish & potato dealer, 121 Whitechapel rd
Williams Henry, painter, 12 Gt. Distaff lane, City
Williams Henry, piece broker, 4 Hoxton Old town
Williams Henry, plane maker, 42 York terrace, Borough rd
Williams Henry, solicitor, 15 Claremont row, Barnsbury rd
Williams Henry, solicitor, 6 Warwick court, Holborn
Williams Henry, tallow chandler, High st. Deptford
Williams Henry, teadealer, 92 Crawford st. Portman sq
Williams Henry N. chemist, 1 Queen's road, Notting hill
Williams Henry Prescott, artist, 37 Chapel st. Pentonville
Williams Herbert, architect, 54 Gt. Ormond st. Queen sq
Williams Hugh, printer, 9 Lower Ashby st. Clerkenwell
Williams Isaac Lloyd, barrister, 8 New sq. Lincoln's inn
Williams James, academy, 23 Gt. Turner st. Commercial rd
Williams James, boot & shoe maker, George st. Camberwell
Williams James, confectioner, 14 Featherstone st. City rd
Williams James, custom house agent, 4 Beer lane, Tower st
Williams James, *Grapes* P.H. 24 Marshall st. Golden sq
Williams James, ironmonger, 5 Samson's place, Bermondsey
Williams James, leather japanner & table cover manufacturer, 9 Marlborough pl. Gt. Peter st. Westminster
Williams James, outfitter, 5 St. George's pl. St. George's east
Williams James, plumber & glazier, 11 Richmond rd. Dalston
Williams James, *Ship* P.H. 16 Glasshouse yd. Aldersgate st
Williams James, silkman, 10 Sclater st. Bethnal green
Williams James, surgeon, 11 Dalston terrace, Dalston
Williams James, tailor, 8 Cambridge pl. Edgware road
Williams James, veterinary surgeon, 3 East India rd. Poplar
Williams James, whalebone manuf. 2 George yard, Bow lane
Williams James, woollendraper, 18 St. Martin's ct. Leices. sq
Williams James Butler, actuary to English & Scottish Law Life Assurance & Loan Association, 12 Waterloo pl
Williams James Dyer, solicitor, Guildhall chambers
Williams James Rogers, surgeon, 158 Grove st. Camden twn
Williams Job, linendraper, silk mercer, &c. 63 Strand
Williams John, attorney, 1 Verulam buildings, Gray's inn
Williams John, baker, 64 Broad st. Ratcliff
Williams John, boot & shoe maker, 46 Carnaby st. Golden sq
Williams John, boot & shoemaker, 6 Church la. Commercial rd
Williams John, boot & shoe maker, 66½ Gt. Guildford st. Boro'
Williams John, builder, Berwick house, Hampstead road
Williams John, candle manufr. 35 Up. Lisson st. Lis. grove
Williams John, coal merchant, 45 York st. York rd. Lambeth
Williams John, coal warehouse, 51 High st. Marylebone
Williams John, comb manufacturer, 19 Mitre st. Blkfrs. rd
Williams John, dairy, 5 Prujean square, Old Bailey
Williams John, dining rooms, 11 Marylebone lane
Williams John, engraver, 11 Pollen st. Hanover sq
Williams John, fishmonger, 32 Park ter. Regent's park rd
Williams John, fruiterer, 178 Whitechapel road
Williams John, gen. clothes salsmn. 44 Union st. Southwark
Williams John, goldsmith, &c. see Nock & Williams
Williams John, grocer & tea dealer, 3 Union road, Rotherhi
Williams John, grocer & cheesemongr. 4 Whitmore rd. Hoxtn
Williams John, lathe & tool maker & cutler, 4 Long acre
Williams John, manufacturers' agent, 3 Copthall chambers
Williams John, oil & colorman, 40 Worship st. Finsbury
Williams John, painter, 42 Gainsford st. Horselydown
Williams John, painter, 6 Queen st. Horselydown
Williams John, pawnbroker, 1 Gt. Chapel st. Westminster
Williams John, jun. pawnbroker, 25 Gt. Smith st. Westminsr
Williams John, plasterer, 32 Colonnade, Brunswick square
Williams John, sec. to Mathematical So. Church st. Spitalfis
Williams John, *Shakspeare* P.H. 29 Marlboro' st. Regent st
Williams John, solicitor, 4 Furnival's inn, Holborn
Williams John, *Spur inn* P.H. Spur inn yard, 97 Boro' High st
Williams John, tailor, 40 Exmouth st. Clerkenwell
Williams John, tailor, 34½ King st. Clerkenwell
Williams John, tailor, 36 Lower st. Islington
Williams John, tailor, 69 Regent st. Lambeth
Williams John, tailor, 59 Wells st. Oxford st
Williams John, tobacconist, 143 Shadwell High st
Williams John, undertaker, 6 Brownlow st. Long acre
Williams John, watch case ma. 56 Gt. Sutton st. Clerkenwll
Williams John Alf. pin & needle ma. see Edelsten & Williams
Williams John Bartlett, grocer, 31 Mid. Grove st. Com. rd. ea
Williams John Chanon, who. coffee dlr. 6 Gt. Tower st

Williams John Chas. solicitor, 18 Gt. George st. Westminstr
Williams John F. coml. agt. 19 Artillery pl. west, Bunhill rw
Williams John Howard, solicitor, see Winter, Williams & Co
Williams John Price, barrister, 1 Plowden buildings, Temple
Williams John Robert, jeweller, 2 King sq. Goswell rd
Williams John Robt. lighterman, 20 Lambeth hill, Doc.com
Williams Joseph, dining rooms, 1 King st. Soho
Williams Joseph, law stationer, 18 Took's ct. Chancery la
Williams Joseph, music printer & publisher, 123 Cheapside
Williams Jsph. *New Inn hotel* P.H. 96 & 97 Bridge rd. Lambth
Williams Joseph, physician, 8 Tavistock square
Williams Joseph, professor of music, 8 Warwick st. Pimlico
Williams Joseph, tailor, 6 Romney ter. Horseferry road
Williams Joseph, teabroker, 35 Jewry st. Aldgate
Williams Joshua, barrister, 3 New square, Lincoln's inn
Williams Lewis Walter, solicitor, 27 Bucklersbury
Williams Llewellyn, coffee rooms, 60 Waterloo road
Williams Louisa (Miss), milliner, 23 Princes st. Hanover sq
Williams Luke, coach spring maker, 14 Up. Marylebone st
Williams Luke, solicitor, 4 Barnard's inn, Holborn
Williams Mark, surgeon, 8 Soley terrace, Pentonville
Williams Martha (Mrs.), baker, 2 Windmill st. Finsbury
Williams Martha (Mrs.), haberdshr. 15 Gt. Ryder st. St. James'
Williams Mary Ann (Mrs.), milliner 110 Gt. Russell st. Blmsb
Williams Mary Arabella (Miss), school, 36 King sq. Goswell rd
Williams Matthew, tailor, 17 Keen's row, Walworth road
Williams Michael, baker, 14 Maryland pl. Gt. Bland st. Dov.rd
Williams Michael, baker, 7 North st. East st. Walworth
Williams Morris, merchant, 27 Mincing lane
Williams Obadiah, hatter, 26 George st. Blackfriars road
Williams Rees, *St. Ann's coffee ho.* P.H. 30 Shoema. rw. Blkfrs
Williams Richard, carpenter, 11 Baynes row, Coldbath sq
Williams Richard, corn dealer, 5 Henry st. Hampstead rd
Williams Richard, merchant, 2 Moorgate st
Williams Richard, silk dyer, 25 Pool terrace, City road
Williams Richard, sculptor, 27 Cadogan st. Chelsea
Williams Richard, umbrella & parasol maker, 44 Ludgate hill
Williams Robert, *Bull's Head* P.H. 8 Broad st. Lambeth
Williams Robert, coffee rooms, 85 Lower Thames st
Williams Robert, grocer & oilman, 22 Old Bailey
Williams Robert, lace, muslin, embroidery, baby linen, ladies' outfitting & hosiery wareho. 57 Mortimer st. Cav. sq
Williams Robert, potato merch. 2 New road, St. George's ea
Williams Robert, physician, 39 Bedford pl. Russell square
Williams Robert, tobacconist, 7 West st. Seven dials
Williams Robert, wood box maker, 48 Compton st. Clerknwl
Williams Robert Bell, wine merchant, see Finzile & Williams
Williams Robt. Sam. *George inn* P.H. Commercial road ea
Williams Robt. Vaughan Wynne, solicr. 3 Paper bldgs. Temple
Williams Samuel, artist, 5 Mabledon place, Burton crescent
Williams Samuel, bootmaker, 42 Mount st. Berkeley square
Williams Samuel, brush & cork dealer, 6 Sloane sq. Chelsea
Williams Samuel, carpenter, Surrey pl. east, Old Kent rd
Williams Samuel, coffee broker, 43 Mincing lane
Williams Samuel, cowkeeper, 43 White st. Borough
Williams Saml. fishmonger, 2 York pl. Portland town
Williams Samuel, fruiterer, 51 Upper George st. Portman sq
Williams Saml. ironmonger, 1 Beaufort ter. ea. King's rd. Chlsa
Williams Saml. *P. Victoria* P.H. 60 Castle st. east, Oxford st
Williams Samuel Andrew, hairdresser, 51 Old street road
Williams Sarah (Mrs.), ladies' school, Deptford High st
Williams Sarah (Mrs.), milliner, 85 Leather lane, Holborn
Williams Sarah (Miss), dairy, 12 Church st. Soho
Williams Sarah (Miss), stay maker, 126 Edgeware road
Williams Selina (Miss), ladies' school, 5 Collier st. Pentonvl
Williams Sophia (Mrs.), beer retailer, Back rd. Kingsland
Williams Stephen, dairy, 12 Fitzroy place, Kentish town
Williams Stephen, solicitor, see Winter, Williams & Co
Williams Stephen, *William the Fourth* P.H. Lit. Chelsea
Williams Sush. (Mrs.), *Plymth. Arms* P.H. 16 Mill la. Tooley st
Williams Theodore T. W. brushmaker, 11 Charing cross
Williams Theodosius, coffee rooms, 26 St. Martin's le grand
Williams Thos. artist, 5 Park road, Notting hill
Williams Thos. *Blackman* P.H. 88 Blackman st. Borough
Williams Thos. boot & shoemaker, High st. Kingsland
Williams Thos. butcher, 8 Baker's row, Walworth road
Williams Thos. butchers' cutler, 14 West Smithfield
Williams Thos. carpenter & builder, 10 King st. Grosvenor sq
Williams Thos. conveyancer, Northumberland house, Charing cross, & 13 Elm tree road, St. John's wood
Williams Thos. dairyman, 5 Silver st. Wood st. City
Williams Thos. india & british shawl wa. 211 & 213 Regent st
Williams Thos. jeweller & pearl work. 28 Whiskin st. Clknwl
Williams Thos. linen draper, 12 Duke st. Manchester sq
Williams Thos. manchester agent, 43 Friday st. Cheapside
Williams Thos. music seller & publisher, 2 Strand
Williams Thos. navigation school, 51 Pennyfields, Poplar
Williams Thos. tailor, 6 Lower Ranelagh st. Grosvenor place
Williams Thos. tailor, 202 Wellington ter. Waterloo road
Williams Thos. tailor, 6 Upper East Smithfield
Williams Thos. tallow chandler, 171 Church st. Shoreditch
Williams Thos. tea dealer, 135 Tottenham court road
Williams Thos. tobacconist, 9 Wardrobe ter. Doctors' commns
Williams Thos. woollendraper, see Dawson & Williams
Williams Thos. Beavan, linendraper, 9 Provost st. City road
Williams Thos. Edward, merchant, 24 Crutchedfriars
Williams Thos. Geo. surveyor, 4 Little St. Thomas Apostle
Williams Thomas Mutlow, preserver of & dealer in birds & animals, 155 Oxford st
Williams Thos. Sheffield, academy, 15 Union st. Deptford
Williams Walter, albion iron warehouse, 10 Up. Thames st
Williams Walter, M.D. pembr. ho. lunatic asylm Mare st. Hkny
Williams Walter, royal mail & railway carriage contractor, Glasshouse yard, Goswell st. & Calthorpe pl. Gray's inn rd
Williams Walter B. wine merchant, 202 Bishopsgate st. without, & 66 Fenchurch st
Williams Wellington, general agent, 31 Gutter la. Cheapsid
Williams (Widow), lighterman, Galley quay, Lw. Thames st
Williams Wm. attorney, 31 Alfred pl. Bedford square
Williams Wm. baker, 35 Upper Albany st. Regent's park
Williams Wm. bookbinder, Duchy place, 137 Strand
Williams Wm. bootmaker, 20 Stockbridge terrace, Pimlico
Williams Wm. *Bull & Butcher* P.H. King st. Deptford
Williams Wm. carpenter & builder, 25 Upper Cleveland st
Williams Wm. carpenter, 20 Berwick st. Pimlico
Williams Wm. carver & gilder, 8 St. James's st. Clerkenwell
Williams Wm. dairy, 103 Park st. Camden town
Williams Wm. electrotechnist, 21 Greville st. Hatton gdn
Williams Wm. goldbeater, 14 Warwick lane
Williams Wm. grocer, Tanner's hill, New town, Deptford
Williams Wm. plumbers' turnr. 15 Providence bdgs. N. Knt. rd
Williams Wm. saddler, 2 Crown row, Mile end road
Williams Wm. saddler & harn ma. 3 Lit. Ryder st. St. James's
Williams Wm. scalemaker, 4 Abchurch yard, & 71 Cannon st
Williams Wm. ship agent, 9 Water lane, Tower st
Williams Wm. silversmith, see Mouslon & Williams
Williams Wm. solicitor, see Currie, Woodgate & Williams
Williams Wm. *Three Johns* P.H 2 Lit. Park st. Westminster
Williams Wm. tobacco pipe maker, 295 Kent st. Borough
Williams Wm. undertaker, 4 Parsonage row, Newington butts
Williams Wm. wholesale teadealer, see Webb & Williams
Williams Wm. wine merchant, 4 Brabant ct. Philpot la
Williams Wm. wine merchant, 6 Rood lane, Fenchurch st
Williams Wm. Charles, oilman, 2 Felix cottages, Liverpool rd
Williams Wm. Cundale, tobacnst. 3 Acton pl. Bgnigg. wells rd
Williams Wm. David, tobaccnst. 1 Gt. Scotland yd. Charingcr
Williams Wm. Edward, builder & undertaker, 7 Little St. Thomas Apostle, City; & 2 Durham pl. east, Hackney rd
Williams Wm. Henry, bricklayer, 21 Kingsland row, Dalston
Williams Wm. J. stay & corset ma. 34 Poland st. Oxford st
Williams Wm. Joseph, boat builder, Creek rd. Deptford
Williams Wm. Lobb, waterproof tailor, 138 Fenchurch st
Williams Wm. Rosser, barrister, 21 Old square, Lincoln's inn
Williams Wm. Thos. cheesemonger, 9c, Lit. Chapel st. Westmr
Williamson & Harrison, who. teadealers, 12 Savage gardens
Williamson & Hill, attorneys, 4 Verulam bldgs. Gray's inn
Williamson & Nash, who. teadlrs. 15 Philpot la. Fenchurch st
Williamson Ambrose Rt. linendraper, 17 & 18 Crawford st
Williamson Chas. carver & gilder, 2 Palace New rd. Lambeth
Williamson Chas. watch tool ma. 3 Northampton pl. Clkwll
Williamson Chas. W. brushmak. 31 Grosvenor row, Pimlico
Williamson Curtis, dining rooms, 312 Oxford st
Williamson David, shoemaker, 29 Lwr. Northampton st. Clkwll
Williamson David, surgeon, 26 Finsbury place north
Williamson David H. builder, 1 Hanover pl. Regent's park
Williamson Edward, attorney, 50 Lincoln's inn fields
Williamson Eliza (Mrs.), strawbon. ma. 41 Wynyatt st. Gos. rd
Williamson Francis Robert, ironmonger, 35 Chiswell st
Williamson Fredk. tailor, 14 Perceval st. Clerkenwell
Williamson George, cornchandler, 87 Bethnal green road
Williamson Henry, engine turner, 22 Perceval st. Clerkenw
Williamson Henry, watchmaker, 9 Frederick pl. Goswell rd
Williamson James, bricklayer, 17 Queen's grdns. Brompton rd
Williamson James, coal merchant, see Stone & Williamson
Williamson James, oilman, 8 Salisbury court, Fleet st
Williamson James, tea dealer, 183 Union st. Southwark
Williamson John, barrister, 3 Raymond bldgs. Gray's inn
Williamson John, boot & shoe maker, 32 Gt. Dover st. Boro'
Williamson John, cheesemonger, see Cory & Williamson
Williamson John, surveyor, 48 Edwardes sq. Kensington
Williamson John, watch & clock ma. 46 Westbourne st. Pimlc
Williamson John Wm. barrister, 16 Carey st. Lincoln's inn

Williamson Joseph, fringe manufactr. 129 Upper st. Islington
Williamson Joshua, merchant, 7 Angel ct. Throgmorton st
Williamson Martha(Mrs.), board & lodg.ho. 1 New ct. Bow la
Williamson Michael, baker, 8 Somerset pl. New rd. Com. rd
Williamson Reuben, upholsterer, see Phenes & Williamson
Williamson Richard, engraver, 14 Gt. Moore pl. Lambeth
Williamson Rd.B. *CampdenArms* P.H. Cmpdn.ter. Knsgtn.rd
Williamson Robert, butcher, 12 New Gravel lane
Williamson Robert, shawl warehouseman, 1 New ct. Bow la
Williamson Sarah (Mrs.), dairy, 53 Park st. Grosvenor sq
Williamson Sarah Amelia(Mrs.), milliner, &c. 10 Brompton rd
Williamson Thomas, academy, 33 King st. Snowhill
Williamson Thomas, hosier, glover & outfitter, 108 Fleet st
Williamson Wm. *Boar's Head* P.H. 66 Fleet st
Williamson Wm. grocer, 36 New rd. St. George's east
Willing James, tobacconist, 17 Mount st. Walworth rd
Willing Philip, *Coach & Horses* P.H. Ring cross, Holloway rd
Willingale Charles, bootmaker, 71 New Compton st. Soho
Willings Susannah (Mrs.), grocer, 25 Edward st. Regent's pk
Willington Robert, bookbinder, 19 Dean st. Soho
Willington Thomas, ironmonger, 1 Willow ter. Kentish town
Willington Wm. bookbinder, 4 Princes st. Fitzroy square
Willins Geo. sol. & notary, 3 Bell ct. Bell yd. Doc. commons
Willinsgale Sam. dyer & scourer, 10 Providence row, Finsby
Willion Fredk. dlr. in brit. & for. securities, Stock Exchange
Willion Wm.Hen. dlr. in brit.& for.securities, Stock Exchange
Willis Alexander & Co. hatters, 358 Strand
Willis Arthur, Son & Co. merchants, 3 Crosby square
Willis Fred. & Chas. *Willis's rooms*, 26 King st. St. James's; & *Thatched House Tavern*, 85 St. James's st
Willis George & Co. clothiers to their Majesties the Queen, the Queen dowager, his royal highness Prince Albert, & the royal family, 18 St. James's st.; & 62 George st. Edinbro'
Willis Henry H. & Co. ship & insurance brokers, 3 Crosby sq
Willis Isaac & Co. musical library, 75 Grosvenor st. Bond st
Willis, Percival & Co. bankers, 76 Lombard st
Willis Wm. & Sons, sheriffs' officers, 25 Cursitor st. Chanc. la
Willis & Wright, vinegar, mustard, acetic acid, & naptha manufacturers, Old st. road, City road
Willis Alexander, wine merchant, 102 Leadenhall st
Willis Alice (Mrs.), oil wareho. 16 Grenville st. Brunswick sq
Willis Ann (Miss), straw hat ma. 9 Huntingdon st. Hoxton
Willis Arthur, printer & stationer, 8 Newgate st. & 36 Throgmorton st
Willis Charles, hairdresser, 24 Gt. Castle st. Regent st
Willis Chas. *Richardson's Arms* P.H. 11 Hampstd.st. Fitz.sq
Willis David, dairyman, 53 Marchmont st. Brunswick sq
Willis Edmund, artist, 9 Rutland st. Hampstead rd
Willis Francis Turber, refiner, 3 Cross st. Goswell st
Willis George, bookseller, Piazza, Covent garden
Willis George, toy maker, 12 Corbet court, Spitalfields
Willis George, *Three Foxes* P.H. Narrow st. Ratcliff
Willis Henry, *Crompton Arms* P.H. 28 Hall pk. Edgwr. rd
Willis Henry, dancing master, 41 Brewer st. Golden sq
Willis Henry, merchant & insur. broker, 37 Old Broad st. City
Willis Henry B. artist, 123 Stanhope st. Hampstead road
Willis Henry H. merchant, 3 Crosby square
Willis James, barrister, 9 Old square, Lincoln's inn
Willis James, fruiterer, 1 Spring st. Marylebone
Willis James, tallow chand. 9 Harper's pl. Back rd. St. Geo.ea
Willis James, tobacconist, 48 Munster st. Regent's park
Willis James, *King's Arms* P.H. 5 Lit. Woodstock st. Maryleb
Willis John, archery & curiosity warehouse, 120 Chancery la
Willis John, architect & draftsman, 4 Nassau st. Middlx. hos
Willis John, coal dealer, 52 Dean st. Soho
Willis John, colorman, 4 Cheshire st. Bethnal green
Willis John, dairy, 14½ Chenies st. Bedford square
Willis John, hairdresser, 33 Gt. Prescot st. Goodman's fields
Willis John, shipowner, 28 Bedford sq. ea. Commercial road
Willis John, smith, 7 Seacoal lane, Skinner st. Snow hill
Willis John Wm. hatter & umbrella maker, 173 High Holborn
Willis Joseph, cheapside dining & refreshment rooms, & dorset ale stores, 114 Cheapside
Willis Joseph, linendraper, 16 Crown row, Walworth road
Willis Joseph Wm. shoemaker, 42 Union st. Middlx. hospital
Willis Joshua, hame manufactr. 20 Turnmill st. Clerkenwell
Willis Maria (Mrs.), fruiterer, Little Chelsea
Willis Mary (Miss), painter, glazier, &c. 47 Essex st. Strand
Willis Mary Ann(Mrs.), confectnr. 5 Charles pl. Ea. st. Walwth
Willis Peter, cowkeeper, Lambeth green, Lambeth
Willis Richd. baker, 140 Upper Whitecross st. St. Luke's
Willis Richd. coffee rooms, 2 Union st. Bishopsgate
Willis Richd. jeweller, 14 Lower Smith st. Northampton sq
Willis Robert, physician, 25 Dover st. Piccadilly
Willis Thos. *Albany Arms* P.H. 295 Albany rd. Camberwell
Willis Thos. enameller, 23 Greenhill's rents, Smithfield bars
Willis Thos. solicitor, 11 Staple inn, Holborn
Willis Thos. H. sec. to the United Service Club, 116 Pall mall
Willis Wm. beer retailer, 1 & 2 Bath st. Newgate st
Willis Wm. dispensing chemist, 14A, Dean st. Soho
Willis Wm. french polisher, 2 Cleveland st. Mile end rd
Willis Wm. fruiterer, 19 Gt. Carlisle st. Portman market
Willis Wm. fruiterer, 21 Lime st. City
Willis Wm. hairdresser & perfumer, 19 Gt. Marlborough st
Willis Wm. livery stables, 36 Claremont mews, Clerkenwell
Willis Wm. oilman, 25A, Tavistock place, Tavistock sq
Willis Wm. tailor, 31 Church st. Chelsea
Willis Wm. George, oilman, 74 Strutton ground, Westmnstr
Willisford Francis Wm. surgeon, 76 Cadogan pl. Sloane st
Williter Charles, wax, &c. chandler, 4 Blandford st. Manch.sq
Williter Wm. Harvey, tallowchand. 24 Clare st. Clare market
Willmer & Stocker, surgeons, 44 Baker st. Portman sq
Willmer John, chandler's shop, 24 Gt. Carlisle st. Portman mkt
Willmer Sarah (Mrs.), newsvender, 72 Seymour st. Euston sq
Willmer Wm. baker, 114 High st. Camden town
Willmore Benj. hat manufr. 2 Princess st. Union st. Boro'
Willmore Graham, barrister, 3 Plowden buildings, Temple
Willmore Jas. T. A.E. landscape engrav. 23 Polygon, Somerst
Willmot Chas. coffee rooms, 19 New road, St. George's ea
Willmott Chas. wholesale brush, &c. mak. 46 Liquorpond st
Willmott Chas. P. beer retailer, 5 Cleaver st. Kenningtn. cr
Willmott Edward, painter, 7 Earl st. east, Lisson gr. north
Willmott Robert, plasterer, 7 Exeter st. Lisson grove
Willmott Thos. machine ruler, 19 & 20 Lit. Bell alley, Coleman st
Willmott Thos. surgeon, 17 Upper Eaton st. Pimlico
Willmott Wm. cheesemonger, 54 Curtain road, Shoreditch
Willmott Wm. chemist & druggist, 83 Borough High st
Willmott Wm. machine ruler, 52 Bartholomew close
Wilmott Wm. James, plumber & glazier, West st. Hackney
Willomatt Benjamin, furniture broker, 186 Whitechapel rd
Willomatt Thomas, appraiser, 45 Hoxton Old town
Willott, Scott & Day, woollen warehousemen, 64 Aldermanbury
Willoughby Alfred & Co. pat. med. wa. 61 Bishopsgt. without
Willoughby Hen. & Edw. attorns. 4 Lancaster pl. Waterloo br
Willoughby & Jaquet, solicitors, 13 Clifford's inn, Fleet st
Willoughby Richard & Co. printers & pub. 86 Aldergate st
Willoughby Benj. billiard table ma. 3 Allen's ct. Oxford st
Willoughby Charles, tailor, 41 Warwick st. Belgrave rd
Willoughby George, cattle salesman, 60 West Smithfield
Willoughby Jane(Mrs.), oyster dealer, 4 Clement's ct. Milk st
Willoughby John, straw hat manufr. 88 Bishopsgate within
Willoughby Lucy A. (Miss), strawhatma. 4 Clemnt's. ct. Milk st
Willoughby Samuel, patten maker, 78 Long la. Bermondsey
Willoughby Solomon, coachmaker, 1 John st. Oxford st
Willoughby Thos. architect, 3 Trafalgar sq. Pall mall east
Willoughby Thomas, butcher, 36 Gt. Windmill st. Haymrkt
Willoughby Thomas, fruiterer, 12 Hertford rd. Kingsland
Wills John & Co. hosiers & ready made linen wa. 371 Oxford st
Wills & M'Dougall, saddlers, &c. 11 & 200 Upper Thames st
Wills Mark & Son, saddlers, 10 Red Lion st. Whitechapel
Wills Elizabeth (Mrs.), coffee rooms, 43 Essex st. Strand
Wills Francis, brick maker, 7 Hope terrace, Notting hill
Wills Harriot (Mrs.), lace mfr. 1 Cripplegate buildings
Wills Isaac, *Feathers* P.H. 25 Grosvenor st. west, Eaton sq
Wills James, mason, 14 Tottenham court, New road
Wills Jane (Miss), milliner, 51 Burlington arcade
Wills John, proctor, 5 Gt. Carter lane, Doctors' commons
Wills John Fisher, oil, &c. merchant, see Gaby & Wills
Wills Orlando S. *Pine Apple tav.* 7 Hungerford st. Strand
Wills Robert, marble, &c. mason, 21 Tottenham ct. New rd
Wills Robert, tobacconist, 88 Bunhill row
Wills Susan (Mrs.), milliner & model wareh. 17 Oxford st
Wills Wm. bricklayer, 19 Webb st. Bermondsey st
Wills Wm. *Crown & Anchor* P.H. 36 King st. Seven dials
Wills Wm. job master, Addington square, Camberwell
Wills Wm. teadealer, &c. 10 Crescent st. Euston sq
Willsea Wm. Geo. boys' school, 72 Long lane, Bermondsey
Willsher George, confectioner, 2 Spring st. Paddington
Willsher John, baker, 35 Grove place, Lisson grove
Willsher Wm. bookseller, &c. 4 Portsdown ter. Kilburn gate
Willshire & Parris, architects, &c. 5 Wolsingham pl. Lambth
Willshire Raymond, stationer, 13 Tyler st. Regent st
Willshire Wm. Hughes, physician, 2 Cecil st. Strand
Willsmore Jas. furn. brok. &c. 13 Royal Hospital row, Chelsea
Willson Rd. & Co. whfngrs. Carpenter Smith's wf. Tooley st
Willson & Tilley, artificial flower makers, 60 King st. Soho
Willson Charles, painter, 12 Bulstrode st. Manchester sq
Willson Charlotte (Mrs.), shape wareh. 22 Sun st. Bishopsgt
Willson Edward, wholes. confectioner, 49 Hoxton Old town
Willson Francis Robt. shoemaker, 10 Exmouth st. Clerkenwll
Willson Geo. tailor, hosier & genl. outfitter, 173 Oxford st
Willson Geo. paper stainer, &c. 30 Norfolk st. Middlsx. hosp

Willson George, upholsterer, 30 Judd place west, New road
Willson George Samuel, engraver, 3 Goldsmith st. Gough square, & 19 Paradise row, Cambridge road
Willson Henry, *Ship* P.H. 47 Charles st. Westminster
Willson Jane (Miss), ladies' seminary, 64 St Paul's churchyd
Willson John, attorney, 3 Raymond buildings, Gray's inn
Willson John, blacking manufr. 5 Marine cres. Bermondsey
Willson John, builder, 130 Gt. Suffolk st. Borough
Willson John, bootmaker, 19 Old Montague st. Whitehapel
Willson John, oil & colorman, 4 Hereford pl. Comerl.rd.east
Willson John, *Old Black Dog* P.H. 13 Denmark st. Ratcff.hwy
Willson John, saw mills, 21 Quaker st. & Phœnix st. Spitalflds
Willson John Barnard, brushma. 32 George st. Portman sq
Willson Joseph, ladies' school, 28 Denbigh st. Pimlico
Willson Martin, tailor, 17 Swan st. Minories
Willson Matthew, upholsterer, 68 Gt. Queen st. Linc.inn flds
Willson Ozwald, undertaker, 17 Cirencester pl. Fitzroy sq
Willson Richard, bruch, clog & patten maker, 211 Shoreditch
Willson Rd. operative chemist, 92 Mount st. Berkeley sq
Willson Robert, flatting mills, 14 Ivy lane, Newgate st
Willson Samuel, curiosity dealer, 14 Bear st. Leicester sq
Willson Thos. stables, 5, 6 & 7 Gt. Cumberland mews, Brynstn.sq
Willson Thomas Moore, grocer, 23 High st. Newington butts
Willson William, baker, Broadway, Deptford
Willson William, baker, New row, Deptford
Willson Wm. lath render, 14 Cleveland st. Fitzroy square
Willson Wm. muffin baker, 4 Charles st. St. George's east
Willson Wm. Brand, profess. of music, 18 Stepney causeway
Willson Wm. Sloman, cooper, see Colyer & Willson
Willy James, straw hat manufr. 25 Cross st. Hatton garden
Willy Joseph, civil engineer, surveyor & architect, 13 Agar st. Strand
Willy Lewis, coal dealer, &c. 19 Lit. Chapel st. Westminster
Willy Wm. ink & blacking manfr. 42 Princes sq. St. George's ea
Willyams Humphry, copper merch. see Sims, Willyams & Co
Wilme Thomas, attorney, 2 Wilmington st. Spafields
Wilmer Wilmer, solicitor, see Currey, Wilmer & Currey
Wilmore Edw. *Ship* P.H. 1 Little Bridge st. Blackfriars
Willmot Charles, blind ma. 36 Northampton st. Clerkenwell
Wilmot Charles, linendraper, 2½ Williams pl. Walworth rd
Wilmot Geo. barometer frame ma. 14 Willow row, Goswell st
Wilmot Hen. stove mkr. & smith, 11 Cross st. Newington butts
Wilmot John Eardley Edwd. barrister, 11 Kg's. Bench wk. Temp
Wilmot Paul, barrister, 3 Elm court, Temple
Wilmot Thos. auctioneer, &c. 18 Grosvenor st. west, Eaton sq
Wilmot Thomas, oil & colorman, & plumber, 2 Creed lane
Wilmott Jas. W. & Co. wax chan. & oilmen, 66 Gracechurch st
Wilmott Charles, stationer & bookseller, 251 Oxford st
Wilmott John, geographic drftsmn. 29 Charlotte st. Pntnvl
Wilmshurst Frederick, smith, Commercial road, Pimlico
Wilmshurst Thomas, baker, 31 Whitehorse lane, Stepney gn
Wilmshurst Thomas, glass stainr. 13 Foley pl. Gt. Portland st
Wilsdon Chas. silk trimming ma. 4 Bacon st. Bethnal green
Wilsher John, coachsmith & springma. 12 Parker st. Drury la
Wilsher Thos. engraver & printer, 11 Old Manor st. Chelsea
Wilshere John, locksmith, &c. 9 Sutton st. Soho
Wilshin Sebastian B. grocer, 86 Albany road, Camberwell
Wilson Alex. & Son, bootmakers, 84 Crawford st. Portman sq
Wilson Alex. & Son, boot & shoe ware. 95 & 97 Holborn hill
Wilson Alex & Sons, letter founders, Gt. New st. Fetter la
Wilson Benjamin William, William, jun. & James, hat manufacturers, 37 Walbrook, & at Denton, Lancashire
Wilson Brothers & Co. importers of french confectionery, foreign fruits, italian articles, & manufacturers of ornaments, 16 Philpot lane
Wilson & Bull, woollen warehousemen, see Bull & Wilson
Wilson & Campbell, woollen drapers, 51 Blackfriars road
Wilson & Cooke, coopers, Russell st. Dockhead, Bermondsey
Wilson Elizh. & John, stables, Laycock's yard, Islington
Wilson, Fisher & Co. surveying, engineering, & draughtsmen, 158 Strand
Wilson, Fox & Co. hat manfs. 33 Bucklersbury & 8 Gt. Tower st
Wilson Geo. & James, & Edward, printers, 6 George ct. 32 Pcdlly
Wilson, Gibb & Co. hat makers, 122 Long lane, Bermondsey
Wilson & Graham, silk & velvet manfrs. 40 Gresham st. City
Wilson & Hall, irish pro. agt. 4 Wellington chmbs. London br
Wilson & Harrison, solicitors, 1 Copthall buildings
Wilson Isaac & Co. tailors, &c. 12 Gt. Hermitage st. Wapping
Wilson James & Son, stockbrokers, 80 Old Broad st. City
Wilson John & Son, butchers, 6 Mason's alley, Basinghall st
Wilson John & Sons, bookbinders, 19 Foley pl. Portland pl
Wilson John & Sons, linendrapers, 159 New Bond st
Wilson John & Sons, thread manufrs. 57 Wood st. Cheapside
Wilson Joseph & Co. cotton manufrs. 27 Noble st. Cheapside
Wilson Joseph John & Isaac, wholesale hosiers, 35 Milk st
Wilson & Lancaster, russia brokers, 80 Old Broad st. City
Wilson & Millson, architects, 2 Portsmouth st. Linc. in. fld
Wilson M. & Co. merchants, 15 Devonshire sq. Bishopsgate
Wilson, Moore & Co. silk manufrs. 31 Milk st. Cheapside
Wilson M. & I. tailors, 18 Old Bond st
Wilson & Ogilvy, printers, 57 Skinner st. Snowhill
Wilson & Plummer, cotton manufacturers, 63 Great Tower st. & manufactory, Golden lane, Barbican
Wilson Richard & Co. lacemen, 159A, Oxford st
Wilson Rd. & Co. oil & russia brokers, 72 Old Broad st. City
Wilson, Richard & Co. wholesale stationers, account book & mill board manufacturers, 26 & 27 St. Martin's court, St. Martin's lane
Wilson Richard Lea & Co. silk manufacturers, 22½ Milk st
Wilson Robert & John, corn factors, 123 Fenchurch st
Wilson Rt. & Wm. who. bath & japan'd ware mnfrs. 95 Wardourst.
Wilson, Seaman & Co. silk manufrs. 30½ St. Paul's churchyd
Wilson & Swale, linendrapers, mercers, &c. to the Queen, 9 & 10 Hanway st. Oxford st
Wilson Thos. & Co. merchts. 6 Warnford ct. Throgmorton st
Wilson Thos. & Son, saddlers & harness makers, 18 & 19 Vere st. Cavendish sq
Wilson Thos. & Son, wholesale stationers, 103 Cheapside
Wilson, Venables & Co. who. stanrs. see Venables, Wilson & Tyler
Wilson, Ware & Co. straw & tuscan manfrs. 11 Aldermanbury
Wilson William & Co. hatters, 11 Wellington street, London bridge, & 104 Fleet st
Wilson Wm. & Saml. cotton spinners, 50 Wood st. Cheapside
Wilson Wm. & Son, watchmakers, 38 Southampton st. Strand
Wilson Wm. & W. J. E. surgeons, 55 Charlotte st. Fitzroy sq
Wilson, Wilson & Co. merchants, 4 Jeffrey's sq. St. Mary axe
Wilson Alexander, arbitrator & accountant, 8 Old Jewry
Wilson Alexander, baker, 14 Duke st. Stamford st
Wilson Alexander, solicitor, 7 Symond's inn, Chancery lane
Wilson Alexander, umbrella maker, 22 Milk st. City
Wilson Alfred, auctioneer, 20 King's road, Bedford row
Wilson Alfred, clockcase & cabinet ma. 17 Perceval st. Clknw
Wilson Alfred Samuel, cooper, 76 Bethnal green road
Wilson Andrew, carpenter, 6 Arlington pl. St. George's east
Wilson Archibald, gasfitter & gunmaker, 141 Drury lane
Wilson Augustus, imp. of berlin wools, canvasses, embroideries, &c. & manfrs. of upholsterer's trimmings, 1 Astey's buildings, Lower rd. Islington, & 48 Newgate st
Wilson Barnabas, academy, 18 Well st. Cripplegate
Wilson Berkley, wholesale fur manufactr. 11 Aldermanbury
Wilson Charles, attorney, 3 Aldermanbury
Wilson Charles, bricklayer, 17 Curtain road, Shoreditch
Wilson Charles, egg merchant, 41 Up. York st. Bryanstone sq
Wilson Charles, grocer, North st. East st. Walworth
Wilson Charles, *Half moon tavern*, 88 Gracechurch st
Wilson Charles, [late J. W. Norie & Wilson], publisher, chart & map seller, bookseller & stationer, to the Admiralty, the Hon. East India Co. & Corporation of the Trinity House, at the Navigation warehouse & naval academy, 157 Leadenhall st
Wilson Charles, *Rising Sun* P.H. 101 Poplar High st
Wilson Charles, shoemaker, 258 Whitechapel road
Wilson Charles, stationer, 37 Wigmore st. Cavendish sq
Wilson Charles, tailor & draper, 81 Aldersgate st
Wilson Charles, woollen warehouseman, 8 Ludgate st
Wilson Charlotte (Mrs.), lodging ho. 1 Thanet pl. Strand
Wilson Cornwall Baron, attorney, 13 Furnival's inn, Holborn
Wilson Daniel, *St. Luke's Head* P.H. 25 Old st.; 151 Upper Whitecross st. St. Luke's
Wilson David, surgeon, 1 Eccleston square, Belgrave road
Wilson Edward, appraiser, 55 Vauxhall walk
Wilson Edward, floor cloth manufacturer, 87 Newgate st
Wilson Edward, sec. to brit. plat. glass co. 1 Albion pl. Blkfrs
Wilson Edward D. *Green Dragon* P.H. 10 St. Andrew's hill
Wilson Edward John, surgeon, &c. 39 Gt. Coram st. Brnswk.sq
Wilson Edwd. Lewell, oil & colorman, 7 Glo'ster pl. Old Kent rd
Wilson Edward Thos. academy, 10 Paradise row, Chelsea
Wilson Effingham, bookseller & statnr. 11 Royal exchange
Wilson Eliza (Miss), seminary, 5 Portland pl. Low. rd. Islngtn
Wilson Elizh. (Mrs.), chandler's shop, 24 Easton st. Spaflds
Wilson Elizh. (Mrs.), childbed linen wa. 7 Lamb's Conduit st
Wilson Elizh. (Mrs.), cotton & yarn mnf. 7 Priest ct. Foster la
Wilson Elizh. (Mrs.), drug grinder, 39 Gt. Sutton st. Clknwell
Wilson Elizh. (Mrs.) fringe ma. 19 Charlotte st. Fizroy sq
Wilson Elizh. (Mrs.), haberdasher, 31 Silver st. Golden sq
Wilson Elizh. (Mrs.), lodging ho. 21 Wakefield st. Brnswk.sq
Wilson Emily (Miss), straw bonnet ma. 80 Bridge rd. Lmbth
Wilson Emma (Mrs.), piecebro. 4 Goodwin's ct. St. Martin's la
Wilson Fletcher, consul gen. for Denmark, 6 Warnford ct
Wilson Francis, mason, 34 Brown's lane, Spitalfields
Wilson Frederick, *Globe tavern*, 30 Finsbury pavement
Wilson Fredk. tobacconist, 6 Samson's pl. Grange rd. Brmndsy

Wilson Fred. wine & spirit merchant, & east india pale ale stores, 9 & 10 Hanway st. & 8 Wells st. Oxford st
Wilson George, ale merchant, 39 Friday st. Cheapside
Wilson George, attorney, 11 New inn, Wych st. Strand
Wilson George, *Beaumont Arms* P.H. White Horse la. Stepny
Wilson George, *Black Jack* P.H. 11 Porstmouth st. Lincoln's inn fields
Wilson George, cabinet ma. 6 Glo'ster pl. King's rd. Chelsea
Wilson George, carp. & buildr, 32 Worship st. Norton folgte
Wilson George, grocer, 100 Goldsmith's row, Hackney road
Wilson George, spectacle maker, 15 Bacon st. Bethnal grn
Wilson George, teadealer, 8 Tothill st. Westminster
Wilson George, patentee & manufacturer of the new paper cutting machine, who.stationer, account book & mill board
Wmanufr. 26 & 27 St. Martin's court, St. Martin's lane
Wilson George John Marris, surgeon, 100 Gt. Portland st
Wilson George Sutell, barrister, 1 Hare court, Temple
Wilson Gilbert, hosier, &c. 140 Oxford st
Wilson Henry, auctioneer & surveyor, 30 Royal exchange
Wilson Henry, bricklayer, 29 Shaftesbury pl. Aldersgate st
Wilson Henry, dining rooms, 31 Brick lane, St. Luke's
Wilson Henry, fruiterer, 101 Drummond st. Euston sq
Wilson Henry, grocer, &c. 1 Union pl. Lower rd. Islington
Wilson Henry, gun stock maker, 1 James st. St. Luke's
Wilson Henry, tailor, 41 Warwick st. Golden sq
Wilson Henry, teadealer, 24 Cable st. Wellclose sq
Wilson Hen. Chas. coal merchant, 46 Chapel st. Edgware rd
Wilson Hen. Chas. sup. reg. of births, Marylebone la. Oxfd. st
Wilson Hen. Walter, barrister, 89 Chancery lane
Wilson Hen. Wm. *Beauvoir Arms* P.H. Hertford rd. Kingslnd
Wilson Jacob, upholsterer, 6 Welbeck st. Cavendish sq
Wilson James, *Alfred's Head* P.H. 38 Union st. Bishopsgate
Wilson James, baker, 26 Red Lion st. Spitalfields
Wilson James, butcher, 60 Tower st. Westminster road
Wilson James, *Chapel House* P.H. 62 Chapel st. Pentonville
Wilson James, *Constitution* P.H. 122 & 123 Drury lane
Wilson James, engineer & patent agent, 117 Chancery lane
Wilson James, linendraper, 33 Wilson st. Finsbury
Wilson James, linendraper, mercer, & manufacturer of bookbinders' cloth, 53 St. John st. Clerkenwell
Wilson James, oil & colorman, 4 Tothill st. Westminster
Wilson James, *Old Axe* P.H. 22 Hackney road
Wilson James, ornamentl. paintr. 30 Myrtle st. Hoxton Old tn
Wilson James, prof. of music 26 Bartlett's bldgs. Holborn
Wilson James, surgeon, see Thompson & Wilson
Wilson James, tailor, 50 Rupert st. Haymaket
Wilson James, undertaker, 18 Little St. Andrew st. 7 Dials
Wilson James Arthur, physician, 28 Dover st
Wilson James Godfrey, engineer, William st. Caledonian rd
Wilson James Peter, racket maker, 12 Weston pl. King's cr
Wilson John, artist, 7 Edward st. Hampstead road
Wilson John, baker, 10 Norfolk st. Borough
Wilson John, barrister, Chapel stairs, Lincoln's inn
Wilson John, barrister, 3 Gray's inn square
Wilson John, barrister, 17 New Boswell court, Lincoln's inn
Wilson John, bootmaker, 4 Back Church lane, Whitechapel
Wilson John, broker & cabinet ma. 12 Broker's alley, Drury la
Wilson John, *Bunch of Grapes* P.H. 5 George st. Minories
Wilson John, cabinet maker, 1 Hop gardens, St. Martin's la
Wilson John, *Clarendon Arms* P.H. 15 Clrndn. ter. Camb. N. rd
Wilson John, coal dealer, 2 Holles st. Clare market
Wilson John, custom ho. & comsn. agt. 12 Harp la. Tower st
Wilson John, floor cloth manf. 8 Pickett st. or 253 Strand
Wilson John, fruiterer, 9 South st. King's road, Chelsea
Wilson John, goldsm. & jeweller, 69 New Compton st. Soho
Wilson John, hop factor, Spur inn yard, 97 Boro' High st
Wilson John, law stationer, 18 Charles st. Middlesex hosp
Wilson John, merchant, 21 Throg norton st
Wilson John, merchant & drysalter, see Judson & Wilson
Wilson John, oil & colorman, 45 Carnaby st. Golden sq
Wilson John, oil & colorman, 6 Weymouth st. New Kent rd
Wilson John, omnibus proprietor, 8 John's yd. Lisson gr. nth
Wilson John, physician, 51 Oxford st
Wilson John, plumber, Stratford, Essex
Wilson John, potato dealer, 18 Red Lion pas. Red Lion sq
Wilson John, seal engraver, 4 Church place, Covent garden
Wilson John, seal engraver & die sinker, 20 Leicester sq
Wilson John, ship & insurance broker & commission agent 33 Nicholas lane, Lombard st
Wilson John, silk velvet manfr. see Cooper & Wilson
Wilson John, surgeon & accoucher, 66 Albany st. Rgnt's pk
Wilson John, tailor, 10 High st. Deptford
Wilson John, tailor, 71 Greenfield st. Commercial rd. east
Wilson John, teadealer, see Moore & Wilson
Wilson John, *Two Spies* P.H. 10 Catherine st. Strand
Wilson John, upholsterer, 1 Liverpool st. Bishopsgate
Wilson John, watch & clockma. 25 Davies st. Berkeley sq
Wilson John, *Woodman* P.H. John st. Old Kent rd
Wilson John, jun. russia mer. 10 Pinner's hall, O. Broad st. City
Wilson John Henry, stationer & bookseller, 22 Gresham st
Wilson John H. surveyor, 15 Southampton row, New rd
Wilson John Iliff, printer, see Bentley, Wilson & Fley
Wilson John James, surgeon, 52 Doughty st. Foundling
Wilson Jonathan, boot & shoe ma. 13 Tottenham st. Fitzroy sq
Wilson Joseph, bookbinder, 33 Ray st. Clerkenwell
Wilson Joseph, bootmaker, 114 Jermyn st. St. James's
Wilson Joseph, chenille & trim. manfr. 31 Sclater st. Bthnl. gr
Wilson Joseph, farrier, 28 Rupert st. Haymarket
Wilson Joseph, sponge seller, 14 Lit. Newport st. Long acre
Wilson Joseph, who. tin manufr. 85 Friar st. Blackfrs. rd
Wilson Joseph, sen. builder, 9 Commercial road east
Wilson Joseph Henry, barrister, 26 Chancery lane
Wilson Joshua, treasr. to Highbury Coll. 4 Blomfield st. Finsb
Wilson Lea, merchant & silk merchant, 124 Wood st. & 13 Goldsmith st. City
Wilson Lewis, undertaker, 85 Rosemary lane, Minories
Wilson Malcolm, tailor, 119 Aldersgate st
Wilson Marmaduke, tailor, 28 Clarges st. Piccadilly
Wilson Mary (Mrs.), coffee rooms, 250 High Holborn
Wilson Mary (Mrs.), furn. brkr. 33 Lit. Pulteney st. Gldn. sq
Wilson Mayor George, artist, Stratford, Essex
Wilson (Miss), ladies' school, 9 Barnsbury st. Islington
Wilson (Miss), ladies' school, 5 Gloucester ter. Cambridge rd
Wilson (Mrs.), ladies' school, 32 Warren st. Islington
Wilson Peter, beer retailer, Maiden lane, King's cross
Wilson Ralph, tailor, 30 Edwards st. Portman square
Wilson Rev. Rd. D.D. Gough ho. school, Paradise row, Chelsea
Wilson Richard, baker, 91 Star st. Edgware road
Wilson Richard, *Marlborough Head* P.H. 36 Drury lane
Wilson Richard, yeast dealer, 91 Aldersgate st
Wilson Robert, cheesemonger, 11 Vigo st. Regent st
Wilson Robert, fishfactor, 103 Lower Thames st
Wilson Robert, surgeon, 177 St. George st
Wilson Robert, tailor, see Woods & Wilson
Wilson Robert F. *White Lion* P.H. 24 James st. Covent grdn
Wilson Robert Henry Hird, attorney, 4 South sq. Gray's inn
Wilson Samuel, leather bottle ma. 11 Lit. Carter la. Drs.' com
Wilson Samuel, ornamental chinadealer, 47 Moorgate st
Wilson Samuel, painter, 1 Eccleston st. south, Pimlico
Wilson Samuel, undertaker, 1 Apollo bldgs. East st. Walwth
Wilson Sam. wheelwright, King's Arms yd. Coal yd. Drury la
Wilson Samuel King, ship agent, see Gallaway & Wilson
Wilson Samuel Serrel, builder, 55 Upper Ebury st. Pimlico
Wilson Sarah (Mrs.), straw hat maker, 2 New st. Brompton
Wilson Sophia (Mrs.), lodgingho. 30 Northumbrld. st. Maryleb
Wilson Stephen Barton, architect, 7 Frederick pl. Gray's inn rd
Wilson Thos. beer retailer, High st. Deptford
Wilson Thos. china & glass wa. 2 Northampton row, Holloway
Wilson Thos. *Coach & Horses* P.H. 17 Gt. Mitchel st. St. Luke's
Wilson Thos. gold lace manufacturer, 31 Lombard st. City
Wilson Thos. *Monument* P.H. 137 Union st. Borough
Wilson Thos. linen merchant, see Banks, Peacock & Co
Wilson Thos. plumber, 102 Old st. St. Luke's
Wilson Thos. tailor, 19 Salisbury st. Strand
Wilson Thos. teacher of dancing, 30 Ship yard, Temple bar
Wilson Thos. warehouseman, see Laurie & Wilson
Wilson Thos. watchmaker, 71 Judd st. Brunswick sq
Wilson Thos. Cutforth, mahogany & timber mer. 13 Greek st
Wilson Thos. Harrington, jun. artist, 1 Lowther arcade
Wilson Thos. H. sen. hairdresser, 15 Lowther arcade
Wilson Thos. Luxmore, solicitor, 43 Bedford row, Bloomsby
Wilson Walter, surgeon, 10 Everett st. & 15 Henrietta st. Brun. sq
Wilson Wm. artist, 48 London st. Fitzroy square
Wilson Wm. beer retailer, 8 Brunswick pl. Old Kent road
Wilson Wm. brassfounder, 4 Peartree ct. Clerkenwell
Wilson Wm. coffee rooms, 8 Clerkenwell green
Wilson Wm. currier, 55 Crucifix lane, Bermondsey
Wilson Wm. dyer, 21 Queen st. Tower hill
Wilson Wm. grocer & cheesemonger, 11 Boswell ct. Queen sq
Wilson Wm. grocer & machinist & engineer, 33 Old change
Wilson Wm. *Hoggs* P.H. 20 Broadwall, Blackfriars rd
Wilson Wm. jeweller, 6 Gloucester st. Queen sq
Wilson Wm. *King's Head* P.H. 49 Chiswell st. Finsbury
Wilson Wm. livery stable keeper, 67 Lower Thames st
Wilson Wm. livery stables, 246 Blackfriars road
Wilson Wm. locksmith, 25 Backchurch lane, Whitechapel
Wilson Wm. *Lord Nelson* P.H. 17 Nelson st. City rd
Wilson Wm. oyster saleseman, 15 Savage gardens, Tower hill
Wilson Wm. perfumer & hairdresser, 277 Strand
Wilson Wm. plasterer, 7 Lambeth High st
Wilson Wm. potato dealer, 6 Lumber ct. Seven dials
Wilson Wm. professor of music, 12 Halton st. Islington

Wilson Wm. straw & tuscan bonnet ma. 10 Yardley st. Clknwl
Wilson Wm. sugar broker, 13 Mincing lane
Wilson Wm. tailor, 79 Watling st
Wilson Wm. tailor, 6 Lower Kennington lane
Wilson Wm. *Three Mariners* P.H. 30 Wapping wall
Wilson Wm. wine & spirit merchant, see Jackson & Wilson
Wilson Wm. sen. plumber & glazier, 7 Chapel st. Bedford rw
Wilson Wm. jun. plumb. paint. &c. 10 Yardley st. Clerkenwl
Wilson Wm. G. vulcan iron wareho. St. Ann'swhf. Earlst. Blkfs
Wilson Wm. George, zinc worker, 14 Cross st. Newingtn. bts
Wilson Wm. Henry, newsvender, 8 Bedford st. Bedford row
Wilson Wm. Jas. timber mer. Iron bridge whf. East India rd
Wilson Wm. John, linendraper, 16 & 17 Crown st. Finsbury
Wilson Wm. Miller, solicitor, 13 South sq. Gray's inn
Wilson Wm. Miller, solicitor, 13 South sq. Gray's inn
Wilson Wm. Richard, ship agent, 2 Pinner's ct. Old Broad st
Wilson Wm. Silvester, barrister, 10 King's Bench walk
Wilson Wm. Thos. linendrap. 10 Bray's bldgs. Lower rd. Islgn
Wilt John Anderson, wine merchant, 125 Leadenhall st
Wilton & Blackman, solicitors, 1 Raymond bldgs. Gray's inn
Wilton Charles, artist, 6 New st. Dorset sq
Wilton George, bootmaker, 9 High st. Deptford
Wilton Geo. Pleydell, solicitor, 1 Raymond bldgs. Gray's inn
Wilton Harry J. plumber, &c. Gibralter row, Lowerrd. Deptford
Wilton James, oil & italian warehouse, 26 Rotherhithe st
Wilton James, jun. plumber & glazier, 1 Emmett st. Poplar
Wilton John, tallow chandler & melter, Stratford broadway
Wilton Mary Ann (Mrs.), bookseller, 11 Jamaica ter. Limeh
Wilton Robt. shellfishmonger, 1 Great Ryder st. St. James'
Wilton Wm. gold size maker, 16 Ray st. Clerkenwell
Wilton Wm. shop fixture dealer, 24 Lambeth lower marsh
Wilton Wm. Burtt, coppersmith, &c. High st. Deptford
Wilton Wm. Wilkins, bookbinder, 6 Bream's bldgs. Chancery la. & 5 Symond's inn
Wilts, Somerset & Southampton Junction Railway Co. 26 Gresham st. City
Wilts, Somerset & Weymouth Railway, 449 West Strand
Wiltsheare James, grocer, 6 Church st. Cheyne walk, Chelsea
Wiltshire Jonathan, cutler, 8 Long lane, Smithfield
Wiltshire & Bawden, milliners, &c. 6 Union st. Berkeley sq
Wiltshire Wm. & Son, writers & grain. 5 William st. Whtchpl
Wiltshire Aaron, butcher, 39 Gt. Guildford st. Borough
Wiltshire Daniel, grocer, 2 Royal Hospital row, Chelsea
Wiltshire John, blacksmith, Nottingham mews, & 2 Nottingham st. Marylebone
Wiltshire John, *Coopers' Arms* P.H. 33 Queen st. Chelsea
Wiltshire John, *Shades* P.H. 28 Charing cross
Wiltshire Wm. butcher, 7 New Park st. Borough
Wiltshire William, *Phœnix* P.H. 26 Norton folgate
Wimant William & Co. cattle salesmen, 17 West Smithfield
Wimble & Allport, ship & ins. brokers, 98 Gracechurch st
Wimbridge Thomas W. colored, fancy & marble paper & card manufr. & who. stationer, &c. 6 Bride court, New Bridge st
Wimburn, Collett, Laurie & Attree, solicitors, 62 Chancery la
Wimbush Samuel & Co. job masters, 315 Oxford st., & Halkin st. Grosvenor place
Wimpey George, baker, 6 Prospect place, Old Brompton
Wimpory Wm. chandler's shop, 96 Church st. Shoreditch
Wimshurst Henry, patent steam ship builder, 2 Cowper's court; Millwall, Poplar; & St. Ann's place, Limehouse
Winbolt Busick Jsph. & Co. account book mks. 172 Aldersgate st
Winch Benjamin, flour factor, 12 Hannibal road, Mile end
Winch Frederick, tobacconist, 20 Lisson grove north
Winch James, *Ship York* P.H. Lower York st. Low. Rotherhth
Winch Thomas, coke contractor, 2 King st. Gravel la. Wapping
Winch William, ivory cutter & turner, 7 North mews, Gray's inn lane, & 10 Gray's inn terrace
Winch William, livery stables, 5 Gt. Windmill st. Haymarkt
Winchester House, 52 Old Broad st. City
Winchester & Capon, ship's hearth ma. 1 & 2 Up. East Smithfld
Winchester John, oilman, 2 Manor pl. sth. King's rd. Chelsea
Winckles Wm. saddler & harness maker, 10 Moor st. Soho
Winckworth Lawrence Hen. solicitor, see Pearce, Phillips & Co
Wincott & Yeats, cheesemongers, 52 Chiswell st. Finsbury
Wincott Henry Robert, butcher, 28 Bread st. hill
Wincott Rufus, cheesemonger, 19 Lime st
Wincott Sophia (Mrs.), butcher, 50 Banner st. St. Luke's
Wind & Elliot, cheesemongers, 128 Jermyn st. St. James's
Windatt Edward, law stationer, 6 Serle's pl. Carey st
Windeatt James, *Stave Porter* P.H. 1 Jacob's st. Dockhead
Windebank Stephen, teadealer, 21, Whitechapel High st. & 10 London ter. Hackney road
Windeler Chas. wool merchant, 33 Wormwood st. Bishopsgt
Winder Henry, boarding house, 9 Wardrobe pl. Doctors' com
Winder Henry, shawl manufr. & furrier, 29 Oxford st
Winder John, surgeon, 154 Up. Whitecross st. St. Luke's
Winder John, window blind ma. 70 & 71 Kingsland road
Winder Robert, carcase butcher, 8 Red Lion alley, Cowcross
Winder Wm. builder, New walk, Shad Thames, Horselydn
Windham Club House (Ths. I. Hampton, sec.), 11 St. James's sq
Windeyer George, law stationer, 12 Castle st. Holborn
Windle & Co. ship & insurance brokers, 10 Gould square
Windle Wm. & Chas. coal mers. Milford wf. Milford la. Strand
Windle Mary (Mrs.), firewood cutter, 1 Leader pl. Chelsea
Windler & Strauss. hattrs. & capmf. 4 Churchla. Whtchpl. Highst
Windmill Ann (Miss), chiropidist, 74 George st. Portman sq
Windley Theodore, carpenter, 3 Appleton pl. Walworth com
Windmill Henry, saddler, see Cockman & Windmill
Windmill Wm. Hill, corn dealer, Stratford broadway
Windover Wm. *Robinson Crusoe* P.H. 43 Earl st. ea. Lisson gr
Window James, notary, 8 Craig's court, Charing cross
Windsor, Ascot & Farnborough Junction Railway Company (J. Morgan, sec.), 11 Adam st. Adelphi
Windsor Brothers, ship & ins. brok. & agts. 20 Gt. St. Helen's
Windsor Edward, barrister, 37 Chancery lane
Windsor Fredk. phial & bottle wa. 37 Bartholomew close
Windsor Henry Thos. colonial broker, 40 Mincing lane
Windsor James, watchmaker, 99 Paul st. Finsbury
Windsor Jane (Mrs.), book & printsel. 44 King st. Seven dials
Windsor John, enamelled card mnfr. 2 Meredith st. Clerknwll
Windsor Richard Vaughan, law stationer, 37 Chancery lane
Windsor Thomas, carpenter, 284 Kent st. Borough
Windsor Thomas, news agent, 99 Bethnal green road
Windsor Wm. artists' colorman, 59 Newman st. Oxford st
Windsor William, billiard rooms, 252 Strand
Windus Thos. & Son, coach & harn. mak. 72 & 73 Bishopsgt. witho
Windus L. (Mrs.) milliner & drs. ma. 1A, Pelham ter. Brompton
Wine Co. of Scotland (Chas. Balfour, sec.), 39 St. James's st
Wine Licence Offi. Excise Offi. Old Broad st. City; hrs. 10 to 3
Winer John Frederick, fishmonger, 52 Minories
Winfield & Simms, camp equipage manfrs. 26 New Bond st
Winfield John, coffee rooms, 22 Farringdon st.
Winfield Robt. W. brass bedsteadmak. & brassfndr. 141 Fleet st
Winfield Wm. auctioneer & estate agent, 18 Gerrard st. Soho
Winfield Wm. carver, 22 Charlton st. Fitzroy square
Winfill George, grocer, 9 Portland pl. south, Clapham rd
Wing Louisa & Emma (Misses), milliners, 6 Goswell st
Wing & Twining, solicitors, 1 Gray's inn square
Wing Charles, baker, 10 College terrace, Chelsea
Wing James, glover to the royal family, 338A, Oxford st
Wing James, orange merchant, 1 East st. Spitalfields markt
Wing John William, barrister, 10 Farrars bldgs. Temple
Wing Mark, watch & clock maker, 2 Goswell st
Wing Ralph, butcher, 7 Goodge st. Fitzroy square
Wing Thomas, glover & shirt mkr. 17 Gt. Newport st. Long ac
Wing Thomas William, wholesale grocer, 20 Eastcheap
Wing William, clock, &c. maker, see Scott, Wing & Co.
Wing William Charles, artist, 44 Dorset st. Manchester sq
Wingate Geo. Theodore, solr. see Chatfield, Wingate & Hart
Wingate Wm. tailor & breeches ma. 11 Tichborne st. Haymkt
Winger John, leather slr. 51 Richardson st. Long la. Brmndsy
Winget William, pianoforte maker, 63 John st. Fitzroy sq
Wingfield James, saddler, 75 Long lane, West Smithfield
Wingfield John, *Fox & Goose* P.H. Brick hill lane, City
Wingfield Joseph, brushmaker, 38 Gt. Portland st. Oxford st
Wingfield Samuel, saddler, 185 Union st. Borough
Wingham James, bricklayer, 6 Upper Bryanstone st
Wingham Thomas, oilman, 44 York terrace, Borough road
Wingrave Jos. & Co. wholes. italian wareh. 80 St. Paul's chyd
Wingrave Caroline (Mrs.), court milliner & dressmaker, 1 Charles st. Grosvenor square
Wingrave George, *Greyhound* P.H. Gretton pl. Bethnal gr
Wingrave George Burton, house decorator, upholsterer, &c. 1 Charles st. Grosvenor square
Wingrave James, bootmaker, 7 Creed lane, Ludgate st
Wingrove David, bookbinder, 44 Commercial road, Lambeth
Wingrove George, backmaker, see Carley, Son & Wingrove
Wingrove George, razor strop ma. 31 King st. Low. rd Islngtn
Wingrove John, dairyman, 34 Queen st. Lower rd. Islington
Wingrove Richard Fownes, refiner, see Browne & Wingrove
Wingrove Walter Fred. coal mer. Augustus st. Regent's pk
Wingrove Wm. butcher, 7 Bedfordbury, Covent garden
Wingrove Wm. engraver, 87 Long lane, West Smithfield
Winkler David, commission agent, 7 Gresse st. Rathbone pl
Winkles Benj. steel plate mnf. 1 Northampton st. Lo. rd. Islgtn
Winkley Luke Wm. ship insur. & cust. ho. agt. 23 Birchin la
Winkley Saml. Jas. stationer & printer, 5 Park st. Boro' mrkt
Winkley Thomas, horse slaughterer, 35 Green st. Blckfrs. rd
Winkley Walter, steam saw mills, 9 Bear lane, Blackfriars
Winks James, baker, 16 Gt. James st. Lisson grove
Winks Thomas, greengrocer, 14 Royal Hospital row, Chelsea
Winks Wm. bread, &c. baker, 6 Royal Hospital row, Chelsea

Winks Wm. *Greyhound* P.H. 5 Brick st. Park lane
Winkworth & Horne, silk warh. 44 Gutter lane, Cheapside
Winkworth John, livery stables, 26 Church st. Camberwell
Winkworth Thomas, engraver & printer, 4 Oxford market
Winmen James, farrier, 144 High st. Camden town
Winmill Geo.Beek,*BlackHorse*P.H.5 Hayfield pl.Mileendrd
Winn Christpr. timber merch. New Crane wf. 202 Wapping
Winn Geo. cowkeeper, 54 Anchor & Hope alley, Wapping
Winn Geo. John, cowkeeper, 54 Lit.Broad st. London Docks
Winn James G. wine & spirit broker, 10 Mark lane
Winn John, brass manufacturer, gasfitter, & gas apparatus
Wmanufacturer, 25 Little Charlotte st. Blackfriars rd
Winn John, commercial agent, see Wells & Winn
Winn Sarah (Mrs.), *White Lion* P.H. 12 Tooley st
Winn Thomas, jeweller, 31 Gt. Pulteney st. Golden sq
Winn Thos. stationer & vellum binder, 10 Sun st. Bishopsgt
Winnett James, worsted dyer, 9½ Hill st. Finsbury
Winning Hen. beer retailer, 60 Back Church la. Whitechapl
Winning Jas. coal merchant, Middle whf. Gt. Scotland yd
Winpenny Richard, surgeon, 57 Fetter lane, Fleet st
Winproy Ann (Mrs.), milliner, 191 Bethnal green road
Winsall Henry, fruiterer, 9 Bedford court, Covent garden
Winsall Joseph, hat manufacturer, 50 Bedford st. Strand
Winsbury John, scalemaker, &c. 107 Bethnal green road
Winser Charles, barrister, 2 New Temple buildings, Mitre ct
Winser Hen. Jas. tin plate wrkr.22 St. Martin's ct.Le'ster sq
Winskip Isabella (Mrs.), grocer, 62 John st. Fitzroy sq
Winskell Robert,*Horse & Groom* P.H.87 St.John's st.Clrkwl
Winskill George, tobacconist, 28 Brydges st. Covent garden
Winskill John, *White Hart* P.H. 7 Giltspur st
Winsland John Anthny.oil wareh.20 Gt.Pulteney st.Goldn.sq
Winsland Nicholas, builder, 17 Duke st. Bloomsbury; & Belvedere road, Lambeth
Winslow Edwd. commissioner in lunacy, 45 Lincoln's inn flds
Winslow Forbes, physician, 45 Guildford st. Russell square
Winslow John, chairmaker, 3 Crown ct. Crown st. Finsbury
Winsor & Newton, artists' colormen, 38 Rathbone pl.; & North London colorworks, Kentish town, & varnishworks, Bell isle
Winsor Charles, dairy, 3 Portsmouth st. Lincoln's inn fields
Winsor Charles, dairyman, 33 Maiden lane, Covent garden
Winsor Emanuel, haberdasher, 2 Thornton st. Dockhead
Winsor Fredk. Albert, barrister, 57 Lincoln's inn fields
Winsor Geo. fellmonger & wool rug ma. Russell st.Bermndsy
Winsor John, *King's Head* P.H. 18 Bear st. Leicester sq
Winsor Josph. lodging houses, 9&10St. Alban's pl.Haymarket
Winstanley Edward & Sons, chemists & druggists, 7 Poultry
Winstanley Jno. S.Jas.&Jno. auctioneers, 10 Paternoster row
Winstanley Jsph.I.&Co.outfitrs.&shirt ma.54KingWm.st.Cy
Winstanley Henry, solicitor, 88 Stanhope st. Hampstead rd
Winstanley James Winckworth, barrister, 26 Chancery lane
Winstanley Richd. Hen. proctor, 6 Godliman st. Doct. com
Winston Charles, special pleader, 2 Paper bldgs. Temple
Winstone Ann&Co. court plaister mfs.20 Bouverie st.Fleet st
Winstone John, bootmaker, 84 Waterloo road, Lambeth
Winstone John, surgeon, 35 Charterhouse square
Winstone Thos. coal mercht. Cannon wf. Cannon rw. Westm
Winter & Bowman, merchants, 2 Walbrook buildings
Winter Charles & Co. hosiers & outfitters, 68 Holborn hill
Winter & Rich, bar iron, tire & nail warehouse, 1 Bank end, Park st. & 7 & 8 Bankside, Southwark
Winter, Williams & Co. solicitors, 16 Bedford row
Winter Arthur, pork butcher, 16 Maiden lane, Covent grdn
Winter Benjamin, bricklayer, 27 Charles st. Hampstead rd
Winter Catherine (Mrs.), embroidress, 18 Poland st.Oxford st
Winter Charles, law stationer, 24 Chancery lane
Winter Charles, painter, &c. 38 George st. Euston square
Winter Deborah (Mrs.), ladies' school, 10 Lower Eaton st. Pim
WinterElizh.(Mrs.),courtmilliner&dressmak.106NewBondst
Winter Frederick, piece brokr. 7 Goodwin's ct.St.Martin's la
Winter Fredk.M. roche ma.&gofferer, 3 Flying horse ct.City
Winter George, *Coopers' Arms*P.H.52Huntingdon st.Hoxtn
Winter George, muffin baker, 2 Charterhouse st
Winter George, wine cooper, 43 Tabernacle walk, Finsbury
Winter Henry, comb & lantern horn maker, 106NewBond st
Winter Henry, solicitor, see Barnes, Winter & Bernard
Winter Henry, solicitor, 12 John st. Adelphi
Winter Hen.John, dyer, &c.19 NewUnion st.Little Moorfields
Winter Henry Louis, sawmills, see Crampern & Winter
Winter James, confectioner, 14 St. George's pl. Cambrwl rd
Winter James, furniture dealer, 100 & 101 Wardour st Soho
Winter James, tailor, Battersea sq. Battersea
Winter John, *Jolly Miller*P.H.51 Millbank st.Westminster
Winter John, plate glass factor, silverer & polisher, 99 Hatton garden, & Robinhood yard, Leather lane
Winter John, tailor, 19 Meredith street, Clerkenwell
Winter John, wine merchant, 8 Duke st. St. James's
Winter Joseph, furrier, 28 Gt. Sutton st. Clerkenwell
Winter Richard, grocer, 3 Norfolk pl. Marlboro' rd.Chelsea
Winter Richard, merchant, 2 Walbrook buildings
Winter Richard, whitesmith, 7 Lr. Queen st. Rotherhithe
Winter Robert, beer retailer, 125 Blackfriars rd
Winter Samuel, baker, 2 Shadwell High st
Winter Samuel, boot maker, 59Back church la.Whitechapel
Winter Sarah (Mrs.), *Robin Hood* P.H. 9 Leather la. Holb
Winter Thomas, baker, 14 Margaret st. Hackney fields
Winter Thomas, *Castle tavern*, 25 High Holborn
Winter Thomas, working optician, 5 Market st. Oxford st
Winter Thomas John, solicitor, 18 Austin friars
Winter William, hairdresser & perfumer, 205 Oxford st
Winter William, marine store dlr. 5 Kingsland row, Dalston
Winterborn James, bedstead&cornice ma. 7 Up.Rathbone pl
Winterborn James, chemist, 14 King David lane, Shadwell
Winterborn surgeon, 1 Clarence pl. Hackney rd
WinterbornWm.leather cutter& shoema.Church st.Hackney
WinterbothamAnn&Hannah,*Hind's Head* P.H.38 Chswll.st
Winterbotham John, *City Arms* P.H. Deptford High st
WinterbothamThos.*Queen's Hd.*P.H.17Freeschl.st.Horslyd
Winterbottom&Peatfield,fencing mstrs.Duchy pl.137Strand
Winterbottom Augustus Abraham, architect & surveyor, 137 Sloane st. & Gresham chambers, 75 Old Broad st. City
Winterbottom Edwin John, dentist, 9 Sloane st
Winterbottom John Frederic, barrister, 13 Old sq. Linc. inn
Winterbourne Henry, linendra.see Grave,Winterbourne&Co
Winterbourne James, law stationer, 6 Serle's pl. Carey st
Winterburn Joseph, firework ma.21 Providence bdgs.Kent rd
Winterbury Wm. mop maker, 21 White st. Lit. Moorfields
Winterflood Elijah, tailor, 16 Charles st. Hampstead rd
Winterflood Geo. potato wareho. 16 Harper st.New Kent rd
Winterhalder Joseph, clockmaker, 99 Bishopsgate without
Winterhalder Leo, wooden, &c. clock ma. 37 Kingsland rd
Winterhalter John & Joseph, clockmks. 44 Tottenham ct. rd
Winterson John, plumber, &c. 16Chichester pl.Wandswh rd
Winterton Thomas, trimming ma. see Sherrard &Winterton
Winthrop Benj. Eveleigh, barrister, 2 Paper bldgs. Temple
Wintle John & Co. wine merchants, 1 Adam st. & Adelphi vaults, Durham st. Strand
Wintle John Marriott, silversmith, 54 Drury lane
Wintle Thomas, *Allsop Arms* P.H. 44 Allsop ter. New rd
Winton David, agt.&com.warehousemn.31Gutter la.Cheapsd
Winton David, stuff manufr. 31 Gutter la. Cheapside
Winton Luke, *Crown* P.H. 151 Borrough High st
Winton Mary Ann (Mrs.), lighterman, Brewer, Chester & Galley quays, Lower Thames st. & 46 Horselydown lane
Winyard Samuel, *Gunmakers' Arms* P.H.Canal rd.Mile end
Wippell John & Son, coal merchants, Red Lion Wharf, 266 Wapping, & 21 Gt. Turner st. Commercial rd. east
Wippermann &Brooke, merchants, 4Jeffrey's sq.St.Mary axe
Wipperman Mary (Mrs.), grocer, 176 Ratcliffe highway
Wire & Child, solicitors, 9 St. Swithin's lane, City
Wire Benjamin, bricklayer & builder, 44 Bethnal green rd
Wire John, carpenter, 4 Fuller st. Church st. Bethnal green
Wisby John, auctioneer & appraiser, 10 Mount st. Lambeth
Wisby John *White Hart* P.H. 8 Market st. Oxford st
Wischusen Henry, furskin drsr.3 Lamb al. Sun st.Bishop-gt
Wisdom Robert, farrier, Cumberland pl. Newington butts
Wisdom Thomas, wholesale hosier, 4 Wood st. Cheapside
Wise James & George, rubbish carters, Ann's pl Hoxton
Wise & Nash, ever-pointed pencil makers, 30 Coppice row
Wise Alphonso Rt. book edge gilder, 18 Bartholomew close
Wise Edwd. cheesmg.100Ratcliffe highway & 2 Cannon st.rd
Wise Edward, barrister, 2 Middle Temple lane
Wise Elizabeth (Mrs.), fruiterer, Long market, Covent gar
Wise James, bootmaker, 22 Leigh st. Burton crescent
Wise James, cowkeeper, 32 King's road east, Chelsea
Wise James, dairyman, 5 Paradise row, Chelsea
Wise James, *Old Red Lion* P.H. 14 Cross st. Finsbury sq
Wise John, chair & sofa maker, see James & Wise
Wise John, grocer, 8 Broadway, St.Thomas's, & cooper, 7 New Weston st. Long lane, Borough
Wise John, tobacconist, 1 Wellington st. London bdg.Boro'
Wise John Gifford, boot & shoe ma. 17 Queen st. Cheapside
Wise Matthew, jun. fishmonger, 6St.Martin's ct.Ludgate hill
Wise Richard, harness maker, 6 Porter's row, Holloway rd
Wise Samuel, fruiterer, 74 Commercial road, Lambeth
Wise Saml. oil&colorman, 1 Cheltenham pl. Westminster rd
Wise Solomon, organ builder, 48 Regent st. Lambeth
Wise Stephen, plumber, 6 Conduit st. Paddington
Wise Thomas, cattle salesman, 17 West Smithfield
Wise Thomas, fruiterer, 39 Millbank st. Westminster
Wise Thomas, dairyman to the Queen, 6Westbourne st.Pmlc
Wise Thomas, surgeon & accoucheur, 44 Frith st. Soho
Wise William, grocer, 1 Norfolk pl. Marlboro' rd. Chelsea

Wise William, wholesale & retail ham & tongue warehouse, 48 Judd st. Brunswick square
Wise Wm. sawmills, North ct. Cowper st. City road
Wisedell John Edward, coffee rooms, 7 Long lane, Smithfield
Wisedill Francis, jeweller, 7 High st. Newington butts
Wiseman & Cole, coachmakers, 57 High st. Kensington
Wiseman John, academy, 1 Grange road, Bermondsey
Wiseman John, baker, 9 Wormwood st. Bishopsgate
Wiseman John, *Blue Anchor* P.H. Blue Anchor rd. Bermondsey
Wiseman John, bricklayer, 23 Crown row, Mile end road
Wiseman John, jun. wheelwright, 12 Artichoke rw. Mile e. rd
Wiseman Richd. horse hair manf. Tyer's gateway, Bermdy. st
Wiseman Robert, *William I V.* P.H. Minervater. Barnsbry. pk
Wiseman Thos. tailor & clock ma. 1 Wilsted st. Somers tn
Wiseman Wm. Cornelius, grocer, 10 Searle's pl. Carey st. & Stratford, Essex
Wiseman Wm. Richd. butcher, 18 Star corner, Bermondsey
Wisewold Thos. rag & bottle dlr. 5 Colonnade, Brunswick sq
Wisewould Harry C. statnr. 13 Belvoir ter. Vauxhall bdg. rd
Wisewould James, tailor, 37 Lower Kennington lane
Wishart & Lloyd, tobacco manufacturers, 21 Coventry st
Wishart William, oilman, 56 Snowsfields, Bermondsey
Wishaw James, barrister, 1 Southampton row, Bloomsbury
Wisker & Reynolds, carpenters, joiners, &c. 2 Greystoke pl. Fetter lane & 5 Dove court, Leather lane
Wisker Butler Bodkin, tailor, 7 Staple inn bldgs. Holborn
Wisker William, carpenter, &c. 2 Greystoke pl. Fetter lane
Wiskin King, butcher, Ferry road, Poplar
Wiss Robert, patent water closet manufr. 38 Charing cross
Wisson Wm. baker, 18 Russell st. Lower Rotherhithe
Whitchurch Mary (Mrs.), bacon drier, 118 Goswell st
Witcomb Charles, bookseller & stationer, 121 Leadenhall st
Witcomb Wm. accountant, 3 Ivy lane, Newgate st
Witford Thomas, baker, 9 Queen's row, Pimlico
Withall Richd. Aug. surveyor & auctioneer, 80 Cheapside
Withall Wm. attorney, 7 Parliament st. Westminster
Withall Wm. Chas. trimming man. 4 Featherstone st. City rd
Witham Henry, barrister, 6 Old square, Lincoln's inn
Witham Henry, zinc & tin plate manufr. 14 Queen st. Chelsea
Witham James, butcher, 7 Back st. Horselydown
Witham William, attorney, 8 Gray's inn square
Withem John, plumber, 55 South Molton st. Bond st
Witheman Joseph, carpenter, 16 Portsmouth st. Linc. inn flds
Witherby Geo. & Wm. Hen. lawstat. 54 Parlmnt. st. & 9 Birchinla
Witherby Charles, land sur. 3 Hemingford cott. Barnsbury rd
Witherby Francis, stockbroker, 7 Throgmorton st
Witherby Richard, fruit & colonial broker, 19 Mincing lane
Witherick Joseph, shoemaker, 4 Abbey st. Bethnal green rd
Witherick Robert, confectioner, 15 Pickett st. or 260 Strand
Witherington William F. R.A. artist, 8 Leigh st. Burton cres
Withers & Osmond, lacemen, 38 Hedge row, Islington
Withers John & James, brushmakers, 18 Union st. Somers town
Withers, Woollatt & Co. who. tea & coff. dlrs. 4 Crownct. Philpt. la
Withers Austin, hosier, 3 Manchester bldgs. Holloway rd
Withers Daniel, bookseller & statnr. 28 Well st. Wellclose sq
Withers David, working jeweller, 71 Marylebone lane
Withers Edward, carpenter, Villa st. Walworth common
Withers Edward, confectioner, 52 Blackfriars road
Withers Edward, who. tea dealer, see Warren & Withers
Withers Esther (Mrs.), butcher, 6 Whitechapel High st
Withers Gabriel, carpenter, 26 Houghton st. Clare market
Withers George, butcher, 20 Park ter. King's road, Chelsea
Withers George, confectioner, 23 George st. Portman square
Withers George, cop. plate printer. 12 Vine st. Horseferry rd
Withers George Wm. baker, 35 Southampton st. Camberwell
Withers Henry, brewer, 3 East side, Camberwell green
Withers Henry, hosier & glover, 9 Poultry
Withers James, baker, 94 East st. Manchester square
Withers Joseph, corn dlr. 100 Grand Junction ter. Edgwre. rd
Withers Joseph, stock broker, 24 Tokenhouse yd. Lothbury
Withers Phineas, *Horn of Plenty* P.H. 18 Globe rd. Mile e. rd
Withers Robert, baker, 6 South place, Dalston
Withers Thomas, seal engraver & die sinker, 4 Noel st. Soho
Withers Thomas Chas. chocolate maker, 71 Blackfriars rd
Withers Thomas Chas. fruiterer, 8 Crosby row, Walworth rd
Withers William, attorney, 36 Titchborne st. Edgeware rd
Withers William, *Bell* P.H. 21 Poppin's ct. Fleet st
Withers William, *Black Bull* P.H. 206 Borough High st
Withers William, *Victory* P.H. 12 Tottenham rd. Kingsld. rd
Withey John, pork butcher, 17 Aylesbury st. Clerkenwell
Withey Thomas, pork butcher, 113 Bishopgate without
Withey William, pork butcher, 37 Gt. Wild st. Drury lane
Withnall Caroline (Mrs.), hairwrkr. 42 Northampton st. Clkw
Withy Thos. wood engraver, 12½ Gough sq. & 1 James place, Alfred road, Vauxhall
Witt Charles, plumber & painter, 51 Liverpool st. Bishopsgat
Witt Charles, surgeon, 30 Spring gardens
Witt Gilbert, cheesemonger, 24 Chenies st. Bedford sq
Witt Thomas, coffee rooms, 3 Lamb's Conduit passage
Witt William, surgeon dentist & cupper, 315 High Holborn
Witt Wm. wine cooper, 62 Mark la. & 9 Collingwood st. Shored
Wittich Conrad, baker, 38 Chicksand st. Whitechapel
Witting Thomas, herald painter, 2 Oxford ter. Commrcl. rd
Witton D. W. & Co. merchants, 2 Crosby sq. Bishopsgate st
Witton John, gunmaker, 82 Old Broad st. City
Witton Joseph, music reed ma. 10 Johnson's pl. Thames bank
Witts Matthew, *Queen Victoria* P.H. 45 Skinner st. Clerknwl
Witty Francis, publisher & news agent, 72 Fleet st
Witty George, baker, 4 Mansfield place, Kentish town
Witty Richard Henry, solicitor, see Campbell & Witty
Wix Charles & Sons, oil & italian warehouse, 22 Leadenhall st
Wix Edward, leather seller & dresser, 41 Greek st. Soho
Wix Frederick, turkey merchant, see Jellicoe & Wix
Wix Samuel, solicitor, 26 Austinfriars
Wix William, clerk, St. Bartholomew's hospital
Wixley Horatio Nelson, bonnet block & stand manufacturer, 14 Long lane, Smithfield
Wodderspoon James, stationer, see Drew & Wodderspoon
Wohlgemuth Conrad, coal mer. Crows nest wf. Lr. Ea. Smthfld
Wohlgemuth Conrad, coal mer. Hope wharf, 238 Wapping
Wohlman Geo. painter & oilman, New road, South Lambeth
Woledge Henry, cheesemonger, 4 Montague pl. Lr. rd. Deptfd
Woley Jeremiah, grocer, 21 Edward st. Star corn. Bermndsy
Wolf & Figg, patent pianoforte & musical instrument makers & importers, 20 St. Martin's le grand (late 79 Cornhill)
Wolf Charles, pastry cook, 28 Crosby row, Walworth road
Wolf Edward Gudge, grocer, 13 John's row, St. Luke's
Wolf Godfrey, baker, 69 Whitechapel High st
Wolfe Brothers, stock & sharebrok. 23 Change alley, Cornhill
Wolfe Fred. Geo. carriage lamp ma. 6 Field pl. St. John st. rd
Wolfe Robert, bootmaker, 1 Northampton st. Clerkenwell
Wolff & Son, chiropodists, 133 Leadenhall st
Wolff Elias & Son, creta lævis inventors, 23 Church st. Spitalfi
Wolff Abraham, surgeon, see Whitaker & Wolff
Wolff Simon, cap manufacturer, 32 Chiswell st. Finsbury
Wollaston Frederick Luard, barrister, 2 Pump ct. Temple
Wollaston Henry Francis, merchant, 9 Gt. St. Helen's
Wollaston Richd. exchange brok. 3 Adam's ct. Old Broad st
Wollastons George, architect, 4 Gt. Titchfield st
Wollen Frederick Charles, tailor, 2 Bath st. City road
Wollen Ruscombe, attorney, 14 New Boswell ct. Lincoln's inn, & 30 Bucklersbury
Wolley John, *Noah's Ark* P.H. 17 Shoe lane, Fleet st
Wolley John, working jeweller, 12 Artillery st. Bishopsgate
Wolsoncroft & Leete, pawnbrokers & silversmiths, 179 Union st. Borough
Wolstenholme Thos. & Jsph. pawnbrokers, 16 Liquorpond st
Wolstenholme Dean, engraver, 22 St. Chad's rw. Gray's inn rd
Wolston Augustus, solicitor, 8 Furnival's inn, Holborn
Wolter William, bookbinder & cork cutter, 52 Drury lane
Wolton Thomas, cattle salesman, see Eve, Wolton & Eve
Womack Ann (Mrs.), baker, 12 Brick lane, St. Luke's
Wombwell George, menagerie, Warkworth ter. Coml. rd. ea
Womersley & Burt, billbrok. 10 & 11 Lombd. st. cha. Clement's la
Womersley Robert, manufacturing chemist, 7 Osborne place, Whitechapel & Bow common
Wonacott William, tailor, 55 Great Portland st. Oxford st
Wonnacott Wm. E. plumber, painter, &c. 62 Coleman st
Wontner Richard, woollen draper, 45 Cloth fair, West Smith
Wontner Thomas, jun. solicitor, 15 Skinner st. Snow hill
Wood Ann & Sons, bootmakers, 101 Newgate st
Wood Arthur & Co. pale ale & stout mer. 16 Clement's la. City
Wood & Barrett, ironfounders, smiths, & stove & range maks. & furnishing ironmongers, 247 Tottenham court road, & Smart's buildings, High Holborn
Wood & Blake, solicitors, 8 Falcon st. Aldersgate
Wood & Borman, bookbinders, 26 Featherstone st. City rd
Wood & Brothers, plate, stuff & paris hat ma. 37 King st. City
Wood Chas. & Co. printers, 18 & 19 Poppin's court, Fleet st
Wood, Field & Wood, hop merchants, 25 Mark lane
Wood & Fraser, attorneys, 78 Dean st. Soho
Wood Frederick John & Co. wine merchants, 13 Crutchedfrs
Wood H. & L. (Misses), ladies' school, 2 Skinner pl. Hollwy. rd
Wood Henry & Co. bottle beer merchants, 26 Chancery lane
Wood Henry & Co. canton merchants, 1 Warwick sq. City
Wood Henry & Thos. & Co. flannel, baize, blanket, drugget, carpet & table cover warehouse, Red Lion ct. Watling st
Wood & Hunt, livery stables, 1 John st. & Barnsbury st. Liverpool rd
Wood & Ivy (late George Wood), manufacturers & importers of musical instruments, &c. 50 New Compton st. Soho
Wood Jas. & Sons, nursery & seedsmen, 1 Nursery pl. O. Kentrd

Wood John & Co. wholesale cabinet & trunk manufacturers & timber merchants, West India docks & 149 Minories
Wood, Jones & Hinde, wholesale straw & chip hat ma. 78 & 79 Newgate st
Wood Joseph, Carter & Co. brewers, 2 Artillery pl, Westmr
Wood & King, who. fancy soapmakers, 23 Radnor st. St. Luke's
Wood Lydia & Son, carpents. & builds. 3 Willow walk, Bermndsy
Wood Matthew & Co. teadlrs. & grocers, 73 Old Broad st. City
Wood & Sharwoods', printers' broks.; type foundrs. columbian & albion press maks. & bookbindrs. tool cuts. 120 Aldersgt. st
Wood & Simpson, colonial brokers, 8 Mincing lane
Wood Stephen Wm. & Jn. law stationers, 52 Carey st. Linc. inn
Wood Thomas & Co. coal merchants, Northumberland whf. Strand, & Kentish town coal whf. & Cardiff, South Wales
Wood & Walker, worsted spinners, Bradford, Yorkshire (Abraham Best, agent), 90 Bermondsey st
Wood William Law & Co. furnishing & export ironmongers, birmingham & sheffield agents & factors, manufacturers of colonial implements, machines, stoves, & of the improved economic kitchen range, brass & iron bedsteads, builders of corrugated iron houses, smiths, &c. 62 Gracechurch st
Wood & Wickham, solicitors, 2 Corbet ct. Gracechurch st
Wood William & Co. tea & coffee dealers, 94 Cannon st
Wood Wm. & Sam. curriers & leathr. cutrs. 32 Bow st. Cov. gardn
Wood & Wormall (Mesdames), boarding ho. 4 North st. Moorflds
Woods & Forests & Land Revenue, Works & Buildings Office of her Majesty, 1 & 2 Whitehall pl.; hours of business 10 to 4
Wood Alex. carver & gilder, 9 Crombie's rw. Comrl. rd. east
Wood Alex. coal merchant, Phœnix whf. Clink st. Bankside
Wood Alex. Fletcher, stock & share bro. 10½ Old Broad st. City
Wood Alfred, pale ale & stout merchant, 24 Mark lane
Wood Ann (Mrs.), chandler's shop, 65 Brook st. Lambeth
Wood Arthur, whipmaker, 1 Princess st. Edgware rd
Wood Benjamin, chandler's shop, 59 Brunswick st. Hackney rd
Wood Benjamin, *Red Lion* P.H. 5 Old Cavendish st. Oxford st
Wood Benjamin, sec. to *Royal Bank of Australia*, 2 Moorgt. st
Wood Benjamin, tailor, 9 Chapel st. Pentonville
Wood Bennett, butcher, 5 New st. Dorset sq
Wood Charles, builder, 8 Charles pl. East st. Walworth rd
Wood Charles, printer, 99 St. George's rd. Borough
Wood Charles Henry, tailor, 88 Albany st. Regent's park
Wood Charles Thomas, *Sun* P.H. 21 Drury lane
Wood Charles William, barrister, 1 Harcourt bldgs. Temple
Wood Chas. Wm. math. inst. ma. 170 Bishopsgate without
Wood Charlte. (Mrs.), *M'Niven's & Carter's tav.* Portugal st
Wood Daniel, awl blade maker, 47½ Seward st. Goswell rd
Wood David, ironmonger, fancy goods dealer, & toy wareman, 15 Whitechapel road, & 56 Newington causeway
Wood Drew, law & general stationer, 81 Basinghall st
Wood Ebenezer, carcase butcher, 25 Newgate new market
Wood Edward, carpent. & undertak. 20 Long alley, Finsbury
Wood Edward, *Grapes* P.H. 9 Bennett st. Fitzroy sq
Wood Edward, rubbish carter, &c. see Spencer & Wood
Wood Edward, varnish maker & colorman, 5 Long acre
Wood Edw. Geo. optician, see Horne, Thornthwaite & Wood
Wood Edw. H. patten ma. 2 Albert pl. Neckinger rd. Bermdsy
Wood Edwin, importer of cigars, 69 King William st. City
Wood Eleanor (Mrs.), pawnbroker, 65 High st. St. Giles's
Wood Eliza (Miss), dressmaker, 33 Gt. Titchfield st. Oxfrd. st
Wood Elizabeth (Mrs.), leather sell. 74 Cable st. Wellclose sq
Wood Elizabeth (Mrs.), lodging house, 6 South st. Grosv'nor sq
Wood Elizabeth (Miss), stationer, 5 Elm terr. Lit. Chelsea
Wood Elizabeth (Mrs.), *Scots Arms* P.H. 10 Lit. Hermitage st
Wood Ezek. boot & shoe ma. 11 Vernon pl. Bagnigge wells rd
Wood Francis, butcher, 35 Elizabeth st. Eaton square
Wood Francis, corn dealer, Globe road, Mile end road
Wood Fras. *Harrison Arms* P.H. 28 Harrison st. Gray's inn la
Wood Frederick, bookbinder, 97 Cornwall road, Lambeth
Wood Frederick, bootmaker, 38 Sidmouth st. Regent sq
Wood Frederick, bootmaker, 38 Sidmouth st. Gray's inn rd
Wood Frederick, fur. ironmonger, 88 Albany st. Regent's pk
Wood Frederick, pawnbroker & salesman, 90 St. George st
Wood Frederick, surgeon, 25 Bedford row, Bloomsbury
Wood Frederick John, barrister, 77 Chancery lane
Wood Frederick John, wine merchant, 13 Crutchedfriars
Wood Frederick Wm. barrister, 1 Hare court, Temple
Wood George, bootmaker, 31 Lit. Charlotte st. Blackfriars rd
Wood George, carman, 17 East lane, Bermondsey wall
Wood George, coal merchant, 18 Penton place, Walworth
Wood George, livery stables, 32 Carey st. Lincoln's inn
Wood George, registrar, 144 Princes road, Lambeth
Wood George, shirt & stock maker, see Dennes & Wood
Wood George, stockbroker, Stock Exchange
Wood George, wine & spirit merchant, 203 Tooley st
Wood George Blamire Goodland, surgeon, 4 Kennington row
Wood George William, surgeon, 53 Great Coram st

Wood Harry P. general agent, 3 New square, Minories
Wood Hen. artist & draughtsmn. 24 Percy st. Tottenham ct. rd
Wood Henry, chemist & druggist, 6 Coleman st
Wood Henry, coffee rooms, 45 High st. Poplar
Wood Henry, fishmonger, 1 Little Saint Thomas Apostle
Wood Henry, fruiterer, 10 Chapel st. Church st. Islington
Wood Henry, glass engraver, 11 Crown court, Fleet st
Wood Hen. grocer & cheesemongr. 14 White Hart st. L. Kngtn. la
Wood Henry, pawnbroker, 25 City road, Finsbury
Wood Henry, solicitor, 14 Bartlett's buildings, Holborn
Wood Henry, tea dealer, 19 Primrose hill, Salisbury square
Wood Henry S. watch & clock ma. 17 Bedford pl. Coml. rd. e
Wood Howard, rope, twine & mat maker, 31 Budge row, City, & Jamaica level, Bermondsey
Wood Isaac, butcher, 10 Newport court, Newport market
Wood Isaac, undertaker, 1 Wilmott place, Old Kent road
Wood Israel John, tin plate worker, 6 Chapel st. Somers tn
Wood James, baker, 27 Saville st. Fitzroy square
Wood James, bookseller, 3 New ct. Coleman st. buildings
Wood James, bootmaker, 7 Bartholomew terrace, St. Luke's
Wood James, copperworks, see Pontifex (Edmd. & Wm.) & Wood
Wood James, dining rooms, 3 Blandford st. Portman sq
Wood James, *Golden Lion* P.H. 272 Kent st. Borough
Wood James, jeweller & registrar, 6 Gt. Russell st. Bloomsby
Wood James, pianoforte & organ key ma. 14 Somers town ter
Wood James, shawl & cloak ma. 27 Marlboro' st. Carnaby st
Wood James, shoemaker, 2 Margaret st. Hackney fields
Wood James Slight, pianoforte maker, 81 Wells st. Oxford st
Wood Jane (Mrs.), *Monument* P.H. 1 Eastcheap
Wood Jeremiah, tallowchandler, 47 Queen st. Ratcliff
Wood John, artist, 65 Charlotte st. Fitzroy square
Wood John, *Black Horse inn*, 32 Coventry st. Haymarket
Wood John, bootmaker, 232 Hoxton Old town
Wood John, bootmaker, 137 Long alley, Finsbury
Wood John, boot & shoe maker, 11 Regent st. Horseferry rd
Wood John, boot & shoe maker, 34 Tothill st. Westminster
Wood John, builder, 46 Shaftesbury st. New North road
Wood John, butcher, 4 Charles place, East st. Walworth
Wood John, carpet manufacturer, see Watson, Wood & Bell
Wood John, carpet manufr. 17 Cumming st. New rd. Pentonville
Wood John, chemist, &c. 11 Queen's bldgs. Knightsbridge
Wood John, coal merchant, see Brown & Wood
Wood John, coffee rooms, 27 Munster st. Regent's park
Wood John, currier & leather cutter, 18 Church st. Shoreditch
Wood John, currier & leather cutter, 102 Shoe lane, Fleet st
Wood John, eel pie house, 7 Rufford's buildings, Islington
Wood John, fruiterer, 2 Pollen st. Hanover square
Wood John, furniture broker, 18 Up. Lisson st. Lisson grove
Wood John, grocer, 3 Hatton wall, Hatton garden
Wood John, lodging house, 9 Castle st. Falcon square
Wood John, meat salesman, 3 New Newgate market
Wood John, naturalist, 29 Crosby Hall chmbrs. Bishopsgate
Wood John, shoe mercer, 8 Little Newport st. Long acre
Wood John, pastrycook, 61 Tottenham court road
Wood John, bird preserver, 1 Northampton rw. Hollwy. rd
Wood John, solicitor, 38 Upper Gower st
Wood John, solicitor, 64 Lincoln's inn fields
Wood John, tailor, 11 Margaret st. Cavendish square
Wood John, tobacconist, 42 & 43 Coleman st. City
Wood John, wholesale coffee dealer, 3 Hatton wall
Wood John East, dining rooms, 54 Gt. Tower st. City
Wood John Mackworth, attorney, 43 Lincoln's inn fields
Wood John Martin, writer & grainer, 62 Waterloo rd. Lmbth
Wood John Richard, solicitor, 1 Hare court, Temple
Wood John T. bird cage maker, 1 Fleet lane, Farringdon st
Wood Jonathan, carpenter, 4 Portland road, Regent's park
Wood Joseph, bootmaker, 4 Bloomfield place, Deptford
Wood Joseph, butcher, 15 Clayton pl. William st. Caledonian rd
Wood Joseph, grocer & teadealer, 37 Shadwell High st
Wood Joseph, shoemaker, 53 Pear tree ct. Clerkenwell
Wood Joseph, walking stick manufacturer, 142 Waterloo rd
Wood Joseph, *White Hart* P.H. Grove st. Deptford
Wood Joseph Thos. publisher & printer, 33 Holywell st. Strand
Wood Lucy (Mrs.), stationer, 25 New Church st. Lisson grove
Wood Luke, *Bricklayers' Ar.* P.H. 3 Jhn. st. Davies st. Bkly. sq
Wood Martin W. sugar refiner, 5 Cleveland st. Mile end rd
Wood Mary (Mrs.), boot & shoemaker, 1 Berners st. Oxford st
Wood Mary (Mrs.), brushmaker, 3 West st. Seven dials
Wood Mary (Mrs.), hairdresser, 15 High st. St. Giles
Wood Matthew, artist, 53 Berners st. Oxford st
Wood Octavius, manchester, &c. warehouseman, see Coates, Ingle & Wood
Wood Octavius, woollen warehouse, 18 Gresham st. City
Wood Peter, straw bonnet mak. 26 Pollard's row, Bethnal grn
Wood Richard, baker, 1 Boundary st. Shoreditch
Wood Robert, butcher, 18 Crisp st. East india road

Wood Robert, foreign oil warehouse, 132 New Bond st
Wood Robert, fruiterer, 64 Anchor & Hope alley, Wapping
Wood Robert, grocer, 24 Houndsditch
Wood Robert, pianofrt.ma.& tunr.26Hastings st.Burton cres
Wood Robt.scale, weight & measure ma.6 & 7WestSmithfield
Wood Robert, whitesmith, 41 Cannon st. road
Wood Rosetta (Mrs.), cutler, 39 Threadneedle st
Wood Ruth (Mrs.), fruiterer, 2 Plumber's row, City rd
Wood Samuel, commercial boarding house, 40 Basinghall st
Wood Samuel, machinist & spring hinges of every description repaired, 13 Prices st. Gravel lane, Borough
Wood Samuel, plumber, 4 Liverpool st. Bishopsgate
Wood Samuel James, pawnbroker, 13 St. John st. rd
Wood Samuel James, pawnbroker, 35 St. John st.Clerknwll
Wood Samuel Stephen, grocer, 49 Fleet la. Farringdon st
Wood Sancton, architect & surveyor, 24 Broad st. buildings
Wood Sarah (Miss), stationer & bookseller, 25 Leather lane
Wood Sarah (Mrs.), undertaker, 204 Bermondsey st
Wood Sarah Ann (Mrs.), butcher, Battersea
Wood Susannah (Mrs.), china wa. 20 Horsefarry rd. Westmr
Wood Thomas, baker, Bolingbroke place, Battersea
Wood Thomas, bookseller, &c. 6 Barnsbury st. Liverpool rd
Wood Thomas, dairyman, 50 Gray's inn lane
Wood Thomas, furrier, 14 York terrace, Commercial rd. ea
Wood Thos. *Jacob's Well* P.H. 13 Charles st. Manchester sq
Wood Thomas, plate glass manufr. 19 Greek st. Soho
Wood Thos. plumber, painter & glazier, 167 St. John st. rd
Wood Thos. straw hat mfr. 11 Chichester pl. Gray's inn rd
Wood Thomas, tailor, 6 Fishmongers' alley, Fenchurch st
Wood Thomas, tailor, &c. 25 Weymouth st. Portland pl
Wood Thomas, tanner, Russell st. Bermondsey, & 1 Artillery st. Horselydown
Wood Thomas, teadealer & grocer, 8 Bridge ter. Harrow rd
Wood Thos. *Westmoreland Arms* P.H. 7 Geo. st.Portmn. sq
Wood Thos.who.sta.engrav.&prntr.24 Milk st.&Godfrey's ct
Wood Thomas Danes, butcher, 99 Upper st. Islington
Wood Thos. Wm. *PrinceRegent* P.H. 130 Regent st.Lambth
Wood Wm. baker, 4 Keen's row, Walworth road, west side
Wood Wm. baker, 8 Maze pond, Tooley st
Wood Wm. bookseller, 39 Tavistock st. Covent garden
Wood Wm. bootmaker, 13 City road, Finsbury sq
Wood Wm. boot & shoe maker, 151 Minories
Wood Wm. bottle warehouse, 22 Lit. Windmill st. Golden sq
Wood Wm. coal & corn dealer, 40 Vauxhall st. Lambeth
Wood Wm. coffee rooms, 6 Borough road, Southwark
Wood Wm. dining rooms, 20 Broad st. Bloomsbury
Wood Wm. wholesale druggist, 25 St. Mary axe
Wood Wm. grocer, 7 Hastings st. Burton crescent
Wood Wm. grocer, 7 Providence pl. Brewer's grn. Westmnr
Wood Wm. grocer & oilman, see Petty, Wood & Tomlin
Wood Wm. *Hoywarden Castle* P.H. 3 Gower pl. Euston sq
Wood Wm. grocer, 17 Hampstead road
Wood Wm. homœpathic veterinarian, 13A, Cannonrw.Westm
Wood Wm. hosier, 11 Crawley st. Oakley sq. Somers town
Wood Wm. linendraper, 59, Tothill st. Westminster
Wood Wm. livery stable keeper, 19 Camomile st. Bishopsg
Wood Wm. japanner, 39 Northampton st. Clerkenwell
Wood Wm. pianoforte maker, see Nutting & Wood
Wood Wm. solicitor, 10 Symond's inn, Chancery lane
Wood Wm. surgeon, 1 Bridge st. Southwark
Wood Wm. tobacconist, 27 Grafton st. Soho
Wood Wm. undertaker, 38 Up. Salisbury place, Locksfields
Wood Wm. Geo. coal merchant, 2 Nile st. Hoxton New town
Wood Wm.Page, queen's counsel, 3 Stone bldgs.Lincoln's inn
Wood Wm. Samuel, bootmaker, 3 Duke st. Chelsea
Woodall Geo. engraver & printer, 16 Gt Chapel st. Oxford st
Woodall Geo. jun. engraver, 65 Poland st. Oxford st
Woodall Henry, berlin wareho. 3 Gt. Russell st. Bloomsbury
Woodall John, coach&harness ma. 28 Orchard st. Portman sq
WoodallWm.Harry, woollen warehsemn.70Bishopsg.without
Woodard Wm. Green, hat manufacturer, 128 Lambeth walk
Woodbine Henry, mill & handscrew maker, 93 Tooley st
Woodbridge, Dyer & Woodbridge, colonial broks. 7Mincing la
Woodbridge Edward, wine mer. see Tennants & Woodbridge
WoodbridgeGeo.Wm. bootmaker, 23Northampton st.Clrknwl
Woodbridge Sarah (Mrs.), grocer, 15 Fleet lane
Woodbridge Thos. corn dealer, 9 Osborne st. Whitechapel
Woodbridge Thos. Anthony, solicitor, 8 Clifford's inn
Woodburn Saml. & Allen, picture dealers, 112 St.Martin's la
Woodcock Robert & Son, builders, 26 Critchill pl. Hoxton
Woodcock Brothers, letter press, copperplate & lithographic printers, & printers by appointment to the medical department of King's college, 27 Brunswick st. Hackney road
Woodcock Alfred, statnr.& account book mnfr. 10 Huggin la
Woodcock Chas. Rodomonte, dental surgn. 29Gt.Pulteney st
Woodcock Cornelius Rd. law statnr. 5 Gt. Carter la. Drs.com
Woodcock John, butcher, 8Ann's terr.Cambrg.heath Hackney
Woodcock John, *Duke of Clarence* P.H. Grundy st. Ea.i.rd
Woodcock Richard, coach builder, 3 York pl. Hackney road
Woodcock Robert, tailor, 4 High st. Kensington
Woodcock Saml. Wm. coal mer. Star wf.King's rd.Camden tn
Woodcock Sarah Ann (Miss), ladies'school.231A, Maida vale
Woodcock Susannah (Mrs.), milliner, 8 High st. Kensington
Woodd Basil & Sons, wine merchants, 108 New Bond st
Wooden Robert, baker, 1 Cleaver st. Kennington cross
Wooder Chas. saddler & harness mak. 61 Fore st. Cripplegate
Wooderson James, carman, 19 Vincent square, Westminster
WoodersonJohnD.tea dlr.&c.144Up.Whitecross st. St.Luke's
Woodfall George & Son, printers, 11 Angel court, Skinner st
Woodfall Francis Wm. tailor, 16 Waterloo place, Pall mall
Woodfall John Ward, physician, 33 Davies st. Berkeley sq
Woodfield Thomas, plumber, 5 Little Ebury st. Pimlico
Woodford James, coffee rooms, 3 Crown court, Pall mall
Woodford James, fruiterer, 14 David st. Marylebone
Woodford Robert, tripe dresser, 47 Bridge road, Lambeth, 116 Edgware road, & 15 Tothill st. Westminster
Woodford Thomas, ladies' school, 2 Oxford terrace
Woodgate Geo. saddler & harness ma.79Curtain rd.Shoredtch
Woodgate Henry, tailor, 113 York road, Lambeth
Woodgate Henry Mark, tailor, 5 Bridge st. Lambeth
Woodgate Hen. Philip, brass manfr. 17 St. George st
WoodgateJohn, *Forester'sArms* P.H.57Seymour pl.Bryans.sq
Woodgate John H. wholes. confectioner, 17 St. George st
Woodgate Thomas, H. law stationer, 71 Coleman st. City
Woodgate Wm. cabinet maker, 34 Hoxton square
Woodgate Wm. solicitor, see Currie, Woodgate & Williams
Woodgate William, upholsterer, 29 Seymour st. Euston sq
Woodgates Margaret(Mrs.), *Bell* P.H.15Friar st.Blackfrs.rd
Woodger John, boot & shoe maker, 18 Warwick st. Pimlico
Woodger Joseph, vetriny. surg.13 &14Market st. Edgware rd
Woodger Thomas, *private hotel*, 18 Albermarle st. Piccadilly
Woodhall Abner, woollendraper, 83 Bridge road, Lambeth
Woodham & Boddy, meat salesmen, 9 Newgate market
Woodham Christ. tobac.&newsvend &c. 9Rosamn.bdgs.Islgtn
Woodham Gabriel, butcher, 13 Ropemakers' fields, Limeho
Woodham John, timber merchant, 213 High Holborn
Woodham Samuel, tobacconist, 2 Albany st. Regent's park
Woodham William, printer, 104 Shoe lane, Fleet st
Woodhams Henry, plumber, &c. Battersea square
Woodhams Joseph, oil & colorman, 60High st.Portland town
Woodhams Joseph, plumber, &c. 47 High st. Portland town
Woodham's Obed. corn dealer, 22 High st. Camberwell
Woodhams Thomas, board & lodging ho. 6Arundel st. Strand
Woodhams William, plumber, 9 Ellis st. Sloane st
Woodhatch Francis, butcher, 23 Fitzroy market
Woodhead Danl. warehouseman & factor, 6Russia rw.Milk st
Woodhead John, carpenter, 8 Denbigh st. Pimlico
Woodherd John, *Duke of Wellington* P.H.12Brook st.Ratclf
Woodhead Joseph, navy agent, 1 James st. Adelphi
Woodhead Thos. merchant, N.&S. Amer. coff. ho.&9Noble st
Woodhead Wm. japanner, 11 Coppice row, Clerkenwell
Woodhouse Hen. & Thos.T.ribbon manufrs.72 Aldermanbury
Woodhouse Mark Jas. & Coventry, colonl.broks.30Mincing la
Woodhouse Geo. Doveton, solicitor, 3 New Boswell court
Woodhouse Henry Wm. solicitor, see Metcalfe & Woodhouse
Woodhouse John, beer retailer, 11 Ferry road west, Poplar
Woodhouse John, butcher, 5 Chapel st. Totnhm. ct. rd
Woodhouse John, tailor, 71 Coleman st
Woodhouse John, tinman, 20 Charlotte row, Walworth rd
Woodhouse John, tin plate worker, 29 Friar st. Blackfrs. rd
Woodhouse Joseph, chandler's shop, Downham rd. Kingsld
Woodhouse Joseph, coffee rooms, 63 King st. Westminster
Woodhouse Joseph, fruiterer, 2 Bath st. Tabernacle square
Woodhouse Samuel, hatter, see Jarritt & Woodhouse
Woodin Dennis, veterinary surgn.2Up.Park pl.Regt's.pk rd
Woodin Henry, baker, 3 Derby st. Parliament st
Woodin John, upholsterer & designer, 16 Soho square
Woodin Samuel, artist & picture dealer, 6 Greek st. Soho
Woodin Wm. *Hen & Chickens* P.H. 17Bath st.Tabernacle sq
Wooding Jas.grocer&cheesemongr.2St.George's st.Albanyrd
Woodland Robert, refiner, 4 Seckforde st. Clerkenwell
Woodland Wm. furn. broker, 5 Henrietta st. Manchester sq
Woodlands Leonard, carpenter, 3 Princes st. Bedford row
Woodley William& John, cornfactors, 7 Crutchedfriars
Woodley Hny. bookslr.& statinr. 24 Lit. Bell alley.Londn wl
Woodley Henry, carcase butcher, 74 Aldgate Hight st
Woodley Jas. birch&alder wood dlr. 20Swan st. Gt.Dover rd
Woodley James, cork cutter, 34 Flint st. East st. Walworth
Woodley John, hair worker, 31 Cursitor st. Chancery la
Woodley Wm. Chas. egg merch. 46 Holland st. Blackfrs.rd
Woodman & Hambridge, orange merchants, 40 Eastcheap & 6 George lane, Botolph lane

Woodman W.& H. *Horseshoe Brewery tap*, 49 Baldwin's gdn
Woodman Augustus, grocer, &c. 9 Compton st. Brunswick sq
Woodman George, tailor, 6 Providence pl. Kentish town
Woodman Henry, coach joiner&trunk makr. 26 Whigmore st
Woodman Hy. Peter, academy. 11 Devonshire st. Bishpgt
Woodman John, grocer, 58 Augustus st. Regent's park
Woodman Joseph, school, 7 Northampton pl. Old Kent rd
Woodman Mary (Mrs.), watch&clk. ma. 29 Paradise rw. Chels
Woodman Peter, cabinet carver, 17 Leonard st. Finsbury
Woodman Philip, academy, 31 Cadogan st. Chelsea
Woodman Richard, carver & gilder, 118 Jermyn st
Woodman Richard, engraver, 5 Gt. College st. Camden town
Woodman Robert, fruiterer, 18 Hayfield place, Mile end rd
Woodman Thomas, artist, Bolingbroke place, Battersea
Woodman Thomas, boys' school, Bolingbroke pl. Battersea
Woodman Thomas (Mrs.), ladies' school, Bolingbroke pl. Batrs
Woodman Wm. cowkeeper, 67 High st. Marylebone
Woodman Wm. leathercase ma. 28 Gt. Cambridge st. Hckny. rd
Woodman Zaccheus, carpenter, 52 Dorset st. Salisbury sq
Woodmancy Geo. hairdresser&wigma. 1 Clifton st. Finsbury
Woodmeston Jane (Mrs.), stationer, 75 Princes rd. Lambeth
Woodnutt John S. fruit salesman, Spitalfields market
Woodridge Richard, wheelwright, see Grove & Woodridge
Woodroff Ann & Elizabeth, straw hat ma. 10 Lambeth wlk
Woodroff Henry, tailor, 84 Salisbury st. Lisson grove
Woodroff John, boot & shoe maker, 32½ Greek st. Soho
Woodroffe Charles, nursery & seedsman, Harrow road
Woodroffe Richard, *Union* P.H. Vassall rd. Camberwll. nw. rd
Woodroffe Thos. chemist, 12 Stanhope ter. Hyde park gdns
Woodroof Fenwick, corn & coal merchant, 54 Crutchedfriars
Woodroof Thos. corn dlr. & coal mer. 38 Worship st. Finsbury
Woodrooffe Wm. attorney&jamaica law agt. 1 New sq. Lin. inn
Woodrough John, *Peacock* P.H. High st. Newington butts
Woodrow John Hockley & Son, tailors, 21 Hatton garden
Woodrow George Alexander, hosier & glover, 38 Cheapside
Woodrow John, *Antigallican & Star* P.H. 117 Tooley st
Woodrow Wm. tailor, see Franklin & Woodrow
Woodruff John&Co. brass&copper founders, 26 Ray st. Clknwl
Woodruffe John, *White Swan* P.H. 26 White st. Lit. Moorfi
Woods & Wilson, tailors, 55 Coleman st
Woods Alfred, beer retailer, Clifton st. Wandsworth rd
Woods Ann (Mrs.), gold frame ma. 19 Rahere st. Goswell rd
Woods Benjamin, baker, 43 Penton st. Walworth road
Woods Benjamin, plumber, &c. 5 Marlborough pl. Kenngtn. cr
Woods Charles, saddlers' ironmonger, see Putland & Woods
Woods Chas. watch case ma. 1 Rahere st. north, Goswell rd
Woods Charles Ray, law stationer, 89 Chancery lane
Woods Chas. Ray, watchmaker, 21 White Lion st. Pentnville
Woods Edmund H. conveyancer, 42 Southampton bdgs. Holbrn
Woods Edwd. manfg. jeweller, 11 Rahere st. north, Goswell rd
Woods George, butcher, 19 Gwynn's place, Hackney rd
Woods George, tailor, &c. 4 Mount place, Whitechapel rd
Woods Hannah (Mrs.), boot & shoema. 35 York st. City rd
Woods Harry Bristow, plumber, 46 Queen Anne's st. Cav. sq
Woods Henry, bootmaker, 38 Bath st. City rd
Woods Henry Thomas, tripe dresser, 10 & 11 Clare st. Clare market; 23 Great hall, Hungerford market; 98 St. John's st. Clerkenwell; 80 London road; 85 Lambeth walk; & 128 Lambeth lower marsh
Woods Isaac, bricklayer & builder, 30 North st. Sloane st
Woods Issachar Thos. upholstr. 2 Westbourne pl. Pimlico
Woods Jas. who. cheesemong. Kentish bdgs. 94 Boro' High st
Woods James, tailor, 23 Conduit st. Regent st
Woods John, china dealer, 21 Clarence st. Rotherhithe
Woods John, fruiterer, 4 Duke st. Manchester sq
Woods John, livery stables, 56 London Wall
Woods Joseph, engineer & sole manufacturer of patent bearings, 3 Barge yard chambers; & Phœnix foundry, 236 Kent st. Borough
Woods Maria (Mrs.), berlin reposty. 82 Judd st. Brunswk sq
Woods Mary Ann (Mrs.), staymaker, 5 Yonl's pl. O. Kent rd
Woods Richd. painter, &c. 13 Market st. Mayfair
Woods Robert, bookbinder & stationer, 47 Duke st. Aldgate
Woods Thomas, tailor, 29 Green st. Church st. Blackfriars
Woods Wm. baker, 126 Shoreditch High st
Woods Wm. birmingham & sheffield wa. 7A, Falcon sq
Woods Wm. *Castle & Falcon hotel*, 5 Aldersgate st
Woods Wm. cheesemonger, 87 Gray's inn lane
Woods Wm. cowkeeper & dairyman, 93 High st. Camden tn
Woods Wm. grocer, 45 Penton st. Pentonville
Woods Wm. ham & tongue dlr. 37 Goodge st. Tottenham ct. rd
Woods Wm. mafr. of military & naval hooks & eyes, steel pens, metallic holes, & wire chains, 1 Queen st. Southwark bridge road
Woods Wm. plumber, painter & glazier, 34 Villiers st. Strand
Woods Wm. steel pen & metallic hole agent, 7A, Falcon sq
Woods Wm. tailor, 55 Brook st. Grosvenor sq
Woods Wm. *Wood's hotel*, Furnival's inn, Holborn
Woodstock Stephen, bootmak. 143 Gt. Saffron hill; 30 Queen st. Ratcliff cross; 58 Ropemaker's fields; & 85 Tooley st
Woodthorpe Edmund, architect; district surveyor for the eastern division of the city of London, Limehouse, Ratcliff, Wapping & St. Katherine's precinct, 30 Jewin st. Cripplegate, & 6 Queen st. Ratcliff cross
Woodthorpe Richard, surgeon, 11 Kingsland pl. Kingsld. rd
Woodward & Castle, newsvenders, 7 Bull head ct. Newgate st
Woodward John&Sons, upholsters. 12 Queen's bldg. Knightsbr
Woodward Thos. & Son, flourfactors, 18 St. Martin's le grand
Woodward Wm. & Co. linendrapers, 34 Hedge row, Islington
Woodward Benjamin Higgins, carpet manufacturer, 315D, Oxford st.; & at Church st. Kidderminster
Woodward Chas. tailor, &c. 2 Pilgrim st. Ludgate hill
Woodward Chas. Fredk. tailor, 9 Grange road, Bermondsey
Woodward Corbet, attorney, 12 Furnival's inn, Holborn
Woodward George, wood turner, 5 Charles st. Hatton garden
Woodward Henry, solicitor, 53 Lincoln's inn fields
Woodward Isabella (Mrs.), lodginghouse, 17 Thayer st. Man. sq
Woodward James, carpenter, 43 Gt. Carlisle st. Portman mkt
Woodward James, builder, 20 Paradise terrace, Lambeth
Woodward James, clogmaker, 14 Bear yd. Linc. inn fields
Woodward James, furn. ironmong. 13 Broadley tr. Blandfd. sq
Woodward James, gunmaker, see Moore & Woodward
Woodward James, grocer, 4 Copenhagen st. Pentonville
Woodward John, brewer&beer ret. Devonshire st. Kenningtn
Woodward John, cattle salesman, 60 West Smithfield
Woodward John, clockmaker, 4 New inn yard, Shoreditch
Woodward John, goldsmith, see Willmore, Yapp&Woodward
Woodward John Thos. optician, 8 Clement's inn pas. Claremkt
Woodward Joseph, corndealer, 1 Chichester pl. Gray's inn rd
Woodward Joseph, potato salesmn. 13 Queen's blgs. Knightsbr
Woodward Maria (Mrs.), baker, 90 Upper st. Islington
Woodward Mary (Mrs.), stayma. 11 Margaret st. Cavendish sq
Woodward Richard, cabinet maker, 12 Kirby st. Hatton gdn
Woodward Richd. *King Henry VIII.* P.H. 54 Lambeth Hi. st
Woodward Robert, attorney, 27 Bouverie st. Fleet st
Woodward Robert, tailor, 11 Lime st. square
Woodward Samuel, merchant, 6 Austinfriars
Woodward Thos. academy, 151 Old Gravel lane, Wapping
Woodward Thos. artist, 31 Conduit st. Bond st
Woodward Thos. auctioneer&ho. agt. 35 Carnaby st. Golden sq
Woodward Thos. tobacconist, 5 Beckford row, Walworth rd
Woodward Thos. tobacconist, 1 City road, Old st
Woodward Wm. carpenter, builder, &c. 73 Cannon st
Woodward Wm. sack collector&cornchndlr. 46 Shad Thames
Woodward Wm. surveyor & steward, 1 Furnival's inn
Woodward Wm. tailor, 18 Ebury st. Pimlico
Woodward Wm. tailor, 4 Glebe place, King's road
Woodward Wm. wire worker, 26 Hosier lane, West Smithfield
Woodwards Ann (Mrs.), beer retailer, Park pl. Old Kent rd
Woodwell Chas. Jsph. newsag. & printer, 9 Castle st. ea. Oxfrd. st
Woodyatt Wm. boot & shoe ma. 6 York bdgs. Rotherhithe
Woodyatt Wm. boot&shoe ma. 6 York pl. Millpond st. Brmndsy
Woodyear Wm. corn chandler, 10 Whitehead's grv. Chelsea
Woodyer Chas. M. coal&corn merchant, 5 Trinity chambers, Water lane, Tower st
Woodyer Henry, architect, 4 Adam st. Adelphi
Woof Maria (Mrs.), stationer, 44 Exmouth st. Clerkenwell
Wookey John, *Blue Last* P.H. 7 Lit. Bell alley, Coleman st
Wool Thos. upholsterer, cabinet ma. &ho. agt. 82 New Bond st
Wool Wm. coachmaker, 38 Margaret st. Cavendish sq
Wooland John, builder, 10 Henrietta st. Manchester sq
Woolcock Henry, silk stocking dyer, 103 Aldersgate st
Woolcombe & Co. shipbrokers, 23 Finch lane, Cornhill
Woolcot John, tailor & habit maker, 1 Wimpole st. Cav. sq
Woolcott George & Son, builders, 51 Doughty st. & Brownlow mews, Gray's inn lane
Woolcott Henry, fringe manfr. 19 Museum st. Bloomsbury
Woolcott Isaac, cheesemonger, 30 Little Newport st
Woolcott James, commission merchant, 6 Gt. Winchester st
Woolcott James, iron agent, fire brick merchant &engineer, 6 Gt. Winchester st. Old Broad st
Wooldridge Edward, surgeon, 171 Union st. Borough
Wooldridge James, apothecary, 14 Jamaica pl. Coml. rd. Limeh
Wooldridge John, chemist, 19 Bath pl. New road
Wooldridge William, surgeon, 6 Jermyn st. St. James's
Wooler Thomas Jonathan, solicitor, 93 Hatton garden
Wooley Charles, silk manufacturer, see Sleigh & Wooley
Woolf Abraham, shoe manufactr. 9 Middlesex st. Aldgate
Woolf Benjamin, glass &china dealer, 136 Whitechapel road
Woolf Benjamin, tailor, 87 Quadrant, Regent st
Woolf Ephraim, slipper maker, 3 New Goulstone st. Whitch
Woolf Henry, china warehouse, 33 London road, Southwark

Woolf George, accountant, 106 Shoe lane, Fleet st
Woolf Henry, military & fancy cap maker, cap peak & strap manufacturer & fancy trimming seller, 103 Houndsditch
Woolf Israel, tobacconist, 95 Drury lane
Woolf John, fur dyer & seal skin dresser, 10 Rose court & 23 New st. Dockhead
Woolf Lewis, earthenware dealer, 161 Shoreditch High st. & potter, 215 Wapping High st
Woolf Lewis, furrier & cap ma. 13 Elder st. Norton Folgate
Woolf Marcus, watchmaker, 2 Castle st. Houndsditch
Woolfe Charles, tinman, 4 Ann's place, Hoxton old town
Woolfe Geo. John, *Antigallican* P.H. Emmett st. Limehse
Woolfe John, tailor, 3 Crombie's row, Commercial rd
Woolfe Thomas, a-la-mode beef ho. 4 Charles st. Midlsx. hsp
Woolfe Thomas, boat builder, 68 Lwr. Shadwell, & New st
Woolford Geo. cheesemngr. & butterman, 21 Goswell road
Woolford John, fruiterer, 18 Foley st. Portland place
Woolford Thomas, grocer, 8 Gravel lane, Southwark
Woolford Wm. coach trimmer, 11 Old North st. Red Lion sq
Woolger Charles, *Pantheon* coffee rooms, 44 Poland st. Oxfd. st
Wool James Francis, merchant, Commercial coffee house
Wooll Mary Ann (Miss), china dealer, 2 Ivy place, Hoxton
Woollams & Carpenter, auctioneers, 16 Old Burlington st
Woollams Jn. & Co. paper hanging manufacturers, 69 Marylebone lane, Oxford st
Woollams Thos. & Co. house decorators, 31 Wigmore st. Cav. sq
Woollams Wm. & Co. paper stainers, 110 High st. Marylebne
Woollams Robert, tailor, 2 Chapel place, Spitalfields
Woollard & Forshaw, law & genl. stationers, 27 Lombard st
Woollard Benjamin, cabinet maker, 224 Whitechapel road
Woollard George, tobacconist, 9 Frederick pl. Old Kent rd
Woollard John, boot & shoe maker, 4 Lisson gr. north, New rd
Woollard Mary (Mrs.), fruiterer, 124 Borough High st
Woollaston & Davison, solicitors, 77 Basinghall st
Woollatt Randall & Frdk. who. tea, &c. dlrs. see Withers & Co
Woollatt Samuel S. & Son, linendrapers, 53 Holborn hill
Woollatt Samuel James, curiosity dealer, 28 Wardour st
Woolcott Thos. builder, 4 Rawstorne st. Goswell road
Woollett & Nephew, ship ins. & custom ho. agts. 1 Lime st. sq
Woollett, Rowe & Clay, woollendrapers, 92 Holborn hill
Woollett Henry, upholsterer, 143 Aldersgate st
Woolley Benj. Z. & Co. soapmakers, 4 Lit. Denmark st. Soho
Woolley & Jones, merchants & general agents, 46 Lime st
Woolley & Cook, printers, 7 St. Benet's pl. Gracechurch st
Woolley & Newnham, surgeons, 8 Brompton row
Woolley Charles, wine merchant, 57 Mark lane
Woolley Chas. Adam, sen. solicitor, 11 New sq. Lincoln's inn
Woolley Fletcher, pat. of the safety camphine & naptha lamps, & ethereal lamp & machine oils, 180 High Holborn
Woolley George, surgeon, 3 Moreton terrace, Kentish town
Woolley Geo. Boyle, straw hat mnfr. see Spurden, Woolley & Co
Woolley Henry, upholder & decorator, 97 New Bond st. & 10 Blenheim st
Woolley James, tailor & habit maker, 77 Cheapside
Woolley John, butcher, 14 Gainsford st. Horselydown
Woolley Rhoda (Mrs.), milliner, 4 Duke st. Grosvenor sq
Woolley Samuel, furn. ironmonger & cutler, 19 Piccadilly
Woolley Thomas, solicitor, 7 Rosamon bldgs. Islington green
Woolley Wm. horse dealer, 7 Gt. Titchfield st. Oxford st
Woolley Wm. manufac. chemist, 17 Regent st. Horseferry rd
Woolley Wm. stockbroker, 2 Hatton ct. & Stock exchange
Woolley Wm. *Windsor Castle* P.H. 9 Windsor st. Islington
Woollford Wm. paper gilder, 10 Belle Sauvage yd. Ludgate hl
Woolloton Rt. Chas. hop mer. Kentish blds. 94 Boro' High st
Woolltorton John, surgeon, 7 Euston place, New road
Woollven Henry, butcher, 12 Lamb st. Spitalfields
Woollven Henry, butcher, 100 Whitehorse st. Stepney
Woollven Richard, butcher, 244 Borough High st
Woolly James, tailor, 7 Stratton st. Piccadilly
Woolmer Alfred Joseph, artist, 7 Cleveland st. Fitzroy sq
Woolmer John, grocer, 11 York place, Kent st. road
Woolmer John, haberdasher & hosier, 73 Aldersgate st
Woolmer Joseph, cheesemngr. 14 Adam's pl. King's rd. Chelsea
Woolmer Joseph, dairyman, 20 Francis st. Tottenham ct. rd
Woolmer Joseph Benson, surgeon, 11 King's rd. Pimlico
Woolmer Robt. beer retailr. 1 Lr. Salisbury st. Lock's flds
Woolmer William, cheesemonger, 6 Duke st. Grosvenor sq
Woolmore Henry, seal engraver, see Groves & Woolmore
Woolmore Mary (Mrs.), milliner, 19 Gt. Marylebone st
Woolmore Thos. coach trimmer, 47 Paddington st. Maryleb
Woolner James & Richard C. cornfactors, 79 Mark lane
Woolner Benjamin, russia broker, 29 Threadneedle st
Woolner Jas. cabinet ma. 4 New yd. Gt. Queen st. Lin. inn flds
Woolnoth Thomas Alfred, artist, 12 Greek st. Soho
Woolnoth Thomas, sen. engraver, 12 Greek st. Soho
Woolnough Chas. bookbinder, 6 Bateman's row, Shoreditch
Woolnough Charles Wingham, marbler, 24 Fleet lane
Woolnough Edwd. Graham, surgeon, 15 St. Thomas st. Boro'
Woolnough Ephraim, corndealer, 9 Wentworth pl. Mile end
Woolnough Robert, tobacconist, 2 South row, New road
Woolnough Samuel, bricklayer, &c. 16 Cursitor st. Chancy. la
Woolnough Stephen, bookbinder, 7 Upp. James st. Golden sq
Woolrich & Ellis, muslin warehousemen, 13 St. Paul's ch. yd
Woolrych Edmd. Humphrey, barrister, 2 Middle Temple la
Woolrych Humphrey Wm. barrister, 2 Hare court, Temple
Woolston John Saml. clothes salesmn. 12 Broadway, Westmr
Woolston Thomas, boot & shoe maker, 8 Botolph alley
Woolven Mary (Mrs.), cheesemonger, 98 Whitehorse st. Stepney
Woolverton E. (Mrs.), *Hole in the Wall* P.H. 2 Kirby st. Hat. gdn
Woolverton James, timber dealer, 45 Broomfields, Deptford
Woolverton Wm. Chas. bootm. 2 Albion pl. Lwr. rd. Rotherhi
Woolvine Sarah (Mrs.), mason, 1 Mary st. New road
Woolwich Police Court, Woolwich, hours 2½ to 5
Woonton Wm. cowkeepr. & fruiterer, 16½ New rd. St. Geo.'s ea
Wooster Jeremiah, dressing case, desk & work box manufacturer, 9 Long lane, Smithfield
Wooster John, carver & gilder, 81 Leman st. Goodman's flds
Wooster Thos. fishmonger, 180 Up. Whitecross st. St. Luke's
Wooster Thos. jun. coal factor, 6 Railway pl. Fenchurch st
Wootten Frederick, news agent, 2 Sherrard st. Golden sq
Wootten James, grocer & oilman, 25 Porter st. Soho
Wootten Thomas, tobacco pipe mak. 12 New Park st. Boro'
Wootton Selina & Elizth. milliners, 3 Devonsh. bldgs. Gt. Dovr. st
Wootton Ann (Mrs.), lodging house, 36 Jermyn st. St. James's
Wootton John, turner, 3 Devonshire bldgs. Gt. Dover st
Wootton John Geo. brush mak. 72 Willow walk, Tabernacle sq
Wootton I. law stationer, 12 Took ct. Chancery lane
Wootton Luke, *Merry Carpenters* P.H. 42 Old st. St. Luke's
Wootton Samuel, jewellery case mak. 23 Pitt st. Fitzroy sq
Wootton Stephen, corn factor, Jack's coffee house, Mark la
Wootton Thomas, attorney, 10 Tokenhouse yard
Wootton Thomas, farrier, 2 Wilton road, Pimlico
Wootton Wm. coal dealer, 1 Boundary st. Shoreditch
Wootton Wm. stationer, see Hill, Wootton & Branston
Woraker Joseph, fruiterer, 24 Charterhouse lane
Worboys John Lowth, butcher, 15 Salmon lane, Limehouse
Worboys Wm. shoemaker, 37 Church road, Coml. rd. east
Worboys Wm. Sanders, druggist, 76 Charlotte ter. New cut
Worcester, Stubbs & Bland, carriers, 24 Glass ho. yd. Aldsgt. st
Worcester, Tenbury & Ludlow Railway Co. (William Putsford, sec.), 5 New Palace yard, Parliament st
Worcester Samuel, tailor, 31 Fetter lane
Wordley George, baker, 15 Seymour place, Camden town
Wordsworth Charles Favell Forth, barrister, 2 Paper bldgs
Wordsworth Henry, solicitor, see Dunn, Wordsworth & Dunn
Wordsworth Wm. oil & colorman, Church st. Hackney
Wordsworth Wm. A. prof. of music, 19 Harpur st. Red Lion sq
Worfell Thomas, coal mer. 6 Chelsea market, Lr. Sloane st
Worger Thomas Clifford, chemist & druggist, 29 Chiswell st
Workman Ann (Mrs.), *Ship* P.H. Stepney green
Workman Emanuel, carpenter, &c. 1 Cleveland st. Mile end
Workman Fred. Wm. linendraper, 32 New rd. St. George's ea
Workman Henry, cheesemonger, Ring cross, Holloway rd
Workman James, cowkeeper, 12 Market st. Ocean rw. Stepny
World of Fashion weekly newspaper, 299 Strand
World Robert, surgeon, 15 City terrace, City rd
Worledge Thomas, newsvender & printer, Church st. Hckny
Worledge Thomas, staymaker, 300 Regent st
Worley Jas. & Co. woollen drapers, 1 Surrey pl. Newington bts
Worley George, butcher, 47 Long lane, Borough
Worley Isaac, *Monument coffee ho. & hotel*, 48 Fish st. hill
Worley Robt. meat, butter, &c. salesm. & prov. ag. 22 Newgate st
Worley Thomas, printer, 14 Rolls buildings, Fetter lane
Worley Wm. coal merchant, 6 New Gloucester place, Hoxton
Worley Wm. ship & insurance bro. see M'Callum, Worley & Co
Worlledge John, barrister, 1 Elm court, Temple
Wormald Henry Burley, tailor, 28 Hyde st. Bloomsbury
Wormald John, *Royal Oak* P.H. 79 Tooley st. Borough
Wormald Thomas, attorney, 4 Gray's inn square
Wormald Thomas, surgeon, 42 Bedford row, Bloomsbury
Wormall Hannah (Madam), boarding ho. see Wood & Wormall
Worman Rt. A. attorney, Moorgate st. chambers, City
Wormleighton Henry, tobacconist, 7 Princess st. Edgw. rd
Worms Lewis & Co. child bed linen wa. 36 Bridge rd. Lambeth
Worms Lewis & Co. warehousemen, 103 to 108 Whitechapel rd
Worms Henry, wholesale boot & shoe maker, 39 Minories
Worms Lewis, appraiser & furniture bro. 176 Kingsland rd
Worms Lewis, furniture broker, 6 Brook hill, Clerkenwell
Worms Morris, furniture broker, 19 Gt. Earl st. Seven dials
Worms Philip, broker & appraiser, 11, 13, 14 Gt. Earl st. 7 dials
Wormull Anthony, sen. cutler, 121 Lambeth walk
Wormull Anthony, jun. surgical inst. ma. 182 Union st. Boro'

Wornell John, artist, 5 Greenland place, Cromer st
Wornum Ralph Nicolson, artist, 1 Bedford pl.Hampstead rd
Wornum Robert, pianoforte maker, 16 Store st. Bedford sq
Worral John, ironmonger, &c. 3 John st. Tottenham ct. rd
Worrall Henry, modeller, 20 Lit. Drummond st. Euston sq
Worrall John, dining rooms, 30 Barbican
Worrall John, watchmaker, 71 Goswell road
Worrall Seth, dining rooms, 91 Holborn hill
Worrall William, cowkeeper, &c. 8 Sutton place, Soho
Worrell John, reg. of births, &c. 28 Hunter st. Brunswick sq
Worrell Joseph, oil & colorman, 56 Golden lane, Barbican
Worrows John, smith & farrier, 12 Three Cup all. Lr. Shadwell
Worsdell George, boot & shoe maker, 2 North Audley st
Worsfold Geo. stationer, 1 Northampton ter. York st. City rd
Worsfold Maria (Mrs.), straw bonnet ma. 8 Dorset st. Clphm. rd
Worsfold Wm. stationer, booksell. & engrav. 161 Regent st
Worship street Police Court, Finsbury ; hours 10 to 5
Worship Wm. engraver, &c. 31 Bridgeho. pl. Newington caus
Worsley John, grocer, 25 Richmond st. Walworth
Worsley John, rag & bottle merc. 24 Brown st. Bryanstone sq
Worsley Peter Owen, saddler, 48A, Mount st. Berkeley square, & 57 South Audley st
Worsley Richard, druggist & chemist, see Collick & Worsley
Worssam Geo. Jervis, millwright, 25 Gt. Mitchell st. St. Luke's
Worster, Stubbs & Bland, carriers & maltsters, 32 Wharf rd City rd. & Golden Horse, Glasshouse yard, Aldersgate st
Worster Henry, bookseller, 167 Bethnal green road
Worster Jacob, gold size maker, 61 New Compton st. Soho
Worster Thos. beer retailer, 7 Hill st. Walworth road
Worster Thos. silver chaser, &c. 34 Monkwell st. Cripplegate
Wort Joseph, fruiterer, 1 Ebury square
Worth Henry, accountant, 12 Redcross square, Cripplegate
Worth Wm. Alfred, painter & glazier, 12 Portsea pl. Edgw. rd
Wortham James, dyer & lace cleaner, 32 Gt. Marlborough st
Wortham John, printer, 313 Strand
Worthington A. J. & Co. sew. silk mfrs. 34 King st. Cheapside
Worthington John C. silk broker, 9 Union ct. Old Broad st
Worthington Nathaniel, optician, 196 Piccadilly
Worthington Thomas, bookbinder, 3 Mayfield pl. Kensington
Wortley & Son, grocers, 54 Up. Baker st. Regent's park
Wortley James, warehouseman, see Castle, Jones & Co
Wortley Hon. Jas. Stuart, M.P. queen's counsel, Twisden bdgs
Wortley Richard, fruiterer, Spitalfields market
Worton Thomas, *Red Lion* P.H. 261 Borough High st
Worts George, cornchndlr. & coal dlr. 81 High st. Marylebon
Worvell James, *Grapes* P.H. 55 St. Mary axe
Wotherspoon & Cuthbert, fur manufr. 60 Cheapside, & 54 & 55 Bow lane
Wotton George, teadealer, 28 Lit. St. Andrew st. Seven dials
Wotton Henry Rendall, surgeon, 32 Fitzroy sq
Wotton John, brazier, &c. King st. Battersea
Woysch Charles Frederick, merchant, Baltic coffee house
Wragg Henry, baker, 3 John st. Cambridge heath, Hackney
Wragg James, porkman, 174 Church st. Shoreditch
Wragg James, saddler & harness maker, 90 Bethnal green rd
Wragg John, butcher, 140 Church st. Shoreditch
Wragg John, livery stables, 31 Finsbury pl. north
Wragg Wm. wine cooper, 62 Greenfield st. Whitechapel
Wrake Jn. Tucker, umbrella ma. & tobacst. 56 York st. Wstmsr
Wrangham Digby Cayley, serjeant-at-law, 1 Serjeant's inn, Chancery lane
Wrangham James, *Three Tuns*, P.H. 63 Broad st. Ratcliff
Wrangham James Frederic, *Rose & Bell*, P.H. 25 Bankside
Wrangham Thomas, butcher, 26 East st. Walworth rd
Wrathall Jas. & Co. printing ink ma. Eliza ter. Whitmore rd
Wrather Wm. civil engineer, 8 Great College st. Westminstr
Wratten James W. beer retailer, 4 Flint st. East st. Walworth
Wray John & Edmond, calico print agt. 8 Friday st. Cheapside
Wray & Roby, tailors, 19 Queen st. Cheapside
Wray Elizabeth (Mrs.), oil & color warehouse, Bow
Wray Fras. livery stable keeper, Barlow's mews, Bruton st
Wray George, solicitor, see Dodd & Wray
Wray Geo. H. manag. of *Ryl. Bank of Australia*, 2 Moorgate st
Wray James, toydealer, 11 Lower rd. Islington
Wray Joseph, cabinet maker, 59 Leonard st. Finsbury
Wray Martin Osterfield, chemist, 118 Holborn hill
Wray Robert, barrister, 60 Chancery lane
Wray Warren Porter, barrister, 60 Chancery lane
Wrede Herman, musical inst. ma. & imp. 5 King st. Snow hill
Wrede Mary (Mrs.), outfitter, 54 Poplar High st
Wreford John & Co. wh. habrdsh. & lacemen, 17 Aldermanbury
Wreford & Lloyd, corspndnts. & advertisement agts. 22 Birchn. la
Wreford, Nicholls & Co. stockbrokrs. 4 Bank cham. Lothbury
Wreford & Pugh, who. haberdashers, hosiers & lacemen, 2 Aldermanbury, & Fountain ct. Aldermanbury
Wren William Weld & Robert, solicitors, 32 Fenchurch st
Wren John baker, 2½ Scott's place, Lower road, Islington
Wren William, butcher, 9 East st. Walworth
Wren Wm. Weld, sec. to London Corn. Ex. 60 Mark lane
Wrenalds Nicholas & Richard, tailors, 20 High st. Islington
Wrench Jacob & Sons, seed merchts. 39 King William st. City
Wrench Edward, optician, 6 Gray's inn terrace
Wrench Wm. dairyman, 7 William st. Manchester sq
Wrench Wm. whiting ma. & corn dlr. 14 Wharf rd. City rd
Wrenn Joseph, coachsmith, 5 Lit. Exeter st. Sloane st
Wrensted Francis, wine mer. 63 Skinner st. Bishopsgate
Wrentmore Isaac, attorney, 19 Lincoln's inn fields, & 11 Cheyne row, Chelsea
Wrentmore John Henry, surgeon, 14 Clarendon sq
Wressell Joseph, *Edinburgh Castle* P.H. 11 Welbeck st
Wrettom John, carpenter, 10½ Felix place, Liverpool road
Wride Nathaniel Blake, *York Arms* P.H. 5 Lt. Shire la. Tem. br
Wrigglesworth John, boot & shoe maker, 31 South Audley st
Wrigglesworth Sophia (Mrs.), grocer, 1 Charles st. Coml. rd
Wrigglesworth Thos. grocer, 1 Arlington st. Hampstd. rd
Wright Alfred & George Wm. forge & house bellows makers, 16 Lit. Alie st. Goodman's fields, & 148 Church st. Shoreditch
Wright Chas. & Co. mftg. perfums. & brush maks. 14 Minories
Wright & Crump, carpet manufrs. 5 New Farringdon st
Wright Edward & John, teadealers, &c. 33 Old Compton st
Wright Geo. & Chas. joiners & cabinet mks. 17 Dartmouth st
Wright & Goodes, newsagents, 106 Crawford st. Marylebone
Wright & Folkard, engravers, 48 Mansell st. Goodman's flds
Wright & Griffith, surgeons, 3 Grenville st. Brunswick sq
Wright & Hanbury, solicitors, 11 Finsbury pl. south
Wright & Harvey, ironmongs. & smiths, 21 & 22 Circus st. New rd
Wright Jas. & Wm. goldbeaters, 26 Holles st. Clare market
Wright & Jeanneret, solicitors, 53 Lincoln's inn fields
Wright Job & Co. russia merchants, 3 Gt. Winchester st
Wright & Kettle, tailors & drapers, 41 Conduit st. Regent st
Wright John & Co. booksellers, 13 Paternoster row
Wright John & Co. druggists & manuf. chemists, 336 Oxford st
Wright John W. & Son, merchants, 52 Old Broad st. City
Wright, Lloyd & Co. coal & Coke mer. Ratcliff wf. Ratcliff crs
Wright & Nash, ironfounders, smiths, &c. 253 Oxford st
Wright & Nash, pat. stove manufactory, 75 Newgate st
Wright & Nephew, fruiterers, 51 Fore st. City
Wright & Sharp, jewellers, 39 Devonshire st. Queen sq
Wright Smith & Shepherd, sol. & parliamnty. agts. 15 Golden sq
Wright Sophia & Eliza, stockmakers, 6 Dyer's ct. Aldermnby
Wright & Westhorp, riggers, Commercial road, Limehouse
Wright Wm. & Co. pat. of imp. leather, 3 Gt Queen st. Linc. in. flds
Wright Wm. Geo. & Jas. coachmaks. 76 & 77 Bridge rd. Lambeth
Wright Wm. & John, carvers, gilders, & picture importers, 22, & antique furniture warehouse, 27 Wardour st
Wright Wm. & Son, looking glass fra. mak. 12 Pitt st. O. Kent rd
Wright Abraham, locksmith, 3 Litchfield st. Soho
Wright Alexander, engraver & printer, 3 Fan st. Aldersgt. st
Wright Ann (Miss), dressma. 47 Up. North pl. Gray's inn rd
Wright Ann (Mrs.), confectioner, 94 Bridge road, Lambeth
Wright Anthony, dining rooms, 6 Rufford's bldgs. Islington
Wright Austin, undertaker, 17 Lit. Coram st. Brunswick sq
Wright Benjamin, house painter, 91 Newman st. Oxford st
Wright Benj. smith & bellhanger, 11 Serles pl. Carey st
Wright Benj. Rt. oil & colorman, 27 Castle st. east, Oxford st
Wright Charles, *Black Bull* P.H. Kingsland High st
Wright Charles, bootmaker, 23 Southampton row, Bloomsby
Wright Charles, cabinet maker, &c. 19 Upper Rathbone pl
Wright Charles, cowkeeper, 23 Leigh st. Burton crescent
Wright Charles, general agent, 1 Water st. Blackfriars
Wright Charles, general mnfr. 6 St. Benet's pl. & Birmingham
Wright Charles, meat salesman, Leadenhall market
Wright Charles, *Red House* P.H. Battersea
Wright Charles, roman cement & plaster of paris works, Somerset wf. Up. Ground st. & 45 Baldwin's grdns. Gray's inn la
Wright Charles, solicitor, 27 Essex st. Strand
Wright Charles, solicitor, 8 Gracechurch st. City
Wright Chas. Edw. mourning collar ma. 16 Pearson st. Kngsld. rd
Wright Chas. Wm. *King's Arms* P.H. 4 Bowling st. Westmr
Wright Charlotte (Mrs.), coffee rooms, see Powter & Wright
Wright Chrisphr. bird dlr. & cage ma. 27 Princes st. Drury la
Wright Daniel, beer retailer, 1 New row, Deptford
Wright David, livery stables, North mews, Nrth. bdgs. Fnsb. cir
Wright Edmund, iron agt. & ship chandler, 61 Wapping High st
Wright Edw. boot & shoe maker, 5 Charles st. Soho sq
Wright Edward, servants' registry, 17 Hemming's row
Wright Elias John, stay & belt maker, 23 Gt. Portland st
Wright Elizh. (Mrs.), coffee rooms, 29 Gt. Marlborough st
Wright Elizh. (Mrs.), soda water ma. 2 So. Island pl. Clphm. rd
Wright Ephraim, builder, &c. 4 Millman st. Bedford row
Wright Frederick, merchant, insurance & commission agent, 20 Pinner's hall, Old Broad st. City, & Lloyd's

Wright Frederick, surgeon, 110 Upper Whitecross st
Wright Freeman John, chemist, 14 Edwards st. Portman sq
Wright Geo. bellows maker, 29 Long lane, West Smithfield
Wright Geo. chairmaker, 12 Chapel st. Somers town
Wright Geo. comb & fan ma. 43 Northampton st. Clerknwll
Wright Geo. commission agent, 70 Mark lane
Wright Geo. dairy, 1 Granby st. Hampstead road
Wright Geo. engineer, 44 Fore st. Limehouse
Wright Geo. fancy work box maker, 40 Seward st. Goswell st
Wright Geo. hairdresser & perfumer, 41 London wall
Wright Geo. hat manufacturer, 76 Redcross st. Borough
Wright Geo. solicitor, 7 Albert square, Commercial rd. east
Wright Geo. tailor, 45 Cornhill
Wright Geo. tailor, 1 Green st. Leicester square
Wright Geo. tailor & draper, 45 Cornhill
Wright Geo. vice maker, 21 Grace's alley, Wellclose square
Wright Geo. wholesale & retail shawl, silk & bandana warehouse, 2 Houndsditch, & 3 Aldgate High st
Wright Geo. Parkinson, woollen draper, see Scott & Wright
Wright Hannah, milliner, 100 New Bond st
Wright Henry, agricultural bookseller, 51 Haymarket
Wright Henry, bath proprietor, 1&4 Winchester row, New rd
Wright Henry, cheesemonger, 93 Edgware rd. Marylebone
Wright Henry, cheesemonger, 44 Leather lane, Holborn
Wright Henry, *Clarendon hotel*, 169 New Bond st. & 19 & 20 Albemarle st. Piccadilly
Wright Henry, glass polisher & silverer, 24 Lit. Saffron hill
Wright Henry, hat manufacturer, 23 Charles st. Blackfrs. rd
Wright Henry, *Horse & Groom* P.H. 1 Keen's rw. Walwrth. rd
Wright Henry, perfumer, 20 Blackfriars road
Wright Henry, tailor, 25 Goswell terrace, Goswell road
Wright Henry, tobacconist, 35 Featherston st. City road
Wright Henry, tobacconist, 9 Horseferry rd. Westminster
Wright Henry, toy dealer, 5 Myddelton st. Clerkenwell, & 12 Great Turnstile, Holborn
Wright Henry, truss & surgical inst. ma. 18 London rd. Sthwk
Wright Henry Wm. pianoforte tuner, 4 Jewin ct. Jewin st.
Wright Hercules, carpenter, 33 East st. Red Lion square
Wright Isaac Wells, surveyor, 8 Harleyford st. Kennington
Wright James, boot & shoe ma. 4 Foxton ter. Thornhill road
Wright James, bootmaker, 29, Stonecutter st. Shoe lane
Wright James, butcher, 3 Compton st. Brunswick square
Wright James, corn dlr. 63 Mount st. & 23 Silver st. Golden sq
Wright James, dairyman, 12 Bridge terrace, Harrow road
Wright James, dentist, 85 Stanhope st. Hampstead road
Wright James, grocer & cheesemonger, 3 Stepney High st
Wright James, hairdresser, 66 Cannon st. City
Wright James, marine store dealer, 72 Redcross st. Borough
Wright James, oilman & brit. wine mer. 33 Lamb's Conduit st
Wright James, *Old Turk's Head coffee house*, 142 Strand
Wright James, plumber & painter, 15 Marshall st. London rd
Wright James, *Queen's Head* P.H. 95 Gt. Titchfield st
Wright James, rigger, 5 Penny fields, Poplar
Wright James, solicitor, 8 New inn, Strand
Wright James, surgeon, 27 Petersburgh pl. Bayswater
Wright James, tailor, 32 Marshall st. Golden square
Wright James, *White Horse & Half Moon* P.H. 55 London wall
Wright James, writer & grainer, 40 Castle st. Holborn
Wright James F. G. chemist, 55A, Gloucester pl. Portman sq
Wright John, barrister, 1 Hare ct. Temple
Wright John, beer retailer, 11 Nowell's bldgs. Liverpool rd
Wright John, blacking maker, see Warren, Russell & Wright
Wright John, bookbinder, 14 & 15 Noel st. Berwick st. Soho
Wright John, boot & shoe maker, 46 Bridge rd. Lambeth
Wright John, boot & shoe maker, 1 Brompton terrace
Wright John, boot & shoe ma. 3 Cross st. Wenlock rd. City rd
Wright John, boot & shoe maker, 8 Crown row, Walworth rd
Wright John, carpenter, 22 Gt. Smith st. Westminster
Wright John, cheesemonger, 9 Clement's inn pass. Clare mkt
Wright John, *Cheshire Cheese* P.H. 48 Crutchedfriars
Wright John, civil engineer, 11 Park st. Westminster
Wright John, coachmaker, 8 Portland st. mews, Soho
Wright John, fruiterer, 3 Star corner, Bermondsey
Wright John, general agent, 2 Cloak lane, City
Wright John, grocer, 52 Orchard st. Westminster
Wright John, grocer & tea dealer, 24 Oxford st
Wright John, *Jolly Anglers* P.H. 42 Bath st. City road
Wright John, map mounter, 4 Bear yd. Lincoln's inn
Wright John, physician, 3 Princes ct. Storey's gate, Westmr
Wright John, picture cleaner & restorer, 22 Wardour st
Wright John, shell fishmonger, 20 Upper St. Martin's lane
Wright John, solr. 7 Rathbone pl. & 6 Cumberland pl. New rd
Wright John, *Star* coffee rooms, 172 St. John st. road
Wright John, straw bonnet ma. 12 Trinity row, Islington
Wright John, tobacconist, 15 Upper East Smithfield
Wright John, upholsterer, 26 Cleveland st. Fitzroy sq
Wright John, watchma. 1 Butler's pl. Chapel st. Pentonville
Wright John, *White Swan* P.H. 124 St. George st
Wright John, jun. ironmonger & smith, 9 Kensington High st
Wright John Baker, solicitor, see Purrier & Wright
Wright John Lawrence, solicitor, 2 South sq. Gray's inn
Wright John Thos. solicitor, 15 London st. Fenchurch st.; secretary to the Andalusian Mining Association, 48 Great Coram st. Russell sq
Wright John White, grocer, 12 Church st. Kensington
Wright John Wm. figure & portrait painter, 5 Gt. Marlboro' st
Wright John W. merchant (Honduras), 52 Old Broad st. City
Wright Jonathan, tailor, 11 Carlton st. Regent st
Wright Joseph, boot & shoe factor, 15 Smithfield bars
Wright Joseph, butcher, 11 Upper area, Hungerford market
Wright Joseph, chemist & druggist, 3 Alexander pl. Brompton
Wright Joseph, railway carriage builder, Gough st. Gray's inn road; 2 Munster st. Regent's pk. & Saltley works, near Birmingham
Wright Joseph, fruiterer, 20 Chapel st. Curtain road
Wright Joseph, merchant, 11 Aldermanbury
Wright Joseph, tobacconist, 5 Wych st. Strand
Wright Joseph, watch enameller, 48 York st. St. Luke's
Wright Joseph Chas. beer retailer, 12 Dacre st. Westminster
Wright Joseph Heywood, law stationer, see Sharp & Wright
Wright Joseph Hornsby, solicitor, see Jones & Wright
Wright Lawrence, *Bull's Head* P.H. 26 Hyde st. Bloomsby. & *Fountain* P.H. 3 Foster lane, Cheapside
Wright Louisa (Miss), *Grotto tav.* 4 Southampton bdgs. Hlbrn
Wright Margaret (Mrs.), baker, 30 Bartholomew ter. City rd. & 30 Powell st. east, King's square
Wright Maria (Mrs.), straw hat manufr. 11 Deptford bridge
Wright Mary (Mrs.), *Harrow* P.H. 23 Whitefriars st. Fleet st. & 21 Primrose hill, Salisbury square
Wright Mary Ann (Mrs.), lodging ho. 3 Eccleston st. south
Wright Mary Ann (Miss), lodging house, 6 Thanet pl. Strand
Wright Michael, carpent. & builder, 14 Gt. Barlow st. Maryleb
Wright Peter, butcher, 22 Little Shire lane, Temple bar
Wright Richard, beer retailer, Penton place, Walworth
Wright Richard, corn dealer, 44 Edgware rd. Marylebone
Wright Richard, stone mason, Vincent sq. Westminster
Wright Richard, surgeon, Platform, 389 Rotherhithe wall
Wright Richard, trimming seller, 66 Berwick st. Soho
Wright Robert, bootmaker, 251 High Holborn
Wright Robert, cornfactor, 48 Mark lane
Wright Robert, fruiterer, 24 & 25 Devonshire st. Lisson grove
Wright Robert, paperhanger, 3 Great Dover st. Borough
Wright Robert, straw hat ma. 5 Artillery terrace, Westmr
Wright Robert, veterinary surgeon, 2 Porter's pl. Holwy. rd
Wright Samuel, cowkeeper, 2 Albion st. Rotherhithe
Wright Stephen, appraiser, &c. 17 Dartmouth st. Westminstr
Wright Stephen, architect, 24 Somerset st. Portman sq
Wright Susan (Mrs.), dressmaker, 3 Judd st. Brunswick sq
Wright Susannah (Mrs.), butcher, 154 Up. Whtcrss. st. St. Luk's
Wright Sydney, coal mercht. Union whf. Millbank st. Westm
Wright Thos. army accoutrem. mak. 9 Dorset pl. Pall mall ea
Wright Thos. baker, Highbury vale
Wright Thos. bookseller & stationer, 42 Mount st. Lambeth
Wright Thos. builder, 20 Gt. Marlborough st. & 48 Poland st
Wright Thos. carcase butcher, 55 Aldgate High st
Wright Thos. chairmaker, 118 Long lane, Bermondsey
Wright Thos. cheesemonger, 9 Blackmoor st. Clare market
Wright Thos. chemist, 35 New road, St. George's east
Wright Thos. coal & wine mer. Bridge wf. & Church st. Hackney
Wright Thos. corn & coal mercht. 16 Millbank row, Westmnr
Wright Thos. grocer & teadealer, 39 Grosvenor row, Pimlico
Wright Thos. house painter, 6 College hill, Upper Thames st
Wright Thos. ironmonger, 104 Lambeth lower marsh
Wright Thos. oil & colorman, 15 St. Mary at hill
Wright Thos. picture dealer, 98 Chancery la. & 86 Hatton ga
Wright Thos. tallowchandler, 15 Gt. Windmill st. Haymarke
Wright Thos. upholsterer, 47 South Molton st. Bond st
Wright Thos. watch & clock maker, 11 Lisle st. Leicester sq
Wright Thos. watch glass maker, 127 Bunhill row
Wright Thos. wholesale cheesemonger, 11 Giltspur st
Wright Thos. wire drawer, 35 Trafalgar st. Walworth road
Wright Thos. B. wind. blind mfr. 14 Nowell's bdgs. Lvrpl. rd
Wright Thos. Henry, prof. of music, 14 Norton st. Fitzroy sq
Wright Thos. Skeeles, solicitor, 13 Cooks court
Wright Uriah, carpenter, 1 Crown court, Pall mall
Wright Wm. architect & surveyor, 18 Palace New rd. Lmbth
Wright Wm. attorney, 11 Furnival's inn, Holborn
Wright Wm. barrister, 6 Stone buildings, Lincoln's inn
Wright Wm. *Black Prince* P.H. 64 Chandos st. Covent gdn
Wright Wm. boot & shoe maker, 29 Fleet la. Farringdon st
Wright Wm. bootmaker, 19 Wells row, Upper st. Islington
Wright Wm. bricklayer, 2 Grange road, Bermondsey

Wright Wm. cabinet maker, 45 Princess st. Portman markt
Wright Wm. cabinet maker, 3 Prospect place, Old Kent rd
Wright Wm. carpenter & bldr. 10 Mount ter. Nw.rd. Whtchpl
Wright Wm. carriers' agent, Rose inn yd. 80 West Smthfld
Wright Wm. carver & gilder, 38 London st. Fitzroy sq
Wright Wm. cheesemonger, see Todd & Wright
Wright Wm. clothes dealer, 19 Cutler st. Houndsditch
Wright Wm. *Coach & Horses* P.H. 1&2 Chester mws. Grosv.pl
Wright Wm. coal merchant, 30 Tooley st
Wright Wm. ironmonger, 7 Goldsmith's row, Hackney road
Wright Wm. *Crown* coffee rooms, 13St.John's sq.Clerknwl
Wright Wm. currier, 1 Rephidim st. Hunter st. Dover road
Wright W. *Duke's Head* P.H. Leman st. Lomond's pond, Boro'
Wright Wm. fruiterer, 5 Snowsfields, Bermondsey
Wright Wm. furn. brok. 85Theobald's rd. Kingsgate st. Hlbn
Wright Wm. gen.agt. & accountant, 14 Cherry gar.st. Brmdsy
Wright Wm. grocer, 12, Park terrace, Camden town
Wright Wm. gunlock polisher, 38 Lambeth st. Lit. Alie st
Wright Wm. manufacturing jeweller, 10 Brewer st. Goswell rd
Wright Wm. map engraver, 1 Bartlett's passage, Holborn
Wright Wm. plumber, &c. 6 Pont st. Belgrave square
Wright Wm. publisher, 13 St. George's road, Southwark
Wright Wm. muffin baker, 8 Barnsbury row, Cloudesley
Wright Wm. shoemaker, 6 Earl st. east, Lisson grove
Wright Wm. smith, 12 Marlborough st. Blackfriars road
Wright Wm. soda water manufr. Bowling green st. Kenngtn
Wright Wm. surgeon aurist, 3Gt. Queen st. Lincoln's inn flds
Wright Wm. tailor, 13 Alfred st. Bedford square
Wright Wm. tailor, 36 Dean st. Soho
Wright Wm. tailor, 30 Earl st. Horseferry road
Wright Wm. tailor, 7 St. George's st. Albany road
Wright Wm. tailor, 20 Stacey st. St. Giles's
Wright Wm. tailor, 26 Portland st. Wardour st
Wright Wm. *Three Crowns* P.H. 5 Old Jewry
Wright Wm. tobacconist. 2 Rufford's bldgs. Islington
Wright Wm. watchmaker, 212 Tooley st
Wright Wm. A printer, 12 Fulwood's rents, Holborn
Wright Wm. Birt, carpenter, Camden place, Peckham
Wright Wm. Charlton, publisher, 3 Warwick square, City
Wright Wm. Dacre, merchant, 3 Cross lane, St. Mary at hill
Wright Wm. Harding, solicitor, see Waterman, Wright & Co
Wright Wm. Hen. vinegar maker, see Willis & Wright
Wright Wm. Jn. *George IV.* P.H. 6Crescent, Southwk.br.rd
Wright Wm. Lee, tailor, 17 Conduit st. Bond st
Wright Wm. N. (late Porter & Wright), bookseller & stationer to their Majesties & the royal family, 60 Pall mall
Wright Wm. N. coal merchant to their Majesties, 60 Pall mall
Wright Wm. Norton, linendraper, 112 Brick la. Spitalfields
Wright Wm. Thrale, carver & gilder, 22 Wardour st. Soho
Wright Wm. Willis, *Coopers' Arms* P.H. 21 Union st. Boro'
Wrightson John, orange merchant, 41 Botolph la. Thames st
Wrigley Jas. & Sons, paper makers, 5 Budge row, Cannon st
Wrinch John, *Nag's Head* P.H. 37 South Audley st
Wrottesley hon. Walter, barrister, 4 Stone bdgs. Linc. inn
Wuest Jno. Fredk. pianoforte ma. 15 Up. York st. Bryanstone sq
Wulcko Charles, tailor, 43 Chandos street
Wulff Geo. Hen. & Jas Fred. merchants, 38 Fenchurch st
Wyard Benj. B. academy, 17 Mornington place, & 14 Harrington street, Hampstead road
Wyatt & Brandon, architects, 75 Gt. Russell st. Bloomsbury
Wyatt (Clement) & Co. wine merchants, 106 Fenchurch st
Wyatt Harriet & Son, wire workers, 192 Oxford street
Wyatt & Norman, tailors & drapers, 12 Duke st. Smithfield
Wyatt, Parker & Co. manufs. of roman cement & tessellated pavement; sole agent for Minton & Co.'s encaustic & other tiles, 9 Albion place, & Holland st. Blackfriars; Irongate wharf, Paddington, & Mill wall, Poplar
Wyatt & Powle, wh. tea & coffee dealers, 2 Blomfield st. Lond. w
Wyatt Thomas & Co. (now Goode & Co.), east india & oil merchants, wholesale dealers in sauces, pickles, &c. & for exportation, 102 Leadenhall street
Wyatt Ann (Mrs.), *Sun* P.H. 4 Foregate, Clement's inn, Strand
Wyatt Anna (Mrs.), milliner, 2 Queen's pl. Queen's rd. Dalston
Wyatt Augustine, builder, 1 Finsbury street, Finsbury sq
Wyatt Charles, beer retailer, Albert rd. Battersea flds
Wyatt Charles, corn dealer, 9 Chiswell st. Finsbury sq
Wyatt Edwd. carver & gilder to her Majesty, 360 Oxford st
Wyatt Edward, drysalter, 10 Gould sq
Wyatt Elizh. (Mrs.), coffee rooms, 26 Drummond st. Euston st
Wyatt Frederick, wine merchant, 6 Mark lane
Wyatt George, *Bull's Head* P.H. 40 Vere st. Clare market
Wyatt George, butcher, 22 Adams row, Hampstead road
Wyatt Hugh Penfold, barrister, 1 Pump court, Temple
Wyatt James, *Queen's Arms* P.H. 4 Marlborough rd. Chelsea
Wyatt James, solicitor, see Husband & Wyatt
Wyatt James, sculptor, 33 Dudley grove, Harrow road
Wyatt James, tailor & reporter of fashions, 36 Frith st. Soho
Wyatt James, sen. *Marqs. of Granby* P.H. 17 Brick st. Picdly
Wyatt Jas. Reeves, brewer, Bowl yd. 37 Broad st. St. Giles's
Wyatt John, barrister, 7 Figtree court, Temple
Wyatt John, iron agt. & grease mer. 2 Weymouth pl. Nw. Kent rd
Wyatt John, jeweller & watchmaker, 46 South Audley st
Wyatt John, *Lord Nelson* P.H. 22 Upper Bryanstone st
Wyatt John, tailor & breeches maker, 26 Gerrard st. Soho
Wyatt John, tobacconist, 408 Oxford st
Wyatt Matthw. Coates, sculptor, 33 Dudley grove, Harrow rd
Wyatt Peter, surgeon, 8 Barnsbury villas, Liverpool road
Wyatt Richard, *White Hart* P.H. Duke st. Chelsea
Wyatt Robert, surgeon, 3 Paulton's ter. King's rd. we. Chlsea
Wyatt Samuel, *Founders' Arms* P.H. 213 Brick la. Spitalflds
Wyatt Samuel, tobacconist, 13 Gt. Queen st. Lincoln's inn fis
Wyatt Thomas Henry, surveyor, Church st. Hackney
Wyatt Valentine, dining rooms, 59 Gt. Tower st
Wyatt Wm. hair cutter & wig ma. 31 Frith st. Soho
Wyatt Wm. locksmith, 5 Manifold pl. Lower Kennington la
Wyatt Wm. silversmith & jeweller, 28 Ebury st. Pimlico
Wyatt Wm. solicitor, see Madox & Wyatt
Wyberd John, *Flower Pot coach Office*, 115 Bishopsgate wthn
Wybourn Augustus, fur. broker, 2 Broomfield pl. Deptford
Wybroo William, cheesemonger, 26 Bridge st. Westminster
Wybrow John, grocer, 85 Upper Ground st. Blackfriars
Wybrow Wm. music seller & publisher, 33 Rathbone pl
Wyburd Joseph, painter, 7 Portsea pl. Connaught square
Wyburd Wm. Francis, coal merchant, 24 & 25 Bryanstone st
Wyburn & Meller (late Hobson), coachmaks. to her Majesty & the Queen Dowager, 121 Long acre, & 9 & 27 Park la. Pcdly
Wyburn James Smalley, stationer & bookseller, 48 Curzon st
Wych Thomas, hairdresser, 19 Beauvoir ter. Kingsland rd
Wyche Thomas Eyre, attorney, 13 George st. Mansion house
Wycliffe School, 6 St. Andrew's ter. Commercial road east
Wye Brothers, merchants, 5 Cooper's row, Crutchedfriars
Wyer Wm. George, baker, 12 Dalgleish pl. Limehouse fields
Wyett Samuel, tailor, 1 Clifford st. Bond st
Wyke Wm. jobmaster, 10 St. Martin's mews, Charing cross, & 16 & 21 Swallow st. Piccadilly
Wyld Benjamin, fruiterer, 46 Curzon st. May fair
Wyld George, bookseller & publisher, see Bruce & Wyld
Wyld James, geographer to her Majesty, 454 West Strand, & 2 Royal exchange
Wyld Joseph, cheesemonger, 30 Shepherd st. Mayfair
Wyld Joseph Woolley, newsvender, 1 White Horse st. Picdly
Wyld Thomas, fishmonger, 172 Sloane st. Knightsbridge
Wylde Alice (Mrs.), milliner, Denmark hill, Camberwell
Wylde Henry, flute maker, 25 Villiers st. Strand

Wylde James, dealer in cotton yarn, &c. 2 Aldermanbury
Wylde Thomas, pork butcher, 16 East st. Walworth road
Wyles John & Co. wholesale coffee dealers, 32 Cannon st
Wylie James & Co. wholesale teadealers, 1 Gt.Tower st. City
Wylie Alex. insur. brok. 3 Crown ct. Philpot la. & Lloyd's
Wylie John, merchant, Lloyd's
Wyllie Robert, wine merchant, 123 Fenchurch st
Wyllie Sidney Alexr. tailor, 45 Conduit st. New Bond st
Wyllie Thos. who. glass dealer, 4 Raven row, Spitalfields
Wyman Ann (Mrs.), fruiterer, Long market, Covent garden
Wyman Charles, printer, 49Cumming st.New rd.Pentonville
Wyman Charles, *Sun* P.H. 47 Curzon st. Mayfair
Wyman David, baker, 105 Crawford st. Portman square
Wyman John, chem. & druggist, 30 Redcross st. Cripplegate
Wyman Joseph, grocer, 23 Market row, Oxford market
Wyman William, furniture broker, 93 Goswell st
Wymark Mark & Son, watch mfrs. 49Perceval st.Clerkenwl
Wymer Christplr. cheesemonger, 1 Wellington pl. Lpool.rd
Wymer James, cowkeeper, 6 Britannia st.Bagnigge wells rd
Wymer William, baker, 70 Leather lane, Holborn
Wynen Widow W.G. & Son, merchts. 49 Commer.sale rooms
Wyness Andrew, hairdresser, 22 Paddington st
Wyndham Edward, stockbroker, 5 Bank chambers, Lothbury
Wynn James & Co. woollen warehousemen, 76 & 77 Wood st
Wynn Elizab.(Mrs.), furn.broker, 38Up.North pl.Gray's inn rd
Wynn Geo. tailor, 41 Skinner st. Bishopsgate without
Wynn James, whitesmith, 7 Pitt place, Drury lane, & 45 Whittlebury st. Euston sq
Wynn Jas. Robt. stationer & bookseller, 3 Bell yd.Docs'.com
Wynn William, druggist, 39 Rotherhithe st
Wynn William, whipmaker, 97 White Lion st. Pentonvillen
Wynne Mrs. & Miss, millins.1 Haberdashers' pl.west, Hoxto
Wynne A. house & estate agt. 10 Sommer's pl. we. New rd
Wynne John Pitchurst, cabinet ma. 5 Theberton st. Islington
Wynne Lewellyn, solicitor, see Delmar & Wynne
Wynne Robert, grocer, 1 Field place, Lark hall la. Clapham
Wynne Robert, grocer, 20 Lambeth walk
Wynne William, pastrycook, 97 Union st. Borough
Wynne William, artist, 5 Hinde st. Manchester square
Wynne William, wholesale stationer, 45 Paternoster row
Wynnick Frederick Jsph. congreve mnfr. 97 Long la. Bmdsy
Wyon Benjamin, medallist & chief engraver of her Majesty's seals, 287 Regent st. Cavendish square
Wyon Edward William, sculptor, 48 Gower st. Bedford sq
Wythe Timothy, builder, 1 Elizabeth place, Kingsland rd
Wyver Henry, grocer, 1 Swan st. Trinity square, Borough

YABLOUSKY Lawrence, metallic pen mfr. 30 Fore st. City
Yabsley Geo. Joseph, hatter, 3 Britannia pl. Com. rd. east
Yale Samuel, grocer, New road, South Lambeth
Yallop John, carpenter, 3 Pritchard's place, Hackney fields
Yallop Moses, grocer & oilman, 88 Mount st. Berkeley sq
Yallop Rowland, solicitor, 8 Furnival's inn Holborn
Yallop Thomas, white lead manfr. see Grace, Yallop & Co
Yallowley & Johnson, surveyors, 17 Redcross st. Cripplegate
Yandall Henry & Co. tailors & drapers, 105 Strand
Yapp George, ladies' shoemaker, 200 Sloane st. Knightsbridge
Yapp John, goldsmith, see Willmore, Yapp & Woodward
Yapp Samuel, tailor, &c. 18 Cromer st. Grays inn road
Yarborough & Adams, solicitors, 44 Lincoln's inn fields
Yarde Giles, chemist & druggist, 28 Lamb's Conduit st
Yardington John, butcher, 34 King's road east, Chelsea
Yardley & Stathan, wholesale & export perfumers & fancy soap makers, original manufacturers of the genuine honey soap, 7 Vine st. Bloomsbury
Yardley Edward, barrister, 7 Serjeants' inn, Fleet st
Yardley James, *Duke of Glo'ster* P.H. 4Glo'ster ter. Hoxton
Yardley James, granary keeper, 32 Rotherhithe wall
Yardley John, plumber, 5 Thorney st. Bloomsbury
Yardley Samuel, *Buck's Head* P.H. 12 James st. Bethnal gr
Yardley William, attorney, 1 Christopher st. Hatton garden
Yardley William, barrister, 2 Brick court, Temple
Yardley Wm. *Halfmoon & Crown* P.H. 37 Bacon st. Bethnal gr
Yarmouth & Norwich Railway Co. (Rd.Till, mgr.) Guildhl.bdg
Yarnold Edwin R. [late Grant & Yarnold], chamois leather dresser, lapland rugs, &c. &c. 9 Lawrence lane, Cheapside (removed from 4 Church court, Old Jewry)
Yarnton George, *Lamb tap* P.H. Hide mrkt. Leadenhl. mkt
Yarnton Willm. undertaker, Denmark hill, Camberwell
Yarrell Wm. bookseller & newsman, see Jones & Yarrell
Yarroll Thos. & Son, tailors & drapers, 8Commercl.pl. City road
Yarroll John, feather ma. 12 Warwick place, Kingsland rd
Yarrow Charles T. agt. to Phœnix Office, 3 Aske ter. Hoxton
Yarrow George, undertaker, 118½ Shoreditch High st
Yarrow John, herald, &c. painter, 16 Wellington st. Goswell st
Yarrow Nicholas, grocer & teadealer, 42 King st. Snow hill
Yate Richard & Son, who. druggists, 91 Blackman st. Boro'
Yates Benj. & Co. who. druggists, 25 Budge row, Cannon st
Yates George & Son, picture gallery, 13½ Old Bond st
Yates John & Co. importers of blacklead, 14 Berry st. Clknw
Yates John & Co. mustard mfrs. & drysalters, 14 Berry st. Clknw
Yates Richd. & Co. braid & stay lace manufacturers, 8 St. Andrew's hill, City, & Pilgrim pl. Walworth common
Yates & Turner, solicitors, 24 Gt. George st. Westminster
Yates & Walton, hop & oil merchants, 60 Barbican
Yates Charles, jeweller, 27 Cross st. Hatton garden
Yates Charles, wholesale grocer, see Bedwell, Yates & Co
Yates Charles Francis, solicitor, 12 Argyle st. King's cross
Yates Clare, cowkeeper, High st. Battersea
Yates Francis, broker, 21 Mincing lane
Yates Francis, cabinetmaker, 65 Myddleton st. Spafields
Yates George, artificial florist, 12Up. Seymour st. Portman sq
Yates George, baker, Bromley, Middlesex
Yates George, cockfounder, 15 Charles st. Hampstead rd
Yates George, plumber & glazier, 243 Tottenham ct. rd
Yates George, tailor, 13 Chapel st. Somers town
Yates George, tailor, 34 Newman st. Oxford st
Yates George Byer, grocer, 3 Lower East Smithfield
Yates James, bookseller, 105 Goswell st
Yates James, copperplate printer, 67White Lion st. Pentnvlle
Yates James, hairdresser, 2 Brook's row, Bagnigge wells rd
Yates John, boot & shoe maker, 250 Whitechapel rd
Yates John, china dealer, 2 Chalcroft ter. New cut, Lambeth
Yates John, stone merchant, 22 York rd. Lambeth
Yates Jno. Thos. grocer & cheesemonger, 8Darkho.la. Billngsgt
Yates Joseph, *Guy Earl of Warwick* P.H.4Crispst.Ea.Ind.rd
Yates Louisa (Miss), ladies' school, 62 Coleman st
Yates Mary A. (Mrs.), fruiterer, 15 & 19 Whitefriars st
Yates Martha (Mrs.), ladies' schl. 14Ladbroke ter. Notting hll
Yates Richard, carver & gilder, 7 Charlotte st. Fitzroy sq
Yates Richard, general outfitter, &c. 8 Shadwell High st
Yates Saul, solicitor, 16 Bury st. St. Mary axe
Yates T. (Mrs.), *Brunswick Arms* P.H. 67 Brunswk.st. Stmfd.st
Yates Thomas, *Black Swan* P.H. 71 Bermondsey st
Yates Wm. barrister, 12 Paper bldgs. Temple
Yates Wm. beer retailer, Albion mews east, Albion st. Hyd.pk
Yates Wm. grocer, 7 Kingsland rd. Dalston
Yates Wm. Holt, physician, 53 Woburn pl
Yates Wm. Thos. engineer & millwright, 1John st. Camb.hth.
Yaxley George, farrier, 5 Bridge row, Pimlico
Yaxley James, beer retailer, 9 Ebury square, Pimlico
Yearron John, hairdresser, 50 Tooley st
Yearsley Ann (Miss), 35 Southampton st. Strand
Yearsley Jas. M.R.C.S.L. aurist, 15 Saville row, Piccadilly

Yearsley John, merchant, 7 Mitre cham. 157 Fenchurch st
Yearwood Henry, *Dun Horse* P.H. 161 Borough High st
Yeates Andrew, optician, 12 Brighton pl. New Kent rd
Yeates Ann (Miss), ladies' school, 130 Mount st. Grosvenr. sq
Yeates Anthony, *Hope* coffee rooms, 74 Goswell st
Yeates Henry, tailor, 7 Lower James st. Golden sq
Yeates Peter Chas. hatter, 7 Cumberland row, Walworth rd
Yeates Robt. tallow chandlr. 15 & 16 Gt. Bell alley, Coleman st
Yeats Thomas, cheesemonger, 12½ Gt. Bell alley, Moorgate st
Yeates Timothy, confectioner, 44 Tothill st. Westminster
Yeates Timothy, ham dealer & confectioner, 23 Strand
Yeates Wm. chandler's shop, 91 Charles st. St. George's east
Yeatherd Wm. wine merchant, 3 Staining lane, Wood st
Yeatman Alex. chemist & druggist, 2 Little Moorfields
Yeatman Charles, shirtmaker, 146½ Leadenhall st
Yeatman David, seedsman, 19 High row, Knightsbridge
Yeatman Morgan, oporto mer. see Taylor, Fladgate & Yeatman
Yeats & Acocks, wholesale cheesemongers, 7 Old Fish st
Yeats James Sebastian, share bro. 6 Bank chambrs. Lothbury
Yeats William, cheesemonger, see Wincott & Yeats
Yeeles John, toy warehouse, 23 Robert st. King's rd. Chelsea
Yeend Jas. Parker, architect, &c. 15 Clifford's inn, Fleet st
Yeldham Stephen, surgeon, 9 Stamford st. Blackfriars rd
Yell John William, tailor, 54 Gt. Dover st. Borough
Yellowlees Wm. artist, 72 Newman st. Oxford st
Yemms Chas. plumber, 10 Up. Copenhagen st. Pentonville
Yems Robt. Thos. *Prince Albert* P.H. Mape st. Bethnal g. rd
Yeo George, stationer, see Eastman & Yeo
Yeo Joseph, birmingham factor, see Jennings & Yeo
Yeoman Benjamin, grocer, 73 Bridport place, New North rd
Yeoman Jas. cornchandlr. & miller, 10 Hall pl. Lr. Kenngtn. la
Yeoman James, livery stables, 87 Guilford st. Russell sq
Yeoman John, livery stables, 24 Eagle st. Red Lion sq
Yeoman Joseph, bricklayer, &c. 73 Bridport pl. New North rd
Yeoman Thos. Harrison, physician, 12 Tavistock pl. Tavstk. sq
Yeoman Wm. *Jolly Sailor* P.H. 27 New Gravel lane
Yeoman Wm. silk shag & hat manfr. 170 Hoxton Old town
Yeomans Jas. gunmaker, 4 Magdalen row, Gt. Prescot st
Yeomans John, fruit salesman, Borough market
Yeomans John, tailor, 65 King st. Boro' High st
Yeowell Francis, brass & cock founder, 20 Litchfield st. Soho
Yeowell William, boot & shoe maker, 38 Barbican
Yerbury Chas. Wm. tobacconist, 21 Kingsland road
Yerbury John, tobacconist, 87 Aldgate High st
Yerbury Walter, baker, 102 Golden lane, St. Luke's
Yerlett Edward, carpenter, &c. 7 Chichester pl. Gray's inn rd
Yerworth William, printer, 259½ Whitechapel road
Yetton Peter John, *Rising Sun* P.H. 1 Globe rd. Mile end
Yetts Joseph Muskett, solicitor, 5 Gray's inn place, Gray's inn
Yetts Thomas, hairdresser, 41 Lombard st. City
Yewd William, attorney, 30 East st. Red Lion square
Yglesias Jose Ramon, merchant, 20 Mark lane
Yglesias Miguel, wine mercht. 9 King's arms yd. Moorgate st
Yolland Thos. appraiser & underta. 15 Cromer st. Brunsk. sq
Yolland Thos. jun. painter, 7 Cromer st. Gray's inn road
Yonge & Hancock, solicitors, 20 Tokenhouse yd. City
Yonge Walter, watchmaker, 156 Strand
Yool Wm. coal merchant, 17 Mill st. Hanover square; 55 Conduit st. Regent st. & Cannon row wharf
York Richard & Co. coal merchants, Crescent road, Millbnk
York Charles, Hy. academy, 12 Cheltenham pl. Westmr. rd
York Henry, wadding manufacturer, 26 Norfolk pl. Curtain road, & 3 New inn, Broadway, Shoreditch
York James, surgeon, Wharncliffe ter. St. John's wood
York Jehoshaphat, builder, 16 Marshall st. Golden sq
York Lucy (Mrs.), marine store dlr. 41 Gt. Wild st. Linc. inn fld
York Richard, *Danl. O'Connell* P.H. 17 New rd. St. Geo. ca
York Wm. brushmkr. York cottage, Caledonian rd. Pntnvl
Yorke John, smith & bellhanger, 29 Wormwood st. Bishpsgt
Yorkshire Fire & Life Insurance Co. (Edward Henwood, agent), 46 Watling st.; see page 2049
Yorkshire & Glasgow Union Railway Co. 3 Park st. Wstm
Yorkshire Society's School, Mead pl. Westminster rd
Yorworth Francis, printer, 21 Ray st. Clerkenwell
Yost Philip, boot & shoe manufr. 127 High st. Shoreditch
Yost Philip, boot maker, 128 Shoreditch High st
Yost Philip, haberdasher, 6 Hoxton Old town
Youatt George, pianoforte mkr. 3 Stanhope st. Hampstd. rd
Youatt Wm. veterinary surgeon, 1 Osnaburgh pl. New rd
Youd Henry, printer, 62 Tottenham court road
Youd John, grocer, 34 Drummond st. Euston square
Youd William, brushmaker, 58 Union st. Lambeth walk
Youens James & Co. china tea wharehouse, 45 Ludgate hill
Youens John, basket maker, New cross
Youens Thomas, *Castle* P.H. 4 Shepherd ct. Up. Brook st
Youhill Jsph. smith & farrier, 1 Portman pl. Globe rd. Mile ed
Youl John Robert, salesman, 5 Newgate market, & 15 West Smithfield, & butcher, 53 Minories
Youl Richard, surgeon, 7 Duke st. Grosvenor square
Youl William, butcher, 1 Dover place, Old Kent road
Youle Wm. commission merchant, 22 Basinghall st
Youle William, practical optician & mathematical instrument maker, wholesale & for exportation, 83 Leadenhall st
Youlton John, tailor, 10 Great Russell st. Bloomsbury
Young & Bainbridge, bottled ale & stout merchants, 87 Upper Thames st
Young (Brown) & Son, glass, oil & color mers. 138 Up. Thames st
Young, Domett & Co. ship biscuit bakers, 35 Narrow st. Limehouse
Young, Dowson & Co. copper mers. & brass founds. 5 George yard, Lombard st. & Emmett st. Poplar
Young George & Co. silk & calico printers, 48 Friday st. Cheapside, & 17 George square, Glasgow
Young, Harrison & Co. mers. 1 Bargeyd. chambers, Bucklersbry
Young Henry & James, wire workers & cage ma. 29 Judd st
Young John & Co. linendrapers, mercers & haberdashers, 5 Albion place, King's cross
Young John & Co. wine merchants, 50 Lime st
Young John & Son, scale makers to her Majesty, 5 Bear st. & 46 Cranbourne st. Leicester square
Young & Peppercorne, blacking manufrs. 19 Cousin lane
Young, Ridge & Co. who. tea & coffee dlrs. 38 Gracechurch st
Young Robt. & Co. sail makers & ship chandlers, 4 Norway place, & Commercial wharf, Limehouse
Young Robert & Daniel, builders, 7 Crown row, Walworth rd
Young Robert & Wm. undertakers, 76 Church st. Shoreditch
Young Thos. & Co. wholesale tea & coffee dealrs. 29 Mark la
Young Thomas & Son, solicitors, 29 Mark lane
Young Thos. & Wm. oil, color & lamp wa. 64 Queen st. Cheapside
Young William & Co. ironmongers, 194 Oxford st
Young, Vallings & Young, solrs. 2 St. Mildred's ct. Poultry
Young Adam, merchant, 8 George yard, Lombard st
Young Adam, upholsterer & underta. 3 Chapel st. Bedford row
Young Adam, jun. insurance brok. 8 George yd. Lombard st
Young Alexander, baker, 10 Southampton st. Camden town
Young Alexander, carman, Maiden lane, Battle bridge
Young Alexander, stockbroker, 3 Bartholomew lane
Young Amelia (Mrs.), embroideress, 1 Duke st. Grosvnr. sq
Young Ann (Miss), corset ma. 14 Mortimer st. Cavendish sq
Young Benjamin, glue, size, hair & leaf ma. Spa rd. Bermsy
Young Charles, linendraper, &c. 7 Britannia pl. Wandswth. rd
Young Charles, oil & italian wareho. 8 High st. Pentonville
Young Charles, prof. of music, 10 Bedford ter. Horsemonger la
Young Charles, solicitor, 10 Warwick square, Newgate st

Young Charles Allen, banker, see Weston & Young
Young Charles C. tailor, 5 York st. St. James's
Young Christiana (Miss), dressmkr. 7 Mount st. Berkely sq
Young Christiana(Mrs.),staymkr.14Up.Baker st.Regent's pk
Young David, grocer, 5 Little College st. Westminster
Young Edward, baker, 1 Richmond st, East st.Walwrth. rd
Young Edward, glasscutter, 2 Hart st. Cripplegate
Young Edward, saddler & harness maker, 432 Oxford st
Young Edward, tailor, 153 Sloane st. Chelsea
Young Eliza (Miss), ladies' school, Lewisham road, Deptford
Young Elizh. (Mrs.), dairy, 52 Charlotte st. Whitechapel
Young Fletcher, baker, 47 Long alley, Finsbury
Young Florance Thomas, cornfactor, see Begbie & Youngs'
Young Frances (Mrs.),berlin ware.4 Lr.Seymour st.Portmn.sq
Young Francis, grocer, 5 Broadway, Deptford
Young Fredk. *Geo. & Dragon* P.H. 121 Vauxhall st. Lambeth
Young Fredk. *Queen's Head* P.H. 68 Marsham st. Westmnr
Young George, baker, 77 Old st. St. Luke's
Young George, *Blue Posts* P.H. 25 Charlotte st. Fitzroy sq
Young George, chandler's shop, 17 Hertford st. Fitzroy sq
Young George, cornfactor, see Begbie & Youngs'
Young George, fruiterer, 11 Finsbury market
Young George, scale maker & lamp maker, 63 London road
Young George Adam, surveyor, 34 Eagle st. Red Lion sq
Young George Fredk. shipbuilder, 15 Church rw. Limehouse
Young Geo. Fredk. merchant, &c. see Curling, Young & Co
Young Geo. Hine, surgeon, 24 Cross st. Blackfriars rd
Young Geo. Johnston, pump mak. Bostock st. Old Gravel la
Young Geo. Midford, pawnbroker, 51 Princes st. Leicester sq
Young Geo. Watson, beer retailer, 64 Compton st. Clerkenwl
Young Gilbert Ainslie, barrister, 28 John st. Bedford row
Young Godfrey, auct. & registrar, 7 Church rw.Newgtn.butts
Young Henry, carman, 10 White horse yard, Coleman st
Young Henry, carpenter, 33 Bayham st. Camden town
Young Hen. grindery dlr. & leather cutr. 14 Dean st. Westmr
Young Henry, solicitor, see Fladgate, Young & Jacksons'
Young Henry, teadealer & grocer, 81 Newgate st
Young Isabella (Mrs.), haberdasher, 23 White Conduit st
Young James, auctioneer & apr. 28 High st. Newington butts
Young James, baker, 2 White Conduit terrace, Islington
Young Jas. boot & shoe ma. 9 James pl. Larkhall la. Claphm
Young James, brushmaker, 29 Kingsland road
Young James, coal dealer, 1 Britannia rw. Lower st. Islingtn
Young James, *Greycoat Boy* P.H. 38 Gt. Peter st. Westmr
Young James, Lowther bazaar, see Graves & Young
Young James, *Roebuck* P.H. 48 Duke st. Aldgate
Young James, *Roebuck* P.H. 108 Tottenham court road
Young James, solicitor, 32 Bloomsbury square
Young James, solicitor, 21 Lower Belgrave place, Pimlico
Young James, tripedresser, 27 Paddington st. Marylebone
Young James, *Two Brewers* P.H. 6 Lit. St.Andrew st. 7 dials
Young James, upholsterer, 2 Arnold place, Walworth
Young James, upholsterer, 12 John st. Oxford st
Young Jas. Forbes, surgeon, 10 Kenningtn.pl.Up.Kenngn. la
Young John, architect & surveyor, 35 King st. Cheapside
Young John, butcher, 46 Pearson st. Kingsland road
Young John, commission agent, 12 Friday st. Cheapside
Young John, dairyman, 75 Manchester st. Gray's inn road
Young John, insurance broker, 68 Old Broad st. City
Young John, *Royal Oak* P.H. 34 Galway st. St. Luke's
Young John, solicitor, see Desborough & Young
Young John, tailor, 33 Duke st. St. James's
Young John, warehouseman, 12 Friday st
Young John, *Windmill* P.H.62 Charlotte ter.Nw.cut.Lmbth
Young John, jun. ironmonger, 18 Blandford st. Manchstr. sq
Young John Andrew, *King's Head* P.H.40 Queen st.Cheapside
Young John Mates, *Bell* P.H. 34 Cumberland row, King's cr
Young John T. plumber, 28 St. Mary at hill, & 12 Walbrook
Young Joseph, cattle salesman, 8 West Smithfield
Young Joseph, linendraper, 8 Bond st. Chelsea
Young Joseph, saddler, &c.24 Middle Queen's bldgs. Knightsbg
Young Joseph Cole, oil & british wine dealer, 6 Edgware rd
Young Joseph John, bootmaker, 6 Greystoke pl. Fetter lane
Young Louis, leather dresser, 14 Russell st. Bermondsey, & 11½ Artillery st. Horselydown
Young Mary (Mrs.) milliner, 8 Lowndes ter. Knightsbridge
Young Mary (Mrs.), stationer, 3 College st. Chelsea
Young Muns, jun. builder, King st. Battersea
Young Peter, plumber & glazier, Stoke Newington road
Young Philip, furrier, & straw hat mfr. 23 Victoria rd. Pimlico
Young Richard, bookseller, 7 York st. Sloane st. Chelsea
Young Richard, bootmaker, 10 King st. Golden square
Young Robert, sail ma. & ship chandler, 4 Norway pl. Com.rd
Young Robert, M.D. surgeon, see Forbes, Browne & Young
Young Samuel, coachmaker, 9 Cockpit yd.Lit.Jas.st.Bdfd.rw
Young Samuel, *Railway* coffee house, 209 Shoreditch
Young Samuel, trimming seller, 3 Peter st. Gt. Saffron hill
Young Sarah (Mrs.), shipchandler & sailmaker, 268 Wapping
Young Thomas, boot & shoe maker, 92 Fore st. Cripplegate
Young Thomas, bootmaker, 14 Sherborne st. Blandford sq
Young Thomas, col. broker, see Kensington, Paines' & Young
Young Thomas, harness ma. 2 Compton mews, Brunswick sq
Young Thomas, lighterman, see Brown & Young
Young Thomas, painter & grainer, 37 Arbour sq. Stepney
Young Thomas, porkman, 45 Whitcomb st. Pall mall east
Young Thomas, surgeon, 42 Piccadilly
Young Thos. Alf. *Crown & Anchor* P.H.34 Up. Albany st. Reg.pk
Young Thomas Bartlett, grocer, 8 Lt.Corum st.Brunswick sq. & baker, Crawley st. Somers town
Young Thomas Bristow, solicitor, see Holme, Loftus & Co
Young William, *Albion* P.H. 6 Vernon place, Bloomsbury sq
Young William, architect, 7 Granby st. Hampstead road
Young William, *Artillery Arms* P.H. 1 Rochester ter. Westm
Young William, *Bell* P.H. 8 Dean st. Commercial road east
Young William, bootmaker, 38 Langley pl. Commrcl. rd. east
Young William, bricklayer, &c. 48 Kinnerton st. Belgrave sq
Young William, furniture broker, 55 Bermondsey st
Young William, grocer, 27 Islington High st
Young William, hatter, 283 Oxford st
Young William, stationer & acct. book ma. 28 Walbrook
Young William, tailor & draper, 52 James st. Oxford st
Young William, *White Horse* P.H. 33 High st. Bow
Young William, jun. hatter, 344 Oxford st
Young William Edward, *Blue Posts* P.H. 81A, Newman st
Young William Henry, tailor, &c. 317 High Holborn
Young William Samuel, solicitor, 30 Parliament st. & 1 Vauxhall bridge road
Young Wm. Thos. haberdasher, 34 Charles st. Hatton gardn
Younge Edward, barrister, 1 New square, Lincoln's inn
Younger Wm. Henry & Son, appraisers & auctnrs. 247 Strand
Young Witherden, architect & surveyor, 35 Gillingham st. Pimlico, & 14 King William st. west, Strand
Younger James, *Old Baptist's Head* P.H. 30 St. John's lane
Younger Matthew, baker, 9 Melbourne place, Old Kent rd
Younger Saml. import. & manufr. of chicory root, 8 Great Tower st
Younger Saml. ship & cust.ho. & gen. commer. agt. 8 Gt. Tower st
Younger Sarah (Mrs.), cabinet ma. 3 Charlotte st. Old st. rd
Younghusband & Ball, wholesale fancy stationers & envelope & enamelled paper manfrs. 80½ Bishopsgate without
Younghusband Henry, biscuit baker, 113 Up. East Smithfield
Younghusband Thomas, *Gerard's Hall tavern*, 2 Basing la
Younghusband Wm. blue manf. 1 Up. Chapman st. Can. st. rd
Youngman Henry, timber mercht. see Eldridge & Youngman

Youngman John, tailor, 8 Weston st. Southwark
Youngman Samuel, mahogany mer. 123 Curtain rd. Shordtch
Youngman Thos. linendraper, &c. 12 Wittam's blds. Old st. rd
Youngman Wm. linendraper, 175 Sloane st. Knightsbridge
Youngs John, tailor, 195 High st. Poplar
Youngs Wm. pork butcher, 46 Three Colt st. Limehouse
Yoxall Richard, butcher, 129 Upper Whitecross st
Yriarte R. de B. of Cadiz, sherry shipper (agent, Joseph Greenstreet), 11 Cullum st. Fenchurch st
Ysasi & Co. (of Xerez de la Frontera), 5 Water la. Gt. Tower st
Yturregui Joseph, grocer, 9 James st. Oxford st
Yuill John, linendraper, 68 Leman st. Goodman's fields
Yuill Wm. tailor, 10 Leadenhall st
Yuille, Shortridge & Co. merchants, 17 Mark lane, & Murdoch, Shortridge, Lundie & Co. Madeira
Yule Chas. hairdresser, 56 Freeschool st. Horselydown
Yule Wm. Trueman & Co. presrv. provis. mer. 31 Wilson st. Finsby

ZACATECAS Mining Co. (A. Godfrey, sec.), 5 Broad st. bdgs
Zaehnsdorf Charles, manfg. jeweller, see Mege & Zaehnsdorf
Zagnani Francis, clock maker, 9 Camden st. Islington
Zaleski Peter Falkenhagen, merchant, 147 Leadenhall st
Zagury Samuel, gen. merchant, 24 Lime st
Zeal John, accountant, 7 King's square, Goswell road
Zetterquist Chas. & Sons, oilmen & blue makers, 60 Blkfrs. rd
Zeitter & Co. manufacturers of all kinds of horizontal & upright pianofortes, by royal letters patent, 4 & 5 New Cavendish st. Portland place
Zillwood Chas. blind school, Trafalgar cottage, Edward pl. Ball's pond
Zimmerman Godfrey, curiosity deal. 48 Albany st. Regent's pk
Zimmerman John Frederick, importer of german & french toys & fancy goods, & english toy manuf. 170 Shoreditch High st
Zizinia Brothers, merchants, 38 Finsbury circus
Zohrab Edward, Ottoman consul general, 1 Bryanston sq
Zonzius Sarah (Mrs.), stationer, 23 John st. Blackfriars rd
Zoological Society's Office (Wm. Ogilby sec.), 11 Hanover sq
Zornlin John Jacob, exchange broker, 72 Old Broad st
Zox Leman, aquatic life cap manufacturer, 46 Drury lane
Zuccani Ernest, looking glass maker, 4 Brick lane, Whtchpl
Zuliani Giacomo, merchant, 11 George st. Minories
Zuliani James, merchant, 11 George st. Minories
Zulueta & Co. merchants, 22 Moorgate st. City

POST OFFICE LONDON

COURT DIRECTORY

FOR 1846.

POST OFFICE LONDON

COURT DIRECTORY

FOR 1846.

ABBISS Rev. John, 5 Northampton sq
Abbot hon. Mrs. 64 Upper Berkeley st
Abbot Mrs. 12 Wellington rd. St.Jns. wd
AbbotW.T.esq.12Welingtn.rd.St.Jns.wd
Abbot Thos. esq. 2 Glo'ster pl. Portman sq. & West hatch, Chigwell, Essex
Abbott hon. Mrs. 3 Upper Grosvenor st
AbbottChas.T.esq.36Gowerst.&8Newinn
Abbott Edwin, esq.1 Lisson grove north
Abbott Francis, esq. 24 Brunswick sq
Abbott Francis, esq. 29 Connaught sq
Abbott Francis George, esq.13 Mecklenburgh square, & Rolls yard
Abbott Geo. esq. 4 Percy st. Bedford sq
Abbott John, esq. 10 Charlotte st
Abbott John, esq. 6 Duke st. Portland pl
Abbott Jsph. esq. 7 Gt.George st. Bmdsy
Abbott Josiah, esq. 21 Earls tr. Knsngtn
Abbott Miss, 10 Charlotte st. Bedford sq
Abbott Rt.esq. 4Glo'ster gr. w.OldBrmtn
Abbott Vernon, esq. 70 Gower st
Abbott Vernon Montagu, esq. 11 Millman st. Bedford rw. & 59 Chancery la
Abdey Rev. James R. Fair st.Horselydn
Abdy Sir Wm. bart. 20 Hill st
Abdy Lt. Col. 2 Earl's terr. Kensington
A'Beckett Gilbert Abbot, esq. 3 Inner Temple lane
A'Beckett Thomas T. esq. 2 Camden cotts. Camden New tn. & 7 Golden sq
A'Beckett Wm. esq. 7 Golden square
Abel John L. esq. 16 Kennington terr
Abel Wm.esq.12Belinda ter.Canonbry.sq
Abell Mrs. 17 New Ormond st
Abercorn Marquis of, K.G.Dudley house, Grosvenor gate, Park lane; Baron's court, Newtown Stewart; Bentley priory, Stanmore, Middlesex; & Ardverkie lodge, Laggan, N.B.
Abercrombie Lord, Airthire castle, near Stirling
Abercrombie John,esq.25A,Kensingtn.sq
Aberdeen Earl of, K.T., P.C., 7 Argyll street; & Haddo house, near Methlic, Aberdeenshire
Abergavenny Earl of, Eridge castle, Tunbridge wells, & Berlin manr.Mdstn
Abernethy Mrs. 14 Chester ter. Rgt.'s pk
Abingdon Earl of, 7 Albermarle street, & Wytham abbey, Oxford
Abinger Lord, 4 New st. Spring gardens; & Abinger hall, Dorking, Surrey
Abinger Dow. Lady, 30 Norfolk st. Pk.la
Ablett Wm. Hen. esq. 19 Lit. Moorfields
Abrahall Bennett, esq. 4 Orme square
Abraham Fras. esq. 48 Gerrard st. Islgtn
Abraham Geo. F. esq. 6 Gt. Marlbro' st
Abraham Henry Robert, esq. Mountfield house, Harrow rd.; & 1 Torrington st
Abraham Rt. esq. 32 York ter. Regent's park; & 1 Torrington st. Russell sq
AbrahamsA.esq.11Welling.rd.St.Jn.'swd
Abrahams Samuel, esq. 19 Cambridge ter. Hyde park, & 4 Lincoln's inn flds
AbrahamsSam.B.esq.1Quality ct.Chan.l
Abram George, esq. 39 Southampton row
Abram J.F.esq.1St.George's ter.Kensgtn
Abram Wm. esq. 18 Norfolk st. Strand
Abrams Clairmonte J.esq.13 Beaufoy ter
Abud Richard, esq. 35 Oxford terrace
Abud Wm. T. esq. 3 James st. Clerknwl
Acheson Viscount, M.P. 59 Grosvenor st. & Worlingham hall, Wangford
AckermannMrs.8Glo'ster rd.OldBrmptn
Ackers James, esq. M.P. 2 Blandford sq. & the Heath, near Ludlow
Acklom Mrs. 81 Cambridge ter. Hyde pk
Ackland Sir Thos. Dyke, bart. M.P. Waterloo hotel, 85 Jermyn st.; & Killerton park, Exeter
Ackland Harding, esq. 3 Park pl.Kntn.cr
Ackland Jas. esq. 38 Spring st. Pdngtn
Acland Thomas Dyke, esq. M.P. 12 Queen st. Mayfair; & Holnicote nr. Minehead, Somerset
Acock Thomas, esq. 16 Sussex gardens
Acosta Antonio, esq. Consul General for the Republic of Bolivia, 47 Lime st
Acott Mrs. 1 Beaufoy ter. Edgware rd
A'Court Capt. Edward Henry, R.N., M.P. 41 St. James's place, & Heytesbury, Wiltshire
A'Court Chas. H.W.esq. 41 St.James's pl
Acret Wm. Henry, esq. 47 Torrington sq
Acton Col. Wm. M.P. 36 Jermyn st
Acton Mrs. 7 Cloudesley sq. Islington
Acton Mrs. 62 Euston square
Acton Wm. esq. 46 Queen Anne st
Acworth Nathaniel B. esq. H1, Albany, & 26 Old sq. Lincoln's inn
Adair Rt. hon. Sir Rt. 11 Chesterfield st
Adair Sir Robt. Shafto, bart. 1 George st. St. James'; Aldeburgh, Suffolk; Flixton hall, Harleston, Norfolk; & Ballymena castle, co. Antrim, Ireland
Adair Alex. Shafto, esq. 23 Dover st
Adair Alex. Shafto, esq. 7 Audley sq
Adair Hugh Edwd. esq. 1 George st. St. James's; 15 Lincoln's inn fields; & Flixton hall, Bungay
Adam Mrs. Larkhall rise, Clapham
Adams Sir George, knt. 83 Jermyn st
Adams Alfd. esq. 62 Brook st. Hanov. sq
Adams Arthur Robarts, esq. 1 Mitre court buildings, Temple
Adams Borlase Hill, esq. 11 New sq. Lincoln's inn, & 36 Lincoln's inn fields
Adams Edward Richards, jun. esq. 33 Woburn square, & 2 Old square
Adams Francis, esq. 6 Victoria villas, Avenue road, Regent's park
Adams Fredk.esq. 11Grove pl. Bromptn
Adams George, esq. 4Burton st. Pimlico
AdamsGeorge,esq.40Up.John st.Ftzry.sq
Adams Henry, esq. 11 Radnor pl. Oxford terrace; & 44 Lincoln's inn fields
Adams James, esq. 7 Victoria villas, Avenue road, Regent's park
Adams Henry, esq. 12 Nottinghill sq
Adams Jas. H. esq. 5 Raymond bldgs. Gray's inn
Adams JamesF.esq. 40Up.John st.Fitz.sq
AdamsJohn,S.L.1Serjeants' inn,Chanc.la
Adams John, esq. 9 Bishopsgate within
Adams John, esq. 21 Connaught square
Adams John. esq. 7 Little Abingdon st
Adams Jno.esq.St.John's hl.Wndswth.rd
Adams Jn. jun. esq. 21 Connaught sq. & 1 Serjeants' inn, Chancery lane
Adams John H. esq. 5 Raymond blds
Adams Jsph. H. esq.5 Chandos st.Cvn.sq
Adams Joseph R. esq. 122 Albany st
Adams Miss, 26 Gibson sq. Islington
Adams Miss, 22 Newintn.pl. Kengtn. rd
Adams Miss, 36 Myddelton square
Adams Mrs. 23 Tibberton sq. Islington
Adams Mrs. S. 8 Torrington square
Adams Mrs. 7 Upper Belgrave place
Adams Mrs. 4 Upper Islington terrace
Adams Moses, esq.29 Hart st.Bloomsby
Adams Rt. esq.24 Pembroke sq.Knsgtn
Adams Samuel, esq. 18 Great Coram st
Adams Thos. esq. 11 Allsop ter. New rd
Adams Th. esq. 14 Alfred pl. Bedford sq
Adams T. G. esq. 38 Chester ter. Rgs. pk
Adams Wm.esq.21Fredk. st.Gray'sinnrd
Adams W. esq. 29 Tavistock st. Cov.gdn
Adams Wm. B. esq. 1 Adam st. Adelphi
Adamson C. T. esq.16 Princes st.Leic.sq
Adamson Jas. esq. 24 Lincoln's inn fields
Adamson James, esq. 29 Ely pl. Holborn
Adamson John, M.D. 13 John st. Adelphi
Adamson J. esq. 9 Princes pl. Kenntn.rd
Adamson Matthew, esq. 14 Arlington st
AdamsonT.esq.5Richmnd ter.Canonbury
Adamthwaite J. Allen, esq. 10 Queen sq
Adare Viscount, M.P. 76 Eaton square, & Dunraven castle, Cowbridge
Addams Jesse, D.C.L. 26 Glo'ster place, New road; & 17 College, Doc. com
Addams Rd. esq. 27 York pl. Portman sq
Adderley Charles Bowyer, M.P. Hams hall, Coleshill
Adderley Rd. Boyle, esq.2 Mdl.Scotld.yd
Addington Henry Unwin, esq. 78 Eaton place, & Foreign Office, Downing st
Addis Charles, esq. 10 Gt. Queen st. Westminster; & 21 Old sq. Linc. inn
Addis Mrs. 16 Soley terrace, Pentonville
Addison Chas. G. esq. 2 Inner Temple la
Addison E.esq.1Montagu pl.Montagu sq
Addison Geo. esq. 8 Mecklenburgh sq
Addison John, esq. 17 St. John's wood rd
Addison John, esq. 6 Delahay st.Westm
Addison Joseph, esq. 7 Dean's yd.Westminster; & 1 King's Bench wk.Temple
Addison the Misses, 26 Doughty st
Addison Mrs. 7 Montague st. Russell sq
Addison Richd. esq. 11 Staple inn, Hlbn
Addison Rt. esq. 2 Warw. vil.Harrow rd
Addison T. M.D. 24 New st.Spring grdns
Ade George, esq.6King's rd.Bedford row

Adey Rev. John, 43 Trinity sq. Borough
Adey Chas. Francis, esq. 5 Barnard's inn
Adey Geo. esq. 10 Manchstr. tr. Lvrpl. rd
Adey Goodson, esq. 5 Barnard's inn
Adkins Mrs. 121 Sloane st
Adkins Jas. esq. 1 South ter. Brompton
Adkyns Miss, 6 Halkin tr. Belgrave sq
Adlard Charles, esq. 32 Gibson sq. Islgtn
Adlard James, esq. Stockwell common
Adney Mrs. 6 Gibson square, Islington
Adolphus John Leycester, esq. 18 Montague st. & 3 Harcourt bldgs. Temple
Agar hon. George, 15 Regent st
Agar hon. Mrs. 1 Dean st. Park lane; & Lanhydrock, near Bodmin, Cornwall
Agar Sir Felix, knt. 7 Stratford place; & Georgiana house, Cheltenham
Agar Wm. esq. Carlton chmbrs. 4 Reg. st
Agar W.T. esq. Elm ldg. King's rd. St. Pan
Agassiz Miss, 7 Allsop terrace, New rd
Agatt Henry, esq. 2 Retreat, So. Lmbth
Ager James, esq. Harrow road
Ager Joseph, M.D. 85 Gt. Portland st
Aggas Wm. esq. 6 River tr. nor. City rd
Agasse Jas. L. esq. 83 Newmn. st. Oxf. st
Aglio Augustine, esq. 2 Osnaburgh st
Aglionby Hen. Aglionby, esq. M.P. 5 Brick court, Temple; & Nunnery, nr. Penrith
Agop Monsieur J. second secretary of Turkish embassy, 1 Bryanstone sq
Ahmuty Mrs. 15 Coleshill st
Ahmuty Major Gen. 38 Chesham place
Aiken Wm. esq 5 Mathon pl. Pentonville
Aikin Arthur, esq. 7 Bloomsbury sq
Aikin Chas. A. esq. 1 Albion st. Hyde pk
Aikin Charles R. esq. 7 Bloomsbury sq
Aikin Geo. esq. 10 Cook's ct. Carey st
Aikin Geo. esq. 31 King st. Holborn
Ailesbury Marquis of, K.T. 41 Grosvenor sq.; Tottenham park, Marlborough; Jerveaux abbey, Middleham, near Bedale; & East Sheen, Surrey
Ailsa Marquis of, K.T. 6 Whitehall gardens; St. Margaret's, Isleworth; & Cassilis castle, Maybole, N.B
Aima B. esq. 1 Belmont ter. Wandsw. rd
Ainger Alfred, esq. 7 John st. Bedfd. rw
Ainger N. esq. 19 Sthmptn. st. Bloomsb
Ainsley Saml. J. esq. 14 Euston pl. Nw. rd
Ainsley Sir Rt. bart. 12 Park st. Westm
Ainslie Rev. Rt. Wyclif cot. Morngtn. rd
Ainslie Hen. Walter, esq. 10 Euston sq
Ainsworth Peter, esq. M.P. 14 Green st. Grosvenor sq. & Smithills hall, Bolton
Ainsworth Rev. Thos. 35 Percy st
Aird Miss, 12 Cadogan place
Airey Joseph, esq. 16 Poland st
Airlie Earl of, Carlton club, 94 Pall mall; & Cortachy castle, by Kirriemuir
Aitken John, esq. 30 Up Belgrave place
Aitkens John, esq. 30 Up. Belgrave pl. Pimlico, & 6 Symond's inn, Chancery la
Aiton John T. esq. Kensington palace
Akerman John Yonge, esq. F.S.A. Lewisham, Kent, & Greenwich Rail off. Londn
Albano Benedict, esq. 24 Essex st. Strnd
Albemarle Earl of, P.C. 12 Berkeley sq. & Quidenam hall, Larlingford, Norfk
Albertazzi Madame, 22 Park rd. Rgt.'s pk
Albin Mrs. 38 Essex st. Strand
Albion Club House (Wm. Abraham, secretary), 35 St. James's st
Albrecht Edmund, esq. 26 Dean st. Soho
Albuquerque de Agostinho J. esq. 46 Mornington place, Hampstead road
Albut James, esq. 75 St. John's wd. ter
Alchin Wm. T. esq. 10 Paulton's square, Chelsea, & Guildhall
Alcock Col. 22 Upper Grosvenor st
Alcock Fred. esq. 12 Dorset ter. Clphm. rd
Alcock Jsph. esq. Euston ho. Drumnd. st
Alcock Samuel, esq. 89 Hatton garden
Aldam Wm. jun. esq. M.P. 3 Plowden bldgs. & Warmsworth, near Doncaster
Alder Rev. Robert, 62 Hatton garden
Alder George, esq. Battersea rise
Alder Mrs. 26 Grosvenor place
Aldersey Jph. Stephens, esq. 8 Gower st
Alderson Sir Edward Hall, knt. 9 Park crescent, Regent's park
Alderson Col. Ralph, 78 Oxford terrace
Alderson Rev. W. 2 Chapel pl. Lg. la. Bmsy
Alderson Jackson, esq. 19 Gt. Quebec st
Alderson J. M.D. 36 Charles st. Brkly. sq
Alderson Thos. J. esq. 7 Barnard's inn
Alderton Wm. esq. 14 Paddington green
Aldin Alfred, esq. 8 Page st. Millbank
Aldis Sir Chas. 13 Old Burlington st
Aldis Chas. J. B. M.D. 13 O. Burlngtn. st
Aldous James, esq. 22 Soho square
Aldous Wm. esq. 28 Argyll st. Regt. st
Aldred Richd. esq. 12 Up. Kennington gn
Aldridge John, esq. 1 Upper Woburn pl. & Hall staircase, Inner Temple
Aldridge J. esq. 42 Gt. Russell st. Blmsby
Aldridge Walter Wm. esq. 10 Gray's in. pl
Aldridge W. esq. 27 Chapel st. Grosvnr. pl
Aldridge Wm. esq. 69 Gt. Portland st
Alepson Martin, esq. 34 Woburn place
Alexander Sir Robert, bart. 11 Charles st. Manchester square
Alexander Boyd, esq. 15 Hanover terr
Alexander Chas. esq. 38 Gt. Coram st
Alexander George, esq. 6 Clement's inn
Alexander George, esq. 40 Gower place
Alexander Geo. esq. 9 John st. Adelphi
Alexander George, M.D. 6 Sussex terr
Alexander Hen. esq. 5 Clarendn. pl. H. pk
Alexander Hen. esq. 6 Cork st. Bond st
Alexander Hen. B. esq. 15 Nottinghl. sq
Alexander Henry, esq. & Lady Louisa, 5 Bolton row
Alexander James, esq. 9 Carlton house terrace, & Somer hill, Tunbridge
Alexander James, esq. 33 Lonsdale sq
Alexander James, esq. 12 Nth. Audley st
Alexander Joseph, esq. 15 Myddelton sq
Alexander Lesley, esq. 6 York ter. Regent's pk. & Foyle park, Londonderry
Alexander Miss, 12 Hanover ter. Regent's pk. & Ballochyle, Mauchline, N.B
Alexander Miss, 26 Hornton st. Knsgtn
Alexander Mrs. Genl. 22 Blandford sq
Alexander Mrs. Joss Dupre, 43 Grosvnr. pl. & Stonehouse, Broadstairs, Kent
Alexander Moses, esq. 11 Bury st. City
Alexander Nathl. esq. M.P. 16 New Bond st. & Portglenone house, Belfast
Alexander Robert, esq. 20 Gloucester pl
Alexander Robert Dupre, esq. 36 Cambridge terrace, Edgware road
Alexander Thos. esq. 7 York pl. Prtmn. sq
Alexander Wm. esq. 11 South tr. Alexr. sq
Alexander Wm. J. esq. Q.C. 7 Figtree ct
Alford Viscount, M.P. 23 Belgrave sq
Alfred Club House (Geo. Biggs, sec.), 23 Albemarle st
Alfred Saml. esq. 4 Nottingham terr
Alfred Wm. esq. 3 Henry pl. Up. Knngtn. la
Alger Owen Tickle, esq. 37 Bedford row
Alison S. Scott, esq. 2 Fitzroy st
Alkin Thos. T. esq. 11 Hemus ter. Chelsea
Allan Capt. Rt. 4 Eccleston st. Chester sq
Allan Sir Wm. R.A. 34 King st. Covent gdn
Allan Alexander, esq. 7 Maddox st
Allan Edwd. Thos. esq. 50 Up. Norton st
Allan James, esq. 59 Gibson sq. Islngtn
Allan Jas. Gordon, esq. 2 Hare ct. Temple
Allan John, esq. 23 Milner sq. Islington
Allan Mrs. 40 Clarges st. Piccadilly
Allan T. R. esq. 1 Mitre ct. bdgs. Temple
Allan William, esq. 8 Hanover sq
Allan Wm. esq. 5 Hollywood pl. Lit. Chels
Allanson Mrs. 6 Angel ter. Islington
Allason Thomas, esq. 1 Connaught sq
Allbrit John, esq. 10 Springfield place, Wandsworth road
Allden Wm. esq. 1 Lloyd st. Lloyd sq
Allder Wm. esq. 21A, Northampton sq
Alldred John, esq. 50 Upper Berkeley st
Allen Chas. Pettitt, esq. 78 Hamilton ter. St. John's wood; & 17 Carlisle st. Soho
Allen Rev. Jn. 8 Cavendish rd. St. Jns. wd
Allen David, esq. 24 Compton ter. Islgtn
Allen Edwd. esq. 19 Albion st. Hyde pk
Allen Geo. esq. 12 South st. Grosvnr sq
Allen Henry, esq. 27 Granville sq
Allen Hen. Geo. esq. 24 Old sq. Linc. inn
Allen Hen. Hughes, esq. 27 Granville sq
Allen Hen. R. esq. 37 Baker st. Lloyd sq
Allen Jas. esq. 22 Cloudesley st. Islgtn
Allen Jas. esq. 18 Harpur st. Red Lion sq
Allen Jas. esq. 15 King st. Portman sq
Allen Jas. M. esq. 37 London st. Fitzry. sq
Allen John, esq. Allen's cot. Eaton ter
Allen John, esq. 14 Haverstock hill
Allen John, esq. 14 Bloomsbury sq
Allen John, esq. 58 Coleshill st
Allen John, esq. 9 Elizabeth st. Eaton sq
Allen John, esq. Upper Coleshill st
Allen J. B. esq. 118 Camden road villas
Allen John Wm. esq. 9 Cavendish rd. St. John's wd.; & 17 Carlisle st. Soho sq
Allen John Wm. esq. 12 Colebrooke row
Allen John Wm. esq. 38 Edwardes sq. Knsg
Allen Joshua J. esq. 19 Bartlett's bldngs
Allen Miss, 3 Devonshire place
Allen Misses, 15 Alfred pl. Alexdr. sq
Allen Mrs. 24 Argyll st. Regent st
Allen Mrs. 10 Elm Tree rd. St. John's wd
Allen Mrs. 28 Guilford st. Russell sq
Allen Mrs. 11 Montague pl. Noel st. Isltn
Allen Mrs. 62 Up. Norton st. Fitzroy sq
Allen Mrs. 72 Oxford terrace
Allen Mrs. 4 Park place, Regent's park
Allen Mrs. 45 Porchester ter. Bayswater
Allen Mrs. 34 South bank, Regent's pk
Allen Mrs. 3 South place, Finsbury
Allen Mundeford, esq. 31 Bedford row
Allen M. C. N. esq. Earl's ct. Old Bromptn
Allen Peter, esq. 29 Fredk. st. Grs. inn rd.
Allen Richd. Wm. esq. 28 Dalbyter. Cty. rd
Allen Mr. Serjeant, 4 Serjeants' in. Flt. st
Allen Thos. esq. 7 King's Bench walk
Allen Thos. esq. 24B, Grafton st. Fitzroy sq., & 4 Holmes ter. Kentish town
Allen Thos. esq. 19 Up. Islington ter
Allen Thos. esq. 24 Wharton st
Allen Wm. esq. 9 Albion pl. Hyde pk. sq
Allen Wm. H. esq. 15 Annett's cr. Islngtn
Allen Wm. H. esq. 50 Porchester terrace
Allen W. J. esq. Up. Hamiltonter. St. Jns. w
Allen William Joseph, esq. L1, Albany
Allenby Hy. esq. 14 George st. Adelphi
Allender Geo. esq. 6 Judd pl. east, New rd
Allerton Rd. esq. 36 Norfolk st. Strand
Alley Mrs. 1 Albany terrace, New rd
Alleyne Dr. 27 Gloucester rd. Hyde pk
Allfrey Mrs. 31 Bryanston sq.; & Salehurst, Robertsbridge; & Banstead, Srry
Allfrey Wm. esq. 36 Lincoln's inn fields
Allison Robert, esq. 29 Berners st
Allison Thos. esq. 23 Torrington square
Alliston Charles, esq. 60 Gower st
Alliston John, esq. 38 Russell square
Allix John Peter, esq. M.P. 57 Montague square, & Swaffham, Norfolk
Allnatt Rchd. H. M.D., F.S.A. 4 Prliamnt. st
Allnutt Geo. S. esq. 30 Chancery lane
Allnutt Miss, 19 Claremont ter. Pntnvl
Allom Thos. esq. 14 Hart st. Bloomsbury
Allport T. esq. 4 Thurloe pl. Old Brmptn
Allsop J. esq. 6 Allsop terrace, New rd
Allway Mrs. 86 Ebury st. Pimlico
Almond Wm. esq. 39 Addison road north
Alport Hen. esq. 1 Annett's cr. Islngtn
Alport Mrs. 11 Ely place, Holborn
Alpres Mrs. 9 Crescent pl. Hampstead rd
Alsager T. M. esq. 26 Queen sq. Bloomsby
Alston Sir Charles, bart. 116 Mount st
Alston James, esq. 18 Bryanstone sq
Alston Rowland, esq. 48 Harley st. & Pishiobury, near Sawbridgeworth
Alvanley Lord, Tarporley, Cheshire
Alvarez Jsph. esq. 13 Argyle st. King's cr
Alves Duncan D. esq. 28 Sackville st
Alves John, esq. 1 Sion villa, Chelsea
Alvey John, esq. 9 Chester pl. Kenn. crs

AmaralJ.T. de, Attaché to the Brazilian Legation, 87 Milton st. Dorset square
Amber Thomas esq. 6 Barnsbury park
AmbroseGoddard, esq.45Up.Seymour st
AmbroseThos. H. esq. 89 Chancery la
Amedroz H.F.esq.44 Charlot.st.Fitzy.sq
Ames John, esq.33 Green st.Grosvnr.sq. & Pinlay house, Lyme Regis
Ames Levi, esq. 14 Hereford st. Oxford st.&The Hyde, St. Alban's Hertfrdsh
Amherst Earl, P. C. 66 Grosvenor st. & Knole, Sevenoaks
Amor Mrs. 4 Eaton terrace, Eaton sq
Amory Wm. esq. 37 Devonshire place
Amos William, esq. 2 Lansdowne villas, Notting hill
Amphlett RichardPaul, esq. 32Wimpole & 5 Old square
Amyot Madame, Amyot ho. Lit. Chels
Amyot Rd.G.esq. 17Chester st.Grosv.pl
Amyot Thos.esq.13 James st.Buckng. gt
Amyot Wm. Henry, esq. 3 Carey st
Ancell H. esq. 3 Norfolk cres. Oxford sq
Anconia J. esq. 15 Chester pl. Kenn. crs
Anderdon J. H. esq. 3 Queen st. Mayfair
Anderdon Thos. Oliver, esq. Q.C. 24 Bedford pl. & 9 Old square
Anders John, esq. 13 Wyndham st
AndersonSirJ.E.M.D.11Nw.Burlngtn.st
Anderson Col. John, 3 Hanover terrace
Anderson Rev.Jas.S.M.14Old sq.Lin.inn
Anderson Alex.esq.17York pl.Portmn.sq
AndersonAndw.esq.9Coborn rd.Mile end
Anderson Charles, esq. 37 Gibson sq
Anderson Edmund. esq. 72 Judd st
Anderson Ed. esq.25 Chapl. st.Grsvnr.sq
Anderson Eustace, esq. 15 Lincoln's inn fields, & Blackheath
Anderson George, esq. 7 Hanover st
Anderson George, esq. 234 Maida vale
Anderson George, esq. 21 Manchester st
Anderson Jas. esq. 28 Parliament street, & 11 New sq. Lincoln's inn
Anderson John, esq. 9 Canonbury villas
Anderson Jn. esq. 1 Euston pl. Euston sq
Anderson J. esq. 18 Maida hill, Edgw. rd
Anderson John, esq. 55 Upper Brook st
Anderson J. C. esq. 3 Queen's pl. Kengtn
Anderson J. F. esq, Inr. Temple hall strs
Anderson J. H. esq. 9 Queen pl. Kengtn
AndersonJ.R. esq.9 Blomfld.rd. Maida hl
Anderson Jsph. esq. Holme villa, Rgt.pk
Anderson Julius, esq. 71 Hamilton ter
Anderson M. esq. 3 Lower Phillimore pl
Anderson Miss, 38 Gibson sq. Islington
Anderson Miss, 46 Southampton row
Anderson Mrs. 2 Beaufoy ter. Edgwr.rd
Anderson Mrs. 38 Claremont square
Anderson Mrs. 36 Hans pl. Sloane st
Anderson Mrs. 4 Smith st. Chelsea
Anderson Mrs. 12 Trevor sq. Knghtsbdg
Anderson R. J. esq.17 Park rd. Rgt.'s pk
Anderson Samuel, esq. 10 Blenheim pl. St. John's wood
Anderson Saml. esq. 55 Upper Brook st
Anderson ThomasPaterson, esq.45Harewood sq. & 2 Adelphi terrace
Anderson Wm. esq. 18 Brompton row
AndersonW.esq.15Cavndsh.rd.St Jns.wd
Anderson Wm. esq.12Chadwell st.Pentvl
AndersonWm. esq.22Up.Seymour st. wst
Anderson Wm. esq. 132 Sloane st
Anderson W.H.esq.5Aberdn.pl.Maida hl
Anderton James, esq. 20 New Bridge st
Andoe Wm. esq. 10 Paddington green
Andover Viscountess, 86 Harley st. & Mintern house, Dorchester
André Jas. P. sen. esq. 5 York pl. City rd
André Jas. Peter, jun.esq.25York pl.Cy.rd
André Peter, esq. 70 Oxford ter. Edg. rd
André Wm. esq. 28 Canonbury villas
AndrewAlexr. esq. 26 Sussex pl. Knsngtn
Andrew Mrs. 2 Wellington st. Islington
AndrewsRev.GerardT.M.A.8Sackville st
Andrews Biggs, esq. Q.C. 36 Hertford st Mayfair, & 4 King's Bench walk, Tem
AndrewsGeorge, esq.30 York pl. City rd
Andrews Mrs. 45 Albion st. Hyde park
Andrews Mrs. 19 Bayswater terrace
Andrews Mrs. 80 Cadogan place
Andrews Mrs. 28 Devonshire st
Andrews Mrs. 1Strahan ter. Liverpool rd
Andrews Mrs. 47 Upper Bedford place
Andrews Mrs. 6 Weymouth st
Andrews Mrs. 4 Wilton st. Grosvenor pl.
Andrews Richard, esq. 96 Crawford st
Andrews Richd. esq. 119 Gt. Russell st
Andrews Richard, esq. 1 South end cottage, Petersburg place, Bayswater
Andrews Saml. esq. 8 Low. Grosvnor pl
Andrews Wm. esq. 1 Albion vils. Lpool.rd
AndrewsWm. esq.2Suffolk pl. Pall mall e
Angel Jsph. esq. 7 Blomfield rd. Edgw.rd
Angell Alfred, esq. 23 Lincoln's inn flds
Angell Joseph, esq. 25 Grove end road
AngellR.M.B.esq.10Cobrg.pl.UpKen.la
Angell Saml. esq. 18 Gower st. Bedford square, & 5 Hatton garden
Angell Wm.Brown, esq. 32 Grove end rd
Angelo Anthony Edwd. esq. 5 Fitzroy sq
Angelo Hen. esq. 16 Upper Wimpole st
Angelo Henry Charles, esq. 10 Bolton row, & 32 St. James st
AngeloMrs.Geo.20Southbank,Regt.'spk
Anger F.J.esq. 26 Chester pl. Kennton. cr
Angerstein Lieut. Col. 70 Jermyn st
Anglesea Marquis of, K.G, G.C B, P.C. Uxbridge house, 1 Old Burlington st., & Beaudesert park, Litchfield; & Plas Newydd, Anglesea
Anglis Wm.esq.7 Richmnd.tr.Cannbry sq
Angus Alexander, esq. 66 Frith st. Soho
Annable John, esq. Mornington road
Annandale Wm. esq. 73 Piccadilly
Annesley Sir James, M.D. 6H, Albany
Annesley Hon. Mrs. 26 Somerset st
AnnesleyGeorge, esq.27 Dorsetplace, Dorset sq. & 64 Lincoln's inn fields
Annesley Mrs. 89 Eaton square
Annett James, esq.2 Chester ter. Eaton sq
Anns Thomas, esq. 8 Pelham rd. Brmpton
Ansall Abrm.esq. 55 Burton st. Brtn. cr
Ansdale Geo. esq. 39 Argyle st. King's cr
Ansell Geo. esq. Blmnt. cot. Morngtn.rd
Ansell Josiah, esq. 3 Mount st
Ansell Miss Susan, 74 Harley st
Ansley Benjamin, esq. 32 Alpha road
Anson Gen.Sir Geo.G.C.B., 2Up.Brook st
Anson Gen.Sir Wm. 32 Devonshire place
Anson Hon. Col. Geo. M.P. 25 Hill st. Berkeley sq. & Newmarket
Anson G. E. esq. & Hon. Mrs. 58 Eaton place
Anstead Wm. esq. 78 Park st. Grosvnr.sq
Ansted Jn.esq. 2Portland pl. Clapham rd
Anstey Geo.esq. 5 Ulster ter. Regnt.'s pk
Anstey Thos. C. esq. 54 Chancery lane
Anstey Wm. Jekyll, esq. 56 Bromptn.cr
Anthony John, esq. 19 Annett's cr. Islgtn
Anthony Mrs. 2 Albion cot. Liverpool rd
Anstruther Lady, 1 Chapel st. Grosv. pl
Anthony John H. esq. 45 Gt. Ormond st
Anton James, esq. 18 Fludyer st
Antrim Earl of, 33 Eaton place
Antrobus Sir Edmnd. bt. 146 Piccadilly; & Lower Cheam, Epsom, Surrey; & Amesbury abbey, Salisbury
Antrobus Edmund, esq. M.P. 146 Piccadilly; & Cheam, Surrey
Antrobus Edmund, esq. Bath lodge, Trafalgar square, Queen's elms
Apel Henry, esq. 5 College st. Chelsea
Aplin Benjamin, esq. 5 Furnival's inn, & Chacombe priory, Banbury, Oxon
Apperley Misses, 19 Harleyford place
Apple John D. esq. 16 Stoke Newngtn.gr
Appleby H. esq. 2 Eldon pl. Kenngtn.la
Appleford Fredk. esq. 30 Cloudesley sq
Applegate Mrs. 52 Newman st. Oxford st
Appleton James, esq. 5 Harrington st.
Appleton Jas. Metcalfe, esq. 45Curzon st
Appleyard Geo. esq. 23 Westbourne pl
AppleyardChas.esq.3York st. Portmn.sq. & 1 New square, Lincoln's inn
Appleyard Mrs. 32 Albion st. Hyde pk
Appleyard Rd. S. esq. 26 Bloomsbury sq
Arabin Mrs. 16 Burton st. Burton crsct
ArberThos. A.esq. 29Brook st.Grosvnr.sq
Arbouin James, esq. 3 Brunswick square
Arbuthnot Visct. Carlton club, 94 Pall mall, & Arbuthnot house, Kincardine
Arbuthnot Lt.Gen. Sir Rd. 16 Grosvnr st
Arbuthnot Hon. Lieut.Gen.Hugh, K.C.B. M.P. H5, Albany & Hatton, Bervie, Kincardineshire
Arbuthnot Henry, esq. & Lady Charlotte, 15 Chester st. Grosvenor place
Arbuthnot Geo. esq. 4 St. George's terr
Arbuthnot Geo. esq. 25 Upper Wimpole st. & Elderslie lodge, Dorking
Arbuthnot John, esq. 25 Up. Wimpole st
Arcedeckne Andrew, esq. 1 Grosvenor sq. & Glevering hall, nr. Wickham market
Archbold Edwd. C. esq. 161 New Bond st
Archbold John Fk. esq. 17Park st. Westminster, & 4 King's Bench wk. Temple
Archbold Rt. esq. M.P. Cox's hotel, & Davidstown, near Castle Dermot
ArchbuttSaml.esq. 4Oakley sq. King's rd
Archbutt Samuel, jun. esq. 9 Sloane sq
Archdall Capt.Mervyn, M.P. A12, Albany & Castle Archdall, Fermanagh
Archer Rev Thomas, 18 Hans place
Archer A. esq. 31 Liverpool st. King's cr
Archer F. esq. 3 Chapel st. Grosvenor pl
Archer F.S.esq. 18 Tavistock st. Cov.gdn
Archer Geo. esq. 17 Harpur st. Red Li.sq
Archer H. G. esq. 8 King's Bench walk
Archer John, esq. 46 Clarendon st
Archer J. esq. 17 Grove pl. Lisson grove
Archer Thomas, esq. 26 Up. Belgrave pl
Archer Wm.esq. 1Montagu st. Portmn.sq
Archibald Thos. D. esq. 5 Torrington sq. & 12 Paper buildings, Temple
Arco Marques del, attaché to the Spanish Legation, 30 Weymouth st
Arden Dow. Lady, 26 St. James's pl.; & Nork house, Surrey; & Lohort castle, Cork
Arden Joseph, esq. 27 Cavendish square, & Rickmansworth park
Arden Richard Edward, esq. 4 Bedford square, & 5 Gray's inn square
Argall Henry Eva, esq. 28 Lloyd square
Argles Frank A. esq. 56 Lincoln's inn flds
Argyle Duke of, 3 Connaught pl. west; & Inverary castle, Inverary, Argyllshire; & Roseneath & Ardencaple castles, Helensburgh, Dumbartonshire
Argles Miss, 41 Waymouth st. Prtld. pl
Ariell S. esq. 15 Maiden la. Cov. garden
Arkwright George, M.P. D2, Albany, & Sutton hall, Chesterfield
Arlington Mrs. 7A, Foley place
Armagh Archbishop of, 30 Charles st. St. James's, & Armagh, Ireland
Armfield G. esq. 15 Princes st. Blackfrs
Armitage Edw. esq. 14 George st. Adlphi
Armour Henry, esq. 20 Old Cavendish st
Armson Francis, esq. 22 Orchard st
Armstead W. esq. 35 Belitha vls. Busby
Armstrong Sir Andrew, bart. M.P. Reform club, 104 Pall mall
Armstrong Capt. 2 Ulster ter. Rgnt's.pk
Armstrong Benjn. John, esq. 2 Southwick cresnt. & Southall green, Middx
Armstrong Charles, esq. 1 Percy circus
Armstrong Chr. esq. 7 Tyndale pl. Islgtn
Armstrong Geo. H. esq. 10 York st. St. James's
Armstrong John E. esq. 102 Gloster pl
Armstrong Miss, 13 New Burlington st
Armstrong Miss, Up. Kennington. green
Armstrong Mrs. 46 Gower st. Bedfd. sq
Armstrong Mrs. 18 Grove ter. St.Jn's.wd
Armstrong Mrs. 9 Manor ter. King's rd
Armstrong Mrs. 1 Pelham cres. Bromptn
Armstrong Mrs. 6 Stanley ter. King's r

Armstrong Mrs. 45 Norland sq. Kensgtn
Armstrong Rd. Baynes, esq. 8 Staple inn
Armstrong Robt. esq. 10 Vauxhall pl
Armstrong Robert Baynes, esq. Q.C. 2 Cloisters, Temple
Armstrong Wm. esq. 11 Claremont pl. New road
Armstrong Wm. M. esq. 38 Red lion sq
Armstrong Wm. Jones, esq. 4 Elm ct
Army & Navy Club House (Thomas Walcott, sec.), 20 James's square
Armytage Sir George, 27 Cambridge sq.; & Kirklees park, Dewsbury
Armytage Lieut. Col. 8 Hyde park st
Arnaud Hen. esq. 6 Queen's hd. la. Islgtn
Arnaud Mrs. 12 York buildings, New rd
Arnell Mrs. 35 Perceval st. Clerkenwell
Arney George Alfred, esq. 35 Foley pl.; & 126 Chancery lane
Arney Hector Wm. esq. 34 George st. Hanover square,& the Close,Salisbury
Arnold Aug. Walter, esq. 31 Golden sq
ArnoldJh.H.esq.7Warwk.vils.Harrowrd
Arnold Mrs. 11 Alpha road, Rgt's. pk
Arnold Mrs. 22 Michael's pl. Brompton
Arnold Mrs. 2 Up. Glo'ster st. Dorset sq
Arnold Thos. Jas. esq. 12 Serjeants' inn
Arnott Jas. M. esq. 2 New Burlington st
Arnott Neil, M.D. 38 Bedford square
ArnouldJsph. esq. 10 Farrar's buildings
ArnouldJsph.esq. 18 Victoria sq.Pimlico
ArpthorpWm. esq. 3 Princes st.Le'str.sq
Arrow Miss, 16 Millman st.Bedford row
Arrowsmith C. esq. 25 Burton crescent
ArrowsmithC. jun.esq. 40 Devonshire st
Arrowsmith G. esq. 11 Up. Islington ter
Arrowsmith Miss, 6 Belgrave terrace
Arrowsmith Miss, 21 Up. Belgrave pl
Arrowsmith Mrs. 24 Burton crescent
Arthur's Club House (James Milner, sec.), 69 St. James's st
Arthy Mrs. 19 Gloucesterroad, Hyde pk
Arundel & Surrey Earl, M.P. 11 Carlton house terrace
Arundel Rev. J. 5 Clarence pl.Claphm.rd
ArundellLord (of Wardour),Union club; & Wardour castle, Shaftesbury
Arundell Dowager Lady, 17 Dover st
Arundell Hon. Henry, 17 Dover st
Arundell Chas. Frans. esq. 3 Cork st
Arundel J. esq. 1 Binfield pl. Clpham.rd
Arundell W. A. H. esq. Mivart's hotel, 44 Brook st. & Lifton park, near Exeter
AscherRev.Simon, 5 Bury st.St.Mary ax
Ash Alfred, esq. 20 Judd pl.west,New rd
Ash C. esq. 3 Beaufoy ter.Edgware road
Ash Geo. esq. 15 Gt. Marlborough st
Ash Geo.S. esq. 11 Albertter.St.Jn's.wd
Ash Matthew, esq. 17 Gt. Ormond st
Ash Mrs. 12 Somerset st. Portman sq
Ash Richd.Holland, esq. 6 Gray's inn sq
Ashbee Mrs. 6 Taunton pl. Regent's pk
Ashburner John, M.D. 55 Wimpole st
AshburnhamEarl, 30 Up. Grosvenor st. & Ashburnham place, Battle, Sussex
AshburnhamDow.Countess,83Eaton sq. &Southwood hou. St.Lawrence, Rmsg
AshburnhamLadyTheodosia,83Eaton sq. &Southwood hou.St.Lawrence,Ram sg
Ashburnham Ladies, 20 Up.Grosvnr. st. & Richmond, Surrey
Ashburnham Hon. Charles, 54 Eaton pl
AshburtonLordP.C. Bath house, 82 Piccadilly, & the Grange, Alresford, & Red hall, Ross
Ashdown Francis, esq. 14 Everett st
AshdownWm.esq.7 Hanover cots.Reg.pk
AsheRev.J.P. 7 Albert ter. Knightsbdge
Ashe Lovat, esq. 15 Petersburgh place
AshenhurstJ.T.esq.41 Up.John st.Fitz.sq
AshfieldEdmundWodley,esq.7Staple inn
Ashford Edmund, esq. 81 Cadogan pl
Ashford Mrs. 2 Brunswick pl. City rd
Ashford Mrs. 70 St. John's wood ter
Ashley Lord, M.P. 49 Up. Brook st. & St. Giles's, near Cranbourne, Dorset
Ashley hon. JohnAnthony, 17 Up.Brook st: & 3 New sq. Lincoln's inn
Ashley hon. Mrs.JohnA. 17 Up.Brook st
Ashley hon. Wm. Stable yd. St. James's, & St. Katherine's lodge, Regent's park
AshleyChas. esq. 7 Dean's pl. so. Lmbth
Ashley James, esq. 3 Gloucester place, New road, & 14 Craven st. Strand
Ashley-Cooper hon. A. H. M.P. Carlton club, & St. Leonard's dale, Windsor
Ashlin Mrs. 2 Southampton pl.Euston sq
AshlingGeo. esq. 68 Oxford ter.Edgw.rd
Ashly Mrs. 47 George st. Euston sq
Ashmore James, esq. 37 Up. Bedford pl. & 3 King's Bench walk,Temple
AshmoreJ. esq. 4 Powell st.w.Goswell rd
Ashmore Thomas, esq. 41 St. James's st
AshmoreW.esq.48Stanhope st.Hmpst.rd
Ashton Henry, esq. 50 Brook st
Ashton Henry, esq. 92 Piccadilly
Ashton Joseph, esq. 59 Up. Stamford st
Ashton John, esq. 10 Up. Barnsbury st
Ashton Mrs. 10 Glo'ster road, Brompton
Ashton Mrs. 6 Old Quebec st. Portmn.sq
AshtonMrs.Sarah, 8 Down st.Piccadilly
Ashton Richard, esq. 34 Burton st
Ashton Rob. sen. esq. 2 Pelham crescent
Ashton Rt. John, esq. 2 Pelham crescent
Ashwell Samuel, M.D. 16 Grafton st
Ashworth F. H. esq. 1Paper bgs. Temple
Ashworth Miss, 36 Chester ter.Regt's.pk
Askew Mrs. 7 Wimpole st
Asling Chas. esq. 37 Allsop ter. New rd
Aspin Jhspht. esq. 24 Stoke Nwngtn. gr
Aspinall John B. esq. 11 Paper buildgs
Aspinwall Col. consul general United States, 1 Bishopsgate churchyard
Aspland A.S.esq. 4Lamb building,Tmpl
Asprey Chas. esq. 46 Markham sq. Chels
Asprey Frederick, esq. 6 Furnival's inn
Aspull Wm. esq. 1 Alfred pl. Bedford sq
Asquith Miss, 27 Oxendon st. Haymrkt
Aste Mrs. 24 Albion ter. Wandsworth rd
Astell Samuel, esq. 9 Bentinck st
Astell Wm. esq. M.P. 51 Old Broad st.; & Everton house, Biggleswade
Astley Lady, 7 Cavendish square
Aston Sir Arthur, bart. 44 Brook st
Aston G. esq.7 Dorset pl.nth.Claphm.rd
Aston Hy. esq. Springfield ho. Wndswth
Aston Mrs. 43 Guilford st. Russell sq
Aston Mrs. 36 South bank, Regent's pk
Aston Thomas, esq. 43 Guilford st
Atcherley David Francis, S.L., F.R.S., 52 Bedford sq.; & Cymman, near Wrexham; & Marton hall, near Shrewsbury
Atchison George, esq. 78 Norton st
Athenæum Club House (Edw. Magrath, sec.), 107 Pall mall
Atherley Mat. esq. 3 Lloyd st. Lloyd sq
Atherly John, esq. 3 Lloyd st
Atherstone Edwin, esq. 7Union pl.Nw.rd
Atherton Miss, 12 Great James st
Atherton Wm. esq. 2 Brick ct. Temple
Atherton Wm. esq. 28 Woburn place
Atholl Duke of, Atholl house, Blair Atholl & Dunkeld
Atkin John H. esq. 30 Cursitor st
Atkin Mrs.&Misses,15Glo'ster rd.Bmptn
AtkinsAbrm. esq. 4 Edwardes pl.Knsing
Atkins Fred. esq.2 Highfield villas,Camden town; & 12 Serjeants' inn,Fleet st
Atkins George, esq. 7 Thurloe square
Atkins Geo. esq.1 Vimiera, Wandswh. rd
Atkins George J. esq. 21 Bruton st
Atkins Miss,Finchley ho. Finchly.Nw.rd
Atkins Mrs. 38 Allsop terrace, New rd
Atkins Rd. 9 Annett's cres. Islington
Atkins Rd. esq. 21 King st. Portman sq
Atkins Saml. E. esq. 21 Artillery pl. west
Atkinson Jasper Sir, 24 Portman sq
Atkinson Francis, esq. 3 Endsleigh st
Atkinson George, esq. 37 Gordon square
Atkinson Geo. esq. 1 Inner Temple lane
Atkinson Hen. esq. 7 Belgrave terrace
Atkinson Hen.Geo.esq. 18Up.Glo'ster pl
Atkinson H.J.esq.2 Bedfd.ter.Claphm.ri
Atkinson Henry T.esq.1 Pump ct.Temple
Atkinson James, esq. 5 Duke st. Westm
Atkinson John, esq. 10 Camden cottages, Camden New town
Atkinson Jonas, esq. 5 Park ter. Highby
Atkinson Miss, 31 Russell square
Atkinson Misses, 8 York terrace
Atkinson Mrs. 3 Binfield pl. Clapham rd
Atkinson Mrs. 2 King's parade, Chelsea
Atkinson Mrs. 3 Park village east
Atkinson Mrs. Porters pl. Holloway
Atkinson Mrs. 5 Soley ter. Pentonville
Atkinson Rd. H. esq. 27 Carey st.&Blkth
Atkinson Rt. esq. 1 Sussex cotts.Cam.tn
Atkinson Rt. M. esq. 14 Soley terrace
Atkinson Saml. esq. 5 New Ormond st
Atkinson Sol. esq. 12 Warwick ct. Hlbn
Atkinson Thos. esq. 8Derby st.Gra.in.rd
AtkinsonWm.esq.35Cheyne wk.Chelsea
AtkinsonWm. esq. 16 Doughty st
AtkinsonWm.esq.32Gordon st.Gordon sq
Atkinson Wm. esq. 31 Great Alie st
Atkinson Wm. esq. 38 Up. Baker st
Atkyns Alfred, 2 Brunswick pl. City rd
Atkyns Miss, 37 Eaton place
Attenborough George, esq. 24 Kenton st
Attfield Rd. esq. 19 Canterbury villas
Atto John, esq. 67 Seymour place
Attree Thomas Augustus, esq. 15 St. James's square, & 62 Chancery lane
Attree Wm. W. esq. 1 Figtree ct. Temple
Attwater Wm. esq. 56 Great Portland st
AttwatersWm.esq.3Beaufort ter.w.Chel
Attwood Benjn. esq. 24 New Bridge st
AttwoodEdwardM.esq.3 Old sq.Linc.inn
Attwood Jas.esq.1 Acacia gds. St. Jns.wd
Attwood Jas.Hen. esq.13 Up. Seymour st
Attwood John, M.P. 25 Park lane, & Highlands park, Chelmsford
Attwood Matthias, M.P. 27 Gracechurch st. & Streatham park
Attwood Matthias Wolverley, esq. 27 Gracechurch st. & Streatham park
Attwood Miss, 17 Brompton row
Attwood Mrs. 7 Lower Grosvenor place
Atty George, esq. 3 Garden ct. Temple
Atwell Joseph, esq. 23 Wilmington sq
Auber Hen. P.esq. 21 Lincoln's inn fields
Aubertin PaulE.esq.60York ter.Rgt's.pk
Aubusson Chas. Wm. esq. 8 Portland rd
Aubrey Sir Thomas Digby, 16 Green st
Auckland, Earl of, G.C.B., P.C. Eldon lodge, Kensington gore
Audley Lord, Sandridge, Chippenham
Auldjo John, esq. Noel ho. Kensingtn.rd
Auldjo Mrs. 26A, Bryanstone square
AuldjoT.R.esq.1 Rutlnd.gate,Knghstbdg
Auriol Rev. Edward, 8 Guilford st
Auriol Miss, 67 Mount st. Berkeley sq
Aust Mrs. 68 Guilford st. Russell sq
Austen Ben. esq. 6 Montague place
Austen Geo. esq. 4 Inner Temple lane
Austen Hy. E. esq. 7 New sq. Linc. inn
AustenWm. esq. 64 Guildford st
Austen Wm. esq. 14 Prospect place, Wandsworth road
Austin Capt. R.N. 10 Alex. sq. Brompton
Austin Charles, esq. 2 Plowden bldgs
Austin G. esq. 16 New Dorst. pl.Clpm.rd
Austin Hy.D.esq.28Winchestr.rw.Nw.rd
Austin Mrs. 36 Gt. James st. Bedford rw
Austin R.W. esq.10Popham tr.Tibrtn.sq
Austin Wm. esq.3 Low. Kennington lane
Austin Wm. Hy. esq. 31 St. Martin's st
Austwick H. esq. Larkhall rise, Clphm
Aveling Frederick, esq. Harrow road
Axford John, esq. 8 Vincent ter. City rd
Ayala Don Rafael de, secretary to the Legation of New Granada, 39 Upper Baker st
Ayers Chas. esq. 8 John st. Berkeley sq
Ayers John, esq. 19 Grosvenor st. west
Ayers Wm. esq. 26 Grafton pl. Euston sq
Ayling James, esq. 7 Westbourn place

Aylesford Earl, 50 Grosvenor st.; & Packington hall, Coventry; & Aylesford, Maidstone
Aylmer General Lord, 15 Eaton square, & Batchacre park, Staffordshire
Aylmer Geo.Wm. esq. 47 Up.Grosvnr.st
Aynsley Joseph B. esq. 4 Noel st. Isltn
Ayres Abrhm. esq. 5 Bartholomew close
Ayres Hen. N.esq.Grove rd. St.John's wd
Ayres Mrs. 37 Jermyn st. St. James's
AyresStephn.esq.12N.Dorset pl.Clpm.rd
Ayrton Edward N.esq.19Old sq.Linc.inn
Ayrton Fredk. esq. 3 Garden ct. Temple
Ayrton William, esq. 39 Dorset square
Ayrton Wm. Scrope, esq. 39 Dorset sq. & Court of Review Registrar's office, Quality court
Ayscough Thos. esq. 4 Raymond bldgs
Aysh Mrs. 5 Park pl. Kennington cross

BABBAGE Charles,esq.F.R.S.1Dorsetst
Baber John, esq. 1 South pl. Knightsbdg
Babington Col.John,2 Glo'ster rd.Reg.pk
Babington Benj. esq. 23 Old sq. Linc. inn
Babington B.G. M.D. 31 Geo. st. Han. sq
Babington Mrs. 3 Addison tr. Knsgtn
Babington Mrs. Wm. 15 Montagu sq
Bacchus Mrs. 50 Oxford terrace
Bach A. esq. 10 Duke st. St. James's
Bachhoffner Wm.esq.28 King st.Holborn
Back Charles, esq. 8 Gray's inn square
Backhouse John, esq. 28 Hans place
Bacon Sir Edmund, bart. 85 Jermyn st
Bacon Charles, esq. 52 Eaton square
Bacon Edmund, esq. 85 Jermyn st
Bacon Frederick, esq. Haverstock hill
Bacon Hy. esq. 2 Stone bldgs. Linc. inn
Bacon J. esq. 36 Bedford pl. & 10 New sq
Bacon Jas. esq. 18 Polygon, Somers tn
Bacon John, esq. 17 Newman st
Bacon John, esq. 25 Rodney st. Pntnvil
Bacon Joshua B. esq. 9 Regent square
Bacon Miss, 1 Bedford row, Clapham rise
Bacon S. esq. 41 Frederic pl. Hmpstd. rd
Bacon Thomas, esq. 26 Great Coram st
Bacon Thomas,esq.18 South st.Grosvn.sq
Bacot J. esq. 4 Portugal st. Grosvenor sq
Bacot Mrs. 29 Portland ter. Regt's.park
Badcock Jsph. esq. 32 Gerrard st. Islgtn
Badcock Wm. esq. 20 Gibson sq. Islingtn
BaddeleyRd.Mumford,esq.5 Chancery la
Baddeley Wm. esq. 29 Alfred st. Islngtn
Badeley E. esq. 3 Paper bldgs. Temple
Badenoch Jas. esq. 16 Cloudesley st
Badger Albert,esq.21 York pl. Fulhm. rd
Badger John,esq.12 Melcombe pl. Dor.sq
Badger Miss M. A. 41 Craven st. Strand
Badham Geo. esq. 4 Verulam buildings
Badillo J. de N.esq. Brunswk. pl.City rd
Bagg Wm. esq. 63 Gower st
Baggallay John, esq. 23 Tavistock sq
Baggallay Rd. esq.11New sq. Lncln. inn
Bagge Richard, esq. Cavendish hotel, 81 Jermyn st. & Gaywood hall, nr. Lynn
Bagge William, esq. M.P. Carlton club; & Stradset hall, near Downham
Baggett John, esq. 27 Tonbridge st. New road
Bagley Wm. esq. 5 Figtree ct. Temple
Bagot Lord, Blithfield house, Rugeley; & Poole park, Ruthin
Bagot hon. Wm. M.P. 23 St. James's sq. & Poole park, Ruthin
Bagot Major, 34 Eaton square
Bagot Mrs. 15 Chapel st. Grosvenor pl
Bagshaw John, esq. 17 Gloucester pl. Portman square; & Harwich, Essex
Bagshaw J. R. esq. 9 York pl. Portman square
Bagshawe Hen. Ridgard, esq. 4 Lamb's Conduit place, & 2 New sq. Linc. inn
Bagster Hen. M. esq. 51 Doughty st
Bagster Wm. esq. 17 Compton st. east
Bague Capt. Geo. R.N. 119 Sloane st
Bague Chas. esq. 19 Coleshill st. Pimlico
Baguley J.E, esq.22 Charlot. st.Bedfd.sq

Bailes Mrs. 5 Wellington ter. Clphm. rise
Bailey Chas. esq. 5 Stratford place
Bailey Edward, esq. 14 Mount st
Bailey Edward S. esq. 5 Berners st
Bailey Fred. esq. 1 Cloisters, Temple
Bailey Geo. esq. 46 Burton st
Bailey Geo. esq. 13 Lincoln's inn fields
Bailey Hen.E.esq.6 King's rd.Bedford rw
Bailey James, esq. 9 Highbury park
Bailey James, esq. 27 Paddington green
Bailey John, esq. 8 Barnard's inn
Bailey Jno. esq. 3 Wellington st. Islgtn
Bailey Joseph, esq. M.P. 26 Belgrave sq. & Glanusk park, Crickhowell
Bailey Joseph, jun. esq. M.P. 26 Belgrave sq. & Easton court, Tenbury
Bailey Mrs. 20 Princes st. Hanover sq
Bailey Mrs. 11 Sidmouth st.Gray's inn rd
Bailey Mrs. John, 35 Wellclose square
Bailey Wm. esq. 5 Stratford place
Bailie John, esq. 26 Connaught square
Baillie Col. H. D. M.P. 34 Mortimer st. & Redcastle Beauly, & Tarradale,N.B
Baillie Lt. Col. 33 Easbourne terrace
Baillie David, esq. 14 Belgrave square; & Hill park, Sevenoaks, Kent
Baillie Hamilton E. esq. 80 Glo'ster pl
Baillie Henry James, esq.M.P.9 Lowndes st.; Tarradale,Ross-shire; & Redcastle Beauly, Inverness-shire
Baillie Jas. esq. 20 Whitehead's grove
Baillie James Evan, esq. 1 Seamore pl. & Redland court, Bristol
Baillie Mrs.E.S. 1 Albion pl. Hyde park
Baillie Mrs. 33 Cavendish square
Baillie Wm. esq. M.P. Carlton club, Pall mall, & Polkemmet, Linlithgowsh
Baillie Wm. Hunter, esq. 33 Cavendish sq. & Duntisbourne, Cirencester
Baily A. esq.4Cumberland pl.Regnt's.pk
Baily Edw. Hodges, esq.R.A.10Percy st
Baily John, jun. esq. 19 Woburn square, & 8 New square, Lincoln's inn
Baily John, sen.esq. 1 Blandford square
Baily Miss, 37 Tavistock place
Bain Alex. esq. 1 Stone bldgs.Lincs. inn
Bain Alex. esq. 35 Northumberland st
Bain Edward Sandys, esq. 12 Chesham place, & 1 Tanfield court, Temple
Bain Henry, esq. 1 Cloisters, Temple
Bainbridge Geo. Mash, esq. Stable yd
Bainbridge Henry, esq. 54 Grosvenor st
Bainbridge JohnN.M.D.86St.Martin's la
Bainbridge Joseph, esq. 22 St.James' st
Bainbridge Mrs. 58 Walcot place east
Baines Fred. W. esq. 16 Hemus ter.Chels
Baines Mat. Talbot, esq. Q.C.2 Tanfld.ct
Baines Robt. esq. 33 Wharton st
Baines Robt. Henry,esq.13Gray's inn sq
Baines Thomas, esq. 15 Thayer st
Baird James, esq.9Leigh st.Red Lion sq
Baird Wm. esq. M.P. 52 Chester square, & Gartsherrie, Lanarkshire
Baker Sir Edward, bart.44St.James's pl
Baker Sir George, bart. 26 Brook st. & Laventor, Totness, Devon
Baker Dowager Lady, 42 Wilton cresct
Baker Col. E. 6 Old Cavendish st. & Salisbury, Wilts
Baker Capt. John V.48 Devonshire st
BakerRev.Wm.Rd.87St.John's wood ter
Baker C.esq.29Harleyford pl.Kenn. com
Baker Charles, esq. 17 Endsleigh st. & 52 Lincoln's inn fields
Baker Charles, esq. 8 Ladbroke villas
Baker Chas. esq.3 Wells st.Gray's inn rd
Baker Edward, esq.50 Walcot place east
Baker Emanuel, esq. 13 Bulstrode st
Baker Frank, esq. 37 Clarges st. Piccad
Baker George, esq. 13 Russell square
Baker George, esq. 3 Regent tr. Chelsea
Baker George Leeke, esq. 1 Hyde park square, & 52 Lincoln's inn fields
Baker Henry, esq. 11 Upper Gower st
Baker Henry S. esq.8 Titchfield terrace, Regent's pk. & 4 Old sq. Lincoln's inn

Baker James, esq. 3 Dalby terr. City rd
Baker James, esq. 39 Mount st
Baker Jn.esq.12 Holloway pl. Holloway
Baker Jn. esq. 52 Park st. Grosvnor. sq
Baker Jsph. esq. 76 Ebury st. Pimlico
Baker Jsph. 15 Westbourne st. Hyde pk
Baker M. B. esq. 4 Albert st. Victoria sq
Baker Mrs. Col. Clontarf lo. Pancras va
Baker Mrs. 25 Alfred st. Bedford sq
Baker Mrs. 2 St. Ann's terr. St. Jn's. wd
Baker Mrs. 69 George st. Euston sq
Baker Mrs. 35 Great St. Helen's
Baker Mrs. 9 King square, Goswell rd
Baker Mrs. 48 Portland place; & Orsett hall, Gray's, Essex
Baker Mrs. 9 Walton place, Brompton
Baker Miss, 20 Charles st. Westbrne.ter
Baker Miss, 9 George st. Hanover sq
Baker Philip, esq. 22 Euston sq. New rd
Baker Rd. G.esq.Earl's ct.OldBrompton
Baker Thos. esq. 13 Bruton st. Bond st
Baker Thos.esq.29 Hunter st.Brnswk. sq
Baker Thos.Eld, esq. 51 Burton crescent
Baker Thos. Hen. esq. 29Spring gardens
BakerT.H.esq.6 Bedford pl.Hmpstead. rd
Baker Wm. esq. 13 Canonbury villas
BakerWm. esq.2Harrington st.Hpstd.rd
Baker Wm. esq. 13Porchester pl.Edg.rd
Baker Wm. Austin, esq. 12 Spencer st
Balcarras Earl of, 21 Berkeley square; & Haigh hall, Wigan
Balderson Abrhm. Thos.esq. 11 Poland st
Balderson Mrs. 24 Manchester st
Baldock Edwd. H. esq. 5 Hyde park pl
Baldwin Capt. 4 Rich terr.OldBrompton
Baldwin Benjamin, esq. 27 Rathbone pl
Baldwin Chas. esq. 29 Sussex square
Baldwin C. B. esq. M.P. 6 Parliament st.; Bovine, King's co.; &Guerston,Totnes
Baldwin Edward, esq. 35 Hyde park sq
Baldwin Hy. esq. 3Trafalgar pl.Clphm. rd
Baldwin Mrs. 14 Kent ter. Regent's pk
Baldwin Mrs. 24 Pelham road, Brompton
Baldwin Robt. esq. 2 Brick ct. Temple
Baldwin S. esq. 16 Claremont ter. Pntnvl
Baldwin Thos. R.esq.14Kent ter.Rgt.'spk
Bale C. S. esq. 71Cambridge ter.Edgw.rd
Balfour Lady Eleanor, 3 Grosvenor sq. & Whittingham ho. Preston kirk
Balfour Batchman, esq. 17 Gibson st
Balfour Buchanan, esq. 17 Gibson sq
Balfour Hen. esq.5Compton ter. Islingtn
Balfour J. M. jun. esq. M.P. 20 Arlington st.; & Whittingham ho. Preston kirk
Balfour Mrs. 8 Grosvenor crescent
Ball Sir Wm. Keith, bt.40Up.Seymour st
Ball Daniel, esq. 42 Brompton square
Ball Edwd. esq. 8 Carlton villas
Ball Fras. L. esq. 24 Grosvenor st. west
Ball Henry, esq. 16 Torrington square, & Hall staircase, Temple
Ball James, esq. 4 Queen's ter. Chelsea
Ball John, esq. 18 Bedford row
Ball John, esq. 3 Davidge ter. Walcot pl
Ball Miss, 6 Bath place, Kensington
Ball Miss, 7 Church st. Kensington
Ball Mrs. 4 Kensington terrace, Kensington gravel pits
Ball Mrs. 34 Cadogan place
Ball Mrs. 11 York place, Pentonville
Ball Thos. P. esq. 15 Chester sq.Pimlico
Ball Wm. esq. Park ho. 1 Glo'ster road
BallantineMajor-Gen.D.Fladong's hotel, 144Oxford st.&Summergrove,Cumbrld
Ballantine Mrs. 118Cmdn. rd.vls.Cmn.tn
Ballantine Wm. sen. esq. 89 Cadogan pl
Ballantine Wm. esq. 19 Frederick st
Ballantine Wm. esq. 5 Inner Temple la
Ballard George, esq. 27 Canonbury sq
Ballard H. esq. 9 Earl's ter. Kensington
Ballard James, esq. 32 Regent square
Ballard Joseph, esq. 6 Paddington green
Ballard Thomas, esq. 81 Connaught ter
Ballin Mrs. 27 Devonshire st. Portland pl
Ballinger John, esq. 40 Coleshill st
Balls A. esq. 12 Blandford pl. Dorset sq

Balls John, esq. 1 Greville pl. Kilburn
Balls Joseph, esq. 92 Albany st
Balmain J. esq. 181 Prospect pl. Maida hl
Baly Price P. esq. 14 Buckingham st. Strn
Baly Wm. M.D. 28 Spring gardens
Bamber Rev. James, 38 Golden square
Bamford C. F. esq. 14 Buckingham st. Strand; & 7 King's Bench wk. Temple
Bamford Thos. esq. 3 Belvoir ter. Vxhall
Bamford Thomas, esq. 47 Gibson square
Bampfield John Westcott, esq. 9 Blenheim place, St. John's wood
Banbury Edwd. esq. 4 Harcourt buildgs
Banbury Wm. esq. 30 Bedford pl. Blms
Banbury Wm. esq. 25 Finsbury pl. north
Bancks A. esq. 15 Albert ter. Kngtsbrdg
Bancks Rt. Olddiss, esq. 11 Cecil st. Strand
Bandinel James, esq. 19 Berkeley sq
Bandon, Earl of, 3 Connaught place; & Castle Bernard, Bandon
Banfield R. S. P. esq. 47 Hunter st
Bangor, Bishop of, Warren's hotel, 1 Regent st.; & the Palace, Bangor
Banister Hen. J. esq. 50 Burton crescent
Banister Miss, 7 Hornsey row, Islington
Banister Mrs. 14 Pelham cres. Fulham rd
Bankes George, esq. M.P. 5 Old Palace yard; & Kingston Lacy, Wimborne; & Studland, Swanage, Dorset
Banks Edward C. esq. 3 Mecklenburgh st
Banks Hopper, esq. 13 York pl. City rd
Banks James, esq. 20 Soley terrace
Banks John, esq. 3 Abbey rd. St. John's wd
Banks John, esq. 44 York st. Portman sq
Banks John P. esq. 51 Devonsh. st. Bloomsb
Banks Wm. esq. 22 Holland pl. Claphm. rd
Banks Wm. L. esq. 12 Melina pl. St. John's r
Bannatyne John, esq. 41 Bernard st
Banner Samuel, esq. 26 Berkeley sq
Bannerman Alexr. esq. M.P. 4 Berkeley st. Berkeley sq.; & Aberdeen
Bannerman Jas. esq. 25 Connaught sq
Banning Thos. esq. Montpelier, Sth. Lmb
Bannister C. G. esq. 13 John st. Bedford rw
Bannister John Hen. esq. 436 Oxford st
Bannister Joseph, esq. 63 Coleshill st
Bannister Mrs. 65 Gower st. Bedford sq
Bannister Mrs. 11 Grenville st
Bannister Thos. esq. 4 Middle Temple la
Banting T. esq. 19 Circus rd. St. John's wd
Banting Wm. esq. 4 Terrace, Kensington
Banton Thos. esq. 3 Ormes sq. Bayswtr
Banton William, esq. 10 Claremont sq
Banyard Wm. H. esq. 7 Blmt. tr. Wands. rd
Bapojee Rungoo, 9 Blandford place
Barber Capt. Jas. 14 Mecklenburgh sq
Barber Rev. John, 11 Lr. Kennington gr
Barber Chas. esq. 2 Lloyd sq. Pentonville
Barber Chas. esq. 4 Princes pl. Kenn. rd
Barber C. C. esq. 11 New sq. Lincoln's inn
Barber C. J. esq. 6 Goulden tr. Barnsby. rd
Barber Edwd. esq. Acacia rd. St. John's wd
Barber John, esq. 10 Gray's inn place
Barber John, esq. 18 Regent sq. Gray's inn road, & 11 Furnival's inn
Barber Joseph, esq. 23 Clapham rise
Barber Samuel, esq. 6 Avenue rd. Rgt.'s pk
Barber Saml. esq. 9 Warwick st. Char. cr
Barber Step. N. esq. Denmk. hill, Cambw
Barber T. B. esq. 42 Newington pl. Kenn. rd
Barber T. H. esq. 4 St. John's vil. Acacia rd
Barber Wm. esq. 10 St. Mary Abbott's ter
Barbrook Wm. esq. 13 Tauntonpl. Rgts. pk
Barchard R. esq. East hill, Wndswth. rd
Barclay Capt. Jas. 14 Burton st. Burton crescent
Barclay Capt. Jas. (late of 88th Regt.), 20 Kenton st
Barclay Archibald, esq. 12 Burton st
Barclay David, esq. M.P. 8 Belgrave sq.; & Eastwick park, Leatherhead
Barclay Henry, esq. 34 Bedford row
Barclay John, esq. 52 Tavistock sq
Barclay R. esq. 8 Holloway pl. Holloway
Barclay Robt. G. 8 Gt. Cumberland st
Bardons John, esq. 27 Bedford st. Bdfd. rw
Bardons P. S. esq. 1 Stanhope st. Hmps. rd
Bardwell Wm. esq. 11 Park st. Westmr
Barfoot Ed. W. esq. 18 William st. Rgt's. pk
Barham Rev. Charles, 144 Oxford st.; & Barming, Maidstone, Kent
Barham Chas. esq. 14 Howard st. Strand
Barham Fras. esq. 6 Warwick ct. Gray's in
Barham Fred. esq. 10 Osnaburgh st
Barham J. esq. 5 Courld. ter. Wandwth. rd
Baring Sir Thomas, bart. 21 Devonshire place; & Stratton park, Winchester
Baring Rt. Hon. Francis Thornhill, M.P. 86 Eaton square
Baring Rt. Hon. W. B. M.P. & Lady Harriett, 12 Great Stanhope st. Mayfair; & Addiscombe farm, Croydon
Baring Henry Bingham, esq. M.P. & Lady Augusta, 13 Eaton place
Baring Henry, esq. 11 Berkeley square; & Cromer hall, Norfolk
Baring Thos. M.P. 40 Charles st. Brkly. sq
Bark John, esq. 2 Bayswater hill
Barker Alexr. esq. 103 Piccadilly
Barker Arthur, esq. 10 Hans place
Barker C. esq. 24 South'ton pl. Eustn. sq
Barker Edgar, esq. 5 Albion pl. Hyde park square; & 40 Edgware road
Barker Edwd. Jas. esq. 59 Lincoln's inn flds
Barker George, esq. 56 Brompton square
Barker George, esq. 41 Russell square, & 1 Gray's inn square
Barker Geo. R. esq. 4 Park st. Grsvnr. sq
Barker Gilbert, esq. 23 Brunswick sq
Barker Hen. esq. 5 Albion pl. Hyde pk. sq
Barker John, esq. 27 Cadogan place
Barker Joseph, esq. 191 Fleet st
Barker Mrs. 55 Cambridge st. Edgw. rd
Barker Mrs. Florence vil. Finchly. nw. rd
Barker Mrs. 28 South bank, Regt's. pk
Barker Mrs. M. R. 5 Highbury grove
Barker Mrs. Raymond, 27 Portman sq
Barker Raymond H. esq. 4 Garden ct. Temple
Barker Richard, esq. 14 Fitzroy square
Barker Samuel, esq. 3 Furnival's inn, & 15 Gray's inn square
Barker Thos. esq. 24 Duncan ter. City rd
Barker T. esq. Florence vil. Finchly. nw. rd
Barker Thos. Alfred, M.D. 15 Grafton st
Barker Walter, esq. 30 South bank, Regent's pk.; & 87 Gt. Portland st
Barker Wm. Ponsonby, esq. 81 Jermyn st. & Kilcooley abbey, John's town, Ireland
Barland A. esq. 11 Southampton st. Fitz. sq
Barlee Edward H. esq. 13 New North st
Barlin Jacob Nath. esq. 15 Bayswa. ter
Barlow Col. 8 Leonard pl. Kensington
Barlow Rev. J. 5 Berkeley st. Berkely. sq
Barlow Dr. 28 Up. Gloster pl. Dorset sq
Barlow Edmund, esq. 31 Torrington sq. & 26 Essex st. Strand
Barlow Francis, esq. 48 Montagu sq. & 45 Lincoln's inn fields
Barlow Fred. Pratt, esq. 17 Rutland gate
Barlow Fredk. P. esq. 24 Kensington sq
Barlow Geo. B. esq. 45 Lincoln's inn fld
Barlow James Pratt, esq. 3 Hyde park gate, Kensington gore; & Doctor's com
Barlow Mrs. 43 Duncan terrace, City rd
Barlow Mrs. 20 Great May's buildings
Barlow Mrs. 11 New Quebec st
Barlow Philip B. esq. 1 Plowden bldgs
Barlow Sir Wm. Owencart, 15 Figtree court, Temple
Barlow Thos. esq. 14 Noel st. Islington
Barlow Thos. esq. 12 Paddington green
Barlow Wm. esq. 11 Paradise ter. Islgtn
Barnard Maj. Gen. Sir A. F. 46 Wilton cres
Barnard Col. 40 Lowndes st. Belgrave sq
Barnard C. E. G. esq. 35 Linc. inn fields
Barnard Charles J. esq. 12 Grove end rd
Barnard E. esq. Belgrave cot. Wndsw. rd
Barnard Edward, esq. 39 Claremont sq
Barnard Edw. Geo. esq. M.P. Deptford grn. Kent; & Gosfield hall, nr. Halstead
Barnard George, esq. 33 Albany st
Barnard George, esq. 85 Gt. Portland st
Barnard George M. esq. 10 Davies st
Barnard Henry Gee, esq. 51 Queen Anne st. & South Cave castle, Yorkshire
Barnard James, esq. 3 Claremont sq
Barnard John, esq. 8 Cross st. Islington
Barnard John A. L. esq. 25 Holloway pl
Barnard M. esq. 28 Sthampton. st. Strand
Barnard Mrs. 5 Guildford pl. Lr. Ken. la
Barnard Philip, esq. 21 Queen Anne st
Barnard Thomas, esq. 4 Southwick cres
Barnard T. B. esq. 51 Lincoln's inn flds
Barnard Wm. esq. 23 Gt. Percy st
Barnard Wm. esq. 36 Vincent square
Barnard Wm. Tyndall, esq. 9 Old sq. Lin. i
Barnard Wm. W. esq. 58 Lincoln's inn fi
Barne Frederick, esq. 37 Grovesnor st
Barne Mrs. Col. 37 Grosvensor t
Barneby John, esq. M.P. 34 Portman sq. & Brockhampton, near Bromyard
Barned Israel, esq. 6 Glo'ster ter. Rgt's. pk
Barnes Lieut. Gen. Sir Jas. 33 Clarges st
Barnes Alfred, esq. 2 Dean st. Park lane; & 12 Copthall court, Throgmorton st
Barnes A. B. esq. King's rd. Chelsea
Barnes C. H. esq. Belle Vue ho. Notting hl
Barnes Geo. esq. Clifton villa, Acacia rd
Barnes Geo. esq. 105 Piccadilly; & 62 Lincoln's inn fields
Barnes John, esq. 6 Clarendon pl. Edg. rd
Barnes John, esq. Park ho. Mile end rd
Barnes John, esq. 15 Regent st
Barnes John, M.D. 32 Tavistock place
Barnes Keith, esq. 8 Up. Portland place, & 7 Spring gardens
Barnes Mrs. 15 Clarges st
Barnes Mrs. 20 George st. Portman sq
Barnes Philip Edward, esq. Botanic garden, Inner circle, Regent's park
Barnes Rt. M.D. 43 Notting hill High st
Barnes Thos. esq. 19 Northumbld. st. Str
Barnes Thos. esq. 3 Upper Park place, Regent's park road
Barnes T. J. esq. 3 Woodstock pl. Avenue rd
Barnett Capt. Wm. 18 Clement's inn
Barnett Rev. Abraham, Gt. St. Helens
Barnett Ebenezer, esq. 12 Barnsbury sq
Barnett Edwd. esq. 4 Belinda tr. Canonby
Barnett Henry, esq. 9 Frith st
Barnett Henry, esq. 2 Halkin st. west
Barnett Henry George, esq. 4 Dorset sq
Barnett John, esq. 26 Barnsbury park
Barnett John, esq. 3 Verulam buildings
Barnett John, M.D. 34 Chesham place
Barnett J. esq. 26 Hemingford tr. Islgtn
Barnett J. esq. 16 Newingtn. pl. Kenn. rd
Barnett Misses, 10 Wilton crescent
Barnett Mrs. 9 Church row, Up. st. Islgt
Barnett Mrs. 4 Dorset square
Barnett Mrs. 1 Gt. Prescot st
Barnett Rd. Clemson, esq. 25 Chester ter. Regent's pk. & Warnham, Horsham
Barnett Robert, esq. 71 Dean st. Soho
Barnett Thos. esq. 168 New Bond st
Barnett Wm. esq. 10 Glo'ster cres. Rgt. pk
Barnewall Geo. W. V. esq. 81 Jermyn st
Barnewall Henry C. esq. 5 Up. Vernon st
Barnewall Miss, 24 Devonshire st
Barnewall Thomas, esq. 15 York terrace
Barney Step. esq. 2 New Temple bldgs
Barns Wm. esq. 6 South sq. Gray's inn
Barnwell Chas. Fred. esq. 44 Woburn pl
Barnwell D. esq. 98 Milton st. Dorset sq
Barnwell Fred. L. esq. 1 Linc. inn fields
Barnwell Wm. esq. 7 Queen Charlott. rw
Barr Misses, 50 Cadogan pl. Sloane st
Barr Mrs. 26 Clapham rise
Barrable John, esq. 3 Park pl. ter. Pad. gn
Barraud Hen. esq. 79 Park st. Grosvr. sq
Barraud Wm. esq. 77A, Park st. Grosvr. sq
Barrel John, esq. 27 Sherrard st. Soho
Barrell Mrs. Mary A. 3 Monument yard
Barrell Zachariah, esq. 82 Mount st
Barrero Don José Maria, Consul gen. for Spain, 37 Old Broad st. & Albany villa, 237 Maida vale, Edgware road

Barrett Capt. Saml. T. 16 Connaught sq
Barrett Edward, esq. 50 Wimpole st
Barrett F. esq. 66 Clarence gdns. Rgt. pk
Barrett Geo. Goodin, esq. 2 Tanfild. ct. Tmpl
Barrett James William, esq. 61 Burton crescent, & 5 Gray's inn square
Barrett Job, esq. 24 River st. Myddltn. sq
Barrett John, esq. 50 Trinity sq. Boro'
Barrett Joseph Radcliffe, esq. 4 Stratford pl. Oxford st.; & 7 Copthall ct
Barrett Joshua, esq. 20 Tibberton sq
Barrett Miss, 3 Albert tr. St. Jn.'s wood
Barrett Mrs. 20 Gerrard st. Islington
Barrett Mrs. 1 Lit. Park st. Westminstr
Barrett Richard, esq. 23 New Bond st
Barrett Sam. esq. 26 Old sq. Lincoln's inn
Barrett Samuel, esq. 176 Sloane st
Barrett Samuel B. C. esq. 25 Sloane st
Barrett Thos. esq. 29 Wellington ter
Barrett Wm. esq. Rosamon house, Islington grn. & 2 Bell yard, Doctors' com
Barringer Mrs. 3 Alfred pl. Bedford sq
Barringer Wm. esq. 1 Onslow tr. Fulhm. rd
Barrington Viscount, M.P. 20 Cavndsh. sq & Beckett house, near Farringdon
Barrington hon. Augustus, 27 Grsvnr. st
Barron Sir Henry Winston, bart. M.P. 13 Grafton st. Bond st. & Belmont house, Waterford
Barron Arthur, esq. 89 Chancery lane
Barron Chas. esq. Denmrk. hill, Cmbrwll
Barron Edwd. esq. 29 Bloomsbury sq
Barron F. W. esq. 27 Northumberland st
Barron Wm. esq. 24 Albion st. Hyde pk
Barrow Sir John, bart. 7 New st. Spring gardens; & Admiralty
Barrow George, esq. Kensington palace
Barrow John, esq. 35 Westbourne ter
Barrow John, esq. 16 York bdgs. New rd
Barrow John George, esq. 48 Davies st
Barrow Mrs. Claremnt. ho. Park pl. Padn
Barrow Mrs. 12 Up. Seymour st. west
Barrow Rich. esq. 6 Raymond buildings
Barrow T. C. esq. 11 Belgrave terrace
Barrowclough Hy. esq. 8 Clifford's inn
Barry A. esq. 13 Smith st. King's rd. Chels
Barry Chas. esq. 25 Charles st. St James's
Barry Chas. esq. R.A. 32 Gt. George st
Barry Chas. esq. 14 Marlborough place, Walworth road, & 3 Brabant ct. City
Barry Chas. R. esq. 1 Stone buildings
Barry Fredk. esq. 7 Dalby ter. City rd
Barry John, esq. 1 Rosedale ter. Notg. hl
Barry Mrs. 10 Gloucester pl. New road
Barry Mrs. 35 Weymouth st. Portland pl
Barstow James, esq. 10 North crescent, Bedford sq. & 7 Figtree court, Temple
Barstow Thos. I. esq. 8 King's bench wk
Barth Capt. J. 11 North ter. Brompton
Barth Geo. esq. 94 Stanhope st. Hamp. rd
Barth W. esq. 12 Chester pl. Knngtn. cr
Bartholomew V. & Mrs. 23 Charlotte st. Portland place
Bartholomew Rt. H. esq. 5 New inn, Strnd
Bartholomew Wm. esq. 3 Gray's inn pl
Barthrop Robt. esq. 2 Glebe pl. King's rd
Bartleet Thos. M. esq. 2 Kent ter. Reg. pk
Bartleman Geo. esq. 74 Westbourne st
Bartlet James, M.D. 10 Bentinck st
Bartlet Jn. esq. 21 Spencer ter. Lower rd. Islington
Bartlett Edw. B. esq. 11 Connaught ter
Bartlett G. esq. 15 Caroline st. Bedford sq
Bartlett G. esq. 5 Holland st. Clpham. rd
Bartlett Michael, esq. 24 Hatton garden
Bartlett Mrs. 3 Malvern ter. Islington
Bartlett Thos. esq. 39 Chancery la
Bartlett T. esq. 8 Holland st. Clpham. rd
Bartlett Thos. J. M. esq. 9 Pall mall east
Bartlett Wm. esq. 35 Mornington cres
Bartlett Wm. esq. 19 Notting hill ter
Bartlett Wm. esq. 15 Park pl. south, Chls
Bartley C. P. esq. 55 Westbourne ter
Bartley George, esq. 11 Woburn square
Barton Rev. Wm. 2 Chesterfield st. Ks. cs
Barton Edward, esq. 27 Hatton garden
Barton Geo. esq. 3 Plowden bdgs. Templ
Barton Geo. H. esq. 6 Bloomfield ter. Pim
Barton Misses, 11 Cambridge tr. Edgw. rd
Barton Mrs. 23 Albion st. Hyde park
Barton Nathl. esq. 3 Sussex sq. Hyde pk
Barton Robt. esq. 22 Connaught ter
Barton Thomas, esq. 17 Buckingham st
Barton Thos. N. esq. 4 Dorchester pl
Barton Wm. esq. 27 Abbey pl. St. John's w
Bartram Chs. esq. 7 Albion pl. Thornhl. rd
Bartram Luke R. esq. Victoria rd. Knsgtn
Bartram Mrs. 3 Upper Fitzroy st
Bartrum Thos. esq. 26 Bolton st
Barwis Wm. H. B. esq. 1 New Boswell ct
Barwise J. esq. 32 Sussex pl. Kens. Nw. tn
Barwise John, esq. Merrington house, Earl's court, Old Brompton
Barwise Mrs. 11 Bedford row, Islington
Barwish Wm. esq. 14 Fortess tr. Kntsh. tn
Basake Miss, 6 Oakley square, Chelsea
Baseley Mrs. Oakley cot. Kng's rd. Chels
Basevi George, jun. esq. 17 Saville row
Basevi Nathaniel, esq. 19 Old sq. Lincoln's inn, & Beechwood, Highgate
Basham George, esq. 7 Staple inn, Hlbn
Basham Wm. Richd. M.D. 17 Chester st
Bashaw Wm. esq. 7 Compton ter. Islgtn
Baskerfield Mrs. 14 Highbury place
Baskerville Thomas B. M. esq. M.P. Carlton club, & Clyro ct. Hay, South Wales
Baskerville Wm. esq. Qn's. rd. St. John's wd
Baskett Wm. esq. 11 Park pl. Kngtn. cross
Basnett Edward, esq. 28 Carey st
Basnett M. H. esq. 31 Alfred st. City rd
Bass James, esq. 7 Fortess tr. Kentish tn
Bass James, esq. 4 Middlesex pl. New rd
Bass Joseph, esq. 62 Nelson square
Bass Mrs. 4 Middlesex pl. New road
Bass Wm. esq. 12 Serjeants' inn, Fleet st
Basset John, esq. 11 Portland pl. Islgt
Basset Mrs. 15 Upper Brook st
Bassett Geo. esq. Glo'ster rd. Regt's. pk
Bassett Hen. esq 7 Powis pl. Hampstd. rd
Bassett H. esq. 1 Southampton st. Fitz. sq
Bastard Capt. 74 Eaton place
Bastard Mrs. 9 Chesterfield st. Mayfair, & Sharpham, Totness, Devon
Bastick Samuel, esq. 2 Brook st
Bastide Francis, esq. 17 Halfmoon st
Batchelor John, esq. 6 Wilton st. Gros. pl
Batchelor George, esq. 40 Harmood st
Bate Mrs. 102 Ebury st. Pimlico
Bateman Lord, 38 Portman square; & Kelmarsh, Northampton; & Shobdon court, Hereford
Bateman Lieut. Col. 46 Stamford st
Bateman Chas. esq. 1 Marlborough sq
Bateman Hen. esq. 3 King st. Finsbury
Bateman John, esq. 4 Castle st. Le'ster. sq
Bateman John, esq. 94 Pall mall
Bateman John Jones, esq. 36 Portland place; 2 New square, Lincoln's inn; & Pentre Mawr, Abergele, Denbighshire
Bateman Joseph, D.C.L. East India rd
Bateman Mrs. 34 Cloudesley square
Bateman H. R. esq. 12 Albert ter. Kngtsb
Bateman Richd. E. M.D. 54 Crawford st
Bateman Sachaveral, esq. Fladong's hotel, 144 Oxford st. & Leachurch vil. Derby
Bateman Thomas, esq. 2 Elm ct. Temple
Bateman Thos. esq. 16 Endsleigh st
Bateman Wm. esq. 30 Alpha rd. Rgnts. pk
Bateman W. esq. 30 Cumming st. Pentonvl
Bates Edward, esq. 3 Union pl. New rd
Bates James, esq. 12 Norfolk st. Strand
Bates Joab, esq. 6 Titchfld. ter. Rgnt's. pk
Bates Joshua, esq. 18 Park sq. Rgnt's. pk
Bates Joshua, esq. 50 Portland place; & East Sheen, Surrey
Bates Robert Makin, esq. 41 Norfolk st
Bates Thos. esq. 4 Old sq. Lincoln's inn
Bates Wm. esq. 18 Abbey pl. St. John's wd
Bateson Saml. esq. 43 Lincoln's inn fields
Bateson Thomas, esq. M.P. 63, Albany
Bathe Anthy. esq. 8 York pl. Walworth rd.; & Swan st. Old Kent road
Bath Charles, esq. 10 Goswell st
Bathurst Earl, 4 Wilton crescent, Belgrave sq.; & Oakley park, Cirencester
Bathurst Lady Georgiana, 4 Wilton crescent, Belgrave square
Bathurst Lady Susan, 8 Cadogan place
Bathurst Gen. Sir James, K.C.B. 1 Devonshire pl. Portland pl
Bathurst hon. Mrs. 8 Grosvenor square
Bathurst hon. Wm. L. 38 Halfmoon st
Bathurst Sir Fredk. bart. 73 South Audley st.; & Clarendon park, Wiltshire
Bathurst Col. Henry, 83 Gloucester pl
Bathurst Mrs. 21 York pl. Portman sq
Batley Henry, esq. 12 Gray's inn sq
Batley Mrs. 5 Windsor ter. Maida hill
Batsford John J. esq. 1 Augustus square
Batson Alfred, esq. 20 Bedford place
Batt John, esq. 8 Highbury grove
Battam John, esq. 41 Oxford terrace
Battam Thomas, esq. 2 Gough square
Battcock Thos. esq. 2 Cheyne wk. Chelsea
Batten Edmd. esq. 5 New sq. Lincln.'s inn
Batten Edmund, esq. 13 Up. Berkeley st
Batthyany Count, 5 Audley square
Batty Mrs. 16 Alexander sq. Brompton
Batty Mrs. M. A. 26 Bloomsbury st
Batty Wm. esq. 1 Sussex gardens, Hyde park; & 26 Charles st. St. James's
Battye Mrs. 15 Wellington ter. St. Jn's. rd
Battye Thomas, esq. 5 Woburn place
Baud Benjamin, esq. 2 Portsmouth st
Baudinet Mrs. 52 Green st. Grosvenor sq
Baughan John Henry, esq. 9 Charing cross
Baughn Mrs. 13 Salisbury pl. New road
Baugniet C. esq. 21 Beaumont st. Marylbn
Bauke G. C. esq. 9 South'ton. st. Fitzroy sq
Bauly Wm. esq. 22 Crawford st
Baumbrough Wm. esq. 16 Prospect pl. Wandsworth road
Baumgartner Edw. J. esq. 3 Plowden bldgs
Baves William, esq. 29 Lloyd square
Bawcomb Mrs. 25A, Grove end road, St. John's wood
Bawden Wm. esq. 1 Alexander sq. Brmptn
Bawtree Geo. F. esq Stoke Newington gn
Bawtree S. C. esq. 3 Walton pl. Brompton
Baxendale J. esq. 16 Park village west; & Woodside, Whetstone, Middlesex
Baxendale Lloyd S. esq. 24 Lincoln's inn fields, & 7 Great Winchester st
Baxter Rev. Rt. Wm. D.D. St. Katherine's, Regent's park
Baxter Chas. esq. 48 Lincoln's inn fields
Baxter Henry, esq. 8 Tibberton square
Baxter Hen. F. esq. 5 George st. Hanvr. sq
Baxter John Cordy, 15 Canterbury vils. & 16 Norfolk st. Middlesex hospital
Baxter Henry J. esq. 5 Essex ct. Temple
Baxter Richard, esq. 3 Garden ct. Temple
Baxter Rt. esq. 7 Michael's grv. Brmptn
Baxter Robt. Michael, esq. 48 Linc. innfld
Baxter Stafford S. esq. 41 Chancery la
Baxter Theodore, esq. 5 Spencer st
Baxter Wm. esq. 31 Park st. Westminster
Bayard Robert, esq. 21 Cornwall terrace
Bayford Aug. Fred. D.C.L. 1 Hornton vils. Kensington; & 8 Bell yd. Docs. coms.
Bayford James, esq. 9 Low. Southwick st
Bayford James Heseltine, esq. 12 & 13 Gt. Knightrider st. & 17 Montpelier rd. Brighton
Bayford Mrs. Hornton vil. Campden hl
Bayley Rev. Frederick, 7 Suffolk st
Bayley Sir John, bart. 3 Poet's corner; 2 Essex ct. Temple; & Updown house, Sandwich
Bayley A. esq. 49 St. John's wood terrace
Bayley Chas. Jn. esq. 3 Essex ct. Temple
Bayley Emilius, esq. 2 Essex ct. Temple, & 3 Poet's corner, Westminster
Bayley Francis, esq. 11 St. George's ter. Cumberland gate, & 21 Old sq. Linc. Inn
Bayley Geo. esq. 36 Green st. Grosvnr. sq
Bayley John D. esq. 52 Lincoln's inn flds
Bayley Miss, 239 Regent st

Bayley Mrs. 37 Harewood square
Bayley Robert, esq. 12 Haymarket
Bayley Thos.esq.1 Hope cot.Wanswth.rd
Bayley Thos. esq. 58 Lincoln's inn fields
Bayley Wm. Kennedy, esq. 12 Haymkt. & 5 New square, Lincoln's inn
Bayley-Wallis Gen. Lewis, 17 Regent st
Baylie John, esq. 5 Cook's ct. Carey st
Baylis Ed. esq. 6 Cambridge ter. Hyde pk
Baylis Edward, esq. 30 Sackville st
Baylis Edward, esq. 28 Trevor square
Baylis James, esq. 52 Beaumont st
Baylis Mrs. & Miss, 8 Addison tr. Nott.hl
Baylis Mrs. 3 Gibson square, Islington
Baylis Thos. esq. 19 James st. Bckngm.ga
Baylis Thos. Hen. esq. 3 Park pl.gardens, Harrow rd. & 11 King's Bench walk
Bayly Bethune, esq. 4 Mitre ct. chmbrs
Bayly Chas. Geo. Villiers, esq. 2 Mount st. & Hampton court palace
Bayly J. H. esq. 5 Essex court, Temple
Bayly Philip Edward, esq. 76 Norton st
Bayly Robt. esq. 3 Harcourt bdgs.Templ
Bayly William, esq. 187 Sloane st
Bayne Ralph, esq. 40 Royal cres. Not. hl
Baynes Sir Wm. bart. 25 Portland place
Baynes Benj. esq. 2 Loraine pl. Hollowy
Baynes J.esq. 48 Duke st.Manchester sq
Baynes Mrs. 9 Dorset pl. Regent's pk
Baynes Thos. M. esq. 41 Burton st
Bayning Rev. Lord, United University club; & Brome rectory, Scole, Norfolk
Bayntin Walter J. esq.28 Lower Eaton st
Baynton Mrs.29 Up.Seymour st. Prtmn.sq
Bazalgette E. esq. 8 Old sq. Lincoln's inn
Bazalgette J.W. esq.24 Gt.Georg.st.Wstm
Bazalgette Lewis, esq. 1 Augusta place, Stockwell common
Bazalgette Miss, 22 Albany st
Bazalgette Miss, 1 Nott'ghm.ter.New rd
Bazalgette Mrs. 86 Gloucester place
Bazett Miss, 65 Gloucester place
Bazett Mrs. 46 Gloucester place
Bazett Mrs. Henry, 19 Up. Southwick st
Beacall Wm.esq.15 Newman st.Oxford st
Beach Jsph. esq. 3 Albion pl. Up.Ken.la
Beach Mrs. Hicks, 20 Portman square
Beach Mrs. 8 Sloane terrace, Sloane st
Beachcroft C. esq. 48 High st. Notting hl
Beachcroft Geo. esq. 81 Milton st
Beachcroft Mrs. 17 Notting hill square
Beachcroft Mrs. Thos. 14 Westbourne st
Beadnell George, esq. 2 Lombard st. & Myfod, near Welshpool
Beadon Wm. Fred.esq. 11 John st. Berkeley sq. & 1 King's Bench walk, Temple
Beake Miss, 30 Albany st. Regent's park
Bealdon Francis, esq. 34 Highbury place
Beale Fred. esq. 13 Albion st. Hyde park
Beale James, esq. 26 Osnaburgh street t
Beale Thos.esq. 13 Chapel pl.Cavndsh.sq
Beale Thos.esq. 53 Up.Norton st. Ftzry.sq
Beales Edmond, esq. 24 Carlton villas, Edgw.rd. & 4 Stone bdgs. Lincoln's inn
Beales John Edwd.esq.7 John st. Adelphi
Beales Wm. esq. Upper Kennington grn
Beall Rd. esq. 4 Windsor ter. Gt. Dovr.rd
Beaman Geo. esq. 32 King st. Covt. gdn
Beames Rev. Thos. 12 Bartlett's bldgs
Beams Wm.esq.7 Augusta pl. Stockwl.cm
Beamish Rev.H.Hamilton, 19 Norfolk crs
Beamish Mrs. 5 Chapel pl. Cavendish sq
Beamish Saml.Geo.esq.16 Kensington sq
Beams Mrs. 4 Park pl. Kennington cross
Beanlands Benj. 14 Cook's ct. Carey st
Beann Miss, 30 Winchester rw. New rd
Beard Francis Carr, esq. 215 Oxford st
Beard Geo. esq. 2 Kenngtn. rw. Kenn. rd
Beard Mrs. 7 Powell st. west, King sq
Beard Richd. esq. 1 Endsleigh st
Beard Thos. esq. 42 Portman pl. Edg. rd
Bearda Miss, 4 Upper Grosvenor st
Beare Capt. 6 Porchester pl. Edgwa. rd
Beare John, esq. 4 Abbey rd. St. John's wd
Beare John, esq. 16 Holborn hill
Beart John, esq. 4 Bouverie st. Fleet st
Beasley William C. esq. 5 Brick court, Temple, & 7 Victoria square
Beaton Thos. esq. 12 Baker st. Pentonvi
Beattie Alex. esq. 4 Sussex pl. Hyde pk
Beattie George, esq. 18 Dover st
Beattie Wm. esq. 74 Gt. Portland st
Beauchamp Earl, 37 Portman square; & Madresfield court, Malvern
Beauchamp J. esq. 14 Up. Seymour st.w
Beauchamp Mrs.29 Cambridge st. Edg.rd.
Beauchamp Mrs. 14 Up. Seymour st. wt
Beauclerk Lord Amelius, 30 Margaret st. Cavendish sq.; & Binfield, Bracknell
Beauclerk Lord Chas.16 Edw.st. Prtmn.sq
Beauclerk Rev. Lord Fredk. 68 Grosvenor st. & Vicarage, St. Michael's, St. Alban's
Beauclerk Capt. G. 23A, Grosvenor st. west
Beauclerk Chas. B. esq. 8 Lr. Belgrave st
Beauclerk Hen. esq. 61 Chester square
Beauclerk Mrs. 7 Eaton place
Beaufort Duke of, K.G. 22 Arlington st; & Badminton house, Gloucestershire; & Troy house, near Monmouth
Beaufort Dow. Duchess, 41 Grosvenor st.; & Stoke Gifford, near Bristol
Beaufort Capt. R.N. 11 Gloucester place
Beaufort Rev. Dan. Aug. 11 Gloucester pl
Beaufort Mrs. 254 Regent st
Beaumier Mrs. 49 South st. Grosvenor sq
Beaumont Lord, 18 Curzon st. May fair, & Carlton hall, Snaith
Beaumont Alf. esq. 5 Beak st. Regent st
Beaumont Benj. esq. 4 Park rd. Reg. pk
Beaumont F. esq 9 Clarendon pl. Maida hl
Beaumont Henry, esq. 5 Beak st. Reg. st
Beaumont Hen. A. esq. 3 Lincoln's in. fds
Beaumont James, esq. Cutler's hall, & 19 Lincoln's fields
Beaumont J. esq. 19 Lincoln's inn fields
Beaumont John Aug. esq. 50 Regent st
Beaumont Jsph. esq. 19 Canonbury vils
Beaumont Miss, 35 Portman square
Beaumont T. W. esq. 144 Piccadilly; & Byewell hall, Newcastle-on-Tyne; & Hexham abbey; & Brittenhall, Wakfld
Beaumont Wm. esq. Mornington road
Beauvale Lord, G.C.B. P.C. 12 Hyde pk. tr
Beavan Chas. esq. 1 New sq. Lincoln's inn
Beavan Edwd. esq. 4 Middle Temple la
Beavan Hen. Wm. esq. 9 Blandford sq. & 2 Royal terrace, Adelphi
Beavan John Phillips, esq. 14 Stratford pl. & Stoughton ldge. St. Neot's, Hunts
Beavers Thos. esq. 29 Gt. Windmill st
Beazley Fredk. esq. 11 Beaufoy ter
Beazley George, esq. 6 Southwick cres
Beazley Samuel, esq. 29 Soho square
Bebb Joseph, esq. 12 Argyll st
Bebb Mrs. 13 Gloucester pl. Portman sq. & Donnington grove, Newbury, Bucks
Beccles Mrs. 5 Wellington pl. St. Jns.wd
Becher Capt. R.N. 29 Up. Gloucester pl
Becher Capt. 33 Lisson grove north
Becher Mrs. 44 Lowndes st. & 20 Wilton pl
Beck Geo. esq. 20 Elm Tree rd. St. Jns.wd
Beck John, esq. 235 Bethnal green road
Becke Geo. esq. 21 Lincoln's fields
Beckett Edward, esq. 19 Hunter st
Beckett Miss, 19 Hunter st
Beckett Rt. Hon. Sir John, bart. & Lady Anne, 11 Stratford pl. Oxford st. & Somerby pk. Gainsbro', Lincolnshire
Beckett Thos. esq. 5 Russell pl. Fitzroy sq
Beckett William, esq. M.P. 18 Up. Brook st. & Kirstall Grange, Leeds
Beckford Fras. esq. 5 Up. Portland pl
Beckford Wm. esq. 5 Upper Portland pl
Beckham Bernard, esq. 106 Sloane st
Beckham Geo. esq. 39 Ebury st. Eaton sq
Beckitt Hen. Hugh, esq. 6 Symond's inn
Beckles Samuel H. esq. 28 Hamilton ter
Beckwith Rev. Edwd. G.A. 1 Calthorpe st
Beckwith Mrs. 52 Eaton place
Bedford Duke of, 6 Belgrave square, & Woburn Abbey; & Endsleigh, Tavistock; & Oakley house, Bedford
Beddall Philip, esq. Gerrard st. Islington
Bedford C.D. esq. 8 Montagu st. Portmn.sq
Bedford C. St. Clare, esq. 2 Dartmouth st
Bedford Dowager Duchess of, Bedford lodge, Campden hill, Kensington; & the Doune, Rothiemurchus, No. B.
Bedford Francis, esq. 28 Granville sq
Bedford Hy. esq. 20 Calthorpe st. Gray's inn road, & 4 Gray's inn square
Bedford Hy. esq. 2 James st. Buckng. gt
Bedford Mrs. 8 Montagu st. Portmn. sq
Bedford W. esq. 14 Dorset pl. no. Clpm. r
Bedwell Lomley, esq. 33 Albion st. Hy.pk
Bedwill Miss, 21 Clapham rise
Beeby James, esq. 6 Smith st. Chelsea
Beech James, esq. 15 Grosvenor place
Beech James, esq. 31 Tibberton square, & Excise Office, Old Broad st
Beech Mrs. 16 Cadogan place
Beecham Rev. John, 11 Lloyd st. Lloyd sq
Beechey Mrs. 10 Duncan ter. City road
Beecroft Thos. esq. 43 Gerrard st. Islgtn
Beedle Thomas, 21 Holles st
Beer T. esq. 7 Cambridge st. Connaught sq
Beere John, esq. 2 Portland pl. Wndswth.rd
Beesley Thos. esq. 2 Vincent ter. Islgton
Beeston Frdk. Robt. esq. 15 Northumberland st. Strand, & Blomfield lodge, Maida hill
Beeston Henry, esq. 26 Lincoln's inn
Beetham Albert Wm. esq. Forest lodge, Tulse hill, & 3 Serjeants' inn, Fleet st
Beetham Francis, esq. 2 Tanfield ct. Temple
Beetham Mrs. 7 Edwardes sq. Kensngtn
Beetholme Geo. esq. 52 Brompton row
Beetholme John Law, esq. 52 Brompton row, & 1 New inn, Strand
Beetson William, esq. 8 Woburn place
Beevor Charles, esq. 49 Berners st
Beevor Fredk. Balders, esq. 3 Dorset sq. & 2 Gray's inn square
Begbie Charles, esq. 27 East st. Red Lion sq. & 2 Love lane, City
Begbie Matthew Benj. 77 Chancery lane
Begg Thos. esq. 35 Duncan ter. City rd
Beggenden John, esq. 14 Milner sq
Beggi Fras. O. esq. 2 Marylebone st. Gldn.sq
Begrex Signor Peter, 6 Jermyn st
Behan William, esq. 16 Euston square
Behnes Wm. esq. 13 Osnaburgh st
Behrends John George, esq. consul for the free city of Frankfort on the Maine, 12 Broad st. buildings
Beioly Richard Wm. F. esq. 14 Stanhope st. Regent's pk. & 9 Old Jewry chambers
Beisley Sidney, esq. 1 Campden hill villas, Kensington, & 1 Lincoln's inn fields
Belcher Alex. Brymer esq. 82 Harley st
Belcher Chas. esq. 38 Baker st. Lloyd sq
Beldam Joseph, esq. 3 Plowden bldgs
Belfour Edmd. esq. 40 Lincoln's inn flds
Belham Mrs. 7 Minerva ter. Brnsby. pk
Belhaven & Stenton Lord, 30 Albemarle st.; & Wishaw house, Hamilton, N.B.
Belinaye Marquise & Marchioness de la, 27 Nottingham place, New road
Belinaye Hen. M.D. 41 King st. Gold. sq
Bell A. esq. 19 Glo'ster gr. wt. O. Brmptn
Bell A. esq. 56 Gordon sq. & 59 Linc. inn fi
Bell Alex. esq. 58 Upper Norton st
Bell C. esq. 1 Lambeth pl. Clapham rd
Bell Chas. esq. 36 Bedford row, Blomsby
Bell Geo. esq. 25 Kensington crescent
Bell Jacob, esq. 15 Langham place
Bell Jacob, esq. 11 Queen st. Oxford st
Bell Jas. esq. 10 Northwich tr. St. Jns. wd
Bell Jas. esq. 18 Portsea pl. Connaught sq
Bell Jas. Thos. esq. 10 Northwich terr
Bell J. C. C. esq. consul for Tuscany, 43 Russell sq. & 15 Angel ct. Bank
Bell John, esq. 28 Craven st. Strand
Bell J. esq. 1 Marlboro' ter. Kens. new tn
Bell John, M.P. 40 Conduit st
Bell John Thos. esq. 18 Russell square
Bell Jn. Wm. esq. 5 Grenvil. st. Brunsk.sq
Bell Mat. esq. 4 Grosvr. cres. Belgrv. s

Bell Matthew, M.P. 35 Wimpole st. & Woolsington, nr. Newcastle-on-Tyne
Bell Miss, 70 Hamilton terrace
Bell Miss, 53 Burton crescent
Bell Mrs. Col. 20 Milton st. Dorset sq
Bell Mrs. 66 Cadogan place
Bell Mrs. 14 Glo'ster st. Queen sq
Bell Mrs. 15 Kensington square
Bell Mrs. 7 Lower Southwick st
Bell Mrs. 18 Pelham cresct. Fulham rd
Bell Mrs. 3 Woburn square
Bell Peter, esq. 6 Dorset square
Bell Rd. esq. 5 Cambridge st. Edgw. rd
Bell Richard, esq. 23 Northampton sq
Bell Robert, esq. 139 Fleet st. & Norris castle, East Cowes, Isle of Wight
Bell Robert, esq. 50 Gower st
Bell Robert, esq. 41 Howland st
Bell Robert Courtney, esq. 3 Woburn sq
Bell Saml. esq. 81 Gower st. Bedford sq
Bell Sydney S. esq. 21 Old sq. Linc. inn
Bell Thos. Wm. esq. 22 Up. Belgrave pl
Bell Wm. M.D. 37 Albemarle st. Piccdly
Bell Wm. esq. 9 Bow churchyard
Bell Wm. esq. 30 Cloudesley st.
Bell Wm. esq. 13 Holles st. Cavendish sq
Bell Wm. esq. 36 Woburn pl. Russell sq
Bellamy Chas. esq. 6 New sq. Linc. inn
Bellamy Chas. esq. 25 Sussex pl. Knsgtn
Bellamy Fredk. esq. 11 Holloway place
Bellamy Henry, esq. 4 Ingram court
Bellamy John, esq. 38 John st. Bedfd. row
Bellamy John, esq. 7 Woburn square
Bellamy Lewis Rt. esq. 4 Frederick pl. Gray's inn rd. & 4 South sq. Gray's inn
Bellamy Mrs. 50 Judd st. Brunswick sq
Bellomy T. esq. 8 Charlotte st. Bedford sq
Bellasis Mrs. Maj. Gen. 81 Oxford ter
Bellasis Mrs. Col. D. H. 31 Grove end rd
Bellasis Mr. Serjt. 17 Bedford square, & 9 New square, Lincoln's inn
Bellew Rd. Montesquieu, M.P. 104 Pall Mall, & Barmeath, county Louth
Bellingham Sir Alan Edward, bart. & Lady, 21 Portman square
Bellingham Edward, esq. 73 Mortimer st
Bellman V. esq. 22 Camden road villas
Bellot Lewis Fredk. esq. 5 Milner st
Belmont Mrs. 7 Aberdeen pl. Maida hill
Beloe Alfred esq. 2 Stanley ter. Chels
Beloe Mrs. C. 19 Michael's pl. Brompton
Belt William, esq. 38 Brunswick square
Benbow John, esq. M.P. 26 Mecklnbg. sq
Benbow John Henry, esq. 50 Doughty st. & 1 Stone buildings, Lincoln's inn
Bencroft William esq. Howard cottage, Mornington road
Bendixen Sigfried, esq. 5 Percy st
Benedict Jules, esq. 2 Manchester sq
Benett John, M.P. Limmer's hotel, & Pyt house, near Hindon, Wilts
Benett Wm. esq. 14 Nottingham place
Benge Frederick, esq. 63 Sloane st
Benham Daniel, esq. 3 Hamilton terr
Benham Ebenezer, esq. 1 Gt. Coram st
Benham Ebenezer, 12 South sq. Gray's inn
Benham E. jun. esq. 13 South sq. Gray's inn
Benham John, esq. 10 St. James's place
Benham Mrs. 28 Frederick st. Gray's i. rd
Benn Robt. esq. 23 Bartholomew close
Benne Major L. 66 Warren st. Fitz. sq
Bennecke Fredk. Wm. esq. Denmark hl
Bennet Ed. esq. 19 Henrietta st. Cov. gd
Bennet Fredk. esq. 9 Pelham pl. Fulm. rd
Bennet Henry, M.D. 9 Cambridge square
Bennet Miss E. H. 5 Upper Porchester st
Bennet Wm. H. esq. 36 Chancery lane, & 19 Camden road villas
Bennett Rev. James, D.D. 49 Gibson sq
Bennett Rev. Wm. J. E. 39 Wilton cresnt
Bennett Abraham, esq. 13 Park pl. Padd
Bennett Charles, esq. 11 Victoria grove
Bennett Charles Graham, esq. 1 Sise la
Bennett Edwd. esq. 7 Stone bldgs. Linc's inn, & 19 Pelham cres. Brompton
Bennett Fred. D. esq. 3 Comml. pl. O. Kt. rd
Bennett J. esq. 21 Charlotte st. Ptlnd. pl
Bennett J. esq. 27 Harleyfd. pl. Kenn. com
Bennett Jas. R. M.D. 24 Finsbury pl. nth
Bennett John, esq. 44 Bloomsbury sq
Bennett John, esq. 14 Heathcote st
Bennett John, esq. 12 Pall mall
Bennett John, esq. 3 Victoria rd. Kensington, & 22 Duke st. Westminster
Bennett John Cole, esq. 1 Princes rd. Not. h
Bennett John Edwards, esq. Wandsworth road
Bennett John J. esq. 5 Melina pl. St. Jns. rd
Bennett John Morris, esq. 46 Up. Bakr. st
Bennett John T. esq. 12 Queen sq. Blmsby
Bennett J. W. esq. 1 Belgrav. st. King's crs
Bennett J. esq. 20 South parade, St. James
Bennett Miss, 87 Sloane st
Bennett Mrs. 31 Cambridge sq. Hyde pk
Bennett Mrs. 20 North bank, Regent's pk
Bennett Nicholas, esq. 2 Bartletts bdgs
Bennett Rowland Nevitt, esq. 2 New sq. & 1 South pl. Camberwell grove
Bennett St. John, esq. 2 Cloisters, Temple
Bennett Thos. esq. Devereux ct. Strand
Bennett Thos. esq. 12 Queen sq. Blmsby
Bennett Wm. esq. Church cott. Brixton
Bennett Wm. esq. 5 Park village west
Bennett Wm. esq. 4 Up. Holland st. Kensgt
Bennett W. S. esq. 15 Russell pl. Fitzr. sq
Bennington Wm. esq. 3 Victoria road, Kensington New town
Benson F. J. esq. 2 Paper bldgs. Temple
Benson John, esq. 13 Park place villas, Paddington
Benson J. L. esq. 41 Up. Seymour st. Eus. sq
Benson Joseph, esq. 6 Gray's inn square
Benson Miss, 14 Chester ter. Eaton sq
Benson Mrs. 6 Hyde park terrace
Benson Mrs. 2 Lr. Phillimore pl. Kensgt
Benson N. esq. 34 Alfred st. City road
Benson Robert, esq. 6 Sussex square
Benson Saml. esq. 8 Argyll pl. Regent st
Benson Thos. Starling, esq. 2 Paper bdgs. & Manor house, Teddington
Benson William, esq. 4 Carey st
Benson Wm. esq. 8 Dorset pl. Dorset sq
Bensusan Jacob Levi, esq. 57 Gordon sq
Bensusan Mrs. 81 Lisson grove north
Bent Mrs. 4 Brompton square
Bent Wm. esq. 15 Gt. Queen st. Westmin
Benthall Rev. J. Lit. Dean's yd. Westmintr
Bentham Mrs. 6 Upper Gower st
Bentinck Lady Frederic, 38 Charles st. Berkeley square
Bentinck Lord Geo. M.P. 19 Cavendish sq
Bentinck Lord Henry, 19 Cavendish sq
Bentinck Col. 12 Halkin st. west
Bentinck Geo. esq. 43A, South st
Bentinck G. A. F. esq. 48 Charles st. Bklysq
Bentinck Miss, 25 Lowndes st. Blgrve. sq
Bentinck Mrs. 25 Hunter st
Bentinck Walter, esq. 81 Gloucester pl
Bentley Edwd. M.D. 35 Trinity sq. Sthwk
Bentley James, esq. St. Bartholomew's hosp. & Wood green, Cheshunt, Herts
Bentley John, esq. 6 Claremont tr. Pntvl
Bentley John, esq. 17 Cross st. Islington
Bentley John, esq. 114 Sloane st
Bentley M. esq. 11 Holland st. Kensingtn
Bentley Michael, esq. 1 Brick ct. Temple
Bentley Miss, 4 Argyle st. King's cross
Bentley Samuel, esq. 38 Southampton row, & 64 & 65 Shoe lane
Bentley Thomas Forbes, esq. 1 Stanhope terrace, Victoria gate, Hyde park
Bentley Wm. esq. 5 River terr. City rd
Bently Mrs. 1 Highbury grange
Bently Rt. esq. 4 Cavendish rd. St. Jn's. wd
Benton Edwd. esq. 22 Alpha rd. Rgnt's. pk
Benyon Miss, 34 Grosvenor square, & Englefield house, near Reading
Benyon Saml. Yates, esq. 15A, Hill st. & Denston house, near Newmarket
Beolchi Chas. LL.D. 48 Upper Albany st
Berens Henry, esq. 19 Queen st. Mayfair, & Sidcup, Footscray, Kent
Berens Richard, esq. 19 Queen st. Mayfair, & Sidcup, Footscray, Kent
Berens Richd. Beauvoir, esq. 18 Bruton st. & 2 New square, Lincoln's inn
Berdmore Thomas, esq. 8 Gt. Ormond st
Beresford Visc. G.C.B., P.C. 16 Cavendish square; & Beresford hall, near Ashbourne; & Bedgebury park, Lamberhurst
Beresford Lady, 53 Portland place
Beresford Hon. Miss, 30 Charles st. St. James's
Beresford Mrs. 3 Pelham rd. Brompton
Beresford William, M.P. 77 Pall mall, & Elsfield, near Oxford
Beresford Wm. esq. 5 Essex ct. Temple
Berger Francis, esq. 6 Wilton place, Knightsbridge, & 23 Mincing la. City
Bergne John Broadhead, esq. 19 Hans. pl
Berkeley, Countess of, 6 Spring gardens
Berkeley Hon. Craven Fitzhardinge, M.P. Berkeley house, 6 Spring gardens
Berkeley Hon. Francis Hen. F. M.P. Berkeley house, Spring gardens, & Cranford house, near Hounslow
Berkeley Hon. Capt. Fredk. Maurice F. R.N., M.P. 15 Halkin st. west
Berkeley Hon. Geo. C. Grantley F. M.P. Berkeley house, 6 Spring gardens, & Beacon lodge, near Christchurch
Berkeley Chas. esq. 25 Montague place, Russell sq. & 52 Lincoln's inn fields
Berkeley Chas. Clement, esq. 5 New square, Lincoln's inn
Berkeley C. R. esq. 35 Lincoln's inn flds
Berkeley G. C. L. esq. 7 Wilton crescent
Berkeley Thomas, esq. 20 Margaret st. Cavendish square, & 2 Falcon court, Fleet st
Berkeley Wm. esq. 1 Park vil. Pk. st. Not. hl
Berkeley Wm. M. esq. Larkhall ri. Clphm
Berkeley Capt. 45 Canonbury sq. Isling
Berkeley Wm. M. esq. Larkhall ri. Clphm
Bernal Ralph, esq. M.P. 75 Eaton square
Bernard Viscount, M.P. 3 Connaught place, & Castle Bernard, Bandon, county Cork
Bernard Lady, 1 Bryanstone place
Bernasconi B. esq. 19 Alfred pl. Bdfd. sq
Bernays Adlph. esq. 4 Powis pl. Blooms. sq
Berrey Geo. Jas. esq. 7 Clarence place, Pentonville, & 61 Chancery lane
Berridge Joseph, esq. 11 Waterloo pl
Berrier Fontaine Camille, M.D. 3 Foley pl
Berriman William, esq. 51 Wharton st
Berry Denham, esq. 4 Tyndale pl. Islngtn
Berry Geo. esq. 17 Avenue rd. Regent's pk
Berry Hnry. esq. 17 Avenue rd. Regent's pk
Berry James esq. 12 Grove pl. Lisson gro
Berry Jas. Wm. M. esq. 1 Paper buildings
Berry the Misses, 8 Curzon st. Mayfair
Berry Miss, 39 Kensington square
Berry Mrs. 7 Fonthill pl. Clapham rd
Berry Mrs. 5 Golden square
Berry Mrs. 74 Grosvenor st. Grosvenor sq
Berry Mrs. 45 Mornington place
Berry Thos. esq. 16 Canonbury villas
Berry Titus, esq. 37 Chester terrace
Berry W. J. esq. 10 Up. Chadwell st. Pntnvil
Berti Auguste, esq. 71 Gt. Portland st
Berti James, esq. 10 North Audley st
Bertie Edwd. esq. 6 Somerset st. Portmn. sq
Bertram Chas. A. esq. 10 Devonshire st
Bertram G. esq. 10 Devnsh. bds Gt. Dvr. rd
Bertram Mon. 8 Glo'ster rd. Old Bromp
Bertrand L. esq. 11 Manchester st
Berwick Rev. Lord, Stable yard, St. James's; Red Rice, Andover; & Attingham house, Shrewsbury
Besant George, esq. 13 Percy st. Bedford sq. & 1 Bond ct
Besant Geo. esq. 13 Percy st. Bedford sq
Besante Hen. esq. 127 Camden rd. villas
Bescoby Fras. esq. 15 Notting hill terr
Besly Sam. P. L. esq. 13 Cmdn. st. Cmdn. tn
Besset J. esq. 8 Glo'ster grve. west, Brmptn

Besborough Earl, P.C. 3 Cavendish sq.; & Besborough house, Carrick on Suir; & Sysonby, near Melton Mowbray; & Roehampton East hill, Wandsworth, Surrey; & Garry hill house, Carlow
Besson Madame, 36 Manchester st
Best Hon. Captain, R.N. 9 Portman sq
Best Miss, 2 Burton st. Burton crescent
Best Mrs. Thanet cottage, Park village
Best Mrs. 28 Welbeck st. & Bayfield hall, Holt, Norfolk
Best Thomas F. esq. 23 Westbourne ter
Best Wm. esq. 35 Lincoln's inn fields
Best Wm. Mawdesley, esq. 89 Chancery la
Betham Mollinieux, esq. 123 Park st
Betham Mrs. 44 Gerrard st. Islington
Bethell James, esq. 3 Bolton st
Bethell James, esq. 10 Connaught pl. west
Bethell Mrs. 43 Upper Grosvenor st
Bethell Richard, esq. Q.C. 3 Stone bldgs. Linc. inn; & Lauderdale house, Highgte
Bethune Capt. 80 Chester square
Bethune John Elliot D. esq. 80 Chester square; & Balfour, Fife, Scotland
Betson Ralph A. esq. 2 Manor grv. Chls
Bettell John, esq. 7 Glo'ster bldgs. O. Kt. rd
Bettridge Mrs. 14 Harpur st. Red Lion sq
Betts Arthur, esq. 3 Brompton grove
Betts Edwd. Ladd, esq. 29 Tavistock sq
Betts Miss, 10 Blandford square
Betts William, esq. 26 Highbury place
Betts Wm. esq. 8 Pembroke sq. Kensingtn
Betty Wm. Hy. W. esq. 1 Robert st. Adelphi
Betzjeman Geo. esq. 6 Upper Ashby st
Bevan Charles D. esq. 3 Paper blds. Tmpl
Bevan Chas. Jas. esq. 70 Portland pl
Bevan David, esq. 42 Upper Harley st.; & Belmont, near East Barnet; & Fosbury, near Hungerford
Bevan Hy. esq. 4 Hamilton pl. Hyde pk. corner, & Cambridge ho. Twickenhm
Bevan John, esq. 13 Trinity sq. Southwrk
Bevan Miss, 52 Devonshire st. Queen sq
Bevan Mrs. Chas. 16 Devonshire place
Bevan Rd. esq. 15 Whitehds. gro. Chelsea
Bevan Robert C. L. esq. & Lady Agneta, 42 Up. Harley st. & Trent park, Enfield
Bevan Thomas, M.D. 20 Finsbury circus
Bevan Wm. esq. 48 Conduit st. Bond st
Bevan Wm. esq. 15 Whitehead's grv. Chels
Beverley, Earl of, P.C. 8 Portman sq
Bevern Mrs. 5 Marlboro' pl. Knngtn. crs
Beverstock James, esq. 56 Gt. Coram st
Beville Chas. esq. 2 Eccleston st. south
Bevir Edward James, esq. 20 Old square
Bewley John, esq. 3 North pl. Kingsld. rd
Bewsher John, esq. 13 Gt. Tower st
Bexley Lord, P.C. 31 Gt. George st. Westminster, & Footscray place, Kent
Bibby Samuel, esq. 9 North Audley st
Bichner O. F. esq. 30 Southampton bdg
Bick Mrs. 11 Newington pl. Kenngtn. rd
Bickerstaff Wm. esq. 6 Brecknock ter
Bickerton John, esq. 18 Gt. George st. Wstr
Bickerton Rd. P. esq. 92 St. John's wd. ter
Bickerton Walter, esq. 8 Pall mall east
Bickley Saml. esq. 11 Albion gr. Thnhl. rd
Bicknell Rev. John, 60 Coleshill st
Bicknell Christr. esq. 48 Manchester st
Bicknell Elhanan, esq. 17 Clapham rise
Bicknell Geo. esq. 18 Dorset pl. Dorset sq
Bicknell Hen. E. esq. 28 Up. Bedford pl
Bicknell Joseph, esq. 1 Staple inn
Bicknell Robert, esq. 38 Bloomsbury sq
Bicknell Samuel, esq. 48 Manchester st
Bicknell Thos. esq. 19 Park pl. Paddingtn
Bidden Jas. esq. 13 Kennington terrace
Bidder Geo. esq. 8 Saville rw. Walwth. rd
Bidder G. P. esq. 24 Gt. George st. Westmr
Biddle Capt. 3 Durham place, Chelsea
Biddle Edwd. esq. 13 Albion ter. Wans. rd
Biddle John, esq. 24 Edwardes square
Biddle Miss, 30 Grove pl. Lisson grove
Biddle Miss, 12 Northwick terrace
Biddlecombe J. esq. 9 Gerrard st. Islgtn
Biddulph Mrs. 2 Alpha rd. Regent's pk
Biddulph John, esq. 43 Charing cross; & Ledbury, Herefordshire
Biddulph Ormus, esq. 44 Charing cross
Biddulph Robert, esq. 31 Eaton place, & Ledbury, Herefordshire
Biden Miss, 22 Holles st. Cavendish sq
Bidgood Mrs. 28 Carlton vills. Edgw. rd
Bidwell John, esq. 2 Park pl. St. James's
Bidwell Mrs. 11 Cloudesley ter. Islgtn
Bidwell Thomas, esq. 99 Gloucester pl. & Paddock, Thetford, Norfolk
Bielefield Samuel Augustus, esq. 11 Southampton place, New road
Bielfeld Henry, esq. 13 Rathbone place
Bielke M. de, sec. to Danish Legation, 52 Wilton crescent
Bieneme Angelo, esq. 22 Newmanst. Fitz. sq
Biers Hugh, sen. esq. Maida va. 244 Edg. rd
Biers Hugh, jun. esq. 12 Dorset pl. Drst. sq
Biffin Jas. esq. 11 Rawstone st. Bmptm
Bifield Miss, 6 Canonbury pl. Islington
Bigg Edward Smith, esq. 45 Tavistock sq.; & 38 Southampton bldgs.; & Hyde, near Crawley
Bigg Fredk. esq. 2 Augusta ter. Clphm. rd
Bigg Richard, esq. 1 Canonbury villas
Bigg Thos. esq. Clevld. vil. Fnchly. nw. rd
Bigg Wm. esq. 20 Hamilton terrace, & 3 Langham place
Bigg Wm. R. esq. 23 Old sq. Lincoln's inn
Bigge Capt. T. E. 19 Bryanstone square
Bigge Arthur, esq. 1 Mitre ct. bldgs. Temp
Bigge Thos. esq. 19 Bryanstone square
Biggers Mrs. 3 Allen ter. Kensington
Biggs Maj. Gen. 10 St. Andrews place, Regent's park
Biggs Rev. Michael, 46 Lincoln's inn flds
Biggs George, esq. 24 Albany st
Biggs Jeremh. esq. 17 Finsbury pl. sth
Biggs Kirkman, esq. 20 Old Quebec st
Biggs Mrs. 24 Cross st. Islington
Bignold Saml. esq. 6 Crescent, N. Brdg. st
Bilke Henry, esq. 12 Stamford st
Billing Allen, esq. 114 Camden rd. villas
Billing Archibald, M.D. 6 Grosvenor gate
Billing Sydney, esq. 2 Church yd. ct. Temp
Billings Rt. Wm. esq. 44 Low. Belgrave pl
Billion Mrs. 50 Notting hill square
Bills Geo. esq. 30 Low. Kennington la
Bilton Sam. Fras. esq. 5 New sq. Lincns. inn
Bilton Saml. Fredk. esq. 24 Regent sq
Binfield Jas. esq. 28 Davies st. Brkly. sq
Bingham Henry, esq. 12 Villiers st
Bingham Miss, 66 Baker st
Bingham Peregrine, esq. 35 Gordon sq
Bingley John, esq. 25 Camden rd. villas
Bingley Mrs. 25 Bloomsbury st
Bingley W. R. esq. 52 Lincoln's inn fields
Binkes — esq. 4 Circus rd. St. John's wd
Binnie Alex. esq. 3 Glo'ster rd. Regt's. pk
Binns Wm. esq. 27 Carey st
Binny W. Scott, esq. 37 Bryanstone sq
Bins Joshua, esq. 24 Grafton st. Eustn. sq
Birch Rev. Sam. D.D. 86 King Wm. st. City
Birch Henry Wm. esq. 68 Lincoln's inn fi
Birch Henry Wm. esq. 49 Welbeck st
Birch James, esq. 46 Lincoln's inn fields
Birch John, esq. 47 Brewer st. Golden sq
Birch John, esq. 66 Wimpole st
Birch John B. esq. 3 Cannon row
Birch John William, esq. 66 Wimpole st
Birch Jonathan, esq. 71 Cadogan place
Birch Jonathan, esq. 45 Upper Gower st
Birch Miss, 22 Avenue rd. Regent's pk
Birch Miss C. 2 Tavistock st. Bedford sq
Birch Mrs. 2 Tavistock st. Bedford sq
Birch Peregrine, esq. 49 Welbeck st
Birch Richard, esq. 14 Clifford's inn
Birch Sam. esq. 1 Park cot. Havrstk. hl
Birch Thos. H. esq. 16 Blandfordst. Ptmn. sq
Birch Thos. Jacob, esq. 16 Blandford st. Portman sq.; & 5 Inner Temple la
Birch Wm. esq. 24 Gt. Russell st. & 3 Little Russell st. Bloomsbury
Birch Wm. J. esq. 20 Park pl. Regt.'s pk
Birch Wm. R. esq. 1 Scarsdale ter. Kngtn
Bircham Francis Thos. esq. 15 Bedford rw
Bircham F. T. esq. 2 Hall pl. St. John's wood
Bircham Wm. esq. 38 Connaught terrace
Bird Col. 39 Howland st
Bird Chas. esq. 1 Bucknm. pl. Old Kent rd
Bird Chas. esq. 4 Stone bldgs. Linc. inn
Bird Charles, esq. 10 Welbeck st
Bird George, esq. 8 Clapham road place
Bird George, esq. 7 Union place, New rd
Bird Golding, M.D. 19 Myddelton sq
Bird Henry, esq. 13 Clapham road place
Bird Henry H. esq. 5 Robert st. Adelphi
Bird H. P. esq. 58 Lin. inn fl. & Tooting com
Bird I. esq. 72 Seymour pl. Bryanstone sq
Bird Jas. esq. 5 New inn & Hammersmh
Bird James, esq. 16 Orchard st. Oxford st
Bird John, esq. 51 Cambridge ter. Edg. rd
Bird John, esq. 89 Hamilton terrace
Bird John, esq. 2 Regent place west
Bird John, esq. 13 Park st. Grosvenor sq
Bird John Lorence, esq. 21 Old square
Bird Miss, 94 High st. Marylebone
Bird S. esq. 28 Hornton st. Kensington
Bird Steph. esq. Hornton vil. Campdn. hl
Bird Wm. esq. 1 Artillery pl. Finsbury
Bird Wm. Fredk. W. esq. 13 Gray's inn sq
Bird Wm. Fredk. W. esq. 5 Verulam bldgs
Bird Wm. Wilberforce, esq. 24 Cambrdg. sq
Birdseye Geo. esq. 36 Royal cres. Nott. hll
Birkbeck Mrs. 10 Glo'ster rd. Hyde pk
Birkbeck Wm. Lloyd, esq. 6 Stone bldgs
Birkenhead John, esq. 22 Manchester st
Birkenhead Miss, 22 Manchester st
Birkhead Joseph, esq. 17 Stamford st
Birkhead Benjn. esq. 34 Hans place
Birt Jacob, esq. 30 Sussex gardens, Hyde park, & 1 Southampton st. Fitzroy sq
Birt John, esq. 1 Coles terr. Barnsby. rd
Bischoff Jas. esq. 20 Highbury terrace
Bishop Sir Hy. R. knt. 13 Cambridge st
Bishop George, esq. South villa, Inner circle, Regent's park
Bishop Hugh, esq. 47 Connaught terrace
Bishop John, esq. 38 Bernard st
Bishop John, esq. 21 Howland st. & 11 Lincoln's inn fields
Bishop John D. esq. 14 John st. Adelphi
Bishop Miss, 38 Albion st. Hyde park
Bishop Mrs. 23 Chapel st. Grosvenor sq
Bishop Wm. esq. 8 Notting hill terrace
Biss Wm. esq. 54 South Molton st. Bond st
Bisse Mrs. 49 Green st. Grosvenor sq
Bisset Andrew, esq. 6 Stone buildings
Bissett Sir J. knt. 1 Tavistock st. Bedfd. sq
Bittleston Adam, esq. 17 Buckingham st. Strand; & 4 Brick ct. Temple
Bitts Mrs. 3 Richmond ter. Canonbury sq
Blaauw Wm. Hy. esq. 3 Queen Anne st
Blaber Miss, 20 Dorset st. Portman sq
Blachford Capt. Hen. 6 Park st. Gros. sq
Black Alexander, esq. 10 Russell sq
Black C. C. esq. 5 Marlboro' rd. S. John's wd
Black John, esq. 111 Camden road villas
Black Mrs. 33 Coleshill st
Black Patrick, M.D. 13 Bedford square
Black Thos. esq. 12 Tavistock st. Bedfd. sq
Black Wm. F. esq. 19 Wilton place
Black Wm. Hy. esq. Mill yard, Leman st. & Rolls house, Chancery lane
Blackall J. G. esq. 14 Henry st. east
Blackall Thos. esq. 13 Queen st. Mayfr
Blackburn Rev. John, 10 Cloudesley st
Blackburn Colin, esq. 5 King's Bench wk
Blackburn Edw. L. esq. 16½ Clement's inn
Blackburn Geo. H. esq. 38 Weymouth st
Blackburn John, esq. 10 Argyle st. New rd
Blackburn John Edw. esq. 106 Mount st
Blackburn Miss, 28 Bloomsbury sq
Blackburn Mrs. 30 Park st. Grosvenor sq
Blackburn Wm. esq. 10 Old sq. Lincs. inn
Blackburne Geo. esq. 20 Lower rd. Islingtn
Blackburne John Ireland, M.P. 2 Park st. Westminster; & Hale, Warrington
Blackburne Miss, 22 Wilton st
Blackdan Henry, esq. 6 Norfolk cresct
Blackden Mrs. 17 Wilton crescent

Blackett Dowager Lady, 16 Portman st. & Thorpe, Lee Egham
Blackett P. C. R.N. 41 Connaught ter
Blackett Mrs.16 Bedford row, Islington
Blackford Edward, esq. 138 Sloane st
Blackith Chas. esq. 9 Stonefield st
Blacklock Joseph, esq. 19 Marlboro' sq
BlacklockWm.J.esq.40London st.Fitz.sq
Blackman Wm. esq. 85 Pratt st. Camden town; & 1 Raymond bldgs. Gray's inn
Blackmore Edwd. esq. 18 Clement's inn, Strand, & Guilford, Surrey
Blackmore Miss, 16 Upper Montagu st
Blackmore Mrs. 7 Eaton square
Blackmore Rd. esq.16 Upper Montagu st
Blackmore Robt. esq. 3 St. Martin's pl
Blackstone Joseph, esq. 31 Bayham ter
Blackstone Wm. S. M.P. 28B, Albemarle st. & Castle Priory, Wallingford
Blackwell John, esq.Cottage rd.Eaton sq
Blackwood Lady, 7 Cornwall terrace
Blackwood Hon. Mrs. 14 Hinde st
Blackwood Mrs. 23 Chesham st. Belg. sq
Bladen Ruspini, esq. 17 Gt. College st
BladesJph.esq.11Cobourg pl.U.Kngtn.la
Blagden Richard, esq. 26 Albemarle st
Blagrave Mrs. 9 Melcombe pl. Dorset sq
Blagrove Charles, esq. 88 Norton st
Blagrove Henry, esq. 71 Mortimer st
Blagrove Hen. John, esq. 34 Harley st
Blagrove Mrs. 21 Welbeck st
Blagrove Wm. esq. 88 Norton st
Blaikley A. esq. 6 Percy st
Blaiklock David, esq. 73 Albany st
Blain John, esq. 30 Connaught terrace
Blair Lieut. Col. Wm. Henry Stopford, 3 Portman square; & Penninghame, Newton Stewart, N.B.
Blair David A.esq.14Pembroke sq.Knsgn
Blair John, esq. 73 Coleshill st
Blair Mrs. 3 Portman sq. & Penninghame, Newton Stewart, Scotland
Blair Rt.esq. 90 Gt. Russell st.Bloomsby
Blake Rt. Hon. Anthony Rd. B4, Albany
Blake Sir Valentine, bart. M.P. 53 Parliament st. & 27 North George st. Dublin, & Munlo castle, Galway
BlakeGen.R.D.8St.George's pl.Hyde pk
Blake Barnabas,esq.6Sussex pl.Hyde pk
Blake Chas. Hy. esq. 15 Devonshire pl
Blake Francis, esq. 37 John st. Bedford row, & 6 King's road
Blake Geo. esq. Carlton cham. 8 Regt. st
Blake Geo. esq.6Sussex pl.Hyde pk.gdns
Blake Jas. esq. 16 Pall mall
Blake Jas. esq.21Theberton st.west,Islng
Blake John Day, esq. 17 Clement's inn
Blake John Day, esq. 4 Stockwell comn
Blake John Goble, esq. F.S.A. 12 Gower st. & 14 Essex st. Strand
Blake Joseph, esq. 11 Hinde st
Blake Mark, M.P. Reform club, & Ballinafad, Mayo
Blake Martin Joseph M.P. Reform club, & Brooke lodge, Dungan, Ireland
Blake Miss, 9 Henrietta st. Cavendish sq
Blake Mrs. 2 Hanover cottages, Park rd
Blake Mrs. 26 Up. Baker st. Regent's pk
Blake Mrs. 22 Up. Berkeley st. west
Blake O. esq. 13 Southampton st. Strand
Blake Thomas, D.C.L. 1College, Doctors' commons, & Coltishall, near Norwich
Blake Thomas, esq. 13 Clifford's inn
Blake Wm. esq. Chancery. chmbs.Qlty.ct
Blake William, esq. 62 Portland place, & Danesbury, Welwyn, Herts
Blake William John, esq. 62 Portland pl. & Danesbury, near Welwyn, Herts
Blakemore Richard, esq. M. P. Club chambers, 15 Regent st. & the Leys, near Monmouth
Blakemore Wm. esq. 21 Grosvenor st
Blakemore Wm. esq. Wandsworth road
Blakeney John, esq. 3 Bedford row
Blakesley Mrs. 5 Dorset ter. Claplm. rd
Blakeway Mrs.16 Radcliffe ter.Goswl.rd
Blaksley H.J.esq.7Clarnce.pl.Clphm.rd
Blakiston Mrs. 2 Charles st. Lowndes sq
Blamire William, esq. 35 Upper Harley st. & the Oaks, Carlisle
Blanchard Thos. esq. 17 Upper Ebury st
Bland George, esq. 8 Suffolk st
Bland Geo.D.esq.Devereux chmbs.Strnd
Bland Hen. Dl. esq.9Duncan ter.City rd
Bland James, 1A, Cadogan st
Bland Mrs. 37 Jermyn st. St. James's
Bland Mrs. 17 Michael's pl. Brompton
Bland Mrs. 71 St. John's wood terrace
Bland Thos. esq. 23 South st. Grosvr. sq
Bland T. esq.8Warwick vil.Maida hl.wst
Blandford Marquis of, 53 Wilton cres
Blandford Silas, esq. R.N. 9 Chester sq
Blane Sir Seymour, bart. 83 Jermyn st
Blane Lieut. Col. 16 Grosvenor st
Blanshard Henry, esq. 37 Gt.Ormond st
Blanshard Hen. jun. esq.5Up.Bedford pl
Blanshard Miss, 19 New Ormond st
Blanshard Rd. esq.64Lincoln's inn fields
Blashfield J. M. esq. 3 Kensington gard
Blatch Hen. esq. 22 River st. Mydltn. sq
Blatherwick S.esq.2Lyon ter.Edgwarerd
Blatspiel Fred. Ernest, esq.25Doughty st
Blaxland Wm.esq. 15 Coles tr.Brnsby.rd
Blaxland Wm. esq. 44 Spencer st
Blaxland Wm. esq.7 Union row,Cmbwll
Blayney Lord, 76 Jermyn st. & Castle Blayney, Monaghan
Blencowe Robt. esq. 1 New Boswell ct
Blenkins Geo. esq. 14 Whiteheads grove
Blenkinsop Jn. esq. 15 John st. Adelphi
Blessington Countess, Kensington gore
Blew Wm. esq.16 Warwick st.Chering cr
Blewitt Octavian, esq. 73 Gt. Russell st
Blewitt R. J. esq. M.P. 7 Mnchstr. bldgs. & Llantarnam abbey, Newport, Mon
Blick Rd. Granger, esq. 4 Guilford st. & 2 Brick court, Temple
Bligh Hon. Col. 13 Bryanstone square
Bligh Misses, 32 Royal cres. Not. hill
Blink Geo. esq. 4 Canonbry. vils. Islgtn
Bliss Hen.esq.11Bentinck st. Mnchstr.sq
Bliss Henry, esq. 30 Mecklenburgh sq. & 11 King's Bench walk
Bliss Jas. esq. 3 Devonshire pl.Edgw.rd
Bliss Mrs.Berkeley house,Cambridge st. Edgw. rd. & Brandon pk. Suffolk
Bliss Mrs. 9 Bryanstone st. Portman sq
Bliss Richd. esq. 2 Albion rd. Holloway
Blizard Lady, 2 Grove ter. Kentish tn
Blizard Allen, esq. 43 Halfmoon st
Blizard Jas. esq. 10 New Cavendish st
Blockey Joseph, esq. 44 Jermyn st
Blofeld R. esq.12 Millman st. Bedford rw
Blogg Fred. esq. 34 Argyle st. King's cr
Blogg Geo. esq. 24 Smith st. Chelsea
Blogg John, esq. 46 Guilford st
Blois Major, 14 St.Alban's pl.St.James's
Blome Mrs. 48 Ebury st. Eaton sq
Blomfield J. esq. 6 Davidg. ter.Walct. pl
Bloomer Thos. esq. 1 Up. Gloucester pl
Bloomfield Lord, 6 Sackville st
BloomfieldRev.Dr.5Up.Robertst.Bmptn
Blore Edward, esq. 7 Welbeck st. & 4 Manchester sq
Blore John, esq. 8 Michael's pl. Brmptn
Blore Mrs. 9 Michael's place, Brompton
Blott Wm. esq.10 Albion gr.Thornhill rd
Blount G. esq. 52 Up.Seymour st.Ptm.sq
Blount Geo. Lane, esq. 84 Baker st
Blount Peter C. esq. Priory, Barnsby.pl
Blount Walter,esq.37 North bk.Rgt.'s pk
Blount W. A. esq. Heralds' coll.Drs.com
Blower John, esq. 23 Old sq.Lincln's.inn
Blower Joseph, esq. 32 Cumming st. Pentonville, & 61 Lincoln's inn fields
Bloxham Chas.J.esq.21Mecklenburgh sq
Bloxam Edward, esq. 2 New Boswell ct
Bloxam James Mackenzie, esq. 40 Cadogan place, & 41 Chancery lane
Bloxam Mrs. 28 Cambridge st. Edgw. rd
Bloxam Richard, esq. 40Cadogan place, Sloane st. & 2 New Boswell court
Bloxam S. esq. 3 Up.Ptlnd. pl. Wands.rd
Bloxam Wm. esq. 28Duke st. Grosvnr. sq
Bloxam Thos. esq. 14 Gt. James st
Bloxam Wm. esq. 10 Shaftesbury cresnt
Bloxsome Geo. Fred. esq. 59 Ebury st
Bluck Thos.Hen. esq.Church rw.Limeho
Bluett J. esq. 5 Bentinck pl. Prtlnd. twn
BluettJohn,esq.5St.Anns villasSt.Jn.'s w
Blumenthal A. esq. 48 Notting hill sq
Blundell Benson, esq. 87 Cadogan place, & 10 Serle st. Lincoln's inn
Blundell Bezer, esq. 1&3Mitre ct.chambs
BlundellEd.Straw,M.D.18Lr.Seymour st
Blundell James, M.D. 1 Gt. George st
Blundell Mrs. 18 Trevor square
Blundstone Mrs. 2 Cloudesley square
Blunt Lady, 26 Eaton place, & Heathfield park, Uckfield
BluntJames T. esq.3 Dorset pl. Dorset sq
Blunt John, esq. 6 Upper Bedford pl
BluntJohnElijah, esq. 4 New sq. Lin. inn
Blunt Jsph. esq. 16 Hertford st. Mayfair
Blunt Jsph. esq. 2 Upper Gower st. & 5 Raymond buildings, Gray's inn
Blunt Mrs. 43 Charlotte st. Prtlnd. pl
Blunt Samuel, esq. 24 Cloudesley sq
Blyde Mrs. 2 Paulton's ter. King's rd. w
Blyth Geo. esq. 9 Cheyne row, Chelsea
BlythJn. esq. Park ho.Grove rd.Mile end
Blyth Miss 1 Bluecoat bdgs. LittleBritn
Blyth Mrs. 9 Theberton st. Islington
Boak Miss, 4 Stockwell vil. Clapham rd
Board Edward, esq. 9 Cadogan terrace
Board John, esq. 3 Polygon, Clarendn. sq
BoardmanMaj.Gen. 12Euston pl.New rd
Bobbit Miss, 50 Jermyn st. St. James's
Bockett D. S. esq. 60 Lincoln's inn fields
Bockett John, esq. 2 Vimiera, Wands. rd
Bockett Miss, 2 Vimiera, Wandswth. rd
BocquetEdwd.esq. 4Thurloe pl.O.Brmpt
BocquetF.esq.2Seymour pl.Wndswth. rd
Bocquet Rd. esq. 59 Trinity sq. Boro'
Boddington Hen. J. esq. 5 Acton st
Boddington Thos. esq. 5 Norfolk crescent
Boddy Edwd. Jph. esq. 10 Calthorpe st
Boddy Wm. esq. 31 Church st. Chelsea
Boden George, esq. 11 Paper buildings
BodenGeo. esq. 18St. Geo.'s ter. Knsngtn
Bodenham Mrs. 7 Alfred st. City road
Bodkin John James, esq. M.P. 41 Piccadilly, & Kilcloony, near Tuam, Ireland
Bodkin Wm. Hen. M.P. 8 Mansfield st.; 4 Paper buildings, Temple; & Lower Heath, Hampstead
Bodman Benj. esq. 23 Up. Southwick st
Bogaerts Peter, esq. 16 Oxford terrace
Bogue David, esq. 39 Lonsdale square
Bohn Jas. esq. 5 Albion ter. Wandsworth
Bohn Miss, 18 Henrietta st. Covent grdn
Boileau Sir John Peter, bart. & Lady Catherine, 20 Upper Brook st. & Ketterington hall, Norwich
Boinville Ernest de, esq. 82Dean st. Soho
BokenhamMrs.15Titchfield tr.Regt. prk
Bokenham Wm. esq. Spring cottage, Stoke Newington green
Boldero Col. 47 Mount st
Boldero Captain Hen. George, M.P. Hurst grove, Reading, Berks
Boldero Charles, esq. 4 Cambridge terrace, Edgware road
Boldero Edwd. Gale, esq. 36 Foley pl
Bolding Jn. Parker, esq. 66 Hamilton ter
Bolingbroke Viscount, 35 Mortimer st. Cav. sq. &Lydiard park, nearSwindon
Bollen Fredk. esq. 21 Claremont ter
BoltonLord, Thomas' hotel; &Hackwood pk. Basingstoke; &Bolton hall,Bedale
Bolton Chas. esq. 2 James st. Adelphi
Bolton Edward, esq. 69 Gibson square
Bolton Geo. Buckley, esq. 9 Pall mall
BoltonJohn,esq. 11 Hill rd. St. John's wd
Bolton John Henry, esq. 1 New square, Lincoln's inn, & Lee park, Blackheath
Bolton Mrs. 29 Winchester row, New rd
Bolton William, esq. 44 Sloane st

Bolton Thos. Whalley, esq. 55 Wigmore st. & 4 Elm court, Temple
BoltonWm.Gillmore, esq. 25Austinfriars
BolusWm.esq.9Clayton pl.Caledonian rd
Bompas Mrs. 11 Park rd. Regent's park
Bonar Jas. esq. 2 Glo'ster st. Portm. sq
Bond A. esq. 3 Holland pk. ter. Notng.hll
Bond C. esq. 11 Portland pl. Clapham rd
Bond Edwd. esq. 84 Oxford ter. Edgw.rd
Bond Hen. esq. 6 Canonbury cot. Islgtn
Bond Miss, 17 Fortess ter. Kentish tn
Bond Mrs. 7 Crescent pl. Hampstead rd
Bond Mrs. 24 Devonshire place
Bond Thos. esq. 7 Figtree court, Temple
Bond Wm. esq. 7 Figtree court, Temple
Bond Wm.H.esq.14Coburg pl.U.Kenn.la
Bond Wm. Henry, esq. 104 Pall mall
Bone Henry P. esq. 12 Percy st
Bone Miss, 1 Pelham terrace, Brompton
Bone Mrs. 6 Brompton grove
Bone Saml.V.esq. 2 Stone bldgs.Linc.inn
Bone Spottiswood, esq. 1 St. James's st
Bone Stanhope, esq. 1 St. James's st
BoneW. jun.esq. 12Percy st.Tottnh.ct.rd
Bones John,esq.3Clarendon pl.Maida hll
Bones Mrs. 22 Grove pl. Lisson grove
Bonham Francis Rbt. esq. 35 Clarges st
Bonham Miss, 35 Clarges st
Bonhote John, esq. 14 Up. Southwick st
Bonner Col. 11A, Gt. Cumberland st
Bonner John, esq. 43 St. John's wood ter
Bonner John Geo. esq. 16 Furnival's inn
Bonnett John C. esq. 29 Queen Anne st
Bonney F. A. esq. 2 Halkin ter. Belgrv.sq
Bonny Geo. esq. 20 Grafton st. Fitzy. sq
Bonsey Miss, 21 Mabledon place
BonwellRev.J.M.A.20Glo'stertr.Nw.rd.e
Boodle Edward, esq. 2 Manchester st. & 23 Old square, Lincoln's inn
Boodle Henry Mitford, esq. 6 Sussex gardens, Hyde park, & 9 Davies st
Boodle John, esq. 42 Connaught sq.; 9 Davies st.; & Heath farm, Watford
Boodle John, jun. esq. 90 Eaton place, & 43 Lower Belgrave place
Boodle Wm. Chilver, esq. 33 Connaught square, & 9 Davies st
Boodle's Club House (John Geo. Fuller, sec.), 28 St. James's st
Booker Robert, esq. 48 Nelson square
Booker Thos. esq. 10 Clapham road pl
Boone Rev. James S. 2 Stanhope st. Hyde park, & 50 Leicester square
Boord Joseph, esq. 24 Mornington cresc
Boosey Thos. esq. 43 Notting hill sq
Boote John, esq. 36 Guilford st
Booth Sir Felix, bart. 43 Portland place, & Ferne hill, near Windsor
BoothChas.B.esq.15 Marlbro'pl.Kenn.cr
Booth Edwin, esq. 3Gt.Queen st.Westmr
Booth George, esq. 4 Newman st
Booth James, esq. 39 Hyde park square
Booth John, esq. 7 Suffolk st.Pall mall e
Booth Miss, 43 Portland place
Booth Mrs. 16 Clarges st
Booth Mrs. 15 New st. Spring gardens
Booth W. esq. 53 Charlotte st. Fitzroy sq
Booth Wm. Joseph, esq. 34 Red Lion sq
Boothby Sir Wm. bart. Fenton's hotel
Boothby Chas. esq. 28Charlotte st.Ftz.sq
Boott Francis, esq. 24 Gower st
Booty J. esq. 4 Devonshire tr. Islington
Booty John G. esq. Brixton hill, & 1 Raymond buildings, Gray's inn
Booty Mrs. 10 Guilford st. Russell sq
Borham Mrs. 16 Church row, Limeho
Borlase Miss, 27 Connaught terrace
Borough Lady, 32 Brook st
Borough Burton, esq. 39 York terrace, & Chetwynd pk. Newport, Shropshire
Borough Mrs. 39 York terrace; & Chetwynd park, Newport, Shropshire; & Hulland hall, nearAshbourne, Drbysh
Borradaile Rev. Abraham, St. Mary's Parsonage, Vincent square
Borrett Francis, esq. 9 Queen Anne st
Borrett Chas. Wm. esq. 9 Queen Anne st. Cavendish sq. & 8 New sq. Lincoln's in
Borrett Thos. esq. 95 Glo'ster pl. Portman sq. & 35 Lincoln's inn fields
Borrow John, esq. 133 Sloane st
Borthwick James A. esq. 56 King sq
BorthwickMichl.A. esq. 1 Furnival's inn
Borthwick Peter, M.P. 94 Pall mall
Borton Edward, esq. 1 New sq. Lin's. in
Bos John, esq. 3 Acton pl. Kingsland rd
Bosanquet Rt. hon. Sir J. B. knt. 12 Montague pl. & the Firs, Hampstead
Bosanquet George, esq. Mivart's hotel, 44 Brook st
Bosanquet Hen. esq. 9 LowerBerkeley st
Bosanquet Jas. esq. 2 Hyde park square
Bosanquet Miss, 13 North Audley st
Bosanquet Mrs. 59 Cambridge st
Bosanquet Mrs. Hen. 5 Orchard st
Bosanquet Mrs. L. P. 46 Up. Harley st. & Dingeston court, Monmouth; & Forest house, Essex
Bosanquet Wm.H.F.esq.1 Innr.Templ.la
Boscawen Lord, 2 St. James's sq. & Woolhampton, Newbury, Berks
Bosier Mrs. Noel st. Islington
Bosfield Chas. esq. 24 Henrietta st
Bosley Mrs. 35 Robert ter. Chelsea
Boss Mrs. 20 Cornwall ter. Regent's pk
Bostock Ellis, esq. 41 Hunter st
Bostock John, M.D. 22 Up. Bedford pl
Boston Lord, Hedsor lodge, Maidenhead; & Llanidan, Anglesey, N.W
Bosville hon. Alexr. & Mrs. 44 Brook st. & Thorpe hall, Slidmere, Yorkshire
Boswick Mrs. 45 Gerrard st. Islington
Boteler Wm. jun. esq. 21 Old sq. Linc.in
Botfield Beriah, esq. M.P., F.R.S. 9Stratton st. & Norton hall, nr. Northampton
Bott A. esq. 6 Berkeley pl. Connaught sq
Bott Mrs. 41 Allsop terrace, New rd
Bott Thos. esq. 29 Beaufoy ter. Edgw. rd
Bottrill Thos. esq. 4Arundel tr. Bnsby.rd
Bouard Alfred F. esq. 5 Chancery lane
Boucher Anthony, esq. 6 Gray's inn sq
BoucherC.esq 6Lawn cottgs.So.Lambth
Boucher Miss, 4 Tibberton square
Boucher Mrs. 18 Chapel st. Pentonville
BoucherWm.R.esq.13Palmerter.Hollwy
Boughey Wm. Fenton, esq. 3 Brick ct
Boughton Henry, esq. 39 Somerset st
Boulcott Jn. Elliker, esq. 8 Hyde pk. sq
Boulcott Jph. esq. 3 Clarence terrace
Boulger John, esq. 1 Robert st. Adelphi
Boullancourt Aug. esq. 19 Frith st. Soho
Boulnois Wm. esq. 12 Abbey road
Boult Jsph. esq. 38 Gower pl. Euston sq
Boult Miss, 13 Bedford st. Covent gdn
Boulter Saml.J.esq.11King's rd. ea.Chels
Boulton Rev. Thos. 44 Essex st. Strand
Boulton Fred. esq. 23 Lit. Knightrider st
Boulton John, esq. 9 St. Pancras vale
Boulton Mrs. 28 York buildings, New rd
Boulton Wm. esq. 2 Leigh st
Boulton Wm. J.esq. 21A, Northamptn.sq
Bourchier Sir Thos. 13 Chapel st. Gro. pl
Bourdillon C. esq. 9 Old sq. Lincoln's inn
Bourdillon Ed. esq. 25 Porchester ter
Bourdillon James, esq. 29 Bedford sq
Bourdillon Mrs. 6 Church st. Kensington
Bourdillon Thos.esq. 3 Stone bdgs.Lin.in
Bourdin D.F.esq.36Bryanstn.st.Prtm.sq
Bourdin Madame, 36 Bryanstone st
Bourdois Mrs. 19 Wimpole st
Bourne Hen. esq. 7 Sussex pl. Canonbry
Bourne Herbert, esq. 45 Lamb's Cndt. st
Bourne James, esq. 7 Somerset st
Bourne John C.esq. 14Buckinghm.st.Str
Bourne Robert, esq. 2 Parliament st
Bourne Wm. esq. 50 King sq. Goswell rd
Bourness Geo. esq. 13 Holloway place
Bouroughs Col. Wm. Rose villa, Alpha pl
Boursot Adolphe, esq. 39 Burton crescnt
Bousfield Rt. esq.4Newingtn. pl.Kenn.rd
Bousfield Wm. esq.6 Colebrooke ter. Isl
Bousfield Wm. C. esq. 12 Gray's inn sq
Bousson J.esq.3Devonshirepl.Wndsth.rd
Boustead John, esq.8UpperGloucester st
Boutcher Wm. esq.Denmk. hill, Cambwl
BouverieHon.Edwd.P. M.P.19Chester st
Bouverie Hon. Philip Pleydell, M.P. 16 Hill st. & 11 Haymarket; & Brymour house, Bridgewater
Bouverie Lieut. Gen. Sir H.F.24Eaton pl
Bouverie, Norman, & Murdoch, 11 Hymkt
Bouverie Mrs. 22 Noel st. Islington
Bouwens Miss, 9 Connaught place
Bovell Jas. esq. East hill, Wandsworth rd
Bovet Charles, esq. 7 Duncan terrace
Bovet Edward, esq. 14 Duncan terrace
Bovill Wm. esq. 11 Paper bldgs, Temple
Bowater Maj. Gen. Sir Ed. 37 Grosvnr. st
Bowden James, esq. 12 St. Helen's place
Bowden Mrs. 17 Grosvenor place
Bowden Mrs. 23 Lonsdale sq. Islington
Bowden Mrs. 36 Kensington square
Bowden Wm. esq. 17 Forston st. City rd
Bowdery Thomas, esq. 4 Canonbury sq
Bowditch James, esq. 45Essex st. Strand, & 70 Chancery lane
Bowdler Rev. Thomas, 79 Chester sq
Bowdler Geo. esq. 5Glo'ster rd. Old Bptn
Bowdon Miss, 11 Hyde park square
Bowen John, esq.19 Circus rd. St. Jn.'s wd
Bowen Joseph, esq. 9 Up. Berkeley st.we
Bower Charles, esq. 52 Welbeck st
Bower Mark Noble, esq. 95 Hatton grdn
Bower Miss, 6 Cheyne walk, Chelsea
Bower Mrs. 20 Lower Belgrave place
Bower Mrs. 1 Powis pl. Gt. Ormond st
Bower Thomas Holme, esq. 62 Doughty st. & 46 Chancery lane
BowerWm.M.esq.5Cmdn.st.sth.Cmdn.tn
Bowerbank Jas. S. esq. 45 Park st. Islgtn
BowernWm.esq.13Nw.Nth.st.Red Ln.sq
Bowes Rev. G.H. 7 Henriett. st. Cov.gnd
Bowers Lt. Col. Chas. Robt. 31 Wilton pl
BowesRev.Wm.B.28Alpha rd.Regt's pk
BowesJn.esq. M.P. 54Conduit st.Bond st. & Streatham castle, near Staindrop
Bowker Hy. Fras. esq. Little Britain
Bowker Jas. esq. 1 Gray's inn square
Bowker Wm. esq. 1 Gray's inn square
Bowlby Thos. Wm. esq. 32Lincoln's inn fi
Bowler Mrs. Col. 128 Albany st
Bowler Rt. Edwen, esq. 17 Judd pl. west
Bowles Rear Adm. C.B. M.P. Admiralty
Bowles Geo. esq. 2Bedford pl. Hmpstd.rd
Bowles G. Rushout, *see* RushoutBowles
Bowles JohnHen.esq.2Middle Temple la
Bowles Mrs. Henry, 6York bldgs. New rd
Bowles Miss, Admiralty
Bowles William, esq. 55 Bernard st
Bowles William, esq. 58 Great Coram st
Bowles William, esq. 23 Haverstock hl
Bowles William, esq. 17 Woburn place
Bowley Mrs. 6 Bayswater hill
Bowley Mrs. 17 Oxford terrace
Bowman Chas. esq. 24 Up. Woburn pl
Bowman Jonas, esq. 2 Barnard's inn
Bowman Joseph, esq. 19 Mecklenbgh.sq
BowmanRobert, esq.17Belindatr.Cannby
Bowman Wm. esq. F.R.S. 14 Golden sq
Bownas the Misses, 28 Cambridge sq
Bowne John, esq. 24 St. James's place
Bowness Wm. esq. 14 Fitzroy st. Fitz.sq
Bowring John, LL.D., F.L.S., M.P. 1 Queen sq. Westminster
Bowring John, esq. 70 Gt. Portland sq
Bowron Mrs. 4 Aberdeen pl. Maida hill
Bowstead Joseph, esq. 1 Gloucester rd. Hyde park, & 5 Essex court, Temple
Bowtell John, esq. 4 Philpott tr. Edg.rd
Bowtell Thos. esq. 51 St. John's wood ter
Bowyer Chas. esq. 5 Eaton pl. Belgr. sq & Farleigh house, Basingstoke
Bowyer George, esq. 21 Old sq. Linc.inn
Bowyer Jas.esq. 8Bernard st. Russell sq
Bowyer Jn. esq. 16 Albion gr. Brnsby.rd
Bowyer Mrs. 13 Seymour pl. New road
Bowzer Mrs. 8Weymouth st. Portland pl
Box John, esq.4Charlotte pl.Up.Kenn.la

Box John, esq.55 Perceval st. Clrkenwll
Boxall Wm. esq.5 Hinde st. Manchstr.sq
Boxill William, esq. 39 Woburn square
BoyceRev.Hen.13Abbey rd.St.John'swd
Boyce George, esq. 24 Barnsbury park
Boyce G. J. esq.5 Park pl. vils. Padngtn
Boyce H. Pitches, esq. 2 Up.Wimpole st
Boyce Jas. esq. 23 Camden cotts.Cam.tn
Boyce Mrs. 6 Beaumont st
Boyce Mrs. 4 Ladbroke pl. Notting hill
Boyd Alex.esq.4Marlboro' pl.St.Jn.'s wd
Boyd Chas. esq. 29 York bdgs. New rd
Boyd Dav.O.esq.3 Elm tree rd.St.Jn.'s w
Boyd E.D. esq. 16Blomfield rd.Maida hl
Boyd Edward, esq. 8 Waterloo place
Boyd Edward Lennox, esq.8Waterloo pl
Boyd George, esq. 35 Chesham place
Boyd Jas.esq. 22 Abbey pl. St.John's wd
Boyd Hy.esq.24A,Grove en.rd.St.Jn.'swd
Boyd John, esq. M.P. 28 Jermyn st. & Dundoan house, Coleraine
Boyd John, esq. 18 Duke st. St. James's
Boyd Mrs.20 Abbey place, St.Jn.'s wood
Boyd Robt. M.D. Marylebone infirmary
Boydell Chas. esq. 41 Queen sq.Blmsby
Boydell Saml. esq. 41 Queen sq. Blmsby
Boyes John,esq. 30 Avenue rd.Regt.'s pk
Boyes Mrs. 2 Langford pl. Abbey road
Boykett Thomas, esq. 1 Belinda terrace
Boyland Mrs. 7 Charles st. St. James's
Boyland James W. esq. 34 Sloane st
Boyle Lady Louisa, 69 Cambridge ter
Boyle Capt. Robert, 3 Hamilton place
Boyle James, esq. 4 Essex court, Temple
BoyleJas.W.esq.48Frederick st.Gr.innrd
Boyle Patrick A. esq. 31 Cardigan st
Boyle Wm. Ansell, esq. 17 Clement's inn
Boyle Wm. Rt. August. esq. 64 Coleshill st. & 5 New square, Lincoln's inn
Boyman Rd. esq. 3 Kingwood pl. South Lambeth
BoyneViscount, 22 Belgrave sq.; & Burwarton house, Bridgenorth; & Stackallan, Meath
Boynton Lady, 12 Connaught square
Boys Daniel, esq. 31 Finchley new road, & 5 & 6 Ely place
Boys Henry, esq. 15Dorset st. Portmn.sq
Boys Mrs. 8 Augusta pl. Stockwell com
Boys Thos.esq. 24Abbey pl. St.John's wd
Boyson Ambrose, esq. 28 Newington pl
Boyson Wm. esq.7Bedford pl.Hmpstd.rd
Brabant Wm. esq. 12 Ladbroke terrace
Brace George, esq. 3 Guilford pl. Russell sq. & 24 Surrey st. Strand
Brace Miss, 15 Surrey st. Strand
Brace Thos. esq. 25 Surrey st. Strand
Bracebridge Edwd. Chas. esq. 6 Barnsbury villas, Liverpool road
Bracebridge Jas. esq. 9 Cloudesley sq
BrackenburyCol. Sir Edwd. 15Regent st
BrackenburyA.esq.6Stanhop.ter.Rgt.pk
Brackenbury Robt. esq. 43 Brompton sq
Brackett Chas.esq.4OldNth.st.Red Ln.sq
Bradbury Hen. esq. 8 Laurie tr.Westmr
Bradbury Mrs. Earl's court ho. Earl's ct
Bradbury Mrs. 67 Sloane st
Bradbury Orlando, esq. 45St.George's rd
Braddon H.esq. 15Cook's ct.Lincoln'sinn
Braddon John, esq. 32 Cirencester place
Bradford, Earl of, 43 Belgrave square, & Castle Bromwich, Birmingham, & Weston hall, Shiffnall
BradleyEdwd.G.esq.11Bernersst.Oxfd st
Bradley Henry, esq. 21 Colebrooke row, Islington, & 2 Harcourt buildings
Bradley J. esq. 12 Buckingham place
Bradley John, esq. 5 Gower pl.Euston sq
Bradley Miss, 80 Wimpole st
Bradley Mrs. 24 Canonbury square
BradleyMrs.2Cunningham pl.St.Jn.'swd
BradleyRd.esq.2Trafalgar pl.Claphamrd
Bradley Rt. esq. 7 Alexander sq. Brmp
Bradley Rt. esq. 49 Pembroke sq.Knstn
Bradley Rt. esq. 1 Pullin's row, Islngtn
Bradley William, esq. 52 Aldermanbury
Bradley W.esq. 54Charlotte st.Fitzry.sq
Bradly J. esq. 1 Brunswick ter.Dover rd
Bradly Mrs. 26 Trinity square, Borough
Bradshaw General, 37 Harley st
Bradshaw Capt. W.C. 22 Bloomfield ter
Bradshaw Jas. esq. M.P. 28 South st
Bradshaw Mrs. 2 Upper Hyde park st
Brady William, esq. 6 Wyndham place
Bradwell William, esq. 63 Torrington sq
Braggiotti D. esq. 11 Porchester terrace
Braham John, esq. 5Glo'ster rd.Hyde pk
Brady Jas. esq. 1 Staple inn, Holborn
Braham Lewis Hen.esq. 101 Chancery la
Braidfield T.J.esq.1Derby st.Westmnstr
Braidley James, esq. 9 Albany st
BraikenridgeWm.esq.16 Bartlett's bldgs
Brailey Chas. esq. 15 Spencer ter. Islgtn
Braine G.H.esq.5 North bank,Regt.'s pk
Braine James W. esq. 5 Cleveland row
BraineWm.esq.20Groveter.St.John's wd
Braithwaite Fredk. esq. 1 Bath pl.Nw.r
Braithwaite Isaac, esq. 18 Meklnbgh. sq
Braithwaite John, esq. 39 Bedford sq
Braithwaite J. esq. 18 Mecklenburgh sq
Braithwaite Jsph. B. esq. 3 New square
Braithwaite Thos. esq. 20 Brecknock pl
Braithwaite Thos. esq. 2 Mitre ct. bldgs
Braithwaite Wm.esq.15 Serjt.'sinn,Flt.st
Brake Wm.L.R.N.2 Priory,Wndswrth.rd
Bramah Edwd. esq. 1Guilford st.Rus. sq
Bramah Edw. Hen. esq. 15 Regent st
Brameld J. W. esq. 7 Coburgh pl.Bayswr
Bramston E.esq. 39 North st.Pentonville
Bramston Miss, 26 Alfred st
Bramston Thos. Wm. M.P. 53 Eaton pl. & Skreens, Chelmsford
Bramston Wm. esq.37 Royal cres.Not.hl
Bramwell George, esq. 7 Artillery pl
Bramwell George, esq. 73 Chester sq. & 6 Furnival's inn
Bramwell Geo. Wm. esq. 2 Paper bldgs
Bramwell Wm.esq.2Gouldentr.Bnsby.rd
Branbury Geo. esq. 16 Old Paradise row
Branch J. esq. 2 Popham tr.Tibberton sq
Brand hon. Miss, 4 Chesterfield st
Brand Capt. Henry, 75 Chester square
Brand Alexander, esq. 22 Bloomsby. st
Brand James, esq. 9 Up. Gloucester st
Brand Mrs. 16 Halfmoon st. Piccadilly
Brand Thos.esq.&hon.Mrs. 49 Piccadilly
BrandardJ.A.esq.50Stanhope st.Hmp.rd
Brandau Fred.Wm.esq.22 Gt.Portland st
Brande Geo. esq. 10 Oxford sq. Hyde pk
Brande Wm. Thos.esq.F.R.S.Royal Mint
Brandon David, esq. 75 Gt. Russell st
Brandon Jacob I. esq. 11 Artillery place
Brandon Joseph I. esq. 1 Wyndham pl
Brandon Miss, 1 Burton crescent
Brandon Raphael, esq. 11 Beaufort bldgs
Brandon Robert, esq. 1 Whyndham st
Brandon Woodthorpe, esq. 30 Berners st
Brandram S. esq. 20 Cumberland terrace
Brandreth Capt. F. 6 Stanhope st. Hy.pk
Brandreth Capt.Hen. R.E. 43 Hyde pk.sq
Brandreth Henry, esq. 102 Jermyn st. & Houghton house, Dunstable
Brandt E. H. 7 Southwick crescent
Brandt E. H. esq.26 York ter.Regt.'s pk
Brandt Fras. F. esq.2 Figtree ct. Temple
Brannan C. esq. 32 Up.Nth.pl.Gry.'s inn
Branscombe Mrs. 14 Beaufoy terrace
Branston Fredk. esq. Wandsworth rd
Brashay Wm. esq.18Lonsdale sq.Islngtn
Brashier E. esq. 16 Blandford st.Ptm.sq
Brashier Miss, 16 Blandford st. Ptm. sq
Brasier Samuel, esq. 2 York terrace
Brassey Rd.J.esq.2 Henrietta st.Brnk.sq
Brawne Houston, esq.2Churchyd.ct.Tmp
Bray Capt.Geo.8Wellington rd.S.Jn.'s w
Bray Hen. M. esq.29 Grove pl.Lisson gr
Bray Miss, 81 Paradise row, Chelsea
Bray Reginald, esq. 57 Gt. Russell st
Bray Mrs. 12Park village east, Reg.'spk
Bray Wm. F. sen. esq 259 High Holborn
Braye Lady, 14 Great Stanhope st. & Stamford hall, Lutterworth
Braybrooke Lord, 10 New Burlington st.; & Audley end, Essex; & Billingbear park, Wokingham
BrayleyEdw.Wedlake,esq 55GtCoramst
Brayne Mrs. 11 Powis pl. Hampstd. rd
Breadalbane Marquis of, K.T. 21 Park lane; & Taymouth castle, Aberfeldie, & Ardmaddy castle, Argyleshire; & Langton Dunse, Berwickshire
Brearey Chas. B. esq. 73 Gt. Portland st
Brearey Thos.esq. 30 Park pl.we.Lvpl.rd
Brecknell Mrs. 22 Lower Islington ter
Brecknock Earl of, 19 Belgrave sq. & Wilderness park, Sevenoaks; & Bayham abbey, Lamberhust, Kent; & Priory, Brecknock
Bredel Charles Alfred, esq. 7 Eaton sq
Bremer Martin F. esq. 33 Cloudesley sq
BremnerHugh,esq.3Nrflk. rd.Avenue rd
Bremridge James, esq. 22 Westbourne st
Bremridge Jas. esq. 1 Pump ct. Temple
Brennan Misses, 12 Lowndes square
Brenner Baron, sec. to the Austrian Embassy, 7 Chandos st. Cavendish sq
Brenchley Wm. Key, esq. 11 Mark lane
Brent Geo. S. esq. 28 Berwick st.Pimlico
Brent Hugh, esq. 51 Manchester st
Brent William Brent, esq. 37 Gower st
Brereton Mrs.16 Michael's pl. Bromp. rd
Brett Lieut. Col. 32 Thurloe sq. Brmptn
Brett Fredk. H. M.D. 24 Brompton sq
Brett Harry, esq. 35 Cadogan place
Brett John Watkins, esq. 2 Hanover sq
Brett Mrs. 35 Newington pl.Kenngtn.rd
Brett Robt. esq. Stoke Newington green
Brett Wilford Geo. esq. 22 Portugal st
Brett Wm. esq.6 Warwick st. Golden sq
Brettell James, 106 Camden road villas
Brettell Janns John, esq. 2 Staple inn
Brettell Jsph. C. esq. 13 Waterloo place
BrettellT. esq. Gt. court, St. Ja's. palace
Brewen Charles, esq. 144 Oxford st. & Oaklands, near Birmingham
Brewer Col. Philip, 20 Pembroke sq
Brewer Rev. J. 63 Queen's rd.Bayswater
Brewer Jno. esq. 6 Coburg pl.Up.Kenn.la
Brewer Jno. H. esq. 8 Up. Bedford pl.; & 4 Pump court, Temple
BrewerThos.Gibson,esq. 13 Gray's inn sq
Brewer Wm. M.D.21 George st. Han. sq
Brewster Edward, esq. 47 Burton cres
Brewster James, esq. 22 Maddox st
Brian Mrs. 40 Michael's pl. Brompton
Brian Thos. H. esq. 26 Penton st. Pntnvl
Briand Fras. esq. 6 Park ter. Highbury
Briant Nathl. esq. 11 Adam st. Adelphi
Briant Wm. esq. 3 Belmont ter. Wandsworth road
BriarlyThos. Ed. esq. 8 King's Bench wk
Brickdale M. I. esq. 4 Stone buildings
Brickenden Rev. Rd. 3 Park row, Knbrg
Brickwood Edw. C. esq. 18 Cornwall pl. Holloway, & 6 Dean's ct. Dcts. com
Brideoake Mrs. 12 Lower Seymour st
Bridge Alfred C. esq. 5 Pump ct. Temple
Bridge Henry, esq. 5 Lamb's Conduit pl
Bridge John E. esq. 24 Essex st. Strand
Bridge Misses, 34 Grosvenor place
Bridge Rev. Stephen, Grove la. Cambwl
Bridgeman Hewitt, esq. M.P. Ennis, Irld
Bridgeman Mrs. Edmund, 91 Eaton pl
Bridger Edwd. esq. 32 Finsbury circus
Bridger Wm. Melton, esq. 4 Cadogan place, & 1 Old square, Lincoln's inn
Bridges Charles, esq. 144 Oxford st. & Cainham court, Ludlow
BridgesJas.esq.18Charles st. Midx. hsptl
Bridges Geo. T. esq. 7 Lincoln's inn flds
Bridges Hen. E. esq. 21 Maida hill west
Bridges Jno.esq.18 Charles st.Midx.hspl
Bridges John, esq. 23 Red Lion sq. & Wallington ho. Carshalton, Surrey
Bridges Jno. Wm. esq. 54 Torrington sq
Bridges Miss, 3 Titchborne st. Edg. rd
Bridges Mrs. 14 Argyle st. King's cross
Bridges Mrs. 4 Burton st. Burton cres

Bridgewater Countess of, 19 Grosvr. sq. & Ashridge, Hemel Hempstead
Bridgman Rev. Henry, A.M. 15 West st. Walworth road
Bridport Lord, 12 Wimpole st. & Cricket St. Thomas, near Chard
Briggs Maj.Gen. 10 St. Andrew's place, & 158 Albany st. Regent's park
Briggs Capt. Fk. R.N. 17 Edward st
Briggs Rev. Wm. 40 Addison road north
Briggs Edward, esq. 75 Harley st. & Park house, Hayes, Middlesex
Briggs Geo. esq. 80 Camden road villas
Briggs James, esq. 30 Edgware road
Briggs JohnH.esq.3 Glo'ster rd.Hyde pk
Briggs Mrs. 5 Cadogan place
Briggs Mrs. 30 Smith st. King's rd.Chels
Briggs Samuel, esq. 18 Cavendish road, St. John's wood
Briggs Thos. esq. 2 Arlington st. Piccadilly, & 55 Lincoln's inn fields
Briggs Thos. Carter, esq. 41 Hans pl
Briggs Thos. Carter, esq. 6 Old square
Briggs Wm. Sturges, esq. 164 Sloane st. & 55 Lincoln's inn fields
Bright Edward, esq. 11 King's bench wlk
Bright Hen. esq. 2 Paper bldgs. Temple
Bright Hen. esq.11 Park pl.villas, Paddtn
Bright James, M.D. 12 Cambridge sq
Bright John, M.P. 20 New st. Spring gdns. & One Ash, Rochdale, Lancashire
Bright John, M.D. 19 Manchester square, & Overton hall, Ashover
Bright John Edwd. esq. 5 Old sq. Linc.inn
Bright Rd.esq.15 Hanover cotts. Rgt.'s pk
Bright Rd. M.D. 11 Saville rw. Piccadilly
Bright Rd. esq. 3 Tanfield ct. Temple
Bright Wm. esq. 11 Baker st. Portmn. sq
Brightman Mrs. 16 Coleshill st. Eatn. sq
Brightwell Mrs. 16 Alfred pl. Bedford sq
Brightwell Thos. esq. 8 Wellington ter
Brigstocke T. esq. 22 James st. Buckm.ga
Brinckman SirT.H.I.bart.10 Langham pl
Brine John, esq. 8 South row, St. Pancras
Brisco Sir Wastell, bart. 11 Beaumont st
Brisco Musgrave, M.P. 38 Devonshire pl. & Coghurst, near Hastings, Sussex
Briscoe John Ivatt, esq. 60 Eaton place; & Foxhill, Chertsey
BrisleyPierce S.esq Grovebank h. Fulhm
Bristead Rd. esq. 27 Rutland st. Hmp. rd
Bristol Marquis of, 6 St. James's sq.; & Ickworth park, Bury St. Edmonds; & Putney heath; & Kemp-town, Brighton
Bristow John, esq. 7 Horselydown lane
Bristow Mrs. 3 Manor gr. King's rd.Chels
Bristow Mrs. 11 Old Dorset pl. Clphm. rd
Bristow Robert, esq. 101 Piccadilly, & Broxmore park, Romsey, Hants
Bristowe Henry F. esq. 18 Linc. inn flds
Bristowe Simon, esq. 3 Essex ct. Temple
Britten Capt. R.N. 5 Alpha pl. Regent's pk
Britten Thomas, esq. 41 Grove end road
BrittenW.S. esq. 28 Henry st.e. Avenue rd
Britton G. esq. 5 Derby st. Gray's inn rd
Britton John, esq. 17 Burton st. Burtn.cs
Broackes Wm. M.D. 1 Cork st. Bond st
Broadbridge Ben. esq. 172 Albany st
Broadfoot Mrs. 28 Albany st. Regent's pk
Broadhead Col. 70 Park st
Broadhead Capt. Henry, R.N. 28 Cavendish road, St. John's wood
Broadhead Alfred, esq. 4 Gray's inn sq
Broadhurst John, esq. Camden hill
Broadhurst Mrs. Lavndr. swps. Wans. rd
Broadhurst Wm. esq. 5 Regent pl. west
Broadley Hen. esq. M.P. 3 Charles st. St. James's, & Norwood house, Beverley
Broadley Mrs. 9 Dorset pl. no. Clphm. rd
Broadwood Capel Thos. esq. 15 Regent st
Broadwood Hen. esq. M.P. 5 Whitehall yd
Broadwood James, esq. 46 Bryanstone square, & Lyne, near Dorking, Surrey
Broadwood Thomas, esq. 17 Cadogan pl. & Holmbush, Crawley, Sussex
Broadwood Walter, esq. 15 Regent st
Brock Ed. esq. 13 King's parade, Chelsea
BrockedonW.esq. 29 Devnsh.st.Queen sq
Brockhardt John C. esq. 8 Ladbroke pl
Brocklehurst John, esq. M.P. 33 Milk st. & Hurdsfield house, near Macclesfield
Brocklesby Charles, esq. 89 Newman st
Brockmer Henry, esq. 30 Millbank st
Brockwell Hy. esq. 33 Baker st. Lloyd sq
Brockwell Josiah, esq. 11 Middlesex pl
Brodbelt Mrs. 24 Queen sq. Bloomsbury
Broderip Fras. esq. 1 Gower st. Bedford sq. & 9 New sq. Lincoln's inn
Broderip Wm. esq. 1 Gower st. Bedford square, & 9 New sq. Lincoln's inn
Broderip Wm. John, esq. F.R.S. 2 Raymond bldgs. & Thames Police court
Brodie Sir Benjamin C. bart. 14 Saville row, & Broome park, Dorking
Brodie Dav.esq. 10 Park pl. ter. Padngtn
Brodie Miss, 19 Somerset st. Portman sq
Brodie Peter Bellinger, esq. 49 Lincoln's inn fields, & Portsmouth st
Brodigan F. esq. 4 Garden court, Temple
Brodribb Hen. esq. 6 Childs pl. Temp. bar
Brodribb Wm. P. esq. 12 Bloomsbury sq
Brodrick Hon. Mrs. 16 Lowndes square
Brodrick Wm. esq. 35 Gt. Ormond st
Brogden John, esq. 10 Sussex gardens
Brogden Thos. esq. 8 Colebrooke row
Bromehead J. Crawford, esq. 3 Old sq
Bromilow Mrs. 8 Wilton pl. Belgrave sq
Bromley Fredk. esq. 5 Brecknock terr
Bromley Joseph Warner, esq. 29 Gt. Coram st. & 1 South sq. Gray's inn
Bromley Thos. esq. 11 St.Mary Abbotts tr
Bromley Wm. jun. esq. 12 Gray's inn sq
Brook Caleb H. esq. 9 Claremont place
Brook Joseph, esq. 6 Portland ter. Rgt's.pk
Brook Richard, esq. South Lambeth
Brook Thos. Geo. esq. 48 Crawford st
Brook Wm. esq. 7 Trinity sq. Tower hill
Brooke Lord, M.P. for South Warwickshire, 7 Carlton gardens; & Warwick castle; & Gatton park, Surrey
Brooke Sir Arthur Brinsley, bart. M.P. Carlton club, 94 Pall mall, & Colebrook house, Fermanagh
Brooke Charles, esq. 29 Keppel st
Brooke Henry Jas. esq. 19 Clapham rise
Brooke Horace J. esq. 19 Thavies inn
Brooke James, esq. 16 Furnival's inn
Brooke Zachary, esq. 17 Featherstone bgs
Brookes Ben. esq. 37 Bedford st. Cov. gn
Brookes the Misses, 75 Cadogan place
Brookes Miss C. 23 London st. Fitzry. sq
Brookes Mrs. 1 Park pl. Regent's park
Brookes Wm. esq. 44 Baker st. Lloyd sq
Brookes Wm. M'Intosh, esq. 6 Adam st
Brooke's Club House (Isaac Halse & Hy. Banderet, secs.), 60 St. James's st
Brookfield Chas. Austin, esq. 3 Minerva pl. Barnsbury park, & 12 Bedford row
Brooking Benj. esq. 7 Bow st. Covent gdn
Brooking John S. esq. 3 Hyde park sq
Brooking Mrs. 20 York st. Portman sq
Brooking Thos. H. 85 Gloucester place
Brooks A. esq. Montgu. vil. Finchly nw.rd
Brooks Fran. esq. 7 Connaught pl. west
Brooks Geo. Hy. esq. 33 Guilford st. & 12 Gt. Knightrider st. Doctors' com
Brooks Hen. esq. 7 Victoria rd. Kensgtn
Brooks James, esq. } 29 John st.
Brooks James Willis, esq. } Bedfordrow
Brooks John, esq. 2 Great James st
Brooks Miss, 6 Lower Chester terrace
Brooks Miss, 19 Milton st. Dorset sq
Brooks Mrs. 2 Chester st. Grosvenor pl
Brooks Mrs. 6 Stranraer pl. Maida hill
Brooks Mrs. 3 Warwick villas, Harrow rd
Brooks Mrs. 45 Bernard st. Russell sq
Brooks Rt. esq. 10 Buckingham st. Strand
Brooks Thos. esq. 11 Rodney st. Pentvlle
Brooks Wm. esq. 13 Percy st. Rthbn. pl
Brooksbank Jas. esq. 1 Essex ct. Temple
Brooksbank Thos. esq. 14 Gray's inn sq. & Tottenham, Middlesex
Brooksbank Theodore, esq. Devereux cha
Brooksbank Thos. C. esq. 39 Cadogan pl
Broom Herbert, esq. 5 Essex ct. Temple
Brophy Peter, esq. 19 South parade, St. James's park
Brophy William Hen. esq. 61 Sloane st
Bros Thos. esq. 16 St. James's place, St. James's, & 10 King's Bench wk. Temple
Brothers Frans. esq. 8 Lr. Phillimore pl
Brothers Jas. esq. 7 Young st. Kensingtn
Brotherton Jas. esq. 11 Crown Office rw
Brotherton Joseph, esq. M.P. 7 Manchstr. bldgs. & Morsborough hall, Chestrfield
Brotherton Miss, 14 Ordnance road
Brotherton Thos. esq. 51 Noel st. Islgt
Brougham Lord, P.C. 4 Grafton st. & Brougham hall, Penrith
BroughamMrs. 21 Park rd. Regent's pk
Brougham William, esq. 19A, Grosvenor square, & 25 Southampton buildings
Broughton Jno.V.esq. 3 Camden st.south
Broughton Mrs. 8 Belmont pl. Wansw.rd
Broughton Robt.Ed. esq. 1 Melcombe pl
Brouncker Mrs. 14 Montagu square
BrowellEdward Marsh, esq. Lord Chamberlain's office, St. James's
BrowellWm.F.esq. 35 Southampton bldgs
Brown Admiral, 39 Hans pl. Sloane st
Brown Genl. George, 56 Eaton square
Brown Rev. Hen. 4 Halkin st. Grosv. pl
Brown Rev. Robt. Wm. 1 Westbourne st
Brown Anthony, esq. 18 Clapham rise
Brown Archd. esq. 16 Brompton cresct
Brown Ben. sen. esq. 49 Howland st
Brown Berry, esq. Up. Hamilton terrace
Brown Burton, esq. 6 Brunswick square
BrownChas. esq. 10 Low. Brompton grov
BrownChas. esq. 36 Oxford ter. Edgware rd. & 22 Duke st. Westminster
Brown C. esq. 12 Buckingham st. Strand
Brown Chas.B. M.D. 38 Hill st. Berkly.sq
Brown Charles James, esq. 6 Nutford pl. Edgward road, & 10 New inn, Strand
Brown Danl. esq. 44 Pembroke sq. Kens
Brown Edward, esq. 44 Hertford st
Brown Edward, esq. 11 Maida hill east
Brown Fred. esq. 32 Francis st. Tot.ct.rd
Brown Fred. esq. 22 Glo'ster cres. Reg.p
Brown Geo. esq. 17 Cloudesley terrace
BrownGeo. esq. 19 Petersburgh pl. Bays
Brown Geo. esq. 24 Portman pl. Edgw. rd. & 19 Southampton st. Bloomsbury
Brown George, esq. 3 Finsbury circus
BrownGeo.A. esq. 20 Gower st. Bedford sq
Brown Geo. Thos. esq. 19 Milner square
Brown H. esq. 8 Ferdinand terrace
Brown Henry, esq. 13 Gloucester grove west, Brompton
BrownHenry E. esq. 36 Essex st. Strand
Brown Henry Hill, esq. 13 Gloucester grove west, Brompton, & 50 Lin.inn flds
BrownIsaac, esq. 27 Oxford sq. Hyde pk
Brown James, esq. 23 Grove pl. Lissn.gr
Brown James, esq. 2 Tibberton square
Brown John, esq. 34 Castle st. Oxford st
Brown John, esq. 4 Charlotte st. Fitz.sq
Brown John, esq. 10 Norfolk st. Strand
Brown John, esq. 25 Norland square
Brown John, esq. 16 Somerset st
Brown John, esq. 26 Tonbridge pl. New rd
Brown John, esq. 34 Upper Berkeley st
Brown John H. esq. 130 Camden rd. vill
Brown John O. esq. 8 Furnival's inn
Brown Joseph, esq. 17 Bedford row, Islington, & 2 Essex court, Temple
BrownJsph. esq. 15 President st. w. Kg.sq
Brown Joseph Hen. esq. 21 North bank, Regent's park
Brown Miss, 7 Barnsbury park
Brown Miss, 6 Holland pl. Kensington
BrownMiss, 35 Montague pl. Russell sq
BrownMiss, 34 Sussex pl. Kensgtn.nw.tn
BrownMiss, 5 Upper Baker st. New rd
Brown Mrs. Col. 20 King st. Portman sq
Brown Mrs. 8 Albion pl. Hyde park sq
Brown Mrs. 25 Bloomsbury sq

Brown Mrs. 29 Blandford square
Brown Mrs. 3 Church row, Limehouse
Brown Mrs. 29 Dorset place, Dorset sq
Brown Mrs. 11 Everett st. Brunswick sq
Brown Mrs. 24 Gt. Percy st
Brown Mrs. 39 Hans place, Sloane st
Brown Mrs. 28 Hertford st. Mayfair
Brown Mrs. 5 Highbury terrace
Brown Mrs. 6 Mornington place
Brown Mrs. 25 Park rd. Regent's park
Brown Mrs. 11 Seymour pl. Euston sq
Brown Philip, esq. 2 Jermyn st. & 8 St. Paul's terrace, Islington
Brown Rd. esq. 5 York pl. Portman sq
Brown Robert, D.C.L. 17 Dean st. Soho
Brown Rt. esq. 58 Gt. Russell st. Blomsby
Brown Robert Chas. esq. 68 Sloane st
Brown Samuel, esq. 24 Bloomsbury sq
Brown Saml. esq. Larkhall rise, Claphm
Brown Thos. esq. 33 Hart st. Bloomsbury
Brown Thos. esq. 24 James st. Oxford st
Brown Thos. esq. 116 Jermyn st
Brown Thos. esq. 5 Muscovy ct. Trinity sq
Brown Thos. esq. 7 Lower Belgrave st
Brown Thos. M.D. 6 Queen Anne st. Cavendish sq. & Brentely hall, Sudbury; & Tostock, Woolpit, Suffolk
Brown Thos. esq. 40 Wharton st
Brown Thos. Boden, esq. 42 Howland st
Brown Thos. esq. 10 King's Bench walk
Brown Wm. esq. 8 Angel terrace
Brown Wm. esq. 1 Manor gr. Kng'srd. Chels
Brown Wm. esq. 12 Spencer terrace, Islington, & 10 Gray's inn place
Brown Wm. esq. 2 Frederick st. Gray'sin.rd
Brown Wm. esq. 29 Chester st
Brown Wm. esq. 69 Goswell road west
Brown Wm. esq. 24 King sq. Goswell rd
Brown Wm. esq. 17 King's parade, Chlse
Brown Wm. Hen. M.D. 13 Bedford st. Bedford square
Brown Wm Mawman, esq. 18 Myddelton sq
Brown Wm. R. esq. 2 Devonport st. Oxf.tr
Brown Wm. R. H. esq. 3 Doughty st
Brown Wm. W. esq. 42 Baker st. Lloyd sq
Brownhill Rev. James, 25 Bolton st
Browne Lady Letitia, 62 Park st
Browne Hon. Maj. George, 29 Lowndes sq
Browne Hon. Wm. M.P. 89 Jermyn st
Browne Capt. B. R.N. 6A, Waterloo place
Browne Capt. John Dean, 20 Jermyn st
Browne Charles Benj. esq. 22 Fleet st
Browne Edward, esq. 17 Regent square
Browne Edwd. Davis, esq. 38 Hunter st
Browne Edward H. esq. 13 Beaufort bds
Browne Frederick, esq. 22 Fleet st
Browne Fredk. esq. 19 Margaret st
Browne G. esq. 37 Euston sq. & 27 Melton st
Browne G. esq. 13 Paradise rw. Rotherhi
Browne Geo. Lathom, esq. 57 Chancery la
Browne Henry Alex. esq. 2 Stratford pl
Browne Henry Nibbs, esq. 46 Baker st
Browne Jas. M.D. 32 Cadogan st. Chelsea
Browne John. esq. 7 Hanover terrace
Browne John esq. 13 Bedford row & Highgte
Browne John O. esq. 8 Furnival's inn
Browne John Markham, esq. 2 Hinde st
Browne Mackley, esq. 21 Parliament st
Browne Misses, 46 Baker st
Browne Miss. 16 Cobourg pl. Up. Kenn.la
Browne Mrs. 6 Petersburgh pl. Bayswr
Browne Mrs. 44 Regent sq. Gray's inn rd
Browne Mrs. John, 3 Old Dorset pl. Clm.rd
Browne Napoleon Buonaparte, esq. 28 Southampton buildings
Browne P. A. esq. 41 Devonshire pl. Portland pl. & Sutton place, Ripley, Surrey
Browne Philip, 32 Bernard st. Russell sq
Browne Richd. L. esq. 13 South square
Browne Rt. Dillon, esq. M.P. Reform club, & Glancorrile, county Mayo
Browne Rt. F. esq. 13 William st. Kntsb
Browne Rowland J. esq. 3 Hare ct. Tmple
Browne Wm. esq. 5 New sq. Linc. inn
Browne Wm. esq. 106 Pall mall
Browne Wm. esq. 28 Southampton bldgs
Browne Wm. M. esq. 27 King st. Cov.grd
Browne Wm. W. esq. 29 Cavendish sq
Browning Charles, esq. 20 Dorset place
Browning Charles, esq. 34 Woburn sq
Browning Geo. esq. 36 Lit. Windmill st
Browning Henry, esq. 4 Glo'ster place
Browning Henry, esq. Stoke Newngtn.gn
Browning Jas. esq. 21 Connaught terrace
Browning Jas. esq. 15 Loraine pl. Holwy
Browning Mrs. 8 Queen's bldgs, Brompt
Browning Miss, 22 Russell pl. Fitz. sq
Browning Ths. esq. 13A, Beaufoyter. Edg.r
Browning Thomas, esq. 6 Whitehall, & 1 Hatton court, Threadneedle st
Browning Wm. esq. 16 Duncan ter. City rd
Browning Wm. esq. 3 Holland pl. Clapm.rd
Brownless A. esq. 9 Richmond ter. Pntvl
Brownless Anth. C. 4 Albion pl. Bnsby.pk
Brownley John, esq. 8 New Boswell ct
Brownley Wm. esq. 14 Harewood square
Brownlow Earl, 12 Belgrave square, & Belton house, Grantham
Brownlow Dow. Lady, 30 Hill st
Brownlow J. esq. 1 Henrietta st. Brsw.sq
Brownlow Wm. esq. 18 Highbury place
Brownlow Wm. esq. 32 Trevor square
Brownrigg Sir Rt. bt. 12 Up. Grosvenr. st
Brownrigg J. S. esq. M.P. 1 Hyde pk. grdns
Brownrigg Mrs. 12 Up. Grosvenor st
Broxholm Mrs. 8 Maida hill east
Bruce Earl, 78 Pall mall, & Savanake lodge, Marlborough
Bruce Rt. Hon. Lord Ernest Augustus Chas. Brudenell, M.P. 7 St. George's pl
Bruce Rt. Hon. Sir Jas. Lewis Knight, knt. Roehampton priory, Surrey
Bruce Sir Harvey, bart. & Lady, Mivart's hotel, 44 Brook st
Bruce A. esq. 26 Montagu st. Portman sq
Bruce Alexander, esq. 14 Up. Bedford pl
Bruce Charles, esq. 4 Edgware road
Bruce Charles Dashwood, esq. & Hon. Mrs. 5 Lowndes st. Belgrave square
Bruce Chas. Lenox C. esq. M.P. 17 Charles st. St. James's sq.; & Dunphail, Forres; & Kinnaird, Falkirk, N.B
Bruce Geo. Stuart, esq. 37 Connaught sq
Bruce Lewis Bruce Knight, esq. the Priory, Roehampton
Bruce Michael, esq. & Lady Parker, 5 Bentinck st. Manchester square
Bruce Miss, 68 Up. Norton st. Fitzroy sq
Bruce Miss, 16 Cavendish rd. St. Jno.'s wd
Bruce Mrs. 77 Gower st
Bruce Norman, esq. 9 Minerva terrace
Bruce Robert N. esq. 18 Chester square
Bruce Wm. esq. 4 Essex court, Temple
Bruce Wm. Downing, esq. 18 Charles st. St. James's, & Ripon, Yorkshire
Bruce Wm. Joseph, esq. 4 Edgware road
Bruck Lewis, esq. 22 Manchester terr
Bruen Col. Henry, M.P. Carlton club, Pall mall, & Oak park, near Carlow
Bruen Randel E. esq. 4 Barnsbury park
Bruff Peter S. esq. 35 Bloomsbury st
Bruges W. H. L. M.P. 3 Suffolk st. Pall mall
Bruggemeyer F. M. esq. 58 Trinity sq. Boro
Bruin George. esq. Hermes hill house, 26 John st. Pentonville
Brumell Charles, esq. 2 Parliament st
Brummell Wm. Chas. esq. 46 Oxford terrace, Edgware road
Brune Mrs. 8 Blenheim pl. St. John's wd
Brunel Isambard K. 18 Duke st. Westm
Brunet J. J. esq. 13 Church row, Limeho
Bruno Cæsar, esq. 27 Euston place
Brunow Baron, Russian Ambassador, 30 Dover st. Piccadilly
Brunswick, Duke of, Brunswick ho. Rg.pk
Brunton Charles, esq. 5 Barnard's inn; & 11 New inn, Strand
Brunton Chas. esq. 11 New inn, Strand
Bryan Col. George, 102 Piccadilly
Bryan Geo. esq. 16 Theberton st. west
Bryan Geo. esq. 38 Vincent square
Bryan Jonathan W. esq. 17 Clement's inn
Bryan Mrs. 9 Omega terrace, Alpha rd
Bryan William, esq. Clapham rise
Bryant Edw. esq. 25 Compton tr. Islngt
Bryant E. esq. 29 Welngtn.rd. St. John's wd
Bryant F. esq. 6 Holloway pl. Holloway
Bryant Geo. esq. 18 Up. Kennington gr
Bryant John, M.D. 50 Edgware road, & Colebrook villa, Finchley
Bryant Mrs. 18 Chester ter. Eaton sq
Bryant Mrs. 24 Loraine pl. Holloway
Bryant Robt. W. W. esq. 40 Pembroke sq
Bryden Wm. esq. 4 New Palace yard
Brydon Hen. esq. 6 Beaufort tr. Chelsea
Brydon Miss, 2 Abbey pl. St. John's wd
Brydon Mrs. 9 Up. George st. Portmn. sq
Bryer Wm. esq. 93 Camden road villas
Brymer Arth. esq. 15 Artillery pl. Finsb
Brymer John, esq. 11 Titchfield terr
Bryson Wm. esq. 4 Grove end rd. St. Jn.wd
Bubb Mrs. Clapham rise
Buccleuch & Queensbury, Duke of, K.G. P.C., Montague ho. Whitehall; & Dalkeith palace, Edinburgh; & Boughton house, Kettering; & Richmond, Surrey; & Drumlanrig castle, Thornhill, N.B.; & Bowhill, Selkirk, N.B.; & Langholm lodge, N.B
Buchan Maj. Gen. Sir John, 39 Up. Harly.st
Buchanan Mrs. 11 Bedford pl. Kensngtn
Buchanan Mrs. 13 Queen sq. Westmins
Buchanan Robt. esq. 6 Richmond tr. Islgt
Buchanan Walter, esq. 2 Sussex place
Buchanan Wm. esq. 1 Lancaster place, Strand, & 12 Little Distaff lane
Buchanan William, esq. 46 Pall mall
Buchanan Wm. R. esq. 4 Montague pl. Old Kent road
Buchannon Maj. Jas. 14 Northwick ter
Buck Geo. esq. 14 Assembly rw. Mile e.rd
Buck Geo. esq. 1 Bloomsbury square
Buck John Oswald, esq. 38 Bow st
Buck Joseph, esq. 16 Smith st. Chelsea
Buck L. W. esq. M.P. & Lady Louisa, 12 Norfolk st. Hartland abbey, & Moreton house, Bideford
Buck Rd. esq. 21 Petersburgh pl. Bayswr
Bucke George, esq. 144 Oxford st
Buckingham & Chandos, Duke of, K.G. P.C. 91 Pall mall; & Stow park, Buckingham; & Wotton, Aylesbury; & Avington house, Winchester; & Auchline house, Killin, Perthshire
Buckingham F. esq. 37 Camden rd. villas
Buckingham J. S. esq. 13 Geo. st. Han.sq
Buckinghamshire Earl of, 1 Spanish pl. & Hampden House, Great Missenden
Buckinghamshire Countess, 18 Brook st
Buckland Rev. Wm. D.D. (Vice President) Geological Society, Somerset house, & Christchurch, Oxford
Buckland Geo. A. esq. Stoke Nwngtn.gn
Buckland Lewis, esq. 24 Avenue road
Buckland Thos. esq. 12 Trinity sq. Boro'
Buckle Henry, esq. 17 Cambridge sq
Buckle Henry, esq. 59 Oxford terrace
Buckle Jno. esq. A8, Albany, & 1 Essex ct
Buckler John, esq. 19 Paradise ter. Islgtn
Buckley Major, 27A, Old Bond st
Buckley Col. Edward P. & Lady C. 12 South Audley st.; & Minstead lodge, Lyndhurst, Hants; & New hall, near Salisbury
Buckley Rev. J. W. M.A. 1 Stanley pl. Paddington green
Buckley J. E. esq. 1 Newman st. Oxfd.st
Buckley Edmd. M.P. 1 Bridge st. Wstm
Buckley John Arth. esq. 2 Gray's inn sq
Buckley Miss, 42 Manchester st
Buckley Miss, 5 Ormes sq. Bayswater
Buckley Mrs. 11 Soley ter. Pentonville
Buckley Richard, esq. 5 Tibberton sq
Buckley Thos. esq. 77 Geo. st. Euston sq
Buckley Wm. A. esq. 28 Bedfd. pl. Knsgtn
Buckmaster Mrs. 16 Holland st. Knsgtn
Buckmaster Wm. esq. 5 Terrace, Knsgtn
Bucknall Wm. esq. 30 Trinity sq. Boro'
Buckstone John B. esq. 6 Brompton sq
Buckwell Mrs. 14 Moor st. Soho square

Buckworth Col. & Lady Mary Payne, 9 York st. Portman square
Budd Chas.H.esq.8 Spring ter.Wndsw.rd
Budd Geo. M.D. 20 Dover st. Piccadilly
Budd Henry, esq. 5 Holles st.Cavndsh.sq
Budd Henry, esq. 35 Russell square, & Marine parade, Brighton
Budd James, esq. 64 Porchester terrace
Budd Miss, 12 Haverstock hill
Budd Thomas William, esq. 13 Norfolk crescent, & 33 Bedford row
Buddell Richard, esq. 90 Cadogan place
Budden Wm. esq. 17 Kensington cres
Buddle Wm.esq.9 Porten's rd. Harrow rd
Bugden Rev. Wm.5 Up. Hollandst. Kngstn
Bulgin Hen.esq.7 Woodld.pl.St.John'swd
Bulkeley Sir Richd. Williams, bart. M.P. 69 Eaton square, & Baron hill, Beaumaris, Anglesea
Bulkeley John M. esq. 38 Cambridge ter
Bulkeley Mrs. 30 Montagu square
Bull Henry Wm. esq. 12 Wilton crescent, & 25 Ely place, Holborn
Bull Mrs. 8 Portman place, Edgware rd
Bull Simeon Thomas, esq. Gordon house, Grove, Kentish town, & 16 Holles st
Bull Thos. esq. 2 Durham place, Chelsea
Bull Thomas, esq. 1 Finchley New road
Bullar John, esq. 11 King's Bench walk
Bullen Benj. esq. 19 Gerrard st. Islngtn
Bullen Edwd. esq. 9 Victoria rd. Kensgtn
Bullen Henry St. John, esq. 24 Judd st
Buller Sir J. B. Y. bt. M.P. 10 New st. Spring gdns. & Lupton ho. nr. Brixham
Buller Lady, Glo'ster gate, Regent's pk
Buller Lady Agnes, 2 Henrietta st. Cav.sq
Buller Gen. 93 Glo'ster pl. Portman sq
Buller Capt. T. W. R.N. 15 Sussex gdns
Buller Chas. jun. esq. M.P. 2 Chester pl. & 5 Hare court, Temple
Buller Edward, esq. M.P. 23 Hertford st. Mayfair, & Dillhorne hall, near Cheadle
Buller James, esq. 14 Arlington st
Buller John, esq. 87 Oxford terrace
Buller John E. esq. 56 Lincoln's inn flds
Buller Wm. Chas. esq. 6 Old sq. Linc.inn
Bulley Mrs. 81 Sloane st
Bullin Benj. esq. 42 Spencer st. Goswl. rd
Bullock Rev. Thos. H. B.A. 8 Everett st
Bullock Edward, esq. 2 Portsmouth st
Bullock Edward, esq. 40 Woburn square, & 10 Farrar's buildings, Temple
Bullock G.G.esq.46 Up.Chrlte.st.Fzry.sq
Bullock Jas. esq. 49 Newingtn.pl.Ken.rd
Bullock Jas. esq. 12 Portland pl. Clpm.rd
Bullock Jas. T. esq. 35 Lincoln's inn flds
Bullock John, esq. 11 Milner sq. Islngtn
Bullock Jonathan, esq. 35 Bryanst. sq. & Faulkbowin hall, Witham, Essex
Bullock Miss, 129 Sloane st
Bullock Mrs. 23 Beaufoy ter. Edgw. rd
Bullock Mrs. 6 Kilburn priory
Bullock Mrs.26 Newington pl.Kenngt.rd
Bullock J. esq. 2 Fredk. pl. Up. Ken. la
Bulmer George, esq. 44 Parliament st
Bulmer Geo. esq. 2 Belle vue, Chelsea
Bulpett George, esq. K3, Albany
Bult James, esq. 88 Blackfriars road
Bulwer Sir Edwd. L. 36A, Hertford st
Bulwer Jas. esq. 44 George st. Prtmn. sq
Bulwer Wm. Lytton, esq. 5 Up. Seymour st. & Heydon hall, Repham, Norfolk
Bumstead Jsph. esq. 32 Hemingford ter
Bumsted David, esq. 19 Tibberton sq
Bumsted John, esq. 33 Portland pl. Islgt
Bunbury Mrs. 14 Crawford st
Bunbury Thos. M.P. St. James's hotel, Jermyn st. & Moyle, co. Carlow, Ireland
Bunce Charles Robert, esq. 2 Mitre ct. buildings, Temple, & Blackheath park
Bunce Jas. esq. 9 Queen Charlotte row
Buncombe Mrs. Up. Kennington green
Bunn Alfred, esq. 11 Fitzroy square
Bunnell Mrs. 17 Tyndal place, Islington
Bunning James B. esq. 34 Guilford st
Bunny Brice Fred. esq.1 New sq. Linc.inn
Bünsen Chevalier, envoy extraordinary & minister plenipotentiary from Prussia, 4 Carlton house terrace
Bunting Rev. Jabez, 30 Middleton sq
Burbidge Edw. esq. 88 Hatton garden
Burbidge Thos. B. esq. 5 St. Thomas's st
Burbidge Wm. esq. 6 Beaufort buildings
Burby Richard, esq. 9 Brecknock cresc
Burch Joseph, esq. 21 Nelson square
Burcham Tho.B.esq.12 Paper blds. Temple
Burchell Major Basil Herne, 4 Hans pl
Burchell Ben. esq. 7 Alfred pl. Brompton
Burchell James, esq. 34 Gordon square
Burchell Wm. esq. 44 Up. Bedford place; 24 Red Lion sq.; & 47 Parliament st
Burchett James Robert, esq. 5 Gordon pl. Gordon sq. & Doctors' commons
Burden Rev. Alfred, M.A. 21 Milner sq
Burden Jn.esq.2 Wellington rd. St. J's.wd
Burden Thos. esq. 17 Jewin crescent
Burder John, esq. 27 Parliament st
Burder Jno. jun. esq. 34 Bloomsbury sq
Burdett-Coutts Miss, 1 Stratton st
Burdett Major Sir Robert, bart. 25 St. James's place; & Foremark hall, Derby; & Ramsbury manor, Wilts
Burdon Cotsford, esq. 23 Old sq. Linc.inn
Bureaud Riofrey, M.D. 68 Wimpole st
Burfield Hen. esq. 43 Norfolk st. Strand
Burfoot Mrs. 24 Henrietta st. Cav. sq
Burfoot Wal. esq. 9 Charlotte pl. Keng.la
Burford Henry Thomas B. 82 Hamilton terrace, St. John's wood
Burford Jno. Court, esq.10 Kg's. Bnc.wk
Burford Mrs. 27 Bryanstone st
Burgass John, esq. 12 Carlton chambers
Burge Hen. esq. 1 Colebrooke ter. Islgtn
Burge John, esq. 19 Dalby ter. City rd
Burge Mrs. 47 Wimpole st
Burge William, esq, Q.C. 47 Wimpole st. & 1 Paper buildings, Temple
Burges Al. esq. 23 Gt. George st. Westmr
Burges Alfred, esq. 2 Lambeth terrace
Burges Mrs. 13 Blandford square
Burgess Rev. Bryant, 1 Dalby ter. City rd
Burgess Rev. Richard, 10 Cadogan pl
Burgess Jno.C. esq. 6 Whiteheads grove
Burgess J.J. esq. 4 Stanley ter. Kings rd
Burgess John H. esq.7 New sq. Lincoln's i
Burgess Mrs. 32 Bryanstone square
Burgess Mrs. 134 Sloane st
Burgess Thos. esq. 35 Essex st. Strand
Burgis Benj. esq. 75 Oxford terrace
Burgon Thomas, esq. 34 Osnaburgh st
Burgoyne Dowager Lady, 31 Grosvnr. pl
Burgoyne Sir John, bart. 27 Up. Brook st. & Sutton park, Biggleswade, Beds
Burgoyne John Chas. esq. 60 Wimpole st. & 160 Oxford st
Burgoyne Thomas, esq. 43 Welbeck st
Burgoyne Thos. Jno. esq. 21 Stratford pl
Burke Col. 1 St. Alban's place
Burke H. esq. 25 Liverpool st. King's cr
Burke James St.George, esq.10 Park st. Westminster, & 44 Parliament st
Burke J. B. esq. 25 Gower st. Bedford sq. & 2 Churchyard ct. Temple
Burke Mrs. 25 Cumberland st
Burke Mrs. 30 Duke st. Bloomsbury
Burke Patk. esq. 13 Upr. Montagu st
Burke Peter, esq. 25 Gower st. Bedford sq. & 2 Churchyard ct. Temple
Burke Peter, 89 Sloane st
Burke T.H. esq.27 Gloucester pl. New rd
Burkett T. A. esq. Rural cot. Clapm.rd.pl
Burkitt Edwd. esq. 29 Highbury place, & 7 London wall
Burleigh Geo. esq.3 Albion pl. Holloway
Burley John, esq. 3 Grove End road
Burley William, esq. 25 York place
Burlington, Earl of, 10 Belgrave square; Holkar hall, Milnthorpe; & Compton place, Eastbourne
Burls Chas. esq.19 New Bridge st. Blkfrs
Burls John, esq. 7 Highbury grove
Burman Richd. esq.22 Whitehead's grove
Burmester Fredk. esq. 15 Upr. Wimpole st. & Gynn house, Woodfrd. brdg. Essex
Burmester John, esq.23 Old sq. Linc.inn
Burmister Mrs. 6 Oxford sq. Hyde park
Burn Henry, esq. 2 Salisbury ct. Fleet st
Burn James, esq. 13 Allsop terr. New rd
Burn John, esq. 18 Adam st. Adelphi
Burn John Ilderton, esq. 6 South square
Burn Wm. esq. 6 Stratton st. Piccadilly
Burnaby John Dick, esq. 2 Pump court, Temple, & Ashfordby, Leicestershire
Burnaby Wm. Dyott, esq. 3 Bow st
Burnand L. esq. 13 St. Mary Abbot's ter
Burnand Geo. esq. 4 Sussex square
Burnell Rev. Samuel, 26 Kensington sq
Burnell Geo. esq. 5 Sussex ter. Hyde pk
Burnell Hen. esq. 20 Cheyne wk. Chelsea
Burnell Thomas, esq. 33 York terrace
Burnet Rev. John, Grove lane, Cmbrwll
Burnett Benj. esq. 6 Waterloo, Kilburn
Burnett Sir Wm. K.C.H. 5 Somerset pl
Burnett Rev. Thos. D.D. 13 Finsbury sq
Burnett Burrow, esq. 5 Upper Harley st
Burnett Chas. F. esq. 19 Park crescent
Burnett D.P. esq. 3 Kendall pl. Vassall rd
Burnett Duncan P. esq. Cowley rd. Nth Brixton & 22 Surrey st. Strand
Burnett H.P.D. esq.15 St. Mary Abbotts tr
Burnett John, esq. 12 Winchester row
Burnett Jno. esq. Egmont ho. Victoria rd
Burnett Rt. French, esq. 19 Cornwall ter. Regent's park, & 10 New sq. Linc. inn
Burnett Wm. H. W. esq. 4 Henrietta st. Cavendish square
Burney Col. Hen. 26 Hamilton terrace
Burney John C. esq. 30 Hemingford ter
Burney Rd. esq.1 Cunninghampl. St. Jn'sw
Burnie Joseph, esq. 54 Chancery lane
Burningham Jas. esq. 13 Liverpool st
Burningham Thos. esq. 14 Cloudesley sq
Burns Capt. 44 St. James's place
Burns Rev. Jabez, 3 Portens rd. Harrow rd
Burns Jas. esq. 1 Willow wk. Kentsh. tn
Burns John, esq. 9 Greville pl. Klbn.pry
Burnside Wm. esq. 6 Lansdowne place
Burr H.D. esq.15 Devonshire pl. Portld.pl
Burr James, esq. 41 Noel st. Islington
Burrage Wm. esq.13 Glo'ster rd. Hyde pk
Burrard Mrs. 2 Rayner pl. Chelsea
Burrell Sir C. M. bart. M.P. 5 Richmond ter. Whitehall, & Knapcastle, Horsham
Burrell Fred. esq. 74 Baker st
Burrell Jas. F. esq. 33 York pl. City rd
Burrell John, esq. 27 Spring gardens
Burrell John Palfrey, esq.1 Gray's inn sq
Burrell J. esq.31 Porchestr.tr. & 7 New sq
Burrell Miss, 44 Queen sq. Bloomsbury
Burrell Mrs. 13 Great Cumberland st
Burrell P. A. esq. 1 White hart ct. City
Burrell Robert, esq. House of Lords, & Birkfield lodge, near Ipswich
Burrell Saml. esq. 10 Vere st. Cavndsh.sq
Burrell Thomas, esq. 18 Pelham place
Burrell W. W. esq. 5 Richmond terrace
Burridge Mrs. 11 Circus, Minories
Burridge Mrs. 39 Upper Gower st
Burridge Wm. esq. 58 Milbank st. Wmr
Burrough Miss, 16 Bedford square, & Laverstock house, Salisbury, Wilts
Burroughes H. N. esq. M.P. Limmer's hotel, & Burlingham hall, Norwich
Burroughs Chas. esq. 20 Montpelier sq
Burroughs Mrs.19 Cobrg.pl. Up. Kenng.la
Burrow Edmund, esq. 2½ Stockwell com
Burrow H.N. esq. Grove ho. Stoke Newgtn
Burrow Mrs. 14 Kensington crescent
Burrow Thos. C. esq. 3 Paper buildings
Burrowes Hon. Mrs. 3 Hill st
Burrows Major, 8 Hamilton terrace
Burrows Arthur, esq. 89 Chancery lane
Burrows Arthur, esq. 3 Torrington st
Burrows Charles, esq. 41 Doughty st. & 20 Lawrence lane, City
Burrows Geo. M.D. esq.45 Queen Anne st
Burrows G. Mann, M.D. 46 Up. Gower st
Burrows John F. esq. 13 Nottingham pl

Burrows Miss, 11 Chapel st. Bedfd. row
Burrows Mrs. 19 Albany st
Burrows Mrs. 16 South Lambeth
Burrows Mrs. 2 Upper Belgrave st
Burry Edward, esq. 16 Ladbroke terr
Bursby Wm. esq.13 St.Geo's. tr. Knsgtn. nw. tn
Bursey Henry, esq.11Chandos st.Strand
Burslem Hy. esq. 14 Kensington gar. ter
Burslem W. M. M.D. 36 Chester pl.west
Burt Capt. Wm. R.N. 86 Lisson gr. north
Burt Geo. esq. 7 Crescent pl. Blackfrs
Burt H. esq. 1 Southmptn. st. Fitzroy sq
Burton Capt. Ryder, R.N. & Hon. Mrs. 15 Park square, Regent's park, & Dunstall Priory, Eynesford, Kent
Burton Arthur, esq. 41 Coleshill st
Burton Archer B.esq.6 King's Bench wk
Burton Decimus, esq. 6 Spring gardens, & Tonbridge wells
Burton Edwd. F. esq. 7 Chancery lane
Burton Henry, M.D. 41 Jermyn st
Burton Jas. esq. 41 Claremont square
Burton Jas. esq. 3 Powis pl. Gt. Ormond st. Queen sq. & Richmond, Surrey
Burton John, esq. 14 South st. Finsbury
Burton Mrs. 7 Cumberland st
Burton Mrs. 23 Maida hill west
Burton Thos. esq. 18 York pl. City road
Burton Thos. Stackhouse, esq. 25 Gloucester pl.Prtmn.sq.&10Salisby.st.Stnd
Burton Wm. esq. 2 Mathon pl. Pentonvl
BurtonW.F.esq.12 Grove rd.St.John'swd
Burton Wm. Warwick, esq. 12 Serle st
Burtt Jsph. esq. 45 Burton st. Burton cr
Bury Viscount, 9 Charles st. Grosvr. sq
Bury Edwd. esq. 1 New sq. Lincoln's inn
Bury Francis, esq.52 Burton crescent
Bury John William, esq. 25 Charles st. St. James's
Bury Mrs. 16 Porchester terrace
Bury Wm. esq. 6 New Bridge st.Blkfrs
Busby Jas. esq. Fonthill ho.Clapham rd
Busch J. A. G. esq. 13 Qn.Charlotte row
Busfeild Wm. esq. M.P. 15 Bury st. St. James's, & Upwood, near Bingley, Yorkshire
Busfield J. esq. 8 St. Mary le Strand pl
Bush Thos. esq. 15 Melbury ter.Drst. sq
Bushby Joseph, esq. 7 Brompton grove
Bushby Mrs. 36 Weymouth st
Bushe Gervas Parker, esq. 78 Eaton sq
Bushell Hen. esq.27Dartmouth st.Wstm
Bushell John,esq. 12 Hall pl. Kengtn.la
Bushell Mrs. 26 Lower Ranelagh st
Bushell Thomas, esq. 117 Crawford st
Bushill Fredk. Wm. esq. 3 Mortimer st
Busk Hans, esq. 1 Gt. Cumberland pl.; Culverden grove; Tunbridge wells; Glenalder, Rhayader; & 28 Brunswick terrace, Brighton
Busk Hans, jun.esq. 1Figtree ct.Temple
Busk HenryWm. esq.7 Powis place, Gt. Ormond st. & 16 Old sq. Lincoln's inn
Buss Chas. esq. 60 Broad st.Bloomsbury
Buss Robt.Wm.esq.29Duke st.Grosv. sq
Buss Rt. Wm. esq. 68 Warren st
Bustead Richard, esq. 26 Up.Marylbn.st
Butcher Geo. esq. 26 York blds. New rd
Butcher Geo.Robert,esq. 51 Welbeck st
Bute, Marquis of, K.T.16Arlington st. & Cardiff castle,Glamorganshire; Dumfries house, Ayrshire; Mount Stuart, Isle of Bute; Luton park, Bedfordsh.; &Kirtling tower, Cambridgeshire
Butler Hon. Sir Ed. 4 Cumberland place
Butler Hon. Charles L. 12 Cornwall ter
Butler Col. Hon.Pierce, M.P.57 York st. York road, Lambeth; & Ballyconra house, Ballyragget
Butler Rev. Daniel, 1A, Wellington rd
Butler Edward, esq. 4 Frith st. Soho
Butler Edwd. Robt. esq. 7 Furnival's inn
Butler Geo. esq. 152 Albany st
Butler Jas. esq.4Up.George st.Prtmn.sq
Butler Jas. esq. 30 Orchard st. Ptmn. sq
Butler James, esq. 118 New Bond st
Butler Jas. esq. 31Winchrtr. rw. New rd
Butler Jas. esq.4Young st. Kensingtn.sq
Butler Jn. esq.10 Cambridge st. Edgr.rd
Butler Jn. esq. 1 Clayland's pl. Clpm. rd
Butler Jn. esq. 8 Clifton pl. Sussex sq
Butler Mrs. 9 Sussex place, Hyde pk
Butler Mrs. 22 Frederick st. Gray's i. rd
Butler Mrs. 19 Manchester st
Butler Mrs. 10 Mary st. Hampstead rd
Butler Mrs. 26 York pl. City road
Butler Miss, 48 Pembroke sq. Kensngtn
Butler Pierce S. esq. M.P. 3 Queen sq. Westminster
Butler Samuel,esq.8Norland pl.Nttg.hll
Butler Thos. esq. 6 Cheyne walk,Chelsea
Butler Tim. esq. 1 Middlesex pl. Nw rd
Butler Wm. esq. 19 Berwick st. Pimlico
ButlerW.esq.12 Blomfield rd.Maida hill
Butt Geo. esq. 41 Up. Berkeley st. west
Butt GeorgeMedd,esq. Q.C. 17 Eaton sq. & 3 Tanfield court, Temple
Butt John, esq. 11 River st.Myddelton sq
Butt Miss, 19 Winchester row, New rd
Butt Mrs. 32 Hyde Park square
Butt Rt. Jas. esq. 97 Gt. Russell st
Butt Thomas, esq. 46 Bedford row
Buttemer Robt.Wm. esq. 27Newingtn. pl
Butterfield B. esq.Retreat, Sth.Lambeth
Butterfield H. esq. 5 River terrace north
Butterfield Walter, esq. 5 Stanhope ter. Hyde park, & 5 Gray's inn sq
Butterfield Wm. esq. 4 Adam st.Adelphi
Butterman George, esq. 9 Clapham rise
Butterworth Rev.J.H.M.A.54Devnshr.st
Butterworth James, esq. 20 Howland st
Butterworth William Henry, esq. Hall staircase, Inner Temple
Buttler C. esq. 5 Bedford pl. Hmpstd. rd
Button Saml. J. esq.4Racquet ct.Fleet st
Butts Thos. esq. 17 Grafton st.Fitzroy sq
Butts Thomas, esq. 5 Up. Fitzroy st
Buxton Lady, 85 Harley st. & Shadwell lodge, Thetford, Norfolk
Buxton Alf. esq. 23 Lincoln's inn fields
Buxton John, esq. 5 Brownlow st. Hlbrn
Buxton Wilmot, esq. 20 Abbey road
Buzaglo Misses, 33 Clapham road pl
Buzzard George, esq. 50 Poland st
By Chas. Wm.esq.26 Terrace,Trinity sq
Byam Wm. Jonathan,esq. 34 Welbeck st
Byard John, esq. 5 Carpenter's buildings
Byers Rev. S. 26 Bedford pl. Kensington
Byers Geo. esq. 8 Addison road north
Byfeld Jas. esq. 11 South cres. Bedfd. sq
Byfeld Misses, 2 North cres. Bedford sq
Byford Thos. esq. 121 Camden rd. villas
Bygrave Thos. esq. 14 Clement's inn
Byham Richard, esq. 87 Pall mall
Byles John Barnard, S.L. 20 Woburn sq. & 6 King's Bench walk, Temple
Byng Hon. Edmund, 10 Clarges st
Byng Hon. Frederick, 37 St. James's pl
Byng George, esq. M.P. 5 St. James's sq. & Wrotham park, near Barnet
Byng Right Hon. George Stevens, M.P. & Lady Agnes, 77 Eaton sq. & Copel house, Bedford
Byng Misses, 25 Charles st. Berkeley square, & Twickenham
BynonJohn, esq.172Prospect pl.Maida hl
Byrn Mrs. 5 Burton crescent
Byrn Oscar, esq. 6 Burton crescent
Byrne Daniel, esq. 33 Duke st. Blmsby
Byrne Edmd. esq. 22 Southampton bdgs
Byrne Mrs. 56 Montagu square
Byrne Wm. Augustus, esq. 94 St. Martin's lane
ByrneWm.Pitt,esq.16Montagu st.Ptn.sq
Byron Lord, Capt. R.N. 21 Eaton place, Ladbroke hall, Southam
Byron Lady Noel, 22 Dover st
Byron Henry, esq. 18 Graham st.Pimlico
Byron J. B. esq. 110 Camden road villas
Byron Miss, 3 Somers pl. Cambridge sq
Byth James, esq. 24 Hyde park gardens
CAARTEN J. M. Bicker, esq. 5 Fig Tree court, Temple
Caballero Madame, 4 Gloucester st
Cabbell Benj. Bond, esq. 52 Portland place; & 1 Brick court, Temple
Cabbell Thomas, esq. 1 Essex ct.Temple
Cabell Thos. S. esq. Larkhall rise,Clphm
Cabell Wm. esq.5Newington pl.Kenn.rd
Caddell Rd.O.F.esq.11Yorkter.Regt.'spk
Cadell Mrs. 36 Weymouth st
Cadman C. esq.1Glo'ster villa,Regt.'s pk
Cadogan Earl, Rear Admiral, 138Picdily
Cadogan Hon. Frederick, 138 Piccadilly
Cadogan Hon. George, 138 Piccadilly
Cadogan Major, 15 St. James's place, & Brinkburn priory, near Morpeth
Cadogan Wm. esq. 2 Essex st
Cafe Henry S. esq. 48Gt.Marlborough st
Cafe Thomas, jun. esq. 80 Newman st
Cafe Thomas S. esq. 80 Newman st
Caffary Patrick J. esq. 17 Titchfield ter
Cahill Thos. M.D.3 William st. Knightsb
Cahlmann Julius, esq. 40 Gt. Coram st
Cahlmann Samson, esq. consul general for Saxe Weimer, 1 Copthall chambers, Throgmorton st
Cahusac John A. esq. F.S.A. 34 Upper Barnsbury st. Islington
Cahusac Thomas, esq. 5 Maida hill
Caillet Jean Pierre, esq. 3 George st. Portman square
CairnsHugh M.C. esq 5New sq.Linc. inn
Calcraft J. H. esq. 12 Carlton house ter. & Rempstone hall, near Corfe Castle
CaldcleughFrs.esq.1Allsop pl.Regt.'s pk
Caldecott Andrew, esq. 24 Russell sq
Calder Sir Henry, bart. & Lady Frances, 18 Sussex place, Regent's park
Calder Alex. esq. 22 Up. Woburn place
CalderF.esq.27Wellington tr.St.Jn.'s wd
Caldwell Sir Jas. K.C.B. 4 Portland pl. & Beachland, Ryde, Isle of Wight
Caldwell Chas. A. esq. 3 Audley sq
Caldwell David, esq. 29 Golden sq
Caldwell Fred. Wm. esq. 29 Golden sq
Caldwell Fred. Wm. esq. Finchley nw. rd
Caldwell George, esq. 33 Thurloe sq
Caldwell John, esq. 78 St. John's wd. ter
Cale Ebenezer, esq. 82 St. John's wd. ter
Caledon Earl, orderly room, Horse grds. & Caledon, County Tyrone, & Boom hall, County Londonderry
Calemard Miss, 62A, Grosvenor st
Caley Mrs. 7 Seymour place, Euston sq
Calf Wm. esq. 12Aberdeen pl. Maida hill
Calkin J. esq. 3Harrington st.Hmpstd.rd
CallSirW.P., Marten&Co. 25 OldBond st
Call Sir W. P. bart. 25 Old Bond st. & Whiteford house, Stoke Climsland, Launceston
Callaghan Daniel, esq. M.P. Reform club, 104 Pall mall, & Lotabeg, near Cork
Calland Mrs. 39 Hertford st. Mayfair
Callander Gen. 41 Bryanstone st
Callander Mrs. 24 Montagu square
Caillard Camille T. esq. 76 Up. Brkley.st
CallcottW.H. esq. The Mall, Kensington
Calley Chas. esq. 38 Hamilton terrace
Callow Chas. esq. 1 Montpelier square
CallowWm.esq. 20Charlotte st.Prtlnd. pl
Calrow Mrs. 33 Up.Gower st. Bedford sq
Calthorpe Lord, 33 Grosvenor square; Elvetham, Hertford bridge; & Ampton, Bury St. Edmunds
Calthorpe hon. Fredk. Gough & Lady Charlotte, 33 Grosvenor sq. & Elvetham, Hertford bridge
Calthorpe hon. Miss, 33 Grosvenor sq. & Elvetham, Hertford bridge
Calton Geo. esq. 8 Blomfld rd. Maida hil
Calvert Chas. Anthony, esq. 9 Harpur s
CalvertChristoph.Alderson,esq. 4Serle s
Calvert Edwd. esq. 14Park pl.Paddingt
Calvert F. esq. 9St.James's pl.&8New s
Calvert John Wm. M.D. 11 Blandford pl

Calvert Miss,16Henrietta st.Brnswck.sq
Calvert Mrs. 30 St. James's place
Calvert Mrs. 37 Up. Berkeley st. west
Calvert Col. Nicolson, & Hon. Mrs. 30 Cavendish sq. & Hunsdon house, Ware
Calvert Nathaniel, esq. 30 Wakefield st
Calvert Wm. esq. 5 Lyon's inn, Strand
Cam William, esq. 1 James st. Adelphi
Camac Col. Sir B. 29 Chas. st. St. Jas.'s
Camara Jose H. Gago da, 32 Sussex gdns
Cambell Lady, 14 Wellington road
Cambridge Duke of, K.G., G.C.B., G.C.H., P.C. Cambridge house, 94 Piccadilly, & Kew
Cambridge, PrinceGeorge of, St.James's palace
Cambridge Mrs. 3 Holland st. Kensngtn
Camden, Marquis of, K.G. 19Belgrave sq.; Wilderness pk. Sevenoaks; Bayham abbey, Lamberhurst;&Brecknockprior
Camden Mrs. 5 Allen ter. Kensington
Cameron Sir D. bart. 144 Oxford st
CameronDugaldEd. esq. 19Bckinghm.st
Cameron Ewen H. esq. 37 Chancery la
Cameron Francis, esq. 50 Beaumont st
Cameron Fred. 50 Beaumontst.Prtlnd.pl
CameronHen.esq. 50Beaumontst.Prtl.pl
Cameron John A. esq. 38 Throgmorton st
Cameron John C. Hampstead heath, & 1 Raymond buildings, Gray's inn
Cameron Mrs. 15 St. George's place
Camoys Lord, 7 Park st. Westminster, & Stonor park, Henley-on-Thames
Campbell Lord P.C. & Lady Stratheden, Stratheden ho. South pl. Knightsbrid
Campbell hon. Capt. Geo. 46 Hertford st
Campbell Gen. Sir Henry, K.C.B., G.C.H. 8 Lowndes square, Knightsbridge
Campbell Sir Hugh Purves Hume, bart., M.P. 72 Portland pl. & Marchmont house, near Dunse, Berwickshire
Campbell Sir Robert, bart., 5 Argyll pl
Campbell Sir John, knt. & Lady, 51 Charles st. Berkeley square
CampbellSirJohn Nicholl Robert, K.C.H. 10 Harley st
Campbell Col. Patrick, 15 Regent st
Campbell Col.Wm. 3 St. George's place
Campbell Lieut. Col.F.W.F.97 Mount st
CampbellMaj. John, 36 Mornington cres
CampbellCapt.G. 19 Chesham st.Belg.sq
Campbell Rev. Arch. M. Rectory house, Park place, Paddington
CampbellRev.JohnB.11King's bench wk
Campbell Alexander, esq. 25 Bernard st
Campbell Alexander (of Monzie), esq. Fenton's hotel, 63 St. James's st. & Monzie, N.B.
Campbell Alexander, esq. 45 Woburn pl
Campbell Alexr. D. esq. 37 Montagu sq
Campbell Archibald, esq. 2 Bentinck st
Campbell Arthur E. esq. 99 Piccadilly
Campbell Colin, M.D. 72 Cambridge ter
Campbell D. esq. 4 Glo'ster rd. O.Brmp
Campbell H. esq. 144 Oxford st. & the Hollies, Stourbridge
CampbellHen. E. esq. 3 New inn, Strand
Campbell Jas. esq. 58 Lincoln's inn flds
Campbell Jas. esq. 45 Portland place
Campbell Jas. esq. 4 Rodney st.Pentvlle
Campbell Jas. esq. 15 Wyndham place, Bryanstone sq. &2New sq.Lincoln's inn
Campbell John, esq. 51 Hans place
Campbell John Henry, esq. M.P. 57 St. James's st. & Sydney lodge, Southptn
Campbell John S. M.D. 16 Weymouth st
Campbell Miss, Finchley new road
Campbell Miss, 27 Queen sq. Bloomsby
Campbell Mrs. Major, 24 Cumberland st
Campbell Mrs. 15 Kensington crescent
Campbell Mrs. 4 Porchester place
Campbell Mrs. 40 Portman square
Campbell Mrs. W. 2 Lowndes st
Campbell P.L.esq. 4 Sydney pl. Fulham r
Campbell R. esq. 128 Camden rd. villas
Campbell Thos. esq. 4 Kensington gore
Campbell Thos. esq. 16 Gt. Marlboro' st & Athenæum club, Pall mall
Campbell Thos. C. esq. 21 Essex st
Campbell Thomas T. esq. 2 Burton cresc
Campbell Wm. Geo. esq. 9 In. Temple la
Campden Viscount, 2 Portman square
Campden Viscount, 169 New Bond st. & Barham court, Maidstone, Kent
Camperdown, Earl of, Lundie & Camperdown ho. Forfar & Bath
CampionJerh. esq. 14 Somer's pl.Hyde pk
Camps Wm. esq. 50 Green st. Grosvr. sq
Camps Wm. H. esq. 22 Goulden terra. Barnsby. road
Camroux Ferdnd. F. esq. 57 Doughty st
CancellorJ.H.esq.32Chester tr.Regts.pk
Candler Sam. esq. 3 Angel ter. Islington
Cane Edward, esq. 105 Piccadilly
Cane Rd. esq. 2 Mitre ct. bldgs, Temple
Caney Miss, 88 Oxford terrace, Hyde pk
CanforM.M.esq.1Cambridge ter.Islngtn
Cankrien Hugh Ker, esq. 23 Old square
Canney T. esq. 5 Percy circus, Pentnvlle
Canning Viscount, 10 Grosvenor square
Canning C. esq. 18 Brnswk pl. Bnsby.rd
Canning Mrs. 15 Glo'ster pl. Portman sq
CanningMrs. 3 Up.Bedford pl. Kensgton
Cannon Edw. Beacon, esq. 5 Cumbrld st
Cannon E. J. esq. 10 Annett's crs. Isling
Cannon Miss, 13 Newngtn.pl. Kengtn.rd
Cannon Rd. esq. 5 Kengtn ter.Up. Kenn
Cannon Robt. esq. 23 Lloyd square
Canofari Mons. G. sec. to the Legation from Sicily, 2 Old Cavendish st
Canterbury, Archbishop of, P.C. Lambeth palace, & Addington park, Croydon
Canterbury Viscount, Rockbeare, Honiton, Devon
Cantilupe Viscount, 17 Up. Grosvenor st. & Buckhurst pk. Tunbridge wells
Cantis Henry, esq. 8 Maddox st
Canton Alfred, esq. 18 Old Bond st
Canton Edwin, esq. 104 St. Martin's la
Canton Geo. A. esq. 40 St. Martin's la
Canton Wm. L. esq. 18 Hanover st.
Cantrell J. T. esq. 21 Old sq. Lincoln's inn
Cantwell Rt. esq. 25 Wimpole st. & 20Gt. Marlboro' st. & 10 Church st. Cambwl
Cape Major, 31 Glo'ster pl. Portman sq
Cape J. esq. 8 Park cot. Park village ea
Cape Lawson, M.D. 64 Brook st
Cape Wm. esq. 13 Portsea pl. Edgwr rd
Capel Vice-Adm. Hon. Sir T.B. 76 Grosvenor st. & Little Cashiobury, Herts
CapelHon.Lt.Gen.14Chas. st.Berkeleyst
Capel Lady Caroline, 23 Chester sq
Capel James, esq. 37 Fitzroy square
Capel John, esq. 32 Russell square
Capel John, esq. 42 Upper Baker st
Capel Mrs. 22 Annetts ter. Islington
Capes George esq. 1 Field ct. & 28 Park st. Grosvenor sq
Capleton J. esq. 1 Up.Southwick st. nrth
CaponsWm. esq.18 Hemingfrd. ter.Islgtn
Caporn Jas. esq. 10 Dyer's buildgs.Holbn
Cappur Ralph T.esq. 8 Brook st. Gros. sq
Capron Fred. esq. 6 Charles st.Grovnr.sq
Capron Geo. esq. 9 New Burlington st. & Saville pl. New Burlington st
Capron Mrs. 35 Finsbury square
Capron Thos. W.esq.24South st.Grosv.sq
Capstick Mrs.20Camdencot.Cmdn.nw.tn
Carbonell John Tuffnell, esq. 25 Oxfd. sq
Carbonell Miss, 4 Hinde st. Manchester sq. & Cottage villa, Old Windsor
Carbonell W.C.esq. Manor ho. Harrowrd
Cardale John B. esq. 2 Tavistock villas
Cardale Edw. Thos. esq. 2 Bedford row
Carden Geo. Fred. esq. 11 Carey st
Carden Rt. Walter, esq. 64 Wimpole st
Cardigan, Earl of, 36 Portman square, & Dean park, Wansford
Cardinali Peter, esq. 31 Gt. Portland st
Cardwell C. esq. 28 Chester ter. Rgt.'s pk
Cardwell Edwd. M.P. 4Whitehall gardens
Cardwell Mrs. 28 Chester ter. Rgt.'s pk
Cardye Mrs. 185 Edgeware road
Careless Mrs. 4 Montagu st. Portman sq
Carew Lord, Castleborough, Wexford
Carew Hon. Robt.S.34 Hill st. & Woodstown, Waterford
Carew Lady Hallowell, 7 Oxford square
Carew Francis, esq. 4 Somers pl.Hydepk
Carew George, esq. 219 Maida vale
Carew Miss Hallowell, 7 Oxford square
Carew Wm. H. P. esq. M.P. 15 Herefrd. st
Carey Jonthn.esq.5Abbeypl.St. John'swd
Carey Lady, 6 Cadogan place
Carey Mrs. General, 44 Cadogan place
Carey Peter Stafford, esq. 15 Bedford sq
Carey Wm. esq. 8 Half moon st
Carfrae Thos. esq. 75 Gloucester place
Cargill, Wm. esq. 2 Sidmouth st
Carless E. B. esq. 39Warwick st.Pimlico
Carleton Hon. Richard, 25 Bruton st
Carleton Dudley Wilmot, esq25Bruton st
Carleton J. W. esq. 15 Regent st.
Carlisle, Earl of, K.G., P.C. 12 Grosvenor pl.; & Castle Howard, Yorkshire; & Naworth castle, near Brampton
Carlisle, Bishop of, University club, Pall mall east, & Rose castle, Carlisle
Carlisle John, esq. 2 Bernard st
Carlisle Nicholas, esq. Antiquarian society, Somerset house
CarlisleSept. E. esq. 20 John st. Adelphi
CarlonJohn, esq.Palace chmbs.St.James' st. & 8 Greville pl. Kilburn priory
Carlow Saml.S.T.C.esq.12Claphamrd.pl
Carlton Club House (James Jephson, sec.), 94 Pall mall
Carlton Wm. T. esq. 12A, Circus rd. St. John's wood
Carlyle Thos. esq. 5 Cheyne rw. Chelsea
Carnaby Mrs. 7 Middlesex pl. New rd
Carnac Cap.Rivett, R.N.46 Devonshire st
Carnarvon, Earl of, 43 Grosvenor sq.; & Highclere hall, Newbury; & Milford the lake, near Newbury; & Pixton Dulverton, Somersetshire
Carne C. esq. 13 Caledonia ter.Caledn.rd
Carne Nicholl, esq. see Nicholl-Carne
Carnegie Hon. Swinfen Thomas, M.P. 94 Pall mall
Carnegie John, esq. 15 St. James's sq
Carnshall Mrs.12A, Lowthr.cot.Livrpl.rd
Carnwath Dow. Countess, 39 Glo'ster pl
Carpenter General, 7 Gt. Cumberland.pl
Carpenter James, esq. 58 Nelson sq
Carpenter Mrs. Major, 20 Norfolk cresc
Carpenter Mrs. North lodge, Avenue rd
Carpenter Mrs. 5 Porchester pl. Edg. rd
Carpenter Mrs. Wm. 10 Nottingham pl
Carpenter Percy, esq. 10 Nottingham pl
Carpenter Richd. esq. 24 Lonsdale sq
Carpenter Richd. C. esq. 99 Guilford st
Carpenter T. esq. 16 Belgravest.New rd
Carpenter Thos. esq. 125 Drummond st
Carpenter William, esq. 73 Hermitage place, St. John st. road
Carpenter Wm. esq. 10 Nottingham pl
Carpenter Wm. jun. esq.10Nottinghm.pl
Carpenter Wm. esq. 13 Salisbury sq
CarpenterWm.G.esq. 1 Westst.Finsbury
Carpmael Wm.esq. 4Old sq.Lincoln's inn
Carpue Joseph, M.D.45Charlot.st.Fitz.sq
Carr Andrew Morton, esq.37Lowndes st
Carr David, esq. 27 Golden square
Carr John, esq. 1Cornwall ter.Gt.Dvr.rd
Carr John, esq. 10 St.James's pl.St.Jas's
Carr J. H. esq. 14Compton st.Brnswk.sq
Carr Geo. B. esq. 7 Cumberland terrace
Carr Matthew esq. 8 Hanoverct.Reg.pk
Carr Miss, 8 Princes ct. Westminster
Carr Mrs. 20 Guilford st. Russell sq
Carr Mrs. 86 Hamilton ter.St.John's wd
Carr Mrs. 4 Kensington gar.ter.Susx.sq
Carr Mrs. 66 Lowndes square
Carr Mrs. 51 Southampton row, Russ.sq
Carr Ralph, esq.14 York ter.Regnt.'s pk. & Barrow point hill, Pinner, Middlsx
CarrThos.esq.3Wellington rd.St.Jn.'s wd

Carr Wm.esq.12Camden cotts.Camdn.tn
Carr Wm. Thos. esq. 15 Halfmoon st. & 89 Chancery lane
Carreras Joseph, esq. 20 Wilsted st
Carrett Miss, 20 Albion st. Hyde park
Carrick A. esq. Oak vill.4 Finchly.nw.rd
Carrick T.esq.43Up. Seymour st.Port.sq
CarrighanT.esq.Henleyldg.St.Pancrs.vs
Carrington Lord, Whitehall yard; & the Abbey, Wycombe; & Gayhurst, New port Pagnell
Carrington Benjamin, esq. 5 Winchester place, Pentonville
Carrington F. A. esq.28Lincoln's inn flds
Carrington Geo. esq.21Up.Brkly.st.west
CarringtonGeo.Wm.esq.14Duke st.Wstr
Carritt Frederick,esq. 11Chapel st.Pentonville, & 10 Basinghall st
Carroll SirG.34Cavendish sq.&Loughton
Carroll John, esq. 91 Oxford terrace
Carroll Mrs. Park cot. Park pl.Paddngtn
Carrow J.M.esq.Hallstaircase,Innr.Tmp
Carruthers Charles, esq. 104 Jermyn st
Carse Alexr. esq. 39 Up.Berkeley st.wst
Carson Mrs. 21 Grove ter. Lisson grove
Carstairs Jsph. esq. 81 Lombard st. City
Carter A. esq. 31 Paradise ter. Lpool. rd
Carter Charles, esq. 11 Gibson square
Carter Daniel, esq. East cottage, Bedford place, Kensington
Carter Edward, esq. Thames bank
Carter Henry, esq. 9 Thanet pl. Strand
Carter Jas. esq. 21 Aberdeen pl.Maida hl
Carter Jas. esq. 3 Middle Temple lane
CarterJas.H.esq.41Gt.Russell st.Blmsby
Carter J. esq. 3 Friedenstn.ter.Hamps.rd
Carter John, esq. 23 Dorset st.Portm.sq
Carter John, esq. 66 Harleyford place
Carter Joshua, esq. 17 Hereford st
Carter Miss, 51 Upper Brook st. & Edgcott house, Banbury, Oxon
Carter Mrs. 2 Camden road villas
Carter Mrs. 41 Great Russell st
CarterMrs.Sussex lodge,Finchley new rd
Carter P.W.esq.29Prtlnd.pl.Lr.rd. Islgn
Carter Robert S. esq.116 Sloane st
Carter Saml. esq.9Up.Robert st.Brmptn
Carter Thomas esq. 21 Canonbury sq
Carter Thomas, esq. 44 Noel st.Islngton
Carter Wm. esq. 238 High Holborn
CarterWm.B esq.Draytoncot.Mrngtn.rd
CarterW.G.esq.21Aberdeen pl.Maida hl
CarterWm.Geo.esq.Templechmb.Fleetst
CarterW.P.esq.2Gt.James st.Bedfordrw
CarterW.P.esq.4 Langfordpl.St.Jn.'s wd
Carthew Edward, esq. 16 Clement's inn
Carthew John, 23 Canonbury villas
Carthew Mrs. 5 St. Mary Abbotts ter
Cartledge Thos. esq. Quality ct.Chan.la
Cartwright Chas. Wm. esq. 22 Fleet st
Cartwright F.esq.3 Pine Apple pl.Mda.v
Cartwright J. esq. 3 New Buckenham pl
Cartwright Mrs. 38 Charlotte st.Fitz.sq
Cartwright Rich. esq.35 Bloomsbury sq
CartwrightS.esq.3Manchestr.st.Grs.i.rd
Cartwright Saml. esq.32 Old Burlington st. & Dele-a-bere, Pangbourne, Berks
Cartwright Sam. jun.esq. 9 Sackville st
Cartwright William Ralph, esq. M.P.17 Hereford st. & Aynhoe hall, Brackley
Carver Rev. James, 28 Finsbury circus
CarverEdwd.T.esq F.R.S.4Robrt.st.Adel
Cary Rev. Hen. F. 21 Bloomsbury st
Cary Fras. S. esq. 21 Bloomsbury st
Cary John, esq. 53 Ebury st. Pimlico
Cary Jsph.esq.Club chmbrs. 15 Regnt.st
Cary Mrs. 19 Allsop terrace, New road
Casamaijor Jas. A. esq.47 Albemarle st
Casanas Michael,esq.7Judd pl.east,New road, & Buenos Ayres, Margate, Kent
CasanasMichael,esq.14Up.Porchester st
Case H. esq. 33 Hemingford ter.Islingtn
Case John,esq.2 Henry pl.Up.Kengtn.la
Case John M. esq. 1 James st. Adelphi
Casey Henry S. esq.17 Great Coram st
CaseyJohnArchibald,esq.17Gt.Coram st

Casley John, esq. 31 Guilford st
Casley Mrs. 3 Beaufort terrace, King's road west, Chelsea
Casse Mrs. 32 Portland ter. Regent's pk
Cassells John, esq. 6 St. John's villas
Cassels Mrs. 7 Wilton pl. Belgrave sq
Cassillis, Earl of, Brixworth, Northampton
Casswell J. esq. 16 Queen's pl. Kenn. rd
Castelcicala Prince, ambassador extraordinary, & minister plenipotentiary from Sicily, 15 Princes st. Cavndh. sq
Castell John, esq. 68 Hamilton ter
Castell John, esq. 26 Hunter st
Castell John, esq. 1 Judd st. Brnswk.sq
Castell Mrs. 18 Russell pl. Fitzroy sq
CastellWm. S. esq.1 Wells st.Jermyn st
Castellain Charles, esq. vice-consul for Belgium, 3 Copthall court
Castellain Hermenegild, esq. consul for Belgium, 3 Copthall court
Castellon Madam,14North bk.Regt.'spk
Casterton James, esq. Parade cottage, Glebe place, King's road, Chelsea
Casterton Miss, 2Regnt.ter.King's rd.wt
Casterton William, esq. Radnor cottage, King's road, Chelsea
Castle Henry, esq. 6 John st. Adelphi
Castle Mrs. 11 Hunter st. Brunswick sq
Castlemain Lord, Conservative club, & Moydrum castle, Athlone
Castlereagh Rt. Hon. Viscount, M.P. 127 Park st. Grosvenor sq
Castro Don Pedro Perez de, attaché to Spanish Legation, 9 Cavendish sq
Caswall Alfred, esq. 3 Paper buildings
Cates James,esq.38Alfred st.Bedford sq
Cathcart Earl, C.B.SeniorUnited Service club, & Schaw park, Clackmanan
Cato J. esq. 48 Cambridge ter.Edgw. rd
Cato Mrs. 1A, Russell square
Caton Rev.R.B.75 Seymour pl.Bryan.sq
Cator Capt. B.R.N.6 Hyde park gardens
Cator Rev.Thomas, 8Bryanstone square
Cator Peter, esq. 5 Old square, Lincoln's inn, & Beckenham, Kent
Catterall Joseph, esq. 4 Essex ct.Temple
Cattermole Rev. Richd. 4St.Martin's pl
Cattermole B. esq.27Northmld.st.Mlebn
Cattermole G.esq. Bedford ter.Clpm.rise
Cattermole John F. 49 Coleshill st
Cattermole Mrs. 4 Paradise ter.Liver.rd
Catterson S. esq. 34 Cloudesley terrace
Cattley Thos.T.esq. 4Vimiera,Wndsw. rd
Cattlin Thos. Magnus, esq. 39 Ely place
Cattlin Wm. esq. 6 Fras. pl. Holloway
Caulet Mrs. 34 Upper Gower st
Caulfield E. T. esq. 6 Albion st. Hyde pk
Caulfield Maj. Gen. C.B.82 Eaton square
Cauvin J. esq. 6 Albert st. Victoria sq
Cavan Jas. esq. 8 Park cresct.Portlnd.pl
Cave Charles, esq. 23 Lowndes st
Cave G. esq. 5 Beaufort ter.King's rd.we
Cave Walter, esq. 108 Sloane st
Cavell John, esq. 16 Guilford st
Cavell Mrs. 12 Annetts cres. Islington
Cavendish Hon. Chas. Compton, M.P. & Lady Catherine, Burlington house, 49 Piccadilly; Latimers, Chesham
Cavendish Col.Hon.Hen.Fred.Compton, Burlington gardens, &Westend house, Hampstead
Cavendish Hon. Geo. Hen. M.P. &Lady, 4 Belgrave sq.&Ashford hall,Bakewell
Cavendish Hon. Mrs. Wm. 1 Belgrave square,& Compton pl. Eastbourne
Cavendish Hon. Richard, 19 Hereford st
Cavendish Fredk. esq. Burlington gar
CavendishGeo. A.esq.43Portmn.pl.Edg.r
Cavendish Jas. esq. 30 Portmn. pl.Edg.r
Cavendish Mrs. 12 Abbeypl.St.John's wd
Cavendish Wm. Geo. esq. 49 Piccadilly
Cawdor Earl, 74 South Audley st.; & Cawdor castle, Nairn, N.B.; & Stackpole court, Pembroke, & Goldengrove, near Llandilo

Cawse Miss, 8 Frith st. Soho
Cawthorn John, esq. 12 New inn, Strand
Cawthorn Thos. esq. 23 Wellington rd
Cayley SirG.bart.20Hertford st.My.fair
Cayley Edward S. esq. M.P. 28 Hertford st. & Wydale, Malton, Yorkshire
Cayley Hy.esq.29 York ter. Regent's pk
Cecil Lord Thomas & Lady Sophia, 62 Eaton place
Cecil W. M.esq.16St.G.ter.Knsntn.nw.tn
Celeste Madame, 18 Suffolk st
Ceronio Mrs. 7 Albert st. Mrngtn. cres
Cevallos Don. J. A Lopez de, attaché to Spanish legation, 30 Weymouth st
Chabot Charles, esq. 7 Thavies inn
Chad Sir Charles, bart. 1 Gloucester sq. & Pinkney hall, Fakenham, Norfolk
Chadwick Edwin, esq. 4 Stanhope st. Hyde pk. & 1 Somerset place, Strand
Chadwick Hy. Strettel, esq. 1 Bury st St. James's; & Swinton hall, near Manchester
Chadwick Wm. esq. 58 Lincoln's inn flds
Chadwick Wm. esq. 29 Montagu square
Chaffe Miss, 4 Belgrave st. King's crs
Chaffers Alex. esq. 43 Bedford row
Chaffin Jas. esq. 2 Bedford st. Strand
Chalk J. G. esq. 45 Bedford row,Blmsby
Chalk Mrs. 9 Kennington pl.Up.Kenn.la
ChalkWm.O.esq.3Nottinghamter.Nw.rd
ChalkWm.Swinborne,esq.6Furnivals inn
Chalklen G.esq. 2Cumberld.ter. Lloyd sq
Challenor Col. 11 Charles st. Berkly. sq. & Portnal park, Virginia water
Challenor Wm. esq. 2 Barnsbury square
Challis Alderman Thomas, 32Wilson st. Finsbury, & Enfield, Middlesex
Chalmer Edmd. esq. 25Cheynewk.Chels
Chalmers Fras. esq.3 Cheyne rw.Chelsea
Chalmers Mrs. 22 Hornton st. Knsgtn
Chalmers Miss, 3 Highbury grove
Chalmers Robert, esq. 50 Thurloe sq
Chalon Alfred E. esq. R.A.10 Wimpole st
Chalon Hen. B. esq. 7 Queen st. Brompth
Chalon John Jas. esq. R.A.10 Wimpole st
Chamberlain Edward Hughes, esq. 7 Norfolk st. Parkla. & 4 Elm ct. Templ
Chamberlain J. H. esq.42 Grafton st.east
Chamberlain Miss,9Compton ter.Islngtn
Chamberlain Phillip, esq. 13 Woburn pl
Chamberlain Rt. esq. 8 Lisson grove nth
Chamberlain Wm. esq. 40 Grafton st. ea
ChamberlayneMiss,7Charlesst.Lowndes square, Knightsbridge
Chamberlayne Alf.F.esq. 31 Gt.James st
ChamberlinWm.esq.13Gresse st.Tot.c.rd
Chambers David, esq. 61 Guilford st
Chambers F. esq. 8 Kensington grdn. ter
Chambers H.esq.6 Paradise ter.Lvrpl.rd
Chambers John David, esq. & Hon.Mrs. 7 Connaught sq. & 6 Old sq. Linc. inn
Chambers Miss, 46 Brook sq. Grsvnr. sq
Chambers Miss, 30 Cumberland terrace, & Garden house, Putney
Chambers Miss,4 Grays bldgs.Kngsld.rd
Chambers Miss, 2 Glo'ster terrace
Chambers Miss, 53 York ter.Regent's pk
Chambers Mrs. 2 Glo'ster terrace
Chambers Mrs. Park place, Paddington
Chambers Mrs. 37 Upper Baker st
Chambers Mrs. 26c, Wellington road
Chambers Mrs. M. 12Liverpool st.Nw.rd
Chambers M. esq. Q.C.3 Child's pl.Tmpl
Chambers Rd. Shafto, esq. 5 Doughtyst
Chambers Robert, esq. 13 Gray's inn sq
Chambers Rt. B. esq. 14 Basinghall st
Chambers Thos.esq. Devereux chambers
Chambers Thomas K. M.D. 42 Curzon st
Chambers Walter,esq. 7 Cheyne rw.Chel
Chambers Wm. Fred. M.D. 46 Brook st
Chambers W. Mellish,esq. 2 Paper bldgs
Chamier Capt. R.N. 14 Halkin st. west
Champ J. esq. 2 Park cot.Haverstock hl
Champ Miss, 21 Cambridge st. Edgw.rd
Champagne Lady Dorcas, 55 Harley st
Champagne Arthur H. esq. 55 Harley st

Champey Danl. esq. 8 Belinda terrace
Champion Charles, esq. 32 Ely place
Champion Mrs. 2 Millman pl. Bedfd. rw
Chance Ed. J. esq. 49½A, Lincoln's inn fl
Chance Henry, esq. 12 Crescent place, Hampstead rd.& 38 Lincoln's inn fields
Chander Mrs. 50 Connaught terrace
Chandler Rev. Dr. 36 Mortimer st. & Deanery, Chichester
Chandler A. esq. 27 Southampton bldgs
Chandler Allen, esq. 3 Harcourt bldgs
Chandler Bentham, esq. 46 Weymouth st
Chandler John, esq. 5 Up. George st
Chandler Miss, 97 Sloane st
Chandler Mrs. 5 Church st. Edgware rd
Chandler Rd.esq. 1 Courld.ter.Wands.rd
Chandless Thomas, esq. 1 Gloucester pl. Portman sq. & 13 Old sq. Lincoln's inn
Channell Wm. Fry, s.L. 2 Clarendon pl. Hyde park, & 2 Serjeant's inn
Chantrey Lady, 2 Gloucester square
Chantry F. esq. 16 Leigh st. Burton cres
Chaplin Edward Amos, esq. 30 Up. Bedford place, & 3 Gray's inn square
Chaplin J. M. esq.3 Newcastle ct.Col.hill
Chaplin Wm. esq. 1 Adelphi terrace
Chaplin Wm. esq. 18 Burton crescent
Chaplin Wm. esq. 37 Gower pl. Euston sq
Chaplyn H. C. esq.53 Lincoln's inn fields
Chaplyn Mrs. 17 Vincent ter. Islington
Chapman Sir Montague Lowther, bart. 81 Jermyn st. & Westmeath, Ireland
Chapman Capt. R.N. 7 Up. Hyde park st
Chapman Rev. John, Priory ho. Kilburn
Chapman Aaron, esq. M.P. 2 Leadenhall st. & 1 Highbury park
Chapman B. L. esq. 3 Stone buildings
Chapman Benj. Jas. M.P. 81 Jermyn st. & Killna castle, Athboy, Westmeath
Chapman Cowdell, esq. 5 Egremont pl. New road, & 2 Cloisters, Temple
Chapman Edward, esq. Clareville cottage, Old Brompton
Chapman Edward, esq. 65 Gibson square
Chapman Geo. esq. 3 Arundel st. Strand
Chapman H. esq.2Tillotson pl.Wtrloo. rd
Chapman John, esq.23Dorset pl. Drst. sq
Chapman John, esq.6A, Lisson grove, nth
Chapman J.esq.25Edwd. st. Langham pl
Chapman J. esq. 25 Milton st. Dorset sq
Chapman J. esq.28Portland ter.Rgt's.pk
Chapman J.esq.7Up.York pl.St.Johns w
Chapman Joseph, esq. 2 Highbury ter
Chapman Miss, 33 Halfmoon st
Chapman Miss, 10 Queen sq. Westmstr
Chapman Mrs. 4 Addison ter. Kensingtn
Chapman Mrs.15Beaumont st.Prtlnd. pl
Chapman Mrs. 31 Lower Belgrave pl
Chapman Mrs. 53 Portman pl. Edgw. rd
Chapman Mrs. 65 St. John's wood ter
Chapman Mrs. 17 Upper North place
Chapman Mrs. 10 Wellington terrace
Chapman Richd. esq. Blenheim st. Chels
Chapman Robt. esq. 3 Canonbury place
Chapman Thos. esq. 3 Arundel st.Strand
Chapman Thos. esq. 14 Montagu place
Chapman Thos. esq. 48 Burton crescent
Chapman T.W.esq. 6 Nelson sq.Blkfs. rd
Chapman Wm.esq.82Albert st.Mrgntn.c
Chapman Wm. esq.7Berwick pl.Grng.rd
Chapman Wm. esq. 64 Oxford terrace
Chapman Wm. esq. 14 Highbury park
Chapman Wm. esq. 54 Wimpole st
ChapmanWm.esq.14Winchester rw.N.rd
ChapmanWm.Hn.esq. 31Lw. Belgrave pl
Chappell Capt. R.N.17Queen st.Mayfair
Chappell Fredk. Patey, esq.14 George st. Hanvr. sq.&ChanceryChambs.Qlity.c.
Chappell Geo. esq. 233 Maida vale
Chappell John Cramer, esq.27Jermyn st
Chappell John Wm. esq.10 Wyndham pl
Chappell Mrs. 14 George st. Hanover sq
Chappell Mrs. 18 Maida hill
Chappell T. B. esq. 1 Farm st. Brkly. sq
Chappell Wm. esq.67Conduit st. Reg. st
Chapple John, esq. 35 King st.Cheapside
Chard Edward, esq. 3 Clifford's inn
Chard William, esq. 3 Clifford's inn
Chard William, esq.21Noel st. Islington
Chardonell Odis, esq. 36 Allsop terrace
Charlemont, Earl of, K.P. 49 Grosvenor st.; & Charlemont house, & Marino, Dublin; & Roxborough, near Moy, & Castle Caulfield, Tyrone
Charles Robert, esq. 23 Endsleigh st
Charlesworth Rev.J.14King st.Finsbury
Charlesworth J. esq.6Bury st.St.James's
Charlesworth Mrs. 10 Montpelier st
Charleville Earl of, 38 St. James's st.; & Charleville castle,Tullamore,King's co
Charleville, Dowager Countess of, 14Cavendish square
Charlewood Col. Benj. 9 St. James's pl
Charlier Joseph, esq. 18 Bayswater ter
Charlton Benoni T. esq. 2 Elm Tree rd
Charlton C. H. esq. 24 Lr. Islington ter
Charlton Chas.Wm. esq.20Harrington st
Charlton Edwin, esq. 42 New Bridge st
Charlton Geo. esq. 21 Beaufoy terrace
Charlton Mrs. 21 Albion st. Hyde park
Charlton Robt. esq. 24 Low.Islington tr
Charman H. esq. 29 Sussex pl.Kens. n. t
Charnock Rd. esq. 5 King's bnch.wk.Tle
Charretie Capt. John, R.N. Claremont cottage, Park village ea. Regent's pk
Charrington C. esq.17Glo'ster rd. Hy.pk
Charrington Harry, esq. 30 Doughty st
Chart S. esq. 2 Charlte. pl.Up.Kngtn. la
Charteris hon. Francis, M.P. 27Chesham st. & Armisfield, Haddington, N.B.
Charter Mrs. 87 Norton st. Fitzroy sq
Chase Major C. M. 31 Nottingham pl
Chase Miss, 37 Beaumont st
Chater Joseph, esq. 12 Finsbury circus
Chatfield Chas. esq. 26 John st. Pntvl
Chatfield Mrs. 76 Sloane st
Chatterley Wm.Weldon, esq. 5 Old Dorset place, Clapham road
ChattertonFrederick,esq.52Gt.Portland
Chatterton J. B. esq. 32 Manchester st
Chatto John, esq. 23 Gt. Coram st
Chauntler Thomas, esq. 2 Roebuck ter. Dover rd. & 8 Gray's inn square
Chauvet Fredk. esq.15Grafton st.Fitz.sq
Cheap John, esq. 12 Tyndale place
Cheere Chas. esq. 11 King's Bench walk
Cheere Robt. esq. 11 King's Bench walk
Cheere Mrs. 19 Montagu square, & Papworth hall, near Caxton
Cheesewright E. esq. 8 Colebrooke ter
Cheffins Chas.F. esq. 6 Castle st. Holbn. & 9 Southampton buildings
Cheley Chas. esq. Lark hall rise, Clphm
ChelseaViscount,M.P.41 Wilton crescent
Chenevix Geo. esq. 28 Sussex gardens
Cheney Capt. Ralph, 4 Audley sq
Cheney Robt. Henry, 4 Audley sq. & Badger hall, Shiffnal, Salop
Cheney Mrs. Gen. 4 Audley sq. & Badger hall, Shiffnall, Salop
Cherer Geo. esq. 10 Lincoln's inn fields
Cherer G. esq. 6 North bank, Regent's p
Cherry Mrs. 9 Montagu square
CheshireW.J. esq. 27 Bedfd. st. Cov. gn
Chesnutt Rev. G. M.A.37Trinity sq. Boro
Chessall Matth. Rd. esq.51 Up. Baker st
Chester, Bishop of, 33 Eaton square, & Palace, Chester
Chester Sir Robert, 2 Upper Seymour st
Chester Edward, esq. 24 Colebrooke rw. Islington, & 11 Staple inn, Holborn
Chester Edward Y. esq. 22 Suffolk st
Chester John R. esq. 11 Staple inn
Chesterfield, Earl of, P.C. Chesterfield house, South Audley st. & Bretby pk. Ashby-de-la-Zouch, Leicestershire
Chesterman Mrs.2 Aberdeenpl.Maida hl
Chesterton E. esq. 18 Gerrard st. Islngt
Chesworth Mrs. 43 King sq. Goswell rd
Cheswright Edgar, esq. 7 Albion grove
Cheswright Henry, esq. 4 Sussex terrace
ChevalierW. esq.24 Tonbridge pl.New rd
Chetwode Sir John, bart. M.P. 47 Montagu sq & Chetwode, nr. Buckingham
Chetwynd Dow. Viscountess, 35 Upper Brook st. Grosvenor square
Chetwynd Sir George, bart. 8 New Palace yard, & Atherstone
Cheveley Jas. esq. 29 Wharton st.
Cheveley Miss, 34 Brompton square
Chevers Forbes M.esq. 26Up. Stamfd. st
Chevers Norman, esq. 26 Up. Stamfd. st
Cheyne Rev. Charles, Little Britain
Cheyne Robt. Romley, esq. 43 Berners st
Cheyney Miss, 10 Hanover pl. Park rd
Chichester Lord John, M.P. 8 St. George's place, Hyde Park corner
Chichester, Earl of, 22 Grosvenor place, & Stanmer park, Lewes
Chichester, Dowager Countess of, 22 Grosvenor place
Chichester Lady Harriet, 19 Portman sq
Chichester, Bishop of, 27 Parliament st. & the Palace, Chichester
Chichester John Hopton Russell, esq. 49 Wimpole st. & 3 Stone bldgs, Linc.inn
Chichester Robert Bruce, esq. 11 Lower Seymour st. & 8 New sq. Lincoln's inn
Chieslie Robert J. esq. 8 Seymour pl
Chilcote Geo. H. esq. 14 George st. City
Chilcote Paul, esq. 12 Golden square
Chilcott Miss, 5 York pl. Fulham road
Chilcott Miss, 8 York pl. Fulham road
Child Rev.V.K. Denmark hill, Cambrwl
Child & Co. 1 Fleet street, Temple bar
Child Geo. Chaplin, M.D. 27 Mortimer st
Child Geo. Harris, esq. 21 Fitzroy sq
Child Mrs. 4 Russell square
Child Robert John, esq. 4 Russell sq. & 32 Bedford row, Bloomsbury
Childe Rev. C.F. 12 Barnsbury pl. Islgn
Childe J. esq. 39 Bedford st. Cov.garden
Childers John W. esq. M.P. 13 Henrietta st. & Cantley hall, near Doncaster
Children John Geo. esq. 48 Torrington sq
Childs Geo. esq. 12Amwell st. Pentonvl
Chilman Geo. esq. 30 St. John's wood ter
Chilton Geo.esq.Q.C.9Crownoff rw.Temp
Chilton Geo. esq.1Sussex pl.Hydepk.gar
Chilton Henry Chas. esq. 7 Chancery la
Chilver Thos.F.esq.14 New Burlington st
Chilvers Mrs. 3 Pembroke sq. Kensingtn
Ching Mrs. 22 Montague pl. Russell sq
Ching Miss, 2 Radnor pl. Oxford terrace
Chinnerworth Edwd. esq.6 Pembroke sq
ChinnockF.esq.14 Norland pl.Notting hl
Chiosso Jas. 55 Liverpool st.King's cross
Chipp John, esq. 5 Ebury st. Pimlico
Chipp Thos. Paul, esq. 109 Albany st
Chippendale Aug.esq.10 John st.Adelphi
Chippendale Chas.esq.22 St.John's wd.rd
Chippendale John, esq. 69 Gt. Queen st
ChippendaleJohn,esq.10 John st.Adelphi
Chippendale Jsph. esq. 14 Claremont rw
Chisholm Alex. B. esq. 32 Devonshire st
Chisholm Hen.esq.30 Bedford pl.Knsgtn
Chisholm Duncan, esq. (the Chisholm of Chisholm),37 Chapel st. Grosvenor pl. & Erchless castle, Inverness-shire, N. B.
Chisholme J. esq.29 Edwd.st.Hmpstd.rd
Chisholme Wm. esq. 77 Oxford terrace, Edgware & 64 Lincoln's inn fields
Chiswick James, esq. 8 Bloomsbury sq
Chitty Thomas, esq. 9 Upper Gower st. & 1 King's Bench walk, Temple
Chitty Tompson, esq. 21 Calthorpe st. & 6 Pump court, Temple
Choice Mrs. 2 Lit. Ormond st. Queen sq
Cholmeley Robt. esq. 6 Old sq. Linc. inn
Cholmeley S. esq. 6 New sq. Lincoln's inn
Cholmley James H.esq. 7 Brompton cres
Cholmley Lewin, esq. 20 Eaton square
Cholmondeley Marquis of, P.C.12 Carltn. ho.ter; Cholmondeley castle, Namptwich; & Houghton hall, nr. Rougham
Cholmondeley hon. Hugh, M.P. 2 Hamilton place, & Vale Royal, Northwich
Cholmondeley Jph. esq. 3 Nottingham pl

Choppin Charles, esq. 15 Gray's inn sq
Chorley Hen. F. esq. 5 Victoria square
Chorley John R. esq. 76 Chester square
Chornor C. esq.9 Camdn.st.sth.Cmdn.tn
Choules Wm. esq. 100 Camden rd. villas
Choveaux Henry, esq. 5 Melcombe pl
Chowne C.E.esq.48 Hertford st.Mayfair
Chowne Jn.A.esq.14A,Princes st. Cav.sq
Chowne Wm. D. M.D. 14A, Princes st
Chreptowitch Count, 44 Brook st
Chreptowitch Countess, 44 Brook st
Chrimes Thomas, esq. 2 Frederick place, Gray's inn road
Christian Chas. T. esq. 8 St. Martin's pl
Christian Chas. T. esq. 5 Montpellier sq
Christian Ed. esq. 32 Friedenstein ter
ChristianJ.A.esq.16 St.MaryAbbott's ter
Christian Mrs. Friedenstein terrace
Christie C.W. esq.5 Old sq.Lincoln's inn
Christie Geo. esq. 14 Allsop ter. New rd
Christie Jas. esq. Engine ct. St. Jas. pal
Christie Jonathan Henry, esq. 12 Upper Berkeley st. & 6 Stone bldgs. Linc. inn
Christie Miss, 19 Sloane st
Christie Mrs. 31 Bouverie st. Fleet st
Christie Mrs. 24 New Ormond st
Christie Mrs. 17 Sussex gardens
Christie Mrs. John, 6 Queen st. Mayfair
Christie Samuel Hunter, esq. Royal Society, Somerset house, & Woolwich
Christie Wm.Dougal, esq. M.P. 5 King's Bench walk, Temple, & Hayes park, Uxbridge, Middlesex
Christmas C. G. esq. 11 Spring gardens
Christmas J.W.esq.6Raymond buildings
Christmas Mrs.4Huntley st.Totnm.ct.rd
Christopher James Charles, esq. 5 Serampore ter.Hammersmith, & 11 John st. Adelphi
Christopher John Danby, esq. 26A, Argyll st. & 30 Penton place, Pentonville
ChristopherR.A.esq. M.P. & Lady Mary, 97 Eaton sq.&Bloxholm hall,Sleaford, & Well vale, nr. Alford, Lincolnshire
Christopher Wm.Thos.esq. 16 Woborn pl
Christopher J. C. esq. 8 Up. Montagu st
Christophers J. C.esq. 26 Gloster place
Christopherson Mrs. 21 Brompton row
Chubb Charles, esq. 8 Barnsbury park
Chubb C.F.esq.4 Raymond bdgs.Gray's i
Chubb Jas. esq. 40 London st. Fitzroy sq
Chubb Jn. esq. 8 Stoke Newington green
ChubbMorley,esq.2 Judd pl.east,New rd
Chubb Thos. esq. 9 Stoke Newington gn
Chumbley J. esq. 4 Park pl. ter. Padgtn
ChumleyThos.esq.2 Glo'ster pl.Regt's pk
Church Edmd. B. esq. 33 Essex st Strand & 39 Long lane, Bermondsey
Church John, esq. 67 Great Portland st
Church JohnThos. esq. 9 Bedford row
Churchill Lord, 2 Upper Wimpole st, & Cornbury park, Whitney, Oxen
Churchill Lady H. S. 5 Gt. George st
Churchill C.esq.12 Sussex pl Regent's pk
Churchill Henry, esq. 2 Harcourt bldgs
Churchill H. B. esq. 2 Raymond bldgs
Churchill John, esq. 1 Petersburgh pl
Churchill Joseph, esq. 9 Bunhill row
Churchill Miss, 6 Manor pl. sth. Chelsea
Churchill Mrs. 36 Argyle square
Churchill Mrs. 12 Sussex pl. Regent's pk
Churchill Mrs. 11 Trinity row Islington
Churchill Sam. esq. 38 Castle st. Holbn
Churchward J. esq.13Gloster tr. O.Brmp
Chute Wm. L. W. esq. M.P. 65 Portland place, & Pickenham hall, near Swaffham, & the Vine house, Basingstoke
Chuter Robt. esq. 16 Beaufoy terrace
City Club House (John ThomasKemble, secretary), 19 Old Broad st. City
Clack Hen. T. Union bank, 14 Argyll pl
Claer Thos. esq. 17 Dalby terr. City rd
Clagett Horatio, esq. 1 Abbey road
Clakson John, esq. 11 Camden rd. villas
Clancarty, Earl of, Garbally park, Loughrea, Ireland
Clanricarde, Marquis of, K.P., P.C. 2 Carlton ho. ter., & Portumna castl. Galway
Clanwilliam, Earl of, 32 Belgrave square & Gill hall, Dromore, Downshire
Clapham Benj. esq. 2 Terrace, O.Knt. rd
Clapham H.C.esq. 29 Francis st. Bdfd.sq
Clapham Wm. Henry, esq. 29 Great Portland st, & Watford, Herts
Clapp Chas.esq.40 Windmill st.Tot.ct.rd
Clapp Robert, esq. 6 Lloyd square
Clapp William, esq. 62 Welbeck st.
Clare, Earl of, P.C. MountShannon, Limerc
Clare, Countess of, Mivart's hotel
Clare H. esq. 8 Up.Chadwell st.Pentnvl
Clare Hen. F. esq. 1 Ladbroke terrace
Clare Miss, 19 St. John's wood road
Clare Mrs. 11 North bank, Regent's pk
Clarence S. esq. 6 Porteus rd.Harrow rd
Clare Samuel, esq. 26 Rodney st
Clarendon, Earl of, G.C.B., P.C. 1 Grovnor. crescent, Belgrave sq. & Grove park, Watford
Clare Thos. esq. 6 Mabledon place
Claridge Chas.esq. Albion rd. Liverpoolrd
Clarke SirJames, bart. M.D. 22B, Brook st
ClarkCapt. R.N. 7Cuninghm.pl.St.Jn's.w
Clark Andrew, esq. 57 Brook street
Clark Chas.esq. 6 Manchester st.Man.sq
Clark Bracy, esq.7 Taunton pl. Rgt.'s pk
Clark Chas. esq. 2 Middle Temple lane
Clark Edwd. esq. 10 Norfolk crescent
Clark Edward, esq. 13 Wigmore st
Clark Frederic, esq.3 Churchyd.ct.Tmpl
Clark Fred. le Gros, esq. 30 Finsbury sq
ClarkGeo.esq.14Hunter st.Brunswick sq
Clark Geo. esq. 5 Seymour pl. Euston sq
Clark Henry, esq. 7 Notting hill sq
Clark Hen. Bingley, esq. 160 Oxford st
Clark Henry M. esq. 27 Great George st
Clark Jas. esq. 11 Dorset ter. Clapm. rd
Clark Jas. esq.34 Lower Belgrave place
Clark Jas. esq. 9 Portland ter. Rgt's pk
Clark James Richd.esq.31 Claremont sq
ClarkJohn, esq.4 Acton pl.Camden nw.tn
Clark John, esq. 44 Alpha road
Clark John, M.D. 12 Beaumont st
Clark John, esq. Denmrk.hill, Cambrwl
Clark John, esq. 25 Hornton st. Knsgtn
Clark John Horn, esq. 23 Paddington gr
Clark John Nassau, esq.26 Tavistock sq
Clark John Patterson, esq.5 Sackville st
Clark Jsph. esq.19 Liverpool st. Kg.'s cr
Clark Jsph.H.esq. 11 Lodge rd. Rgt's pk
ClarkM.esq.15 Manchester ter.Lvrpl.rd
Clark Matthew, esq.6Sussexpl.Rgt.'s pk
Clark Mrs.1 Brecknock cres.Camden tn
Clark Mrs. 35 Brompton square
Clark Mrs. 18 Claremont pl. New road
Clark Mrs.18 Compton st.Brunswick sq
Clark Mrs. 4 Grove ter. St. John's wood
Clark Richd. esq. Cloisters, Westminstr
Clark Richd. F. esq. 20 Cloudesley ter
Clark Robert, esq. 27 Finchley New rd
Clark Robert, esq. 7 Finsbury square
Clark Robert, esq. 57 Up Marylebone st
Clark Sam. esq. 38 Craven st. Strand
Clark Thos. esq. 36 Burton st. Burtn.cres
Clark Thos. esq. 23 Park village east
Clark Wm. esq. 12 Green's row, Chelsea
Clark Wm. esq. 25 Stamford st. Blackfrs
Clark Wm. Cosmo, esq. 4 Brompton pl
Clark Wm.H. esq. 11 Leonard pl.Knsgtn
Clarke Sir Simon H. bart. 144 Oxford st.; & Oak hill, East Barnet
Clarke Gen. 48 Charlotte st. Fitzroy sq
Clarke Capt. Stanley, 5 Suffolk st. Pall mall east
Clarke Mr. Serj. 53 Up. Bedford pl. & 5 Brick ct. & Handsworth, Staffordshire
Clarke Rev. O. 2 Vernon sq.Bagng.wl.rd
Clarke Abraham, esq. 20 Spencer st
Clarke Chas. esq. 14 Cloudesley terrace
Clarke Chas.esq.11 Grove road, St.John's wood; & 20 Lincoln's inn fields
Clarke C. E. esq. 10 Lower Grosvenor pl
Clarke Edwd. esq. 5 Featherstone bldgs
Clarke Edwd. esq. 9 Chapel st. Bedford row & Waltham cross, Herts
Clarke Edward, esq. 2 Pump ct. Temple
Clarke Fran. esq. 9 Mrylebone la. Oxf. st
Clarke Fredk. esq. 61Grosvenor st
Clarke Fred. C.esq.9Chapel st. Bedfd.rw
Clarke Geo. esq. 2 Campdn. ter. Kensing
Clarke Georg Rochfort, esq. 2 Spring garden ter.; 1Mitre ct. bldgs. Temple; & Chesterton lodge, near Bicester
Clarke H.esq.13Springfld.pl.Wndswh.rd
Clarke Henry, esq. 21 Portman square
Clarke Hy. Booth, esq. 22 Chancery la
Clarke Hyde, esq. 10 Great Ormond st. & 9 St. Michael alley
ClarkeJacobA.esq.11Warwick st.Blgve.r
Clarke James, esq. 26 Carlton villas
Clarke James F. esq. 23 Gerrard st
Clarke JamesLangton, esq.35Southampton buildings
Clarke John, esq. Bayham st.Pancras rd
Clarke John, esq.7 Beaufoy ter. Edgw.rd
Clarke John, esq. 4 Heathcote st
Clarke John, esq. 7 Leonard pl.Kensngtn
Clarke John, esq. 12 Lloyd st. Lloyd sq
Clarke John J. esq. 2 Harleyford place
Clarke Jsph.esq.2 Porchester ter. Byswr
Clarke Joseph Saml. esq. 50 Sloane st
Clarke Miss, 5 Cambridge ter. Edgw. rd
Clarke Mrs. Col. 26 Porchester terrace
Clarke Mrs. 22 Albion ter. Wndswth. rd
Clarke Mrs. 3 Canonbury park
Clarke Mrs. 18 Earls ter. Kensington
Clarke Mrs. 4 Lisson grove south
Clarke Mrs. 21 Portman st. Portman sq
Clarke Mrs. 76 Warren st
Clarke Mrs. C. 40 Upper Harley st
Clarke Mrs. Sarah, 8 Serle st. Linc. inn
Clarke N. esq. Amyott ho. Lit. Chelsea
Clarke Richard, esq. 94 Jermyn st
Clarke Richard, esq. 17 Kensington sq
Clarke Rd. esq. 25 George st. Hanovr.sq
Clarke Robt.esq. 7 Jermyn st.St.James's
Clarke Robert George, 43 Craven st
Clarke Seymour, esq. 2 Eastbourne ter
Clarke Seymour, esq. 23 Blomfield rd
Clarke T.esq.16 Charles st.Westbrne. ter
Clarke Thos. esq. Ordnance Office, Pall mall, & Highgate hill
Clarke Thos. Rt. esq. 76 Hamilton terr
Clarke Thos. Sydenham, esq. 36 Glo'ster pl. Portman sq. & 6 New sq. Linc. inn
Clarke Thos. T. esq. 34 Upper Brook st. & Bury st. Rieslip, near Uxbridge
Clarke Wm. esq. 33 Bloomsbury square
Clarke Wm. esq. 9 Milner sq. Islington
Clarke Wm. esq. 54 Chancery lane
Clarke Wm.B.esq.9 Chapel st. Bedfd.rw
Clarke Wm. Hislop, esq.4 New sq. Lin.in
Clarke Wm. Tredway, esq.30 Gt.James st
Clarkson Henry, esq. 2 Brecknock cres
Clarkson Thomas, esq. 55 Euston square
Clarkson Wm. esq. 53 Euston sq.; A1, Endsleigh st. & 1 Paper bdgs. Temple
Clarkson Wm. Geering, esq. 13 Leonard pl. Kensington, & Doctors' commons
Classon Geo. esq. 23 Winchtr.rw.New rd
Clater Thomas, esq.11 Whitehead's grove, Sloane st
Clavering Col. Henry, 64 Sloane st
Clavey Wm. R. esq. 12 Little Queen st
Claxson Mrs. 57 St. John st. road
Claxton Marshall, esq. 6 Up. Sthmptn. st
Clay SirWm. bt. M.P. 17 Hertford st. Mayfair, & Fulwell lodge, nr. Twickenham
Clay Richd. esq. 20 Park ter. Highbury
Clay Robt. esq. 12 Kent ter. Regent's pk
Claydon Chas. Broadbelt, esq. 20 Glo'ster cresc. Regt's. pk. & 2 Hare ct. Temple
Claypon Joseph, esq. 9 Westbourne st
Clayton Col. Sir Wm. Robt. bart. 79Gloucester pl. Portman sq.; & Marden park, Godstone; & Whitehall, Watton; & the Cottage, Harleyford, near Marlow
Clayton James, esq. 3 Percy st. Bedfd.sq

Clayton James Henry, esq. 17 Gt. James st. Bedford row, & 3 Hare ct. Temple
Clayton John, esq. 72 Hamilton terrace, & 10 Lancaster place, Strand
Clayton J. jun. esq. 38 Elizbth.st. Eatn.sq
Clayton John Lloyd, esq. 11 Portman sq
Clayton Michael, esq. 17 Up. Wimpole st.; & 6 New sq. Lincoln's inn; & Charlwood park, Crawley
Clayton the Misses, 4 Gloucester terrace
Clayton Mrs. 6 Hyde park st
Clayton Mrs. 9 New Ormond st. Queen sq
Clayton Nath. esq. 7 Suffolk st. Pall mall ea. & Chesters, Wexham, Northumbld
Clayton Oscar, esq. 3 Percy st
Clayton Rice Richard, M.P. 11 Portman sq. & Hedgerley park, Beaconsfield
Clayton Wm. esq. 22 Spencer ter. Islngt
Cleary Thos. esq. 12 Alfred pl. Bedford sq
Cleasby Anthony, esq. 3 King's bnch. wk
Cleasby A. esq. 1 Spring garden terrace
Cleasby Richard, esq. 5 Harley pl. Nw. rd
Cleave H. esq. 11 Porteus ter. Harrow rd
Cleere Hen. Wm. esq. 3 Retreat. So. Lmbth
Cleeve Geo. esq. Dunsany pl. Wandsw. rd
Clegg Edm. esq. 3 Devonshire ter. Marylb
Clegg Jas. esq. 3 Devonshire ter. Marylb
Clegg S. esq. 16 Sidmouth st. Gray's inn rd
Cleghorn T. K. esq. 20 Paradise tr. Livpl. rd
Cleland Miss, 10 Church row, Islington
Clement John T. esq. 444 Strand
Clements Viscount, M.P. 19A, Davies st. & Lough Rhynn, Mohill, Ireland
Clements Lady Elizabeth, 2 Grosvnr. sq. & Long Ditton, nr. Kingston, Surrey
Clements Rd. esq. 2 Up. Baker st. Lloyd sq
Clementson F. esq. 6 Warwick vil. Harrw. rd
Clementson John, esq. 23 Abingdon st
Clendinning John, M.D. 16 Wimpole st
Clendon Chitty, esq. 15 Conduit st
Clentworth Viscountess, 10 Cambridge sq
Cleoburey T. M. esq. 30 Sackville st
Clephan J. esq. 18 Warwick st. Charing cr
Clerc Peter Bernard, esq. 20 Granville sq
Clerical Club (Richard Hayes, secretary), 13 Henrietta st. Covent Garden
Clerk Rt. Hon. Sir Geo. bart. M.P. 8 Park st. Westmr. & Penicuick ho. Edinburgh
Clerk John, esq. 9 King's Bench w. Tmple
Clerk Misses, 6 Upper Montagu st
Clerke Sir Wm. Hy. 73 Baker st. Portn. sq
Clerke Major Shadwell, 4 Brmptn. grove
Clerke Miss, 1 Myddelton square
Cleveland Duke of, K.G. 17 St. James's sq. & Raby castle, Darlington, Durham
Cleveland Dow. Duchess, 2 Seamore pl
Cleveland Mrs. 4 Taunton pl. Park rd
Clewer Miss, 22 Bentinck st
Clews John, esq. 9 Craig's ct. Charing crs
Clifford Lord, Ugbrook park, Chudleigh
Clifford Sir Augustus, 74 Eaton sq. & Westfield house, Ryde, Isle of Wight
Clifford John, esq. 35 Osnaburgh st
Clifford Mrs. 17 Elizabeth st. Eaton sq
Clifford Wm. esq. 36 Lincoln's inn fields
Clift Wm. esq. F.R.S. 40 Lincoln's inn fields, & Stanhope cottages, Morngtn. rd
Clift James, esq. 30 Bloomsbury sq
Clift Wm. esq. Thames parade, Thames bk
Clifton Maj. Gen. Sir Arthur, 15 Old Bond st. & Barton lodge, Nottingham
Clifton Sir Juckes, bart, 144 Oxford st. & Clifton hall, Nottingham
Clifton Abel, esq. 1 Brompton grove
Clifton Chas. esq. 32 York st. Portmn. sq
Clifton Edward, esq. 37 Dorset square
Clifton Eugene, esq. 37 Canonbury sq
Clifton Hen. C. esq. Finchley new road
Clifton John T. M.P. 5 Wilton crescent
Clifton Joseph, esq. 2 Addison rd. south
Clifton Mrs. 14 Leicester place
Clifton Thos. esq. 16 Hyde park gardns. & Lytham hall, Lancashire
Clifton Waller, esq. 6 Thurloe place
Clinch John, esq. 19 Loraine pl. Hollowy
Clint Alfd. esq. 42 Robert st. Hmpstd. rd
Clint George, esq. 4 Keppel st
Clint Mrs. 12 Calthorpe st. Gray's inn rd
Clintock Wm. esq. 5 Brick court, Temple
Clinton Lord, 18 Upper Grosvenor st. & Hinton, Devonshire
Clinton Lord Thos. C. 16 Carlton villas
Clinton Dow. Lady, 28 St. James's pl
Clinton Gen. Sir W. H. G.C.B. & La. Louisa, 6 Audley sq. & Cockennach, Royston
Clinton Lieut. Col. 66 Eaton place
Clinton John, esq. 14 Greek st. Soho
Clipperton John, esq. 17 Bedford row
Clissold E.A. esq. 5 Manchestr. st. Gray's inn road
Clissole H. esq. Montpelier, Sth. Lmbth
Clitherow Lieut. Gen. 18 Up. Harley st
Clitherow the Misses, 31 Wimpole st
Clitherow Robert, esq. 31 Wimpole st
Clive Viscount, M.P. 45 Berkeley sq
Clive Hon. R. H. M.P. & Lady Harriet, 53 Grosvenor st.; & Oakley park, near Ludlow; & Hewell Grange, Broomsgr
Clive Geo. esq. 18 Grafton st. Bond st
Clive Jsph. esq. 28 Chester st. Grvnr. pl
Clively Chas. esq. 11 Compton st. east
Clode Chas. Mathew, esq. 7 Staple inn
Clogher, Bishop of, the Palace, Clogher
Clonbrock Lord, 23 Dover st. & Clonbrock, Galway
Cloncurry Lord, Brookes' club, 60 St. James's st.; & Lyons castle, Kildare; & Rathcoole, Dublin
Clonmel Dow. Countess of, 18 Eaton sq
Close Major, 10 Montagu square
Close D. esq. 1 Bedford pl. Kensington
Close John, esq. Clapham rise
Close Mrs. 1 Bedford pl. Kensington
Clossman F. F. esq. 16A, Park lane
Clothier Rt. esq. 13 Gt. James st. Bedfrd. rw
Clough Mrs. 8 Crescent pl. Burton cres
Clover Joseph, esq. 85 Newman st
Clow Leonard, esq. 25 Cloudesley st
Clowes Ellis, esq. 10 King's Bench walk
Clowes John Ellis, esq. 7 Brunswick sq. & 10 King's Bench walk
Clowes Wm. esq. 32 Bedford pl. Russell sq
Clowes William, esq. 24 Parliament st
Cluer John, esq. 57 Spencer st
Cluff Jas. esq. 24 Steward st. Spitalfields
Cluney Alex. esq. Larkhall rise, Clapham
Clutterbuck Hy. M.D. 1 Crescent, Blkfrs
Clutton Henry, esq. 8 Whitehall place
Clutton John, esq. 48 Borough High st
Clutton Miss, 20 Queen st. Mayfair
Clutton O. esq. 46 Newington pl. Kngtn. rd
Clutton Robert, esq. 8 Whitehall place
Clyatt C. J. esq. 2 Park pl. Kengtn. cros
Coad Hugh C. esq. 13 Grafton st. Fitzroy sq
Coates Chas. esq. Queen's rd. St. John's wd
Coates D. esq. 1 Ladbroke vils. Nottng. hill
Coates Ed. esq. 17 Park pl. vils. Padngtn
Coates E. J. esq. 11 Devonshire st
Coates Geo. esq. 43 Hart st. Bloomsbury
Coates John M. esq. 8 Woodlnd. pl. St. Jn. w
Coates Mrs. 42 Regent square
Coates Mrs. 32 Michael's pl. Brompton
Coates Thomas, esq. 42 Bedford square
Coats Edward, esq. 35 Bernard st
Coats Jno. esq. 24 Alfred pl. Bedford sq
Coatswith T. W. esq. 9 Connaught pl. west
Cobb Hen. esq. 18 Lincoln's inn fields
Cobb John, esq. 10 Northmblnd. st. Strd
Cobb Mrs. 45 George st. Euston sq
Cobb Mrs. 8 Fitzroy st. Fitzroy sq
Cobb Mrs. 75½ Manchester st. Gray's inn rd
Cobb Rt. esq. 10 Frederick's pl. Hmpstd. rd
Cobb Richd. esq. 6 Upper Woburn place
Cobbe Chas. esq. 45 Bedford pl. Kensngtn
Cobbe Thomas, esq. 12 Queen Anne st. & 22 Portugal st. Lincoln's inn fields
Cobbett Jas. Paul, esq. 17 Chancery la
Cobbett J. M. esq. 4 Figtree ct. Temple
Cobbett Wm. esq. 20 Bruton st. Bond st. & Sunbury, Middlesex
Cobbold Alfred, esq. 7 Lincoln's inn flds. & at Ipswich
Cobden Richd. M.P., 20 New st. Spring gardens, & 32 Norfolk st. Strand, & Kay st. Manchester
Cobley Thomas, esq. 6 Gt. Prescot st
Cochran Mrs. 7 St. Ann's vils. Acacia rd
Cochran Thomas, esq. 56 Glo'ster pl
Cochrane Hon. Mrs. 30 Sussex sq. Hyde pk. & Largo, Fifeshire, N.B.
Cochrane Col. Adjutant Genl.'s office
Cochrane Col. Wm. 9 Pall mall
Cochrane Alex. Dndas. Ross W. B. esq. M.P
Cochrane C. esq. 26 Devonshire pl. Portland pl. & Firtrees farm, Southampton
Cochrane George, esq. 77 Chancery lane
Cochrane John Geo. esq. 49 Pall mall
Cochrane Mrs. 20 Wilton st
Cochrane Robert, esq. 24 Clarges st
Cock Rev. T. A. 19 Chapel st. Pentnvl
Cock Edwd. J. esq. 19 Chapel st. Pntnvl
Cock Mrs. 4 Norland pl. Notting hill
Cock Rd. S. esq. 62 Lincoln's inn fields
Cockburn Rt. Hon. Sir Geo. G.C.B., M.P. Admiralty, & High Beech, Essex
Cockburn Sir James, knt. 45 Harley st
Cockburn & Co. 4 Whitehall
Cockburn Alexander Jas. Edmund, esq. Q.C. 3 Harcourt buildings, Temple
Cockburn Danl. esq. 22 South bk. Rgt.'s pk
Cockburn Patrick H. esq. 9A, Circus rd
Cocke Archibald, esq. 7 Ulster pl. Rgt.'s pk
Cocke Arthur, esq. 32 Howland st
Cocke C.A. esq. 10 Queen's bldgs. Bmptn
Cockell James, esq. 36 Bernard st
Cocker Alf. R. esq. 11 Nassau st. Soho
Cocker Miss, 46 Charlotte st. Portld. pl
Cockerell Hon. Lady, 147 Piccadilly
Cockerell Sir Chas. brt. 60 Grosvnr. st
Cockerell Geo. W. esq. St. John's lodge, Wandsworth road
Cockerell Jas. Chas. esq. Lavender hill
Cockerell Jno. esq. 12 Hyde pk. gdns
Cockerell the Misses, 45 Hertford st
Cockerell Saml. Pepys, esq. 45 Hertford st. Mayfair, & 7 Old sq. Lincoln's inn
Cockin Jno. esq. 1 Fredk. pl. Up. Kngtn. la
Cockings Miss, 18 Soley terrace
Cockle Jas. esq. 19 Devereux ct. Strand
Cockle Jas. esq. 18 New Ormond st
Cockle John, M.D. 107 Guilford st
Cocks Hon. Col. 57 Beaumont st. Marylbn
Cocks & Biddulph, 43 Charing cross
Cocks Jas. esq. 7 Chesterfield st. Mayfair
Cocks Mrs. Thomas S. 15 Hereford st
Cocks Robt. esq. 3 Ladbroke terrace
Cocks Thos. Somers, esq. 47 Harley st
Cocks Thos. Somers, esq. 15 Hereford st
Cocks Thos. S. jun. esq. 15 Hereford st
Codd Capt. J. E. 1 Up. Bdfrd. pl. Knsgtn
Codd Edw. Septimus, esq. 15 Fludyer st
Codd Wm. esq. 42 Allsop ter. New road
Codrington Sir Christopher Wm. bart. M.P. & Lady Georgiana, 3 Park pl. St. Jas. & Doddington pk. nr. Chippenham
Codd Mrs. Harrison, 10 Campden hill villas, Kensington
Codrington Admiral Sir Edward, G.C.B. 92 Eaton square
Codrington Sir W. R. bart. 5 Christopher st. Finsbury, & Manor of La Boullaye, near Mortford, Brittany
Codrington Miss, 17 Wilton st. Grosv. pl
Coe Matt. Wm. esq. Cmdn. hill, Kensgtn
Coe Richard B. esq. 9 Adam st. Adelphi
Coe Wm. esq. 42 Alpha rd. Regent's pk
Coeharn Thomas, esq. 56 Glo'ster place
Cogdon Saml. esq. 23 Up. Gloucester pl
Cogger John, esq. 9 Wharton st. Lloyd sq
Coghlan Capt. R.N. 7 Albert terrace, St. John's wood
Coglan Hen. Thos. esq. 14 Hyde pk. grdns
Coham J.J. esq. 27 Dorset st. Portman sq
Cohen Albert, esq. 34 Nottingham pl
Cohen Alexander, 54 Guilford st
Cohen Daniel W. M.D. 5 Highbury pl
Cohen Henry, esq. 5 Southwick cres
Cohen Henry H. esq. 21 Westbourne terr

Cohen Isaac, esq. 32 Norfolk st. Park la
Cohen Isaac, esq. 23A, Park lane
Cohen John, esq. 26 Soho square
Cohen Louis, esq. 5 South st. Finsbury
Cohen Mrs. J. 34 Nottingham place
Cohen Soln. esq. 12 Canonbury pl. Islng
Coilett T. A. esq. 18 Hemus ter. Kngs.rd
CokeleyThos.J.esq.1Thurloe pl.O.Bmptn
Colborne Lord, 19 Hill st. & West Harling, Norfolk
Colborne hon.Wm.Nicholas Ridley, M.P. 19 Hill st. & West Harling, Norfolk
Colborn Wm.esq.7Granbyst.Hampstd.rd
Colburn Joshua, esq. 75 Ebury st
Colchester Lord Capt. R.N. 7 Charles st. Berkly. sq. & Kidbrooke, E. Grinstead
Colchester Dow. Lady, 64 Up. Berkly.st
ColchesterChs.esq.3 Milton pl.Wands.rd
Colchester C.jun.esq.2Miltonpl.Wnds.rd
Colclough Mrs. 53 Westbourne terrace
Coldrey Thos.esq. 5 Stoke Newingtn.grn
Coldwell T. esq. 10 Queen's pl. Kenn. rd
Cole Lady Elizabeth, 13 Chester st
Cole Lady Frances, 65 Lowndes sq
Cole Capt. H. 23 Chester pl. Kenngtn.cr
Cole Rev. Henry, 39 Highbury place
Cole Chas. esq. 58 Stanhope st. Hpst. rd
Cole Charles, esq. 34 Sussex gardens
Cole Chas. Nicholas, esq. 13 Doughty st
Cole Cole John, esq. 43 Up. Bedford pl
Cole George, esq. 73 Edgware road
Cole Geo. B. esq. 13 Chester st.Grosvr.pl
Cole Hen.esq.24 Petersbrgh. pl.Bayswtr
Cole Henry Thos. esq. 2 Elm ct. Temple
Cole H.W.esq.5Chester sq.&40Chncry.la
Cole James, esq. 25 Harley st
Cole James H. esq. 65 Lowndes square
Cole John, esq. 4 Adelphi terrace
Cole J. G. esq. 8 Charles st. Berkeley sq
Cole Miss, 60 Margaret st. Cavendish sq
Cole Mrs. 20 Gower place, Euston square
Cole Mrs. 17 Park sq. east, Regent's pk
Cole Mrs. 3A, Pelham road, Brompton
Cole Rd. Wm. esq. 39 St. John st. road
Cole Robt. esq. 57 Norton st. Fitzroy sq
Cole Robert, esq. 12 Old Quebec st
Cole Thos. esq. 73 Manchester st. Gr.i.rd
Cole William, esq. 31 Lit. Russell st
Cole Wm. Robt. esq. 1 Elm ct. Temple
Colebrooke SirThos.Edw.bt.M.P.18Park lane, & Abington, Lanarkshire, N.B
ColegraveWm.esq.5 Warwick sq.Knsgtn
Coleman C.R.esq. Riches villa, Finchley
Coleman Geo. esq. 11 Guilford st.Rus.sq
Coleman Jas. esq. 47 St. John st. road
Coleman Mrs. 72 Baker st. Portman sq
Coleman Mrs. 31 Upper Phillimore pl
Coleman Jsph. esq. 3 Sidmouth st
Coleman Josh. F. esq. 27 Wharton st
Coleman Joshua, esq. 10 Howland st
Coleraine Lady, Ridgmount pl. Hpstd.rd
Coleridge hon. Sir J. T. knt. 4 Montague place, & Heath's court, near Honiton
Coleridge Mrs.10 Chester pl.Regent's pk
Coles Rev. George, 25 Wellington ter
Coles C. B. esq. 4 Alpha pl. Regent's pk
Coles H. B. esq. 25 Portman sq.; & Middleton ho. Whitchch.; & Rickmanswth
Coles James, esq. 14 Buckingham st.Str
Coles Wm. esq.7 Elm. tree rd.St.Jn's.wd
Coles Wm. esq. 1 Manor ter. Chelsea
Collard Chas. esq. 30 Carlton villas
Collard Fredk.Wm.esq. 14 Carlton villas
Collard W. esq. 32 Gt. Castle st.Regt.st
Collen Geo. Wm. esq. Heralds' college
Collen H.esq.29 Somerset st.Portman sq
Collett Charles M. esq. 62 Chancery la
Collett John, esq. M.P. 7Up. Belgrave st
Collett John, esq. 15 Up. Charlton st
CollettWm.R.esq. M.P.2A, St. James's sq
Collette Chas. Hastings,esq. 3 Porchester pl. Edgw. rd. & 57 Lincoln's inn fields
ColleyRd.B.esq.8Bentinck ter.Regt.'spk
Collick Chas. esq. 7 North ter. Alex. sq
Collier Charles, M.D. 20 Fitzroy sq
Collier J. P. esq. 1 Madeley vil. Knsgtn

Collier George Fredk. M.D. 32 Spring gardens, & Bohemia house, Chiswick
Collier Miss, 1 Hornsey row, Islington
Collier Thomas, esq. 21 Gloucester place, Portman sq. & 3 Brick ct. Temple
Collin Miss, 29 Maddox st. Regent st
Collindon Thomas, esq. 5 Kensington sq
Collingridge Mrs. 55 Thurloe sq
Collingwood Hon. Mrs. N. 30 York pl
Collingwood Edmund, esq. 11 Harper st
Collingwood John W. esq. 51 King sq
Collingwood Mrs. 37 Welbeck st
Collins C. G.esq. 53 Thurloe sq.O.Brmtn
Collins Geo.Wm.esq. 1 New sq. Linc.inn
Collins G. W. esq. 16 King st. Prtm sq
Collins J. esq. 23 Annett's cres. Islington
Collins Jas.esq. 5 Rufford's rw. Islington
Collins John, esq. 60 Cambridge st
Collins John, esq. 5 Crescent pl. Blkfrs
Collins John, esq. 32 Nelson sq
Collins Julius, esq. 89Mary st.Regt.'s pk
Collins Miss, 9 Burton crescent
ollins Miss, 8 Cambridge st. Edgw. rd
Collins Mrs. 1 Alfred pl. Alex. sq
Collins Mrs. 26 Manchester sq
Collins Robert, esq. 3 Barton st.Westmr
Collins Stephen, esq. 57 Coleshill st
Collins T. esq. 13 Cobourg pl. Kenngtn
Collins Whitfield, esq. 39 Elizabeth st
Collins Wm.esq.59 Cambridge ter. Hy.pk
Collins Wm.esq.Cambridge vil. Finchley
Collins Wm.esq.1 Devonport st. Hyde pk
CollinsWm.esq.Lavndr.hl.Wandswth. rd
Collins Wm.esq.23Pembroke sq.Knsgtn
Collins Wm. esq. M.P. 18 Pall mall, & Warwick
Collins Wm.A.esq.23Abbeypl. St.Jns.wd
Collins Wm. A. esq. 3 Old sq. Linc. inn
Collinson George, esq. 4 Ladbroke ter.
Collinson H. esq. Hall stair. In. Temple
Collis Edwd. esq. 6 New Ormond st
Collis Jas. esq. 10 Berkeleyst.Clerkenwl
Collis Jas. esq. 2 Shaftesbury cres. Pimlico, & Frederick pl. Blackheath
Collis Joseph, esq. 59 Russell sq
Collison Brown, esq. 47 Guilford st
Collisson Wm. esq. 83 Camden rd. villas and 28 Gt. James st. Bedford row
Collmann LeonardW.esq.24Halfmoon st
Colls Mrs. 27 Avenue rd. Regent's park
Colls Rd. esq. 18 Charles st. St. James's
Collyer Geo. esq. 50 Little Britain
Collyer Geo. S. esq. 9 Park pl. St. James
Collyer John, esq. 8 Alfred place, Bedford square & 10 Serle st
Collyer Mrs. 4 Queen sq. Bloomsbury
Collyer Saml. esq. 42 Southampton bdgs
Colman Geo. Aug. esq. 2 New inn, Strand
ColmanWm.Gooding,esq.2 New in.Strnd
Colombine David E.esq.7 Thistle gr.Lit. Chelsea, & 8 Carlton chmbs. Regent st
Colquhoun Gideon, esq. Walmer lodge, Avenue road, Regent's park
Colquhoun James, LL.D., K.S.M., consul general for Saxony, & diplomatic agent & consul general for Hanseatic republics of Lubeck, Bremen & Hamburg, 12 St. James's place; Penshurst, Tonbridge, Kent; & consulate office, 76 Cornhill
Colquhoun John C. M.P. 8 Chesham st.& Putney heath, & Killermount, Dumbartonshire
Colquhoun Mrs. 4 Hornsey row, Islntn
Colquhoun Mrs. 48 Vincent square
Colquhoun Patrick, LL.D. 12St.James' pl
Colquhoun Wm. H. esq. 144 Oxford st. & Elston lodge, Bedford
Colson Jesson, esq. 26Store st. Bedford sq
Coltman Sir Thos. knt. 8 Hyde prk. gdns
Colvile Andrew, esq. 32 Curzon st. Mayfair, & Craigflour, Dunfermline
Colvile Charles Robert, M.P. 10 St. James's place, and Duffield hall, Derby
ColvileJ. W. esq.32Curzon st. & 9 New sq
Colvill Mrs. 33 York bldgs. New road

Colville Lord, 29 Portland place
ColvilleWm.esq. 3North bank,Regt.'s pk
Colvin Alex. esq. 6Clarendon pl.Hyde pk
Colvin Alex. John, esq. 64 Glo'ster pl
Colvin Jas. esq. 55 Manchester st. & the Grove, Woodbridge, Suffolk
Colvin John R. esq. 41 Sussex gardens
Combe Boyce, esq. Clerkenwell police court, & Acton
Combe Boyce, esq. 32 Gower st
Combe BoyceHarvey,esq.11 NewBond st
Combe Hen. esq.2 Caroline st.Bedford sq
Combe John, esq. 4 South row, St. Pancras, & 9 Staple inn, Holborn
Combermere Viscount, G.C.B., G.C.H., P.C., 48 Belgrave sq. & Combermere abbey, Namptwich
Comerford Chas. esq. 21 Oxford square, Hyde park, and 72 Old Broad st
Comerford J.esq.7St. Andrew's pl.Rgt.pk
Comfort Jas. esq. 4 Milner st. Islington
Comfort J. esq. 5 Straham ter. Livrpl. rd
Comfort Wm. esq.25 Loraine pl.Hollowy
Commercial Bank of London, 6 Henrietta st. Covent garden
Commerell John William, esq. 5 Lower Berkeley st. & Stroud park, Horsham
Compton Earl, 145 Piccadilly & Castle Ashby, near Northampton
Compton Lord William, 145 Piccadilly, & Castle Ashby, Northamptonshire
Compton Sir H. knt. 26 Hyde pk. grdns
ComptonGeo.Wm.esq.5Southmptn.bldgs
Compton Henry Combe, esq. M.P, 34 Up. Eaton st. & Manor house, Lyndhurst
Compton Mrs. 15 Millman st. Bedfd. rw
Compton Mrs. 4 Whitehead's grove
Comrie Alex. esq. 2 Bridge st. Westmins
Comte Geo. esq. 4 Down st. Piccadilly
Comyn Sir Robt. B. 9New st.Spring gdns
Comyn Fitzwilliam, esq. 6 Caroline place, Mecklenburgh sq. & Bush lane
Comyn Mrs. 10 Mecklenburgh square
Comyn Mrs. 14 Norfolk st. Strand
Conant John Edw. esq.19 Up. Wimpole st
Concanen Geo. esq. 5 Lincoln's inn fields
Condell Mrs. 57 Sloane st
Conduitt E. F. esq. 3 Up. Bedford place
Condy Mrs. 135 Sloane st
Congleton Lord, 24 Coles terrace, Barnsbury road
Coningham Mrs. 8 Up. Gower st
Coningham Wm. esq. 42 Porchester ter
Connell Hen. esq.4 South bank,Rgt.'s pk
Connell John, esq. 36 St. James's place, & 21 Fludyer st. Westminster
Connell Miss, 3 York gate, Regent's pk
Conner Daniel, esq. 9 Orme sq. Bayswtr
Connop Rev. John, 7 Whitehall, & Bradfield hall, Reading, Berks
Connop Henry, esq. 32 Porchester ter
Connop Newell, esq. 7 Whitehall
Connor Geo. esq.4 Henriettast.Covt.gdn
Conolly Colonel Edward Michael, M.P. Payne's hotel, Jermyn st.; Castletown, Celbridge; & Cliff, Donegal
Conolly C. J. T. esq. & Mrs. Cavendish hotel, 81 Jermyn st. & Hartham park, Wilts
Connor Mrs. 6 Chandos st. Cavendish sq
Connor Mrs. 20 Hornton st. Kensington
Conquest John, esq. 38 Woburn square
Conquest John T. M.D. 13B, Finsbury sq
Conroy Sir John, bart. K.C.H. Vicarage pl. Knsngtn. & Arborfield hall, Berks
Conroy Miss, 19 York st. Portman sq
Consett Mrs. 2 Hans pl. Sloane st
Conservative Club House (E.C.Hampton, sec.), 47 St. James's st
Constable Jn. esq. 14A, Wellington road
Constable Jn. esq. 17 Westbourne ter
Constable John C. esq. 31 Hyde park sq
Constable Miss, 16 Cunningham place
Constable T. esq. 7 Colebrooke row
ConstantineThos.Wm.esq.8N.Ormond st
Constantine Wm. esq. 7 Stafford st. Plco

Conway Col. 18 North bank, Regent's pk
Conway Wm. Shipley, esq. 104 Piccadilly, & Bodryddan, St. Asaph, Flintsh
Conyers Thos. G. esq. 33 New Bridge st
Conyngham, Marquis of, K.P., G.C.H., P.C.. 5 Hamilton pl. Piccadilly; & Slane castle, Meath; & Mountcharles, Donegal
Conyngham, Marchioness of, Mivart's hotel, 41 Brook st
Conyngham, Dowager Marchioness of, 5 Hamilton pl. & Bifrons, Canterbury
Conyngham Lord Albert Denison, 5 Hamilton pl. & Mickleham hall, Drking
Coode Mrs. 23 Gt. Smith st. Westminstr
Cook Capt. Wm. 1 Bond st. Pentonville
Cook Chas. esq. Adelaide vil. Finchley
Cook Chas. esq. 23 Carlton villas
Cook Chas. esq. Montpelier, So. Lambth
Cook Charles, esq. 1 New inn, Strand
Cook Edwd. Rd. esq. 35 Lincoln's in. flds
Cook Fras. esq. 21 Park square east
Cook George Simon, esq. 56 Up. Norton st. Fitzroy sq. & 18 New Bridge st
Cook Geo. W. F. esq. 46 York st. Portman sq
Cook Gregory, esq. 1 Canterbury villas
Cook Hy. esq. 13 Devonshire pl. Edgw. rd
Cook Hy. Lover, esq. 49 London st. Fitz. sq
Cook John, esq. 9 Pelham ter. Brompton
Cook John, esq. 4 Rosedale ter. Ntng. hl
Cook John, esq. 25 Stonefield st. Islingtn
Cook John Richard, esq. 12 Sackville st
Cook John D. esq. 12 John st. Adelphi
Cook Joshua, esq. 109 Mount st. Grsnr. sq
Cook Mrs. 3 Blomfield rd. Maida hill
Cook Mrs. 4 St. Agnes villas, Bayswater
Cook Rd. esq. 2 Abbey rd. St. John's wd
Cook Rt. esq. 18 Warwick st. Golden sq
Cook Samuel R. esq. 14 Denbigh st. Pmlco
Cook Thomas Fredk. esq. 3 New st. sq
Cook Wm. esq. 23 Baker st. Lloyd sq
Cook William, esq. 3 Charlotte place, Upper Kennington lane
Cook Wm. esq. 20 Clapham rise, & Royden hall, near Maidstone
Cook Wm. esq. 25 Gloucester rd. Hyde pk
Cook Wm. esq. 2 Grange ter. Brompton
Cook Wm. esq. 2 Stanhope pl. Hamp. rd
Cooke Lady, 9 Arlington st. Piccadilly
Cooke Colonel, 45 Upper Brook st
Cooke Charles, esq. 71 Coleshill st
Cooke Charles, esq. 45 Doughty st
Cooke Chs. esq. 7 Swinton st. Gray's inn rd
Cooke Charles John, esq. 3 Staple inn
Cooke Edward, esq. 3 Elm court, Temple
Cooke Edward, esq. 4 Doughty st
Cooke Ed. esq. 8 Southampton buildings
Cooke Edwd. esq. 2 Taviton st. Gordon sq
Cooke Geo. esq. 81 Jermyn st. & Bristol
Cooke George Fred. esq. 4 Elm ct. Temple
Cooke George Wingrove, esq. 9 Inner Temple lane
Cooke Grattan, esq. 34 Foley place
Cooke John, esq. 1 Warwick pl. Bedfd. rw
Cooke John, A. esq. 7 Old sq. Lincoln's inn
Cooke Jn. C. M.D. 4 Caroline st. Bedford sq
Cooke John Hy. esq. 26 Old sq. Lincoln's inn
Cooke Masta Joscelin, esq. 20 Halfmoon st
Cooke Mrs. 67 Park st. Grosvenor sq
Cooke Mrs. 16 Portsea pl. Connght. sq
Cooke Thos. esq. 92 Great Portland st
Cooke Wm. esq. 8 Lodge rd. Rgnt.'s pk
Cooke W. H. esq. 3 Brick court, Temple
Cooke Wm. Henry, esq. 4 Elm ct. Templ
Cookes John, esq. 17 Glo'ster grove west
Cookes Mrs. 10 Provdnce. pl. U. Knngtn. la
Cookes Russell, esq. 144 Oxford st. & Woodhampton, Oxfordshire
Cookney J. T. esq. 5 Lamb's conduit pl
Cooksey Sl. esq. 2 St. Peter st. Islington
Cookson J. esq. 9 Frederick pl. Up. Kenn. la
Cookson Mrs. 28 Hunter st. Brunswick sq
Cookson William Strickland, esq. 24 Bedford sq. & 6 New sq. Lincoln's inn
Coombe Henry, esq. 13 Tibberton sq
Coombe Misses, 3 Hertford st. May fair
Coombe Mrs. 5 Up. Phillimore pl. Kensn
Coombes James, esq. 5 Kennington row
Coombs Mrs. 19 Spencer ter. Islington
Coombs Miss, 51 Brompton row
Cooper Dowager Lady, 57 Portland pl. & Isleworth house, Middlesex
Cooper Rev. Allen, 7 Hereford st
Cooper A. sen. esq. R.A. 19 Nw. Millman st
Cooper A. esq. 3 Albion ter. Wandswrth. rd
Cooper A. D. jun. esq. 19 Nw. Millman st
Cooper A. H. esq. 191 Blackfriars road
Cooper Bransby B. esq. 2 Nw. st. Spng. gdn
Cooper C. esq. 50 Guildford pl. Lr. Kenn. la
Cooper Chas. P. esq. Q.C. 7 New Boswell ct
Cooper Daniel, esq. Denmark hill
Cooper Edward, esq. 17 Howland st
Cooper Edw. P. esq. 27 Southampton buildings, & 7 Old sq. Lincoln's inn
Cooper F. C. esq. 37 Dorset st. Portman sq
Cooper Geo. esq. 15 Addison rd. Kensgtn
Cooper Geo. esq. 3 Liverpool st. King's cr
Cooper Geo. Edw. esq. 57 Burton crescnt
Cooper Geo. Lewis, esq. 35 Keppel st
Cooper Henry, esq. 20 Moore st. Soho
Cooper Henry, esq. 9 Paddington green
Cooper Hy. esq. 1 Up. Vernon st. Lloyd sq
Cooper Henry, esq. 25 Wilmington sq
Cooper H. S. esq. 3 Paper bldgs. Temple
Cooper Jas. W. esq. 9 Park st. vil. Notng. hl
Cooper John, esq. 10 Claremont pl. Pntnv
Cooper John, esq. 21 Gt. Percy st
Cooper John, esq. 10 Park pl. St. Jas's
Cooper John, esq. 27 Duke st. Westmnr
Cooper John, esq. 2 Euston grove
Cooper John, esq. 48 King sq. Goswell rd
Cooper John, esq. Paradise ter. Liverpl. rd
Cooper Jn. esq. 15 St. Ann's vil. St. Jn.'s wd
Cooper John Edward, esq. 10 Crown office row, Temple
Cooper John Eggar, esq. 13 Gt. Coram st. & Sessions House, Old bailey
Cooper Michael, esq. 1 Essex ct. Temple
Cooper Mrs. 39 Sloane st
Cooper Mrs. Col. 58 Up. Seymour st
Cooper Mrs. 74 Cadogan place
Cooper Mrs. 6 Gloucester grove west
Cooper Mrs. Chester, 32 Glo'ster place
Cooper Mrs. 21 Maida hill, Edgware rd
Cooper Mrs. 9 Paddington green
Cooper Mrs. 14 Southampton rw. New rd
Cooper Misses, 14 Clapham rise
Cooper Miss, Stoke Newington green
Cooper Miss, 10 Sussex pl. Knsgtn. nw. tn
Cooper Miss, 20 Wharton st. Lloyd sq
Cooper Montague O. esq. 8 Gt. James st
Cooper Rd. esq. 6 Stanhope st. Glo. gate
Cooper Rd. esq. 19 Sussex pl. Knsgtn. nw. tn
Cooper Rd. S. esq. 2 Stanley pl. King's rd. w
Cooper Samuel, esq. 7 Woburn place, & Shepperton, Middlesex
Cooper S. M. esq. 9 Old Cavendish st
Cooper Stephen, esq. 2 Lloyd st
Cooper Thos. esq. 184 Fleet st
Cooper Thos. esq. 24 Lincoln's inn fields
Cooper T. S. esq. 16 Wellingtn. tr. St. Jn'swd
Cooper Wm. esq. 27 Claremont sq. Pntnvl
Cooper Wm. esq. Denmark hill, Cambrwl
Cooper Wm. esq. 13 Park village east
Cooper Wm. esq. 11 Lonsdale sq. Islngtn
Cooper Wm. esq. 26 Up. Berkeley st. west
Cooper Wm. esq. 2 Vincent sq. Westmr
Cooper Wm. Bush, esq. 5 Heathcote st
Cooper Wm. H. esq. 1 Verulam bds. Gry's. in
Cooper Wm. F. esq. 5 Grove end rd. St. Jns. w
Cooper Wm. Salmon, esq. 38 Montagu sq
Cooper Wm. Wellington, esq. 18 Heathcote st. & 60 Chancery lane
Cooper Wm. White, esq. 2 Tenterden st
Coote Lady Mary, 4 Chapel st. Grosv. sq
Coote Sir Chas. Henry, bart. M.P. 5 Connaught place, Carlton club, & Ballyfin, near Montrath
Coote Capt. Chas. Chidley, 81 Jermyn st & Mount Coote, Killmalloch, Ireland
Coote Chas. John, esq. 5 Verulam bldgs
Coote David, esq. 40 Claremont square
Coote Holmes, esq. 24 Argyll st. Regt. st
Coote John, esq. 48 Lincoln's inn fields
Coote Rd. esq. 6 Gray's inn square
Coote Rd. Holmes, esq. 1 Stone bdgs. & the Grove, Blackheath
Coote Rt. esq. 2 Lambeth pl. Clapham rd
Cope Rev. Wm. H. Cloisters, Westminstr
Cope Charles, esq. 58 Euston sq
Cope E. esq. 4 Pelham ter. Brompton
Cope Francis, esq. 1 Stockwell common
Cope Mrs. 4 Brecknock cres. Camden tn
Cope Thos. S. esq. 5 Mitre ct. chbs. Fleet st
Cope William, esq. 3 Pump court, Templ
Copeland Col. F. 1 Park pl. Paddington
Copeland R. esq. 4 Stanley pl. Paddtn. gn
Copeland John, esq. 25 Portland place
Copeland Wm. Taylor, Alderman & M.P. 4 Park st. west, & 37 Lincoln's inn fields, & Lee House, Littlebury & Layton, Essex
Copland & Burnett, 22 Surrey st. Strand
Copland Jas. M.D., F.R.S. 5 O. Bulngtn. st
Copland Misses, 22 Surrey st. Strand, & Sudbury lodge, near Harrow
Copley Edward Joseph, esq. 81 Jermyn street, & Tees cottage, Darlington
Coppard George, esq. 43 King st. Stepny
Coppock James, esq. 3 Cleveland row
Copus Chas. esq. 5 Coburg pl. Bayswater
Corbally Matthew Elias, M.P. Cox's hotel, 55 Jermyn st. & Corbalton hall, Dunshaughlin, Ireland
Corbaux Miss Fanny, 59 Up. Norton st
Corbet Robert, esq. 17 Mount st
Corbett Chas. Hen. esq. 5 Caroline place
Corbett Geo. esq. 27 Bartlett's buildings
Corbett Mrs. 54 Green st. Grosvenor sq
Corbett Mrs. Mary, 23 Beaumont st
Corbett Uvedale, esq. 7 Suffolk st. Pall mall east; & 22 Old sq. Lincoln's inn; & Tettenhall wood, Wolverhampton
Corbett Wm. esq. 2 Maida hill, Edgwr. rd
Corbyn Capt. J. P. 1 Thanet pl. Spa rd. Berm
Corbould Edwd. esq. 21 Rutlnd. gte. Hd. pk
Corbyn Thos. J. esq. 6 New Palace yard
Corder Jas. esq. 6 Bow st. Covent garden
Corderoy Geo. esq. 98 High st. Marylebn
Corderoy J. esq. 1 Chester pl. Kenn. crs
Corderoy Wm. esq. 98 High st. Marylebo
Core Miss, 34 Harley st
Corfield Chas. Leopold, esq. 88 Chancery lane, & 14 Lamb's Conduit st
Corfield Geo. Keates, esq. 20 Harley st
Corfield Mrs. 75 Wimpole st
Corfield Wm. esq. 2 Robert st. Adelphi
Cork & Orrery, Earl of, K.P. 3 Hamilton pl. Piccadilly, & Marston hall, Frome
Corles T. B. esq. 12 Featherstone bldgs
Corley John, esq. 4 Verulam buildings
Cormack T. esq. 1 Arundel ter. Barnsby. rd
Cormick Miss, 51 Beaumont st
Cornelius Wm. esq. 10 Howard st. Strand
Cornell Geo. esq. 66 Up. Norton st
Cornell Saml. esq. 16 Whitehead's grove
Cornell Thos. esq. 11 Baron st. Pentnvll
Cornell Thos. esq. 16 Cloudesley ter
Corner Rd. J. esq. 2 Tanfield ct. Temple
Cornewall Frederic Henry, esq. Fenton's hotel, & Delbury hall, Ludlow
Cornewall Miss, 102 Mount st
Cornick John, esq. 59 Spencer st. Gos. rd
Cornish John Rt. esq. 11 Paper bdgs. Tem
Cornish Wm. esq. 1 Stonefield st. Islngtn
Cornthwaite Daniel, esq. 11 Middlesex pl
Cornwall Hon. Mrs. 37 Grosvenor place
Cornwall A. R. esq. 13 Egremont pl. New rd
Cornwall Hen. Cobb, esq. 3 Barnard's inn
Cornwallis Marchioness, 12 Park cresct
Cornwallis Earl, 6 Hill st. Berkeley sq. & Linton pl. Linton, near Maidstone
Cornwell Lieut.-Col. 60 Cadogan place
Corpe Alf. esq. 33 Sussex pl. Kensington
Corpe George, esq. 3 Lincoln's inn fields
Corpe Mrs. 12 Cambridge st. Edgware rd
Correvon A. P. A. esq. 32 Wilmington sq
Corri Mrs. 3 Barrow hill pl. Regent's pk
Corrie Adam, esq. 47 Upper Norton st

Corrie Edgar, esq. 29 Mincing lane, & Purley lodge, Croydon
Corrie Thos. S. esq.36Bedford st.Cvt.gdn
Corrie W. esq. 54 Gower st. & 1 Pump ct
Corry Rt.Hon.Hen. Thos. Lowry,M.P. & Lady Harriett,Admiralty,24Grosvenor sq.; & Castle Cool, near Enniskillen
Cort Henry H. esq. 34A,York st.Ptmn.sq
Cort John, esq. 48 Lower Belgrave pl
Corvan J. esq. 11 Ehrenburg ter.Reg. pk
Cory Hen. esq. 1 New square, Linc. inn
Cory Wm.esq.2Verulam bldgs.Gray's inn
Cory Wm. Hanrott, esq. 8 Air st.Regt. st
Cosens Mrs. 19 Chester pl. Kenngtn. crs
Cosgreave Peter, esq. 34 Norfolk st
CossartWm.esq.2Lennard pl.St.John'swd
Cossins Wm. esq. 7 Chester ter. Eaton sq
Costall Mrs. 5 Albion grove,Thornhill rd
Costello Thos. esq. 4 Charles st. Islingtn
Costello William B. esq. 10 Golden sq
Costar Francis, esq. 12 Frederick st
Costar Mrs. 12 Frederick st.Gray's inn rd
Costello Dudley, esq. 14 St. Ann's villas
Coster John, esq. 2 Glo'ster pl. New rd
Coster Thos. esq. 27York ter.Regent's pk
Cotes Chas. esq. 61 Russell sq.Bloomsby
Cotes John, esq. 24 Grosvenor st. & Woodcot, Shiffnall, Staffordshire
Cotes Misses, 24 Grosvenor st
Cotes Miss, 24 Lower Grosvenor st
Cotes Miss, 15 Barnsbury park, Islngtn
Cotes Wm. esq. 11 Tyndale pl. Islington
Cother Dunbar J. esq. 4 Harcourt bldgs
Cother Wm. esq. 4 Garden ct. Temple
CotmanJ.S.esq.8Henriettast.Brunswk.sq
Cottam George, esq. Manor house, Acacia road, St. John's wood
Cottée Henry, esq. 13 Crawford st
Cottee Mon. Felix, attaché to the French embassy, 20 Manchester square
Cottenham Lord, P.C. 15 Park lane; & Copse hill, Wimbledon
Cotterell Chas. Jas. esq. 57 Warren st
Cotterell George, esq. 13 Bruton st
Cotterell John, esq. 17 Nottingham st
Cotterell Miss, 1 Allen ter. Kensington
Cotterill Wm. Hen. esq. 48 Bedford sq
Cottin Miss, 86 Wimpole st
Cottingham John, esq. 10 Lancaster pl
CottinghamL.N.esq.43Basing pl.Wtrl.rd
Cotton Sir Willoughby, knt. G.C.B. & Lady Augusta, 15 Lowndes square
Cotton Capt. Ed. 25 Bedford pl. Knsgtn
Cotton Capt. 12Bentinck st.; &Convent, Kingsgate, Isle of Thanet
Cotton Francis, jun. esq. 27 Hackney rd
Cotton George, esq. 17 Maida hill
Cotton Geo. Vernon, esq.2Raymond bdgs
Cotton John, esq. 30 Upper Harley st
Cotton Mrs. Thomas, 25 Bryanstone square, & Ham common, Surrey
Cotton Mrs. 49 Cambridge ter. Edg. rd
Cotton Miss, 5 Montagu place
Cotton Miss, 19 Stonefield st. Islington
Cotton Philip, esq. 8 Clement's inn,Strd
Cotton Richard, esq. 10 Kensington sq
Cotton Wm. esq. 2 Orme sq. Bayswater
Couch Rd. esq. 7 Mitre court chambers
Couchman Jas. esq.5 Hornton st.Kngstn
Coule Charles, esq. 21 Gt. May's bldgs
Coulbrook Lady, 22 Westbourne st
Couling Edwd.esq.Queen's rd.St.Jn.'s wd
Coulon Mons. Eugene,47Gt.Marlboro' st
Coulson Jukes, esq. 15 Circus rd.St.J.wd
CoulsonWalter,esq.7New sq.Lncln's. inn
Coulthard Edward, esq. 4 Gray's inn sq
Coulthard Mrs. 3 Albion grove, Islngtn
Coulthurst Hen. Utrick, esq. 13New inn
Coulthurst Nicholas, esq. 13 New inn
Coulthurst Wm.Matthew, esq. 6 New st. Spring gardens, & Streatham lodge
Couper Col. SirGeorge,bart.5Lowndes sq
Court Jsph.esq.16Buckingham st.Strand
Courtenay Lord, M.P. 4 Bryanstone sq. & Powderham castle, Exeter
Courteany Lady Elizh. 4 Bryanstone sq
Courtenay Chas. B. esq. 82 Cadogan pl
Courtenay F. B. esq. 289A, Regent st
Courtenay James, esq. 90 Guilford st
Courtenay Miss, 26 Chapel st. Grosvr. pl
Courtenay P.W. esq. 10Crown office row
Courthope, Wm. esq. Heralds' college
Courtney Henry Thos. F. esq.1 Lloyd sq
Courtney John esq. 3 York cott. Brmtn
Courtney William, esq. 54 Oxford ter
Courtney Wm. C.esq.26Up.Southwick st
Courtown, Earl of, 11 Green st.; &Courtown house,Wexford; &Gorey,Ireland
CourtonHenry,esq.17North bk.Rgt.'s pk
Courtoy Geo. esq. 27 Hamilton terrace
Courtoy Mrs. 14 Wilton crescent
Cousens Mrs. 10 Derby st.Gray's inn rd
CousensR.T.esq.8Hydepk.gt.Knsgtn.gre
Cousens W. esq.4Compton st.ea.Bruns.sq
Cousins Hen. esq. 15 Osnaburgh st
Cousins Lewis, esq. 8 Mabledon place
Cousins Robt. esq. 14 Gerrard st. Islgtn
Cousins Sam. esq. A.R.A.15Osnaburgh st
Cousins Thos. esq.10Park ter.Liverpl.rd
Coutts & Co. 59 Strand
Coutts Miss Burdett, 1 Stratton st
Couzens Charles, esq. 38 Up.Berkeley st
Coventon Wm. G. esq.12 Highbury park
Coventry Right Hon. & Rev. John, 8 Albert terrace, Knightsbridge
CoventryM.esq.St.John'shi.Wndswth.rd
Coventry Mrs. 4 Kensingtn. palace gdns
Coventry Mrs. 2 Wilton place
Coventry Thomas, esq. 5 Tavistock sq.; & 5 Old sq. Lincoln's inn; & Swindon
Cover Mrs. 38 Kirby st. Hatton garden
Coverdale John, esq. 4 Bedford row, & Oak lodge, Kilburn
Coverdale Mrs. & Misses, 35 Chester ter
Covey J. esq. 2 Lowther cot.Liverpool rd
Covey Wm. Henry, esq.42 Charing cross
CowanMalcolm, esq.4Devnprt.st.Hy.pk. & 1 New Temple buildings, Mitre ct
Cowan Mrs. 4 Devonport st. Hyde park
Cowan Mrs. 34 Burton crescent
Coward Chas. esq. 9 Smith st. Chelsea
Coward Geo. esq. 6 Woburn buildings
Coward James, esq. 91 Sloane st
Coward Wm.esq.8Dorset ter.Claphm. rd
Cowburn Wm. esq.10 Lincoln's inn flds.; & Sydenham, Kent; & Warren's Gill, Hever, Kent
Cowell Mrs. 7 Great Cumberland st
Cowell Thos. Wm. esq. 1 St. George's pl
Cowell Wm. esq.4 Chester pl. Oxford sq
Cowey Mrs. 18 Nw. Church st.Lisson gro
Cowie Hen. Chas. esq. 16 Burton cresct
Cowland Miss, 1Albion cotgs.Lvrpool.rd
Cowlard Hen.esq. 14 Lincoln's inn fields
Cowles Capt. R.N. 51 Connaught terrace
Cowles Fred. esq. 5 Holywell st. Millbnk
Cowley Lord, G.C.B., P.C. 12Grosvenr.st
Cowley John C. esq.1Park cres.Ptlnd. pl
Cowley Saml. N. esq. 1 Park crescent
Cowper, Earl of, 1 Gt. Stanhope st.; & Panshanger, Hertford; & Moat house, Wingham
Cowling John, esq. 2 Mitre ct. buildings
Cowper Hon. Spencer, 29 Up. Brook st
Cowper Hon. W. Francis, M.P. 39 South st. Grosvenor sq
Cowper Edwd.esq. 6 Campden hill villas
Cowper Edward, esq. 24 Petersburgh pl. Bayswater, & King's college
Cowper Frederick, esq. 65 Russell sq
Cowper John, esq. 19 Stamford st. Blkfrs
Cox Alfred, esq. 7 Barnard's inn, Holbn
Cox Algernon, esq. 22 Portugal st
Cox Charles & Lady Wood, esq. 6 Chesham place
Cox Chas. Edwd. esq. 44 Hatton garden
Cox Chas. James, M.D. 3 Beaumont st
Cox Chas. John, esq.43 Lincoln's inn fds
Cox Edwd. esq. 6 Elm tree rd. St. Jno.wd
Cox Edward Lewton, esq. 1 Hyde park st. & 62 Lincoln's inn fields
Cox Ed. Truslove, esq. 8 Duke st. St. Jas
Cox Edwd. Wm. esq. 3 Crown Office row
Cox Edward, esq. 1 Torrington sq
Cox Edward Wm. esq. 1 Torrington sq
Cox Fredk. esq. 10 Chester st. Grosv. pl
Cox Geo. esq. 4 Coleshill st. Eaton sq
Cox Jas. M. esq. 12 Hanway st.Oxford st
Cox John, esq. 10 Brompton sq
Cox John, esq. 9 Gibson sq. Islington
Cox John, jun. esq. 1 Hyde park st
Cox John, sen. esq. 1 Hyde park st
Cox Miss, 33 Chapel st. Grosvenor pl
Cox Miss, 91 Gloucester place
Cox Miss, 49 Park st. Grosvenor sq
Cox Miss, 6 Up. Glo'ster st. Dorset sq
Cox Mrs. 28 Belvedere road, Lambeth
Cox Mrs. 21 Brompton crescent
Cox Mrs. 7 Rich terrace, Old Brompton
Cox Mrs. 10 Smith st. Chelsea
Cox Mrs. 2 Southampton row, New rd
Cox Mrs. 16 Southampton st. Fitzroy sq
Cox Mrs. 15 Southwick crescent
Cox Philip Z. esq. 24 Gloucester place
Cox Richard Henry, esq. 8 Grosvenor pl. & Hillingdon house, Uxbridge
Cox Rd. Sawrey, esq. 2 Up. Woburn pl
Cox Rd.W. esq. 52 Liverpool st.King's cr
Cox Rt. esq. 12 Whitehead's gro. Chelsea
Cox Samuel, esq. 13 Weymouth st
Cox Stephen, esq. 22 Nottingham st New rd. & Merton lodge, Turnham grn
Cox Thos. esq. 29 Charlotte st. Portl. pl
Cox Travers, M.D. 2 Stanhope place, Connaught square
Cox Wm. esq. 3 Clarendon square
Cox Wm. esq. 29 Essex st. Strand
Cox Wm. esq. 82 Oxford terrace
Cox Compton Miss, 52 Guilford st
Coxe L. esq. 4 Brunswick pl.Regent's pk
Coxe Philip Smith, esq. 12 Park road
Coxhead Geo.esq. 5 Gt.College st.Westm
Coxhead John, esq. 47 Myddelton sq
Coxwell H. esq. 10 Claremont rw. Islgtn
Coyel Thos. esq. 24 Hans pl. Sloane st
Coyle Ignatious, esq. 21 Alexander sq
Coyne Henry, esq. 26 Smith st. Chelsea
Coyne Mrs. 13 Craven st. Strand
Coyne Phineas, esq. 13 Bulstrode st
Crabb George esq. 103 Mount st
Crabb Geo. esq. 16 Southampton bldngs
Crace Fred. esq. 19 Glo'ster pl. New rd
Crace Hen. W. esq. 19B, Buckingham st
Cracknel Geo. esq. 15 Noel st. Islington
Cracknell Stephen, esq. 157 Albany st
Craddock C.esq.6Chapel pl.Cavendish sq
Craddock Chas. Rd. esq. 5 Gray's inn sq
Crafer Edwin Turner, esq. Treasury, & 2 St. Ann's terrace, North Brixton
Cragg Joseph, esq. 21 Queen sq. Blmsby
Cragg Joseph esq. 11 Bayham ter. Camden town, & 22 Bedford rw. Bloomsbury
Cragg Miss, 58 Burton crescent
Cragg Misses, 14 Brompton sq
Cragg Wm. esq. 1Cumberland pl.New rd
Craggs Mrs. 24 Glo'ster grove w.O.Brptn
Craghill Wm. esq. 24 Theberton st. Islgtn
Craig Rd. Davis, esq. 23 Earl's terrace, Kensington, & 3 Stone bldgs. Lin. inn
Craig Wm. Gibson, jun. esq. M.P.27Grosvenor pl. & Riccarton, near Edinburgh
Crainers Mrs. 11 Upper Baker st
Crake John, esq. 4 Regent st
CrakeVanderleurB.esq.6King'sBench wk
Crake Wm. esq. 10 Stanhope st.Hyde pk. & Pelham pl. Hastings
Cramer F.esq.37 Charlotte st.Fitzroy sq
Crampern J. B. esq. 6 King st. Finsbury
Crampten Wm. esq. 53 St.Martin's lane
Crampton Mrs. 189 Sloane st
Cranage John, esq. 19 Tavistock sq
Crane Miss, 16 Scarsdale ter. Knsgton
Craneley Viscount 100 Mount st
CranleyMrs.19Smith st.King's rd.Chels
Cranstoun Lord, A2,Albany; Brompton villa, OldBrompton; Sundridge, Torquay, Devonshire; Arrasaig, FortWilliam; & Rose hall, Sutherlandshire, N.B.

Cranmer Mrs. 33 Percy st. Bedford sq
Craufurd Rev. Alex. 21 Up. Gower st
Craufurd Miss, 56 Up. Berkeley st
Craufurd W.P. esq. 56 Up. Berkeley st
Craths Jas. esq.3Stanhope st.Regt.'s pk
Craven, Earl of, 16 Charles st. Berkeley sq.; & Coombe abbey, Coventry; & Hampstead park, Bracknell, Berks
Craven Hon.F.K.16Charles st.Berkly.sq
Craven Arron,esq.16George st.Prtmn.sq
Craven Miss,18 Gt. Ormond st.Queen sq
Crawcour Abraham, esq. 31 Nelson sq
Crawcour Edward,esq.43 Porchester ter
Crawcour Moses, esq. 69 Connaught ter
CrawcourS.esq.33Beckfordrw.Wlwth.rd
Crawford Rev. J.R.North ter. Bromptn
Crawford Geo. Morland, esq. 3 Old sq
Crawford James, esq. 25 Manchester st
CrawfordMervyn,M.D.62Up.Berkeley st
Crawford Mrs. 70 Aldermanbury
Crawford Mrs.11 Weymouth st.Port. pl
Crawford Miss,28Abbeypl.St.John's wd
Crawford Rt.M.esq.51 Lincoln's inn flds
Crawford Wm. esq. 6 Gt. Winchester st
Crawford Wm.esq. 2 Raymond buildings
CrawfordWm.Sharman,M.P.Crawfordsburn, near Bangor, Ireland
Crawhall Mrs. 11Henrietta st. Cavdh. sq
Crawley A. G. esq. 12 Southampton bdg
Crawley Geo. A. esq. 20 Whitehall pl
Crawshay George, esq. 1 Montague st. Russell sq. & Colney hatch, Middlesex
Crawter Hy. esq. } 7 Southamptn.bdgs
Crawter Thos. esq. } &Cobham,Surrey
Crealock Wm. Belton, esq. 3 Stanhope place, Hyde park, & 4 Regent st
Crease Orlando, esq. 12 Amwell terrace
CreaserThos.Wm.esq.4Lamb bldg.Tmpl
Creasy E. S. esq. 2 Mitre ct. chambers
Creasy Miss, 8 Park pl. villas, Paddgtn
Cree David, esq. 42 University st
Cree Thos. esq. 26 Mornington place; & 3 Verulam buildings, Gray's inn
Cree Thos. jun.esq. 3 Verulam buildings
Creed Mrs. 1 Chesham pl.Belgrave sq.; Ripley, Surrey; & Cheltenham
Creed Rd. esq.7 Norfolk cres.Oxford sq
Creighton Mrs. 18 Smith st. Chelsea
Crellin Wm. esq. 19 Wellington road
Cremer John, esq. 5 Sussex pl. Knsngtn
Cremorne Lord, Dawtrey house, Cootehill, Monaghan
Cremorne Dow. Lady, 3Gt. Stanhope st
Cresswell Sir Cresswell, knt. Fleming house, Old Brompton,&Judges' chambers, Rolls' garden
Cresswell A.J.B.esq.M P. Eltham, Kent, & Cresswell, nr. Morpeth, Nrthmbrlnd
Cresswell Hen. esq. 23 Hemingford ter
Cresswell Mrs. 48 Southampton st.Pent
Cresswell Thos esq.1Brecknock ter
Cresswell Wm. esq. 5 Sussex gardens
Creswell Edw.esq.5 Albert ter.Kngtsbdg
Creswell Miss, 57 Euston square
Creswick J. esq.Russell cot.Morngtn.rd
Creswick Thos.esq. 8 Linden gr. Knsngn
Crew Thos. Fras.esq. 38 Essex st. Strnd
Crewe Lord, 2 Hill st.; & Crewe hall, Nantwich
Crewe Sir Geo. bart.Brunswick hotel,52 Jermyn st. & Calke abbey, nr. Derby
Cribb G. esq. 65 Gt.Russell st. Blmsbry
Crichton Jas. esq. 51 Gibson sq. Islngtn
Crichton John, esq. 17King st.Prtmn.sq
Crichton John, esq. 44 Upper Gower st
Crichton P.C. esq.Buckingham st.Strnd
Crick Mrs. 3A, Sussex ter.Old Bromptn
Criddle Mrs. 3 Upper Belgrave pl
Cridland Richd. esq. 12 Montpelier st
Crighton Mrs. 5 Stanhope st.Glo'ster gt
Crippa Joseph, esq. 5 Up. Belgrave tr
Cripps Henry Wm.esq. 11Walton place, Brompton, & 13 Serle st.Lincoln's inn
Cripps Wm. esq. M.P.38 St.James's pl.; & Cirencester
Crispen Hen.M.esq.6Bedford pl.Knsngtn
Crivelli Dominico F. esq. 71 U.Norton st
Crocker Edwd.esq.2Belgrave rd.Pimlico
Crocker Hen. esq. 7 Castle st. Holborn
Crockett Chas. esq. 10 Linc. inn fields
Crockford Edw. esq. 1 Clapham rise
Crockford Fredk. esq. 6 Seamore place
Crockford Geo. esq.11 Cmptn.st.e.Rgt.sq
Crockford Joshua, esq. 34 Alfred pl
Crockford Mrs. 6 Seamore place
Croft Dowager Lady, 35 Queen Anne st
Croft Sir Archer Denman, bt. 14 Southwick cr.; & Master's offi.Mtre.ct.Tmpl
Croft Major, 15 Regent st
Croft Chas. esq. 11 Canonbury villas
Croft Geo.Wm. Hen.esq. 95Gt.Russell st
Croft Rd. esq. 11 Portland ter.Regt.'spk
Croft Rd. Henry, esq. 39 Park st
Croft Wm. esq.1 Bayham cot.Camden tn
Croft Wm. esq. 8 Surrey pl. Kennington
Crofton Lord, 12 Bryanstone sq. & Mote park, Roscommon
Crofton Anth. esq. 7 New sq. Linc. inn
Crofton Geo. esq. 61 Bartholomew close
Crokatt Charles, esq. 14 Connaught sq
Croker Mrs. Kensington palace
Crombie Lewis, esq. 9 Sussex pl.Hyde pk
Crombie Mrs. 12 York tr. Regent's park
Cromelin Thos. esq. 31 Blandford sq
Crompton Chas.esq.10 Endsleigh st. Tavistock sq. & 1 Paper bldgs. Temple
Crompton Mrs. 29 Howland st
Cronin Denis, M.D. 113 Strand
Crook Geo. esq. 22 Torrington square
Crook James M.esq.17Brook st.Grosv.sq
Crook John, esq.17 Clement's inn,Strand
CrookJno.C.esq.6Cunnghm.pl.StJn's.wd
Crook Miss, 30 Percy st. Bedford sq
Crookes John Farrar, esq. 5 Suffolk pl. Pall mall east
Crookes Joseph, esq. 4 Park village ea
Crookes Willam, esq. 13 Montague pl
Croome Chas. Jas. esq. 126 Albany st
Croome John Daniel, esq. 20 Albany st
Cropley John, W. esq. 31 Wilmington sq
Cropper Joseph Almond, esq. 2 South sq
Crosbie Arthur, esq. 52 Nelson sq
Crosby James, esq.3 Church ct.OldJewry
Crosby John, esq. 15 Sloane st
Crosby Rd. esq.15 Camden st.Islngtn.gn
Crosby Walter, esq. 4 Plowden buildgs
Crosdill Col. John, 45 Berners st
Crosley John, esq. 5 South bnk. Rgt. pk
Cross Benj. B. esq. 38 Southampton blds
Cross Geo. esq. Courlnd.lodge, Wndsw.rd
Cross Henry W. esq. 5 New inn, Strand
Cross James, esq. 7 Frederick st. Gray's inn road, & 9 Staple inn
Cross John, esq. 14 Canonbury villas
Cross John, esq. 13 Victoria square, & 5 Hare court, Temple
Cross Mrs. 4 Cunninghm.pl.St.John's wd
Cross Mrs. 10 Up. Glo'ster st. Dorset sq
Cross Mrs. 119½ Upper st. Islington
Cross Osborn P. esq. 7 Durham pl.Chels
Cross Rt. esq. 8 Lawn pl. South Lambth
Cross Robert, M.D. 21 Leicester sq
Cross Thos. esq. 15 Bedford row, Islgtn
Cross Wm. A. esq. 1 New Temple bldgs
Cross William Henry, esq. 28 Surrey st. Strand, & Barnes, Surrey
Cross Wm. S. 7 King's Bench.wk.Temple
Crosse Miss, High st. Kensington
Crosse Misses, 10 Norland pl. Notting h
Crosse Robt. esq. 4 Bell yd. Doctors' com
Crosse Robt. Fredk. esq. 7 New Temple buildings, Mitre court, Temple
Crosse Robert Jennings, esq. 11 Serjeants' inn, Fleet st
Crossland J. M. esq. 21 Shaftesbury ter
Crotch Wm. esq.24 Bedford pl.Knsngtn
Crouch Christr. esq. 37 Souhamptn.bdgs
Crouch Daniel, N. esq. 15 Chancery lane
Crouch D.N.esq.13Sthmptn.pl.Eustn.sq
Crouch Fredk. esq. 75 Gt. Titchfield st
Croucher Jph. esq. 6 James st. Bknghm gate; 3Trafalgar sq.&31 New Broad st
Crouch Mrs. 28 Tavistock pl. Tavstk. sq
Crowder Geo. Augustus, esq. 11 Pall mall east, & 57 Coleman st. City
Crowder Rd. Budden, esq. Q.C. 11 Pall mall east, & 1 Brick court, Temple
Crowe Rev. Henry, 38 Hatton garden
Crowe Mrs. 1 George st. Euston square
Crowe P. esq. 33 Gloucester st.Queen sq
Crowgey Robt. esq. 46 Threadneedle st
Crowley E. esq. Lavender hill, Wands.rd
Crowley Jas. esq. Stoke Newington grn
Crowley N. esq. R.H.A. 13 Up. Fitzroy st
Crowther Rev. J. 3 Chester pl. Kenn.crs
Crowther Mrs. 5 Mornington crescent, & Ware hill, Ware, Herts
Crowther Rt.W.esq.1 Trinity pl.Char. cr
Croxton Major Thos. 32 Upper Baker st
Croysdill H. esq. 37King st.&33 O.Jewry
Crozier H. R. esq. 93 Milton st.Dorset sq
Cruden Wm. esq. 33 York st. Baker st
Cruickshank F. esq. 56 Devonshire st. Portland place
Cruickshank George, esq. 23 Amwell st
Cruickshank Pat. esq.20 Hyde pk. gard. & Harbord house, Richmond, Surrey
Cruickshank Robt. esq. 66 Gray's inn la
Cruickshanks John, esq. 21 Milton st
Crumling Thomas, esq. 7 Grove end rd
Cruse Edw. esq. 66 Ebury st. Pimlico
Cruttwell Chas. J.esq.9 New sq. Linc.inn
Cubison Wm. esq. 8 Grenville st. Brns. sq
Cubison Wm. Henry, esq. 8 Grenville st
Cubitt Jsph. esq. 12 Manchester bldgs
Cubitt Lewis, esq. 77 Gt. Russell st.Blm
Cubitt Thomas, esq. 53 Doughty st
Cubitt Wm. esq. 7 Charles sq. Hoxton
Cubitt Wm. esq. 6 Great George st
Cubley John, esq. 53 Walcot pl.Lambeth
Cuell Miss, 9 Gloucester place, New rd
Cuff Christopher, esq. 12 Half moon st
Cuff G. E. esq. 5 Victoria vil. Avenue rd
Cuff Joshua H.esq. 35 Gt. Dover st. Boro'
Cuff Mrs. 7 Gt. Ryder st. St. James's
Cuff Mrs. Col. 29 Norfolk st. Park lane
Cuffe Rev. T. 2 Chester pl. Kenngtn. crs
Cuisset Frank Frs. esq. 11 Bentinck st
Culham James, esq. 103 Drummond st
Culiford John, esq. 12 President st. west
Cull Rd. esq. 13 Tavistock st. Bedford sq
Cullen Chas. esq. 3 Wellington terrace
Cullen Danl. Robt. esq. 31 Cloudesley st
Cullerne C. esq. 6 Air st. Piccadilly
Culley Sam. esq. 2 Hyde park terrace
Cullimore Mrs. 5 Vxhall. pl.So.Lambeth
Cullington Daniel, jun. esq. 2 Craven st. & 2 Terrace, Hammersmith
Cullington Daniel, esq. 2 Craven st. & 2 Terrace, Hammersmith
Cullum Wm. esq. 8 Kilburn priory
Culmer Mrs. 16 Grafton st. Fitzroy sq
Culpeper John B. esq. 7 Stanhope st
Culverwell Mrs. 16 Rodney st
Culverwell Robert, esq. 4 Rathbone pl
Culverwell R.J.M.D.21&23Arundel st.Str
Culverwell Saml. Hen. esq. 21 Norfolk st
CumberJn.esq.31Frederick st.Gry'sinnrd
Cumberland Duke of (King of Hanover) St. James's palace
Cumberland Mrs. 9 Brompton row
Cumberlege Charles Nathaniel, esq. 15 Sussex place, & 5 John st. Adelphi
Cumberlege Nathl.esq 3 York tr.Reg.pk
Cuming Hugh, esq. 80 Gower st
Cuming Miss, 46 Up. Albany st. Reg.pk
CummingLt.Genl.SirH.J.15Up.Grosv.st
Cumming Rev. John, M.A. 7 Hunter st
Cumming Arthur, esq. 1Burlington gdns
Cumming Jas.C.M.D.27 Lowndes st.Blg.s
Cumming Wm.esq.23Nth.bank,Rgt.'s pk
Cundell Chs. esq. 4 Warwick sq. Knsngtn
Cundell Rd. esq. 3 Grenville pl. Kilburn
Cundy Chas. Fishlake, esq. 8 Regent st
Cundy Thos. esq. 13 Chester sq. Pimlico
Cunliffe-Offley, Hon. Mrs. 16 Up. Brook st. & Madley Manor, Newcastle, Staffrd
Cunliffe Jas. esq. 32 Duncan ter. City rd

Cunliffe Roger, esq. 21 Highbury place
Cunningham Charles, esq. 4 Clarges st
CunninghamRt.esq.15Dorst.ter.Clpm.rd
Cunningham Rt. esq. 30 Howland st
Cunynghame Lady, 12 Saville row
Cunynghame Capt.19Bury st.St.James's
Cunynghame Geo.A. F.esq. 12Saville rw
Cure Capel, esq. 2 Devonshire place, Portland pl. & Blakehall, Ongar, Esx
Cureton Rev. Wm. 37 Queen Anne st
Curie Paul Francis, M.D. 30 Brook st
Curle Wm. esq. 34 Westbourne place
Curling Rev. Wm. 44 Trinity sq. Boro'
Curling Daniel, esq. 15Park st. Grosnr.sq
Curling Mrs. Canonbury pl. Islington
Curling Robt. esq. 15 Buckingham st. Strand, & 2 George yard, Lombard st
Curling Wm.esq.Denmark hill,Cambrwl
Curling William, esq. 15 Regent st
Curran JohnP.esq.36 Southampton bdgs
Curran Mrs.Adams pl.King's rd. Chelsea
Curran Mrs. 11 Bedford st. Bedford sq
CurrerWm.esq.2 Harcourt bldgs.Temple
Currey B. esq.6 Old Palace yd.& Eltham
Currey Fredk. esq. 3 New sq. Linc. inn
Currey Henry, esq. 22 Brook st
Currey Wm. esq.23 Abingdon st. Westm
CurreyWm.Saml.12Bucknghm.st.Adlph
Currie A. esq.Clyde vil.Qn's. rd.St.Jn.wd
Currie Arthur, esq. 12 Cavendish square
Currie Henry, esq.23 Park st. Grosnr. sq
Currie Jas. esq. 32 Lincoln's inn fields
Currie John G. esq. 39 Upper Brook st
Currie Mrs. 28 Coleshill st
Currie Mrs. 38 Wimpole st. & Bush hill, Enfield, Middlesex
Currie Raikes, M.P. & Hon. Mrs. 4 Hyde park ter. & Albyns, Romford, Essex
Currie Thos. esq. 1 Whitehead's grove
Currie Wm. B. esq. 59 Westbourne ter
Curry Thos. esq. 11 Circus rd. St. Jn's.wd
Cursham George, M.D. 5 Saville row
Curteis Herbert B.esq. M.P. 19 Bridge st. Westmnstr. & Windmill hill, nr. Battle
Curteis Wm. Calverley, D.C.L. 12 Montague st. Russl.sq.&14 College, Doc. co
Curteis John, esq. 39 Devonshire place
Curteis Reginald, esq. 49 Eaton place
Curtis Sir Wm. bart. 61 Portland place, & Cliff house, Ramsgate
Curtis Capt. Hen. 11 Bayswater terrace
Curtis George, esq. 54 Harley st
Curtis James, esq. 23 Hanover square
Curtis James John, esq. 13 Blandford st
Curtis John, esq. 41 Woburn place
Curtis John Harrison, esq. 2 Soho square
Curtis Jsph. esq.1 St.James' ter.Cmdn. tn
Curtis Mrs. 40 Albion st. Hyde park
Curtis Mrs. 39 Clapham road place
Curtis Mrs. Denmark hill, Camberwell
Curtis Mrs. 23 Lwr. Belgrave pl. Pimlico
Curtis Mrs. 7 New Cavendish st
Curtis Mrs. Villa, Up. Kennington lane
Curtis Thos. esq. 2 Kilburn priory
Curtis Wm.esq. 11 Dorset pl. n.Clapm.rd
Curtis Wm. esq. 9 Portugal st. Grosv. sq
Curtiss I.C. esq. 7 Marlboro' pl. Abbey rd
Curtiss John Alfred, esq. 32 Beaumont st
Curtois Rev. Peregrine, 3 Tenterden st. & Long hills, near Lincoln
Curtois Mrs. 8 Devonshire pl. Edgw. rd
Curwood John, esq. 17 Clifford's inn
Curzon Viscount, 8 South Audley st. & Pennhouse, Amersham
Curzon Hon. Edwd. Cecil, 17 Connaught terrace, & 7 New sq. Lincoln's inn
Curzon Hon. Fras.Jas.3Brick ct.Temple
Curzon Hon. Robert & Baroness de la Zouche,24 Upper Brook st.; &Hagley, Litchfield; & Parham park, Petworth
Curzon Hon. Miss, 50 Berkeley square
Cusel Herman, esq.18 Dalby ter.City rd
CustHon.Chas.Hen.4Lowndesst.Belg.sq
Cust Hon. Miss, 30 Hill st. Berkeley sq
Cutbill Alfred R. esq. 6 Henrietta st. Covent Garden, & 6 Lothbury
Cuthbert Rev. Dr. Wm. 16 Abbey road
Cuthbert Louis M. esq. 8 South Bank
Cuthbert Miss, 4 Manor grove,King's rd
Cuthbert Rd. esq.48Wharton st.Lloyd sq
Cuthell John, esq.10 Cavendish road,St. John's wood,&13A,Avery row,Bond st
Cutland Wm. esq. 26 Grove end road
Cutler Edwd. esq. 15 New Burlington st
Cutler Edwd. esq.Park vil. ea.Regt.'spk
Cutler Edward R. esq. 3 Furnival's inn
Cutler Frederick, esq. 16 Furnival's inn
Cutler John, esq. 37 Hamilton terrace
Cutler Miss, 55 Brompton square
Cutler Miss, 12 Devonshire st. City
Cutten C.esq. 8 Frederick pl.Up.Kenn.la
Cuttill Richd. esq. 3 Camden cottages
Cuttill Rd. Jas. 19 Camden cottages
Cutting Jn. esq. 42 London st.Fitzroy sq

DA COSTA Antonio,vice-consul for the Brazils,3 Howford bldgs.Fenchurch st
Da Costa Moses M. esq.2River ter.north
Dacre Lord, 2 Chesterfield st.&the Hoo, Welwyn, Herts
Dacre Col. 28 York pl. Portman square
Dacre George, esq. Stratford, Essex
Dacre Life, esq. 8 Harley st
Dacre Misses, 5 Albert ter. St. Jn's. wd
Dacre Mrs. 2 Baker st. Portman square
Dadley Wm.esq.20Chester pl.Knngtn.cr
DaftPhillip,esq.3 Albion cotgs.L'pool.rd
Daggett Mrs. 6 Radcliffe terrace
Dagley James, esq. 45 Connaught sq
Dagley Mrs. 45 Connaught square
Dakeyne Henry C. esq. 14 Hamilton ter
Dakin Mrs. 41 Finsbury square
Dakins Rev. Dr. Dean's yd. Westminstr
Dakins Rev. John H. 29 Gloucester cres
Dalbiac Lt. Gen. Sir Chas. A13, Albany
Dalbiac Hen. esq.10 Duke st. St.James's
DaleRev.Thos.2Amen ct.Paternoster rw
Dale John, esq. 15 Park ter. Highbury
Dale Joseph Langham, esq. 8 Stanhope st. Hampstead rd. & 8 Furnival's inn
Dalgleish Robt. esq. 3 Bloomsbury pl
Dalhousie Earl of, P.C. 21 Hyde park gardens,& Dalhousie castle,Edinburgh
Dallas Hon. Lady,18Henrietta st.Cav.sq
Dallas Hon. Lady, 59 Up. Seymour st
Dallas Lady, 16 Park sq. Regent's park
Dallas Sir RobertC.bt.59Up.Seymour st
Dallas SirRt.C.bt.18Henrietta st.Cav.sq
Dallas Capt. P. W.17 Upper Harley st
Dallas Mrs. 13 Cloudesley st. Islington
Dallet Mrs. 14 Scarsdale ter. Knsgtn
Dalley John, esq. 26 Clapham rd. place
Dalling Sir William Windham, bart. 12 Manchstr.sq.&Earshamhouse,Bungay
Dalling Capt. R.N. 12 Manchester sq
Dalliston Robt. esq. 19 Burton crescent
Dalmahoy Mrs. 13 Nottingham terrace
D'Almaine Thos. esq. 12 Brompton cres
Dalmeny Lord, M.P. 20 Charles st. Berkeley square, & Dalmeny park, near Edinburgh
Dalrymple Col.Sir Adolphus John, bart. 129 Park st. & Delrow house, Watford
Dalrymple Capt. John,M.P. 6 Bolton st. & Culham house, Stranrear
Dalrymple John, esq. 56 Grosvenor st
Dalrymple John, esq. 56Lr.Grosvenor st
Dalrymple Mrs. 4 Colebrook row
Dalrymple Robt. F. esq. 15 Bedford row
Dalston Jonathan N.esq.8A, Hertford st
Dalton Rev.C. B.Chapel stairs,Linc.inn
Dalton Chas. esq. 2 Robert st. Adelphi
Dalton E. esq. 5 Fitzroy st
Dalton John, esq. Pembroke sq. Knsgtn
Dalton Joseph, esq. 21 Bernard st
Dalton Peter J. esq. 6 John st. Adelphi
Dalton Thomas, esq. 6 Artillery pl. west
Daly F. H. esq. 3 Brick court, Temple
Daly Charles Y. esq. 20 Montagu st. Portman square
DalyChas. Y.esq. 20 Mntge. st. Ptmn. sq
Dalzell Mrs. 5 Rosedale ter. Notting hl
Damer Rt. Hon. Col. G. L. D. M.P. 6 Tilney st. Park lane; Came house, Dorchester; & Iron Mills, Queen's county
Dames Capt. 3 St. Alban's pl. St. James'
Dampier C.E. esq. 31 Ladbroke sq. Notg. hill, & 48 Lincoln's inn fields
Dampier John Lucius, esq. 24 Montague place, Russell square
Danby Sam.esq. 4Henrietta st. Brnsk.sq
Dance Charles, esq. Hereford house, 1 Earl's court, Old Brompton
Danford Saml. esq. 14 Margt. st. Cav.sq
Dangerfield Abm. esq. 68 Chancery la
Dangerfield A. E. T. esq. 123 Albany st
Dangerfield John, esq. 26 Craven st. Stnd
Dangerfield John, esq. 68 Chancery lane
Dangerfield John, esq.3Kent ter.Reg.pk
Daniel Edwd. esq. 10 Spencer st. Islgtn
Daniel Geo. Rt. esq. 3 Park sq. Reg. pk
Daniel Henry, esq. 36 Clarges st
Daniel Wm. Thomas Shave, esq. 24 John st. Bedford row, & 41 Chancery lane
Daniell Col. 45 Baker st. Portman sq
Daniell Alfred, esq. 44 Harewood sq
Daniell Alfred B. esq. 31 Cambridge st
Daniell George, esq. 14 Elm Tree road
Daniell Mrs. 7 Brecknock ter. Cmdn. tn
Daniell Mrs. 8 Cloudesley st. Islington
Daniell Mrs. 9 Hertford st. Mayfair
Daniell N. esq. 15 Charlotte st. Fitzr. sq
Daniell Richd. P. esq. 18 Wigmore st
Daniels Abm. esq. 14 Alexandr.sq. Brmp
Daniels Arthur, esq. 16 Annetts cr. Islg
Daniels David, esq. 12 Addison rd. nrth
Daniels Moses. esq. 45 Gt. Coram st
Daniels Mrs. 13 Paddington st. Maryleb
Daniels Mrs. 14 Up. Berkeley st
Dann Henry, esq. 46 Duke st. St. Jas.'s
Dansey Wm. esq. 2 Canterbury villas
Dansey Wm. esq. 41 Green st. Grov. sq
Danvers Fred. D. esq. Duchy of Lancaster off. Lancaster pl. Waterloo bridge
Darby Elde, esq. 5 Queen sq. Westminr
Darby Geo. esq. M.P. 21 Duke st. Westminster; 1 Fig tree ct. Temple; & Markly Warbleton, near Uckfield
Darby Mrs. 6 Charlotte pl. Up. Kenn. la
Darby Mrs. 24 Michael's pl. Brompton
Darby Mrs. 13 Up. Ranelagh st. Pimlico
Darby Walter, esq. 19 Fortess tr. Knt. tn
Darby Wm. A. esq. 3 Charles st. Westbourn terrace
Darcy Alex. esq. 4 Pump ct. Temple
D'Arcy Rev. Charles, 78 Dean st. Soho
D'Arcy Jas. Joseph. esq. 19 Clarendon sq
D'Arcy Wm.A.esq.23Denbigh st. Pmlco
Dardis Capt. R.N. 1 Old Quebec st
Dare Mrs. 31 Hyde park gardens
Dare Rd.W. esq. 10 Harleyford pl. Kngt
Dare Sam. esq. 22 Norfolk cresc. Oxford square, & 8 Old sq. Lincoln's inn
Dark Jas. Hen. esq. 29 St. John's wd. rd
Darke Rt. esq. 4 Devonshire pl.Edgw.rd
Darley Major Gen. 24 North bk.Regt.pk
Darley Capt. Henry, 9 Abbey road
D'Arley Mrs. 23 Hornton st. Kensington
Darling Rev. Thomas, 6 Russell square
Darling George, M.D. 6 Russell square
Darnell Nicholas, esq. 11 New. sq. Lin. in
Darnton Mrs. 28 Lr. Islington terrace
Darnton Wm. esq. 43 Cross st. Islington
Darricarrére A. esq.9 KingWm. st. Stnd
Dart Hen. esq. 15 Warwick villa, Harrow road
Dart Joseph Henry, esq. 20 Southampton buildings
Dart Richd. esq. 43 Albion st. Hyde pk
Dartnell Edw. T. esq. 31 Addison rd. n
Darthez Laurent, esq. 15 Austinfriars
DartiguenaveVictor, esq. 199 Piccadilly
Dartmouth Earl, 23 St. James's sq.; & Sandwell park, Birmingham; &Woodsome, Huddersfield
Dasent Bury esq. 11 Pall mall
Dasent John B. esq. 2 Serjeant's in. Flt.st
DashwoodCapt. 3Westbourne st. Hy. pk

Dashwood Lady Ann, 9 Seamore place, Mayfair, & Hallcott, Bexley, Kent
Dashwood Francis, esq, 9 Seamore pl & Hallcot, Bexley, Kent
Dashwood George Henry, M.P. 248 Oxford st. & West Wycombe pk. Bucks
Dashwood Miss, 4 Dean st. Park lane
Dashwood William Halsey, esq. 3 Clifford's inn, & Cheshunt, Herts
Date John Wm. esq. Kensington palace
Daugars Rev. Wm. G. Parsonage house, St. Martin's-le-grand
Daugart Rev. Wm. Earl's ct.OldBromp
Daukes Mrs. The Elms, Avenue road
Daun Miss, 14 Gloucester rd. Hyde pk
DavenallThos.esq.19Warwick st.Chrg.cr
DavenportB.esq.11Russell pl. Fitzroy sq
DavenportEdw.Davies, esq. 28 Brook st; & Capesthorne, Congleton, Cheshire; & Calverley hall, Tarporley; & Court garden, Great Marlow
Davenport John, esq. 10 Salisbury sq. Fleet st.; & Westwood hall, Leek
DavenportMrs.4 Ordnance tr.St.Jn's.wd
Davenport William, esq.21 Ely place
Davey Lady, 26 Park st. Grosvenor sq
Davey Henry, esq. 6 King st. St.James's
DaveyJ.M. esq. 5 Up.Charles st. Westmr
Davey Mrs. 14 Manchester st. Gra.in.rd
Davey Peter, esq. 1 Sussex pl.Regt.'s pk
DaveyRt. esq.19 Gt.Ormond st.Queen sq
DavidJohn, esq. 24 Brewer st. Golden sq
Davidge John H. esq. 2 Clapham rise
Davidge Mrs. 1 Davidge ter. Walcot pl
DavidsWm.Henry, esq. 49 Brompton rw
Davids Wm. Thos. esq. 5 Coventry st
DavidsonChas. esq. 15 Duke st. Adelphi
DavidsonChs. esq. 6 Stone bdgs.Linc.inn
Davidson Henry, esq. 9 Lime st. sq
Davidson Jas. esq. 36 Essex st. Strand
Davidson M. S. esq. 38 Bloomsbury sq
Davidson Meyer, esq. 36 Gordon sq
Davidson Mrs. 3 Lower Calthorpe st
Davidson N. esq. 40 North st.Mnchtr.sq
DavidsonSeptimus, esq. 22 Basinghall st
Davidson Thos. esq. 13 St. George's pl
Davidson T. P. esq. 4 Theberton st.west
Davidson Walter Stevenson, esq. 16 St. Jas. st. & Inchmarlo, Branchory, N.B
DavidsonW. esq. 10 Portland place
Davie Mrs. Capt. 34 Bedford pl. Knsntn
DaviesSirDavid,M.D.,K.C.H.2Berkley st
DaviesLieut.Col. 8 Coburg pl. Up. Kenn
Davies Rev. Dr. Stepney col.Stepney gn
Davies Rev. Henry, 26 Blandford sq
Davies Rev. John, 43 Horselydown lane
Davies Rev. Rd. 8 Walton pl. Brompton
Davies Daniel, esq. 21 Warwick st
DaviesDaniel Henry, esq. 21 Warwick st
Davies David, esq. 9 Essex st. Islington
Davies David, esq. 18 Euston square
Davies David, esq. 17 Lower Belgrave st
Davies David A. S. esq. M.P. University club, Pall mall east, & Pentrie, Carmarthen
DaviesDavid, esq. 4 Henrietta st.Cov.gr
Davies Dd. esq. 6 Queen sq. Bartholm.cl
Davies Frederick, esq. 19 Up. Gower st
DaviesGeo. esq. 2 Belmont pl.Wandsw.rd
Davies George, esq. 24 Clapham rise
Davies Hy. esq. 4 Grenville st
Davies Hen. M.D. 18 Saville row,Piccdy
Davies Jas. esq. 68 Connaught terrace
Davies HenryTudor, esq. 18 Saville row, & Hall staircase, Inner Temple
Davies Jas. esq. 20 Holland pl.Clapham r
Davies John, esq. 33 Tavistock place
Davies John E. esq. 3 Leonard pl. Kensington, & Irish chambers, Guildhall
Davies John Jones, M.D. 46 Finsbury sq
Davies Miss, 7 Brompton square
Davies Mrs. 5 Craven st. Strand
Davies Miss, 47 Grove place, Brompton
Davies Mrs. 6 Euston grove, Euston sq
Davies Mrs. 20 Northumberland st.Stnd
Davies Mrs. 9 Paradise row, Chelsea
Davies Mrs. Stoke Newington green
Davies P. esq. 18 Glo'ster cresc.Glstr.gt
Davies Thos. esq. 9 Clapham road place
DaviesThos.esq.1Hamilton pl.St.Jn's.wd
DaviesThos. Hugh, esq. 2 Spanish place
DaviesWm. esq. 15 Earl st. ea. Lis.gr.no
Davies Wm.Brisset, esq. 21 Red Lion sq
DaviniereWm.T. esq. 25North bk.Rg.pk
Davis —, esq.2 Melbourne pl.St.Jn's.wd
Davis Abrm. esq. 227 Maida vale,Edg.r
Davis Alex. esq. 22 Addington pl. Cmwl
DavisAllen, esq. 5 Blomfld.rd.Maida hill
Davis Edwd. esq. 17 Up. Belgrave place
Davis Edw. 17 Russell pl. Fitzroy sq
Davis Edwd. esq. 5 Shaftesbury cresc
Davis Elias, esq. 35 Finsbury circus
Davis Geo. esq. 6 Church row, Limeho
Davis George, esq. 119 New Bond st
Davis Grif. esq. 12 Palmer ter. Holloway
Davis Hart, esq. 17 Oxford square
Davis Henry, esq. 52 Up. Bedford pl
DavisHen.jun.esq.6Lansdowne vil.Ng.hl
Davis Hen. Edwin, esq. 33A, Red Lion sq
Davis Horatio Nelson, esq. 16 Russell sq
Davis Isaac, esq. 24 St. James's square
DavisJacob, esq. 8 Artillery pl.Finsbury
Davis Jas. esq. 23 Adams rw.Hmpstd.rd
Davis Jas. esq. 12 Charlotte st. Pntnvl
Davis James, esq. 4 Up. Ranelagh st
Davis Jas. B. esq. 6 Quickset rw. New rd
Davis Jas. Edwd. esq. 1 Elm ct. Temple
Davis John, esq. 9 Baker st. Lloyd sq
Davis Jno. esq. 11 Cloudesley st. Islgtn
Davis Jno. esq. 45 Lr. Belgrave pl. Pmlc
Davis Jno. esq. 14 Palmer ter. Hollwy
Davis John Hall, M.D. 17 Russell place
Davis Joseph, esq. 29 Lower Belgrave st
Davis Joseph, esq. 123 Pall mall
Davis Misses, 10 Hart st. Bloomsbury
Davis Miss, 52 Cumming st. Pentonville
Davis Mrs. 6 Augusta ter. Stockwl. com
Davis Mrs. 2 Clarendon ter. Nttng. hill
Davis Mrs. 18 Great Percy st
Davis Mrs. 20 King st. Finsbury
Davis Mrs. 18 Loraine place, Holloway
Davis Mrs. 49 Notting hill square
Davis Mrs. 5 Park road, Regent's park
Davis Mrs. 73 Portland place
Davis Mrs. 23 Portland ter. Regent's pk
Davis Mrs. 44 Upper Harley st
Davis Mrs. 34 Wharton st. Lloyd sq
Davis Richd. esq. 14 Marlbro' sq. Chels
Davis Richd. esq. 9 St. Helen's pl. Bpsgt
Davis Rd.B. esq. 9 Bedford pl.Kensingtn
Davis Richard S. esq. 13 Chancery lane, & 12 Mecklenburgh sq
Davis Richd.Vaughan, esq.Excise office, Broad st. & Hampstead heath
Davis Robt. esq. 1 Worship sq. Finsbury
Davis Rt.K. esq. 2 Bayham cot.Cmdn. tn
Davis Stephen J. esq. 43 Lonsdale sq
Davis Thos. esq. 40 Beaufort st. Chelsea
Davis Thos. esq. 69 Brook st. & Steeple Aston, Woodstock
DavisThos. John, esq. 5 Bloomsbury pl
DavisThos.Rooke,esq.33North bk.Rg.pk
Davis Val. esq. 4 King Edward st. Islgtn
Davis Walter H. esq. 1 New Boswell ct
DavisWm. esq.24Portland pl.Lr.rd.Islgt
Davis Wm. G. esq. 17 Up. Belgrave pl
Davison Hen. esq. 21 Bury st. St.James's
Davison Hen. esq. 10 King's Bench walk
Davison Miss, 1 Grove end place
Davison Nicholas Fras.M.D.30Russell sq
Davison Wm. esq. 21 Bloomsbury sq
Davison Wm. esq. 12 York st.Covent gdn
Davy SirWm.Gabriel, bart. 83 Jermn. st
Davy Christopher, esq. 11 Furnival's in
DavyDl. esq. 91 Stanhope st.Hmpstd. rd
Davy Jas. G. esq. 26 College st. Islington
Davy John, esq. 32 Myddelton sq
Dawes Richard, esq. 12 Bernard st
Dawes Richd. esq. 5 Blenheim terrace
Dawes S. esq. 17 Goulden ter.Brnsby. rd
DawesWm. esq. 23A, Grove end road, St. John's wood
Dawes W. esq. 15 Serjeants' inn, Fleet st
Dawkins Edw. Jas. esq. 36 Up. Brook st
Dawkins Miss, 31 Upper Grosvenor st
DawsonLadyAnnaM.17Green st.Grov.sq
Dawson Rt. Hon. G. R. 16 Upper Grosvenor st.&CastleDawson,Londonderry
Dawson Hon. Capt. T. V. M.P. 2 Great Stanhope st
Dawson C. esq. 1 Hopkin's bdgs. Islngtn
Dawson Fras. Dennis M. esq. 6 Pump ct
Dawson Fred. esq. 2 Pump ct. Temple
Dawson Fred. esq.3Union pl.Lr.rd.Islgn
DawsonHen.esq.10Farrar's bdgs.Temple
Dawson John, esq. 25 Albemarle st. & Saville place, New Burlington st
Dawson Jno. esq. 5 Mitre ct. chambers
Dawson John, esq. 35 Regent square
Dawson J.W.J. esq. 7 Bloomsbury st
Dawson Mrs. 3 Albion st. Hyde park
Dawson Mrs. 4 Hereford st. Park lane
Dawson Mrs. 4 North pl. Kingsland rd
Dawson Rd. C. esq. 7 Queen sq. Westmr
Dawson Rt. esq. 43 Spencer st. Goswl.rd
Dawson Rt. esq.7 Up.Robert st.Bromptn
Dawson Vesey T. esq.11 New sq. Linc.inn
Dawson Wm. esq.10Holland pl.Clapm.rd
Dawson Wm. esq. 51 Lamb's Conduit st
Dawson Wm.esq. 9Nw.Dorset pl.Clpm.rd
Dawson Wm. esq. 2 Oddy's row, Islntn
Dax Thomas, esq. 70 Connaught terrace, & 8 Old square, Lincoln's inn
DayRev.John,M.A.13A,Plhm.pl.Flhm.rd
Day Abram. esq.15 Egremont pl. New rd
Day Arthur G. esq. 4 Adam st. Adelphi
Day Geo. esq. 3 Lower Southwick st
Day Geo. Thos. esq. 18 Ranelagh grove
Day Hamilton, esq. 41 Camden st. south
Day Henry,esq.4 Somerset st.Portman sq
Day Henry,esq. 36 Michael's pl. Brmptn
Day John, esq. 19 Margaret st
Day John, esq. 20St.John's vil. Acacia rd
Day John, esq. 10 Sussex square
Day Lewis, esq. 9 Salisbury square
Day M. esq. 41 Holywell st. Westminsr
Day Miss, 21 Mornington place
Day Mrs. 22 Liverpool st. King's cross
Day Mrs. 28 Montague st. Russell sq
Day Mrs. 1 Park row, Knightsbridge
Day Mrs. 19 Up. Charles st. Northton. sq
Day Wm. esq. 11 Baker st. Lloyd sq
Day Wm. esq. 55 Lincoln's inn fields
Day Wm. esq. 1 Queen st. Mayfair
Daycock John, esq. 33 King square
Dayman C.O. esq.10 South sq.Gray's inn
Dayment Geo. esq.18Glo'ster st.Queen sq
Deacon Capt. R.N. 12 Leonard pl. Knsng
Deacon Harry C. esq. 68 Up. Norton st
Deacon Hen. esq. 70 Basing pl.Watrlo.pl
Deacon Hen. H. esq. Rectory, Grove, Clapham, & Doctors' commons
Deacon Jas. Wm. esq. 1 Southwick pl
Deacon John, esq. 4 Portman square, & Mabledon park, Tunbridge, Kent
Deacon John, esq. 38 Stamford st. & Ashbridge house, Aldershot, Hants
Deacon Mrs. 156 St. John st. road
Deakins Jas. esq. 57 Gibson square
Deal Mrs. 25 Harleyford pl. Knngtn. cm
De Allex T. M.D. 7Nottingham ter.Nw.rd
Dealtry Miss, 8 Bedford square
Dean Arth. esq.Broad Sanctuary,Westmr
Dean Charles, esq. 435 Oxford st
Dean Chas. esq. 2 St. Agnes villa. Baysw
Dean Geo. esq. 18 Portland pl. Islington
Dean Geo. esq. 4 River ter. City road
Dean Jas. Wm. esq.16 Essex st. Strand
Dean John Colpitts, esq. 36 Chancery la
Dean Rd. Betenson, esq. 31 Albemarle st
Dean Richard Rider, esq. 31 Albemarle st. & 2 New square, Lincoln's inn
Dean Thos. esq. 2 Albion gr. Thrnhl. rd
Dean Thomas, esq. 14 Brunswick sq
Dean Thomas, esq. 435 Oxford st
Dean William, esq. 16 Essex st. Strand
Dean Wm. esq. 109 Guildford st
Deane Rev. John B. 31 Finsbury circus

Deane Chas. esq. 8 Blandford pl. Dorst.sq
Deane Chas. esq. 61 Lincoln's inn fields, & Keekle grove, Whitehaven
Deane Jas. Parker, D.C.L. 6 Porchester ter. Baysw. & 17 College, Doctors' com
Deane Miss, 24 Lower Phillimore pl
Deane Wm. W. esq. 4 York pl. City rd
Deans John, esq. 48 Connaught terrace
Deans Thomas, esq. 23 Fludyer st. Westm
Dear Chas. esq. 85 Milton st. Dorset sq
Dear Rev. Robt. 4 Clement's inn, Strand
Dear Thos. esq. 47 Wharton st. Lloyd's sq
Deare Chas. esq. 8 King's Bench walk
Deare Mrs. Col. 44 Gloucester place
Dearie Charles, esq. Highgate rise
Dearie Chas. esq. 13 Old Jewry chmbrs
Dearie Wm. esq. 15 Portland rd. Regt's.pk
Dearlove Mrs. 32 Orchard st. Prtmn. sq
Dearmer Thos. esq. 2 James st. Haymarkt
Dearsly Hen. Rd. esq. 3 Plowden bldgs
Deason Jas. esq. 31 Keppel st. Russell sq
De Ayala Don R. sec. to Legation from NewGrenada, 39 Up. Baker st. Regts. pk
Debary Miss, 24 Newman st. Oxford st
Debary Peter Fras. esq. 35 Mount st
De Bathe Sir Wm. bart. 27A, Portmn. sq
De Beauvoir Rd. Benyon, esq. 34 Grosvenor sq.; & Englefield house, Reading; & Culford hall, Bury St. Edmunds
Debenham William, esq. 12 Welbeck st
De Berg Monsr. first secretary to the Russian embassy, 30 Dover st
De Bernardy Constne, esq. 21 Cork st
De Blaquiere Lady, 3 Spanish place
DeBlaquiere Hon. John, 3 Spanish place
De Blaquiere Hon. Wm. B. 3 Spanish pl
Deboos Geo. esq. 183 Brick la. Spitalfi
De BoteBaron, 18 Grove end rd. St. Jns. wd
De Bruyn Henry, esq. 34 Hyde park sq
De Burgh Hubert, esq. 44 Brook street, & West Drayton, Hounslow
De Butts Gen. Sir A. 14 Cambridge sq
De Calabrella Baroness, 5 Berkeley sq
Du Cane Capt. Charles, R.N. 64 Lowndes sq. Belgrave square
De Carvalho Custodio P. esq. 2 Ulster pl
De Carvalho Joaa O. esq. 2 Ulster pl
De Castro Don Pedro Perea, attaché to the Span. Legation, 30 Weymouth st
De Castro Hananel, esq. 19 South st. Finsb
De Cetto Baron, envoy extraordinary & minister plenipotentiary from Bavaria, 3 Hill st. Berkeley sq
De Chatelain Le Chevalier Ernest, 27 Grafton pl. Euston sq
De Costa Maurice, esq. 23 Pelham cresc
De Crouy Count, 36 Connaught terrace
De Crouy Countess, 36 Connaught ter
De Daubrawa Henry, esq. 10 Trevor sq
Dedel Monsieur, minister from Holland, 25 Wilton crescent
Dedman William, esq. 22 Bryanstone st
De Dunstanville Lady, 10 Charles st. Berkeley square
Deed John, esq. 20 Mornington cresc
DeedesHn. Chs. esq. 10 Davies st. Brkly. sq
Deedes John, esq. 1 Essex ct. Temple
Deedes Wm. esq. M.P. 68 Eaton place, & Sandling, Kent
Deedes Wm. Henry, esq. 52 Chester sq
DeeleyRd. esq. 9 Belmont pl. Wndswth. rd
Deer Miss, 12 Glo'ster gr. we. O.Brmptn
Deering John Peter, esq. 40 South st.; & the Lee, Great Missenden, Bucks
Deey Rev. Wm. 7 St. Thomas st. Boro'
Deffell Geo. H. esq. 7 King's Bench walk
Deffell Henry, esq. 17 Queen Anne st
Deffell John Henry, esq. 38 Up. Harley st
De Freyne Lord, 45 Oxford ter. Edgware rd.; & French park, Roscommon
Defries N. esq. 26 Grafton st. Fitzroy sq
Degex Edw. esq. 44 Hunter st. Brnswk. sq
Degex John P. esq. 5 New sq. Lin. inn
De GreyEarl, K.G., K.P., P.C. 4 St. James's sq.; West pk. Silsoe; Cowes; Putney heath; & Newby hall, Boroughbridge
De GuichyP. esq. 1 Diddington pl. Cldn. rd
De Hagne John, esq. 26 Cross st. Islntn
De Horsey Spencer Horsey, esq. 8 Up. Grosvenor st
Deinhard Chas. esq. 2 Albert pl. Vict. rd
De Koudriaffsky M. secretary to the Russian embassy, 30 Dover st
De la Beche Sir Hen. T. knt. 5&6 Craig's ct
Delacourt Thos. esq. King's rd. Chelsea
Delafeld Count & Lady Cecil, 44 Brook st
Delafield Wm. esq. 4 Stanhope pl. Hy. pk
Delafosse Fras. esq. 32 Oxford terrace
De Lagos Baron, 10 Southwick crescent
De la Grange le Comte, attaché to the French embassy, 20 Manchester sq
Delamere Lord, 33 Upper Brook street; & Vale Royal, Northwich
De Lancy Col. 68 Haymarket
Delane Wm. Fred. Aug. esq. 4 Chatm. la
Delaney Andrew, esq. 1 London st. City
De Lannoy Wm. esq. 42 Guilford st
Delany E. M.D. 98 Chalton st. Somers tn
Delap Col. 42 Harley street, & Stoke park, Guilford
Delarue Daniel, esq. 15 Judd place east
De la Torre Mrs. 22 Gloucester place
DelavanteJ. esq. 3 Kimbolton pl. Brmptn
Delawarr Earl, P.C. 7 Up. Grsvnr. st; Caxton; & Buckhurst pk. TunbridgeWells
De la Zouche Baroness, 24 Upper Brook st. & Barham, Petworth
De Leiros A. esq. 41 York st. Portmn. sq
De LeonI. M. esq. 12 Carlton vil. Edgw. rd
Delepierre Octave, esq. attaché to the Belgium Embassy, 50 Portland place
Delepierre Octavius, esq. 44 Welbeck st
Delepierre Madame, 44 Welbeck st
Delferier Wm. esq. 40 Sloane square
Delille Charles J. esq. 32 Ely place
Delille Mons. 33 Michael's pl. Bromptn
De L'Isle & Dudley Lord, G.C.H. 16 New Burlington st. & Penshurst, Tonbridge
De Lisle Ferd. esq. 16 Devonshire sq
De Lisle Fredk. esq. consul general for Monte Video, 1 York pl. Portman sq
De Lisle Peter, esq. 33 Gibson square
Dell John, esq. 5 Burton st. Burton crsnt
Dell Jph. esq. 3 Bedford pl. Hampstd. rd
Dell Leonard, esq. 11 Halkin st. west
Dell Wm. Westly, esq. 5 Augustus sq
Delmar Baldock, esq. 10 New inn, Strnd
Delmar George, esq. 49 Devonshire st. Portland place, & 46 Lincoln's inn flds
De Lowenburgh Baron, 44 Brook st
Delplanque Louis, esq. 75 Baker st
Delves Wm. esq. 18 Avenue rd. Rgts'. pk
DemaidSam. esq. 8 Southmptn. row. Nw. r
DemantSam. esq. 28 Maddox st. Regent st
De Mattos Thomas, esq. 73 Regent st
De Mauley Lord, Clarendon hotel, 169 N.Bond st. & Canford house, Wimborne
De Medina Hen. A. esq. 10 Argyle sq
Demole Issabel, esq. Courland, Wnds. rd
De Moncorvo Baron da Torre, Portuguese envoy extraordinary, 57 Upper Seymour st. Portman square
De Moray Mrs. 1 Orme square, Bayswtr
De Morgan Aug. esq. 7 Cmdn. st. south
De Morgan Geo. esq. 13 Titchfield terr. Regent's park, & 30 Lincoln's inn flds
De Morgan Mrs. 17 Manchester st
De Mounteney T. J. B. esq. 16 Pelham rd
Dempsey Geo. D. esq. 101 Gt. Russell st
Denbigh Earl of, P.C. 44 Eaton square; Newnham Paddox, Lutterworth; & Upper lodge, Bushy park, Middlesex
Denby Thomas, esq. 37 Cloudesley ter
Dence Robert, esq. 3 Stonefield st
Dendy S. esq. 16 Montague st. & Dorking
Dene Geo. B. esq. 10 Hemingford terr
DenewJas. esq. 30 Charles st. Berkeley sq
Denham Rev. Joshua Fredk. 1 New inn
Denham John Charles, esq. 89 Pall mall
Denison Edmund Beckett, esq. M.P. 8 Duke st. Westminster; 10 New sq. Lincoln's inn; & Doncaster
DenhamJ. C. esq. Mulberry ho. Lit. Chls
Denison John Evelyn, M.P. Burlington house, 49 Piccadilly, & Ossington hall, Tuxford, Notts
Denison Step. Chas. esq. 4 Harcourt blgs
Denison Wm. Joseph, esq. M.P. 90 Pall mall, & Denbies, near Dorking
Denman Lord, P.C. 38 Portland place, & Stoney Middleton, Bakewell, Derby
DenmanHon. Capt. Josph. 38 Portland pl
Denman Hon. Richd. 50 Torrington sq. & 3 Paper buildings, Temple
Denman George L. esq. 4 Curzon st
Denman John, esq. 74 Upper Norton st
Denman Miss, 74 Up. Norton st. Fitz. sq
Denman Thos. esq. 83 Quadrant, Regent st. & 7 Buckingham st. Fitzroy sq
Denne W. esq. 6 Lower Berkeley st
Dennington Jas. esq. 24 Northampton sq
Dennis Geo. esq. 7 Gt. Vine st. Regt. st
Dennis James, esq. 8 King's Bench walk
Dennis John, esq. 18 Up. Southwick st
Dennis Mrs. 34 Bryanstone st. Prtmn. sq
Dennis Wm. esq. Pembrok vil. Caledn. rd
Dennison Robert, esq. 9 Gray's inn sq
Dennison Wm. esq. 3 Prtld. ter. Wndsw. rd
Dennistoun John, esq. M.P. 29 Grosvenor square, & Glasgow
Denny Capt. 32 Cambridge ter. Hyde pk
Denny Thomas A. esq. 2 Lr. Southwick st
Dennys Nicholas, esq. 40 Mornington pl
De Noailles Count Louis, sec. to the French embassy, 20 Manchester sq
De Noual Baroness, 24 Up. Phillimore pl
Dent Edwd. J. esq. the Mall, Kensington
Dent Miss, 8 Fitzroy square
Dent Miss, 18 New st. Dorset square
Dent Mrs. 10 Hertford st. Mayfair, & Barton cottage, Christchurch, Hants
Dent Richd. esq. 28 Bayham terrace
Dent Thomas, esq. 8 Hyde park terrace
Dent Wm. esq. 10 Clarence pl. New rd
DentVilliers, esq. 7 Clarendon pl. Hydepk. sq. & Avon cottage, Ringwood, Hants
Denton Henry, esq. 60 Lincoln's inn fields, & 6 New square, Lincoln's inn
Denton John, esq. 3 Garden court, Temple, & Plassdraw, Ruthin
Denton John Bailey, esq. 9 Gray's inn sq
Denton Sam. jun. esq. 15 Gray's inn sq. & 8 Camden cottages, Camden town
Denton Sam. esq. 10 Park village east
Denys Sir George Wm. bart. 15 Stratford place
Denys Misses, 9 Wellngtn. tr. St. Jn's. wd
De Paiva M. Augustus, secretary to Brazilian embassy, 16 Milton st. Dorset sq
De PedrorenaDonMiguel, 3 Up. Gordon st
De Pedrorena Don Victoriano, sec. of Spanish Legation, 9 Cavendish sq
De Pinna Joseph, esq. 15 Tavistock sq
De PinnaJoshua, esq. 38 Alpha rd. Rgt. pk
De Pollon Count Nomis, envoy extraordinary & minister plenipotentiary from Sardinia, 11 Low. Grosvenor st
De Pontigny Mrs. 42 Tavistock square
De Prati Joachim, M.D. 23 Cloudesley sq. Islington, & 4 Mortimer st. Cav. sq
De Preville Miss R. 25 Dorchester place
Derbishire John, esq. 3 Grafton st
Derby, Earl of, K.G., P.C. 23 Grosvenor sq. & Knowsley hall, Prescot, Lancashire
Derby Wm. esq. 12 Osnaburgh st
Derby Cobbett, esq. 2 George st. Portman sq. & Houghton
Derby Cobbett, esq. 2 Harcourt bldngs
Derick J. M. esq. 12 Buckingham st. Strd
De Riemer G. esq. 4 Manor pl. Chelsea
Dering Sir Edwd. Chomley, 81 Jermyn st. & Surrenden, Dering, Kent
Dering Cholmeley C. W. esq. 2 Chapel st. Grsv. sq. & Ayott, St. Lawrence, Welwyn
Dermer Edward Corduit, esq. 23 Albion terrace, Wandsworth road
Dermer Mrs. 20 Hemus ter. Chelsea
Dermott G. D. esq. 16 Bloomsbury st

De Ros Lord, Adjt. Genl.'s office, Horse Guards, & Strangford, Downshire
De Ros Hon. Capt. 116 Piccadilly
De Rothschild Baron A. Grosvenor pl. & Gunnersburg park, Ealing
De Rothschild L. N. esq. consul gen. for Austria, 2 New ct. St. Swithin's lane
De Russett Geo. esq. 27 Grove end road
De St. Croix Jasper, esq. 21 Hans place
Desanges Sir Francis, knt. 30 Upper Seymour st. Portman square
De Saumarez Lord, United University club, & Cheltenham
De Sausmarez J. esq. 1 Fig tree ct. Temple
Desbarres Misses, 19 Up. Phillimore pl
Despard Henry P. esq. 5 Durham pl. Chls
D'Este Sir Augustus, 35 Up. Berkeley st
De Starck Adml. 10 Kensingtn. crescent
Desvignes Elise H. esq. 2 Golden sq
Des Vœux Sir Chas. bart. 7 Belgrave sq
De Symons Aaron, esq. 24 Glo'ster rd. Hy. p
De Symons S. L. esq. 9 Cumberland st
De Tabley Lord, 10 Grosvenor sq. & Tabley house, Knutsford, Cheshire
Dethier Mrs. 30 Edwards st. Portman sq
Dettmar Geo. esq. 25 Mecklenburgh sq
Dettmer Saml. esq. 3 Brecknock cr
Dettmer Wm. 60 Howland st
Devall Mrs. 46 Upper Berkeley st. west
DeVandes Count, 144 Oxford st. & Hastngs
Devarley Madame, 16 Up. Berkeley st. w
Devas Thos. esq. 23 Finchley new rd
De Vear Thos. esq. 8 Kensington cresc
Devenish Mrs. 14 Cambridge st. Edg. rd
Devenport Hen. D. esq. 50 Lincoln's i. fds
Deverell John, esq. 5 Gray's inn square
De Vesci Viscount, Abbey Leix, Queen's county, Ireland
Devey Fredk. Nicholls, esq. 34 Ely place
Devey Wm. esq. 6 Dorset pl. no. Clpm. rd
Devils Louis, esq. 12 Brunswick par
Devisme Mrs. 6 St. Andrew's pl. Regt's. pk
De Vitery Jsph. esq. 6 Duncan tr. City rd
De Vitre M.T. D. esq. 9 Southwick cresct
Devon Earl of, 4 Bryanstone square; & Powderham castle, Exeter
Devon Chas. esq. 36 Queen sq. Bloomsby
Devonald Eras. L. esq. 71 Gt. Titchfild. st
Devonshire, Duke of, K.G., P.C. 78 Piccadilly; Chiswick; Chatsworth & Hardwick, Derbyshire; & Lismore castle, Waterford
Dew James, esq. 10 Claremont terrace
Dew Mrs. 11 Smith st. Chelsea
Dewar David, esq. 16 Tyndale pl. Islngtn
DewarDav. A. B. esq. 25 York ter. Regts. pk
Dewar Jas. esq. 6 Charles st. Lowndes sq
Dewar Miss, Larkhall rise, Clapham
Dewdney Wm. esq. 2 Green's rw. Chels
Dewey Geo. esq. 60 Myddelton square
Dewey John, esq. 1 Cavendish road
Dewhurst Thomas, esq. 21 Stonefield st
Dewick Edwin, esq. 3 Belinda terrace
Dewint Peter, esq. 40 Upper Gower st
De Wuits Count, 37 York st. Portman sq
Dexter Sam. esq. 22 King sq. Goswell rd
D'Eyncourt Rt. Hon. Charles Tennyson, M.P. 1 John st. St. James's, & Baynes manor, Market Raisin
D'Eyncourt Louis C.T. esq. 11 Paper bldgs
De Zoete Sam. esq. 41 Gower st
Diamond Hugh W. esq. F.S.A. 22 Frith st
DiamondWmB. esq. 17 Weston st. Smrs. tn
Dibbin F. W. esq. 22 Chester pl. Kenngtn
DibdinRv. T.F. D.D. 28A, Up. Yk. st. Bry. sq
Dibdin Rev. R. W. 7 Caroline st. Bedfd sq
Dibdin T.C. esq. 23 Charltt. st. Fitzroy sq
Dick Chas. Geo. esq. 2 Cloisters, Temple
Dick J. esq. 8 North crescent, Bedford sq
Dick Mrs. 9 Eaton terrace, Eaton sq
Dick Mrs. 47 Upper Harley st
Dick Quintin, esq. M.P. 20 Curzon st. & Layer Marney hall, Kelvedon
Dick Robert, M.D. 12 Bentinck st
Dick Wm. Fleming, esq. 3 Sussex place
Dicken Rev. Chas. R.M.A. Charterhouse
Dickens Mrs. 13 Scarsdale tr. Kngstn
Dickens Thomas, esq. 1 Kilburn priory
Dickens Wm. Saml. esq. 18 Tibberton sq
Dickenson Genl. 3 Norland pl. Nttg. hl
Dickenson Lowes, esq. 114 New Bond st
Dickenson Robt. esq. 114 New Bond st
Dickenson William, esq. 2 Kingswood pl. South Lambeth
Dicker Wm. esq. 2 Beaufort pl. Chelsea
Dickerson Capt. Thos. R.N. 38 Groveend rd
Dickerson Mrs. 5 Princes ct. Westmnr
Dickie Miss Maria, 29 Clapham rise
Dickinson Rev. Wm. Hen. 5 Maddox st
Dickinson Fras. Henry, esq. M.P. 8 Upper Harley st. & King weston, Somerton
Dickinson Fredk. esq. 15 Gibson square
Dickinson Jas. esq. 24 Old sq. Linc. inn
Dickinson James, esq. 17 Wigmore st
Dickinson John, esq. 4 Furnival's inn
Dickinson Mrs. 8 New Millman st
Dickinson Mrs. 12 Gt. Coram st
Dickinson Mrs. 55 Russell square
Dickinson Nodes, esq. 17 Wigmore st
Dickinson Wm. esq. 7 Curzon st
Dickinson Wm. esq. 37 Sloane st
Dickinson Wm. jun. esq. 19 Lowndes st
Dickinson Wm. R. esq. 2 Ladbroke villas
Dickinson Wm. R. esq. 19 Lowndes st
Dickman D. esq. 14 Porchester place
Dickman Jas. esq. 5 North ter. Brmptn
Dicksee Rt. J. esq. 53 O. Cmptn. st. Soho
DickseeT.F. esq. 23 Howland st. Fitzroy sq
Dickson Commr. R.N. 18 Adam st. Adelphi
Dickson Major, 11 Pembroke sq. Knsgtn
Dickson Alfred, esq. 51 Hunter st
Dickson Edw. S. esq. 24 Old sq. Lin. inn
DicksonGeo. F. esq. consl.-gen. for Buenos Ayres, 20 Hanover ter. Regent's pk. & 1 Winchester bdgs. City; & Abbots Reading, Ulverstone
Dickson Peter, esq. 5 Chester terrace
Dickson Robert, M.D. 5 Curzon st
Dickson Samuel, M.D. 28 Bolton st
Dickson Thos. esq. 23 Nottingham pl
DicksonWm. esq. 7 Ladbroke pl. Notng. hi
Dickson Wm. Hen. esq. 32 Doughty st
Diether Miss, 28 Everett st. Brnswk. sq
Dietrischen Mrs. 78 Newman st
D'Iffanger Mrs. 8 New Quebec st
Digby Earl of, 35 Brook st. Grosvenor sq. & Sherborne castle, Dorset
Digby Col. 6 Chapel st. Grosvenor sq
Digby Mrs. 15 Aberdeen pl. Maida hill
Digby Edward St. Vincent, esq. & Lady Theresa, 31 Old Burlington st. & Minterne house, Cerne, Dorsetshire
Diggles George, esq. 4 Great College st. Westminster
Dighton Isaac, esq. 40 Torrington sq
Dighton Robt. esq. 1 Brompton grove
Dighton Thos. D. esq. 2 Lr. Grosvenr. pl
Dighton Wm. E. esq. 40 Torrington sq
Dilke Capt. R.N. 15 Chapel st. Grosvnr. sq
Dilke Chas. W. esq. 9 Lr. Grosvenor pl
Dilke Mrs. 15 Chapel st. Grosvenor sq
Dilke Wentworth, esq. 76 Sloane st
Dillon Viscount, 16 Halkin st. west, Belgrave square; & Loughlyn house, Loughlyn, Ireland; & Ditchley, Oxon
Dillon Dowager Visc. 49 Wilton cres
Dillon Hon. Arthur, 6 Lr. Belgrave st
Dillon Hon. Gerald, 49 Wilton crescent
DillonHon. Mrs. 12 Grafton st. Nw. Bond st
Dillon Capt. Sir W. H. R.N. 22 Arundel st. & Heath lodge, Hanwell
Dillon John, esq. 5 Kensington grdn. ter
Dimes Wm. esq. 46 Lincoln's inn fields
DimondC. J. esq. 10 Henrietta st. Cvnsh. sq
Dimsdale Fredk. esq. 17 Clement's inn
DimsdaleJ. esq. 5 Brunswick pl. Regt.'s pk
Dimsdale Hon. Baron & Baroness, Mivart's hotel, & Camfield pl. nr. Hatfield
Dines Mrs. 12 Woburn buildings
Dingle John K. esq. 31 Upper Eaton st
Dingle Miss, 26 Up. Eaton st. Pimlico
Dingley Miss, 24 Paddington green
Dinorben Lord, 75 South Audley st. & Kinmell park, St. Asaph
Disbrowe the Misses, Kensington palace
Dismore Thos. esq. 1 Milner st. Islngtn
Disney Gen. Sir Moore, K.C.B. 26 Up Brook st. & Manor house, East Acton
Disney Geo. C. esq. 24 Duke st. Foley pl
Disney James Cathrow, esq. Heralds' college, Doctors' commons
Disney Mrs. 4 Up. Eaton pl. Havrstk. hl
D'IsraeliBenj. esq. M.P. 1 Grosvenor gate, & Bardenham house, High Wycombe
Ditchfield James, M.D. 4 Gordon st
Dive Major, 3 Tavistock st. Bedford sq & Millwick hall, near Stone
Ditchburn Thos. esq. 18 St. John's wd. rd
Divett Edw. esq. M.P. 79 Eaton sq. & Bystock, Exmouth, Devonshire
DixC. esq. 10 Claremont rw. Barnsbury rd
Dix John E. esq. 2 Bedford st. Euston sq
Dix Rd. esq. 10 Symond's inn, Chancery la
Dixey Alf. esq. 36 Gibson sq. Islington
Dixon Lieut. Col. 33 Harley st
Dixon Col. 97 Mount st. Berkeley sq
Dixon Edward, esq. 66 Wardour st. Soho
Dixon Fred. Seekamp, esq. Radnor cot. King's rd. Chelsea, & 1 Angel ct. Bank
Dixon George, esq. 7 Kennington ter
Dixon James, esq. 19 Cambridge sq
Dixon Jas. Hen. esq. Tollington park, Hornsey rd. & 13 St. Swithin's lane
Dixon John, esq. 37 Broad st. buildings
DixonJohn, esq. 16 Clapham rd. pl. Claphm
Dixon John, esq. 48 Doughty st
Dixon Joseph, esq. 3 Macclesfield st
DixonJ.B. esq. 2 Crescent pl. Burton cresc
Dixon Mrs. 15 Canonbury square
Dixon Mrs. 15 Portland ter. Regent's pk
Dixon Robt. esq. 26 Canonbury villas
Dixon Thos. esq. 33 Cloudesley st. Islngtn
Dixon Thomas Henry, esq. 31 Mornington crescent, & 5 New Boswell court
DixonWm. esq. 26 Southampton rw. Rus. sq
DixonWm. H. esq. 2 Wellington tr. St. Jn's w
Dixon, Brooks & Dixon, 25 Chancery la
Doane Chas. esq. 14 Berners st
Doane Rich. esq. 2 New inn bldgs. Strand
Dobbing Rt. esq. 21 York pl. City road
Dobell John, esq. 11 Upper Fitzroy st
Dobie Alexander, esq. 4 Hyde park terrace, & 2 Lancaster place, Strand
Dobie John, esq. 45 Wilmington sq. Spafields, & 2 Raymond bldgs. Gray's inn
Dobinson Jas. Geo. esq. 10 Gray's inn sq
Dobinson Joseph, esq. 15 Regent st
Dobles Walter, esq. 6 Lodge rd. Regt's pk
DobreeBonamy, esq. 16 Gt. Cumberland st
Dobree Geo. jun. esq. 22 Hart st. Bloomsby
Dobree Geo. esq. 19 Russell pl. Fitzroy sq
Dobson Sir Richard, 47 Gloucester pl
Dobson Rev. J. 37 Edward st. Hmpstd. rd
Dobson Henry, esq. 7 New Millman st
Dobson Wm. esq. 3 Verulam buildings
Docksey John, esq. 61 Doughty st
Dod Charles, esq. 16 Gt. Marlborough st
Dod Jn. Coucher, esq. 3 Manor ter. Chelsea
Dodd George, esq. M.P. 9 Grosvenor pl
Dodd Grantham Robt. esq. 13 Claremont sq. & 26 New Broad st. City
Dodd John, esq. 12 Portman st. Portman sq. & 1 Bryanstone st
Dodd Miss C. 51 Dorset st. Salisbury sq
Dodd Miss, 14 Judd pl. east, New rd
Dodd Moses, esq. 18 Albion gr. Thrnhl. rd
Dodd Mrs. 8 York buildings, New rd
Dodgson Geo. esq. 21 Mornington pl
Dodgson Geo. esq. 4 Up. Bedford pl. Kens
DodgsonHassardH. esq. 7 King's Bnch. wk
DodsJas. Maitland, esq. 102 St. Martin's la
Dodson Sir John, knt. LL.D. 12 Hertford st. Mayfair; & 14 College, Doctors' com.; & Hurstperpoint, Sussex
Dodson George Peter, esq. 20 Southampton bldgs. Chancery la. & 14 College sq
Dodson Jas. esq. 7 Warwick vil. Maida h
DodsworthRev. Wm. Glo'ster gt. Rgt.'s pk

Dodwell Miss, 21 Woburn place
Doery Miss, 59 St. John's wood terrace
Dolan Laurence, esq. 8Judd pl.ea.New rd
Dolber Mrs. 24 Paddington st
Dolby Misses, 79 Harley st. & Brizes, Brentwood, Essex
Dolby Mrs. & Miss, 61 Berners st
Dole Mrs. 9 Dalby terrace, City road
Dollard Rev. Jas. 2 Acton pl. Camden rd
Dolman Fredk. Wm. esq. 27 Carey st
Dolman Jas. esq. 1 Augusta ter. Stockwl
Dolman James, esq. 14 Clifford's inn
Doman Mrs. 8 Charlotte st. Pimlico
Domvile Sir Compton, bart. 5 Grosvenor sq. & Santry house, Dublin
DomvilleWm.H.esq.31Charlesst.Bkly.sq
Donaldson George, esq. Hawthorn cottage, 21 Park village east
Donaldson Geo. Hay, esq. 39Harewood sq
Donaldson Henry, esq. 28 Sackville st
Donaldson John, esq. 1Highbury pk. nth
Donaldson John, esq. 39 Westbourne ter
Donaldson Stuart, esq. 4 Up. Hyde pk. st
Donaldson Thos. L. esq. 71 Russell sq. & 3 Pelham terrace, Brompton
Donaldson Wm. L. esq. 18 Southampton st. Bloomsbury
Donegal Dowager Marchioness, 15 Chesham place, Belgrave square
Donegal, Marquis of, G.C.H., P.C. 28 Lowndes st. Belgrv. sq.; & Ennishawen, County Donegal; & Carrickfergus, County Antrim; & Ormeau, Belfast
Donelan John, esq. 9Fonthill pl.Clapham
Doneraile Viscount, Limmers' hotel, & Doneraile house, Mallow
Donidieu Alcide, esq. 8 Duke st. St.Jas.'s
Donkin Bryan, esq. F.R.S. 6 Paragon New Kent road
Donkin John, esq. Corrie pl. Old Kent rd
Donkin Mrs. 10 Porchester pl. Edgw. rd
Donne Edward, esq. 50 Upper Harley st
Donne John, esq. 2Powis pl.Gt.Ormnd.st
Donne John Geo. esq. 22 Up.Seymour st. & Whitlands, near Lyme Regis
Donne Miss, 186 Blackfriars road
Donnelly Mrs. 51 Charlotte st. Prtld. pl
Donoughmore, Earl of, K.P. Knocklofty house, Clonmel; & Palmerstone house, Dublin
Donovan Mrs. 4 Ladbroke pl. Notting hl
Donthorn John Wm. esq. 18 Hanover st
Doran Rev. Dr. John, 16 Lonsdale sq
Dorchester Lord, Stuffings, Maidenhead
Doria A. A. esq. 4 Old sq. Lincoln's inn
Dorington Jas.Thos. esq.16Parliament st
Dorington Jn. E. esq. 11 Queen sq.Wstm
DormerLord, Peterley house, Amersham, & Grove park, Warwick
Dorrell E. esq. 43 Warren st. Fitzroy sq
D'Orsay Count, Gore ho. Kensingt. Gore
Dosell Jas. esq. 3 South ter. Alxndr. sq
D'Ossuna Duke, Mivart's hotel
Doswell Thos. esq, 17 Upper Charles st
Dotasio Chas. esq. 19 Grosvenor st. west
Dottin Capt. A. R. 31 Argyll st. Regent st. & Bugle hall, near Southampton
Doubleday George, esq. 16 Gerrard st
DoubledayWm.esq. 20Kensington cresct
Douce Capt. 17 St.Alban's pl. St.James's
Douce John, esq. Nw.Nth.st. RedLion sq
Doudney E.P.esq. 18Paradise ter.Lvp.rd
Dougal Capt. George, 24 Tibberton sq
Dougan Jas. esq. New chambers, Foregate, Clement's inn
Doughty Ed.esq.4William st.Lowndes sq
Doughty John, esq. 38 Duncan terrace
Doughty Mrs. 8 Elm ter. Lit. Chelsea
Doughty Thos. N. esq. 15 Queen's bdg. Brompton
Douglas Marquis, 12 Portman square
DouglasLord, 6St.George's pl.Hyd.pk.cr. & Douglas & Bothwell castles, Lanark
DouglasSir Howard, bt. G.C.M.G., C.B., M.P., F.R.S., 15 Green st. Grosvenor square, & Carr, Perthshire
Douglas Hon. Chas. 6 St. George's pl
Douglas Sir C. E. M.P. 27 Wilton cres
Douglas Admiral J. E. 34 Charles st. Berkeley square
Douglas Rev. Alexander H. 69 Chester sq
Douglas Archibald, esq. 44 Brook st
Douglas Chas. esq. 12 America square
Douglas James, esq. 16Hyde park square, & Chilston park, near Maidstone, Kent
Douglas J. D. S. esq. M.P. Jun. United Service club, & Chilstone park, Maidstone
Douglas John M. esq. 36A, Belvedere rd
Douglas Jsph. esq. 4 Garden ct. Temple
Douglas Jsph. esq. 3 Trevor ter. Kntsbrg
Douglas Miss, 32 Chapel st. Grosvnr. pl
Douglas Mrs. 65 Eaton pl. Belgrave sq. & Burseldon house, Southampton
Douglas Mrs. 11 Milton st. Dorset sq
Douglas Mrs. 21 New Ormond st
Douglas Sholto J. esq. 10 Farrar bldgs
Douglass Hon. Mrs. 11 Queen sq. Blmsby
Douglass J. A. esq. 11 Queen sq. Blmsby
Douglass Robt. Johnstone, esq. 144 Oxford st. & Coton house, Rugby
Douglass Robt. esq. Stoke Newington gr
Douro Marquis of, M.P. 3Up.Belgrave st
DouseWm.Hen.esq.51Grove pl.Bromptn
Doutty John, esq.33 Belitha vl.Bnsby.rd
Dove John, esq. 27 Bernard st. Russell sq
Dove Joseph, esq. 9 New Millman st
Dove Mrs. 51 George st. Portman sq
Dove Wm. Spencer, esq. 20 Milner sq
Dover Lady, Dover house, Whitehall
Dover Henry John, esq. 2 Everett st
DoverHen. J. esq. 12South sq.Gray's inn
Dover Mrs. 33 Claremont square
DovetonMaj.Gen.SirJ.K.C.B.5 Sussex sq
Doveton Maj. 50 Norland sq. Notting hl
Doveton Bazett, esq. 37 Gloucester pl
Dow Miss, 13 Albert ter. Knightsbridge
Dow Mrs. 19 High row, Knightsbridge
Dow Wm. Alex. esq. 13 Nelson sq. & 9 King's Bench walk, Temple
Dowbiggin Major, 5 Bayswater ter
Dowbiggin Thomas, esq. Abercorn lodge, Up. Hamilton ter. St. John's wood
Dowdall John, esq. 20 Great Quebec st
Dowden Mrs. 11 Bulstrode st
Dowdeswell Rev.Dr. 48Up.Grosvenor st. & Stanford Rivers, Ongar, Essex
Dowdeswell Geo. M. esq.5 Crown off. rw
Dowdeswell John Edm. esq. 7 Park pl. St. James's; & Masters' off. Southampton bldgs.; & Pull ct. Tewkesbury
Dowdeswell Wm. esq. M.P. 7 Park pl. St. James's & Pull ct. near Tewkesbury
Dowding Chas. esq. 55 Oxford terrace
Dowding Miss, 24 Mecklenburgh square
Dowding Wm. esq. 15 Cross st. Islingtn
Dowers Mrs. 32 York pl. Portman sq
DowglassT. esq. 2 Marlbro'pl.St.Jn.'swd
Dowland Mrs. 8 Hill road, St.John's wd
Dowley John, esq. 35 Howland st.Fitz.sq
Dowling Capt. 2 Stafford row, Pimlico
Dowling Mr. Serjeant, Tanfield chambs
Dowling James, esq. 38 Foley place
Dowling Thos. esq. 4 Princes st. Hnvr. sq
Dowling Vincent G.esq. 4 Norfolkst.Strd
Downard Thos. esq. 3 Gerrard st. Islngt
Downe Viscount, 30 Upper Brook st.; & Benningborough Hall, York; &Cowick hall, Snaith; & Danby lodge, Gainsborough; & Sessay, Thirsk, Yorkshire
Downer Campbell J.esq.6&7NwBridge st
Downes Lord, K.C.B. Carlton Club & Bert House, Athy, Kildare
Downes Commander Henry, R.N. United Service Institution, Middle Scotland yard, & 8 Ladbroke ter. Notting hill
Downes C. esq.14 Warwick st.Charingcr
Downes Edwd. esq. 30Hyde pk. sq.; Furnivals inn; & Mardock's house, Ware
Downes John, esq. 6 Bedford pl. Russ. sq
Downes John Jas. esq. 1 College ter. Isl
Downes Mrs. 61 Harley st
Downes Thos. Rd.esq.16 p.Belgravepl
Downham Wm.esq.22York pl.Fulhamrd
Downing Charles, esq. 57 Gt. Coram st
Downing F. esq. 22 Camden tr.Camdentn
Downing Fras. esq. 13 King's rd. Bdfd rw
Downing Geo. esq. King's rd. Chelsea
Downing Miss, 1 Up.Ranelagh st. Pimlico
Downing Thomas, esq. 74 Sloane st
DownshireMarquisof, K.P.21Hanoversq.; & Hillsborough castle, Hillsborough, Downshire; & Easthampstead park, Bracknell, Berks
Dowse T. esq. 39 Charlotte st. Fitzroy sq
Dowse Wm. H. esq. 77 Chancery lane
Dowson Joseph, esq. 22 Grove end road
Dowson Mrs. 3 Sebbons bldgs Islngtn
Doxat Chas. esq. 15 Somers pl.Cambgesq
Doxat L. esq. 30 Henrietta st. Cov. grdn
Doxat Mrs. 3 Lavender hill tr.Wdswh.rd
Doyel Miss, 3 Melcombe pl. Dorset sq
Doyl John, esq.17Cambrdge.ter.Edgw.rd
Doyle Lady, 30 Baker st
Doyle Sir Francis Hastings, bt. 17 Serjeants' inn, & 20 Grafton st. Bond st
Doyle Edward, esq. 48 Bedford row
Doyle Miss, 16 Arlington st
Doyle Miss, 18 Charles st. Berkeley sq
Doyle Mrs. Gloucester cottage, Gloucester gate, Regent's park
Doyley John, esq 36 Up. Barnsbury st
Doyley Wm. esq. 6 John st. Adelphi
D'Oyly Maj.-Gen. 25 Eaton square
D'Oyly Thomas, S.L. 2 Upper Harley st. & Rottingdean, Brighton
Draffen Jsph. W. esq. 78 Cambridge ter
Drake Lieut. Col. 21 Harley st
Drake Fras. esq. 34 Bouverie st. Fleet st
Drake John, esq. 6 Pelham crescent
Drake J. Collard, esq. 19 Elm tree rd
Drake Joseph, esq. 14 Camden road villas
Drake Philip, esq. 42 Leicester square
Drake Richard, esq. 3 Brompton place
Drake Thomas, esq. 14 Keppel st
Drake Thomas Tyrwhitt, esq. 29 Belgrave sq.; & Bucknell, Bicester; & Shardeloes, Amersham
Draper Hastings D. esq. 45 Vincent sq
Draper Hen. esq. 7 Brunswickpl.Bnsy.rd
Draper Mrs. 58 Charlotte st. Portland pl
Draper Mrs. 8 Grove ter. St. John's wd
Draper Mrs. 142 Sloane st. Chelsea
Drax John S. Wanley Sawbridge E. esq. M.P. Coulson's hotel, 45 Lwr. Brook st
Draycott Hy. Rd.esq. 4 Lr.Phillimore pl
Drayton Thos. esq. Park Village east
Dreager B.esq.7 Up.Chadwell st.Pntnvl
Dresden Edw. Zadoc, esq. 39 Woburn pl
Drew Rev. Geo. Smith, 14 Burton cresc
Drew David, esq. Inrolment Off.Chan.la
Drew Henry, esq. 79 Gower st
Drew Henry, esq. 33 Torrington square
Drew James P. esq. 8 Howland st
Drew J. W. esq. 4 Low.Chesterter.Eatonsq
Drew Mrs. 18 Abbey pl. St. John's wood
Drew Mrs. 7 Delahay st. Westminster
Drew Mrs. 7 Hamilton ter.St.John's wd
Drew Mrs. 48 Wharton st. Lloyd square
Drew Thomas, esq. 186 Sloane st
Drew Walter, esq. 79 Gower st
Drew William, esq. 17 Coleshill st
Drew Wm. esq. 67 Hamilton terrace
Drewry Charles Stewart, esq. 5 New sq. Lincoln's inn, & 4 Park rd. Nottinghill
Drewry Edward, esq. 8 Park ter. Highbry
Drewry H. esq. 5 St.John's vil. Acacia rd
Drinkald Joseph, esq. 18 Blandford sq
Drinkwater Wm. Leece, esq. 8 Mecklenburgh st. & 3 Paper buildings
Driscoll Rev.C.M.A.5 Omega tr.Alpha rd
Driver Edward, esq. 8 Richmond terr
Driver George N. esq. 8 Richmond terr
Driver Hy. Austin, esq. 18 Barnsbury pk
Driver Mrs. Montpelier, So. Lambeth
Drory Geo. Wm. esq. 38 Westbourne terr
Drouet Charles, esq. sec. to Belgian Legation, 9A, Weymouth st

Drouhet Amédée, esq. 4 Finsbury circus
Druce Chas. esq. Denmark hill, Cmbrwl
Druce John, esq. 27 Cheyne walk, Chelsea
Druce Mrs. 2 Oakley square, Chelsea
Druce Wm. esq. 22 Cheyne walk, Chelsea
Druitt Henry, esq. 53 Myddelton square
Druitt Robert, 39A, Curzon st
Drummond Gen. Sir Gordon, G.C.B. 25 Norfolk st. Park lane
Drummond Lady Caroline, 12 Fitzroy st
Drummond Col. B. 23 Charles st. Bkly. sq
Drummond Col. Wm. 107 Sloane st
Drummond & Co. 49 Charing cross
Drummond A. Mortimer, esq. & Lady Emily, 49 Charingcr. & Tile ho. Denham
Drummond Andrew Robert, esq. & Lady Elizabeth, 2 Bryanstone sq. & Cadland, nr. Southampton
Drummond Charles, esq. & hon. Mrs. 17 Stratton st. & Dower hall, Haverhill, Essex, & Roehampton, Surrey
Drummond Hen. Home, esq. M.P. Carlton club, & Blairdrummond, Stirling
Drummond Hen. esq. & Lady Harriet, Albury park, Guildford
Drummond Geo. esq. 11 Wilton crescent
Drummond Hen. esq. 103 Gloucester pl
Drummond Misses, 78 Wimpole st
Drummond Miss, 5 Chesham place
Drummond Mrs. 18 Hyde park gardens
Drummond Mrs. 6 Sloane terr. Chelsea
Drummond Spencer, esq. 5 Chesham pl
Drury Jas. esq. 42 Alpha road, Rgt.'spk
Drury Mrs. 102 Guilford st
Dry Chas. esq. 19 Cambridge st. Edg. rd
Dry Mrs. 32 Up. Bedford pl. Russell sq
Dry Thomas, esq. 21 Lincoln's inn fields
Dryden C. B. esq. 31 Cambridge terrace, Edgw. rd. & 21 Lincoln's inn fields
Dryden Rt. esq. 28 Brown's la. Sptlflds
Du Bois Edward, esq. 16 Sloane st. & 12 Abingdon st. Westminster
Du Bois Mdm. 23 Middle Queen's blds
Dubois Danl. esq. 65 Princes st. Lstr. sq
Dubois Hill E. F. esq. 1 Mitre ct. Fleet st
Dubois Mrs. 22 Walcot pl. east, Lambeth
Dubourg Chas. S. esq. 25 Shaftesbury cr
Du Cane Captain, R.N. 64 Lowndes sq. & Braxted lodge, Wickham, Essex
Du Carron Joseph, esq. 11 Chesterfield st. King's cross
Ducie, Earl of, 24 Belgrave sq. & Woodchester pk. Gloucestershire, & Ampney pk. Cirencester
Duckworth Sir John Thos. B. bart. M.P. Fenton's hotel, & Weirhouse, Exeter
Duckworth Samuel, esq. 11 Hyde park st. & Masters' Off. 25 Southampton bdgs
Dudden Edmnd. esq. 17 Addison rd. Knstn
Dudden Jacob, esq. 1 Churchrd. Kngsld. rd
Dudgeon R.E. M.D. 82 Glo'ster st. Ptm. sq
Dudley Jos. esq. 1 Crescent pl. Hamps. rd
Dudley Mrs. 6 Up. Fitzroy st. Fitzroy sq
Dudley Pedro, esq. 10 Wellington ter
Dufaur Antonine, esq. 3 Bedford row
Dufaur Frederick, esq. 23 Queen Anne st. Cavendish sq.; 13 South sq. Gray's inn, & Howton hall, near Ipswich
Duff Alexander M. esq. 2A Welbeck st
Duff George, esq. 15 Arlington st
Duff James, esq. M.P. 30 Pall mall, & Delgaty castle, Turiff, Aberdeenshire
Duff Gordon James, esq. 10 Devonport st
Duff Miss, 20 Brook st. Grosvnr. sq
Duff Mrs. 10 Russell square, & Corsinday, near Aberdeen
Duff Thos. esq. 3 Theberton st. we. Lpl. rd
Duff Wm. esq. 10 South bank, Rgnt.'s pk
Duff Wm. esq. 15 Red Lion sq. Holborn
Duffell Mrs. 3 Conduit st. wst. Hyde pk
Duffield Francis, esq. 81 Jermyn st. & Townhill house, Bradford, Yorkshire
Duffield Mrs. & Miss, 81 Jermyn st. & Townhill house, Bradford, Yorkshire
Duffield Miss, 47 Grosvenor st
Duffield Miss M. 4 Lower Seymour st
Duffin Edward W. esq. 14 Langham pl
Duffy Bernard, M.D. 6 Up. Seymour st
Dufferin Lord, 29 Brook st. Grsvnor. sq
Dugard Julian, esq. 5 Park pl. ter. Pad. gr
Dugmore Wm. esq. 7 Cravenhill lodge, Bayswater, & 4 New sq. Lincoln's inn
Dujardin John, esq. 5 Westbourne place
Duke Sir James, knt. alderman, M.P. 23 Botolph lane, & Field place, Manor Horsham
Dukinfield Rev. Sir Henry Robert, bart. 6 St. Martin's place, Trafalgar square
Dulcken Hy. Augustus, esq. 80 Harley st
Dulcken Madame, 80 Harley st
Dumergue Chas. esq. 37 York pl. Portm. sq
Dumergue Francis, esq. 13 Old square, Lincoln's inn, & Acton
Dumergue Mrs. 4 Trafalgar sq. Chelsea
Dunalley Lord, Union club, & Dunalley castle, Tipperary
Dunbar David, esq. 15 Elizabeth st. south
Dunbar Mrs. 16 Brompton row
Dunbar Wm. Geo. esq. 11 Montagu place, Montagu square
Duncan Visct. M.P. 15 Hill st. Berkeley sq. & Camperdown, Forfarshire, & Sidney place, Bath
Duncan Hon. Hamelton, 70 Jermyn st
Duncan Andrew, esq. 14 Albert terrace
Duncan Andw. esq. 11 Featherstone bds
Duncan Edward, esq. 2 Mornington pl
Duncan Geo. esq. M.P. 26 Gt. George st. Westminster
Duncan John, esq. 7 Belgrave road
Duncan John B. esq. 2 Tanfield ct. Temple
Duncan John Francis, esq. 14 Claremt. sq
Duncan J. esq. 13 Chester pl. Knngtn. cr
Duncan Miss, 77 Gower st
Duncan Peterkin, esq. 15 Beaufoy ter
Duncan Thos. esq. Paulton sq. Chelsea
Duncannon Viscount, M.P. 3 Cavendish sq
Duncombe Hon. Arthur, Capt. R.N., M.P. 22 Grosvenor square, & Kilnwick Percy, Bradford, Yorkshire
Duncombe Hon. Octavius, M.P. & Lady Coroline, 24 Arlington st. & Waresley park, Caxton
Duncombe Fred. esq. 18 Devereuxct. Stnd
Duncombe Hy. Haynes, esq. 6 Lyon's inn
Duncombe James, esq. 4 Gray's inn pl. & Woodcock hill, Berkhampstead
Duncombe John, esq. 13 Wharton st
Duncombe Philip Duncombe Pauncefort, sen. esq. 14 Bryanstone, sq. & Brick hill, Manor, Fenny Stratford
Duncombe Slingsby, esq. 3 Bryanstone square, & Langford, Newark, Notts
Duncombe Thos. S. esq. M.P. F3, Albany
Dundas Rt. Hon. Wm. 45 Grosvenor st. & Quarry castle, St. Leonard's-on-Sea
Dundas Hon. John Chas. M.P. 19 Arlington st. & Oran, Catterick
Dundas Admiral, M.P. & Hon. Mrs. 4 Lower Berkeley st.; Barton court, near Hungerford; & Ashton hall, Hawarden
Dundas D. esq. Q.C. M.P. 13 King's Bch. wk
Dundas E.W. esq. 8 Charles st. Trevor sq
Dundas Fredk. esq. M.P. 24 Hanover sq
Dundas Miss Charlotte, 24 Hanover sq
Dundonald, Earl of, 8 Chesterfield st. & 2 Victoria square
Dunfermline Lord, P.C. 7 Brook st. & Stubbing court, near Chesterfield; Colington house, Edinburgh
Dungannon Viscount, 3 Grafton st. Bond st. & Brynkinalt, near Denbigh
Dungarvon Viscountess, 3 Hamilton pl
Dunhill Mathew, esq. 54 Gt. Coram st
Dunkin Mrs. 26 Torrington square
Dunlap James, M.D. 42 Baker st
Dunlop Donald Mackenzie, esq. 10 Chancery lane
Dunlop John, esq. 77 Park st. Grsvnr. sq
Dunlop Mrs. 27 Russell square
Dunlop Mrs. 22 Wilton pl. Belgrave sq
Dunlop Wm. esq. 23 Fludyer st. & 4 Lower Belgrave st
Dunmore, Earl of, 1 Grafton st. Bond st. & Dunmore park, Falkirk
Dunn Rev. Ed. Alex. 2 Up. Belgrave pl. & 11 Chatham place, Blackfriars
Dunn Edward, esq. 38 Highbury place
Dunn Geo. esq. 129 Stanhope st. Hampstead rd. & 2 Raymond bldgs. Gray's in
Dunn Mrs. 3 Connaught square
Dunn Mrs. 49 Noel st. Islington
Dunn Ralph, esq. 2 Comptn. ter. U. st. Islgtn
Dunn Robert, esq. 15 Norfolk st. Strand
Dunnage Rev. James Arthur, Tower
Dunn-Gardner, see Gardner-Dunn
Dunraven, Earl of, 76 Eaton square; & Dunraven castle, Cowbridge; & Adare abbey, Limerick
Dunsany Lord, Carlton club, & Dunsany castle, Dunshaughlin, Meath
Dunsford G.W. esq. 32 Mornington cresc
Dunsford Harris, M.D. 44 Upper Seymour st. Portman square
Dunster Hy. esq. 4 Cumberland ter. Pentv
Dunster Wm. H. esq. 34 Gt. Marylebone st
Dunsterville Edward, esq. 2 Springfield place, Wandsworth road
Dunt John Ebenezer, esq. 25 St. James sq
Du Pasquier Francis, esq. 62 Pall mall
Du Pasquier John M. esq. 8 Regent st. & 62 Pall mall
Du Pasquier Mrs. 62 Pall mall
Du Pasquin Mrs. 16 King's parade, Chelsea
Dupleix Hen. esq. 61 Lincoln's inn flds
Duplex Geo. esq. 28 Guilford st. Rusl. sq
Dupons Mrs. 32 Claremont square
Du Pré Caledon George, M.P. 40 Portland pl. & Wilton park, Beaconsfield
Du Pré James, esq. 40 Portland place, & Wilton park, Beaconsfield, Bucks
Dupree Miss, 5 Lr. Duncan pl. City rd
Dupuy Rev. Henry, 33 Cadogan st. Chels
Dupuy Mrs. 31 Welbeck st. & Felbridge park, East Grinstead, Surrey
Dupuy Mrs. M. 23 Tonbridge pl. New. rd
Durant Major General, 7 Hyde park gate, Kensington
Durant Edwin F. esq. 15 Old Cavendish st
Durant Enoch, esq. 12 Mansfield st. Portland pl. & High canons, Shenley, Herts
D'Urban Mrs. 9 Hamilton pl. St. John's wd
Durham Right Rev. Lord Bishop of, 4 Upper Portland place, & Auckland castle, Bishops Auckland, Durham
Durham Cornelius, esq. 191 Regent st
Durham Edwd. esq. 36 Singleton st. Hxtn
Durham Jsph. esq. 6 North cres. Bedfrd. sq
Durham Mrs. 9 Blandford st Portman sq
Durham Thos. esq. 32 Percy st
Durham Thos. esq. 9 Up. Seymour st. w
Durlacher Louis, esq. 15 O. Burlingtn. st
Durnford J. C. esq. 10 Up. Phillimore pl
Durnford Misses, 13 Southmptn. rw. Nw. rd
Durrant Lieut. Col. Wm. 20 Wimpole st
Durrant Rev. Jas. 9 Soley ter. Pntnville
Durrant Jas. esq. 9 Argyle st. King's crs
Durrant John M. B. esq. 6 Gray's inn sq
Dustan Wm. esq. 21 Highbury terrace
Dutchman Mrs. 12 Lr. Phillimore place, Kensington
Duthoit D. esq. Bellmont cot. Brnsb. pk
Duthoit Jonathan, esq. 11 Compton ter. Upper st. Islington
Dutton Douglas, esq. 73 Connaught ter
Dutton Miss, 6 Portland pl. Clphm. rd
Dutton Wm. esq. 58 Ebury st. Pimlico
Dutton Jas. esq. 10 Grove ter. St. Jhn's. wd
Dutton Mrs. 17 Norfolk cresc. Oxford sq
Dutton Thos. G. esq. Bales cot. Wndsw. rd
Dutton Wm. C. esq. 5 Duncan ter. City rd
Duval Hy. esq. 14 Charlotte st. Bedfd. sq
Duval Mrs. 19 Burton st. Burton cresc
Duval P.S. esq. 5 Regent sq. Gray's inn rd
Duvall John, esq. 3 Nrthumbrlnd. st. Strnd
Duvall Mrs. 6 Cadogan st. Chelsea
Dwelly Thomas, esq. 26 Vincent square

Dwarris Sir Fortunatus, knt. 5 James st Buckinghamgt.&Queen'sBnch.offi.Tpl
Dyce Rev. Alexander, 9 Gray's inn sq
Dyce Wm. esq. School of Design, Somerset house, & 1A, Adelphi terrace
Dyer Dr. Henry, 3 Cambridge terrace, & Pytchey Grange, near Kettering
Dyer Charles, esq. 36 Guilford st
Dyer G.esq.3Windsor cots.Havrstck.hill
Dyer James, esq. 27 Ely pl. Holborn
Dyer Mrs. 1 Allen terrace, Kensington
Dyer Mrs. 6 Omega terrace, Alpha rd
Dyer Mrs. 16 Park st. Westminster
Dyer Thos. esq. 37 Up. Marylebone st
Dyer William, esq. 71 Gloucester pl
Dyer Wm. Geo. T. esq. 23 Sackville st
Dyke Decimus, esq. 5Mount st.Brkly.sq
Dyke Fras. H. esq. 1 Tilney st. Park la. & 5 Deans court, Doctors' commons
Dyke John, esq. 4 Grange vil. Bromptn
Dyke Thomas, esq. 82 Sloane st
Dykes Lamplugh B.esq. 1 Elm ct. Tmpl
Dymant John, esq. 20 Up. Montagu st
Dymoke Hon. Mrs. 9 Norfolk st.Park la
Dymoke Sir Henry, bart. 46 Wimpole st
Dyne Edward, esq. 6 Moccas cottages, Camden Nw. tn. & 61 Linc. inn fields
Dyne Wm. W. esq. 7 Hamilton pl.King's cross, & 61 Lincoln's inn fields
Dynevor Lord, 34 Dover st.; & Dynevor castle, Llandillo, Carmarthenshire
Dyson Maj. Gen. 5 Spanish pl. Mnchstr. sq.; & Manor ho. Swinshead, Lincolnshire ; & Cowbit, Spalding, Lincolnsh
Dyson Edward, esq. 98 Guilford st
Dyson Jas. Armstrong F. esq.36Carey st
Dyson Henry, esq. Acacia vil. Acacia rd
Dyson Mrs. 10 Manchester st
Dyson Thomas, esq. 14 Calthorpe st. & 21 Bedford row, Bloomsbury
Dyson T.esq.7Chepstow pl. Cmbrwl.n.rd
Dyson Thomas, esq. 25 Parliament st
Dyson Wm. esq. 33 Southampton row, Russell square, & 19 Chancery lane
Dyte Henry, esq. 2 Hare ct. Temple

EADE William A. esq. 1 Albany, Piccadilly, & 10 Old square
Eagle Fras.King,esq.4 New sq. Linc. inn
Eagle Wm.esq.3 Plowden bldgs.Temple, & Lakenheath hall,Mildenhall,Suffolk
Eagles W. B. esq. 31 Tavistock place
Eales Chr. esq. 4 Chapel pl. Cavend. sq
Eales Christphr. esq. 21 Cork st. Bond st
Eales Mrs. 17 Milner sq. Islington
Eales Wm. esq. 23 Parliament st
Eams Mrs. 43 Connaught terrace
Eames Mrs. 13 Connaught square
Eardley John, esq. 23 Bloomsbury st
Earith Chas. esq. 21 Myddelton square
Earl Jas.esq. 8 Belinda cott. Canonby.sq
EarleJames,esq.35Albany st.Regent's pk
Earle Joseph, esq. 1 Kensington gardens
Earle Mrs. 28 George st. Hanover sq
Earle Thos.esq. 72 Up. Ebury st.Pimlico
Earnshaw Geo.esq. 16 Gerrard st. Islgtn
EarnshawWm.esq.2Fitzroypl.Kentish tn
Earnshaw Wm. esq. 14 Kennington ter
Earnsteign Francis, esq. 7 Scarsdale terrace, Kensington
Eason Mrs. 24 Upper Ebury st. Pimlico
Easson Jas. U. esq.1A,Bedford pl.Rus.sq
East Rt. Hon. Sir Edward Hyde, bart. Sherwood lodge, Battersea
East Charles, esq. 33 Sloane st
East Geo. esq. 1 Straunear pl. Maida hl
East James Buller, esq.M.P. 99 Eaton sq
East Hy.V.esq.14 Canterbury vls.Edg.rd
East Jsph.esq.25Newingtonpl. Kenngtn.r
East W.Fred.esq.7Winchester pl. Newrd
Easthope Sir John, bart. M.P. 19Grafton st. & Firgrove, Weybridge, Surrey
Eastlake Charles Locke, esq. R.A. 7 Fitzroy sq. &Gwydir house, Whitehall
Eastnor Viscount, M.P. Carlton club, & Eastnor castle, near Tewkesbury

Easton Arthur, esq. 44 Hyde park sq
Easton Jas.esq. 6 Hamilton pl. St.John's wood, & 6 New sq. Lincoln's inn
Easton John, esq.31 Edwardes sq.Knsgn
Easton Thomas, esq. 1 Hare ct. Temple
Eastly Nl. esq. 3 Virginia tr. Gt. Dr. rd
Eastwick Captn. jun. 22 Sloane st
Eastwick Cap.Rt.Wm.sen.R.N.33Hanspl
Eastwick John, esq.3 Elm court, Temple
Eaton Rd. Jefferson, M.P. Stetchworth park, near Newmarket
Eaton David, esq. 44 Bloomsbury sq
Eaton Henry, esq. 35 Ebury st. Eaton square, & 10 New inn, Strand
EatonH.W.esq.9 Glo'ster ter.Regent's pk
Eaton Mrs. 11 Lower Belgrave st
EavestaffWm.esq.1 Howleypl.vils.Pdtn
Eayre Wm.esq.10 Portsea pl.Connght.sq
Ebbetts Danl. esq. 7 Canonbury villas
Ebbrell Thos. esq. 21 Chapel st. Blgr. sq
Ebdell Mrs. 20 Dalby terrace, City rd
Ebrington Visct. M.P. 17 Grosvenor sq
Ebsworth Chs. esq. 18 Surrey sq. O.K.rd
Ebsworth Miss, 2 Upper ter. Islington
Ebsworth R.M.esq. 28Cloudesly st.Islgn
Eccles Henry, esq. 14 Park st
Eccles John, esq. 2 Sussex terrace
Echlin Wm. Leahy,esq. 56 Dean st.Soho
Eckett Rev. Robt. 6 Argyle sq. New rd
Eckstein Geo. F. esq. 13 High Holborn
Eddels James C. esq. 5 Finchley new rd
Eddes J.esq. 14 Ampton st.Gray's inn rd
Eddis Arth. S. esq.28 Southampton bldgs
Eddis Eden Upton, esq. 78 Newman st. & 1 Barnsbury st. Islington
Eddison Wm. Edward, esq. 69 Euston sq
Eddrup Edw. C.esq. 4 Tunbridge pl.N.rd
Ede John Rt. esq. 1 Mathon pl. Pntnvl
Ede Mrs. 29 Upper Harley st. & Lordship lane, Tottenham, Middlesex
Eden Hon. & Rev.Robt.Vicarage,Batters
Eden Lt.Col.G.M.14 William st.Kntsbdg
Eden Leonard, esq. 3 College ter. Islgtn
Eden Ralph, esq. 28 Abingdon st
Eden Thomas,esq. 3 Salisbury st. Strand
Eden Wm. esq. 10 Norfolk st. Strand
Edgar Hy.Rt.esq. 7 Caroline st. Bedfd.sq
Edgar Thos. esq. 7 Up.Glo'ster st.Drst.sq
EdgcombJsph. esq. 5Bedfd. rw.Clphm.ri
Edgcumbe Richd.esq.26Shaftesbury cres
Edge Thos. esq.61 Walcot pl. ea.Lambth
Edge Thomas, esq. 39 Vincent square
EdgellAlex.esq.4Verulam bdgs.Gray's in
Edgell Harry, esq. 21 Cadogan place
Edgell Henry P. esq. 13 Bouverie st
Edgell Miss Wyatt, 40 Grosvenor st
Edgington Benjamin, esq. Abingdon lodge, Wandsworth road
Edgson Jas. esq. 21 Salisbury st Lson. gr
Edison Jno. Sibbald,esq. 3 Plowden bdgs
Edkins Rt. Pitt, esq. 4 Mathon pl.Pntnvl
Edlin Ed. esq. 9 Queen's row, Pentonvil
Edlin Mrs. 3 Taunton pl. Regent's park
Edlin Peter, esq. 91 Jermyn st
Edmands Thos.esq.26 Bury st. St. James
Edmond John, esq. 60 Margaret st
Edmonds Chas. Henry, esq. 8 Trevor sq
Edmonds E. esq. 19 Seymour pl.Brys.sq
Edmonds H.esq. 1 Devonsh.pl.Edgw. rd
Edmonds Jno. Thos. esq. 27 George st. Hanover sq.& Rose cot.Hammersmith
Edmonds Mrs. 44 Cloudesley tr. Islgton
Edmonds Mrs. 57 Stamford st. Blackfrs
EdmondsT.R.esq.3 Henrietta st.Brsw.sq
Edmonds Wm. esq. 8 St. James's place
Edmonstone Neal B. esq.31 Sussex gdns
Edmunds Alfred S. esq. 16 Heathcote st
EdmundsAlf.S.esq.12 South sq.Gray's in
Edmunds George, esq. Wandsworth road
Edmunds Leonard, esq. 4 Grafton st. & Crown office, Rolls' yard
Edmunds Mrs. 14 Maddox st. Regent st
Edmunds Mrs.8 Portld.pl.Wandswth.rd
EdridgeMiss,35Devonshire st.Portlnd.pl
Edridge Thos. esq. Mornington road
Edwards Hon. Geo. 49 South Audley st

Edwards Capt. 5 Montagu square
Edwards Rev. Howel Holland, M. A. 13 Dean's yard,& Pennant,LlanrwstN.W
Edwards Rev.Joseph, 37 Bloomsbury sq
Edwards Chas. esq. 26 Bell yard
Edwards Chas. esq.2 George st.Eustn.sq
Edwards David,esq.22 King st. Cov.gar
EdwardsD.O.esq.15 Cheyne wk.Chelsea
EdwardsE.esq.11Gouldn.ter.Barnsby rd
EdwardsEd.Hugh,esq.14Park st.Wstmr
Edwards Edwin, esq. 1 Bennett's hill
EdwardsEd.W.esq. 26 Bell yd.Templ.br
EdwardsFras.esq.17Hart st.Bloomsbury
Edwards Fras.esq. 38 Moorgate st. City, & 8 Delahay st. Westminster
Edwards Fras. esq. 57 Westbourne ter
Edwards Frederic, esq. 9 South terr. Alexander sq.& 4 Brick court, Temple
EdwardsFredk.esq33 Pelham rd.Bmptn
Edwards Geo. esq. 13 George st. Adelphi
Edwards George, esq. 10 Maida hill west
EdwardsGeorge,esq.3Montagu pl.Islntn
Edwards George N. esq. 7 Keppel st
Edwards Henry, esq. 67 Edgware road
Edwards Henry, esq. 8 Ely pl. Holborn
Edwards Henry, esq. 4 Park cottages, Park village east, Regent's park
Edwards JefferyJ.esq.51 Lincoln's inn fi
Edwards John, esq. 34 Upper Eaton st
Edwards John esq. 96 Wimpole st
EdwardsJ.H.esq.4Torrianno tr.Kntsh.tn
Edwards John A.esq. 1 Oakley sq.Chels
Edwards John Chas. esq. 59 Conduit st
EdwardsJn.S.esq.89Glo'ster pl.Kntsh.tn
Edwards Jno.esq.King's road west, Chel
EdwardsJsph.esq.40Robert st.Hmpstd.r
Edwards Miss, 19 Great Carter lane
Edwards Miss, 32 Hyde park square
Edwards Miss, 13 Michael's pl. Brmptn
Edwards Mrs. 50 Bedford square
Edwards Mrs. 13 Belgrave st.King's crs
Edwards Mrs. Denmark hill, Cambrwll
Edwards Mrs. 2 George st. Euston sq
EdwardsMrs.11Gt.James st. Bedfd.row
Edwards Mrs. 13 Hans place, Sloane st
Edwards Mrs. 16 Milton st. Dorset sq
Edwards Rd.esq. 1 Green's row, Chelsea
Edwards Rt. esq. 90 Oxford ter. Edg. rd
Edwards Tenison, esq. 77 Chancery lane
Edwards Thomas, esq. 4 Clement's inn
Edwards Thos. esq. 28 Gt. Ormond st
EdwardsT.esq. 2Grevle.pl.Kilbrn.priory
Edwards Thos. esq. 1 Hamilton terrace
Edwards Thos. esq. 8 Moorgate st. City, & 8 Delahay st. Westminster
Edwards Thos. esq. 37 Noel st. Islngton
EdwardsThos.esq.21 Union st.Clrndn.sq
EdwardsThos.G.esq.8York ter.Rgt.'s pk
Edwards Thos.K.esq. 1 Raymond bldgs
EdwardsWm.esq.19Chapel st.Grosvr.sq
Edwards Wm. esq. 36 Highbury place
Edwards Wm. 7 New inn, Strand
Edwards Wm.esq. 2York gate,Rgt.'s pk
Edwards Wm. H.esq.1 MiddleTemple la
Edye John,esq. 9 Mecklenburgh square
Edye Thos.esq.1St.John's vills.Acaca.rd
Edye Walter Oke, esq. 13 King's Bench walk, Temple
Effendi Hassen, attaché to Turkish Embassy, 1 Bryanstone square
Effendi Sarim, Turkish Ambassador, 1 Bryanstone square
Effendi Edib, secretary to Turkish Embassy, 1 Bryanstone square
Effingham, Earl of, G.C.B. 57 Eaton pl. & Grange, Rotherham
Egan Chas. esq. 26 Bell yard
Egan Edward, esq. 11 Grove end road
Egan Wm. esq. 58 Lincoln's inn fields
Egan J. esq. 27 Cavendish rd.St. Jno's.wd
Egerton Rt. Hon. Lord Francis, M.P. 18 Belgrave sq. ; & Worsley hall, Manchester ; & Hatchford, near Cobham
Egerton Sir Philip de Malpas Grey,bart. M.P. 111 Jermyn st. & Oulton park, near Middlewich

Egan Mrs. 11 Grove end rd. St. John's wd
Egerton Gen. Sir Chas. 16 Chesham pl
Egerton Henry, esq. 13 Hanover terrace, Regent's pk. & 6 Old sq. Lincoln's inn
Egerton Wilbraham, esq. 7 St. James's sq. & Tatton park, Knutsford
Egerton Wm. Tatton, esq. M.P. & Lady Charlotte, 30 Eaton place, & Puddington hall, Neston, Chester
Egg Augustus, esq. 30 Gerrard st. Soho
Eggbrecht Miss, 15 Paddington green
Eggleton Miss, 41 Cheyne walk, Chelsea
Egleton John, esq. 9 Oxford terrace
Egley Wm. esq. 75 Connaught ter. Hyde pk
Eglington Robert, esq. 29 Woburn sq. & Demoore castle, Argylshire
Eglinton Earl of, Clarendon hotel, New Bond st.; & Eglinton castle, Ayrshire
Eglinton Robert, esq. 10 Hyde Park sq. & Dunoon castle, Argylshire
Egmont Earl of, 43 Berkeley sq.; & Cowdery lodge, Petworth; & Burgh house, Epsom
Eicke Chas. esq. 3 Norfolk st. Park la
Eicke John, esq. 65 Gower st. Bedford sq
Eilgy Miss, 21 Paddington green
Eilsart F. esq. 9 Harrington square
Eisenberg John, esq. 14 Cockspur st
Eivers John, esq. 12 Buckingham st. Str
Ekins Admiral Sir Chas. 69 Cadogan pl
Ekins William, esq. 20 Kensington gore
Elam Benj. esq. 13 Endsleigh st. Tav. sq
Elam John, esq. 4 Charlotte st. Bedfd. sq
Elam Thos. Henry, esq. 33 Sackville st
Eland Richard, esq. 26 Northampton sq
Elderton Chas. Merrick, esq. 15 Abbey pl. St. John's wood, & 9 New sq. Linc. inn
Elderton Miss, Belgrave cot. Wndsw. rd
Eld Howard, esq. 67 Mortimer st. Cav. sq
Eldon Earl of, 1 Hamilton place; & Encombe house, Wareham, Dorset; & Shirley, Croydon
Eldred Chs. esq. 2 Richmond tr. Cannby. sq
Eldred Edgar, esq. 2 Up. Barnsbury st
Eldred Mrs. 37 York st. Portman sq
Eldridge Mrs. 8 Kennington pl. U. Ken. la
Eldridge William, esq. 36 Carey st
Elen Philip, esq. 6 Portens rd. Harrow rd
Eley Mrs. 3 Alfred pl. Alexander sq
Elger Miss, 3 Belgrave pl. Wandswth. rd
Elgie Chas. Wm. esq. 7 Warwick ct. Hlbn
Elgie Thos. esq. 3 Upper ter. Islington
Elgood John G. esq. 97 Wimpole st
Elin John Bloxam, esq. 7 Kent ter. Rgt.'s pk
Eliot G. H. esq. 17 Charlotte st. Portlnd. pl
Elkin Ben. esq. 20 Upper Bedford pl
Elkington Hen. esq. 17 Liverpl. st. King's cr
Elkins Alf. esq. 30 Foley pl. Portland pl
Elkins Edward, esq. 19 Park village west, Regent's pk.; & 59 Newman st
Elkins H. esq. 29 Crescent st. Euston sq
Elkins Mrs. 62 George st. Portman sq
Elkins Wm. Morris, esq. 7 Addington pl. Camberwell road
Ella John, esq. 70 Mortimer st
Ellaby Mrs. 35 Doughty st
Ellaby Wm. Francis, esq. 2 Bedford row
Ellamby Wm. Frs. esq. 15 Plhm. rd. Brmptn
Ellcock Mrs. 2 Melina pl. St. John's wd
Ellenborough Earl, G.C.B., P.C. 12 Charles st. Berkeley sq. & Southam house, Cheltenham
Ellerby J. esq. 3 Brunswick ter. Dover rd
Ellerby Thos. esq. 13 Victoria gr. Knsntn
Ellerman C. F. esq. 21 Pelham pl. Fulhm. rd
Ellerman T. esq. 21 Pelham pl. Fulham rd
Ellerton John Lodge, esq. & Lady Harriet, 6 Connaught place
Ellerton Mrs. 8 Sussex pl. Knsngtn. nw. tn
Ellery Edmund B. esq. 12 Gray's inn sq
Ellery James, esq. 15 Grafton st. east
Ellice Right Hon. Edward, M.P. 18 Arlington st
Ellice Edwd. jun. esq. M.P. 130 Park st. Grosvenor square; Invergarry; & Glenquoich lodge, Fort Augustus
Ellice Charles, esq. 57 Park st. Grsvr. sq
Ellice Mrs. 12 Great Cumberland st
Ellice Russell, esq. 5 Portman square
Ellicombe Geo. B. esq. 15½ Parliament st
Ellicombe Rd. R. esq. 16 Parliament st
Ellinthorpe Misses, 4 Hall pl. St. Jhn's. wd
Elliot Rev. Wm. Henry, 12 Wharton st
Elliot Henry, esq. 27 Fitzroy square
Elliot Miss, 10 Chandos st. Strand
Elliot T. esq. 17 Up. Glo'ster pl. Dorset sq
Elliot Thos. Frederic, esq. 37 Chesham place, & 9 Park st. Westminster
Elliot Wm. esq. 15 New Ormond st
Elliotson John, M.D. 37 Conduit st
Elliott Charles, esq. 47 Portland place
Elliott C. A. esq. Retreat, Old Brompton
Elliott Geo. Percy, esq. 2 Plowden bldgs
Elliott Hen. esq. 14 Tavistock st. Cov. gdn
Elliott J. A. esq. Retreat, Old Brompton
Elliott John Sam. esq. 7 Park rd. Reg. pk
Elliott John Shearman, esq. 7 Canterbury villas, Edgware road
Elliott Mrs. 9 Belgrave road
Elliott Mrs. 63A, Montagu square
Elliott Thos. esq. Ambassador's ct. St. Jas'
Elliott Thomas, esq. 2 Claremont sq
Elliott Thos. esq. 2 Regt. sq. Gray's inn rd
Elliott W. T. esq. Cowper ho. Old Bromptn
Elliott Wm. T. esq. 44 Gt. Russell st. Bmsby
Ellis Sir Henry, knt. 79 Gt. Russell st. & Antiquarian Soc. Somerset house
Ellis Capt. Wm. 46 Cadogan place
Ellis Rev. F. W. M.A. 10 Portland road
Ellis Rev. John J. 116 Bishopsgate within
Ellis Rev. Wm. W. 8 Grafton st. Bond st
Ellis Alfred, esq. 13 Hornton st. Knsgtn
Ellis Arthur, esq. 48 Conduit st
Ellis Chas. esq. 7 Cavendish rd. St. Jn's. wd
Ellis Chas. esq. 1 Russell ct. St. James's
Ellis Chas. esq. 2 Stone bldgs. Linc. inn
Ellis Chas. Heaton, esq. 49 Harley st
Ellis Cydwelyn, esq. 31 Howland st
Ellis Edward, esq. 32 Harley st. & Grove house, Hendon, Middlesex
Ellis Edwd. esq. 14 Henry st. Pentonvl
Ellis Edw. esq. 10 Melbury terrace
Ellis Edwd. Smith, esq. 3 Hyde Park st
Ellis Frederick, esq. 6 Pump ct
Ellis Geo. esq. 53 Cumming st. Pentnvl
Ellis Geo. esq. Larkhall rise, Clapham
Ellis Geo. Henry, esq. 7 Spring gardens, & Lavender hill, Wandsworth
Ellis Henry, esq. 40 Bernard st
Ellis James, esq. 10 Alfred place, Newington causeway
Ellis James, esq. 9 Claremont ter. Pntvl
Ellis John, esq. 12 Clement's lane, City
Ellis Miss, 21 Upper Eaton st
Ellis Mrs. 40 Bernard st. Russell sq
Ellis Mrs. Col. 56 Sloane st
Ellis Mrs. 52 Connaught terrace
Ellis Mrs. 3 Cumberland pl. New rd
Ellis Mrs. 10 Melbury ter. Dorset sq
Ellis Mrs. 16 New Millman st
Ellis Mrs. 63 Westbourne tr. Sussex gdns
Ellis Richd. 4 St. Peter st. River la
Ellis Robt. esq. 59 Brompton crescent
Ellis Rd. 1 Warwick pl. St. John's wd
Ellis Samuel, esq. 7 Burton crescent
Ellis Sam. H. esq. 16 Keppel st. Russell sq
Ellis Thos. esq. 4 Bennett st. St. James's
Ellis Thomas Flower, esq. 15 Bedford place, Bloomsby. & 3 Elm ct. Temple
Ellis Welbore, esq. E2, Albany
Ellis Wm. esq. 15 Park pl. ter. Paddingtn
Ellis Wm. esq. 27 Portlnd. pl. Lr. rd. Islngtn
Ellis Wm. Rt. esq. 7 Park pl. vils. Paddngtn
Ellis Wm. Robert, esq. 24 Chancery la
Ellis Wynn, esq. M.P. 30 Cadogan place, & Ponsbourn park, near Hertford
Ellison Cuthbert, esq. 1 Whitehall gardens, & Hebbern hall, Gateshead
Ellison Cuthbert Edwd. esq. 4 Hare ct
Ellison Geo. T. esq. 9 Halfmoon st. & 1 Lincoln's inn fields
Ellison Jas. esq. 22 Notting hill sq
Ellison M. esq. Club chambs. 15 Rgnt. st
Ellison Thomas, esq. 4 New Boswell ct
Ellison Wm. esq. 45 Warwick st. Pimlico
Ellman Rev. John H. 11 Bryanstone sq
Elmer Mrs. 32 Nutford pl. Bryanstone sq
Elmes H. L. esq. Gordon st. Gordon sq
Elmore A. W. esq. 19 Charles st. Mid. hsptl
Elmore John Rd. M.D. 9 Nw. Cavendish st
Elmore Thos. John, esq. 9 New Caven. sq
Elmsley Wm. esq. 8 Old sq. Lincoln's inn, & 37 Bedford pl. Bloomsbury
Elmslie Edmund W. esq. 50 Berners st
Elmslie James, esq. 6 Endsleigh st
Elmslie John Foster, esq. 1 Dorset pl
Elmslie Mrs. 1 Dorset pl. Dorset sq
Elmslie Wm. esq. 24 York st. Portmn. sq
Elphick Jas. Hy. esq. 2 Ladbroke tr. Not. hl
Elphicke Miss, 59 Torrington sq
Elphinstone Sir Howard, bart. 13 Norfolk st. Park lane, & Ore place, Hastings
Elphinstone Hon. Mountstuart, A4, Albny
Elphinstone Howard, D.C.L., M.P. 19 Eaton pl. & 7 College, Doctors' commns. & Ridge cottage, Hastings
Elphinstone John F. esq. 23 York terrace, & Ford farm, near East Grinstead
Elphinstone Miss, 3 Chesham pl. Belg. sq
Elphinstone Mrs. 26 Lonsdale square
Elrington Col. Wm. Fred. 12 Wyndham pl
Elrington Gerrad, esq. 37 Weymouth st
Elsam Mrs. 39 Frederick st. Gray's inn rd
Elsegood Henry, esq. 91 Park st
Elsegood Hen. Chas. esq. 14 Up. Brook st
Elsey Joseph R. esq. 2 Lonsdale square
Elster Derrick J. esq. 5 John st. Adelphi
Elster James Godfrey, esq. 54 Hans pl
Elstob Dryden, esq. 48 Dover st
Elstob Dryden, esq. 48 Dover st
Elstone H. esq. 47 Perceval st. Clerknwl
Eluics Mrs. 24 Alfred st. Bedford sq
Elwes George C. esq. 10 Eaton place
Elwes Henry, esq. 34 Portman square, & Colesbourne, Gloucestershire
Elwick George, 16 Henry st. Pentonvl
Elwin M. esq. Chapel stairs, Linc. inn
Elwyn Jeken, esq. 33 Pembroke sq
Ely Bishop of, 37 Dover st. Piccadilly, & the Palace, Ely, Cambridgeshire
Ely Joseph, esq. 8 Cadogan st. Chelsea
Ely Mrs. Queen's rd. St. John's wd
Elyard James, esq. 5 Millbank row
Emanuel Michael, esq. 5 Hanover sq
Emerson J. esq. 3 Blenheim ter. Chelsea
Emery Geo. esq. 89 Norton st. Fitzroy sq
Emery Mrs. 22 Broad st. buildings
Emly Hen. esq. 3 New sq. Lincoln's inn
Emlyn Viscount, M.P. 6 Eaton place
Emmens Thos. esq. 13 St. Ann's vls. St. J. wd
Emmens Wm. esq. 5 Lothbury, City
Emmerson Thos. esq. 20 Stratford place
Emmerton Mrs. 36 Glo'ster st. Queen sq
Emmet Geo. N. esq. 14 Bloomsbury sq
Emperor John, esq. 10 Grove end road
Empson Rev. John, 17 Cecil st. Strand
Empson J. W. esq. 26 Up. Seymour st. Portman square
Enderby Mrs. Geo. 2 Park sq. Regent's pk
Enfield Henry, esq. 45 Lincoln's inn fields
Engel Jsph. esq. 25 Castle st. Le'ster sq
England Jsph. esq. 3 Up. Phillimore pl
England Thos. esq. 87 Guilford st
Engleheart Wm. H. esq. 3 Gt. Knightrdr. st
English Edward, esq. 41 Guilford st
English Henry Scale, esq. 4 Barnsbury ter. Liverpool rd. & 33 Old Jewry
English Miss, 40 Brompton row
English Wm. esq. 38 Cadogan pl. Belg. sq
English Wm. esq. 2 Cardign. pl. Kengtn. crs
Enniskillen Earl of, Athanæum club, & Florence court, Fermanagh
Ennever Mrs. 5 Hanover cotgs. Rgnt.'s pk
Enoch Capt. John, 31 Coleshill st
Enoch Geo. esq. 21 Edward st. Portmn. sq
Enot Auguste, esq. 37 Foley place
Enson T. R. esq. 31 Fortess ter. Kntsh. tn
Ensor T. R. esq. 14 South sq. Gray' inn

Enthoven John Henry, esq. 50 Euston sq
Entwisle John, esq. 1 Russell square
Entwisle Thomas, esq. 4 Cambridge sq
Entwisle Wm. esq. M.P. 25Cambridge sq
Epps George N.esq. 79 South Audley st
Epps John, M.D.89Gt.Russell st.Blmsby
Eppy C. W. esq. 21 Lincoln's inn fields
Epworth B. H. esq. 14South ter. Alex. sq
Erat Wm. esq. 5Cmden. rd.villas, Cmdn.tn
Erby Mrs. 5 Cloudesley sq. Islington
Erck W. E. esq. Priory cot. Wandsw. rd
Erectheum Club House (William Holl, sec.), 8 York st. St. James's
Ericksen Eric, esq. 11 Albany st
Erichsen John Edwd. esq. 48Welbeck st
Ericsson Mrs. 39 Glo'ster pl. New road
Eriach Count of, 23 Beaumont st
ErlamJohnJ.esq.Marlboro'rd.St.Jn's.wd
Erlam Mrs. 16 Elm tree rd. St. Jn's. wd
Erle Peter, esq. 15 Chester terrace, Regent's park, & 2 New sq. Lincoln's inn
Erle Wm. esq. Q.C. 20 Bedford square
Erne Earl of, Irish Rep. Peer
Errington Jno.E.esq.11 Adam st.Adelphi
Errington Rowland, esq. 10 Hill st. & Newnham Paddox, Lutterworth
Errol Earl of, K.T., P.C. St.James's palace, & Slains castle, Aberdeens.; & Richmond park, Surrey
Erskine Lord, 35 University st. & 137 Marine parade, Brighton
Erskine Lady Harriet, 6 Grosvenor pl
Erskine Alexander, esq. 29 Bryanstone square, & Bell hall, Forfarshire, N.B
Erskine Henry D. esq. 93 Mount st
Erskine Hy. T. esq.3Stone bldgs.Linc.inn
Erskine Miss, 45 Chester square
Escott Bickham, esq. M.P. 9 John st. Berkeley square; & Harlow court, Taunton
Escreet T. esq. 8 Hornsey row, Islington
Esdaile Jas. esq. 24 Up. Bedford place
Esdaile Jsph.esq.Park ho.Old Brompton
Esmonde Sir Thomas, bart. M.P. 151 Regent st. & Gorey, Wexford
Espartero Gen.(Duke of Victory), Abbey lodge, Park road, Regent's park
Espin John, esq. 3 Elm court, Temple, & 3 New Boswell court
'Espinasse J.esq. 13 South sq. Gray's inn
Essex Earl of, 3 Chapel st. Grosvenor square, & Cashiobury park, Watford
Essex Dow. Countess of, 9 Belgrave sq
Essex John, H. esq. 52 Berners st
Essex Rd. H. esq. 13 York bldgs.New rd
Essex Thomas, esq. 20 Camden rd. villas
EssexTim.*mus.doc.* 13York bldgs.New rd
Essex Wm. esq. 5 Gordon st. Gordon sq
Essex Wm. esq. 32 Compton st. Brnsk. sq
Estcourt T. G. B. D.C.L., M.P. 82 Eaton place, & Estcourt, near Tetbury
Este Dr. Michael Lambton, 01, Albany
Esterhazy Count Anthony, attaché to the Austrian embassy, 7 Chandos st. Cavendish square
Etheridge J.esq. 7 Essex st. Noel st.Islgt
Etheridge Jsph. esq. 5 Angel ter. Islgtn
Etty Wm. esq. R.A. 14 Buckingham st
Etwall Ralph, esq. M.P. Oxford & Cambridge club, & the Mount Nursling, Southampton
Etwell Wm. esq. 3 St. James's place
Eude Isaac, esq. 219 Bethnal green rd
Eustace Maj. Gen. Sir Wm.25 Grosvenor pl. & Sampford hall, Braintree, Essex
Evans Gen.Sir de Lacy, 26 Bryanstone sq
Evans Capt. R.A. 15 Upper Porchester st
Evans Capt. Chas. 2 Malcomb pl. Clapm
Evans Benj. esq.2 Barnsbury st.Lvrpl.rd
Evans Benj esq.10 Stonefield st.Islington
Evans Benj. F. esq. 2 Charles st.Gibsn.sq
Evans C.esq. 23 Cole's ter. Barnsbury rd
Evans Chas. esq. 9 Grosvenor st. west
Evans Chas. esq. 9 Park pl. Kengtn. cr
Evans Charles, esq. 2 Tavistock place, Russell square, & 2 Gray's inn square
Evans Edward, esq.54 Poland st.Oxfd.st
Evans Edwin, esq.11 Caroline st.Bedfd.sq
Evans Fredk. Hodgson, esq. 4 Stone blds
Evans Griffith F. D. M.D. 21A, Hill st
Evans Henry Jas. esq. 76 Leman st. Goodman's fields
Evans Hugh, esq. 5 New sq. Linc. inn
Evans Jas. Cook, esq. 15 Chancery lane
Evans Jeremiah, esq. St. John's lodge, Clapham rise
Evans John, esq. Box farm, King's rd.Chl
Evans John, esq. 2 Dalby ter. City rd
Evans John, esq. 3 Francis pl. Holloway
Evans John, esq.Q.C. St.Katharine's, Regent's pk.& 11 Crown office rw. Temple
Evans John, esq. 32 Hertford st. Mayfair
Evans John, esq.8 Richmond ter.Pentonville, & 5 New sq. Lincoln's inn
Evans John, esq. 6 South sq. Gray's inn
Evans John, esq. 41 Torrington square, & 51 Lincoln's inn fields
Evans, John E. esq. 155 St. John st.road
Evans John Llewellyn, esq. 1 Wardrobe pl. Doctors' com. & 1 Mitre ct. chmbs
EvansJoseph P. esq. 1 Mecklenburgh ter
Evans M. M. esq. Box farm, King's road Chelsea
Evans Mrs. 11 Caroline st. Bedford sq
Evans Mrs. 45 Devonshire st. Queen sq
Evans Mrs. 19 Dorset st. Portman sq
Evans Mrs. 22 Eaton square, & Portrane house, Dublin
Evans Mrs. 184 Prospect pl. Edgware rd
Evans Mrs. 6 Sussex ter. Old Brompton
Evans Mrs. 29 Tonbridge pl. New rd
Evans Mrs. Wm. 34 Baker st. Portm. sq
Evans Richard, esq. 17 Newman st
Evans Richd. esq. 9 Southmptn. rw. Nw.r
Evans Robt. esq. 15 Glo'ster rd. Hyde pk
Evans Thomas, esq. 89 Blackfriars road
Evans T. esq. 20 Cambrdg. st. Edgwr. rd
Evans Ths. esq. 20 Portland ter. Regts.pk
Evans T. jun. esq. 1 Charles st.Gibson sq
Evans Wm. esq. 3 Chesham st
Evans Wm. esq. 19 Mornington crescent
Evans Wm. esq. M.P. Park house, Kensington gore, & Allistree hall, nr. Derby
Evans Wm.esq. 55 Walcotpl. ea. Lambeth
Evans Wm. David, esq. 5 New square
Evans Wm.J.M.D.25Henrietta st.Cavd.sq
EvansWm.L. esq. 13 Stonefield st. Islgtn
Eveningstar Wolfe, esq. 82 New Bond st
Everall Rd. esq. 11 Ecclestone st. south
Everett Edwd. J. esq. 105 St. Martin's la
Everett Henry, esq. 5 Pump ct. Temple
Everett Miss, 19 Bedford square
Everett Mrs. Acacia cot. Acacia rd
EveringhamJs.esq.9Cmden.cot.Cmdn.tn
Everingham Thos. esq. 3 Onslow terrace
Everington Wm. esq. 8 Endsleigh st
Everington W. esq. 1 Gloucester terrace
Eves Miss, Aberdeen villa, Maida hill
Evett Miss, 26 Coleshill st. Eaton square
Evezard Rev. Geo. 7 York bldgs. New rd
Evill Thos. esq. 8 Park sq. Regent's pk
Evill William, esq. 51 Berners st
Ewart Francis, esq. 4 Brick court, Tmpl
Ewart Geo. esq. 8 Powis pl.Hampstead rd
Ewart Hen. Larkins, esq. 7 Duchess st
Ewart John, esq. 19 Upper Woburn pl
Ewart Joseph, esq. 87 Jermyn st
Ewart Miss, 27 Wimpole st
Ewart Mrs. 53 Burton crescent
Ewart Wm. esq. M.P. 6 Cambridge sq
EwbankThos.H.esq.3South sq.Gray's inn
Ewbanke Mrs. 15 New Broad st. City
Ewens Creasy, esq. 28 Myddelton sq
Ewer Walter, esq. 23 Hanover square
Ewing J.esq. 18Park crescent, Portlnd.pl
Exeter Marquis of, K.G., P.C., 36 Grosvenor sq. & Burghley house, Stamford
Exeter Bishop of, Athenæum club, & the Palace, Exeter
Exmouth Viscount, Carlton club, 94 Pall mall; Canonteign house, Exeter; & Treverry, Teignmouth, Cornwall
Exeter John, esq. 6 Chester pl. Ken. crs
Eyles Chas. esq. 11 Brownlow st. Holbn
Eyles JohnB.esq. 1 St.Andrew's ct.Holbn
Eyles Richd. S.esq. 1St.Andrw's.ct.Hlbn
Eyre Count, 7 Hinde st
Eyre Sir James, M.D. 11 Brook st
Eyre Col. Hen. Saml. 22 Bryanstone sq
Eyre Lieut. Col. G. W. 68 Haymarket
Eyre Rev.M.V.Chapel house, Cadogan tr
Eyre Edwin, esq. 43 Devonshire st
Eyre Fredk. E. esq. 22 Bryanstone sq
Eyre George John, esq. 11 Bedford row
Eyre Geo. L. P. esq. 69 Lincoln's inn flds
Eyre Miss, 37 Michael's pl. Brompton
Eyre Mrs. George, 29 Eaton place
Eyre Stratford A. esq. 3 Fitzroy st
Eyre Walpole, esq. 22 Bryanstone square
Eyre William, esq. 16 Bernard st.&1Bond ct. Walbrook
Eyre Wm. V. esq. 16 Bernard st
Eyston George esq. 9 Montagu st. Portman sq. & 5 Gray's inn square
Eyton B. esq. 7 Michael's grove, Brmptn

FABER Augustus, esq. 29 Finsbury sq
Faber Chas. Waring, esq.23Chancery la
Fabries Antonio, esq. 10 Titchfield ter
Fache Chas.J.esq.51Cummingst.Pntnvl
Fagan J. H. esq.14 Gloster rd.O.Brmptn
Fagan Mrs. 9 Albion st. Hyde park
Fagan Mrs. 54 Gibson square, Islington
Fagan Stephen, M.D.9Albion st.Hyde pk
Fagg Edwin, esq. 1 Clarement pl. Grove end, Lisson gr. & 73 New Church st
Fagg Robert, esq. 14 Wilmington square
Fahey Jas. esq. 15 York pl. Fulham rd
Faija G. esq. 23 Sloane st. Chelsea
Fair Maj.Gen. C.B.5 South cres.Bdfd. sq
Fairbairn Thos. esq. 7 Furnival's inn
Fairbrother Mrs. 12 Lit. Stanhope st
Fairchild Mrs. 16 Alfred pl. Brompton
Fairfax Capt. Jas. 1 James st. Adelphi
Fairfoot Henry Spence, esq. 25 Lloyd sq
Fairholt Mrs. Grosvn. cot. Park vil. ea
Fairland Mrs. 33 Lowndes st.Belgrve. sq
Fairland Rd. esq. 5 Powis pl. Hmstd. rd
Fairland Thos. esq.Pembroke sq.Knsntn
Fairman Wm. G. esq. 150 St. John st. rd
Faithfull E. C. esq. 5 King's rd. Bdfd. rw
Faithfull W. esq. 11 Strahan tr. Lpool. rd
Falcon Henry, esq. 4 Elm court, Temple
Falcon Hy. esq. 35 Royal cr. Notting hill
Falconer Christie, esq. 7 Wilton st
Falconer F. esq.A.M.42Dorsetst.Ptm. sq
Falkiner Sir Rigge, bart. 5 Suffolk st. Pall mall east
Falkland Viscount, G.C.H. P.C. Scuttiskelfe, Stoksley
Falkner Edwd. esq. 6 Arthur st. east
Fallow Rev.Thos.Mount, 70 Margaret st
Fallowdown Chas. S. esq. 42 Claremont sq. & 2 Paper buildings, Temple
Fallowdown C. S. esq. 58 Myddelton sq
Fallowfield Rev. Wm. 49 Warren st
Fallows Joseph, esq. 198 Piccadilly
Falmouth Earl of, 2 St. James's square; & Tregothnan, Truro, Cornwall; & Woolhampton house, Newbury, Berks
Fane Lady Georgiana, 5 Up. Brook st
Fane Hon. Mrs. 23 Wimpole st
Fane Cecil, esq. 4 Upper Brook st
Fane Vere, esq. 11 Nottingham place
Fane Wm. Dashwood, esq. 21 Old square
Fanning Miss, Cavendish hotel, 81 Jermyn st. & 3 Circus, Bath
Fano Jaco, esq. 10 Portld. pl. Clapm. rd
Fanshaw Miss, 70 Harley st
Fanshawe Col. 14 Cumberland terrace
Faraday Michael, esq. 21 Albemarle st
Farden Saml. esq. 24 Spencer tr.Lr.rd.Is
Farebrother Mr. Ald. 9 Lancaster place
Farebrother Mrs. 32 Millbank st
Farenden Miss, 26 Avenue rd. Regt's. pk
Farey John, esq. 35 Guilford st
Fargues Hy. F. esq. 26Alfred pl.Bedfd.sq
Fargues J. P. esq. 1 Albion gr. Thrnhl. rd

Faris Mrs. 53 Oxford terrace
Farish James, esq. 8 Lancaster pl.Strand
Farish Jas.esq.7Northwk.ter.St.Jn.'s wd
Farland Chas.esq.3Strutton grd.Westmr
Farlar Miss, Chichester cot. Wands. rd
Farley Chas. esq. 37 Southampton row
Farmer Miss, 5 North cresct. Bedfd. sq
Farmer Mrs. 31 Alfred st. Bedford sq
Farmer Mrs. 3 Mornington place
Farmer Mrs. 5 North cresct. Bedford sq
Farmer Rt. esq. Fortess ter. Kentish tn
Farmer Wm. esq.4 River ter. nth.City rd
Farn Edward, esq. 14 Gray's inn square
Farncomb Thomas (Alderman), 12 Harleyford place, Kennington common
Farnham Lord, K.P. Carlton club,94Pall mall, & Farnham, county Cavan
Farnham Edward B. esq. M.P. 63 St. Jas. st. & Quorndon ho. Loughborough
Farques Hy. F. esq.26Alfred pl.Bedfd. sq
Farquhar Sir Walter Rockliffe, bart. & Lady Mary, 41 Grosvenor st
Farquhar Lady, 18 King st. St. James's
Farquhar Harvie, esq.18 King st.St. Jas'
FarquharThos.Newman,esq.27Abingdon st. Westminster, & 65 Moorgate st
Farquharson Mrs. 19 Alpha road
Farr Henry Fuller, esq. 13 Gray's inn sq
Farr Wm. W. esq. 1 Paper bldgs. Temple
Farran Major Chs. 10 Chester pl. Ken. cr
Farran Miss, 16 Thayer st. Manchstr. sq
Farrance Jas. esq. 26 Lr. Phillimore pl
Farrance Mrs. 47 Mount st
Farrant Geo. B. esq. 7 Figtree court
Farrant Jsph. esq.3 King Wm. st. Strand
Farrant Miss, 25 Woburn square
Farrant Thos. esq.17 Montagu st.Ptm.sq
Farrar Edward, esq. 48 Guilford st
Farrar Fredk. esq. 12 Godliman st. Doct. comns. & Halfway house, near Esher
FarrarHy.W.esq.7Cumbrld.ter.Lloyd sq
Farre Arthur, M.D. 22 Curzon st
Farre John Rd. esq. 3 Elm ct. Temple
Farre John Richard, M.D.7 Queen's row, Pentonville, & 4 Charterhouse square
Farrell Capt. S.7 Bentinck ter. Rgt's. pk
Farrell Jas. esq. 48 York st. Portman sq
Farrell John, esq. 18 Rupert st
FarrellWm.esq.10Ehrenbg.ter.Morng.rd
Farren George, esq. 1 Symond's inn
Farren Wm. esq. 30 Brompton square
Farrer Major Gen. Jas. 5 Up. Glo'ster st
Farrer Hy.esq.15 Albert rd.Glo'str. gate
Farrer Jas. Wm. esq. 7 John st. Berkeley sq.; & Masters' off.25 Southampton bldgs.;&Ingleborough,Settle,Yorkshir
Farrer Mrs. 20 Michael's pl. Brompton
Farrer Mrs.Thos.3 Glo'ster ter. Regt. pk
Farrer Misses, 4 Upper Glo'ster st
FarrerOliverWm.esq.8King'sBench wlk. Temple, & 7 John st. Berkeley sq
Farrer Wm.L. esq. 66 Lincoln's inn fields
Farrier Chas. esq.2 Manor ter. nth. Chels
Farsyde Geo.Jas. W.esq.3 Elm ct.Templ
Farthing Thos. esq.2 Markham sq. Chels
Fasson Benjn. esq. 17 Lime st. City
Faucher Frs. esq. 7 Half Moon st. Pcdly
Faulconer Thos. esq. 69 Westbourne ter
Faulder Joseph, esq. 15 Fitzroy square
Faulkes Mrs. 62 Drummond st
Faulkes William, esq. 39 Coleshill st
Faulkner Rev.W.E.L.7Rodney st.Pntnv
Faulkner Benj. R. esq. 23 Newman st
Faulkner George, esq. 1 Bedford row
Faulkner George, esq. 41 St. James's st
Faulkner Thomas,esq.7Lw.Phillimore pl
Fauntleroy John, esq. 14 Gt. Portland st
Fauquier Edw. esq. 26 Charles st. St. Jas
Fauquier Wm. esq. 30 Dorset square
Favell Mrs. 27 Clapham rise
Favenc Mrs. 4 Augusta pl. Stkwl. com
Fawcett Edwd. esq. 5 Pump ct. Temple
Fawcett Walter Thos. esq. 11 Addison rd
Fawcett William, esq. 15 Finsbury sq
Fawcett Wm. esq. 23 Mornington cresc
Fawkener J. esq. 14Essex st.& Chatham
Fawlkner C.esq.11 Norland pl.Notng. hl
Fawssett Mrs. 11 Connaught square
Faxon Samuel Walton, esq. 6 Belmont terrace, Wandsworth road
Fay Rd. esq. 9 Lowther cottgs. Livpl. rd
Fayerman Edmd. R. esq. 8 Edwardes sq
Fayrer Rev. Robert Emanuel, Parsonage, Camberwell road
Fearn John Geo. esq. 2 Cumberland pl
Fearnhead Peter, esq.17 Clifford's inn, & 26Ely place,Holbrn.&17Ironmonger la
Fearnley Rev. J. 47 Lincoln's inn fields
Fearnside Tarva Rd. esq. 50 Ebury st. Pimlico, & 11 Spring gardens
Fearon J.P.esq.1 Cumberld.pl.Regts.pk. 1 Crown office row,&8Fig tree ct.Temp
Fearon Mrs. 4 Clapham rise
Fearon Saml. John esq. 1 Gray's inn sq
Featherstone Wm. esq. 42 Albemarle st
Featon Edward Dickons, esq. 2 Myddelton square
Febvre Mrs. 24 Grove pl. Lisson grove
Feeny Patrick M. esq. 63 Waterloo road
Feetham Thos. esq. 4 Millbank st
Feilden Wm. esq. M.P. 18 Hanover sq. & Fenniscowles, near Blackburn
FeildingLadyEliz.31Sckville.st.&Lacock abbey, Chippenham, Wilts
Feldwick Chas. esq. 5 Marchmont st
Felking Rt. esq. 11Loraine pl. Holwy.rd
Fell Rev. Francis Hunter, M.A. Cloudesley parsonage, Thornhill road
Fell Rev. F. H. 1 Albion ctgs. Islington
Fell Miss, 20 Tavistock place
Fell Robert, esq. 3 Raymond buildings
Fell Wm. esq. 15 Everett st. Brunswk. sq
Fellowe Rice G. esq. 1 Park village east
Fellowes hon. Newton & LadyCatherine, 41 Bryanstone square, & Eggesford, Oakhampton, Devon
Fellowes Rev. Dr. 31 Dorset square
Fellowes A. Wm. esq. 144 Oxford st.; & Chumleigh, Devon
Fellowes Edw. esq. M.P. 15 Low. Berkeley st.; & Haverling hall, Norfolk; & Ramsey abbey, Huntingdon
Fellowes Mrs. 29 Glo'ster pl. Portman sq & Mortimer house, Reading, Berks
Fellowes Mrs. 15 Lower Berkeley st
Fellowes Mrs. 8 Montagu square
Fellowes Miss, 38 Brompton row
Fellowes Thos. esq. 41 Baker st. Lloyd sq
Fellows Chas. esq. 30 Russell square
Fellows James, esq. 64 Pall mall
Feltham Mrs. 43 Upper Baker st
Feltham John, esq. 7 Canonbury square
Feltham Wm. esq.12King's parade,Chels
Felton Wm. John, esq. 7 Halkin st. west
Fencott Miss, 4 Marlboro' rd. St.Jn's. wd
Fendall Mrs. 1 Harewood sq. Dorset sq
Fendall Thomas H. esq. 1 Harewood sq
Fenhoulhet Andw. esq. 26 Kensingtn. cr
Fenn B. esq. 9 Titchfield ter. Regent's pk
Fenn Thos. esq. 2 Staple inn, Holborn
Fenn Thomas, esq. 25 Up. Grosvenor st
Fenn Wm. Hugh,esq.136St.John st. road
Fennell Edwd. Fras.esq.34UpperBedford place, Russell sq. & 32 Bedford row
Fenner Hen. esq. 13Park pl.Up.Baker st
Fennessey Robert, esq. Belgrave st. sth
Fenning Chas. W. esq. 49 Connaught sq
Fenning Miss, 89 Pall mall
Fennings Wm. esq. 21 Wilmington sq
Fenoulhet James, esq. 65 Hatton garden
Fenoulhet Wm. esq. 10Grafton st. Fitz.sq
Fenton Edward, esq. 2 Queen sq. Westmr
Fenton Mrs. 2 Nottingham tr. New rd
Fenton Thos. J. esq. 2 Goswell road
Fenwick Henry, esq. 6King'sBench walk
Fenwick Joseph, esq. 8 Blandford sq
Fenwick Thos. esq. 1 Hare court, Temple
Ferard Miss, 26 Gower st. Bedford sq. & Ascot place, Winkfield, Berks
Ferguson Sir R. A. bart. M.P. United University Club, Pall mall east, & the Farm, near Londonderry
Ferguson Col. Hen. Rt. 48 Wilton crest
Ferguson Capt. Geo. R.N. & Hon. Mrs. 37 Charles st. Berkeley sq. & Pitfour Mintlow, Aberdeen, N. B.
Ferguson Lieut.-Col. Robt. M.P. 46 Clarges st. & Raith, near Kirkaldy
Ferguson Rev. Jas. 35Albert sq.Coml.rd
Ferguson Jas. esq. 3 Markhm. sq. Chels
Ferguson James Wm. esq.28Chancery la
Ferguson J. esq. 13 Colebrooke rw. Isln
Ferguson M. esq. Larkhall rise, Clapm
Ferguson Mrs. 4 Chester st. Grsvnr. pl
Ferguson Mrs. 3 Clifton vil. Maida vale
Ferguson Mrs. 18 Portman square
Ferguson Robt. M.D. 9Queen st.Mayfair
Ferguson Wm. esq. 18 Wharton st
Fergusson F. esq. 35 Dorset pl. Dorset sq
Fergusson J.M.D.21Cvndsh.rd.St.Jn'swd
Fergusson Wm. M.D. 21 Grove end road
Fergusson Wm. esq. 8 Dover st
Fergusson Wm.esq.4Nelson sq.Blkfrs.rd
Fergusson Wm.esq.27Park rd.Regt.'s pk
Fermor James, esq. 6 Fitzroy st
Ferrand Wm. Busfeild, M.P. Carlton club, & HardenGrange,Bingley,Yorks
Ferrand Mrs. 32 Wimpole st
Ferrar Mrs. Sarah, 21 Hunter st
Ferrers Earl, 24 Dover st. & Chartley castle, Lichfield
Ferrers Wm. Edwd. esq. 43 Hertford st
Ferrey Benj. esq. 7Bedford st. Bedford sq
Ferrier Alexander, esq. 46 Bernard st
Ferrier Robert, esq. 14 Lwr. Charles st
Ferris Josephus, esq. 11 Duncan terrace
Ferris Rd. esq. 8 Victoria gr. Kensingtn
Fesenmeyer John FrederickWilliam,esq. 12 Denmark st. Pentonville
Fesenmeyer Fk. esq. 20 Up. Islington ter
Feversham Lord, 25 Belgrave square, & Duncombe park, Helmsley,Yorkshire
Feversham Dow. Lady, 24 Arlington st
Few Chas. esq. 2 Henrietta st. Cov. gar
Few Charles, esq. 41 Jermyn st
Few Wm. Edward, esq. 41 Jermyn st
Few Rt. esq. 3 Henrietta st. Covent gar
Fewester A. esq.1 Stratton vil. Acacia rd
FfaringtonEdmd.F.esq.4Gardenct.Templ
Ffinch Rev. Benjn. Church st. Deptford
Ffrench Mrs. 5 Spencer tr. Lr. rd.Islgtn
Ffolliott John, esq. M.P. Carlton club, & Holybrook, Boyle, Ireland
Fickus Mrs. 15 Upper Baker st
Fickus Wm. esq. 21 Up. Islington terr
Fiddes Jas. esq. 4 St. Ann's vls. Acacia rd
Fiddes Jas. esq. 1 Wellington terrace
Fiddey Chas. esq. 3 Paper blds. Temple
Fidler Wm. esq. 17 Stonefield st. Islgtn
Fido Robt.esq.24 Winchester row,Newrd
Field Ben. esq. 3 Bdfd. ter.Clapham rise
Field Ben. esq. 4 Lincoln's inn fields
Field Chas.esq.6 Bentinck ter. Regt.'s pk
Field Chas. esq. 5 Nottingham place
Field Chas. esq. 1 Up.Robert st.Brmptn
Field Chas. esq. Wandsworth road
Field Edward, esq. 5 Raymond bldgs
Field Edwin Wilkins, esq. 41 Bedfd. rw
FieldFras.esq.8Chester pl. Regent's park
Field Jas. esq. 1 Harleyford pl.Ken.com
Field Henry J. esq. 22 Penton pl. Pentvl
Field John, esq. 5 Bennett st. St.James's
Field John, esq. 10 Cross st. Hatton gdn
Field John, esq. 9 Guilford st. Russell sq
Field John, esq. 2 Strand
Field John, esq. 9 Trinity sq. Southwark
Field John, esq. 36 Trinity sq. Tower hl
Field John, esq. 15 Upper Gower st
Field John, esq. 25 Upper Seymour st
Field Joshua, esq. 13 Park crescent, Portland place; & Weston, Malton; & Helmsley lodge, near York
Field Michael, esq. 89 Albany st
Field Mrs. 6 Bentinck ter. Regent's pk
Field Mrs. 13 Brompton crescent
Field Mrs. 8 Compton st. ea. Brunswk.sq
Field Mrs. 29 Grafton st. Fitzroy sq
Field Mrs. 1 Salcombe's pl. Regent pk

Field O.A. esq. 4 Stanhope ter. Hyde pk
Field Rt. esq. 25 Tibberton sq. Islington
Field Sam. esq. 13 Beaufort bdgs. Strand
Field Wm. esq. Carlton chambs. Regt. st
Field Wm. esq. 20 Nottinghill square
Field Wm. Hy. esq. 3 Ladbroke pl. Not. hl
Fielden John, esq. M.P. 7 Wilton place, & Todmorden, near Rochdale
Fielden Mrs. 17 Somerset st. Portman sq
Fielder Geo. esq. 23 Manchester st
Fielder John, esq. Nelson lodge, Trafalgar sq. Queen's elms, Chelsea
Fielder Thos. esq. 23 Manchester st
Fielding Copley, esq. 26 Newman st
Fielding Danl. esq. 42 Cloudesley ter
Fielding Fredk. esq. 23 Upper Brook st
Fife Earl of, K.T., G.C.H. Union club, Trafalgar sq. & Duff house, near Banff, N.B
Figge Fred. esq. 4 Lawn cott. Sth. Lambth
Figgins Vincent, esq. 19 Park ter. Highbry
Filder Edwd. esq. 1 Ladbroke pl. Nttg. hl
Filer A.J.D. esq. 4 Spencer st. Goswell rd
Filica Chas. esq. 24 Park cresct. Portlnd. pl
Filkin Rd. M.D. 28 Coventry st. Haymkt
Fillans James, esq. 82 Baker st
Filmer Sir Edmund, bart. M.P. 72 Eaton sq. & East Sutton park, nr. Maidstone
Filmer Thos. esq. 30 Harleyford place
Finch Hon. Daniel, 33 Chesham place
Finch Lady Elizabeth, 33 Chesham place
Finch Lady Frances, 33 Chesham place
Finch Chas. esq. 2 Madeley villas, Knsgtn
Finch Francis O. esq. 51 Charlotte st
Finch George, esq. 68 Acton st. Gr. inn rd
Finch George Wm. esq. 20 Oxford ter
Finch J.W. esq. 17 Southampton pl. Euston sq. & Duncroft cottage, Staines
Finch Geo. Wm. esq. 57 Linc. inn fields
Finch John, esq. 47 Cambridge terrace, Edgware road, & 21 Old Jewry
Finch John, esq. 22 Guilford st
Finch John, esq. 21 Percy st. Bedford sq
Finch John, esq. 27 Woburn place
Finch John, jun. esq. 22 Guilford st
Finch Misses, 49 Charles st. Berkeley sq
Finch Mrs. Benj. 10 Albany st
Finch Thos. esq. 20 Theberton st. Islngtn
Finch Wm. Hen. esq. 32 Lonsdale square
Fincham George, esq. 5 Spring gardens
Fincham Geo. T. M.D. 38A, Curzon st
Fincher Jos. esq. 2 Trafalgar sq. Chelsea
Finden E. esq. 18 Sthmptn. pl. Eustn. sq
Finden John, esq. 25 Regent st
Finden Thos. esq. 9 John st. Adelphi
Finden Wm. esq. 49 Camdn. st. s. Cmdn. tn
Findin John esq. 24 Dorset place
Findon Wm. esq. 16 Hanover ter. Regt. pk
Fingall Earl of, Brookes's club, & Killeen castle, Meath, Ireland
Finlason Hen. esq. 41 Edwards sq. Knsgtn
Finlason Wm. esq. 5 Essex ct. Temple
Finlay Captain Thos. R.N. 50 Hunter st
Finlay Fred. esq. 26 Duke st. Westm
Finlay T. esq. 79 Cambridge tr. Edgwr. rd
Finlayson John, esq. 5 Philpott tr. Edg. rd
Finmore Mrs. 3 Vassal cot. Addison rd
Finnelly Wm. esq. 20 Old sq. Linc. inn
Finney Douglas, esq. 76 Welbeck st
Finney John D. esq. 6 Furnival's inn
Finnimore B. K. esq. 5 Leonard pl. Knsgtn
Finnis Mrs. 3 Bath pl. Kensington
Finnis Rt. F. esq. 21 Hart st. Bloomsbury
Finny John, esq. 5 Bedfd. pl. Kensington
Fippard Thos. esq. 34 Glo'ster pl. New rd
Firby Jas. esq. 8 Pelham pl. Fulham rd
Firth Wm. H. esq. 23 Charles st. Westm
Fish John, esq. 12 Sloane terrace
Fish Saml. esq. 18 Highbury terrace
Fish Saml. Chas. C. esq. 2 Hare ct. Temple
Fisher Rev. Jas. M. M.A. Lr. Grv. Brmtn
Fisher Capt. S. 2 Park cottages, Pk. vil. ea
Fisher Francis, esq. 36 Bloomsbury sq. & 3 Austinfriars
Fisher Henry, esq. 83 St. John's wood ter
Fisher Henry Wm. esq. 21 Argyll st
Fisher James, esq. Denmark hill
Fisher Jas. esq. 29 York place, City rd
Fisher John, esq. 32 Somerset st. Ptm. sq
Fisher John C. esq. 57 Pratt st. Camden town, & 3 Mitre ct. Ely place
Fisher John Philip, esq. 16 Gt. Ryder st
Fisher Joseph, esq. 38 Cloudesley ter
Fisher Miss, 33 Dorset square
Fisher Mrs. 14 George st. Portman sq
Fisher Mrs. 39 Gower place, Euston sq
Fisher Mrs. 7 Hornton st. Kensington
Fisher Mrs. Knightsbridge green
Fisher Octavius, esq. 8 Brompton sq
Fisher Rd. jun. esq. 35 Queen square
Fisher R. T. esq. 30 Eaton pl. & 3 Stone bdgs
Fisher Robert, esq. 13 Highbury park
Fisher Rt. A. esq. 1 Churchyd. ct. Temple
Fisher R. H. esq. 16 James st. Buckingham gate, & Bentworth hall, nr. Alton
Fisher S. esq. 6 Montagu pl. Clapham rd
Fisher Thomas, esq. 8 Wilton crescent
Fisher Thos. J. esq. 1 Churchyd. ct. Tmpl
Fisher William, esq. 19 Doughty st
Fisher William esq. 1 Camden st. south
Fisher Wm. esq. 2 Verulam bldgs. Gray's in
Fisher William, esq. 4 Cork st. Bond st
Fisher W. esq. St. Leonards ctg. Acacia rd
Fisher Wm. esq. Yorkvil. Finchley newrd
Fisher Wm. Richd. esq. 13 Gray's inn sq
Fisk Rev. Geo. 12 Finchley New road
Fisk Wm. esq. 31 Blomfield road. Maidahl
Fisk Wm. esq. 13 Howland st. Fitzroy sq
Fitch Col. Geo. 36 York terrace, Reg. pk
Fitch Geo. esq. 15 New Bridge st
Fitch Mrs. 8 Haydon sq. Minories
Fitness John, esq. 64 Stafford pl. Pimlico
Fitter Godfrey, esq. 7 Up. Grosvenor st. & at 9 Marine parade, Dover
Fitton Henry Wm. esq. 53 Up. Harley st
Fitz Mrs. 10 Albert ter. Knightsbridge
Fitzclarence Lord Adolphus, Ambassador's court, St. James's palace
Fitz Gerald Lord William, 45 Green st
Fitzgerald Sir John, bart. 5 Montagu st. Portman sq
Fitzgerald Col. 16 Hereford st & Maperton house, Wincanton, Somersetshire
Fitzgerald — esq. 15 North bk. Reg. pk
Fitzgerald C. R. esq. 15 Northbk. Regtspk
Fitzgerald Edward, esq. 45 Davies st
Fitzgerald Frederic, esq. 22 Jermyn st
Fitzgerald Jas. David, esq. 20 Somerset st
Fitz Gerald John, esq. 39 Portland pl. & Boulge hall, Woodbridge, & Naseby Northants, & Little Island, Waterford, & Castle Irwell, Manchester
Fitzgerald M. esq. 12 Buckingham st. Str
Fitzgerald Mrs. 17 Wellington road
Fitzgerald Stephen James, esq. 4 Regent's vls. Avenue rd. & 53 Chancy. la
Fitz Gerald Thomas, esq. 2 Portland pl & Muntham park, Worthing, Sussex
Fitz Gerald Wm. Rt. Seymour, esq. 17 Whitehall place, & Church porch chambers, Farrar's bdgs. Temple
Fitzgibbon Hon. Col. Richard Hobart, 64 Eaton sq. & Mount Shannon, near Castle Connell, Ireland
Fitzgibbon Mrs. 2 Cambridge st. Edgw. rd
Fitzhardinge Earl, Berkeley house, 6 Spring gardens, & Berkeley castle
Fitzherbert E. H. esq. 25 Torrington sq
Fitzherbert E. H. esq. 1 Paper bdgs. Tpl
Fitzherbert John K. esq. 2 Davies st
Fitzherbert Miss, 112 Mount st
Fitzherbert Thos. esq. 23 Hanover sq
Fitzherbert Wm. M.D. 1 Paper buildings
Fitzhugh Mrs. 18 Orchard st. & Bannister's lodge, Southampton
Fitzhugh Thos. esq. 2 Gt. Stanhope st. Mayfair, & Plaspower, Wrexham
Fitzhugh Wm. esq. 21 Green st. Gros. sq
Fitzmaurice Hon. Wm. Edward, M.P. 4 Chesham st. Belgrave sq. & Taplow, Maidenhead, Bucks
Fitzmaurice Hon. Mrs. 4 Chesham st
Fitzmaurice Rev. Jas. 13 Walcot pl. eas
Fitzmaurice G. L. esq. 97 Gloucester pl
Fitzpatrick Fras. esq. 27 Up. Lisson st
Fitzpatrick Henry James, esq. 3 Cook's ct. Carey st. & 29 Cranbourne st
Fitzpatrick Jas. esq. 2 N. Temple bdgs
Fitzpatrick M. J. esq. 21 Gt. Marlbro' st
Fitzpatrick Richd. esq. 1 Elm. ct. Temp
Fitzpatrick Rd. Wm. esq. 18 Glo'ster rd
Fitzroy Rt. Hon. Lord Chas. M.P. 3 Burlington gds. & Salcey ldge. Nmptn
Fitzroy Lord Charles, 47 Clarges st
Fitzroy Lord Frederick, 47 Clarges st
Fitzroy Lord John, 2 Halfmoon st
FitzRoy Hon. Capt. Geo. 70 Jermyn st
FitzRoy Hon. Henry, M.P. 42 Up. Gros. st
Fitzroy Lady Laura, 47 Clarges st
Fitzroy Hon. Mrs. 58 Grosvenor st
Fitzwilliam Earl, Mortimer house, Halkin st. & Wentworth ho. Rotherham
Fitzwilliam Hon. Geo. Wentworth, M.P. Halkin st. & Wentworth ho. Rotherhm
Fitz Wygram Sir Robert, bart. 10 Connaught pl.; & Belmont lodge, Malvern; & Clifford house, near Wexford
Flack Mrs. 11 Argyle st. King's cross
Fladgate Fran. esq. 8 Lr. Brompton gr
Fladgate Mrs. 6 Queen sq. Westminster
Fladgate Wm. Mark, esq. 37 Craven st
Flanders Wm. esq. 8 Up. Woburn place
Flather John, esq. 39 Hastings st. & 24 Old square, Lincoln's inn
Flavell Thos. Wm. esq. 21 Bedford row
Flaws James, esq. 10 Old North st
Flaxland Chas. esq. 23 Vincent ter. Islgtn
Fleeming Hon. Mrs. Elphinstone, 1 Lyall st. Belgrave square
Fleet Mrs. 42 Hemingford ter. Islington
Fleet Saml. esq. 8 Clement's inn, Strand
Fleetwood Sir Peter Hesketh, bart. M.P. 107 Pallmall; & Rossall hall, Fleetwd
Fleetwood Geo. esq. 9 Connaught terrace
Fleming Arthur C. esq. & Mrs. Cavendish hotel, 81 Jermyn st
Fleming James, esq. 15 Norfolk st. Park lane, & 25 Old sq. Lincoln's inn
Fleming Mrs. Warwick ho. Lit. Chelsea
Flemming Jph. esq. 3 Alpha pl. Regt.'s pk
Fletcher Chas. esq. 6 Glo'ster rd. Reg.'s pk
Fletcher Chas. Wm. esq. 8 Notting hill sq
Fletcher Edwd. esq. 125 Park st. Grosvenor sq.; & Pierremont, Isle of Thanet; & Lime grove, Putney
Fletcher J. B. esq. 17 New Burlington st
Fletcher John D. esq. 5 Essex court
Fletcher Joseph, esq. 27 Sackville st
Fletcher Miss, 8 Argyle st. King's cross
Fletcher Mrs. 16 Alpha rd. Regent's pk
Fletcher Mrs. 34 Duke st. St. James's
Fletcher Mrs. 36 Golden square
Fletcher Mrs. 15 London st. Fitzroy sq
Fletcher Robert, esq. 22 Finsbury sq
Fletcher Wm. esq. 17 Gerrard st. Islgtn
Flexon Mrs. 55 Coleshill st. Eaton sq
Flight E. G. esq. 1 Adam st. & Bridport
Flight Thomas, esq. 22 Up. Brook st
Flint Lady, 77 Cadogan pl. Sloane st
Flint George, esq. 229 Maida vale
Flintoff Thos. esq. 73 Gt. Titchfield st
Flockton G. esq. 1 Cambridge ter. Edg. rd
Flockton Mrs. 35 Beaufort st. Chelsea
Flockton Stephn. esq. 21 Westbourne st
Flood Fred. Solly, esq. St. John's lodge, 8 Alpha rd. Regt.'s pk. & 1 Pump ct
Flood C. esq. 10 Clarendon pl. Maida vale
Flood Luke T. esq. Bellevue lodge, Chels
Flood Mrs. 4 Addison rd. Kensington
Florence Hen. esq. 18 Cobourg pl. Up. Kenningten lane
Flower Sir James, bart. M.P. 15 Wimpole st. & Eccleshall, Larlingford, Norfolk
Flower Edward, esq. 69 Chancery lane
Flower Henry, esq. 3 Upper Ground st
Flower Mathw. esq. 14 Norfolk crescent
Flower Thomas, esq. 96 Hatton garden
Flower William, esq. 14 Furnival's inn
Flowerdew Mrs. 2 Albert ter. Knightsb

Flowers Geo. Fredk. esq. 3 Keppel st
Flowers Henry, esq. 39 Regent square
Floyer Wm. Humberstone Cawley, esq. 2 Great Cumberland place, & Hints, Tamworth, Staffordshire
Flude Mrs. 15 Marlborough sq. Chelsea
Fluder Geo. esq. 1 Egremont pl. New rd
Fludyer Sir Sam.bart.16Gt.Cumberland place, & Felixtow, near Ipswich
Fludyer Col.Wm.123 Mount st.Berkeley sq.& Hasting hall, near Uppingham
Foden Strethill, esq. 31 Essex st. Strand
Fogarty Fred. Wm. esq. 31 Gt. Percy st
FoggoDavid,esq. 10 Chathampl.Blackfrs
Foggo Fras. Alexander,esq, 14 Craven st
Foggo George, esq. 62 Upper Norton st
Foley Lord, P.C. 26 Grosvenor square
Foley Edwd. esq. 59 George st.Euston sq
Foley Edwd. Thos. esq.&Lady Emily, 31 Portmn.sq.&StokeEdith pk.Worcester
Foljambe Mrs, 2 Glo'ster vil. Glo'ster gt
Folkard A. esq. 49 Clifton st. Finsbury
Folkard George, esq. 3 Lyon's inn
Folkard Geo. esq.21South bank,Rgts.pk
Follett Brent Spencer, esq. 25 Norfolk crescent, & 22 Old sq. Lincoln's inn
Follett John, esq. 46 Half moon st. & 1 Sambrook court
Follett Robt. B. esq. 25 Norfolk crescent
Follett Wm. esq. 13 Manchr.tr.Lpool.rd
Follit C. esq. Raleigh cot.Mornington rd
Folquah J. L.esq. 15 Kensingtn.grdn.ter
Fonblanque Albany, esq. 48 Connght.sq
Fonblanque John Saml. M. esq. 19 Hamilton terrace & Bankruptcy Court
Fonblanque John Wm.M.esq. 19 Hamilton terrace, St. John's wood, & 30 Chancery lane
FonnereauMrs.8Grove end rd.St.Jn's.wd
Fontana S. esq. 25 Charlottest. Portld.pl
Fonvielle Ferdinand Georges de, esq. 9 King William st. Strand
Fonvielle Hyde, esq. 9 KingWm.st.Stnd
Fooks W. esq. 3 Figtree court, Temple
Fooks Wm. esq. 25 Lonsdale sq. & 30 Chancery lane
FoordThos. J. esq. 45 Gt. Portland st
Foot Jas. esq. 4 Grove rd. St. John's wood, & Holley park, near Dublin
Foot James A. esq. 5 Brick ct. Temple
Foot Jeffery, esq. 3 Madeley villas, Kensington New town
Foote John, esq.36Tavistock st.Cov.gdn
Foote Keppel, esq. 102 Camden rd.villas
Forbes Viscountess, 32 Grosvenor place
Forbes Sir Chas. bart. 9 Fitzroy square, & New & Edinglassie, Strathdon,N.B
Forbes Sir Charles Fergusson, K.C.H., M.D. 23 Argyll st. Regent st
Forbes Lady, 3 Fitzroy square
Forbes Lt. General, 21 Sloane st. & Auchernach Strathdon, Aberdeenshire
Forbes Capt. Chas. 1 Hy.pk. gt.Kensgtn
Forbes C. D. esq. 8 Chapel pl. Cavend. sq
Forbes Charles, esq. 3 Elm ct. Temple
Forbes Bartholomew, esq. 18 Sloane st
Forbes Duncan, esq. 5 Burton crescent
Forbes Geo. esq.26 Chester ter.Regt's.pk
Forbes George, esq. 3 Titchfield terrace
Forbes John, esq. 4 Allen ter. Kensngtn
Forbes John, esq. 12 Old Burlington st
Forbes John, esq. 44 Sackville st
Forbes John Gregory, esq. 52 Oxford ter
Forbes Miss, 2Hydepk. gt. so.Knsgtn.gr
Forbes Mrs. 4 Belgrave ter. Pimlico
Forbes Mrs. 14 Glo'ster ter. O. Bromptn
Forbes Mrs. 80 Sloane st
Forbes Rt. esq. 48 Glo'ster pl. Ptmn. sq
Forbes Rt. esq.1 Hyde pk. gt. so. Knsgtn
Forbes Thos. esq. 50 St. John's wood ter
Forbes Wm. esq. 11 Gray's inn square
Forbes Wm. esq. M.P. Carlton Club, & Callender house, Falkirk, Stirlingshire
Ford Lady, 123 Park st. Grosvenor sq
Ford Capt. R.N. 4 Warwickvils. Harrowrd
Ford Capt Robt. 8 Lincoln's inn fields
Ford Rev. Fredk. 3 Sussex ter. Hyde pk
Ford Rev. Joseph, 48 Canonbury sq
Ford Charles, esq. 5 Bloomsbury sq
Ford Chas. esq. 19 Chester ter. Eaton sq
Ford Chas. B. esq.18Somersetst.Prtm.sq
Ford Fred. esq. 14 York pl. Pentonville
Ford GeorgeSaml.esq. 3Henrietta st.Covent gdn.; & 46Brunswicksq.Brighton
Ford Henry, esq. 4 Argyle sq. New road
Ford James, esq. 4 Argyle sq. New road
Ford John, esq. 10 Retreat, So. Lambeth
Ford John, esq. 61 St. John's wood ter
Ford Matthew, esq. 9 Keppel st. Rusk.sq
Ford Matthew, esq.8 Lincoln's inn fields
Ford Miss, 24 Upper Baker st
Ford Miss, 9 Keppel st. Russell square
Ford Wm. esq. 1 Essex ct
Ford Wm. esq. Millbrook house,Kentish town, & 4 South sq. Gray's inn
Ford Wm. esq. 61 Red Lion st. Holborn
FordWm.Aug.esq. 8Henrietta st.Cov.gd
Fordati James, esq. 27 Up. Bedford place
Foreman Rev. John, 8 Paddington green
Foreman H.R.esq.Ordnance offi. Pall mll
Foreman John, esq. 12 Clifford's inn
Forest Robert, esq. Brunswick lodge, Wandsworth road
Forester Lord, P.C.21Charlesst.Berkeley sq. & Willeypark,Broseley, Shropshire
Forester Hon. G. C. W. M.P.21 Charles st. Berkeley sq.; & Willey park, Shropshire
Forester Major, 31 St. James's place
Forester Francis, esq. 31 St. James's pl. & Somerby,MeltonMowbray,Le'stersh
Forman Miss, 17 Bryanstone st
Forman Mrs. 22 Upper Montagu st
Forman Rd. esq. 8 Chester pl. Knngtn. cr
Forman Thos.Seaton,esq.M.P.E5,Albany
Forman W. Henry, esq. E5, Albany
Forrest John, esq. 1 Surrey pl. Strand
Forrest Mrs. 3 Gloucester st. Queen sq
Forrest Thos. esq. 3 Park rd. Regt.'s pk
Forrester Henry, esq. 1 Minerva terrace
Forrett Dl. esq. Park cot. Barnsbury pk
Forshall Rev. Josiah, British Museum
Forster Rev. John, 5 Lancaster pl. Strnd
Forster Christopher, esq. 13 Brmptn. sq
Forster John, esq. 33 Canonbury square
Forster John, esq. 2 Highbury grove
Forster John, esq. 58 Lincoln's inn fields
Forster M. esq. 3 Dorset pl. Clapham rd
Forster Matthew, esq. M.P. 5 New City chambers, & Belsise, Hampstead
Forster Miss, 40 Duke st. St. James's
Forster Mrs. 9 Halkin st. west
Forster Mrs. 27 South st. Grosvenor sq
Forster Ralph Wm. E. esq. 4 Stone blds
Forster Robert Edward, esq. 182 Strand
Forster Sam. esq. 6 New sq. Lincoln's inn, & South end, Lewisham, Kent
Forster Thomas, esq. 3 Clarges st
Forster Thos. H. esq. 37 Smith st. Chelsea
Forster William, esq. 4 Carey st
Forsyth Geo. esq. 8 Stanhope pl. Hyde pk
Forsyth Mrs. 7 Upper Baker st. Lloyd sq
Forsyth Osborn, esq. Clapham rise
Forsyth Wm. esq. 3 St. Andrew's pl. Regent's pk. & 1 Paper bdgs. Temple
Forsyth Wm. esq. 25 Finchley New rd
Forsyth Wm. esq. 455 West Strand
Fort Mrs. 11 Nelson square
Forteath Geo. Alexr. esq. 7 Gt. Ryder st
Fortescue Earl, P.C. 17 Grosvenor sq. & Castle hill, South Molton
Fortescue Hon. Dudley Francis,17 Grosvnr.sq.& Castle hl. South Molton, Devon
FortescueHon.JohnWm.17Grosvenor sq. & Castle hill, South Moulton, Devon
Fortescue Geo. esq. 2 Hanover st. Islgtn
Fortescue Matthew, esq. 28 Regent sq. Gray's inn rd. & 2 Elm court, Temple
Fortescue Mrs. 1 Keppel st. Russell sq
Fortescue Mrs. 28 Regent square
Fortey Jas. esq. 1 Stanley pl. Kgs. r. Chls
Forth John, esq. 240 Oxford st
Fortune John, esq. 2 President st. west
Fortune Miss, 2 Bedford pl. Kensington
FortuneThos.esq.16Suthmptn.st.Blmsby
Forwood Mrs. 31 College st. Chelsea
Fosbrooke L. esq. 12 King's Bench walk
Foster Rt. Hon. Sir Augustus John, bart. & Lady Albinia, 1 New st. Spring grd
Foster Chas. esq. 6 Earl's ct. O. Brmptn
Foster Chas. 15 Michael's pl. Brompton
Foster Chas. esq.1 Willow tr. Canonby.sq
Foster Chas.J.esq.5Stone bldgs. Linc.inn
Foster Edwd. esq. 24 Glo'ster pl. New rd
Foster Edward, esq. 30A, Soho square
Foster Edward, esq. 43 Wakefield st
FosterEdwd.W.esq.4Barnard'sinn,Holbn
Foster Frederick Thos. esq. 32 Pall mall
Foster Geo. esq. 7 Vincent ter. Islington
Foster Hen. esq. 13 Frith st. Soho
Foster John, esq. 5 Addison tr. Kensgtn
Foster John, esq. 2 Montague pl. Islgtn
Foster John, esq.66 Jermyn st. St. James'
Foster M. B. esq. 4 Stranrear pl. Maida hl
Foster Mrs. 2 Cadogan st
Foster Mrs. 48 Hunter st. Brunswick sq
Foster Peter Le Neve, esq.92Chancery la
Foster Robt. C. esq.28 John st.Bedfrd.rw
Foster Saml. esq. 3 Up. Gore, Kensingtn
Foster Thos. esq. 11 Crown Office row
Foster Thos. Gregory, esq.12 King'sB.wk
Foster Wm. esq. 2 Soley ter. Pentonville
Fosters'Wm.C. esq. 28 John st.Bedfrd.rw
Fothergill Capt. Thos. 37 Bedford sq
Fothergill Fras. esq. 18 Cambridge st
Foulger Chas. esq. 46 Welclose sq. & 2 Tanfield ct. Temple
Foulger James, esq. 277 Regent st
Foulger Thomas, esq. 15 Ladbroke terr
Foulis Sir Wm. bart. & Lady, Mivart's hotel, 44 Brook st
Foulis Sir Wm. 7 Grosvenor place
Foulkes Griffith, esq. Denbigh cottage, Finchley New road, St. John's wood
Foulkes Wm. L. esq. 5 King's B. wlk. Templ
Fountain John M. esq. 29 Porchester ter
Fountain W. esq. 8 Regent's vil. Avenue rd
Fountaine Andrew, esq. 4 Albemarle st. & Narford hall, Swaffham, Norfolk
Fourman Mrs. 59 Great Prescot st
Foveaux Genl. 21 York bldgs. New rd
Fowell Frs. K. esq. 5 Alpha rd. Regts. pk
Fowke Anthony H. esq. 6 Stone bldgs
Fowke Frederic, esq. 6 Berkeley square
Fowke Fredk. T. esq.7 King's Bench wk
Fowke Gustavus W. esq. 6 Stone bldgs
Fowke Wm. Villiers, esq. 77 Chancery la
Fowle C. esq. 22 Southwark bridge road
Fowle Geo.Fred. esq.7King's Bench wlk
Fowle Geo. F. esq.93 Jermyn st. St. Jas's
Fowler Rev. Hy. Rt. 7 Manchester sq
Fowler Rev. Joseph, 10 Harpur st
Fowler Benj. esq. 17 Loraine pl. Hollwy
Fowler Charles, esq. 1 Gordon square
Fowler Chas. Slater, esq. 4 Fitzroy sq
Fowler Francis, esq. 28 Sackville st
Fowler Fras. E. H. esq. 28 Sackville st
Fowler Geo. esq. 10 Coles ter. Barnby.rd
Fowler Henry, esq. 27A, Grosvenor pl
Fowler John Coke, esq. 11 Paper bldgs
Fowler Mrs. 2 Rich ter. Old Brompton
Fowler Wm. esq. 11 Eccleston st. south
Fowlis Thos. esq. 85 Guilford st
Fownes Hen. esq. Poplar ho. Battersea
Fownes John, esq. Grange ter. Brompton
Fox Lady Caroline Lane, 1 Chesham st
Fox Hon. Miss, Lit. Holland ho. Knsngtn
Fox Col.CharlesRichd.M.P.&LadyMary, Lit. Holland ho. Addison rd. Knsngtn
Fox Chas. esq. 17 Edwardes sq. Knsngtn
Fox Chas. esq.65 Westbourne ter.Sussex gardens, Hyde park, & Trafalgar sq
Fox Chas. Jas. M.D. 30 New Broad st
Fox Edw. Buckley, esq. 33 Montague pl
Fox Edwin G. esq. 13 Gt. James st
Fox George, esq. 5 Bedford row, Islngtn
Fox John, esq. 21 New Bridge st. & Southgate, Middlesex

Fox John, esq. 8 Gibson sq. Islington
Fox Miss, 4 University st
Fox Mrs. 5 Beaumont st
Fox Mrs. George Lane, 36 Curzon st
Fox Mrs.S.2 Sand's bldgs.Up.st.Islngtn
Fox Sackville Lane, M.P. 3 St. James's sq. & Oran house, Catterick, Yorkshire
Fox Wm. esq. 30 Chester ter.Regt.'s pk. & 16 Gt. Knightrider st
Fox Wm.J.esq.5 Charlotte st. Bedfd. sq
Foxhall Edward Martin, esq. 18 South Audley st. & 14B, South st.Grosvnr.sq
Foxhall Miss, 4 Grove end place
Foy Miss, Burleigh house, Lit. Chelsea
Fradelle H. esq. 44 Cirencester place
Fradelle Hon. J. esq. 9 Percy st.Tot.ct.rd
Fradgley John, esq.7 Bedford row,Islgtn
Framton Thos. esq. 8 High st. Maryleb
Frampton John DeKewer,esq.6Stone bds
FramptonWm.H.esq.2South sq.Gray'sin
France James, esq. 17 Clarendon sq
France Jn. F.esq. 88Cadogan pl.Chelsea
France Mrs. 69 Edgware road
France Thomas, esq. 42 Upper Bedford place, Russell sq. & 24 Bedford row
France Wm. esq. 63 Cadogan place
Francillon Jas.esq. 10 Southampton blds
Francis Rev. Geo.135 Long lane,Bermny
Francis Alf.esq.2Encombe ter.Wndsw.rd
Francis Charles, sen. esq. Belgrave house, Wandsworth road
Francis Chas. L.esq. 1 Lawn,Sth.Lmbth
Francis Edward, esq. 50 Gt. Ormond st
Francis Frederick John, esq. 2 Cork st. Bond st
Francis John, esq. 53 Chancery lane
Francis John, esq. 1 New Boswell court, & 2 Portland ter. Wandsworth road
Francis John, esq. 56 Albany st
Francis Lewis, esq. 64 Newman st
Francis Mrs. 50 Great Ormond st
Francis Mrs. 9 Norfolk cres. Oxford sq
Francis Mrs. 10 St. George's terrace
Francis Philip, esq. 50 Great Ormond st
Francis Stephen, esq. 14 Montpelier sq
Francis Thos. Chs. esq. 23 Cloudesley st
Francis T. D. esq. 27 Mornington place
Francklyn Alexr. A. esq. 18 Hereford st
Franco Geo. F.esq. 34 Glo'ster pl.Ptmn.sq
Frankfort Viscount, Theydon bower, Epping; & Newlands, Dublin
Frankfort de Montmorency Viscountess, 24 Wilton place
Franklin Mrs. 9 Paradise ter. Islington
Franklin Wm. esq. 8 Bedford pl. Kensgtn
Franklyn H. G.esq.17Princes st.Hanv.sq
Franklyn Mrs. 46 Fredk. st. Gray's inn rd
Franklyn Rd.esq.25Gt.Quebec st.Newrd
Franklyn Rd.esq. 44Oxford ter. Hyde pk
Franks Charles, esq. 27 Cumberland st. Portman sq. & Dacre lodge, Barnet
Franks George T. esq. 45 Drummond st
Franks Jas. esq.1 Melbrne.pl.St. Jn.'swd
Franks John Fred. esq. 29 Cadogan pl
Franks Mrs. 29 Cadogan place
Franks Wm. esq.9 Winchester rw.Nw.rd
Frankum Hy. esq. 6 John st. Adelphi
FrankumMrs.24Up.George st.Brynst.sq
Frankum Richard, esq. 17 Albemarle st
Frankum R. F. esq. 24 Upper George st
Fraser Lieut.Gen. 37 Bury st. St.James's
Fraser Major R. 5 Titchfield ter.Reg.pk
Fraser Rev. Peter, 18 New st. Spring gardens, & Rectory, Kegworth
Fraser Alexr. esq. 65 Upper Seymour st
FraserJames,esq.10Park sq.west,Reg.pk
Fraser John, esq. 78 Dean st. Soho
Fraser John, esq.2 Gothic cot.Park vl. ea
Fraser J.esq. Harcourt vil. Finchly N.rd
Fraser John, esq. 22 King st. Covent gdn
Fraser John, esq. 35 York terrace, Regent's pk.& Bunchrew, Inverness, N.B.
Fraser John Farquhar, esq. 15 Eaton pl
Fraser Michael, esq. 2 Furnival's inn
Fraser Miss, 18 Camden road villas
Fraser Mrs. 25 Argyll st
Fraser Mrs. 12 Sussex sq. Hyde park
Fraser Patrick, M.D. 62 Guilford st
Fraser Roderick, esq. 15 Harley st
Frazer Chas. esq.41 Glo'ster pl.Ptmn. sq. & Williamston house, Aberdeen
FrazerJohn,esq.32Hamiltn.tr.St.Jn's.wd
Frazer Thomas, esq. 25 Glo'ster crescent
Frazier Mrs. 106 Milton st. Dorset sq
Fread Mrs. 30 Park rd. Regent's pk
Freake Chas. esq. 1Sydney pl.Fulham rd
Freake Jas. esq. 20 Chester ter. Eaton sq
Freeborn Joseph,esq. 4 Hanovr. st.Islgtn
Free Trade Club House (Edward John Evans, sec.), 27 Regent st
Frederick Mrs. Col. 52 Berkeley square
Frederick T. esq. 3 Michael's gr. Brmptn
Free Peter, esq. 7 Hyde park place west
Freebairn Alfred, esq. 23 Mornington pl
FreebodyWm.Yates,esq.9Duke st.Wstm
Freeborn H. L. esq.Nw.chmbs.Forgt. Str
Freeland H. W. esq. 42 Chancery lane
Freeland H.W.esq.19Duke st.St.James's
Freeling Chas. Rivers, esq.43 Weymouth st. & 4 New square, Lincoln's inn
Freeling John Clayton, esq. 41 Harley st
Freelone Mrs. 1 Bifrons vil. Acacia rd
FreemanA.esq.14Spencer tr.Lr.rd.Islgtn
Freeman Chas. esq. 14 Arundel st.Strand
Freeman George, esq. 29 Euston square
Freeman Henry,esq.3 Albion rd.Lvrpl.rd
FreemanJohn,esq.10Albert tr.St.Jn.'s wd
Freeman Joseph,esq.6Newingtn.pl.Keng
Freeman Joseph, esq. 21 Spring gardens
Freeman Miss, 30 Nutford pl. Edgw. rd
Freeman Mrs. 30 Upper Southwick st
Freeman Philip,esq. 24 Edwards st.Pt.sq
Freeman Rd. M. esq. 4 Great James st
FreemanWm.esq. 19Cloudesley ter. Islg
Freemantle Mrs.25 Claremont sq.Pentvll
Freer George, esq. 3 Coleshill st
Freeth Lieut. Col. 80 Coleshill st
Freeth Chas. esq.16St.Ann's vl.Acacia rd
Freeth Geo. esq. 24 Wellington road
Freeth George, esq. 4 Spring garden ter. & 63 Lincoln's inn fields
Freeth Thos. Jacob, esq. 4 Inn.Temple la
Fremantle Rt.Hon.SirThomas Fras.bart. M.P.2 Eaton pl. & Swanbourne, Winslow, & the Secretary's lodge, Phœnix pk. Dublin
Fremantle Sir Wm. Hen. bart. 6 Great Stanhope st. & Holly gve.Wndsr.gt.pk
Fremantle Mrs. Gen. 5 Tilney st. &Cranford bridge, Hounslow
Fremantle Miss, 29 Charles st. Berk. sq
French Baroness, 43 Cadogan place
French Fitzstephen, esq. M.P. 54 Parliament st. & French park, Roscommon
French Geo. esq. 64 Lincoln's inn fields
FrenchGeo.R.esq.18Sussex gdn. Hde. pk
French Henry, esq. 1 King square
French Joseph, esq. 10 New Palace yard
French John G. esq. 41 Gt. Marlboro' st
French Mrs. 5 Glo'ster pl. Glo'ster cresc
French Mrs. 6 Park cottage, Park vil. ea
French Ph. esq. 3 Egremont pl. New rd
French Thos. esq. 19 Cornwall terrace, Regt's. pk. & Poland cottage, Odiham
French Thomas, esq. 5 Up. Islington ter
French William, esq.10 John st. Bedfd.rw
Frend A. B. esq. 14 Buckingham st. Adph
Frend Geo. esq.25 Park pl.west, Lpool.rd
Frend HenryT.esq.28 Southampton bdgs
Frere Bartholomew, esq. 24 Saville row
Frere Bartle John L. esq. 45 Bedford sq. & 6 New sq. Lincoln's inn
Frere Edward, esq.53 Lincoln's inn fields
Frere George, esq. 45 Bedford sq. & 6 New square, Lincoln's inn, & Twyford house, Bishop's Stortford, Herts
Frere Jas. Hatley, esq. 2 Poet's corner
Freret Victor, esq. 10 Baker st.Lloyd sq
Freshfield Henry Ray, esq. 42 Devonshire st. Portland pl. & 5 New Bank buildings, City
Freshfield J. W. esq. 15 Regent st
Fretwell Rt. R. esq. 1 Staple inn, Holbrn
Frewer S. esq. 27Winchester rw. New rd
Frewin Mrs. 84 Lisson grove north
Fricker F. esq. 15 Glo'ster crs. Glostr.gt
Friend John Banks, esq. 23 Cambrdg.sq
Friend Wm. esq. 11 Egremont pl.New rd
Frineby Fredk. R. esq. 7 Claremont ter
Fripp George, esq. 92 Albany st
Frisby Mrs. Bedford ter. Clapham rise
Friswell Wm. esq. 93 Wimpole st
Frith Chas. esq.14Park vil.wst. Rgt.'s pk
Frith Miss, 41 Park ter. Regent's park
Frith Mrs. 31 Charlotte st. Fitzroy sq
Frith Wm. P. esq.31 Charlotte st.Fitz.sq
Frodsham Wm. Jas.esq. Stk.Newngt.grn
Froggatt John, esq. 16 Clifford's inn
Froggatt Thomas, esq. 75 Regent st
Frooms Robt. esq. 21 Gibson sq. Islngtn
Frost C. M. esq. 5 Ladbroke pl. Nottnhl
Frost J. esq. 12 Up.North pl.Gray's inn rd
Frost Mrs. 23 Cecil st. Strand
Frost Mrs. 21 Compton st. Brunswick sq
Frost Mrs. 6 Leonard pl. Kensington
Frost Mrs.30 Mornington pl.Hmpstd.rd
Frost Wm. Edwd. esq. 55 Berners st
Frostick Charles, esq. 9 Broadley terr
Fructuozo Jsph. A. esq. 69 Portland pl
Fry Alfrd.Augustus,esq.6Pump ct.Tmpl
Fry Geo. jun.esq.6Ordnance rd.St.Jn's.w
Fry Misses, 16 New Manor pl. Chelsea
Fry Mrs.5 Manor pl. so. King's rd. Chels
Fry Peter Wickens, esq. 14 Montague st. Russell sq. & 80 Cheapside
Fry Thos. esq. 22 Bedford square east
Fryer Jas. J. esq. 9 Hanover cot.Rgts.pk
Fryer Mrs. 15 Portland ter. Regent's pk
Fryer Mrs. 14 Queen st. May fair
Fuge James, esq. 111 Sloane st
Fukes Mrs. 35 Theberton st. Islington
Fulcher Capt. R. P. 144 Oxford st. & 35 Brunswick square, Brighton
Fulford Mrs. 9 Cumberland tr. Lloyd sq
Fulford Wm. esq. 16 Cross st. Islington
Fullarton John, esq. 12 Hyde park st
Fuller Gen. Sir Joseph, 10 Bryanstone sq. & High grove, Pinner, Middlesex
Fuller Capt. R.N. 27 Montagu square
Fuller Rev. Thomas, 1 Eaton place
Fuller Augus. Eliot, M.P. 16 Clifford st.; & Rosehill, Robertsbridge; & Ashdown house, East Grinstead
Fuller Chris. esq. 26 Paradise ter. Islgtn
Fuller Ed. I. esq. 16 Fortess ter.Kntsh.tn
Fuller Ed.Wm.esq.6 Linden gro. Kensgtn
Fuller Francis, esq. 8 Parliament st
Fuller Fredk. esq. Carlton chmbrs.Rgt.st
Fuller Fred. Jas. esq. 12 Regent st
Fuller F.J. esq. Maida vale, 238 Edgw. rd
Fuller Hen. Peter, esq. 111 Piccadilly
Fuller John, esq. 18 New Bond st
Fuller J. esq. 31Northumberld.st.Nw.rd
Fuller John Geo. esq. 28 St. James's st
Fuller Jsph.esq. 3Warwick vils.Maida hl
Fuller Miss, 49 Manchester st
Fuller William, esq. 8 Kensington gore
Fulton J.A.esq. Stamford hou.So.Lmbth
FultonM.esq.70Hermitage pl.St.Jn.st.rd
Fulton Thomas, esq. 22 Tibberton sq
Ferguson Jas. esq. 3 Markhm.sq.Chelsea
Furmage Geo. S. esq. 5 Mecklenburgh st
Furnell Mrs. 42 Gerrard st. Islington
Furner Frederick, esq. 42 Southampton bldgs. & 3 Eastman pl. Old Kent road
Furner Robert, esq. 39 Fitzroy square
Furnivall Jno.J. M.D.3Weymth.st.Por.pl
Furse John, esq. 21 Upper Woburn pl
Furze Jno.esq.1 Addison rd.so.Kensingtn
Fussell A. esq. 29 Argyle st. King's cr
Fussell Joseph esq. 20 Sidmouth st
Fust, *see* Jenner-Fust Rt.Hon.Sir Herbert
Futvoye C.F.esq. 3 Lt.James st.Bedfd.rw
Futvoye Edw.esq. 23 John st.Bedford rw
Fyler George, esq. 4 Pump ct. Temple
Fynmore Arth. esq. 13 Up. Porchester st
Fynmore Thos.Geo.esq. 12 Fitzroy sq. & 43 Cravenst. Strand

GABRIEL B. esq. 60 Walcot place east
Gabriel Christr. esq. 26 Glo'ster crescent
Gabriel Francis H. esq. 58 St. James's st
Gabriel Jas. Alex. esq. 19 Lincoln's inn fi
Gabriel Wm. Wallace, esq. 44 Linc. inn flds
Gadd Mrs. 7 Queen's bldgs. Brompton
Gadderer Chas. esq. 23 Craven st. Strand
Gaddesden Aug. Wm. esq. 21 Woburn sq
Gadsden Roger, esq. 14 Furnival's inn
Gadsden Roger, esq. 1 Maida hill west
Gael Samuel Higgs, esq. 2 Old square
Gaerth Charles, LL.D. 9 Essex st. Strand
Gaffin Edw. esq. 63 Quadrant, Regnt. st
Gage Visc. 4 Whitehall, & Firle pl. Lewes
Gage Vice Adml. Sir Wm. H. Admiralty
Gage Sir Thomas, bart. 35 Pall mall
Gage John, esq. 8 Eaton place
Gaine Mrs. 7 Crescent pl. Burton cresc
Gaines C. esq. 1 Caroline st. Bedford sq
Gainsborough, Earl of, 9 Cavendish sq.; Barham court, Maidstone; & Exton park, near Stamford
Gairdner G. esq. & Mrs. 17 Hamilton ter
Gairdner Wm. M.D. 12 Bolton st
Gaisford John, esq. 32 Up. Seymour st
Gaisford Richd. esq. 9 Bartlett's buildgs
Gaitskell Henry, esq. 19 York place
Galalier Rev. Geo. F. 32 Sackville st
Gale Charles James, esq. 12 South bank, Regent's park, & 1 Mitre court bldgs
Gale Henry, esq. 2 Berkeley square
Gale James, esq. 5 Park village east
Gale John, esq. 12 Nelson sq. Blkfrs. rd
Gale J.H. esq. 4 Up. Queen's bdgs. Brmptn
Gale Joseph W. esq. 9 John st. Adelphi
Gale Samuel, esq. 5 Bedford row, & Charlton, near Cheltenham
Gale Thos. A. esq. 13 Queen sq. Bloomsby
Gael Wiliam, esq. 44 Berners st
Gale Wm. esq. 6 Wellington rd. St. Jn.'sw
Galeari Michl. M.D. 6 Walton pl. Brmptn
Galindo Mrs. 4 Park place, Paddington
Gall Thos. esq. 20 King sq. Goswell rd
Gallaway Alexander, esq. 30 Canonbry. sq
Galliers J. esq. 1 Cumbrlnd. ter. Lloyd sq
Galloway, Earl of, Galloway ho. Wigton
Galloway Col. Archibald, C.B. 19 Upper Harley st
Galloway F. esq. 12 Albion tr. Canonbry
Galloway Thomas, esq. 19 Serjeants' inn; & 50 Fleet st
Galpin Thos. Carter, esq. 62 Haymarket
Galsworthy John, esq. 19 Ely pl. Holbn
Galsworthy John, esq. 33 Gordon sq. & 9 Cook's ct. Lincoln's inn
Galsworthy Wm. esq. 19 Ely pl. Holbrn
Galton Ed. Herbert, esq. 23 Portman sq. & Warley hall, Halesowen, Salop
Galton Theodore H. esq. 3 Figtree ct. Temple, & Hadzor, Droitwich
Galway Viscount, Coulson's hotel, 45 Brook st. & Serlby hall, near Bawtry
Gamage Mrs. 7 Melcombe place
Gambardella S. esq. 10 Pelham crescent
Gambert Madame, 9 Avenue rd. Rgts. pk
Gambier Capt. Mark, 50 Up. Seymour st
Gambier Mrs. 9 Harley st
Gamble Harpur, M.D. 7 Dukest. Portld. pl
Gamel Ernest, esq. 5 Victoria ter. Chels
Gamlen Robert, esq. 3 Gray's inn sq
Gamlen Thomas, esq. 7 Mecklenburgh st. & 7 Furnival's inn
Gammell Major, 105 Piccadilly
Gandell John, esq. 1 Mecklenburgh st
Gane Wm. esq. 35 Manchester st
Gane W. T. esq. 17 Charles st. Wstbn. tr
Gann Amos, esq. 6 Caroline st. Bedfd. sq
Gann Amos, esq. 31 Norfolk st. Strand
Gannon Jno. esq. 1 Dean's rw. Walw. rd
Gannon John Pahie, esq. 4 Elm ct. Tmp
Gapes Thos. esq. 9 Gt. Ormond st.
Gapp John B. esq. 8 Albion gr. Thornh. rd
Garcia Mad. 6 Glo'ster rd. Old Brmptn
Gardener Thos. esq. 14 Cambridge ter
Gardener Wm. esq. 11 Sussex gs. Hyde pk
Gardiner Lt. Gen. Sir J. K.C.B. 23 Eaton pl
Gardiner Maj. Gen. Sir Rt. K.C.B. & K.C.H. Gun house, North par. St. James's pk. & Esher
Gardiner Lieut. Col. 9 Gt. George st
Gardiner John, esq. 20 Whitehall pl
Gardiner K. esq. 24 Moscow rd. Bayswtr
Gardiner Mrs. 18A, Portman square
Gardiner Roger C. esq. 13 Cheyne wk
Gardiner Saml. W. esq. 18A, Portman sq
Gardiner Thos. esq. 5 Grove ter. Kntsh. tn
Gardiner Wm. esq. 7 Tavistock st. Bfd. sq
Gardiner Wm. J. esq. 29 Southamptonrow
Gardner Lord, 46 Dover st. Piccadilly
Gardner Lady, 75 South Audley st
Gardner Hon. Major Gen. Wm. Henry, 64 Cadogan place
Gardner Hon. Edwd. 10 North Audleyst
Gardner John, esq. 49A, Gt. Portland st
Gardner John, esq. 10 Grovepl. Lisson gr
Gardner John Arthur, esq. 10 Chancery la
Gardner J. esq. 1 Minerva pl. Barnsbry
Gardner J.E. esq. Elm gr. ho. Notting hl
Gardner Miss, 21 Abbeyrd. St. John'swd
Gardner Mrs. 4 Addison road north
Gardner Mrs. 5 York ter. Regent's park
Gardner Rd. esq. 4 Kimboltn. pl. Brmptn
Gardner Robt. esq. 2 Grove cot. Grove rd
Gardner W. H. esq. 42 Addison rd. north
Gardner-Dunn John, esq. M.P., 14 Grosvenorst. & Chatteris house, Isle of Ely
Garey Edw. B. esq. 9 Powis pl. Hmpstd. rd
Garey Edw. B. esq. 24 Southampton bdgs
Gargrave R. B. esq. 19 Buckingham st
Garland Henry esq. 1 Barnsbury ter
Garland Jas. W. esq. 33 Cross st. Islington
Garland Mrs. 2 Albion place, Holloway
Garland Mrs. 5 Up. Berkeley st. west
Garland Robt. esq. 12 Cloudesly square
Garland Robt. esq. 17 New Millman st. & 11 John st. Adelphi
Garle Thomas, esq. 80 Hamilton ter
Garlike Wm. esq. 42 Theobald's road
Garling Henry, esq. 27 Bedford row
Garman Corns. E. esq. 1 University st
Garment J. esq. 32 Connaught terrace
Garnault Mrs. 33 Francis st. Bedford sq
Garner Maj. Gen. 35 North bank, Regt. pk
Garner E.S. esq. 29 George st. Portmn. sq
Garner Jonathan, M.D. 3 Maida hill we
Garner Jsph. S. esq. 49 High st. Kensngtn
Garner Wm. esq. 14 Holloway place
Garnett Rev. Richard, 22 Mabledon place, and British Museum
Garnett Wm. esq. 49 Thurloe sq. O. Brmptn
Garnett T.E. esq. 27 Portman pl. Edg. rd
Garnick Mrs. 73 Cambridge terrace
Garnier Lady Harriet, 6 Grafton st
Garod Mrs. 3 Belgrave st. south, Pimlico
Garrard Rev. G. 4 Queen's bdgs. Brmptn
Garrard Stephen, esq. 13 Suffolk st. & 18 Nottinghill square, Kensington
Garratt Henry John, esq. 53 Welbeck st
Garratt Miss, Stoke Newington green
Garratt Thomas, esq. Stoke Newington
Garrett Edward, esq. 19 Cloudesley st
Garrett J. esq. 30 Portland ter. Regt's pk
Garrett Mrs. 10 Southampton pl. Eus. sq
Garrett Richd. esq. 62 Torrington sq
Garrett Sam. esq. 7 St. Agnes vls. Baysw
Garrett William, esq. 12 Milner square
Garrick Club House (James Winston, secretary), 35 King st. Covent garden
Garry Wm. Henry, esq. 39 Chancery la
Garth Capt. Thomas, 30 Hans place
Garth Mrs. 11 Hill st. Berkeley sq. & Haines hill, Hurst, Middlesex
Garvagh Lord, 26 Portman square
Garvagh Rt. Hon. Lady, 26 Portman sq. & Garvagh, Londonderry
Garwood Rev. John, 5 Church pas. Sptlf
Garwood Mrs. 2 Haberdasher st. Hoxton
Garwood Mrs. 6 Soley ter. Pentonville
Gascoigne Col. 14 Lowndes square
Gascoyne Mrs. Gen. 71 South Audley st
Gaselee Binstead, esq. 26 Montague pl. Russell sq. & 2 New sq. Lincoln's inn
Gaselee Stephen, S.L. 2 Cambridge sq. Hyde park, & 3 Serjeants' inn
Gaskell Fredk. esq. 1 Masham sq. Chelsea
Gaskell James Milnes, M.P. 72 Lower Grosvenor st. & Thornes ho. Wakefield
Gaskell John D. esq. 1 Brick ct. Temple
Gaskell T. esq. 1 Markham sq. Chelsea
Gaskell Wm. P. esq. 32 Eastbourne ter
Gaskoin George, esq. 34 Cambridge ter. & 7 Upper Southwick st. north
Gaskoin John S. esq. 32 Clarges st
Gaspey T. esq. 6 Tavistock st. Bedford sq
Gasquet Raymond, esq. 11 Burton cres
Gass David, esq. 8 & 9 Bayswater ter. & 166 Regent st
Gates Miss, 29 Mornington crescent
Gates Mrs. 24 Cloudesley ter. Islgtn
Gates Wm. esq. 31 South bank, Regt.'s pk
Gatty Charles, esq. 31 Doughty st
Gatty Edw. esq. Northwick ter. St. Jn.'swd
Gatty Edward, esq. 1 Red Lion square
Gatty Geo. esq. 6 Marlbro' tr. Kensgtn
Gaudri J. esq. 15 Henrietta st. Cyndsh. sq
Gauffier Madame, 2 Russell pl. Fitz. sq
Gaugain Philip A. esq. 138 Tottenham ct. rd
Gaulter Mrs. 20 Sloane terrace
Gaunt John, esq. 2 Bridgewater gardens
Gaunt Thos. esq. 10 Dalby ter. City rd
Gauntlett Miss, 3 Adelphi terrace
Gaussen Fredk. Chas. 2 Harcourt bldgs
Gaussen R. W. esq. 44 Brook st
Gaussen Wm. esq. 3 King's Bench walk
Gautier Fred. esq. French vice consul, 22 Princes st. Cav. sq. & 3 Copthall bgs
Gavaron Mrs. 27 Tavistock square
Gaven D. esq. 15 St. Geo's. ter. Knsgn. N. tn
Gawdery Misses, 4 Bayswater hill
Gawen Mrs. 17 Waterloo place
Gawthern Mrs. 17 Upper Gower st
Gawtress William, esq. 161 Fleet st
Gaye Ed. R. esq. 32 Up. George st. Prtmn. sq
Gayleard John, jun. esq. 56 Beaumont st
Gear Handel, esq. 26 Newman st
Gear Jn. Wm. esq. 5 Charlotte st. Ftzr. sq
Gear Mrs. 7 Maida hill, Edgware road
Gear Robert, esq. 19 Oxford square
Geary Francis, esq. 8 Figtree ct. Temple
Geary S. esq. 10 Hamilton pl. King's cross
Geddes Alex. esq. Parade ho. Thames bk
Geddes Andrew, esq. A.R.A. 15 Berners st
Gedye N. esq. 9 Saville row, Walworth rd
Gee George, esq. 7 Trevor ter. Knightsbdg
Gee James, esq. Fladong's hotel, Oxford st. & Holywood, near Stockport
Gee John, esq. 9 Belinda tr. Canonbry. sq
Gee John, esq. 5 Victoria rd. Kensingtn
Gee Miss, 5 Hyde park terrace
Gee Mrs. 18 Lowther cottages, Islngtn
Geeves Thos. esq. 26 Southbank, Regt.'s pk
Geesin William, esq. 34 Golden square
Geldart Thos. Chas. esq. 43 Bryanstone square, & 18 Old square, Lincoln's inn
Gell John Hy. esq. Lit. Cloisters, Westm
Gell Fras. Thomas, esq. 8 Regent st. & Devonshire st. Portland place
Gell Mrs. 1 Abbey pl. St. John's wood
Geller Wm. O. esq. 4 Crescent pl. Hmpsd. rd
Geller W. O. esq. 4 Stanhope pl. Mornington crescent
Gelston Capt. W. 61 Glo'ster pl. Portman sq
Genese Sam. esq. 2 Artillery ct. Chswll. st
Gent George William, esq. 4 Orchard st. & Moyne's pk. Ridgwell, Halstead
Gent Mrs. 6 Tavistock st. Bedford sq
George Edwd. esq. 4 Stucley ter. Camdn. tn
George Hen. esq. 4 Hornton vil. Kensngtn
George Jas. esq. 22 Calthorpe st. Gray's in. r
George John, esq. 56 Cadogan place
George Miss, 6 Clapham rise
George Mrs. 15 Nottingham st
George Mrs. 16 Tibberton square
German Andrew, jun. esq. Maida pl. Mile e
Gerrans James George, esq. 6A, Wyndham place, & 37 Crawford st
Gerret F.J. esq. 2 Queen's bldgs. Brompton
Ghrimes Saml. esq. 71 Baker st. Ptmn. sq

Ghrimes Wm. esq. 19 Westbourne place
Giampietro Monsr. 14 North bank
Gibb Mrs. 9 Argyle square, King's cross
Gibbes Charles, esq. 24 Cavendish sq
Gibbes Thomas, esq. 36 Tavistock place
Gibbins Jsph. esq. 11 Friedenstein ter
Gibbins Mrs. 17 Belmont pl. Wandsw. rd
Gibbins Mrs. 36 Lonsdale sq. Islington
Gibbon Benj. Phelps, esq. 89 Albany st
Gibbon Edwd. Howard, esq. Heralds' col
Gibbon E.H. esq. 1 John st. St.James's sq
GibbonsSirFredk.20Montaguest.Ptmn.sq
Gibbons Arthur Danl. esq. 58 Warren st
Gibbons David, esq. 5 Kennington place
Gibbons David, esq. 1 New ct. Temple
Gibbons Geo. esq. 20 Old Cavendish st
Gibbons John, esq. 17 Hanover terrace
Gibbs Rev. Michael, King Edward st
Gibbs Andw. esq.178 Prospct.pl.Edgw.rd
Gibbs Dickson, esq. 14 Addison road
Gibbs Hen. C. esq. 23 Colebrooke rw.Isln
Gibbs Humphrey, esq. 47 Half Moon st
Gibbs James, esq. 67 Connaught terrace
Gibbs James, esq. 4 Storey's gate, Westr
Gibbs John, M.D. 6 Baker st
Gibbs Joseph, esq. 5 Hare court, Temple
Gibbs Joseph, esq. 2 Queen sq. pl. Westr
Gibbs Michael, esq. 33 Walbrook
Gibbs Miss, 45 Devonshire st. Portld. pl
Gibbs Miss, 42 St. James's place
Gibbs Mrs. 11 Bedford square
Gibbs Mrs.5Up.Portland pl.Wandswh.rd
Gibbs Sam. esq. 7Compton st.e. Brnsk.sq
Gibbs Thos. esq. Brompton lodge, O.Brmp
Gibbs William, esq. 13 Hyde park st
Gibbs Wm. esq. 19 King's rd. Bedford rw
Gibbson Miss, 39 Pembroke sq. Knsgtn
Giberne John, esq. 5 Gray's inn sq
Giblett John, esq. 14 Barnsbury villas
GibsonRev.J.M.A.4Westbournepl.Eat.sq
Gibson Rev. John E. M.A. Bermondsey st
Gibson Alex. esq. 18 Chestr.pl.Kengtn.cr
Gibson Anthony, esq.15 Canonbury villas
Gibson Chs. esq. 5 Holland pl. Clapm. rd
GibsonChas.F. esq. Glo'ster pl.Glo'ster gt
Gibson Chas. Wm. esq. 10 Alpha road
Gibson E. M.D. 1 Hawley ter.Hampstd.rd
Gibson Daniel, esq. 11 Sloane terrace
Gibson John, esq. 5 Bernard st
Gibson John R. esq. 115 Holborn hill
Gibson Jsph. esq. 39 Swinton st.Grs.in. rd
Gibson Miss, 2 Hamilton ter. St. Jn's. wd
Gibson Rowland, esq. 160 Albany st
Gibson Thos. Milner, M.P. 50 Wilton crescent, & Theberton house, Saxmundham
Gibson Wm. esq. 64 Lincoln's inn fields
Gibson Wm. esq.1 Marlboro'rd. St.Jn's.w
Giesler Wm. esq. 80 Oxford terrace
Giffard Francis, esq. 47 Vincent square
Giffard George M. esq. 26 Chancery lane
Giffard John Walter De L. esq. Hall staircase, Inner Temple
Giffard Miss, 5 Clarges st. Piccadilly
Giffard Stanley L. LL.D. 39 Myddelton sq
Gifford Lord, Kyer house, Tenbury
Gifford James, esq. 10 Hanover cottages, & 39 Alpha rd. Regent's park
Gigner Mrs. 38 Michael's pl. Brompton
Gilbank Thos. esq. 10 New Millman st
Gilbert Rev. C. 25 Manchr.ter.Livrpl.rd
Gilbert Rev. Edw. 11 Duke st. Prtlnd.pl
Gilbert George, esq. 46 Bernard st
Gilbert John, esq. 1 Cloudesley square
Gilbert John, esq. 2 Notting hill square
Gilbert Mrs. 4 Annetts cr. Lr. rd. Islgtn
Gilbert Mrs. 9 Belgrave st. King's cross
Gilbert Mrs. 83 Mount st. Berkeley sq
Gilbert Richard, esq. 70 Euston square
Gilbert Wm.J.esq.6 Gt.Smith st.Westmr
Gilbertson Henry, esq. Tudor lodge, Finchley new road
Gilchrist Miss, 45 Norland sq. Nott. hl
Gilchrist Mrs. 10 Heathcote st
Gildder Chas. esq. 27 Lverpl.st.King's cı
Gilder Wm, T. esq. 14 Queen Anne st
Giles Edw. Galley, esq. 1 Gray's inn sq
Giles Frank, esq. 45 Lincoln's inn flds
Giles George, esq. 7 Gray's inn square
Giles Geo. K.esq.52Cambrdg.st.Edgw.rd
Giles John E. esq. 38 Lincoln's inn flds
Giles JohnW. esq.27Stanhope st.Hmp.rd
Giles Mrs. 31 Granville sq. Clerkenwell
Giles Mrs. 5 Tavistock place, Russell sq
GilesNetlam, esq.4Verulambdgs.Gray's i
Giles R. H. esq. 11 Burton st. Brtn.crest
Giles Sl. esq. 12 Powell st. we.Goswell st
Giles Sam. esq.4 Sussex ter.Old Brmptn
Gilfillan Wm. esq. 6 Mathon pl. Pentnvl
Gilham John, esq. 24 Bartletts bldgs
Gill Edmd. esq. 40 Frederick pl.Hmps.rd
Gill Edwd. esq. 35 Argyle sq. King's cr
Gill Edwd.esq.5 Dean's pl. Sth. Lambeth
Gill Mrs. 29 Hemingford ter. Islington
Gill Mrs. 10 Strahan ter. Liverpool rd
Gill Thomas, esq. M.P. Reform club, & the Crescent, Plymouth
Gill T. esq. 12 Harrington st. Hmpstd.rd
Gill Wm. S. esq.29 WhiteLion st.Pntnvl
Gillan Wm. Campbell, esq. 20 Upper Woburn pl. & 44 Parliament st
Gillard Wm. esq. 4 Gower st.nth.New rd
Gillbee Mrs. 9 Melina pl. St. John's wd
Gillen Mrs. 12 Compton ter. Islington
Gillespie Alexr. esq. 13 America square
Gillespie Rt. esq. 33 York pl. Portm. sq
Gillespy Mrs. 7 Upper Gloucester place
Gillespy Richd. esq. 16 Grafton st. ea
Gillespy Saml. esq. 16 Grafton st. ea
Gillett Chas. esq.Up. 16 Seymour st. west
Gillett Gabriel, esq. 25 Guilford st
Gillett Geo. esq.2 Grosvnr. gate, Park la
Gillett Jn. esq. 1 Tavistock st. Bedfd. sq
Gillett Wm. S. esq. 16 Wilton st
Gillies Miss, 45 Mortimer st. Cavend. sq
Gillies Miss, 36 Parliament st
Gillies Mrs. 43 Allsop terr. New rd
Gillies Mrs. 12 Hinde st. Manchester sq
Gillies Richard M.esq. 3 Bayswater hill
Gillies Wm. esq. 14 Chestr. pl.Kengtn.cr
Gilligan Fras. E. esq. 8 Oxford terrace
Gilling Miss Catherine, 35 Albemarle st
Gillioli Joseph, M.D.46 Gt. Marlbro' st
Gillman Mrs. Clapham rise
Gillman Wm. esq. 11 South st.Grsvnr.sq
Gillot Arthur, esq. 45 Haymarket
Gillot Benj. esq. 70 Edgware road
Gilman Mrs. 1 Sussex pl. Canonbury sq
GilmourCol.Chas.15Elizabethst.Eatn.sq
Gilpen Mrs. 11 Westbourne pl. Pimlico
Gilpin Wm. Edw. esq. 28 Westbourne pl
Gimblett Capt. R.N. 14 Norfolk st.Strnd
Gimingham John, esq. 41 Westbourne ter
Gimingham Wm.esq.5 Duke st.Adelphi
Ginger Miss, 14 Hornton st. Kensington
Giorgi Peter, esq. 31 Smith st. Chelsea
Gipps Hen. Plumptre, esq. 9 Montagu place, Montagu sq. & 77 Chancery la
Gipps Thos. esq. 63 Lincoln's inn fields
Giraud Richard Hervé, esq. 21 Swinton st. & 7 Furnival's inn
Girdler T. S. esq. 8 Loraine pl.Holloway
Girdwood Gilbert F. esq. 177 Prospect pl. Edgware rd. & 1 Southwick cresct
Giro James, esq. 15 Regent st
Girvane John, esq. 6 Milner sq. Islgtn
Gisborne Thomas, jun. esq. M.P. Park house, Kensington gore, & Horwich house, Buxton, Derbyshire
Girton Stephen J. esq. 23 York pl.City rd
Giubilei T. V. esq. 2 Charlott. st.Bedfd.sq
Giuseppi M.esq. 103 Milton st. Dorset sq
Gladstone Rt. Hon. Wm. Ewart, M.P. 13 Carltine house terrace, & Fasque, Kincardine
Gladstone Capt. John N. R.N. M.P. 80 Eaton place, & Fasque, Fettercairn
Gladstone Lieut. J. R.N. 6 Carlton gardens, & Fasque, Fettercairn, N.B.
Glasgow Earl of, Lieut. R.N. Clarendon hotel; & Hawkhead, Renfrewshire; & Boroughbridge, Yorkshire; & Kelburn castle, Ayrshire
Gladstone Thos. esq. 1 Up. Belgrave st
Glanfield Geo. esq. 14 Grove end road
GlasierW.B. esq. 84 Milton st. Dorset sq
Glasse Mrs. 30 Cambridge st. Conght.sq
Glasse Wm. Bulkeley, esq. 7 South cres. Bedford sq. & 10 New sq. Lincoln's inn
Glegg John Baskervyle, esq. 24 Albemarle st. & Wilkington hall, Monksheath, Cheshire
Glehn Robert, esq. 34 Upper Harley st
Glemm Mrs. 4 Bedford pl. Kensington
Glen Adam, esq. Old Brompton
Glen Miss, the Mall, Kensington grvl.pts
Glen Wm. Cunningham, esq. 3 Essex ct
Glen Wm. C. 7 Egremont pl. New road
Glendinning Fryer, esq. Devon villa, Finchley New road
Glendinning Wm. esq. 34 Clapham rd.pl
Glenelg Lord P.C. H4, Albany, & Waternish, Invernesshire
Glengall Earl, 34 Grosvenor st. & Caher castle, Tipperary
Glenlyon Lord, Carlton club, & Blair Athol, Perthshire
Glennie Rev. John D. 51 Green st
Glennie John Irving, esq. 15 Devonshire st. Portland place, & 19 Bennett's hill
Glindining M.S.esq.6 Queen's bgs.Brmtn
Glindon Robert, esq. 3 River la. Islingtn
Gloucester, H.R.H. Duchess of, Park la
Gloucester & Bristol, Bishop of, Little Cloisters, Westminster, & Palace, Gloucester
Glover Geo. A. esq. 5 Paddington green
Glover John H. esq. 4 Stafford rw. Piml
Glover Mrs. 18 Brook st
Glover Thomas, esq. 47 Myddelton sq
GloverT.W.esq.3Harringtonsq.Hmps.rd
GloverWm.S.L. 2 Serjeants'inn, Chncy.la
Glyn Sir Richd. Plumtre, bt.37 Up. Brook st. & Gaunt house, Wimbourne, Dorset
Glyn Capt.Richd.Henry, 2 St.James's pl
GlynClaytonWm.F.esq.5Hare ct.Temple
Glyn Geo. Carr, esq. 1 Upper Eccleston st. & Combe house, Croydon
Glynne Sir Stephen Richard, bart. M.P. 4 Spring gardens, & Hawarden castle, Chester
Glynne Lady, 13 Carlton house terrace
Goad Mrs. 7 Melcombe place, Dorset sq
Goatly Walter Ephraim, esq. 3 Cork st
Goblet H.F.esq. 8 Chesterfield st.Kng's.c
Godbee Wm. esq. New chambers, Foregate, Clement's inn, Strand
Godbold Thomas, esq. 5 Barnsbury st
Godby Mrs.22Southampton pl.Euston sq
Goddard Rev. Dr. 11 Cadogan pl.Sloane st. & Andover, Hants
Goddard Rev.G.F. 6 Dover st.Piccadilly
Goddard Alfd. esq. 2 Bedford pl.Clpm.rd
Goddard Geo. esq. 3 Kensington cresnt
Goddard H. esq. 29 Gerrard st. Islingtn
Goddard Jas. esq. 13 Park rd.Rgnt.'s pk
Goddard John, esq. 13 Tyndale place, Upper st. Islington
Goddard John, esq. 3Surrey pl.O.Kent rd
Goddard Mrs. 2 Manor terrace, Chelsea
Goddard Rt.H.esq.8Williamst.Caledn.rd
Godden Henry James, esq. 3 John st. Bedford row
Godden John, esq. 3 John st.Bedford rw
Godden Mrs. 6 St. George's terrace
Godebert Peter, esq. 15 Oxford terrace
Godet Julas, esq. 28 Wakefield st. Rgt.sq
Godfrey Alfred, esq. 14 Canonbury sq. Islington, & 5 Broad st. buildings
Godfrey Charles, esq. 43 Vincent sq
Godfrey John, esq. 17 Porchester ter
GodfreyJ.B.esq.21Henriettast.Brnsw.sq
Godfrey Joseph S. esq. 10 New sq. Linc.i
Goding J.esq. & Lady Jane, 2 Belgrave sq
Goding Jas. sen. esq. 9 St. George's pl
Goding Miss, 9 St. George's place
Goding Miss, 12St. George's pl.Hyde pk
Godlee Rickman, esq. 3 New sq. Linc.in
Godrich Francis, esq. Little Chelsea

Godolphin Lord, Brookes's club, & Gog Magog hills, near Cambridge
Godsell William, esq. 6 Furnival's inn
Godson Ralph, esq. 40 Lonsdale square
Godson Rd.esq. Q.C.M.P.,30 Grosvenor pl
Godson Septimus Holmes, esq. 14 Rutland gate, & Tenbury, Worcestershire
Godson Stphn.H.esq.11 King'sBench wk
Godson Wm.Coker,esq. 8 Harrington sq
Godwin Rev. John H. Highbury college
Godwin Col. Henry, C.B., 12 Pall mall
Godwin George, esq. 24 Alexander sq
Godwin Geo.esq.11Pelham cres. Brompt
Godwin Jas. esq. 34 Maiden la. Cov. gdn
Godwin Wm. esq. 12 Upper Baker st
Goepel Mrs. 16 Stonefield st. Islington
Goff Mrs. 15 Brompton row
Gold Henry, esq. 7 Trinity square, Borough, & 164 High st. Borough
Golden Mrs. 50 Frederick st. Gr's. inn rd
Golden Mrs. 64 Gibson square, Islington
Golden Thomas, esq. 49 Burton crescent
Golden Thos.H.esq.9 Burton st.Brtn.cres
Goldfinch Genl. 11 Up. Wimpole st
Goldfinch Hen. Rt. esq. 44 Chancery la
Goldfinch Hy. Rt. esq.11Up.Wimpole st
Goldham J. jun. esq.27 Love la. Eastchp
Goldie John, esq. 39 Baker st
Golding Bailie, esq. 38 Park st. Gro. sq
Golding Benj. M.D.29KingWm st.Strand
Golding Miss,8Hamilton pl.St.Jhn's.wd
Golding M. esq. 2 Vassl. ctgs. Kensngtn
Goldshede Bernardo,esq.8Dukest.St.Jas
Goldsmid Sir Isaac Lyon, bart.St.John's lodge, Inner circle, Regent's park, & the Wick, Brighton
Goldsmid Lieut. Col. 2 Park crescent
Goldsmid Aaron, esq. 10 Lr.Southwk. st
Goldsmid Aaron Asher, esq.8 Cavndh.sq
Goldsmid Andrew,esq.10 Crown office rw
Goldsmid Augustus, esq. 79 Wimpole st
Goldsmid Chas. esq. 9 Duke st. Westmr
Goldsmid Charles, esq. 79 Wimpole st
Goldsmid Edward, esq.41 Up. Harley st
Goldsmid Elias, esq. 10 Lr. Southwk. st
Goldsmid Fras. esq. 15 Upper Harley st
Goldsmid Francis Henry, esq. 15 Upper Harley st.&5Stone bldgs. Lincoln's inn
Goldsmid Fred. D. esq. 50 Harley st
Goldsmid John, esq. 14 New Dorset pl. Clapham road
Goldsmid Nathl. esq. 74 Upper Berkeley st. & 3 Figtree court, Temple
Goldsmid Sampson,esq.39Mecklnbgh. sq
Goldsmith C.esq.13Montaguepl.Clpm.rd
Goldsmith Geo. esq. 6 Trevor terrace, Knightsbridge,& 9 New sq. Lincn's. in
Goldsmith Misses, 2 Up. Gloucester st
GoldsmithW.esq.1Prospectpl.Wndsw.rd
Gole Abraham, esq. 15 Paradise row, Chelsea, & 455 West Strand
Gole George, esq. 37 Park st. Islington
Gole Thomas, esq. 39 Canonbury square
Golightly E. esq. 1 Verulam buildings
Golledge Edw.esq. 2 Bedford row,Islgtn
Gomes F. M.D. 49 George st. Euston sq
Gomm J. esq. 31 Edwards st. Prtmn. sq
Gomme Stephen, jun. esq. 65 Regent st
Gompertz Benj. esq. 1 Kennington ter
Gompertz Isaac, esq. 45 Ebury st
Gonne Chas.esq.19Glo'ster pl. Portm. sq
Gonzales Carlo,LL.D.33Londonst.Fitz.sq
Gooch D. esq.8 Warwick vils.Harrow rd
Gooch Edward W.esq.42 Connaught ter
Gooch John, esq.25 Banner st. St.Luke's
Gooch John,esq.16Albert ter. Knightsbg
GoochJohn,esq.8Thurloe pl.w.O.Brmptn
Good John,esq.14 Theberton st. Islngtn
Good Jsph. Hen. esq. 12 Beaufoy ter
Good Jph. Hy.esq. Palace green Kensngt
Good Joseph Hy. jun.esq.75 Hatton gdn. & High st. Bow
Good Miss, 46 Burton crescent
GoodairGeo.W.esq.24Conduit st.Bond st
Goodall Chas. esq. 5 Canterbury villas
Goodall E.esq.Gro.cot.Albert st.Morn.cr
Goodall John, esq. 10 Panton sq.Hymkt
Goodall Miss, 4 Glo'ster pl. New road
Goodall Mrs. 9 Hyde park square
Gooday Edward Wm. esq. 14 Doughty st. & 14 South square, Gray's inn
Gooday John C.esq.16 Claremont pl.Pvl
Goodban John, esq. 19 Beaufort st.Chls
GoodbehereG.T.esq.4 Park ter.Highbry
Goodbody James P. esq. 6 Barnsbury pl
Goodburn Wm. esq. 8 Tyndale place, Upper street, Islington
Goodchap Wm. esq. 84 Hatton garden
GoodchapW.esq.6Montft.cr.Barnsby pk
Goodchild Mrs.21 Elmtree rd.St.Jn's.wd
Goodchild Mrs. 30 Woburn square
Goodchild Thomas, esq. 70 Warren st
Goodday H.esq.48 Baker st.Portman sq
Goode Rev.William,31 Charterhouse sq
Goode Benjn. esq. 44 Howland st
Goode Frederick, esq. 15 Surrey st. Strand, & Stockwell common
Goode Miss, 21 Dalby terrace, City rd
Goode Mrs. 45 Howland st. Fitzroy sq
Goode Philip, esq. 43 Howland st
Gooden James, esq. 33 Tavistock square
Goodes Mrs. 9 Allsop pl. Regent's park
Goodes Mrs. 33 Upper Baker st
Goodeve John,esq.1 Raymond buildings
Goodeve Joseph, esq. 41 Kensington sq. & 9 Old sq. Lincoln's inn
Goodfellow Major Gen. 19 Fitzroy sq.
Goodfellow Mrs. Capt. 7 Carlton villas
Goodford Henry,esq.32 Montague place
Goodger Wm. Fredk.esq.13 Bentinck st
Goodhart Alfred H. esq. 12 Brecknock crescent, Camden town
Goodhart Jacob E. esq. 21 Doughty st
Goodheart John,esq.3 Courland terrace, Wandsworth road
Gooding Jas. esq. 28 Baker st. Lloyd sq
GoodlakeH.esq.5Montagu pl.Claphm.rd
Goodman Alfd.esq. 94 Camden rd. villas
Goodman Abm. A.esq. 5 Nottingham ter
Goodman Arnold,esq.20 Trinity sq.Boro
Goodman Hiller, esq. 63 Lincoln's inn fls
Goodman John,esq.13 Kent ter.Rgt.'s pk
Goodman John, esq. 12 Regent st
Goodman Jn. esq. 5 Vincent ter.City rd
Goodman Miss, 10 Woburn place
Goodman Richd. Alf. esq. 3 South sq
Goodrich Rich. esq. 35 Amwell street, & Queen's Bench office, Temple
GoodmanS.R.esq.1 Devnsh.tr.Thornh.rd
Goodman Thomas,esq.6Up.Barnsbury st
Goodrich W. esq. 16 River st.Mydltn.st
Goodson John, esq.7 Bartlett's buildings
Goodwin J.esq. 3 Devonshire ter. Islngn
Goodwin JohnThs.esq. 3 President st. ea
Goodwin Mrs. 12 York pl. Portman sq
Goodwin Mrs. 34 Beaumont st
Goodwin Wm.esq.18 Chapel st.Grosv.pl
GoodyJas.esq 3Circus rd.St.John's wood
Goolden Rd. Hen. M.D.8 John st.Adelphi
Gorden Mrs. 2 Allsop pl. Regent's park
Gordon Capt. Lord Francis, 20 Chapel st. Belgrave square
GordonLd.Hen.9 St.George's ter.Kensgt
Gordon Lady Alicia, Admiralty
Gordon Lady Charlotte, 52 Hans place
Gordon Lady Duff, 34 Hertford st
Gordon Hon. Douglas, 7 Argyll st
Gordon Hon. Capt. A. 7 Argyll st
Gordon Hon. Wm. Capt. R.N. M.P. Admiralty, & Haddo house, Aberdeen
Gordon Sir Alex. Cornewall Duff, bart. 8 Queen sq.Westm.& Crombie,Banffsh
Gordon SirFrancisDuff,8 Queen sq.West
Gordon Alexr. esq. 22 Fludyer st
Gordon Alex. jun. esq. 6 Quality court
Gordon C. esq. 22 Hemingford ter. Islngt
Gordon Geo. Huntley, esq. 30 Aberdn. pl
Gordon James, esq. 15 Mabledon place
Gordon Jas. Alex. M.D. 71 Grosvenor st
GordonJohn,esq. 12Paper bldgs. Temple
Gordon Miss, 22 Chester ter. Eaton sq
Gordon Miss, 1 Dean's pl. South Lmbth
Gordon Miss, 6 Stanhope pl. Hyde pk
Gordon Mrs. Col.4Charles st.Lowndes sq
Gordon Mrs. 45 Brompton square
Gordon Mrs. 3 Hyde pk. ter. Kensngtn
Gordon Mrs. 7 Mortimer st
Gordon Mrs. 31 Upper Gower st
Gordon Patk. esq. 29 Cambridge ter. Edgware road, & 3 Symond's inn
Gordon Peter, esq. 8 Barnsbury st
Gordon Theodore, M.D. 8 Norfolk cres
Gordon Wm. esq. 23 Queen st. Mayfair, & Fyvie castle, Aberdeenshire
Gore Hon. Mrs. 21 Wilton crescent
Gore Hon. Robt. M.P., Commander, R.N. 21 Wilton crescent
Gore Hon. Wm. 21 Wilton crescent
Gore Col. Fras. 15 Grosvenor st. west
Gore John Ralph Ormsby, esq. 66 Portland place
Gore Miss, 23 Wilton st. Grosvenor pl
Gore Montagu, M.P. 8 Mount st. & Barrow court, near Bristol
Gore Wm. Ormsby, esq. M.P. 66 Portlnd. pl. & Porkington hall, Oswestry
Gore Wm. Rd. O. M.P. 66 Portland pl
Goren Jas. esq. 29 South Molton st
Goring Charles, esq. M.P. 26 Pall mall, & Wiston, near Steyning
Gorman Michael, esq. 56 Baker st
Gorman Mrs. 35Up.Norton st.Fitzroy sq
Gorst Jas. esq. 12 Polygon, Clarendon sq
Gortz Mrs. 70 Regent st
Gorway Richd. esq. 47 Adam st. west
Gosford Earl of, G.C.B., P.C. Brookes's club, 60 St. James's st.; Worlingham hall,Beccles; &Gosford castle,Armagh
Goslett Alfd. esq. 10 Addison rd. north
Goslett Wm. esq. 20 Porchester terrace
Gosling Capt. 33 Montagu square
Gosling Bennett, esq. 15 St. James's sq
Gosling Francis, esq. 11 Arlington st. & Manor house, Sutton, Surrey
Gosling John, esq. 25 Glo'ster pl. Nw. rd
Gosling Miss, 34 Beaumont st
Gosling Richard, esq. 67 Lowndes sq. & North Cray, Kent
Gosling Robt. esq. 5 Portland place; & Botley's pk.Chertsey,Surrey; & Hassobury, Bishop's Stortford, Essex
Gosling T.esq.10Chandos st.Cavendsh.sq
Gosling & Sharpe, 19 Fleet st
Gosnell John, esq. 17 Highbury place
Goss J. esq. 17 Alfred pl. Alexander sq
Goss Misses, Vicarage pl. Kensington
Gosset Mrs. 4 Montagu pl. Montagu sq
Gosset Montague, esq.5Trinity ter.Boro'
GossetRev.T.S.13Cornwall tr.Regt.'s pk
Gostling A. esq. D.C.L. 60 Montagu sq
GostlingH.esq.1Seymour pl.Wndswth.rd
Gostling the Misses, 1 Bedford sq. & Whitton place, near Isleworth
Gostling Wm. Fred. esq. 7 Hyde pk. st
Goter Wm. Henry, esq. 3 Victoria sq
Gotobed Mrs. 82 Gt. Russell st. Blmsby
Gottheimer L. esq. 27 Alfred st. Bed. sq
Gougenheim Aug. esq. 36 King st. Soho
GougerHen.esq.3A Montagupl.Clapm.rd
Gouger J. esq. 15 Albion ter. Wndswh.rd
Gough —, esq. 10 Lancaster pl. Strand
Gough Fras. J. esq.32East st.RedLion sq
Goulburn Rt. Hon. Henry, M.P. 11 & 12 Downing st.&Beechworth ho.Dorking
Goulburn Fredk. esq. 12 Downing st
Goulburn Mr. Serjeant,62 Up. Seymour st.&Court of Bankruptcy, Basinghll. st
Gould Joseph,esq.4 Cleveland sq.St.Jas'
Gould Miss, 7 Bentinck st
Gould Miss, 16 Gt. Castle st. Regent st
Gould Mrs. 75 Gower st. Bedford sq
Gould Mrs. 4 Queen st. Mayfair
Gould Mrs.9Up.Chadwell st.Pentonville
Gould Nathaniel, esq. 4 Tavistock sq
Gould Thos. esq. Porter's pl. Holloway
Goulding Mrs. 1 Clarence pl. Claphm. rd
Goulding Robert, esq. 25 Clapham rise
Gouldsmith Edmund,esq,12Highbury ter

GoundryGeo.A.esq.2 Lawn cot.S.Lmbth
Gover Wm. 44 Roebuck pl. Gt.Dover rd
Gover Wm.G. esq. 8 Chester sq Pimlico
Govett Edward, esq.4 Cook's ct.Linc.inn
Govett John C. esq.10 & 22 Linc.inn flds
Gow Chas. esq. 61 Charlotte st. Prtld.pl
Gow Niel, esq. 1 Gray's inn place
Gowan Geo. esq. 20 Park crst.Portlnd.pl
Gowan Mrs. 8 Albert rd. Glo'ster gate
Gowan Wm. esq. 8 Albert rd.Glo'ster gt
Gowen James Rt. esq. 41 St. James's st
GowerEdwin,esq.11Hanover ter.Rgts.pk
Gower Mrs. 20 York ter. Regent's park
Gower Robt. Fred. esq. 13 Devonshire pl
Gower Wm. Leveson, esq. 20A, Hill st. Berkeley sq. & Clapham common
Gower Wm. Leveson, jun. esq.33 Brook st. & Titsey pl. near Godstone, Surrey
GowersJas.W.esq.18King's rd.Bedfd.rw
Gowing Geo.esq.32 Theberton st.Islngtn
Gowland Capt. 11½ Myddelton square
Grabowski Count & Countess, 11 Bentinck terrace, Regent's park
Grace Capt. Percy, R.N. 10 Mount st
Grace Henry, esq. 9 Stockwell common
Grace John, esq. 73 Cadogan place
Grace Richard, esq. 65 Leman st
Grady Standish Grove, esq. 1 Pump ct. Temple, & 4 Lambeth terrace
Graeff John Geo. esq. 12 Furnival's inn
Graff Mrs. 17 Heathcote st
Grafton, Duke of, 47 Clarges st.; & Euston hall, Thetford; & Wakefield lodge, Stoney Stratford
Grafton Maj. 27 Bedford pl. Kensington
Graham Rt.hon. Sir Jas.R.G. bart. M.P. 31 Hill st. & Netherby hall, Carlisle
Graham Sir Bellingham, bt. 131 Park st. & Norton Convers, near Ripon
Graham SirSandford,bart. 1 Portland pl
Graham Major George,2 Cumberland st
Graham LadyCarl. 2 Portugal st.Gro.sq
Graham Charles, esq. 17 Chester square
GrahamChas.esq.67George st.Euston sq
Graham Chas.Jas. esq.3 Plowden bldgs
Graham Chas. W. jun.esq.10 Chester sq
Graham David, esq. 13A,Up.Woburn pl
Graham Edward, esq. 23 Hanover sq. & the Hall, Worth, near Crawley
Graham Edwin, esq. 29 Trevor sq.Kgtsb
Graham Geo.esq. 31 Albany st.Rgt.'spk
Graham Geo.J.esq. 32 Mecklenburgh sq
Graham Geo.Wm. esq. 31 Burton cresct
Graham Geo.Wm.esq.7Manor ter. Chlsa
Graham Jas. B. esq. 27 Sussex gardens
Graham Jas.esq.23Cmbrdg.ter.Edgw.rd
GrahamJ.esq.7Newingtn.pl.Kenngtn.rd
Graham John, esq. 60 Moorgate st. & 6 Thurloe pl. Brompton
Graham Joseph, esq.15 Portland place, Clapham road
Graham Miss, 38 Euston square
Graham Miss,32Hamiltn.tr.St.John'swd
Graham Miss, 44 Park st. Grosvenor sq
Graham Mrs. 10 Cottage rd. Eaton sq
Graham Mrs. Old Brompton road
Graham P.esq.Angelo villa,6Glo'ster rd
Graham Rt. esq.33 Cumberland terrace
Graham Rt. esq. 13A, Up.Woburn place
Graham Rt. Hay, M.D. 47Gt.Portlnd.st
Graham Thos. esq. Old Brompton, & 1 & 3 Mitre court chambers
Graham Thos.esq. 5Montague pl.Islngn
Graham Thomas, esq.9 Torrington sq
Grahame Archd. esq. 30 Gt. George st
Grainger Abm. T. esq. 2 Lr. Belgrave pl
GraingerChas.G.esq.16Adam st.Adelphi
Grainger Hen.esq. 2Glo'ster rd.Hyde pk
Grammar S.esq.22 Colebrooke rw.Islngn
Grammar Mrs. 18 Theberton st. Islngtn
Granby, Marquis of, M.P. 5 St. James's place, & Belvoir castle, Grantham
Grane William, esq. 23 Bedford row
Granfield Mrs. 14 Aberdeen pl. Mda. hl
Grange Stphn. esq. 16 St. John's wd. rd
Granger Thos.C.M.P. 12 King's bench wk
Grant Sir Lewis, K.C.H. 31 Harley st
Grant Gen. Sir William Keir, K.C.B. 20 Chapel st. Grosvenor place
Grant Mrs. Col. 9 Kent ter. Regent's pk
Grant Alexander, esq. 12 Arlington st. & Aberlour, Banffshire
Grant Alex. Lorent, esq. 6A, Waterloo pl
Grant Alex. Wm. esq. 13 King's road, Gray's inn, & 36 Lincoln's inn fields
Grant deVaux A.R.esq.19Buckingham st
Grant Charles esq. 23 Fitzroy square
Grant Daniel,esq.30 Clifton st. Finsbury
Grant Edward,esq. 7 Highbury place
Grant Francis, esq. A.R.A. Sussex villa, Sussex place, Regent's park
Grant F.J.esq.15Sussex pl.Kensgtn.N.tn
Grant F.A. esq. 13 King's rd. Bedford rw
Grant Geo. esq. 8 Carpenter st.Grsvnr.sq
Grant Jas.esq. 2 Plowden bldgs. Temple
Grant John, esq. 5 Coleshill st. Eaton sq
Grant John, esq. 35 Noel st. Islington
Grant Jsph. esq. 20 Palmer ter. Hollowy
Grant Klein, M.D. 73 St. James's st
Grant Madame,6Up.Geo.st.Bryanstn.sq
Grant Miss, 16Cumberland ter. Rgt.'s pk
Grant Miss, 15 Guilford st. Russell sq
Grant Miss, 60 Sloane st
Grant Miss, 92 Oxford ter. Edgware rd
Grant Mrs. Lit. Dean's yd. Westminster
Grant Mrs. 15 Torrington square
Grant Nath. M.D. 21 Thayer st
Grant Robert, esq. 5 Raymond buildings
Grant R. E. M.D. 10 Grafton pl.Eustn. sq
Grant T.W. esq. 41 Nutford pl.Bryans.sq
Grant Wm. esq. 27 Cambridge terrace, & Litchborough, Northamptonshire
Grant Wm. 5 Pump court, Temple
Grant Wm. Neill, esq. 36 Smith st.Chels
Grantham Rd. B. esq.2Robert st.Adelphi
Grantham Rd. B. esq. 68 Torrington sq
Grantley Lord, 94 Pall mall; & Wonersh, Guildford; & Grantley hall, Ripon
Granville Earl of, G.C.B., P.C. 16 Bruton street
Granville Augustus B. M.D. 109 Picadly
Granville Edward, esq. 16 Granville sq
Granville Walter, esq. 109 Piccadilly
Grasett Elliot, esq. 6 Chesham st
Grason Thos. esq. 15 Mornington cresct
Grasswell R.A. esq. 31 Carltn.vls.Edg.rd
Grattan Hen. esq. M.P. 40 Piccadilly, & Stephen's green, Dublin
Grattan James, esq. 1 Sackville st. & Tinnehinch, near Bray, co. Wicklow
Gravatt Wm. esq. 34 Parliament st
Grave William L. esq. 13 Bruton st
Gravenor Chas. esq. 36 Ely pl. Holborn
Graves Benj. esq. 2 Lower Belgrave st
Graves Chas. Gray, esq. 59 Montagu sq
Graves Fras. esq. 16 Camden rd. villas
Graves Geo. Christr. esq. 25 Eastcheap
Graves Henry, esq. 6 Pall mall
Graves John Thos. esq. 8 Gray's inn sq
Graves Mrs. 2 Lower Belgrave st
Graves Mrs. 24 Manchester ter.Lvrpl.rd
Graves Ph. esq. 10 Lit. New st. Shoe la
Gray Lord, St. George's hotel, 34 Albemarle st. & Kinfauns, Perth
Gray Abraham, esq. 10 Aberdeen pl
Gray Adam, esq.40Hemingfrd.ter.Islgtn
Gray Alex. esq.51 Upper Marylebone st
Gray Ben.esq, 12 Grove pl. Lisson grve
Gray Ben.esq.22Hamilton ter.St.Jns.wd
Gray Ben. C. T. esq. 13 Burton crescent
Gray Chas.W.esq.3Crescent pl.Burtn.cr
Gray Charles, esq. Devereux chambers, Devereux court, Strand
Gray David, esq. 20 Lincoln's inn fields
Gray David, esq. 34 Wilmington sq
Gray Fredk. Hen. esq. 9 Eccleston sq
Gray Geo. E.esq.7Dorset ter. Claphm.rd
Gray Geo. Mounsey, esq. 7 Upper Bedford place, & 9 Staple inn, Hoborn
Gray Jas. esq. 7Glo'ster rd.O. Bromptn
Gray Jas. esq. 7 Gordon st. Gordon sq
Gray Jas.esq.1Harrington sq.Hamps.rd
Gray John, esq. 8 Crown office row
Gray John, esq. 9 Hemus ter. Chelsea
Gray John, esq. 4 Lonsdale sq. Islingtn
Gray John, esq. 25 Old Burlington st. & Brighton, Sussex
Gray John, esq. 7. Up. Geo.st.Brystn. sq
Gray John Edwd. esq. British Museum
Gray Rev. J.D.D.10South cres.Bdfrd. sq
Gray Miss, 2 Kensington gore
Gray Mrs. 36 Trevor sq. Knightsbridge
Gray Mrs. 8 Wilton st. Grosvenor pl
Gray Mrs. 20 York place, Portman sq
Gray Mrs. Robert, 45 Brompton row
Gray Robert, esq.17 Brompton crescent, & 7 New inn, Wych st. Strand
Gray Sam. esq.5Brecknock cr.Camdn.tn
Gray Thomas, esq. 91 Piccadilly
GrayThos.M.esq.36Gt.George st.Westm
Gray Thomas Wm.esq. 8Wilton st. Belgrave sq. & 7 John st. Adelphi
Grayson George, esq. 39 Little Britain
Grazebrook John Warrell, esq. 8 St. John's wood road
Gream G. T. esq.42 Hertford st.Mayfai
Gream H. S. esq. 6 Northwick ter. St John's wood
Greasley Miss, 14 Regent square
Greated Timothy, esq. 13 Ely place
GreatheadCapt.Edward,44St.James's pl
Greathed Mrs. 23 Chapel st. Grosvnr. pl
Greatheed John, esq. 133 Piccadilly
Greatorex Jer. esq. 6 Tibberton square
GreatorexJohn,esq.Titchfild.ho.Regt.pk
Greatorex Wm. Anthony, esq. 70 Up. Norton st. & Kingsbury, Middlesex
Greaves Chas. esq. 43Cheyne walk,Chel
Greaves Chas. Sprengel, esq. 11 Blandford sq.&1Harcourt buildings, Temple
Greaves John, esq. 33 Euston square, & Irlam hall, Warrington
Green Sir Andrew, Capt. R.N. 9 James st. Buckingham gate
Green B. R. esq.62Charlotte st.Ptlnd.pl
Green Bevis E.esq.5 Kensngtn. pal.gdns
Green Chas. esq.13Blandford st.Prtm.sq
Green Charles, esq. 43Gibson sq.Islngtn
Green Chas.P.esq.44Southampton bldgs
Green Fras. esq. 3 Canonbury cottages
Green Francis Edmd. esq.4 Gray's in. sq
Green Francis Gwinnett, esq.45A, Queen Anne st. Cav. sq. & 18 Portugal st
Green Fred. esq. 10 King's Bench walk, & 10 Angel ct. Throgmorton st
Green Fred. esq. 17 Up. Southwick st
Green G. F. esq. Clare cot. King's road
Green George, esq. 28 Upper Harley st
Green Geo. P.esq. 27 Lamb's Conduit st
Green Henry T. esq. 2 Ebury st. Pimlico
Green James, esq. 21 Tavistock place
Green John,esq.23Alpha rd.Regent's pk
Green John, esq. 4 Bedford row, Islngtn
Green John, esq.26Liverpl. st. King's cr
Green J. esq. 4Marlbro'tr.Kensgtn.nw.tn
Green John, esq. 33 Soho square
Green John, esq. 40 Southampton row
Green John esq.5 Up.Yorkpl.St.John'swd
Green J. G. esq. 10 Sussex ter. Hyde pk
Green John Harry, esq. 26 Golden sq
Green Miss, 28 Rodney st. Pentonville
Green Mrs.Col.3Wyndham pl.Bryans.sq
Green Mrs. 3 Albert ter. Knightsbridge
Green Mrs. 24 Beaumont st. Portland pl
Green Mrs. 1 Broadley ter. Blandford sq
Green Mrs. 13 Charles st. Trevor sq
Green Mrs. 27 George st. Portman sq
Green Mrs. 10 Green st. Grosvenor sq
Green Mrs. 11Queen's pl. Kennington rd
Green Mrs. 52 Russell square
Green Mrs. 5 Smith st. Chelsea
Green Mrs. 21 Tavistock pl. Russell sq
Green Philip J. esq.4Dorset pl. Dorset sq
Green Thos. esq. 35 York pl. Portmn. sq
Green W. esq. 12 Smith st. Kg's. rd. Chls
Green W. esq. H3, Albany, Piccadilly
Green Wm.esq.1Camden cot.Cmdn.N.tn
Green Wm. esq. 59 George st. Euston sq

Green Wm. esq. 12 Noel st. Islington
Green Wm. A. esq. 4 Jamesst. Bckinghm. gt
Green Wm. Frost, esq. 5 Gibson square
Green W. H. esq. Larkhall rise, Claphm
Greenaway Edw. esq. 9 River ter. City rd
Greene Benjamin, esq. 45 Russell sq. & Bury St. Edmunds, Suffolk
Greene Benj. Buck, esq. 52 Woburn pl
Greene Edward, esq. 77 Coleshill st
Greene F. N. esq. 10 Bernard st. Russl. sq
Greene Miss, 12 Southampton rw. Newrd
Greene Thomas, esq. M.P. 19 Duke st. Westminster, & Whittington hall, Burton, Westmoreland
Greene Thos. Alex. esq. 2 Churchyard ct
Greene Thomas Webb, esq. 17 Gower st. & 9 New square, Lincoln's inn
Greenhalgh Rt. esq. 66 Charlt. st. Fitz. sq
Greenhill G. esq. 18 Cunningham pl
Greenhill Wm. W. esq. 23 Hunter st
Greening Henry, esq. 3 Harcourt bldgs
Greening Henry, esq. 20 Up. Albany st
Greening Rich. Jas. esq. 2 Harcourt bgs
Greenland James, esq. 11 Elm Tree rd
Greenough George Bellas, esq. Grove house, Park road, Regent's park
Greensill Francis, esq. 3 Essex ct. Temple
Greenville Major Wm. 62 Ebury st
Greenway Geo. esq. 9 Lonsdale sq. Islgt
Greenway Jsph. esq. 2 Gibson sq. Islingtn
Greenwell S. esq. 20 Park sq. Rgnts. pk
Greenwell Walpole E. esq. 2 Beaumont st
Greenwood Col. Wm. 2 St. James's place
Greenwood Major Julius, 14 Gt. Queen st. Westminster
Greenwood Chas. esq. 103 Camdn. rd. vils
Greenwood Chas. esq. 26 Holywl. st. Wesm
Greenwood John, esq. 10 Bayswater ter
Greenwood John, esq. 3 Pump ct. Temple
Greenwood John, esq. 11 Chester sq
Greenwood John, esq. 53 Chester sq
Greenwood John, esq. 51 Hamilton ter
Greenwood John, esq. 53 Wigmore st
Greenwood John Beswicke, esq. 4 Woburn sq. & Clerkenwell Police court
Greenwood Michael, esq. 12 Lowther cottages, Liverpool road
Greenwood Mrs. 21 Cumberland terrace
Greenwood Samuel, esq. Lavender hill
Greenwood Thos. esq. 14 Gt. Queen st
Greenwood T. esq. 54 Liverpool st. Kg's. cr
Greg Robt. Hyde, esq. Burlington hotel, & Norcliffe, Wilmslow, Manchester
Gregg Henry, esq. 20 Gt. Marlboro' st
Gregg Miss, 32 Percy st. Tottnhm. ct. rd
Gregg Mrs. 5 Park square, Regent's pk
Gregg Rt. A. S. esq. Marlbro' pl. Druryla
Gregg Thos. H. esq. 8 Grafton st. Fitz. sq
Gregory Barnard, esq. 15A, N. Audley st
Gregory Edward, esq. 5 Claremont sq
Gregory E. esq. 6 Cmptn. st. ea. Bnswk. sq
Gregory Edward, jun. esq. 13 South sq
Gregory Geo. M.D. 31 Weymouth st
Gregory Geo. J. esq. 21 John st. Adlphi
Gregory George B. esq. 1 Bedford row
Gregory John, esq. 7 Harley pl. New rd
Gregory John, esq. 13 Up. Kenningtn gr
Gregory John S. 41 Bedford sq. & 1 Bedfd. row, & Shoreham cottage, Dartford
Gregory Jonas, esq. 5 Up. Montague street, & 12 & 13 Clement's inn
Gregory Mrs. 8 Porchester terrace, Bayswater
Gregory Thos. esq. 12 & 13 Clement's inn
Gregory Wm. Hen. M.P. 14 Parkst. Grsv. sq
Gregory Wm. Hen. esq. 5A, Cork st. Bond st
Gregson John, esq. 18 Bedford row
Gregson Sam. esq. 11 Upper Harley st
Gregson Wm. esq. 2 Tanfield ct. Temple
Greig Alexander, esq. 10 Lowndes st
Greig James, esq. 37 Tonbridge place
Greig Mrs. 12 Seymour place, New rd
Greig Rt. Reed, esq. 13 King's rd. Gray's inn
Greig Woronzow, esq. 14 Lower Belgrave st. & 6 King's Bench walk
Greive Wm. R. esq. 3 Waterloo, Kilburn
Greives Jas. esq. 24 Haverstock hill
Grellet Hen. Rd. esq. 7 Lloyd st. Lloyd sq
Grellet Saml. esq. 13 Markham pl. Chel
Grenall Peter, M.P. 45 Pall mall, & St. Helen's, Lancashire
Grenfell Chas. P. esq. 38 Belgrave sq
Grenfell Mrs. 27 Connaught terrace
Grenfell Pascoe, esq. 14 Hyde park sq
Grenside Chas. Knowlys, esq. 10 Serle st
Grenville Hon. & Rev. Geo. Neville & Lady Charlotte Neville, 23 Hill street, Berkeley sq.; Bufleigh ct. Glastonbury; & Magdalen lodge, Cambridge
Grenville Lady, 33 Charles st. Berkeley square, & Dropmore, Beaconsfield
Grenville Lady Anne, 91 Pall mall, & Stowhouse, Buckingham; Wotton ho. Aylesbury; & Avington ho. Wnchster
Grenville Rt. Hon. Thos. 2 Hamilton pl
Grenville Mrs. 1 Glo'ster gr. w. Brmptn
Gresham Club House (William Best, sec.), 1A, King William street, City
Gresham Wm. esq. 42 Notting hill sq
Gresley Richard, esq. 11 Oxford sq
Gressier Miss, 12 Maddox street
Gretis Miss, 1 St. Ann's ter. St. John's wd
Grevill Henry, esq. 2 Hobart pl. Pimlic
Greville Lady Charlte. 42 Grosvnr. pl
Greville Lady Louisa C. A. & Lady Charlotte M. 46 Eaton pl. Belgrave sq
Greville Hon. Mrs. 18 Lr. Belgrave st
Greville Capt. 64 Cambridge ter. Edg. rd
Greville A. F. esq. 42 Grosvenor place
Greville Brook, esq. 2 Hill st. Brkly. sq
Greville Brooke, esq. 24 Holles st
Greville Chas. C. esq. 40 Grosvenor pl
Greville Fulke, esq. 57 Eaton square
Greville Henry, esq. 2 Hobart pl. Ea. sq
Greville P. G. esq. 37 Hemingfd. tr. Isln
Grey Earl, P.C. 30 Belgrave sq. Howick hall, Alnwick, Northumberland, & Datchet lawn, Slough
Grey Countess Dowager, 48 Berkeley sq. & Howick hall, near Alnwick
Grey Rt. Hon. Sir Chas. E. G.C.H. Clarendon hotel, New Bond st. & The Oaks, Carshalton, Surrey
Grey Rt. Hon. Sir George, bart. M.P. 14 Eaton place
Grey Hon. Lady, 13 Hertford st. & Falloden, Alnwick, Northumberland
Grey Dowager Lady, 14 Eaton place
Grey Hon. William Booth, 43 Charles st. Berkeleysq. & the Hall, Berkhamstead
Grey Hon. Mrs. W. 60 Upper Berkeley st
Grey Chas. esq. 6 Chester st. Grosvnr. pl
Grey Ed. esq. 4 Linden gr. Kensgtn. gr. pts
Grey Mrs. 110 Guilford st. Russell sq
Grey Mrs. 1 Hornton st. Kensington
Grey Wm. P. esq. 3 Abbey pl. S. John's wd
Grey Wm. Hen. esq. 10 South Lmbth. pl
Grey Wm. Scurfield, esq. 1 Cloisters, Templ
Gribble Henry, esq. 3 Raymond bldgs
Gribble Miss, 89 Sloane street
Gribble Thos. esq. 3 Hamiltn. pl. S. Jn's. wd
Gribble Wm. esq. 3 Raymond bldgs
Gridley Hy. Gillett, esq. 20 Jermyn st. & 5 Southampton st. Bloomsbury
Griellier Richd. esq. 11 Dalby ter. City rd
Grieve Jas. esq. 87 Hamilton terrace
Grieve Jas. esq. 3 Wilton st. Grosvnr. pl
Griffin Alfred, esq. 1 New sq. Lincoln's inn
Griffin George, esq. 4 Burton cres
Griffin George, esq. 26 Northumbrlnd. st
Griffin Henry Horatio, esq. Inner Temple hall staircase
Griffin John, esq. 21 Bedford place
Griffin John Alex. esq. 26 Austinfriars
Griffin John Palk, esq. 7 Clapham rise
Griffin Miss, 11 Up. Robert st. Brmptn
Griffin Mrs. 3 Kennington place
Griffin Nathl. esq. 2 Cloisters, Temple
Griffin S. esq. 2 Parliament st
Griffin Thos. esq. Chichester pl. Wnds. rd
Griffin Thos. esq. 14 Paradise ter. Islgtn
Griffith Edwd. C. esq. 5 Lincoln's inn fi
Griffith Edwd. esq. Common Pleas office Chancery lane
Griffith Edward C. esq. 19 Lincoln's inn fi
Griffith Edward Geo. esq. 2 Paper bldgs
Griffith Henry, esq. 9 Gray's inn square
Griffith Jas. esq. 6 Raymond bdgs. Gray's in
Griffith John, esq. 9 Church st. Kensgn
Griffith Mrs. Brompton hall, Old Brmptn
Griffith Samuel C. esq. 19 Brunswick sq
Griffith Thomas, esq. 11 Gray's inn pl
Griffith T. esq. Steward's off. Gray's inn
Griffith W. esq, 1 Blmsbry. pl. Blmsby. sq
Griffith Wm. esq. 31 Lower Belgrave st
Griffiths Captain, 2 Clarence tr. Regt.'s pk
Griffiths Rt. Rev. Dr. 35 Golden square
Griffiths Edward, esq. 13 Gt. James st
Griffiths Edward, esq. 144 Oxford st. & Newcourt, near Ledbury
Griffiths John, esq. 1 Pleasant pl. Kg. cr
Griffiths Mrs. 17 Brompton row
Griffiths Mrs. 24 Camden cottages Camden New town
Griffiths Mrs. 14 Coleshill st. Eaton sq
Griffiths Mrs. 10 Glo'ster pl. Glo'ster gt
Griffiths Mrs. Derby, 35 Grosvenor st
Griffiths Miss, 8 Cambridge st. Cnght. sq
Griffiths Misses, 3 Sussex ter. Brompton
Griffiths Richd. esq. 23 Clapham rd. pl
Griffiths Rich. Clewin, esq. 10 Gower st
Griffiths —, esq. 13 Wellington ter. St. John's wood
Griffits Henry, esq. 3 Crescent place, New Bridge st
Griggs William, esq. 20 Aberdeen place
Grignon Mrs. 15 Rodney st. Pentonville
Grimsdale T. esq. 10 Hemus ter. Chelsea
Grimsditch Thomas, esq. M.P. Ginger's hotel, Bridge st. Westminster, & Brook park, near Macclesfield
Grimshaw Edmund, esq. 6 Stone buildings, Lincoln's inn
Grimshaw George G. esq. 20 John st. Adlphi
Grimstead Lady, 1 Hanover terrace
Grimston Hon. & Rev. Edward H. 42 Grosvenor sq. & Pebmarsh Hatstead, Essex
Grimston Hon. Miss, 6 Chesterfield st. & Prae house, St. Alban's, Herts
Grimston Hon. Miss, 14 Upper Grosvenor st. & Berkhampstead castle, Herts
Grimston Hon. Robert, 42 Grosvenor sq
Grimstone Mrs. 9 Charles st. Hatton gar
Grindall Mrs. 19 Judd pl. west, New rd
Grindlay Captain, 16 Cornhill, & 8 St. Martin's place, Charing cross
Grindle G. esq. Linden gr. Knsgtn. gr. pts
Grindle Mrs. Earl's court, Old Brompton
Grissell Hen. esq 3 River terrace, City rd
Grissell Thomas, esq. Lavender sweeps, Wandsworth road
Grissell Thos. D. esq. 10 Stockwell com
Grinsted Hy. esq. 2 Verulam tr. Maida hl
Gritten Henry, esq. 16 Pelham pl. Fulm. rd
Gritten Hen. F. esq. 16 Denbigh st. Pimlc
Grogan Edmund N. esq. 9 Cambridge st
Grogan Edward, esq. M.P. Carlton club, Pall mall, & Harcourt st. Dublin
Grogan Nichs. esq. 6 Princes st. Cav. sq
Gronow Rev. Thos. 29 Brompton square, & Court Herbert, Glamorganshire
Groom Arthur, esq. 15 Up. Seymour st
Groom Arth. P. esq. 4 Henrietta st. Cavn. sq
Groom Fras. H. esq. 4 Burton st. Eaton sq
Groom Rd. esq. 3 Henrietta st. Cavn. sq
Groom Robert, esq. 13 Myddelton sq
Groombridge Hy. esq. 16 Seymr. pl. N. w. rd
Groome Mrs. 26 Aberdeen pl. St. John's wd
Grose Rev. Thos. 12 Trinity sq. Tower hl
Grose Thos. esq. 23 Sudeley st. Islington
Grossmith Geo. esq. 3 Essex ct. Temple
Grosvenor Rt. Hon. Lord Robt. M.P. 107 Park st. Grosvenor st
Grosvenor Gen. 42 Grosvenor st.; & Upper Harepark, Newmarket; & Mount Ararat, Surrey; & Warren lodge, Loughton, Essex

Grosso R. esq. 15 Regent st
Grosvenor John, esq. Liverpool tr. Islgn
Grote George, esq. 4 Upper Eccleston st. Belgrave square; & East Burnham, near Slough
Grove Rev. E. H. 16 Lowndes st. Belgrve. sq
Grove Chas. Houblon, esq. 49 Chancery la
Grove John, esq. 8 Duke st. St. James's
Grove John, esq. 6 Henrietta st. Cavn. sq
Grove J. esq. 8 Portland pl. no. Claphm. rd
Grove Jsph. esq. 6 Up. Seymour st. west
Grove Wm. Robt. esq. 27 Upper Glo'ster pl. Dorset sq. & 4 Hare ct. Temple
Grover John Thos. esq. 50 Bedford row
Groves Jas. esq. 25 Charlotte st. Bdfd. sq
Groves Jas. jun. esq. 25 Charlt. st. Bdf. sq
Groves Jeremiah, esq. 18 Queen st. Mayfr
Groves Mrs. 58 Beaumont st. Portld. pl
Groves Mrs. 38 Jermyn st. St. James's
Groves Thos. esq. Thurlow ter. Wands. rd
Groves William, esq. 38 St. John st. road
Gruaz Hy. C. esq. 14 Buckingham st. Stnd
Grubb Edw. esq. 35 Lincoln's inn fields
Grubb John E. esq. 19 Old sq. Linc. inn
Grubb Mrs. 7 Claremont row, Barnsby
Grundy Mrs. 1 Earl st. Horseferry rd
Gruneisen Chas. L. esq. 16 Surrey st
Gruner L. esq. 59 Gt. Russell st. Blmsby
Grut Nicholas, esq. 7 Waterloo place
Guards' Club House (Thomas Robinson, secretary), 49 St. James's st
Guazzaroni J. B. esq. 3 Terrace, Kensngton
Gubbins Mrs. 17 Lower Berkeley st
Gudalla Haim, esq. 15 Kennington terr
Gudge James Wm. esq. 31 Burton st. Pimlico, & Inner Temple
Guedella Moses, esq. 4 Canonbury sq
Guenigault Louis S. esq. 11 Wharton st
Guest Sir Josiah John, bart. M.P. & Lady Charlotte, 8 Spring gardens, & Dowlais house, near Merthyr Tydvil
Guest E. esq. 19 Whiteheads gr. Chelsea
Guest Edwin, esq. 4 Kng's. Bnch. wk. Tmpl
Guest Mrs. 16 Chapel pl. Cavendish sq
Guest Mrs. 36 Hamilton ter. St. John'swd
Guest Mrs. 25 Tavistock square
Guichard Charles, esq. Vernon villa, Finchley new road
Guignard Albert, esq. 2 Foley place
Guilford, Rev. Earl of, 23 Dover st.; & Waldershare park, Dover; & Old Alresford, Hants
Guillaume Monsieur J. J. 36 Elizabeth st. Eaton square
Guillemard Mrs. 27 Gower st. & Woodford
Guillod Thos. esq. 11 Cadogan st. Chels
Guimaraens M. P. esq. 1 Northwick ter
Guinness Rd. esq. 58 East st. Marylebone
Guiton Miss, 14 York buildings, New rd
Guise Lieut. Gen. Sir Jno. W. bart. 48 Eaton pl. & Rendicombe park, Cirencester
Gullan Thos. esq. 4 Dean's yard, Wstmstr
Gulliford Jno. B. esq. 16 Salisbury st
Gulston Mrs. 20 Grosvenor square; & Durwydd, near Llandilo; & Knuston hall, Northamptonshire
Gundry Thos. esq. 41 Wakefield st
Gunn Wm. esq. 17 Bernard st. Russell sq
Gunnell Rd. Pickering, esq. 31 Oxford sq
Gunner Thomas, esq. 2 Stone buildings
Gunning A. T. esq. New Church st. Lis. gr
Gunning Capt. Matthew, 98 Glo'ster pl
Gunning Fred. esq. 17 Serjts.' inn, Flt. st
Gunning Joseph Waldegrave, esq. 7 Trafalgar sq. Chelsea, & St. George's hsp
Gunning Miss, 2 Rosedale vil. Notng. hl
Gunning Mrs. 9 Trafalgar sq. Chelsea
Gunning Thos. W. esq. 36 Lincoln's inn fds
Gunston William, esq. 127 Piccadilly
Gunter Robt. esq. Earls ct. Old Bromptn
Gunter Thos. Wm. esq. 28 Beaufoy terr
Gunthorpe Capt. R.N. 38 Brompton sq
Gunthorpe Col. J. 28 Connaught terr
Gunton John, esq. 11 Cadogan terrace
Gurden Chas. esq. 42 Camden st. south
Gurdon Thorney T. esq. 89 Glo'ster pl
Gurdon Wm. esq. 11 Crown Office row
Gurney Lady, 34 Lincoln's inn flds
Gurney Chas. esq. 3 Up. Islington terr
Gurney Fred. esq. 52 Cambrdg. tr. Edgw. rd
Gurney Hudson, esq. 9 St. James's sq. & Keswick hall, Norwich
Gurney J. esq. Lavend. hl. Wndswrth. rd
Gurney Russell, esq. Q.C. 34 Lincoln's inn fields, & 2 Inner Temple lane
Gurney Sidney, esq. 34 Lincoln's inn fields, & 6 Portugal st
Gurney Thos. esq. 8 Canonbury cottages
Gurney T. esq. 4 Devnshr. pl. Wandsw. rd
Gurney Thos. esq. 21 Glo'str. pl. New rd
Gurney Wm. esq. 24 Up. Berkeley st. wst
Gurney Wm. B. esq. 26 Abingdon st Westminster, & Denmark hl. Camwll
Gurrier Wm. esq. 14 Lonsdale sq. Islngtn
Gurwood Lieut. Col. 70 Lowndes square
Gustard Edwd. esq. 3 Kensington gore
Gustard Geo. Edw. esq. 3 Lincoln's inn flds
Gustard John, esq. 7 Up. Cheyne rw. Chlsa
Gutch Geo. esq. Bridge house, Harrow rd
Guthrie David Chas. esq. 30 Portland pl
Guthrie George Jas. esq. 4 Berkeley st
Gutteridge Wm. esq. 28 Up. Montagu st
Gutteres George, esq. 28 Southampton buildings, & 1 Brabant court
Guy Edward, esq. 3 King's Bench walk
Guy Hen. esq. 21 Dorset pl. Dorset sq
Guy Jas Wm. esq. 8 Palmer ter. Holowy
Guy John, esq. 30 Bury st. St. James's
Guy John, esq. 10 Great Queen st. Westminster; & Hampton wick, & Kingston, Surrey
Guy Thos. esq. 17 Portland ter. Rgt's. pk
Guy Wm. A. M.D. 15 Bloomsbury sq
Guydickens Miss, 49 Connaught terrace
Gwatkin Fred. esq. 26 Guilford st. Russell sq. & 9 New square, Lincoln's inn
Gwatkin Hen. esq. 26 Guilford st. Rus. sq
Gwatkin Rd. Wm. esq. 26 Guilford st
Gwatkin Robt. esq. 7 Wellington st. Str
Gwennap Thos. esq. 5 St. John's wd. grov
Gwilt John S. esq. 20 Abingdon st
Gwilt Joseph, esq. 20 Abingdon st
Gwilt Misses, 10 Norland ter. Notng. hl
Gwyn Daniel, esq. 23 Up. Seymour st
Gwyn Robt. Thompson, esq. 7 Portman st
Gwynne Sampson, esq. 126 Chancery la
Gyde Chas. esq. 17 Albion gr. Barnsby. rd
Gye Edwin, esq. 2 Belmont pl. Wndswth. rd
Gye Fred. esq. 9 Lawn pl. South Lmbth
Gyles H. esq. 10 Thurloe pl. we. O. Brmptn
Gyles John, esq. 16 Regent st. City rd
Gyles Mrs. 64 Upper Seymour st
Gyll Sir Rt. knt. Walgrove ho. Chelsea
Gyll Sir Rt. knt. 26 Charles st. St. James's
Gyll Gordon W. esq. 7 Lr. Seymour st
Gyll Mrs. 7 Lr. Seymour st. Ptmn. sq
Gyll Mrs. 13 Marlboro' ter. Kensington

HABBERTON Miss, 3 Regent pl. east
Hackbock Wm. esq. Denmark hill
Hacket Chas. A. esq. 14 Maida hill west
Hackett Jas. Thos. esq. 52 Theobald rd
Haddan John C. esq. 11 Up. Woburn pl
Haddan Mrs. 8 Belgrave st. King's cross
Haddan Thos. H. esq. 6 New sq. Linc. inn
Hadden Geo. esq. 15 Highbury terrace
Hadden George E. esq. 8 Furnivals inn, & 35 King st. Cheapside
Hadden John, esq. 29 Liverpool st. Kgs. cr
Haddington Earl, P.C. Admiralty, & Tyninghame ho. Preston Kirk, N.B.
Haddo Lord, 7 Argyll st. Regent st
Hadley Benj. esq. 13 Warren st. Fitzry. sq
Hadley George, esq. 14 Sloane terrace
Hadow Patrick, esq. 43 Upper Harley st
Hadow Patk. D. esq. 5 Essex court
Hadwen Rich. S. esq. 30 George st. Cmbwl
Hadwen Mrs. 37 Cross st. Islington
Haedy Christopher, esq. Bedford office, Montague st. Bloomsbury
Haedy Chr. esq. 76 Gt. Russell st. Blmsb
Haes David, esq. 50 Upper Bedford pl
Haes Hen. esq. 1 Priory, Wandswth. rd
Hagan John, esq. 60 Baker st. Portman sq
Hagan Thos. esq. 29 Glo'ster pl. New rd
Hagart Thomas C. esq. 169 New Bond st
Haggard John, D.C.L. 4 College, Drs. com
Haggard Wm. D. esq. 8 Sussex terrace, Hyde park
Hagger Mrs. 13 Low. Phillimore place
Haggitt Mrs. 69 Wimpole st. & Ditton, near Cambridge
Haghe Lewis, esq. 6 Upper Belmont pl
Hague Miss, 15 Scarsdale ter. Kensgtn
Hague Thos. esq. 12 King's rd. Bedfd. rw
Haig Jas. esq. 1 Stone bldgs. Lincoln's inn
Haig John B. esq. 49 Guilford st. Russl. sq
Haines A. esq. 1 Cobourg pl. Up. Kngtn. la
Haines Ed. W. esq. 21 Montagu st. Russl. sq
Haines Hy. esq. 13 Loraine pl. Holloway
Haines Henry, esq. 44 Sussex gardens
Haines Hen. Jn. esq. 24 Up. Belgrave pl
Haines Jas. esq. 38 Gt. James st. Bedfd. rw
Haines Saml. esq. 21 Montague st. Rsl. sq
Haines Wm. esq. 24 Noel st. Islington
Hair Quintin B. esq. 288 Regent st
Hake Wm. A. G. esq. 5 Crown office row
Hakes James, esq. 28 Duke st. Mchr. sq
Hakewell Edwd. Chas. esq. 8 Craig's ct
Hakewell John Henry, esq. 8 Craig's ct
Hakewell Mrs. 8 Thurloe sq. O. Bromptn
Hakewell Miss, 106A, Crawford st
Hakewell Thomas, esq. 18 Welbeck st
Halcombe John, S.L. 3 Serjeants' inn
Haldane Alexr. esq. 4 Carey st
Haldane Geo. esq. 6 Stone buildings, Lincoln's inn
Haldane George, esq. 19 Montpelier sq
Haldane James, esq. 65 Warren st
Haldimand George, esq. 31 Belgrave sq
Haldren Joshua, esq. 13 Chas. sq. Hoxtn
Hale Venble. Archdeacon, Charter house
Hale Hon. Mrs. 5 Grosvenor pl
Hale Bernard, esq. 13 Bruton st. Bond st
Hale F. jun. esq. 28 Charterhouse sq
Hale John Rd. W. esq. 23 Chancery lane
Hale John W. esq. 18 Park pl. we. Livrpl. rd
Hale Matthew, esq. 35 Connaught ter. Edgware road, & 6 Ely place, Holborn
Hale Miss, 70 Grosvenor st
Hale Mrs. 3 Park place, Paddington
Hale Rt. Blagden, M.P. 15 Boulton st. & Alderley park, Wootton-under-edge
Hale Robert Hale Blagden, esq. 81 Jermyn st; Alderly house, Glocestershire; & Castlerea, Roscommon
Hales Lady, 54 Montagu square, & Hales place, Canterbury
Haley Wm. esq. 72 Ebury st. Pimlico
Halfhide Captain, 45 Sloane st
Halford Sir Henry, bart. M.P. 8 Bolton st. & Wistow hall, near Leicester
Halford Rev. Thomas, 2 Hanover sq
Halford Chas. Douglas, esq. 29 Grsvnr. sq
Halford Thos. F. esq. 8 Duke st. St. James'
Haliva Rev. Abraham, 23 Bury st. St. Mary axe
Hall Sir Benjamin, bart. M.P. 24 Portman square; Llanover court, Abergavenny; & Abercarne, Newport, Mon
Hall Sir John, K.C.H. consul general for Hanover, St. Katharine's Dock house; & Stannington, Yorkshire; & Woodford, Essex; Consulate, 6 Circus, Minories
Hall Col. Chas. 24 Curzon st. Mayfair
Hall Capt. Chas. F. 16 Maida hill west
Hall Mrs. Colonel, 78 South Audley st
Hall Capt. John, 33 Burton crescent
Hall Rev. Peter, 39 Smith st. Chelsea
Hall Rev. Sam. M.A. 42 Duncan tr. City rd
Hall Rev. Thos. Grainger, 72 Chester sq
Hall Rev. Wm. Jn. 3 Amen ct. Patrnstr. rw
Hall Alfred, esq. 40 Doughty st. & 19 Southampton buildings, Chancery la
Hall Barton P. esq. 2 & 3 Kensington sq
Hall Benjamin, esq. 2 Verulam buildings, Gray's inn, & Buxstead, Uckfield
Hall Capel, esq. 30 Somerset st, Portmn. sq

Hall Benjamin Ed. esq. 22 Paddington green, & Cilgwyn, Cardiganshire
Hall Chas. esq. 4 Stone bldgs. Lincoln's inn, & Petersburgh ho. Bayswater hill
Hall Cheslyn, esq. 16 New Boswell ct
Hall Fredk. esq. 37 Keppel st
Hall Fredk. Jas. esq. 5 Old sq. Linc. inn
Hall George, esq. 78 Albany st
Hall George, esq. 10 Kensington terrace
Hall George, esq. 11 New Boswell ct
Hall Giles, esq. 3 Elm ct. Temple
Hall Giles, esq. 6 Barnard's inn, Holborn
Hall Hen. esq. 5 Mansfield st. Portlnd. pl
Hall Hen. esq. 20 Gt. Marlborough st
Hall Hen. esq. 16 New Boswell ct
Hall Hen. esq. 10 Upper Kennington la
Hall Horatio Wm. esq. 23 Rupert st
Hall James, esq. 40 Brewer st. Golden sq
Hall James, esq. 82 Camden road villas
Hall James, esq. Clarendon hotel, New Bond st. & Scarbro', near Beverley
Hall JamesChas.esq.2York bdgs.Islngtn
Hall John, esq. 7 Artillery place west
Hall John, esq. 43 Myddelton square
Hall John, esq. 68 South Audley st
Hall John, esq 13 Wilton st
Hall John Charles, esq. 8 Bloomsbury place, & 64 Lincoln's inn fields
Hall JohnHancock, esq.67Up.Berkeley st
Hall JohnO.esq.1Brunswick rw.Blmsby
Hall John Robert, esq. 40 Grove end rd. & 25 Parliament st
Hall Jhn.Wm.esq.6Marlboro sq. Chelsea
Hall Marshall, M.D. 14 Manchester sq
Hall Miss, 70 Albany st. Regent's pk
Hall Miss, 7 Portland rd. Regent's pk
Hall Mrs. 6 Brecknock cres. Camden tn
Hall Mrs. 12 Cheyne walk, Chelsea
Hall Mrs. 9 Nottingham ter. New rd
Hall Mrs. 35 Pembroke sq. Kensington
Hall Mrs. 19 Portman pl. Edgware rd
Hall Mrs. 20 Smith st. Chelsea
Hall Mrs. 1 Victoria terrace, Chelsea
HallMrs.Foley,1James st.Buckinghm.gt
Hall Mrs. Richard, 28 Portland place, & Copped hall, Totteridge, Herts
Hall Peter B. esq. 68 Cadogan place
Hall Richard, esq. 21 Chesham st
Hall Rt. esq. 8 Dean's yd. Westminster, & 1 New ct. Middle Temple
Hall R. esq. 1 Park lane, Hyde park
Hall Rt. T. esq. 5 Aldermanbury postern
Hall S. Carter, esq.:Rosery, O.Brompton
Hall Sam.G.esq.4Aldermanbury postern
Hall Stphn.esq.49Frederick st.Gry's.i.rd
Hall Sydney esq.2Gt.George st.Westmr
HallThos.esq.22Elm tree rd.St.Jhn.'s wd
Hall Thos. Henry, esq. 48 Finsbury sq
Hall Thos. Henry, esq. 49 Tavistock sq. & 19 Old square, Lincoln's inn
Hall Thomas James, esq. 1 Brunswick square, & Bow st. Police court
Hall Walter, esq.1James st.Bnknghm.gt
Hall Wm. esq.10Michael's grv.Bromptn
Hall Wm. esq. 6 Myddelton sq
Hall Wm. John, esq. 23 Wilton crescent
Hallam Henry, esq. 24 Wilton crescent
Hallen Capt. 1 Charles st. Trevor esq
Hallen Mrs. 46 Sloane st
Hallen Samuel, esq. 52 Stamford st
Hallett Chas.Wm. esq. 18 Abingdon st. & 14 Great George st. Westminster
Hallett George, esq. 40 Stamford st
Hallett Henry Hughes, esq. 7 Staple inn
Hallett Jas.esq. 6William st. Knghtsbdg
Hallett Mrs. 7 Osnaburgh ter. Regt.'spk
Hallett Thomas Perham Luxmoore, esq. 31 Bedford pl. & 2 New sq. Linc. inn
HallettWm.esq.38 Clarence gds.Rgts.pk
Hallett Wm. esq. 30 Up. Gloucester pl
Hallett Wm. T. esq. 1 Plowden bldgs
HallidayHen.esq 35Chalton st.Somrs.tn
HallidayM.esq.15Buckingham st.Strnd
Hallifax Thomas, esq. 67 Portland pl. & Chadacre hall, nr. Bury St. Edmunds
Hallifax Thos. jun. esq. 20 Berkeley sq
Halling Mrs. 37 Connaught terrace
Hallion John W. esq. 64 Warren st
Halliwell Richard, esq. 10 Fitzroy st. & 4 Great Ryder st. St. James's
Hallowes William, esq. 5 Woburn sq. & 39 Bedford row
Halls J. J. esq. 29 Cadogan st. Chelsea
HallsWm. esq. 5 St. James pl.St.James's
Hallyburton Lord Fredk. John Gordon, G.C.H., M.P., & Lady Augusta, Kensington palace
Halse Isaac, esq. 60 St. James's st
Halse Isaac, esq. 1 Park pl. St. James's
Halse John, esq.48 Markham sq.Chelsea
Halse John, esq. 20 Paddington green
HalsonRev.Chas.A.8 Norfolk st.Park la
Haly Capt. 9 St. Alban's pl.St.James's
Ham Mrs. 44 King sq. Goswell road
Hambleton Rev. John, 21 Compton ter. Upper st. Islington
Hambley Wm. esq. 2 Aston pl. Holwy
Hamblin Miss, 21 St. James's st
Hambro Chas. jun. esq. 1Up.Portland pl
Hambro Jsph. sen. esq. 1 Up.Portland pl
Hamer Misses, 52 Cadogan place
Hamer Mrs, 5 Chester pl.Kenningtn.crs
Hamer Samuel, esq. 74 Wimpole st
Hamerton Charles, esq. 10 Spencer st
Hamerton Jno. esq. 2 Essex ct. Temple
Hamerton Mrs. 21 Maddox st. Regent st
Hamilton, Duke of, K.G., P.C.12Portman sq.; Hamilton palace, Hamilton, Lanark; Ashton hall, Lancaster; & Easton hall, Woodbridge, Suffolk
HamiltonLord Claude,M.P.Haddo house, Methlick, Aberdeen
Hamilton Lady, 15 James's st. Buck. gt
Hamilton Lady H. 21 New st.Spring gar
Hamilton Dowager Lady, 19 Baker st. Portman sq. & Woodbrook, Tyrone
Hamilton Rear Adm. Sir Edward, bart. K.C.B. 17Cumberland ter.Regent's pk. & Trebinsheen house, Crickhowell
Hamilton Sir Fredk. bt. 59 Portland pl
Hamilton Sir Jas. John, bart. 10 Glo'ster pl. Portman sq. & Woodbrook, Tyrone
Hamilton Col. 116 Park st
HamiltonMajor,6 Camden st.nth.Cmd.tn
Hamilton Capt. Chas.John Baillie, M.P. 21 New st. Spring gardens, & Thame park, near Tetsworth
Hamilton Capt.A.P. R.N. 48 Wimpole st
Hamilton Capt. F. W. 59 Gloucester pl
Hamilton Capt. H. 20 Wilton st
Hamilton Capt.J.Cavendish hotel,81Jermyn st. & Sackville st. club, Dublin
Hamilton Capt. Wm. B. R.N. 21 New st. Spring gardens, & Admiralty
Hamilton Rev. Geo. 32 Burton crescent
Hamilton Rev. James, 7 Lansdowne pl
Hamilton Rev.T.N.86 Gt. Tower st. City
Hamilton De LukW.esq.12 Gt.May's bg
Hamilton Edward M.D. 22 Grafton st. Bond st
Hamilton Frs.Geo.esq.34 Gibson square
Hamilton Geo. A. esq. M.P. 20 Chester sq & Hampton hall, Balbriggan, Ireland
Hamilton Geo. Wm. esq. 2 New Burlington st
Hamilton Hen. esq. 18 Francis st
Hamilton James Hans, esq. M. P. Carlton club, 94 Pall mall & Abbotstown, Castle Knock, Ireland
Hamilton John, esq. 58 Oxford terrace
Hamilton John Edwd. esq. 17 Cumberland ter. Regent's park
Hamilton John, esq. 88 Regent st
Hamilton the Misses, 19 Orchard st
Hamilton Miss, 28 Portman pl. Edg. rd
Hamilton Mrs. 14 Queen st. Westmnstr
Hamilton Mrs. 5 Nottingham st
Hamilton Mrs. 85 St. John's wood ter
Hamilton Otho, esq.15 James st.Bckm.gt
Hamilton Richard, esq. 22 Down st
Hamilton Sydney D. esq. 63 Judd st
Hamilton Terrick, esq. 121 Park st
Hamilton William, esq. 15 Woburn sq
Hamilton Wm. John, esq. M.P. & Hon. Mrs. 14 Chesham place, Belgrave sq
Hamilton William R. esq. 12 Bolton rw
HammersleyChas.esq.25Park cr.Rgt.pk
Hammersley Misses, 23 Up. Berkeley st
Hammerton John, esq. St. George's hospital, & 1 St.George'spl.Hyde pk.cornr
Hammerton Mrs. 25 St. John's wood ter
Hammerton Thomas, esq. 111 Piccadilly
Hammick Sir S.L. bart. 36 Cavendish sq
Hammill Mrs.17A, Montpelier sq.Brmtn
Hammond Lady, 78 Upper Berkeley st
Hammond Gen. Sir Fras.Thomas, G.C.H. 7 Dean st. Park lane, & Plumpton, near Bury St. Edmunds, Suffolk
Hammond Rev.Edw.Ranson, 38 Gillingham st. Vauxhall bridge road
Hammond Chas. esq.12 Midx.pl.New rd
Hammond Freelove, esq. 29 Norfolk st
Hammond G.esq.56Gt.Carlse.st.Ptm.mt
Hammond George, esq. 22 Portland pl
Hammond Henry, esq. 16 Furnival's inn, Holborn; Hampstead; & Finchley
Hammond Mrs. 10 Albion st. Hyde pk
Hammond Mrs.1 Barrow hill pl.Rgt.'spk
Hammond Mrs. 106 Glo'ster place
HammondParker, esq.Batt's hot.Dovr.st
Hammond Wm. esq. 10 Kennington ter
Hammond Wm. esq.9 Queen sq. Blmsby
Hammond Wm. esq. 3 Russell square
Hamon Peter G. esq. 33 Jermyn st
Hampden Renn, esq. M.P. 59 St. James's st. & Marlow house, Little Marlow
Hampshire Wm. esq. 16 Sussex place, Kensington New town
Hampson James, esq. 7 Dorset square
Hampton E. C. esq. 74 St. James's st
Hampton J.esq.4Granville pl.Bagng.wls
Hamrock John, esq. 4 Francis st
Hamstede Fredk. Wm. esq. 3 Adam st. Adelphi
Hamston Mrs.12 Hornton st. Kensingtn
Hanbury Gen. Sir John, K.C.H. & Lady, 15 Charles st. Berkeley square
Hanbury Chas. esq. 77 Connaught ter
HanburySam.esq.9Judd pl.east, New rd
Hanbury-Tracy Misses, 35 Dover st
Hanby J.esq. Almonry off. Md.Sctlnd.yd
Hanby Wm. esq. 30 Coleshill st.Eaton sq
Hance Chas. esq. 1Harcourt blds. Tmple
Hance Chas. esq. 17 Alexander sq
Hancks Edw. C. esq. 18 Gt. Portland st
Hancock Chas. esq. 8 Halkin st. west
HancockChas.esq.5Michael's pl.Brmptn
Hancock Henry, esq. 59 Harley st
Hancock Mrs. 6 Hamilton pl. King's cr
Hancock Mrs. 12 Milton st. Dorset sq
Hancock Mrs. 2 Vernon pl. Bloomsbury
Hancock Sam. esq. 1 Waterloo, Kilburn
HancockThos. Wm. esq. 31 Coventry st
Hancorne Robt. esq. 4 Euston sq. Nw. rd
Hand Fredk. Jas. esq. 89 Chancery lane
Hand Thomas, esq. 40 Chancery lane
Handcock Capt. 10 St. George's terrace, Kensington New town
Handford N.esq.16Cheyne walk, Chelsea
Handley Major, 14 Suffolk st. Pall mall
Handley Mrs. 12 Winchester pl. Pentnvl
Hands Decimus, esq. 22 Thayer st.
Hands Joseph, esq.23Duke st.Grosvnr.sq
Hankey Col. SirFredk.G.C.M.G.30Queen Anne st. Cavendish sq. & 14 Brunswick terrace, Brighton
Hankey Lieut. Fred. 30 Queen Anne st. & 14 Brunswick terrace, Brighton
Hankey Beaumont, esq. 11 Old Bond st
Hankey John Alex. esq. 36 Brook st. Grosvenor square, & Finchley
Hankey J. T. esq. 2 Claremont rw. Islng
Hankey Mrs. John, 8 Grosvenor square, & Grass farm, Finchley
Hankey Misses, 20 Up. Berkeley st
HankeyThomson, jun.esq.72Sth.Audly.st
Hankey Wm. A. esq. 5 Hyde park gdns
Hanley Wm. esq. Stoke Newington green

Hanley W. Lucas, esq. 1 Park ter. Highby
Hanmer Sir John, bart. M.P. 59 Eaton pl. & Bettisfield pk. Whitchurch, Salop
Hanmer Col. 7 Devonshire pl. Portlnd. pl.: & Stockgrove, Fenny Stratford; & Hare place, Maidenhead, Berks
Hanmer Job W. esq. 3 Old sq. Linc. inn
Hanmer Thos. esq. 4 Harcourt buildings
Hannam Rev. Edward Pett, 2 Sussex cottages, Camden New Town
Hannam Miss, 5 Onslow ter. Fulham rd
Hannen James, esq. 1 King's bench walk
Hanney Dav. esq. 23 Friedenstein ter
Hannington Mrs. 11 Howley pl. villas
Hanrott Hen. A. esq. 29 Queen sq
Hanrott Philip August. esq. 29 Queen sq
Hansard Geo. esq. 22 Old sq. Linc. inn
Hansard James, esq. 7 Southampton st. Bloomsbury, & Hendon, Middlesex
Hansard Luke J. esq. 7 Southampton st
Hansard Mrs. 2 Kensington garden ter
Hansard Mrs. 1 Chatham pl. Blckfrs
Hansard Rd. esq. 15 Motcomb st. Belgrv. sq
Hansard Thos. C. esq. 1 Chatham pl. Blkfrs
Hanslar Henry S. esq. 19 Linc. inn flds
Hansler Capt. 2 Holland pk. ter. Notng. hil
Hanslip Chas. esq. 20 Thavies inn, Holbrn
Hanson Alf. esq. Chpl. stairca. Linc. inn
Hanson Geo. esq. 50 Woburn pl. Russl. sq
Hanson Jas. H. esq. 9 Blandford st. Manchester square
Hanson John, esq. 4 Mornington road
Hanson John, esq. 346A, Strand
Hanson John F. esq. Hyde pk. gate sth
Hanson John Oliver, esq. 9 Dorset sq
Hanson Mrs. 17 Millbank rw. Westmstr
Hanson Miss, 44 Russell square
Hanson Saml. esq. 15 Trinity sq. Tower hill
Harben Chas. Hy. esq. 9 John st. Minories
Harber Mrs. 68 Margaret st. Wilmngtn. sq
Harbert Mrs. 98 Sloane st
Harbin Peter Tait, esq. 11 Retreat, South Lambeth, & 12 Clement's inn
Harborough, Earl of, Stapleford park, Melton Mowbray
Harborow John, esq. 15 Cockspur st
Harbour James, esq. 24 Oxford terrace
Harcourt Capt. Vernon, 47 Cadogan pl
Harcourt Hon. Egerton V. 40 Grvnr. sq
Harcourt George Granville, esq. M.P. 24 St. James's place; & Nuneham park, near Oxford; & East Sheen, Surrey
Harcourt Miss G. V. 40 Grosvenor sq
Harcourt O. V. esq. 29 Devonshire pl
Hardcastle Mrs. New cross, Deptford
Harden Charles, esq. 9 Fleet st
Harden Mrs. 66 Newman st
Hardenberg Miss, 9 Norland terrace
Hardess Mrs. 5 Sidmouth st. Gray's inn rd
Harding Sir Chas. 3 Chester pl. Hyde pk
Harding Chas. T. esq. 37 Wm. st. Hmstd. rd
Harding Ernest A. esq. 95 Paul st. Finsbry
Harding Geo. esq. 15 Montague st. Russell square, & 57 Gt. Russell st
Harding Jas. Duffield, esq. 4 Gordon sq
Harding Mrs. 3 Melina pl. St. John's wd
Harding Mrs. 42 Up. George st. Portmn. sq
Harding Philip, esq. 5 Earl's ct. Old Brmpt
Harding Rt. T. esq. 24 Portland st. Soho
Harding Saml. esq. 3 Marlboro' rd. Chels
Harding Wm. esq. 47 Newington pl. Kngtn
Harding Wm. esq. 4 Percy st. Bedford sq
Harding Wm. esq. 7 Johnson's ct. Fleet st
Harding Wm. M. esq. 23 Tonbridge st
Hardinge Rev. Thomas H. 23 Park lane
Hardingham Geo. G. esq. 28 Blandford sq. & 61 Carey st. Lincoln's inn
Hardisty Edw. B. esq. 43 Gt. Marlboro' st
Hardman John, esq. 6 Harrington sq
Hardman J. esq. 30 Upper Phillimore st
Hardwick Alfd. M.D. 28 Lr. Phillimore pl
Hardwick Bedjn. esq. 22 Basinghall st
Hardwick John, D.C.L.K. 5 Albany, & Marlborough street police court
Hardwick Miss, 2 Kennington place
Hardwick Philip, esq. R.A. 60 Russell sq
Hardwicke Earl of, Capt. R.N. Wimpole hall, Arrington, Cambridge
Hardwicke John, esq. 20 Regent square
Hardy Capt. 8 Tavistock st. Bedford sq
Hardy Benjamin, esq. 61 Chancery lane
Hardy Gathorne, esq. 35 Eaton square, & Inner Temple lane
Hardy James, esq. 4 Upper Baker st
Hardy John, esq. 43 Canonbury square
Hardy John, esq. M.P. 3 Portland place, & Worty park, near Winchester
Hardy John, sen. esq. 12 Cumberland ter
Hardy John V. esq. 45 Camden st. south
Hardy J. F. esq. 23 Rutland gate
Hardy Miss, 17 Highbury park
Hardy Mrs. 52 Porchester ter. Bayswtr
Hardy Robt. esq. 8 South ter. Alexander sq
Hardy Sam. 17 Southampton blgs. Chcy. la
Hardy Wm. esq. 41 Gllingham st
Hardy Wm. Wells, esq. 28 Cadogan st
Hare Sir John, bart. 11 Langham place
Hare Sir Thomas, bart. 15 Waterloo pl. & Stow hall, Downham market
Hare Col. 34 South st. South Audley st & Norton Disney, near Newark
Hare Chas. John, M.D. 9A, Langham pl
Hare Geo. esq. 33 Up. Berkeley st. west
Hare Launcelot, esq. 13 Up. Gower st
Hare Mrs. 13 Upper Gower st
Hare Miss, 32 Up. Phillimore pl. Kensgn
Hare Philip, esq. 7 Belinda cottages. Isln
Hare Reginald, esq. 144 Oxford st. & the Wilderness, Dartmouth, Devon
Hare Richd. esq. 5 South sq. Gray's inn
Hare Robt. esq. 14 Charlotte st. Pimlico
Hare Robert esq. 13 Upper Gower st
Hare Samuel esq. 9A, Langham place
Hare Thomas, esq. 23 Chancery lane, & 1 Pelham place, Fulham road
Hare William, esq. 72 Gt. Portland st
Hare William esq. 19 Spring gardens
Harenc Chas. J. esq. 12 King's Bench wk
Harenc Hen. Ben. esq. 12 King's Benchwk
Harewood, Earl of, 13 Hanover square, & Harewood house, near Leeds
Harford Chas. Robt. esq. 9 Rutland gate
Hargrave John F. esq. 4 Campden hill villas, Kensington
Hargrave John F. esq. 59 Chancery lane
Hargrave Mrs. 193 Sloane st
Hargreave Chas. J. esq. 69 Chancery la
Hargreave Oliver esq. 2 Bloomsbury pl
Hargreaves Hy. esq. 40 South bnk. Reg. pk
Harington Sir John, 14 Hyde park st
Harington Lady, 14 Hyde park st
Harington Mrs. Henry, 35 Hans place
Harker John, esq. 26 Cadogan st
Harker John, esq. 24 Upp. Barnsbury st
Harland Sir Robt. bart. 3 Richmond ter. Whitehall, & Orwell pk. near Ipswich
Harland Thos. Wm. esq. 28 Trinity sq. Boro
Harle Ezra, esq. 109 Chancery lane
Harley George, esq. 4 Augustus square
Harley James, esq. 23A, Davies st
Harley John Pritt, esq. 14 Up. Gower st
Harley Miss, 30 Harley st. & Cowley, near Urbridge
Harley Mrs. 12 Coleshill st. Eaton sq
Harley Mrs. 26 Manchester st. Manch. sq
Harling Mrs. 1 Eaton square
Harlowe Stephen, esq. 2 Northbk. Rgt.'s pk
Harman Chas. esq. 14 Baker st. Lloyd sq
Harman C. H. esq. 4 Winkwrth. blds. Cityrd
Harman Henry, esq. 34 Clarges st
Harman John, esq. 2 Falcon ct. Fleet st
Harman John, esq. 11 Chester pl. Ken. crs
Harman Miss, 14 Liverpool st. King's crs
Harman Thos. R. esq. 11 Bedford place
Harmer James, esq. 139 Fleet street, & Ingress Abbey, Kent
Harmer William, esq. 19 Endsleigh st
Harms G. A. esq. 10 Thornhill pl. Caledn. rd
Harmston T. esq. 5 Princes rd. Notting hl
Harnage Edward, esq. & Lady, 18 Beaufoy terrace, Edgware road
Harnden Jas. Cooper, esq. 167 Albany st
Harness H. esq. 1 Kimbolton pl. Brmptn
Harness Rev. W. 19 Heathcote st
Harnett John, esq. 45 Museum st
Harnett Wm. C. esq. 40 Up. Bedford pl
Harper Charles, esq. 15 Compton st. east
Harper E. Norton, esq. 21 Kensington sq
Harper John, esq. 11 Howland st
Harper John A. W. esq. 13 Mitre ct. chmbrs
Harper Mrs. 12 Angel ter. Islington
Harper Mrs. 23 Suffolk st. Haymarket
Harper Mrs. 166 Albany st. Regent's pk
Harper Miss, 5 Wyndham pl. Brynstn. sq
Harper Thomas, esq. 23 Alexander sq
Harper T. jun. esq. 32 Argyle st. New rd
Harper Wm. esq. 17 Camden cot. Cmdn. tn
Harpur Hen. esq. 17 Cobourg pl. Up. Ken. la
Harratt Chas. esq. 4 Highbury terrace
Harrington, Earl of, Whitehall gardens; & Elvaston castle, Derby; & Gawsworth, near Macclesfield
Harrington Mrs. 46 Beaumont st
Harrington Mrs. 21 Michael's place
Harriott Mrs. W. H. 14 Sussx. pl. Regt's pk
Harris Lord, 30 Albemarle st. & Belmont, near Faversham, Kent
Harris Lieut. Col. Sir Noel Thomas, 24 South bank, Regent's park
Harris Hon. Capt. Edward Alfred John, R.N., M.P., Whitehall gardens
Harris Capt. R.N. 59 Brompton square
Harris Capt. 23 Cambridge st. Edgw. rd
Harris Capt. 38 Allsop terrace, New rd
Harris Rev. Jas. Spicer st. Spitalfields
Harris Chas. esq. 76 Guilford st
Harris Fredc. esq. 14 Warwick ct. Hlbrn
Harris George, esq. 28 Charles st. Westm
Harris Geo. esq. 9 King's Bench wk. Tm
Harris Geo. F. esq. 12 Bernard st
Harris Hen. esq. 6 Claremont pl. Pentnvl
Harris Hen. esq. 13 Kensington crescent
Harris Hen. esq. 28 Up. Southwick st
Harris John, esq. 22 Argyll st. Regent st
Harris John, esq. 17 Red lion square
Harris John, esq. 34 Sandwich st
Harris J. esq. 40 Sidmouth st. Gray's innrd
Harris John, esq. 2 York pl. Walworth rd
Harris John, M.D. 28A, Albemarle st
Harris John Greathed, esq. 2 Old Palace yard, & 33 Lincoln's inn fields
Harris John H. esq. 8 Tonbridge pl. Nw. rd
Harris J. esq. 34 Compton ter. Islngtn
Harris Langley H. esq. 12 Furnival's inn
Harris Mrs. 51 Coleshill st
Harris Mrs. 3 Paddington green
Harris Mrs. 40 Portman pl. Edgware rd
Harris Mrs. 3 Rayner place, Chelsea
Harris Mrs. 36 Upper Berkeley st
Harris Mrs. 4 Up. Montagu st. Montagu sq
Harris Mrs. 28 Upper Southwick st
Harris Mrs. 7 York place, Walworth rd
Harris Miss, 15 Theberton st. Islington
Harris Rd. esq. Astronomical soc. Smst. h
Harris Rd. D. esq. 23 Geo. st. Euston sq
Harris Sydney, esq. 22 Grove terrace, St. John's wood
Harris Thomas, esq. 62 Connaught ter
Harris Wm. esq. 18 Hart st. Bloomsbury, & 5 Stone bldgs. Lincoln's inn
Harris Wm. esq. Larkhall rise, Claphm
Harris Wm. esq. 31 Northbank, Regt.'s pk
Harris William, esq. 55 Park st
Harris Wm. esq. 10 Saville rw. Walwth. rd
Harriskine W. esq. 8 Seymour pl. Eustonsq
Harrison Rev. T. 6 Albion ter. Wndsw. rd
Harrison Rev. Wm. King Edward st. City
Harrison A. esq. 16 Haverstock hill
Harrison Charles, esq. 7 Cambridge sq. & 19 Bedford row
Harrison C. esq. 13 Fortess tr. Kntsh. tn
Harrison Chas. T. esq. 12 Savage gardns
Harrison Dan. C. Rogers, esq. 1 Doughty st
Harrison David, esq. 1 Kennington pl
Harrison E. esq. 3 St. George's ter. Knsgtn
Harrison Ed. esq. 9 Berkeley st. Piccadilly, & 19 Bedford row
Harrison Edwd. M. esq. 44 Chancery la

Harrison Edwin,esq.13Grove ter.St.J's.w
Harrison Frank, esq. 3 Verulam buildgs
Harrison Fredk. esq. 44 Bloomsbury sq. & 10 Beaufoy terrace, Edgware road
Harrison Fredc. esq. 51 Gt. Coram st
Harrison Fredc.esq.22Oxford sq. Hydepk
Harrison Fredk. esq. 11 Westbourne st
Harrison Geo. esq. 67 Brook st
Harrison Geo. esq. 16 Carlton house ter
Harrison George, esq. 15 Foley place
Harrison Geo. M. esq. 22 Hart st. Blmsb
Harrison George Harrison Rogers, esq. Herald's college,Bennett's hill, Drs. c
Harrison Hen. esq. 8 Egremont pl. Nw.rd
Harrison Hen. esq. 35 Hill st
Harrison Hen. esq. 1 Percy pl. Bedfrd.sq
Harrison Hen. Austen, esq. 33 Burton st
Harrison Jas.esq.6Westbourne pl.Eat. sq
Harrison James P. esq. 11 Chancery la
Harrison John, esq. 5 Barnsbury square
Harrison John, esq. 9 Cambridge terrace
Harrison John, esq. 1 Albany court yard
Harrison John, esq. 32 Green st
Harrison John, esq. 3 Grosvenor gate
Harrison John, esq. 2 Haverstock hill
Harrison John, esq. 11 Staple inn
Harrison John, esq. 5 New inn, Strand, & Ensham, Oxon
Harrison John, esq. 162 St. John st. rd
Harrison John, esq. 6 Upper Vernon st
Harrison John, esq. 4 Waterloo, Kilburn
Harrison John S. esq. 89 Chancery lane
Harrison Matth. esq. 70 Cambridge ter
Harrison Matth. esq. Highbury park sth
Harrison Mrs. Cintra villa, Finchley New road
Harrison Mrs. 9 Edward's sq. Kensingtn
Harrison Mrs. Mable E. 33 Welbeck st
Harrison Mrs. 23 Millbank st. Westminr
Harrison Mrs. 12 New Manor pl. Chelsea
Harrison Miss, 7 Tibberton square
Harrison Misses, 11 Charlotte st. Bedford square
Harrison Pryce I. esq. 2 Inner Temple la
Harrison Ralph, esq. 6 Old sq. Linc. inn
Harrison Richard, esq. 55 Doughty st. Mecklenburgh sq. & 2 Gray's inn sq
Harrison Rd. H. esq. 3 Tanfield ct. Templ
Harrison Rich. T. esq. 2Pump ct.Temple
Harrison Rt. esq. 20Sussex pl.Regt.'s pk
Harrison Thos. esq. 36 Alpha rd. Regt.'s park, & Garden cott. Cheshunt, Herts
Harrison Thomas, esq. 21 Gower st
Harrison Thos. esq. 11 Bloomfield ter
Harrison Thos. esq. Lark hall rise
Harrison Thomas C. esq. 31 York ter
Harrison Wm. esq. 35 Burton st. Brtn. cr
Harrison Wm. esq. 60 Oxford terrace
Harrison Wm. esq. 13Stockwell common
Harrison Wm. A. esq. 34 Keppel st
Harrisom Wm. H. esq. 2 New sq.Lin.inn
Harrison Wm.R.esq.2 Marsham st.Wsmr
HarrisonWm.Tennant,esq.2Gray's inn sq
Harrison — esq. 8 Albert ter.St. John's w
Harrowby, Earl of, P.C. 39 Grosvenor sq. & Sandon hall, near Stafford
Harry Mrs. 9 Vincent terrace, City rd
Harston A. D.esq. 22Trinidad pl. Lvpl.rd
Hart Sir Hen. knt. Capt. R.N.34 York ter
Hart Lady, 34 York terrace, Regt.'s pk
Hart Abr.S.esq.6Lowndes ter.Knightsbr
Hart Chas. esq. 82 Guilford st. Russell sq
Hart Edwd. esq. 24Guilford st.Russellsq
Hart Fred. esq. 13 King st. Goswell rd
Hart Fred. esq. 11 Stanhope pl.Hyde pk
Hart Hen. esq. 2 Portsmouth st
Hart Hen. esq.5Portlandter.Wndswth.rd
Hart Hen. A. esq. 9 Devonshire st.Qn. sq
Hart Lemon, esq. 4 Cambridge place, Regent's park
Hart Maurice, esq. 6 Haydon square
Hart Mrs. 6 Haydon square, Minories
Hart Robert, esq. 2 Middle Temple lane & Dripshill lodge, Worcestershire
Hart Sol. A.esq. R.A.22Chas.st.Midsx.hl
Hart Wm. esq. 14 Portland pl. Islington

Harting James, esq. 79 Cadogan place
Harting Jas. Vincent, esq. 24 Linc. inn fl
Harting Jsph. Thos. esq. 24 Linc. inn fl
Hartley Major, 44 St. James's place
Hartley Lieut. Col. 139 Sloane st
Hartley James, esq. 40 Mecklenburgh sq
Hartley Jas. esq.27New Bridge st. Blkfrs
Hartley Perceval, esq. 27 New Bridge st
Hartley Robt. esq. 12 Holland st. Knsgtn
Hartley T.esq.109Stanhopest.Hmpstd.rd
HartleyWm.esq.6Southampton st.Blmsy
Hartman Mrs. 31 Devonshire pl.Prtld.pl
Hartmann C.F.esq. 3Vimiera, Wndsw.rd
Harton George, esq. 42 Grove end road
Harton Wm. Hy. esq. 2 Rodney st. Pentonville, & 15 Clifford's inn, Fleet st
Harvey Archd. esq. 20 Colebrooke row
Harvey Brydges, esq. 9 Staple inn
Harvey Chas. esq. 40 Smith st. Chelsea
Harvey Daniel W. esq. 26 Old Jewry
Harvey E. esq. 21 Paradise tr. Lvrpl. rd
Harvey John, esq. Barnsbury cottage, Thornhill road, Islington
Harvey John, esq.5Circus rd.St.Jn.'s wd
Harvey John,esq.Rushhill, Wandswth.rd
HarveyJsph.esq.8James st.Bcknghm. gt
Harvey Mrs. 17 Cadogan ter. Sloane st
Harvey Mrs. 126 Long la. Bermondsey
Harvey Mrs. 174 Prospect pl. Edgw. rd
Harvey Richd. esq. Wandsworth road
Harvey Wm. esq. 48 Lonsdale square
Harvey Wm. esq. 42 Gt. Queen st
Harvey Wm. Edw. esq. 4 Barnard's inn
Harvey Wm. Legg, esq. 44 Stamford st
Harwood Charles, esq. 89 Chancery la. & 15 Park row, Greenwich
Harwood Geo. esq. 12 Tnbrdg.pl. New rd
Harwood Jas. sen. esq. 12 Tonbridge pl
Harwood Miss,13Nw.Dorset pl.Clpm.rd
Hase Henry, esq.4 Duncan place, City rd
Haselwood Mrs. 6 Manor ter. Chelsea
Hasker Rev. Geo. Hen. 3 Southwick cres
Haslem John, esq. 34 Old Bond st
Hasler John, esq. 19 Rgt.sq.Gray's inn rd
Haslock Mrs. 22 Gt. Percy st. Lloyd sq
Hassall A. H. esq. 32 Addison road north
Hassan Effendi, second secretaryof Turkish embassy, 1 Bryanstone sq
Hassan J. esq. 21Harleyford pl.Ken.com
Hasswell E. S. esq. Gore lodge, Old Brompton
Hastelow Mrs. 12 Wakefield st
Hastie Archd. esq. M.P. 3 West st. Finsbury, & 5 Rutland gate, Knightsbridge
Hastings Lord, 7 Cavendish square; & Melton Constable, Norfolk; &Seaton Delaval, Northumberland
Hastings Sir Chas. Abney, 6 Cavend. sq. & Willesley hall, Ashby-de-la-Zouch
Hastings Captain Sir Thomas, Ordnance office, Pall mall
Hastings Edward, esq. 63 Up.Norton st
Hastings John, M.D. 14 Albermarle st
Hastings Wm. Warren, esq. 3 Harpur st
Hatch Mrs.14A,St.Geo.'s pl.Hyde pk.cor
Hatch Thomas, esq. 9 Gloucester grove west, Old Brompton
Hatchard Jas. esq. 37 Low. Belgrave pl
Hatchett C. esq. Bellevue ho. Chelsea
Hatchett John, esq. 20 John st. Adelphi
Hatfield Alex. esq. 1 Hyde pk. terrace
Hatfield Chas. esq. 10 Romney terrace
Hatfield Rd. esq. 7 Camdn. cot.Cmdn.tn
Hatfield Richd. P. M.D. 41Cleveland st
Hathaway Mrs.15NewDorset pl.Clph.rd
Hatherly John, esq. 13 Alfred place, Bedford sq. & 5 Gt. Marlboro' st
Hatherton Lord, P.C. Teddesley hall, Penkridge
Hathorn Capt.Geo.R.N.40Brunswick sq
Hathorn George, esq. 40 Brunswick sq
Hatton Fredk. esq. 21 Gt.George st.Wstr
Hatton Mrs. 27 Stoke Newington green
Hatton Richard, esq. 29 Albany st
Hatton V. F. Capt. R.N., M.P. United Service club, & Delgarry, Wicklow

Haughton Moses,esq.5Percy st.Bedfd.sq
Haurie Calixto, esq. 41 St. James's st
HaurieJhn.C.esq.Yorkcham.41St.Jas.'st
Hauxwell Mrs.3Stanhope ter.Regt.'s pk
Havell Wm. esq. 16 Bayswater terrace
Haverfield H. D. esq. 28 Bloomsbury st
Haviland Edwd. esq. 1 Southwick cresnt
Haviland Robt. esq. 66 Sloane street
Hawarden Viscount, 5 St. George's pl. Hyde park corner, &Dundrum, Cashel
Hawarden Dowager Viscountess, 10 Glo'ster terrace, Regent's park
Hawarth — esq. Fladong's hotel, 144Oxford street, & Sale lodge, nr. Manchstr
Hawden Miss, 32 Allsop ter. New road
Hawes Benj. jun. esq. M.P. 9 Queen sq. St. James's park
Hawes Benj. esq. 36 Brunswick square
Hawes Miss, Lavender hill, Wandswh.rd
HawesT.esq.Lavender hill, Wandswth.rd
Hawes Wm. esq. 17 Montague place
Hawes Wm. jun. esq. 12KingWm.st.Strd
Hawes Wm. sen. esq. 7 Adelphi terrace
Hawke Lord, 11St.James's square,&Womersley park, Pontefract
Hawker Admiral, 25 Cavendish square
Hawker Col. Peter, 2 Dorset place, & Longparishhouse, Whitechurch, Hants
Hawker Lady Lucy, 1Radnor pl.Hyd.pk
Hawker Edwd. esq. 4 Wilton st. Grsvr.pl
Hawker Joseph, esq. F.S.A. 23Alfred pl. Bedford sq.&College of Arms, Bennett's hill
Hawker Rd. esq. 48 Park street
Hawker Wm. esq.42Gower pl.Euston sq
Hawkes Major, 8 Orme sq. Bayswater
Hawkes John,esq.12Up.Kennington grn
Hawkes Mrs. 23Pelham pl. Fulham road
HawkesS.esq.5Dorset pl.nth.Claphm.rd
Hawkes S. M. esq. 50 Chancery lane, & 1 Tavistk. vils. Tavistk. sq
Hawkesworth Amorey, esq.9Pembrke.sq
HawkeyWm.H.esq.34Burtonst.Pimlico
Hawkins Col. 33 St. James's place
Hawkins Rev. Ernest, 79 Pall mall
Hawkins Rev. Wm. B.23Gt.Marlboro'st
Hawkins Alex. N. esq. 10 Montagu pl
Hawkins Bisset, M.D. 30 Golden square
Hawkins Cæsar H. esq. 26 Grosvenor st
Hawkins Charles, esq. 2 Albany ct. yd
Hawkins Chas. B. esq. 47 Gt. Coram st
Hawkins Chas. B. esq. 33 Hastings st
Hawkins Edward, esq. British Museum
Hawkins Edward, esq. 7 Russell sq
Hawkins Edwd.esq.2South sq.Gray's inn
Hawkins Enoch, esq. 18 Gloucester pl. New road
Hawkins Fras. M.D. 18 Bolton st
Hawkins George, esq. B2, Albany
Hawkins Geo. esq.2Egremont pl.New rd
Hawkins Hy. esq. 4 Crown Off. rw.Tmpl
Hawkins Henry, esq. 5 Gt. Woodstock st
Hawkins H. A.esq.6St.Ann's tr.St.Jn.wd
Hawkins James, esq. 58 Hatton garden
Hawkins John, esq. 5 Upper Gower st
Hawkins John, esq. 2 New Boswell ct
Hawkins J. V. esq. 63Geo.st.Portman sq
Hawkins John Wm. esq. 46 Margaret st
Hawkins J. esq. 15Albion gr.Thornhill rd
Hawkins Joseph, esq. 54 Nelson sq
Hawkins Mrs. 23 Gt. Marlborough st
HawkinsMrs.10Montagu pl.Montagu sq. & the Gaer, Newport, Monmouthshire
Hawkins Mrs. 2 Onslow ter. Fulham rd
Hawkins Mrs. 8 Somers pl.Cambridge sq
Hawkins Mrs. 1 Regent st. & Bignor park, Petworth, Sussex
Hawkins Rt.RalphA.esq.59Chancery la
Hawkins Wm. esq. 22 Camden cottages
Hawkridge Mrs. 22 Victoria rd. Knsgtn
Hawks Edw. esq. 5 Hemingford tr.Islgn
Hawksley Thos. esq.4Derby st.King's +
Hawksley T. esq. 57 Margaret st. Cav.sq
Hawley Sir Joseph, bt. 34 Eaton place, & Leybourn grange, Maidstone
Hawley Alf. esq. 15 Stoke Newingtn. gr

Hawthorn Robert, esq. 34 Gower st
Hay Capt. James, 6 Victoria sq. Pimlico
Hay Charles, esq. 1 Terrace, Kensington
Hay George Gun, esq. 127 Sloane st. & 44 Lincoln's inn fields
Hay James, esq. 33 Nottingham place
Hay JamesGordon, esq.2Fig tree ct.Tmpl
Hay John Holman, esq.7 Up.Seymour st
Hay Mrs. 19 Gloucester rd. Hyde park
Hay Mrs. 5 Ladbroke villas, Notting hl
Hay Wm. esq. 8 Clifford st. Bond st
Haydn Joseph, esq. 44 Carey st
Haydon B. R.esq.14Burwood pl. Edg.rd
Haydon Geo. esq. Larkhall rise, Claphm
Haydon Saml. Jas. B. esq.79Newman st
Hayes Lady, 7 Harewood's square
Hayes Sir Edmd. Saml. bart. M.P. 15 Chesham st. & Drumboe castle, near Stranorlar, Ireland
Hayes Capt. 7 St. George's ter. Hyde pk
Hayes Chas. Wm. esq.17NewBoswell ct
Hayes Geo. esq. 3 Garden ct. Temple
Hayes Henry, esq. 5 Great May's buildings, & 12 Bedford court, Covent grdn
Hayes John, esq. 1 Frith st. Soho
Hayes Joseph, esq. 12 Soho square
Hayes Joseph, esq. 12 Regent st
Hayes Rd. esq. 31 Mornington place
Hayes Robt. esq. 9 Clement's inn, Strnd
Hayes Samuel, esq. 40 Wilmington sq
Hayes T. esq. 50 Sthamptn. st. Pentnvl
Hayes Thomas Porrett, esq. 22 Russell square, & 33 Bedford row
Hayes Wm. esq.3 Avenue rd. Rgnt.'s pk
Hayes William, esq. 20 Bolton st
Hayes William, esq. Cloisters, Temple
Hayes Wm. esq.43 Queen sq. Bloomsby
Haygarth Mrs. 54 Up. Berkeley st
Hayley Rev. Burrell, 10 Portland road
Hayman Wm.esq.80Judd st. Brnswk. sq
Hayne Saml. H. T. esq. 33 Gt. James st
Haynes Ambrose, esq. 7East st.Rd.Ln.sq
Haynes Ambrose, esq.3Grange vil.Brmtn
Haynes C. esq.10 Belmont ter.Wands.rd
Haynes Freeman O.esq. 29 Torrington sq
Haynes J. esq.20 Chadwell st.Mydltn.sq
Haynes Joseph, esq. 14 Avenue road, & Palace chambers, St. James's st
Haynes Mrs. 15 Devonshire pl.Edgw.rd
Haynes Mrs. 3 Lower Belgrave place
Haynes Mrs. 2 Norland sq. Notting hill
Haynes Rt. esq.Queen's rd. St. John's wd
Haynes Richard, jun. esq. 2 Hunter st
Haynes R. L. esq. Ring cross, Hollwy.rd
Haynes Samuel, esq. 71 St. James's st
Haynes Thos. Wm. esq. 41 Arlington st Camden town
Haynes Wm. esq. 101 Camden rd. villas
Hayter Sir Geo. knt. 9 Stratford place
Hayter Geo. esq. 18 Park ter. Highbury
Hayter John, esq. 13 Manchester square
Hayter Wm. G. esq. M.P. 11 Hyde park terrace, & Wells, Somersetshire
HaywardAbrm.esq.Q.C.11King'sBen.wk
Hayward Hy.esq.18 Edwards st.Prtm.sq
Hayward James, esq. 17 Myddelton sq
Hayward Jas. R. esq. 16 Parliament st
Hayward Jn. esq. 3 Francis st. Tot.ct.rd
Hayward Miss, 16 Notting hill square
Hayward Mrs. 11 Church st. Paddingtn
Hayward Mrs. 79 Guilford st
Hayward Mrs. 18 Porchester terrace
Hayward Philip, esq. 13 Furnival's inn, Holborn, & Marden, Devizes
Hayward Thos. esq. 80 Guilford st
HaywardThos.esq.10River st.Mydeltn.sq
Haywood D.esq.18Newington pl.Ken.rd
Haywood Mrs.13Hanover cots.Rgt.'spk
Haywood Mrs. 19 Newington pl.Ken.rd
Haywood Rt.esq.3 Lowther cot. Lvrpl.rd
HaywoodWm.T.esq.6Chesterter.Eatn.sq
Hazard Danl. esq. 9 Barnsbury villas
Hazelgrave Rev. Jas. 23 Duncan terrace
Hazell John, esq. 9 Gresse st. Tot. ct. rd
Head SirEdmd.bart.2Chesterpl.H.pk.sq
Head Arthur J.esq.17 Southampton blds
Head Frank S. esq. 8 Gloucester sq
Head Geo. esq. 18 Park rd. Regent's pk
Head John, esq. 14 Hemus terr. Chelsea
Headford Marquis of, K.P.Brookes' club, St.James's st.& Headfort house, Meath
Headland Edward, esq. 32 Guilford st
Headland John, esq.16 Lodge rd. Reg.pk
Headland Miss, 5 Harley st. Caven. sq
Headley Henry, esq. 35 Gloucester pl
Heal Mrs. 14 Notting hill terrace
Heald Henry, esq. 15 Doughty st. & 19 & 20 Austinfriars
Heale Josiah, esq. 3 Gray's inn square
Heales Mrs. Stoke Newington green
Healey Francis, esq. 7 Euston grove
Healey Thos. Piers, esq. 3 Elm court
Heap John C. esq. 13Millman st.Bdfd.rw
Heard Hon. Lady, 10 Kent ter. Regt.'spk
HeardRev. Jas.N.10 Kent ter.Rgnt.'s pk
Hearder John E. esq. 35 Nelson square
Hearle Pomeroy, esq. 21 Kenton st
Hearn Rev. Edward, 24 Foley place
Hearns Miss, 71 George st. Portman sq
Heatch Miss, 6 Orme's sq. Bayswater
Heath John Benjamin, esq. consul genl. forSardinia,66Russellsq.&31OldJewry
Heath Chas. esq. 6 Seymour pl. Eust. sq
Heath Christopher, esq. 38 Gordon sq
Heath Douglas D. esq. 11 Chancery la
Heath George, esq. 11 Chancery lane
Heath George Craufurd, esq. 14 Albany
Heath Hen. B. T. esq. 123 Edgware road
Heath John, esq. C6, Albany
Heath John, esq. 11 Albemarle st
Heath John, esq. 11 Theberton st. Isltn
Heath Mrs. 37 Theberton st. Islington
Heath Thos. esq. 2 Albert st. Pimlico
Heath Thomas, esq. 4 Porchester ter
Heath Wm, esq. 6 Hampstead st. Fitz. sq
Heathcoat John, esq. M.P. 5Warwick st. Charingcross & Bolham, near Tiverton
Heathcote Sir Gilbert, bart. 12 Langham place; & Normanton park, near Stamford; & Durdans, Epsom
Heathcote Sir Wm. bart. M.P. 43 Eaton place; & Hursley park, Winchester
Heathcote Gilbert John, esq. M.P. 47 Lower Brook st.; & Stocken hall, near Grantham
Heathcote John E. esq. 9 Grenville st. & 1 King's Bench walk, Temple
Heathcote Lionel, esq. 34 Grove end rd
Heathcote Mrs. 33 Brompton square
Heathcote Mrs.41 Chas. st. Berkeley sq
Heathcote Unwin, esq. 7 Suffolk st
Heathcote — esq. Boscombe lodge, Finchley new rd
Heather J. esq. 3 Bedford ct. Cov. gard
Heather James, esq. 17 Paternoster row
Heather John, esq. 25 Brompton cres
Heather John, esq. 26 Hans pl. Sloane st
Heathfield Rd. 76 Oxford ter. & 1 New sq
Heathfield William, esq. 8 Featherstone buildings, Holborn
Heatley Mrs. 38 Hertford st. Mayfair
Heaton Chas. Hord, esq. 3 Mid. Templela
Heaviside Capt. Richd.15 Regent st
Heawood J. esq. 18 Manchester tr. Isltn
Hebard Chas. esq. 5 St. John's wood rd
Hebden Miss, 14 Brompton crescent
Hebden Mrs. 12 Perceval st. Clerknwl
Hebden Wm. esq. 14 Brompton crescent
Hebbert Mrs. 17 Queen's pl. Kenngtn.rd
Hebeler Bernhard, esq. Prussian & Wirtenberg consul general, 15 York place, Baker st. & 106 Fenchurch st
Heberden Chas. esq. 10 Old sq. Linc.inn
Heberden Thos. M.D. 11 Upper Brook st
Hecker Saml. Hen.T.esq. 26 Lowndes st
Heckford J. esq. 6 Diddington pl. Isltn
Heddington Mrs. 28 York place, City rd
Hedge Edward, esq. 10 King's Bench walk, & Paradise row, Stoke Newington
Hedge Geo. esq. 91 Milton st. Dorset sq
Hedgeland John, esq. 2 Grove pl. Liss.gr
Hedger Wm. esq. 9 Kensington gore
Hedges E. esq. 3 St. Vincent pl. City rd
Hedges Killingworth, esq. 9 Carey st
Hedges R. W. esq. 10 Earl's ter. Kngstn
Hedgman Jas.esq.4Crescent pl.Burt.cres
Hedley Capt. 50 Charles st. Berkeley sq
Hedley P. esq. 1 Up. Glo'ster pl. Chelsea
Hedley Thomas, esq. 4 Elm ct. Temple
Hefferman Jas. esq. 35 Coleshill st
Hegell Wm. esq. 10 Cross st. Islington
Heigham Chas.W. esq.19Old sq.Linc.inn
Heimsath Mrs. 7 Omega ter. Alpha road
Heisch Rev J.G.Mountfort ho.Brnsby.sq
Heisch Mrs. 38 Newington pl. Kengtn.rd
Helder George esq. 26 York st. Portman square, & 17 Clement's inn
Helder Wm. esq. 3 Aberdeen place
Helder Wm. esq. 10 Lancaster pl. Strand
HeleWm.Selby, esq.2Avenue rd.Rgt's.pk
Hellands Mrs. 50 Cumming st. Pentnvl
Hellier E. esq. 4 Edwardes sq. Kensngtn
Hellyer Wm. Varlo, esq. 1 Coleshill st. Eaton sq. & 4 King's Bench walk
Helme J. esq.4 Raymond bdg. Gray's inn
Helphouse S. esq. 17 Maida hill west
Helps Arthur, esq. 46 Chester square
Helps John, esq.26 Pelham cres.Brmptn
Helps John, esq.429Strand&Claphamcom
Helps Thomas, esq. 12 Furnival's inn
Helps Thomas Williams, esq.9Dean's yd. Westminster, & 3 Plowden bds.Temple
Helten Mrs. 12 New Millman st
Hemans Bathurst, esq.5 Raymond bldgs. & 12 St. George's ter. Edgware road
Hembery Jph. H. esq.2Bedfrd.st.Bdf.sq. & Finchley
Hembrow Mrs. 44 Warren st. Fitzroy sq
Heming Rd. esq. 4 Marlboro' sq.Chelsea
Hemings Mrs. 31 Up. Berkeley st. west
Hemingway Alex. esq. 39 Bryanstone st
Hemming F. H. esq. 38 York st. Ptmn.sq
Hemming John, esq. 8 North bk. Rgt.pk
Hemming Mrs. 3 St. John's wood villas, Finchley new road
Hemsley Wm. esq. 75 Lower Sloane st
Henderson Major, 15 Norfolk crescent
Henderson Rev. Dr. 11 Park ter.Highby
Henderson Alex. esq. M.D. 6 Curzon st
Henderson Andrew, esq. 2 Montagu sq
Henderson Ben.C. esq.18 Sth.bnk.Rg.pk
Henderson Cooper, esq.3 Lmb's.Condt.pl
Henderson David, 23 St. John's wood rd
Henderson Gilbert, esq. 2 Harcourt bdgs
Henderson Hen. esq. 18 Carlton villas
Henderson Hugh, esq. 15 Ebury st
Henderson Jas. esq. 55 Green st
Henderson Jas.esq.1 Powis pl.Hampd.rd
Henderson Jas.Hy.esq.31 Bloomsbury sq
Henderson John, esq. 64 Hamilton ter
Henderson John, esq. 4 Hare ct. Temple
Henderson John, esq. R.N.9Lwr.Eaton st
Henderson John, esq. 2 Montagu sq
Henderson John, esq. 3 Montagu st
Henderson John, esq. 26 Poland st
Henderson John, esq. 2 Stranrear pl. Maida hill
Henderson J. P. esq. 18 Manchester sq
Henderson Miss, 64 Hamilton terrace
Henderson Mrs. 21 Earl's ter. Kensngtn
Henderson Rt. esq. 22 Alfred pl.Bedfd.sq
Henderson Robt. esq. 33 Clapham rise
Henderson Rt.esq.3Montagupl.Mont.sq. & 36B, Charlotte st. Fitzroy sq
Henderson Thomas Wingate, esq. D4, Albany, & Allan park, Stirling, N.B
HendersonWm.esq.5Stanhopest.Hydepk
Henderson Wm.esq.16 Upper Gloucester pl. Dorst. sq. & 10 Lancstr. pl. Strand
Hendrey Mrs. 10 Lisson grove south
Hendry Wm.esq.27 Alfred pl.Bedford sq
Heneage Edwd. esq. M.P. 12 Devonshire pl. Marylebone, & Hainton hall, Lincoln
Heneage Geo. Feiske, esq. 39 Charles st. Berkeley sq. & Hainton hall, Lincoln
Heneage Geo. Heneage Walker, M.P. 41 Dover st. & Compton Basset, Calne
Henfrey Mrs. 5 Claremont terrace

Henley Capt. 9A, Kensington gore
Henley Joseph Warner, esq. M.P. 22 Gt. George st. & Waterperry, Wheatley
Henley Mrs. 12 Norland ter. Notting hill
Henman Charles, esq. 12 Clifford's inn
Henman Charles, esq. 4 Henman ter. Prince of Wales road, Haverstock hill
Hennege Dudley, esq. 39 Sth.bnk. Rgt.pk
Hennell Chas. T. esq. 1 Harcourt bldgs
Hennell Mrs. 3 Edwardes pl. Kensington
Hennen John, M.D. 24 Up. Southwick st
Hennet Geo. esq. 16 Duke st. Westmstr
Henniker Lord, M.P. 49 Portland pl. & Thornham hall, Stoneham, Suffolk
Henniker Aldborough, esq. 70 Chanc.la
Henning John, esq. 13 Coleshill st
Henning John, jun. esq. 17 Lr. Belgrave pl
Henning J. esq. 11 Grafton pl. Euston sq
Henning Mrs. 7 Chester pl. Regent's pk
Henriques David, esq. 14 Woburn sq
Henriques Jph. G. esq. 71 Westbourne ter
Henry Alex. esq. 33 John st. Bedford row
Henry Edward, esq. 9 King st. Finsbury
Henry Mrs. 43 Bernard st. Russell sq
Henry Mrs. 53 Conduit st
Henry Mrs. 8 Duncan terrace, City rd
Henry Stephen, esq. 16 Hunter st
Henry Thos. esq. 26 Charles st. St. Jas.'s
Henshaw Charles, esq. 41 Up. George st
Henshaw Frazer B. esq. 2 Lr. Seymour st
Henshaw F. H. esq. 13 Charlotte st. Fitz. sq
Henshaw Ths. esq. 27 Charlotte st. Fitz. sq
Henshaw Thos. esq. 60 Connaught ter
Hensley Jhn. Isaac W. esq. 35 Tavistock sq
Hensley Lewis, esq. 3 Gt. James st
Henslow Stephen Wade, esq. 4 Regent pl. west, Gray's inn rd. & 13 Clement's inn
Henson Jas. esq. 27 Chester pl. Ken. crs
Hentsch George, esq. 17 New Boswell ct
Henty Jas. esq. 20 Pelham pl. Fulham rd
Henzel Edward, esq. 2 Gt. Quebec st
Hepburn Sir Thomas Buchan, bart. M.P. Carlton club, 94 Pall mall, & Smeaton, Preston Kirk
Hepburn Joseph G. esq. 12 Trinity ter. Trinity sq. & 12 Copthall court, City
Hepburn Rt. esq. 8 Davies st
Hepburne Peter, esq. 25 Camden cott
Heppel Mrs. 6 Radnor place, Hyde pk
Hepworth Geo. esq. 31 Theberton st. Isl
Herapath John, esq. Bedford lodge, Upper Bedford place, Kensington
Heraud John A. esq. 28 Burton st
Herbert Sir Thos. R.N., K.C.B., A5, Albany; & York cott. Killarney, Ireland
Herbert Hon. Mrs. Chas. 8 Berkeley st
Herbert Hon. Mrs. 11 Hereford st. Park la
Herbert Rt. Hon. Sidney, M.P. 5 Carlton gard. & Wilton house, near Salisbury
Herbert Francis, esq. 7 Sloane terrace, Chelsea, & 10 Staple inn
Herbert Geo. esq. 55 Burton crescent
Herbert Henry Arthur, esq. 3 Grosvenor crescent, Belgrave sq. & Muckrass abbey, Killarney
Herbert Horatio, esq. 7 Clifton place
Herbert James, esq. 8 Newman st
Herbert John Maurice, esq. 10 Connaught square, & 24 Southampton buildings, Chancery lane
Herbert J. R. 1 Glo'ster rd. Old Brompton
Herbert Miss, 20 Glo'ster rd. Hyde park
Herbert Mrs. 6 Portland road
Herbert Mrs. 6 Royal hl. Qun's. rd. Byswtr
Herbert Wm. esq. 87 Albany st
Herbst Misses, 15 Queen sq. Bloomsby
Hercy John, esq. 20 Baker st. Portmn sq. & Hawthorn hill, Maidenhead, Berks
Hercy Mrs. 14 Cunningham pl. St. Jn. wd
Hereford Viscount, 12 Portland place, & Tregoyd, Hay, Breconshire
Hereford, Bishop of, 17 Hill st. Berkeley square, & the Palace, Hereford
Hering Fred. esq. 23 Duke st. Portld. pl
Hering G. E. esq. 4 Sthmptn. st. Fitzroy sq
Hering Wm. esq. 38 Mortimer st
Herington Edward, esq. 5 Bath pl. Knsgtn
Heriot Wm. esq. 15 Belgrave st. Kng.'scr
Heritage Thos. esq. 25 Sherborne st
Hermon John, esq. 4 Windsor ter. Edgw. rd
Hermon Rd. esq. 16 Groveend rd. St. Jn. wd
Hermon Rd. jun. esq. 17 Grove end road
Herne Mrs. 38 Beaumont st
Heron Sir Robt. bart. M.P. Brookes' club, & Stubton hall, near Grantham
Heron Mrs. 21 Montagu square
Herries Rt. Hon. John Charles, 14 Waterloo place, Pall mall
Herries Col. Sir Wm. Lewis, C.B., K.C.H. 14 Bolton st. Piccadilly, & Audit office
Herries, Farquhar, Davidson, Chapman & Co. 16 St. James's st
Herring Chas. esq. 1 Lodge road, Regt.'s pk
Herring Geo. esq. 4 Titchfld. ter. Rgt. pk
Herring Wm. esq. St. John's hl. Wandsw. rd
Herschel Sir John Fred. William, bart. Hawkhurst, Kent
Herschell Rev. Ridley H. 60 Gibson square
Hertford Marquis, Dorchester house, Park lane; Ragley park, Alcester; & Sudbourne hall, Woodbridge
Hertslet Charles, esq. 1 Grange villas, Brompton
Hertslet Chas. esq. 31 Norfolk st. Strand
Hertslet C. esq. 13A, Pelham pl. Fulhm. rd
Hertslet C. J. B. esq. 31 Norfolk st. Strnd
Hertslet Lewis, esq. 16 Gt. College st. Westmr. & Claygate, Esher, Surrey
Hertslet Lewis C. esq. 1 Greek st. Soho
Hertz Bram, esq. 11 Gt. Marlborough st
Hervey Lord Alfred, M.P. 6 St. James's square; 5 King's Bench walk, Temple; Ickworth park, Bury St. Edmunds; and Kemp town, Brighton
Hervey Misses, 3 Chester square
Hervey Mrs. 27 Clapham road place
Hervieu Auguste, esq. 7 Percy st. Bdfd. sq
Heselrige Lady Maynard, 23 Up. Brook st. & Hillingdon, near Uxbridge
Heseltine Edw. esq. 3 the Lawn, So. Lambh
Hesketh Rt. esq. 13 Arundel st. Strand
Heskett Miss, 15 Upper Seymour st
Heslop John R. esq. 9 Retreat. So. Lambeth
Hessey Francis, esq. 27 Kensington sq
Hestor John, esq. 42 Southwk. bdge. rd
Hetherington Jn. esq. 16 Connaught ter
Hetherington Wm. esq. 19 Connaught tr
Hetherington Wilson, esq. 13 Hyde park sq. & 3 New square, Lincoln's inn
Heuland Henry, esq. 31 Red Lion sq
Heusch Charles, esq. 34 Bedford square
Heward Rev. T. 13 Ladbroke tr. Notting. hl
Hewat Richd. Jas. esq. 17 Colebrooke rw
Hewetson John, esq. 48 Wardour st
Hewetson John, esq. 41 Woburn square
Hewett Mrs. Capt. 6 Barkham ter. Boro'
Hewett Prescott G. esq. 4 Vigo st
Hewett Mrs. 44 Piccadilly
Hewitt Edwd. esq. 12 Vauxhll. pl. S. Lmbth
Hewitt Henry, esq. 5 Stockwell common
Hewitt Isaac, esq. 51 Gt. Marlboro' st
Hewitt Isaac, esq. 10 Rich ter. Bromptn
Hewitt Mrs. 4 Henry pl. Up. Kenngton. la
Hewitt Thomas, esq. 54 Burton crescent
Hewlett Dan. esq. 24 King st. Clerknwl
Hewlett Hen. Wm. esq. 34 Gt. James st
Hewlett John, esq. 22 Upper Baker st
Hewlett John C. esq. 15 Chancery lane
Hewlett Mrs. 55 Hunter st. Brnswk. sq
Hewlett Mrs. 14 Up. Robert st. Bromptn
Hewson Rev. Frank, 74 St. James's st. & Southhall, Middlesex
Hewson Thos. Ansaldo, esq. 6 Woburn pl
Hewson Wm. B. esq. 6 King's Bench walk
Hext Samuel Hen. esq. 12 Gray's inn sq
Heylyn Edward, esq. 68 Haymarket
Heys Mrs. West cottage, Lodge pl. Reg. pk
Heytesbury Lord, G.C.B., P.C. The Castle, Dublin, & Heytesbury hou. Warminster
Heywood Sir Benjamin, bart. 9 Hyde park gardens, & Claremont, Lancash
Heywood John, esq. 3 Finsbury st
Heywood John P. esq. 6 Connaught pl. west, & Norris green, near Liverpool
Heywood Oliver, esq. 29 Oxford square
Heywood Peter, esq. 14 Oxford sq. Hyde pk
Heywood Wm. esq. Stoke Newington grn
Hibbard Charles, esq. 5 Furnival's inn
Hibbat Mrs. 45 Great Prescot st
Hibbert Geo. esq. L4, Albany, Piccadilly
Hibbert John, esq. 47 Great Ormond st. & 8 New sq. Lincoln's inn
Hibbert John, esq. 13 Lowndes square, & Chalfont park, Bucks
Hibbert Mrs. & Miss, 6 Hyde park sq
Hibbert Mrs. 5 Brompton grove
Hibbert Robert, esq. 13 Welbeck st
Hibbert Samuel, esq. 11 Sussex square
Hibbert Thos. esq. 25 Hyde park gardns. & Birtles hall, Cheshire
Hibbert Wm. Titlow, esq. Denmark hill
Hibbit Wm. esq. 48 Carey st
Hickinbotham Dd. esq. 4 Manchester st
Hicklenton J. esq. 14 Goulden ter. Islngn
Hickley Miss, 11 Sloane st
Hickman Edwd. esq. 10 Southampton rw
Hickman John, esq. 10 Duke st. St. James's
Hickman Mrs. 23 Petersburgh pl. Baysw
Hickman Philip Devereux, esq. 18 Lincoln's inn fields
Hicks Cecil, esq. 46 Vincent sq. Westmr
Hicks Francis, esq. 16 Bartlett's bldgs. Holborn; & West Meon, Hants
Hicks Fdk. M.D. 119 Stanhope st. Hmp. rd
Hicks F. E. esq. 7 Henrietta st. Cvndsh. sq
Hicks John, esq. 6 South cres. Bdfd. sq
Hicks Leonard, esq. 5 Gray's inn square
Hicks Mrs. 33 Regent square
Hicks Mrs. 17 Somerset st. Portman sq
Hicks Richd. esq. 1 Bedford pl. Clapham rd
Hicks Rd. esq. 7 Argyle sq. King's cros
Hicks Sam. esq. 25 Cumbrlnd. ter. Rgt.'spk
Hicks Thos. esq. 7 Somers place west, New rd. & 10 Clifford's inn, Fleet st
Hicks Wm. esq. Lavnder. sweeps, Wnds. rd
Hickson Mrs. 49 Bernard st
Hickson Samuel, esq. 9 Brunswick sq
Hickson Samuel, esq. The Cottage, 3 Pleasant row, York ter. Regent's park
Hidson Durant, esq. Larkhall lane
Higginbotham Mrs. 2 Thurloe sq. O. Bmptn
Higgins Col. Sir S. G. 34 Chapel st. Grsnr. pl
Higgins C. esq. 10 New North st. Red Lion sq
Higgins Edw. Townsend, esq. 17 Montagu st. Russell sq. & 3 Tanfield ct. Temple
Higgins Jas. White, 15 Furnival's inn
Higgins J. W. esq. Grove ho. Kentish tn
Higgins Matthew Jas. esq. 105 Piccadilly
Higgins Wm. esq. 11 Abbey pl. St. John's w
Higgins Wm. M. esq. 92 Guilford st
Higginson Col. George & Lady Frances, 9 Wilton crescent
Higginson Edmund, esq. 144 Oxford st. & Saltmarshe castle, Bromyard
Higgs Edwd. esq. 8 Rodney st. Pentnvll
Higgs James B. esq. Finchley lodge, Finchley New road
Higgs Thos. esq. 34 Newington pl. Kennington road
Higgs Wm. esq. 48 Newington pl. Kenn. rd
Higham Charles, esq. 46 Davies st
Higham James, esq. 6 Woburn square
Higham J. W. esq. 13 Tavistk. st. Befd. sq
Higham Mrs. 35 Baker st. Lloyd sq
Highmoor Mrs. 14 Campden hill villas
Highmore Mrs. 13 Golden square
Higins Rev. Thos. 4 York st. Portman sq
Hilbert John, esq. 60 Glo'ster pl. Portm. sq
Hilder James J. esq. 8 Gresham st
Hilder Rd. esq. 25 Stanhope st. Hmpted. rd
Hilditch Geo. esq. 2 Barnsbury villas
Hilditch John Frederick, esq. 55 Gower st. & 1 Brook green, Hammersmith
Hildyard Rev. James, 15 St. James's sq
Hildyard Francis, esq. 4 Inner Temple la
Hildyard George, esq. 8 Furnival's inn
Hildyard John, esq. 8 King's Bench wk
Hildyard Rt. Chas. esq. Q.C. 11 Paper bdgs

Hilhouse Richard, esq. Denmark hill
Hill Viscount.Thomas'shotel,25Berkeley square; & Hardwickegrange, Shrewsbury; & Hawkstone, Market Drayton
Hill Lord Arthur Marcus C.M.P.2 Chesham st. Belgrave square
Hill Hon. Miss, 18 Westbourne st
Hill Hon.Wm.N.Cox's hotel,55Jermyn st
Hill Rev. Robert, 11 King square
Hill Rev. T. B. 20 Portland pl. Islngtn
Hill Almon, esq. 13 Park sq.Regent's pk
Hill Arthur, esq. 3 Bedford rw.Clphm.ri
Hill Chas. Hamor, esq.Canonbury tower, Canonbury sq. & 10 Chancery lane
Hill David, esq. 5 John st. Adelphi
Hill David, esq. East India House, & Southend, Sydenham
Hill Edw. esq. 6 The Lawn, So. Lambeth
Hill George, esq. 31 Cloudesley square
Hill Geo. esq.13 Burwood pl. Edgware rd
Hill George, esq. 24 Portland place
Hill Henry, esq. 20 Brompton square
Hill Henry, esq. 38 Camden road villas
Hill Henry, esq. 45 Parliament st
Hill Henry, esq. 4 Verulam buildings
Hill Hen. esq. 5Verulam bdgs.Gray's inn
Hill Henry Munton, esq. 13 Orchard st
Hill Henry Reginald,esq. 62 Moorgate st
Hill Hugh, esq. 2 Osnaburgh terrace, Regent's park, & 1 Inner Temple lane
Hill James, esq. 10 Adelphi ter. Strand
Hill James, esq. 27 Finsbury square
Hill James, esq. 30 Glo'ster st.Queen sq
Hill James, esq. 58 Newman st
Hill Jas. esq. 19 Hermes st. Pentonville
Hill Jas. B. esq. 2 Guilford pl.Foundling
Hill James H. esq. 11 Mansfield st.Portland pl. & 6 New square, Lincoln's inn
Hill John, esq. 23 Claremont square
Hill John, esq. 26 Duncan terr. City rd
Hill John, esq. 1 Lodge pl. Regent's pk
Hill John, esq. 10 Stanhope pl. Hyde pk
Hill John, esq. 12 Up. Southwick st
Hill John Fredk. esq. 5 Inner Temple la
Hill John R. esq. 28 Upper Stamford st
Hill Marcus L. esq. 23 Suffolk st.Pall ml
Hill Matthew D. esq. 44 Chancery lane, & England's lane, Hampstead road
Hill Miss, 38 Charlotte st. Portland pl
Hill Miss, 10 Michael's place, Brompton
Hill Miss Noel,10 Montagu st.Portmn.sq
Hill Miss, 9 Springfield pl. Wandsw. rd
Hill Mrs. 42 Brompton row
Hill Mrs. 43 Cambridge st. Edgware rd
Hill Mrs. 10 Holland st. Kensington
Hill Mrs. 13 Orchard st. Portman sq
Hill Mrs. 7 Salisbury place, New rd
Hill Mrs.Seymour,6York gate,Regt.'spk
Hill Mrs. 14 York place, City road
Hill Patrick Y.esq.7Gt.College st.Wstmr
Hill Samuel, esq. Albion villas, Albion rd
Hill Samuel, esq. 14 Barnsbury park
Hill Samuel, esq. 1 St. Peter st. Islgntn
Hill Saml. esq. 26 Up. Berkeley st. west
Hill Thos. esq. 5 Eaton ter. Eaton sq
Hill Thos. esq. 1A, Sussex ter. Hyde pk
Hill Wm. Alfred, esq. 3 Gray's inn sq
Hill Wm. Alfred, esq. 29 Lonsdale sq
Hillas Capt.2 St. Andrew's pl. Regt.'s pk
Hilldrup J. esq. 14Caroline st.Bedford sq
Hillerston Frederick Edward,esq.2 Stafford st. Bond st. & Barnes, Surrey
Hillery Geo. esq. 2 Montagu st. Portm. sq
Hilliard Mrs.15 Southampton st.Blmsby
Hilliard Wm. Edw.esq.2 Raymond bldgs
Hillier Edward,esq.38 Cumming st. Pentonville,& 6 Raymond bldgs.Gray's inn
Hillier Hen. Bentinck C.esq. 85 Gower st
Hillier Mrs. 10 Alfred place, Bedford sq
Hillier Wm. esq. 12 Carthusian st
Hillman Mrs. 6 Upper Berkeley st
Hillman Wm. esq. 1 Argyll st. Regt. st
Hillman Wm.Aug.esq. 1 Argyll st.Reg.st
Hills Miss, 1 Trevor sq. Knightsbridge
Hillstead Wm.esq.104 East st. Manchr.sq
Hillyard Edwd. esq. 10 Burton crescent
Hillyer Mrs. 10 Soley ter. Pentonville
Hinchliff J. esq. 1 Notting hill terrace
Hinchliff John E. esq. 5 Mornington pl
Hinchliff Mrs. 22 Howland st. Fitzy. sq
Hinchliffe Edwin Stanley, esq. 3 North terrace, Alexander sq. Brompton
Hind Geo. Wm. esq. 66 Gower st
Hinde John H. esq. M.P. 13 Up. Brook st. & Acton house, Felton, Northmbrlnd
Hinde Mrs. 39 Chester ter. Regent's pk
Hinde Pelley, esq. 1 Cloisters, Temple
Hindley Charles, M.P. 1 Dartmouth st. Westminster,& Dunkinfield lodge, near Ashton-under-Lyne
Hindley C. esq. 34 Trevor sq. Kngtsbrdg
Hindmarch William Mathewson, esq. 7 King's Bench walk, Temple, & Bishops Wearmouth
Hindmarsh James, esq. 15 Tibberton sq
Hinds Mrs. 69 Baker st. Portman sq
Hine Rev. Geo. Hy. A.M. 5 Belgrave ter
Hine James, esq. 6 Heathcote st
Hine James, esq. 11 Paper bldgs.Temple
Hine William, esq. 26 Charterhouse sq
Hingeston Samuel, esq. 58 Chancery la
Hinton Rev. Jas.5 Grove rd.St.John's wd
Hinton Rev. J. H. 13 Liverpool st. City
Hinton John, esq. 3 Up. Brunswick ter
Hinxman John, esq. 27 Queen Anne st.; & 34 Soho square; & Sampford park, Finchinfield, Essex
Hippisley Sir John Stuart, bart. 7 Stratton st. Piccadilly, & West Cowes
Hippisley Miss Wyndham, 6 Chester sq
Hird Charles, Clevedon cot. Glo'ster place, Glo'ster crescent, Regent's pk
Hird C. esq. 49 Up.Marylebone st.Fitz.sq
Hird C. W. esq. 49 Up.Marlbe. st. Fitz.sq
Hird David, esq. 5 Lloyd sq. Pentonville
Hirschfeld Ferdind. esq. 26 Nelson sq
Hislop Lady, 36 Wilton crescent
Hislop Hardy,esq. 14South bank,Reg.pk
Hitchcock Rev. Roger, 8 Brompton cres
Hitchcock Frederic, esq. 3 Carey st
Hitchcock Mrs. Priory lodge, Kilburn
Hitchcock Miss, 41 Cadogan place
Hitchcock Rd. Jas. esq. 38 Davies st
Hitchcock Wm. esq. 23 John st. Bedford row, & 28 Duncan terrace, City road
Hitchcock Wm. esq. 22 Low. Belgrave st
Hitchcock Wm. H. esq. 2 St.Ann's villas, Acacia road, St. John's wood
Hitchcock Wm. H. esq.16 Highbury pk
Hitchins Capt. Hen. 43 Queen Anne st. & Adlicott house, Shipston on Stour
Hitchman Mrs. 30 Sussex pl. Kensingtn
Hitt Thos. esq. 112 Goswell rd. ea. side
Hoares & Co. 37 Fleet st
Hoare Sir Hugh Rich. bart. 100 Eaton square, & Lillingstone, Towcester
Hoare Charles, esq. 37 Fleet street, & Luscombe, Dawlish, Devon
Hoare Chas. Aug. esq. 30 Kensington sq. & Horton hall, Bucks
Hoare Chas. Richard, esq. 15 Tavistock st. Bedford sq. & 9 New sq. Linc. inn
Hoare Clotworthy O. esq.6 Symond's inn
Hoare Edwd. esq. 29 Percy st. Fitzroy sq
Hoare Francis B. esq. 20 Beaumont st
Hoare Fras. B. esq. 30 Lincoln's inn flds
Hoare Henry, esq.& Lady Mary, 14 New st. Spring gardns. & Staplehurst, Kent
Hoare Hen. Chas. esq. 7 York st. St. James's & Wavendon house, Newport Pagnell
Hoare Hen. M. esq.31 York pl. Prtmn. sq
Hoare Jsph. esq. 22 Loraine pl. Holloway
Hoare Peter R. esq. & Lady Sophia, Bird cage walk, St. James's park
Hoare Wm. esq.1 Southampton st.Fitzy.sq
Hobart Benj. Paul, esq. 24 Brompton cres
Hobbs John, esq. 35 Southampton row
Hobbs John W.esq. 38 Hart st. Bloomsby
Hobbs Stphn. esq. 1 Portsea pl. Congh. sq
Hobhouse Arthur, esq. 30 Lincoln's inn fls
Hobhouse Hen. esq. 9 King's Bench walk
Hobhouse Thos. Ben. esq. 5 Brick court
Hobhouse Rt. hon. Sir John Cam. M.P. 42 Berkeley sq. & Earl Stoke park, Devizes
Hobler Francis, esq. 47 Canonbury sq
Hoblyn Ed.esq.11St.Ann's vils.Acacia rd
Hoblyn F. esq. 12 Princes rd. Notting hill
Hoblyn Mrs. 2 Sussex pl. Regent's park
Hobson Campbell Wright, esq. 1 Gordon pl. Gordon sq. & 4 Raymond bldgs
Hobson Jas. E. esq.Courland,Wandsw. rd
Hobson Nich. G. esq. 5 Gt.Marylebone st
Hobson Rd. M.D. 68 Mount st. Berkeley sq. & Park house, Leeds
Hobson William, esq. 43 Harley st
Hoby Rev. James, D.D. 31 Gt. Coram st
Hoby Chas. esq. 115 Camden road villas
Hocken Edwd. O. M.D. 13 Bloomsby. sq
Hockin Chas.esq. 29A venue rd.Regts.pk
Hockley Mrs. 41 Berners st
Hodder Miss, Circus cot. St. John's wd
Hodding Wm. H. esq. 67 Glo'ster place
Hodge John, esq. 35 Upper Gower st
Hodge John W. esq.12 Buckingham st.Std
Hodge Langford Lovell, esq. 2 Upper Seymour st. west, Connaught sq
Hodges Lieut.Col.H.W.61 Cambridge ter
Hodges Capt. Thomas, 65 Connaught ter
Hodges Henry, esq. 6 Grove pl. Lisson gr
Hodges J. G. esq. 61 Millbank st
Hodges Miss, 73 Hamilton terrace
Hodges Mrs. 15 Cumberland ter. Rgt. pk
Hodges Richd. esq. 17 Up. Barnsbury st
Hodges Septs. esq. 20 Maida hill west
Hodges Thomas, esq. 104 Guilford st
Hodges T.Twysden, esq.Clarendon hotel, 169 New Bond st. & Sandgate, Kent
Hodges Wm. esq. 16 Southampton st. Bloomsbury,& 6 Figtree court, Temple
Hodges William, esq. 8 Virginia place, Great Dover road
Hodges Wm. Robt. esq. 49 Leicester sq
Hodgkin Thomas, M.D. 9 Brook st
Hodgkins T. esq.16 Clarmnt. rw. Brnsby.r
Hodgkinson Ed. esq. 15 Kilburn priory
Hodgkinson E.esq.15 Park pl.Paddington
Hodgkinson Geo. esq. Grove, Kentsh. tn
Hodgkinson Geo. esq. 7 York ter. Rgt. pk
Hodgkinson George, esq. 10 Stamford st
Hodgkinson John, esq. 6 Highbury ter
Hodgkinson S. esq.54 Upper Seymour st
Hodgkinson Thomas, esq. 41 Wimpole st
Hodgkinson T. esq.56 Burton crescent
Hodgkinson Wm. esq. 56 Burton crescent
Hodgson Lieut. Gen. 63 Welbeck st
Hodgson Rev. H. 18 Lit. Queen st. Wstm
Hodgson Rev. Rd. 17 James st. Buck. gt
Hodgson Chas. F. esq. 21 Wharton st
Hodgson Christophr. esq. 3 Gt. Dean's yd
Hodgson Fred. esq. M.P. 3 Carlton grdns
Hodgson Hy. John, esq. 3 Pump ct. Tmp
Hodgson Henry W. esq. 59 Chancery la
Hodgson Jas. esq. 11 Regent sq. Gray's inn road, & 5 Lincoln's inn fields
Hodgson John, esq. Q.C. 4 New sq. Linc. inn, & the Cedars, South Lambeth
Hodgson John, esq. 15 Queen Anne st. & Bowles house, Chigwell, Essex
Hodgson John H. esq. 52 Up. Norton st. Portland place
Hodgson K.D. esq.1 Clifton pl. Sussex sq
Hodgson Mrs. 4 Burwood pl. Edgware rd
Hodgson Mrs. 25 Clarges st
Hodgson Mrs. 4 Islington green
Hodgson Rd. esq. M.P. 13 Up. Brook st. & Stellinghall, near Newcastle-on-Tyne
Hodgson Richard, esq. 9 Highbury place
Hodgson Rd. esq. 10 Salisbury st.Strand
Hodgson R.J.esq.13 Frederick st.Gr.inn r
Hodgson Samuel, esq. 1 Regent's villas, Avenue road
Hodgson Thomas, esq. 3 Brecknock ter
Hodgson Wm. esq. 8A, Red Lion square
Hodgson Wm. H. esq. 5 Hare ct. Temple
Hodson Hen. B. esq. 13 New Ormond st
Hodson Jas. esq. 3 Amwell st. Pntnville

Hodson Robert, esq. 7 Maida hill west
Hodson Wm. esq. 24 Penton st.Pntnvill
Hodson Wm.esq. 19 King's rd.Bedfd.row
Hofferman Henry, esq. 2 Augusta place, Stockwell common, Clapham road
Hoffman Lewis, esq. 11 South sq.Gray's in
HoffmannF.esq. 6 Gloucester pl.Rgt.'spk
HoffmannJohn, esq. 6 Hanover ter.Rg.pk
Hoffstrutter Chas. esq. 52 Thurloe sq
Hogar Mrs.74Manchestr.st.Gray's inn r
Hogg Jas. Weir, M.P. 40 Up. Grosvnr.st
Hogg John, M.D. 71 Gower st
Hogg John, esq. 12 King's bench walk
Hogg Miss, 56 Chester square
Hogg Miss, 27 Highbury place
Hogg Rt. esq. 24 Sussex pl. Kensington
Hogg Thomas, esq. 231 Maida vale
Hogg Thomas J. esq. 3 Plowden bldgs
Hoggins C. A. esq. 4 Lamb bldg. Temple
Hoghton Sir Hen. B. bart. 7 Park cres. & Hoghton tower, Lancashire
Holbech William, esq. 44 Brook st. Grosvnr. sq. & Farnborough, Banbury
Holbeck Jas. 75 St. John's wood terrace
Holbeck Jas. esq. 21 Princes st.Hnvr. sq
Holborn Robert Major, esq. Northampton lodge, Canonbury square
Holcombe I. Jsph. esq. 15 Somers pl. ea
Holcombe W. A. esq. 28 Chancery lane
Holcroft Thomas, esq. 1 Clifford's inn
Holden Rev. Henry A. 23 Gower st
Holden Mrs.6 Hennington ter.U.Kngtn.l
Holdgate Mrs. 8 Upper George st
Holding Charles, esq. 13 New Bridge st
Holding John, esq. 12 Ehrenburg terrace
Holdship Jas. Michael, esq. 4 Regent sq
Holdship John, esq. 11 Upper Bedford pl
Holdship Mrs. 11 Upper Bedford place
Holdstock Rev. Jas. 29 Polygon, Clar. sq
Holdsworth Rev. Wm. 39 Royal crescent
Holdworth J.E. esq. 1 Figtree ct.Temple
Hole Miss, 11 Highbury terrace
Holford Maj. Gwynne, 31 Grosvenor sq. & Buckland, near Brecon, & Kilgwyn, Carmarthen
Holford Jas. esq. Holford house, Rgt. pk
Holford Robert Steiner, esq. 15 Bolton st. & Westonbirt house, Tetbury
Holford Ths.Wm.esq. 61 South Audley st
Holiday Geo. H. esq. 2 Hampstead st
Holiwell John, esq. 67 Geo. st. Euston sq
Holl Joseph, esq. South Lambeth
Holl Wm. esq. 8 York st. St. James's
Holland Dowager Lady, 9 Gt. Stanhope st.; & Kensington; & Ampthill park
Holland Lord, minister at Florence
Holland Captain, 27 Upper Berkeley st
Holland Rev. Edmd. 33 Hyde pk. gardns
Holland Chas. M.D. 16 Queen st.Mayfair
Holland Edmd. C. esq. 38 Lincln. inn flds
Holland G. S. O. esq. 9 Inner Temple la
Holland Henry, M.D. 25 Brook st
Holland Hen. esq. 11 John st. Adelphi
Holland Henry, esq. 46 Montagu square
Holland Henry L. esq. 11 Harley st
Holland James, esq. 11 Osnaburgh st
Holland Mrs.37 Frederick st.Gray's in.rd
Holland Mrs. 3 Grove ter. Kentish town
Holland Mrs. 32 Hyde park gardens
Holland Mrs. Ann, 36 York pl. City rd
Holland P. esq. 2 Maynard pl. Chelsea
Holland Rd.esq. Acacia villa, Avenue rd
Holland Robt. esq. M.P. 63 Portland pl. & Allegria, near St.Leonard's, Sussex
Holland Rt.G.M.D.44 Clerkenwell green
HollandWm.esq.4Clarendon pl.Maida hl
Holland W. F. esq. 9 Inner Temple lane
Hollier Chas. esq. 4 Cumbrlnd.pl. Nw.rd
Hollingbury Miss, 24 Haydon st. Minrs
Hollingsworth Nathaniel, esq. 22 Gower st. & 24 Cateaton st
Hollingworth Arch. D.D. 20 Finsbury sq
Hollingworth J. G. esq. 41 Gt. James st
Hollins John, esq. 47 Berners st
Hollis Rev. Benj. Sam. 29 Gibson sq
Holliwell Jn. esq. 67 George st. Eust. st
Holloway Rev. Jas.Thos. D.D. 6 Hanover ter. Ladbroke sq. Notting hill
Holloway J.esq. 13 Albert ter.St Jn's. wd
Holloway J. esq.12 Hemus ter. King's rd
Holloway Wm. esq. 8 New sq. Linc. inn
Hollyer M. H. esq. 20 Haverstock hill
Hollyer Mrs. 33 Great Portland st
Holman John B. esq. 38 Harewood sq. & 47 Coleman st. City
Holman Mrs. 7 Princes pl.Kenningtn. rd
Holmden John Geo. esq. 53 King sq
Holme Bryan, esq. 13 Brunswick sq. & 10 New inn, Strand
Holme Wm.esq. 15 Nassau st.Middx. hos
Holmes Hon. Wm. Hen. Ashe A'Court, M.P. 19 Cork st. & Westover, Newport, Isle of Wight
Holmes Alex. 26 Charles st. St. James's
Holmes Alf.G.esq.25Gt.Jamesst.Bedf.rw
Holmes David, esq. 31 Up. Berkeley st
Holmes Edward, esq. 5 Raymond buildings, & Bury St. Edmunds
Holmes Edward C. esq. 31 Bedford row
Holmes Geo. esq. 34 Eastbourne ter
Holmes Henry esq. 11 Camden cottages
Holmes Hen. esq. 26 Terrace, Trinity sq
Holmes Jas. esq. 4 New Ormond st
Holmes Jas. esq. 15 Wilton st. Grosvr. pl
Holmes Mrs. 15 Alfred st. Bedford sq
Holmes Mrs. 1 Clarence ter. Regent's pk
Holmes Mrs. 6 Marlboro'pl.St.John'swd
Holmes Mrs. 22 New Millman st
Holmes Mrs. 10 Pelham rd. Brompton
Holmes Mrs. 9 Stanhope st.Glos'ter gate
Holmes Mrs. 4 St. George's ter. Kensgt
Holmes Mrs. 29 Theberton st. Islington
Holmes Miss, 2 Caroline pl. Mecklnb. sq
Holmes P.esq.2Windsor cot.Haverstk.hl
Holmes Rayner, esq. 9 Compton st. east
Holmes Robt. esq. 4 Great Coram st
Holmes Saml. esq. 14 Coles tr. Brnsby.rd
Holmes Thos. esq. 36 Thurloe sq. Brmptn
Holmes Thomas Knox, esq. 10 Grafton st. Bond st. & 18 Fludyer st
Holmes Wm. esq.43 Alpha rd. Regt.'s pk
Holmes William, esq. 15 Brunswick sq
Holmes Wm. esq. 25 Great James st
Holmes Wm. esq. & Lady Strong, 10 Grafton st. Bond st. & 6 Church rw.Fulham
Holmes Wm. Hen. esq. 36 Beaumont st
Holmesdale Visct. 66 Grosvenor street
Holmsted Arthur, esq. 40 Bedford row
Holroyd Edward esq. 82 Basinghall st. & Wimbledon, Surrey
Holt Barnard W. esq. 30 Abingdon st
Holt Chas. esq. 14 Guilford st. Russ. sq
Holt John, esq. 28 Grove pl. Lisson gr
Holt John, esq. 3 Lyon ter. Edgware rd
Holt John Eyre, esq. 47 Lambeth st
Holt Mrs. 13 Earl's terrace, Kensington
Holt N. J. W. esq. 2 Kensington pk. vils
Holt Raymond B. esq. 1 Harcourt bldgs
Holt William, esq. 77 Chancery lane
Holt Thomas Littleton, esq. 32 Great Coram st.; & Elms, Watford
Holt Wm. John, esq. 13 Chatham place
Holthouse Crasten, esq. 2 Serle st
Holthouse Hy. J. esq. 1 Harcourt bldgs
Holtmeyer H. esq. 2Ladbroke pl.Notg.hl
Holworthy Chas. esq. 11 Grove terrace
Home, Earl of, 6 Hamilton pl. & Hirsel, Coldstream, Berwickshire
Home Chas.esq.21 Annett's cresc. Islgtn
Homershaur S.C. esq. 20 Lr.Belgrave pl
Homes John, esq. 20 Wood st. Spitalflds
Homfray Hen. R. esq. 18 Margaret st
Homfray Mrs. 21 Duke st. Westminster
Honey Andrew, esq. 12 Newngt. pl. Ken
Honyman Sir Orde John, bt. 95 Mount st
HonymanGeo. Essex, esq.6Pump ct.Tem
Hood Viscount, 44 Bryanstone square, & Barton Seagrave, Kettering
Hood Hon. Capt. 19 Hanover square
Hood Hon. Mrs. 37 Nottingham place
Hood Edwd. T. esq. 60 Chancery lane
Hood J. L. esq.15Elm treerd.St.John'swd
Hood Joseph, esq. 15 Soley ter. Pentvlle
Hood Miss, 4 North ter. Alexander sq
Hood Peter, esq. 15 Lower Seymour st
Hood Thos. esq. 22 Panton st.Haymket
Hood William, esq. 17 Burton crescent
Hood Wm. esq. 23 Up. Bedford place
Hoof W. esq. Madeley ho. Kensington
HookJas.esq.4Sidmouth st.Gray's inn rd
Hook James Charles, esq. 70 Newman st
HookJohn, esq. 3 Ladbroke villas,Not.hl
HookJohn, esq. 13 St.Geo.ter.Hyde park
Hook John, esq. 54 Welbeck st
Hook Mrs. 21 College st. Chelsea
Hook Mrs. 17 Welbeck st
Hook Rd. esq. 17 Shaftesbury ter. Piml
Hook Rt. esq. 9 Arlington st. Piccadilly
Hooke Ben. esq. 53 Bernard st
Hooker Jas. esq. 38 Walcot ter. Lambeth, & 8 Bartlett's bldngs. Holborn
Hoole Rev. Elijah, 8 Myddelton square
Hoole Henry, esq. 50 Gerrard st. Islgtn
Hooper Alfred, esq. 64 Connaught ter
Hooper Fras. Philip, esq. 11 Sackville st. & Acton, Middlesex
Hooper Geo. H. sen. esq. 19 Bloomsbury sq.; & New Shoreham; & Stanmore, Middlesex
HooperGeo.H.jun.esq.8Old sq. Linc.inn
Hooper Harvey B. esq. 60 Lin.inn fields
Hooper John, esq. 42 Burton crescent
HooperJn. esq.12Glo'ster rd. Old Brmtn
Hooper Mrs. Capt. 2 New Dorset place
Hooper Mrs. 26 Glo'ster grove w.Bmptn
Hooper Mrs. 27 Lr.Phillimore pl.Kenstn
HooperNathaniel, esq. 5 Pump ct. Temp
Hooper Richd. esq. 1 Highbury place
Hooper Wm. esq. 2 Albion vil.L'pool rd
HooperWm.esq.10Frdk.st.Gray's inn rd
Hooper Wm. L. esq. 1 Noel st. Islington
Hoopwood Capt. 69 Park st. Grosvr.sq
HopeHon.Lady, 35 Charles st.Berkly.sq
Hope Lady, 5 Park st. Westminster
Hope Lady Frances, 4 Belgrave square
Hope Lady Mildred, 1 Connaught pl
Hope Sir John, bart. M.P. 57 St.James's st. & Craighall, Fifeshire
Hope Rev. Fred.Wm. 56 Up.Seymour st
Hope Adrian John, esq. 4 Carlton gdns
Hope Alex.Jas. B.esq. M.P. 1 Connaught pl. & Bedgbury park, Goudhurst, Kent
Hope Chas. esq. 19 Montagu st.Prtm.sq
Hope George Wm. esq. M.P. & Hon. Mrs. 14 Curzon st. Mayfair, & Luffness, near Haddington, Scotland
Hope Henry Thos. esq. 1 Mansfield st. Portland place; & Deepdene, near Dorking, Surrey; & East Looe, Cornwall; & Betchworth castle, Surrey
Hope Hugh, esq. 14 St. James's place, & 19 Fludyer st. Westminster
Hope J. R. D.C.L.35 Charles st.Berkeley square, & 3 Paper buildings, Temple
HopeJohnThos.esq.& 37Up.Seymour st.; & Netley, Shrewsbury; & Southend
Hope-Vere Lady Elizabeth, 20 Park la.; & Cragie hall, Cramond, Edinburgh; & Blackwood, Lanarkshire
HopeWm.esq. 17 Montpelier sq.Brompt
Hope Wm. esq. 48 Hans pl. Sloane st
Hopetown Countess, Niddry ldg. Campden hill, Kensington
HopgoodFrs.esq.8 St.Agnes vil.Baysw.r
Hopgood Jas. esq. 93 Eaton place, & 14 King William st. Strand, & Clapham
HopkinsA.esq.5 Devonshire pl.Wand.rd
Hopkins Danl. esq. 57 Connaught ter
Hopkins John, esq. Lavinham cottage, Mornington road, Regent's park
Hopkins John D. esq. 25 Bedford square
Hopkins John M. M.D. 1 Elizabeth st
Hopkins John Wm. esq. 240 Maida vale
Hopkins Mrs. 72 Myddelton square
Hopkins Mrs. 50 Hans place, Sloane st
Hopkins Mrs. 4 Portland pl.Clapham rd
Hopkins Mrs.17 Up. Phillimore place
Hopkins T. esq. De Beauvoir rd. Kingsl

Hopkins Wm. esq. 12 Chesterfid. st. Kg's. cr
Hopkins Wm. Alex. esq. 25 Bedford sq
Hopkinson Col. Sir Chas. 5 Waterloo pl
Hopkinson Charles & Co. 3 Regent st
Hopkinson Charles, esq. 39 Eaton place
Hopkinson Edward, esq. 10 Tibberton sq
Hopkinson Jonathan, esq. 55 Chester sq
Hopkinson Luke, esq. 10 Bedford row
Hopkinson Mrs. 33 Cadogan place
Hopkinson W. esq. 4 Hamiltn. pl. King's cr
Hoppe Henry, esq. 53 Connaught ter
Hopper Anthony, esq. 12 Porchester ter. Bayswater
Hopper Thos. esq. 1 Bayswater hill
Hopper Thos. esq. 40 Connaught terr
Hopperton Wm. esq. 83 Ebury st. Pimlico
Hoppus Rev. J. 39 Camden st. so. Cmdn. tn
Hoppus John, esq. 39 Camden st. south
Hopwood John S. S. esq. 47 Chancery la
Hopwood Robert, esq. 81 Jermyn st. & Blackburn, Lancashire
Hopwood Wm. esq. 56 Liverpool st. Kg's. cr
Hora Mrs. 43 High st. Notting hill
Horden John, esq. 1 Malvern ter. Islgtn
Horder J. G. esq. 20 Coles ter. Barnsby. rd
Horder Wm. Geo. esq. 16 Howard st. Strnd
Hore Chas. F. esq. 6 Lincoln's inn fields
Hore Henry, esq. 1 Raymond buildings
Hore Jas. esq. 1 Duchess st. Portland pl
Hore James, esq. 6 Lincoln's inn fields
Hore Jas. Fraser, esq. 24 Old sq. Linc. inn
Hore John, esq. 32 Portland pl. Islgtn
Horn Henry, esq. 51 Upper Bedford pl. & 2 Hare court, Temple
Horn Hen. Geo. esq. 7 Heathcote st
Horn Mrs. 4 Hemingford ter. Islington
Horn Mrs. Edward, 15 Cumberland st
Horn Wm. esq. 12 Clarendon pl. Maida hill
Hornby John, M.P. 10 Dover st
Hornby Mrs. 41 Portland place, & Hook house, Titchfield, Hants
Hornby Thos. esq. 27 Euston square, & 31 St. Swithin's lane
Hornby William, esq. 41 Portland place, & Hook house, Titchfield, Hants
Horncastle T. esq. 8 Retreat, So. Lmbth
Horne Sir Wm. knt. Q.C. 49 Up. Harley st.; & the Masters' office, Southampton buildings, Chancery lane; & Epping house, near Hertford
Horne Rev. Thos. Hartwell, 4 Nicholas la
Horne Benj. Worthy, esq. 3 Bedford pl
Horne Chas. esq. 5 Verulam bldgs. Gr. inn
Horne Geo. esq, 6 Cavendish rd. St. Jns. wd
Horne Henry, esq. 26 Montagu square
Horne James, jun. esq. Wandsworth rd
Horne Jas. Thos. esq. 5 Grosvenor cresc. & Swerford house, Euston, Oxon
Horne Miss, 110 Sloane st
Horne Miss, 11 Tunbridge pl. New rd
Horne Mrs. 13 Canterbury villas
Horne Mrs. E. 15 Cumberland st. Ptmn. sq
Horner Rev. John, 14 Grosvenor place
Horner Anthony, esq. 96 Camden rd. villas
Horner Charles B. esq. 144 Oxford st. & Mells park, near Frome
Horner Leonard, esq. 2 Bedford place
Horner Miss, 12 Park place, Paddington
Horner Mrs. 60 Charlotte st. Portld. pl
Hornidge Sam. G. esq. 16 Bloomsbury sq
Hornidge Thos. esq. 10 Mitre ct. chmbrs
Horning James, esq. 2 Torrington sq
Horry Sidney C. esq. 126 Chancery lane
Horsburgh Jas. esq. 4 Adam st. Adelphi
Horsey Geo. esq. 39 Hemingford ter. Isln
Horsey Mrs. 19 Hemingford ter. Islngtn
Horsfield Thos. esq. 20 Stonefield st. Islgtn
Horsley Chas. esq. 2 Staple inn, Holborn
Horsley George, esq. South Lambeth
Horsley Joseph. C. esq. 7 Clement's inn
Horsley Thos. B. esq. 34 Southampton row
Horsman Edwd. esq. M.P. 6 Up. Brook st
Horsnaile Mrs. 26 Portmn. pl. Edgw. rd
Hort Jas. esq. 9 Bedford row, Islington
Hort Miss, 22 Devonshire pl. Portld. pl
Horton Alexander, esq. 3 Abbey road
Horton Benj. esq. 16 Trinity sq. Tower
Horton Edward John, esq. 5 Canning pl. Kensington New tn. & 11 Frnivl's. inn
Horton Hen. Geo. esq. 11 Highbury grove
Horton Mrs. 30 Paddington green
Horton Mrs. 9 Park place, Paddington
Horton Mrs. 15 Paradise ter. Livrpl. rd
Horton Robert, esq. 8 Brecknock ter
Horwood Mrs. 3 Eaton square
Horwood Thomas, esq. 1 New ct. Temple, & Sydenham grove, Sydenham
Horwood T. R. esq. 12 Canonbury villas
Hosack John, esq. 6 King's bench walk
Hosking Wm. esq. 23 Woburn square
Hoskins Geo. Alex. esq. 54 Eaton square, & 9 King's bench walk
Hoskins Kedgwin, esq. M.P. 90 Sloane st. & Birch house, near Ross
Hotchkin L. esq. the Mall, Kensington
Hotham Lord, M.P. 7 Hill st. Berkeley sq. & South Dalton hall, Beverley
Hotham Lady, Hereford house, Earl's ct
Hough Thos. Geo. esq. 16 Brunswick sq
Houghaton Jthn. esq. 5 King st. Prtmn. sq
Houghton Chs. G. G. esq. 6 Carlton villas
Houghton Jas. esq. 20 Charterhouse sq
Houghton Jas. Rt. esq. 2 Earl st. Blackfriars
Houghton Miss, 49 Park st. Grosvr. sq
Houghton, Wm. esq. 4 Verulam buildings
Houlditch John, esq. 78 Harley st
Houldsworth Thos. esq. M.P. 16 Suffolk st. & Portland place, Manchester
Houle J. W. C. esq. Warwick ct. Holborn
Houlston T. esq. 5 Belinda cot. Canonby
Houlton Jsph. esq. 87 Lisson grove north
Houlton Wm. esq. 7 Up. Spring st. Prtm. sq
Houndle Ed. esq. 8 Radnor pl. Oxford ter
Houseley S. esq. 11 Glo'ster ter. Regt's. pk
Housley Geo. esq. 28 Sussex pl. Kensgtn
Houson Jsph. esq. 19 Lincoln's inn fields
Houston Col. Sir Geo. bart. 19 Chapel st. Grosvenor square
Hovell James, esq. 5 South sq. Gray's inn
Hovenden John Eykyn, esq. 8 Oxford sq. & 9 Somerset pl. Somerset house
How Henry, esq. 7 Loraine pl. Holloway
How Jermh. esq. 8 Lonsdale sq. Islingtn
How Miss, 2 Swan walk, Chelsea
How Mrs. 27 South bank, Regent's pk
How Thos. esq. 26 Norton st. Fitzroy sq
How Wm. esq. 39 Albion st. Hyde park
Howard Lord Edward, 21 St. James's sq
Howard Lady C. 34 Lowndes st. Belg. sq
Howard Lady Julia, 124 Park st
Howard Lady Mary, 12 Grosvenor pl
Howard Hon. Col. Fulke Greville, 16 Grosvenor square; & Ashstead park, Epsom; & Castle Rising, Lynn, Norfolk; & Elford, Litchfield; & Levens, Milnthorpe, Westmoreland
Howard Hon. Capt. E. G. G. R.N., M.P. 86 Eaton place, & Castle Howard, Yorks
Howard Hon. C. W. M.P. 56 Park st. Gros. sq. & Naworth castle, Brampton
Howard Hon. Hen. Geo. 56 Park st. Gros. sq
Howard Hon. Rd. Edw. 3 Garden ct. Templ
Howard Sir Ralph, bt. M.P. 17 Belgrave sq. & Bushy pk. near Bray, Ireland
Howard Rev. W. H. 5 Oakley sq. Chelsea
Howard Abraham, esq. 2 Eccleston sq. Pimlico
Howard Alfred, esq. 2 Harewood square, & 28½ Basinghall st. City
Howard Chas. esq. 24 Aberdeen place
Howard E. esq. 4 Brunswick pl. Brnsby. rd
Howard E. B. esq. 15 Regent st
Howard Fredk. J. esq. & Lady Fanny, 1 Belgrave square
Howard Hen. esq. R.A. 5 Newman st
Howard James Peter, esq. 32 Lownds. sq
Howard Jonathan, esq. 28 New Bridge st
Howard Miss, 5 Newman st
Howard Mrs. 57 Brompton square
Howard Mrs. 47 Brooke st. Grosvenor sq
Howard Mrs. 25 Gibson sq. Islington
Howard Mrs. 5 Glos'ter ter. Old Bromptn
Howard Mrs. 11 York pl. Portman sq. & Norfolk cottage, Pinner, Middlesex
Howard Philip Henry, esq. M.P. 15 Gloucester pl. & Corby castle, near Carlisle
Howard Robt. 6 Up. Glo'ster st. Dorset sq
Howard Stanley, esq. 15 Regent st
Howard Thomas, esq. 52 Fleet st
Howard Thomas, esq. 23 Leicester sq
Howard Thos. esq. 7 Norfolk st. Strand
Howard Thos. B. esq. 7 Norfolk st. Strand
Howard Wm. esq. 9 Porchester terrace
Howard Wm. esq. 4 St. George's place, & Whitehead's wood, Southampton
Howard Wm. esq. 4 Melina pl. St. Jhn's. wd
Howard de Walden, Lord, G.C.B. Ambassador at Lisbon
Howarth Rev. Henry, 15 Grosvenor st
Howden Lord, 13 Hereford st. Park la. & Grimstone park, Tadcaster
Howden Lady, 13 Hereford st
Howe Earl, G.C.H., P.C. Curzon house, 8 South Audley st.; Gopsall hall, Leicester; & Penn house, near Amersham
Howe Misses, 3 Albert rd. Regent's pk
Howe Mrs. 16 Cadogan ter. Sloane st
Howe Mrs. 5 Lower Belgrave st
Howe Mrs. 49 Smith st. Chelsea
Howell Charles, esq. 38 Woburn pl
Howell Geo. esq 22 Oxford terrace
Howell Jas. esq. 1 Vincent sq. Westmstr
Howell John, esq. 41 Hatton garden
Howell John, esq. 30 Lincoln's inn fields, & 24 Bernard st. Russell sq
Howell John, esq. 7 Rutland gt. Knightsbridge, & West Wickham, Bromley, Knt
Howell Sidney, esq. Mid. Scotland yd
Howell Thos. esq. 5 Portland ter. Reg. pk
Howell V. esq. 68 Park st. Grosvenor sq
Howes Edw. esq. 1 Old sq. Lincoln's inn
Howes G. esq. 26 Blomfield rd. Maida hl
Howes William, esq. 13 South Lambeth
Howlet Hen. esq. 18 Bartlett's buildings
Howlett Rev. J. H. 9 Young st. Kensgtn
Howlett H. esq. 18 Cambridg. tr. Edg. rd
Howlett Samuel B. esq. 83½ Pall mall, & 34 Smith st. Chelsea
Hows Edwd. esq. 17 York st. Portman sq
Howse Rt. esq. 34 Beaufort st. Chelsea
Howton Benjamin, esq. 31 Thayer st
Hoy H. B. esq. 14 St. Pancras va. Hmpstd. rd
Hoyes Mrs. 39 Brompton row
Hoyland C. W. esq. 23 York st. Portman sq
Hoyle John, esq. 40 Gt. Portland st
Hoyle Joseph, esq. 2 Highbury pk. west
Hubback John, esq. 5 New sq. Linc. inn
Hubback John, esq. 42 Torrington sq
Hubbard John Gillebad, esq. & Hon. Mrs. 28 Sussex square, Hyde park
Hubbuck Thomas, esq. 44 Wellclose sq
Huburt Mrs. 11 Brompton square
Hucklebridge Miss M. 103 Up. Ebury st
Hucks Jn. esq. 4 Belgrave pl. Wndswth. rd
Huckvale Robert, esq. 3 Regent's villas, Avenue road
Huddleston J. W. esq. 5 Inner Temple la
Huddleston Misses, 2 Bulstrode st
Huddleston Purefoy, esq. 2 Bulstrode st
Huddleston Edward, esq. 6 Lowndes sq
Hudlestone Col. 12 Euston sq
Hudson George, esq. M.P. 24 Gt. George st
Hudson Franklin, esq. 24 Alexander sq
Hudson Hen. esq 14 Manor pl. nth. Chls
Hudson John C. esq. 5 Thurloe pl. O. Bmptn
Hudson John Godfrey, esq. 5 Essex ct
Hudson John G. B. esq. 5 St. George's ter. Hyde pk. & Verulam pl. Hastings
Hudson James, esq. 12 Hanover square
Hudson Robert, esq. 4 Pembroke square
Hudson Thomas, esq. 6 Park crescent, & Cheswardine hall, near Market Drayton
Hudson Thos. esq. 9 Caroline pl. Mecklenburgh sq. & 2 New sq. Linc. inn
Hudson T. B. esq. 30 Wellgtn. tr. St. Jn's. wd
Hudson Wm. esq. 2 Bloomsbury sq

Hudswell Mrs. Mahala, 23 London wall
Hue Clement, M.D. 9 Bedford square
Hue Mrs. 74 Little Britain
Huggard Richard, esq. 30 Trevor sq
Huggins Albany, esq. Victoria villa, Queen's road, St. John's wood
Huggins C. esq. 10 Northamptn.ter.Isln
Huggins Geo esq. 7 Earl st. Blackfriars
Huggins Hen. esq. 99 Camden rd. villas
Hughan Mrs. 33 Grosvenor pl
Hughan Thomas, esq. 33 Grosvenor pl
HughesCap. 21 Cumberland st.Prtmn.sq
Hughes Rev. Hugh, 59 Red lion st.Clkwl
HughesRev.Hen.12Gordon st.Gordon sq
HughesA.R.esq. Adelaide rd.Havrstk.hl
Hughes Benj. esq. 50½ Trinity sq.Boro'
Hughes David, esq. 9 Canonbury square
Hughes Edward, esq. 7 Dover st
Hughes F. B. esq. 3 Lit.Geo. st. Westmr
Hughes Fred. B. esq. 57 Walcot pl.east
Hughes Geo.esq.14 Seymour pl.Eusn.sq
Hughes Henry, esq. H2, Albany; & 13 Clement's inn, & Bradbourn, Sevenoaks
Hughes Hen. P.esq.20 Canonbury villas
Hughes Jas. esq. 12 Heathcote st
Hughes John, esq. 10 Chapel st.Bedfd.rw
Hughes John, esq. 14 Tyndale pl. Isln
Hughes John Carlyon, esq. 6 Eaton ter
Hughes Miles, esq. 14 Grafton st.Fitz.sq
Hughes Miss, 7 Portland pl. Clapm. rd
Hughes Mrs. 18 Coles ter. Barnsbury rd
Hughes Mrs. 10 Devonshire pl. Edgw.rd
Hughes Mrs. 1 Edwardes sq. Kensington
Hughes Mrs. 4 Green's row, Chelsea
Hughes Mrs. 13 Greville st. Hatton gard
Hughes Mrs. 1 Norwood pl. Kensington
Hughes Mrs. 10 Upper Harley st
Hughes Mrs. 29 Up.Ph llimore pl.Knstn
Hughes Philip, esq. 25 Fitzroy square
Hughes Rd. esq. Albion pl.Up. Kenn. la
Hughes Saml.esq.7 & 8 Duke st.Westmr
Hughes Sam.esq.10 Farrar's bdgs.Tmpl
Hughes Seneca, esq. 15 Bedfd.st.Cov. gdr
Hughes Thos. 13 Goulden ter. Brnsby. rd
Hughes Thos. esq. 19 Margaret st
Hughes Thos. esq. 14 Prtmn.pl.Edgw.rd
HughesWalter, esq. 5 York gate, Rgt.'s pk
Hughes Wm. esq. 26 Frederick st
Hughes Wm. esq. 7 Montagu pl. Islingt
Hughes Wm.esq. 6 North terr. Alexdr. sq
Hughes Wm. esq. 35 Northampton sq
Hughes Wm.esq. 9 Old sq. Lincoln's inn, & Pond st. Hampstead
Hughes Wm. Bulkeley, esq. M.P. Carlton club, & Plas Coch, Anglesea
HughesWm.Hughes, esq. 12 King's bnch. wk. & BelleVue house, Ryde, Isle of Wgt
Hughes Wm.H.jun.esq.11 Brunswick sq
HughesWm.H.jun.esq.12Kng.'sbnch.wk
Hughes Wm. P. esq. 4 Devonshire st
HughesWm.T.esq.8Seymour pl.Wnds.rd
HughesWm.W.esq.16 Victoria gro.Kens
Hughs Mrs. 58 Harley st
Hugman Wm. C. esq. 23 New North st. Red lion square
Huish John, esq. 74 Albany street
Hulbert Henry, esq. 21 Chester square
Hulbert J.esq. 5 Bedford ter. Claphm.rd
Hull Alonzo, M.D. 54 Upper Brook st
Hull Mrs. Gen. 31 Norfolk st. Park lane
Hull P.T.esq. 40 Camden rd.vill.Camn.tn
Hull Wm. W. esq. 1 Tavistock square
Hullah Chas. M. esq. 7 Doughty st
Hullah John, esq. 20 St. James's pl
Hullah John, esq. 101 St. Martin's lane
Hulm Edwyn St. J. M.D. 1 Tonbridge pl
HulmeH.esq.5NewDorset pl.Claphm.rd
Hulme Henry, esq. 30 Regent st
Hulme Miss, 19 Brunswk. pl. Blls. P. rd
Hulme Robert esq. 9 Old Burlington st
HulseSir Chas. bart. 4 New Burlington st. & Breamore house, Salisbury, Wilts
Hulse Chas.esq.23 Chester st.Grosvnr.pl
Humber Richard, esq. 40 Burton st
Humbert Dennis F.esq. 29 Connaught tr
Humbert Fras. Jsph. esq. 299 Oxford st
Humbert L. esq. 1 Belmont pl. Wnds.rd
HumbleW.E.M.D.6Manchr.ter.Livrpl.rd
HumbyEdwin, esq. 1 Windsor ter. Maida h
Humby George, esq. 8 Regent st
Humby George, esq. 69 Up. Norton st
Humby Mrs. 69 Up. Norton st. Fitzroy sq
Humby Wm. esq. 18 Up. Wellington st
HumbyWm.W.esq.18Sthmptn.st.Ftz.sq
Hume Adolphus W. esq. 15 Blandford sq
Hume Fitzwilliam, esq. 5 Suffolk st
Hume George, esq. 10 Great James st
Hume Henry, esq. 44 Lincoln's inn fields
Hume John P.esq. 29 Allsop ter. New rd
Hume John Robert, M.D. 9 Curzon st
Hume Joseph, esq. M.P. 6Bryanstone sq. & Somerton hall, near Gt. Yarmouth
Hume Joseph Burnley, esq. 10 Old sq
Hume Thos. esq. 6 King's parade, Chelsea
Hume Wm. F. esq. 4 Park pl. St. James st
Humfrey Lebbens Charles, esq. Q.C. 11 Gt. Queen st. Westminster, & 5 Brick ct
Hummerston Mrs. 5 Gt. Smith st. Westm
Humpage Hen. esq. 39 Gt. James st
Humphery Ald. John, M.P. Hay's wharf, Tooley st. & Clapham common
HumphreyMiss, 19 Victoria gro. Kens
Humphrey Mrs. 36 Gower pl. Euston sq
HumphreyW.J.esq.4York pl.Up.st.Islng
Humphreys Erskine, esq.24Sthampt.bgs
Humphreys John Jas. H. esq. 14 Serle st
Humphreys Henry Noel, esq. 20 Dorchester pl. Blandford square
Humphreys James, esq. Lansdown cottage, Wandsworth road
Humphreys Thos. esq. 14 Carey st
HumphreysWm.esq. 8 Foley st. Portld.pl
Humphreys Wm. C. esq. 17 Guilford st
Humphreys Wm.E.esq.21 Up.Sthwick.st
HumphriesF.esq.17Greenter.Nw.Rvr.hd
Humphris Mrs. 29 Grove end road
Humphry Joseph, esq.4New sq. Linc.inn
HumphryJsph.Thos.esq. 8Chancery lane
Humphrys George, esq. 2 Clifton place, Sussex square, & 43 Chancery lane
Humphrys Harry, esq. 12 Gray's inn sq
Humphrys Josiah, esq. 1 Featherston bgs
Humphrys Misses, 22 Upp. Wimpole st
Hundley F. esq. 1 Retreat, Sth.Lambeth
Hungerford Henry, esq. 18 New Bond st
Hunloke Sir Hen. bart. 81 Jermyn st. & Wingerworth hall, near Chesterfield
Hunnard John, esq. 10 Lloyd st.Lloyd sq
Hunt Rev.Wm. 7 Spanish pl. Manchr.sq
Hunt Chas. esq. 7 Blandford square
Hunt Chas. Edwd. esq. 2 Barnard's inn
Hunt Ed.Marklew, esq. 8 Nw. Boswell ct
Hunt Geo.esq. 8 Beaufoy ter. Edgware rd
Hunt Gideon, esq. 10 Clifford's inn
Hunt Henry, esq. 19 Highbury place
Hunt Henry, M.D. 68 Brook st
Hunt Holdsworth, esq. 3 Tanfield court
Hunt Jas.esq. Bridge ho. Vauxhall bdg.rd
Hunt Jas. esq. 11 Dean's yard, Westmr
Hunt John, esq. 13Dorset st. Portman sq
Hunt John, esq. 156 New Bond st
HuntJsph.esq.9Lit.Woodstock st.Mylbn
Hunt Joseph B.esq. 25 John st. Bedfrd.rw
Hunt Miss, 4 Spanish pl. Manchester sq
Hunt Miss, 6 Victoria grove, Kensington
Hunt Mrs. 45 Gower place, Euston sq
Hunt Mrs. 27 Halfmoon st
Hunt Mrs. 62 Stanhope st. Hampstd. rd
Hunt Mrs. 12 Torrington square
HuntR.esq.24Harrison st.Gray's inn road
Hunt Richard Rt. esq. 10 Cadogan st
Hunt Rt. esq. 6 Craig's ct. Charing cross
Hunt Thos.esq.29 Cloudesley st. Islingtn
Hunt Thomas, esq. 26 Upper Harley st
Hunt Thomas, esq. 11 Manchester sq
Hunt Wm.esq. 18 Elmtree rd.St.Jn.'swd
Hunt Wm.esq.62 Stanhope st.Hamps.rd
Hunt William, esq. 10 Whitehall
Hunt William Ogle, esq. 10 Whitehall
Hunter Sir Claudius Stephen Paul, bart. 23 Euston sq. & Mortimer hill, Reading
Hunter Rev. John, Battersea
HunterSirRd.knt. 8Gt.Stanhope st.Park lane; Dulaney cot. Patching, Sussex; & 4 Grand parade, Brighton
Hunter Rev. Joseph, 30 Torrington sq
Hunter Arch. esq. 20 Upper Baker st
Hunter David, esq. 49 Gower st. Bedfd .sq
Hunter Geo. esq. 43 Hans pl. Sloane st
Hunter George, esq. 43 Mornington pl. Hampstead road
Hunter Henry L. esq. 16 Queen Anne st
Hunter James, esq. 24 Bloomsbury st
Hunter Jas. esq. 1 Compton ter. Islington
Hunter Jas. esq. 10 Milner sq. Islington
Hunter Jameson, esq. 28 Mecklenburg sq
Hunter Job, esq. 16 Compton ter. Upper street, Islington
Hunter John, esq. 11 Hart st. Blmsbry
Hunter John, esq. 4 Church row, Islngtn
Hunter John, esq. 6 Lamb's Conduit st
Hunter John C. esq. 30 Wilton place
Hunter Mrs. Glebe pl. King's rd. Chelsea
Hunter Mrs. 12 Titchfield ter. Reg. pk
Hunter Mrs. 4 William st. Lowndes sq
Hunter Mrs. 47 York st. Portman sq
Hunter Mrs. Holmes, 23 Baker st. Ptm.sq
Hunter Richard, esq. 29 Brunswick sq
Hunter Richard, esq. 9 New sq. Lin. in
Hunter Ridley, esq. 6 Montague pl.Islgn
Hunter Robt. esq. 1 Bouverie st. Fleet st
Hunter Robt. M.D. 6 Gt. Queen st. Westm
Hunter T. D. esq. 8 Union ter. Notting hl
Hunter Thos. Orby, esq. 47Grosvenor pl. & Lydiard park, Swindon, Wilts
Hunter Alderman Wm. 10 Finsbry. circ
Hunter William, M.D. 86 Sloane st
HunterWm. esq. 23 Mortimer st. Cav.sq
Hunter Wm. esq. 10 Bloomsbury st
Huntingdon, Earl of, Union club, Trafalgar sq. & Gaultier cot. Waterford
Huntingdon Lady, 24 South bank
HuntingdonH. esq. 16Devonsh.pl.Edg.rd
Huntly, Marquis of, K.T. 24Chapel st. Belgrave sq. & Aboyne castle, Aberdeenshire, & Orton, Huntingdon
Huntly J. esq. 5 Addison ter. Notting hill
HuntleyW. S. esq. 5 Addison ter. Notg.hl
Huntsman Francis, esq. 19 Linc. inn fls
Hurd Philip, esq. Lodge, Kentish town
Hure Louis Adolphe, esq. 31 Mount st
Hurle Mrs. 39 Sussex grdns. & Ramsbury
Hurley Hen.W. esq. 7 Alpha rd. Rgt. pk
Hurley John, esq. 7 Argyll pl. Regent st
Hurley Mrs. 7 Park pl. terr. Padngtn. gr
Hurley Richard, esq. 25 Fitzroy square
Hurlock Miss, 14 Mabledon place
Hurlstone Edw. T. esq. 7 Crown Of. row
Hurlstone F. esq. 9 Chester st. Belgr. sq
Hurlstone Wm. esq. 3 Millman st
Hurly Mrs. 13 Guilford st. Russell sq
Hurndall Wm. esq. 37 Burton crescent
Hurrell John, esq. 2 Pump ct. Temple
Hurrell Mrs. 4 Princes rd. Notting hill
Hurry Edward, esq. 85 Oxford terrace
Hurry PaulWm. esq. 1 Vernon sq. Pentnv
Hurst D. esq. 28 Charlotte st. Portld. pl
Hurst John, esq. 3 Clapham rise
Hurst Miss, 14 Abbey rd. St. John's wd
Hurst Robert Henry, esq. M.P. 68 St. James's st. & Horsham park, Sussex
Hurst Robert Hy. esq. 2 Brick ct. Temple
Hurst Wm. esq. 19 Wilmington square
Hurt Edward N. esq. 34 Dorset square
Husband James, esq. 13 Bayswater terrace, & 11 Gray's inn square
Husband Mrs. 42 Edwardes sq. Kensgtn
Husey Henry, esq. 6 Upper Grosvenor st. Grosvenor square
Husey-Hunt Bernard, esq. 2 New inn
Husey Ralph, esq. 18 Abbey rd. St. Jn's.w
Huskinson L. esq. 39 Penton pl. Pentvl
Huskinson R. esq. 39 Penton pl. Pentvl
Huskisson Lieut. Gen. 10 Mount st
Huskisson Mrs. 2 Carlton gardens, & Eartham house, Petworth, Sussex
Huson Geo. John, esq. 7 Ironmonger lane
Huson Miss, 8 Southampton pl. Eust. sq

Huson Mrs. 14 Northampton square
Hussey Ambrose, esq. M.P. 8 Park st. & New st. Salisbury
Hussey Edwd. esq. 122 Park st
Hussey Henry, esq. 6 Up. Grosvenor st
Hussey Geo. Wm. esq. 30 Halfmoon st Piccadilly, & 20 Basing lane, City
Hussey Mrs. 122 Park st. Grosvenor sq. & Scotney castle, Lamberhurst, Kent
Hussey Thomas, M.P. 42 St. James's pl. & Lyme Regis, Dorset
Hussey W. esq.6 Quality ct. Chancy. la
Hussey Wm. esq. 4 Upper Woburn pl
Hustler Jas. D. esq. 53 Park st. Gro. sq
Hutchings James A. esq. 7 Maddox st
Hutchins Mrs. 19 St. Mary Abbott's terrace, Kensington
Hutchins Jas. esq.23A,Southbk.Rgt. pk
Hutchins Miss, 33 Chapel st. Grosv. pl
Hutchins William, esq. 25 Hanover sq. & Streatham common, Surrey
Hutchinson Cp.R.N.7Grove rd.St.Jn.wd
Hutchinson Benjamin, esq. Sussex villa, Queen's road, St. John's wood
Hutchinson Berry, esq. 26 Portland ter
Hutchinson Bury,esq.7 Staple inn, Hlbn
Hutchinson Jas. esq. 6 Highbury park
Hutchinson Jas. esq.10 Tyndale pl. Islgn
Hutchinson Jas. A. esq. 36 Theberton st
HutchinsonJ.esq.105 Milton st.Dorset sq
Hutchinson Mrs. 6 Canonbury villas
Hutchinson Mrs. 5 Elm tree road
Hutchinson Wm. B. esq. 40 Guilford st
Hutchinson C. esq.17 Holland st.Kensgn
Hutchison John, esq. 27 Lloyd square
Hutchison John, esq. 8 River ter. north
Hutchison P. esq. 28 Gerrard st. Isltn
Hutchison Wm. esq. 8 Shaftesbury cres
Hutchons Jas.esq.2Clarence tr.Rgt's pk
Huth Chas. Fred. esq. 25 Upper Harley st; & 10 Moorgate st. City
Huth Frederick, esq.33Upper Harley sq
Hutin John A. esq. 11 Trevor square
Hutt Wm. esq. M.P. & Dow. Countess of Strathmore, 39 Maddox st. & Gibside, Durham
Huttner John Christn.esq. 11 Fludyer st
Hutton Rev. Dr.5Hamilton pl.King's cr
Hutton Rev. F. H. 50 Hamilton terrace
Hutton C. esq. 3 Churchyard, Temple
Hutton Charles, M.D. 25 Motcomb st
Hutton Robert, esq. Denmark hill
Hutton Wm.esq. 4 Camden cott.Cam.tn
Hutton Wm. esq. Larkhall rise, Clphm
Huxley Geo. esq. 41 North bk. Regt.pk
Huxley Hen.Thos.esq.3Pump ct.Temple
Huxley Jas. esq. Stoke Newington grn
Huxley Mrs. 26 Welbeck st
Huxley Thos. esq. 3 Pump ct. Temple
Hyam Hyam, esq. 53 Upper Gower st
Hyam John, esq. 6 Hans pl. Sloane st
Hyam Moses, esq. 29 Tavistock place
Hyatt Mrs. 61 Connaught terrace
Hyde Chas. esq. 25 Sussex gardens
Hyde Chas. esq. 33 Ely place, Holborn
Hyde Chas. T. esq.4 Adam st. Adelphi
Hyde Edwd. esq. 18 Park pl. Paddngtn
Hyde Henry, esq. 33 Ely place, Holborn
Hyde Mrs. 3 Harewood square, & 6 Park villa, Cheltenham
Hyndman John Benj.esq.7Hyde park sq
HyronsE.esq.29NewNorth st.RedLionsq

I'ANSON Mrs. 4 Cirencester place
Ibbetson Hen. esq.34Chester tr.Rgt's.pk
Ibbetson L.L.B. esq.22 Up. Phillimre.pl
Ibbetson Mrs. 37 Wilton crescent
Ibbotson Geo. Aug. esq. 66 Brook st
Idle John,esq.8Newington pl.Kengtn. rd
Idle Mrs. 59 Gower st. Bedford square
Ifill Benjamin, esq. 59 Welbeck st
Ifold Wm. esq. 33 Manchester st
Ifold Wm. esq.33 Bedford pl.Kensington
Iggulden John, esq. 8 Russell square
Ilbery Miss, 13 Dalby terr. City road
Ilbery Wm. esq. 14 Dalby terr. City rd
Ilchester, Earl of,31 Old Burlington st.; Melbury house; & Abbotsbury castle, Dorchester
Ilderton Hen. D. esq.7 Lincoln's inn flds
Iliffe John, esq. 2 Bedford row
Illidge Thomas Henry, esq. 33 Bruton st
Illingworth Rev.E.A. 43 Burton cresent
Illingworth Hy. S. esq. 1 Arlington st
Illingworth Rd. S. 18 Chester st.Grov.pl
Illingworth Rd. S. esq. 6 Connaught sq
Imeson Joseph, esq. 23 Park st
ImhoffLt.Gen.SirC.6Portugal st.Grsvnr. sq. & Daylesford ho. Chipping Norton
Imms Mrs.30 Frederick st.Gray's inn rd
Impey E. esq.17 Cumberland st.Ptmn.sq
Impey Francis, esq. 17 Bedford row
ImpeyMchl.E.esq.4Duchess st.Prtlnd.pl
Imrie William, esq. 16 Saville row
Ince Jas. esq. 5 Blenheim pl.St. Jn's.wd
Ince J.B. esq.55Up.Seymour st.Ptmn.sq
Ince John, esq. 3 Lower Grosvenor pl
Ince Joseph M.esq.9 George st.Ptmn.sq
Ince Thomas, esq. 29 Argyll st
Ince Wm. esq.31Southampton st.Strand
Indermaur J. G. esq. 8 Howland st
Inderwick A. esq.4 Michael's gr.Brmtn
Ingall Chas. esq. 6 Stoke Newington gn
Ingall Frederick B. esq. Larkhall lane
Ingall Samuel, esq. 21 Barnsbury park
Ingestre Viscount, C.B., Capt.R.N.,M.P. Brompton park,& Ingestre hall, Staffordshire
Ingham Jas.Taylor, esq.7 Brunswick pl. Regent's park, & 5 Inner Temple lane
Ingham Robt.esq. 13 King's Bench walk, Temple, & Westoe, near South Shields
Ingleback L. E. esq. 30 Brompton cresc
Ingleby Charles, esq. 306 Regent st
Ingles Jas.esq.4New Dorset pl.Clapm.rd
Inglis Sir Robt.Harry,bart.D.C.L.,M.P.7 Bdfd.sq.&Milton Bryan, near Woburn
Inglis John B. esq. 21Upper Montagu st
Inglis P. esq. 1 Curzon place, Knsgtn.rd
Inglis Wm. esq. 65 Camden road villas
Ingolby Fredk. esq. 5 King Edward ter
Ingpen E. esq.2 Brecknock ter.Cmdn.tn
Ingram Benj. jun. esq. 7 Providence row
Ingram Edw.Russell, esq.1Lancaster pl
Ingram James, esq. 68 Lincoln's inn flds
Ingram James,esq.8 Sussex pl.Rgt.'s pk
Ingram Miss, 42 St. John's wood ter
Ingram Mrs. 35 Myddelton square
Ingram Mrs.17 Osnaburg st.Regent'spk
Ingram Thomas, esq. 48 Coleshill st
Ings E. esq.2 Verulam blds. Gray's inn
Inman Wm. S.esq.5 Up.Kensington gore
Innes Charles, esq. 3 Bayswater terrace
Innes Edward,esq.10 Park ter.Highbury
Innes George Arch. esq. 2 Plowden bldgs
Innes John, esq. 46 Porchester terrace
Innes Mrs. 51 Guilford st. Russell sq
Innes RobertWm.esq. 23 Oxford terrace
Innes Wm. John, esq. 15 St. James's sq
InnisC.esq.9Euston sq.&15 Linln.'s inn fi
Innis Thomas, esq. 29 Fitzroy square
Insoll Robert, esq. 27 Alpha road
Instone Mrs. 18 Westbourne place
Instone Thomas, esq. 17 Westbourne pl
Inverness Duchess of,Kensington palace
Ion Matthew, esq 25 Colebrook row
Ireland Alexn. J. esq. 33 Rathbone place
Ireland John J. 17 Marchmont st
Ireland Mrs. 16 Titchfield ter. Rgt.'s pk
Ireson Mrs. 40 St. James's place
Irons Rev. Wm. J. B.D. 12 Michael's gr Brompton
Irons Thomas, esq.19Brompton crescent
Ironside Mrs. 24 Guilford st. Russell sq
Irton Samuel, esq. M.P. Carlton club, & Irton hall, near Ravenglass
Irton Samuel, esq. 35 Piccadilly
Irvine Alex. Robt. esq. 18 Wilton place
Irving Major, 70 Jermyn st
Irving Henry, e sq. 70 Jermyn st
Irving James C. esq. 89 Chancery lane
Irving Mrs. 50 Bernard st. Russell sq
Irving Thos. esq. 7 Sussex ter. O. Brompt
Irving Wm. esq.4 Gt.George st.Westmst
IrwinAnth.Wellington, esq. 11 King's rd
Isaac William esq. 48 Brompton row
Isaacs I. esq. 2 Blenheim pl.St.John's wd
Isaacs John, esq. 42 Gordon square
Isaacs Miss, 23 York bldgs. New road
Isaacs Mrs. 34 Bernard st. Russell sq
Isaacs Samuel, esq. 7 Upper Gower st
Isaacson John Fredk. esq. 40 Norfolk st
Isham the Misses, 17 Bayswater terrace
Israel Aaron, esq. 4 Sussex gardens
Israel Isr. esq. 11 Southampton st.Strnd
Ivall David, esq.14 Blomfld.rd.Maid. hll
Ive Wm. James, esq.21 Northampton sq
Ivens Wm. H. esq. 12 Lloyd sq. Pentnvl
Ives Jeremiah Robt. esq. 41 Hertford st
Ives Mrs. 71 Mount street, Grosvenor sq
Ivimey Joseph. esq. 1 Ampthill square, Hampstead road, & 26 Chancery lane
Ivory Thos. esq. 25 Old sq. Lincoln's inn
Ivy Thos. J. esq. 43 Princes st. Ptm.mkt
Ivyleafe Jas. esq. 3 Park village west
Jack Miss, 41 Sloane st
Jackaman Simon, esq. 1 Bartlett's bldgs
Jackson Admiral, 21 Hornton st.Kensgtn
Jackson Col. 52 Coleshill st. Eaton sq. & 3 Waterloo place
Jackson Rev. J. 17 Radcl. ter. Goswl. rd
Jackson Rev. Joseph, Kensington palace
Jackson Rev. Thomas, Battersea
JacksonAbram, esq. 9 Barking churchyd
Jackson Albert Fras. esq. 1 Tanfield ct
Jackson A. esq. 2 Montague pl. Clpm. rd
Jackson C. R. esq. 37 Gloster rd. Hd.pk
JacksonChas.Rt.M.Chapel stairs,Lin. in
JacksonEdwd.esq.23South bank,Rgt.pk
Jackson George, esq. 44 Nelson square
JacksonGeorge,esq.26Welgtn.ter.S.J.wd
Jackson Geo. B.W. esq. 9 Gray's inn sq
Jackson Hugh, esq. 12 Essex st. Strand, & Terrace, Hampstead
Jackson Jas. esq. 5 Church pl.Covnt.gdn
Jackson John,esq. 2 Lodge pl.St.Jn.'swd
Jackson Jn. esq.27 Comptn. ter. Islingtn
JacksonJohn esq.12 Essex street,Strand, & Terrace, Hampstead
Jackson John, esq. 4 Grosvenor st. west
JacksonJn.esq. 2 Robert st. Hampstd. rd
Jackson John, esq. 12 Upper Belgrave pl
Jackson Joseph, esq. 3 Cloudesley square
Jackson Miss,53 Frederick st.Gray.in. rd
Jackson Mrs. 17 Albany street
Jackson Mrs. 2 Albion pl. Up. Kengtn.la
JacksonMrs. 12 Crescent pl. Burton cres
Jackson Mrs. 37 Elizabeth st. Eaton sq
Jackson Mrs. 23 Glo'ster pl. Portman sq
Jackson Mrs. 30 Lonsdale square
Jackson Mrs. 36 Harewood square
Jackson Paul, esq. 18 Thayer street
Jackson Peter, esq. 5 Falcon square
Jackson Rd. esq. 14 Craven st. Strand
Jackson Rd. esq. 19 Webb's County terr
Jackson Robert, esq. 41 Bedford row
Jackson Sl. esq. 6 Stonefield st. Islgt
Jackson Sam. B. esq. 9 New inn, Strand
Jackson Stephen, esq. 2 Bridgewater sq
Jackson Thos.esq.5 Alfred pl.Bedford sq
Jackson Thos. esq. 21 Baker street
Jackson Thos. esq. 33 Trevor square
Jackson Wm. esq. 14 Vincent ter. Islgtn
Jackson Wm.Oliver, esq. 11 John street, Adelphi
JacksonWm.W.esq. 2 Field ct.Gray's inn
Jacob Wm. esq. 31 Cadogan pl. Sloane st
Jacobs Jacob, esq. 55 Upp. Berkeley st
Jacobs F. N. esq.6 Rufford's row, Islgtn
Jacobs John, esq. 164 Strand
Jacobs Levi, esq. Tenter house, Tenter ground, Goodman's fields
Jacobs Mrs. 27 Westbourne pl. Sloane sq
Jacobs Wm. esq. 10 Carter st. Walworth
Jacobs Wm. esq. 25 Clarges st
Jacox Francis, esq. 1 Bayswater terrace
Jaffray John Richmond, esq.28 Eaton sq
Jakins Isaac N. esq. 32 Osnaburgh st

Jalfon Isaac, esq.6 Sydney pl. Fulhm. rd
JamesSirW.C. bart. M.P. 11 Whitehll. pl
James Rev. Hy.20James st.Bckinghm.gt
James Andrew, esq. 15 Heathcote st
James David, esq. 3 Old sq. Lincoln's inn
James Edward, esq. 2 Elm ct. Temple
James Edwd. esq. 28 Gordon st. Gordn.sq
James Edwin, esq. 3 Inner Temple lane
James Francis, esq. 51 Lincoln's inn flds
James Henry, esq. 34 Brunswick sq
James Henry, esq. 6 Old sq.Lincoln's inn
James Hen. C. esq.12 Princes pl.Kenn.rd
James James, esq. 5 Gray's inn square
James John, esq. 31 Botolph lane
James John, esq.2Cornwall ter.Rgts.pk
James John, esq. Harrow road
James John, esq. 6 Hatfield st.Stamfd.st
James John, esq. 34 Brunswick square
James John, jun. esq.58Lincoln's inn flds
James John K. esq. 13 Stratton st. Picd
James Michael, esq. 58 Fleet st
James Miss, 2 Addison road, Kensington
James Miss, 12 Bedford pl. Russell sq
James Miss, 7 Clarges st. Piccadilly
James Miss, 19 Lonsdale sq. Islington
James Miss, 54 Cumming st.Pentonville
James Miss, 1 Grove rd. St. John's wood
James Mrs. & Miss, 13 Mabledon place
James Mrs. 1 Bulstrode st. Manchstr.sq
James Mrs.85Hamilton ter.St.John's wd
James Mrs. 20 Harleyford pl. Kenn.com
James Mrs. 5 Montagu st. Portman sq
James Rd. esq.9 Seymour pl. Euston sq
James Richard,esq.14Low.Phillimore pl
James Rich.esq.4Marlbro'.rd.St.Jn.'swd
James Sam. esq. 2 Old sq. Lincoln's inn
James Theodore, esq. 9 Staple inn, Hlbn
James Thomas, esq. 21 Burton crescent, & 11 Gray's inn square
James Thomas, esq. 46 Doughty st
James Thomas, esq. 1 Bulstrode st
James Trevenen, esq. 36 Tavistock sq
James Wm.esq.13 Blomfield rd.Maida hl
James William, esq. 70 Hatton garden
James Wm. esq. 42 Norfolk st. Strand
James Wm. esq. M.P. 15 Regent st. & Barrack lodge, near Carlisle
James Wm.esq 6Westbourne st.Hyde pk
James Wm. Boyce, esq. 5 Basinghall st
James Wm. Henry, esq. 15 Bridge st. Blackfriars, & 2 Whitefriars st
James Wm. Milbourne,esq. 6 Stone bdgs
James Wm. M. 29 Fortess tr. Kentsh. tn
James Wm. Roberts, esq. 23 Ely place
JamesWm.R.esq. 1 Omega ter.Alpha rd
Jamieson Alex.esq.131Grove st.Cmdn.tn
Jamieson A. LL.D.13Beaufort st. Chelsea
Jamieson Andrew, esq. 5 Hyde park st
Jamieson John Y.esq. 9 Allsop tr. New rd
Jannaway Mrs. 12 Maida hill, Edgw. rd
Janson J. esq. 16 Hemingford ter. Islng
Janvin Francis, esq. 27 Devonshire pl
Jaques John, esq. 8 Ely place
Jaques Miss, 96 Sloane st
Jaques Mrs. 8 Kennington terrace
Jacquet Philip, esq. 4 Pine Apple place, Maida vale, & 13 Clifford's inn
Jaquier Lewis,esq.24 Baker st.Ptmn. sq
Jardine Sir William, bart. 81 Jermyn st. & Jardine hall, Lockerby, N.B
Jardine David, esq. 23 Cumberland ter. Regent's park & Bow st. police court
Jardine Jas. esq. 8 Liverpool st.King's cr
Jardine James Bell, esq. 44 Drury lane, & 1 Leigh st. Burton crescent
Jardine John, esq. 3 Whitehead's grove
Jarman Geo. F. esq. 21 Up. Berkeley st. & Brindley house, Faversham, Kent
Jarman John Boykett, esq. 83 Grosvenor st. & Rosenan, near Windsor
Jarman Thos. esq. 3 New sq. Linc. inn
Jarna L. esq. 2 Hemingford ter. Islgtn
Jarnac, Count de, sec. to French Embassy. 20 Manchester square
Jarrett Mrs. 14 Princes st. Cavendish sq
Jarvis John, esq. 6 Circus rd. St.Jn.'swd
Jarvis John, esq. 13 Hart st. Bloomsbry
Jarvis Mrs. 3 Milner st. Islington
Jarvis Rd. esq. 58 Connaught terrace
Jarvis Richd. Hayter, esq. 12Up.Gwr. st
Jarvis Thomas, esq. 46 Leicester square
Jater Mrs. 3 Upper Ranelagh st.Pimlico
Jay Rev. Robt. 6 Alexander sq. Brmptn
Jay Cyrus, esq. 15 Serjeants' inn, Fleet st
Jay Edwd. esq. 51 Park st. Grosvnr. sq
Jay Geo. H. esq. 23 Stoke Newington gn
Jay Henry, esq. 42 Sloane st
Jay Jno. esq. 7 Thurloe pl.we.O.Brompn
Jay Saml. esq. 11 Norfolk st. Park la. & 10 Old square, Lincoln's inn
Jaycock W.esq.6 Devonshire pl.Wnds. rd
Jayne Thomas, esq. Esher villa, Finchley New road
Jays Mrs. 3 St. Ann's ter. Acacia road
Jeaffreson Hen. M.D. 2 Finsbury square
Jeafferson J. esq. 10 Trinity rw. Islng
Jeaffreson Saml. J. M.D. 22 Halfmoon st
Jeaffreson Wm. esq. 21 South Audley st
Jeanneret Hy. esq. 53 Lincoln's inn flds
Jearrad Rt. Wm. jun. esq. 260 Oxford st
Jebb Maj. R.E. 7 Somers pl. Cambridge sq. Hyde park, & 45 Parliament st
Jebb Richard, esq. 9 New sq. Linc. inn
Jee Alfred S. esq. 6 John st. Adelphi
Jee J. esq. 2 Churchyard ct. Temple
Jeeks Wm. esq. 4 College ter. Islington
Jefferson J. esq. 2 Francis pl. Holloway
JeffersonRt.esq. 3 Polygon,Clarendon sq
Jeffery Rev. J. 30 Chester pl. Kenn. crs
Jeffery John, esq. 10 Weymouth st
Jeffery Miss, 13 Up. Seymour st. west
Jeffkins George, esq. 10 Loraine place
Jeffkins John, esq. 3 Loraine place
JeffordWm.esq.13 Petersburgh pl.Bysw
Jeffray E. esq. 11 Bedford st. Bedford sq
Jeffray Jas. esq.11 Bedford st.Bedford sq
Jeffree Thos. L. esq. Pullam ter. Chelsea
Jeffreys Rev. C. 16 Dorset pl. Dorset sq
Jeffreys James, esq. 13 Chadwell st
Jeffreys J. esq. 25A, Norfolk crescent
Jeffreys Mrs. 16 Eaton pl. Belgrave sq
Jeffries Edwd. esq. 2 Lamb's Conduit pl
Jeffries G. esq. 5 Marlbro' ter. Knsgtn
Jekyll Edwd. esq. 2 Grafton st. Bond st
Jelf Geo. esq. 26 Upper Brook st. & 13 Gt. George st.Westminster; & Manor house, East Acton
Jellico G. esq. 20 Hemingford ter. Islng
Jellicoe George, esq. 156 Albany st
JellicoeMrs.3 Grove end pl.St. John's wd
Jellicoe Joseph, esq. 13 Up. Wimpole st
Jenings Chas. E. esq.2 Terrace,Kensington, & 1 Mitre court buildings
Jenings John, esq. 1 Mitre court bldgs
Jenkin Charles, esq. 34 Lonsdale sq
Jenkin E. A. esq. 5 Norfolk st. Park la
Jenkins Sir Richd. G.C.B. 7 Mansfield st. Portland pl. & Bicton hall, Shrewsbry
Jenkins Rev. George, 25 Bolton st. Picdl
Jenkins Abel, esq. 4 Upper Montague st. Russell sq. & 8 New inn, Strand
Jenkins D. esq.4 Bretten ter.King's rd. w
Jenkins E. esq. 7 Harleyford pl.Ken.com
Jenkins Fielder, esq. 47 Woburn place
Jenkins Geo.T. esq. 43 Lincoln's inn flds
Jenkins H. esq. 8 Caroline st. Bedford sq
Jenkins Jsph. J.esq.8Caroline st. Bdfd.sq
Jenkins Mrs. 21 Goulden ter. Barnsby
Jenkins Rt. esq. 22 Huntley st. Bdfd. sq
Jenkins Thos. L. esq. 22 Chancery lane
Jenkins Wm. esq. 25Coleshill st.Eaton sq
Jenkins Wm.jun.esq. 20 Bartlett's bldgs
Jenkins Wm.K. esq. 1 Sussex ter.Bayswr
Jenkinson Miss,11Petersburg pl.Byswtr
Jenkyn Rev. Thomas Wm. D.D. Byng place, Torrington square
Jenkyn James, esq. 11 John st. Adelphi
Jenkyns Ed. esq. Park cot King's rd. we
Jenner-Fust Rt. Hon. Sir Herbert, knt. D.C.L. 1 Chesterfield st. Mayfair; & 4 College, Doctors' commons; & Chiselhurst & Hill court, Gloucestershire
Jenkyns John, esq.14 Red Lion square, & Botley hill, Southampton
Jenner Chas. esq. 4 Victoria ter. Chelsea
Jenner E.F.esq.7 Lowndes st.Belgrave sq
Jenner George, esq. 31 Adam st. west
Jenner Hen. esq. 44 Gt. Dover st. Boro'
Jenner Wm. esq. 14 Albany st.Regt.'s pk
Jennings Rev. John, Smith sq. Westmr
Jennings —, esq. 16 Maida hill,Edgw.rd
Jennings David, esq. 71 Whitechapel rd
Jennings Edmund John, esq. 4 Elm ct
Jennings Edward, esq. 26 Tonbridge pl. New road, & 16 Chancery lane
Jennings F. W. esq. 12 Nottingham ter
Jennings H. esq. 12 Nottingham terrace
Jennings John, esq. 26 Grove pl. Lis. gro
Jennings John, esq.64 Judd st.Brnswk.sq
Jennings Jsph. esq.14 King st. Portmn.sq
Jennings Miss, 42 Gibson square
Jennings Miss, 25 Portland ter. Regt. pk
Jennings Mrs. 53 Gibson square
Jennings Mrs. 12 Nottingham terrace
Jennings Mrs. 29 Welbeck st
Jennings P. esq. 43 Mecklenburgh sq
Jennings Samuel, esq. 52 Gibson square
Jennings Samuel, esq. 1 Poland st
Jennings T. F. esq. 1 Notting hill High st
Jennings Wm. Geo. esq. 83A, Guilford st
Jenour Geo. esq. 2 Field ct. Gray's inn
Jenvey Thomas, esq. 3 Trinity sq. Boro'
Jephson Lady, 12 Pelham cres. Fulhm.rd
Jephson Rev. William, 40 Vincent sq
Jephson Jas. esq. 21 Charles st. Hyde pk
Jepson Rev. Geo. 36 Lincoln's inn fields
Jepson Miss, 31 St. John's wd. terrace
Jeremy George, esq. 7 Guilford st
Jermyn Rt. Hon. Earl, M.P. 47 Eaton pl. & Ickworth park, Bury St. Edmunds
Jermyn Rev. Hugh, 25 Kensington sq
Jermyn Geo.A.esq.15 Buckingham st.Str
Jerningham Hon. Henry S. 69 Eaton pl
JerninghamEdm.esq.16Park rd.Rgt.'spk
Jerningham Edward, esq. 69 Pall mall
Jerome A. esq. 91 Gt. Russell st.Blmsby
Jerran George, esq. 45 Lonsdale sq
Jerrall Thomas, esq. 72 Cadogan place
Jersey Earl of, P.C. 38 Berkeley square, Middleton pk. Bicester, & Osterley pk
Jervis Major, 9 Regent's villas, Avenue rd
Jervis Jervis John, esq.3 New sq. Lin.'s in
Jervis John, esq. Q.C., M.P., 3 Old Palace yd. Westmnstr.& Fairhill,nr.Tonbridge
Jervis J. J. jun. esq. 14 Tavistock place
Jervis Mrs. 25 Hans place
Jervis Swynfen, jun. esq, 3 Whitehall pl. & Darlaston hall, near Stone, Stafford
Jervis Thos.esq.16 Orchard st.Portmn.sq
Jervis Wm. Paxton, esq. 59 Cadogan pl
Jervoise Rev. Sir Sam. C. 15 Hanover sq
Jerwood Rd. esq. 10 Vincent ter. City rd
Jerwood Thos. John, esq.1 Walbrook bgs. City, & 12 Elm Tree rd. St.John's wood
Jesson Henry, esq. 2 Middle Temple la
Jessopp Joseph, esq. 12 Clifford's inn
Jeudwine Geo. esq. 10 Gray's inn sq
Jewes Francis F. esq. 22 Bedford row
Jewesson R. esq. 25 Chester pl.Kenn.crs
Jewitt J. W. esq. 14 Sthmptn.st.Blmsbry
Jewson F. B. esq. R.A. 60 Berners st
Jeyes Fras.F.esq.4 Harpur st.RedLion sq
Joachim Miss, 27 York bldgs. New road
Jobbins Jn. Rd. esq.3 Warwick ct.Holbn
Jocelyn Viscount, M.P. 35 Curzon st. Mayfair, & Tullamore pk. Dunkald, Ireland, & Hyde hall, Sawbridgeworth
Jodrell Sir Richard Paul, bart. 64 Portland pl.; & Sall park, Reepham; & Nethercoate house, Tetsworth
Jodrell Col. Edmund, 7 Bryanstone st
Johnes A. J. esq. 24 Southampton bldgs
Johnes John H. esq. 3 Upper Spring st
Johnson Sir Edward, knt. 16 Suffolk st
Johnson Gen. William Augustus, M.P. 7 Suffolk st. Pall mall, & Wytham hill, Bourne, Lincolnshire
Johnson Lieut. Col. Fred. A10, Albany

Johnson Rev. Arthur, 36 Canonbury sq
Johnson Rev.Wm.B.D.29Trinity sq.Boro'
Johnson Adolphus P.esq.77 Hamilton ter
Johnson Cuthbert, esq. 11 Avenue road
Johnson C.E.esq.22 London st.Fitzroy sq
Johnson Cuthbert W.esq.14Gray's inn sq
Johnson Edwd.M.D.42Carnaby st.Gldn.sq
Johnson E. esq. 20 Manchstr. ter. Lpl.rd
Johnson Edwd.M.D.18 NewBurlington st
Johnson Francis, esq. 46 Jewin st
Johnson Fredk. Wm. esq. 45 Gibson sq
Johnson Geo. esq. 4 Grove pl. Brompton
Johnson Geo. esq.86 Guilford st. Brunswick sq. & 7 King's bench walk
Johnson Geo. esq. 3 Heathcote st
Johnson G. esq. 1 Thornhill pl. Pntnvl
JohnsonGeo.jun.esq.7King's bench walk
Johnson Geo. H. esq. 67 Ebury st
Johnson Geo.L. esq. 6 Park village east
Johnson Groves W.esq.25Clapham rd.pl
Johnson Hy.esq. 4 Caroline st. Bedfd. sq
Johnson Henry, esq. 15 Essex st. Strand
Johnson Henry, esq. 20 Petersburgh pl
Johnson Hen. esq.3 Stanhope ter. Hy.pk
Johnson Hen. Chas. esq. 6 Saville row
Johnson Hen.J. esq.8Suffolk pl.Pall mall
Johnson J. esq. 23 Park pl.we. Livrpl. rd
Johnson Jas. M.D. 12 Park village west
Johnson John,esq.28Bury st. St. James's
Johnson John, esq. 27 Doughty st
Johnson John, esq. 12 Gerrard st. Islng
Johnson John, esq.4 Millbank row,Wmr
Johnson John, esq. 11 Notting hill ter
Johnson John, esq. 47 Notting hill sq
Johnson John,esq.42Southampton bldgs
Johnson J.E.esq.52Newington pl.Ken.rd
Johnson John, esq. 9 John st. Adelphi
Johnson John J. esq.19 Duke st.St. Jas's
Johnson John J. esq. 10King's bench wlk
Johnson John J. esq. 12 Chester place, Hyde park; 19 Southampton bldgs.; & 22 Duke st. Grosvenor square
Johnson Jsph.White, esq.5Cambridge pl
Johnson Miss, 31Up. Seymour st.Ptm.sq
Johnson Mrs. 10 Allsop ter. New road
Johnson Mrs. 44 Edward st. Regent's pk
Johnson Mrs. 25Edwarde sq.Kensington
Johnson Mrs. 27Grove end rd.St.Jn.'swd
Johnson Mrs. 79 John st. Fitzroy square
Johnson Mrs. 53 Notting hill square
Johnson Mrs.2Palace pl.Gt.Scotland yd
Johnson Mrs. 13 Queen st. Brompton
Johnson Mrs.29Thurloe sq. Old Bromptn
Johnson Mrs. 5 Tavistock row, Cov. gdn
Johnson Mrs.39Wakefield st. Brnswk.sq
Johnson Mrs.2 Warwick pl.St.John's wd
Johnson Misses, 9 Tibberton square
Johnson Miss, 83 Cambridge terrace, Edgware road
Johnson Miss, 79 Connaught terrace
Johnson Miss, 89 Strand
Johnson Percival N.esq.38 Mecklnbg.sq
Johnson Philip esq. 57 Linc. inn fields. & 1 Upper Fitzroy pl. Kentish town
Johnson Rd. esq. 46 Gerrard st. Islgtn
Johnson Richd. Wm.esq.23Holloway pl
Johnson Robt. E. esq. 16 Hamilton ter. St. John's wood.& 7 Gt. Winchester st
Johnson SaffreyWm.esq.2Verulam bdgs. & 5 Gray's inn square
Johnson Samuel, esq.14 Up. Ranelagh st
Johnson T. esq.2 Woodstock pl. Avnu.rd
Johnson Thomas, esq. Harrow road
Johnson Thos.Ed. esq. 58Lincoln's inn fi
Johnson T.W.esq.5Buckinghm.pl.Fitz.sq
JohnsonWm.esq.12Chestr.pl.Hydepk.sq
Johnson Wm. esq. 14 Queen's pl. Ken. rd
Johnson Wm. esq. Stoke Newington grn
Johnson Wm. F. esq. 8 Connaught sq
Johnson Wm. Hy.esq.4 Cresc.N.Bdge.st
JohnsonWm.Hy.esq.29Thurloe sq. Brom
Johnson Wm. Henry, esq. 7 Chancery la
Johnson Wm. John, esq. 14 Serle st
Johnston Right Hon. Sir Alex. knt. 19 Gt. Cumberland pl.; & Carnsalloch, Dumfries; & York house, Twickenhm
Johnston Major G. 73 Oxford terrace
Johnston Rev. Jas.A.96 Up. Stamfrd. st
Johnston Alexander, esq. 14 Bernard st
Johnston Alex. Duguid, esq. 1 Pump ct
Johnston Andrew, esq. 9 Cursitor st
Johnston David M. 27 Abingdon st
Johnston Fras. G. esq. 4 Beak st
Johnston Hen.esq.64 Warren st. Ftzry.sq
Johnston James, esq. 100 Chancery lane
Johnston J.esq.5 Canonbury la. Islingtn
Johnston John, esq.51Gloucester pl.Portman sq. & 24 Cateaton st
Johnston John, esq. 16 Dover st. Picdlly
Johnston Miss, 9 Belgrave square
Johnston Mrs. 19 Portman pl. Edgw. rd
Johnston Mrs. 3 Princes rd. Notting hill
Johnston Mrs. 16 Regent sq.Gray's inn rd
Johnston Nathaniel, esq. 20 Oxford sq
Johnston P. esq.19 Gt.Cumberland place
Johnston T. esq.3Goulden ter.Brnsby. rd
Johnston T. E. esq.12 Park village west
Johnston Thos. H. esq.16 Cecil st. Strand
Johnston Wm. esq. 51 Mortimer st
Johnstone Sir Jno.Vanden Bempde, bart. M.P. 27 Grosvenor square, & Hackness hall, Scarborough, Yorkshire
Johnstone Hon. Henry Butler, 24 Park st
Johnstone Col. 37 Green st. Grosvenor sq
Johnstone Lieut. Col. G. 17 Eaton place
Johnstone David G. esq. 13 Serle st. Lincoln's inn, & 42 Lothbury
Johnstone Edw. esq. 10 Crown Office rw
Johnstone George, esq. 53 Tavistock sq
Johnstone Geo. Fras. esq. 21 Saville row
Johnstone James, esq. 26 Cloudesley sq
Johnstone John James Hope, esq. M.P. Carlton club, & Rayhill, Moffat, N. B
Johnstone J. esq.3 Albion vil. Livpl. rd
Johnstone Miss, 31 Upper Montagu st
Johnstone Mrs. 57 Glo'ster pl. Portm. sq
Johnstone Mrs. 28 Gower st
Johnstone Robt. esq. 4 Camden st. south
Jolley Thomas, esq. 35 Burton crescent
Jollands Charles, esq. 25 Russell square, & Buxshall, Lindfield, Sussex
Jolliffe Sir Wm. Geo. H. bt. M.P. Carlton club, 94 Pall mall; Merstham, Surrey; & Heath house, Petersfield
Jolliffe Miss, 41 Devonshire st. Portld. rd
Jolliffe Wm. P. esq. 41 Regent square, & 6 New square, Lincoln's inn
Jolly Thomas, esq. Larkhall rise, Clphm
Jolly Mrs. 40 Bedford place, Kensington
Jones Hon. Miss, 3 Bolton row, Mayfair
JonesMajorN.1 Lennard place,St.Jn's.wd
Jones Rev. D. B.D. 20 Union st. Deptford
Jones Rev.HughH.10 Brides pas.Fleet st
Jones Rev. Jn. 10 Up. John st. Golden sq
Jones Rev. Thomas, 103 Fenchurch st. & Canant house, Globe road, Mile end rd
Jones Alfred, esq. 44 Canonbury sq
Jones Alfred, esq. 64 Grosvenor st
Jones Bence, M.D. 30 Grosvenor st
Jones Benj. esq. 23 Cheyne walk, Chels
Jones Benj. esq. 19 Park road, Rgt.'s pk
Jones Charles, esq. 27 Cumberland ter
Jones Charles, esq. 7B, Manchester sq
Jones Charles, esq. 144 Oxford st. & Wrexham, Denbighshire
Jones C. C. S.L. 3 Serjeants' inn, Fleet st
Jones Charles Gwillim, esq. 11 Gray's inn square, & 6 Craven hill, Bayswatr
Jones Charles T. esq. 5 Symonds inn
Jones D. esq.9 Hemingford cot. Brnsb.rd
Jones D.esq.15Southampton pl. Eustn.sq
Jones Evan, esq. 1 Friedenstein terrace
Jones Edward, esq. 8 Canonbury park
Jones Edwd. Chester, esq. 4 Stone bldgs
Jones Edward A. esq. 20 Gt. Russell st
Jones Fras.W.Reeve,esq.10Brunswick sq
Jones Frederick, esq. 5 Old sq. Linc. inn
Jones F. P. esq. 16 Radnor pl. Oxford ter
Jones Geo. esq. 42Cambridge st. Edgw.rd
Jones Geo. esq. 5 Haydon sq. Minories
Jones Geo. esq. 17 Paradise ter. Liv. rd
Jones Geo. esq. Royal Acad. Trafalgar sq
Jones Geo. esq. 6 Thurloe sq. Brompton
JonesGeo.J.esq.27Margaretst.Cavdsh.sq
Jones Geo. R. esq. 5 Palsgrave pl. Strand
Jones Handfield, M.D. 54 Sloane st
Jones Harvey B. esq. 51 Montagu sq
Jones Hen. esq. 26 New Bridge st. Blkfrs
Jones Henry, esq. 7 Pall mall
Jones Hen. esq. 22 Seymour st. Euston sq
Jones Henry D. esq. 23 Soho square
Jones Hy. J. esq. 2 Church ct. Clements la
Jones H.G. S.L. 1Serjeant's inn, Chncy. la
Jones Horace, esq. 16 Furnival's inn
Jones Hugh, esq. 55 Upper Berkeley st
Jones Isaac, esq. 7Thebertonst.we.Lpl.rd
Jones Isaiah, esq. 129 Strand
Jones Jas. esq.2 Albert ter. St. John's wd
Jones Jas. esq. 69 Berners st. Oxford st
Jones Jas. esq. 70 Judd st. Brunswick sq
Jones Jenkin, esq. 3 Coles ter. Brnsby. rd
Jones Jn. esq. 3 Fonthill pl. Clapham rd
Jones John, esq. 68 Gibson sq. Islington
Jones John, esq. 3 Pump court, Temple
Jones John, esq. 38 Sandwich street
Jones John, esq. 11 Tavistock st.Bdfd. sq
Jones John Edwd. esq. 8 Cannon row
Jones John G. 11 Tavistock st. Bedfd.sq
Jones John Harper esq. 14 South sq
Jones John Oliver, esq. 4 Upper Bedford place, & 1 John st. Bedford row
Jones John W. esq. 24 Stonefield street
Jones L. esq. 6 St.Ann's villas, Acacia rd
Jones Michael, esq, 33 Mount street
Jones the Misses, 15 Salisbury square
Jones Miss, 54 Coleshill st
Jones Miss, 58 Doughty st
Jones Miss, 3 Duke st. Portland place
Jones Miss, 34 Gerrard st. Islington
Jones Miss, 16Northwick ter. St.Jn's. wd
Jones Mrs. 20 Barnsbury park
Jones Mrs. 19 Bernard st. Russell sq
Jones Mrs. 44 Brompton row
Jones Mrs. 17 Camden road villas
Jones Mrs. 29 Dalby terrace, City road
Jones Mrs. 5 Chester pl. Regent's park
Jones Mrs. 15 Edgware road
Jones Mrs. 9 Gt. College st. Westminster
Jones Mrs. 18 Michael's pl. Brompton
Jones Mrs. 12 New st. Spring gardens, & North Shoebury house, Essex
Jones Mrs. 43 Up. Norton st. Fitzroy sq
Jones Mrs. 10 Pelham pl. Fulham road
Jones Mrs. 7 Portland ter. Regent's pk
Jones Mrs. 21 Queen Anne st
Jones Mrs. 24 Salisbury st. Strand
Jones Mrs. 9 Terrace, Kensington
Jones Mrs. 25 Theberton st. Islington
Jones Mrs. 5 University st. Tott. ct. rd
Jones Owen, esq. 9 Argyll pl. Regent st
Jones Rd. esq. 14 Chapel st.Grosvenor pl
Jones Rd. esq. 12 Fortess ter. Kntsh. tn
Jones Richard, esq. 40 Parliament st
Jones Rd. esq.32 Tonbridge pl.New road
Jones R. L. esq. Creamhall, Highb. vale
Jones Rt. esq. 5 Milton pl. Wndswrth.rd
Jones Rt. Henry, esq. 7 Weymouth st
Jones R. esq. 24 Warwick st. Golden sq
Jones Rymer, esq.120 Camden rd. villas
Jones Sidney, esq. 49 Davies st
Jones Theobald Capt. R.N., M.P. 30Chas. st. St.Jms.'s; & 18Harcourt st. Dublin
Jones Thos.esq.2 Grove endpl.St Jhn's. w
Jones Thos. esq. 5 Argyle st. King's cross, & 10 Brunswick square
Jones Thomas, esq. 21 Clapham rd. pl
Jones Thos.esq.6King's bench wk. Tmple
Jones Thos. esq. 4 Millman pl. Foundling
Jones Thos. esq. 24 Milton st. Dorset sq
Jones Thos. esq. 16 York pl. Fulham rd
Jones T. jun. esq. 2 Curzon pl. Kensgt.rd
Jones T. W. esq. 35 George st. Hanover sq
Jones Thos. Wm. M.D.19Finsbury pavem
Jones Wm. esq. 1 Bridge row, Pimlico
Jones Wm. esq.14 Buckingham st. Strnd
Jones Wm. esq. 27Clipstone st. Fitzry.sq
Jones Wm. esq. Clytha hou. 19 Rutland gate&Clytha hou.Ragland, nr. Monmth

Jones Wm.esq.39 Frederick st.Gra.inn rc
Jones Wm. esq. 34 Gt. Marylebone st
Jones Wm. esq. 6 King Edward ter. Islı
Jones William, esq. 11 Parliament st. & Madox cottage, Greenwich
Jones Wm. esq. 56 St. John st. road
Jones Wm. esq. 34 Upper Baker st
Jones W.esq.4Up.Belmont pl.Wandsw. 1
Jones Wm. esq. 9 Alpha pl. Regt.'s park
Jones Wm. esq. 13 Salisbury st. Strand
Jones Wm. esq. 32 York pl. City road
Jones Wm. H. esq. 4 Field ct. Gray's inn
Jones Wm. Henry, esq. 36 Brompton rw
Jones Wm. Henry, esq. 14 Up. Ebury st
Jones Wm. Hughes, esq. 11 Stonefield st
Jones Wm. J. esq. 4Portugal st.Linc.inn
Jones Wm. Sl.esq.16Chester ter.Regt.pk
Jonson Geo. C. esq. 1 Grosvenor st. west
Joplin Miss, 1 Lit. George st. Wesminstr
Jopling Chs. esq. 4 Pelham cr. Fulham rd
Jopling Joseph, esq. 29 Wimpole st
Jordan Lewis, esq. 19 Berners st. Oxfd. st
Jordan Mrs. 43 London st. Fitzroy sq
Jordon Octavius, esq. 12 John st. Adlph
Jordan Richard, esq. 11 Keppel st
Jordan R. esq. 27 Montague st. Blmsby
Jordan T. B. esq. 11 Cottage rd. Eaton sq
Jordan Wm. Prue, esq. 9 Lr. Belgrave st
Jorden Mrs. 1 Bernard st. Russell sq
Jorden Rd. esq. 3 Lit.George st.Westmst
Jorge John, esq. 46 Clarendon sq
Jortin Lee, esq. 43 Lincoln's inn fields
Jortin Mrs. 7 Charlotte st. Bedford sq. & Nibley ho. nr. Wotton under edge
Joseph Aaron, esq. 1 Fitzroy square
Joseph Edwd. esq. 15 Gt. Marylebone st
Joseph Joseph, esq. 2 Montague place
Joseph Mrs. 2 Heathcote st
Joseph Solomon N. esq. 10 Cres. Minrs
Joshua John, esq. 4 Palmer ter. Hollwy
Josi Charles, esq. 99 Gt. Portland st
Jourdain F. J. esq. 10 Sebbons bdgs. Islg
Jourdain Miss, 19 Portland pl. Islngtn
Jowett Josh. esq. 13 Green's rw.Chelsea
Joy John, esq. 1 Staple inn, Holborn
Joy Miss, 10 Fitzroy square
Joy Thos. esq. 24 South ter. Brompton
Joy Thos. M. esq. 4 Russell pl. Fitzroy sq
Joy William, esq. 51 Nelson square
Joyce Frncs.esq.3 Dean's pl.Sth.Lambth
Joyner John C.esq. Denmark hl.Cambwl
Juby Rt.esq. 36 Gt.Percy st.Pentonville
Judd Mrs. 58 York ter. Regent's park
Judd S. esq. 2Malvern ter.Richm.rd.Islg
Judd William, esq. Curzon lodge, Old Brompton, & Richmond hill, Surrey
Judd Wm.esq.11Hamilton pl.King's cros
Judd Wm. C. esq. 4 Middle Temple lane
Judd Wm. Hy. esq. 9 Little Maddox st
Judkin Rev. Thos. James, 48 Euston sq
Judson Wm. esq. 30 Lower Ranelagh st
Juitt George, esq. 35 Euston square
Juler Philip, esq. 157 High Holborn
Julians Thomas, esq. 12 Stonefield st
Julien Louis G. esq. 214 Regent st
Julius Alfred Alex. esq. 19 Buckingham st. Adelphi, & Richmond, Surrey
Junior United Service Club (Thomas Hatch, sec.), 11 Charles st. St. James's
Jupe Mrs. 16 Bulstrode st
Justus Mrs. 1 Ionian cot. Park village ea
Jutsum Mrs. 9 Princes st. Cavendish sq

KAIN Mrs. 36 Up.Bedford pl.Russell sq
Karslake Henry, esq. 6 Queen square, Bloomsbury, & 4 Regent st
Kater Edward, esq. F.R.S. 1 Somers pl. Hyde park
Kater Edward, esq. 7 Up. Porchester st
Kay Sir Wm. 2 Rutland gate, Kngtsbdg
Kay Joseph, esq. 6 Gower st. Bedford sq
Kay Miss, 1 Woodstock pl. Avenue road
Kay Mrs. Hyde park gate, Knsngtn.gore
Kay Mrs. 8 Sebbons buildings, Islington
Kaye Sir John L. L. bart. 54 Portland pl. & Denbey grange, Wakefield
Kay Mrs. 24 York terrace, Regent's pk
Kaye John, esq. 14 Cork st. & Fulmer grove, Gerard's cross
Kaye Mrs. 15Pelham crescent, Fulham rd
Kaye Mrs. 2 Stanley pl. Paddington gn
Kayes Henry, esq. 4 Surrey st. Strand, & North Brixton
Keal John, esq. 24 Woburn pl. Russell sq
Keane Lord, United Service club, Pall mall, & Burton lodge, Christchurch
Keane Daniel, esq. 36 Lincoln's inn flds
Keane David D. esq. 51 Lincoln's inn fl
Kearney Col. Chas. 10 Cumberland st
Kearney Joshua, esq. 32 Albany st
Kearns Wm. Mosson, esq. 5 Red Lion sq
Kearse Mrs. 48 Foley st
Kearsey Frs. esq. 31 Mecklenburgh sq
Kearsley Mrs. 25 Alfred pl. Bedford sq
Keate Col. 32 Halfmoon st. Piccadilly
Keate Robert, esq. 15 Albemarle st
Keates Mrs. Col. 18 Up. Seymour st.wst
Keating Hen. Singer, esq. 1 Paper blds
Keating Wm. esq. 9 Inner Temple lane
Keats Frederick, esq. 4 Oxford ter. & 182 Piccadilly
Keats Thos. P. esq. 23 Spencer ter. Islgtn
Keaven Jas.esq. 4 Cumbrld.st.Portmn.sq
Keays Fred. esq. 6 Cloudesley st. Islntn
Kebbell J. sen. esq. 10 Mayfld. pl. Dlstn
Keeble John, esq. 1 Ranelagh rd.Pimlico
Keech Wm.esq.25 Alpha rd.Regent's pk
Keed William, esq. 7 York pl. Fulham rd
Keeley Jas. esq.2 Newington pl.Ken.com
Keeley Robert, esq. 19 Brompton sq
Keeling Edwd.H.esq.8Earl's ter.Kensgtn
Keeley Rt. esq. 10 Charlotte st. Bdfd.sq
Keen Jas.esq. 22 Up. Geo. st.Brynstn. sq
Keen Mrs. 37 Bedford pl. Kensington
Keen Thos. esq. 15 Manor pl. nth. Chels
Keene Chas. esq. 1 New sq. Lincoln's inn
Keene Chas. esq. 4 Sussex pl.Regt.'s pk
Keene John, esq. 33 London st.Fitzry.sq
Keene J.J.esq.9Cunninghm.pl.St.Jn.'swd
Keene Rev. Chas. E. R. 38 Charles st. Berkeley square, & Swincomb house, Henley on Thames
Keene Mrs. 49 Queen st. Edgware road
Keene Mrs. 4 Sussex pl. Regent's park
Keene Thos.esq.4Stanhope ter.Regt's.pk
Keer Thos. esq. 6 Sussex pl. Canonby. sq
Kehoe Thomas, esq. 1A, Woburn place
Keighley Thos. David, esq. 32 Myddelton sq. & 77 Basinghall st
Keightley Archibald, esq. 43 Chancery lane, & Charterhouse
Keil Wm. esq. 34 Cadogan st. Chelsea
Keily Rd. esq. 6 Cleveland row, St. Jas's
Keith Viscountess, 110 Piccadilly
Keith Hon.Wm.Mivart's hot.44Brook st
Keith Alexander, esq. 195 Piccadilly
Keith John, esq. 15 Hans pl. Sloane st
Keith Wm. esq. 1 York bldg.Marylebone
Kekewich S. J. esq. 44 Brook st
Kekewich Geo.G. 3 Paper bldgs. Temple
Kelk John, esq. 22 Circus rd. St.John's w
Kell Chas. esq.7 Glo'ster rd.Regnt.'s pk
Kell Lionel P. esq. 8 Bridge st. Westmr
Kell Wm. Ghrimes, esq. 43 Bedford row
Kellman J. esq.34 Petersburgh pl. Bayswr
Kellner Mrs. 2 Porchester pl. Edgw. rd
Kelly Sir Fitzroy, knt. S.G. M.P. 19New st. Spring gdns. & 8 Figtree ct. Temple
Kelly Lt. Col. 58 Cambridge tr. Hyde pk
Kelly Rev. A.P. M.A. 12 Charles sq. Hoxtn
Kelly Rev. Denis, M.A. 96 Farringdon st
Kelly Rev. John, 9 Polygon, Clarendon sq
Kelly Charles, esq. 9 Gray's inn square
Kelly Edwd. Robt. esq. M.A. 8 Cook's ct. Carey st. & 12 King's parade, Chelsea
Kelly Frederick, esq. 60 Fetter lane
Kelly Frederick, esq. 49 Hunter st. Brunswick sq. & New ho. Northfleet, Kent
Kelly Henry Lindsay, esq. 8 Cook's ct. Lincoln's inn, &2Albion vils. Hamrsmth
Kelly James, esq. M.P. Erina house, County of Clare
Kelly James Birch, esq. 10 Somers pl. Hyde park, & 1 Inner Temple lane
Kelly Lucius, esq. 8 Cook's ct. Lincoln's inn, & 9 Essex st. Strand
Kelly Miss, 8 Bryanstone st
Kelly Miss, 73 Dean st. Soho
Kelly Miss, 8 Northumberland st. Strnd
Kelly T.W.esq. 33 Beaumont st. Portld.pl
Kelly W.K.esq.17Wellingtn.tr.St.Jn's.w
Kelly Wm. esq. M.R.C.S. 8 Cook's court, Carey st
Kelly Wm. esq 7 David st. Marylebone
Kelly Wm. Hy. esq. 33 Manchester st
Kelly Wm. Hy. esq. 34 Porchester ter
Kelly Wm. Rt. esq. 6 Montagu pl. Mntgu.sq
Kelsy Mrs. 15 Connaught terrace
Kemball V.C.esq. 6 Chester pl.Oxford sq
Kember Geo. esq. 5 Amwell ter. Pntnvll
Kember Jas.esq.8Lowther cot.Liverpl.rd
Kemble C.esq.10 Montagu pl.Clapham rd
Kemble H. esq. M.P. Grove hill, Cambrwl
Kemble Horatio, esq. 1 Oxford square
Kemble John M.esq.13Bruton st.Bond st
Kemble Mrs.St.John's hill, Wandswth.rd
Kemp Rev. George, 41 Weymouth st
Kemp Chas. esq. Asylum rd.Old Kent rd
Kemp Edward, esq.9Trevor sq.Kngtsbdg
Kemp GeorgeB.esq. 23 Duke st.Westmn
Kemp John Abbott, esq, 36 Coleshill st
Kemp John H.esq. 1 Acton pl.Camden rd
Kemp John Young, esq. 41 Weymouth st. Cavndsh. sq. & 4 Stone bdgs.Linc.'s inn
Kemp Joseph, esq.7 Bloomfield ter.Pimlic
Kemp Mrs. 62 Margaret st. Cavendish sq
Kemp Mrs. 18 Tonbridge pl. New road
Kemp Thos.esq.3Up.Albanyst.Regt.'spk
Kemp T. Reginald, esq. 3Abchurch la. & Kemp villa, Loampit hill, Kent
Kemplay Jas. esq. 1 King's Bench walk
Kempson Carteret J. esq. 7 Princes ct
Kempson Geo. S. esq. 31 Abingdon st
Kempster John, esq.3Park cot.Havrstk.hl
Kempster W.H.esq.4Fredk.pl.U.Kngt.la
Kempt Rt. Hon. Sir James, 32 South st
Kempton Mrs.41Frederick st.Grays' i. rd
Kenah Maj. Gen. Thos. 35 Albemarle st
Kendal John, esq. 28 Kensington square
Kendall Hen. Edwd. esq. 17 Suffolk st. Pall mall, & Kemptown, Brighton
Kendall Hen. E. jun.esq.33Brunswick sq
Kendall Wm. esq. 31 Gibson sq. Islingto
Kendrick John, esq. 12 Manchester st
Kendrick M.esq.28Grafton st. Fitzroy sq
Kenmare, Earl of, 11 Belgrave square, & Killarney, county Kerry
Kennard Thomas, esq. 12 Providence pl. Upper Kennington lane
Kennedy Hon. John, 24B, Bryanstone sq
Kennedy Rev.W.J. M.A. 9Cmdn.hl.vil.Kns
Kennedy A.esq.3NewDorsetpl.Clphm.rd
Kennedy Chas.R.esq.10CrownOffice row
Kennedy Denham Wm. esq. 26 Soho sq
Kennedy James, esq. 17 Tavistock sq
Kennedy Langford, esq. 11 Devonshire pl
Kennedy Lewis, esq. 5 Alexander sq
Kennedy Mrs. 16 Loraine pl. Holloway
Kennedy Thomas, esq. 100 Chancery la
Kennell J. F.esq. 2Southmptn. st.Fitz. sq
Kennett Chas.esq. 2Duke st.Portland pl
Kennett Miss, 24 Wakefield st
Kennett Mrs. 42 Hans place, Sloane st
Kennett Thomas, esq. 7 Chatham place
Kennington Mrs. 28 Glo'ster st. Queen sq
Kennion Miss, Leonard cot. Brnsby. pk
Kennion Mrs. 10Devonshire st.Bishopsgt
Kennion Robt. W. esq. 43 Oxford terr. & 23 Old sq. Lincoln's inn
Kenrick Rev. George, 26 Regent sq
Kenrick Wm. esq. 9 Davies st. Berkly.sq
Kensett Wm. esq.32Southbank, Reg.'spk
Kensington A.esq.22Glo'ster rd. Hyde pk
Kensington Edward. esq. 13 Chancery la
Kensington Miss, 28 Bryanstone square
Kensington Mrs. 32 New Bridge st
Kensit Henry, esq. 29 Bedford row
Kensit Henry, jun. esq. 29 Bedford row

Kent, H. R. H. the Duchess of, Clarence house, Stable yard, St. James's
Kent Adolphus, esq. 38 Lonsdale sq
Kent Geo. esq. 9 Tonbridge pl. New rd
Kent Hen. esq. 9A, Warwick vil. Harw. rd
Kent John King, esq. 28 Essex st. Strand
Kent the Misses, 43 Woburn place
Kent Robert T. esq. 5 Crown Office row
Kent Robt. T. esq. 8 Trinity sq. Southwk
Kent Thos. esq. 6 Glo'ster ter. Old Bromptn
Kent Thos. esq. 20 Southmptn. pl. Euston sq
Kent Thos. F. esq. 87 Ebury st. Pimlico, & 6 Serle st. Lincoln's inn
Kent Wm. Dixon, esq. 28 Essex st. Strand
Kentish James, esq. 23 Wharton st
Kentish Joshua, esq. 2 York st. Prtmn. sq
Kentish Wm. esq. 12 Claremont ter. Pntnvll
Kenyon Lord, 9 Portman sq.; & Gredington hall, near Whitchurch, Salop; & Peel hall, near Bolton
Kenyon Hon. E. L. 30 Charles st. St. Jas
Kenyon John, esq. 40 York ter. Regt.'s pk
Kenyon John Rt. esq. 11 New sq. Linc. inn
Keogh Dennis, esq. 69 Millbank st. Westmr
Keogh Geo. D. esq. 12 Grove tr. St. John's wd
Keogh Thomas, esq. 20 Orchard st. Prtm. sq. & Stamp & Tax Office, Somerset ho
Keonig M. N. esq. 2 Up. Portland place, Wnds. road
Kepp Rd. esq. 33 Gower st. Bedford sq
Keppel Major the Hon. G. 11 Grosvnr. sq
Keppel Major Edwd. Geo. W. 3 Grange ter. Brompton, & Lexham hall, Norfolk
Ker Lady Selina, 11 Grosvenor st
Ker Capt. Thos. 21 Oxford terrace
Ker Alan, esq. 7 New sq. Lincoln's inn
Ker Chas. Hy. Bellenden, esq. 8 Old sq. Lincoln's inn, & Swiss cottage, Cheshunt, Herts
Ker David Stewart, M.P. 11 Grosvenor st. & Portavoe, near Donaghadee
Ker Mrs. Bellenden, 7 South bk. Regt.'s pk
Ker Thos. C. esq. 5 Verulam buildings
Ker Thomas C. esq. 46 Woburn place
Kerby John, esq. 13 Hemus ter. Chelsea
Kerby John, esq. 7 Porchester terrace
Kerby J. esq. 11 Providence pl. Up. Ken. la
Kerie Jedediah, esq. 70 Glo'ster place
Kerie Jedediah, jun. esq. 36 York place
Kerkman Hyde, esq. 29 Somerset st
Kerly Edward John, esq. 5 Gray's inn sq
Kernot John, esq. 7 Welbeck st
Kerr Alfred, esq. 22 North bank, Rgnt.'s pk
Kerr Charles, esq. 18 Devonshire place
Kerr C. D. esq. 4 Kensington garden ter
Kerr James, esq. 19 Cloudesley square
Kerr Mrs. 31 Clapham rise
Kerrison Lt. Genl. Sir Edwd. bart. G.C.H., K.C.B., M.P. 13 Gt. Stanhope st.; 27 Brunswick terrace, Brighton; & Oakley park, near Eye
Kerrison Robt. M. M.D. 12 New Burlington st. & Frognal, Hampstead
Kerry, Countess of, 3 Cavendish sq
Kerry William, esq. 9 Upper Brook st
Kerschner J. esq. 4 Middle Temple lane
Kerschner Joseph, esq. 2 Davidge terr
Kersey John, esq. 24 Euston square
Kershaw Rev. J. 46 Cumming st. Pentnvll
Kershaw Mrs. 1 Walcot ter. Lambeth
Kershaw Wm. esq. 2 Stonefield st. Islng
Kester Mrs. 8 St. Geo.'s tr. Knsgtn. N. w. tn
Kesteven Mrs. 19 Holloway pl. Holloway
Kettle Hen. Fred. esq. 16 Calthorpe st
Kettle John Lucena Ross, esq. 19 Duke st. St. James's; & 89 Chancery lane; & Orchardleigh house, Isle of Wight
Kettle Rupert, esq. 1 Plowden bdgs. Temp
Key John, esq. 14 Chester st. Grosvnr. pl
Key Joseph, esq. 7 Up. Phillimore place
Key Thos. esq. 48 Camden st. south
Key Wm. esq. 17 River st. Myddelton sq
Keyes Aaron, esq. 14 Duke st. Lin. in. flds
Keymer Jas. esq. 7 Queen's pl. Kengtn
Keys F. esq. 1 Chelsea pk. cot. Lt. Chelse
Keys Henry Lent, esq. 6 Regent square
Keyser Alf. esq. 21 Norfolk crescent
Keyser Chas. esq. 1 Chester pl. Hyde pk
Keyser Hen. esq. 1 Plowden bdgs. Temp
Kiallmark Alfred, esq. 17 Aberdeen pl
Kiallmark Geo. Fredk. esq. 29 Percy st
Kibblewhite James, esq. 6 Gray's inn pl
Kibblewhite James, esq. 9 Langham pl
Kidd Geo. esq. 41 Albion st. Hyde park
Kidd Robt. Chas. esq. 1 Hyde park gate, Lower Kensington gore
Kidd Wm. esq. 25 Acton st. Gray's in. rd
Kiernan F. esq. 30 Manchester st. Mnchr. sq
Kilgour Geo. A. esq. 69 Hamilton ter. St. John's wood, 47 Parliament st. & 24 Red Lion square
Kilgour Patrick, esq. 54 Hamilton terrace, & Woodside, Aberdeenshire
Killett Wm. Hy. esq. 16 Percy st. Bedfd. sq
Kilmaine Lord, 31 South st. South Audley st.; & Golstow pk. Rochford bridge, Westmeath, Ireland
Kilmaine Dowager Lady, 26 Chester st. Grosvenor place
Kilmansegge Count, Hanoverian ambassador, 44 Grosvenor place
Kilner Thomas, esq. 9 Albion grove
Kilpin Wm. H. esq. 7 Holland pl. Clphm. rd
Kimber Mrs. 20 High row, Knightsbridge
Kime William Thomas, esq. 24 Woburn square, & 4 Essex court, Temple
Kimpton Fras. esq. 1 Rich ter. Old Brmptn
Kincaid Jn. D. esq. 9 Princes st. Spitalfi
Kinder Wm. S. esq. 23 Southampton bldgs
Kinder Wm S. esq. 5 Thurloe sq. Bromptn
Kinderley Geo. H. esq. 10 Bedford square, & 6 New square, Lincoln's inn
Kindersley Edward C. esq. 35 Harley st
Kindersley Miss, 51 Wimpole st
Kindersley Rd. T. esq. Q.C. 3 Stone buildings, Lincoln's inn, & 18 Hyde park sq
Kindred Miss, 41 Newington pl. Ken. rd
King Lady M.P. L. 5 Park cresc. Regt.'s pk
King Lady, 38 Dover st. Piccadilly, & Woburn park, Chertsey
King Hon. P. J. Locke, 38 Dover st
King Hon. Miss, 20 South Audley st
King Sir Hen. bart. 7 Sussex ter. Hyde prk
King Sir R. D. bart. 13 Halkin st. west
King Colonel, 18 Aberdeen pl. Maida hl
King Colonel, 40 Hans place, Chelsea
King Captain John D. 5 Ehrenburg ter
King Captain George St. Vincent, 13 Halkin st. west, Belgrave square
King Alfred, M.D. 4 Gray's inn lane
King Alfred, esq. 10 Lyon's inn, Strand
King C. esq. 4 Sion vil. King's rd. we. Chel
King Charles, esq. 24 University st
King Charles Allen, esq. 7 Gray's inn sq
King Chas. S. esq. 21 Camden cot. Camden town, & 15 Serjeants' inn
King Edward Bolton, esq. 44 Grosvenor sq. & Umbersdale park, Warwickshire
King Frederick Sidney, esq. 9 Lr. Eaton st
King George, esq. 3 Lloyd square
King Henry esq. 9 King's bench wk. Tem
King James, esq. 4 Tavistock pl. Russell sq
King James, esq. 39 Foley place
King John, esq. 1 Belgrave pl. Wndsw. rd
King John, esq. 20 Grosvenor place
King John, esq. 10 Pall mall east
King John, esq. 10 Portland ter. Rgts. pk
King John, esq. 23 Tonbridge pl. New rd
King John, esq. 4 Trinity pl. Charing crs
King John, esq. 3 Upper Seymour st. wst
King J. esq. 4 Windmill st. Tott. ct. rd
King John, esq. 1 Woodland pl. St. Jn. wd
King John Dl. 3 Elm court, Temple
King John Wm. esq. 40 Gerrard st. Soho
King Jsh. esq. 9 Northwick ter. St. Jns. wd
King M. esq. 43 Frederick st. Gray's inn rd
King Miss, 29 Alfred st. Bedford sq
King Mrs. 7 Barnsbury square, Islington
King Mrs. 6 Bedford row, Islington
King Mrs. 38 Cambridge st. Edgware rd
King Mrs. 4 Cardigan pl. Kennington crs
King Mrs. 8 Clarendon square
King Mrs. 29 Kensington square
King Mrs. 226 Maida hill, Edgware rd
King Mrs. 8 New Manor pl. King's rd. Chels
King Mrs. 14 Park road, Regent's park
King Mrs. 41 Smith st. King's road, Chel
King Mrs. 12 Wilton place, Belgrave sq
King Mrs. 50 Upper Gower st. Bedford sq
King Mrs. 9 York place, Fulham road
King Osmer, esq. 37 Bernard st
King Pitman, esq. 3 Argyle sq. New rd
King Richard, esq. 7 Park ter. Highbury
King Richard, esq. 27 Sackville st
King Rob. esq. 9 Albion ter. Canonby sq
King Robert, esq. 28 Chester st. Grosv. pl
King Samuel, esq. 22 Wilmington sq
King Thomas, esq. 34 Store st. Bedford sq
King Thomas Bennet, esq. 9 Gray's inn sq
King Thomas K. esq. 10 Southampton blds
King Thomas Wilkinson, esq. 36 Bedford sq
King Thos. Wm. esq. Heralds' col. Drs. com
King Wm. esq. 2 Duncan terrace, City rd
King Wm. esq. 10 Southampton bldgs
King Wm. esq. 9 Osnaburgh st. Regent's pk
King William Chas. esq. 20 Westbourne st. Hyde park gardens, & 1 New square, Lincoln's inn
King William, esq. 27 Lincoln's inn fields
King Wm. Charles, esq. 1 New sq. Lincoln's inn
King Wm. Read esq. 1 New sq. Lincoln's in
Kingdom James, esq. 3 Hemus ter. Chels
Kingdom William, esq. 32 Westbourne ter
Kingdom William, esq. 15 Regent st
Kingdon Richard, esq. 16 Clifford's inn
Kingdon Thos. Kingdon, esq. 3 St. John's villas, Acacia rd. & 5 Hare ct
Kingdon Wm. esq. 5 Hare ct. Temple
Kingdon William, esq. 13 Bedford row
Kingdon Wm. esq. 6 New Palace yard
Kinglake Alex. Wm. esq. 24 Old sq. Lin. inn
Kinglake John A. S.L. 3 Hobart place, Eaton square, & 3 Brick court, Temple
Kingscote Hen. esq. 10 Up. Grosvnr. st
Kingsford James, esq. 23 Essex st. Strand, & Sydenham, Kent
Kingsley Rev. C. Rectory house, Chelsea
Kingsmill Miss, 4 Warwick vil. Maida hl
Kingsmill Parr, esq. 50 Cloudesley ter
Kingston, Earl of, Michaelstown castle, Cork
Kingston, Dowager Countess of, 35 Alpha rd. & Mountain lodge, cnty. Cork
Kingston John, esq. 6 Grove end road
Kingston Lacy Hy. esq. 8 York gt. Reg. pk
Kingston Mrs. 10 Clarence ter. Reg. pk
Kingston P. N. M.D. 27 Curzon st
Kingston Wm. esq. 2 York bldgs. New rd
Kington John Parnet, esq. 4 Smith sq
Kinloch Dowager Lady, 20 Eaton place
Kinloch Henry A. esq. 13 New inn, Strand
Kinloch Wm. esq. 3 Lr. James st. Goldn. sq
Kinlock Jas. J. esq. 21 Glo'ster rd. Hyd. pk
Kinnaird Lord, P.C. 33 Grosvenor st. & Rossie priory, Inchture, Perthshire
Kinnaird Dow. Lady, 28 Up. Grosvnr. st
Kinnaird Hon Arthur, 35 Hyde pk. sq
Kinnear George, esq. 5 Gower st
Kinnoull Earl, 58 Green st. & Dublin castle, Perth
Kinsey Mrs. 23 Edward st. Langham pl
Kinsey William, esq. 20 Bloomsbury sq
Kinsman John, esq. 27 Trevor square
Kirby Charles, esq. 12 Blandford sq
Kirby Geo. Goldsmith, esq. 11 Waterloo pl
Kirby Fred. esq. 30 Milton st. Dorset sq
Kirby John Blake, esq. 9 Devonshire st. Portland pl. & 5 Elm court, Temple
Kirby Mrs. 54 Cambridge ter. Edgw. rd
Kirchhoff Dominique, esq. 14 Grafton st. e
Kirk Peter, esq. M.P. Carlton club, 94 Pall mall, & Thornefield, near Carrickfergus
Kirk Thomas, esq. 10 Symond's inn
Kirk Thos. esq. 50 Guilfd. st. Russell sq
Kirkaldy James, esq. 144 Oxford st. & Blackness house, Dundee
Kirkby Mrs. 103 Guilford st

Kirkham John, esq. 3 Tonbridge place, New road
Kirkland Sir John, 80 Pall mall, & East Horsley park, Leatherhead
Kirkland Mrs. 21 Cadogan st
Kirkman Hyde, esq. 50Green st.Grvr.sq
Kirkman Joseph, esq. Harrow road
Kirkman Mrs. 39 Clarendon square
Kirkmann Wm. esq. Kennington house, Upper Kennington green
Kirkmann Abraham, esq. 89Chancery la
Kirkpatrick Geo. esq. 21 Cloudesley st
Kirkpatrick John, esq.5King'sBench wk
Kirkup Alfred, esq. 7 Vigo st. Regent st
Kirkwood John, esq. 12 Aldenham ter. Pancras road, & 77 Brewer st
Kirton Mrs. 5 Goulden ter. Barnsbury rd
Kirwan Andrew V. esq. 73 Glo'ster pl. Portman sq. & 9 Inner Temple la
Kisch Abm. esq. 12St.Alban's pl.St.Jas's
Kitchener Mrs. 3 George st. St. James's
Kitchiner Mrs. 24 Allsop ter. New road
Kitchiner Mrs. 14 Wilton place
KitchingJonathan, esq.3Northampton sq
Kitching Joseph Francis, esq. 16 Gloucester grove west, Old Brompton
Kitching Mrs. 8 Goulden ter. Brnby. rd
Kitchingman Rev. P.69Park st.Grosv.sq
Kitley Rev.Jsph.27Charles st.Berkley sq
Kitsell Mrs. 11 Glo'ster pl. Regent's pk
Kittoe H. esq. 2 Chandos st. Cavnd. sq
Klingemann Charles, esq. secretary to the Hanoverian Embassy, 4 Hobart pl
Klose Mrs. 39 Beaumont st
Knaggs H. esq. 3St.James's ter.Cmdn. tn
Knaggs John, esq. 1 Mornington crescent
Knapp Charles, esq. 2 Brick ct. Temple
Knapp George, esq. 33 Stamford st
Knapp Hambly, esq. 50 Brook st
Knapton Rt.W.esq. 27Nth. bk.Regnt.pk
KnatchbullNorton, esq. 169 New Bond st
Knesebeck Capt. Baron, 35 Halfmoon st
Knevitt Lieut.Thos.L.R.N.13Red Lion sq
Knight Capt. Edw. 41 St. James's pl
Knight Alf. esq. 4 Pullin's rw. Islngtn
KnightC.esq.Walpole ldg.Fnchly.Nw.rd
Knight Fred. A. esq. 1 Mitre court blds. Tmpl. & 19 Kepple st. Russell sq
Knight Fred. Winn, M.P. 10 Dover st. & Wolverley house, near Kidderminster
Knight George, esq. & Dow. Countess Nelson, Duchess of Bronte, 5 Great Cumberland st
Knight George, esq. 46 Regent sq
Knight Geo. esq. 95 Sloane st. & Weybourne house, Farnham, Surrey
KnightH.esq.3Mortimer pl.DeBeauvr.sq
Knight Hen. Gally, esq. M.P. 69 Grvnr. st. & Firbeck hall, near Rotherham
Knight H. O. esq. 13 Grove end road
Knight J. esq.Lavender hill,Wndswth.rd
Knight J.P.esq. R.A. 20 James st.Pmlico
Knight Morrison, esq. 47 Dover st
Knight Miss, 14 Gloucester pl. New rd
KnightMiss,13Grve. end rd.St.Jno.'s wd
Knight Miss, 14 King st. Covent garden
Knight Miss, 7 Norfolk st. Park lane
Knight Mrs. Gen. 14 Portman st
Knight Mrs. 10 Crescent pl. Burton cres
Knight Mrs. 47 Dover st
Knight Mrs. 28 Glo'ster cres. Regnt. pk
Knight Mrs. 10 Thayer st
Knight Rd. esq. 19 Beaufoy ter.Edgw. rd
Knight Robert, esq. 44 Grosvenor sq. & 3 Clarence terrace, Leamington
Knight Sam. esq. 4 Dalby ter. City rd
KnightS.esq.Songhurst cot.Wndswth.rd
Knight V. esq. 3 Cornwell ter.Regt.'s pk
Knight Wm. esq. 1 Canonbury pl.Islngtn
Knight William, esq. 47 Dover st. Piccadilly, & 9 Inner Temple lane
Knight Wm. esq. 10Glo'ster ter.O.Brptn
Knight Wm.Palmer, esq.35Grove end rd
Knightley Sir Charles, M.P. 10 Up.Brook st. & Fawksley park, near Daventry
Knipe Miss, 11 Hans place, Sloane st
Knoble Edw. esq. 69 Lincoln's inn fields. & 25 Abbey place, St. John's wood
Knott Rev. R.R. 25 Cumming st. Pntnvl
Knott Geo. esq. 18 Penton pl. Pentonvill
KnottR.esq.jun.14Chichesterpl.Wands.r
Knott R.esq.sen.14Chichester pl.Wand.r
KnottWm.esq.3Newington pl.Kengtn.rd
Knowles Sir Francis Charles, F.R.S. 2 Harcourt buildings, Temple
KnowlesChas.Jas.esq.Q.C.1Brick ct.Tem
Knowles John, esq. 3 Highbury park
Knowles John, esq.14Park pl.Regt.'s prk
Knowles Mrs. 3 Church st. Kensington
Knowles T. esq. 15 Devereux ct. Strand
Knowles TownleyR.esq.3Raymond bldgs
Knowles Wm. esq. 9 Wilton st. Grvnr. pl
KnoxHon.Col.Jas.10Cheshm. st.Belg.sq
Knox Lady Fra. 22 Park st. Grosvnr. sq
Knox Hon. Capt. 12 Montagu sq
Knox Col. 15 King st. James's
Knox Lt. Col. Brownlow, 28 Wilton cres
Knox Chas. Geo. esq. 26 Old sq. Linc.inn
Knox C.G. esq.Hermitage,Finchley nw.r
Knox Geo. esq. 7 Cloudesley st. Islngtn
Knox Geo. esq. 4 Bloomsbury sq
Knox Geo. Frederick, esq. 39 Davies st
Knox Miss, 20 Russell pl. Fitzroy sq
Knox Miss, 9 Welbeck st. Cavendish sq
Knox Rt. esq. White's cottage, Earl's ct. Old Brompton
Knox Vicesimus, esq. 8 Stratford pl.; 3 King's Bench walk; & Whittle lodge, Chelmsford
Knyvett Carey Seymour, esq. 3 Regt. st
Knyvett Chas. esq. 39 St. James's pl
Koe J. H. esq. Q.C. 28 Bedford sq. & 19 Old square
Koch Christian, esq. 16 Adam st. Adelphi
Koecker Leonard, esq. 5 Conduit st
Kohler Mrs. 8 Marlborough pl. Ken. crs
Kolbe John G.esq. 34 Conduit st.Bond st
Koller Baron, councillor to the Austrian Embassy, 7 Chandos st. Cavendish sq
Konig Charles, esq. British Museum
Koudriaffsky M.de, sec. to Russian Embassy, 30 Dover st. Piccadilly
Kraeutler William, esq. 2 Albemarle st
Kreeft Christph. esq. 35 Claremont sq
Krehmer George, esq. consul general for Russia, 15 Saville row, & 2 Winchester buildings
Kübeck Baron, attaché to the Austrian embassy, 7 Chandos st
Kuhff Henry, esq. 11 Cross st. Islington
Kuper Rev. Dr. the Lodge, Sth. Lambth
Kusel Samuel, esq. 32 Gt. Alie st
Kyd Colonel, 6 Blandford pl. Dorset sq
Kyle Henry S. esq. 12 Melbury terrace, Dorset sq. & 2 Old sq. Lincoln's inn
Kynaston Mrs. 1 Albionpl. Albn.rd.Hllwy
Kynaston Roger, esq.jun.33St.James's pl
Kyne Rev. John, 54 Lincoln's inn fields
Kyrle Rev. William Money, Cavendish hotel, 81 Jermyn st
Kyrls Rev. Jas. S. M. Cavendish hotel, 81Jermyn st.& Yatesbry. rectory, Wilts

LABALMONDIERE Mrs. 46 Harley st
La Beaume Michael, esq. 11 Argyll st
Lablache Signor F. 21 Albany st
Lablache Signor M. 148 Albany st
Labouchere Rt. Hon. Hen. M.P.&Mrs.27 Belgrave sq. & Stowey, Bridgewater
Lacey Misses, 2 Church row, Islington
Lacey James, esq. 3 Trafalgar sq.Chelsea
Lacey Walter, esq. 20 Edwardes sq
Lacey Wm. Chas. esq. 28 New Bridge st
Lack Mrs. 24 Cecil st. Strand
Lachlan Robt.Hen.esq.91 Camden rd.vil
Lackerstein Aug. esq. 1 Circus road
Lackresteen Jas. esq. 1 Gerrard st. Isl
Lacroix J.B.esq.51 Up.Norton st.Fitz.sq
Lacy Chas. esq. 5 Wilton st. Grosvnr.pl
Lacy T. esq. 6 Tavistock pl.Tavistock sq
Ladbury Geo. esq. 19 Tyndale pl. Isling
Ladbury J. Edwd. esq. 7 Up. Fitzroy st
Ladell Richard, esq. 17 Claremont place
Laforest Edwd.esq.26John st.Bedford rw
Laforest William, esq. 8 Bedford row
Lahee C.esq.16 Manor pl.north, Chelsea
Lahee Jas. esq. 7 Ulster pl. Regent's pk
Lahee Samuel, esq. 32 Hans pl.Sloane st
Laidlaw Mrs.14 Powell st.w. Goswell rd
Laidlow Miss, 17 Up. Seymour st. west
Laing Rev. D.M.A.,F.R.S. 1 Cambdg.ter
Laing Allan Stewart, esq. 3 Tanfield ct
LaingGeo.Edwd.esq.Carlton ch.12Rgt.st
Laing Samuel, esq. 8 King's bench walk
Lainson Wm. esq.Up.Cheyne rw.Chelsea
Lake Viscount, 76 Gloucester place, & Aston Clinton, Aylesbury
Lake Edward Wm. esq. 40 Oxford ter. Edgware rd. & 30 Bury st. St.James's
Lake Geo.esq.19 Gt. Charter la.Doc.com
Lake H. esq.3Mcklnbrgh. sq.&10New sq
Lake Jas. esq. 3 King's rd. ter. Chelsea
Lake Jas.P.esq.22 Portugal st. Linc.inn
Lake John, esq. 10 New sq.Lincoln's inn
Lake John, esq. Whitmore rd. Hoxton
Lake Josiah, esq.109 Stanhope st.Hm.rd
Lake Mrs. Eyre vil.Queen's rd.St.Jn's.wd
Lake Wm. esq. 8 New sq. Lincoln's inn
Laking Fras. esq. 13 Addison rd.Knsgtn
Laking Fred.esq.12 Marlbro' rd.Chelsea
Laking Henry, esq. 48 Curzon st
Laking Mrs. 27 Brompton crescent
Lalande Mrs. 20 Sloane st
Lamb Sir Chas. bart. 169 New Bond st
Lamb Edwd. B. esq. 26 Charlotte st. Portland place
Lamb James, esq. 25 Hyde park square
Lamb John S. esq. 22 Maida hill
Lamb Miss, 13 Bryanstone st.Portmn. sq
Lamb Mrs. 3 Glo'ster pl. Glo'ster cresct
Lamb Mrs. 20 Osnaburgh st.Regnt's.pk
Lamb Mrs. 2 York place, City road
Lamb Wm. esq. 55 Earl st. east, Lis. gr
Lamb Wm.esq.4Prtland.ter.Wndswth.rd
Lambe Alfred, esq. 7 Bethnal green
Lambert Lady Henrietta, 71 Euston sq
Lambert LadyJulia, 71 Euston sq.Nw.rd
Lambert Maj. Gen. 11 South Audley st
Lambert Rev.Wm. 15Belmnt.pl.Wnds.rd
Lambert Chas. esq. 6Cheyne row, Chlsea
Lambert Daniel, esq. 77 Chancery lane
Lambert Edwd. esq. 4 Raymond buildings, Gray's inn
Lambert Edward, esq. 4South sq.Gray's i
Lambert Francis John, esq. 6 Kensington garden terrace, Sussex square
Lambert Geo. esq. 7 Albion st. Hyde pk
Lambert Geo. Hall, esq. 105 Albany st
Lambert Harry, esq. 24 Marlborough sq
Lambert H. E. F. esq. 4 Hare ct. Temple
Lambert Henry Wm. esq. 28A, Devonshire st. Portland place
Lambert John, esq. 60 Lisson gro. nrth
Lambert John, esq. 2 Stockwell common
Lambert John, esq. 32 Tavistock square
Lambert John Wallace, esq.57 Berners st
Lambert Jos. esq. 32 Lower Belgrave pl
Lambert Mrs. 21 Norfolk st. Park lane, & Fowlers, Hawkhurst, Kent
Lambert Mrs. Regent vil. Finchley nw.rd
Lambert Rd. esq. 32 John st. Bedford rw
Lambert Thomas, esq. 4 Harrington sq
Lamborn Chas. esq. 18 Scarsdale ter
Lamborn Capt. 14 Sussex pl. Kensingtn
Lambton Hedworth, esq. M.P. 20 Wilton pl. Belgrave sq
Lambton Wm. Hy. esq. 41 Chesham pl
Laming Jas. esq. 5Warwick vil.Maida hl
LamminWm.Henry, esq.5John st.Adelph
Lamotte John Laquier, esq. 9 Searle st
Lamoureux Miss, 23 Green st
Lamplough Wm. esq. 5 Barnsbury villas
Lampton W. esq. 2 Up. Queen's buildings, Brompton
Lancaster B. esq. 40 Chester ter.Regt.pk
Lancaster Mrs. 9Weymouth st.Portld. pl
Lancaster Thos. J. esq. 88 Hamilton ter
Lancaster Wm. C. esq. 11 Red Lion sq

Lance John Henry, esq. 4 Plowden bldgs
Lance Miss, 71 Warren st. Fitzroy sq
Lancefield Thos. esq. 3 Augustus sq
Land T. esq. 6 Queen Charlotte row, N.rd
Lander James, esq. 17 Marlborough sq
Lander J. G. esq. 9 Middlesex pl. New rd
Lander Mrs. 7 Manor terrace, Chelsea
Landon Arthur J. esq. 1 Old sq. Linc. inn
Landon Mrs. 30 Westbourne place
Landon Wm. esq. 11 Halfmoon st
Landseer Chas. esq. 8 Sthmptn.st. Fitz.sq
Landseer Edwin, esq. R.A. 1 St. John's wd.rd
Landseer J. esq. 8 Sthmptn.st. Fitzry.sq
Landseer Thos. esq. 10½ Cunningham pl
Landzelle Wm. C. esq. 22 Grosvenor st
Lane Burton, esq. 5 Osnaburgh terrace
Lane Edwd. esq. 11 Annetts crs. Lr.rd. Islg
Lane Geo. esq. 18 South par. St. James's pk
Lane Geo. D. esq. 22 Gt. Russell st. Cov.gdn
Lane James, esq. 63 Chancery lane, & Herne hill, Surrey
Lane Jas. H. M.D. 13 North st. Westmr
Lane John, esq. 22 Keppel st. Russell sq
Lane John, esq. 23 Montpelier sq. Brmptn
Lane Miss, 4 Weymouth st. Portland pl
Lane Mrs. 39 Canonbury square
Lane Mrs. 41 Queen Anne st
Lane R. J. esq. 11 Chester pl. Regent's pk
Lane Rd. Kirkman, esq. 29 Argyll st. & 8 Upper Robert st. Brompton
Lane Samuel, esq. 60 Greek st. Soho
Lane Sam. esq. 1 Grosvenor pl. Hyde pk
Lane Wm. esq. 4 Bedford pl. Russell sq
Lane Wm. esq. 8 Palsgrave pl. Strand
Lang Alf. esq. 12 Buckingham st. Strand
Lang Chas. E. esq. 18 Adam st. Adelphi
Lang Charles Von, M.D. 41 Newman st
Lang Charles Von, M.D. 32 Bedford sq
Lang Gabrl. H. esq. 37 Gt. George st
Lang Henry, esq. 35 Montagu square
Lang Mrs. 33 Charterhouse square
Lang Mrs. 9 Sussex square
Lang Wm. Tilteman, esq. 20 Gt. Percy st
Langdale Lord, P.C. 37 South st. Grosvenor sq. & Templeton house, Roehampton
Langdale Hon. Chas. 10 Mansfield sq. & Houghton hall, nr. Market Weighton
Langdale Rev. Wm. J. 33 Camdn.rd. villas
Langdale Alfred, esq. 4 Hamilton ter. St. John's wood road
Langdale Marmaduke Rt. 38 Gower st
Langdale Mrs. 11 Ladbroke pl. Notng.hl
Langdale Wm. A. esq. 7 Gray's inn sq
Langdon Wm. esq. 12 Brompton square
Langford Dowg. Lady, 47 Berkeley sq
Langford Miss, 7 Hyde park gardens
Langford Mrs. 2 Lyall st. Belgrave sq
Langford Rd. esq. 5 Paradise ter. Islgt
Langham Jas. G. esq. 10 Bartlett's bldgs
Langham Sam. F. esq. 10 Bartlett's bldgs
Langhorne Jas. esq. Cowly cot. Wndsth.rd
Langley Col. 34 Hamilton ter. St. Jn.'s wd
Langley Capt. 17 Cecil st. Strand
Langley C. esq. 3 Charlotte st. Bedford sq
Langley H. esq. 3 Charlotte st. Bedford sq
Langley John, esq. 10 Howland st
Langley Mrs. 4 Old Quebec st. Portmn.sq
Langley Thos. esq. 28 Prtmn. pl. Edg.rd
Langley Wm. esq. 40 Glo'ster pl. Prtm.sq
Langley Wm. Hilliar, esq. 9A, Davies st
Langley W. H. esq. 27 John st. Bedford rw
Langley Wm. T. 11 Bedford st. Bedford rw
Langlois Claude, esq. 24 Trevor square
Langmaid Henry, esq. 122 Regent st
Langmore John C. esq. 15 Upper George st. Bryanstone square
Langmore Wm. M.D. 40 Finsbury sq
Langstaff Jsph. esq. 9 Cambridge sq
Langston James Haughton, M.P. & Lady Julia, 143 Piccadilly, & Sarsden house, Chipping Norton, Oxfordshire
Langton Daniel, esq. 34 Clapham rise
Langton D. jun. esq. 7 Furnival's inn
Langton Wm. Gore, M.P. 12 Grosvenor sq. Newton park, near Bath, & Acton, Middlesex
Langton Francis, esq. 7 Glo'ster crescent
Langton H. esq. 5 Queen's Head row, Isltn
Lankester Edwin, M.D. 19 Golden sq
Lansdowne Marquis of, K.G., P.C. 54 Berkeley sq.; & Bowood, near Calne
Lansdowne Mrs. 34 Bedford place
Langslow Robt. esq. 3 Harcourt bldgs
Lanza George, esq. 75 Newman st
Lapidge Edw. esq. 2 Derby st. Parlmnt.st
Laplume Geo. P. esq. 15 Lodge rd. Rgt.'s pk
Laport Mrs. 33 Church st. Spitalfields
Lapoulide P. esq. 2 Clarence pl. Clapm.r
Large Wm. Henry, esq. 140 Sloane st
Larkin Mrs. 18 Bryanstone st. Portman sq
Larkins John Pascal, 67 Chester square
Larkins Mrs. 14 Bedford square
Larkman J. B. esq. 12 Egremont pl. Kg.cr
Laroch John, esq. 45 Clarendon square
Laroche Capt. R.N. 83 Jermyn st
La Roche Philip, esq. 1 Old Quebec st
Lascelles Col. 35 Upper Grosvenor st
Lascelles John, esq. 4 Brick ct. Temple
Lascelles Miss, 35 Up. Grosvenor st
Lascelles Mrs. 37 Hans pl. Sloane st
Lascells Hon. Edwin, 4 Belgrave sq
Lashmar Henry, esq. 8 Cambridge terr
Last Burnard, esq. 12 Portland terrace
Last Fredk. esq. 16 Old sq. Lincoln's inn
Last Wm. esq. 12 Lodge rd. St. John's wd
Latchford Mrs. 4 Alexandr. sq. Brmptn
Laterriere P. esq. 3 Park cot. Pk. vil. ea
Lateward Rev. Jas. F. 10 Notting hill sq
Latham Alfd. esq. 23 Norfolk st. Park la
Latham John H. esq. 5 Cornwall terrace
Latham Jn. Wm. S. M.D. 14 Devonsh. st
Latham Oliver, esq. 44 Jermyn st
Latham Peter Mere, M.D. 36 Grosvnr.st
Latham Rd. esq. 65 Queen's rd. Bayswater
Latham Rt. Gordon, M.D. 29 Up. Suthwk.st
Latimer Mrs. 11 Gloucester crescent
Latimer Sturman, esq. 20 King Wm. st. Str
Latouche Lt. Col. 5 Charles st. Lowndes st
Latreille H. esq. 4 Chapman pl. Gt. Dov.st
Latrobe Rev. Peter, 33 Ely place
Latten R. esq. 4 Grafton st. ea. Tot.ct.rd
Latter Major Gen. 12 Sussex ter. Hy.pk
Latter Chas. esq. 3 Hanover st. Islgtn
Latter Henry, esq. 5 Adelphi terrace
Latter Mrs. 19 Up. Baker st. Regent's pk
Latter Mrs. 48 Park st. Grosvenor sq
Latter Thomas, esq. 16 Grove pl. Liss.gr
Lattey Abraham H. H. esq. 41 Baker st
Lattey Park P. esq. 29 Harley st
Lattey R. J. esq. 2 Claremont pl. St. Jn.'sw
Lattimer Miss, 12 Bridgewater square
Lauder R. S. esq. 35 Charlot.st. Fitzry. sq
Lauder Wm. P. esq. 8 Sloane st
Lauderdale Earl, Warren's hotel, Regent st.; & Thirlstane castle, Berwick; & Dunbar house, East Lothian
Laugher E. C. esq. 17 Sussex pl. Kens.nw.tn
Laurence Mrs. 59 Wimpole st
Laurie Sir Peter, 7 Park sq. Regent's pk
Laurie Geo. esq. 14 Albert rd. Rgnt.'s pk
Laurie George, esq. 62 Chancery lane
Laurie James R. esq. 17 Euston square
Laurie John, esq. 10 Charles st. St. Jas.'s
Laurie John, esq. 1 Hyde park place
Laurie Joseph, M.D. 12 Lr. Berkeley st
Laurie Mrs. 40 Duncan terr. City road
Laurie Peter, esq. 6 Park sq. Regent's park, & 1 Paper buildings, Temple
Laurie Robert, esq. Heralds' college
Laurie Swinton, esq. 36 Argyle st. Nw.rd
Laurier Adolph, esq. 20 Nottingham st
Lauriere Richd. esq. 33 Pembroke sq
Lavenu Louis Henry, esq. 48 Greek st
Laver Hen. esq. 53 Hunter st. Brunsw.sq
Laver Mrs. 53 Hunter st. Brunswick sq
Lavers Wm. esq. 5 Park st. Islington
Lavie Germain, esq. 12 Queen sq Wstmnstr
Lavis John, esq. 4 Gt. George st. Westmnr
Law Hon. Chas. Ewan, Q.C., M.P. 10 Hyde park ter. & Farrar's bldgs. Temple; & Springfield lodge, Taplow, Maidenhead
Law Edmund, esq. 38 Lincoln's inn fields
Law Geo. esq. 5 Montague pl. Russell sq. & 10 New square, Lincoln's inn
Law Geo. Still, esq. 3 New sq. Linc. inn
Law Jas. esq. 18 Fluyder st. Westminstr
Law John Halsey, esq. 8 New sq. Linc. inn
Law Joseph, esq. 90 Blackman st. Boro'
Law Miss, 13 Haberdashers' wk. Hoxton
Law Mrs. 18 Portland place, & Cannon hill, Maidenhead, Berks
Law Mrs. 7 Upper terrace, Islington
Law William, esq. 4 Brunswick square
Law Wm. esq. 15 Fludyer st. Westmnstr
Law Wm. esq. 50 Devonshire st. Portl.pl
Law Wm. John, esq. 63 Up. Seymour st. & Horsted place, near Uckfield
Lawes Serjeant, esq. 40 Woburn place
Lawes Edward, esq. 5 Pump ct. Temple
Lawes Edwd. H. V. S.L. 82 Basinghall st
Lawes Edwd. 15 Nw. Millman st. Bruns.sq
Lawes Miss, 9 Millman st. Bedford row
Lawes Mrs. Londown rd. St. John's wood
Lawes Thos. esq. 5 Canonbury vil. Islgtn
Lawford Lady, 30 Grove end road
Lawford Mrs. 2 Marlboro' pl. Kngtn.crs
Lawless Hon. Cecil, 55 Jermyn st
Lawley Hon. Francis, 29 Berkeley sq
Lawley Hon. Stephen, 29 Berkeley sq
Lawley Sir Francis, bt. 18 Grosvenor sq. Burton cottage, Wenlock, Shropshire; & Myddleton hall, near Fazeley
Lawley B. esq. 4 Up. Vernon st. Lloyd sq
Lawley Hon. Beilby, 29 Berkeley sq
Lawley Hon. Robt. 29 Berkeley square
Lawrance Richard, esq. 27 Arundel st
Lawrance Rd. M. M.D. 27 Arundel st
Lawrell Horatio, esq. 77 Gloucester pl
Lawrell Horatio, esq. 21 Up. Seymour st
Lawrence Rev. Geo. 15 Allsop ter. Nw.rd
Lawrence Capt. John, 15 Regent st
Lawrence B. esq. 79 Camden road villas
Lawrence Charles, esq. 83 Jermyn st
Lawrence Edward B. esq. 2 Mortimer st
Lawrence Effingham, esq. 44 Chancery la
Lawrence George, esq. 52 Cadogan place
Lawrence John, esq. 29 Lincoln's inn fields
Lawrence J. esq. 2 Norwood pl. Kensgtn
Lawrence Harry H. esq. 5 South sq. Gray's i
Lawrence Miss, 11 Bloomsbury square
Lawrence Miss M. 11 Myddelton square
Lawrence M. esq. 6 Blomfield rd. Maida hl
Lawrence Mrs. 6 Marlboro' rd. St. Jhn.'s wd
Lawrence Mrs. 21 Princes st. Hanover sq
Lawrence Mrs. 16 Vincent ter. Islington
Lawrence Mrs. 5 Walcot pl. west, Lmbth
Lawrence Philip Hen. esq. 13 Gray's in sq
Lawrence Thomas, esq. Denmark hill
Lawrence Tertius, esq. 15 Gray's inn sq
Lawrence Wm. esq. 56 Geo. st. Euston sq
Lawrence Wm. esq. 32 Sidmth. st. Gr's.in.r
Lawrence William, esq. 18 Whitehall place, & Ealing park, Middlesex
Lawrie James, esq. 55 Trinity sq. Boro'
Laws Rt. esq. 2 Stanhope ter. Hyde pk
Lawson Andrew, esq. M.P. 26 Pall mall, & the Hall, Boro'bridge, Yorkshire
Lawson Chas. L. esq. 46 Howland st. Fitz s
Lawson Edw. esq. 3 Gower st north
Lawson Hen. esq. 4 Fortess tr. Kntsh.tn
Lawson Jn. Edwd. esq. 49 Trinity sq. Boro
Lawson Martin, esq. 55 Beaumont st
Lawson Miss, 46 Gt. Ormond st. Queen sq
Lawson Thos. esq. 144 Oxford street
Lawson Wm. esq. 13 Cleveland st. Fitzr.sq
Lawson Wm. esq. 19 Stoke Newington gr
Lawton Hugh, esq. 9 Warwick vils. Har.rd
Laxe Mrs. Glo'ster lodge, Regent's pk
Laxton Henry, esq. 145 Strand
Laxton Wm. esq. 10 Fludyer st. Westmr
Lay Joseph, esq. 8 Bolton row, & Dudley
Layard Capt. B. V. M.P., Reform club, & Upper Mount st. Dublin
Layard Capt. R.N. 9 St. Alban's pl. St. James's
Laycock Henry S. esq. 43 Lincoln's inn fi
Layton G. esq. 74 Mount st. Berkeley sq
Layton Thos. esq. 23 Down st

Lazar Rev. N. 70 George st.Portman sq
Lazarus Solomon, esq. 21 Carlton villas
Lea Rev. Henry, 50 Noel st. Islington
Lea John, esq. 22 Ebury st. Pimlico
Lea Miss, 13 Abbey place, St. John's wd
Lea Thos. esq. 28 Cambridge ter.Edg.rd
Lea Wm. esq. 23 Albany st. Regent's pk
LeaWm.L.esq.9Ehrenburgh tr.Mrngtn.r
LeachRev.Wm.Jas.J.13Up.Southwickst
LeachGeo.esq.10 Melina pl.St.John's wd
Leach Joseph,esq.31 Duncan ter.City rd
Leach Mrs. 16 Albion st. Hyde park
LeachR.H.G.esq.44 Cambridge tr.Egw.r
LeachS.F.esq.34 Gloucester st. Queen sq
Leach Thos. esq. 26 Russell square
Leach Thos. jun. esq. Chapel strs. Lnc.in
LeachWm. esq. 3 Windsor ter. Edgw.rd
LeachmanJph.esq.13Compton ter.Up.st
LeachmanJoseph,esq. 18 Aldermanbury
LeachmanThs.esq.20Compton ter.Up.st
Leadbeater Benjn.esq.1Camden rd.villas
Leadbitter Geo. esq. 50 Coleshill st
Leadbitter Thos. esq. 6 Frederick place, Gray's inn road, & 7 Staple inn
LeaderWm.esq.36High st.Camden town
Leaf Edwin,esq. 13 Cumbld.st.Portm.sq
Leahy David, esq.1 Mitre ct.bldgs.Tmpl
Leahy Henry Cane,esq. 5 St.James's sq
Leahy Edward Daniel,esq.13 Berners st
Leake Col.Wm.Martin,50 QueenAnne st
Leake Edwd.Leach,esq.4 Kensington sq
Leake Frederick, esq. 52 Regent st
Leake Geo.esq.2 Titchfield ter.Rgt.'s pk
LeakeStephenR.M.esq.15Nottingham pl
Leake William,esq.45A,UpperHarley st. & Mount Ararat, Wimbledon, Surrey
Lean Lieut. R.N. 70 Lower Thames st
Lean Fras. esq. 10 Park pl. Kenngtn.crs
Lear Chas.H.esq.35London st.Fitzroy sq
LearmonthW.esq.4 Blnhm.pl.St.Jn's.wd
Learmouth Thos. Young, esq. 1B, Albany
Leary John Fredk. esq. 2 Abingdon st
Leath James, M.D. 11 Nottinghill square
Leath J. G. M.D. 11 Nottinghill square
Leatherdale John, esq. 16 Brnsbry. pk
Leathley Mrs. 22 Hyde park gardens
Le Blanc Chas. esq. 23 Grosvenor pl
Le Blanc Chas. esq. 44 Lincoln's inn flds
Le Blanc Chas. esq. 1 Up. Grosvenor st
Le Blanc Geo. esq. 17 Gt.Cumberland st
Le Blanc Wm. E. esq. 18 New Bridge st
Le Blance Miss, 36 Montagu square
Le Blond Abraham, esq. 7 Grove, Tollington park, Hornsey road
Le Blond Robert, esq. 7 Grove, Tollington park, Hornsey road
Le Breton Rev. Philip, 19 Charlotte st
Le Breton Frs. esq. 21 Sussex pl.Reg.pk
Le Breton Php. Hemery, esq. 24 Upper Seymour st. & 44 Castle st.Leicester sq
Lecaan Miss, 7 South st. Finsbury
LeCappelain J.esq. 45 Edwd.'s sq.Kensn
Lechmere Chas. esq. 12 Duke st. Westr
LechmereWm.esq.22Sthmptn. st.Blmby
Leckie Mrs. 2 Kensgtn.ter. Ken.grvl.pts
LeCointeJn.Fras. esq. 33 Up.Bedford pl
Ledgard H. esq. 6 Bedford pl. Russell sq
Ledger Geo. esq. 13 Hamilton pl.New rd
Ledger Rt. esq. 5 Canonbury cottages
Le Despencer Baroness, 2 St.James's sq
Le Dieu Thos. F. esq. 17 College st.Islg
Lee Sir George, 24 Norfolk crescent
Lee —, esq. 2 Marlboro' rd.St.John's wd
Lee Charles, esq. 20 Golden square
Lee Daniel James, esq. 4 Bedford row
Lee Edward, esq. 42 Bryanstone square, & Ditton house, Maidenhead, Berks
Lee Edwd. Stphn. esq. 43 Linc. inn flds
Lee Fras. Valentine, esq. 1 Chester pl. Regent's pk. & 1 King's bench walk
Lee Geo. esq. 5 St.Martin's pl.Chang.cr
LeeH. M.D. 21 Bloomsbury st.St.Giles's
LeeH.J. esq. 6 Claremont row,Barnsb.rd
Lee John, D.C.L. 5 College, Doctors' commons, & Hartwell ho. Aylesbury
Lee John, esq. 8 St.Martin's pl.Chrng.cr
Lee John Benj. esq. 3 Gt.Dean's yard,& Neasdon, near Willesden, Middlesex
LeeJortinWm.esq.25 Cadgn. pl.Sloane st
Lee John Would, esq. 34 Hunter st
Lee Miss, 4 Albert ter. Knightsbridge
Lee Miss, 174 Blackfriars road
Lee Mrs. 10 Cumberland place, New rd
Lee Mrs. 28 Down st. Piccadilly
Lee Mrs. 10 Essex st. Strand
Lee Mrs. 1 Goswell road, west side
Lee Mrs. 58 Sloane st
Lee Mrs. Peter, 71 Myddelton square
Lee Robert, esq. 27 Regent square
Lee Rd. esq. 12 Weymouth st. Prtlnd.sq
Lee Rt. esq. 1 Regent pl.west,Regent sq
Lee Robert, M.D. F.R.S. 4 Saville row
Lee Saml. esq. 13 Claremont ter. Pentvl
Lee Thos. esq. 85 Blackfriars road
Lee Thos. 5 Somers pl. Hyde park
LeeThos.S.esq.2Up.Gordon st.Euston sq
Lee Timothy, esq. 27 Barnsbury park
LeeW. esq. 4 Old Dorset pl.Clapham rd
LeeWm. esq. 17 Chesham st.Belgrave sq
Lee Wm. esq. 16 Howland st. Fitzroy sq
Lee Wm. esq. Q.C. 58 Chancery lane
LeeWm.A.esq.29Chapel st.Grosvenor pl
Leece Mrs. 40 Queen Anne st
Leech Edward, esq. 32 Brompton row
LeechJohn, esq. 3 Felix pl. Liverpool rd
LeechJohn,esq. 9 Powispl.Gt.Ormond st
Leech Mrs. 26 Michael's pl. Brompton
Leeds, Duke of, Clarendon hotel, New Bond st. & Hornby castle, Catteric
Lee Gassick John, esq. 221 Maida vale
LeesJas. esq. 1 Elm tree rd.St.John's wd
Leese Jn. esq. 8 Haberdashers' pl. west
Leeson J. esq. 6 Edwards sq. Kensington
Leete J. esq. 10 Foster lane
Lefebure Miss, 42 York st. Portman sq
Lefevre Rt. Hon. Charles Shaw, M.P. 71 Eaton sq. & Heckfield pl.Hartford bdg
LefevreSirGeo.M.D. 60 Brook st.Gros.sq
Lefevre Hen. Shaw, esq. 31 Hertford st
Lefevre Mrs. 1 Claremont ter. Pentnvle
LefroyAnthony, M.P. 18 Chesham place, Belgrave sq. & Carrickglass, Longford, Ireland
Lefroy Geo. Bentinck, esq. 217 Piccadil
LefroyThos.Ed.P. esq. 5 Pump ct.Temp
Leftley Chas. D. esq. 1 Carlisle st. Soho
Legg Cyrus, esq.1Berwick pl.Grange rd
Legg George, esq. 10 South sq. Gray's inn, & 239 Maida vale
Legg Miss, 2 Melcombe pl. Dorset sq
Leggat Benj. esq. 5 Annett's cres. Isln
Legge Richard Henry, esq. Grove villa, 6 Finchley New road
Leggett Wm.esq.8 Union st.Berkeley sq
Legh Edward, esq. 95 Regent street, & the Limes, Lewisham, Kent
Legh Geo. Cornwall, M.P.Carlton club, 94 Pall mall,& High Legh,Warrington
Legh Mrs. 26 Bedford square
Legh Thomas, esq. 68 Mount st
Legrand Mrs. 11 Up. Glo'ster pl.Chelsea
Legrew Misses,1Ladbroke pl.Notting hl
Leifchild Rev. J. DD.6 Camden st. south
Leifchild Miss, 7 University st
Leifchild W. esq. 3 Montague pl.Rusl.sq
Leigh Lord,30 Portman square,& Stoneleigh Abbey, Coventry
Leigh Hon. Mrs. 30 Portman square
Leigh Hon. Mrs. George, Great court St. James's palace
Leigh Col. Great ct. St. James's palace
Leigh Henry,esq.1New sq. Lincoln's inn
Leigh Rev. Jas. 15 Up. Kennington gn
Leigh Rev. Thos. 39 King Wm. st. City
Leigh Jas. esq. Willow cott. Acacia rd
Leigh Percival, esq. 10 Bedford st
Leighton Mrs. 2 Surrey st. Strand
Leinster, Duke of, P.C. 6 Carlton house terrace, & Carlton house, Maynooth
Leitch Rd. jun. esq. 25 Mornington pl
Leith Jas. esq.21 Alpha rd. Regent's pk
Leith Mrs. 26 Connaught terrace
Leith Mrs. 2 Glo'ster cresct. Regent's pk
Leith W.H.esq.15Montagu st.Portmn.sq
Leitrim, Earl of, K.P. 18 Great Cumberland pl.& Killadoon,Celbridge,Ireland
Lemale T. esq. 62 Chandos st. Covt.gard
Leman Henry, esq. 44 York terrace, Regent's pk. & 51 Lincoln's inn fields
Leman James, esq. 29 Chester terrace, Regent's pk. & 51 Lincoln's inn fields
Lemann Chas. Morgan, M.D. 34 Soho sq
Le Marchant Sir Denis, 7 Harley street, & Chobham park, Surrey
Le Marchant Mrs. 28 Wimpole st
Lemare Joshua, esq. 8 Highbury place
Le Moinne Lewis, esq. 29 Poultry, & 20 Coventry st. Haymarket
Lemon Sir Chas. bart. M.P.46Charles st. Berkeley sq. & Carlew, near Penryn
Lemon Miss, 6 Upper Porchester st
Lemon Misses, 8 Upper Brook st
Lemon Mrs. 6 Camden cottages
Lemon Mrs. 10 Chesterfield st. New rd
Lemon Robert, esq. 62 London wall
Lemon Robt. esq. 6 Stafford rw. Pimlico
Lemoyne Misses, Loudoun villa, Loudoun road, St. John's wood
Lennard Sir Thos. Barrett, bart. 40 Bryanstone sq. & Belhus, near Ongar
Lennard Geo. Barrett, esq. 1 Figtree ct
Lennard John B. esq.12York gt.Regt.pk
Lennard Mrs. 17 Norfolk st. Park lane
Lennard Thomas Barrett, esq. 9 Hyde park terrace, & Rottingdean, Sussex
Lennox Lord Arthur, M.P. & Lady, 10 Chesham place, Belgrave square
Lennox Lord George, 33 St James's st
Lennox Lord Wm. Pitt, 1 Berkeley sq
Lenthall Edmund Hy. esq. 10 Staple inn
Lenthall Frank Kyffin, esq. 33 Mount st
Lenton Chas. S. esq. 33 Leicester square
Leon Joseph Isaac, esq.28 Hyde park sq
Leonard James, esq.18 Craven st.Strand
Leonard Wm. S. esq. 3 York place, Fulham road, & 34 Bedford st.Cov.garden
Leonino I. esq. 10 Gt. Cumberland st
LeopardJohn,esq.Sidney house,Wheeler place, Hampstead road
LepardSaml.esq.31Nwngtn.pl. Kngn. rd
Lépée Edward,esq. 90Upper Seymour st
Lerew Fredk.H.esq.17Edwd.st.Hamp.rd
Lerew Wm. H. esq. 41 Upper Norton st
Lerew Wm. K.esq.10North st. Edgw. rd
Le Roy Mademoiselle,42 Upp.Norton st
Leslie Charles P.esq.M.P. 3 Upper Harley st. & Glasslough, Monaghan
Leslie C.R.esq.12PineApple pl.Edgw.rd
Leslie D.A.esq. 9 Brunswick para. Pntvl
Leslie Francis S. esq. 113 Piccadilly
Leslie James, esq. 34 Kensington square
Leslie John, esq.7 Mitre court chambers
Leslie Mrs. 3 Upper Harley street, & Glasslough castle, Ireland
Leslie Patrick, M.D. 27 Wilton place
Leslie R. esq.17ElmTree rd.St.John's wd
Leslie T.C.esq.9Brunswick para. Pntnvl
Lester Mrs.2 Bullingham pl. Kensgtn
Lester Rd. esq. 10 Litchfield st. Soho
L'Estrade Alex. esq. 12 Burton crescent
L'Estrange Lieut.Gen.77 Sth. Audley st
L'Estrange Francis, esq. 12 Gower st. north, & 28 Euston place, Euston sq
Lett Mrs. 1 Stockwell cres. Claphm. rd
Lettis John W. esq. 39 Noel st. Islngtn
Letts Rev. John, 8 Hart st. Crutchedfrs
Letts John,esq.8 Bartlett's bldgs. Holbn
Letts Mrs. 3 Montague pl. Clapham rd
LettsomWm.N.esq.14Lowndes st.Blg.sq
Leuty John A. esq. 30 Up. Berkeley st
Leven & Melville Earl, 3 Arlington st. & Melville house, Cupar, Fife
Lever Chas. esq. 10 King's rd. Bedfd. rw
Lever Mrs. 44 St. James's place
Leveson Visct. M.P. 16 Bruton st. & Aldenham, near Bridgenorth
Leveson Gower Hon. F. 16 Bruton st
Levesque Peter, esq. 29 Guilford st

Levet Philip S. esq. 6 Albert road
Levi Samuel M. esq. 149 Leadenhall st
LevienC.esq.5 Calthorpe st.Gray's inn rd
Levien Edw.esq.13 Upper Woburn place
Levison Saml. esq. 9 Sussex gardens
Levy Abraham, esq. 32 Finsbury sq
Levy Abraham, esq. 46 Gt. Coram st
Levy Jonas, esq. 55 Tavistock square
Levy Joseph, esq. 41 Gt. Coram st
Levy Joseph, esq. 6 South st. Finsbury
Levy Joseph Moses, esq. 41 Gt.Coram st
Levy Laurence, esq. 28 Finsbury square
Levy Lewis, esq. 55 Tavistock square
Levy Mrs. 7 Haydon square, Minories
Levy Mrs. 13 North buildings, Finsbury
Levy Nathaniel, esq. 22 Woburn place
Levy S. A. esq. 37 Upper Gower st
Levyson Montague, esq. 18 Queen sq
Lewellin Danl. esq. 15 Cook's ct. Serle st
LewellinR.esq.1Up.Georgest.Bryston.sq
Lewer Wm. Hen.esq.3 Duke st. Westmr
Lewes E. F. M.esq.16Lower Belgrave st
Lewin Geo.esq.7 Circus rd.St.John's wd
Lewin Geo. H. esq. 42 Pall mall
Lewin Hen.esq.30 Pelham rd.Brompton
LewinHy.esq.8St.Martin's pl.Char.cross
Lewin Mrs. 20 Sussex gardens, Hyde pk
Lewin Thos. esq. 34 Harleyfrd. pl. Kngn
Lewin Thos. esq. 21 Old sq.Lincoln's inn
Lewis Thomas, esq.4 Raymond bldgs
Lewis Rt. Hon. Thomas Frankland, 21 Grafton st. & Harpton ct. nr. Kington
Lewis Capt.Chas.A.25Wilton pl.Belg.sq
Lewis Rev. Benj. 56 Trinity sq. Boro'
Lewis Rev. Geo. Wm. 65 Up. Stamfd. st
Lewis Rev. T. 15 Compton ter. Islingtn
Lewis Rev. Thos. 7 Suffolk st. Pall mall
Lewis Rev.Wm.47 Westbornetr.Hyde pk
Lewis A.J.esq.29Hanspl.&58Chancery la
Lewis Benj. esq. 22 Carlton vils. Edg. rd
Lewis Benjamin, esq.9 Gray's inn square
Lewis B.L.esq.14Cornwall ter.Rgt.'s pk
Lewis Chas. esq. 4 Belgrave st. south
Lewis Chas. esq. 9 Grosvenor st.Bond st
Lewis Chas. esq. 7 Lodge rd.Regent's pk
Lewis Chas. V. esq. 25 Woburn pl. & 14 Warwick court, Gray's inn
Lewis David,esq.4Chesham pl.Belgrave square, & Stradey, near Llanelly
Lewis Edward, esq. 7 Adam st. Adelphi
Lewis Edward, esq. 8 Kensington sq
Lewis Fred. esq. 64 St. John's wood terr
Lewis Fred. esq. 7 Lyon's inn, & 6 London terrace, Hackney road
LewisF.C.esq.53Charlotte st.Portlandpl
Lewis Geo. esq. 25 Park st.Grosvenor sq
Lewis Geo. esq. Queen's mews, Pimlico
Lewis Geo. C. esq. South pl.Knightsbdg. & Grove mill ho. Watford, Herts
Lewis Geo. Coleman Hamilton, esq. 25 Woburn place, & 10 Ely place
Lewis Geo.Hen. esq. 2 Campden hill ter
Lewis Geo. R. esq. 61 Up. Norton st. Fitzroy square
Lewis Geo. Vallancey, esq. 11 Warwick ct. Gray's inn, & 25 Woburn place
LewisHarmanH.esq.8Gt.Queen st.Wsm
Lewis Hen. esq. 7Devonshire st.Prtld.pl
Lewis Hen. Rt. esq. 12 Up. Montagu st
Lewis Jas. esq. 25 Park st.Grosvenor sq
Lewis James, esq. 20 University st
Lewis JamesGraham, esq. 10 Ely place, & 25 Woburn place
Lewis Jas. Henry F. esq. 28 Essex st
Lewis Jn.esq.23Southampton pl.Eust.sq
Lewis John, esq. 7 Arundel st. Strand
Lewis Jn. esq. 13 Crescent pl. Morn.crst
Lewis John, esq. 5 Park pl. Regent's pk
Lewis John R. esq. 2 Field ct.Gray's inn
Lewis Kensington, esq. 18 Stratford pl
Lewis Miss, 1 Trafalgar sq. Chelsea
Lewis Miss, 25 Wilton pl. Belgrave sq
Lewis Mrs. Col. 22 Cadogan place
Lewis Mrs. Bedford pl. Clapham rise
Lewis Mrs. 4 Campden hill ter. Knsgtn
Lewis Mrs. 7 Edwardes sq. Kensington
Lewis Mrs. 27 Grosvenor place
Lewis Mrs. 21 Grove place, Brompton
Lewis Mrs. 71 Harley st. Cavendish sq
Lewis Mrs.Prospect house, Earl's court
Lewis Mrs. 10 Porchester terrace
Lewis Owen, esq. Clapham rise
Lewis Richd.J.esq.8Percy st.Bedford sq
Lewis Samuel, esq. 20 Highbury place
Lewis Thos. esq.70Baker st.Portman sq
Lewis Thos. esq. 2 Percy st. Bedford sq
LewisThos.A.esq.10Dean's pl.So.Lmbth
Lewis Thos. Day, esq. 58 Cadogan pl
Lewis T.E.esq.14 Wellngtn.tr.St.Jns.wd
Lewis Thos. H. esq. 9 John st. Adelphi
Lewis Thos.H.jun.esq.70Bakr.st.Ptm.sq
Lewis Wm.esq.2Blomfield rd.Maida hill
Lewis Wm. esq. 24 Up. Seymour st.west
Lewis William, esq. 4 Woburn place, & 6 Raymond buildings, Gray's inn
LewisWm.Dav.esq.3New sq.Lincln.'sin
Lewis Wm. Stone, esq. 5 Sussex place, Regent's park; 14 New Bridge st.; & Wood hall, Shenley, Herts
Ley Henry, esq. 51 Chester square
Ley John Hen. esq. & Lady Frances, 4 Richmond ter. & Tray hill, Exeter
Ley Mrs. 5 Bloomfield ter. Pimlico
Ley Walter, esq. 23 New Millman st
Ley William, esq. 15 Queen st.Mayfair, & Woodlands, near Exeter
Leybourn Mrs.17A,Holland pl.Clapm.rd
Leyburn Wm. esq. 84 Cadogan place
Leyland Mrs. 27 Tibberton square
Lichfield Earl of, P.C. at present abroad
Lichfield & Coventry,Bishop of,39 Harley st. & Castle, Eccleshall
Liddard Wm.esq. 2 Park villas,Not.hill
Liddel Howard, esq. 24 Milner sq. Isln
Liddel Hon.Adolphus, 17 Serjeants' inn, Fleet st
Liddell Hon. Capt. & Mrs.17 Lowndes st
Liddell Hon. Henry Thos. M.P. Carlton club, & Ravensworth castle, Durham
Liddell John, esq. 1 Manchester sq
Liddell Joseph, esq. 56 Connaught ter
Liddell Wm. esq. 3 Harcourt buildings
Lidderdale Halliday, M.D. 6 Blandford sq
Liddiard Thos. esq. 11 St. George's ter
Lievesley Morris,esq.Foundling hospital, & 49 Camden road vils. Cmdn. town
Liggins Joseph, esq. Addison rd. south
Lightfoot Geo. esq. 16 North bk. Rgt. pk
Lightfoot Hen.W. esq. 26 Castlest.Lei.sq
Lightfoot Mrs. 8 Upper Baker st
Lightfoot Patrick T. esq. 14 James st. Buckingham gate
Lightfoot Saml. esq. 8 Claremont ter
Lightfoot Thos.esq. 10 OldBurlingtn. st.; 26 Castle st. Leicr.sq.; Crowle Thorne, Yorkshire; & Seven Oaks, Kent
Lightfoot Wm. Herbert, esq. 5 Charles st. Westbourne terrace
Lilburn Mrs. 24 Harley st
Liley Chas. esq. 3 Bloomfield ter. Pimli
Lilford Lord, 10 Grosvenor place; & Lilford hall, Oundle; & Bewsay hall, Warrington
Lilley John, esq. 19 Newman st
Lilleyman John, esq. 24 Claremont sq
Lilly Jn. esq. 16½ Church st. Spitalfields
Lilly Samuel, esq. 9 Inner Temple lane
Lincoln, Rt. Hon. Earl of, M.P. 19 Whitehall pl. & Ranby hall, near Retford
Lincoln, Bishop of, 1 Regent st.; & Willingham, Market Raisin
Lincoln Abrm. esq. 33 Highbury place
Lincoln Stroud, esq.8 Alexr.sq.Bromptn
Lindesay Miss. 58 Up. Seymour st
Lindley John, esq. 21 Regent st
Lindley Rt. esq. 22 Percy st. Bedford sq
Lindley William, esq. 8 Adelphi terrace
Lindly Miss, 6 Ladbroke villas, Not.hl
Lindo Benj. E. esq. 31 Queen Anne st
Lindo Moses Da Costa, esq. 24 Finsb. sq
Lindo Nethaneel, esq. 24 Finsbury sq
Lindon Wm. esq. 11 Sussex ter. Hyde pk
Lindsay Lady Charlotte, 47 Green st
Lindsay Lord, 21 Berkeley square
Lindsay Capt.7 Stanhope ter. Hyde pk
Lindsay Hon. Mrs. 22 Berkeley sq
LindsayHon.Capt.Jas.M.P.21Berkely.sq
Lindsay Col. & Mrs. 11 Grosvenor sq
Lindsay Edwd. esq. 14 Mornington cres
Lindsay Fred. Hugh, esq. 13 Montagu st
Lindsay Hugh H. M.P. 22 Berkeley sq
Lindsay Jas. esq. 54 King sq. Goswell rd
Lindsell Henry, esq. 33 Grove end road
Lindsell John, esq. 24 Old sq. Linc. inn
Lindsell John, esq. 27 Torrington sq
Lindsell Wm. esq. 8 Fortess tr. Kentsh.tn
Lindsey, Earl of,Uffington,nearStamford
Lindsey Mrs. 14 Dorset pl. Dorset sq
Lindsey Mrs. 30 Upper Seymour st
Lindsey Mrs. 7 York st. Portman sq
Lindsey Thos. esq. 7 Baker st. Clerkenwl
Line John, esq. 6 Hanover st. Hanover sq
Line John, esq. 11 Addle st. Wood st
Lineker Mrs. 17 Beaufort st. Chelsea
Lingard Rd. B. M. esq. 7 Furnival's inn
Lingen Ralph Rt.W. esq. 25 Lincoln's inn
Linnell John, esq. 38 Porchester terrace
Linton John, esq. 70 Coleshill st
Linton Wm. esq. 7 Lodge pl. Lodge rd
Lintott Thos. esq. 12 Colebrooke ter
Lintott Wm. Henry, esq. 69 Welbeck st
Linwood Js. esq. 13 Cole's tr. Barnsb. rd
Lisboa Commandeur Marquess, envoy extraordinary & minister plenipotentiary from H. M. the emperor of Brazil, 10 York place, Portman square
Lismore Viscount, Farrance's hotel, Belgrave st. & Shanbally castle,Tipperary
List Thomas M. esq. 14 Clifford's inn
Lister Daniel, esq. 23 Berkeley square
Lister Daniel Neale, esq. 3 Gray's inn sq
Lister IsaacS.esq.6Rodneyst.Pentonville
ListerJ. esq. 25 Edward st. Langham pl
Lister Mrs. 37 Claremont sq. Pentonville
ListerNath.M.D.15Manchr.bdgs.Westmr
Lister Wm. esq.15 Manchr.bdgs.Westmr
Liston John, esq. 14 St. George's pl
Lister Wm. esq. 14 Annetts cres. Isln
Liston Robt. esq. 5 Clifford st. Bond st
Listowel, Earl of, M.P. Kingston house, Knightsbridge, & Fermoy, Ireland
Listowel,Dowag.Countess of,78Eaton sq
LitchfieldCapt.R.N.31Glo'ster pl.New rd
Litchfield Chas. esq. 2 Nottingham pl
Litchfield Elijah, esq. 89 Chancery lane, & 12 Kensington square
Litherland John, esq. 22 Brunswick st. Barnsbury rd
Litt Miss, 42 Kensington square
Little Rev. J. 19 Rutland st. Hampst. rd
Little Augustus Fdk. esq. 1 Dorset sq
Little George, esq. 11 New sq. Linc. inn
LittleThos.esq.36 Nrthmbrld.st.Maryleb
Little William, esq. 17 Portland place
Little Wm. esq. 49½ Trinity sq. Boro'
Little Wm. John, esq. M.D. 10 Finsby.sq
Littledale Lady, 5 Bedford square
Littledale Charles, esq. 42 Portland pl
Littledale Henry, esq. 33 Harley street, & Cardington, Bedfordshire
Littledale H. A. esq. 8 King's bench wk
Littler Rev. Robert, 14 Cloudesley st
Littler Reading, esq. 10 Eaton terrace
Littlewood John, esq. 14 Lowr. Eaton st
Littlewood J. esq. 13 Barnsbury villas
Littlewort Chas. J. esq. 12 NewBridge st
LiveingCapt.W. 183 Prospect pl. Edg. rd
Liverpool, Earl of, P.C. Middle Scotland yard; Buxted park, Uckfield; & Pitchford hall, Shrewsbury
Livesey Joseph, esq. 42 Sackville st. Piccadilly
Living Mrs. 18 Clapham rd. place
Lizardi I. de Manuel, esq. 81 Harley st
Llandaff, Bishop of, Deanery, St. Paul's, & Hardwick house, Chepstow
Llewellyn Miss,1Eldon pl.Up.Kengtn la. & Hardwick house, Chepstow

Lloyd Capt. 3 Upper Brook st. Grosv.sq
Lloyd Rev. Wm. 144 Oxford st. & Norbury rectory, Newport, Shropshire
Lloyd Dd. esq. 51 London st. Fitzroy sq
Lloyd Edmund, esq. 22 Lowndes st
Lloyd Edward, esq. 34 Bedford place
Lloyd Edwd. esq. 27 Gt.College st.Westr
Lloyd Edward John, esq. 9 Old sq. Lincoln's inn, & Coom's hill, Blackheath
Lloyd Eusebius A. esq. 14 Bedford row
Lloyd Francis, esq. 27 Bedford square
Lloyd Francis, esq. 10 Crown office row, Temple, & Beaufort house, Chelsea
Lloyd F. B. M.D.4Up.Phillimr.pl.Knsgtn
Lloyd George John, esq. 49 Doughty st
Lloyd Hy. esq. 22 Gt. James st.Bdfd.rw
Lloyd Henry, esq. 59 Lincoln's inn fields
Lloyd Hen. esq. 9 St. James's place
Lloyd Hen. esq. 44 Weymouth st.Portl.pl
Lloyd Hen. Evans, esq. 12 Charterho. sq
Lloyd Hubert, esq. 11 Gt. St. Helens
Lloyd Hugh, esq. 34 Gerrard st. Soho
Lloyd J. H. esq. 25Nthumbrld.st.New rd
Lloyd John Horatio, esq. 15 Park place, Regent's park, & 1 King's bench walk
LloydMorgan,esq.N.Temp.bdgs.Mitre ct
Lloyd Miss, 4 Glo'ster rd. Vic. gt. Hy.pk
Lloyd Mrs. 112 Glo'ster pl. Portman sq
LloydMrs.22Gt.May's bdgs.St.Mrtn.'s la
Lloyd Mrs. 27 Oxford ter. Edgware rd
Lloyd Mrs. 8 Warwick court, Holborn
Lloyd Mrs. 22 Westbourne pl. Pimlico
Lloyd Mrs. S. 19 Clapham road place
Lloyd Rt. esq. 29 Cambridge sq.Hyde pk
Lloyd Thomas, esq. 55 York ter. Reg. pk
Lloyd Thomas Wm. esq. 97B, Regent st
Lloyd Thos. E. esq. 5 New sq. Linc. inn
Lloyd Wm. F. esq. 4 Highbury park west
Lloyd Wm. Fras.Hen. esq. 35 Lonsdale sq
LloydWm. Horton,esq.1 Park sq.Rgt.pk. & Lordship ho. Gt.Hadham,near Ware
LoadenWm. esq. 32 Gt. James st.Bdfd.rw
Loch James, esq. M.P. 12 Albemarle st. & Wimbledon common, Surrey
Loch Wm. Adam, esq. 12 Albemarle st. & 21 Old square, Lincoln's inn
Lochner Chrstphr. Pelley, esq. Grove ho. Old Brompton, & 12 Gt. Carter lane
Lock Capt. Robert, 84 Wimpole st
Lock Jas. esq. 19 Buckingham st. Strnd
Lock Mrs. 6 Up. Cheyne row, Chelsea
Lock Rob. Fred. esq. 8 New inn, Wych st. & Castelnau, Barnes, Surrey
Lock Thos. A. esq. 18 Surrey st. Strand
Locke Capt. John, 2Up.Fitzroy st.Fitz.sq
Locke J. esq. 25James st. Buckingham gt
Locke Jn. esq. 2 Harcourt bdgs. Temple
Locke Joseph, esq. 6 Chester terrace, Regent's park, & 11 Adam st. Adelphi
Locke Mrs. 48 Sloane st
Locke Mrs. 32 London st. Fitzroy sq
Locke W. esq. 2 Judd st. Brunswick sq
Locket Geo. esq. 6 Acton pl. Camden rd
Lockett Jn.Wm.esq.27Pelham cre.Ful.rd
Lockett Mrs. 16 Southampton pl. Eust.sq
Lockey C. esq. 24 Percy st. Bedford sq
Lockhart John Gibson, esq. 24 Sussex pl
Lockhart William, M.P. Carlton club, 94 Pall mall, &Milton Lockart,nr.Lanark
LockleyThos.esq.6 St.George's pl.Kngtsb
Lockman E. esq. 3 Prospect pl.Wndsw.rd
Lockwood Jsph.esq.6Child's pl.Tmpl.bar
Lockwood Mrs. 13 St. John's wood road
Lockwood Wm. Joseph, esq. 66 Pall mall
Lockyer E. L. esq. Cavendish hotel, 81 Jermyn st. & Maids causeway, Cmbg
Lockyer Jas. esq. 19 Sthamptn.st. Fitz.sq
Lockyer John, esq. 17 Colebrooke row
Locock Charles, M.D. 26 Hertford st
Locock George, esq. 8 Noel st. Islngtn
Loder Edwd. esq. Grove ter. Kentish tn
Loder Mrs. 27 Grove pl. Lisson grove
Loder John, esq. 165 Albany st
Lodge Adam, esq. 5 Brick court, Temple
Lodge Saml. esq. 7 Coles ter. Brnsby. rd
Loft James, esq. 29 Clipstone st
Loftus James, esq. 10 New inn, Strand
Loftus Wm. esq. 10 Devonsh. st.Queen sq
Logan Col. Queen's road, St. John's wd
Logan Hart, esq. 4 York gate, Rgnt.'spk
LoganWm. Thos. esq. Up.Kennington gn
Lomas Wm. esq. Deans pl. South Lamth
Lomax Edm.esq. Leonard vil. St.Jhn.'swd
Lomax Edwd. esq.Circus rd. St.Jhn.'swd
Lomax Henry, esq. 13 Old Quebec st
Lomax Jas. esq. 40 Dorset st. Portman sq
Lomax John, esq. 21 Paddington green
Lomax Mrs. 21 Montpelier sq. Brompton
London, Bishop of, P.C. 22 St. James's square, & Palace, Fulham
London Mrs. Addison ctg. Addison road
LondonW.J.G.esq.23Old sq.Lincoln's inn
London & Dublin Bank, 46 Piccadilly
London Joint Stock Bank (western branch), 69 Pall mall
London & Westminster Bank (western branches), 1 St. James's square, & 4 Stratford place
Londonderry, Marquis of, G.C.B.,G.C.H., B.E.,S.P.,P.C. Holderness house, Park lane; Wynyard park, Stockton; Seaham hall, Sunderland; Rose Bank, Fulham; and Mount Pleasant, Newtonards, Ireland
Loney T. C. esq. 26Wakefield st.Regt. sq
Long Major, 29 Wilton pl. Belgrave sq
Long Rev. Thos. 78 Dean st. Soho
Long Charles, esq. 103 Ebury st
Long Chas. E. esq. 88 Mount st.Grosvr.sq
Long Fred. B. esq. 35 Lincoln's inn fields
Long Fredk. B. esq. 7 Campden hill vils
Long F. J. esq. 16 Up.Phillimore pl.Knsn
Long Gainsford, esq. 43½ Vincent square
Long Geo. esq. 4 Charles st. Mnchstr. sq
Long Geo. esq. 81 Wimpole st. & Marylebone police court
Long H.H. esq. 16Up. Phillimore pl.Knsn
Long John, esq. 56 Clarendon square
Long John, esq. Harrow road
Long John, esq. 12 Symons st. Chelsea
Long John, esq. 7 Windmill st. Tot. ct. rd
Long JohnWakeman, esq. 44 Linc's. inn fi
Long Miss, 24 Beaufort st. Chelsea
Long Miss, 18 Spencer ter. Lr. rd. Islgn
Long Mrs. 2 Derby st. Gray's inn road
Long Mrs. 2 Harcourt st
Long Pierce, esq. 25 New Millman st
Long Walter, esq. M.P.29 Hill st. Berkeley sq. & Rood Ashton, nearTrowbridge
Long Thomas, esq. 1 Philpot lane
Long Wm.esq.31 Brook st. Grosvenor sq
Long Wm. esq. 47 Nelson square
LongWm.esq.5Queen's pl.Kennington rd
LongWm.C.esq.21Southamptn.st.Blmby
Longbottom Robt. esq. 5 Cavendish sq
Longbottom Robt.Isaac,esq.10 Cornwall crescent, Camden town; 309 Regent st.; & 5 Cavendish square
Longbottom Robt. Joseph, esq. 7 Moccas cottages, Camden New town
Longbourne Wm. Thos. esq. 4 South sq. Gray's inn, & Grays Thurrock, Essex
Longden Geo.esq.37 Argyle st.King's crs
Longden Thos. H. esq. 1A, Hyde pk. pl
Longdon Jno. esq. 14Lr.Ashby st. Clkwl
Longe Mrs. 22 Allsop terrace, New rd
Longfellow Misses, 11Up.Berkeley st. w
Longford, Countess of, 24 Bruton st. & Pakenham hall, Westmeath
Longford, Earl of, 24Bruton st.& Pakenham hall, Westmeath
Longhurst Wm. esq. 28 Norfolk st
LonglowRt.esq.6 Powis pl.Gt.Ormond st
Longman Mrs. 24 Coleshill st. Pimlico
Longman Mrs.13 Dorset pl.n.Clapham r
Longman Wm. esq. 36 Hyde park sq
LongmanThos. esq.2Hanover ter.Rgt.pk
Longmore Geo. esq. 2 Lansdowne place
Lonsdale, Earl of, P.C., F.R.S., F.S.A. 14 Carlton house terrace; Lowther castle, Penrith; & Whitehaven castle, Cumberland
Lonsdale Edward F. esq. 82 Guilford st
Lonsdale Jas. J.esq.52 Lincoln's inn flds. & 7 Park cottages, Park village east
Lonsdale Mrs. 31 Henrietta st. Cov. gn
Lonsdale Rd. esq.7 Park cots. Regt.'s pk
Lonsdale Richd. esq. Temple chambers, Fleet st.&2 St.Alban's pl.Hammersmh
LonsdaleWm.esq.D evnshre.pl.Wdsth.rd
Lonsdale Wm.esq.5Old sq. Lincoln's inn
Loosley Wm.esq. 12 Strahan ter. Lvpl.rd
Lopes Sir Ralph, M.P. 46 Up. Grosvenor st. & Maristow, Plymouth
Lopez D.Juan Antonio, 30 Weymouth st
Lopez Ramon de B. esq. 14 Sussex grdns
Lorant Lewis, esq. 7 Seymour crescent
Lord James, esq. 3 Elm court, Temple
Lord Jas. esq. 1 Lonsdale sq. Islington
Lord Jno. esq. Augus.cot. Park vil. east
Lord Jn.esq.4Howley pl. villas, Padngtn
Lord Mrs. 5 Baker st. Portman square
Lord Mrs. 13 Pembroke sq. Kensington
Lord Wm. Hind, esq. 17 Brunswick sq
Lorkin John, esq. 24 Aldersgate st
Lorton Viscount, 18 Chesham place, & Rockingham, Boyle, Roscommon
Lothian Mrs. Loudoun rd. St.John's wd
Lott Mrs. 17 Petersburgh pl. Bayswater
Louch Wm. esq. 12 Buckingham st
Loudon Mrs. 3 Porchester ter. Bayswatr
Loudonsack & Case,1 James st. Adelphi
Lough John G. esq.42 Harewood square
Loughborough Vis. 6 Grosvenor place
Louis Jas. esq. 44 Leicester square
LousadaGeo.E.B.esq.9Glo'ster rd.Hy.pk
Lousada Mrs. 16 Sussex pl. Regent's pk
Lovaine Lord, 8 Portman square
Lovat Lord, Brooke's,& Beaufort house, Beauly, N.B.
Lovat Saml. esq. 14 Montagu st. Portman sq. & 2 Stone blds. Lincoln's inn
Love James, esq. 11 Grosvenor row,Piml
Love John, esq. 12 Brook st. Grosvn. sq
Love Mrs.17 Southampton st. Bloomsby
Love Mrs. 49 Upper Berkeley st
Lovekin Mrs. 21 Regent's vils.Avenue rd
Lovelace Earl,10 St.James's sq.; & Ockham park, Ripley, Surrey; & Ashleycombe, Postock, Somerset
Loveland Miss, 24 Park pl. west Lvl. rd
Loveland Thos. M. esq. 6 Lincoln's inn fields, & Shawfield cottage, King's rd. Chelsea
LovellChas.H.esq.14South sq.Gray's inn
Lovell Chas. Wells, esq. 14 Rodney st. Pentonville, & 14 South square
Lovell Geo. esq. 12 Ely place, Holborn
Lovell Geo. Wm. esq. 6 Mornington cres
Lovell Miss, 125 Albany st. Regent's pk
Lovell Mrs. 34 Theberton st. west
Lovell Wm. esq. 45 Cumming st. Pntnvl
Lovell Wm. esq. 4 Gt. Ryder st. St.Jas's
Lovell Wm. jun. esq. 20 Swinton st
Lovelock Edwd. esq. 9 Milner st. Isling
Loveridge John,esq. 11 Grove pl. Lis. gr
Lovesy Conway W. esq. 4Brick ct.Templ
Lovett Mrs. Sycamore cot. Lit. Chelsea
Lovewell Capt. John, 15 Regent st
Lovibond G. B. M. esq. 23 Manchester sq
Lovibond Hen. esq. Manor vil.Wndw.rd
Low Archd. M'Arthur,esq.65Chanceryln
Low David, esq. 47 Berners st
Low James, esq. 39 Museum st. Blmsby
Low Joseph, esq. 28 Lower Smith st
Low Robt. esq. 24 Keppel st. Russell sq
Low Wm. Francis, esq. 67 Wimpole st
Lowden John Dawson, esq.42Doughty st
Lowe John, esq. 7 Montague pl. Russell sq. & 2 Tanfield court, Temple
Lowe John, esq. 26 Norfolk crescent
Lowe John Wm. esq. 1 Park cottages, Regent's park, & 3 Elm ct. Temple
Lowe Mrs. 230 Maida vale, Edgware rd
Lowe Mrs. 13 Park st. Westminster
Lowe Robert Manley, esq. 10 Mecklenburgh st. & 2 Tanfield court, Temple
Lowe Wm. esq. 2 Allsop ter. New road

LoweWm.esq. 3 Buckingham pl.O.Kt.rd
Lowe Wm. esq. 11 Montague st. Russell square, & 2 Tanfield ct. Temple
LowerEdwd.Wm.esq.23Parkwk.Chelsea
Lowless Joseph, esq. 33 Gordon st. Gordon sq. & 2 Hatton ct. Threadneedle st
Lowman Hen. esq. 6Powis pl.Hmpstd.rd
Lowndes Alfred, esq. 31 St. Mary axe
Lowndes John Jas. esq. 5 Hare ct. Temp
Lowndes Mrs. 34 Connaught terrace
Lowndes Robt. esq. 34 Connaught ter
Lowndes Thos. Mee, esq. 84 Eaton pl
Lowndes Wm. Loftus, esq Q.C. 22 Qn.sq. Blmsbury. & 23 Old square, Linc. inn
Lowndstone Wm. F. esq. 144 Oxford st. & Brightwell park, near Tetsworth
Loury E.L.esq.17Harringtn.st.Hmptd.rd
Lowry John, esq. 17 Chester ter. Eaton sq
Lowry Misses, 1 Glo'ster cres. Rgt.'s pk
Lowth Mrs. 4 John st. Berkeley square, & Winchester
Lowther Hon. Lt. Colonel H. C. M.P. & Lady Eleanor, 31 Bruton st. Berkeley square, & Borleythorpe, Oakham
Lowther Sir John Henry, bart. M.P. 32 Grosvenor sq.; Swillington hall, near Leeds; & Wilton castle, nr. Guisboro'
Lowther Jas. esq. 7 South ter. Alexr. sq
Lowther Mrs. 5 Up. Chadwell st. Pentnv
Lowthian J.esq.5Clrmnt.rw.Barnsbry.rd
Lowthian Mrs. 10 Colebrooke ter. Islntn
Loyd Lewis, esq. 19 Grosvenor square, & Overton hall, Northampton
Loyd Mrs. 13 Portland pl. Clapham rd
Loyd Samuel Jones, esq. 22 Norfolk st. Park la. & Wickham park, Bromley
Luard Henry, esq. 10 Up. Wimpole st
Lubbock Sir John Wm. bart. 23 St. James's pl.; Mitcham grove, Surrey; & High elms, Farnborough, Kent
Lubbock Dowager Lady, 23 St. James's pl. St. James's, & Mitcham gr. Surrey
Lubbock Miss, 78 Coleshill st. Eat. sq
Lucan, Earl of, 20 Hanover square, & Laleham, near Chertsey
Lucas Rev. Richard, 39 Bryanstone sq
Lucas C. esq. 54 Berner st
Lucas C. R.esq.5Arlington st.Camden tn
Lucas Edward, esq. Cavendish hotel, 81 Jermyn st. & the Castle, Dublin
Lucas Fras. esq. 10 New sq. Lincoln's inn
Lucas Fred. esq. 3 Brydges st. Cov. gar
LucasFredk.esq.25Pembroke sq.Knsgtn
Lucas Geo.O.esq.23Nw.Church st.Lis.gr
Lucas Geo. esq. 12 Manchester terrace
Lucas Henry, esq. 144 Oxford st. & The Green, Newport Pagnell, Bucks
LucasHubertH.esq.2Childs pl.Temp.bar
Lucas John, esq. 3 St. John's wood rd
Lucas Jn. esq. 176 Prospect pl. Edgw. rd
Lucas John, esq. 39North bank, Regent's park, & 9 Argyll st. Regent st
Lucas John, esq. 3 St. John's wood road
Lucas Joseph, esq. 8 Gray's inn square
Lucas Lewis, esq. 19 Hyde Park gardns
Lucas Mrs. 2 Bedford row, Clapham rise
Lucas Mrs. 12 Eccleston street south
Lucas Mrs. 7 Winchester row, New rd
Lucas Orton, esq. 1 St. Martin's pl.Chg.c
Lucas PhilipBennett,esq.8Manchester st
Lucas Rd. Cockrell, esq. 29 Devonshire st. Portland place
Lucas Robt. esq. 42 Bloomsbury square
Lucas Saml. esq. 3 Figtree ct. Temple
Lucas Thos. esq. 27 Canonbury villas
Lucas William, sen. esq. 130 Sloane st
LucasWm.O.esq.8&9Tauntonpl.Rgt.'s pk
Lucca H.R.H. Duke of, 44 Brook st
Lucena James L. esq. 4 Garden ct.Templ
Lucena Stephen L. esq. Guildhall chmbs. Basinghall st. & Clayhill, Enfield
Lucet J. S.esq.49Weymouth st.Prtlnd.pl
Luck John Kinton, esq. 9 St. Mary le Strand place, Old Kent road
Luckie Miss, 13 Tonbridge pl. New rd
Luckombe Chas. C. esq. 56 Doughty st
Lucombe Miss, 12 Torrington square
LucquetJohnB.esq. 34York st.Portmn.sq
Lucy Chas. esq. Albert st. Morningtn.cres
Lucy James, esq. 27 Burton st
Lucy John G. esq. 7 Francis pl. Hollowy
Ludlam Jsph.Thos.esq. 7 Up. Berkeley st
Ludlam Joseph, esq. 5 Notting hill ter
Ludland Mrs. 7 Stanhope st. Regnt.'s pk
Ludlow John M. esq. 69 Chancery lane
Ludlow Mrs. 86 Cadogan pl. Sloane st
Luffman A. esq. 7 Bell's blgs. Slsbry. sq
Luigi John, esq. 54 Rathbone place
Luke Mrs. 63 Gibson square, Islington
Luking Wm.esq.45Portmn.pl.St.Jn.'s wd
Lumb Fred. esq.41Argyle st.King's cross
Lumley Lt. Gen. Hon. Sir Wm. bart. 38 Green st. & Winkfield pl. near Windsr
Lumley Benjamin, esq. 46 Parliament st
Lumley Henry, esq. 32 Rathbone place
Lumley Robt. Wheatley,esq.9Charles st. Berkeley square, & 18 Carey st
Lumley W. Golden, esq. 32 Park road, Regent's park, & Somerset house
Lumsden Mrs. 5 Kensington gore
Lund Henry, esq. 6 Figtree court
Lundie Rt. S. esq. 28 Maddox st. Rgt. st
Lunn Joseph, esq. 7 Craven st. Strand
Lupton Thos.esq. 4 Keppel st. Russell sq
Lurgan Lord, Burlington hotel, Cork st. & Lurgan, Ireland
Luscombe John Teed, esq. 53 Linc. inn
Luscombe Wm. esq. 3 Manor grove,Chel
Lush James Wilmot, esq. Montpelier house, South Lambeth
Lush Robert, esq. 34 Mecklenburgh sq. & 4 Inner Temple lane
LushW.esq.173Prospect pl. St.John's wd
Lushington Rt. hon. Stephen, D.C.L. 29 Gt. George st.; 8 College, Doctors' commons; & Merryhill, near Watford
Lushington Sir Henry, 32 Montagu sq
Lushington Major Gen. Sir James Law, 26 Dorset sq. & Acton green lodge, Mddx
Lushington Charles, esq. Chapel pl. Duke st. Westminstr. & Hill house, Edgware
LushingtonChas.esq.1Kensington palace gardens, Bayswater
Lushington Chas. M. esq. 9 Pall mall ea
Lushington Hy.esq.2Mitre ct.bdgs.Temple, & Park house, Maidstone, Kent
Lushington Misses, 4 York pl. Portm. sq
Lushington Stephen G. esq. 9 Pall mall e
Lutterell John, esq. 4 Rutland gate
Luttrell Hy. Fownes, esq. 164 Albany st. Regent's park
Luttrell Henry L. esq. 31 Brompton sq
Lutwidge R.W.S.esq.10 Old sq. Linc.inn
Lutwyche A.J.P. esq.6 Pump ct.Temple
Luxmoore Coryndon H. esq.21Keppel st
Luxmore Wm. T. esq.75Camden. rd.vils. Camden town & 5 Albany court yard
Luxton J.esq. 2 Thornhl. pl. Caledon. rd
Lyall C. esq. 33 Westbourne tr. Hyde pk
Lyall George, M.P. 17 Park crescent, Portland pl.; &Findon, nearShoreham; & Nutwood lodge, near Gatton
Lyall Mrs. 32 Craven st. Strand
Lycett Francis, esq. 7 Milner sq. Isln
LycettWm.esq.22 Compton tr.Up.st.Islg
Lyddon Wm. esq. 24 Carey st
Lyddon Spencer, esq. 12 Mabledon pl
Lyde Capt.S. Sid villa, Earl's ct.Brmptn
Lyde Lionel, esq. 291 Regent st
Lydekker Gerard Wolfe, esq. 4 Hare ct
Lye John, esq.19Walcot pl.east, Lambeth
Lyell Chas. esq. F.R.S.16 Hart. st.Blmsb
Lyell Mrs. 10 Ladbroke pl. Notting hill
Lygon Lady Louisa, 12 Up. Brook st
Lygon Hon. Maj. Gen. H.B. M.P. 16 Grosvenor pl. & Springhill, near Broadway
Lyle Mrs. 16 Bedford pl. Kensington
Lyle Wm. G. esq. 10 Bloomsbury st
Lynam Rev. Robert, 4 Bridgwater sq
Lynch A. H. esq.33 Queen sq.; 25 Southampton bldgs.; & the Castle, Galway
Lynch Jas. esq.3 Stanley ter. King's rd.w
Lynch Jas. H. esq. 31 Polygon, Som's. tn
Lynch Rt. M.D. 15 Somerset st. Prtm. sq
Lynch William, esq. 35 Devonshire pl
Lynde Jas. G. jun. esq. 33 Gt. George st
Lynde Jas.G.sen.esq.16 Gt.Queen st.Wst
Lyndhurst Lord, P.C., F.R.S. 25 George st. Hanover sq. & Turville park, Henley
Lyndon C. esq. New chambers, Foregate, & 2 Harcourt bldgs. Temple
Lyne Fras. esq. 6 Hunter st. Brnswk. sq
Lynn Hon. Mrs. 8 Berkeley st. Piccadly
Lynn Jas. esq. 3 Pennsbury, Wndswh. rd
Lynn Rt. esq. 3 Wilton pl. Belgrave sq
LynneT. W. esq.York chm. 41 St. Jas. st
Lynott Rd.Wm. esq.24 Camden rd.villas
Lyon Capt. Wm. 44 Upper Grosvr. st
Lyon Rev. P.Wm. 31Edwd. st.Hmpst.rd
Lyon Charles, esq. 6 Piccadilly
Lyon David, esq. 44 Upp. Grosvenor st. & North Brook house, Goring, Sussex
Lyon Edwd. esq. 23 Sussex pl. Knsgtn
Lyon Geo. Wm. esq. 1 Brick ct. Temple
Lyon Jas. esq. Bedford ter. Claphm. rise
Lyon James Wittit, esq. 7 Spring gardens; and 39 Belgrave square; & Misserdine park, Cirencester
Lyon Miss, 6 Euston grove, Euston sq
Lyon Mrs. 4 Belmont pl. Wandsworth rd
LyonWm.T.esq.15Southampton st.Strnd
Lyons Abraham, esq. 33 Woburn place
Lyons Miss, 5 Weymouth st. Portland pl
Lyons Misses, 3 Stanhope st. Hyde pk
Lys Miss, 14 Notting hill sq
Lysley Wm. John, esq. 3 In. Temple la.; & Pewsham, Wilts; & Mimwood, near Hatfield, Herts
Lyster Hy. esq. 9 Spring ter. Wandsw. rd
Lythgoe Rev. Randal, 25 Bolton st
Lyttelton Lord, 39 Grosvenor place, & Hagley park, Stourbridge
Lyttelton Dow. Lady, 39 Grosvenor pl. & Hagley hall, Stourbridge

MABERLY Lieutenant Colonel William Leader, 15 Manchester square
Maberly Joseph, esq. 17 Harley st. & 17 King's road, Bedford road
McAdam Sir James, 22 Whitehall pl
McAdam Sir James Nicholl, 40 Charing cross, & Tindon & Thaxted, Essex
McAdam Sir J. 23 Grove end rd. St. Jn.w
Macalpine Lieut. Col. Jas. 90 Eaton sq. & Castlebar, county Mayo, Ireland
Macalpine C. esq.1 Albert ter. Knghtsbdg
Macalpine C. esq.17 High row, Knghtsbg
McAlpine Mrs. 9 Stranrear pl. Maida hl
Macan Mrs. 10 Lowndes square
Macarthur Col. 16 Carlton house terr
McArthur John, esq. 17 Mount st
Macarthur Mrs. 40 Hunter st. Brunswick square, & the Cottage, Heston
MacaulayColinCampbell,esq.15Regnt.st
Macaulay James, esq. 28 Chancery la
MacaulayKenneth,esq. 4 Harcourt bdgs
M'Aulay Mrs. 20 St. John's wood road
MacauleyKennth.esq.21So.Prade.St.Jas
Macauley Rt. hon. T.B. M.P., E1, Albany
Macauley Jas. esq. 2 Brick ct. Temple
M'Bean Misses, 9 Carlton vil. Edgwr. rd
M'Beath Wm. John, esq. 2 Duchess st
Maccabe Charles, esq. 80 Wimpole st
M'CabeJas.E. esq. 35 Castle st. Holborn
M'Cabe Robt. esq. 1 Guilford pl. Rusl. sq
MacCabeWm. B. esq. 29 Up. Belgrave pl
M'Callan J.esq.5William st. Knightsbrdg
M'Calmont Robert, esq. 30 Eaton sq
M'Cann Mrs. 24 Sloane st
M'Cann Nicholas, esq. 50 Parliament st
M'Carthy D. esq. 10 Park pl.vil. Padgtn
M'Caul George, esq. 43 Kensington sq
M'Causland M. esq. 14 Low. Berkeley st
Macclesfield, Earl of, 9 Conduit st. & Sherborne castle, Oxfordshire
M'Christie Thos.Y. esq. 37 Gt. James st. & 4 Old square, Lincoln's inn
M'CleanJohnR.esq.17Gt.George st.Wm

M'Clise Dan. esq. 14 Russell pl. Fitzy. sq
M'CormickG.esq.12Richmond ter.Pntvl
M'Cracken Robert De Crez, esq. 26 Southampton pl. New road, Euston sq
M'Culloch John, esq. 47 Beaumont sq
M'Culloch J.R.esq.Statny.off.Buckm.gt
M'Culloch Rt. esq. 26 Colebrooke row
M'Cullom John, esq. 26 Up. Bedford pl
M'Curdy J. esq. 39 Tonbridge pl. New rd
M'Cutcheon J.esq.13Prospt. pl.Wnsw.rd
M'Cutcheon Jno. esq. 18 Canterbury vill
MacannArthur,esq.22 King st.Portm. sq
Macdermot Mrs. 49 St. John's wood ter
Macdonald Lord G.Wm.W. c5, Albany & Armidale castle, Isle of Skye, N.B.
Macdonald Lady, 84 Eaton sq. & Kirkley hall, Northumberland
Macdonald Lt.Gen.Sir John,23Bruton st
Macdonald Sir Archibald,1 St. James's st
Macdonald Colonel D. 65 Sloane st
Macdonald Captain, 44 Jermyn st
Macdonald Alex. esq. 182 Regent st
Macdonald Daniel, esq. 18 Halfmoon st
MacdonaldJ.C.esq.3Churchyd.ct.Templ
Macdonald Mrs. 65 Sloane st
M'Donald Mrs.6Cmdn.tr.w.Cmdn.nw.tn
McDonald Mrs.4Cobourg pl.U.Kngtn.la
M'Donald Mrs. 12 St. John's wood road
Macdonald Reginald, esq. 166 Piccadilly
MacdonaldWm. esq.23Princes st.Cav. sq
MacdonaldW.R.esq.19King's pa.Chelsea
Macdonell Patk.esq.36 Percy st.Bdfd. sq
M'Donnell Archibald, esq. 13 Regent sq
M'Donnell Edmund, esq. 44 Brook st. & Glenarm castle, Antrim
M'Donnell Eneas, 16 Up. Phillimore pl
M'Donnell Geo. esq. 28 Terrace, Twr. hill
M'DonoughWm.esq.20Bernardst.Rus.sq
M'Dougal Thos. esq. 2 Mornington crst
M'Dougall A. esq. 10 Edwarde sq.Knsgn
Macdougall Alex. H. esq.31 Park st
Macdougal Thomas St. Clair, esq. 4 Minerva terrace, Barnsbury park
M'Dougul Col. Sir Duncan, 94 Eaton sq
M'Dowell James, esq. 46 Portland place, & East Brechford, Bingham, Notts
Macdowall John, esq. 65 Baker st
M'Duff Chas. esq. 37 Castle st. Holborn
Macdowell Patk. esq. 75A, Margaret st
Macduff Miss,25Winchester row,New rd
M'Ewen James, esq. 178 Albany road
M'Ewen Robt.esq.2Ladbrokepl.Notg.hil
Macey C. esq.2Ehrenburg ter.Mrngtn.rd
Macey Mrs. 51 St. John st. road
Macfarlane Major Jas. 20 Cambridge sq. Hyde pk. & Frant, Tunbridge wells
Macfarlane Jas. esq. 41 York ter.Rgt.pk
M'Farlane A. esq. 29 Southampton bdgs
M'Farquaher Rev. W. P. 47 Euston sq
Macfarren Geo. Alex. esq. 73 Berners st
Macfarren Walter C. esq. 73 Berners st
M'Garel Charles, esq. 14 Wimpole st
Mac Greachy Foster Alleyne, esq. M.P. 33 St. James's pl. & Windsor terrace, Clifton
M'Gedy Francis, esq. 36 Keppel st
M'Gedy Francis, esq. 7 Oxford terrace
M'George Mrs. 3 Wilton crescent
M'Ghie Willoughby, esq. 2 New inn
M'Gill James, esq. 4 Euston pl. New rd
M'Gill Mrs. 4 Euston place, New road
M'Gill Mrs. 2 Grange villas, Brompton
M'Glashan Rev. A. 20 Bedford sq. east
M'Glew Robert, esq. Clapham rise
M'GraHon.Mrs. C.10Radnor pl.Hyde pk
M'Grath Miss, 5 Albion ter. Chelsea
Macgregor Lady, 3 Glo'ster st. Ptmn.sq
Macgregor Alex. esq. 3 Arlington st
McGregor Alex.esq.31Chester st.Grsv.pl
MacGregor John, esq. 3 Lowndes sq
MacGregor Duncan, esq. 3 Lowndes sq
MacGregor Jsph. Al. J. esq.26 Suffolk st
M'Gregor Mrs.3Clarendon ter.Nottng.hl
MacGrigorC.R.esq.17Charles st.St.Jas's
M'Grigor Sir James, bart. 3 Harley st
M'Grigor W. G. J. esq.Chapel strs.Lin.in
M'Haffie A. esq. 2 Hanover ter. Notg. hl
Machaon Daniel, M.D. 12 Tavistock pl
Machell George, esq. 2 Carlisle st. Soho
Machen John, esq. 10 Nottingham ter
Machen Mrs. 10 Nottingham ter. New rd
Machin John M. esq.16 Craven st.Strand
Macilwain Geo. esq. 3 Albany court yd
Macintosh Alex.esq.12Duncan ter.Cityrd
M'Intosh David, esq. 39 Bloomsbury sq
M'Intosh J. esq. 4 Richmond ter. Pntnvl
M'Intosh Robt. esq. Hornton vils.Knsgtn
MacintyreP.esq.13Grevle. pl.Kilb.priory
Macintyre Robert, esq. 3 Barnsbury sq
MacIntyre William, M.D. 84 Harley st
Mackay Adm. Hon. D. H. A11, Albany
Mackay Alex. esq. 28 Charles st.Westm
Mackay Donald, esq. 56 Porchester ter
Mackay Hugh, esq.18Downham rd.Islg
Mackay Miss, 47 Baker st. Portman sq
Mackay Mrs.17 Scarsdale ter.Kensngtn
Mackay Rt. Wm. esq. 41 Hamilton ter
Mackay Spencer, esq. 55 Up. Harley st
Mackdonnell Capt. J. 67 Up. Norton st
M'Kean Hugh,esq.13Cambridge terrace, Edgware road, & 7 Pall mall
Mackell Jas. esq. 14 Park la. Piccadilly
M'Kellar Wm. esq. 7 Lonsdale sq. Islgtn
M'KellarDuncan,esq.Grovcho.Battersea
M'Keller Mrs. 38 Hemingford ter.Islgtn
Mackenzie Lady, 17 Clarges st. & Avoch, near Inverness, N.B
Mackenzie Hon. Mrs. 5 Grosvenor gate, Park lane
Mackenzie Major L. 12 Southwick cres
Mackenzie Alex. esq. 36 Devonshire pl
Mackenzie C. A. esq. 5 Hyde pk. pl.west
Mackenzie Fred.Wm.esq.3Bayswater ter
Mackenzie Geo. esq. Canonbury villas
Mackenzie Harry, esq. 17 Cornwall ter
MackenzieHy.esq.3Claremont rw.Brn.rd
Mackenzie John, esq. 17 New Ormond st
Mackenzie John,esq.13Alfred pl.Brmptn
Mackenzie John, esq. 1 Verulam bldgs
Mackenzie Mrs. K.8Bedford st.Bedfd. sq
Mackenzie Mrs. 16 South Bank, Reg. pk
Mackenzie Mrs. 45 Mecklenburgh sq
Mackenzie Mrs. 84 Gloucester place
Mackenzie Mrs. 4 Glo'ster ter. O. Brmp
Mackenzie Rt. S. D.C.L. 22 Grafton st. e
Mackenzie Roderick, esq. 15 Hunter st
Mackenzie Rowld.H.M.D.68Mortimer st
Mackenzie Thos. esq. M.P. 17 Clarges st. & Applecross, near Dingwall, Scotland
Mackenzie Thos.esq.23Soley ter.Llyd. sq
M'Kenzie Wm.esq.5Warwick sq.Belgr.rd
M'KenzieWm.B.esq.23Loraine pl.Holwy
Mackenzie Wm. F. esq. 5 St. Alban's pl. St. James's
Mackenzie Wm. Forbes, esq.M.P.Carlton club, & Portmore, Eddleston, N.B
Mackeson Edwd. esq. 16 Serjeants' inn
Mackeson L. esq. 10 Old sq. Lincoln's inn
Mackey A. A. esq. 2 Clifton vil.Maida va
Mackie Rev. John Wm. 27 Up. Baker st. Regent's park, & Christchurch, Oxon
Mackie J. esq.50Newington pl.Kngtn. rd
Mackie John, esq. 3 Eccleston st
Mackillop James, esq. 4 Montagu sq
M'Kinnell Miss, 15 Billiter st
Makinnon Alpin, esq. 30 Gibson sq
Mackinnon Dr. Leo. 23 Brompton cresc
Mackinnon W. A. esq. M.P. 4 Hyde pk.pl
Mackintosh A.esq.27 Duncan ter.City rd
Mackintosh Eneas, esq. 17 Montagu sq
Mackintosh Geo. esq. 27 Up. Seymour st
Mackintosh George D. esq. 12 Regent st
Mackintosh James, esq.4 Adam st.Adelp
Mackintosh Jas.S.M.D.32Wiltonpl.Knsb
Mackintosh Mrs. 1 Encombe ter.Wdsw.r
Macklew Andrew, esq. 4 Burlington gar
Macklin H. N. esq. 21Suffolk st. Pall ml
Mackmurdo Ed. L. esq. 23 Finsbury circ
M'Knight Wm. esq. 38 Wilmington sq
Mackrell Wm. Thos. esq. 25 Abingdon st
MackrellWm.T.esq.54Millbankst.Westm
Mackrill Wm. N. esq.1Little Carter lane
Mackworth Dow.Lady, 2 Up. Bedford pl
M'Laggen George, esq. 2 Poland st
M'Lane Louis, esq.United States Minister, Harley st
M'Laren David, esq. 13Park ter. Highby
Maclaren Mrs, 38 Tavistock square
M'Laughlen Edwd. esq. 46 Nelson sq
McLaughlen Walter esq. 78 Seymour pl
Maclean Gen. Sir F. bart. 53 Cadogan pl
Maclean Gen. Sir H. 3 Northwick ter
M'Lean Lt. Gen. Sir John, 26 Argyll st. Regent st. & Hithe hill, Colchester
Maclean Allen, esq. 14 Cork st. Bond st
Maclean Alex. esq. 4 Sebbon's bdgs. Islg
Maclean Archibald esq. 41 St. James's pl
Mac Lean Donald, esq. 37 Brunswick sq
Mac Lean John Geo.esq.37 Brunswick sq
Maclean Donald, esq. M.P. United University club; 28 Upper Brook st.; 1 New court, Temple; & Witton castle, Bishops Auckland
Maclean John, M.D. 29 Up. Montagu st
Maclean Mrs. 22 Wilton crescent
Maclean Miss, 1Cambridge pl.Edgwr.rd
Maclean R. esq. 32 Carlton vils.Edgw.rd
M'Leod Major Gen. Daniel, 3 Clifton place, Sussex square
Macleod Gen. Sir John, 18 Montagu st
Macleod Major Gl. Chas. 6 Gloucester pl
Macleod Rev. Rodk.D.D.58Dean st.Soho
Macleod John, esq. 1 Stanhope st. Vic. gt
Mac Leod Mrs. of Mac Leod, 18 Great Cumberland st
M'Leod George D. esq. 6 Furnival's inn
M'Leod Misses, 9 Wilton pl. Belgrave sq
Macleod Miss, 4Foley place, Portland pl
Macleod Roderick, M.D.1Lw. Seymour st
Maclure Rev. Robt. 14 Bulstrode st
Maclure William, esq. 14 Harley st
M'Mahon Edwd. esq. 78 Cadogan place
M'Mahon Jas. esq. 11 Paper bdgs.Temple
M'Mahon John,esq.4Glo'ster pl.Glo'st.cr
Mac Mahon P. esq. 10 Farrars bdgs
Mac MahonW.esq.10Crescentpl.Hmp.rd
M'Morris Samuel, esq. 12 Up. Fitzroy st
M'MullinJn.esq.Lavender hl.Wandsw.rd
McMurray Robt. esq. 18 Clement's inn
Macnab J.esq.2Mountfort ter.Brnsby.pk
Macnaghten Lady, 29 Hertford st
Macnaghten Steuart, esq. 29 Hertford st. Mayfair, & 4 Old sq. Lincoln's inn
Macnaghten Francis,esq.10Hyde park st
McNair Capt. R.N. 5 Kensington crescent
McNair Capt. R. 9 Belgrave st. south
Macnama Mrs. 155 Sloane st
Macnamara H. T. J. esq. 9In.Temple lane
Macnamara Wm.Nugent, M.P.11Charles st. & Doolin, near Ennistimon
Macnaughten Wm. esq. 31 Bernard st
M'Neal Rev.M.Cha.ho.Gro.r.St.Jn.'s wd
M'Neil Rt. Hon. Duncan, M.P. Lord Advocate, 9 Charles st. Grosvenor sq
M'Neill Forbes, esq. 44 Finsbury circus
Macneill Sir John, LL.D. 9 Whitehall place, & Southwood cottage, Highgate
M'Nish Mrs. 16 Belinda ter. Canonby.sq
M'Nicol George, esq. 122 Pall mall
Maconochie Robt. esq. 30 Devonshire pl
M'Pherson Alex. esq. 9 Cadogan place
M'Quoid Saml. esq. 3 Stanley pl.Chelsea
Macpherson Mrs. 7 Noel st. Islington
Macpherson Wm. esq. 3 Stone buildings
Macqueen John F. esq. 27 Westbourne grove, Bayswater, & 4 Old sq. Linc.inn
Macqueen Mrs. 19 Euston place, New rd
Macqueen Mrs. 38 Kensington sq
M'Quige Thomas, esq. 3 Staple inn
M'Rae Jas. Layton, esq.1New inn,Strand
Macray Mrs. 18 Victoria gro. Kensngtn
Macready Wm. Chas. esq. 5 Clarence ter
M'Swiney Eugene, esq. 26 Dorset place
M'Taggart Sir John, bart. M.P. 22Mnchr. sq. & Ardwell, near Wigtoun, Scotland
M'Taggart Mrs. 43 Gloucester place
M'Whinnie Andrew M. esq. 5 Crescent, New Bridge st. Blackfriars

MacVicar J.D.esq.9Sussex pl.Regt.'s pk
M'Whinnie Jas. esq. 29 Osnaburgh st
M'Whinnie J. esq.25 Beaufort st.Chelsea
Mactire Alex. W. esq. 8 Duke st. St. Jas
Macy Chas. esq. 27 Bury st. St. James's
Madan Capt.5 Northwick ter.St.Jn.'s wd
Madan Miss, 2 Northwick ter.St.Jn.'s wd
Madden Sir Frederick, British Museum
Madden Jas. esq. 23 Artillery pl. Finsbury
Madden Mrs. 17 Wells st. Oxford st
MaddisonRd.T.esq.48Lincoln's inn fields
Maddock Alfred B. M.D. 10 Hunter st
Maddock Alfred B. M.D. 22 Harley st
Maddock Henry Fredk. esq. 2 Lyons inn
Madeley G.E.esq.4 Warwick sq. Kensng
Madeley Mrs. Cumberland lodge, Caroline place, Hampstead road
Madeley Miss, 2 Warwick sq. Kensingtn
Madge Thomas, esq. 5 Highbury grange
Madgwick Edward,esq.13 Canonbury sq
Madigan Richd. esq. 10 St. Pancras vale
Madot Adolphus, esq. 31 Upper Baker st
Madox Wm.esq. 154Albany st.Rgnt.'s pk
Magan Capt.Wm.Hen.St.Mary Abbott's terrace, Kensington
Magee Very Rev. 9 Romney terrace
Magenis Mrs. 13 Grosvenor place
Mageniss Peter, esq, 29 Chichester pl
Maggioni Manfred, esq. Portland road
Maggs Felix, esq. 66 St. John's wood ter
Maggs John, esq. 11 Green st.Grosv. sq
Magnay Mrs. 67 Oxford ter. Hyde park
Magrini R. F. esq. 43 Warren st. Fitz. sq
Maguire C. esq. 18 Tavistock st.Bdfd. sq
Maguire George, esq. 38 Bryanstone st
Maher N. esq.M.P.Cox's hotel,Jermyn st
Mahon Viscount, M.P. 41 Grosvenor pl. & Chevening pk. nr. Seven Oaks, Kent
Mahony John, esq. 72 Paradise rw. Chls
Mahony Rev. Fras. 16 Gt. Marlboro' st
MaidesWm. esq.4Petersburg pl.Bayswtr
Maidlow Chas.esq. 76 St. John's wd. ter
Maidstone Viscount, White's club, St. James's st
Main Rev. Robert, Somerset house
Mair Geo. esq.18Charlotte st.Bedford sq
Mainwaring Mrs.68 Milton st. Dorset sq
Mainwaring Townshend, esq.M.P.94 Pall mall, & Murchwell hall, Denbigh
MainwairingGeorge, esq.23 Blandford sq
Mair William, esq. 46 Notting hill sq
Maire P.F.esq.3 St. Agnes vils.Bayswtr
Maitland SirThomas,12 Knsngtn.gdn.ter
MaitlandChas.esq.3Omega ter. Alpha rd
Maitland Collier, esq.27York st.Ptmn.sq
Maitland David A. esq. 16 Victoria sq
Maitland David John, esq.105 Jermyn st
Maitland D.M. esq. 45 York st.Ptmn. sq
Maitland Fred.Charles, esq.91 Jermyn st
Maitland John G.esq.8 New sq.Linc.inn
Maitland Mrs. 35 Upper George st
Maitland Thomas, esq. M.P. Dundreman
MaitlandThomas F.esq.51Up.Seymour st
MaitlandThomas F. esq. 6 Pump ct.Tem
Maitland Wm.esq.4 Portland pl.Wnds.rd
MaitlandP.esq.21Newington pl.Kngtn.rd
Major Rev. J. R. D.D. 40 Bloomsbury sq
Major Charles Jas.esq. 13 Barnsbury pk
Major Geo.T.esq.9 Grove rd.St.John's wd
Major Job,esq.14 Thayer st.Manchstr.sq
Major Mrs.Raby house,Finchley New rd
Majoribanks Edwd.esq. 13 Cavendish sq
Majoribanks Mrs.3 Upper Wimpole st
Makeham John P. esq. 10 Dartmouth st
Makins Mrs. 2 Campden hill,Kensington
Malcolm SirChas.4 Mount st. Berkeley sq
Malcolm Lady, Earl's ct. Old Brompton
Malcolm John, esq. 7 Gt. Stanhope st. & Lamorbey, Eltham, Kent
Malcolm John George,esq.34 Torrington square, & 4 Lamb building, Temple
Malcolm Neill, esq. 7 Gt. Stanhope st. ; Kilmarton house, Lochgilphead, N.B. ; & Duntroon castle, Argyleshire, N.B.
Malden Hen. esq.20 Alfred pl. Bedfrd.sq
Malet Lady, 3 Mount st. Berkeley sq
Malcolmson James, esq. West lodge, Campd. hl. Knsngtn. & 9 King William st. City
MalimGeorge,esq.11 South sq.Gray's inn
MalingCol.Thos.6Osnaburg ter.Rgt.'spk
MalingHy.esq.15 Glo'ster gr.w.O.Brmtn
Maling Mrs. 8 Manor ter.King's rd.Chls
Malins Richard, esq. 35 Bedford place, Russell sq.&6Stone bdgs.Lincoln's inn
Malkin Arthur Thos. esq. 21 Wimpole st
MallMajorJames,1Norland pl.Notting hl
Mallam Mrs.2Wellington ter.Clphm.rise
Mallan Edward, esq. 155 Oxford st
Mallan James M. esq. 63 Fleet st. & 19 Bouverie st
MallanJohn, esq. 59 Brook st. Grosv. sq
Malleson John, esq. 34A, Charles st. Berkeley sq. & Wimbledon, Surrey
Mallett Fred. esq. 59 Wardour st. Soho
Mallett Hen. esq. 2 Baker st. Lloyd sq
Mallett Thos. esq.25 Lower Islington ter
MallockJas.esq.8 Southampton st.Blmbs
Malpas Mrs. 32 Fortess ter. Kentish tn
Malpas Wm. esq. 29 Camden road villas
Malmesbury Earl, Whitehall gardens; & Heron ct. Christchurch; & Durnford, near Salisbury
Maltby Brough G. esq.11 Stockwell com
Maltby C.F.esq.19Took's ct.Chancery la
Maltby Edward Harvey,esq. G3, Albany
Maltby Henry, esq. 38 Eaton square
Maltby Mrs. 3 Hornsey row, Islington
Malton Chas. J.A. esq.9 Up.Seymour st
Malton William, esq. 36 Wimpole st. & 60 Carey st. Lincoln's inn
Malyn John,esq.12 James st.Bknghm.gt
Malyon James, esq. 37 Wilmington sq
Man Mrs. 5 Princes place,Kennington rd
Man Henry, esq. 21 Hamilton terrace
Manas Geo.esq.Eaton ho.Haverstock hl
Manby Charles, esq. 25 Great George st
Manby Mrs. 7 Fredk. pl. Up. Knngtn. la
Manby John, esq. 25 Great George st
ManbyJosephLane,esq.32 Bucklersbury
Manchester, Duke of, Athenæum club; Kimbolton castle, Kimbolton; & Tandregee, Ireland
Manchester, Dean of, 11 Hereford st
Mander Henry Waterland, esq. 16 Tavistock sq. & 7 New square, Lincoln's inn
Mander Jas. esq.49 Bedford row,Blmsby
Manders Geo. esq. 5 Grove pl. Lisson gr
Mandeville Viscount, 129 Mount st
Mangles Capt. R.N. 66 Cambridge terr
Mangles Ross D.esq. M.P. 17 Arundel st. Haymkt. & Woodbridge, near Guildfd
Mangold Chas. esq.37Hunter st.Bswk.sq
Manisty Hy.esq. 7 Caroline pl.Mcklbg.sq
Mann Arthur, esq. 8 Woburn square
Mann Chas. esq. 16 Albion rd. Liverpl.rd
Mann ChristopherW.esq. 20 Blandford st
Mann Geo.esq. 10 Cloudesley ter.Islngtn
Mann Geo. esq. 13 Porchester tr.Bayswt
Mann John, esq. 10 Stafford rw. Pimlico
Mann Mrs. 51 New Church st. Lisson gr
Mann Miss, 1 Cornwall ter.Regent's pk
Mann Thos. esq. 1 Up. ter. Up. st. Islgtn
Mann Wm. esq. 15 Duke st. St. James's
Manners Lord, 56 Upper Brook st. & Farnham park, Bury St. Edmunds
Manners, Lord Charles Somerset, M.P. E3, Albany, & Belvoir castle
Manners,LordJohnJ.R. M.P., C4,Albany, & Belvoir castle
Manners Capt. Russell Henry, R.N. 8 Henrietta st. Cavendish square
Manners Arthur, esq. 20 Rutland gate
Manners Mrs. 32 Upper Montagu st
Manners-Sutton Hon. John H. T. M.P. Home office, & King st. Norwich
Manett Jn.esq. 20 Up.Chas.st. Nthm.sq
Mannin John, esq. 28 Percy st. Bedfd. sq
Mannin Mrs. 28 Percy st. Totten. ct. rd
Manning Capt. J. S. 15 Regent st
Manning Augustus, esq. 8A, Hertford st
Manning Chas. J. esq. 3 New Bank bdgs
Manning Fred. Jno. esq. 30 Craven st
Manning Jas. S.L. 22 Up. Southwick st. & 3 Serjeants' inn, Chancery lane
Manning Mrs. 9 Sloane ter. Chelsea
Manning Mrs. 6 Euston square
ManningRt.esq. 7Montague pl.Clapm.rd
Manning Saml. jun. esq. 17 Newman st
Manning Saml. esq. 9 York pl. City road
Manning T. esq. 28 Theberton st.Islngtn
Manning W.O. esq. 3 Haverstock hill
ManningW.O.esq.3Paragon,Nw.Kent rd
Manning Wm. Thos. esq. 21 Thavies inn
Manningham Chas.esq. 47 QueenAnne st
Manningham Mrs. 13 Chesterfield st
Mansel Charles Grenville,esq. B3,Albany
Mansel John, esq. 44 St. James's place
ManselJsph.esq.24Fredk.st.Gray's inn rd
Mansel Mrs. 8 Gloucester pl. New road
Mansell Mrs. 19 Claremont place,Pntnvl
Mansfield, Earl of, K.T. Caen wood, Hampstead; & Mansfield; & Scone palace, Perth; Comlongon, Dumfriesshire; & Shaw park, Clackmannan
Mansfield,Countess of,13Langham place
Mansfield Henry, esq. 59 Nelson square
Mansfield Jas. esq. 20 John st. Bedfd.row
Mansfield John Smith,esq. 3 Essex court
Mansfield Mrs. 51 Grosvenor st
Mansfield Wm. esq. 16 Dorset pl. north
MansfieldWm.C.esq.20John st.Bedfd.rw
Manson Miss, 51 Devonshire st
Manson William, esq. 5 Portugal st. Grosvenor sq. & 8 King st. St. James's
Manson Wm. Pitt, esq. 45 Duncan terr
Mantell Gideon A. esq. 19 Chester sq
Manton Mrs. 46Up.Berkeley st.Portm.sq
Manvers, Earl, 13 Portman square, & Thoresby park, Ollerton, Notts
Manwell Geo. esq. 12 Up. Southwick st
ManwellHen.esq. 100Milton st.Dorset sq
Maples Capt. R.N. 3 Kilburn priory
Mapleson Jas. esq. 25 Essex st. Strand
Mapleson John, esq. 19B, Golden square
Mapleton Rev. John H. 48 Stamford st. Blackfriars road
MapletopMiss, 20North bank,Regt.'s pk
Marcer Chas. esq. 16 Park village east
March, Earl of, M.P. Molcombe cottage, Chichester
March George, esq. 2 James st. Adelphi
March Wm.esq.26Cumbrlnd.tr.Reg.'spk
MarchantJonathan,esq. 24 Wellngtn.ter
MarchantMrs.20Glo'ster gr.wc.O.Bmtn
Marcus Rev. Lewis, B.A. 30 Paddtn.gr
Marcus Rev. M. 16 Caroline st.Bedf.sq
MardonThos. Todd, esq. 30 Wimpole st
Mardon Wm. esq. 56 Hunter st
Mare Charles, esq. 25 Westbourne ter
Mares Chas.esq. 4 South sq. Gray's inn, & 1 Grafton pl. Kentish town
Mareschal Geo.esq. 45 Park st.Grosv.sq
Marett Chas. esq. 3 Stone bdgs. Linc.inn
Margarey Miss, 38 Sussex gardens
MargaryJoshuaJ.L.esq.112 New Bond s
MargaryThomas George, esq. 1 Quality ct. & 7 Southwood lane, Highgate
Margetson P. esq. 3 Adelaide st. Strand
MargotyCapt.E. R.N. 25Up.Berkeley st
Maris Andrew, esq. 45 Burton crescent
Maris Andrew, esq. 6 Tonbridge place
Majoribanks Edwd. esq. 34 Wimpole st
Majoribanks Stewart, M.P. & Dowager Lady Rendelsham, 6 Charles st. Berkeley sq. & Bushey grove, Watford
Mark Henry, esq. 36 University st
MarkJohn, esq. 5 Portland pl.Clapm.rd
MarkbyJas.esq.22Aberdeen pl. Maida hl
MarkhamArthur B. esq.10 Crow.Offi.rw
Markham Edw. esq. 10 Marylebone st
Markham Mrs. 4 Kennington place
MarkhamMrs.4 Kngtn.pl.Up.Knngt.la
MarksRev.D.W.51 Burton st.Burton cs
Marks Chas. esq. 1 Cumming st. Pntnvl
Marks Charles, esq. 14 Tibberton square
Marks Edmd. esq. 5 Seymour pl. Nw.rd
MarksJob, esq. 6 Up.Spring st.Portm.sq

Marks J. I. esq. Russell cot. Morngtn.rd
Marks Mrs. 20 Holles st. Cavendish sq
Markwick Alfred, esq. 19 Langham pl
Marlay Mrs. 14 Cavendish square
Marlborough, Duke of, 16 Eaton square, & Blenheim park, Woodstock
Marley Miles, M.D. 11 Cork st. Bond st
Marley Mrs. 57 Cambridge ter. Edgwr.rd
Marnock Rt. esq. 11 Hanover cots. Reg. pk
Marquet Jas. 9 Manor pl. south, Chelsea
Marr A. J. esq. 11 Princes st. Spitalfiel
Marr Edw. esq. 75 Hamilton ter. St. Jn's. w
Marrable Sir Thomas, Gt. Court, St. James's palace
Marrable Fred. esq. 1 Lancaster pl. Strand
Marrable John, esq. 13 Bruton st
Marrinell Geo. esq. 5 Newland st. Eaton sq
Marriot T. esq. 12 Windsor ter. City rd
Marriott Fred. esq. 3 Eastbourne ter
Marriott Fredk. esq. 19 Up. Albany st
Marriott Robt. esq. 8 Argyle sq. New rd
Marriott Robt. esq. 7 New inn, Strand, & Colchester
Marriott Thos. W. esq. 10 Montpelier sq
Marris J. G. esq. 2 Park pl. ter. Padntn. gr
Marris William, esq. 5 Gray's inn sq
Marryatt J. esq. 6 Richmond ter. Whtch
Mars Madame, 14 Suffolk st. Pall mall
Marschan A. esq. 35 Charlotte st. Prtld. pl
Marsden Jsph. D. esq. 14 Furnival's inn
Marsden Rt. esq. 14 Hanover ter. Reg. pk
Marsden Wm. M.D. 65 Lincoln's inn flds
Marsh Rd. Jas. esq. 22 Lr. Belgrave pl
Marsh Rich. esq. 6 Stockwell common
Marsh Robert, esq. 12 Haymarket
Marsh Thomas C. esq. 2 Harcourt bldgs
Marsh Wm. esq. 8A, Milton st. Dorset sq
Marshall Sir Chapman, 42 Russell sq
Marshall Sir Charles, knt. 29 Albion st
Marshall Major, & the Hon. Mrs. 27 Albion st. Hyde park
Marshall Rev. Chas. 9 South st. Finsbry
Marshall Rev. Wm. Deptford High st
Marshall Chas. esq. 52 Gt. Marlboro' st
Marshall Chas. esq. 9 Montague pl. Isln
Marshall Edward, esq. 13 Fitzroy sq
Marshall F. esq. 3 Campd. hl. vls. Knsgtn
Marshall George, esq. 12 Hyde park sq
Marshall James, esq, 4 Allsop ter. Newrd
Marshall Jas. esq. 27 Southampton bdgs
Marshall James, esq. 23 Up. Woburn pl
Marshall J. esq. 8 Crescent pl. Hmptd. rd
Marshall John, esq. 32 Gt. Portland st
Marshall John, esq. 22 Portugal st
Marshall J. esq. 15 Portland pl. Islngtn
Marshall John, esq. 4 Swan walk, Chlsea
Marshall John, esq. 41 Upper Grosvenor street; Hallstead, near Penrith; & Headingley, near Leeds
Marshall Mrs. 6 Arundel ter. Bnsby. rd
Marshall Mrs. 20 Queen st. Mayfair
Marshall Mrs. 1 St. Ann ter. St. John's wd
Marshall Mrs. Stoke Newington green
Marshall Mrs. 1 Wilton st. Grosvnr. pl
Marshall Peter, esq. 53 Greek st. Soho
Marshall Ralph, esq. 11 Bloomsbury sq
Marshall R. esq. 23 Newington pl. Kngtn. rd
Marshall T. esq. 23 Grafton st. Fitz. sq
Marshall Wm. esq. 6 Albion ter. Kg's. rd. Ch
Marshall Wm. esq. 50 Noel st. Islngtn
Marshall Wm. esq. 1 Princes st. Stmfd. st
Marshall Wm. esq. 15 Tyndale pl. Islgtn
Marshall Wm. esq. M.P. 41 Upper Grosvenor street; & Patterdale hall, near Carlisle; & Edge grove, Watford
Marshall Wm. esq. 215 Upper Thames st
Marshall W. esq. Wellington tr. St. Jn's. wd
Marshall Wm. C. esq. 6 Up. Belgrave pl
Marshall W. F. esq. 1 Fig Tree ct. Temple
Marshall Wm. H. esq. 17 St. George's pl
Marshall W. Skinner, esq. 4 Hyde pk. sq
Marsham Lady Emily, 2 Grosvenor pl
Marshman Joshua Ryland, esq. 9 Chester terrace, Eaton sq. & 1 In. Temple lane
Marsland Hen. esq. M.P. Reform club, & Wood bank, near Stockport

Marston Hen. esq. 19 Baker st. Lloyd sq
Marston J. esq. 6 Devonshire st. Ptld. pl
Marston Miss, 23 Hans place, Sloane st
Marston Mrs. 14 Lowther cottages, Liverpool road, Islington
Marston Thos. esq. Ampthill square, & 10 Norfolk st. Strand
Martell Chas. esq. 5 Dyers bldgs. Holbn
Martelli Chas. Hen. A. esq. 9 Serle st
Martelli Chas. H. A. esq. 19 Up. Berkeley st
Marten Geo. Robt. esq. 25 Old Bond st
Marter Wm. I. esq. 5 Furnival's inn
Martin Admiral Sir George, 51 Berkeley square, & Lee, Kent
Martin Admiral Sir Thomas Byam, G.C.B. 53 Wimpole st
Martin Col. John, 13 Vigo st. Regent st
Martin Major Joseph J. 39 St. James's pl
Martin Capt. 24, Beaufoy terr. Edgw. rd
Martin Capt. H. Byam, R.N. 53 Wimpole st
Martin Rev. Frs. 1 Euston gr. Euston sq
Martin Rev. Saml. 1 Chester pl. Pimlic
Martin Charles, esq. 17 Salisbury sq
Martin Chas. Wykeham, esq. M.P. 55 Up. Seymour st. & Leeds castle, Maidstone
Martin D. W. esq, 7 Charlton pl. Islgtn. gn
Martin Edwd. esq. Radnor pl. Oxfd. ter
Martin Edwd. H. esq. 4 Tanfield ct. Temple
Martin Edw. W. esq. 61 Up. Seymour st. & Burchwood house, Croydon, Surrey
Martin E. M. esq. 10 Crown Off. rw. Templ
Martin Fras. esq. Her. col. Bennett's hill
Martin Francis Offley, esq. 3 Stone bldgs. & 29 Chesham st. Belgrave sq
Martin Geo. esq. 24 Connaught terrace
Martin G. esq. 8 Newlnd. cot. Finch. N. rd
Martin Hen. esq. 9 Green's row, Chelsea
Martin Henry, esq. 11 Mornington pl
Martin Hen. esq. 8 Portland ter. Rgt.'s pk
Martin J. esq. 33 Blomfield rd. Maida hl
Martin Jas. esq. 21 Kensington gore
Martin J. F. M. esq. 77 Norton st
Martin James R. esq. 71A, Grosvenor st
Martin J. K. L. esq. 30 Allsop ter. New rd
Martin John, esq. M.P. 14 Berkeley sq. & Ledbury, Herefordshire
Martin John, esq. 9 New Manor pl. Chelse
Martin John, esq. 2 New sq. Lincoln's inn, & 40 Bedford place, Russell square
Martin John, esq. 5 Stanhope ter. Rgt.'s pk
Martin John, esq. 1 Wilmington square
Martin Josiah, esq. 4 Nottingham pl
Martin Marcus, esq. 40 Bedford place, Russell sq. & 2 New sq. Lincoln's inn
Martin Miss, 1 Harley place, New road
Martin Mrs. 8 Albion ter. Wandwth. rd
Martin Mrs. 13 Bedford place, Knsngtn
Martin Mrs. 82 Cambridge ter. Edgw. rd
Martin Mrs. 28 Euston square
Martin Robert, esq. 21 Eaton square
Martin Robert, esq. 8 Gt. Newport st
Martin Robt. T. esq. 43 Old Compton st
Martin Samuel, esq. Q.C. 18 Wimpole st & 1 Essex court, Temple
Martin Thomas, esq. 4 Hanover square
Martin Thos. esq. 3 South sq. Gray's inn
Martin T. B. esq. M.P. 2 Trinity pl. Charing cross, & Ballinahinch, near Outerard
Martin Wm. esq. 20 Artillery pl. west
Martin Wm. esq. 15 Hyde park square
Martin Wm. Byam, esq. 6 Hyde park ter
Martindale Benj. esq. 19 Cecil st. Strand
Martindale Mrs. 51 Trinity sq. Borough
Martindale S. M. esq. 10 Old sq. Lncln.'s in
Martineau Alfred, 1 Mitre ct. buildings
Martineau Hubert, esq. 2 Raymond buildings, Gray's inn
Martineau Misses, 12 Montagu pl. Clap. rd
Martineau Mrs. 55 Guilford st
Martineau Peter, esq. 16 Highbury terr
Martineau Philip, esq. 29 Montague pl
Martineau Richard, esq. 17 Westbourne st. & Lenton house, Nottingham
Martinez Sebastian Gonzalez, esq. 1 Cumberland terrace, Regent's park, & West cliff house, Brighton

Martins Sir Wm. 3 Hyde park gardens
Martins Sir Wm. Stable yard, St. James's
Martiny Mrs. 9 Camden rd. vils. Camd. tn
Marton Geo. esq. M.P. 16 Park square, & Capernwray hall, near Lancaster
Martyn Chs. C. esq. 2 Whitehall gardens
Martyn Miss, 39 Brompton square
Martyn Patrick, esq. 18 Spring gardens
Martyn Wm. esq. 14 Brompton row
Martyn Wm. esq. 38 Davies st. Berkeley sq. & 7 Thayer st. Manchester square
Martyne Capt. F. M. 17 Charles st. Berkeley sq. & Fern cottage, near Windsor
Martyr Chs. esq. 8 Circus rd. St. John's wd
Marx Francis, esq. 15 Wilton crescent
Marx Mrs. M. 15 Wilton crescent
Mascall Francis, sen. esq. 22 Red Lion square, & Eppleton, Durham
Mascall Francis, jun. esq. 7 New sq. Lincoln's inn, & 10 Powis pl. Queen sq
Mascall J. jun. esq. 10 Powis pl. Gt. Orm. st
Mash Miss, 8 Seamore place, Curzon st
Maslin Thomas, esq. 7 Old Quebec st
Mason Augustus, esq. 8 Delahay st. Westminster, & 8 Moorgate st
Mason Chas. esq. 27 Argyll st. Regent st
Mason Edw. esq. 30 Duncan terr. City rd
Mason Geo. Wm. esq. 61 York ter. Rgt.'s pk
Mason G. W. W. esq. 12 Stockw. c. Clp. rd
Mason Jas. esq. 6 Cannon row, Westmstr
Mason James, esq. 61 Brompton square
Mason James, esq. 38 Doughty st
Mason John Chas. esq. 44 Burton crscnt
Mason Mrs. 2 Endsleigh st
Mason Mrs. 9 Grove ter. St. John's wd
Mason Nathl. esq. 17 Compton ter. Islgt
Mason Nathaniel, esq. 23 Red Lion sq
Mason Saml. esq. 23 Nottinghm. st. N. w. rd
Mason Thomas, esq. 65 Oxford st
Mason Thos. esq. 134 St. John st. road
Mason Thos. esq. 48 St. John's wd. terr
Mason Ths. esq. 2 Warwk. vils. Maida hill
Mason Wm. esq. 21 Albemarle st
Mason Wm. esq. 20 Brownlow st. Holborn
Mason Wm. esq. 69 Gt. George st. Brmnsy
Massall Mrs. 4 Earl's ct. Old Brompton
Massareene & Ferrard Viscount, 10 Albemarle st.; & Ovel Temple, Louth; & Antrim castle, Antrim
Massey Hon. Maj. 19 Cumberland st
Massey Lady, 52 Upper Brook st
Massey John, esq. 6 Brunswick place, Regent's park, & 33 Lincoln's inn flds
Massey Jonathan, esq. 50 Cambridge tr
Massey Mrs. 220 Maida vale
Massey R. M. O. esq. 8 Queen st. Mayfair
Massey Wm. N. esq. 1 Pump ct. Temple
Massingberd C. L. esq. 20 Hyde park sq
Masson John George, esq. 14 Jermyn st
Masson Miss, 86 Great Portland st
Master Geo. esq. 22 Duke st. Grosvnr. sq
Master Stephen, esq. 53 Davies st
Masterman John, M.P. 35 Nicholas lane, & Knott's green, Leyton, Essex
Masterman Mrs. 34 Noel st. Islington
Masterman Wm. S. esq. 4A, Wine Office court; & 6 Hind court, Fleet st.; & 9 Durham place east, Hackney road
Masters George, esq. 3 Amwell terrace
Masterson Hen. W. esq. 4 Clarence ter
Matcham Nelson, esq. 13 Bruton st
Matcham Nelson, esq. 8 New sq. Linc. in
Mate Wm. esq. 2 Scarsdale ter. Kensngtn
Mather Geo. esq. 4 Bayswater terrace
Mather Miss, 32 Aberdeen place
Mathers Robert, esq. 30 Nelson sq
Matheson Rev. Jas. 4 Blomfield st
Matheson Rev. Jas. 5 Palmer ter. Hollwy
Matheson James, esq. M.P. Stornaway house, 13 Cleveland row, St. James's; Coul house, Dingwall; & Stornaway, Lewis, Ross-shire
Mathew J. M. esq. 4 Gray's inn square
Mathew Mrs. 25 Howland st
Mathews Edmund, esq. 31 Somerset st
Mathews Hen. esq. 53 Dorset st. Salsb. sq

Mathews James, esq. 103 Jermyn st
Mathews John, esq. 1 Mitre ct. Temple
Mathews John, esq. 1 New Temple bdgs
Mathews John, esq. 3 Highbury grange, & 1 Essex court, Temple
Mathews Mrs. 11 Clapham road place
Mathews Mrs. 36 Sloane st
Mathews Peter, esq.14 Clement's in.Strd
Mathews Richard, esq. 15 Clapham rise
Mathews T. esq. 28 Hemingford ter.Isln
Mathews Wilkinson, esq. Q.C. 16 Old sq
Mathias George, esq. 30 Gt. Portland st
Mathias J.E.esq.13 Up.King st.Blomsby
MathisonG.F.G.esq.112Parkst.Grvnr.sq
Mathison Mrs. 112 Park st. Grosvnr. sq
Matson Vice Adml. Rd. 14 Cavendish road, St. John's wood
Matson Major Edward, R.E. 30 Norfolk crescent, Oxford square
Matson Capt. Hy. R.N. 25 Westbourne place, Pimlico
Matson Charles, esq. 25 Westbourn pl
Matson Mrs. 30 Baker st. Clerkenwell
Matthew Thos. esq.1 Church st.Edgw.rd
Matthews John, esq. 6 Charles st.Clar.sq
Matthews J. esq. Lavender hl.Wndsw.rd
Matthews J.S.esq.4 Saville row,Walw.rd
Matthews Miss, 11 Barnsbury park
Matthews Miss, 16 Westbourne st.Hy.pk.
Matthews Mrs.23Glo'ster gr.we.O.Brmpl
Matthews Mrs. 3 Sloane ter. Chelsea
Matthews Peter, esq. 15 High st.Marylb
Matthews Richd. esq. 5 Belitha villas, Barnsbury pk. & 4 Brick ct. Temple
Matthews Robt.H.esq.10 Lr.Seymour st
Matthews Thos. esq.35 Devonsh.st.Qn.sq
Matthias Miss, 53 Green st. Grosvenr.sq
Matthie Mrs.53 Hans pl.&HighWycomb
Matts Thos.esq.23Regent sq.Gray'sin.rd
Matts Wm. esq. 17Belgrave st.King's crs
Maturin W. S. esq.31 Bedford pl.Kensgn
Maude Hon. Capt. F. R.N.10 Glo'ster ter
Maude Hon. Miss, 10 Gloucester terrace
Maude Arthur Grey, esq.14Gt.George st. Westmnstr. & Sessions ho. Clkwl. grn
Maude Fred. P.esq.3,Kg.'sBch.wk.Tmpl
Maude Hartwell J. esq. 14 Gt. George st
Maude Hen. Hallett, esq. 6 New sq
MaudeJ.R.esq.8 St. Andrew pl.Rgt.'s pk
Maugham G. esq. Lee cot. Old Bromptn
Maugham Rt. esq. Law Socity.Chncy.la
Maugham Thos. esq. 70 Myddelton sq
MaughamW.esq.51Guilfd.pl.L.Kngtn.la
Maughan Edward, esq.55 Nelson sq
Maul John C. esq. 5 Pump ct. Temple
Maule Sir Wm. Hen. 22 Hyde park gardens, & Rolls garden, Chancery lane
Maule Rt. Hon. Fox, M.P. 19 Pall mall, & Birnam lodge, near Dunkeld
Maule Geo. esq. 18 Wilton crescent, & Gwydir house, Whitehall
Maule Wm. esq. 7 Gt.George st.Westmn
Maund Geo. esq. 8 Omega ter. Alpha rd
Maunder Samuel, esq. 67 Gibson square
Maunsell Garnett P. esq. 8 Bentinck st
Maunsell Thos. Philip, esq. M.P. Carlton club, & Thorp, Malson, nearKettering
Maunsell Wm.T. esq. 1 Pump ct.Temple
Maurice Rev.M. D.D. 7 Ladbroke villas, Notting hill
Mawby Lieut.Gen.76 Baker st. Porm.sq
Mawby Miss, 75 Upper Berkeley st
MawdittThos.esq.Ambassad.'s ct.St.Jas'
Mawdsley John, esq. 9 Hanover square
Mawe Thos. Jones, esq. 4 New Bridge st
Mawley Hy. esq. 43Gower st.Bedford sq
Mawson Mrs. 21 Duke st. Manchester sq
Maxse James, esq. & Lady Caroline, 49 Upper Grosvenor st
Maxwell Lt. Gen. Sir Chas.24Chester st
Maxwell Capt. the Hon. Jas.Pierce, M.P. Carltn.club, Pallmall, & Fanham, Cavan
Maxwell Captain, R.N. 69 Harley st
Maxwell Acheson, esq. 8 Up.Belgrave pl
Maxwell Edward, esq. 39 Hatton gardn
Maxwell John, esq.27 Tysoe st.Spafields
Maxwell Mrs. Major, 8 Gloucester pl
Maxwell Mrs. 86 Norton st. Fitzroy sq
Maxwell Peter B. esq.3 Thurloe pl.west
Maxwell Pet.B.esq.4Stone bdgs.Linc.inn
Maxwell Wm. Edward, esq. 53 Woburn place, & 6 Gray's inn square
Maxwell Wm. Jas. esq. 9 Wimpole st
May Sir John, K.C.B. 15 Hyde park st
May Edward Collett, esq. 141 Sloane st
May Jas.Bowen, esq.14Queen sq. Blmsb
May John William, esq. consul general for the Netherlands, Holland lodge, 31 Portland ter. & 123 Fenchurch st
May John Wm.esq. Portland ter.Rgt.pk
May Leon, esq.32 Gt.Russell st. Blmsby
May Mrs.3 Camden rd.villas, Camden tn
May Oliver, esq. 4 Sloane ter. Chelsea
May Thomas, esq. 2 Middle Temple lane
May Thos.Baker, esq.35Lincoln's inn flds
May Thos. Erskine, esq. 60 Chester sq
May William, esq. 8 Prospect cottages, Thornhill road, Islington
Maybank Mrs. 16 Stafford st. Lisson gr
Maybery Chas. esq.3Earl's ct.OldBromp
Mayhew A. esq. 129 Albany st. & 26 Carey st
Mayhew Chas. esq.14 Argyll st. Regt.st
Mayhew Fredk. esq. 4 Verulam buildings, Gray's inn
Mayhew Henry, esq. 355 Strand
Mayhew Jas.esq.35Cambridg.ter.Edg.rd
Mayhew Jas. esq. 37 Portman pl.Edg.rd
Mayhew James G. esq. 14 Argyll st
Mayhew Joshua, esq. 16 Fitzroy square, & 26 Carey st. Lincoln's inn
Maynard Viscount, 38 Grosvenor sq. & Easton, near Dunmow, Essex
Maynard Hen. esq. 17 Park terrace
Maynard John, esq. 1 Maynard pl.Chels
Maynard J. A. esq. 2 Mitre ct. bldgs
Maynard Joseph, esq. 43 Tavistock sq
Maynard Mrs. 29 Bernard st. Russell sq
MayneCap.R.N.Manr.ho.Stanmore, Mdx
Mayne Edward, esq. 16 Norfolk crescent
Mayne Henry Blair, esq. 74 Jermyn st
Mayne Mrs. 35 York st.Portman square
Mayne R.esq.13 New st. Spring gardens
Mayne Wm. Hen. esq.2 Lisson gr. south
Mayo, Earl of, G.C.H. 24 Norfolk street, & Palmerston house, Naas, Kildare
Mayo John, esq. 31 Connaught terrace
MayoJn.Ryall, esq.37 Bedford st.Cov.gdn
Mayo Newman K. esq. 7 Canonbury pk
Mayo Thomas, M.D. 56 Wimpole st
Mayor George, esq. 12 New Ormond st
Mayor Hen. esq. 115 Upper st. Islington
Mayor Mrs. 14 Compton terrace, Up. street, Islington
Maysey Mrs. 4 Highbury place
Mazzinghi Thos. John, esq.28 Green st. Grosvenor sq. & Devereux chambers
MeacherJ.esq. 33 Fredk. st.Gray's inn rd
Meacher Mrs. 26 Green st. Grosvenor sq
Mead Hon. Gen. 48 Bryanstone square
Mead Jas.P.esq.4Ladbroke vils.Nottg.hl
Mead JosephC.S. esq.11 Bedford st. Bdfd. row, & 25 East st. Red Lion sq
Mead Miss, 22 Claremont sq.Pentonville
MeadRichd. esq.2Ordnanceter.St.Jn.'s w
Meade Major Roach, 28 Trevor square
Meade Capt. Edwd. 55 Jermyn st
Meade John, esq.2Dorchester pl.Bldfd.sq
Meaden Mrs. 7 Wellington terrace
Meadows Drinkwater, esq. 82 Ebury st
Meares John, esq.15Holland pl.Clapm.rd
Meares John, esq. 1 Park lane
Measure John, esq. 19 Avenue road, Regent's park, & 4 Serle st. Linc. inn
Meason Capt. G. L. 2 Hyde park gate
Medcalf Robt. esq. 20 Lincoln's inn fields
Medford Robt. esq. 44 Porchester ter
MedleyGeo. Bowley, esq.2 Milner st.Isltn
Medlicott Edwd. H. esq. 6 Middle Nw. st
Medlicott Mrs. 29 Paddington green
Mee Arthur, esq. Carlton chm.12 Reg.st
Mee George, esq. 25 Hemingford ter. Isl
Mee James, esq.27Up.Barnsbury st. Isln
Mee Joseph, esq. 33 Allsop ter. New rd
Meehan JamesPatk.esq.15Clement's inn
Meek George, esq. 29 Russell square
Meek Wm.esq.9John st.Holland st.Blkfs
Meeres Charles, esq. 9 Westbourne pl
Meeson Roger, esq. 2 Pump ct. Temple
Mege John, esq. 30 Keppel st. Russell sq
Meggeson George, esq. 79 Cannon st.City
Meggy Robert, esq. 33 Trinity sq. Boro', & 15 London st. Fenchurch st
Meier F. esq. 15 Camden road villas
Meikleham Wm. esq. 23 Parliament st
Meilan Miss, 11 Albion st. Hyde pk
Meinertzhagan Daniel, esq. 28 Devonshire place, Portland place
Melbourne Viscount, P.C. 39 South st. Grosvenor sq.; Brocket hall, Welwyn; & Melbourne hall, near Derby
Meldola Rev. David, 6 Great Alie st
Melia Rev. Dr. 54 Lincoln's inn fields
Meller Hen. Jas. esq. 10 Clifford's inn
Meller Thos. Wm. esq. Denmark hill
Mellis J. esq. M.D.169Prospect pl.Edg.rd
Mellish G. esq. 3 Harcourt bdgs. Temple
Mellish Miss, 11 Gt. Stanhope st. & Hamells park, near Puckeridge, Herts
Mellish Mrs. 7 Addison rd. Kensington
Mellish Richd. Chas. esq. 62 Chester sq
Melliship G. W. esq. 13 Paddington grn
Melliss Mrs. 9 St. George's ter. Knsgtn
Mellor John, esq. 21 Endsleigh st. Tavistock sq. & 10 Farrar's bldgs. Temple
Melton Wm. esq. 6 Bedford row
MelvillRev.Henry, Rectory house, Tower
Melvill P. esq. 4 Clarendon pl. Hyde pk
Melville Viscount, K.T., P.C. Somerset house, & Melville castle, Edinburgh
Melville Hon. Wm. L. 3 Arlington st
Melville Rev. Edmund, 40 St. James's pl
Melville Gansevoort, esq. sec. of American Legation, Harley st
Melville Jas. esq. 5 Lansdwn. vil. Not.hl
Melville John, esq. 16 Upper Harley st
Melville Robt. A. esq. 47 Noel st. Islgtn
Melville Robt. W. esq. 8 Suffolk st
Melville White, esq. 47 South st. Gro. sq
Mendam Robert, esq. 32 Clapham rise
Mendes Aug. esq. 10 Carlton vil. Edg. rd
Mendibil Mrs. 8 Burton st
Menetone Mrs.15Newington pl.Kngtn.rd
Menetrier Emile, esq. 35 York pl.City rd
Menetrier Mrs. 1 Cumberland pl. New rd
Menham B. esq.16Holloway pl.Holwy.rd
Menham Hen.esq.39East st.Manchstr.sq
Mercer Col. 53 Queen Anne st
Mercer George, esq. 54 Queen Anne st. & Teddington, Middlesex
Mercer Jas. esq. 11 Argyll pl. Regent st
Mercer Misses, 54 Queen Anne st. & Teddington, Middlesex
Mercraken Jas. J. esq. 13Bedfordrw. Islg
Meredeth Mrs. 4 Connaught square
Meredith Charles, esq. 67 Queen's road, Bayswater, & 8 New sq. Lincoln's inn
Meredith E. T.esq.15 Chas.st.Wstbrne.tr
Meredith Fras.esq.47 Cumming st.Pntvl
MeredithH.B.esq.47 Cumming st.Pentvl
Merewether Henry Alworth, S.L. Guildhall, & Castlefield, Calne
Merewether Henry Alworth, jun. esq. 2 Inner Temple lane, & 5 Victoria sq
Meriton Mrs. 9 Canterbury villas
Merivale Herman, esq. 2 Cambridge pl. Regt.'s pk. & 3 Harcourt bldgs. Templ
Merlet P. F. esq. 15 Southampton st. Fitzroy square
MerphyG.esq.Branden vil.Morningtn.rd
Merrick Wm. esq. 33 Northampton sq
Merriman J. N. esq. 1 Young st. Knsgtn
Merriman John, esq. 45 Kensington sq
Merriman William, M.D. 34 Brook st
Merriman Saml. B.esq.8 Broad st.bldgs
Merry Thos. esq. 6 York pl. City road
MerrydueW.esq.8A, Melina pl.St.Jn's w
MerryweatherJas.esq.54 Connaught ter

Mertens Henry, esq. 30 Addison rd. north
Meryon Edward, esq. 4 Bolton st
MestayerR.esq.68Hermtge.pl.St.Jn.st. r
Messitter Thomas, esq. 15 Harewood sq
Metaxa, Countess of, 33 Gloucester pl
Metcalfe Lord, G.C.B., P.C., Governor General of Canada
MetcalfeChas.T.P.esq.3Victoria ter.Chel
Metcalfe Geo.esq.5 Richmond ter.Pntnv
Metcalfe Hy. esq. 32 Hill st. Berkeley sq. & Hawstead house, BurySt.Edmund's
Metcalfe J. esq. 13 Clarndn.pl.Maida hl
Metcalfe Mrs. 58 Brompton square
Metcalfe Mrs. 21 Up. Gloucester place
Metcalfe Thomas, esq. 10 Conduit st
Metcalfe Wm. esq. 1 Upper Bedford pl. & 2 Stone buildings, Lincoln's inn
Meteyard Horace Wm.esq. 4 Gray's inn square, & 8 Chatham place
Metherell J. esq. 7 Swan st. Southwark
Methley Rev. Jas. 12 Virgina tr. Dov. rd
Methold Henry, esq. 18 Nottingham pl
Methold Mrs. 8 Park pl. Up. Baker st
Methuen Lord, 128 Park st. & Corsham house, Chippenham, Wilts
Meux Sir Henry, 41 Upper Brook st
Meux Sir Hen. 19 Gt. Russell st. Bloomsbury, & Theobald's park, Herts
Mew George, esq. 40 Gt. James st
Mew Geo.esq.12 King's Bench wk.Temp
Mewburn Bowyer, esq. 9 Green ter. New River head, & 9 Gt. Winchester st
Mewes Mrs. 22 Dalby terrace, City road
Mexborough, Earl of, 33 Dover st. Piccadilly, & Methley park, Leeds
Meyer Edward S. esq. 1 Lavender hill terrace, Wandsworth road
MeyerFred.esq.2Lavendr.hl.tr.Wdsw.rd
MeyerF.J.esq.30Up.North pl.Gry's.in.rd
Meyer John, esq. 45 Baker st. Lloyd sq
Meyer John, esq. 4 Wilton place
Meyer Louis, esq. 24 Nottingham st
Meyer Philip J. esq. 23 Judd place west
Meyers Barnett, esq. 17 Crutchedfriars
Meyers Wm. esq. 38 Sackville st
MeyersWm.esq. Queen's mews, Pimlico
Meymott Fred.W.esq.3 Figtree ct.Temp
Meymott John Clarke, esq. 11 Glo'ster rd. Hyde park, & 86 Blackfriars rd
Meymott John G.esq. 86 Blackfriars rd. & 44 Lincoln's inn fields
Meymott Wm.esq.24 Gibson sq. Islngtn
Meynell Capt. Hen.R.N., M.P. 14 Hill st
Meynell Mrs. 7 Upper Wimpole st
Meyrick Col.Wm. Henry & Lady Laura, 30 Curzon st. & Orbery's, nr. Sudbury
Meyrick Miss, 14 Gloucester crescent
Meyrick Owen Fuller, esq.16 Clifford st
Meyrick Wm. esq. 15 Cambridge ter. Edgware road, & 2 Furnival's inn
Meyrick Wm. esq. 7 King's bench walk
Michael Jacob, esq. 9 Red lion square
Michau Madame Louis, 19 Dover st
MicheleJohn G.esq. 23 Russell pl. Fitz.sq
Michelie Chas. E. esq. 3 Lancaster pl
Michell Mrs. 8 Baker st. Portman sq
Michell Mrs. 7 Eccleston st. Chester sq
Michell Mrs. 38 Howland st. Fitzroy sq
Michell Mrs. 8Lr.Southwick st. Hyde pk
Michie Miss, 50 Up. Baker st. Regt. pk
Micholls Edward Emanuel, esq. 13 New Broad st. City
Mickle David, esq. 37 Queen st. Blmsby
Mickle John, esq. 23 Bloomsbury sq
Micklem Edwd. esq. 3 Edgware road
Micklethwaite Col. 49 South st. Gro. sq
Micklethwait F. N. esq. 30 Chancery la
Micklethwayt Sir S.B.P.49 Albemarle st. & Iridge place, Hurst green
Middleditch W. esq. 26 Woburn place
Middlemas Rt. H. esq. 4 St. Andrew's pl. Regt. pk. & West Barns, E. Lothian
Middlemist Miss, 95 Great Russell st
Middlemist Rt. Law, esq. 7 Gt.Coram st
Middleton Lord, 11 Montagu st. Portman sq.; & Wollaton hall, nr. Nottnghm
Middleton Sir William Fowle, bart. & Hon. Lady, 13 Whitehall place, & Shrubland park, near Ipswich
Middleton Chas. J. esq. 63 Oxford ter. & 2 Godliman st. Doctor's commons
Middleton James, esq. 7 Furnival's inn
Middleton James G. esq. 76 Newman st
Middleton Jesse, esq. 8 Burton crescent
MiddletonJ.esq. 8Norland ter.Notting hl
Middleton Jsph. esq. 4 Essex ct. Temple
Middleton J.H.esq. 15 Radnor pl.Oxfd.tr
Middleton Mrs. 6 Lamb's Conduit place
Middleton Mrs. 36 Cadogan place
Midlam Wm. G. esq. 3 Spring gar.Chr.cr
Midwinter Wm. esq. 24 Wilmington sq
MiévilleAmêdee F. esq.32 Nottingham pl
MiévilleAndw. Amêdee, esq.67 Gower st
Miéville Fredc. L. esq. 23 Hanover sq
Miéville Louis, esq. 23 Hanover square
Milbanke Richd.Tyler,esq. 8 Burwood pl
Milburn Alex. esq. 117 Chancery lane
Milburn Geo.Wm.A.esq. 117Chancery la
Mildmay Sir Hen.St.John, bart. 6 Halkin ter. Belgrave sq. & Dogmers field pk. Hartford bridge
Mildmay Capt. Geo.St.John,36Chshm.pl
Mildmay Humphrey St. John, M.P. 46 Berkeley sq. & Oxford ct. Shoreham
Mileham Wm. esq. 42 Mincing lane
MilesCol. Northvilla, Park rd.Regt.'s pk
Miles Lt.R.N. 3Springfld.pl.Wandswh.rd
Miles Rev. John, 6Abbey rd.St.Jhn.'s wd
Miles Charles, esq. 15 St. James's sq
Miles Chas. esq.11 Somerset st. Prtmn.sq
Miles Fred. esq. 7 Henriet. st.Brnswk.sq
Miles George, esq. 18 Edwardes square
Miles Henry, esq. 23 Harley st
Miles Henry, esq. 2 Raymond buildings, Gray's inn
Miles Miles, esq.6Up.Phillimore pl.Knsg
Miles Misses, 31 Baker st
Miles Mrs. 22 Everett st. Brunswick sq
Miles Mrs. 7 Henrietta st. Brunswick sq
Miles Philip John, esq. 7 Hamilton pl. & Abbotsleigh, Somerset
Miles P. W. S. esq. M.P. 7 Hamilton pl. Piccadilly, & Leigh ct. near Bristol
Miles Thos. esq. 65 George st. Euston sq
Miles Wm. esq. 27A, Howland st
Miles William, M.P. 7 Hamilton place, Piccadilly, & Kingsweston, nr. Bristol
Miles Wm. esq. 45 York st. Portman sq
Milford Hen. esq. 5 Woburn pl. Russl.sq
Mill John, esq. 1 Plowden blds. Temple
Millard James, esq. 5 Soley ter. Pntnvl
Millard Richd. esq. 12 Craven st. Strand
Millbank Sir John, 88 Gt. Portland st
Millen Mrs. 11 Up. Southwick st. north
Miller Capt. 9 Dean's pl. South Lambth
Miller Andrew, esq. 5 Canonbury park
Miller Chas.esq.Ambassador's ct. St.Jas'
MillerEdward, esq. 1 York gt.Regt.'s pk. & Poet's lodge, Bushy heath, Stanmore
Miller Felix M. esq. 6 Lower Eaton st
Miller George, esq. 16 Bryanstone sq
MillerHen. esq. 55 Nwngtn. pl. Kngtn. rd
Miller Ingleby Thomas, esq. 12 Upper Bedford place
Miller James, esq.32Church st. Spitalflds
MillerJas.esq.1Guildfd.pl.Lr.Kenngtn.la
Miller James, M.D. 40 Welbeck st
Miller John, esq. 2 Parliament st
Miller John, esq. 4St.John's wood grove
Miller Joseph, esq.44Michl's. pl.Brmptn
Miller Mark Blowers, esq. 1 Windsor cottages, Haverstock hill, & 2 Clfds. in
Miller Misses, 22 Grosvenor st. west
Miller Miss, 9 Doughty st
Miller Miss, 80A, Dean st. Soho
Miller Mrs. 50 Smith st. Chelsea
Miller Rt. esq. 16 Albany st.Regent's pk
Miller Robt. esq. 25 Artillery pl. west
Miller Robert, esq. 32 Essex st. Strand
Miller Samuel, esq. 4 New sq. Lincoln's inn, & St. John's, Fulham
Miller Saml.Fredk.esq.10Duke st.St.Jas
Miller Thos. esq. 2Petersburgh pl. Bysw
Miller T. J. esq. 7 Millbank st. Westmr
Miller Walter, esq.15Carlton vils.Edg.rd
Miller Wm. esq. Larkhall rise, Claphm
Miller Wm. esq. 27 King st. St. James's
Miller Wm. esq. 46 Leicester square
Miller Wm. esq. 2Minerva ter.Brnsby.pk
Milligan Chas. esq. 19 Craven st. Strand
Milligan James, esq. 5 Finsbury circus
Milliken Wm. esq. 25 Burton st
Millingan Thomas, esq. 23 Glo'ster cres
Millington Mrs. 6 Lonsdale sq. Islington
Mills Arthur, esq. 2 Paper buildings
Mills Chas. esq. Camelford house, Oxford st. & Hillingdon, Uxbridge
Mills Chas. esq. 40 Tavistock st. Cov.gn
Mills Daniel, esq. 3 Eaton ter. Eaton sq
Mills Edward, esq. 5 Bryanstone square
Mills Francis, esq. 3 New st. Spring gdns
Mills Fredk. R. esq. 11 Cunningham pl
Mills Geo. esq. 14 Up. Berkeley st. west
Mills Geo. I. esq. 28 Francis st.Tot.ct.rd
Mills Henry, esq. 10 Maida hill
Mills Henry, esq. 4 Pump court, Temple
Mills Jas. esq. 8Claremont pl. Judd st
Mills John H. esq. 27 Keppel st. Russell square, & 1 Paper buildings, Temple
Mills Jn. Jas. esq. 20 King's par. Chlsea
Mills Miss 14 Hans place, Sloane st
Mills Mrs. 32 Cloudesley st. Islington
Mills Mrs. 12 Coles ter. Barnsbury rd
Mills Mrs. 18 Kensington square
Mills Mrs. 8 Park village east
Mills Mrs. 10 Theberton st. Islington
Mills Mrs. 21 Winchester row, New rd
Mills Samuel, esq. 20 Russell square
Millward Mrs. 6Trevor sq. Knightsbridge
Milman Major Genl. 9 Berkeley sq
Milman Rev. H. Lit. Dean's yd. Westmr
Milman Wm. esq. 27 Keppel st. Russell sq. & 11 Paper buildings, Temple
Milne Alexander, esq. 1 Whitehall
Milne Alfred, esq. 4 Garden ct. Temple
Milne Frank, esq. 4 Raymond buildings
Milne John, esq. 15 Cumming st.Pntnvl
Milne Mrs. 8 Bolton st. Piccadilly
Milne Mrs. 12 Brunswick square
Milne Nathaniel C. esq. 22 Endsleigh st. & 2 Harcourt buildings, Temple
Milne Wm. esq. 3 Old sq. Lincoln's inn
Milner Isaac, esq. Bale's cottage, Chichester place, Wandsworth road
Milner Jas. esq. 12 Addison rd. Knsgtn
Milner J.esq. Arthur's club, 69 St.Jas.st
Milner Miss, 18 Charles st. Berkeley sq
Milner Mrs. 47 Upper Seymour st
Milner Mrs. Geo. 3Ulster ter. Regt's. pk
MilnerWm.E.M.esq.75Eatn.pl.Belgra.sq
Milnes Richard Monckton, M.P. 26 Pall mall, & Frystone hall, Ferrybridge
Milnes Thos. esq. 3 Judd pl. east, Nw. rd
Milroy Gavin, M.D. 30 Fitzroy square
Milsom G. P. H. esq. 70 Tottenhm.ct.rd
Milson Rd.esq.40 Somerset st.Portmn.sq
Milton Viscount, 4 Grosvenor square, & Wentworth house, near Rotherham
Milton Mrs. 8 Charlotte pl. Up.Kngtn.la
Milton Mrs. Heckfield lodge, Little Chls
Minasi Henry S. esq. consul gen. for Sicily, 15 Cambridge st. Connaught sq
Minchin Geo. Howard, esq. 32North bnk
Minchin O.esq.18St.Geo's.pl.Hyd.pk.cor
Ming Thos. esq. 6 OldDorset pl.Clapm.rd
Minnet W.esq.1 Warwick vils. Harrow rd
Minney John, esq. 29 Brompton crescent
Minnikin Jas. esq. 3 Minerva ter. Islgtn
Minot Misses, 11 North crsnt. Bedfd. sq
Minshaw Rd. esq. 30 Theberton st. Islgtn
Minshull Rd. esq. 10 Pelham ter. Bromp
Minshull Samuel, esq. 51 Margaret st
Minto Earl of, G.C.B., P.C. Farrance's hotel, 11 Upper Belgrave st. & Minto house, Roxburgh
Miranda Mrs. 27 Grafton st. Fitzroy sq
Mirehouse John, esq. 60 Up. Seymour st. Banjeston, & Brownslade, Pembrokesh

Mirfin George H. esq. 12 Gray's inn pl
Mirfin Rd. esq. 2 Devonsh.ter. Thornh.rd
Mitcalfe Henry, esq. M.P. 1 Manchester buildings, & Whitley, Morpeth
Mitcalfe William, esq. 40 Fitzroy sq
Mitchel E. esq. 8 Charles st. Lowndes sq
Mitchell Col. 29Cavendish rd. St. Jn's wd
Mitchell Lady Harriet, 25 Queen Anne st
Mitchell Fras. esq. 12 Upper Wimpole st
Mitchell George, esq. 21 Motcomb st
Mitchell Geo. esq. 13 Charles st. Gro. sq
Mitchell Geo. esq. 3 Cadogan row, Chels
Mitchell Geo. M. esq. 4 Strtfd.pl Oxford st
Mitchell James, esq. 58 Chancery lane
Mitchell Jas. Hy. esq. 17 Up. Wimpole st. & Stapleford hall, near Nottingham
Mitchell John, esq. 42 Charles st. Berkeley square, & 9 New Broad st
Mitchell John, esq. 3 Mylne st. Pentonvl
Mitchell John, esq. 4 Portsmouth st
Mitchell John W. esq. 3 Hanover st
Mitchell Miss, 10 Bolton st. Piccadilly
Mitchell Miss, 42 Charles st. Berkeley sq
Mitchell Mrs. 19 Cheyne walk, Chelsea
Mitchell Mrs. 15 Great George st. Westmr
Mitchell Mrs. 17 Upper Wimpole st. & Stapleford hall, near Nottingham
Mitchell Mrs. 1 Whitehall
Mitchell Mrs. Forbes, 18 Upper Gower st
Mitchell Mrs. Jas. 8 Portugal st. Gros. sq
Mitchell Mrs. M. 26 Arundel st. Strand
Mitchell Rowland, esq. 17 Up. Wimpole st
Mitchell T. esq. 55 Holywell st. Millbnk
Mitchell Thomas esq. 3 River ter. north
Mitchell Thos. A. M.P. 30 George st. Han. sq
Mitchell V. C. esq. 1 Vxhall. pl. Sth. Lmbh
Mitchell William, esq. 21 Lloyd square
Mitchison Mrs. 31 Compton ter. Islingtn
Mitchinson Wm. esq. 23 Upper Charles st
Mitford Hon. Miss, 6 Park pl. St. Jas's
Mitford Robert, esq. 34 Russell square
Mitthofer John C. esq. 21 Upper Ebury st
Mitton Thos. esq. 23 Southampton bldgs. & Lampton hall, Middlesex
Mittonnette Fred. esq. 16 Queen sq. Blmy
Mivart Jas. E. esq. 16 Addison rd. Kensing
Mivart James E. esq. 39 Brook st
Moat W. C. esq. 28 Upper Berkeley st
Mobbs Sam. esq. 2 Alfred place, Bromptn
Mocatta Abraham, esq. 2 Woburn place
Mocatta David, esq. 32 Brunswick sq
Mocatta E. esq. 7 Devonport st. Hyde pk
Mocatta Miss, 13 Woburn square
Mocatta Mrs. 31 Woburn place
Mocatta Moses, esq. 33 Russell square, & 122 King's road, Brighton
Moeller Mrs. 23 Park road, Regent's pk
Moffatt Capt. W. R.N. 6 Addison rd. south
Moffatt George, esq. M.P. 85 Eaton sq
Moffatt T. J. esq. 6 Catherine ct. Tower hl
Moffatt Wm. Bonython, esq. 20 Spring gardens, & Manby cottage, Kenningtn
Mogford Ths. esq. 16 Norton st. Portland pl
Moggridge Wm. H. esq. 13 O. Burlingtn. st
Moginee Dan. esq. 4 Thornhl. pl. Caled. rd
Moginie John, esq. 23 Lr. Phillimore pl
Moginie N. C. esq. 5 St. Andrew's ct. Holbn
Mogue A. esq. 26 Queen's row, Pimlico
Moira Edward, esq. 28 Devonshire st
Mole Wm. esq. 41 D, Park st. Grosvenor sq
Molesworth Sir Wm. bt. M.P. 1 Lowndes sq. Belgrave square, & Pencarrow, Bodmin
Molesworth Dowager Lady, 41 Lowndes st
Molling Godfrey, esb. 12 Connaught pl
Molloy Charles, esq. 1 Gray's inn square, & 8 New square, Lincoln's inn
Mollison Crawd. esq. 3 Grove tr. St. Jn. w
Molloy Mrs. 7 Beaumont st. Marylebone
Molloy Mrs. 23 Upper Baker st
Molony Mrs. 5 Lower Chester terrace
Molyneux the Ladies, 21 Arlington st. & Stoke Farm, Slough, near Windsor
Molyneux Anthony Lancaster, esq. 23 Dorchester pl. Blandford square
Molyneux Edw. E. esq. 6 Pump ct. Tem
Molyneux Mrs. 8 Wyndham st. New rd

Monaghan Patk. esq. 8 Surrey st. Strand
Monck Sir Charles, bart. & Lady Mary, 20 Duke st. Westminster, & Belsay castle, Newcastle-on-Tyne
Monck Lady Elizabeth, 18 St. James's pl. & Hampton court palace
Monckton Edwd. esq. 23 Saville row, & Somerford hall, Wolverhampton
Monckton Wm. C. esq. 33 Norfolk st. Strn
Moncreiff A. esq. 30 Gt. George st. Westr
Money Geo. Henry, 3 Furnival's inn
Money Mrs. 5 Osnaburgh ter. Regt's. pk
Money W. esq. Corinthn. vil. Finchley rd
Mongredien J. P. esq. 10 South st. Finsby
Monins Richard, esq. 2 Warwick st. Gol. sq
Monkhouse Cyril John, esq. 3 Craven st
Monkhouse Geo. esq. 15 Pelham pl. Ful. rd
Monkhouse Richd. esq. 10 Halfmoon st
Monro Cecil, esq. 76 Cambridge terrace
Monro Edward Thomas, M.D. 87 Harley st. & Clay hill, Bushy
Monro Hen. esq. 8 Up. Seymour st. west
Monson Hon. Miss Charlotte, 22 Chapel st. Grosvenor sq
Monson Lord, 1 Lincoln's inn fields
Montagu Lord, 6 Hamilton place, & Ditton park, Windsor
Montagu Hon. Col. Hen. 1 Up. Berkeley st. & Hazlewood, King's Langley, Herts
Montagu Hon. Miss, 1 Up. Berkeley st
Montagu Hon. Spencer, 61 Cadogan pl
Montagu Basil, esq. Q.C. 2 Princes ct. Storey's gate, Westminster
Montagu Edgar, esq. 4 New sq. Lin. inn
Montagu Mrs. 2 Prince's ct. Storey's ga
Montague Hon. Mrs. S. 61 Cadogan pl
Montague Capt. 8 Eccleston st
Montague H. S. esq. Larkhl. rise, Clpm
Montague F. esq. Willowcot. Sth. Lambth
Montague Miss, 25 Artillery pl. Finsbury
Montanary N. esq. 9 Albion ter. Chelsea
Monteagle Lord, P.C. 37 Brook st. & Mount Trenchard, near Shanagolden
Montefiore Sir Moses, F.R.S. 7 Grosvenor gate, Park lane, & East cliff lodge, Ramsgate
Montefiore Jsph. esq. 4 Gt. Stanhope st
Montefiore H. Jsph. esq. 8 Devonport st
Montefiore Moses, jun. esq. 31 Woburn pl
Montefiore Mrs. 4 Gt. Stanhope st. & Worth park, Crawley, Sussex
Monteith Wm. esq. 2 Paper buildings
Monterio L. A. esq. 9 Radnor pl. Oxfd. ter
Montfort Lord, 24 Upper Montagu st
Montfort Lady, 20 Lower Eaton st. & Monk's grove, St. Ann's hill, Chertsey
Montgomery Rev. R. A.M. 51 Torringtn. sq
Montgomery Alfred, esq. 63 Eaton pl
Montresor Hen. esq. 2 Albion ter. Chlsa
Montresor Thos. esq. 36 Lincoln's inn fi
Montrose Duke of, K.T. P.C. 45 Belgrave square, & Buchanan house, Stirling
Monypenny T. G. esq. 15 Regent st
Moody Rev. Peter, 81 St. John's wood ter
Moody James, esq. 33 Hunter st
Moody John Doble, esq. 11 Curzon st
Moody Mrs. 23 Walcot sq. Lambeth
Moody Wm. esq. 6 King's bench wlk. Temp
Moon Fras. G. esq. 19 Finsbury square
Moon James, esq. 4 Adam st. Adelphi
Moon James, esq. 1 Millman st. Bed. rw
Moon Jthn. G. esq. 5 Dorset pl. Dorset sq
Moore Col. 24 Grove end rd. St. Jno.'s wd
Moore Col. Wm. Geo. 38 Curzon st
Moore Major Arthur, 33 Queen Anne st
Moore Capt. Fred. 29 Southampton st. Strd
Moore Rev. Dr. Jas. 16 Upper Gower st
Moore Rev. Robt. 45 Charles st. Berkly. sq. & Hunton, near Maidstone
Moore Ambrose, esq. 12 Endsleigh st
Moore Andw. esq. 22 Pelham cres. Fulm. rd
Moore A. esq. 9 Coles ter. Barnsbury rd
Moore Augustus H. esq. 23 Calthorpe st
Moore Augusts. H. esq. 7 Sth. sq. Gry.'s inn
Moore Charles Henry, esq. 45 Wimpole st. & 36 Lincoln's inn fields

Moore B. esq. 15 Cunningham pl. St. Jn.'s w
Moore Chas. W. esq. 15 Burtn. st. Brtn. cres
Moore Christopher, esq. 22 Howland st
Moore David, esq. 11 Up. Ranelagh st
Moore Edmund F. esq. L2, Albany, & 11 New square, Lincoln's inn
Moore Edwd. esq. 10 King sq. Goswell rd
Moore Edw. esq. 4 Seamore pl. Curzon st
Moore Edwd. D. esq. 10 Arlington st
Moore Geo. esq. 64 Lincoln's inn fields
Moore Geo. esq. 17 Canterbury villas
Moore George, esq. 55 Ebury st
Moore G. B. esq. 19 Southmptn. pl. Eustn. sq
Moore Hen. esq. 10 Connaught terrace
Moore John, esq. 77 Camden rd. villas
Moore John, esq. 39 Chester sq. Pimlico
Moore John, esq. 4 Maida hill west
Moore John, esq. 30 Regent sq. Gray's inn road, & 1 New sq. Lincoln's inn
Moore John A. esq. 3 Hunter st. Brnswik. sq
Moore John C. esq. 37 Hertford st. Mayfair
Moore Jnthn. esq. 2 Field ct. Gray's inn
Moore Joseph, esq. 10 Saville row
Moore Joseph S. esq. 5 Stone blds. Lin. in
Moore Josph. W. esq. Sandon lo. Avenue rd
Moore Josiah, esq. 6 Up. Islington ter
Moore Mrs. 19 Beaumont st. Marylebo
Moore Mrs. 48 Cadogan place
Moore Mrs. 13 Marlboro' pl. Kengtn. cross
Moore Mrs. 12 Mornington crescent
Moore Mrs. 51 Portman pl. St. John's wd
Moore Mrs. 10 York pl. Fulham road
Moore Morris, esq. 27 Grafton st. Fitzry. sq
Moore R. W. esq. 2 Chas. st. Eastborn terra
Moore Regnier W. esq. 1 New sq. Linc. inn
Moore Rich. esq. 16 Grove ter. Lisson grov
Moore Robt. O. esq. 19 Sussex pl. Rgt.'s pk
Moore S. esq. 13 Lowther cottgs. Livrpl. rd
Moore Thomas, esq. 23 Bedford sq
Moore Thomas, esq. 5 Dorset sq
Moore Thos. esq. 8 Grove pl. Brompton
Moore Thomas, esq. 31 Sackville st
Moore White J. esq. 22 Harrington st
Moore Wm. esq. 68 Chester sq. Pimlico
Moore Wm. esq. 11 Cheyne walk, Chelsea
Moore Wm. esq. 16 Park pl. Paddington
Moore Wm. E. esq. 2 Noel st. Islington
Moores Sam. esq. 68 Myddelton square, & 25 Throgmorton st
Moorson Capt. R. 68 Lowndes square
Moorson Capt. Wm. 8 Sussex sq. Hyde prk
Moran Edwd. R. esq. 24 Webb's county ter
Morant George, esq. 95 Wimpole st
Moray Earl of, K.T. 7 Stratford pl. Oxford st.; & Darnaway castle, Forres; & Donibristle house, Aberdour; & Doune lodge, Doune, Perthshire; & Castle Stuart, Cambletown, Invernessshire
Mordan S. esq. 15 Cloudesley ter. Islgtn
Mordaunt Lady, 41 Eaton place, & Waltonhall, Stratford-on-Avon
Mordaunt Fred. esq. 11 Addison rd. nrth
Mordaunt Misses, 4 Upper Wimpole st
Mordaunt Mrs. 41 Charlotte st. Portlnd. pl
Mordaunt Octavius D. esq. 22 Bolton st
More Mrs. 19 Lower Phillimore place
Moreing Charles, esq. 31 Saville row
Morell Mrs. Clifton cot. Mornington rd
Moreno Don Manuel, Envoy Extraordinary, & Minister Plenipotentiary from Rio de la Plata, 23 Upper Wimpole st
Morel Dominique, esq. 1 Langham pl
Moresby Wm. esq. 11 South sq. Gray's inn
Moret Pet. esq. Ambassad's. ct. St. James's
Morewood Rev. J. B. St. Geo.'s hospital
Morgan Sir Charles, bart. 70 Pall mall, & Tredegar, Newport, Monmouthshire
Morgan Lady, 11 William st. Knightsbg
Morgan Alfred, esq. 6 Manchester sq
Morgan Arthur, esq. F.R.S. New Bridge st
Morgan Cadogan, esq. 3 Plowden bldgs
Morgan Charles, esq. 44 & 45 Bedford row
Morgan Charles, esq. 14 Cadogan place
Morgan Chas. M. R. esq. M.P. 70 Pall mall, & Ruperra, near Newport, Monmouth

Morgan Chas. O. S. esq. M.P. 70 Pall mall,&Tredegar, Newport, Monmouth
Morgan Chas.Robt.esq.39Up.Bedford pl
Morgan Francis, esq. 51 Bedford square, & Oakfield lodge, Reading, Berks
Morgan Jas. A. esq. 36 Gamden rd.villas
Morgan John,esq.22Chapel st.Grosvn.pl
Morgan John, M.D. 19 Northampton sq
Morgan Joseph, esq. 45 Bedford row
Morgan Miss, 62 Burton crescent
Morgan Mrs. 47 Coleshill st. Eaton sq
Morgan Mrs. 9 Lr. Phillimore pl.Kensng
Morgan Mrs. 6 Manchester square
Morgan Mrs. 1 Montagu pl. Montagu sq
Morgan Mrs. 84 Sloane st
Morgan Moses, 12 Charlotte st. Bedford square, & 71 St. Martin's lane
Morgan Moses, esq. 40 Millbank st
Morgan Richd. esq. 4 New sq. Linc. inn
Morgan Rd. esq. 29 Northampton sq
Morgan Rt. esq. 2 Strahan ter. Livpl. rd
Morgan Samuel, esq. 22 Mornington pl
Morgan Thomas, esq. 13 Rutland gate
Morgan Wm.esq. 3Dorchestr.pl.Blndf.sq
Morgan Wm. esq. 9 Hemingfd.ter.Islntn
Morice Jno. Chas. esq. 116Camden rd.vil
Morier Greville, esq. 106 Mount st
Morier James, esq. 22 Charles st. Berkeley sq. & 17 Marine parade, Brighton
Morier John Phillip, esq.20Up. Harley s
Morier Miss, 53 Devonshire st
Morison Sir Alexr. M.D. 26 Cavendish sq
Morison Rev. Dr. J. 1 Walton pl. Bromp
Morison Geo.esq.6 Southbank, Regt's.pk
Morison John, esq. 18 Park village west
Morison Mrs. 16 Tonbridge pl. Euston sq
Morland Mrs. 102 Glo'ster pl. Portm.sq
Morlet John, esq. 24 Blomfield road
Morley Earl of, Kent house, Knightsbridge, & Saltram, Plympton
Morley George, esq. 35 Michael's place, Brompton, & 15 Serle st. Linc. inn flds
Morley Hen.esq.16Hanover cot.Rgt.'spk
Morley John,esq.24 Charles st. Brkly.sq
Morley Thos.Wm. esq.11NewCavendh.st
Morley Wm. Hart, esq. 15 Serle st
Morman J.esq.1Portland pl. Clapham rd
MorningtonEarl,Mivart's hotel,Brook st
Morpeth Viscount, 12 Grosvenor place
Morphett Geo. esq. 5 Lloyd st. Lloyd sq
Morphett Nathaniel, esq. 3 Bream's buildings, Chancery lane
Morphy Fras.esq.9 Montague pl.Russ.sq
Morrah James, esq. 62 Sloane st
Morrell Rev. D. 35 Sackville st
Morrell Chas. esq. 118 Sloane st
Morrell Henry, esq. 9 Bloomsbury sq
Morrell Miss, 19 Upper Seymour st
Morren Mrs. 9 Allen terrace, Kensington
Morrice George, esq. 6 Highbury grove
Morrice John, esq. 4 Cumberland ter
Morris Rev. R. 74 Gt. Russell st. Blmsby
Morris Lieut.Gen. J. 28 Hyde park grdns
Morris David, esq. M.P. 8 St. James's place, & King st. Carmarthen
Morris Charles, esq. 7 Connaught place
Morris Chas. esq. 7 Portugal st. Gros. sq
Morris Edwd. esq. B6, Albany, Picadily
MorrisEvan,esq.2Harcourt bdgs.Temple
Morris Fredk. P. esq. 26 Old sq.Linc. inn
Morris Henry, M.D. 26 Sackville st
Morris Henry S. esq. 26 Sackville st
Morris Henry Wm. esq. 1 Lancaster pl
Morris James, esq. 15 Belgrave sq
Morris James, esq. 12 Crescent, Minories
Morris John,esq.7Chapel pl.Cavendh. sq
Morris John,esq.4 Child's pl.Temple bar
Morris John, esq. 41 Vincent sq
Morris Jn. esq. Wheeler pl. Hampstd. rd
Morris Jsph. esq. Ambass.ct. St.James's
Morris Mowbray, esq. 2Stone bdg.Lin.in
Morris Miss, 1 Child's place, Temple bar
Morris Mrs. 44 Camden st. south
Morris Mrs. 7 Charlotte pl. Up. Ken. la
Morris Mrs. 7 Portugal st. Grosvenor sq
Morris Mrs. 20 Up. George st. Prtmn.sq
Morris Mrs. 10 Wilton st. Grosvenor pl
Morris Rd. esq. Wright's la. Kensington
Morris Robert, esq. 13 Cadogan terr
Morris Thomas, esq. 5 Albert road
Morris Thos.esq.21Devonshr.pl.Edgw.rd
Morris Thomas, esq. 58 Warren st
Morris Thos. esq. 17 Sthamptn. st. Strnd
Morris V. esq. The Retreat, Battersea
Morris Wall J.esq. 35Baker st.Prtmn.sq
MorrisW.Geo.esq.25Michael's pl.Bmptn
Morris Wm. Henry, esq. 38 Finsbury sq
Morrison Major-Gen. W. C.B. M.P. 16 Saville row; & Greenfield, Alloa, Clackmannan
Morrison Alexr.esq.6Milner st.Islington
Morrison Alex. esq. 10 Camden rd.villas
Morrison Geo. esq. 13 Whitehds. gr.Chel
Morrison Jas.esq.M.P. 57 Up.Harley st.; &Fonthill,Hindon; & Basildon,Reading
Morrison Jsph. esq. 3 Lonsdale sq. Islntn
Morrison Mrs. East hill, Wandswrth. rd
Morrison Mrs. 41 Michael's pl. Bromptn
Morrison Miss, 18 Cadogan pl. Sloane st
Morriss James,esq.32 Oxford sq.Hyd.pk
Morritt Aaron, esq. Clarence cottage, Gloucester gate, Regent's park
Morson Henry, esq. 106 Regent st
Mortan Frederick, esq. 18 Beaumont st
Mortimer Alfred, esq. 23 Burton cresnt
Mortimer Chas. esq. 38 Argyle st.Nw.rd
Mortimer Ed. esq.83 Oxford ter. Hyd.pk
Mortimer John, esq. 43 Doughty st. Mecklenburg sq.; & 17 Clifford's inn
Mortimer John, esq. 14 Hanover square, &Pippinford pk.EastGrinstead,Sussex
MortimerJno.esq.14Pelham pl.Fulhm.rd
MortimerJsph.esq.7Glo'str.gr.w.O.Bmp
Mortimer Thomas, esq. 4 Albany ct. yd
Mortimer T. esq. 10 Greville pl. Kilburn
Mortimer Thos. Hill, esq.4 Albany ct. yd
MortimerW.Hy.esq. 12 Harley st.Cav.sq
MortisJohn,esq.Springfield pl.Wndsw.rd
Mortlock Sir John, 18 Dorset square
Mortlock Wm. esq. 28 Essex st. Strand
Mortlock Wm. esq. 33 Finchley New rd
Morton, Earl of, 7 Old Palace yard; & Dalmahoy, near Edinburgh
Morton And. esq. Larkhill rise, Claphm
Morton Andrew, esq. 21B, Soho sq
Morton Edwd. esq. 25 Craven st. Strand
Morton Edwd. M.D. 7 York pl. Kntsh. tn
Morton Edw. esq. 48 Gower st
Morton Francis, esq. 19 Maida hill west
Morton George, esq. 14 Wharton st
Morton Jph. esq. 15 Dorset pl. n.Clap.rd
Morton Thos. esq. 6 Glo'ster st.Portm.sq
Morton Thos. esq. 7 Woburn place
Moscheles Ignece, esq. 3 Chester place
Moseley Rev. Dr. W. 18 Bloomsbury st
Moseley Andrew, esq. 53 Gt. Ormond st
Moseley George, esq. D4, Albany
MoseleyHen. esq. 57 Charlotte st. Fitz.sq
Moseley Joseph, esq. 1 Mitre ct. bldgs
Moseley Mrs. 57 Charlotte st. Fitzroy sq
Moseley Rd. esq. 8 Pine Apple place
MoseleyRobt.esq. 4 John st.Bedford row
Moseley Thos. esq. 13 Bedford st.Cov. gr
MoseleyWm.esq.13Cmbrlnd.ter.Rgts.pk
MoseleyWm. esq.17 New st. Covent gdn
Mosely Ephraim, esq. 32 Haymarket
Mosely Lewin, esq. 12 Berners st
Mosely Simeon, esq. 29 Duke st. St. James's, & 32 Haymarket
Moser Richard, esq. 24 Trinity sq. Boro'
Moser Robt. esq.2 Gordon pl. Gordon sq
Moser Robert, esq. 30 Tavistock square
MoserWm.esq.9Robert st.Hampstead rd
Moses Abraham L. esq. 11 Finsbury circ
Moses Hen. esq. 41 Trinity sq.Tower hill
Moses Hy.esq.1Up.Prtlnd. pl.Wndsw.rd
Moses Jn. esq. 4Up.Prtlnd. pl. Wndsw.rd
Mosley Oswald, esq. 10 Cumberland ter
Mosquera Don Manuel Maria, chargé d'affaires of New Grenada, 52 Baker st
Moss Edwin, esq. 71 Wimpole st
Moss JohnThos. esq.2Dyers's bldgs.Hbn
Moss Matthew, esq. 18 Greek st. Soho
Moss Mrs.71Hermitage pl.St. John st.rd
Moss Mrs. 83 New Bond st
Moss Wm. esq. 11 Serjeants' inn, Fleet st
Mosse Rd. B. esq. 2 Princes st.Westmstr
Mostyn Lord, 9 Lower Seymour st. & Pengwern, St. Asaph
Mostyn Hon. Edward M. Lloyd, 9 Lr. Seymour st. & Mostyn, Holywell
Mostyn Chas.Browne, esq.3 Montagu st. Portman sq.& Kiddington ho.Woodstk
Mostyn Hen. esq.83Baker st.Portman sq
Mostyn Llewellyn,esq.36 Nottingham pl
Mostyn William, esq. 36 Nottingham pl
Mott Richd. esq. 6 Gordon st. Gordon sq
Motte Standish, esq. 55 Lincoln's inn flds
Mouat Charles, esq. 12 Finsbury pl. so
Moucher Mrs. 7 Stranrear pl. Maida hl
MouelWm.esq.32Cambridge st.Edgw.rd
Mouflet C. esq. 10 Queen st. Mayfair
Mould Mrs. 12 Keppel st. Russell sq
Mould Thomas, esq. 45 Brompton row
Moule Henry, esq. 43 Hunter st
Moule Thos. esq. Stable yd. St. Jas.Pala
Moule Wm. esq. 34 Canonbury square
Moultrie E. M. esq. 4 Serle st. Linc. inn
Mount Edward Shaw, esq. 41 Carey st
Mount Miss, 18York terrace,Regent's pk
MountainThos esq.7 Claremont pl.Ptnv
Mountcashel,Earl of, Conservative club, & Moore park, Kilworth, county Cork
MountcastleR.esq.4U.York pl.St.Jns.wd
Mountford John, esq. 14 Gt. Coram st
Mountnorris Countess, 39 Chesham pl
Mourilyan Jsph. N. esq. 2 Verulam bdg
Mousley Wm. Eaton, esq. 5 Stone bdgs
Moutry Mrs. 4 Earl st. Horseferry road
Mouzon Geo. A. esq. 237 Bethnal gr. rd
Mowatt Francis, esq. 14 Devonshire pl
Mowatt Mrs.22 Up.Glo'ster pl.Dorset sq
Mower Mrs. 29 St. James's place
Moxon Hen. esq. 9 Marlbro' pl.Kngtn.cr
Moxon Henry, esq. 2 Tanfield ct.Temple
Moxon John,esq.8Hanover ter.Rgt.'s pk
Moxon Wm. esq.10 New sq Lincoln's inn
Moy Mrs. 49 Sloane st
Moyes Mrs.3Belmont pl.Wandsworth rd
Moyse Edw. esq. 9 Angel ter. Islington
Muckarsie G. J. esq. 18 King st. Holborn
Muddle Mrs. 54 Welbeck st
Mudell John, esq. 7 Canonbury ctgs. Isln
Mudford Wm. esq. 5 Harrington sq
Mudry Monsieur, 51 Bernard st. Russ. sq
Muggeridge S. esq. 13 Paradise ter. Isln
MuirheadLadyJane,15Park rd.Rgt.'s pk
Mulcaster Lieut. General Sir Fred.W. 8 Hyde pk. pl. w.; & Carlton,Cantrbry
Mulgrave, Earl of, 1 St. James's st
Mullane Mrs.1Frederick st.Gray's inn rd
MullenMiss,1 Acacia place, St.John's wd
Mullens James D. esq. 16 Cambridge sq
Mullens Rd. esq.8 Spencer st.Goswell rd
Muller Frederick, esq. 46 Hans place
Muller William, esq. 180 Blackfriars rd
Mullett John, esq. 3 Allsopp ter.New rd
Mulligan James, esq. consul general of Venezuela, 16 Tokenhouse yard
Mulliner Mrs.11Rodney ter.ea.Mile e.rd
Mullings Mrs. 4Wellington tr.St.Jn.'swd
MullinsEdw.esq.1 Gt.James st. Bedfd.rw
Mullins G. esq. Bartholomew pl.Kntsh.tn
Mulock Mrs. 1 Lamb's Conduit place
Mulready William, esq. R.A. 1 Linden grove, Kensington gravel pits
Mumbray John, esq. 12 York pl. Pentvl
Mumby Mrs. 19 Theberton st. Islington
Mumby Mrs. 7 Spring ter. Wandswth rd
Munday Edward Miller, M.P. 19 Pall mall, & Shipley hall, Derby
Munday Jas. esq. 8 Albion ter.Canby.sq
Munday Mrs. 31 Portland place,Islngtn
Munday Mrs. Charles, 135 Sloane st
Munday William, esq. 61 Carey st
Mundell Rt.esq.1Cambridge pl.Rgt.'spk
Mundell Wm.A.esq. 9 Park village east
MundyRearAdml.SirGeo.2Grosvnr.st.w

Mundy General, 1 Hobart pl. Eaton sq
Mundy William, esq. 44 Queen Anne st. & Markeaton, Derbyshire
Munn Hen. esq. 7 Lr. Duncan pl. City rd
Munnings Miss, 2 Windsor ter. Maida hl
Munro Sir Hugh, 21 Manchester square, & Fowlis castle, Dingwall, N.B
Munro Lady, 27 Eaton place, Belgrave sq
Munro Gordon, esq. 4 Charles st. St. Jas. sq
Munro Hugh Andrew J. esq. 113 Park st
Munro Mrs. 6 Belgrave st. south, Pimlico
Munster Henry, esq. 41 Brompton sq
Muntz Geo. Frd. esq. M.P. 6 Mnchstr. bdgs. & Ley hall, near Birmingham
Murch Rev. W. H. D.D. 11 Blgrv. st Kg's. cr
Murchison Rodk. I. esq. 16 Belgrave sq
Murchison Simon, esq. 21 Holles st
Murcott Wm. H. esq. 30 Henrietta st. Cvt. g
Murdoch James Gordon, esq. 11 Haymarket, & 23 Chester ter. Regent's pk
Murdoch Thomas W. C. esq. 44 Harley st
Murdock James, esq. 7 Staple inn, Holb
Murdock Thomas, esq. 8 Portland place
Mure Robt. esq. Blandford lo. Blandfd. sq
Murgatroyd Frederick, esq. Little Britain
Muriel Charles, esq. 10 Clapham rise
Murietta F. esq. 7 Pineapple pl. Edgw. rd
Murley C. esq. 8 Victoria vils. Avenue rd
Murphy Adolphus, esq. 83 Baker st. Portman square
Murphy Don Jsph. 1st sec. of legation for Mexico, 7 Sussex pl. Regent's prk
Murphy Don Thomas, Mexican minister, 7 Sussex place, Regent's park
Murphy Edward Wm. M.D. 12 Henrietta st
Murphy Francis Stack, S.L., M.P. 3 Serjeants' inn, Chancery lane
Murphy Mrs. 33 Cambridge st. Conght. sq
Murphy Mrs. 4 Claremont row, Islngtn
Murray Rt. Hon. Lieutenant General Sir George, 5 Belgrave square
Murray Hon. Lady Ann, 63 Wimpole st
Murray Sir A. bt. 11 Upper Berkeley st
Murray Hon. Miss A. 30 Chesham st. Belgrave square
Murray Hon. Capt. W. 13 Chesham st. Belgrave square
Murray Hon. Gen. 4 Up. Seymour st
Murray Hon. Major Chas. 13 Chesham st
Murray Hon. John J. 3 Rutland gate
Murray Hon. Miss, 13 Chesham st
Murray Hon. Mrs. 14 Great Stanhope st
Murray Captain James, 28 Soho square
Murray Rev. Thos. Boyles, 77 Guilford st
Murray Adam & Sons, 47 Parliament st
Murray Chas. Knight, esq. 5 Whitehall pl. & 25 Eastbourne terrace, Bayswater
Murray C. R. S. esq. 11 Cavendish square, & Danesfield, Great Marlow, Bucks
Murray Edward, esq. 27 Camden rd. villa
Murray Geo. esq. 3 Acton pl. Camden rd
Murray George M. esq. 6 Hereford st. Park lane, & Heathfield lodge, Acton
Murray Hy. esq. 72 Milton st. Dorset sq
Murray H. S. esq. 38 Lincoln's inn fields
Murray James, esq. 36 Queen Anne st
Murray James Archibald, esq. 28 Porchester terrace, & 7 Whitehall place
Murray James B. esq. 35 Lr. Belgrave pl
Murray John, esq. 8 Canterbury villas, Edgware road, & 7 Whitehall place
Murray John, esq. 55 Lincoln's inn fields
Murray John, esq. 2 Salisbury pl. New rd
Murray John C. esq. 35 Craven st. Strand
Murray Miss, 25 Argyle st. King's cross
Murray Mrs. 4 Acton place, Holloway
Murray Mrs. 27 Cloudesley sq. Islngtn
Murray Mrs. 3 Gothic cott's. Park vil. ea
Murray Mrs. 35 Thayer st. Mnchster. sq
Murray Mrs. Scott, 11 Cavendish sq
Murray Robt. H. esq. 1 Fitzroy st. Fitz. sq
Murray Robt. H. esq. 5 New sq. Linc. inn
Murray Thos. esq. 10 Lonsdale sq. Islngtn
Murray Thomas Lamie, esq. 16 George st. Hanover square
Murray Wm. esq. 11 Cambridge sq. Hy. pk
Murray Wm. esq. 3 Garden ct. Temple
Murray Wm. esq. 2 John st. Berkeley sq
Murray Wm. P. esq. 59 Chancery lane
Murrell Mrs. 23 Woburn pl. Russell sq
Murrieta C. de, esq. 21 Kensington gdns
Murrough John P. esq. 7 New inn, Strnd
Murry Mrs. 45 Gower st
Murton Jn. M. esq. 3 Somers pl. wst. Nw. rd
Musgrave Hon. Mrs. 17 Hill st. Berkly. sq
Musgrave Geo. esq. 6 Gordon square
Musgrave Hon. Mrs. 56 Harley st
Musgrave Thos. esq. 5 Chatham place
Musgrove Richd. esq. 29 Granville sq
Muspratt John Petty, esq. 21 Russell sq
Muston Miss Fanny, 40 Myddelton sq
Mutlow Miss, 16 Paradise ter. Islingtn
Muzy Peter A. L. esq. 2 Union pl. New rd
Myatt Archipher, esq. 94 Albany st
Myatt Wm. esq. 7 North crescent, Bedford sq. & 35 Throgmorton st
Myddleton Miss, 48 Upper Brook st. & Chirk castle, Denbighshire
Myer C. esq. 32 Newingtn. pl. Kenngtn. rd
Myers Sir Fras. W. 7 Chester st. Grosvnr. pl. & Pentlow hall, Sudbury, Suffolk
Myers Henry, esq. 94 Milton st. Dorset sq
Myers Lawrence, esq. 33 Bedford place
Myers Mrs. 2 Acacia gardens, Acacia rd
Myers Mrs. Arlington vil. Finchley Nw. rd
Myers Mrs. 53 Burton st
Myers Miss, 12 Green st. Park lane
Myers Miss, 2 Petersburgh pl. Bayswtr
Myhill Hy. esq. 7 Spencer tr. Lw. rd. Islgtn
Mylne James Wm. esq. 4 Bloomsbury pl. & 10 Old square, Lincoln's inn
Mylne Rt. Wm. esq. Carlton cham. 8 Rgt. st
Mylne Wm. C. esq. New River head
Myson James, esq. 12 Oxford terrace

NAINBY Miss, 10 Canonbury pl. Isingtn
Nairne Rt. M.D. 44 Charles st. Berkeley sq
Naish Mrs. 2 Charlotte row, Islington
Nalder Fras. esq. 8 South st. Finsbury
Nalder Fras. esq. 2 Waterloo, Kilburn
Nalder Fred. Harris, esq. 58 Gordon sq
Nalder H. esq. 11 Greville pl. Kilburn
Nall Mrs. 12 Hemngfrd. cots. Brnsbry. rd
Namarcy T. esq. 2 Queen's pl. Knngtn. rd
Napier Capt. Henry, 62 Cadogan place
Napier Commodore Sir Charles, knt. G.C.B., M.P. Royal Naval club house, 160 New Bond st. & Merchistoun hall, Horndean, Hants
Napier Miss, 57 Green st. Grosvenor sq
Nappi Paul, esq. 31 Newman st
Narroway John J. esq. 5 Dorchester pl
Nash Benj. esq. 40 George st. Euston sq
Nash Charles, esq. 16 Claremont sq
Nash Charles, esq. 74 Mortimer st
Nash David Wm. esq. 26 Bedford pl
Nash Davyd Wm. esq. 3 Essex ct. Temple
Nash Mrs. De Lacy, 15 Motcmb. st. Blgrv. sq
Nash Geo. esq. 1 Belinda cot. Canonbury sq
Nash Henry, esq. 30 Woburn place
Nash Hen. J. esq. 17 High rw. Knightsbdg
Nash J. E. esq. 11 New Ormand st
Nash John, esq. 1 Queen sq. Bloomsbry
Nash John, esq. 14 South sq. Gray's inn
Nash John Howell, jun. esq. 14 South sq. Gray's inn, & Wycombe, Bucks
Nash Joseph, esq. 3 Thames parade
Nash Mrs. 15 Bulstrode st
Nash Sebastian, esq. 11 St. John's wd. rd
Nash Thos. esq. 14 Richmond tr. Pntnvl
Nash Thos. esq. 18 Stoke Newington gr
Nash Thos. esq. 13 Thornhill Bridge pl
Nash Tyndale J. esq. 19 Blandford sq
Nash Wm. esq. St. Pancras vale, Hmpt. rd
Nash Wm. Wed. esq. Denmark hill, Cmbrw
Nasmyth A. esq. 13A, George st. Hnovr. sq
Nasmyth Mrs. 29 Regt. sq. Gray's inn rd
Nathan Baron, esq. 10 Kenningtn. cross
Nathan Henry, esq. 13 Lit. Stanhope st
Nathan Lawrence I. esq. 2 Cecil st. Strnd
Nathan Phineas, esq. 44 Bedford sq
Natili Angelo, esq. 3 Green's row, Chelsea
Nation Rd. esq. 4A, Orchard st. & 23 Somerset st. Portman sq
Natt Thomas, esq. 36 Mecklenburgh sq
Navone Dominick, esq. 11 Lloyd sq
Nayler Richd. esq. 12 Nelson ter. City rd
Naylor Maj. Jas. F. 40 Devonshire st
Naylor Capt. T. 31 Eastbourne tr. Pdntn
Naylor Elisha, esq. 13 Mornington pl
Naylor Miss E. A. 16 York pl. City rd
Naylor Mrs. 31 Eastbourne ter. Padngtn
Naylor Richard, esq. 4 Diddington pl. Islgn
Naylor Samuel, esq. 10 Park village, wst
Naylor Saml. jun. esq. 10 New sq. Linc. inn
Neal John, esq. 23 Wilton place
Neal John, esq. 23 Wyndham st
Neal Wm. esq. 5 Glo'ster grv. w. Old Bmpt
Neal Wm. esq. 1A, Park rd. Regent's pk
Neal Wm. esq. 14 Park sq. Regent's pk
Neale Edwd. V. esq. 66 South Audley st. & 4 New sq. Lincoln's inn
Neale Jas. esq. 19 Manchstr. tr. Livpl. rd
Neale Mrs. 8 Chandos st. Cavendish sq
Neale Mrs. 11 Woburn pl. Tavistock sq
Neale Wm. Johnson, esq. 5 King's bench walk, & 1 Churchyard ct. Temple
Neale Wm. Michael, esq. 8 Sloane sq
Neall C. esq. 20 Devonshire pl. Edgwr. rd
Neall John, esq. 4 Berwick pl. Grange rd
Nealor Wm. esq. 18 Lower Stamford st. & 23 Southampton buildings
Neame John Austin, esq. 3 Vincent ter. Islg
Neatby Jsph. esq. 20 Newingtn. pl. Ken. rd
Neate Chas. esq. 12 Manchester st
Neate Rowland, esq. 57 Lincoln's inn flds
Neate Rowland, esq. 10 Tavistock sq
Neave Sir Thomas, bart. 6 Albemarle st. & Dagnam park, Romford, Essex
Neave Digby, esq. & Hon. Mrs. 17 Dover st
Neave Mrs. Robert, 29 Burton crescent
Neave Thos. esq. 27 Park pl. wst. Lvrpl. rd
Neck Robert, esq. 13 Howard st. Strand
Neech Geo. esq. 41 Pembroke sq. Knsgtn
Needham Hon. —. 6 Addison rd. Knsngt
Needham Joseph, esq. 11 Paper buildings, & 5 Titchfield ter. Regent's park
Needham Miss Hermitage house, Linden grove, Kensington gravel pits
Needham Mrs. 11 Judd pl. east, New rd
Needham Wm. esq. 12 South sq. Gray's in
Neeld John, esq. M.P. 6 Grosvenor sq. & Red lodge, near Cricklade
Neeld Joseph, esq. M.P. 6 Grosvenor sq. & Grittleton ho. near Chippenham, & Kelston park, Bath, Somerset
Neeld Mrs. 101 Glo'ster pl. Portman sq
Neele Mrs. 23 Theberton st. Islington
Neeton Geo. esq. 20 Kensington gore
Neil Jas. esq. 6 Cornwall cr. Camdn. Nw. tn
Neild John C. esq. 5 Cheyne walk, Chelsea
Neilson Andw. esq. 9 Burwood pl. Edgw. rd
Neilson Mrs. 27 Cambridge st. Edgw. rd
Nellan Andw. F. esq. 6 St. George's tr. Islgt
Nellis Mrs. 2 Brompton square
Nelson Earl of, Carlton club, 94 Pall mall, & Trafalgar house, Salisbury
Nelson Countess, Duchess of Bronte, 5 Great Cumberland street
Nelson Rev. Edward, B.A. 19 St. John's villas, Acacia road, St. John's wood
Nelson Rev. Edward H. 19 Acacia road
Nelson Duckworth, esq. 19 Acacia road
Nelson George, esq. 10 New inn, Strand
Nelson Geo. esq. 8 Providence pl. Up. Ken. la
Nelson John, esq. 8A, Gloucester place
Nelson John, esq. 4 Hemus ter. King's rd
Nelson Jsph. esq. 4 Circus pl. London. wl
Nelson Joseph, esq. 4 St. John's wd. rd
Nelson Miss, 8 Providence pl. Up. Kngtn. la
Nelson Mrs. 30 Hyde park gardens
Nelson Park, esq. 11 Essex st. Strand, & Fulham lodge, Fulham
Nelson Rd. Albany, esq. 37 Oxford tr. Edgware road; & 25 Old sq. Lincoln's inn
Nelson Thos. esq. 11 Camden st. south
Nelson Thos. A. esq. 41 George st. Prtmn. sq
Nelson Thomas, esq. 10 Sidmouth st

Nelson Thos. M. esq. 3 Chas. st. St. Jas'
Nelson Thomas Wright, esq. 23 Gloucester place, New road, & 2 Gresham pl
Nelson Wm. esq. 5 Furnival's inn, Holbn
Nelson Wm. Benford, esq. 11 Essex st. Strd
Nembbard Miss, 6 Hyde park square
Nerinck Rev. John, 51 Clarendon sq
Nesbet John, esq. 9 Oxford square
Nesbett Cosby T. esq. 1 Elm ct. Temple
Nesbitt Lieut. Col. 62 Harley st
Nesbitt Mrs. 33 Devonshire st
Nesham Thos. esq. 15 Harpur st. Red Ln. sq
Ness Jas. esq. 2 Upper Gloucester st. St. John st. rd.; & 4 Dyer's bldgs. Holbn
Nethersole Henry, esq. 3 New inn, Strand, & Cedars, South Lambeth
Nettleship Rd. H. esq. 15 Clifford's inn
Nettleship Sam. esq. 14 Chapel st. Grosvenor sq. & North Cray pl. Kent
Nettleship Thomas, esq. 63 Harley st. & 4 Trafalgar square
Neumann Baron, envoy extraordinary & minister plenipotentiary from Austria, Chandos house, 7 Chandos st. Cavendish square
Neve William, esq. 10 Godliman st
Neves A. R. esq. 47 Upper Berkeley st
Nevett Chas. Shaw, esq. 192 Oxford st
Nevett Mrs. 17 Spencer st. Goswell rd
Nevill Charles, esq. 144 Oxford st. & Nevill hall, Market Harborough
Nevill Mrs. 11 Highbury place
Nevill William, esq. 15 Regent st
Neville Hy. Reginald, esq. 22 Saville row
Neville Miss, 6 Camden rd. villas, Cmd. tn
Neville Mrs. 13 Gerrard st. Islington
Neville Mrs. 93 Great Portland st
Neville Ralph, esq. M.P. 23 Hill st
Nevinson Charles D. M.D. 39 Montagu sq
Nevinson Edwd. esq. 24 Old sq. Linc.'s inn
Nevinson Geo. H. esq. 2 Elm ct. Temple
New Rev. Fras. T. 12 Chester pl. Regnt.'s pk
New Geo. Rd. esq. 6 Dorchst. pl. Blandf. sq
New Mrs. 5 Gt. Ormond st. Queen sq
Newbery Lt. Gen. 16 Earl's ter. Brmptn
Newbery Col. 10 Hereford st. Oxford st
Newbery W. M. esq. 23 Charlot. st. Bdfd. sq
Newburgh, Countess of, 35 Wilton crescent
Newby Mrs. 16 Mecklenburgh square
Newcastle, Duke of, K.G. 17 Portman sq. Clumber park, & Worksop Manor
Newdegate C. N. esq. M.P. 44 Brook st. & Arbury park, Coventry
Newdigate Mrs. 44 Brook st. & Harefield place, Middlesex
Newell Miss, 31 Cambridge st. Edgw. rd
Newell Miss, 5 Hanover st. Islington
Newell Mrs. 24 York buildings, New rd
Newell Wm. esq. 23 Noel st. Islington
Newell Sam. esq. 6 Grove rd. St. Jn.'s wd
Newen Geo. esq. 1 Hyde park terrace
Newenham Fred. esq. 14 Kensngtn. sq
Newham Mrs. 10 Red Lion square
Newington Wm. esq. 44 Lincoln's inn flds
Newland John, esq. 3 Tanfield ct. Temple
Newland M. esq. 29 Southampton st. Strand, & 1 Stanley terrace, King's road west, Chelsea
Newland Wm. esq. 21 Soley terrace
Newman Alfred, esq. 5 Mortimer st
Newman Alfred, esq. 78 Jermyn st
Newman Chas. esq. 28 Up. Phillimore pl
Newman Francis Chas. esq. 29 Sloane st
Newman Geo. esq. 38 Bedford pl. Knsngtn
Newman Jas. esq. 3 Cardigan pl. Knngtn. cr
Newman Jsph. esq. 3 Arundel st. Haym
Newman Mrs. 35 Cloudesley tr. Islngtn
Newman Mrs. 25 Dalby terrace, City rd
Newman Mrs. 17 Frederick st. Gray's in. r
Newman Mrs. 8 Pelham cresc. Fulham rd
Newman Mrs. 21 Pelham rd. Brompton
Newman Orlando, esq. 5 Francis pl. Hollw
Newman Rd. esq. 9 Fortess ter. Kntsh. tn
Newman William, esq. 43 Lincoln's inn fields, & Esher, Surrey
Newnham Nath. esq. 15 Cornwall ter
Newnham Ths. esq. 24 Chapel st. Gros. sq
Newnham Wm. esq. 4 Park cres. Prtlnd. pl
Newport Viscount, M.P. 30 Wilton cresc
Newport Miss, 8 Vauxhall pl. S. Lambeth
Newport Mrs. 3 North pl. Gray's inn la
Newry Viscount, M.P. Carlton club, Morne park, Rostrevor, Ireland
Newsom Samuel, esq. 3 Bloomsbury sq
Newsom Wm. esq. 22 Holloway pl. Holwy
Newstead Wm. Hen. esq. 18 Ely place
Newth John A. 116 Jermyn st. St. James
Newton Sir William John, 6 Argyll st
Newton — esq. 9 Regent's vills. Avenue rd
Newton Capt. Wm. 39 Dover st. Piccadilly, & Heldon, near Thetford
Newton Chas. esq. 13 Cvndsh. rd. St. Jn.'s w
Newton Chas. esq. 3 Middle Temple la
Newton Chas. esq. 2 Mount st. Grosvnr. sq
Newton Edward, esq. 26 Howland st
Newton Henry, esq. Harrow road
Newton James, esq. 83 Norton st
Newton James, esq. 13 South sq. Gray's in
Newton Jsph. esq. 10 Princes' pl. Ken. rd
Newton Lancelot, esq. 15 Albion st. Hyde park, & 31 Gutter lane
Newton L. van der V. M.D. 72 Milton st. Dorset square
Newton Miss, 11 Percy st. Bedford sq
Newton Mrs. 15 Albion st. Hyde park
Newton Mrs. 23 Up. Phillimore pl. Knsg
Newton Morris, esq. 3 Cambrdg. st. Edg. rd
Newton Morris, esq. 10 Lancaster pl. Strd
Newton W. esq. 23 Glo'ster rd. Hyde pk
Newton Wm. esq. 74 Cambridg. tr. Edg. rd
Newton William, esq. 39 Dover st. Piccadilly, & Heldon, near Thetford
Newton Wm. esq. 42 Queen sq. Blmsbry
Newton Wm. esq. 75 Westbourne terrace
Newton Wm. E. esq. 21 Granville sq. Pntvl
Newton Wm. T. esq. 13 Cavendish rd. St. John's wood
Nichol John G. esq. 27 Up. Phillimore pl
Nicholas Geo. esq. 18 Haverstock hill
Nicholes Mrs. 20 Suffolk st. Pall mall ea
Nicholl Rt. Hon John, D.C.L., M.P. 33 Belgrave square, & Merthyrmawr, near Bridgend
Nicholl Lieut. Col. 13 Beaumont st
Nicholl Fred. J. esq. 24 Bentinck st
Nicholl George, esq. 88 Piccadilly
Nicholl G. W. esq. 3 Plowden bdgs. Temple
Nicholl Fredk. Iltid, esq. 18 Carey st
Nicholl Hen. Iltid, D.C.L. 3 College, Doctors' commons, & Upper Clapton,
Nicholl John, esq. 18 Cross st. Islington
Nicholl John Iltid, esq. Upper Clapton, & 11 Godliman st. Doctors' commons
Nicholl Wm. G. esq. 1 Grftn. st. ea. Fitz. sq
Nicholles John, esq. 34 Bruton st
Nicholls C. esq. 11 Cornwall ter. Reg. pk
Nicholls Francis, esq. 43 St. Martin's la
Nicholls George, esq. 17 Hyde park st
Nicholls James, esq. 48 Bedford row
Nicholls James, jun. esq. 48 Bedford row
Nicholls John, esq. 21 Park pl. w. Lvrpl. rd
Nicholls John E. esq. 9 Thurloe pl. north
Nicholls John George, esq. 13 Gibson sq
Nicholls Mrs. 3 Delahay st. Westmnstr
Nicholls Mrs. 3 Paradise terrace, Islgtn
Nicholls Nathl. esq. 36 Harleyford place
Nicholls Rd. P. esq. 22 Brompton square
Nicholls Thomas, esq. 13 Castle st. Hlbrn
Nicholls Thos. esq. 48 Upper Berkeley st
Nicholls Thos. jun. esq. 13 Castle st. Hlb
Nichols David, esq. 15 Allsop ter. Newrd
Nichols Geo. esq. 52 Wharton st. Lloydsq
Nichols Hen. esq. 2 Stone bdgs. Linc. inn
Nichols Jas. esq. 12 Leicester pl. Lester. sq
Nichols John, esq. 9 Cook's ct. Carey st
Nichols Mrs. 20 Cobourg pl. Up. Kngtn. la
Nichols Mrs. 8 Park pl. ter. Padgtn. gn
Nichols Wm. esq. 15 Queen st. Brynstn. sq
Nichols Wm. esq. 3 Inner Temple lane
Nicholson Capt. 16 Grosvenor st
Nicholson Rev. Thos. Maling, 81 Jermyn st. & Pampisford hall, Cambridge
Nicholson Alex. esq. 18 Cloudesley sq
Nicholson Frdk. Wm. esq. 17 Gt. College st
Nicholson George, esq. 21 Abingdon street
Nicholson George, esq. 3 St. Peter st
Nicholson George Henry, esq. 89 Chanc. la
Nicholson George James, esq. 5 Raymond buildings, Crouch hill, Hornsey
Nicholson George S. esq. 6 Godliman st
Nicholson Henry, esq. 6 Barnard's inn
Nicholson Henry, esq. 13 Lloyd square
Nicholson Isaac, esq. 54 Hunter st
Nicholson James, esq. 141 New Bond st. & 3 Park villas, Park road, Holloway
Nicholson John, esq. 29 Burton st. Piml
Nicholson John, esq. 4 Brick ct. Temple
Nicholson John, esq. 7 Hanover st. Isltn
Nicholson Joseph, esq. 28 Chancery lane
Nicholson Jsph. esq. 12 George st. Adelphi
Nicholson Mrs. 7 Upper Seymour st. west
Nicholson Miss, 51 Baker st. Lloyd sq
Nicholson Miss, 54 Hunter st
Nicholson Miss, 69 Myddelton square
Nicholson Mrs, 150 Albany st. Rgnt.'s pk
Nicholson Mrs. 26 Oxford terrace
Nicholson Robert, esq. 81 Jermyn st. & Pampisford hall, Cambridgeshire
Nicholson Wm. esq. 8 Lincoln's inn flds
Nicholson Wm. N. esq. 44 Chancery la
Nickols John, esq. 16 Queen's row, Pntvl
Nicol James Dyce, esq. 23 Portland place, & at 7 Mincing lane, City
Nicol Miss, 12 Hans place, Sloane st
Nicol William, esq. Lord Steward's Pay office, St. James's palace
Nicolas Sir Nicholas Harris, G.D., M.G., K.H. 55 Torrington square
Nicolas Jose de, } 34 Brunswick
Nicolas y Badillo Jose de, } pl. City road
Nicolas John T. esq. 7 Conduit st. Regent st
Nicolay Rev. G. F. L. St. Kthrine.'s Rgt. pk
Nicolay Christian Wm. esq. 2 Oxford sq
Nicoll Alex. esq. 2 Seymour pl. Euston sq
Nicoll Henry, esq. 3 Staple inn
Nicoll John, esq. 12 Theberton st. Islgtn
Nicols John, esq. 7 Blandford pl. Rgt. pk
Nicolson Sir F. bart. 15 Wm. st. Knightsbd
Nicolson Lady, 15 William st. Knightsbg
Nicolson Rev. Hugh, 6 John st. Adelphi
Nightingale Chas. esq. 22 Park vil. east
Nightingale Miss, 13 Manor pl. n. Chlse
Nightingale Mrs. 41 Geo. st. Portman sq
Nightingall Lady, 29 York place
Nimmo Thos. esq. 6 Regent pl. w. Rgt. sq
Nisbett Geo. esq. 10 Charlotte st. Pimlico
Nisbett Mrs. 33 Devonshire st. Portland pl
Nitsch Ferdinand, esq. 6 Macclesfield st
Niven Rev. Wm. 5 Walton place, Bromp
Nixon Chas. esq. 10 Upper Belgrave pl
Nixon Edwd. H. esq. Bladen lodge, Earls court, & Dome house, Bognor, Sussex
Nixon Jas. Edwd. esq. 3 Lyon's inn, Stnd
Nixon Jas. H. esq. 4 Robert st. Hmpstd. rd
Nixon John, esq. 13 Clifford's inn
Nixon Mrs. Col. 13 Upper Montague st
Nixon Richard, esq. 6 Saville row
Noad Captain, 4 Cecil st. Strand
Noad Richard, esq. 113 Camden rd. villas
Noakes J. T. esq. 14 Harleyfd. pl. Kntn. com
Noakes Miss, 2 Albert st. Regent's park
Noakes Rt. esq. 7 Hemus ter. Chelsea
Noaks Mrs. 103 Sloane st
Noble Benjamin W. esq. 15 Up. Bedford pl
Noble Chas. esq. Clement's inn chambers
Noble Francis, esq. 3 Up. Porchester st
Noble G. J. L. esq. 3 Tavistock pl. Russell sq
Noble Hen. esq. 117 Gt. Russell st. Blmsby
Noble James, esq. 45 Halfmoon st
Noble John, esq. 22 Newman st. Oxfd. st
Noble John, esq. 90 Gloucester place
Noble J. esq. 15 Up. Bedford pl. Rusl. sq
Noble John Padmore, esq. 25 Regent sq
Noble John T. esq. 7 Carpenter's bldgs
Noble Mrs. 22 Cumberland ter. Rgt. prk
Noble Mrs. 26 Trevor sq. Knightsbridge
Noble Richd. Hatt, esq. Home office, & Little Fife house, Mid. Scotland yard

Noble Richard P. esq. 56 Long acre
Noble Thos.esq.6 Minerva ter.Brnsby.rd
Nocera Joseph, esq. 39 Devonshire st
Nock Geo. esq. 4 Church st. Kensington
Nockells Christr. esq. 84 Jermyn st
Nodder Banks R. esq. 4 Lt.Smith st.Wst
Nodes Sydenham, esq. 16 Up. Bedford pl
Nodes Wm. esq. 16 Upper Bedford pl
Noding John Henry, esq. 51 Euston sq
Nokes John, esq.74 Guilford st. Rusl. sq
Nolan Edw. esq. 13 Kensington grdn. ter
Nolan William, esq. 32 Southampton st. Covent garden
Norbury, Earl of, 6 Lowndes st
Norbury, Countess of, 34 Belgrave sq. & Durrow abbey, King's county
Norbury John, esq. 5 Finsbury square
Norcliffe Colonel, 61 Charing cross
Norcott Thomas Gascoigne,esq.34 Qn.sq
Norfolk, Duke of, P.C. Norfolk house,21 St. James's sq. & the Castle, Arundel
Norgate Miss, 3 Tavistock vil. Tavisk.sq
Norman Henry, esq.21 Chester st.Grosvenor place,& 11 Haymarket
Norman H.esq.11 Henrietta st.Cvndh.sq
Norman H. B. esq. 3 Duchess st
Norman James,esq.59 George st.Ptmn.sq
Norman James Ormond,esq.89 Chancery lane, & 2 Norfolk crescent, Oxford sq
NormanJohn,esq.14Dorset ter.Clphm.rd
Norman John,esq.18Stonefield st.Islngtn
Norman John P. esq 9 King's bench wk
Norman Mrs. 2 Norfolk cresc.Oxford sq
Norman Richard, esq. 30 Bryanstone sq
Norman Richard, esq. 2 New Broad st
Norman Robert, esq.24 Craven st.Strand
Normanby, Marquis of, P.C. Clarendon hotel,& Mulgrave castle, Whitby
Normansel Mrs. 41 Camden road villas
NormansellHn.T.esq.1Glo'sterst.Ptm.sq
Normanton, Earl of, 3 Seamore place, Curzonst.&Somerley,Ringwood,Hants
NormanvilleW.J.esq Glyn cot.Park vil.e
Norreys Lord, M.P. 18 Grosvenor st
Norreys Sir Denham Jephson, bart. M.P. Union club, Trafalgar square, & the Castle, Mallow, county Cork
Norris Anthony, esq. 2 Bedford sq. & 3 Grove road, St. John's wood
Norris Caleb,esq.10 Lancaster pl.Strand
Norris Henry,esq. 23 Lincoln's inn flds
Norris Henry James,esq.22 Up.Gower st
NorrisJohn Thomas,esq.23 Myddelton sq
Norris Mrs. 21 Compton st. Burton cres
Norris Thomas, esq. 3 Grove road, St. John's wood, & 2 Bedford row,Blmsby
Norris Wm. esq. 30 Dorset pl.Dorset sq
Norris Wm. J. esq.19 Bedford pl.Blmsby
Norsworthy Mrs. 65 Oxford terrace
North Lady Lucy, 24 Manchester sq
North Colonel JohnSydney&LadySusan, 16 Arlington st. ; Putney hill, Surrey ; & Wroxton abbey, near Banbury
North John, esq. 18 King st. Portman sq
North Mrs. 11 Noel st. Islington
North Wm. M.D. 5 Green's row, Chelsea
Northage William,esq.10Upper Gower st
Northam John, esq. 44 Brompton sq
Northam Mrs.39 Gibson square
Northampton, Marquis of, 145 Piccadilly ; & Castle Ashby, Northampton ; & Compton Winyates, Shipston on Stour
Northcote H. S. sen. esq. 13 Devonshire st. & Pyne's house, Exeter
Northcote S. esq. 19 John st. Bedford rw
Northcote S. H. jun.esq.13Devonshire st
Northey Capt.William B.St.Kath.Rt.pk
Northey Misses, St. Katherine's, Rgt.pk
Northie F. esq. 4 Elm court, Temple
Northland Viscount, M.P. 40 Berkeley square, & Northland house,Dunganon
Northover T. E.esq.15 Park pl,Livrpl.rd
Northwick Lord, 44 St. James's place,& Northwick park, Moreton in Marsh
Northwood George, esq. 22 Dorset st
Norton Hon. Mrs. 3 Chesterfield st
Northumberland, Duke of, K.G., P.C. Northumberland house, Charingcross; & Sion house, Isleworth ; & Alnwick castle ; & Werrington pk. Launceston
Norton the Hon.Geo.Chapple, 10 Wilton place ; & Kettlethorpe hall,Wakefield
Norton Edward, esq. 29 Upper Baker st
Norton John,esq. 1 St. George sq. Piml
Norton John, esq.88 St. John's wood ter
Norton John, esq. 46 Wharton st.Pntnvl
Norton J.E. esq. 21 St.Mary le Strand pl
Norton Mat. esq. 16 Glo'ster pl. New road, & 29 Upper Baker st
Norton Mrs. 16 Manor pl. nth. Chelsea
Norton Wm. Fletcher Norton, esq. 6 Mansfield st. & Elton manor, Grantham & Hastings
Norton Peter, esq. 25 Soho square
Norton Rd.esq.33 Liverpool st. King's cr
Norton Wm. esq. 1 Barnsbury villas
Norton Wm.esq.11 South sq. Gray's inn
Norwich, Bishop of, 38 Brook st. Grosvenor sq. & the Palace, Norwich
Norwood Wm. esq. 45 Notting hill sq
Nossoc Alex. esq. 26 Percy st. Tot. ct.rd
NosworthyWm.Saml.esq.3 Clarendon sq
Notley Mrs. 13 Annett's cres. Islington
Nowell Philip,esq.51 Lower Belgrave pl
NoyesMiss,3Northamptn.pl.Cannbry.sq
Noyes Mrs. 34 York place, City road
Noyes Saml. Fredk. esq. 43 Chester sq
Noyes Samuel F. esq. 5 Lincoln's inn fields, & 19 Hart st. Bloomsbury
Nugee Fras. Jas. esq. 107 Glo'ster place
Nugent Lord, 1 Alpha pl. Regent's pk. & Lillies, Aylesbury, Bucks
Nugent Lady, 4 Grosvnr. gate, Park la
Nugent Lieut. Col. G.E. 22 Hill st
Nugent Major, 38 Nottingham place
Nugent Chas. esq. 5 Suffolk st.Pall mall
Nugent Edmund, esq. 22 Chancery lane
Nugent Edmund, esq. 62 Oxford terrace
Nugent Edmund Lynch, esq. Chichester chambers, 22 Chancery lane
Nugent Miss, 46 George st. New road
Nunn John, esq. 16 New Ormond st
Nunn Mrs. 144 Oxford st
Nunn Robt. R. esq. 33 Cardington st
Nunn Saml.esq. 6 Duke st. Westminster
Nurse Mrs. 9 Chester pl. Regent's park
Nurse Wm. esq. 4 Up. Gore, Kensington
Nussey John, esq. 4 Cleveland row
Nutter Richard W. esq. 27 Mansell st
Nutting Hen. esq. Stoke Newington grn
Nye Wm.esq. 1 Harrington st.Hmptd.rd

OAK Wm. esq. 3 Brompton rw.Bromptn
Oakes Captain, 29 Nottingham place
Oakes John,esq. 3 Popham tr.Tibbrtn.sq
Oakes Mrs. 6A, Waterloo pl. Pall mall
Oakes Mrs. 42 Up. Wharton st. Lloyd sq
Oakey John, esq. 21 King st. Finsbury
Oakley Mrs. 88 Sloane st
Oakley Octavius, esq. 3 Bentinck st
Oakley Mrs. 3 Bentinck st. Manchest.sq
Oates Miss, 7 Barnsbury st. Islington
Oates P. esq. 17 Tavistock place
Obrê H. esq. 31 Grove pl.Lisson gro.nth
O'Brien Capt. D. 16 Glo'ster rd.Hyde pk
O'Brien Capt.H.R.A.41Green st.Grsvr.sq
O'Brien Aug. Stafford, M.P. 175 Piccadilly, & Blatherwick house, Wansford
O'Brien Cornelius, M.P. 8 Gray's inn place, & Ennistimon, Ireland
O'Brien John, esq. M.P. Reform club,& Ennis County Clare
O'Brien Michael Wm. esq. Gray's inn pl
O'Brien Wm.esq.4 Charles st. Westbrn.tr
O'Brien Wm. Smith, esq. M.P. Oxford & Cambridge club, & Cahirmoyle, Rathkeale
O'Byrne Major, 35 Tichborne st. Edg. rd
O'Callaghan Hon. George, 13 Clarges st
O'Connell Daniel, esq. M.P. Merrion sq. Dublin ; & Darrynane abbey, near Cahirciveen, Ireland
O'Callaghan Hon. Geo. P. 3 Lowndes st
O'Connell DanielJas. esq.1 Stone bldgs. Lincoln's inn
O'Connell John, esq. M.P. Merrion sq. Dublin
O'Connell Maurice,esq. M.P. Merrion sq. Dublin
O'Connell Morgan John, esq. M.P. 6 King st. St. James's, & Greena, near Killarney
O'Connor Wm.esq.21George st.Portm.sq
O'Connor Wm. esq. 18 Hatton wall
O'Connor Rev. Wm. 54 Lincoln's inn flds
O'Connor Miss, 7 Melina pl.St. John's wd
O'Conor Denis, esq. (the O'Conor Don), M.P. Brooke's club, St. James's st. & Cloonalis,near Castlerea, Roscommon
Oddie Hen. esq.2 Somer's pl. Cambrdg.sq
Oddie Henry Hoyle, esq.65Portland pl.; 18 Carey st. ; Barnwell castle,Oundle ; & Colney house, near Barnet
Oddie Richd. H. esq. 1 New ct. Temple
Odell Chas. esq. 7 Lawn, South Lambth
Odell John esq. 42 Holywell st Millbnk
Odling Francis, esq. 26 Oxford st
O'Ferrall Richd. More, esq. M.P. Cox's hotel, Jermyn st. & Ballyna house bridge, near Clonard
Offley Geo. esq. 24 Henrietta st. Covt.gn
Offord Rt. esq. 3 Norland ter.Notting h
O'Flaherty Mrs. 75 Gt. Portland st
O'Flynn Miss, 2 Clarendon square
Ogelvie J. esq,25 Pelham cresct. Brmtn
Ogg Danl. esq. Percy cot. South Lmbth
Ogg George, esq. 2 Pelham ter. Brmptn
Ogier John Creuzé H. esq. 46 Carey st
Ogier Peter, esq. 46 Carey st
Ogilby Mrs. 3 Gt. Cumberland st
Ogilby Wm. esq. 19Gower st.Bedford sq
Ogilby Wm.L. esq.25 Sussex pl.Regt.pk
Ogillvie James, esq. 3 Old Quebec st
Ogillvie Mrs. 3 Old Quebec st
Ogilvie Robert A. esq. 15 Wharton st
Ogilvy Alexander, esq. 13 Montagu sq
Oglander Sir Wm. bart. 25 Berkeley sq. & Nunwell, Isle of Wight
Oglander Henry, esq. 18 New Bond st
Ogle Rev. John S. & Lady Macdonald, 84 Eaton square
Ogle Capt. Chaloner, 44 Eaton place
Ogle Chalenor B. esq. 8 Up.Wimpole st
Ogle Edw. esq. 25 South st. Grosvn. sq
Ogle Jas. Wm. esq. 5 Chester pl.Oxfd.sq
Ogle John, esq. 12 Hunter st
Ogle Miss, 8 Rich. terr. Old Brompton
Ogle Mrs. 64 Eaton pl. Belgrave square
Ogle Richd. esq. 2 Paper bldgs. Temple
Ogle Robert, esq. 14 Gray's inn square
Ogle Savile C. H. esq.M.P. 84 Eaton sq & Kirkley hall, Newcastle, north
Old Thos. T. esq. 18 David st. Marylebo
Oldaker T. esq. 1 Brnswk. pl. Regt.'s pk
Oldershaw Aug. P. 11½ Gt. Carter lane
Oldershaw J. esq. 14 Park terr. Highby
Oldershaw Robert, esq. Lower road, Islington, & 18 King's arms yard
OldershawWm.esq.9 Canonbury pl.Islgl
Oldfield Chas. esq. 35 Porchester terrace
Oldfield D. esq.19Wellingt.ter.St.Jn.'sw
Oldfield Edmd. esq.35 Lincoln's inn flds
Oldfield Geo. esq. 16 Adam st. Adelphi
Oldfield Jonathan, esq. 3 Alexander sq
Oldfield Mrs. 3 Frederick pl.Up.Kenn.la
Oldham Miss, 42 Bernard st. Russell sq
Oldham Thos. esq.17Abbey pl.St.Jn.'s w
Oldknow Saml.esq.1Chapel st.Bedfd.rw
Oldmixon Geo.esq.28Abbey pl.St.Jn.'s w
Oldroyd Jph.esq.7 Colebrooke ter.Islgtn
Oliphant G.Hy.Hewit,esq.1Elm ct.Tmpl
OliphantT.H.esq.15Hamilton ter.S.Jn.w
Olive Jeremiah, esq. 4 York terrace
Olive Jsph.esq. 3 Warwick pl.Bedfd row
Oliveira Benjamin, esq. 8Up. Hyde pk.st
Oliveira Miss, 4 Gt. Cumberland st
Oliver Capt.J.R.N. 4Grove pl.Lisson grv
Oliver Capt. Richd. Silver, D3, Albany

Oliver Benj. M. esq. 52 Upper Gower st
Oliver Edward,esq.85Lisson grove north
Oliver Geo. esq. 26 Henrietta st.Cov.gar
Oliver Geo. esq. 2 Paradise ter. Islngtn
Oliver Henry, esq.6Park rd.Regent's pk
Oliver James, esq. Harrow road
Oliver John B. esq. 7 Linden grv.Knsgtn
Oliver JohnStanlend, esq.3 Blandford sq
Oliver Jsph. Y. esq. 54 Hatton garden
Oliver Lewis B. esq. 7 Addison terrace
Oliver Lionel,esq. 4 Old sq.Lincoln's inn
Oliver Miss, 28 College st. Chelsea
Oliver Miss,12Gloucester place, New rd
Oliver Mrs. 63 Connaught terrace
Oliver Mrs. 10 Devonshr.pl.Portland pl
Oliver Mrs. 4 Lansdowne ter. Notng. hl
Oliver Mrs. 6 Park road, Regent's park
Oliver Samuel, esq. 83 Hatton garden
Oliver Thos. Fras. esq. 1 Plowden bdgs
Oliver Wm. esq.8Hamilton pl. King'scrs
Oliver Wm. esq. 39 Manchester st
Oliver Wm.D.esq.3 Plowden bdgs.Tmpl
Oliver Wm. Elliott, esq. 19 Halfmoon st
Olivie Wm. Geo. esq. 2 Cavendish rd
Oliverson Richard, esq. 14 Portland pl
Oliverson Rt. esq. 6 Raymond buildings
Olivieri Domenico A. esq. 18 Wardour st
Ollerenshaw Edwd. esq. 6 Augustus sq
Olley J. esq. 7 Union place, NewKent rd
Ollive Edward, esq. 6 West st. Finsbury
O'Loghlin Mrs. 1 Bentinck street, & the Grange, Gerrard's cross, Bucks
O'Malley Peter F. esq. 11 Chester sq. & 1 New ct. Temple
Ommaney Lady, 1 Upper Wimpole st
Ommaney O. esq. 22 Norfolk st. Strand
O'NealRev.J.Chapelho.Groverd.Rgt.'sp
O'Neil Earl, K.P. United Service club, & Shane's castle, Antrim
O'Neil Charles, esq. 33 Golden square
O'Neil John,esq. 8 Green's row, Chelsea
Ongley Lord, 144 Oxford street, & Old Warden, near Bedford
Onley Savill Mrs. 12 Chester terrace
Onslow, Earl of, Richmond, & Clandon, near Guildford, Surrey
Oom Adolphus K. esq. 1 Burlington gar
Oppenheim Mrs. 13 Compton st. east, Regent square
Oram J. esq. 3 Belgrave st. King's cross
Oram James,esq. 30 Gerrard st. Islngtn
Oranmore Lord, 3 St. James's place, & Hampton court
Orchard Mrs. 1 Gt. Woodstock st
Orchard Mrs. 22 Liverpool ter. Liv. rd
Orchard Thomas, esq. 15Hatton garden ; & 4 Grove, Kentish town
Ord John Chas. esq. 2 Cumberland ter
Ord John Hy. esq. 2 Highbury grange
Ord Mrs. 2 Cumberland ter. Regent's pk
Ord Mrs. Wm. 47 York ter. Regent's pk
Ord Ralph, esq. 59 Up. Berkeley st
Ord Wm. esq. M.P. 17 Berkeley square, & Whitfield hall, Haydon bridge, Northumberland
Ord Wm. M.D. 9 Warwick st. Pimlico
Orde Sir John Powlett, bt. 50 N. Bond st
Ordish Frederick, esq. 9 John st. Adelph
O'Reilly Edmd. esq. 2 Robert st. Adelphi
Orford Earl of, White's club, & Wollerton park, near Aylsham
Orford John, esq. 11 Park pl. Paddingtn
Orger Thos. LL.D. 28 York st. Portmn.sq
Oridge Mrs. 29 Mecklenburgh square
Oriel C. G. C. esq. 36 Alfred pl. Bedfd. sq
Oriel Fredk. esq. 21 Alfred pl. Bedfd sq
Oriental Club House (F.A. Sturt, sec.), 18 Hanover square
Orkney Earl of, Limmer's hotel, George st. Hanover square, & Taplow court, Maidenhead
Orlebar Chs. Dl. esq. 27 Gt. Portland st
Orlebar Wm. esq. 6 George st. Hanover sq. & Dorset cottage, Chiswick
Orme Edward, esq. 6 Fitzroy sq. & Milton, Kent
Orme Cosmo, esq. 15 Bryanstone sq
Orme Francies, esq. 6 Fitzroy square, & 54 Chancery lane
Orme H. esq. 5 Charles st. Midx. hosptl
Orme Jonthn. esq. 5 Fredk. pl. Up. Ken. la
Orme Malcolm, esq. 15 Sussex square
Orme Mrs. 15 Bryanstone square
Orme Mrs. 24 Liverpool st. King's cross
Orme Mrs. 36 Edwardes sq. Kensington
Orme Mrs. 16 Wyndham pl. Bryanstn.sq
Ormonde Marquis of, 14 Weymouth st. & Kilkenny castle
Ormonde Marchess. of, 14 Weymouth st
Ormsby Mrs. 70 South Audley st
Ormsby Rt. esq. 24Portland ter. Rgt.'s pk
Ormsby Watt, esq. 54 Manchester st
Orr Capt. 16 Westbourne pl. Eaton sq
Orr Johnson, esq. 48 Burton st. Burton cr
Orr Mrs. Genl. 63 Glo'ster pl. Portm. sq
Orr Wm. esq. 21 Russell pl. Fitzroy sq
Orris John, esq.32 Pembroke sq. Knsngtn
Orriss J. B. esq. 53 Holywell st. Milbnk
Orrok Mrs. 11 Alexander sq. Brompton
Osbaldeston Geo. esq. 29 South bk. Rgt. pk. & Ebberston lodge, Malton, Yorks
Osbaldeston Wm. esq. 6 Furnival's inn
Osbaldeston Wm. esq.21 U. Phillimre. pl
Osbaldeston Wm.S. esq.7 Park pl. Padg
Osborn Sir John, bart. Earl's court, Old Brompton, & Audit Off. Somerset house
Osborn Hen. esq. 2 King's rd. Bedfrd rw
Osborn Robert, esq. 20 Clarendon square
Osborn Robert W. esq.6 Gower st. north
Osborn Thomas, esq. 13 Sidmouth st
Osborne Lord Sidney, 83 Jermyn st
Osborne Hon. D'Arcy G. 12 Paper bldgs
Osborne Edward, esq. 7 Lit. Abingdon st
Osborne John, esq. 22 Sussex gardens, Hyde park, & 22 Old sq. Lincoln's inn
Osborne Miss, 37 Baker st. Portman sq
Osborne Ralph B. esq. M.P. 32 Albemarlest
Osgood Geo. esq. 3 Raymond buildings, & 2 Alexander sq. Brompton
Osgood Mrs. 2 Alexander sq. Brompton
O'Shaughnessy Wm. esq. 54 Glos'ter pl
Osmond Fredk. esq. 5 Halfmoon st
Ossulston Lord, M.P. 17Southst. Grsvr.sq. & Walton, Esher ; & Chillingham castle, near Belford
Ostell Thos. esq. Queen's rd. St. John'swd
Oswald Alexd. esq. M.P. Thomas's hotel, Berkeley sq. & Cavens, Dumfries, N.B
Oswald James, esq. M.P. 14 Arlington st. ; 52 Claremont place, Glasgow ; Auchincruive, Ayrshire ; Cavens, Kircudbrightshire, & Holy Isle, Arran
Oswald Edwd. esq. 7 Berkeley st. Pcdly
Oswell Edward, esq. 52 Linc. inn fields
Oswin Charles, esq. 72 Harley st
Ottaway Henry, esq. 5 Powell st. west
Otter Chas. esq. 28 Brompton crescent, & 6 King's bench walk
Ottey Francis F. esq. 18 Jermyn st
Ottley Drewry, esq.5 Bedford pl. Blmsby
Ottley Sir Richd. 50 York st. Portmn. sq
Ottley Warner, esq.28 York ter. Regt.pk
Otto Lieut. Col. 7 Queen st. Mayfair
Otway Admiral Sir Robert Waller, bart. K.C.B. 2 Hyde park gardens
Otway Lieut. Gen. Sir Loftus, 13 Grosvenor square
Oughton Fk. esq.7Southamptn st. Cmbwl
Oulton J. esq. 27 William st. Lisn. gro
Ousby Mrs. 16 Sloane terrace Chelsea
Ousely Lady, 39 Lowndes st. Belgrv. sq
Outram B. F. M.D., F.R.S. 1 Hanover sq
Outhwaite Mrs. 38 Canonbury square
Ouvry Mrs. 49 Oxford ter. Edgware rd
Ouvry Rev. Peter T. 49 Oxford terrace
Ovens Edward, esq. 6 Pump ct. Temple
Over Jno. esq.11 Lo. Charles st. Nortn.sq
Over Mrs. 15 Richmond tr. Pentonville
Overbury Rev. Rt. W. 5 Wakefield st
Overbury Benj. esq. 6 Highbury grange
Overend Wm. esq. 3 Paper bldgs. Templ
Overstall Mrs. 8 President st. we. Kg. sq
Overton Mrs. Rose cot. King's rd. w. Chls
Ovey Rd. esq. 31 Avenue rd. Regts. pk
Owen Sir John, bart. M.P. 69 St. James's st. & Purton house, Swindon
Owen Colonel, 47 Connaught square
Owen Lieut. Col. 73 Cambridge terrace
Owen Rev. H. J. 8 Amelia pl. Fulham rd
Owen Rev. William, 10 Gibson square
Owen Chas. S. esq. 9Hunterst. Brnswksq
Owen David, esq.54Cambridge st. Edg.rd
Owen Foster, esq. 15Chester ter. Eatonsq
Owen Herbert, esq.25 Cambridge terrace, Edgware rd. & 10 King's bench walk
Owen Hugh, esq. 8 Coles ter. Barnsby. rd
Owen Misses, 25 Cross st. Islington
Owen O. T. esq. 19Guilford st. Russell sq
Owen Richd esq. 40 Lincoln's inn fields
Owen Wm. esq.14Bedfordplace, Russellsq
Owen Wm. esq. 10 Canonbury villas
Owen Wm. esq. 21 Cloudesley sq. Islingtn
Owlett Tim. esq. 23 Milton st. Dorset sq
Owthwaite John, esq. 22 Highbury ter
Oxendon Geo. Chichester, esq. 44 Brook st. & Broome park, Canterbury
Oxberry Wm. esq. 30 St. John's wood rd
Oxenford Edw. esq. 44 Mecklenburgh sq
Oxenford Wm. esq. 16 John st. Bedfd.rw
Oxenham Geo. N. esq. 43 Torrington square, & 61 Chancery lane
Oxenham Saml. esq. 4 Chester terrace
Oxford, Earl of, Eywood & Brampton Brian, near Kington, Herefordshire
Oxford, Bishop of, 61 Eaton place
Oxford & Cambridge University Club (Wm. Geo. Morris, sec.), 71 Pall mall
Oxlad Rev. Robt. 30 Holywell st. Milbnk
Oxley John, esq. 134 St. John st. Smithfld
Oxley Miss, 29 Norfolk cres. Oxford sq
Oxley Mrs. 113 Gt. Russell st. Blmsbry
Oxley Wm. Hy. esq. 28 Gibson sq. Islngtn
Oxtoby T. esq. 7 Goulden ter. Brnsby.rd

PAAS Mrs. 94 Guilford st. Russell sq
Pacifico Emanuel, esq. 38 Burton crescent
Packe Chas. W. esq. M.P. 7 Richmond ter. & Prestwold hall, nr. Loughboro'
Packe E. esq. 1 Stanhope pl. Hyde park
Padday J. esq. 5 Norland ter. Notting hl
Paddison Rd. esq. 1 Gt. James st. Bdfd.rw
Paddison Rd. esq. 34 Mornington crescent
Padgett John, esq. 69 Coleshill st
Padmore J. esq. 19 Up. Seymour st. west
Pagani H. esq. Holywell ho. Havstk.hill
Page Rev. Cyril, Lit. Cloisters, Westmr
Page Chas. esq.40Cambridge tr. Edgw.rd
Page Miss, Little Cloisters, Westminster
Page Philip F. esq. 28 Sackville st. Picdy
Page Philip N. esq.14King's rd. Bedfd.rw
Page S. esq.5 Up. Belmont pl. Wandsw.rd
Page Thomas, esq. 38 Hyde park gardens, & Ely, Cambridgeshire
Page Thos. esq. 2 Middle Scotland yard
Page Wm. esq. 3 Ulster pl. Regent's pk
Page Wm. Emmanuel, M.D. 43Curzon st
Page Wm. Jas. esq. 33Duke st. Manch. sq
Page Wm. J. esq.3 Marlboro' pl. St Jn.'s wd
Paget Lord Alfred Hen. M.P. Uxbridge house, & 1 Old Burlington st
Paget Lord Clarence, 1 Old Burlington st
Paget Lord George, 1 Old Burlington st
Paget Lady Adelaide, 1 Old Burlington st
Paget Lieut. Col. Frederick, M.P. 5 John st. Berkeley square
Paget Capt. Chas. 3 Sussex gdns. Hyde pk
Paget Rev. Edw. Brit. hot. 83 Jermyn st
Paget Charles, esq. 9 Clement's inn
Paget John, esq. 7 Gordon pl. Gordon sq
Paget John, esq. 3 Middle Temple lane
Paget Mrs. & Miss, 38 Cadogan place
Paget Wm. esq.7Gt. Percy st. Pentonville
Pagett Jas. esq.26Westbourne pl. Eatn.sq
Paice John, esq. 13 Fashion st. Dockhd
Paillet P. esq. 12 Scarsdale ter. Kensgtn
Pain Charles, 17 Surrey st. Strand
Pain Edwd. esq. 5 Great Marlborough st. & 83 Basinghall st

Pain Solomon J. esq. 9 New inn, Strand
Pain Thos. jun.esq.Chapel stairs Linc.in
Paine C. Mountford house,Barnsburypk
Paine Jn.esq.10 NewDorset pl.Clapm.rd
Paine Wm. D. esq. 17 Canonbury villas
Paine Wm. Steph. esq. 4 Furnival's inn
PainterC.B.esq.22Comptonst.Brnswk sq
Painter James, esq. 26 Howland st
Painter James, esq. 41 Berners st
Painter Rd. esq. 4 Broadway,Westmnstr
Palva A. Augustus De, secretary to the Brazilian embassy, 10 York pl.Prtm.sq
Pake Geo. Hussey, esq. 41 Charles st. Berkeley sq.&Caythorphall,Grantham
Pakington John Somerset, esq. M.P. 55 Eaton pl. & Westwood pk. Droitwich
Pakington Miss,13 Westbourne st.Hyde park, & Westwood park, Droitwich
Palethorpe Thomas, M.D.13 Up.Baker st
Paley Captain, 21A, Hill st. Berkeley sq
Paley Thomas, esq. 18 Fitzroy sq
Palgrave Sir Francis,Record office,Rolls yard,Chancery la. & Hampstead green
Palgrave Robert, esq. 18 Brompton cres
Palin Richard, esq. 13 Artillery pl. west
Palin Robert, esq. 25 George st. New rd
Palk Lady Elizabeth, 30 Bruton st. & Rectory house, Enfield, Middlesex
PalkChas.esq.Kennington vil.Up.Ken.la
Pallavicino Marquis, 11 Grosvenor st
Palle Mrs. 9 North terrace, Brompton
Pallister Miss, 22 Kensington square
Palmby J. esq. 42 Frdk. st. Gray's inn rd
Palmer Sir Wm. Roger, bt. 56 Portland place, & Kenure park, county Dublin
PalmerRev.Geo.3Cumberland st.Ptm.sq
Palmer AlfredWm.esq.6Hanovr.st.Islgt
Palmer Charles James, esq. 24 Endsleigh st. & 24 Bedford row
Palmer Clarkson, esq. 105 Glo'ster pl
Palmer Ebzr. esq. 3 Charles st.Gibson sq
Palmer Edward H. esq. 7 Chesham pl
Palmer Francis, esq. 8 Burlington st. & Nazing park, Waltham cross
Palmer Francis, esq. 8 Old Burlington st
Palmer Fred. esq. 9 Mitre ct. chambers
PalmerGeorge, esq. M.P. 8 Old Burlington st.; 11 King's arms yard, & Nazing park, Waltham cross
PalmerGeo.esq.1 Lowndes st.Belgrave sq
Palmer George, esq. 15 Regent st
Palmer Geo. esq. 17 Brownlow st. Holbn
Palmer George, esq. 12 Upper Woburn pl
Palmer Hen. esq. 9 Mitre ct. chambers
Palmer Hen. G.esq.4Youl's pl.O.Kent rd
Palmer J.esq.15Porchester pl. Edgrw. rd
Palmer J. esq. 4 Chatham pl.Walwth. rd
PalmerJacob, esq.41 Princess st.Pt.mkt
PalmerJohnH.esq.16Old sq.Lincoln's inn
Palmer Michl. esq. 20 Portland pl.Islgtn
Palmer Miss, 12 Bedford row, Islington
Palmer Mrs. 12 Belgrave st.King's cross
Palmer Mrs. 42 Lowndes st. Belgrave sq
Palmer Mrs. 10 Queen Anne st
Palmer Mrs. 12 Russell place,Fitzroy sq
Palmer Mrs. 4 Spring gardens
Palmer Mrs.30Tonbridge place, New rd
Palmer Mrs. 17 Trevor sq. Knightsbdg
Palmer Mrs.46Up.George st.Portman sq
Palmer Mrs. E. 15 Gt. Cumberland st
Palmer Mrs. P. P. 42 Gower st
Palmer Nathal. esq. 18 Southampton rw
Palmer Nathaniel, esq. 1 Paper bldgs
Palmer Robert, esq.M.P.Mould's hotel, 6 Suffolk st. & Holme pk. near Reading
Palmer Robert, esq. 14 Devereux court
Palmer Robt.Samuel, esq. 19 Devonshire st. Portland place, & 4 Trafalgar sq
PalmerRoundell,esq.11 New sq.Linc. inn
Palmer T. esq. 4 Felix place,Liverpool rd
Palmer T. esq. Rolls chapel, Chancery la
Palmer William, esq. 35 Dorset square
Palmer Wm. esq. 6 King's Bench walk
Palmer Wm. esq. 3 George st. Euston square, & 7 Gray's inn square
Palmer William, esq. 50 South st
PalmerWm. esq.3Victoria vls.Avenue rd
Palmer Wm. Henry, esq. 24 Endsleigh st.Tavistock square, & 24 Bedford row
Palmer Wm. Spencer, esq. 15 Keppel st
Palmerston Right hon. Viscount, G.C.B., M.P. 5 Carlton house terrace, & Broadlands, Romsey, Hants
Palsgrave Sir Fras.Rolls yd.Chancery la
Pamplin T. esq. 8 Cambridge ter.Islngtn
Pampling Miss, Lavender hill,Wands. rd
PanchaudThos.Jas.esq.4Homerpl.Nw.rd
Paneti Edward, esq. 8 Thanet pl. Strand
Pank Thomas, esq.123 Praed st.Padngtn
Panmure Lord, 9 Cornwall ter. Regent's park, & Brechin castle, Forfarshire
Pannell Charles, esq. 50 Eaton square
Pannizzi Antonio, esq. British Museum
Panormo Robert, esq. 60 Judd st
Panter John Edwd. esq. 58 Chancery la
Panter John Leech, esq. 22 Whitehall place, & North end lodge, Fulham
Panton Charles, esq. 24 Hunter st
PapineausW.M.esq.14Marlbro'pl.Ken.cr
PapworthJ.W.esq.10Caroline st.Bdfd.sq
PapworthW.A.esq.10Caroline st.Bdfd.sq
Parbury Geo. esq. Mansfield house, Russell sq. & West house, Brighton
Pardoe George, M.D. 2 Cavendish sq
Parfit Mrs. 5 York buildings, New rd
Paris Charles Snell, esq. 121 Regent st
Paris John Ayrton, M.D. 27 Dover st
Parish Sir Woodbine, K.C.H. 5Glo'ster pl
Parish Chas. esq.Carltn.chmbs.12Regt.st
ParishHy.H.esq.7Chesham st.Belgrv.sq
Parish Wm. esq. 29 Great Ormond st
Park, Alex. A. esq. Common Pleas office, Chancery la. & Merton grove, Surrey
ParkMrs.21Sussex pl.Kensngtn.new twn
Park Patrick, esq. 13 Bruton st
Park Thos. esq. 70 Gt.Russell st. Blmsby
ParkeRightHon.Sir James,knt. 56 Park st. Grvnr. sq. & Ampthill park, Beds
Parke Colonel, 203 Regent st
Parke Henry, esq. 36 Sussex gardens
Parke James, esq. 33 Curzon st. May-fair, & 63 Lincoln's inn fields
Parke John, esq. 1 Park ter. Regent's pk
Parken John P. esq. 13 New Boswell ct
Parken Wm. Palmer, esq. 13Nw. Boswell ct. & 3 Linden grove, Kensington
Parker Viscount, 9 Conduit st
Parker Viscountess, 9 Conduit st
Parker Lady Louisa, 9 Conduit st
Parker Captain, 13 Dorset square
Parker Rev.J.M.A.21Bedford pl.Kensgtn
ParkerAlfred, esq.28Park rd. Regt.'s pk
ParkerChas.esq.16Tavistock st.Bedfd.sq
Parker Charles, esq. 41 Upper Bedford place, & 1 Lincoln's inn fields
Parker Ed. esq. 7Up.Barnsbury st. Islng
Parker Frederick Henry, esq. 82A, Mount st. & 11 Portugal st. Grosvenor sq
ParkerG.R.esq.51Fredk.st.Gray's inn rd
Parker Hiam, esq. 12, Albany, Piccadilly
ParkerHy.esq.3Raymond blds.Gry.'s inn
Parker Isaac, esq. 5 Lr. Belgrave pl
Parker James, esq. Q.C. 21 Chester ter. Regent's pk. & 2 New sq. Lincoln's inn
Parker John, esq. M.P. Athenæum club, & Woodthorpe, Sheffield
Parker John, esq. 4 Cloudesley ter
ParkerJohn H. esq. 1Argyle sq. New rd
Parker John J. esq. 26 Cloudesley st
Parker Joseph, esq. 20 Ely place
Parker Kenyon Stevens, esq. Q.C. 40 Gower st. & 13 New sq. Lincoln's inn
Parker Miss, 45 Upper Harley st
Parker Mrs. 2 Ampthill sq. Hampstd.rd
Parker Mrs. 71 Baker st. Portman sq
ParkerMrs.12Dorset pl.north,Claphm.rd
Parker Mrs. 13 Dorset square
Parker Mrs. 2 King st. Finsbury sq
ParkerMrs.10North bank,Regent's park
ParkerMrs.10Wellington rd.St.Jno.'s wd
ParkerR.A.esq.11Canonbury pl.Islingtn
Parker Rd. esq. 57 Museum st. Blmsbry
ParkerRobt.esq.22Kenton st.Brnswik.sq
ParkerThos.esq.20Hanover cot.Rgt.'s pk
ParkerThos.esq.Maida hl.villa,Maida hil
Parker Thos. esq. 4 Clapham rise
Parker Thos. esq. 6 Lincoln's inn fields
Parker Thos. jun. esq. 5 Henrietta st. Brunswick sq. & 6Old sq. Lincoln's inn
ParkerT. H.esq.35Spencer st.Goswell rd
Parker T. L. esq. 44 Brook st
Parker Thomas M. esq. 3 New inn Strnd
Parker Wm. esq. 34 Claremont square
Parker Wm. esq. 23 Throgmorton st
Parker Wm.P.esq.12Up.Robt. st.Bmptn
Parker Wilmot, esq. 36 Carey st
Parkes Charles H. esq. 25 Parliament st
Parkes Joseph, esq. 21 Great George st
Parkes Josiah, esq. 11 Gt. College st
Parkes Thos. esq. Lavndr. hl. Wandsw.rd
Parkes Thos. Wm. esq. 13 Bedford row
Parkes Wm. esq. 12 Bedford row
Parkes Wm. B. M.D. 31 Gt. Marlboro' st
Parkhurst Rodie, esq. 44 Sackville st
ParkInG.P.esq.12Regnt.sq.Gray's inn rd
Parkin John, esq.20Whitehd's. gr. Chels
Parkin Peter S. esq. 3 Clifford's inn
ParkinP. S. esq. 2 Falcon court, Fleet st
Parkin William, esq. 13 Notting hill ter. Notting hill, & 43 Chancery lane
Parkins Edw.esq.40 Weymouth st. Portland pl. & Chesfield lodge, Stevenage
Parkins Wm. esq. 8 Albion ter. Chelsea
ParkinsWm.esq.13Camdenctgs.Cmdn.tn
Parkinson Rev. Richard, M.A.10Orme sq
Parkinson Col. 9 Glo'ster pl. Portman sq
Parkinson Fredk. K. esq. 13 Hunter st. Brnswk.sq. &4 Raymd. bdgs. Gray's in
Parkinson Geo.esq. 1 Racquet ct.Fleet st
Parkinson John, esq. 2Gray's inn square, & 66 Lincoln's inn fields
Parkinson John, esq. 80 Cambridge ter
Parkinson John,esq.1Ulster ter.Regent's park, & 9 Argyll st. Regent st
Parkinson J. jun.esq.24Earls ter.Knsgtn
Parkinson John H. esq. 36 Sackville st
Parkinson John L. esq. 26 Cloudesley tr
Parkinson Joseph, esq. 41 Sackville st
Parkinson Miss, 6 Ulster ter. Regt. prk
Parkinson Mrs. 46 Bedford square
Parkinson Mrs. 9 Norland pl. Notng. hl
Parkinson Mrs. 79 St. John's wood ter
Parkinson Mrs. 27 Surrey st. Strand
Parkinson Rt. Hy. esq. Beaufoy tr.Ed.rd
Parkinson Saml. esq. 15 Up.Barnsbury st
Parks Jas.Hamilton,esq.& Mrs.44 Brook st. & Stonewell park, Penshurst, Kent
ParkynsThos.G.A.esq. 31Lr.Belgrave st
ParlbyMaj. Gen.C.B.18Rutlandgt.Kngtb
ParlbyMaj.12St.Geo's.ter.Kngstn.nw.tn
Parlby Mrs. 15A, North Audley st
Parlett David, esq. 13 Gower place
ParlourMrs.23 Manchester. ter.Lpool.rd
Parmenter John H. esq. 4 St. Alban's pl
Parnell Chas. Octavius, esq.2 Norfolk st
Parnell John Jessopp, esq. 12 Clifford's inn; & Waltham Abbey
Parnell Misses, 22 Beaufort st. Chelsea
Parnell Paul, esq. 3 Hare court Temple
Parnell Thos. Hugh, esq. 57 Nelson sq
Parnther Michael S. esq. 9 Charlotte st
Parnther Robert, esq.5 Grafton st. Bond st. & Bird's place, Hatfield
Parr John E. esq. 11 Paper bldgs.Temple
Parratt Edw. esq. 12 Church st. Wstmr
Parratt Edw. esq. 63 St. James's st. & Berkeley cottage,Fishbourne,Chichstr
ParrattGeo. F.esq.6 Chas.st.Grosvnr.sq
Parratt James, esq 18 Mount st
Parrell W.esq.25New North st.Rd.Ln.sq
Parrett John, esq. 144 Oxford st. & Aylesbury, Bucks
Parris Edm. T. esq. 17Graftonst.Bond st
Parrott Edward, esq. House of Lords
ParrottJsph.esq.32Fredk. st.Gray'sinnrd
Parrott Mrs. 1 Cavendish square
Parry Col. 12 Westbourne place
Parry Rev. Elias, 2 Holford sq. Pntnvl

Parry Arthur, esq. 22 Northampton sq
Parry D.esq.13Cunninghm.pl.St.Jn.'swd
Parry Edwd. esq. 8 Up. Glo'ster place
Parry Geo. Jn. esq. 20 Myddelton square
Parry John, esq. 4 Collier st.Pentonville
Parry John, esq. 31 Great Russell st
Parry John B.esq.Q.C.11Gt.Cumberland place, & 9 New sq. Lincoln's inn
Parry Jn.jun. esq. 17 Tavistk.st. Bdf. sq
Parry John H. esq. 35 Southampton blds
Parry Mrs. 18 Montpelier sq. Brompton
Parry Mrs. 7 Portman square, & Powis lodge, Hendon, Middlesex
Parry Mrs. 4 York buildings, New road
Parry Owen, esq. 11 Trevor square
Parry Owen,esq.Avenue rd.Regent's prk
Parry Thos. esq. 10 Barnsbury square
Parry Thos.esq.11 Warwickvil.Harrowrd
Parry Wm. esq. 2 Harcourt bdgs.Temple
Parry Wm. B. esq. 5 Addison road north
Parry Wm. T. esq. 11 Colebrooke row
ParsHen. Wm.esq.7 Princes rd.Notng.hl
Parsey Arthur, esq. 2Spur st. Leicstr. sq
Parsey John, esq. 1 Swan walk, Chelsea
Parsey John, esq. 6 Hemus ter. Chelsea
Parson John, esq. 24, Red Lion square, & 47 Parliament st
Parson Thos.E.esq.61 Lincoln's inn fields
Parsons Lady, 22 Somerset st.Portm. sq
Parsons Ambrose, 2 Gray's inn square
Parsons Chas.esq.Temple chmbs.Fleet st
Parsons Edwd.esq.35Dartmouth st.Wmr
Parsons Geo. esq.4 Manchester bgs.Wmr
Parsons Jacob,esq. 11 Edwardes square, Kensington
Parsons John, esq. Earl's ct. Old Brmtn
Parsons John, esq. 34 Finsbury square
Parsons John M. esq. 6 Raymond bldgs
Parsons Joseph, esq. 20 Claremont pl
Parsons Mrs. 41 Alpha road, Regent's pk
Parsons Thos. esq. 24 Old sq. Linc.'s inn
Parsons Wm.esq.34 Halfmoon st. Picdly
Part J.esq.2Cambridge ter.Camdn.nw.tn
Parthenon Club House, 16 Regent st. James Hall Daly, secretary
Partington Edward, esq. 49 Ebury st. Pimlico, & 9 Davies st. Berkeley sq
Partridge E. esq.11Spring ter. Wands.rd
Partridge John, esq. 21 Brook st
Partridge the Misses, 2 York pl. Prtm.sq
Partridge Mrs.3Up.Belmont pl.Wands.rd
Partridge Rd. esq. 17 New st.Spring gds
Partridge Samuel John, esq. 3 Elm ct
Partridge S. T. M.D.2York pl.Portmn.sq
Partridge Wm.esq. 12 York st. Ptmn. sq & 10 Farrar's buildings
Parvavicini Baron Jas. P. 15 Regent st
Pascall Jas. esq. 1 Queen's row, Pntnvl
Pascall Steph. esq.27 Bartholomew close
Pascall W. L. esq.17Charlotte st.Fitz.sq.
Paschall Maj.Geo.F.14Green's rw.Chlsea
Pasfield Mrs. 18 Cloudesley st. Islingtn
Pashley Robt. esq. 12 King's bench wk
Pask John, esq. 3 Pelham rd. Brompton
Paskin Charles, esq. 13 Gt. College st
Paskin W. esq. 11Thurloe sq.Old Bmptn
Pasley Maj.Gen.12 Norfolk cres.Oxfd.sq
Pasmore Dan. esq. 2 Gower pl. Eust.sq
Pasmore J. F. esq. 2 Gower pl.Euston sq
Pass Hen.esq.45 Cambridge ter.Hyde pk
PassauOwen H.esq.14Glo'ster gro.w.Bm
Passell Rt. esq. 7 Calthorpe st.Gr.inn rd
Pasteur Adolphus, esq. 213 Regent st
Patch John, esq. 51 Upper Gower street, & 2 Pump ct. Temple
Patching Robt. esq. 23 River st. Pntnvl
Patching Wm. esq. 23 River st. Pntnvl
Pater J.esq.16Gt.Randolph st.Camdn.tn
Pater Wm. F. esq. 22 Coles ter. Islngtn
Paternoster Jn. esq. 30 Norfolk st.Strnd
Paternoster Rd. esq. 2 Essex ct. Temple
Paterson John, esq. 29 Colebrook row, & 57 Cannon st. city
Paterson J. esq.6 Portld. pl.Wndswth.rd
Paterson Richd.esq.7 Tilney st. Park la. & Eliot place, Blackheath
Paterson Wm.esq. 1 New Mitre ct.bldgs
Paterson Wm. esq. 2 Albion st. Hyde pk
Paterson Wm. esq. 24 Orchard st
Paterson Wm S. esq. 7 Bouverie st
Paton Geo. esq. 4 New sq. Lincoln's inn
Paton Thos. esq.7 Richmond ter. Pntnvl
Patrick Hy.esq.18Montpelier sq.Brmptn
Patrick John A. esq. 3 Clifford's inn
Patrick John G.esq. 98 Camden rd.villas
Patrick Mrs. Ladbroke pl. Notting hill
Patrick Wm.B.esq.11Church rw.Limeho
Patten George, esq. 59 Berners st
Patten Hen. esq. 12½ Bishopsgate wthn
Patten James, esq. 17 Upper Woburn place, & 41 Ely place, Holborn
Patten John Wilson, esq. M.P.24Hill st. Berkely sq.; & Light Oaks, Cheadle, Staffordsh.; & Bank hall, Warrington
Patten Joseph,esq.3Bentinck ter.Rgt.pk
Patten Wm. V. esq. 27 Howland st
Patterson Hy.esq.4Lodge rd.Regnt.'s pk
Patterson Jas. esq. 6 Cornwall terrace
Patterson M. esq. 5 Norfolk st. Park la
Patterson Peter, esq. 36 Duncan terrace
Patteson Sir John, knt. 33 Bedford sq.; Judges' chambers, Rolls' gardens; & Feniton court, Devon
Pattinson J. esq. 15 Vincent ter.Islingtn
Pattison Jas. esq.27 Carlton vls. Edg.rd
Pattison Jas. esq. 51 Gerrard st. Islgtn
Pattison Jas. M.P. 37 Upper Harley st
Pattison Mrs. 172 Albany st. Regt.'s pk
Pattison Thos. esq. 6 Tyndale pl. Islgtn
Patton Capt. Hugh, R.N. 6Dean st.Pk.la
Patton Capt. Robt. R.N. 6 Dean st. Park lane, & Fareham, Hants
Patton Philip E. esq. 6 Dean st. Park la
Paty Colonel, 24 Regent st
Paul Sir John Dean, bart. 218 Strand, & Hill house, Rodborough, Glo'stershire
PaulMajr.Gl.T.H.4Melcombe pl.Drst.sq
Paul Col. M. 8 Melcombe pl. Dorset sq
PaulRev.R.B.OldChapel row,Kentish tn
Paul Mrs. 4 Hamilton pl. Piccadilly
Paul John Dean, esq. 218 Strand, & Ivy cottage, Parsons green
Paul Peter, esq. 2 Upper Islington ter
Paulett Lord Geo. D. 1 Albany, Piccadly
Pauli Edward, esq. 7 Park village east
Paull Rev. H.A. 15 Foley pl. Portland pl
Paull Arch. esq. 33 Devonsh.pl. Prtld.pl
Pavey Geo. esq.9 Lo.Chas.st.Nrthptn.sq
Pavey Hen.esq. 4 Newcastle pl.Edgw.rd
Pavitt George, esq. 2 Gray's inn square
Pawle Francis, esq. 12 Park ter. Highby
Pawle Robt. esq. 1 Amwell ter. Pentonv
Pawley George, esq. 35 St. Martin's la
Paxon Francis, esq. 18 Featherstone buildings, & Hampstead
Paxon William, esq. 9 Gray's inn terrace
Paxton Wm. Gill, esq. 11 Buckingham st. & Grove house, Neesdon, Middx
Payler Col. A9, Albany, Piccadilly
Payn Sir Coventry, 27 Sloane st
Payne Edward, esq. 24 Cloudesley st
Payne George, esq. 124 Albany st
Payne Geo.esq.19Charlotte st.Portlnd.pl
PayneGeo.esq.Steven'sho.18NewBondst
Payne Jsph. esq. 1 Harpur st.RedLion sq
Payne Jsph. esq. 1 Church yd. ct.Temple
Payne Julian, esq. 1 Clifford's inn
Payne Mrs. 4 Belmont ter.Wandswth. rd
Payne Randolph, esq. 125 Sloane st
Payne Rt. Hy. esq. 5 Suffolk pl.Pall mall
Payne Thos. esq. 7Titchfield ter.Regt.pk
Payne Wm. esq. 1 Church yd. ct.Temple
Payne Wm. esq. 26 Brunswick square
Payne Wm. esq. 16 Nelson square
Paynter Frs.E.esq.2Gt.Jamesst.Bdfd.rw
Paynter Mrs. Denmark hill, Cambrwl
Paynter Ths. esq. 2 Addison cot. Knsgtn
Paynter Wm. esq. 21 Belgrave square, & Richmond, Surrey
PeabodyGeo.esq.11 Devonshr.st.Ptld.pl
Peachey James, esq. 39 Brunswick sq. & 17 Salisbury square, Fleet st
Peachey Fras.esq. 4 George st. Hanvr.sq
PeacheyJohn,esq.4 George st.Hanovr.sq
Peacock Rev.J.7Owen's rw.St.Johnst.rd
Peacock Barnes, esq. 59 Gordon square, & 1 Harcourt buildings, Temple
Peacock Francis, esq. 4 Essex ct. Temple
Peacock Jsph. esq. 31 East st.RedLion sq
Peacock Miss, 80 St. John's wood ter
Peacock Lewis, esq. 43 Lincoln's inn flds
Peacock Mrs. 22 Albany st. Regent's pk
Peacock Mrs. 5 Grosvr. pl. Cambrwl. rd
Peacock Mrs. Field ctg. Haverstock hill
PeacockRt.Wm.esq.5Bellina vil.Kntsh.t
PeacockThos.B.M.D.Finsbury pavement
PeacockThos. L. esq. 22 John st. Adelphi
Peacocke Gen. Sir Warren, 45 Brook st
Peake James, esq. 38 Clarges st
Peake Mrs. 22 Porchester terrace
Peake Mrs. 17 Torrington square
Peake Rt. esq. 1 Glo'ster pl.Glo'ster cres
Peake Robt. Wm. esq. 11 New Palace yard, Westminster
PeakeThos. esq.33Glo'ster cres.Rgt.'s pk
Peal Edwd. esq. 4 Bryanstone st
Peal Mrs. 4 Bryanstone st. Portman sq
Pearce Geo. esq. 16 Liverpool st. Bpsgate
Pearce John, esq. 27 Connaught square
Pearce John, esq. 225 Maida vale
PearceJohn,esq.2Hydepk.gt.Knsgn.gore
Pearce Mrs. 27 Connaught square
Pearce Mrs. 8 Stanhope st. Regent's pk
Pearce S. esq. Queen's mews, Pimlico
Pearce S. jun.esq.Queen's mews,Pimlico
PearceThos.esq. 19South bank,Rgt.'s pk
Pearce Wm. esq. 34 Pembroke square
Pearce Wm. esq. 10 Whitehall place, & 11 Great George st
Pearsall Jas.esq. 15 Claremont ter.Pnvl
Pearse Brice, esq. 12 Gloucester place
Pearse Christopher, esq. 35 Lowndes st
Pearse George, esq. 46 Marsham street, & 5 Regent street, Westminster
Pearse Henry, esq. 9 Manchester square
Pearse John, esq. 27 Connaught square
Pearse Miss, 16 Lower Seymour street
Pearse Mrs. 9 Norfolk street, Strand
Pearson Charles, esq. Guildhall yard, & 7 Old Jewry
Pearson Chas. Hill, esq. 5 Serjeant's inn
Pearson Geo. esq. 14 Beaumont street
Pearson Henry, esq. 5 Brick ct. Temple & 58 Welbeck street
Pearson Hy. Robt.esq.46 Hyde park sq
Pearson John, esq. 76 Gower street
Pearson John, esq. 17 Myddelton street
Pearson John, esq. 3 New sq. Linc. inn
Pearson John, esq. 21 New Millman st
Pearson John, esq. 31 Up. Barnsbury st
Pearson John L. esq. 31 Keppel street
Pearson Michael, esq. 43 Gordon sq
Pearson Miss, 19 St. James's place
Pearson Mrs. 31 Clapham road place
Pearson Mrs. 2 Kensington crescent
Pearson Mrs. 4 Lowndes square
Pearson Mrs. 5 Rodney st. Pentonville
Pearson Mrs. 10 Up. Gloucester place
Pearson Thos. esq. 40 Argyle sq. Nw.rd
Pearson Thos. esq. 22 Essex st. Strand
Pearson Wm. esq. 17 White Conduit st
Pechell Sir John Brooke, bart. 27 Hill st. Berkeley sq. & Hampton court
Pechell Augustus,esq. 4 Harcourt bldgs
Pechell George Richard,Capt.R.N.,M.P. & Hon. Mrs. 4 Spring gardens, & Castle Goring, near Worthing
Peckett Charles, esq. 25 Barnsbury pk
Peckett George, esq. 25 Barnsbury pk
Peckham Robt. esq. 7 Wardrobe ter
Peckham Wm.Scott,esq.3 New Boswell court, Lincoln's inn, & 72 Euston sq
Peckover Edmd. esq. 1 Stanhope terrace
PedderRobt.esq.31Thurloe sq.Old Bmpt
Pedley Henry, esq. 59 Fenchurch street
Pedley Jph.esq. 5 Carlton vls.Edgwr.rd
PedleyJph.esq.19Morningtn.pl.Hamp.rd
Pedley Robert,esq.59 Park st.Grosvr.sq

Pedrorena Don Victoriano de, sec. of Legation of Spain, 30 Weymouth st. Portland place
Peck James, esq. 8 Finsbury square
Peck Mrs. 7 Westbourne place
Peck Robert, esq. 3 Finchley new road
Peel Rt. Hon. Sir Robert, bart. M.P., 3 Whitehall gardens, & Drayton Manor
Peel Col. Jonathan, M.P. & Lady Alice, 8 Park place, St. James's, & Marble hall, Twickenham
Peel Rev. Fred. Fladong's hotel, 144 Oxford st. & Willingham, nr. Gainsbro'
Peel Rev. John, 44 Brook street, & Worseley house, Stourport
Peel Bolton L.esq.Rolls yd.Chancery la
Peel Jas. esq. 4 Barton st. Westminster
Peel Jonathan, esq.2 Elm court, Temple
Peel Jonathan, esq. 4 Oxford square
Peel Joseph, esq. Fladong's hotel, 144 Oxford st.& Hardwk.hill,nr.Chepstow
Peel Jsph. esq. 20 Loraine pl. Holloway
Peel Lawrence, esq. 83 Jermyn street
Peel Wm. Yates, esq. & Lady Jane, 63 St. James's st. & Bone hill, Tamworth
Peele Mrs. 2 Woburn square
Peer Mrs. 5 Park place, Paddington
Peers Capt. 130 Jermyn street
Peet Thos. esq. 26 Sudeley st. Islington
Peet Thos. esq. 5 Gutter lane,Cheapside
Pegler Francis, esq. 54 Euston square
Pegler Moses, esq. 54 Euston square
Pegler Wm. H. esq. 10 Gt. Portland st
Peile Solmn.esq. 1 Cumberld.st. Port.sq
Peile Thomas Hanson, esq. 26 Fitzroy sq & 6 Gt. Winchester street
Peirce C. J. esq. 5 Madeleyvil.Kensingtn
Peirson Geo. C. esq. 35 Southampton bds
Peirson James, esq. 11 Furnival's inn
Peirson Mrs. 5 Barnsbury park, Islngtn
Pelham Lady Emily, 43 Up. Brook st
Pelham the Ladies, 22 Grosvenor place
Pelham Hon. Capt. R.N. 22 Grosvenor pl
Pell Bennet, esq. 12 Finsbury pl. north
Pellatt N. esq. 64 Dorset st. Salsby. sq
Pelletier Augustus, esq. 46 Howland st
Pellew Capt. Hon. Sir F. 7 Grafton st
Pemberton-Leigh Rt. Hon. Thos. Q.C. 3 Spring garden terrace, Whitehall, & Hindley hall, Lancashire, & Toory hill, Sittingbourne, Kent
Pemberton Charles, esq. 4 Symond's inn
Pemberton Christph. R. esq. 37 Eaton pl
Pemberton Edward Leigh, esq. 17 Russell square, & 20 Whitehall place
Pemberton N. esq. 10 William st. Knghb
PembertonMrs.14St. Geo. ter. Kensingtn
PembertonW.Aug.S.esq.4 Symond's inn, & 5 St. George's ter. Kensng. Nw. twn
Pembroke Earl of, 7 Carlton house terrace, & Wilton house, near Salisbury
PembrokeCountess, 1 Grafton st.Bond st. & Wilton house, near Salisbury
Penell Wm. esq. 1 Elm court, Temple
Pendarves Edward Wm.Wynne,esq.M.P 36 Eaton pl. & Pendarves, near Truro
Pendrell Miss, 34 Duke st. Grosvr. sq
Pendry Chas. esq. 54 George st. New rd
Penfold Rev. Geo. Saxby, D.D. 15 Dorset sq. & King's Winford, Dudley
Penfold Thos. E. esq. 42 Mecklnbrgh. sq
PengellyRev.Jn. C. Chapel house City rd
Penhall J. esq. 11 Sprngfld. pl. Wnds.rd
Penkivil Wm. J. esq. 9 Finsbury pl.south
Penleaze Capt. Henry, 13 Bruton street
Penley Major, 9 Ladbroke vls. Nottinghl
Penn Edward, esq. 22 Essex st. Strand
PennGrenvileJ. esq. 48 Duke st. St. Jas's
Penn Richard, esq. F.R.S. 6 Whitehall, & Richmond hill, Surrey
Penn Wm. esq.13 Lo. Chas. st. Nthpt. sq
Penn Wm. D. esq. 10 Bedford rw. Islngtn
PennantLieut. Col. Hon. E.G. D. M.P. 36 Belgrave sq. & Penrhyn castle, Bangor. & Wicken park, Stoney Stratford
Pennant Mrs. Dawkins, 8 Wimpole st.
PennellJ.W.C.esq.6Princes st.Hanv.sq
Pennell Wm. esq. 9 Cumberland terrace
Penney Wm. esq. 4 Northwick terrace
PenneyWm. Page, esq. Westbourne villa, Finchley new rd
Pennington Geo. J. esq. 20 Cumbrlnd. st
PenningtonRt.Reney,M.D.15Portman sq
Pennington Wm. esq. 21 Montagu pl
Penny Rev. Hy. 12 Upper Phillimore pl
Penny Rev. J. Millbank prison
PennyAlfd. esq 9 Colebrooke rw.Islngtn
Penny Frederick, esq. 49 Edgware road
Penny Geo. esq. 91 Guilford st. Russ. sq
PennyHy.esq.1Langford pl.St. John's wd
Penny Henry Harwood esq. 1 Elm court, Temple, & 5 Oxford square
Penny John, esq. 28 Mornington place
PennyMiss, 11 Gt. James st. Bedford row
Penny Miss, 91 Guilford st. Russell sq
Penny Rd. esq. 11 Vauxhall pl. S. Lmbth
Penrose Thos. esq. 119 Camden rd. villas
Pensam Miss, 18 Alfred pl. Bedford sq
Pensam Philip, esq. 41 St. James's st
Penson Miss, 4 Kennington place
Pentland Mrs. 18 Wellington ter.St.Jn.w
Peplow Jph. esq. 13 Tottenham court rd
Pepoli Count C. 11St.Geo's. ter. Kensgtn
Pepper Chas. Bailey, esq. 7 Gt.Queen st
Pepper John, esq. 10 Up. Ranelagh st
Peppercorn Jas.esq.12Lower Belgrave st
Pepperell Mrs. 31 Pembroke square
PepysSirWm.Weller,bart.36Bryanstone sq. & Tandridge ct. Godstone, Surrey
Pepys Edmund, esq. 7 Upper Harley st
Pepys John, esq. 8 Lower Berkeley st
Pepys Mrs. C. 5 St. Andrew's pl.Regt.pk
Pepys Wm. H. esq. 11 Earl's ter. Kngstn
Perceval Lieut. Col. Alex. 137 Regt. st. & Temple ho. nr. Ballymote, Ireland
Perceval Capt.Spencer,13Cleveland row
Perceval Dudley M. esq. 16 Wilton st
Perceval Misses, 91 Eaton sq.; Crofton hall, Bromley, Kent; & 7 Brunswick terrace, Brighton
Perceval Philip, esq. 3 Chester place
Percival Richard, esq. 2 Highbury park
Percival Spencer,esq.6York st.St.Jas.sq
Percival Thomas, esq. 1 Cleveland row
Percival Wm. esq.20George st. Hanov.sq
Percy Hon. Joycelyn, 8 Portman square
Percy Capt. A. 31 Charlotte st. Portl. pl
Percy Benj. esq. 8 Alfred pl. Alexand.sq
Percy Mrs. 24 Arundel st. Strand
Percy SidneyR.esq.11Johnson st.Som.tn
Percy Thos. esq. 1 Alfred pl. Bedford sq
Peregrine John P. esq. 3 Halfmoon st
Peregrine Thos. esq. 17Mount st.Bkly.sq
Pereira General, 18 Woburn square
Pereira Chevalier de, Attaché to Brazilian Legation, 10York pl.Portman sq
PereiraAntonio, esq.11Park cres.Rgt.pk
Pereira José, esq. 17St.MaryAbbotts ter
Pereiro de Rodrigo, 29 York st. Prtm. sq
Perex Sixto, esq. 20Gt. Marylebone st
Perfect Alfred, esq. 40Brook st.Grosv. sq
Perigal Edwd. esq.22Portland ter.Rg.pk
Perigal Geo. esq. 109 Camden rd. villas
Perigal Henry,esq.5Avenue rd.Rgt.'s pk
Perior James, esq. 15 Maida hill west
Perkin Rt. J. T. esq.81 Camden rd.villas
Perkins AngelMarch,esq 21Gt.Coram st
Perkins Augustus Saml. esq. 26Eaton sq
Perkins Charles, esq. 1 Up. Harley st
Perkins Hen. esq. 3 Berkeley st.Berkly. sq. & Hanworth park, Middlesex
Perkins Houghton, esq. 25 Mortimer st
Perkins John, esq. Larkhall rise, Clphm
Perkins Miss,11 Cambridge st.Edgw. rd
Perkins Mrs. 2 Bentinck st. Manchst. sq
Perkins Mrs. 2 North pl. Hampstead rd
Perkins Richard, esq. 15 Regent sq
Perkins Rd.esq. 19 Park sq.Regent's pk
PerkinsWm.esq.11Titchfield tr.Rgt.'spk
Perrat Madame Adele, 27A, Davies st
Perrin Thomas, esq. 1 Powell st. west
Perrin Wm. esq. 4 Cloudesley sq. Islgtn
Perring Rev. Chas. 1 Verulam buildgs
Perring Claude, esq. 19Lincoln's inn fld
PerringMrs.Jackson,13Parkvillage wess
PerringPhilip, esq.19Devnshr.pl.Ptld.pt
Perring Rt. esq. 9 Rich ter. Old Brmptn
Perry Benj. esq.10Augusta pl.Stock.com
Perry Benj. esq. Perry st. Somers town
Perry Danl. esq. 16 Baker st. Lloyd sq
Perry Edward, esq. 41 Gibson square
Perry George, esq. 71 Berners st
Perry George, esq. 1 Tenterden st
Perry Henry James, esq. 6 Gt. James st. Bedford row, & Quality ct. Chanc. la
Perry James, esq. 62 Carey st
Perry John, esq. 2 Gray's inn place
Perry John, esq. 4 Eaton square
Perry J. esq. 11 Albion ter. Canonbury
Perry J.B. esq.12Holland pl.Clapham rd
Perry John Geo. esq. 16 Carlton hou. ter
Perry Jsph. esq. 14 Bury st. Bloomsby
Perry Louis, esq. 19 Berners st
Perry Miss,18Chester ter. Regent's park
Perry Miss,33Tonbridge place,New road
Perry Richd. esq.18Chester ter. Rg's. pk
Perry Richd. esq. 7 Old sq. Lincoln's inn
PerryRichd.Wm.esq.3Perry's pl.Oxfd.st
Perry S. esq. 6Woodland pl.St.John's wd
Perry Thos. W. esq. 1 Tuffnell pl. Islgtn
Perry William, esq. 54 Tavistock square
Pery Hon. E. 6 Hinde st. Manchester sq
Pesley Frdk.Chs. esq.44 Southmptn. bds
Peter Edmd. esq. 4 Cloudesley st.Islngtn
Peter Jn. Tho. Hen.esq.4 InnerTemple la
Peterborough Bishop of, 27 Parliament st. & the Palace, Peterborough
Peters Chas. esq.Orleans cot. Morng. rd
Peters John,esq.16 Cobourg pl.Bayswatr
Peters John, esq. 8 Manor ter. Chelsea
Peters Rt. esq. 24 Paradise ter. Islingtn
Peters Thos. jun. esq. 36 Albion st.Hy.pk
Petersdorff Chas. esq. 1 Tanfield ct.Tmpl
Petersdorff Edward, esq.11Gray's inn sq. & 1 Tanfield court, Temple
Peterson Andr. T. T. esq.1 Essex ct.Tmp
Peterson Mrs. Queen's rd. St. John's wd
Pether Harry,esq.2 Spring tr. Wndsw. rd
Petherick Wm. esq. 5Camdn. cot.Cmd.tn
Petit Louis H. esq.9 New sq. Lincoln's in
Petit Louis Peter, esq. 10 Gray's inn sq. & 7 New square, Lincoln's inn
Peto Samuel Morton, esq. 47 Russell sq
Petre Lord, 3 Mansfield st. & Thorndon hall, near Brentwood, Essex
Petre Hon. Edw. 26 Wilton crescent
Petre Hon. Mrs. 26 Wilton crescent
Petre Henry, esq. 33 Portman square, & Dukenhalgh, Blackburn, Lancashire
Petrie Miss, 3 George st. Portman sq
Petrie Sam. esq. 46 Ebury st. Pimlico
Pettat Sam. esq. 7 Cumbrlnd.pl. Nw. rd
Pettet Wm. esq. 10 Lancaster place
Pettigrew Thos. Jsph. esq. 8 Saville row
Pettigrew Wm. V. M.D. 30 Chester st
Pottingal Mrs.29 North bank,Regt.'s pk
Pettit James, esq. 16 Allsop ter. New rd
Pettit Wm. esq. 7 Stonefield st. Islng
PettittChas.A.esq.1Chester ter.Rgt.'s pk
Peyron Hy. esq. 5 Southmptn. pl. Eus.sq
Peyton Sir Henry, bart. 19 Grosvenor pl. & Swift's house, Bicester, Oxfordshire
Peyton Rev. Algernon, 32 Chester st. & Doddington, near Chatteris
Peyton Richd. esq. 10 Cook's ct.Carey st
Pfeil AdolphL.esq. 2Carlton vls.Edgr. rd
Phare George, esq. 17 South Lambeth
Pheasant Miss, 24 York place, City rd
Phelp Miss, 1 Berkeley pl.Connaught sq
Phelps Abel Peyton, esq. 10 Regent st
Phelps Abel Peyton, esq. 162 Albany st
Phelps Miss, 16 St. George's pl.Hyde pk
Phelps Mrs. 11 Somers pl. Cambridge sq
Phelps Saml. esq 8 Canonbury st. Islgtn
Phelps Wm. esq. 18 Montague place
Phelps William, esq. 14 Red Lion sq
Phene John, esq. 8 Catherine ct. Tow.hill
Phene Phineas, esq. 51 Woburn place

Philipe George Peter De Rhe, esq. & 38 Amwell st. Pntnvl. & 9 Gray's inn sq
Philipps Sir Rd. Bulkeley Philipps, bart. M.P. Brown's hotel, 23 Dover st. & Picton castle, near Haverfordwest
Philipps Chas. S. M. esq. 3 Stone bldgs
Philipps Rt. N. esq, 9 King's bench walk
Philips Sir George, bart. 2 Hill st. Brkly. sq. & Weston house, Warwick
Philips Geo. Rd. M.P. & Hon. Mrs. 12 Hill st. & Weston, near Chipping Norton
Philips Chas. F. esq. 11 Adam st. Adelphi
Philips John Burton, esq. 65 Wimpole st. & Heath house, Cheadle, Staffordshire
Philips Joseph, esq. 1 New Temple bdgs
Philips Mark, esq. M.P. 60 James's st. & the Park, near Manchester
Philips Trenham W. esq. 1 Whitehall yd
Phillimore Capt. Chas. 50 New Bond st
Phillimore Augustus, esq. 22 Portman st
Phillimore Charles B. esq. 22 Prtman. st
Phillimore John George, esq. 6 Pump ct. Temple, & 14 Albion st. Hyde park, & Shiplake house, near Reading
Phillimore Robert, D.C.L. 42 Clarges st. & 15 College, Doctors' commons
Phillimore Greville, esq. 22 Portman st
Phillimore Joseph, esq. D.C.L. 15 College, Doctors' commons; & 22 Portman st.; & Shiplake house, near Reading
Phillimore Wm. Rt. esq. 38 South st. Grosvenor sq
Phillip Mrs. 21 Portman pl. Edgware rd
Phillipe John, esq. 14 Camden st. Islg. grn
Phillips Thomas, esq. 74 Grosvenor sq
Phillipps John, esq. 5 Regent's villas, Avenue road
Phillipps S. M. esq. 16 Cumberland ter
Phillipps Wm. Phillipps, esq. 50 Strand
Phillips Sir Thos. 11 King's bench walk
Phillips Rev. Howell J. 42 Up. Seymour st. & Hartwell rectory, Aylesbury
Phillips Ben. esq. F.R.S. 17 Wimpole st
Phillips Ben. esq. 15 Coborg pl. U. Ken. la
Phillips Chas. Hy. esq. 6 Trafalgar sq. Chelsea, & 11 Cleveland row, St. James's
Phillips Chas. V. esq. 42 Up. Gower st
Phillips Edmund, esq. 25A, Bedford row
Phillips Edwd. esq. 29 Canonbury sq
Phillips Edw. R. esq. 76 Gt. Titchfield st
Phillips G. B. C. esq. Denmrk. hill, Cmbrwl
Phillips Hen. esq. 24 Dorchester place
Phillips Henry, esq. 35 Hart st. Blmsbry
Phillips H. W. esq. 8 George st. Hnvr. sq
Phillips Jas. esq. 15 Baker st. Lloyd sq
Phillips John, esq. 17 Chancery lane
Phillips John, esq. 11 Cleveland row
Phillips John, esq. 32 Wilton place
Phillips John E. esq. 11 Canterbury vill
Phillips Joseph, esq. 20 Cambridge terrace, Edgware road
Phillips Jsph. esq. 41 Up. North pl. Grs. inn
Phillips J. Hen. esq. 96 Charlotte st. Fitz. sq
Phillips J. S. esq. 96 Charlotte st. Fitz. sq
Phillips J. S. esq. 18 Fortess ter. Kntish. tn
Phillips Lawrence, esq. 18 Cornwall ter
Phillips Lewis, esq. 13 Up. Islington ter
Phillips Mark, esq. 10 Finsbury pl. sth
Phillips Mrs. 37 Albion st. Hyde park
Phillips Mrs. 7 Chester pl. Kennington cr
Phillips Mrs. 12 Gibson sq. Islington
Phillips Mrs. 14 Holland pl. Clapham rd
Phillips Mrs. 42 Upper Seymour st
Phillips Miss, 5 Foley place
Phillips Philip, esq. 29 Milton st
Phillips Revell, esq. 3 Harcourt buildings
Phillips Revel, esq. 27 Kensington sq
Phillips Rd. esq. 1 Angel ter. New rd
Phillips Richard, esq. 5 & 6 Craig's ct
Phillips Rt. esq. 4 Glo'ster rd. Regt. pk
Phillips S. esq. 10 Chester ter. Regent's pk
Phillips S. esq. 7 Hamilton pl. St. John's wd
Phillips Thos. esq. 7 Albion tr. Wandsw. rd
Phillips Thos. esq. 5 Brunswick square
Phillips Thos. esq. 24 Circus rd. St. Jn.'s wd
Phillips Thomas, esq. 74 Grosvenor st
Phillips Thos. esq. 1 River terrace, City rd
Phillips T. G. esq. 44 Albion st. Hyde park
Phillips Thos. Joddrell, esq. 7 New sq
Phillips Wm. esq. 1 Richmond tr. Canby
Phillips Wm. esq. 25 St. John's wood rd
Phillips Wm. Edward, esq. 21 Dorset sq
Phillips Wm. J. esq. 16 College st. Islgtn
Phillipson Chas. esq. 34 Up. Montagu st
Phillipson Montague, esq. 7 Burton st
Phillott Lieut.-Col. 2 Up. Gore, Kensingtn
Phillott Arthur, esq. 4 Wimpole st
Phillott Johnson, esq. 13 Charterhouse sq
Phillpott Hy. esq, 2 Livrpl. st. King's cross
Phillpotts John, esq. M.P. Reform club, & Porthgwidden, Truro, Cornwall
Phillpotts Thos. G. esq. 8 Earl st. Blkfrs. & Newport, Monmouthshire
Philp F. C. M.D. Kensington ho. Knsgtn. rd
Philp Fras. Richd. M.D. 28 Grosvenor st
Philp William, esq. 27 King st. Holborn
Philpot Fred. esq. 19 Charles st. Hyde pk
Philpot J. jun. esq. 3 Southampton st
Philpotts Miss, 10 U. Spring st. Portman sq
Philps Mrs. 13 Lower Belgrave place
Phinn Thos. esq. 1 New court, Temple
Phipps Hon. Edmd. 64 Mount st. & 6 Figtree court, Temple
Phipps John, esq. 3 Palace pl, G. Sctlnd. yd
Phipps Miss, 22 Portlnd. pl. Lr. rd. Islngtn
Phipps Rt. esq. 54 St. John's wood terrace
Phipson Thos. Weatherley, esq. 1 Hare ct
Phipson W. esq. 1 Hare ct. Temple
Physick Ed. G. jun. esq. 20 Up. Glo'ster pl
Picard Fras. esq. 35 Robert st. Hampstd. rd
Picciotto Moses, esq. 3 Dean st. Finsbury
Pichione Madame, 9 Kensington gdn. ter
Pickar Miss, 2 Weymouth st. Portlnd. pl
Pickard Mrs. 3 Southamptn. pl. Euston sq
Picken Andrew, esq. Friedenstein ter
Pickering Edwd. Rowland, esq. 4 Stone buildings, Lincoln's inn, & Clapham
Pickering George Smith, esq. 4 Stone buildings, & Clapham
Pickering J. S. esq. 1 Union cr. Nw. Kt. rd
Pickering Percival A. esq. 2 Paper bdgs
Pickersgill F. R. esq. 8 Leigh st. Brtn. cres
Pickersgill Hen. W. esq. R.A. 18 Soho sq
Pickersgill John, esq. 31 Tavistock sq
Pickett John, esq. 10 Bridgewater sq
Pickstock Thos. esq. 10 Trinity square, Borough, & 39 Clement's lane
Pico John, esq. 26 Holloway pl. Holloway
Pidcock J. H. esq. 9 Devonprt. st. Hyde pk
Pidduck Isaac, M.D. 22 Montague st
Pidgeon J. S. esq. 33 Myddelton sq
Pierce Capt. G. 17 Albion rd. Liverpl. rd
Pierce Sl. esq. 9 Warwk. villas, Maida hil. w
Piercy Mrs. 19 George st. Hanover sq
Piercy Wm. esq. 26 Burton st. Burtn. cres
Pierpoint Mrs. 21 Upper Belgrave pl
Pierrepont Right Hon. Henry Manvers, 20 Great Cumberland place, & Conhalt park, Andover
Piesse Chas. A. J. esq. 12 Maida hill wst
Piggott Simon F. esq. 10 Old sq. Lin. inn
Pigot Rt. Hon. D. R. M.P. 3 Queen sq. Westmnstr. & 8 Merrion sq. sth. Dublin
Pigot Sir Robert, bt. M.P. 16 Hertford st. & Patishull, near Stafford
Pigot Henry Becher, esq. 8 Milner st
Pigott Gillery, esq. 14 Keppel st
Pigott Gillery, esq. 3 Pump ct. Temple
Pigott John Allen, esq. 8 Heathcote st
Pigott Miss, 101 Mount st
Pigott Mrs. G. F. 4 Cambridge tr. Rgt.'s pk
Pigou Fredk. esq. 11 Albert ter. Kngtsbdg
Pike Charles Andrew, 1 Cursitor st
Pike Rev. John Josiah, 5 U. Seymour st. w
Pike Francis Wm. esq. 26 Bedford row
Pike John, esq. 26 Old Burlington st
Pike John Leon, esq. 72 Gt. Prescot st
Pike Warburton, esq. 12 King's bench wlk
Pike Wm. esq. Caroline pl. Hampstd. rd
Pilcher Jeremiah, esq. 46 Russell sq
Pilcher Mrs. 9 Cornwall cr. Cmdn. nw. tn
Pilcher Rt. esq. 9 Charles st. Manch. sq
Pile S. esq. 93 Hatton grdn. & 41 Castle st
Pilgrim Chas. H. esq. 17 York terrace
Pilgrim Charles, jun. esq. 17 York ter
Pilkington John, esq. 2 Alpha pl. Rgt.'s pk
Pilkington Wm. esq. 1 Vincent sq. Wstm
Pilkington William Ormond, esq. (Eyrefield), 18 Finchley New road
Pilleau Miss, 39 Newington pl. Kengt. rd
Pilleau Mrs. 12 Kengtn. ter. U. Kengtn. la
Pimlott John, esq. 3 Inner Temple la. & Grafton cottage, Camden pl. Peckham
Pinckard Hen. esq. 3 Argyle st. Kng's. crs
Pinckard Mrs. 18 Bloomsbury square
Pinckard Geo. Hen. esq. 78 Gt. Russell st
Pincott Jas. esq. 12 Hamilton terrace
Pinder John, esq. 10 York gate, Regt.'s pk
Pine Mrs. Genl. 35 Manchester st
Pinero John Dl. esq. 16 Lr. Calthorpe st
Pinfold Miss, 77 Wimpole st
Pinhorn Chas. esq. 12 Portland pl. Islgtn
Pink John, esq. 15 Blomfld. rd. Maida hill
Pink Miss, 15 Gt. James st. Bedford rw
Pinkard Richard, M.D. 18 Bloomsbury sq
Pinkus Henry, esq. 36 Maddox st
Pinn Wm. esq. 17 South bank, Regent's pk
Pinney John, esq. 5 Upper Berkeley st
Pinney John Fred. esq. 30 Berkeley sq.; Somerton house, Somerton; & Pinney house, Lyme Regis
Pinney Wm. esq. 30 Berkeley square; Somerton house, Somerton; & Pinney house, Lyme Regis
Pinniger John, esq. 28 John st. Bed. rw
Pinniger John, esq. 3 Raymond buildings
Pinto John F. esq. 4 Suffolk pl. Haymrkt
Pinto-de-Soveral Monsieur L. A. attaché to the Portuguese embassy, 92 Milton st. Dorset square
Piper Thos. esq. Byng place, Torrington sq. & Denmark hill, Camberwell
Pirie Wm. esq. 7 New sq. Lincoln's inn
Pistor Wm. Jas. esq. 2 Tanfield ct. Tmpl
Pitcher Augustus E. esq. 89 Guilford st
Pitcher Chas. esq. 6 Hanover cot. Rgt.'s pk
Pitcher Hen. J. esq. 11 Godliman st
Pitcher Rt. esq. 5 York ctgs. Old Bmptn
Pitcher Wm. esq. 6 Guilford st. Russll. sq
Pitches Miss, 4 Harleyford pl. Ken. com
Pither Mrs. 15 Alfred pl. Bedford sq
Pithouse Mrs. 13 Portland ter. Rgt.'s pk
Pitman Rev. Jno. R. 10 Young st. Knsgtn
Pitman Rev. Wm. M.A. 21 St. Jhn.'s wd. rd
Pitman Ed. Dix, esq. 3 New sq. Lin. inn
Pitman H. A. esq. 28 Montague place
Pitman Mrs. 28 Montague place
Pitman Mrs. 87 Chiswell st
Pitman Wm. esq. Stoke Newington grn
Pitt Hon. Horace, 2 Tilney st
Pitt Col. George Dean, 32 Cadogan pl
Pitt Jas. esq. 9 Cheyne walk, Chelsea
Pitt Miss, 31 Kensington square
Pitt Mrs. 2 Belmont tr. Wandsworth rd
Pitt Steph. esq. Vicarage pl. Kensington
Pittendreigh Saml. John, esq. 13 Green ter. New Riverhead, & 14 South sq
Pittkin Edm. esq. 26 Winchstr. rw. Nw. rd
Pittman John, esq. 1 New Ormond st. & 32 Lamb's Conduit st
Pittman John, esq. 2 Pullin's pl. Islngtn
Pittman Richd. esq. 31 Paddington grn
Pittman Thos. esq. 18 Charlotte st. Ptld. pl
Pittock Mrs. 8 Portsea pl. Connaught sq
Pitts Joseph, esq. 77 Ebury st. Pimlico
Pitts Thos. esq. 8 Melina pl. St. John's wd
Pitts Wm. esq. 77 Ebury st. Pimlico
Pix John, esq. 1 Chatham pl. Walwth. rd
Pizey Rev. Edwd. 38 Hatton garden
Pizzala F. A. esq. 3 Highbury park west
Place Francis, esq. 21 Brompton sq
Place John, esq. 21 Marlboro' sq. Chels
Place Rd. esq. 21 Marlboro' sq. Chelsea
Place Thos. esq. 106 Dorset st. Fleet st
Planché Jas. R. esq. Michaels gr. Brmptn
Plank George, esq. 4 Gibson sq. Islgtn
Planta Rt. Hon. Joseph, 52 Queen Ann st. Cavendish square

Plasket Thos. H. esq. 18 Clifford st. Bond st. & Sidcup pl. Footscray, Kent
Plaskett Hen. esq. 27A, Wellington rd
Plater Fk. esq. 6 Chesterfield st. King cr
Plater J. esq. Blossom's inn, Lawrence la
Platt Sir Thomas Joshua, knt. 39 Tavistock square
Platt Edward, esq. 3 Hare court, Temple
Platt J. esq. 6 Albrt. tr. Queen'srd. St. Jn. w
Platt John, esq. 22 Park sq. east, Reg. pk
Platt Mrs. 22 Alexander sq. Brompton
Platt Saml. esq. 33 Keppel st. Russell sq
Platt Saml. esq. 10 Hyde park gardens
Platt Saml. esq. 33 Royal cr. Notting hl
Platt Thos. esq. 4 Stone bldgs. Linc. inn
Player J. P. esq. 2 Porteus rd. Harrow rd
Playor Joseph, esq. 12 Connaught ter
Pledger Wm. esq. 3 Blomfield st. City
Plestow C. B. esq. 14 Princes st. Cavn. sq
Plestow Mrs. 10 Lower Berkeley st
Plews Jn. esq. 3 Claylands pl. Clapm. rd
Plimpton Rd. esq. 14 Alpha rd. Rgnt.'s pk
Plimpton Richard, esq. 236 Maida vale
Plinke Hy. esq. 2 Addison tr. Kensingtn
Plomer Wm. esq. 14 Welbeck st
Plowden Chas. esq. 15 York st. Portmn. sq
Plowden Miss, 11 Dorset pl. Dorset sq
Plowden Wm. H.C. esq. 8 Devonshire pl
Plowes John, esq. 5 Endsleigh st
Plowman Richard, esq. 17 Brompton sq
Plowman Rd. esq. 2 Upper Wellington st
Plowman Wm. esq. 3 Derby st. Gray's inn r
Plucknett Geo. esq. 19 Fred. st. Gray's inn r
Plucknett Geo. esq. 19½ Fred. st. Gray's inn r
Plucknett James, esq. 18 Tavistock square, & 17 Lincoln's inn fids
Plum T. W. esq. 3 Addington pl. Cambwl. rd
Plumer John, esq. 11 Harleyford. pl. Ken. co
Plumer T.H. esq. Examiners' offi. Rolls yd
Plummerward Robert, esq. 2 Up. Brook st
Plumley Charles, esq. 35 Brunswick sq
Plumley Wm. D. esq. 44 Mornington pl
Plummer Miss, 4 Blandford pl. Rgnt.'s pk
Plumptre Ch. J. esq. 3 Churchyard ct
Plumptre Edward H. esq. 4 Lamb bldgs. Temple, & 20 Queen sq. Bloomsbury
Plumptre John Pemberton, esq. M.P. 3 Great George st. & Fredville, Wingham
Plumridge Cpt. J. H. R.N., M.P. 66 Chstr. sq
Plunket Lord, P.C. Old Connaught, Wckw
Plunket Mrs. 32 Dorset pl. Dorset sq
Pochin Mrs. 17 Lower Seymour st
Pocklington Joseph, esq. Camberwell grn
Pocock Sir George, 1 York st. Portman sq
Pocock Rev. George, 4 Osnaburgh ter
Pocock Augustus, esq. 153 Piccadilly
Pocock Geo. P. esq. 10 Norfolk st. Strand
Pocock John Carne, esq. 27 Lincoln's inn fi
Pocock John Innes, esq. St. Katherine's, Regent's park, & 27 Lincoln's inn fields
Pocock Lewis, esq. F.S.A. 29 Montague st. & 4 Trafalgar square
Pocock Samuel esq. 27 Bloomsbury sq
Pocock Thos. esq. 9 Ladbroke ter. Notg. hl
Pocock Thomas W. esq. 4 Brompton row
Pocock William F. esq. 10 Trevor ter. Ktsb
Poett Joseph G. esq. 75 Great Portland st
Poignand Charles, esq. 113 Sloane st
Poignand John R. esq. 62 Torrington sq
Pointer G. A. esq. 132 Drummond st. Eu. sq
Pol Paris, esq. 23 Dalby terrace, City rd
Poland Peter, esq. 57 Russell square
Pole Sir Peter, bart. 41 Welbeck st
Pole Chas. esq. 4 Craig's ct. Charing cr. & Wyck hill house, Morton in Marsh
Pole Chales Richard, esq. 14 Park cresc
Pole Edward Sacheverell Chandos, esq. 93 Eaton sq. & Radborne, near Derby
Pole Lambert, esq. 23 Upper Harley st
Pole Miss, 36 Upper Harley st. & Aldenham abbey, Watford, Herts
Pole William, esq. M.A., F.R.S. 66 Brook st. Grosvenor sq. & 8 New sq. Linc. inn
Pole Wm. E. esq. 1 New sq. Lincoln's inn
Polhill Frederic, M.P. 10 King Wm. st. Strand, & Howbury hall, nr. Bedford
Polhill Rd. esq. 8 North ter. Brompton
Polidori G. esq. 15 Park village east
Pollard Charles, esq. 1 Brompton sq
Pollard Charles Fk. esq. 26 Brompton cr
Pollard Edward Wm. esq. 1 Brompton sq
Pollard James Prince, esq. 51 Upper John st. Fitzroy square
Pollard John, esq. 42 Sussex gardens
Pollard John D. esq. 9 Little Abingdon st
Pollard the Misses, Brompton crescent
Pollard Rt. B. esq. Blemell ho. O. Bromptn
Pollett Charles, esq. 3 Furnival's inn
Pollett Hugh, esq. 1 Furnival's inn
Pollington Viscount, M.P. 2 Bolton row, & Methley park, Wakefield, Yorkshire
Pollock Rt. Hon. Sir Frederick, knight, Lord Chief Baron, Queen sq. house, Guildford st. & Hatton, near Hounslow
Pollock Captain, 6 St. Geo.'s ter. Knsgtn
Pollock C. E. esq. 5 Childs pl. Temple bar
Pollock Chas. M. I. esq. 19 Gt. George st
Pollock David, esq. Q.C. 20 Montagu st. Russell square
Pollock George K. esq. 19 Gt. George st
Pollock Geo. Fred. esq. 2 Brick ct. Temp
Pollock Mrs. 12 Glo'ster road, Hyde pk
Pollock R. esq. 5 Child's pl. Temple bar
Pollock Timothy, esq. 26 Hatton garden
Pollock Wm. Fred. esq. 1 King's Bench walk, & 21 Torrington square
Pollok Maj. Gen. C.B. 6 Kent ter. Park rd
Pollon Count, Sardinian minister, 11 Grosvenor st
Poltimore Lord, 25 Grosvenor sq.; Poltimore, Exeter; & Court hall, North Molton, Devon; & Hardington, Bath
Polwarth Lord, 94 Pall mall, & Merton house, Berwick-on-Tweed
Polwarth Mrs. 30 Lower Belgrave st
Pond the Misses, 46 Southampton row
Ponder S. esq. 26 Camden cot. Camden tn
Ponsford Rev. S. Courlnd. gro. Wands. rd
Ponsford Henry, esq. 8 New inn, Strand
Ponsford Jn. esq. 17 Grove ter. St. Jn.'s wd
Ponsford Mrs. 2 River st. Pentonville
Ponsford T. esq. 1 Conduit st. w. Hyde pk
Ponsonby Viscount, 15 Great Stanhope st. & Bishop's court, Kildare
Ponsonby Hon. Chas. Fredk. Ashley-Cooper, M.P. 24 George st. Hanover sq & Canford house, near Wimbourne
Ponsonby Hon. Fred. G. B. 10 Farrars buildings
Pontet Mrs. 4 Pelham road, Brompton
Pontifex John, esq. 5 St. Andrew's ct. Hlbn
Pontifex R. esq. 2 Brunswick ter. Dover rd
Ponting Paul, esq. 1 Cambrdg. st. Edg. rd
Ponton Mrs. John, 18 Portman st
Ponton Thomas, esq. 4 Hill st
Pook Thos. esq. 2 Stratton vil. St. Jn's. wd
Pool Burnett M. esq. 16 Goulden ter. Islgtn
Poole Mrs. 5 Canonbury pl. Islington
Poole Moses, esq. 7 Rgnt. villas, Avenue rd. & 4 Old sq. & 13 Serle st. Lincln.'s in
Poole Thomas, esq. 6 South sq. Gray's inn
Poole Thomas Evered, esq. 43 Carey st
Poole Thos. E. esq. 18 Kensington cres
Poole William, esq. 36 Great Ormond st
Poole Wm. H. esq. 10 Gray's inn place
Pooley James, esq. 1 Lincoln's inn fields
Poore Montague, esq. 3 Princes st. Cav. sq
Poore Mrs. 3 Princes st. Cavendish sq
Poore Wm. D. esq. 2 Childs pl. Temple bar
Pope George, esq. 12 Gray's inn square
Pope J. R. esq. 3 Manchester sq. & Hanwell
Pope Misses, 123 Sloane st
Pope Robt. esq. 63 Guilford st. Russell sq. & 2 Raymond buildings, Gray's inn
Pope Samuel, esq. 2 Barnsbury st
Pope Thos. esq. 3 Richmond ter. Islgtn
Popham Mrs. Genl. 39 York st. Portmn. sq
Popham Mrs. Col. 1 Blue coat buildings
Popham Mrs. 11 Scarsdale ter. Kensgtn
Pople Wm. esq. 95 Stanhope st. Hmpst. rd
Popoff Rev. Eugenius, 32 Welbeck st
Poppe Fredk. esq. 8 Hemus ter. Chelsea
Popplewell Mrs. 4 Thames parade
Portal B. B. esq. 20 Claremont square
Portal Melville, esq. 3 Clifford st. & Freefolk Priors, Overton, Hants
Portal Wm. A. esq. 10 Clifford's inn
Portbury Edwd. esq. 12 Claremont row
Porter Capt. R.N. 17 Albemarle st
Porter G. esq. 10½ Kenngtn. rw. Kengtn. rd
Porter Henry, esq. 41 Cambridge ter
Porter John, esq. 4 St. Andrew's place, Regent's park, & 22 Lincoln's inn fields
Porter Lieut. Col. 18 New Bond st
Porter Jn. esq. 10 Belmont pl. Wandsw. rd
Porter Joseph Long, esq. 43 Sloane st
Porter Mrs. 7 Grove ter. St. John's wood
Porter Mrs. 4 Holland pl Clapham rd
Porter Mrs. 10 Manchester st. Grs. inn rd
Porter Mrs. 23 Nottingham st
Porter Rd. esq. 10 Holloway pl. Holloway
Porter Rt. esq. 40 Wilson st. Finsbury
Porter Thomas, esq. 32 Euston square
Porter Thos. Hen. esq. 19 Granville sq
Portington Mrs. 31 St. John's wood rd
Portland, Duke of, P.C. 19 Cavendish sq.; Welbeck abbey, Worksop; & Fullarton house, Troon, Ayrshire
Portland Club House (John William Walsh, secretary), 1 Stratford place
Portman Lord, 38 Bryanstone square, & Bryanstone, Blandford, Dorset
Portman Hon. Mrs. 5 Dean st. Parklane
Portman Mrs. 2 Gt. Cumberland st
Portsmouth, Earl of, Hurstborne park, Whitchurch, Hampshire
Post H.O. esq. Montpelier, Sth. Lambeth
Postance Mrs. 18 Lodge road, Rgt.'s pk
Postlethwaite J. L. esq. 32 Denbigh st
Potochi Count Alfred, Attaché to the Austrian embassy, 7 Chandos st. Cavendish sq
Pott Rev. Archdeacon, 20 Woburn place
Pott Chas. esq. Foundling hospital, & Bridge st. Southwk. & Bromley, Kent
Pott Frederick William, esq. 18 John st. Bedford row, & 13 Godliman st
Pott Mrs. 111 Glo'ster pl. Portman sq
Pott Wm. H. esq. 11 Victoria rd. Kensgtn
Potter Cipriani, esq. 9 Baker st. Portm. sq
Potter Geo. esq. 5 Spring ter. Wandsw. rd
Potter Geo. Wm. Killett, esq. 30 Henrietta st. Brnswk. sq. & 5 Basinghall st
Potter Jas. esq. 4 Bedford rw. Claphm. ri
Potter Mrs. 18 Marlbro' sq. Chelsea
Potter Rd. esq. 11 Henrietta st. Brnsk. st
Potter Rd. esq. 3 Upper Hamilton ter
Potter Robt. esq. 2 Canonbury villas
Potter Rt. esq. 34 Glo'ster cres. Regt. pk
Potter Sam. esq. 37 Newingtn. pl. Ken. rd
Potter Rt. Jas. esq. 2 James st. Adelphi
Potter Wm. esq. 32 Albion st. Hyde pk
Potter Wm. esq. 28 Clapham road pl
Potter Wm. S. esq. 7 Sussex gdns. Hyde pk
Potticary Miss, 35 Upper Baker st
Pottinger Sir Henry, bart. 67 Eaton pl
Pottinger Charles, esq. 72 Hermitage pl
Pottle Miss, 5 Cobourg pl. Up. Kengtn. la
Potts Edwd. esq. 8 Serjeants' inn, Fleet st
Potts George, esq. 52 Walcot place east
Potts George B. esq. 28 Pall Mall
Potts Lawrence H. M.D. 9 Buckingham st
Potts Wm. esq. 8 Serjeants' inn, Fleet st
Potts Wm. esq. 27 South Audley st
Poulden Geo. esq. 1 Figtree ct. Temple
Poulett Earl, Hinton St. George, Crewkerne, Somerset
Poullett Hon. Adml. G. 69 Sou. Audley st
Poulteney Mrs. 21 Whitehead's grv. Chels
Poulter John Sayer, esq. 5 King's Benchwk
Poulter Miss, Lark hall rise, Clapham
Pouncey Miss, 4 Hyde park gardens
Pound Matt. esq. 33 Orchard st
Povah Mrs. 25 Stoke Newington green
Powell Col. Wm. Edwd. M.P. 7 Hyde pk. ter. & Nanteos house, nr. Aberystwith
Powell Arthur, esq. 19 Hanover ter
Powell Benj. esq. 2 Stanhope ter. Rg. pk

Powell Caleb, M.P. Reform club, & Clanshavoy, co. Limerick
Powell CalebEdwd. esq.11 South parade, Chelsea, & 5 Raymond buildings
Powell C.G. esq.5Ordance ter. St.Jns.wd
Powell Edward Joseph, esq. 8 Gordon st. Gordon sq. & 5 Raymond buildings
Powell Fred. esq. 22 Alfred st. Bedfd. sq
Powell Geo. esq.8 Beaufort bdgs. Strand
Powell Geo. esq. 1York bdgs. Islgtn.grn
Powell Geo. esq.3Raymond bdgs.Gra.'sin
Powell James, esq. 16 Gt. Coram st
Powell James, esq. 74 Hamilton terrace
Powell James, esq. 36 Lwr. Belgrave pl
Powell Jas. Richd. esq. 27A, Howland st
Powell Jesse, esq. 13 Glo'ster st. Qun. sq
Powell John Allan, esq. 7 George st. Hanover square, & 9 New sq. Linc.inn
Powell John Clarke, esq.16 St.Helen's pl
Powell John H. esq. 33 Old Burlington st. & Hengrave hall, BurySt.Edmunds
Powell Lewis, M.D. 12John st.Berkly. sq
Powell Miss, 1 Cheyne walk, Chelsea
Powell Miss, 16 Water st. Blackfriars
Powell Mrs. 16 Kent ter. Regent's park
Powell Mrs. 42 York ter. Regent's park
Powell Rd. esq.19Abbeypl. St. John's wd
Powell Rt. esq. 13 Beaufort bldgs. Stnd
Powell Thos. esq. 52 Portmanpl. Edgw.rd
Powell Whiston, esq. 13 Burton st
Powell Wm. esq. 3 Barnard's inn, Holbrn
Powell Wm.esq.6 Mylne st.Claremont sq
Powell Wm.esq.38 Theberton st. Islgton
Power David, esq. 1 Cloisters, Temple
Power James, esq. M.P. 151 Regent st. & Edermine house, near Wexford
Power Jas.esq.M.P.Cox's hotl.55Jerm. st
Power John, M.D.9 Gt. Queen st.Westm
Power Mrs. 22 Buckingham st. Strand
Power Robt. F.M.D.11Queen st.May fair
Power Wm. esq. 18 St.Mary Abbott's ter
Powis Earl of, K.G. 45 Berkeley sq.; & Walcot, Ludlow; & Powis castle, Welshpool
Powis Capt. 13Campden hl.vils.Kensgtn
Powis Mrs. 33 Spring gardens
Powis Thos.esq.11Pelham rd. Brompton
Powis Wm.esq.18Blomfield rd. Edgw.rd
Powis Wm. esq.4 Carey st
Powlett Lord Wm. Vane, 19 Curzon st.; Downham hall, Brandon, Suffolk; & Somerton, Melton Mowbray
Pownall Charles Edward, esq. 5 Lower Phillimore place, Kensington, & 28 Nicholas lane
Pownall George, esq. 5 Gordon square, 7 Bedford row, & 14Up.King st.Holbn
Pownall Henry, esq. 63 Russell square, & Spring grove, Hounslow
Pownall Henry, jun. esq. 63 Russell sq. & Spring grove, Hounslow
Pownall John Fish, esq. 19 Old sq. Lincoln's inn; & Spring grove, Hounslow
Pownall William, esq. 8 & 9 Staple inn
Powys Bransby Wm. esq. 78 Guilford st. Russell square, & 8 Staple inn
Powys Littleton, esq. 5 St. James's pl
Powys Philip L.esq.2Harcrt.bldgs.Templ
Poyce Wm.M.esq.5 Camdenst.So.Cmd.tn
Poyer John P. esq. 7 Russell pl. Fitz. sq
Poynder Rev. Fredk. M.A. Charterhouse
Poynder John,esq.Montpelr.Sth.Lambth
Poynder Thomas, esq. 52 Wimpole st
Poynder Thos. Allen, esq. 83 Harley st
Poynder Thos. H.A.esq.13New sq.Lnc.in
Poynter Ambrose, esq. 1 Poet's corner
Poynter Mrs. 10 Bedford pl.Hampstd.rd
Poynter Thos. esq. 96 Gloucester pl
Poynter Wm. esq.2 South sq. Gray's inn
Pradey Patrick, esq. 11 Old Quebec st
Praed, Fane, Praed & Johnston, 189Flt. st
Praed William Tyringham, esq. M.P. 35 St.James's pl. & Trevethow, Truro
Praed Mrs. Winthrop, 64 Chester sq
PranceMilesHammett,esq.3 Gray's in.sq
Pranckard Mrs. 15 St. John's wood rd
Prandi F. esq. 13 Davies st. Brkly. sq
Prater Charles, esq. 71 Portland place
Prater Mrs. 5 Cloudesley ter. Islington
Pratt Rev. Jermyn, 12 Suffolk st
Pratt Rev. Josiah, jun.13 Finsbry. circus
Pratt David, esq. 25 Old Fish st
Pratt Frederic Thos. D.C.L. 2 College, Doctors' commons
Pratt Geo.esq.7Portld.pl.Lr.rd. Islington
Pratt Geo. esq. 38 Tonbridge pl. New rd
Pratt Henry, esq. 2 Hill rd.St.John's wd
PrattJno.esq.2Chelsea pk.cot.Lt.Chelsea
Pratt John, esq. 29 Beaumont st
Pratt John Tidd, esq. 5 Bolton st.; 54 Russell sq.; & Cecil ho. Margate
Pratt Miss, 18 York buildings, New rd
Pratt Miss de Montmorency, 83 Piccadilly, & Cabard castle, Cavan, Ireland
Pratt Saml. esq. 10 Bentinck ter. Rgt.pk
Pratt Saml.P. esq. 55 Lincoln's inn fields
Pratt Thos. esq. 35 King st. Westminstr
Pratt Wm. M.D. 34 Southampton bldgs
Pratten Miss, 25 Southampton pl. Eu. sq
Preece Richard M. esq.24 Park sq. east
Preedy John, esq. 28 Oxford terrace
Preiston Mrs. 28 Cloudesley square
Prendergast Harris, esq. 48 Beaumont st. & 4 Old sq. Lincoln's inn
Prendergast J. esq. 13 Camden rd. villas
Prendergast M.esq.32 Castle st. Holborn
Prendergast Mrs. 3 Upper Seymour st
Prendeville Mrs. 17 Henrietta st. Bk. sq
Prentice Samuel, esq. 4 Essex ct. Temple
Prentice Saml. esq. 57 Trinity sq. Boro'
Prentice Wm.esq.10Lowthr.cot.Lpool.rd
Prentis Edwd. esq.9Hornton st.Knsngtn
Presbury Geo. esq. 19 Rodney st. Pntnvl
Prescott Fredk. Jsph. esq. 13 Oxford sq
Prescott G.F.esq.6 Holland pl.Clphm.rd
Prescott Hen. Jas. esq. 22 Chester st
Prescott Mrs. 22 Chester st. Grosvnr. pl
Prescott W.G.esq.8 Rutland gt. Kngtsbr
Presig Mrs. 2 Augustus sq. Regent's pk
Presland Mrs. 17 Cole's ter. Barnsby.rd
Pressly Chas. esq. 13 Montague st
Prest John, esq. 19 Chenies st.Bedfd. sq
Prest Miss, 10 Avenue rd. Regent's pk
Preston Chas. Jas.esq.13Park st.Westm
Preston Edwd.esq. 31 Burlington arcade
Preston Hen. J. esq. 43 Bloomsbury sq
Preston John, esq.41 Allsop terrace, New road, & Tokenhouse yard, City
Preston J. K. esq. 8 Osnaburgh st
Preston Miss, 11 Barnsbury sq
Preston Miss, 19 Nottingham place
Preston Mrs. 68 George st. Euston sq
Preston Richard, esq. Q.C. Lee house, Chumleigh, North Devon; & Inner Temp
Peston S. Tolver, esq. 12 Nw.Boswell ct
Preston Wm. T. esq. 2Figtree ct. Temple
Prestwich Joseph, esq. 20 Mark lane
Pretty Wm.esq.Maude cot. Morngtn. rd
Prevost George, esq. vice-consul for Switzerland, 24A, Gresham st
Prevost John Lewis, esq. consul-general for Switzerland, 3 Suffolk place, Pall mall east; & 24A, Gresham st
Prevost Louis A. esq. 122 Crawford st
Price Sir Robert, bart. M.P. Waterloo hotel, Jermyn st.; & Foxley, near Hereford
Price Sir Robert, bart. 85 Jermyn st
Price Rev. Edwd. 54 Lincoln's inn flds
Price Capt. R.N. 60 St. John's wood ter
Price Edwin P. esq. 2 Inner Temple la
Price George, esq. Caledonian road
Price Geo. P.esq.7 Holloway pl. Hollowy
Price Geo.R. esq.29 Lower Islington ter
PriceHenry,esq.26 Cambridge ter.Edg.rd
Price Henry, esq.2 Gt.Queen st.Westm
Price Jas. esq. 6 Clarence ter. Rgnt.'s pk
Price John, esq. 42 Beaufort st. Chelsea
Price John B. esq. Priory, Barnsbury pl
Price J. D. esq. 4 King's rd. Bedford rw
Price Miss, 23 Harleyford pl. Ken. com
Price Mrs. 4 Norfolk cr. Oxford square
Price Mrs. 2 Up. Holland st.Kensington
Price Richard, esq. M.P. United University club, Pall mall east; & Norton house, Presteign
Price Rd.esq 5 the Lawn, South Lambth
Price Rd. Alex. esq. 3 Brick ct. Temple
Price Rt. esq. 3 Caroline pl. Mcklbg. sq
Price Rt. Alex. esq. 14 John st. Adelphi
Price Thomas, esq. 7 Highbury terrace
Price Thomas, esq.13 Millbank rw.Wmr
Price Thos.esq.14 Petersburgh pl.Byswtr
Price Thos. esq. 29 Upper Bedford place
Price Timothy, esq. 19 Trevor square
Price Wm. esq. 6 Allsop pl. Regent's pk
Price Wm. esq. 34 Craven st. Strand
Price Wm. esq. 2 St. George's terrace
Price Wm. esq. 46 Warren st. Fitzroy sq
Price Wm. F. esq. 34 Craven st. Strand
Price Wm. Fraser, esq. 6 Regent's villas, Avenue road
Price Wm. Thos. esq. 36 Up. George st. Edgware road
Prichard Hen. esq.3 Duncan ter.City rd
Prichard Hen. esq. 57 Lincoln's inn flds
Prichard Wm.B. esq.15 St. John's wood road, Regent's park; & 24 & 27 Wilmington square
Prideaux Chas. Grevile, esq. 2 Elm ct
Prideaux Fredk. esq. 28 Chancery lane
Prideaux Walter, esq. 12 Park la. Piccadilly, & Goldsmiths' hall, Foster la.Cty
Prideaux Wm. Fras. esq. 7 Avenue rd
PridhamCapt.R.N.82Ebury st. Eaton sq
Pridmore Rd. esq.47 Cantrbry.st. Lmbth
Pridon Madame, 80 South Audley st
Priest Benjn. esq. 9 Holland pl. Knsgtn
Priestley J. esq. 12 Nthmptn. ter. Islgtn
Priestly Mrs. 22 Charlotte st. Portld. pl
Prime Miss, 22 Clapham rise
Prince Alexr. esq. 68 Russell square
PrinceFredk.W.esq.13Lodge rd.Rgt.'s pk
Prince George, esq. 8 & 9 NewPalace yd
Prince Jas.esq. 9 Albert ter.St.John's wd
Prince Miss, 27 Edward st. Portmn. sq
Prince Wm. esq. 127 Gt. Portland st
Prince William, esq. 16 Pall mall
Pring John, esq. 5 Union pl. City road
Pring Thomas Jas. esq. 33 Bouverie st
Pringle Capt. Alexander, 45 Pall mall
Pringle Alexander,esq.M.P.43 Pall mall, & Yair, near Selkirk, N.B
Pringle the Misses,4Bentinck st. Man.sq
Pringle Mrs. 10 Argyll st. Regent st
Pringle Mrs. 8 Lloyd st. Lloyd square
Pringle Wm. esq. 3 King's rd. Bedfd.row
Prinsep Hen. T. esq. 37 Hyde pk. gardns
Prinsep Mrs. 6 Gt. Cumberland st
Prinsep Wm. esq. 26 Cambridge square
Prior Edw. esq. 48 York ter. Regent's pk
Prior Harvey Morris, esq. 5 Hans place
Prior Hen. esq. 36 Cumming st. Pentnvl
Prior James, esq. 14 Oxford terrace
PriorJohnVenn,esq.9Old sq.Lincln.'s inn
Prior Martin, esq. 36 Charltt. st. Fitz.sq
Prior Thos. Young, esq. 1 Elm ct.Temple
Prior Wm. esq. 7 Myddelton square
Prior Wm.H.esq.18Liverpool st. New rd
Pritchard Rev. Geo. 4 York pl. Pentonv
Pritchard Chas. esq. 6 Portman st
Pritchard Edward, esq. 9 Staple inn
Pritchard Edwd. esq. 35 Tavistock pl
Pritchard George, esq. 45 St. James's pl
Pritchard George Berry, esq. 10 Albion ter. Wandsworth road
Pritchard John, esq. 111A, Jermyn st
Pritchard John,esq.52Lincoln's inn fields
Pritchard Mrs. 82 Milton st. Dorset sq
Pritchard Mrs.6Princes ct. Storey's gate
Pritchard T. esq. 9 Albert ter. Kntsbrdg
Pritchard Thos. K. esq. 20 Manchestr. st
Pritchard Wm. esq. 6 College, Doctors' commons; Town hall, Southwark; & Walton, Surrey
PritchardWm.T.esq.8Chester.pl.Oxfd.sq
Pritt Geo. esq. 4 Btnck.ter. Regt.'s pk
Pritt George, esq. 44 Parliament st

Probart Ed. esq.2Ebenezer ter.Ken.com
Probyn Capt. R.N. 21 Bryanstone sq
Procter Bryan Waller. esq. 13 Up. Harley st. & 4 Gray's inn square
Procter Christr. esq.10New sq. Linc. inn
Procter Mrs. 19 Compton ter. Islington
Procter Wm.esq.9South bank,Regt.'s pk
Proctor Dowager Lady Beauchamp, 11 Hertford street, Mayfair
Proctor Fras. sen. esq. 26 Lisson gr. nth
Proctor John, M.D. 17 Whitehead's grv
Proctor Joseph, esq. 24 Pall mall
Proctor S. M. D.7Norland pl.Notting hill
Profitt Mrs. 24 Westbourne pl. Eaton sq
Prole Wm. W. 51 Thurloe sq. Brompton
Propert John, esq. 6 New Cavendish st
Prosser S. esq. 6Hamilton ter.St.Jn's.wd
Prosser Wm. esq. 26 Petersburgh place
Protat Peter, esq. 37 Charlotte st. Prtl.pl
Prothero Thos. esq. 13Lyon ter.Edgw.rd
Prothero Thomas, esq. 4 Furnival's inn
Protheroe Edward, jun. esq. M.P. 12 Cottage road, Chester square, & Turnwood, Blandford, Dorset
Prout Wm. M.D. 40 Sackville st
Prout John Wm. esq. 57 Chancery lane
Provis Wm. Alex. esq. 24 Abingdon st
Prowett D. esq. 8 Up.Portld.pl.Wdsw.rd
Prowett Edward, esq. 18 Clement's inn
Prowett Miss,9Up.Portland pl.Wdsw.rd
ProwettRobt.esq.16Up.Berkeley square
Prudence Wm. esq. 12 Rodney st.Pntnvl
Prudhoe Lord, Capt. R.N. 5 Whitehall gardens,& Stanwick park, Darlington
Prujean Francis, esq. 5 Staple inn
Pryme Saml. S.esq.7Radnor pl.Hyde pk
PryorFelix,esq.St.John's hl.Wndswth.rd
Pryor John, esq. 33 Finsbury circus
Pryor Mrs. 123 Broad street buildings
Pryor Robt. esq. 109 Glo'ster pl. Portman square, & 7 Old sq. Lincoln's inn
Pryor Saml. esq. 43 Cumming st. Pntvl
Pryor Stephen A. esq. 5 Rayner pl.Chls
Pryor Wm. S. esq. 23 Broad st.buildings
Pryse Pryse, esq. M.P. Limmer's hotel, 1 George st. Hanv.sq. & Aberystwith, & Buscot park, Faringdon
Puddick Mrs. 35 Alfred st. Bedford sq
Puddick Rd. esq. Lavender hl.Wands. rd
Puddicombe Edw.D.esq.1Warwick vills. Maida hill west, & 3 Furnival's inn
Pudney Mrs. 8 Aberdeen pl. Maida hill
Puffer Peter, esq. 15 Sloane terrace
Puget Capt. R.N. 14 Finchley new road
Pugh Chas. esq. 13 King's rd. Bedfrd. rw
Pugh Chas. esq. 1 Up. Hamilton terrace
Pugh David, esq. 5 King's bench walk
Pugh John, esq. 157 Regent st
Pugh John, esq. 17 Wilton pl. Knightsb
Pugh Jsph. esq. 48 Porchestr. ter. Baysw
Pugh Joshua R. esq. 17 York pl. City rd
Pugh Mrs.33 Bernard st. Russell sq
Pugh Rd. esq. 4 Hollywood pl. Chelsea
Pugh Rd. esq. 11 Salisbury st. Strand
Pugh Robt. esq.12Salisbury st. Strand
Pugh Thos. B. esq. 6 Dorset ter.Clpm.rd
Pulbrook Lott, esq. 3 Clarnce. pl.Clm.rd
Pulford Richd. esq. 58 Clarendon square
Pulham Jas. esq. 7 Gower st. nth.Nw.rd
Pulleine James, esq. 77 Harley st. & 1 King's bench walk
Pullen John Stephen, esq. 15 Woburn pl
Pullen John, esq. 21 Bedford st. Cov. gn
Pullen Wm. esq. 37 Maiden la. Cov. gn
Pullen Lady Giles,30Grosvenor square, & Youngsbury, Ware
Puller Christr. W. esq. 30 Grosvenor sq
Pulley Wm. M. esq. 34 John st. Bedf. rw
Pullin Mrs. 9 Beaufoy ter. Edgw. road
Pullin Sml. Jn. esq.29Park rd.Regt's.pk
Pulling Rev. John, 19 Union st. Deptford
Pulling Alex. esq. 6 Crown office row
Pulling Chas. esq. 11 Trinity sq. Boro'
Pulling Robt. esq. 39 Up. Thames st
Pulling W. esq. 39 Upper Thames st
Pullinger Wm. G. esq. 3 Ehrenburg ter
PulmanJs.esq.Heralds'col.Bennett's hl.; Ho. of Lords; & East hill,Wandsworth
Pulman John, esq. 4 Elm court, Temple, & Shore house, Hackney
Pulsford Mrs. 29 Hyde park gardens
Pulsford Rt. esq. M.P. 6 Up. Belgrave st
Pulsford Wm. esq. 11 Hyde park terrace
Pulteney Lady, 97 Piccadilly
Pulteney John, esq. 36 Grosvenor place, & Northerwood house, Lyndhurst
Puncher Wm. esq. 19 Parliament st
Purcell Rd. H.esq. 6 Cambge. st.Edg. rd
Purchase Col. H.A. 14 Geo. st.Hanov. sq
Purday Isaac, esq. 52 Frederick st
Purdey Wm. esq.7Royal hill, Bayswatr
Purdue John, esq.14Hemingfrd. ter.Isln
Purdue John, esq.33Newingtn.pl.Ken.rd
Purdy Rt. esq.17 St.George's ter. Knsgn
Purling John C. esq. 24 York pl. Prtm. sq
Purvis Fredk. esq.26Bayham ter.Cmd.tn
Purvis Thos. esq. Q.C. 8 Michael's grove, Brompton, & 2 Stone bldgs. Linc. inn
Pusey Lady Lucy, 35 Grosvenor square
Putnam Geo.esq.1Up.Spring st.Prtm sq
Putnam George P. esq. 21 Euston sq
Puxon Wm. esq. 10 Charterhouse sq
Puzey Robt. esq. 33 Park rd.Regt's. pk
Puzey Thomas, esq. 65 Myddelton sq
Puzzi Giovanni, esq. 38 Jermyn st
Pybus Marmaduke, esq. 3 Grosvnr. st.w
Pycroft Chs. esq. 18 Paulton sq. Chelsea
Pye George, esq. 15 Regent st
Pye John, esq. 42 Cirencester pl. Fitz.sq
Pye Wm. esq. 46 Cambridge ter. Edg. rd
Pyeman S. esq. 22 Fortess tr.Kentish tn
Pyke George, esq. 11 Kent ter. Park rd
Pyke George, esq. 43 Lincoln's inn fields
Pyle John, esq. 56 Oxford terrace
Pym Sir Wm. 55 Charlotte st.Portld. pl
Pym Rev. Wollaston, 139 New Bond st
Pym Alexr. esq. 12 George st. Hanv. sq
Pym Chas. esq. 15 Montague pl.Blmsby
Pym Miss, 12 George st.Hanover square
PyneGeo.H.esq.1A.,Middlesex pl.Newrd
Pyne Hen. esq. 12 Porchester pl. Edg. rd
Pyne Wm. esq. 4 Inner Temple lane
Pyrke John S. esq.7Lloyd sq.Pentonville

QUAIN John Rd. esq.2 Essex ct. Templ
Quain Richard, esq. 23 Keppel st
Quarles William, esq. 21 Red Lion sq
Queckett John, esq. 21 Regent st
Quennell Mrs. 54 Bernard st. Russell sq
Quentin Lieut. Gen. Sir George A. C.B., K.C.H. 11 Gt. Cumberland st
Quick Jas.C.esq.Denmark hill,Cambrwl
Quick John,esq.30 Glos'ter crs.Regt's.pk
Quiddington Nath.esq.17 King st.St.Jas'
Quilter James, esq. 1 York terrace, Regent's park, & 7 Gray's inn square
Quilter Jas. esq 11 Cobourg pl.Bayswa
Quilter Mrs.5 Campden hl. vl.Kensingtn
Quilter Wm. esq. 83 Finsbury square
Quin Capt. R.N. 18 Albion rd.Liverpl. rd
Quin Fred. Foster, M.D. 4 Arlington st
Quincey Joseph, esq.22 Burton crescent
Quincey Wm. esq. 27 Brunswick sq
Quintin Madame, 12 Lyon ter. Maida hl

RAAB John Hen. esq. 10 Carburton st
Rabaccdy Monseiur de, 20 Manchestr.sq
Rabaudy George de, esq. Chancelier to French Legation, 20 Manchester sq
Rabbeth Wm. esq 6 Clement's inn, Strnd
Raby Mrs. 5 Southampton row, New rd
Rackham P.esq,24Pelham cr.Fulham rd
Rackham Willoughby, esq.35 St.Jas.'sst
Racster Martin, esq. 6 Up. ter. Islington
Racster Wm. esq. 6 Upp. terr. Islington
Radburn Mrs. 4 South cres. Bedford sq
Radcliffe Lady, 22 Cambdg. tr. Edgw. rd
Radcliffe Capt.17 St.Alban's pl.St. Jas's
Radcliffe Derwentwater, esq. 32 Strand
Radford J. esq.8 Howley pl.vils. Hrw.rd
Radford Wm. esq. 4 Lansdowne villas
Radford Wm. M.D. 21 Suffolk st
Radford Wm. esq. 14 Kilburn priory
Radiger Charles, esq. 39 Argyle square
Radiger N.Chas.esq.1 Churchyd.ct.Tmpl
Radley John esq. Denmark hill, Cmbrwl
Radmall John, esq. 1 Bedford rw. Islgtn
Radnor, Earl of, 52 Grosvenor st. & Coleshill house, Farringdon, Berkshire, & Longford castle, Salisbury
Radstock Lord, 26 Portland place
Rae James, esq. 16 Manchester square
Rae Joseph John, esq. 4 Bedford row, & 4 Stoke Newington green
Rae Miss, 9 Somerset st. Portman sq
Raffles Thos. Stamford, esq. 3 Hare ct
Ragan Adolphin, esq. 9 Gower st. north
Ragg Robt. esq. 38 King sq. Goswell rd
Raggatt Wm.esq.6 Aberdeen pl.S.Jn.'sw
Raggett Geo. P. esq. 38 University st
Ragget Misses, 1 Ulster place, New rd
Railton Mrs. 10 Baker st. Portman sq
Railton Wm. esq.Carlton chm. 12 Rgt. st
Raimbach D. M. esq. 99 Stanhope st. Hampstead road
Raimondi John F. esq. 36 Linc. inn fields
Raimondi Willoughby, esq. 23 Surrey st. Strand, & 14 South square, Gray's inn
Raines William, esq. 1 New ct. Temple
Rainey Col. Henry, 64 Welbeck st
Rainey Geo. esq. 31 Cumberland terrace
Rainforth Miss, 27 Berners st
Rainger Wm. esq. 6 Ebury st. Pimlico
Rainsford Mrs. 19 St. George's place
RalfeJohnE.esq.12Lonsdale sq.Islington
Rallett Jas. esq. Hereford rd. Bayswater
Ralli Antonio, esq. 42 Finsbury circus
Ralli Eustratios, esq. 17 Hyde park sq
RalliPandia,esq.consul forGreece,5Connaught pl. west, & 25 Finsbury circus
Ralph Mrs. 41 St. John's wood terrace
Ralph Mrs. 71 Sloane st
Ralph T. S. esq. 8 Charlotte st. Fitz. sq
Ram Mrs. 28 Gloucester place
Ram Stephen, esq. 8 Hereford st
Ramadge Fras. H. M.D. 24 Ely place
Rammell Thomas Wm. esq. 15 Regent st
Ramsay Capt. R.N. 46 Leicester square
Ramsay James, esq. 12 Newman st
Ramsay Mrs. 25 Southampton st. Strand
RamsayT.esq.21Gloster.gro.wt.O.Bmptn
Ramsbotham Jsph. M. esq. 15 Amwell st
Ramsden Lady, 140 Piccadilly, & Barham, Ferrybridge, Yorkshire
Ramsden Capt. & Lady Annabella, 3 Up. Eccleston st. Belgrave square, & Lotherton hall, Tadcaster, Yorkshire
Ramsden Hon. Mrs. Isabella, 6 Upper Brook st. & Byram, Ferrybridge, & Buckden, near Skipton, Yorkshire
Ramsden Sir John, bart. 6 Upper Brook st. & Byram, Ferrybridge, & Buckden, near Skipton
Ramsden Charles, esq. & Hon. Mrs. 45 Eaton pl. & Cantley hall, Doncaster
Ramsden Geo. esq. R.N. 12 Clifford's inn
Ramsden Jn. esq. 14 Norfolk st. Park la
Ramsden Jno. G. esq. 7 New sq. Linc.in
Ramden Miss, 10 Lowndes st. Belgr. sq
Ramsden Rd. esq. 3 Compton ter. Islgtn
Ramsden Mrs. 67 Mortimer st. Cav. sq
Ramsey Rev. Septimus,103St.Martin'sla
Ramsey Alex. esq. 7 South sq.Gray'sinn
Ramsey John, esq. 9 Endsleigh st
Ramshay Wm. esq. 2 Hare ct. Temple
Rancliffe Lord, Mivart's hotel,44 Brook st. & Bunney park, Nottingham
Rand John, esq. 37 Howland st
RandalJ.L.esq.2Providnc.pl.U.Kngtn.la
Randall Edmd. Geo. esq. 56 Welbeck st
Randall Hy. Claremnt. vil. Finchley N.r
Randall John, esq.10 King's bench wlk
Randall John, esq. 19 Up. Bedford pl
Randall Miss, 66 Charlotte st. Ftzry. sq
Randall Mrs. 2 Chesham pl. Belgrv. sq
Randall Mrs. 7 Regent sq. Gray's inn rd
Randall N. T. esq. 2 Parade, Harleyfd.rd
Randall Richard, esq. 20 Bridgwater sq
Randall Saml. esq. 19Bury st.St.James's

Randall Thos. esq. 8 Castle st. Holborn
Randell George, esq. 41 Burton crescent
Randell Hen. esq. 11 New sq. Linc. inn
Randell John, esq. 9 Mecklenburgh st
Randle Mrs. 12 Charles st. Manchstr. sq
Randoll Philip, esq. 74 Goswell road
Randolph Rev. Thomas, 15 Regent st
Randolph John, esq. 55 Marshm. st. Wstm
Randolph John Jas. esq. 24 Old sq. Linc. inn
Ranelagh Viscount, 3 Bolton row
Ranfurly Earl of, 40 Berkeley sq.; Barham ho. Elstree, & Dungannon, Tyrone
Ranger Robt. A. esq. 15 Duke st. Adelphi
Ranger Wm. esq. 13 Pelham place, Brompton, & College, Putney
Ranken Chas. esq. 4 South sq. & Dulwich
Rankin Rt. esq. 9 Devonshire pl. Edg. rd
Rankine Robert, esq. 17 Woburn square
Rankley Alfred, esq. 37 Brompton row
Rankley James, esq. 3 Hans pl. Sloane st
Ransom & Co. 1 Pall mall east
Ranyard Wm. esq. 6 South sq. Gray's inn
Raper Chas. esq. 5 Chapel st. Grosvr. sq
Raper Hen. esq. 18 Tavistock place
Raphael Alexander, esq. 10 Great Stanhope st. & Ditton lodge, Ditton, Surrey
Raphael John, esq. 45 Finsbury circus
Raphael L. esq. 1 & 2 Argyle st. King's cr
Raphael Lewis, esq. 18 Bedfrd. pl. Rsl. sq
Rappallo E. esq. 8 Springfld. pl. Wndsw. rd
Rasch Arthur Aug. esq. 46 Up. Bedford pl
Rasch Frederic Carne, esq. 30 Cambridge sq. & 4 Old sq. Lincoln's inn
Rasch Oswald Lee, esq. 1 Staple inn
Rashleigh Wm. jun. M.P. 16 Stratford pl. & Menabilly ho. Fowey, Cornwall
Rashleigh Wm. sen. esq. 3 Cumberland ter. Regent's park; & Menabilly ho. Fowey, Cornwall
Rastrick John U. esq. 46 Eaton square; 454 Strand, & 1 Robert st. Adelphi
Ratcliff Jas. T. esq. 6 Dorset tr. Gt. Dvr. rd
Ratcliffe Mrs. 10 Finchley new road
Ratcliffe Wm. esq. 19 Sloane terrace
Rathbone B. esq. Queen's rd. St. John's wd
Rathbone John, esq. 2 South bk. Rgt.'s pk
Rathbone Misses, 15 Lr. Phillimore pl
Rathbone Wm. esq. 4 King's bench wlk
Ratliff Joseph, esq. 20 River st. Pentonv
Ratray Mrs. 3 Barnsbury pl. Islington
Ratton Joseph, esq. 3 Park ter. Highbury
Raven Hen. esq. Charltt. cot. Cadogan ter
Raven Hen. esq. 18 Hunter st. Brnsw. sq
Raven Hen. Baldwin, esq. 102 Sloane st
Raven Hen. Taylor, esq. 2 Harcourt bdgs
Raven Richd. esq. 2 King's bnch. wk. Tmpl
Raven Richard, esq. 53 Norland sq. Ntg. hl
Raven S. jun. esq. 6 Northampton pl. Islgtn
Raven Thomas, esq. 8 Euston square
Ravenscroft Hy. Wm. esq. 21 Guilford st
Ravenscroft Mrs. 12 Portland place
Ravenshaw Mrs. 40 Harley street
Ravenshaw Mrs. 13 Wimpole st
Ravensworth Lord, Percycross, Fulham, & Ravensworth castle, Gateshead
Raw Joseph, esq. 5 Furnival's inn
Raw Thomas, esq. 40 Noel st. Islington
Rawbone Geo. esq. 17 Manor pl. Chelsea
Rawden Lieut. Col. John Dawson, M.P. & Dowager Lady Cremorne, 3 Great Stanhope st. Mayfair
Rawlings Chas. esq. 17 Cheyne walk
Rawlings J. esq. Albt. vil. Finchley nw. rd
Rawlings Joseph, esq. 1 Inner Temple lane, & Tottenham park
Rawlings Wm. esq. 8 Comptn. ter. Islingtn
Rawlings Wm. esq. 70 Mount st
Rawlins Rev. Rd. Rectory ho. Limehouse
Rawlins Geo. esq. Langley cot. So. Lambth
Rawlins Hen. A. esq. 1 Francis ter. Ken. tn
Rawlins John, esq. 51 Oxford terrace
Rawlins Joseph, esq. 6 Norland tr. Ntg. hl
Rawlins Samuel George, esq. Hermitage, Sth. Lambth. & 15 Salisbury st. Strand
Rawlins Wm. M.D. York gt. Regt.'s pk
Rawlinson Christr. esq. 1 Essex ct. Temple
Rawlinson E. A. esq. 24 Glo'ster cr. Reg. pk
Rawlinson John, esq. 42 Wimpole st. & New place, Alresford, Hants
Rawlinson Wm. H. esq. 20 Gt. Marlboro' st
Rawnsley Hen. C. esq. 5 Robert st. Adelph
Rawson Misses, 4 Tilney st. South Audley st. & Nidd hall, Knaresborough
Ray Charles, esq. 7 Elizth. st. Eaton sq
Ray Edmund Barker, esq. 13 Montagu pl
Ray Geo. esq. 44 Fredk. st. Gray's inn rd
Ray Geo. esq. 2 Woodland pl. St. John's wd
Ray Hen. Belward, esq. 28 Hill st. Brkly. sq. & Serjeants' inn, Chancery lane
Ray Mrs. 41 Gt. James st. Bedford row
Ray Mrs. 28 Wilton pl. Knightsbridge
Ray Walter J. esq. 23 Lincoln's inn fields
Rayleigh Lord, United University club, & Terling place, Witham, Essex
Rayley Richard, esq. 16 Upper Berkeley st. Portman sq. & Old sq. Linc. inn
Raymond George, esq. 18 Pall mall east
Raymond John, esq. 9 King's bench wk
Raymond Misses, 17 Bedford pl. Kensgn
Raymond Thos. esq. 2 Angel ter. Islngtn
Raymond Wm. esq. 4 Upper Glo'ster pl
Rayner Jph. esq. 18 Belmnt. pl. Wands. rd
Rayner William, esq. 6 Barnard's inn, & 22 Bridge road, Southwark
Raynolds John, esq. 4 Albion st. Hyd. pk
Raynsford Mrs. 7 Keppel st. Russell sq
Raynsford Thos. Alex. esq. 5 Devons. pl
Read Lieut. Geo. R.N. 28 Gt. Coram s
Read Alexander, esq. 2 Dorset square
Read David, esq. 6 Lincoln's inn
Read Edmund, esq. 7 Furnival's inn
Read Henry, esq. 12 South st. Finsbury
Read Miss, 12 Earl's ter. Kensington
Read Mrs. 5 Cadogan ter. Sloane st
Read Mrs. 49 Gloucester place
Read Mrs. 11 Norland ter. Notting hill
Read Rd. esq. 1 Douro cotgs. St. John's wd
Read T. P. esq. 18 Hornton st. Kensgn
Read T. R. esq. 10 Hunter st. Brnswk. sq
Read Wm. Hen. esq. 4 Dyer's bldgs. Hlbrn
Reade James, esq. 13 Lower Berkeley st
Reardin Mrs. 2 Colebroke ter. Islington
Reading Cyrus, esq. 10 Hill rd. St. Jn.'s wd
Reading Wm. Hy. esq. 16 Paddington gn
Ready Mrs. 4 Albion pl. Up. Kenngtn. la
Reardon Rev. Timothy, 7 Spanish place
Reay Lord, Arthur's club, 69 St. James's st. & Goldens, near Hertford
Rebecca John B. esq. 8 Dukest. St. James'
Rebello Francisco, esq. vice consul for Portugal, 16 Upper Woburn place, & 26 Mark lane
Rebow Lieut. Gen. 12 Gt. Cumberland pl. & Wivenhoe park, Colchester
Rebow John Gurdon, esq. 12 Gt. Cumberland pl. & Wivenhoe pk. Colchester
Reckless Mrs. 304 Regent st
Reddick Wm. esq. Fitzroy cot. Morngtn. rd
Reddish John, esq. 10 Myddelton square
Redesdale Lord, 6 Park pl. St. James's st. & Batsford, Morton in Marsh
Redford George, esq. 32 Golden square
Redford S. esq. 8 Thornhill pl. Pentnvl
Redgrave A. esq. 2 Ionian cot. Park vil. ea
Redgrave James F. esq. 95 Albany st
Redgrave Saml. esq. 7 Hyde park gate sth
Redgrave Wm. esq. 95 Albany st. Rgt.'s pk
Redhead L. esq. 24 Holland pl. Clapm. rd
Redhead R. esq. 1 Ordnance ter. St. Jn.'s w
Redington Thomas Nicholas, esq. M.P. & Kilcoran, near Oranmore, Ireland
Redmaine G. esq. 13 Somerset st. Ptm. sq
Redman John B. esq. 5 New Palace yd
Redmayne Leonard, esq. 2 Pine Apple pl
Redwood Mrs. 15 Dorset pl. Dorset sq
Redwood T. esq. 19 Montague st. Blmsby
Reece Geo. esq. 45 Sussex gar. Hyde pk
Reece Richard Marsden, esq. 8 Calthorpe st. Gray's inn road, & 2 Furnival's inn
Reece Wm. esq. 50 Connaught square
Reed Charles, esq. 32 New Broad st. City
Reed Edwd. esq. 80 Milton st. Dorset sq
Reed George, esq. 5 Glo'ster st. Queen sq
Reed Mrs. 40 Kensington square
Reed Robert, esq. 2 Robert st. Adelphi
Reed Thos. G. esq. Western ho. Earl's ct
Reeks Trenham, esq. 4 Craig's court
Rees David, M.D. 8 Craven st. & New cross
Rees Geo. Owen, M.D. 59 Guilford st
Rees Josiah, esq. 59 Guilford st
Rees Miss, 5 Euston square, New road
Reeve Ellis, esq. 43 Montague square
Reeve Hen. esq. 16 Chester sq. Pimlico
Reeve Henry, esq. Privy Council office, Downing st
Reeve James, esq. 21 Broad st. buildings
Reeve Jn. Forster, esq. 34 Gt. Ormond st
Reeve Miss, 10 Chapel st. Grosvenor sq
Reeve Mrs. 19 Holland pl. Clapham rd
Reeve Mrs. 45 Montagu square
Reeve Mrs. 24 New Broad st. City
Reeve Mrs. John, 46 Brompton row
Reeve Philip, esq. 4 Lincoln's inn fields, & 8 New square, Lincoln's inn
Reeve Rd. F. esq. 13 Milman st. Bedford rw
Reeve Thomas, esq. 17 Calthorpe place
Reeves C. esq. 2 Devonshire pl. Wnds. rd
Reeves Henry, esq. 5 Gt. Coram st
Reeves Jas. esq. 20 Holloway pl. Hollwy
Reeves Mrs. 12 Brompton row, Bromptn
Reeves Mrs. 10 Somerset st. Portman sq
Reeves Miss, 13 Brompton row
Reeves Misses, 3 Bulstrode st
Reeves Wm. esq. 6 Lyon's inn, Strand
Reeves Wm. esq. Upper Kennington gr
Reform Club House (Wm. Henry Bond, secretary), 104 Pall mall
Rehausen Baron, chargé d'affaires for Sweden & Norway, 14 Halkin st. west
Reichenbach Mrs. 38 Devonsh. st. Qn. sq
Reid Col. Geo. Alex. 31 Cavendish sq
Reid Sir John Rae, bart. M.P. 4 Eaton pl. Belgrave sq. & Ewell grove, Surrey
Reid Curtis, esq. 41 St. Mary Axe
Reid Edw. M. esq. 13 Northwk. tr. St. Jn.'s w
Reid Fredk. M.D. 25 Duke st. Westminster
Reid Fredk. esq. 57 Burton st. Brtn. cres
Reid Geo. esq. 8 Clarence ter. Regent's park, & Woodmanstone, near Epsom
Reid Jas. esq. 2 Arundel ter. Brnsby. rd
Reid James, M.D. 10 Bloomsbury sq
Reid John, esq. 6 Crescent pl. Burtn. cresnt
Reid John William, esq. 29 Sloane st
Reid Mrs. 4 Alber ter. Qn.'s rd. St. Jn.'s w
Reid Mrs. 16 Cornwall ter. Regent's pk
Reid Mrs. 47 Weymouth st. Portland pl
Reid Mrs. 21 York terrace, Regent's pk
Reid the Misses, 31 Cavendish square
Reid Wm. Ker, esq. 26 Claremont square
Reierson Mrs. 34 Upper Harley st. & Woodhill, Ripley, Surrey
Reilly Hugh, esq. 3 North row, Park lane
Reily Chas. esq. 21 Loraine pl. Holloway
Reily Mrs. 8 Dean's place, South Lmbth
Remington D. esq. 6 Montague st. Rusl. sq
Remington Geo. esq. 18 Adam st. Adelphi
Remmett Robert, esq. 1 Paper bdgs. Temp
Remmington Mrs. 16 Bolton st
Remnant Mrs. 41 Tavistock square
Remnant Fredk. esq. 2 Pullin's rw. Islgtn
Renaud Charles, esq. 2 George st. Han. sq
Renaud P. T. esq. 15 South ter. Alexand. sq
Rendall Chas. esq. 41 York st. Westmnr
Rendall Simon, esq. 16 Clement's inn
Rendel Jas. M. esq. 8 Gt. George st
Rendlesham, Right Hon. Lord, M.P. 17 Bruton st. Berkeley square
Rendlesham Dowager Lady, 6 Charles st. Berkeley sq. & Bushy grove, Watford
Rendlesham Lady Sophia, 17 Bruton st
Renell Wm. T. esq. 10 Tonbridge pl. Nw. rd
Rennalls Wm. Rodon, esq. 13 Tavistock square, & 1 Elm court, Temple
Rennell Chas. John, esq. 2 Plowden bldgs
Rennick Fras. esq. 36 Northampton sq
Rennie Sir John, knt. 15 Whitehall place
Rennie George, esq. 21 Whitehall place, & Holmwood, Dorking, Surrey

Rennie James, esq. 6 Whitehall
Rennie Matthew Bolton, esq.6Whitehall
Renolds Mrs. 37Cambridge ter.Edgw.rd
Renshaw Thomas Charles,esq.15 Milner sq. Islington, & 5 Stone buildings
Renton Alex. esq. 2 Coleshill st.Eaton sq
Repton Rev.Edwd. Lit.Cloisters,Westmr
Repton Rev.G.H.Lit.Cloisters,Westmst
Repton George Stanley, esq. & Lady Elizabeth, 27 Norfolk st. Park lane
Repton George Wm. John, esq. M.P. 27 Norfolk st. Park lane
Repuke John, esq. 72 John st. Tot. ct. rd
Reseigh Thos.esq. 40 King sq.Goswell rd
Réuss,the Count Henry, 9 Barnard's inn
Revel Count, secretary of Sardinian legation, 26 Mount st. Berkeley sq
Revel Count, secretary of Sardinian legation, 11 Grosvenor st
Reveley Mrs. 17 Queen sq. Bloomsbury
Revell Henry, esq. 28 Burton crescent
Reventlow Count, envoy extraordinary & minister plenipotentiary of his majesty the king of Denmark, 52 Wilton crescent
Rew Mrs. 2 Duncannon st.Charing cross
Rew Mrs. 37 Tavistock square
Rew Wm.Andrew,esq.3Tanfield ct.Tmpl
Reynal G.T.R. esq. Denmark hill, Cmbw
Reynard Francis, esq. 9 Davies st
Reynardson Lt.Col.B.2Mill st. Hanvr.sq
ReynardsonHen.B.esq.5King'sBenchwk
Reynardson Miss, 47 Charles st. Berk.sq
Reynell John Griffiths, esq. 42Chancy.la
Reynett Sir James, 13 Harley st
Reynold T.esq. Albion road,Liverpool rd
Reynolds Captain P.A. 23 Sussex gardns
Reynolds Chas. esq. 19 Carlisle st. Soho
Reynolds F.esq. Warwk.cot. Addisn.rd.so
Reynolds HenryRevell,sen. esq. 5Upper Wimpole st. & 33 Lincoln's inn fields
Reynolds HenryRevell, jun. esq. 51 Upper Harley st. & 10 Whitehall
Reynolds John H. esq. 77 Chancery la
Reynolds Joseph, esq. 21 Chadwell st
Reynolds J.esq.14Hamilton pl. Kng.'s cr
Reynolds Joseph, esq. 131 Piccadilly, & Severn house, Colebrook dale
ReynoldsJsph. esq, 10 York pl. Pentnvl
Reynolds Mrs. 24 Gt. College st. Westmr
Reynolds Mrs. 9 Lodge rd. Regent's prk
Reynolds Mrs. 15 Maida hill, Edgwr. rd
Reynolds Mrs. 10 Maida hill east
Reynolds Mrs. 11 Park pl. Regent's park
Reynolds Sl. esq. 15½ Holland st. Knsgtn
Reynolds Samuel, esq. 28A, Howland st. & 22 Haverstock hill
Reynolds Thomas, esq. 11 Calthorpe st
Reynolds William, esq. 38 Myddelton sq
Rhodes Abraham esq. 26 Granville sq
Rhodes Charles Henry, esq. 63Chancery lane, & Denmark hill, Camberwell
Rhodes Geo. esq. 2Queen's Hd.rw.Islgtn
Rhodes Henry, esq. 26 Margaret st
Rhodes John, esq.5 Beaufoy ter.Edgw.rd
Rhodes John, esq. 7 Clapham road pl
Rhodes Mrs.23Cumberland st.Portmn.sq
RhodesSam.esq.22Sussexpl.Kens.Nw.tn
Rhodes Thomas.esq.9Davies st.Berkeley square, & Muswell hill, Highgate
Riadore Evans, M.D. 73 Harley st
Ribeiro Chevalier Marcal José, (sec. of Portuguese Legation), 57 Upper Seymour st
Ricardo Albert, esq. 38 Lowndes st
Ricardo Francis, esq. 22 Up. Harley st
Ricardo John L. esq. M.P. 31 Lowndes sq
Ricardo Miss, 38 Lowndes st
Ricardo Mortimer, esq. 44 Brook street, & Pudlicot house, Chipping Norton
Ricardo Osman, esq. 71 Eaton place, & Broomsharrow place, Tewkesbury
Ricardo Sampson, esq. 38Lowndes street, & Titness park, Sunning hill
Rice Sir Ralph, knt. 4 Hanover terrace
Rice Hon. Chas. Spring, 37 Brook st
Rice Chas. esq.10 Paragon,New Kent rd
Rice Edward Royd, esq. M.P. United University club, & Dane ct. Sandwich
Rice Henry,esq.39Jermyn st. St.James's
Rice Henry, esq. 24 Notting hill sq
Rice Miss, 14 New Ormond st. Queen sq
Rice Mrs. 10 Blomfield rd. Edgware rd
Rich Sir Geo. 43 Lowndes st. Belgrave sq
Rich Francis, esq. 5 Manchester st
Rich Henry, esq. 47 Mount st
Rich Mrs. 5 Albert st. Pimlico
Rich Mrs. 31 Chapel st. Grosvenor pl
Rich Solomon, esq. 2Lodge rd. Regt.'s pk
Richard Ed. Wm. esq. 18 Gt. Newport st
Richards Rev. Upton, 169 Albany st
Richards Arthur A. esq. 31 King square
Richards Ed. Lewis, esq.4Essexct.Temple
Richards Ed. V. esq. 8Wellington st.Stnd
Richards Hen. esq. 1 Bennett st. St.Jas's
Richards Hen. esq.7 Chandos st. Cav.sq
RichardsH.esq.12Cornwall cr.Cmd.N.tn
Richards Henry, esq. 31 King sq
Richards Hen. B. esq. 53 Albemarle st
Richards H. C. esq.33 Lincoln's inn flds
Richards Jas. esq. Stoke Newington grn
RichardsJohn, esq. 36 Addison rd. north
RichardsJohn,esq.9Chapel st. Bedford rw
Richards John, esq.5Devonshire sq. Bpsg
Richards John, esq. 65 Welbeck st. Cavendish sq.; 3 Craig's court, Charing cross, & 63 Threadneedle st
Richards Jph.esq.28 Newcastle st.Strand
Richards Miss, 16 Colebrooke row
Richards Mrs. 30 Blomfield rd. Maida hl
Richards Mrs.15Grove ter. St.John's wd
Richards Mrs. 1 Park pl. Glo'ster gate
Richards Mrs. 156 Sloane st
Richards Mrs. 6 Stanhope tr. Hd. pk.gdns
Richards Oliver, esq. 16 Warwick st
Richards Owen, esq. 194 Fleet st
Richards Rich. esq. M.P. 21 Park cres.; 1 Tanfield ct.; & Caerynwch, Dolgelly
Richards Rd. esq. 10 Victoria rd. Knsgtn
Richards Rt. Sam. esq. 1 Churchyard ct
Richards Rt. Vaughan, esq. Q.C. 14 Whitehall place
Richards Samuel, esq. 39A, Bedford sq
Richards Stephen, esq. 2 Tavistock sq
Richards Thomas, esq. 46 Drummond st
Richards Thomas, esq.18Up. Ranelagh st
Richards T. esq. 1 Victoria rd.Kens.N.tn
Richards William John, esq. 26 Great College st. Camden town
Richardson Capt. R.N. 30 Cambridge ter
RichardsonCapt.W. 6 Charlotte st. Bd.sq
Richardson Major, 51 York st. Portm. sq
Richardson Alex. esq. 8 Up. Islington ter
RichardsonB. esq. 13 Suffolk st. Pall mall
Richardson Bernard, esq. 12 Judd pl. ea
Richardson Charles, esq. 19 Bruton st. & 28 Golden square
Richardson C. esq. 15 Charles st. St.Jas'
Richardson Chas. esq. 32 Blandford sq
Richardson Chas. Geo. esq. 3 Tanfield ct
RichardsonChas. J. esq. 22 Brompton crs
Richardson Edwd. esq. 39 Stamford st
Richardson Edwd. T. esq. 3 Parliamt. st
Richardson E. W. esq. 18 Gt.Newport st
Richardson Fras. esq. 6 Up. Portland pl
Richardson Geo. G. esq. 10 Thurloe sq
Richardson Henry, esq. 68 Jermyn st
Richardson Henry, esq. 69 Jermyn st
Richardson Henry, esq. 10 Oxford terr
Richardson Hen. esq. 22 York pl.City rd
Richardson Hen. B. esq. F.S.A. 26 Gothic cotts. Park vill. ea. & 9 Gray's inn sq
Richardson H. F. esq. 4 Belgr.tr.Up.Hol
Richardson J. esq. 8 Queen's pl. Kenng.rd
Richardson Jas. esq. 12 John st. Bedfd.rw
Richardson Jas. S. esq. 9 Hans pl.Slne.st
Richardson John, esq. 47 Beaumont st
Richardson John, esq. 21 Fludyer st. & Kirklands, Jedburgh, Roxburghshire
Richardson John, esq. 7 Up. North place, Gray's inn road
Richardson John, esq. 10 Oxford terrace
Richardson Miss, 7 Brompton row
Richardson Miss, 41 Up. Seymour st
Richardson Mrs. 33 Alfred pl. Bedford sq
Richardson Mrs. 17 Melbury pl. Dorset sq
Richardson Mrs. 85 Jermyn st
Richardson Mrs. 17 York bldgs. New st
RichardsonMalcott J. J. esq. 9 Rodneyrd
Richardson Rd. esq. 5 Cumming place
Richardson Rd. esq. 4 Soley ter. Pntnvl
Richardson Robert, M.D. 19 Gordon st
RichardsonSaml. esq. 1 West pl. Islgtn.gn
Richardson Thos. esq. Denmark hill
RichardsonWal.esq. 43 Royal cr.Notg.hl
Richardson Walter, esq. 15 Regent st
Richardson Wm. esq. 47 Bedford row
RichardsonWm. esq. 38A, Edwd.st. Hms.r
RichardsonWm. esq.4 Lyon's inn, Strand
Richardson Wm. esq. 19 Oxford terrace
RichardsonWm. esq. 7 St. Geo.ter. Kens
RichardsonWm.Geo. esq. 5 Pembroke sq
Richardson W. S. esq. 3 Tanfield court
Richbell Mrs. 10 O. Dorset pl. Claphm.rd
Riches Wm. esq. 6 Belmont pl. Wandsworth road
RichfordW.H.esq. 14 Tonbridge pl. Nw.rd
Richman E. C. esq. 2 Farm st. Berkely sq
Richmond, Duke of, K.G., P.C. 51 Portland place; Goodwood, near Chichester; & Gordon castle, near Fochabers; & Glenfiddick lodge, Dufftown, N.B
Richmond Geo. esq. 10 York st. Prtm.sq
Richmond Thomas, esq. 16 Beaumont st
Richmond James, esq. 14 Millbank row
Richmond John, esq. 54 Ebury st
Richmond Mrs. 56 Burton st
RichmondMiss, 6 Onslow ter. Fulham rd
Richmond Rt.esq. 10 King's bench walk, & Gothic cottage, North end, Hampstd
Richmond Robt. esq. Larkhall la. Clphm
RichmondWm. esq. 6 Pelham pl. Fulm.rd
Richter Adolps. esq. 55 Greek st. Soho
Richter Thomas, esq. Cottage, Sloane st
Rickards Edw. H. esq. 8 Cumberland ter. Regent's park, & 29 Lincoln's inn fids
Rickards F. esq. 6 Union st. Clarendn.sq
Rickards Geo. K. esq. 4 Elm ct. Temple
Rickards John, esq.4 Wharncliffe terrace
Rickards Robert, esq. 2 Chiswell st
Rickerby Wm. esq. 73 Sloane st
Ricketts Chas. S. esq. 2 Hyde park ter. & Darton house, Thame, Oxfordshire
Ricketts Edward, esq. 78 Chester sq
Ricketts Fredk. esq. 37 Porchester ter
Rickford Wm. esq. 23 New st. Spring gardens, & Aylesbury, Bucks
Rickman E. esq. Retreat cot. Sth. Lmbh
Rickman Jas. esq. Courlnd.ho.Wndsw.rd
Rickman Miss, 10 Wharton st. Lloyd sq
RickmanWm.C.esq. 21 Park side, Kngtsb
Riddell Sir Walter Buchanan, 13 Old sq
Riddell David, esq. 27A, Francis st
Riddell Fras. H. 19 Old sq. Lincoln's inn
Riddell Hy. Matt. esq. 8 New sq. Lin.inn
Riddell Mrs. 61 Montagu square
Riddell the Misses, 2 Grosvenor place
Riddell Wm. esq. 10 Westbourne st
RiddleJohn, esq. 5Up. Montagu st. Mon.sq
Riddle Thomas, esq. 40 Gibson square
Rider William, esq. 28 Sackville st
Ridge E. esq. 9 Northampton pl. Canonb
Ridge John, esq. 7 Alpha pl. Regent's pk
Ridge Joseph, M.D. 37 Cavendish sq
Ridge Wm. esq. 36 Cross st. Islington
Ridgeway Mrs. 5 Park cot. Park vil.east
Ridgway Alex. F. 19 Grove end road
Ridgway Alex. F. esq. 42 Leicester sq
Ridgway Geo. Spencer, esq. 1 Bolton row
Ridgway Rich. B. H. esq. 4 Trafalgar sq
Riding Roger, M.D. 36 Euston square
RidleyDow.Lady, 5 Seamore pl. Mayfair
Ridley Sir Matthew White, bart. 10 Carlton house terrace, & Heaton hall, Blagdon, Newcastle-upon-Tyne
Ridley Lt. Col. 4 Chester pl. Chester sq
Ridley Anthony, esq. 8 Queen sq. Blmby
Ridley Chas. esq. 14 Bedford st. Bedfd.sq

RidleyGeo. esq. 2 Charles st.Berkeley sq
Ridley Geo. esq. 5 Pump ct. Temple
Ridley Miss, Lawn cottage, Battersea
Ridley Stephen H. esq. 8 Lit.Tufton st
Ridley Wm. esq. 20 Noel st. Islingtn
Ridout George, esq. 11 Wimpole st
RidoutJn. esq. 10 Montague st.Russell sq
RidoutMiss, 63 Hamilton ter. St.Jn.'swd
Ridsdale Francis James, esq.35 Doughty st. & 5 Gray's inn square
Ridsdale Geo. esq. 1 Gower pl.Euston sq
Rigby Edw. M.D. 23 New st. Spring gar
Rigby Joseph D. esq. 15 Cadogan place
Rigby Mrs. 14 Southampton st. Strand
Rigg Bentick, esq. 28 Albion st. Hyde pk
Rigg Chas. M. M.D. 22 York pl.Portm.sq
Rigg John, esq. 51 Tavistock square
Rigge John, esq. 8 St. Mary Abbott's ter
Rigge Jonathan, esq. 30 Brompton row
Rigge Miss, 5 Hunter st. Brunswick sq
Riggs Thos. esq.30 Up.Berkeley st. west
Rigby William, esq. 7 John st. Adelphi
RigleyHy.Adol.esq.5 Crescent pl.Blkfrs
Rigmaiden Lt. R.N. 6 Harley pl. New rd
Riley Benj. esq. 95 Camden road villas
Riley Chas.esq. 21 Loraine pl. Holloway
Riley Mrs. 15 Tavistock pl. Tavistock sq
Riley Thos. esq. 24 Clapham road place
Rimbault Edward, L.L.D., F.S.A., Grosvenor cottage, 17 Park village east
Rimington Mrs. 16 York st. Portman sq
Ring David B. esq. 3 Brick ct. Temple
RingD.B. esq. 32 Glo'ster cres. Regt.'spk
Ring Frederick, esq. 26 Cheapside
Ring George, esq. 3 Gt. Knightrider st
Ring John, esq. 13 Trinity sq. Tower hill
RintoulWm. esq. 33 Southampton st.Strd
Riordan Mrs. 32 Southampton row
Ripley Fredk. Peter, esq. 12 Woburn pl
Ripley Mrs. 30 Clapham rise
Ripley Mrs. 18 Hanover terrace
Ripley Mrs. Philip, 9 York terrace
Ripley Wm. Rd. esq. 7 Whitehall pl
Ripon, Earl of, P.C. 1 Carlton gardens ;& Noctonhl.Sleaford; &Putny.hth.Surry
Ripon, Bishop of, 27 Parliament st. & the Palace, Ripon
Ripon, Dean of, 16 Gt.Dean's yard, Westminster, & theDeanery, Ripon, Yorksh
Rippin Mrs. 64 Charlotte st. Portland pl
Rippon Abrahm. esq. 18 Charterhouse sq
Risdon John, esq. 5 Lansdowne place, & Kingsmore house, Gt. Parndon, Essex
Risdon John, esq. 33 Osnaburgh st
Risley Shuckburgh, esq.14Furnival's inn
Ritchie Capt.Alexr.10 Taunton pl.Rt.pk
Ritchie A. M. esq.3 Churchyd.ct.Temple
Ritchie Jas.esq.3 Arundel ter. Brnsby.rd
Ritchie Miss, 45 York ter. Regent's pk
Ritchie Samuel, esq. 32 Torrington sq
Ritchie T. esq. 3 Took's ct. Chancery la
Ritterbrandt Dr. Louis A. 32 Gerrard st
Rivers Lord, 10 Chester st. & Rushmore lodge, Dorset
Rivers Dowager Lady, 10 Chester st
Rivers Andrew, esq. 14 Clapham rd. pl
Rivers Mrs. 1 York cottages,OldBrmptn
Rivett Samuel, esq. 3 Artillery pl. west
Riviere Dan. V. esq. 8 Cirencester place
Riviere Hy.P.esq.13 North cres. Bdfd. sq
Riviere Wm. esq. 46 Cirencester place
Rivington Charles, esq. 7 Queen square, Bloomsbury, & 1 Fenchurch buildings
Rivolta D. A. esq. 44 Bloomsbury sq
Rix Frederick John, esq. 49 Gt.Coram st
Rixon A.H.esq.4 Mountford cr.Bnsby.pk
Rixon A.W.esq.1 Kingswd.pl.Sth.Lmbth
Roach Jas. esq. 22 Stonefield st. Islngtn
Roake Geo. esq. 5 Robert st. Adelphi
Robarts Abraham, esq. 26 Hill street, & Besborough house, Roehampton
Robarts Henry, esq. 28 Brunswick sq
Robarts Hy. Pratt, esq. 11 Gt. Coram st
Robarts James, esq.& Mrs.57 Welbeck st
Robarts Miss, 12 Eaton pl. Belgrave sq
Robarts Mrs. 5 Manor pl. south,Chelsea
Robb Robert, esq. 95 St. Martin's lane
Robedore Miss, 20 Whitehead's grove
Roberdeau Col. Wm. 72 Sloane st
Roberts Chas. esq. 38 Baker st
Roberts C. esq. Earl's court,Old Bromptn
Roberts Chs.Julius, M.D.,31 Nw.Bridge st
Roberts Dav. esq.7 Fitzroy st. Fitzroy sq
Roberts Edwd. esq. 36 Blomfield road
Roberts Elliott, esq. 40 Park st. Gros. sq
RobertsE.W.esq.Brunswick ho.O.Knt.rd
Roberts H. esq. 13 Suffolk st. Pall mall
Roberts H. T. esq. 2 Bridge court, New Bridge street
Roberts J.esq.10 Up.Robert st. Brompton
Roberts John, esq. 4 Barnsbury park
Roberts John, esq. 18 Brompton square, & 2 Inner Temple lane
Roberts J. H. esq.Norfolk vil.St.Jn.'s wd
Roberts Miss, 10 Queen Charlotte row
Roberts Miss, 75 Upper Berkeley st
Roberts Mrs. 17 Allsop terrace, New rd
Roberts Mrs. 6 Devonshire pl. Edgw. rd
Roberts Mrs. 34 Doughty st
Roberts Mrs. 53 Green st. Grosvenor sq
Roberts Mrs. 10 Northmptn.pl.Canonbry
Roberts Mrs. 8 Nottingham place
Roberts Mrs. 28 Tonbridge pl. New rd
Roberts Mrs. 22 Wharton st
Roberts Mrs. 44 Vincent square, Westr
Roberts Mrs. 11 Winchester row,New rd
Roberts Mrs. Thomas, 57 Montagu sq
Roberts Philip, esq. 28 Carey st
Roberts R. B. esq. 7 New sq. Lncln.'s in
Roberts Rd. John, esq. 17 Linc. inn fields
Roberts Rd. Rbt. esq. 8 Trinity ter.Boro'
Roberts Robert, esq. 33 Bryanstone st
Roberts Rt. esq. 15 Claremont pl. Pntvl
Roberts Sam. E. esq. 13 cross st. Islngtn
Roberts Thomas, esq. 87 Goswell road
Roberts Thomas, esq. 17 Spring gardens
Roberts Thos. esq. 7 Vernon pl. Blmsby
Roberts William, esq. 68 Chancery lane
Roberts Wm. H. esq. Hall stairca. Tmpl
Roberts Wm.P.esq. 2 Robert st. Adelphi
Robertson Hon. Mrs. 23 Osnaburg st
Robertson Maj. Gen. A. 53 Baker st
Robertson Rev. Thomas, 4 Blandford sq
Robertson Alex. esq. 85 Jermyn st
Robertson Alex. esq. 11 Porchester pl
Robertson David, esq. 27 Gt. George st
Robertson Divie, esq.22 Bedford square
Robertson E. esq.11 Paradise rw. Chlsa
Robertson Eben. Wm. esq. 26 Chester sq
Robertson Erasmus R. G. esq. 9 Serle st
RobertsonG.esq.5 Stranraer pl. Maida hl
Robertson George, esq. 4 Bayham cottages, Camden New town
Robertson George, esq. 24 Doughty st
Robertson Hy. esq. 7 Salisbury st.Strand
Robertson Hy.esq. 4 Bath pl. Kensngton
Robertson Hy. esq. 3 Hornton vls. Knsg
Robertson H. esq.1 Prince's pl. Cov.gdn
Robertson Jas. esq. 11 Melcombe place
Robertson Jas.esq.44 Southampton bds. & Parkshot house, Richmond, Surrey
Robertson James, esq. 6 Bentinck street
RobertsonJas. Court, esq. 116 Jermyn st
RobertsonJ.R.esq.26Glo'ster rd.Hyde pk
Robertson J. esq. 26 Glo'ster rd. Hyde pk
Robertson John, esq. 3 Coventry street
Robertson John,esq. 27 Great George st. Westminster
Robertson John esq. 313 Regent street
Robertson John esq. Stuartfield cottage, Acre lane, Brixton
RobertsonJ.E.P. D.C.L.16 Col.Drs.com
Robertson Jsph. C. esq. 11 Serjeants' inn
Robertson the Misses, 4 Bath pl.Kensgn
Robertson Miss, 5 Keppel st. Russell sq
Robertson Miss, 17 Argyll st. Regent st
Robertson Mrs. 6 Bentinck st. Wigm. st
Robertson Mrs. 5 Brompton square
Robertson Patrk. F. esq. 10 Hanover ter
Robertson Rd. esq. 47 Devonshire street
Robertson Richd. H. esq.36Albermarle st
Robertson Wm. esq. 5 Blandford place
Robertson Wm. esq. Woodbine cottage, Albion road, Liverpool road
Robertson Wm. esq. 3 New sq. Linc. in
Robertson Wm. Parish, esq. Peruvian consul, 17 St. Helen's place
Robillard Emanuel, esq. 19 Rathbone pl
Robins Edmund, esq.Piazza, Covent gdn
Robins Edmund,esq. 21 Mornington cres
Robins Geo. esq. 31 Bedford st.Cov. gar
Robins Geo.esq.26Park crsc.Portland pl
Robins Jas. esq. Piazza, Covent garden
Robins J.W.esq.4 Edward st. Hmpstd.rd
Robins Mrs. 7 Addison ter. Kensington
Robins Thomas, esq. 5 Myddelton sq
Robins Thomas Fras. esq. 55 Gibson sq
Robins Wm. esq. 16 Up. Southwick st
RobinsWm.L.T.esq.36Bury st.St.James'
Robinson Lieut.Col. 53 Montagu square
Robinson Ven.Archdeacon, 14 Euston sq
Robinson Rev. John, Park village east
Robinson Rev. John T. 3 St.Andrew's ct
Robinson Alex. esq. 1 Wellington road
Robinson Alfred, esq. 17 Orchard street
Robinson Augustin, esq. 73 Eaton place
Robinson Benj.C.esq. 3 Inner Temple la
Robinson Chas. esq. 6 Dorset pl. Drst.sq
Robinson Chas. esq. 2 Essex ct. Temple
Robinson Chas. Fras. esq. 24 Wimpole st
Robinson C. F.esq.1 Crescent pl. Brtn.cr
RobinsonE esq.2 Kimbolton pl.Bromptn
Robinson Edwd. esq. 13 Clapham rise
Robinson Edw. esq. 5 Upp. Belgrave pl
Robinson Edwd. esq. 11 Up.Belgrave pl
Robinson Francis, esq. 36 Jermyn street
Robinson Francis Barlow, esq. 16 Bedford pl. Russell sq. &26 Essex st.Strnd
Robinson Fred. esq. 11 Crown office row
Robinson George, esq. 9 Heathcote st
Robinson George, esq. 28 Paradise terrace, Liverpool road
Robinson Geo. esq. 10 St.George's place
Robinson Geo. esq. 3 Shaftesbury cres
Robinson Geo. esq. 20 Tonbrdg.pl.Nw.rd
Robinson Geo. esq.23 Up. Brkly. st. west
Robinson Geo. R.esq.27 Chester terrace
Robinson Henry, esq. 64 Baker street
Robinson H. esq.4 Cambrdg.st.Goldn.sq
Robinson Hen.esq.9 Chesham st.Belg.sq
Robinson Hen. esq. Low. Kennington la
Robinson Henry, esq. 69 Pall mall
Robinson Hen.esq.5 St.Agnes vlls.Bysw
Robinson H. C. esq. 2 Caledonian place
Robinson Hen. Crabb, esq.30 Russell sq
Robinson H. G. esq. 5 Essex ct. Temple
Robinson Hy. G. esq. 6 Halfmoon street
Robinson Hen. J.esq. 25 Upper Baker st
Robinson Jas.esq.7 Gower st. Bedford sq
Robinson John, esq. 28 Sackville street
Robinson John Henry, esq. 6 Warwick villas, Maida hill west
Robinson John Thos. esq. 43 Clarges st
Robinson Jonathan, esq. 10 Pine apple pl
Robinson Marmaduke,esq. 3Chandos st. Cavendish sq. & 14 Gt. George st
Robinson Miss, 72 St. John's wood terr
Robinson Mrs. Major, 14 Cumberland st
Robinson Mrs. 1 Brompton row
Robinson Mrs. 1 Carlton vil. Edgware rd
Robinson Mrs. 170 Edgware road
Robinson Mrs. 2 Hyde park place
Robinson Mrs. 34 King sq. Goswell rd
Robinson Mrs. 7 NewDorset pl.Clphm. rd
Robinson Mrs.15NewManor pl.King's rd
Robinson Mrs. 27 Pall mall
Robinson Mrs.170 Prospect pl. Edgw. rd
Robinson Mrs. 7 Park pl.Kennington crs
Robinson Mrs. 32Weymouth st.Prtld. pl
Robinson Miss, 3 York pl. Portman sq
Robinson Richard, esq. 25 Blomfield rd
Robinson Samuel, esq. 12 Gt.Marlbro' st
Robinson Thomas, esq. 35 Cross st.Islgtn
Robinson Thomas, esq. 55 Sloane st
Robinson Thomas F. esq. 6 Doughty st
Robinson William, esq. 46 Connaught sq
Robinson Wm. esq. 1 Hemus ter.Chelsea
RobinsonWm.esq.3Up.Yorkpl.St.Jns.wd

RobinsonWm. D.C.L.7Coll.Doctors' com
Robinson Wm. Fred. esq. 53 Coleshill st
Robinson Wm. R. esq. 7A, Portman sq. & Coombe end, Gloucestershire
RobinsonW.T. 5 Moccas cotts.Cmd.N.tn
Robinson Wm.T. esq. 5 Camden ter.west
RobbleyHen.esq.5Clarendon pl.Edgw.rd
Robson Chas. esq. 9 Loraine pl. Holloway
Robson Chas. esq.51Liverpool st.Kgs.crs
Robson Christopher, esq. 7 Cambridge ter. Hyde park, & 13 Clifford's inn
RobsonGeo.esq.46Cambridgest.Edgw.rd
RobsonGeorgeYoung, esq.46 Cambridge st. Hyde park, & 49 Chancery lane
Robson Hy. esq. 26 Castlest.Leicester sq
Robson Jacob, esq. 4 Mornington cres
Robson John,esq.71Castle st. ea.Oxfd. st
Robson John, esq.7Clarence ter.Regent's park, & 26 Castle st. Leicester sq
Robson J. esq. 3 Hamilton pl. King's cr
Robson Miss, 7 Albion place, Hyde park
Robson Mrs. 7 Cambridge ter. Hyde pk
RobsonRd.esq.17Margaret st.Cvndsh.sq
Robson Wm. Froggatt, esq. 25 Brompton sq. & 10 Lancaster place, Strand
Rochard Francis T. esq. 40 Foley place
Rochard Simon J. esq. 281 Regent st
Rochas Henry, esq. 52 Gower st
Roche Sir David, bart. Reform club, 104 Pall mall, & Carass house, near Croom, Ireland
Roche Antonin,esq. 20Brook st.Grosv.sq
Roche Edmund Burke, esq. M.P. Reform club, &Trabolgan, near Cloyne, Ireland
Roche Garrard, esq. 2 Up.Wellington st
Roche James, esq. 103 Guilford st
Rochester, Bishop of, 55 Eaton place, & Bromley palace, Kent
Rochford Mrs. 61 Wimpole st
RockGeorge,esq.7Cloudesley ter.Islngtn
Rock Mrs. 13 Princes road, Notting hill
Rodd Lady Tremayne, 40 Wimpole st
Roden, Earl of, K.P.,P.C. United Service club ; Hyde hall, Sawbridgeworth ; & Tallymore park, Castlewellan, Ireland
Roden Thos. esq.11Clement's inn, Strand
Rodgers A.R.esq.121Stanhp.st.Hmps.rd
RodgersThomas, esq. 9 Devonshire sq. & 37 King st. Cheapside
Rodney Lord, 67 Harley st. & Barrington, Leominster, Herts
Rodney Hon. Mortimer, 7 Kensingt gore
Rodney Hon. Thos. Harley, 67 Harley st
Rodwell Edgar K.esq.1New court,Tmple
Rodwell Geo. H. esq. 1 Thurloe pl. west
Rodwell Henry, esq. 3 Notting hill sq
Rodwell Hunter, esq. 11 York st. Portman sq. & 1 New court, Temple
Rodwell Lionel, esq. 66 Gt. Portland st
Rodwell the Misses,15 Tavstk.st.Bdfd.sq
Rodwell Miss, 39 Clarges st
Rodwell Richard, esq. 23 Brompton sq
Rodwell W. esq. 6 St.Agnes vil.Bayswtr
Roe Sir Fred. Adair, bart. 96 Piccadilly
Roe Edward, esq. 1 Albion pl.Canonb.sq
Roe Francis, esq. 6 Notting hill ter
Roe Geo. Hamilton, M.D. 6 Hanover sq
Roe John, esq. 18 Gower pl. Euston sq
Roe John, esq. 5 Grafton st. Fitzroy sq
Roe Miss, 46 Smith st. Chelsea
Roe Peter, M.D. 1 Porteus ter. Paddgtn
Roe Thos. esq. Temple chmbrs. Fleet st
Roe Thos. esq. 37 Doughty st
Roe Wm.H.esq.21Princes st. Cavndsh.sq
Roebuck Geo. S. esq. 62 Cambridge ter
Roebuck John Arthur, esq. M.P. 12Victoria sq. Pimlico, & 3 Essex ct. Temple
Roebuck Mrs.62Cambridge ter.Edgw.rd
Roempke Jn. esq. 2 Dorset ter.Clapm. rd
Roffey Thos. esq. 20 Walcot pl.ea.Lmbth
Rogers Sir John L. bart. 18New Bond st
Rogers Arnold, esq. 296 Regent st
Rogers Chas. esq. 9 Lyon ter. Edgw. rd
Rogers Chas. esq. 22 Manchester buildings, & 12 Cannon row
Rogers Chas. esq. 2 Cork st. Bond st
Rogers Colin, M.D. 29 Dorset square
Rogers Edmund, esq. 35 Brompton row
Rogers Francis Norman Jas. esq. Q C. 6 Up.Hyde park st.& 4 Inner Temple la
Rogers Fred. esq. 76 Connaught ter
Rogers Fred. esq. 12Paper bldgs. Temple
Rogers Fred. Wm. esq. 5 Sackville st
Rogers Geo. esq. 23 Up.Seymour st.west
Rogers James, esq. 22 Manchester buildings, & 6 Dean's yard
Rogers John, esq. 18 Finsbury square
Rogers John, esq. 1 Halfmoon st. Picdy
Rogers John, esq. 40 Jermyn st
Rogers John J.esq. 11 King's bench walk
Rogers Joseph, esq. 79 Wardour st. Soho
Rogers Miss, 5 Hanover ter. Regent's pk
Rogers Misses, 85 Cadogan place
Rogers Mrs. 31 Aberdeen pl. Maida hill
Rogers Mrs. 35 Sloane st
Rogers Mrs. 25 Petersburgh pl. Baysw
Rogers Rt.esq. 3Moccas cot.Cmdn.nw.tn
Rogers Rt. A. esq.6Park pl.vils.Paddgtn
Rogers Samuel, esq. 22 St. James's pl
Rogers Simon, esq. 7 Greville pl. Kilbn
Rogers Thos.esq. 11 Blandford st.Man.sq
Rogers Wm. esq. 40 Bedford square, & 2 Stone buildings, Lincoln's inn
Rogers Wm. esq. 21 Camden road villas
Rogers Wm.esq. 7 Portland pl. Wnds. rd
Rogerson John, esq. 50 Lincoln's inn flds
RogersonJsp.esq.15Camdn.cot.Cam.n.tn
Roget Peter Mark, M.D. 18 Up. Bedfd.pl
Rohde Samuel, esq. 13Radnor pl. Hyde p
Rokeby Lord, Montagu ho. Up. Berkeley st
Rolfe Sir Robert Monsey, knt. 8 New st. Spring gardens, & Rolls garden
Rolfe Rev. John, 22 Finsbury circus
Rolfe Chas. Wells, esq. 12 South square, Gray's inn, & 2 Linden grove, Kensington gravel pits
RolfesWm. G.esq.Ship la.Walcot pl.east
Rolle Lady, 18 Upper Grosvenor st. & Bicton house, near Sidmouth
Rolleston Col. L. 3 St. James's place
Rolleston Col. Lancelot, M.P. 8 Hertford st. Mayfair, & Watnall hall, near Nottingham
Rollo Lord, Carlton club, & Duncrub, Dunning, Perthshire
Rollo Mrs. 64 George st. Euston sq
RollsJ.G.esq.Cook's gds.King's rd.Chels
Rolls Mrs. 45 Gloucester pl. Portman sq
Rolt Col. 5 Great Cumberland place
Rolt John, esq. 50 Chancery lane, & 6 Stone buildings, Lincoln's inn
Rolt Peter, esq. 23 Hyde park gardens
Romaine Wm. Govet,esq.4Harcourt bdg
Romer Frank, esq. 11 Harrington st
Romer John, esq. 10Cambdg.ter.Reg.pk
Romilly Capt. Fred. 29 Wilton crescent
Romilly Chas. esq. & Lady Georgiana, 29 Wilton crescent
Romilly Edw. esq. 14 Stratton st.Piccadilly, & Porthkerry, near Cardiff
Romilly John, esq. Q.C. 32 Gordon sq. & 6 New sq. Lincoln's inn
Romney Earl, 45 Wilton crescent, & the Mote, near Maidstone, Kent
Ronald Mrs. 14 Belgrave st. King's cross
Ronald Rowand, esq. 5 Manchester sq
Ronalds Chas. esq. 1 Verulam buildings
Ronalds Edmd.esq.Grove,Canonbury sq
Rood J. W. esq. 17 Albion tr. Wndswh.rd
RoodsHen.C.esq.67Gt.Russellst.Blmsby
Roof Miss, 69 Torrington square
Rook Mrs. 36 Connaught square
Rooke George, esq. 144 Oxford st
Rooke Michl. esq.5 Hanover cot.Rgt.pk
Rooke Peter Hy. esq. 9 Serle st
Rooke Thos. Jas. esq. 3 Raymond bldgs. & 5 Colebrooke row, Islington
Rooke Wm. esq. 74 Newman st
Room Hen. esq. 23 Charles st. Berners st
Room Henry, esq.2 York cot.Old Brmptn
Roome Maj.Gen.19Cadogan pl.Sloane st
Roope Cabel, esq. 36 Woburn square
Rooper George,esq.68Lincoln's inn fields
Rooper George, esq. 23 Sussex place, Regent's park,& 68 Lincoln's inn fields
Roose Francis, esq. 33 Up. Montagu st
Roots Augustus, esq.1 Tanfield ct.Templ
Roots Chas.O.esq.48Skinner pl.Hollwy.rd
Roots George, esq. 1 Tanfield ct. Temple
Roots Hen.Shuckburgh,M.D.2Russell sq
Roots Miss, 30 Southampton row
Roper David, esq. 3 Gt. Coram st
Roper Francis, esq.5 Mitre ct.chambers, Mitre ct. Fleet st
Roper George, esq. 3 Queen sq.Bloomsby
Roper Giles S. esq. 5 Ossulston st
Roper Joshua, esq.1 Staple inn, Holborn
Roper Thos. Hen. esq. 26 Chancery lane
Roper Wm. esq. 32 Sackville st
Roper Wm. J. esq. 14 Osnaburgh st
Roques Alex. esq. 56 High Holborn
RoräuerJas.esq.21Glo'ster cres. Rgt.'spk
Roscoe Rd. esq. 16 Millman st. Bedfd.rw
Roscoe Robert, esq. 14 Torrington sq
Rose Rt.Hon. Sir Geo.Hen.7 Old Palace yd. & Sandhills, near Christchurch
Rose Hon. Sir Geo. knt. & Lady, 4 Hyde park gardens, & Masters' office, 25 Southampton buildings
Rose Danl.G.esq.8 Church st.Paddingtn
Rose Ethelbert B.esq.62 Burton crescent
Rose George, esq. 43 Lincoln's inn fields
Rose Geo.Fred.esq.28North bk.Rgt.'spk
Rose GeorgeJames,esq.6New inn,Strand
Rose Hector, esq. 18 Hamilton terrace
Rose James, esq. 12 Argyll st. Regent st
Rose James, esq. 5 Belinda tr. Canonby
Rose James, esq. 48 Gower pl. Euston sq
Rose James, esq. 65 Trinity sq. Boro'
Rose John, esq. Filacers' office, Queen's Bench office, Temple
Rose John, esq. 28 North bank, Regt. pk
Rose John B. C. esq. 43 Parliament st
Rose John M.esq. 6 Park rd. Notting hill
Rose Joseph Franklin, esq. 16½ Blackfriars road, & 60 Stamford st
Rose Philip, esq. 22 Hans place
Rose Samuel, esq. 31 Westbourne place
Rose Thomas Wm. esq. 34 Myddelton sq
Rose Wm.esq.Ho.of Lords,&11 Mount st
Rose Wm. esq. 10 Torrington square, & 1 Hare court, Temple
Rose Wm. Rose, esq. 35 Eaton place, & Wolston heath, nr. Coventry, Warksh
Rosebery, Earl of, K.T., P.C. 139 Piccadilly; Dalmeney park, Linlithgow ; & Warren wood, Hatfield, Herts
Rosher Edward, esq. 20 Mornington rd
Rosher Henry, esq. 20 Hunter st
Roskell Joseph Kaye, esq. 3 Cork st
Roskell Robt. esq. 6 Terrace, Kensingtn
Roskilly R.esq.8 Portland pl.Nw.Knt.rd
Rosling A. esq. 2 Newington pl. Kenn.rd
Ross Maj. Gen. Sir P. 34 Connaught sq
Ross Sir Wm. C. knt. R.A. 38 Fitzroy sq
Ross Alexander, esq. 47 Finsbury circus
Ross Chs.esq.& Lady Mary,60 Prtlnd.pl
Ross Chas. esq.5 Campden hl.ter. Knsgtn
Ross Daniel, esq. 29 Addison rd. north
Ross David Robt. esq. M.P. 15 Gt. Ryder st. ; Reform club ; & Rosstrevor, Irelnd
Ross George, esq. 4 Trafalgar square
Ross Hen.esq.15WineOff.ct.&36Careyst
Ross Hugh, esq. 13 Chancery lane
Ross Hugh, esq. 24 Russell pl. Fitz. sq
Ross John, esq.3 Furnival's inn, Holborn
Ross JohnW.esq.Yorkchmbs.St.Jas.'s st
Ross Mrs. General, 60 Portland place
Ross Mrs. 37 Albany st. Regent's park
Ross Mrs. 2 St. John's wood grove
Ross William, esq. 4 Howard st. Strand
Ross Wm.A.esq. York chmbs.St.Jas.'s st
Rosse, Earl of, Birr castle, Parsonstown, Ireland
RossellotyBthw.esq.3Warwickst.Chng.c
Rosser Richard, esq.36Southampton row, &Mount St.John, Wilden, Bedfordshire

Rosser Arch. Rd.F.esq.63 Lincoln's inn fi
Rosser William Henry, esq. 2 Dyer's blds
RossettiGabl.esq. 50 Charlt.st.Portlnd.pl
Rossiter James Marmaduke, esq. 4 Kennington terrace, Upper Kennington la
Rosslyn, Earl of, P.C. 6 Grosvenor place, & Dysart house, Fife
Rossmore Lord, Brookes's club, St. James' st.; Dell, Windsor; & Rossmore park, county of Monaghan
Rosson John, esq. 6 St. Martin st
Rostin Mrs. 15 Glo'ster rd. Old Bromptn
Rotch Benjamin, esq. 1 Furnival's inn, & Lowlands, Harrow-on-the-hill
Rotch Mrs. 8 Sidmouth st. Gray's inn rd
Rothburn Geo. Valentine, esq. Mornington cottage, Mornington road
Rothery Rev. Joseph, 71 Aldermanbury
Rothery William, esq. 10 Stratford place
Rothery William, jun. esq. 18 James st
Rothman Rd. Wellesley, esq. A6, Albany
Rothpletz T. esq. 18 Henry st. Pentonvil
Rothschild Baron Lionel, Austrian consul general, 148 Piccadilly, & 3 New court, St. Swithin's lane
Rothschild Baroness, 107 Piccadilly, & Gunnersbury park, Acton
Rothschild Baron de A. 38 Grosvenor pl
Rothschild Mayer, esq. 107 Piccadilly
Rothwell Rt. R. esq. 6 Alfred pl. Bdfd.sq
Rothwell Rd. esq. 31 Devonshire st
Rottier Jules, esq. 33 South bk. Rgt.'s pk
Rouge John, esq. 54 Rathbone place
Rougemont Alex. esq. 23 Kensington sq
Rougemont George, esq. 9 Chester ter
Rough Mrs. 7 Smith square, Westminstr
Rough Wm. H. esq. 1 Paper bldgs. Tem
Roughmont Mrs. Wright's lane, Kensgtn
Rought George, esq. 3 Cloudesley ter
Roulente Mrs. 59 Brompton square
Roumieu John, esq. 8 Regent's sq. Gray's inn road, & 9 New square, Lincoln's inn
Roumieu R. L. esq. 10 Lancaster pl. Strd
Round Charles Grey, esq. M.P. 25 Upper Brook st. & Birch hall, near Colchester
Round Edmund, esq. 4 Harcourt bldgs
Round Fredk. Peel, esq. 15 St. James's sq
Round John, esq. M.P. 15 St. James's square, & Danbury park, near Chelmsfd
Round Oliver Stphn. esq. 36 Lincoln's innfi
Round Winfield S. esq. 36 Lincoln's inn fi
Roupell Charles Morris, esq. 15 Welbeck st. & 13 Old sq. Lincoln's inn
Roupell George Leith, M.D. 15 Welbeck st
Roupell John Stuart, esq. 5 New sq. Linc.in
Roupell Mrs. G. B. 15 Welbeck st. & Chartham park, East Grinstead, Sussex
Roupell Rt. P. esq. Q.C. 103 Piccadilly, & 5 New square, Lincoln's inn
Rourke George, esq. 7 Grafton st. east
Rous Hon. Henry John, Captain, R.N., M.P. 23 Grafton st. Bond st
Rous Mrs. George, 28 Charles st. Berkeley square, & 42 Brunswick ter. Brighton
Rous Thomas Bates, esq. 28 Charles st. Berkeley square, & Courtyralla, Cardiff
Rouse Miss, 42 Woburn place
Rouse Mrs. 13 Soley terrace, Pentonvil
Rouse Mrs. 18 York place, Portman sq
Rouse Mrs. 30 York terrace, Regent's pk
Rouse Rt. esq. 4 Devonshire pl. Wndsw.rd
Rouse Wm. esq. 16 Canterbury vill. Edg.rd
Rousham William Henry, esq. 53 George st. Euston square
Routh Sir Randolph, bart. 19 Dorset sq
Routh Martin J. esq. 53 Lincoln's inn flds
Routh Miss, 19 Dorset square
Routh Robert A. esq. 53 Lincoln's inn fi
Rouw Mrs. 12 Devonshire pl. Edgware rd
Rouw Peter, esq. 80 Norton st. Fitzroy sq
Rovedino Thomas, esq. 16 Osnaburgh st
Row Geo. esq. 32 Alfred st. Bedford sq
Row Mrs. 16 Kensington crescent
Rowan Col. Charles, 17 Bolton street, & 4 Whitehall place
Rowcliffe G. esq. Meadow pl. Sth. Lambth
Rowdon Hen. M. esq. 24 Bayham ter
Rowe Chas. Geo. esq. 8 Up. ter. Islingtn
Rowe Geo. Robt. M.D. 2 Golden sq
Rowe J. esq. 16 Manchstr. ter. Lvrpool.rd
Rowe Mathias, esq. 24 Woburn place, & Gloucester rd. Regent's park
Rowe Mrs. 2 Canonbury cotgs. Islington
Rowe Mrs. 47 Pembroke sq. Kensington
Rowe Rd. esq. 17 Beaufoy ter. Edgw. rd
Rowe Rbt. esq. 36 John st. Bedford row
Rowe Wm. esq. 38 Milk st. Cheapside
Rowe W. Carpenter, esq. 2 Pump ct. Tmpl
Rowed Henry, esq. 4 Up. Belgrave place
Rowell E. esq. 1 Loraine pl. Holloway
Rowland A. esq. 29 George st. Euston sq
Rowland Alex. Wm. esq. 39 Guilford st
Rowland Charles, esq. 10 Eccleston sq
Rowland Daniel, esq. 28 Grosvenor pl
Rowland James, esq. 30 Albion st. Hyde pk
Rowland Rd. M.D. 9 Woburn pl. Russell sq
Rowlands David, esq. 57 Wimpole st
Rowlands Ed. esq. 17 Prospect pl. Wnds.rd
Rowlatt Rev. Jn. Hen. 16 Gower st
Rowlatt Rev. Wm. Hen. 16 Gower st
Rowlatt Saml. esq. 43 Lamb's Conduit st
Rowley Mrs. 3 Ordnance ter. St. John's wd
Rowley Robt. M.D. 37 King Wm. st. City
Rowley Thos. esq. 25 Carlton vils. Edg.rd
Rowney G. esq. 5 Cornwall crs. Cmdn.nw.tn
Rowsell Evan E. esq. 14 Kennington row
Rowsell S. W. esq. Lavender hl. Wndsth.rd
Roxberry Mrs. 28 Blomfield rd. Maida hl
Roxburgh Wm. M.D. 38 Gloucester pl
Roxburgh, Duke of, K.T. Thomas's hotel, 25 Berkeley sq. & Fleurs castle, Kelso
Roxburgh Harriet, Dowager Duchess of, Thomas's hotel, 25 Berkeley sq. & Broxmouth park, Dunbar
Roxburgh Fras. esq. 89 Chancery lane
Roxby Rev. Henry R. 20 Connaught sq
Roy Mrs. & Miss, 16 Bentinck street
Roy Richard, esq. 37 Gt. George street, Westmr. & Grove fields, Cheltenham
Royal Naval Club House (David Foggo, secretary), 160 New Bond st
Royds John, esq. 3 Kensington gdn. ter
Royle J. Forbes, M.D., F.R.S. 4 Bulstrode st
Rozea Mrs. 95 Milton st. Dorset sq
Rubbi Signor, 25 Gt. Pulteney st
Ruck John, jun. esq. 9 Crescent, Minories
Ruck Wm. D. esq. 9 Vauxhl. pl. Sth. Lmbth
Rucker John Anthony, esq. 31 Hunter st
Rudall G. esq. 52 Charlotte st. Prtld. pl
Rudall John, esq. 13 Highbury terrace, & 4 Stone bdgs. Lincoln's inn
Rudall William, esq. 50 Chancery lane
Rudd Eric, esq. 29 Lincoln's inn fields
Rudd Jas. esq. 49 Southampton row
Rudd John, esq. 12 Qn. Char. row, New rd
Rudd Miss, 2 Windsor ter. Maida hill
Ruddick John, esq. 39 Up. Baker st
Ruddiman Capt. Thomas, 298 Regent st
Rudge Edward, esq. 44 Wimpole st. & Abbey Manor house, Evesham
Rudge Edwd. John, esq. 52 Up. Harley st
Ruding Clement, esq. 10 Judd pl. east
Ruding Rogers, esq. 24 Nottingham pl
Rudlin Wm. esq. 14 Paradise row, Chls
Rudsdell Mrs. 29 Curzon st. Mayfair
Ruff William, esq. 33 Doughty st
Ruffell Mrs. 20 Wellington rd. St. Jn.'swd
Rugg Hen. H. esq. 15 Broadly tr. Blndf.sq
Ruggles Miss, 9 Sussex ter. Hyde park
Ruggles Mrs. 4 Colebrooke ter. Islington
Rule Chas. esq. 21 Up. Bedford pl. Russell sq. & 2 New sq. Lincoln's inn
Rule Miss, 21 Sloane ter. Sloane st
Rule Wm. Noble, esq. 21 Up. Bedford pl
Rumball Sampson A. esq. 27 Pembroke sq
Rumbelow W. esq. 8 Devonsh. st. Queen sq
Rumbold Chas. Edmd. M.P. 13 Bury st. St. James's, & Preston Candover, Basingstoke
Rumsey Lacy, esq. 14 Sloane st
Rumsey Robt. C. esq. 2 Arthur st. Gry.'sin.r
Runciman C. esq. 18 Oxford ter. Hyde pk
Rush John, esq. 16 Alfred st. Bedford sq
Rush John, esq. 74 Ebury st. Pimlico
Rush John Rogers, esq. 11 Tavistock sq
Rush Miss, 12 St. Ann's villas, Acacia rd
Rush Thos. esq. 7 Manor pl. south, Chelsea
Rush Wm. esq. 6 Up. Robert st. Brompton
Rushbitter Joseph, esq. 6 Addison ter
Rushbury Hy. D. esq. 3 Mitre ct. Ely pl
Rushforth Rd. esq. 40 Howlnd. st. Fitzry.sq
Rushforth R. W. esq. 12 Westbourne st
Rushout-Bowles George, esq. Hyde park barracks
Rushworth Chas. H. esq. 10 Staple inn
Rushworth Chs. Poulett, esq. 4 Qn. Anne st
Rushworth Edmd. esq. 29 Carlton villas
Rushworth Geo. A. esq. 10 Staple inn
Ruskin John, esq. Denmark hill, Cambwl
Russell Lord Edward, M.P. 8 Park lane
Russell Lord William, 35 Grosvenor pl
Russell Right Hon. Lord John, M.P. 32 Chesham pl. & Unstead wood, Godalmin
Russell Sir Robert Frankland, bart. 15 Cavendish sq. & Chequers court, Wendover, & Thirkleby park, Thirsk
Russell Rev. John, D.D. 3 Devonshire sq
Russell Rev. Whitworth, 26 Cumberld.st
Russell Alex. esq. 3 Holywell st. Millbank
Russell Chas. M.P. 27 Charles st. St. Jas.'s, & Swallowfield, Reading, Berks
Russell Edwd. esq. 6 Durham pl. Chelsea
Russell Frs. esq. 2 Figtree ct. Temple
Russell Fras. Wm. esq. 19 Westbourne st
Russell Geo. Lake, esq. & Lady Caroline, 4 Mansfield st. & 21 Old sq. Linc. inn
Russell Hen. esq. 14 Park pl. vil. Paddgtn
Russell H. esq. 24 Wilton st. Grosvnr. pl
Russell Henry Ed. esq. 12 Dartmouth st
Russell Henshaw S. esq. 43 Manchester st. & 1 & 3 Mitre court chambers, Temple
Russell James, esq. 57 Gloucester place
Russell Jas. esq. 24 Goulden ter. Islington
Russell James, esq. 20 Grove end road
Russell Jas. esq. 99 Milton st. Dorset sq
Russell Jas. esq. Q.C. 40 Rusl. sq. & 6 Old sq
Russell James Thomas, esq. 37 Percy st
Russell Jse. Dav. W. esq. M.P. 9 Chesham pl
Russell Jesse W. esq. 169 New Bond st
Russell John, esq. 11 Claremont square
Russell John, esq. 3 Fredk. st. Gray's in.rd
Russell John, esq. 12 South Lambeth
Russell Jn. A. esq. 1 Child's pl. Temple bar
Russell John Henry Cromwell, esq. 25 Wharton st. & 8 Gray's inn square
Russell Mrs. 10 Chesterfield st. Mayfair
Russell Mrs. 28 Curzon st. Mayfair
Russell Mrs. 10 Dorset pl. no. Clapm. rd
Russell Mrs. 18 Lowndes st. Belgrv. sq
Russell Mrs. 21 Nottingham pl. New rd
Russell Robert W. esq. 1 New ct. Temple
Russell Thomas, esq. 1 Printinghouse sq
Russell Wm. esq. 50 Belgrave square, & Accountant-General's office, Chancy.la
Russell Wm. esq. 180 Prospect pl. Edgw.rd
Russell W. H. esq. 1 New court, Temple
Rust Miss, 4 Montagu st. Portman sq
Ruston David, esq. 1 Somers pl. wst. Nw.rd
Rutherford Geo. S. M.D. 23 Devonsh. st
Rutherford James, esq. 9 Nottingham pl
Rutherford Jn. esq. 6 Hanover st. Hanv.sq
Rutherfurd Right Hon. Andrew, M.P. Groves hotel, 49 Albemarle st. & St. Colme st. Edinburgh
Rutland Duke of, K.G. 85 Pall mall; & Belvoir castle; & Palace, Newmarket; & Longshaw lodge; & Stantonwood house, Bakewell, Derbyshire
Rutland James, esq. 49 Mortimer st
Rutley Thos. esq. 84 St. Martin's lane
Rutlidge Thos. esq. 3 Mountfort tr. Islgtn
Rutt Thos. Prentice, esq. 16 Canonbury sq
Rutter G. esq. 4 Wellington st. Islington
Rutter John, esq. 26 Friedenstein terrace
Rutter John Champley, esq. 4 Ely pl
Rutter Miss, 5 Allsop ter. New road
Rutter Valentine, esq. 9 Park ter. Higby
Rutter W. esq. 1 Albert st. Mornington cr

Rutty John, esq. 3 Maida hill, Edgw. rd
Rutty Wm. esq. 32 Cloudesley sq. Islgtn
Ryall Hy. Thos. esq. 1 Robert st. Adelphi
Ryan Rt. Hon. Sir Edward, 5 Addison rd
Ryan James, M.D. 28 Somerset st. Ptmn. sq
Ryan John, esq. 23 Up. North pl. Gray's i. rd
Ryan Jsph. esq. 3 Gordon pl. Tavistock sq
Ryan Madame, 20 Edwards st. Prtmn. sq
Ryan Mrs. 33 Fitzroy square
Ryan Wm. esq. 15 Shaftesbury terrace
Ryde Wm. esq. 23 Bedford pl. Russell sq
Ryder Hon. G. D. M.P. 39 Grosvenor sq. & Westbrook, Hemel Hempstead
Ryder John B. esq. 159 Sloane st
Ryder Mrs. 14 Chancery lane
Ryder Thos. esq. Devereux chmbrs. Strnd
Rydon Hen. esq. 1 North bdgs. Finsbury
Rye Edw. esq. 14 King's parade, Chelsea, & 16 Golden square
Ryland Archer, esq. 36 Carey st
Ryler Edwd. Chas. esq. 3 Inner Temple la
Ryley Robt. Ralph, esq. 3 Inr. Temple la
Rymell Mrs. 44 Bernard st. Russell sq
Rymer Alf. esq. 7 Glo'ster ter. O. Brmptn
Rymer James Malcm. esq. 18 Woburn pl
Rymer John Snaith, esq. 7 Whitehall pl
Rymer Wm. Hy. esq. 59 Chancery lane
SABIN Rev. John Edwd. 101 Sloane st
Sabin Edward L. esq. 4 South sq. Gray's inn
Sabin Mrs. 12 Circus rd. St. John's wood
Sacre Mrs. 24 Park road, Regent's park
Sadd Mrs. 2 Vauxhall pl. Sth. Lambeth
Sadgrove Alfred, esq. 3 Broad st. bldgs
Sadler Rev. Jas. Hayes, 1 Portman sq. & Keynshambury, Cheltenham
Sadler Edward, esq. 3 Lincoln's inn fields
Sadler Jsph. esq. 6 Gordon pl. Tavistock sq
Sadler Miss, 2 Compton st. ea. Brnswick. sq
Sadler Nathl. esq. Queen's mews, Pimlico
Sadler Robert R. esq. 28 Golden sq
Sadler Seymour, esq. 8 Regent st
Saeed Alli Ben Nassur, special envoy from the Imaun of Muscat, 95 Great Portland st
Saenz José Maria, vice consul for Mexico, 3 Winchester buildings
Saenz José M. esq. 4 Canterbury villas
Safford Mrs. 2 Sussex pl. Canonbury sq
Sage Geo. esq. 3 Cloudesley st. Islington
Sagrini Luigi, 46 Up. Norton st. Fitzroy sq
St. Alban's, Duke of, 80 Piccadilly; & Holly lodge, Highgate; & Redburn hall, Brigg
St. Amand Mrs. 1 Up. Porchester st. Edg. rd
St. André Durant, esq. French consul general, 44 Montagu square, & 3 Copthall buildings
St. Asaph, Bishop of, 44 Portland place, & Palace, St. Asaph
St. Aubyn James P. esq. 5 Furnival's inn
St. Aulaire Count de, French ambassador, Hertford ho. 20 Manchester sq
St. Bauzel Henry, esq. 56 High Holborn
St. Clair P. esq. 5 William st. Hmpstd. rd
St. David's, Bishop of, 27 Parliament st. & Aberguilli palace, Carmarthen
St. George Lady, 6 York st. Portman sq
St. George Mrs. 4 Notting hill square
St. George's Chess Club House (George Walker, secretary), 5 Cavendish sq
St. Germans, Countess of, 22 Park crescent, Portland place
St. Germans, Earl of, P.C. 36 Dover st. & Port Eliot, St. Germans
St. James's Club House (William Simmonds, sec.), 50 St. James's st
St. John Lord, Melchbourn, Kimbolton
St. John Jas. A. esq. 9 Northbank, Regt.'s pk
St. Leger Captain John, 22 Baker st
St. Leger Anthony B. esq. 10 Berkeley sq
St. Martin de la Tour Countess, 9 Upper Gloucester place, Dorset square
St. Maur Lord Archibald, 14 Arlington st
St. Quintin William, esq. 27 Bruton st.; Scampstone hall, near Malton; & Lowthorpe lodge, Driffield
St. Vincent Viscount, 60 St. James's st. & Meaford, near Stone
St. Vincent W. esq. 73 Westbourne ter
Saker Sl. esq. 20 Prospect pl. Wndswth. rd
Salaman Charles, esq. 36 Baker st
Salaman Miss, 36 Baker st. Portman sq
Salaman Reuben, esq. 3 Up. Hyde park st
Salaman Simeon K. esq. 36 Baker st
Sale Miss, 12 William st. Knightsbridge
Salisbury Marquis, K.G. P.C. 20 Arlngtn. st.; Childwell hall, Liverpool; & Hatfield house, Herts
Salisbury, Bishop of, 40 Chesham place, & the Palace, Salisbury
Salisbury, Dean of, 7 Saville row
Salisbury Mrs. 51 Westbourne terrace
Salkeld Joseph, esq. 14 Up. Woburn pl
Salmon Genl. 27 Park st. Grosvenor sq
Salmon Chas. esq. 8 Eccleston st. south
Salmon Edwd. esq. 4 King's bench walk
Salmon Henry, esq. 284 Regent st
Salmon Mrs. 13 Chesham pl. Belgrave sq
Salmon Mrs. 42 Ebury st. Pimlico
Salmon Mrs. 16 Kensington gore
Salmon Thomas Deere, esq. 123 Chanc. la
Salmon Wm. W. esq. 9 Park sq. Regt.'s pk
Salomon Jsph. C. esq. 7 Windml. st. Tot. c. r
Salomon Mrs. 100 Gloucester place
Salomons Aaron, esq. 22 Cambridge sq
Salomons Philip, esq. 4 Crosby square
Salomons P. J. esq. 18 Upper Wimpole st
Salomonson Mrs. 9 Portland pl. Wand. rd
Salt Isaac, esq. 3 St. George's terrace
Salt John, M.D. 53 Hamilton ter. St. Jn.'s wd
Salt John, esq. 10 Upper Woburn place
Salt Mrs. 9 Russell square, & Weeping cross, Stafford
Salter Major Genl. 22 Dorset square
Salter Geo. esq. 8 Alpha pl. Regent's pk
Salter Mrs. 47 Charing cross
Salter R. F. esq. 8 Park pl. vil. Padngtn
Salter William, esq. 51 Pall mall
Salter Wm. esq. 1 Bullingham pl. Kensng
Saltoun Lord, K.C.B., G.C.H. 1 Gt. Cumberland st. & Philorth house, Frazerburgh
Saltwell Miss Sarah, 28 Fitzroy square
Saltwell Wm. Hy. esq. 12 Regent st
Salusbury Thos. esq. 27 Halfmoon st
Salvin Capt. Jeffery, 4 Nottingham st
Salvin Capt. John, 4 Nottingham st
Salway Joseph Eisdell, esq. 117 Sloane st
Sambourne Edward, esq. 15 Lloyd square
Samler George, esq. 22 University st
Samler Henry, esq. 3 Raymond bdgs
Samler Wellington, esq. 3 Raymond bds
Sampson Geo. esq. 12 Chester st. Grov. pl
Sampson S. esq. 12 Albion ter. Wands. rd
Sampson Saml. esq. 13 King's bench walk
Sampson Saml. esq. Glo'ster rd. Rgt.'s pk
Sampson William, esq. 87 Eaton square
Sampson Wm. esq. 34 London st. Fitzry. sq
Samrach Chas. esq. 164 St. George st
Sams Joseph, esq. 56 Gt. Queen st
Sams Mrs. 21 Halfmoon st. Piccadilly
Samson Augs. Fras. esq. 6 Gt. Coram st
Samson Louis, esq. 67 Cambridge ter
Samson Lewis A. esq. 23 Oxenden st
Samson Mrs. S. 6 Gt. Coram st. Brunswk. sq
Samuel Alfred, esq. 4 Nottingham ter
Samuel Alfred, jun. esq. 17 Keppel st
Samuel Denis M. esq. 26 Sussex pl. Reg. pk
Samuel Mrs. 6 Henrietta st. Brunswk. sq
Samuel Mrs. 33 Woburn pl. Russell sq
Samuel Philip, esq. 1 Bedford pl. Russl. sq
Samuel S. M. esq. 29 Park cres. Portlnd. pl
Samuel Simon, esq. 30 Glo'str. pl. Portm. sq
Samuels David, esq. 18 Little Alie st
Samuels Miss, 18 Guilford st
Sanways Jas. esq. 28 Low. Belgrave pl
Samwell Francis, esq. 52 Margaret st
Sancton Philip, esq. 9 Gower st
Sandall D. esq. 10 Newingtn. pl. Kenng. rd
Sandell J. esq. 12 Regent's vil. Avnue. rd
Sandeman Geo. Glas. esq. 13 Highbury pl
Sandeman Hugh F. esq. 14 Dorset sq
Sander Jph. esq. 9 Elm Tree rd. St. John's wd
Sanders Rev. J. W. 1 Mount pl. Lndn. hspt
Sanders Frederick, esq. 13 Albion grove, Thornhill road
Sanders Geo. esq. 25 Allsop ter. New rd
Sanders Geo. W. esq. Rolls yd. Chancery la
Sanders John Thos. esq. 11 Gray's inn sq
Sanders Mrs. 3 Augusta pl. Stockwl. com
Sanders Mrs. 4 Dean's pl. South Lambeth
Sanders Mrs. 16 South ter. Alexander sq
Sanders Rd. esq. 40 Allsop terr. New road
Sanders Rt. B. esq. 20 Hart st. & 1 New inn
Sanders Thomas, esq. 37 Guildford st. Russell sq. & 10 Crown office row
Sanders Thomas, esq. 58 Guilford st. Russell square, & 3 Elm court, Temple
Sanders Thos. esq. 10 Crown office row
Sanders Wm. esq. 18 New Millman st
Sanderson Rev. Chas. 31 Northamptn. sq
Sanderson Cornelius, esq. Sherborne cottage, Park village ea. Regent's pk
Sanderson John, esq. 15 Cambridge sq
Sanderson Mrs. 43 Baker st. Lloyd sq
Sanderson Mrs. 9 Howland st. Fitzroy sq
Sanderson Mrs. 13 Park place ter. Pdgtn
Sanderson Richard, esq. M.P. & Hon. Mrs. 46 Belgrave sq. & Gunton park, Aylsham
Sandford Rev. John, 4 Connaught place
Sandford Edward, esq. 77 Chancery la
Sandham John, esq. 49 Hans place
Sandiland Rev. R. S. 20 Hans place
Sandiland Wm. esq. 8 Stepney green
Sandon Viscount, M.P. 39 Grosvenor sq.; & Norton, near Campden; & Sandon, Stafford
Sandon Fred. esq. 14 Orchard st. Ptmn. sq
Sandoz Frederick, esq. 46 Canonbury sq
Sands Miss, 13 Sloane st
Sandwich Earl, 32 Dover st. & Hinchinbroke, near Huntingdon
Sandwith Major Gen. 27 Holles st
Sands E. esq. 25 Fortess ter. Kentish tn
Sandy Saml. esq. 7 Soley ter. Pentonvle
Sandys Lord, 48 Curzon st. Mayfair, & Ombersley court, Worcester
Sandys Rev. John, 8 Canonbury place
Sandys Mrs. 66 Hamilton ter. St. Jn's. wd
Sandys Richd. Hill, esq. 89 Chancery la
Sandys Wm. esq. 5 Serjnt's. inn, Fleet st. & 25 Devonshire st. Portland place
Sanford Feake, esq. 20 John st. Adelphi, & 17 Connaught square
Sanford Henry, esq. 37 Mecklenburgh sq
Sanford Wm. esq. Northcot ldg. Glostr. pl
Sang Fredk. esq. 27 Portland ter. Reg. pk
Singer Wm. esq. 23 Grafton place, Euston sq. & 4 Essex court, Temple
Sangiovanni B. esq. 23 Nassau st. Mdx. hos
Sangster David, esq. 11 Kennington ter
Sansom Mrs. 2 Cloudesley st. Islington
Sansom Samuel, esq. 56 Judd st
Sanson Miss, 23 Fortess ter. Kntsh. tn
Sant James, esq. 19 Soho square
Santa Maria Constant, esq. 15 Regnt. st
Santagnello the Misses, 40 Cambridge st
Sapte Francis, esq. 70 Eaton place
Saquille C. esq. 3 Ladbroke pl. Notng. hl
Sardi Ths. G. esq. 51 Cambridge st. Edg. rd
Sargant Mrs. 13 Up. Glo'ster pl. Dorst. sq
Sargeant Rd. esq. 10 Norfolk st. Strand
Sargent Edmund, esq. 21 Margaret st
Sargent Geo. F. esq. 5 Bouverie st. Fleet st
Sargent Rd. esq. 7 Kensington gard. ter
Sargent T. esq. 21 Cambridge ter. Edg. rd
Sargood T. A. esq. 11 South sq. Gray's inn
Sarim Effendi, ambassador extraordinary, & minister plenipotentiary from Turkey, 1 Bryanstone square
Sarjent Geo. R. esq. 3 Charlotte st. Fitz. sq
Sarl Abraham, esq. 50 Gibson square
Sarl William, esq. 44 Gibson square
Sarratt Mrs. 1 Russell place, Fitzroy sq
Sass Hen. esq. 25 Henrietta st. Brnswk. sq
Satchwell Mrs. 66 Warwick st. Fitzroy sq
Satterthwaite Miss, 4 Artillery place
Saumarez Capt. Rich. R.N. 45 Hans pl
Saunder Wm. D. esq. 33 Baker st

Saunders Rev. A. P. D.D. Charterhouse
Saunders Rev. J. Helmet row, St. Luke's
Saunders Chas. esq. 3 Hare ct. Temple
Saunders C. esq. 1 Princes pl. Kenngtn. rd
Saunders Edwin, esq. 16 Argyll st
Saunders James, esq. 50 New Bond st
Saunders Jas. Eben. esq. 16 Finsbury sq
Saunders James Edward, esq. 5 Linden grove, Kensington gravel pits
Saunders John, esq. 8 Cloudesley square
Saunders John, esq. 2 Gt. Knightrider st
Saunders John, esq. 2 Norland place
Saunders Miss, 1 Charles st. Westbn. ter
Saunders the Misses, 22 Mornington cres
Saunders Mrs. 25 Paddington green
Saunders Mrs. Anthony, 47 Mornington pl
Saunders Nthel. esq. 5 Stockwell villas
Saunders Richd. E. esq. 14 Millman st
Saunders Robert, esq. Cavendish hotel, 81 Jermyn st.; Northwood park, Cowes; & Blackheath, Kent
Saunders Saml. esq. 3 Mid. Temple lane
Saunders Simon, esq. 2 Up. Bedfrd. pl Ksgtn
Saunders Simon, esq. 51 Geo. st. Eust. sq
Saunders Thos. Bush, esq. 16 Brompton square; & 19 Lincoln's inn fields
Saunders Thos. J. esq. 31 Maddox st. Rgt. st
Saunders Thos. Wm. esq. 1 Cloisters, Temp
Saunders Wm. esq. 14 Staffrd. st. Lisn. gr
Saunderson E. esq. 1 Angel st. St. Mt's. le gr
Saurm Cap. R.N. & Lady Mary, 19 Wilton cr
Savage Hen. esq. 34 Dorset pl. Dorset sq
Savage James, esq. 31 Essex st. Strand
Savage Jas. Hy. esq. 23 Avnu. rd. Regt.'s pk
Savage John, esq. 2 Clarges st. Piccdly
Savage Miss, 2 River terrace, City road
Savage Mrs. 11 Duke st. Portland place
Savage Rt. esq. 11 Montague pl. Russl. sq
Savage Robt. C. esq. 22 Wellington rd
Savage Wm. esq. 12 Furnival's inn, Holbrn
Savage Wm. Henry, esq. 68 Gower st
Savill Onley Mrs. 12 Chester terrace
Saville Robt. esq. Park village east
Savio Mrs. 20 Chapel st. Grosvenor sq
Savory Thos. F. esq. 22 Sussex pl. Rgt.'s pk
Saward James T. esq. 4 Hare ct. Temple
Saward Michl. esq. 9 Chatham pl. Blkfrs
Sawer Thos. esq. 1 Lion ter. Edgware rd
Sawkins Miss, 3 Park ter. Regent's pk
Sswtell Edwin, esq. 14 Hanov. cot. Pk. rd
Sawtell Geo. Hen. esq. 12 New inn, Strand
Sawyer Edmund, esq. 2 Pump court
Sawyer Edw. esq. 18 Canonbury villas
Sawyer George, esq. 1 Myddelton sq
Sawyer Geo. Hen. esq. 21 Tibberton sq
Sawyer Henry J. esq. 46 Carey st. Lin. in
Sawyer John J. esq. 101 Park st. Grov. sq
Sawyer Robert Henry, esq. 18 Endsleigh st.; & 2 Staple inn
Sawyer Wm. Hy. esq. 30 Burton crescent
Saxby Mrs. 21 Portland pl. Lwr. rd. Islngtn
Saxton Edward, esq. 4 Highbury park
Saxon Mrs. 39 Gower st. Bedford sq
Say Eusebius, esq. 7 Bury st. St. James's
Say Frederick Richd. esq. 18 Harley st
Say Mrs. Eleanor, 7 Foley place
Saye & Sele Lord, 43 Grosvenor st.; Belvedere, Erith, Kent; & Broughton castle, Banbury
Sayer Augustin, M.D. 28 Up. Seymour st
Sayer Charles, esq. 19 Old Cavendish st
Sayer Miss, 5 Judd place east, New rd
Saywell Rt. esq. Temple chambs. Fleet st
Scace Robt. esq. 26 New Church st. west
Scadding Edwin, esq. 2 Gordon st
Scadding Edwin Ward, esq. 3 Gordon st
Scafe Mrs. 6 Michael's place, Bromptn
Scaife Francis, esq. 9A, Upper Brook st
Scale Thomas, esq. Wellesley house, Finchley new road
Scales Henry, esq. 7 St. John's wood rd
Scales Jsph. esq. Summit pl. Up. Claptn
Scales Thomas, esq. 6 River ter. City rd
Scanlan Capt. 44 Markham sq. Chelsea
Scanlan Edwd. esq. 18 Park place villas
Scanlan Robt. esq. 63 Burton crescent
Scannell Danl. esq. 6 Upper Ranelagh st
Scappa Guiseppe, esq. 18 Manchester st
Scarborough, Earl of, 41 South st. Grosvenor sq.; Sandbeck park, Rotherham; & Rufford hall, Ollerton
Scarborough, Dow. Cts. of, 14 Portman sq
Scarborough-White Cornelius S. esq. 27 Montagu place, Russell square
Scard John, esq. 2 North cres. Bedfrd. sq
Scarfe A. W. esq. 23 Princes st. Hanvr. sq
Scargill John, esq. 23 Montagu place
Scarisbrick Chas. esq. 11 Suffolk st
Scarlet Miss, 23 New Ormond st
Scarman Mrs. 16 Pembroke sq. Kensgtn
Scarman Wm. esq. 10 George st. Hnvr. sq
Scarnell Joseph, esq. 1 Gibson square
Scarsdale Lord, Keddlestone hall, Derby
Scatcherd Mrs. 19 Portland ter. Reg. pk
Scatliff John P. esq. 48 Sloane square
Schaezler Adolphus Fred. esq. Bavarian consul, 11 Bury court, St. Mary Axe
Scharf Geo. esq. 14 Francis st. Tott. ct. rd
Schaw Capt. F. D. R.N. 24 Porchester ter
Scheels Mrs. 17 Compton st. Brunswk. sq,
Schelch Vernon, esq. Glendearg lodge Queen's road, St. John's wood
Scheydt Peter, esq. 11 Elm ter. Lit. Chlsea
Schilizzi John, esq. 37 Finsbury circus
Schill Louis, esq. 15 Maddox st
Schleneker T. esq. 10 Mount pl. Whtchpl. rd
Schmack Augustus, esq. 17 Stockwl. com
Schmidt Henry, esq. Camberwell green
Schmidt Henry, esq. 14 Piccadilly
Schmitz Leonard, Ph.D. 9 Glo'ster cres
Schneidau Mrs. 28 Henrietta st. Brnswk. sq
Schneider Hen. Wm. esq. 4 Harewood sq
Schofield Jas. esq. 12 Up. Islington ter
Schofield Joseph, esq. 63 Warren st
Schofield Mrs. 19 Cirencester place
Schofield Mrs. 18 Gt. College st. Westmr
Scholey John, esq. 36 Westbourne ter
Scholey Wm. S. esq. Larkhall rise, Clapm
Scholfield Edmund, esq. 45 Lime st
Scholfield Edm. esq. 4 Up. Chadwell st
Schomberg Joseph T. esq. 40 Chancery lane, & 16 Pelham crescent, Fulham rd
Schonswar Capt. J. S. 9 Chapel st. Grosv. sq
Schooling Jas. esq. 13 Artillery pl. Finsbry
Schott Fredk. esq. 7 Cottage rd. Eaton sq
Schrimshaw Wm. 11 Upper Glo'ster st. Dorset sq
Schröder Alfred, esq. 13 Bruton st
Schroder Ludolf, esq. 14 Tavistock sq
Schulz Edw. esq. 30 Maddox st. Rgt. st
Scobell Rev. Edward, 14 Blandford st
Scoffern J. M.D. 10 Henry st. ea. Avenue rd
Scoles Jsph. J. esq. 11 Argyll pl. Regt. st
Scoles Mattw. esq. 14 Melton st. Eust. sq
Scollick Jonathan, jun. esq. 35 Beaufort st. Chelsea
Score Charles, esq. 43 Carey st. Linc. inn
Score Chas. Call. esq. 43 Carey st
Scorer Charles, 18 Mornington crescent
Scotland C. H. esq. 1 Pump ct. Temple
Scotland Mrs. 1 Bath place, Kensington
Scott Hon. Chas. G. 25 Chesham st. Blg. sq
Scott the Ladies, 18 Eaton square
Scott Hon. Francis, M.P. Carlton club, 94 Pall mall, & Snowdenham, Guildford
Scott Sir Claude, bart. & Co. 1 Cavndsh. sq
Scott Sir David, bart. 54 Porchester ter & the Elms, Kingston on Thames
Scott Sir Edwd. bart. 45 Bryanstone sq
Scott Sir Samuel, bart. 5 Mount st
Scott Capt. Jas. 10 Grove pl. Brompton
Scott Rev. John, 23 City road
Scott Anthony, esq. 58 Gower st
Scott Chas. esq. 6 Winchester row, New rd
Scott Chas. Davison, esq. 31 Gordon st. Gordon sq. & 7 Furnival's inn
Scott Claude Edward, esq. 29 Bruton st
Scott David, esq. 20 Sherrard st. Golden sq
Scott Edmund John, esq. 8 St. Mildred's court, Poultry
Scott Fredk. esq. 12A, Myddelton sq
Scott Geo. esq. 4 Dorset ter. Gt. Dover rd
Scott Geo. esq. 12 Pembroke sq. Kensngtn
Scott Geo. esq. 1 St. Agnes vils. Bayswtr
Scott Geo. G. esq. 12 Avenue rd. Regt. pk
Scott Geo. G. esq. 20 Spring gardens
Scott George Walter, esq. 23 Doughty st
Scott Hen. D. esq. 12 Grosvenor st. west
Scott James, esq. 65 Cadogan place
Scott James, esq. 1 Eccleston st
Scott James, esq. 25 Lincoln's inn fields
Scott James, esq. 29 Lisson grove north
Scott James, M.D. 369 Strand, & 37 Grove end road, St. John's wood
Scott James John, esq. 1 Cloisters, Temp
Scott Ja. Wm. P. esq. 2 Southmptn. bldgs
Scott John, esq. 8 Chancery lane
Scott John, esq. 9 Clifford's inn, Fleet st
Scott John, M.D. 12 Bedford sq
Scott John, esq. 32 Harleyfrd. pl. Kngtn
Scott John, esq. 53 High st. Camden tn
Scott John, esq. 4 Hyde park st
Scott John, esq. 17 Park lane
Scott John, esq. 11 Princes sq. St. Geo. ea
Scott John, esq. 1 River st. Myddelton sq
Scott John, esq. 86 St. Martin's lane
Scott John, esq. 83 Sloane st
Scott John, esq. 6 Spring ter. Wandswth. rd
Scott John F. esq. Thurlow cot. Wandsw. rd
Scott John G. esq. 16 Clapham rise
Scott John Steward, esq. 54 Edgware rd
Scott Joseph, esq. 62 Charing cross
Scott Matt. Rd. esq. 17 Devonshire pl
Scott Miss, 14 Maddox st. Hanover sq
Scott Miss, 17 Notting hill terrace
Scott Miss, 11 Park vill. ea. Regnt.'s prk
Scott Mrs. 23 Cambridge st. Edgware rd
Scott Mrs. 26 Gilbert st. Grosvenor sq
Scott Mrs. 73 Guilford st. Russell sq
Scott Mrs. 3 Hereford st
Scott Mrs. 6 Hornsey row, Islington
Scott Mrs. 30 John st. Bedford row
Scott Mrs. 12A, Myddelton sq
Scott Mrs. 10 Park road, Regent's park
Scott Mrs. 43 Somerset st. Portman sq
Scott Mrs. 32 University st. Tottm. court rd
Scott Mrs. 10 Westbourne pl. Sloane sq
Scott Montague, esq. 19 Devereux ct. Strnd
Scott Montague, esq. 369 Strand
Scott Rd. Ashley, esq. 9 Up. Woburn pl
Scott Rt. esq. M.P. 7 Manchester bldngs
Scott Rt. esq. 9 Upper Barnsbury st
Scott T. esq. 2 Montagu pl. Montagu sq
Scott Thos. sen. esq. 23 Doughty st
Scott William, esq. 23 Bolton st
Scott Wm. esq. 2 Dean's yard, Westmnstr
Scott Wm. esq. 4 Golden sq
Scott Wm. esq. 3 Hall pl. St. John's wd
Scott Wm. esq. 11 Park village east
Scott Wm. esq. 3 Strahan ter. Liverpl. rd
Scott Wm. Pulteney, esq. 5 Sydney pl. Pelham cres. & 31 Norfolk st. Strand
Scoular Wm. esq. 92 Dean st. Soho
Scovell Geo. esq. 8 Chester st. Grosvnr. pl
Scovell James, esq. 5 Ulster pl. New rd
Scrase Mrs. 7 Chesterfield st. King's cr
Scrimgeour Miss, 11 Brompton cresce
Scriven John, esq. 2 Elm court, Temple
Scrivener Rev. F. H. 7 Smith st. Chelsea
Scrivener John Fred. P. esq. 30 Bedford square, & Ramridge house, Andover
Scrivens James, esq. 15 Millbank row
Scrivner Miss, 8 King's parade, Chelsea
Scrope Geo. Poulett, M.P. 13 Belgrave sq. & Castle Combe house, near Chipnhm
Scrope William, esq. 13 Belgrave sq. & Cockering hall, Louth, Lincolnshire, & Chelton, Hungerford
Scudamore Sir Chas. M.D. 6 Wimpole st
Scudamore Fitzroy, esq. 170 Albany st
Scully Francis, esq. 44 Lincoln's inn flds
Sculthorpe Walter, esq. 6 South sq. Gr. inn
Sculthorpe Wm. esq. 6 Grafton st. east
Seabrook Chas. esq. 32 Pelham rd. Bmtn
Seabrook Isaac, esq. 43 Regent sq
Seafield Earl, 17 Charles st. St. James's, & Castle Grant, Grantown, Invernessshire, & Cullen house, Cullen, Banffshire

Seabrook Wm. esq. 4 Francis pl. Holowy
Seaford Lady, 2 Audley square, & Wood end, Chichester, Sussex
Seagar J. L. esq. Carrown ho. Soth. Lambth
Seager John, esq. 3 Osnabugh st. Regnt. pk
Seale Dowager Lady, 16 Hans place
Seale Sir John Hen. bart. 42 Cadogan place, & Mount Boone, Dartmouth
Sealy Edward Forward, esq. 11 Linc. inn fld
Seaman Benj. Cruttall Pierce, esq. 4 Upper Gower st. & Rotherby, Leicestershire
Seaman Chas. esq. 15 Hornton st. Knsingtn
Seare Thomas, esq. 2 South sq. Gray's inn
Seargeant John, esq. 28 Claremont sq
Searle F. B. esq. 10 Southampton st. Blsby
Searle Geo. esq. 42 Cumming st. Pentnvl
Searle John, esq. 94 Glo'ster pl. Ptmn. sq
Searle Jsph. esq. 15 George st. Ptmn. sq
Searles Robt. T. esq. Terrace, O. Kent rd
Seater Jas. esq. 42 King sq. Goswell rd
Seaton Lord, G.C.B.G.C.H. Govnr. of Corfu
Seaton Edward, esq. 77 Sloane st
Seaton Jas. esq. 8 Bridge st. Westmnstr
Seaton Mrs. 24 Lowndes st. Belgrave sq
Seaton Rt. esq. 1 Up. Brnswk. tr. Brnsby. rd
Seaton Rt. esq. 72 Up. Norton st. Fitzry. sq
Seaward Jas. esq. 15 Beaufort st. Chelsea
Seaward Mrs. 5 Hanway st. Oxford st
Seaward Mrs. 14 Middlesex pl. New rd
Sebbon Miss, 2 Sebbons buildings, Islgtn
Sebright Sir John, bart. 88 Jermyn st. & Beechwood, Herts
Secker Isaac O. esq. 5 Pump ct. Temple
Secker John, esq. St. Katherine's, Rgt. pk
Secretan Fred. esq. 47 Oxford terrace
Seddon Samuel, esq. Springfield lodge, Wandsworth road
Sedgwick John Ball, esq. Pall mall east
Sedgewick Mrs. 20 Portman st. Portmn. sq
Sedgeley Fred. esq. 2 Allen terr. Kensingtn
Sedgwick George, esq. 8 Furnival's inn
Sedgwick Mrs. 3 Church st. Kensington
Sedgwick Mrs. 3 Glo'ster ter. O. Bromptn
Sedgwick Samuel, M.D. 19 Pembroke sq
Sedgwick Wm. esq. 14 Westbourne pl
Sedingham Joseph, esq. 11 Kensngtn sq
Seeley Rt. B. esq. 11 Powis pl. Gt Ormondst
Sefton, Earl of, 37 Belgrave sq. & Croxteth park, Liverpool
Sefton, Dowager Countess, 21 Arlington st. Piccadilly, & Stoke farm, Slough
Sefton Richard, esq. 59 Connaught ters
Sefton Wm. esq. 6 Queen's pl. Kenngtn. rd
Seguare Hilra, esq. 13 Euston pl. New rd
Seguier Mrs. 70 Sloane st
Seguin Arthur, esq. 45 Duke st. St. Jas
Seguin Wm. H. esq. 43 Curzon st. Mayfair
Selby Geo. esq. 16 Serjeant's inn, Fleet st
Selby Hy. esq. 8 York cotgs. Old Brmptn
Selby John, esq. 13 York pl. Portman sq
Selby Mrs. 8 Connaught terrace
Self Mrs. 1 Devonshire pl. Wndswth. rd
Selfe Chas. esq. 4 Chester pl. Kenngtn
Selfe Hen. Selfe, esq. 6 Grenville st
Selkirk, Earl of, St. Mary's isle, Krcdbght
Seller Jas. esq. 4 Portland pl. Lr. rd. Isln
Sellick Philip, esq. 18 Grove pl. Lis. grv
Selot John Frs. esq. 27 Duke st. St. James's
Selsby James, esq. 3 Clifford's inn
Selsey Lady, 71 Chester square
Selwyn Chas. Jasper, esq. 7 Old sq. Linc. inn, & Pagoda house, Richmond, Surrey
Selwyn Mrs. 4 Earl's terr. Kensington
Selwyn Wm. esq. Q.C. 7 Old square, & Pagoda house, Richmond, Surrey
Semple Alex. esq. 11 Portman pl. Edgw. rd
Semple Rt. esq. 2 Ruffords row, Islgtn
Semple Robt. H. esq. 3 Sands bldgs. Islgtn
Senior Bernard M. esq. 3 Barnsbury st
Senior Jas. esq. 14 Leonard pl. Knsgtn
Senior Nassau Wm. esq. 5 Hyde pk. gate, Kensgtn. go. & 25 Southampton bldgs
Seppings N. L. esq. 6 York pl. Pentonvl
Sercumbe R. esq. 6 Pine Apple pl. Mada. vl
Sergeant Fred. Thos. esq. 2 New sq. Linc. inn, & 8 Springfield ter. Camberwl. grv
Serin Madame, 38 Oxford terrace
Serny John B. M.D. 8 Nottingham ter
Serocold Rev. E. S. P. 26 Norfolk st. Pk. la
Serrall D. esq. 4 North bank, Rgnt.'s pk
Serrell Dalton H. esq. 3 South sq. Grs. in
Seton Jas. Garden, esq. 1 Kent terrace, Regent's pk. & 12 George st. Adelphi
Seton C. M. esq. & the Honble. Mrs. 2 Park place villas, Paddington
Seton Wilmot, esq. 58 Chester square
Setree Henry, esq. 10 Bernard st
Severn John Percy, esq. 2 Inner Temp. la
Severn Jsph. esq. 21 James st. Buckm. gt
Severne Samuel Amy, esq. 11 Portland pl. Wallop hl. Salop, & Thenford, Nthmptn
Seville Mrs. 11 Lower Grosvenor place
Seward Hy. Hake, esq. 10 Sth. Audley st
Seward Miss, 44 Notting hill square
Sewell Charles, esq. 49 Clarendon square
Sewell C. esq. 9 Portland pl. Clphm. rd
Sewell George, esq. 8 Sussex gardens
Sewell Henry, esq. 13 Gray's inn square, & Newport, Isle of Wight
Sewell Henry, esq. 24 Welbeck st
Sewell John, esq. 7 Finsbury tr. City rd
Sewell Mrs. 21 Up. Albany st. Regt.'s pk
Sewell Mrs. 10 York place, City road
Sewell Richard Clarke, D.C.L. 4 Garden court, Temple
Sewell Thos. 8 Bedford pl. Hampstd. rd
Seymour Lord, M.P. 18 Spring gardens, & Burton hall, Loughborough
Seymour Sir Horace Beauchamp, knt. M.P. & Dowager Lady Clinton, 28 St. James's pl. & Stoke house, Chichester
Seymour Lady Robert, 27 Portland pl
Seymour Capt. Francis, 8 Park lane
Seymour Frederick, esq. 83 Jermyn st
Seymour E. J. M.D. 13 Chas. st. Brkly. sq
Seymour E. R. esq. 13 Chas. st. Brkly. sq
Seymour Hen. esq. 39 Up. Grosvenor st.; Brook ldg. Exeter; & Knoyle ho. Hindn
Seymour Mrs. 12 Markham pl. Kng.'s rd
Seymour Wm. esq. 19 Montague place
Seymour Wm. Digby, esq. 11 Doughty st
Seymour Wm. Henry, esq. 9 Coleshill st
Shadwell Rt. Hon. Sir Lancelot, kt. Vice-Chancellor of England's court, Linc. inn, & Barn Elms, Barnes, Surrey
Shadwell Cayley, esq. 8 Stanhope ter. Hyde park, & 4 Carey street
Shadwell Charles, esq. 21 Blandford sq. & 4 South square, Gray's inn
Shadwell Lancelot, esq. 1 Nottingham place; & 4 Old square, Lincoln's inn
Shadwell Louis Henri, esq. 3 King's bench wk. Temple, & Barn Elms, Surrey
Shadwell Mrs. 8 Stanhope ter. Hyde pk
Shadwell Thos. M. esq. 18 Lloyd sq
Shaftesbury Earl, P.C. 24 Grosvenor sq.; & St. Giles house, Woodyates, Dorset
Shairp Walter, esq. 29 Sussex gardens
Shakerley Sir Chas. bart. Mivart's hotel
Shakespear Wm. esq. 29 King st. Holborn
Shallis John, jun. esq. 4 Lowther cottages
Shancke John J. esq. 11½ Addison rd
Shank Hen. esq. 62 Glo'ster pl. Portman sq. & Laurencekirk, N.B.
Shannon, Earl of, Castle Martyr, Ireland
Shannon Mrs. Ann, 9 Calthorpe st
Shapland Jsph. esq. 4 Pump ct. Temple
Shappard, Mrs. 7 Walton pl. Brompton
Shapter Henry D. esq. 5 Verulam bdgs
Shapter John. esq. 20 Devonshire pl. Portland pl. & 8 New square
Sharman Miss, 74 John st. Fitzroy sq
Sharp Benj. esq. 15 Northwick terrace
Sharp Dan. T. esq. 27 Glo'ster cres. Rgt. pk
Sharp E. esq. 2 Devonshire ter. Marylebn
Sharp Geo. Oxford villa, St. John's wd
Sharp Henry L. esq. 39 Porchester ter
Sharp James, esq. 7 Endsleigh st
Sharp John, esq. 3 Alpha rd. Regent's pk
Sharp John, esq. 10 Grenville st
Sharp Joseph, esq. 3 Gt. Knightrider st
Sharp Miss, 10 Grenville st. Brunswk. sq
Sharp Mrs. 4 Church st. Paddington
Sharp Mrs. 4 Lloyd st. Pentonville
Sharp Mrs. 5 South ter. Alexander sq
Sharp Mrs. 48 Upper Seymour st
Sharp Samuel, esq. 37 Ely pl. Holborn
Sharp Samuel, esq. 32 Highbury place
Sharp Thos. esq. 25 Albany st. Regnt.'s pk
Sharp Thos. esq. 27 Burton crescent
Sharp Thomas, esq. 3 Tibberton sq
Sharp Wm. esq. 19 Ely place, Holborn
Sharp William, esq. 2 Verulam bldgs
Sharpe Daniel, esq. 2 Adelphi terrace
Sharpe James, esq. 21 Grosvenor st. west
Sharpe John, esq. 10 Lisson grove north
Sharpe John, esq. 3 Thornhill rd. Islng
Sharpe John, esq. 8 Vine st. Regent st
Sharpe Joseph, esq. 27 Colebrooke row
Sharpe Joseph, esq. 79 Dean st. Soho
Sharpe J. A. esq. 22 Lit. Knightrider st
Sharpe Wm. esq. 1 Prospect pl. Chelsea
Sharpe Wm. esq. 22 Woburn sq. & 41 Bedford row
Sharpe Wm. esq. 22 Woburn square
Sharpey Wm. M.D. 35 Glos'ter cr. Rgt.'s pk
Sharwood Langton, esq. 16 Furnival's inn
Shave John, esq. 3 Petersburgh pl. Byswr
Shaw Rt. Hon. Fredk. M.P. 5 Chester st. & Kimmage house, near Dublin
Shaw Sir John, bt. 33 Sussex gdns. Hydepk
Shaw Mrs. Gen. 18 Baker st. Portman sq
Shaw A. esq. 23 Henrietta st. Cavndsh. sq
Shaw Alexander, esq. 53 Berners st
Shaw Benj. esq. 13 Cambridge sq. Hyd. pk
Shaw Benj. esq. 9 Priory cottgs. Kilburn
Shaw Edward, esq. 40 Little Britain
Shaw Frederick, esq. 102 London wall
Shaw George, esq. 45 Myddelton square
Shaw Geo. John, esq. 8 Furnival's inn
Shaw George L. esq. 27 Trinity sq. Boro'
Shaw Henry, esq. 37 Southampton row
Shaw Hugh Thos. esq. 18 Ely pl. Holborn
Shaw John, esq. 5 Berners st
Shaw John Thos. esq. 15 Clapham rd. pl
Shaw Miss, 21 Brunswick square
Shaw Miss, 25 Canonbury sq. Islington
Shaw Miss, 175 Prospect pl. Edgware rd
Shaw Mrs. 21 Brunswick square
Shaw Mrs. 7 Upper Montagu st
Shaw Richard, esq. 10 Clifford's inn
Shaw Robt. Elgie, esq. 8 Powell st. west
Shaw Thos. C. esq. 8 New st. sq. Fetter lane
Shaw Wm. esq. 34 Bloomsbury st. Bloomsb
Shaw Wm. esq. 6 Hyde park ter. Kensg
Shaw Wm. esq. 7 King's rd. Bedford rw
Shaw Wm. A. esq. Wycombeldg. Cmdn. hil
Shaw Wm. E. esq. 15 John st. Minories
Shawe Col. Chas. Augustus, 24 Eaton sq
Shea Capt. 31 Connaught square
Shea Alex. esq. 8 Featherstone bldgs
Shealier Wm. esq. 9 Stanhope pl. Hyde pk
Shearman Charles, esq. 2 Gray's inn sq
Shearman M. esq. 1 Trinity pl. Charingers
Shearman Wm. M.D. 30 Northampton sq
Shears A. esq. 28 Upp. Berkeley st. west
Shears D. T. esq. 4 Lawn, South Lambh
Shearsby Miss, 49 Beaumont st
Shearwood Bailey, esq. 6 Kenningtn. rw
Shedden George, esq. 6 Bedford square, & Spring hill cottage, Cowes
Shedden Peter, esq. 7 Claremont square
Shee Sir Martin Archer, knt. P.R. A32, Cavendish square
Shee Martin Archer, esq. 63 Chancery la
Shee Wm. S.L. 5 Sussex pl. Hydeparkgardens, & 2 Serjeants' inn, Chancery la
Shee Wm. Archer, 17 Up. Seymour st
Sheehan John, esq. 4 Hare ct. Temple
Sheen Jas. esq. 3 Acacia grdn. St. Jn.'swd
Sheepshanks John, esq. 24 Rutland gate
Sheffield, Earl of, 20 Portland place, & Sheffield park, Uckfield
Sheffield Sir Robt. bart. 35 Portland pl. & Normanby hall, Brigg, Lincolnshire
Sheffield Isaac, esq. 12 Wigmore st
Sheffield John, esq. 35 Canonbury sq
Sheffield John, esq. 23 Old sq. Linc. inn

Sheffield Thos. esq. 32 Canonbury sq
Sheffield Wm. esq. 68 Old Broad st
Sheil Rt. Hon. Richard Lalor, M.P. 73 Eccleston sq. & Long Orchard, Tipperary
Sheldon Edw. esq. 9 Brompton sq
Shelburne, Earl of, M.P. 54 Berkeley sq. & Bowood, near Calne, Wiltshire
Sheldon Solomon, esq. 9 Tavistock sq
Shelford Leonard, esq. 3 Brick ct. Tmpl
Shelley Sir John, bart. 35 Belgrave sq. & Lonsdale ho. Fulham; & Maresfield Uckfield; & Brockholes, Preston. Lan
Shells Fred. esq. 11 Lit. Queen st. West
Shepard B. esq. 9 Henrietta st. Cov. gar
Shepard John, esq. Church st. Chelsea
Shepard Mrs. 27 Lower Ranelagh st
Shepard Peter Wm. esq. 27 Cloudesley st
Shepard Saml. esq. 5 Grove pl. Bromptn
Shepburn Mrs. 5 Sloane st. Chelsea
Shephard Fredk. esq. 10 Wellington rd
Shephard Robert, esq. 34 Tavistock sq
Shephard Wm. esq. 9 Wellington road
Shepheard Chas. esq. 3 Lewis pl. Fulham fields, & 21 Old Jewry
Shepheard George, esq. 100 Guilford st
Shepheard G. W. esq. 34 Gt. James st. Bedford row
Shepheard L. H. esq. 100 Guilford st
Shepherd Rev. Geo. D.D. 14 Russell sq
Shepherd Rev. Henry, D.D. 13 Keppel st
Shepherd Rev. Rd. Herne, 11 Chatham pl. Blackfriars, & 9 Palace st. Pimlico
Shepherd Edward, esq. 26 Green st
Shepherd Hen. John, esq. Q.C. & Lady Mary, 3 Hyde pk. ter. & 4 Old sq. Lin. in
Shepherd John, esq. 15 Golden square
Shepherd John, esq. 7 Kensington sq
Shepherd John, esq. 11 Wilton st
Shepherd Miss, 127 Albanyst. Regent'spk
Shepherd Mrs. 11 Bartlett's buildings
Shepherd Mrs. Howell, 30 Devonshire st
Shepherd Sam. esq. F.A.S. 20 Marlbro' sq
Shepherd Thos. esq. 6 New sq. Linc's. inn
Shepherd Wm. esq. 47 Wilton crescent
Sheppard T. B. esq. 2 Tuffnell pl. Islgtn
Sheppard Alf. B. esq. 18 Lincn's. inn flds
Sheppard Chas. esq. 6 Lyon's inn, Strnd
Sheppard Chas. Halford, esq. 3 Plowdn. bg
Sheppard Edmund, esq. 47 Howland st
Sheppard Ed. esq. 5 Ladbroke pl. Notng. hl
Sheppard Edw. H. esq. 4 Wyndham pl
Sheppard Fred. S.W. esq. 22 Grosvnr. st
Sheppard Geo. esq. 15 Cook's ct. Linc. inn
Sheppard Miss, 77 Cambridge terrace
Sheppard Thos. esq. M.P. 20 Gt. George st. Westminster, & Hampstead
Sheppard Wm. esq. 4 Bloomfield terrace
Shepperd Robt. esq. 7 New Palace yard
Shepperson M. esq. 19 Victoria rd. Piml
Sherborn Hen. esq. 24 Mornington pl
Sherborne Lord, 15 Hyde park gardens, & Sherborne lodge, Northleach
Sheridan Rd. B. M.P. 18 Spring gardens
Sherlock Geo. esq. 2 Cadogan rw. Chlsea
Sherrard Jas. C. esq. 2 Gt. Geo. st. Wstmnr
Sherrard Mrs. 35 East st. Red Lion sq
Sherrard Richard, esq. 8 New Bond st
Sherratt Thos. Hy. esq. 47 Mornington pl
Sherson Mrs. 9 York buildings, New rd
Sherwin Frank, esq. 14 Bruton st
Sherwood George, esq. Grove, St. John's park, Kentish town
Sherwood John, esq. 9 King's bench wk
Sherwood Joseph, esq. 44 Parliament st. & 4 Mecklenburgh square
Sherwood Jph. esq. 35 Trevor sq. Kgtsb
Sherwood Mrs. 4 Omega ter. Alpha rd
Sherwood Thomas, esq. 4 Mecklenburgh square, & 19 Dean st. Borough
Sherwood Thomas, esq 31 Woburn square, & 1 Serjeants' inn, Chancery lane
Shew Mrs. 61 Westbourne ter. Hyde pk
Shew Wm. esq. 13 Up. Marylebone st
Shewell John, esq. 83 Hamilton terrace
Shewell Mrs. 28 Norfolk crescent
Shick J. esq. 8 Hemingfd. ct. Brnsby. rd
Shield Wm. esq. 118 Park st. Camden
Shiell Qeely, esq. 40 Clarges st
Shiffner Thomas, esq. 30 Pall mall
Shilcock Jn. esq. 1 Southamptonst. Blmby
Shilletto Mrs. 2 Alfred pl. Bedford sq
Shillinglaw John, esq. 3 Waterloo pl
Shillito Mrs. 222 Maida vale, Edgwr. rd
Shinn Benj. H. esq. 15 Up. Phillimore pl
Skinner Mrs. 25 Brompton row
Shipley Mrs. Col. 104 Piccadilly
Shirley Evelyn John, M.P. 20 Belgrave sq. & Eatington park, near Shipston; & Lough Fea, Carrickmacross, Ireland
Shirley Evelyn Phillip, M.P. 95 Eaton sq. & Lower Eatington park, near Shipston; & Lough Fea, Carrickmacross, Ireland
Shirreff Chas. I. esq. 7 Lincoln's inn fields
Shirreff Miss, 60 Upper Berkeley st. & Grove mills, near Watford
Shirress J. esq. 48 Chapel st. Pentonvl
Shirt Mrs. 14 Edwardes sq. Kensington
Shirt Samuel, esq. 11 New Millman st
Shoesmith Robt. esq. 37 Clapham rd. pl
Shoobridge Thos. esq. Larkhall rise
Shoolbred James, esq. 49 Euston square
Shore Geo. esq. 43 Sussex gdns. Hyde pk
Shore John, esq. 23 Guilford st. Russl. sq
Shorno A. esq. 6 Southmptn. rw. New rd
Short Lieut. Col. 1 Albert ter. Knghsbdg
Short Rev. Wm. 43 Gt. Ormond st
Short John, esq. 1 Philpot ter. Edgw. rd
Short Mrs. 4 Osnaburgh terrace
Shoubridge Chas. Jn. esq. 3 Bedford row
Shoubridge Mrs. 18 Oxford square
Shoveller John, LL.D. 50 Finsbury sq
Shrewsbury, Earl & Countess of, Clarendon hotel, 169 New Bond st.; & Heythrop house, Oxfordshire; & Alton towers, Cheadle, Staffordshire
Shrewsbury, Dow. Ctss. of, 49 Montagu sq
Shrimpton Chas. Ths. esq. 130 St. Johnst. rd
Shrimpton Henry, esq. 20 Bentinck st
Shrimpton Rt. esq. 2 Devnshr. pl. Edgw. rd
Shrubb Mrs. 15 Smith st. Chelsea
Shubrick Genl. British ho. 83 Jermyn st
Shuckburgh Sir Fras. bt. Pavilion, Hans pl. & Shuckburgh park, Warwickshire
Shum Robt. esq. 3 King's rd. Bedford rw
Shurr Miss, 28 Brompton square
Shury Geo. esq. 28 George st. Euston sq
Shury John, esq. 7 Seymour pl. Wands. rd
Shute Robert, esq. 27 Mecklenburgh sq
Shute T. M.D. 21 Wellingtn. rd. St. Jhn.'swd
Shuter John David, esq. 67 Millbank st
Shuter Richd. esq. 66 St. Martin's lane
Shuter Richard, sen. esq. 120 Sloane st
Shuttleworth Capt. Hen. 31 Regent sq
Shuttleworth Geo. E. esq. 2 Mecklnbrgh. st
Shuttleworth James Philip Kay, esq. Vere lodge, Old Brompton
Shuttleworth J. B. esq. 4 Harley pl. N.w. rd
Shuttleworth Mrs. 29A, York st. Portm. sq
Shuttleworth Saml. esq. 3 Priory, Wandsw
Sibley Chas. 6 Russell pl. Fitzroy sq
Sibley Hen. esq. 5 Wharton st. Lloyd sq
Sibley Mrs. 182 Sloane st
Sibley Robert, esq. 39 Gt. Ormond st
Sibson Hy. esq. 18 Wellington rd. St. J.'sw
Sibthorp Col. Chas. De Laet Waldo, M.P. 27 Chester st. & Canwick hall, Lincoln
Sibthorp Mrs. 24 Howland st. Fitzroy sq
Sicer Miss, 2 Baker st. Portman square
Sichart John G. esq. 6 Trinity sq. Boro'
Siddons Geo. John, esq. 10 Harewood sq
Sidebotham Miss, 73 Up. Norton st
Sidebottom Alex. Radclyffe, esq. 47 Sloane st. & 2 New square, Lincoln's inn
Sidebottom Edward Venner, esq. 28 Avenue rd. & 4 New sq. Lincoln's inn
Sidford John, esq. 16 Marlborough sq
Sidmouth Rev. Visct. P.C. Albury, near Guildford
Sidney Algernon, esq. 58 High st. Cmdn. tn
Sidney George, esq. 13 South sq Gray's inn
Sidney John Apsley, esq. 53 Beaumont st
Sidney P. J. M. esq. 4 Mitre ct. Temple
Sidwell Rd. esq. 21 River st. Pentonville
Sievier Rt. W. esq. 12A, Hnriet. st. Cav. sq.
Sigismund S. M.D. 3 Gt. Marlborough st
Sigmond Geo. Gabriel, M.D. 31 Baker st. Portman sq
Silk Hen. esq. 1 Wheeler pl. Hampst. rd
Silk John A. esq. 2 Brunswick square
Sillitoe Purney, esq. 25 Bedford pl. & Pelwall hall, Market Drayton, Salop
Sillitor T. esq. 15 Cambridge pl. Edgw. rd
Sills Geo. esq. 21 Victoria gro. Kensgtn
Silva E. esq. 54 Newingtn. pl. Kenngtn. rd
Silva Moses Gomes, esq. 7 Sydney pl. Pelham cres. Fulham rd. & 19 E. I. chambers
Silva John, esq. 40 Regent square
Silva Edward D. M.D. 30 Berners st
Silver Fred. esq. 10 James st. Buckg. gt
Silver Jas. esq. 18 Addison rd. so. Kensgtn
Silver Stephen W. esq. 10 Abbey road
Silver William, esq. 3 Elm ct. Temple
Silvertop Geo. esq. 158 New Bond st. & Minster acres, Newcastle-on-Tyne
Sim John C. esq. 9 Clifton pl. Hyde pk. gdn
Sim Wm. esq. 8 King's Bench walk, Tmp
Simes Thos. esq. 2 Highbury park north
Simes Wm. esq. 14 Ebury st. Pimlico
Simkin Hen. esq. 4 Sand's blds. Islington
Simmonds A. esq. 3 Portland pl. Wndsw. rd
Simmons Edw. Rt. esq. 13 Clifford's inn, & Glo'ster lodge, Croydon, Surrey
Simmons George, esq. 13 Judd st
Simmons John, esq. 59 Bshpsgt. without
Simmons John, esq. 29 Cmptn. ter. Up. st
Simmons Mrs. 3 Cumberland pl. Rgt.'s pk
Simmons Miss, 8 Elmtree rd. St. Jn.'s wd
Simmons Mrs. 65 Edgware road
Simmons Mrs. 39 Lower Belgrave pl
Simmons Rd. esq. 3 Cumberland place
Simmons Thos. esq. Cloudesley villa
Simmons Wm esq. 10 King's Bench wlk
Simms Thos. esq. 12 Panton sq. Hymrkt
Simner Abel, esq. 19 Coles ter. Islington
Simon Henry A. esq. 2 Middle Temple la
Simon John, esq. 3 Brick court, Temple
Simon John, esq. 11 Wellington st. Strand
Simonds Major Wm. 17 Fitzroy square
Simonds Wm. esq. 13 Dorset pl. Dorset sq
Simonds W. H. esq. 7 Bury sq. St. Mary ax
Simons Nich. esq. 11 New sq. Linc. inn
Simpkin Wm. esq. 83 Blackfriars road
Simpkinson Sir John Aug. F. knt. Q.C. 21 Bedford pl. Rusl. sq. & 8 Old sq. Lin. inn
Simpson Charles, esq. 26 Bernard st
Simpson C. esq. 12 Cambridge st. Gldn. sq
Simpson Chas. M.D. 5 Eccleston st. south
Simpson Charles, esq. 10 Carlisle st. Soho
Simpson Charles John, esq. G1, Albany, & Litchfield, Staffordshire
Simpson George, esq. 26 Bernard st
Simpson Geo. esq. 6 Bedford st. Bedford sq
Simpson Geo. esq. 19 Old square, Lincoln's inn, & Clapham rise
Simpson Jas. esq. 33 Great George st. Westminster, & Chelsea Waterworks
Simpson James, esq. 21 King st. Cmdn. tn
Simpson James, esq. 18 Osnaburgh st
Simpson James G. esq. 27 Red Lion sq
Simpson Jas. esq. 25 Queen's sq. Bloomsby
Simpson John, esq. 10 Carlisle st. Soho sq
Simpson John, esq. 6 Compton ter. Islngtn
Simpson John, esq. 5 Furnival's inn
Simpson John, esq. 10 Henrietta st. Cav. sq
Simpson John, esq. 43 Newingtn. pl. Kenng
Simpson John, esq. 3 Oxford terrace
Simpson John, esq. 12 Powis pl. Havstk. hl
Simpson John W. esq. 3 Churchyd. ct. Tmpl
Simpson Jsph. esq. 11 Argyle sq. King's cr
Simpson Miss, 17 Newington pl. Kenngtn
Simpson Mrs. 19 Alexander sq. Brompton
Simpson Mrs. 7 Glo'ster road, Hyde pk
Simpson Mrs. 47 Lower Belgrave place
Simpson Mrs. 45 Mecklenburgh square
Simpson Mrs. 13 Mornington crescent
Simpson Mrs. 42 Oxford terrace

Simpson Mrs. 3 Portman st. Portman sq
Simpson Mrs. 47 Windsor ter. City rd
Simpson Palgrave, esq. 27 Guilford st. & 19 Bartlett's buildings, Holborn
Simpson Percy, esq. 5 Mitre ct. chambers
Simpson Pinder, esq. 24 Cambridge terrace, Edgware road, & 29 Saville row
Simpson Robert, esq. 45 Beaumont st
Simpson Thomas, esq. 17 Lonsdale sq
Simpson Thomas, esq. 9 Notting hill ter
Simpson Thomas B. esq. E6, Albany
Simpson W. esq. Belgrave road, Pimlico
Simpson Wm. esq. 4 High st. Bloomsbury
Simpson Wm. C. esq. 8 Lr. Belgrave pl
Simpson William Woolley, esq. 8 Montague place, Russell square
Sims Davis, esq. 29 Lr. Kennington la
Sims Hen. Chas. esq. 7 Angel ter. Pntvnl
Sims Mrs. 13 Pelham cresc. Fulham road
Sims Rt. esq. 2 Albion pl. Canonbury sq
Simson Rev. Robt. 3 Colebrooke rw. Islgn
Simson Alexander, esq. 8 Highbury pk
Simson Mrs. 39 Bernard st. Russell sq
Simson Mrs. 67 Sloane st
Simson William, esq. 15 Cork st. Bond st
Simson William, esq. 12 Sloane st
Sinclair Lord, United Service Club; & Herdmanstown, Haddington; & Torquay, Devonshire
Sinclair Capt. Charles, 13 Bruton st
Sinclair Venble. Archdeacon John, M.A. Rectory, Vicarage place, Kensington
Sinclair Mrs. 6 Beaufoy ter. Edgware rd
Sinclair Wm. esq. 42 Gerrard st. Soho
Sindall Mrs. 16 Notting hill terrace
Sinderby Miss, 168 Albany st. Regt.'s pk
Sindrey Mrs. 31 Harleyford pl. Kenng.com
Singer G. esq. 12 Prospect pl. Wandsw.rd
Singer Miss, 20 Upper Montague st
Singer Samuel Weller, esq. 7 Upper Belmont place, Wandsworth road
Singleton Lady Mary, 17 Sussex place
Singleton Chas. esq. 130 St. John st. rd
Singleton Cuthbert, esq. 21 Gt. James st
Singleton J. esq. & Hon. Mrs. 6 Wilton cres
Singleton Miss, 2 Dean's yd. Westminster
Singleton Mrs. 2 Dorset st. Portman sq
Sinkins Jn. esq. 10 Charles st. Manch.sq
Sintzenich Edwd. R. esq. 31 Grosvenor st. & the Elms, Ashford, nr. Chertsey
Sintzenich G.E. esq. 3 Princes st. Fitzy.sq
Sisk Rev. Thos. Chapel ho. Cadogan ter
Sismey Thomas, esq. 11 Serjeants' inn
Sissmore Col. B. 1 Norland ter. Notg. hl
Sisson C. esq. 4 Minerva pl. Barnsby. pk.
Sisson J. esq. 12 Belmont ter. Wandsw.rd
Sisson Miss, 32 Allsop terrace, New road
Sisson William, esq. 46 Leicester square
Sitwell Edwd. Degg, esq. 41 Wigmore st
Sivewright Mrs. 23 Montagu square, & Blakesley, Northamptonshire
Sivrac Charles A. G. esq. 8 St. Martin's pl
Skardon John, esq. 11 Victoria rd. Pimlco
Skeel David, esq. 42 Norfolk st. Strand
Skeel Thos. esq. 42 Norfolk st. Strand
Skeet Chas. esq. 4 Dorset st. Portmn. sq
Skeet Robert, esq. 4 Dorset st. Portman square, & 16 Furnival's inn
Skeet Robert, esq. Hill rd. Abbey rd
Skegg Robert, esq. 2 St. Martin's place
Skegg Wm. Harper, esq. 39 Brudenell pl
Skekel Capt. J. 36 Pembroke sq. Knsngtn
Skelding Thomas, esq. 11 Euston square
Skelmersdale Lord, 55 Portland place, & Latham house, Ormskirk
Skelton Benj. F. esq. 1 Bath ter. St. Geo's.e
Skelton John D. esq. 11 Clement's inn
Skelton Mrs. 5 Suffolk pl. Haymarket
Skelton Misses, 14 St. John's wood road
Skelton Miss, 32 London st. Fitzroy st
Skerrett Jas. esq. 43 Smith st. Chelsea
Skey Fred. Chas. esq. 13 Grosvenor st
Skillbeck John Jsph. esq. 15 Highbury pl
Skilbeck Wm. esq. 19 Southampton bldgs. & 15 Highbury pl. Islington
Skingley Geo. D. esq. 19 Sackville st
Skinner Rev. John, 8 Ebrenburg terrace
Skinner Allan M. esq. 1 Pump ct. Temple
Skinner D. esq. 11 Sebbons bldgs. Islngtn
Skinner Fitzowen, esq. 25 Keppel st. & 1 New square, Lincoln's inn
Skinner Hy. esq. 12 Glo'ster cr. Rgt.'s pk
Skinner Mrs. 15 Burton crescent
Skinner Mrs. 35 Hunter st. Brunswk sq
Skinner Mrs. 44 Southampton row
Skinner Mrs. 15 Hemus terrace, Chelsea
Skinner Saml. esq. 31 Norfolk crs. Hy. pk
Skinner T. esq. 18 Annett's cres. Islgtn
Skinner T. esq. 3 Comptn. st. ea. Brunk. sq
Skipper Charles, esq. 28 Russell square
Skipper T. esq. 12 Campden hill villas
Skipwith Lionel, esq. 15 Regent st
Skipworth Geo. B. esq. 8 New sq. Linc.'s in
Skirrow Charles F. esq. Eldon chambers, Devereux court, Strand
Skirrow Chas. Fras. esq. 11 Bedford row
Skirrow Walker, jun. esq. 3 Pump ct. Tmpl
Skottowe A. esq. 42 Pembroke sq. Kngstn
Skottowe Mrs. Barn cotge. O. Brompton
Skottowe Mrs. 16 Somers pl. Oxford sq
Skrine Hen. esq. 48 Green st. Grosvenor sq.; Feltham, Bognor, Sussex; Stubbings ho. Maidenhead; & Warleigh, nr. Bath
Skrine Wm. esq. 68 Glo'ster pl. Ptmn. sq
Skurray Francis, esq. 12 Stanhope pl
Skynner Hy. esq. 46 Gt. Portland st
Skynner Miss, 2 Connaught square
Skynner Robert, esq. 42 Mortimer st
Skynner Wm. Hy. sen. esq. 75 Gt. Tichfield st. & 42 Mortimer st. Cavendish sq
Slack Wm. G. esq. 10 Union st. Berkly. sq
Slade Fredc. Wm. esq. 2 Cadogan place, & 2 Pump ct. Temple
Slade Frederick Wm. esq. 2 Cadogan pl
Slade Miss, 6 Alfred pl. Bedford square
Slade Rd. esq. 1 Glo'ster st. Portmn. sq
Slade Steph. esq. 8 Argyll st. Regnt. st
Slade Wm. esq. Walcot pl. east, Lmbth
Slade Wm. B. esq. 2 Foregate, Clemnt.'s in
Sladen St. Barbe, esq. 6 South terrace, Brompton, & 14 Parliament st
Slaney William Henry, esq. 16, Albany, & 13 Gray's inn square
Slate Jno. esq. 14 Belmont pl. Wands.rd
Slater Edw. esq. 31 York bldgs. New rd
Slater Jph. esq. 33 London st. Fitzroy sq
Slater Mrs. 48 George st. Euston square
Slater Mrs. 66 Hermitage pl. St. Jn.'s st.rd
Slater Mrs. 2 Old Dorset pl. Clapham rd
Slater Mrs. 4 Ranelagh grove
Slater S. M. esq. 2 Paulton's sq. Chelsea
Slater Wm. esq. Larkhall lane, Clapham
Slaton John, esq. 95 Guilford st
Slaughter E. esq. 5 Duchess st. Portld. pl
Sleap John Gifford, esq. 65 Hermitage place, St. John street road
Sleap Jonathan T. esq. 2 Mid. Temple la
Sleath Rev. Dr. 4 Hertford st. Mayfair
Sledge Thomas, esq. 36 Clapham rd. pl
Slee Thos. esq. Larkhall lane, Clapham
Sleigh John, esq. 25 Mary st. Hampstd.rd
Sligo Marquis of, 2 Mansfield street, & Westport, Ireland
Slingsby Sir Charles, 40 Upper Brook st
Slingsby Miss, 40 Upper Brook st
Slingsby Mrs. 40 Upper Brook st
Sloane Geo. esq. 6 Pump court, Temple
Sloane John, esq. 21 Northumberland st
Sloane William, esq. 37 Wimpole st
Slodden Thomas, esq. 35 Beaumont st
Sloman Henry, esq. 2 Kennington ter
Sloman Mrs. Stoke Newington green
Sloper John W. esq. 6 Vernon pl. Blmsby
Slough T. esq. 10 Southampton st. Strnd
Slous Fred. L. esq. 11 Crescent pl. Ham.rd
Slouse Gideon, esq. 1 Oval rd. Regt.'s pk
Slyfield Hen. esq. 14 Milbank st. Wesmr
Smale Henry, esq. 34 Fitzroy square
Smale John, esq. 1 New square, Lincoln's inn, & Highgate
Smale Thos. jun. esq. 187 High Holborn
Smale Wm. Adderley, esq. 30 Arundel st
Small Mrs. 22 Bedford pl. Russell sq
Small Robert, esq. 26 Devonshire st
Small Robert, esq. 37 York terrace, Regent's park, & Beaulieu, Hastings
Smallbone G. esq. Albion rd. Stk. Newgtn
Smalley Rev. C. 12 Orme's sq. Bayswtr
Smalley Miss, 2 Southend cot. Bayswtr
Smart Sir Geo. knt. 91 Gt. Portland st
Smart Ben. Humph. esq. 55 Connaught ter
Smart Charles esq. 1 Gray's inn square
Smart James, esq. 3 Furnival's inn
Smart Jno. esq. 5 Montague street, Russell square, & 56 Lincoln's inn fields
Smart John, esq. 3 North pl. Hampstd rd
Smart Mrs. 7 Sebbons buildings, Islngtn
Smart Robert King, esq. 38 Sloane sq
Smart Wm. esq. 2 Figtree court, Temple
Smartt Thos. L. esq. 25 Sun st. Bishopsg
Smedley Francis, esq. 40 Jermyn st
Smedmor Mrs. 35 New st. Dorset sq
Smee Capt. 61 Baker st. Portman sq
Smee Alfred, esq. 7 Finsbury circus
Smeeton Thos. esq. 168 St. John street rd
Smellie Jas. M.D. 42 Brewer st. Somers tn
Smethurst Mrs. 12 Oxford sq. Hyde pk
Smethurst John, esq. 18 Mornington pl
Smidt Percy, esq. 36 Glo'ster cres. Rgt.'s pk
Smiley Wm. Rt. esq. 47 Hertford st. Mayfa
Smirke Sir Robert, Royal Academy, Trafalgar square, & Stanmore
Smirke Ed. esq. West cot. Bedfd. pl. Knsgt
Smirke Ed. esq. 3 (nth.) King's Bench wk
Smirke Miss, 3 St. John's wood grove
Smirke Sidney, esq. 24 Berkeley sq
Smith Sir Benjamin, knt. 312 Regent st
Smith Rt. Hon. Rt. Vernon, M.P. 20 Saville row, & Farmingwoods, nr. Thrapstone
Smith Rt. Hon. Thomas, B. C. M.P. 19 Eaton sq. Pimlico, & 8 Merrion square, Dublin
Smith Lady, 29 Oxford square
Smith Lady, 21 Pelham crsnt. Fulham rd
Smith Major, 9 Park pl. Regent's park
Smith Col. 34 Thurloe sq. Old Brompton
Smith Capt. 19 Cavendish rd. St. Jn.'s wd
Smith Capt. T. 18 New Suffolk st. Com.rd.e
Smith Capt. Timothy, 68 Cambridge ter
Smith Rev. C. A. J. A.M. 14 Mount place, Whitechapel road
Smith Rev. Jas. 5 Brunswick ter. Dovr.rd
Smith Rev. Jn. C. 15 Motcomb st. Belgr.sq
Smith Rev. Jno. James, 12 Hereford st
Smith Rev. Richd. Soden, 12 Hereford st
Smith Rev. Saml. 129 Camden rd. villas
Smith Rev. Theyre T. 13 Notting hill sq
Smith Abel, M.P. 39 Berkeley square, & Woodhall park, near Ware
Smith Albert, esq. 14 Percy st
Smith Andrew, M.D. 7 Pelham crescent
Smith Archbd. esq. 25 Old sq. Lincoln's inn
Smith Arthur, esq. 1 Grove ter. Kenth.tn
Smith Arthur, esq. 58 Lincoln's inn flds
Smith Attwood Hy. esq. 8 Park pl. Padngtn. & 108 Dorset st. Salisbury square
Smith A. H. esq. 108 Dorset st. Salsby. sq
Smith Benjamin, M.P. 5 Blandford square, & Hastings
Smith Benjn. esq. 41 Canonbury square
Smith Chas. esq. 29 Charles st. St. James
Smith Chas. esq. 6 Middle Temple lane
Smith Chas. esq. 31 Osnaburgh st. Rg. pk
Smith Chas. esq. Park cottage, Acacia rd
Smith Charles, esq. 8 Queen Charlotte row, New rd. & 37 Gloucester pl. New rd
Smith Charles, esq. 19 Russell square
Smith Charles, esq. 17 Nottingham st
Smith Charles, esq. 1 Surrey st. Strand
Smith Chas. esq. 30 Tavistock st. Cov.gdn
Smith Charles C. esq. 22 Arlington st
Smith C. H. esq. 5 Thurloe pl. we. O. Brmptn
Smith Charles Henry, esq. 13 Duke st. Manch. sq.; & 32 North bank, Reg. pk
Smith Chas. D. esq. 5 Terrace, Gr.'s in. la
Smith Chas. M. esq. 61 Lincoln's inn flds
Smith Chas. R. esq. 37 Glo'ster pl. New rd
Smith Christ. esq. 29 Carter st. Walwth

SmithChrist.esq.13Up.North pl.Gr.'s in.r
Smith Clement, esq. 28 Colebrk. rw. Islg
Smith David, esq. 7 Mabledon place
Smith David. S. esq. 8 Devonshire st
Smith Duncan, esq. 5 Wilmington sq
Smith Edward, esq. 2 Barnsbury park
Smith Edward, esq. 9 Tyndale place, Islington, & 5 Chancery lane
Smith Edw. esq. 2 Chester pl.Rgnt.'s pk
Smith Edward, esq. 2 Copthall court
Smith Edw.esq.9Pelham cres.Fulham rd
Smith Edw. esq. 26 Sussex grdns. Hi.pk
Smith Edwin, esq. 12 Gray's inn place
Smith Edwin D. esq. 7 Hertfrd.st.Mayfr
Smith E. esq. Ecclesbl. cot.Morningtn.rd
Smith Francis, esq. 14 Furnival's inn
Smith Francis, esq. 27 Mortimer st
Smith Fras. Redhead, esq. 17 Bethnal green east side, & 6 Barnard's inn
Smith Frederick Garle, esq. 37 Cornhill
Smith Fred. Thomas, esq. 32 Sloane sq
Smith Fredk. Jas. esq. 1 New ct. Tmple
Smith Fred. Wickings, esq.63 Linc.inn fi
Smith George, esq. 4 Stone bldgs. Lincoln's inn, & 27 Norfolk cres. Hyde pk
Smith Geo. esq. 3 Bennett st. St. James's
Smith. George, esq.12 Canterbury villas, Edgware road, & 5 Southampton bdgs
Smith George, esq. 24 Golden square
Smith George, esq. 15 Park pl. vil. Padn
Smith George, esq. 15 Gillingham st
Smith Geo. A. esq. 5 Upper Hyde park st
Smith Geo. Fred. esq. 15 Golden square
Smith Geo. Jas. P. esq. 12 Hereford st. Park lane, & 1 King's Bench walk
Smith Geo. Morgan, esq. 28 Golden sq
Smith Geo. Robt. esq. 4 Gt. Cumberland pl. & Selsden, near Croydon, Surrey
Smith Geo. S. esq.17 Henrietta st.Cav.sq
Smith Geo.S.esq.85 Baker st.Portman sq
Smith George W. esq. 17 Bloomsbury sq
Smith Hen. esq. 97 Camden road villas
Smith Hen. esq. 107 Camden road villas
Smith Hen. esq.2 Portsmouth st.Linc.in
Smith Hy.esq. 17Henrietta st. Cavdh. sq
Smith Henry, esq. 67 Torrington sq
Smith Henry, esq.53 Trinity sq.Borough
Smith Henry Jsph. esq. 12 Hereford st
Smith Hy. Nelson, esq. 18 Gt. Russell st
Smith Hy. P.esq.3 Crescent, N.Bridge st
Smith Hy. Smith, esq. 80 New Bond st
Smith Hy. Stone, esq.3 Smith sq.Westmr
Smith Hy. Valentine, esq. 37 Golden sq
Smith Herbert, esq. 2 Sloane ter.Chelsea
Smith Hugh, esq. 3 Bedford row
Smith Hugh Wallis, esq. 19 Old square
Smith Isaac, esq. 5 Albany vil.Lvrpl. rd
Smith Jas. esq. 30 Alfred pl. Bedford sq
Smith Jas. esq. 22 Margaret st
Smith Jas.esq. 1 Prospect cot.Thornhl.rd
Smith Jas. esq. (of Deanston) 13 Queen square, Westminster
Smith Jas. esq. 5 Retreat, Sth Lambeth
Smith Jas. esq. 14 Soho square
Smith Jas. B. esq. 7 Cleveland st.Fitz.sq
Smith James Bogle, esq. Wandsworth rd
Smith Jas. Wm. esq. 8 Chester ter. Regent's park, & 48 Lincoln's inn fields
Smith Jas.Wm.esq.14Montagu pl.Clphm
Smith J.esq.Elm tree ho.13 Havrstck. hl
Smith John, esq. 1 Field ct. Gray's inn
Smith John, esq. 3 Gt. Percy st
Smith John, esq. 7 Highbury grange
Smith John, esq. 11 King's bench walk, Temple, & Newhouse, Sutton Coldfield
Smith John, esq. 74 Oxford terrace
Smith John, esq. 5 Porchester terrace
Smith John, esq. 37 Regent square
Smith John, esq. 2 St. Mary Abbotts ter
Smith John, esq. 16 Spencer ter. Islgtn
Smith John, esq. 9 Spring gardens
Smith John Abel, esq. M.P. 47 Belgrave sq. & Dale park, Arundel
Smith John Bell, esq. 10 Sackville st
Smith Jn.E.esq.40Newngtn.pl.Kenngt.rd
Smith JohnF.esq.6 Albion gr.Barnsby.rd
Smith John H. esq. 1 Blandford st
Smith John Henry, esq. 26 Spring gardens, & Heathfield lodge, Croydon
Smith John Hood, esq. 4 Wyndham pl
Smith John J. esq. 17 Haverstock hill
Smith John Shaw, esq. 41 Chester ter
Smith John Spry, esq. 9 Woburn square
Smith John T. esq.51 East st. Manch.sq
Smith J.V.esq. 1 Vassal cot.Addisn.rd.so
Smith John Wm. esq. 2 Mitre crt. bldgs
Smith J. W. B.esq. 1 Plowden bdgs.Tem
Smith Joseph, esq. 1 Field ct. Gray's inn
Smith Joseph, esq. 6 Finsbury terrace
Smith Joseph, esq. 21 Holloway place
Smith Jsph. esq. 12 Marshall st. Gldn.sq
Smith Josiah William, esq. 8 Old sq
Smith Kennard,esq.2 Chapel st.Prtlnd.pl
Smith L. esq. 19 Hanover cot. Regt's.pk
Smith M. esq.40Gordon sq.&5 Berners st
Smith Martin T. esq. 13 Up. Belgrave st
Smith Miss, 30 Alfred st. Bedford sq
Smith Miss, 27 Beaufort st. Chelsea
Smith Miss, 42 Beaumont st. Portland pl
Smith Miss, 6 Chester pl. Regent's park
Smith Miss, 6 Eaton square, Pimlico
Smith Miss, 23 Friedenstein ter. Reg.pk
Smith Miss, 9 Green st. Grosvenor sq
Smith Miss, 1 Halfmoon st. Piccadilly
Smith Miss, 22 Hunter st. Brunswick sq
Smith Miss, 3 Rufford's row, Islington
Smith Miss, 48 Weymouth st. Portld. pl
Smith Mrs. 3 Aston place, Holloway
Smith Mrs. 10 Avenue rd. Regent's pk
Smith Mrs. 2 Barrow hill pl. Regt's. pk
Smith Mrs. 16 Beaufort st. Chelsea
Smith Mrs. 19 Bedford place, Kensingtn
Smith Mrs. 10 Brompton row
Smith Mrs. 21 Charterhouse square
Smith Mrs. 9 Chapel st. Grosvenor place
Smith Mrs. 7 Coleshill st
Smith Mrs. 20 Connaught ter. Edgw. rd
Smith Mrs. 24 Craven st. Strand
Smith Mrs. 3 Eaton place, Belgrave sq
Smith Mrs. 49 Edgware road
Smith Mrs. Elm cottage, O. Bromptn.rd
Smith Mrs. 37 Glo'ster st. Queen sq
Smith Mrs. 56 Green st. Grosvenor sq
Smith Mrs. 10 Henrietta st. Brunsw. sq
Smith Mrs. 1 Hollywood pl. Lit. Chelsea
Smith Mrs. 4 Hyde park place, west
Smith Mrs. 11 Mabledon pl. Burton cres
Smith Mrs 8Montague pl. Noel st.Islgtn
Smith Mrs. 10 Mornington crescent
Smith Mrs. 16 Mornington crescent
Smith Mrs. 39 New Bond st
Smith Mrs.1 Osnaburgh ter. Regent's pk
Smith Mrs. 24 Norfolk street, Park lane, & Birstead lodge, Bognor, Sussex
Smith Mrs. 2 Park ter. Regent's park
Smith Mrs. 5 Park ter. Regent's park
Smith Mrs. 6 Pelham pl. Fulham rd
Smith Mrs. 6 Portland place, & Mapledurham, Reading
Smith Mrs. 7 Scarsdale ter. Kensington
Smith Mrs. 94 Sloane street
Smith Mrs. 37 Sussex gardens, Hyde pk
Smith Mrs. 3 Swan walk, Chelsea
Smith Mrs. 13 Tavistock pl. Russell sq
Smith Mrs. 5 & 6 Tenterden st. Hanvr. sq
Smith Mrs. 25 Trevor square
Smith Mrs. 1 Upper Seymour st. west
Smith Mrs. 20 Upper Southwick street
Smith Mrs. 94 Wimpole street
Smith Mrs. J. C. 28 Brompton square
Smith Mrs. James, 28 Southampton row
Smith Mrs. Joseph, 12 Hereford street
Smith Mrs. N. 38 Glo'ster st. Queen sq
Smith Mrs. Phillis, 8 Albion st. Hyde pk
Smith Mrs. Thos. 10 Mornington crescnt
Smith Mrs.Tower, 8 John st. Berkeley sq
Smith Montague E. esq. 3 Paper bldgs
Smith Octavius H. esq. Thames bank
Smith Percy Robert, esq. 20 Saville row & Cheam, near Epsom
Smith Peter, esq. 11 Hornton st. Kensgtn
Smith Peter, esq. 2 Finchley new road
Smith Pillett, esq.5Terrace, Gray's in. la
Smith Protheroe, esq. 15 Jhn. st. Bdfd.rw
Smith Ralph C. esq. 9 New sq. Linc. inn
Smith Richard esq. 44 Berners street
Smith Rd. esq. 57 Guilford st. Russ. sq
Smith Rd. esq. 12Harpur st.&67Chanc.la
Smith Rd. esq. Lark hall rise, Clapham
Smith Richard, esq. 162 New Bond st
Smith Rich. jun.esq.27 Baker st. Lloyd sq
Smith Rd. sen. esq. 29 Baker st. Lloyd sq
Smith Rd.Edgar,esq.12Serjnt.'s in.Flt.st
Smith Robert, esq. 2 Percy circus
Smith Robt. esq. 10 Green's rw. Chelsea
Smith Robert, esq. 8 Hunter st
Smith Robert, esq. 2 Lombard st
Smith Robert, esq. 29 Myddelton sq
Smith Rt. esq. 15 Percy st. Bedford sq
Smith Rt. Edwd. esq. 20 Endsleigh st
Smith Robert George, esq. 7 Lower Eaton st. & 5 New inn, Strand
Smith Sam. esq. Elm cot. Thames bank
Smith Sam. esq. 17 Hyde park gardens
Smith Samuel, esq. 6 Whitehall
Smith Sebastian, esq. 1 Connght. pl. west
Smith Seth, esq. 33 Eaton square
Smith Sidney, esq. 68 St. John's wood terrace, & 8 Barnards' inn
Smith Sidney esq. 3 Noel st. Islington
Smith Sidney, esq. 10 Woburn square
Smith S. esq. 9Providence pl.Up.Ken.lan
Smith Spencer, esq. 6 Portland place, & Bocklings, near Southampton
Smith Strother, esq. 12 George st. Eus.sq
Smith T.esq.4Dorset pl.NorthClaphm.rd
Smith Thomas esq. 15 Furnival's inn
Smith Thos. esq. 15 Maddox st. Regnt. st
Smith Thomas, esq. Woodfield villa, Queen's road, St. John's wood
Smith Thos. Assheton, esq. 13 Hyde park gardens, & Tedworth, Andover; & Vaynol house, Bangor
Smith Thomas Chas. esq. 23 Hanover sq
Smith Thos.C.esq.8 Duke st. St. James's
Smith Thos.C.esq.5King'sBnch.wk.Tmp
Smith T.G.esq.7Dorchestr.pl.N.Northrd
Smith Thos. Geo. esq. 29 Doughty st
Smith Thos. Geo. esq. 24 Montague st
Smith Thos.H.esq.7A,Miltn.st.Dorset sq
Smith Thos. W. esq. Chapel pl. Westmr
SmithThos.Southwood, M.D.38 Fnsbry.sq
Smith Toulmin, esq. 12 King's bench wk
Smith Toulmin J. esq. 1 Hare ct. Temple
Smith Turberville, esq. 9 Gt.Marlboro' st
Smith Tyler, esq. 9 Bolton st
Smith Vincent, esq. 5 Hyde park terr. Kensington gore,&5Stone blds. Linc.in
Smith Wade,esq.16Avenue rd.Rgnt.'s pk
Smith Walter, esq. 9 St. Mildred's court
Smith Wm. esq. Adelaide cot. Adelaide road, Haverstock hill
Smith Wm. LL.D. 16 Barnsbury villas
Smith Wm. esq. 2 Bedford square
Smith Wm. esq. 1 Canonbury pk. Islgtn
Smith Wm. esq. 21 Charlotte st. Fitz.sq
Smith Wm. esq. 9 Connaught square
Smith Wm. esq. 2 Francis st. Golden sq
Smith Wm. esq. 11 Holland pl. Claph.rd
Smith Wm. esq. Larkhall rise, Clapham
Smith Wm. esq. 103 St. Martin's lane, & Hampstead
Smith Wm. esq. 2 Torrington st. Russ. sq
Smith Wm. esq. 20 Upper Southwick st
Smith Wm. esq. 4 Woodland pl.St.Jn.wd
Smith Wm. Bowyer, esq.29Up.Grosvr.st
Smith Wm.C.esq.12 Hereford st. Park la
Smith Wm. Hen.esq.10Adam st.Adelphi
Smith Wm. Hen. esq. 12 Bedford row
Smith Wm. Hen. esq. 76 Harley st
Smith Wm. Hen. esq. 27 Norfolk crscnt
Smith Wm. H. LL.D. New sq. Lincoln's inn, & 37 Myddelton sq
Smith Wm. Henry, esq. 23 Russell sq
Smith Wm.W.esq.24Fortess tr.Knsh.tn
Smith Wm. W. esq. 16 Sthmpt. st. Blmb
Smithe Wm. F. esq. 46 Lincoln's inn flds
Smithers Mrs. 22 Doughty st

Smithies Mrs. 14 Compton st. east
Smithyman Mrs. 2 Brompton row
Smollett Alexr. M.P. 43 Pall mall, & Cameron house, Dumbarton
Smowton Wm. esq. 4 New Millman st
Smyth Lady Carmichael, 40 Sussex gds
Smyth Lady Elizabeth, 96 Eaton square
Smyth Sir Edwd. Bowyer, bart. 9 Grosvenor square; & Hill hall, Epping; & Attleborough hall, Norfolk
Smyth Sir George Henry, bart. M.P. 1 George st. Hanover square, & Berechurch hall, Colchester
Smyth Capt. J. W. 10 Up. Porchester st
Smyth Capt. W. H. R.N. Somerset house
Smyth Edward, esq. 85 Newman st
Smyth George, esq. 43 Sackville st
Smyth Geo. Lewis, esq.2 Derby st.Wstm
Smyth James Richd. M.D. 43 Sackville st. & Cross, near Londonderry
Smyth John George, esq. & Hon. Mrs. 17 Lowndes square
Smyth Leigh C. esq. 6 Ehrenburg ter. Regent's park, & 18 Carey st
Smyth Miss, 32 Charles st. Berkley sq
Smyth Miss, 6 Lower Phillimore pl
Smyth Mrs. Watson, 25 Eaton pl
Smythe Hn.Geo.A.F.P.S.M.P.68 Hrly.st
Smythe Capt. R.N.3 Cheyne wk.Chelsea
Smythe Owen Mrs. 9 Gt. Cumberland st
Smythe Mrs. 6 Great Cumberland pl
Smythe Thos. esq. 49 Chancery lane
Smythe Wm. esq. 22 John st.Bedford rw
Smythe Wm. Mead, esq. 47 Up.Brook st
Smythies Charles, esq. 20 Hereford st. & Villa François, Colchester, Essex
Smythies John K. esq. 35 Sthmptn.bldgs
Smythies Mrs. Wm. 19½ Tavistock sq
Snape Rt. Jas. esq. 12 Paper bldgs.Tmp
Snee Edmund L. esq. 15 Colebrooke rw
Snee Frederick, esq. 21 Canonbury villas
Snee John Adolphus, esq.13Grenville st. Brunswick sq. & 3 Brick ct. Temple
Snee Mrs.12Northampton pl.Canonby.sq
Snelgar Homer, esq. 48 Myddleton sq
Snelgar William, esq. 4 Percy circus
Snell George B. esq. 14 Abingdon st. Westminster, & 36 Chancery lane
Snell Wm. esq. 48 Eaton square
Snell Wm. Philip, esq. Carlton chambers, 8 Regent st
Snelling Jas. esq. 3 Queen's hd. rw. Isln
Snelling Mrs. 7 New Ormond st
Snelling Richd.esq.22East st.RedLion sq
Snewin Chas. esq. 32 Baker st. Lloyd sq
Sneyd Mrs.6 Glo'ster rd.Vic.gt.Hyde pk
Snipe Mrs. 10 Southampton row, New rd
Snitch Charles James, esq. 33 Brydges st
Snook Mrs. 132 London wall
Snoulton O. esq. 31 Sussex pl. Kensingtn
Snow John, esq. 54 Frith st. Soho
Snow Jsph.esq.12Hanvr. cotgs.Rgt.'s pk
Snow Mrs. 9 Saville row, Piccadilly
Snow Paul Robt. esq.7 Lr. Grosvenor pl
Snow Robt. esq. 9 Saville row, Piccadilly
Soady Brooking, esq. 5 Hamilton place, St. John's wood, & Audit office
Soady Rt. Williams, esq. 46 St. John's wood terrace, & 5 New square
Soames Geo. esq. 15 Euston pl. New rd
Soames Jas. esq. 14 Titchfield terrace
Soames Jsph. esq. 38z, Park st. Grov. sq
Soare Chas. esq. Manor pl. so. Chelsea
Soares Manuel, esq. 36 Fitzroy square
Soden Jas. Benj. esq. 25 Canonbury vill
Sola Alfred, esq. 21 Charlotte st
Sola Chas.M.esq.21Charlotte st.Fitzy.sq
Solari Mrs. 13 Belmont pl. Wandswth. rd
Sole William Charles, esq. 31 Oxford terrace, & 68 Aldermanbury
Solly Edward, esq. 38 Bedford row
Solly Richard H. esq. 48 Gt. Ormond st
Solly Samuel, esq. 48 Upper Gower st
Solomon Aaron, esq. 23 Bevis marks
Solomon Henry, esq. 73 Leman st
Solomon Joel Woolf, esq. 1 Strand
Solomon Miss, 8 Finsbury circus
Solomon Morrice, esq. 16 Mansell st
Solomon Moses E. esq. 22 Mansell st
Solomons Abra. esq. 22 Claremont ter
Solomons Benj. esq. 39 Albemarle st
Solomons Coleman, esq. 2 Haydon sq
Solomons Samuel, esq. 39 Albemarle st
Solomons Mich. Moses, esq. 13 Euston sq
Somers Earl,45Grosvenor place; & Eastnor castle, Tewkesbury; & Priory, Reigate
Somers Dowager Countess, 28 Norfolk st
Somers J. P. M.P. Reform club, & Sligo
Somerset, Duke of, K.G. Park lane; & Bradley house, Mere, Wilts; & Stobec house, Newton Abbot
Somerset Ld. Fitzroy, 5 Gt. Stanhope st
Somerset Rt. Hon. Lord Granville Chas. Henry, M.P. 8 Clarges st
Somerset Lord John, 69 Glo'ster place
Somerset Lady Charles, 132 Piccadilly
Somerset Arthur E. esq.3 Pump ct.Tmpl
Somerset A. E. esq. 9 King st. St. James'
Somerton Viscount, M.P. 3 Seamore pl. Mayfair, & Somerley, nr. Ringwood
Somervail Charles Rt. esq. 40 Argyle st
Somerville Lord, the hall, Berkhampstd
Somerville Sir William Meredyth, bart. M.P. Somerville, near Ashbourne, Ireland
Somerville Capt. 2 Park rd. Notting hll
Somerville J. C. esq. 11 Lincoln's inn flds
Somerville Mrs. 2 Taunton place
Somes Fredk. esq. 15 Highbury park
Sondes Lord, 18 St. James's sq.; & Elmham, Dereham, Norfolk; & Leeds court, Kent
Sonper Thos. E. esq. 3 Savoy st. Strand
Soper Ebenezer, esq. 14 Gibson square
Sophia H.R.H. Princess, Vicarage place, Kensington
Sotheby Capt. R.N. 16 Manchester sq
Sotheby Misses, 3 Portugal st. Grosv. sq
Sotherby Mrs. 14 Cadogan terrace
Sotheron Thomas Henry Sutton, esq. M.P. 51 Eaton place, & Bowden park, near Chippenham
Sotomayor Duke of, Spanish minister, 30 Weymouth st
Soul Joseph, esq. 20 Brunswick parade
Soulsby John, esq. 18 Essex st. Strand
Soundy Henry, esq. 2 Circus, Minories
South Sir James, knt. Observatory, Campden hill, Kensington
South Rev. Robt. King Edward st. City
South Miss, 236A, Maida vale, Edgwr.rd
South Anthony, esq. 24 Avenue road
South Thos. esq. 8 Judd st. & 6½ Hunter st. Brunswick square
South Wm. esq. 1 Alpha rd. Regent's pk
Southam Hy. esq.17 Berwick st. Pimlico
Southampton Lord, 66 Mount st. & Whittlebury lodge, Towcester
Southcombe Miss, 45 Pembroke square
Southee Robert, esq. 16 Ely pl. Holborn
Southeland John, esq. 11 South bank
Southern Thos. esq. 12 Tibberton square
Southey Geo. esq. 5 Waterloo, Kilburn
Southey Henry Herbert, M.D. 1 Harley st
Southey Misses, 19 Torrington square
Southey Pearce, esq. 11 Kilburn priory
Southey Thos. esq. 23 Compt. ter. Islgn
Southey Thos. esq. 2 Wharncliff terr
Southgate Ephm.esq.7Up. Baker st.Pnvl
Southgate F. T. esq. 10 Gray's inn place
Southgate Thos. esq. 89 Chancery lane
Southwell Mrs. 13 Brooksby st.Lvrpl.rd
Southwood Walter, esq. 30 Somerset st. & 13 Maida hill, Edgware road
Southwood Wm.esq.8Charles pl.York rd
Soward J. jun.esq. 1 Bedford st.Bedfd.sq
Sowell Benj.Lawrence, esq. 109Regent st
Sowerby Colonel, 11 North Audley st
Sowerby Col. Thomas, 44 Wilton cresent
Sowerby James de Carle, esq. Botanic garden, inner circle, Regent's park
Sowerby Mrs. 11 Bolton st. Piccadilly
Sowray Geo. esq. 69 Ebury st. Pimlico
Sowter Jas. esq. 2 Palmer ter. Holloway
Sowton James, esq. 27 Great James st
Sowton W.March, esq. 6 King's Bench w
SpaethChas.Benj.esq. 126 Camden rd.vil
Spaibam Henry M. esq. 123 Chancery la
Spain Mrs.F.5Cunningham pl.St.Jn.'swd
Spalding Hy. esq. Fortress ter.Kntsh.tn
Spalding T. esq. 6 Fortress ter.Kntsh.tn
Spall John, esq. 27 Cloudesley terrace
Spankie Mrs. 36 Russell square
SparkeG.Y.esq. 11 Warwick ct.Gry.'s in
Sparkes Charles, esq. 16 Aberdeen pl
Sparks Joseph, esq. 2 Thavies inn
Sparks Jsph.esq.3Low.John st.Golden sq
Sparrow Lady Olivia, 22 Dover st
Sparrow Mrs. 32 Alfred pl. Bedford. sq
Sparrow Mrs. 9 Stafford row, Pimlico
Sparrow Mrs. 10 Park pl. Up. Baker st
Sparshot Capt. E. R.N. 12 Elm ter.Chels
SparshottCapt.R.N. Marlboro'rd.StJ.wd
Spawforth B.esq. 6 Rochester sq.Cam.rd
Spawforth G. B. esq. 2 Tollington park
Spear John, esq. 31Park rd. Regent's pk
Spearman Sir Alex. Y. 38 Grosvenor pl
Spedding Jas.esq. 60 Lincoln's inn fields
Speed John, esq. 22Soley terrace, Pentnvl
Speed Joseph, esq. 17 Grafton st. east
Speed Wm. esq. 92 Camden road villas
Speed William, esq. 9 New square, & 92 Camden vil. Camden New town
Speer Edward, esq. 7 John st. Adelphi
Speer E.esq.Ashley vil.Qn.'s rd.St.Jn's w
Speight Mrs. 6 Philpott ter. Edgware rd
SpellerNewman, esq.6Stanhopepl.Hy.pk
Spence George, esq. Q.C. 42 Hyde park sq. & 2 Stone buildings, Lincoln's inn
Spence Miss, 27 St. John's wood road
Spencer Earl, 27 St. James's pl.; Althorp, Northamptn. & Wiseton, Bawtry
Spencer John, esq. 49½A, Linc. inn fields
Spencer Geo. E.esq. 13Addison road, nrth
Spencer Geo. E. esq. 6 Lincoln's inn flds. & 5 Blnhm.ter. De Beauvoir sq.Kngld
Spencer Hy. esq. 3 Everett st. Brnsk. sq
Spencer J. esq. Swiss vil. Glo'str.cr.Rg.p
SpencerMrs.20Scarsdale terrace, Knsgn
Spencer Mrs. 4 Up.Albany st.Regt.'spk
Spencer Rd.esq.1Verulam bdgs.Gry.'s in
SpencerThos.esq. 17 Marlboro' pl.Ken.cr
Spencer Thomas, esq. 3 St. James's pl
Spencer Thomas, esq. 31 Myddleton sq
Spettigue Edmund, esq. 24 Lloyd square
Spice Mrs. 4 Notting hill terrace
Spicer Chas. Wm. esq. 28 Portman sq
Spicer Hen. esq. 18 Bedford row, Islgtn
Spicer Jas. esq. 44 Newington pl.Ken.rd
Spicer Jsph. esq. 13 Church st. Edgw.rd
Spicer Mrs. 45 Markham square, Chels
Spicer Mrs. Henry, 28 Portman square
Spicer Thos. G. esq. 26 Gerard st. Soho
Spicer Wm. esq. 42 Canonbury square
Spicer W. H. esq. 15 Regent st
Spiers Jsph. esq. 4 Carlton vils. Edgw.rd
Spike Edward, esq. 77 Upper Ebury st. Pimlico, & 15 Clifford's inn, Fleet st
Spiller Fred.Tremlett, esq. 5Gray's inn sq
Spiller Miss, 15 Upper Southwick st
Spilsbury F.G. esq. 9 Hill rd.St.Jn.'s wd
SpinksFrederic L.esq.2Chchyd.ct.Templ
Spinks John, esq.27Gt.James st.Bdfd.rw
Spitta Hen. E. esq. Larkhall rise, Clphm
Spittal Francis, esq. 16 Compton st. ea
Spooner Fredk. W. Park cot. Battersea
Spooner Isaac, esq. 2 Old square, Linc.in
Spooner Jn. esq. 8 Glo'ster cr. Regt.'s pk
Spooner Richard, M.P. 39 St. James's pl
Spooner Wm.esq. 17 Chapel st.Grsvnr.pl
Spooner Wm. esq. 4 Elm court, Temple
Sporle Nathl. J. esq.5 North crs.Bedf.sq
Spottiswoode Andrew, esq. 17 Carlton house terrace, & Broome hall, Dorking
Spottiswoode John, esq.16 Gt.George st. & Spottiswoode house, Lauder, N.B
Sprado Wm.L.esq.25River st.Mydltn.sq

Spragg Mrs. 32 Sloane st
Spranger Rev. Dr.30Green st.Grosvr. sq
Spratt C. esq. 3 Stranrear pl. Maida hl
Spratt George,esq.6Dean's pl.so.Lambth
Spratt Miss, 3 Chester terrace, Eaton sq
Spratt Mrs.& Miss,3Chester ter.Eaton sq
Spreadbury Mrs.44 Portman pl.Edgw.rd
Spredbury E.esq.2 Charltn.pl.Gt.Dov.rd
SpriggeJ.esq.18Up.North pl.Gry's.inn rd
Spring Rev. Geo. Thos. 1 Milner sq. Islg
Springbett J. esq. 21 Cloudesley ter
Springall John, esq. 3 Raymond bldgs
Springate Samuel, esq. 45 London wall
Springate William, esq. 7 UpperAshby st
Springett Misses, 7 Canonbury pl
Springford Thos. esq. 26 Great Prescot st
Sprowl Hen.esq. 13Edwardes sq. Knsgtn
Spry Sir Sam. Thos. knt.M.P.8Arlington st. Piccadilly, 15 Avenue rd. Regent's park, & Tregolls, near Truro
Spry Rev. J. H. D.D. 22 York terrace
Spry Wm. esq. 54 Warren st. Fitzroy sq
Sprye Rd. esq. 26 Charles st. St. James's
Spurgin John, M.D. 38 Guilford st. Russell square, & Orplands Bradwell, Essex
Spurling John, esq. 3 Bedford row, Islgtn
Spurling Mrs.16Compton st.Brunswk.sq
Spurr John, esq. 36 Portman pl. Edgw.rd
Spurr Strafford, esq. 43 Burton st
Spurrell Benj. esq. 21 Cheyne wk. Chlse
Spurrier J. W. esq.7Charles st.Trevor sq
Spurrier J. W. esq. 25 Old sq. Linc. inn
Spurway Fredk.J.B.esq.1Wrwck.ct.Hbn
Spyer Jones, esq. 3 Lansdowne place
Spyres John, esq. 7 Bedford place
Squair Mrs. 29 Chester pl. Kengtn. crs
Squance Rev. T.H.19Wood st.Spitalflds
Squibb George J. esq. 6 Orchard st
Squibb Mrs. Saville row, Piccadilly
Squire Alfred, esq. 18 Nelson square
Squire John, esq. 3 Pall mall east
Squire Peter, esq. 20 Duke st. Grsvr. sq
Stabb Ewen, esq. 7 Retreat, Sth. Lmbth
Stable David Henry, esq. 7 Hatton grdn
Stables John, esq. 5 Bridge st. Wstmr
Stacey Mrs. 12 Howard st. Strand
Stacpoole F. esq. 2 Calthorpe st
Stacy Mrs. 50 Tavistock square
Staff James, esq. 58 Stamford st
Stafford Lord, Pulteney hotel, Albemarle st. & Cossey park, Norwich
Stafford Hy. esq. 24 Cumming st. Pntnv
Stafford Mrs. 9 Bolton st. Piccadilly
Stafford Mrs. 2 Devonshire st. Portl. pl
Stafford Rd. A. esq.28 Old Burlington st
Stafford Robt. esq. 5 Smith sq. Westmnr
Stafford Wm. esq. 13 Buckingham st
Stagg Roland, esq. 52 Noel st. Islgtn
Staines Edwd.esq.9 Salisbury pl. New rd
Staines Mrs. 18 Pelham rd. Brompton
Stains Rd. esq. 5 Middlesex pl. New rd
Stainsby Peter, esq. 44 Finsbury sq
Stainton John, esq. 3 Claremont terrace
Stair, Earl of, 6 Upper Brook st. & Oxenfoord castle, Ford, Edinburghshire
Stalker Mrs. 2 Prospect pl.Wndswth.rd
Stallwood Nathaniel, esq.13Calthorpe st
Stalman Henry, esq. 28 Oxford square, Hyde park, & 23 Old sq. Lincoln's inn
Stalman Hy. esq. 15 Gt. Coram st
Stamford & Warrington Earl, 33 Hill st.; Dunham Massey, Altrincham; & Enville hall, Stourbridge, Staffordshire
Stammers Edward, esq. 1 Avenue road
Stammers Joseph, esq. 31 Canonbury sq
Stammers Joseph, esq. 5 Chancery lane
Stamp Rev. J.S.41Westmorlnd.pl.City r
Stamp William Hy.esq.12Pall mall east
Standen Mrs.3 Montpelier sq. Brmpton
Standing Mrs. 14 Kenton st. Brunswk.sq
Standing Thos. esq. 53 Dorset st. Fleet st
Standish Charles, M.P. Standish hall, near Wigan
Standish Mrs. 7 Montagu square
Standfast Wm.G.esq.Temple cha.Fleet st
Stanfield Clarkson, R.A. 48 Morningt. pl
Stanfield George C. jun.esq.48Mrngtn.pl
Stanford Mrs. 4 Stockwell common
Stanger Samuel, esq. 1 Lower Charles st
Stanhope Earl, 20 Charles st. Berkeley square, & Chevening, Sevenoaks
Stanhope Lady Elizth. 51 Harley st
Stanhope Hon.&Rev. Fitzroy,3Trevor sq
Stanhope Hon. Col. Leicester, Ashburnham house, King's road west, Chelsea
Stanhope Hon.Henry, 23 Spring gardens
Stanhope Colonel Spencer,310 Regent st
Stanhope Mrs. Spencer, 8 Langham pl
Staniforth Charles, esq. 2 Connaught pl
Staniforth Miss, 7 Bulstrode st
Staniland Samuel, esq. 9 Bouverie st
Stanislaus Mrs. 2 Park pl. Regent's pk
Staniewiez E. esq.11Marlboro' pl.Ken.cr
Stanley Lord (of Alderley), 40 Dover st.; & Alderley park, near Congleton, Cheshire; & Penrhos', Holyhead
Stanley Lord (of Bickerstaffe), P.C. 8 St. James's square, & Stanley lodge, Bally-Histeen, Tipperary
Stanley Hon.Col.Charles,23Grosvenor sq
Stanley Hon. Edward John, 2 Grosvenor crescent,&Alderley park,nearCongletn
Stanley Hon. William Owen, M.P. 40 Dover st. & Penrhos', Holyhead
Stanley Sir Wm. Massey, bart. 10 Stratton st.Piccadilly, &Booton hall, Chstr
Stanley Caleb R. esq. 25 Gt. Maddox st
Stanley Edward, esq. & Lady Mary, 14 Grosvenor square
StanleyEdw.esq. 23A, Brook st.Grosv.sq
Stanley Edward, esq. M.P. Carlton club, & Ponsonby hall, near Whitehaven
Stanley Harold, esq. 3 Bedford row
Stanley Henry, esq. 5 Euston grove
Stanley John M. esq. 36 Berkeley sq
Stanley Mrs. Bale's cotts. Wandswth.rd
Stanley Mrs. 18 Cumberland st
StanleyMrs.28Grove end rd.St.John's wd
Stanley T. esq.12 Victoria gro.Kns. N.tn
Stanley William, esq. 11 Carthusian st
Stanley Wm.Sloane,esq.& Lady Gertrude S. 21 Curzon st. & Paulton's, Romsey
Stanly Harold esq. 18 Park village ea
Stannard Thos.esq.5River st.Mydeltn.sq
Stanser Robert B. esq.Park village east
Stansfield William Rookes Compton, M.P. 22 Charles st.Berkeley square, & Esholt hall, near Leeds
Stanton Alexander, esq. 8 Milner sq
Stanton Mrs. 6 Annett's crs.Lr.road,Islg
Stanton William Henry, M.P. Reform club, 104 Pall mall, & Stroud
Staple Moses William, esq. 5 South square, Gray's inn, & Norwood, Surrey
Staples Robert P. esq. 10 Chesterfield st
Staples Samuel, esq. 69 Newman st
Stapleton Hon.Thomas, 13 Wilton place
Stapleton Augs. esq. 35 Clapham rise
Stapleton William, esq. 10 Pembroke sq
Stapleton W.H. esq. 23 Stonefield st.Isln
Stapylton H.R.C. esq. 18 Devonshire st
Stapylton Robert George, esq. 3 New sq
Stapylton Robert M.esq.11Harewood sq
Starbuck Edward F.esq.2Walbrook, Cty
Starey Richard, esq. 18 Noel st. Islngtn
Starie William, esq.6 Paulton's sq.Chels
Stark Alex.esq.21 Spencer st.Goswell rd
Stark Hugh, esq. Old Brompton
Starkie Mrs. 36 Keppel st. Russell sq
Starkie Thos.esq.Q.C. 31 Bedford sq. ; 1 Hare ct. Templ.;&Downing coll.Camb
Starling Edward, esq. 7 Sackville st
Starling George Aug.esq.40 Leicester sq
Starr Thomas, esq. 3 Garden ct. Temple
Startridge C.esq.14Tavistock st.Bedfd.sq
States Charles, esq. 1A, Adelphi terrace
States George S. esq. 1A, Adelphi terrace
States William, esq. 1A, Adelphi terrace
Statham Wm.esq.9 Gt.Chapel st.Westm
Staunton Sir George Thomas, bart. M.P. 17 Devonshire st.&Leigh park, Havant
Staunton Edwd.esq.10 Norfolk st.Strand
Stavely Thos. esq.20 Earl's ter. Kensgtn
Stavers Mrs. 2 Albany ter. New road
Stavordale Lord, 31 Old Burlington st. & Melbury house, Dorchester
Stead Thomas, esq.25Glo'ster st.Queen sq
Steavenson John, esq. 15 Lonsdale sq
Stebbing Rev. Dr.St.Jas's.pl.Hmpstd.rd
Stedman Francis, esq.10Baron st.Pntnvl
StedmanJohn, esq.11New sq.Lincoln's in
Stedman Silas, esq. 60 Guilford st
StedmanWm.Charles,esq.31Mnchestr.st
Steed Mrs. 15 Fitzroy st. Fitzroy sq
Steel George, esq.9Carey st. Lincoln's in
Steel J. esq. 13A, Lowther ct. Lpool. rd
Steel James E. esq. 25 Baker st.Lloyd sq
Steele Col. Thomas & Lady Elizabeth, 21 Up. Brook st. & the Castle, Kimbolton
Steele Adam Rivers, esq. 1 Lincoln's inn fields, & Oakland house, Cricklewood
Steele Misses, 5Grove en. rd.St. Jn's.wd
Steele Miss, 32 Hunter st. Brunswk. sq
Steele Richard, esq. 32 Hunter st
Steell Jas. esq. 44 Bernard st. Russell sq
Steer George, esq. 11 Queen Anne st
Steer Mrs. 11 Queen Anne st
Steere William, esq. 14 Egremont place, New road, & 92 Chancery lane
Steern David, esq. 92 Gloucester place
Steet George, esq. 25 Gt. Ormond st
Steggall Robt.esq.31B, Sth.bnk. Rgt. pk
Stein Chas.esq.32 Holywell st. Millbank
Stein Fred.Wm.esq.4 Loraine pl. Hollwy
SteinkopffRev.C.F.A.D.D.Savoyst.Strnd
Stephen Sir Geo. knt. 3 Furnival's inn
Stephen Mrs. 7 William st.Knightsbrdge
Stepheney John, esq. 6 Tonbridge place
Stephens Andrew, esq. 107 Hatton gdn
Stephens Archd. Jn. esq. 61 Chancery la
Stephens Charles Lyne, esq. 32 Portman sq. & Chicksands priory, Bedfordshire
Stephens Edwd. esq. 36 Porchester terr
Stephens E. B. esq. 1A, Hampstead st
Stephens E. B.esq. 27 Upper Belgrave pl
Stephens George, esq. 11 Carey st
Stephens Gilbert, esq. 30 Chapel street, Grosvenor place, & 13 Northumberland st. Strand
Stephens Henry Lewis, esq. 49 Baker st. Portman square, & Treganna castle, St. Ives, Cornwall
Stephens John, esq. 2 Church st. Chelsea
Stephens John, esq. 1 Elm ct. Temple
Stephens John, esq. 3 Raymond buildgs
Stephens Miss, 35 Pembroke square
Stephens Mrs. 49 Baker st. & Weston cottage, Plymouth
Stephens Mrs. 7 Onslow pl. Fulham rd
Stephens Mrs. 30 Clapham road place
Stephens Mrs. 5 Petersburgh pl. Byswtr
Stephens Mrs. 29 Craven st. Strand
Stephens Richard, esq. 21 Lonsdale sq
Stephens S. J. esq. 3 Stanley pl. Pad. gn
Stephens Richd. esq. 12 York pl. City rd
Stephens Samuel Josiah, esq. 4 & 5 Charlotte st. Portland place
Stephens T. esq. 6 Campden hl.ter.Knsn
Stephens T. esq. 23 Gouldn.ter. Brnsby.rd
Stephens Thomas, esq. 30 Highbury pl
Stephens Wm. esq. 30 Bedford row
Stephens Wm.esq.1 Trafalgr. pl.Clpm.rd
Stephenson Capt. D. 30 Guilford st
Stephenson Chs. esq. 3 Oxford square
Stephenson Edwd.S.esq. 12 Gt. Queen st
Stephenson Frank, esq. 13 Bruton st
Stephenson Geo. esq. 24 Gt. George st
Stephenson Geo. H. esq. 10 St.Helen's pl
Stephenson Henry Frederic esq. & Lady Mary, 5 Arlington st. Piccadilly
Stephenson J. esq. 42 Southamptn.bldgs & Brotherton, Ferrybridge, Yorkshire
Stephenson Misses, Kensington palace
Stephenson Mrs.83 Albany st. Regt.'s pk
Stephenson Mrs. 34 Euston square
Stephenson Robt. esq. 15 Cambridge sq
Stephenson Robt. esq. 24 Gt. George st
Stephenson Robt. esq. 10 St. Helen's pl

Stephenson Rt. esq. 6 Low. Southwick st
Stephenson Wm. Hy. esq. 12 Bolton row
Stericker Walter, esq. 6 Canonbury pk
Sterkey Mrs. 4 Victoria sq. Pimlico
Sterling Capt. 2 South pl. Knsngtn. rd
Sterling Edwd. esq. 24 Brompton row
Sterry Henry, esq. 42 Trinity sq. Boro'
Sterry Mrs. 6 Grove ter. St. John's wood
Steven Robt. esq. 1 Bridge st. Blackfrs
Stevens Sir Geo. 14 Porchester terrace
Stevens Major Hen. 19 Thurloe sq. Bmp
Stevens Rev. John, 15 Huntley st. Bdfd. st
Stevens Charles, esq. 20 Mabledon pl
Stevens Geo. esq. 26 Paddington basin
Stevens Hen. esq. 6 Alfred pl. Alexn. sq
Stevens Henry, esq. 30 Chancery lane
Stevens John, esq. 2 Brompton grove
Stevens John, esq. 6 Clement's inn
Stevens John, esq. 21 John st. Bedford row
Stevens J. esq. 2 St. John's vil. Acacia rd
Stevens John, esq. 260 Oxford st
Stevens John, esq. 39 Torrington square
Stevens Miss, 4 Hunter st. Brunswick sq
Stevens Mrs. 84 Ebury st. Pimlico
Stevens Mrs. 4 Elm Tree rd. St. John's w
Stevens Mrs. 4 Hunter st. Brunswick sq
Stevens Mrs. 6 Kennington place
Stevens Mrs. M. 4 Southamptn. row, Nw. rd
Stevens Nathaniel, esq. 3 Euston grove, & 1 Gray's inn square
Stevens Rd. jun. esq. 120 Waterloo road
Stevens Richd. Geo. esq. 46 Albion st
Stevens Sam. esq. 20 Henrietta st. Br. sq
Stevens Thos. esq. 47 Markham sq. Chel
Stevens Thomas, esq. 25 Mornington cres
Stevens Thomas, esq. 12 New Boswell ct
Stevens William, esq. 18 South Lambeth
Stevenson Benjamin, esq. 5 Argyle sq
Stevenson Cha. esq. 1 Park pl. grds. Pdgtn
Stevenson D. esq. 10 North ter. Bromptn
Stevenson E. esq. 7 Cambridge terrace
Stevenson John, esq. 35 Marchmont st. Brnswk. sq. & 3 King's rd. Bedford row
Stevenson John M. esq. 3 Cork st
Stevenson Mrs. 3 Cadogan place
Stevenson Mrs. 11 Maida hill west
Stevenson Mrs. M. H. 100 Park st. Grosv. sq
Stevenson Thos. M.D. 37 Up. Grosvenor st
Stevenson Wm. esq. 22 Milner square
Steward Col. Rt. 44 Norland sq. Notg. hl
Steward Rev. Geo. 26 Artillery pl. west
Steward Jas. esq. 13 Southwick crescet
Steward J. esq. 10 Marlborough pl. Ken. crs
Steward John, esq. 20 Mortimer st
Steward Mrs. 12 River st. Myddelton sq
Steward Samuel, esq. 23 Connaught square, & 59 Lincoln's inn fields
Steward Thos. F. esq. 12 Dean's yard
Steward W. esq. 2 Little Stanhope st
Stewart Hon. Edward & Lady Katherine, 9 Bryanstone square
Stewart Sir Wm. Drummond, bart. 78 Grosvenor st. & Murthley castle, Perth, N.B
Stewart Lady Caroline, 37 Cadogan pl
Stewart Lady Shaw, 42 Belgrave sq. & Argowan, Greenock; & Carnack, Falkirk; & Castle Newark, Pt. Glasgow
Stewart Alex. Rt. esq. 35 Sackville st
Stewart Archibald, esq. 13 Bruton st
Stewart Charles, esq. 57 Curzon st
Stewart Charles, esq. 2 Paper bldgs
Stewart Daniel, esq. 8 Clapham rise
Stewart David, esq. 94 Gt. Russell st
Stewart Edward, esq. 14 Chesterfield st
Stewart Jas. esq. 3 Gloucester crescent
Stewart Jas. esq. 5 Michael's gr. Bmptn
Stewart Jas. esq. 9 Somerset pl. Somst. ho
Stewart John, esq. M.P. 2 Albany, & 3 Cambridge st. Edgware road
Stewart J. esq. 3 Cambridge ter. Edg. rd
Stewart John, esq. 9 Circus rd. St. Jn.'s wd
Stewart John, esq. 6 Cirencester place
Stewart John, esq. 22 Portman square; & Belladrum, Beauly; & Carnousie, Banff
Stewart Leonard, M.P. 28 Keppel st
Stewart Miss, 20 St. John's wood road
Stewart Miss, 11 Taunton place
Stewart Mrs. 59 Baker st. Portman sq
Stewart Mrs. 55 Cadogan place
Stewart Mrs. 10 Cadogan ter. Chelsea
Stewart Mrs. 3 Chester st. Grosv. place
Stewart Mrs. 3 Grove pl. Lisson grove
Stewart Mrs. 6 Kensington square
Stewart Patrick, esq. 57 York terrace
Stewart Pat. M. esq. M.P. 17 Finsby. circ
Stewart Richd. H. esq. 2 Blandford pl
Stewart Robert, esq. 94 Gt. Russell st
Stewart Robt. esq. 13 Park pl. St. James
Stewart Spencer, esq. 2 Northwick ter
Stewart Rd. H. esq. 2 Blandford pl. Rgt. pk
Stibbert Giles, esq. 44 Connaught square
Stickney Jno. esq. 4 Albion ter. Wndwth
Stiebel Samuel, esq. 39 Russell square
Stiebel Sigismund, esq. 75 Guilford st
Stiff Thomas, esq. 47 Manchester st
Stiles Miss, 1 Stanhope pl. Hampstd. rd
Stiles Mrs. 84 Gower st
Still Robt. esq. 5 New sq. Lincoln's inn
Stillwell Edwd. esq. 8 Furnival's inn
Stillwell G. esq. 21 Prospect pl. Wdswth. rd
Stillwell Thos. esq. 22 Arundel st. Strand
Stinton Jsph. esq. 5 New sq. Lincoln's inn
Stirling Sir Walter, bart. 29 Portman sq
Stirling John, esq. 32 Ebury st. Pimlico
Stirling Walter, esq. 18 Upper Baker st. Pirbright lodge, Guildford; & Cornbrook bank, near Manchester
Stobie Mrs. 25 Connaught square
Stock Maj. 3 Arundel st. Coventry st
Stock Edwd. esq. Poplar ho. Poplar Hi. st
Stock John Shapland, esq. 2 Plowden bldgs
Stock J. LL.D., M.P. 14 Manchester bldgs
Stock Mrs. 3 Sussex pl. Canonbury sq
Stock Mrs. 7 Upper Brook st
Stockdale Hen. M. esq. 19 Linc. inn flds
Stocken Thomas, esq. 37 Albany st
Stocker John, esq. 93 Oxford terrace, & Carey street, Lincoln's inn
Stocker John P. esq. 2 New Boswell ct
Stocker Richard, esq. 44 Baker st
Stocker Thos. esq. 22 Wellington terrace
Stockler Mrs. 11 Lyon ter. Maida hill
Stockley J. esq. 20 Victoria gr. Kns. N. tn
Stockwell George, esq. 81 Jermyn st. & Brunswick square, Brighton
Stodart George, esq. 11 Russell square
Stoddart Sir John, knt. D.C.L. 22 Pelham place, Brompton
Stoddart J. esq. 15 Porteus rd. Harrw. rd
Stoddart Sam. esq. 34 Alpha rd. Regt. pk
Stodhart Rev. Rt. Providence pl. Isling
Stokes Charles, esq. 65 Brook st
Stokes Charles, esq. 4 Verulam bldgs. Gray's inn, & 23 Threadneedle st
Stokes Chas. Wm. esq. 14 Radnor pl. Hy. pk
Stokes Fras. esq. 9 Hamilton pl. New rd
Stokes Mrs. 38 Hans place, Sloane st
Stokes Robert, esq. 15 Parliament st
Stoll Fredk. esq. 10 Gt. College st. Westmr
Stone Rev. Wm. M.A. 1 Church st. Spitalfds
Stone A. F. esq. 18 Alfred pl. Alexndr. sq
Stone David Henry, esq. 2 Trinity square, Borough, & 24 Poultry
Stone Edwd. esq. Campden hill, Kensgtn
Stone Mrs. 6 Somers pl. west, New road
Stone Frank, esq. Tavstk. ho. Tavstk. sq
Stone Geo. esq. 2 Courland ter. Wands. rd
Stone Geo. esq. 57 Jermyn st. St. James'
Stone Geo. G. esq. 3 Hanover ter. Nottg. hl
Stone Hen. C. esq. 4 Howley pl. Belvdr. rd
Stone Humphrey J. esq. 3 Burton st
Stone John, esq. 4 Euston grove
Stone Miss, 21 Henrietta st. Cavdsh. sq
Stone Mrs. 25 Aberdeen pl. Maida hill
Stone Mrs. 39 Hill st. Berkeley sq
Stone Rd. esq. 6 Oxford ter. Edgware rd
Stone Saml. esq. 13 Winchester rw. New sq
Stone Thomas A. M.D. 16 Curzon st
Stone Thos. W. esq. 104 Camden rd. villas
Stone William, esq. 25 Golden square
Stone Wm. Hen. esq. 10 Barnsbury villas
Stonebridge Joseph, esq. 31 Wyndham st
Stonestreet Rev. Geo. G. 35 Gower st. & Halton house, Hastings
Stonestreet Fetherston, esq. 35 Gower st
Stonhill Rd. esq. 13 New Manor pl. Chels
Stonor Henry, esq. 4 New Boswell court
Stooks Rev. Thos. Fredk. 9 Suffolk pl
Stooks Thomas, esq. 8 Bedford place
Stopford Lt. Col. E. 16 Edward st. Ptm. sq
Stopford Capt. Robert F. 7 Chester sq
Stopford Mrs. 18 Lower Phillimore pl
Stopher Rd. esq. Harmood st. Camden tn
Storer Egbert, esq. 19 York pl. City rd
Storey Andrew, esq. 5 Gray's inn place
Storey Chas. esq. 10 Lower Belgrave st
Storey Mrs. 19 Winchester row, New rd
Storey Wm. J. C. esq. 23 Shaftesbury cres
Storks Henry, S.L. 44 Gower st. & 3 Serjeant's inn, Chancery lane
Storks Robt. R. esq. 44 Gower st. Bdfd. sq
Storr Wm. esq. 36 Gt. Coram st
Storrar John, M.D. 6 Holles st. Cavdh. sq
Storrs Mrs. 37 Addison rd. nth. Nottg. hl
Story Col. Edmd. R. 31 Trevor sq. Knghtsbd
Story Jas. Hamilton, esq. 17 Bryanstone square, & Relagh lodge, Enniskillin
Story Mrs. & Miss, 1 Wilton crescent
Stoughton Rev. John, 6 Kensington cr
Stoughton William, esq. 39 Welbeck st
Stourton Lord, 10 Mansfield st. & Allerton park, Green Hammerton, York
Stourton Hon. Charles, 10 Mansfield st.; & Cafe Castle, South Cafe, Yorkshire; & Biddleston castle, Hexham; & Allerton park, Knaresborough
Stourton Joseph, esq. 79 Coleshill st
Stout William, esq. 18 Maida hill west
Stovel Rev. Chas. 5 Stebon ter. Coml. rd
Stovell Frederick, esq. 2 Gt. Percy st
Stovell Mrs. 30 Sidmouth st. Gray's inn rd
Stovin Maj. Gen. Sir Frederick, bt. K.C.B. 20 Finchley N. rd
Stovin Chas. Fredk. esq. 6A, Waterloo pl
Stovin Wm. esq. 2 Duchess st. Portld. pl
Stow George, esq. 7 Nottingham place
Stowers Nowell, esq. 26 Albion st. Hy. pk
Strachan Mrs. 7 Belgrave st. King's crs
Strachan William, esq. 15 Regent st
Strachey Sir Hen. 115 Mount st. Berkeley sq. & Sutton court, Old Down
Stradbroke Earl of, 18 Queen st. Mayfair, & Henham hall, Wangford
Stradbroke Countess of, 33 Hertford st
Strafford Lord, G.C.B., G.C.H., P.C., 6 Portman square
Strahan Paul, Paul & Bates, Temple bar without, 217 Strand
Strahan William, esq. 34 Hill st.; 218 Strand; & Ashurst, near Dorking
Straight Robt. M. esq. 1 Mid. Temple la
Strange John C. esq. 1 Park pl. Kenn. crs
Strange J. T. esq. 11 Pelham pl. Fulhm. rd
Strange Mrs. 2 Thornton vil. Kensngtn
Strange Mrs. 60 Cambridge ter. Edgw. rd
Strangford Viscount, G.C.B., G.C.H., P.C. 68 Harley st. & Westenhanger house, Hythe, Kent
Strangwayes D'Arcy, esq. 4 Barnard's inn
Strangways Lady Caroline Fox, 31 Old Burlington st
Strangways Hon. John George Charles Fox, 31 Old Burlington st
Strangways Ths. H. esq. 11 King's rd. Bed. r
Stratenus M. de, esq. sec. to legation from the Netherlands, 90 Cadogan pl
Stratenus A. J. L. esq. 90 Cadogan place
Stratford Hon. Col. John W. 12 Stratford place, & Addington place, Maidstone
Stratford Lady Emily, 40 Wilton cresct
Stratford Lieut. Wm. 6 Notting hill sq
Stratford Jas. esq. 3 Lit. George st. Westr
Stratford J. esq. 13 South bank, Rgt.'s pk
Stratford Mrs. 20 Charlotte st. Bedford sq
Strathallan Viscount, 44 Charles st. Berkeley square, & Castle Strathallan, Auchterarder, N.B

Stratheden Lady, Stratheden house, South place, Knightsbridge, & Ashstead house, near Epsom
Strathmore Dowager Countess of, 39 Maddox st. Regent st
Stratton Rev. James, 65 Hamilton terr
StrattonJn.T.esq.11Carlton vill Edgw.rd
Stratton Mrs. 9 Portugal st. Grovnr. sq
Stratton Sam. esq. 27 Lincoln's inn flds
Stratton Thos. esq. 2 Old sq. Lincoln's inn
Strauchan F. esq. 2 South ter. Bromptn
Stray John, esq. 58 Rupert st
Streatfield Thos. esq. 16 Stockwell comn
StreckerEdwd.esq. 4 Mid. Scotland yard
Strecker Jacob, esq. 15 Park st
Street Hy. esq. 34 Beaufort st. Chelsea
Street J. P. esq. 13 Colebrooke tr.Islgtn
Street Mrs. 2 Edwardes sq. Kensington
Street Mrs. 104 Milton st. Dorset sq
Street Wm. J. esq. 69 Lincoln's inn fields
Streeten Fras. Towers, esq. 5 Quality ct
Streeter John S. esq. 20 Harpur st
StretchWm.esq.1Oxford pl.Marlboro' rd
Stretton Chas.M.esq.18Southmptn.bldgs
Stretton Geo. esq.36 Albany st. Regt. pk
Stretton Hen. esq. 3 Lincoln's inn fields
Stretton Henry, esq. 2 Claremont ter
Stretton Mrs. 9 Claremont row
Strick Edward, esq. 10 Doughty st
Strickland Sir Geo. bart. M.P. 1 Spring gardens; &Boynton, nearBridlington; & Newton, near Malton, Yorkshire
Strickland Fdk. esq. 10 John st. Adelphi
Strickland Samuel West, esq. Kensington palace gardens, Bayswater road
Strickland W. esq. 4 Addison tr. Notg. hl
Stride James, esq. 13 Fludyer st
Strike John, esq. 6 Eccleston st. south
Strode Mrs. 5 Rich ter. Old Brompton
Strode Wm. esq. 3 South st. Finsby
Strong Lady, 10 Grafton st. Bond st
Strong Rev. Thos. L. 20 Up. Seymour st
Strong Chas.W.esq.10Grafton st.Bond st
Strong Hy.Linwood, esq.5Brickct.Templ
Strong Jsph. esq. 14Stoke Newington grn
Strong Thomas, esq. 20 Upper Seymour st. & Sedgefield, near Durham
Strong Wm.esq.12Park pl.ter.Padgtn.gn
Strong Wm. Oswald, esq. 37 Sloane sq
Stroud Geo. esq. 11 Kennington row
Stroud Wm. M.D. 20 Great Coram st
Strutt Chas. E. esq. 4 Adelaide st. Strnd
Strutt Edward, esq. M.P. 42 South st. Grvnr. sq. & St. Helen's, near Derby
Strutt John, esq. 18 Buckingham st.Stnd
Strutt Wm. esq. 8 Lodge pl. Regent's pk
Stuart Lord Dudley, 34 St. James's pl
Stuart de Decies Lord, Long's hotel, 16 New Bond st. & Dromana, Cappoquin
Stuart de Rothesay Lord, Ambassador at
Stuart Lord Patrick Crichton, M.P. 6 Whitehall pl. & Cardiff castle, Cardiff
Stuart Lady George, 5 Elizabeth st. Eaton square
Stuart Lady Louisa, 108 Glo'ster place
Stuart Lieut. Col. Chas. 74 Chester sq
Stuart Abel, M.D. West cottage, Sth.bnk
Stuart Chas. esq. 20 Norfolk st. Park la
Stuart D. esq. 1 Brick court, Temple
Stuart Daniel, esq. 9 Upper Harley st. & Wykham park, Banbury, Oxon
Stuart Henry, esq. M.P. 18 Hill st. Berkeley sq. & the Lodge, Bedford
Stuart John, esq. 49 Russell square, & 1 Field court, Gray's inn
Stuart John, esq.Q.C.19Hertford st.Mayfair, & 12 Old square, Lincoln's inn
Stuart John Arch. esq. 6 New inn, Strnd
Stuart Mrs. 13 Bolton row, Piccadilly
Stuart Mrs. 10 South tr. Alexander sq
Stuart Wm. esq. 18Hill st. Berkeley sq. & Aldenham abbey, Watford
Stuart Wm. esq. 8 Frederick st. Gray's inn road, & 6 Gray's inn square
Stuart Wm. Villiers, esq. M.P. 16 New Bd. st. & Droman ho. Cappoquin
Stubbs Charles, esq. 31 Lonsdale sq
Stubbs Joseph, esq. 46 Mecklenburgh sq
Stubbs J. esq. 23 Wellington terrace, St. John's wood
Stubbs Mrs. 1 Maddox st. Regent st
Stubbs Mrs. 51 Sloane st. Chelsea
Stubbs Morton, esq. York cham. St. Jas. st
Stubbs Wm. Edw. esq. 15 Furnival's inn
Stuck John, esq.166Grove st. Camden twn
Stuckey Mrs. 36 Bloomsbury square
Stulz John, esq. 2 Saville row
Stump Samuel John, esq. 7 Cork st
Sturch Miss, 21 York ter. Regent's pk
Sturdy Daniel, esq. Wandsworth road
Sturgeon Chas.esq.5 Eldon pl.Up.Ken.la
Sturgeon Chas. esq. 8 Southampton bdgs
Sturgeon Mrs. 3 Nottingham st
Sturges John, esq. 35 Connaught sq
Sturges S.esq.39Charlotte st.Portland pl
Sturt LadyMaryAnn, 38 Up.Seymour st
Sturt Hen. Chas. esq. M.P. & LadyCharlotte, 16 Portman square; & Critchell house, near Woodyates, Dorsetshire
SturtGeo. esq.5 Arundel ter.Barnsby. rd
Sturt Mrs. 1 Tibberton square
Stuteley Edward Reeder, esq. 18 Charles st. Westbourne terrace
Stutely Martin, esq. 6 Cambridge ter
Stutely Martin J. esq. 2 Gower st
Stutfield W. esq. 1 Montague place
Stuttard John, esq. 3 Colebrooke ter
Stutzer Henry Lewis, esq. 19 Euston sq
StyanThomas,esq.8Harpurst.Red Lionsq
Styan Wm.esq.15 Albion rd.Liverpool rd
Suart John, esq. 9 Leonard pl. Kensngtn
Such George, M.D. 27 New st. Dorset sq
Sudeley Lord, 35 Dover st. & Winchcombe, Gloucestershire
Sudlow John James J. esq. 20 Chancery lane, & Coombe Burycot.Kingston hill
Sudlow John Jas. J. esq. 2 Pelham pl
Sudlow Jno. J.J.jun.esq.6NewPalace yd
Suffield Lord, 12 Gt. Marlborough st.; & Gunton park, Norwich; & Middleton hall, Manchester
Suffield Lady, 2 Wilton st. Grosvenor pl
Suffolk, Earl of, 9 Clarges st. & Charlton park, Malmesbury
Sullivan J. esq. 101 Guilford st. Rus. sq
SullivanM.Wogan,esq.9Alfred pl.Bdf.sq
Sullivan Mrs. Stuart, 23 Devonshire pl
Summers Charles, esq. 60 Euston sq
Summers Mrs. 2 Cambridge place
SummersWm.H.esq.66Princesst.Lstr.sq
Sumner Chas.esq.10 Farrar's bdgs.Templ
Sundborg Fred. esq. 58 Greek st. Soho
Surman Wm. Harry, esq. 13 John st. Berkeley sq. & 11 New sq. Lincoln's in
Surr Joseph, esq. 70 Gibson square
Surrey, Earl of, M.P. 15 Chesham pl
Surtees Alfred W. esq. 40 St. James's pl
Surtees F.Rd.esq.3 Plowden bdgs.Templ
Surtees Robert L. esq. 1 Sackville st
Surtees Wm. Edw. esq. 3 Plowden bdgs
Sutcliffe Wm. esq. 23 Low. Islngton ter
Suter Edward, esq. 58 Gibson square
Sutherland, Duke of, K.G. Stafford house, St. James's; & Trentham pk. Stafford; & Lilleshall, Salop; & Dunrobin castle, Sutherlandshire
Sutherland Gen.Sir Jas.8 Cumberland st
Sutherland Alex. J. M.D. 1Parliament st
Sutherland Alex. R. M.D. 1Parliament st
Sutherland Miss, 28 Albany st
Sutherland Mrs. 62 Gibson square
Suttaby Rt. esq. 40 Cumming st. Pntnvl
Sutton Hon. J. H. M. M.P. *See* Manners Sutton
Sutton Frank, esq. 33 Wimpole st
Sutton Daniel, esq. 25Earl's ter. Knsgtn
Sutton E. P. esq. 40 Gt. Ormond st
Sutton Isaac, esq. 7 Amwell terrace
Sutton James, esq. 10 St. John's wood rd
Sutton Miss, 10 Stonefield st. Islington
Sutton Mrs. Evelyn, 35 Berkeley sq
Sutton Mrs. J. 17 Chapel st. east, Mayfr
Sutton Mrs.Nassau, 3 LowerBerkeley st
Sutton Mrs. 7 Sussex pl.Kensgtn. nw. tn
Sutton Mrs. 11 York buildings, New rd
Sutton Robert, esq. 79 Hamilton ter
Swaine Wm. Edward, M.D. 43 Foley pl
Swainson Mrs. 3 Queen sq. Westminster
Swales Thos.esq.18Circus rd. St. Jns. wd
Swallow Miss, 112 Sloane st
Swan Joseph, esq. 6 Tavistock square
Swan Miss, 19 Aberdeen pl. Maida hill
Swan Robt. esq. 4 Serjeants' inn, Fleet st
Swann Charles, esq. 1 Hare ct. Temple
Swann Miss, 17 Radnor pl. Hyde park
Swann Mrs. 2 Ranelagh grove
Swann Mrs. 1 Upper Ebury st. Pimlico
Swanston C.T.esq.Q.C.51&52Chancery la
Swanwick Mrs. 27 Woburn square
Swayne Geo. esq. 2 Circus rd. St. Jn.'s wd
Sweatman Mrs. 15 South bank, Regt.'s pk
Swedish & Norwegian Consulate, 2 Crosby square
Sweedland Lady, 10 Bedford pl.Kensgtn
Sweet George, esq. 11 Mecklenburgh st & 60 Chancery lane
Sweet Mrs. 10 Dorset square
Sweeting Chs. esq. 22 Southampton bds
SwenyM.H.Capt.R.N.4Up.Robrt.st.Bmp
Swift Fred. G. esq. 34 Cross st. Islington
Swift Hy. E. esq. Breda cot. Acacia rd
Swift Mrs. 22 Earl's terrace, Kensingtn
Swift Rd. esq. 16 Palmer ter. Holloway
Swift Richard, esq. 87 Hatton garden
Swift Richd. F. esq.66 St.John st. Clkwl
Swift Rd.L.esq.Rolls chbs.89Chancery la
Swift Wm. Hen. esq. 41 Cloudesley ter
Swinbourn Mrs. 30 Oxford terrace
Swinburne Sir John Edward, bart. 18 Grosvenor pl.; & Capheaton, Newcastle-upon-Tyne; & Mounces, Hexham
SwinburneThos.esq.11South sq.Gray's in
Swincow Wm. esq. 75 Blackfriars road
Swindell John, esq. 9 Clapham rise
Swinden Miss, 19 Kensington gore
Swindley J.esq. 1 Church la.Kns. gvl.pts
Swinfin Mrs. 5 Connaught square
Swinton Edulf, esq. 5 Surrey st. Strand
Swinton James R. esq. 5 Bulstrode st
Swinton Mrs. 2 Sussex gardens
Sydney Viscount, 3 Cleveland square, & Frognall, Footscray, Kent
Sydney Mrs. 31 Cambridge pl. Edgw. rd
Syer Jas. J. esq. 29 New Bridge st. Blkfs
Syers Robert M. esq. 2 Notting hill ter
Sykes Lady, 21 St. James's place
Sykes Rear-Admiral, 51 Wilton crescent
Sykes Lieut. Col. 47 Albion st. Hyde pk
Sykes Edwd. esq. 2 Inner Temple lane
Sykes J. esq. 4 Mountfort ter. Brnsby.pk
Sykes Miss, 71 Euston square
Sykes Wm. esq. 2 Hyde park place, west
Sylvester J. J. esq. 26 Lincoln's inn fields
Sylvester John, esq. 96 Gt. Russell st
Sylvester Nathl. esq. 43 Connaught sq
Sylvester Wm. esq. 9 Lloyd st. Lloyd sq
Symes Edmund S. esq. 77 Grosvenor st
Symes J. esq. 8 Porteus ter. Paddingtn
Symes John Coles. 55 Montagu square
Symes Wm. M.D. 3 Tavistock sq
Symm Joseph, esq. 12 Doughty st
Symonds Capt. Sir Wm. R.N., F.R.S., 4 Somerset place, & Jersey
Symonds Arthur, esq. 3 Trafalgar sq
Symonds Arthur, esq. 31 Up. Bedford pl
Symonds Chas. E. esq. 5 Horselydown la
Symonds John, esq. 43 Nelson square
Symons Jelinger C. esq. 1 Harcourt bdgs
Symons Mrs. 3 Glo'ster pl. Portman sq
Sympson Joseph Dyer, esq. 7 Golden sq
Sympson Jsph. D. esq. 28 Manchester st
Synnet R. M.D. 8 Westbourne pl. Sloane sq
Szechni Count, Mivart's ho. 44 Brook st
Szulozewski Lieut. Charles, 10 Duke st. St. James's

TABER Fredk. esq. 5 Bayswater hill
Tabor Chas. William, esq. 58 Russell sq

Tabor Mrs. 25 Finsbury square
Tabram W. esq. 11 Northamptn. ter. Islng
Tackley Mrs. 3 OldQuebec st. Portmn. sq
Taft J. esq. 38 Blomfield road, Maida hl
Tagart Rev. Edward, 33 Porchester ter
Tagart Chas. Fortescue, esq. 3 Boxworth gr. Up. Islngtn. & 1 Raymond's bldgs
Tagliabue Mrs. 9 Goulden ter. Islington
Tahourdin Chas. esq. 25 Lincoln's inn flds
Tait Alex. esq. 15 Albert ter. St. Jn.'s wd
Tait Miss, 86 Jermyn st
Tait Wm. esq. 43 Upper Gower st
Talbot Earl, K.P., P.C. 10 Great George st. & Ingestre hall, Stafford
Talbot de Malahide Lord, Long's hotel, & Malahide castle, Ireland
Talbot Hon. John C. 10 Gt. George st. Westminster, & 1 New ct. Temple
Talbot Hon. & Rev. R. 44 Brook st
Talbot Sir George, bart. 21 Grosvenor sq
Talbot A. esq. 4 Brecknock ter. Cmdn. tn
Talbot Charles, esq. 71 Margaret st
Talbot Clere, esq. 36 Upper Baker st
Talbot C. R. M. esq. M.P. & Lady Charlotte, 40 Belgrave sq. & Penrice castle, Swanse
Talbot Fred. esq. 8 John st. & 47 Bedfd. rw
Talbot Henry Fox, esq. 31 Sackville st
Talbot Matt. D. esq. 15 George st. Port. sq
Talbot the Misses, 25 Curzon street
Talbot Misses, 15 Upper Berkeley street
Talbot Miss, 2 Foundling ter. Gra. in. rd
Talbot Wm. esq. 37 Bury st. St. James's
Talfourd Field, esq. 68 Newman street
Talfourd Thomas Noon, S.L. 56 Russell sq. & 3 Serjeants' inn, Chancery lane
Tallant Miss, 6 Charles st. Manchester sq
Tallemach Richard, esq. 13 Serle street
Talmadge Wm. esq. 1 Cloisters, Temple
Tamplin Geo. esq. 6 King's rd. Bedford rw
Tamplin Rd. Wm. esq. 29 Great Queen st.
Tancred Charles, esq. 1 Furnival's inn, & Arden hall, Thirsk, Yorkshire
Tancred Hen. Wm. esq. M.P., Q C. Reform club, 104 Pall mall
Tankerville Earl of, P.C. 65 Lower Grosvenor st.; & Walton, Esher, Surrey; & Chillingham castle, near Belford, Northumberland
Tanley John, esq. 11 Nottingham st
Tanner Thomas, esq. 13 St. James's pl
Tanner Wm. esq. 84 Blackfriars road
Tannock James, esq. 16 Newman street
Tansley Saml. esq. 19 Ranelagh grove
Tanswell John, esq. 5 King's bench walk
Taplin John, esq. 23 Connaught terrace
Tapling Thos. esq. 41 Duncan ter. Islgtn
Tappenden Jas. esq. 15 Great College st
Tappenden Jas. esq. 26 Suffolk st. Pall ml
Tapping Thos. esq. 8 Mitre ct. chambers, Mitre court, Fleet street
Taprell S. esq. 4 Clarendon pl. Maida hill
Taprell Wm. esq. 8 Caroline pl. Mecklenburgh sq. & 1 Harecourt, Temple
Tarleton Thos. S. esq. 9 Brompton cresc
Tarling H. J. esq. 12 Petersburgh pl. Bayswr
Tarn Wm. esq. 8 Millman st. Bedford row
Tarrant Sam. esq. 14 Portland ter. Rgt. pk
Tarring J. esq. 23 Chas. st. Middx. hsptl
Tart John, esq. 6 Lower Grosvenor pl
Tarver John, esq. 2 Coles ter. Barnsby. rd
Tasker Joseph, esq. 3 York bldgs. New rd
Tasker Mrs. 36 Up. Norton st. Fitzroy sq
Tassie Wm. esq. 8 Upper Phillimore pl
Tatchell Mrs. 37 Argyle sq. King's crs
Tatchell Mrs. 20 Goulden tr. Barnsby. rd
Tate John P. esq. 40 Trinity sq. Boro'
Tate Miss, 21 Grosvenor pl.; & Burleigh, Loughborough; & Langdown, Southhampton
Tate Miss, 32 Westbourne pl. Pimlico
Tate Wm. esq. 19 Charles sq. Hoxton
Tate Wm. esq. Vendome cottage, Park village ea. Rgt.'s pk, & 10 Basinghall st
Tatem E. C. esq. 30 Portland pl. Islingtn
Tatham A. C. esq. 11 Staple inn, & Highgate
Tatham Fredk. esq. 17 Newman st
Tatham John Lawrence, esq. 6 New sq. Lincoln's inn, & Highgate hill
Tatham Joseph, esq. 10 New sq. Lincoln's inn, & North end, Hampstead
Tatham Meaburn, esq. 24 Lincoln's inn fields, & Morton lodge, Highgate hill
Tatham Mrs. 17 Albion street, Hyde pk
Tatham Mrs. 65 Guilford street
Tatham Montagu, esq. 45 Cambridge st
Tatham Thos. Jas. esq. 27 Bedford place Russell sq. & Three Ash cott. Maldon
Tatham Thos. Trevor, esq. 11 Staple inn
Tatham Wm. esq. 61 Oxford ter. & 22 Throgmorton street
Tatham Wm. Hen. esq. 6 Albion pl. Islgtn
Tatlock Paul, esq. 41 Upper Gower street; Bramfield, near Saxmundham; and Highbeach, Essex
Tattersall Geo. esq. 51 Cadogan place
Tattersall George, esq. 42 Pall mall
Tattersall Miss, 22 Bloomsbury square
Tattersall Richard, esq. 99 Sloane street
Tattershall Edwd. B. esq. 9 Gt. James st
Tatum Thos. esq. 3 George st. Hanover sq
Taunton John C. esq. 48 Hatton garden
Taunton Thos. esq. 14 Devonport st
Tavenor Jas. esq. 11 Pine Apple place
Taverner Lewin, esq. 18 Highbury park
Tavistock, Marquis of, 6 Belgrave sq
Tawney James D. esq. 21 Regent sq
Tay Mrs. 17 New street, Dorset square
Tayler James Geo. esq. 23 Norfolk cres
Tayler Mrs. 81 Hamilton terrace
Tayler Wm. esq. 17 Park st. Grosvenor sq
Tayler Wm. esq. 5 Warwick st. Charing cross, & 6 Stone blds. Lincoln's inn
Taylor Lady, St. Katharine's lodge, Rg. pk
Taylor Rt. Hon. Sir Brook, G.C.H. 68 Etn. pl
Taylor Maj. Gen. 3 Clarendon pl. Hyde pk
Taylor Col. Pringle, 15 St. James's pl
Taylor Colonel, 72 Dean st. Soho
Taylor Capt. Herbert, 62 Lowndes sq
Taylor Rev. Wm. 77 Westbourne terrace
Taylor Alf. H. esq. 72 Charltt. st. Fitzy. sq
Taylor Alf. S. esq. 3 Cambdge. pl. Regt. pk
Taylor Abraham, esq. 4 Spur st. Le'str. sq
Taylor A. esq. 5 Augusta pl. Stckwl. com
Taylor Bridges, esq. 8 Lowndes st
Taylor Chas. esq. 76 Westmoreland pl
Taylor C. A. esq. 42 Duke st. St. James's
Taylor Ebenezer, esq. 1 Canonbury sq
Taylor Edward, esq. 10 Craven st
Taylor G esq. 40 Frederick st. Gray's in rd
Taylor Geo. esq. 4 Gower st. Bedford sq
Taylor Geo. esq. 32 St. John's wood ter
Taylor Geo. esq. 9 John st. Bedford row
Taylor George Henry, esq. 14 Abbey pl. St. John's wd. & 23 Lincoln's inn flds
Taylor Geo. L. esq. 45 Hyde park square, & 3 Trafalgar square
Taylor G. T. esq. 18 Featherstone bldgs
Taylor Henry Villiers de Billinghurst, esq. 3 New square, Lincoln's inn
Taylor I. C. esq. 12 Coborg pl. Up. Ken. la
Taylor Jas. esq. 39 Allsop ter. New rd
Taylor Jas. esq. 8 Essex st. Noel st. Isln
Taylor James, esq. 1 Mecklenburgh sq. & 15 Furnival's inn
Taylor James, esq. 24 Upper Harley st
Taylor James Arthur, esq. M.P. Carlton club, & Moseley hall, near Birminghm
Taylor Jas. E. esq. 2 Paddington green
Taylor James Molyneux, esq. 20 York place, City road, & 11 Furnival's inn
Taylor James Wells, esq. 28 Gt. James st
Taylor Jasper Wilson, esq. 62 Coleshill st
Taylor John, esq. 14 Albion grove, Islgn
Taylor John, esq. Sheffield house, Church st. Kensington, & 2 Duke st. Adelphi
Taylor John, esq. 2 Castle st. Holborn
Taylor John, esq. 4 Ely place, Holborn
Taylor John, esq. 13 Glo'ster rd. O. Brmptn
Taylor John, esq. 7 Gray's inn square
Taylor John, esq. 46 Green st. Grsvnr. sq
Taylor John, esq. 10 Harrington sq
Taylor John, esq. 17 Kent ter. Regt.'s pk
Taylor John, esq. 18 Keppel st. Russell sq
Taylor John, esq. Loudoun rd. St. Jn.'swd
Taylor John, esq. 11 St. Geo. pl. Hyde pk
Taylor John, esq. 30 Upper Gower st
Taylor Jno. jun. esq. 61 Queen's rd. Byswtr
Taylor J. E. esq. 35 Frederick st. Gr. in. rd
Taylor John F. esq. 2 Verulam buildings
Taylor John Henry, esq. 22 Parliament st.; 22 Queen st. Cheapside; & Warner ter. Tottenham high cross
Taylor John H. esq. 10 South pl. Fnsby. sq
Taylor John Hockley, esq. 13 Old sq
Taylor John Pitt, esq. 1 Plowden bldgs
Taylor John S. esq. 46 Portmn. pl. Edg. rd
Taylor Joseph, esq. 82 Albany st
Taylor Joseph, esq. 9 New Bridge st
Taylor Jph. esq. 6 Somers pl. Cambdge. sq
Taylor Josiah, esq. 58 Pall mall
Taylor Mark, esq. 48 Upper Baker st
Taylor Miss, 6 Scarsdale ter. Kensingtn
Taylor Misses, 5 Harewood sq. Dorset sq
Taylor Mrs. 4 Abbey pl. St. John's wood
Taylor Mrs. 23A, Bruton st. Berkeley sq
Taylor Mrs. 22 Glo'ster gr. we. Old Brom
Taylor Mrs. 10 Great Titchfield st
Taylor Mrs. 10 Lloyd square, Pentonvill
Taylor Mrs. 6 North cres. Bedford sq
Taylor Mrs. 26 Orchard st. Portman sq
Taylor Mrs. 4 Staple inn, Holborn
Taylor Mrs. 20 Sussex pl. Knsngtn. N w. tn
Taylor Mrs. 5 Up. Eccleston st. Belg. sq
Taylor Mrs. 10 Up. Seymour st. west
Taylor Richard, esq. 31 Alpha rd. Regt. pk
Taylor Richard, esq. 6 Charterhouse sq
Taylor Richd. esq. 1 Constitution row
Taylor Rd. Stephens, esq. 3 Field court, & 3 Raymond's buildings, Gray's inn
Taylor Samuel, esq. 14 John st. Bedfrd rw
Taylor Silas, esq. 35 Regent square
Taylor Stpn. esq. 14 Albion ter. Wand. rd
Taylor Stephen, esq. 1 Goulden terrace
Taylor Thomas, esq. 15 Bryanstone st
Taylor Thomas, esq. 21 Gt. Titchfield st
Taylor Thomas, esq. 9 New Bridge st
Taylor Thomas, esq. 1A, Terrace, Adelphi
Taylor Thos. Ed. esq. MP. Carlton club, 94 Pall mall, & Argellan castle, co. Dub
Taylor Thos. H. esq. 7 South sq. Gray's in
Taylor Well, esq. 13 Foley place
Taylor Wm. esq. 1 Blenheim pl. St. Jn.'swd
Taylor Wm. esq. 8 Marchmont st
Taylor Wm. esq. 15 Porchester ter. Bayswr
Taylor Wm. esq. 15 Stamford st. Blkfrs
Taylor Wm. Chs. esq. 6 Theberton st. west
Taylor Wm. G. esq. 14 John st. Bdfd. rw
Tayspill Miss, 3 Woodland pl. St. Jn.'s wd
Teagle Geo. W. esq. 55 Gloucester pl
Teague C. esq. 10 Portland pl. Wndsw. rd
Teague Jas. esq. 8 & 9 Beaumont st
Teague Jas. A. esq. 28 Spencer st. Gos. rd
Teakle Chas. esq. 35 Camden road villas
Teakle Oliver Edwd. esq. 9 New inn, Strnd
Teape H. esq. 37 Trinity sq. Tower hill
Teast Mrs. 33 Westbourne pl. Sloane sq
Tebbs Chas. esq. 9 Eccleston st. Eaton sq
Tebbs Mrs. 9 St. George's ter. Hyde pk
Tebbs William, esq. 24 Essex st. Strand
Teed George, esq. 40 Chancery lane
Teed John Godfrey, esq. Q.C. 14 Upper Harley st. & 3 New sq. Lincoln's inn
Teed Mrs. 55 Devonshire st. Portland pl
Teede George, esq. 5 Sloane ter. Chelsea
Teesdale John, esq. 80 Park st. Grosv. sq
Teesdale John, esq. 5 Russell square
Teesdale Lady, 33 Upper Baker st
Teevan Jas. esq. 30 Chesham pl. Belgr. sq
Teevan William, esq. 23 Bryanstone sq
Tegart Edward, esq. 37 Bryanstone st
Tegart Edward, esq. 39 Pall mall
Teignmouth Lord, 19 Portland place, & St. Leonard's, Sussex
Teil Geo. esq. 1 Albert rd. Glo'ster gate
Telford Rev. J. 7 Spanish pl. Manch. sq
Temple Christopher, esq. Q.C. 4 Lansdowne pl. Brunswick sq.; 22 Old sq. Lincoln's inn; & Hall place, Dulwich

Tellick Miss, 5 Chester ter. Eaton sq
Temple Christ. jun. esq. 4 Lansdowne pl
Temple Fred. James Henry, esq. 3 Dean st. Park lane, & 16 Furnival's inn
Temple Henry, esq. 3 Elm ct. Temple
Temple Henry, esq. 33 Mornington pl
Temple Stephen, esq. 30 Bernard st
Temple Stephen, esq. 3Hare ct. Temple
Temple Wm. esq. 4 Winchester pl. Pntvl
Temple Wm. Woods, esq. 4 Blomfield st
Templeman James, esq. 73 Mount st
Templeman J. R. esq. 5 Cumberland ter
Templemore Lord, 9 Up. Grosvenor st. & Dunbrody park, county Wexford
Templemore Dow. Lady, 12 Bryanstone sq
Templer John Chas. esq. 10 Farrars bdgs
Templeton A. esq. 15 Hemingford ter. Isl
Templeton J. esq. 7 Norland ter. Notg. hl
Templeton Patrick S. esq. 10 Poland sq
Templeton T. esq. 6 Frederick st. Gr. inn rd
Templetown Viscount, 15 Berkeley sq. & Castle Upton, Templepatrick, Belfast
Tennant Rev. Wm. 10 Dean's yd. Wstmstr
Tennant Charles, esq. 62 Russell square, & 2 Gray's inn square
Tennant George, esq. 12 Paper buildgs
Tennant Henry, esq. 5 New sq. Lincoln's
Tennant Mrs. 62 Russell square, & Cadoxton lodge, Neath, Glamorganshire
Tennant Richard D. esq. 29 Berners st
Tenniel John B. esq. 22 Glo'ster. pl. New rd
Tenterden Lord, 12 Wilton st. & Hendon
Tepper L. esq. 9 Montague pl. Claphm. rd
Ternouth John, esq. 9 Lr. Belgrave pl
Terrail John, esq. 2 Verulam buildings
Terrell Robert H. esq. 14 Gray's inn sq
Terrell Thomas H. esq. 10 New sq. Linc. inn
Terrell Wm. Hull, esq. 4 Stone bldgs
Territt Mrs. Isabella, 8 Allsop terrace
Terry Capt. C. 16 Montepelier sq. Brmptn
Terry H. esq. 9 Chesterfield st. King's cr
Terry Miss & Miss E. 32 Blandford sq
Terry Mrs. 10 Cornwall ter. Regt.'s pk
Terry Mrs. 8 Grove place, Lisson grove
Terry Wm. esq. 45 Southampton bldgs
Teschemacher Fk. esq. 2 Park ter. Highby
Teulon Peter, esq. 22 Queen st. Golden sq
Teulon Samuel S. esq. 18 Millman st
Teuten C. esq. 4 Scarsdale tr. Kensgtn
Tewart Edwd. jun. esq. 16 York pl. Port. sq
Tewart John, esq. 34 York pl. Portman sq. & Coupland castle, Wooler
Teynham Lord, Leamington
Thacker Wm. esq. 25 Euston square
Thackeray Martin, esq. 88 Gloucester pl
Thackthwaite Rt. esq. 24 Essex st. Strand; Westmoreland; & Skipton castle, Yorks
Thanet, Earl of, 78 Glo'ster pl.; Hothfield pl. near Maidstone; Appleby castle, Westmorland, & Skipton castle, Yorkshire
Thatcher A. esq. 5 Devnsh. pl. Edgw. rd
Thatcher Chas. esq. 2 Park pl. Paddingtn
Theaker Edw. esq. 39 Camden rd. villas
Theakstone Geo. H. esq. 27 Allsop terrace
Théleur Edw. A. esq. 26 Manchester st
Thellusson Hon. Miss, 17 Bruton st
Thellusson Thos. R. esq. 16 Hyde park st
Thelwall Rev. A. S. 33 Cumming st
Theobald John, esq. 12 Camden rd. villa
Theobald John P. esq. 16 Furnival's inn
Theobald Mrs. 10 Minerva ter. Brnby. pk
Theobald Wm. esq. 21 Cambridge square
Theobalds Thomas, esq. 81 London wall
Thesiger Sir Frederic, knt. M.P. Attorney General, 11 Bryanstone sq. & 2 King's bench walk
Thesiger Mrs. 24 Cambridge st. Edgw. rd
Thew Major, 11 Hyde park gate, south
Thickbroom Theop. esq. 63 Millbank st
Thickbroom Wm. esq. 19 College st. Wstm
Thicke Misses, 17 Duke st. Portland pl
Thile Baron, secretary to the Prussian legation, 4 Carlton house terrace
Thistlethwayte Henry Frederick, esq. 14 St. Mary Abbott's terrace
Thiselton Aug. U. esq. 7 Blmsbury. pl
Thistlethwayte Thos. esq. 8 Connaught pl. & Southwick park, Fareham, Hants
Thodey Edwd esq. 3 Belinda cot. Islngtn
Thomas Dow. Lady, 31 Chapel st. Gros. pl
Thomas Capt. 19 Petersburgh pl. Bysw
Thomas Alex. esq. Rozel cot. Brnsby. pk
Thomas Charles E. esq. 11 Jermyn st
Thomas Chas. S. esq. 35 Sussex gardens
Thomas David, esq. 21 Duncan terrace
Thomas Fredk. esq. 3 Annett's cresc. Isln
Thomas Geo. Evan, esq. 3 St. James's sq
Thomas Geo. Pollard, esq. 3 Bolton row
Thomas Griffith, esq. Denmark hill
Thomas Griffiths, esq. 4 Claremont sq
Thomas H. esq. 4 Albion cot. Liverpl. rd
Thomas Henry, esq. 2 Doughty st. Foundling; & 35 Lincoln's inn fields
Thomas Jas. esq. 3 Portland pl. Islngtn
Thomas John, esq. 8 Addison rd. Knsgtn
Thomas John, esq. 1 Delahay st. Westm
Thomas John, esq. 48 Upper Harley st
Thomas John Evan, esq. 7 Lr. Belgrave pl
Thomas Maurice, esq. 6 New Boswell ct
Thomas Mrs. 20 Brompton row
Thomas Mrs. 40 Brompton row
Thomas Mrs. Betsy, 11 Clapham rise
Thomas Mrs. 7 Hamilton ter. St. Jn.'s wd
Thomas Mrs. 8 Harleyford pl. Ken. com
Thomas Mrs. 9 Holles st. Cavendish sq
Thomas Mrs. 26 Lower Belgrave place
Thomas Mrs. 6 Sussex pl. Knsngtn. Nw. tn
Thomas Mrs. 11 Tibberton sq. Islington
Thomas Mrs. 4 Upper Seymour st. west
Thomas Miss, 12 Clapham rise
Thomas Miss, 4 Highbury grove
Thomas Miss, 8 Onslow ter. Fulham rd
Thomas Miss, 30 Upper Montagu st
Thomas Ralph, esq. 7 Devonshire st. Queen sq. & 7 South sq. Gray's inn
Thomas Ralph, esq. 16 Chancery lane, & Grove cottage, Chiswick
Thomas Robt. esq. 17 Hamltn. pl. Kg's. cr
Thomas S. esq. 75 Cambridge ter. Edg. rd
Thomas Thos. esq. 8 Addison tr. Knsngtn
Thomas Thomas, esq. 64 Berners st
Thomas Wm. esq. 5 Acton pl. Camden rd
Thomas Wm. esq. 3 Ely pl. Holborn
Thomas Wm. esq. 18 Granville square
Thomas Wm. esq. 25 Granville square
Thomas Wm. esq. 30 Porchester terrace, Bayswater, & 129 Cheapside
Thomas W. C. esq. 6 Gt. James st. Bdfd. rw
Thomas Wm. L. esq. 3 King's bench walk
Thomond Marquis of, K.P. 41 Belgrave square; & Rostellan castle, Cork; & Taplow house, Maidenhead, Berks
Thompson Col. T. P. 21 Old square
Thompson Capt. 3 Dorset ter. Clphm. rd
Thompson Rev. Edwd. Gothic villa, Finchley new road, & North Mimms park, Barnet, Herts
Thompson Wm. esq. Alderman, M.P. 12 Whitehall pl. & Penydarran house, Merthyr Tydvil, Glamorganshire
Thompson Benj. esq. 8 Trafalgar sq. Chel
Thompson Chas. esq. 6 Church st. Liss. gr
Thompson Chas. esq. 20 Kensington sq
Thompson Chas. J. esq. 22 Geo. st. Han. sq
Thompson C. R. esq. 4 Blomfld. rd. Maida hi
Thompson Darius, esq. 128 Strand
Thompson Fras. esq. 12 King's Bnch. wk
Thompson Fras. esq. 2 Westbourne ter
Thompson F. esq. Hollywood cot. Chelsea
Thompson Fred. esq. 5 Brick ct. Temple
Thompson Fred. esq. 4 Malvern ter. Isln
Thompson Fred. esq. 19 Robert ter. Chel
Thompson Fred. E. esq. 4 Alpha road, Rgt.'s pk. & 3 Raymond bldgs. Gray's inn
Thompson Geo. esq. Eccleston st. east
Thompson Geo. esq. 6A, Waterloo place
Thompson Geo. G. esq. 26 Devonshire st
Thompson Hen. esq. 4 King's rd. ter. Chel
Thompson Hen. esq. 16 Northwick ter
Thompson James, esq. 7 Burwood place
Thompson James, esq. 12 Furnival's inn
Thompson Jas. esq. 21 Grove pl. Liss. gr
Thompson James, esq. 12 Orchard st
Thompson John, esq. 3 Albion ter. Chel
Thompson John, esq. 1 Middle Temp. la
Thompson John, esq. 14 O. Burlington st
Thompson John, esq. 14 Old Burlington st. & 19 Lincoln's inn fields
Thompson John C. esq. 22 Geo. st. Han. sq
Thompson John C. esq. 6 Noel st. Islngtn
Thompson J. J. esq. 35 Glo'ster rd. Hyde pk
Thompson Jsph. esq. 2 John st. Bedfrd. rw
Thompson J. V. S.L. 4 Up. Belgrave st
Thompson Mrs. Major, 34 Royal crescent, Notting hill
Thompson Mrs. 31 Chester pl. Ken. cros
Thompson Mrs. 36 Cloudesley ter. Isln
Thompson Mrs. 11 Colebrooke ter. Islngtn
Thompson Mrs. 18 Connaught square
Thompson Mrs. 25½ Dalby ter. City rd
Thompson Mrs. 4 Harrington st. Ham. rd
Thompson Mrs. 7 Sloane st
Thompson Misses, 11 King's parade, Chel
Thompson Miss, Addison rd. so. Knsngtn
Thompson Miss, 10 Burton st
Thompson Miss, 18 Sackville st
Thompson M. W. esq. 18 Kent ter. Rgt.'s pk
Thompson Robt. M. esq. 181 Blackfrs. rd
Thompson Sam. esq. 103 Hatton garden
Thompson Seth, M.D. 19 Brook st
Thompson Theophilus, M.D. 3 Bedfd. sq
Thompson Thos. esq. 109 Chancery lane, & Lower Tulse hill, Brixton
Thompson Thos. esq. 5 Devonshire st. Queen square
Thompson Thos. Charles, esq. 6 Pump ct
Thompson Thos. C. esq. R.H.A. 76 Welbeck street
Thompson Thos. K. esq. 33 Mecklenbrg. sq
Thompson Thomas P. Edwd. esq. 21 Old sq
Thompson Wm. esq. 44 Burton st. Brtn. crs
Thompson Wm. esq. 2 Conduit st. west
Thompson Wm. M.D. 28 Osnaburgh st
Thompson Wm. esq. 6A, Waterloo pl. P. ml
Thompson Wm. Henry, esq. 48 Margaret st
Thompson Wm. Jas. esq. 30 Brunswick sq
Thoms Hen. esq. 3 Philpott ter. Edgw. rd
Thomson Anthy. Todd, M.D. 30 Welbck. st
Thomson Benj. R. esq. 56 Myddelton sq
Thomson Chas. esq. 6 Addison rd. north
Thomson Fred. Hale, esq. 48 Berners st
Thomson Greig, esq. 29 Grosvenor st
Thomson Hy. T. esq. 117 Camdn. rd. vill
Thomson Henry U. M.D. 123 Piccadilly
Thomson James, esq. 97 Albany st
Thomson Jas. esq. 57 Devonsh. st. Prtld. pl
Thomson Jn. esq. 7 Burwood pl. Edgw. rd
Thomson John Duffin, esq. 68 Linc. inn fi
Thomson John S. esq. 17 John st. Bdfd. rw
Thomson Miss, 82 Paradise row, Chelsea
Thomson Miss, 15 Montagu place
Thomson Mrs. 27 Fredk. st. Gray's inn rd
Thomson Mrs. 44 Doughty st
Thomson Mrs. 25 New Bond st
Thomson Mrs. 16 Northampton square
Thomson Mrs. 17 Up. Montagu st
Thomson Robt. esq. 4 Rufford's row, Islgn
Thomson Rt. Wm. esq. 18 Adam st. Adelphi
Thomson Wm. esq. 51 Charlotte st. Fitz. sq
Thomson Wm. G. esq. 33 Glo'ster road, Hyde park
Thorburn Rt. esq. 77 Upper Berkeley st
Thorby Thomas, esq. 1 Wharncliff ter
Thoream Miss, 25 Up. Gloucester place
Thorn Geo. R. esq. 1 Albion ter. Chelsea
Thorn Hen. esq. 4 Albion pl. Canonby. sq
Thorn Rd. L. esq. 31 Upper Belgrave pl
Thorndike Andrew S. esq. 11 Staple inn
Thorne Jas. esq. Mawby ho. Sth. Lmbth
Thorne Jn. esq. 4 Mylne st. Claremont sq
Thorne John M. esq. Turrett ho. South Lmb
Thorne Jsph. S. esq. 7 Park pl. Highby. va
Thorne Mrs. 17 Devereux court, Strand
Thorne Mrs. 88 Great Portland st
Thorne William, esq. 44 Connaught ter
Thorne Wm. esq. 22 Maida hill west
Thornely Thos. esq. M.P. 24 Regent st

Thornes Thos. Wm. esq. 19 Connaught sq
Thornhill Major, K.H. 43 York tr. Rgt.'s pk
Thornhill C. E. esq. 21 Princes st. Cav. sq
Thornhill Geo. esq. M.P. 17 Grosvenor st. & Diddington ho. nr. Buckden, Hunts
Thornhill Mrs. 49 Berkeley square
Thornley J. esq. 1 Polygon, Clarendon sq
Thornthwaite Thos. esq. 30 Gordon st
Thornton Major Gen. Sir Chas. Wm. Great court, St. James's palace
Thornton Lieut. Col. 5 Queen Anne st
Thornton Major, 34 Bedford pl. Blmsby
Thornton Capt. R.N. 12 Up. Glo'ster. pl
Thornton Butler E. esq. 21 Lowndes st
Thornton Edwd. esq. Stone bdg. Linc. inn
Thornton Ed. esq. 3 Up. Woburn pl. Tav. sq
Thornton Henry, esq. 2 Albert rd. Rgt.'s pk
Thornton Hy. esq. 6 Park pl. Up. Baker st
Thornton Hy. Milnes, esq. 215 Regt. st
Thornton Miss, 31 York st. Portman sq
Thornton Mrs. 91 Norton st
Thornton Mrs. 29 South st. Grosvr. sq
Thornton N. F. esq. 3 Montpelier st. Bmtn
Thornton Philip, esq. 3 Museum st
Thornton William, esq. 5 Mountfort crescent, Barnsbury park
Thornton Wm. T. esq. 58 Up. Berkeley st
Thorogood John, esq. 6 Maida hill
Thorold Mrs. 5 Albany ter. New road
Thoroton Mrs. 8 Cornwall ter. Regent's pk
Thorowgood Edwd. J. esq. 38 Argyle sq
Thorp Alf. esq. 55 Cambridge ter. Edg. rd
Thorpe Major S. 10 Exeter hall
Thorpe Rev. Wm. D.D. & Dow. Countess of Pomfret, 9 Upper Belgrave st
Thorpe Geo. esq. 38 Gt. Percy st. Lloyd sq
Thorpe J. esq. 22 Rutland st. Hampstd. rd
Thorpe Jas. esq. 32 Bury st. St. James's
Thorpe Jhn esq. 2 Maida hill w. Edg. rd
Thorpe T. C. esq. 16 Chapel st. Grosvnr. pl
Thorpe Wm. J. esq. 7 New sq. Lincoln's inn
Thoyts Lieut. Col. John, 71 Wimpole st
Thredder J. esq. 3 Princes pl. Kengtn. rd
Threlkeld Dacre, esq. 8 Connaught pl. w
Thring Hen. esq. 30 Lincoln's inn fields
Throckmorton Sir Robt. G. bart. 5 Up. Belgrave st. & Buckland, Farringdon
Thrupp Chas. esq. 1 Hyde park pl. west
Thrupp Fredk. esq. 30 Glo'ster pl. N. w. rd
Thrupp John, esq. 6 Spanish place, & 2 Winchester buildings, City
Thrupp John Aug. esq. 6 Spanish place
Thrupp Joseph Wm. esq. 50 Up. Brook st. & 160 Oxford st
Thrupp Misses, 4 Hamiltn. pl. St. Jn.'s wd
Thrupp Mrs. 50 Welbeck st. Cavend. sq.
Thurgood Mrs. 14 Grove tr. St Jn.'s wd
Thurkle Miss, 7 River ter. City road
Thurlow Lord, Burlington hotel, & Ashfield lodge, Woolpit, Suffolk
Thurlow Thos. esq. 25 Wellington road
Thursby Mrs. 76 Wimpole st. Cavend. sq
Thurston John, esq. 2 Gray's inn square
Thurston John, esq. 29 Hornton st. Knsgtn
Thurston Simon, esq. 9 Sthampt. st. Blmbs
Thwaites Lieut. Col. Geo. Saunders, National Gallery, Trafalgar square, Pall mall east
Thwaites Mrs. 17 Hyde park gardens
Thwaites Wm. Gray, esq. 4 Lyon's inn
Thyne Mrs. 4 Seymour pl. Wandsworth. rd
Thynne Lady Caroline, 15A, Up. Brook st
Thynne Lady Edw. 2 Richmond terrace
Thynne Fred. esq. 11 Gt. George st. Westm
Tiarks Rev. J. G. 67 Gt. Prescot st
Tibbs John, esq. 4 Canonbury park
Tiarks Henry Fred. esq. consul general for Oldenburgh, 4 Park ter. Regent's park, & 48 Fenchurch st
Tibbs R. Wm. esq. 4 Glo'ster st. Queen sq
Tibson Arthur, esq. 1 Spring st. Pdgtn
Tibson Chas. esq. 38 Southbank, Reg. pk
Tickell Hen. esq. 27 Charterhouse sq
Tickell Mrs. 17 Charlotte st. Bedfd. sq
Tickell Mrs. 123 St. John street road
Tiddpratt John, esq. 54 Russell square
Tidd Wm. esq. 59 Walcot pl. Lambeth
Tidey Alfred, esq. 29 Edwards st. Ptmn. sq
Tidman Rev. Arthur, 27½ Finsbury sq
Tidmarsh S. H. esq. 5 Taunton pl. Pk. rd
Tielens John Anthony, esq. 7 Euston sq
Tierney Geo. esq. 28 Regent st
Tilbury Mrs. 26 Tibberton sq. Islington
Tilbury Thos. esq. 12 Friedenstein ter
Tilghman Miss, 44 Devonsh. st. Portl. pl
Tilke Samuel W. esq. 8 Thayer st
Till Mrs. Hy. 16 Notting hill sq. Bayswtr
Tiller Miss, 7 Glo'ster rd. Hyde pk. gar
Tillett John, esq. 7 Upper Portland pl. Wandsworth road
Tillett Saml. esq. 4 Inner Temple lane
Tilley Mrs. 13 Drummond st. Euston sq
Tilling Rt. esq. 37 Alpha rd. Regt.'s pk
Tillotson Wm. esq. 2 Stone bldgs. Linc. inn
Tillotson Wm. esq. 83 Wimpole st
Tilly Mrs. 2 Salisbury street, Strand
Tilt Edw. Wm. M.D. 10 Norfolk st. Park la
Tilt William, esq. 19 Claremont square
Tiltman Miss, 35 Harleyfd. pl. Ken. com
Timbury F. esq. 6 Hemingfrd. cot. Islngtn
Timbury John, esq. 6 Spencer ter. Islgtn
Times Henry G. esq. 41 South bnk. Reg. pk
Timm Jsph. esq. Stamp & Tax office, Somerset ho. & Champion hill, Cambrwl
Timms Mrs. 28 Paddington green
Tindal Rt. Hon. Sir Nicolas Conyngham, knt. 43 Bedford sq.; & Rolls garden, Chancery lane
Tindal Chas. John, esq. 36 Linc. inn flds
Tindal Thomas, esq. 36 Doughty street, & 10 New square, Lincoln's inn
Tindal Wm. esq. 36 Doughty st. Mecklenburgh sq. & 2 Tanfield ct. Temple
Tindale Henry, esq. 26 Up. Montagu st
Tindale John T. esq. Dunsany pl. Wnds. rd
Tindale Mrs. 5 Craig's court
Tindall Geo. esq. 20 Lloyd sq. Pentnville
Tindall Wm. esq. 5 New inn, Strand
Tingle Saml. esq. 12 Notting hill ter
Tinling Lieut. Col. 18 Chapel st. Gros. sq
Tinney Wm. Henry, esq. Q.C. 31 Montague pl. Russell sq. & 9 Old sq. Lincoln's inn
Tinslay John, esq. 2 Rolls buildings
Tiplady Wm. Henry, esq. 31 Gower st
Tipple Mrs. 4 Barnsbury st. Islington
Tisdall J. T. esq. 26 Charles st. Brkly. sq
Tisley Samuel, esq. 112 Chancery lane
Titchfield, Marquis of, 19 Cavendish sq
Tite Wm. esq. 25 Upper Bedford place
Titford Richd. V. esq. 122 Camden rd. vil
Titt Miss, 8 St. James's pl. St. James's
Titt Richard, esq. 34 Addison road north
Tobitt Timothy, esq. 8 Northampton sq
Tod Dav. esq. 5 Sol's row, Hampstead rd
Tod Mrs. 6 Cumberland ter. Regt.'s pk
Tod Wm. esq. 5 Sol's row, Hampstead rd
Todd Anthony, esq. 14 Claremont terr
Todd Hen. John, esq. Larkhall la. Claphm
Todd James Ruddell, esq. 33 Portland pl
Todd John, esq. 1 Elm court, Temple
Todd John, esq. 23 Thavies inn, Holborn
Todd Mrs. 12 Bedford pl. Hampstead rd
Todd Mrs. 3 Earl's terrace, Kensington
Todd Mrs. 10 Noel st. Islington
Todd Mrs. 171 Prospect pl. Edgware rd
Todd Ralph, esq. 20 Cecil st. Strand
Todd Robert, esq. 20 Alpha rd. Regt.'s pk
Todd R. J. esq. Rochfort villa, Glo'ster rd
Todd Rt. Bentley, M.D. 26 Parliament st
Todd Wm. esq. 2 Minerva pl. Brnsbry. pk
Todhunter John, esq. 44 Tavistock sq
Toe David, esq. 66 Millbank st
Tolcher Rt. Hooper, esq. 59 Chancery la
Tollemache Lady E. 11 Chesham place
Tollemache Hon. Chs. 38 Charles st. Bk. sq. & Harrington Rothwell, Kettering
Tollemache Hon. Frederick James, M.P. Athenæum club; & Ham ho. Surrey
Tollemache John, esq. M.P. 40 Wilton crescent, & Tilstone lodge, Tarporley, Cheshire; & Helmington hall, Ipswich
Toller S. B. esq. 23 Old square; & Church row, Hampstead
Toller Thomas, esq. 6 Gray's inn square
Tomalin C. esq. 10 Rodney st. Pentnvl
Tomes John, esq. 41 Mortimer st
Tomes Mrs. 2 Belgrave pl. Wandswth. rd
Tomkies Edw. esq. 3 Malcolm pl. Claphm
Tomkins Rev. Saml. A.M. Stepney collge
Tomkins F. P. esq. 3 Lambeth place, Clapham road
Tomkins John, esq. 11 Gray's inn square
Tomkins John N. esq. 8 Russell pl. Fitz. sq
Tomkins Saml. esq. 4 Albert rd. Regt.'s pk
Tomkins William, esq. 50 Nelson square
Tomkison Thomas, esq. 16 Portland rd
Tomline Geo. M.P. 1 Carlton house ter.; & Riby grove, nr. Brigg, Lincolnshire
Tomlins Philip N. esq. 9 Little Trinity la
Tomlinson J. esq. 34 Henrietta st. Cov. gdn
Tomlinson John, esq. 10 Gt. Maddox st
Tomlinson Thomas, esq. 28 Gt. George st. Westminster; & 3 (north) King's bench walk, Temple; & Heysham, near Lancaster
Tompson Edwd. esq. 4 Stone blds. Linc. inn; & 21 Sussex gardens, Hyde park
Tompson Fred. O. esq. 3 Hyde park pl
Tompson George, esq. Camden villa
Toms Mrs. 16 Belmont pl. Wandswrth. rd
Toms Mrs. 12 Pelham pl. Fulham road
Tonge George, esq. 21 Tavistock sq
Tonna Lewis H. J. esq. United Serv. Inst. Mdle. Scotld. yd. & 8 Park row, Blckhth
Toogood Jas. 27 Elizabeth st. south, Pml
Toogood Hen. esq. 18 Charles st. St. James's; & 22 Parliament st
Toogood Hen. C. esq. 3 Camden ter. west
Toogood William, esq. 18 Charles st. St. James's; & 22 Parliament st
Tooke Thomas, esq. 31 Spring gardens
Tooke Wm. esq. 12 Russl. sq. & 39 Bedfd. rw
Tooker Mrs. 58 Welbeck st
Tookey Wm. esq. 3 River st. City rd
Toombs Hy. esq. 30 Dudley gro. Harrw. rd
Topham Benj. G. esq. 18 Baker st. Lloyd sq
Topham Wm. esq. 7 Figtree ct. Temple
Toplis Jas. esq. 30 New Bridge st. Blkfrs
Toplis Jas. jun. esq. 22 Fitzroy square
Topping Mrs. 4 Cornwall tr. Gt. Dover rd
Torey John, esq. 7 Gibson sq. Islington
Torkington P. Thos. esq. 22 New Bridge st
Torr J. S. esq. 27 Compton ter. Islington
Torre John, esq. 15 Bernard st. Rusll. sq
Torre Mrs. 15 Bernard st. Russell sq
Torrens Mrs. Genl. 18 Cambridge sq
Torriano Wm. Harcourt, esq. 4 George st. Euston sq. & 6 Stone bldgs. Lincoln's inn
Torrington Viscount, 5 Gt. Cumberland st. & Yotes court, Tonbridge
Torrington Mrs. 13 Oxford terrace
Tosswill C. S. 20 Mecklenburgh square
Tothill F. D. esq. 8 Charles st. St. James's
Tottie Charles, esq. consul general for Sweden & Norway, 52 Montagu sq. & Consulate office, 2 Crosby square
Tottie Mrs. 52 Montagu square
Tottie Wm. esq. vice-consul for Sweden & Norway, 2 Crosby square
Tottie Wm. esq. 6 Melcombe pl. Dorset sq
Tottingham Miss, 21 Upper Harley st
Toulmin Mrs. 8 Doughty st
Toulmin Sam. Simpson, esq. 8 Doughty st
Toulson Rd. esq. 10 Gerrard st. Islgtn
Tourle John Jos. esq. 13 Southampton bldgs
Tourner Robert Chas. esq. 273 Strand
Tourrier Jn. esq. 69 Charlotte st. Portlnd. pl
Toussaint John, esq. 21 Wellington ter
Tout Thomas, esq. 1 Stockwell common
Tow James, esq. near Church, Battersea
Tower Christopher, esq. M.P. 23 Belgrave sq. & Huntsmore park, Iver, Bucks
Tower Mrs. 9 Eaton pl. Belgrave sq
Tower Robt. esq. 9 Eaton pl. Belgrave sq
Tower Thos. esq. 4 King's bench wk. Tmple
Towers Wm. C. esq. 31 Montagu square
Towgood Henry, esq. 35 Woburn square

Towgood John, esq. 64 Chancery lane
Towle Fredk. Wm. esq. 190 Sloane st
Town Charles, esq. 103 New Bond st
TowneJosiah,esq.9William st.Knightsbg
Towneley John, esq. M.P. 76 Eaton place, & Towneley hall, Lancashire
Towneley Peregrine Edwd. esq.7 Park st. Westminstr.&Towneley hall, Burnley
Townend John, esq. 18 Compton terrace
Townley Col. Chas. 36 St. James's st
Townley Rev.H. 3 Highbury pl.Highbry
Townley Charles, esq. & Lady Caroline, 3 Tilney st. South Audley st. & Townley hall, Burnley
Townley George, esq. L5, Albany
Townsend John A. esq. 48 Finsbury circ
Townsend Jsph. esq. 5 Geo. st. Euston sq
Townsend Mrs. 9 Eccleston st. south
Townsend S. esq. 5 Wilmot st. Brnswk. sq
Townsend Wm. esq. 9 Clarence terrace
Townsend William Charles, esq. 37 Torrington sq. & 3 Figtree court, Temple
Townshend Lord Charles, 23 Cavendish sq. & Raynham hall, Fakenham; & Tamworth castle
Townshend Marchioness, 1 Hunter st. & Hemmingford Grey lodge, St. Ives
Townshend John, esq. 19 Grove ter. St. John's wood, & 17 Howland st
TownshendSml.I.esq.54Walcot pl.e.Lmb
Towse Wm. B. esq. Fishmongers' hall
Towsey Edw. esq.16 Chestr.pl.Kengtn.cr
Toynbee Joseph, esq. 12 Argyll place
Tozer John, esq. 2 Churchyd. ct. Temple
TracyG.M.esq.8St.Ann'svil.St.John's wd
TracyWm.M. esq. 13 Hill st.Berkeley sq
Trafford Miss, 9 Cambridge ter.Rgt.'s pk
TraherWm.esq.Gothic cot.Wandswth.rd
Trail Archd.esq.69 Gt.Russell st.Blmsby
TrailGeo.M.P.Steven's ho.18Nw.Bond st
Trail George Wm. esq. 23 Hanover sq
Trail John, esq. 20 Upper North place, Gray's inn road, & 4 Hare ct. Temple
Traile Mrs. 10 Addison ter. Kensington
Traill Jas. esq. Union hall police court, & Morden hill, Blackheath
Train Geo. esq. 5 John st. Bedford row
Train Mrs. Wm. 5 John st. Bedford row
Trant Hen. D. esq. 2Charles st.Grosv.sq
Travellers' Club House(William Browne, secretary), 106 Pall mall
Travers Ben. esq. 12 Bruton st. Bond st
Travers Benj. jun. esq. 6 St. Thomas's st
Travers Geo. F. esq. 9 Russell pl. Fitzroy sq. & Fairfield lodge, Exeter
Travers Hen.Ths.esq.3 Park rd. Notg. hl
TreacherW.esq.1St.Ann'svils.St.Jn.'swd
Trebeck James, esq. 29 Green st
Treble J.esq. 3A, Marlboro' pl.St.Jn.'swd
Trecothick Barlow, esq. 40 York st
Trecothick Jas. esq. 15 Connaught ter
Tree Mrs. 3 Torrington square
Treeby John Wright, esq. Elizabethan villa, Finchley new road
Tregelles Sam. P. esq 5 Theberton st. we
Treherne David, esq. 48 Haymarket
Treherne Edm. esq. 14 St. George's ter
Trelawney Harry Brereton, esq. 30 Hertford st. Mayfair
Trelawney John Salusbury, esq. M.P. 1 Lower Grosvenor place
Tremenheere John Henry, esq. 1 New sq
Tremenhere Col. 33 Somerset st
Trench Major Gen. Sir Fred.Wm. K.C.H., M.P.85 Pall mall,& Moyvannon castle, near Athlone, Ireland
Trench Mrs. 24 Oxford square
Trenery T. esq. 4 Salisbury st. Lissn. gr
Trent Mrs. 11 Lowndes st. Belgrave sq
Trestail Rev. Fredk. 48 Gibson square
Trevelyan Lt.Col.Waltr.2 St. James's pl
Trevor Hon. Geo. Rice Rice, M.P. 11 Hyde pk.gardens,&Bromhall, Bedford
Trevor Lt.Gen. Hon.Hy.O.75 Chester sq
Trevor And. esq. 27 Glo'ster pl.Portm.sq
TrevorChas. esq.15 Gower st.Bedford sq
Trevor Mrs. 72 Coleshill st. Eaton sq
Trezevant Peter, esq. 31 Chester terrace
Trezise Mrs. 4 Montague pl. Noel st. Isln
Tribe Edward, esq. 34 Foley place, & 6 Barge yard, Bucklersbury
TribemanHy.C.esq.19Maida hl.Edgw.rd
Triebener F. esq.10 Hornton st. Kensgtn
Trigg M. esq. 1 Sebbon's bldgs. Islingtn
Trigge Saml. esq.3 Bernard st.Russell sq
Trimen Andw. esq.1 Durham pl.Chelsea, & 9 Adam st. Adelphi
Trimen Rd. esq. 3 Park pl. vil. Padgton
Trimleston Lord, 24 Park lane, & Turvey house, county Dublin
Trimmer Mrs.12St.George's ter.Hyde pk
Trimming Edwin L. esq.16 Barnard's inn
Trinder Wm.Hen.esq.1John st.Bedfd.rw
Trinery Ed.esq.4 Holland st. Brixton rd
Tringham Misses, 9 St. John's wood rd
Tringham William, esq.11 Cavendish rd. St. John's wood, & Long cross, Surrey
Tripp Richd.S.esq.24Oldsq.Lincoln's inn
TrippStevens,esq.34Cumming st.Pntnvl. & 2 Adelaide place, London bridge
TriquetT.M.esq.3Spring tr.Wandswh.rd
Triston John Hovell, esq.40 Southampton buildings, Chancery lane
Tritton Henry, esq. 32 Portland place
Trivett Mrs. 30 Osnaburgh st.Rgnt.'s pk
Trollope Sir John, bt.M.P. 17 Gt.Cumberland place
Trollope Edward, esq. 59 Doughty st. & 60 Carey st
Trollope Wm. esq.2 Grenville st.Brun. sq
Trotman Ebenezer, esq. 13 Furnival's inn
Trott Wm. esq. 8 Elizabeth st. Eaton sq. & 1 Crown court, Threadneedle st
Trotter Lady Coutts, 11 Grosvenor sq
Trotter Alex.esq.8 Montagu pl.Mntgu.sq
Trotter Dixon T. esq. 13 Ehrenburgh ter
Trotter Fredk.esq.16 Old sq.Lincoln's inn
Trotter John, esq. 13 Connaught place, & Durham park, near Barnett
Trotter John, M.P. 28 Eaton place, Belgrave sq. & Horton place, Epsom
Trotter Miss, 28 Eaton pl. Belgrave sq
Trotter Miss, 11 Grosvenor square
Troubridge Admiral Sir Edward Thomas, M.P. K.C.B. 11 Eaton pl. Belgrave sq
Trotter Thos. Dixon Marr, esq. 4 Ely pl
Troup Captn. John Rose, 11 Bernard st
Troward Thomas, esq. 67 Baker st
Troughton Richard Zouch, esq. 16 Dorset terrace, Clapham road
Trower Chas. Fras. esq. 6 New sq.Lin.inn
Trower Fredk. esq. 4 Clifton pl. Susx. sq
Trower George S. esq. 10 St. James's pl
Trower Mrs. 1 Up. Montague st.Russ. sq
Trubee Henry, esq.2Kemp's row, Pimlico
Trueman Joseph, esq. 9 Highbury grove
Trufitt Mrs. 5 Burwood pl. Edgware rd
Trulock Thos. esq. 13 Bruton st.Berk. sq
Truman Edwin, esq. 40A, Haymarket
Truman C. esq. 5 Westbourne st.Hyde pk
Trundle Geo. esq. 18 Gt.Queen st.Westm
Trundle Miss, 18 Brunswick square
Truscott Jas. esq. 9 Colebrooke ter.Islgtn
Truwhitt George, esq. 2 Cook's court, Carey st. & Long lodge, Finchley
Try Henry, esq. 7 Stockwell common
Trye Edward, esq. 13 Clifford's inn
Trye Jas.Hen.esq.7Palmer ter.Holloway
Trye Mrs. 22 Gibson square, Islington
Tuach Wm. A. esq. 24B, Davies st
Tubb Edward, esq. 3Took's ct.Chanceryla
Tubb Robert, esq. 46 Queen Anne st
Tubb Wm. Hen. esq.6Racquet ct.Fleet st
Tuck Hen. Ed.esq.24Grftn.st.e.Fitzry.sq
Tucker Benj. esq. 35John st. Bedford row
Tucker Edward, esq. 53 Davies st
Tucker E. esq. 24 Edward's ter.Caledn.rd
Tucker Fredk. John, esq.6Raymond bdgs
Tucker G. W. esq. 11 Paper bdgs.Temple
Tucker Hen. St. Geo. esq. 3 Up. Portl. pl
Tucker Jedediah S. esq. 5Pump ct.Temple
Tucker Jervis, esq.35John st.Bedford row
Tucker John Hodges, esq. 38 Berners st
Tucker Joseph, esq. 41 Finsbury circus
Tucker Mrs. 18 Goulden ter.Barnsby. rd
Tucker Mrs. 35 John st. Bedford row
Tucker Mrs. 8 Scarsdale ter.Kensington
Tucker Richard, esq. Charterhouse
Tucker Rt. C. esq. 6 Coleshill st.Eatn. sq
Tucker Thos. esq. 28Bury st. St. James's
Tucker Wm. esq. 28 South Molton st
Tucker Wm. esq.11 Oxford st.Marlbro' rd
Tuckey Geo. esq.10Grove rd. St.Jn.'s wd
Tuckey Mrs. 1 Victoria sq. Pimlico
TuderWm.esq.144Oxford st.&Tenby,S.W
Tudor Capt. Robt. Owen, 30Blandford sq
Tudor George, esq. 41 Portman square
Tudor Henry, esq. 6 Conduit st
Tudor Henry, esq. 39 Gordon square
Tudor Owen Davies, esq. 30 Chancery la
Tudor Owen Davies, esq. 30 Blandford sq
Tudway Clement, esq. 1 John st.Bdfd.rw
Tudway Clement, esq. 4 Endsleigh st
Tufnel Nathl. esq. 16Park pl.ter.Pad.grn
Tufnell Henry, esq. M.P. Brookes' club
Tufnell John Jolliffe, esq. 49 Albemarle st. & Langley's, Chelmsford
Tufton Lady E. 11 Cumberland st
Tuite Hugh Morgan, esq. M.P. 2 Princes pl. St. James's, & Sonna, Westmeath
Tuke Wm. esq. 36 Northbank, Regt.'s pk
Tull Hen. esq. 81 Jermyn st. & Newbury
Tull Rd. esq. 14 Stockbridge ter. Pimlico
Tullett Rd. esq. 34 Camden rd. villas
Tulloch James, esq. 16 Montague place
Tulloh James, esq. 3 Agar st. Strand
TumbridgeJ.esq.1Regentter.King'srd.we
Tunley Wm. esq. 43 Camden st. south
Tunno Edwd. Rose, esq. 19 Upper Brook st.; & Amport house, Andover, Hants; & Llangennick park, Carmarthen
Tunno Miss, 65 Upper Berkeley st
Tunstall B. esq.48Portman pl.Maida hill
Tupper H. esq. 1 Warwick sq.Kensingtn
Tupper Martin, esq. 5 New Burlington st. & Albury, Guildford, Surrey
Tupper Mrs. 7 Onslow ter. Fulham rd
Tupper Nants, esq. 313 Regent st
TurckHermanC.esq.40Queen st.Blmsbry
Turck Mrs. 4 Marlbro' pl.Kenngtn. cross
Turle James, esq. Cloisters, Westminster
Turle John, esq. 2 Richmond ter. Pntnvl
Turnbull Alexander, M.D. 48 Russell sq
Turnbull John George, esq. 2 Sussex sq
Turnbull Thos. esq. 47 Clarendon sq
Turnbull Thos. esq. 18 Portland terrace
Turnbull Thos. esq. 14 Trinity square
Turnbull Wm. esq. K2, Albany, Piccadilly
Turner Sir Gregory O. Page, bart. 27 Up. Harley st. & Battersden pk.nr.Woburn
Turner Col. F. H. 32 Argyll st. Regent st
Turner Major, 4 Montagu pl. Clapham rd
Turner Capt. Herbert, 46 Hamilton ter
Turner Rev.John, D.D. 19 Up.Montagu st
Turner Rev. C. 2 Cobourg.pl.Up.Kenn.la
Turner Rev. Michael, 4 Vigo st
Turner Alfred, esq. 32 Red lion square
Turner Brooke, esq. 12 Devonport st
Turner Brooke, esq. 1 Red lion square
Turner Charles, esq. 2 Euston square
Turner Chas.esq.2 Michael'sgr.Brompton
Turner Chas. esq. 21 Westbourne place
Turner Chas. Robt. esq. 17 Chester ter. Regent's pk. & 2 Mitre ct. Temple
Turner Edmund, esq. M.P. 18 Dover st. & Truro
Turner Edward, esq. 4 Bolton row
Turner Francis, esq. 86 Newman st
Turner Francis, esq. 15 Queen square, Westminster, & 7 New sq.Lincoln's inn
Turner Frederick John, esq. 7 New sq
Turner George, esq. 6 Harley st. Cav. sq
Turner George, esq. 35 Northampton sq
Turner George Jas. esq. Q.C. 6 Harley st. Cavendish sq. & 11 New square
Turner Henry, esq. 10 Bedford pl. Russell sq. & Nutfield, Surrey
Turner Henry, esq. 1 Belle vue, Chelsea

Turner Henry, esq. 32 Crown st. Soho
Turner Henry John, esq. 27 Percy st
Turner Henry N. esq. 1 Up. Belgrave pl
Turner Henry Scott, esq. 57 Jermyn st
Turner Henry W. esq.10 Crown office row
Turner John, esq. 31 Conduit st
Turner John, esq. 49 Gt Ormond st
Turner John, esq. 10 Bedford pl. Blmsby
Turner John, esq. 43 Lower Belgrave pl
Turner John, esq. 16 Mabledon place
Turner John, esq. 2 North bank, Rgt. pk
Turner Joseph, esq. 63 Borough road
Turner Joseph H. esq. 20 Montague pl. & 8 Chancery lane; & Frith Grange, Hindon
Turner Joseph Mallord William, esq. R.A. 47 Queen Anne st. Cavendish sq
Turner Marshal, esq. 52 Torrington sq. & 24 Gt. George st. Westminster
Turner Miss, 21 Upper Wimpole st
Turner Mrs. 26 Gt. James st. Bedford rw
Turner Mrs. 16 Great Ormond st
Turner Mrs. 10 Kensington garden ter
Turner Mrs. 30 Oxford sq
Turner Mrs. 12 Radcliffe ter. Goswell rd
Turner Mrs.6 Up.Chadwell st. Pentonville
Turner Rd. esq. 9 Dorset ter. Clapham rd
Turner Richard Edward, esq. 23 Chester ter. Eaton sq. & 2 Tanfield ct. Temple
Turner Samuel, esq. 9 Gray's inn square
Turner Thos. M.D. 31 Curzon st. Mayfair
Turner Thos. esq. 32 Milton st. Dorset sq
Turner Thos. esq. 7 Old sq. Lincoln's inn, & Fenton house, Hampstead
Turner Thos. Preregrine, esq. 2 Field ct. Gray's inn, & 19 Lloyd square
Turner William, esq. 32 Red lion square
Turner Wm. esq. 27 Sussex pl. Kensingtn
Turner Wm. esq. 7 Ulster terrace
Turner Wm. L. esq. 25 Cambridge st
Turnley Hen. esq. 4 Bishopsgate within
Turnor Christr. esq. M.P. 12 Up. Belgrave st. & Stoke Rochfort, Lincolnshire
Turnour T.G. esq. 11 Charlt.pl.Up.Ken.la
Turpin Chas. esq. Salvador ho. Bshpsgte
Turquand Alex. esq. 245 Regent st
Turton Rt. esq. 24 Northumberland st
Tuson Ed. W. esq. 10 Russel pl. Fitzroy sq. & Preston house, Harrow, Middlx
Tussaud Fras. esq. 10 Salisbury pl. Nw.rd
Tustin Edwd. Erskine, esq. 8 Fludyer st. Westminster, & 4 New Bridge st. Bfrs
Tuvey Mrs. 26 Brompton square
Twait O. esq. 2 Powis pl. Hampstead rd
Twallin Mrs. 15 Gerrard st. Islington
Tweddell John, esq.3 Mitre ct. Hattn. gdn
Tweed John J. jun. esq. 9 Gilbert st
Tweed John J. sen. esq. 4 Alfred pl. Bdfd.sq
Tweeddale, Marquis of, K.T. Yesterhouse, Haddington
Tweedie Alex. M.D. 30 Montague place
Tweedy Mrs. 26 Tavistock place
Twells Philip, esq.1 New sq. Lincoln's inn
Twemlow Thos. F. esq. 54 Davies st. & 2 Stone buildings, Lincoln's inn
Twentyman Rd. esq. 9 Coburg pl. Kngtn.la
Twentyman Wm. Holme, esq. 11 Regent villa, Avenue road, Regent's park
Twining Richard, George John Aldred, Richard Samuel Harvey, & William Brewster, 215 Strand
Twining Aldred, esq. 1 Gray's inn square
Twining Richard, esq. 13 Bedford pl
Twining Wm. M.D.13 Bedford pl. Russ.sq
Twisden Thos. Edwd. esq. 5 Verulam bldgs. Gray's inn, & 1 Lincoln's inn flds
Twiselton Edward, esq. 122 Pall mall
Twiss Rev. Robert, LL.D. 39 Cambridge ter. Edgware rd. & Hoseley, Flintshire
Twiss Horace, esq. Q.C. 5 Park place, St. James's, & 56 Chancery lane
Twiss Mrs. 4 Trevor sq. Knightsbridge
Twiss Rd. esq.39 Cambridg. ter. Edgw.rd
Twiss Travers, D.C.L. B5, Albany, & 9 Godliman st. Doctors' commons
Twopeny Wm. esq. 4 Lamb bldg. Temple

Twycross Rev. John, 42 Hunter st
Twyford Samuel, esq. 2 Harley st
Twysden Sir Wm.41 Dorset st. Portmn.sq
Tyars Fras. esq. 17 Bread st. Cheapside
Tyas Isaac Henry, esq. 13 Beaufort bdgs
Tyas John, esq. 19 Essex st. Strand
Tyas Richard, esq. 13 Beaufort buildings
Tyas Richard, esq. 34 Bedford pl. Blmsby
Tyerman Thomas, esq. 12 Queen's bdgs. Brompton, & 6 Chancery lane
Tylee Charles, esq. 17 Hans place
Tylee Edward, esq. 29 Oxford square, Hyde park, & 14 Essex st. Strand
Tyler Rev. James Endell 18 Bedford sq
Tyler Henry Fredk. esq. 47 Bedford row
Tyler James, esq. 15 Holloway pl. Holwy
Tyler John, esq. 3 Staple inn, Holborn
Tyler Joseph, esq. 7 South sq. Grays' inn
Tyler Miss, 18 Brunswick pl. Barnsbury
Tyler Peter, esq. 4 Alfred pl. Brompton
Tyler Wm. esq. 25 Duncan ter. City rd
Tyler Wm. esq. 2 Warwick sq. Kensngtn
Tymms Henry W. esq. 13 Maddox st
Tyndale Capt. C. W.20 Alfred pl. Brmptn
Tyndale John W. esq.11 Lincolns' inn flds
Tyndale Mrs. 19 Blandford square
Tynte Miss, 66 Porchester ter. Bayswtr
Type Matthew, esq. 16 Cloudesley sq
Tyrell Sir John Tyssen, bart. M.P.4 Cleveland sq. & Boreham ho. Chelmsford
Tyrie John G. esq. 11 Kensington gar.ter
Tyrrell Edward, esq. 3 Hinde st
Tyrrell Richd. esq. 79 Oxford terrace
Tyrrell Thos. esq. 17 Blomfield road
Tyrwhitt Lady, 51 Eaton square
Tyrwhitt Capt. Chas. 51 Eaton square
Tyrwhitt Chas. esq. 1 Charles st. Bkly.sq
Tyrwhitt Robert Philip, esq. 5 Eccleston sq. & 4 Brick court, Temple
Tyson Wm. esq. 37 University st
Tytler Peter F. esq. 34 Devonshire place

UDALL Henry, esq.3 Figtree ct. Temple
Ude Louis Eustace, esq. 2 Albemarle st
Udney Mrs. 16 Blandford square
Uffell Mrs. 39 Kenton st. Brunswick sq
Ullathorne Mrs.3 Up. Eaton pl. Hmpstd.rd
Ullathorne Wm. esq. Moundho. Nottng.hl
Ulyat Wm. Phillips, esq.20 Claphm.rd.pl
Umney Alfred, esq. 12 Woburn square
Underdown Mrs. 28 Allsop ter. New rd
Underdown Robt. esq.3 Warwick sq. Knsg
Underwood Col. John, 6 Harewood sq
Underwood Charles, esq. 25 Ely place
Underwood Chs. esq.10 Egremont pl. N.w.r
Underwood Chs. esq. 75 Gt. Titchfield st
Underwood Jn. Wm. esq. 7 Manchestr.st
Underwood John M. esq. 4 Salisbury pl. New rd
Underwood Mrs. 14 Glo'ster pl. Prtm sq
Underwood Mrs.25 Norland sq. Notng.hl
Underwood T. esq.45 Gt. Marlborough st
Union Bank of London (Regent st. branch), Argyll place, Regent st. (Charing cross branch), 4 Pall mall ea
Union Club House (John Mackenzie, sec.), Trafalgar square
United Service Senior Club Ho. (Thos. Hen. Willis, sec.), 116 Pall mall
United University Club House (Wm. Hoys, sec.), Pall mall east
Unitt Mrs. 4 Canonbury ctgs. Islngtn
Unthank John, esq. 46 Torrington sq
Unwin Joseph, esq. 4 Calthorpe st
Unwin Mrs. 10 Blandford pl. Regent's pk
Unwin Wm. esq. 90 Milton st. Dorset sq
Upcher Miss, 1 Titchfield tr. Regt.'s pk
Upcroft John M. 4 Salisbury pl. New rd
Upham C. esq. 7 Mylne st. Claremont sq
Upjohn Saml. esq.7 Church st. Knsngtn
Upperton Wm. esq. 4 Everett st. Brswk.sq
Uppleby Geo. esq. 4 Elm ct. Temple
Upton Hon. Gen. Arthur, G2, Albany
Upton Hon. Arthur, 15 Berkeley sq
Upton Hon. Geo. 15 Berkeley square
Upton Hon. Henry Montague, 18 Albemarle st. Piccadilly
Upton Hon. Miss Sophia, 5 Chesterfield st

Upton Archer T. esq. 24 Lincoln's inn flds
Upton Edwd. esq. 17 Euston pl. New rd
Upton Geo. esq. 24 Queen's rw. Pntnvll
Upton Mrs. 9 London st. Fitzroy sq
Upton Robert B. esq. 5 Guilford st. Russell sq. & 44 Parliament st
Upward J.W. esq. 12 Hamiltn.pl. New rd
Ure Alex. esq. 13 Charlotte st. Bedfd. sq
Ure Andw. M.D. 13 Charlotte st. Bedfd.sq
Ure Masterton, esq. 16 Brook st
Urling Geo. F. esq.16 Glo'ster cres. Glo.'gt
Urlwin P.W. esq.1 Brunswick pl. Walw.rd
Urquhart Alex. esq. 44 Linc. inn fields
Urquhart Jn. esq. 2 Charles st. Brkly. sq
Usborne Major, 9 Upper Bedford place
Usborne John, esq. 3 Halkin st. Grosvnr. pl.; & Holden, nr. Tunbridge, Kent; & Woodlands, near Bagshot, Surrey
Usborne Mrs. 48 Queen Ann st. Cav. sq
Usborne Thos. esq. 14 Montague pl.; & Gillwell house
Usborne Thos. Hen. esq. 14 Montague pl
Usherwood Thomas, esq. 29 Alpha road
Usiglio Angelo, esq. 53 London st. Fitz.sq
Uster Henry L. T. Von, 3 Berkeley sq
Uwins James, esq. Victoria rd. Knsgtn
Uxbridge, Earl of, P.C., Uxbridge house, 1 Old Burlington st.; & Tewin Water, Wellyn, Herts
Uzielli Matthew, esq. 1 Euston square

VACHELL Col. York chamb. 41 St. Jas.st
Vachell Mrs. 9 Union st. Berkeley sq
Vacher Thos. B. esq. 9 Alfred pl. Alex.sq
Vade John Knox, M.D. 8 Up. Seymour st
Vade Walpole, R.H. esq. 38 Up. Brook st
Vage Thos. esq. 28 Alfred pl. Bedford sq
Vaizey John, esq. 2 South sq. Gray's inn
Vaker Thos. esq. 34 Tavistock st. Cov.ga
Valdez Mons. Antonio Travassos, Delahay st. Westminster
Vale John, esq. 7 Devonshire pl. Edgw.rd
Vale John, esq. 10 Radcliffe ter. Goswl.rd
Valentine Francis, esq. 6 Keppel st
Valentine Mrs. 16 Berwick st. Pimlico
Valiant Mrs. 26 Keppel st. Russell sq
Vallance Henry, esq. 20 Essex st. Strand
Vallance Hy. W. esq. 112 Camden rd. vils
Vallance James, esq. 35 Cavendish sq
Vallance Jas. esq. 4 King's Bench walk
Vallance John, esq. 20 Essex st. Strand
Valletti Madame, 4 Portland tr. Rgt. pk
Vallings Fred. esq. 2 Euston pl. New rd
Vallotton C.H. esq. Clifton ho. O. Brmptn
Vallotton Mrs. 24 Myddleton square
Valpy Abraham John, esq. 6 St. John's wood road, & Brighton
Valpy Rd. esq. 19 Earl's ter. Kensingtn
Van Butchell Edwin M. esq. 14 Broad st
Van Butchell Sidney J. esq. 27 Baker st
Vance John E. esq. 12 Serle st. Linc. inn
Vance Mrs. 17 Dorset square
Vance Thos. esq. 2 Hare court, Temple
Vandenhoff J. esq.34 Northbank, Rgt.'s pk
Vandeput Geo. H. esq. 17 Up. Bedford pl
Vandercom J.F. esq. 10 Mecklenburgh sq
Vanderkiste Robt. esq. 15 Calthorpe st
Vanderpant Hy. C. esq.51 Margt. st. Cav.sq
Van de Weyer M. Sylvian, envoy extraordinary, & minister plenipotentiary from Belgium, 50 Portland pl.; office, 9A, Weymouth st
Vanderpant J. esq. 5 Minerva ter. Islntn
Vandiest F. G. esq.14 Stockwell common
Vane Lord Harry Geo. M.P. 29 Grosvenor place, & Raby castle, Durham
Vane Hen. M. esq. Carlton chm. 12 Regt.st
Van Fowinkle Miss, 85 Hamltn. tr. St. J's.w
Van Heythusen Richard Edward, esq. 31 John st. Bedford row
Van Millingen Joseph, esq. 26 Albany st
Vannett Madame, 15 York bldngs. New.rd
Van Oven Barnard, esq. 30 Gower st
Van Sandau Andr. esq.4 Ampton pl. Gr.i.rd
Vann Edwd. esq.16 Providence rw. Fnsby
Vansittart Hon. Mrs. 1 Halkin st. west

Vansittart Capt. Rt. 1 Halkin st. west
Vanvoorst Mrs. 36 Gt. James st. Bedfd. rw
Van Zeller le commandeur Francisco Ignacio, consul general for Portugal, 40 Dorset square, & 5 Jeffery sq
Vardon Mrs. 22 Holywell st. Millbank
Vardon Mrs. 33 Oxford terrace
Vardon Wm. esq. 41 Halfmoon st. & Eaton hall, Congleton
Varicas Mrs. 19 Tonbridge pl. New road
Varicas Robert A. esq. 29 Woburn pl
Varley C. esq. 1 Charles st. Clarendn. sq
Varley Mrs. 37 Edwardes sq. Kensington
Varley Mrs. 4 Parham pl. Chelsea
Varnham Mrs. 16 Milton pl. Belgrave sq
Varty Thos. esq. 1 Villiers st. Strand
Vaughan Col. G. H. 144 Oxford st
Vaughan Sir Chas. R. 5 Hertford st. Myfr
Vaughan Col. Thos. 15 Rutland gate, Knightsbridge; & Woodstone, Huntingdonshire
Vaughan Geo. esq. 28 Cumberland ter
Vaughan Henry, esq. 28 Cumberland ter
Vaughan H. Halford, esq. Devereux ct. Tm
Vaughan John, esq. 14 Lloyd square
Vaughan Mrs. 28 Cumblnd. ter. Rgt. pk
Vaughan Miss, 17 Glo'ster cr. Regts. pk
Vaughan Samuel B. esq. 16 Argyl st. Newrd
Vaughan Samuel B. esq. 4 Furnival's inn
Vaux of Harrowden Lord, 1 Halkin st. west
Vaux Chris. esq. 9 Fred st. Gray's inn rd
Vaux Mrs. 7 Kennington pl. Up. Kengn. la
Vaux Mrs. 23 Up. Grosvenor st
Vavasseur Mrs. 3 Newington pl. Kent rd
Vawser G. R. jun. esq. 35 Graham st. Pimlc
Vawser G. R. sen. esq. 35 Graham st. Pimlc
Vawser Miss, 35 Graham st. Pimlico
Veal Jas. esq. 19 Abingdon st. Westminster
Veal Rd. esq. 2 Stockwell vil. Clapham rd
Veale George, esq. 13 Adam st. Adelphi
Veale Wm. esq. St. Ann's vils. Acacia rd
Vedy Madame, 2 Victoria ter. Chelsea
Veitch Jas. M.D. 33 Kensington square
Venables Adolphus, esq. 74 Newman st
Venables Chs. J. esq. 8 Glo'ster rd. Vic. gt
Venables Geo. S. esq. 2 Mitre ct. buildgs
Venables Miss, 13 Nottingham terrace
Venables Rt. M.D. 5 St. Vincent pl. City rd
Venn John, esq. 7 Highbury park
Venn John, esq. 12 Canonbury square
Venn Thos. esq. 54 Warren st. Fitzroy sq
Venner Thos. esq. 62 George st. Eustn. sq
Venning James M. esq. 3 Cambridge sq. Hyde pk. & Cock fosters, East Barnet
Venning Saml. B. esq. 4 Lindsey row, Chls
Venour Stephen Chas. esq. 5 Gray's inn sq
Vere James, esq. 48 Oxford terrace
Verey Geo. esq. 13 Gloster cr. Regent's pk
Verey Hen. esq. 12 Cavndsh. rd. St. Jn.'swd
Verey Mrs. 41 Portman pl. Edgware rd
Verinder Henry, esq. 6 Falcon square
Verity Major I. L. 21 South ter. Alex. sq
Verner Col. Wm. M.P. 68 Eaton square, & Church hill, near Moy, Ireland
Verner Lt. Col. 49 Cadogan place
Verney Hen. Robt. esq. 10 Goswell road
Vernon Hon. Miss, 18 Albemarle st
Vernon Lord, 12 Gt. Marlborough st.; & Sudbury hall, Derbyshire; & Poynton hall, Cheshire; & Widdrington Castle, Northumberland
Vernon Capt. R.N. 41 St. James's st
Vernon Granville Harcourt, esq. M.P. c2, Albany, & the Grove, Ea. Retford
Vernon John Y. esq. 48 Tavistock sq
Vernon Joseph, esq. 10 Hamilton terrace
Vernon Joseph, esq. 12A, Up. Woburn pl
Vernon Robert, esq. 50 Pall mall, & Ardington house, Wantage, Berks
Verralls John, esq. 17 Noel st. Islington
Verry George, esq. 14 Tonbridge place
Verschoyle Robert, esq. 98 Eaton sq
Vertigans Edward, esq. 15 Belinda ter
Vertue Geo. esq. Middle Scotland yard
Verulam Earl of, 42 Grosvenor square, & Gorhambury, St. Alban's

Vesey Hon. Thos. M.P. & Lady Emma, 1 Grafton st. Bond st
Vevers Mrs. 3 Cumming st. Pentonville
Vezey Jsph. esq. 9 Park pl. ter. Pdgtn. gr
Vialls Mrs. 59 Chester square
Vian Wm. esq. 49 Duke st. St. James's
Vibert John Este, esq. 10 Colebrooke row
Vickerman Chas. R. esq. 4 South square, Gray's inn, & Priory, Blackmow, Ingatestone
Vickers J. esq. 24 Holloway pl. Holloway
Vickers J. esq. 1 Park pl. vills. Padding
Vickers Samuel, esq. 35 Park st. Islngtn
Vickers Wm. esq. 12 Radnor pl. Hyde pk
Vickers Wm. Randall, esq. 32 Baker st
Vickery Thos. M. esq. 25 Lincoln's inn fi
Victory Duke of (Gen. Espartero), Abbey lodge, Park road, Regent's park
Vidgen Mrs. 33 Up. Berkeley st. Portmn. sq
Vieyres Anth. esq. 9 Glo'ster rd. O. Brmptn
Vigers Wm. Revell, esq. 50 Russell sq
Vignatti G. esq. 3 Glo'ster rd. Old Bmtn
Vigne Felix Wm. esq. 5 York st. Portmn. sq
Vigne Mrs. 5 Cambridge sq. Hyde park
Vignoles Charles, esq. 4 Trafalgar sq
Vigurs Ed. Beverley, esq. 20 Morningtn. pl
Vile Oliver, esq. 1 St. James's square
Villebois Henry, esq. 83 Glo'ster pl. Portman sq. & Marsham house, Downham
Villiers Viscount, M.P. 38 Berkeley sq. & Upton park, Banbury
Villiers Lord & Lady, 38 Berkeley sq
Villiers Hon. A. J. C. 110 Piccadilly
Villiers Hon. Charles Pelham, M.P. Brook's club, & Rolls yard, Chancery la
Villiers Hon. Edward Ernest, 22 Rutland gate, Hyde park, west side
Villiers Hon. Mrs. Geo. South pl. Knightsbr
Villiers John F. esq. 7 New sq. Linc. inn
Vilmet Fk. esq. 7 Petersburgh pl. Byswr
Vinall John, esq. 1 Churchyd. ct. Temple
Vinaw George, esq. 25 Haverstock hill
Vincent Lady, 8 Berkeley st. Piccadilly
Vincent General, L6, Albany
Vincent George, esq. 2 Dartmouth st. Westminster, & 3 Trafalgar square
Vincent Geo. esq. 9 King's bench walk
Vincent Geo. esq. 109 Sloane st. Chelsea
Vincent Geo. Giles, esq. 3 Broad sanctry
Vincent George G. esq. 8 Castle st. Hlbn
Vincent Hen. D. esq. 1 Up. Phillimore pl
Vincent Hen. Wm. esq. Thornwood lodge, Campden hill, Kensington
Vincent Jacob, esq. 10 South sq. Gray's inn, & 5 Canonbury sq. Islington
Vincent Jas. esq. 31 Paddington green
Vincent John, esq. 4 Inner Temple la. Temple
Vincent John R. esq. 3 St. Mary Abbott's ter
Vincent Miss, 11 Southampton pl. Blmsby
Vincent Mrs. 2 Curzon st. Mayfair
Vincent Mrs. 2 Up. Eaton pl. Haverstk. hill
Vincent Mrs. 56 Hans place, Sloane sq
Vincent Rt. esq. 2 Harper st. Red Lion sq
Vincent Thomas, esq. 16 Old Quebec st
Vincent Wm. esq. 1 Up. Eaton pl. Hvstk. hl
Vincent Wm. esq. 51 Smith st. Chelsea
Vine William, esq. 157 John st. road
Vines Samuel, esq. 47 Upper Gower st
Vining James, esq. 14 Hanover st. Hanv. sq
Violet Madame, 42 Upper Norton st
Vipan Edward James, esq. 50 Jermyn st
Virgo John, esq. 34 Essex st. Strand
Virtue George, esq. 2 Northampton sq
Vivian Lord C. Arthur's club, & Glynn, near Lostwithiel
Vivian Captain Hon. John C. W. M.P. Arthur's club, 69 St. James's st
Vivian Rev. James Wm. D.D. 56 Guilford st
Vivian J. esq. 27 Aberdeen pl. Maida hill
Vivian J. E. esq. M.P. 35 Jermyn st. & Truro
Vivian John Henry, esq. M.P. Arthur's club & Singleton, near Swansea
Vizard William, esq. 16 New st. Spring gardens; 91 Lincoln's inn fields; & Little Farringdon, Lechlade

Vizard Wm. jun. esq. 51 Lincoln's inn fields
Vizard Wm. sen. esq. 51 Lincoln's inn fields
Vizer Wm. esq. 35 Gibson sq. Islington
Vizetelly H. esq. 11 Sussex place, Knsgtn
Voelecker George, esq. 6 Loraine pl. Holwy
Vokins William, esq. 67 Margaret st
Von Mille William, esq. 1 Bedford terrace, Clapham rise
Von Zandt Baroness, 6 Clarges st
Vouillon Francis, esq. 13 Stratford pl
Voules William James, esq. 5 Pelham pl. Fulham road, & 9 Inner Temple lane
Vredenburgh Mrs. 23 South st
Vulliamy Lewis, esq. 13 Saville row
Vyner Capt. & Lady Mary, 4 St. James's sq
Vyner Robert, esq. 57 Grosvenor st. & Grantley park, St. Leonards
Vyse Capt. George Howard, 5 Chesham st
Vyvyan Sir Richard Rawlinson, bt. M.P. St. Dunstan's villa, Regent's park, & Trelowarren, Cornwall
Vyvyan E. W. esq. 11 Cambridge st. Edg. rd
Vyvyan Mrs. 10 Notting hill terrace

WACE Mrs. 3 Barnsbury park
Wackerbarth A. F. D. esq. 10 Staple inn
Wadd Mrs. William, 3A, Cleveland row
Waddell Mrs. 23 Cambridge st. Edgw. rd
Waddilove Alfred D.C.L. 5 Gt. Knightrider st. & 8 Ladbroke place, Notting hl
Waddilove Henry Jesse, esq. 3 Great Knightrider st
Waddington Misses, 29 Upper Berkeley st
Waddington Harry Spencer, esq. M.P. Arthur's club, & Cavenham, Ipswich
Waddington Horatio, esq. 3 King's bnch. wk
Waddington James, esq 119 London wall
Waddy Cadwallader F. esq. 103 Jermyn st. & 13 Fludyer st. Westminster
Wade Colonel, Sir Claude Martin, C.B. Groves hotel, Albemarle st. & Corston house, Ryde, Isle of Wight
Wade Rev. N. M.A. Artillery place west
Wade Field, esq. 8 Albion vils. Lpool. rd
Wade Chas. J. esq. 3 Churchyard ct. Temp
Wade James, esq. 16 Stockbridge ter
Wade Mrs. 17 Buckingham st. Fitzroy sq
Wade Rd. P. esq. 50 Upper Seymour st
Wade Robert, esq. 68 Dean st. Soho
Wade Thomas, esq. 2 Upper Phillimore pl
Wadeson Edw. W. esq. 12 Tavistock sq
Wadeson Mrs. 7 Milner st
Wadmore Thos. esq. 3 Dorset st. Man. sq
Wadsworth G. B. esq. 28 Broad st. Gldn. sq
Wageman M. A. esq. 25 Mount st. Berkly. sq
Wageman Thomas, esq. 25 Mount st
Wagg John, esq. 72 Gloucester place
Wagner George, esq. 13 Bloomsbury sq
Wagner James, esq. 14 York pl. Fulham rd
Wagner John, esq. 35 Grosvenor rw. Pmlco
Wagstaff James, esq. 1 Albion ter. Canob. sq
Wagstaff William, esq. 24 Lr. Belgrave pl
Waide Captain, 5 Quickset row, New rd
Wailes George, esq. 1 Cloisters, Temple
Wain Richard, esq. 45 Manchester st
Wainewright Arnold, esq. Devonshire place, Portland place
Wainewright John, esq. 3 Hyde park pl
Wainewright Wm. esq. 20 Fludyer st
Wainwright Chas. esq. 12 Nrth. bnk. Rg. pk
Wainwright Geo. esq. 9 Albert road
Waite Charles, esq. 3 Old Burlington st
Waite George, esq. 2 Old Burlington st
Waite John, esq. 12 Sackville st
Waite John, esq. 8 Welbeck st
Waite Mrs. Anne, 3 Old Burlington st. & Sion lodge, Richmond
Waite Richard, esq. 34 Brompton row
Waite Wm. Hen. esq. 9 Foley st
Waites John C. esq. 3 Paddington green
Waithman Hen. esq. 4 Kent ter. Regt.'s pk
Wake Mrs. 4 Moccas cottages, Cam. new. tn
Wake Wm. esq. 3 Cobourg pl. Up. Kngtn. la
Wakefield Danl. esq. Q.C. 5 Cambridge ter. Edgware rd. & 12 New sq. Linc. inn; & Hare Hatch cott. Maidenhead

Wakefield Edw. G. esq. 9 Broad st. bldgs
Wakefield George, esq. 27 Ossulston st
Wakefield Henry, esq. 1 Lansdowne place
Wakefield H. esq. 6 Albion pl. King's cross
Wakefield Mrs. 59 Burton crescent
Wakefield Thos. esq. 11 Belinda terrace
Wakefield Thos. esq. 16 Judd place west
Wakely George, esq. St. James's palace
Wakely Geo. esq. Queen's door, St. Jas. pa
Wakeman Sir Offley, bart. 10 Pall mall
Wakeman Wm. F. esq. 13 Aberdeen pl. Maida hill
Wakley Thos. esq. M.P. 35 Bedford sq & Romans, Southall, Middlesex
Walcot Thomas, esq. 10 Sloane st. & Army & Navy club, St. James's sq
Walcot Thos. esq. 1 Churchyard court, Temple, & Acre lane, Brixton
Walcot Thomas, esq. 20 St. James's sq
Walcot Stphn. esq. 8 York st. Prtmn. sq
Waldegrave Earl, 25 Berkeley sq
Waldegrave Hon. Capt. Wm. R.N. 4 Hrly. st
Waldegrave Hon. Miss, 4 Park sq. Regt. pk
Waldener John, esq. 9 Suffolk st. Pall mall
Waldo Mrs. 73 Ebury st. Pimlico
Waldron Miss, 12 Wm. st. Knightsbridge
Walenn Wm. esq. 6A, Lodge rd. St. Jn.'swd
Wales Geo. Ed. esq. 20 Wellington ter
Walesby Fras. P. esq. 10 Farrar's bdgs. Temp
Waley Jacob, esq. 69 Chancery lane
Waley Soloman J. esq. 22 Devonshire pl
Walford Rev. Oliver, 2 Rutland place, Charterhouse square
Walford Arthur, esq. 27 Bolton st
Walford Edwd, esq. 1 Bolton st. Mayfair
Walford F. esq. 2 Thurloe pl. we. O. Brmptn
Walford Fras. J. G. esq. 1 New sq. Lin. inn
Walford Fredk. esq. 1 Norfolk crescent, Oxford sq. & 4 King's bench walk
Walford Fred. H. esq. 27 Bolton st
Walford George, esq. 8 Grafton st. Bond st. & Bellevue lodge, Fulham
Walford G. H. J. esq. 8 Clarendon pl. Edg. rd
Walford Misses, 1 Bolton st
Walford Rd. esq. 15 Charlotte st. Bdfd. sq
Walford Thomas, esq. 27 Bolton st
Walford Thomas, esq. 14 Clarges st
Walford Weston S. esq. 2 Plowden bldgs
Walhouse Misses, 4 Halkin terrace
Walker Lady, 7 Sussex square
Walker Sir Geo. bart. 7 Sussex square
Walker Major-Genl. 23 Gt. Quebec st
Walker Lieut-Col. Edw. 2 Wilton crest. & Manor house, Bushy, Herts
Walker Lieut-Col. Edw. W. F. 2 Wilton cr
Walker — esq. 7 Wellington rd. St. Jn'swd
Walker Arthur, esq. 16 Tavistock place, Tavistock sq. & 13 King's rd. Bdfd. rw
Walker C. L. esq. & Mrs. Cavendish hotel, 81 Jermyn st. & Redlands, near Bristol
Walker Charles, esq. 5 New inn, Strand
Walker Deane F. esq. 7 Camden rd. vills
Walker Edmund, esq. 8 Old sq. Lincoln's inn, & Manor ho. Fryern, Barnet
Walker Edward, esq. 71 Oxford terrace, & 8 New square, Lincoln's inn
Walker Geo. F. esq. 9 Harewood square
Walker George Alfred, esq. 11 St. James's place, & 101 Drury lane
Walker Greaves, esq. 11 Beaufort bldgs
Walker Hen. esq. 5 Southmptn. st. Blmsby
Walker Hen. G. esq. Stoke Newngtn. grn
Walker Holden, esq. 13 Furnival's inn
Walker James, esq. 23 Gt. George st
Walker Jas. E. esq. Devereux ct. Strand
Walker John, esq. 47 Bernard st. Russell sq
Walker Jno. esq. 32 Cambridge sq. Hydepk
Walker John, esq. Q.C. 3 Old sq. Linc. inn
Walker Jno. esq. 4 St. Mary Abbott's terr
Walker John, esq. 20 Up. Seymour st. wst
Walker John Thos. esq. 14 Serle st. Linc. inn
Walker J. Goldie, esq. 81 Jermyn st. & Terrace, Aberystwith
Walker J. T. esq. 1 Park row, Knightsbg
Walker Laurence, esq. 46 Welbeck st. & 13 King's road, Gray's inn

Walker Joshua, esq. 2 Park pl. gardens
Walker Micajah H. esq. 8 Red Lion sq
Walker Miss, 47 Bernard st. Russell sq
Walker Miss, 13 Kensington square
Walker Miss, 46 Wigmore st. Cavendish sq
Walker Mrs. 14 Beaufort bldgs. Strand
Walker Mrs. 49 Bedford sq. & Arno's grove, Southgate, Middlesex
Walker Mrs. 9 Bloomfield ter. Pimlico
Walker Mrs. 8 Cleveland row, St. James's
Walker Mrs. 1A, Fitzroy square
Walker Mrs. 52 Hamilton ter. St. Jn.'swd
Walker Mrs. 13 York ter. Regent's park
Walker Richard, esq. M.P. 5 Great Ryder st. St. James's, & Bury, Lancashire
Walker Rd. esq. 7 Grove end pl. St. Jn.'swd
Walker Robt. O. esq. 21 Bedford square
Walker Saml. esq. 29 Lincoln's inn fields, & 6 Rutland gate, Knightsbridge
Walker S. G. esq. 121 Pall mall
Walker Stott, esq. 7 Paradise ter. Livp. rd
Walker Thos. esq. 13 Cloudesley ter
Walker Thos. esq. 26 Euston sq. New rd
Walker Thos. esq. 9 Holloway pl. Hollwy
Walker Thos. esq. 17 Old Quebec st
Walker Thos. esq. 3 Regent square, Gray's inn road, & 12 Furnival's inn
Walker Thos. esq. 4 Stanhope st. Glo'str. g
Walker Thos. Geo. esq. 1 Essex ct. Temple
Walker Wm. esq. 1 King's bnch. wk. Tmpl
Walker Wm. esq. 21 Judd place west
Walker Wm. esq. 10 Ladbroke ter. Not. hl
Walker Wm. esq. 29 Lincoln's inn fields
Walker Wm. F. esq. 3 South sq. Gray's inn
Walker Wm. H. esq. 10 Sthmptn. st. Strd
Walker W. Newton, esq. 28 Gt. Ormond st
Wall Rev. Wm. M.A. Harrow road
Wall Chas. Baring, M.P. 44 Berkley sq. & Norman court, Stockbridge, Hants
Wall John Prichard, esq. 6 Mount st
Wall Joseph, esq. Addison rd. south
Wall Mrs. 24 East st. Red Lion square
Wall Wm. esq. 56 Perceval st. Clknwll
Wallace Andrew, esq. 40 Windsor ter
Wallace David, esq. 55 Oxford terrace
Wallace Dav. esq. 8 Whitehead's gr. Chls
Wallace Ed. J. esq. 57 Chancery lane
Wallace Geo. esq. 72 Gower st. Bedford sq. & 10 New sq. Lincoln's inn
Wallace John, esq. 53 Gloucester place
Wallace Miss, 2 North ter. Brompton
Wallace Mrs. 18 Hanover ct. Regt.'s pk
Wallace Mrs. 32 Queen Anne st
Wallace Robert, esq. 41 Parliament st
Wallace Wm. esq. 8 Up. Brnsbry. st. Islgn
Wallace Wm. esq. 89 Oxford terrace
Wallace Wm. B. esq. 28 Torrington sq
Wallas Gilbert I. esq. 10 Crown Off. row
Wallbancke John Brock, esq. Riches villa, Finchley new road
Waller Sir Wathen, bt. 8 New Caven. st
Waller Major Jas. K.H. 15 St. James's sq
Waller Arthur, esq. 4 Myddelton sq
Waller Benj. esq. 4 Beaufoy ter. Edgw. rd
Waller Frederick, esq. 17 Clement's inn
Waller Geo. esq. 3 Granville square
Waller Geo. jun. esq. 24 Finsbury circus
Waller Geo. sen. esq. 24 Finsbury circus
Waller John, esq. 51 Ebury st. Pimlico
Waller Jn. G. esq. 20 Charles st. Fitz. sq
Waller Miss, 78 Sloane st
Waller Thos. esq. 2 Churchyd. ct. Temple
Waller Thos. esq. 8 Lyon ter. Edgware rd
Waller Thos. Geo. esq. 1 Essex ct. Temple
Waller Wm. esq. 53 Upper Seymour st. & 5 Clement's inn, Strand
Wallinger Arnold, esq. 16 Torrington square, & 3 Inner Temple lane
Wallington J. esq. 4A, Salsbry. pl. Nw. rd
Wallis Chas. Edw. esq. 44 Gt. Marlboro' st
Wallis Ed. esq. 15 Bryanston st. Ptmn. sq
Wallis Hen. esq. 48 Tavistock square
Wallis Mrs. 23 Beaufort st. Chelsea
Wallis Mrs. 3 South bank, Regent's park
Walls John, esq. 44 Bloomsbury square, & Tyvyree cottage, North end, Fulham

Wallop Wm. esq. 10 Highbury terrace
Walls John, esq. 17 Kensington gore
Walls Wm. Albt. esq. 44 Bloomsbury sq & Mill field lane, Highgate
Walmesley Richard, esq. 14 Serle st
Walmisley Edwd. esq. 68 Chancery la
Walmisley F. esq. 18 Cowley st. Westmr
Walmisley John A. sen. esq. 7 Clapham rise, & 40 Parliament st
Walmisley John Angus, esq. 12 North st. Smith sq. & 40 Parliament st
Walmisley John R. L. esq. 12 North st
Walmisley Wm. E. esq. 1 Adam st. Adelphi
Walmsley John W. esq. 6 Sidmouth st
Walmsley John W. esq. 100 Chancy. la
Walmsley Mrs. 21 Upper Southwick st
Walmsley Thos. esq. 6 Figtree ct. Temple
Walne Daniel Henry, esq. 72 Guilford st
Walond Capt. 2 Bifron's vil. Acacia rd
Walpole Lord Horace, 7 Grafton st
Walpole Rev. Rt. B.D. 43 Harewood sq
Walpole Chas. esq. 11 South st. So. Aud. st
Walpole Edward, esq. 22 Saville row
Walpole Francis, esq. 39 Up. Seymour st
Walpole Miss, 15 Princes st. Cavdsh. sq
Walpole Spencer Horatio, esq. 6 Serle st
Walsh Sir John Benn. M.P. & Lady Jane, 28 Brkly. sq. Travellers' club, 106 Pallmall, & Warfield pk. nr. Bracknell
Walsh Aubray, esq. 4 Fredrck. st. Gr's. in. rd
Walsh Chas. Robt. esq. 42 Halfmoon st
Walsh Finey, N. esq. 9 Parliament st
Walsh Frank N. esq. Thurlow cot. Wand. rd
Walsh Fredk. esq. 3 Up. Queen's bldgs
Walsh Frederick, esq. 42 Gt. Ormond st
Walsh James, esq. 49 Stamford st
Walsh Jas. Wm. esq. 68 Lincoln's inn fields, & 17 Park place, Paddington green
Walsh Mrs. 6 George st. Euston square
Walsh William, esq. Harrow road
Walsh Wm. Jas. esq. 17 Park pl. Paddngtn
Walshe W. H. M.D. 47 Charlte. st. Fitz. sq
Walsingham Lord, 7 Upper Portland place, & Merton hall, Thetford, Norfk
Walstab A. J. G. esq. 45 Cambdge. tr. Egw. r
Walter Chas. esq. 28 Gt. Marylebone st
Walter H. D. esq. 1 New Boswell court
Walter James, esq. 26 Burton crescent
Walter John, esq. 47 Ebury st. Pimlico, & 4 Symond's inn, Chancery lane
Walter John, esq. 8 Charing cross, & Bearwood, Binfield, Berks
Walter John F. M.D. 23 New Bridge st
Walter Mrs. 9 Devonshire pl. Portland pl
Walter Mrs. 12 Abingdon st. Westminstr
Walters Edmd. Thos. esq. 25 Duke st. S. Jas
Walters Gregory S. esq. 2 Artillery pl
Walters John Eldad, esq. 15 Campden hill villas, Kensington, & 9 New sq. Linc. inn
Walters T. esq. 11 New Dorset pl. Clph. rd
Walters Thos. esq. 60 Up. Charlotte st
Walters Wm. esq. 61 Queen's rd. Bayswtr
Walthew Fred. Jas. esq. 5 Furnival's inn
Walthew Richard, esq. 5 Furnival's inn
Walton Col. 49 Upper Seymour st
Walton Henry, esq. 74 Long acre
Walton H. esq. 12 Sidmouth st. Gry's. in. r
Walton Henry H. esq. 6 Bernard st
Walton John, esq. 3 Albion pl. Cannbry. sq
Walton John, esq. 9 Barnsbury square
Walton Jn. esq. 14 Elizabeth st. Eaton sq
Walton John, esq. 32 Woburn square
Walton John W. esq. 27A, Old Bond street
Walton Miss, 5 Radnor pl. Oxfd. terrace
Walton Mrs. 23 Michael's pl. Bromptn
Walton Wm. esq. 9 Fitzroy st. Fitzroy sq
Walton Wm. Hen. esq. 34 Queen Anne st & 8 Old square, Lincoln's inn
Walwyn Major James, 16 Cork st
Wansey George, esq. 30 Ely pl. Holbrn. & 3 Moorgate street
Wansbrough Thos. W. esq. Kg.'s rd. w. Chl
Warburton Maj. Garnet, 8 Bentinck st
Warburton A. esq. 7 Allen ter. Kensingtn
Warburton C. esq. 15 Prospect pl. Wnds. rd
Warburton Henry, M.P. 45 Cadogan pl

Warburton Mrs. 26 Park rd. Regent's pk
Warburton Thos. esq. 23 Parker. Rgt.'s pk
Warburton Thos. Acton, esq. 10 Serle st
Ward Lord, Mivart's hotel, 44 Brook st. & Himley hall, Wolverhampton
Ward Lady, Mivart's hotel, 44 Brook st
Ward Hon. Dudley, Mivart's h. 44 Brook st
Ward Major, 5 Manor terrace, Chelsea
Ward Capt. 19 Park pl. villas, Pddngtn
Ward Rev. John Giffard, 197 Piccadilly
Ward Rev. Rich. 24 Cadogan pl. Sloane st
Ward Benjmn. esq. 5 Noel st. Islington
Ward Chas. esq. 13 Grove rd. St. John's wd
Ward Chas. esq. 2 Marlbro' ter. Knsgtn
Ward Davis Jas. esq. 14 Park village ea
Ward Edward, esq. 1 Claremont sq
Ward George Henry, esq. 81 Jermyn st. & Northwood pk. Cowes, Isle of Wight
Ward Geo. Raphael, esq. 31 Fitzroy sq
Ward Henry, esq. 51 Lincoln's inn fields, & Richmond, Surrey
Ward Henry Geo. esq. M.P. 99 Mount street, and Much Hadham, Ware
Ward James, esq. 39 Essex st. Strand
Ward Jas. esq. 2 Victoria vil. Avenue rd
Ward Jas. Kippoth, esq. 12 Furnival's inn
Ward John L. G. esq. 10 New sq. Lincoln's inn, & 22 Lincoln's inn fields
Ward Matthew, esq. 36 Osnaburgh st
Ward Miss, Blacklands house, Marlborough rd. King's rd. Chelsea
Ward Miss, 5 Grove ter. St. John's wd
Ward Mrs. 26 Baker st. & Worthing
Ward Mrs. 4 Compton ter. Up. st. Islington
Ward Mrs. 18 Petersburgh pl. Bayswatr
Ward Mrs. 18 Wilmot st. Russell st
Ward Ogier, esq. 21 Low. Phillimore pl
Ward Richard, esq. 17 Lloyd square
Ward Rich. C. esq. 15 Cloudesley st
Ward Rd. Danvers, esq. 40 North bank, Regent's park, & 12 Clement's inn
Ward Rt. P. esq. 14 Claremont pl Pntnvl
Ward Saml. esq. 98 Guilford st. Rusl. sq
Ward Thomas, esq. 59 Sloane st
Ward Thos. Lawrence, esq. 50 Conduit st
Ward Wm. esq. 19 Abbey rd. St. Jn.'s wd
Ward William, esq. A3, Albany
Ward Wm. esq. 14 Wyndham place
Ward Wm. esq. 1 Plowden bdgs. Temple
Ward Wm. esq. 4 Tavistock st. Bedfd. sq
Ward Wm. John. esq. 26 Baker st. Ptmn. sq
Warde Mrs. Col. 35 Southbank, Regt.'s pk
Wardell Capt. Chas. 43 Westbourne ter
Wardell John Lyod, esq. 25 Brunswk. sq
Wardell Mrs. 12 Allsop terrace, New rd
Wardell Wm. esq. 22 Henrietta st. Cov. gn
Warden Capt. 28 Bryanstone square
Warden Francis, esq. 28 Bryanstone sq
Wardrop Jas. esq. 2 Charles st. St. James
Wardroper Wm. esq. 45 Welbeck st
Ware Arch. esq. 22 Beaufoy ter. Edg. rd
Ware Martin, esq. 51 Russell square
Ware Miss, 11 Clarence ter. Regt. park
Ware Miss, 1 Woburn square
Ware Samuel, esq. 34 Portland place, & Hendon hall, Hendon, Middlesex
Ware Samuel, esq. 1 Tavistock place, Russell square, & 5 Gray's inn square
Warhurst J. esq. 23 Henrietta st. Brnsw. sq
Waring Richd. esq. 11 Spencer ter. Islgt
Waring John E. Esq. 42 Chester square
Waring Mrs. 4 Kensington palace grdns
Waring Thos. esq. 9 Caroline st. Bedfd. sq
Warman C. F. esq. 17 Spencer ter. Islingtn
Warmsley John, esq. 54 Chester square
Warmsley Mrs. 1 Clarendon pl. Hyde pk
Warmsley Rd. esq. 1 Earl's ter. Knsngtn
Warne Mrs. 9 Bedford pl. Russell sq
Warne Wm. esq. 25 South ter. Alexndr. sq
Warneford Hon. Mrs. Mivart's hotel, 44 Brook st. & Warneford place, Wilts
Warneford Richd. esq. 6 Symond's inn
Warner George, esq. 9 Kensington sq
Warner James, esq. 10 Canonbury square
Warner John, esq. 4 Montague st. Bloomsbury, & 11 King's Bench walk, Temple
Warner Robt. esq. 19 Charterhouse sq
Warner Robt. Wm. esq. 16 Euston pl. N.w.
Warre A. esq. 4 Milton pl. Wandswh. rd
Warre Henry Rupert, esq. 15 St. Jas.'s sq
Warre John A. esq. 54 Lowndes sq. Belg. sq
Warre Mrs. James, 26 Oxford square
Warren Capt. Geo. 1 Thurloe sq. Brmptn
Warren Adolphus, esq. 106 Shoe land
Warren Augustus, esq. 6 Up. Montague st
Warren Chas. esq. 1 Pembroke sq. Knsngtn
Warren Edw. esq. 18 Burton st
Warren E. esq. 12 Sthamptn. pl. Euston sq
Warren Jas. esq. 6 Walcot pl. we. Lambth
Warren John, esq. 34 Allsop ter. New rd
Warren John, esq. 32 George st. Hanr. sq.
Warren Mrs. Geo. 33A, York st. Prtm. sq
Warren Mrs. 26 Upper Grosvenor st
Warren Mrs. B. 2 Regent villas, Avenue rd
Warren Robert, esq. 87 Gloucester pl
Warren Saml. esq. F.R.S. 35 Woburn pl. & 12 King's Bench walk, Temple
Warren Thomas, esq. 6 Belinda cottage, Canonbury sq
Warren Thos. P. esq. Highbury pk. south
Warren Wm. esq. 235 Maida vale, Edgw. rd
Warren Wm. esq. 13 Noel st. Islington
Warring Mrs. 29 Westbourne place
Warrington Capt. T. 66 Upper Berkeley st
Warrington J. esq. 21 Kensington cresc
Warrington Mrs. 16 Edwardes sq
Warry George, esq. 7 New inn, Strand
Warsup Richard, esq. 27 Orchard st
Warter Henry de Grey, esq. 1 Carey st. & the Grove, Highgate
Warton Wm. Hen. esq. 24 Highbury pl
Warwick Chas. esq. 16 Highbury place
Warwick Earl, K.T. 7 Carlton gardens, & Warwick castle
Warwick Guy, esq. 29 Cloudesley sq
Washbourn John, esq. 22 Theberton st
Wass Charles W. esq. 1A, Adelphi terrace
Wass Wm. esq. 73 Charlotte st. Fitzr. sq
Waterfield Thos. esq. 6 Gt. Dean yd. Wstm
Waterford, Marquis of, Mivart's hotel, & Curraghmore, Waterford
Waterhouse George, esq. 10 Gloucester grove west, Old Brompton
Waterhouse Jas. esq. 18A, Glo'ster grv Brm
Waterman Thos. esq. 23 Trinity sq
Waterman Wm. esq. 23 Essex st. Strand
Waterpark Dow. Lady, 18 Hertford st
Waters George, esq. 34 Wellclose square
Waters John, M.D. 2 South cres. Bedfrd. sq
Waters Mrs. 13 New Quebec st
Waters Thos. esq. 3 Upper Chadwell st
Waters Wm. L. esq. 1 South bk. Rgt.'s pk
Waters Wm. Rd. esq. 67 Castle st. east, Oxford st
Wathen Geo. Hen. esq. 12 Regent st
Wathen John B. esq. 61 Torrington sq. & 28 St. Swithin's lane
Wathen Josiah Iles, esq. 47 Bedford sq
Wathen Nathaniel, esq. 41 Gordon sq
Watherston J. H. esq. 12 Sussex pl. Knsgtn
Watkin Mrs. 14 Up. Islington terrace
Watkins Alex. esq. 34 High st. Mrylbne
Watkins B. esq. 14 George st. Portmn. sq
Watkins Danl. esq. 6 John st. Regent's pk
Watkins G. esq. 7 Blenheim pl. St. Jn.'s rw
Watkins Hen. Geo. esq. 13 Low. Islgn. ter
Watkins Jesse V. esq. 25 Myddelton sq
Watkins John, esq. 21A, Saville row
Watkins Mrs. 14 Addison road north
Watkins Mrs. 27 Broadley terrace
Watkins Rd. esq. 44 Bedford pl. Kensgtn
Watkins Thomas, esq. 47 Doughty st
Watkins Thomas, esq. 41 Harewood sq
Watkins William, esq. 1 Vincent terrace
Watkins William, esq. 13 Wilton crescent, & 11 Sackville st
Watling Arthur, esq. 33 Great Coram st
Watlington Geo. esq. 45 Upper Bedford place, & Caldicott hill, near Stanmore
Watson Maj. Gen. Sir Hen. 7 Portland pl
Watson Lieut. Col. Sir Fredk. 7 Prtlnd. pl
Watson Sir Fred. Beilbey, 4 Albany tr. N. rd
Watson Capt. Wm. 14 Gt. Cumberland pl
Watson Lt. David Hy. 14 Clement's inn
Watson Rev. Thomas, 67 Myddelton sq
Watson — esq. 52 New Church st. Lissn. gr
Watson Alexr. esq. 13 Church st. Soho
Watson Andrew K. esq. 2 Plowden blgs
Watson Barclay Farquharson, esq. 16 Cambridge terrace, Edgware road, & 36 Lincoln's inn fields
Watson Carroll, esq. 4 Pump ct. Temple
Watson Chas. esq. 5 Devonport st. Hy. pk
Watson Daniel, esq. 8 Gray's inn square
Watson David, esq. 1 John st. Brkly. sq
Watson Fras. Pagett, esq. 8 Thavies inn
Watson George, esq. 1 Essex st. Noel st
Watson George, esq. Nine elms, Vauxhl
Watson Henry, esq. 4 Halfmoon st. Pcdly
Watson Jas. esq. 23 Bedford pl. Knsgtn
Watson James, esq. 30 Mornington cresc
Watson Jas. esq. 12 Clarence ter. Rgt.'s pk
Watson James, esq. 2 Cursitor st
Watson Jas. Eyre, esq. 36 Up. Gower st
Watson John, esq. 10 Henrietta st. Cv. gn
Watson John, esq. 30 George st. Han. sq
Watson John, esq. 53 Gower st
Watson J. jun. esq. 10 Henrietta st. Cv. gn
Watson J. sen. esq. 10 Henrietta st. Cv. gn
Watson John, esq. 19 Hyde park square
Watson John, esq. 6 Park pl. Paddingtn
Watson John, esq. 5 Red Lion st. Holbn
Watson John, esq. 13 Sthmptn. st. Blmsb
Watson John, esq. 15 Stockwell common
Watson John B. esq. 39 Manchester st
Watson Jsph. esq. 4 Hyde pk. gate, Knsgtn
Watson Jsph. esq. 4 Hyde pk. gdns. Knsgtn
Watson Joseph, esq. 6 Christopher st
Watson Jsph. Heapy, esq. 28 Bedford pl
Watson Mrs. 9 Aberdeen pl. Maida hill
Watson Mrs. 10 Cambridge tr. Edg. rd
Watson Mrs. 11 Fitzroy st. Fitzroy sq
Watson Mrs. 7 Glo'ster pl. Portman sq
Watson Mrs. 24 Hamilton terrace
Watson Mrs. 54 Marchmont st. Bnswk. sq
Watson Mrs. 7 Northmptn. pl. Cannbry. sq
Watson Mrs. 3 Portland ter. Regt's. pk
Watson Mrs. 1 Up. Yardley st. Clknwll
Watson the Misses, 1 John st. Brkly. sq
Watson Miss, 32 Gloucester pl. New rd
Watson M. L. esq. 13 Upper Glo'ster st. Dorset square
Watson Robert, esq. 12 Bouverie st. & Hammersmith
Watson Robert, esq. 24 Canonbury vills
Watson Saml. esq. 38 Royal cr. Nttg. hill
Watson Saml. Wm. esq. 37 Welbeck st
Watson Seth. B. M.D. 16 Norfolk st. Park. la
Watson Stewart, esq. 91 Dean st. Soho
Watson Thos. esq. 87 Blackfriars road
Watson Thos. esq. 17 Claremont square
Watson Thos. esq. 42 Park st. Grosvenor sq
Watson Thos. M.D. 16 Henriett. st. Cav. sq
Watson Thos. esq. 12 Norton st. Fitzr. sq
Watson Tho. Simons. esq. 42 Halfmoon st
Watson Wm. esq. 14 Colebrooke row, Islgt
Watson Wm. esq. 10 Gordon st. Gordon sq
Watson Wm. esq. 40 London st. Tott. ct. rd
Watson Wm. esq. 27 Porchester terrace
Watson Wm. Davy, esq. 10 Crown Off. rw
Watson Wm. Hy. esq. 1 Newntn. pl. Ken. rd
Watson Wm. Henry, M.P., Q.C. 38 Wilton crescent, & 3 King's Bench walk
Watson Wm. Webster, esq. 1 Pump ct. Tmp
Watt Geo. esq. 5 Tyndale pl. Up. st. Islgt
Watt James, esq. 10 Lodge rd. Rgt.'s pk
Watt Richd. esq. 49 Charlotte st. Fitz. sq
Watt Thos. esq. 8 Claremont pl. Pntnvl
Watters John N. esq. 25 Bedfordbury
Watters Roger, esq. 10 New sq. Lincoln's in
Watton John, esq. 9 Albert st. Morngtn. cr
Watt Alfred, esq. 6 Belgrave st. New rd
Watts Alaric Alex. esq. 17 Berners st
Watts Benj. esq. 1 Harriet st. Sloane st
Watts Edm. esq. 9 Hamilton ter. St. Jns. wd
Watts Francis, esq. 1 Warwick sq. Belgrave rd. Pimlico, & 45 Parliament st
Watts Geo. esq. 10 River st. Pentonville

Watts Hy. esq. 5½ Bell yd. Doctors' coms
Watts Mrs. 30 Claremont sq. Pentonville
Watts Mrs. 34 Kenton st. Brunswick sq
Watts Mrs., Cottage, Swinton st. Gra. i. rd
Watts Mrs. Robt. 68 St. Paul's churchyd
Watts Walter, esq. 19 Ely place, Holbrn
Watts Walter, esq. 5 Colebrooke ter
Watts Walter, esq. 7 Orme's sq. Bayswtr
Watts Wm. esq. 5 Albion pl. Thornhill rd
Watts Wm. esq. 45 Cirencester pl. Ftzry. sq
Watts William, esq. 16 New Quebec st
Wauchope Mrs. 23 Eaton square
Waudby Mrs. 3 Whrnclff. tr. St. Jns. wd. rd
Waugh George, esq. 5 Gt. James st
Waugh Mrs. 6 Mecklenburgh st
Waugh Wm. esq. 20 Surrey st. Strand
Waugh Wm. Neil, esq. 14 Surrey st. Strand
Wawn John T. M.P. 25 Bridges st. Westmr
Way Albert, esq. 12 Rutland gate, Kntsb
Way Jas. esq. 25 Melton st. Euston sq
Way Miss, 9 Chandos st. Cavendish sq
Way Miss, 25 Melton st. Euston square
Way Mrs. 9 Chandos st. Cavendish sq.; & Glympton park, Woodstock; & Denham rectory, Uxbridge
Way Wm. esq. 8 Boyne ter. Notting hill
Waymouth Major, 19 Up. Grosvenor st
Waymouth Henry, esq. 17 Bryanstone sq
Waynman James, esq. 12 Claremont sq
Weale Mrs. 19 York buildings, New rd
Weall Wm. esq. 20 Margaret st. Cavendish sq. & 2 Falcon court, Fleet st
Weare Rev. Thos. Wm. Little Dean's yd
Wearing Wm. Alfred, esq. 28 Chancery la
Weatherall E. esq. 4 Kng. Edw. tr. Livpl. rd
Weatherall Edw. esq. 7 King's bench wk
Weatherall Miss, 60 Torrington square
Weatherby Chas. esq. 6 Old Burlingt. st
Weatherby Jas. esq. 6 Old Burlington st. & 21 Notting hill square
Weatherhead Geo. H. M.D. 63 Guilford st
Weatherhead W. esq. 3 Montague pl. O. K. r
Weathers Geo. esq. 41 High st. Cmdn. tn
Weaver Thos. esq. 31 Baker st. Lloyd sq
Webb Capt. J. R. R. R.N. 24 Shaftesbury cr
Webb Charles, esq. 86 Gt. Titchfield st
Webb Francis, esq. 53 Russell square
Webb Frederick, esq. 17 Clapham rd. pl
Webb Fredk. Hen. esq. 53 Nelson sq
Webb Geo. esq. 31 Allsop ter. New rd
Webb Geo. esq. 43 Holford sq. Pentnvl
Webb George Bush, esq. 3 Mortimer st
Webb Hy. esq. 22 Sackville st. Piccadly
Webb Henry B. esq. 31 Gt. Queen st
Webb Jas. esq. 18 Wilton st. Grosvnr. pl
Webb John B. esq. 21 Portland ter. Reg. pk
Webb John W. esq. 25 Wardour st
Webb Jsph. esq. 34 Hastings st. Brtn. cr
Webb Miss, 48 Eaton place, & Adwell house, Tetsworth, Oxfordshire
Webb Miss, 2 Park place, Up. Baker st
Webb the Misses, 6 Clapham road pl
Webb Mrs. 17 Alfred pl. Newington cau
Webb Mrs. 17 Baker st. Lloyd square
Webb Mrs. 48 Eaton place, & Adwell house, Tetsworth, Oxfordshire
Webb Mrs. 28 Edwards st. Portman sq
Webb Mrs. 1 Landfears villas, Albion rd
Webb Mrs. 13 Portland pl. Lower rd. Islgtn
Webb Mrs. 12 Queen's pl. Kennington rd
Webb Mrs. 12 Up. Gloucester st. Dorset sq
Webb Mrs. 15 Westbourne pl. Eaton sq
Webb Orlando, esq. 22 Sackville st
Webb Rd. Holden, esq. 66 Gloucester pl
Webb Robt. esq. 61 Stafford pl. Pimlico
Webb Samuel, esq. 10 Eccleston st. south
Webb Thomas R. esq. 18 Wyndham st
Webb Valentine B. esq. 14 Duke st. Adelphi
Webb Wm. esq. 15 Harleyford pl. Knngtn
Webb Wm. esq. 63 Lincoln's inn fields, & 3 Arundel st. Strand
Webb Wm. esq. 7 Pelham pl. Fulham rd
Webber Alex. esq. 47 Up. Baker st. Reg. pk
Webber Chas. Geo. esq. 5 Up. Woburn pl
Webber Henry, esq. 13 Bruton st
Webber Jas. esq. 2 York cot. Old Brmptn
Webber Jn. H. esq. 3 Caroline st. Bedfd. sq
Webber Miss, 28 Nottingham place
Webber Martin, esq. 11 Aberdeen place
Webber Mrs. Col. Rosebank cottage, Finchley New road
Webber Mrs. 23 Bryanstone st. Prtm. sq
Webber Mrs. 15 Bury st. St. James's
Webber Thos. esq. 55 St. John's wd. ter
Weber Albert, esq. 36 Harley st
Weber Frederic, M.D. 8 Grosvenor st
Webster Col. Sir Hen. bt. 31 Up. Brook st
Webster Rev. Wm. Church ct. Old Jewry
Webster Rev. William, King Edward st
Webster Benjamin, esq. 3 Old Brompton
Webster B. esq. 18 Suffolk st. Pall mall
Webster Chas. esq. 24 Brook st. Grosvenor sq. & 13 New Boswell court
Webster Edw. esq. 3 Old sq. Lincoln's inn, & South lodge, Ealing, Middlesex
Webster E. esq. 4 Courland ter. Wandsw. rd
Webster George, esq. 78 Connaught ter
Webster George, esq. 26 Great George st. & Sudbury priory, Harrow, Middlesex
Webster Geo. esq. 31 Lower Kennington la
Webster Hy. esq. 13 Stanhope st. Regt.'s pk
Webster Jas. C. esq. 4 Trinity sq. Boro'
Webster John, M.D. 24 Brook st. Grsvnr. sq
Webster John, esq. 35 Mecklenburgh sq
Webster Mrs. 12 Chapel st. Bedford row
Webster Mrs. 39 Michael's pl. Bromptn
Webster Mrs. 9 Pelham road, Bromptn
Webster Mrs. 38 Queen Anne st
Webster Mrs. 1 River ter. north, City rd
Webster Mrs. 10 Sthamptn. row, New rd
Webster Mrs. 14 Warwick court, Hlbrn
Webster R. H. esq. 26 Suffolk st
Webster Ridley M. esq. 1 River ter. n. Cityr
Webster Thomas, esq. 22 Chester square, Pimlico, & 2 Pump court, Temple
Webster Thomas, esq. 20 Euston square
Webster Thos. esq. Mall, Ken. Gravel pits
Webster Thomas, esq. 1 Old palace yard
Webster Wm. esq. 26 Alpha rd. Reg. pk
Webster Wm. M. esq. 15 New Boswell ct
Weddison Mrs. 24 Dalby terrace, City rd
Wedgwood Hensley, esq. 42 Chester tr. Regent's park
Wedgwood Hensleigh, esq. 7 Park st. Gro. sq. & 3 Princes st. Storey's gate
Wedgwood Ralph, esq. 3 Landsdowne villas, Notting hill
Wedlake H. B. esq. 13 Camden st. south, Camden town
Wedlake Hy. B. esq. 10 King's bench walk
Weeden Frederick, esq. 1 Porchester ter
Weeden Wm. esq. 1 Surrey place, Strand
Weeding Thos. esq. 47 Mecklenburgh sq
Weedon Edwd. esq. Temple chamb. Fleetst
Weedon Fras. esq. 19 Duncan ter. Cityrd
Weedon F. P. esq. 29 Lower st. Islington
Weedon Henry Wm. esq. 14 Stonefield st
Weedon Wm. esq. 26 Harleyford pl. Kngtn
Weekes Henry, esq. 29 Lr. Belgrave pl
Weeks Hen. esq. 12 Cook's ct. Linc. inn
Weems Robt. esq. 30 Gt. George st. Westmr
Wegg William, M.D. 5 Maddox st. Bond st
Weguelin G. esq. 6 Grafton st. Fitzry. sq
Weguelin Wm. A. esq. 39 Weymouth st
Wehnert E. H. esq. 23 Charlot. st. Bedfd. sq
Wehnert N. esq. 23 Charlotte st. Bedfd. sq
Wehnert Misses, 2 Up. Robert st. Brmptn
Weigall C. H. esq. 13 Michael's pl. Brmptn
Weight Chas. esq. 24 Up. Albany st
Weightman Hugh, esq. 1 Paper bldngs
Weightman Js. M. esq. 1 Warwick ct. Hlbn
Weippert John, esq. 21B, Soho square
Weippert Wm. esq. 24 Ernest st. Regt.'s pk
Weir Mrs. 7 Mecklenburgh square
Weir Mrs. 41A, Park st. Grosvenor sq
Weiss Frederick F. esq. 33 Chester terr
Weiss Joseph, M.D. 28 Sackville st
Weiss Miss, 33 Chester terrace
Weiss Mrs. 14 Connaught terrace
Welbank Richd. esq. 102 Chancery lane
Welbank Robert, esq. 1 Furnival's inn
Welborne Wm. esq. 49 Dover st. Piccdly
Welby Sir Wm. E. bt. 8 Upper Belgrave st. & Denton house, Grantham
Welby Glynne Earle, esq. M.P. 8 Up. Belgrave st. & Newton house, nr. Flknghm
Welch Arthur Henry, esq. 2 Plowden buildings & 4 Stone buildings
Welch John, esq. 7 Charles st. Westminster, & 3 King's bench walk
Welch John W. esq. 9 New Broad st
Welch Martial L. esq. 13 Wyndham pl
Welch Mont. S. esq. 7 King's bench walk
Welch Mrs. 17 Annett's cre. Lr. rd. Islgtn
Welch Mrs. 179 Regent st
Welch Patk. Robt. esq. 2 Churchyard ct. & Newtown Welch, co. Kilkenny
Welch Mrs. 18 Torrington square
Welch Wm. Geo. esq. 390 Strand
Welchman Mrs. 3 Brnswk. row, Blmsby
Weld Chas. R. esq. Royal Soc. Somrst. ho
Weld Erasmus, esq. 25 Notting hill sq
Welford Fredk. esq. 11 Lower Ashby st
Welford Richd. G. esq. 6 Chancery lane
Wellard Mrs. 43 Upper Albany st
Wellbeloved Wm. F. esq. 10 Margaret st
Wellby Dan. esq. 33 George st. Eustn. sq
Weller Edwd. esq. 11 Green's row, Chls
Weller Geo. esq. 8 King's rd. Bedford ro
Weller Wm. esq. 68 Ebury st. Pimlico
Welles Edward, esq. 1 Cadogan place
Welles Mrs. 14 Gower st. Bedford sq
Wellesley Marchioness, 22 Rutland gate
Wellesley Lieut. Col. Lord Charles, M.P. Apsley house, 149 Piccadilly
Wellington Duke of, K.G., G.C.B., P.C., D.C.L. Apsley house, 149 Piccadilly; Strathfieldsaye, Hants; & Walmer castle, Kent
Wellington G. esq. 1 Verulam tr. Maida hi
Wellington W. esq. 5 St. Ann's tr. Acacia rd
Wells Lieut. Col. John, 11 Lowndes sq
Wells Rev. Algernon, 4 Blomfield st
Wells Rev. John Tighe, 14 Newman st
Wells Fredk. esq. 5 Gerrard st. Islgtn
Wells Fredk. O. esq. 22 Montagu sq
Wells G. W. esq. 10 St. Ann's vil. Acacia rd
Wells Hardy, esq. 6 Serjeants' inn, Fleet st
Wells Henry, esq. 31 London st. Fitz. sq
Wells John, esq. 53 Cambridge ter. Egw. rd
Wells John, esq. 23 Percy st. Bedford sq
Wells John, esq. 18 Up. Phillimore place
Wells John R. esq. 11 Charlotte st. Fitz. sq
Wells Jonah, esq. 4 Milner sq. Islington
Wells M. L. esq. 6 Serjeants' inn, Fleet st
Wells Mrs. 21 Chapel st. Grosvenor sq
Wells Mrs. 46 Gibson sq. Islington
Wells Mrs. 42 Great Ormond st
Wells Nthl. esq. 25 Hamilton ter. St. Jn.'s w
Wells Robert, esq. 29 Nelson square
Wells Saml. esq. 6 Serjeants' inn, Fleet st
Wells Wm. esq. 5 St. James's pl. St. James's
Wells William, esq. 144 Oxford st. & Redleaf, Penshurst, Kent
Wells Wm. esq. 8 Victoria rd. Kensgtn
Wellton Henry, esq. 6 Cumberland ter
Welsby Wm. Newland, esq. 14 Clarendon pl. Maida hl. & 2 Elm ct. Temple
Welsh Edwd. esq. 5 Dalby terrace, City rd
Welsh Edward, esq. 17 Union pl. Blackheath, & 16 Old Jewry
Welstead Chas. esq. 66 Berners st
Welstead Mrs. 126 Park st. Grosvnr. sq
Welton Mrs. 11 Maida hill, Edgware rd
Wemyss & March, Earl of, 19 Stratford pl.; & Gosford house, near Haddington; & Nidpath castle Peeblesshire; & Stanway hall, Broadway
Wemyss Maj. Gen. 11 Clarges st. Pcdly
Wemyss James Erskine, Capt. R.N., M.P. 14 St. Alban's place, St. James's; & Wemyss castle, Kirkaldy; & Torrie house, Dunfermline
Wenham John, esq. 9 Grove pl. Lisson gr
Wenham Mark, esq. 6 Melina pl. St. Jn.'s w
Wenham Miss, 6 Melina pl. St. Jhn.'s wd
Wenlock Lord, 29 Berkeley square, & Escrick park, near York

Wenlock Lady, 8 Carlton house terr. & Canwell hall, near Sutton, Coldfield
Wentworth Fred. Vernon, esq. & Lady Augusta, 11 Connaught place; & Aldborough lodge, Suffolk; & Stoke park, Towcester; & Wentworth castle, Barnsley
Wertheimer Jn. esq. 5 West st.Finsbury
Werner Louis, esq. 37 Upper Gower st
Wesley Rev. C. Stable yd. St.Jas. palace
Wesley Matthias E. esq. 50 Wharton st
West Adml. Sir John, K.C.B.18 Berkeley sq. & Braywich lodge, Maidenhead
West Benj. esq. 26 Mornington crescent
West Hon. Fred. 38 Up. Grosvenor st.; Cullum court, Henley-on-Thames; & Ruthin castle, Denbighshire
West Col.C.A. 1Aberdeen pl.Maida hill, & Landguard fort, Suffolk
West India (Thos.Ellis),61 St.James's st
West Benjamin, esq. 25 Tavistock place
West Chas. esq. 37 Charterhouse square
West Dl. esq. 16 & 17 Egremont pl. N. rd
West Edwd. esq.3 Robert ter. Chelsea
West Fred.esq. 1 Winchester rw. New rd
West John, esq. 65 Albany st.Regnt.'spk
West John J. esq.25 Lower Belgrave pl
West J. T. esq. 1 Hollywood ho.Lt.Chels
West Jsph. John, M.D. 6 Warwick villas
West J. R. esq. Cavendish hotel, 81 Jermyn st. & Alscot pk.Warwickshire
West Martin, esq. & Lady Maria, 5 New st. Spring gardens
West Mrs. 27 Bryanstone square
West Mrs. 17 Cloudesley st. Islington
West Mrs. Lavender hill, Wandswth. rd
West Mrs. 21 Liverpool st. King's cross
West Mrs. 6 Lower Duncan pl. City rd
West Mrs. 9 Park rd. Regent's park
West Mrs. 2Park village east, Regt.'spk
West Mrs. 25 Tavistock pl. Russell sq
West Miss, 10 Powis pl. Hampstead rd
West Miss, 2 Upper Grosvenor st
West Robert, esq. 13 Sloane terrace
West Samuel, esq. 78 Newman st
West Thomas, esq. 15 Connaught sq
West Thos.esq.5Wellington rd. St.Jn's.w
West Wm. esq. 16 & 17 Egremont place, New road
West William, esq. 38 Ely pl. Holborn
West Wm. esq. 6 Holywood pl. Lt.Chels
West Wm. John, esq. 18 Calthorpe st
Westall Mrs. 45 Trinity square, Boro'
Westall Sam.esq.18 Clement's inn,Strnd
Westbroom Joseph, esq. 6 Salisbury st
Westby Nich. esq. & Hon. Mrs. 9 York gardens, Regent's park
Westcott J.H. esq. 2 Leonrd. pl.Knsgtn
Westenra Lieut. Col.Hon.J.Craven, M.P. 60 St. James's st. & Sharavogue castle, near Roscrea, Ireland
Western Chas. F. esq. 7 Gt. James st
Western Ed. esq. 1 Caroline pl.Mekln.sq
Western James, esq. 7 Gt. James st
Western Wm. esq.28Portland pl. Islngtn
Westgarth Miss, 19 Park village east
Westhorp Isaac, esq. 155 Albany st
Westhorp Joseph, esq. 155 Albany st
Westley Wm. esq. North lodge, Rgt.'spk
Westmacott Sir R. 14 South Audley st
Westmacott George, esq. 6 & 7 Howley place villas, Paddington
Westmacott Hen. S. esq.28 John st.Bedford row, & 4 Park pl. villas, Maida hl
Westmacott Richd. jun. esq.21Wilton pl
Westmacott S. esq. 17 Nottingham st
Westmacott Wm. esq. 37 Charlotte st. Portland place
Westmacott Wm. esq. Counciloff.Whteh
WestmeathMarquis of,Sr.UnitedService club, & Clonyn, Castledon, Delvin, Ireland
Westmeath Marchioness of, 95 Piccadilly, & Great court, St. James's
Westminster Dowager Marchioness of, 33 Upper Grosvenor st
Westminster Marquis of, K.G. 15 Grosvenor sq.; & Eaton hall, Chester; & Halkin castle, Flintshire; & Motcombe house, Shaftesbury
Westmore Lieut. Col. 21 Avenue rd
WestmorelandEarl of,K.C.B.,P.C.,G.C.H., D.C.L. ambassador at Berlin; 12 Up. Harley st. & Apthorpe, near Wansfrd
Westmoreland Countss.of,12Up.Hrley.st
Westmoreland Isaac, esq. Camberwell gn
Westoby Wm. Amos S. esq. 5 Old sq. Lincoln's inn, & 2A, Hyde park place
Weston Ambrose, esq. 30 Hamilton ter
Weston Chas. Henry, esq. 35 Gt. Coram st. & 3 Harcourt bldgs. Temple
Weston Edw. J. esq.14Southptn.pl.Nw.r
Weston George, esq. 10 Highbury grove, & 7 New square, Lincoln's inn
Weston Henry, esq. 15 Mecklenburgh sq
Weston James, esq. 81 Blackfriars road
Weston James, esq. 6 Hyde park gate, Kensington, & 31 Fenchurch st
Weston John, esq. 28 Woburn square
Weston Miss, 18 Albion st. Hyde park
Weston Mrs. 21 Bentinck st
Weston Mrs. Webb, 63 Montagu square
Weston Sam.Chas.esq.7Up.Montague st
Weston Thos. Eyre, esq. 43 Lincoln's in.fi
Weston Wm. esq. 15 Marlborough place, Walworth road
Westphal Sir Geo. knt.Capt.R.N.14 Up. Seymour st.&2Brunswick sq.Brighton
Westroff James, esq. 27 Henrietta st
Westron Miss, 14 King st. St. James's
Westron Rt.esq.1Warwick sq. Knsingtn
Westrop Hy. esq. 19 Great Percy st
Westropp Berkeley, esq.16Manchestr. st
Westwood Mrs. 2 Finsbury st
Westwood Wm. esq. 8 Gray's inn square
Westwood Wm. Hy. esq.13Powell st.wst
Wetherell Sir Chas. knt. Q.C.5 Stone bgs
Wetherell Nathl. esq. 3 Old sq. Linc.inn
Wetherfield G. M. esq. 5Union pl.City rd
Wetherfield J.esq.1Henrietta st.Cvt.gdn
Wetherhead Thos. esq. 13 Up. Baker st
Wetherill Charles, esq. 5 Powis st
Wetherill Mrs. 5 Powis pl.Gt.Ormond st
Wetten John Luke, esq. 15 Regent st. & 48 Conduit st
Wetten Robt.G.esq.6Gt.College st.Wstr
Wettenhall J. esq.24Chester pl. Knngtn
WettigJohnF.esq.72Albany st.Regt.'s pk
Weyland John, esq.52Charles st. Brkly. sq. & Woodrising hall, Attleborough
Weymouth John, esq. 74 Gower st
Weymouth J.esq.23James st.Bucknm.gt
Weymouth Jonathan, esq. 89 Chancry.la
Whale Simon, esq. 18 LowerBelgrave pl
Whaley H. J. esq. 17 Lower cot. Lvrpl.rd
Whalley Geo. Hammond, esq. 4 Serjeants' inn, Fleet st
Whalley Mrs. 11 Claremont ter. Pntnvl
Whalley Wm. esq. 14 Gray's inn square
Whapham Mrs. 15 Russell square
Wharncliffe Lord. P.C. 15 Curzon st.; Wortley hall, Sheffield; & Belmont castle, Dundee
Wharton Hon. Mrs. 6 Upper Wimpole st
Wharton Rev. Thos. St. John's wood rd
Wharton Gerrard Blisson, esq. D6, Albany, & 8 Lincoln's inn fields
Wharton John, esq. 7 Elm ter.Lt.Chelsea
Wharton John J. S. esq. 36 Linc.inn flds
Wharton Robert, esq. 31 Upper Harley st. & 1 Tanfield court, Temple
Whateley Wm. esq. Q. C. & Lady Henry Spencer Churchill, 5 Gt. George st. Westmr. & 3 Tanfield court, Temple
Whatley Thos. Denman, esq. 9 St. Andrew's pl. Regt.'s park; & 8 New sq. Lincoln's inn
Whatman Wm. G. esq. 34 Montague pl
Wheatley Maj. Gen. Sir Henry, Ambassadors' court, St. James's palace, & Hampton court green
Wheatley Joel, esq. 105 Sloane st
Wheatley L. L. esq. 12 Nottingham pl
Wheatley Mrs.25 Baker st. Portman sq
Wheatly R. Ben. esq.3Roll's yd.Chanc.la
Wheatly R. B. esq. 24 Rodney st. Pntnvl
Wheeler Geo. esq. 56 Queen's rd. Byswt
Wheeler Hy. Jas. esq. 27 Hyde pk.grdns
Wheeler Miss, 28 Mornington crescent
Wheeler Miss, 22 Chester ter. Rgt.'s pk
WheelerMrs.2Gloucester rd.O.Bromptn
Wheeler Mrs.12Montagu pl.Montagu sq
Wheeler Mrs. Wrwck. cot.Addison rd.so
Wheeler Rt. W. esq. Eldon chambers, Devereux court
Wheeler Samuel, esq. 67 Cadogan place
Wheeler William O. esq. 3 Guilford st
Wheelock Joseph, esq. 3 Suffolk place, Lr. road, Islington, & 10 Chancery la
WheelwrightWilliam,esq.21Gt.Coramst
Wheildon Jas. esq. 28 Wt.Lion st.Pntnvl
Whelan WilliamCurteis,esq.8 Montague st.Blmsby. & Herrenden ho. Tenterden
Wheler Mrs. 17 Duke st. Manchester sq
Whelin Mrs. 28 Wharton st
Whetton Wm. esq.53Margaret st.Cav.sq
Whewell Rev. William, D.D. University club, & Trinity college, Cambridge
Whichcote Benj. esq. 40 Devonshire pl
Whichelo Jn.esq.26Charles st.St.James'
Whidborne George F. esq. 28 Queen sq
WhiffenE.H.esq.104Gt.GrandJunction tr
WhiffinW.H.esq.3St.Ann's vil.Acacia rd
Whigham James, esq. 5 Plowden bldgs
Whimper E.esq.7Gt.Moore place,Lmbth
WhiphamTheodoreW.esq.10Kngs.bh.wk
Whish Captain, R.N. 23 Welbeck st
WhishawChas.J.esq.1South sq.Gray's in
Whishaw Francis,esq.19John st.Adelphi
WhishawHenry,esq.1 South sq.Gray's in
Whishaw James, esq.1Southampton row
Whiskin James, esq.10 Upper Bedford pl
WhitakerAlfd.H.esq.4 Field ct.Gray's in
Whitaker Edward T.esq.12 Lin.inn fields
Whitaker Joseph, esq. 7 Furnival's inn
Whitaker Thomas, esq.56 Upper John st
WhitbreadLadyGrove ho.Kensington gor
Whitbread Gordon,esq.8Newsq.Linc.inn
Whitbread Samuel Charles, esq.22Eaton place, & Cardington, Bedfordshire
Whitchurch James, esq. 16 Norland pl
Whitcombe James, esq. 2 Bolton st
Whitcombe Nathaniel James, esq. 12 Bedford st. Bedford square
White Lieut. Gen. 17 Upper Berkeley st
White Col 25 UpperSeymour st.Ptmn.sq
White Colonel Henry, M.P. 44 Belgrave square, & St. Helen's, near Dublin
White Captain,R.N.,7 Hans pl.Sloane st
White Captain, 4 Leonard place, Knsgtn
White Captain, 11 Park sq. Regent's pk
White CaptainB.12 Loraine place,Holwy
White Captain Hammond, R.N. Carlton chambers, 8 Regent st
White Rev. Arnold, 16 Mornington pl
White's Club House (Henry Raggett, secretary), 37 & 38 St. James st
White Alfred, esq. 15 Cloudesley sq
White Andrew, esq. 14 Hertford st
White Anthony, esq. 5 Parliament st
White Charles,esq.32Mortimer st.Cav.sq
WhiteChas.F.esq.9A,Church st.Edgw.rd
WhiteD.esq. 6 Augusta pl.Stckwll.com
White Edmund,esq. 59 York terrace
White Edward, esq.8 Cambridge square, & 12 Gt. Marlborough st
White Edward, esq.73Lamb's Conduit st
White Edward G. esq. 24 Charlotte st. Bedford sq. & 1 New sq. Lincoln's inn
White Edward M. esq. 15 Up. Albany st
White Fred.T.esq.6 Stone bldgs.Linc.inn
White George, esq, 54 Brompton square
White George, esq. 12 Hatton garden
White George,esq.10Leonard pl. Knsgtn
WhiteGeorge,esq.14Lodge pl.Regent'spk
White George Francis, esq. 8 Haymrkt
WhiteGeorgeHarton,esq.69Dean st.Soho
White George Towry, esq.25 Old square

White Henry, esq. 3 Mountford crescent
White Henry A. esq. 18 King's par. Chels
White Henry Hopley, esq. 13 Old sq
White H. J. esq. 7 Hemingford cot. Islgtn
White John, esq. 2 Albion ter. Canonby
White John, esq. 7 Park place, Regt.'s pk
White John, esq. 1 St. Andrew's pl. Rgt.'s pk
White John, esq. 1 Devonshire place, north, & Westbourne green, Paddington
White John, esq. 34 Montagu square
White John, esq. 1 Princess st. Westmnst
White John, esq. 2 Up. Charles st. West
White John Meadows, esq. 35 Lincoln's inn fields & 7 Whitehall place
White John Charles, esq. 32 Mortimer st
White John Thomas, esq. 11 Bedford row
White John Wm. esq. 34 Montagu sq.; & 10 Godliman st. Doctors' commons
White Jonathan W. esq. 40 Up. Norton st
White Jph. esq. 10 Elizabeth st. Eaton sq
White Joseph, esq. 68 Lamb's Conduit st
White Jsph. esq. 19 Portland pl. Islngtn
White Miss 20 Brunswick square
White Miss, 4 Lyon ter. Edgware road
White Mrs. Col. 25 Upper Seymour st. Portman square
White Mrs. 4 Augusta ter. Stockwell
White Mrs. 7 Bayswater ter
White Mrs. 77 Chester square
White Mrs. 6 Clarendon ter. Notting hill
White Mrs. 6 Francis st. Bedford sq
White Mrs. 3 New Ormond st
White Mrs. 36 Sidmouth st. Gry's in. rd
White Mrs. 4 Strahan ter. Liverpool rd
White Mrs. 1 Tavistock row, Covent gdn
White Mrs. Arth. 15 Coleshill st. Eaton sq
White Rd. esq. 2 Cumberland pl. New rd
White Rd. esq. 14 Essex st. & Acton hill
White Rd. esq. 2 Lawn, South Lambeth
White Richd. Saml. esq. 4 Gordon pl. Gordon sq.; & 11 Lincoln's inn fields
White Richd. S. esq. 22 Old sq. Linc. inn
White Robert, esq. 24 Sussex gardens
White Samuel, esq. 5 Lower Ranelagh st
White Samuel, M.P. Reform club, Pall mall; & Killakee, near Dublin
White Sl. G. esq. 4 Sion college gardens
White Stephen, esq. 1 Lamb's Conduit st
White Stephen P. esq. 2 Old sq. Lin. inn
White Thomas, esq. 11 Bedford row
White Thos. A. esq. 30 Botolph la. City
White Thomas R. esq. 12 Cloudesley st
White Walter, esq. 6 Chancery lane
White Wm. esq. 8 Holland pl. Kensingtn
White William esq. 11 Montague place, Clapham road
White Wm. esq. 9 Seymour pl. Wandsworth road
White Wm. esq. 26 Woburn square
White Wm. A. A. esq. 14 College st. Westminster; & Castor, near Great Peterborough
White Wm. Fred. esq. 10 Camden st. south
White Wm. Fredk. esq. 15 Regent st
White Wm. G. S. esq. 14 Took's court
White Wm. Hy. esq. 18 Artillery pl. Finsby
White W. Foster, esq. 134 St. John st
Whitear Thos. esq. 36 Bedford pl. Knsgtn
Whitehead C. esq. 15 Milton st. Dorset sq
Whitehead Geo. esq. 2 Boyle st. Savillerw
Whitehead Hy. esq. 7 Whitehead's grove
Whitehead Jn. esq. 56 High st. Portld. tn
Whitehead Jno. esq. Terrace, OldKent rd
Whitehead Mrs. 55 Hans pl. Sloane st
Whitehead Mrs. 163 Sloane st
Whitehead Mrs. 13 Westbourne place
Whitehead Thos. M. esq. 2 Gt. James' st. Bedford row
Whitehead William Henry, esq. 7 South sq. Gray's inn; & 82 Basinghall st
Whitehorne Jas. esq. 4 Glo'st. cr. Glo'st. gt
Whitehouse Jsph. esq. 1 Francis st. Bedford sq.; & 36 Lincoln's inn fields
Whitehouse Richd. esq. 7 Chancery la
Whitehouse Richd. esq. 7 Ladbroke ter
Whitehurst Chas. H. esq. Q.C. 1 Brick ct
Whitehurst Mrs. 179 Prospect pl. Ed. rd
Whitehurst Mrs. St. John's hill, Wandsw
Whitehurst Thomas, esq. Hartington cottage, Devonshire pl. Wandsworth rd
Whiteley Geo. esq. 3 Middle Temple la
Whiteley Geo. esq. 18 Milner sq
Whitelock Geo. esq. 8 Harewood sq
Whitelock Miss, 8 Harewood sq
Whitelow Mrs. A. 14 NewManor pl. Chel
Whiteman John C. esq. 7 Bryanstone sq.; & the Grove, Epping, Essex
Whiteside Wm. esq. 7 Lowndes sq.; & 63 Lincoln's inn fields
Whiteway John H. esq. 51 Linc. inn flds
Whitfield Chs. esq. 2 Grove ter. St. Jns. wd
Whitfield Geo. esq. 9 Alexander sq
Whitfield Richd. G. esq. 8 St. Thos. st. Boro'
Whitfield Wm. B. esq. 64 Lamb's Condt. st
Whitgreave Geo. Thos. esq. 29 Eaton sq.; & Moseley court, nr. Wolverhampton
Whitherby Fras. esq. 3 Highbury ter
Whiting Chas. esq. 8 Montaguepl. Clpm. rd
Whiting Fras. esq. 2 Mecklenburgh sq
Whiting Frederic, esq. 11 New inn
Whiting Geo. esq. 3 Stockwell vil. Clpm
Whiting Mathew, esq. Lavender sweeps, Wandsworth road
Whiting M. esq. 9 Spencer ter. Islington
Whiting Thos. esq. 10 Chapel st. Gros. sq
Whiting Thos. esq. 17 Nelson square
Whitley Mrs. 11 Bolton st. Piccadilly
Whitley Wm. esq. 214 Up. Thames st
Whitlow Chas. esq. 69 Oxford terrace
Whitmarsh Fras. esq. Q.C. 1 Henry st. Vauxhall, & 3 Serle st. Linc. inn
Whitmarsh Fras. jun. esq. 8 Nw. Boswl. ct
Whitmarsh Mrs. 41 Great Ormond st
Whitmarsh Thos. W. esq. 55 Brmptn. crs
Whitmore Alfred, esq. 29 Queen Anne st
Whitmore Chas. S. esq. 12 King'sbnch. wlk
Whitmore Edwd. esq. 53 Torrington sq
Whitmore Geo. esq. 63 Park st. Grosv. sq
Whitmore John, esq. 6 Cadogan terrace
Whitmore John, esq. 125 Oxford st
Whitmore Robert, esq. 31 Portland pl. & 9 New square, Lincoln's inn
Whitmore Thomas Greenslaid, esq. 3 Seymour place, Wandsworth road
Whitmore Wm. W. esq. 1 Dorset st. Ptm. sq. & Dudmaston hall, nr. Bridgenorth
Whitshed Adml. Sir J. H. 18 Cavendish sq
Whitt John, esq. 72 East st. Manchester sq
Whittaker Geo. B. esq. 20 Up. Phillimorepl
Whittaker John Hen. esq. 20 Nelson sq
Whittaker Mrs. 20 Allsop ter. New rd
Whittam George, esq. 54 Cadogan place
Whitter Mrs. 4 Ulster ter. Regent's pk
Whittington Miss, 21 Upper Baker st
Whittle Bramley, esq. 43 Norfolk st. Strd
Whitworth Rt. esq. 5 New sq. Linc. inn
Whorwell Thos. esq. Mount villa, Mountfort crescent, Barnsbury sq. Islington
Whyatt Wm. esq. 7 Harrington square
Whyte Mark B. esq. 4 Garden ct. Temple
Whyte Wm. John. esq. 61 Russell square
Whytt Ebenezer, esq. 34 Baker st. Llyd. sq
Wick Mrs. 19 Upper Kennington green
Wickens Hen. esq. 23 Old Burlington st
Wickens Jas. S. esq. 35 Mortimer st. & 1 Chandos st. Cavendish square
Wickens John, esq. 7 New sq. Linc. inn
Wickes Mrs. 42½ Clarendon square
Wickham Hy. L. esq. 15 Chesterfield st
Wickham Wm. esq. 15 Cadogan terrace
Wicking Matt. esq. 81 Milton st. Dors. sq
Wickings Mrs. 1 Barnsbury pl. Islington
Wickings Wm. esq. 3 Finsbury terrace
Wicklow Earl of, 2 Cavendish square; & Shelton abbey, Arklow, Ireland; & Stanmore park, Middlesex
Wicks George, esq. 83 Upper Ebury st
Wicks Richard, esq. 46 King square
Widdowson Mrs. 100 Sloane st
Widdowson George, esq. 89 Norton st
Widnell C. esq. 21 Judd pl. west, New rd
Widnell Josiah, esq. 33 Southampton. rw
Wigan Edwd. esq. 17 Highbury terrace
Wigan G. esq. 42 Somerset st. Mnchstr. sq
Wigan Miss, 19 Highbury terrace
Wigg Francis, esq. 7 Bedford row, Bloomsbury, & Frogmore, St. Alban's
Wigg George, esq. 22 Mecklenburgh sq
Wigg Smith Spencer, esq. 9 Tavistock pl. Russell sq. & 12 South sq. Gray's inn
Wiggins Edw. esq. 33 Jewry st. Aldgate
Wiggins John, esq. 30 Tavistock place
Wiggins S. esq. 14 Albert ter. Knightsb
Wight Alex. esq. 4 Pall mall east, & 4 Hanover terrace, Notting hill
Wight A. jun. esq. 6 Clarendn. ter. Nott. hl
Wight Geo. John. esq. 56 Gt. Marylebone st
Wight Jas. Lane esq. 38 Bedford place
Wight John, esq. 9 Sussex pl. Kensingtn
Wight Robert, esq. 6 Finsbury circus
Wight Thos. esq. 25 Percy st. Bedfd. sq
Wightman Sir Wm. knt. 38 Eaton pl. Belgrave square; Roll's garden, Chancery lane; & St. Alban's bank, Hamptn
Wightman Rev. J. St. Katherine's, Rgt. pk. & Saltford rectory, Bath
Wightman W. B. esq. 10 Montaguepl. Isln
Wigle Hen. esq. 5 Hanover ter. Notting hl
Wigley Charles Geo. esq. Harrow road
Wiglesworth Thomas, esq. 42 Gloucester place, & 5 Gray's inn square
Wigney William, esq. 20 Wilton place
Wigram Rt. Hon. Sir James, knt. V.C. 68 Portland place
Wigram Edwd. esq. 2 Connaught pl. west
Wigram George V. esq. 14 Gt. Percy st
Wigram Henry Loftus, esq. 27 Brook st
Wigram Loftus Tottenham, esq. Q.C. 4 Stone buildings, Lincoln's inn
Wigram Wm. esq. 56 Upper Harley st. & Bennington park, Stevenage
Wilberforce Wm. esq. 7 James st. Buckingham gate, & Highwoodhill, Hendon
Wilbraham Edw. esq. Q.C. 44 Torrington sq. & 11 Old square, Lincoln's inn
Wilbraham Geo. esq. & Lady Anne, 23 Brook st. & Grosvenor sq. & Delamere house, near Knutsford
Wilbraham Misses, Wilton st. Belgr. sq
Wilby Hy. esq. 27 Theberton st. Islingtn
Wilcocks John W. esq. North ho. Rgt.'s pk
Wilcox Brodie, esq. 24 Dorset square
Wilcox James A. esq. 25 Long la. Bermndsy
Wilcox John, esq. 86 Gt. Titchfield st
Wild Edw. Archer, esq. 13 Duke st. Wstmr
Wild James Wm. esq. 9 Argyll pl. Regentst
Wild Wm. esq. 3 Tyndalepl. Up. st. Islingtn
Wildbore Saml. esq. 6 Kensington ter
Wilde Sir Thos. knt. Q.C., M.P. 29 Dover st. Piccadilly; 9 Serjeants' inn, Fleet st.; & Bowes manor, nr. Southgate, Middlesex
Wilde Chas. Rt. Claude, esq. 29 Dover st. & 9 Serjeants' inn, Fleet st
Wilde Claude, esq. 29 Dover st. Piccadly
Wilde George, esq. 1 Cambridge sq. Hyde park, & 9 New sq. Lincoln's inn
Wilde Hy. S. esq. 3 Serjeants' in. Fleet st
Wilde Jas. P. esq. 1 Serjeants' in. Chanc. la
Wilde Miss, 44 Clarges st
Wilde Sam. F. T. esq. 10 Serjt'. inn, Fleet st
Wilde Thos. Montague C. esq. 29 Dover st. & 9 Serjeants' inn, Fleet st
Wilden Chas. esq. 35 Cumming st. Pntnv
Wilder Lady, 8 York place, Portman sq
Wilder Mrs. 13 Sussex pl. Regent's pk
Wilder Wm. Saml. esq. 15 Kenton st
Wildes Rev. Wm. 10 Up. John st. Gold. sq
Wilding T. esq 5 Chesterfieldst. King's cr
Wildman Lieut. Col. J. 39 Brook st
Wildman Richard, esq. 12 Lowndes sq. & 1 New court, Temple
Wildsmith J. P. esq. 14 Alfred st. Bfd. sq
Wilk John, esq. 24 Cheyne walk, Chelsea
Wilkes Francis, esq. 16 Craven st
Wilkie Miss, 29 York st. Portman sq
Wilkie Thos. esq. 3 Charles st. Lowndes sq
Wilkin Geo. esq. 3 Essex court, Temple

Wilkin Henry, esq. 20 Newman st
Wilkin James, esq. 217 Piccadilly
Wilkin John, esq. 10 Spring gardens
Wilkin Thos. M. esq. 11 Amwell ter. Pentonville, & 3 Furnival's inn, Hlbrn
Wilkins Chas. esq. 8 King's bench walk
Wilkins Chas. esq. 7 Terrace, Kensngtn
Wilkins James, esq. 26 Soho square
Wilkins J. esq. 41 Bedford pl. Kensgtn
Wilkins Miss, 40 Baker st. Portman sq
Wilkins Rt. esq. 19 Haverstock hill
Wilkins R. H. esq. 18 Wilton st. Grosv. pl
Wilkins Wm. esq. 2Richmondpl. Hamp. rd
Wilkins Wm. Bushby, esq. 89Chanceryla
Wilkinson Sir Gardner, knt. 34Conduit st
Wilkinson Major, 9 Upper Phillimore pl
Wilkinson A. esq. 1 Marlboro'pl. Kenn.cs
Wilkinson Anthony, esq. 3 Lodge place
Wilkinson Arthur O. esq. 5 Highbury pk
Wilkinson Chas. M.D. 27 Liverpool ter
Wilkinson Chas. esq. 8 Canonbury villas
Wilkinson Edwd. esq. 28 Dorset square
Wilkinson Edwd. S. esq. 51 Notting hl. sq
Wilkinson Frdk. esq. 1Stone bdgs. Lnc. in
Wilkinson G. esq. 4 Albion vil. Livrpl. rd
Wilkinson Green, esq. 39 Wimpole st
Wilkinson Hy. esq. 127Stanhope st. Hd. rd
Wilkinson Henry, esq. 27 Brompton sq
Wilkinson Jas. J. G. esq. 13 Store st
Wilkinson Jas. John, esq. 23 Barnsbury park, & 1 Pump court, Temple
Wilkinson John, esq. 5Belgrave st. Nw. rd
Wilkinson John, esq. 2 James st. Adelphi
Wilkinson John, esq. 49 Sloane st
Wilkinson Josiah, esq. 8 Bedford row, Islington, & 7 Lincoln's inn fields
Wilkinson Josiah, esq. 36 Compton ter
Wilkinson Michl. E. esq. 4 River st. Islg
Wilkinson Mrs. 1 Addison ter. Knsgtn
Wilkinson Mrs. 31 Blandford square
Wilkinson Mrs. 29 Cumming st. Pntnvl
Wilkinson Mrs. 11 Dean's pl. So. Lmbth
Wilkinson Mrs. 41 Montagu square
Wilkinson Mrs. 50 New Bond st
Wilkinson Mrs. 28 St. John's wood road
Wilkinson Mrs. 40 Sloane st
Wilkinson Mrs. 40 Tavistock square
Wilkinson Norman, esq. 15 Regent st
Wilkinson Rt. esq. 22 Cumberland ter
Wilkinson Rt. H. esq. 25 Old sq. Linc. in
Wilkinson Thos. esq. 6 Canterbury villas
Wilkinson Thos. esq. 20 Grosvenor st. wt
Wilkinson Thos. esq. 12 Kensington gore
Wilkinson Wm. M. esq. 26 Camden rd. villas, Camden town, & 44 Linc. inn fld
Wilkinson Wm. Smith, esq. 21 Coles terrace, Barnsbury road, Islington
Wilks Rev. Saml. Chas. 6 Grove end pl
Wilks Geo. Aug. F. M.D. 19 Hart st
Wilks John, esq. 3 Finsbury square
Wilks Joseph, esq. 3 Harley pl. New rd
Wilks Miss, 11 Stoke Newington green
Willan Edward, esq. 35 Bedford row
Willan Jacob, esq. 9North pl. Gray's inn la
Willan Thos. esq. 38 Albany st. Rgt.'spk
Willan Wm. esq. 13 Green st. Grosvnr. sq
Willcock John Wm. esq. 6 Stone bldgs. Linc. inn, & Retreat, Kentish town
Willes Irwin L. esq. 4 Maddox st. Regt. st
Willes Jas. esq. 13 Somers pl. Cambdg. sq
Willes James Shaw, esq. 3InnerTemple la
Willes Mrs. 10 Manor place, S. Chelsea
Willes William G. esq. 27 Hans place
Willet Joseph, esq. 52 Gloucester place
Willett Geo. esq. 9 Howley pl. vill. Padn
Willett Jas. esq. 20 York bldgs. New rd
Willett Henry Ralph, esq. K4, Albany
Willett Miss, 19 Charles st. Berkeley sq
Willett Mrs. 25 Somerset st. Portman sq
Willett Robt. esq. 9 Whitehead's grove
Willey James, esq. 15 Beaufort bldgs
Williams Sir Jas. H. bart. & Lady Mary, 21 Up. Grosvenor st.; Clovelly court, Bideford; & Edwinsford, Carmarthen
WilliamsSirJohnHay, bart. Mivart's hot. 44 Brook st. & Bddwyddan, St. Asaph
Williams Sir John, knt. 28 Grosvenor sq
Williams Lady, 25 Cavendish square, & Burwood house, Cobham, Surrey
Williams Major Lewis, 10Up. Seymour st
WilliamsCapt. A. W. 5John st. Berkeley sq
Williams Capt. Percy, 10 Up. Seymour st
Williams Capt. Rd. R.N. 27 Artillerypl. wt
Williams Rev. Alfred, 33 Guilford st
Williams Rev. Danl. 3 Chas. sq. Hoxton
Williams Rev. H. G. 16 Up. Seymour st
Williams Rev. John, 11 Mecklenburgh sq
Williams Rev. T. 28 Compton ter. Islngtn
Williams Albert, esq. 1 Notting hill sq. & 38 Lincoln's inn fields
Williams Benjamin, esq. 4 Whitehall
Williams Benjamin B. esq. 2Wyndham pl
Williams Charles, esq. 13 John st. Adelphi, & 19 Ely place, Holborn
Williams Chas. esq. 6 Lyon ter. Edgw. rd
Williams Chas. esq. 5 Loraine pl. Hollwy
Williams Chas. esq. 23 Park sq. Regts. pk
Williams Chas. J. B. M.D., F.R.S. 7 Holles st. Cavendish square
Williams Chas. esq. Kent cot. Park vil. ea
Williams Chas. R. esq. 62Lincoln's inn fi
Williams David, esq. 9 Goswell road
Williams D. E. esq. 29Charlot. st. Fitz. sq
Williams Edmd. esq. 5Glo'ster pl. New rd
Williams Edward, esq. 47 King square
Williams Edw. esq. 3 Southampton row
Williams E. sen. esq. 100 Cromer st
Williams Edwd. Vaughan, esq. 1 Park st. Westminster, & 2 Inner Temple la
Williams Evan, esq. 15 Goulden terrace
Williams E. H. esq. East Temple chambs
Williams Francis, esq. 13 Newman st
Williams Frederick, esq. 88 Chancery la
Williams Fred. S. esq. 53 Chancery lane
WilliamsGeo. esq. 9Granby st. Hampst. rd
Williams George Henry, esq. 12 New North st. Red Lion square
Williams Geo. Thos. esq. 4 King's bench walk, Temple, & Limington house, Somerset
Williams H. esq. 17Chester pl. Kenn. crs
Williams Henry, esq. 64 Connaught terr
Williams Hen. esq. 39Cross st. Islington
Williams Hen. esq. 3 Stafford pl. Liss. gr
Williams Hen. esq. 15Clarmnt. row. Islgtn
Williams H. P. esq. 37 Chapel st. Pntnvl
Williams Isaac L. esq. 8New sq. Linc. inn
WilliamsJas. D. esq. 18Milton st. Dorsetsq
WilliamsJohn, esq. 8Abbey rd. St. Jn's. wd
Williams John, esq. 11 Barnsbury villas
Williams John, esq. 6 Cobham rw. Clkw
Williams John, esq. 80 Eaton square, & Boons, near Brasted, Kent
Williams John, esq. 19 Gibson square
Williams John, esq. 238 Oxford st
Williams John, esq. 1 Verulam bldgs
Williams J. esq. 4 Westbourne st. Hy. pk
Williams J. C. esq. 18Gt. George st. Wstmr
Williams John D. esq. 49 Myddelton sq
Williams John Howard, esq. 2 Albany ter. Regent's park, & 16 Bedford row
Williams John P. 1 Plowden bldgs
Williams Jsph. esq. 8Warwick st. Pmlco
Williams Joshua, esq. 16 Devonport st. & 3 New square, Lincoln's inn
Williams Luke, esq. 4 Barnard's inn
Williams Miss, 75 Milton st. Dorset sq
Williams Mrs. Col. 8 Cambridge terrace
Williams Mrs. 14Albion rd. Liverpool rd
Williams Mrs. 4Chapel st. west, Mayfair
Williams Mrs. 110 Gt. Russell st
Williams Mrs. 14 Halton st. Islington
Williams Mrs. 12 Marlbro' pl. Kenn. crs
Williams Mrs. 14 Michael's pl. Bromptn
Williams Mrs. 75 Milton st. Dorset sq
Williams Mrs. 1 Mornington place
Williams Mrs. 38 Noel st. Islington
Williams Mrs. 11 North Audley st
Williams Mrs. 8 Park road, Regt.'s pk
Williams Mrs. 1 Salisbury st. Strand
Williams Mrs. 158 Sloane st
Williams Mrs. 3 Spencer st. Goswell rd
Williams Mrs. 10Spring ter. Wndswth. rd
Williams Mrs. 5 Stanley ter. King's rd. w
Williams Mrs. 2Wellington pl. St. Jn.'swd
Williams Mrs. 8 York place, City road
Williams Rhys, esq. 34 Mornington pl
Williams Rd. esq. 27 Cadogan st. Chels
Williams Rd. esq. 55 Crutchedfriars
Williams Rd. esq. 2 Duke st. Adelphi, & Dulwich
Williams Richard, esq. 2 Pall mall east
Williams Robt. M.D. 39 Bedford place
Williams Robt. esq. 16 Whitehall place
Williams Robt. jun. esq. 16 Whitehall place, & Bridehead, near Dorchester
Williams Robt. F. esq. 76 Coleshill st
Williams Rt. Wynne, esq. 29Bedford pl. Russell sq. & 3 Paper bldgs. Temple
Williams Stephen, esq. 16 Bedford row, & Clapham common, Surrey
Williams Thos. esq. 21 Cornwall terrace
Williams Thomas, esq. 13 Elm Tree road, St. John's wd. & Northumberland house
Williams Thos. esq. 11 Felix ter. L'pl. rd
Williams Thomas, esq. 2 Grove end rd
WilliamsThos. esq. 4Lambeth pl. Clpm. rd
WilliamsThos. esq. 5Park rd. Notting hill
Williams T. esq. 19 Pelham pl. Fulham rd
WilliamsThomasEdward, esq. 13Milnr. sq
Williams Thomas Peers, esq. M.P. 41 Berkeley sq.; Temple house, Marlow; & Craigydon, nr. Bangor, Nth. Wales
Williams Wm. esq. 2 Addison ter. Not. hill
Williams Wm. esq. 31 Alfred pl. Bdfd. sq
Williams Wm. esq. 32 College st. Chelsea
Williams Wm. esq. 15 Earl's ter. Knsngtn
Williams Wm. M.P. 12Pk. sq. west, Rgt. pk
Williams Wm. esq. 9 Upper Porchester st. & 32 Lincoln's inn fields
WilliamsWm. esq. 9Windmill st. Tot. ct. rd
Williams Wm. H. esq. 8 Amwell terrace
Williams Wm. R. esq. 21 Old sq. Linc. inn
Williams Wm. S. esq. 3 Campden hill ter
Williamson Rev. Dr. 15 Dean's yd. Westm
Williamson Christopher, esq. 17 Soley ter
Williamson Edwd. esq. 44 Smith st. Chelsea, & 50 Lincoln's inn fields
Williamson E. esq. 16 Trinity sq. Southw
Williamson Friend, esq. 27 Dorset sq
Williamson Jas. esq. 39 Hunter street, Brunswick sq. & 4 Verulam buildings
Williamson J. esq. 11 Robert st. Hamp. rd
Williamson John, esq. 3 Raymond bldgs. & the Woodlands, Harrogate
Williamson John Wm. esq. 16 Carey st
Williamson Miss, 27 Hertford st
Williamson Mrs. 54 Frith st. Soho
Williamson Mrs. 7 Pelham rd. Brompton
Williamson Mrs. 32 Polygon, Clrndn. sq
Williamson Wm. esq. 66 Gibson sq. Islgn
Willich Chas. M. esq. 25 Suffolk st
Willink Mrs. 39 Cumming st. Pentonvil
Willion Geo. esq. 9 Up. Kennington la
Willis Basil C. esq. 52 Quadrant, Rgt. st
Willis Edmd. esq. 9Rutland st. Hmpstd. rd
Willis H. B. esq. 123Stanhope st. Hpstd. rd
Willis Jas. esq. 9 Old sq. Lincoln's inn
Willis John esq. 4Nassau st. Middlsx. hos
Willis Misses, Palace gn. Kensington
Willis Mrs. 48 Charlotte st. Portland pl
Willis Mrs. 13Heathcote st
Willis Mrs. 4 Hill st. Berkeley square
Willis Mrs. 49 Up. Norton st. Fitzroy sq
Willis Robert, M.D. 25 Dover st. Picedly
Willisford John, esq. 2Hollywood ho. Chls
Willisford Fras. W. esq. 76 Cadogan pl
Willitts Benj. esq. 10 Belgrave terrace
Willmer Henry, esq. 44 Baker st
Willmore Graham, esq. 3 Plowden bldgs
Willmore J. T. esq. 23 Polygon, Somers tn
Willmott Thos. esq. 17 Upper Eaton st
Willoby John, esq. 13 Cloudesly sq
Willock Major G. Vicarage pl. Kensgtn
Willock Mrs. 30 St. James's st
Willoughby de Broke Lord, 21 Hill st. & Compton Verney, Kineton
Willoughby Sir Henry, bart. 63 Brook st

Willoughby D'Eresby Lord, P.C. 142 Piccadilly; & Grimsthorpe, Bourne; Drummond castle, Crieff, N.B.; & Gwydyr, Llanelly
Willoughby Sir Nesbit Josiah, Capt. R.N 2 Montagu st. Portman square
Willoughby Benj. Edward, esq. 38 Upper Bedford place, & 13 Clifford's inn
Willoughby D. esq. 11A, Cunningham pl
Willoughby Edwd. esq. 4 Lancaster pl
WilloughbyG.esq.12Stoke Newingtn.gn
Willoughby Hen. esq. 4 Lancaster pl
Willoughby Thos. esq. 3 Trafalgar sq
Willoughby Wm. esq. 2 Gordon square
Wills Felix, esq. 118 St. John st. road
Wills Frs. esq.4 Hanover cotgs.Rgt.'spk
Wills John, esq.2Chatham pl.Walwth.rd
Wills Richd. esq. 6 Claremont square
Wills Thos. esq. 23 Webb's county ter
Wills William, esq. 22 Nelson square
Willshire Wm. H. M.D.2 Cecil st.Strand
Willson Geo. esq. 26 Gt. College st. Wstr
WillsonJsph.Wm.esq.Elm cot.Up.Ken.la
Willson Mrs. 2 Harrington square
Willson John, esq. 3 Raymond buildings
Willy Joseph, esq. 13 Agar st. Strand
Wilme Thomas, esq. 2 Wilmington st
Wilmer Wilmer, esq. 6 Old Palace yard
Wilmer Wilmer, esq. 34 Wilton crescent
Wilmot Major Eardley, 15 Mount st. & Rosebank, Great Malvern
Wilmot Charles Foley, esq. A1, Albany
Wilmot John E. E. 11 King's Bench walk
Wilmot Mrs. 7 Cadogan pl. Sloane st
Wilmott Mrs.21Up.George st.Bryanst.sq
Wilmot P. esq. 16 Welbeck st.&3 Elm ct
Wilmot-Horton Lady, 44 Upper Brook st. & Catton hall, Derbyshire
Wilmsburst T. esq. 31 George st.Eust. sq
Wilshere Wm. M.P. 11 Stratton st. & the Hermitage, Hitchin, Herts
Wilson Sir Giffin, knt. Q.C. 2 Stratford place; 25 Southampton buildings; & Woburn house, Beaconsfield, Bucks
Wilson Col. 9 Somers pl. Cambridge sq
Wilson Capt. 5 Kent ter. Regent's park
Wilson Rev. Danl. M.A. 9 Barnsbury pk
Wilson Rev. Francis C. 8 Stonefield st
Wilson Rev.Jno.M.A. 6 Green's row,Chls
Wilson Rev. John, 1 Raymond bldgs
Wilson Rev. Josias, 2 Gibson square
Wilson Alex. esq. 34 Bryanstone square
Wilson Alex. esq. 25 Lr. Phillimore st
Wilson Alex. esq. 7 Symond's inn
Wilson Charles, esq. 14 Buckingham st
Wilson Chas. Heath, esq.24 Brompton sq
Wilson Chas. M. esq. 22 Connaught sq
Wilson Cornelius Lea, esq 25 St. Paul's church yard, & Beckenham, Kent
Wilson Cornwall B.esq. 3 Woburn place
Wilson Cornwell B.esq. 13 Furnival's inn
Wilson David, esq. 1 Eccleston square
Wilson EdwardJohn,esq.39 Gt.Coram st
Wilson Forester, esq. 20 Up. Wimpole st
Wilson Fras. esq. 3 Green st. Grosvnr. sq
Wilson Fred. J.esq.10 Bloomfield tr. Pim
Wilson Geo. esq. 5 Gt. Queen st. Westm
Wilson George, esq. 106 London wall
Wilson Geo. esq. 8 Maida hill, Edgw. rd
Wilson George, esq. 11 New inn, Strand
Wilson Geo. Hy.esq.17 Arundel st.Strand
Wilson Geo. J.M. esq.100 Gt.Portland st
Wilson Geo. S. esq. 1 Hare ct. Temple
Wilson G. S. esq. 11 Alfred pl. Brompton
Wilson Hy. Vickery, esq.26 Pembroke sq
Wilson Hen. Walter, esq. 89 Chancery la
Wilson Horace H. esq. 14Up.Wimpole st
Wilson James, esq. 117 Chancery lane
Wilson Jas. esq. 1 Grove cott. Grove rd
Wilson James, esq. 14 Highbury terrace
Wilson Jas. esq. 17 Lodge road, Regt.'spk
Wilson Jas. esq.15 Hertford st. May fair, Reform club, & 6 Wellington st. Strand
Wilson Jas. esq. 20 Tyndale pl. Islington
Wilson Jas. Holbert, esq. 18 Clarges st. & York chambers, 41 St. James's st
Wilson James Arthur, M.D. 28 Dover st
Wilson John, esq. 66 Albany st.Regt.'spk
Wilson John, esq. 32 Eaton square
Wilson John, esq. 47 Gower st
Wilson John, esq. 3 Gray's inn square, & 4 Kilburn priory
Wilson Jno. esq.15 Henrietta st. Brnsk.sq
Wilson Jno. esq. 14 Loraine pl. Holloway
Wilson John, esq. 17 New Boswell ct
Wilson John, esq. 24 Osnaburgh st
Wilson John, M.D. 51 Oxford st
Wilson Jno. esq.1 Phillimore ter.Knsgtn. & Chapel stairs, Lincoln's inn
Wilson John, esq. 7 South sq. Gray's inn
Wilson Jno.H.esq.15Sthmpt.row,New rd
Wilson John Hy. esq. 3A, Portland ter
Wilson Jonath. S. esq. 15 Wilmington sq
Wilson Joseph, esq. Highbury hill
Wilson Joseph Hen.esq.26Chancery lane
Wilson Joshua, esq. 35 Highbury place
Wilson Lestock Peach, esq. 1 North Audley st. & the Grove, Epping, Essex
Wilson Melville, esq.16 Montagu square
Wilson Miss, 10 Brompton crescent
Wilson Miss, 17 Halfmoon st
Wilson Mrs. 16Devonshire st.Portlnd. pl
Wilson Mrs. 1 Francis st. Bedford sq
Wilson Mrs. 6 Gerrard st. Islington
Wilson Mrs. 14 Gower st. north, New rd
Wilson Mrs. 1 Highbury grove
Wilson Mrs. 12 Highbury place
Wilson Mrs. 11 Manchester st.Gra.in.rd
Wilson Mrs. 81 Norton st. Fitzroy sq
Wilson Mrs. 38 Piccadilly
Wilson Mrs. 37 Pembroke sq. Kensngn
Wilson Mrs. 9 St. James st
Wilson Mrs. 20 Upper Wimpole st
Wilson Mrs. 3 Vauxhall pl. Sth. Lmbth
Wlison Mrs. 15 Winchester row, New rd
Wilson Ralph, esq. 21 Allsop ter.New rd
Wilson Rd. esq. 9 Maida hill, Edgw. rd
Wilson Rt. esq. 2 Binfield pl. Clphm. rd
Wilson Rt. H.H.esq.4 South sq.Gray's in
WilsonSam.esq.Aldmn.25St.Paul'sch.yd
Wilson Sam. esq. 57 St. John's wood ter
Wilson Step. B. esq.7Fredk.pl.Gry.'sin.r
Wilson Thos. esq.2 Charles st.Trevor sq
Wilson Thos. esq. 12 Dalby ter. City rd
Wilson Thomas, esq. 2 Up. Eccleston st
Wilson Thos. H. esq. 1 Lowther arcade
Wilson Thomas L. esq. 43 Bedford row
Wilson Walter, esq. 15 Henrietta st. & 10 Everett st. Brunswick square
Wilson Wm. esq.40 Beaumont st.Port.pl
Wilson Wm. esq. 19 Canonbury square
Wilson Wm. esq. 55 Charlotte st. Fitz.sq
Wilson William, esq. 8 Clapham rise
Wilson Wm. esq. 48 London st. Fitz. sq
Wilson W.J.E.esq.55Charlotte st.Fitz.sq
Wilson William Miller, esq. 13 South sq
Wilson Wm. S. esq. 10 King's Bench wa
Wilson-Henniker Jn. esq. Chelsea park
Wilson-Patten Mrs. 9 Lowndes square
Wilthew Edw. esq. 3 Gloucester grove,w
Wilton Earl of, P.C. 7 Grosvenor square; Heaton house, near Manchester; & Egerton lodge, Melton Mowbray
Wilton Benjamin, esq. 32A, Pembroke sq
Wilton Charles, esq. 6 New st. Dorset sq
WiltonDav.W.esq.23Claremont tr.Nw.rd
Wilton George P. esq. 1 Raymond bldgs
Wilton Joseph R. esq. 57 Oxford terrace, Edgware road, & 1 Raymond bldgs
Wiltshire Geo. C. esq. 15 River st. Pntv
Wimbush Samuel, esq. 2 Halkin st
Winchester Bishop of, 19 St. James's sq. & Palace, Winchester, & Farnham castle
Winchester Marquis of, P.C. Amport house, Andover
Winchester Mrs. 7 Stafford row, Pmlco
Winchilsea & Nottingham Earl of, 20 Wilton crescent, & Eastwell park, Ashford, Kent; & Haverholm priory, Sleaford
Winckworth J. R. esq.23Northumbrld.st
Winckworth L. H. esq.10 St.Swithin's la
Winckworth Miss, 49 York st. Portm. sq
Windeler Chas. esq.18 Rodney st.Pntnvl
Winders Jas. esq. Lavender hi. Wndswth
Windeyer Edw. esq. 4 Essex ct. Temple
Windham Club House (Thomas I. Hampton, sec.), 11 St. James's sq
Windham Joseph Smith, esq. 14 Connaught place, & Waghen, Beverley
Windle Mrs. 6 Osborne st. Whitechapel
Windmill Miss, 74 George st.Portman sq
Window Jas. esq.Uplands, Lavender hill, Wandsworth, & 8 Craig's ct.Charing cr
Windsor Chas. Geo. Price, esq. 79 Pall mall, & 4 Victoria road, Kensington
Windsor Edward, esq. 37 Chancery lane
Windsor Other Richard, esq. 4 St. Ann's terrace, Acacia rd. & 37 Chancery la
Windsor William, esq. 59 Newman st
Winfield Chas. Hen. esq. 56 Tavistock sq
Wing John William, esq. 6 Connaught sq. & 10 Farrars buildings, Temple
Wing Mrs. 13 Chesterfield st. New rd
Wing Mrs. 4 Up. Fitzroy st. Fitzroy sq
Wing Thomas, esq. 1 Gray's inn square
Wing William Charles, esq. 44 Dorset st. Manchester square
Wingfield Francis. esq. 10 Allsop place
Wingfield John T. esq. 36 Newington pl
Wingfield Mrs. 35 Pall mall
Wingfield Mrs. 39 Oxford terrace
Wingfield Rd. Baker, esq. 2 Lowndes sq
Wingfield William, esq. Q.C.73 Eaton sq. & Masters' off, 25 Southampton bldgs
WingraveJ.H.esq.3 Eldonpl.Up.Kngt. la
Wingrove Wm.esq.7 Albert rd.Regt.'spk
Winkfield Jas. esq. 9 Addison tr. Not. hi
Winkfield Mrs. 2 Zion cottages, Camden terrace west, Camden new town
Winkle Mrs. 16 Henrietta st.Manchr. sq
Winn Hon. Mrs. 26 Upper Phillimore pl
Winn Jas. esq. 14 Victoria gro. Kensgtn
Winn Jas. G. esq. 22 Canonbury villas
Winn Mrs. 7 Princes st. Hanover sq
Winn Thos. esq. 9 Holland pl. Clphm. rd
Winnington Sir Thos. Edwd.bart.M.P. 16 Suffolk st. Pall mall, & Stanford ct. Bewdley
Winser Chas. esq. 10 Cheyne row, Chels
WinserChas.esq.2 New Temple buildings
Winser Mrs. 13 Hinde st. Manchester sq
Winsland Nicholas, esq. 9 Montague st
Winslow Arthur, esq. 3 Harcourt bldgs
Winslow Edward, esq. 7 Torrington sq. & 45 Lincoln's inn fields
Winslow Thos. esq. 40 Camden st. south
Winsor Fred.Albert, esq.57Linc.inn fields
Winsor Philip, esq.R.N. 12 Cambridge ter
Winstanley Clement, esq. 15 Regent st
Winstanley Henry, esq. 88 Stanhope st. Hampstead road
Winstanley Jas. W. esq. 26 Chancery la
Winstanley John, esq. 38 Regent square
Winstanley Miss, 7 Edwards st.Ptmn. sq
Winstanley Mrs. 41 Mecklenburgh sq
Winstanley Newman, esq. 12 Somers pl
WinstanleyRd.H.esq.41Mecklenburghsq
Winstanley T.esq.13 Dorset ter.Clpm. rd
Winstanley Wm. esq. 27 Halfmoon st
Winston Rev. Benjmn. 64 Torrington sq
Winston Chas. esq. 64 Torrington sq. & 2 Paper buildings, Temple
Winstone Mrs.19A, Albion gr. Thornhl.rd
WinterChas.Wm.esq.3Up.Kennington la
Winter Geo. esq.21 George st.Euston sq
Winter Henry, esq. 12 John st. Adelphi
Winter John, esq. 13 Lower Eaton st
Winter J.G.esq.8Brunswick pl.Brnsby.rd
Winter Mrs. 18 Bernard st. Russell sq
Winter Mrs. 30 Burton st. Pimlico
Winter Mrs. 50 Cambridge st. Edgwr. rd
Winter Mrs. 1 Edwardes pl. Kensington
Winter Mrs.62Hamilton tr.St.John's wd
Winter Mrs. 10 Trinity sq. Tower hill
Winter Rd. esq. 23 Hamilton terrace
Winter Rt. esq. 16Bedford rw.& Brighton
Winter W.esq.4 Lavender hl.Wandsw. rd

Winterbotton A. A. esq. 137 Sloane st. & Gresham chambs. Old Broad st. City
Winterbottom Edw. J. esq. 9 Sloane st
Winterbottom John Fred. esq. 13 Old sq
Winterbottom Rd. T. esq. 22 Hertford st
Winterburn Rd. esq. 47 Portman place
Winterton Earl of, 37 Portland pl. & Shillinglee park, Petworth, Sussex
Winterton Dowager Countess of, 7 North bank, Regent's park, & 65 Grand parade, Brighton
Winthrop Benj. esq. 48 Up. Bedford pl
Winthrop Benj. Eveleigh, esq. 2 Paper bdg
Winthrop Wm. 15 Regent st
Wintle Robt. H. esq. 20 Beaufort st. Chels
Winton David, esq. 4 Richmond tr. Islgt
Winton Mrs. 6 Grosvenor st. west
Winward Sam. esq. 32 Up. Berkeley st
Wise Edward, esq. 2 Middle Temple lane
Wise Mrs. 5 Portland pl. Wandsworth rd
Wise Thos. esq. 4 Albion gro. Thornhl. rd
Wise Thomas, esq. 44 Frith st. Soho
Wishaw Jas. esq. 1 Southampton rw. Hlbn
Wiseman Mrs. 4 North bdgs. Finsbry cir
Wishart Mrs. 40 Up. Baker st. Rgt.'s pk
Wiss John Anth. esq. 33 Connaught ter
Withall William, esq. 7 Parliament st
Witham Capt. Fras. 6 Cottage rd. Eaton sq
Witham Hen. esq. 78 Gower st. & 6 Old sq
Witham Henry, esq. 25 Montague st
Witham Misses, 78 Gower st
Witham William, esq. 12 Bedford row
Witham William, esq. 49 Eaton square, & 8 Gray's inn square
Witherby Charles, esq. 3 Hemingford cottages, Pentonville
Witherby Geo. esq. 10 Highbury park
Witherby Richard, esq. 22 Canonbury sq
Witherby Wm. Hen. 16 Park ter. Hibry
Witherington Wm. F. esq. 8 Leigh st
Withers Rev. Edwd. 31 Lr. Phillimore pl
Withers Jsph. esq. 15 Kent ter. Regt.'s pk
Withers Jsph. esq. 20 Up. Berkeley st. w
Withers Wm. esq. 36 Titchborne st. Edg. rd
Witt Charles esq. 30 Spring gardens
Witt Wm. esq. 314 High Holborn
Witter Thos. esq. 2 Westbourne st. Hy. pk. g
Whittich Wm. esq. 47 Warren st. Fitz. sq
Witty Rd. Henry, esq. 37 Essex st. Strand
Wix Rev. Saml. St. Bartholomew hospital
Wix Miss, 3 Kennington ter. Up. Keningtn
Wix Saml. esq. St. John's hill, Wndswth. rd
Wixcey Wm. esq. 10 Paradise ter. Islgtn
Woad Mrs. 21 Osnaburgh st. Regent's pk
Wodehouse Lord, Fenton's hotel, 63 St. James's street; & Kimberley, Wymondham; & Witton park, Norfolk
Wodehouse Hon. Edwd. Thornton, Capt. R.N. 13 South Audley st. Grosvenor sq
Wodehouse Edmond, esq. M.P. Limmer's hotel, & Thorpe, Norwich
Wodehouse Mrs. 20 Montagu sq
Wolfe J. L. esq. 52 Guildford pl. Lr. Ken. la
Wolfe Lewis, esq. 13 Connaught terrace
Wolfe Misses, 13 Torrington sq
Wolfe Mrs. 29 Half moon st. Piccadilly
Wolfe Mrs. 6 York cotts. Old Brompton
Wolfe Sl. esq. 13 Vauxhall pl. Sth. Lmbth
Wolford Arthur, esq. 66 Lowndes sq
Wolker John, M.D. 11 Chester st. Gro. pl
Wollaston Col. 144 Oxford st. & Shewton hall, near Hinckley, Leicestershr
Wollaston Rev. C. H. 10 Bryanstone st. & East Dereham, Norfolk
Wollen Fred. esq. 1 Belmont pl. Wndswh. rd
Wollaston Fredk. Luard, esq. 5 Chester pl. Pimlico, & 2 Pump court, Temple
Wollen Ruscombe, esq. 14 New Boswell court, & 30 Bucklersbury
Wolston Augustus, esq. 8 Furnival's inn
Wombwell Sir Geo. bart. 88 Eaton sq
Wombwell Chas. O. esq. 47 Grosvenor pl
Wombwell Geo. esq. 15 George st. Hanvr. sq. & Newburgh pk. Easingwold, Yorks
Wontner Miss, 28 Tibberton sq
Wontner Thomas, esq. 17 Barnsbury pk
Wontner T. jun. esq. 15 Skinner st. Snowhl
Wood Lady, 16 Southwick crescent
Wood Lady, 25 Sussex square. Hyde pk
Wood Sir A. agent for Ionian States, Colonial office, 13 Downing st
Wood Sir Gabriel, knt. & Lady, 81 Jermyn st. & 3 Circus, Bath
Wood Col. M.P. & Lady Caroline, 4 Cavendish sq. & Littleton ho. nr. Staines
Wood Lieut.-Col. Thos. M.P. 4 Cavendish sq. & Littleton house, near Staines
Wood Capt. R.N. 17 Queen st. Mayfair
Wood Capt. Clapham rise
Wood Capt. R.N. 23 Ladbroke sq. Nott. hl
Wood Rev. David, M.A. 32 York buildings, New road
Wood Rev. Robert, 39 Sloane square
Wood Rev. William, 27 Harley st
Wood Chas. esq. 65 Cambridge ter. Edg. rd
Wood Chas. Alex. esq. 12 King's bench wlk
Wood Chas. Jas. esq. 78 Dean st. Soho
Wood Chas. Wm. esq. 1 Harcrt. bdgs. Tmpl
Wood Frederick, esq. 25 Bedford row
Wood Fredk. John, esq. 77 Chancery la
Wood Fredk. Wm. esq. 1 Hare ct. Temple
Wood Geo. esq. 43 Beaufort st. Chelsea
Wood Geo. Wm. esq. 53 Great Coram st
Wood Geo. W. esq. 2 Hollywd. pl. Lit. Chls
Wood Hamilton, esq. 19 Paddington grn
Wood Henry, esq. 14 Bartlett's buildgs
Wood Henry, esq. 24 Percy st. Bedfd. sq
Wood Hugh, esq. 26 Green st. Grsvnr. sq
Wood Jas. esq. 28 Aberdeen pl. Maida hill
Wood Jas. esq. 6 Sebbon's bldgs. Islgtn
Wood Jno. esq. 2 Bedford pl. Vauxhl. bdg. r
Wood John, esq. 65 Charlotte st. Fitzroy sq
Wood John, esq. 20 Doughty st
Wood John, esq. 52 Hunter st. Brnswk. sq
Wood John, esq. 64 Lincoln's inn fields
Wood John, esq. 23 Oxford square
Wood John esq. Stable yd. St. Jas.'s pala
Wood John, esq. 38 Up. Gower st
Wood John Mackworth, esq. 5 Golden square, & 43 Lincoln's inn fields
Wood John Richd. esq. 1 Hare ct. Temple, & Woodbridge, Suffolk
Wood Joseph, esq. 57 Cadogan place
Wood Lewis, esq. 4 Barnsbury square
Wood Matthew, esq. 53 Berners st
Wood Misses, 31 Green st. Grosvenor sq
Wood Mrs. 35 Addison road north
Wood Mrs. 12 Alexander sq. Brompton
Wood Mrs. 9 Cottage road, Eaton sq
Wood Mrs. 5 Derby street, King's cross
Wood Mrs. 6 Ladbroke villas, Notng. hl
Wood Mrs. 17 Manchester tr. Livpl. rd
Wood Mrs. Somerville, 27 Charlotte st
Wood Richard, esq. 28 Red Lion square
Wood Rd. esq. 21 Whitehead's grv. Chls
Wood Robt. esq. 23 Duke street, Manchester square, & Back lane, Fulham
Wood Robert H. esq. 21 Green st
Wood Robt. W. esq. 5 Lodge pl. Regt.'s pk
Wood Saml. James, esq. 41 Wigmore st
Wood Thomas, esq. 39 Craven st. Strand
Wood Thos. esq. 11 Lowther cotgs. Islgn
Wood Thos. esq. Alderman, 5 York pl. Walworth road
Wood Thos. C. esq. 1A, Sussex tr. Hd. pk. gds
Wood Weston, esq. 9 Up. Hyde park st
Wood Wm. esq. 10 Symond's inn
Wood Wm. esq. 9 Wilmot st. Russell sq
Wood Wm. B. esq. 41 Bloomsbury sq
Wood Wm. Page, esq. Q.C. 12 Gt. George st. Westminster, & 3 Stone buildings
Woodall Francis, esq. 8 St. Pancras vale
Woodall John, esq. 83 Jermyn st
Woodbridge Thos. A. esq. 8 Clifford's inn
Woodburn Samuel, esq. 1 Park lane
Woodcock Chas. Rt. esq. 29 Gt. Pultney st
Woodcock Miss, 6 Rich ter. Old Brmptn
Woodcock Thos. esq. 29 Paradise ter
Woodd Basil T. esq. 14 Gt. Cumberland st
Wooden Mrs. 1 Lower Southwick st
Woodfall Hen. D. esq. 14 Gt. Dean's yd
Woodfall H. T. esq. 13 East st. Rd. Lion sq
Woodfall John W. M.D. 38 Davies st
Woodford General, 21 Somerset st
Woodford J. R. esq. 3 York pl. City rd
Woodford Mrs. Box cot. King's rd. Chels
Woodford Mrs. 19 Porchester terrace
Woodford Thos. esq. 27 Piccadilly
Woodgate Septimus, esq. 69 Albany st
Woodgate Wm. esq. 18 Cumberland ter. Regent's park, & 32 Lincoln's inn flds
Woodhead Joseph, esq. 6 Montagu sq. & 1 James st. Adelphi
Woodhead Thos. esq. 66 Camden rd. vil
Woodhouse Geo. D. esq. 3 New Boswell ct
Woodhouse Henry, esq. 58 Torrington sq
Woodhouse Henry Wm. esq. 10 Regent sq. & 5 New square, Lincoln's inn
Woodhouse Jas. esq. 7 Bayswater hill
Woodhouse Mrs. 9 Coburg pl. Bayswtr
Woodhouse Richd. esq. 56 Torrington sq
Woodifield Rt. D. esq. 11 Ormes sq. Baysw
Woodin Mrs. 25 Aberdeen pl. Maida hill
Woodley John, esq. 13 Millbank row
Woodman Geo. esq. 10 Upper Charles st
Woodrooffe Wm. esq. 1 New square, Lincoln's inn, & Hampstead
Woodrow John H. esq. 4 Upper ter. Islgtn
Woods A. W. esq. Heralds' col. Drs. coms
Woods F. F. esq. 20 Stanhope st. Hmpstd. rd
Woods F. J. esq. 13 North cres. Bdfrd. sq
Woods Hen. esq. 15 Upper Gloucester pl
Woods John, esq. 30 Up. Montagu st
Woods Mrs. 5 Goswell rd. west side
Woods Mrs. 1 Lit. Titchfield st. Portld. pl
Woods Mrs. 36 Up. George st. Brynstn. sq
Woodward Chas. esq. 10 Compton ter
Woodward Corbet, esq. 12 Furnival's inn
Woodward Hen. esq. 53 Linc. inn fields
Woodward Isaac, esq. 19 Edwardes sq
Woodward John, esq. 27 Beaufoy ter
Woodward John, esq. 4 Davidge ter. Lbth
Woodward Mrs. 1 Islington green
Woodward Mrs. 75 Milton st. Dorset sq
Woodward Mrs. 11 Palmer ter. Hollwy
Woodward Mrs. 3 Up. Glo'ster st. Dorset sq
Woodward Robert, esq. 27 Bouverie st
Woodward Thomas, esq. 31 Conduit st
Woodward Wm. esq. 1 Furnival's inn
Woodward Wm. J. esq. Lowlnds. Wand. rd
Woodyard Rev. B. 18 Glo'ster ter. Comcl. rd
Woodyatt Mrs. 6 Bulstrode st
Woodyer Hen. esq. 4 Adam st. Adelphi
Wool Thomas, esq. 50 Brompton row
Woolcott George, esq. 54 Doughty st
Wooldridge Wm. esq. 6 Jermyn st. St. Jas
Woollacott Rev. C. 31 Glo'ster st. Queen sq
Woollams Wm. esq. 12 Thayer st. Mnch. sq
Woollett Geo. esq. 2 Red Lion square
Woolley Chas. Adam, sen. esq. 3 Clarnc. pl. Nw. rd. & 11 New sq. Lincoln's inn
Woolley George, esq. 8 Brompton row
Woolley Geo. esq. 31 Burton st. Burton crst
Woolley Geo. esq. 14 Kensington gore
Woolley Geo. Boyle, esq. 17 Canonbury sq
Woolley Hen. esq. 12 Goulden terrace
Woolley Miss, 4 Leicester pl. Leics. sq
Woolley Samuel, esq. 15 Hastings st
Woolltorton Jno. esq. 7 Euston pl. New rd
Woolmer A. J. esq. 7 Cleveland st. Fitzy. sq
Woolmer Joseph B. esq. 11 King's rd. Pimli
Woolmore Lady, 15 Bruton st
Woolnoth T. A. esq. 12 Greek st. Soho
Woolrych Edmund H. esq. 2 Eccleston st. & 2 Middle Temple lane
Woolrych Humphrey W. esq. 2 Hare ct
Woolsey Brien B. esq. 49 Westbourne tr
Woolsey Mrs. 2 Ampton pl. Gray's inn rd
Wootton Thos. esq. 23 Circus rd. St. Jn.'s w
Worcester, Bishop of, 24 Grosvenor pl.; Hartlebury castle, Stourport; & Palace, Worcester
Worcester Timothy, esq. 243 Maida vale
Wordsworth C. F. F. esq. 2 Paper buildings
Wordsworth Hen. esq. 27A, Avenue rd
Worgan Geo. esq. 12 Camden st. so. Cden. tn
Worley John, esq. 15 New Cavendish st
Worley Miss, 12 Chester square, Pmlco

Worlledge John, esq. 56 Ebury st. Pimlico, & 1 Elm court, Temple
Worlledge John, esq. 56 Ebury st. & 1 Elm court, Temple
Wormald John, esq. Highbury lodge
Wormald Rd.esq.11Blmfield.rd.Maida hl
Wormald Thos. esq. 42 Bedford row
Wormald Thomas, esq. 4 Gray's inn sq
Wormley Capt. R.N. 3 Gordon square
Worms Solomon B. esq. 27 Park cresnt
Wornell J. esq. 5 Greenland pl. Cromer st
Wornum Rt.esq.2Camden st.so.Cmdn.tn
Wornum R.N.esq.1Bedford pl.Hmptd.rd
Worrell Edwd. esq. 55 Cambridge st
Worrell Miss, 43 Jermyn st
Worrell Septimus, esq. 11 Portman st
Worsdell Thomas, esq. 48 Mortimer st
Worsley Lord, M.P. 17 Arlington st. & Manby, near Brigg, Lincolnshire
Worsley P. esq. 4 Taviton st. Gordon sq
WorsleyRt.esq.1Marlboro' pl.St.Jn.'s wd
Worthington Rev. Dr. 1 Sidmouth pl
Worthington John, esq. 37 Sidmouth st
Wortley Hon. James Stuart, Q.C., M.P. 19 Grosvenor st. Bond st. & Twisden buildings, Temple
Wortley Hon. John Stuart, M.P. & Lady Georgiana, 15 Curzon st. Mayfair, & Wortley hall, Sheffield, Yorkshire
Wortley Jas. esq. 3 Canonbury pl
Wortley Mrs. 23 Allsop ter. New road
Wotton Henry Rendall, esq. 32 Fitzr. sq
Wrangham Digby C. S.L. 1 Serjeants' inn, Chancery lane
Wrangham Mrs. 9 Bernard st
Wrather Wm. esq.8Gt.Collegest.Westmr
Wrather Wm. esq.3 Paulton's sq.Chelsea
Wray John, esq. 6 Suffolk pl.Pall mall ea
Wray Mrs. 5 Glo'ster rd. Regent's park
Wray Robt. esq. 22 Queen sq. Bloomsbury, & 60 Chancery lane
Wray Wm. esq. 27 Mornington crescent
Wray Warren P. esq. 60 Chancery lane
Wreford Samuel, esq. 15 Oxford square
Wreford Wm. esq. 5 Pullin's row, Islgtn
Wren William Weld, esq. 73 Gower st
Wrentmore Isaac, esq. 19 Lincoln's inn fields, & 11 Cheyne row, Chelsea
Wrentmore John H. esq. 14 Clarendon sq
Wright Capt. Geo. T. 33 Gt. Portland st
Wright Rev. John, 67 Westbourne ter
Wright Alf. esq. 2 Belgrave st.King's cr
Wright Augustus, esq. 10 Clarendon sq
Wright Chas. esq. 27 Essex st. Strand
Wright Edgar, esq.8Grove rd.St.Jn.'s wd
Wright Edwd. esq. 18 Allsop ter. New rd
Wright Geo. esq. 49 Gerrard st. Islngtn
Wright Geo. esq. 53 Lincoln's inn fields
Wright Henry, esq. 22 Brunswick sq
Wright Henry T. esq. 84 Hamilton ter
Wright J. esq. 27 Petersbrg. pl. Bayswtr
Wright Jas. esq. Grove hall, Larkhall la
Wright James, esq. 8 New inn, Strand
Wright J. esq. 85 Stanhope st.Hmpstd.rd
Wright James, esq. 29 Tibberton square
Wright John, esq. 18 Aldermanbury
Wright John, esq, 1 Canonbury cottages
Wright Jn. esq. 6 Cumberland pl.New rd
Wright John, esq. 1 Hare court, Temple
Wright John, esq. 13 Pall mall
Wright John, esq. 11 Park st. Westminr
Wright John, M.D.3Princes ct.Storey gt
Wright John, esq. 7 Rathbone place, & 6 Cumberland place, New road
Wright John, esq. 4 Torrington st
Wright John, esq. 6 Wharton st
Wright John L.esq. 2South sq.Gray's inn
Wright John W. esq. 19 Cumberland ter
Wright Miss, 12B, Old Cavendish st
Wright Miss, 11 Gloucester pl. New rd
Wright Mrs. 10 Addison ter. Notting hill
Wright Mrs. 20 Brompton crescent
Wright Mrs. 9 Carlisle st. Soho
Wright Mrs. 10 Clarendon square
Wright Mrs. 18 Gibson sq. Islington
Wright Mrs. 7 Porteus road, Harrow rd
Wright Mrs. 56 St. John's wood terrace
Wright Mrs. 24 Somerset st.Portman sq
Wright Mrs. 37 Woburn square
Wright Peter, esq. 40 Upper George st. & Hatfield priory, Essex
Wright Rd. esq. 7 Barnsbury vils. Islgtn
Wright Rd. esq. 11 Gloucester pl.New rd
Wright Richd. Seaton, esq. 15 Golden sq
Wright Robt. esq. 22 Baker st. Lloyd sq
Wright Robert, esq. 44 Gerrard st. Soho
Wright Robt. esq. 22 Lonsdale sq. Islgtn
Wright Samuel, esq. 14 Bryanstone st
Wright Stephen, esq. 24 Somerset st
Wright ThomasS.esq.13Cook's ct.Lin.inn
Wright Wm. esq. 56 Coleshill st.Eaton sq
Wright Wm. esq.9Gt.Queen st.Lin. inn fls
Wright Wm. esq. Flag yd. St.James's pal
WrightWm.esq.6Frederick pl.Up.Knn.la
Wright William, esq. 11 Furnival's inn
Wright Wm.esq.3Grenville st.Brnswk.sq
Wright Wm. esq. 6 Stone bldgs.Linc. inn
Wright Wm. H. esq. 23 Essex st.Strand, & Highgate hill
Wrighton Wm. Thos.esq.15 Edwardes sq
Wrightson Richd. esq. 7 Up.Portland pl
Wrightson T. B. esq. 44 Lincoln's inn flds
Wrightson Wm. Battie, esq. M.P.22 Up. Brook st.; & Cusworth park, near Doncaster
Wrottesley Lord, 1 Albemarle st. & Wrottesley hall, Wolverhampton
Wrottesley Hon. Walter, 4 Chester sq. Pimlico, & 4 Stone bdg. Lincoln's inn
Wyand Mrs. 10 Lyon ter. Edgware rd
Wyatt Albert, esq.12 Chapel st.Grosv.sq
Wyatt Alf.esq. 52 Stanhope st.Hamps.rd
Wyatt George, esq.11 Glo'ster sq.Hy.pk
Wyatt Henry John, esq. 18 Sloane ter
Wyatt Hugh Penfold, esq. 1 Pump ct
Wyatt Jas. esq. 33 Dudley gr.Harrow rd
Wyatt James, esq. 11 Gray's inn square
Wyatt James, esq. 3 Radnor pl.Hyde pk
Wyatt John, esq. 7 Figtree ct. Temple
Wyatt Matthew, esq. 5 Porteus terrace
Wyatt Matthew, esq. 1 Up. Hyde pk.st
Wyatt Matthew Coates, esq. Dudley grove house, Harrow road
Wyatt Mrs. 5 Albion st. Hyde pk
Wyatt Mrs. 13 Chester ter. Regent's pk
Wyatt Mrs. 3 Notting hill terrace
Wyatt Peter, esq. 8 Barnsbury villas
Wyatt Robt. esq.3 Paultons ter. Chelsea
Wyatt Rbt.esq.12Suffolk st.Pall mall ea
Wyatt Thos. Hen. esq. 75 Gt.Russell st. Bloomsbury, & Church st. Hackney
Wyburn Jas. esq. 38A, Porchester ter
Wye Geo. Wm. esq. 2 Princes place, Kennington road
WyldJas.esq.8Park village wt. Regt.'s pk
Wyld Wm.esq.Chichester pl.Wndsworth
Wylde Henry, esq. 32 Upper Gower st
Wylde James, esq. 15 Stonefield st
Wylde John, esq. 3 Argyle st. King's crs
Wylde Miss, 6 Lr. Belgrave pl. Pimlico
Wylie Alexander, esq. 6 Burwood place
Wylie Alexander, esq. 8 Stanhope ter
Wylie James, esq. 40 Burton crescent
WylieJn.esq.2Up.Belmont pl.Wndsth.rd
Wyllie Mrs. 24 Tavistock pl. Russell sq
Wyllie Wm. esq. 19 Notting hill sq
Wyndham Hon. Mrs. 72 Connaught terr
Wyndham Col. 4 Grosvnr.pl. & Petworth house, Sussex; &East lodge, Brighton
Wyndham Edwd. esq. 14 Blandford sq
Wynford Lord, Leesons, nr. Chiselhurst
Wynn Rt. Hon. Chas. Watkin Williams, M.P. 20 Grafton st. Bond st. & Llangedwyn hall, near Oswestry
Wynn Sir Watkin Williams, bart. M.P. 36 Hill st. Berkeley sq. & Wynnstay, Wrexham, Denbighshire
Wynn SirWm.bart.3Suffolk st.Pall mall
Wynn Miss Williams, 104 Piccadilly
Wynne Chas. Wynne Griffith, esq. 39 Portman sq.; & Cefnamwlch, Carnarvonshire; & Pentrevolus, Nth. Wales
WynneG.esq.25Glo'stergrv.w.O.Brmptn
WynneL.esq.10Cunningham pl.St.Jnswd
Wynne Lewellyn,esq. 46 Linc's.inn field
Wynne Mrs. 8 Earl's ter. Kensington
Wynne Wm.esq.5 Hinde st.Manchstr.sq
Wynne William, esq. 56 Euston square
Wyon Benjamin, esq. 287 Regent st
Wyon Benj. esq. Marlboro' rd.St.Jns.wd
Wyon E.W. esq. 48 Gower st, Bedford sq
Wyse Thos. M.P. 17 Wilton pl. Belgrave sq.; Brookes's & Reform clubs; Manor of St. John, near Waterford; & Cuddagh, near Montrath, Queen's county
YALLOP Mrs.6 Canonbury sq.Islington
Yallop Rowland, esq. 8 Furnival's inn
Yallop Thomas, esq. 61 Myddelton sq
Yapp Thos. esq. 108 Goswell road east
Yarborough, Earl of, 17 Arlington st.; Appuldercombe park, Isle of Wight; & Brocklesby, Brigg, Lincoln
Yarborough Rd.C. esq. 44 Linc.inn flds
Yardley Charles, esq. 3 Bayham cottgs. Camden New town
Yardley Ed. esq.7 Serjeants' inn,Fleet st
Yardley Mrs. M.4Coles ter.Barnsbry. rd
Yardley Wm. esq. 1 Christopher st. Hatton grdn. & 5 Nelson ter. Stoke Newgn
Yardley W. esq. 2 Brick court, Temple
Yarnold Mrs. 23 Gibson sq. Islington
Yates Rev. Harry, 18 King st. Finsbury
Yates Chas. esq. 5 Mecklenburgh square
Yates Chas. Frs.esq.12Argyle st.Kngs.cr
Yates Edwd. esq. 30 Compton ter. Islngn
Yates Fredk.esq.14Duke st.Westminster
Yates Fredk. esq. 24 Gt. George st. Wmr
Yates Geo. esq.14 Ladbroke ter. Notg. hl
Yates Geo. sen. esq.2Earl's ct.OldBrmtn
Yates John, esq. 5 Gower st. nth. New rd
Yates John Ashton, esq. 33 Bryanstone sq. & Dinglehead, near Liverpool
Yates Miss, 2 Bryanstone st.Portman sq
Yates Mrs. 10 Alfred pl. Alexander sq
Yates Mrs. 12 Alpha road, Regent's pk
Yates Thos. esq. 28 Chester pl.Kenntn.cr
Yates Thomas B. esq. 15 Euston square
Yates Wm. esq. 12 Paper bldgs. Temple
Yates Wm. Holt, M.D. 53 Woburn place
Yatman Wm. esq. 18 Norfolk crescent, Hyde park
YearsleyJas.esq.M.R.C.S.L.15Saville row
Yearsley James, esq. 32 Sackville st
Yearsley Mathew, esq. 37 Lonsdale sq
Yeates Mrs. 15 Upper Seymour st. west
Yeatman Morgan, esq. 34 Fenchurch st. & Richmond, Surry
Yeats J. S. esq.2Montague pl.Clphm.rd
Yeats J.S.jun.2Montague pl.Clapham rd
Yeend Jas. Parker, esq. 15 Clifford's inn
Yellowlees Wm. esq. 72 Newman st
Yems Miss, 12 Albion st. Hyde park
Yeo Robt. esq. 58 St. John's wood ter
Yeoman Thos. H.M.D. 12 Tavistock pl
Yerbury Geo. esq.Ambass. ct.St. James's
Yetts Joseph M. esq. 5 Gray's inn pl
Yewd Wm. esq. 30 East st. Red Lion sq
Yglesias Joseph Ramon, esq.9 Gordon st
Yockney Rev. John, 9 Highbury terrace
Yonge Geo. esq. 1 Crescent pl. Blackfrs
York, Archbishop of, P.C. 40 Grosvenor sq.; Bishopthorpe palace, near York; & Nuneham park, Oxford
York J.esq.Wharncliffe ter.St.John's wd
Yorke Hon. Eliot Thos. M.P.15 Wilton pl
Yorke Hon. Mrs. Charles, 28 Bruton st. Bkly. sq. & Hatfield Woodside, Herts
Yorke Lieut. Col. P.89Eaton pl.Belgr.sq
Yorke Edmd. esq.4 St.Vincent pl.City rd
Yorke Henry Redhead, esq. M.P. & Hon. Mrs. 81 Eaton square
Yorke Miss,10 New Ormond st.Queen sq
Yorke Miss, 48 Sloane st
Youdan Miss, 11 Low. Phillimore place
Youl Richd.esq.7 Duke st.Grosvenor sq
Young Sir Charles George, knt. F.S.A. Heralds' college
Young SirWm.bt.7Westbourne st.Hy. p

Young Rev. Robt. 17 Beaumont st
Young Capt. R.N. 12 Victoria rd. Kensgtn
Young Alex. esq. 1 Hanover cots. Rgt.'s pk
Young A. D. esq. 5 College ter. Islingtn
Young Anthy. esq. 12 Sudeley st. Islgtn
Young Chas. esq. 16 Lr. Phillimore pl
Young Chas. esq. 23 Grosvenor place
Young Chas. Baring, esq. 5 Langham pl
Young Chas. M. esq. 121 Gt. Prtlnd. st
Young Geo. esq. 4 Camden road villas
Young Geo. esq. Denmark hill, Cambwll
Young Geo. esq. 30 Paradise ter. Islngtn
Young Geo. A. esq. 34 Eagle st. Rd. Lion sq
Young Geo. W. esq. 22 Kennington oval
Young Geo. Wm. esq. 37 Mortimer st
Young Gilbert A. esq. 28 John st. Bdfrd. rw
Young Henry, esq. 12 Essex st. Strand
Young Henry, esq. 2 Lower Berkeley st
Young James, esq. 32 Bloomsbury sq
Young James, esq. 21 Lower Belgrave pl
Young John, esq. 2A, Burton st. Eaton sq
Young John, M.P. 19 Chesham place, & Bailieborough castle, Ireland
Young John, esq. 25 Paradise ter. Islgtn
Young John, esq. 69 Stanhope st. Hmpstd. r
Young John, esq. 19 York ter. Regt.'s park
Young John Adolphus, esq. 13 Great Ormond st. & Harehatch lodg. Maidnhd
Young John William, esq. 3 Euston sq
Young Jsh. esq. 4 Union pl. New rd
Young Mrs. 16 Cumberland st. Prtmn. sq
Young Mrs. 6 Maida hill west
Young Mrs. 15 Palmer ter. Holloway
Young Mrs. 37 Trevor sq. Knightsbridge
Young Rd. esq. 87 Milton st. Dorset sq
Young Richard, esq. 29 Mornington pl
Young Robert, M.D. Camberwell green
Young Robt. esq. 38 Nelson sq. Blkfrs. rd
Young Rt. Lake, esq. 9 Sebbons bdgs. Isl
Young Samuel, esq. 1 Vauxhall bridge road, & 30 Parliament st
Young Thomas, esq. 13, Albany
Young Thos. esq. 1 Dorset ter. Clphm. rd
Young Thomas, esq. 42 Piccadilly
Young Thos. Bristowe, esq. 22 Bernard st. Russell square, & 10 New inn
Young Thos. F. esq. 9 Gt. Cumberland pl. & Shottesbrooke park, Maidenhead
Young Wm. esq. 7 Granby st. Hmpstd. rd
Young Wm. esq. 4 Highbury grange
Young Wm. esq. 12 Taunton pl. Regt.'s pk
Young Wm. Sl. esq. 1 Vauxhall bridge road, & 30 Parliament st
Young Wm. Sawer, esq. 9 Cross st. Islgtn
Young Witherden, esq. 35 Gillingham st. Pimlico & 14 King Wm. st. W. Strand
Younge Edward, esq. 1 New sq. Linc. inn
Younge Miss, 4 Gothic cottages, Park village east, Regent's park
Younghusband Thos. Wm. esq. 1 Lansdowne villas, Notting hill
Ysasi Manuel G. de, esq. 15 Regent st
Yung Mrs. 17 Radnor pl. Glo'ster square

ZANCHI Mrs. 20 Regent st
Zeitter Fred. esq. 6 Nottingham terrace
Zetland, Earl of, 19 Arlington st.; Aske hall, Richmond, Yorkshire; Marsk hall, Cleveland, Yorkshire; & Kerse house, Falkirk, Scotland
Zohrab Edward, esq. Ottoman consul general, & 1st attaché to the embassy, 1 Bryanstone square
Zorhab Edwd. esq. 16 Camden cot. Cm. tn
Zornlin John Jacob, esq. 10 Bethel pl. Camberwell road
Zulueta Pedro de, esq. 29 Cumberl. ter
Zulueta Peter John de, esq. 29 Cumberland terrace, Regent's park

PARLIAMENTARY DIRECTORY.

Second Parliament of Her Majesty Queen Victoria.

Corrected to September, 1846.

CONTENTS.

HOUSE OF PEERS.

PEERS of the BLOOD ROYAL, 3; ARCHBISHOPS, 3; DUKES, 20; MARQUISES, 22; EARLS, 137; VISCOUNTS, 28; BISHOPS, 27; BARONS 211........................ } Total 451, of whom 12 are MINORS.

The undermentioned Noblemen sit as Peers of reat Britain by an inferior title to that by which they are usually addressed.

Superior Title.	*sits as*	*Superior Title.*	*sits as*	*Superior Title.*	*sits as*
E. Aberdeen	V. Gordon	M. Drogheda	V. Moore	M. Londonderry	E. Vane
D. Argyll	L. Sundridge	E. Eglinton	L. Ardrossan	M. Lothian	L. Kerr
D. Atholl	E. Strange	E. Egmont	L. Lovell	E. Meath	L. Chaworth
E. Balcarras	L. Wigan	M. Ely	L. Loftus	V. Midleton	L. Brodrick
L. Belhaven & Stenton	L. Hamilton	E. Enniskillen	L. Grinstead	D. Montrose	E. Graham
E. Besborough	L. Ponsonby	E. Errol	L. Kilmarnock	E. Moray	L. Stuart
D. Buccleuch	E. Doncaster	V. Falkland	L. Hunsdon	E. Mornington	L. Maryboro'
M. Clanricarde	L. Somerhill	V. Ferrard	L. Oriel	E. Roden	L. Clanbrassil
E. Clare	L. Fitzgibbon	E. Galloway	L. Stewart	D. Roxburgh	E. Innes
V. Clifden	L. Mendip & Dover	E. Glasgow	L. Ross	E. Shannon	L. Carleton
		E. Haddington	L. Melros	M. Sligo	L. Monteagle
M. Conyngham	L. Minster	D. Hamilton	D. Brandon	E. Stair	L. Oxenfoord
E. Cork	L. Boyle	M. Headfort	L. Kenlis	V. Strangford	L. Penshurst
E. Courtown	L. Saltersford	M. Huntly	L. Meldrum	M. Thomond	L. Tadcaster
M. Donegal	L. Fisherwick	E. Kinnoul	L. Hay	E. Uxbridge	L. Paget
E. Donoughmore	V. Hutchinson	E. Leitrim	L. Clements	M. Waterford	L. Tyrone
M. Downshire	E. Hillsboro'	E. Limerick	L. Foxford		

In the following list the above are arranged under the titles by which they sit, their superior title being placed immediately after in parenthesis; but in the alphabetical arrangement they will be found under that title by which they are ordinarily known.

PEERS ARRANGED ACCORDING TO THEIR ORDER OF PRECEDENCE.

Marked thus * are Irish Representative Peers. Marked thus † are Scotch Representative Peers.

PEERS OF THE BLOOD ROYAL (3).

	Creation.
His Royal Highness Albert Edward Prince of Wales, K.G. (*a minor*)	1841
His Royal Highness Ernest Augustus Duke of Cumberland and Teviotdale, K.G., P.C., King of Hanover	1799
His Royal Highness Adolphus Frederick Duke of Cambridge, K.G., P.C.	1801

ARCHBISHOPS (3).

Style, *His Grace.*	Consecrated.	Translated
Right Hon. Dr. William Howley, Lord Archbishop of Canterbury, P.C.	1813	1828
Right Hon. Dr. Edward Harcourt, Lord Archbishop of York, P.C.	1791	1807
Right Hon. Lord John George Beresford, Lord Archbishop of Armagh, P.C.	1806	1822

DUKES (20).

Style, *Most Noble, His Grace.*

Name.	Title.	Creation.	Title by Courtesy of Eldest Sons.
Henry Charles Howard	Norfolk, P.C.	1483	E. of Arundel & Surrey
Edward Adolphus St. Maur	Somerset, K.G.	1546	L. Seymour
Charles Gordon-Lennox	Richmond, K.G., P.C.	1675	E. of March
Henry Fitzroy	Grafton	1675	E. of Euston
Henry Somerset	Beaufort, K.G.	1682	M. Worcester
William Aubrey de Vere Beauclerck	St. Albans	1684	E. of Burford
Francis Godolphin d'Arcy Osborne	Leeds	1694	M. of Carmarthen
Francis Russell	Bedford	1694	M. Tavistock
William Spencer Cavendish	Devonshire, K.G., P.C.	1694	M. Hartington
George Spencer Churchill	Marlborough	1702	M. Blandford
John Henry Manners	Rutland, K.G.	1703	M. of Granby
Alexander Hamilton	Brandon (and Hamilton), K.G., P.C.	1711	M. Douglas
William Henry Cavendish Scott Bentinck	Portland, P.C.	1716	M. Titchfield
George Montagu	Manchester	1719	V. Mandeville
Henry Pelham Pelham-Clinton	Newcastle, K.G.	1756	E. of Lincoln
Hugh Percy	Northumberland, K.G., P.C.	1766	E. Percy
Arthur Wellesley	Wellington, K.G., P.C.	1814	M. of Douro
Richard Plantagenet Temple Nugent Brygdes-Chandos-Grenville	Buckingham and Chandos, K.G., P.C.	1822	M. of Chandos
George Granville Leveson-Gower	Sutherland, K.G.	1833	M. of Stafford
Henry Vane	Cleveland, K.G.	1833	E. of Darlington

MARQUISES (22).

Style, *Most Honourable.*

Name.	Title.	Creation.	Title by Courtesy of Eldest Sons.
John Paulet	Winchester	1551	E. of Wiltshire
†George Hay	Tweeddale, K.T.	1694	E. Gifford
Henry Petty Fitzmaurice	Lansdowne, K.G., P.C.	1784	E. Shelburne
George Ferrers Townshend	Townshend	1787	E. of Leicester
James Brownlow William Gascoigne Cecil	Salisbury, K.G., P.C.	1789	V. Cranbourne
John Alexander Thynne	Bath (*a minor*)	1789	V. Weymouth
James Hamilton	Abercorn, K.G., P.C.	1790	V. Hamilton
Richard Seymour Conway	Hertford, K.G.	1793	E. of Yarmouth
John Crichton Stuart	Bute, K.T.	1796	L. Mountstuart
Brownlow Cecil	Exeter, K.G., P.C.	1801	L. Burghley
Spencer Joshua Alwyne Compton	Northampton	1812	E. Compton
George Charles Pratt	Camden, K.G.	1812	E. Brecknock
Henry William Paget	Anglesey, K.G., G.C.B., K.P., P.C.	1815	E. Uxbridge
George Horatio Cholmondeley	Cholmondeley, P.C.	1815	E. Rocksavage
Paulyn Reginald Serlo Rawdon-Hastings	Hastings (*a minor*)	1816	E. Rawdon
Charles Brudenell-Bruce	Ailesbury, K.T.	1821	E. Bruce
*George Thomas John Nugent	Westmeath	1822	L. Delvin
Frederick William Hervey	Bristol	1826	E. Jermyn
Archibald Kennedy	Ailsa	1831	E. Cassillis
John Campbell	Breadalbane, K.T.	1831	E. Ormelie
Richard Grosvenor	Westminster	1831	E. Grosvenor
Constantine Henry Phipps	Normanby, P.C.	1838	E. Mulgrave

EARLS (137).

Style, *Right Honourable.*

John Talbot	Shrewsbury	1442	L. Talbot
Edward Smith Stanley	Derby, K.G.	1485	L. Stanley
Francis Theophilus Henry Hastings	Huntingdon	1529	L. Hastings
Robert Henry Herbert	Pembroke & Montgomery	1551	L. Herbert
William Courtenay	Devon	1553	L. Courtenay
Thomas Howard	Suffolk & Berkshire	1603	V. Andover
William Basil Percy Feilding	Denbigh, P.C.	1622	V. Feilding & Callan
John Fane	Westmoreland, P.C., G.C.B., G.C.H., D.C.L.	1624	L. Burghersh
George Augustus Frederick Albemarle Bertie	Lindsey	1626	L. Bertie
George Harry Grey	Stamford & Warrington (*a minor*)	1628	L. Grey of Groby
George William Finch-Hatton	Winchilsea & Nottingham	1628	V. Maidstone
George Augustus Frederick Stanhope	Chesterfield, P.C.	1628	L. Stanhope
Henry Tufton	Thanet	1628	L. Tufton
John William Montagu	Sandwich	1660	V. Hinchinbroke
Arthur Algernon Capel	Essex	1661	V. Malden
James Thomas Brudenell	Cardigan	1661	L. Brudenell
George Howard	Carlisle, K.G., P.C.	1661	V. Morpeth
Walter Francis Montagu-Douglas-Scott	Doncaster, K.G., P.C. (D. of Buccleuch,)	1662	E. of Dalkeith
Cropley Ashley-Cooper	Shaftesbury, P.C.	1672	L. Ashley
Montagu Bertie	Abingdon	1682	L. Norreys
John Lumley-Savile	Scarborough	1690	V. Lumley
William Charles Keppel	Albemarle, P.C.	1696	V. Bury
George William Coventry	Coventry (*a minor*)	1697	V. Deerhurst
George Child Villiers	Jersey, P.C.	1697	V. Villiers
John Poulett	Poulett	1706	V. Hinton
†George Sholto Douglas	Morton	1458	L. Aberdour
†Alexander Home	Home	1605	L. Dunglas
†David Ogilvy	Airlie & Lintrathen	1639	L. Ogilvy
†David Leslie-Melville	Leven & Melville	1641	V. Balgonie
†Dunbar James Douglas	Selkirk	1646	L. Daer
†Thomas John Hamilton Fitzmaurice	Orkney	1696	V. Kirkwall
†Francis William Grant	Seafield	1701	V. Reidhaven
Edward Harley	Oxford & Mortimer	1711	L. Harley
Washington Sewallis Shirley	Ferrers	1711	V. Tamworth
William Legge	Dartmouth	1711	V. Lewisham
Charles Augustus Bennet	Tankerville, P.C.	1714	L. Ossulston
Heneage Finch	Aylesford	1714	L. Guernsey
George Augustus Frederick Cowper	Cowper	1718	V. Fordwich
Philip Henry Stanhope	Stanhope	1718	V. Mahon
Robert Sherard	Harborough	1719	L. Sherard
Thomas Parker	Macclesfield	1721	V. Parker
George William Richard Fermor	Pomfret	1721	L. Leominster
James Graham	Graham (D. of Montrose) K.T., P.C	1722	E. of Kincardine
William Waldegrave	Waldegrave, C.B.	1729	V. Chewton
Bertram Ashburnham	Ashburnham	1730	V. St. Asaph
Charles Stanhope	Harrington	1742	V. Petersham
John Charles Wallop	Portsmouth	1743	V. Lymington
Henry Richard Greville	Brooke & Warwick, K.T.	1746	L. Brooke
George Robert Hobart-Hampden	Buckinghamshire	1746	L. Hobart
Charles William Wentworth-Fitzwilliam	Fitzwilliam	1746	V. Milton
Rev. Francis North	Guilford	1752	L. North
James Mann	Cornwallis	1753	V. Brome
Charles Philip Yorke	Hardwicke	1754	V. Royston

Name.	Title.	Creation.	Title by Courtesy of Eldest Sons.
Henry Stephen Fox-Strangways	Ilchester	1756	L. Stavordale
George John Sackville West	De La Warr, P.C.	1761	V. Cantilupe
William Pleydell-Bouverie	Radnor	1765	V. Folkestone
Frederick Spencer	Spencer, P.C.	1765	V. Althorp
Henry George Bathurst	Bathurst	1772	L. Apsley
Arthur Wills Blundell Sandys Trumbull Windsor Hill	Hillsborough (M. of Downshire)	1772	E. Hillsborough
George William Frederick Villiers	Clarendon, P.C.	1776	L. Hyde
William David Murray	Mansfield and Mansfield, K.T.	1776	V. Stormont
Rev. William Nevill	Abergavenny	1784	V. Nevill
Charles Chetwynd Talbot	Talbot, K.G., K.P., P.C.	1784	V. Ingestre
Geo. Augustus Fred. John Murray	Strange (D. of Atholl)	1786	M. of Tullibardine
Ernest Augustus Edgecumbe	Mount-Edgecumbe	1789	V. Valletort
Hugh Fortescue	Fortescue, P.C.	1789	V. Ebrington
Edward Digby	Digby	1790	V. Coleshill
George Percy	Beverley	1790	L. Louvaine
Henry John George Herbert	Carnarvon	1793	L. Porchester
Charles Cecil Cope Jenkinson	Liverpool, G.C.B., P.C.	1796	L. Hawkesbury
George Cadogan	Cadogan	1800	V. Chelsea
James Howard Harris	Malmesbury	1800	V. Fitzharris
*Francis William Caulfeild	Charlemont (L. Charlemont, in England)	1763	V. Caulfeild
*Stephen Moore	Mountcashel	1781	L. Kilworth
*John Bourke	Mayo	1785	L. Naas
*John Crichton	Erne	1789	V. Crichton
*William Howard	Wicklow, K.P.	1793	L. Clonmore
*John Otway O'Connor Cuffe	Desart	1793	V. Cuffe
*George Charles Bingham	Lucan	1795	L. Bingham
*John Bruce Richard O'Neill	O'Neill	1800	L. O'Neill
*James Bernard	Bandon, G.C.B.	1800	V. Bernard
*Du-Pré Alexander	Caledon	1800	V. Alexander
James Alexander St. Clair Erskine	Rosslyn, P.C.	1801	L. Loughborough
William Craven	Craven	1801	V. Uffington
Arthur George Onslow	Onslow	1801	V. Cranley
Charles Marsham	Romney	1801	V. Marsham
Henry Thomas Pelham	Chichester	1801	L. Pelham
Thomas Egerton	Wilton, P.C.	1801	V. Grey de Wilton
Edward Herbert	Powis, K.G.	1804	V. Clive
Horatio Nelson	Nelson, G.C.B.	1805	V. Trafalgar
*Archibald Acheson	Gosford P.C. (L. Worlingham, in England)	1806	V. Acheson
*William Parsons	Rosse, K.P.	1806	L. Oxmantown
*Charles William Bury	Charleville	1806	L. Tullamore
Charles Herbert Pierrepoint	Manvers	1806	V. Newark
Horatio Walpole	Orford	1806	L. Walpole
Henry Grey	Grey, P. C.	1806	V. Howick
William Lowther	Lonsdale, P. C.	1807	V. Lowther
Dudley Ryder	Harrowby, P.C.	1809	V. Sandon
Henry Lascelles	Harewood	1812	V. Lascelles
Gilbert Elliot Murray Kynynmound	Minto, P.C., G.C.B.	1813	V. Melgund
Charles Murray Cathcart	Cathcart, K.C.B.	1814	L. Greenock
James Walter Grimston	Verulam	1815	V. Grimston
John Cust	Brownlow	1815	V. Alford
Edward Granville Eliot	St. Germans, P.C.	1815	L. Eliot
Edmund Parker	Morley	1815	V. Boringdon
George Augustus Frederick Henry Bridgeman	Bradford	1815	V. Newport
John Reginald Pindar	Beauchamp	1815	V. Elmley
*Richard Butler	Glengall	1816	V. Caher
Thomas Philip De Grey	De Grey, K.G., K.P., P.C.	1816	L. Lucas
John Scott	Eldon	1821	V. Encombe
George Henry Boscawen	Falmouth	1821	L. Boscawen
Richard William Penn Curzon-Howe	Howe, P.C.	1821	V. Curzon
John Somers Somers Cocks	Somers	1821	V. Eastnor
John Edward Cornwallis Rous	Stradbroke	1821	V. Dunwich
*Windham Henry Wyndham-Quin	Dunraven	1822	V. Adare
Charles William Vane	Vane, G.C.B., P.C. (M. of Londonderry)	1823	V. Seaham
William Pitt Amherst	Amherst, P.C.	1826	V. Holmesdale
John Frederick Campbell	Cawdor	1827	V. Emlyn
William George Fitzclarence	Munster	1831	V. Fitzclarence
William Cavendish	Burlington	1831	L. Cavendish
Robert Dundas Duncan Haldane	Camperdown	1831	V. Duncan
Thomas William Anson	Lichfield, P.C.	1831	V. Anson
George Frederick D'Arcy Lambton	Durham (*a minor*)	1833	V. Lambton
Frederick John Robinson	Ripon, P.C.	1833	V. Goderich
Granville George Leveson-Gower	Granville	1833	L. Leveson
Henry Howard	Effingham	1837	L. Howard
Henry George Francis Reynolds Moreton	Ducie	1837	L. Moreton
Charles Anderson Worsley	Yarborough	1837	L. Worsley
James Henry Robert Innes Ker	Innes, K. T. (D. of Roxburgh)	1837	M. of Beaumont
Thomas William Coke	Leicester	1837	V. Coke
William King	Lovelace	1838	V. Ockham
Thomas Dundas	Zetland	1838	L. Dundas
George Eden	Auckland, G.C.B., P.C.	1840	L. Eden
Charles Noel Noel	Gainsborough	1841	V. Campden
William Fitzhardinge Berkeley	Fitzhardinge	1841	L. Segrave
Edward Law	Ellenborough, G.C.B., P.C.	1844	V. Southam
Francis Egerton	Ellesmere, P.C.	1846	V. Brackley

VISCOUNTS (28).

Style, *Right Honourable.*

Name.	Title.	Creation.	Title by Courtesy of Eldest Sons.
Robert Devereux	Hereford, P.C.	1550	
†John Arbuthnot	Arbuthnot	1641	
†James Andrew John Laurence Chas. Drummond	Strathallan	1686	
Henry St. John	Bolingbroke	1712	
George Byng	Torrington	1721	
Augustus Frederick Fitzgerald	Leinster, P.C. (D. of Leinster)	1747	M. of Kildare
Henry Maynard	Maynard	1766	
John Robert Townshend	Sydney	1789	
Francis Wheler Hood	Hood (*a minor*)	1796	
*John Vesey	De Vesci	1776	
*Hayes St. Leger	Doneraile	1785	
*Cornwallis Maude	Hawarden	1793	
Edward Jervis Jervis	St. Vincent	1801	
Robert Saunders Dundas	Melville, K.T., P.C.	1802	
Rev. William Leonard Addington	Sidmouth	1805	
*Robert Edward King	Lorton	1806	
Warwick Lake	Lake	1807	
George Hamilton Gordon	Gordon, K.T. P.C. (E. of Aberdeen)	1814	L. Haddo
Edward Pellew	Exmouth	1816	
John Hely-Hutchinson	Hutchinson, K.P. (E. of Donoughmore)	1821	V. Suirdale
William Carr Beresford	Beresford, G.C.B., P.C.	1823	
William Thomas Le-Poer-Trench	Clancarty (E. of Clancarty)	1823	V. Dunlo
Stapleton Stapleton-Cotton	Combermere, G.C.B., P.C.	1826	
Charles John Canning	Canning, P.C.	1828	
Charles John Manners-Sutton	Canterbury	1835	
John Brabazon Ponsonby	Ponsonby, G.C.B.	1839	
Rowland Hill	Hill	1842	
Henry Hardinge	Hardinge, G.C.B., P.C.	1846	

BISHOPS (27).

Style, *Right Reverend.*

The Bishop of Sodor and Man (Dr. Thomas Vowler Short, consecrated 1841) has no vote.

The Bishops of London, Durham, and Winchester take precedence in right of their respective sees; the other Bishops in the order of their consecration.

		Consec. Translated.
Right Hon. Dr. Charles James Blomfield	London, P.C.	1824—1828
Dr. Edward Maltby	Durham	1831—1836
Dr. Charles Richard Sumner	Winchester	1826—1827
Dr. George Murray	Rochester	1813—1827
Dr. John Kaye	Lincoln	1820—1827
Dr. Christopher Bethel	Bangor	1824—1830
Hon. Dr. Hugh Percy	Carlisle	1827—1827
Dr. Edward Copleston	Llandaff	1828
Dr. John Bird Sumner	Chester	1828
Hon. Dr. Richard Bagot	Bath and Wells	1829—1845
Dr. James Henry Monk	Gloucester and Bristol	1830
Dr. Henry Phillpotts	Exeter	1830
Dr. Charles Thomas Longley	Ripon	1836
Dr. Edward Denison	Salisbury	1837
Dr. Edward Stanley	Norwich	1837
Dr. Thomas Musgrave	Hereford	1837
Dr. Henry Pepys	Worcester	1839—1841
Dr. George Davys	Peterborough	1839
Dr. Connop Thirlwall	St. Davids	1840
Dr. Ashhurst Turner Gilbert	Chichester	1842
Dr. John Lonsdale	Lichfield	1843
Dr. Thomas Turton	Ely	1845
Dr. Samuel Wilberforce	Oxford	1845
	St. Asaph	

and three Irish Representative Bishops.

BARONS (211.)

Style, *Right Honourable.*

William Lennox Lascelles De-Ros	De-Ros	1264
Jacob Henry Delaval Astley	Hastings	1290
George Edward Thicknesse Tuchet	Audley	1296
Charles Rodolph Trefusis	Clinton	1299
Thomas Brand	Dacre	1307
Thomas Miles Stapleton	Beaumont	1309
Peter Robert Drummond-Willoughby	Willoughby d'Eresby, P.C.	1313
Thomas Stonor	Camoys	1383
William Stourton	Stourton	1448
Henry Wilson	Berners	1455
Henry Peyto Verney	Willoughby de Broke	1492
George Browne-Mostyn	Vaux of Harrowden	1523

Name.	Title.	Creation.	Title by Courtesy of Eldest Sons.
Henry Paget	Paget, P.C. (E. of Uxbridge)	1550	L. Paget
St. Andrew Beauchamp St. John	St. John	1558	
Charles Augustus Ellis	Howardde Walden & Seaford	1597	
William Francis Henry Petre	Petre	1603	
William Thomas Twisleton-Fiennes	Saye and Sele	1603	
Henry Benedict Arundell	Arundell of Wardour	1605	
John Stuart Bligh	Clifton (E. of Darnley) *a minor*	1608	L. Clifton
Joseph Thaddeus Dormer	Dormer	1615	
George Henry Roper Curzon	Teynham	1616	
George William Stafford Jerningham	Stafford	1640	
George Anson Byron	Byron	1643	
William Ward	Ward	1664	
Hugh Charles Clifford	Clifford of Chudleigh	1672	
†Alexander George Fraser	Saltoun, K.C.B., G.C.H	1445	
†Charles St. Clair	Sinclair	1489	
†John Colville	Colville (of Culross)	1609	
†Eric Mackay	Reay	1628	
†John Rollo	Rollo	1651	
†Henry Francis Hepburn Scott	Polwarth	1690	
Edmund Boyle	Boyle, K.P. (E. of Cork and Orrery)	1711	V. Dungarvan
Thomas Robert Drummond-Hay	Hay (E. of Kinnoul)	1711	V. Dupplin
Digby Willoughby	Middleton	1711	
William John Monson	Monson	1728	
Henry Bromley	Montfort	1741	
George William Frederick Brudenell-Bruce	Bruce (E. Bruce)	1746	
John William Ponsonby	Ponsonby, P.C. (Earl of Besborough)	1749	V. Duncannon
George John Milles	Sondes	1760	
Nathaniel Curzon	Scarsdale	1761	
George Irby	Boston	1761	
Henry Edward Fox	Holland	1762	
George James Perceval	Lovell and Holland (E. of Egmont)	1762	V. Perceval
George John Warren	Vernon	1762	
John Douglas Edward Henry Campbell	Sundridge and Hamilton (D. of Argyll)	1766	M. of Lorne
Edward Wm. Harvey Hawke	Hawke	1776	
Thomas Henry Foley	Foley, P.C.	1776	
George Talbot Rice	Dynevor	1780	
Thomas De Grey	Walsingham	1780	
William Bagot	Bagot	1780	
Charles Fitzroy	Southampton	1780	
Fletcher Norton	Grantley	1782	
Robert Dennett Rodney	Rodney	1782	
John Thynne	Carteret	1784	
Richard Noel Hill	Berwick	1784	
John Dutton	Sherborne	1784	
Henry De-la-Poer-Beresford	Tyrone, K.P. (M. of Waterford)	1786	E. of Tyrone
Richard Boyle	Carleton (E. of Shannon)	1786	V. Boyle
Edward Vernon Harbord	Suffield	1786	
Guy Carleton	Dorchester	1786	
George Kenyon	Kenyon	1788	
Richard Griffin	Braybrooke	1788	
George Hamilton Chichester	Fisherwick (M. of Donegal)	1790	E. of Belfast
Charles Douglas	Douglas	1790	
Henry Edward Hall Gage	Gage (V. Gage)	1790	
Edward Thomas Hovell Thurlow	Thurlow	1792	
George William Lyttelton	Lyttelton	1794	
Henry Agar-Ellis	Mendip and Dover (V. Clifden)	1794	
Francis Stuart	Stuart, K.T. (E. of Moray)	1796	L. Doune
Randolph Stewart	Stewart (E. of Galloway)	1796	V. Garlies
James Thomas Stopford	Saltersford (E. of Courtown)	1796	V. Stopford
George Alan Brodrick	Brodrick (V. Midleton)	1796	
George Gough Calthorpe	Calthorpe	1796	
Robert John Carington	Carington	1797	
Henry William Powlett	Bayning	1797	
William Orde Powlett	Bolton	1797	
John Wodehouse	Wodehouse	1797	
John Rushout	Northwick	1797	
Thomas Atherton Powys	Lilford	1797	
Thomas Lister	Ribblesdale, *(a minor)*	1797	
John Fitz-Gibbon	Fitzgibbon, K.P., G.C.H., P.C. (E. of Clare)	1799	V. Fitzgibbon
*Edward Wadding Plunkett	Dunsany	1461	
*Cadwallader Davis Blayney	Blayney	1621	
*Henry Maxwell	Farnham K. P.	1756	
*Robert Dillon	Clonbrock	1790	
*Edward Crofton	Crofton	1797	
*Henry Prittie	Dunalley	1800	
Henry Francis Seymour Moore	Moore (M of Drogheda)	1801	V. Moore
John Henry Loftus	Loftus (M. of Ely)	1801	V. Loftus
John Proby	Carysfort (E. of Carysfort)	1801	L. Proby
William Arden	Alvanley	1801	
George Ralph Abercromby	Abercromby	1801	
John Thomas Freeman Mitford	Redesdale	1802	
George Pitt-Rivers	Rivers	1802	
Arthur Moyses William Hill	Sandys	1802	
George Aug. Fred. Charles Holroyd	Sheffield (E. of Sheffield)	1802	L. Pevensey

Name.	Title.	Creation.	Title by Courtesy of Eldest Sons.
David Montagu Erskine	Erskine	1806	
George John Browne	Monteagle, (M. of Sligo)	1806	E. of Altamont
Archibald William Montgomerie	Ardrossan (E. of Eglinton)	1806	L. Montgomerie
James Maitland	Lauderdale (E. of Lauderdale)	1806	V. Maitland
George Arthur Forbes	Granard (E. of Granard), *a minor*	1806	V. Forbes
Hungerford Crewe	Crewe	1806	
Alan Legge Gardner	Gardner	1806	
John Thomas Manners-Sutton	Manners	1807	
John Alexander Hope	Hopetoun (E. of Hopetoun), (*a minor*)	1809	L. Hope
*Richard Handcock	Castlemaine	1812	
James Andrew Broun Ramsay	Dalhousie (E. of Dalhousie)	1815	L. Ramsay
George Gordon	Meldrum, K.T. (M. of Huntly)	1815	E. of Aboyne
James Carr Boyle	Ross (E. of Glasgow)	1815	V. Kelburne
William Willoughby Cole	Grinstead (E. of Enniskillen)	1815	V. Cole
William Lamb	Melbourne, P.C. (V. Melbourne)	1815	
Francis George Spencer	Churchill	1815	
George Harris	Harris	1815	
William Henry Tenison Pery	Foxford (E. of Limerick)	1815	L. Glentworth
Algernon Percy	Prudhoe	1816	
Charles Abbot	Colchester	1817	
William Schonberg Robert Kerr	Kerr (M. of Lothian), *a minor*	1821	E. of Ancrum
Francis Nathaniel Conyngham	Minster, K.P. P.C., (M. of Conyngham)	1821	E. of Mountcharles
John Butler	Ormonde K.P. (M. of Ormonde)	1821	E. of Ossory
Francis Wemyss-Charteris-Douglas	Wemyss (E. of Wemyss)	1821	L. Elcho
Robert Jocelyn	Clanbrassil, K.P., P.C. (E. of Roden)	1821	V. Jocelyn
Robert King	Kingston (E. Kingston)	1821	V. Kingsborough
Edward Michael Pakenham	Silchester (E. of Longford)	1821	
William Pole Tylney Long Wellesley Pole	Maryborough, (E. Mornington)	1821	
John Skeffington-Foster	Oriel (V. Massareene & Ferrard)	1821	
Thomas Henry Liddell	Ravensworth	1821	
Thomas Cholmondeley	Delamere	1821	
John George Weld Forester	Forester, P.C.	1821	
John James Strutt	Rayleigh	1821	
*Ulysses Burgh	Downes, G.C.B.	1822	
Nicholas Vansittart	Bexley, P.C.	1823	
Robert Francis Gifford	Gifford	1824	
Percy Clinton Sydney Smythe	Penshurst, G.C.B., P.C. (V. Strangford)	1825	
James O'Brien	Tadcaster, G.C.H. (M. of Thomond)	1826	E. Inchiquin
Ulick John De-Burgh	Somerhill, K.P., P.C. (M. of Clanricarde)	1826	L. Dunkellin
James Lindsay	Wigan (E. of Balcarras)	1826	L. Lindsay
Thomas Knox	Ranfurly (E. of Ranfurly)	1826	V. Northland
George Warren	De Tabley	1826	
John Stuart-Wortley	Wharncliffe	1826	
William Duncombe	Feversham	1826	
John Singleton Copley	Lyndhurst, P.C.	1827	
James Duff	Fife, K.T. (E. of Fife)	1827	V. Macduff
John Henry Abbott	Tenterden	1827	
William Conyngham Plunket	Plunket, P.C.	1827	
Thomas Hamilton	Melros, P.C. (E. of Haddington)	1827	L. Binning
Henry Wellesley	Cowley, G.C.B., P. C.	1828	
William A'Court	Heytesbury, G.C.B., P.C.	1828	
Archibald John Primrose	Rosebery, K.T., P.C. (E. of Rosebery)	1828	L. Dalmeney
Richard Meade	Clanwilliam (E. of Clanwilliam)	1828	L. Gilford
Edward Bootle-Wilbraham	Skelmersdale	1828	
William Samuel Best	Wynford	1829	
Henry Brougham	Brougham and Vaux, P.C.	1830	
William George Hay	Kilmarnock (E. of Errol)	1831	L. Kilmarnock
Arthur James Plunkett	Fingall (E. of Fingall)	1831	L. Killeen
Charles William Molyneux	Sefton (E. of Sefton)	1831	V. Molyneux
George William Fox Kinnaird	Rossie (L. Kinnaird)	1831	
Nathaniel Clements	Clements, K.P. (E. of Leitrim)	1831	V. Clements
Thomas Taylor	Kenlis, K.P. (M. of Headfort)	1831	E. of Bective
John Chambre Brabazon	Chaworth, K.P. (E. of Meath)	1831	L. Brabazon
Charles Adolphus Murray	Dunmore (E. of Dunmore), *a minor*	1831	V. Fincastle
Robert Montgomery Hamilton	Hamilton (L. Belhaven & Stenton)	1831	
John Hobart Caradoc	Howden	1831	
William Maule	Panmure	1831	
George Warwick Bampfylde	Poltimore	1831	
Edward Pryce Lloyd	Mostyn	1831	
Henry Spencer Chichester	Templemore	1831	
William Lewis Hughes	Dinorben	1831	
Valentine Browne Lawless	Cloncurry	1831	
James Saumarez	De Saumarez	1831	
Francis Godolphin Osborne	Godolphin	1832	
Lucius Cary	Hunsdon, P.C. (V. Falkland)	1832	
Edward Geoffrey	Stanley of Bickerstaffe, P.C.	1832	
Thomas Denman	Denman, P.C.	1834	
Robert Campbell Scarlett	Abinger	1835	
Philip Charles Sidney	De L' Isle and Dudley	1835	
Alexander Baring	Ashburton, P.C.	1835	
Charles Grant	Glenelg, P.C.	1835	
Edward John Littleton	Hatherton, P.C.	1835	
John Byng	Strafford, G.C.B	1835	
Charles Christopher Pepys	Cottenham, P.C.	1836	

Name.	Title.	Creation.	Title by Courtesy of Eldest Sons.
Henry Bickersteth	Langdale, P.C.	1836	
Edward Berkeley Portman	Portman	1837	
Thomas Alexander Fraser	Lovat	1837	
William Bateman-Hanbury	Bateman	1837	
Francis Alexander Keith-Falconer	Kintore (E. of Kintore) *a minor*	1838	L. Inverury
Cornelius O'Callaghan	Lismore (V. Lismore)	1838	
Henry Robert Westenra	Rossmore	1838	
Robert Shapland Carew	Carew	1838	
William Francis Spencer Ponsonby	De Mauley	1838	
John Wrottesley	Wrottesley	1838	
Charles Hanbury-Tracy	Sudeley	1838	
Paul Methuen	Methuen	1838	
Frederick James Lamb	Beauvale, G.C.B., P.C	1839	
James Abercromby	Dunfermline, P.C.	1839	
Richard Wogan	Furnival (L. Talbot de Malahide)	1839	
John Thomas Stanley	Stanley of Alderley	1839	
Henry Villiers Stuart	Stuart de Decies	1839	
Chandos Leigh	Leigh	1839	
Paul Beilby Thompson	Wenlock	1839	
Charles Brownlow	Lurgan	1839	
Nicholas William Ridley Colborne	Colborne	1839	
Arthur French	De Freyne	1839	
Thomas Spring-Rice	Monteagle, P.C.	1839	
John Colborne	Seaton, G.C.B	1840	
Edward Arthur Wellington Keane	Keane	1840	
John Campbell	Campbell, P.C	1841	
John Hamilton Dalrymple	Oxenfoord (E. of Stair)	1841	V. Dalrymple
Valentine Browne	Kenmare (E. of Kenmare)	1841	V. Castlerosse
Charles Crespigny Vivian	Vivian	1841	
John Parnell	Congleton	1841	
Hugh Gough	Gough, G.C.B.	1846	

OFFICERS OF HOUSE OF PEERS.

Clerk of the Parliament, Right hon. Sir George H. Rose, 7 Old Palace yard
Clerk Assistant, John William Birch, esq
Additional Clerk Assistant, Benjamin Currey, esq. 6 Old Palace yard
Reading Clerk & Clerk of the Private Committees, William Rose, esq
Counsel to the Chairman of Committees, Robert Palk, esq
Clerk of Journals, Edward Parratt, esq
Chief Clerk, Henry Stone Smith, esq
Clerk of Engrossments, William Elyard Walmisley, esq
Librarian, John Frederic Leary, esq. F.S.A.
Clerk of Enrolments, George John Dike, esq
Other Clerks in the Office, Messrs. William Atkinson Green, Lionel Hill Thompson, Edward Courtenay, William Frederick White, Andrew Guisti Flint, Peregrine Birch, George Mitchell, James Nicholas Birch, Edward Meredith Parratt, Michael Halliday, Bartholomew Samuel Rowley Adam, William Henry Dike, William Henry Haines, Frederick Vane, Charles Congreve, Owen E. Grant, John Harding Robinson, Augustus W. Du Bourg, Henry Walmisley, William Malony, Charles William Green, William J. Thoms
Assistant Librarian, Mr. James Heard Pulman
Collecting Clerk, Mr. Thomas William Couch
Offices of Enrolments & Engrossments, Mr. James Kilpin,
Doorkeeper to Library, Samuel Lethbridge
Keeper of Parliament Office, Mrs. Mary Truscott
Messengers, James Batterbee, Henry Norris
Gentleman Usher of the Black Rod, Sir Augustus William Clifford, bart
Yeoman Usher, James Pulman, esq. F.S.A.
Serjeant at Arms, Colonel Percival
Deputy, Mr. George Goodbody
Receiver of Fees, Mr. Gerard John Oldrini
Short-hand Writer, William Brodie Gurney, esq
Assistant, Mr. Joseph Gurney
Principal Doorkeepers, Messrs. Thomas Stamp, Frederic Shells, Gerrard John Oldrini, Abraham Grainger, Robert Hogwood, John Maggs, Robert Moody
Assistant Doorkeepers, Messrs. Herman Muhlenkamp, William Moyes, John Royal, William Howard, Anthony Allan, William Dean, James Whitton
House Porter, John Gurr
Messengers, James Lilly, William Manning
Housekeeper, Mrs. Brandish
Deputy, Mrs. Jane Bennett
Necessary Woman, Mrs. Oldrini
Fire Lighter, Mrs. Theresa Poisnel
Bishops' Doorkeeper, John Gurr

HOUSE OF PEERS,

ALPHABETICALLY ARRANGED.

Created.

1790. Abercorn Marquis of, K.G., P.C., *Groom of the Stole in the Household of H. R. H. Prince Albert*, Dudley house, Grosvenor gate, Park lane, and Priory, Stanmore, Middlesex, and Barons court, New Town Stewart, Tyrone, Ireland, and Ardverkie lodge, Laggan, N.B

1801. Abercromby Lord (no address in London), Airthrie castle, near Stirling

1682. Aberdeen Earl of, in the peerage of Scotland, sits as Viscount Gordon (1814) in that of the United Kingdom, K.T., P.C., Lord Lieut. of Aberdeenshire, Keeper of Greenwich Park, 7 Argyll street, and Haddo house, near Methlic, Aberdeenshire

1784. Abergavenny Earl of (no address in London), Eridge castle, Tunbridge wells, & Berlin Manor, Maidstone, Kent

1682. Abingdon Earl of, Lord Lieutenant of Berkshire, 7 Albemarle street, and Wytham abbey, Oxford

1835. Abinger Lord, 4 New street, Spring gardens, and Abinger hall, Dorking, Surrey

1821. Ailesbury Marquis of, K.T., 41 Grosvenor square, and Tottenham park, Marlborough, and East Sheen, Surrey, and Jerveaux abbey, Middleham, near Bedale

1831. Ailsa Marquis of, 1 Whitehall gardens, & St. Margarets, Isleworth; Cassillis castle, Maybole, Ayrshire

1639. Airlie and Lintrathen Earl of, Scotch Representative Peer, Lord Lieut. of Forfarshire, Carlton club, and Cortachy castle, by Kirriemuir

1696. Albemarle Earl of, P.C., 12 Berkeley square, and Quidenham hall, Larlingford, Norfolk

1801. Alvanley Lord (abroad), Brown's hotel, 24 Dover street, and Tarporley, Cheshire

1826. Amherst Earl, P.C., 66 Grosvenor street, and Knole, Sevenoaks

1815. Anglesey Marquis of, K.G., K.P., G.C.B., P.C., *Master General of the Ordnance*, Lord Lieut. of Anglesey, a General in the Army, Col. of the Royal Horse Guards Blue, Uxbridge house, 1 Old Burlington street, and Beaudesert park, Lichfield, Staffordshire, and Plas Newydd, Anglesey

1641. Arbuthnot Viscount, Scotch Representative Peer, Lord Lieut. of Kincardineshire, Carlton Club, 94 Pall Mall and Arbuthnot house, Bervie, Kincardineshire

1701. Argyll Duke of, in the Peerage of Scotland, sits as Lord Sundridge and Hamilton (1766) in that of the United Kingdom, Hereditary Lord Steward of Scotland, Hereditary Sheriff of Argyllshire, 3 Connaught place west, Hyde park, and Inverary castle, Inverary, Argyllshire, and Roseneath and Ardencaple castles, Helensburgh, Dumbartonshire

Armagh Archbishop of, Primate of all Ireland, and Metropolitan, 30 Charles street, St. James's, and Armagh, Ireland

1605. Arundell Lord (of Wardour), Union club, Trafalgar square, and Wardour castle, Shaftesbury, Wiltshire

1730. Ashburnham Earl of, 30 Upper Grosvenor street, and Ashburnham place, Battle, Sussex

1835. Ashburton Lord, P.C., Bath house, 82 Piccadilly, and the Grange, Alresford, and Red hall, Ross

1703. Atholl Duke of, in the Peerage of Scotland, sits as Earl Strange (1786) in the Peerage of the United Kingdom, Hereditary Sheriff of Perthshire, Carlton club, Atholl house, Blair Atholl, and Dunkeld, Perthshire, and Mona castle, Isle of Man

1840. Auckland Earl of, G.C.B., P.C., *First Lord of the Admiralty*, Eden lodge, Kensington Gore

1296. Audley Lord (no address in London), Sandridge, Chippenham, Wiltshire

1714. Aylesford Earl of (no address in London), Packington hall, Coventry, and Aylesford, Maidstone

1780. Bagot Lord (no address in London), Blithfield house, Rugeley, and Poole park, Ruthin, Denbighshire

1650. Balcarras Earl of, in the Peerage of Scotland, sits as Baron Wigan (1826) in that of the United Kingdom, 21 Berkeley square, and Haigh hall, Wigan

1800. Bandon Earl of, Irish Representative Peer, Lord Lieut. of Co. Cork, 6 Hyde park ter. & Castle Bernard, Bandon

Bangor Bishop of, consecrated 1824, translated 1830, Warren's hotel, Regent street, and the Palace, Bangor

1837. Bateman Lord, 38 Portman square, and Kelmarsh, Northampton, and Shobdon court, Leominster

Bath and Wells Bishop of, consecrated Bishop of Oxford, 1829, translated 1845, 16 Grosvenor square, and the Palace, Wells

1772. Bathurst Earl, 4 Wilton crescent, Belgrave sq., and Oakley park, Cirencester

1797. Bayning Lord, is in holy orders, and has taken the surname Powlett in lieu of Townshend, University club, and Brome rectory, Scole, Norfolk

1815. Beauchamp Earl, has taken the surname Pindar in lieu of Lygon, 37 Portman sq., and Madresfield ct. Worcester

1682. Beaufort Duke of, K.G., 22 Arlington street, and Badminton house, Gloucestershire, and Troy house, near Monmouth

1309. Beaumont Lord, 18 Curzon street, Mayfair, and Calton hall, Snaith, Yorkshire

1839. Beauvale Lord, G.C.B., P.C., 12 Hyde park terrace

1694. Bedford Duke of, P.C., 6 Belgrave sq., and Woburn Abbey, and Endsleigh, Tavistock, and Oakley House, Bedford

1647. Belhaven and Stenton Lord, in the Peerage of Scotland, sits as Lord Hamilton (1831) in that of the United Kingdom, 30 Albemarle street, Piccadilly, and Wishaw house, Hamilton, N.B.

1823. Beresford Viscount, G.C.B., P.C., General in the Army, Colonel of the 16th Foot, Governor of Jersey, 16 Cavendish square, and Bedgebury park, near Lamberhurst, Kent, and Beresford Hall, near Ashbourne

1455. Berners Lord, British hotel, Cockspur street, and Kirby-cane Hall, near Bungay

1784. Berwick Rev. Lord, Rector of Berrington, Shropshire, Stable yard, St. James's palace, and Red Rice, Andover, and Altringham house, Shrewsbury

1739. Besborough Earl of, in the Peerage of Ireland, sits as Baron Ponsonby (1749), and Baron Duncannon (1834) in that of the United Kingdom, P.C., *Lord Lieutenant of Ireland*, Lord Lieutenant of Kilkenny county, a Commissioner for building Churches, &c., The Castle, Dublin, and 3 Cavendish square, and East hill, Wandsworth, Surrey, and Garryhill house, Carlow, and Besborough house, Pilltown, Carrick-on-Suir

1790. Beverley Earl of, P.C., Colonel of Northumberland Militia, 8 Portman square

1823. Bexley Lord, P.C., a Commissioner for building Churches, 31 Gt. George st. Westminster, & Footscray place, Kent

1621. Blayney Lord, Irish Representative Peer, St. James's hotel, 76 Jermyn street, and Castle Blayney, Monaghan

1712. Bolingbroke Viscount, 35 Mortimer street, Cavendish square, and Lydiard park, Swindon, Wiltshire

1797. Bolton Lord, Thomas's hotel, and Hackwood park, Basingstoke, and Bolton Hall, Bedale

1761. Boston Lord, United Service Club, and Hedsor Lodge, Great Marlow, Bucks, and Llanidan, Anglesey

1815. Bradford Earl of, 43 Belgrave square, and Castle Bromwich, Birmingham, and Weston hall, Shiffnall

1788. Braybrooke Lord, Hereditary Visitor of Magdalen college, Cambridge, 10 New Burlington street, and Audley End, Essex, and Billingbear park, Wokingham

1831. Breadalbane Marquis of, K.T., Lord Lieutenant of Argyllshire, 21 Park lane, and Taymouth castle, Aberfeldie, Perthshire, and Ardmaddy castle, Argyleshire, and Langton, Dunse, Berwickshire

1826. Bristol Marquis of, Hereditary Steward of Bury St. Edmunds, 6 St. James's square, and Ickworth park, Bury St Edmunds, and Putney heath, and Kemp town, Brighton

1830. Brougham & Vaux, Lord, P.C., 4 Grafton street, Bond street, and Brougham hall, Penrith

1815. Brownlow Earl, Lord Lieutenant, and Custos Rotulorum of the county of Lincoln, Colonel of South Lincoln Militia, 12 Belgrave square, and Belton house, Grantham

Created.

1746. Bruce Earl, by courtesy, being the eldest son of the Marquis of Ailesbury, summoned to the House of Peers, during the lifetime of his father, by the title Baron Bruce, 78 Pall mall, and Savanake lodge, Marlborough

1663. Buccleuch and Queensberry Duke of, in the Peerage of Scotland, sits as Earl of Doncaster (1662) in the Peerage of the United Kingdom, K.G., P.C., High Steward of Westminster, Lord Lieut. of Edinburgh county, Lord Lieutenant of Roxburghshire, Montagu house, Whitehall, and Dalkeith palace, Edinburgh, and Boughton house, Kettering, and Richmond, Surrey, and Drumlanrig castle, Thornhill, N.B., and Bowhill, Selkirk, N.B., and Langholm lodge, N.B.

1822. Buckingham and Chandos Duke of, K.G., P.C., 91 Pall mall, and Stow park, Buckingham, and Wotton, Aylesbury, Bucks, and Avington house, Winchester, and Auchline house, Killin, Perthshire.

1746. Buckinghamshire Earl of, 1 Spanish place, Manchester square, and Hampden house, Great Missendn, Bucks

1831. Burlington Earl of, 10 Belgrave square, and Holkar hall, Milnthorpe, and Compton place, Eastbourne.

1796. Bute Marquis of, K.T., Lord Lieut. of the county of Bute and of Glamorganshire, Colonel of the Glamorganshire Militia, 16 Arlington street, Piccadilly, and Cardiff Castle, Glamorganshire, and Kirtling Tower, Cambridgeshire, and Mount Stuart, Rothsay, Isle of Bute, and Luton park, Bedfordshire, and Dumfries house, Cumnock, Ayrshire

1643. Byron Lord, Capt. R.N., *Lord in Waiting to Her Majesty*, 21 Eaton place, Belgrave square, and Ladbroke hall,

1800. Cadogan Earl, a Rear Admiral, 138 Piccadilly [Southam, Warwickshire.

1800. Caledon Earl, Irish Representative Peer, 5 Carlton terrace, and Caledon, county of Tyrone, and Boom hall, county of Londonderry

1796. Calthorpe Lord, 33 Grosvenor square, and Ampton, near Bury St. Edmunds, Suffolk, and Elvetham, Hertford bridge

1801. Cambridge Duke of, K.G., G.C.B., G.C.H., P.C., Field Marshal in the army, Col. of the Coldstream Guards and of the 60th Foot, Ranger of Richmond Park, and Lord Warden of the New Forest, Cambridge House, 94 Piccadilly, and Kew [hurst, Kent, and Brecknock priory

1812. Camden Marquis of, K.G., 19 Belgrave square, and Wilderness park, Sevenoaks, and Bayham abbey, Lamber-

1383. Camoys Lord, *a Lord in Waiting to Her Majesty*, 7 Park street, Westminster, and Stonor park, Henley on Thames, Oxfordshire

1841. Campbell Lord, P.C., *Chancellor of the Duchy of Lancaster*, Stratheden house, South place, Knightsbridge

1831. Camperdown Earl of (no address in London), Camperdown house, Dundee, Forfarshire, and Lundie and Gleneagles,

1828. Canning Viscount, P.C., 10 Grosvenor square [Perthshire, and Sydney place, Bath

Canterbury, Archbishop of, P.C., consecrated Bishop of London 1813, translated 1828; a Lord of Trade and Plantations, a Commissioner for building new Churches; Lambeth palace, and Addington park, Croydon

1835. Canterbury Viscount (no address in London), Rockbeare, Exeter, Devon

1661. Cardigan Earl of, 36 Portman square, and Deene Park, Wansford

1838. Carew Lord, Lord Lieutenant of Co. Wexford, 21 Hertford street, Mayfair, Castleborough, Wexford

1797. Carington Lord, Lord Lieutenant of Buckinghamshire, Colonel of the Buckinghamshire Militia, Whitehall yard, and the Abbey, Wycombe, and Gayhurst, Newport Pagnell, Buckinghamshire [Brampton

1661. Carlisle Earl of, K.G., P.C., 12 Grosvenor place, and Castle Howard, Yorkshire, and Naworth Castle, near

Carlisle Bishop of, consecrated Bishop of Rochester 1827, translated 1827, University club, 4 Pall mall east, and Rose castle, Carlisle [Pixton, Dulverton, Somersetshire

1793. Carnarvon Earl of, 43 Grosvenor square, and Highclere hall, Newbury, & Milford the Lake, near Newbury, and

1784. Carteret Lord, P.C. (no address in London), Hawnes house, Ampthill

1789. Carysfort Earl of, in the Peerage of Ireland, sits as Lord Carysfort (1801), and Baron of Norman Cross, in that of the United Kingdom, a Lieut. General in the Army, (no address in London), Elton hall, Stilton, Hunts, and Glenart castle, Wicklow

1812. Castlemaine Lord, Irish Representative Peer, Carlton club, and Moydrum Castle, Athlone, county Westmeath

1814. Cathcart Earl, K.C.B., Governor-General of Canada, Lieut.-General in the army, Col. of the 11th Hussars, Senior United Service Club, and Inversleith house, Edinburgh

1827. Cawdor Earl, 74 South Audley street, and Cawdor castle, Nairn, and Stackpole court, Pembroke, and Golden [Grove, near Llandillo, Carmarthenshire

1763. Charlemont Earl of, K.P., Irish Representative Peer; also Lord Charlemont in the Peerage of England, Lord Lieut. of county Tyrone, 49 Grosvenor street, and Charlemont house, and Merino, Dublin, and Roxborough, near Moy, Co. Armagh, and Castle Caulfield, Co. Tyrone [more, King's county

1806. Charleville Earl of, Irish Representative Peer, White's club, 38 St. James's street, and Charleville castle, Tulla-

Chester Bishop of, consecrated 1828 (no address in London), Palace, Chester

1628. Chesterfield Earl of, P.C., Chesterfield house, South Audley street, and Bretby park, Ashby-de-la-Zouch,

1801. Chichester Earl of, 22 Grosvenor place, and Stanmer park, Lewes [Derbyshire

Chichester Bishop of, consecrated 1842, 27 Parliament street, and Palace, Chichester

1815. Cholmondeley Marquis of, P.C., Joint Hereditary Great Chamberlain of England, 12 Carlton house terrace, and Cholmondeley castle, Namptwich, and Houghton hall, near Rougham, Norfolk

1815. Churchill Lord, 2 Upper Wimpole st. and Cornbury park, near Witney, Oxon

1803. Clancarty Earl of, in the Peerage of Ireland, sits as Viscount Clancarty (1823) in that of the United Kingdom, (no town residence), Garbally park, Loughrea, Ireland

1825. Clanricarde Marquis of, in the Peerage of Ireland, sits as Baron Somerhill (1826) in that of the United Kingdom, K.P., P.C., *Postmaster-General*, Lord Lieut. of Galway, Col. of Galway Militia, 2 Carlton house terrace, & Portumna castle, Galway

1776. Clanwilliam Earl of, in the Peerage of Ireland, sits as Baron Clanwilliam (1828) in that of the United Kingdom, 32 Belgrave square, and Gill hall, Dromore, Down

1795. Clare Earl of, in the Peerage of Ireland, sits as Baron Fitzgibbon (1799) in that of the United Kingdom, K.P., G.C.H., P.C., 35 Lowndes square, and Mount Shannon, Limerick

1776. Clarendon Earl of, G.C.B., P.C., *President of the Board of Trade*, 1 Grosvenor crescent, Belgrave square, and

1833. Cleveland Duke of, K.G., 17 St. James's square, and Raby Castle, Darlington [Grove park, Watford

1781. Clifden Viscount, in the Peerage of Ireland, sits as Baron Mendip and Dover (1794), in that of the United Kingdom, *Lord of the Bedchamber to Prince Albert* (no address in London), Gowran castle, and Ringwood, Kilkenny

1672. Clifford Lord (of Chudleigh), Ford's hotel, 13 Manchester street, Manchester square, & Ugbrook park, Chudleigh

1299. Clinton Lord (no address in London), Heanton, Satchville, Devonshire

1790. Clonbrock Lord, Irish Representative Peer, 23 Dover street, and Clonbrock, Galway

1831. Cloncurry Lord, Brookes's club, St. James's street, and Lyons castle, Kildare, and Rathcoole, near Dublin

1839. Colborne Lord, 19 Hill street, and West Harling, Norfolk.

1817. Colchester Lord, Captain R.N., 7 Charles street, Berkeley square, and Kidbrooke, Tonbridge Wells

1609. Colville Lord, Scotch Representative Peer, Admiral of the Blue, *Extra Lord of the Bedchamber to H. R. H. Prince Albert*, 29 Portland place

1826. Combermere Viscount, G.C.B., G.C.H., P.C., General in the Army, Colonel of the 1st Life Guards, Governor of Sheerness; 48 Belgrave square, and Combermere Abbey, Namptwich

1841. Congleton Lord, (no address in London)

1816. Conyngham, Marquis, K.P., G.C.H., P.C., in the Peerage of Ireland, sits as Baron Minster (1821) in that of the United Kingdom, 5 Hamilton place, Piccadilly, and Slane castle, Meath, and Mountcharles, Donegal

Created.

1620. Cork and Orrery Earl of, K.P., in the Peerage of Ireland, sits as Lord Boyle (1711) in that of the United Kingdom, General in the Army, 3 Hamilton place, and Marston hall, Frome
1753. Cornwallis Earl, 6 Hill street, Berkeley square, and Linton place, Linton, near Maidstone
1836. Cottenham Lord, P.C., *Lord High Chancellor of England*, a Commissioner for building new Churches, 15 Park lane, and Copse hill, Wimbledon, Surrey
1762. Courtown Earl of, in the Peerage of Ireland, sits as Baron Saltersford (1796) in that of the United Kingdom, 11 Green street, Grosvenor square, and Courtown house, Wexford, and Gorey, Ireland
1828. Cowley Lord, G.C.B., P.C., letters go to the Foreign office
1718. Cowper Earl, 1 Great Stanhope street, and Panshanger, Hertford, and Moat house, near Wingham, Kent
1801. Craven Earl of, 16 Charles st. Berkeley sq. and Coombe abbey, Coventry, and Hampstead park, Bracknell, Berks
1806. Crewe Lord, 2 Hill street, Berkeley square, and Crewe hall, Nantwich
1797. Crofton Lord, Irish Representative Peer, 12 Bryanstone square, and Mote Park, Roscommon
1799. Cumberland and Teviotdale, Duke of, K.G., P.C., G.C.B., G.C.H., King of Hanover; St. James's palace
1307. Dacre Lord, 2 Chesterfield street, and the Hoo, Welwyn, Herts
1633. Dalhousie Earl of, in the Peerage of Scotland, sits as Lord Dalhousie (1815) in that of the United Kingdom, P.C., *Lord Registrar of Scotland*, 21 Hyde park gardens, & Dalhousie castle, Lasswade, Edinburgh
1711. Dartmouth Earl of, Colonel of the Staffordshire Militia, 23 St. James's square, and Sandwell park, Birmingham and Woodsome, Huddersfield
1839. De Freyne Lord, 45 Oxford terrace, Edgware road, and French park, Ireland
1816. De Grey Earl, K.G., K.P., P.C., Lord Lieutenant of Bedfordshire, and Colonel of Yorkshire Yeomanry Cavalry, 4 St. James's square; West park, Silsoe, Beds., and Cowes, Isle of Wight, and Putneyheath, and Studley park, near Ripon, York
1821. Delamere Lord, 33 Upper Brook street, and Vale Royal, Northwich
1761. De La Warr Earl, P.C., 17 Upper Grosvenor street, and Bourn Hall, Caxton, Cambridgeshire, and Buckhurst park, Tonbridge Wells, Sussex
1835. De L'Isle and Dudley Lord, G.C.H., 16 New Burlington street, and Penshurst, near Tunbridge
1838. De Mauley Lord, 169 New Bond street, and Canford house, near Wimborne, Dorset
1622. Denbigh Earl of, P.C., G.C.H., 44 Eaton square, and Newnham Paddox, Lutterworth, and Upper Lodge, Bushy park, Middlesex
1834. Denman Lord, P.C., Lord Chief Justice of the Queen's Bench, 38 Portland place, and Stoney Middleton, near Bakewell
1485. Derby Earl of, K.G., P.C., Lord Lieutenant of Lancashire, Colonel of Lancashire Militia, 23 Grosvenor square and Knowsley hall, Prescot, Lancashire
1264. De Ros Lord, Premier Baron of England, a Lieut.-Col. in the Army, Adjutant General's Office, Horse Guards, and 25 Chester street, Grosvenor place, and Strangford, Down Co.
1793. Desart Earl of, Irish Representative Peer (no address in London), Desart, Kilkenny
1831. De Saumarez Lord, United University club, and Cheltenham
1826. De Tabley Lord, Mivart's hotel, 44 Brook street, and Tabley house, Knutsford, Cheshire
1776. De Vesci Viscount, Irish Representative Peer, Christie's hotel, 57 St. James's st. and Abbey Leix, Queen's County
1553. Devon Earl of, High Steward of the University of Oxford, 4 Bryanstone square, and Powderham castle, near Exeter
1694. Devonshire Duke of, K.G., P.C., Lord Lieutenant of Derbyshire, 78 Piccadilly, Chatsworth and Hardwick, Derbyshire; Chiswick, Middlesex; and Lismore castle, Waterford
1790. Digby Earl of, Lord Lieutenant of Dorsetshire, and Colonel of the Dorset Militia, 35 Brook street, and Sherborne castle, Dorset
1831. Dinorben Lord, Major Commandant of the Royal Anglesea Militia, 75 South Audley street, and Kinmell park, St. Asaph
1791. Donegal Marquis of, in the Peerage of Ireland, sits as Baron Fisherwick (1790) in that of the United Kingdom Lord Lieut. of County Antrim, G.C.H., P.C., 28 Lowndes street, Belgrave square, and Ennishowen, county Donegal, and Carrickfergus, county Antrim, and Ormeau, Belfast, Ireland
1785. Doneraile Viscount, Irish Representative Peer, Limmer's hotel, George street, Hanover square, and Doneraile house, Mallow
1800. Donoughmore Earl of, in the Peerage of Ireland, sits as Viscount Hutchinson (1821) in that of the United Kingdom, K.P., Lord Lieutenant of Tipperary, 6 Sackville street, Piccadilly, and Knocklofty house, Clonmel, and Palmerston house, Dublin
1786. Dorchester Lord, Capt. 7th Hussars (no address in London), Stuffings, Maidenhead, Berkshire
1615. Dormer Lord, (no address in London) Peterley house, Amersham, and Grove park, Warwick
1790. Douglas Lord, Hereditary Sheriff of Forfarshire, 6 St. George's place, Hyde park corner, and Douglas and Bothwell castles, Glasgow
1822. Downes Lord, Irish Representative Peer, K.C.B., Major General in the Army, Carlton club, Pall mall, and Bert House, Athy, Kildare
1789. Downshire Marquis of, in the Peerage of Ireland, sits as the Earl of Hillsborough (1772) in that of the United Kingdom, Hereditary Constable of Hillsborough fort, 21 Hanover sq. and Hillsborough castle, Hillsborough, Downshire, and Easthampstead park, Bracknell, Berks
1791. Drogheda Marquis of, in the Peerage of Ireland, sits as Viscount Moore (1801) in that of the United Kingdom (no address in London)
1837. Ducie Earl of, *a Lord in Waiting to Her Majesty*, Limmer's hotel, George street, Hanover square, and Woodchester park, Gloucestershire, and Ampney park, Cirencester
1800. Dunalley Lord, Irish Representative Peer, Union club, Trafalgar square, and, Dunalley castle, Tipperary
1839. Dunfermline Lord, P.C. (no address in London), Colinton house, Edinburgh, and Stubbing court, Chesterfield
1822. Dunraven & Mountearl Earl of, Irish Representative Peer, Lord Lieutenant of Co. Limerick, 76 Eaton square, and Dunraven castle, Cowbridge, South Wales; and Adare abbey, Limerick
1461. Dunsany Lord, Irish Representative Peer, Lord Lieutenant and Custos Rotulorum of Meath County, Carlton Club, and Dunsany castle, Dunshaughlin, Meath

Durham Bishop of, consecrated Bishop of Chichester 1831, translated 1836, 4 Upper Portland place, and Auckland castle, Bishop's Auckland, Durham

1780. Dynevor Lord, Lord Lieutenant of Carmarthen county, 34 Dover street, and Dynevor castle, Llandillo, Carmarthenshire
1837. Effingham Earl of, 57 Eaton place, and the Grange, Rotherham
1507. Eglinton Earl of, in the Peerage of Scotland, sits as Baron Ardrossan (1806) in that of the United Kingdom, Lord Lieutenant of Ayrshire, Colonel of the Ayrshire Militia, 10 St. James's square, and Eglinton castle, Irvine, Ayrshire
1733. Egmont Earl of, in the Peerage of Ireland, sits as Baron Lovell and Holland, (1762) in that of the United Kingdom, a Captain in the Royal Navy (no address in London), Burgh House, Epsom, and Cowdry lodge, Petworth
1821. Eldon Earl of, 1 Hamilton place, Piccadilly, and Encombe house, Wareham, Dorset, and Shirley, Croydon
1844. Ellenborough Earl, G.C.B., P.C. (no address in London), Southam house, Cheltenham
1846. Ellesmere Earl of, P.C., 18 Belgrave square, and Hatchford, near Cobham, Surrey, and Worsley hall, near Manchester

Created.

1800. Ely Marquis of, in the Peerage of Ireland, sits as Baron Loftus (1801) in that of the United Kingdom, (no address in London) Ely lodge, Enniskillen

Ely Bishop of, 37 Dover street, Piccadilly, and the Palace, Ely

1789. Enniskillen Earl of, in the Peerage of Ireland, and Baron Grinstead (1815) in that of the United Kingdom, Athenæum club, Pall mall, and Florance court, Fermanagh

1789. Erne Earl of, Irish Representative Peer, Lord Lieutenant of County Fermanagh, and Colonel of the Fermanagh Militia (no address in London), Croom Castle, Fermanagh

1453. Errol Earl of, in the Peerage of Scotland, sits as Baron Kilmarnock (1831) in that of the United Kingdom, Hereditary Lord High Constable of Scotland, Slains Castle, Aberdeenshire, and Richmond park, Surrey

1806. Erskine Lord (no address in London) 137 Marine Parade, Brighton

1661. Essex Earl of (no address in London), Cashiobury park, Watford, Hertfordshire

1801. Exeter Marquis of, K. G., P.C. Hereditary Grand Almoner, Lord Lieut. of Northamptonshire, and Rutlandshire, 36 Grosvenor square, aud Burghley house, Stamford

Exeter Bishop of, consecrated 1830, Athenæum club, and the Palace, Exeter

1816. Exmouth Viscount, Carlton club, and Treverry, Teignmouth, Cornwall, and Canonteign house, near Exeter

1620. Falkland Viscount, in the Peerage of Scotland, sits as Baron Hunsdon (1832) in that of the United Kingdom, G. C. H., P.C., *Captain of H. M.'s Yeomen of the Guard*, Scuttiskelfe, Stokesley, Yorkshire

1821. Falmouth Earl of, High Steward of Wallingford, 2 St. James's sq. Tregothnan, Truro, Cornwall and Woolhampton house, Newbury, Berkshire

1756. Farnham Lord, K.P., Irish Representative Peer, Carlton club, 94 Pall mall, and Farnham, County Cavan

1711. Ferrers Earl, Brown's hotel, 24 Dover street, Piccadilly, and Chartley castle, Litchfield

1826. Feversham Lord, 25 Belgrave square, and Duncombe park, Helmsley, Yorkshire

1759. Fife Earl of, in the Peerage of Ireland, sits as Baron Fife (1827) in that of the United Kingdom, K.T., G.C.H., *Lord in Waiting to Her Majesty*, Ld. Lt. of Banffshire, Union club, Trafalgar sq., & Duff house, near Banff, N.B.

1628. Fingall Earl of, in the Peerage of Ireland, sits as Baron Fingall (1831) in that of the United Kingdom, Brookes's club, and Killeen castle, Meath

1841. Fitzhardinge Earl, Lord Lieutenant of Gloucestershire, and Colonel of the South Gloucestershire Militia, Berkeley house, Spring gardens, and Berkeley castle, Gloucestershire

1746. Fitzwilliam Earl, Mortimer house, Halkin street, Grosvenor place, and Wentworth house, Rotherham

1821. Forester Lord, P.C., 21 Charles street, Berkeley square, and Willey park, Broseley, Shropshire

1776. Foley Lord, P. C., *Capt. of Her Majesty's Hon. Corps of Gentlemen at Arms*, 26 Grosvenor square

1789. Fortescue Earl, P.C., *Lord Steward of Her Majesty's Household*, Lord Lieutenant of Devonshire, Colonel of the East Devon Militia, 17 Grosvenor square, and Castle hill, Southmolton

1720. Gage Viscount, in the Peerage of Ireland, sits as Baron Gage (1790) in that of the United Kingdom, 4 Whitehall yard, and Firle place, Lewes

1841. Gainsborough Earl of, 9 Cavendish square, and Barham court, Maidstone, and Exton Park, near Stamford

1623. Galloway Earl of, in the Peerage of Scotland, sits as Lord Stewart of Garlies (1796) in that of the United Kingdom Lord Lieutenant of the counties of Kircudbright and Wigton (no address in London), Galloway house, Wigton and Cumloden cottage, Newtown Stewart, N.B

1806. Gardner Lord, 46 Dover street, Piccadilly

1824. Gifford Lord, (no address in London) Kyer house, Tenbury

1703. Glasgow Earl of, in the Peerage of Scotland, sits as Baron Ross (1815) in that of the United Kingdom, Lieut. R.N. Lieut. and Sheriff Principal of Renfrewshire, Clarendon hotel, 169 New Bond street, and Hawkshead, Paisley, Renfrewshire, and Boroughbridge, Yorkshire, and Kelburne castle, Largs, Ayrshire

1835. Glenelg Lord, P.C., H4, Albany, Piccadilly, and Waternish, Inverness-shire

1816. Glengall Earl of, Irish Representative Peer, Colonel of the Tipperary Militia, 34 Grosvenor street, and Caher castle, Caher, Tipperary

Gloucester and Bristol Bishop of, consecrated 1830, Little Cloisters, Westminster, and Palace, Gloucester

1832. Godolphin Lord, Brookes's club, 60 St. James's street, and Gog Magog hills, Cambridge

1806. Gosford Earl of, G.C.B., P.C., in the Peerage of Ireland, and Baron Worlingham (1835) in that of the United Kingdom, an Irish Representative Peer, Lord Lieutenant of Co. Armagh, Brookes's club, 60 St. James's street, and Worlingham hall, Beccles, Suffolk, and Gosford castle, Armagh

1846. Gough Lord, G.C.B., Commander-in-Chief in India (abroad at the time of publication)

1675. Grafton Duke of, Hereditary Ranger of Whittlebury Forest, Colonel of the West Suffolk Militia, 47 Clarges street, and Euston hall, Thetford, and Wakefield lodge, Stoney Stratford

1782. Grantley Lord, Carlton club, 94 Pall mall, and Wonersh, Guildford, Surrey, and Grantley hall, Ripon, Yorkshire

1833. Granville Earl of, P.C., *Master of Her Majesty's Buckhounds*, 16 Bruton street, Berkeley square

1806. Grey Earl, P.C., *Secretary of State, Colonial Department*, 30 Belgrave square, and Howick hall, near Alnwick

1752. Guilford Earl of, Rector of Southampton, 23 Dover street, Piccadilly, and Waldershare park, near Dover, and Old Alresford, Hants

1619. Haddington Earl of, P.C., in the Peerage of Scotland, sits as Baron Melros (1827) in that of the United Kingdom, an Elder Brother of the Trinity house, 43 Berkeley sq., and Tyninghame castle, Preston kirk, Haddingtonshire

1643. Hamilton Duke of, in the Peerage of Scotland, sits as Duke of Brandon (1711) in that of the United Kingdom, K.G., P.C., Premier Peer of Scotland, Hereditary Keeper of Holyrood house, Lord Lieutenant of Lanarkshire, Colonel of the Lanarkshire Militia, 12 Portman square, and Hamilton palace, Hamilton, Lanarkshire, and Ashton hall, Lancaster, Lancashire, and Easton hall, Woodbridge, Suffolk.

1719. Harborough Earl of (no address in London), Stapleford park, Melton Mowbray

1846. Hardinge Viscount, G.C.B., P.C., Governor-General of India (abroad at the time of publication)

1754. Hardwicke Earl of, Capt. R.N., Lord Lieutenant of Cambridgeshire, Patterson's hotel, 48 Brook street, and Wimpole hall, Arrington, Cambridge

1812. Harewood Earl of, Lord Lieut. West Riding of Yorkshire, 13 Hanover square, and Harewood house, near Leeds

1742. Harrington Earl of, a Colonel in the army, Whitehall gardens, and Elvaston castle, Derby, and Gawsworth Macclesfield, Cheshire

1815. Harris Lord, 30 Albemarle street, and Belmont, Feversham

1809. Harrowby Earl of, P.C., a Commissioner for building churches, 39 Grosvenor square, and Sandon hall, Stafford

1290. Hastings Lord, 7 Cavendish square, and Melton Constable, Norfolk, and Seaton Delaval, Northumberland

1835. Hatherton Lord, P.C. (no address in London), Teddesley hall, Penkridge

1793. Hawarden Viscount, Irish Representative Peer, 5 St. George's place, Hyde park corner, and Dundrum, Cashell

1776. Hawke Lord, Windham club, 11 St. James's square, and Womersley house, Pontefract

1800. Headfort Marquis of, in the Peerage of Ireland, sits as Baron Kenlis (1831) in that of the United Kingdom, K.P., Lord Lieutenant of Cavan county, Colonel of the Meath Militia, Brookes's club, 60 St. James's street, and Headfort house, Meath

1550. Hereford Viscount, in Holy Orders, Premier Viscount of England, 12 Portland place, & Tregoyd, Hay, Brecknockshire

Hereford Bishop of, consecrated 1837, 17 Hill street, Berkeley square, and the Palace, Hereford

1793. Hertford Marquis, K.G., Dorchester house, Park la, & Ragley pk. Alcester, & Sudbourne hall, Woodbridge, Suffolk

Created.
1828. Heytesbury Lord, G.C.B., P.C., Burlington hotel, Cork street, Bond street, and Heytesbury, house, Wiltshire
1842. Hill Viscount, Lord Lieutenant of Shropshire (no address in London), Hawkstone, Market Drayton, and Hardwicke grange, Shrewsbury.
1762. Holland Lord, Minister at Florence (letters go to the Foreign Office, Downing street)
1605. Home Earl of, Scotch Representative Peer (no address in London), Hirsel, Coldstream, Berwickshire
1597. Howard-de-Walden & Seaford Lord, G.C.B. Ambassador at Lisbon (letters go to the Foreign Office, Downing street)
1831. Howden Lord, a Colonel in the army, 13 Hereford street, Park lane, and Grimstone park, Tadcaster
1821. Howe Earl, G.C.H., P.C., Lord Chamberlain to the Queen Dowager, Curzon house, 8 South Audley street, and Gopsall hall, Leicester
1529. Huntingdon Earl of, Union club, Trafalgar square, and Gaultier cottage, Waterford
1599. Huntly Marquis of, K.T., in the Peerage of Scotland, sits as Baron Meldrum (1815) in that of the United Kingdom, 24 Chapel street, Belgrave square, and Aboyne castle, Aboyne, Aberdeenshire, and Orton, Huntingdon
1756. Ilchester Earl of, 31 Old Burlington street, and Melbury house, Dorchester, and Abbotsbury castle, Dorchester
1697. Jersey Earl of, P.C., 38 Berkeley square, and Middleton park, Bicester, Oxford, and Osterley park, Hanwell, Middlesex
1840. Keane Lord, Major in the army, Junior United Service Club, 11 Charles street, St. James's, and Burton lodge, Christchurch, Hants
1800. Kenmare Earl of, in the Peerage of Ireland, sits as Baron Kenmare (1841) in that of the United Kingdom, Lord Lieutenant of the county of Kerry, Colonel of the Kerry Militia, 11 Belgrave sq. and Killarney, County Kerry
1788. Kenyon Lord, a Commissioner for building Churches, 9 Portman square, and Gredingtonhall, Whitchurch, Shropshire, and Peel hall, near Bolton
1768. Kingston Earl of, in the Peerage of Ireland, and Baron Kingston (1821) in that of the United Kingdom, (no address in London) Mitchelstown castle, County of Cork
1682. Kinnaird Lord, in the Peerage of Scotland, sits as Baron Rossie (1831) in that of the United Kingdom, P.C. 33 Grosvenor street, Grosvenor square, and Rossie Priory, Inchture, Perthshire
1633. Kinnoul Earl of, Lord Lyon King of Arms, in the Peerage of Scotland, sits as Baron Hay (1711) in that of the United Kingdom, G.C.B., Lord Lieut. of Perthshire, & Colonel of the Perth Militia, 58 Green st. & Duplin castle, Perth
1807. Lake Viscount, 76 Gloucester place, Portman square, Aston Clinton, Aylesbury, Buckinghamshire
1836. Langdale Lord, P.C., Master of the Rolls, 37 South street, Grosvenor square, and Templeton house, Roehampton
1784. Lansdowne Marquis of, K.G., P.C., *Lord President of the Council*, Lord Lieutenant of Wilts, a Trustee of the British Museum, a Commissioner for building Churches, 54 Berkeley sq., and Bowood, near Calne, Wiltshire
1624. Lauderdale Earl, in the Peerage of Scotland, sits as Baron Lauderdale (1806), in that of the United Kingdom; Hereditary Standard-bearer, and Marshal of the Household of Scotland, Lord Lt. of Berwickshire, Warren's hotel, Regent street, and Thirlstane castle, Lauder, Berwickshire, and Dunbar house, Dunbar, Haddingtonshire
1694. Leeds Duke of, Clarendon hotel, New Bond street, and Hornby castle, Catterick
1837. Leicester Earl of, Lord Lieutenant of Norfolk, and Custos Rotulorum (no address in London), Holkham hall, Lynn, Norfolk
1839. Leigh Lord, 30 Portman square, and Stoneleigh abbey, Coventry, Warwickshire
1766. Leinster Duke of, in the Peerage of Ireland, sits as Viscount Leinster (1747) in that of the United Kingdom; P.C., Lord Lieutenant of Kildare, 6 Carlton house terrace, and Carton house, Maynooth
1795. Leitrim Earl of, in the Peerage of Ireland, sits as Baron Clements (1831) in that of the United Kingdom, Lord Lieutenant of Leitrim, Colonel of the Donegal Militia, 18 Great Cumberland place, and Killadoon, Ceibridge, Ireland
1641. Leven and Melville Earl, Scotch Representative Peer, Capt. R.N., 8 George street, Hanover square, & Melville house, Cupar, Fife
1831. Lichfield Earl of, P.C., (abroad at the time of publication)
Lichfield and Coventry Bishop of, consecrated 1843, 39 Harley street, Cavendish square, and the Castle, Eccleshall
1797. Lilford Lord, 10 Grosvenor place, and Lilford hall, Oundle, Northamptonshire, and Bewsay hall, Warrington
1803. Limerick Earl of, in the Peerage of Ireland, and Baron Foxford (1815) in that of the United Kingdom, Conservative club, 74 St. James's street, and Southill park, Bracknel, Berks
Lincoln Bishop of, consecrated Bishop of Bristol 1820, translated 1827, Warren's hotel, 1 Regent street, and Willingham, Market Raisin
1626. Lindsey Earl of, (no address in London), Uffington, near Stamford, Lincolnshire
1806. Lismore Viscount, in the Peerage of Ireland, and Baron Lismore (1838) in that of the United Kingdom, Farrance's hotel, Belgrave street, and Shanbally castle, Tipperary
1796. Liverpool Earl of, G.C.B., P.C., Middle Scotland yard, and Buxted park, near Uckfield, and Pitchford hall, Shrewsbury
Llandaff Bishop of, consecrated 1828, Deanery, St. Paul's, and Hardwick house, Chepstow
London Bishop of, P.C., consecrated Bishop of Chester 1824, translated 1828, a Lord of Trade and Plantations, a Commissioner for building Churches, 22 St. James's square, and Palace, Fulham
1816. Londonderry Marquis of, in the Peerage of Ireland, sits as Earl Vane (1823) in that of the United Kingdom, G.C.B., G.C.H., B.E., S.P., P.C., Lord Lieutenant of the County of Durham, a General in the army, Colonel of 2nd Regiment of Life Guards, Holderness house, Park lane, and Wynyard park, Stockton, and Rose Bank, Fulham, and Mount Stewart, Newtonards, Ireland, and Seaham hall, Sunderland
1785. Longford Earl of, in the Peerage of Ireland, sits as Baron Silchester (1821) in that of the United Kingdom 24 Bruton street, Berkeley square, and Pakenham Hall, Westmeath
1807. Lonsdale Earl of, P.C., F.RS., F.S.A., Lord Lieutenant of Cumberland and Westmoreland, 14 Carlton house terrace, and Lowther castle, Penrith, and Whitehaven, Cumberland
1806. Lorton Viscount, Irish Representative Peer, General in the ar my, Lord Lieutenant of Roscommon, Colonel of the Roscommon Militia, 18 Chesham place, and Rockingham, Boyle, Roscommon
1837. Lovat Lord, Brookes's club, 60 St. James's street, and Beaufort house, Beauly, Invernessshire
1838. Lovelace, Lord Lieutenant of Surrey, Lieutenant-Colonel of the Surrey Yeomanry Cavalry, 10 St. James's square, and Ockham park, Ripley, Surrey, and Ashley Combe, Postock, Somerset
1795. Lucan Earl of, Irish Representative Peer, Lord Lieutenant of Sligo, a Colonel in the army, 20 Hanover square, and Laleham, near Chertsey
1839. Lurgan Lord, (no address in London), Lurgan, Ireland
1827. Lyndhurst Lord, P.C., F.R.S., High Steward of the University of Cambridge, 25 George street, Hanover square, and Turville park, Henley, Buckinghamshire
1794. Lyttelton Lord, Lord Lieutenant of Worcestershire, 17 St. James's place, and Hagley park, Stourbridge
1721. Macclesfield Earl of, 9 Conduit street, and Sherbourne castle, Oxford
1800. Malmesbury Earl of, 8 Whitehall gardens, and Heron court, Ringwood, and Durnford, near Salisbury
1719. Manchester Duke of, Athenæum club, and Kimbolton castle, Kimbolton, and Tandregee, Ireland
1807. Manners Lord, 56 Upper Brook street, and Farnham hall, Bury St. Edmunds
1776. Mansfield and Mansfield Earl of, K.T. Ken Wood, Hampstead, and Scone palace, Perth, and Comlongon castle, Dumfries, and Shaw park, Clackmannan
1806. Manvers Earl, 13 Portman square, and Thoresby park, Ollerton, Nottinghamshire
1702. Marlborough Duke of, Lord Lieutenant of Oxfordshire, 16 Eaton square, and Blenheim park, Woodstock

Created.
1797. Massareene & Ferrard Viscount, in the Peerage of Ireland, sits as Baron Oriel (1821) in that of the United Kingdom, York hotel, 10 Albermarle street, and Oriel Temple, Louth, and Antrim castle, Antrim
1766. Maynard Viscount, Lord Lieutenant of Essex, 38 Grosvenor square, and Easton, near Dunmow, Essex
1785. Mayo Earl of, Irish Representative Peer, G.C.H., Colonel of the Kildare Militia, 24 Norfolk street, Park lane, and Palmerston house, Naas, Kildare
1627. Meath Earl of, in the Peerage of Ireland, sits as Baron Chaworth (1831), in that of the United Kingdom, K.P., Lord-Lieutenant of Dublin county (no address in London), Kilruddery house, Wicklow
1781. Melbourne Viscount, in the Peerage of Ireland, sits as Baron Melbourne (1815) in that of the United Kingdom P.C., a Commissioner for building Churches, an Elder Brother of the Trinity House, 39 South street, Grosvenor square, and Brocket hall, Welwyn, Herts, and Melbourne Hall, Derbyshire
1802. Melville Viscount, K.T., P.C., Lord Privy Seal in Scotland, an Elder Brother of the Trinity house, Somerset house and Melville castle, Lasswade, Edinburgh
1838. Methuen Lord, Capt. R.N., 128 Park street, and Corsham house, Chippenham, Wilts
1711. Middleton Lord, 11 Montagu street, Portman square, and Wollaton hall, near Nottingham
1717. Midleton Viscount, in the Peerage of Ireland, sits as Baron Brodrick (1796) in that of the United Kingdom, (no address in London), Pepper Harrow park, Godalming
1813. Minto Earl, G.C.B., P.C., *Lord Privy Seal*, Minto house, Hawick, Roxburghshire
1728. Monson Lord (letters delivered at 1 Lincoln's inn fields), and Burton hall, near Lincoln, & Chart lodge, Sevenoaks
1839. Monteagle Lord, P.C., 37 Brook street, and Mount Trenchard, near Foynes, Ireland
1741. Montfort Lord, 24 Upper Montagu street
1707. Montrose Duke of, in the Peerage of Scotland, sits as Earl Graham (1722) in that of the United Kingdom, K.T., P.C., Lord Lt. of Stirlingshire, 45 Belgrave square and Buchanan house, Stirlingshire (post town, Dumbarton)
1561. Moray Earl of, K.T., in the Peerage of Scotland, sits as Baron Stuart (1796) in that of the United Kingdom, 7 Stratford place, Oxford street, and Donibristle house, Aberdoun, Fifeshire, and Darnaway castle, Forres, Morayshire, & Doune lodge, Doune, Perthshire, and Castle Stuart, Cambletown, Inverness-shire
1815. Morley Earl of, *Lord in Waiting to Her Majesty*, Colonel of South Devon Militia, Kent house, South place, Knightsbridge, and Saltram, Plympton
1760. Mornington Earl, in the Peerage of Ireland, sits as Baron Maryborough (1821), in that of the United Kingdom (no address in London), Wanstead, Essex
1458. Morton Earl of, Scotch Representative Peer, 7 Old Palace yard, and Dalmahoy, near Edinburgh
1831. Mostyn Lord, 9 Lower Seymour street, and Pengwern, St. Asaph
1781. Mountcashel Earl of, Irish Representative Peer, Conservative club, 74 St. James's st. & Moore park, Kilworth, Cork
1789. Mount Edgecumbe Earl of, P.C., Colonel of Cornwall Militia, 31 Sackville street, & Mount Edgecumbe, Plymouth
1831. Munster Earl of, a Lieutenant in the Life Guards (no address in London), Windsor barracks
1805. Nelson Earl, Carlton club, 94 Pall mall, and Trafalgar house, Salisbury, Wiltshire
1756. Newcastle Duke of, K.G., 17 Portman square, and ClumberPark, and Worksop Manor, Notts
1483. Norfolk Duke of, P.C., *Master of the Horse to Her Majesty*, Premier Duke and Earl, Hereditary Earl Marshal, Norfolk house, St. James's square, and the Castle, Arundel
1838. Normanby Marquis of, P.C., ambassador at Paris, Mulgrave castle, Whitby
1812. Northampton Marquis of, President of the Royal Society, 145 Piccadilly, and Castle Ashby, near Northampton, and Compton Wynyates, near Shipston-on-Stour, Warwickshire
1766. Northumberland Duke of, K.G., P.C., Lord Lieut. of Northumberland; Chancellor of the University of Cambridge; Northumberland house, Charing cross, and Sion house, Isleworth, and Alnwick castle, Northumberland, and Werrington park, Launceston, Cornwall
1797. Northwick Lord, 44 St. James's place, and Northwick park, Morton-in-Marsh, Gloucestershire
Norwich Bishop of, consecrated 1837, 38 Brook street, and the Palace, Norwich
1800. O'Neill Earl, Irish Representative Peer, a Lt. Gen. in the army, United Service club, and Shane's castle, Co. Antrim
1801. Onslow Earl of, Clarendon hotel, 169 New Bond street, & Richmond, Surrey, & Clandon, near Guildford, Surrey
1806. Orford Earl of, Colonel of the West Norfolk Militia, White's club, and Wolterton park, near Aylsham, Norfolk
1696. Orkney Earl of, Scotch Representative Peer, Limmer's hotel, George st. Hanover sq. & Taplow court, Maidenhead
1825. Ormonde Marquis of, in the Peerage of Ireland, sits as Baron Ormonde (1821) in that of the United Kingdom, K.P., 14 Weymouth street, and Kilkenny castle
1711. Oxford Earl of, (and Mortimer Earl,) Blenheim hotel, 94 New Bond street, and Eywood, and Brampton, Brian, near Kington, Herefordshire
Oxford Bishop of, consecrated 1845, Chancellor of the Most Noble Order of the Garter, 61 Eaton place, Belgrave square, and Cuddesdon palace, Wheatley, Oxon
1831. Panmure Lord, 9 Cornwall terrace, Regent's park, and Brechin castle, Brechin, Forfarshire
1551. Pembroke Earl of, 7 Carlton house terrace, and Wilton house, Salisbury
Peterborough Bishop of, consecrated 1839, 27 Parliament street, and the Palace, Peterborough
1603. Petre Lord, 3 Mansfield street, and Thorndon hall, near Brentwood, Essex
1827. Plunket Lord, P.C. (no address in London), Old Connaught, Wicklow
1831. Poltimore Lord, Colonel of the North Devon Militia, 25 Grosvenor square, and Poltimore, near Exeter, and Court hall, North Molton, Devonshire, and Hardington Park, 9 miles from Bath, Somerset.
1690. Polwarth Lord, Scotch Representative Peer, Carlton club, 94 Pall mall, and Merton house, St. Boswell's, Berwick-upon-Tweed
1721. Pomfret Earl of, 100 Mount st. Berkeley square, Easton-Neston, Towcester, and Twinsted hall, Halstead, Essex
1839. Ponsonby Viscount, G.C.B., ambassador at Vienna, Bishop's court, Kildare
1716. Portland Duke of, P.C., 19 Cavendish square, and Welbeck abbey, Worksop, and Fullarton house, Troon, Ayrshire
1837. Portman Lord, Lord Lieutenant of Somerset, 38 Bryanstone square, and Bryanstone, Blandford, Dorset
1743. Portsmouth Earl of (no address in London), Hurstborne park, Whitchurch, Hampshire
1706. Poulett Earl, Colonel of the Somerset Militia, 12 Charles st. Berkeley sq. and Hinton St. George, Crewkerne, Somerset
1804. Powis Earl of, K.G., Lord Lieutenant of Montgomeryshire, 45 Berkeley square, and Walcot, Ludlow, and Powis castle, Welchpool
1816. Prudhoe Lord, Capt. R.N., 2 Whitehall gardens, and Stanwick park, Darlington
1765. Radnor Earl of, 52 Grosvenor street, and Longford castle, Salisbury, and Coleshill house, Farringdon, Berkshire, and Longford castle, Salisbury
1831. Ranfurly Earl of, in the Peerage of Ireland, sits as Baron Ranfurly (1826) in that of the United Kingdom, 40 Berkeley square, and Barham house, Elstree, Edgware, and Dungannon, Tyrone
1821. Ravensworth Lord, Percy's cross, Fulham, and Ravensworth castle, Gateshead, Durham
1821. Rayleigh Lord, United University club, and Terling place, Witham, Essex
1628. Reay Lord, Scotch Representative Peer, Arthur's club, 69 St. James's street, and Goldings, Hertford
1802. Redesdale Lord, 6 Park place, St. James's, and Batsford, Morton-in-Marsh, Gloucestershire
1675. Richmond Duke of, K.G., P.C., Lord Lieut. of Sussex, Col. of the Sussex Militia, 51 Portland place, and Goodwood, near Chichester, Sussex, and Gordon castle, Fochabers, and Glenfiddich lodge, Dufftown, N.B.
1833. Ripon Earl of, P.C., a Lord of Trade and Plantations, 1 Carlton gardens, Putney heath, Surrey; and Nocton hall, Sleaford, Lincolnshire

Created.

Ripon Bishop of, consecrated 1836, 27 Parliament street, and the Palace, Ripon

1802. Rivers Lord, *Lord in Waiting to Her Majesty*, 10 Chester st., Grosvenor pl., and Rushmore lodge, Dorsetshire

Rochester Bishop of, consecrated Bishop of Sodor and Mann 1813, translated 1827, 55 Eaton place, and Danbury palace, Chelmsford

1771. Roden Earl of, in the Peerage of Ireland, sits as Baron Clanbrassill (1821) in that of the United Kingdom, K.P., P.C., United Service club, and Hyde hall, Sawbridgeworth, Herts, and Tallymore park, Castlewellan, Ireland

1782. Rodney Lord (no address in London), Barrington, Leominster, Herefordshire

1651. Rollo Lord, Scotch Representative Peer, Carlton club, 94 Pall mall, and Duncrub, Dunning, Perthshire

1801. Romney Earl, 45 Wilton crescent, and the Mote, near Maidstone, Kent

1703. Rosebery Earl of, in the Peerage of Scotland, sits as Baron Rosebery (1828), in that of the United Kingdom, K.T, P.C., Lord Lieutenant of Linlithgowshire, 139 Piccadilly, and Dalmeney park, South Queenferry, Linlithgowshire, and Warren wood, Hatfield, Hertfordshire

1806. Rosse Earl of, Irish Representative Peer, Lord Lieut. of King's County, and Colonel of King's County Militia, (no address in London), Parson's town castle, Parson's town, King's county

1801. Rosslyn Earl of, P.C., Lieut. Col. of the 9th Lancers, 6 Grosvenor place, and Dysart House, Fief

1838. Rossmore Lord, Lord Lieut. of Co. Monaghan, Brookes' club, St. James's street, and Dell, Windsor, and Rossmore park, county Monaghan

1707. Roxburgh Duke of, in the Peerage of Scotland, sits as Earl Innes (1837) in that of the United Kingdom, K.T. Thomas's hotel, 25 Berkeley square, and Fleurs castle, Kelso, N.B.

1703. Rutland Duke of, K.G., Lord Lieut. of Leicester, Col. of Leicestershire Militia, 85 Pall mall, and Belvoir castle, Grantham, and Palace, Newmarket, and Longshaw lodge, and Stantonwood house, Bakewell, Derbyshire

1684. St. Alban's Duke of, Hereditary Grand Falconer, and Hereditary Registrar of the Court of Chancery, 80 Piccadilly, and Holly lodge, Highgate, and Redburn hall, Brigg

St. Asaph Bishop of, the Palace, St Asaph

St. David's Bishop of, consecrated 1840, 7 Half Moon street, Piccadilly, and Palace, Aberguili, Carmarthen

1815. St. Germans Earl of, P.C., 36 Dover street, and Port Eliot, St. Germans, Cornwall

1558. St. John Lord, Carlton club, 94 Pall mall, and Melchbourn, Kimbolton

1801. St. Vincent Viscount, Ellis's hotel, 59 and 60 St. James's street, and Meaford, near Stone, Staffordshire

1789. Salisbury Marquis, K.G., P.C., Lord Lieutenant of Middlesex, Colonel of the Hertfordshire Militia, 20 Arlington street, and Hatfield house, Hatfield, Hertfordshire, and Childwell hall, Liverpool

Salisbury Bishop of, consecrated 1837, 40 Chesham place, Belgrave square, and the Palace, Salisbury

1445. Saltoun Lord, K.C.B., G.C.H., Scotch Representative Peer, 1 Gt. Cumberland st. and Philorth house, Fraserburgh, N.B

1660. Sandwich Earl of, Lord Lieutenant of Huntingdonshire, 32 Dover st. Piccadilly, and Hichinbroke, near Huntingdon

1802. Sandys Lord, Colonel in the Army, 48 Curzon street, and Ombersley court, Worcester

1603. Saye and Sele Lord, 43 Grosvenor street, and Belvedere, Erith, Kent, and Broughton castle, Banbury, Oxon

1690. Scarborough Earl of, Lord Lieutenant of Nottinghamshire, 41 South street, Grosvenor square, and Sandbeck park Rotherham, Yorkshire, and Rufford hall, Ollerton, Nottinghamshire

1761. Scarsdale Lord (no address in London), Keddleston hall, Derby

1701. Seafield Earl, Scotch Representative Peer, Lord Lieutenant of Inverness-shire, Colonel of Inverness-shire Militia, 17 Charles street, St. James's, and Cullen House, Banff, Banffshire, and Castle Grant, Grantown, Inverness-shire

1840. Seaton Lord, G.C.B., G.C.H., a Lieut. General in the army and Colonel of the 26th foot, and Governor of the Island of Corfu, Senior United Service Club, 116 Pall mall, and Kitley, near Yealmpton, Devon

1771. Sefton Earl of, in the Peerage of Ireland, sits as Baron Sefton (1831) in that of the United Kingdom, 37 Belgrave square, and Croxteth park, Liverpool

1646. Selkirk Earl of, Scotch Representative Peer (no address in London), and St. Mary's Isle, Kirkcudbright

1672. Shaftesbury Earl of, P.C., 24 Grosvenor square, and St. Giles's house, Woodyates, Dorsetshire

1756. Shannon Earl of, in the Peerage of Ireland, sits as Baron Carleton (1786) in that of the United Kingdom, 44 Brook street, and Castle Martyr, Cork, Ireland

1816. Sheffield Earl of, in the Peerage of Ireland, sits as Baron Sheffield (1802) in that of the United Kingdom, 20, Portland place, and Sheffield Park, Uckfield

1784. Sherborne Lord, 15 Hyde park gardens, and Sherborne lodge, Northleach, and Standish house, Stroudwater, Gloucester

1442. Shrewsbury Earl of, Hereditary Lord High Steward of Ireland, Clarendon hotel, 169 New Bond street, Heythrop house, Oxfordshire, and Alton towers, Cheadle, Staffordshire

1805. Sidmouth Rev. Viscount, (no address in London) Albury, near Guildford, Surrey

1489. Sinclair Lord, Scotch Representative Peer, United Service Club, and Herdmanstown, Haddington, and Torquay

1828. Skelmersdale Lord, 55 Portland place, and Latham house, Ormskirk

1800. Sligo Marquis of, in the Peerage of Ireland, sits as Baron Monteagle (1806) in that of the United Kingdom, Colonel of the South Mayo Militia, 2 Mansfield street, and Westport house, County Sligo, Ireland

1821. Somers Earl, Lord Lieutenant of Herefordshire, Colonel of the Herefordshire Militia, 45 Grosvenor place, and Eastnor castle, Tewkesbury, & Priory, Reigate

1546. Somerset Duke of, K.G., Park lane, and Bradley house, Mere, Wilts, and Stobec house, Newton Abbot

1760. Sondes Lord, 18 St. James's square, and Elmham, near Dereham, Norfolk, and Leeds Court, Kent

1780. Southampton Lord, 66 Mount street, Berkeley square, and Whittlebury lodge, Towcester

1765. Spencer Earl, Capt. R.N., P.C., *Lord Chamberlain of Her Majesty's Household*, Spencer house, 27 St. James's place, and Althorp, Northampton, and Wiseton, Bawtry, Yorkshire

1640. Stafford Lord, (no address in London), Cossey park, Norwich

1703. Stair Earl of, in the Peerage of Scotland, sits as Baron Oxenfoord (1841) in that of the United Kingdom, Keeper of the Great Seal of Scotland, 6 Upper Brook street, and Oxenfoord castle, Ford, Edinburghshire

1718. Stanhope Earl (no address in London), Chevening, Sevenoaks

1839. Stanley Lord, *of Alderley*, 40 Dover street, Piccadilly, & Alderley park, near Congleton, Cheshire, & Penrhos', Holyhead

1832. Stanley Lord, *of Bickerstaffe*, P.C., the eldest son of the Earl of Derby, summoned to the House of Peers during the lifetime of his father, Trustee of the British Museum, 8 St. James's square, and Stanley lodge, Bally-Histeen, Tipperary, Ireland

1448. Stourton Lord, 10 Mansfield street, and Allerton park, Green Hammerton, York

1821. Stradbroke Earl of, Lord Lieutenant of Suffolk, and Col. of the East Suffolk Militia, 18 Queen street, May Fair, and Henham hall, Wangford

1835. Strafford Lord, G.C.B., G.C.H., P.C., Lieut. Gen. in the Army, Col. of the 29th foot, 44 Grosvenor street

1628. Strangford Viscount, in the Peerage of Ireland, sits as Baron Penshurst (1825) in that of the United Kingdom G.C.B., G.C.H., P.C., 68 Harley street, and Westenhanger house, Hythe, Kent

1686. Strathallan Viscount, Scotch Representative Peer, 44 Charles street, Berkeley square, and Castle Strathallan, Auchterarder, N. B.

1839. Stuart de Decies Lord, Lord Lieutenant of the County Waterford, Colonel of the Waterford Militia, Long's hotel, 16 New Bond street, and Dromana, Cappoquin, Ireland

Created.
1838. Sudeley Lord, 35 Dover street, and Winchcomb, Gloucestershire
1786. Suffield Lord, 12 Great Marlborough street and Gunton park, Norwich, and Middleton hall, Manchester
1603. Suffolk & Berkshire, Earl of, 9 Clarges street, Piccadilly, and Charlton park, Malmesbury
1833. Sutherland Duke of, K.G., Lord Lieut. of Shropshire and Sutherlandshire, Stafford house, St. James's, and Trentham park, Staffordshire, and Lilleshall, Salop, and Dunrobin castle, Sutherlandshire
1789. Sydney Viscount, 3 Cleveland square, and Frognall, Footscray
1784. Talbot Earl, K.G., K.P., P.C., Lord Lieutenant of Staffordshire, 10 Great George street, and Ingestre hall, Stafford
1831. Talbot de Malahide Lord, in the Peerage of Ireland; sits as Baron Furnival (1839) in that of the United Kingdom, Long's hotel, New Bond street, and Malahide castle, Ireland
1714. Tankerville Earl of, P.C. (no address in London), Walton, Esher, Surrey, and Chillingham castle, near Belford, Northumberland
1831. Templemore Lord, 9 Upper Grosvenor street, and Dunbrody park, County Wexford
1827. Tenterden Lord, 12 Wilton street, Belgrave square, and Hendon, Middlesex
1616. Teynham Lord, Somerset house, Strand
1628. Thanet Earl of, Hereditary Sheriff of Westmoreland, 78 Gloucester place, and Hothfield place, near Maidstone, and Appleby castle, Westmoreland, and Skipton castle, Yorkshire
1801. Thomond Marquis of, in the Peerage of Ireland, and Baron Tadcaster (1826) in that of the United Kingdom, Vice Admiral, G.C.H. (no address in London), Taplow house, Maidenhead, Berkshire, and Rostellan castle, Cork
792. Thurlow Lord, Burlington hotel, Cork street, Bond street, and Ashfield lodge, Woolpit, Suffolk
1721. Torrington Viscount (no address in London), Yotes court, Tonbridge
1787. Townshend Marquis (no address in London)
1694. Tweeddale Marquis of, Scotch Representative Peer, K.T., C.B., Governor of Madras, Lieut. General in the army, Lord Lieut. of Haddingtonshire, Hereditary Chamberlain of Dunfermline (letters go to the India house), Yester house, Haddington
1550. Uxbridge Earl of, by courtesy, being the eldest son of the Marquis of Anglesea, summoned to the House of Peers during the lifetime of his father, by the title of Baron Paget, P.C., a Lieut. Col. in the army, Uxbridge house, 1 Old Burlington street, and Tewin Water, Welwyn, Herts
1523. Vaux, *of Harrowden* Lord (no address in London), Coughton court, Bromsgrove
1762. Vernon Lord, 12 Great Marlborough street, and Sudbury hall, Derbyshire, and Poynton hall, Cheshire, and Widdrington castle, Northumberland
1815. Verulam Earl of, Lord Lieut. of Hertfordshire (no address in London), Gorhambury, St. Albans
1841. Vivian Lord, Arthur's club, 69 St. James's street, and Plasgwyn, Anglesea, and Glyn, Bodmin, Cornwall
1729. Waldegrave Earl, C.B., Capt. R.N., 4 Harley street
1780. Walsingham Lord, 7 Upper Portland place, and Merton hall, Thetford, Norfolk
1664. Ward Lord, Mivart's hotel, 41 Brook street, and Himley hall, Dudley, Wolverhampton
1746. Warwick Earl, K.T., Lord Lieutenant of Warwick County, and Col. of the Warwickshire militia, 7 Carlton gardens and Warwick castle
1789. Waterford Marquis of, in the Peerage of Ireland, sits as Baron Tyrone (1786) in that of the United Kingdom, K.P., Mivart's hotel, Brook street, Grosvenor square, Curraghmore, Waterford
1814. Wellington Duke of, K.G., G.C.B., P.C., D.C.L., General and Commander in Chief of the Forces, Lord Lieutenant of Hampshire, and of the Tower Hamlets, Field Marshal in the army, Col. of the Grenadier Guards and of the Rifle Brigade, Constable of the Tower and of Dover castle, Warden of the Cinque Ports, Chancellor of the University of Oxford, an Elder Brother of the Trinity House, Apsley house, 149 Piccadilly, & Strathfieldsaye, Hants, & Walmer castle, Kent
1633. Wemyss and March Earl of, in the Peerage of Scotland, sits as Baron Wemyss (1821) in that of the United Kingdom, Lord Lieutenant of Peebles-shire, 19 Stratford place, and Gosford house, near Haddington, East Lothian, N.B., and Nidpath castle, Peebles-shire, and Stanway hall, Broadway, Worcestershire
1839. Wenlock Lord, Lord Lieut. and Custos Rotulorum of the East Riding of the County of York, 29 Berkeley square and Escrick park, near York
1822. Westmeath Marquis of, Irish Representative Peer, Lord Lieutenant of Westmeath County, and Col. of the Westmeath Militia, Senior United Service Club, 116 Pall mall, and Clonyn, Castle town, Delvin, Ireland
1831. Westminster Marquis of, Lord Lieutenant of Cheshire, 15 Grosvenor square, and Eaton Hall, Chester, and Halkin Castle, Flint, and Motcomb house, Shaftesbury, Dorset
1624. Westmoreland Earl of, P.C., G.C.B., G.C.H., D.C.L., Lieut. General in the army, Colonel of the 56th Foot, Ambassador at Berlin, 12 Upper Harley street, and Apthorpe, near Wandsford
1826. Wharncliffe Lord, Lieut.-Col. South West Regiment, Yorkshire Yeomanry Cavalry, 15 Curzon street, and Wortley hall, Sheffield, and Belmont castle, near Dundee
1793. Wicklow Earl of, Irish Representative Peer, K.P., Lord Lieutenant of Wicklow county, 2 Cavendish square, and Shelton abbey, Arklow, Ireland, and Stanmore park, Middlesex
1492. Willoughby de Broke Lord, 21 Hill street, and Compton Verney, Kineton
1313. Willoughby d'Eresby Lord, P.C., Joint Hereditary Great Chamberlain of England, Lord Lieut. of Carnarvon Co. 142 Piccadilly, and Grimsthorpe, Bourne, and Drummond castle, Crieff, Perthshire, and Gwydyr, Llanelly, Carnarvonshire
1801. Wilton Earl of P.C., 7 Grosvenor square, and Heaton house, near Manchester, and Egerton lodge, Melton Mowbray
Winchester Bishop of, consecrated Bishop of Llandaff 1826, translated 1827, 19 St. James's square, and the Palace Winchester, and Farnham castle
1551. Winchester Marquis of, Premier Marquis of England, Colonel of the North Hants Militia, 158 New Bond street, and Amport house, Andover
1628. Winchilsea and Nottingham Earl of, 20 Wilton crescent, Belgrave square, and Eastwell park, Ashford, Kent, and Haverholm, Priory, Sleaford, Lincolnshire, and Kirkby hall, Northamptonshire
1797. Wodehouse Lord, Fenton's hotel, 63 St. James's street, Kimberley, Wymondham, and Witton park, Norfolk
Worcester Bishop of, consecrated Bishop of Sodor and Man 1839, translated 1841, 24 Grosvenor place; Hartlebury castle, Stourport; and the Palace, Worcester
1838. Wrottesley Lord, Everall's hotel, 1 Albemarle street, Wrottesley hall, Wolverhampton
1829. Wynford Lord (no address in London), Leesons, near Chiselhurst, Kent
1837. Yarborough Earl of, 17 Arlington street, and Brocklesby, Brigg, Lincoln, and Appuldercombe park, Isle of Wight
York Archbishop of, P.C., consecrated Bishop of Carlisle 1791, translated 1807, a Commissioner for building Churches, 40 Grosvenor square, and Bishopsthorpe palace, near York, and Nuneham park, near Oxford
1838. Zetland Earl of, Lord Lieutenant of North Riding of Yorkshire, and of Orkney and Shetland, 19 Arlington street, and Aske hall, Richmond, Yorkshire, and Upleathum, Gisborough, and Marsk hall, Cleveland, Yorkshire, and Kerse house Falkirk, N.B.

ALPHABETICAL LIST OF
THE MEMBERS OF THE HOUSE OF COMMONS,
WITH THEIR VARIOUS OFFICES; THE PLACES FOR WHICH THEY SIT; RESPECTIVE TOWN RESIDENCES, & PRINCIPAL COUNTRY SEATS.

SPEAKER, The Right Honourable Charles Shaw Lefevre.

Acheson Viscount	*Armagh County*	59 Grosvenor street, and Worlingham hall, near Wangford, Suffolk.
Ackers James, Esq.	*Ludlow*	2 Blandford square, and the Heath, near Ludlow
Acland Sir Thomas Dyke, Bart	*North Devonshire*	Waterloo hotel, 85 Jermyn street, and Killerton park, Exeter, Devonshire.
Acland Thomas Dyke, Esq.	*West Somersetshire*	12 Queen street, Mayfair, and Holnicote, Minehead, Somerset.
A'Court Edward Henry, Capt. R.N.	*Tamworth*	41 St. James's place, and Heytesbury, Wiltshire.
Acton Col. William,	*Wicklow County*	36 Jermyn street, St. James's.
Adare Viscount	*Glamorganshire*	76 Eaton square & Dunraven castle, Cowbridge.
Adderley Charles Bowyer, Esq	*North Staffordshire*	30 Portman square, and Hams hall, Coleshill
Aglionby Henry Aglionby, Esq.	*Cockermouth*	5 Brick court, Temple, & Nunnery, near Penrith.
Ainsworth Peter, Esq.	*Bolton*	13 Portman st. Portman sq. & Smithills hall, Bolton
Aldam William, jun. Esq.	*Leeds*	13 Henrietta street, Cavendish square, and Warmsworth, near Doncaster.
Alexander Nathaniel, Esq.	*Antrim County*	Long's hotel, 16 New Bond street, and Portglenone house, near Belfast, Ireland.
Alford Viscount	*Bedfordshire*	23 Belgrave square.
Allix John Peter, Esq.	*Cambridgeshire*	57 Montagu square, and Swaffham.
Anson Hon. Colonel George, *Clerk of the Ordnance*	*South Staffordshire*	25 Hill street, Berkeley square, and Newmarket
Antrobus Edmund, Esq.	*East Surrey*	146 Piccadilly, and Cheam, Surrey.
Arbuthnot Hon. Lieut. Gen. Hugh, K.C.B.	*Kincardineshire*	H 5 Albany, & Hatton, Bervie, Kincardineshire
Archbold Robert, Esq.	*Kildare County*	Cox's hotel, 55 Jermyn street, and Davidstown near Castle Dermot, Ireland.
Archdall Capt. Mervyn	*Fermanagh County*	Carlton Club, 94 Pall Mall, and castle Archdall, Fermanagh.
Arkwright George, Esq.	*Leominster*	D 2 Albany, and Sutton hall, Chesterfield.
Armstrong Sir Andrew, Bart.	*King's County*	Reform club, 104 Pall mall.
Arundel and Surrey Earl	*Arundel*	11 Carlton terrace.
Ashley-Cooper Hon. Anthony Henry	*Dorchester*	Carlton club & Clewer lodge, near Windsor
Astell William, Esq	*Bedfordshire*	51 Old Broad st. & Everton house, Biggleswade.
Attwood John, Esq.	*Harwich*	25 Park lane, and Highlands park, Chelmsford.
Attwood Matthias, Esq.	*Whitehaven*	27 Gracechurch street, & Streatham park.
Austen Colonel Thomas	*West Kent*	(no address in London), Kippington, Seven Oaks
Bagge William, Esq.	*West Norfolk*	Carlton club, and Stradset hall, near Downham.
Bagot Hon. William	*Denbighshire*	23 St. James's square, and Pool Park, Ruthin.
Bailey Joseph, Esq.	*Worcester*	26 Belgrave sq. & Glanusk pk. near Crickhowell
Bailey Joseph, jun. Esq.	*Herefordshire*	26 Belgrave sq. & Easton court, near Tenbury, Worcestershire
Baillie Colonel Hugh Duncan	*Honiton*	34 Mortimer street, and Redcastle, Beauly, Inverness-shire, & Tarradale, Ross-shire, Scotland.
Baillie William, jun. Esq.	*Linlithgowshire*	Carlton Club, 94 Pall Mall, and Polkemmet, Linlithgowshire
Baillie Henry James, Esq.	*Invernesshire*	9 Lowndes st. Knightsbridge; Tarradale, Ross-shire; and Redcastle, Beauly, Ross-shire.
Baine Walter, Esq	*Greenock*	45 Pall mall, and Greenock.
Baldwin Charles Barry, Esq.	*Totness*	6 Parliament st. & Bovine, King's County, Ireland, and Guerston park, Totness, Devon.
Balfour James Maitland, jun. Esq.	*Haddington*	25 St. James's place, and Whittingham House, Preston Kirk, Haddingtonshire.
Bankes George, Esq.	*Dorsetshire*	5 Old Palace yard, & Kingston Lacy, Wimbourn & Studland, Swanage, Dorset.
Bannerman Alexander, Esq.	*Aberdeen*	4 Berkeley street, Berkeley square, and Aberdeen
Barclay David, Esq.	*Sunderland*	8 Belgrave sq. & Eastwick park, Leatherhead.
Baring Rt. Hon. Francis Thornhill	*Portsmouth*	86 Eaton square.
Baring Rt. Hon. Henry Bingham	*Marlborough*	13 Eaton place.
Baring Rt. Hon. William Bingham	*Thetford*	12 Great Stanhope street, May fair, & Addiscombe farm, Croydon, Surrey.
Baring Thomas, esq.	*Huntingdon*	40 Charles street, Berkeley square
Barkly Henry, Esq.	*Leominster*	50 Eaton place, Belgrave square.
Barnard Edward George, Esq.	*Greenwich, &c.*	Deptford Green, and Gosfield hall, Halstead.
Barneby John, Esq.	*East Worcestershire*	34 Portman sq. & Brockhampton, near Bromyard.
Barrington Viscount	*Berkshire*	20 Cavendish sq. & Beckett house, near Farringdon
Barron Sir Henry Winston, Bart	*Waterford*	(no address in London), Belmont house, Waterford
Baskerville Thos. Baskerville Mynors, Esq.	*Herefordshire*	(no address in London), Clyro court, Hay, Radnorshire
Bateson Thomas, Esq.	*Londonderry County*	C 3 Albany
Beckett William, Esq.	*Leeds*	18 Upper Brook street, & Kirstall Grange, Leeds
Bell John, Esq.	*Thirsk*	Limner's hotel, 1 George st. Hanover sq.
Bell Matthew, Esq.	*South Northumberland*	35 Wimpole st. and Woolsington, near Newcastle

Bellew Richard Montesquieu, Esq	*Louth County*	Reform club, 104 Pall mall, and Barmeath, near [Dunleer, co. Louth.
Benbow John, Esq	*Dudley*	26 Mecklenburgh sq
Benett John, Esq	*South Wiltshire*	Limmer's hotel, 1 George street, Hanover square, and Pyt house, near Hindon, Wiltshire.
Bennet Philip, jun. esq	*West Suffolk*	8 Cleveland row, St. James's, and Rougham hall, Bury St. Edmonds, Suffolk.
Bentinck Lord George William Frederick Cavendish	*Lynn Regis*	19 Cavendish square.
Bentinck Lord Henry William	*North Nottinghamshire*	19 Cavendish square
Beresford William, Esq	*Harwich*	77 Pall Mall
Berkeley Hon. Craven Fitzhardinge	*Cheltenham*	Berkeley house, Spring gardens.
Berkeley Hon. Francis Henry Fitzhardinge	*Bristol*	Berkeley house, Spring gardens, and Cranford house, near Hounslow.
Berkeley Hon. George Charles Grantley Fitzhardinge	*West Gloucestershire*	Berkeley house, Spring gardens, and Beacon lodge, near Christchurch, Hants.
Berkeley Hon. Maurice Fred. Fitzhardinge, Capt. R.N. *a Lord of the Admiralty*	*Gloucester*	15 Halkin street west.
Bernal-Osborne, see Osborne Ralph, Esq		
Bernal Ralph, Esq	*Weymouth*	75 Eaton square.
Bernard Viscount	*Bandonbridge*	6 Hyde park ter. and Castle Bernard, Cork.
Blackburne John Ireland, Esq	*Warrington*	2 Park st. Westmnstr. & Hale hall, nr. Warrington
Blackstone William Seymour, Esq	*Wallingford*	28 Albemarle st. St. James's, and Castle priory near Wallingford.
Blake Martin Joseph, Esq	*Galway*	Reform club, 104 Pall mall, and Brook lodge, Dungan [lin, & Munlo castle, Galway
Blake Sir Valentine, Bart	*Galway*	154 Oxford street, & 27 North George st. Dub-
Blakemore Richard, Esq	*Wells, Somerset*	Club chambers, 15 Regent street, Waterloo place, and The Leys, near Monmouth.
Blewitt Reginald James, Esq	*Monmouth, &c*	7 Manchester buildings, and Llantarnam abbey, near Newport, Monmouthshire.
Bodkin John James, Esq	*Galway County*	41 Piccadilly, and Kilcloony, near Tuam, Ireland
Bodkin William Henry, Esq	*Rochester*	4 Paper buildings, Temple, & 8 Mansfield street, Portland place, & Lower Heath, Hampstead
Boldero Captain Henry George	*Chippenham*	Hurst Grove, near Reading, Berks
Borthwick Peter, Esq	*Evesham*	Carlton club, 94 Pall mall.
Botfield Beriah, Esq. F.R.S.	*Ludlow*	9 Stratton street, & Norton hall, Northampton.
Bouverie Hon. Edward Pleydell	*Kilmarnock*	19 Chester street, Grosvenor place
Bowes John, Esq	*South Durham*	54 Conduit street, Regent street, and Streatlam [castle, near Staindrop.
Bowles Rear Admiral, C.B.	*Launceston*	8 Hill st. Berkeley sq.
Bowring John, LL.D	*Bolton*	1 Queen square, Westminster.
Boyd John, Esq	*Coleraine*	2 Pall mall, and Dundooan house, Coleraine
Bradshaw James, Esq	*Canterbury*	28 South street, Grosvenor square
Bramston Thomas William, Esq	*South Essex*	53 Eaton place, and Skreens, near Chelmsford.
Bridgeman Hewitt, Esq	*Ennis*	(No address in London) Ennis, Ireland.
Bright John, Esq	*Durham City*	Free Trade club, 27 Regent street, & One Ash, Rochdale, Lancashire
Brisco Musgrave, Esq	*Hastings*	38 Devonshire place & Coghurst
Broadley Henry, Esq	*East Riding of Yorkshire*	3 Charles st. St. James's square, and Norwood [house, near Beverley
Broadwood Henry, Esq	*Bridgewater*	5 Whitehall yard
Brocklehurst John, Esq	*Macclesfield*	33 Milk st. & Hurdsfield house, near Macclesfield.
Brooke Lord	*South Warwickshire*	7 Carlton gardens
Brooke Sir Arthur Brinsley, Bart	*Fermanagh*	Carlton club, 94 Pall mall, and Colebrooke house, Brookborough, Ireland.
Brotherton Joseph, Esq	*Salford*	7 Manchester buildings, and Morsborough hall, [Chesterfield.
Brown William, Esq	*South Lancashire*	(No address in London) Richmond hill, Liverpool
Browne Robert Dillon, Esq	*Mayo County*	Reform club, 104 Pall mall, and Glancorrile, Co. [Mayo.
Browne Hon. William	*Kerry County*	89 Jermyn street, St. James's.
Brownrigg John Studholme, Esq	*Boston*	19 Great Cumberland street
Bruce Rt. Hon. Lord Ernest Augustus Chas. Brudenell	*Marlborough*	7 St. George's place, Hyde Park corner.
Bruce Charles Lennox Cumming, Esq	*Elginshire and Nairnshire*	17 Charles street, St. James's, and Dunphail, Forres, and Kinnaird, Falkirk N.B.
Bruen Colonel Henry	*Carlow County*	Carlton club, Pall mall, & Oak park, near Carlow
Bruges William Heald Ludlow, Esq	*Devizes*	3 Suffolk street, Pall mall east.
Buck Lewis William, Esq	*North Devonshire*	12 Norfolk st. Park lane, & Hartland Abbey, & Moreton house, near Bideford, Devonshire.
Buckley Edmund, Esq	*Newcastle, Staffordshire*	Ginger's hotel, 1 Bridge street, Westminster.
Bulkeley Sir Richard Williams, Bart	*Flint, &c*	69 Eaton sq. & Baron hill, Beaumaris, Anglesea.
Buller Charles, jun. Esq. *Advocate General & Judge Martial*	*Liskeard*	2 Chester pl. Pimlico, & 5 Hare court, Temple.
Buller Edward, Esq	*Stafford*	23 Hertford st. May-fair & Dilhorne hall, near Cheadle.
Buller Sir John Buller Yarde, Bart	*South Devonshire*	39 Belgrave square, & Lupton house, near Brix- [ham, Devonshire.
Burrell Sir Charles Merrik, Bart	*New Shoreham, &c.*	5 Richmond ter. Whitehall, and Knapp castle, near Horsham, Sussex.
Burroughes Henry Negus, Esq	*East Norfolk*	Carlton club, Pall mall, and Burlingham hall, [near Norwich
Busfeild William, Esq	*Bradford, Yorkshire*	15 Bury st. St. Jas's. & Upwood, nr. Bingley, Yorks
Butler Pierce Somerset, Esq	*Kilkenny County*	23B, Grosvenor street west.
Byng George, Esq	*Middlesex*	5 St. James's sq. and Wrotham park, near Barnet.
Byng Right Hon. George Stevens, *Secretary to the Board of Control*	*Chatham*	77 Eaton square, and Cople house, Bedford, Bed.
Cabbell Benjamin Bond, Esq	*St. Albans*	52 Portland place, and 1 Brick court, Temple
Callaghan Daniel, Esq	*Cork*	Reform club, 104 Pall mall & Lotabeg, near Cork.
Campbell Sir Hugh Purves Hume, Bart	*Berwickshire*	72 Portland place, and Marchmont house, near Dunse, Berwickshire.

Cardwell Edward, Esq.	*Clitheroe*	3 Whitehall gardens
Carew Hon. Robert Shapland	*Waterford County*	28 Belgrave square, & Woodstown, Waterford.
Carew William Henry Pole, Esq	*East Cornwall*	13 King street, St. James's
Carnegie Hon. Swynfen Thomas	*Stafford*	Carlton club, 94 Pall mall
Castlereagh Rt. Hon. Viscount	*Down County*	127 Park street, Grosvenor square.
Cavendish Hon. Charles Compton	*Youghall*	Burlington house, 49 Piccadilly, Latimers, near Chesham, Bucks.
Cavendish Hon. George Henry	*North Derbyshire*	4 Belgrave square, and Ashford hall, near Bakewell, Derbyshire.
Cayley Edward Stillingfleet, Esq.	*North Riding of Yorkshire*	20 Hertford st. Mayfair, and Wydale, Malton.
Chandos Marquis of	*Buckinghamshire*	91 Pall mall
Chapman Aaron, Esq.	*Whitby*	34 Leadenhall street and Highbury park
Chapman Benjamin James, Esq	*Westmeath County*	81 Jermyn st. & Killna castle, Athboy, Westmeath.
Chelsea Viscount	*Reading*	Putney heath.
Chichester Lord John	*Belfast*	8 St. George's place, Hyde park corner
Cholmondeley Hon. Hugh	*Montgomery*	2 Hamilton place, and Vale Royal, Northwich.
Christie William Dougal, Esq	*Weymouth*	3 Eccleston st. & Hays park, Uxbridge
Christopher Robert Adam, Esq	*North Lincolnshire*	97 Eaton square, & Bloxholme hall, near Sleaford, and Well vale, Alford, Lincolnshire
Churchill Lord Alfred Spencer	*Woodstock*	16 Eaton square, & Blenheim park, Woodstock
Chute William Lyde Wiggett, Esq	*West Norfolk*	(No address in London) Pickenham hall, near Swaffham, & the Vine house, Basingstoke, Hants.
Clay Sir William, Bart	*Tower Hamlets*	17 Hertford street, Mayfair, and Fulwell lodge, Twickenham.
Clayton Rice Richard, Esq	*Aylesbury*	11 Portman sq. & Hedgerley park, Beaconsfield
Clements Viscount	*Leitrim*	(No address in London) Lough Rhynn, Mohill, Ireland.
Clerk Rt. Hon. Sir George, Bart	*Stamford*	8 Park street, Westminster, and Penicuich house, Edinburgh.
Clifton John Talbot, esq	*North Lancashire*	5 Wilton crescent, Belgrave square
Clive Hon. Robert Henry	*South Shropshire*	53 Grosvenor street, & Oakley park, near Ludlow, and Hewel, Broomsgrove, Worcestershire.
Clive Viscount	*North Shropshire*	45 Berkeley square
Cobden Richard, Esq	*Stockport*	(No address in London) Kay st. Manchester
Cockburn Rt. Hon. Sir George, G.C.B.	*Ripon*	Admiralty, Whitehall, and High Beech.
Codrington Sir Christopher Wm., Bart	*East Gloucestershire*	3 Park place, St. James's, and Doddington park near Chippenham, Wilts.
Cole Hon. Henry Arthur	*Enniskillen*	109 Jermyn street, St. James's
Colebrooke Sir Thomas Edward, Bart	*Taunton*	18 Park lane, & Abington, Lanarkshire, N. B.
Collett John, Esq	*Athlone*	7 Upper Belgrave street
Collett William Rickford, Esq	*Lincoln*	2A, St. James's square.
Collins William, Esq	*Warwick*	18 Pall Mall, & Warwick.
Colquhoun John Campbell, Esq	*Newcastle, Staffordshire*	8 Chesham street, and Killermount, Glasgow.
Colvile Charles Robert, Esq	*South Derbyshire*	10 St. James's place, and Duffield hall, Derby.
Compton Henry Combe, Esq	*South Hampshire*	34 Upper Eaton st. & Manor house, Lyndhurst.
Conolly Colonel Edward Michael	*Donegal County*	Brunswick hotel, 52 Jermyn st. & Castletown, near Celbridge, & Cliff, County Donegal.
Cooper Hon. Anthony Henry. See *Ashley-Cooper.*		
Coote Sir Charles Henry, Bart	*Queen's County*	Carlton club. & Ballyfin, near Montrath, Ireland
Copeland William Taylor (Alderman of London)	*Stoke upon Trent*	37 Lincoln's-inn-fields, & Lee house, Littlebury, & Leyton, Essex.
Corbally Matthew Elias, Esq	*Meath*	Cox's hotel, 55 Jermyn street, & Corbalton hall, Dunshaughlin, Ireland.
Corry Rt. Hon. Henry Thomas Lowry	*Tyrone County*	24 Grosvenor square, and Castle Cool, near Enniskillen, Ireland.
Courtenay Lord	*South Devonshire*	4 Bryanstone sq. & Powderham castle, Exeter
Cowper Hon. Wm. Francis, *a Lord of the Admiralty*	*Hertford*	39 South street, Grosvenor square.
Craig William Gibson, jun. Esq., *a Lord of the Treasury*	*Edinburgh*	27 Grosvenor place, & Riccarton, near Edinburgh.
Crawford William Sharman, Esq	*Rochdale*	Reform club, Pall mall, and Crawfordsburn, near Bangor, Ireland.
Cresswell Addison John Baker, Esq	*North Northumberland*	Carlton club, 94 Pall mall, and Cresswell, near Morpeth, Northumberland
Cripps William, Esq.	*Cirencester*	38 St. James's place, & Cirencester.
Currie Raikes, Esq	*Northampton*	4 Hyde park terrace
Curteis Herbert Barrett, Esq	*Rye*	16 Waterloo place, & Windmill hill, near Battle, Sussex
Dalmeny Lord	*Stirling, &c.*	20 Charles street, Berkeley square, & Dalmeny park, near Edinburgh.
Dalrymple Captain John	*Wigtonshire*	6 Bolton st. Piccadilly, & Culhorn house, Stranraer Wigtonshire.
Damer Rt. Hon. Col. Geo. Lionel Dawson	*Portarlington*	6 Tilney street, Park lane, and Came house, near Dorchester; and Roscrea, and Iron Mills, Queen's County.
Dashwood George Henry, Esq	*Wycombe*	Gloucester coffee ho. 248 Oxford st. & West Wycombe Park, Bucks.
Davies David Arthur Sanders, Esq	*Carmarthenshire*	University club, Pall mall east, and Pentrie, near Carmarthen
Dawson Hon. Captain Thomas Vesey	*Louth County*	3 Great Stanhope street.
Deedes William, Esq.	*East Kent*	21 Lower Belgrave street, & Sandling, Kent
Denison Edmund Beckett, Esq.	*West Riding of Yorkshire*	8 Duke street, Westminster, and Doncaster.
Denison John Evelyn, Esq.	*Malton*	Burlington house, 49 Piccadilly, and Ossington, hall, Tuxford, Notts.

Denison William Joseph, Esq.	*West Surrey*	90 Pall Mall, and Denbies, near Dorking.
Dennistoun John, Esq.	*Glasgow*	3 Grosvenor place houses, and Glasgow.
D'Eyncourt Right Hon. Charles Tennyson	*Lambeth*	35 Pall mall, and Baynes manor, near Market Raisin, Lincolnshire.
Dick Quintin, Esq.	*Maldon*	20 Curzon st.&Layer Marney hall,near Kelvedon.
Dickinson Francis Henry, Esq.	*West Somerset*	8 Up. Harley st. and King Weston, Somerton.
Disraeli Benjamin, Esq.	*Shrewsbury*	1 Grosvenor gate, Park lane
Divett Edward, Esq.	*Exeter*	79 Eaton square & Bystock, near Exmouth.
Dodd George, Esq.	*Maidstone*	9 Grosvenor place.
Don the O'Conor, see O'Conor Denis, Esq.		
Douglas James Douglas Stoddart, Esq.	*Rochester*	Jun. United Serv. Club,& Chilston pk.Maidstone
Douglas Sir Charles Eurwiche, Knt. *Commissioner of Greenwich Hospital*	*Warwick*	27 Wilton crescent, and Grenewich Hospital
Douglas Sir Howard, Bart., G.C.B., G.C.M.G., F.R.S.	*Liverpool*	15 Green st. Grosvenor sq. and Carr, Perthshire.
Douro Marquis of	*Norwich*	3 Upper Belgrave street, Belgrave square.
Dowdeswell William, Esq.	*Tewkesbury*	7 Park pl. St. James'&Pull Court, nr. Tewkesbury
Drax Joh^{n} Samuel Wanley Sawbridge Erle, Esq.	*Wareham*	Coulson's hotel, 45 Brook street, and Chadborough park, Blandford, Dorset, & Holnest house, near Sherborn, Dorset
Drummond Henry Home, Esq.	*Perthshire*	Carlton club, and Blairdrummond, Stirling.
Duckworth Sir John Thomas Buller, bart.	*Exeter*	Fenton's hotel, and Weir house, Exeter
Duff James, Esq.	*Banffshire*	31 Lowndes sq. and Delgaty castle, Turriff, N.B.
Dugdale William Stratford, Esq.	*North Warwickshire*	21 St. James's place.
Duke Sir James, Knt. Alderman.	*Boston*	1 Devonshire terrace, & Field place manor, near Horsham.
Duncan George, Esq.	*Dundee*	26 Gt. George st. Westminster.
Duncan Viscount	*Bath*	15 Hill st. Berkeley sq. and Sydney place, Bath, and Camperdown house, Dundee, Forfarshire.
Duncannon Viscount	*Derby*	3 Cavendish square.
Duncombe Hon. Arthur, Captain, R.N.	*Bassetlaw*	22Grosvenorsq.&Kilnwick Percy,Bradford,Yorks
Duncombe Hon. Octavius	*North Riding of Yorkshire*	24 Arlington st. & Waresley park, Caxton,Hunts.
Duncombe Thomas Slingsby, Esq.	*Finsbury*	F. 3 Albany, Piccadilly.
Dundas Admiral James Whitley Deans, *a Lord of the Admiralty*	*Greenwich*	4 LowerBerkeley st.&Barton court, near Hungerford, Berkshire, and Aston hall, Hawarden, North Wales.
Dundas David, Esq. *Solicitor General*	*Sutherlandshire*	13 Kings bench walk, Temple.
Dundas Frederick, Esq.	*Orkney and Zetland*	24 Hanover square.
Dundas Hon. John Charles	*Richmond, Yorkshire*	(no address in London) Oran, Catterick, Yorkshire.
Dunn-Gardner John, Esq. see Gardner-Dunn		
Du Pré Caledon George, Esq.	*Buckinghamshire*	40 Portland pl.&Wilton park,Beaconsfield,Bucks.
East James Buller, Esq.	*Winchester*	99 Eaton square.
Easthope Sir John, Bart.	*Leicester*	19 Grafton street, and Fir Grove, Weybridge.
Eastnor Viscount	*Reigate*	Carlton club, & Eastnor castle, nr. Tewkesbury
Eaton Richard Jefferson, Esq.	*Cambridgeshire*	6 Chesham pl. Belgrave sq. & Stetchworth park, Newmarket.
Ebrington Viscount, *a Lord of the Treasury*	*Plymouth*	17 Grosvenor square.
Egerton Sir Philip de Malpas Grey, Bart.	*South Cheshire*	(no address in London) Oulton pk.nr.Middlewich.
Egerton William Tatton, Esq.	*North Cheshire*	43Wilton cresnt.&Puddington hll. Neston,Chester
Ellice Right Hon. Edward	*Coventry*	13 Great Cumberland street
Ellice Edward, jun. Esq.	*Crail, St. Andrew's, &c.*	130 Park st. Grosvenor square, Invergarry & Glenquoich Lodge, Fort Augustus.
Ellis Wynn, Esq.	*Leicester*	30 Cadogan place, & Ponsbourn park, Hertford.
Elphinstone Sir Howard, Bart. D.C.L.	*Lewes*	19 Eaton place, and Ridge cottage, Hastings
Emlyn Viscount	*Pembrokeshire*	6 Eaton place.
Entwisle William, Esq	*South Lancashire*	1 Sussex square, & Rusham house, near Manchester
Escott Bickham, Esq.	*Winchester*	9 John st.Berkeley sq.&Hartrow court,Taunton.
Esmonde Sir Thomas, Bart.	*Wexford*	151 Regent street, and Gorey, Wexford.
Estcourt Thos. Grimston Bucknall, D.C.L.	*Oxford University*	82 Eaton place, and Estcourt, near Tetbury.
Etwall Ralph, Esq.	*Andover*	Oxford and Cambridge club, 71 Pall mall, and the Mount, Nursling, Southampton.
Evans Gen. Sir De Lacy, K.C.B.	*Westminster*	26 Bryanstone square.
Evans William, Esq.	*North Derbyshire*	Park house, Kensington gore, and Allistree hall near Derby.
Ewart William, Esq.	*Dumfries*	6 Cambridge square, Hyde park
Farnham Edward Basil, Esq.	*North Leicestershire*	Fenton's hotel,63 St.James's street, and Quorndon house, near Loughborough.
Feilden William, Esq.	*Blackburn*	18 Hanover sq. & Fenniscowles, near Blackburn.
Fellowes Edward, Esq.	*Huntingdonshire*	(no address in London), Ramsey Abbey, Huntingdonshire, & Haverling hall, Norfolk.
Ferguson Lieut.-Col. Robert	*Kirkaldy*	46 Clarges street, Mayfair, and Raith, Kirkaldy
Ferguson Sir Robert Alexander, Bart.	*Londonderry*	United University club, Pall mall east, and Th Farm, near Londonderry.
Ferrand William Busfeild, Esq.	*Knaresborough*	St. James's hotel, 76 Jermyn st. & Harden grange, Bingley, Yorkshire.
Ffolliott John, Esq.	*Sligo County*	Carlton club, 94 Pall Mall, & Holybrook, Boyle.
Fielden Sir John, Bart.	*Oldham*	31 Arundel st. Strand, & Todmorden, Rochdale.
Filmer Sir Edmund, Bart.	*West Kent*	72 Eaton sq. & East Sutton park, near Maidstone.
Finch George, esq.	*Rutlandshire*	29 Hill street, Berkeley square, & Burleigh-on-the-hill, Rutlandshire
Fitzgerald Richard Albert, Esq.	*Tipperary County*	(No address in London), Muckeridge house, County Cork.
Fitzmaurice Hon. William Edward	*Buckinghamshire*	4 Chesham street, Belgrave square, & Taplow, Maidenhead, Bucks.
Fitzroy Right Hon. Lord Charles	*Bury St. Edmunds*	3 Burlington gardens,& Salcey lodge, Northamptn

Fitzroy Hon. Henry, Capt. R.N.	*Lewes*	42 Upper Grosvenor street [Rotherham,
Fitzwilliam Hon. George Wentworth	*Peterborough*	Halkin st. Grosvenor pl. and Wentworth house.
Fleetwood Sir Peter Hesketh, Bart.	*Preston*	Athenæum club, 107 Pall mall, and Rossall hall, Fleetwood, near Preston.
Flower Sir James, Bart	*Thetford*	15 Wimpole street, Cavendish square, and Eccles hall, Larlingford, Norfolk.
Floyer John, Esq	*Dorsetshire*	5 Old Palace yard, Westminster, and West Stafford, Dorchester.
Forbes William, Esq	*Stirlingshire*	Carlton club, 94 Pall mall, and Callender house, Falkirk, Stirlingshire.
Forester Hon. George Cecil Weld	*Wenlock*	Regent's park barracks, & Willey pk. Shropshire
Forman Thomas Seaton, Esq.	*Bridgewater*	E 5, Albany. [Hampstead.
Forster Matthew, Esq.	*Berwick*	5 New City Chambers, Bishopsgate, and Belsise,
Fox Col. Charles Richard, *Surveyor-General of the Ordnance*	*Tower Hamlets*	Little Holland house, Addison road, Kensington
Fox Sackville Lane, Esq.	*Ipswich*	3 St. James' sq. and Oran house, Catterick
French Fitzstephen, Esq.	*Roscommon*	54 Parliament st. & French park, near Roscommon
Frewen Charles Hay, Esq	*East Sussex*	43 Pall mall, and Cold Overton hall, Leicestershire, and Northiam, Staplehurst.
Fuller Augustus Eliott, Esq.	*East Sussex*	16 Clifford st. and Rosehill, Robertsbridge, and Ashdown house, near East Grinstead, Sussex.
Gardner-Dunn John, Esq	*Bodmin*	14 Grosvenor st. and Chatteris, Isle of Ely
Gaskell James Milnes, Esq.	*Wenlock*	72 Grosvenor street, and Thornes house, near Wakefield, Yorkshire.
Gibson Thomas Milner, Esq. *Vice President of the Board of Trade*	*Manchester*	[mundham. 50 Wilton crescent, and Theberton house, Sax-
Gill Thomas, Esq	*Plymouth*	Reform club, 104 Pall mall, & the Crescent, Plymouth. [Buxton, Derbyshire.
Gisborne Thomas, jun. Esq.	*Nottingham*	(No address in London), Horwich house, near
Gladstone Sir John Neilstone, Bt. Capt. R.N.	*Ipswich*	80 Eaton place, & Fasque, Fettercairn, N.B.
Glynne Sir Stephen Richard, Bart.	*Flintshire*	13 Carlton terrace, & Hawarden castle, Chester
Godson Richard, Esq	*Kidderminster*	30 Grosvenor place. [tlesham, Suffolk
Gooch Edward Sherlock, Esq	*East Suffolk*	32 St. James's street, and Beacon hill, Mar-
Gordon Hon. William, Capt. R.N	*Aberdeenshire*	35 Hertford st. Mayfair, & Haddo ho. Aberdeen.
Gore Hon. Robert, Commander R.N.	*New Ross*	21 Wilton crescent.
Gore Montague, Esq	*Barnstaple*	39 Mount street, and Barrow court, near Bristol.
Gore William Richard Ormsby, Esq.	*Sligo County*	66 Portland place.
Gore William Ormsby, Esq.	*North Shropshire*	66 Portland pl. & Porkington hall, near Oswestry.
Goring Charles, Esq	*New Shoreham*	26 Pall mall, and Wiston near Steyning.
Goulburn Right Hon. Henry	*Cambridge University*	11 & 12 Downing street, and Beechworth house, near Dorking, Surrey.
Graham Rt. Hon. Sir James Robert George, Bart.	*Dorchester*	31 Hill street, Berkeley square, and Netherby hall, near Carlisle, Cumberland.
Granby, Marquis of	*Stamford*	5 St. James's place, and Belvoir castle, Grantham
Granger Thomas Colpitts, Esq.	*Durham City*	12 King's bench walk, Temple.
Grattan Henry, Esq.	*Meath County*	40 Piccadilly, & Stephen's green, Dublin.
Greene Thomas, Esq	*Lancaster*	19 Duke st. Westminster, and Whittington hall, Burton, Westmoreland, & Slyne, Lancaster
Gregory William Henry, Esq.	*Dublin City*	14 Park street, Grosvenor square.
Grey Right Hon. Sir George, Bart. *Sec. of State (Home Department)*	*Devonport*	14 Eaton place, Belgrave square
Grimsditch Thomas, Esq	*Macclesfield*	Ginger's hotel, Bridge street, Westminster, and Brook Park, near Macclesfield.
Grogan Edward, Esq	*Dublin City*	Carlton club, 94 Pall mall, & Harcourt st. Dublin
Grosvenor Rt. Hon. Lord Robt. *Treasurer of Her Majesty's Household*	*Chester*	107 Park street. [Merthyr Tidvil·
Guest Sir Josiah John, Bart.	*Merthyr Tidvil*	8 Spring gardens, and Dowlais house, near
Hale Robert Blagden, Esq.	*West Gloucestershire*	15 Bolton street, Piccadilly, and Alderley park, near Wootton-under-edge.
Halford Sir Henry, bart.	*South Leicestershire*	8 Bolton st. Piccadilly, & Wistow hall, Leicester.
Hall Sir Benjamin, Bart.	*Marylebone*	2 St. James's place, St. James's street, and Llanover Court, Abergavenny, and Abercarne, near Newport, Monmouth.
Hall Lieut. Col. Robert	*Buckingham*	(No address in London), Windsor barracks.
Hallyburton Lord John Fred. Gordon G.C.H. Capt. R.N.	*Forfarshire*	Kensington palace.
Halsey Thomas Plumer, Esq.	*Hertfordshire*	Carlton club, & the Hall, Great Berkhampstead
Hamilton Capt. Charles John Baillie	*Aylesbury*	21 New street, Spring gardens, & Thame park, near Tetsworth, Oxon. [Ireland
Hamilton George Alexander, Esq.	*Dublin University*	20 Chester square, & Hampton hall, Balbriggan
Hamilton James Hans, Esq.	*Dublin County*	Carlton club, 94 Pall Mall, Abbotstown, Castle
Hamilton Lord Claude	*Tyrone*	19 Eaton square [Knock, Ireland.
Hamilton William John, Esq.	*Newport, Isle of Wight*	14 Chesham place, Belgrave square.
Hampden Renn, Esq.	*Great Marlow*	Ellis's hotel, 59 St. James's street, and Marlow House, Little Marlow, Bucks.
Hanmer Sir John, Bart.	*Hull*	59 Eaton pl. & Bettisfield park, Whitchurch, Salop.
Harcourt George Granville, Esq	*Oxfordshire*	24 St. James's place, and Nuneham park, near Oxford, and East Sheen, Surrey.
Hardy John, Esq	*Bradford*	3 Portland place, and Warty park, Winchester
Harris Hon. Edward Alfred J. Capt. R.N.	*Christchurch*	8 Whitehall gardens, and Christchurch, Hants
Hastie Archibald, Esq.	*Paisley*	5 Rutland gate, Knightsbridge, & 3 West st Finsbury circus.
Hatton Villiers Francis, Captain, R.N.	*Wexford County*	United Service club, and Delgarry, Wicklow
Hawes Benjamin, jun. Esq., *Under Sec. of State (Colonial Depart.*	*Lambeth*	6 Queen square, St. James's park

Hay Col. Sir Andrew Leith, Knt........	*Elgin, &c. district of Burghs*	Reform club, 104 Pall mall
Hayes Sir Edmund Samuel, Bart.......	*Donegal County*	15 Chesham street, Belgrave square, & Drumboe castle, near Stranorlar, Ireland.
Hayter William Goodenough, Esq......	*Wells*..................	11 Hyde park terrace, and Wells, Somersetshire.
Heathcoat John, Esq..................	*Tiverton*	5 Warwick street, Charing cross, and Bolham, near Tiverton.
Heathcote Gilbert John, Esq..........	*Rutlandshire*	(No address in London), Stockenhall, Grantham
Heathcote Sir William, Bart..........	*North Hampshire*.........	43 Eaton place, and Hursley park, Winchester.
Heneage Edward, Esq..................	*Great Grimsby*	12 Devonshire place, Marylebone, and Hainton hall, near Lincoln. [Calne, Wiltshire.
Heneage George Heneage Walker, Esq.	*Devizes*...................	(No address in London), Compton Basset, near
Henley Joseph Warner, Esq...........	*Oxfordshire*	22 Gt. George street, Westminster, & Waterperry, near Wheatley, Oxfordshire.
Hepburn Sir Thomas Buchan, Bart.....	*Haddingtonshire*	Carlton club, 94 Pall mall, and Smeaton, Prestonkirk, Scotland.
Herbert Rt. Hon. Sidney	*South Wiltshire*	5 Carlton gardens, & Wilton house, Salisbury
Heron Sir Robert, Bart...............	*Peterborough*	Brookes's club, and Stubton hall, near Grantham.
Hervey Lord Alfred....................	*Brighton*	6 St. James' square, and Ickworth park, Bury St. Edmond's, and Kemp Town, Brighton
Hildyard Thos. Blackborne Thorston, Esq.	*South Nottinghamshire*	60 Grosvenor street, Grosvenor sq. and Flintham
Hill Lord Edwin.......................	*Down County*..............	21 Hanover square .... [hall, Newark
Hill Rt. Hon. Lord Arthur Marcus Cecil *Comptroller of H. M. Household*..	*Evesham*	2 Chesham street, Belgrave square.
Hinde John Hodgson, Esq.............	*Newcastle-on-Tyne*	13 Upper Brook street, and Acton house, Felton, Northumberland
Hindley Charles, Esq.................	*Ashton-under-Lyne*........	Dartmouth house, 1 Dartmouth st. Westminster, and Dukinfield Lodge, nr. Ashton-under-Lyne.
Hobhouse Rt. Hon. Sir John Cam, Bart. *President of the Board of Control*	*Nottingham*..............	42 Berkeley square, and Earl Stoke park, near Devizes.
Hodgson Frederick, Esq..............	*Barnstaple*	3 Carlton gardens [castle-on-Tyne.
Hodgson Richard, Esq................	*Berwick-on-Tweed*.........	13 Up. Brook st. and Stelling hall, near New-
Hogg Sir James Weir, Bart............	*Beverley*	40 Upper Grosvenor street.
Hollond Robert, Esq..................	*Hastings*	63 Portland place, and the Allegria, near St. Leonard's-on-Sea, Sussex.
Holmes Hon. Wm. Henry Ashe A'Court	*Isle of Wight*	Burlington hotel, 19 Cork street, and Westover near Newport, Isle of Wight.
Hope Alexander James Beresford, Esq..	*Maidstone*................	1 Connaught place, and Bedgbury park, Goudhurst, Lamberhurst, Kent
Hope George William, Esq............	*Southampton*	14 Curzon street, May fair, and Lufness, Haddington, N. B.
Hope Sir John, bart..................	*Edinburghshire*	14 St. James's place, and Craighall, Fifeshire.
Hornby John, Esq.....................	*Blackburn*................	10 Dover street, Piccadilly
Horsman Edward, Esq.................	*Cockermouth*.............	6 Upper Brook street. [fordshire.
Hoskins Kedgwin, Esq.................	*Herefordshire*	90 Sloane st. & Birch house, near Ross, Here-
Hotham Lord..........................	*East Riding of Yorkshire*...	7 Hill street, Berkeley square, and South Dalton hall, near Beverley, Yorkshire.
Houldsworth Thomas, Esq............	*North-west Nottinghamsh*..	16 Suffolk street, Pall mall east, and Portland place, Manchester.
Howard Hon. Charles Wentworth George	*East Cumberland*..........	56 Park street, Grosvenor square, and Naworth Castle, Brampton
Howard Hon. Edward George Granville, Capt. R.N.	*Morpeth*	86 Eaton place, & Castle Howard, Yorkshire.
Howard Hon. Henry Thomas	*Cricklade*.................	(No address in London), Charlton pk. Malmesbury
Howard Hon. James Kenneth..........	*Malmesbury*	(No address in London), Charlton pk. Malmesbury
Howard Philip Henry, Esq.............	*Carlisle*..................	15 Gloucester place, and Corby castle, near Carlisle.
Howard Sir Ralph, Bart...............	*Wicklow County*	17 Belgrave square, and Bushy park, near Bray, Wicklow County.
Hudson George, Esq..................	*Sunderland*	Albert gate, Knightsbridge, and York
Hughes William Bulkeley, Esq.........	*Carnarvon*	Carlton club, and Plâs-Coêh, Anglesey.
Hume Joseph, Esq.....................	*Montrose, &c*.............	6 Bryanston sq. & Somerton hall, Yarmouth Norfk
Humphery John, Esq..................	*Southwark*	Hay's wharf, Tooley street, & Clapham common
Hurst Robert Henry, esq..............	*Horsham*	(No address in London) Horsham park, Surrey
Hussey Ambrose, Esq..................	*Salisbury*.................	4 Upper Woburn place, and New st. Salisbury
Hussey Thomas, Esq..................	*Lyme Regis*...............	42 St. James's place, and Lyme Regis, Dorset.
Hutt William, Esq....................	*Gateshead*	39 Maddox st. Regent st. & Gibside, Gateshead
Ingestre Viscount, C.B., Capt. R.N.	*South Staffordshire*	Carlton club, 94 Pall mall, and Brompton park, Middlesex, and Ingestre, Staffordshire
Inglis Sir Robert Harry, Bart. D.C.L....	*Oxford University*	7 Bedford sq. and Milton Bryan, near Woburn.
Irton Samuel, Esq....................	*West Cumberland*	Carlton club, 94 Pall mall, and Irton hall, near Ravenglass.
James Sir Walter Charles, Bart........	*Hull (Kingston upon)*......	11 Whitehall place.
James William, Esq...................	*East Cumberland*	15 Regent street, & Barrack lodge, near Carlisle.
Jermyn Rt. Hon. Earl.................	*Bury St. Edmunds*	47 Eaton place, Belgrave square, and Ickworth park, Bury St. Edmunds.
Jervis Sir John, Knt. *Attorney General*	*Chester*	42 Eaton square, and 3 Old Palace yard.
Jocelyn Viscount.....................	*Lynn Regis*...............	35 Curzon street, May fair, & Tullamore park, Dundalk, Ireland, & Hyde hall, Sawbridgeworth.
Johnson Gen. William Augustus........	*Oldham*	21 Suffolk street, Pall mall east, and Wytham hill, Bourne, Lincolnshire.
Johnstone John James Hope, Esq......	*Dumfriesshire*............	(No address in London), Rayhill, Moffat, Scotland
Johnstone Sir John Vanden Bempde, Bart.	*Scarborough*.............	27 Grosvenor sq. and Hackness hall, Scarbro'.
Jolliffe Sir William George Hylton, Bart.	*Petersfield*	Carlton club, 94 Pall mall, & Merstham, Surrey, and Heath house, Petersfield
Jones Theobald, Capt, R.N.............	*Londonderry County*	30 Charles street, St. James', and 18 Harcourt street, Dublin

Lawless Cecil, Esq	*Clonmel*	(No address in London)
Kelly Sir Fitzroy, Knt. Q.C	*Cambridge*	8 Figtree court, Temple
Kelly James, Esq.	*Limerick City*	(no address in London), Erina house, county Clare.
Kemble Henry, Esq.	*East Surrey*	Grove hill, Camberwell.
Ker David Stewart, Esq.	*Downpatrick*	11 Upper Grosvenor st. & Portavoe, near Donaghadee
Kerrison Lieut. Gen. Sir Edward, Bart. G.C.H., K.C.B.	*Eye*	13 Great Stanhope st. Mayfair, and 27 Brunswick terrace, Brighton, and Oakley park, near Eye.
Kirk Peter, Esq	*Carrickfergus*	Carlton club, 94 Pall mall, and Thornfield, near Carrickfergus.
Knight Frederick Winn, Esq.	*West Worcestershire*	10 Dover st. & Wolverly house, Kidderminster.
Knightley Sir Charles, Bart.	*South Northamptonshire*	10 Upper Brook st. & Fawsley pk. near Daventry,
Labouchere Right Hon. Henry, *Chief Secretary for Ireland*	*Taunton*	27 Belgrave square, and Stowey, Bridgewater, and the Castle, Dublin.
Lambton Hedworth, Esq.	*North Durham*	Farrance's hotel, 11 Upper Belgrave street
Langston James Haughton, Esq.	*Oxford*	143 Piccadilly; Sarsden house, Chipping Norton
Langton William Gore, Esq.	*East Somersetshire*	12 Grosvenor sq. & Newton park, near Bath, & Acton, Middlesex.
Lascelles Hon. Edwin	*Ripon*	4 Belgrave sq. & Harewood house, Leeds, Yorks
Lascelles Hon. William Sebright	*Wakefield*	Bute house, Campden hill, Kensington
Law Hon. Charles Ewan, M.A. *Recorder of London*	*Cambridge University*	72 Eaton place, and Farrar's bldg. Temple
Lawson Andrew, Esq.	*Knaresborough*	26 Pall mall, and the Hall, Boroughbridge.
Layard Capt. Brownlow Villiers	*Carlow*	Reform club, & Upper Mount street, Dublin.
Leader John Temple, Esq	*Westminster*	Putney hill, Surrey.
Lefevre Rt. Hon. Charles Shaw	*North Hampshire*	SPEAKER OF THE HOUSE OF COMMONS, 71 Eaton sq. and Heckfield pl. Hartford bridge.
Lefroy Anthony, esq	*Longford*	18 Chesham place, Belgrave square, and Carrickglass, Longford, Ireland.
Legh George Cornwall, Esq	*North Cheshire*	Carlton Club, & High Legh, Warrington.
Le Marchant Sir Denis, Bart.	*Worcester*	7 Harley street, and Chobham place, Surrey
Lemon Sir Charles, Bart.	*West Cornwall*	46 Charlesstreet, Berkeley square, & Carlew, near Penryn.
Lennox Lord Henry Charles George	*Chichester*	51 Portland place
Leslie Charles Powell, Esq.	*Monaghan*	(no address in London) Glasslough, Monaghan.
Liddell Hon. Henry Thomas	*North Durham*	6 Eaton place, and Ravensworth Castle, Gateshead, Durham.
Lincoln Rt. Hon. Earl of	*Falkirk, &c.*	19 Whitehall pl. and Ranby hall, near Retford, Notts
Lindsay Hugh Hamilton, Esq	*Sandwich*	22 Berkeley square
Lindsay Hon. Capt. James	*Wigan*	21 Berkeley square
Loch James, Esq	*Wick, Kirkwall, &c.*	12 Albemarle street, and Wimbledon common
Lockhart Allan Eliott, Esq	*Selkirkshire*	4 Down st. Piccadilly, & Borthwick-Brae, Selkirk.
Lockhart William, Esq	*Lanarkshire*	Carlton club, 94 Pall mall, and Milton-Lockhart, near Lanark
Long Walter, Esq.	*North Wiltshire*	29 Hill street, and Rood Ashton, near Trowbridge.
Lopes Sir Ralph, Bart.	*Westbury*	46 Upper Grosvenor st. & Maristow, Plymouth
Lowther Lieut.-Col. Hon. Henry Cecil	*Westmoreland*	31 Bruton street, and Borleythorpe, Oakham.
Lowther Sir John Henry, Bart.	*York*	32 Grosvenor square, and Swillington hall, near Leeds, and Wilton castle, near Guisboro'
Lyall George, Esq	*London*	17 Park crescent, Portland place, and Findon, near Shoreham, and Nutwood lodge, Gatton.
ygon Hon. Maj. Gen. Henry Beauchamp	*West Worcestershire*	16 Grosvenor pl. and Springhill, near Broadway, Worcestershire.
M'Carthy Alexander, Esq.	*Cork*	(no address in London), Up. Fitzwilliam st. Dublin
M'Clintoch William Bunbury, Esq	*Carlow County*	Moyle, County Carlow
M'Donnell Joseph Myles, Esq	*Mayo*	(No address in London)
Macaulay Rt. Hon. Thomas Babington, *Paymaster General of the Forces*	*Edinburgh*	E 1 Albany.
MacGeachy Forster Alleyne, Esq.	*Honiton*	33 St. James's place, and Windsor terrace, Clifton, Gloucestershire.
Mackenzie Thomas, Esq.	*Ross and Cromartyshires*	17 Clarges street, Piccadilly, & Applecross, near Dingwall, Scotland
Mackenzie William Forbes, Esq.	*Peeblesshire*	Carlton club, and Portmore, near Eddleston, N.B.
Mackinnon William Alexander, Esq.	*Lymington*	4 Hyde park place, Cumberland gate
Maclean Donald, Esq	*Oxford*	28 Upper Brook street, 1 New court, Temple, United University club, Pall Mall East, and Witton castle, Bishops-Auckland.
Macnamara William Nugent, Esq.	*Clare County*	Junior United Service club, 11 Charles street, St. James's, and Doolin, near Ennistimon, Ireland.
M'Neill Rt. Hon. Duncan	*Argyllshire*	9 Charles street, Grosvenor square.
M'Taggart Sir John, Bart.	*Wigtoun, &c.*	22 Manchester sq. and Ardwell, near Wigtoun.
Maher Nicholas, Esq	*Tipperary County*	Reform club, 104 Pall mall
Mahon Viscount	*Hertford*	41 Grosvenor place, & Chevening park, Seven Oaks, Kent
Mainwaring Townshend, Esq.	*Denbigh*	Carlton club, 94 Pall mall, & Murchwell hall, Denbigh.
Maitland Thomas, Esq. *Solicitor-General for Scotland*	*Kircudbright*	105 Jermyn st. & Dundrennan, Kircudbright
Mangles Ross Donnelly, Esq	*Guildford*	17 Arundel st. Haymkt. & Woodbridge, Guildford
Manners Lord Chas. Somerset	*North Leicestershire*	E 3 Albany, & Belvoir castle, near Grantham.
Manners Lord John James Robert	*Newark*	C 4 Albany, & Belvoir castle, near Grantham.
Manners-Sutton Hon. John Henry Thos.	*Cambridge*	11 Southwick cres. & King st. Norwich.
March Earl of	*West Sussex*	(No address in London) Molcombe cottage, Chichester.
Marjoribanks Stewart, Esq.	*Hythe*	6 Charles st. Berkeley sq. & Bushey grove, Watford
Marshall William, Esq	*Carlisle*	55 Lowndes square, and Patterdale hall, near Penrith, and Edge grove, Watford.
Marsland Henry, Esq.	*Stockport*	Reform Club, & Wood Bank, near Stockport
Martin Charles Wykeham, Esq.	*Newport, Isle of Wight*	(No address in London) Leeds castle, nr. Maidstone
Martin John, Esq.	*Tewkesbury*	14 Berkeley sq., and Ledbury, Herefordshire.

Martin Thomas Barnwell, Esq.	*Galway County*	2 Trinity place, Charing Cross, and Ballinahinc near Onterard, Galway, Ireland. [Lancaster
Marton George, Esq.	*Lancaster*	(No address in London) Capernwray hall, near
Masterman John, Esq.	*London*	35 Nicholas la. & Knotts green, Leyton, Essex.
Matheson James, esq	*Ashburton*	Stornaway house, 13 Cleveland row & Coul house, Dingwall & Stornaway, Lewis, Ross-shire
Maule Right Hon. Fox, *Secretary at War*	*Perth*	38 Grosvenor street, and Birnam lodge, Dunkeld, Perthshire, Scotland.
Maunsell Thomas Philip, Esq	*North Northamptonshire*	Carlton club, and Thorp Malson, Kettering.
Maxwell Capt. the Hon. James Pierce	*Cavan*	Carlton club, 94 Pall mall, and Farnham, Cavan.
Meynell Henry, Captain R.N., *Groom in Waiting to Her Majesty*	*Lisburn*	14 Hill street, Berkeley square.
Mildmay Humphrey St. John, esq	*Southampton*	46 Berkeley sq. & Oxford court, Shoreham, Kent
Miles Philip William Skynner, Esq.	*Bristol*	44 Belgrave square, & Kingsweston, near Bristol.
Miles William, Esq	*East Somersetshire*	7 Hamilton pl. and Kingsweston, near Bristol.
Milnes Richard Monckton, Esq	*Pontefract*	26 Pall mall, and Frystone hall, near Ferrybridge.
Milton Viscount	*Malton*	4 Grosvenor sq. & Wentworth house, Rotherham.
Mitcalfe Henry, Esq	*Tynemouth*	8 Delahay street, and Whitley, Morpeth.
Mitchell Thomas Alexander, Esq	*Bridport*	B 6 Albany.
Moffatt George, Esq	*Dartmouth*	85 Eaton square
Molesworth Sir William, Bart.	*Southwark*	1 Lowndes square, and Pencarrow, Bodmin
Morgan Charles Morgan Robinson, Esq.	*Brecon*	70 Pall mall, & Ruperra castle, Newport, Mnmth.
Morgan Charles Octavius Swinnerton, Esq	*Monmouthshire*	70 Pall mall, and Tredegar, Newport, Monmouth.
Morison Major Gen. Wm. C.B	*Clackmannan & Kinross*	16 Saville row, and Greenfield, Clackmannan.
Morpeth Right Hon. Viscount, *First Commissioner of Woods & Forests*	*West Riding of Yorkshire*	12 Grosvenor place
Morris David, Esq	*Carmarthen*	8 St. James's place, and King street, Carmarthen.
Morrison James, Esq.	*Fortrose, &c.*	57 Upper Harley street, and Fonthill, Wilts, and Basildon, Reading, Berkshire.
Mostyn Hon. Edward Mostyn Lloyd	*Lichfield*	9 Lower Seymour st. & Mostyn, Holywell, Flintshire
Munday Edward Miller, Esq	*South Derbyshire*	19 Pall mall, and Shipley hall, Derby.
Muntz George Frederick, Esq	*Birmingham*	5 St. James's sq. & Ley hall, near Birmingham
Napier Commodore Sir Chas. Knt. K.C.B.	*Marylebone*	8 Duke street, St. James's, and Merchistoun hall, Horndean, Hants. [lade, Wiltshire.
Neeld John, Esq	*Cricklade*	(no address in London), Red lodge, near Crick-
Neeld Joseph, Esq	*Chippenham*	6 Grosvenor sq. & Grittleton house, Chippenham, & Kelston park, Bath, Somersetshire
Neville Ralph, Esq.	*Windsor*	15 Cavendish square
Newdegate Charles Newdegate, esq	*North Warwickshire*	3 Arlington st. St. James's, and Harefield place, near Uxbridge, & Arbury park, Coventry.
Newport Viscount	*South Shropshire*	30 Wilton crescent, Belgrave square.
Newry Viscount	*Newry*	Carlton club, & Morne park, Rostrevor, Ireland.
Nicholl Rt. Hon. John, D.C.L.	*Cardiff, &c.*	33 Belgrave square, & Merthyrmawr, near Bridgend, Glamorganshire, S.W.
Norreys Sir Denham Jephson, Bart	*Mallow*	Union club, and The Castle, Mallow, Cork.
Norreys Lord	*Oxfordshire*	18 Grosvenor street, Grosvenor square.
Northland Viscount	*Dungannon*	40 Berkeley sq. & Northland house, Dungannon.
O'Brien Augustus Stafford, Esq	*North Northamptonshire*	175 Piccadilly, & Blatherwick park, Wansford.
O'Brien Cornelius, Esq	*Clare County*	8 Gray's inn place, and Ennistimon, Ireland.
O'Brien John, Esq.	*Limerick City*	Reform club, 104 Pall mall, & Ennis, County Clare
O'Brien Timothy, Esq.	*Cashel*	(No address in London) & Merrion square, Dublin
O'Brien William Smith, Esq.	*Limerick County*	Oxford & Cambridge club, 71 Pall mall, & Cahirmoyle, near Rathleake, Co' Limerick, Ireland.
O'Connell Daniel, Esq.	*Cork County*	British hotel, 83 Jermyn st. & Merrion square, Dublin, & Darrynane abbey, near Cahirciveen.
O'Connell Daniel, Jun. Esq.	*Dundalk*	(No address in London)
O'Connell John, Esq.	*Kilkenny*	British hotel, Jermyn st. & Merrion sq. Dublin.
O'Connell Maurice, Esq.	*Tralee*	Merrion square, Dublin
O'Connell Morgan John, Esq.	*Kerry County*	Reform Club, Pall mall, & Greena, Killarney
O'Conor Denis, Esq. (The O'Conor Don) *a Lord of the Treasury*	*Roscommon*	British hotel 83 Jermyn street, and Cloonalis near Castlerea, Roscommon.
O'Ferrall Richard More, Esq	*Kildare County*	British hotel, 83 Jermyn st. & Brookes' club, St. James's street, & Ballyna house bridge, near Clonard, Ireland
Ogle Savile Craven Henry, Esq	*South Northumberland*	41 St. James's street, & Kirkley hall, Newcastle
Ord William, Esq.	*Newcastle-on-Tyne*	17 Berkeley sq. & Whitfield hall, Haydon bridge,
Osborne Ralph, Esq.	*Wycomb*	(No address in London) [Northumberland
Ossulston Lord	*North Northumberland*	17 South street, Grosvenor square, and Walton Esher, and Chillingham castle, near Belford.
Oswald Alexander, Esq.	*Ayrshire*	(No address in London), Cavens, Dumfries.
Oswald James, Esq.	*Glasgow*	14 Arlington st. Piccadilly; 52 Claremont pl. Glasgow; Auchincruive, Ayrshire; Cavens, Kircudbrightshire; & the Holy Isle, Arran
Owen Sir John, Bart., *Lord Lieut. of Pembrokeshire*	*Pembrokeshire*	Arthur's club, 69 St. James's street, and Taynton house, Newent, Gloucestershire
Packe Charles William, Esq.	*South Leicestershire*	7 Richmond terrace, Whitehall, and Prestwold hall, near Loughborough, & Glenn, nr. Leicester
Paget Lieut. Col. Frederick	*Beaumaris*	5 John street, Berkeley square.
Paget Lord Alfred Hy. *Clerk Marshall & Chief Equerry to Her Majesty*	*Lichfield*	Uxbridge house, 1 Old Burlington street.
Paget Lord William	*Andover*	Hotel de Provençe, 18 Leicester sq. [Droitwich.
Pakington Sir John Somerset, Bart.	*Droitwich*	55 Eaton place, and Westwood park, near
Palmer George, Esq.	*South Essex*	11 King's arms yard, and Nazing park, near Waltham cross, Essex.
Palmer Robert, Esq.	***Berkshire***	**Mould's hotel, 16 Suffolk st. Pallmall east, & Holme park, Reading.**

Palmerston Right Hon. Viscount, G.C.B. *Secretary of State for Foreign Affairs*	*Tiverton*	3 Carlton house terrace, & Broadlands, Romsey.
Parker John, Esq. *Secretary of the Treasury*	*Sheffield*	Athenæum club, and Woodthorpe, Sheffield.
Patten John Wilson, Esq.	*North Lancashire*	24 Hill st. Berkeley sq. and Light Oaks, Cheadle, Staffordshire, and Bank hall, Warrington.
Pattison James, Esq.	*London*	37 Upper Harley street.
Paulet Lord William	*St. Ives, Cornwall*	19 Curzon street, Mayfair.
Pechell George Richard, Capt. RN	*Brighton*	4 Spring gardens, & Castle Goring, near Worthing
Peel Col. Jonathan	*Huntingdon*	8 Park pl. St. James's & Marble Hall, Twickenham
Peel Right Hon. Sir Robert, Bart.	*Tamworth*	4 Whitehall gardens, and Drayton Manor house near Fazeley, Tamworth.
Pendarves Edward William Wynne, Esq.	*West Cornwall*	36 Eaton place, and Pendarves, near Truro.
Pennant Lieut. Col. Hon. Edward Gordon Douglas	*Carnarvonshire*	36 Belgrave sq. & Penrhyn castle, Bangor, and Wicken park, Stoney Stratford
Philipps Sir Richd. Bulkeley Philipps, Bt	*Haverfordwest*	23 Dover street and Picton castle, near Haverfordwest
Philips George Richard, Esq.	*Poole*	12 Hill street, Berkeley square, and Weston house, near Chipping Norton, Oxon.
Philips Mark, Esq	*Manchester*	Brooke's club, 60 St. James's street, and The Park, near Manchester.
Phillpotts John, Esq	*Gloucester*	Reform club, 104 Pall mall, and Porthgwidden, [Truro.
Pigot Sir Robert, Bart.	*Bridgenorth*	30 Albemarle street, Piccadilly, and Patishull, near Stafford
Plumptre John Pemberton, Esq.	*East Kent*	University club, Pall mall east, and Fredville, near Wingham.
Plumridge James Hanway, Capt. R.N.	*Penryn and Falmouth*	66 Chester square.
Polhill Frederic, Esq	*Bedford*	10 King William st. Strand, and Huwbery hall, near Bedford.
Pollington Viscount.	*Pontefract*	2 Bolton row, and Methley park, Wakefield.
Ponsonby Hon. Chas. Fred. Ashley Cooper.	*Poole*	24 George street, Hanover square
Powell Caleb, Esq.	*Limerick County*	Reform club, and Clanshavoy, County Limerick.
Powell Col. William Edward, *Lord Lieut. of Cardiganshire*	*Cardiganshire*	7 Hyde park terrace, and Nanteos house, near Aberystwith, South Wales.
Power James, Esq.	*Wexford County*	151 Regent st. & Edermine house, near Wexford
Price Richard, Esq	*Radnor (New)*	United University club, Pall mall east, and Norton house, near Presteign, Radnorshire.
Price Sir Robert, Bart.	*Hereford*	Waterloo hotel, Jermyn st. & Foxford, nr. Hereford
Protheroe Edward, jun. Esq	*Halifax*	12 Cottage road, Chester square, & Turnwood, Blandford, Dorset.
Pryse Pryse, Esq.	*Cardigan*	Limmer's hotel, 1 George st. Hanover sq. and Aberystwith, and Buscot park, Farringdon.
Pulsford Robert, Esq	*Hereford*	6 Upper Belgrave street, Belgrave square.
Pusey Philip, Esq.	*Berkshire*	35 Grosvenor sq. & Pusey house, near Farringdon
Rashleigh William, jun. Esq.	*East Cornwall*	16 Stratford place, Oxford st. & Menabilly, near Fowey, Cornwall.
Rawdon Lieut. Col. John Dawson	*Armagh*	3 Gt. Stanhope st. Mayfair, & Linton, Devonshire
Reid Sir John Rae, Bart.	*Dover*	4 Eaton place, Belgrave square, & Ewell grove, Surrey.
Reid Lieut. Col. George Alexander	*Windsor*	Bulstrode park, Buckinghamshire.
Rendlesham Rt. Hon. Lord	*East Suffolk*	11 Hertford street, May fair
Repton George William John, Esq	*St. Albans*	27 Norfolk street, Park lane.
Ricardo John Lewis, Esq	*Stoke-upon-Trent*	31 Lowndes square, Knightsbridge.
Rice Edward Royd, Esq.	*Dover*	United University club, Pall mall east, and Dane court, Sandwich, Kent.
Rich Henry, Esq., *a Lord of the Treasury*	*Richmond, Yorkshire*	7 Mount street, Berkeley square.
Richards Richard, Esq	*Merionethshire*	21 Park crescent, and Caerynwch, near Dolgelly.
Roche Edmund Burke, Esq.	*Cork County*	Reform club, 104 Pall mall, and Trabolgan, near Cloyne, Ireland.
Roebuck John Arthur, Esq	*Bath*	12 Victoria sq. Pimlico, & 3 Essex court, Temple.
Rolleston Col. Lancelot	*South east Nottinghamshire*	8 Hertford st. Mayfair, & Watnall hall, near Nottingham.
Romilly John, Esq.	*Bridport*	32 Gordon square, & 6 New square, Lincoln's inn
Ross David Robert, Esq.	*Belfast*	Reform club, Pall mall, and Rosstrevor, Ireland.
Round Charles Gray, Esq.	*North Essex*	25 Upp. Brook st. & Birch hall, near Colchester.
Round John, Esq.	*Maldon*	(No address in London), 15 Brunswk. sq. Brightn
Rumbold Charles Edmund, Esq.	*Yarmouth*	13 Bury street, St. James's, and Preston, Candover, near Basingstoke, Hants.
Russell Charles, Esq.	*Reading*	27 Charles st. St. James's, and Swallowfield, near Reading.
Russell Jesse David Watts, Esq	*North Staffordshire*	9 Chesham place, Belgrave square
Russell Lord Edward	*Tavistock*	8 Park lane.
Russell Right Hon. Lord John, *First Lord of the Treasury*	*London*	32 Chesham place, Belgrave square
Rutherfurd Right Hon. Andrew, *Lord Advocate of Scotland*	*Leith, &c*	Grove's hotel, 49 Albemarle st. & St. Colme st. Edinburgh.
Ryder Hon. Granville Dudley	*Hertfordshire*	39 Grosvenor sq. & Westbrook, Hemelhempsted.
Sanderson Richard, Esq.	*Colchester*	46 Belgrave square, and Gunton Park, Aylsham.
Sandon Viscount	*Liverpool*	39 Grosvenor square, and Norton, near Campden, and Sandon, Stafford.
Scott Hon. Francis	*Roxburghshire*	Carlton club, and Anglesea villa, Gosport
Scott Robert, Esq	*Walsall*	7 Manchester buildings.
Scrope George Poulett, Esq.	*Stroud*	13 Belgrave square, & Castle Combe house, Chip- [penham.

Seymer Henry Ker, Esq	*Dorsetshire*	(No address in London), Hanford house, Dorsetshire
Seymour Lord	*Totness*	18 Spring gardens, & Burton Hall, Loughborough.
Seymour Sir Horace Beauchamp, K.C.H.	*Antrim County*	28 St. James's pl. and Stoke house, Chichester.
Shaw Right Hon. Frederick, *Recorder of Dublin*	*Dublin University*	(No address in London), Kimmage house, near Dublin.
Sheil Right Hon. Richard Lalor, *Master of the Mint*	*Dungarvon*	73 Eccleston sq. and Long Orchard, Tipperary
Shelburne Earl of	*Calne*	54 Berkeley sq. & Bowood, near Calne, Wiltshire.
Sheppard Thomas, Esq	*Frome*	20 Great George st. Westminster, & Hampstead.
Sheridan Richard Brinsley, Esq	*Shaftesbury*	18 Spring gardens.
Shirley Evelyn John, Esq.	*South Warwickshire*	20 Belgrave sq. & Eatington park, Shipston on Stour and Loughfea, Carrickmacross, Ireland.
Shirley Evelyn Philip, Esq	*Monaghan County*	95 Eaton sq. & Lower Eatington pk. near Shipston on Stour; & Lough Fea, Carrackmacross, Ireland
Sibthorp Col. Charles De Laet Waldo	*Lincoln*	27 Chester street, Grosvenor square, & Canwick hall, near Lincoln.
Smith Abel, Esq	*Hertfordshire*	39 Berkeley sq. and Woodhall park, near Ware.
Smith Benjamin, Esq	*Norwich*	5 Blandford square, and Hastings, Sussex.
Smith John Abel, Esq	*Chichester*	47 Belgrave square, and Dale park, Arundel
Smithwick Richard, Esq	*Kilkenny County*	11 Beak street, Regent street
Smollett Alexander, Esq	*Dumbartonshire*	43 Pall mall, & Cameron house, Dumbarton.
Smyth Sir George Henry, Bart	*Colchester*	Limmer's Hotel, 1 George street, Hanover square, and Berechurch hall, near Colchester.
Smythe Hon. George Augustus Frederick Percy Sydney	*Canterbury*	68 Harley street.
Somers John Patrick, Esq	*Sligo*	Reform club, 104 Pall Mall and Sligo.
Somerset Rt. Hn. Lord Granville Chs. H.	*Monmouthshire*	8 Clarges street, Piccadilly.
Somerton Viscount	*Wilton*	3 Seamore place, Mayfair, and Somerley, near [Ringwood
Somerville Sir William Meredyth, Bart *Under Sec. of State (Home Dep.)*	*Drogheda*	8 Lowndes street, Belgrave square, and Somerville, near Ashbourne, Ireland.
Sotheron Thomas Henry Sutton, Esq	*North Wiltshire*	51 Eaton place, & Bowden park, near Chippenham.
Spooner Richard, Esq	*Birmingham*	40 Duke street, St. James's
Spry Sir Samuel Thomas, Knt	*Bodmin*	8 Arlington street, Piccadilly, & Alfred club, 23 Albemarle st., & Tregolls, nr. Truro, Cornwall
Standish Charles, Esq	*Wigan*	(No address in London), Standish hall, Wigan.
Stanley Edward, Esq	*West Cumberland*	Carlton club, & Ponsonby hall, Whitehaven.
Stanley Hon. William Owen	*Anglesey*	40 Dover street, Piccadilly, & Penrhos, Holyhead.
Stansfield William Rookes Crompton, Esq.	*Huddersfield*	22 Charles street, Berkeley square, and Esholt hall, near Leeds.
Stanton William Henry, Esq	*Stroud*	Reform club, 104 Pall mall, and Stroud.
Staunton Sir George Thomas, Bart	*Portsmouth*	17 Devonshire street, Portland place, and Leigh park, near Havant, Hampshire.
Stewart John, Esq	*Lymington*	F 2 Albany, & 3 Cambridge terrace, Edgware [road.
Stewart Patrick Maxwell, Esq	*Renfrewshire*	17 Finsbury circus.
Strickland Sir George, Bart	*Preston*	1 Spring gardens, and Boynton, near Bridlington, Yorkshire, and Newton, near Malton.
Strutt Edward, Esq	*Derby*	42 South st. Grosvenor sq. & St. Helens, near Derby
Stuart Henry, Esq	*Bedford*	18 Hill st. Berkeley sq. & The Lodge, Bedford.
Stuart John, Q.C	*Newark*	19 Hertford street, May fair, and 12 Old sq. Lincoln's inn, and Kinlockleven, Argyleshire
Stuart Lord Patrick Jas. Herbert Crichton	*Ayr, &c.*	6 Whitehall place, and Cardiff Castle, Cardiff.
Stuart William Villiers, Esq	*Waterford County*	Long's hotel, 16 New Bond street, and Droman house, near Cappoquin, County Waterford.
Surrey, Earl, *see Arundel and Surrey*		
Sutton, *see Manners Sutton*		
Talbot Christopher Rice Mansel, Esq.	*Glamorganshire*	40 Belgrave sq. & Penrice castle, near Swansea, and Wargram park, Taibach, South Wales.
Tancred Henry William, Esq.	*Banbury*	Reform club, 104 Pall Mall.
Taylor James Arthur, Esq	*East Worcestershire*	Carlton club, 94 Pall mall, & Moseley hall, nr. [Birmingham.
Taylor Thomas Edward, Esq	*Dublin County*	Carlton club, 94 Pall mall, and Argellan castle, Co. Dublin.
Thesiger Sir Frederic, Knt. Q.C.	*Abingdon*	11 Bryanstone sq. & 2 King's bench walk, Temple.
Thompson Wm. Esq. (Alderman of London)	*Westmoreland*	12 Whitehall place, and Penydarran house, Merthyr Tidvil, Glamorganshire, and Underley [hall, Westmoreland
Thornely Thomas, Esq	*Wolverhampton*	24 Regent street.
Thornhill George, Esq.	*Huntingdonshire*	17 Grosvenor st. & Diddington house, Buckden.
Tollemache Hon. Fred. James	*Grantham*	Athenæum club, and Ham house, Surrey.
Tollemache John, Esq	*South Cheshire*	40 Wilton crescent, and Tilstone lodge, Tarporley, Cheshire, & Helmington hall, Ipswich, Suffolk.
Tomline George, Esq	*Shrewsbury*	1 Carlton house terrace, & Riby grove, Brigg, Lincolnshire.
Towneley John, Esq	*Beverley*	76 Eaton place, and Towneley hall, Burnley, [Lancashire.
Tower Christopher, Esq.	*Buckinghamshire*	2 Little Ryder street, & Huntsmore park, Iver, [Bucks
Trail George (of Ratter), Esq	*Caithnessshire*	Stevens's hotel, 18 New Bond street.
Trelawny John Salusbury, Esq	*Tavistock*	5 Lower Grosvenor place
Trench Major Gen. Sir Fred. Wm. K.C.H.	*Scarborough*	85 Pall mall, & Moyvannon castle, near Athlone.
Trevor Hon. George Rice Rice	*Carmarthenshire*	11 Hyde park grdns. & Bromham hall, Bedford
Trollope Sir John, Bart	*South Lincolnshire*	17 Great Cumberland place.
Trotter John, Esq	*West Surrey*	28 Eaton place, and Horton place, Epsom.
Troubridge Adml. Sir Edward Thos. Bart.	*Sandwich*	11 Eaton place, Belgrave square
Tufnell Henry, Esq. *Joint Secretary of the Treasury*	*Devonport*	Brooks' club, 60 St. James' street
Tuite Hugh Morgan, Esq	*Westmeath County*	2 Princes place, St. James's, and Sonna, West [meath

Turner Edmund, Esq.	*Truro*	12 Lower Belgrave street, Pimlico, and Truro.
Turnor Christopher, Esq.	*South Lincolnshire*	(No address in London), Stoke Rochfort, Lincoln.
Tyrell Sir John Tyssen, Bart.	*North Essex*	4 Cleveland square, St. James's, Carlton club, & Boreham house, near Chelmsford.
Vane Lord Harry George.	*South Durham*	29 Grosvenor place, and Raby Castle, Durham.
Verner Colonel Sir William, Bart.	*Armagh County*	68 Eaton sq., and Churchhill, near Moy, Ireland.
Vernon Rt. Hon. Robert	*Northampton*	20 Saville row, & Farming woods, nr. Thrapstone
Vernon Granville Harcourt, Esq.	*Bassetlaw*	22 Hertford street, May fair, & the Grove, East Retford.
Vesey Hon. Thomas	*Queen's County*	1 Grafton street, Bond street.
Villiers Viscount	*Cirencester*	38 Berkeley square, and Upton park, Banbury
Villiers Hon. Charles Pelham	*Wolverhampton*	Brooks' club, 60 St. James's street
Vivian Capt. Hon. John Cranch Walker	*Penryn & Falmouth*	Arthur's club, 69 St. James's street
Vivian John Ennis, Esq.	*Truro*	35 Jermyn street, St. James's, and Truro.
Vivian John Henry, Esq.	*Swansea*	Arthur's club, 69 St. James's street, & Singleton, near Swansea.
Vyse Capt. Henry Richard Howard	*South Northamptonshire*	Limmer's hotel, 1 George st. Hanover square, and Stokeplain, Northamptonshire.
Vyvyan Sir Richard Rawlinson, Bart.	*Helstone*	St. Dunstan's villa, Regent's park, & Trelowarren, Cornwall
Waddington Harry Spencer, Esq.	*West Suffolk*	Arthur's club, and Cavenham, Suffolk.
Wakley Thomas, Esq.	*Finsbury*	35 Bedford square, Bloomsbury
Walker Richard, Esq.	*Bury, Lancashire*	5 Gt. Ryder st. St. James's, & Bury, Lancashire.
Wall Charles Baring, Esq.	*Guildford*	44 Berkeley sq. and Norman court, Stockbridge
Walpole Spencer Horatio, Esq. Q.C.	*Midhurst*	6 Serle street, Lincoln's inn
Walsh Sir John Benn, Bart. Lord Lieut. of Radnorshire	*Radnorshire*	28 Berkeley square, & Warfield park, Bracknell.
Warburton Henry, Esq.	*Kendal*	45 Cadogan place, Sloane street
Ward Henry George, Esq. *Secretary to the Admiralty*	*Sheffield*	99 Mount street, & Much Hadham, Ware, Herts
Watson William Henry, Esq. Q.C.	*Kinsale*	38 Wilton crescent.
Wawn John Twizell, Esq.	*South Shields*	Reform club, 104 Pall mall
Welby Glynne Earle, Esq.	*Grantham*	8 Upper Belgrave street, and Newton house, Folkingham, Lincolnshire
Wellesley Lieut.-Col. Lord Charles	*South Hampshire*	Apsley house, Piccadilly.
Wemyss James Erskine, Capt. R.N.	*Fifeshire*	14 St. Alban's place, St. James's, and Wemyss castle, Kirkaldy, & Torrie house, Dunfermline
Westenra Lieut. Col. Hon. John Craven	*Kings County*	Brookes's club, 60 St. James's st. & Sharavogue castle, near Roscrea, Ireland.
White Colonel Henry	*Longford County*	(No address in London), St. Helen's, Booters, near Dublin.
White Samuel, Esq.	*Leitrim County*	Reform club, and Killakee, near Dublin
Whitmore Thomas Charlton, Esq.	*Bridgenorth*	(No address in London), Cotsbrook, nr. Shiffnall.
Williams Thomas Peers, Esq.	*Great Marlow*	41 Berkeley square, and Temple house, Marlow, and Craigydon, near Bangor, North Wales.
Williams William, Esq.	*Coventry*	12 Park square west, Regent's park.
Wilshere William, Esq.	*Yarmouth*	11 Stratton street, Piccadilly, and The Hermitage, Hitchin, Hertfordshire.
Winnington Sir Thomas Edward, Bart.	*Bewdley*	(No address in London), Stanford court, near Bewdley.
Wodehouse Edmond, Esq.	*East Norfolk*	Limmer's hotel, 1 George street, Hanover square, and Thorpe, near Norwich.
Wood Rt. Hon. Charles, *Chancellor of the Exchequer*	*Halifax*	Treasury, and Hickleton hall, Doncaster
Wood Lieut.-Col. Thomas	*Middlesex*	26 Hyde park gardens, & Littleton house, near Staines.
Wood Colonel Thomas	*Breconshire*	26 Hyde park gardens, & Littleton house, near Staines.
Worcester Marquis of	*East Gloucestershire*	27 Berkeley square
Wortley Rt. Hon. Jas. Archibald Stuart	*Buteshire*	29 Berkeley sq. and Twisden blds. Inner Temple.
Wrightson William Battie, Esq.	*Northallerton*	22 Upper Brook street, and Cusworth park, near Doncaster.
Wyndham Col. Charles	*West Sussex*	(No address in London), Rogate lodge, Petersfield.
Wyndham John Henry Campbell, Esq.	*Salisbury*	57 St. James's st. & Sydney lodge, Southampton
Wynn Right Hon. Chas. Watkin Williams	*Montgomeryshire*	20 Grafton street, Bond street, and Llangedwyn hall, near Oswestry.
Wynn Sir Watkin Williams, Bart.	*Denbighshire*	18 St. James's square, and Wynnstay, near [Wrexham.
Wyse Thomas, Esq., *Secretary to the Board of Control*	*Waterford*	17 Wilton place, Belgrave sq. Brookes' & Reform clubs, & Manor of St. John, near Waterford, & Cuddagh, near Montrath, Queen's Co. Ireland.
Yorke Henry Redhead, Esq.	*York*	81 Eaton square
Yorke Hon. Eliot Thomas	*Cambridgeshire*	15 Wilton place, Belgrave square
Young John, Esq.	*Cavan County*	19 Chesham place, Belgrave square, and Bailieborough castle, Bailieborough, Ireland.

HOUSE OF COMMONS.

ALPHABETICAL LIST OF THE BOROUGHS, CITIES, & COUNTIES

RETURNING MEMBERS TO PARLIAMENT.

ENGLAND and WALES, 498; IRELAND, 105; SCOTLAND, 53; TOTAL, 656.

ENGLAND AND WALES.

498 MEMBERS.

Abingdon, Berkshire.
Sir Frederic Thesiger, knt. Q.C

Andover, Hampshire.
Ralph Etwall, Esq., *and*
Lord William Paget.

Anglesey, North Wales.
Hon. William Owen Stanley.

Arundel, Sussex.
Hon. Henry Granville Howard, *commonly called* the Earl of Arundel and Surrey

Ashburton, Devonshire.
James Matheson, Esq.

Ashton-under-Line, Lancashire.
Charles Hindley, Esq.

Aylesbury, Buckinghamshire.
Capt. Charles John Baillie Hamilton, *and*
Rice Richard Clayton, Esq.

Banbury, Oxfordshire.
Henry William Tancred, Esq.

Barnstaple, Devonshire.
Frederick Hodgson, Esq., *and*
Montague Gore, Esq.

Bassetlaw, Nottinghamshire.
Hon. Arthur Duncombe, Capt. R.N. *and*
Granville Harcourt Vernon, Esq.

Bath, Somersetshire.
Hon. Adam Duncan, *commonly called* Viscount Duncan, *and*
John Arthur Roebuck, Esq.

Beaumaris district (comprising Beaumaris, Amlwch, Holyhead, and Llangevin) Anglesey.
Lieut.-Col. Frederick Paget.

Bedford, Bedfordshire.
Frederic Polhill, Esq., *and*
Henry Stuart, Esq.

Bedfordshire.
William Astell, Esq., *and*
Hon. John Hume Cust, *commonly called* Viscount Alford.

Berkshire.
Robert Palmer, Esq., *and* Viscount Barrington, *and* Philip Pusey, Esq.

Berwick-on-Tweed.
Richard Hodgson, Esq., *and*
Matthew Forster, Esq.

Beverley, Yorkshire.
Sir James Weir Hogg, Bart., *and*
John Towneley, Esq.

Bewdley, Worcestershire.
Sir Thomas Edward Winnington, Bart.

Birmingham, Warwickshire.
George Frederick Muntz, Esq. *and*
Richard Spooner, esq

Blackburn, Lancashire.
Wm. Fielden Esq., & John Hornby, Esq.

Bodmin, Cornwall.
Gardner-Dunn John, esq. *and*
Sir Samuel Thomas Spry, Knt.

Bolton, Lancashire.
Peter Ainsworth, Esq., *and*
John Bowring, LL.D.

Boston, Lincolnshire.
John Studholme Brownrigg, Esq., *and*
Alderman Sir James Duke, Knt.

Bradford, Yorkshire.
John Hardy, Esq., *and*
William Busfeild, Esq.

Brecon, Breconshire.
Charles Morgan Robinson Morgan, Esq.

Breconshire.
Colonel Thomas Wood.

Bridgenorth, Shropshire.
Thomas Charlton Whitmore, Esq., *and*
Sir Robert Pigot, Bart.

Bridgewater, Somersetshire.
Henry Broadwood, Esq., *and*
Thomas Seaton Forman, Esq.

Bridport, Dorsetshire.
Thomas Alexander Mitchell, Esq., *and*
John Romilly, Esq

Brighton, Sussex.
Geo. Richard Pechell, Capt. R.N., *and*
Hon. Alfred Hervey, *commonly called* Lord Alfred Hervey

Bristol, Gloucestershire.
Philip William Skynner Miles, Esq., *and*
Hon. Frncs. Hen Fitzhardinge Berkeley

Buckingham, Buckinghamshire.
Lieut. Col. Robert Hall, *and*
Hon. Richard Plantagenet Campbell Temple Nugent Brydges Chandos Grenville, *commonly called* Marquis of Chandos

Buckinghamshire.
Caledon George Du Pré, Esq., *and*
Hon. Wm. Edward Fitzmaurice, *and*
Christopher Tower, Esq.

Bury, Lancashire.
Richard Walker, Esq.

Bury St. Edmunds, Suffolk.
Lord Charles Fitzroy, *and* Rt. Hon. Frederick Wm. Hervey, *commonly called* Earl Jermyn.

Calne, Wiltshire.
Rt. Hon. Henry Petty Fitzmaurice, *commonly called* Earl of Shelburne.

Cambridge, Cambridgeshire.
Hon. John Henry Thomas Manners-Sutton, *and* Sir Fitzroy Kelly, Knt.

Cambridge University.
Right Hon. Henry Goulburn, *and*
Hon. Charles Ewan Law, M.A.

Cambridgeshire.
Hon. Eliot Thomas Yorke, *and*
Richard Jefferson Eaton, Esq., *and*
John Peter Allix, Esq.

Canterbury, Kent.
James Bradshaw, Esq., *and*
Hon. George Augustus Frederick Percy Sydney Smythe.

Cardiff district (comprising Cardiff, Cowbridge, Llantrissant, Aberdare, and Llandaff) Glamorganshire.
Rt. Hon. John Nicholl, D.C.L.

Cardigan district (comprising Cardigan, Aberistwith and Llampeter, Cardiganshire.
Pryse Pryse, Esq.

Cardiganshire.
Col. William Edward Powell.

Carlisle, Cumberland.
Philip Henry Howard, Esq., *and*
William Marshall, Esq.

Carmarthen and Llanelly, Carmarthenshire.
David Morris, Esq.

Carmarthenshire.
Hon. Geo. Rice Rice Trevor, *and*
David Arthur Sanders Davies, Esq.

Carnarvon district (comprising Carnarvon, Conway, Pwllheli & Bangor) Carnarvonshire.
William Bulkeley Hughes, Esq.

Carnarvonshire.
Hon. Edward Gordon Douglas Pennant.

Chatham, Kent.
Right Hon. George Stevens Byng.

Cheltenham, Gloucestershire.
Hon. Craven Fitzhardinge Berkeley.

Cheshire (North).
William Tatton Egerton, Esq., *and*
George Cornwall Legh, Esq.

Cheshire (South).
Sir Philip de Malpas Grey Egerton, Bart. &
John Tollemache, Esq.

Chester, Cheshire.
Right Hon. Lord Robert Grosvenor, *and*
Sir John Jervis, Knt. A.G.

Chichester, Sussex.
John Abel Smith, Esq., *and*
Hon. Henry Charles George Lennox, *commonly called* Lord Henry Lennox

Chippenham, Wiltshire
Joseph Neeld, Esq., *and*
Henry George Boldero, Esq.

Christchurch, Hampshire.
Hon. Edw. Alfred John Harris, Capt. R.N.

Cirencester, Gloucestershire.
William Cripps, Esq. *and*
Hon. George Augustus Frederick Villiers *commonly called* Viscount Villiers

Clitheroe, Lancashire.
Edward Cardwell, Esq.

Cockermouth, Cumberland.
Henry Aglionby Aglionby, Esq., *and*
Edward Horsman, Esq.

Colchester, Essex.
Richard Sanderson, Esq., *and*
Sir George Henry Smyth, Bart.

Cornwall (East).
William Rashleigh, jun., Esq. *and*
William Henry Pole Carew, Esq.

Cornwall (West).
Edward William Wynne Pendarves, Esq. *and* Sir Charles Lemon, Bart.

Coventry, Warwickshire.
Right Hon. Edward Ellice, *and*
William Williams, Esq.

Cricklade, Wiltshire.
John Neeld, Esq., *and*
Hon. Henry Thomas Howard.

Cumberland (East).
Hon. Charles Wentworth George Howard, *and* William James, Esq.

Cumberland (West).
Samuel Irton, Esq. & Edward Stanley, Esq.

Dartmouth, &c. Devonshire.
George Moffatt, Esq.

Denbigh district, (comprising Denbigh, Holt, Ruthin, & Wrexham), Denbighshire.
Townshend Mainwaring, Esq.

Denbighshire.
Hon. William Bagot, *and*
Sir Watkin Williams Wynn, Bart.

Derby, Derbyshire.
Edward Strutt, Esq., *and*
Hon. John George Brabazon Ponsonby, *commonly called* Visct. Duncannon

Derbyshire (North).
Hon. George Henry Cavendish, *and*
William Evans, Esq.

Derbyshire (South).
Edward Miller Munday, Esq., *and*
Charles Robert Colvile, Esq.

Devizes, Wiltshire.
George Heneage Walker Heneage, Esq. *and* Wm. Heald Ludlow Bruges, Esq.

Devonport, Devonshire.
Right Hon. Sir George Grey, Bart., *and*
Henry Tufnell, Esq.

Devonshire (North).
Sir Thomas Dyke Acland, Bart., *and*
Lewis William Buck, Esq.

Devonshire (South).
Sir John Buller Yarde Buller, Bart., *and*
Hon. Wm. Reginald Courtenay, *commonly called* Lord Courtenay.

Dorchester, Dorsetshire.
Hon. Anthony Henry Ashley-Cooper, *and*
Rt. Hon. Sir James Robert George Graham, Bart.

Dorsetshire.
George Bankes, Esq. *and*
Henry Ker Seymer, Esq., *and*
John Floyer, Esq

Dover, Kent.
Sir John Rae Reid, Bart., *and*
Edward Royd Rice, Esq.

Droitwich, Worcestershire.
Sir John Somerset Pakington, Bart.

Dudley, Worcestershire.
John Benbow, Esq.

Durham (City).
Thomas Colpitts Granger, Esq., *and*
John Bright, Esq.

Durham County (North).
Hedworth Lambton, Esq., *and*
Hon. Henry Thomas Liddell.

Durham County (South).
Lord Harry George Vane, *and*
John Bowes, Esq.

Essex (North).
Sir John Tyssen Tyrell, Bart., *and*
Charles Gray Round, Esq.

Essex (South).
Thomas William Bramston, Esq., *and*
George Palmer, Esq.

Evesham, Worcestershire.
Rt. Hon. Lord Arthur Marcus Cecil Hill, *and*
Peter Borthwick, Esq.

Exeter, Devonshire.
Edward Divett, Esq., *and*
Sir John Thomas Buller Duckworth, bart.

Eye, Suffolk.
Lieut. Gen. Sir Edward Kerrison, Bart.

Finsbury, Middlesex.
Thomas Wakley, Esq., *and*
Thomas Slingsby Duncombe, Esq.

Flint district, (comprising Flint, Overton, Rhyddlan, Holywell, Mold, and St. Asaph), Flintshire.
Sir Richard Williams Bulkeley, Bart.

Flintshire.
Sir Stephen Richard Glynne, Bart.

Frome, Somersetshire.
Thomas Sheppard, Esq.

Gateshead, Durham.
William Hutt, Esq.

Glamorganshire.
Christopher Rice Mansel Talbot, Esq., &
Hon. Edward Richard Wyndham Quin, *commonly called* Viscount Adare.

Gloucester, Gloucestershire.
John Phillpotts, Esq., *and*
Hon. Maurice Frederick Fitzhardinge Berkeley, Capt. R.N.

Gloucestershire (East).
Sir Christopher William Codrington, Bart., *and* Hon. Henry Somerset, *commonly called* Marquis of Worcester

Gloucestershire (West).
Hon. Geo. Chas. Grantley Fitzhardinge Berkeley, & Robert Blagden Hale, Esq.

Grantham, Lincolnshire.
Glynne Earle Welby, Esq., *and*
Hon. Frederick James Tollemache.

Greenwich, &c. Kent.
Admiral Jas. Whitley Deans Dundas, *and* Edward George Barnard, Esq.

Grimsby (Great), Lincolnshire.
Edward Heneage, Esq.

Guildford, Surrey.
Charles Baring Wall, Esq., *and*
Ross Donnelly Mangles, Esq.

Halifax, Yorkshire.
Rt. Hon. Charles Wood, *and*
Edward Protheroe, jun. Esq.

Hampshire (North).
Rt. Hon. Chas. Shaw Lefevre, SPEAKER, *and* Sir William Heathcote, Bart.

Hampshire (South).
Henry Combe Compton, Esq., *and*
Lieut.-Col. Hon. Charles Wellesley, *commonly called* Lord Charles Wellesley.

Harwich, Essex.
John Attwood, Esq., *and*
William Beresford, Esq.

Hastings, Sussex.
Robert Hollond, Esq. *and*
Musgrave Brisco, Esq.

Haverfordwest district, (comprising Haverfordwest, Fishguard, Narbeth, and St. David's) Pembrokeshire.
Sir Rd. Bulkeley Philipps Philipps, Bt.

Helstone, Cornwall.
Sir Richard Rawlinson Vyvyan, Bart.

Hereford, Herefordshire.
Robert Pulsford, Esq., *and*
Sir Robert Price, Bart.

Herefordshire.
Kedgwin Hoskins, Esq., *and*
Thomas Baskerville Mynors Baskerville, Esq. *and*
Joseph Bailey, jun. Esq.

Hertford, Hertfordshire.
Hon. Phillip Henry Stanhope, *commonly called* Viscount Mahon, *and*
Hon. William Francis Cowper.

Hertfordshire.
Abel Smith, Esq., *and*
Hon. Granville Dudley Ryder, *and*
Thomas Plumer Halsey, Esq.

Honiton, Devonshire.
Colonel Hugh Duncan Baillie, *and*
Forster Alleyne Mac Geachy, Esq.

Horsham, Sussex.
Robert Henry Hurst, Esq.

Huddersfield, Yorkshire.
Wm. Rookes Crompton Stansfield, Esq.

Hull (Kingston upon), Yorkshire.
Sir Walter Charles James, Bart., *and*
Sir John Hanmer, Bart.

Huntingdon, Huntingdonshire.
Col. Jonathan Peel, *and*
Thomas Baring, Esq.

Huntingdonshire.
Edward Fellowes, Esq., *and*
George Thornhill, Esq.

Hythe, Kent.
Stewart Marjoribanks, Esq.

Ipswich, Suffolk.
Sackville Lane Fox, Esq., *and*
Sir John Neilstone Gladstone, Bart. Capt. R.N.

Kendal, Westmoreland.
Henry Warburton, Esq.

Kent (East).
John Pemberton Plumptre, Esq. *and*
William Deedes, Esq.

Kent (West).
Sir Edmund Filmer, Bart. *and*
Colonel Thomas Austen.

Kidderminster, Worcestershire.
Richard Godson, Esq.

King's Lynn. See *Lynn Regis.*

Knaresborough, Yorkshire.
Andrew Lawson, Esq., *and*
William Busfeild Ferrand, Esq.

Lambeth, Surrey.
Benjamin Hawes, jun. Esq., *and*
Rt. Hon. Charles Tennyson D'Eyncourt

Lancashire (North).
John Wilson Patten, Esq., *and*
John Talbot Clifton, Esq.

Lancashire (South).
William Entwisle, Esq., *and*
William Brown, Esq.

Lancaster, Lancashire.
Thomas Greene, Esq., *and*
George Marton, Esq.

Launceston, Cornwall.
William Bowles, Esq. C.B. Rear-Admiral of the Blue

Leeds, Yorkshire.
William Beckett, Esq., *and*
William Aldam, jun. Esq.

Leicester, Leicestershire.
Sir John Easthope, Bart. *and*
Wynn Ellis, Esq.

Leicestershire (North).
Lord Charles Somerset Manners, *and*
Edward Basil Farnham, Esq.

Leicestershire (South).
Sir Henry Halford, bart., *and*
Charles Wm. Packe, Esq.

Leominster, Herefordshire.
George Arkwright, Esq., *and*
Henry Barkly, Esq.

Lewes, Sussex.
Sir Howard Elphinstone, bt. D.C.L., *and*
Hon. Henry Fitzroy.

Lichfield, Staffordshire.
Lord Alfred Henry Paget.
Hon. Edward Mostyn Lloyd Mostyn

Lincoln, Lincolnshire.
Colonel Charles De Laet Waldo Sibthorp, &
William Rickford Collett, Esq.

Lincolnshire (South).
Christopher Turnor, Esq., *and*
Sir John Trollope, Bart.

Lincolnshire (North).
Robert Adam Christopher, Esq., *and*
One vacancy.

Liskeard, Cornwall.
Charles Buller, junior, Esq.

Liverpool, Lancashire.
Hon. Dudley Ryder, *commonly called* Viscount Sandon, *and*
Sir Howard Douglas, Bart. G.C.B.

London, Middlesex.
John Masterman, Esq., *and*
George Lyall, Esq. *and*
Rt. Hon. Lord John Russell, *and*
James Pattison, Esq.

Ludlow, Shropshire.
Beriah Botfield, Esq., *and*
James Ackers, Esq.

Lyme Regis, Dorsetshire.
Thomas Hussey, Esq.

Lymington, Hampshire.
John Stewart, Esq., *and*
William Alexander Mackinnon, Esq.

Lynn Regis, Norfolk.
George William Frederick Cavendish Bentinck, Esq., *commonly called* Lord George Bentinck, *and*
Hon. Robert Jocelyn, *commonly called* Viscount Jocelyn

Macclesfield, Cheshire.
John Brocklehurst, jun. Esq., *and*
Thomas Grimsditch, Esq.

Maidstone, Kent.
Alexander James Beresford Hope, Esq., &
George Dodd, Esq.

Maldon, Essex.
Quintin Dick, Esq., *and* John Round, Esq.

Malmesbury, Wiltshire.
Hon. James Kenneth Howard.

Malton, Yorkshire.
John Evelyn Denison, Esq. *and*
Hon. Thomas Spencer Wentworth Fitz-William, *commonly called* Viscount Milton

Manchester, Lancashire.
Mark Philips, Esq., *and*
Thomas Milner Gibson, Esq.

Marlborough, Wiltshire.
Rt. Hon. Lord Ernest Augustus Chas. Brudenell Bruce, *and*
Rt. Hon. Henry Bingham Baring

Marlow (Great), Buckinghamshire
Thomas Peers Williams, Esq., *and*
Renn Hampden, Esq.

Marylebone, Middlesex.
Sir Benjamin Hall, Bart., *and*
Commodore Sir Charles Napier, K.C.B.

Merionethshire.
Richard Richards, Esq.

Merthyr Tydvil, Glamorganshire.
Sir Josiah John Guest, Bart.

Middlesex.
George Byng, Esq., & Lieut. Col. Thos Wood.

Midhurst, Sussex.
Spencer Horatio Walpole, Esq. Q.C.

Monmouth district, (comprising Monmouth, Newport, and Usk), Monmouthshire.
Reginald James Blewitt, Esq.

Monmouthshire.
Rt. Hon. Ld. Granville C. H. Somerset, *and*
Chas. Octavius Swinnerton Morgan, Esq

Montgomery district, (comprising Montgomery, Llanfyllin, Llanidloes, Machynlleth, Newtown, and Welchpool), Montgomeryshire.
Hon. Hugh Cholmondeley.

Montgomeryshire.
Rt. Hon. Chas. Watkin Williams Wynn.

Morpeth, Northumberland.
Hon. Edward George Granville Howard, Capt. R.N.

Newark-on-Trent, Nottinghamshire.
Lord John James Robert Manners, *and*
John Stuart, Q.C.

Newcastle-under-Lyne, Staffordshire
Edmund Buckley, Esq., *and*
John Campbell Colquhoun, Esq.

Newcastle-on-Tyne, Northumberland.
William Ord, Esq., *and*
John Hodgson Hinde, Esq.

Newport, Isle of Wight, Hampshire.
Charles Wykeham Martin, Esq., *and*
William John Hamilton, Esq.

Norfolk (East).
Edmond Wodehouse, Esq. *and*
Henry Negus Burroughes, Esq.

Norfolk (West).
William Bagge, Esq., *and*
William Lyde Wiggett Chute, Esq.

Northallerton, Yorkshire.
William Battie Wrightson, Esq.

Northampton, Northamptonshire.
Right Hon. Robert Vernon, *and*
Raikes Currie, Esq.

Northamptonshire (North).
Thomas Philip Maunsell, Esq., *and*
Augustus Stafford O'Brien, Esq.

Northamptonshire (South).
Sir Charles Knightley, Bart., *and*
Capt. Henry Richard Howard Vyse

Northumberland (North).
Hon. Charles Bennet, *commonly called* Lord Ossulston, *and*
Addison John Baker Cresswell, Esq.

Northumberland (South).
Matthew Bell, Esq., *and*
Savile Craven Henry Ogle, Esq.

Norwich, Norfolk.
Hon. Arthur Richard Wellesley, *commonly called* Marquis of Douro, *and*
Benjamin Smith, Esq.

Nottingham, Nottinghamshire.
Right Hon. Sir John Cam Hobhouse, Bt., *and* Thomas Gisborne, Esq.

Nottinghamshire (North-west).
Thomas Houldsworth, Esq., *and*
William Henry Cavendish Bentinck, Esq., *commonly called* Lord Henry Bentinck

Nottinghamshire (South-east).
Col. Lancelot Rolleston, *and* Thomas Blackborne Thorston Hildyard, Esq.

Oldham, Lancashire.
Sir John Fielden, Bart., *and*
Gen. William Augustus Johnson.

Oxford, Oxfordshire.
Donald Maclean, Esq., *and*
James Haughton Langston, Esq.

Oxford, University.
Thos. Grimston Bucknall Estcourt, D.C.L. *and*
Sir Robert Harry Inglis, Bart. D.C.L.

Oxfordshire.
Montagu Bertie, Esq., *commonly called* Lord Norreys, *and* Geo. Granville Harcourt, *and* Joseph Warner Henley, Esqs.

Pembroke district, (comprising Pembroke, Tenby, and Milford), Pembrokeshire.
Sir John Owen, Bart.

Pembrokeshire.
Hon. John Frederick Vaughan Campbell, *commonly called* Viscount Emlyn.

Penryn (and Falmouth), Cornwall.
Capt. John Cranch Walker Vivian, *and*
James Hanway Plumridge, Capt. R.N.

Peterborough, Northamptonshire.
Sir Robert Heron, Bart., *and*
Hon. George Wentworth Fitzwilliam.

Petersfield, Hampshire.
Sir William George Hylton Jolliffe, Bart

Plymouth, Devonshire.
Thomas Gill, Esq., *and*
Hon. Hugh Fortescue, *commonly called* Viscount Ebrington.

Pontefract, Yorkshire.
Richard Monckton Milnes, Esq., *and*
Hon. John Charles George Saville, *commonly called* Viscount Pollington.

Poole, Dorsetshire.
Hon. Chas. Fred. Ashley Cooper Ponsonby & George Richard Philips, Esq

Portsmouth, Hampshire.
Rt. Hon. Francis Thornhill Baring, *and*
Sir George Thomas Staunton, Bart.

Preston, Lancashire.
Sir Peter Hesketh Fleetwood, Bart., *and*
Sir George Strickland, Bart.

Radnor district, (comprising Radnor, Knighton, Rhayadr, and Presteign) Radnorshire.
Richard Price, Esq.

Radnorshire.
Sir John Benn Walsh, Bart.

Reading, Berkshire.
Charles Russell, Esq. *and*
Hon. Henry Charles Cadogan, *commonly called* Viscount Chelsea.

Reigate, Surrey.
Hon. Charles Somers Somers Cocks, *commonly called* Viscount Eastnor.

Retford (East). See *Bassetlaw.*

Richmond, Yorkshire.
Hon. John Charles Dundas, *and*
Henry Rich, Esq.

Ripon, Yorkshire.
Rt. Hon. Sir George Cockburn, G.C.B, & Hon. Edwin Lascelles

Rochdale, Lancashire.
William Sharman Crawford, Esq.

Rochester, Kent.
James Douglas Stoddart Douglas, Esq., *and* William Henry Bodkin, Esq.

Rutlandshire.
Gilbert John Heathcote, Esq., *and*
George Finch, Esq.

Rye, Sussex.
Herbert Barrett Curteis, Esq.

St. Alban's, Hertfordshire.
George William John Repton, Esq. *and*
Benjamin Bond Cabbell, Esq.

St. Ives, Cornwall.
Hon. William Paulet, *commonly called* Lord William Paulet

Salford, Lancashire.
Joseph Brotherton, Esq.

Salisbury, Wiltshire.
Ambrose Hussey, Esq. *and*
John Henry Campbell Wyndham, Esq.

Sandwich, Deal, & Walmer, Kent.
Sir Edward Thomas Troubridge, Bart., & Hugh Hamilton Lindsay, Esq.

Sarum (New). See *Salisbury.*

Scarborough, Yorkshire.
Maj.Gen.Sir Frederick W. Trench, K.C.H., *and* Sir John Vanden Bempde Johnstone, Bart.

Shaftesbury, Dorsetshire.
Richard Brinsley Sheridan, Esq.

Sheffield, Yorkshire.
John Parker, Esq., *and*
Henry George Ward, Esq.

Shoreham (New), Sussex.
Sir Charles Merrik Burrell, Bart., *and*
Charles Goring, Esq.

Shrewsbury, Shropshire.
Benjamin Disraeli, Esq., *and*
George Tomline, Esq.

Shropshire or *Salop (North).*
William Ormsby Gore, Esq., *and* Hon. Edward James Herbert, *commonly called* Viscount Clive

Shropshire or *Salop (South).*
Hon. Robert Henry Clive, *and* Hon. Orlando George Charles Budgeman, *commonly called* Viscount Newport

Somersetshire (East).
William Gore Langton, Esq., *and*
William Miles, Esq.

Somersetshire (West).
Thomas Dyke Acland, Esq., *and*
Francis Henry Dickinson, Esq.

Southampton, Hampshire.
George William Hope, Esq., *and*
Humphrey St. John Mildmay, esq

South Shields, Durham.
John Twizell Wawn, Esq.

Southwark, Surrey.
John Humphery, Esq., *and*
Sir William Molesworth, Bart.

Stafford, Staffordshire.
Edward Buller, Esq., *and*
Hon. Swynfen Thomas Carnegie

Staffordshire (North).
Jesse David Watts Russell, Esq., *and*
Charles Bowyer Adderley, Esq.

Staffordshire (South).
Hon. Henry John Talbot, Capt. R.N. *commonly called* Viscount Ingestre, *and* Hon. Col. Geo. Anson.

Stamford, Lincolnshire.
Rt. Hon. Charles Somerset Manners, *commonly called* Marquis of Granby, *and* Rt. Hon. Sir George Clerk, Bart.

Stockport, Cheshire.
Henry Marsland, Esq., *and*
Richard Cobden, Esq.

Stoke-upon-Trent, Staffordshire.
William Taylor Copeland (Alderman of London), & John Lewis Ricardo, Esq.

Stroud, Gloucestershire.
George Poulett Scrope, Esq., *and*
William Henry Stanton, Esq.

Suffolk (East).
Rt. Hon. Lord Rendlesham, *and*
Edward Sherlock Gooch, Esq.

Suffolk (West).
Harry Spencer Waddington, Esq. *and*
Philip Bennet, jun. esq.

Sunderland, Durham.
David Barclay, Esq., *and*
George Hudson, Esq.

Surrey (East).
Henry Kemble, Esq., *and*
Edmund Antrobus, Esq.

Surrey (West).
William Joseph Denison, Esq., *and*
John Trotter, Esq.

Sussex (East).
Augustus Eliott Fuller, Esq. *and*
Charles Hay Frewen, Esq.

Sussex (West).
Hon. Charles Henry Gordon Lennox, *commonly called* Earl of March, *and*
Col. Charles Wyndham

Swansea district (comprising Swansea, Aberavon, and Neath), Glamorganshire.
John Henry Vivian, Esq.

Tamworth, Staffordshire.
Right Hon. Sir Robert Peel, Bart., *and*
Edward Henry A'Court, Capt. R.N.

Taunton, Somersetshire.
Rt. Hon. Henry Labouchere, *and*
Sir Thomas Edward Colebrooke, Bart.

Tavistock, Devonshire.
Lord Edward Russell, *and*
John Salusbury Trelawny, Esq.

Tewkesbury, Gloucestershire.
William Dowdeswell, Esq., *and*
John Martin, Esq.

Thetford, Norfolk.
Hon. William Bingham Baring, *and*
Sir James Flower, Bart.

Thirsk, Yorkshire.
John Bell, Esq.

Tiverton, Devonshire.
John Heathcoat, Esq., *and*
Rt. Hon. Viscount Palmerston, G.C.B.

Totness, Devonshire.
Hon. Edward Adolphus Seymour, *commonly called* Lord Seymour, *and*
Charles Barry Baldwin, Esq.

Tower Hamlets, Middlesex.
Colonel Charles Richard Fox, *and*
Sir William Clay, Bart.

Truro, Cornwall.
John Ennis Vivian, Esq., *and*
Edmund Turner, Esq.

Tynemouth and North Shields, Northumberland.
Henry Mitcalfe, Esq.

Wakefield, Yorkshire.
Hon. William Sebright Lascelles

Wallingford, Berkshire.
William Seymour Blackstone, Esq.

Walsall, Staffordshire.
Robert Scott, Esq.

Wareham, Dorsetshire.
John Samuel Wanley Sawbridge Erle Drax, Esq.

Warrington, Lancashire.
John Ireland Blackburne, Esq.

Warwick, Warwickshire.
Sir Chas. Eurwiche Douglas, Knt. *and*
William Collins, Esq.

Warwickshire (North).
William Stratford Dugdale, Esq., *and*
Charles Newdegate Newdegate, Esq.

Warwickshire (South).
Evelyn John Shirley, Esq. *and*
Hon. George Guy Greville, *commonly called* Lord Brooke

Wells, Somersetshire.
Richard Blakemore, Esq., *and*
William Goodenough Hayter, Esq.

Wenlock, Shropshire.
Hon. George Cecil Weld Forester, *and*
James Milnes Gaskell, Esq.

Westbury, Wiltshire.
Sir Ralph Lopes, Bart.

Westminster, Middlesex.
John Temple Leader, Esq., *and*
Gen. Sir De Lacy Evans, K.C.B.

Westmoreland.
Lieut.-Col. Hon. Henry Cecil Lowther, &
William Thompson (Aldrmn. of London)

Weymouth & Melcombe Regis, Dorset.
Ralph Bernal, sen., Esq., *and*
Wm. Dougal Christie, Esq.

Whitby, Yorkshire.
Aaron Chapman, Esq.

Whitehaven, Cumberland.
Matthias Attwood, Esq.

Wigan, Lancashire.
Charles Standish, Esq. *and*
Hon. Capt. James Lindsay.

Wight (Isle of), Hampshire.
Hon. Wm. Hen. Ashe A'Court Holmes.

Wilton, Wiltshire.
Hon. James Charles Herbert Welbore Ellis Agar, *commonly called* Viscount Somerton.

Wiltshire (North).
Walter Long, Esq., *and*
Thomas Henry Sutton Sotheron, Esq

Wiltshire (South).
John Benett, Esq., *and*
Hon. Sidney Herbert.

Winchester, Hampshire.
James Buller East, Esq., *and*
Bickham Escott, Esq.

Windsor (New), Berkshire.
Ralph Neville, Esq. *and*
Lt. Col. Geo. Augustus Reid

Wolverhampton, Staffordshire.
Thomas Thornely, Esq., *and*
Hon. Charles Pelham Villiers.

Woodstock, Oxfordshire.
Hon. Alfred Spencer Churchill, *commonly called* Lord Alfred Spencer Churchill

Worcester, Worcestershire.
Joseph Bailey, Esq., *and*
Sir Denis Le Marchant, Bart.

Worcestershire (East).
John Barneby, Esq., *and*
James Arthur Taylor, Esq.

Worcestershire (West).
Maj.Gen. Hon. Hen. Beauchamp Lygon *and* Frederick Winn Knight, Esq.

Wycombe, Buckinghamshire.
George Henry Dashwood, Esq., *and*
Ralph Osborne, Esq.

Yarmouth (Great), Norfolk.
Charles Edmund Rumbold, Esq., *and*
William Wilshere, Esq.

York, Yorkshire.
Sir John Henry Lowther, Bart., *and*
Henry Redhead Yorke, Esq.

Yorkshire (East Riding).
Henry Broadley, Esq., & Lord Hotham.

Yorkshire (North Riding).
Edward Stillingfleet Cayley, Esq., *and*
Hon. Octavius Duncombe.

Yorkshire (West Riding).
Edmund Beckett Denison, Esq., *and*
Rt. Hon. George William Frederick Howard, *commonly called* Viscount Morpeth

IRELAND.

105 MEMBERS.

The places marked C. are in the Province of Connaught; those marked L. in the Province of Leinster; M. in the Province of Munster; and U. in the Province of Ulster.

Antrim County, U.
Nathaniel Alexander, Esq. *and*
Sir Horace Seymour Beauchamp, K.C.B.

Armagh, County of Armagh, U.
Lieut. Col. John Dawson Rawdon.

Armagh County, U.
Archibald Acheson, *commonly called* Viscount Acheson, & Col. Sir Wm. Verner, Bart.

Athlone, County of Westmeath, L.
John Collett, Esq.

Bandonbridge, County of Cork, M.
Hon. Francis Bernard, *commonly called* Viscount Bernard.

Belfast, County of Antrim, U.
David Robert Ross, Esq., *and*
Hon. John Chichester, *commonly called* Lord John Chichester.

Carlow City, L.
Capt. Brownlow Villiers Layard.

Carlow County, L.
Colonel Bruen, *and*
William Bunbury M'Clintoch, Esq.

Carrickfergus, County of Antrim. U.
Peter Kirk, Esq.

Cashel, County of Tipperary, M.
Timothy O'Brien, Esq.

Cavan County, U.
John Young, Esq., *and*
Capt. the Hon. James Pierce Maxwell

Clare County, M.
Wm. Nugent Macnamara, Esq., *and*
Cornelius O'Brien, Esq.

Clonmel, County of Tipperary, M.
Cecil Lawless, Esq.

Coleraine, County of Londonderry, U.
Boyd John, Esq.

Cork City, County of Cork, M.
Daniel Callaghan, Esq., *and*
Alexander M'Carthy, Esq.

Cork County, M.
Daniel O'Connell, Esq., *and*
Edmund Burke Roche, Esq.

Donegal County, U.
Colonel Edward Michael Conolly, *and*
Sir Edmund Samuel Hayes, Bart.

Down County, U.
Rt. Hon. Fred. Wm. Robt. Stewart, *commonly called* Viscount Castlereagh, *and* Hon. Arthur Edwin Hill, *commonly called* Lord Edwin Hill.

Downpatrick, County of Down, U.
David Stewart Ker, jun., Esq.

Drogheda, County of Louth, L.
Sir William Meredyth Somerville, Bart.

Dublin, L
Edward Grogan, Esq., *and*
William Henry Gregory, Esq.

Dublin University, L.
Right Hon. Frederick Shaw, *and*
George Alexander Hamilton, Esq.

Dublin County, L.
James Hans Hamilton, Esq., *and*
Thomas Edward Taylor, Esq.

Dundalk, County of Louth, L.
Daniel O'Connell, Esq., Jun.

Dungannon, County of Tyrone, U.
Hon. Thomas Knox, *commonly called* Viscount Northland.

Dungarvon, County of Waterford, M.
Right Hon. Richard Lalor Sheil.

Ennis, County of Clare, M.
Hewitt Bridgeman, Esq.

Enniskillen, County of Fermanagh, U.
Hon. Henry Arthur Cole.

Fermanagh County, U.
Capt. Mervyn Archdall, *and*
Sir Arthur Brinsley Brooke, Bart.

Galway, County of Galway, C.
Martin Joseph Blake, Esq., *and*
Sir Valentine Blake, Bart.

Galway County, C.
John James Bodkin, Esq., *and*
Thomas Barnwell Martin, Esq.

Kerry County, M.
Morgan John O'Connell, Esq., *and*
Hon. William Browne.

Kildare County, L.
Richard More O'Ferrall, Esq., *and*
Robert Archbold, Esq.

Kilkenny, County of Kilkenny, L.
John O'Connell, Esq.

Kilkenny County, L.
Pierce Somerset Butler, Esq., *and*
Richard Smithwick, Esq.

King's County, L.
Lieut. Col. Hon. John Craven Westenra, *and* Sir Andrew Armstrong, Bart.

Kinsale, County of Cork, M.
William Henry Watson, Esq., Q.C.

Leitrim County, C.
Samuel White, Esq., *and*
Hon. Sidney Clements, *commonly called* Viscount Clements.

Limerick, County of Limerick, M.
John O'Brien, Esq., *and*
James Kelly, esq.

Limerick County, M.
William Smith O'Brien, Esq., *and*
Caleb Powell, Esq.

Lisburn, County of Antrim, U.
Henry Meynell, Capt. R.N.

Londonderry, Coy. of Londonderry, U.
Sir Robert Alexander Ferguson, Bart.

Londonderry County, U.
Theobald Jones, Capt. R.N., *and*
Thomas Bateson, esq.

Longford County, L.
Anthony Lefroy, Esq., *and*
Col. Henry White.

Louth County, L.
Richard Montesquieu Bellew, Esq., *and*
Hon. Capt. Thomas Vesey Dawson.

Mallow, County of Cork, M.
Sir Denham Jephson Norreys, Bart.

Mayo County, C.
Robert Dillon Browne, Esq., *and*
Joseph Myles M'Donnell, Esq

Meath County, L.
Henry Grattan, Esq., *and*
Matthew Elias Corbally, Esq.

Monaghan County, U.
Charles Powell Leslie, Esq., *and*
Evelyn Philip Shirley, Esq.

New Ross, County of Wexford. L.
Hon. Robert Gore, Commander, R.N.

Newry, County of Down, U.
Hon. Francis Jack Needham, *commonly called* Viscount Newry.

Portarlington, King's County, L.
Rt. Hon. Col. Geo. Lionel Dawson Damer.

Queen's County, L.
Sir Charles Henry Coote, Bart., *and*
Hon. Thomas Vesey.

Roscommon County, C.
Fitzstephen French, Esq., *and*
The O'Conor Don (Denis O'Conor, Esq.)

Sligo, County of Sligo, C.
John Patrick Somers, Esq.

Sligo County, C.
Wm. Richd. Ormsby Gore, Esq., *and*
John Ffolliott, Esq.

Tipperary County, M.
Nicholas Maher, Esq., *and*
Richard Albert Fitzgerald, Esq

Tralee, County of Kerry. M.
Maurice O'Connell, Esq.

Tyrone County, U.
Rt. Hon. Hen. Thos. Lowry Corry, *and*
Lord Claude Hamilton.

Waterford, County of Waterford, M
Sir Henry Winston Barron, bart., *and*
Thomas Wyse, Esq.

Waterford County, M.
Wm. Villiers Stuart, Esq., *and*
Hon. Robert Shapland Carew.

Westmeath County, L.
Hugh Morgan Tuite, Esq., *and*
Benjamin James Chapman, Esq.

Wexford, County of Wexford, L.
Sir Thomas Esmonde, Bart.

Wexford County, L.
James Power, Esq., *and*
Villiers Francis Hatton, Capt. R.N.

Wicklow County, L.
Sir Ralph Howard, bart. *and*
Col. William Acton.

Youghall, County of Cork, M.
Hon. Charles Compton Cavendish.

SCOTLAND.

53 MEMBERS.

Aberdeen, Aberdeenshire.
Alexander Bannerman, Esq.

Aberdeenshire.
Hon. William Gordon, Capt. R.N.

Andrews (St.) See *St. Andrews, &c.*

Argyllshire.
Rt. Hon. Duncan M'Neill.

Ayr, Irvine, Campbelltown, Inverary and Oban district of Burghs.
Lord Patrick James Herbert Crichton Stuart.

Ayrshire.
Alexander Oswald, Esq.

Banffshire.
James Duff, Esq.

Berwickshire.
Sir Hugh Purves Hume Campbell, Bart

Buteshire.
Rt.Hon.James ArchibaldStuartWortley

Caithness-shire.
George Traill, jun. (of Ratter), Esq.

Clackmannanshire and Kinross.
Major Gen. William Morison, C.B.

Crail, &c. See *St. Andrews.*

Dumbartonshire.
Alexander Smollett, jun.

Dumfries district of Burghs, comprising Dumfries, Annar, Kirkcudbright, Lochmaben and Sanquhar.
William Ewart, Esq.

Dumfriesshire.
John James Hope Johnstone, Esq.

Dundee, Forfarshire.
George Duncan, Esq.

Dysart. See *Kirkaldy, &c.*

Edinburgh.
William Gibson Craig, jun., *and*
Rt. Hon. Thomas Babington Macaulay

Edinburghshire.
Sir John Hope, bart.

Elgin district of Burghs, comprising Elgin, Banff, Cullen, Inverary, and Peterhead.
Col. Sir Andrew Leith Hay, Knt.

Elginshire and Nairnshire.
Charles Lennox Cumming Bruce, Esq.

Falkirk district of Burghs, comprising Falkirk, Airdrie, Hamilton, Lanark, and Linlithgow.
Rt. Hon. Henry Pelham Fynes Pelham Clinton, *commonly called* Earl of Lincoln

Fifeshire.
James Erskine Wemyss, Capt. R.N.

Forfar, Forfarshire. See *Montrose, &c.*

Forfarshire.
Lord John Frederick Gordon Hallyburton, G.C.H., Capt. R.N.

Fortrose, Inverness, Nairn, & Forres district of Burghs.
James Morrison, Esq.

Glasgow, Lanarkshire.
James Oswald, Esq., *and*
John Dennistoun, Esq.

Greenock, Renfrewshire.
Walter Baine, Esq.

Haddington, Dunbar, North Berwick, Lauder, and Jedburgh d. of Burghs.
James Maitland Balfour, jun., Esq.

Haddingtonshire.
Sir Thomas Buchan Hepburn, Bart.

Inverness. See *Fortrose, &c.*

Inverness-shire.
Henry James Baillie, jun.

Kilmarnock, Dumbarton, Renfrew, Rutherglen, and Port Glasgow, &c. district of Burghs.
Hon. Edward Pleydell Bouverie

Kincardineshire.
Hon. Lt. Gen. Hugh Arbuthnot, K.C.B.

Kirkaldy, Dysart, Kinghorn, and Burntisland district of Burghs.
Lieut. Col. Robert Ferguson.

Kircudbright (Stewartry).
Thomas Maitland, Esq.

Lanarkshire.
William Lockhart, Esq.

Leith, Musselburgh, and Portobello district of Burghs.
Rt. Hon. Andrew Rutherfurd.

Linlithgowshire.
William Baillie, jun. Esq.

Montrose, Aberbrothwick, Brechin, Forfar, and Inverbervie district of Burghs.
Joseph Hume, Esq.

Orkney and Zetland (Isles).
Frederick Dundas, Esq.

Paisley, Renfrewshire.
Archibald Hastie, Esq.

Peeblesshire.
William Forbes Mackenzie, Esq.

Perth, Perthshire.
Rt. Hon. Fox Maule.

Perthshire.
Henry Home Drummond, Esq.

Renfrew. See *Kilmarnock.*

Renfrewshire.
Patrick Maxwell Stewart, Esq.

Ross and Cromartyshires.
Thomas Mackenzie, Esq.

Roxburghshire.
Hon. Francis Scott.

St. Andrews, Anstruther, Crail, Cupar, Pittenweem & Kilrenny district of Burghs.
Edward Ellice, junior, Esq.

Selkirkshire.
Allan Eliott Lockhart, Esq

Stirling, Culross, Dunfermline, Inverkeithing, & Queensferry.
Hon. Archibald Primrose, *commonly called* Lord Dalmeny.

Stirlingshire.
William Forbes, Esq

Sutherlandshire.
David Dundas, Esq.

Wick, Cromarty, Dingwall, Kirkwall and Tain district of Burghs.
James Loch, Esq.

Wigtoun, Whithorn, Stranraer, Galloway, &c. district of Burghs.
Sir John M'Taggart, Bart.

Wigtounshire.
Captain John Dalrymple.

*** One vacancy for North Lincolnshire.

CLERKS AND OFFICERS OF THE HOUSE OF COMMONS.

Clerk of the House of Commons—John Henry Ley, esq. (4 Richmond terrace)
Clerk Assistant—William Ley, esq. (15 Queen st. Mayfair)
Second Clerk Assistant—Henry Ley, esq. (4 Richmond terr)
Public Business Office and for the Collection of the Fees, 43 Parliament street
Clerk of Fees—John Edward Dorington, esq
Clerks—Mr. Arthur Jones, Mr. Robert Marriott, Mr. Edward Ley, Mr. William Rose
Accountant—Mr. John James Wilkinson

Committee Clerks and Election Office, House of Commons.

Committee Clerks—Robert Chalmers, George Whittam, George Dyson, Robert Gibbons
Clerks—Mr. John Rose, Mr. Charles Pole, Mr. Charles Gunnell, Mr. Charles Frere, Mr. Henry H. Creed, Mr. Littleton Powys, Mr. George Walgrave, Mr. Charles Eales, Mr. Augustus Palk

Journal Office, and for the Votes and Proceedings of the House, 43 Parliament street.

Clerk of the Journals—James Gudge, esq
Clerks—Mr. Charles Rowland, Mr. Joseph Postlethwaite, Mr. Charles Gray, Mr. Wm. Ley, Mr. James Bull, Mr. Richard Dickinson
First Clerk of Engrossing Office—Samuel Gunnell, esq
Clerks—Mr. George Gunnell, Mr. William Ginger

Private Bill Office, 2 Parliament street.

First Clerk in Private Bill Office—Mr. William Hawes
Clerks—Mr. William Hodgkin, Mr. Henry Mayne, Mr. Joseph Johnson, Mr. Samuel Burgess Gunnell
Examiner of Election Recognizances, & Counsel to the Speaker—James Booth, esq
Clerk of Election Recognizances—Charles Brooksby, esq
Librarian—Thomas Vardon, esq
Assistant—Thomas Erskine May, esq
Messenger to Library—William Kay
Short-hand Writer—William Brodie Gurney, esq
Serjeant at arms—Sir William Gosset
Deputy—John Clementson, esq
Assistant—Ralph Allen Gosset, esq

Vote Office.

Deliverer of Votes and Printed Papers—Chas. Paskin, esq
Clerks—Mr. Robert Collins, Mr. Robert Joseph Collins, Mr. James Jeremiah Collins
Deputy Housekeeper—Mr. Wilbraham Taylor
Assistant—Mr. Edmund Bellamy
Door Keepers—Mr. John Pratt, Mr. Francis Williams
Messengers—Mr. Chas. Stein, Mr. William Cook, Mr. Robert Baily, Mr. Hugh Mallons, Mr. Wm. Bellamy, Mr. James Poingdestre
Superintendent of Members' Waiting Room—Mr. Thomas Collett
Assistant—Charles Warman
Receiver of Post Letters—Wilbraham Taylor
Assistant—William Kendall
Chaplain to the House of Commons—Rev. Gerrard Thomas Andrewes, M.A. 8 Sackville street
Secretary to the Speaker—Charles Edward Lefroy, esq House of Commons, and Farnham, Surrey
Train Bearer—Mr. Robert Baily
Printers of the Journals, &c.—James & Luke Jas. Hansard
Printers of the Votes—John B. Nichols and Son

PEERESSES
IN THEIR OWN RIGHT.

Name.	*Title.*	*Creation.*
Mary Frances Elizabeth Stapleton	Baroness Le Despencer	1264
Sophia Russell	Baroness de Clifford	1299
Harriet Anne Curzon	Baroness De la Zouche of Haryngworth	1308
Barbara Rawdon Hastings	Baroness Grey de Ruthyn	1324
Sarah Otway Cave	Baroness Braye	1509
Susan Doyle	Baroness North	1554
Maria Janet	Baroness Sempill (Scotland)	1494
Frances Basset	Baroness Basset	1797
Margaret Mercer Elphinstone	Baroness Keith & Nairne	1803
Sophia Elizabeth Wykeham	Baroness Wenman	1834
Mary Elizabeth Campbell	Baroness Stratheden	1836
Cecilia Letitia Underwood	Duchess of Inverness	1840

ALPHABETICAL LIST OF

THE SURNAMES OF THE PEERS OF GREAT BRITAIN.

Abbot, Colchester *l.*
Abbott, Tenterden *l.*
Abercromby, Abercromby *l.*
Abercromby, Dunfermline *l.*
Acheson, Gosford *e.*
A'Court, Heytesbury *l.*
Addington, Sidmouth *v.*
Agar-Ellis, Clifden *v.*
Alexander, Caledon *e.*
Amherst, Amherst *e.*
Anderson-Pelham, Yarboro' *e.*
Anson, Lichfield *e.*
Arbuthnot, Arbuthnot *v.*
Arden, Alvanley *l.*
Arundell, Arundell of Wardour *l.*
Ashburnham, Ashburnham *e.*
Ashley-Cooper, Shaftesbury *e*
Astley, Hastings *l.*
Bagot, Bagot *l.*
Bampfylde, Poltimore *l.*
Baring, Ashburton *l.*
Bateman-Hanbury, Bateman *l.*
Bathurst, Bathurst *e.*
Beauclerk, St. Albans *d.*
Bennet, Tankerville *e.*
Bentinck, Portland *d.*
Beresford, Beresford *v.*
Beresford, Waterford *m.*
Berkeley, Fitzhardinge, *e.*
Bernard, Bandon *e.*
Bertie, Abingdon *e.*
Bertie, Lindsey *e.*
Best, Wynford *l.*
Bickersteth, Langdale *l.*
Bingham, Lucan, *e.*
Blayney, Blayney *l.*
Bligh, Darnley *e.*
Bootle-Wilbraham, Skelmersdale *l.*
Boscawen, Falmouth *e.*
Bourke, Mayo *e.*
Bouverie, Radnor *e*
Boyle, Cork & Orrery *e.*
Boyle, Glasgow *e.*
Boyle, Shannon *e.*
Brabazon, Meath *e.*
Brand, Dacre *l.*
Bridgeman, Bradford *e.*
Brodrick, Midleton *v.*
Bromley, Montford *l.*
Brougham, Brougham & Vaux *l.*
Browne, Kenmare *e.*
Browne, Sligo *m.*
Browne-Mostyn, Vaux of Harrowden *l.*
Brownlow, Lurgan *l.*
Brudenell, Cardigan *e.*
Brudenell-Bruce, Ailesbury *m*
Brudenell-Bruce, Bruce *e*
Brydges-Chandos-Grenville, Buckingham & Chandos *d.*
Burgh, Downes *l.*
Bury, Charleville *e.*
Butler, Glengall *e.*
Butler, Ormonde *m.*
Byng, Strafford *l.*
Byng, Torrington *v.*
Byron, Byron *l.*
Cadogan, Cadogan *e.*
Calthorpe, Calthorpe *l.*
Campbell, Argyll *d.*
Campbell, Campbell *l.*
Campbell, Breadalbane *m.*
Campbell, Cawdor *e.*
Canning, Canning *v.*
Capel, Essex *e.*
Caradoc, Howden *l.*
Carew, Carew *l.*
Carington, Carington *l.*
Carleton, Dorchester *l.*
Cary, Falkland *v.*
Cathcart, Cathcart *e.*
Caulfeild, Charlemont *e.*
Cavendish, Burlington *e.*
Cavendish, Devonshire *d.*
Cecil, Exeter *m.*
Cecil, Salisbury *m.*
Chichester, Donegal *m.*
Chichester, Templemore *l.*
Churchill, Marlborough *d.*
Cholmondeley, Cholmondeley *m.*
Cholmondeley, Delamere *l.*
Clements, Leitrim *e.*
Clifford, Clifford of Chudleigh *l.*
Cocks, Somers *e.*
Coke, Leicester *e.*
Colborne, Colborne *l.*
Colborne, Seaton *l.*
Cole, Enniskillen *e.*
Colville, Colville, *l.*

Compton, Northampton *m.*
Conway, Hertford *m.*
Conyngham, Conyngham *m.*
Copley, Lyndhurst *l.*
Courtenay, Devon *e.*
Coventry, Coventry *e*
Cowper, Cowper, *e.*
Craven, Craven *e.*
Crewe, Crewe *l.*
Crichton, Erne *e.*
Crofton, Crofton *l.*
Curzon-Howe, Howe *e.*
Curzon, Scarsdale *l.*
Curzon, Teynham *l.*
Cust, Brownlow *e.*
Dalrymple, Stair *e.*
De-Burgh, Clanricarde *m.*
De Grey, De Grey *e.*
De Grey, Walsingham *l.*
Denman, Denman *l.*
De-Ros, De-Ros *l.*
Devereux, Hereford *v.*
Digby, Digby *e.*
Dillon, Clonbrock *l*
Dormer, Dormer *l.*
Douglas, Douglas *l.*
Douglas, Morton *e.*
Douglas, Selkirk *e.*
Drummond, Strathallan *v.*
Drummond-Hay, Kinnoul *e.*
Drummond-Willoughby, Willoughby d'Eresby *l.*
Duff, Fife *e.*
Duncombe, Feversham *l.*
Dundas, Melville *v.*
Dundas, Zetland *e.*
Dutton, Sherborne *l.*
Eden, Auckland *e.*
Edgecumbe, Mount-Edgecumbe, *e.*
Egerton, Wilton *e.*
Eliot, St. Germans *e.*
Ellis, Howard de Walden *l.*
Ellis, Seaford *l.*
Erskine, Erskine *l.*
Erskine, Rosslynn *l.*
Fane, Westmoreland *e.*
Feilding, Denbigh *e.*
Fermor, Pomfret *e.*
Finch, Aylesford *e.*
Finch-Hatton, Winchilsea *e.*
Fitzclarence, Munster *e.*
Fitzgerald, Leinster *d.*
Fitz-Gibbon, Clare *e.*
Fitzmaurice, Lansdowne *m.*
Fitzmaurice, Orkney *e.*
Fitzroy, Grafton *d.*
Fitzroy, Southampton *l.*
Foley, Foley *l.*
Forbes, Granard *e.*
Forester, Forester *l.*
Fortescue, Fortescue *e.*
Fox, Holland *l.*
Fox-Strangways, Ilchester *e.*
Fraser, Lovat *l.*
Fraser, Saltoun *l.*
French, De Freyne *l.*
Gage, Gage *v.*
Gardner, Gardner *l.*
Gifford, Gifford *l.*
Gordon, Aberdeen *e.*
Gordon, Huntly *m.*
Gough, Gough
Graham, Montrose *d.*
Grant, Glenelg *l.*
Grant, Seafield *e.*
Greville, Warwick *e.*
Grey, Grey, *e.*
Grey, Stamford *e.*
Griffin, Braybrooke *l.*
Grimston, Verulam *e.*
Grosvenor, Westminster *m.*
Haldane, Camperdown *e.*
Hamilton Abercorn *m.*
Hamilton, Belhaven *l.*
Hamilton, Haddington *e.*
Hamilton, Hamilton *d.*
Handcock, Castlemaine .
Harbord, Suffield *l.*
Hanbury-Tracy, Sudeley *l.*
Hardinge, Hardinge *v.*
Harley, Oxford *e.*
Harris, Harris *l.*
Harris, Malmesbury *e.*
Hastings, Huntingdon *e.*
Hawke, Hawke, *l.*
Hay, Errol *e.*
Hay, Tweeddale *m.*
Hely-Hutchinson, Donoughmore *e.*
Herbert, Carnarvon *e.*
Herbert, Pembroke *e.*
Herbert, Powis *e.*
Hervey, Bristol, *m.*
Hill, Berwick *l.*
Hill, Downshire *m.*
Hill, Hill *v.*
Hill, Sandys *l.*
Hobart-Hampden, Buckinghamshire *e.*
Holroyd, Sheffield *e.*
Home, Home *e.*
Hood, Hood *v.*
Hope, Hopetoun *e.*
Howard, Carlisle *e.*
Howard, Effingham *e.*
Howard, Norfolk *d.*
Howard, Suffolk *e.*
Howard, Wicklow *e.*
Hughes, Dinorben *l.*
Irby, Boston *l.*
Jenkinson, Liverpool *e.*
Jerningham, Stafford *l.*
Jervis, St. Vincent *v.*
Jocelyn, Roden *e.*
Keane, Keane *l.*
Keith-Falconer, Kintore *e.*
Kennedy, Ailsa *m.*
Kenyon, Kenyon *l.*
Keppel, Albemarle *e.*
Ker, Roxburgh *d.*
Kerr, Lothian *m.*
King, Kingston *e.*
King, Lorton *v.*
King, Lovelace *e.*
Kinnaird, Kinnaird *l.*
Knox, Ranfurly *e.*
Kynynmound, Minto *e.*
Lake, Lake *v.*
Lamb, Beauvale *l.*
Lamb, Melbourne *v.*
Lambton, Durham *e.*
Lascelles, Harewood *e.*
Law, Ellenborough *e.*
Lawless, Cloncurry *l.*
Legge, Dartmouth *e.*
Leigh, Leigh *l.*
Lennox-Gordon, Richmond *d.*
Le-Poer-Trench, Clancarty *e.*
Leslie-Melville, Leven & Melville *e.*
Leveson-Gower, Granville *e.*
Leveson-Gower, Sutherland *d*
Liddell, Ravensworth *l.*
Lindsay, Balcarras *e.*
Lister, Ribblesdale *l.*
Littleton, Hatherton *l.*
Lloyd, Mostyn *l.*
Loftus, Ely *m.*
Lowther, Lonsdale *e.*
Lumley-Savile, Scarboro' *e.*
Lyttelton, Lyttelton *l.*
Mackay, Reay *l.*
Maitland, Lauderdale *e.*
Mann, Cornwallis *e.*
Manners, Rutland *d.*
Manners-Sutton, Canterbury *v.*
Manners-Sutton, Manners *l.*
Marsham, Romney *e.*
Maude, Hawarden *v.*
Maule, Panmure *l.*
Maxwell, Farnham *l.*
Maynard, Maynard *v.*
Meade, Clanwilliam *e.*
Metcalfe, Metcalfe *l.*
Methuen, Methuen *l.*
Milles, Sondes *l.*
Mitford, Redesdale *l.*
Molyneux, Sefton *e.*
Monson, Monson *l.*
Montagu, Manchester *d.*
Montagu-Douglas-Scott, Buccleuch *d.*
Montagu, Sandwich *e.*
Montgomerie, Eglinton *e.*
Moore, Drogheda *m.*
Moore, Mountcashel *e.*
Moreton, Ducie *e.*
Murray, Atholl *d.*
Murray, Dunmore *e.*
Murray, Glenlyon *l.*
Murray, Mansfield *e.*
Nelson, Nelson *e.*
Nevill, Abergavenny *e.*
Noel, Gainsborough *e.*
North, Guilford *e.*
Norton, Grantley *l.*
Nugent, Westmeath *m.*
O'Bryen, Thomond *m.*
O'Callaghan, Lismore *v.*
Ogilvy, Airlie *e.*
O'Neill, O'Neill *v.*
Onslow, Onslow *e.*
Osborne, Godolphin *l.*
Osborne, Leeds *d.*
Paget, Anglesey *m.*
Paget, Uxbridge *e.*
Pakenham, Longford *e.*
Parker, Macclesfield *e.*
Parker, Morley *e.*
Parnell, Congleton *l.*
Paulet, Winchester *m.*
Pelham, Chichester *e.*
Pelham-Clinton, Newcastle *d.*
Pellew, Exmouth *v.*
Pepys, Cottenham *l.*
Perceval, Arden *l.*
Perceval, Egmont *e.*
Percy, Beverley *e.*
Percy, Northumberland *d.*
Percy, Prudhoe *l.*
Pery, Limerick *e.*
Petre, Petre *l.*
Petty, Lansdowne *m.*
Phipps, Normanby *m.*
Pierrepoint, Manvers *e.*
Pindar, Beauchamp *e.*
Pitt-Rivers, Rivers *l.*
Plunket, Plunket *l.*
Plunkett, Dunsany *l.*
Plunkett, Fingall *e.*
Ponsonby, Besborough *e.*
Ponsonby, De Mauley *l.*
Ponsonby, Ponsonby *v.*
Portman, Portman *l.*
Poulett, Poulett *e.*
Powlett, Bayning *l.*
Powlett, Bolton *l.*
Powys, Lilford *l.*
Pratt, Camden *m.*
Primrose, Rosebery *e.*
Prittie, Dunalley *l.*
Proby, Carysfort *e.*
Quin, Dunraven *e.*
Ramsay, Dalhousie *e.*
Rawdon-Hastings, Hastings *m.*
Rice, Dynevor *l.*
Robinson, Ripon *e*
Rodney, Rodney *l.*
Rollo, Rollo *l.*
Rous, Stradbroke *e.*
Rushout, Northwick *l.*
Russell, Bedford *d.*
Ryder, Harrowby *e.*
St. Clair, Sinclair *l.*
St. John, Bolingbroke *v*
St. John, St. John *l.*
St. Leger, Doneraile *v.*
St. Maur, Somerset *d.*
Saumarez, De Saumarez *l.*
Scarlett, Abinger *l.*
Scott, Eldon *e.*
Scott, Polwarth *l.*
Sherard, Harborough *e.*
Shirley, Ferrers *e.*
Sidney, De L'isle & Dudley *l.*
Skeffington-Foster, Ferrard *v.*
Smythe, Strangford *v.*
Somerset, Beaufort *d.*
Spencer, Churchill *l.*
Spencer, Spencer *e.*
Spring-Rice, Monteagle *l.*
Stanhope, Chesterfield *e.*
Stanhope, Harrington *e.*
Stanhope, Stanhope *e.*
Stanley, Derby *e.*
Stanley, Stanley of Alderley *l.*
Stanley, Stanley of Bickerstaffe *l.*
Stapleton, Beaumont *l.*
Stapleton-Cotton, Combermere *v.*
Stewart, Galloway *e.*
Stonor, Camoys *l.*
Stopford, Courtown *e.*
Stourton, Stourton *l.*
Strutt, Rayleigh *l.*
Stuart, Bute *m.*
Stuart, Moray *e.*
Stuart, Stuart de Decies *l.*
Stuart-Wortley, Wharncliffe *l.*
Talbot, Shrewsbury *e.*
Talbot, Talbot *e.*
Taylor, Headfort *m.*
Thompson, Wenlock *l.*
Thurlow, Thurlow *l.*
Thynne, Bath *m.*
Thynne, Carteret *l.*
Townshend, Sydney *v.*
Townshend, Townshend *m.*
Trefusis, Clinton *l.*
Tuchet, Audley *l.*
Tufton, Thanet *e.*
Twisleton-Fiennes, Saye & Sele, *l.*
Vane, Cleveland *d.*
Vane, Londonderry *m.*
Vansittart, Bexley *l.*
Verney, Willoughby de Broke
Vesey, De Vesci *v.*
Villiers, Clarendon *e.*
Villiers, Jersey *e.*
Vivian, Vivian *l.*
Waldegrave, Waldegrave *e.*
Wallop, Portsmouth *e.*
Walpole, Orford *e.*
Ward, Ward *l.*
Warren, De Tabley *l.*
Warren, Vernon *l.*
Wellesley, Cowley *l*
Wellesley, Wellington *d.*
Wellesley-Pole, Mornington *e.*
Wemyss-Charteris-Douglas, Wemyss *e.*
Wentworth-Fitzwilliam, Fitzwilliam *e.*
West, De La Warr *e.*
Westenra, Rossmore *l.*
Willoughby, Middleton *l.*
Wilson, Berners *l.*
Wodehouse, Wodehouse *l.*
Wogan, Furnival *l.*
Wrottesley, Wrottesley *l.*
Yorke, Hardwicke *e.*

TITLES OF THE ELDEST SONS OF PEERS.

THE eldest Sons of Dukes, Marquises, and Earls assume (by courtesy) the second title of their fathers.—The younger Sons of Dukes and Marquises take the title of Lord.
The younger Sons of Earls take the title of Honourable.
All Daughters of Dukes, Marquises, and Earls take the title of Lady.
All Sons and Daughters of Viscounts and Barons take the title of Honourable.

The following are the titles borne by the eldest Sons of Peers, with the titles of their fathers:—

[Those marked thus * are the second titles of Irish Representative Peers. Those marked thus † are the second title of Scotch Representative Peers].

*Aberdour *l.* Morton *e.*
Aboyne *e.* Huntly *m.*
*Acheson *v.* Gosford *e.*
*Adare *v.* Dunraven *e.*
*Alexander *v.* Caledon *e.*
Alford *v.* Brownlow *e.*
Altamont *e.* Sligo *m.*
Althorp *v.* Spencer *e.*
Ancrum *e.* Lothian *m.*
Andover *v.* Suffolk *e.*
Anson *v.* Lichfield *e.*
Apsley *l.* Bathurst *e.*
Arundel & Surrey *e.* Norfolk *d.*
Ashley *l.* Shaftesbury *e.*
†Balgonie *v.* Leven & Melville *e.*
Beaumont *m.* Roxburgh *d.*
Bective *e.* Headfort *m.*
Belfast *e.* Donegal *m.*
*Bernard *v.* Bandon *e.*
Bertie *l.* Lindsey *e.*
*Bingham *l.* Lucan *e.*
Binning *l.* Haddington *e.*
Blandford *m.* Marlborough *d.*
Boringdon *v.* Morley *e.*
Boscawen *l.* Falmouth *e.*
Boyle *v.* Shannon *e.*
Brabazon *l.* Meath *e.*
Brecknock *e.* Camden *m.*
Brome *v.* Cornwallis *m.*
Brooke *l.* Warwick *e.*
Bruce *e.* Ailesbury *m.*
Brudenell *l.* Cardigan *e.*
Burford *e.* St. Alban's *d.*
Burghersh *l.* Westmoreland *e.*
Burghley *l.* Exeter *m.*
Bury *v.* Albemarle *e.*
*Caher *v.* Glengall *e.*
Campden *v.* Gainsborough *e.*
Carmarthen *m.* Leeds *d.*
Cantilupe *v.* De La Warr *e.*
Cassillis *e.* Ailsa *m.*
Castlereagh *v.* Londonderry *m.*
Castlerosse *v.* Kenmare *e.*
Cavendish *l.* Burlington *e.*
*Caulfeild *v.* Charlemont *e.*
Chandos *m.* Buckingham *d.*
Chelsea *v.* Cadogan *e.*
Chewton *v.* Waldegrave *e.*
Clements *v.* Leitrim *e.*
Clive *v.* Powis *e.*
*Clonmore *l.* Wicklow *e.*
Coke *v.* Leicester *e.*
Cole *v.* Enniskillen *e.*
Coleshill *v.* Digby *e.*
Compton *e.* Northampton *m.*
Courtenay *l.* Devon *e.*
Cranbourne *v.* Salisbury *m.*
Cranley *v.* Onslow *e.*
Crichton *v.* Erne *e.*
Curzon *v.* Howe *e.*
†Daer *l.* Selkirk *e.*
Dalkeith *e.* Buccleuch *d.*
Dalmeny *l.* Rosebery *e.*
Darlington *e.* Cleveland *d.*
Deerhurst *v.* Coventry *e.*
*Delvin *l.* Westmeath *m.*
De Montâlt *l.* Hawarden *v.*
Douro *m.* Wellington *d.*
Douglas *m.* Hamilton *d.*
Doune *l.* Moray *e.*
Duncan *v.* Camperdown *e.*
Duncannon *v.* Besborough *e.*
Dundas *l.* Zetland *e.*
Dungarvan *v.* Cork *e.*
Dunglas *l.* Home *e.*
Dunkellin *l.* Clanricarde *m.*
Dunlo *v.* Clancarty *e.*
Dunwich *v.* Stradbroke *e.*
Dupplin *v.* Kinnoul *e.*
Eastnor *v.* Somers *e.*
Ebrington *v.* Fortescue *e.*
Eden *l.* Auckland *e.*
Elcho *l.* Wemyss *e.*
Eliot *l.* St. Germans *e.*
Elmley *v.* Beauchamp *e.*
Emlyn *v.* Cawdor *e.*
Encombe *v.* Eldon *e.*
Euston *e.* Grafton *d.*
Feilding *v.* Denbigh *e.*
Fincastle *v.* Dunmore *e.*
Fitzclarence *v.* Munster *e.*
Fitz Gibbon *v.* Clare *e.*
Fitzharris *v.* Malmesbury *e.*
Folkstone *v.* Radnor *e.*
Forbes *v.* Granard *e.*
Fordwich *v.* Cowper *e.*
Garlies *v.* Galloway *e.*
†Gifford *e.* Tweeddale *m.*
Gilford *l.* Clanwilliam *e.*
Glenluce *l.* Stair *e.*
*Glentworth *l.* Limerick *e.*
Goderich *v.* Ripon *e.*
Granby *m.* Rutland *d.*
Greenock *l.* Cathcart *e.*
Grey de Wilton *v.* Wilton *e.*
Grey of Groby *l.* Stamford *e.*
Grosvenor *e.* Westminster *m.*
Grimston *v.* Verulam *e.*
Guernsey *l.* Aylesford *e.*
Haddo *l.* Aberdeen *e.*
Hamilton *v.* Abercorn *m.*
Harley *l.* Oxford *e.*
Hartington *m.* Devonshire *d.*
Hastings *l.* Huntingdon *e.*
Hawkesbury *l.* Liverpool *e.*
Herbert *l.* Pembroke *e.*
Hinchinbroke *v.* Sandwich *e.*
Hillsborough *e.* Downshire *m.*
Hinton *v.* Poulett *e.*
Hobart *l.* Buckinghamshire *e.*
Holmesdale *v.* Amherst *e.*
Hope *l.* Hopetoun *e.*
Howard *l.* Effingham *e.*
Howick *v.* Grey *e.*
Hyde *l.* Clarendon *e.*
*Inchiquin *e.* Thomond *m.*
Ingestre *v.* Talbot *e.*
Inverury *l.* Kintore *e.*
Jermyn *e.* Bristol *m.*
Jocelyn *v.* Roden *e.*
Kelburne *v.* Glasgow *e.*
Kildare *m.* Leinster *d.*
Killeen *l.* Fingall *e.*
Kilmarnock *l.* Errol *e.*
*Kilworth *l.* Mountcashel *e.*
Kincardine *e.* Montrose *d.*
Kingsborough *v.* Kingston *e.*
†Kirkwall *v.* Orkney *e.*
Lambton *v.* Durham *e.*
Lascelles *v.* Harewood *e.*
Leicester *e.* Townshend *m.*
Leominster *l.* Pomfret *e.*
Leveson *l.* Granville *e.*
Lewisham *v.* Dartmouth *e.*
Lincoln *e.* Newcastle *d.*
Lindsay *l.* Balcarras *e.*
Loftus *v.* Ely *m.*
Lorne *m.* Argyll *d.*
Loughborough *l.* Rosslyn *e.*
Louvaine *l.* Beverley *e.*
Lowther *v.* Lonsdale *e.*
Lucas *l.* De Grey *e.*
Lumley *v.* Scarborough *e.*
Lymington *v.* Portsmouth *e.*
Macduff *v.* Fife *e.*
Mahon *v.* Stanhope *e.*
Maidstone *v.* Winchilsea *e.*
Maitland *v.* Lauderdale *e.*
Malden *v.* Essex *e.*
Mandeville *v.* Manchester *d.*
March *e.* Richmond *d.*
Marsham *v.* Romney *e.*
Melgund *v.* Minto *e.*
Milton *v.* Fitzwilliam *e.*
Molyneux *v.* Sefton *e.*
Montgomerie *l.* Eglinton *e.*
Moore *v.* Drogheda *m.*
Morpeth *v.* Carlisle *e.*
Moreton *l.* Ducie *e.*
Mountcharles *e.* Conyngham *m.*
Mountstuart *l.* Bute *m.*
Mulgrave *e.* Normanby *m.*
*Naas *l.* Mayo *e.*
Nevill *v.* Abergavenny *e.*
Newark *v.* Manvers *e.*
Newport *v.* Bradford *e.*
Norreys *l.* Abingdon *e.*
North *l.* Guilford *e.*
Northland *v.* Ranfurly *e.*
Ockham *v.* Lovelace *e.*
†Ogilvy *l.* Airlie *e.*
Ormelie *e.* Breadalbane *m.*
Ossory *e.* Ormonde *m.*
Ossulston *l.* Tankerville *e.*
Oxmantown *l.* Rosse, *e.*
Paget *l.* Uxbridge *e.*
Parker *v.* Macclesfield *e.*
Pelham *l.* Chichester *e.*
Perceval *v.* Egmont *e.*
Percy *e.* Northumberland *d.*
Petersham *v.* Harrington *e.*
Pevensey *v.* Sheffield *e.*
Porchester *l.* Carnarvon *e.*
Proby *l.* Carysfort *e.*
Ramsay *l.* Dalhousie *e.*
Rawdon *e.* Hastings *m.*
†Reidhaven *v.* Seafield *e.*
Rocksavage *e.* Cholmondeley *m.*
Royston *v.* Hardwicke *e.*
Sandon *v.* Harrowby *e.*
St. Asaph *v.* Ashburnham *e.*
Segrave *l.* Fitzhardinge *e.*
Seymour *l.* Somerset *d.*
Shelburne *e.* Lansdowne *m.*
Sherard *l.* Harborough *e.*
Southam *v.* Ellenborough *e.*
Stafford *m.* Sutherland *d.*
Stanhope *l.* Chesterfield *e.*
Stanley *l.* Derby *e.*
Stavordale *l.* Ilchester *e.*
Stopford *v.* Courtown *e.*
Stormont *v.* Mansfield *e.*
Suirdale *v.* Donoughmore *e.*
Talbot *l.* Shrewsbury *e.*
Tamworth *v.* Ferrers *e.*
Tavistock *m.* Bedford *d.*
Titchfield *m.* Portland *d.*
Trafalgar *v.* Nelson *e.*
Tufton *l.* Thanet *e.*
*Tullamore *l.* Charleville *e.*
Tullibardine *m.* Atholl *d.*
Tyrone *e.* Waterford *m.*
Uffington *v.* Craven *e.*
Uxbridge *e.* Anglesey *m.*
Valletort *v.* Mount-Edgecumbe *e.*
Villiers *v.* Jersey *e.*
Walpole *l.* Orford *e.*
Weymouth *v.* Bath *m.*
Wiltshire *e.* Winchester *m.*
Worcester *m.* Beaufort *d.*
Worsley *l.* Yarborough *e.*
Yarmouth *e.* Hertford *m.*

Of the above list, the following have been summoned to the House of Peers during the lifetime of their fathers —

Title by Courtesy.	*Summoned as*
Earl of Bruce	Lord Bruce.
Lord Stanley	Lord Stanley of Bickerstaffe.
Earl of Uxbridge	Lord Paget.

IRISH REPRESENTATIVE PEERS [28],

ELECTED FOR LIFE,

Of whom three are also Peers of England—their English title is added in a parenthesis.

The dates given are those of their creation as Peers of Ireland, but they only rank as Peers of Great Britain from the Union.

	MARQUISES OF	Creation.	Title by Courtesy of Eldest Son.
George Thomas John Nugent	Westmeath	1822	L. Delvin
	EARLS OF		
Francis William Caulfeild	Charlemont (L. Charlemont, in England)	1763	V. Caulfeild
Stephen Moore	Mountcashel	1781	L. Kilworth
John Bourke	Mayo	1785	L. Naas
William Howard	Wicklow, K.P.	1793	Clonmore
John Otway O'Connor Cuffe	Desart	1793	V. Cuffe
George Charles Bingham	Lucan	1795	L. Bingham
John Crichton	Erne	1789	V. Crichton
James Bernard	Bandon	1800	V. Bernard
John Bruce Richard O'Neill	O'Neill	1800	
Du-Pre Alexander	Caledon	1800	V. Alexander
Archibald Acheson	Gosford, G.C.B. (L. Worlingham, in Englnd)	1806	V. Acheson
Charles William Bury	Charleville	1806	L. Tullamore
William Parsons	Rosse, K.P.	1806	L. Oxmantown
Richard Butler	Glengall	1816	V. Caher
Windham Henry Wyndham-Quin	Dunraven	1822	V. Adare
	VISCOUNTS.		
John Vesey	De Vesci	1776	
Hayes St. Leger	Doneraile	1785	
Cornwallis Maude	Hawarden	1793	
Robert Edward King	Lorton	1806	
	BARONS.		
Edward Wadding Plunkett	Dunsany	1461	
Cadwallader Davis Blayney	Blayney	1621	
Henry Maxwell	Farnham K.P.	1756	
Robert Dillon	Clonbrock	1790	
Edward Crofton	Crofton	1797	
Henry Prittie	Dunalley	1800	
Richard Handcock	Castlemaine	1812	
Ulysses Burgh	Downes, K.C.B.	1822	

SCOTCH REPRESENTATIVE PEERS [16],

ELECTED EVERY PARLIAMENT.

The dates given are those of their creation as Scotch Peers, but they only rank as Peers of Great Britain from the Union

	MARQUIS OF	Creation.	Title by Courtesy of Eldest Son.
George Hay	Tweeddale, K.T.	1694	E. Gifford
	EARLS.		
George Sholto Douglas	Morton	1458	L. Aberdour
Alexander Home	Home	1605	L. Dunglas
David Ogilvy	Airlie and Lintrathen	1639	L. Ogilvy
David Leslie Melville	Leven and Melville	1641	V. Balgonie
Dunbar James Douglas	Selkirk	1646	L. Daer
Thomas John Hamilton Fitzmaurice	Orkney	1696	V. Kirkwall
Francis William Grant	Seafield	1701	V. Reidhaven
	VISCOUNTS.		
John Arbuthnot	Arbuthnot	1641	
James Andrew John Laurence Charles Drummond	Strathallan	1686	
	BARONS.		
Alexander George Fraser, K.C.B., G.C.H.	Saltoun	1445	
Charles St. Clair	Sinclair	1489	
John Colville	Colville (of Culross)	1609	
Eric Mackay	Reay	1628	
John Rollo	Rollo	1651	
Henry Francis Hepburn Scott	Polwarth	1690	

POSTAL DIRECTORY.

INDEX.

GENERAL POST OFFICE,

ST. MARTIN'S LE GRAND.

CHIEF OFFICERS.

POSTMASTER-GENERAL FOR THE UNITED KINGDOM. } The Right Hon. Edward Granville, Earl of St. Germans.
SECRETARY.—Lieut.-Col. Wm. Leader Maberly.
Assistant Secretary.—Thomas Lawrence, Esq.
Solicitor.—Mark Beauchamp Peacock, Esq.
Private Secretary to the Postmaster-General.—Gustavus Charles Cornwall, Esq.
Chief Clerk to the Secretary.—James Campbell, Esq.
Superintending President of Inland and Foreign Office.—William Bokenham, Esq.
Superintending President of London District Office.—Robert Smith, Esq.
Surveyor and Superintendent of Mail Coach Department.—George Stow, Esq.
Receiver-General.—Thomas Young, Esq. *Chief Clerk.*—George Edward Hide, Esq.
Accountant General.—Charles Thomas Court, Esq. *Deputy.*—Charles Compton, Esq.
President of Money Order Office.—William Barth, Esq.
Inspector of Dead and Returned Letter Office.—Charles Newton, Esq.
Inspector of Ship Letter Office.—George Richard Huddlestone, Esq.

For other officers of the Post Office, see "OFFICIAL DIRECTORY."

LETTERS

whether containing Coin or not, can be

REGISTERED

on payment of a registration fee of ONE SHILLING, *in addition to the ordinary rates of Postage* on Inland and Colonial as well as on Ship or Foreign Letters, or Letters. On those for delivery *within France*, the charges, *besides the registration fee of one shilling*, will be *the English rate to France*, in addition to *double the French rate* to the place to which the Letter is addressed. The same regulation applies to registered letters passing through France. A printed acknowledgment torn out of the receipt book, and stamped with the office stamp, will be given to any person registering a Letter. Registered Letters, to pass by the Evening Mails will be taken at the Receiving Houses in London (for list of which see page 787) until five o'clock, p.m., and by Postmasters throughout the United Kingdom, until within half an hour of the closing of the Box for the particular Mail or Bag by which they are to be despatched. Registered Letters bearing a sufficient number of Stamps will be considered Paid Letters, but the *registration fee of one shilling must always be paid in money.*

LETTERS REGISTERED FOR DELIVERY WITHIN THE LIMITS OF THE LONDON DISTRICT (formerly the Two-penny) Post, must be posted half an hour before the departure of the particular Despatch by which they are intended to pass. The Receivers have instructions to retain letters put in later, until *the next despatch*. For hours of despatch see page 784.

In the case of Foreign, Colonial, or Ship Letters, it must be clearly understood, that Registration cannot extend beyond the Port of despatch in the United Kingdom, though parties, if they wish it, may register such Letters *as far as* the Port of despatch. Letters, however, addressed to France, and Letters passing through France, are exceptions to this rule, the French Post Office undertaking to provide for their security till they shall have been delivered, *if addressed to France*, and so long as they remain in the French territory, *if passing through France*.

The arrangements for carrying out the system of Registration have been made with the view of ensuring the punctual delivery of Registered Letters; on their delivery the parties to whom they may have been addressed will be required to acknowledge in writing their receipt.

The system of Registration provides a secure mode of transmitting *Bank Notes, Bank Post Bills, Drafts, &c., &c.*, and persons having occasion to send by Post *small sums* will avoid risk by sending the money through the medium of

THE MONEY ORDER OFFICE,

carried on, on the Public account, at the General Post Office. The commission chargeable for Money Orders is *three-pence on sums not exceeding two pounds*, and on sums above two, and *not exceeding five pounds, sixpence.*

No Order will be given for sums beyond this amount. It will be in most cases a convenience to parties in

LONDON

that Money Orders in their favour should be drawn on the Money Order Offices, nearest to their residences, as Orders on *London only* are not payable at any other than the General Post Office in St. Martin's le Grand. The "*Index to the Street Directory*" in the *complete* edition of this work has a list of Streets, Squares, and Places in the Metropolis and its vicinity, and in every case the *nearest* Money Order Office is indicated. It is, therefore, only necessary to turn to that Index to ascertain on what particular Office a Money Order, in favor of any one resident in the Metropolis or its vicinity should be drawn.

TIME AT WHICH MONEY ORDERS MAY BE HAD OR CASHED,

Orders are issued and paid in *London* and *within the three mile* circle, between the hours of Ten a.m. and Four p.m., and in *other places* between the hours of Nine a.m. and Six p.m., except during the short intervals of time when the Letter Boxes are closed for the receipt of *paid* Letters.

These economical modes having been devised expressly with a view to the security of property, it may reasonably be expected that all persons having occasion to transmit money, will avail themselves of the opportunity of securing it and in no case, *by committing property* UNREGISTERED *to the Letter boxes*, RISK ITS LOSS.

If, however, persons are willing to incur such risk, should the articles forwarded be Notes, or Cheques payable at sight they should be cut in halves, and the second halves should not be despatched until the receipt of the first has been acknowledged. The numbers, dates, and amounts should also be carefully taken.

Money Orders may be obtained at the GENERAL POST OFFICE; at the several BRANCH OFFICES in *Lombard street, Charing Cross, Old Cavendish street,* and *Blackman street, Borough;* and at the following RECEIVING HOUSES:—

Battle Bridge	No.1 Pleasant row	Hackney	No. 8 Church st.	Oxford Street	No. 210.
Bloomsbury	No.1 Broad street	Islington	86 Upper street	Paddington	No.116 Edgware rd
Brompton	No.5 Brompton pl.	Kennington Cross	No. 2.	Piccadilly	No. 65.
Camberwell Green		Kensington	High street, opposite the church.	Pimlico	28 Queen's Row.
Camden Town	No. 98 High street			Ratcliff	No. 77 Broad st.
Chelsea	No.79 Paradise row	Kingsland Road	4 Orchard place.	Strand	No. 180.
City Road	No. 36 near Old st.	Lambeth	No.33 Mount st.	Tottenham Court Rd.	No. 103.
Dockhead	No. 11.	Limehouse	No.5 Three Colt st	Upper Baker Street	No. 54.
Gray's Inn road	No.43 Up. North pl.	Old Kent Road	No.9 Northptn. pl.	Whitechapel Road	No. 1.

BEYOND THE THREE MILE CIRCLE.

Barking; Barnet; Bexley; Brentford; Bromley, Kent; Clapham; Croydon; Deptford; Dulwich; Edgware; Edmonton; Enfield; Foot's Cray; Greenwich; Hammersmith; Hampstead; Harrow; Highgate; Hounslow; Kingston; Lewisham; Norwood; Putney; Richmond, Surrey; Romford; Shooter's Hill; Southall; Stanmore; Stratford; Sydenham; Tooting; Waltham Cross; Woodford; Woolwich.

OF ALL POSTMASTERS, AND OF MANY OF THE CHIEF DEPUTY POSTMASTERS THROUGHOUT THE UNITED KINGDOM;

For list of places within the delivery of the London District Post, see pages 785 & 786.

(For List of Post Towns and Principal Places throughout England and Wales, see pages 733 *to* 754.*)*

Scotland, see pages 754 *to* 759. *Ireland, see pages* 760 *to* 765.

Money Orders may be drawn payable, as well as issued, at the above mentioned offices, except the London Branch Office of Lombard Street, which *only* GRANTS Orders.

*** In cases where personal attendance is inconvenient, if the Order is receipted by the person to whom it is made payable and the party presenting it for payment can afford full information as to the *Christian name, Surname, Address* and *Occupation* of the person WHO ORIGINALLY OBTAINED THE ORDER, payment will be made, but unless these conditions are strictly complied with, it must be refused.

PEERS AND MEMBERS OF PARLIAMENT

Members of either House are entitled to receive, free of charge Petitions to Parliament, provided that each Petition is sent without a cover, or in a cover open at the sides, and does not exceed the weight of *Thirty-two Ounces*

ADDRESSES TO HER MAJESTY PASS FREE.

With these exceptions, **ALL INLAND LETTERS OR PACKETS,** including those from the Channel Isles and the Isle of Man, if PREPAID, are subject to the following

RATES OF POSTAGE:

Not exceeding Half an Ounce in Weight .... **One Penny**
One Ounce .... **Two Pence**
Two Ounces .... **Four Pence**
Three Ounces .... **Six Pence,** *and so on,* **Two Rates** being added for every ounce up to **Sixteen Ounces,** beyond which, *with the following* exceptions, NO PACKET, *whether subject to postage or not,* CAN BE RECEIVED.

1. PARLIAMENTARY PETITIONS and ADDRESSES TO HER MAJESTY.
2. PARLIAMENTARY PROCEEDINGS.
3. LETTERS and PACKETS *addressed to or received from Places beyond Sea.*
4. LETTERS and PACKETS *to and from* PUBLIC OFFICERS AND PUBLIC DEPARTMENTS.
5. DEEDS if sent open, or in covers open at the sides. They may be tied with string and sealed in order to prevent inspection of the contents, but they *must be open at the sides* that it may be seen that they ar entitled to the privilege.
6. BANKERS' PARCELS *despatched from London,* and specially delivered at the General Post Office, under certain regulations.

With these exceptions, ALL PACKETS ABOVE THE WEIGHT OF SIXTEEN OUNCES *will be forwarded to the* DEAD LETTER OFFICE.

INLAND LETTERS OR PACKETS PUT INTO THE UNPAID LETTER BOXES ARE CHARGED DOUBLE THE AMOUNT OF POSTAGE TO WHICH, HAD THEY BEEN PREPAID, THEY WOULD HAVE BEEN LIABLE. The Scale of Weight in force for General Post Letters is equally applicable to Letters passing through the local penny posts throughout the Kingdom and to those pasing through the *local Posts* of LONDON, DUBLIN and EDINBURGH. They are subject to the *same Rules* and *the same Charges* as General Post Letters, and must be paid in advance, or they will be liable to double the rate to which they would otherwise be subject.

The same Regulation applies to Letters pre-paid by Money, where the full and proper rate of Postage has not bee paid in advance.

POSTAGE STAMPS.

Letters written on Stamped Paper or enclosed in Stamped Covers, or having Stamps (whether labels or medallion heads) affixed to them, the Stamps in every such case being equal to the rates of Postage chargeable on such Letters if pre-paid, will pass *Free* of all other Postage charge in whatever part of the UNITED KINGDOM they may be posted.

In those cases where the Value of Stamps on the Letter is less than the Amount of the Postage to which it would be now liable, if pre-paid, the letter will be charged Double the Amount of such difference on delivery. An Inland Letter, for example, weighing more than Half-an-Ounce, and not exceeding an Ounce, if bearing only a Penny Stamp, will be charged Two Pence on delivery.

Stamps may be used for *Printed Votes* and *Proceedings in Parliament;* if the Stamps, however, should be less in value than the proper rate of Postage to which these documents are subject, only the difference, and not Double the difference, is charged.

Stamps *(provided they cover the whole postage)* may also be used on Foreign, Colonial, and Ship Letters, &c. *outwards.* If any Letter, however, addressed to Places beyond Sea, to which pre-payment is compulsory, shall bear an insufficient number of Stamps, it will be sent to the Dead Letter Office, to be returned, in all practicable cases, to the writer. Stamps are *not* permitted to be used on Letters arriving in the United Kingdom *from the Colonies or Foreign Countries.* In such cases, therefore, Letters will be chargeable with the same rates as they would be if not bearing Stamps.

All these Regulations will be applicable to Newspapers in those cases where they are liable to Postage.

Note—Adhesive Stamps should be placed on the Front of the Letter and upon the right-hand corner on the upper side. Should this direction not be attended to, from the rapidity with which the duty must be performed, Letters which bear Stamps will frequently be taxed, while the Parties receiving them will be put to much trouble in obtaining a return of the Postage improperly charged. In all cases of complaint, whether of overcharge or of any other irregularity, the Covers of the Letters must invariably be kept and sent to the Post Office, as affording the only means of investigating the complaint.

ADHESIVE STAMPS AND ENVELOPES.

Every Postmaster, Sub-Postmaster, or Letter-Receiver, without exception, will sell the Postage *Label* Stamps, Stamped Envelopes, and Stamped half-sheets of paper to the Public at the following Prices:—

The Penny Label Stamps............at 1d. each.
The Twopenny ditto ....at 2d. „
The Penny Envelopes ....24 for 2s. 3d. or 2 for 2¼d.
The Twopenny ditto ....12 „ 2s. 2d. „ 3 „ 6½d.
Stamped Half sheets of Paper 1¼d. each, or the quire of 24 for 2s. 3d.

They are also sold at the Chief Office in St. Martin's le Grand, and at the Branch Offices at Lombard Street, Charing Cross, Old Cavendish Street, and the Borough.

LETTERS TO PASS BY THE INLAND EVENING MAILS

can be posted at the Receiving Houses till 5 30 P.M.; by the Letter Carriers ringing bells (on payment of one penny with each) from 4 30 to 5 30 P.M.; at the Branch Post Offices, at Charing Cross; Old Cavendish Street, and 108 Blackman Street, Borough, till 6 P.M.; and with a *fee* of *one penny* (which must be paid by a *Stamp affixed to the letter*) until 6 45 P.M.; at the Branch Post Office in Lombard Street, till 6 P.M.; and till 7 P.M., with a fee paid by means of a *penny Stamp affixed to the letter;* at the General Post Office, St. Martin's le Grand, until 6 P.M. and until 7 P.M. upon payment of a fee of one penny (or an *affixed Stamp*), in addition to the postage, which must *then* be paid in advance, and from 7 till half-past 7 upon payment of a fee of 6d. with each. For Morning Mails, see page 789.

FOREIGN MAILS.

Letters are received for despatch by the mails to France and Belgium on every *Monday*, *Wednesday*, *Thursday*, and *Saturday*, at the same hours as by the Inland Evening Mails. For *all the Continental Mails* on *Tuesdays* and *Fridays*, at the Branch Offices, Charing Cross; Old Cavendish Street, and 108, Blackman Street, Borough, and at all the Receiving Houses, until 8 P.M.; at the General Post Office, St. Martin's le Grand, and at the Branch Office in Lombard Street, until 10 P.M.; *and at St. Martin's le Grand only* from 10 until a quarter past 10 P.M. on payment of *a fee of one penny*, and until half-past 10 P.M. *on payment of a fee of sixpence.*

Letters for Holland are in time if posted on Wednesday and Saturday *mornings*, at the different Offices, at the hours appointed, for the reception of Letters to be forwarded by the *Morning Mails*, for which see page 789.

*** For all other Foreign Mails the hours are the same as for Inland Letters.

FOREIGN AND SHIP LETTERS ADDRESSED LONDON ONLY,

for persons whose residences are not known, are copied into lists which are hung up daily in the hall of the General Post Office. Parties writing their addresses opposite to their names will receive their letters on the following morning.

NON-COMMISSIONED OFFICERS, CAPTAINS' AND PURSERS' STEWARDS, CLERKS' ASSISTANTS, SEAMEN, AND SOLDIERS,

sen and receive Letters, to and from the East Indies by the Overland Mails, "*viâ* Southampton," under the weight nalf an ounce, on their own private concerns only, while they are employed on her Majesty's Service, or in the service of the East India Company, for one penny.

Letters coming from a Seaman, or from a Serjeant, Corporal, Trumpeter, Fifer, or Private Soldier.	The Penny must be paid at the time the letter is put into the Post Office. The name of the Soldier or Sailor, his Class or Description, and the name of the Ship or Regiment, Corps or Detachment, to which he belongs, must be specified. And the Officer having the Command must sign his name, and sp cify the name of the Ship or Regiment, Corps or Detachment, he commands.
Letters going to Seamen or Soldiers.	The Penny must be paid at the time it is put into the Post Office, and the direction must specify the class of person, and the Ship, Regiment, or Corps to which he belongs.

The postage upon Soldiers' and Seamen's letters received from parts beyond sea, without the penny having been prepaid, is twopence in addition to the Ship Letter gratuity, if received by Private Ship.

Threepence Postage is charged on Letters addressed to Soldiers and Seamen to either of the following places:—River Gambia, Sierra Leone, Goree, Senegal, Cape Coast Castle, Fernando Po, Coast of Africa, Ascension (Isle). To St. Helena, the East Indies, New South Wales, Cape of Good Hope, Mauritius, Hong-Kong, and China, one penny. Seamen's and Soldiers' Letters from Abroad by private Ships are chargeable with 3d. each.

*** WARRANT OFFICERS either in the ARMY or NAVY, or MASTER'S MATES i the NAVY, are not entitled to receive or transmit Letters at less than the usual rates of Postage.

Soldiers' and Seamen's Letters are not liable to any additional rate upo re-direction; but all other

LETTERS RE-DIRECTED—

become, on re-direction, subject to new rates of postage, which (except to those places abroad to which payment is compulsory) may either be paid in advance or upon delivery.

The *pre-paid* rate *only* is charged upon re-directed letters.

Re-directed Letters for Commissioned Officers in the Army or Navy, when addressed in the first instance to or from a place abroad, are, in the event of such Officers being removed upon service (whether at home or abroad), forwarded without any additional charge for Postage.

OVERCHARGED LETTERS.

Overcharges returned between the hours of ten and four, on presenting the overcharged letters at the window in the Hall of the General Post Office. Or the letter may be sent to the Office by the letter-carrier of the district, and the overcharge will be returned with the letter in two days.

PRINTED VOTES AND PROCEEDINGS OF THE IMPERIAL PARLIAMENT, OR OF THE COLONIAL LEGISLATURES,

are charged	Under Four Ounces	One Penny.
	Above Four and under Eight Ounces..........	Two Pence.
	Above Eight and under Twelve Ounces	Three Pence, and so on.

Such Votes and Proceedings, whether paid or unpaid, pass at these rates between places in the United Kingdom as well as to the Colonies *by packet.* To those places to which there are no packets—the Cape, for instance—they may be forwarded "by Private Ships," at *double* the above rates. They are not, however, forwarded to the East Indies, *viâ* Southampton and Alexandria, nor to places through France *under the full rates of Letter Postage.* The Post-master General is authorised (if he shall see fit) to delay the transmission of Printed Votes and Proceedings in Parliament for any space not exceeding Twenty-four hours from the time at which the same would otherwise have been forwarded.

DELIVERY OF LETTERS IN LONDON.

The morning delivery of General Post Letters (including despatches from every Post Town and place in the United Kingdom, and those Foreign, Ship, and Packet letters which have arrived in sufficient time) commences in every district within three miles of St. Martin's le Grand at about nine o'clock, A. M., and is completed in about two hours, except on Mondays, or on other days when there are large arrivals of Foreign or Ship Letters, when the period of commencing and concluding the delivery is unavoidably retarded for a space varying from thirty to sixty minutes. Letters by the day mails arrive at 2 P.M. They are delivered in Upper Thames street, St. Paul's Church yard, Newgate street, Cloth Fair, Aldersgate street, Redcross street, Finsbury place, Eldon street, New Broad street, Bishopsgate within, Houndsditch, Minories, Haydon square, and Tower hill, and in all places within the limits of those streets, by the General Post Letter Carriers, and the delivery is completed within about two hours from the time of the arrival of the Mail. All despatches by the Day Mails for places beyond the above limits are sent out by the three and four o'clock District Post deliveries. Those by the Gravesend Day Mail, which arrive at a quarter past Four P.M., are sent out by the District Post five o'clock delivery. Foreign Mails arriving after the morning despatch of the Letter Carriers are (provided they arrive before two o'clock, P.M.) sent out within the before-mentioned limits by the General Post Letter Carriers, who complete their deliveries in about an hour from the time of their despatch. For places beyond those limits, all Foreign letters arriving subsequent to the Morning despatch of the Letter Carriers, are delivered by the District Post Letter Carriers, as are all *Letters which arrive later than half past two* P.M. *by any Foreign Mail.*

COIN SHOULD NOT, UNLESS IN REGISTERED LETTERS, BE SENT BY POST.

The great increase in the number of *Money Letters* having rendered it impossible, without hazard to the punctual despatch of the Mails, to continue the former practice of entering the addresses of such Letters, and of taking receipts for them on delivery to the parties to whom they were addressed; such practice being now adopted in the case of Registered letters *only.*

ARTICLES WHICH MAY NOT BE SENT BY POST.

Letters or Packets cannot be forwarded, conveyed, or delivered by the Post Office containing any of the following enclosures, viz., any Glass or Glass Bottle, any Razor, Scissors, Knife, Fork, or other sharp or pointed instrument, any Leeches, Game, Fish, Flesh, Fruit, Vegetable, or other perishable substance, any Bladder, or other vessel containing liquid or any article, matter, or thing whatsoever which might, by pressure or otherwise, be rendered injurious to the Officers of the Post Office, or to the contents of the Mail bags.

LETTER STAMPS.

The date shows when the letters were received at the Post Office.

The circular stamp of black or red ink, at the back of the letter, is used when the postage is to be paid on delivery.

Ditto of red ink, on the face of the letter, with the word "paid," when the postage has been paid at the time of posting the letter.

NEWSPAPERS AND SUPPLEMENTS TO NEWSPAPERS.

It is not compulsory to send Newspapers or Supplements to Newspapers by the Post, but those that are intended to be so transmitted, and are entitled to pass free, must be put into the Receiving Houses before 5 P.M.; at the Branch Post Offices, before half-past 5 P.M.; or at the General Post Office, St. Martin's le Grand, before 6 P.M. Each Newspaper given with a penny to the Letter Carriers ringing bells, from 4.30 to 5.30 P.M.; or put into one of the late Newspaper Windows, at St. Martin's le Grand, from 6 until half past 7 P.M., with a halfpenny, will be despatched the same evening. *Newspapers for the Colonies and Foreign Countries cannot be received after* 6 P.M. For Newspapers by *Morning Mails*, see page 789. All Newspapers must be sent in covers, open at the sides, and no words or communication may be printed on such papers after the same shall have been published, nor must there be any writing or marks upon any Newspaper, or the cover, other than the name and address of the person to whom it is sent; nor any paper or thing enclosed or concealed in, or with such newspaper, or the cover, nor any printed words or communication on the cover, except that Newsvenders *only* may *print* their names and addresses thereon. Newspapers may be examined by the Officers of the Post Office; and if there be any breach of the above regulations, the packet is chargeable with treble the amount of postage which a letter of the same weight would have been liable to. And any person who shall write or enclose anything in any Newspaper or the cover thereof, or shall print any words or communication on a Newspaper, after it shall have been published, *to be sent by the Post*, or any person who shall knowingly send, or cause to be sent, by the Post, a Newspaper in respect of which any one of those offences has been committed, may, at the option of the Postmaster General, be prosecuted as for a Misdemeanor.

⁂ As the mere affixing a Newspaper Stamp on any *new* periodical publication will not entitle it, *as a matter of course, to pass free by the Post*, those who may be about to publish, for the *first* time, any such paper, should submit a copy to the Postmaster-General, in order that it may be determined whether the publication is of a nature that will entitle it to pass free of postage.

Clause of the Act of 1st *Victoria, cap.* 34, *sec.* 32.

" And be it further enacted, that in all cases in which a question shall arise, whether a printed Paper is entitled to the " privileges of a Newspaper or other Publication hereby privileged, so far as respects the transmission thereof by the " Post under the Post Office Acts, the question shall be referred to the determination of the Postmaster-General, whose " decision, with the concurrence of the Lords of the Treasury, shall be final."

NEWSPAPERS

DIRECT FROM THE BRITISH COLONIES BY PACKET

are delivered free of Postage at any place within the British dominions (except those from Canada, which are charged ½d. upon delivery): those for Persons who have removed may be forwarded by Post, free of charge, provided they have not been opened at the place to which they were originally addressed.

NEWSPAPERS TO THE BRITISH COLONIES AND FOREIGN PARTS.

NEWSPAPERS liable to the Stamp Duty may be forwarded direct to the British Colonies and Possessions by Her Majesty's Packet Boats, free of the duty of Postage, provided the same be duly stamped and made up open at the ends, and put into the Office within seven days after the day of Publication: to some Foreign Parts free, and to others for a Postage of One Penny or Twopence each, to be paid at the time of putting in, under the same regulations as to date, &c.

For days of despatch, Rates of Postage, &c. &c. *see* " UNIVERSAL RATES OF POSTAGE," pages 777 to 782.

NEWSPAPERS TO FRANCE AND BELGIUM

are forwarded free of charge to the sender. A rate of four centimes (nearly equivalent to One Halfpenny) will be charged upon delivery in France and Belgium.

NEWSPAPERS FROM ABROAD,

vide " *Universal Rates of Postage*," pages 777 to 783, the charge being the same each way, except on those *from* FRANCE and BELGIUM which are charged One Halfpenny each.

All Newspapers from abroad must be printed in the language of the Country from which they are sent, unless in cases *specially* exempted by the *Lords of the Treasury*.

Those for Persons who have removed may be re-directed to them at any place within the United Kingdom, without extra Postage, *provided they have not been opened* at the place to which they were originally addressed; but *a Newspaper which has been opened is charged at the same rate as if it were a letter, from the place of redirection to the place at which it may ultimately be delivered.*

NEWSPAPERS BY PRIVATE SHIPS,

if put into the Office within seven days after the date of publication, are forwarded to the Cape of Good Hope, Mauritius, or Isle of France, Sydney, New South Wales, Van Diemen's Land, Swan River, South Australia, Chili, Peru, Guatemala, and the Western Coast of America, and the East Indies, on payment of one penny with each paper; to St. Helena and the Western Coast of Africa, viz.: St. Mary's, River Gambia, Sierra Leone, Cape Coast Castle, Fernando Po, and Ascension (Isle), at the same rate; to Hong Kong 1d., and to other parts of China, and places not British, *on payment of twopence each*, under the above regulations as to date, &c.

⁂ All Newspapers forwarded through the Ship Letter Office, except those between Ports in Great Britain and Ireland, must be paid for when put in.

THE UNDERMENTIONED PRINTED PRICES CURRENT,

having obtained the sanction of the Lords of the Treasury, pass through the Post Office to the *Colonies* and *Foreign Parts* at one penny each, provided they contain simply the names and prices of articles; the names and addresses on the parties dealing in such articles must be excluded.

- Annual Supplement to Price Current
- British ships entered inwards and cleared outwards from and to places within the limits of the East India Company's charter
- Commercial Daily List
- Lloyd's List
- London New Price Current
- London Mercantile Price Current
- Mercantile Journal
- Nicholson's New Price Current
- Prince's Price Current
- Sound List
- Trades List
- Universal Corn Reporter
- Wetenhall's Course of the Exchange

Each copy to be made up in the same form as a Newspaper, with covers open at the end.

The title of the publication must be written or printed immediately above the address; and any other writing than such address, name, initial, or mark for reference of any kind, calculated to convey information as to the party by whom such publication is forwarded, will subject the same to full letter rates of postage.

Every Price Current to be posted within *seven* days after its publication; and no one can be forwarded a *second* time without being charged with full letter postage.

All other Prices Current, and Commercial Lists, published in the United Kingdom, *if duly stamped*, and *under the weight of two ounces*, will be treated as Newspapers, and enjoy the Newspaper privileges; *the sanction of the Postmaster General having been previously obtained.* See "Newspapers and Supplements to Newspapers," preceding page.

Printed Prices Current, and Commercial Lists, from the British Colonies, France, Belgium, and Holland are now admitted into the United Kingdom at the reduced rate of One Penny each, whether conveyed by Packet or Private Ship.

Printed Prices Current, and Commercial Lists, from any foreign country, except France, Belgium, Holland and China, are admitted into the United Kingdom at the reduced rate of Two Pence each.

Prices Current, and Commercial Lists, *from* the British Colonies, *passing through* the United Kingdom, are liable to a Postage of Twopence each, to be paid at the time of being posted.

Prices Current, and Commercial Lists, from the British Colonies, passing through France, Belgium or Holland to the United Kingdom, are liable to a Postage of Two Pence each.

Printed Prices Current, and Commercial Lists, to China, *viâ* Southampton, 4d. each; *viâ* Marseilles, 5d. each. From China, *viâ* Southampton, 3d. each; *viâ* Marseilles, 5d. each.

NORTH AMERICA AND BRITISH AND FOREIGN WEST INDIA ISLANDS.

The Mails for North America are forwarded by Steam Packets, which leave *Liverpool* twice a month immediately after the arrival of the London night Mails of the 3rd and 18th, unless either of these should fall on a Sunday, and then on the succeeding day. During the winter months, viz. *Dec. Jan. Feb.* and *March*, but one Mail, that of the 3d, is despatched.

WEST INDIA, AND AMERICAN LETTERS.	PACKET RATES, Paying the Postage optional, excepting those Places marked thus *, which must be paid with. Not exceeding ½ Oz.	Not exceeding 1 Oz.	Not exceeding 2 Oz.	For SHIP LETTER RATES See 'Ship Letters' on this page.
	s. d.	s. d.	s. d.	
North America, viz.:—Quebec, Montreal, and all Parts of †Canada, Nova Scotia, (Halifax excepted), Prince Edward's Island, and New Brunswick, *conveyed direct by the contract Packets* (being one shilling packet postage, and two-pence Uniform internal Colonial Rate)	1 2	2 4	4 8	
Halifax, Newfoundland, * New York, the Bermudas, and the * United States	1 0	2 0	4 0	
British West Indies, &c., including Kingston (Jamaica), Barbadoes, New Providence, Turk's Island, Bahamas, Antigua, Cariacou, Demerara, Dominica, Grenada, St. Lucia, Monserrat, Nevis, St. Vincent's, St. Kitt's, Tobago, Tortola and Trinidad	1 0	2 0	4 0	
Foreign West Indies, including *Guadaloupe, *Martinique, *St. Thomas, *Curaçoa, *St. Martin's, *St. Croix and Porto Rico	1 5	2 10	5 8	
Jamaica (all the island except the Packet-Port Kingston) & Berbice	1 2	2 4	4 8	

Letters to the West Indies are forwarded at the above Uniform rates from all parts of the United Kingdom.

All Letters addressed to North America will be considered as intended to be forwarded by the *Contract Steam Packets*, and charged accordingly, unless the words *"By Private Ship"* be plainly written on them.

RATES OF POSTAGE WITHIN BRITISH NORTH AMERICA.

Letters forwarded to or from British North America by the Liverpool Packets, or by Private Ships, passing direct between the United Kingdom and British America, are charged with an Uniform *Colonial rate* of *Two Pence the half ounce* when posted or delivered at any other towns than the Ports of Halifax (Nova Scotia), or St. John's (Newfoundland).

SHIP LETTERS.

The single uniform rate on Letters between the United Kingdom and places beyond Sea, (except those for France, Belgium, Holland, Hamburgh, Brunswick and Hanover, to which places the Rates are the same as by Packet,) when conveyed by Private Ships, is 8d., in whatever part of the United Kingdom the Letters may be posted or delivered. This is the rate now taken on Letters between the United Kingdom and the East Indies, &c. &c. *when conveyed by Private Ship*, the former distinction between these and other descriptions of Ship Letters having been abolished.

The rates of Postage on "Ship" as on other Letters are taken by weight:—

Not exceeding half an ounce .... Single.
,, an ounce .... Double.
,, two ounces .... Quadruple.
,, three ounces .... Sextuple, and so on.

PERSONS EXEMPT FROM SHIP LETTER POSTAGE.

The Owners, Charterers, or Consignees (resident in the United Kingdom), and the Owners, Consignees, and Shippers of Goods on board Vessels inward bound, are entitled to receive their Letters free from Sea Postage, to the extent collectively of Six ounces in weight, by any One Vessel to any One such Person. In the case of Vessels coming from *Ceylon, the Mauritius, the East Indies*, or the *Cape of Good Hope*, for an Owner, Charterer, or Consignee of such Vessel, the letters may be collectively Twenty ounces in weight. The Owner, Charterer, or Consignee must be described as such on the address and superscription; and in the case of Owners, Shippers, or Consignees of goods, it must also appear by the Ship's Manifest that they have Goods on board the Vessel. Such persons are entitled to have their Letters which come within the above Conditions before the Master of the Vessel delivers the other Letters in his charge to the Post Office.

*** Every Person who shall, with intent to evade any Duty of Postage, falsely superscribe a Letter as being the Owner or the Charterer, or the Consignee of a Vessel conveying the same, or as the Owner, or the Shipper, or the Consignee of Goods shipped in such Vessel, shall for every such offence forfeit Ten Pounds.

LEGHORN, CIVITA VECCHIA, NAPLES, MALTA, SYRA, ATHENS, SMYRNA, CONSTANTINOPLE, AND ALEXANDRIA.

TABLE of the Route of the FRENCH STEAM PACKETS, with the Rates of Postage (*on letters posted within France*) from Marseilles; Time occupied during the Voyage, and Time of Stopping at each Place from Marseilles to Alexandria.

	Postage.	Time of Voyage.		Stop.	
	Franc.	Days.	Hours.	Days.	Hours.
To Leghorn	1	1	10	..	7
Civita Vecchia	1	2	2	..	8
Naples	1	2	23	..	6
Malta	1	4	22	1	
Syra	2	8	..	..	12
Athens	2	8	10	..	14
Smyrna	2	8	21	1	
Constantinople	2	10	13	1	15
Alexandria	2	10	16	1	18
From Alexandria to Syra		2	16	..	12
Athens	1	3	2	..	14
Smyrna	1	3	13	1	
Constantinople	1	5	5	1	15
Malta	2	5	18		
Naples	2	7	17	..	6
Civita Vecchia	2	8	14	..	6
Leghorn	2	9	16		
Marseilles	2	10	16		

The Packet leaves Marseilles the 1st, 11th, and 21st of each Month, at 5 p.m., and Alexandria the 6th, 16th, and 26th, at 4 p.m. Letters intended to be sent by these Packets must be addressed "*viâ* Marseilles" "per French Packet."

Packets are also dispatched on the 4th and 24th of each month from Marseilles direct to Alexandria, touching at Malta only.

MAILS MADE UP IN LONDON.

Letters for the Continental Mails are received at the Branch Offices, Charing Cross; Old Cavendish street, and 10, Blackman street, Borough, until 8 o'clock at Night, on Tuesday and Friday, and till 10 at St. Martin's-le-Grand and Lombard street: at St. Martin's-le-Grand only they will be received *after* 10, *and up to a quarter past* 10 P.M. *on payment of a fee of one penny; and until half-past* 10 P.M., *on payment of a fee of sixpence.*

*** For full particulars as to the hours for posting Colonial and Foreign Letters and Newspapers, see "UNIVERSAL RATES OF POSTAGE," pages 777 to 783.

	When made up in London.	*When Due.*
France	Daily	Daily.
Belgium	Daily	Daily.
Holland	Wednesday and Saturday *mornings*	Monday and Thursday.
Hamburg, Sweden and Norway	Tuesday and Friday	Tuesday and Saturday, but usually arrive on previous day.
Dublin	Twice a Day	Twice a Day.
Guernsey and Jersey, (now sent *viâ* Southampton)	*Mornings* of Saturdays, Tuesdays, and Thursdays	Monday, Wednesday and Friday.

Lisbon, Madeira, Vigo, Coruna, Cadiz, Oporto and Gibraltar	On the mornings of the 7th, 17th, and 27th of each month, unless those dates fall on a Sunday, and then on the following *morning*.
Malta, Greece, and Ionian Islands, *viâ* Southampton	Twice in each Month, viz.:—On the 3rd *morning* of every month, and on the 20th *morning* of every month unless these dates fall on a Sunday, and then on the PREVIOUS *evening*.
Syria, Egypt and India, *viâ* Southampton	*Mornings* of the 3rd and 20th in every month.
Brazil, Buenos Ayres, Madeira, and Canary Islands	1st Tuesday in each month.
British North America, Bermuda, and United States	3rd and 18th of every Month, except in the Winter Months. December, January, February, and March, and then on the 3rd only.
Jamaica, Leeward Islands, Hayti, Porto Rico, Cuba, Venezuela & New Granada	*Mornings* of the 2nd and 17th of every month.
Mexico	*Morning* of the 2nd of every month.
Panama	*Morning* of the 17th of every month.

The Mails despatched on the mornings of the 7th, 17th, and 27th of each month for Coruna, Vigo, Oporto, Lisbon, Cadiz, and Gibraltar are forwarded by Steam Vessels from Southampton to Gibraltar.

The Mails of the *third and twentieth days* in each month are forwarded by the same Packet from Southampton to Alexandria; leaving Mails at Malta.

The Mails for Greece and the Ionian Islands (*viâ* Southampton) are sent from hence on the mornings of the 3rd and 20th of each month, and are conveyed from Malta by Steam Packets, which start after the arrival of the Mails from England.

The Mails for Egypt and India are forwarded *direct from Southampton* on the 3rd and 20th *mornings* of each month by Steam Packets.

From *August* to *January* inclusive, the Brazil Packet touches at PERNAMBUCO and BAHIA, on her *outward* passage to RIO JANEIRO, and the other Six months on her *homeward*.

POST TOWNS AND PRINCIPAL PLACES,

WITH THE NAMES OF THE RESPECTIVE POSTMASTERS

IN

ENGLAND AND WALES, SCOTLAND, AND IRELAND.

To each place is prefixed the time at which letters *from London* should be delivered, and after each is stated that at which the box closes *for letters to London*. By these tables the "RETURN OF POST" from any place in the United Kingdom can be readily ascertained. In the Towns where the delivery is at 7 a.m. in summer, it is usually an hour later during the winter months. Those which grant and pay

MONEY ORDERS

are marked thus *. A Money Order intended for a person residing at a place in which there is no Money Order Office should be drawn upon the Post Town nearest to it which may have a Money Order Office.

Throughout the list is stated the Post Town through which any place not a Money Order Office receives its *London* letters and its distance from such Post Town. Thus, "Abbotts Anne" being 2½ miles from Andover, any one residing at the former place and receiving a Money Order, could obtain cash for the same at Andover, provided the Order be drawn upon that Office, and so on. *Abergavenny, *being marked (*) is a Money Order Town*, and in that place, as in all others so marked, Money Orders can be obtained or cashed.

ENGLAND AND WALES.

Letters from London delivered at h. m.	Town. Postmaster.	Box for London closes at h. m.
8. 0 a.m	Abbotts-Anne, 2½ miles from Andover	6. 0 p.m
7. 0 a.m	Abbots Bromley, 6 miles fm. Rugeley	6.45 p.m
10. 0 a.m	Abbotsbury, 10 miles frm. Dorchester	3.30 p.m
8.30 a.m	Abbotts-Langley, 5 miles from Hemel Hempstead	6. 0 p.m
8. 0 a.m	Abbots-Leigh, 4 miles from Bristol	4.30 p.m
11. 0 a.m	Abbotts-Roding, 8 miles from Ongar	3. 0 p.m
3.45 p.m	Aberavon, 1 mile from Taibach	8.30 a.m
1.30 p.m	Aberayron, 16 miles from Aberystwith	12.45 p.m
4. 0 p.m	Abercarne, 10 m. from Newport, Mon.	9. 0 a.m
7.15 p.m	Aberdare, 4 m. from Merthyr-Tydvil.	10. 0 p.m
4.30 p.m	Aberdovey, 10 mi. from Machynlleth	7.30 a.m
10.20 a.m	Aberffraw, 19 miles from Bangor	2. 0 p.m
10.20 a.m	Aberford, 7 miles from Tadcaster	2.35 p.m
7.30 a.m	*Abergavenny, Mrs. Margaret Price	6. 0 p.m
8. 0 a.m	Abergele, 39 miles from Chester	3.30 p.m 10. 0 p.m
9.30 p.m	*Aberystwith, Miss Anne Cox	8.30 a.m
11. 0 a.m 9.30 p.m	*Abingdon, George Shepherd	9.15 a.m 10. 0 p.m
9.40 a.m	Abington, 8 miles from Cambridge	7.15 p.m
7. 0 a.m	Abridge, 7 miles from Romford	5.15 p.m
10. 0 a.m	*Accrington, Robert Holt	4.30 p.m 9. 0 p.m
9. 0 a.m	Ackworth, 8 miles from Wakefield	3.45 p.m
8. 0 a.m	Acle, 12 miles from Norwich	2.30 p.m
9. 0 a.m	Acomb, 2¼ miles from York	4.15 p.m
9. 0 a.m	Acton-Burnel, 8 mi. fr. Shrewsbury	2. 0 p.m
9. 0 a.m	Adderbury, 3½ miles from Banbury	7. 0 p.m
8.45 a.m	Addingham, 9 miles from Otley	2.30 p.m
9. 0 a.m 12. 0 a.m	Addington place, 2 miles from Ramsgate	7. 0 a.m 7.30 p.m
7. 0 a.m	Addlestone, 2 miles from Chertsey	6. 0 p.m
8.15 a.m	Aigburth, 3½ miles from Liverpool	3.30 p.m
11. 0 a.m	Albrighton, 7 mi. fr. Wolverhampton	5. 0 p.m
7. 0 a.m	Albury, 5 miles from Guildford	4.30 p.m
10. 0 a.m	Alcester, 8 m. f. Stratford-on-Avon	4.45 p.m
9.45 a.m	Alconbury, 5 miles from Huntingdon	4.15 p.m
12.45 p.m	Aldborough, 12 miles from Hull	12.35 p.m
7. 0 a.m	Aldborough, Sfflk. 7 m. f. Saxmundham	6.15 p.m
8. 0 a.m	Aldbourne, 8 miles from Hungerford	6. 0 p.m
11.25 a.m	Aldbrough, 7 miles from Darlington	7.30 p.m
7. 0 a.m	Aldbury, 3 miles from Tring	6. 0 p.m
10. 0 a.m	Aldermaston, 9 miles from Newbury	4.30 p.m
9. 0 a.m	Alderton, 9 miles from Woodbridge	4.15 p.m
8. 0 a.m	Aldridge, 4 miles from Walsall	4. 0 p.m
12 noon	*Alford, Lincolnshire	1.30 p.m
7. 0 a.m	*Alfreton, John Smedley	8. 0 p.m
10.10 a.m	Allendale, 7 miles from Haydonbridge	9. 0 p.m
7. 0 a.m	Allesley, 2 miles from Coventry	8.30 p.m
11. 0 a.m	Allonby, 23 miles from Carlisle	10.45 a.m
10.30 a.m	Almondbury, 2 m. from Huddersfield	2.30 p.m
8.15 a.m	Almondsbury-Hill, 7 m. from Bristol	3.15 p.m
7.50 a.m	Alne, 11 miles from York	5. 0 p.m
5. 0 p.m	Alnmouth, 5½ miles from Alnwick	7.50 a.m
8. 0 a.m 2.30 p.m	*Alnwick, Robert Anderson	11. 5 a.m 5.15 p.m
7. 0 a.m	Alphington, 1½ miles from Exeter	7. 0 p.m
7. 0 a.m	*Alresford, Miss Ann Keene	8.30 p.m
8. 0 a.m	Alrewas, 5 miles from Lichfield	5.15 p.m
5. 0 p.m	*Alston, John Dryden	8.25 a.m
11. 0 a.m	Alstonfield, 8 miles from Ashbourne	3.50 p.m
9. 0 a.m	Althorne, 7 miles from Maldon	5. 0 p.m
7. 0 a.m	*Alton (Hants), Robert Baker	7.30 p.m
11.30 a.m	Alton, 5 miles from Cheadle	4.45 p.m
8.35 a.m	*Altrincham, Geoffrey Wilde	5. 0 p.m
7. 0 a.m	Alvaston, 4 miles from Derby	7.25 p.m
8. 0 a.m	Alvechurch, 3 miles from Redditch	5. 0 p.m
10. 0 a.m	Alvescot, 6½ miles from Lechlade	4.15 p.m
4.50 p.m	Amble, 9 miles from Alnwick	9. 0 p.m
11.30 a.m	*Ambleside, Mrs. Agnes Nicholson	1.40 p.m
7.30 a.m	*Amersham, Mrs. Eleanor Priest	7.30 p.m
8.30 a.m	*Amesbury, Wm. Cox	6.30 p.m
9.30 a.m	Amlwch, 24 miles from Bangor	3. 0 p.m
7.30 a.m	Amport, 3 miles from Andover	6.30 p.m
8. 0 a.m	*Ampthill, Mrs. Ann Shaw	6. 0 p.m
9. 0 a.m	Ampton, 6 miles from Bury (Suffolk)	5. 0 p.m
7.55 p.m	Ancroft, 6 miles from Berwick	3.20 p.m
8. 0 a.m	Andenshaw, 4½ mi. from Manchester	5.45 p.m
7. 0 a.m	*Andover, George Marcer	8. 0 p.m
8. 0 a.m	*Andover-Road, John Roblin Wolfe	9.45 p.m
7. 0 a.m	Andoversford, 7½ mi. from Northleach	8.30 p.m
12. 0noon	Antony, 5 miles from Devonport	8.45 a.m
11.20 a.m 1.20 p.m	*Appleby, Ths. Robertson Lidderdale	10.40 a.m 12.30 p.m
7. 0 a.m	Appleby, 9 miles from Atherstone	6.30 p.m
12. 0noon	Appledore, 3 miles from Bideford	1.20 p.m
9. 0 a.m	Appledore, 6 miles from Tenterden	4. 0 p.m
8. 0 a.m	Appleshaw, 5 miles from Andover	6. 0 p.m
8. 0 a.m	Appleton, 5 miles from Abingdon	5. 0 p.m
9.15 a.m	Appleton-Wiske, 8 mi. f. Northallerton	3.40 p.m
9. 0 a.m	Ardingly, 6 miles from Cuckfield	5. 0 p.m
8. 0 a.m	Ardleigh, 5 miles from Colchester	8. 0 p.m
10. 0 a.m	Arnold, 4 miles from Nottingham	5.25 p.m
10. 0 a.m	Arreton, 4 miles from Newport, I.W.	3. 0 p.m
8. 0 a.m	*Arrington, Mrs. Jane Meyer	9. 0 p.m
7. 0 a.m	*Arundel, Charles Weller	7.30 p.m
7.30 a.m	Ash, 4 miles from Farnham	4.45 p.m
7. 0 a.m	Ash, 3 miles from Sandwich	8. 0 p.m
8.45 a.m	*Ashbourn, John Howell	5.30 p.m
8. 0 a.m	*Ashburton, William Barons	6. 0 p.m
7.45 a.m	*Ashby-de-la-Zouch, Thos. Wayte	5. 0 p.m
8.15 a.m	Ashby-Parva, 3½ mi. fm. Lutterworth	5.15 p.m
8. 0 a.m	Ashcott, 5 miles from Glastonbury	5.25 p.m

Letters from London delivered at h. m.	Town. Postmaster.	Box for London closes at h. m.
7. 0 a.m 3. 0 p.m	*Ashford (Kent), John Tunbridge..	9.45 a.m 10. 0 p.m
10. 0 a.m	Ashford, 4 miles from Chertsey	4.30 p.m
8. 0 a.m	Ashill, 8 miles from Taunton	8. 0 p.m
9. 0 a.m	Ashover, 89 miles from Chesterfield	4. 0 p.m
7.30 a.m	Ashton, 8 miles from Warrington	5.30 p.m
10.30 a.m	Ashton-Kynes, 5½ m. fr. Cirencester	3.50 p.m
8.30 a.m	*Ashton-under-Lyne, Alfred Saxon..	5.30 p.m 8.30 p.m
8. 0 a.m	Ashwell, 4 miles from Baldock	6. 0 p.m
11.15 a.m	Askern, 7 miles from Doncaster	3. 0 p.m
2. 0 p.m	Askrigg, 5 miles from Hawes	10.35 a.m
2.40 p.m	Aspatria, 8 miles from Wigton	10. 5 a.m
8. 0 a.m	Aspley, 2 miles from Woburn	6. 0 p.m
11.30 a.m	Aston, 11 miles from Ludlow	1.15 p.m
8. 0 a.m	Aston-Clinton, 2¾ miles from Tring..	8. 0 p.m
7. 0 a.m	*Atherstone, John Morewood	7.30 p.m
9. 0 a.m	Attercliffe, 2 miles from Sheffield	6.10 p.m
8. 0 a.m	*Attleborough, Samuel Caley	6. 0 p.m
9.15 a.m	Audlem, 7½ miles from Nantwich	6. 0 p.m
9.15 a.m	Audley, 7½ miles fr. Newcastle, Staff.	4.30 p.m
9. 0 a.m	Avebury, 8 miles from Marlborough..	3.15 p.m
8.15 a.m	Aveley, 8 miles from Romford	5.15 p.m
7.30 a.m	Avening, 6 miles from Stroud	4.30 p.m
12. 0noon	Aveton-Gifford, 6 m. from Ermebridge	1.15 p.m
7. 0 a.m	Axbridge, 10 miles fr. Wells Somerset	5.30 p.m
8. 0 a.m	*Axminster, William Slyfield	5.25 p.m
11.30 a.m	Aycliffe, 5 miles from Darlington	7. 0 p.m
7. 0 a.m	*Aylesbury, Samuel Payne	7.30 p.m
7. 0 a.m	Aylesford, 4 miles from Maidstone ..	6.30 p.m
9. 0 a.m	*Aylsham, Miss Mary Nobbs	4. 0 p.m
7.30 a.m	Aynhoe, 5 miles from Brackley	5.30 p.m
7. 0 a.m 11.15 a.m	Backbarrow, 15 miles from Milnthorp	2.20 p.m 9.30 p.m
10. 0 a.m	Bacton, 6 miles from Stowmarket ..	4. 0 p.m
11. 0 a.m	Bacup, 7 miles from Rochdale	3.30 p.m
9. 0 a.m	Baddingham, 7 m. from Saxmundham	5. 0 p.m
7. 0 a.m	Badminton, 10 miles fr. Chippenham	7.45 p.m
9. 0 a.m	Bagillt, 2¼ miles from Holywell	3.45 p.m
7. 0 a.m	*Bagshot, Frederick Mumford	8. 0 p.m
6. 0 a.m	*Bakewell, Joseph Swaine	5.45 p.m
1.30 p.m	Bala, 14 miles from Corwen	7.30 a.m
10. 0 a.m	Balcombe, 4 miles from Cuckfield ..	4. 0 p.m
8. 0 a.m	*Baldock, Mrs. Sarah Stocken	9.30 p.m
9.30 a.m	Balsham, 3 miles from Linton	4.45 p.m
9.10 a.m	Bamber-Bridge, 3½ miles fr. Preston	5.20 p.m
7. 0 p.m	Bamborough, 5 miles from Belford ..	2. 0 p.m
8.30 a.m	Bampton, 5 miles from Witney	6. 0 p.m
7. 0 a.m	*Bampton, Devon, John Catford	6. 0 p.m
8. 0 a.m 5. 0 p.m	*Banbury, William Brain	7. 0 a.m 6.15 p.m
7. 0 a.m 1.15 p.m	*Bangor, Robert Pritchard	12. noon 7.45 p.m
10.30 a.m	Banham, 6 miles from Attleborough.	4. 0 p.m
12.15 p.m	Banstead, 3½ miles from Epsom	5. 0 p.m
8. 0 a.m	Banwell, 15 miles from Wells	4.45 p.m
9. 0 a.m	Bardfield, 9 miles from Braintree ..	4. 0 p.m
2. 5 p.m	Bardsea, 3 miles from Ulverstone	10. 0 a.m
8. 0 a.m	Barford, 3½ miles from Warwick	4.45 p.m
7. 0 a.m	Barford St. Martin, 6m. from Salisbury	7. 0 p.m
8.30 a.m	Barham, 6 miles from Canterbury ..	5. 0 p.m
9. 0 a.m	Barkston, 4 miles from Grantham ..	3.30 p.m
9. 0 a.m	Barkway, 4 miles from Royston	6.30 p.m
8. 0 a.m	Barlborough, 8 mi. from Chesterfield	5.30 p.m
8. 0 a.m	Barley, 3 miles from Royston	7.30 p.m
7. 0 a.m	Barming, 2½ miles from Maidstone	7. 0 p.m
5. 0 p.m	Barmouth, 41 miles from Corwen	10. 0 p.m
10.30 a.m	*Barnard-Castle, Thomas Kipling.	1.45 p.m 4.30 p.m
	*Barnet, *see* "London District Off."	
0.30 a.m	Barningham, 11 miles from Bury, S.	4.15 p.m
7. 0 a.m 16.50 p.m	*Barnsley, Thomas Lister	7.15 p.m 10. 0 p.m
19.15 a.m	Barnsley, 4 miles from Cirencester ..	4. 0 p.m
8.15 a.m	*Barnstaple, William Petter	4.20 p.m
0.10 a.m	Barrow, 10 miles from Ulverstone	2.50 p.m
0.10 a.m	Barrow-on-Humber, 4 miles fr Hull	1.50 p.m
9. 0 a.m	Bartley, 8 miles from Southampton	6.30 p.m
12.30noon	*Barton-on-Humber, Wm. Morley ..	1.15 p.m
8.30 a.m	Barton, 8 miles from Lichfield	4.45 p.m
0.30 a.m	Baschurch, 8 miles from Shrewsbury	2. 0 p.m
19. 0 a.m	Basford, 3 miles from Nottingham ..	5. 0 p.m

Letters from London delivered at h. m.	Town. Postmaster.	Box for London closes at h. m.
7. 0 a.m 1. 0 p.m	*Basingstoke, Robert Cottle	9.45 a.m 8.30 p.m
7. 0 a.m	Baslow, 8 miles from Chesterfield ..	5.30 p.m
8. 0 a.m	Bassingbourn, 3 miles from Royston	6.45 p.m
9. 0 a.m	Batcombe, 7½ mi. fr. Shepton-Mallet	5. 0 p.m
7. 0 a.m 3. 0 p.m	*Bath, Thomas Moore Musgrave ..	8. 0 a.m 10. 0 p.m
10. 0 a.m	Bath-Easton, 2 miles from Bath	7. 0 p.m
11. 0 a.m	Bathford, 3 miles from Bath	7. 0 p.m
9. 0 a.m	Batley, 2 miles from Dewsbury	3.30 p.m
7. 0 a.m	*Battle, Francis William Ticehurst..	9.15 p.m
8. 0 a.m	*Bawtry, William Adams	5. 0 p.m
8.25 a.m	Bayford, 5½ miles from Hertford	5.30 p.m
9. 0 a.m	Baythorn-End, 12 miles from Halstead	4.30 p.m
4.30 p.m	Beachley, 4 miles from Chepstow	7. 0 a.m
7. 0 a.m	*Beaconsfield, Thomas Everett	6.45 p.m
12. 0noon	Beaford, 16 miles from Oakhampton	12. 0noon
8. 0 a.m	*Beaminster, C. Frampton	4.15 p.m
7. 0 a.m	Bearstead, 2½ miles from Maidstone..	7.15 p.m
7. 0 a.m	Beaulieu, 16 miles from Southampton	6.45 p.m
7.45 a.m	*Beaumaris, Thomas Byrne	5.30 p.m
7.30 a.m	*Beccles, John Crickmay	5.45 p.m
7. 0 a.m	Beckermont, 9 miles from Whitehaven	3. 0 p.m
9.45 a.m	Beckford, 6 miles from Tewkesbury..	3. 0 p.m
10. 0 a.m	Beckingham, 5 miles from Newark ..	3. 0 p.m
7. 0 a.m	Beckington, 18 miles from Chippenham	7.30 p.m
9.45 a.m	Beckley, 5 miles from Oxford	4.20 p.m
10. 0 a.m	*Bedale, Mrs. Mary Place	3.45 p.m
4.10 p.m	Beddgelert, 13 miles from Carnarvon	8.45 a.m
8.30 a.m	Bedfont, 3 miles from Hounslow	4.30 p.m
8. 0 a.m	*Bedford, Charles Bithrey	9.30 p.m
3.40 p.m	Bedlington, 5 miles from Morpeth	9. 0 a.m
6.30 a.m	Bedminster, 1¼ miles from Bristol ..	5.30 p.m
8. 0 a.m	Bedwin (Gt.) 8 miles fr. Marlborough	4.30 p.m
7. 0 a.m	Bedworth, 5 miles from Coventry ..	9. 0 p.m
8.15 a.m	Beeding, 2 miles from Steyning	4.20 p.m
10. 0 am.	Beer, 8 miles from Axminster	2.45 p.m
2.30 p.m	Beeralston, 6 miles from Tavistock..	8.30 a.m
8. 0 a.m 3. 0 p.m	Beeston, 2¼ miles from Leeds	4.30 p.m 9. 0 p.m
10.15 a.m	Beeston, 5 miles from Nottingham ..	4.25 p.m
9.30 a.m	Begelly, 5 miles from Tenby	4. 0 p.m
10.30 a.m	*Belford, John Macdonald	9.30 a.m
8.30 a.m	Bellbroughton, 5 m. from Stourbridge	5.30 p.m
7. 0 p.m	Bellingham, 16 miles from Hexham..	8. 0 a.m
8. 0 a.m 5. 0 p.m	*Belper, Mrs. Hannah Haslam	8.30 p.m 10. 0 p.m
9. 0 a.m	Belton, 2¾ miles from Grantham	4. 0 p.m
10. 0 a.m	Bembridge, 5 miles from Ryde	4.45 p.m
7. 0 a.m	Benenden, 4 miles from Cranbrook..	7.30 p.m
8. 0 a.m	Bensington, or Benson, 2 miles from Wallingford	7. 0 p.m
9.30 a.m	Bentham, 15 miles from Lancaster ..	4. 0 p.m
8. 0 a.m	Bentley, 4 miles from Farnham	6. 0 p.m
9.30 a.m	Bentworth, 4 miles from Alton	4.30 p.m
12.30 p.m	Benwell, 3 m. from Newcastle-on-Tyne	9.20 p.m
9. 0 a.m	Bere-Regis, 8 miles from Blandford	5. 0 p.m
9. 0 a.m	Berkeley, 6 miles from Dursley	4.30 p.m
7. 0 a.m 11. 0 a.m	*Berkhempstead, George John Scott	11. 0 a.m 9. 0 p.m
11. 0 a.m	Berriew, 5 miles from Welchpool	2. 0 p.m
8.50 p.m	*Berwick, James Forster	7.45 a.m
2.30 p.m	Bethesda, 5 miles from Bangor	9.45 a.m
9. 0 a.m	Betley, 8 m. fr. Newcastle-under-Lyne	4.15 p.m
10.10 a.m	*Beverley, Michael Ellis	3.45 p.m
8. 0 a.m	Bevois-Hill, 2 mi. from Southampton	7. 0 p.m
7. 0 a.m	*Bewdley, John Bate Rowley	6. 0 p.m
8.30 a.m	Bexhill, 6 miles from Battle	5.30 p.m
	*Bexley, *see* "London District Office"	
	Bexley Heath, *see* "Lon. District Office"	
9.30 a.m	Bibury, 5 miles from Fairford	4.30 p.m
8. 0 a.m	*Bicester, John Walford	4.40 p.m
7. 0 a.m	Bicknoller, 13 miles from Taunton ..	6.30 p.m
8. 0 a.m	Biddenden, 5 miles from Cranbrook..	6. 0 p.m
10.30 a.m	*Bideford, John Lee	2.40 p.m
8.30 a.m	Bidford, 7 m. from Stratford-on-Avon	3.15 p.m
7. 0 a.m	*Biggleswade, William Wright	10. 0 p.m
8.20 a.m	Bildeston, 5 miles from Hadleigh	6.30 p.m
7. 0 a.m	*Billericay, W. Curtis	7.30 p.m
10. 0 a.m	Billesdon, 9 miles from Leicester ..	9. 0 a.m 4.15 p.m
7. 0 a.m	Billinghurst, 7 miles from Horsham.	8. 0 a.m

Letters from London delivered at h. m.	Town. Postmaster.	Box for London closes at h. m.
7. 0 a.m 4. 0 p.m	*Bilstone, Edward Ingle	9. 0 p.m
4. 0 p.m	Binbrook, 10 mi. fr. Market Raisin	9.30 a.m
10.30 a.m	Bingham, 10 miles from Nottingham	7.30 a.m 2.30 p.m
9.20 a.m	Bingley, 6 miles from Bradford, York	3.30 p.m
9. 0 a.m	Birch, 8 miles from Ross	3.30 p.m
10. 0 a.m	Bircham, 8 miles from Rougham	3. 0 p.m
8. 0 a.m	Birchington, 4 miles from Margate	6.30 p.m
8. 0 a.m	*Birkenhead, George Kirkby	8. 0 p.m
7.30 a.m 4. 0 p.m	*Birmingham, Miss G.M. Gottwaltz	7. 0 a.m 10.30 p.m
9. 0 a.m	Birstall, 7 miles from Leeds	8.30 p.m
9.30 a.m	*Bishop Auckland, Wm. H. Walton	2.50 p.m 5.50 p.m
11.20 a.m	Bishop Middleham, 10 m.f. Darlington	1.20 p.m
10.30 a.m	*Bishop's Castle, Edward Griffiths	1.30 p.m
9.30 a.m	Bishop's Caundle, 4½ mi. fr. Sherborne	2. 0 p.m
11. 0 a.m	Bishop's Cleeve, 3½ m. fr. Cheltnhm	6. 0 p.m
8. 0 a.m	Bishop's Clyst, 3 mi. from Topsham	5 0 p.m
7. 0 a.m	Bishop's Hull, 1½ miles from Taunton	6. 0 p.m
7. 0 a.m	Bishop's Lydeard, 5 m. from Taunton	7.45 p.m
7. 0 a.m 1.15 p.m	*Bishop's Stortford, Thos. Bradfield	9.30 p.m 10.15 a.m
11. 0 a.m	Bishop's Tawton, 2¼ m. f. Barnstaple	12. 0noon
9. 0 a.m	Bishop's Teignton, 2½ m. f. Teignmouth	4.15 p.m
10. 0 a.m	Bishop's Thorpe, 3 miles from York	4.15 p.m
7. 0 a.m	*Bishop's Waltham, John Mansell	8. 0 p.m
	Bishop's Wearmouth, *see* Wearmouth	
9. 0 a.m	Bishopstoke, 7 m. from Winchester	4.15 p.m
1.40 p.m	Bishopton, 6 miles from Stockton	3.35 p.m
10. 0 a.m	Bisley, 4 miles from Stroud	3. 0 p.m
8. 0 a.m	Bittern, 3 miles from Southampton	5.15 p.m
8.20 a.m	Bitton, 7 miles from Bristol	3.45 p.m
7. 0 a.m	Blackboys, 4½ miles from Uckfield	9. 0 p.m
8. 0 a.m	Blackbirds-Stapleton, 1½ m. f. Bristol	4. 0 p.m
8.55 a.m 7.30 p.m	*Blackburn, Thomas Butterfield	5. 0 p.m 10. 0 p.m
10.15 a.m	Blackpool, 18 miles from Preston	3. 0 p.m
11. 0 a.m	Black Torrington, 14 mi.f. Oakhampton	2. 0 p.m
7.15 a.m	Blackwater, 4½ m. from Bagshot	6.30 p.m
9. 0 a.m	Blackwater, 2 m. from Newport I. W.	3.30 p.m
5. 0 p.m	Blackwood, 14m. from Newport, Mon.	8. 0 a.m
10. 0 a.m	Blagdon, 13 miles from Bristol	1.30 p.m
11.30 a.m	Blakeney, 6 miles from Holt	1.15 p.m
8. 0 a.m	Blakeney, 3½ miles from Newnham	4.15 p.m
7. 0 a.m	*Blandford, William Shipp	8. 0 p.m
11. 0 a.m	Bleadon, 19 m. from Wells, Somerset	2.30 p.m
7. 0 a.m	Blean, 2 miles from Canterbury	7.30 p.m
7. 0 a.m	Bletchingley, 7 miles from Reigate	7.15 p.m
9. 0 a.m	Bletsoe, 6 miles from Bedford	3.15 p.m
9. 0 a.m	Blewbury, 6 miles from Wallingford	6.15 p.m
7.30 am.	Blisworth, 4 miles from Northampton	6. 0 p.m
7. 0 a.m	Blockley, 3 m. from Moreton-in-Marsh	7.15 p.m
10.30 a.m	Blofield, 7 miles from Norwich	3.30 p.m
8. 0 a.m	Bloxwich, 2 miles from Walsall	6. 0 p.m
7. 0 a.m	Blunham, 6½ miles from St. Neots	7.30 p.m
8. 0 a.m	Bluntisham, 4 miles from St. Ives	7.30 p.m
3. 0 p.m	Blyth, 10 miles from North-Shields	6.15 p.m
10. 0 a.m	Blyth, 7 miles from Worksop	2.55 p.m
8. 0 a.m	Bocking, 1 mile from Braintree	6. 0 p.m
10. 0 a.m	Bodedern, 18 miles from Bangor	2. 0 p.m
11.45 a.m	Bodenham, 7 miles from Leominster	1. 0 p.m
12. 0noon	*Bodmin, Thomas Pearse	12.50 p.m
7. 0 a.m	*Bognor, Henry Hounsom	7.30 p.m
8.30 a.m	Bolsover, 8 miles from Chesterfield	3.55 p.m
12. 0noon	Boldon, 8 miles from Gateshead	8. 0 p.m
10. 0 a.m	Bolingbroke (New), 12 m. fr. Boston	3. 0 p.m
11. 0 a.m	Bolingbroke (Old), 12 mi. fr. Boston	3. 0 p.m
2. 0 p.m	Bollington, 4 miles from Macclesfield	10.45 a.m
8. 0 a.m 8.45 p.m	*Bolton, Miss Elizabeth Campbell	4.30 p.m 9.45 p.m
8. 0 a.m	Bolton-le-Sands, 4 m. from Lancaster	5.40 p.m
9. 0 a.m	Bolton-Percy, 4 miles from Tadcaster	3.45 p.m
9. 0 a.m	Bonsall, 2 miles from Matlock	4. 0 p.m
3.30 p.m	Bonvilstone, 8 miles from Cardiff	8. 0 a.m
9.40 a.m	Bootle, 3½ miles from Liverpool	3.30 p.m
7. 0 a.m	Bootle, 22 miles from Ulverstone	5.20 p.m
8.40 a.m	Boreham, 8 miles from Battle	7.30 p.m
9. 0 a.m	Boreham, 4 miles from Chelmsford	6. 0 p.m
9.15 a.m	*Boroughbridge, William Hirst	3.55 p.m
11. 0 a.m	Borough-Bridge, 7½ m. fr. Bridgewater	4. 0 p.m

Letters from London delivered at h. m.	Town. Postmaster.	Box for London closes at h. m.
8. 0 a.m	Borough-Green, 6 m. fr. Newmarket	6.30 p.m
10. 0 a.m	Borrowby, 5 miles from Thirsk	3.20 p.m
10. 0 a.m	Bosbury, 7 miles from Malvern	2.45 p.m
8. 0 a.m	Boscastle, 5 miles from Camelford	7. 0 p.m
8. 0 a.m	Boscombe, 22 miles from Salisbury	5.30 p.m
9.30 a.m	*Boston, Mrs. Sarah Creasey	4.30 p.m
7. 0 a.m	Botesdale, 16mi. fr. Bury St. Edmund's	6. 0 p.m
8. 0 a.m	Botley, 7 miles from Southampton	5.15 p.m
10. 0 a.m	Bottisham, 6 miles from Newmarket.	5. 0 p.m
8. 0 a.m	Boughton, 4 miles from Feversham	7. 0 p.m
7. 0 a.m	*Bourn, Mrs Wm. Emmitt	9.30 p.m
9. 0 a.m	Bournmouth, 5 miles from Poole	5.15 p.m
9.35 a.m	Bourton on the Water, 8 m.fr. Moreton	5. 0 p.m
7. 0 a.m	Bourton, 5 miles from Bristol	4.15 p m
8. 0 a.m	Bourton, 4 miles from Wincanton	5.30 p.m
8. 0 a.m	Bovey-Tracey, 4 m. from Chudleigh	5.30 p.m
9. 0 a.m	Bovingdon, 4 m. fr. Hemel-Hempstead	6.30 p.m
8.10 a.m	Bow, 7 miles from Crediton	4.30 p.m
9. 0 a.m	Bower's Gifford, 21 m. fr. Ingatestone	3.45 p.m
12.30 p.m	Bowes, 4 miles from Barnard-Castle	12.15 p.m
11.25 a.m	Bowness, 9 miles from Kendal	2.10 p.m
8. 0 a.m	Box, 7 miles from Chippenham	5. 0 p.m
8.15 a.m	Boxford, 13 miles from Colchester	5.30 p.m
7. 0 a.m	Boxmoor, 1½ m. fr. Hemel-Hempstead	7. 0 p.m
2. 0 p.m	Bozeat, 12 miles from Northampton	2. 0 p.m
9. 0 a.m	Brabourne, 5 miles from Ashford	5.30 p.m
7. 0 a.m. 3. 0 p.m	*Brackley, Robert Bartlett	8. 0 a.m 6.30 p.m
7. 0 a.m	*Bracknell, Miss Esther Maslin	6.30 p.m
10.30 a.m	Bracon-Ash, 7 miles from Norwich	3.45 a.m
7.45 a.m	Bradfield, 3 miles from Manningtree	7. 0 p.m
7. 0 a.m	*Bradford, Wilts, Charles Johnson	7.40 p.m
7. 0 a.m 8. 0 a.m	*Bradford, Yorksh. William Coates	4.50 p.m 6.15 p.m
8.30 a.m	Bradford, 4 miles from Taunton	5. 0 p.m
10. 0 a.m	Bradford-Abbas, 2 m. fr. Sherborne	2. 0 p.m
10. 0 a.m	Brading, 4 miles from Ryde, I.of.W.	5. 0 p.m
7. 0 a.m	Bradninch, 2½ miles from Cullompton	7. 0 p.m
10.30 a.m	Bradwell, 15 miles from Maldon	3. 0 p.m
8.15 a.m	Bradwell, 4 m. from Stoney-Stratford	5. 0 p.m
11.15 a.m	Brailes, 5 miles from Shipston	1. 0 p.m
7. 0 a.m	*Braintree, Joseph Watson	7. 0 p.m
8.30 a.m	Bramdean, 5 miles from Alresford	6.15 p.m
7.30 a.m	Bramfield, 8 mi. from Saxmundham	6.45 p.m
8.30 a.m	Bramford, 3 miles from Ipswich	6. 0 p.m
8. 0 a.m	Bramford-Speke, 4 miles from Exeter	6.30 p.m
9.10 a.m	Bramham, 5 miles from Tadcaster	3.45 p.m
8. 0 a.m	Bramley, 3 miles from Guildford	5.30 p.m
10. 0 a.m	Bramley, 4 miles from Leeds	5. 0 p.m
2 0 p.m	*Brampton, Joseph Coulthard	11.30 a.m
8. 0 a.m	Brampton, 2 miles from Huntingdon	8.45 p.m
12. 0noon	Brampton-Bryan, 10 m. from Ludlow	1.15 p.m
10. 0 a.m	Brancaster, 22 miles from Lynn	3.45 p.m
9.38 a.m	Brancepeth, 4½ miles from Durham	8.30 p.m
9. 0 a.m	Brandeston, 12 mi. from Woodbridge	4. 0 p.m
7. 0 a.m	*Brandon, John Clark	10. 0 p.m
10. 0 a.m	Brandsburton, 8¼ miles from Beverley	10.30 a.m
11. 0 a.m	Brant-Broughton, 8 m. from Newark.	2. 0 p.m
7.15 a.m	Brasted, 4½ miles from Seven-Oaks	6.15 p.m
7.45 a.m	Braunston, 3 miles from Daventry	6.15 p.m
11. 0 a.m	Braunton, 5 miles from Barnstaple	2. 0 p.m
8 30noon	*Brecknock, Mrs. Anne Morgan	3.30 p.m
9. 0 a.m	Brenchley, 9¼ miles from Cranbrook	5. 0 p.m
9.30 a.m	Brent, 8 miles from Ashburton	3. 0 p.m
7. 0 a.m 12. 0noon	*Brentwood, Mrs. Maria Taylor	11.50 a.m 10. 0 p.m
8.45 a.m	Brewood, 8 miles from Wolverhampton	5.45 p.m
8. 0 a.m	Brickhill, 3 m. from Fenny-Stratford	6. 0 p.m
8. 0 a.m	Bridestowe, 6 miles from Oakhampton	3. 0 a.m
8. 0 a.m	Bridge, 3 miles from Canterbury	6.30 p.m
11. 0 a.m	*Bridgend, Philip Price	1.30 a.m
12. 0noon	Bridgerule, 20 mi. from Oakhampton	10. 0 a.m
7.30 a.m	*Bridgenorth, James Shipman	6.30 p.m
7. 0 a.m	*Bridgewater, Alfred Saunders	9.30 p.m
1.45 p.m	*Bridlington, Robert Thomas Brown	12.15noon
12. 0noon	Bridlington-Quay, 1¼ m. f. Bridlington	11..45 am
9. 0 a.m	*Bridport, Harry Warr	3 45 p.m
9.40 a.m	Bridport-Harbour, 2 mi. fr. Bridport	3·15 p.m
9. 0 a.m	Brierley, 6 miles from Barnsley	2·50 p.m
7. 0 a.m	Brierley-Hill, 12½ mi. fr. Birmingham	8· 0 p.m
2. 0 p.m	*Brigg, Frederick Horatio Atkinson	12. 0noon
10.30 a.m	Brighouse, 4 miles from Huddersfield	12. 0noon

Letters from London delivered at h. m.	Town. Postmaster.	Box for London closes at h. m.
8.30 a.m	Brightlingsea, 10 m. from Colchester.	5.45 p.m
7.30 a.m 1. 0 p.m	*Brighton, John Wm. Ferguson	10.45 a.m 9.30 p.m
10.30 a.m	Brigstock, 6 miles from Thrapstone	2.30 p.m
10. 0 a.m	Brill, 7 miles from Thame	5.30 p.m
10. 0 a.m	Brimpton, 7 miles from Newbury	5. 0 p.m
9. 0 a.m	Brimscombe, 2½ miles from Stroud	4.30 p.m
8. 0 a.m	Brinkley, 6 miles from Newmarket	6.30 p.m
8.45 a.m	Brinklow, 7½ miles from Coventry	4.15 p.m
11. 0 a.m	Brinningham, 14 miles from Dereham	2.30 p.m
7. 0 a.m	Brislington, 3 miles from Bristol	7.15 a.m 5.45 p.m
7. 0 a.m 3.30 p.m	*Bristol, Thomas Todd Walton, jun.	7.10 a.m 9.15 p.m
8.30 a.m	Brittal-lane, 1 mile from Stourbridge	6.30 p.m
10.15 a.m	*Brixham, Mrs. Harriet Tozer	2.45 p.m
10.30 a.m	Brixton (I.W.) 7 miles from Newport	2.30 p.m
9. 0 a.m	Broad-Chalk, 8 miles from Salisbury	8. 0 p.m
8. 0 a.m	Broad-Clist, 5½ miles from Exeter	5.30 p.m
10. 0 a.m	Broadhembury, 6 miles from Honiton	2. 0 p.m
8. 0 a.m	Broadstairs, 2 miles from Ramsgate	7. 0 p.m
7. 0 a.m	Broadwas, 6½ miles from Worcester	6.30 p.m
7. 0 a.m	Broadwater, 1 mile from Worthing	6.30 p.m
7. 0 a.m	*Broadway, John Dimock	6.15 p.m
9.30 a.m	Broadwinsor, 3 mi. from Beaminster	2. 0 p.m
8. 0 a.m	Brockenhurst, 3 mi. from Lyndhurst	8. 0 p.m
7. 0 a.m	Brockley, 9 miles from Bristol	3.45 p.m
9. 0 a.m	Bromham, 7½ miles from Chippenham	6. 0 p.m
	*Bromley, Kt. *see* London District Off.	
7.30 a.m 3. 0 p.m	Brompton (Kent), 1¼ m. from Chatham	8. 0 p.m
8.15 a.m	Brompton, 2 miles from Northallerton	4.35 p.m
11.30 a.m	Brompton, 8 miles from Scarboro	1.40 p.m
8. 0 a.m	*Bromyard, Thomas Griffiths	5. 0 p.m
1. 0 p.m	Bronllys, 7 miles from Hay	11. 0 a.m
10. 0 a.m	Brook-End, 4 miles from Lydney	2. 0 p.m
8.20 a.m	Brooke, 7 miles from Norwich	5.10 p.m
7. 0 a.m	Brookland, 6 miles from Romney	8. 0 p.m
9. 0 a.m	Broomfield, 3 miles from Chelmsford	6. 0 p.m
7. 0 a.m	*Broomsgrove, Wm. Johnson	9.15 p.m
8. 0 a.m	Broseley, 2 miles from Ironbridge	5.15 p.m
9.30 a.m	Brotherton, 1½ mi. from Ferrybridge	2. 0 p.m
11. 0 a.m 2.35 p.m	*Brough, John Lancaster	10.10 a.m 2. 0 p.m
8. 0 a.m	Broughton, 3 miles from Stockbridge	5. 0 p.m
7. 0 a.m	Broughton, 10 miles from Ulverstone	6.50 p.m
9. 0 a.m	Broxbourne, 5 m. from Waltham-Cross	6. 0 p.m
9.45 a.m	Bruntingthorpe, 5½ m. fr. Lutterworth	4.45 p.m
8. 0 a.m	Bruton, 23 miles from Bath	7.15 p.m
11.30 a.m	Brynmawr, 8 mi. from Abergavenny	12.30 p.m
11.40 a.m	Bubwith, 8 miles from Selby	2. 0 p.m
7.30 a.m	Buckden, 4 miles from Huntingdon	9. 0 p.m
8. 0 a.m	Buckfastleigh, 3 mi. from Ashburton	5. 0 p.m
7.30 a.m 1.30 p.m	*Buckingham, Wm. Stallworthy	9. 0 a.m 7.15 p.m
8.30 a.m	Buckland, 1 mile from Dover	6.30 p.m
8.30 a.m	Buckland, 4 miles from Farringdon	5.30 p.m
1.20 p.m	Bude, 32 miles from Oakhampton	8.45 p.m
9.15 a.m	Budleigh-Salterton, 7 mi. fr. Sidmouth	4.30 p.m
5.30 p.m	*Builth, Mrs. Anne Gwillim	5. 0 a.m
10. 0 a.m	Bulwell, 4 miles from Nottingham	5. 0 p.m
8. 0 a.m	Bunbury, 5 miles from Tarporley	5.45 p.m
7.30 a.m	*Bungay, Daniel Stock	6.30 p.m
9.30 a.m	Bunny, 7 miles from Nottingham	4. 0 p.m
7. 0 a.m	*Buntingford, William Hampton	9.30 p.m
7. 0 a.m	Burbage, 6 miles from Marlborough	7. 0 p.m
8. 0 a.m	Bures, 9 miles from Colchester	7.30 p.m
9. 0 a.m	*Burford, Ben. Geo. Olivet Matthews	4. 0 p.m
3. 0 p.m	Burgh, 8 miles from Spilsby	8. 0 p.m
9. 0 a.m	Burlesdon-Bridge, 6 m. f. Southampton	4. 0 p.m
10. 0 a.m	Burley, 2 miles from Otley	3. 0 p.m
9. 0 a.m	Burnham, 8 miles from Bridgewater	5.30 p.m
8. 0 a.m	Burnham, Bucks, 3 mi. fr. Maidenhead	6.45 p.m
9.30 a.m	Burnham, Essex, 15 mi. from Maldon	4. 0 p.m
11. 0 a.m	Burnham, Norfolk, 28 miles fr. Lynn	3. 0 p.m
7.30 a.m 10.45 a.m	*Burnley, Thomas Sheppard Dewhirst	3. 7 p.m 7.45 p.m
8.30 a.m	Bursledon, 5 mi. from Southampton	4.30 p.m
8. 0 a.m	*Burslem, Jabez Wilson	7.20 p.m
1. 0 p.m	Burton-Agnes, 28 miles from Hull	12.30 p.m
10.30 a.m	Burton-Bradstock, 3 m. fr. Bridport	2.45 p.m
11.30 a.m	Burton Latimer, 6½ m. f. Highm. Ferrars	3.30 p.m

Letters from London delivered at h. m.	Town. Postmaster.	Box for London closes at h. m.
8. 0 a.m	*Burton-on-Trent, John Whitehurst	5.45 p.m
8.20 a.m	*Burton, Westmoreland, T. Rallinshaw	5.15 p.m
10.30 a.m	Burwarton, 10 mi. from Bridgenorth	2.30 p.m
8. 0 a.m	Burwash, 4 miles from Hurst-Green	9. 0 p.m
9. 0 a.m	Burwell, 4 miles from Newmarket	7. 0 p.m
10. 0 a.m	Bury, Hunts, 11 m. from Huntingdon	3. 0 p.m
8.30 a.m	Bury, Sussex, 4½ miles from Arundel	4.30 p.m
9.30 a.m	*Bury, Lancash. James Whitehead.	5. 0 p.m 8.30 p.m
7. 0 a.m 5.30 p.m	*Bury St. Edmund's, Henry Newson	9. 0 p.m 6. 0 a.m
8. 0 a.m	Bushey, 1 mile from Watford	7. 0 p.m
7.30 a.m	Butleigh, 4 miles from Glastonbury	5.30 p.m
8. 0 a.m	Butterley, 3 miles from Alfreton	5.30 p.m
6.30 a.m	Buxted, 2 miles from Uckfield	7.45 p.m
9.30 a.m	*Buxton, Mrs. Mary Anne Moore	4. 0 p.m
9. 0 a.m	Buxton, 10 miles from Norwich	4.30 p.m
1.30 p.m	Bwlch, 8 miles from Brecon	10.30 a.m
9. 0 a.m	Byfield, 7 miles from Daventry	4.45 p.m
7. 0 a.m	Byfleet, 2 miles from Cobham S.	6. 0 p.m
3.15 p.m	Caerphilly, 7½ miles from Cardiff	7.45 a.m
8. 0 a.m	Cainscross, 1¼ mile from Stroud	5. 0 p.m
3.30 p.m	Caistor, 9½ miles from Brigg	10.30 a.m
10.15 a.m	Calbourne, 5 m. from Newport, I. W.	3. 0 p.m
7.10 a.m	Calderbridge, 10 m. from Whitehaven	3. 0 p.m
12.30 noon	*Callington, Mrs. Grace Peter	12.50 noon
7. 0 a.m	*Calne, Edwin Baily	8.30 p.m
1. 0 p.m	Calstock, 6 miles from Tavistock	9. 0 a.m
11.45 a.m	Calverton, 7 miles from Nottingham	4.30 p.m
4.30 p.m	Camborne, 14 miles from Truro	7.15 a.m
7.30 a.m 2.45 p.m	*Cambridge, William Barsham	9.15 a.m 10. 0 p.m
8.30 a.m	Cambridge Inn, 4 miles from Dursley	4.20 p.m
11.50 a.m	*Camelford, John Jones	12.40 p.m
7.30 a.m	*Campden, Mrs. Sarah Barnes	6.15 p.m
1.15 p.m	Candlesby, 4 miles from Spilsby	8. 0 a.m
9. 0 a.m	Canewden, 6 miles from Rochford	4. 0 p.m
7. 0 a.m	Canford, 2 miles from Wimborne	7. 0 p.m
11.30 a.m	Cann-Office, 15 miles from Welchpool	1. 0 p.m
7.30 a.m	Cannington, 3½ mi. from Bridgewater	7. 0 p.m
9. 0 a.m	Cannock, 8 miles from Walsall	4.45 p.m
7. 0 a.m 5.15 p.m	*Canterbury, John Callaway	9.15 a.m 8.45 p.m
8.45 a.m	Capel, 7 miles from Ipswich	4.30 p.m
9. 0 a.m	*Cardiff, William Bird	4. 0 p.m
8. 0 p.m	*Cardigan, Mrs. Mary Jones	9.30 p.m
9. 0 a.m	Carisbrooke, 1 m. from Newport, I. W.	4.30 p.m
3.30 a.m	Carleon, 3 miles from Newport, Mon.	9. 0 a.m
7. 0 a.m 3. 0 p.m	*Carlisle, William Forster	10.39 a.m 6. 6 p.m
8. 0 a.m	Carlton, 7½ miles from Newmarket	6.30 p.m
9.30 a.m	Carlton, 4 miles from Worksop	3.45 p.m
10. 0 a.m	Carlton-Scroop, 6 m. from Grantham.	3.15 p.m
10.30 a.m	Carlton-on-Trent, 7 miles from Newark	2. 0 p.m
5. 0 p.m	*Carmarthen, John Matthews	7. 0 a.m
7.45 a.m 2. 0 p.m	*Carnarvon, Robert Edwards	11. 0 a.m 5.15 p.m
8.40 a.m	Carnforth, 6 miles from Lancaster	5.10 p.m
8. 0 a.m	Carrington, 2 miles from Nottingham	5. 0 p.m
12. 0 noon	Cartmell, 14 miles from Milnthorpe	1.35 p.m
9. 0 a.m	Castle-Bromwich, 6 m. fr. Birmingham	4.45 p.m
8. 0 a.m	Castle-Cary, 26 miles from Bath	5.45 p.m
11. 0 a.m	Castle-Camps, 6 miles from Linton	4. 0 p.m
8. 0 a.m	Castle-Combe, 6 m. from Chippenham	5. 0 p.m
8. 0 a.m	Castle-Donington, 9 mi. from Derby	6. 0 p.m
11. 0 p.m	Castle-Eden, near Durham	6.45 p.m
10. 0 a.m	Castleford, 3 miles from Pontefract	3.30 p.m
10. 0 a.m	Castle-Howard-Inn, 16 m. from York	2.50 p.m
	Castle-Hedingham, *see* Hedingham	
8. 0 a.m	Castle-Rising, 4 miles from Lynn	6. 0 p.m
7.30 a.m	Castle-Thorpe, 3 m. f. Stoney-Stratford	6.30 p.m
10.30 a.m	Castleton, 14 miles from Bakewell	3. 0 p.m
7.15 a.m	Castletown, 10 m. fr. Douglas, I. of Man	4.45 p.m
8. 5 a.m	Caton, 4 miles from Lancaster	5.30 p.m
8.30 a.m	Catsfield, 4 miles from Battle	8. 0 p.m
10.30 a.m	*Catterick, James Young	3. 5 p.m
9. 0 a.m	Cattistock, 9 miles from Dorchester	4. 0 p.m
8. 0 a.m	Catton, 2 miles from Norwich	5.30 p.m
9.40 a.m	Cave (North), 2 miles from Howden	3.15 p.m
10. 0 a.m	Cave (South), 12 miles from Howden	2.50 p.m
8. 0 a.m	Cavendish, 5 miles from Sudbury	5. 0 p.m
11.20 a.m	Cawood, 5 miles from Selby	3. 5 p.m

Letters from London delivered at h. m.	Town. Postmaster.	Box for London closes at h. m.
1.30 p.m	Cawsand, 4½ miles from Devonport..	1.15 p.m
7. 0 a.m	*Caxton, Samuel Fordham..........	9. 0 p.m
9.15 a.m	Caythorpe, 9 miles from Grantham..	3. 0 p.m
8.40 a.m	Cefn-y-bedd, 4 miles from Wrexham.	3.45 p.m
11.30 a.m	Cemmaes, 28 miles from Bangor	1.45 p.m
2. 0 p.m	Cemmes, 31 miles from Welchpool ..	10. 0 a.m
12.15 noon	Cerrig-y-druidon, 32 mi. fr. Oswestry	12.30 p.m
9. 0 a.m	Cerne-Abbas, 8 m. from Dorchester..	4.30 p.m
7. 0 a.m	Chacewater, 5 miles from Truro	7. 0 p.m
9.30 a.m	Chaddesley-Corbett, 5 miles from Kidderminster	4. 0 p.m
11. 0 a.m	Chagford, 16 miles from Chudleigh..	3. 0 p.m
9. 0 a.m	ChalfontSt.Giles, 4 m. from Gerrards ×	5.30 p.m
9. 0 a.m	ChalfontSt.Peters, 1½m.f.Gerrards crs.	6. 0 p.m
7. 0 a.m	*Chalford, Miss Mary Ann Cother	3. 0 p.m 8.30 p.m
7. 0 a.m	Chalk, 1½ miles from Gravesend	7. 0 p.m
8. 0 a.m	Chapel-Allerton, 3 miles from Leeds..	5.45 p.m
11. 0 a.m	Chapel-in-le-Frith, 6 mi. fr. Buxton ..	1.30 p.m
8. 0 a.m	Chapel-Town, 7 miles from Sheffield.	3. 0 p.m
7. 0 a.m	*Chard, John Toms................	6.30 p.m
8. 0 a.m	Charing, 13 miles from Maidstone ..	5.30 p.m
8. 0 a.m	Charlbury, 3 miles from Enstone	5.45 p.m
14. 0 p.m	Charlestown, 1½ m. from St. Austell..	9. 0 a.m
1. 0 a.m	Charlton-Kings, 2 m.fr. Cheltenham .	6.45 p.m
9. 0 a.m	Charlton-Mackrel, 3 m.fr. Somerton..	4. 0 p.m
7.30 a.m	Charlwood, 3½ miles from Crawley ..	6. 0 p.m
8. 0 a.m	Charminster, 2 miles from Dorchester	5.30 p.m
9.30 a.m	*Charmouth, John Carter	3.30 p.m
9.15 a.m	Charter-House-Hinton, 6 m.fr. Bath.	9. 0 p.m
8. 0 a.m	Chartham, 3½ miles from Canterbury.	7. 0 p.m
7. 0 a.m	Chasewater, 5 miles from Truro	8. 0 p.m
7. 0 a.m 2.30 p.m	*Chatham, Isaac John Dadd	11.45 a.m 9. 0 p.m
8. 0 a.m	*Chatteris, David Rowley	8. 0 p.m
5.30 p.m	Chatton, 5 miles from Belford	7. 0 a.m
9.15 a.m	*Cheadle Staffords, Samuel Keys ..	7. 0 p.m
8.30 a.m	Cheadle, 7 miles from Manchester ..	5.30 p.m
10. 0 a.m	Cheam, 3 miles from Epsom	3.15 p.m
10. 0 a.m	Checkendon, 7 miles from Henley ..	4. 0 p.m
8. 0 a.m	Cheddar, 8 miles from Wells........	6. 0 p.m
8. 0 a.m	Chedzoy-Lane, 1½ mi. fr. Bridgewater	6. 0 p.m
7.30 a.m	Cheetham-Hill, 2½ m.fr. Manchester.	5.30 p.m
7. 0 a.m	*Chelmsford, Abjohn Joseph Stokes.	9. 0 p.m
10.15 a.m	Chelsfield, 7 miles from Bromley	5.30 p.m
7.45 a.m 4.45 p.m	*Cheltenham, John Nicholson	6.30 a.m 9.45 p.m
9. 0 a.m	Chenies, 4½ miles fm. Rickmansworth	4.30 p.m
9. 0 a.m	*Chepstow, Mrs. Mary Hedgius	7. 0 p.m
7.30 a.m	Cheriton, 3 miles from Alresford	7. 0 p.m
9.30 a.m	Cheriton-Fitzpaine, 6½ m.fr. Crediton	3. 0 p.m
9.30 a.m	Cherrington, 4 miles from Shipstone.	2. 0 p.m
7. 0 a.m	*Chertsey, Samuel Toll Bidwell	7. 0 p.m
7. 0 a.m	*Chesham	7.10 p.m
7.30 a.m	Cheshunt-Street, 2 m.fr. Waltham +	7. 0 p.m
9. 0 a.m	Chessington, 4 miles from Kingston..	2. 0 p.m
7. 0 a.m 5.15 p.m	*Chester, William Palin	3.45 a.m 9. 0 p.m
8. 0 a.m 5.30 p.m	*Chesterfield, John Roberts	7.45 p.m 10. 0 p.m
2.30 p.m	*Chester-le-street, W. Cuthbertson	9.45 a.m
7.30 a.m	Chesterton, 1½ m. from Cambridge ..	7. 0 p.m
7. 0 a.m	Chesterton, 5 miles from Stilton	7. 0 p.m
10.15 a.m	Chetnole, 7½ miles from Sherborne ..	1.30 p.m
8. 0 a.m	Cheveley, 4 miles from Newmarket..	8. 0 p.m
8. 0 a.m	Chevely, 4 miles from Newbury	5. 0 p.m
2. 0 p.m	Chewbent, 13 m. from Manchester ..	9. 0 a.m
9. 0 a.m	Chewmagna, 7 miles from Bristol ..	3.30 p.m
9.30 a.m	Chew-Stoke, 8 miles from Bristol....	3. 0 p.m
9. 0 a.m	Chewton-Mendip, 15 miles from Bath	4. 0 p.m
7. 0 a.m	*Chichester, John Attree Fuller	9. 0 p.m
10. 0 a.m	Chideock, 3 miles from Bridport....	3. 0 p.m
10.30 a.m	Chilbolton, 4½ miles from Andover ..	5. 0 p.m
8. 0 a.m	Chilcompton, 12 miles from Bath ..	6. 0 p.m
8. 0 a.m	Chilham, 6 miles from Canterbury ..	6. 0 p.m
7. 0 a.m	Chilmark, 12 miles from Salisbury ..	6.30 p.m
9.30 a.m	Chinnor, 5 miles from Tetsworth ...	5.45 p.m
7. 0 a.m 2.30 p.m	*Chippenham, Miss Ann Elliott ..	8.40 a.m 10. 0 p.m
7. 0 a.m	Chippenham, 5 m. from Mildenhall..	7. 0 p.m
8. 0 a.m	*Chipping-Norton, James Prestidge	8.30 p.m
	Chipping-Sodbury, see Sodbury	

Letters from London delivered at h. m.	Town. Postmaster.	Box for London closes at h. m.
7. 0 a.m	Chipstead, miles from Seven Oaks.	7. 0 p.m
9. 0 a.m	Chipstead, 6 miles from Reigate	4.30 p.m
11. 0 a.m	Chirbury, 6½ miles from Welchpool ..	1. 0 p.m
9.30 a.m	*Chirk, Mrs. Hannah Maria Williams	3. 0 p.m
7.30 a.m	Chiselhurst, 3 miles from Bromley ..	7. 0 p.m
8. 0 a.m	Chislet, 7 miles from Canterbury....	5.30 p.m
9. 0 a.m	Chobham, 4 miles from Bagshot	5. 0 p.m
8. 0 a.m	Cholderton, 11 miles from Salisbury.	5.45 p.m
7. 0 a.m	Cholsey, 2 miles from Wallingford...	7. 0 p.m
7.30 a.m	*Chorley, Horatio N. Lawson	6.55 p.m
8. 0 a.m	Chorleywood, 2½ m.f. Rickmansworth	5. 0 p.m
8. 0 a.m	*Christchurch, Abraham Pike......	6.30 p.m
10. 0 a.m	Christow, 9 miles from Exeter......	1. 0 p.m
7. 0 a.m	*Chudleigh, John Petherick........	6.30 p.m
9.30 a.m	*Chumleigh, Mrs. Mary Howell....	3.45 p.m
11. 0 a.m	Church-Eaton, 7 miles from Stafford.	4.45 p.m
8.30 a.m	Church-Gate, 1¾ m.f. Waltham-Cross	7.30 p.m
10. 0 a.m	Churchill, 12 miles from Bristol	1.30 p.m
2.30 p.m	Churchingford, 8½ m. from Taunton.	12.15 p.m
10. 0 a.m	Church-Stoke, 9½m. from. Welchpool	2.30 p.m
11.30 a.m 4.45 p.m	Church-Stretton, 13 m.f. Shrwsbry.	11.15 a.m 4.15 p.m
9.15 a.m	Cinderford, 4 miles from Newnham..	3. 0 p.m
7. 0 a.m 2.30 p.m	*Cirencester, Thomas Squires	8. 0 a.m 10. 0 p.m
8. 0 a.m	Clandon, 4 miles from Guildford.....	5.30 p.m
10.30 a.m	Clapham, 6 miles from Settle	3. 0 p.m
8.30 a.m	*Clare, George Hammond	4.30 p.m
9. 0 a.m	Clatford, 2 miles from Andover	6. 0 p.m
12.30 a.m	Clay, 4½ miles from Holt	1.30 p.m
9. 0 a.m	Clay-Cross, 5 miles from Chesterfield	4.30 p.m
7. 0 a.m	Claydon, 4 miles from Ipswich......	8. 0 p.m
10. 0 a.m	Clearwell, 4 miles from Coleford	12.45 p.m
9. 0 a.m	Cleckheaton, 10 miles from Leeds ..	3. 0 p.m
7. 0 a.m	Cleeve, 10 miles from Bristol........	3.30 p.m
9. 0 a.m	Clenchwarton, 2 miles from Lynn ..	5. 0 p.m
8. 0 a.m	Cleobury-Mortimer, 8 m. f. Bewdley.	5. 0 p.m
7. 0 a.m	Clevedon, 12 miles from Bristol	2.45 p.m
8.40 a.m	Clifford, 4 miles from Tadcaster	4.20 p.m
7. 0 a.m 4.10 p.m	Clifton, 2 miles from Bristol	5.30 a.m 9. 0 p.m
10. 0 a.m	Clipstone, 5 mi. fr. Market Harbro'..	3.15 p.m
8. 0 a.m 10. 0 a.m	*Clitheroe, Henry Whalley	3.20 p.m 8.10 p.m
3. 0 p.m	Clovelly, 11 miles from Bideford....	9. 0 a.m
2.30 p.m	Clun, 17 miles from Ludlow	9. 0 a.m
4.15 p.m	Clynnog, 9½ miles from Carnarvon ..	9. 0 a.m
11.30 a.m	Coatham, 4 miles from Darlington ..	7.20 p.m
7. 0 a.m	*Cobham, Surrey, Charles Newland.	7.15 p.m
8. 0 a.m	Cobham, 4 miles from Gravesend ..	6. 0 p.m
7. 0 a.m	Cobridge, 5 m. f. Newcastle, Stafford.	7.30 p.m
11.15 a.m 2.50 p.m	*Cockermouth, John Birkett	10.40 a.m
8.30 a.m	Cockfield, 11 miles from Sudbury ...	5.30 p.m
9.30 a.m	Cocking, 9 miles from Chichester ..	4.15 p.m
8.30 a.m	Coddenham, 7 miles from Ipswich ..	6. 0 p.m
8.15 a.m	Codford St.Mary, 3½ m.f. Heytesbury	5. 0 p.m
7. 0 a.m	Coggeshall, 3 miles from Kelvedon..	8.30 p.m
7. 0 a.m	*Colchester, Joseph Verlander......	9. 0 p.m
1.40 p.m	Cold-Conistone, 7 miles from Skipton	1. 0 p.m
7. 0 a.m	Cold-Harbour, 4 miles from Swindon	8.30 p.m
9.30 a.m	Cold-Overton, 3½ miles from Oakham	3.15 p.m
9.15 a.m	*Coleford, William Nicholson	2.45 p.m
7.30 a.m	*Coleshill, James Dale	7.30 p.m
9. 0 a.m	Colford, 5 miles from Crediton......	4. 0 p.m
7. 0 a.m	Collingbourne, 10½ m. f. Marlborough	6.30 p.m
9.30 a.m	Collingham, 6 miles from Newark...	3.30 p.m
8. 0 a.m	Colnbrook, 4 miles from Slough	6.45 p.m
11. 0 a.m	Colne. 6 miles from Burnley........	2.30 p.m
7.15 a.m	Coltersworth, 13 miles fr. Stamford..	5.45 p.m
9. 0 a.m	Coltishall, 7½ miles from Norwich ..	5. 0 p.m
7. 0 a.m	Colton, 2 miles from Rugeley	6.15 p.m
8. 0 a.m	Colwall, 3 miles from Malvern......	4. 0 p.m
9. 0 a.m	Colyton, 6 miles from Axminster ...	3.15 p.m
2. 0 p.m	Comb-Martin, 5 mi. from Ilfracombe..	7. 0 a.m
8. 0 a.m	Comb St. Nicholas, 2½ mi. from Chard	2. 0 p.m
12.30 p.m	Compton, 2 miles from Plymouth....	2.30 p.m
10. 0 a.m	Compton, 3½ miles from Sherborne ..	2. 0 p.m
8.45 a.m	Compton, Sussex, 7 m. fr. Petersfield	4.30 p.m
8. 0 a.m	*Congleton, Thomas Steele	7.15 p.m
7. 0 a.m	Congresbury, 12 miles from Bristol..	2.45 p.m
8.30 a.m	Conisbrough, 5½ mi. from Doncaster	3.35 p.m

Letters from London delivered at h. m.	Town. Postmaster.	Box for London closes at h. m.
7. 0 a.m 2. 0 p.m	*Conway, Thomas Roberts	11. 0 a.m 9.30 p.m
2.40 p.m	Coniston, 9 miles from Ambleside	10. 0 p.m
8. 0 a.m	Cookham, 3½ m. from Maidenhead	7. 0 p.m
9. 0 a.m	Cookley, 3 miles from Kidderminster	5. 0 p.m
8. 0 a.m	Coombe-Bissett, 3 mi. from Salisbury	6.30 p.m
7.30 a.m	Copdock, 4 miles from Ipswich	5. 0 p.m
8.30 a.m	Copplestone, 4 miles from Crediton	4. 0 p.m
7.30 a.m	Corbetstay, 5 miles from Romford	6. 0 p.m
3.10 p.m	Corbridge, 16 mi. fr. Newcastle, Tyne	6.30 p.m
6.10 p.m	Corby, 5 miles from Carlisle	9. 0 a.m
7. 0 a.m	Corfe-Castle, 5 miles from Wareham	5.30 p.m
7.30 a.m	Corfe-Mullen, 3 miles from Wimborne	5. 0 p.m
9. 0 a.m	Corse-Lawn, 6 miles from Tewkesbury	4. 0 p.m
7.30 a.m	Corsham, 4 miles from Chippenham	6.15 p.m
8. 0 a.m	Corsley, 4 miles from Warminster	4.45 p.m
11.30 a.m	*Corwen, John Owen Lewis	1.15 p.m
7. 0 a.m	Coseley, 2¾ miles from Bilston	6.30 p.m
7. 0 a.m	Cosgrove, 2 m. from Stoney Stratford	7.30 p.m
8.15 a.m	Cosham, 5 miles from Portsmouth	5.30 p.m
10.30 a.m	Cossey, 4½ miles from Norwich	4.45 p.m
8. 0 a.m	Cossington, 4 miles from Bridgewater	6. 0 p.m
9. 0 a.m	Cossington, 7 miles fr. Loughborough	7.15 p.m
2.10 p.m	Cotherstone, 4 m. from Barnard Castle	10. 0 a.m
9. 0 a.m	Cottenham, 7 miles from Cambridge	4. 0 p.m
9.15 a.m	Cottesmore, 5 miles from Oakham	3.30 p.m
12.10 p.m	Cottingham, 5 miles from Hull	2.15 p.m
8. 0 a.m	Coulsdon, 5½ miles from Croydon	6. 0 p.m
7.30 a.m	Coute, 4 miles from Worthing	5.30 p.m
7. 0 a.m 2. 0 p.m	*Coventry, Timothy Peters Glennan	8.30 a.m 10. 0 p.m
10.15 a.m	*Cowbridge, Thomas Lister	10.15 a.m
9. 0 a.m	Cowden, 5 miles from East-Grinstead	4.15 p.m
8.15 a.m 5. 0 p.m	*Cowes, Mrs. Ann Roach	4.15 p.m
9. 0 a.m	Cowfold, 7 miles from Horsham	4.30 p.m
6. 0 a.m	Cowley, 2 miles from Exeter	7. 0 p.m
7. 0 a.m	Cowley, 1 mile from Uxbridge	7. 0 p.m
10. 0 a.m	Cowlinge, 8 miles from Newmarket	6. 0 p.m
1.30 p.m	Crabtree, 2 miles from Plymouth	2. 0 p.m
10. 0 a.m	Cradley, 4 miles from Malvern	2.50 p.m
7. 0 a.m	Cranborne, 7 mi. from Fordingbridge.	8. 0 p.m
7. 0 a.m	*Cranbrook, Eli Pethurst	9.30 p.m
8.30 a.m	Cranfield, 5 miles fr. Newport-Pagnell	4.45 p.m
8. 0 a.m	Cranford-Bridge, 3 m. from Hounslow	5. 0 p.m
9.15 a.m	Cranley, 9 miles from Guildford	4. 0 p.m
7. 0 a.m	*Crawley, Sussex, William Mitchell	9.30 p.m
7. 0 a.m	Crawley, 3 miles from Winchester	8.45 p.m
9. 0 a.m	Crawley's Down, 5½ mi. from Crawley	4.30 p.m
9. 0 a.m	Credenhill, 5 miles from Hereford	3.15 p.m
7. 0 a.m	*Crediton, Francis Shute	6. 0 p.m
9. 0 a.m	Creech-St.-Michael, 4 mi fr. Taunton	4.30 p.m
9. 0 a.m	Crewe, 5 miles from Nantwich	6.20 p.m
7. 0 a.m	*Crewkerne, John Budge	5.30 p.m
17. 0 a.m	Cribb's-Causeway, 6 mi. from Bristol	5. 0 p.m
0. 0 a.m	Crich, 5 miles from Alfreton	5.30 p.m
8.30 a.m	Crick, 4 miles from Chepstow	3.15 p.m
7. 0 a.m	*Crickhowell, Thomas Williams	5.15 p.m
7. 0 a.m	Cricklade, 8½ miles from Swindon	7.45 p.m
8.30 a.m	Crockernwell, 12 miles from Exeter	7. 0 a.m
10.50 a.m	Croft, 3 miles from Darlington	8.10 p.m
10.30 a.m	*Cromer	3. 0 p.m
9.10 a.m	Crondall, 3½ miles from Farnham	5. 0 p.m
11. 0 a.m	Crosby, 7¾ miles from Liverpool	2.45 p.m
8.30 a.m	Cross, 12 miles from Wells, Somerset	5.45 p.m
7. 0 a.m	Cross-Brook Street, 1 m. fr. Waltham +	7. 0 p.m
7.30 a.m	Cross-Hands, 11 miles from Bristol	4.30 p.m
7. 0 a.m	Cross Hands, 12 m. from Chippenham	7.20 p.m
7. 0 a.m	Cross-in-Hand, 12 m. fr. Hurst-Green	7.30 p.m
10.20 a.m	Crosshills, 5 miles from Skipton	2.50 p.m
6.15 p.m	Cross-Inn, 7 miles from Llandilo	6. 0 a.m
6.30 a.m	Crowcombe, 11 miles, from Taunton	7. 0 p.m
9. 0 a.m	Crowland, 9 miles from Peterborough	4.45 p.m
12.30 p.m	Crowle. 20 miles from Bawtry	1. 0 p.m
	*Croydon, *see* "London District Office"	
8. 0 a.m 1. 0 p.m	*Cuckfield Samuel Mitchell	10. 0 a.m 9.30 p.m
10. 0 a.m	Cuckney, 7 miles from Mansfield	3.30 p.m
8. 0 a.m	Cudworth, 3 miles from Barnsley	3.50 p.m
1.45 p.m	Cullercoates, 2 m. from North-Shields	7.30 p.m
7. 0 a.m	*Cullompton, Thomas Mitchell	8.45 p.m
1.30 a.m	Culworth, 7 miles from Banbury	12.15 p.m

Letters from London delivered at h. m.	Town. Postmaster.	Box for London closes at h. m.
9.30 a.m	Curdworth, 9 miles from Birmingham	4. 0 p.m
9.30 a.m	Curry-Rivell, 2 miles from Langport.	3.45 p.m
1. 0 p.m	Cwmcellyn, 12 mi. fr. Abergavenny	11. 0 a.m
8. 0 a.m	Dagenham, 3 miles from Romford	6. 0 p.m
7. 0 a.m	Daglingworth, 3 m. from Cirencester	7.30 p.m
9.30 a.m	Dale, 10 miles from Milford	3.30 p.m
9.30 a.m	Dalham, 6½ miles from Newmarket	6.30 p.m
8. 0 a.m	Dallinghoo, 4 miles from Woodbridge	6. 0 p.m
7.10 a.m	Dalston, 5 miles from Carlisle	11.50 a.m
8.10 a.m	Dalton, 5 miles from Ulverstone	4.50 p.m
7. 0 a.m	Damerham, 3 miles fr. Fordingbridge	8.30 p.m
7. 0 a.m	Danbury, 5 miles from Chelmsford	7. 0 p.m
7. 0 a.m	Darlaston, 2 miles from Wednesbury	9. 0 p.m
8.15 a.m	*Darlington, George Johnson Wilson	4.20 p.m 10. 0 p.m
7. 0 a.m 12. 0 noon	*Dartford, William Pittock	1.30 p.m 8.30 p.m
11.30 a.m	*Dartmouth Miss Mrgt. Fosse Sparke	2.12 p.m
7.45 a.m 11.55 a.m	Darwen, 4 miles from Blackburn	7.30 a.m 2.15 p.m
8. 0 a.m	Datchet, 2½ miles from Slough	7.15 p.m
8. 0 a.m	Davenham, 2 miles from Northwich	6.45 p.m
7. 0 a.m 1.30 p.m	*Daventry, Matthew Sharman	8.45 a.m 8.45 p.m
7.30 a.m	Dawley-Green, 4¾ m. from Shiffnal	5.30 p.m
7.30 a.m	*Dawlish, John Lowe	5.30 p.m
8. 0 a.m	*Deal, John Norris	10. 0 p.m
7.30 a.m	Debenham, 5 miles from Stoneham	6.30 p.m
7. 0 a.m	Deddington, 10 m. from Woodstock	7. 0 p.m
7. 0 a.m	Dedham, 7 miles from Colchester	6.30 p.m
8. 0 a.m	Deene, 12 miles from Wansford	5. 0 p.m
10. 0 p.m 6.30 a.m	Delph, 15 miles from Manchester	1.30 p.m 8. 0 p.m
9. 0 a.m	*Denbigh, Edward Roberts	3.30 p.m
12.40 p.m	Dent, 11 miles from Kirby-Lonsdale	12.40 p.m
9.30 a.m	Denton, 5 miles from Harlestone	4.30 p.m
8.45 a.m	Denton, 5½ miles from Manchester	5. 0 p.m
7.30 a.m	Denver, 1 mile from Downham	6. 0 p.m
9.15 a.m	Deptford-Inn, 7 mi. from Heytesbury	4. 0 p.m
7. 0 a.m 5. 0 p.m	*Derby, Thomas Parker Bainbrigge	6. 0 a.m 9. 0 p.m
7. 0 a.m	*Dereham, Miss Sarah Bone	6. 0 p.m
5. 0 p.m	Devils-Bridge, 12 mi. fr. Aberystwith	10. 0 p.m
7. 0 a.m	*Devizes, Thomas Burrough Smith	7.30 p.m
10.15 a.m	*Devonport, James Waller Coffin	3. 5 p.m
4. 0 p.m	Devorau, 5 miles from Truro	6.30 p.m
7.30 a.m	*Dewsbury, Paul Fletcher	5. 0 p.m
8. 0 a.m	Didsbury, 6 miles from Manchester	5.30 p.m
7. 0 a.m	Dinton, 9 miles from Salisbury	8. 0 p.m
12.15 p.m	Disley, 7 miles from Stockport	3.15 p.m
8. 0 a.m	*Diss, Miss Mary Ann Musgrave	8. 0 p.m
9.30 a.m	Distington, 4½ mi. from Whitehaven	3.55 p.m
9.30 a.m	Ditchling, 8 miles from Lewes	4.30 p.m
10. 0 a.m	Dobcross, 12 miles from Manchester.	1.30 p.m
11. 0 a.m	Docking, 13 miles from Rougham	2.30 p.m
9. 0 a.m	Doddescombsleigh, 6 m. from Eris	2. 0 p.m
7. 0 a.m	Doddington, 3 miles from Chater	8. 0 p.m
4.30 p.m	Dolgelly, 32 miles from Corwen	10. 0 p.m
8. 0 a.m	*Doncaster, Jn. Barnard Sheardow	5.45 p.m
8. 0 a.m	Donhead, 4 miles from Shaftesbury	6. 0 p.m
9.15 a.m	Donington, 10 miles from Spalding	4. 0 p.m
8.30 a.m	*Dorchester, John Pett	6. 0 p.m
9. 0 a.m	Dorchester, 4 miles from Wallingford	5. 0 p.m
7. 0 a.m	*Dorking, Robert Best Ede	8.30 p.m
10. 0 a.m	Dorrington, 7 miles from Shrewsbury	2.15 p.m
¾ of an hour from the arrival of the packet in summer, two hours in winter.	*Douglas, Isle of Man — Noble Macadam	7.20 a.m. summer and one hour previous to the sailing of the packet in winter.
7. 0 a.m 4. 0 p.m	*Dover, William Norwood	9. 0 a.m 10. 0 p.m
8.30 a.m	Dover-Court, 2 miles from Harwich	4.30 p.m
2. 0 p.m	Dowlais, 1½ miles from Merthyr	9.30 a.m
8. 0 a.m	Down, 6 miles from Bromley	2. 0 p.m
10. 0 a.m	Downend, 5 miles from Bristol	3. 0 p.m
5. 0 a.m	*Downham, Edward Hutson	8.30 p.m
7. 0 a.m	Downton, 6 miles from Salisbury	8. 0 p.m
10.40 p.m	*Driffield, Miss Catherine Laybourne	2. 0 p.m
7. 0 a.m	*Droitwich, Richard Smith	8.45 p.m
9. 0 a.m	Dronfield, 6 miles from Sheffield	5.30 p.m
8. 0 a.m	Droxford, 4½ mi. from Bp. Waltham	6.30 p.m
9.30 a.m	Duddington, 5 miles from Stamford	4.15 p.m

Letters from London delivered at h. m.	Town. Postmaster.	Box for London closes at h. m.
7.30 a.m	*Dudley, George Dalton	8.30 p.m
9. 0 a.m	Duffield, 4 miles from Derby	5.45 p.m
9. 0 a.m	Dukinfield, 1 m. f. Ashton-under-Lyne	4. 0 p.m
7. 0 a.m	Dullingham, 4 mi. from Newmarket.	6.45 p.m
8.30 a.m	Dulverton, 6 miles from Bampton ..	5.30 p.m
9.30 a.m	Dumbleton, 6 miles from Evesham ..	3.15 p.m
7.30 a.m	*Dunchurch, William Sedgley......	6.30 p.m
8.30 a.m	Duncton, 5 miles from Petworth....	4.50 p.m
11.30 a.m	Dunham, 16 miles from Newark	2. 0 p.m
9.30 a.m	Dunkirk, 8 miles from Tetbury	2.45 p.m
7.30 a.m 6. 0 p.m	*Dunmow, John Perry Gunn	6. 0 p.m 7.30 a.m
10.10 a.m	Dunnington, 4½ miles from York....	3.30 p.m
8. 0 a.m	*Dunstable, Joseph Squire..........	7. 0 p.m
7.30 a.m	Dunster, 22 miles from Taunton	5.30 p.m
7. 0 a.m 9. 0 p.m	*Durham, William Caldcleugh	3.30 p.m 9.20 p.m
7. 0 a.m	*Dursley, John Owen	6. 0 p.m
7. 0 a.m	Durweston, 2½ miles from Blandford	7. 0 p.m
11. 0 a.m	Duxford, 9½ miles from Cambridge ..	3. 0 p.m
7. 0 p.m	Dyffryn, 47 miles from Corwen......	10. 0 p.m
7. 0 a.m	Dymchurch, 5 miles from Hythe	9. 0 p.m
10.30 a.m	Eardisland, 5 miles from Leominster	1.15 p.m
2.15 p.m	Eardisley, 6 miles from Kington	9. 0 a.m
8.30 a.m	Earls-Colne, 3½ miles from Halstead	4. 0 p.m
9. 0 a.m	Earl Shelton, 4 miles from Hinckley	4. 0 p.m
9. 0 a.m	Earl-Soham, 14 miles fr. Woodbridge	6. 0 p.m
2. 0 p.m	Earsdon, 9 mi. fr. Newcastle-on-Tyne	8.30 a.m
12.30 noon	Easington Lane, 9 miles from Durham	6.30 p.m
9.30 a.m	Easingwold, 13 miles from York	3.40 p.m
1. 0 p.m	East-Ayton, 5 miles fr. Scarborough	1.25 p.m
7. 0 a.m	*Eastbourne, George Cook..........	7. 0 p.m
8. 0 a.m	East-Bergholt, 9 miles fr. Colchester	6. 0 p.m
8. 0 a.m	East-Clandon, 8 miles fr. Leatherhead	5. 0 p.m
10.30 a.m	East-Coker, 2½ miles from Yeovil....	4.15 p.m
8.30 a.m	East-Cowes, 1 mile from Cowes	5. 0 p.m
7. 0 a.m	East-Farleigh, 2½ miles fr. Maidstone	6.30 p.m
12.45 noon	East-Gate, 24 miles from Durham ..	5.10 p.m
7. 0 a.m	*East-Grinstead, Th. Jackson Palmer	6.45 p.m
7.30 a.m	Eastham, 10 miles from Chester	6. 0 p.m
9. 0 a.m	East-Hanham, 4 miles from Bristol..	4.30 p.m
10. 0 a.m	East-Harptree, 11 miles from Bristol.	2. 0 p.m
9. 0 a.m	East-Hoathley, 16 mi. fr. Hurstgreen	6. 0 p.m
10.30 a.m	East-Ilsley, 10 miles from Newbury ..	4. 0 p.m
9.45 a.m	Eastington, 5 miles from Stroud	3.15 p.m
11.15 a.m	East-Lulworth, 6 miles from Wareham	3. 0 p.m
8. 0 a.m	East-Malling, 5 miles from Maidstone	6. 0 p.m
8. 0 a.m	East-Meon, 5 miles from Petersfield	6. 0 p.m
8. 0 a.m	East Moulsey, 4 miles from Kingston	6.30 p.m
8. 0 a.m	Easton, 2¼ miles from Stamford	4.30 p.m
8. 0 a.m	Easton, 8 miles from Woodbridge ..	5. 0 p.m
8. 0 a.m	East Peckham, 7 miles fr. Tunbridge	5.45 p.m
9.15 a.m	East Pennard, 5 m. fr. Shep. Mallett	5.30 p.m
11. 0 a.m	East-Rudham, 5 miles from Rougham	2. 0 p.m
10. 0 a.m	Eastry, 2 miles from Sandwich......	6. 0 p.m
7.30 a.m	East-Stratton, 3 m. from Andover road	7. 0 p.m
10. 0 a.m	Eastwood, 8½ miles from Nottingham	4. 0 p.m
8. 0 a.m	East-Woodhay, 5 miles fr. Newbury	4.30 p.m
7. 0 a.m	Eaton Socon, 1 mile from St. Neots..	8. 0 p.m
11. 0 a.m	Eccles, 4 miles from Manchester	2.30 p.m
8. 0 a.m	Ecclesfield, 5 miles from Sheffield ..	3. 0 p.m
8. 0 a.m	*Eccleshall, Mrs. Louisa Williams ..	9. 0 p.m
10. 0 a.m	Eccleshill, 2½ mi. fr. Bradford, Yorks.	3. 0 p.m
9.30 a.m	Eckington, 7 miles from Chesterfield	4. 0 p.m
10.30 a.m	Eckington, 4 miles from Pershore ..	3.30 p.m
9.30 a.m	Eden-Bridge, 12 mi. from Seven-Oaks	4. 0 p.m
7. 0 a.m	Edgbaston, 2½ miles fr. Birmingham	6. 0 p.m
9.30 a.m	Edge-Hill, 2 miles from Liverpool ..	4. 0 p.m
	*Edgware, *see* "London District Office"	
8. 0 a.m	Edgeworth, 7 miles from Cirencester	6. 0 p.m
9. 0 a.m	Edith-Weston, 6 miles from Stamford	4.50 p.m
8. 0 a.m	Edmonscote, 1 mile from Warwick ..	5.30 p.m
7.45 a.m	Effingham, 3 miles from Leatherhead	6. 0 p.m
8. 0 a.m	Egham, 4 miles from Chertsey......	6. 0 p.m
8.10 a.m	Eglingham, 7 miles from Alnwick ..	9.50 a.m
9.10 a.m	Eglwyswrw, 6 miles from Cardigan..	2.25 p.m
9. 0 a.m	Egremont, 3 miles from Liverpool ..	3.30 p.m
7.40 a.m	Egremont, 3 miles from Whitehaven	2.30 p.m
10. 0 a.m	Elham, 11 miles from Canterbury ..	4. 0 p.m
9. 0 a.m 4. 0 p.m	Elland, 3 miles from Halifax	9. 0 a.m 5.30 p.m
9. 0 a.m	*Ellesmere, Thomas Lowe	5.30 p.m
8. 0 a.m	Ellesmere-Port, 8 miles from Chester	3.45 p.m
4. 0 p.m	Ellington, 7 miles from Morpeth	8.15 a.m
8. 0 a.m	Elmdon, 7 miles from Birmingham ..	5. 0 p.m
9. 0 a.m	Elmdon, 7 miles from Royston	5. 0 p.m
10.30 a.m	Elmham, 5 miles from Dereham	4.30 p.m
10. 0 a.m	Elmsall, 12 miles from Wakefield ..	1.55 p.m
7. 0 a.m	Elmstead, 4 miles from Colchester ..	6.30 p.m
7. 0 a.m 3. 0 p.m	*Ely, John Clements	2.45 p.m 10. 0 p.m
6.45 p.m	Embleton, 10 miles from Alnwick....	10. 0 p.m
7. 0 a.m	*Emsworth, James Cobby	9.45 p.m
7. 0 a.m 11.15 a.m	Enfield, 2 miles from Accrington ..	2.45 p.m 9.10 p.m
9. 0 a.m	Englefield-Green, 6 mi. from Chertsey	5.45 p.m
8. 0 a.m	Enmore, 5 miles from Bridgewater ..	6. 0 p.m
8. 0 a.m	Ensham, 6 miles from Oxford	4.30 p.m
7. 0 a.m	*Enstone, William Kibble	9.15 p.m
12. 0 noon	Epperstone, 11 miles fr. Nottingham	3.25 p.m
7. 0 a.m	*Epping, John Judges..............	8.30 p.m
8.40 a.m	Epping-Green, 6½ miles from Hertford	5.30 p.m
7. 0 a.m	*Epsom, Wm. Chase Morrish Andrews	9.30 p.m
12. 0 noon	Epworth, 14 miles from Bawtry	3. 0 p.m
9. 0 a.m	*Ermebridge, John Gillard	3. 0 p.m
7. 0 a.m	*Esher, William Collett	9. 0 p.m
8.40 a.m	Escrick, 6 miles from York	4.30 p.m
9.30 a.m	Essenden, 5½ miles from Hertford ..	5. 0 p.m
7. 0 a.m	Etchingham, 1¾ m. from Hurst-Green	9. 0 p.m
8. 0 a.m 12.30 p.m	Eton, 1 mile from Windsor........	11. 0 a.m 9.30 p.m
7. 0 a.m	Etruria, 2 mi. f. Newcastle-under-Lyne	7.45 p.m
10. 0 a.m	Etwall, 12 miles from Uttoxeter	4.30 p.m
7.45 a.m	Evercreech, 4 mi. fr. Shepton Mallet	5.45 p.m
8. 0 a.m	Eversholt, 2 miles from Woburn	6. 0 p.m
9.30 a.m	Evershot, 13 miles from Dorchester..	3.30 p.m
7.30 a.m	Eversley, 3 miles fr. Hartfordbridge	7. 0 p.m
8. 0 a.m	Everton, 2¾ miles from Lymington..	5. 0 p.m
7. 0 a.m	*Evesham, Robert Cooper	6.30 p.m
10. 0 a.m	Ewell, 3¼ miles from Dover..........	5.30 p.m
8. 0 a.m	Ewell, 2 miles from Epsom..........	8. 0 p.m
9.30 a.m	Exbourne, 6 miles from Oakhampton	3. 0 p.m
8. 0 a.m	Exbury, 16 miles from Southampton	5. 0 p.m
7. 0 a.m	*Exeter, Paul Measor..............	8. 6 p.m
6. 0 a.m	Exminster, 4 miles from Exeter....	7. 0 p.m
7.45 a.m	*Exmouth, Miss Elizabeth Wyer	5.45 p.m
7.30 a.m	Exning, 2 miles from Newmarket....	8. 0 p.m
9. 0 a.m	Exton, 5 m. from Bishopswaltham ..	6. 0 p.m
10. 0 a.m	Exton, 4½ miles from Oakham	3.25 p.m
9.15 a.m	Eyam, 6½ miles from Bakewell......	3.50 p.m
8. 0 a.m	*Eye, Richard Nurse..............	8. 0 p.m
9.30 a.m	Eythorne, 7 miles from Sandwich....	4.45 p.m
7. 0 a.m 4. 0 p.m	*Fairford, John Wilson	7.30 a.m 7.15 p.m
7. 0. a.m	*Fakenham, Charles Lulman.......	4.45 p.m
3.30 p.m	*Falmouth, Miss Jane Seymour Wood	9.11 a.m
7. 0 a.m	*Fareham, Augustus Nicholson	8.15 p.m
8. 0 a.m	Farnborough, 5 miles from Bagshot...	5.30 p.m
8. 0 a.m	Farnborough, 4½ miles from Bromley	2.30 p.m
8.10 a.m	Farndon, 8 miles from Chester......	3.15 p.m
7. 0 a.m 1. 0 p.m	*Farnham, Surrey, Robert Nichols.	8. 0 p.m 10. 0 a.m
10. 0 a.m	Farnham, 9 miles from Woodbridge..	5.30 p.m
9. 0 a.m	Farnham-Royal, 2½ miles from Slough	7. 0 p.m
8.30 a.m	Farningham, 5 miles from Dartford..	6. 0 p.m
8. 0 a.m	Farnworth, 6 miles from Warrington	5.30 p.m
9.30 a.m	Farnworth, 3 miles from Bolton......	2.30 p.m
7. 0 a.m 2.30 p.m	*Farringdon, John Haines........	9. 0 a.m 9. 0 p.m
7. 0 a.m	Farrington, 3 miles from Alton......	6.30 p.m
9. 0 a.m	Farrington-Gurney, 13 m. from Bristol	3.30 p.m
8.30 a.m	Farway, 6 miles from Honiton	5. 0 p.m
7. 0 a.m	Fawley, 16 miles from Southampton..	7.45 p.m
7. 0 a.m	*Fazeley, Richard Sadleir	7.30 p.m
9. 0 a.m	Feckenham, 8 miles from Bromsgrove	4.30 p.m
7. 0 a.m	Felstead, 10 miles from Chelmsford..	7. 0 p.m
8.30 a.m	Feltham, 3 miles from Hounslow.....	4.30 p.m
8. 0 a.m 1. 0 p.m	*Felton, Mrs. Sarah Hine	12. 0 noon 6.30 p.m
9.30 a.m	Feltwell, 6 miles from Brandon......	5.30 p.m
9. 0 a.m	Feniton, 5 miles from Honiton	4. 0 p.m
7. 0 a.m 11.45 a.m	*Fenny-Stratford, John Turner.....	10. 0 a.m 9. 0 p.m
7.30 a.m	Fenstanton, 2 mi. fr. St. Ives, Hunts.	7. 0 p.m

Letters from London delivered at h.m.	Town. Postmaster.	Box for London closes at h.m.
5. 0 p.m	Feock, 8 miles from Truro	5.30 p.m
5.35 p.m	Ferriby, 7½ miles from Hull	7.20 a.m
8. 0 a.m	*Ferrybridge, Thomas Arnall.........	2.45 p.m
12.10 p.m	Ferry-Hill, 12 miles from Darlington	12.10 p.m
7.30 a.m	Ferryside, 9 miles from Carmarthen ..	4.15 p.m
9. 0 p.m	Festiniog, 29 miles from Carnarvon ..	7. 0 a.m
7. 0 a.m	Fetcham, 1½ from Leatherhead	7.30 p.m
7. 0 a.m 4. 0 p.m	*Feversham, Jn. Bunyer Sharp	10.30 a.m 8. 0 p.m
12. 0 a.m	Filby, 18 miles from Norwich	2.15 p.m
2.40 p.m	Filey, 8 miles from Scarboro'	11.30 a.m
9.30 a.m	Fillongley, 7 miles from Coventry....	3.45 p.m
8. 0 a.m	Filton, 4 miles from Bristol..........	4. 0 p.m
7.30 a.m	Fincham, 6 miles from Downham. ..	5.30 p.m
9.30 a.m	Finchingfield, 10 mi. from Braintree	3.30 p.m
8.30 a.m	Findon, 7 miles from Shoreham......	3.45 p.m
10. 0 a.m	Finedon, 4 miles from Higham Ferrars	4. 0 p.m
10.30 a.m	Finningham, 8 mi. from Stowmarket..	3.30 p.m
7. 0 a.m	Fishbourne, 1½ mi. from Chichester..	7. 0 p.m
7.30 a.m	Fishguard, 15 mi. fr. Haverfordwest..	4.30 p.m
8. 0 a.m	Fittleworth, 3 miles from Petworth..	6. 0 p.m
10.30 a.m	Five-Lanes, 8 miles from Launceston	2.30 p.m
6. 0 a.m	Flax-Bourton, 6 miles from Bristol..	4. 5 p.m
9.20 a.m	Flaxton, 10 miles from York	4. 5 p.m
8. 0 a.m	Fleet, 12 miles from Wisbeach	6.45 p.m
9.20 a.m	*Fleetwood, David Dixon Neeve....	3.45 p.m
8. 0 a.m	Fletching, 4 miles from Uckfield	6.30 p.m
7. 0 a.m	Flimwell, 3 miles from Hurst-Green	8.30 p.m
11. 0 a.m	Flintham, 7 miles from Newark	2. 0 p.m
8.30 a.m	Flint, 15 miles from Chester	5.30 p.m
10. 0 a.m	Flixton, 8 miles from Manchester ..	5. 0 p.m
10. 0 a.m	Flockton, 7½ miles from Wakefield ..	4. 0 p.m
12.15 p.m	Flookborough, 16 mi. from Milnthorp	1. 0 p.m
4.30 p.m	Flushing, 1 mile from Falmouth	7.30 a.m
7. 0 a.m	Foleshill, 3 miles from Coventry	9.30 p.m
7. 0 a.m	*Folkingham, Robert Ward..........	8.30 p.m
7. 0 a.m 3.30 p.m	*Folkstone, John Punnett........	9.15 a.m 10. 0 p.m
	*Footscray, *see* London District Office	
6. 0 a.m	Ford, 5½ miles from Chippenham ...	8. 0 p.m
7.30 a.m	Fordham, 5 miles from Mildenhall ..	6.30 p.m
8. 0 a.m	*Fordingbridge, Mrs. Elizth. Pleden	8.30 p.m
10. 0 a.m	Fordstreet, 9 miles from Halstead ...	3. 0 p.m
7.30 a.m	Fornham, 2 mi. from Bury S. Edmds.	6. 0 p.m
7. 0 a.m	Forrest-Row, 12 m. f. Tunbridge Wells	7.15 p.m
7.30 a.m	Forton, ¾ of a mile from Gosport....	6.30 p.m
8.45 a.m	Fosbrook, 7 miles from Stone.	7.45 p.m
9. 0 a.m	Fostersbooth, 3½ mi. from Towcester	8. 0 p.m
8. 0 a.m	Four-Forks, 4½ mi. from Bridgewater	6. 0 p.m
8. 0 a.m	Fovant, 10 miles from Salisbury	5. 0 p.m
3.30 p.m	*Fowey, John Bate	8.10 a.m
11. 0 a.m	Fownhope, 6½ miles from Hereford ..	1. 0 p.m
7. 0 a.m	Fox, 8 miles from Woodstock	8. 0 p.m
8. 0 a.m	Framlingham, 11 mi. fr. Woodbridge	7. 0 p.m
8.30 a.m	Frampton, 6 miles from Dorchester	4.15 p.m
8.45 a.m	Frampton-Cotterell, 7 mi. fr. Bristol	3. 0 p.m
9.30 a.m	Frampton-on-Severn, 6 mi. fr. Dursley	3. 0 p.m
7. 0 a.m	Frant, 3 mi. fr. Tunbridge Wells ...	7. 0 p.m
7. 0 a.m	Frating, 7 miles from Colchester....	6. 0 p.m
7.30 a.m	Freckenham, 3¾ mi. from Mildenhall	7.15 p.m
9.30 a.m	Fremington, 3 miles from Barnstaple	4. 0 p.m
9. 0 a.m	Frensham, 6 miles from Farnham....	5. 0 p.m
12. 0 a.m	Freshford, 5 miles from Bath	2.30 p.m
10. 0 a.m	Freshwater, 7 miles from Lymington	2.45 p.m
10. 0 a.m	Freshwater-Norton, 6 m. f. Lymington	3. 0 p.m
8. 0 a.m	Fressingfield, 4 mi. from Harlestone	4.15 p.m
8. 0 a.m	Freston, 4 miles from Ipswich	7. 0 p.m
9. 0 a.m	Frimley, 4 miles from Bagshot	5. 0 p.m
7. 0 a.m	Frodsham, 4 miles from Prestonbrook	6.45 p.m
7. 0 a.m	Frogmore-End, 2 m. fr. H. Hempstead	7. 0 p.m
7. 0 a.m	*Frome, John Stevens Jones	6.30 p.m
7. 0 a.m	Froxfield, 2 miles from Hungerford..	6. 0 p.m
8.20 a.m	Froyle, 3½ miles from Alton	5.3 p.m
10. 0 a.m	Fulbeck, 11 miles from Grantham ..	2.45 p.m
9. 0 a.m	Fulbourne, 5½ mi. from Cambridge ..	4. 0 p.m
8. 5 a.m	Fulford, 2 miles from York.	5. 0 p.m
8. 0 a.m	Fulmer, 3 miles from Gerrards-Cross	5. 0 p.m
11. 0 a.m	Gainford, 8 miles from Darlington. ..	2. 0 p.m
8.30 a.m	*Gainsborough, Adam Stark	3.30 p.m
8.40 a.m	Galgate, 4 miles from Lancaster	5. 0 p.m
8.30 a.m	Gannicks-Corner, 2 mi. from Barnet	5.30 p.m
9.20 a.m	Garboldisham, 12 mi. from Thetford	3.45 p.m

Letters from London delivered at h.m.	Town. Postmaster.	Box for London closes at h.m.
9.30 a.m	Gardner-Street, 10 miles from Battle	6.30 p.m
11.30 a.m	Gargrave, 4 miles from Skipton	2.30 p.m
8. 0 a.m	*Garstang, Miss Sarah Clarke	5.30 p.m
7. 0 a.m 9 45 a.m	*Gateshead, Thomas Douglas	2.45 p.m 10. 0 p.m
11. 0 a.m	Gayton, 8 miles from Lynn.........	3. 0 p.m
9. 0 a.m	Gazeley, 5 miles from Newmarket...	6.45 p.m
8. 0 a.m	Gedney, 11 miles from Wisbeach ...	6.15 p.m
9. 0 a.m	Gee-Cross, 9 miles from Manchester	5. 0 p.m
9.30 a.m	Gelmpton, 7 miles from Torquay	3.45 p.m
10.30 a.m	Germoe, 7 miles from Helston	3. 0 p.m
7. 0 a.m	*Gerrard's-Cross, Miss Elizabeth Hunt	7. 0 p.m
7. 0 a.m	Giddyhall, 4 miles from Chippenham	8. 0 p.m
11.50 a.m	Gilling, 3 miles from Richmond, York	5.10 p.m
10.45 a.m	Gilling, 18 miles from York	3.10 p.m
8.30 a.m	Gillingham, 6½ miles from Wincanton	4.45 p.m
8. 0 a.m	Gillingham, 2 miles from Chatham ..	7.30 p.m
7. 0 a.m 4.50 p.m	Gilsland, 18 miles from Carlisle	10. 0 p.m 4.30 p.m
8. 0 a.m	Gisburn, 7 miles from Clitheroe	2. 0 p.m
9. 0 a.m	Gislingham, 5 miles from Eye	5. 0 p.m
7.10 p.m	Glanton, 10 miles from Alnwick.	10. 0 p.m
12.30 p.m	Glasbury, 4 miles from Hay	11.30 a.m
7. 0 a.m	*Glastonbury, William Cruse	6.45 p.m
3. 0 p.m	Glentham, 3 miles from Spittal......	9. 0 a.m
9. 0 a.m	Glossop, 15 miles from Manchester	3.30 p.m
7. 0 a.m 3.30 p.m	*Gloucester, Frederick Woodcock	7.30 a.m 10. 0 p.m
9. 0 a.m	Glynde, 3 miles from Lewes........	5. 0 p.m
3. 0 p.m	Glynneath, 11 miles from Neath	8.30 p.m
7. 0 a.m 2. 0 p.m	*Godalming, James Edwards	9.30 a.m 7. 0 p.m
8. 0 a.m	Godmanchester, 1 mi. fr. Huntingdon..	9. 0 a.m
9. 0 a.m	Godmersham, 8 mi. from Canterbury	5. 0 p.m
9.20 a.m	Godshill, 25 miles from Southampton.	3.15 p.m
7. 0 a.m	*Godstone, 7 miles from Reigate	7.15 p.m
10. 0 a.m	Goldhanger, 4½ miles from Maldon ..	4. 0 p.m
9. 0 a.m 5. 0 p.m	Gomersal, 8 miles from Leeds......	3. 0 p.m 8. 0 p.m
7. 0 a.m	Goodneston, 2½ miles from Wingham	6.30 p.m
9.15 a.m	Goodrich, 5 miles from Ross	2.45 p.m
7.30 a.m	*Goole, David Cass	4.50 p.m
8.30 a.m	Goring, 3½ miles from Worthing	5. 0 p.m
11. 0 a.m	Gorlestone, 2¼ miles from Yarmouth.	3. 0 p.m
10. 0 a.m	Gorton, 3½ miles from Manchester ..	6. 0 p.m
9. 0 a.m	Gosberton. 6 miles from Spalding....	4.30 p.m
7. 0 a.m	Gosford, 4 miles from Oxford	6. 0 p.m
7. 0 a.m	Gosforth, 12 mi. from Whitehaven..	3.30 p.m
7. 0 a.m 3.30 p.m	*Gosport, Mrs. Elizabeth Legg	7.50 a.m 10. 0 p.m
8. 0 a.m.	Goudhurst, 4 miles from Cranbrook	6.15 p.m
4.15 p.m	Grampound, 6 miles from St. Austle..	8.30 a.m
8.30 a.m 5.30 p.m	*Grantham, Thomas S. Lawrence	4. 0 p.m
7. 0 a.m 1. 0 p.m	*Gravesend, Chas. Solomon Couves	1. 0 p.m 9. 0 p.m
9. 0 a.m	Grays, 12 miles from Romford	4.30 p.m
11.45 a.m	Greatham, 8 miles from Stockton....	1.20 p.m
12.20 p.m	Great Ayton, 3 miles from Stokesley	12.40 p.m
7. 0 a.m	" Baddow, 2 m. from Chelmsford	7.30 p.m
7. 0 a.m	" Barford, 6 miles from St. Neots	6.30 p.m
7.30 a.m	" Barr, 5 miles from Birmingham	5.15 p.m
8. 0 a.m	" Bedwin, 8 mi. fr. Marlborough	4.30 p.m
7. 0 a.m	" Bentley, 8 mi. from Colchester	6. 0 p.m
11. 0 a.m	" Bircham, 10 m. from Rougham	3. 0 p.m
7. 0 a.m	" Bookham, 2½ m. fr. Leatherhead	6. 0 p.m
8.30 a.m	" Budworth, 4 mi. fr. Northwich	5.45 p.m
9. 0 a.m	" Chesterford, 4 miles from Saffron-Walden................	6. 0 p.m
9. 0 a.m	" Clacton, 16 mi. from Colchester	3.30 p.m
9. 0 a.m	" Easton, 2½ miles from Dunmow	4.45 p.m
9.30 a.m	" Ellingham, 2½ m. fr Attleborough	4. 0 p.m
7.30 a.m	" Gaddesden, 3 mi. fr. Hempsted	5.30 p.m
8. 0 a.m	" Glen, 6 miles from Leicester ..	6. 0 p.m
8. 0 a.m	" Hadham, 7 miles from Ware..	6. 0 p.m
9.30 a.m	" Hazeley, 5 mi. from Wheatley	5.30 p.m
7. 0 a.m	" Haywood, 4 mi. from Rugeley..	6.30 p.m
10. 0 a.m	" Hendred, 5 miles from Wantage	4. 0 p.m
9.30 a.m	" Massingham, 2 mi. fr. Rougham	3.30 p.m
10. 0 a.m	" Oakley, 6 miles from Harwich .	3. 0 p.m
3.30 a.m	" Smeaton, 7 m. fr. Northallerton	3.10 p.m
7.30 a.m	" Stanghton, 5 m fro St. Neots	8. 0 p.m

Letters from London delivered at h. m.	Town. Postmaster.	Box for London closes at h. m.
8. 0 a.m	Great Stukeley, 2 m. from Huntingdon	5.30 p.m
9. 0 a.m	" Swaffham, 6 m. fr. Newmarket	6.30 p.m
8. 0 a.m	" Tew, 4 miles from Enstone ..	6. 0 p.m
7. 0 a.m	" Waltham, 5 m. from Chelmsford	7. 0 p.m
8. 0 a.m	" Warley, 2 miles from Brentwood	6.30 p.m
10. 0 a.m	" Witley, 11 miles fr. Worcester	4.45 p.m
9.15 a.m	Green-Acres Moor, 7½ m. fr. Mchester.	2.15 p.m; 9. 0 p.m
9.30 a.m	Green-Hammerton, 10 mi. from York.	4. 0 p.m
9. 0 a.m; 4. 0 p.m	Green-Hithe, 3 mi. from Dartford ...	1 15 p.m
8. 0 a.m	Green-Street, 3 mi. fr. Sittingbourne.	7. 0 p.m
7. 0 a.m	Gresford, 3 miles from Wrexham....	6. 0 p.m
4.20 p.m	Gretabridge, 4 mi. fr. Barnard-Castle	11.50 p.m
5. 0 p.m	Greysouthen, 4 mi. fr. Cockermouth.	5.30 p.m
3.35 p.m	Greystoke, 5 miles from Penrith....	7. 0 a.m
7. 0 a.m	Griesbeck, 6 miles from Ulverstone ..	8.10 p.m
4. 0 p.m	*Grimsby, William Skelton	9.30 a.m
10. 0 a.m	Gringley, 6 miles from Bawtry......	4. 0 p.m
8.15 a.m	Groby, 4 miles from Leicester	5.45 p.m
7. 0 a.m	Groombridge, 4 m. fr. Tunbridge-Wells	7. 0 p.m
8. 0 a.m	Grundisburgh, 3 mil. from Woodbridge	6. 0 p.m
Letters delivered on the arrival of the Packet on Sundays Wednesdays & Fridays	*Guernsey, Arthur Forrest — Sunday, Tuesday, Thursday	10. 0. a.m
7. 0 a.m; 1. 0 p.m	*Guildford, William Pook..........	10. 5 a.m; 7.30 p.m
11.30 a.m	Guilsfield, 5 miles from Welchpool..	1.15 p.m
9. 0 a.m	Guiseley, 9 miles from Leeds........	4. 0 p.m
10.30 a.m	Guist, 8 miles from Dereham........	3.15 p.m
11. 0 a.m	Gunnislake, 4 miles from Tavistock..	2. 0 p.m
7.30 a.m	Gussage-All-Saints, 11m.f. Fordingbri	6. 0 p.m
9.15 a.m	Gwyndu, 15 miles from Bangor	3. 0 p.m
10.30 a.m	Haddenham, 7½ miles from Ely......	4.15 p.m
8. 0 a.m	*Hadleigh, Suffolk, J. P. Ellisdon ..	8. 0 p.m
9. 0 a.m	Hadleigh, Essex, 7 mi. from Rochford	2. 0 p.m
8. 0 a.m	Hadlow, 4 miles from Tunbridge....	6.30 p.m
8.30 a.m	Hagley, 2 miles from Stourbridge ..	5.30 p.m
7. 0 a.m	Hailsham, 20 miles from Hurst-green.	7.30 p.m
8. 0 a.m	Hale, 11 miles from Warrington.....	4.30 p.m
7.30 a.m	Hales-Owen, 7½ mi. fr. Birmingham..	5.30 p.m
7.30 a.m	*Halesworth, Thos. Jno. Bird Bedwell	6.45 p.m
9. 0 a.m	Halfway-house, 8 m. from Canterbury	5. 0 p.m
7.30 a.m; 9. 0 a.m	*Halifax, Mrs. Charlotte Akers...	3.45 p.m; 10. 0 p.m
9. 0 a.m	Halliford, 3 miles from Chertsey....	6. 0 p.m
10. 0 a.m	Hallingbury, 4 m. from Bps. Stortford	6. 0 p.m
7.30 a.m	Halnaker, 4 miles from Chichester..	7. 0 p.m
8. 0 a.m	*Halstead, Essex, Mrs. Lydia Anderson	6.20 p.m
8.30 a.m	Halstead, Kent, 6 mi. fr. Seven-Oaks	4.45 p.m
7. 0 a.m	Halton, 3 miles from Prestonbrook..	7.30 p.m
7. 0 a.m; 4.40 p.m	Haltwhistle, 20 miles from Carlisle..	9.30 p.m; 4. 0 p.m
9.30 a.m	Halwell, 6 miles from Totness.......	3. 0 p.m
9. 0 a.m	Ham, 4 miles from Hungerford	5. 0 p.m
8.30 a.m	Hamble, 6 m. fr. Southampton	4.30 p.m
8. 0 a.m	Hambledon, 4½ miles from Henley ..	5. 0 p.m
8.30 a.m	Hambledon 6 miles from Horndean..	6.45 p.m
8. 0 a.m	Hambrook, 6 miles from Bristol......	3.30 p.m
8. 0 a.m	Handcross, 4½ miles from Crawley..	6. 0 p.m
12. 0noon	Hand & Pen, 8 miles from Exeter ..	1.45 p.m
6.45 a.m	Handley, 8 miles from Chester.......	6. 0 p.m
8. 0 a.m	Handley, 11 miles from Fordingbridge	5. 0 p.m
7. 0 a.m	Handsworth, 3 m. from Birmingham	9. 0 p.m
10.15 a.m	Handsworth, 9 miles from Sheffield..	2.50 p.m
8. 0 a.m	Hanham, 3½ miles from Bristol	4.45 p.m
7. 0 a.m; 6. 0 p.m	*Hanley, Geo. Rhodes	7.30 p.m
10. 0 a.m	Hanney, 4 miles from Wantage	3.30 p.m
9.30 a.m	Hanworth, 4½ miles from Aylsham..	3.30 p.m
10.30 a.m	Hanworth, 3 miles from Hounslow...	4. 0 p.m
7.45 a.m	Harberton, 1¾ miles from Totness ..	4.15 p.m
8. 0 a.m	Harborne, 3½ m. from Birmingham..	5. 0 p.m
7. 0 a.m	Hardingstone, 2 mi. f. Northampton..	7. 0 p.m
9. 0 a.m	Hare street, 10 miles from Romford .	6. 0 p.m
10. 0 a.m	Haresfield, 6 miles from Gloucester..	3.45 p.m
9. 0 a.m	Harewood, 7 miles from Leeds	5. 0 p.m
9. 0 a.m	Harewood-End, 5 miles from Ross ..	4.15 p.m
7.30 p.m	Harlech, 39 miles from Carnarvon ..	10. 0 p.m
7. 0 a.m	*Harleston, James Caley	7. 0 p.m
8. 0 a.m	Harling, 8 miles from Thetford.....	7. 0 p.m

Letters from London delivered at h. m.	Town. Postmaster.	Box for London closes at h. m.
9. 0 a.m	Harlington, 4 miles from Hounslow..	4. 0 p.m
7. 0 a.m	*Harlow, David Whittaker..........	9. 0 p.m
9. 0 a.m	Harpenden, 5 miles from St. Albans.	5.30 p.m
10. 0 a.m	Harpley, 4 miles from Rougham.....	3. 0 p.m
10. 0 a.m	Harpole, 7 miles from Weedon......	4. 0 p.m
8.30 a.m	Harpurhey, 2 m. from Manchester..	6. 0 p.m
8. 0 a.m	Harrietsham, 7½ m. from Maidstone..	7. 0 p.m
5.30 a.m	Harrington, 2½ m. from Workington..	8. 0 a.m
1. 0 p.m	Harrington, 7 miles from Spilsby....	1. 5 p.m
10. 0 a.m	Harrold, 12 miles from Bedford	3. 0 p.m
10. 0 a.m	*Harrowgate, Pickersgill Palliser ..	4. 0 p.m
9. 0 a.m	Hartest, 9 miles from Bury	4. 0 p.m
7. 0 a.m	Hartfield, 8 m. f. Tunbridge-Wells..	6. 0 p.m
7. 0 a.m	*Hartfordbridge, Jas. Murray Stone	8.30 p.m
8. 0 a.m	Harting, 4 miles from Petersfield ...	6.30 p.m
5. 0 p.m	Hartland, 13 m. from Bideford......	8. 0 a.m
8. 0 a.m	Hartlebury, 2 miles from Stourport ..	5. 0 p.m
12. 0noon	*Hartlepool, Mrs. Mary A. Wilkinson	2.15 p.m
2.30 p.m	Hartley-Pans, 6 mi. f. North-Shields	7. 0 p.m
10. 0 a.m	Harwell, 7 miles from Abingdon	5. 0 p.m
7.30 a.m	*Harwich, Wm. Baggott Nalborough	6. 0 p.m
12. 0noon	Haselbury, 12 m. from Blandford ...	3. 0 p.m
10. 0 a.m	Haselbury, 2 miles from Crewkerne..	4. 0 p.m
9. 0 a.m	Hasfield, 7 miles from Gloucester....	3.30 p.m
7. 0 a.m	*Haslemere, Thos. Lambert	7. 0 p.m
9.30 a.m	Haslingden, 17 m. from Manchester..	3.45 p.m
7. 0 a.m; 6.30 p.m	*Hastings, John Woods	7. 0 a.m; 10. 0 p.m
7. 0 a.m	Hatch, 6 miles from Taunton	8. 0 p.m
8. 0 a.m	*Hatfield, Mark Powell	9.30 p.m
8.30 a.m	Hatfield, 7 miles from Doncaster. ..	5. 0 p.m
8. 0 a.m	Hatfield Bd. Oak, near Harlow	5.30 p.m
10. 0 a.m	Hatfield-Peverell, 6½ m. f. Chelmsford	5.30 p.m
9. 0 a.m	Hatherleigh, 7 mi. from Oakhampton	4. 0 p.m
10. 0 a.m	Hathersage, 10 miles from Bakewell	3. 0 p.m
9. 0 a.m	Haughley, 3 miles from Stowmarket.	4.15 p.m
7. 0 a.m	*Havant, Arter Frederick Randall...	10. 0 p.m
7. 0 a.m	*Haverfordwest, Mrs. Marianne Relly	10. 0 p.m
9.15 a.m	Haverhill, 17 miles from Halsted....	5.15 p.m
8. 0 a.m	Havering, 3 miles from Romford	7. 0 p.m
7. 0 a.m; 11. 0 p.m	Hawarden, 9 miles from Chester ..	10. 0 p.m; 6.30 p.m
3. 0 p.m	*Hawes, Miss Hannah Clarke......	11. 5 a.m
7. 0 a.m	Hawkhurst, 9 miles from Staplehurst	8.20 p.m
1. 0 p.m	Hawkshead, 5 miles from Ambleside.	8.10 a.m
9.30 a.m	Haworth, 10 mi. from Bradford, Yorks.	1.45 p.m
10.15 a.m	Haxey, 10 miles from Bawtry	2.45 p.m
11.45 a.m	*Hay, Benjamin Watkins	12.10 p.m
12. 5noon	*Haydon-Bridge, William Walton..	1. 0 p.m
9.30 a.m	Hayes, 3½ miles from Uxbridge......	6.15 p.m
7. 0 a.m; 12. 0noon	Hayes, Kent, 2 m. from Bromley ..	2.45 p.m; 6.45 p.m
10.30 a.m	Hayfield, 11 miles from Stockport ..	3. 0 p.m
5. 0 p.m	*Hayle, Richd. Barlow	7. 0 a.m
8. 0 a.m	Hayling-Island, 4 miles from Havant	6. 0 p.m
10. 0 a.m	Hayton, 2 miles from Pocklington ..	3.40 p.m
9. 0 a.m	Hazelgrove, 3 miles from Stockport..	2.30 p.m
9. 0 a.m	Heacham, 14 miles from Lynn......	5. 0 p.m
9.50 a.m	Headcorne, 9 miles from Maidstone ..	2.30 p.m
8. 0 a.m	Headington, 2½ miles from Oxford ..	5.30 p.m
7. 0 a.m	Heathfield, 10 m. from Hurst-Green..	9. 0 p.m
8. 0 a.m	Heavitree, 1 mile from Exeter	6.30 p.m
8. 0 a.m; 1. 0 p.m	Hebdenbridge, 8 m. from Halifax ..	12. 0 a.m; 5. 0 a.m
9. 0 a.m	Heckington, 5 miles from Sleaford..	4.30 p.m
9.30 a.m; 5. 0 p.m	Heckmondwicke, 10½ m. f. Leeds...	2.30 p.m; 7.30 p.m
9. 0 a.m	Hedgerley, 2½ m. f. Gerrards-Cross..	4. 0 p.m
8. 0 a.m	Hedingham (Castle), 4 m. f. Halsted	5. 0 p.m
8. 0 a.m	Hedingham (Sible), 3 m. f. Halsted..	5.15 p.m
10.10 a.m	Hedon, 6 miles from Hull	3.10 p.m
1.20 p.m	Heddon on the Wall, 7 m. f. NewcastleT	8.30 p.m
1. 0 p.m	Heighington, 7 miles from Darlington	6.15 p.m
10. 0 a.m	Helmingham, 8 miles from Stonham.	5.30 p.m
11. 0 a.m	Helmsley, 23 miles from York	2.10 p.m
11.15 p.m	Helperby, 5 miles fr. Boroughbridge.	1.30 p.m
10. 0 a.m	Helpringham, 8 miles from Sleaford..	4. 0 p.m
4.40 p.m	*Helstone, Samuel Drew...........	7.10 a.m
7. 0 a.m; 2. 0 p.m	*Hemel-Hempstead, Geo. Coupland	9. 0 p.m
7.30 a.m	Hemingford-Grey, 2 mi. fr. St. Ives..	7. 0 p.m
8.15 a.m	Hemsworth, 8 miles from Wakefield.	3.10 p.m

etters from London delivered at h. m.	Town. Postmaster.	Box for London closes at h. m.
8. 0 a.m	Henbury, 5 miles from Bristol	4.30 p.m
9.30 a.m	Henfield, 6 miles from Steyning	3. 0 p.m
9.30 a.m	Henham, 5 miles from Bp. Stortford .	6.30 p.m
7. 0 a.m	*Henley-on-Thames, Wm. Hickman	7.30 p.m
7. 0 a.m	Henley-in-Arden, 8 miles fr. Stratford	7.15 p.m
10.30 a.m	Henlow, 5½ miles from Baldock	6. 0 p.m
9.30 a.m	Henstridge, 8 miles from Wincanton	4. 0 p.m
8.45 a.m	*Hereford, Miss Elizabeth Bennett ..	3.15 p.m
8. 0 a.m	Herne-Bay, 9 miles from Canterbury	6.30 p.m
7. 0 a.m	Herne-Street, 6 miles fr. Canterbury	7. 0 p.m
8. 0 a.m	Herongate, 3 miles from Brentwood..	6. 0 p.m
8.30 a.m	Hersham, 2 miles from Esher	6. 0 p.m
8. 0 a.m 2. 0 p.m	*Hertford, Thomas Adkins.........	10.20 a.m 9.30 p.m
7.45 a.m	Hertingfordbury, 1½ m. from Hertford	6.45 p.m
11.30 a.m	Hessle, 5 miles from Hull	2.10 p.m
9.30 a.m	Hethersett, 3½ m. from Wymondham	3.30 p.m
10.15 a.m	Hever, 10 miles from Seven-Oaks ..	3. 0 p.m
8.30 a.m	Hevingham, 9 miles from Norwich..	5. 0 p.m
11.15 a.m	Heworth, 3½ miles from Gateshead ..	8.15 p.m
9. 0 a.m	Heworth, 1½ miles from York	5. 0 p.m
11.45 a.m 2.15 p.m	*Hexham, William Bell	10.30 a.m 6.10 p.m
9. 0 a.m	Heybridge, 1 mile from Maldon	5.45 p.m
9.10 a.m	Heysham, 6 miles from Lancaster ..	3.45 a.m
7. 0 a.m	*Heytesbury, John Compton........	6.30 p.m
8. 0 a.m	Heywood, 3 miles from Rochdale....	3.30 p.m
9.25 a.m	Hickleton, 6 miles from Doncaster ..	3.45 p.m
7.30 a.m	*Higham Ferrers, Robert Grindell ..	1. 0 p.m
8. 0 a.m	Highbridge, 6 mi. fr. Bridgewater ..	6. 0 p.m
5.30 a.m	Higher-Broughton, 2 m. f. Manchester	2.30 p.m
9. 0 a.m	High-Ercall, 5 m. fr. Wellington, Salop	4. 0 p.m
9. 0 a.m	Higher-Wambrook, 2¼ m. fr. Chard..	2. 0 p.m
11. 0 a.m	High-Fell, 2 miles from Gateshead ..	9.40 a.m
9. 0 a.m	High-Field, 2¼ m. from Southampton	6. 0 p.m
9.30 a.m	High-Hampton, 10 mi. fr. Oakhampton	3.30 p.m
7. 0 a.m	High-Hesket, 9 miles from Penrith..	7.40 p.m
7. 0 a.m 5. 0 p.m	*Highworth, Office vacant	5.30 p.m 7.30 p.m
	*High-Wycombe, *see* Wycombe.	
7. 0 a.m	Hilborough, 9 miles from Brandon ..	8.15 p.m
8.30 a.m	Hilgay, 4 miles from Downham	5.30 p.m
7. 0 a.m	Hillingdon, 1¼ mile from Uxbridge ..	7. 0 p.m
9.15 a.m	Hillington, 7 miles from Lynn	4.15 p.m
10. 0 a.m	Hilton, 3½ miles from St. Ives, Hunts.	5.30 p.m
7. 0 a.m	*Hinckley, William Tomlinson	7. 0 p.m
8. 0 a.m	Hindley, 3 miles from Wigan........	3.45 p.m
7.30 a.m	*Hindon, Tho. Harrison	5.30 p.m
10. 0 a.m	Hingham, 6 miles from Attleborough	4. 0 p.m
8.30 a.m	Hinton-Martell, 5 mi. fr. Wimborne..	6.30 p.m
6.45 a.m	Hinton St. George, 3 m. fr. Crewkerne	6. 0 p.m
10 .0 a.m	Hinxton, 7 m. from Saffron-Walden..	5. 0 p.m
2.45 p.m	Hipperholme, 4 mi. fr. Halifax	12.10 p.m 5.30 p.m
2.30 p.m	Hirwain, 6 m. from Merthyr-Tydvil..	9. 0 a.m
8. 0 a.m	Histon, 3½ miles from Cambridge....	4.30 p.m
7.30 a.m	*Hitchin, John Palmer	9. 0 p.m
8.30 a.m	Hoathley (West), 5 m. fr. E. Grinstead	4.45 p.m
7. 0 a.m	*Hobbs-Point, Sarah Williams	10. 0 p.m
7. 0 a.m	Hockley, 11 miles from Birmingham	8.15 p.m
7. 0 a.m	Hockliffe, 4 m. fr. Leighton-Buzzard	7.30 p.m
7. 0 a.m 1. 0 p.m	*Hoddesdon, George Allen	2. 0 p.m 9. 0 p.m
7.30 a.m	Hodnet, 5 miles from Market Drayton	5.15 p.m
7. 0 a.m	*Holbeach, Edward Hoff	5.45 p.m
9. 9 a.m	Holbrook, 6 miles from Ipswich	5.45 p.m
8. 0 a.m	Holford, 11 miles from Bridgewater.	6. 0 p.m
10.45 a.m	Holkham, 28 miles from Lynn	2.45 p.m
9.15 a.m	Hollesley, 8 miles from Woodbridge .	5. 0 p.m
9. 0 a.m	Hollins-Green, 6 m. from Warrington	4.15 p.m
8 30 a.m	Hollinwood, 5 mi. from Manchester	2.30 p.m 9.30 p.m
7. 0 a.m 10.50 a.m	Hollytroyds, 1½ mi. fr. Accrington	3.10 p.m 9.30 p.m
12.10 p.m	Holm, 8 miles from Pocklington	1. 0 p.m
9. 0 a.m	Holme-Pierrepoint, 8 m. fr. Nottingham	5.30 p.m
8.30 a.m	Holmes-Chapel, 4 miles f. Middlewich	5.45 p.m
11.0 a.m	Holmfirth, 6 mi. from Huddersfield	8. 0 a.m 2.30 p.m
8.45 a.m	Holnicote, 28 miles from Taunton ..	4.30 p.m
11. 0 a.m	Holsworthy, 21 miles from Oak-hampton	5. 0 p.m

Letters from London delivered at h. m.	Town. Postmaster.	Box for London closes at h. m.
7. 0 a.m	*Holt, Norfolk, Jeremiah Wm. King	4. 0 p.m
7. 0 a.m	Holt, 10 miles from Chippenham....	8. 0 p.m
7. 0 a.m	Holt, 6 miles from Woodstock	8.45 p.m
7.30 a.m	Holt-Chapel, 3½ mi. fr. Wimborne ..	6.30 p.m
7. 0 a.m	Holybourne, 1½ mile from Alton	6.30 p.m
8. 0 a.m 6. 0 p.m	*Holyhead, Wm. Bulkeley Jones..	6.15 a.m 5.10 p.m
8.30 a.m	*Holywell, Mrs. Margaret Hughes..	5. 0 p.m
7. 0 a.m	*Honiton, Richard Tucker..........	7.27 p.m
8. 0 a.m	Honiton-Clyst, 4 miles from Exeter..	4. 0 p.m
11. 0 a.m	Honley, 3½ miles from Huddersfield .	2.30 p.m
9.15 a.m	Hoogreen, 8 miles from Warrington..	4. 0 p.m
8. 0 a.m	Hook, 4 miles from Hartfordbridge.	6. 0 p.m
10. 0 a.m	Hook-Norton, 5 m. f. Chipping Norton	5. 0 p.m
8. 0 a.m	Hooton-Pagnell, 6½ m. from Doncaster	2. 0 p.m
10.30 a.m	Hopton, 9 miles from Thetford......	3. 0 p.m
9.30 a.m	Horbling, 4 miles from Folkingham..	4.15 p.m
8.30 a.m	Horbury, 3 miles from Wakefield....	5. 0 p.m
8. 0 a.m	Horfield, 2½ miles from Bristol	4.30 p.m
7. 0 a.m	Horksley, 4 miles from Colchester ..	7. 0 p.m
8.30 a.m	Horley, 5 miles from Crawley	5. 0 p.m
8.40 a.m	Hornby, 9 miles from Lancaster	5. 0 p.m
9. 0 a.m	*Horncastle, Henry Boulton..........	4.28 p.m
7. 0 a.m	Hornchurch, 2 miles from Romford..	6. 0 p.m
7. 0 a.m	*Horndean, Thomas Stephens	8.30 p.m
9. 0 a.m	Horndon, 16 miles from Romford....	4.15 p.m
9.30 a.m	Horningsham, 4½ m. from Warminster	3. 0 p.m
7.30 a.m 3.30 p.m	Hornscross, 2 miles from Dartford..	1. 0 p.m
12.10 p.m	Hornsea, 18 miles from Hull	1. 0 p.m
2.40 p.m	Horrabridge, 10 miles from Plymouth	8.15 a.m
7. 0 a.m	Horsebridge, 19 mi. fr. Hurst-Green	8. 0 p.m
10. 0 a.m	Horseferry-bridge, 5 m. from Gloster	4. 0 p.m
8. 0 a.m	Horseforth, 5 miles from Leeds....	4.30 p.m
9. 0 a.m	Horsemonden, 8 miles from Cranbrook	5.30 p.m
7. 0 a.m	*Horsham, John Tugwell	9. 0 p.m
9. 0 a.m	Horstead-Keynes, 8 m. f. E. Grinstead	4. 0 p.m
8. 0 a.m	Horton-Kirby, 4 miles from Dartford	6.30 p.m
10.20 a.m	Horwich, 6 miles from Bolton	2. 0 p.m
8. 0 a.m	Hothfield, 15½ miles from Maidstone	5.15 p.m
7.30 a.m	Hoton, 3 miles from Loughboro'	8.30 p.m
8. 0 a.m 5. 0 p.m	Hotwells, 1¼ miles from Bristol	5. 0 a.m 9. 0 p.m
	*Hounslow, *see* "London District Offi."	
8.30 a.m	Houghton, 4 miles from Huntingdon	6. 0 p.m
9.45 a.m	Houghton, 6 miles from Rougham ..	3. 0 p.m
9.45 a.m	Houghton le Spring, 6½ mi. f. Durham	8. 0 p.m
9. 0 a.m 4. 0 p.m	Hove, 2½ miles from Brighton	5.45 p.m
9.30 a.m	Hoveton-St.-John, 8 m. from Norwich	5.30 p.m
11.30 a.m	Hovingham, 20 miles from York	1.30 p.m
8. 0 a.m	*Howden, John Sugden	6. 0 p.m
12.40 a.m	Howdon-Pans, 6 m. fr. Newcastle T..	7.40 p.m
8. 0 a.m	Hoxne, 2½ miles from Scole	7. 0 p.m
9. 0 a.m	Hoyland, 10 miles from Sheffield	2.15 p.m
8.30 a.m	Hubberston, 1 mile from Milford	4. 0 p.m
9. 0 a.m	Hucknal-Torkard, 8 m. f. Nottingham	5.30 p.m
8. 0 a.m	*Huddersfield, William Moore	5.15 p.m 12.30 ngt
9.30 a.m	*Hull, Richard Mosey	5. 0 p.m 9. 0 p.m
4.10 p.m	Humshaugh, 6 miles from Hexham..	9.30 a.m
7. 0 a.m	*Hungerford, Mrs. Anne Hincks	7.45 p.m
2.15 p.m	Hunmanby, 8 miles from Bridlington	11. 0 a.m
7. 0 a.m	Hunsden, 5 miles from Ware........	6.30 p.m
9.15 a.m	Hunstanton, 17 miles from Lynn	4.15 p.m
8. 0 a.m	*Huntingdon, James Hatfield	9.30 p.m
9.30 a.m	Hunton, 5 miles from Maidstone	3.30 p.m
8. 0 a.m 2.15 p.m	Hunton-Bridge, 4 miles fr. Watford	10.15 a.m 6.45 p.m
9. 0 a.m	Huntspill, 6 miles from Bridgewater..	4. 0 p.m
7.30 a.m	Hursley, 5 miles from Winchester....	8. 0 p.m
7. 0 a.m	Hurstbourne-Priors, 8 miles from Andover-road	7. 0 p.m
9. 0 a.m	Hurstbourne-Tarrant, 6 m. f. Andover	5. 0 p.m
11. 0 a.m	Hurst-Pierpoint, 10 miles fr. Brighton	3. 0 p.m
7. 0 a.m 4. 0 p.m	*Hurstgreen, Jno. Wood	9. 0 a.m 10. 0 p.m
11.10 a.m	Hurstgreen, 4 miles from Clitheroe ..	1.35 p.m
11.10 a.m	Hurworth, 3½ m. from Darlington....	7.50 p.m
9.45 a.m	Hutton, 8 miles from Berwick	2.40 p.m
10. 0 a.m	Hutton, 17 mi. fr. Wells, Somerset ..	3.45 p.m

Letters from London delivered at h. m.	Town. Postmaster.	Box for London closes at h. m.
10.15 a.m	Hutton-Rudby, 16 miles from Thirsk	2.15 p.m
7. 0 a.m	Huyton, 2 miles from Prescot	5. 0 p.m
9. 0 a.m	Hyde, 7 miles from Manchester......	5. 0 p.m
7. 0 a.m	*Hythe, Mrs. Lydia Mercer Fisher ..	10. 0 p.m
7. 0 a.m	Hythe, 1½ miles from Colchester	7. 0 p.m
8. 0 a.m	Hythe, 12 miles from Southampton...	8. 0 p.m
10.30 a.m	Ibstock, 6 m. from Ashby-de-la-Zouch	3.15 p.m
9. 0 a.m	Ickleton, 5 m. from Saffron Walden..	5.30 p.m
7. 0 a.m	Ide, 2 miles from Exeter...........	6. 0 p.m
8. 0 a.m	Ideford, 3 miles from Chudleigh	5. 0 p.m
10.30 a.m	Idle, 3½ miles from Bradford, Yorksh.	3. 0 p.m
7.30 p.m	Ifley, 1½ mile from Oxford..........	6. 0 p.m
7.45 a.m	Ightham, 6 miles from Seven Oaks..	5.15 p.m
10. 0 a.m	Ilam, 5 miles from Ashbourne	4.50 p.m
8.30 a.m	*Ilchester, Philip Handover	4. 0 p.m
11.25noon	*Ilfracombe, Edward Hearson......	2.35 p.m
9.30 a.m	Ilkeston, 8 miles from Nottingham ..	4. 0 p.m
10.30 a.m	Ilkley, 6 miles from Otley	2.10 p.m
7. 0 a.m	*Ilminster, William Hagley	7.10 p.m
10.30 a.m	Ilsley, 9 miles from Newbury	4. 0 p.m
7. 0 a.m	*Ingatestone, John Whichcord	9. 0 p.m
9. 0 a.m	Ingham, 4 m. from Bury-St.-Edmond's	5. 0 p.m
9.30 a.m	Ingleby-Cross, 12 miles from Thirsk..	3.20 p.m
11.40 a.m	Ingleton, 18 miles from Lancaster....	1.50 p.m
10. 0 a.m	Instow, 6 miles from Barnstaple......	3.15 p.m
7. 0 a.m	*Ipswich, Wm. Stevenson Fitch	10. 0 p.m
9. 0 a.m	Iron-Acton, 10 miles from Bristol...	3. 0 p.m
8. 0 a.m	*Iron-Bridge, Thomas Bayliss......	5.30 p.m
9.45 a.m	Ironville, 7 miles from Alfreton	4.45 p.m
7.30 a.m	Isfield, 3 miles from Uckfield........	7.30 p.m
9. 0 a.m	Isleham, 5 miles from Mildenhall....	6. 0 p.m
	*Isle-of-Man, *see* Douglas	
	Isle-of-Wight, *see* Cowes, Newport, Ryde, and Yarmouth.	
9. 0 a.m	Islip, 6 miles from Oxford..........	4.45 p.m
7. 0 a.m	Itchenferry, 1 m. from Southampton	6.45 p.m
7.30 a.m	Ivinghoe, 4 miles from Tring........	6. 0 p.m
8. 0 a.m	Iver 2½ miles from Uxbridge........	6.30 p.m
8.25 a.m	*Ivy-Bridge, John Bird	4.23 p.m
9.30 a.m	Iwerne-Minster, 6¼ m. from Blandford	4. 0 p.m
8. 0 a.m	Ixworth, 7 m. from Bury St. Edmund's	7. 0 p.m
12. noon	Jarrow, 6 miles from Gateshead....	7.20 p.m
Sun. Wed. & Fridays; hours depending on the arrival of H.M. packets	*Jersey (Isle) Robert Fullerton	9. 0 p.m on Sunday, Tus.&Thrs
12. 0 a.m	Jump, 5 miles from Plymouth	10. 0 a.m
8. 0 a.m	Kegworth, 11 miles from Derby......	6. 0 p.m
8.15 a.m	*Keighley, J. Cooke	3.30 p.m
10. 0 a.m	Keinton-Mandeville, 5 miles from Somerton	3. 0 p.m
8. 0 a.m	Kelsall, 8 miles from Chester.........	3.15 p.m
7. 0 a.m	*Kelvedon, Mrs. Ann Crampin......	10. 0 p.m
8.30 a.m	Kelweston, 8 miles from Bristol......	4.30 p.m
9. 0 a.m	Kemerton, 4 miles from Tewksbury..	4. 0 p.m
7. 0 a.m	Kempsey, 4 miles from Worcester...	6.30 p.m
8. 0 a.m	Kempstone, 1½ miles from Bedford ..	5.30 p.m
8.30 a.m 2.30 p.m	Kemp-Town, 1 mile from Brighton	8. 0 p.m 10.45 a.m
10. 0 a.m	Kemsing, 6 miles from Seven-Oaks..	6.30 p.m
7. 0 a.m 9.30 a.m	*Kendal, Mrs. Elizabeth Fenton ..	4.10 p.m 10. 0 p.m
7. 0 a.m 3. 0 p.m	*Kenilworth	7.30 a.m 9.30 p.m
7. 0 a.m	Kennford, 4 miles from Exeter	7. 0 p.m
9. 0 a.m	Kenninghall, 12 miles from Thetford	4. 0 p.m
10.30 a.m	Kentchurch, 13 miles from Hereford	1. 0 p.m
7. 0 a.m	Kenton, 7 miles from Exeter.........	6.30 p.m
1.40 p.m	Kenton, 3 miles from Newcastle T...	7.50 p.m
9.30 a.m	Kenyon, 13 miles from Manchester..	2.30 p.m
7.30 a.m	Keston, 3 miles from Bromley	6.30 p.m
1.30 p.m	*Keswick, Cumberland, Jas. Atkinson	12. 0noon
8. 0 a.m	Keswick, 3 miles from Norwich	6. 0 p.m
8. 0 a.m	*Kettering, Miss Sarah Stockburn ..	5.55 p.m
7. 0 a.m	Ketley, 1½ mi. from Wellington, Salop	5.15 p.m
8. 0 a.m	Ketton, 3 miles from Stamford	6. 0 p.m
9. 0 a.m	Keynsham, 5 miles from Bristol....	5. 0 p.m
7. 0 a.m	Key-Street, 2 mi. from Sittingbourne	6.30 p.m
8.30 a.m	Kibworth Beauchamp, 9 m. fr. Leicester	5. 0 p.m
7. 0 a.m	*Kidderminster, George Friend	6.30 p.m
8.30 a.m	Kidwelly, 9 miles from Carmarthen..	3.30 p.m
9. 0 a.m	Kiln-Green, 6 miles from Maidenhead	6. 0 p.m
8. 0 a.m	Kilsby, 5 miles from Daventry	5.30 p.m

Letters from London delivered at h. m.	Town. Postmaster.	Box for London closes at h. m.
8. 0 a.m	*Kimbolton, George Craddock	7. 0 p.m
8.30 a.m	*Kineton, Mrs. Eleanor Worrall....	3.30 p.m
4.30 p.m	Kingerby, 5 miles from Market Raisin	8. 0 a.m
11.30 a.m	*Kingsbridge, Charlotte Cranch	2.50 p.m
8.30 a.m	Kingsbromley, 5¾ m. from Lichfield..	3.30 p.m
9.30 a.m	Kingsclere, 7 miles from Newbury...	4.30 p.m
8. 0 a.m	Kingscliffe, 6 miles from Wansford ..	5. 0 p.m
9. 0 a.m	Kingscote, 5 m. f. Wotton-under-Edge	4. 0 p.m
9. 0 a.m	Kingskerswell, 3 m. f. Newton-Abbot	4. 0 p.m
8.30 a.m	King's Norton, 8 m. from Birmingham	4.30 p.m
7.30 a.m	King's Langley, 4 m. f. Hemel-Hempsted	6.30 p.m
8.40 a.m	Kingstanley, 4 miles from Stroud..	4. 0 p.m
10.30 a.m	Kingston, 3½ miles from Taunton....	4.30 p.m
	*Kingston, Surry, *see* "London Dis. Offi."	
9. 0 a.m	Kingston, 2 miles from Portsmouth	6. 0 p.m
8.30 a.m	Kingston Blount, 4 m. from Tetsworth	6.15 p.m
8.30 a.m	Kingston-Inn, 6 miles from Abingdon	4.45 p.m
10. 0 a.m	Kingston-Lisle, 5 miles from Wantage	4.30 p.m
8. 0 a.m	Kingswinford, 5 miles from Dudley..	5.45 p.m
9. 0 a.m	Kingswood, 4 miles from Epsom	5.15 p.m
9. 0 a.m	Kingswood-Hill, 4 miles from Bristol	3. 0 p.m
11. 0 a.m	*Kington, James Pugh	1. 0 p.m
9. 0 a.m	Kinson, 5 miles from Wimborne	6. 0 p.m
7. 0 a.m	Kintbury, 3 miles from Hungerford..	6.30 p.m
10. 0 a.m	Kinver, 4 miles from Stourbridge....	5.30 p.m
11. 0 a.m	Kippax, 6 miles from Pontefract....	2.45 p.m
7.30 a.m	Kirby, 15 miles from Colchester	4.45 p.m
1.40 p.m	Kirby-Malzeard, 8 miles from Ripon	3.20 p.m
12. 0noon	Kirby-Moorside, 29 miles from York	1.30 p.m
4. 0 p.m	Kirby-Stephen, 4½ miles from Brough	8.50 a.m
10.30 a.m	Kirkburton, 5 mi. from Huddersfield	2.15 p.m
9.45 a.m	*Kirkby-Lonsdale, John Foster	3.30 p.m
4. 0 p.m	Kirkbythore, 8 miles from Penrith ..	9.30 a.m
11.40 a.m	Kirkella, 5 miles from Hull	2.20 p.m
8.50 a.m	Kirkham, 9 miles from Preston......	4. 0 p.m
1.50 p.m	Kirklington, 7 miles from Ripon	3.30 p.m
6.10 p.m	Kirklinton, 8 miles from Carlisle	7.50 a.m
4. 0 p.m	Kirkoswald, 8 miles from Penrith....	8.25 a.m
8. 0 a.m	Kirkstall, 3 miles from Leeds	5. 0 p.m
5.15 p.m	Kirmington, 8½ miles from Brigg.....	8.15 a.m
9.30 a.m	Kirtling, 7 miles from Newmarket ..	7. 0 p.m
10.45 a.m	Kirton, 4 miles from Boston	3. 0 p.m
3. 0 p.m	Kirton-Lindsey, 18 miles from Lincoln	11. 0 a.m
9.50 a.m	*Knaresborough, Elizabeth Taylor ..	3.45 p.m
7. 0 a.m	Knighton, 2 miles from Chudleigh ..	6. 0 p.m
1. 0 p.m	Knighton, 6 miles from Presteign ..	12.15 p.m
11.15 a.m	Knockers Knowle, 3 m. from Plymouth	2. 0 p.m
9. 0 a.m	Knottingley, 1¼ mile from Ferrybridge	2.15 p.m
7. 0 a.m	Knowle, 7 miles from Birmingham ..	8. 0 p.m
8. 0 a.m	Knowle, 2 miles from Bristol........	4.45 p.m
8.30 a.m	Knoyle 2½ miles from Hindon	4.15 p.m
7.45 a.m	*Knutsford, Miss Marian Dakin....	6.30 p.m
5. 0 p.m	Laceby, 16 miles from Brigg........	8.30 a.m
7. 0 a.m	Lacock, 3 miles from Chippenham ..	10. 0 p.m
8. 0 a.m	Ladock, 7 miles from Truro	9. 0 p.m
10.30 a.m	Lake, 7 miles from Ryde	2.30 p.m
8. 0 a.m	Laleham, 2 miles from Chertsey....	6. 0 p.m
7.30 a.m	*Lamberhurst, Thos. Roberts	7.30 p.m
8.30 a.m	Lambourn, 8 miles from Hungerford	5.20 p.m
4. 0 p.m	*Lampeter, Evan Evans	7.15 p.m
8. 0 a.m 7.15 p.m	*Lancaster, Mrs. Elizabeth Moffat Glasson	6. 5 p.m 10. 0 p.m
11. 0 p.m	Lanchester, 8 miles from Durham ..	7. 0 p.m
7. 0 a.m	Lancing, 2 miles from Shoreham	6. 0 p.m
9. 0 a.m	Landbeach, 5 miles from Cambridge	5. 0 p.m
9. 0 a.m	Landford, 12 miles from Fordingbridge	4.30 p.m
7.30 a.m 4. 0 p.m	Landport, 1 mile from Portsmouth	4. 0 p.m 10. 0 p.m
1.30 p.m	Landrake, 8 miles from Devonport ..	7. 0 a.m
7. 0 a.m	Lane-Delph, 4 miles fr. Newcastle, S.	7.45 p.m
7. 0 a.m	*Lane-End, John Glover	7.30 p.m
9. 0 a.m	Langford, 11 miles from Bristol	2.15 p.m
10.30 a.m	Langford, 8 miles from Heytesbury..	3. 0 p.m
10.30 a.m	Langham, 7 miles from Haverfordwest	4. 0 p.m
9. 0 a.m	Langham, 2 miles from Oakham	4. 0 p.m
8. 0 a.m	Langley, 4 miles from Maidstone....	5.30 p.m
8.30 a.m	Langley, 4 miles from Slough	5.30 p.m
8. 0 a.m	Langport, 6 miles from Somerton......	4.50 p.m
7. 0 a.m	Langton Green, 3 mi. fr. Tunbridge Wells	8. 0 p.m
9. 0 a.m 4. 0 a.m	Lansdown, 1 mile from Bath........	7. 0 p.m
12. 0noon	Lapford, 9 miles from Crediton......	2. 0 p.m

Letters from London delivered at h. m.	Town. Postmaster.	Box for London closes at h. m.
7.30 a.m	Larkfield, 4 miles from Maidstone....	6.10 p.m
7.30 a.m	Larlingford, 8 miles from Thetford ..	7. 0 p.m
8. 0 a.m	Latchingdon, 5 miles from Maldon ..	5. 0 p.m
8. 0 a.m	Laugharne, 3 miles from St. Clears..	5. 0 p.m
9.30 a.m	*Launceston, Thos. Melhuish Truscott	3.10 p.m
8. 0 a.m	Lavenham, 7 miles from Sudbury ..	5.30 p.m
9.15 a.m	Lavington (Market), 7 mi. fr. Devizes	6. 0 p.m
9.30 a.m	Lavington (West), 8½ mi. fr. Devizes	5.45 p.m
11. 0 a.m	Lawhitton, 3 miles from Launceston..	2.15 p.m
8. 0 a.m	*Lawton, Miss Sarah Peake	7. 0 p.m
9. 0 a.m	Laxfield, 12 miles from Woodbridge	6. 0 p.m
10. 0 a.m	Laxton, 4 miles from Howden.......	4. 0 p.m
4. 0 a.m	Laycock, 4 miles from Chippenham..	9. 0 p.m
7. 0 a.m	Lea, 5 miles from Ross	5.45 p.m
10. 0 a.m	Leadenham, 12 miles from Grantham	2.30 p.m
7.30 a.m 2.30 p.m	*Leamington, Edward Enoch	7.30 a.m 8.45 p.m
7. 0 a.m	*Leatherhead, Thomas Hill	9. 0 p.m
7. 0 a.m 3.30 p.m	*Lechlade, John Charles Lockwood	8. 0 a.m 7.45 p.m
10. 0 a.m	Lechmore-Heath, 4 mi. from Watford	5.30 p.m
10.15 a.m	Leckhampton, 1½ m. from Cheltenham	6. 0 p.m
7. 0 a.m	*Ledbury, William Taylor	5.15 p.m
7.30 a.m	*Leeds, James Anderson	6. 0 p.m
9. 0 a.m	*Leek, George Nall	6.15 p.m
9.30 a.m	Lees, 8½ miles from Manchester....	1.50 p.m 8.50 p.m
7.30 a.m 3.30 p.m	*Leicester, William Parsons	7.45 a.m 10. 0 p.m
8. 0 a.m	Leigh, 4½ miles from Rochford	3.30 p.m
7. 0 a.m	Leigh, 3 miles from Tunbridge	7. 0 p.m
8.30 p.m	Leigh, 13 miles from Manchester....	5.30 p.m
7. 0 a.m 12.15 p.m	*Leighton-Buzzard, Wm. Doggett..	10.30 a.m 8.40 p.m
11.15 a.m	Leintwardine, 8 miles from Ludlow..	1.15 p.m
7.30 a.m	Leiston, 4 miles from Saxmundham..	5.30 p.m
5.30 p.m	Lelant, 3 miles from Hayle	10. 0 p.m
7.30 a.m	Lenham, 9 miles from Maidstone....	6.15 p.m
8. 0 a.m	Lenton, 2 miles from Nottingham....	5.45 p.m
9.30 a.m	*Leominster, Francis Went	3.15 p.m
7. 0 a.m	Letterstone, 9½ mi. fr. Haverfordwest	5.15 p.m
10. 0 a.m	Letton, 11½ miles from Hereford	1.30 p.m
9.50 a.m	Leven, 6½ miles from Beverley......	10.50 a.m
11. 0 a.m	Lewdown, 11 miles from Oakhampton	2.15 p.m
7. 0 a.m 2.30 p.m	*Lewes, Thomas Saxby, junior.....	8.45 a.m 8.30 p.m
7. 0 a.m	Lexden, 1¾ miles from Colchester ..	7. 0 p.m
12.20 p.m	Leyburn, 12 miles from Bedale ...	12.20 p.m
10.40 a.m	Leyland, 4 miles from Chorley......	2.20 p.m
8. 0 a.m	*Lichfield, John Proffitt.........	6. 0 p.m
10.30 a.m	Lidgate, 8 miles from Newmarket ..	5. 0 p.m
11. 0 a.m	Lifton, 4 miles from Launceston ..	2. 0 p.m
4. 0 p.m	Limber, 10 miles from Brigg........	9.45 a.m
7.30 a.m	Limpsfield 12 miles from Reigate....	5.45 p.m
8.15 a.m	*Lincoln, John Wold Drury	5.30 p.m
7. 0 a.m 10.30 a.m	Lindal, 9 miles from Milnthorp....	3. 5 p.m 9. 0 p.m
8. 0 a.m	Lindfield, 4 miles from Cuckfield....	5. 0 p.m
8.30 a.m	*Linton, Cambridge, John Adcock	7. 0 p.m
7. 0 a.m	Linton (Kent), 6 miles fr. Staplehurst	8. 0 p.m
7. 0 a.m	*Liphook, Mrs. Mary Hobbs	8.30 p.m
9.30 a.m	Liscard, 4 miles from Liverpool	3. 0 p.m
2. 0 p.m	*Liskeard, Miss Mary Rawe Ede	6.30 a.m
9. 0 a.m	Liss, 4 miles from Petersfield........	6.30 p.m
9.30 a.m	Litcham, 8 miles from Swanham.....	3.45 p.m
7. 0 a.m	Little-Bentley, 8 mi. from Colchester.	6. 0 p.m
9. 0 a.m	Little-Berkhamstead, 7 m. f. Hertford	5. 0 p.m
8. 0 a.m	Littleborough, 3½ mi. from Rochdale.	3.30 p.m
8. 0 a.m	Littlebury, 2 m. from Saffron-Walden	7. 0 p.m
7. 0 a.m	Little-Canford, 2½ mi. fr. Wimborne	6. 0 p.m
9.30 a.m	Little Chesterford, 3½ m. f. S. Walden	6.30 p.m
0 a.m	Little-Gaddesden, 4 miles fr. Hemel-Hempstead	5. 0 p.m
9.30 a.m	Little-Glemham, 8 m. fr. Woodbridge	6. 0 p.m
8. 0 a.m	Littlehampton, 5 miles from Arundel	6 15 p.m
8.30 a.m	Little-Harrowden, 3 m. f. Wellingboro	5.30 p.m
10.15 a.m	Little-Haven, 7 mi. fr. Haverfordwest	4. 0 p.m
0.30 a.m	Little-Hulton, 5½ miles from Bolton...	1.45 p.m
9.30 a.m	Little-Massingham, 2½ m. f. Rougham	3.30 p.m
9. 0 a.m	Little-Port, 5 miles from Ely........	5.30 p.m
9. 0 a.m	Little-Stukeley, 3 m. from Huntingdon	5. 0 p.m
10. 0 a.m	Little-Swaffham, 6 m. fr. Newmarket	5.30 p.m

Letters from London delivered at h. m.	Town Postmaster.	Box for London closes at h. m.
9. 0 a.m	Little-Waltham, 5 mi. fr. Chelmsford	5. 0 p.m
7. 0 a.m	Littlewick-Green, 4 miles from Maidenhead	7. 0 p.m
9.55 a.m	Livermere, 7 miles from Bury, Suff.	4. 0 p.m
8.30 a.m 6.30 p.m	*Liverpool, William Banning	1.30 p.m 6. 0 a.m
10.30 a.m	Llanasa, 8 miles from Holywell	1.45 p.m
7.15 a.m	Llanbedr, 51 miles from Corwen	11. 0 p.m
7. 0 p.m	Llanbrynmair, 17 miles fr. Newtown	10. 0 p.m
2. 0 p.m	Llandaff, 2 miles from Cardiff	8.45 a.m
12.51 p.m	*Llandilo, Hugh Evans	11.45 a.m
11.25 a.m	*Llandovery, David Rice Rees	1.15 p.m
8.30 a.m	Llandudno, 4 miles from Conway....	4.45 p.m
9.30 a.m	Llandyssil, 14 miles from Lampeter..	2. 0 p.m
3.30 p.m	*Llanelly, Mrs. Jane Chalinder......	8. 0 a.m
8.30 a.m	Llanerchymed, 18 miles from Bangor	4. 0 p.m
11. 0 a.m	Llanfair, 8 miles from Welchpool ..	2. 0 p.m
11.30 a.m	Llanfyllin, 15 miles from Oswestry..	1. 0 p.m
2. 0 p.m	*Llangadock, Henry Evans	12.45 noon
7.30 a.m	Llangefin, 11 miles from Bangor	5. 0 p.m
10.40 a.m	*Llangollen, Mrs. Lucy Davies	2.20 p.m
2.30 p.m	Llanidloes, 14 miles from Newtown...	9. 0 a.m
11.15 a.m	Llanrhaiadr, 14 miles from Oswestry	1.30 p.m
11.45 a.m	Llanfihangel-Crucorney, 4 miles from Abergavenny..............	12.50 p.m
1.30 p.m	Llanrwst, 12 miles from Conway....	5.40 p.m
8. 0 a.m	Llansantffraid, 3 miles from Conway	5.45 p.m
10.30 a.m	Llansantffraid, 9 miles from Oswestry	2. 0 p.m
5.15 p.m	Llantrissant, 10 miles from Cardiff ..	10. 0 p.m
2.30 p.m	Llantwit-Major, 5 m. from Cowbridge	7. 0 a.m
10. 0 a.m	Llanybldwell, 7 miles from Oswestry	2. 0 p.m
10. 0 a.m	Llanymynech, 5½ miles from Oswestry	2.15 p.m
9.15 a.m	Locking, 17 miles fr. Wells, Somerset	4.15 p.m
10.30 a.m 6.30 p.m	Lockwood, 1 m. from Huddersfield	8. 0 a.m 3. 0 p.m
9. 0 a.m	Loddon, 14 miles from Norwich......	4.30 p.m
7. 0 a.m	Lodsworth 4 miles from Petworth ..	6.30 p.m
3.30 p.m	Lofthouse, 9 miles from Guisboro' ..	8.50 a.m
8. 0 a.m	London-Colney, 8 miles fr. St. Albans	6. 0 p.m
9. 0 a.m	London-Elm, 12 miles from Salisbury	4. 0 p.m
7. 0 a.m	Long-Ashton, 3 miles from Bristol....	4.30 p.m
12.40 p.m	Long-Benton, 3½ m. from Newcastle T.	9.45 a.m
8. 0 a.m	Long-Bredy, 8 miles from Dorchester	5.35 p.m
9. 0 a.m	Long-Buckby, 5 miles from Daventry	5.30 p.m
9. 0 a.m	Long-Compton, 5 miles from Chipping Norton	3.30 p.m
7. 0 a.m	Long-Crendon, 1½ miles from Thame	7. 0 p.m
	Long-Ditton, *see* London District offi.	
9.30 a.m	Longdon, 5 miles from Tewkesbury ..	4.35 p.m
8.30 a.m	Longdon, 4 miles from Lichfield	4.20 p.m
8. 0 a.m	Longham, 4 miles from Wimborne ..	5.30 p.m
4.10 p.m	Long-Horsley, 7 miles from Morpeth	9. 0 a.m
2.50 p.m	Long-Hurst, 3 miles from Morpeth ..	9.25 a.m
11.15 a.m	Long-Marston, 7 miles from York....	2.15 p.m
8. 0 a.m	Longmelford, 4 miles from Sudbury..	5.45 p.m
8. 0 a.m	Long-Parish, 6 m. fr. Andover-road	6. 0 p.m
7. 0 a.m	Longport, 3 miles from Newcastle S.	7.45 p.m
12.40 p.m	Long-Preston, 4 miles from Settle ..	12.30 p.m
8. 0 a.m	*Long-Stratton, George Barnes	8. 0 p.m
8. 0 a.m.	Long-Sutton, 9 miles from Wisbeach	6.15 p.m
7. 0 a.m 3.50 p.m	*Longtown, Robert Little	10. 0 a.m 4. 0 p.m
10. 0 a.m	Long-Wittenham, 5 mi. fr. Abingdon	4.45 p.m
5. 0 p.m	Looe (East & West), near Liskeard ..	4.30 a.m
7.30 a.m	Loose, 7 miles from Staplehurst	8.30 p.m
1.25 p.m	*Lostwithiel, William Probert	9. 0 a.m
8. 0 a.m	Loudwater, 2½ m. fr. High-Wycombe	6.30 p.m
7. 0 a.m 3.15 p.m	*Loughborough, Samuel Lee.....	7. 0 a.m 10. 0 p.m
6. 0 p.m	Loughor, 4 miles from Llanelly......	10. 0 p.m
9. 0 a.m	Loughton, 4 m. from Stoney-Stratford	5. 0 p.m
12. 0 noon	*Louth, Thomas Simons...........	1.45 p.m
3.30 p.m	Lower-Chapel, 5 miles from Brecon..	8. 0 a.m
10. 0 a.m	Lower-Wallop, 8 miles from Andover	4. 0 a.m
7.30 a.m	*Lowestoff, Thomas Pratt	6. 0 p.m
10.30 a.m	Low-Harrogate, 1 m. f. H. Harrogate	3.15 p.m
10. 0 a.m	Low-Moor, 3 mi. fr. Bradford, Yorks.	3. 0 p.m
9.30 a.m	Lowick, 2 miles from Thrapston	3.30 p.m
8.35 p.m	Lowick, 10 miles from Berwick	2.50 p.m
7.50 a.m	Low-Wortley, 3 miles from Leeds ..	5. 0 p.m
7. 0 a.m	Luddenden, 4 miles from Halifax ...	6. 0 p.m
8. 0 a.m	Ludford, 5 miles from Market-Rasen	11.20 a.m

Letters from London delivered at h. m.	Town. Postmaster.	Box for London closes at h. m.
11. 0 a.m	Ludgershall, 6 miles from Andover ..	4. 0 p.m
10. 0 a.m	*Ludlow, Miss Elizabeth Sankey ...	3. 0 p.m
7. 0 a.m	Ludwell, 3 miles from Shaftesbury ..	6.40 p.m
9.30 a.m	Lullington, 6 mi. fr. Burton-on-Trent	3.45 p.m
9. 0 a.m	Luppitt, 5 miles from Honiton	2. 0 p.m
8. 0 a.m	*Luton, Gresham Puddephatt	7. 5 p.m
7. 0 a.m	*Lutterworth, William Vears, jun. ..	8.30 p.m
10. 0 a.m	Lydbrook, 7 miles from Ross	2.15 p.m
7. 0 a.m	Lydd, 6 miles from New Romney....	7. 0 p.m
8.45 a.m	Lydney, 7 miles from Newnham	3.30 p.m
8. 0 a.m	*Lyme, Mrs. Elizabeth Lock	4.30 p.m
7. 0 a.m	*Lymington, William L. Galpine....	7.30 p.m
9.45 a.m	Lymm, 6 miles from Warrington	4.15 p.m
10.30 a.m	Lympsham, 19 mi. fr. Wells, Somerset	2. 0 p.m
7.15 a.m	Lympstone, 8 miles from Exeter	6.15 p.m
7. 0 a.m	*Lyndhurst, John Smith	8.30 p.m
10.30 a.m	Lyneham, 10 miles from Chippenham	3. 0 p.m
7.30 a.m	*Lynn, Robinson Cruso...........	6.30 p.m
9. 0 a.m	Lytchett-Minster, 5 miles from Poole	5. 0 p.m
9.30 a.m	Lytham, 13 miles from Preston......	3. 5 p.m
9.30 a.m	*Macclesfield, James Sargent	5.45 p.m
2.40 p.m	Machynlleth, 38 miles fr. Welchpool	10. 0 a.m
9. 0 a.m	Madely, 4 m. from Newcastle, S.....	5. 0 p.m
5. 0 p.m	Maesteg, 9 miles from Bridgend	10.30 p.m
9.15 a.m	Maghull, 8 miles from Liverpool....	4.45 p.m
7. 0 a.m 12. 0noon	*Maidenhead, Mrs. Rose Robinson..	11.15 a.m 9. 0 p.m
9. 0 a.m	Maiden-Newton, 8 mi. fr. Dorchester	4. 0 p.m
7. 0 a.m 3.15 p.m	*Maidstone, George Jury	10.30 a.m 9. 0 p.m
8.30 a.m	Maisemore, 2½ miles from Gloucester	5. 0 p.m
8. 0 a.m	*Maldon, John Polley	7. 0 p.m
	Malling, *see* Town-Malling	
1. 0 p.m	Mallwyd, 26 miles from Welchpool..	11.30 a.m
7. 0 a.m	*Malmsbury, Mr. Hauks	6.45 p.m
7.30 a.m	Malpas, 15 miles from Chester......	5.15 p.m
8. 0 a.m	Maltby, 6 miles from Rotherham....	6. 0 p.m
8.30 a.m	*Malton, George Barnby	4. 0 p.m
7. 0 a.m	*Malvern (Great), John Mason	5.30 p.m
8. 0 a.m	Malvern Link, 1½ mi. from Malvern	4.45 p.m
8. 0 a.m	Malvern Wells, 2½ mi. f. Gt. Malvern	4.30 p.m
8. 0 a.m 6.15 p.m	*Manchester, Robt. Peel Willock ..	12 night 6.30 p.m
9. 0 a.m	Manewden, 5 mi. from Bp. Stortford	6.30 p.m
7. 0 a.m	*Manningtree, Thomas Taylor	8. 0 p.m
7.15 a.m	*Mansfield, William Holt	6.30 p.m
7.30 a.m	Mansfield-Woodhouse, 4m. f. Mansfield	3. 0 p.m
	*Marazion, *see* Market-Jew	
7. 0 a.m	*March, Charles Bates	9. 0 p.m
7. 0 a.m	Marcham, 3 miles from Abingdon ..	6. 0 p.m
7.30 a.m	Marchwood, 8 m. from Southampton	8.30 p.m
8. 0 a.m	Marden, 3½ miles from Staplehurst ..	7. 0 p.m
7. 0 a.m	Maresfield, 2 miles from Uckfield....	7. 3 p.m
7. 0 a.m 7.15 p.m	*Margate, Frederic Gore	8. 0 p.m
10. 0 a.m	Market-Bosworth, 8 mi. fr. Hinckley	3.30 p.m
7. 0 a.m	*Market-Deeping, John Wherry	10. 0 p.m
7. 0 a.m	*Market-Drayton, Richard Grant ..	8.45 p.m
8. 0 a.m	*Market-Harborough, T. G. Goward	6.30 p.m
6. 0 p.m	*Market-Jew, or Marazion, Miss Amelia Gluyas	10. 0 p.m
2. 0 p.m	*Market-Raisin, John Lau. Thornton	11. 0 a.m
7. 0 a.m	*Market-Street, Thomas Norcutt....	6. 0 p.m
9.30 a.m	*Market-Weighton, James Holmes..	3.20 p.m
9.45 a.m	Markfield, 8 miles from Leicester....	4.40 p.m
7. 0 a.m	*Marlborough, Wm. Wootten Lucy..	8. 0 p.m
12.15 p.m	Marlboro', 4 miles from Kingsbridge	8.30 a.m
7. 0 a.m	*Marlow, James Field	7.30 p.m
9. 0 a.m	Marple, 4 miles from Stockport	3.30 p.m
9. 0 a.m	Marr, 4 miles from Doncaster	4.30 p.m
11.30 a.m	Marsden, 3½ miles from Burnley	3. 0 p.m
10.30 a.m	Marsden, 7 miles from Huddersfield ..	1.30 p.m
8. 0 a.m	Marshfield, 10 m. from Chippenham	5. 0 p.m
2.10 p.m	Marsk, 6 miles from Guisborough ..	10.30 a.m
10.50 p.m	Marske, 5 mi. fr. Richmond, Yorks.	6.25 p.m
11.10 a.m	Marston, 6 miles from York	2.20 p.m
9. 0 a.m	Martock, 2½ miles from So. Petherton	4.10 p.m
11.15 a.m	Marton, 6 miles from Skipton	2. 0 p.m
11.15 a.m 4.30 p.m	*Maryport, Miss Jane Kitchen	9.10 a.m 10.22 a.m
11.25 a.m	Masham, 7 miles from Bedale	1. 0 p.m
4.15 p.m	Matten, 16 m. fr. Newcastle-on-Tyne	5.50 p.m

Letters from London delivered at h. m.	Town. Postmaster.	Box for London closes at h. m.
8. 0 a.m	*Matlock, Miss Frances Shore	6. 0 p.m
9. 0 a.m	Matlock-Village, 2 m. from Matlock	4. 0 p.m
9.30 a.m	Mattersea, 5 miles from Bawtry	3.45 p.m
10. 0 a.m	Mattishall, 5 miles from Dereham ..	2.15 p.m
9.15 a.m	Mayfield, 9 miles from Uckfield	4.45 p.m
8. 0 a.m	Measham, 12 miles from Atherstone	6. 0 p.m
8. 0 a.m	Melbourn, 3 miles from Royston	7. 0 p.m
7. 0 a.m	Melbourne, 8 miles from Derby	6.15 p.m
	Melcomb-Regis, *see* Weymouth	
7. 0 a.m	*Melksham, John Bullock.	8.30 p.m
9. 0 a.m	Mells, 3 miles from Frome..........	5. 0 p.m
1.50 p.m	Melmerby, 10 miles from Penrith....	9.35 a.m
6.10 p.m	Melton, 7 miles from Hull..........	10. 0 p.m
7.30 a.m	*Melton-Mowbray, Miss Anne Wright	7.15 p.m
9. 0 a.m	Meopham, 5½ miles from Gravesend..	4.30 p.m
8.30 a.m	Mere, 7 miles from Wincanton......	4.45 p.m
8. 3 a.m	Mereworth, 7 miles from Maidstone.	5.30 p.m
7. 0 a.m	Meriden, 6 miles from Coventry	8.30 p.m
7. 0 a.m	Merriott, 2 miles from Crewkerne ...	6. 0 p.m
7.15 a.m	Merrow, 2 miles from Guildford	6. 0 p.m
8. 0 a.m	Mersham, 4 miles from Ashford .. .	5. 0 p.m
7.30 a.m	Merstham, 3 miles from Reigate	6. 0 p.m
10.30 p.m	*Merthyr-Tydvil, Rhys Davis	2. 0 p.m
11. 0 a.m	Merton, 13 miles from Oakhampton	1. 0 p.m
8. 0 a.m	Messing, 3 miles from Kelvedon	6. 0 p.m
3.30 p.m	Mevagissy, 6 miles from St. Austle..	9. 0 a.m
10. 0 a.m	Mexborough, 9 miles from Rotherham	3. 0 p.m
7. 0 a.m	Micheldever, 3 miles from Andover rd.	7. 0 p.m
8.45 a.m	Middle-Claydon, 3¼ m. from Winslow	4.30 p.m
12. 0noon	Middleham, 10 miles from Bedale ..	12.45noon
9.30 a.m 6.20 p.m	*Middlesborough	3.20 p.m 6.20 p.m
3.15 p.m	Middleton-Teesdale, 10 miles from Barnard Castle	8.45 a.m
8. 0 a.m	Middleton, 5½ m. from Manchester ..	5.50 p.m
8. 0 a.m	Middleton Cheney, 3 m. from Banbury	2.45 p.m
12.10 p.m	Middleton One Row, 7 m. f. Darlington	6.50 p.m
9. 0 a.m	Middle-Wallop, 7 miles from Andover	4.45 p.m
7. 0 a.m	*Middlewich, Miss Elizth. Nicklin ..	7.30 p.m
8. 0 a.m	*Midhurst, Henry Goodner	6.15 p.m
8. 0 a.m	Midlavant, 2 miles from Chichester..	7. 0 p.m
7. 0 a.m	Midsummer-Norton, 10 m. from Bath	7.45 p.m
9. 0 a.m	Milborn-Port, 12 mi. fr. Shaftesbury	3.45 p.m
7.50 a.m	Milbourne S. Andrew. 8m. f. Blandford	6. 0 p.m
9.30 a.m	Milbridge, 9 miles from Leeds	2.30 p.m
7. 0 a.m	*Mildenhall, Charles Brown.........	8. 0 p.m
7.30 a.m	*Milford (Pembrk.) Mrs. C. A. Pritchard	5.30 p.m
9. 0 a.m	Milford, 4 miles from Lymington....	4.45 p.m
7.30 a.m	Millbrook, 2 miles from Southampton	9. 0 p.m
7. 0 a.m 9.30 a.m	*Milnthorpe, George Whitaker....	4.10 p.m 11. 0 p.m
8.30 a.m	Milnthorp-Toll-Bar, 3 m. f. Wakefield	5. 0 p.m
8. 0 a.m	Milton, 3½ miles from Cambridge ..	5. 0 p.m
7. 0 a.m	Milton, 1 mile from Sittingbourne ..	9. 0 p.m
9.30 a.m	Milton, 5 miles from Christchurch ..	5. 0 p.m
7.30 a.m	Milton, 2 miles from Pewsey........	5.45 p.m
8.30 a.m	Milton-Abbas, 6 miles from Blandford	5. 0 p.m
12. 0noon	Milton-Abbott, 7 m. from Launceston	1. 0 p.m
9.30 a.m	Milton-Ernest, 5 miles from Bedford	3.30 p.m
8. 0 a.m	Milverton, 4 m. fr. Wellington, Somerset	7.30 p.m
7. 0 a.m	Minchinhampton, 2 mi. fr. Chalford	6.15 p.m
7.15 a.m	*Minehead, Elizabeth Preddy	5. 0 p.m
8.30 a.m	Minster, 5 miles from Ramsgate	6.30 p.m
11. 0 a.m	Minsterley, 10 m. from Shrewsbury..	1.30 p.m
8.30 a.m	Mirfield, 5 miles from Dewsbury....	3.30 p.m
9. 0 a.m	Miserdine, 8 miles from Cirencester..	5.30 p.m
7.30 a.m	Missenden, 6 miles from Amersham	6.40 p.m
12. 0noon	Mitchell, 7 miles from Truro........	2. 0 p.m
7. 0 a.m	Mitchell-Dean, 5½ miles from Ross ..	5. 0 p.m
2.30 p.m	Mitford, 2 miles from Morpeth......	10.20 a.m
7. 0 a.m	Mochdrai, 9 miles from Conway	10. 0 p.m
11. 0 a.m	Modbury, 3 miles from Ermbridge ..	3.10 p.m
7.30 a.m	*Mold, John Catherall	6. 0 p.m
12. 0noon	Molesworth, 11 mi. from Huntingdon	2. 0 p.m
9. 0 a.m	Monksheath, 8 mi. from Congleton..	5.30 p.m
8.30 a.m	Monksilver, 15 miles from Taunton..	4.30 p.m
8.30 a.m	Monkton, 3½ miles from Taunton....	5.30 p.m
7. 0 a.m 8.30 p.m	*Monmouth, William Alfred Cossens	7.30 p.m
10. 0 a.m	Montacute, 4½ miles from Yeovil....	4. 0 p.m
11.30 a.m	Montgomery, 10 mi. from Welchpool	1.15 p.m
11. 0 a.m	Morchard Bishop, 7 m. from Crediton	2. 0 p.m

Letters from London delivered at h. m.	Town. Postmaster.	Box for London closes at h. m.
10. 0 a.m	Morden, 6 miles from Royston	6. 0 p.m
7. 0 a.m	*Moreton-in-Marsh, John Heath	7.30 p.m
9.30 a.m	Moretonhampstead, 11 m.f.Chudleigh	4.45 p.m
4.40 p.m	Morland, 8 miles from Penrith	7. 0 a.m
8. 0 a.m	Morley, 4 miles from Leeds	3.40 p.m
11.15 a.m	*Morpeth, James Jobling	1. 0 p.m
7. 0 a.m	Moseley, 3½ miles from Birmingham.	5. 0 p.m
10. 0 a.m	Mottram, 11 miles from Manchester.	5.45 p.m
8. 0 a.m	Moulton, 3 miles from Newmarket	7.30 p.m
8. 0 a.m	Moulton, 4 miles from Spalding	5. 0 p.m
8. 0 a.m	Mount-Lane, 7 mi. from Launceston	7.30 p.m
12. 0noon	Mounts, 11½ miles from Totness	2. 0 p.m
8.15 a.m	Mountsorrel, 4½ m. f. Loughborough	8. 0 p.m
11. 0 a.m	Mousehole, 3 miles from Penzance	2.30 p.m
8.30 a.m	*Much-Wenlock, Thomas Lawley	4.50 p.m
8.30 a.m	Muddeford, 2 miles from Christchurch	6.30 p.m
9.30 a.m	Mulbarton, 5½ miles from Norwich	4.30 p.m
7.15 p.m	Mumbles, 6 miles from Swansea	5. 0 a.m
8. 0 a.m	Mundford, 5 miles from Brandon	8.45 p.m
8. 0 a.m	Mundon, 3 miles from Maldon	5.30 p.m
12. 0noon	Mundsley, 21 miles from Norwich	1.30 p.m
8.45 a.m	Musbury, 5 miles from Axminster	4.15 p.m
12.30 p.m	Myfod, 8 miles from Welchpool	1. 0 p.m
5. 0 p.m	Mylor, 2½ miles from Falmouth	7. 0 a.m
11. 0 a.m	Naburn, 5 miles from York	3.20 p.m
9. 0 a.m	Nacton, 5 miles from Ipswich	6. 0 p.m
6.30 a.m	Nailsea, 9 miles from Bristol	3.30 p.m
7. 0 a.m	Nailsworth, 4½ miles from Stroud	5. 0 p.m
7.30 a.m	*Namptwich, E. H. Griffiths	8. 0 p.m
11.30 a.m	Nantyglo, 9 miles f. Abergavenny	12.30 p.m
10. 0 a.m	Napton, 5 miles from Southam	3.15 p.m
8.30 a.m	*Narbeth, John Williams	10. 0 p.m
9. 0 a.m	Narborough, 6 miles from Leicester	5. 0 p.m
11.15 a.m	Navenby, 9 miles from Grantham	1. 0 p.m
7.45 a.m	Nayland, 6 miles from Colchester	6.30 p.m
9. 0 a.m	Nazing, 6½ miles from Waltham-Cross	5. 0 p.m
11.30 a.m	Neasham, 3 miles from Darlington	7.30 p.m
1.30 p.m	*Neath, Matthew Whittington	11.30 a.m
9. 0 a.m	Neatshead, 14 miles from Norwich	5. 0 p.m
8. 0 a.m	Needham-Market, 8 miles fr. Ipswich	7. 0 p.m
7.30 a.m	Needingworth, 2 miles from St. Ives	8. 0 p.m
7.45 a.m	Neston, 10 miles from Chester	4.45 p.m
4. 0 p.m	Netherwitton, 8 miles from Morpeth.	8. 0 a.m
8. 0 a.m	Nettlebed, 6 m. f. Henley-on-Thames	6. 0 p.m
8. 0 p.m	Nevin, 6½ miles from Pwllheli	5. 0 a.m
8. 0 a.m	*Newark, Thomas Burgin	4.45 p.m
4.40 p.m	Newbiggin, 9 miles from Morpeth.	8. 0 a.m
4.30 p.m	Newbridge, 11 mi. fr. Newport, Mon.	8.10 a.m
10. 0 a.m	New-Brighton, 5 miles from Liverpool	2.30 p.m
10.30 a.m	New-Buckenham, 5 mi. fr. Attleboro'	4. 0 p.m
7.30 a.m	*Newbury, George Barnes	6.45 p.m
7. 0 a.m 11.10 a.m	Newby-Bridge, 14 mi. fr. Milnthorpe.	2. 0 p.m 9.50 p.m
11.10 p.m	Newby-Wiske, 7 miles from Thirsk	1.50 p.m
9. 0 a.m	Newcastle-Emlyn, 19 m.f.Carmarthen	5. 0 p.m
7. 0 a.m 10. 0 a.m	*Newcastle-on-Tyne, Lambton Loraine	2.30 p.m 10. 0 p.m
7. 0 a.m	*Newcastle-under-Lyne, Miss Elizbth. Brothers	9. 0 p.m
11. 0 a.m	New-Church, 10 miles from Rochdale	3. 0 p.m
7. 0 a.m	Newenden, 14 m. from Staplehurst	7. 0 p.m
7. 0 a.m	Newent, 9 miles from Gloucester	5.15 p.m
8. 0 a.m	Newhaven, 6 miles from Lewes	6. 0 p.m
5. 0 p.m	New-House, 6 miles from Totness	8. 0 a.m
8.45 a.m	Newick, 4½ miles from Uckfield	5.15 p.m
8. 0 a.m	Newington, 3 mi. from Sittingbourne	6. 0 p.m
9.30 a.m	Newland, 2 miles from Coleford	2. 0 p.m
10. 0 a.m	Newlyn, 1½ miles from Penzance	3.30 p.m
10. 0 a.m	Newlyn, 8 miles from Truro	11. 0 a.m
7. 0 a.m 4. 0 p.m	*Newmarket, William Le Pla	7.30 a.m 10.10 p.m
10. 0 a.m	New-Mills, 8 miles from Stockport	3.15 p.m
7.30 a.m	*Newnham, Richard Morse	9. 0 p.m
8. 0 a.m	Newnham, 6 miles from Sittingbourne	5.30 p.m
9. 0 a.m 6. 0 p.m	*Newport, (Isle of Wight), Miss Tabitha Wavell	3. 0 p.m
8. 0 a.m	*Newport, Mon. Marmaduke Brewer	5.15 p.m
7.30 a.m	*Newport, Salop, John Justice	5.30 p.m
9.30 a.m	Newport, 1 mile from Barnstaple	4. 0 p.m
9. 0 a.m	Newport, 9 mi. fr. Bishop's Stortford	7.30 p.m
9.20 a.m	Newport, 9 miles from Howden	3.30 p.m
8.50 a.m	Newport, Pembroke, 11m.f. Cardigan	3. 0 p.m

Letters from London delivered at h. m.	Town. Postmaster.	Box for London closes at h. m.
7. 0 a.m 1.15 p.m	*Newport Pagnell, Thos. Edwd. Staines	9. 0 a.m 8.30 p.m
4.15 p.m	New-Quay, 6 miles fr. Aberayron	8.30 a.m
11. 0 a.m	New-Quay, 7 miles from St. Columb	4. 0 p.m
12. 0noon	New-Radnor, 6½ miles from Kington.	12.30 p.m
8. 0 a.m	Newton, 3 mi. from Burton-on-Trent	5.30 p.m
10.40 a.m	Newton, 11 miles from Milnthorpe	3. 0 p.m
11.15 a.m	Newton, 15 miles from Newark	2.30 p.m
7. 0 a.m	Newton, 4½ miles from Warrington	6. 0 p.m
8. 0 a.m	*Newton Abbot, Thomas K. Sweeting	5.15 p.m
9. 0 a.m 6. 0 p.m	Newton-Heath, 3 mi.fr. Manchester	2.30 p.m 9.30 p.m
9. 0 a.m	Newton Moor, 9 mi. from Manchester	4.30 p.m
7. 0 a.m	Newton St. Cyres, 4½ m. from Exeter	7. 0 p.m
7. 0 a.m	Newton St. Looe, 3½ miles from Bath	6.30 p.m
	New-Romney, *see* Romney	
12. 0noon	*Newtown, Miss Ann Williams	1. 0 p.m
8. 0 a.m	Ninfield, 5 miles from Battle	8. 0 p.m
10.30 a.m	Niton, 9 m. fr. Newport Isle of Wight	2. 0 p.m
8. 0 a.m	Nonnington, 4 mi. from Wingham	6. 0 p.m
8.30 a.m	Norham, 8 miles from Berwick	1.30 p.m
9.30 a.m	Normanton-Station, 5 m.f. Wakefield	4.10 p.m
7.45 a.m	*Northallerton, Henry Harrison	4.40 p.m
12. 0noon	Northam, 1½ miles from Bideford	2. 0 p.m
7. 0 a.m 1.30 p.m	*Northampton, George N. Wetton	9.30 a.m 10. 0 p.m
10.15 a.m	Northaw, 5 miles from Barnet	4.30 p.m
8.30 a.m	North-Brook, 2 miles from Exeter	7. 0 p.m
8. 0 a.m	North Cadbury, 29 miles from Bath	5. 0 p.m
	North-Cave, *see* Cave.	
9.15 a.m	North-Cerney, 4 m. from Cirencester	4. 0 p.m
8. 0 a.m	North-Chapel, 5 mi. fr. Petworth	5. 0 p.m
9. 0 a.m	North-Crowley, 3 m.f. Newport Pagnel	6.30 p.m
11. 0 a.m	North-Currey, 7 miles from Taunton	4. 0 p.m
8. 0 a.m	Northfield, 6 miles from Birmingham	4.15 p.m
7.30 a.m	Northfleet, 1½ miles from Gravesend	7. 0 p.m
11.30 a.m	North-Grimston, 4 miles fr. Malton	2.20 p.m
7. 0 a.m	Northiam, 16 miles from Staplehurst.	7. 0 p.m
7. 0 a.m	*Northleach, Elizabeth Smith	5.15 p.m
10.20 a.m	North-Lopham, 15 miles from Thetford	3.15 p.m
7. 0 a.m	North Nibley, 2 m.f. Wotton-und.-edg.	5.15 p.m
8. 0 a.m	North-Ockenden, 7 mi. fr. Romford	5.30 p.m
7. 0 a.m	Northop, 11½ miles from Chester	5.30 p.m
2. 0 p.m	Northowram, 2½ miles from Halifax	4. 0 p.m
8.15 a.m	North-Petherton, 4 m. f. Bridgewater	5.15 p.m
	North-Shields, *see* Shields (North)	
8.10 p.m	North-Sunderland, 8 m. from Belford	10. 0 p.m
9. 0 a.m	North-Tawton, 12 m. from Crediton	4. 0 p.m
9.30 a.m	North-Walsham, 15 mi. fr. Norwich	3.45 p.m
7. 0 a.m	*Northwich, William Fryer	8.30 p.m
10.30 a.m	Norton, 8 miles from Mansfield	3.25 p.m
10. 0 a.m	Norton, 5 miles from Sheffield	2. 0 p.m
11. 0 a.m	Norton, 1 mile from Stockton	1.10 p.m
7. 0 a.m 5.30 p.m	*Norwich, William Power Hicks	10. 0 p.m 5.55 p.m
8. 3 a.m	Norwood-Green, 2½ m.from Hounslow	6.30 p.m
7. 0 a.m 4.30 p.m	*Nottingham, John Crosby	7.30 p.m
7. 0 a.m	Nuneaton, 8 miles from Coventry	8.30 p.m
10. 0 a.m	Nuneham, 5 miles from Oxford	4.30 p.m
8.30 a.m	Nunney, 3½ miles from Frome	4. 0 p.m
7.30 a.m	Nursling, 4 miles from Southampton	7.30 p.m
6.40 a.m	Nuthurst, 2 miles from Horsham	7. 0 p.m
7.50 a.m	Oakengates, 3½ m.f. Wellington, Salop	5.10 p.m
9.30 a.m	Oakford, 8½ mi. fr. Tiverton	4.30 p.m
8. 0 a.m	*Oakham, Miss Jane Stimson	6. 0 p.m
8. 0 a.m	*Oakhampton, Richard Crotch	4.45 p.m
7. 0 a.m	Oakhill, 15 miles from Bath	8. 3 p.m
	*Oakingham *see* Wokingham	
8.15 a.m	Oakley, 7 miles from Thame	5. 0 p.m
10. 0 a.m	Ockbrook, 6 miles from Derby	5.20 p.m
9.30 a.m	Odell, 10 miles from Bedford	3. 0 p.m
7. 0 a.m	*Odiham, Adelaide Webb	6.30 p.m
10. 0 a.m	Old-Buckenham, 3 m.from Attleboro'	5. 0 p.m
7. 0 a.m	Oldbury, 5 miles from Birmingham	7. 0 p.m
7.30 a.m	Old-Down, 5 miles from Radstock	5.30 p.m
8. 0 a.m	Old-Hall-Green, 5 miles from Ware	6.30 p.m
9. 0 a.m	*Oldham, William Bamford	5. 0 p.m 9. 0 p.m
8. 0 a.m	Old-Hurst, 6 miles from Huntingdon	4. 0 p.m
7.30 a.m	Old-Passage, 12 miles from Bristol	5. 0 p.m
10. 0 a.m	Old-Swan, 3¼ miles from Liverpool	4.30 p.m

Letters from London delivered at h. m.	Town. Postmaster.	Box for London closes at h. m.
9. 0 a.m	Old-Windsor-Green, 2 m. fr. Windsor	4.45 p.m
10.15 a.m	*Ollerton, Thomas Roe	3. 0 p.m
8. 0 a.m	Olney, 5 mi. from Newport-Pagnell	5.45 p.m
9. 0 a.m	Olveston, 10 miles from Bristol	2.15 p.m
9. 0 a.m	Ombersley, 6 miles from Stourport	4. 0 p.m
8.30 a.m	*Ongar, Miss Anna Maria Scruby	5.30 p.m
11. 0 a.m	Onibury, 5 miles from Ludlow	2. 0 p.m
7.30 a.m	Openshaw, 3 miles from Manchester	6.15 p.m
11.30 a.m	Oreston, 1 mile from Plymouth	2.40 p.m
8.30 a.m	Orford, 16 miles from Woodbridge	6. 0 p.m
1. 0 p.m	Ormesby, 6½ miles from Stockton	12.30 p.m
8. 0 a.m	*Ormskirk, Miss Alice Wignall	4. 0 p.m
9.30 a.m	Orpington, 6 miles from Bromley	5.30 p.m
8. 0 a.m	Orrell, 4 miles from Wigan	6. 0 p.m
9. 0 a.m	Orset, 14 miles from Romford	4.30 p.m
11.30 a.m	Osmington, 4 miles from Weymouth	3. 0 p.m
9.30 a.m	Osmotherley, 11 miles from Thirsk	3.15 p.m
8. 0 a.m	Ossett, 4 miles from Wakefield	5. 0 p.m
10.30 a.m	Oswaldkirk, 20 miles from York	2.50 p.m
10. 0 a.m	*Oswestry, Miss Sarah Babington	3.30 p.m
7.30 a.m	Otford, 4 miles from Seven Oaks	2.30 p.m
7.45 a.m	Otham, 3½ miles from Maidstone	6. 0 p.m
8.30 a.m	*Otley, Mrs. Sarah Holmes	4.15 p.m
9. 0 a.m	Otley, 8 miles from Ipswich	5. 0 p.m
8. 0 a.m	Otterbourne, 4 m. from Winchester	6. 0 p.m
9. 0 a.m	Ottershaw, 2½ miles from Chertsey	6. 0 p.m
9. 0 a.m	Otterton, 3 miles from Sidmouth	4.15 p.m
7.30 a.m 7.30 p.m	Ottery-St.-Mary, 6 miles fr. Honiton	6.30 a.m
9. 0 a.m	Oulton, 5 miles from Leeds	3.30 p.m
7. 0 a.m	*Oundle, Miss Ann Everest	10. 0 p.m
9.30 a.m	Ouseburn, 12½ miles from York	4.10 p.m
7. 0 a.m	Ouseley, 3 miles from Windsor	4.30 p.m
10. 0 a.m	Outwell, 6 miles from Wisbeach	3.30 p.m
10. 0 a.m	Overseal, 4½ m. fr. Ashby-de-la-Zouch	3.15 p.m
7.30 a.m	*Overton, Hants, William Beale	7.30 p.m
10. 0 a.m	Overton, Flints, 5 mi. from Ellesmere	3.45 p.m
9. 0 a.m	Ovingdean, 4 miles from Brighton	5. 0 p.m
4.30 p.m	Owersby, 6 miles from Market Raisin	8. 0 a.m
10.30 a.m	Owsden, 7 miles from Newmarket	5.30 p.m
12. 0noon	Owston, 14 miles from Bawtry	9. 0 a.m
9.30 a.m	Oxenden, 3 mi. from Market Harboro'	4. 0 p.m
7. 0 a.m 1.30 p.m	*Oxford, Joseph Warne	9.30 a.m 10. 0 p.m
7. 0 a.m	Oxted, 10 miles from Reigate	6.15 p.m
9. 0 a.m	Oxton, 2 miles from Birkenhead	4. 0 p.m
7. 0 a.m 12.30 p.m	Padiham, 3 miles from Burnley	1.30 p.m 8.30 p.m
2.20 p.m	Padstow, 15 miles from Bodmin	7.45 a.m
9.30 a.m	Paglesham, 8 miles from Rochford	3.30 p.m
9. 0 a.m	Paington, 3 miles from Torquay	3.30 p.m
7.30 a.m	Painswick, 6 miles from Glo'ster	5. 0 p.m
8. 0 a.m	Pangbourne, 6 miles from Reading	6. 0 p.m
9. 0 a.m	Parkgate, 12 miles from Chester	4. 0 p.m
6. 0 a.m	Parkgate, 5 miles from Maidstone	7. 0 p.m
7. 0 a.m	Parkstone, 1¾ miles from Poole	6.30 p.m
10.30 a.m	Parndon, 9 m. from Waltham Cross	4. 0 p.m
8. 0 a.m	Passingford-Bridge, 7 m. fr. Romford	7. 0 p.m
1.30 p.m	Pateley-Bridge, 12 miles from Ripon	7.15 a.m
12. 0 p.m	Patrington, 16 miles from Hull	1.30 p.m
8. 0 a.m	Pattingham, 6 m. fr. Wolverhampton	6. 0 p.m
9.45 a.m	Paulton, 12 miles from Bristol	3. 0 p.m
8.40 a.m	Paxton, 5 miles from Berwick	3.15 p.m
9. 0 a.m	Peasenhall, 6 mi. from Saxmundham	5. 0 p.m
7. 0 a.m	Peasmarsh, 22 miles from Staplehurst	5.30 p.m
8.30 a.m	Peas-Pottage Gate, 6 mi. fr. Crawley	5.30 p.m
7.30 a.m	Peel, 12 mi. fr. Douglas, Isle-of-Man	4.30 p.m
7. 0 a.m	Pemberton, 2½ miles from Wigan	6. 0 p.m
9. 0 a.m	Pembrey, 5 miles from Llanelly	2.45 p.m
12. 0noon	Pembridge, 8 miles from Leominster	12.30 p.m
7. 0 a.m	*Pembroke, John Ormond	10. 0 p.m
8. 0 a.m	Pembroke Dock, 1 m. fr. Pembroke	8.30 p.m
8. 0 a.m	Pembury, 5 miles from Tunbridge	5.30 p.m
8.30 a.m	Pencraig, 4 miles from Ross	4. 0 p.m
11. 0 a.m	Penistone, 8 miles from Barnsley	3. 0 p.m
7. 0 a.m	Penketh, 3 miles from Warrington	6.15 p.m
8. 0 a.m 4. 0 p.m	*Penkridge, Miss Mary Scarlett	9. 0 p.m
7. 0 a.m 12. 0noon	Pennybridge, 18 m. from Milnthorp	1.50 p.m 9.10 p.m
7. 0 a.m 1. 0 p.m	*Penrith, Martindale Scott	12.50 p.m 7.50 p.m

Letters from London delivered at h. m.	Town. Postmaster.	Box for London closes at h. m.
3.30 p.m	*Penryn, Francis Bice	9.20 a.m
8. 0 a.m	Pensford, 6 miles from Bristol	4. 0 p.m
8.30 a.m	Penshurst, 6 miles from Tunbridge	6. 0 p.m
9. 0 a.m	Penton-Mewsey, 3 mi. fr. Andover	5. 0 p.m
8.30 a.m	Pentraeth, 7 miles from Bangor	4.30 p.m
12.30 p.m	Pentre-Voelas, 15 miles from Corwen	12. 0noon
12.30 a.m	Pen-ybont, 10 miles from Rhayader	11.30 a.m
6. 0 p.m	*Penzance, Miss Ellen C. Swain	10. 0 p.m
7. 0 a.m	Perry-Street, 1½ miles from Gravesend	7.30 p.m
7. 0 a.m	*Pershore, William Workman	6. 0 p.m
7. 0 a.m	*Peterborough, Thomas Crane	10. 0 p.m
1. 0 p.m	Peterchurch, 13 miles from Hereford	6. 0 a.m
7. 0 a.m	*Petersfield, William Minchin	8.45 p.m
7. 0 a.m	*Petworth, George Arnold	7.15 p.m
11. 0 a.m	Petrockston, 12 m. fr. Oakhampton	2. 0 p.m
10. 0 a.m	Pevensey, 6 miles from Eastbourne	4.45 p.m
7. 0 a.m	*Pewsey, Frederick Banning	6. 0 p.m
8. 0 a.m	Phillips-Norton, 7 miles from Bath	11. 0 a.m
10. 0 a.m	*Pickering, Mrs. Frances Wilsthorp	2.50 p.m
8.20 a.m	Piddletown, 11 miles from Blandford	5.15 p.m
10. 0 a.m	Piecomb, 6 miles from Brighton	4. 0 p.m
10.40 a.m	Pierse-Bridge, 5½ m. from Darlington	2.30 p.m
8.30 a.m	Pill, 6 miles from Bristol	4. 0 p.m
11.30 a.m	Pillgwenlly, 1 mile fr. Newport, Mon.	12.30 p.m
10.15 a.m	Pilton, ½ mile from Barnstaple	5. 0 p.m
7. 0 a.m	Pilton, 3 miles from Shepton-Mallet	6.30 p.m
9.30 a.m	Pinkneys-Green, 2 m. fr. Maidenhead	6. 0 p.m
8.15 a.m	Pinner, 5 miles from Watford	6. 0 p.m
8. 0 a.m	Plaxtole, 6 miles from Seven-Oaks	5.30 p.m
9.55 a.m	*Plymouth, Charles Markes	3.15 p.m
9.30 a.m	*Plympton, Miss Emma Duley	3.30 p.m
9. 0 a.m	*Pocklington, Lucy Scaife	4.15 p.m
5. 0 p.m	Polperro, 12 miles from Liskeard	9. 0 p.m
11. 0 a.m	Ponsanooth, 2 miles from Truro	9.15 a.m
6. 0 p.m	Ponterdulais, 9 miles from Swansea	10. 0 p.m
8. 0 a.m	*Pontefract, James Lucas	6. 0 p.m
3.10 p.m	Ponteland, 7 m. from Newcastle-Tyne	6.25 p.m
10. 0 a.m	Pontesbury, 7½ miles from Shrewsbury	2.30 p.m
10.30 a.m	Pontypool, 7 miles from Usk	12.15 p.m
3.30 p.m	Pontypridd, 12 miles from Cardiff	6.30 a.m
7. 0 a.m	Pool, 11 miles from Truro	7.30 p.m
7.30 a.m	*Poole, Mrs. Jane Elizbth. Moores	7.15 p.m
2.20 p.m	Pooley-Bridge, 5 miles from Penrith	8.20 a.m
9. 0 a.m	Porlock, 32 miles from Taunton	3.30 p.m
9.30 a.m	Portbury, 7 miles from Bristol	3.10 p.m
7. 0 a.m	Portchester, 3 miles from Fareham	6.30 p.m
10. 0 a.m	Portesham, 8 miles from Dorchester	4. 0 p.m
9. 0 a.m	Porthleaven, 3 miles from Helstone	4.30 p.m
10.10 a.m	Portishead, 11 miles from Bristol	2. 0 p.m
12. 0noon	Portland, Isle, 5 mi. from Weymouth	3. 0 p.m
6. 0 p.m	Portmadoc, 21 miles from Carnarvon	7. 0 a.m
	Portsea, *see* Portsmouth	
8.30 a.m	Portslade, 3 miles from Shoreham	6. 0 a.m 6. 0 p.m
7. 0 a.m 4. 0 p.m	*Portsmouth, George Welch	7.30 a.m 10. 0 p.m
8.30 a.m	Pottern, 2 miles from Devizes	6.30 p.m
9.30 a.m 1.30 p.m	Pottersbarr, 3½ miles from Barnet	8. 0 a.m 3. 0 p.m 5.30 p.m
9. 0 a.m	Potton, 5 miles from Biggleswade	7.30 p.m
9.10 a.m	Poulton, 12 miles from Preston	3.40 p.m
8.30 a.m	Poulton-le-Sands, 4 m. from Lancaster	4.30 p.m
7. 0 a.m	Powburn, 11 miles from Alnwick	11.20 a.m
7. 0 a.m	Powick, 3 miles from Worcester	6.30 p.m
9.30 a.m	Prees, 15 miles from Shrewsbury	2. 0 p.m
7. 0 a.m	*Prescot, John Culshaw	7.25 p.m
8. 0 a.m	Prestbury, 1½ miles from Cheltenham	7. 0 p.m
11. 5 a.m	*Presteign, Miss Mary Askey	1.45 p.m
8. 0 a.m 6.30 p.m	*Preston, Rachael Hardman	6.30 p.m 10. 0 p.m
9.30 a.m	Preston 1½ mile from Yeovil	5. 0 p.m
8. 0 a.m	Preston, 2 miles from Brighton	5. 0 p.m
9. 0 a.m	Preston-Bissett, 5 m. fr. Buckingham	5.30 p.m
7. 0 a.m 4.45 p.m	*Preston-Brook, Miss Charlotte Bosworth	3. 0 a.m 8.10 p.m
9. 0 a.m	Preston-Candover, 7 m. fr. Andover rd	6. 0 p.m
7. 0 a.m	Princes-Risborough, 11 m. from Tring	7. 0 p.m
7.30 a.m	Prittlewell, 3 miles from Rochford	4.15 p.m
10. 0 a.m	Probus, 5½ miles from Truro	9. 0 p.m
3. 5 p.m	Prudhoe, 10 m. fr. Newcastle-on-Tyne	7.18 a.m
8. 0 a.m	Puckeridge, 6 miles from Ware	6.30 p.m

Letters from London delivered at h. m.	Town. Postmaster.	Box for London closes at h. m.
9.30 a.m	Pucklechurch, 8 miles from Bristol..	2. 0 p.m
8.30 a.m	Pudsey, 6 miles from Leeds	3.10 p.m
8.30 a.m	Pulborough, 6 miles from Petworth..	5.30 p.m
1.45 p.m	Pumpsaint, 12 m. from Llandovery..	7. 0 a.m
8. 0 a.m	Purbrook 6½ miles from Portsmouth	5. 0 p.m
8.30 a.m	Purfleet, 9 miles from Romford	4.30 p.m
9. 0 a.m	Purleigh, 4½ miles from Maldon	4.15 p.m
9.30 a.m	Purton, 6 miles from Swindon	6.45 p.m
8.15 a.m	Putsom, 12 miles from Bridgewater	6. 0 p.m
10. 0 a.m	Puttenham, 4½ miles from Guildford	4.30 p.m
10.30 a.m / 5.30 p.m	*Pwllheli, Evan Evans	7.30 a.m / 2.30 p.m
3.30 p.m	Pyle, 5½ miles from Bridgend	8. 0 a.m
7. 0 a.m	*Queenborough, Mrs. Isabella Hall..	7.30 p.m
11. 0 a.m	Queen-Camel, 7 miles from Sherborne	2. 0 p.m
8.15 a.m	Quendon, 6½ m. f. Bishop's Stortford	7.45 p.m
8.30 a.m	Radcliffe, 7 miles from Nottingham..	6. 0 p.m
	Radnor, *see* New-Radnor	
6. 0 a.m	Radstock, 8 miles from Bath	9.30 p.m
8.30 a.m	Ragland, 8 miles from Monmouth	3.15 p.m
8.30 a.m	Rainford, 7 miles from Prescot	3. 0 p.m
7.30 a.m / 2. 0 p.m	Rainham, 5 miles from Romford..	2. 0 p.m / 6. 0 p.m
9.30 a.m	Rainham, 6 m. from Sittingbourne..	8. 0 p.m
7. 0 a.m	Rainhill, 2 miles from Prescot	5.45 p.m
11.30 a.m	Raithby, 2 miles from Spilsby	2.30 p.m
1. 0 p.m	Ramsbottom, 4 miles from Bury, Lancashire	3. 0 p.m
18. 0 a.m	Ramsbury, 4 miles from Hungerford.	6.45 p.m
1. 0 a.m	Ramsey, 12 miles from Huntingdon..	3. 0 p.m
8.30 a.m	Ramsey, 16 miles from Douglas, I.M.	3.30 p.m
9. 0 a.m	Ramsey, 4 miles from Harwich	4. 0 p.m
7. 0 a.m / 7. 0 p.m	*Ramsgate John Barnet Hodgson	8.30 p.m
2. 0noon	Ratcliffe, 7 miles from Manchester..	12. 0noon
9.30 a.m	Raunds, 4 miles from Thrapstone	3. 0 p.m
7. 0 a.m	*Ravenglass, John Brown	4. 0 p.m
12.30 p.m	Ravensworth, 6 m. f. Richmond, Yorks.	4.20 p.m
9.50 a.m	Rawcliffe, 3 miles from Selby	3.35 p.m
8.30 a.m	Rawdon, 7 miles from Leeds	4.30 p.m
8. 0 a.m	Rawmarch, 4 miles from Rotherham	5. 0 p.m
9.30 a.m	Rawtenstall, 17 m. f. Manchester..	4. 0 p.m
7. 0 a.m	Rayleigh, 15 miles from Ingatestone.	6. 0 p.m
7. 0 a.m	Rayne, 2 miles from Braintree	6. 0 p.m
7. 0 a.m / 1. 0 p.m	*Reading, John Berry Clacy	10.30 a.m / 8.30 p.m
11. 0 a.m	Rearsby, 8 miles from Leicester	2. 0 p.m
7. 0 a.m	Redbridge, 4 miles from Southampton	9. 0 p.m
8. 0 a.m	Redburn, 4½ miles from St. Alban's..	6.15 p.m
2. 0 p.m	Redcar, 7 miles from Guisboro'	10.40 a.m
7. 0 a.m	*Redditch, Miss Elizabeth Taylor	7.15 p.m
7. 0 a.m	Redhill, 1½ mile from Reigate	7. 0 p.m
9.30 p.m	Redmarley, 5 miles from Ledbury..	2.30 p.m
4. 0 p.m	*Redruth, Miss Mary Michell	8. 0 a.m
9.15 a.m	Reepham, 12 miles from Norwich	4. 0 p.m
11.50 a.m	Reeth, 10 m. f. Richmond, Yorkshire	5.45 p.m
7. 0 a.m / 12.30 p.m	*Reigate, James Alexander Brewer	11.30 a.m / 9. 0 p.m
7.30 a.m	Rendham, 2 miles from Saxmundham	5.30 p.m
8.30 a.m	Repton, 3 mi. from Burton-on-Trent	4.45 p.m
9.30 a.m	*Retford, Mrs. Elizabeth Suter	4. 0 p.m
10. 0 a.m	Rewe, 5 miles from Exeter	4. 0 p.m
11. 0 a.m	Reynoldstone, 13 miles from Swansea	3.30 a.m
2. 0 p.m	*Rhayader, Miss Mary Jones	10. 0 a.m
8.30 a.m	Rhosymedre, 6½ miles from Wrexham	3. 0 p.m
10.20 a.m	Rhuddlan, 3 miles from St. Asaph..	7.30 p.m
11. 0 a.m	Rhyl, 6 miles from St. Asaph	6.45 p.m
1. 0 p.m	Rhymney, 6 miles from Merthyr	10.45 a.m
9.35 a.m	*Richmond, Yorkshire, Mrs. Alice Metcalfe..	3. 0 p.m / 8. 0 p.m
7. 0 a.m / 2.45 p.m	*Rickmansworth, Miss Susannah Newman	9.45 a.m / 6. 0 p.m
11. 0 a.m	Ridge, 4 miles from Barnet	4.30 p.m
8. 0 a.m	Ridgemount, 3 miles from Woburn..	5.30 p.m
8.30 a.m	Ridgewell, 10 miles from Halstead..	4.30 p.m
3.30 p.m	Ridingmill, 15 miles fr. Newcastle T.	6.50 p.m
7.30 a.m	Ringmer, 3 miles from Lewes	6.30 p.m
7. 0 a.m	*Ringwood, John Benson	9.30 p.m
7. 0 a.m	*Ripley, Surrey, James Gwinn	7.45 p.m
9.15 a.m	Ripley, 6 miles from Alfreton	5.15 p.m
10. 0 a.m	*Ripon, Thomas Procter	3. 5 p.m / 6. 0 p.m
11.15 a.m	Ripley, 4 miles from Harrogate	2.15 p.m
3.30 p.m	Risca, 7 miles from Newport	9.15 a.m
9.30 a.m	River, 2½ miles, from Dover	6. 0 p.m
7. 0 a.m	Riverhead, 1½ mile from Seven-Oaks	6.45 p.m
8.30 a.m	Roade, 5 miles from Northampton..	5.30 p.m
7. 0 a.m	*Robertsbridge, Robert Marchant..	8.45 p.m
7.30 a.m	Robertsend-Street, 1½ mi. f. Worcester	4.30 p.m
6. 0 p.m	Robinhoods-Bay, 6½ m. from Whitby	8. 0 a.m
7. 0 p.m / 9. 0 a.m	*Rochdale, Edmund Wrigley	5. 0 p.m / 10. 0 p.m
4. 0 p.m	Roche, 5 miles from St. Austle	8.45 a.m
7. 0 a.m / 2. 0 p.m	*Rochester, Edward Finch	11.45 a.m / 9. 0 p.m
8. 0 a.m	*Rochford, Thomas White	5. 0 p.m
8. 0 a.m	*Rockingham, Miss Ann Hunter	4.30 p.m
7.30 a.m	Rodney-Stoke, 5 mi. fr. Wells, Som.	6.30 p.m
7.30 a.m	Rogate, 4 miles from Petersfield	6.45 p.m
7. 0 a.m	Rolvenden, 7 miles from Cranbrook..	7. 0 p.m
2.30 p.m	Romald-Kirk, 6 m. fr. Barnard Castle.	9.30 a.m
	*Romford, *see* "London District Offi."	
7. 0 a.m	*Romney (New), James Vidgen	9. 0 p.m
7. 0 a.m	*Romsey, Moses Pepper	9. 0 p.m
8. 0 a.m	Ropley, 4 miles from Alresford	6.30 p.m
7. 0 a.m	*Ross, William Paine	8.30 p.m
5. 0 p.m	Rothbury, 15 miles from Morpeth..	10. 0 p.m
8. 0 a.m	Rotherfield, 7 m. fr. Tunbridge-Wells	5.30 p.m
9. 0 a.m	Rotherfield-Peppard, 3 m. fr. Henley	5. 0 p.m
7. 0 a.m / 6. 0 p.m	*Rotherham, Mrs Martha Wilson..	10. 0 p.m / 7.15 p.m
9. 0 a.m	Rothwell, 4 miles from Kettering	4. 0 p.m
9. 0 a.m	Rothwell, 4 miles from Leeds	3.15 p.m
9.30 a.m	Rottingdean, 4½ miles from Brighton	4.30 p.m
8. 0 a.m	*Rougham, James Rayner	6. 0 p.m
7. 0 a.m	Rowde, 2 miles from Devizes	6. 0 p.m
9. 0 a.m	Roxwell, 6 miles from Chelmsford..	5. 0 p.m
9. 0 a.m	Roydon, 4 miles from Ware	5. 0 p.m
7. 0 a.m	*Royston, Thomas Daintry, jun.	9. 0 p.m
10. 0 a.m	Royton, 2 miles from Oldham	1.20 p.m
8. 0 a.m	Ruabon, 5 miles from Wrexham	4.45 p.m
9. 0 a.m	Ruddington, 5 miles from Nottingham	5. 0 p.m
8.30 a.m	Rudgeway, 8 miles from Bristol	3. 0 p.m
10. 0 a.m	Rudgwick, 7 miles from Horsham..	3.45 p.m
7. 0 a.m / 2. 0 p.m	*Rugby, George Ashby	9. 0 a.m / 9. 0 p.m
7. 0 a.m	*Rugeley, Matthew Woodward	8. 0 p.m
	Rumford, *see* "London District Offi."	
7. 0 a.m	*Runcorn, Thomas Chantler Stelfox	7. 0 p.m / 10. 0 p.m
12.30 p.m	Rushyford, 5 miles fr. Bp. Auckland.	8.20 a.m
9. 0 a.m	Ruislip, 4 miles from Uxbridge	6. 0 p.m
9.30 a.m	*Ruthin, Samuel Jones	3.45 p.m
11. 0 a.m	Ruyton, 10 miles from Shrewsbury.	1.30 p.m
9. 0 a.m / 4.30 p.m	*Ryde, Isle of Wight, Philip Thomas Hellyer..	6. 0 p.m
7.15 a.m	*Rye, Alfred Miller	7.15 p.m
1.20 p.m	Ryton, 6 miles from Newcastle	7. 0 p.m
7. 0 a.m / 2. 0 p.m	*Saffron-Walden, Francis Turner..	9. 0 p.m / 9.45 a.m
8. 0 a.m	St. Agnes, 9 miles from Truro	5. 0 p.m
7. 0 a.m / 4. 0 p.m	*St. Alban's, George Ward	7.50 a.m / 7. 0 p.m
11.20 a.m	St. Anthony, 4½ mi. from Devonport.	9. 0 a.m
12. 0noon	St. Arvans, 2 miles from Chepstow..	10.0 a.m
7. 0 a.m / 9.15 a.m	*St. Asaph, Mrs. Margaret Lodge.	3.30 p.m / 10. 0 p.m
2.30 p.m	*St. Austle, Joseph Drew	10. 0 a.m
11.10 a.m / 6.10 p.m	St. Bees, 4 miles from Whitehaven.	10. 0 p.m / 2.50 p.m
5. 0 p.m	St. Blazey, 5 miles from St. Austle..	8. 0 a.m
11.15 a.m	St. Briavels, 9½ mi. fr. Monmouth..	12.45 p.m
6. 0 p.m	*St. Clear's, David Morris	10. 0 p.m
7.30 a.m	St. Clements, 1 mile from Oxford..	6.30 p.m
2. 0 p.m	*St. Columb, Mrs. Elizabeth George..	10. 0 a.m
7. 0 a.m	St. Cross, 1 mile from Winchester..	7. 0 p.m
8. 0 a.m	St. David's, 16 mi. fr. Haverfordwest	3.50 p.m
7. 0 a.m	St. Day, 7 miles from Truro	6. 0 p.m
8. 0 a.m	St. Faith, 4 miles from Norwich	4.45 p.m
8. 0 a.m	St. George's, 2¾ miles from Bristol..	5.15 p.m
9. 0 a.m	St. George's, 6½ miles from Bristol..	3.30 p.m
12. 0noon	St. German's, 10 m. from Devonport.	8. 0 a.m
7.15 a.m	*St. Helen's Lancashire, Miss Helen Greenhalgh	6.30 p.m

Letters from London delivered at h. m.	Town. Postmaster.	Box for London closes at h. m.
10. 0 a.m	St. Helen's, 4½ miles from Ryde	2. 0 p.m
5.45 p.m	St. Ives, Cornwall, 6 m. f. Truro....	9.30 p.m
7. 0 a.m	*St. Ives, Hunts, John Frank	9. 0 p.m
7. 0 a.m	St. John's, 1 mile from Worcester...	7. 0 p.m
1.45 a.m	St. John's Chapel, 28 m. fr. Durham	4.10 p.m
12. 0noon	St. John's Common, 10 m. fr. Brighton	7.25 p.m
12. 0noon	St. Just, 7 miles from Penzance	2. 0 p.m
12. 0noon	St. Keverne, 14 mi. fr. Helstone	12. 0noon
8.15 a.m	St. Lawrence, 1 mile from Ramsgate	8. 0 p.m
7. 0 a.m 6. 0 p.m	*St. Leonard's on Sea, Charles Heywood Southall	9.35 p.m 7.15 a.m
10. 0 a.m	St. Mary Bourne, 7 m. from Andover	4. 0 p.m
10. 0 a.m	St. Mary Church, 2 m. from Torquay	3. 0 p.m
9. 0 a.m	St. Mary Cray, 5 miles from Bromley	5.45 p.m
7.30 p.m	St. Mawes, 19 miles from St. Austle..	9.30 p.m
7. 0 a.m	*St. Neots, John Barker	8. 0 p.m
3.30 p.m	St. Nicholas, 6 miles from Cardiff ..	8.50 a.m
8. 0 a.m	St. Osyth, 12 miles from Colchester .	4.30 p.m
7. 0 a.m	St. Peter's, Thanet, 2 m. fr. Margate	7.15 p.m
4.30 p.m	St. Roche, 6 miles from St. Austle..	8. 0 a.m
2.45 a.m	Salcombe, 6 miles from Kingsbridge	7.45 a.m
7.45 a.m 6.45 p.m	Salford, by Manchester	5.45 .am 2.40 p.m
8. 0 a.m	Saling, 5 miles from Braintree	5. 0 p.m
7. 0 a.m	*Salisbury, Alexr. Hayward Minty ..	10. 0 p.m
12.30 p.m	Saltash, 5 miles from Plymouth	7. 0 p.m
7. 0 a.m	Saltford, 4 miles from Bath	7. 0 p.m
7. 0 a.m	*Sandbach, Richard Eachus........	8. 0 p.m
9. 0 a.m	Sanderstead, 3 miles from Croydon..	2.45 p.m
8. 0 a.m	Sandford, 1½ miles from Crediton....	5. 0 p.m
7.45 a.m	Sandgate, 2 miles from Folkstone ..	10. 0 p.m
8. 0 a.m	Sandhurst, 12 m. from Staplehurst..	7.30 p.m
9.10 a.m	Sandhutton, 3 miles from Thirsk	3.40 a.m
7. 0 a.m	Sandling, 1 mile from Maidstone....	7. 0 p.m
10.35 a.m	Sandown, 6 miles from Ryde.........	2.30 p.m
6.30 a.m	Sandway, 9 miles from Maidstone ..	6.30 p.m
8. 0 a.m	*Sandwich, Thomas Bowes	9.30 p.m
9 10 a.m	Sarre, 8 miles from Margate	5. 0 p.m
8.15 a.m	Saundersfoot, 3 miles from Tenby ..	4.45 p.m
8. 0 a.m	*Sawbridgeworth, Charles Norris ...	9.30 p.m
10. 0 a.m	Sawston, 7 miles from Cambridge....	4. 0 p.m
9. 0 a.m	Sawtry, 4 miles from Stilton........	6. 0 p.m
9.30 a.m	Saxlingham, 8 miles from Norwich..	3.45 p.m
7 30 a.m	*Saxmundham, James Smy	7.45 p.m
10. 0 a.m	*Scarborough, John Gillott	3. 0 p.m

Scilly (Islands). The packet "Lionesse," leaves Penzance for the Scilly Isles every Friday at 9, a.m.; arrives with a brisk fair wind in 4 or 5 hours; and with a brisk contrary wind, in 10 or 12 hours. Leaves Scilly for Penzance every Monday at 11, a.m. Clement Mumford.

Letters from London delivered at h. m.	Town. Postmaster.	Box for London closes at h. m.
8. 0 a.m	*Scole, Henry Haynes	9. 0 p.m
11.30 a.m	Scorton, 3 miles from Catterick	1.15 p.m
9. 0 a.m	Scottow, 10 miles from Norwich	4.30 p.m
7.25 p.m	Scremerston, 5 miles from Berwick..	3.50 p.m
9. 0 a.m	Seacombe, 1½ miles from Liverpool ..	4. 0 p.m
8.30 a.m	Seaford, 12 miles from Lewes	5.20 p.m
10. 0 a.m	Seaforth, 4½ miles from Liverpool ..	3. 0 p.m
10.45 a.m	*Seaham	7. 0 p.m
8. 0 a.m	Sea-House, 2 miles from Eastbourne.	6.20 p.m
7. 0 a.m	Seal, 2 miles from Seven-Oaks......	6.30 p.m
9.30 a.m	Seaton, 8 miles from Axminster	3.25 p.m
12. 0noon	Seaton, 9½ miles from Stockton......	1. 0 p.m
10.30 a.m	Sea-View, 3½ miles from Ryde	4. 0 p.m
11. 0 a.m	Sedburgh, 25 miles from Lancaster..	2.40 p.m
8.30 a.m	Seddlescombe, 4 miles from Battle ..	6. 0 p.m
10. 30a.m	Sedgefield, 54 miles from York......	2. 0 p.m
7. 0 a.m	Seend, 4 miles from Melksham	6. 0 p.m
8. 0 a.m	Selborne, 4 miles from Alton........	5. 0 p.m
8. 0 a.m	*Selby, Francis Hutchinson	6.30 p.m 9.30 p.m
9. 0 a.m	Selling, 4 miles from Feversham	6. 0 p.m
12.15 p.m	Senny, 9 miles from Brecon	11.45 a.m
9. 0 a.m	Setch, 8 miles from Downham	5. 0 p.m
11.15 a.m	*Settle, John Gibbins	2.15 p.m
7. 0 a.m	*Seven-Oaks, Henry Morris........	8.30 p.m
7. 0 a.m	Severn-Stoke, 7½ miles from Worcester	6. 0 p.m
7. 0 a.m	Shadingfield, 4 miles from Wangford	6.30 p.m
7. 0 a.m	*Shaftesbury, Richard Buckland	7.30 p.m
9. 0 a.m	Shaldon, 1½ miles from Teignmouth.	4.15 p.m
11. 0 a.m	Shalfleet, 9 miles from Lymington ..	2. 0 p.m
8. 0 a.m	Shalford, 1 mile from Guilford	6.45 p.m
11. 0 a.m	Shanklin, 9 miles from Ryde........	2. 0 p.m

Letters from London delivered at h. m.	Town. Postmaster.	Box for London closes at h. m.
3.10 p.m	Shap, 10 miles from Penrith........	10.50 a.m
7.45 a.m	Shapwick, 7 miles from Glastonbury	5.10 p.m
7. 0 a.m	Shardlow, 7 miles from Derby......	6. 0 p.m
9.30 a.m	Sharnbrook, 8 miles from Bedford....	3.30 p.m
10.30 a.m	Shaw, 3 miles from Oldham	1. 0 p.m
9.45 a.m	Shawbury, 7½ miles from Shrewsbury	3.45 p.m
9. 0 a.m	Shedfield, 5 miles from Fareham....	5. 0 p.m
8.10 a.m	Sheepshead, 4 m. from Loughborough	8. 0 p.m
10.30 a.m	Sheepwash, 12 m. from Oakhampton	2. 0 p.m
7. 0 a.m	Sheepy, 3 miles from Atherstone	7.30 p.m
7. 0 a.m.	*Sheerness, William Knewstub.....	7. 0 p.m
7.30 a.m 6.15 p.m	*Sheffield, Miss Ellen Wreaks	7.30 p.m 10. 0 p.m
8. 0 a.m	Shefford, 6 miles from Biggleswade..	8.30 p.m
9. 0 a.m	Shelford, 5 miles from Cambridge ..	5. 0 p.m
7. 0 a.m	Shelton, 4mi. fr. Newcastle-under-Lyne	7.45 p.m
11.30 a.m	Shenington, 6½ miles from Banbury..	2. 0 p.m
9. 0 a.m	Shenley, 5½ miles from Barnet	4.15 p.m
7. 0 a.m	*Shepton-Mallet, Elijah Merchant ..	8.15 p.m
10. 0 a.m	*Sherborne W. Rutter	4. 0 p.m
11.30 a.m	Sherbourne, 7 miles from Ferrybridge	12.20 p.m
11. 0 a.m	Sheriff-Hutton, 14 miles from York..	2.45 p.m
7. 0 a.m	Sherrington, 2 m. fr. Newport-Pagnel	7. 0 p.m
11.30 a.m	Sheviock, 6 miles from Devonport....	8.30 p.m
7.30 a.m 10.30 p.m	*Shields (North), Joseph Peart.....	2.15 a.m 8. 0 p.m
8. 0 a.m 10. 0 a.m	*Shields (South), George Hen. Wilson	3. 0 p.m 8.30 p.m
10. 0 a.m	Shiere, 6 miles from Guildford	4. 0 p.m
7. 0 a.m 5.30 p.m	*Shiffnal, Miss Frances Adam	7.25 p.m
10. 0 a.m	Shildon, 9 miles from Darlington....	2.40 p.m
7.30 a.m	Shillingstone, 6 miles from Blandford	6. 0 p.m
8.30 a.m	Shipdham, 17 miles from Thetford ..	7. 0 p.m
10. 0 a.m	Shipley, 3 miles from Bradford, Yorks.	3.45 p.m
8.30 a.m	*Shipston-on-Stour, Richard Brain..	4.15 p.m
7 0. a.m	Shipton, 18 miles from Marlborough	6. 0 p.m
8.45 a.m	Shirehampton, 5 miles from Bristol..	7.15 p.m
8.30 a.m	Shirley-Common, 2 m. from South'ton	6. 0 p.m
7.15 a.m	Shirleywich, 7 miles from Rugeley ..	6.30 p.m
11. 0 a.m	Shobden, 8 miles from Leominster....	2. 0 p.m
	*Shooter's Hill, *see* "Lon. District Offi."	
8. 0 a.m 1.30 p.m	*Shoreham (Sussex), Mrs. E. Crumb.	8.45 p.m
10.30 a.m	Shoreham (Kent), 9 miles fr. Dartford	4. 0 p.m
7.30 a.m	Shorne, 3½ miles from Gravesend....	6.30 p.m
10. 0 a.m	Shorwell, 5 miles from Newport	3. 0 p.m
10. 0 a.m	Shotley, 10 miles from Ipswich	4. 0 p.m
8. 0 a.m	Shottisham, 4 miles from Woodbridge	5. 0 p.m
12. 0noon	Shotley-Bridge, near Durham	6. 0 p.m
8.15 a.m 8. 0 p.m	*Shrewsbury, John William Towers	5.30 p.m
10.30 a.m	Shrewton, 13½ miles from Devizes ..	4.45 p.m
9.30 a.m	Shrivenham, 5½ mi. from Farringdon	5. 0 p.m
10.30 a.m	Shurdington, 4 miles fr. Cheltenham	5.30 p.m
11.30 a.m	Sibford, 7 miles from Banbury	2. 0 p.m
8. 0 a.m	Sible-Hedingham, 3 m. from Halstead	5. 0 p.m
9.30 a.m	Sibsey, 5 miles from Boston	4.30 p.m
7.30 a.m	Sidbury, 6 miles from Honiton	6. 0 p.m
8.45 a.m	Sidcot, 11 miles fr. Wells, Somerset	5.30 p.m
8. 0 a.m	*Sidmouth, Reuben Barratt	5. 0 p.m
9.29 a.m	Silkstone, 4 miles from Barnsley	4.30 p.m
8. 0 a.m	Silsoe, 4 miles from Ampthill	5. 0 p.m
8. 0 a.m	Silverton, 5 miles from Cullompton..	6. 0 p.m
8.15 a.m	Singleton, 5 miles from Chichester ..	5.30 p.m
7. 0 a.m 3. 0 p.m	*Sittingbourne, William Marsh	11. 0 a.m 9.30 p.m
11. 0 a.m	Skelmanthorp, 8 m. from Huddersfield	1. 0 p.m
1.54 p.m	Skelton, 4 miles from Guisborough..	11. 0 a.m
9.40 a.m	Skelton, 4 miles from York	4. 0 p.m
11.15 a.m	*Skipton, Thomas Naylor Cockshott	2.45 p.m
11. 0 a.m	Skirlaugh, 9 miles from Hull.......	2.20 p.m
11. 0 a.m	Slaithwaite, 4½ mi. from Huddersfield	2.30 p.m
3. 0 p.m	Slapton, 7 miles from Dartmouth....	11. 0 a.m
8. 0 a.m	*Sleaford, Samuel Obbinson	7.30 p.m
12.30noon	Sledmere, 12 miles from Malton	1.30 p.m
11. 0 a.m	Slindon, 4 miles from Arundel	4.30 p.m
8.30 a.m	Slinfold, 4 miles from Horsham	4.30 p.m
11.50 a.m	Slingsby, 18 miles from York	1.10 p.m
7. 0 a.m 11.15 a.m	*Slough, Mrs. Maria Luff........	12. 0noon 10. 0 p.m
10. 0 a.m	Smallbridge, 2 miles from Rochdale..	4. 0 p.m

Letters from London delivered at h. m.	Town. Postmaster.	Box for London closes at h. m.
9. 0 a.m	Smarden, 8 miles from Cranbrook ..	4.45 p.m
8.30 a.m	Smeeth, 4½ miles from Ashford......	6. 0 p.m
7. 0 a.m	Smethwick, 4 miles from Birmingham	7. 0 p.m
1.20 p.m	Snainton, 12 miles from Malton......	2.10 p.m
9.15 a.m	Snaith, 7½ miles from Selby	3.45 p.m
9. 0 a.m	Snettisham, 10 miles from Lynn	5. 0 p.m
7. 0 a.m	Sodbury, 15 miles from Chippenham	6.30 p.m
8. 0 a.m	Soham, 9 miles from Mildenhall	6. 0 p.m
7. 0 a.m	*Solihull, Thomas Harborne.........	8.30 p.m
7. 0 a.m	Solva, 12 miles from Haverfordwest	5.15 p.m
10. 0 a.m	Somerby, 6 miles from Oakham	2.30 p.m
10. 0 a.m	Somerford-Magna, 8m.fr.Chippenham	4. 0 p.m
8.30 a.m	Somersham, 6 mi. fr. St. Ives, Hunts	6.30 p.m
8. 0 a.m	*Somerton, Thomas Hitchings Davies	5.45 p.m
7.30 a.m	Sompting, 4 miles from Shoreham...	5.30 p.m
8. 0 a.m	Sonning, 4½ miles from Reading	6.15 p.m
	*Southall, *see* "London District Office."	
8. 0 a.m	*Southam, Miss Ann C. Pettifer	6.45 p.m
7. 0 a.m 3. 0 p.m	*Southampton, Robert Lankester...	8.30 a.m 10. 0 p.m
7.30 a.m	Southborough, 3 m.fr.TunbridgeWells	6. 0 p.m
7.30 a.m	Southbourne, 1 mile from Eastbourne	6.30 p.m
11.30 p.m	South-Brent, 17 mi. f. Wells Somerset	2. 0 p.m
	South Cave, *see* Cave	
7. 0 a.m	Southend, 5 miles from Rochford....	4. 0 p.m
9. 0 a.m	Southery, 7 miles from Downham....	5. 0 p.m
7.30 a.m	South-Fleet, 3 miles from Gravesend	7. 0 p.m
8.50 a.m	South-Hayling, 5½ m. from Havant..	5. 0 p.m
8. 0 a.m	South-Luffenham, 7 mi. fr. Stamford.	6.30 p.m
8. 0 a.m	South-Mimms, 3½ miles from Barnet	6.30 p.m
9.30 a.m	Southminster, 12 miles from Maldon .	3.30 p.m
8. 0 a.m	*Southmolton, John Thomas	5.30 p.m
8.30 a.m	South-Moreton, 3 m. from Wallingford	7. 0 p.m
11.15 a.m	South-Newington, 6 mi. fr. Banbury	1.30 p.m
8. 0 a.m	South-Newton, 5 mi. from Salisbury	6. 0 p.m
8. 0 a.m	South-Ockendon, 8 m. from Romford	5.30 p.m
8. 0 a.m	*South-Petherton, John Daniel	5.10 p.m
11.30 a.m	Southport, 9 miles from Ormskirk ..	2.45 p.m
	South-Shields, *see* Shields, (South)	
10.10 a.m	Southshore, 19 m. from Preston	2.30 p.m
9.30 a.m	Southwell, 8 miles from Newark....	3.30 p.m
9. 0 a.m	Southwick, 4 miles from Fareham	4. 0 p.m
8. 0 a.m	Southwick, 2 miles from Shoreham ..	7. 0 p.m
8. 0 a.m	Southwold, 3½ miles from Wangford..	5.45 p.m
7. 0 a.m 11.50 a.m	Sowerby-Bridge, 2 m. fr. Halifax..	12. 0noon 6.35 p.m
8. 0 a.m	*Spalding, Thomas North	6.10 p.m
10. 0 a.m	Spaldwick, 7 miles from Huntingdon	5. 0 p.m
8. 0 a.m	Speen, 1 mile from Newbury.........	5.30 p.m
11.50 a.m	Spennithorne, 11 miles from Bedale. .	12.50 p.m
10.45 a.m	*Spilsby, John Morton	3. 0 p.m
9.30 a.m	*Spittal, Joseph Keyworth	4.30 p.m
4.30 p.m	Spittal, 1 mile from Berwick	9. 0 p.m
8.15 a.m	Spondon, 3½ miles from Derby......	6. 0 p.m
8. 0 a.m	Springfield, 1½ miles from Chelmsford	7. 0 p.m
11.10 a.m	Sproatley, 7 miles from Hull........	2. 0 p.m
10.30 a.m	Stadhampton, 6 m. from Wallingford	5. 0 p.m
8. 0 a.m 5. 0 p.m	*Stafford, Thomas D. Weaver......	6. 0 a.m 10. 0 p.m
11.40 a.m	Staindrop, 13 miles from Darlington..	1.15 p.m
7. 0 a.m	*Staines, Miss Jane Caroline Evitts	7.30 p.m
9. 0 a.m 4. 0 p.m	Stainlaind, 4½ miles from Halifax....	4.20 p.m
5.30 p.m	Staithes, 14 miles from Guisborough	7.35 a.m
10. 0 a.m	Stalbridge, 9 miles from Wincanton..	3.30 p.m
8.30 a.m	*Staley-Bridge, D. Cheetham	5.15 p.m
11. 0 a.m	Stalham, 14 miles from Norwich....	2. 0 p.m
7. 0 a.m	*Stamford, Richard Capon Reynolds	6.30 p.m
11.20 a.m	Stamford-Bridge, 8 miles from York..	2. 0 p.m
2.20 p.m	Stamfordham, 14 mi. fr. Newcastle T.	7.30 a.m
8. 0 a.m	Standford, 4 miles from Hythe......	6. 0 p.m
8. 0 a.m	Standish, 3½ miles from Wigan......	3.45 p.m
10. 0 a.m	Standlake, 5½ miles from Witney....	5. 0 p.m
10.30 a.m	Stanford in the Vale, 4m.f.Farringdon	12.30 p.m
7.30 a.m	Stanford-Rivers, 9 mi. from Romford	6. 0 p.m
12. 0noon	Stanhope, 21 miles from Durham....	6. 8 p.m
8. 0 a.m	Stanley, 1½ miles from Wakefield ..	5. 0 p.m
7.50 a.m	Stanningley, 6 miles from Leeds	4.30 p.m
8. 0 a.m	Stanstead, 3 m. from Bishop's Stortfd.	8. 0 p.m
7. 0 a.m	Stanstead, 2 miles from Ware.......	7. 0 p.m
9. 0 a.m	Stanton, 9 miles from Bury	5. 0 p.m
9. 0 a.m	Stanton-Drew, 7½ miles from Bristol	3. 0 p.m

Letters from London delivered at h. m.	Town. Postmaster.	Box for London closes at h. m.
8.30 a.m	Stanwell, 2½ miles from Staines......	6. 0 p.m
8.20 a.m	Staplefield-Common, 5½ m.fr.Crawley	5. 0 p.m
10. 0 a.m	Stapleford, 6 miles from Nottingham	12. 0noon
9.30 a.m	Stapleford, 5 miles from Cambridge..	4.30 p.m
7. 0 a.m 2.30 p.m	*Staplehurst, Thomas Humphrey ..	10.15 a.m 9. 0 p.m
7.30 a.m	Stapleton, 3 miles from Bristol	8. 0 p.m
7. 0 a.m	Starcross, 8 miles from Exeter	6.30 p.m
10.30 a.m	Staveley, 5 miles from Borobridge ..	2. 0 p.m
9. 0 a.m	Staveley, 4 miles from Chesterfield..	6. 0 p.m
10. 0 a.m	Staveley, 4½ miles from Kendal	3.30 p.m
8. 0 a.m	Stebbing, 14 miles from Chelmsford	5.30 p.m
11. 0 a.m	Steeple, 9 miles from Maldon	2. 0 p.m
9. 0 a.m	Steeple-Ashton, 4 mi. fr. Trowbridge	5. 0 p.m
10.30 a.m	Steeple-Bumpstead, 3 m. fr.Haverhill	4. 0 p.m
7. 0 a.m	Stetchworth, 3½ mi. from Newmarket	7.30 p.m
7. 0 a.m	*Stevenage, Mrs. Charlotte Aldham	9. 0 p.m
8.45 a.m	Steventon, Hants, 5 m. fr. Andover rd.	4. 0 p.m
7. 0 a.m	Stewkley, 6 mi. fr. Leighton Buzzard	8. 0 p.m
7.30 a.m	*Steyning, Zaccheus Steer	5.15 p.m
7. 0 a.m	Stickelpath, 19 miles from Exeter...	6. 0 p.m
9.30 a.m	Stickney, 9 miles from Boston	4. 0 p.m
8. 0 a.m	Stifford, 10 miles from Romford	5. 0 p.m
9.10 a.m	Stillington, 10 miles from York......	4. 0 p.m
8. 0 a.m	*Stilton, Charles Stokes	8.30 p.m
9.30 a.m	Stock, 3 miles from Ingatestone	7. 0 p.m
7. 0 a.m	*Stockbridge, Wm. Tyrrell Coakley	7.45 p.m
9. 0 a.m	Stockland, 8 miles from Honiton	5. 0 p.m
8.15 a.m 8.15 p.m	*Stockport, Edward Holme	5.30 p.m 9.30 p.m
3.15 p.m	Stocksfield, 13 miles from Newcastle-upon-Tyne	7. 0 a.m
7. 0 a.m 9.40 a.m	*Stockton-on-Tees, Mrs. Isab. Dunn	3.15 p.m 6.30 p.m
11.30 a.m	Stockwith, 6 mi. from Gainsborough .	2. 0 p.m
8. 0 a.m	Stogumber, 13 miles from Taunton ..	5. 0 p.m
10.30 a.m	Stogursay, 9 miles from Bridgewater	3.30 p.m
7. 0 a.m	*Stoke-upon-Trent, Miss Ann Wigley	7.45 p.m
6. 0 p.m 8.30 a.m 15. 0 p.m	Stoke, 2 miles from Gosport	6. 0 p.m
1. 0 a.m	Stoke, 6 miles from Yeovil	3. 0 p.m
7.30 a.m	Stoke-by-Nayland, Suffolk, 9 miles from Colchester	6.30 p.m
11. 0 a.m	Stoke, 1 mile from Devonport	2.30 p.m
9. 0 a.m	Stoke, 12 miles from Halstead	3.45 p.m
10. 0 a.m	Stoke, 4 miles from Newark	3. 0 p.m
10. 0 a.m	Stoke-Canon, 4 miles from Exeter ..	4.30 p.m
1.15 p.m	Stoke-Climsland, 3 mi. fr. Callington	10.45 a.m
7. 0 a.m	Stoke-ferry, Norfolk, 10 m. f. Brandon	7.15 p.m
1. 0 p.m	Stoke-Fleming, 2½ m. fr. Dartmouth	10. 0 a.m
9.30 a.m	Stoke-Green, 2 miles from Slough....	6.30 p.m
9. 0 a.m	Stoke-Holy Cross, 5 m. fr. Norwich	4.45 p.m
7. 0 a.m	*Stokenchurch, Wm. Holmes	7.30 p.m
3.30 p.m	Stokenham, 9½ miles from Dartmouth	7.30 a.m
9. 0 a.m	Stokescroft, 1 mile from Bristol	8.45 p.m
10.50 a.m	*Stokesley, Mrs. Catherine Wilstrop	2.30 p.m
8. 0 a.m 5. 0 p.m	*Stone, Staffordshire, Mrs. S. Key ..	9.30 p.m
12. 0noon	Stone, 7 miles from Dursley.........	10. 0 a.m
7. 0 a.m	Stonebridge, 8 miles from Coventry..	8. 0 p.m
8.30 a.m	Stone-Easton, 7 miles from Bath	4.45 p.m
9. 0 a.m	Stonehouse, 3 miles from Stroud....	4. 0 p.m
8. 0 a.m	Stoney-Cross, 5 miles from Lyndhurst	6.50 p.m
9. 0 a.m	Stoney-Middleton, 5 m.from Bakewell	4.15 p.m
7. 0 a.m 12.30 p.m	*Stoney-Stratford, Miss Elizabeth Richardson	9.35 a.m 8.30 p.m
7. 0 a.m	*Stonham, James Gurr	10. 0 p.m
7.30 a.m	Stonham-Aspall, 2 mi. from Stonham	6.30 p.m
9.30 a.m	Storrington, 10 miles from Petworth	4.45 p.m
8. 0 a.m	Stotfold, 3 miles from Baldock......	6. 0 p.m
7. 0 a.m	*Stourbridge, Miss Sophia Coltman...	7.30 p.m
7. 0 a.m	*Stourport, Thomas Wheeldon......	6. 0 p.m
8. 0 a.m	Stower, 5½ miles from Shaftesbury ..	5.30 p.m
7.30 a.m	Stowey, 8 miles from Bridgewater...	6.30 p.m
10. 0 a.m	Stowmaries, 6½ miles from Maldon ..	5. 0 p.m
8. 0 a.m	*Stow-Market, Ths. Brackett Woolby	6.30 p.m
7. 0 a.m	Stow-on the-Wold, 4 miles from Morton-in-Marsh	7. 0 p.m
10. 0 a.m	Stradbrooke, 20 m. fr. Woodbridge ..	4.45 p.m
12. 0noon	Stranton, 11 miles from Stockton ..	1.10 p.m
7.30 a.m	Stratford St. Mary, 7 m. fr. Colchester	6.45 p.m

Letters from London delivered at h. m.	Town. Postmaster.	Box for London closes at h. m.
7.30 a.m 7.30 p.m	*Stratford-on-Avon, John Lane	5. 0 a.m 5.45 p.m
1. 0 p.m	Stratton, 21 miles from Oakhampton	9. 0 a.m
8.30 a.m	Stratton, 3 miles from Dorchester	4.40 p.m
9.30 a.m	Streatley, 10 miles from Reading	4.30 p.m
7.30 a.m	Street, 2 miles from Glastonbury	5.45 p.m
10. 0 a.m	Strensham, 5 miles from Tewkesbury	4. 0 p.m
8.30 a.m	Stretford, 4 miles from Manchester	6. 0 p.m
8.30 a.m	Stretham, 4 miles from Ely	6. 0 p.m
9. 0 a.m	Stretton, 8 miles from Coventry	3.45 p.m
7.20 a.m	Stretton, 4 miles from Warrington	5.15 p.m
8. 0 a.m 2. 0 p.m	Strood, Kent, by Rochester	8. 0 p.m
7. 0 a.m 4. 0 p.m	*Stroud, Gloucestershire, Mrs. S. Hambidge	7. 0 a.m 9.30 p.m
7. 0 a.m	Studley, 9 miles from Broomsgrove	7. 0 p.m
10. 0 a.m	Sturminster-Marshall, 5m.fr.Wimborne	4. 0 p.m
8.30 a.m	Sturminster-Newton, 10 m. f. Blandfd.	5.45 p.m
7. 0 a.m	Sturry, 2½ miles from Canterbury	7.30 p.m
9. 0 a.m	Stutton, 8 miles from Ipswich	5. 0 p.m
10. 0 a.m	Sudborough, 3 miles from Thrapstone	3.15 p.m
7. 0 a.m	*Sudbury, Alexander Frost	6 45 p.m
9. 0 a.m	Sudbury, 5 miles from Uttoxeter	5.45 p.m
7.30 a.m 10. 0 a.m	*Sunderland, Mrs. Arabella Robinson	2.45 p.m 8.10 p.m
7.30 a.m	Sundridge, 4 miles from Seven-Oaks	6.30 p.m
8. 0 a.m	Sunning-Hill, 9 miles from Chertsey	5. 0 p.m
7.40 a.m	Surbiton-Hill, 1½ m. from Kingston	2.45 p.m
10. 0 a.m	Sutterton, 10 miles from Spalding	3.15 p.m
9. 0 a.m	Sutton, 6 miles from Ely	6. 0 p.m
9. 0 a.m 12. 0noon	Sutton, 5 miles from Epsom	8.30 a.m 3.30 p.m
11.40 a.m	Sutton, 4 miles from Hull	2.20 p.m
7.30 a.m	Sutton, 5 miles from Woodbridge	5.30 p.m
8. 0 a.m	Sutton-in-Ashfield, 3 mi. f. Mansfld.	7. 0 p.m
8.30 a.m	Sutton-Bridge, 12 mi. from Wisbeach	4.45 p.m
7. 0 a.m	Sutton-Coldfield, 8 m. fr. Birmingham	8.30 p.m
8.30 a.m	Sutton-Benger, 4 m. fr. Chippenham	6. 0 p.m
8. 0 a.m	Sutton-at-Hone, 3 mi. from Dartford.	6.30 p.m
10.20 a.m	Sutton-on-Derwent, 10 mi. fr. York	2.50 p.m
9. 0 a.m	Sutton-on-the-Forest, 8 mi. fr. York	4.20 p.m
8.30 a.m	Sutton-Scotney, 7 m. f. Andover-Road	6. 0 p.m
9. 0 a.m	Sutton-Valance, 6 mi. fr. Maidstone	4. 0 p.m
8.30 a.m	*Swaffham, William Parson	5.15 p.m
11.10 a.m	Swainby, 37 miles from York	2. 0 p.m
9.30 a.m	Swanage, 12 miles from Wareham	4.15 p.m
7. 0 a.m	Swanbourne, 9 miles from L. Buzzard	7.30 a.m
12.30 p.m	Swanland, 8 miles from Hull	1.20 p.m
6.30 a.m	Swanmore, 1½ m. f. Bishop's Waltham	7. 0 p.m
9. 0 a.m	Swanscombe, 4 miles from Dartford	12. 0noon
2. 0 p.m	*Swansea, John Davies	10.30 a.m
8. 0 a.m	Swathling, 3 mi. from Southampton	5.30 p.m
8.30 a.m	Swavesey, 6 miles from St. Ives	6. 0 p.m
5.20 p.m	Swinbridge, 4½ miles from Barnstaple	2. 0 p.m
7. 0 a.m 2. 0 p.m	*Swindon, Thomas Rose	9. 0 a.m 9.15 p.m
7.30 a.m 2.30 p.m	Swindon-Station, 1½ mi. fr. Swindon	8.27 a.m 8.27 p.m
12.40 p.m	Swine, 7 miles from Hull	1.20 p.m
10. 0 a.m	Swinefleet, 3 miles from Goole	2.45 p.m
11. 0 a.m	Swineshead, 14 miles from Spalding	3. 0 p.m
10. 0 a.m	Swinton, 5 miles from Manchester	2. 0 p.m
9.30 a.m	Swinton, 7 miles from Rotherham	3.30 p.m
10.30 a.m	Sydling, 9 miles from Dorchester	3. 0 p.m
8. 0 a.m	*Tadcaster, John Hartley	5.30 p.m
12. 0noon	*Taibach, John Snook	12.20noon
11.30 a.m	Talsarn, 6 miles from Lampeter	12. 0noon
12. 0noon	Tamerton, 5 miles from Plymouth	1.30 p.m
7. 0 a.m	*Tamworth, Joseph Atkins	7.15 p.m
2.25 p.m	Tanfield, 7 mi. fr. Chester le-Street	4.40 p.m
7. 0 p.m	Tanybwlch, 23 miles fr. Carnarvon	6. 0 a.m
7. 0 a.m	Taphouse, 8 miles from Exeter	6.30 p.m
7. 0 a.m	Taplow, 2 miles from Maidenhead	7. 0 p.m
1. 0 p.m	Tarleton, 9 miles from Ormskirk	1.10 p.m
7. 0 a.m	*Tarporley, John Gregory	7.45 p.m
10.30 a.m	Tarrant-Gunville, 5 m. from Blandford	4. 0 p.m
7. 0 a.m	Tarring, 2 miles from Worthing	6. 0 p.m
7.30 a.m	Tarvin, 5 miles from Chester	3.30 p.m
8. 0 a.m	Tattenhall, 9 miles from Chester	5. 0 p.m
10. 0 a.m	Tattingstone, 6 miles from Ipswich	4. 0 p.m
7. 0 a.m	*Taunton, Miss Elizabeth Reed Owen	9. 0 p.m
10.30 a.m	*Tavistock, Mrs. Agnes Martin	2.50 p.m

Letters from London delivered at h. m	Town. Postmaster.	Box for London closes at h. m.
10.15 a.m	Tean, 2½ mi. from Cheadle, Staffords.	4.45 p.m
6.30 a.m	Teffont, 10 miles from Salisbury	6. 0 p.m
8. 0 a.m	*Teignmouth, E. & W., Jn. Wreyford	5.15 p.m
9. 0 a.m	Temple-Cloud, 10 miles from Bristol	3.45 p.m
9. 0 a.m	Temple-Comb 5 m. from Wincanton	5. 0 p.m
4. 0 p.m	Temple-Sowerby, 6½ m. fr. Penrith	8.30 a.m 3.30 p.m
7. 0 a.m	Tempsford, 5 miles from St. Neot's	7.30 p.m
8.45 a.m	*Tenbury, Benjamin Home	3. 0 p.m
8.30 a.m	*Tenby, Mrs. Martha Morgan	10. 0 p.m
7. 0 a.m	*Tenterden, William Bourner	6.45 p.m
10.30 a.m	Terrington, 18 miles from York	2.20 p.m
9.30 a.m	Terrington, 5 miles from Lynn	3.45 p.m
7.15 a.m	Teston, 4 miles from Maidstone	6.45 p.m
7.30 a.m	*Tetbury, Thomas Home	5.30 p.m
7. 0 a.m	*Tetsworth, Thomas Jones	9. 0 p.m
7. 0 a.m	Tettenhall-Regis, 2 m. fr. Wolverhptn	6.30 p.m
7. 0 a.m	*Tewkesbury, John Spurrier	6.45 p.m
7. 0 a.m	*Thame, Miss F. W. Parsons	7.15 p.m
7.30 a.m	Thames-Ditton, 2 m. from Kingston	7. 0 p.m
8.30 a.m	Thatcham, 3 miles from Newbury	5.30 p.m
10. 0 a.m	Thaxted, 6 miles from Dunmow	3.45 p.m
10. 0 a.m	Theobalds, 6 mi. from Waltham cross	5.30 p.m
7. 0 a.m	*Thetford, Wm. Christopher	10. 0 p.m
9. 0 a.m	Thickthorn, 15 mi. fr. Fordingbridge	4. 0 p.m
8. 0 a.m 9.10 p.m	*Thirsk, Robert Peat	5.10 p.m 10. 0 p.m
11. 0 a.m 7. 0 p.m	Thongsbridge, 5 m. fr. Huddersfield	8. 0 p.m 2.30 p.m
9.30 a.m	Thornbury, 12 miles from Bristol	2.15 p.m
10.30 a.m	Thorncombe, 7 miles from Chard	2. 0 p.m
9. 0 a.m	*Thorne, Mrs. Ann Mason	4. 0 p.m
8.30 a.m	Thorney, 7 miles from Peterborough	5. 0 p.m
10.40 a.m	Thorngumbald, 8 miles from Hull	2.35 p.m
10. 0 a.m	Thornham, 21 miles from Lynn	4. 0 p.m
8.30 a.m	Thornham, 3½ miles from Eye	6.30 p.m
10.15 a.m	Thornton, 4 mi. fr. Bradford, Yorks.	2.50 p.m
12 0noon	Thornton, 6 miles from Skipton	1.45 p.m
12.20 p.m	Thornton, 3 miles from Pickering	10.20 a.m
12.10 p.m	Thorp, 4 miles from Stockton	5. 0 p.m
8.20 a.m	Thorp-Arch, 4 miles from Tadcaster	4.50 p.m
7. 0 a.m	Thorpe, 12 miles from Colchester	5. 0 p.m
7. 0 a.m	Thorpe, 2 miles from Chertsey	6.45 p.m
10. 0 a.m	Thorpe-St.-Andrews, 2½ m.fr.Norwich	4. 0 p.m
8.30 a.m	Thorverton, 8 miles from Cullompton	5.15 p.m
7. 0 a.m	*Thrapstone, Henry Collier	10. 0 p.m
8.30 a.m	Thurlow, 9 miles from Newmarket	5.30 p.m
3.20 p.m	Thursby, 6 miles from Carlisle	10.20 a.m
7.30 a.m	Thwaite, 5 miles from Stoneham	6.15 p.m
8. 0 a.m	Ticehurst, 4 miles from Hurst-Green	7. 0 p.m
6.30 a.m	Tickenham, 10 miles from Bristol	3.20 p.m
8. 0 a.m	Tickhill 4 miles from Bawtry	5.30 p.m
8. 0 a.m	Ticknall, 10 miles from Derby	6. 0 p.m
8. 0 a.m	Tid, 6 miles from Wisbeach	6.30 p m
11. 0 a.m	Tiddenham, 3 miles from Chepstow	1. 0 p.m
8. 0 a.m	Tiddington, 2 m. f. Stratford-on-Avon	4.15 p.m
10. 0 a.m	Tideswell, 7 miles from Bakewell	4. 0 p.m
7. 0 a.m	Tidworth, 15 miles from Marlboro'	7. 0 p.m
10. 0 a.m	Tillingham, 14 miles from Maldon	3. 0 p.m
9.30 a.m	Tilshead, 10 miles from Devizes	5. 0 p.m
1. 0 p.m	Timsbury, 8 miles from Bath	4. 0 p.m
9. 0 a.m	Tingewick, 3 miles from Buckingham	5.30 p.m
1.30 p.m	Tintern-Abbey, 5½ m. from Chepstow	9.15 a.m
7. 0 a.m	*Tipton, Miss Martha Partridge	8.45 p.m
8.45 a.m	Tisbury, 4 miles from Hindon	4. 0 p.m
8. 0 a.m 5.30 p.m	Titchfield, 2 miles from Fareham	5. 0 p.m
7. 0 a.m	*Tiverton, Miss Emma Tucker	7.50 p.m
9. 0 a.m	Tixover, 6 miles from Stamford	4.55 p.m
8. 0 a.m 11.30 p.m	*Todmorden, James Newell Walton	12.30 a.m 4.40 p.m
10. 0 a.m	Tolleshunt-D'Arcy, 7 mi. fr. Maldon	4. 0 p.m
7. 0 a.m	Topcliffe, 4 miles from Thirsk	7. 0 p.m
7. 0 a.m	*Topsham, John Swale Harrison	6.45 p.m
9.15 a.m	Tor, 1 mile from Torquay	3.30 p.m
11.30 a.m	Torpoint, 1½ miles from Devonport	1.45 p.m
9.30 a.m	*Torquay, Samuel Row	3.45 p.m
11.15 a.m	*Torrington, James Rude	1.30 p.m
9. 0 a.m	Tortworth, 4 m. f. Wotton-under-Edge	3.30 p.m
9.30 a.m	*Totness, Jane Kelland Hannaford	3.45 p.m
10. 0 a.m	Totterdown, 1 mile from Bristol	4. 0 p.m
10.15 a.m	Tottington, 3½ miles from Bury, Lan.	3. 0 p.m

Letters from London delivered at h. m.	Town. Postmaster.	Box for London closes at h. m.
7. 0 a.m	Totton, 4 miles from Southampton ..	8. 0 p.m
8. 0 a.m	Tovil, 1 mile from Maidstone	6. 0 p.m
7. 0 a.m 2. 0 p.m	*Towcester, George Gurney	9. 0 a.m 9.30 p.m
8.30 a.m	Town-Malling, 6 mi. from Maidstone	5.45 p.m
5. 0 p.m	Towyn, 14 miles from Machynlleth..	6.30 a.m
8.45 a.m	Toxteth-Park, 1 mile from Liverpool.	3.30 p.m
1. 0 p.m	Trecastle, 12 miles from Brecknock	11. 0 a.m
1. 0 p.m	Tredegar, 12 mi. from Abergavenny..	10.30 a.m
8. 0 p.m	Tregaron, 12 miles from Lampeter ..	11. 0 a.m
5. 0 p.m	Tregony, 9 miles from St. Austle	8. 0 a.m
6. 0 p.m	Tremadoc, 20 miles from Carnarvon..	7.45 a.m
8. 0 a.m	Trentham, 5 m.f. Newcastle, (Stafford)	7. 0 p.m
10. 0 a.m	Trimley, 9 miles from Ipswich	4. 0 p.m
7. 0 a.m 1. 0 p.m	*Tring, Miss Elizabeth Montague.	9.30 a.m 8.30 p.m
7. 0 a.m	*Trowbridge, David Walker........	8. 0 p.m
8. 0 a.m	Trull, 1½ miles from Taunton........	6. 0 p.m
8. 0 a.m	Trumpington, 2½ mi. from Cambridge	5.45 p.m
2.35 p.m	*Truro, Richard Andrews..........	9.50 a.m
9.30 a.m	Trysull, 6 miles from Wolverhampton	3.45 p.m
11.30 a.m	Tuckenhay, 3 miles from Totness....	2. 0 p.m
9.30 a.m	Tugby, 7 miles from Uppingham	5. 0 p.m
7. 0 a.m 1.45 p.m	*Tunbridge, William Ware	11. 0 a.m 9.30 p.m
7. 0 a.m 2.30 p.m	*Tunbridge Wells, Robert Nash ..	10. 0 a.m 8.15 p.m
7. 0 a.m	Tunstall, 5 miles from Newcastle S...	7.10 p.m
8. 0 a.m	Tunstall, 8 miles from Woodbridge ..	6. 0 p.m
9.30 a.m	Turgis, 6 miles from Hartfordbridge..	5. 0 p.m
8.30 a.m	Turnershill, 1½ m. from Waltham-Cross	7.30 p.m
8.30 a.m	Turvey, 7 miles from Newport-Pagnell	4. 0 p.m
9.30 a.m	Turville, 8½ miles from Henley	4. 0 p.m
9. 0 am.	Tutbury, 5 mi. from Burton-on-Trent	5. 0 p.m
11. 0 a.m	*Tuxford, Thomas Andrews	2.30 p.m
9. 0 a.m	Twerton, 2 miles from Bath	5. 0 p.m
7. 0 a.m	Twycross, 6 miles from Atherstone ..	7. 0 p.m
8.30 a.m	Twyford, 5 miles from Reading......	6. 0 p.m
8. 0 a.m	Twyford, 3½ miles from Winchester..	6. 0 p.m
8.30 p.m	Tyldesley, 12 miles from Manchester	5.30 a.m
10.30 a.m 1.30 p.m	Tynemouth, 1 mile from North Shields	11. 0 a.m 8. 0 p.m
6. 0 p.m	Tywardreth, 5 miles from St. Austle..	7. 0 a.m
7. 0 a.m	*Uckfield, Benjamin Piddington	8.30 p.m
9. 0 a.m	Uffculme, 5 miles from Cullompton ..	5. 0 p.m
5. 0 p.m	Ugborough, 11 miles from Totness ..	7. 0 a.m
8. 0 a.m	Uley, 2 miles from Dursley	4.40 p.m
8. 0 a.m	Ullesthorpe, 3½ mi. from Lutterworth	5.30 p.m
7. 0 a.m 12.30 p.m	*Ulverstone, Moses Mawson......	1. 0 p.m 8. 0 p.m
7.30 a.m	Upham, 2½ mi. fr. Bishop's Waltham	6.30 p.m
10.20 a.m	Uphill, 19 m. from Wells, Somerset ..	3.20 p.m
8. 0 a.m	Upholland, 4 miles from Wigan......	5. 0 p.m
9. 0 a.m	Uplyme, 1 mile from Lyme	4. 0 p.m
7.15 a.m	Upminster, 3 miles from Romford....	6. 0 p.m
1. 0 a.m	Upottery, 5 miles from Honiton	3. 0 p.m
10.30 a.m	Upper-Chute, 8 miles from Andover..	4.15 p.m
8. 0 a.m	Upper-Gornal, 2 miles from Dudley..	7. 0 p.m
9.45 a.m	Upper-Mill, 12 miles from Manchester	1.45 p.m
7.30 a.m	*Uppingham, Walter Leak..........	5.15 p.m
9.15 a.m	Upton, 5 miles from Birkenhead	3.45 p.m
8. 0 p.m	Upton-Scudamore, 4 m.fr. Warminster	10. 0 p.m
7.30 a.m	Upton-on-Severn, 10 mi.fr. Worcester	5.45 p.m
7. 0 a.m	Upton-St.-Leonard's 3 mi. fr. Glo'ster	6. 0 p.m
8.30 a.m	Upway, 4 miles from Dorchester	5.45 p.m
1. 0 a.m	Upwell, 6 miles from Wisbeach......	3.15 p.m
10. 0 a.m	*Usk, Owen Mathews..........	5.30 p.m
12. 0noon	Usworth, 5½ miles from Gateshead ..	7.15 p.m
8.30 a.m	*Uttoxeter, Robert Richards........	6. 0 p.m
7. 0 a.m 1. 0 p.m	*Uxbridge, Thomas Man Lake.....	9.45 a.m 9. 0 p.m
0. 0 a.m	Ventnor, I.W. 28 mi. fr. Southampton	3.30 p.m
8. 0 a.m	Waddesdon, 6 miles from Aylesbury..	5.45 p.m
2. 0 p.m	Wadebridge, 7 miles from Bodmin ..	10. 0 p.m
7. 0 a.m	Wadesmill, 2 miles from Ware......	7. 0 p.m
8.15 a.m	Wadhurst, 7 miles from Hurst-Green	5. 0 p.m
2. 0 noon	Wainfleet, 18 miles from Boston	2. 0 p.m
7.30 a.m 7.30 p.m	*Wakefield, Rowland Hurst......	7. 0 p.m 12. 0night
9. 0 a.m	Wakering, 6 miles from Rochford ..	3. 0 p.m
9. 0 a.m	Wakes-Colne, 6 miles from Halstead	3.45 p.m
9.30 a.m	Walberton, 3½ miles from Arundel ..	5. 0 p.m

Letters from London delivered at h. m.	Town. Postmaster.	Box for London closes at h. m.
9. 0 a.m 4. 0 p.m	Walcot, 1 mile from Bath	7.45 p.m
7.30 a.m	Waldron, 14 miles from Hurst-Green	7. 0 p.m
11. 0 a.m	Walkeringham, 9 miles from Bawtry	3. 0 p.m
7.30 a.m 1. 0 p.m	*Wallingford, John Childs	9.30 p.m 10. 0 a.m
12.25 p.m	Wallsend, 5 miles fr. Newcastle T. ..	9. 0 p.m
7. 0 a.m	Walmer, 6 miles from Dover........	10. 0 p.m
7. 0 a.m	Walmer-road, 1 mile from Deal	7. 0 p.m
10.30 a.m	Walpole-St.-Andrew, 9 mi. fr. Lynn	3. 0 p.m
7. 0 a.m 4. 0 p.m	*Walsall, Thomas Hill	6.30 a.m 9.30 p.m
9.15 a.m	Walsham-le-Willows, 12 m. f. Bury S.	4.15 p.m
11. 0 a.m	Walsingham, 5 miles from Fakenham	2.30 p.m
10. 0 a.m	Waltham, 5 mi. fr. Melton Mowbray	9. 0 a.m
	Waltham-Abbey & *Waltham-Cross, *see* London District Office	
7.15 a.m	Walton, 3½ miles from Glastonbury	5.40 p.m
10.30 a.m	Walton, 6 miles from Epsom........	5. 0 p.m
6.45 a.m	Walton, 12 miles from Bristol	2.40 p.m
10. 0 a.m	Walton, 10 miles from Ipswich	4. 0 p.m
8. 0 a.m	Walton-on-Thames, 4 miles fr. Esher	6. 0 p.m
8.45 a.m	Walton-on-the-Hill, 3 m. fr. Liverpool	5.30 p.m
8.20 a.m	Walton-le-dale, 1½ mi. from Preston	5.20 p.m
7.30 a.m	Walton-le-Soken, 17 m. fr. Colchester	5. 0 p.m
8. 0 a.m	Wambrook, 2 miles from Chard	2. 0 p.m
7. 0 a.m	*Wangford, Ezekiel Read	7.15 p.m
7. 0 a.m	*Wansford, George Dexter	7.30 p.m
7. 0 a.m	*Wantage, Joseph Lewis	7. 0 p.m
10. 0 a.m	Warbleton, 3 miles from Arundel	5. 0 p.m
9. 0 a.m	Warborough, 2½ mi. fr. Wallingford..	5. 0 p.m
9. 0 a.m	Warboys, 8 miles from Huntingdon..	4. 0 p.m
7. 0 a.m 2. 0 p.m	*Ware, George Price	1.30 p.m 8.30 p.m
8. 0 a.m	*Wareham, Peter Selby	6. 0 p.m
7.30 a.m	Wargrave, 3 miles from Henley......	6.30 p.m
4.40 a.m	Warkworth, 7½ miles from Alnwick..	7.50 a.m
12. 0noon	Warlingham, 5 miles from Croydon ..	2. 0 p.m
7. 0 a.m	*Warminster, Mrs. Fanny Strode....	6.30 p.m
10. 0 a.m	Warmley, 5 miles from Bristol	2.30 p.m
7. 0 a.m	Warnham, 3 miles from Horsham....	7. 0 p.m
7. 0 a.m 5. 0 p.m	*Warrington, William Robson.....	7.45 p.m 10. 0 p.m
7.30 a.m 2.30 p.m	*Warwick, Henry Baly	7.30 a.m 8.45 p.m
7 30 a.m	Washford, 18 miles from Taunton....	6.15 p.m
9.45 a.m	Washington, 11½ miles from Shoreham	3.30 p.m
8. 0 a.m	Watchet, 20 miles from Taunton	5.15 p.m
9. 0 a.m	Waterbeach, 6 miles from Cambridge	4. 0 p.m
9. 0 a.m	Waterhead-Mill, 9 mi. fr. Manchester	2.20 p.m
8. 0 a.m	Wateringbury, 5 miles fr. Maidstone..	6.15 p.m
7.30 a.m	Waterstock, 3 miles from Wheatley..	6. 0 p.m
7. 0 a.m 11.30 a.m	*Watford, William Hearn.........	11.45 a.m 9. 0 p.m
9. 0 a.m	Wath-upon-Dearne, 6 m.f. Rotherham	4. 0 p.m
8. 0 a.m	Watlington, 6 miles from Tetsworth..	6.15 p.m
9.30 a.m	Watnall, 6 miles from Nottingham ..	4.45 p.m
8.30 a.m	Watton, 6 miles from Ware	6.30 p.m
8.30 a.m	Watton, 12 miles from Thetford......	7.10 p.m
9.40 a.m	Wavertree, 3 miles from Liverpool ..	3.45 p.m
8.30 a.m 12.30 p.m	Wearmouth, 1½ m. from Sunderland	12.30 p.m 7.30 p.m
2.30 p.m	Wearhead, 30 miles from Durham ..	3.30 p.m
9.30 a.m	Weathersfield, 7 miles from Braintree	3.15 p.m
8.30 a.m	Weaverham, 4 miles from Northwich	5.45 p.m
12. 0noon	Wedmore, 10 mi. fr. Wells, Somerset	12.0noon
7. 0 a.m 3.30 p.m	*Wednesbury, Martin Worcester....	8.45 p.m
7. 0 a.m 1. 0 p.m	*Weedon, Richard Andrew	9.45 a.m 10. 0 p.m
7. 0 a.m	Weeley, 10 miles from Colchester	5.30 p.m
9.45 a.m	Welbourne, 12 miles from Grantham	2. 0 p.m
9. 0 a.m	Welbury, 7 miles from Northallerton	3.52 p.m
10. 0 a.m	*Welchpool, Thomas Clarke	2.30 p.m
9. 0 a.m	Weldon, 15 miles from Wandsford....	3.30 p.m
7. 0 a.m	*Welford, Mrs. Ann Spencer	7. 0 p.m
8.30 a.m	Welford, 7 miles from Newbury	4. 0 p.m
7. 0 a.m	*Wellingborough, Miss Eliz. Spong..	10. 0 p.m
10. 0 a.m	Wellingore, 14 miles from Grantham	2. 0 p.m
7. 0 a.m 8. 0 p.m	*Wellington, Salop, Benjamin Smith	6.30 p.m
7. 0 a.m	*Wellington, Somerset, James Hewett	8.45 p.m

Letters from London delivered at h. m.	Town. Postmaster.	Box for London closes at h. m.
11. 0 a.m	*Wells, Norfolk, John Southgate	2.30 p.m
7. 0 a.m	*Wells, Somerset, George Lawrence..	7.15 p.m
7.15 a.m	Wellsbourne, 5 mi. fr. Stratford Avon	4.15 p.m
8. 0 a.m	Wellsbridge, 5 miles from Bristol....	5. 0 p.m
6.10 p.m	Welton, 10 miles from Hull	10. 0 p.m
8. 0 a.m	*Welwyn, James Freshwater	9. 0 p.m
9. 0 a.m	Wem, 11 mi. fr. Whitchurch, Salop..	3. 0 p.m
7. 0 a.m	*Wendover, James Senior	7.45 p.m
7.30 a.m	Wennington, 7 miles from Rumford..	5.30 p.m
10.15 a.m	Weobley, 12 miles from Hereford....	1.15 p.m
8. 0 a.m	Wereham, 2 miles from Stoke	6. 0 p.m
1. 0 p.m	West-Alvington, 1 m. fr. Kingsbridge	9. 0 a.m
10. 0 a.m	West-Ashling, 4½ mi. fr. Chichester..	5. 0 p.m
11.40 a.m	West-Auckland, 3 m. f. Bshp. Aucklnd	4. 0 p.m
7. 0 a.m 3.30 p.m	*West-Bromwich, Samuel Sutton ..	9. 0 p.m
1.10 p.m	West-Burton, 20 miles from Bedale..	11.20 a.m
7. 0 a.m	*Westbury, Miss Elizabeth Cowdall..	7.30 p.m
7. 0 a.m	Westbury, 4 m. from Wells Somerset.	6.30 p.m
9. 0 a.m	Westbury, 10 m. from Shrewsbury ..	4. 0 p.m
7. 0 a.m	Westbury-on-Severn, 3 m. f. Newnham	5.30 p.m
8. 0 a.m 4. 0 p.m	Westbury-on-Trym, 4 m. f. Bristol.	12. 0noon 5. 0 p.m
11. 0 a.m	West-Clayton, 10 m. fr. Huddersfield	1.30 p.m
11. 0 a.m	West-Coker, 3 miles from Yeovil....	3.15 p.m
9. 0 a.m	West-Dean, 5 miles from Chichester..	5.30 p.m
10. 0 a.m	West-Derby, 5 miles from Liverpool..	4. 0 p.m
8.15 a.m	West-Drayton, 3 m. from Uxbridge..	6.30 p.m
9.30 a.m	West-End, 3 miles from Slough......	6. 0 p.m
9. 0 a.m	West-End, 3½ m. from Southampton.	5. 0 p.m
7.30 a.m	*Westerham	6. 0 p.m
8. 0 a.m	West-Farleigh, 4 mi. from Maidstone	5. 0 p.m
9.30 a.m	Westfield, 7½ miles from Battle......	5. 0 p.m
9. 0 a.m	West-Firle, 4½ miles from Lewes.....	5. 0 p.m
10. 0 a.m	West-Grinstead, 7 m. from Horsham	3.30 p.m
9. 0 a.m	West-Haddon, 8 miles from Daventry	5. 0 p.m
8. 0 a.m	Westley Waterless, 6 m. f. Newmarket	6.30 p.m
	West-Malling, see Town-Malling	
9. 0 a.m	West-Marden, 8 m. from Petersfield..	4.30 p.m
9. 0 a.m	West-Meon, 8 miles from Petersfield.	5. 0 p.m
8. 0 a.m	West-Moulsey, 4 m. from Kingston..	6. 0 p.m
12.30 p.m	West-Sockwith, 12 miles fr. Bawtry	1.45 p.m
7. 0 a.m	West-Tarring, 1½ m. from Worthing.	6.30 p.m
12.20 p.m	Westoe, 2 miles from South Shields..	1. 0 p.m
10.30 a.m	Weston, 2 miles from Bath..........	6. 0 p.m
8. 0 a.m	Weston-Green, 3 m. from Kingston..	6.45 p.m
10. 0 a.m	*Weston super Mare, Miss M. Gibbons	4. 0 p.m
3. 0 p.m	West-Rasen, 3 m. from Market-Rasen	9.30 a.m
1. 0 a.m	West-Tilbury, 16 miles from Rumford	12.45 p.m
7. 0 a.m	West-Town, 8 miles from Bristol....	4. 0 p.m
10.30 a.m	West-Wratting, 5 miles from Linton..	3.45 p.m
8. 0 a.m	West-Wycombe, 2½ m. fr. H. Wycombe	6.30 p.m
5.40 p.m	Wetheral, 4 miles from Carlisle	9.20 a.m
8.20 a.m	*Wetherby, John Smith	4.15 p.m
10.30 a.m	Weybridge, 6 miles from Esher	5. 0 p.m
9. 0 a.m	Weyhill, 3 miles from Andover......	6.30 p.m
9.30 a.m	*Weymouth, John Harvey	5.15 p.m
12.50 p.m	Whaley-Bridge, 11 m. f. Stockport..	2. 0 p.m
9. 0 a.m	Whalley, 7 miles from Blackburn...	3.45 p.m
4.40 p.m	Whalton, 6 miles from Morpeth	8. 0 a.m
9. 0 a.m	Whaplode, 6 miles from Spalding....	4. 0 p.m
8.30 a.m	Wheathamstead, 5 m. fr. St. Alban's	6. 0 p.m
7. 0 a.m	*Wheatley, William Lovelock	8.30 p.m
9. 0 a.m	Wheddon-Cross, 7 miles fr. Minehead	4. 0 p.m
8. 0 a.m	Wheelock, 1½ miles from Sandbach..	7. 0 p.m
12.40 p.m	Whickham, 4 miles from Gateshead	9.15 a.m
7. 0 a.m	Whiddon-Down, 16 mi. from Exeter.	5.30 p.m
12. 0noon 2. 0 p.m	Whimple, 8 miles from Exeter	11. 0 a.m 1. 0 p.m
9.15 a.m	Whippingham-Street, 2 m. f. Cowes..	3.15 p.m
1.10 p.m	Whitburn, 3½ miles from Sunderland	8. 0 a.m
2.40 p.m	*Whitby, Richard Rodgers	10.30 a.m
7. 0 a.m	*Whitchurch, Hants, John Wm. Wise	8.30 p.m
8. 0 a.m	*Whitchurch, Salop, Richard Crosse	7. 0 p.m
8. 0 a.m	Whitchurch, 3 miles from Bristol....	4.30 p.m
10. 0 a.m	Whitchurch, 6½ miles from Ross	2.40 p.m
8. 0 a.m	Whitchurch, 5 miles from Blandford	6.30 p.m
8. 0 a.m	Whitchurch, 5 miles from Aylesbury	5.30 p.m
8.15 a.m	Whitchurch, 6 miles from Reading ..	5. 0 p.m
11.30 a.m	Whitchurch-Canonicorum, 6 miles from Bridport	2. 0 p.m
8. 0 a.m	Whitehart, 3 miles from Uxbridge ..	6. 0 p.m

Letters from London delivered at h. m.	Town. Postmaster.	Box for London closes at h. m.
10. 0 a.m	White-Parish, 7 miles from Salisbury	4. 0 p.m
8.30 a.m 4.30 p.m	*Whitehaven, John Gibson........	8.50 a.m 2.30 p.m
9.55 a.m	Whitfield, 8 m. from Haydon-Bridge	2.20 p.m
10. 0 a.m	Whitminster, 7 miles from Dursley..	2.45 p.m
8. 0 a.m	Whitstable, 6 miles from Canterbury.	6. 0 p.m
6.15 p.m	Whittingham, 8 miles from Alnwick.	10. 0 p.m
10. 0 a.m	Whittington, 3 miles from Oswestry.	2.15 p.m
8. 0 a.m	Whittlesea, 6½ m. from Peterborough	6.30 p.m
10.30 a.m	Whittlesford, 8 mi. from Cambridge.	3.30 p.m
10. 0 a.m	Whittle-le-Woods, 3 mi. fr. Chorley.	3.20 p.m
8.30 a.m	Whittwell, 5 miles from Welwyn....	6. 0 p.m
9.30 a.m	Whitwell, 12 miles from York	3.55 p.m
7. 0 a.m	Whitwell, 5 miles from Worksop	6. 0 p.m
12. 0noon	Whitwick, 8 m. fr. Ashby de la Zouch	2.30 p.m
9.30 a.m	Wichampton, 5 miles from Wimborne	5. 0 p.m
7. 0 a.m	Wickford, 11 miles fr. Ingatestone ..	6.20 p.m
7.15 a.m	Wickham, 4 miles from Fareham...	6. 0 p.m
11. 0 a.m	Wickham-Brook, 12 m. fr. Newmarket	4.45 p.m
7. 0 a.m	Wickham-Market, 5 m. f. Woodbridge	7.45 p.m
8. 0 a.m	Wickwar, 3½ m. f. Wotton-under-edge	4.30 p.m
8. 0 a.m	Widford, 6 miles from Ware........	6.30 p.m
7. 0 a.m 7. 0 p.m	*Wigan, Robert Acton	6.30 p.m 9.45 p.m
9. 0 a.m	Wigston-Magna, 4 m. from Leicester	5.30 p.m
12.45 p.m. 4. 0 p.m.	*Wigton, Joseph Messenger	9.23 a.m 11.45 a.m
8.55 a.m	Wilberfoss, 8½ miles from York......	4.30 p.m
9.15 a.m	Wiley, 7 miles from Heytesbury	4. 0 p.m
7.30 a.m	Willenhall, 3 miles from Walsall	3.30 p.m
7. 0 a.m	Willesborough, 2 m. from Ashford ..	7. 0 p.m
9.30 a.m	Willingale, 4 miles from Ongar	4. 0 p.m
7. 0 a.m	Willingdon, 28 m. from Hurst-Green.	7. 0 p.m
10, 0 a.m	Willingham, 8 miles from St. Ives ..	5.30 p.m
4.30 p.m	Willington, 7 miles from Durham ...	8.10 a.m
12.30 p.m	Willington, 6 miles fr. Newcastle T..	9. 0 p.m
7. 0 a.m	Williton, 16 miles from Taunton	6.15 p.m
3.30 p.m	Willmington, 3 miles from Honiton..	10.15 a.m
8. 0 a.m	Willsbridge, 6 miles from Bristol....	4.45 p.m
9.30 a.m	Wilmslow, 12 mi. from Manchester..	4. 0 p.m
8. 0 a.m	Wilsden, 5 m. from Bradford, Yorksh	3. 0 p.m
7. 0 a.m	Wilton, 3 miles from Salisbury......	7.30 p.m
7. 0 a.m	*Wimborne, John Vey	8. 0 p.m
8. 0 a.m	*Wincanton, Jno. Cletsome Musgrave	5.45 p.m
8. 0 a.m	Winchcombe, 7 mi. fr. Cheltenham ..	5. 0 p.m
8. 0 a.m	Winchelsea, 4 miles from Rye	5.10 p.m
7. 0 a.m 2.30 p.m	*Winchester, John Tilley	9. 0 a.m 10. 0 p.m
7. 0 a.m	Windlesham, 1 mile from Bagshot ..	6.30 p.m
7.30 a.m 12. 0noon	*Windsor, Henry Cook	11.30 a.m 10. 0 p.m
8. 0 a.m	Winford, 7 miles from Bristol	3. 0 p.m
11.40 a.m	Winfrith, Newbgh. 9 m. f. Dorchester	2. 0 p.m
7. 0 a.m	*Wingham, John Beal..............	8. 0 p.m
9.30 a.m	Winkfield, 11 miles from Chertsey ..	4. 0 p.m
11. 0 a.m	Winkleigh, 17 miles from Crediton..	2. 0 p.m
7. 0 a.m	Winkton, 6½ miles from Ringwood ..	8. 0 p.m
12.50 p.m	Winlaton, 5½ m. fr. Newcastle-on-Tyne	7.50 p.m
8. 0 a.m	Winsford, 4 miles from Middlewich..	6.15 p.m
9. 0 a.m	Winsham, 4 miles from Chard	1. 0 p.m
7. 0 a.m	*Winslow, Grant King..............	6.30 p.m
8. 0 a.m	Winster, 6 miles from Matlock......	3. 0 p.m
8. 0 a.m	Winterborne-Abbas, 4½ m. f. Dorchstr	5.45 p.m
9. 0 a.m 5. 0 p.m	Winterbourne, 24 mi. from Marlboro'.	4.30 p.m
8.30 a.m	Winterbourne, 7 miles from Bristol..	3.15 p.m
5. 0 p.m	Winterton, 10 miles from Brigg....	9. 0 a.m
9. 0 a.m	Winthorpe, 2 miles from Newark....	4. 0 p.m
7. 0 a.m	Winwick, 3 miles from Warrington..	6. 0 p.m
8.15 a.m	*Wirksworth, Miss Mary Jane Brace	5. 0 p.m
8.45 a.m	*Wisbeach, John Goward	5.15 p.m
7. 0 a.m	Wisborough-Green, 10 m. fr. Horsham	6. 0 p.m
7. 0 a.m	*Witham, William Garrett	10. 0 p.m
3. 0 p.m	Witheridge, 10 miles from Crediton..	7.30 a.m
11.10 a.m	Withnall, 6 miles from Chorley	2.50 p.m
7. 0 a.m	Withyham, 7 m. from Tunbridge-Wells	7. 0 p.m
7. 0 a.m	*Witney, Joseph Masters	10. 0 p.m
7.30 a.m	Wittersham, 16 mi. from Staplehurst	4.30 p.m
12.45 p.m	Witton-le-Wear, 4 miles from Bishop-Auckland	2.50 p.m
7. 0 a.m	*Wiveliscombe, Wm. John Hancock	7.15 p.m
7. 0 a.m	Wivenhoe, 4½ miles from Colchester..	7. 0 p.m

Letters from London delivered at h. m.	Town. Postmaster.	Box for London closes at h. m.
7. 0 a.m	*Woburn, Stephen Dodd	7. 0 p.m
8. 0 a.m	Woburn, 3 miles from Beaconsfield..	5.30 p.m
8. 0 a.m	Woddesdon, 5 miles from Aylesbury..	5.30 p.m
8. 0 a.m	Woking, 3 miles from Ripley	6. 0 p.m
7.30 a.m	*Wokingham, Thomas Spencer	6.15 p.m
8. 0 a.m	Wollaston, 4 miles from Wellingboro'	5. 0 p.m
7. 0 a.m	Wolseley-Bridge, 3 miles fr. Rugeley	7.30 p.m
11.20 a.m	Wolsingham, 16 miles from Durham	7. 0 a.m
8. 0 a.m 8.30 p.m	*Wolverhampton, Mr. Elwell	6. 0 a.m 10.15 p.m
8. 0 a.m	Wolverton station, 2m. fr. S.Stratford	5.45 p.m
11.50 a.m	Wolviston, 5 miles from Stockton....	12.55 p.m
7.30 a.m	Womborne, 4 miles f. Wolverhampton	6.15 p.m
6.0 a.m	Womersley, 5 miles from Pontefract..	4. 0 p.m
8. 0 a.m	Wonersh, 5 miles from Guildford	5. 0 p.m
7. 0 a.m	*Woodbridge, John Loder	9. 0 p.m
8. 0 a.m	Woodbury, 7 miles from Exeter	6. 0 p.m
7. 0 a.m	Wood-Chester, 2½ miles from Stroud	5. 0 p.m
8. 0 a.m	Woodchurch, 3 miles from Tenterden	4.30 p.m
9. 0 a.m	Wooden-Box, 7 m. f. Burton-on-Trent	3.45 p.m
5.30 p.m	Woodford-Bridge, 11 mi. fr. Bideford	7. 0 a.m
7. 0 a.m	*Woodstock, William Howels	10. 0 p.m
7. 0 a.m	Wookey, 2 mi. from Wells, Somerset	7. 0 p.m
10. 0 a.m	Wool, 5 miles, from Wareham	4. 0 p.m
4. 0 p.m	Wooler, 9 miles from Belford........	8. 0 p.m
10. 0 a.m	Woolhampton, 7 miles from Newbury	4. 0 p.m
8. 0 a.m	Woolpit, 8 miles f. Bury St. Edmunds	6. 0 p.m
8.30 a.m	Woolston, 6 miles from Coventry....	4.30 p.m
10.30 a.m	Woolton, 6 miles from Liverpool	2.45 p.m
8. 0 a.m	Woolverston, 5 miles from Ipswich..	5. 0 p.m
8.30 a.m	Woore, 7½ miles fr. Market-Drayton	4.15 p.m
7. 0 a.m	Wootton-Bassett, 6 miles fr. Swindon	8. 0 p.m
11. 0 a.m	Wootton-Bridge, 3½ miles from Ryde	3. 0 p.m
7. 0 a.m	*Worcester, John Hill	7.45 p.m
10.15 a.m	Wordsley, 2 miles from Stourbridge..	6.25 p.m
7. 0 a.m	Worfield, 10 mi. fr. Wolverhampton	7. 0 p.m
10.22 a.m 3.30 p.m	*Workington, James Kirkconel	9.45 a.m
8.30 a.m	*Worksop, Miss Elizabeth Haykin ..	5.35 p.m
8.45 a.m	Worle, 18 miles from Wells, Somerset	4.15 p.m
7. 0 a.m	Worlington, 1 mile from Mildenhall..	7. 0 p.m
9.15 a.m	Worlingworth, 18 m. from Woodbridge	5.15 p.m
10. 0 a.m	Wormbridge, 8½ miles from Hereford	1.30 p.m
8.30 a.m	Wormley, 4 mi. from Waltham-Cross	6.15 p.m
10. 0 a.m	Worstead, 12 miles from Norwich....	3. 0 p.m
10.15 a.m	Worthenbury, 8 m. from Wrexham ..	2.50 p.m
7. 0 a.m 2. 0 p.m	*Worthing, Miss Caroline Plumer..	7.15 p.m 10. 0 a.m
9. 0 a.m	Wortley, 9 miles from Sheffield.......	2. 0 p.m
7. 0 a.m	*Wotton-under-edge, Henry Cogswell	6. 0 p.m
1.30 p.m	Wragby, 11 miles from Lincoln	1. 0 p.m
6. 0 a.m	Wraxhall, 8 miles from Bristol	3.40 p.m
8.50 a.m	Wray, 10 miles from Lancaster	4.40 p.m
6.45 a.m	Wrecclesham, 1½ miles from Farnham	7. 0 p.m
7. 0 a.m	Wrentham, 3½ miles from Wangford	7. 0 p.m
7.30 a.m.	*Wrexham, Richard Hughes.........	5.30 p.m
8. 0 a.m	Wrington, 11 miles from Bristol	2.15 p.m
8. 0 a.m	Writtle, 2½ miles from Chelmsford ...	6. 0 p.m
9. 0 a.m	Wrotham, 7 miles from Seven-Oaks...	4. 0 p.m
8. 0 a.m	Wroughton, 3 miles from Swindon ...	7.30 p.m
9.15 a.m	Wroxton, 3 miles from Banbury	3.30 p.m
7. 0 a.m	*Wycombe (High), George Harman..	8.30 p.m
8. 0 a.m	Wye, 4½ miles from Ashford	6.30 p.m
11.40 a.m	Wykeham, 15 miles from Malton....	1.45 p.m
10.50 a.m	Wyke-Regis, 1½ mi. from Weymouth	4.50 p.m
7.15 a.m	Wymeswold, 5 miles from Loughboro'	6.55 p.m
8. 0 a.m	*Wymondham, Richard Francis	10. 0 p.m
9.20 a.m	Wymondham, 7 miles from Oakham..	3. 0 p.m
8.15 a.m	Yalding, 6 miles from Maidstone.....	4.30 p.m
10. 0 a.m	Yarcombe, 6 miles from Chard.......	2. 0 p.m
9. 0 a.m 4.30 p.m	*Yarm, Mrs. Elizth. Stonehouse....	3.30 p.m 6.30 p.m
9. 0 a.m	Yarmouth, I. W 4 m. fr. Lymington	3.30 p.m
8.35 a.m	*Yarmouth, Norfolk, David Hogarth	5. 0 p.m
9.30 a.m	Yateley, 5 miles from Hartfordbridge	6. 0 p.m
7.30 a.m	Yatton, 12 miles from Bristol	3.20 p.m
7.40 a.m	Yaxley, 2 miles from Eye	7. 0 p.m
8. 0 a.m	Yaxley, 3 miles from Stilton.........	6. 0 p.m
9. 0 a.m	Yeadon, 8 miles from Leeds	4.30 p.m
8.40 a.m	Yealand-Conyers, 9 m. from Lancaster	5. 0 p.m
11. 0 a.m	*Yealmpton, Samuel Brock	1.30 p.m
8.30 a.m	Yeldham, 7 miles from Halstead	4.45 p.m
9. 0 a.m	*Yeovil, Robert Jennings	5.30 p.m
9.45 a.m	Yetminster, 6 miles from Sherborne	1. 45 p.m
8. 0 a.m 8. 0 p.m	*York, Joshua Oldfield.............	5.15 p.m 10. 0 p.m
7. 0 a.m	York-Town, 3½ miles from Bagshot..	6.30 p.m
8.45 a.m	Youl-Greave, 4 miles from Bakewell	4. 0 p.m
10. 0 a.m	Yoxall, 8 miles from Lichfield	3.15 p.m
7. 0 a.m	Yoxford, 4 miles from Saxmundham	7.30 p.m

SCOTLAND.

	*Aberbrothwick, *see* Arbroath	
4.15 p.m	Aberchirder, 9 miles from Banff ...	3.40 p.m
7. 0 a.m 5.20 p.m	*Aberdeen David Stewart........	4.20 a.m 2. 0 p.m
9. 0 a.m 7. 0 p.m	*Aberdour Peter Kennedy........	3.30 p.m 10. 0 p.m
4.30 p.m	*Aberfeldy, James Kippen	8. 0 a.m
2. 0 p.m	Aberfoyle, 20 miles from Stirling....	9.30 a.m
11. 0 a.m	Aberlady, 5 miles from Haddington..	4.30 p.m
3.45 p.m	Aberlour, 2 miles from Craigellachie	10. 0 p.m
11.30 a.m 4. 0 p.m	Abernethy, 3½ miles from Newburgh Fife	10. 0 a.m 3.30 p.m
10. 0 a.m	Abington, 18 miles from Moffat....	12.20 p.m 7.30 p.m
11.40 a.m	*Aboyne, George Cromar, jun.......	10. 0 a.m
6.15 p.m	Advie, 4 miles from Ballindalloch ..	10. 0 p.m
8. 0 a.m	*Airdrie, Mary Torrance	8.30 p.m
8. 0 a.m	Alexandria, 3½ mi. from Dumbarton	5.30 p.m
11. 0 a.m	Alford, 26 miles from Aberdeen	10. 0 a.m
10. 0 a.m	*Alloa, Matthew Brydie	3. 0 p.m 9. 0 p.m
12.25 p.m	Almond Bank, 5 miles from Perth...	2.15 p.m
7. 0 a.m	Alness, 3 miles from Invergordon....	9. 0 p.m
10.30 a.m	Alva, 7 miles from Stirling	1.45 p.m
2.15 p.m	Alyth, 3½ miles from Meigle........	4.50 p.m
5. 0 p.m	Amulrie, 10 miles from Dunkeld....	8. 0 a.m
8. 0 a.m 4.45 p.m	*Annan, George Tool	8.20 a.m 1.45 p.m
12.30noon	*Anstruther, John Murdoch........	6. 0 p.m
8. 0 a.m	*Appin, Duncan Clark	9. 0 p.m
7. 0 a.m 12. 0noon	*Arbroath, Robert Findlayson......	9.45 a.m 7.30 p.m
7. 0 a.m 6.15 p.m	*Ardersier, John Currie...........	5.15 p.m 9.30 p.m
10.30 a.m.	Ardentinny, 20 miles from Greenock	12.15noon
4.30 p.m	Ardnamurchan, 30 mi. fr. Strontian..	8.30 a.m
9. 0 a.m 6.45 p.m	*Ardrossan, James Stevens	3.45 p.m
5. 0 p.m	Ardwell Inn, 12 mi. from Stranraer..	8.20 a.m
10. 0 a.m	Arisaig, 40 miles from Fort-William..	9. 0 p.m
4. 0 p.m	*Aross, David Fletcher	9. 0 p.m
	Arran, *see* "Brodick" and "Lamlash"	
9. 0 a.m	Arrochar, 36 miles from Glasgow....	3. 0 p.m
2. 0 p.m	Ascog, 3 miles from Rothesay	3. 0 p.m
9.30 a.m	Ashkirk, 7 miles from Hawick......	11.40 a.m
3. 0 p.m	Assynt, 51 miles from Golspie	10. 0 p.m
7.45 a.m	Auchenblae, 5 mi. fr. Laurence Kirk	2.30 p.m
9. 0 a.m	Auchencairn, 8½ m. fr. Castle-Douglas	3. 0 p.m
12. 0noon	Auchenleek, 1 mile from Cumnock..	1.30 p.m
7.30 a.m 5.40 p.m	Auchmill, 3½ miles from Aberdeen ..	1. 0 p.m
8. 0 a.m	Auchnacraig, 18 miles from Aross ..	9.30 a.m
11.40 a.m	*Auchterarder, James Stewart......	5. 0 p.m
8. 0 a.m 11.30 a.m	*Auchtermuchty, Margaret Laing	10. 0 a.m 10. 0 p.m
9.45 a.m	Auchtertore, 3¾ miles from Kirkcaldy	3.30 p.m
7. 0 a.m	Auldearn, 3 miles from Nairn	4.30 p.m
7.45 p.m	Auldgirth-Bridge, 8 m. fr. Dumfries	3. 0 p.m
8. 0 a.m 7.15 p.m	*Ayr, Elizabeth Davidson..........	4.15 p.m 9.30 p.m
8.30 a.m 8. 0 p.m	*Ayton, Mary Thompson	2. 0 p.m 10. 0 p.m
11.30 a.m	Balbeggie, 5 miles from Perth	7.15 p.m
8.10 a.m	Balblair, 6 miles from Tain	6. 5 p.m
9.30 a.m 7.45 p.m	*Balerno, William Walker..........	5.15 p.m
12.30 a.m 5.15 p.m	Balgonie, 1½ miles from Markinch	12.15noon 5. 0 p.m

Letters from London delivered at h. m.	Town. Postmaster.	Box for London closes at h. m.
0.30 a.m	Balfron, 20 miles from Glasgow	2.15 p.m
8. 0 a.m	Ballachelish Ferry, 14 miles fr. Appin	6. 0 p.m
8. 0 a.m	Ballachelish Village, 15½ m. fr. Appin	4.30 p.m
8. 0 a.m 6.30 p.m	*Ballantrae, John Millar	5.30 p.m 9.45 p.m
1.30 p.m	*Ballater, Donald Farquharson	8.30 a.m
7. 0 p.m	Ballieston, 5½ miles from Glasgow	9. 0 p.m
7. 0 a.m 5.20 p.m	*Ballindalloch, James Burgess	4.20 p.m 10. 0 p.m
3.40 p.m	Balquhidder, 13 miles from Callander	8. 0 a.m
9.30 a.m	Banchory, 18 miles from Aberdeen	11.45 a.m
7. 0 a.m 1.10 p.m	*Banff, Alexander Smith	7.30 a.m 2. 0 p.m
2. 0 p.m	Bankend, 6 miles from Dumfries	2.45 p.m
2. 0noon	Bankfoot, 9 miles from Perth	2.30 p.m
9. 0 a.m	Bannockburn, 2½ miles from Stirling	2.45 p.m
11. 0 a.m	Barr, 8 miles from Girvan	3. 0 p.m
10.30 a.m	Barrhead, 7 miles from Glasgow	12.30noon
13.30 p.m	Barrhill, 12 miles from Girvan	11. 0 a.m
7.30 a.m 6. 0 p.m	*Bathgate, Margaret Jamieson	8.30 p.m
On Arrival of the Packet	Battasound, near Lerwick, Zetland	Uncertain
7. 0 a.m	*Beauly, Peter Fraser	10. 0 p.m
8. 0 a.m 6. 0 p.m	*Beith, Robert Wilson, jun.	6. 0 p.m
10. 0 a.m	Bellshill, 8 miles from Glasgow	4. 0 p.m
8. 0 a.m	Beltonford, 3 miles from Dunbar	7. 0 p.m
7. 0 a.m 2.30 p.m	*Bervie James Souter	7. 0 a.m 5.15 p.m
2. 0 p.m	*Biggar, Andrew Nichol	9. 0 a.m
8. 0 a.m	Bishopbriggs, 3½ miles from Glasgow	8. 0 p.m
8. 0 a.m	Bishopton, 6 miles from Paisley	10. 0 p.m
8. 5 a.m	Blackburn, 4 miles from Kintore	1. 0 p.m
9.30 a.m	Blackburn, 2 miles from Whitburn	2.40 p.m
2.35 p.m	Blackford, 4½ miles fr. Auchterarder	3.15 p.m
1.30 p.m	Blackhillock, 5 miles from Keith	10. 0 p.m
9.30 a.m	*Blackshiels, William Pearson	9.45 a.m
8.30 a.m 7. 0 p.m	*Blair-Adam, James Stewart	6. 0 p.m 10. 0 p.m
3. 0 p.m	*Blair-Athole, William Robertson	11.30 a.m
9. 0 a.m	Blair-Drummond, 6 miles fr. Stirling	3.15 p.m
1.30 p.m	*Blairgowrie, Robert Ayson	5.30 p.m
9.30 a.m	Blairlogie, 3½ miles from Stirling	3. 0 p.m
10. 0 a.m	Blantyre, 3 miles from Hamilton	6.15 p.m
7. 0 a.m	Bogroy, 8 miles from Inverness	8. 0 p.m
5.45 p.m	Bohally, 12 miles from Petlochrie	5. 0 p.m
10. 0 a.m	*Bonar-Bridge, Alexander Ross	4.30 p.m
6.30 p.m	*Bonaw, John Cameron	10. 0 p.m
4. 0 p.m	Bonchester-Bridge, 7 miles f. Hawick	10. 0 p.m
8. 0 a.m	Bonhill, 4 miles from Dumbarton	5. 0 p.m
11. 0 a.m	Borgue, 6 miles from Kirkcudbright	3.30 p.m
10.30 a.m	*Borrowstouness, Margt. Anderson	11.15 a.m 8.15 p.m
1. 0 p.m	Bothwell, 2 miles from Hamilton	9. 0 a.m
8. 0 a.m	*Bowmore, Duncan McAllister	12.30noon
10. 0 a.m	*Braco, Robert Whyte	7.30 p.m
Irregular	Brae, near Lerwick, Zetland	Uncertain
4.30 p.m	Braemar, 18 miles from Ballater	10. 0 p.m
7. 0 a.m 4. 0 p.m	*Brechin, William Low	4.20 p.m 9.30 p.m
8.45 a.m	Bridge of Allan, 3¼ miles fr. Stirling	8.30 p.m
10.30 a.m	*Bridge of Earn, Daniel Campbell	4.30 p.m 10. 0 p.m
8. 0 a.m	Bridge of Weir, 6 miles fr. Paisley	4.30 p.m
8.20 p.m	*Broadford, George MacPhail	3. 0 p.m
12. 0noon	Brodick (Arran), 16 mil. fr. Ardrossan	3.30 p.m
11.15 a.m	Brora, 5 miles from Golspie	3.30 p.m
8. 0 a.m 1.30 p.m	Broughty-Ferry, 4 miles fr. Dundee	9. 0 a.m 7.15 p.m
9.30 a.m	*Broxburn, Jane Mather	4. 0 p.m
12.45 p.m	Brucklaw, 5½ miles from Mintlaw	7. 0 p.m
3.30 p.m	Buchlyvie, 14½ miles from Stirling	9.30 a.m
10. 0 a.m	Buckhaven, 6 miles from Kirkcaldy	8. 0 p.m
7. 0 a.m	*Buckie, John Reid	10. 0 p.m
10.10 a.m	Burghead, 9 miles from Elgin	10.50 a.m
6. 0 p.m	Bunessan, 30 miles from Aross	9. 0 p.m
7.30 a.m 6. 0 p.m	*Burntisland, Elizabeth Ross	3. 0 p.m 10. 0 p.m
regular	Burravoe, near Lerwick, Zetland	Uncertain
8.30 a.m 6. 0 p.m	Busby, 6 miles from Glasgow	10. 0 p.m

Letters from London delivered at h. m.	Town. Postmaster.	Box for London closes at h. m.
3.15 p.m	Byth, 9 miles from Turriff	10. 0 p.m
11. 0 a.m	Cairndow, 50 miles from Glasgow	9.30 a.m
Uncertain	Cairnish, 13 miles from Lochmaddy	Uncertain
8. 6 a.m 5. 0 p.m	Cairnryan, 6 miles from Stranraer	4. 0 p.m 9. 0 p.m
11. 0 a.m	*Callander, Anne McEwan	1.30 p.m
9. 0 a.m	Cambuslang, 4 miles from Glasgow	1.45 p.m
12.20 a.m	Camelon, 1 mile from Falkirk	3.30 p.m
8.30 p.m	*Campbelton, Alexander Lowthian	10. 0 p.m
8. 0 a.m 4. 0 p.m	*Canonbie Agnes, Donaldson	4. 0 p.m 10. 0 p.m
7. 0 a.m	Carbost, 23 miles from Broadford	8.30 a.m
8.30 a.m	Carluke, 5 miles from Lanark	1. 0 p.m
10.30 a.m	Carnock, 3½ miles from Dunfermline	3.45 p.m
7. 0 a.m 11.30 a.m	*Carnoustie, Alexander Balfour	9.45 a.m 7.15 p.m
10. 0 a.m	Carnwath, 7 miles from Lanark	4. 0 p.m
7. 0 a.m	*Carrbridge, Alexander Ellis	10. 0 p.m
11.30 a.m	Carron, 2 miles from Falkirk	3. 0 p.m
1.30 p.m	Carronshore, 3 miles from Falkirk	2. 0 p.m
2.15 p.m	Carsphairn, 25 miles from Ayr	11.45 a.m
7. 0 a.m 2. 0 p.m	*Castle-Douglas, William Green	10. 0 p.m
9.30 a.m	Castleton, 5 miles from Thurso	5. 0 p.m
7.30 a.m	Cathcart, 3½ miles from Glasgow	2.15 p.m
9. 0 a.m	Catrine, 2¼ miles from Mauchline	2.30 p.m
7.45 a.m	Cawdor, 6 miles from Nairn	1.45 p.m
9. 0 a.m 12.15 p.m	*Chance Inn, David Todd	9. 5 a.m 7.15 p.m
10.15 a.m	Charleston, 4 miles fr. Dunfermline	3.25 p.m
8. 0 a.m	Chirnside, 5 miles from Ayton	5 10 p.m
3.30 p.m	Clackmannan, 1½ miles from Alloa	10. 0 a.m
8. 0 p.m	Closeburn, 12 miles from Dumfries	2.15 p.m
9.30 a.m	Cluny, 15 miles from Aberdeen	11.45 a.m
8. 0 a.m 5. 0 p.m	Coatbridge, 8 miles from Glasgow	8.30 p.m
8. 0 a.m 10. 0 a.m	*Cockburnspath, James Crooks	12 noon 9.30 p.m
10. 0 a.m	Coldingham, 4 miles from Ayton	3.45 p.m
10. 0 a.m	*Coldstream, John Halliburton	10. 0 p.m
11.30 a.m	*Colinsburgh, Elizabeth Ronald	6. 0 p.m
8.30 a.m 4.45 p.m	*Colinton, David Girdwood	6.45 p.m
Uncertain	Coll, 20 miles from Tobermory	Uncertain
8.30 a.m 3.30 p.m	Colmonell, 5½ miles from Ballantrae	8.45 a.m 3.30 p.m
11. 0 a.m	Comrie, 6¾ miles from Crieff	4. 0 p.m
3.20 p.m	Cornerhouse, 2 miles from Stranraer	9.50 a.m
4. 5 p.m	Cornhill, 8 miles from Banff	12.30 p.m
11. 0 a.m	Corpach, 4 miles from Fort William	1. 0 p.m
8. 0 a.m	Corran (Ardgour), 19 miles fr. Appin	4. 0 p.m
8. 0 a.m	Corrance, 10¾ miles from Dumfries	3. 0 p.m
9.30 a.m 6.30 p.m	*Corstorphine, Andrew Henderson	2.30 p.m 10. 0 p.m
12.25 p.m	Cortes, 5 miles from Fraserburgh	7. 0 a.m
7. 0 a.m 3.30 p.m	*Craigellachie, James Cumming	2.30 p.m 10. 0 p.m
1. 0 p.m	*Crail, James Key	5. 0 p.m
7. 0 a.m 5. 0 p.m	*Cramond, John Gourlay	7.30 p.m
2.45 p.m	Crathie, 8 miles from Ballater	10. 0 p.m
8. 0 a.m	*Creetown, Alexander M'Kean	10. 0 p.m
11.30 a.m	*Crieff, Anne Macqueen	7. 0 a.m 6.10 p.m
8. 0 a.m	Crinan, 5 miles from Lochgilphead	3. 0 p.m
8. 0 p.m	Crocketford, 9 miles from Dumfries	10. 0 p.m
9.15 a.m	*Cromarty, Margaret Ross	5. 0 p.m
12.30noon	Crook, 18 miles from Noblehouse	9.10 p.m
9. 0 a.m	Crossgates, 4 m. from Inverkeithing	11. 0 a.m 6.30 a.m
12.45noon	Crosshill, 3 miles from Maybole	12. 0noon
8. 30 a.m	Crossmichael, 4 miles from Castle Douglas	5.30 p.m
7. 0 a.m	Cruden, 9 miles from Ellon	9. 0 a.m
9.15 a.m	Culbokie, 9 miles from Dingwall	5.45 p.m
7. 0 a.m	*Cullen, Alexander Anderson	9.30 a.m 10. 0 p.m
Irregular	Cullivoe, nr. Lerwick, Zetland	Uncertain
9. 0 a.m 8. 0 p.m	*Culross, Robert Henderson	4. 0 p.m 9. 0 a.m
9.30 a.m	Cumbernauld, 15 miles from Glasgow	1.30 p.m
2. 0 p.m	Cummistown, 5½ miles from Turriff	6.45 a.m

Letters from London delivered at h. m.	Town. Postmaster.	Box for London closes at h. m.
10. 0 a.m	*Cumnock, Archibald Sliman	1.30 p.m
1. 0 p.m	*Cupar (Angus), Andrew Stevenson	6. 6 p.m
9.20 a.m	*Cupar (Fife), Thomas Pratt	12. 5noon
8.30 a.m 6.45 p.m	*Currie, William Frier	6.15 p.m
3. 0 p.m	Dailly, 7 miles from Maybole	3.30 p.m
9.30 a.m	Dairsie, 3 miles from Cupar (Fife)	8.30 p.m
9.30 a.m 1. 0 p.m	Dalbeattie, 13¾ m. from Dumfries	6. 0 p.m
10.30 a.m 2. 0 p.m	Daljarroch, 9½ mi. from Ballantrae	11.20 a.m 2. 0 p.m
9. 0 a.m 5.30 p.m	*Dalkeith, John Goldie	9.30 p.m
7. 0 p.m	Dalmally, 16 miles from Inverary	10. 0 p.m
12.15noon	Dalmellington, 15 miles from Ayr	1. 0 p.m
7.30 a.m	Dalmuir, 8½ miles from Glasgow	7.30 p.m
4. 0 p.m	Dalnacardoch, 11 m. fr. Blair Athole	10.30 a.m
8. 0 a.m 6. 0 p.m	Dalry, 5 miles from Beith	5.40 p.m
10. 0 a.m	Dalry, 16 miles from Castle-Douglas	4. 0 p.m
11.15 a.m	Dalrymple, 6 miles from Ayr	1.45 p.m
2.30 p.m	Dalswinton, 7½ miles from Dumfries	7.30 a.m
10. 0 a.m	Damhead, 6½ miles from Kinross	5. 0 p.m
9.40 a.m	Denholm, 6 miles from Hawick	4.30 p.m
8. 0 a.m	*Denny, William Cousland	5.45 p.m
8. 0 a.m	Dennyloanhead, 16 miles fr. Glasgow	6. 0 p.m
7. 0 a.m	*Dingwall, John MacPhail	10. 0 p.m
11.50 a.m	Dirleton, 9 miles from Haddington	3.45 p.m
12.40noon	Dollar, 7 miles from Alloa	7. 0 p.m
12.45noon	Dolphington, 9 miles from Noblehouse	6.30 a.m
8.45 a.m	*Dornoch, Alexander Davidson	5.30 p.m
8. 0 a.m 1. 0 p.m	*Douglas, Thomas Tassie	9. 0 a.m 7. 0 p.m
9.30 a.m	*Doune, 8 miles from Stirling	3.15 p.m
6.15 p.m	Dromore, 20 miles from Stranrear	7. 0 a.m
9.15 a.m	Drumlithie, 7 miles from Stonehaven	5.45 p.m
7. 0 a.m	Drumnadrochit, 14 miles fr. Inverness	11.30 a.m
10.30 a.m	Drymen, 12 miles from Dumbarton	1.50 p.m
11.30 a.m 6. 0 p.m	Duddingstone, 1½ miles f. Portobello	7. 0 p.m
8. 0 a.m 6. 0 p.m	*Dumbarton, Margaret Davidson	6.20 p.m
10. 0 a.m 6.30 p.m	*Dumfries, John Thorburn	7. 0 a.m 12.45 p.m
8. 0 a.m 11. 0 a.m	*Dunbar, Alexander Barclay	11.10 a.m 10. 0 p.m
3.30 p.m	*Dunbeath, William Sinclair	11.20 a.m
9. 0 a.m	*Dunblane, Anne Dawson	8.30 p.m
7. 0 a.m 11.20 a.m	*Dundee, Robert Bell	10. 0 a.m 9. 0 p.m
8.30 a.m	Dundonald, 5 miles f. Kilmarnock	2.30 p.m
11.30 a.m	Dundrennan, 7½ miles f. Kirkcudbright	3.30 p.m
8. 0 a.m 7. 0 p.m	*Dunfermline, Catherine Angus	5.15 p.m 10. 0 p.m
8. 0 a.m	Dunglas, 12 miles from Glasgow	7. 0 p.m
1. 0 p.m	*Dunkeld, John Mathew	1.45 p.m
10.15 a.m	Dunnett, 9 miles from Thurso	2.45 p.m
12.10noon	Dunning, 5 miles from Auchterarder	5.45 p.m
10.30 a.m	*Dunoon, —— McPhee	12. 0noon
9. 0 p.m	Dunscore, 9 miles from Dumfries	5. 0 p.m
8. 0 a.m	*Dunse, Magdalane Selby	4. 0 p.m
10. 0 a.m	Duntocher, 9½ miles from Glasgow	6. 0 p.m
7. 0 a.m	*Dunvegan, David MacDonald	10. 0 p.m
7.30 a.m	Durness, 65 miles from Thurso	10.45 a.m
8.30 a.m 8.15 p.m	Dysart, 2 miles from Kirkcaldy	1. 0 p.m 9. 0 p.m
10. 0 a.m	Eaglesham, 9 miles from Glasgow	12.30noon
8.30 a.m	Earlston, 4½ miles from Melrose	4.15 p.m
9.30 a.m	Easdale, 16 miles from Oban	12.30noon
9. 0 a.m 1. 0 p.m	*Ecclefechan, William Johnstone	3. 0 p.m 9. 0 p.m
15.35 a.m	Echt, 12½ miles from Aberdeen	7.50 a.m
11.30 a.m	*Eddleston, Margaret Thornburn	8.30 a.m
7.30 a.m 12. 0 p.m	*Edinburgh, Sir Edward S. Lees, Bart., *Secretary*	7. 0 a.m 9.30 p.m
9.15 a.m	Edzell, 6 miles from Brechin	1.45 p.m
7.15 a.m 3.15 p.m	*Elgin, John Forsythe	2.15 p.m 10. 0 p.m
2.45noon	Elie, 3 miles from Colinsburgh	4.45 p.m
9.30 a.m	*Ellon, John Rae	9.30 a.m
7. 0 a.m	*Errol, William Adam	9.30 p.m
11.50 a.m	Etal, 6 miles from Coldstream	3.30 p.m

Letters from London delivered at h. m.	Town. Postmaster.	Box for London closes at h. m.
7. 0 a.m	*Evanton, Donald Ross	9.30 p.m
9. 0 a.m	Eyemouth, 2½ miles from Ayton	4.45 p.m
11. 0 a.m	Fairlie, 2¾ miles from Largs	1.45 p.m
11. 0 a.m 4.30 p.m	*Falkirk, Henry Salmon	3. 0 p.m 10. 0 p.m
10.30 a.m	Falkland, 4 miles from Kettle	11. 0 a.m
1.45 p.m	Farr, 31 miles from Thurso	9.45 a.m
8. 0 a.m	Fearn, 5 miles from Tain	6. 0 p.m
8. 0 a.m	Fenwick, 18 miles from Glasgow	9.30 p.m
8 10 a.m	Ferrintosh, 6 miles from Dingwall	6.50 p.m
11.15 a.m	Ferryport-on-Craig, 3 miles from Newport	8.15 a.m
8. 0 a.m	*Fettercairn, James Austin	2.15 p.m
9. 0 a.m	Findhorn, 5 miles from Forres	12.45noon
3. 0 p.m	Finhaven, 6½ miles from Forfar	10. 0 p.m
9. 0 a.m	Fintry, 18 miles from Glasgow	2.45 p.m
9. 0 a.m 5. 0 p.m	Fisherrow, ½ mile from Musselburgh	7.45 p.m
7. 0 a.m 1.45 p.m	*Fochabers, Mary Marquis	7. 0 a.m 1. 0 p.m
9.30 a.m 7.30 p.m	*Ford, John Otto	7. 0 p.m
12.35noon	Ford, 6 miles from Coldstream	12. 5noon
10.30 a.m 2. 0 p.m	*Forfar, John Thomson	6.30 a.m 6.20 p.m
3.15 p.m	Forgue, 7½ miles from Huntly	9.30 a.m
7. 0 a.m 4.20 p.m	*Forres, Robert Watson	3.30 p.m 9.30 p.m
8. 0 p.m	*Fort-Augustus Wm. Mac Kinnon	10. 0 p.m
7. 0 a.m 6.45 p.m	Fort-George, 1¾ miles fr. Ardersier	4. 0 p.m 8. 0 p.m
7.40 p.m	Fortingal, 9 miles from Aberfeldy	10. 0 p.m
7. 0 a.m	*Fortrose, Christian Bain	7.15 p.m
10. 0 a.m	*Fort-William, James Taylor	4. 0 p.m
1. 0 p.m	*Fraserburgh, Margaret Fraser	6.15 a.m
10. 0 a.m	Fruchie, 2 miles from Kettle	11.30 a.m
8. 0 a.m 1. 0 p.m	*Fushie-Bridge, James Craik	9. 0 a.m 10. 0 p.m
10.15 a.m 8.30 p.m	*Fyvie, Sarah Rose	10.30 a.m 4. 0 p.m
11.30 a.m	Gairlochead, 7½ miles f. Helensburgh	12.30noon
8. 0 a.m 11.30 a.m	*Galashiels, Janet Haldrane	9.45 a.m 9. 0 p.m
10. 0 a.m 8.45 p.m	Gallowtown, 2 miles from Kirkcaldy	5. 0 p.m
9. 0 a.m	Galston, 5 miles from Kilmarnock	2.30 p.m
Uncertain	Garderhouse, nr. Lerwick, Zetland	Uncertain
8.35 a.m	*Garlieston, John Pollock	6. 0 p.m
3.30 p.m	Garmouth, 5 miles from Fochabers	11.15 a.m
3.15 p.m	Gartmore, 23 miles from Stirling	8.45 a.m
7.30 a.m	Garve, 14 miles from Dingwall	12.10 p.m
8. 0 a.m	*Gatehouse, Janet McKeard	10. 0 p.m
11.40 a.m	Gifford, 4½ miles from Haddington	7. 0 p.m
8. 0 a.m	Gilston, 4 miles from Castle-Douglas	3.30 p.m
8. 0 a.m 1.30 p.m	*Girvan, Thomas Davidson	12.30 p.m 7. 0 p.m
3.30 p.m	Glammis, 5½ miles from Forfar	4.35 p.m
10. 0 a.m 4. 0 p.m	Gladsmuir, 4 miles from Haddington	3.30 p.m
7.30 a.m 2. 0 p.m	*Glasgow, J. W. Sebright	8.15 a.m 10. 0 p.m
1. 0 p.m	Glencaple, 5 miles from Dumfries	3.15 p.m
7. 0 a.m	Glencarse, 6 miles from Perth	10. 0 p.m
8. 0 a.m	Glendaruel, 80 miles from Glasgow	6. 0 p.m
7.20 p.m	Glenelg, 6 miles from Lochalsh	11.50 a.m
7.20 p.m	Glenlivat, 6 miles from Ballindalloch	2.45 p.m
8. 0 a.m	Glenlocher, 4 mi. fr. Castle-Douglas	5. 0 p.m
8. 0 a.m	*Glenluce, Sarah Hawthorn	8. 0 p.m
12. 0noon	Glenmorriston, 6 m. fr. Fort Augustus	8. 0 a.m
10.45 a.m	*Golspie, Robert Hill	4. 0 p.m
11. 0 a.m	Gortlech, 14 miles from Fort Augustus	10.30 a.m
8.30 a.m 5.30 p.m	Gourock, 3 miles from Greenock	6.45 p.m
9. 0 a.m 4. 0 p.m	Govan, 2½ miles from Glasgow	6.45 p.m
11. 0 a.m	Grahamstown, 1 mile from Falkirk	3.30 p.m
11. 0 a.m 5.45 p.m	*Grangemouth, George Gibson	11.45 a.m 9. 0 p.m
8. 0 a.m 4.30 p.m	Granton Pier, 3 miles from Edinburgh	2.20 a.m 4.20 p.m
7. 0 a.m 7.15 p.m	*Grantown, John Grant	10. 0 p.m

Letters from London delivered at h. m.	Town. Postmaster.	Box for London closes at h. m.
11.30 a.m	Greenlaw, 8 miles from Dunse	1.15 p.m
7.30 a.m / 2.30 p.m	*Greenock, Ralph Logan	8.30 p.m
8. 0 a.m / 4. 0 p.m	Gretna, 9½ miles from Carlisle	9.45 a.m / 5. 0 p.m
10. 0 a.m	Guardbridge, 5 mi. from Cupar (Fife)	8.30 p.m
11.20 a.m	Gullan, 7 miles from Haddington	4.15 p.m
8. 0 a.m / 12.15noon	*Haddington, Peter Martin	10. 0 a.m / 10. 0 p.m
8. 0 a.m	Halkirk, 6 miles from Thurso	5.45 p.m
10. 0 a.m / 2. 0 p.m	*Hamilton, James Roxburgh	9.30 a.m / 9. 0 p.m
2.30 p.m	Harriotfield, 12 miles from Perth	8. 0 a.m
Uncertain	Harris, 40 miles from Portree	Uncertain
Uncertain	Harroldswick, near Lerwick	Uncertain
8. 0 a.m	Haugh of Urr, 4 m. fr. Castle Douglas	4. 0 p.m
3.30 a.m / 7. 0 p.m	*Hawick, Robert Armstrong	12.45noon / 10. 0 p.m
10. 0 a.m	*Helensburgh, James Breingan	3.30 p.m
12.45 p.m	Helmsdale, 17 miles fr. Golspie	2.0 p.m
8. 0 a.m	Hermiston, 5 miles from Edinburgh	4. 0 p.m
7. 0 a.m / 4. 0 p.m	Hillside, 8 miles from Aberdeen	3.20 p.m / 10. 0 p.m
Uncertain	Hillswick, near Lerwick, Zetland	Uncertain
7.15 p.m	Hollywood, 3½ miles from Dumfries	3. 0 p.m
9.30 a.m	*Holytown, 4 miles from Airdrie	5. 0 p.m
9.10 a.m	Hopeman, 7 miles from Elgin	9. 0 a.m
9. 0 a.m	Horndean, 9 miles from Coldstream	10. 0 p.m
8. 0 a.m	Houston, 6 miles from Paisley	4. 0 p.m
Uncertain	Howmore, 37 miles fr. Lochmaddy	Uncertain
9.15 p.m	Huna, 18 miles from Wick	Uncertain
10.20 a.m / 11.30 a.m	*Huntly, James Lawson	9.30 a.m / 10.45 a.m
9. 0 a.m	Hurlet, 6 miles from Glasgow	1.30 p.m
7. 0 a.m	*Inchture, Thomas Reid	10. 0 p.m
8.15 a.m	Innerkip, 6 miles from Greenock	4. 0 p.m
2. 0 p.m	Innerleithen, 6½ miles from Peebles	9. 0 p.m
1.10 p.m	Insch, 3½ miles from Old Rain	8. 0 a.m
2. 0 p.m	*Inverary, Catherine Maclean	7.50 a.m
7. 0 a.m	Invergarry, 7½ m. fr. Fort-Augustus	Uncertain
7. 0 a.m	*Invergordon, Wilson Mackenzie	9. 0 p.m
Uncertain	Inverie, 54 miles fr. Fort-Augustus	Uncertain
7.45 a.m / 6. 0 p.m	*Inverkeithing, James Angus	7. 0 p.m / 10. 0 p.m
7. 0 a.m / 7.45 p.m	*Inverness, William Hay	9.30 p.m
7.45 a.m / 6.45 p.m	*Irvine, John Deans	5. 0 p.m
7. 0 a.m	Isle, Ornshay, 9 miles from Broadford	11.45 a.m
9.15 a.m	Isle of Withorn, 3½ miles fr. Whithorn	3.15 p.m
10.50 a.m	*Jedburgh, William Renwick	4. 0 p.m
8.15 a.m / 6.15 p.m	Johnshaven, 5 miles from Bervie	12.40 p.m
8. 0 a.m / 5. 0 p.m	Johnstone, 10 miles from Glasgow	7.40 p.m
3. 0 p.m	Johnstone-Bridge, 10 miles fr. Moffat	9. 0 p.m
12. 0noon	Jura, 27 miles from Lochgilphead	9. 0 p.m
12.50 p.m / 9.20 a.m	*Keith, John Keith	8. 0 a.m / 12. 0noon
9. 5 a.m	*Keith-Hall, David Masson	12. 0noon
11.30 a.m	*Kelso, Peter Darling	10. 0 p.m
8. 0 a.m	Kelton Hill, 2 miles f. Castle-Douglas	4. 0 p.m
5.30 p.m	Kenmore, 6 miles from Aberfeldy	6.40 a.m
3.20 p.m	Kennethmoat, 10 miles fr. Old-Rain	10. 0 p.m
11.30 a.m	Kennoway, 3½ miles fr. Markinch	11. 0 a.m / 6. 0 p.m
8.30 a.m	*Kettle, John Inglis	12.30noon
8. 0 a.m	Kilbarchan, 6 miles from Paisley	5. 0 p.m
9.15 a.m / 7.15 p.m	Kilbirnie, 3 miles from Beith	3.30 p.m
Uncertain	Kilbride, 57 miles f. Lochmaddy	Uncertain
11. 0 a.m	Kilbride-East, 8 miles from Glasgow	12.30noon
9. 0 a.m	Kilbride-West, 5 miles f. Ardrossan	2. 0 p.m
2.30 p.m	Kilchrenan, 14 miles from Inverary	10. 0 p.m
9. 0 p.m	Kilfinnan, 80 miles from Glasgow	2. 0 p.m
10. 0 a.m	Killearn, 16½ miles from Glasgow	2.30 p.m
6.40 p.m	Killin, 22 miles from Callander	10. 0 p.m
8. 0 a.m / 7. 0 p.m	*Kilmarnock, David Rankin	4.30 p.m / 10. 0 p.m
8. 0 a.m	Kilmaurs, 2 miles from Kilmarnock	3.30 p.m
9.15 a.m	Kilmuir, 21 miles from Portree	3.45 p.m
12.45noon	Kilmun, 12 miles from Greenock	8.30 a.m

Letters from London delivered at h. m.	Town. Postmaster.	Box for London closes at h. m.
9.30 a.m	Kilpatrick (New), 6 m. f. Glasgow	1. 0 p.m
8. 0 a.m	Kilpatrick (Old), 10 miles f. Glasgow	7. 0 p.m
8. 0 a.m	Kilsyth, 12 miles from Glasgow	6.30 p.m
8.30 a.m / 6.30 p.m	Kilwinning, 3 miles from Irvine	5.15 p.m
1. 5 p.m	Kincaldrum, 9½ miles from Dundee	7.30 p.m
9.40 a.m	*Kincardine, Margaret Finlay	3.30 p.m / 9.30 p.m
10.40 a.m	Kincardine O'Neil, 26 m. f. Aberdeen	11. 0 a.m
10.30 a.m	Kingairloch, 9 miles from Strontian	11.30 a.m
3.30 p.m	King-Edward, 6 miles from Banff	11.30 a.m
8. 0 a.m	*Kinghorne, James Greig	2.40 p.m / 10. 0 p.m
8. 0 p.m	*Kingussie, Ewen Davidson	6.30 a.m
7. 0 p.m	Kinlock-Moidart, 20 miles f. Strontian	10. 0 p.m
9. 0 a.m / 7.20 p.m	*Kinross, James Simpson	5.30 p.m / 10. 0 p.m
8.40 a.m	*Kintore, William Smith	12.30 p.m
11.30 a.m	Kippen, 12 miles from Stirling	12.30noon
4. 0 p.m	Kirkbank, 5 miles from Kelso	10.30 a.m
1.45 p.m	Kirkbean, 12 miles from Dumfries	5.15 p.m
8. 0 a.m / 7.15 p.m	*Kirkcaldy, John Paton	2. 0 p.m / 10. 0 p.m
1.30 p.m	Kirkconnell, 4 miles from Sanquhar	11. 0 a.m
12.30noon	Kirkcowen, 7½ m. f. Newton-Stewart	2.30 p.m
9. 0 a.m / 4. 0 p.m	*Kirkcudbright, Chas. Jas. Finlayson	7.30 p.m
8. 0 a.m	Kirkintulloch, 7 miles from Glasgow	7.30 p.m
8. 0 a.m	*Kirkliston, Andrew Peebles	5.30 p.m
1. 0 p.m	Kirkmahoe, 3 miles from Dumfries	9. 0 p.m
4.15 p.m	Kirkmichael, 14 miles fr. Blairgowrie	7.45 a.m
9. 0 a.m	Kirkmichael, 3½ miles from Maybole	4.30 p.m
11. 0 a.m	*Kirknewton, Andrew Braid	12.15noon / 7.45 p.m
8. 0 a.m	Kirkinner, 3 miles from Wigtown	7. 0 p.m
9. 0 a.m / 8. 0 p.m	Kirkpatrick, 9 mi. fr. Castle-Douglas	6.30 p.m
Uncertain, generally about mid-day.	*Kirkwall, Archibald Garioch	2.30 p.m
3. 0 p.m	*Kirriemuir, James Dickson	5.30 p.m
12. 0noon	Kirtlebridge, 8½ miles fr. Ecclefechan	12. 0noon
6.15 p.m	Knockando, 9 miles fr. Craigellachie	10.30 a.m
10.30 a.m	Knome, 9 miles from Newton-Stewart	3.40 p.m
10.30 a.m	Laggan, 11 miles from Kingussie	1.45 p.m
8. 0 a.m	Laggavoulin, 17 miles fr. Boromore	6.30 a.m
9.15 a.m	Lairg, 19 miles from Golspie	11. 0 a.m
12.30noon	Lamlash, 20 miles from Ardrossan	3. 0 p.m
4. 0 p.m	Lammington, 7 miles from Biggar	10. 0 p.m
7.30 a.m	*Lanark, Archibald Huddon	6.30 p.m
9. 0 a.m / 4.30 p.m	*Langholme, John Nicol	8.30 a.m / 3.30 p.m
12. 0noon	Larbert, 3 miles from Falkirk	2. 0 p.m
10.40 a.m	Largo, 3 miles from Leven	7. 0 p.m
10. 0 a.m	*Largs, William McColl	2. 0 p.m
7. 0 a.m / 10. 0 a.m	Larkhall, 3 miles from Hamilton	10.45 a.m
8.30 a.m / 5.30 p.m	*Lasswade, John Buckham	8.30 p.m
8.15 a.m	*Lauder, Janet Romanis	6. 0 p.m
7. 0 a.m	*Laurencekirk, George Watt	3.45 p.m
9. 0 a.m	Laurieston, 6 mi. fr. Castle Douglas	4. 0 p.m
11. 0 a.m	Laurieston, 1¼ mile from Falkirk	5.15 p.m
3. 0 p.m	*Leadhills, Robert Martin	9. 0 p.m
8. 0 a.m / 4. 0 p.m	*Leith, George Goodlet	6. 0 a.m / 9.30 p.m
12. 0noon	Leithlumsden, 34 miles fr. Aberdeen	9. 0 a.m
11.50 a.m	Leitholm, 6 miles from Coldstream	11.20 a.m
8. 0 a.m / 6. 0 p.m	Lennoxtown, 9 miles from Glasgow	6. 0 p.m
On arrival of the Packet.	*Lerwick, Wm. Ray Duncan	According t circumstances.
9.15 a.m	Leslie, 3 miles from Markinch	12. 0noon
8. 0 a.m / 12. 0noon	*Lesmahagow, Robert Telfer	10. 0 a.m / 8.30 p.m
4. 0 p.m	Lethaw, 6 miles from Forfar	10. 0 a.m
10.30 a.m	Leuchars, 7 miles from Cupar (Fife)	8. 0 p.m
10.30 a.m	*Leven, Margaret Howden	9.20 a.m / 7.40 p.m
2.15 p.m	Lhanbryde, 4 miles from Elgin	10. 0 p.m
9. 0 a.m	*Libberton, William Kerr	1. 0 p.m / 10. 0 p.m

Letters from London delivered at h. m.	Town. Postmaster.	Box for London closes at h. m.
9.15 a.m	Lilliesleaf, 6 miles from Selkirk	4. 0 p.m
10. 0 a.m	Limekilns, 3 miles from Dumfermline	3.45 p.m
8. 0 a.m	Lindores, 2 miles from Newburgh	6.30 p.m
Uncertain	Linkshouse, near Lerwick	Uncertain
10. 0 a.m	*Linlithgow, Robert Speeden	1. 0 p.m 10. 0 p.m
11.15 a.m	Linton, 3 miles from Noblehouse	8. 0 a.m
8.40 p.m	Linwilg, 9 miles from Kingussie	10 0 p.m
1.30 p.m	Lismore, 7 miles from Appin	9. 0 p.m
3. 0 p.m	Loan, 3 miles from Linlithgow	3. 0 p.m
10.15 a.m 6.15 p.m	*Loanhead, William Begg	8.50 p.m
5. 0 p.m	*Lochalsh, David Logan	9.30 p.m
1.30 p.m	Lochcarron, 15¾ miles from Lochalsh	10. 0 p.m
3.50 p.m	Lochearnhead, 14 miles fr. Callander	10. 0 p.m
7.45 a.m 12.45 p.m	Lochee, 2½ miles from Dundee	11. 0 a.m 8. 0 p.m
11. 0 a.m	Lochgelly, 8 miles from Kirkcaldy	2. 0 p.m
4.30 p.m	*Lochgilphead, Catherine Munro	9. 0 p.m
5. 0 p.m	Lochinver, 65 miles from Golspie	10. 0 p.m
9.45 a.m	Lochmaben, 4 miles from Lockerby	2.30 p.m
On arrival of the packet	*Lochmaddy, Malcolm McLeod	Uncertain
8. 0 a.m 5.30 p.m	Lochwinnock, 8 miles from Paisley	6.30 p.m
9.15 a.m 5.15 p.m	*Lockerby, Thomas Walker	4.30 p.m 9. 0 p.m
2.30 p.m	Logierait, 8¾ miles from Dunkeld	10. 0 a.m
Uncertain	Longhope, 16 miles from Kirkwall	Uncertain
5.15 p.m	Lossiemouth, 6 miles from Elgin	11.45 a.m
8. 0 a.m	Luss, 13 miles from Dumbarton	4.30 p.m
4.15 p,m	Lybster, 13 miles from Wick	10 0 a.m
8. 0 a.m 1.45 p.m	Macduff, 1¼ miles from Banff	6.35 a.m 11.45 a.m
8.15 a.m	*Markinch, William Hutchinson	1. 0 p.m 4.45 p.m
10. 0 a.m	Marycutter, 7¼ miles from Aberdeen	11.50 a.m
8. 0 a.m 4.30 p.m	Maryhill, 4 miles from Glasgow	1.45 p.m
7. 0 a.m	Mary-Kirk, 6 miles from Montrose	4.45 p.m
8.30 a.m	*Mauchline, Hugh Wilson	3. 0 p.m
8. 0 a.m 11.30 a.m	*Maybole, William Rennie	2. 0 p.m 8.15 p.m
1.40 p.m	*Meigle, James Donaldson	5. 0 p.m
8. 0 a.m	*Melrose, W. M. Pringle	6.30 p.m
10.45 a.m	Melvich, 18 miles from Thurso	12.40 p.m
10. 0 a.m	Menstrie, 5 miles from Stirling	2.30 p.m
10.15 a.m	Methlic, 22 miles from Aberdeen	11. 0 a.m
7. 0 a.m	Methven, 6 miles from Perth	4.30 p.m
11.10 a.m	Mey, 12 miles from Thurso	2. 0 p.m
11.40 a.m	*Midcalder, Ann Cruickshank	11.15 a.m 6.45 p.m
6. 0 p.m	Millport, 5 Miles from Largs	7.30 a.m
9.30 a.m 7.50 p.m	Milnathort, 1¾ miles from Kinross	5. 0 p.m 9. 0 p.m
10.30 a.m 5.30 p.m	Milngavie, 7 miles from Glasgow	12.30noon
8. 0 a.m	Milton of Campsie, 9 mi. fr. Glasgow	6.30 p.m
1.20 a.m	*Mintlaw, Bathia Levay	7.50 a.m
9. 0 a.m	*Moffat, Thomas Grieve	1. 0 p.m 9. 0 p.m
10.45 p.m	Moneymusk, 19 miles from Aberdeen	7.45 a.m
9. 0 a.m	Moniaive, 8 miles from Thornhill	9. 0 a.m
8.30 a.m	Monkton, 4 miles from Ayr	4. 0 p.m
12.55 p.m 7. 0 a.m	*Montrose, James Valentine	8.10 a.m 6. 0 p.m
11,45 a.m 5. 0 p.m	Moodiesburn, 7 miles from Glasgow	4. 0 p.m
4. 0 p.m	Morebattle, 8 miles from Kelso	8.30 a.m
9.40 a.m	Morenish, 8 miles from Tobermory	12.20noon
5.30 p.m	Mortlach, 6 miles from Craigellachie	8. 0 p.m
2. 0 p.m	Morvern, 19 miles from Oban	1.30 p.m
12. 0noon	Mossatt, 33 miles from Aberdeen	8.45 a.m
Uncertain	Mossbank, near Lerwick, Zetland	Uncertain
7. 0 a.m	Moy, 12 miles from Inverness	10. 0 p.m
2. 0 p.m	Muchart, 10 miles from Alloa	4. 0 p.m
8. 0 a.m 4.45 p.m	Muirdrum, 2 miles from Carnoustie	8.15 a.m 5. 0 p.m
5. 0 p.m	Muirkirk, 10 miles from Douglas	10. 0 p.m
7. 0 a.m	Munlochy, 12 miles from Beauly	8.45 p.m
9. 0 a.m 5. 0 p.m	*Murrayfield	5. 0 p.m

Letters from London delivered at h. m.	Town. Postmaster.	Box for London closes at h. m.
9. 0 a.m 1. 0 p.m	*Musselburgh, John Leitch	8.30 a.m 10. 0 p.m
11. 0 a.m	Muthill, 3 miles from Crieff	6.30 p.m
7. 0 a.m 5.30 p.m	*Nairn, Flora Ann MacIntosh	4.15 p.m 9.30 p.m
9.30 a.m	Neilston, 10 miles from Glasgow	12.15 p.m
1. 0 p.m	New-Abbey, 7¼ miles from Dumfries	6. 0 p.m
3.10 p.m	New-Aberdour, 8 m. from Fraserburgh	5.15 p.m
8.30 a.m 12. 0noon	*Newburgh, Fife, J. M. Sharp	2.15 p.m 5.30 p.m
12. 0noon	Newcastleton, 9 mi. fr. Langholm	3. 0 p.m
12. 0noon	Newcumnock, 5 miles from Cumnock	2.30 p.m
1.15 p.m	New-Deer, 29 miles from Aberdeen	8. 5 a.m
10. 0 a.m	New-Galloway, 14 miles from Castle Douglas	4.30 p.m
8.30 a.m 5. 0 p.m	Newhaven, 2 miles from Edinburgh	8. 0 p.m
10. 0 a.m	Newmills, 8 miles from Kilmarnock	1.30 p.m
2.30 p.m	New-Pitsligo, 10 miles from Mintlaw	5.45 p.m
10. 0 a.m	*Newport, Charles Mitchell	7. 0 p.m
8. 0 a.m	Newton, 7 miles from Glasgow	8. 0 p.m
8. 0 a.m	*Newton-Stewart, Marion Paterson	10. 0 p.m
3. 0 p.m	Newtyle, 6 miles from Cupar Angus	3.45 p.m
8.30 a.m	Nigg, 6 miles from Park-Hill	5.45 p.m
10.25 a.m	*Noblehouse, George Williams	11.14 a.m
12.15noon 7.30 p.m	*North-Berwick, James Hislop	3. 0 p.m
7. 0 a.m 5.30 p.m	*North Queensferry, Alison Brown	7.30 p.m 10. 0 p.m
Uncertain	Nunton, 22 miles from Lochmaddy	Uncertain
8. 0 p.m	*Oban, Anne Rankin	10. 0 p.m
12. 0noon	Ochiltree, 4 miles from Cumnoch	12. 0 noon
7.45 a.m 5.45 a.m	Old-Aberdeen, 1½ miles from Aberdeen	1.50 p.m 4.15 p.m
9.30 a.m 7.30 p.m	*Old-Meldrum, Jane Forbes	11.30 a.m 5.30 p.m
10.15 a.m	*Old-Rain, Ann Horne	11. 0 a.m
Uncertain	Ollaberry, near Lerwick, Zetland	Uncertain
10.15 a.m	Ormiston, 2½ miles from Tranent	2. 0 p.m
2.40 p.m	Orton, 10 miles from Keith	6.45 p.m
8. 0 a.m 1.40 p.m	*Paisley, Alexander Hart	10. 0 p.m
8. 0 a.m	Parkgate, 8 miles from Dumfries	3. 0 p.m
9. 0 a.m	Parkhead, 2 miles from Glasgow	12. 0noon
7. 0 a.m	*Parkhill, Helen Maclean	8. 15 p.m
9. 0 a.m	Parton, 6 miles from Castle-Douglas	5. 0 p.m
8. 0 a.m 5. 0 p.m	Partick, 3 miles from Glasgow	10.15 a.m 8. 0 p.m
8.15 a.m 8. 0 p.m	Pathhead, 1 mile from Kirkcaldy	1.30 p.m 9.30 p.m
11.30 a.m	Patua, 10 miles from Ayr	2,15 p.m
12.15noon	*Peebles, Nancy Williamson	8. 0 a.m
10.30 a.m	Pencaitland, 3½ miles from Tranent	1. 0 p.m
9.30 a.m 6.45 p.m	*Pennycuick, Michael Jenkinson	7.45 p.m
10.45 a.m 9.30 p.m	*Perth, Charles Graham Sidey	3.15 p.m 11. 0 p.m
11.33 a.m	*Peterhead, Thomas Knox	7.30 a.m
9.40 a.m	Pitcaple, 4 miles from Keith-Hall	11.30 a.m
1.30 p.m	Pitlessie, 4 miles from Cupar, (Fife)	7.45 a.m
2.25 p.m.	*Pitlochrie, James Gibson	12.15 p.m
12.15noon	*Pittenween, Robert Morris	5.30 p.m
8.30 a.m 5. 0 p.m	Pollockshaws, 3 miles from Glasgow	5.40 p.m
2. 0 p.m	Polmont, 3½ miles from Falkirk	4. 0 p.m
8.30 a.m	Polnackie, 6 miles fr. Castle-Douglas	3. 0 p.m
7. 0 a.m	Poolewe, 67 miles from Dingwall	8.30 a.m
7. 0 p.m	*Portaskaig, James McNab	3. 0 p.m
2. 0 p.m	Port Barnatyne, 3 miles fr. Rothesay	3. 0 p.m
8. 0 a.m 2. 0 p.m	*Port-Glasgow, Alexander Wood	9. 0 p.m
5.30 p.m	Port-Logan, 14 miles from Stranraer	8. 0 a.m
9.15 a.m	Portmahomac, 12 miles from Tain	4.45 p.m
11.30 a.m	Port-Monteith, 15 miles from Stirling	11. 0 a.m
8.45 a.m 4.30 p.m	*Portobello, James Scott	8. 0 p.m
8. 0 a.m	*Port-Patrick, Alexander Niven	6.22 p.m
7. 0 a.m	*Portree, Alexander MacDonald	10.30 a.m
7. 0 a.m 11.15 a.m	*Portsoy, John Crawford	9.30 p.m 10.30 a.m
8. 0 a.m	*Port-William, 10 miles from Wigtown	4. 0 p.m
8.15 a.m	Poyntzfield, 7 miles from Fortrose	6. 0 p.m

Letters from London delivered at h. m.	Town. Postmaster.	Box for London closes at h. m.
2. 0 p.m	Preston, 13 miles from Dumfries	5.10 p.m
10.30 a.m	*Prestonkirk, Janet Gibb	10. 0 p.m
10. 0 a.m 6. 0 p.m	*Prestonpans, Thomas Cleugh	8. 0 p.m
11.30 a.m	*Rachan-Mill, James Horne	9.30 a.m
9.30 p.m	Rannoch, 21 miles from Pitlochrie	1.45 p.m
Uncertain	Rasay, 14 miles from Broadford	Uncertain
10. 0 a.m	*Ratho, James Hepburn	1.10 p.m 9. 0 p.m
9. 0 a.m	Reay, 11 miles from Thurso	2.30 p.m
11.30 a.m	Redgorton, 4 miles from Perth	3.15 p.m
8. 0 a.m 5. 0 p.m	Renfrew, 3 miles from Paisley	6. 0 p.m
8. 0 a.m	Renton, 2½ miles from Dumbarton	6. 0 p.m
12.45 p.m	Rhynie, 9 miles from Huntly	8. 0 a.m
8. 0 a.m	Riccarton, 1 mile from Kilmarnock	3.30 p.m
10.30 a.m	Ringford, 5 miles from Kircudbright	4. 0 p.m
3.30 p.m	Roberton, 6 miles from Hawick	4.30 p.m
2.45 p.m	Rosehearty, 4½ miles fr. Fraserburgh	10.45 a.m
10.15 a.m	Roseneath, 3½ miles from Helensburgh	1.40 p.m
9. 0 a.m 6. 0 p.m	*Roslin, Thomas Wilson	8.15 p.m
2.45 p.m	Rothes, 3 miles from Craigellachie	9.30 p.m
12.30noon	*Rothesay, Duncan McCorkindale	1.30 p.m 10. 0 p.m
1.40 p.m	Rothiemay, 6½ miles from Huntly	6. 5 p.m
10. 0 a.m	Row, 2½ miles from Helensburgh	2.15 p.m
8.15 a.m	Rutherglen, 2 miles from Glasgow	8.45 p.m
11.20 a.m	*St. Andrews, George Cruickshanks	7.30 p.m
8. 0 a.m	*St. Boswells Green, Catherine Scott	6. 0 p.m
7. 0 a.m 1.15 p.m	St. Cyrus, 6½ miles from Montrose	6. 0 p.m 10. 0 p.m
When the Runner arrives fr. Burwick.	St. Margarets Hope, 12 miles from Kirkwall	7.45 p.m Varies according to the arrival of the Runner.
1. 0 p.m	St. Monance, 1½ miles f. Pittenween	4.20 p.m
8.30 a.m	St. Ninians, 1¼ mile from Stirling	3.45 p.m
11.15 a.m	Saline, 7 miles from Dunfermline	2.45 p.m
11. 0 a.m	Salsburgh, 7 miles from Airdrie	3. 0 p.m
9. 0 a.m 7. 0 p.m	*Saltcoats, Hugh Baird	3.45 p.m
11.30 a.m	Salton, 6 miles from Tranent	12.30noon
Uncertain	Sanday, 20 miles from Kirkwall	Uncertain
4.15 p.m	Sandhead, 8 miles from Stranraer	9. 0 a.m
Uncertain	Sandness, near Lerwick, Zetland	Uncertain
12.15noon	*Sanquhar, John Holliday	5.30 p.m
11.15 a.m	Scone, 2 miles from Perth	7.40 p.m
7. 0 a.m	Scoucer, 12 miles from Broadford	1. 0 p.m
8. 0 p.m	Scourie, 72 miles from Golspie	2.30 p.m
Uncertain	Seafield, near Lerwick, Zetland	Uncertain
8.15 a.m 12.15noon	*Selkirk, Jean Buchan	11.30 a.m 9. 0 p.m
9.20 p.m	Shielhouse, 12¼ miles fr. Lochalsh	10.45 a.m
11. 0 a.m	Shotts, 7½ miles from Whitburn	2.30 p.m
8. 0 a.m	Shuttleston, 4 miles from Glasgow	9.30 p.m
8.15 a.m	Skene, 8 miles from Aberdeen	12.45 p.m
7.30 a.m 5.15 p.m	*Slateford, James Frier	7.45 p.m
8. 0 a.m	Sorby, 12 miles from Wigtown	5.30 p.m
11. 0 a.m	Sorn, 4 miles from Mauchline	12. 0noon
7.15 a.m 5.15 p.m	*South-Queensferry, Elizbeth. Meikle	7. 0 p.m 10. 0 p.m
2.30 p.m	Southwick, 16 miles from Dumfries	4.45 p.m
3. 0 p.m	Spittalfield, 6 miles from Dunkeld	9.30 a.m
7. 0 a.m 4.30 p.m	Springbank, 2 miles from Glasgow	3. 0 p.m
8.30 a.m	Springburn, 2¼ miles from Glasgow	9. 0 p.m
12. 0noon	Stanley, 7 miles from Perth	10. 0 a.m
8.30 a.m	Steventson, 12 miles from Kilmarnock	3.45 p.m
9. 0 a.m	*Stewarton, 6 miles from Kilmarnock	2. 0 p.m
8. 0 a.m 6. 0 p.m	*Stirling, John Shearer	4.40 p.m 9.30 p.m
7. 0 a.m 3.25 p.m	*Stonehaven, Charles Mechie	5.30 a.m 3.50 p.m
4. 0 p.m	Stoneykirk, 6 miles from Stranraer	9.15 a.m
12.15 p.m 8. 0 p.m	Stonehouse, 7½ miles fr. Hamilton	10. 0 a.m
On arrival of the Packet	*Stornoway, ohn Mac Aulay	Uncertain
8. 0 a.m 11.30 a.m	*Stow, Robert Brown	10. 0 a.m 10. 0 p.m

Letters from London delivered at h. m.	Town. Postmaster.	Box for London closes at h. m.
4.30 p.m	Strachur, 60 miles from Glasgow	10. 0 p.m
10. 0 a.m	Straiton, 7 miles from Maybole	2.30 p.m
8. 0 a.m	*Stranraer, William Campbell	7. 0 p.m
1. 0 p.m 9. 0 p.m	Strathaven, 7 miles from Hamilton	1.45 p.m
8. 0 a.m	Strathblane, 11 miles from Glasgow	4.45 p.m
3.30 p.m	Strathdon, 45 miles from Aberdeen	8.30 p.m
8. 0 a.m	Strathmiglo, 9 miles from Kinross	10. 0 p.m
8.15 a.m	Strathpeffer, 6 miles from Dingwall	6.45 p.m
1.45 p.m	Strichen, 7 miles from Mintlaw	10. 0 p.m
5.45 p.m Uncertain	Stromness, 15 miles from Kirkwall	11.30 a.m Uncertain
Irregular	Stronsay, 15 miles fr. Kirkwall	Uncertain
10. 0 a.m	*Strontian, Donald Cameron	2. 0 p.m
7. 0 a.m	Struan, 27 miles from Broadford	10. 0 p.m
10.15 a.m	Struy, 12 miles from Beauly	1.45 p.m
12.30 p.m	Stuartfield, 3 miles from Mintlaw	6.30 a.m
8.25 a.m	Summerhill, 10 miles from Aberdeen	12.20noon
2.10 p.m	Swinton, 6 miles from Coldstream	1.40 p.m
9. 0 a.m	Symington, 6 miles from Kilmarnock	2. 0 p.m
7. 0 a.m	*Tain, Harriet Calder	7.45 p.m
Uncertain	Tangwick, near Lerwick, Zetland	Uncertain
2. 0 p.m	*Tarbert, John McLaghlan	8. 0 a.m
9.30 a.m	Tarbolton, 9 miles from Kilmarnock	1.30 p.m
1.30 p.m	Tarland, 6 miles from Aboyne	8. 0 a.m
8. 0 a.m	Tayinloan, 18 miles from Tarbert	9. 0 p.m
3. 0 p.m	Teviothead, 9 miles from Hawick	9. 0 p.m
8.40 a.m 11. 0 a.m	*Thornhill, Samuel McKinnell	7.30 p.m
10. 0 a.m	Thornhill, 10½ miles from Stirling	1.30 p.m
8.30 a.m 5.30 p.m	Thornliebank, 5 miles from Glasgow	4. 0 p.m
10.25 a.m	Thornton, 4 miles from Keith	5.50 p.m
10. 0 a.m	Thornton, 4 miles from Kirkcaldy	5. 0 p.m
8.30 p.m	*Thurso, Donald MacKay	6.25 a.m
11.45 a.m	Tillicoultry, 3 miles from Alloa	7.30 p.m
Uncertain	Tiree, 30 miles from Tobermory	Uncertain
7. 0 p.m	*Tobermory, James Graham	3.30 p.m
9.10 a.m	Tomintoul, 18 m. f. Ballindalloch	11. 0 a.m
1.25 p.m	Tomnavonlin, 10 mi. fr. Ballindalloch	1. 0 p.m
4.30 p.m	Tongue, 45 miles from Thurso	10. 0 p.m
6. 0 p.m	Torphichen, 4 miles from Linlithgow	10. 0 p.m
6. 0 p.m	Torrance, 6 miles from Glasgow	8.40 a.m
10.20 a.m 7.35 p.m	Torryburn, 5 miles fr. Dunfermline	5. 0 p.m 7.50 p.m
8. 0 a.m 1. 0 p.m	*Tranent, Thomas Simson	9. 0 a.m 9.30 p.m
8.30 a.m 6.45 p.m	Troon, 6 miles from Irvine	4.30 p.m
9. 0 a.m	Tullibody, 5 miles from Stirling	3.15 p.m
7. 0 a.m 12. 0noon	*Turriff, Alexander Chisholm	9.30 a.m 3.30 p.m
10. 0 a.m	Twynholm, 4 miles fr. Kirkcudbright	4.30 p.m
8. 0 a.m	Tyndrum, 36 miles from Callander	10. 0 p.m
9. 0 a.m	Udney, 13½ miles from Aberdeen	12. 0noon
8. 0 p.m	*Ullapool, Susan MacKenzie	10. 0 p.m
11. 0 a.m	Ulva, 10½ milest rom Aross	1. 0 p.m
12. 0noon	Unachan, 9 milest rom Fort-William	10. 0 a.m
10.30 a.m	*Uphall, William Brown	3.30 p.m
Uncertain	Uyeasound, near Lerwick, Zetland	Uncertain
Uncertain	Voe, near Lerwick, Zetland	Uncertain
Uncertain	Walls, near Lerwick, Zetland	Uncertain
12. 0noon	Waterbeck, 4½ mi. fr Ecclefechan	1.30 p.m
6.30 p.m	Watten, 6 miles from Wick	7.30 a.m
9.30 a.m	Wemyss, 4½ miles from Kirkcaldy	8. 0 p.m
9. 0 a.m	*Wenchburgh, Margaret Hughes	4.30 p.m
1.45 p.m	West-Calder, 5 m. fr. Mid Calder	4.30 p.m
Uncertain	Westray, 24 miles from Kirkwall	Uncertain
Uncertain	Westsandwick, nr. Lerwick, Zetland	Uncertain
8.10 a.m	*Whitburn, Alexander Wilson	4.30 p.m
10.15 a.m	Whitehouse, 22 miles fr. Aberdeen	11. 0 a.m
8. 0 a.m	*Whithorn, Elizabeth Ford	4.50 p.m
6.10 p.m	*Wick, William Craig	8.40 a.m
11.45 a.m	Windygates, 2½ miles from Leven	11.30 a.m 5.15 p.m
8. 0 a.m	*Wigton, Thomas Tait	7.35 p.m
12. 0noon	Wishaw, 5 miles from Hamilton	2. 0 p.m
5. 0 p.m	Wiston, 8 miles from Biggar	10. 0 p.m
7.30 a.m 5.45 p.m	Woodside, 2 miles from Aberdeen	1.30 p.m 7.30 p.m
4.30 p.m	Yetholm, 8 miles from Kelso	8.30 a.m

IRELAND

Letters from London delivered at h. m.	Town. Postmaster.	Box for London closes at h. m.
1.42 p.m	Abbeyfeale, 12¾ miles from Newcastle	10.52 a.m
6.24 p.m	*Abbeyleix, John Warburton	7. 0 a.m
10.30 a.m	*Adair, Ann O'Regan..............	2. 0 p.m
2.45 p.m	Aghadowey, 5¾ miles fm. Ballymoney	10. 0 a.m
7.20 a.m	*Ahascragh, Miss Jane Fallon......	5. 0 p.m
1.15 p.m	Ahoghill, 4 miles from Ballymena ..	1. 0 p.m
9.40 a.m	Allihees, 7 miles from Castletown ..	12.20 p.m
10. 0 a.m	Annahilt, 4 miles from Hillsborough .	5.15 p.m
7.20 a.m	Annamoe, 8¾m.f.Newtown.Mt.Kendy.	4.40 p.m
8.10 p.m	Annascall, 7¼ miles from Tralee	9. 0 p.m
9.30 a.m	*Antrim, George Goold	3.20 p.m 9.30 p.m
7. 0 a.m	Ardagh, 5 miles fm. Edgeworthstown	5.20 p.m
8.10 p.m	*Ardara, Andrew Young	9.30 p.m
7. 0 a.m	Ardaragh, 6¼ miles from Newry	8.45 p.m
7. 0 a.m	*Ardee, William Brunker..........	9.30 p.m
6.40 p.m	Ardfert, 5 miles from Tralee	9. 0 p.m
9. 0 a.m	Ardfinan, 8¾ miles from Clonmel	2.46 p.m
8.30 a.m	Ardglass, 12¾ miles from Clough	3.10 p.m
8.30 a.m	Ardloher, 4½ miles from Killeshandra	3.25 p.m
4.20 p.m	Ardmore, 12¾ miles from Dungarvan.	7.35 a.m
11.20 a.m	*Ardrahan, George Taylor	1. 0 p.m
7. 0 a.m	*Arklow, Mrs. Frances Murphy	8.30 p.m
7. 0 a.m 8.30 p.m	*Armagh, Robt. Birch	7. 0 p.m 9.30 p.m
4.45 p.m	Armoy, 11¾ miles from Ballymoney..	7.15 a.m
9.30 a.m	Artane, 4 miles from Dublin	2.45 p.m
10.25 a.m	*Arthurstown, William Gordon	1.35 p.m
3.30 p.m	Articlave, 4 miles from Coleraine ..	8.45 a.m
9. 0 a.m	Arva, 13¾ miles from Cavan	2.45 p.m
9.20 a.m	*Ashbourne, Robert McAulay	3.30 p.m
10.10 a.m	Ashfield, 3 miles from Dromore	6.15 p.m
7. 0 a.m	*Ashford, Alexander Hall..........	8.30 p.m
11.56 a.m	Askeaton, 16¾ from Limerick	12.20 p.m
7.30 a.m	*Athboy, Mrs. Elizabeth Molloy....	5.15 p.m
10.40 a.m	Athenry, 5 miles from Craughwell ..	4.50 p.m
9.40 a.m	Athleague, 5½ miles from Roscommon	2.45 p.m
7. 0 a.m	*Athlone, Miss Ann Pakenham	7.20 p.m
3.35 p.m	*Athy, Thos. Sheill	10. 0 a.m
7. 0 a.m	Augher, 7 miles from Aughnacloy ..	5. 0 p.m
7. 0 a.m	*Aughnacloy, Rowland Betty	6.45 p.m
7. 0 a.m	*Aughrim, Patrick Clarke..........	5.45 p.m
7. 0 a.m	Aughrim, 7½ miles from Rathdrum ..	6.15 p.m
7. 0 a.m 5.20 p.m	*Bagnalstown, James Byrne........	8.20 p.m 8.10 a.m
8.15 a.m	*Bailyborough, Henry Adams	4.25 p.m
7. 0 a.m 10.15 a.m	*Balbriggan, Henry Joyson	2.35 p.m 9. 0 p.m
9.10 a.m	Baldoyle, 7 miles from Dublin	3.45 p.m
2.50 p.m	Balla, 6½ miles from Ballyglass	9.40 a.m
8.15 a.m	Ballacolla, 3½ miles from Durrow....	5. 5 p.m
9.40 a.m	*Ballaghaderin, Thomas Dillon	2.30 p.m
8. 0 a.m	*Ballibay, Henry Nesbitt	5.20 p.m
9.30 a.m	Ballicarry, 5¾ miles fm. Carrickfergus	3.10 p.m
2.25 p.m	*Ballina, Annesley Knox	9.30 a.m
3.47 p.m	Ballinacally, 11¼ miles from Ennis ..	8.33 a.m
8.45 a.m	Ballinafad, 4¾ miles from Boyle	3.55 p.m
8.45 a.m	Ballinakill, 3¾ miles from Abbeyleix	4.40 p.m
7.30 a.m	Ballinalee, 7 mi. fr. Edgeworthstown	4.40 p.m
10. 0 a.m	Ballinamallard, 6 mi. fr. Enniskillen	2. 0 p.m
9.30 a.m	BallinamoreBridge, 7½ m. f. Ahascragh	2.40 p.m
7. 0 a.m	*Ballinasloe, Richard Carroll	5.45 p.m
5.12 p.m 8.52 a.m	*Ballincollig, Thomas Sloane	9. 0 p.m 2. 0 p.m
7. 0 a.m	Ballinderry, 8 miles from Lurgan....	5.20 p.m
12.30 p.m	*Ballingarry, Catherine Humphreys	11.30 a.m
7. 0 a.m	Ballingarry, 5½ miles from Shinrone	4.20 p.m
9.18 a.m	Ballinhassig, 9¾ miles from Cork....	1.37 p.m
2. 0 p.m	*Ballinrobe, David Elligot	10. 0 a.m
2.30 p.m	Ballintra, 7 miles from Ballyshannon	10.10 a.m
8.50 a.m	Ballybrack, 10 miles fm. Cahirciveen	10.35 a.m
7. 0 a.m	*Ballybrittas, William Arthur......	9. 0 p.m
7. 0 a.m	Ballycarney, 3¼ miles from Ferns ..	9. 0 p.m
3.45 p.m	*Ballycastle, Archibald McDonnell..	8.25 a.m
7.10 p.m	Ballycastle, 10 miles from Killala ..	9. 0 p.m
10.15 a.m	Ballyclare, 12¾ miles from Belfast ..	2.20 p.m
8.30 a.m	*Ballyconnell, Ralph Montgomery..	3.30 p.m
7. 0 a.m	Ballycumber, 3¾ miles from Clara ..	6.35 p.m
4.55 p.m	Ballydehob, 8½ miles from Skibbereen	9. 0 p.m
10.35 a.m	Ballyfarnon, 8¾ miles from Boyle....	1.40 p.m
7. 0 a.m	*Ballygawley, Peter Montague	6.25 p.m
12.50 p.m	*Ballyglass, John McEvely	11.30 p.m
8.10 a.m	Ballygowan, 4 miles from Comber ..	3.10 p.m
7. 0 a.m	Ballyhaise, 4½ miles from Cavan	5. 0 p.m
2.10 p.m	Ballyhaunis, 11½ m. fr. Claremorris..	9.50 a.m
7.28 p.m	Ballyheigue, 11¼ miles from Tralee ..	9. 0 p.m
7.30 a.m	*Ballyjames-Duff, Thomas Morrow..	5.15 p.m
4. 0 p.m	Ballykelly, 4 m. f. Newtown-Limavady	8.20 a.m
8. 0 a.m	Ballylinan, 3¾ miles from Athy	4.10 p.m
4.45 p.m	Ballylongford, 5 miles from Tarbert	9. 0 a.m
8.30 a.m	Ballymacarrett, 1½ mls. from Belfast	4.45 p.m
7.20 a.m	*Ballymahon, William Lee	4. 0 p.m
7.15 a.m	Ballymascanlan, 4 miles fm. Dundalk	5.45 p.m
10.40 a.m	*Ballymena, George Dugan	2. 0 p.m 9.30 p.m
11.10 a.m	Ballymoe, 5½ miles from Castlerea..	1. 0 p.m
1. 0 p.m	*Ballymoney, Richard Hamilton ..	11.45 a.m 9.30 p.m
7. 0 a.m	Ballymore, 7 miles from Moate	4.50 p.m
8.25 a.m	Ballymore-Eustace, 4½m.f.Blessington	3.10 p.m
10.18 a.m	*Ballymote Joseph Lougheed	2. 0 p.m
7. 0 a.m	*Ballynacargy, Phillip Murray	6.10 p.m
7. 0 a.m	Balrynahinch, 11½ miles fr. Dromore	5.15 p.m
9.55 a.m	*Ballynamore, Thomas Fitzsimon ..	2. 0 p.m
10.58 a.m	Ballyporeen, 19¾ from Clonmel......	1.18 p.m
7.40 a.m	Ballyragget, 5½ miles fr. Castlecomer	4.50 p.m
6. 0 p.m	Ballyroan, 5 miles from Abbeyleix ..	5.40 p.m
10.40 a.m	Ballysadare, 2 miles from Collooney	1.50 p.m
1.15 p.m	*Ballyshannon, John O'Donnell	11.15 a.m
7. 0 a.m	*Ballytore, James Kelly............	8.30 p.m
4.20 p.m	Ballyvary, 7½ miles from Castlebar..	7.55 a.m
12.15 p.m	Ballywalter, 10 mi. fr. Newtownards	12.45 p.m
9.30 a.m	Ballyward, 9¾ miles from Rathfriland	4. 0 p.m
9.15 a.m	Balrath, 9 miles from Drogheda	4.15 p.m
4.20 p.m	Baltimore, 7 miles from Skibbereen	9. 0 p.m
1. 0 p.m	*Baltinglass, William Condell......	6.10 p.m
8.40 a.m	*Banagher, Richard Sharpe	3.30 p.m
7. 0 a.m 4.20 p.m	*Banbridge, Miss Margaret Mitchell	9.15 a.m 8.30 p.m
6.45 p.m 10.45 a.m	*Bandon William H. Shine	10. 0 p.m & noon
9.30 a.m	*Bangor, James Graham	2.50 p.m
7. 0 a.m	Bangor, 26 miles from Ballina	5.25 p.m
1.15 p.m	Bannow, 8¼ miles from Taghmon....	8.30 a.m
11. 0 a.m	Bansha, 18½ from Clonmel..........	1.30 p.m
5. 0 p.m	*Bantry, Thomas Jenkins	9. 0 p.m
12. 4 p.m	Barna, 4½ miles from Galway	8.55 a.m
11.10 a.m	Barringtons'bridge, 5¾m.f.CastlConnl	12.50 p.m
9.15 a.m	Bawnboy, 5 miles from Ballyconnell	2.30 p.m
12.15 p.m	Beleek, 4 miles from Ballyshannon..	12.15 p.m
7.30 a.m 7.30 p.m	*Belfast James Dickey............	6. 0 a.m 5.30 p.m
12.10 p.m	Bellaghy, 3 miles from Castledawson	11.30 a.m
7. 0 a.m	Bellenanagh, 5¼ miles from Cavan ..	5. 0 p.m
8.30 a.m	*Belmullet, Arthur Rose	2.15 p.m
7. 0 a.m	*Belturbet, Richard Wright........	4.45 p.m
10.15 a.m	Beragh, 7¾ miles from Omagh	1.15 p.m
10.15 a.m	Bettystown, 5¾ miles from Drogheda	5.45 p.m
10.15 a.m	Blacklion, 11¾ miles from Enniskillen	2. 0 p.m
8.15 a.m	*Blackrock, Mrs. Mary Warren	2.30 p.m
8. 0 a.m 3.45 p.m	Blackrock, 2¾ miles from Cork	5.30 p.m
7. 0 a.m	Blackwatertown, 2½ miles from Moy.	5.20 p.m
6.10 p.m	Blennerville, 1½ miles from Tralee ..	9. 0 p.m
10.45 a.m	*Blessington, Thomas Boothman....	4.30 p.m
7. 0 a.m	Blue-Ball, 6 miles from Tullamoore..	5.50 p.m
8.15 a.m	*Booterstown, George Burnett......	2.30 p.m
7.20 a.m	Borris, 4¼ miles from Goresbridge ..	4.50 p.m
7.26 a.m	*Borrisakane, Thomas Gardiner	4. 0 p.m
7. 0 a.m	*Borris-in-Ossory, George Pratt	8.30 p.m
7.53 a.m	*Boyle, William Laurence..........	4. 0 p.m
9.30 a.m	*Bray, Miss Jane Millar	2.55 p.m
5.30 p.m	Bready, 7 miles from Strabane......	8.35 a.m
10.30 a.m	Bridgetown, 10 miles from Wexford	12.30 p.m
10.50 a.m	Broadford, 10¼ miles from Limerick	1.40 p.m
10.30 a.m	Broadway, 10 miles from Wexford ..	12.30 p.m
8.30 a.m	*Brookborough, MissSusanArmstrong	3.50 p.m
11.45 a.m	Broughshane, 3¾ mi. from Ballymena	12.40 p.m
11. 0 a.m	*Bruff, Richard Fogarty............	1.20 p.m
7. 0 a.m.	Bryansford, 3 mi. from Castlewellan	5.15 p.m

Letters from London delivered at h. m.	Town. Postmaster.	Box for London closes at h. m.
4. 0 p.m	*Buncrana, Miss Mary Armstrong	7.30 a.m
2.25 p.m	Bundoran, 3¾ mi. from Ballyshannon	10. 0 a.m
12.10 p.m	Bunmahon, 5¼ mi. fr. Kilmacthomas	8. 0 a.m
11.18 a.m	Bunnanaden, 5½ mi. from Ballymote	11.36 a.m
10.15 a.m	*Bunratty, Patrick Keane	2.33 p.m
2.30 p.m	Burnfoot, 5 miles from Derry	9. 0 a.m
4.10 p.m	Burrin, 15 miles from Gort	7. 0 a.m
8. 5 a.m	Burrosoleigh, 5¾ mi. fr. Templemore	3.50 p.m
4. 0 p.m	*Bushmills, Samuel Steel	8.25 a.m
8. 5 a.m	Butler's-Bridge, 3¾ miles from Cavan	3.50 p.m
8.20 a.m 1.28 p.m	*Buttevant, Michael Guinee......	10.52 a.m 2. 0 p.m
8.45 a.m	*Cabinteely, William Staunton	3.40 p.m
7. 0 a.m	*Caherciveen, John Fitzgerald......	2. 0 p.m
7. 0 a.m 10. 0 a.m	*Cahir, John M. Bowen	1. 0 p.m 9. 0 p.m
11.40 a.m	Cahirconlish, 8¾ miles from Limerick	12.50 p.m
7. 0 a.m	*Caledon, John Wilson	5. 0 p.m
7.20 a.m	*Callan, Eliza Nowlang...........	6.38 p.m
7.30 a.m 3.45 p.m	Camlough, 3 miles from Newry	8.45 a.m 6.15 p.m
7.20 a.m	*Camolin, Cassandra Keogh........	6.56 p.m
7. 0 a.m	Camp, 11¾ miles from Tralee........	9. 0 p.m
11. 0 a.m 1.40 p.m	*Cappoquin, Hannah Dodsworth...	10.20 a.m 1. 0 p.m
4. 0 p.m	Cappawhite, 9½ miles from Tipperary	8.20 a.m
7.35 a.m	Carlingford, 12 miles from Newry...	5.40 p.m
7.30 a.m 3.15 p.m	*Carlow, William Carey	10. 0 a.m 10. 0 p.m
5.15 p.m	*Carn, Mrs. Mary Carey	9.30 p.m
1. 0 p.m	Carncastle, 5¾ miles from Larne	10.45 a.m
8.30 a.m	*Carnew, Richard Goodison	3.30 p.m
7. 0 a.m	Carney, 7½ miles from Sligo	5.40 p.m
8. 0 a.m	Carnmoney, 5 miles from Belfast....	4.45 p.m
9.15 a.m	Carrick, 10 miles from Killybegs	5.45 p.m
8.50 a.m	*Carrickfergus, George Erskine	3.40 p.m
7. 0 a.m	*Carrickmacross, Wm. C. M'Auley..	9.30 p.m
7. 0 a.m	*CarrickonShannon, ArthurH. Bourns	5.15 p.m
8. 0 a.m	*Carrick-on-Suir, John Leech	4.10 p.m
7. 0 a.m	Carrigaholt, 16¼ miles from Kilrush	4. 5 p.m
8.30 a.m	Carrigahorig, 5½ mi. fr. Borrisakane..	3.10 p.m
10.22 a.m 6.10 p.m	Carrigaline, 12 miles from Cork....	1. 0 p.m 9.30 p.m
9.15 a.m	Carrigallen, 6¼ mi. from Killeshandra	2.45 p.m
3.35 p.m	Carrigans, 5¾ miles from Derry	8.55 a.m
6.50 p.m	Carrigart, 23¼ miles from Letterkenny	1.45 p.m
8.22 a.m	Cashcarrigan, 10m.fr.CarrickShannon	4.16 p.m
7.30 a.m 11. 0 a.m	*Cashel, William Ryall	1.30 p.m 9.30 p.m
2. 3 p.m	*Castlebar, Miss Margaret Foy	10. 0 a.m
7. 0 a.m 12.30 p.m	*Castlebellingham, Miss Mary Ann Miller	11.30 a.m 9.30 p.m
8. 7 a.m	*Castleblakeney, Roderick Rabit....	4. 0 p.m
7. 0 a.m 8. 0 p.m	*Castleblaney, John Smith	9.30 p.m
8.25 a.m	Castlecaulfield, 4 mi. fr. Dungannon..	3.45 p.m
7.30 a.m	*Castlecomer, Patrick B. Kenna	8.30 p.m
8.25 a.m	*Castleconnel, Stephen Hall	3.50 p.m
11.30 a.m	*Castledawson, Miss Anne Oliver....	12.30 p.m
5.15 p.m	Castlederg, 10 miles from Strabane ..	7.40 a.m
1.55 p.m	*Castledermot, George Graham	8.30 p.m
11.45 a.m	*Castlefin, William McLoughlin	12.15 p.m
7.40 p.m	Castlegregory, 16¾ miles from Tralee	9. 0 p.m
3.20 p.m	Castleisland, 14¾ m. from Newcastle	9.20 a.m
8.35 a.m	Castleknock, 5 miles from Dublin....	3.45 p.m
1.30 p.m	Castlelyons, 2½ m. from Rathcormack	11.10 a.m
10. 0 a.m 6.15 p.m	*Castlemartyr, Joseph Taylor	3.50 p.m 9. 0 p.m
7.15 a.m	*Castlepollard, Thomas M. Riggs.....	5.30 p.m
9.11 a.m	*Castlerea, Peter Dillon...........	2.20 p.m
7.20 a.m	*Castletown, Nathaniel Spencer	2.40 p.m
7.30 a.m	Castletown, 7½ m. from Kilbeggan ..	4.40 p.m
7. 0 a.m	Castletown, 1¾ mile from Mountrath	5.40 p.m
7. 0 a.m	*Castletowndelvin Patrick Fegan	7.30 p.m
7.40 a.m	Castletown-Roche, 8¾ m. fr. Fermoy	2.50 p.m
4.10 p.m	Castletownsend, 4 m. fr. Skibbereen..	7.15 a.m
7. 0 a.m	*Castlewellan, James O'Neill	6.30 p.m
8.40 p.m	Causeway, 11¼ miles from Tralee....	4.20 p.m
7. 0 a.m	*Cavan, James Parker	7.15 p.m
4. 0 p.m	Cecilstown, 7¾ miles from Mallow....	8.10 a.m
9.21 a.m	*Celbridge, James Leslie............	3.10 p.m
8. 6 a.m	Chapelizod, 3¾ miles from Dublin....	4.20 p.m

Letters from London delivered at h. m.	Town. Postmaster.	Box for London closes at h. m.
12.30 p.m	*Charleville, Cornelius Graham	11.40 a.m
11. 5 a.m	Church-Hill, 12 m. from Enniskillen..	1.30 p.m
4.25 p.m	Church-Hill, 9 m. from Letterkenny..	7.45 a.m
3.15 p.m	Clady 9 miles from Derry	8. 0 a.m
7.25 a.m	Clane, 5½ miles from Naas	5.15 p.m
7. 0 a.m	*Clara, Thomas Norris	6.50 p.m
5. 5 p.m	Clare, 7½ miles from Galway	7.18 a.m
2.35 p.m	*Claremorris, Sarah Collins	9.45 a.m
9.55 a.m	Clarina, 5½ miles from Limerick	2.10 p.m
12.20 p.m	Clashmore, 6¾ miles from Youghall	1.50 p.m
7.15 p.m	*Clifden, Catherine Thomas	9. 0 p.m
5.30 p.m	Cliffoney, 14 miles from Ballyshannon	8. 0 a.m
7.47 a.m	*Cloghan, James Devery	4.20 p.m
10.35 a.m	*Clogheen, James Sandford	1.30 p.m
7.15 a.m	*Clogher, Miss Martha Crooks	4.25 p.m
8.50 a.m	Clogher-Head, 8½ miles fr. Drogheda	4. 0 p.m
12. 8 p.m 8.40 p.m	*Cloghnakilty, Dinah O'Conner ..	10.47 a.m 9.30 p.m
8.10 a.m	Cloghran, 7 miles from Dublin	4. 0 p.m
7. 0 p.m	*Clonard, Bartholomew Herbert ..	8.30 a.m
8.27 a.m	Clonaslee, 9 miles fr. Mountmellick	4.50 p.m
4.50 p.m	Clonbur, 9½ miles from Ballinrobe ..	7.25 a.m
8.20 a.m	*Clonee, Patrick Fitzpatrick	4.20 p.m
8.46 a.m	Clonegal, 17¾ from Carlow	4. 0 p.m
7.15 a.m	*Clones, Benjamin Thompson	4.50 p.m
8.40 a.m	*Clonmel, William P. Worrall	3.30 p.m
9.25 a.m	Clonmellon, 5 miles from Athboy ..	3.45 p.m
8.30 a.m	Clontarf, 3¾ miles from Dublin	4.45 p.m
7. 0 a.m	*Clough, Mrs. Margaret Mc Cartan	5.35 p.m
12.45 p.m	Clough, 7½ miles from Ballymena ..	7.40 a.m
7. 0 a.m	*Cloughjordan, Miss Jane Wilson ..	5. 0 p.m
10.25 a.m 8.15 p.m	*Cloyne, Sarah Collins	3.30 p.m 9. 0 p.m
9.54 a.m	Coachford, 16 miles from Cork	1.16 p.m
10.45 a.m	Coagh, 3¾ miles from Moneymore ..	7.30 a.m
7.35 a.m	Coalisland, 5 miles from Dungannon	4.30 p.m
7. 0 a.m	Colehill, 5 miles from Ballymahon ..	5.15 p.m
2.15 p.m	*Coleraine, Mrs. Margaret Galt ..	10. 0 a.m 9.30 p.m
7. 0 a.m	Collon, 6¾ miles from Drogheda	9.30 p.m
10.10 a.m	*Collooney, Miss Jane Benson	2.10 p.m
9.15 a.m	*Comber, Joseph Shean............	2.30 p.m
4. 0 p.m	Cong, 6½ miles from Ballinrobe	8.25 a.m
2.20 p.m	Convoy, 3 miles from Raphoe	9.15 a.m
8.40 a.m	*Cookstown, Miss Margaret Pattison	3.25 p.m
12. 0 a.m	Coolany, 6½ miles from Collooney ..	12.25 p.m
8.10 a.m	Coolattin, 2½ miles from Carnew	4. 0 p.m
7.20 a.m	Coolrain, 4¾ miles from Mountrath ..	5.40 p.m
7. 0 a.m	*Cootehill, Miss Mary Wallace	5.45 p.m
8. 0 a.m 3. 0 p.m	*Cork, John Macdonnell	10. 0 a.m 5.30 p.m
8.15 a.m	Courtownsharbour, 3¼ m. from Gorey	6.20 p.m
10.20 a.m 5. 5 p.m	*Cove, Jane Ensor	12.20 p.m 9.30 p.m
9. 8 a.m	*Craughwell, John Briscoe	3.10 p.m
4.50 p.m	Creeslough, 15½ m. from Letterkenny	7.20 a.m
7. 0 a.m	Cretteyard, 9½ miles from Carlow ..	6.30 p.m
7.55 p.m	Crookhaven, 24¾ m. from Skibbereen	9. 0 p.m
2.30 p.m	Crookstown, 25¾ miles from Cork....	8.30 a.m
10.50 a.m	Croome, 10½ miles from Limerick ..	2. 0 p.m
2.25 p.m	Cross, 4 miles from Derry	9. 0 a.m
7.50 a.m	Crossakeale, 6¼ miles from Kells....	4.20 p.m
7. 0 a.m	*Crossdoney, Francis Galligan	5.45 p.m
9. 0 a.m	Crossgar, 6¼ miles from Down	3. 0 p.m
7.40 a.m 6.15 p.m	Crossmaglen, 8¼ miles from Castle-blaney	4.45 p.m 9.30 p.m
4.15 p.m	Crossmolina, 8 miles from Ballina ..	8.10 a.m
7.30 a.m	*Crumlin, James Campbell	4.30 p.m
11.30 a.m	Crusheen, 7½ miles from Gort	11. 5 a.m
7. 0 p.m	Culdaff, 5 miles from Carn..........	3.15 p.m
11.45 a.m	Cullybackey, 3¾ m. from Ballymena	12.45 p.m
3.35 p.m	*Curofin, Martin Mullins	8.25 a.m
3.10 p.m	*Cushendall, Miss Anne Mc Donnell	9.20 a.m
8.15 a.m	Dalkey, 2½ miles from Kingstown ..	10.25 a.m
9. 5 a.m	*Dangan, Jno. Gannon	3.20 p.m
10.33 a.m	*Delgany, Hugh McLinden	2. 0 p.m
12.10 p.m	*Derry, Mrs. Elizabeth Peoples....	12. noon 1. 5 p.m
11. 5 a.m	Derrygonnelly, 11½ m. fr. Enniskillen	1. 5 p.m
10.20 a.m	Derrylin, 6 miles from Ballyconnell..	1.45 p.m
2. 0 p.m	Dervock, 4½ miles from Ballymoney..	10.40 a.m
7. 0 a.m	*Dingle, John Griffin	9. 0 p.m

Letters from London delivered at h. m.	Town. Postmaster.	Box for London closes at h. m.
10. 5 a.m	Donabate, 2¼ miles from Malahide ..	3. 0 p.m
10. 0 a.m	*Donaghadee, Daniel J. Curtis	1. 0 p.m
7.30 a.m	Donaghmore, 2½ m. fr. Dungannon ..	4. 0 p.m
10.40 a.m 3. 0 p.m	Donaghmore, 5 miles from Newry	10.15 a.m 3. 0 p.m
3.35 p.m	*Donegal, Mrs. Anne Dillon	8.30 a.m
7.20 a.m 8.45 p.m	*Doneraile, John Haycroft	3. 0 p.m 9. 0 p.m
8.50 a.m 3.35 p.m	Douglas, 2 miles from Cork	1.50 p.m 9. 0 p.m
7. 0 a.m	*Down, Benjamin Mc Ivor	5. 0 p.m
2.40 p.m	Draperstown, 3¾ mi. fr. Tobbermore	9.10 a.m
7. 0 a.m 10.50 a.m	*Drogheda, John Shaw McCulloch	2.30 p.m 9. 0 p.m
12.55 p.m	Dromahair, 9¾ miles from Collooney	7. 0 a.m
7. 0 a.m	Dromara, 6¼ miles from Dromore ..	6.10 p.m
7. 0 a.m	*Dromod, James Fenton	6.40 p.m
11. 0 a.m	Dromore, 10 miles from Omagh	1.15 p.m
7. 0 a.m	*Dromore, Michael Bodell	8.15 a.m 7.30 p.m
12.30 p.m	*Dromore-West, Wm. Rutledge	12.0 noon
9.30 a.m	Drum, 9 miles from Clones	2.25 p.m
2.30 p.m	Drumcollogher, 9¾ from Charleville	8.30 a.m
7.30 a.m	Drumcondra, 2½ miles from Dublin	4.30 p.m
8.30 a.m	Drumconra, 5 miles from Ardee	6. 0 p.m
7. 0 a.m	Drumcree, 5 mi. fr. Castletowndelvin	6.40 p.m
12.10 p.m	Drumkeer, in 19¾ miles from Carrick-on-Shannon	8.30 p.m
7.20 p.m	Drumlish, 5 miles fr. Newtonforbes	5.40 p.m
11. 0 a.m	Drumquin, 9 miles from Omagh	1.15 p.m
8.58 a.m	Drumshambo, 9 m. f. Carrick Shannon	3.35 p.m
7. 0 a.m	*Drumsna, Mrs. Mary Gilroy	6. 5 p.m

*Dublin,
Augustus Godby, esq. *Secretary*

Hours of Closing the Letter Box at the Principal Office in Dublin.

	Boxes close.
For London Mail	6. 0 a.m
For Local Posts, & Dublin delivery of Local Letters	7. 0 a.m
For Holyhead, Kilkenny, & Belfast Day Mails	8. 0 a.m
For Cork Day Mail	10. 0 a.m
For Dublin delivery of Local Letters, & Booterstown, Blackrock, & Kingstown bags	12. 0noon
For Dublin delivery of Local Letters	1.45 p.m 4. 0 p.m
For Liverpool Mail	5. 0 p.m
For Mails for the interior, & Dublin delivery of Local Letters	6. 0 p.n.

At the Dublin Receiving Houses.

For Dublin delivery of Local Letters	11. 0 a.m 1. 0 p.m 3. 0 p.m
For Liverpool Mail	4.30 p.m
For Mails to the interior, & Dublin delivery of Local Letters	5.30 p.m
For London Mail & first Dublin delivery of Local Letters	10. 0 p.m

Letters from London delivered at h. m.	Town. Postmaster.	Box for London closes at h. m.
3. 0 p.m	Dugort, 29½ miles fr. Newport Mayo,	8.40 a.m
8. 0 a.m	Duleek, 5 miles from Drogheda	5.25 p.m
1.10 p.m	Dunamanagh, 7½ miles fr. Strabane ..	7.45 a.m
10.48 a.m	Duncannon, 2¼ miles fr. Arthurstown	1.18 p.m
7. 0 a.m 1. 0 p.m	*Dundalk, James Parks	12.15 p.m 9.30 p.m
8.15 a.m	Dundonald, 5 miles from Belfast	4.15 p.m
8.14 a.m	Dundrum, 4½ miles from Dublin	4. 0 p.m
11.30 a.m	Dundrum, 6 miles from Cashel	5.50 p.m
6. 0 p.m	*Dunfanaghy, Robert Wilkinson	9. 0 p.m
7. 0 a.m	*Dungannon, Samuel Hughes	5.30 p.m
12.30 p.m	*Dungarvan, B. G. Dyer	11.45 a.m
4.45 p.m	*Dungiven, David Mitchell	9.30 p.m
11. 0 a.m	Dungloe, 26¾ miles from Ardara	9.30 p.m
5.45 p.m	Dunkaneely, 12¼ miles from Donegal	9.30 p.m
7. 0 a.m	Dunlavin, 6½ miles from Kilcullen	6. 0 p.m
7. 0 a.m 11.50 a.m	*Dunleer, George Govers	1.40 p.m 9.30 p.m
3.40 p.m	Dunmanway, near Bandon	7.20 a.m
1.42 a.m	Dunmore, 9 miles from Tuam	12.30 p.m

Letters from London delivered at h. m.	Town. Postmaster.	Box for London closes at h. m.
10.38 a.m	Dunmore-East, 16¼ m. fr. Waterford	1.20 p.m
8. 0 a.m	Dunmurry, 3½ miles from Lisburn ..	5.15 p.m
10. 0 a.m	*Dunshaughlin, Thomas Devitt	3. 0 p.m
8.45 a.m	*Durrow, Edward Harte	4.10 p.m
2.55 p.m	Easky, 4½ miles from Dromore-West	10.40 a.m
7. 0 a.m	*Edenderry, Mrs. Bridget Nowlan ..	6. 0 p.m
12. 0noon	Ederny, 2¾ miles from Kesh	12. 0noon
7. 0 a.m	*Edgeworthstown, William Morgan	8.45 p.m
7.40 a.m	*Elphin, Miss Margaret Crawford ..	4. 5 p.m
7. 0 a.m	*Emo, Samuel Holmes	8.45 p.m
7. 0 a.m	*Emyvale, Alexander McDowell	7.30 p.m
7. 0 a.m	*Enfield, Mrs. Johana Furg	9. 0 p.m
12.0 noon	*Ennis, George Crow	12.10 p.m
7.20 a.m	*Enniscorthy, W. D. Fayle	5.20 p.m
3.42 p.m	Enniskean, 8½ miles from Bandon ..	8.32 a.m
9.30 a.m	Enniskerry, 12 miles from Dublin ..	2.40 p.m
9. 0 a.m	*Enniskillen, Richard Ball	3·30 p.m
4.10 p.m	*Ennistimon, Bridget McDonough	7.40 a.m
8.35 a.m	*Eyrecourt, Miss Mary Eyre	3.30 p.m
3.10 p.m	Fahan, 10 miles from Derry	8.25 a.m
8.30 a.m	Fairview, 2 miles from Dublin	5. 0 p.m
7. 0 p.m	Falcaragh, 7 miles from Dunfanaghy	9.30 p.m
11.40 a.m	Feakle, 15 miles from Killaloe	12.10 p.m
9.31 a.m	Fenagh, 2½ miles from Ballinamore..	3. 0 p.m
7.50 a.m	Fenagh, 6¼ miles from Leighlinbridge	4.50 p.m
7. 5 a.m	Ferbane, 4½ miles from Cloghan	6.25 p.m
8. 0 a.m 12.25 p.m	*Fermoy, Jonathan Dann	12.30 p.m 8.30 p.m
7.20 a.m	*Ferns, Joseph Haughton	6.30 p.m
9.50 a.m	*Fethard, Tipperary, Patrick Stokes	1. 5 p.m
11.36 a.m	Fethard, 7¼ miles from Arthurstown	12.30 p.m
7.40 a.m	Finea, 5½ miles from Granard	3.40 p.m
8. 0 a.m	Finglas, 3¾ miles from Dublin	5. 0 p.m
9.50 a.m	Fintona, 8¼ miles from Omagh	2.20 p.m
9.30 a.m	Fivemiletown, 6¼ m. fr. Brookborough	3. 0 p.m
5.50 a.m	Florence-Court, 8 m. from Enniskillen	1.40 p.m
7. 0 a.m 2. 0 p.m	*Flurrybridge, John Gosson	11.30 a.m 9.30 p.m
7.45 a.m	Forkhill, 5¾ miles from Dundalk	5.40 p.m
4.24 p.m	Foxford, 9¼ miles from Ballina	8. 0 a.m
11. 0 a.m	Foxhall, 7½ miles from Tuam	1.40 p.m
12.56 p.m	Foynes, 23¾ miles from Limerick	11.20 a.m
7.15 a.m	*Frankford, Miss Anna Maria Haslam	4.30 p.m
8.38 a.m	*Frenchpark, Thomas Coleman	3.20 p.m
7.20 a.m	*Freshford, Richard Stone	5.20 p.m
10.46 a.m	*Galway, Robert Dudley Persse	1.10 p.m
11. 0 a.m	Garristown, 6¼ miles fr. Ashbourne ..	1.45 p.m
12.45 p.m	*Garvagh, James Wallace	11.15 a.m
7.55 a.m	Geashell, 5 miles from Philipstown ..	3.40 p.m
7. 0 a.m	*Gilford, Kennedy Cochrane	6.20 p.m
7. 0 a.m	Glaneely, 3¾ miles from Ashford	5.40 p.m
8. 0 a.m 3. 0 p.m	Glanmire, 4 miles from Cork	2.45 p.m 9. 0 p.m
7.30 a.m	Glasslough, 6¼ miles fr. Monaghan ..	4.40 p.m
8.30 a.m	Glassnevin, 3¾ miles from Dublin ..	2. 0 p.m
9. 0 a.m	Glasson, 6½ miles from Athlone	2.55 p.m
9. 0 a.m	Glasthule, 2 miles from Kingstown	3.50 p.m
12.40 p.m	Glenarm, 11¾ miles from Larne	11.50 a.m
7. 0 a.m	Glenavy, 12¾ miles from Lurgan	4.50 p.m
7. 0 a.m	Glenbegh, 26½ miles from Tralee	4.45 p.m
7. 0 a.m	Glengariff, 9 miles from Bantry	6.50 p.m
12.40 p.m	Glennamaddy, 16 miles fr. Castle-blakeney	8.40 a.m
7. 0 a.m	Glenties, 6 miles from Ardara	4.40 p.m
7. 0 a.m 5. 0 p.m	Glounthaun, 6 miles from Cork	10. 0 a.m 6. 0 p.m
2.20 p.m	Glin, 32 miles from Limerick	9.54 a.m
11.30 a.m	Golden, 4½ miles from Cashel	5.50 p.m
8.54 a.m	Golden-Ball, 8¾ miles from Dublin ..	3.20 p.m
7.20 a.m	*Goresbridge, Catherine Nolan	7.20 p.m
7.20 a.m	*Gorey, Anne Ponder	7.45 p.m
10.30 a.m	*Gort, Thomas F. Morris	1.30 p.m
11. 0 a.m	Gortin, 9 miles from Omagh	1.15 p.m
7.20 a.m	*Gowran, Catherine Shortall	7.30 p.m
11.25 a.m	Grace-Hill, 2½ miles from Ballymena	1. 0 p.m
8.20 a.m	Graig, 10½ miles from Goresbridge ..	5.50 p.m
7. 0 a.m	*Granard, William Stephenson	5. 0 p.
7. 0 a.m	Greenan, 3 miles from Rathdrum	6.40 p.m
5.40 p.m	Greencastle, 2½ miles from Moville ..	8.45 p.m
11 0 a.m	Grey-Abbey, 6¼ mi. fr. Newtownards	2.10 p.m
8.35 a.m	Hacketstown, 8½ miles fm. Baltinglass	3.20 p.m
12.20 p.m	*Headford, Christopher Jameson	7.15 a.m

Letters from London delivered at h. m.	Town. Postmaster.	Box for London closes at h. m.
7. 0 a.m 8. 0 p.m	*Hillsborough, Mrs. Sarah Lutton ..	7.45 a.m 7.15 p.m
7.30 a.m	Hilltown, 3 miles from Rathfriland..	6. 0 p.m
11.56 a.m	*Hollymount, Christopher Bowen ..	12.20 p.m
7.30 a.m	*Hollywood, James Greenfield......	3.50 p.m
9.10 a.m	Holycross, 4 miles from Thurles	3. 0 p.m
12.15 p.m	Hospital, 5 miles from Bruff	8.45 a.m
9.30 a.m	*Howth, Miss Ellen Sweetman......	3.30 p.m
5. 0 p.m	Inishcroane, 7¾ miles from Ballina ..	7.20 a.m
9. 2 a.m	Inniscarra, 8½ miles from Cork......	1.53 p.m
10. 0 a.m 6.10 p.m	*Innishannon, Johnston McIntosh..	12.50 p.m 9. 0 p.m
7.20 a.m	*Innistiogue, George Armstrong	5.30 p.m
10.30 a.m	Island-Magee, 9½ m. f. Carrickfergus	7.45 a.m
7.34 a.m	*Johnstown, Thomas Pick	4.30 p.m
12. 0 noon	Julianstown, 4 miles from Drogheda..	1.45 p.m
3.50 p.m	*Kanturk, Benjamin Savage	8.20 a.m
7.15 a.m	Katesbridge, 5 miles fm. Rathfriland.	5.15 p.m
9.30 a.m	Keadue, 8¾ mi. fm. Carrick-on-Shannon	3. 0 p.m
7.30 a.m	*Keady, Watson Kidd.............	7. 0 p.m
7. 0 a.m	*Kells, Miss Catherine Dyas........	9. 0 p.m
7. 0 a.m	Kells, 7 miles from Antrim	1.15 p.m
7. 0 a.m	Kells, 2½ miles from Stoneyford	5. 0 p.m
9. 0 a.m	Kenagh, 5 miles from Ballymahon ..	3.40 p.m
7. 0 a.m	*Kenmare, Denis Downing	9. 0 p.m
7. 0 a.m	*Kilbeggan, William Gannon	9. 0 p.m
7. 0 a.m	*Kilcock, Mrs. Eliza Allen	9. 0 p.m
11.50 a.m	Kilcolgan, 5½ mi. fm. Oranmore	12.40 p.m
8. 0 a.m	Kilconnell, 3¾ miles from Aughrim..	4.10 p.m
1.45 p.m	*Kilcullen, William Henry Delany ..	11.45 a.m
7. 0 a.m	*Kildare, Charles Dunne	9. 0 p.m
7.20 a.m 4.55 p.m	*Kildorrery, Samuel Piddle	4.15 p.m 9. 0 p.m
4.40 p.m	*Kildysart, Patrick Macnamara	7.40 a.m
5.40 p.m	Kilfenora, 5½ miles from Ennistimon.	9. 0 p.m
3. 5 p.m	Kilfinan, 5¾ miles from Kilmallock..	8.50 a.m
7.30 p.m	Kilkee, 8¾ miles from Kilrush	9. 0 p.m
8.20 a.m	*Kilkeel, Stephen Byrne	6. 0 p.m
8. 0 a.m 6.15 p.m	*Kilkenny, R. D. Matthews........	7.20 a.m 7. 0 p.m
7. 0 a.m	Kill, 3¾ miles from Naas	6.40 p.m
4.15 p.m	*Killala, Robert Poke.............	7.45 a.m
8.30 a.m	*Killaloe, Margaret Thompson......	3.45 p.m
2.50 p.m 5.40 p.m	*Killarney, John Doherty	7. 0 a.m
7. 0 a.m	Killashee, 5 miles from Longford....	6.10 p.m
10.26 a.m	Killeagh, 7 miles from Castlemartyr.	3.10 p.m
7. 0 a.m	Killeigh, 5 miles from Tullamore....	5.40 p.m
7.15 a.m	*Killeshandra, Thomas McCabe	4.30 p.m
6.45 p.m	Killetter, 14½ miles from Strabane ..	9.30 p.m
10.10 a.m	Killinardrish, 20¼ miles from Cork ..	12.39 p.m
8.15 a.m	Killinchy, 6¼ miles from Killyleigh ..	3.45 p.m
9.30 a.m	Killiney, 3 miles from Kingstown ...	4.10 p.m
8.58 p.m	Killorglin, 20¼ miles from Tralee....	6. 7 p.m
7.45 a.m	Killough, 10 miles from Clough.....	3.40 p.m
7. 0 a.m	Killucan, 4 miles from Kinnegad....	9. 0 p.m
7. 5 p.m	*Killybegs, Francis Rogers	9.30 p.m
12.10 p.m	Killygordon, 10 miles from Strabane	12. 0 noon
7. 0 a.m	Killylea, 6¼ miles from Armagh	5.45 p.m
7.50 a.m	*Killyleigh, Miss Ellen Thompson ..	4. 0 p.m
10.35 a.m	Killymor, 8 miles from Eyrecourt ..	1.40 p.m
10. 8 a.m	Killynaule, 6¼ miles from Littleton..	1.20 p.m
10.10 a.m	Kilmacow, 5 miles from Waterford ..	1.50 p.m
2.35 p.m	Kilmacrennan, 6¼ mi. fr. Letterkenny	8.40 a.m
10.40 a.m	*Kilmacthomas, Thomas Brown	1.20 p.m
3. 0 p.m	Kilmain, 6½ miles from Hollymount..	8.45 a.m
11.41 a.m	*Kilmallock, M. M. M'Connel	12.39 p.m
8.30 a.m	Kilmoganny, 13¼ miles fr. Kilkenny	4.30 p.m
9.30 a.m	Kilmuckridge, 19¼ miles from Gorey	1.20 p.m
9.25 a.m	Kilnaleck, 5 mi. fr. Ballyjames-Duff	3.45 p.m
4.50 p.m	Kilrea, 15 miles from Coleraine	7.25 a.m
6. 0 p.m	*Kilrush, W. Brew	10. 0 p.m
4.50 p.m	Kiltemagh, 13 miles from Ballyglass	7.40 a.m
7.25 a.m	Kiltegan, 5 miles from Baltinglass ..	4.30 p.m
8.55 a.m	Kiltormer, 5 miles from Eyrecourt ..	3.25 p.m
12.15 p.m	*Kilworth, David Quain............	noon
8.15 a.m	*Kingscourt, Mrs. Anne Anderson ..	4.20 p.m
7. 0 a.m	*Kingstown, Miss Rebecca Bagnall..	5.20 p.m
7. 0 a.m	*Kinnegad, William Clarendon......	9. 0 p.m
8.15 a.m	Kinnetty, 8 miles from Parson town .	3.40 p.m
12. 0 noon 6.15 p.m	*Kinsale, John Wadle	noon & 10. 0 p.m

Letters from London delivered at h. m.	Town. Postmaster.	Box for London closes at h. m.
3. 5 p.m	Kinvara, 9 miles from Gort	7.55 a.m
11.45 a.m	Kircubbin, 8 miles from Portaferry..	1.25 p.m
11.15 a.m	*Kish, John Acheson	12.40 p.m
6.20 p.m	*Knock, Denis Culligan...........	9. 0 p.m
4.10 p.m	Knocknacarry, 5 mi. fr. Cushendall	8.30 a.m
7.10 a.m	Knocktopher, 3¾ miles fr. Stoneyford	4.40 p.m
9.30 a.m	Kyle, 8½ miles from Enniscorthy....	3.30 p.m
7. 0 a.m	Lanesborough, 10 miles fr. Longford	5.40 p.m
11. 0 a.m	*Larne, James Cooch	1.45 p.m
4.24 p.m	Lahinch, 2 miles from Ennistimon ..	7.26 a.m
7. 0 a.m	Laurencetown, 2½ mi. fr. Banbridge .	7.25 p.m
7.55 a.m	Laurencetown, 4 miles fr. Eyrecourt	4.25 p.m
7.20 a.m 4.10 p.m	*Leighlinbridge, Cecilia Magee	9.30 a.m 9.30 p.m
9. 8 p.m	*Leixlip, Anthony Bacon	3.20 p.m
1.45 p.m	*Letterkenny, Mrs. Catherine Lyle..	11.30 a.m
7. 0 a.m	Licarrow, 8¾ miles from Roscommon	5.40 p.m
11. 0 a.m	Lifford, 1 mile from Strabane	1.15 p.m
9. 8 a.m	*Limerick, Patrick M'Namara	2.45 p.m
10.10 a.m	Lisbellaw, 5 miles from Enniskillen..	1.25 p.m
7. 0 a.m 7.30 p.m	*Lisburn, Samuel Gamble	7.15 a.m 6.45 p.m
10.30 a.m 2.10 p.m	*Lismore, Richard Huddy	9.50 a.m 1.30 p.m
9.30 a.m	Lisnagry, 1¾ miles from Castleconnel	2.40 p.m
7.20 a.m	*Lisnaskea, John Smyth	5. 0 p.m
4.30 p.m	*Listowel, John G. Church	7.40 a.m
9. 0 a.m	*Littleton, John Goring............	2.20 p.m
	*Londonderry. *See* Derry.	
7. 0 a.m	*Longford, William Beatty	7.40 p.m
9. 0 a.m	Lorrha, 7¾ miles from Borrisakane..	2.40 p.m
7. 0 a.m 4. 0 p.m	*Loughbrickland, Nath. O'Flatherty	9.30 a.m 8.45 p.m
7.30 a.m	*Loughgall, William Addy	4.40 p.m
10.50 a.m	Loughglyn, 7½ miles fr. Frenchpark	1.15 p.m
2.20 p.m	Loughill, 27¾ miles from Limerick .,	9.54 a.m
8.18 a.m	*Loughrea, Guy Armstrong	3.45 p.m
7.40 p.m	Louisbourgh, 12¾ miles fr. Westport	8.40 p.m
8.50 a.m	Louth, 7 miles from Dundalk	5. 0 p.m
10.20 a.m	*Lowtherstown, Samuel Douglas....	1.40 p.m
8.42 a.m	*Lucan, James Lynch..............	3.45 p.m
7. 0 a.m	*Lurgan, William B. Morris........	6.30 p.m
10.10 a.m	Lusk, 11½ miles from Balbriggan....	3. 0 p.m
11. 6 a.m	*Macroom, Peter Williams	11.50 p.m
11.20 a.m	*Maghera, David Thompson........	12.45 p.m
10.20 a.m	*Magherafelt, Joshua Adams	2. 0 p.m
9.50 a.m	Magheramorne, 9 m. fr. Carrickfergus	2.30 p.m
7.45 a.m	Maguire's-bridge, 2½ mi. fr. Lisnaskea	4.35 p.m
9. 0 p.m 9.40 a.m	*Malahide, Miss Elizh. Alicia Batty	3.15 p.m 9. 0 p.m
6. 0 p.m	Malin, 3¾ miles from Carn..........	9.45 p.m
8.20 a.m 3.30 p.m	*Mallow, Robert Lynch............	9.40 a.m 1.40 p.m
12.25 p.m	Manor-Cunningham, 12 m. f. Strabane	11.15 a.m
11.45 a.m	*Manor-Hamilton, Simon Armstrong	12.10 p.m
7. 0 a.m 6.15 p.m	*Markethill, Miss Susanna Penny ..	7.55 p.m 9.30 p.m
9.10 a.m	Marlfield, 2½ miles from Clonmel....	3.35 p.m
7. 0 am	*Maryborough, John Miller	9.40 p.m
7. 0 a.m	*Maynooth, John Maclean	9. 0 p.m
9. 0 a.m 6.50 p.m	*Middleton, Joseph Brabazon	4.40 p.m 9. 0 a.m
8.15 a.m	Middletown, 2½ miles from Tynan ..	4. 0 p.m
4.10 p.m	Milford, 4½ miles from Ramelton	7.15 a.m
12.19 p.m	*Millstreet, R.B. Wynne	10.36 a.m
8.20 a.m	Miltown, 3¾ miles from Belturbet ..	3.15 p.m
12.28 p.m	Miltown, 6½ miles from Tralee	6.43 p.m
5.10 p.m	*Miltown-Malbay, Robert Maroney..	9. 0 p.m
7.20 a.m 12.40 p.m	*Mitchelstown, Edward Thornhill ..	8.50 a.m 9.30 p.m
7. 0 a.m	*Moate, George Gurd	8.45 p.m
7. 0 a.m	*Mohill, Mrs. Honoria Brady	5.10 p.m
6.30 p.m	Moincoim, 5¾ miles from Piltown....	3.43 p.m
7.30 a.m	*Moira, Miss Elizabeth Bamber	4.25 p.m
7. 0 a.m	*Monaghan, Thomas Wright........	8. 0 p.m
7. 0 a.m	*Monastereven, William Morgan....	9. 0 p.m
7. 0 a.m	*Moneygall, Samuel Goulding	7.10 p.m
9.30 a.m	*Moneymore, David Richey	2.40 p.m
12. 5 p.m	Monivea, 10½ miles from Craughwell	12.25 p.m
4.40 p.m 9.30 a.m	Monkstown, 8¼ miles from Cork	1. 5 p.m 9. 0 a.m
9.15 a.m	Monkstown, ½ mile from Kingstown..	4. 0 p.m

Letters from London delivered at h. m.	Town.	Postmaster.	Box for London closes at h. m.
2.45 p.m	Mosside, 8¼ miles from Ballymoney . .		9.45 a.m
4.20 p.m	Mountcharles, 3¾ miles from Donegal		8 20 a.m
10.25 a.m	Mountfield, 7 miles from Omagh		1.45 p.m
7. 0 a.m	*Mountmellick, William Thacker . .		6.15 p.m
7. 0 a.m	Mountnorris, 4½ mi. from Markethill		6. 0 p.m
8.40 a.m	*Mountnugent, Henry Spinks		4.30 p.m
7. 0 a.m	*Mountrath, Daniel Egan		9. 0 p.m
11. 5 a.m	Mountshannon, 15 miles fr. Killaloe		12.20 p.m
10.40 a.m	Mount-Talbot, 8¾ mi. fr. Roscommon		1.45 p.m
4.50 p.m	*Moville, John Anderson		7.15 a.m
7. 0 a.m	*Moy, Thomas Wilford		6.30 p.m
7. 0 a.m	Moyallon, 2½ miles from Gilford		5.45 p.m
12.45 p.m	Moycullen, 8¾ miles from Galway . .		12.15 p.m
10. 0 a.m	Moylough, 6½ m. fr. Castleblakeney		2.10 p.m
7. 0 a.m	Moynalty, 4½ miles from Kells		6.20 p.m
7.40 a.m	Moyvore, 6 miles from Ballynacargy		4. 0 p.m
2.30 p.m	Muff, 6¼ miles from Derry		9.25 a.m
2.30 p.m	Muff-don, 6¼ miles from Derry		9.40 a.m
7.15 a.m	Mullinahone, 5 miles from Callen . .		5. 0 p.m
7. 0 a.m	*Mullingar, Edward Gordon		9. 0 p.m
5.10 p.m	Mullinavat, 8¾ miles from Waterford		9. 0 p.m
8. 0 a.m	Multifarnham, 7½ mi. from Mullingar		4.40 p.m
8.50 a.m	Myshall, 10 mi. from Leighlinbridge		4.50 p.m
12.55 p.m	*Naas, Miss Jane Parsons		12.45 p.m
9.15 p.m	Narin, 7 miles from Ardara		4.40 p.m
7. 0 a.m	*Navan, John Mullen		9. 0 p.m
8. 0 a.m	*Nenagh, Patrick Cane		5.30 p.m
10.10 a.m	New-Birmingham, 3¾ mi. fr. Littleton		12.50 p.m
8.30 a.m	Newbliss, 5 miles from Clones		3.20 p.m
7. 0 a.m	*Newbridge, Thomas Dowling		9. 0 p.m
7.40 a.m	Newbridge, 6½ miles from Rathdrum		5.40 p.m
12.10 p.m	*Newcastle, Hugh Murray Green . .		12.14 p.m
8. 0 a.m	Newcastle, 4¾ mi. from Castlewellan		4.30 p.m
10. 0 a.m	Newcastle, Tipperary, 9 m. fr. Clonmel		1.46 p.m
7.10 a.m	Newmarket, 4½ miles from Kanturk		4.15 p.m
10.58 a.m	*Newmarket-on-Fergus, M. Shannon		1.40 p.m
7. 0 a.m	Newmills, 3¾ miles from Dungannon .		5.15 p.m
8.50 a.m	*Newport (Tipperary), Daniel Ryan		3.10 p.m
4.20 p.m	*Newport (Mayo), Mrs. Margt. Arthur		7.30 a.m
7. 0 a.m 3. 0 p.m	*Newry, James Moore		10.45 a.m 9.30 p.m
9. 0 a.m	*Newtownards, Miss Jane Pollock . .		2.50 p.m
7.28 a.m	*Newtown-Barry, Paul Kennedy		4.10 p.m
8.30 a.m	Newtownbreda, 3¾ miles from Belfast .		4. 0 p.m
8.40 a.m	Newtown-Butler, 6½ miles fr. Clones.		3.25 p.m
4.25 p.m	Newtown-Cunninghm, 12¾ m. f. Derry		7.20 a.m
7. 0 a.m	*Newtown-Forbes, John Bonny		7.40 p.m
7.25 a.m 5.10 p.m	Newtown-Hamilton, 10 miles from Castleblaney		7. 0 a.m 5.10 p.m
4.15 p.m	*Newtown-Limavady, Miss Letitia Ross		8.45 a.m 8.20 p.m
10.57 a.m	*Newtown-Mount-Kennedy, Patrick Lamb		1.40 p.m
9.15 a.m	*NewtownStewart, ClarkeMatthewson		3. 0 p.m
9.25 a.m	Nobber, 9¾ miles from Kells		4.30 p.m
9.20 a.m	O'Briensbridge, 2¾ m. fr. Castleconnel		2.50 p.m
7.30 a.m	*Oldcastle, Mrs. Eleanor Kenna		5.40 p.m
8.40 a.m	*Omagh Miss Margaret Wallace		4. 0 p.m
7. 0 a.m	Omeath, 6¼ miles from Newry		6.25 p.m
10.10 a.m	*Oranmore, Henry Griffin		2.10 p.m
9. 0 a.m	Oulart, 13¾ miles from Gorey		2.10 p.m
2. 3 p.m	Outerard, 17½ miles from Galway		10.50 a.m
12. 0 noon	Pallasgreen, 14¼ miles from Limerick		12.35 p.m
11.55 a.m	Pallaskenry, 12½ miles from Limerick		12.20 p.m
7. 0 a.m	*Parsonstown, Thomas Dooley		5.15 p.m
10.50 a.m	Passage, 6¾ miles from Waterford . .		1.20 p.m
9.25 a.m 4.25 p.m	Passage-West, 6¾ miles from Cork . .		1.15 p.m 9. 0 p.m
9.40 a.m	Patrickswell, 4¾ miles from Limerick.		3. 0 p.m
12.0 noon	Pettigo, 5 miles from Kesh		12.10 p.m
3.20 p.m	Pharis, 7 miles from Ballymoney		8.45 a.m
7. 0 a.m	*Philipstown, Mrs. Catherine Ellis. .		5.45 p.m
8.30 a.m	*Piltown, John Anthony		3.40 p.m
8.35 a.m	Pomeroy, 9 miles from Dungannon . .		2.45 p.m
7.15 a.m	*Portadown, Richard Edgar		6. 0 p.m
8.50 a.m	*Portaferry, Charles Press		3. 0 p.m
7. 0 a.m	*Portarlington, Michael Carroll		5.40 p.m
1. 0 p.m	*Portglenone, Thomas Madden		12. 0noon
4. 0 p.m	Portrush, 5 miles from Coleraine . .		8.10 a.m 6.40 p.m
3.10 p.m	Portstewart, 4½ mi. from Coleraine		9. 0 a.m 7.30 p.m

Letters from London delivered at h. m.	Town.	Postmaster.	Box for London closes at h. m.
9.20 a.m	Portlaw, 7¼ miles fr. Carrick-on-Suir		3.10 p.m
9. 0 a.m	*Portumna, Miss Margaret Manahan		2.20 p.m
7. 0 a.m	Poyntz-Pass, 3¾ mi. fr. Loughbrickland		7.15 p.m
9.28 a.m	Priesthaggard, 5 mi. fr. Arthurstown		2.38 p.m
3.25 p.m	Quigley's Point, 11½ miles from Derry		8.40 a.m
12. 5 p.m	Quin, 5 mi. fr. Newmarket-on-Fergus		8.30 a.m
8.40 a.m	Raheny, 4¼ miles from Dublin.		4.30 p.m
3.30 p.m	*Ramelton, Robert Gillespie		8.15 a.m
10. 0 a.m	*Randalstown, Alexander McDowell		2.20 p.m
1.30 p.m	*Raphoe, Samuel Kerr		10. 0 a.m
7. 6 a.m	*Rathangan, Michael Mylod		5.20 p.m
11.40 a.m	*Rathcoole, Office vacant		2. 0 p.m
7.20 a.m 12.50 p.m	*Rathcormack, Mary Ann Langstaff		12.16 p.m 8.16 p.m
7.58 p.m	*Rathdowney, William Carr Perry . .		5.30 p.m
7. 0 a.m	*Rathdrum, Joseph Walker		9. 0 p.m
9. 0 a.m	Rathfarnham, 5 miles from Dublin . .		3.15 p.m
7. 0 a.m	*Rathfriland, John Fegan		8. 0 p.m
11.20 a.m	*Rathkeale, John Hammond		1.19 p.m
6.10 p.m	Rathlacken, 6½ miles from Killala . .		8.30 p.m
5.30 p.m	Rathmullen, 6½ miles from Ramelton		9.30 p.m
7. 0 a.m	Rathnew, 1 mile from Ashford		8. 0 p.m
7. 0 a.m	*Rathowen, James Murray		9. 0 p.m
7.50 a.m	Red-Hills, 8½ miles from Cavan		3.40 p.m
7.30 a.m	Rich-Hill, 5 miles from Armagh		4.40 p.m
7. 0 a.m	Richmond Harbour, 5 mi. fr. Longford		6.50 p.m
10.15 a.m	Riverstown, 8 miles from Ballymote		2.15 p.m
7. 0 a.m	Robertstown, 8¾ miles from Naas . .		4.40 p.m
7. 0 a.m	*Rochfortbridge, Patrick Geraghty		9. 0 p.m
8.35 a.m	Rock, 8 miles from Dungannon		2.45 p.m
8.40 a.m	Rockcorry, 5¼ miles from Ballibay . .		4.35 p.m
1.15 p.m	*Roscarbery, Stephen Legoe		9.40 a.m
8. 0 a.m	*Roscommon Richard Johnston		4.20 p.m
7. 0 a.m	*Roscrea, Miss Ellen Short		7.40 p.m
8.40 a.m	Roslea, 5¾ miles from Clones		3.25 p.m
7.30 a.m	*Ross (or New Ross), John Williams.		4. 0 p.m
7. 0 a.m	*Rostrevor, Ruthven Emerson		7.30 p.m
8.30 p.m	Roundstone, 12½ miles from Clifden		8.30 p.m
9. 0 a.m	Rush, 8¼ miles from Balbriggan		3.45 p.m
7. 0 a.m	Ruskey, 1½ mile from Dromod		6.15 p.m
7.35 a.m	Saintfield, 7½ miles from Comber		4.20 p.m
3.50 p.m	Saint-Johnstown, 7½ miles from Derry		8.35 a.m
7.40 a.m	Santry, 3¾ miles from Dublin		4.25 p.m
9.45 a.m	Scariff, 9¼ miles from Killaloe		1.50 p.m
7. 0 a.m	Scarva, 3 miles from Loughbrickland		7.45 p.m
8.25 a.m	Scrabby, 12 miles from Cavan		2.45 p.m
7. 0 a.m	Seaforde, 1¼ miles from Clough		5. 0 p.m
11.45 a.m	Shanagarry, 4¼ miles from Cloyne . .		1.40 p.m
1.30 p.m	Shanagolden, 23½ miles from Limerick		10.30 a.m
8.25 a.m	Shercock, 7¾ mi. fr. Carrickmacross		4.45 p.m
7. 0 a.m	*Shinrone, Thomas A. Doolan		5.50 p.m
11.20 a.m	*Sixmilebridge, Lucinda O'Halloran.		1. 0 p.m
10. 0 a.m	Sixmilecross, 10 miles from Omagh . .		1.20 p.m
8. 0 a.m	Skerries, 4 miles from Balbriggan . .		5. 0 p.m
2.45 p.m	*Skibbereen, Daniel Crowley		8.10 a.m
5.45 p.m	Skull, 13¾ miles from Skibbereen		9. 0 p.m
7. 0 a.m	*Slane, John McOwen		9.30 p.m
11. 0 a.m	*Sligo, Hugh McSweeny		1. 0 p.m
7.55 a.m	Smithborough, 6¼ mi. fm. Monaghan.		6. 0 p.m
9.25 a.m	Sneem, 15¼ miles from Kenmare		2.50 p.m
6.40 p.m	Spa, 3¾ miles from Tralee		9. 0 p.m
3.10 p.m	Spenag, 7½ miles from Derry		8.20 a.m
1. 5 p.m	Spiddle, 11 miles from Galway		7.50 a.m
8.30 a.m	Stackallan, 5 miles from Navan		5.45 p.m
7.50 a.m	*Stewartstown, Joseph Dudgeon		4.10 p.m
8.20 a.m	Stillorgan, 5½ miles from Dublin		4.15 p.m
7.20 a.m	*Stoneyford, William Davis		5.26 p.m
10.50 a.m	*Strabane, Andrew Jenkins		1.40 p.m
4.31 p.m	*Stradbally, Thomas Connell		5.40 p.m
7. 0 a.m	*Stradone, Joseph Bridgewood		7.40 p.m
9.55 a.m	Straffan, 3½ miles from Celbridge . .		2.40 p.m
7.40 p.m	Straid, 6¼ miles from Carn		2.45 p.m
8.30 a.m	Strangford, 7½ miles from Down		3.30 p.m
12.50 p.m	*Stranorlar, Samuel Brown		11.15 a.m
2.20 p.m	Stratford, 4½ miles from Baltinglass. .		4.30 p.m
7. 0 a.m	*Strokestown, Miss Jane Fearns		5.40 p.m
7. 0 a.m	Summerhill, 7 miles from Kilcock . .		6.40 p.m
10.25 a.m	Swanlinbar, 10 miles fr. Ballyconnell		1.45 p.m
11.55 a.m	Swatragh, 5 miles from Maghera		12.25 p.m
5.51 p.m	*Swinford, Peter Cawley		8.30 p.m
7. 0 a.m 8.30 a.m	*Swords, 3¾ miles from Malahide . .		3.30 p.m 6.10 p.m

Letters from London delivered at h. m.	Town. ostmaster.	Box for London closes at h. m.
10.20 a.m	*Taghmon, Ellen Corish	12.40 p.m
9.15 a.m	*Tallaght, Andrew Armstrong	3.30 p.m
8.20 a.m 3. 0 p.m	*Tallow, Anne Mellsop	9. 0 a.m 5.40 p.m
6. 0 p.m	Tamney, 13 miles from Ramelton	9.30 p.m
7. 0 a.m	*Tanderagee, Richard Trotter	7. 0 p.m
2.50 p.m	*Tarbert, John Creagh	9.22 a.m
7.20 a.m	*Templemore, James Lanigan	4.40 p.m 9.30 p.m
9. 0 a.m	Templeogue, 5 miles from Dublin	3.50 p.m
8.30 a.m	Templepatrick, 5 miles from Antrim	4. 0 p.m 9.30 p.m
8.20 a.m	Templetuohy, 5 mi. from Templemore	3.35 p.m
12. 0 noon	Tempo, 10 miles from Enniskillen	12. 0noon
7.55 a.m	Termonfeckin, 5¾ mi. from Drogheda	4.45 p.m
7.20 a.m	*Thomastown, Alicia Duke	6.12 p.m
7.20 a.m 8.30 a.m	*Thurles, Thomas Burke	3.30 p.m 9. 0 p.m
9. 0 a.m	Timahoe, 7½ miles from Maryborough	5.40 p.m
1.40 p.m	Timoleague, 7¼ miles from Bandon	9. 0 p.m
7.12 a.m	*Tinahely, Miss Mary Ann Morton	5.40 p.m
11.50 a.m	*Tipperary, Richard Molloy	12.55 p.m
10.45 a.m	*Tobbermore, Alexander Christie	1.15 p.m
10.50 a.m	Toome, 6¾ miles from Randalstown	1.40 p.m
5.30 p.m	*Tralee, William Mason	7. 0 a.m
10. 0 a.m	Tramore, 7¾ miles from Waterford	2.20 p.m
11.30 a.m	Trillick, 11¾ miles from Enniskillen	1. 0 p.m
7. 6 a.m	*Trim, Samuel Allen	5.20 p.m
10. 1 a.m	*Tuam, John Sandford	2.15 p.m
12. 6 p.m	Tubbercurry, 10¾ miles fr. Ballymote	12.24 p.m

Letters from London delivered at h. m.	Town. Postmaster.	Box for London closes at h. m.
12.20 p.m	Tulla, 19 miles from Limerick	12.10 p.m
7. 0 a.m	*Tullamoore, John A. Bradley	6.20 p.m
7.15 a.m	*Tullow, William Nourse	6.30 p.m
8.25 a.m	Tullyhogue, 2½ miles fr. Stewartstown	4.10 p.m
7. 0 a.m	Tullyvin, 3¾ miles from Cootehill	6.45 p.m
7.24 a.m	Tulsk, 6½ miles from Strokestown	4.55 p.m
7.15 a.m	*Tynan, Miles Magrath	4.40 p.m
7. 0 a.m	Tyrrella, 4½ miles from Clough	4.30 p.m
7. 0 a.m	*Tyrrellspass, Miss Anne Glanville	9. 0 p.m
3.20 p.m	Union-Hall, 6½ mi. fr. Roscarbery	8. 0 a.m
7.54 a.m	Urlingford, 2¼ miles from Johnstown	4.16 p.m
7.10 a.m	Valentia, 48 miles from Tralee	12.20 p.m
7.30 a.m	Verners-Bridge, 5 miles from Moy	5. 0 p.m
7. 0 a.m	*Virginia, Miss Mary Anne Shegog	9.30 p.m
7. 0 a.m	Waringstown, 6¼ mi. from Banbridge	7,20 p.m
7. 0 a.m	*Warrenspoint, Mrs. Jane Forres	7.50 p.m
9. 0 a.m	*Waterford, Thomas Parsons	3. 0 p.m
7.46 p.m 9.56 a.m	Watergrass-Hill, 13½ mi. from Cork	2. 0 p.m 9. 0 p.m
3.30 p.m	*Westport, Miss Elizabeth Hildebrand	9. 0 a.m
7.50 a.m	*Wexford, John Greene	3. 0 p.m
12. 5 p.m	Whitegate, 5¼ miles from Cloyne	1.20 p.m
7.20 a.m	Whitehall, 2½ mlies from Gowran	5.50 p.m
8. 0 a.m	Whitehouse, 3¾ miles from Belfast	5. 0 p.m
7. 0 a.m	*Wicklow, Michael Byrne	7.20 p.m
8.30 a.m	Wilkinstown, 6¼ miles from Navan	5.15 p.m
12.15noon	Woodford, near Loughrea	12. 0noon
9.50 a.m 4.50 p.m	*Youghall, Archibald Merry	7. 0 a.m 3.45 p.m

OBLITERATING STAMPS.

It sometimes occurs that the Stamps on letters used to denote the places at which such have been posted are not sufficiently plain In such cases the *stamp used to obliterate the postage label* may supply the information. The shape of the stamp and its number will prove the office in which it has been used. The following are *fac similcs* of the obliterating stamps:—

Used in London District Office and in places within its delivery.

Used in the London Office for letters passing by the *General* Post.

Used in all places in England and Wales except London and the London District.

Used in Scotland.

Used in Ireland.

The London District Obliterating Stamp is used at the following places. The *number* on the stamp indicates the particular Office

Highgate,

Finchley, and so on. The *number* in the centre of the stamp denoting the particular office in which it has been used.

1 Highgate
2 Finchley
3 Whetstone
4 Hampstead
5 Hendon
6 Edgware
7 Stoke Newington
8 Tottenham
10 Edmonton
11 Enfield
12 Bow
13 Stratford
14 Leyton
15 Woodford
16 Chigwell
17 Ilford
18 Deptford
20 Greenwich
21 Woolwich
22 Eltham
23 Bexley
24 Dulwich
25 Sydenham
26 Beckenham
27 Clapham
8 Tooting
29 Mitcham
30 Carshaltonq
31 Wandsworth
32 Putney
33 Mortlake
34 Richmond
35 Twickenham
36 Hampton
37 Brompton
38 Kensington
39 Hammersmith
40 Acton
41 Brentford
42 Paddington
43 Charing Cross
44 NorthRow(Branch office)
45 Portland Street
46 Stepney
47 Southwark
48 Shoreditch
49 Sidmouth Street, (Branch office)

The Country Obliterating Stamp

is used as follows. The *number* in the centre of the stamp denoting the town in which it has been used.

1 Abergavenny
2 Aberystwith
3 Abingdon
4 Wantage
5 Accrington
6 Alfreton
7 Crich
8 Alnwick
10 Alresford
11 Alton
12 Altrincham
13 Ambleside
14 Amersham
15 Chesham
16 Missenden
17 Amesbury
18 Ampthill
20 Silsoe
21 Andover
22 Andover-Road
23 Whitchurch
24 Overton
25 Appleby
26 Arrington

27 Arundel
28 Ashbourne
29 Ashburton
30 Ashby-de-la-Zouch
31 Ashford
32 Ashton-under-lyne
33 Atherstone
34 Attleborough
35 Axminster
36 Colyton
37 Seaton
38 Aylesbury
39 Aylsham
40 Bagshot
41 Bakewell
42 Baslow
43 Stoney-Middleton
44 Tideswell
45 Baldock
46 Banbury
47 Bangor
48 Barnard's Castle
49 Barnsley
50 Barnstaple
51 Barton-on-Humber
52 Basingstoke
53 Bath
54 Battle
55 Bawtry
56 Gringley
57 Beaconsfield
58 Beaumaris
59 Beccles
60 Bedale
61 Bedford
62 Belford
63 Wooler
64 Belper
65 Berkhempstead
66 Berwick
67 Beverley
68 Bewdley
69 Bicester
70 Bideford
71 Biggleswade
72 Billericay
73 Bilstone
74 Birkenhead
75 Birmingham
76 Campden
77 Halesowen
78 Henley-in-Arden
79 Knowle
80 Bishop's Auckland
81 Stanhope
82 Bishop's Castle
83 Bishop's Stortford
84 Canterbury
85 Bishop's Waltham
86 Blackburn
87 Blandford
88 Bodmin
89 Wadebridge
90 Padstow
91 Bognor
92 Bolton
93 Boroughbridge
94 Boston
95 Alford
96 Stickney
97 Bury St. Edmond's
100 Bottesdale
101 Ixworth
102 Woolpit
103 Bourn
104 Brackley
105 Bracknell
106 Bradford, Wilts
107 Bradford, Yorkshr
108 Carnarvon
110 Keighley
111 Bingley
112 Braintree
113 Brampton
114 Brandon
115 Stoke-Ferry
116 Brecknock
117 Trecastle
118 Brentwood
120 Bridgend
121 Pyle
122 Bridgenorth
123 Bridgewater
124 Bridlington
125 Bridlington Quay
126 Hunmanby
127 Bridport
128 Beaminster
129 Brigg
130 Calstor
131 Limber
132 Brighton
133 Catterick
134 Bristol
135 Caxton
136 Brixham
137 Broadway
138 Bromyard
139 Broomsgrove
140 Redditch
141 Studley
142 Brough
143 Temple-Sowerby
144 Bromley
145 Buckingham
146 Builth
147 Bungay
148 Buntingford
149 Burford
150 Burnley
151 Colne
152 Burton-on-Trent
153 Burton, Westmld
154 Bury, Lancashire
155 Buxton
156 Chapel-le-Frith
157 Calne
158 Cambridge
159 Chard
160 Camelford
161 Five Lanes
162 Cardiff
163 Ponty-pridd
164 Cardigan
165 Carlisle
166 Haltwistle
167 Carmarthen
168 Kidwelly
170 Newcastle-Emlyn
171 Chalford
172 Minchinhampton
173 Chatham
174 Chatteris
175 Cheadle
176 Chelmsford
177 Cheltenham
178 Chepstow
179 Chertsey
180 Chester
181 Abergele
182 Hawarden
183 Mochdrai
184 Neston
185 Northop
186 Chesterfield
187 Staveley
188 Chester-le-Street
190 Chichester
191 Chippenham
192 Malmsbury
193 Sodbury
194 Charmouth
195 Chipping-Norton
196 Chirk
197 Ruabon
198 Chorley
200 Christchurch
201 Chiselhurst
202 Chudleigh
203 Chumleigh
204 Cirencester
205 Dunkirk
206 Clare
207 Clitheroe
208 Cobham
209 Cockermouth
210 Colchester
211 Boxford
212 Coleford
213 Coleshill
214 Cullompton
215 Coltersworth
216 Congeton
217 Monksheath
218 Conway
219 Corwen
220 Bala
221 Barmouth
222 Dolgelly
223 Coventry
224 Cowbridge
225 Cowes
226 Cranbrook
227 Biddenden
228 Crawley
229 Crediton
230 Crewkerne
231 Crickhowell
232 Cuckfield
233 Darlington
234 Smeaton
235 Staindrop
236 Dartford
237 Dartmouth
238 Daventry
239 Dawlish
240 Deal
241 Denbigh
242 Derby
243 Melbourne
244 Ticknall
245 Dereham
246 Brinningham
247 Elmham
248 Guist
249 Devizes
250 Devonport
251 St. Germain's
252 Torpoint
253 Dewsbury
254 Diss
255 Doncaster
256 Dorchester
257 Dorking
258 Dover
259 Walmer
260 Downham
261 Driffield
262 Droitwich
263 Dudley
264 Dunchurch
265 Dunmow
266 Dunstable
267 Durham
268 Seaham
269 Dursley
270 Berkeley
271 Eastbourne
272 East-Grinstead
273 Eccleshall
274 Ellesmere
275 Ely
277 Emsworth
278 Enstone
279 Epping
280 Epsom
281 Ermebridge
282 Modbury
283 Esher
284 Evesham
285 Exeter
286 Exmouth
287 Eye
288 Fakenham
289 Walsingham
290 Falmouth
291 Fareham
292 Farnham
293 Farringdon
294 Fairford
295 Highworth
296 Lechlade
297 Fazeley
298 Felton
299 Fenny-Stratford
300 Ferry-Bridge
301 Feversham
302 Folkingham
303 Folkestone
304 Fordingbridge
305 Fowey
306 Frome
307 Gainsborough
308 Garstang
309 Gateshead
310 Gerrard's-Cross
311 Glastonbury
312 Gloucester
313 Lea
314 Painswick
315 Thornbury
316 Godalming
317 Godstone
318 Bletchingley
319 Goole
320 Gosport
321 Grantham
322 Gravesend
323 Grimsby
324 Guernsey
325 Guildford
326 Guisborough
327 Gretabridge
328 Hadleigh
329 Halesworth
330 Halifax
331 Sowerby-Bridge
332 Todmorden
333 Northowram
334 Halstead
335 Haverill
336 Harleston
337 Harlow
338 Harrowgate
339 Hartfordbridge
340 Harwich
341 Haslemere
342 Hastings
343 Hatfield
344 Havant
345 Haverfordwest
346 Hawes
347 Hay
348 Bruntless
349 Glasbury
350 Haydonbridge
351 Helstone
352 Hayle
353 Hemelhempstead
354 King's Langley
355 Henley-on-Thms
356 Nettlebed
357 Hereford
358 Eardisley
359 Hertford
360 Hexham
361 Heytesbury
362 Deptford Inn
363 Higham-Ferrers
364 High Wycombe
365 Hinckley
366 Hindon
367 Hitchin
368 Hobbs Point
369 Hoddesdon
370 Holbeach
371 Holt
372 Blakeney
373 Clay
374 Holyhead
375 Holywell
376 Honiton
377 Ottery-St.-Mary
378 Horncastle
379 Bolingbroke (Old)
380 Horndean
381 Horsham
382 Howden
383 Hull
384 Filey
385 Hedon
386 Barrow-on-Humber
387 Huddersfield
388 Marsden
389 Slaithwaite
390 Hungerford
391 Aldbourne
392 Lambourne
393 Ramsbury
394 Hounslow
395 Southall
396 Huntingdon
397 Buckden
398 Hythe
399 Ilchester
400 Ilfracombe
401 Ilminster
402 Ingatestone
403 Rayleigh
404 Wickford
405 Ipswich
406 Ironbridge
407 Isle of Man
408 Ivy Bridge
409 Jersey
410 Kelvedon
411 Kendal
412 Bowness
413 Keswick
414 Kettering
415 Kidderminster
416 Kimbolton
417 Kineton
418 Kingsbridge
419 Kingston
420 Pennybont
421 Radnor
422 Kington
423 Kirkby-Lonsdale
424 Knaresborough
425 Knutsford
426 Lamberhurst
427 Hawkhurst
428 Hurst Green
429 Newenden
430 Northiam
431 Peasmarsh
432 Rolvenden
433 Sandhurst
434 Lampeter
435 Aberayron
436 Lancaster
437 Kirkby-Stephen
438 Sedbergh
439 Launceston
440 Holsworthy
441 Stratton
442 Bude
443 Lawton
444 Leamington
445 Leatherhead
446 Ledbury
447 Leeds
448 Leek
449 Leicester
450 Leighton-Buzzard
451 Lewes
452 Newhaven
453 Seaford
454 Leominster
455 Pembridge
456 Shobden
457 Lichfield
458 Lincoln
459 Kirton-in-Lindsey
460 Wragby
461 Linton
462 Liphook
463 Liskeard
464 Looe
465 Polperro
466 Liverpool
467 Llandilo
468 Llandovery
469 Llanelly
470 Ponterdulais
471 Llangadock
472 Llangollen
473 Long-Stratton
474 Lostwithiel
475 Loughborough
476 Mountsorrel
477 Louth
478 Lowestoff
479 Ludlow
480 Knighton
481 Leintwardine
482 Luton
483 Lutterworth
484 Lyme
485 Lymington
486 Yarmouth
487 Lyndhurst
488 Lynn
489 Burnham
490 Holkham
491 Macclesfield
492 Maidenhead
493 Maidstone
494 Maldon
495 Malton
496 Sledmere
497 Malvern, (Great)
498 Manchester
499 Glossop
500 Haslingden
501 Rawtenstall
502 Staley Bridge
503 Manningtree
504 Mansfield
505 March
506 Margate
507 Marazion
508 Market-Deeping
509 Market-Drayton
510 Woore
511 Market-Harbro'
512 Market-Raisin
513 Market-Street
514 Market-Weighton
515 South-Cave
516 Marlborough
517 Great-Bedwin
518 Marlow
519 Maryport
520 Matlock
521 Melksham
522 Melton-Mowbray
523 Merthyr-Tydvil
524 Middlewich
525 Holmes-Chapel
526 Winsford
527 Midhurst
528 Mildenhall
529 Milford
530 Milnthorpe
531 Mold
532 Monmouth
533 Ragland
534 Moreton-in-Marsh
535 Stow-in-the-Wold
536 Winchcomb
537 Morpeth
538 Namptwich
539 Narbeth
540 Neath
541 Newark
542 Southwell
543 Carlton-on-Trent
544 Newbury
545 Newcstl.-on-Tyne
546 Newcastle-under-Lyne
547 Stoke
548 Tunstall
549 Hanley
550 Cobridge
551 Burslem
552 Lane-Delph
553 Lane-End
554 Etruria
555 Long-Port
556 Shelton
557 Newmarket
558 Newnham
559 Lydney
560 Newport, I. of W
561 Newport, Mnmth
562 Caerleon
563 Tredegar
564 Newport-Pagnell
565 Newport-Salop
566 New-Romney
567 Newton-Abbott
568 Newtown
569 Northallerton
570 Northampton
571 Northleach
572 Andoversford
573 North Shields
574 Northwich
575 Norwich
576 Acle
577 Cromer
578 Loddon
579 North-Walsham
580 Reepham
581 Scattow
582 Worstead
583 Nottingham
584 Bingham
85 Ilkeston
586 Stapelford
587 Oakham
588 Oakhampton
589 Hatherleigh
590 Odiam
591 Oldham
592 Ollerton
593 Ormskirk
594 Southport
595 Oswestry
596 Cerrig-y-Druidon
597 Llanrwst
598 Pentre Voylas
599 Otley
600 Addingham
601 Oundle
602 Ongar
603 Oxford
604 Pembroke
605 Penkridge
606 Penrith
607 Alston
608 Penryn
609 Penzance
610 Scilly
611 Pershore
612 Peterborough
613 Petersfield
614 Petworth
615 Fitticworth
616 Pulborough
617 Storrington
618 Pewsey
619 Pickering
620 Plymouth
621 Plympton
622 Pocklington
623 Pontefract
624 Poole
625 Portsmouth
626 Prescot
627 Presteign
628 Preston
629 Fleetwood
630 Preston-Brook
631 Frodsham
632 Pwllheli
633 Queenborough
634 Ramsgate
635 Reading
636 Redruth
637 Reigate
638 Retford
639 Rhayader

640 Devil's Bridge
641 Richmond, Yorksh
642 Ravenglass
643 Rickmansworth
644 Ringwood
645 Ripley
646 Ripon
647 Robertsbridge
648 Rochdale
649 Littleborough
650 Rochester
651 Rochford
652 Rockingham
653 Romsey
654 Ross
655 Rotherham
656 Wath
657 Rougham
658 Royston
659 Rugby
660 Rugeley
661 Great-Heywood
662 Shirlewich
663 Wolseley-Bridge
664 Rushyford
665 Ruthin
666 Ryde, Isle of Wght
667 Rye
668 Romford
669 Saffron-Walden
670 St. Austell
671 Grampound
672 St. Mawes
673 Mevagissey
674 Tregoney
675 St. Alban's
676 St. Asaph
677 St. Clear's
678 St. Columb
679 St. Helen's
680 St. Ives Hunts
681 Somersham
682 St. Leonard's
683 Salisbury
684 Downton
685 Wilton
686 St. Neot's
687 Sandbach
688 Sandwich
689 Sawbridgeworth
690 Saxmundham
691 Aldborough
692 Yoxford
693 Scarborough
694 Scole
695 Selby
696 Settle
697 Seven-Oaks
698 Shaftsbury
699 Sheerness
700 Sheffield
701 Shepton-Mallet
702 Sherborne
703 Queen-Camel
704 South-Shields
705 Shiffnall
706 Shipston
707 Shoreham
708 Shrewsbury
709 Church-Stretton
710 Llanidloes
711 Wem
712 Sidmouth
713 Sittingbourne
714 Skipton
715 Cross-Hills
716 Sleaford
717 Slough
718 Colnbrook
719 Solihull
720 Somerton
721 Langport
722 Southam
723 Southampton
724 South-Molton
725 South-Petherton
726 Martock
727 Spalding
728 Spilsby
729 Spittal
730 Stafford
731 Stilton
732 Stockbridge
733 Stockport
734 Disley
735 Hazlegrove
736 Stockton
737 Castle-Eden
738 Stokenchurch
739 Stokesley
740 Ingleby
741 Staines
742 Stamford
743 Stevenage
744 Steyning
745 Stone
746 Stoneham
747 Thwaite
748 Stoney-Cross
749 Stoney-Stratford
750 Stourbridge
751 Stourport
752 Stowmarket
753 Needham-Market
754 Stratford-on-Avon
755 Alcester
756 Henly-in-Arden
757 Stroud
758 Kingscote
759 Uley
760 Sudbury
761 Sunderland
762 Swaffham
763 Swansea
764 Brinmawr
765 Reynoldstone
766 Swindon
767 Cricklade
768 Wotton-Basset
769 Wroughton
770 Stanmore
771 Shooter's Hill
772 Tadcaster
773 Taibach
774 Tamworth
775 Tarporley
776 Taunton
777 Williton
778 Dunster
779 Minehead
780 Tavistock
781 Callington
782 Teignmouth
783 Tenbury
784 Tenby
785 Tenterden
786 Tetbury
787 Tetsworth
788 Tewkesbury
789 Thame
790 Thetford
791 Harling
792 Larlingford
793 Shipdam
794 Walton
795 Thirsk
796 Osmotherley
797 Thorne
798 Thrapstone
799 Tipton
800 Tiverton
802 Bampton
803 Dulverton
804 Topsham
805 Torquay
806 Torrington
807 Totness
808 Towcester
810 Tring
812 Risborough
813 Trowbridge
814 Truro
815 Cambourne
817 St. Ives
818 Tunbridge
820 Tunbridge-Wells
821 Tuxford
822 Uckfield
823 Hailsham
824 Ulverstone
825 Uppingham
826 Usk
827 Uttoxeter
828 Abbot's Bromley
829 Sudbury
830 Uxbridge
831 Wakefield
832 Wallingford
833 Benson
834 Walsall
835 Waltham-Cross
836 Wangford
837 Wrentham
838 Southwold
839 Wansford
840 Deane
841 Weldon
842 Ware
843 Wareham
844 Corfe-Castle
845 Swanage
846 Warminster
847 Warrington
848 Warwick
849 Watford
850 Wednesbury
851 Weedon
852 Welchpool
853 Machynlleth
854 Montgomery
855 Chirbury
856 Churchstoke
857 Welford
858 Wellingborough
859 Wellington, Salop
860 Wellington, Somst
862 Milverton
863 Wells Norfolk
864 Wells Somerset
865 Welwyn
867 Wendover
868 West Bromwhich
870 Westbury [Mare
871 Weston - super -
872 Wetherby
873 Weymouth
874 Wheatley
875 Whitby
876 Whitchurch Salop
877 Whitehaven
878 Wigan
879 Wigton
880 Allonby
882 Wimborne
883 Wincanton
884 Henstridge Ash
885 Milborne Port
887 Stalbridge
888 Winchester
890 Windsor
892 Eton
893 Wingham
894 Winslow
895 Wirksworth
897 Wisbeach
900 Witham
902 Witney
903 Wivelisoombe
904 Wokingham
905 Wolverhampton
906 Wooburn
907 Woodbridge
910 Woodstock
912 Deddington
913 Woodyates
914 Cranbourn [Edge
915 Wotton - under -
917 Wickwar
918 Worcester
920 Upton-on-Severn
921 Workington
922 Worksop
923 Worthing
924 Wrexham
925 Wymondham
926 Yarm
927 Yarmouth
928 Yealmpton
929 Yeovil
930 York
931 Easingwold
932 Escrick
933 Hamerton
934 Helmsley
935 Kirby Moorside
936 Whitwell
937 Barnet
938 Croydon
939 Staplehurst
940 Alne
941 Burton Agnes
942 Bradbury
943 Beaminster
944 Lynton
945 Runcorn
946 Middlesborough
947 Hartlepool
948 Bruton
950 Kenilworth

SCOTLAND.

The Scotch Obliterating Stamp

is used as follows. The *number* in the centre of the Stamp denoting the town in which it has been used.

1 Aberdeen
2 Aberfeldy
3 Aberdour
4 Aboyne
5 Aberchirder
6 Alford
7 Alloa
8 Aberlour
10 Alness
11 Annan
12 Auchenblae
13 Arbroath
14 Ardersier
15 Ardrossan
16 Abington
17 Airdrie
18 Arisaig
20 Arrochar
21 Auchnacraig
22 Anstruther
23 Aross
24 Appin
25 Auchterarder
26 Auchtermuchty
27 Ayr
28 Ayton
29 Assynt
30 Alyth
31 Ballater
32 Crathie
33 Ballantrae
34 Ballindalloch
35 Banchory
36 Banff
37 Macduff
38 Bathgate
39 Beauly
40 Beith
41 Biggar
42 Blackshields
43 Bervie
44 Blair-Athole
45 Dalnacardoch
46 Blairgowrie
47 Blair-Adam
48 Bonaw
49 Bonar-Bridge
50 Bogroy
51 Blackburn
52 Borrowstouness
53 Bowmore
54 Braco
55 Blackhillock
56 Braemar
57 Brechin
58 Edzell
59 Broadford
60 Bridge of Earn
61 Buckie
62 Burntisland
63 Brucklaw
64 Callander
65 Campbelton
66 Canonbie
67 Carluke
68 Cairnryan
69 Carnwarth
70 Carsphairn
71 Castle-Douglas
72 Cairndow
73 Coldingham
74 Coldstream
75 Carrbridge
76 Carnoustie
77 Chance-Inn
78 Colinsburgh
79 Comrie
80 Crail
82 Craig-Ellachie
83 Creetown
184 Crieff
85 Cromarty
87 Cullen
88 Culross
90 Cumnock
91 Cupar (Angus)
92 Cupar (Fife)
93 Cluny
94 Castleton
95 Crinan
96 Cruden
97 Cockburnspath
98 Dalkeith
100 Dalmally
101 Dalry
102 Denny
103 Dingwall
104 Dornoch
105 Dunbeath
106 Douglas
107 Doune
108 Dumfries
110 Dumbarton
111 Dunbar
112 Dunblane
113 Dunfermline
114 Dundee
115 Broughty-Ferry
116 Lochee
117 Kincaldrum
118 Dunkeld
120 Dunning
121 Dunoon
122 Dunse
123 Dunvegan
124 Durness
125 Dunnett
126 Drumnadrochit
127 Dysart
128 Eaglesham
129 Earlston
130 Ecclefechan
131 Edinburgh
132 Eddleston
133 Elgin
134 Ellon
135 Elie
136 Errol
137 Evanton
138 Eyemouth
139 Falkirk
140 Falkland
141 Fenwick
142 Fettercairn
143 Fochabers
144 Forfar
145 Forres
146 Fort-Augustus
147 Fortrose
148 Fort-William
149 Fort-George
150 Fraserburgh
151 Fushie Bridge
152 Finhaven
153 Farr
154 Fyvie
155 Galashiels
156 Garlieston
157 Gatehouse
158 Girvan
159 Glasgow
160 Glenluce
161 Grangemouth
162 Greenlaw
163 Greenock
164 Glenlivat
165 Glammis
166 Grantown
167 Golspie
168 Brora
170 Glenmorriston
171 Haddington
172 Halkirk
173 Hamilton
174 Hawick
175 Helmsdale
176 Helensburgh
177 Harris
178 Huntly
179 Holytown
180 Huna
181 Inverary
182 Inverkeithing
183 Inverness
184 Inchture
185 Invergordon
186 Irvine
187 Jedburgh
188 Johnstone
190 Jura
192 Keith
193 Kelso
194 Keith-Hall
195 Kettle
196 Kenmore
197 Kennoway
198 Killin
200 Kingussie
201 Kintore
202 Kilsyth
203 Kilmarnock
204 Kincardine
205 Kinghorne
206 Kinross
207 Kirkwall
208 Kippen
209 Kirkcudbright
210 Kirkaldy
211 Kirkintulloch
212 Kirriemuir
213 Kirkmichael
214 Kincardine O'Neil
215 Lanark
216 Langholme
217 Largs
218 Lauder
219 Laurencekirk
220 Leadhilis
221 Leith
222 Leithlumsden
223 Lerwick
224 Linwilg
225 Laggan
226 Lochcarron
227 Lochearnhead
228 Lesmahagow
229 Leven
230 Linlithgow
231 Lochalsh
232 Lochgilphead
233 Lockerby
234 Lochmaddy
235 Lochmaben
236 Lochinver
237 Lairg
238 Longhope
239 Luss
240 Lybster
241 Markinch
242 Mauchline
243 Maybole
244 Melrose
245 Meigle
246 Melvich
247 Mey
248 Mintlaw
249 Methlic
250 Moneymusk
251 Montrose
252 St. Cyrus
253 Mossat
254 Mortlach
255 Midcalder
256 Moffat
257 Moniaive
258 Morvern

259 Moy
260 Muirdrum
261 Munlochy
262 Muirkirk
263 Musselburgh
264 Nairn
265 Newburgh
266 New-Galloway
267 New-Deer
268 New-Pitsligo
269 Newport
270 Newton-Stewart
271 Noblehouse [ferry
272 North-Queens-
273 Oban
274 Old-Meldrum
275 Old-Rain
276 Orton
277 Paisley
278 Parkhill
279 Peebles
280 Perth
281 Peterhead
282 Pitcaple
283 Pittenweem
284 Pitlochry
285 Poolewe
286 Portaskaig
287 Port-Glasgow
288 Port-Patrick
289 Portree
290 Portsoy
291 Port-William
292 Poyntzfield
293 Prestonkirk
294 Rachan-Mill
295 Renfrew
296 Rhynie
297 Rothes
298 Rothesay
299 Rothiemay
300 St. Andrew's
301 St. Boswell's Green
302 Saltcoats
303 Sanquhar
304 Scourie
305 Selkirk [ferry
306 South-Queens-
307 Stewarton
308 Stirling
309 Stonehaven
310 Stornoway
311 Stow
312 Stranraer
313 Strathaven
314 Strathdon
315 Strichen
316 Stromness
317 Strontian
318 Skene
319 St. Magaret's Hope
320 Tain
321 Tarbert
322 Tarland
323 Thornhill
324 Thurso
325 Tobermory
326 Tomintoal
327 Tomnavoulin
328 Tongue
329 Tranent
330 Troon
331 Turriff
332 Tyndrum
333 Udney
334 Ullapool
335 Watten
336 Kilbride (West)
337 Whitburn
338 Whithorn
339 Wick
340 Whitehouse
341 Wigton
342 Wishaw
343 Ford
344 Lasswade
345 Loanhead
346 North-Berwick
347 Pennycuick
348 Portobello
349 Prestonpans
350 Slateford

IRELAND.

The Irish Obliterating Stamp  is used as follows. The *number* in the centre of the Stamp denoting the town in which it has been used.

1 Abbeyleix
2 Adair
3 Ahascragh
4 Ardara
5 Ardee
6 Ardglass
7 Ardrahan
8 Armagh
10 Arklow
11 Arthurstown
12 Arva
13 Ashbourne
14 Ashford
15 Athboy
16 Athenry
17 Athleague
18 Athlone
20 Athy
21 Aughnacloy
22 Aughrim
23 Antrim
24 Askeaton
25 Bagnalstown
26 Bailyborough
27 Balbriggan
28 Ballaghaderin
29 Ballina
30 Ballibay
31 Ballinakill
32 Ballinasloe
33 Ballincollig
34 Ballinderry
35 Ballingarry
36 Ballinrobe
37 Ballycastle
38 Ballyclare
39 Ballyconnell
40 Ballybrittas
41 Ballygawley
42 Ballyglass
43 Ballyhaise
44 Ballyjames-Duff
45 Ballymahon
46 Ballymena
47 Ballymoe
48 Ballymoney
49 Ballymore
50 Ballymote
51 Ballynacargy
52 Ballynahinch
53 Ballynamore
54 Ballyragget
55 Ballyshannon
56 Ballytore
57 Banagher
58 Banbridge
59 Bandon
60 Bangor
61 Bantry
62 Belfast
63 Bellaghy
64 Belmullet
65 Belturbet
66 Broadford
67 Blackwatertown
68 Blackrock
69 Blessington
70 Boyle
71 Booterstown
72 Bray
73 Broadway
74 Brookborough
75 Broughshane
76 Bruff
77 Buncrana
78 Bunratty
79 Burrin
80 Borrisakane
81 Burrosoleigh
82 Borris-in-Ossory
83 Bushmills
84 Buttevant
85 Baltinglass
86 Cabineteely
87 Caherciveen
88 Caherconlish
90 Cahir
92 Caledon
93 Callan
94 Camolin
95 Cappoquin
96 Carlingford
97 Carlow
100 Carn
101 Carnew
102 Carrickfergus
103 Carrickmacross
104 Carrick-on-Shannon
105 Carrick-on-Suir
106 Cashel
107 Castlebar
108 Castlebellingham
110 Castleblakeney
111 Castleblaney
112 Castlecomer
113 Castleconnel
114 Castledawson
115 Castlederg
116 Castledermot
117 Castlefin
118 Castlemartyr
120 Castlepollard
121 Castlerea
122 Castletown
123 Castletowndelvin
124 Castletown-Roch
125 Castlewellan
126 Cavan
127 Celbridge
128 Charleville
129 Church-Hill
130 Clane
131 Clara
132 Clare
133 Clashmore
134 Clifden
135 Cloghan
136 Clogheen
137 Clogher
138 Cloghnakilty
139 Clonard
140 Clonee
141 Clones
142 Clonmel
143 Clough
144 Cloughjordan
145 Cloyne
146 Coachford
147 Coalisland
148 Colehill
149 Coleraine
150 Collon
151 Collooney
152 Cong
153 Comber
154 Cookstown
155 Cootehill
156 Cork
157 Cove
158 Carrigart
159 Craughwell
160 Creeslough
161 Crookstown
162 Crossakeale
163 Crossdoney
164 Crossmolina
165 Croome
166 Crumlin
167 Curofin
168 Cushendall
170 Dangan
171 Delgany
172 Derry
173 Dervock
174 Dingle
175 Donaghadee
176 Donegal
177 Doneraile
178 Down
179 Drogheda
180 Dromod
181 Dromore
182 Dromore-West
183 Drumcree
184 Drumsna
185 Draperstown
186 Dublin
187 Dundalk
188 Dunfanaghy
190 Dundrum
192 Dromara
193 Dungannon
194 Dungarvan
195 Dungiven
196 Dunlavin
197 Dunleer
198 Dungloe
200 Dunmanway
201 Dunmore
202 Dunmore-East
203 Dunshanghlin
204 Durrow
205 Edenderry
206 Edgeworthstown
207 Elphin
208 Emo
209 Emyvale
210 Enfield
211 Ennis
212 Enniscorthy
213 Enniskerry
214 Enniskillen
215 Ennistimon
216 Eyrecourt
217 Ferbane
218 Fermoy
219 Ferns
220 Fethard (Tip.)
221 Fethard (Wexford)
222 Fintona
223 Fivemiletown
224 Florence-Court
225 Flurrybridge
226 Forkhill
227 Foxford
228 Foynes
229 Frankford
230 Frenchpark
231 Freshford
232 Galway
233 Garvagh
234 Geashell
235 Gilford
236 Glasslough
237 Glenarm
238 Glenavy
239 Glin
240 Golden
241 Golden-Ball
242 Gort
243 Gorey
244 Gowran
245 Graig
246 Granard
247 Grey-Abbey
248 Goresbridge
249 Headford
250 Hillsborough
251 Hollymount
252 Hollywood
253 Howth
254 Inistiogue
255 Innishannon
256 Johnstown
257 Kanturk
258 Keady
259 Kells
260 Kenmare
261 Kilbeggan
262 Kilcock
263 Kiconnell
264 Kilcullen
265 Kildare
266 Kildorrery
267 Kildysart
268 Kilkeel
269 Kilkenny
270 Killala
271 Killaloe
272 Killarney
273 Killinardrish
274 Killeagh
275 Killucan
276 Killybegs
277 Killyleigh
278 Killynaule
279 Killeshandra
280 Killinchy
281 Killough
282 Kilmacrennan
283 Kilmallock
284 Kilrea
285 Kilrush
286 Kilworth
287 Kilmacthomas
288 Kingscourt
289 Kingstown
290 Kinsale
291 Kinnegad
292 Kinnetty
293 Kircubbin
294 Kish
295 Knock
296 Knocktopher
297 Kinvara
298 Lanesborough
299 Larne
300 Leighlinbridge
301 Leixlip
302 Letterkenny
303 Limerick
304 Lisburn
305 Lismore
306 Lisnaskea
307 Listowel
308 Littleton
309 Longford
310 Loughbrickland
311 Loughgall
312 Loughrea
313 Lowtherstown
314 Louth
315 Lucan
316 Lurgan
317 Macroom
318 Maghera
319 Magherafelt
320 Malahide
321 Mallow
322 Manor-Hamilton
323 Markethill
324 Maryborough
325 Maynooth
326 Middleton
327 Millstreet
328 Miltown
329 Miltown-Malbay
330 Mitchelstown
331 Moate
332 Mohill
333 Moira
334 Monaghan
335 Monastereven
336 Moneygall
337 Moneymore
338 Mountmellick
339 Mountnugent
340 Mountrath
341 Mount-Talbot
342 Moville
343 Moy
344 Moynalty
345 Mullingar
346 Naas
347 Narin
348 Navan
349 Nenagh
350 New-Birmingham
351 Newbliss
352 Newbridge
353 Newcastle
354 Newmarket-on-Fergus
355 Newport, Mayo
356 Newport, Tip
357 Newry
358 Newtownards
359 Newtown-Barry
360 Newtown-Forbes
361 Newtown-Hamltn
362 Newtown-Limavady
363 Newtown-Mountkennedy
364 Newtown-Stewart
365 Nobber
366 Oldcastle
367 Omagh
368 Oranmore
369 Pallasgreen
370 Pallaskenry
371 Parsonstown
372 Passage-West
373 Philipstown
374 Piltown
375 Portadown
376 Portaferry
377 Portarlington
378 Portglenone
379 Portlaw
380 Portumna
381 Ramelton
382 Randalstown
383 Raphoe
384 Rathangan
385 Rathcoole
386 Rathcormack
387 Rathdowney
388 Rathdrum
389 Rathfarnham
390 Rathfriland
391 Rathkeale
392 Rathowen
393 Red-Hills
394 Rich-Hill
395 Rochfortbridge
396 Roscommon
397 Roscrea
398 Ross
399 Roscarbery
400 Rostrevor
401 Ruskey
402 Saintfield
403 Scariff
404 Scrabby
405 Shanagolden
406 Shinrone
407 Sixmilebridge
408 Skibbereen
409 Slane
410 Sligo
411 Stewartstown
412 Strabane
413 Stradbally
414 Stradone
415 Strangford
416 Stranolar
417 Strokestown
418 Stoneyford
419 Summerhill
420 Swinford
421 Swords
422 Taghmon
423 Tallaght
424 Tallow
425 Tanderagee
426 Tarbert
427 Templemore
428 Thomastown
429 Thurles
430 Tinahely
431 Tipperary
432 Toome
433 Tralee
434 Trim
435 Tuam
436 Tubbermoore
437 Tulla
438 Tullamore
439 Tullow
440 Tynan
441 Tyrrellspass
442 Valentia
443 Virginia
444 Warrenspoint
445 Waterford
446 Waringstown
447 Westport
448 Wexford
449 Wicklow
450 Youghall
451 Clonegal
452 Dunamanagh

CITIES AND PRINCIPAL PLACES THROUGHOUT THE WORLD

TO WHICH MAILS ARE DESPATCHED FROM LONDON.

On reference to the Kingdom or Country in "*Universal Rates of Postage*" (the list immediately following this), full information with reference to the despatch of *Letters* and *Newspapers* will be found. For instance—"Aalborg, Denmark" under the head "DENMARK" in "Universal Rates of Postage" are the various modes of despatch, the postage by each route, and instructions as to the manner in which letters should be addressed.

Aalborg........Denmark
Aalen........Wirtemburg
Aarburg.......Switzerland
Aarhus........Denmark
Abach........Bavaria
Abahides........Spain
Abancay........Peru
Abano .....V. Lombardy
Abbehausen...Oldenburg
Abbeville........France
Abisca........Peru
Abkhas..Prov. of Russia
Abo........Russia
Abofeira........Portugal
Aboukir........Egypt
Abousir........Egypt
Aboutig........Egypt
Abox........Spain
Abrantes........Portugal
Abruzzo..Prov. of Naples
Abu Shehr........Persia
Abydos........Turkey
Abyssinia...see Abyssinia
Acadera........Spain
Acapulco........Mexico
Accum........Oldenburg
Acheen........Sumatra
Achim........Hanover
Acqs........France
Acqui........Sardinia
Acre or Acoha........Syria
Adalia........Turkey
Adana........Turkey
Adelaide........Australia
Adelfors........Sweden
Ademuz........Spain
Aden........Arabia
Aderbijan..Prov. of Persia
Adrianople........Turkey
Adventure Bay, Van Dieman's Land
Afghanistan.....see India
Africa........see Africa
Agades........Africa
Agen........France
Agincourt........France
Agra..Province of Bengal
Agra........Spain
Agram........Croatia
Agria........Hungary
Aguilar de Campos..Spain
Ahlhorn........Oldenburg
Ahmedabad........Guzerat
Ahmednaggur .Hindostan
Aibling........Bavaria
Aichach........Bavaria
Aichstaedt........Bavaria
Aigle........Switzerland
Aiguebelle........Sardinia
Aigueperse........France
Aiguesmortes........France
Aime........Sardinia
Ain....Dept. of France
Ainsa........Spain
Airaines........France
Aire-sur-l'Adour...France
Aire-sur-la-Lys....France
Airolo........Switzerland
Aisne....Dept. of France
Aitkirch........France
Aix........France
Aix........Southern Italy
Aix les Baines...Sardinia
Aix la Chapelle..Prussia
Ajaccio........Corsica
Ajmeer Prov. of Hindostan
Akhmym........Egypt
Akiska........Turkey
Ak-shehr........Turkey
Alabama........one of the United States
Alagoas..Prov. of Brazil
Alais........France
Alassio........Sardinia
Alba, in Albe.....Sardinia
Albania, country of Turkey
Albano........Papal States
Albany........New York
Albenga........Sardinia
Albion........Illinois
Albisola........Sardinia
Alby........France
Alcacerdo........Portugal
Alcantara........Spain
Alcaraz........Spain
Alcira........Spain
Aldea........Portugal
Aldingen....Wirtemburg
Alearcal........Portugal
Alemtejo........Prov. of Portugal
Alençon........France
Aleppo........Turkey
Alessandria........Sardinia
Alet........France
Alexandretta........Turkey
Alexandria........Egypt
Alexandria, Syria........see Aleppo
Alexandria, United States
Alexandrie........Sardinia
Alfeld........Hanover
Algarve, Prov. of Portugal
Algeria........see France
Algesiras........Spain
Algiers........Algeria
Algoa Bay........Africa
Alhama........Spain
Alicante........Spain
Alkmaar........Holland
Allahabad Prov. of Bengal
Allaman ....Switzerland
Allendorf........Hesse
Alles........Spain
Allier...Dept. of France
Alliers........France
Almaden........Spain
Almado........Portugal
Almagro........Spain
Almanza........Spain
Almarez........Spain
Almazan........Spain
Almazarron........Spain
Almedixor........Spain
Almeida........Portugal
Almendra........Spain
Almeria........Spain
Alost........Belgium
Alpirsbach...Wirtemburg
Alps (Lower), Dept. of France
Alps (Upper), Dept. of France
Alsace...Prov. of France
Alsfeld........Hesse
Altea........Spain
Altenburg Saxe Altenburg
Alteneschi....Oldenburg
Altenhuntorf...Oldenburg
Altenoylhe....Oldenburg
Altona........Holstein
Altorf........Switzerland
Alt Otting........Bavaria
Altshausen, Wirtemburg
Alt-Sittenbach...Bavaria
Alt-Strelitz, Mecklenburg
Altstaetten.. Switzerland
Alvacagua, Prov. of Chili
Alvarado........Mexico
Alverdissen........Lippe-Detmold
Alzey........Hesse
Amantea........Naples
Amapalla........Mexico
Amarante........Portugal
Amberg........Bavaria
Ambert........France
Amboyna........Moluccas
Amelunxhorn, Brunswick
Amercote........Hindostan
Amersfort........Holland
Amherstburg........Canada
Amiens........France
Amoeneburg........Hesse
Amol........Persia
Amoy........China
Ampfing........Bavaria
Amritsir........Lahore
Amsterdam........Holland
Amsterdam (New) Berbice
Ancenis........France
Ancona.....Papal States
Andalusia, Prov. of Spain
Andelfingen, Switzerland
Andelys (les)........France
Andierne........France
Andreasberg....Hanover
Andujar........Spain
Anduze........France
Angaraes..Prov. of Peru
Angelica...United States
Angers........France
Angola........Africa
Angornou, Central Africa
Angora........Turkey
Angostura........Venezuela
Angoulême........France
Anguilla...Brit. W. Indies
Anhalt........Germany
Anklam........Prussia
Anjou....Prov. of France
Ankum........Hanover
Anloze........Sardinia
Annapolis...Nova Scotia
Annapolis........Maryland
Annecy........Sardinia
Annonay........France
Anspach........Bavaria
Antequera........Spain
Antibes........France
Antigua...Brit. W. Indies
Antioch........Turkey
Antioquia..New Granada
Antraia........France
Antwerp........Belgium
Anusco........Spain
Aosta........Sardinia
Apen........Oldenburg
Apenrade........Denmark
Appenzell..Swiss Canton
Apt........France
Aquadilla For. West Indies
Aquila........Naples
Aquino........Naples
Arabia........see India
Aracena........Spain
Aragon....Prov. of Spain
Aranda........Spain
Aranjuez........Spain
Arau........Switzerland
Arberg........Switzerland
Arboga........Sweden
Arbon........Switzerland
Arburgh........Switzerland
Archangel........Russia
Archipelago....see Archipelago
Arcis-sur-Arbe....France
Arcot........Hindostan
Ardebil........Persia
Ardèche..Dept. of France
Ardennes. Dept. of France
Ardres........France
Ardrah........Africa
Areeivo, For. West Indies
Arega........Portugal
Arensburgh....Denmark
Arensberg........Prussia
Arequipa........Peru
Arevalo........Spain
Arezzo........Tuscany
Argelès........France
Argençon........France
Argentan........France
Argenton Chateau France
Argos........Greece
Argovia ..Swiss Canton
Arica........Peru
Arisch, El........Egypt
Arispe........Mexico
Arkansas....one of the United States
Arlenay........France
Arles........France
Arma (L')........Sardinia
Armenia. Prov. of Turkey
Arnay-le-Duc....France
Arnedo........Spain
Arnheim........Holland
Arnstadt ..Schwarzburg
Aroa........Venezuela
Arona........Sardinia
Arracan........see India
Arras........France
Arriège..Dept. of France
Arroeskiöbing..Denmark
Art........Switzerland
Arta........Albania
Artois....Prov. of France
Arttenburg........Hanover
Ascension (Isle)..Africa
Aschaffenburgh..Bavaria
Aschendorf........Hanover
Ascoli........Papal States
Asendorf........Hanover
Asfeld........France
Ashantee........Africa
Assam........India
Assen........Holland
Assens........Denmark
Assumption........Brazil
Astante....Prov. of Chili
Asti........Sardinia
Astorga........Spain
Astrabad........Persia
Astrachan, Prov. of Russia
Asturias...Prov. of Spain
Atens........Oldenburg
Athens........Greece
Atooi..Sandwich Islands
Ath........Holland
Attigny........France
Au........Bavaria
Aube.... Dept. of France
Aubenas........France
Auberive........France
Aubeterre........France
Aubigny........France
Aubonne........Switzerland
Aubusson........France
Auburn.... United States
Auch........France
Aude....Dept. of France
Augsburg........Bavaria
Augusta........Maine
Auma........Saxe-Weimar
Aurich........Hanover
Aurillac........France
Aurunzabad....Hindostan
Austerlitz........Austria
Australasia..see Australia
Australind. see Australasia
Autun........France
Auvergne. Prov. of France
Auvernier........Switzerland
Auxerre........France
Auxonne........France
Auzance........France
Ava (or Birman Empire), India
Aveiro........Portugal
Avellino........Naples
Avenches........Switzerland
Aversa........Naples
Avesnes........France
Avestad........Sweden
Aveyron..Dept. of France
Avigliana........Sardinia
Avignon........France
Avila........Spain
Avranches........France
Ax........France
Axiarcollar........Spain
Ayamonte........Spain
Ayua........Spain
Azamor........Morocco
Azelio........Sardinia
Azof........Russia
Azores........see Azores
Azua........St. Domingo
Azutan........Spain
Baalbec........Turkey
Babenhausen........Hesse
Bacharach..West Prussia
Backnang....Wirtemburg
Backum........Oldenburg
Badajos........Spain
Badhergen........Hanover
Baden........see Baden
Baden........Switzerland
Baeza........Spain
Baffin's Bay....Columbia River
Bagdad......Pachalic of Turkey
Bagnara........Naples
Bagnasco........Sardinia
Bagneres-en-Bigorre France
Bagneres de Luchon France
Bahamas....see Bahamas
Bahar....Prov. of Bengal
Bahawulpoor. -Hindostan
Bahia.....Prov. of Brazil
Bahrdorf........Brunswick
Bahus........Sweden
Baierdissen........Bavaria
Baigneux-les-Juifs France
Bakitchiserai........Russia
Balaclava........Crimea
Balagaut ....Hindostan
Balaguer........Spain
Balaruc........France
Balavano........Havana
Balbastro........Spain
Baleares.......see Balearic Islands
Balfroosh........Persia
Balhary........Hindostan
Balingen........Wirtemburg
Ballaigne........Switzerland
Bally..E. In. Archipelago
Bally........see India
Baloochistan........see India
Balstall........Switzerland
Baltimore........Maryland
Bamberg........Bavaria
Banca........Sumatra
Band........France
Bangalore....Hindostan
Bankapore........Hindostan
Banya........Hungary
Bapaume........France
Bar........Hindostan
Baracoa, For. West Indies
Baralonetta........Spain
Barbadoes. Br. West Indies
Barbary........see Barbary
Barbelroth........Bavaria
Barbezieux........France
Barbuda..... West Indies
Barcelona........Spain
Barcelonette........France
Bardenfleth....Oldenburg
Bardewisch....Oldenburg
Bareilly........Delhi
Barenburg........Hanover
Barfleur........France
Bari........Prov of Naples
Barjac........France
Bar-le-Duc........France
Barletta........Naples
Barnaul........Siberia
Barneville........France
Barnstorf........Hanover
Barntrup. Lippe-Detmold
Baroach........Hindostan
Baroda........Guzerat
Barramahal ..Hindostan
Barrano........Spain
Barssec........Oldenburg
Bas-sur-Seine........France
Basbeck........Hanover
Basilicata, Prov. of Naples
Basle........Switzerland
Basques, Les........France
Bassano. Venet. Lombardy
Basseterre........Guadaloupe
Basseterre......St. Christopher's
Bassora........Turkey
Bassum........Hanover
Bastia........Corsica
Batavia........Java
Bate........Hindostan
Bathurst........Australia
Battenberg........Hesse
Bau........Podolia
Bauge........France
Baumes-les-Dames France
Bautzen........Saxony
Bavaria .....see Bavaria
Bayazid........Armenia
Bayeux........France
Bayona........Spain
Bayonne........France
Bayreuth........Bavaria
Baza........Spain
Bazas........France
Beaucaire........France
Beaufort........France
Beaulieu........France
Beaune........France
Beaupreau........France
Beauvais........France
Beauvoir-sur-Mer. France
Bebra........Hesse
Bedarrieux........France
Bederkesa........Hanover
Bednore........Hindostan
Beeder Prov. of Hindostan
Beerfelden........Hesse
Befort........France
Beinum........Hanover
Beira....Prov. of Portugal
Beja........Portugal
Bejapoor........Hindostan
Bela........Hindostan
Belem........Portugal
Belem........Brazil
Belgirate........Sardinia
Belgium......see Belgium
Belgrade........Servia
Belize........Honduras
Bellac........Austria
Bellegam........Ceylon
Bellegard........France
Belle-Isle........France
Bellesme........France
Belley........France
Bellinzone....Switzerland
Belluno...Venetian Lombardy
Belnhausen........Hesse
Beloochistan ....see India
Benares...Prov. of Bengal
Benavente........Spain
Benavento........Brazil
Bencoolen........Sumatra
Bender........Russia
Bene........Sardinia
Benedict Beuern..Bavaria
Benevente........Portugal
Benevento....Papal States
Bengal ....Presidency of India
Benguela........Africa
Benisuef........Egypt
Bentheim........Hanover
Berar........Hindostan
Berbice (Guiana) West Indies
Berchtesgaden....Bavaria
Berdyczew......Volhynia
Bergamo..Venetian Lombardy
Bergedorf........Hanover
Bergen........Hanover
Bergen..Prof. of Norway
Bergen-op-Zoom. Holland
Bergerac........France
Bergzabern........Bavaria
Berhe......Saxe-Weimar
Berlin........Prussia
Bermuda....see Bermuda
Bernay........France
Berne........Switzerland
Berne........Oldenburg
Berneck........Bavaria
Berri.... Prov. of France
Berthoud........Switzerland
Besançon........France
Bessarabia. Prov. of Russia
Bessingheim. Wirtemburg
Betanzos........Spain
Bethune........France
Betlis........Turkey
Bevaix........Switzerland
Bevern........Brunswick
Beverstadt........Hanover
Bex........Switzerland
Beyrout........Syria
Beziers........France
Bhatgong ....Hindostan
Bhownuggur..Hindostan
Bhurtpore........Agra
Bialystock ....Lithuania
Biasca........Switzerland
Bibbiena........Tuscany
Biberbach........Bavaria
Biberbach....Wirtemberg
Bidjeegar........Hindostan
Bieberich........Nassau
Bickenbach........Hesse
Biekenkopf........Hesse
Bielefield........Prussia
Biella........Sardinia
Bienne........Switzerland
Bienenbüttell....Hanover
Bilboa........Spain
Billom........France
Bingen........Hesse
Birbhoom........Bengal
Birkenfeld....Oldenburg
Birrwyl........Switzerland
Biscay....Prov. of Spain
Bischhaussen........Hesse
Bischoffzell...Switzerland
Biserta........Tunis
Bissunpoor....Hindostan
Bitche........France
Blanheuern..Wirtemburg
Blanfelden...Wirtemburg
Blangy........France
Blankenburg..Brunswick
Blankenhain........Saxe-Weimar
Blaye........France
Bleckede........Hanover
Blet........France
Blexen........Oldenburg
Bliescastel........Bavaria
Blois........France
Blomberg. Lippe-Detmold
Boa Vista........Brazil
Bobbio........Sardinia
Bochma........Gallicia
Bockenem........Hanover
Bockhorn.....Oldenburg
Bodenteich........Hanover
Bodenwerder........Hanover
Bœblingen...Wirtemburg
Bogense........Denmark
Boglipoor........Bengal
Bogota.......New Granada
Bohemia......see Austria
Bohmte........Hanover
Bohol....Philippine Isles
Bois-le-Duc........Holland
Boizenburg..Mecklenburg
Bolivia........see Peru
Bologna ....Papal States
Bolsano........Tyrol
Bolswaert........Holland
Bombay......Hindostan
Bommel........Holland
Bona or Bone....Algeria
Bonn......West Prussia
Bonneval........France
Bonneville........Sardinia
Boodroom........Turkey
Boorhampoor ..Candeish
Bootan........Hindostan
Bopfingen....Wirtemburg
Borabura..Society Islands
Bordeaux........France
Bordighera........Sardinia
Borghelto........Sardinia
Borgo-Manero....Sardinia
Borgo-Masino....Sardinia
Borgo San Dalmazzo ....Sardinia
Borgo-Sessia ....Sardinia
Borgo-Ticino........Sardinia
Borken........Hesse
Borneo........East Indian Archipelago
Bornou....Central Africa
Bort........France
Bösingfelde .. Lippe-Detmold
Bosna-Serai ......Bosnia
Bosnia...Country of Turkey
Bosse........France
Boston ....Massachusetts
Botany Bay........Australia
Botilla........Spain
Botzen........Tyrol
Bouches du Rhône . Dept of France
Boudevilliers. Switzerland
Boudry........Switzerland
Boujeiah........Algeria
Boukow ....Mecklenburg
Boulak........Egypt
Boulogne........France
Bourbonne........France
Bourbon l'Archambault.. France
Bourbon Laney....France
Bourbon Vendee....France
Bourbon, Isle of, see Africa
Bourbonnois ....Prov. of France
Bourganeuf........France
Bourg (Ain)........France
Bourgas........Turkey
Bourg d'Oysans....France
Bourges........France
Bourg-en-Bresse...France
Bourg la Reine....France
Bourgistein..Switzerland
Bourgoin........France
Bourgneuf, Le........France

Bourg St. Maurice...Sardinia
Bourmont......France
Bourra......Turkey
Boussac......France
Bouton..Molucca Islands
Boyne......France
Bra......Sardinia
Bracke......Oldenburg
Braga......Portugal
Braganza......Portugal
Brainçon......France
Bramsche......Hanover
Bramstedt......Denmark
Branback......Nassau
Brandenburg....Mecklenburg
Brandenburg....Prussia
Brantôme......France
Braslaw......Lithuania
Braunau......Austria
Braunsburg......Prussia
Brazil......see Brazil
Breda......Holland
Bredstedt......Denmark
Bregenz......Tyrol
Breglio......Sardinia
Bregueli......Switzerland
Bremen......see Bremen
Bremervorde......Hanover
Bremmgarten, Switzerland
Brensback......Hesse
Brescia.....V. Lombardy
Bresciano....Prov. of V. Lombardy
Breslau......Prussia
Bressuire......France
Brest......France
Breteuil......France
Breton (Cape)......British America
Briansk......Russia
Bridgetown... Barbadoes
Bridgetown......Maryland
Bridgetown..New Jersey
Brienne......France
Brienz......Switzerland
Brieviesca......Spain
Briey......France
Brignais......France
Brignolles......France
Brigue......Switzerland
Brill......Holland
Brindisi......Naples
Brinkum......Hanover
Brioude......France
Brittany, Prov. of France
Brixen......Tyrol
Brod......Transylvania
Brody......Gallicia
Broken Bay, Australasia
Bromberg......Prussian Poland
Brome......Hanover
Broni......Sardinia
Brooklyn...Massachusets
Brooklyn......New York
Broons......France
Brotterode......Hesse
Brou......France
Bruchhausen....Hanover
Bruck......Styria
Bruckenau......Bavaria
Bruckhausen......Bavaria
Bruges......Belgium
Brugg......Switzerland
Brüggen......Hanover
Brühl......Mecklenburg
Brunn......Moravia
Brunnen......Switzerland
Brunsbuttel....Denmark
Brunswick......Brunswick
Brussels......Belgium
Brzest......Lithuania
Buchan......Wirtemburg
Bucharest......Turkey
Büchen......Denmark
Buchloe......Bavaria
Buckeburg..Schaumburg Lippe
Buda......Hungary
Budingen......Hesse
Budissin......Saxony
Budweis......Bohemia
Buenavista, For.W.Indies
Buenos Ayres, see Buenos Ayres
Buffalo......New York
Bugia......Algeria
Bujalance......Spain
Bulac......Egypt
Bulalach....Switzerland
Bulgaria, part of Turkey
Bulle......Switzerland
Bulzow....Mecklenburg
Bumm......Russia
Bunde......Hanover
Bundelcund...Allahabad
Burdwan, Dis. of Bengal
Buren......Switzerland
Burg......Denmark
Burgan......Bavaria
Burgdorf......Hanover
Burgdorf......Switzerland
Burghausen......Bavaria
Burghane......Oldenburg
Burglenyenfeld..Bavaria
Burgos......Spain
Burgundy, Prov. of France
Burgwinheim....Bavaria
Burlington....New Jersey
Burlington......Vermont
Buronzo......Sardinia
Bursa......Turkey
Busca......Sardinia
Busbire......Persia
Bussora......Turkey
Büttlar.....Saxe-Weimar
Butzback......Hesse
Buxthude......Hanover
Cabello......Venezuela
Cabes......Tunis
Cabra......Spain
Cabrera....Balearic Isles
Cabul......Afghanistan
Caceres......Spain
Cachoeira......Brazil
Cadiz......Spain
Cadoritho....V. Lombardy
Caen......France
Caffraria......Africa
Cagliari......Sardinia
Cahors......France
Caifong......China
Cairo (Grand)......Egypt
Cairo......Sardinia
Calabria......Naples
Calahorra......Spain
Calais......France
Calatayud......Spain
Calatrava......Spain
Calcutta......Bengal
Calicut......Hindostan
California......a State of Mexico
Callao......Peru
Callinger......Bengal
Calmar......Sweden
Caltanisetta......Sicily
Caluso......Sardinia
Calvados, Dept. of France
Calvi......Corsica
Calvi......Naples
Calvirde......Brunswick
Calw......Wirtemburg
Caly......New Granada
Camarinas......Spain
Cambourg....Saxe-Meiningen
Cambrai......France
Camp......Nassau
Campeachy......Mexico
Campen......Hanover
Campobasso......Naples
Canada......see British America
Canale......Sardinia
Canary......see Canary Islands
Canavara......Spain
Candahar......Prov. of Afghanistan
Candeish......Prov. of Hindostan
Candia (Isle).... Turkey
Candy......Ceylon
Canelli......Sardinia
Cannes......France
Cannstadt...Wirtemburg
Canobbio......Sardinia
Canourgue (la)...France
Canso......Nova Scotia
Cantal..Dept. of France
Cantena......Greece
Canton......China
Cape Town......Africa
Cape Breton......British America
Cape Coast Castle, Africa
Cape Cruz, For.W.Indies
Cape Gracias......Mexico
CapeHaytien, StDomingo
Cape Henri, For.W.Indies
Capitanata......Prov. of Naples
Cappeln......Denmark
Cappeln......Oldenburg
Capraja......Sardinia
Captieux......France
Capua......Naples
Caraccasor....Venezuela
Caraglio......Sardinia
Caraman......Turkey
Carcare......Sardinia
Carcassonne......France
Cardona......Spain
Carentan......France
Carentoire......France
Carhaix......France
Cariaçou....West Indies
Carignano......Sardinia
Carinthia......see Austria
Carlisle......Jamaica
Carolina..see North and South
Carlsbad......Austria
Carlscrona......Sweden
Carlshafen......Hesse
Carlshamm......Sweden
Carlsruhe......Baden
Carlstadt......Croatia
Carmagnold......Sardinia
Carmona......Spain
Carolina......Spain
Carpentras......France
Cartago......Mexico
Cartana......Spain
Carthagena......Spain
Carthagena Columbia... see Chagres
Casa Velha......Brazil
Casal......Sardinia
Casalborgone...Sardinia
Casalle......Sardinia
Casbin......Persia
Casco Bay, Massachusets
Cashmere......Dist. of Hindostan
Cassel......France
Cassel......Hesse Cassel
Cassel......near Mayence
Cassine......Sardinia
Casteggio......Sardinia
Castel Branco..Portugal
Castellamare......Naples
Castellamonte....Sardinia
Castellane......France
Castellazzo......Sardinia
Castello..Southern Italy
Castello Branco, Portugal
Castelnau......France
Castelnaudary....France
Castelnuovo......Sardinia
Castile (Old and New).. Provinces of Spain
Castillones......France
Castle Jaloux....France
Castres......France
Castro Marino..Portugal
Catabaw...SouthCarolina
Catalonia, Prov. of Spain
Catania......Sicily
Catanzaro......Naples
Cateau (le)......France
Catherinoslav....Prov. of Russia
Catlenburg......Hanover
Catmandoo...Hindostan
Cattaro......Dalmatia
Catus......France
Caub......Nassau
Caucasus, Prov. of Russia
Caussade......France
Cavaglia......Sardinia
Cavaillon......France
Cavanas, For. West Indies
Cavellar Maggiore...... Sardinia
Cavour......Sardinia
Cawnpoor......Bengal
Cayenne, For. West Indies
Cayocca......Spain
Cazères......France
Cebegin......Spain
Cedar Point....Maryland
Celebes, E.I. Archipelago
Celle......Hanover
Celle......Sardinia
Centalle......Sardinia
Céphalonia, IonianIslands
Ceram......Moluccas
Ceret......France
Cerigo....Ionian Island
Cerlier......Switzerland
Cervera......Spain
Cervin......France
Cesena..Southern Italy
Cespedas......Spain
Ceva......Sardinia
Ceylon (Isle)...see India
Cezubranca......Portugal
Chablis......France
Chagres......see Chagres
Chalamont......France
Chalonnes......France
ChalonssurMarne, France
Chalons surSaône, France
Chalus......France
Chambery......Sardinia
Chambon......France
Champagne......Prov. of France
Champlemi......France
Champlitte......France
Chandernagore....Bengal
Chang-hai......China
Chantilly......France
Chan-tong, Prov.of China
Chao-hing......China
Chao-tcheo......China
Charcas...Buenos Ayres
Chaource......France
Charcas......Peru
Charcof......Russia
Charente, Dept. of France
Charente (Lower)..Dept. of France
Charenton......France
Charité (la)......France
Charleroi......Belgium
Charleston..S. Carolina
Charleville......France
Chartres......France
Châtaignerage....France
Châteaubriant....France
Châteaudun......France
Château d'Oex, Switzerl'd
Château-du-Loir..France
Châteauneuf......France
Chateauroux......France
Château Thiery...France
Châtelleraült......France
Chat Gontier......France
Chatham, NewBrunswick
Chatillon......France
Chatillon......Sardinia
Chat Meillant....France
Chat Regnault....France
Chat Solins......France
Chatel St. Denie, Switzerland
Chaudesaignes...France
Chaumont......France
Chateaulin......France
Chaux de Fonds. Switzerland
Chaves......Portugal
Chedura......Bengal
Chely d'Ap......France
Chemnitz......Saxony
Chenit (le)..Switzerland
Cher....Dept. of France
Cherasco......Sardinia
Cherburg......France
Cherchel......Algeria
Cherson......France
Cherson, Prov. of Russia
Chester....Pennsylvania
Chiapa......Mexico
Chiasse......Switzerland
Chiavari......Sardinia
Chiclana......Spain
Chicland......Spain
Chieri......Sardinia
Chieti......Naples
Chihuahaa......Mexico
Chili......see Chagres
Chillicothe......Ohio
Chiloe....Prov. of Chili
China......see China
Chinca......Pèru
Chinchilla......Spain
Chinon......France
Chiusa.....V. Lombardy
ChittagongDist.ofBengal
Chivasso......Sardinia
Chivray......France
Choco......Colombia
Cholet......France
Cholula......Mexico
Christeansfelt..Denmark
Christiana......Norway
Christianburg...Virginia
Christianople......Sweden
Christiansand....Norway
Christianstadt...Sweden
Chuquisaca......Peru
Chur......Switzerland
Chusen......China
Cigliano......Sardinia
Cinaloa..Prov. of Mexico
Cincinnati......Ohio
Cinfuegos..For.W.Indies
Cintra......Portugal
Circassia, Prov. of Russia
Cirie......Sardinia
Ciudadela, Balearic Isles
Ciudad Real......Spain
Ciudad Real......Mexico
Ciudad Rodrigo....Spain
Cividadella......Minorca
Civita Vecchia......Papal States
Clagenfurt......Illyria
Clairvaux......France
Clamecy......France
Clausenburg....Hungary
Clausthal......Hanover
Clermont......France
Cleverns......Oldenburg
Cleves......Prussia
Clisson......France
Cloppenbourg, Oldenburg
Cluny......France
Cluses......Sardinia
Coblentz....WestPrussia
Coburg......Saxe-Coburg
Cobre Mines..For. West Indies
Cocconato......Sardinia
Cochabamba......Bolivia
Cochin......Hindostan
Cochin China....see India
Cognac......France
Cohahuila, State of Mexico
Coimbra......Portugal
Coire......Switzerland
Co-king......China
Colchagua, Prov. of Chili
Colding......Denmark
Colima..State of Mexico
Colinac......France
Collioure......France
Colmar......France
Cologne....West Prussia
Colombia......Switzerland
Colombo......Ceylon
Columbia District, one of the United States
Columbia, South Carolina
Columbus......Ohio
Comayagua......Mexico
Combreux......France
Commercy......France
Como......V. Lombardy
Comorn......Hungary
Compeigne......France
Compostella......Spain
Concepcion, Prov. of Chili
Concize......Switzerland
Concord, New Hampshire
Concord......Massachusets
Concots......France
Condé......France
Condottieri, Papal States
Conflans......France
Conflans......Sardinia
Confolens......France
Congo......Africa
Congoon......Persia
Coni......Sardinia
Connecticut, one of the United States
Constance......Baden
Constance, Swiss Canton
Constantina......Algeria
Constantinople..Turkey
Cooperstown......United States
Copenhagen......Denmark
Copiapo......Chili
Coppenbrugge....Hanover
Coppet......Switzerland
Coquimbo, Prov. of Chili
Corbeil......France
Corbigny......France
Cordova......Spain
Corfu......IonianIslands
Coria......Spain
Corinth......Greece
Coro......Venezuela
Corolles......France
Corrèze..Dept. of France
Corsica..Prov. of France
Corsoer......Denmark
Cortemiglia....Sardinia
Cortona......Tuscany
Corunna......Spain
Corvijal......Spain
Corvo......Azores
Corydon......Indiana
Cosenza......Naples
Coslin......Prussia
Cosne......France
Cossacks(Country of the), Russia
Cossimbuzar......Bengal
Cosson......France
Cossonay....Switzerland
Costa Rico......Chagres
Côte d'Or, Dept.of France
Côte St. Andre....France
Côtes du Nord..Dept. of France
Coudom......France
Coulanges......France
Coulommiers......France
Courland, Prov.of Russia
Courtagnon......France
Courtenay......France
Courtray......Belgium
Coutances......France
Couterne......France
Coutras......France
Couvet......Switzerland
Craelsheim..Wirtemburg
Cracow......see Cracow
Crakow....Mecklenburg
Craon......France
Creance......France
Crecy......France
Cremona..V. Lombardy
Crempe......Denmark
Crepy......France
Crescentino......Sardinia
Crest......France
Creuze...Dept. of France
Crevecœur......France
Criewitz....Mecklenburg
Crimderod......Hanover
Crimea..Southern Russia
Croatia......see Hungary
Crodo......Sardinia
Cronborg......Denmark
Cronstadt......Russia
Cröpelin....Mecklenburg
Cruseilles......Sardinia
Cuba, see St. Jago de Cuba
Cuddalore......Hindostan
Cuella......Spain
Cuença......Spain
Cuença......Colombia
Culiacan......Mexico
Cullar......Spain
Cully......Switzerland
Cumana......Venezuela
Cuorgne......Sardinia
Curaçoa, DutchW. Indies
Cutch, Prov.of Hindostan
Cuttack, Prov.ofHindostn
Cutwa......Bengal
Cuxhaven......Hamburg
Cuyaba......Brazil
Cuzco......Peru
Cydonia......Turkey
Cyprus (Isle)....Turkey
Czernigov......Russia
Czervenitz......Hungary
Czirnitz......Austria
Dacca......Bengal
Dachau......Bavaria
Dahllenbourg....Hanover
Dahomey......Africa
Daleburg......Sweden
Dalecarlia, Prov.of Swedn
Dalia....Prov. of Sweden
Dalmatia......see Austria
Damanour......Egypt
Damascus......Turkey
Damietta......Egypt
Dammartin......France
Damme......Oldenburg
Dampiere-sur-Salon...... France
Damville......France
Dannenburg....Hanover
Dantzic......Prussia
Danville......Kentucky
Danville, North Carolina
Daroca......Spain
Dardanelles (the), Turkey
Dargun....Mecklenburg
Darmstadt......Hesse Darmstadt
Dassel......Hanover
Dassow....Mecklenburg
Daswang......Bavaria
Daughistan......Prov. of Russia
Dauphine, Prov.of France
Davos......Switzerland
Dax......France
Deba......Spain
Debretzin......Hungary
Deccan......Hindostan
Decize......France
Deckendorf......Bavaria
Dedesdorf......Oldenburg
Delaware......one of the United States
Délemont....Switzerland
Delft......Holland
Delhi, Prov. of Hindostan
Delmenhorst..Oldenburg
Demacar......Spain
Demerara, BritishGuiana
Demonte......Sardinia
Dendermonde......Belgium
Denia......Spain
Denmark...see Denmark
Dermback..Saxe-Weimar
Deseada, FrenchW.Indies
Detmold, Lippe-Detmold
Dettelback......Bavaria
Dettingen......Bavaria
Detroit......Michigan
Deux Ponts......Bavaria
Deventer......Holland
Diana-Marina..Sardinia
Diarbekir, Prov.of Turkey
Die......France
Dieburg......Hesse
Diepholy......Hanover
Diepenau......Hanover
Dieppe......France
Diessenhofen, Switzerland
Dietfurth......Bavaria
Dietz......Nassau
Digne......France
Dijon......France
Dillenburg......Nassau
Dillengen......Bavaria
Dimizance......Greece
Dinan......France
Dinant......Belgium
Dinkelsbuhl......Bavaria
Dinklage......Oldenburg
Dirschau......Prussia
Dischengen, Wirtemburg
Dissen......Hanover
Dissen......Hesse
Dissentis......Switzerland
Dobberan...Mecklenburg
Dobhertin..Mecklenburg
Doemetz....Mecklenburg
Dogliani......Sardinia
Dokum......Holland
Dolce-Acqua......Sardinia
Dôle......France
Domberg......Hesse
Domfront......France
Dominica, BrtshW.Indies
Domme......France
Domo d'Ossola..Sardinia
Domremy......France
Donas......Sardinia
Donauworth......Bavaria
Donjon (le)......France
Donneloie....Switzerland
Donzenac......France
Doongurpoor..Hindostan
Dorak, ArabianKhusistan
Dordogne Dept. of France
Dorthagen......Hanover
Dorlingen......Oldenburg
Dorpat......Russia
Dort, or Dordrecht...... Holland
Dortan......France
Dorum......Hanover
Douai......France
Doubs..Dept. of France
Douglas, New Brunswick
Doulens......France
Douvaine......Sardinia
Dover......Delaware
Dowlatabad....Hindostan
Draguignan......France
Dransfeld......Hanover
Drenthe, Prov.of Holland
Dresden......Saxony
Dreux......France
Drohobitz......Gallicia
Drôme...Dept. of France
Dronero......Sardinia
Drontheim......Norway
Dubno......Volhynia
Dubrowna......Lithuania
Duderstadt......Hanover
Dunkerque......France
Durango......Spain
Durango, State of Mexico
Durazzo......Turkey
Durckheim......Bavaria
Durrenaesch..Switzerland
Düsseldorf, West Prussia
East Flanders..Prov. of Belgium
East Indies......see India
Easton......Maryland
Easton......Massachusets
Easton......Pennsylvania
Eauze......France
Ebeltoft......Denmark
Ebersdorf......Reuss
Ebingen......Wirtemburg
Ebron......France
Ebstorf......Hanover
Echelles (les)....Sardinia
Echtenach......Holland
Ecija......Spain
Eckenfirde......Denmark
Eckrenforde......Denmark
Eckwarden......Oldenburg
Ecuador......see Chagres
Edenburg......Hungary
Edessa......Turkey
Edewecht......Oldenburg
Edington..United States
Eger......Bohemia
Eggenfelde......Bavaria
Egletons......France
Eglisau......Switzerland
Eglofsheim......Bavaria

Egypt...see Egypt
Ehingen ...Wirtemburg
Eichstœdt ...Bavaria
Eilsen,Schaumburg Lippe
Eimbeck ...Hanover
Eimeo...Society Islands
Eisenach ...Prussia
Eisenach ..Saxe Weimar
Eisenburg,SaxeAltenburg
Eisenstadt...Hungary
Eisfeld...Saxe Meiningen
Eisleben ...Prussia
Eiterfeld ...Hesse
Ekaterinoslav ..Prov. of Russia
Ekaterinoslaw ..Government of Russia
Elba ...see Tuscany
Elberfeldt..West Prussia
Elbing ...West Prussia
Elbingerode ...Hanover
Elbœuf...France
Elche...Spain
Eldena ...Mecklenburg
El Escurial...Spain
Eleusis...Greece
Elfsborg...Sweden
Elgg ...Switzerland
Elizabeth Town...New Jersey
Ellingen ...Bavaria
Ellwangen..Wirtemburg
Ellwurden ...Oldenburg
Elma...Russia
Elmshorn ...Denmark
El Prado...Spain
Else ...Hanover
Elseneur...Denmark
Elsfleth...Oldenburg
El Tersorera ...Spain
Eltville...Nassau
Elvas ...Portugal
Embrach...Switzerland
Embrun...France
Emden...Hanover
Ems...Nassau
Emskirchen ...Bavaria
Engadin ...Switzerland
Engelholm...Sweden
Enghien...Belgium
Enkhuysen...Holland
Enköping ...Sweden
Enos ...Turkey
Entlebuck...Switzerland
Entraigues...France
Entre Douro e Minho... Prov. of Portugal
Entrevaux ...France
Entzerstorf...Austria
Epernay ...France
Ephesus ...Turkey
Epinal...France
Equator, see New Granada
Erbach...Hesse
Erdingor...Bavaria
Erekli ...Turkey
Erfurt...Prussia
Ergolsbach...Bavaria
Erie...Pennsylvania
Eriswyl...Switzerland
Erlangen...Bavaria
Erlau...Hungary
Erzeroum...Armenia
Escalona...Spain
Escheburg...Denmark
Eschede ...Hanover
Eschenau...Bavaria
Eschershausen,Brunswck
Eschwege...Hesse
Esens...Hanover
Esenschamm..Oldenburg
Esné...Egypt
Espalion...France
Espinar...Spain
Espiritu Santo..Prov. of Brazil
Espital...Spain
Esposenda...Portugal
Essek...Hungary
Essek...Sclavonia
Esselbach...Bavaria
Essen...Oldenburg
Essequibo Guiana,British West Indies
Esslingen ..Wirtemburg
Estawayer ..Switzerland
Estella...Spain
Esthonia, Prov. of Russia
Estremadura ...Prov. of Portugal
Estremadura...Prov. of Spain
Etain ...France
Etampes...France
Eu ...France
Eupen ...Belgium
Euratsburg...Bavaria
Eure...Dept. of France
Eure et Loir...Dept. of France
Eutin ...Denmark
Evian ...Sardinia
Evora...Portugal
Evreux...France
Eylau...Prussia
Eymoutiers ...France
Faaberg ...Denmark
Fahlköping ...Sweden
Fahlun ...Sweden
Fahrwanger, Switzerland
Fairfield...Connecticut
Falaise...France
Falkland Isles...see Falkland Isles
Fallersleben...Hanover
Falmouth ...Jamaica
Falsterbo ...Sweden
Fanjeaux...France
Fano ...Papal States
Faoug ...Switzerland
Farnbach...Bavaria
Faro (Isle of) ...Sweden
FaroeIslands,see Denmark
Fars...Prov. of Persia
Farsala ...Greece
Farshout...Egypt
Fatsa...Turkey
Fauquemburg...France
Faverges...Sardinia
Fayal...Azores
Fay Billot...France
Fayzabad ...Oude
Fécamp...France
Fedderwarden,Oldenburg
Feira...Portugal
Feldberg ..Mecklenburg
Feldkirch...Tyrol
Feldstellen..Wirtemburg
Felipe ...Spain
Felizzano ...Sardinia
Felletin ...France
Felsberg ...Hesse
Fenestrelle...Sardinia
Ferabad ...Persia
Fère (la) ...France
Fermo...Papal States
Fernando Po...Africa
Ferney ...France
Ferozabad ...Persia
Ferra ...Afghanistan
Ferrara...Papal States
Ferro ...Canary Isle
Ferrol ...Spain
Ferryland,Newfoundland
Feucht...Bavaria
Feuchtwarz...Bavaria
Fez...Morocco
Fichbach ...Bavaria
Fiesole...Tuscany
Figeac...France
Figueras ...Spain
Finale-Marina...Sardinia
Finisterre,Dept.of France
Finland..Prov. of Russia
Finmark,Prov.ofLapland
Fiume ...Illyria
Fladstrand ...Denmark
Flanders (French), Prov. of France
Fleaurance ...France
Flensburg...Denmark
Fleurien...Switzerland
Flix ...Spain
Florac ...France
Florence...Tuscany
Flores ...Azores
Florida,one of the United States
Flushing ...Holland
Foggia ...Naples
Foglizzo...Sardinia
Foix...France
Fokein...Prov. of China
Fontainebleau ...France
Fontarabia...Spain
Fontello ...Portugal
Fontenay ...France
Fontenoy...Belgium
Foreali ...Spain
Forcalguier ...France
Forcheim ...Bavaria
Forli ...Papal States
Formentera,BalearicIsles
Formosa, Island of China
Fort de l'Ecluse ..France
Forteventura,CanaryIsles
Fossano...Sardinia
Fougères...France
Fou-tcheou ...China
Frabertsheim ...Bavaria
France ...see France
France (Isle of)...see Mauritius
Franche-Comte..Prov. of France
Franeker ...Holland
Frangy...Sardinia
Frankenberg ...Hesse
Frankenfeld, Switzerland
Frankenthal ...Bavaria
Frankfort (Mayn) ...see Frankfort
Frankfort (Oder),Prussia
Frankfort...Kentucky
Frascati ...Papal States
Frauenfeld...Switzerland
Frederickshall ...Norway
Fredrickshaven,Denmrk
Fredericksund,Denmark
Fredericton,N.Brunswick
Fredonia...United States
Frejus ...France
Freudingen ...Bavaria
Frenay (le) Vicomte ...France
Frendenstadt, Wirtembrg
Frenes...France
Freren ...Hanover
Fresnillo ...Spain
Freudenthal ...Austria
Freyberg ...Saxony
Freyburg ...Baden
Freylingen...Nassau
Freysengen ...Bavaria
Freysing ...Bavaria
Freyung ...Bavaria
Frias ...Spain
Friburg...SwissCanton
Frick ...Switzerland
Fridrickshafen, Wirtemburg
Friedverg ...Austria
Friedeberg ...Bavaria
Friedeberg ...Hesse
Friedeburg...Hanover
Friedensburg...Denmark
Frederica...Denmark
Friedrickshafen,Denmrk
Friedrickstadt, Denmark
Friederikensiel, Oldenbrg
Friederwalde ...Hesse
Friendly Islands...see Sandwich Islands
Friesland,Prov.of Hollnd
Friesoythe...Oldenburg
Frio...Brazil
Fritzlar ...Hesse
Frutigen ...Switzerland
Fuentelsauca...Spain
Fuerteventura...Canary Isle
Fulda...Hesse Cassel
Fumel ...France
Funchal ...Madeira
Funen,Island of Denmark
Fünfkirchen...Hungary
Furfeld ...Hesse
Furfeld ...Wirtemburg
Furstenau ...Hanover
Furstenburg..Brunswick
Furstenburg, Mecklenbrg
Furstenfeldbruck,Bavaria
Furstenzell...Bavaria
Furth...Bavaria
Furth...Hesse
Fussen...Bavaria
Futtipoor ...Hindostan
Gaabense...Denmark
Gacé...France
Gadebusch..Mecklenburg
Gaëta ...Naples
Gabel ...Bohemia
Gaillac...France
Gaisa ...Saxe-Weimar
Galaxidi ...Greece
Galicia...Prov. of Spain
Galacz ...Turkey
Galistea ...Spain
Gallicia ...see Austria
Gallipoli...Naples
Gallipoli...Turkey
Galtinara ...Sardinia
Galveston...Texas
Gambia (River)...Africa
Gand ...Belgium
Ganderkesee...Oldenburg
Gandersheim, Brunswick
Gandia ...Spain
Ganges...France
Ganjam...Hindostan
Gannat ...France
Gap...France
Garching ...Bavaria
Gard ...Dept. of France
Garding...Denmark
Garessio...Sardinia
Garinera ...Spain
Garlasco ...Sardinia
Garlin...France
Garonne (Upper)..Dept. of France
Gartow ...Hanover
Gascony, Prov. of France
Gaspé, District of Canada
Gassino ...Sardinia
Gaudalupe ...Spain
Gavi ...Sardinia
Gaya...Bengal
Gaza ...Turkey
Geestendorf ...Hanover
Gefle ...Sweden
Gefleburg,Prov.ofSweden
Géfrées ...Bavaria
Geisenfeld...Bavaria
Geislingen...Wirtemburg
Gelnhausen ...Hesse
Geneva ...Switzerland
Geneva ...United States
Genoa ...Sardinia
Génolhac ...France
Georgetown...Columbia District
George Town..Demerara
George Town ..Van Diemen's Land
Georgia..Prov. of Russia
Georgia ...One of the United States
Georgiewsk...Russia
Gera ...Reuss
Germany...see Germany
Germesheim...Bavaria
Gerona...Spain
Gers ...Dept. of France
Gersau ...Switzerland
Gerzensee...Swiss
Gex ...France
Ghent ...Belgium
Ghilan ..Prov. of Persia
Ghuznee...Afghanistan
Giaveno ...Sardinia
Gibraltar ...see Gibraltar
Gien...France
Giesen ...Hesse
Gifhorn ...Hanover
Gijon ...Spain
Gilolo ...Moluccas
Gilserburg...Hesse
Ginjee...Hindostan
Girgenti...Sicily
Giromagny...France
Gironde, Dept. of France
Girshe ...Egypt
Giurgevo ...Turkey
Gizon ...Spain
Gladenbach...Hesse
Glandorf...Hanover
Glaris or Glarus...Swiss Canton
Glatz...Prussia
Gleidingen...Hanover
Gleussen...Bavaria
Glückstadt...Holstein
Gmünd...Wirtemburg
Gnesna..PrussianPoland
Gniolle...France
Gnoyen ...Mecklenburg
Goa ...Hindostan
Godens...Hanover
Goes ...Holland
Goiana...Brazil
Golconda ...Hydrabad
Goldberg ...Mecklenburg
Goldenstedt...Oldenburg
Gombroon...Russia
Gomera ...Canary Isle
Gonaives...St. Domingo
Gondar ...Abyssinia
Gondrecourt ...France
Goppingen...Wirtemburg
Goree ...Africa
Görlitz...Prussia
Gorze ...France
Goshen ...Connecticut
Goshen ...New York
Goslar...Hanover
Gosnitz...Saxe-Altenburg
Gossau...Switzerland
Gotha...Saxe-Coburg-Gotha
Gottenburg ...Sweden
Gottingen ...Hanover
Gottlieben...Switzerland
Gouda ...Holland
Gourdon...France
Gourin ...France
Gournay...France
Goyaz...Prov. of Brazil
Gozo, an island nearMalta
Gozzano ...Sardinia
Grabowo ...Mecklenburg
Graciosa ...Azores
Gradisca...Transylvania
Grafenau ...Bavaria
Graffenburg...Bavaria
Graham's Town ...Africa
Græfenthal ...Saxe-Meiningen
Gramat...France
Gran ...Arabia
Gran ...Hungary
Granada..Prov. of Spain
GrandCanary,CanaryIsle
Grand Pré...France
Grande Terre...For. West Indies
Grandson...Switzerland
Grandville ...France
Grandvilliers...France
Graslitz ...Bohemia
Grasse ...France
Gratz...Austria
Gratz...Prussia
Grave ...Holland
Gravelines...France
Gray ...France
Great Novogorod, Russia
Grebenstein...Hesse
Greece ...see Greece
Greencastle,Pennsylvania
Greene...Brunswick
Greenfield...Massachusets
Greetsyl...Hanover
Greiz ...Reuss
Grenaa ...Denmark
Grenada, Bri.West Indies
Grenade-sur l'Adour ...France
Grenade-sur-Garonne...France
Grenna...Sweden
Grenoble ...France
Grevismuhlen,Mecklenbg
Griefensée...Switzerland
Grisons ...Swiss Canton
Grodno ...Lithuania
Gröningen, Prov.Holland
Grossalmerode...Hesse
Grossander...Hanover
Grosselo...Tuscany
Grossenmeer ..Oldenburg
Grossfedderwarden ...Oldenburg
Grossgeran...Hesse
Grosswaradin ..Hungary
Grünburg...Hesse
Grüningen ...Saxony
Grüningen ...Switzerland
Grunstadt...Bavaria
Gruyère ...Switzerland
Guadalajara ...Mexico
Gudalaxara ...Spain
Guadaloupe, Fr.W.Indies
Guadaloupe...Spain
Guamanga...Peru
Guanaxuato ...Mexico
Guarda...Portugal
Guaropas...Brazil
Guastalla ..V. Lombardy
Guatemala ...Mexico
Guaxaco ...Mexico
Guayanilla,For.W.Indies
Guayaquil ...Equator
Guaymas...Mexico
Guayra...see La Guayra
Gudensburg ...Hesse
Gueldres,Prov.of Holland
Gueldres ..West Prussia
Guérande ...France
Guéret...France
Guienne, Prov. of France
Guingamp ...France
Guise ...France
Gujerat,Prov.of Hindostn
Gumbinuen ...Prussia
Gundwana ...Prov. of Hindostan
Guns...Hungary
Guntersblum...Hesse
Gunzbourg...Bavaria
Gunzenhausen...Bavaria
Guocin...Spain
Gurupa ...Brazil
Gustavia,St.Bartholomew
Gustrow...Mecklenburg
Guzelhissar...Turkey
Guzerat,Prov.of Hindostn
Gwalior ...Agra
Gy...France
Gyula ...Hungary
Haagl...Bavaria
Haarburg...Bavaria
Haarlem...Holland
Hackenburg...Nassau
Hacolalpam ...Mexico
Hadamar ...Nassau
Hademsdorf ...Hanover
Hage...Hanover
Hagenburg...Hanover
Hagenow...Mecklenburg
Hague (The)...Holland
Haguenau...France
Haiger...Nassau
Haigerloch..Wirtemburg
Hainau, Island of China
Hainault,Prov.ofBelgium
Halberstadt ...Prussia
Halicz...Gallicia
Halifax...Nova Scotia
Halle ...Prussia
Halle...Tyrol
Halle ...Wirtemburg
Hallwyl...Switzerland
Halmstadt...Sweden
Halpuxotoa...Mexico
Halsdorf ...Hesse
Halte ...Hanover
Ham...France
Hamadan ...Persia
Hamah ...Turkey
Hambach ...Bavaria
Hamburg...see Hamburg
Hameln...Hanover
Hamfelde...Denmark
Hammelburg ...Bavaria
Hammelwarden,Oldenbrg
Hammerfest ...Lapland
Hanau ...Hesse Cassel
Hanerau ...Denmark
Hang Yang ...China
Hanover...Hanover
Hanover ..United States
Han-tchong ...China
Harburg ...Hanover
Harebrouck ...France
Harfleur...France
Harlingen...Holland
Haro ...Spain
Harrisburg,Pennsylvania
Harsefelde ...Hanover
Hartford...Connecticut
Hartford, North Carolina
Hartford ...Kentucky
Hartmannshof...Bavaria
Harzburg...Brunswick
Hasbergen...Oldenburg
Haselüne ...Hanover
Hassan Kela...Armenia
Hasselfelde...Brunswick
Hassfurt ...Bavaria
Hatten...Oldenburg
Hattersheim ...Nassau
Havana ...see Havana
Haverhill...Massachusets
Haverhill,NewHampshire
Havre de Grace...France
Hawaii,Sandwich Islands
Hayti ...St. Domingo
Hebron...Maine
Hechingen ..Wirtemburg
Hechthausen...Hanover
Hêdé...France
Heide ...Denmark
Heidelburg ...Baden
Heidenheim..Wirtemburg
Heilbronn ...Wirtemburg
Heiligenhafene, Denmark
HeilsbronnCloster,Bvaria
Helder (The) ...Holland
Heligoland,see Heligoland
Hellin ...Spain
Helmstagd ...Brunswick
Helsa ...Hesse
Helsenving...Sweden
Helsingfors...Finland
Helvoetsluys...Holland
Hennebon...France
Hepperheim ...Hesse
Heppers...Oldenburg
Herat...Afghanistan
Herault, Dept. of France
Herborn ...Nassau
Herisau...Switzerland
Hérisson ...France
Hermanstadt...Hungary
Hernosand ...Sweden
Herrenbreitungen...Hesse
Herrenburg..Wirtemburg
Herrira...Spain
Hersfeld ...Hesse
Herzburg ...Hanover
Herzogenbusch..Holland
Hesdin ...France
Hesse, see German States
Hessel...Hanover
Hessen ...Brunswick
Hetzkirch...Switzerland
Hildburghausen...Saxe Meinengen
Hildesheim ...Hanover
Hillah...Turkey
Hillerod ...Denmark
Himmelpforten ..Hanover
Hindostan...see India
Hing-hou...China
Hinoiosa ...Spain
Hiörring ...Denmark
Hirchau ...Bavaria
Hirschberg, Mecklenburg
Hirschberg ...Prussia
Hirschholm ...Denmark
Hispaniola,seeStDomingo
Hitzacker...Hanover
Hoai-king ...China
Hoai-ngan ...China
Hoang-tcheou ...China
HobartTown,VanD.Land
Hobro...Denmark
Hochiem...Nassau
Hocksiel...Oldenburg
Höckst ...Nassau
Höckst...Hesse
Hodeida ...Arabia
Hof ...Bavaria
Hofgeismar ...Hesse
Hohegeis...Brunswick
Hoheneggelsen..Hanover
Hohenkirchen,Oldenburg
Hohenlinden ...Bavaria
Hohenlohe ..Wirtemburg
Hohenzollern ..Germany
Hohnsen ...Hanover
Ho-kien ...China
Holbeck...Denmark
Holland ...see Holland
Holle ...Oldenburg
Holstebro...Denmark
Holstedt...Denmark
Holzkirchen...Bavaria
Holzminden...Brunswick
Hollfeld ...Bavaria
Holstein,Prov.of Denmrk
Homburg,HesseHomburg
Homburg ...Bavaria
Honau ...Prov. of China
Honda...New Granada
Honduras ...see Honduras
Honfleur...France
Hong Kong,BritishChina
Hoogly ...Bengal
Hoopte...Hanover
Hoorn ...Holland
Horbe ...Wirtemburg
Horneburg...Hanover
Horsens...Denmark
Hospital ...Switzerland
Houdan...France
Houquang, Prov.of China
Huanchaco ...Peru
Hude ...Oldenburg
Hudson...New York
Hudson's Bay ...see Columbia River
Hudwickswald ...Sweden
Hué ...Cochin-China
Huebla...Spain
Huelva ...Spain
Huesca...Spain
Hünfeld ...Hesse
Hungary...see Austria
Hungen ...Hesse
Huntlosen...Oldenburg
Huntsville...Alabama
Huntsville,Nrth.Carolina
Husum ...Denmark
Hydra ...Isle of Greece
Hydrabad ...Scinde
Hyères ...France
Iade ...Oldenburg
Ibila ...Turkey
Iburg ...Hanover
Iceland (Isle of) ...see Denmark
Idstein...Nassau
Iesberg ...Hesse
Iever...Oldenburg
Iglau...Moravia
Iglo ...Hungary
Igualada ...Spain
Igurqui...Chagres
Ildefonso...Spain
Illano ...Spain
Illerdiessen ...Bavaria
Illingen ...Wirtemburg
Illinois ...one of the United States
Illyria...see Austria
Ilmenau ...Saxe-Weimar
Imeretia, Prov. of Russia
Immendstadt ...Brunswick
Immenstadt ...Bavaria
India...see India (East)
Indiana ...one of the United States
Indianopolis...Indiana
Indre...Dept. of France
Indre et Loire ...Dept. of France
Ingelheim ...Hesse
Ingoldstadt ...Bavaria
Ingouville ...France
Ingrande ...France
Innspruck ...Tyrol
Ins...Switzerland

Insterburg ....Prussia
Interlacken..Switzerland
Intra ....Sardinia
Ionian Isles ...see Ionian Islands
Irak....Prov. of Persia
Irkoutsk....Siberia
Irlomitz ....Volhynia
Isère....Dept. of France
Isigny....France
Islamabad....Chittagong
Isle en Jourdain (l') .... France
IsleofFrance,seeMauritius
Isle of France ...a Prov. of France
Isle et Vilaine ..Dept. of France
Ismail....Turkey
Isny....Wirtemburg
Isola ....Austria
Ispahan ....Persia
Issoire ....France
Issoudun ....France
Is-sur-Tille....France
Italy Northern ....see Venetian Lombardy
Itzepæ ....Denmark
Ivenack....Mecklenburg
Iviça....Balearic Isles
Ivory Coast....see Africa
Ivrea ....Sardinia
Ivry-sur-Seine....France
Ixar....Spain
Jaca....Spain
Jackson ....Mississippi
Jacmel....St. Domingo
Jaen....Spain
Jaffa....Turkey
Jägerndorf ....Moravia
Jamaica,BritishW.Indies
Jarnage....France
Jaroslav...Prov. of Russia
Jaroslaw....Gallicia
Jassy....Moldavia
Jault....France
Java .... see Archipelago, East Indian
Javat ....Persia
Jefferson....Missouri
Jegerndorf ....Austria
Jellalabad ....Seistan
Jena....Saxe-Weimar
Jenné....Central Africa
Jerusalem....Palestine
Jhalrapatun....Malwa
Joannina....Albania
Jodar ....Spain
Johannisburg....Prussia
John's Town....Antigua
Joigny....France
Joinville ....France
Jonkoping ....Sweden
Jonzac ....France
Jorjan ....Persia
Joudpoor....Hindostan
Jovols ....France
Juanpoor....Hindostan
Jucatan....Mexico
Judda....Arabia
Jumella....Spain
Jura ....Dept. of France
Jussey ....France
Jutland ....see Denmark
Juvigne....France
Jyenagur....Ajmeer
Kahla....Saxe-Altenburg
Kahlert...Saxe-Meiningen
Kaisarieh....Turkey
Kaiserslautern....Bavaria
Kaiserstuhl ..Switzerland
Kalisch ....Poland
Kallundberg ...Denmark
Kalouga ....Russia
Kaminiec....Podolia
Kamm ....Bavaria
Kano ....Central Africa
Kappeln ....Denmark
Karpfheim ....Bavaria
Karlstadt ....Bavaria
Kasan....Russia
Kaschau....Hungary
Kastel....Bavaria
Kaufbeuren....Bavaria
Kehl....Baden
Kej ....Mekran
Kelat....Beloochistan
Kellinghusen....Denmark
Kempten ....Bavaria
Kentucky ....one of the United States
Kerman...Prov. of Russia
Kermanshah ....Persia
Kerstenhausen....Hesse
Keuzenach ....Prussia
Khars ....Armenia
Khorassan,Prov.of Persia
Khusistan, Prov.of Persia
Kiachta....Siberia
Kiangnan, Prov.of China
Kiangsee, Prov. of China
Kief....Prov. of Russia
Kiel ....Holstein
Kielce ....Poland
Kiew ....Prov. of Russia
King George's Sound.... see Australia
Kingston ....Canada
Kingston ....Jamaica
Kioge ....Denmark
Kipfenberg ....Bavaria
Kirberg ....Nassau
Kirchberg ....Switzerland
Kirchberg... Wirtemburg
Kircheimboland..Bavaria
Kirchhain ....Hesse
Kirchheim...Wirtemburg
Kirkagatch ....Turkey
Kirklissa....Turkey
Kirn....Bavaria
Kitzingen....Bavaria
Kiutayah ....Turkey
Klosterlaussnitz S. .... Altenburg
Kloster Neuburg, Austria
Klütz ....Mecklenburg
Knonau ....Switzerland
Koeitchoo,Prov. of China
Kolding....Denmark
Kolhorn....Holland
Kolomna....Russia
Konieh ....Turkey
Königsberg ....Prussia
Königsgratz....Bohemia
Königshafen ....Bavaria
Königslutten, Brunswick
Königstein ....Nassau
Königstein ....Saxony
Koordistan....Prov. of Turkey
Köping ....Sweden
Korn Neuburg ..Austria
Korsör ....Denmark
Koslamboul ....Turkey
Kostroma,Prov.of Russia
Kotah ....Malwa
Koursk..Prov. of Russia
Kowno ....Lithuania
Kraissen ....Bavaria
Krakow....Mecklenburg
Kranichfeld,SaxeWeimar
Krefeld....Prussia
Kremnitz....Hungary
Krempe....Denmark
Krems ....Austria
Kriewitz....Mecklenburg
Kronach....Bavaria
Kröpelin ...Mecklenburg
Kuhstedt....Hanover
Kulm ....Switzerland
Kulmback ....Bavaria
Kunselsau...Wirtemburg
Kursk...Prov. of Russia
Kussel....Bavaria
Kyburg....Switzerland
La Bouliere ....France
Lacaune ....France
La Charite ....France
La Châtre....France
Lachen ....Switzerland
La Ciota ....France
La Cliva ....Spain
La Fera ....France
La Ferte Bernard, France
La Ferte Milon....France
Lafferde ....Hanover
La Flèche ....France
Lage ....Mecklenburg
La Gesta....Spain
Lagos ....Portugal
La Grasse ....France
La Guayra ....Venezuela
La Guerche ....France
Laguna....Brazil
Laguna....Teneriffe
La Haye....France
La Herradura....Spain
Laholm....Sweden
Lahore,Prov.ofHindostan
Lahsa,a District of Arabia
L'Aigle ....France
La Linde ....France
La Mancha,Prov.of Spain
Lambesc ....France
Lamego....Portugal
La Mezquita ....Spain
LaMota deBelmont,Spain
Lampa ....Peru
Lampspringe....Hanover
La Mure....France
Lancaster....Ohio
Lancaster ..Pennsylvania
Lancerola, Canary Island
Landau ....Bavaria
Landerneau ....France
Landerou ....Switzerland
Landes...Dept. of France
Landrecy ....France
Landsberg....Bavaria
Landshut ....Bavaria
Landshut....Prussia
Landsthul ....Bavaria
Lanes ....Spain
Langeac....France
Langelsheim...Brunswick
Langen ....Hesse
Langenburg, Wirtemburg
Langenselbold....Hesse
Langensenn ....Bavaria
Langförden...Oldenburg
Langlethal ...Switzerland
Langlingen ....Hanover
Langnau ....Switzerland
Langogne ....France
Langres ....France
Languedoc,Prov.ofFrance
La Guna ....Venezuela
La Guna de Terminos.... Honduras
Langwarden...Oldenburg
Lannilis....France
Lannion....France
Lanslebourg....Sardinia
Lanzo....Sardinia
Laon....France
La Parra....Spain
La Paz....Bolivia
Lapland....see Sweden
La Plata, see BuenosAyres
Lar ....Prov. of Persia
La Réole....France
Largentiere....France
Largue....France
Lari....Persia
Larissa....Greece
La Rochelle ....France
LaRochefoucauld, France
La Roche Posay, France
La Rua ....Spain
Lassaraz....Switzerland
Lastrup....Oldenburg
La Tete-de-Buch, France
Lathen ....Hanover
Lauenburg....Holstein
Laufen....Bavaria
Lauffenburg, Switzerland
Launceston....Van Dieman's Land
Laupheim....Wirtemburg
Laurvig....Norway
Lausanne ....Switzerland
Lauterbach....Hesse
Laval ....France
La Valetta....Malta
Lavaur ....France
Laybach....Illyria
Le Barp ....France
Le Blanc....France
Lebrija ....Spain
Le Cateau....France
Lecce ....Naples
Lechfeld....Bavaria
Lectoure ....France
Le Dorat....France
Leedam....Holland
Leer ....Hanover
Leese....Hanover
Leghorn ....Tuscany
Lehe ....Hanover
Lehornia ....Spain
Leignitz....Prussia
Leimuden ....Holland
Leipzig ....Saxony
Leiria ....Portugal
Le Luc ....France
Le Mans....France
Lemberg ....Gallicia
Lemforde ....Hanover
Lemgo....Lippe-Detmold
Lemwerder....Oldenburg
Lensburg....Switzerland
Leogane ....St. Domingo
Leon....Mexico
Leon ....Prov of Spain
Lepanto ....Greece
Le Palisse ....France
Le Puy en Velay, France
Lerida ....Spain
Lerma ....Spain
Le Russey ....France
Les Cayes ..St. Domingo
Les Mees ....France
Lesa....Sardinia
Lesparre....France
Lesum....Hanover
Le Tour-du-Pin....France
Leuchtenfels ....Bavaria
Leupoldstein ....Bavaria
Leurey....France
Leutkirch....Wirtemburg
Leuwarden ....Holland
Levant. see Levant (The)
Levanto ....Sardinia
Le Vigan ....France
Levroux....France
Lexington ....Georgia
Lexington ....Kentucky
Lexington..Massachusets
Lexington ....Virginia
Leyden ....Holland
L'Hôpital ....France
Libau ....Russia
Libourne....France
Lich ....Hesse
Lichtenau ....Hesse
Lichtenstein....Germany
Liebenstein....Saxe-Meiningen
Liechdenstaeg,Switzerlnd
Liege ....Belgium
Liestall ....Switzerland
Liea (le) ....Switzerland
Lignières....France
Lignitz ....Silesia
Ligny ....Belgium
Ligny....France
Lille ....France
Lima ....Peru
Limburg ....Nassau
Limburg,Prov.ofBelgium
Limoges....France
Limone ....Sardinia
Linares....Spain
Lindaw ....Bavaria
Linde (la)....France
Lindern ....Oldenburg
Lingen ....Hanover
Linkiang ....China
Linköping ....Sweden
Lintz ....Austria
Lipari ....Sicily
Lippe-Detmold....see German States
Lisbon ....Portugal
Lisieux....France
Lisle ....France
L'Isle Jourdain ...France
Lissa....Prussian Poland
Lithuania (Russian Poland)....see Russia
Littau....Austria
Little Rock ....Arkansas
Liverpool....Australasia
Liverpool....Nova Scotia
Livignac....France
Livonia...Prov. of Russia
Loadicea ....Turkey
Loana ....Sardinia
Lobau ....Saxony
Lobeinstein....Reuss
Locana....Sardinia
Locarno....Switzerland
Loches ....France
Locle (le) ....Switzerland
Lodene ....France
Lodi, Venetian-Lombardy
Lodomiria (Austrian Poland)....see Austria
Loesch....Switzerland
Logrono....Spain
Loheia ....Arabia
Lohne ....Oldenburg
Loire....Dept. of France
Loire (Lower)...Dept. of France
Loire (Upper)...Dept. of France
Loir et Cher....Dept. of France
Loiret...Dept. of France
Lombes....France
Lombardy ...see Venetian Lombardy
Lombok....East Indian Archipelago
Lomello ....Sardinia
Long Island....New York
Longny ....France
Longueville ....France
Loningen ....Oldenburg
Lons le Saunier ..France
LooChoo, Island of China
Lora....Spain
Lorca ....Spain
Lorch ....Wirtemburg
Loretto....Papal States
L'Orient ....France
Lorraine, Prov. of France
Lot....Dept. of France
Lot et Garonne, Dept. of France
Loudéac ....France
Loudun ....France
Louhans ....France
Louisiana ....one of the United States
Louisville ....Georgia
Louisville....Kentucky
Louvain ....Belgium
Louviers....France
Lowell....Massachusets
Lozère...Dept. of France
Lubeck ....see Lubeck
Lublin ...Prov. of Poland
Lubthen....Mecklenburg
Luc (le) ....France
Lucca....Southern Italy
Lucca ....Saxe-Altenburg
Lucens....Switzerland
Lucerne....Switzerland
Luchon ....Hanover
Lucknow....Oude
Luçon....France
Luçon....Philippines
Luditz ....Austria
Ludwigsburg, Wirtemburg
Lugano ....Switzerland
Lugo ....Spain
Lugumskslosten,Denmrk
Luishausen...Wirtemburg
Lulea ....Sweden
Lund ....Sweden
Lunden....Denmark
Luneburg....Hanover
Lunenburg...Nova Scotia
Luneville....France
Lüneburg....Hanover
Lure....France
Luthen....Oldenburg
Lützenburg....Denmark
Lutlen....Brunswick
Lutry....Switzerland
Lutzen ....Saxony
Luxemburg....Prov. of Holland
Luxeuil ....France
Luzarches....France
Luzy....France
Lyonnois,Prov. of France
Lyons....France
Mabrishstadt....Bavaria
Macao ....China
Macassar,E.I. Archipelago
Macerata ....Papal States
Machias....Maine
Maçon....France
Madagascar (Isle),Africa
Madeira....see Madeira
Maden....Turkey
Madison....Indiana
Madras ....Hindostan
Madrid....Spain
Madridejas ....Spain
Madrigal....Spain
Maennedorf..Switzerland
Maestricht ....Holland
Magadino....Switzerland
Magadoxa ....Africa
Magdeburg....Prussia
Magnesia....Turkey
Magny ....France
Mahé....Hindostan
Mahon....Balearic Isles
Mainatchin....Siberia
Mainbenheim ....Bavaria
Maine..one of the United States
Maine et Loire..Dept. of France
Maine et Perche....Prov. of France
Maintenon....France
Majacella ....Spain
Majorca....Balearic Isles
Malacca....see India
Malaga....Spain
Malchin ....Mecklenburg
Malmo....Sweden
Malaunay....France
Maldonado..Monte Video
Maletroit ....France
Malines or Mechlin....Belgium
Malmedy ....Prussia
Malmo....Sweden
Malta....see Malta
Malwa,Prov.of Hindostan
Mamers ....France
Manche, Dept. of France
Manchineel....Jamaica
Mangalore ....Hindostan
Manilla,E.I. Archipelago
Mannheim....Baden
Mans (le)....France
Mansle ....France
Mansoura ....Egypt
Mantua,VenetianLombdy
Manzanillo,For.W.Indies
Maracaybo....Venezuela
Maragha....Persia
Maranham,Prov. of Brazil
Marans....France
Marbella ....Spain
Marbourg ....Hesse
Marcellin....France
Marennes....France
Mareuil ....France
Margaux ....France
Margritta....Venezuela
Mariager ....Denmark
Maribo ....Denmark
Marie Galante....French West Indies
Marienbourg ....Belgium
Marienburg....Saxony
Marienburg,West Prussia
Marienhave ....Hanover
Marienwerder,W. Prussia
Marignano, V. Lombardy
Markausen ...Oldenburg
Marksubl...Saxe Weimar
Marktel....Bavaria
Marlow ....Mecklenburg
Marmande ....France
Marnaud....Switzerland
Marne....Denmark
Marne ..Dept. of France
Marne (Upper)..Dept. of France
Marnitz ....Mecklenburg
Marolles ....France
Marsala....Sicily
Marseilles....France
Marsilly ....France
Martel ....France
Martha Brac....Jamaica
Martignes....France
Martigny....Switzerland
Martinique, French West Indies
Martinsburg....Virginia
Martinsville ....Virginia
Marvejois ....France
Maryland....one of the United States
Massachussets, one of the United States
Masserano ....Sardinia
Massiac....France
Masulipatam...Hindostan
Matamores ....Mexico
Matanzas....Cuba
Mataro ....Spain
Matilla....Spain
Matto Grosso....Prov. of Brazil
Matura....Ceylon
Maubeuge....France
Mauleon ....France
Mauritius....see Mauritius
Maurs....France
Mauzé....France
Maxenne ....France
Mayaques, For. W. Indies
Mayence,HesseDarmstadt
Mayenne, Dept.of France
Mazamet ....France
Mazanderan ....Prov. of Persia
Mazatlan ....Mexico
Meaux ....France
Mecca ....Arabia
Mechlin, or Malines .... Belgium
Mechoacan ....a State of Mexico
Mecklenburg,see Northern States of Europe
Medina ....Arabia
Medina Del Campo,Spain
Medinet ....Egypt
Medoc ....France
Meerut ....Delhi
Megara ....Greece
Mehallet ....Egypt
Mehun ....France
Meilen ....Switzerland
Meiningen ....Saxe-Meiningen
Meissen....Saxony
Meissenheim....Hesse Homburg
Meisterschwarden.... Switzerland
Meitengen....Bavaria
Mekran, Prov.of Hindstn
Melasso ....Turkey
Meldorf....Denmark
Melides ....Portugal
Melle....France
Mellendorf ....Hanover
Mellesimo ....Sardinia
Mellingen....Switzerland
Meloui....Egypt
Melun ....France
Memel ....Prussia
Memmingen ....Bavaria
Mende....France
Mendoyd ...Buenos Ayres
Mendrisio....Switzerland
Menouf....Egypt
Menselwitz,Saxe-Altenbg
Mengen....Wirtemburg
Mengkosen....Bavaria
Menin ....Belgium
Mentone....Sardinia
Menzaleh....Egypt
Meppen....Hanover
Mequinenza ....Spain
Mequinez ....Morocco
Mera ....Spain
Merat ....Delhi
Merching ....Bavaria
Merdin ....Turkey
Mergenthieim,Wirtembrg
Merida ....Spain
Merida....Venezuela
Merou ....Persia
Merseburg ....Prussia
Méru ....France
Meshed....Persia
Messina....Sicily
Metoulis....Egypt
Metz....France
Metzingen ..Wirtemburg
Meulan....France
Meurthe, Dept. of France
Meuse...Dept. of France
Mexico....see Mexico
Meyreurs ....France
Mezen ....Russia
Mezières ....France
Miana....Persia
Michigan ....one of the United States
Middleburg....Holland
Middleburg....Vermont
Middefarth ....Denmark
Middoge....Oldenburg
Miesback....Bavaria
Milan, Venetian-Lombrdy
Milhau....France
Milledgeville,Georgia,US
Milo....Isle of Greece
Milsungen ....Hesse
Miltenberg ....Bavaria
Mimigin ....France
Minas Geraes..a Prov. of Brazil
Mindanao ....Philippines
Mindelheim....Bavaria
Minden....West Prussia
Mindoro....Philippines
Mingrelia,Prov.of Russia
Minorca ....Balearic Isles
Minsen....Oldenburg
Minsk ....Lithuania
Minyet ....Egypt
Mirambeau ....France
Miramichi,NewBrunswck
Miramont ....France
Miranda de Vita,Portugal
Mirande....France
Mirandella ....Portugal
Mirandola....Modena
Mirecourt ....France
Mirow ....Mecklenburg
Mirzapore ....Bengal
Mischkoks....Hungary
Misitra....Greece
Mississippi ....one of the United States
Missolonghi ....Greece
Missouri....one of the United States
Mittau ....Russia
Mittelpöllnitz....Saxe Weimar
Mittlewald ....Bavaria
Mitylene (Isle) ....Turkey
Mobile ....Albama
Mocha....Arabia
Modane....Sardinia
Modena....see Italy
Modon ....Greece
Mogadore....Morocco
Moghilev....Podolia
Moguer ....Spain
Mohilow....Lithuania
Moissac ....France
Moldavia ..a Principality of Turkey
Molibergen....Oldenburg
Mölln ....Denmark
Molsheim ....France
Moluccas,EI.Archipelago
Momo....Sardinia
Mompox....Venezuela
Monaco ....Sardinia
Monasteer ....Tunis
Monasterio ....Spain
Moncalieri....Sardinia
Moncalvo ....Sardinia

Monclova ....Mexico
Moncontour.......France
Moncug...........France
Mondoubleau......France
Mondovi..........Sardinia
Monghir..........Bengal
Monheim..........Bavaria
Monlieu..........France
Monosque ....France
Mons.............Belgium
Monsarez ....Portugal
Montabaner.......Nassau
Montaigu.........France
Montargis........France
Montauban ....France
Montaubun........Spain
Montbach ....France
Montbazon........France
Montbéliard......France
Montbrison ......France
Montcenis........France
Mont Dauphin ....France
Mont-de-Marsan...France
Montdidier.......France
Montechiaro......Sardinia
Montego Bay......Jamaica
Montelimart......France
Montereau........France
Monte Video...see Buenos Ayres
Montfort.........France
Monthey .....Switzerland
Monticello..United States
Montier ....France
Montilla.........Spain
Montlouis ....France
Montluçon........France
Montluel.........France
Montmatre........France
Montmedy ....France
Montmeillant ...Sardinia
Mont Mirail......France
Montmorillon ....France
Montpelier.......France
Montpelier.......Vermont
Montprevevee, Switzerlnd
Montreal ....a district of Canada
Montreuil ....France
Montsalvy ....France
Montserrat, B.WestIndies
Moorburg......Oldenburg
Moorfields ......Virginia
Moorshedabad ....Bengal
Moosa ....Arabia
Moosh .....a Pachalic of Turkey
Moquehua..........Peru
Mora ....Sweden
Morat.......Switzerland
Moravia.......see Austria
Morbihan,Dept.of France
Morella ....Spain
Moretta ....Sardinia
Morgenthal ..Switzerland
Morges ....Switzerland
Morienne.......Sardinia
Moringen ....Hanover
Morlaix ....France
Morocco.......see Barbary
Moron ....Spain
Morschen.........Hesse
Mortagne..........France
Mortain ....France
Mortara..........Sardinia
Moscow...........Russia
Moselle..Dept. of France
Moss ....Norway
Mostar ....Turkey
Mostoles ....Spain
Mosul.......a Pachalic of Turkey
Motiers-Travers..Switzerland
Motril.............Spain
Moudon.......Switzerland
Moulins ....France
Moultan,Prov.ofHindostn
Moura...........Portugal
Moussoul ....Turkey
Moutiers..........Sardinia
Mowee, Sandwich Islands
Muhldorf..........Bavaria
Muhlhausen.......Prussia
Mühlenbech...Brunswick
Mühlenbech,Mecklenburg
Mujacar............Spain
Mulhausen.........France
Munchberg........Bavaria
Munchwylen, Switzerland
Munda ....Spain
Munden ....Hanover
Munich ....Bavaria
Munsinger...Wirtemburg
Münster.......Switzerland
Münster.....West Prussia
Murano .....V. Lombardy
Murat ....France
Murcia.....Prov. of Spain
Mure (la) ....France
Muret ....France
Muri ....Switzerland
Muriac.............France
Murnau...........Bavaria
Murom............Russia
Murviedro ....Spain
Muscat ....Arabia
(Letters for Muscat should be directed to the care of an agent at Aden)
Mustizlawl ....Lithuania
Muttra ....Bengal
Mysore.Prov.ofHindostan
Naarden...........Holland
Nachschou .....Denmark
Nagold.........Wirtemburg
Nagpoor ......Hindostan
Najerd...........Spain
Namur ....Belgium
Nancy............France
Nandere,Prov.ofHindostn
Nanking ....China
Nantes............France
Nantucket,Massachusetts
Naples.............Italy
Naplous.........Palestine
Narbonne.........France
Narva ....Russia
Nashville.......Tennessee
Nassau ....Bahamas
Nassau,*see* German States
Nastatten ....Nassau
Natal.........*see* Africa
Natchez.......Mississippi
Natchitoches,UnitdStates
Naumberg ....Hesse
Naumburg ....Prussia
Nauplia ....Greece
Navarino..........Greece
Navarre...Prov. of Spain
Navarreins........France
Naxos .....Isle of Greece
Negapatam....Hindostan
Negropont, Isle of Greece
Nejin ....Russia
Nellenbruck ......Bavaria
Nelson.........New Zealand
Nemours...........France
Nentershausen.......Hesse
Nepaul ....Hindostan
Neresheim....Wirtemburg
Nesselwang.......Bavaria
Nestyed ....Denmark
Netra ....Hesse
Neu-Brandenburg, Mecklenburg
Neu Buckow, Mecklenbrg
Neuburg ....Bavaria
Neuenbrock.....Oldenburg
Neuenhaus ......Hanover
Neuf-Brisach .....France
Neufchâteau ......France
Neufchâtel ....France
Neufchatel ..Switzerland
Neuhalden...Mecklenburg
Neuhans...........Bavaria
Neuhaus ....Hanover
Neuhirchen ......Bavaria
Neuhof...........Hesse
Neuhof...........Nassau
Neuilly...........France
Neukirchen ....Hesse
Neukloster..Mecklenburg
Neumarck ....Bavaria
Neumunster......Denmark
Neundorf...........Hesse
Neunhunlorf ..Oldenburg
Neusatz ....Hungary
Neusol ....Hungary
Neusses ....Bavaria
Neustadh-Goedens.....Hanover
Neustadt ....Bavaria
Neustadt.........Denmark
Neustadt.........Hanover
Neustadt....Mecklenburg
Neustadt.....Saxe Coburg Gotha
Neu-Strelitz,Mecklenburg
Neuve Lyre ....France
Neuveville ....Switzerland
Nevers............France
Nevis,British West Indies
New Barcelona,Venezuela
Newbern..North Carolina
New Britain..Australasia
New Brunswick....British America
New Caledonia, Australia
NewCastile,Prov.of Spain
Newcastle, NewBrunswck
Newfoundland,B.America
New Granada....*see* New Granada
New Hampshire.....one of the United States
Newhaven......Connecticut
New Hebrides, Australia
New Holland ....*see* Australia
New Jersey....one of the United States
New Leon.......a State of Mexico
New Mexico ..a State of Mexico
New Orleans ..Louisiana
New Providence,Bahamas
New South Wales.......*see* Australia
New York .....one of the United States
New Zealand..........*see* Australia
Neyva......New Granada
Niagara ....Canada
Nibel ....Denmark
Nicasia...........Cyprus
Nice ....Sardinia
Nickerie.........Demarara
Nicolaief, Prov. of Russia
Nicopoli..........Turkey
Nidda...........Hesse
Niederolm.........Hesse
Nienburg.........Hanover
Nictenau ....Bavaria
Nieuport ....Belgium
Nievre...Dept. of France
Nimeguen.........Holland
Ning-po ....China
Nions..............France
Niort ....France
Nishegorod ....Russia
Nismes ....France
Nivernois,Prov. of France
Nizni Novogorod..Russia
Nocera ....Naples
Noé ....France
Noerten ....Hanover
Nogaro ....France
Nogent-le-Roi.......France
Nogent-le-Retrou, France
Noirmoutier.........France
Nolay ....France
Noli ....Sardinia
Nomery ....France
None'............Sardinia
Nontron ....France
Noorkoping ....Sweden
Nora..............Sweden
Nord......Dept. of France
Nordburg..........Denmark
Nordheim..........Hanover
Nordlingen ....Bavaria
Nordtorf ....Denmark
Norfolk ....Virginia
Norfolk Island..........*see* Australia
Normandy,Prov.ofFrance
Norresundby.......Denmark
Norridgewick....U. States
NorthAmerica,*see*U.States
North Brabant....Prov. of Holland
North Carolina.....one of the United States
Norway.........*see* Norway
Novara............Sardinia
Nova Scotia,Brit.America
Novi..............Sardinia
Novogorod,Prov.ofRussia
Noyon..............France
Nozay..............France
Nubia ....*see* Nubia
Nuevitas,For.West Indies
Nuits..............France
Nuremberg.........Bavaria
Nurtingen.....Wirtemburg
Nus................Sardinia
Nutschof....Mecklenburg
Nyburg...........Denmark
Nydau..........Switzerland
Nyeborg..........Denmark
Nykiobing ....Denmark
Nyköping ....Sweden
Nyon..........Switzerland
Nystedt...........Denmark
Oaxaca, a State of Mexico
Oberaula ....Hesse
Ober Gunzborg ..Bavaria
Oberkaufungen.......Hesse
Obernbourg ....Bavaria
Oberndorf..........Bavaria
Oberndorf......Wirtemburg
Obernkirchen ....Hesse
Obernstein .....Oldenburg
Obidos ....Portugal
Ocana.............Mexico
Ocana..............Spain
Ochsenfurth ....Bavaria
Ochsenhausen,Wirtemburg
Odensee,Island ofDenmrk
Odessa ....Russia
Œdenburg ....Hungary
Oehringen ..Wirtemburg
Oettingen..........Bavaria
Oeyras ....Brazil
Ofen..............Hungary
Offenbach,HesseDarmstdt
Offerburg ....Baden
Ogdensburg.....New York
Oggersheim ....Bavaria
Ohio ..one of the United States
Ohrdruf ....Saxe-Coburg Gotha
Oise ....Dept. of France
Okhotsk............Siberia
OldCastile, Prov. of Spain
Oldenbrock.....Oldenburg
Oldendorf...........Hesse
Oldenburg.........Denmark
Oldenburg, *see* Oldenburg
Oldersum ....Hanover
Oldesloke ....Denmark
Oleggio ....Sardinia
Olinda ....Brazil
Oliva ....Spain
Olivenza ....Portugal
Olmutz..............Moravia
Olonetz..Prov. of Russia
Oloron ....France
Olten..........Switzerland
Oltmutz.............Austria
Ombo................Egypt
Omegra ....Sardinia
Oneglia............Sardinia
Oodipoor ....Hindostan
Oojein..............Malwa
Ooscat..............Turkey
Oporto............Portugal
Oppeln..............Prussia
Oppenheim ....Hesse
Oran ....Algeria
Orange..............France
Orangeburg ..S. Carolina
Orangetown ....Maine
Orangetown.......New York
Orbe..............Switzerland
Orbec...............France
Orduna...............Spain
Orebro ....Sweden
Oregrund ....Sweden
Orel......Prov. of Russia
Orenburg, Prov. of Russia
Orense ....Spain
Orfa, Pachalic of Turkey
Orford..........Connecticut
Orgon................France
Orihuela..............Spain
Orissa ..Prov. of Bengal
Orizaba..............Mexico
Orléannois,Prov.ofFrance
Orleans...............France
Ormea ....Sardinia
Ornans ....France
Orne.....Dept. of France
Ornavasso..........Sardinia
Oron...........Switzerland
Oropesa ....Spain
Ororu ....Bolivia
Orta ....Sardinia
Orthez ....France
OsiumKarahissar, Turkey
Osma...................Spain
Osnabruck..........Hanover
Ossuna ....Spain
Ostend ....Belgium
Osterby ....Sweden
Osterhagen........Hanover
Osterkappeln.......Hanover
Osternhosen ......Bavaria
Osterode...........Hanover
Ostersund ....Sweden
Ostia...........Papal States
Ostrog..............Volhynia
Oswego .....United States
Otaheite..Society Islands
Othfresen ....Hanover
Otranto...............Naples
Ottenstein.......Brunswick
Otterndorf.........Hanover
Oude...a Prov. of Bengal
Oufa.................Siberia
Oulk ....Sardinia
Ourique ....Portugal
Ovado ....Sardinia
Ovelgönne........Oldenburg
Overyssel,Prov.ofHolland
Oviedo...............Spain
Owhyhee,SandwichIslnds
Oythe...............Oldenburg
Pacaudiere (la) ..France
Pachuca ....Mexico
Packins............Oldenburg
Padua .....V. Lombardy
Paimbœuf..........France
Paimpol ....France
Palamcotta.....Hindostan
Palembang ....Sumatra
Palencia ....Spain
Palenzuela...........Spain
Palermo ....Sicily
Palestine..........*see* Turkey
Palisse (la) ....France
Pallanza............Sardinia
Palma........Canary Isles
Palma..............Majorca
Palma di Solo...Sardinia
Palos.................Spain
Pamiers...............France
Pamplona....New Grenada
Pamplona.............Spain
Panama ....Venezuela
Papal States.......*see* Italy
Papenburg ....Hanover
Pappenheim.........Bavaria
Papua.............Australia
Para........Prov. of Brazil
Paracuta.............Brazil
Paraguay,*see*Buenos Ayre
Paraiba....Prov. of Brazil
Paramaribo,For.W.Indies
Paramatta ......Australia
Parana.....Prov. of Brazil
Parchim.......Mecklenburg
Parilla................Peru
Paris ....France
Parma...............*see* Italy
Paros..........Isle of Greece
Parsdorf............Bavaria
Parthenay...........France
Pas de Calais ..Dept. of France
Pasa ....Persia
Passgaut..........France
Passau...............Bavaria
Pasto..............Colombia
Paterno..............Sicily
Patna...............Bengal
Patras................Greece
Pattensen..........Hanover
Pau ....France
Pavia, Venetian Lombardy
Payern ....Switzerland
Pays de Vaud,Switzerland
Payta..................Peru
Paz (la)...............Bolivia
Peage (le) ....France
Pearaza ....Spain
Pechelee..Prov. of China
Pedrasa...............Spain
Pegnitz ....Bavaria
Peina ....Hanover
Peiss ....Bavaria
Pekin.................China
Pembroke ...Massachusets
Penang,Prince of Wales's Island
Penaranda..............Spain
Peniscola..............Spain
Pennsylvania...one of the United States
Pensacola.............Florida
Penza.................Russia
Penzlin.........Mecklenburg
Pera...................Turkey
Pergamino, Buenos Ayres
Périgueux ....France
Perm ....Russia
Pernambuco,Prov.ofBrazl
Pernau ....Russia
Péronne...............France
Perpignan ....France
Persia..............*see* Persia
Perth...............Australia
Peru................*see* Peru
Perugia ....Tuscany
Pesaro.......Papal States
Pescara...............Naples
Peshawar..........Hindostan
Pesth...............Hungary
Petersburg..........Russia
Petersburg ....Georgia
Petersburg,NewHampshr
Petersburg ....Virginia
Peterwaradin.....Hungary
Peyrehorade.........France
Pezenas ....France
Pfaffenhosen ......Bavaria
Pfatten..............Bavaria
Phalsbourg..........France
Pharsa ....Greece
Philadelphia, Pennsylvan
Philippeville.........Algeria
Philippeville.........France
Philippines (the) ....E.I. Archipelago
Piauhy....Prov. of Brazil
Picenza........*see* Placentia
Picardy..Prov. of France
Pico ....Azores
Pictou.........Nova Scotia
Pierre Buffiere.......France
Pietra (la)..........Sardinia
Pieve (la)...........Sardinia
Pignerol ....Sardinia
Pillau...............Prussia
Pilsen...............Bohemia
Pilstling...............Bavaria
Pina.................Spain
Pisa ....Tuscany
Pisco ....Peru
Pistoia...............Tuscany
Pitea ....Sweden
Pithimiers ....France
Pittsburg...............Ohio
Pittsfield....Massachusets
Pittstown..............Maine
Pittstown.....New Jersey
Piverone............Sardinia
Place.........Mecklenburg
Placencia.............Spain
Placentia.........*see* Italy
Plate Forme, St.Domingo
Platling..............Bavaria
Plattsburg, United States
Pleinfelden.........Bavaria
Ploermel.............France
Plombieres...........France
Plon...............Denmark
Plymouth, Massachusetts
Podgorce ....Poland
Podolia, (Polish Ukraine) *see* Russia
Podolsh ....Russia
Point de Galle.....Ceylon
PointManato,ForWIndies
Point de Nipe..For.West Indies
Point Porto Rico.....For. West Indies
Point Tanamo, For. West Indies
Point Xibra....For. West Indies
Poirino..............Sardinia
Poitiers...............France
Poitou, *or La Vendée*.... Prov of France
Poix ....France
Pola ....Dalmatia
Poland ....*see* Poland
Polignano............Naples
Poligny ....France
Poltawa...Prov. of Russia
Pomerania,Prov.ofPrussa
Ponce...For. West Indies
Poncin................France
Pondicherry ..Hindostan
Pons...................France
Pont-à-Marg.........France
Pontarlier...........France
Pont Audemer.......France
Pont-Cananesé ..Sardinia
Pont-de-Beauvoisin ...... Sardinia
Pont d'Ouilly.........France
Ponte-Grande.......Sardinia
Pont-Gibaud.........France
Pontivy ....France
Pont l'Eveque ....France
Pont (le)....Switzerland
Pontoise ....France
Pontorson............France
Ponts (les) ..Switzerland
Pont-St. Esprit ..France
Pont-sur-Yonne ..France
Poonah ....Bombay
Popayan............Venezuela
Poppenhausen ......Bavaria
Porrentry .....Switzerland
Porta ....Portugal
Portalegre..........Portugal
Port Antonio.......Jamaica
Port-au-Prince ....St. Domingo
Port Dalrymple......Van Dieman's Land
Port de Vaux ....France
Port Huasco.......Mexico
Port Mahon.......Minorca
Port Haytien,St.Domingo
Port Jackson....Australia
Portland ....Maine
Port Louis ....Mauritius
Port Macquarie.......Van Dieman's Land
Port Maurice.......Sardinia
Port Nicholson.......New Zealand
Port Penn.......Delaware
Port Philip, *see*PortPhilip
Porto Bello.....Venezuela
Porto Rico.........Spanish West Indies
Port Royal.........Jamaica
Port Royal....Martinique
Porto Plata, St. Domingo
Porto del Principe...For. West Indies
Porto Seguro.....Prov. of Brazil
Portsmouth,N Hampshire
Portugal......*see* Portugal
Posega...............Sclavonia
Posen, a Prov. of Prussia
Posneck, Saxe-Meiningen
Possenheim ....Bavaria
Potosi ....Bolivia
Potsdam ....Prussia
Povoa ....Portugal
Pouzanges ....France
Prades...............France
Prades...............Spain
Præsto...............Denmark
Prague...............Bohemia
Prairie.......Lower Canada
Prato.................Tuscany
Prats de Molo.......France
Pré St. Didien..Sardinia
Presburg ....Hungary
Prez-en-Pail........France
Prince Edward's Island.. British North America.
Prince of Wales Island... *see* India
Princeton..............Illinois
Privas.................France
Provence, Prov. of France
Providence .....Bahamas
Providence, Rhode Island
Provincetown,Massachust
Provins...............France
Prussia ....*see* Germany
Przemyzl ....Gallicia
Pskof....Prov. of Russia
Puebla...................Spain
Puebla de los Angelos... Mexico
Puerto Cabello,Venezuela
Puerto de Lamar, Bolivia
Puerto Espana..Trinidad
Puget Theniers, Sardinia
Puis Laurens.......France
Pullicate.........Hindostan
Pultowa..............Russia
Punderpoor ...Hindostan
Purchena..............Spain
Puy de Dôme...Dept. of France
Puy (le) ....France
Pyrenees (Eastern), Dept. of France
Pyrenees (Lower)..Dept. of France
Pyrenees (Upper)..Dept. of France
Quackenbruick..Hanover
Quagliuzzo ....Sardinia
Quangsee, Prov. of China
Quebec ....Canada
Quedlinburgh ....Prussia
Queretaro ....Mexico
Quillan...............France
Quimper...............France
Quimperlé ....France
Quingey.............France
Quito................Colombia
Quito..............the Equator
Raab ....Hungary
Rabat ....Morocco
Racconigi..........Sardinia
Radow...............Poland
Rafat.................Spain
Ragatz ....Switzerland
Ragusa ....Dalmatia
Raleigh ...North Carolina
Ramaru................France
Rambouillet..........France
Rampoor...............Delhi
Ramslok ....Oldenburg
Randers..............Denmark
Rangoon ....Hindostan
Raon l'Etape.........France
Rapallo..............Sardinia
Rapperschwyl,Switzerlnd
Rastadt...............Baden
Rastede...........Oldenburg
Ratisbon............Bavaria
Ratzeburg ....Denmark
Ravenna.....Papal States
Ravières..............France
Ravensburg, Wirtemburg
Rawa..................Portugal
Recco................Sardinia
Recife...............Brazil
Redon..................France
Redefin.........Mecklenburg
Rees....................Prussia
Regan..................Russia
Regen.................Bavaria
Regensberg ..Switzerland
Regensburg..........Bavaria

Regensburg ......Bavaria
Reggio ....Modena
Reggio ....Naples
Rehburg.........Hanover
Rehna.......Mecklenburg
Reichenhal ....Bavaria
Reichensachsen ....Hesse
Reidlingen ..Wirtemburg
Reinach ......Switzerland
Reinheim...........Hesse
Remberviller .....France
Remiremont.........France
Remmels........Denmark
Rempelin....Mecklenburg
Renan ....Switzerland
Rendsburg .....Denmark
Renneroth ....Nassau
Rennes ....France
Réole (la) ....France
Requena ....Spain
Rethel ....France
Rethem ....Hanover
Retimo ....Candia
Rena...................Spain
Reuss..see German States
Reutlingen ..Wirtemburg
Revel.................Russia
Revilla ....Mexico
Reyden.......Switzerland
Rheims ....France
Rheinfelden..Switzerland
Rheinigg.........Switzerland
Rhine (Lower)..Dept. of France
Rhine (Upper)..Dept. of France
Rhine ....Prov. of Prussia
Rhode Island..one of the United States
Rhodes (Isle) ....Turkey
Rhodez ....France
Rhone...Dept. of France
Riaisân...Prov. of Russia
Ribadavia.............Spain
Riben..............Denmark
Riberac................France
Ribnitz.........Mecklenburg
Richmond............Virginia
Richterschwyl,Switzerlnd
Rieux ....France
Riez ....France
Riga ....Russia
Rimini.......Papal States
Ringkiobing.....Denmark
Rinteln........Hesse Cassel
Rio Grande do Norte.... Prov. of Brazil
Rio Grande do Sul ..... Prov. of Brazil
Rio Hacha ......Venezuela
Rio Janeiro..........Brazil
Rio Pardo..............Brazil
Riom ....France
Ripen ....Denmark
Ritzbüttel ....Hamburg
Rir[illegible]ella ....Spain
Riva[illegible] ....Sardinia
Rivesaltes..........France
Rivoli...............Sardinia
Roanne ....France
Robbio ....Sardinia
Robel ....Mecklenburg
Roccasterone ....Sardinia
Rocella ....Naples
Roche.........Switzerland
Roche (la) ....Sardinia
RocheBernard(la),France
Rochechouart........France
Rochefort ....France
Rochefort ....Switzerland
Rochefoucauld(la)France
Rochejean ....Turkey
Rochelle (la) ....France
Rochester ....New York
Rocky Mount.....Virginia
Rocroy ....France
Roeskilde.........Denmark
Rodack......Saxe-Coburg-Gotha
Rodbye ....Denmark
Rodenberg ....Hesse
Rodenkirchen, Oldenburg
Rodez ....France
Rôdome ....France
Rodrigues...see Mauritius
Rohilcund ....Hindostan
Rohrback ....Bavaria
Rolle ....Switzerland
Romagnano.......Sardinia
Romainmotier, Switzerlnd
Roman States....see Italy
Rome.........Papal States
Romhild, Saxe Meiningen
Romney ....Virginia
Romenay ....France
Romont ....Switzerland
Romorantin ....France
Romrod ....Hesse
Roncesvalles...........Spain
Ronda ....Spain
Ronne...............Denmark
Ronneburg, Saxe-Altenbg
Roquefort ....France
Rorschack ...Switzerland
Rosas.....................Spain
Roschild ....Denmark
Roseau ....Dominica
Rosenheim.........Bavaria
Rosoy ....France
Rossano.................Naples
Rossbrunn.........Bavaria
Rossetta ....Egypt
Rosshaupten........Bavaria
Rossiniere....Switzerland

RostockMklnbrg.Schwern
Rostrenen ....France
Rota..................Spain
Ro[illegible] ....Bavaria
Rothen[illegible] ....Hanover
Rothenburg [illegible]
Rothenburgh.......Bavaria
Rotterdam ....Holland
Rotthenburg,Wirtemburg
Rottingen..........Bavaria
Rottweill....Wirtemburg
Rotz...............Bavaria
Rouen..............France
Rougemont...Switzerland
Roumelia, Part of Turkey
Roussillon,Prov.ofFrance
Roveredo...........Illyria
Rovigo, Venetian Lombdy
Roxbury....Massachusets
Royan ....France
Roye..................France
Rudesheim..........Nassau
Rudolstadt..Schwarzburg
Rudkioping......Denmark
Rue ....France
Rued..........Switzerland
Ruerderthal...Switzerland
Ruffec...............France
Rugeleo ....France
Rukersdorf ....Bavaria
Rumelia, Prov. of Turkey
Rumilly ....Sardinia
Rungpoor ....Bengal
Ruremonde ....Holland
Rusoer ....Norway
Russia ....*see* Russia
Rutland....Massachusets
Rutland ....Vermont
Rutshuk...........Turkey
Saal.................B[illegible]
Saalfeld, Saxe-[illegible]
Saalmuster ....Hesse
Saanen.........S[illegible]tzerland
Saarbruck...... Prussia
Saba..Dutch West Indies
Sable ....France
Sables (les).........Fra[illegible]
Sables d'Olonne ..Fran[illegible]
Saby ....Denm[illegible]
Sacket's Harbour, N.York
Saffi ....Morocco
Saigong ....Hindostan
St.Affrique.........France
St.Agreve ....France
St.Aignau.........France
St.Amand ....France
St.Ambrogio........Sardinia
St.Andre ....Portugal
St.Andrew's,N.Brunswck
St.Anna..........Venezuela
St.Anna de Tamantipin... Chagres
St.Anne............Jamaica
St.Antonin ....France
St.Antonio..........Brazil
St.Aubin du Cormier .... France
St.Aubin.....Switzerland
St.Augustine .....Florida
St.Avolot ....France
St.Barraux ....France
St.Bartholomew ...Sp.W. Indies
St.Beat ....France
St.Begnigno .....Sardinia
St.Benoit du Sault,France
St.Blaise .....Switzerland
St.Bonnet ....France
St.Brieux ....France
St.Calais...........France
St.Catherine,Prov.ofBrazl
St.Cere.............,France
St.Chamond........France
St.Christo[illegible]her's, or St. Kitts
St.Clai[illegible] ....France
St.Clo[illegible] ....France
Sainte Croix, Switzerland
St.Croix,Danish W.Indies
St.Damiano .....Sardinia
St.Denis ....France
St.Die-sur-Loire....France
St.Domingo........*see* St. Domingo
St.Dorothy ......Jamaica
St.Esprit..........France
St.Etienne ....France
St.Eustatia....Dutch W. Indies
St.Eustatius ....British West Indies
St.Florentin........France
St.Flour............France
St.Gall ....Swiss Canton
St.Gaudens ....France
St.Geniez ....France
St.George ....Azores
St.George ....Demerara
St.George ....Grenada
St.Germain ....France
St.Germano ....Sardinia
St.Gilles ....France
St.Gingolph, Switzerland
St.Giorgio ....Sardinia
St.Girons ....France
St.Helena ....Africa
St.Hippolyte........France
St.Imier.......Switzerland
St.Jago,*see*St.Jago deCuba
St.Jago de Compostella .. Spain
St.Jean ....France
St.Jean-de-Luz ....France
St.Jean-de-Roi ......France

St.Jean-de-Maurienne ... Switzerland
St.Joao del Rey ...Brazil
St.John's, Newfoundland
St.John's, NewBrunswick
[illegible] W. Indies
St.Juan ......Porto Rico
St.Juan de Nicaragua ... Honduras
St.Julien ....Sardinia
St.Julien ....France
St.Julien de Chep, France
St.Junien ....France
St.Kitt's,Brit.WestIndies
St.Lèonard............France
St.Lô ....France
St.Lorenzo ....Spain
St.Lorenzo ....Majorca
St.Lucar ....Spain
St.Lucia, Brit WestIndies
St.Luis de Potosi, Mexico
St.Lys....................France
St.Malo ....France
St.Marie ....France
St.Martina ....Sardinia
St.Martin's,F.WestIndies
St.Mary ....Azores
St.Matthews ....Brazil
St.Maurice ..Switzerland
St.Maximim ....France
St.Michael's ....Azores
St.Mihiel ....France
St.Nicholas .....Belgium
St.Omer..............France
St.Papoul ....France
St.Peray ....France
St.Petersburg .....Russia
St.Pierre.............France
St.Pierre .....Martinique
St.Pierre d'Albigny ..... Sardinia
St.Pons ....France
St.Pourcain ....France
St.Quentin.........France
S[illegible] Rambert ....France
[illegible] Rer[illegible] ....Sardinia
[illegible].Remy ....France
St.Romain ....France
St.Salvador, or Bahia
St.Salvador ....Honduras
St.Salvadore de Bayamo... For. West Indies
St.Salvatore ....Sardinia
St.Saphorin..Switzerland
St.Savin ....France
St.Sebastian ....Spain
St.Sernin ....France
St.Seven ....France
St.Stephono Marina ..... Sardinia
St.Sulpice ....France
St.Sulpice ......Switzerland
St.Thomé d'Angostura .. Venezuela
St Thom[illegible]...Danish West Indies
S[illegible]on ....Belgium
St[illegible]pez ......France
St.[illegible]es ....Portugal
St.Vallery ....France
St.Vallien ....France
St.Vincent de Tyrosse ... France
St.Vincent's ..West Indies
St.Yrieux ....France
Saintes...........France
Sala ....Sweden
Salamanca..........Spain
Salamis...........Greece
Saldana ....Spain
Sale de-Castelnuoro ...... Sardinia
Salem..........Hindostan
Salem.......Massachusets
Salem ....New Jersey
Salerno ....Naples
Salinas ....Spain
Salins ....France
Sallanches ......Sardinia
Salle (la)..........Sardinia
Sallee ....Morocco
Saluzzo...........Sardinia
Salon ....[illegible]rance
Salona..............[illegible]reece
Salonica ....[illegible]reece
Salswedel ....[illegible]russia
Salvatierra.......Portugal
Salzburg ....Austria
Salzg[illegible] ....Hano[illegible]
Salzungen,Saxe-Me[illegible]ingen
Samar..........Phi[illegible]ppines
Samara ....Russia
Samarang..............Java
Sambor ....Gallicia
Samer ....France
Samos Isle ....Turkey
Sana ....Arabia
Sanazzaro..........Sardinia
San Blas ....Mexico
San Blas Guadalaxa .... Mexico
Sancerre.............France
Sandel...........Oldenburg
Sandomier,Prov, [illegible]and
San Felipe ....Spain
San Francisco........Brazil
San Juan de Nicaragua... *see* Chagres
San Juan de Porto Rico. Porto Rico
San Justo ....Spain
San Luis Potosi ..a State of Mexico
San Marino, Papal States

San Paulo, Prov. of Brazil
San Salvador.......Mexico
SantaCruz,CanaryIslands
Santa Cruz de la Sierra.. Peru
Santa Cruz del Quiche... Mexico
Santa Fè de Bogotá .... New Grenada
Santa Fé ....Mexico
Santa Fé............Spain
Santa Martha, *see* Chagres
SantaMaura,IonianIslnds
Santander............Spain
Santarem ....Portugal
Santhia............Sardinia
Santiago...Prov. of Chili
Santiago..............Spain
Santiago...........Venezuela
Santiago de Cuba...Cuba
Santillana.............Spain
Santona.................Spain
Saône (Upper)..Dept. of France
Saone and Loire, Dept. of France
Saragossa ....Spain
Sardinia ......*see* Sardinia
Sardval.............Portugal
Sargel..................Algeria
Sarlat ....France
Sarmenstorf..Switzerland
Sarnen ....Switzerland
Sarrebourg...........France
Sarreguemines ......France
Sarrion ....Spain
Sarthe...Dept. of France
Sassari..............Sardinia
Saulieu ....France
Saumur................France
Sauze ....France
Savana la Mar....Jamaica
Savanilla.........Venezuela
Savannah ....Georgia
Savenay...............France
Saverne ....France
Savigliano ....Sardinia
Savigné ....France
Savona ....Sardinia
Sax Kiolung.......Denmark
Saxe-Altenburg.... } *see* German States
Saxe Coburg Gotha }
Saxe-Meiningen.... }
Saxe-Weimar........ }
Saxony,*see*NorthernStates
Sazzana.............Sardinia
Scala Nova ....Turkey
Scarana ....Sardinia
Scarborough.........Tobago
Sceaux ....France
Schaafstedt ....Denmark
Schaffhausen, Switzerland
Schambach..........Bava[illegible]a
Schapen..............Hanov[illegible]r
Scharrel ....Oldenbu[illegible]
Scharzfeld ....Hanover
Schaumberg Lippe...... German States
Schelestat ....France
Schellersage ....Hanover
Schemnitz ....Hungary
Scheveling ....Holland
Schiedam ....Holland
[illegible]nznach...Switzerland
Schirwan, Prov. of Russia
Schlachtern ....Hesse
Schladen ....Hanover
Schleswig..........Denmark
Schlitz...................Hesse
Schmalkalden.........Hesse
Schmölla,Saxe-Altenburg
Schnackenburg...Hanover
Schoefftland, Switzerland
Schoenenwerth, Switzrlnd
Schonberg.............Bavaria
Schönberg..........Denmark
Schönberg ...Mecklenburg
Schönemoos.....Oldenburg
Schöngau ....Bavaria
Schonram ....Bavaria
Schöppenstadt,Brunswick
Schorndorf ...Wirtemburg
Schortens ....Oldenburg
Schrobenhausen..Bavaria
Schumla ....Turkey
Schwabach ....Bavaria
Schwalbach ....Nassau
Schwan ....Mecklenburg
Schwandorf ....Bavaria
Schwartzburg Rodolstadt, *see* German States
Schwartzburg Sonderhausen ..*see* German States
Schwarzenburg, Switzrlnd
Schwarzenfeld........Bavaria
Schweidnitz..........Prussia
Schweinfurth........Bavaria
Schwerin ....Mecklenburg
Schweitz.....Swiss Canton
Sciglio..................Naples
Scinde,Prov.of Hindostan
Scio (Isle)............Turkey
Scituate ......Massachusets
Sclavonia.....*see* Hungary
Scutari...near Constantinople
Scutari ...Upper Albania
Seara......Prov. of Brazil
Sebastopol.............Russia
Sebeneco ....Dalmatia
Secadon ....Spain
Sechuen ...Prov. of China
Sechura ....Peru
Sedau ....France

Seefeld ....Oldenburg
Seengen.......Switzerland
Seenpach .....Switzerland
Segeberg ....Denmark
Segorbe ....Spain
Segovia.................Spain
Ségré....................France
Sehweyburg ..Oldenburg
Seignes..................France
Seine...Dept. of France
Seine(Low)Dept.ofFrance
Seine et Marne..Dept. of France
Seine et Oise......Dept. of France
Seistan,a Prov.of Hindostn
Seligenstadt..........Hesse
Semenhoud...........Egypt
Semlin.......Transylvania
Semur ....France
Senegal...............Africa
Sengwarden ..Oldenburg
Senlis ....France
Sennaar...............Nubia
Sens...................France
Serampore ....Bengal
Serdao ....Portugal
Seregipe, a Prov. of Brazil
Seringapatam ..Hindostan
Serpa ....Portugal
Serravalle ....Sardinia
Sert....................Turkey
Servia ....*see* Austria
Sestri ....Sardinia
Seteef ....Algeria
Settimo-Torrinese,Srdinia
Settimo Vittone, Sardinia
Setubal ....*see* St. Ubes
Severac..............France
Seville...................Spain
Sevres Deux .....Dept. of France
Seychelles (the) ....*see* Mauritius
Seyja ....Portugal
Seyssel..............Sardinia
Seyssel...............France
Sezanne ....France
Shahjehanpoor .....Delhi
Shanghai.............China
Shantung, Prov. of China
Shawnee Town....Illinois
Shensee ..Prov. of China
Shiraz..................Persia
Shoa (*Letters should be addressed to the care of an agent at Aden*).
Siak ....Sumatra
Siam ....*see* India
Siberia ....*see* Russia
Sicilies (Two) ...*see* Italy
Sicyon.................Greece
Sidon ....Syria
Sienna ....Tuscany
Sierra Leone....*see* Africa
Sierre ....Switzerland
Signeville ....France
Silesia...Prov. of Prussia
Silicia.............*see* Austria
Silistria................Turkey
Sillenstede ....Oldenburg
Silves ....Portugal
Simbach ....Bavaria
Simbirsk ....Russia
Singanfou ....China
Singapore, *see* East Indies
Singhofen.............Nassau
Sinigaglia ..Papal States
Sinope.................Turkey
Sins.................Switzerland
Sion ....Switzerland
Siout.....................Egypt
Sissach..........Switzerland
Sisteron.................France
Skanderburg ...Denmark
Skara....................Sweden
Skielskiör ....Denmark
Slangemp.............Denmark
Sleswick ....Denmark
Slobodes Ukraine...Prov. of Russia
Slugs ....Holland
Smolensko,Prov of Russia
Smyrna ....*see* Turkey
Society Islands.............*see* Sandwich Islands
Soissons...............France
Soleure,....Swiss Canton
Soller...................Majorca
Solon ....United States
Soltau ....Hanover
Sombreretti............Mexico
Sommariva ....Sardinia
Somme...Dept. of France
Sommershausen ..Bavaria
Sommieres ....France
Sonceboz........Switzerland
Sonderburg .....Denmark
Sonneberg,Saxe-Meiningen
Sonora & Cinalio ....a State of Mexico
Sontra ....Hesse
Soolso..E. I. Archipelago
Sophia..................Turkey
Sorèze..................France
Soria ....Spain
Soröe..................Denmark
Sospello...............Sardinia
Sourabaya ....Java
Souterraine ....France
South Australia..........*see* Australia
South Brabant....Prov. of Belgium

South Carolina ....one of the United States
Spa.......................Belgium
Spaichingen, Wirtemburg
Spain..................*see* Spain
Spalatro................Dalmatia
Spandan ....Prussia
Spangenberg...........Hesse
Spanish Town ..Jamaica
Speir ....Bavaria
Spencer's Gulf, Australia
Spezia..................Sardinia
Spezzia.....Isle of Greece
Splugen.........Switzerland
Sprackensehl.......Hanover
Springe ....Hanover
Stade....................Hanover
Stadt-Oldendorf,Brunswk
Staeffa.............Switzerland
Staffelbach ..Switzerland
Stalwang.............Bavaria
Stanislaus ....Gallicia
Stantz.............Switzerland
Stargard...............Prussia
Starnberg ....Bavaria
Staten Island...New York
Statesburg,SouthCarolina
Statesville,NorthCarolina
Stavelot ....Holland
Stavenhagen, Mecklenbrg
Steckboren....Switzerland
Steenbergen...........Holland
Stege ....Denmark
Stein ....Bavaria
Stein ....Switzerland
Steinau..................Hesse
Steinbach ....Hesse
Steinfeld ......Oldenburg
Steinbœring............Bavaria
Stendahl ....Prussia
Sternberg......Mecklenburg
Stettfeld...............Bavaria
Stettin ....Prussia
Steyer ....Austria
Stockey ....Hanover
Stockholm ....Sweden
Stollhamm ....Oldenburg
Stolpe ....Prussia
Storchedinge......Denmark
Stottel..................Hanover
Stralsund...............Prussia
Stratford ....Connecticut
Stramhino ....Sardinia
Strasburg...............France
Straubing..............Bavaria
Strelitz.........Mecklenburg
Stresa...................Sardinia
Strohhausen ..Oldenburg
Stronstadt................Sweden
Stry........................Gallicia
Stubbekiobing...Denmark
Stuhlweissemberg........ Hungary
Sturamger ....Hungary
Stuttgard.......Wirtemburg
Styria ....*see* Austria
Suderfors ....Sweden
Suez.......................Egypt
Suhlingen...........Hanover
Sully ....France
Sulzbach.............Bavaria
Sülze ....Mecklenburg
Sumatra..*see* Archipelago East Indian
Summiswald..Switzerland
Sundswall.............Sweden
Surat.....................Guzerat
Surinam, For.West Indies
Sursee...........Switzerland
Susa.....................Sardinia
Swally..................Guzerat
Swan River; *see* Australia
Sweaborg ....Russia
Sweden ....*see* Sweden
Swendborg ....Denmark
Switzerland,*see* Switzerlnd
Sycke ....Hanover
Sydney..............Australasia
Sydney..........Cape Breton
Sympheropol..........Russia
Syra ....Isle of Greece
Syracuse..................Sicily
Syria ....*see* Syria
Szarnygrod..........Podolia
Szegedin ....Hungary
Taas.......................Arabia
Tabasco..................Mexico
Tabor ....Bohemia
Tabreez..................Persia
Tacna ....Peru
Taganrog ....Russia
Talavera ....Spain
Talchauno..............Chagres
Tallahassee ....Florida
Talmont..................France
Taman ....Russia
Tamaulipas......a State of Mexico
Tambof..Prov. of Russia
Tampico ....Mexico
Tangier..................Barbary
Tanjore...............Hindostan
Tanta ....Egypt
Tappahannoc.......Virginia
Tarançon ....Spain
Tarascon.................France
Tarbes ....France
Tarento.....................Naples
Targowitz.................Podolia
Tarifa........................Spain
Tarma.........................Peru
Tarn........Dept. of France
Tarn et Garonne, Dept. of France

Tarnopol ....Gallicia
Taro. ....Portugal
Tarragona ....Spain
Tarsas ....Turkey
Tasco ....Mexico
Tatta............Scinde
Taunda ....Hindostan
Taurida..Prov. of Russia
Tauris...........Persia
Tavasthus ....Russia
Tay-yuen-fou ......China
Tchekiang, Prov.of China
Tcherkask.........Russia
Tchernigow......Prov. of Russia
Tching-tou-fou ....China
Tchusan Islands ...China
Tecali...........Mexico
Teflis...........Georgia
Teheran.............Irak
Tehuantepec.......Mexico
Teisendorf.......Bavaria
Tejuco............Brazil
Tellicherry ....Hindostan
Temeswar......Hungary
Teneriffe, Canary Islands
Tenda.............Sardinia
Tennessee......one of the United States
Tepic..............Mexico
Terceira ....Azores
Ternovo ....Turkey
Terracini ....Papal States
Terra del Greco...Naples
Teruel ....Spain
Tessin ......Mecklenburg
Tessin ....Swiss Canton
Tête-de-Buch......France
Teterow.....Mecklenburg
Tettens...........Oldenburg
Tetuan...........Morocco
Texas ....*see* Texas
Texel ....Holland
Tezcuco ....Mexico
Theaki....Ionian Islands
Themar..Saxe Meiningen
Theresopol.......Hungary
Thiedennuese ...Hanover
Thiel ....Holland
Thiers..............France
Thimers............France
Thionville..........France
Thisted..........Denmark
Thizy ....France
Thonon...........Sardinia
Thorigny ....France
Thouars...........France
Thumbach........Bavaria
Thun.........Switzerland
Tiensing...........China
Tilsit ....Prussia
Timbuctoo,Central Africa
Timor..E. I. Archipelago
Tinchebray ....France
Tinghai ....China
Tinnevelly.....Hindostan
Tittmaning ....Bavaria
Tivoli ......Papal States
Tlascala,a State of Mexico
Tobago, Brit. West Indies
Tobolsk ....Siberia
Tocat ....Turkey
Toggenburg..Switzerland
Tokat..............Turkey
Tokay.............Hungary
Tokerem.........Belgium
Toledo ....Spain
Tolesburg ....Russia
Tolna ....Hungary
Tolosa ....Spain
Tolu.............Venezuela
Tolz ....Bavaria
Tondern ....Denmark
Tongchoo..........China
Tongres..........Belgium
Tonnene ....France
Tönningen ......Denmark
Tonquin....Cochin China
Tonsberg...........Norway
Toolombah ....Hindostan
Töplitz.........Bohemia
Tordesillas..........Spain
Torgau............Russia
Toro ....Spain
Torres Vedras...Portugal

Tortola, Brit. West Indies
Tortona ....Sardinia
Tortosa.............Spain
Totana...............Spain
Toul ....France
Toulon..............France
Toulouse............France
Touraine, Prov. of France
Tour-du-Pin (le)..France
Tournay...........Belgium
Tournon ....France
Tournus.............France
Tours ....France
Toury ....France
Tralleborg ....Sweden
Trancasco ....Portugal
Tranckiaer......Denmark
Trani...............Naples
Tranquebar....Hindostan
Transylvania, *see* Hungary
Trapani ....Sicily
Tras os Montes...Prov. of Portugal
Traunick...........Turkey
Traustein ....Bavaria
Traves.........Switzerland
Trebisond..........Turkey
Trecate............Sardinia
Treignac.............France
Trelawney..........Jamaica
Trenchin ....Hungary
Trent..............Illyria
Trenton ......New Jersey
Trenton....North Carolina
Treport..............France
Treves .....West Prussia
Treviso,VenetianLombrdy
Treysa ....Hesse
Trichinopoly ..Hindostan
Trieste ....Illyria
Trincomalee ...Hindostan
Trinidad,British W.Indies
Trinidad de Cuba ...For. West Indies
Trino.............Sardinia
Tripoli.........*see* Barbary
Tripoli ....Syria
Tripolizza............Greece
Trogen ....Switzerland
Trois Rivières ....Dist. of Canada
Troja ....Naples
Troki............Lithuania
Troppau.............Moravia
Trouse ....Denmark
Troy .... [illegible] York
Troy .... [illegible]
Troyes ... [illegible]
Truns ... [illegible]
Truxi[illegible]
Truxi[illegible]
Truxi[illegible]
Truxi[illegible]
Tub[illegible]
Tübi[illegible]
Tude[illegible]
Tuej[illegible]
Tula... [illegible]
Tulle... [illegible]
Tunis... [illegible]
Tunja... [illegible]
Turchei[illegible]
Turenne........... [illegible]
Turin........... [illegible]
Turkey .... [illegible]
Turk's Isl[illegible]
Turnan.......... [illegible]
Tuscaloosa.......Alabama
Tuscany ....*see* Italy
Tuttlingen.. Wirtemburg
Tuy..................Spain
Tver......Prov. of Russia
Tyre..............Syria
Tyrol ....*see* Austria
Ubeda ....Spain
Uchte...........Hanover
Uddervalla..........Sweden
Udina,Venetian-Lombrdy
Uelsen..............Hanover
Uetersen ....Denmark
Uffenheim ....Bavaria
Ukraine, Prov. of Russia
Ulaardingen, East Indian Archipelago
Ulietea ..Society Islands

Ulm.........Wirtemberg
Ulsingen ....Nassau
Ulyssingen ......Holland
Umea................Lapland
United States ....*see* United States
Unity............Maryland
Unterbrück ....Bavaria
Untersen ....Switzerland
Unterwalden, SwissCantn
Upsal ....Sweden
Urbana ....Ohio
Urbana............Virginia
Urbino.......Papal States
Urburg ....Denmark
Urgel ....Spain
Uri.........Swiss Canton
Ursern...........Switzerland
Uruguay, Prov. of Brazil
Urumea ....Persia
Ushant, Island of, France
Uslar...............Hanover
Ussel ....France
Utelle..............Sardinia
Utica...........New York
Utrecht.............Holland
Uzel................France
Uzerche ....France
Uzes ....France
Vacha.......Saxe-Weimar
Vaiges..............France
Vaison..............France
Valais........Swiss Canton
Valangin..........Switzerland
Valdivia ..Prov. of Chili
Valença ....Portugal
Valençay ....France
Valence.. ....France
Valencia...Prov. of Spain
Valencia ....Venezuela
Valenciennes.......France
Valenza............Sardinia
Valetta (la)...........Malta
Valladolid ....Mexico
Valladolid............Spain
Valmy ....France
Valognes.............France
Valparaiso..............Chili
Valpelline.........Sardinia
Valtablado.............Spain
Vandalia ....Illinois
Van Dieman's Land....*see* Australia
Vannes ....France
Var.......Dept. of France
Varallo ....Sardinia
Varel ....Oldenburg
Varennes ....France
Varesdin ....Croatia
Vargos ....Spain
Varinas...........Venezuela
Varna ....Turkey
Varzi ....Sardinia
Vassy ....France
Vaucluse, Dept.of France
Vaucouleurs..........France
Vaud ....Swiss Canton
Vaulion.......Switzerland
Vaumarcus.....Switzerland
Vechta ....Oldenburg
Veichtach ....Bavaria
Velannera...........Spain
Velez-Malaga.........Spain
Vendée...Dept. of France
Vendôme ....France
Venerie ....Sardinia
Venetian-Lombardy ...*see* Venetian-Lombardy
Venezuela ...*see* Venezuela
Venice,Venetian-Lombrdy
Venlo...............Holland
Ventimiglia........Sardinia
Vera Cruz.........Mexico
Vera Paz............Mexico
Veragua...........Venezuela
Vercelli ....Sardinia
Verden ....Hanover
Verdun ....France
Verdun................Spain
Vermanton...........France
Vermont...........one of the United States
Verneuil ....France
Vernex ....Switzerland
Vernon ....**France**

Verona .....V. Lombardy
Verres ....Sardinia
Verrières ....Switzerland
Versailles ....France
Versetz ....Hungary
Vertus ....France
Verviers ....Belgium
Vervins..............France
Vesoul ....France
Vesprim...........Hungary
Vevay.........Switzerland
Viana ....Portugal
Viatka ....Russia
Vicenza......V. Lombardy
Vichney-Voloshok........ Russia
Vico Canavese ..Sardinia
Vic Tezensac.........France
Viege ....Switzerland
Vienna................Austria
Vienne ....France
Vienne ..Dept. of France
Vienne (Upper), Dept. of France
Vierzon..............France
Vigevano..........Sardinia
Vigo ....Spain
Vihiers...............France
Vilboel ....Hesse
Villach..............Illyria
Villa Bella ....Brazil
Villa Boa............Brazil
Villaconancia ....Spain
Villacosta...............Spain
Villa del Principe...Cuba
Villa Franca.....Portugal
Villa Franca.....Sardinia
Villa Nova........Portugal
Villa Nuova.......Sardinia
Villa Real...........Spain
Villa Viçosa........Portugal
Ville Contal ....France
Villedieu.............France
Villefort ....France
Villefrauche ....France
Villeneuve...........Sardinia
Villeneuve....Switzerland
Villeneuve-de-Berg........ France
Villeneuvre............France
Villers Coterets ...France
Villmergen ..Switzerland
Vilscibourg........Bavaria
Vilshofen............Bavaria
Vimiero ....Portugal
Vinaroz ....Spain
Vincennes ....France
Vincennes............Indiana
Vire...................France
Virgin Islands, W. Indies
Virginia ......one of the United States
Visbeck............Oldenburg
Viseu.................Portugal
Vistrorio............Sardinia
Viterbo..........Papal States
Vittoria ....Spain
Vitre ....France
Vitry le Français, France
Vivero ....Spain
Viviers ....France
Vivonne.................France
Vizini.....................Sicily
Vladimir, Prov. of Russia
Voghera ....Sardinia
Vogogna.............Sardinia
Voiron................France
Volhynia(Polish Ukraine) *see* Russia
Volkmarsen ....Hesse
Volmar ....Russia
Vologda ....Russia
Volpiano ....Sardinia
Volterra ....Tuscany
Voltri...............Sardinia
Vorchleim ....Bavaria
Voronetz, Prov. of Russia
Vorsfelde.......Brunswick
Vosges ..Dept. of France
Vouchang ....China
Vouziers...............France
Wabern ....Hesse
Waddens ....Oldenburg
Waddewarden, Oldenburg
Wadesborough,N Carolina

Waging...............Bavaria
Wahleroth.........Nassau
Waihlingen, Wirtemburg
Walburg..............Hesse
Walcheren ......Holland
Waldenburg, Switzerland
Waldenbuch,Wirtemburg
Waldheim ....Saxony
Waldkappel..........Hesse
Waldmunchen....Bavaria
Waldsassen ....Bavaria
Walkenried......Brunswick
Wallachia....Principality of Turkey
Wallenstatt..Switzerland
Walmeroth ....Nassau
Walpole, New Hampshire
Walsrode............Hanover
Walterswyl....Switzerland
Wandshedi.......Denmark
Wanfried..............Hesse
Wangen ....Wirtemburg
Warde...............Denmark
Wardenburg...Oldenburg
Waren.......Mecklenburg
Warfleth ....Oldenburg
Warnemünde,Mecklenbrg
Warsaw...............Poland
Washington ..Mississippi
Wassenburg .....Bavaria
Wassermungenau, Bvaria
Waterloo..............Belgium
Watertown, United States
Wattwyt ....Switzerland
Waxholm ....Sweden
Wecnen...............Hanover
Weesen...........Switzerland
Weilbach ....Nassau
Weile...............Denmark
Weilheim ....Bavaria
Weimar ....Saxe-Weimar
Weinfelden ..Switzerland
Weisham.............Bavaria
Weissemburg.......France
Weissenburgh ......Bavaria
Weissensfels ....Prussia
Weissenstadt.......Bavaria
Welle ....Hanover
Wels...................Austria
Wemding ....Bavaria
Wenersburg........Sweden
Werneck.............Bavaria
Wertheim ....Baden
Wertign ....Bavaria
Wesenberg...Mecklenberg
Wesenburg...........Russia
Westeras.............Sweden
Westerstede....Oldenburg
West Flanders...Prov. of Belgium
WestIndies,*see*WestIndies British and Foreign
Westphalia ...Province of Prussia
Westrum.......Oldenburg
Westuffeln..............Hesse
Wetten ....Hesse
Wheeling.............Virginia
Wiborg ....Denmark
Wiborg ....Russia
Widin ....Turkey
Wiefels ....Oldenburg
Wiefelstede ...Oldenburg
Wieliczca ....Gallicia
Wiesbaden ....Nassau
Wilbad............Wirtemburg
Wilkes....North Carolina
Williamstadt .....Holland
Willisau ....Switzerland
Wilmington........Delaware
Wilmington, N. Carolina
Wilmington ....Ohio
Wilna ....Lithuania
Wilster ....Denmark
Winbryholt........Denmark
Windecken ....Hesse
Windsheim............Bavaria
Windsor.......Australasia
Windsor .....Nova Scotia
Windsor ....Vermont
Winsen ....Hanover
Wintherthur, Switzerland
Wirtemburg..*see* German States
Wismar.....Mecklenburg

Witepsk............Lithuania
Wittenburg ......Prussia
Wittenburg, Mecklenburg
Wittengen............Hanover
Witzenhausen...........Hesse
Wlodimir ....Volhynia
Wohlen ......Switzerland
Woldegk ...Mecklenburg
Wolfegg ......Wirtemburg
Wolfhagen ....Hesse
Wollin....................Prussia
Wologda, Prov. of Russia
Wordinburg....Denmark
Worms, Hesse Darmstadt
Wôrrstadt...........Hesse
Wredenhagen, Mecklnbrg
Wunziedel..........Bavaria
Wüppels ....Oldenburg
Wurgan ....Bavaria
Wurges ....Nassau
Wurstorf ....Hanover
Wurtzbourg........Bavaria
Wurzach ....Wirtemburg
Wustrow..............Hanover
Wyl ....Switzerland
Xalapa..............Mexico
Xalisco.........a State of Mexico
Xeres ....Spain
Yakoutsh ....Siberia
Yarmouth....Nova Scotia
Yembo ....the Port of Medina
Yemen.........a District of Arabia
Yenne ....Sardinia
Yezd ....Persia
Yezdikhast ....Persia
Yniesta...................Spain
Yonne...Dept. of France
York.......................Canada
Ypres..................Belgium
Yssingeaux..........France
Ystad ....Sweden
Yucatan.......*see* Jucatan
Yunan....Prov. of China
Yverdun.......Switzerland
Yvetot ....France
Zaandam.............Holland
Zabea ....Spain
Zacatecas..........a State of Mexico
Zambor ....Hungary
Zamora....................Spain
Zandvoost..........Holland
Zanesville ....Ohio
Zante .....Ionian Islands
Zara......................Dalmatia
Zarrentin..Mecklenburgh
Zauxa ....Peru
Zealand, Prov. of Holland
Zealand,Island of Denmrk
Zebu............Philippines
Zelaya...............Mexico
Zella, Saxe-Coburg-Gotha
Zeres ....Mexico
Zeres ....Spain
Zetet...............Oldenburg
Zettlitz ....Bavaria
Zeulenroda............Reuss
Zeuz.......................Spain
Zeven..................Hanover
Ziegenhain ....Hesse
Zierenberg.............Hesse
Zieriksee............Holland
Zittau ....Saxony
Zizana ....Spain
Zlaczow.............Gallicia
Znaym ....Moravia
Zoffingen.....Switzerland
Zorge................Brunswick
Zorneding ....Bavaria
Zug.................Switzerland
Zurescel ....Bavaria
Zurich.........Switzerland
Zurita......................Spain
Zurzach ....Switzerland
Zusmarshausen ..Bavaria
Zutphen..............Holland
Zuybruck ....Bavaria
Zwiefalten...Wirtemburg
Zwischenalm..Oldenburg
Zwoll..................Holland

RATES OF POSTAGE UPON LETTERS INWARDS,

FROM *FRANCE*, AND FROM COUNTRIES THROUGH FRANCE, TO THE UNITED KINGDOM.—*(The Channel Islands excepted).*

COUNTRY		Combined British and Foreign Rates. Weighing under a ¼ oz.	Weighing ¼ and under ½ oz.	Weighing ½ and under ¾ oz.	Weighing ¾ and under 1 oz.	Weighing 1 oz. and under 1¼ ozs.
		s. d.	s. d.	s. d.	s. d.	s. d.
‡ **FRANCE & ALGERIA.**	British	0 5	0 5	0 10	0 10	1 8
	Foreign	0 5	0 10	1 3	1 8	2 1
	Total	0 10	1 3	2 1	2 6	3 9
Places in the Mediterranean, by the French Packet	British	0 5	0 5	0 10	0 10	1 8
	Foreign	0 10	1 8	2 6	3 4	4 2
	Total	1 3	2 1	3 4	4 2	5 10
German States served by the Office of Tour & Taxis	British	0 5	0 5	0 10	0 10	1 8
	Foreign	0 10	1 8	2 6	3 4	4 2
	Total	1 3	2 1	3 4	4 2	5 10
Northern States forwarded through the office of Tour & Taxis	British	0 5	0 5	0 10	0 10	1 8
	Foreign	1 3	2 6	3 9	5 0	6 3
	Total	1 8	2 11	4 7	5 10	7 11
Poland and Southern Russia	British	0 5	0 5	0 10	0 10	1 8
	Foreign	1 1	2 2	3 3	4 4	5 5
	Total	1 6	2 7	4 1	5 2	7 1
Two Sicilies, by the French Packet.	British	0 5	0 5	0 10	0 10	1 8
	Foreign	0 9	1 6	2 3	3 0	3 9
	Total	1 2	1 11	3 1	3 10	5 5
Greece, by French Packet	British	0 5	0 5	0 10	0 10	1 8
	Foreign	1 0	2 0	3 0	4 0	5 0
	Total	1 5	2 5	3 10	4 10	6 8
Turkey in Europe, and Scutari, through the Austrian offices	British	0 5	0 5	0 10	0 10	1 8
	Foreign	1	3 0	4 6	6 0	7 6
	Total	1 11	3 5	5 4	6 10	9 2
Southern Italy, Ionian Islands, & Greece	British	0 5	0 5	0 10	0 10	1 8
	Foreign	0 10	1 8	2 6	3 4	4 2
	Total	1 3	2 1	3 4	4 2	5 10
Austria, Belgrade & Cracow	British	0 5	0 5	0 10	0 10	1 8
	Foreign	1 0	2 0	3 0	4 0	5 0
	Total	1 5	2 5	3 10	4 10	6 8
Spain & Portugal, Sardinia, Tuscany & Lucca, Belgium, Holland, Prussia, Baden & Bavaria	British	0 5	0 5	0 10	0 10	1 8
	Foreign	0 5	0 10	1 3	1 8	2 1
	Total	0 10	1 3	2 1	2 6	3 9
Switzerland	British	0 5	0 5	0 10	0 10	1 8
	Foreign	0 6	1 0	1 6	2 0	2 6
	Total	0 11	1 5	2 4	2 10	4 2
Colonies & Countries, beyond sea	British	0 5	0 5	0 10	0 10	1 8
	Foreign	0 10	1 8	2 6	3 4	4 2
	Total	1 3	2 1	3 4	4 2	5 0

NEWSPAPERS.
* From Continental States .... } Two-pence each Newspaper.
‡ From the Mediterranean & Countries beyond Sea }
From France, Algeria & Belgium .... One Halfpenny each Newspaper.

(*) Spain excepted, from which country Newspapers are charged ½d. each.
(‡) Greece excepted, from which country Newspapers are charged 1d. each, when brought by the French packets

N.B. Periodical works not strictly Newspapers, are chargeable with the same Rates Inwards (from France, Holland and Belgium only), as similar publications which have *previously* received the sanction of the Postmaster General, are liable to Outwards; viz., not exceeding 2 oz., 1d.; exceeding 2 oz. and not exceeding 3 oz., 6d., and 2d. additional for each oz. afterwards up to 16 oz. beyond which weight packets *cannot be received.*

CLOSED MAILS.

COUNTRY		Combined British and Foreign Rates. Weighing under a ¼ oz.	Weighing ¼ and under ½ oz.	Weighing ½ and under ¾ oz.	Weighing ¾ and under 1 oz.	Weighing 1 oz. and under 1¼ oz
		BY FRENCH PACKET.				
		s. d	s. d.	s. d.	s. d.	s. d.
MALTA	British	0 5	0 5	0 10	0 10	1 8
	Foreign	0 8	1 4	2 0	2 8	3 4
	Total	1 1	1 9	2 10	3 6	5 0
Alexandria & Ionian Islands *Newspapers*, Two-pence each.	British	0 5	0 5	0 10	0 10	1 8
	Foreign	0 10	1 8	2 6	3 4	4 2
	Total	1 3	2 1	3 4	4 2	5 10
		BY BRITISH PACKET.				
MALTA	British	0 10	0 10	1 8	1 8	3 4
	Foreign	0 5	0 10	1 3	1 8	2 1
	Total	1 3	1 8	2 11	3 4	5 5
Alexandria & Ionian Islands	British	1 3	1 3	2 6	2 6	5 0
	Foreign	0 5	0 10	1 3	1 8	2 1
	Total	1 8	2 1	3 9	4 2	7 1
INDIA *Newspapers* Three-pence each.	British	1 5	1 5	2 10	2 10	5 8
	Foreign	0 5	0 10	1 3	1 8	2 1
	Total	1 10	2 3	4 1	4 6	7 9

‡ The *French* uniform rate of 5d. single, and so on in proportion, has reference to those Letters only the postage upon which is paid on delivery in the United Kingdom. If the French rate be paid in France, it then *varies* according to the distance, in conformity with the laws of France.

Hours for Posting Foreign and Colonial Letters and Newspapers.

LETTERS.

Throughout the following list it is to be understood, that where the despatch is stated to take place

In the Evening,

Letters can be posted at the Receiving Houses throughout the Metropolis until 5 30 P.M., *by the Letter Carriers ringing bells, on payment of one penny with each, from* 4 30 *to* 5 30 P.M., *at the Branch Post Offices at Charing Cross, Old Cavendish Street, and* 108, *Blackman Street, Borough, until* 6 P.M., *and with a fee of one penny (which must be paid by a Stamp affixed to the Letter) until* 6 45 P.M.; *at the Branch Post Office, in Lombard Street, until* 6 P.M., *and until* 7 P.M., *with a fee paid by means of a Penny Stamp affixed to the Letter; at the General Post Office, St. Martin's-le-Grand, until* 6 P.M., *and until* 7 P.M. *on payment of a fee of one penny (or an affixed Stamp), in addition to the postage (which must then be paid in advance), and from* 7 *until* 7 30 P.M., *upon payment of a fee of six-pence with each Letter. On*

TUESDAYS AND FRIDAYS.

Letters for France, Belgium, Holland, or Hamburg, or for the Mails passing through those places, are taken at the various Receiving Houses, and at the Branch Post Offices, Charing Cross, Old Cavendish Street; and Blackman Street, until 8 P.M.; *at the General Post Office, St. Martin's-le-Grand; and at the Branch Post Office, Lombard Street, until* 10 P.M.; *and at St. Martin's-le-Grand* ONLY, *from* 10 *until a quarter past* 10 P.M., *on payment of a fee of one penny, and until half-past* 10 P.M. *on payment of a fee of six-pence. For those Mails despatched in the*

MORNING,

Letters are in time at the Receiving Houses, and at the Charing Cross, Old Cavendish street, and Borough Branch Offices, until 8 A.M.; *at the General Post Office, and at the Branch Office, in Lombard Street, until* 8 30 A.M.

NEWSPAPERS

For those Mails despatched in the EVENING, *must be posted at the Receiving Houses before* 5 P.M.; *by the Letter Carriers ringing bells (on payment of one penny with each) from* 4 30 *to* 5 30 P.M.; *at the Branch Post Offices, before* 5 30 P.M.; *and at the General Post Office, St. Martin's-le-Grand, before* 6 P.M. *Those for Mails despatched in the* MORNING, *must be posted at the Receiving Houses before* 7 A.M.; *at the Branch Offices, Charing Cross, Old Cavendish Street, and Borough, before* 7 30 A.M.; *and at the General Post Office, and Branch Office, in Lombard Street, at a quarter before* 8 A.M.

Letters and Newspapers brought by the Mails, arriving in London, are always forwarded by those Colonial and Foreign Mails made up on the SAME MORNINGS.

UNIVERSAL

RATES OF POSTAGE

ON LETTERS AND NEWSPAPERS TO THE COLONIES AND FOREIGN PARTS,

WITH ROUTES OF MAILS AND DAYS OF THEIR DESPATCH.

The time of despatch stated is in all cases FROM LONDON.

All Newspapers to the Colonies or Foreign Parts must be posted within *seven* days from the date of publication; and to all places to which Newspapers are not sent free, the Postage on them must be paid in advance.

*** *Unpaid Letters specially addressed to be forwarded by routes which require postage to be paid in advance will not, if there be any means of transmitting them, be opened and returned to the writers for the payment of such postage, but will be despatched, if possible, by other routes, unpaid.*

The List of Cities and Principal Places throughout the World commences at page 1717.

Abyssinia.—No regular Mails. *Letters* should be addressed to the care of an agent at "Malta," or Aden, as opportunities for direct communication seldom occur.

Africa.—To the places in Africa not mentioned in this list, there are no regular Packets. Mails are despatched through the Ship Letter Office by every Outward-bound Vessel. Postage, 8d. not exceeding ½ an oz., and so on.

Newspapers to British Settlements in Africa, 1d. each. Other places (Algeria excepted) 2d. each.

Algeria. *See* FRANCE.

Alexandria.—*Letters* may be sent *unpaid* by the *French* Packet-boats, which leave *Marseilles* on the 1st, 4th, 11th, 21st and 24th of each month, at 5 P.M.; or may be *paid to destination*, 1s. 3d. under ¼ oz., 2s. 1d. under ½ oz., 3s. 4d. under oz., 4s. 2d. under 1 oz., 5s. 10d. under 1¼ ozs., and so on. Or *unpaid* by *British* packets, by Closed Mail from *Marseilles*, *paid to destination*, 1s. 8d. under ¼ oz., 2s. 1d. under ½ oz., 3s. 9d. under ¾ oz., 4s. 2d. under 1oz., 7s. 1d. under 1¼ ozs *By the Closed Mails*, which leave London on the 7th and 24th of each month (unless that should happen on a Sunday, and then the *following* day), *Letters are always forwarded*, unless otherwise directed. Letters may be forwarded *viâ* Southampton on the *mornings* of the 3d and 20th of each month (unless they fall on a Sunday, and then the *previous evening*), 1s. 6d. not exceeding ½ oz., *paid* or *unpaid*, and so on. For this route Letters should be addressed, "*viâ Southampton.*"

Newspapers, 2d. each by Southampton or by *French* Packet, and 3d. each by Closed Mail.

America. *See* UNITED STATES.

Arabia. *See* INDIA (EAST).

Archipelago (The Grecian), *viâ* France, *Letters* must be *paid* to Calais, 5d. not exceeding ½ an oz. and so on; or may be paid as far as *Trieste*, 1s. 3d. under ¼ oz.; 2s. 1d. under ½ oz.; 3s. 4d. under ¾ oz.; 4s. 2d. under 1 oz.; 5s. 10d. under 1¼ ozs., and so on. *See also* GREECE.

Newspapers, free by Packet; 1d. *viâ* France; 3d. by Closed Mail.

Archipelago (The East Indian).—Sumatra, Borneo, The Molucca (or Spice) Islands, and the Phillipines —No regular Mails. *Paid* Letters are forwarded through the *Ship Letter Office* "by private Ship," at every opportunity; or *viâ* Southampton, *if specially so addressed*, they may be forwarded by the Overland Indian Mail, *viâ* Marseilles; postage, *viâ* Marseilles, under ¼ oz., 2s. 2d. nnder ½ oz., 2s. 7d. under ¾ oz., 4s. 9d. under 1 oz. 5s. 2d. under 1¼ ozs. 9s. 1d.; *viâ* Southampton, not exceeding ½ oz., 1s. 4d. not exceeding 1 oz., 2s. 8d. above 1 oz. 5s. 4d., and so on.

Newspapers, by Ship, 2d.; *viâ* Southampton, 4d.; *viâ* Marseilles, 5d.

To JAVA, *Letters* may be forwarded *viâ* Holland *paid*, 1s. not exceeding ½ oz., and so on. *Newspapers*, 1d.

Australia.—Letters are sent through the Ship Letter Office "by Private Ship," 8d. not exceeding ½ oz. Or (*if specially so addressed*) they can be forwarded "*by Sydney Packet*" on the last day of every month, Postage 1s. not exceeding ½ oz.; or if so addressed, by the Overland Mails, *viâ* Southampton and Marseilles, postage, under ½ oz.. 2s 2d under ½ oz., 2s. 7d. under ¾ oz., 4s. 9d. under 1 oz. 5s. 2d. under 1¼ ozs. 9s. 1d.; *viâ* Southampton, not exceeding ½ oz., 1s. 4d. not exceeding 1 oz., 2s. 8d. above 1 oz., 5s. 4d. and so on.

Newspapers, by Private Ship, one penny each. If addressed "by Sydney Packet," *free*. *Viâ* Southampton, 2d.; [*viâ* Marseilles, 5d.

Australia (South).—*Letters*, unless otherwise addressed, are sent by the Sydney Packets, on the last day of every month, postage, 1s not exceeding ½ oz., and so on; or, by Private Ship, 8d. not exceeding ½ oz., and so on; or if so addressed by Overland Mail, *viâ* Marseilles, 2s. 2d. under ¼ oz., 2s. 7d. under ½ oz., and so on; or, *viâ* Southampton 1s. 4d. not exceeding ½ oz., and so on.

Newspapers, by Sydney Packet, *free*; by Private Ship, 1d.; *viâ* Marseilles, 5d.; *viâ* Southampton, 2d. each.

Austrian Dominions, and City of Belgrade.—Letters forwarded daily, *viâ* France, *unpaid* or *paid to destination*, 1s. 5d. under ¼ oz., 2s. 5d. under ½ oz., 3s. 10d. under ¾ oz., 4s. 10d. under 1 oz., 6s. 8d. under 1¼ ozs. And on Tuesday and Friday, if so addressed, *viâ* Hamburgh, 1s. 8d. not exceeding ½ oz., *paid in advance*, and so on. Or *viâ* Holland, if addressed "*by Rotterdam*," 8d. not exceeding ½ oz., *paid in advance*; or *viâ* Belgium, if addressed "*by Ostend*," and *paid* 8d.; from any other place but London the postage, *viâ* Hamburgh, is 1s. 10d. not exceeding ½ oz., and so on.

Newspapers, 2d. each.

The Austrian Dominions include the following Provinces:—

Austria (Upper and Lower), Bohemia, Dalmatia, Gallicia, Hungary, Illyria, Lombardy and the Venetian Provinces, Military Frontiers, Moravia, Silesia, Styria, Transylvania, Tyrol, Northern and Southern.

Azores.—*Letters*, which must be *paid*, are forwarded on the 7th, 17th, and 27th of each month, "*viâ Southampton*," unless those dates should fall on the Sunday, and then on the following *morning*. Postage, 1s. 9d. not exceeding ½ oz., and so on.

Newspapers, 2d. each.

Baden.—*Letters* are sent on Tuesdays and Fridays, *viâ* Hamburgh, postage 1s. 8d. not exceeding ½ oz., or through France daily (*if so addressed*), *unpaid*, or *paid to Calais* 5d. not exceeding ½ oz., or paid *to destination* 1s. 1d. under ¼ oz., 1s. 9d. under ½ oz., 2s. 10d. under ¾ oz., 3s. 6d. under 1 oz., 5s. under 1¼ ozs., and so on; or by Belgium, if so addressed, postage 8d. not exceeding ½ an oz., or *viâ Holland*, on the mornings of Wednesday and Saturday, if so addressed, 8d., not exceeding ½ oz.; from any other place but London the postage, *viâ* Hamburgh, is 1s. 10d. not exceeding the ½ oz., and so on.

Newspapers, 2d. each.

Bahamas (The).—Mails despatched on the *mornings* of the 2nd and 17th of every month (excepting when those dates fall on a Sunday; in such cases the Mail of the 2nd is despatched on the *evening* of the 1st, and the Mail of the 17th on the *morning* of the 18th), *viâ* Southampton, 1s. not exceeding ½ oz., *paid or unpaid*, and so on.

Newspapers, free.

Balearic Islands.—*Letters*, which must be *paid* (for Rates of Postage, *see* SPAIN), forwarded daily *viâ* France, unless specially directed "*viâ* Southampton," when they are forwarded on the 7th, 17th, and 27th of each month, unless those dates should fall on the Sunday, and then on the following morning.

Newspapers, 2d. each.

Barbary.—No regular Packets. *Letters* are despatched by *private* Ship *when* opportunities occur; but these being but seldom, Letters should be addressed to an Agent at "Malta," or Gibraltar, which *see*.

Bavaria.—*Letters* are sent on Tuesdays and Fridays, *viâ* Hamburgh, postage 1s. 8d. not exceeding ½ oz., or through France daily (*if so addressed*), *unpaid*, or may be *paid to Calais*, 5d. not exceeding ½ oz.; or *to destination*, 1s. 8d. under ¼ oz., 2s. 11d. under ½ oz., 4s. 7d. under ¾ oz., 5s. 10d. under 1 oz., 7s. 11d. under 1¼ ozs., and so on. Or by Belgium (*if so addressed*), postage 8d. not exceeding ½ an oz.; or *viâ* Holland, on the mornings of Wednesday and Saturday (*if so addressed*), postage 8d. not exceeding ½ an oz.; from any other place but London the postage, *viâ* Hamburgh, is 1s. 10d. not exceeding the ½ oz., and so on.

Newspapers, 2d. each.

Belgium.—*Letters*, paid or unpaid, are despatched daily, to Ostend; postage 1s. under ¼ oz., 1s. 4d. under ½ oz., 2s. 4d. under ¾ oz. and 2s. 8d. under 1 oz., and so on. Or, if so addressed, daily, *viâ* France: *must be paid* to Calais, 5d. not exceeding ½ oz.; or may be paid *through France*, 10d. under ¼ oz., 1s. 3d. under ½ oz., 2s. 1d. under ¾ oz., 2s. 6d. under 1 oz., 3s. 9d. under 1¼ ozs., and so on.

Newspapers, free.

Bermuda.—*Letters, paid* or *unpaid*, forwarded *viâ* Liverpool on the *evenings* of the 3rd and 18th of each month, except in December, January, February, and March, and then on the 3rd only; or specially directed "*viâ* Southampton" or "by West India Packet," *throughout the year* on the *morning* of the 17th (or, in the event of the 17th falling on a Sunday, on the *morning* of the 18th) of every month. Postage *paid* or *unpaid* by either route 1s. not exceeding ½ oz. and so on.

Newspapers, free.

Beyrout.—By French Packet, *viâ* Marseilles, *paid* or *unpaid*, 1s. 3d. under ¼ oz., 2s. 1d. under ½ oz., 3s. 4d. under ¾ oz., 5s. 10d. if weighing an ounce, and so on.

Newspapers, 2d. each.

Bohemia. *See* AUSTRIA. **Bolivia.** *See* PANAMA.

Brazil.—*Letters*, which must be *paid*, are despatched in Sailing Packets, *viâ* Falmouth, on the *evening* of the 1st Tuesday in every month, 2s. 9d. (from Falmouth 2s. 7d.) not exceeding ½ oz. & so on. *From* AUGUST *to* JANUARY *inclusive, the Packet touches at* PERNAMBUCO *and* BAHIA, *on her* OUTWARD *passage to* Rio Janeiro, *and the other six months on her* HOMEWARD.

Newspapers, free.

Bremen (Free City of).—Mails by which Letters may be *paid to destination*, 8d. not exceeding ½ oz., and so on, or sent *unpaid*, are despatched every Tuesday and Friday night, by Thames Packet to Hamburgh. Or letters addressed "*viâ* France," may be sent daily *unpaid* or *paid to destination*, 1s. 3d. under ¼ oz., 2s. 1d. under ½ oz., 3s. 4d. under ¾ oz., 4s. 2d. under 1 oz., 5s. 10d. under 1¼ ozs. and so on.

Newspapers, free by Packet; 2d. *viâ France*.

British Colonies in West Indies. *See* WEST INDIES.

British North America.—*Letters* are despatched, in *Steam* Packets, *viâ* Liverpool, on the *evenings* of the 3rd and 18th of every month, (unless those dates fall on the Sunday, in which case on the *following evenings*), except December, January, February, and March, and in those months on the 3rd *only*, 1s. not exceeding ½ oz., *paid* or *unpaid*. To Upper and Lower Canada, Prince Edward's Island, New Brunswick, and Nova Scotia (Halifax excepted) the *uniform* rate is 1s. 2d.; this includes the internal colonial rate of 2d. per ½ oz. Bermuda, *see* "BERMUDA." *Letters* are likewise despatched through the Ship Letter Office by Private Ships. *Letters* for Canada are forwarded by the United States Mail if so addressed, postage 1s. not exceeding ½ oz., and so on, *which must be paid in advance*.

Newspapers, by Ship 1d.; by Packet (Canada excepted) free; Canada one halfpenny each *charged upon delivery*.

Brunswick.—*Letters* forwarded by Hamburgh Mail every Tuesday and Friday night, postage (the payment of which is optional) 9d. for a letter not exceeding 2 ozs., 1s. 6d. not exceeding 1 oz., and so on.

Newspapers, 1d. each. *See* also NORTHERN STATES OF EUROPE.

Buenos Ayres.—*Letters*, which must be *paid*, are despatched in Sailing Packets *viâ* Falmouth on the *evening* of the 1st Tuesday in every month, 2s. 7d. (2s. 5d. from Falmouth) not exceeding ½ oz. and so on.

Newspapers, free.

Canada. *See* BRITISH NORTH AMERIC

Canary (or Fortunate) Islands.—*Letters*, which must be *paid*, are despatched by *Brazil* Packet, *viâ* Falmouth on the first Tuesday in every month, 1s. 10d. not exceeding ½ oz. and so on.

Newspapers, 2d. each.

Ceylon. *See* INDIA EAST.

Chagres.—Mails, by which the *Letters* must be *paid*, despatched *on the morning* of the 17th (or in the event of the 17th falling on a Sunday, on the *morning* of the 18th) of every month, *viâ* Southampton, 1s. not exceeding ½ oz. and so on.

Newspapers, 2d. each by Packet; 1d. by Private Ship.

Chili. *See* PANAMA.

China.—*See* HONG KONG.

Colombia, divided into *Equator (Republic)*, *New Granada*, and *Venezuela*, which latter *see*.—

Columbia River & Hudson's Bay.—No regular Mails. Letters, &c. forwarded by the Ship Letter Office at every opportunity; or they may, if specially so addressed, be forwarded *prepaid viâ* New York.

Constantinople.—*Letters* may be sent *unpaid* by the French Packets, which leave Marseilles on the 1st, 11th, and 21st of each month, at 5 P.M.; *or paid to destination*, 1s. 3d. under ¼ oz., 2s. 1d. under ½ oz., 3s. 4d. under ¾ oz., 4s. 2d under 1 oz., 5s. 10d. under 1¼ ozs., and so on.

Newspapers, 2d. each.

Cracow (Free City of).—By Packets from London, *viâ* Hamburgh, every Tuesday and Friday *evening*, 1s. 8d. not exceeding ½ oz., paid in advance. Or if addressed *viâ* France may be sent daily, *unpaid or paid to destination*, 1s. 5d. under ¼ oz., 2s. 5d. under ½ oz., 3s. 10d. under ¾ oz., 4s. 10d. under 1 oz., 6s. 8d. under 1¼ ozs., and so on. From any other place but London the postage, *viâ* Hamburgh, is 1s. 10d. not exceeding the ½ oz., and so on.

Newspapers, 2d. each.

Cuba. *See* ST. JAGO DE CUBA; also HAVANA.

Dalmatia. *See* AUSTRIA.

Dardanelles. *See* TURKEY.

Denmark.—*Paid Letters* despatched on every Tuesday and Friday, by Packets from London *viâ Hamburgh*, 1s. 8d. not exceeding ½ oz. Or may be sent through France *unpaid* or paid *to destination*, 1s. 8d. under ¼ oz., 2s. 11d. under ½ oz., 4s. 7d. under ¾ oz., 5s. 10d. under 1 oz., 7s. 11d. under 1¼ oz., and so on. Letters intended to pass through France should be so directed. From any other place but London the postage, *viâ* Hamburgh, is 1s. 10d. not exceeding the ½ oz., and so on.

Newspapers, free by Packet; 2d. *viâ* France.

Egypt.—Closed Mails are made up on the *evenings* of the 7th and 24th of each month (unless they should happen on a Sunday, then the *following* evening), and despatched *viâ Marseilles*; Letters must be *prepaid*, 1s. 8d. under ¼ oz. *By this route all Letters are forwarded, unless otherwise addressed. Letters* addressed "*viâ* Southampton," will be forwarded by the Mails on the *mornings* of the 3d and 20th of each month, unless they should be on a Sunday, when the Mails are made up on the *previous evening*; 1s. 6d. not exceeding ½ oz. and so on. By the *French* Packets, which leave *Marseilles* on the 1st, 4th, 11th, 21st, and 24th of each month, at 5 P.M., 1s. 3d. under ¼ oz., 2s. 1d. under ½ oz., 3s. 4d. under ¾ oz., 4s. 2d. under 1 oz., 5s. 10d. under 1¼ ozs., and so on. To all places in Egypt except Alexandria Letters must be paid.

Newspapers, by closed Mail, 3d.; by Southampton or by French Packet, 2d.

Equador (Republic of). *See* PANAMA.

Falkland Isles.—No regular Mails. *Letters* are despatched by the "*Ship Letter Office*" at every opportunity 8d. not exceeding ½ oz. Or, *if specially* so addressed, by Brazil Packet *viâ* Falmouth, 2s. 9d. not exceeding ½ oz., and so on

Newspapers, 1d. each by Private Ships. Free by Packet.

Foreign West Indies. *See* WEST INDIES.

France & Algeria.—Daily, *viâ* Dover. *Letters* may be sent unpaid, or paid to destination.

COMBINED BRITISH AND FRENCH RATES.

Weighing under a ¼ oz.	Weighing ¼ oz. and not exceeding ½ oz.	Exceeding ½ oz. and under ¾ oz.	Weighing ¾ oz. and not exceeding 1 oz.	Exceeding 1 oz. and under 1¼ oz.
s. d.	s. d.	s. d.	s. d.	s. d.
British .. 0 5	British... 0 5	British .. 0 10	British .. 0 10	British .. 1 8
French .. 0 5	French .. 0 10	French .. 1 3	French .. 1 8	French .. 2 1
Total .. 0 10	Total.. 1 3	Total.. 2 1	Total.. 2 6	Total.. 3 9

*** The *French* uniform rate has reference to those Letters only, *the postage upon which is paid in the United Kingdom*. If a Letter be despatched unpaid, the French charge upon delivery *varies* according to the distance, in conformity with the laws of France.

Newspapers, free by Packet; 1d. by Private Ship.

Frankfort (Free City of). *See* GERMAN STATES.

Gallicia (Austrian Poland). *See* AUSTRIA.

German States, *served by the Office of Tour and Taxis*, through France.

Bremen. } Free Cities.	Hesse-Homburg.	Saxe-Meiningen.
Frankfort. } Free Cities.	Lippe-Detmold.	Saxe-Weimar.
Hamburg. } Free Cities.	Nassau.	Schaumberg-Lippe.
Lubeck. } Free Cities.	Reuss.	Schwartzburg-Rudolstadt.
Hesse Darmstadt.	Saxe-Altenburg.	Schwartzburg-Sonderhausen.
Hesse (*Electoral*).	Saxe-Coburg-Gotha.	Wirtemburg.

Letters to these States are forwarded on Tuesdays and Fridays by the Hamburgh Mail, unless otherwise addressed; postage from London to (Hamburg, Bremen and Lubeck excepted) 1s. 8d. not exceeding ½ oz., 3s. 4d. not exceeding 1 oz., and so on. From any other place 1s. 10d. not exceeding ½ oz., 3s. 8d. not exceeding 1 oz., and so on, which must be paid in advance. Letters for Hamburg, Bremen and Lubeck are forwarded by Hamburg Mail, postage to Hamburg and Lubeck, 6d. not exceeding ½ oz., 1s. not exceeding 1 oz.; to Bremen 8d. not exceeding ½ oz., 1s. 4d. not exceeding 1 oz. When specially so addressed, the Letters for any of the German States may be sent every evening *viâ* France or Belgium, and on the mornings of Wednesday and Saturday *viâ* Holland.—*viâ* France, the postage is 1s. 3d. under ¼ oz., 2s. 1d. under ½ oz., 3s. 4d. under ¾ oz., 4s. 2d. under 1 oz., 5s. 10d. under 1¼ ozs., payment optional; *viâ* Holland or Belgium, 8d. not exceeding the ½ oz. The postage must be paid in advance in the two latter cases.

Newspapers to Bremen, Hamburg, and Lubeck, pass *Free by Packet*. To Frankfort and the "German States' they are charged 2d. each.

Germany. *See* GERMAN STATES.

Gibraltar.—*Letters* are despatched on the mornings of the 7th, 17th, and 27th of every month, unless those dates fall on a Sunday, and then on the following *morning*, *viâ* Southampton, and by the India Mail, *viâ* Southampton, on the 3rd and 20th of every month, 1s. not exceeding ½ oz. and so on, *paid* or *unpaid*.

Newspapers, free.

Greece.—*Letters, prepaid*, are despatched daily, *viâ* France, and twice monthly from Southampton. On the *morning* of the 3d and 20th, unless they happen to fall on a Sunday, when the Mails are made up on the *previous evening*—postage, 1s. 6d. not exceeding ½ oz.; or *may be paid* to Calais, 5d. not exceeding ½ oz.; or *as far as Trieste*, 1s. 3d. under ¼ oz., 2s. 1d. under ½ oz., 3s. 4d. under ¾ oz., 4s. 2d. under 1 oz., 5s. 10d. under 1¼ oz. and so on; or may be sent *unpaid* by *French* Packets, which leave *Marseilles* on the 1st, 11th, and 21st of each month, at 5 P.M.; or by the same route may be paid *to destination*, under ¼ oz., 1s. 5d. under ½ oz., 2s. 5d. under ¾ oz., 3s. 10d. under 1 oz. 4s. 10d. under 1¼ ozs. 6s. 8d. and so on. *Letters* intended to be sent "*by French Packet*" should be so directed.

Newspapers, one penny each, *viâ Marseilles*, or free by Packet.

Guatemala. *See* HONDURAS.

Hamburg (Free City of).—*Letters*, which must be *paid*, forwarded every Tuesday and Friday night from London 6d. not exceeding ½ oz. *See* also GERMAN STATES.

Newspapers, free.

Hanover. *Letters* forwarded by Hamburgh Mail every Tuesday and Friday *night*, postage (the payment of which s *optional*), 9d. for a Letter not exceeding ½ oz., 1s. 6d. not exceeding 1 oz., and so on. *See* also NORTHERN STATES OF EUROPE.

Newspapers, 1d. each.

Havana.—Mails by which the *Letters* must be *paid* despatched on the *morning* of the 2nd (or in the event of the 2nd falling on a Sunday, on the *evening* of the 1st) of every month, *viâ* Southampton, 2s. 3d. not exceeding ½ oz., and so on.

Newspapers, 2d. each.

Heligoland.—*Letters*, which must be *paid*, forwarded by Packets from London every Tuesday and Friday night, *viâ Hamburg*, Postage 6d. not exceeding ½ oz.

Newspapers, free.

Hesse (Electoral), Hesse-Darmstadt, and Hesse-Homburg. *See* GERMAN STATES.

Hindostan. *See* INDIA (EAST).

Holland.—*Letters* forwarded by Packets from London every Wednesday and Saturday *morning*, 1s. not exceeding ½ oz. *paid* or *unpaid*. For Countries on the Continent of Europe, *viâ* Holland, 8d. not exceeding ½ oz., which *must be paid* in advance. Letters for Holland, if addressed *viâ* France, may be sent daily, *paid to Calais*, 5d. not exceeding ½ oz., or *through France*, 10d. under ¼ oz., 1s. 3d. under ½ oz., 2s. 1d. under ¾ oz., 2s. 6d. under 1 oz., 3s. 9d. under 1¼ ozs., and so on.

Newspapers, to Holland, or passing through—*By Packet*, 1d.; *viâ* France, 2d.

Honduras.—Mails, by which the *Letters* may be *paid* or *unpaid*, are despatched on the *morning* of the 2nd (or in the event of the 2nd falling on a Sunday, on the *evening* of the 1st) of every month, *viâ Southampton*, 1s. not exceeding ½ oz., and so on.

Newspapers, free.

Hong-Kong & China. *Letters* are forwarded by the Overland Mails *viâ* Marseilles on the *evening* of the 24th of each month, unless that date falls on a Sunday, then on the *evening* of the 25th: postage under ¼ oz. 1s. 10d., under ½ oz. 2s. 3d., under ¾ oz. 4s. 1d., under 1oz. 4s. 6d., and so on; or *viâ* Southampton on the *morning* of the 20th of each month, unless that date falls on a Sunday, then the *evening* of the 19th; postage 1s. not exceeding ½ oz., 2s. not exceeding 1 oz., and so on; *Letters* for China must be *pre-paid*, but the *pre-payment* of postage to Hong-Kong is *optional*.

Newspapers to Hong-Kong free, by Southampton to China, 2d. *viâ* Marseilles, 3d. to Hong-Kong and China.

N.B. The *Letters*, &c. may be addressed *viâ* Bombay, Calcutta, or Madras; but such address will subject them to an additional rate of 4d. per *Letter*, and 2d. per *Newspaper*.

Hungary. *See* AUSTRIA.

Illyria. *See* AUSTRIA.

India (East.)—Closed Mails are made up on the 7th and 24th of each month, unless they should happen on a Sunday, and then the *following* day, and despatched *viâ Marseilles*, whence they are forwarded by *British* Steam Boats. *All* paid *Letters are sent by this route unless otherwise addressed.* Must be paid to *Bombay*, 1s. 10d. under ¼ oz., 2s. 3d. under ½ oz., 4s. 1d. under ¾ oz., 4s. 6d. under 1 oz., 7s. 9d. under 1¼ oz. and so on. Mails for India are likewise forwarded *viâ Southampton* on the *mornings* of the 3rd and 20th of every month, unless they should happen on *Sunday*, then the *previous evening*; 1s. not exceeding ½ oz. and so on. On Letters for places *within the territory of the East India Company*, addressed "*viâ* Southampton," the payment is optional; the postage on all other Letters addressed to India, as well as on all Letters addressed to Countries beyond India (the Colony of HONG KONG excepted), by whatever route they may be forwarded, must be paid in advance.

Newspapers by British Packets from *Marseilles*, 3d.; Free *viâ Southampton*.

Ionian Islands.—Mails by which the postage is 1s. not exceeding ½ oz. and *payment optional*, are forwarded *viâ Southampton* on the *mornings* of the 3rd and 20th of every month (unless they should happen on a Sunday, then the *previous evening*). Or daily *viâ France*, paid to *Trieste*, 1s. 3d. under ¼ oz., 2s. 1d. under ½ oz., 3s. 4d. under ¾ oz., 4s. 2d. under 1 oz., 5s. 10d. under 1¼ ozs. and so on. Or *paid to destination* by *French* Packets from *Marseilles*, at the *same rates*. Or may be paid *to Calais*, 5d., not exceeding ½ oz., and so on. Letters are forwarded by *Closed Mail* on the 7th and 24th of every month, *viâ Marseilles*, in *British* Packets, 1s. 8d. under ¼ oz., 2s. 1d. under ½ oz., 3s. 9d. under ¾ oz., 4s. 2d. under 1 oz., 7s. 1d. under 1¼ oz., and so on. All *paid* Letters for the Ionian Islands *not otherwise directed* are forwarded *viâ Trieste*. None can be despatched unpaid but *viâ Southampton*.

Newspapers, free by Southampton Packet, or if addressed "*viâ Trieste*,"; 2d. by French Packets *viâ* Marseilles 3d. by British Packet (Closed Mail.)

Italy (Northern), *See* VENETIAN LOMBARDY.

Italy (Southern) including—Papal States, Two Sicilies (Naples & Sicily), Modena, Parma & Placentia.—*Letters* forwarded daily, *viâ* France, may be paid only as far as Calais, 5d. not exceeding ½ oz., and so on; or to the frontier towns of Casal Pusterlengo or San Benedetto 1s. 3d. under ¼ oz., 2s. 1d., under ½ oz., 3s. 4d. under ¾ oz., 4s. 2d. under 1 oz., 5s. 10d. under 1¼ ozs., and so on. *See also* "LUCCA" and "TUSCANY." Or *Letters* for the Papal States or Two Sicilies may, if addressed "*viâ Marseilles* by *French* packet," be forwarded unpaid by the packets which leave *Marseilles* on the 1st, 11th, and 21st of each month, at 5 P.M.; or *paid to destination* by the same route. *Papal States*, 1s. 7d. under ¼ oz., 2s. 9d. under ½ oz., 4s. 4d. under ¾ oz., 5s. 6d. under 1 oz., 7s. 6d. under 1¼ oz. and so on. Naples, and Sicily 1s. 9d. under ¼ oz., 3s. 1d. under ½ oz., 4s. 10d. under ¾ oz., 6s. 2d. under 1 oz., 8s. 4d. under 1¼ oz. and so on.

Newspapers, 2d. each.

Jamaica.—*Letters, paid* or *unpaid*, forwarded on the *mornings* of the 2nd and 17th (or in the event of the 2d falling on a Sunday, on the *evening* of the 1st, or if the 17th fall on a Sunday on the *morning* of the 18th) of every month, *viâ Southampton*, at the uniform rate of 1s. 2d. not exceeding ½ oz. and so on. Letters addressed to or posted at Kingston (the packet port in Jamaica), not being liable to *inter-colonial* postage, are charged only 1s. per ½ oz. and so on

Newspapers, free.

La Guayra. *See* VENEZUELA.

La Plata. *See* BUENOS AYRES.

Leeward Islands.—The Mails are despatched with those for Jamaica; arrangements the same. *Letters, paid* or *unpaid*, 1s. not exceeding ½ oz., and so on.

Newspapers, free.

Lippe-Detmold. *See* GERMAN STATES.

Lombardy. *See* VENETIAN LOMBARDY.

Lubeck (Free City of).—*Paid Letters* forwarded by Packet from London every Tuesday and Friday night, 6d ot exceeding ½ oz., and so on. *See* also GERMAN STATES.

Newspapers, free.

Lucca.—*Letters* forwarded daily:—may be paid *through France*, 10d. under ¼ oz., 1s. 3d. under ½ oz., 2s. 1d. under ¾ oz., 2s. 6d. under 1 oz., 3s. 9d. under 1¼ oz., and so on. Or may be paid *as far as Sarzane*, the *Italian frontier* of Sardinia, 1s. 4d. under ¼ oz., 2s. 3d. under ½ oz., 3s. 7d. under ¾ oz., 4s. 6d. under 1 oz., 6s. 3d. under 1¼ ozs. and so on.

Newspapers, 2d each.

Madeira.—*Letters*, which must be *paid*, 1s. 9d. not exceeding ½ oz. and so on, forwarded on the mornings of the 7th, 17th, and 27th of each month, unless those dates should fall on a Sunday, and then on the following *morning*, *viâ Lisbon*; first Tuesday in every month, by Brazil Mail, 1s. 10d. (from Falmouth 1s. 8d.) not exceeding ½ oz., and so on; and on the *mornings* of the 2nd and 17th (or in the event of the 2d falling on a unday, on the *evening* of the 1st or if the 17th fall on a Sunday on the *morning* of the 18th) day of every month, *viâ* Southampton by West India Mail, at the same rates.

Newspapers, 2d. each.

Malta.—Closed mails are made up in London on the 7th and 24th of each month (unless they should happen on a Sunday, and then the *following* day) by which *Letters* may be forwarded by *British* packets, *viâ Marseilles*, either *unpaid* or *paid to destination*, 1s. 3d. under ¼ oz., 1s. 8d. under ½ oz., 2s. 11d. under ¾ oz, 3s. 4d. under 1 oz., 5s. 5d. under 1¼ oz., and so on. *Letters are always sent by this route, unless otherwise addressed.*

Mails are made up to be sent, *viâ Southampton*, on the *mornings* of the 3d and 20th of each month (unless they should happen on a Sunday, when the Mail is made up on the *previous evening*), 1s. not exceeding ½ oz., *paid* or *unpaid*, and so on.

Letters may also be forwarded to Malta by *French* Packets, which leave *Marseilles* on the 1st, 4th, 11th, 21st, and 24th of each month at 5 P.M., *unpaid* or *paid to destination*, 1s. 1d. under ¼ oz., 1s. 9d. under ½ oz., 2s. 10d. under ¾ oz., 3s. 6d. under 1 oz., and 5s. under 1¼ oz. For this route Letters should be addressed "per *French* packet, *viâ Marseilles*."

Newspapers, free, by *Southampton* Packet—*French* Packet, 2d.; British Packet (*Closed Mail*), 3d.

Mauritius.—No regular Packets. Mails are despatched through the *Ship Letter Office*, by every *private* vessel bound to, or touching at, the Mauritius. *Letters* may be forwarded *viâ Marseilles*, "by *Overland Mail*," or *viâ Southampton*, if *specially addressed*, postage *viâ* Marseilles, under ¼ oz. 2s. 2d., under ½ oz. 2s. 7d., under ¾ oz. 4s. 9d., under 1 oz. 5s. 2d., under 1¼ oz. 9s. 1d.; *viâ* Southampton, under ½ oz. 1s. 4d., under 1 oz. 2s. 8d., above 1 oz. 5s. 4d., and so on. The usual mode, however, is through the *Ship Letter Office*, "by Private Ship," 8d. not exceeding ½ oz.

Newspapers, 1d. by ship, 2d. *viâ* Southampton, and 5d. *viâ* Marseilles.

Mediterranean. *See* MALTA, GREECE, or IONIAN ISLANDS.

Mecklenburg-Schwerin. } *See* NORTHERN STATES OF EUROPE.
Mecklenburg-Strelitz. }

Mexico.—Mails, by which *Letters must be paid*, despatched on the *morning* of the 2nd (or in the event of the 2d. falling on a Sunday, on the *evening* of the 1st) of every month, *viâ* Southampton, 2s. 3d. not exceeding ½ oz. and so on.

Newspapers, 2d. each.

Modena. *See* SOUTHERN ITALY.

Moldavia. *Viâ* France daily, *unpaid* or *paid to destination*, 1s. 9d. under ¼ oz., 3s. 1d. under ½ oz., 4s. 10d. under ¾ oz., 6s. 2d. under 1 oz., 8s. 4d. under 1¼ oz., and so on.

Newspapers, 2d each.

Molucca Islands. *See* ARCHIPELAGO (THE EAST INDIAN).

Moravia. *See* AUSTRIA.

Morocco. *See* BARBARY.

Naples. *See* SOUTHERN ITALY.

Nassau (Germany). *See* GERMAN STATES. **Nassau (New Providence.)** *See* BAHAMAS.

Newfoundland. *See* BRITISH NORTH AMERICA.

New Granada.—Mails, by which *Letters* must be *paid*, despatched on the *mornings* of the 2nd and 17th day of every month, *viâ* Southampton, 2s. 3d. not exceeding ½ oz., and so on. In the event of the 2nd falling on a Sunday or the *evening* of the 1st, or if the 17th falls on a Sunday, the Mails are despatched on the *following morning*.

Newspapers, free.

New South Wales. *See* SYDNEY and AUSTRALIA.

New Zealand. *See* SYDNEY.

Northern States of Europe.—(*Forwarded through the Office of Tour & Taxis*), through France, daily, Brunswick; Denmark; Hanover; Mecklenburg-Schwerin; Mecklenburg-Strelitz; Oldenburg; Saxony; Sweden and Norway. May be sent *unpaid* or *paid to destination*, 1s. 8d. under ¼ oz., 2s. 11d. under ½ oz., 4s. 7d. under ¾ oz., 5s. 10d., under 1 oz., 7s. 11d. under 1¼ oz. *Letters* are forwarded by Packet to Hamburg, every Tuesday and Friday, postage from London 1s. 8d. not exceeding ½ oz.; from any other place 1s. 10d. not exceeding the ½ oz.; or *viâ* Belgium daily, or *viâ* Holland on the mornings of Wednesday and Saturday, postage 8d. not exceeding ½ oz., 1s. 4d. not exceeding 1 oz., and so on. Those intended to pass, *viâ* France, Belgium, or Holland, should be so directed. *See also* "BRUNSWICK," *also* HANOVER.

Newspapers, Denmark free, *viâ* Hamburgh; other states, 2d. each.

North America. *See* UNITED STATES and BRITISH NORTH AMERICA.

Norway & Sweden. *See* NORTHERN STATES OF EUROPE.

Nova Scotia. *See* BRITISH NORTH AMERICA.

Nubia.—No regular Mails. *Letters* should be addressed to the care of an agent at Malta, or Aden, as opportunities of direct communication seldom occur.

Oldenburg.—Mails, by which *Letters* must be *paid*, despatched on every Tuesday and Friday, by Thames Packet, to Hamburg, 6d. not exceeding ½ oz., and so on. Or may be sent *unpaid* if forwarded, *viâ* France, for which route, *see* NORTHERN STATES OF EUROPE.

Newspapers, free by Packet; *viâ France*, 2d. each.

Panama & Western Coast of America, including Chili, Peru, Bolivia, and Equador, &c. &c.; postage, not exceeding ½ oz. 2s., not exceeding 1 oz. 4s., and so on.

Newspapers free.

Mails dispatched from London on the mornings of the 17th of every month, unless the 17th should fall on a Sunday, and then on the following morning.

Papal States. *See* SOUTHERN ITALY; and *Letters* may be paid to Calais 5d. not exceedlng ½ oz., or forwarded, *unpaid*, by *French* Packets, from *Marseilles*, or *paid to destination*, 1s. 7d. under ¼ oz., 2s. 9d. under ½ oz., 4s. 4d. under ¾ oz., 5s. 6d. under 1 oz., 7s. 6d. under 1¼ oz., and so on. For this Route Letters should be addressed, per *French* Packet *viâ Marseilles*.

Newspapers, 2d. each.

Parma & Placentia. *See* SOUTHERN ITALY.

Persia.—*Letters*, which must be *paid*, are forwarded, *viâ* Alexandria and Beyrout. *See* **ALEXANDRIA.**

Peru. *See* PANAMA.

Poland.—Mails, by which the *Letters* must be *paid*, postage 1s. 8d. from London, not exceeding ½ oz., from any other place 1s. 10d. not exceeding ½ oz., and so on, despatched every Tuesday and Friday, *viâ* Hamburg. *Letters specially so directed* may be forwarded to the Provinces of Cracow, Lublin and Sandomier, daily *viâ* France, *unpaid* or *paid* to Podgorce 1s. 6d. under ¼ oz., 2s. 7d. under ½ oz., 4s. 1d. under ¾ oz., 5s. 2d. under 1 oz., 7s. 1d. under 1¼ ozs. They may also be forwarded, *viâ Holland* or *Belgium*, prepaid 8d. not exceeding ½ oz., if so addressed.

Newspapers, 2d. each.

Port Phillip.—*Letters* are despatched on the last day of each month *by Packet* to Sydney, (whence there is an Overland Post to Port Phillip,) 1s. not exceeding ½ oz., and so on. Or specially so addressed may be sent "*by Private Ship*," 8d. not exceeding ½ oz. and so on All Letters must be *paid*. *See* AUSTRALIA.

Newspapers, free by Packet; by Private Ship 1d. each.

Portugal.—Mails, by which *Letters* must be *paid*, despatched on the *mornings* of the 7th, 17th, and 27th of each month, unless those dates fall on a Sunday, and then on the following *morning*, *viâ Southampton*, 1s. 9d. not exceeding ½ oz., or daily, *if so directed*, *viâ* France; paid through France, 10d. under ¼ oz., 1s. 3d. under ½ oz., 2s. 1d. under ¾ oz., 2s. 6d. under 1 oz., 3s. 9d. under 1¼ ozs. and so on.

Newspapers, 2d. each.

Prussia.—*Letters* are despatched on Tuesdays and Fridays, *viâ* Hamburg, postage from London 1s. 8d. not exceeding ½ oz., from any other place 1s. 10d. not exceeding ½ oz., and so on; or *viâ* France, daily, *if so addressed, must be paid* as far as Calais, 5d. not exceeding ½ oz.; or *through France*, 10d. under ¼ oz., 1s. 3d. under ½ oz., 2s. 1d. under ¾ oz., 2s. 6d. under 1 oz., 3s. 9d. under 1¼ oz., and so on. Also, if so addressed, daily, *viâ* Belgium, postage 8d. not exceeding ½ oz.; or on Wednesday and Saturday *mornings, viâ* Holland, 8d. not exceeding ½ oz. **By either route the** Postage must be paid in advance.

Newspapers, 2d. each.

Reuss. *See* GERMAN STATES.

Roman States. *See* PAPAL STATES.

Russia (Northern).—Mails, by which the *Letters* must be *paid*, despatched every Tuesday and Friday, by Thames Packet to Hamburg, postage from London, 1s. 8d. not exceeding ½ oz., from any other place 1s. 10d. not exceeding ½ oz., and so on. They may also be forwarded by Holland, if addressed "*viâ Rotterdam*," or by Belgium, if "*viâ Ostend*." Postage 8d. not exceeding ½ oz. in either case.

Newspapers, 2d. each.

Russia (Southern).—Including the Governments of

Abkhas	Cossacks of the Don	Koursk	Taurida
Astrakhan	Daughistan	Mingrelia	Tchernigow
Bessarabia	Ekaterinoslaw	Nicolaw	Ukraine
Caucasus	Georgia	Podolia	Volhynia
Circassia	Imeretia	Poltowa	Voroney
Cossacks of the Black Sea	Kiew	Schirwan	

Letters, if specially so directed, despatched daily *viâ* France, *unpaid* or *paid to destination*, 1s. 6d. under ¼ oz., 2s. 7d., under ½ oz., 4s. 1d. under ¾ oz., 5s. 2d. under 1 oz., 7s. 1d. under 1¼ ozs., and so on. Or by the Thames Packets to Hamburg, by which the postage must be *paid* from London, 1s. 8d., from any other place 1s. 10d. not exceeding ½ oz., and so on, despatched every Tuesday and Friday. They may also be forwarded *viâ* Holland, 8d. not exceeding ½ oz., if addressed "*by Rotterdam*," or *viâ* Belgium, if addressed "*by Ostend*," 8d. not exceeding ½ oz.

Newspapers, 2d. each.

St. Domingo.—For *Letters*, see WEST INDIES (Foreign).

Newspapers, free.

St. Helena.—No regular Packets. *See* AFRICA.

St. Jago de Cuba.—Mails, by which the *Letters* must be *paid*, despatched *viâ* Southampton, on the mornings of the 2d and 17th of every month, 2s. 3d. not exceeding ½ oz., and so on. Whenever the *2d of the month falls on Sunday* the Mails are made up and despatched on the *previous evening*; and whenever the *17th of the month falls on Sunday* the Mails are made up and despatched on the following *morning*.

Newspapers, 2d. each.

Sandwich Islands.—No regular Mails. *Letters* despatched by private ships at every opportunity, 8d. not exceed. ½ oz.

Newspapers, 1d. each.

Sardinia.—*Letters* must be *paid*, and are forwarded daily *through France*, 10d. under ¼ oz., 1s. 3d. under ½ oz., 2s. 1d. under ¾ oz., 2s. 6d. under 1 oz., 3s 9d. under 1¼ ozs., and so on; *or to destination*, 1s. 1d. under ¼ oz., 1s. 9d. under ½ oz., 2s. 10d. under ¾ oz., 3s. 6d. under 1 oz., 5s. under 1¼ oz., and so on.

Newspapers, 2d. each.

Saxe-Altenburg, Saxe-Coburg-Gotha, Saxe-Meiningen, & Saxe-Weimar. *See* GERMAN STATES.

Saxony. *See* NORTHERN STATES OF EUROPE.

Schaumberg-Lippe, Schwartzburg-Rudolstadt, & Schwartzburg-Sonderhausen. *See* GERMAN STATES

Siberia. *See* RUSSIA.

Sicilies.—i. e. Naples and Sicily, *see* SOUTHERN ITALY; and *Letters* may be forwarded *unpaid* by *French* Packets from Marseilles; or *paid to destination*, 1s. 9d. under ¼ oz., 3s. 1d. under ½ oz., 4s. 10d. under ¾ oz., 6s. 2d. under 1 oz., 8s. 4d. under 1¼ ozs., and so on. For this route, letters should be addressed per *French* Packet *viâ Marseilles*.

Sierra Leone.—No regular Packets. *See* AFRICA.

Silesia. *See* AUSTRIA.

Singapore. *See* INDIA (EAST).

South Australia. *See* AUSTRALIA (SOUTH).

Southern Italy. *See* ITALY (SOUTHERN).

Spain.—Mails, made up on the *mornings*, of the 7th, 17th, and 27th of every month, unless those dates fall on the Sunday, and then on the following *morning*, and despatched, *viâ* Southampton, 2s. 2d. not exceeding ½ oz., and so on. *Letters* may be sent daily, *viâ Calais*, 10d. under ¼ oz., 1s. 3d. under ½ oz., 2s. 1d. under ¾ oz., 2s. 6d. under 1 oz., 3s. 9d. under 1¼ oz., and so on. By either route the Postage *must be paid*.

⁂ Letters for Spain, not specially addressed (with the exception of Cadiz, Coruna, and Vigo, which are sent *viâ* Southampton) are forwarded through France.

Newspapers, by Southampton Packet, free; *viâ* France, one halfpenny each.

Styria. *See* AUSTRIA.

Swan River. *See* AUSTRALIA.

Sweden & Norway. *See* NORTHERN STATES OF EUROPE.

Switzerland.—*Letters* despatched daily through France. Postage, the *pre-payment* of which is *optional*, 11d. under ¼ oz., 1s. 5d. under ½ oz., 2s. 4d. under ¾ oz., 2s. 10d. under 1 oz., 4s. 2d. under 1¼ oz., and so on.

Newspapers, 2d. each.

Sydney.—Mails despatched *from London* by sailing Packets on the last day of every month, unless that should happen on a Sunday, and then the day following. Postage (*which must be paid in advance*), 1s. not exceeding ½ oz.

and letters, if *specially so directed*, may be sent "by Private Ship," 8d. not exceeding ½ oz., and so on. Or by India, if specially addressed, postage, *viâ* Marseilles, under ¼ oz. 2s. 2d., under ½ oz. 2s. 7d., under ¾ oz. 4s. 9d., under 1 oz. 5s. 2d., under 1¼ ozs. 9s. 1d.; *viâ* Southampton, not exceeding ½ oz. 1s. 4d., not exceeding 1 oz. 2s. 8d., above 1 oz. 5s. 4d., and so on.

Newspapers, free by Packet; by Private Ship, one penny each; *viâ* Marseilles, 5d.; *viâ* Southampton, 2d. each.

Syra. *See* GREECE.

Syria.—Closed Mails are made up in London on the 7th and 24th of each month (unless they should happen on a Sunday, then the *following* day), and despatched to *Marseilles*, whence they are forwarded by *British* Packets. *All Letters to Syria are sent by this route, unless otherwise addressed*, 1s. 8d. under ¼ oz. Mails are despatched, *viâ Southampton*, on the *mornings* of the 3d and 20th of every month (unless they happen on a Sunday, and then the Mails are made up on the *previous evening*). 1s. 6d. not exceeding ½ oz. Letters for this route should be addressed *viâ Southampton* and all must be *paid*. For Letters addressed Beyrout *olny*, see "BEYROUT."

Newspapers, by closed Mail, 3d. each; by Southampton or by French Packet, 2d. each.

Texas.—No regular Mails. Letters, &c., forwarded by private ships at every opportunity. Postage 8d. not exceeding ½ oz. and so on.

Newspapers, 1d. each.

Transylvania. *See* AUSTRIA.

Tripoli & Tunis. *See* BARBARY.

Turkey in Europe (with the Town of SCUTARI in Asia), Daily *viâ* FRANCE, *unpaid* or *paid to destination*, 1s. 11d. under ¼ oz., 3s. 5d. under ½ oz., 5s. 4d. under ¾ oz., 6s. 10d. under 1 oz., 9s. 2d. under 1¼ oz.; except Belgrade, which is 1s. 5d. under ¼ oz., 2s. 5d. under ½ oz., 3s. 10d. under ¾ oz., 4s. 10d. under 1 oz., 6s. 8d. under 1¼ ozs., and so on.

Newspapers, 2d. each.

Turkey in Asia (except SCUTARI).—Letters, which *must be paid*, 1s. 8d. under ¼ oz., 2s. 1d. under ½ oz., 3s. 4d under ¾ oz., 4s. 2d. under 1 oz., 5s. 10d. under 1¼ ozs., are forwarded with those for Alexandria *viâ* Marseilles.

Newspapers, 2d. each.

Letters to Smyrna, the Dardanelles, and Constantinople, may be forwarded by the *French* Packets, which leave *Marseilles* on the 1st, 11th, and 21st of every month, at 5 P.M., *unpaid*, or *paid to destination*, 1s. 3d. under ¼ oz., 2s. 1d. under ½ oz., 3s. 4d. under ¾ oz., 4s. 2d. under 1 oz., 5s. 10d. under 1¼ ozs., and so on. They should be addressed, "*viâ Marseilles*, by *French* Packet."

Newspapers, 2d. each.

Tuscany.—*Letters* forwarded daily; must be paid *through France*, 10d. under ¼ oz., 1s. 3d. under ½ oz., 2s. 1d. under ¾ oz., 2s. 6d. under 1 oz., 3s. 9d. under 1¼ ozs., and so on. Or may be paid *as far as Sarzane*, the *Italian frontier* of Sardinia, 1s. 4d. under ¼ oz., 2s. 3d. under ½ oz., 3s. 7d. under ¾ oz., 4s. 6d. under 1 oz., 6s. 3d. under 1¼ ozs., and so on. Or may be sent *unpaid* by *French* packet boats from Marseilles, or *paid to destination* by the same route, 1s. 9d. under ¼ oz., 3s. 1d. under ½ oz., 4s. 10d. under ¾ oz., 6s. 2d. under 1 oz., 8s. 4d. under 1¼ oz., and so on.

Newspapers, 2d. each.

Tyrol (Northern and Southern). *See* AUSTRIA.

United States.—Mails, by which the *Letters* must be *paid*, despatched by Steam Packets from Liverpool on the 3d and 18th of each month, except in Dec. Jan. Feb. and March, when on the 3rd *only*, 1s. not exceeding ½ oz., and so on. Letters, addressed "*by Private Ship*," may also be despatched through the Ship Letter Office, by any outward-bound vessel. Postage 8d. not exceeding ½ oz.

Newspapers, 2d. each.

Van Diemen's Land. *See* AUSTRALIA.

Venezuela.—Mails, by which the Letters must be *paid*, despatched *on the morning* of the 2nd and 17th (or, in the event of the 2nd falling on a Sunday, on the *evening* of the 1st, or if the 17th fall on a Sunday on the *morning* of the 18th) of every month, *viâ Southampton*, 1s. 0d. not exceeding ½ oz., and so on. Or by private Ship 8d. not exceeding ½ oz., and so on.

Newspapers, free by Packet; 1d. by private Ship.

Venetian Lombardy.—Daily, through France. *Unpaid* or paid *to destination*, 1s. 5d. under ¼ oz., 2s. 5d. under ½ oz., 3s. 10d. under ¾ oz., 4s. 10d. under 1 oz., and so on.

Wallachia.—*Viâ* France, daily, *unpaid* or *paid to destination*, 1s. 9d. under ¼ oz., 3s. 1d. under ½ oz., 4s. 10d. under ¾ oz., 6s. 2d. under 1 oz., 8s. 4d. under 1¼ ozs., and so on.

Newspapers, 2d. each.

West Indies (British), except for Bahamas, and Bermuda (which see), the Mails are despatched on the *mornings* of the 2nd and 17th (or, in the event of the 2d falling on a Sunday, on the *evening* of the 1st, or if the 17th fall on a Sunday on the *morning* of the 18th) of every month, *viâ* Southampton, 1s. not exceeding ½ oz., and so on, *paid* or *unpaid*. To Jamaica (the *Packet Port* Kingston excepted) and Berbice, the postage is 1s. 2d. not exceeding ½ oz. This includes the inter-colonial rate of 2d. the ½ oz.

Newspapers, free.

West Indies (Foreign), except for Havana (which see), the Mails are forwarded with those for the West Indies (British). Letters and Newspapers received until the same hours. Letters *must be paid* 1s. 5d. not exceeding ½ oz, and so on.

Newspapers, 2d. each.

Wirtemburg. *See* GERMAN STATES.

LETTERS NOT TO BE SEALED WITH WAX WHEN SENT TO WARM CLIMATES.

The practice of Sealing Letters passing to and from the *East* and *West Indies*, and other warm Climates, with Wax is attended with much inconvenience, and frequently with serious injury to the Letters, in consequence of the Melting of the Wax, and Adhesion of the Letters to each other.

In the case of Mails received from *India*, considerable delay is occasioned; and notwithstanding the greatest care is taken in separating the Letters, which, owing to the cause already mentioned, adhere closely together, many are much damaged and torn; the public are therefore recommmended in all cases to use Wafers in preference to Wax in securing their Letters sent to *India* or other warm Climates, and also to advise their Correspondents in those Countries to pursue the same course.

LONDON DISTRICT (LATE TWOPENNY) POST OFFICE.

The Principal Office is at the General Post Office, St. Martin's-le-Grand, where Letters may be posted One Hour later **up to 12 o'clock, and** ¾ of an hour later from 12 to 6 o'clock, at each Despatch than at the Receiving Houses.

There are 10 Deliveries of Letters in London daily, and at the following places in the Environs of London, within the circle **of three miles** from the General Post Office. There are 6 Deliveries, viz.: *Camberwell*; *Camden Town*;

Dalston; Hackney; Holloway; Islington; Kent Road (Old); Kennington; Kentish Town; Kingsland; Newington Butts; Pentonville; Shacklewell; South Lambeth; Somers' Town; Vauxhall; and *Walworth*.

Letters, posted at the Receiving Houses in London before 6 o'clock, are delivered at all Places within the circle of Three Miles from the General Post Office the same evening.

By a recent Regulation, an additional Delivery has been extended to all places within Six Miles of the General Post Office, so that Letters posted at the Receiving Houses in London before 5 o'clock, or at the Principal Office before ¼ to 6 o'clock, are delivered within this limit the same evening.

The Times by which Letters should be put into the Receiving Houses, or the Principal Office, for each Delivery of the Day, and the time at which they are despatched for Delivery, are as follows:—

Letters going from one part of the Town to another.

If put into the Receiving Houses by	Hours.	Or the Principal Office by	Hours.	Are sent out for Delivery at	Hours.
Morning	8	Morning	9	Morning	10
Morning	10	Morning	11	Morning	12
Noon	12	Noon	¼ before 1	Noon	1
Afternoon	1	Afternoon	¼ „ 2	Afternoon	2
Afternoon	2	Afternoon	¼ „ 3	Afternoon	3
Afternoon	3	Afternoon	¼ „ 4	Afternoon	4
Afternoon	4	Afternoon	¼ „ 5	Afternoon	5
Afternoon	5	Evening	¼ „ 6	Evening	6
Evening	6	Evening	7	Night	8
Night	8	Night	8	Next Morning	8

And each Delivery should be completed within One Hour and a Quarter after the stated hour of Despatch, according to distance and number of Letters.

From London to the Country.—Places having Five Deliveries daily.

If put into the Receiving Houses by	Hours.	Or the Principal Office by	Hours.	Are dispatched at	Hours.
Morning	8	Morning	9	Morning	10
Noon	12	Afternoon	¼ before 1	Afternoon	1
Afternoon	3	Afternoon	¼ „ 4	Afternoon	4
Afternoon	5	Afternoon	¼ „ 6	Evening	6
Evening	6	Evening	7	Night	8

Places having Four Deliveries Daily.

If put into the Receiving Houses by	Hours.	Or the Principal office by	Hours.	Are despatched at	Hours.
Morning	8	Morning	9	Morning	10
Noon	12	Afternoon	¼ before 1	Afternoon	1
Afternoon	3	Afternoon	¼ „ 4	Afternoon	4
Evening	6	Evening	7	Night	8

Places having Three Deliveries Daily.

Morning	8	Morning	9	Morning	10
Afternoon	3	Afternoon	¼ before 4	Afternoon	4
Evening	6	Evening	7	Night	8

The Deliveries in the Country should be completed from within one hour and a half to three hours after the stated hour of despatch, according to the distance from the General Post Office.

From the Country to London.

Letters put into the Post in time for the Morning Despatch, are sent out at 12 from the Principal Office, for Delivery in all parts of London. If put in for the Noon Despatch, they are sent out for Delivery at 3 o'clock. If for the Afternoon Despatch, they are sent out for Delivery at 8 o'clock in the Evening; and if put in for the Night Collection, they are despatched the following Morning, and are sent out for Delivery at 10 o'clock.

From one Part of the Country to another.

If going from one part of a Ride or District to another part of the same Ride or District, and put in for the Morning Despatch, they are delivered, through the means of a Bye-Post arrangement, the same Day at Noon. If put in for the Afternoon Despatch, they are delivered the same Evening, where an Evening Delivery is given. If going to parts not belonging to the same Ride, they come to London: such Letters put into the Post for the Morning Despatch, are delivered in the Country the same Evening, where an Evening Delivery is given; if for the Afternoon Despatch, the next Morning, where a Morning Delivery is given; or otherwise at Noon. The Deliveries given to each will be found in the List of Places.

STAMPS.

The Date Stamp on Letters, or, if there be more than one, that having the latest hour, shows the Day and time of Day they were despatched for Delivery. Persons having occasion to complain of the Delay of their Letters, are requested to transmit to the Superintendent President (R. Smith, Esq.) the Covers, with a statement of the Time of Delivery, as the Date and Stamp will assist materially in tracing their course.

Newspapers

pass free by the London District Post, except in those cases where they shall be posted and delivered within a circle of three miles, from the General Post Office, when the postage is one Penny on each Newspaper.

Letters not to be Delivered Back.

And to prevent the possibility of Letters being surreptitiously obtained from the Offices where put in, Office-keepers are strictly forbid returning, to any persons whatsoever, Letters that may be applied for, under whatever circumstances the recovery may be urged. This is moreover forbid by the established principle, that the instant a Letter is committed to the Post, it is no longer the property of the Sender.

Penalties.

By the 1st Victoria, cap. 36, sec. 2, any Person illegally conveying Letters incurs a Penalty of £5 for every offence, and £100 for every Week the practice is continued. The Sender also incurs a Penalty of £5 for every offence, with full costs of Suit.

COUNTRY DELIVERY.

The ountry limits is confined to a circle of Twelve miles, from the General Post Office, with the exception of Hampton CoCurt, Hampton and Sunbury, which are included in the limits, although more than Twelve miles from London. The following is a list of the places, showing the number of deliveries at each place, with the hours of despatch from the General Post Office, and the latest time at which letters can be posted at the Receiving Houses to be sent in the London bas.

LIST OF PLACES IN

THE COUNTRY DELIVERY

OF THE LONDON DISTRICT POST:

Showing also the Deliveries given Daily at each place: and in the following Columns, the Time fixed for the Departure of the Post from *such as have Receiving Houses.—Those having no Time stated have no Receiving Houses*

MONEY ORDER OFFICES.

B	Barking.	Cc	Croydon.	G	Greenwich.	Kb	Kingston.	Sb	Southall.
Bb	Barnet.	Da	Deptford.	H	Hackney.	L	Lewisham.	Sc	Stanmore.
Bc	Bexley.	Db	Dulwich.	Ha	Hammersmith.	N	Norwood.	Sd	Stratford.
Bd	Brentford.	Ea	Edgeware.	Hb	Hampstead.	Pa	Paddington.	Se	Sydenham
Be	Bromley, Kent.	Eb	Edmonton.	Hc	Harrow.	Pb	Putney.	T	Tooting.
Bf	Brompton.	Ec	Enfield.	Hd	Highgate.	Ra	Richmond.	Wa	Waltham cross.
Ca	Chelsea.	Ed	Epsom.	He	Hounslow.	Rb	Romford.	Wb	Woodford.
Cb	Clapham.	F	Footscray.	Ka	Kensington.	Sa	Shooters' Hill.	Wc	Woolwich.

At the above places marked thus * in the following list,

MONEY ORDERS

are granted and paid. They are not so at any other places in the Country Delivery of the London District Post. Prefixed to each place in the following list is a reference corresponding to that affixed to the place in the above list to which it is nearest. Therefore any person wishing to remit money to any place in the Country delivery of the London District Post, can readily ascertain on which Money Office the Order should be drawn.

The Country Delivery of this Office has been extended to a circle of twelve miles from the General Post-office.

Letters stamped Ten o'clock, are for the Delivery at Noon; One o'clock, for Delivery in the Afternoon; Four o'clock, for Delivery the same Evening; and Eight o'clock, for Delivery next Morning. Bye letters having in the Date Stamp the Letters Mg. should be delivered at Noon; those having the Letters Ev. the same Evening, where an Evening Delivery is given.

N.B. The number of Deliveries is regulated by the number of despatches from the General Post Office, which will be found marked against each place.

	PLACES.	Hours of Despatch from the General Post Office.					Number of Despatches from the country, with the latest Time at which Letters can be posted for the London Bag.				
		Morning.	Afternoon.	Afternoon.	Evening.	Night.	Morn h. m.	Noon h. m.	Aftern. h. m	Aftern. h. m	Ngt h. m
Bd	ACTON	10	1	4		8	8 30	1 0	4 0		7 30
d	Acton, East ...	10		4		8	8 15		3 45		
Ha	Apperton	10				8					
Cb	Balham	10	1	4	6	8	9 30	1 15	2 30	4 15	7 30
*	Barking	10	1	4		8	8 30	12 45	3 30		7 0
Ha	Barnes........	10	1	4		8	8 30	12 30	3 45		7 30
*	Barnet	10		4		8	8 45		3 45		
Ca	Battersea.	10	1	4	6	8	9 0	12 15	4 0		7 30
Ka	Bayswater	10	1	4	6	8	9 15	1 15	4 15	5 30	8 0
Be	Beckenham	10		4		8	8 45	12 30	3 45		
Cc	Beddington ...	10		4		8	8 15		3 15		
*	Bexley........	10		4		8	8 30		3 30		
Bc	Bexley Heath ..	10		4		8	8 0		3 0		
G	Blackheath....	10	1	4	6	8	9 15	1 0	4 45		8 0
Bc	Blendon	10		4		8			See Bexley		
Sd	Bow..........	10	1	4	6	8	9 45	1 45	4 45		7 45
*	Brentford	10	1	4		8	9 0	1 0	4 15		8 0
Bc	Bridging.......	10		4		8			See Bexley		
*	Bromley, Kent	10	1	4		8	8 30	12 45	3 30		
Sd	Bromley, Midd.	10	1	4	6	8			See Bow.		
*	Brompton	10	1	4	6	8	9 30	2 0	3 30	5 0	8 30
Ec	Bush Hill	10	1	4		8			See Enfield.		
Cc	Carshalton.....	10		4		8	8 45		3 45		
Wc	Charlton.......	10	1	4	6	8	9 0		4 15		
We	——— New...	10	1	4							

	PLACES.	Hours of Despatch from the General Post Office					Number of Despatches from the country, with the latest Time at which Letters can be posted for the London Bag.				
		Morning.	Afternoon.	Afternoon.	Evening.	Night.	Morn h. m.	Noon h. m.	Aftern. h. m	Aftern. h. m	Ngt h. m
Ed	Cheam........	10		4		8	8 15		3 15		
*	Chelsea	10	1	4	6	8	9 0	1 30	3 0	4 30	8 0
Wb	Chigwell	10		4		8	8 15		3 15		
Wb	Chigwell Row..	10		4		8	8 0		3 0		
Wb	Chingford.....	10		4		8	8 30		3 30		
F	Chiselhurst	10				8			2 45		
Ha	Chiswick.......	10	1	4		8	9 0	1 0	4 15		8
*	Clapham.......	10	1	4	6	8	9 45	1 30	3 0	4 30	8
H	Clapton........	10	1	4	6	8	9 30	1 45	4 33		
Bb	Colney Hatch..	10		4		8	8 30		3 30		
Bc	Crayford......	10		4		8	7 45		2 45		
Hd	Crouch End...	10	1	4	6	8	9 0	1 30	4 0		
*	Croydon......	10	I	4		8	8 45	12 30	3 45		
Rb	Dagenham....	10				8			2 30		
*	DeptfordBrdw.	10	1	4	6	8	9 30	1 0	4 45		8 0
*	Dulwich......	10	1	4	6	8	9 0	1 45	4 30		7 30
Bd	Ealing	10	1	4		8	8 15	12 15	3 30		7 15
Bd	Ealing, Little..	10	1	4		8					
Bb	East Barnet...	10		4		8	8 30		3 30		
Sd	East Ham.....	10		4		8	8 30		3 30		
Ra	East Sheen....	10	1	4		8	9 0	1 0	4 0		7 30
*	Edgware	10		4		8	8 45		3 45		
Eb	Edmonton, Lr. .	10	1	4		8	9 15	1 0	4 15		7 30
Eb	——— Uppr..	10	1	4		8	9 30	1 15	4 30		8 0
Ea	Elstree.......	10				8			3 0		

	PLACES.	Morning.	Afternoon.	Afternoon.	Evening.	Night.	Morn h. m.	Noon h. m.	Aftern. h.m.	Aftern. h.m.	Ngt h.m.
Sa	Eltham	10		4		8	9 0			4 0	
*	Enfield	10	1	4		8	9 0	12 45		4 0	7 0
Ec	Do. Highway..	10	1	4		8	8 0	12 0		3 0	8 0
Bc	Erith	10				8				2 30	
Hd	Finchley......	10		4		8	9 0			4 0	
*	Foot's Cray ..	10				8				2 45	
Bb	Fryern Barnet.	10		4		8	See Colney Hatch.				
Pb	Fulham	10	1	4	6	8	9 15	1 15		4 15	8 0
Hb	Golder's Grn..	10		4		8	See Hendon.				
Hc	Greenford	10				8	7 0			2 30	
*	Greenwich	10	1	4	6	8	9 0	1 0		4 45	8 0
Bb	Hadley	10		4		8	See Barnet.				
Ra	Ham	10		4		8	8 15			3 15	
*	Hammersmith.	10	1	4	6	8	9 15	1 30		4 30	8 0
*	Hampstead ..	10	1	4	6	8	9 30	2 0		4 30	8 0
Kb	Hampton	10		4		8	8 15			3 15	
Kb	Hamptn.Court.	10		4		8	8 0			3 0	
Kb	Hamptn.Wick.	10		4		8	8 30	3 30			
Bd	Hanwell	10	1	4		8	8 0	12 0		3 15	8 0
*	Harrow	10		4		8	9 0			4 0	
Be	Hayes, Kent ..	10				8				2 45	
Hb	Hendon.......	10		4		8	9 0			4 0	
He	Heston	10		4		8	8 15			3 30	
Wb	High Beech .	10	1	4		8	7 20			2 45	
*	Highgate	10	1	4	6	8	9 30	2 0		4 30	8 0
Bb	Highwood	10		4		8					
Pa	Holdsden Grn..	10		4							
H	Homerton	10	1	4	6	8	9 30	1 45		4 30	8 0
Hd	Hornsey......	10	1	4	6	8	8 50	1 15		3 50	
*	Hounslow	10		4		8	8 30	12 45		3 45	
Bc	Hurst	10		4		8	See Bexley.				
Ea	Hyde	10				8	8 0			3 30	
Ba	Ilford	10	1	4		8	9 15	1 15		4 15	8 0
Ba	Ilford, Little..	10	1	4		8					
Bd	Isleworth	10	1	4		8	8 30	12 30		3 30	8 0
Pa	Kensall Green..	10		4		8	9 30			4 30	
*	Kensington ..	10	1	4	6	8	9 30	1 45	3 15	4 30	8 30
Be	Keston	10				8	See Hayes, Kent.				
Bd	Kew	10	1	4		8	8 30	12 30		2 30	8 0
Pa	Kilburn	10	1	4	6	8	10 0	2 0			5 0
Ea	Kingsbury	10				8	See Hyde.				
	Kingston	10	1	4		8	8 45	12 30		3 45	
He	Lampton	10		4		8	See Hounslow.				
L	Lee	10	1	4	6	8	8 30			3 45	
*	Lewisham.....	10	1	4	6	8	9 15	1 0		4 30	7 45
Wb	Leyton	10	1	4	6	8	9 0	12 30		4 0	
Wb	Leytonstone ..	10	1	4	6	8	9 30	1 15		4 30	8 0
Pa	Lisson Grove..	10	1	4	6	8	10 0	1 45	3 30	4 45	8 0
Be	Locksbottom..	10				8					
Wb	Loughton ...	10				8	8 0			3 0	
Kb	Maldon, Surrey	10					See Cheam.				
T	Merton	10		4		8	9 0			4 0	
Ea	Mill Hill......	10		4		8	8 15			3 15	
T	Mitcham, Lr...	10	1	4	6	8	9 0	12 15		4 0	7 20
T	Mitcham, Upr..	10	1	4		8	9 15	1 0		4 15	7 30
T	Morden	10		4		8	8 45			3 45	
Ra	Mortlake.	10	1	4		8	8 45	12 45		4 0	7 30
Hd	Muswell Hill..	10	1	4	6	8	8 15			4 0	
Pa	Neasden......	10		4							
Da	New Cross ...	10	1	4	6	8	9 30	1 0		4 45	8 0
H	Newgtn. Stoke	10	1	4	6	8	10 0	1 45		5 0	8 0
Bc	North Cray ..	10				8	See Foot's Cray.				
Ha	Noh. End, Flhm.	10	1	4	6	8	9 0	1 15		4 0	8 0
* Hb	North End, Hampstead..	10	1	4	6	8					
Hc	Northol	10				8	See Greenford.				
*	Nrwood, Surry.	10	1	4	6	8	9 15	1 15		4 0	7 30
Sb	Norwoo , Mid.	10		4		8	8 0			3 15	
Sd	Old For	10	1	4	6	8					
*	Paddington ..	10	1	4	6	8	10 0	1 45	3 30	5 0	8 0
Eb	Palmers' Grn..	10		4		8					
Pb	Parsons' Grn..	10	1	4	6	8	9 15	1 0		4 15	7 45
	Peckham	10	1	4	6	8	9 15	1 30		4 15	7 45
Hc	Perrivale	10									

	PLACES.	Morning.	Afternoon.	Afternoon.	Evening.	Night.	Morn h. m.	Noon h. m.	Aftern. h.m.	Aftern. h.m.	Ngt h.m.
Ra	Petersham....	10		4		8	8 0			3 30	
Sd	Plaistow, Essex	10		4		8	9 0	1 0		4 0	
Be	Plaistow, Kent.	10		4		8	See Bromley.				
Wc	Plumstead. ..	10				8	8 15			3 30	
Ec	Ponder's End. .	10	1	4		8	8 30	12 15		3 30	7 30
Pa	Portland Twn..	10	1	4	6	8	9 45	1 45	3 15	4 30	8 0
Bb	Potter's Bar ..	10				8	8 0			3 0	
*	Putney	10	1	4		8	9 30	1 15		4 30	8 0
Bf	Queen's Elm ..	10	1	4	6	8	9 0	1 30	3 0	4 30	8 0
Rb	Rainham, Essex	10								2 0	
*	Richmond. ...	10	1	4		8	9 0	12 45		4 0	8 0
Pb	Roehampton ..	10	1	4		8	9 0	12 30		4 0	
*	Romford.	10		4		8	8 45			3 45	
Wa	Sewardston ..	10				8					
Ha	Shephd's. Bush.	10	1	4	6	8	8 45	1 0		4 0	
*	Shooter's Hill...	10		4		8	8 0			3 15	8 0
F	Sidcup	10				8	See Foot's Cray.				
Wb	Snaresbrook ..	10	1	4		8					
*	Southall	10		4		8				2 45	
Be	Southborough..	10				8	See Bromley.				
Sa	S. End, Eltham..	10		4			See Eltham.				
L	S.E., Lewishm..	10		4		8	8 45			3 45	
Eb	Southgate	10		4		8	8 30			3 30	
H	Stamford Hill..	10	1	4	6	8	9 45	1 45		4 45	7 45
*	Stanmore	10		4		8	8 0			3 0	
F	St. Mary Cray...	10				8				2 15	
Cb	Stockwell	10	1	4	6	8	9 45	1 30	3 0	4 30	8 0
F	St. Paul's Cray.	10				8	See St. Mary's Cray.				
Bd	Strand undr. Gn	10	1	4		8					
*	Stratford .. .	10	1	4	6	8	9 30	1 45		4 30	8 0
N	Streatham	10	1	4	6	8	9 0	12 45		4 0	8 0
Kb	Sunbury.	10				8	7 20			2 45	
Ed	Sutton.. Surry	10		4		8	8 30			3 30	
He	Sutton... Midd.	10		4		8	See Heston.				
Ha	Sutton, Little..	10		4		8					
*	Sydenham ...	10		4		8	9 0	1 0		4 0	
Kb	Teddington. ..	10		4		8	8 0			3 0	
Cc	Thornton Hth...	10		4		8	8 30			3 30	
T	Tooting, Lower.	10	1	4	6	8	9 30	1 15		4 30	7 30
T	Tooting, Upper.	10	1	4	6	8	9 15	1 0		4 15	7 15
Eb	Tottenham. ..	10	1	4		8	9 45	1 30		4 45	7 30
Bb	Totteridge .. .	10		4		8	8 30			30	
Bd	Turnham Grn...	10	1	4		8	9 0	1 15		15	8 0
Ra	Twickenham ..	10	1	4		8	8 45	12 30		3 45	8 0
Sd	Upton, Essex...	10	1	4		8					
Bc	Upton, Kent ..	10		4		8	See Bexley.				
Cc	Waddon	10		4		8					
Ha	Walham Grn..	10	1	4	6	8	9 30	12 45		4 30	7 30
Cc	Wallington....	10		4		8					
Wa	Walthm. Abby..	10	1			8		12 0		2 45	
*	Waltham Cros.	10	1			8		12 30		3 0	
Wb	Walthamstow .	10	1	4	6	8	8 45	12 30		3 45	
Pb	Wandsworth ..	10	1	4	6	8	9 30	1 0		4 30	8 0
Wb	Wanstead	10	1	4		8	9 0	12 45		4 0	
Sa	Welling	10		4		8	7 30			2 45	
Hc	Wembly	10		4							
Hb	West End, Hampstead...	10		4	6	8					
Sd	West Ham	10	1	4	6	8	9 20	1 30		4 20	
Sd	Ditto Abbey...	10	1	4	6	8					
Bb	Whetstone. ...	10		4		8	9 0			4 0	
Wb	Whips' Cross..	10	1	4	6	8	9 0	12 45		4 0	
Ea	Whitchurch ..	10				8	See Edgware.				
Bd	Whitton	10		4			7 45			2 45	
Sa	Wickham, Ea..	10		4		8	Slee Welling.				
Be	Wickham, W...	10				8				2 15	
Be	Widmore	10				8	See Bromley.				
Hc	Wilsdon	10		4			9 30			4 30	
Pb	Wimbledon ...	10		4		8	8 30			3 30	
Eb	Winchmre. Hl..	10		4		8	8 40			3 40	
*	Woodford	10	1	4		8	9 15	1 0		4 15	8 0
Wb	Woodfrd. Bdg..	10		4		8	9 0			4 0	
*	Woolwich	10	1	4		8	9 0	12 45		4 0	8 0
Bd	Worton	10		4							

N.B.—Letters despatched from the General Post Office at 8 o'clock p.m. are delivered in the Country Districts the following morning.

THE GENERAL & LONDON DISTRICT POST RECEIVING HOUSES

are for the receipt of General, Foreign, Ship, and London District Post Letters, both paid and unpaid, with the exception of the Receiving Houses at 24 Cornhill, 21 Charing Cross, and 313 Regent Street, near Langham Place, at which places General Post Letters cannot be received. Unpaid Letters, and Letters bearing adhesive stamps, or enclosed in stamped covers, must be dropped into the box, and Paid Letters taken into the Office. *General Post Letter* posted after *half-past* 5 *o'clock* cannot be forwarded the same evening. *Newspapers* intended to pass by the General Post THE SAME NIGHT must be put in *before* 5 *o'clock.*

⁂ General Post Letters for the Day Mails can be put into the Receiving Houses till eight o'clock in the morning of the day on which the Mails are despatched.

LIST OF RECEIVING HOUSES,

WITHIN THE TOWN DISTRICTS OF THE LONDON DISTRICT (LATE TWOPENNY) POST.

At these offices Letters are despatched for the London Delivery, Ten times daily; viz., 8, 10, and 12 in the morning and 1, 2, 3, 4, 5, 6, 8, in the afternoon; and for the Country, at 8 and 12 morning, and 3, 5, and 6 o'clock, afternoon.—

⁂ *Those in* CAPITALS *are Money Order Offices.*

No. NORTH.

54 Amwell street, Clerkenwell
Bagnigge wells, 9 Acton place
31 Barbican
BATTLE BRIDGE, 1 PLEASANT RW
81 Bunhill row
City road, Anderson's buildings, opposite the Orphan School
36 CITY RD. NEAR OLD STREET RD
City road, 31 Ashley crescent
41 Clerkenwell green
39 Cleveland street, Fitzroy square
1 Crawley street, St. Pancras
7 Exmouth street, Clerkenwell
5 Goswell street
40 Goswell road
109 Goswell street
43 UP. NORTH PL. GRAY'S INN RD
Hampstead road, 37 Frederick place, corner of Edward street
13 High st. Islington, corner of White Lion st
54 Leather lane
103 Old street
Pancras, 27 Judd pl. west, New rd
6 St. John street, Clerkenwell
10 Smithfield bars
10 Tabernacle square
Whitecross street, *in the prison*

SOUTH.

Belvedere pl. Southwark Bridge rd. *(within the Queen's Bench prison)*
BERMONDSEY, 9 DOCKHEAD
Bermondsey, 4 Salmon pl. Grange rd
203 Bermondsey street
111 Blackfriars road
231 Blackfriars road
106 Blackman street, Borough
Horselydown, 22 Back street
55 Borough
Dover road, Alsop buildings
1 Gillingham street, Vauxhall br road
Horselydown, 22 Back street
Kent street road, 7 York place
Kent rd. (New), 5 Providence bldgs
5 Knightrider street (Little)
Lambeth, 93 Bridge road
Lambeth, 60 Commercial road
Lambeth, 38 High street
Lambeth, 66 Lower Marsh
LAMBETH, 33 MOUNT STREET
Lambeth, 2 Saville place
128 London road, Southwark
4 New Park street, Southwark

No.

Newington Causeway, 36 Bridge house place
12 Rotherhithe wall
Ditto, 50 Lower Queen street
54 St. Thomas' place, Gt. Dover street
196 Tooley street
48 Union street, Southwark

EAST.

27 Aldgate
141 Bethnal green road*
72 Bishopsgate within
160 Bishopsgate without
Blackwall, opposite the Plough*
51 Brick lane, Spitalfields
77 Cable street
102 Cheapside
37 Clifton street, Finsbury market
Commercial road, E. 8 Prince's place
Commercial road, E. 38 Colet place
Commercial road, 2 Waterloo terr
24 *Cornhill, for London District Post Letters only*
12 East Smithfield (Upper)
136 Fenchurch street
5 Finsbury place, north
99 Fore street, Cripplegate
36 Great Tower street
8 Hackney road
Hackney road, 16 Wade's place
Hackney road, 13 Gwynn's place*
139 Hoxton Old town, High street*
Hoxton New town, 3 Haberdasher's p
65 King William street, City
26 Leadenhall street
LIMEHOUSE, 5 THREE COLT ST
Limehouse bridge, opposite the church
8 Mansell street, Goodman's fields
Mile end road, 4 Freeman's place
Mile end, 6 Ireland row
Mile end (New) 2 doors west of Grove road*
104 Minories
60 Moorgate street
26 New road, St. George east
27 Norton folgate
234 Poplar High street*
70 Queen street, Cheapside
RATCLIFF CROSS, 77 BROAD ST
221 Shadwell High street
211 Shoreditch
2 Stepney High street
83 Thames street (Lower)
21 Throgmorton street

No

9 Wapping wall
340 Wapping
1 WHITECHAPEL ROAD
133 Whitechapel road

WEST.

99 Albany st. Regent's park
87 Berwick street, Soho
7 Blackmoor st. Clare market
5 Blandford st. Manchester sq
25 Bridge street, Westminster
1 BROAD STREET, BLOOMSBURY
8 Broadway, Westminster
61 Brook street, Hanover square
9 Bruton street
38 Castle st. Leicester sq
93 Chancery lane
8 Chapel st. Grosvenor place
15 *Charing Cross, for London District Letters only*
3 Charles st. (Upper), Westminster
6 Connaught terrace, Edgware road
25 Crawford street
27 Cromer street
48 Curzon street, Mayfair
37 Devonshire st. Portland place
88 Drummond st. Euston sq
148 Drury lane
12 Duke street, Manchester square
5 Eccleston street
63 Edgware road
72 Farringdon street
117 Fetter lane
31 Fleet street
84 Fleet street
32 Gray's Inn lane
57 Great Coram street, Russell square
7 Great Mary-le-bone street
51 Great Portland street
21 Great Russell st. Covent garden
43 Great Russell st. Bloomsbury
47 Greek street, Soho
16 Grenville st. Brunswick sq
55 High street, St. Giles's
44 High Holborn
116 High Holborn
14 Holborn bars
107 Holborn hill, corner of Hatton Grd
30 Jermyn street
132 Jermyn street
2 King street, Covent Garden
Knightsbridge, 32 St. George's pl
52 Lamb's Conduit street
3 Leigh street, Burton crescen
33 Little Newport street

There is no 8 o'clock night collection from these offices.

No.
41 Long Acre
35 Ludgate street
4 Lyall place, Eaton square
19 Maddox st. Hanover square
23 Mary-le-bone st. Golden sq
2 Millbank street, Westminster
5 Mount street, Grosvenor sq
49 Newman street
24 Osnaburgh st. Regent's park
21 Oxford street
98 Oxford street
152 Oxford street
210 OXFORD STREET
119 Pall Mall
35 Park street, Grosvenor square
18 Park terrace, Regent's park road

No
PIMLICO, 28 QUEEN'S ROW
Pmlico, 1 Ranelagh terrace
65 PICCADILLY
119 Piccadilly, corner of Down st
17 Portugal street
61 Princes st. Leicester sq
52 Red Lion street
189 Regent street, St. James's
11 Regent pl. Horseferry rd. Westmin
313 *Regent st., near Langham place,*
3 St. James's street
27 Skinner street, Snowhill
161 Sloane street*
179 Sloane street
27 Southampton row, Russell sq
16 South Audley street
34 South Audley street

No.
38 Store street, Bedford square
49 Strand
104 Strand
180 STRAND
338 Strand
7 Sussex pl. (Little) Hyde pk. gardens
Temple, 2 Devereux court
29 Thayer st. Manchester sq
1 Torrington place
57 Tottenham court road
103 TOTTENHAM COURT ROAD
132 Tottenham court road
54 UPPER BAKER ST. NEW ROAD
70 Upper Berkeley st. Portman sq
19 Upper Berkeley street west
2 Vigo street

* There is no 8 o'clock night collection from this office.

AT THE FOLLOWING RECEIVING HOUSES (WITHIN THE THREE-MILE CIRCLE) LETTERS ARE DESPATCHED AT THE HOURS STATED IN EACH COLUMN.

	MORNING.						AFTERNOON.							
	h.	m.	h.	m.	h.	m.	h.	m.	h.	m.	h.	m.	h.	m.
Albany road, Kent road	7	45	9	45	11	30	1	45	3	30	4	45		
Balls Pond road, No. 4 North place	7	45	9	45	11	15	1	45	3	15	4	45		
Brixton (North) 14 Claremont place	7	30	9	15	11	0	1	15	3	0	4	45		
Brixton road, 18 Commerce place	7	45	9	30	11	15	1	45	3	15	5	0		
Caledonian road	7	30	9	45	11	45	1	30	3	45	4	45		
Camberwell green, 1 New terrace	8	0	10	0	11	15	2	0	3	15	5	0	7	45
Camberwell grove, 22 Church street	7	45	9	45	11	0	1	45	3	0	4	45		
Camberwell New road, 5 Leicester place	7	30	9	15	11	15	1	30	3	15	4	45		
Camberwell road, 3 Clarence place	7	45	9	45	11	20	1	45	3	20	4	45		
Camberwell, 3 Edward place, Southampton street	7	45	9	45	11	10	1	45	3	10	4	45		
Camden Town, 89 High street	8	0	10	0	11	30	2	0	3	30	5	0	7	30
Camden New Town, 2 Great Randolph street	7	45	9	45	11	30	1	45	3	30	4	45		
Camden Town, Park street	7	45	9	45	11	0	1	30	3	0	4	45		
Clarendon square (7), Somers town	8	0	10	0	11	45	2	0	3	45	5	0	7	30
Clapham road, 2 Holland place	7	30	9	30	11	15	1	30	3	15	5	0		
Dalston, 1 Victoria place	7	45	9	45	11	30	1	45	3	30	4	45		
Highbury, No. 1 Park terrace	7	15	9	45	11	15	1	45	3	15	4	45		
Holloway, 6 Pleasant place	7	15	9	45	11	15	1	45	3	15	4	45		
Holloway road, 17 Wells row	7	30	10	0	11	15	2	0	3	15	5	0		
Hackney, Church street	7	45	9	45	11	15	1	45	3	15	4	45	7	45
Hackney, Mare street	7	45	9	30	11	30	1	45	3	30	4	40		
Islington, 9 Lower road	7	45	9	45	11	30	1	45	3	30	4	45		
Islington, Liverpool road, 10 Felix terrace	7	45	9	45	11	15	1	45	3	15	4	15		
Islington, 13 High street	8	0	10	0	11	30	2	0	3	30	5	0	8	0
Islington, 3 Brunswick terrace, Barnsbury road	8	0	9	45	11	30	2	0	3	30	5	0		
Islington, 86 Upper street	7	45	9	45	11	30	1	45	3	30	4	45		
Kentish town, 10 Providence place	7	45	9	45			1	45	3	15	4	45		
Kennington, 3 Octagon place	7	45	9	30	11	30	1	45	3	30	5	0		
Kennington cross (2)	7	45	9	30	11	30	1	45	3	30	5	0		
Kent road, 9 Northampton place	8	0	10	0	11	45	2	0	3	45	5	0	7	30
Kent road, 18 Sussex place	7	45	9	45	11	15	1	45	3	15	4	45		
Kingsland green, No. 1	8	0	10	0	11	15	2	0	3	15	5	0	7	30
Lambeth, 5 East place	7	45	9	30	11	15	1	45	3	15	4	45		
Newington Butts, 22 High street	8	0	10	0	11	30	2	0	3	30	5	0	7	0
Pancras road, 6 Aldenham terrace	7	50	9	40	11	45	1	50	3	15	4	45		
Penton street (44), Pentonville	7	45	9	45	11	30	1	45	3	30	5	0		
Shacklewell, 7 High street	7	45	9	45	11	0	1	45	3	0	4	45		
Vauxhall	8	0	10	0	11	30	1	45	3	45	5	0	7	30
Walworth road, 10 Staverton row	7	45	9	45	11	45	1	45	3	45	4	45		
Walworth road, 13 Bolingbroke row	7	45	9	45	11	30	1	45	3	30	4	45		
Walworth, 23 Crosby row	8	0	10	0	11	30	2	0	3	30	5	0	8	0
South Lambeth	7	45	9	45	11	15	1	30	3	30	4	30		

MAILS.

LIST OF POST TOWNS TO WHICH LETTERS AND NEWSPAPERS ARE FORWARDED BY THE

MORNING AS WELL AS BY THE EVENING MAILS.

Abingdon
Accrington
Alnwick
Andover Road
Appleby
Ashford
Attleborough
Aylesbury
Banbury
Bangor
Barnsley
Basingstoke
Bath
Battle
Beaumaris
Belford
Belper
Berkhempstead
Berwick
Bilstone
Birmingham
Bishops Stortford
Blackburn
Bolton
Brackley
Bradford, Yorksh.
Brandon
Brentwood
Bridgewater
Brighton
Bristol
Brough
Buckingham
Burnley
Bury St. Edmunds
Cambridge
Canterbury
Carlisle
Carnarvon
Chatham
Chelmsford
Cheltenham
Chepstow
Chester
Chesterfield
Chippenham
Chorley
Cirencester
Clitheroe
Cockermouth
Colchester
Conway
Coventry
Cowes
Cranbrook
Cuckfield
Darlington
Dartford
Daventry
Derby
Dorking
Dover
Downham
Dunmow
Durham
Dursley
Ely
Exeter
Fairford
Fareham
Farringdon
Felton
Fenny Stratford
Feversham
Folkstone
Gateshead
Gloucester
Godalmin
Gosport
Grantham
Gravesend
Guernsey
Guildford
Halifax
Hastings
Hemel Hempstead
Hertford
Highworth
Hoddesdon
Holyhead
Holywell
Huddersfield
Hurst Green
Hythe
Ipswich
Jersey
Kelvedon
Kendal
Kenilworth
Lancaster
Leamington
Lechlade
Leeds
Leicester
Leighton Buzzard
Lewes
Liverpool
Loughborough
Lynn
Maidenhead
Maidstone
Manchester
Margate
Maryport
Melton Mowbray
Milnthorpe
Mold
Monmouth
Morpeth
Newcastle, Staff.
Newcastle on Tyne
Newmarket
Newport, I. of W
Newport Pagnell
Northallerton
Northampton
North Shields
Nottingham
Norwich
Oxford
Penkridge
Penrith
Portsmouth
Preston
Preston Brook
Pwlheli
Ramsgate
Reading
Reigate
Rickmansworth
Ripon
Rochdale
Rochester
Rotherham
Rugby
Ryde
Rye
Saffron Walden
Seven Oaks
Sheffield
Shiffnall
Shoreham
Shrewsbury
Sittingbourne
Slough
Southampton
South Shields
Staplehurst
St. Albans
St. Asaph
St. Leonards
Stafford
Stockport
Stone
Stony Stratford
Stratford-on-Avon
Stroud
Sunderland
Swindon
Taunton
Tenterden
Tetbury
Thetford
Thirsk
Towcester
Tring
Tunbridge
Tunbridge Wells
Ulverstone
Uxbridge
Wakefield
Wallingford
Walsall
Ware
Warrington
Warwick
Watford
Wednesbury
Weedon
Wellington Salop
Wellington, Som.
West Bromwich
Whitehaven
Wigan
Wigton
Winchester
Windsor
Witham
Wolverhampton
Workington
Worthing
Wooton-under-Edge
Wymondham
Yarmouth
York

All Ireland
All Scotland

For all the above places the Letter Boxes at the Receiving Houses will be open till 7 A.M. for Newspapers, and 8 A.M. for letters; and those at the Branch Offices, Charing Cross, Old Cavendish street, and the Borough, for the reception of Newspapers, until half past 7 A. M. and for Letters until 8 A.M. At the General Post Office and the Branch Office in Lombard street, the boxes will close for Newspapers at a quarter before 8 A.M., and for Letters at half past 8 A.M.

LONDON MAILS.

HOURS OF ARRIVAL AND DEPARTURE: — The Lancaster, Preston, Liverpool and Manchester MORNING MAIL (by Birmingham, Grand Junction, and North Union Lancaster Railway), which conveys despatches to Ireland, leaves the General Post Office at *half past nine in the morning;* the Brighton and Dover (DAY) MAILS at ten. The Bristol, Cheltenham and Exeter (DAY) leave at thirty minutes past nine. The Portsmouth and Southampton (Day), at ten, and the Cambridge, Ipswich and Yarmouth (Day), at eleven. The Evening Mails leave London at eight o'clock. They all arrive between the hours of five and seven in the morning, with the exception of the Portsmouth and Southampton (Day), which arrive about five minutes past one o'clock; the Brighton (Day), about fifty-five minutes past one; the Bristol and Cheltenham (Day), about forty-five minutes past one; the Lancaster, Preston and Liverpool and Manchester (Day), at twenty-eight min. past one; the Dover (Day), about fifty-five min. past one; and the Yarmouth (Day), at one *in the afternoon.*

Dublin Morning Mail from London.

The despatches are forwarded by the Birmingham Railway to Liverpool. They arrive at 5. 20 p.m. The packet sails immediately afterwards, and is about 12 hours on its voyage. The letters are delivered in Dublin on the morning following the one on which they were despatched from London.

Dublin Evening Mail from London.

The Mails are forwarded by the Birmingham Railway to Birkenhead, where they arrive at 4. 46 A.M. The Packet sails immediately on the arrival of the Irish Mails, and is about 12 hours on its voyage. The Letters for Dublin and the vicinity are delivered shortly after the arrival of the Packet, and those for the Provinces forwarded by the Mails of the same evening.

Edinburgh Morning Mail from London.

The letters are forwarded by the Birmingham Railway. They arrive at Newcastle at 11. 15 p.m., and are despatched at midnight, and the Mail arrives in Edinburgh at 1. 35 p.m., having been 28 hours and five minutes on its journey from London.

Edinburgh Evening Mail from London.

The Mails are forwarded by the Birmingham and Midland Railways. They arrive at Newcastle at 8. 45 on the following morning, and are despatched immediately, and the Mail arrives in Edinburgh at 9. 33 P.M. having been 25 hours 33 minutes on its journey. The Letters for places beyond Edinburgh are forwarded by various Mails, for which see "CROSS ROAD MAILS," in which the routes can be traced.

Glasgow Morning Mail from London.

The letters are forwarded by the Birmingham Railway. They arrive at Lancaster at 6. 35 p.m., and are despatched 7. 0 p.m., and the Mail arrives in Glasgow at 11. 41 a.m., having been 26 hours and 11 minutes on its journey from London.

Glasgow Evening Mail from London.

The Mails are forwarded by the Birmingham Railway. They arrive at Lancaster at 6. 39 on the following morning, and are at 6. 49 forwarded to Carlisle, where they arrive at 1. 39 P.M. The despatch from Carlisle takes place at 2. 20 P.M. and the Mail arrives in Glasgow at 11. 50 P.M. having been 27 hours 50 minutes on its journey from London.

RAILWAY MAILS.

		Distance from the Railway Stations.		Starts from place in first column at	Arrives at destination at	Sets out on return at	Arrives at place in first column at
		miles.	frlongs.	h. m.	h. m.	h. m.	h. m.
LONDON	AND BIRMINGHAM .	111	6	10 0 a m	1 30 p m	8 32 a m	1 0 p m
LONDON	AND BIRMINGHAM .	111	6	8 30 p m	12 57 a m	1 5 a m	5 32 a m
LONDON	AND BRIGHTON	50	4	10 30 a m	12 35 p m	11 30 a m	1 30 p m
LONDON	AND BRIGHTON	50	0	10 30 a m	12 5 p m	11 30 a m	1 30 p m
LONDON	AND BRISTOL	118	2	10 15 a m	2 30 p m	8 40 a m	1 5 p m
LONDON	AND BRISTOL	118	2	8 55 p m	1 10 a m	12 25 a m	4 45 a m
LONDON	AND COLCHESTER..	51	0	8 30 p m	10 49 p m	2 45 a m	5 4 a m
LONDON	AND DOVER	88	5	8 30 p m	12 15 a m	1 30 a m	5 0 a m
LONDON	AND IPSWICH	70	0	11 0 a m	3 25 p m	8 55 a m	1 11 p m
LONDON	AND PETERBORO' ..	111	0	8 30 p m	1 15 a m	12 45 a m	5 32 a m
LONDON	AND PORTSMOUTH..	87	0	8 35 p m	1 17 a m	11 0 p m	6 0 a m
LONDON	AND SOUTHAMPTON	77	0	8 35 p m	11 57 a m	2 15 a m	5 25 a m
LONDON	AND SOUTHAMPTON	77	0	11 0 a m	2 0 p m	9 0 a m	12 30 p m
LONDON	AND YARMOUTH....	146	0	11 30 a m	6 30 p m	5 30 a m	12 45 p m
LONDON	AND YARMOUTH....	146	0	8 40 p m	3 51 a m	10 17 p m	5 22 a m
BIRMINGHAM	AND DERBY........	41	2	12 5 a m	1 50 a m	11 0 p m	12 45 a m
BIRMINGHAM	AND BRISTOL	90	4	1 10 a m	5 30 a m	7 5 p m	11 30 p m
BIRMINGHAM	AND LIVERPOOL ...	97	2	1 50 p m	5 20 p m	4 9 a m	8 12 a m
BIRMINGHAM	AND LIVERPOOL....	97	2	11 22 a m	3 22 p m	11 10 a m	3 31 p m
BIRMINGHAM	AND LIVERPOOL ...	97	2	1 17 a m	5 10 a m	8 27 p m	12 45 a m
BISHOP'S STOKE ..	AND GOSPORT.......	15	0	11 44 p m	12 32 a m	1 38 a m	2 19 a m
BRISTOL........	AND EXETER	75	0	1 20 a m	4 0 a m	9 35 p m	12 15 a m
BRISTOL	AND EXETER........	75	0	8 0 a m	10 45 a m	3 15 p m	5 50 p m
BRISTOL	AND EXETER........	75	0	2 45 p m	5 20 p m		
CARLISLE.......	AND NEWCASTLE ..	59	0	12 5 p m	3 0 p m	9 50 a m	1 15 p m
CHESTER	AND BIRKENHEAD..	14	4	4 16 a m	4 46 a m	8 59 p m	9 29 p m
COVENTRY	AND LEAMINGTON .	8	6	1 15 p m	1 40 p m	8 35 a m	9 0 a m
CREWE..........	AND BIRKENHEAD..	35	4	3 26 a m	4 46 a m	8 59 p m	10 21 p m
CREWE..........	AND CHESTER	21	0	3 26 a m	4 11 a m	9 34 p m	10 21 p m
CREWE..........	AND CHESTER	21	0	3 50 p m	4 50 p m	4 45 a m	5 45 a m
DUNDEE	AND ARBROATH....	17	0	10 30 a m	11 20 p m	10 10 a m	11 0 a m
EDINBURGH.....	AND GLASGOW......	46	0	8 30 a m	10 0 a m	8 30 a m	10 0 a m
EDINBURGH.....	AND GLASGOW	46	0	1 0 p m	2 30 p m	1 0 p m	2 30 p m
EDINBURGH.....	AND GLASGOW	46	0			3 0 p m	4 40 p m
EDINBURGH.....	AND GLASGOW	46	0	10 0 p m	12 30 a m	10 0 p m	12 30 a m
GLASGOW.......	AND AYR	40	0	4 30 p m	6 30 p m	11 0 a m	1 0 p m
GLASGOW.......	AND GREENOCK....	22	4	1 20 p m	1 0 p m	9 30 a m	10 26 a m
GLASGOW.......	AND GREENOCK....	22	4	3 0 p m	4 0 p m	12 30 p m	1 26 p m
GLASGOW.......	AND GREENOCK....	22	4	5 0 p m	6 0 p m	3 30 p m	4 26 p m
GLASGOW.......	AND PAISLEY	7	0	1 30 p m	1 46 a m	9 0 p m	9 20 p m
LEEDS	AND HULL	54	0	4 0 a m	6 30 a m	6 0 p m	8 25 p m
LIVERPOOL......	AND MANCHESTER .	30	0	8 45 a m	10 10 a m	9 0 a m	10 15 a m
LIVERPOOL......	AND MANCHESTER .	30	0	10 30 a m	12 20 p m	11 15 a m	1 15 p m
LIVERPOOL......	AND MANCHESTER .	30	0	2 0 p m	3 15 p m	2 0 p m	3 15 p m
LIVERPOOL......	AND MANCHESTER.	30	0	7 45 p m	9 30 p m	5 0 p m	6 15 p m
MANCHESTER....	AND HULL	98	5	10 9 p m	8 21 a m	10 0 p m	6 6 a m
MANCHESTER....	AND LEEDS	60	0	10 24 a m	1 14 p m	10 46 a m	1 31 p m
NORMANTON......	AND LEEDS	9	6	4 36 a m	5 0 a m	7 30 p m	8 0 p m
OXFORD	AND DIDCOTE......	10	0	10 45 a m	11 10 a m	12 12 p m	12 38 p m
OXFORD	AND DIDCOTE.	10	0	2 20 a m	2 49 a m	10 53 p m	11 16 p m
PARKSIDE	AND LIVERPOOL.....	18	0			3 20 p m	4 35 p m
PARKSIDE	AND PRESTON......	22	2	4 50 p m	5 40 p m	3 37 a m	4 37 a m
PARKSIDE	AND PRESTON......	22	2	4 44 a m	5 34 a m	8 3 p m	8 53 p m
GOSPORT	AND BISHOPSTOKE..	15	0	8 30 a m	9 11 a m	1 37 p m	2 25 p m
PRESTON	AND LANCASTER ..	20	1	5 44 a m	6 29 a m	7 8 p m	7 53 p m
PRESTON	AND LANCASTER ..	20	1	5 50 p m	6 35 p m	2 42 a m	3 27 a m
REIGATE	AND DOVER.........	67	0	12 23 p m	3 5 p m	9 30 a m	12 17 p m
RUGBY	AND NEWCASTLE ...	220	1	11 50 p m	8 45 a m	3 25 p m	1 10 a m
RUGBY	AND NEWCASTLE....	220	1	1 30 p m	11 0 p m	10 50 p m	9 30 a m
STOCKTON........	AND DARLINGTON..	12	0	4 5 p m	4 45 p m	7 40 a m	8 15 a m
SWINDON........	AND GLO'STER	37	0	11 52 p m	1 10 a m	12 15 a m	1 50 a m
SWINDON........	AND GLO'STER	37	0	1 15 p m	2 40 p m	8 30 a m	10 13 a m
WARRINGTON	AND MANCHESTER.	19	2	4 25 a m	5 8 a m	4 9 a m	4 57 a m
WARRINGTON	AND MANCHESTER.	19	2	2 28 p m	3 13 p m	11 10 a m	11 5 p m
WARRINGTON	AND MANCHESTER.	19	2	4 25 p m	5 15 p m	8 28 p m	9 15 p m

CROSS ROAD MAILS.

		Distance.		Starts from place first column at	Arrives at destination at	Sets out on return at	Arrives at place in first column at
		miles.	frlongs.	h. m.	h. m.	h. m.	h. m.
ABERDEEN	AND BALLATER	42	0	7 15 a m	12 50 p m	9 0 a m	2 35 p m
ABERDEEN	AND INVERNESS.....	106	7	7 10 a m	7 10 p m	2 34 a m	2 30 p m
ABERDEEN	AND PETERHEAD ..	34	0	7 0 a m	11 3 a m	8 0 a m	12 3 p m
ABERGAVENNY ..	AND MERTHYR......	20	0	6 45 a m	9 45 p m	3 0 p m	6 0 p m
BARNSTAPLE....	AND BIDEFORD	9	4	8 54 a m	10 14 a m	3 24 p m	4 40 p m
BARNSTAPLE....	AND ILFRACOMBE ...	11	0	8 44 a m	10 14 a m	3 20 p m	4 50 p m

CROSS ROAD MAILS—*continued.*

	Distance.		Starts from place in first column at	Arrives at destination at	Sets out on return at	Arrives at place in first column at
	miles.	frlongs.	h. m.	h. m.	h. m.	h. m.
BARNSTAPLE .... AND LAUNCESTON...	41	1	2 30 p m	8 45 p m	4 30 a m	10 45 a m
BEGELLY .....AND HAVERFORDWEST	15	1	6 41 p m	9 21 p m	3 20 a m	6 0 p m
BEWDLEY........ AND STOURPORT....	3	3	5 30 a m	5 55 a m	6 50 p m	7 15 p m
BIRMINGHAM.... AND HOLYHEAD.....	150	6	2 0 a m	5 32 p m	6 45 a m	10 41 p m
BIRMINGHAM.... AND LUDLOW	45	0	2 15 a m	8 40 a m	4 0 p m	10 25 p m
BIRMINGHAM.... AND SHREWSBURY..	44	4	2 0 p m	7 0 p m	6 45 a m	11 45 a m
BOSTON......... AND HULL...........	66	0	8 45 a m	5 14 p m	7 50 a m	4 49 p m
BRISTOL......... AND HEREFORD....	52	4	3 30 p m	9 48 p m	6 0 a m	12 8 noon
BRISTOL......... AND SWANSEA	89	0	8 0 a m	7 0 p m	6 0 a m	5 0 p m
CAMBRIDGE..AND BURY ST. EDMUNDS	28	0	1 30 p m	5 0 p m	6 0 a m	9 30 a m
CAMBRIDGE..... AND HOLBEACH	58	0	11 45 p m	7 12 a m	6 18 p m	1 45 a m
CARLISLE........ AND EDINBURGH...	94	2	2 20 p m	12 13 a m	1 39 a m	11 19 a m
CARLISLE .... AND GLASGOW......	94	7	2 11 a m	11 41 a m	9 0 a m	6 30 p m
CARLISLE .... AND GLASGOW	94	7	2 20 p m	11 50 p m	1 39 a m	11 9 p m
CARLISLE .... AND DUMFRIES	33	5	2 20 p m	5 43 p m	7 56 a m	11 19 a m
CARLISLE .... AND PORT PATRICK	85	2	2 20 p m	4 21 a m	6 52 p m	11 19 a m
CARLISLE .... AND WHITEHAVEN.	42	6	12 0 noon	4 46 p m	8 44 a m	1 30 p m
CARMARTHEN ... AND CARDIGAN	31	0	2 15 p m	6 45 p m	5 40 a m	10 40 a m
CARNARVON...... AND PWLLHELI	21	0	2 0 p m	5 0 p m	8 0 a m	11 0 a m
CARNARVON ..... AND TANYBWLCH ..	27	0	2 0 p m	6 18 p m	6 45 a m	11 3 a m
CHELTENHAM ... AND ABERYSTWITH	116	7	3 20 a m	4 58 p m	7 0 a m	8 46 p m
CHESTER .... AND CARNARVON ..	75	0	5 15 a m	1 34 p m	11 41 a m	8 0 p m
CHICHESTER .... AND PORTSMOUTH..	17	6	9 0 a m	11 15 a m	4 0 p m	6 15 p m
COLCHESTER .... AND NORWICH	62	0	11 9 p m	6 18 a m	7 16 p m	2 25 a m
COVENTRY........ AND LEICESTER....	26	7	9 0 a m	12 45 p m	4 30 p m	8 15 p m
CREWE........... AND HOLYHEAD	106	2	3 50 p m	7 32 a m	6 0 p m	5 45 a m
DERBY .... AND LINCOLN	54	0	2 30 a m	8 54 a m	4 0 p m	10 24 p m
DERBY .... AND MANCHESTER..	63	6	8 20 a m	4 30 p m	10 30 a m	6 40 p m
DONCASTER..... AND ROTHERHAM...	12	0	6 45 p m	8 15 p m	5 0 a m	6 30 a m
DORCHESTER..... AND WEYMOUTH.....	8	0	7 15 a m	8 15 a m	5 45 p m	6 45 p m
DUMFRIES .... AND PORTPATRICK.	85	2	6 13 p m	4 21 a m	6 52 p m	5 0 a m
EDINBURGH ..... AND ABERDEEN....	133	5	4 15 p m	6 37 a m	3 0 p m	5 30 a m
EDINBURGH ..... AND ABERDEEN....	111	1	5 0 a m	4 25 p m	5 0 a m	4 33 p m
EDINBURGH ..... AND DUMFRIES	71	2	8 23 a m	4 28 p m	5 27 a m	1 57 p m
EDINBURGH...... AND PERTH	44	4	5 30 a m	10 16 a m	4 30 p m	9 16 p m
EXETER.......... AND DARTMOUTH ..	39	4	5 20 a m	10 38 a m	2 42 p m	8 0 p m
EXETER.......... AND DEVONPORT...	49	7	11 30 a m	5 0 p m	8 55 a m	2 30 p m
EXETER .... AND DEVONPORT....	49	7	5 0 a m	9 45 a m	3 50 p m	8 35 p m
EXETER.......... AND FALMOUTH....	100	4	5 0 a m	3 14 p m	10 6 p m	8 20 p m
EXETER.......... AND FALMOUTH....	104	6	4 6 p m	4 29 a m	8 24 p m	8 50 a m
FRASERBURGH .. AND BURNESS......	22	0	6 38 a m	9 22 a m	9 25 a m	12 9 p m
GAINSBOROUGH .. AND SHEFFIELD....	33	0	4 15 p m	8 45 p m	3 30 a m	8 0 a m
GLOUCESTER .... AND CARMARTHEN .	112	7	1 45 a m	1 37 p m	11 23 a m	11 15 p m
GLOUCESTER .... AND CARMARTHEN.	112	7	5 0 a m	5 45 p m	5 0 a m	5 45 p m
GLOUCESTER .... AND PEMBROKE ..	163	0	1 45 a m	8 14 p m	4 16 a m	11 15 p m
GRANTHAM....... AND NOTTINGHAM..	24	0	8 0 a m	10 54 a m	1 45 p m	4 39 p m
GRANTHAM ...... AND YARMOUTH	124	1	6 30 p m	9 0 a m	4 30 p m	6 55 a m
HEREFORD .... AND BRECON	37	0	8 30 a m	1 25 p m	10 30 a m	3 25 p m
HEREFORD....... AND SHREWSBURY .	52	7	7 0 a m	12 49 p m	3 0 p m	8 49 p m
HULL .... AND HORNSEA.......	18	0	7 30 a m	10 10 a m	2 5 p m	4 45 p m
HULL .... AND PATRINGTON..	16	0	7 30 a m	9 55 a m	2 30 p m	4 45 p m
HULL .... AND SCARBOROUGH	54	4	7 30 a m	1 40 p m	10 50 a m	5 0 p m
INVERNESS ...... AND THURSO	142	4	1 20 a m	7 49 p m	6 45 a m	1 24 a m
IPSWICH .... AND YARMOUTH....	54	0	1 30 p m	7 41 a m	5 54 p m	12 4 a m
KESWICK........ AND WIGTON	19	3	8 30 a m	11 0 a m	1 30 p m	4 0 p m
LANCASTER ...... AND CARLISLE	66	3	6 49 a m	1 39 p m	11 59 a m	6 48 p m
LANCASTER ...... AND CARLISLE	66	3	7 0 p m	1 51 a m	7 0 p m	1 57 a m
LANCASTER ...... AND SETTLE	25	0	7 11 a m	10 46 a m	2 45 p m	6 20 p m
LANCASTER ...... AND ULVERSTONE ..	37	0	7 21 a m	12 6 p m	1 35 p m	6 20 p m
LANCASTER ...... AND WHITEHAVEN.	79	3	7 11 a m	4 1 p m	9 20 a m	6 30 p m
LEEDS ....AND KNARESBOROUGH	19	4	6 0 a m	8 0 a m	4 19 p m	6 38 p m
LEEDS .... AND SKIPTON	29	4	6 0 a m	9 19 a m	3 11 p m	6 30 p m
LEICESTER ...... AND GRANTHAM....	31	1	2 0 p m	5 7 p m	8 0 a m	11 26 a m
LIVERPOOL ...... AND SOUTHPORT....	22	0	8 0 a m	10 50 a m	3 0 p m	5 50 p m
LLANELLY .... AND SWANSEA	11	0	9 45 a m	11 25 a m	1 15 p m	2 50 p m
LOUTH .... AND GRIMSBY	16	0	12 15 p m	2 15 p m	10 0 a m	12 0 noon
NEWCASTLE...... AND EDINBURGH...	121	7	11 14 a m	11 57 p m	12 10 a m	1 30 p m
NEWCASTLE...... AND EDINBURGH. ..	121	7	11 20 p m	12 55 p m	8 0 a m	9 35 p m
NEWPORT .... AND ABERGAVENNY	22	4	7 0 a m	10 15 a m	2 30 p m	5 45 p m
NORTHALLERTON AND HAWES	39	0	6 45 a m	1 15 p m	11 5 a m	5 30 p m
NORWICH........ AND CROMER	22	6	7 0 a m	10 5 a m	3 45 p m	6 45 p m
NOTTINGHAM.... AND STAMFORD....	45	2	7 0 a m	12 32 p m	1 0 p m	6 32 p m
PENRITH .... AND DARLINGTON..	57	4	8 25 a m	3 15 p m	9 30 a m	4 5 p m
PERTH .... AND INVERNESS	117	0	10 36 a m	12 39 a m	1 57 a m	4 0 p m
PETERBORO' .... AND HULL........	88	0	1 45 a m	12 33 p m	1 22 p m	12 10 a m
PLYMOUTH ...... AND LAUNCESTON..	29	0	4 30 p m	8 6 p m	5 30 a m	9 6 a m
SHREWSBURY .... AND ABERYSTWITH.	74	2	7 0 a m	4 45 p m	8 0 a m	5 36 p m

CROSS ROAD MAILS—*continued.*

	Distance.		Starts from place in first column at		Arrives at destination at		Sets out on return at		Arrives at place in first column at	
	miles.	frlongs.	h. m.		h. m.		h. m.		h. m.	
SOUTHAMPTON .. AND EXETER.......	109	7	12 32	a m	12 52	p m	12 56	p m	1 30	a m
STAPLEHURST.... AND HASTINGS......	29	0	1 55	p m	5 30	p m	7 15	a m	10 50	a m
STILTON .... AND LEEDS.........	114	5	3 56	a m	4 31	p m	8 9	a m	9 35	p m
STILTON .... AND SALISBURY ..	114	0	3 56	a m	4 31	p m	8 9	a m	9 35	p m
SWANSEA......... AND MERTHYR.....	32	2	10 0	a m	2 30	p m	10 15	a m	2 45	p m
SWINDON......... AND SALISBURY....	42	0	2 20	a m	8 15	a m	4 50	p m	10 45	p m
TIVERTON........ AND BARNSTABLE..	36	1	3 50	a m	8 24	a m	5 10	p m	9 40	p m
TRURO .... AND PENZANCE	26	7	2 35	p m	5 35	p m	7 10	a m	10 30	a m
TRURO .... AND PENZANCE	28	0	4 0	a m	8 0	a m	5 0	p m	9 0	p m
WELCHPOOL ..... AND NEWTOWN...	14	0	9 30	a m	11 5	a m	1 30	p m	3 5	p m
WOLVERTON..... AND BANBURY	27	5	11 45	a m	3 19	p m	7 30	a m	10 44	a m
YORK .... AND HULL..........	40	2	7 0	a m	11 43	a m	1 37	p m	6 20	p m
YORK......... AND KIRBY MOORSIDE	29	0	7 0	a m	11 38	a m	2 40	p m	6 18	p m
YORK............ AND RIPON.........	24	0	7 0	a m	9 38	a m	3 37	p m	6 15	p m